Tolley's Yellow Tax Handbook 2017–18

58th Edition Part 2a

Tolley's Yellow Tax Handbook 2017–18

58th Edition

Part 2a

Secondary legislation relating to—
direct taxes, including:
income tax
corporation tax
capital gains tax

Consultant Editor

Anne Redston MA (Oxon) LLB FCA CTA(Fellow), Barrister

LexisNexis®

Members of the LexisNexis Group worldwide

United Kingdom	RELX (UK) Limited, trading as LexisNexis, 1-3 Strand, London WC2N 5JR
Australia	LexisNexis Butterworths, Chatswood, New South Wales
Austria	LexisNexis Verlag ARD Orac GmbH & Co KG, Vienna
Canada	LexisNexis Butterworths, Markham, Ontario
Czech Republic	Nakladatelství Orac sro, Prague
France	LexisNexis SA, Paris
Germany	LexisNexis Deutschland GmbH, Frankfurt and Munster
Hong Kong	LexisNexis Butterworths, Hong Kong
Hungary	HVG-Orac, Budapest
India	LexisNexis Butterworths, New Delhi
Italy	Giuffrè Editore, Milan
Malaysia	Malayan Law Journal Sdn Bhd, Kuala Lumpur
New Zealand	LexisNexis Butterworths, Wellington
Singapore	LexisNexis Butterworths, Singapore
South Africa	LexisNexis Butterworths, Durban
Switzerland	Stämpfli Verlag AG, Berne
USA	LexisNexis, Dayton, Ohio

First published in 1962

Published by LexisNexis UK

ISBN: 9781474304092 (for set); 9781474304139 (for Part 2a)
A CIP Catalogue record for this book is available from the British Library.

Visit Tolley at www.tolley.co.uk or email the editorial department on: yellowandorange@lexisnexis.co.uk

Contents

PARTS 1A, 1B, 1C

NATIONAL INSURANCE CONTRIBUTIONS

TAX CREDITS

PETROLEUM REVENUE TAX

List of abbreviations

AEA 1925	Administration of Estates Act 1925
ACT	Advance Corporation Tax
APRT	Advance petroleum revenue tax
art	article(s)
ATED	annual tax on enveloped dwellings
BES	Business Expansion Scheme
CAA	Capital Allowances Act
CCAB	Consultative Committee of Accountancy Bodies
C&E	Customs & Excise
CGT	Capital gains tax
Ch	Chapter of statute
CIOT	Chartered Institute of Taxation
col	column(s)
Comrs	Commissioners
CPA 1947	Crown Proceedings Act 1947
CRCA 2005	Commissioners for Revenue and Customs Act 2005
CRT	Composite rate tax
CT	Corporation tax
CTA 2009/2010	Corporation Tax Act 2009/2010
CTD	Certificates of tax deposit
CTT	Capital transfer tax
Dir	EC Directive
DLT	Development land tax
DPT	Diverted Profits Tax
DTR	Double taxation relief
EC	European Community/Communities
edn	edition
EEC	European Economic Community
EEIG	European Economic Interest Grouping
EIS	Enterprise Investment Scheme
ESC	Extra-statutory concession
et seq	(et sequens) and the following
EU	European Union

FA	Finance Act
FII	Franked investment income
FIMBRA	Financial Intermediaries, Managers and Brokers Regulatory Association
F(No 2)A	Finance (No 2) Act
FSA	Friendly Societies Act
FYA	first-year allowance
GAAR	General Anti-abuse Rule
HL	House of Lords
HM	Her Majesty
HMRC	Her Majesty's Revenue & Customs
HMSO	Her Majesty's Stationery Office
IA	Interpretation Act
IA 1986	Insolvency Act 1986
ICAEW	Institute of Chartered Accountants in England & Wales
IHT	Inheritance tax
IR	Inland Revenue
IR Comrs	Commissioners of Inland Revenue
IT	Income tax
ITA 2007	Income Tax Act 2007
ITEPA 2003	Income Tax (Earnings and Pensions) Act 2003
ITTOIA 2005	Income Tax (trading and Other Income) Act 2005
LAUTRO	Life Assurance and Unit Trust Regulatory Organisation
LIFFE	London International Financial Futures and Options Exchange
NB	(nota bene) note well
NI	National insurance
NIC	National insurance contributions
NRCGT	Non-resident capital gains tax
OJ	Official Journal of the European Communities
OTA	Oil Taxation Act
para	paragraph(s)
PAYE	Pay as you earn
PCTA 1968	Provisional Collection of Taxes Act 1968
PR	Press release
PRP	Profit-related pay
PRT	Petroleum revenue tax
PSO	Pension Schemes Office

Pt	Part(s)
QCB	Qualifying corporate bond
r	rule(s)
RD	Revenue decision
reg	regulation(s)
R&D	research & development
RI	Revenue Interpretation
s(s)	section(s)
SAYE	Save as you earn
Sch	Schedule
SSA	Social Security Act
SSAA 1992	Social Security Administration Act 1992
SS(C)A	Social Security (Contributions) Act
SSCBA 1992	Social Security Contributions and Benefits Act 1992
SS(No 2)A	Social Security (No 2) Act
SI	Statutory Instrument
SP	Statement of Practice
SSAP	Statement of Standard Accounting Practice
STC	Simon's Tax Cases
sub-para	sub-paragraph(s)
sub-s	sub-section(s)
SWTI	Simon's Weekly Tax Intelligence
TA	Income and Corporation Taxes Act
TaA 2000	Transport Act 2000
TCGA 1992	Taxation of Chargeable Gains Act 1992
TIOPA 2010	Taxation (International and other Provisions) Act 2010
TMA 1970	Taxes Management Act 1970
TPA 2014	Taxation of Pensions Act 2014
UCITS	Undertakings for Collective Investment in Transferable Securities
UK	United Kingdom
VAT	Value added tax
VCT	Venture capital trust
vol	volume(s)
WDA	writing down allowance
WRA	Welfare Reform Act

TAX TABLES

INCOME TAX ALLOWANCES

	2017–18	*2016–17*
Personal allowance	£	£
basic allowance	11,500	11,000
income limit*	100,000	100,000
Personal savings allowance**		
basic rate taxpayers	1,000	1,000
higher rate taxpayers	500	500
Dividend allowance***	5,000	5,000
Trading allowance	1,000	—
Property income allowance	1,000	—

* Where income is above £100,000, the personal allowance is reduced by £1 for every £2 of income above the £100,000 limit.

** The personal savings allowance is not available to additional rate taxpayers. Savings income exceeding the allowance is taxable at the basic or higher rate as appropriate. The allowance is not a deduction in arriving at taxable income.

*** The dividend allowance is available to all taxpayers. It is not a deduction in arriving at taxable income. For the rates of tax on dividend income above the allowance, see below.

TRANSFERABLE MARRIAGE ALLOWANCE*

Maximum amount of allowance	£1,150	£1,100

* Available to married couples and civil partners who are not in receipt of married couple's allowance. A spouse or civil partner who is not liable to income tax, or not liable at the higher or additional rates, can transfer this amount of their unused personal allowance to their spouse or civil partner. The recipient must not be liable to income tax at the higher or additional rates. Relief is given at 20% (maximum of £230 for 2017–18).

MARRIED COUPLE'S ALLOWANCE* (RELIEF AT 10%)

either partner born before 6 April 1935*	8,445	8,355
income limit	28,000	27,700
minimum where income exceeds limit	3,260	3,220

* Available for civil partners.

BLIND PERSON'S ALLOWANCE

Blind person's allowance	2,320	2,290

INCOME TAX RATES

Non-savings income

Taxable income £	*Band £*	*Rate %*	*Tax on band £*	*Total tax £*
2017–18				
0–33,500	33,500	20	6,700	6,700
33,501–150,000	116,500	40	46,600	53,300
Over 150,000	—	45%	—	—
2016–17				
0–32,000	32,000	20%	6,400	6,400
32,001–150,000	118,000	40%	47,200	53,600
Over 150,000	—	45%	—	—

Trust rate of income tax for 2016–17 and 2017–18 is 45%.

Scottish Income Tax

From April 2017, the Scottish Parliament has the power to set all income tax rates and bands (except the personal allowance, which remains reserved) that will apply to Scottish taxpayers' non-savings, non-dividend income. The Scottish rates and bands are set annually by the Scottish Parliament.

Scotland: non-savings income

Taxable income £	*Band £*	*Rate %*	*Tax on band £*	*Total tax £*
2017–18				
0–31,500	31,500	20	6,300	6,300
31,501–150,000	118,500	40	47,400	53,700
Over 150,000	—	45%	—	—

Where income is above £100,000, the personal allowance is reduced by £1 for every £2 of income above the £100,000 limit.

Starting rate for savings income

Taxable income £	*Band £*	*Rate %*	*Tax on band £*	*Total tax £*
2017–18				
0–5,000	5,000	0	0	0
2016–17				
0–5,000	5,000	0	0	0

Where taxable non-savings income exceeds £5,000 the special 0% starting rate for savings income does not apply.

Income taxable at the starting rate for savings does not fall within the personal savings allowance (see above).

Dividend tax rates

Taxable income £	*Rate %*
2017–18	
0–33,500	7.5
33,501–150,000	32.5
Over 150,000	38.1
2016–17	
0–32,000	7.5
32,001–150,000	32.5
Over 150,000	38.1

A 0% rate applies to dividend income within the dividend allowance (see above).

The dividend trust rate is 38.1% for 2017–18 and 2016–17.

NATIONAL INSURANCE CONTRIBUTIONS 2017–18

Class 1 (Earnings related)

Employees	
Weekly earnings	
First £157	Nil
£157.01 £866	12%
Over £866	2%
Employers	
Weekly earnings	
First £157	Nil
Over £157	13.8%

Employers' rates for employees under 21 and apprentices under 25 are nil on earnings up to £866 per week.

Employment allowance (per employer): £3,000 a year.

Class 1A and 1B: 13.8%.

Class 2 (self-employed): flat rate £2.85 a week (small profits threshold £6,025 a year).

Class 3 (voluntary contributions): £14.25 a week.

Class 4 (self-employed): 9% of profits between £8,164 and £45,000 a year (2% of profits above £45,000 a year).

Budget 2016 announced the Government's intention to abolish Class 2 contributions from April 2018.

APPRENTICESHIP LEVY

	2017–18	*2016–17*
	£	£
Allowance (per employer)	15,000	—
Rate	0.5%	—

Effectively applies to UK employers' pay bills in excess of £3 million.

INDIVIDUAL SAVINGS ACCOUNTS

	Annual limit	*Junior ISA annual limit*	*Lifetime ISA annual limit*	*Help to Buy ISA monthly limit*
	£	£	£	£
2017–18	20,000	4,128	4,000	200
2016–17	15,240	4,080	—	200

Savings are exempt from income tax and capital gains tax.

CAPITAL GAINS TAX

	2017–18	*2016–17*
Annual exempt amount	£	£
Individuals, disabled trusts, personal representatives for year of death and two years thereafter	11,300	11,100
Trusts generally	5,650	5,550
Rates		
Individuals		
Standard rate	10%	10%
Higher rate	20%	20%
Trustees and personal representatives	20%	20%
Gains on residential property and carried interest		
Standard rate	18%	18%
Higher rate	28%	28%

Entrepreneurs' relief and investors' relief: qualifying gains charged at 10% (subject to £10 million lifetime limit).

CORPORATION TAX

Financial year to—	*31 March 2018*	*31 March 2017*
Rate	19%	20%

The main rate for ring-fence profits is 30% and the small profits rate for ring-fence profits is 19%. Ring fence profits above £300,000 but not exceeding £1.5m attract marginal relief. The marginal relief ring-fence fraction is 11/400.

BANK LEVY

	1.1.2011–28.2.2011	1.3.2011–30.4.2011	1.5.2011–31.12.2011	1.1.2012–31.12.2012	1.1.2013–31.12.2013
short-term chargeable liabilities	.05%	.1%	.075%	.088%	.130%
long-term chargeable equity and liabilities	.025%	.05%	.0375%	.044%	.065%

	1.1.2014–31.3.2015	1.4.2015–31.12.2015	1.1.2016–31.12.2016	1.1.2017–31.12.2017	1.1.2018–31.12.2018
short-term chargeable liabilities	.156%	.21%	.18%	.17%	.16%
long-term chargeable equity and liabilities	.078%	.105%	.09%	.085%	.08%

CAR BENEFIT

CO_2 emissions (2017–18) grams per kilometre	*% of list price*	
	Petrol	*Diesel*
50	9	12
51 75	13	16
76–94	17	20
95	18	21
100	19	22
105	20	23
110	21	24
115	22	25
120	23	26
125	24	27
130	25	28
135	26	29
140	27	30
145	28	31
150	29	32
155	30	33
160	31	34
165	32	35
170	33	36
175	34	37
180	35	37
185	36	37
190 and above	37	37

A 9% charge applies for cars incapable of producing CO_2 emissions.

CAR FUEL BENEFIT

For 2017–18, car fuel benefit is calculated by applying the above car benefit percentage to a figure of £22,600.

TAX-FREE MILEAGE ALLOWANCES

Employee's own vehicle

Motorcars and vans	*2017–18*
Up to 10,000 business miles	45p
Over 10,000 business miles	25p
Passenger making same trip	5p
Motorcycles	24p
Cycles	20p

Advisory fuel rates for company car (from 1 September 2017)

Cylinder capacity	*Petrol*	*LPG*
Up to 1,400 cc	11p	7p
1,401 cc to 2,000 cc	13p	8p
Over 2,000 cc	21p	13p
	Diesel	
Up to 1,600 cc	9p	
1,601 cc to 2,000 cc	11p	
Over 2,000 cc	12p	

Hybrid cars are treated as petrol or diesel cars accordingly.

INHERITANCE TAX

Transfers made after 5 April 2017 and before 6 April 2018.

Death rates	
Nil-rate band	£325,000
Residence nil-rate band	£100,000
Rate of IHT on excess	40%

Unused nil-rate/residence nil-rate band is transferable to spouse or civil partner.

Chargeable lifetime transfers are initially charged at 20%.

Annual gifts of up to £3,000 per donor are exempt.

A reduced rate of 36% applies where 10% or more of the net estate is left to charity.

The residence nil-rate band is phased in from 6 April 2017, set at £125,000 for 2018–19, £150,000 for 2019–20 and £175,000 for 2020–21. The basic nil-rate band will remain at £325,000 until 5 April 2021. After that, both nil-rate bands will increase in line with CPI.

STAMP TAXES

Shares and marketable securities	.5%*

* Rounded up to the nearest multiple of £5 and subject to exemption where consideration is less than £1,000 or nil.

STAMP DUTY LAND TAX

Residential	*Rate*
Up to £125,000	Nil
£125,001–£250,000	2%
£250,001–£925,000	5%
£925,001–£1,500,000	10%
Over £1,500,000	12%

Rates are charged on the **portion** of the consideration that falls within each rate band.

For residential property, where consideration exceeds £500,000 a 15% rate applies if purchase by, or by a partnership including, a company or collective investment scheme enveloping the property.

Rates are increased by 3 percentage points for certain purchases including purchases of additional residential properties by individuals. Transactions under £40,000 are excluded.

Non-residential	*Rate*
Up to £150,000	Nil
£150,001–£250,000	2%
Over £250,000	5%

Rates are charged on the **portion** of the consideration that falls within each rate band.

Leases

Residential	*Non-residential*	*Rate*
Up to £125,000	Up to £150,000	Nil
Over £125,000	£150,001 to £5,000,000	1%
—	Over £5,000,000	2%

Rates are charged on the **portion** of the net present value that falls within each rate band.

LAND AND BUILDINGS TRANSACTION TAX (SCOTLAND)

Residential	*Rate*
Up to £145,000	Nil
£145,001–£250,000	2%
£250,001–£325,000	5%
£325,001–£750,000	10%
Over £750,000	12%

Rates are charged on the **portion** of the consideration that falls within each rate band.

Non-residential	*Rate*
Up to £150,000	Nil
£150,001–£350,000	3%
Over £350,000	4.5%

Rates are charged on the **portion** of the consideration that falls within each rate band.

Leases

*Residential**	*Non-residential*	*Rate*
—	Up to £150,000	Nil
—	Over £150,000	1%

*Generally, leases of residential property are exempt from LBTT.

Rates are charged on the **portion** of the net present value that falls within each rate band.

ANNUAL TAX ON ENVELOPED DWELLINGS

Property value	*Charge for the tax year 2017–18*	*Charge for the tax year 2016–17*
Over £500,000 to £1m	£3,500	£3,500
£1m – £2m	£7,050	£7,000
£2m – £5m	£23,550	£23,350
£5m – £10m	£54,950	£54,450
£10m – £20m	£110,100	£109,050
£20m +	£220,350	£218,200

VAT

Standard rate	20%
Lower rate	5%
Registration level from 1 April 2017	£85,000 pa
Deregistration limit from 1 April 2017	£83,000 pa

VAT CAR FUEL SCALE CHARGES FROM 1 MAY 2017

Description of vehicle: vehicle's CO_2 emissions figure	*VAT inclusive consideration for a 12 month prescribed accounting period (£)*	*VAT inclusive consideration for a 3 month prescribed accounting period (£)*	*VAT inclusive consideration for a 1 month prescribed accounting period (£)*
120 or less	563	140	46
125	842	211	70
130	901	224	74
135	955	238	79
140	1,013	252	84
145	1,068	267	88
150	1,126	281	93
155	1,180	295	98
160	1,239	309	102
165	1,293	323	107
170	1,351	337	111
175	1,405	351	116
180	1,464	365	121
185	1,518	379	125
190	1,577	393	131
195	1,631	408	136
200	1,689	422	140
205	1,743	436	145
210	1,802	449	149
215	1,856	463	154
220	1,914	478	159
225 or more	1,969	492	163

CAPITAL ALLOWANCES

	Rate %
Dredging (straight-line basis)	
Writing-down allowance	4
Know-how (reducing-balance basis)	
Writing-down allowance	25
Mineral extraction (reducing-balance basis)	
Writing-down allowances	
General	25
Acquisition of mineral asset	10
Patent rights (reducing-balance basis)	
Writing-down allowance	25
Plant and machinery (reducing-balance basis)	
Annual investment allowance (max £200,000)	100
First-year allowances	
Energy-saving or environmentally beneficial assets	100
New low-emission cars	100
New zero-emission goods vehicles	100
New assets for use in designated areas of enterprise zones	100
New electric charge-point equipment	100
Writing-down allowances	
General	18
Cars (other than low-emission cars)	8
Special rate expenditure (including integral features and thermal insulation)	8
Long-life assets	8
Research and development	
Allowance	100

REGISTERED PENSION SCHEMES

2017–18	£
Annual allowance	40,000
Income limit	150,000
Minimum where income exceeds limit	10,000
Lifetime allowance	£1,000,000

2016–17	£
Annual allowance	40,000
Income limit	150,000
Minimum where income exceeds limit	10,000
Lifetime allowance	£1,000,000

Any unused annual allowance can be carried forward for up to three years.

The annual allowance is tapered by £1 for every £2 of income over £150,000 (income including pension contributions), subject to a maximum reduction of £30,000.

TAX CREDITS

Annual amounts	*2017–18*	*2016–17*
	£	£
Child tax credit		
Family element	545	545
Child element (for each child)	2,780	2,780
Addition for disabled child	3,175	3,140
Severely disabled child enhancement	1,290	1,275
Working tax credit		
Basic element	1,960	1,960
Lone parent and couple element	2,010	2,010
30-hour element	810	810
Disability element	3,000	2,970
Severe disability element	1,290	1,275
Childcare element (up to 70% of costs)	Weekly	Weekly
maximum eligible cost (1 child)	175	175
maximum eligible cost (2 or more children)	300	300
Income thresholds		
Income threshold	6,420	6,420
eligible for child tax credit only	16,105	16,105
Withdrawal rate	41%	41%
Income rise disregard	2,500	2,500
Income fall disregard	2,500	2,500

Part 2a

Statutory Instruments

Contents

Chronological list of printed Statutory Instruments

Note—

For an alphabetical list of the printed statutory instruments, and a chronological list of current and amending statutory instruments, *see below*.

Scottish statutory instruments are listed separately below (in a separate section at the end of Part 2a).

SI 2000/1093 Finance Act 1999, Schedule 10, Paragraph 18, (First and Second Appointed Days) Order 2000
SI 2000/2004 Finance Act 1999, Section 59(3)(b), (Appointed Day) Order 2000
SI 2000/2074 Donations to Charity by Individuals (Appropriate Declarations) Regulations 2000
SI 2000/2076 Individual Learning Accounts (Separate Employers Under the Crown) Regulations 2000
SI 2000/2080 Income Tax (Benefits in Kind) (Exemption for Welfare Counselling) Regulations 2000
SI 2000/2082 Finance Act 2000, Section 108(3), (Appointed Day) Order 2000
SI 2000/2089 Insurance Companies (Overseas Life Assurance Business) (Excluded Business) Regulations 2000
SI 2000/2090 Employee Share Ownership Plans (Partnership Shares—Notice of Effects on Benefits, Statutory Sick Pay and Statutory Maternity Pay) Regulations 2000
SI 2000/2129 Tonnage Tax (Training Requirement) Regulations 2000
SI 2000/2303 Tonnage Tax Regulations 2000
SI 2000/2875 Orders for the Delivery of Documents (Procedure) Regulations 2000
SI 2000/3158 Controlled Foreign Companies (Designer Rate Tax Provisions) Regulations 2000
SI 2000/3315 Exchange Gains and Losses (Miscellaneous Modifications) Regulations 2000
SI 2001/56 Income Tax (Electronic Communications) (Incentive Payments) Regulations 2001
SI 2001/253 Finance Act 1989, Section 178(1), (Appointed Day) Order 2001
SI 2001/391 Investment Trusts (Approval of Accounting Methods for Creditor Relationships) Order 2001
SI 2001/1122 Capital Gains Tax (Gilt-edged Securities) Order 2001
SI 2001/1123 Income Tax (Car Benefits) (Reduction of Value of Appropriate Percentage) Regulations 2001
SI 2001/1156 Double Taxation Relief (Taxes on Income) (Underlying Tax on Dividends and Dual Resident Companies) Regulations 2001
SI 2001/1163 Double Taxation Relief (Surrender of Relievable Tax Within a Group) Regulations 2001
SI 2001/1757 General Insurance Reserves (Tax) Regulations 2001
SI 2001/2541 Capital Allowances (Energy-saving Plant and Machinery) Order 2001
SI 2001/3973 Friendly Societies (Provisional Repayments for Exempt Business) (Amendment) Regulations 2001
SI 2001/3974 Individual Savings Account (Insurance Companies) (Amendment) Regulations 2001
SI 2002/205 Income Tax (Exemption of Minor Benefits) Regulations 2002
SI 2002/653 Scottish Water (Transfer of Functions, etc) (Tax Provisions) Order 2002
SI 2002/680 Income Tax (Employments and Electronic Communications) (Miscellaneous Provisions) Regulations 2002
SI 2002/1596 Income Tax (Benefits in Kind) (Exemption for Employment Costs resulting from Disability) Regulations 2002
SI 2002/1966 Relief for Community Amateur Sports Clubs (Designation) Order 2002
SI 2002/1967 Corporation Tax (Finance Leasing of Intangible Assets) Regulations 2002
SI 2002/1969 Exchange Gains and Losses (Transitional Provisions and Savings) Regulations 2002
SI 2002/1970 Exchange Gains and Losses (Bringing into Account Gains or Losses) Regulations 2002
SI 2002/2661 Venture Capital Trust (Exchange of Shares and Securities) Regulations 2002
SI 2002/2849 Capital Gains Tax (Gilt-edged Securities) Order 2002
SI 2002/3047 Statutory Payment Schemes (Electronic Communications) Regulations 2002
SI 2003/96 Community Investment Tax Relief (Accreditation of Community Development Finance Institutions) Regulations 2003
SI 2003/282 Income and Corporation Taxes (Electronic Communications) Regulations 2003
SI 2003/1830 Income Tax (Authorised Unit Trusts) (Interest Distributions) Regulations 2003
SI 2003/2076 Capital Allowances (Environmentally Beneficial Plant and Machinery) Order 2003
SI 2003/2082 Insurance Companies (Calculation of Profits: Policy Holders' Tax) Regulations 2003
SI 2003/2172 Finance Act 1995, Section 127(12) (Designated Transactions) Regulations 2003

SI 2005/3452 Registered Pension Schemes (Discharge of Liabilities under Sections 267 and 268 of the Finance Act 2004) Regulations 2005
SI 2005/3453 Employer-Financed Retirement Benefits Schemes (Provision of Information) Regulations 2005
SI 2005/3454 Registered Pension Schemes (Accounting and Assessment) Regulations 2005
SI 2005/3455 Registered Pension Schemes and Employer-Financed Retirement Benefits Schemes (Information) (Prescribed Descriptions of Persons) Regulations 2005
SI 2005/3456 Registered Pension Schemes (Audited Accounts) (Specified Persons) Regulations 2005
SI 2005/3458 Registered Pension Schemes (Restriction of Employers' Relief) Regulations 2005
SI 2006/129 Registered Pension Schemes (Relevant Annuities) Regulations 2006
SI 2006/130 Registered Pension Schemes (Uprating Percentages for Defined Benefits Arrangements and Enhanced Protection Limits) Regulations 2006
SI 2006/131 Registered Pension Schemes (Enhanced Lifetime Allowance) Regulations 2006
SI 2006/132 Armed Forces and Reserve Forces (Compensation Scheme) (Excluded Benefits for Tax Purposes) Regulations 2006
SI 2006/133 Registered Pension Schemes (Co-ownership of Living Accommodation) Regulations 2006
SI 2006/134 Registered Pension Schemes (Authorised Payments) (Transfers to the Pension Protection Fund) Regulations 2006
SI 2006/135 Registered Pension Schemes (Meaning of Pension Commencement Lump Sum) Regulations 2006
SI 2006/136 Pension Benefits (Insurance Company Liable as Scheme Administrator) Regulations 2006
SI 2006/137 Registered Pension Schemes (Authorised Member Payments) Regulations 2006
SI 2006/138 Pension Schemes (Reduction in Pension Rates) Regulations 2006
SI 2006/184 Taxation of Chargeable Gains (Gilt-edged Securities) Order 2006
SI 2006/206 Pension Schemes (Categories of Country and Requirements for Overseas Pension Schemes and Recognised Overseas Pension Schemes) Regulations 2006
SI 2006/207 Pensions Schemes (Application of UK Provisions to Relevant Non-UK Schemes) Regulations 2006
SI 2006/208 Pension Schemes (Information Requirements—Qualifying Overseas Pension Schemes, Qualifying Recognised Overseas Pensions Schemes and Corresponding Relief) Regulations 2006
SI 2006/209 Registered Pension Schemes (Authorised Payments) Regulations 2006
SI 2006/210 Employer-Financed Retirement Benefits (Excluded Benefits for Tax Purposes) Regulations 2006
SI 2006/211 Registered Pension Schemes (Surrender of Relevant Excess) Regulations 2006
SI 2006/212 Pension Schemes (Relevant Migrant Members) Regulations 2006
SI 2006/333 Tonnage Tax (Exception of Financial Year 2006) Order 2006
SI 2006/364 Registered Pension Schemes (Modification of the Rules of Existing Schemes) Regulations 2006
SI 2006/365 Registered Pension Schemes (Unauthorised Payments by Existing Schemes) Regulations 2006
SI 2006/497 Taxation of Judicial Pensions (Consequential Provisions) Order 2006
SI 2006/498 Registered Pension Schemes (Block Transfers) (Permitted Membership Period) Regulations 2006
SI 2006/499 Registered Pension Schemes (Transfer of Sums and Assets) Regulations 2006
SI 2006/567 Registered Pension Schemes (Provision of Information) Regulations 2006
SI 2006/568 Registered Pension Schemes (Prescribed Manner of Determining Amount of Annuities) Regulations 2006
SI 2006/569 Registered Pension Schemes (Splitting of Schemes) Regulations 2006
SI 2006/570 Registered Pension Schemes and Overseas Pension Schemes (Electronic Communication of Returns and Information) Regulations 2006
SI 2006/571 Registered Pension Schemes (Authorised Member Payments) (No 2) Regulations 2006
SI 2006/572 Taxation of Pension Schemes (Transitional Provisions) Order 2006
SI 2006/573 Pension Schemes (Transfers, Reorganisations and Winding Up) (Transitional Provisions) Order 2006
SI 2006/574 Registered Pension Schemes (Authorised Surplus Payments) Regulations 2006
SI 2006/575 Pension Protection Fund (Tax) Regulations 2006

SI 2007/2483 Finance Act 2007 (Schedules 13 and 14) Order 2007

SI 2007/2485 Sale and Repurchase of Securities (Modification of Schedule 13 to the Finance Act 2007) Regulations 2007

SI 2007/2486 Sale and Repurchase of Securities (Modification of Enactments) Regulations 2007

SI 2007/2532 Finance Act 2007, Schedule 25 (Commencement and Transitional Provisions) Order 2007

SI 2007/2709 Tribunals, Courts and Enforcement Act 2007 (Commencement No 1) Order 2007

SI 2007/3000 Income Tax (Benefits Received by Former Owner of Property) (Election for Inheritance Tax Treatment) Regulations 2007

SI 2007/3104 Tax Avoidance Schemes (Penalty) Regulations 2007

SI 2007/3175 Police and Criminal Evidence Act 1984 (Application to Revenue and Customs) Order 2007 (revoked)

SI 2007/3186 Corporation Tax (Implementation of the Mergers Directive) Regulations 2007

SI 2007/3278 Energy-Saving Items (Income Tax) Regulations 2007

SI 2007/3338 Securitisation Companies (Application of Section 83(1) of the Finance Act 2005: Accounting Standards) Regulations 2007

SI 2007/3402 Taxation of Insurance Securitisation Companies Regulations 2007

SI 2007/3425 Real Estate Investment Trusts (Joint Venture Groups) Regulations 2007 (revoked)

SI 2007/3426 Scientific Research Organisations Regulations 2007

SI 2007/3507 Recovery of Foreign Taxes Regulations 2007

SI 2007/3532 Registered Pension Schemes (Authorised Member Payments) Regulations 2007

SI 2007/3537 Employer-Financed Retirement Benefits (Excluded Benefits for Tax Purposes) Regulations 2007

SI 2008/403 Serious Crime Act 2007 (Disclosure of Information by Revenue and Customs) Order 2008

SI 2008/562 Income Tax (Purchased Life Annuities) Regulations 2008

SI 2008/568 Finance Act 2007, Schedule 24 (Commencement and Transitional Provisions) Order 2008

SI 2008/1464 (Taxation of Benefits under Government Pilot Schemes (Up-Front Childcare Fund) Order 2008

SI 2008/1520 Energy-Saving Items (Corporation Tax) Regulations 2008

SI 2008/1579 Corporation Tax (Implementation of the Mergers Directive) Regulations 2008

SI 2008/1588 Taxation of Chargeable Gains (Gilt-edged Securities) Order 2008

SI 2008/1926 Financing-Arrangement-Funded Transfers to Shareholders Regulations 2008

SI 2008/1936 Finance Act 2008 Section 135 (Disaster or Emergency) Order 2008

SI 2008/1942 Friendly Societies (Transfers of Other Business) (Modification of the Corporation Tax Acts) Regulations 2008

SI 2008/1948 Taxes (Fees for Payment by Telephone) Regulations 2008

SI 2008/2353 Serious Crime Act 2007 (Specified Anti-fraud Organisations) Order 2008

SI 2008/2603 Taxation of Benefits under Government Pilot Schemes (Better off in Work Credit) Order 2008

SI 2008/2646 Group Relief for Overseas Losses (Modification of the Corporation Tax Acts for Non-resident Insurance Companies) Regulations 2008

SI 2008/2682 Income Tax (Deposit-takers and Building Societies) (Interest Payments) Regulations 2008

SI 2008/2698 Tribunal Procedure (Upper Tribunal) Rules 2008

SI 2008/2834 Appeals from the Upper Tribunal to the Court of Appeal Order 2008

SI 2008/2835 First-tier Tribunal and Upper Tribunal (Composition of Tribunal) Order 2008

SI 2009/56 Transfer of Tribunal Functions and Revenue and Customs Appeals Order 2009

SI 2009/273 Tribunal Procedure (First-tier Tribunal) (Tax Chamber) Rules 2009

SI 2009/275 Appeals (Excluded Decisions) Order 2009

SI 2009/403 Finance Act 2008, Schedule 39 (Appointed Day, Transitional Provision and Savings) Order 2009

SI 2009/404 Finance Act 2008, Schedule 36 (Appointed Day and Savings) Order 2009

SI 2009/511 Finance Act 2008, Schedule 41 (Appointed Day and Transitional Provisions) Order 2009/511

SI 2009/571 Finance Act 2008, Schedule 40 (Appointed Day, Transitional Provisions and Consequential Amendments) Order 2009

SI 2011/22 Dormant Bank and Building Society Accounts (Tax) regulations 2011
SI 2011/23 Finance Act 2008, Section 39(7) (Commencement) Order 2011
SI 2011/132 Finance (No 3) Act 2010, Schedule 11 (Appointed Day) Order 2011
SI 2011/711 Taxes, etc (Fees for Payment by Internet) Regulations 2011 (revoked)
SI 2011/712 Qualifying Care Relief (Specified Social Care Schemes) Order 2011
SI 2011/976 Penalties, Offshore Income etc. (Designation of Territories) Order 2011
SI 2011/1079 International Mutual Administrative Assistance in Tax Matters Order 2011
SI 2011/1157 Skipton Fund Limited (Application of Sections 731, 733 and 734 of the Income Tax (Trading and Other Income) Act 2005) Order 2011
SI 2011/1295 Taxation of Chargeable Gains (Gilt-edged Securities) Order 2011
SI 2011/1752 Registered Pension Schemes (Lifetime Allowance Transitional Protection) Regulations 2011
SI 2011/1783 Registered Pension Schemes (Relevant Income) Regulations 2011
SI 2011/1784 Corporation Tax Act 2010 (Factors Determining Substantial Commercial Interdependence) Order 2011
SI 2011/1791 Registered Pension Schemes (Modification of Scheme Rules) Regulations 2011
SI 2011/1792 Registered Pension Schemes (Prescribed Requirements of Flexible Drawdown Declaration) Regulations 2011
SI 2011/1793 Registered Pension Schemes (Notice of Joint Liability for the Annual Allowance Charge) Regulations 2011
SI 2011/1797 Registered Pension Schemes (Provision of Information) (Amendment) (No.2) Regulations 2011
SI 2011/1798 Employer Supported Childcare (Relevant Earnings and Excluded Amounts) Regulations 2011
SI 2011/2391 Finance (No 3) Act 2010, Schedule 10 and the Finance Act 2009, Schedule 55 and Sections 101 to 103 (Appointed Day, etc) (Construction Industry Scheme) Order 2011
SI 2011/2401 Finance Act 2009, Section 103 (Appointed Day) Order 2011
SI 2011/2446 Taxes and Duties, etc (Interest Rate) Regulations
SI 2011/2696 Employment Income Provided Through Third Parties (Excluded Relevant Steps) Regulations 2011
SI 2011/2833 Money Laundering (Amendment No.2) Regulations 2011
SI 2011/2931 MARD Regulations 2011
SI 2011/2999 Investment Trust (Approved Company) (Tax) Regulations
SI 2012/286 Research and Development (Qualifying Bodies) (Tax) Order 2012
SI 2012/458 Bank Levy (Double Taxation Relief) Regulations 2012
SI 2012/459 Bank Levy (Double Taxation Arrangements) (Federal Republic of Germany) Regulations 2012
SI 2012/689 Taxes, etc. (Fees for Payment by Telephone) Regulations 2012 (revoked)
SI 2012/701 London Legacy Development Corporation (Tax Consequences) Regulations 2012
SI 2012/735 Finance Act 2010, Schedule 6, Part 1 (Further Consequential and Incidental Provisions etc) Order 2012
SI 2012/736 Finance Act 2010, Schedule 6, Part 2 (Commencement) Order 2012
SI 2012/764 Postal Services Act 2011 (Taxation) Regulations 2012
SI 2012/822 Income Tax (Pay As You Earn) (Amendment) Regulations 2012
SI 2012/847 Data-gathering Powers (Relevant Data) Regulations 2012
SI 2012/1258 Finance Act 2004, Section 180(5) (Modification) Regulations 2012
SI 2012/1836 Tax Avoidance Schemes (Information) Regulations 2012
SI 2012/1843 Taxation of Chargeable Gains (Gilt-edged Securities) Order 2012
SI 2012/1868 National Insurance Contributions (Application of Part 7 of the Finance Act 2004) Regulations 2012
SI 2012/1898 Business Investment Relief Regulations 2012
SI 2012/2933 Bank Levy: International Tax Enforcement Arrangements (Federal Republic of Germany) Order 2012
SI 2012/3008 Friendly Societies (Modifications of the Tax Acts) Regulations 2012
SI 2012/3009 Insurance Companies (Transitional Provisions) Regulations 2012
SI 2012/3024 Controlled Foreign Companies (Excluded Territories) Regulations 2012
SI 2012/3041 Controlled Foreign Companies (Excluded Banking Business Profits) Regulations 2012
SI 2012/3044 Insurance Companies and CFCs (Avoidance of Double Charge) Regulations 2012

SI 2015/448 Childcare Payments (Eligibility) Regulations 2015
SI 2015/522 Childcare Payments Regulations 2015
SI 2015/549 Finance Act 2014 (High Risk Promoters Prescribed Information) Regulations 2015
SI 2015/616 Market Value of Shares, Securities and Strips Regulations 2015
SI 2015/725 Community Amateur Sports Clubs Regulations 2015
SI 2015/866 Offshore Asset Moves Penalty (Specified Territories) Regulations 2015
SI 2015/878 International Tax Compliance Regulations 2015
SI 2015/1449 Cultural Test (Television Programmes) (Amendment) Regulations 2015
SI 2015/1540 Housing and Regeneration Transfer Schemes (Tax Consequences) Regulations 2015
SI 2015/1783 Police and Criminal Evidence Act 1984 (Application to Revenue and Customs) Order 2015
SI 2015/1790 Taxation of Chargeable Gains (Gilt-edged Securities) Order 2015
SI 2015/1948 Income Tax (Approved Expenses) Regulations 2015
SI 2015/1983 Lloyd's Underwriters (Transitional Equalisation Reserves) (Tax) Regulations 2015
SI 2015/1986 Enforcement by Deduction from Accounts (Prescribed Information) Regulations 2015
SI 2015/2002 Qualifying Private Placement Regulations 2015
SI 2015/2047 Capital Allowances (Designated Assisted Areas) Order 2015
SI 2016/44 Enforcement by Deduction from Accounts (Imposition of Charges by Deposit-takers) Regulations 2016
SI 2016/208 Proceeds of Crime Act 2002 (Cash Searches: Code of Practice) Order 2016
SI 2016/209 Proceeds of Crime Act 2002 (Investigations: Code of Practice) (England and Wales and Northern Ireland) Order 2016
SI 2016/222 Proceeds of Crime Act 2002 (Investigative Powers of Prosecutors: Code of Practice) (England and Wales and Northern Ireland) Order 2016
SI 2016/237 Taxes (Base Erosion and Profit Shifting) (Country-by-Country Reporting) Regulations 2016
SI 2016/333 Fees for Payment of Taxes, etc. by Credit Card Regulations 2016
SI 2016/350 Income Tax (Travel Expenses of Members of Local Authorities etc) Regulations 2016
SI 2016/566 Banking Surcharge (Information) Regulations 2016
SI 2016/751 Capital Allowances (Designated Assisted Areas) Order 2016
SI 2016/771 Major Sporting Events (Income Tax Exemption) Regulations 2016
SI 2016/1005 Registered Pension Schemes (Bridging Pensions) and Appointed Day Regulations 2016
SI 2016/1181 Corporation Tax Act 2010 (Profits Arising from the Exploitation of Patents) Foreign Taxes Designation Regulations 2016
SI 2016/1195 Donations to Charity (Gift Aid Declarations) Regulations 2016
SI 2016/1212 Bank Levy (Double Taxation Relief) (Single Resolution Fund Levy) Regulations 2016
SI 2016/1244 Annual Tax on Enveloped Dwellings (Indexation of Annual Chargeable Amounts) (No 2) Order 2016
SI 2016/1250 Sporting Testimonial Payments (Excluded Relevant Step) Regulations 2016
SI 2017/10 Taxation of Chargeable Gains (Gilt-edged Securities) Order 2017
SI 2017/292 Investment Allowance and Cluster Area Allowance (Investment Expenditure) Regulations 2017
SI 2017/334 Asset-based Penalty for Offshore Inaccuracies and Failures (Reductions for Disclosure and Co-operation) Regulations 2017
SI 2017/345 Penalties Relating to Offshore Matters and Offshore Transfers (Additional Information) Regulations 2017
SI 2017/377 Capital Gains Tax (Annual Exempt Amount) Order 2017
SI 2017/446 Scottish Infected Blood Support Scheme (Application of Sections 731, 733 and 734 of the Income Tax (Trading and Other Income) Act 2005) Order 2017
SI 2017/614 Major Sporting Events (Income Tax Exemption) Regulations 2017
SI 2017/692 Money Laundering, Terrorist Financing and Transfer of Funds (Information on the Payer) Regulations 2017
SI 2017/876 Facilitation of Tax Evasion Offences (Guidance About Prevention) Regulations 2017
SI 2017/904 Infected Blood Schemes (Application of Sections 731, 733 and 734 of

Alphabetical list of printed Statutory Instruments

Note—

For the chronological list of printed statutory instruments, *see above*.

SI 2004/1450 Child Trust Funds Regulations 2004
SI 1998/3132 Civil Procedure Rules 1998 (Orders 53, 55, 77 and 91 only)
SI 2015/725 Community Amateur Sports Clubs Regulations 2015
SI 2003/96 Community Investment Tax Relief (Accreditation of Community Development Finance Institutions) Regulations 2003
SI 2000/3158 Controlled Foreign Companies (Designer Rate Tax Provisions) Regulations 2000
SI 2012/3041 Controlled Foreign Companies (Excluded Banking Business Profits) Regulations 2012
SI 1998/3081 Controlled Foreign Companies (Excluded Countries) Regulations 1998
SI 2012/3024 Controlled Foreign Companies (Excluded Territories) Regulations 2012
SI 2011/1784 Corporation Tax Act 2010 (Factors Determining Substantial Commercial Interdependence) Order 2011
SI 2016/1181 Corporation Tax Act 2010 (Profits Arising from the Exploitation of Patents) Foreign Taxes Designation Regulations2016
SI 1992/3066 Corporation Tax Acts (Provisions for Payment of Tax and Returns) (Appointed Days) Order 1992
SI 2009/3313 Corporation Tax (Exclusion from Short-Term Loan Relationships) Regulations 2009 (revoked)
SI 2002/1967 Corporation Tax (Finance Leasing of Intangible Assets) Regulations 2002
SI 2009/3173 Corporation Tax (Financing Costs and Income) Regulations 2009 (revoked)
SI 2007/3186 Corporation Tax (Implementation of the Mergers Directive) Regulations 2007
SI 2008/1579 Corporation Tax (Implementation of the Mergers Directive) Regulations 2008
SI 1998/3175 Corporation Tax (Instalment Payments) Regulations 1998
SI 2009/2037 Corporation Tax (Land Remediation Relief) Order 2009
SI 2004/2502 Corporation Tax (Notice of Coming within Charge—Information) Regulations 2004
SI 1999/2975 Corporation Tax (Simplified Arrangements for Group Relief) Regulations 1999
SI 2007/678 Corporation Tax (Surrender of Terminal Losses on Films and Claims for Relief) Regulations 2007
SI 2007/1050 Corporation Tax (Taxation of Films) (Transitional Provisions) Regulations 2007
SI 2009/3217 Corporation Tax (Tax Treatment of Financing Costs and Income) (Acceptable Financial Statements) Regulations 2009 (revoked)
SI 1999/358 Corporation Tax (Treatment of Unrelieved Surplus Advance Corporation Tax) Regulations 1999
SI 1981/233 Crown Proceedings (Northern Ireland) Order 1981
SI 2013/1831 Cultural Test (Television Programmes) Regulations 2013
SI 2015/1449 Cultural Test (Television Programmes) (Amendment) Regulations 2015
SI 2014/1958 Cultural Test (Video Games) Regulations 2014
SI 1995/1370 Deposit-takers (Interest Payments) (Discretionary or Accumulation Trusts) Regulations 1995
SI 1994/236 Distraint by Collectors (Fees, Costs and Charges) Regulations 1994
SI 2009/3314 Distributions (Excluded Companies) Regulations 2009
SI 2000/2074 Donations to Charity by Individuals (Appropriate Declarations) Regulations 2000
SI 2016/1195 Donations to Charity (Gift Aid Declarations) Regulations 2016
SI 2001/1163 Double Taxation Relief (Surrender of Relievable Tax Within a Group) Regulations 2001
SI 1999/3330 Double Taxation Relief (Taxes on Income) (Foreign Interest and Dividends) Regulations 1999
SI 1993/1957 Double Taxation Relief (Taxes on Income) (General) (Manufactured Overseas Dividends) Regulations 1993
SI 1970/488 Double Taxation Relief (Taxes on Income) (General) Regulations 1970
SI 2001/1156 Double Taxation Relief (Taxes on Income) (Underlying Tax on Dividends and Dual Resident Companies) Regulations 2001
SI 1997/57 Electronic Lodgement of Tax Returns Order 1997
SI 2000/2090 Employee Share Ownership Plans (Partnership Shares—Notice of Effects on Benefits, Statutory Sick Pay and Statutory Maternity Pay) Regulations 2000
SI 2006/210 Employer-Financed Retirement Benefits (Excluded Benefits for Tax Purposes) Regulations 2006
SI 2010/4 Employers' Duties (Implementation) Regulations 2010
SI 2010/5 Employers' Duties (Registration and Compliance) Regulations 2010

SI 2007/2532 Finance Act 2007, Schedule 25 (Commencement and Transitional Provisions) Order 2007
SI 2009/404 Finance Act 2008, Schedule 36 (Appointed Day and Savings) Order 2009
SI 2009/403 Finance Act 2008, Schedule 39 (Appointed Day, Transitional Provision and Savings) Order 2009
SI 2009/571 Finance Act 2008, Schedule 40 (Appointed Day, Transitional Provisions and Consequential Amendments) Order 2009
SI 2009/511 Finance Act 2008, Schedule 41 (Appointed Day and Transitional Provisions) Order 2009/511
SI 2009/3024 Finance Act 2008, Section 128 and Part 2 of Schedule 43 (Appointed Day, Transitional Provision and Savings) Order 2009
SI 2008/1936 Finance Act 2008 Section 135 (Disaster or Emergency) Order 2008
SI 2014/2395 Finance Act 2009, Schedule 55 (Penalties for failure to make returns) (Appointed Days and Consequential Provision) Order 2014
SI 2010/466 Finance Act 2009, Schedule 56 (Appointed Day and Consequential Provisions) Order 2010
SI 2010/1878 Finance Act 2009, Sections 101 to 103 (Appointed Day and Supplemental Provision) Order 2010
SI 2015/549 Finance Act 2014 (High Risk Promoters Prescribed Information) Regulations 2015
SI 2015/131 Finance Act 2014 (Schedule 34 Prescribed Matters) Regulations 2015
SI 2010/1187 Financial Assistance Scheme (Tax) Regulations 2010
SI 2008/1926 Financing-Arrangement-Funded Transfers to Shareholders Regulations 2008
SI 2010/2655 First-tier Tribunal and Upper Tribunal (Chambers) Order 2010
SI 2008/2835 First-tier Tribunal and Upper Tribunal (Composition of Tribunal) Order 2008
SI 1977/1143 Friendly Societies (Life Assurance Premium Relief) Regulations 1977
SI 1980/1947 Friendly Societies (Life Assurance Premium Relief) (Change of Rate) Regulations 1980
SI 2005/2014 Friendly Societies (Modification of the Corporation Tax Acts) Regulations 2005
SI 2012/3008 Friendly Societies (Modifications of the Tax Acts) Regulations 2012
SI 2001/3973 Friendly Societies (Provisional Repayments for Exempt Business) (Amendment) Regulations 2001
SI 1008/1942 Friendly Societies (Transfers of Other Business) (Modification of the Corporation Tax Acts) Regulations 2008
SI 2001/1757 General Insurance Reserves (Tax) Regulations 2001
SI 2009/1926 General Insurers' Technical Provisions (Appropriate Amount) (Tax) Regulations 2009
SI 1999/2118 Gifts for Relief in Poor Countries (Designation of Kosovo) Order 1999
SI 1998/1868 Gifts for Relief in Poor Countries (Designation) Order 1998
SI 2014/1327 Government Alternative Finance Arrangements Regulations 2014
SI 2006/3389 Group Relief for Overseas Losses (Modification of the Corporation Tax Acts for Non-resident Insurance Companies) (No 2) Regulations 2006
SI 2008/2646 Group Relief for Overseas Losses (Modification of the Corporation Tax Acts for Non-resident Insurance Companies) Regulations 2008
SI 2015/1540 Housing and Regeneration Transfer Schemes (Tax Consequences) Regulations 2015
SI 2003/3143 Income and Corporation Taxes (Electronic Certificates of Deduction of Tax and Tax Credit) Regulations 2003
SI 2003/282 Income and Corporation Taxes (Electronic Communications) Regulations 2003
SI 2015/1948 Income Tax (Approved Expenses) Regulations 2015
SI 2003/1830 Income Tax (Authorised Unit Trusts) (Interest Distributions) Regulations 2003
SI 2002/1596 Income Tax (Benefits in Kind) (Exemption for Employment Costs resulting from Disability) Regulations 2002
SI 2000/2080 Income Tax (Benefits in Kind) (Exemption for Welfare Counselling) Regulations 2000
SI 2007/3000 Income Tax (Benefits Received by Former Owner of Property) (Election for Inheritance Tax Treatment) Regulations 2007
SI 1992/10 Income Tax (Building Societies) (Audit Powers) Regulations 1992
SI 1990/2231 Income Tax (Building Societies) (Dividends and Interest) Regulations 1990 (revoked)
SI 2001/1123 Income Tax (Car Benefits) (Reduction of Value of Appropriate Percentage) Regulations 2001

SI 1995/1730 Insurance Companies (Taxation of Reinsurance Business) Regulations 1995
SI 2003/1828 Insurance Companies (Taxation of Reinsurance Business) (Amendment) Regulations
SI 2012/3009 Insurance Companies (Transitional Provisions) Regulations 2012
SI 2015/878 International Tax Compliance Regulations 2015
SI 2007/2126 International Mutual Administrative Assistance in Tax Matters Order 2007
SI 1997/168 International Organisations (Miscellaneous Exemptions) Order 1997
SI 2014/520 International Tax Compliance (Crown Dependencies and Gibraltar) Regulations 2014
SI 2015/878 International Tax Compliance Regulations 2015
SI 2013/1962 International Tax Compliance (United States of America) Regulations 2013 (revoked)
SI 2014/1506 International Tax Compliance (United States of America) Regulations 2014 (revoked)
SI 2017/292 Investment Allowance and Cluster Area Allowance (Investment Expenditure) Regulations 2017
SI 2014/April Investment Manager (Investment Transactions) Regulations 2014
SI 2009/May Investment Manager (Specified Transactions) Regulations 2009 (revoked)
SI 2006/1959 Investment-regulated Pension Schemes (Exception of Tangible Moveable Property) Order 2006
SI 2014/685 Investment Transactions (Tax) Regulations 2014
SI 2006/1182 Investment Trusts and Venture Capital Trusts (Definition of Capital Profits, Gains or Losses) Order 2006
SI 2001/391 Investment Trusts (Approval of Accounting Methods for Creditor Relationships) Order 2001
SI 2009/2034 Investment Trusts (Dividends) (Optional Treatment as Interest Distributions) Regulations 2009
SI 1997/265 Life Assurance and Other Policies (Keeping of Information and Duties of Insurers) Regulations 1997
SI 2013/1820 Life Insurance Qualifying Policies (Statement and Reporting Requirements) Regulations 2013
SI 1997/405 Lloyd's Underwriters (Double Taxation Relief) Regulations 1997
SI 2006/3262 Lloyd's Underwriters (Double Taxation Relief) (Corporate Members) Regulations 2006
SI 2009/2039 Lloyd's Underwriters (Equalisation Reserves) (Tax) Regulations 2009 (revoked)
SI 1997/2681 Lloyd's Underwriters (Partnerships) (Tax) 1997
SI 1995/353 Lloyd's Underwriters (Special Reserve Funds) Regulations 1995
SI 1999/3308 Lloyd's Underwriters (Special Reserve Funds) Regulations 1999
SI 1995/351 Lloyd's Underwriters (Tax) Regulations 1995
SI 2005/3338 Lloyd's Underwriters (Tax) Regulations 2005
SI 2015/1983 Lloyd's Underwriters (Transitional Equalisation Reserves) (Tax) Regulations 2015
SI 2004/3271 Loan Relationships and Derivative Contracts (Change of Accounting Practice) Regulations 2004
SI 2004/3256 Loan Relationships and Derivative Contracts (Disregard and Bringing into Account of Profits and Losses) Regulations 2004
SI 2006/843 Loan Relationships and Derivative Contracts (Disregard and Bringing into Account of Profits and Losses) Regulations 2006
SI 2014/3188 Loan Relationships and Derivative Contracts (Disregard and Bringing into Account of Profits and Losses) (Amendment) Regulations 2014
SI 2005/3422 Loan Relationships and Derivative Contracts (Exchange Gains and Losses using Fair Value Accounting) Regulations 2005
SI 2012/701 London Legacy Development Corporation (Tax Consequences) Regulations 2012
SI 2010/2913 London Olympic Games and Paralympic Games Tax Regulations
SI 2007/304 Long Funding Leases (Elections) Regulations 2007
SI 2016/771 Major Sporting Events (Income Tax Exemption) Regulations 2016
SI 2017/614 Major Sporting Events (Income Tax Exemption) Regulations 2017
SI 1997/993 Manufactured Dividends (Tax) Regulations 1997
SI 1996/1826 Manufactured Overseas Dividends (French Indemnity Payments) Regulations 1996
SI 1995/3036 Manufactured Payments and Transfer of Securities (Tax Relief) Regulations 1995

SI 2016/209 Proceeds of Crime Act 2002 (Investigations: Code of Practice) (England and Wales and Northern Ireland) Order 2016
SI 2016/222 Proceeds of Crime Act 2002 (Investigative Powers of Prosecutors: Code of Practice) (England and Wales and Northern Ireland) Order 2016
SI 2013/420 Profits from Patents (EEA Rights) Order 2013
SI 2015/130 Promoters of Tax Avoidance Schemes (Prescribed Circumstances under Section 235) Regulations 2015
SI 2014/834 Public Bodies (Merger of the Director of Public Prosecutions and the Director of Revenue and Customs Prosecutions) Order 2014
SI 2011/712 Qualifying Care Relief (Specified Social Care Schemes) Order 2011
SI 2015/2002 Qualifying Private Placement Regulations 2015
SI 2006/2867 Real Estate Investment Trusts (Assessment and Recovery of Tax) Regulations 2006
SI 2006/2864 Real Estate Investment Trusts (Breach of Conditions) Regulations 2006
SI 2006/2865 Real Estate Investment Trusts (Financial Statements of Group Real Estate Investment Trusts) Regulations 2006
SI 2006/2866 Real Estate Investment Trusts (Joint Ventures) Regulations 2006 (revoked)
SI 2007/3425 Real Estate Investment Trusts (Joint Venture Groups) Regulations 2007 (revoked)
SI 2009/3315 Real Estate Investment Trusts (Prescribed Arrangements) Regulations 2009
SI 2004/674 Recovery of Duties and Taxes etc Due in Other Member States (Corresponding UK Claims, Procedure and Supplementary) Regulations 2004
SI 2007/3507 Recovery of Foreign Taxes Regulations 2007
SI 2005/3454 Registered Pension Schemes (Accounting and Assessment) Regulations 2005
SI 2006/570 Registered Pension Schemes and Overseas Pension Schemes (Electronic Communication of Returns and Information) Regulations 2006
SI 2013/1741 Registered Pension Schemes and Relieved Non-UK Pension Schemes (Lifetime Allowance Transitional Protection) (Notification) Regulations 2013
SI 2014/1842 Registered Pension Schemes and Relieved Non-UK Pension Schemes (Lifetime Allowance Transitional Protection) (Individual Protection 2014 Notification) Regulations 2014
SI 2006/137 Registered Pension Schemes (Authorised Member Payments) Regulations 2006
SI 2007/3532 Registered Pension Schemes (Authorised Member Payments) Regulations 2007
SI 2006/571 Registered Pension Schemes (Authorised Member Payments) (No 2) Regulations 2006
SI 2006/209 Registered Pension Schemes (Authorised Payments) Regulations 2006
SI 2009/1171 Registered Pension Schemes (Authorised Payments) Regulations 2009
SI 2006/614 Registered Pension Schemes (Authorised Payments—Arrears of Pension) Regulations 2006
SI 2006/134 Registered Pension Schemes (Authorised Payments) (Transfers to the Pension Protection Fund) Regulations 2006
SI 2006/1465 Registered Pension Schemes (Authorised Reductions) Regulations 2006
SI 2006/574 Registered Pension Schemes (Authorised Surplus Payments) Regulations 2006
SI 2006/498 Registered Pension Schemes (Block Transfers) (Permitted Membership Period) Regulations 2006
SI 2007/826 Registered Pension Schemes (Bridging Pensions) Regulations 2007
SI 2016/1005 Registered Pension Schemes (Bridging Pensions) and Appointed Day Regulations 2016
SI 2006/133 Registered Pension Schemes (Co-ownership of Living Accommodation) Regulations 2006
SI 2006/131 Registered Pension Schemes (Enhanced Lifetime Allowance) Regulations 2006
SI 2010/650 Registered Pension Schemes etc (Information) (Prescribed Descriptions of Persons) Regulations 2010
SI 2006/1957 Registered Pension Schemes (Extension of Migrant Member Relief) Regulations 2006
SI 2011/1752 Registered Pension Schemes (Lifetime Allowance Transitional Protection) Regulations 2011
SI 2006/135 Registered Pension Schemes (Meaning of Pension Commencement Lump Sum) Regulations 2006
SI 2006/364 Registered Pension Schemes (Modification of the Rules of Existing Schemes) Regulations 2006

SI 2017/1022 Tax Collection and Management (Administration) (Wales) Regulations 2017

SI 2008/2603 Taxation of Benefits under Government Pilot Schemes (Better off in Work Credit) Order 2008

SI 2003/2339 Taxation of Benefits under Government Pilot Schemes (Return to Work Credit and Employment Retention and Advancement Schemes) Order 2003

SI 2008/1464 Taxation of Benefits under Government Pilot Schemes (Up-Front Childcare Fund) Order 2008

SI 1996/2396 Taxation of Benefits under Pilot Schemes (Earnings Top-up) Order 1996

SI 2006/184 Taxation of Chargeable Gains (Gilt-edged Securities) Order 2006

SI 2008/1588 Taxation of Chargeable Gains (Gilt-edged Securities) Order 2008

SI 2010/416 Taxation of Chargeable Gains (Gilt-edged Securities) Order 2010

SI 2012/1843 Taxation of Chargeable Gains (Gilt-edged Securities) Order 2012

SI 2013/13 Taxation of Chargeable Gains (Gilt-edged Securities) Order 2013

SI 2013/2983 Taxation of Chargeable Gains (Gilt-edged Securities) (No 2) Order 2013

SI 2014/1120 Taxation of Chargeable Gains (Gilt-edged Securities) Order 2014

SI 2015/1790 Taxation of Chargeable Gains (Gilt-edged Securities) Order 2015

SI 2017/10 Taxation of Chargeable Gains (Gilt-edged Securities) Order 2017

SI 1995/2902 Taxation of Income from Land (Non-residents) Regulations 1995

SI 2007/3402 Taxation of Insurance Securitisation Companies Regulations 2007

SI 2006/497 Taxation of Judicial Pensions (Consequential Provisions) Order 2006

SI 2006/572 Taxation of Pension Schemes (Transitional Provisions) Order 2006

SI 2013/3209 Taxation of Regulatory Capital Securities Regulations 2013

SI 2004/1864 Tax Avoidance Schemes (Information) Regulations 2004 (revoked)

SI 2012/1836 Tax Avoidance Schemes (Information) Regulations 2012

SI 2007/3104 Tax Avoidance Schemes (Penalty) Regulations 2007

SI 2009/2033 Tax Avoidance Schemes (Prescribed Descriptions of Arrangements) (Amendment) Regulations 2009

SI 2004/1863 Tax Avoidance Schemes (Prescribed Descriptions of Arrangements) Regulations 2004

SI 2006/1543 Tax Avoidance Schemes (Prescribed Descriptions of Arrangements) Regulations 2006

SI 2004/1865 Tax Avoidance Schemes (Promoters and Prescribed Circumstances) Regulations 2004

SI 2017/1022 Tax Collection and Management (Administration) (Wales) Regulations 2017

SI 1990/2361 Tax-exempt Special Savings Account Regulations 1990 (lapsed)

SI 1995/3239 Tax-exempt Special Savings Account (Relevant European Institutions) Regulations 1995

SI 2009/3333 Tax Credits (Excluded Companies) Regulations 2009

SI 2010/1879 Taxes and Duties (Interest Rate) Regulations 2010

SI 2016/237 Taxes (Base Erosion and Profit Shifting) (Country-by-Country Reporting) Regulations 2016

SI 2010/1904 Taxes (Definition of Charity) (Relevant Territories) Regulations 2010

SI 2014/1807 Taxes (Definition of Charity) (Relevant Territories) (Amendment) Regulations 2014

SI 2011/711 Taxes, etc (Fees for Payment by Internet) Regulations 2011 (revoked)

SI 2008/2008 Taxes (Fees for Payment by Telephone) Regulations 2008

SI 2009/3073 Taxes, etc (Fees for Payment by Telephone) Regulations 2009 (revoked)

SI 1989/1297 Taxes (Interest Rate) Regulations 1989

SI 1992/42 Taxes (Relief for Gifts) (Designated Educational Establishments) Regulations 1992

SI 2014/3066 Tax Relief for Social Investments (Accreditation of Social Impact Contractor) Regulations 2014

SI 2013/2892 Tax Treatment of Financing Costs and Income (Excluded Schemes) Regulations 2013 (revoked)

SI 2010/2929 Treatment of Financing Costs and Income (Available Amount) Regulations 2010 (revoked)

SI 2004/1819 Thalidomide Children's Trust (Application of Section 329AA of the Income and Corporation Taxes Act 1988) Order 2004

SI 2000/2303 Tonnage Tax Regulations 2000

SI 2006/333 Tonnage Tax (Exception of Financial Year 2006) Order 2006

SI 2007/850 Tonnage Tax (Exception of Financial Year 2007) Order 2007

SI 2005/1449 Tonnage Tax (Further Opportunity for Election) Order 2005

Chronological list of Statutory Instruments

Note—

The following is the list of current and amending instruments.

For the list of current instruments which are reproduced in this work, *see above*.

For an alphabetical list, *see above*.

SI 1986/387 CGT (Parallel Pooling) Regulations 1986
SI 1986/482 *IT (Building Societies) Regulations 1986* (see SI 1990/2231; SI 1991/512)
SI 1986/2211 Charitable Deductions (Approved Schemes) Regulations 1986
SI 1987/352 *Pension Scheme Surpluses (Administration) Regulations 1987* (lapsed)
SI 1987/412 *Pension Scheme Surpluses (Valuation) Regulations 1987* (lapsed)
SI 1987/530 IT (Entertainers and Sportsmen) Regulations 1987
SI 1987/844 *IT (Building Societies) (Amendment) Regulations 1987* (amend SI 1986/482)
SI 1987/1513 *Occupational Pension Schemes (Maximum Rate Lump Sum) Regulations 1987* (lapsed)
SI 1987/1749 *Occupational Pension Schemes (Additional Voluntary Contributions) Regulations 1987* (lapsed)
SI 1987/1765 *Personal Pension Schemes (Provisional Approval) Regulations 1987* (lapsed)
SI 1988/88 *DTR (Taxes on Income) (Foreign Loan Interest) Regulations 1988* (revoked)
SI 1988/266 CGT (Definition of Unit Trust Scheme) Regulations 1988
SI 1988/267 IT (Definition of Unit Trust Scheme) Regulations 1988
SI 1988/504 *Occupational Pension Schemes (Rate of Tax under Paragraph 2(2) of Part II of Schedule 5 to the Finance Act 1970) Order 1988* (see TA 1988 s 598)
SI 1988/993 *Personal Pension Schemes (Establishment of Schemes) Order 1988* (amends TA 1988 s 632)
SI 1988/1012 Personal Pension Schemes (Minimum Contributions under the Social Security Act 1986) Regulations 1988
SI 1988/1013 Personal Pension Schemes (Relief at Source) Regulations 1988
SI 1988/1014 *Personal Pension Schemes (Transfer Payments) Regulations 1988* (revoked)
SI 1988/1347 *IT (Interest Relief) (Housing Associations) Regulations 1988* (lapsed)
SI 1988/1436 *Occupational Pension Schemes (Transitional Provisions) Regulations 1988* (lapsed)
SI 1989/469 Personal Equity Plan Regulations 1989 (revoked)
SI 1989/992 *Transfer of Functions (Economic Statistics) Order 1989* (amend SI 1987/412)
SI 1989/1115 Personal Pension Schemes (Transfer Payments) (Amendment) Regulations 1989 (amend SI 1988/1014) (revoked)
SI 1989/1297 Taxes (Interest Rate) Regulations 1989
SI 1989/1299 IT (Stock Lending) Regulations 1989 (revoked)
SI 1989/2290 *Pension Scheme Surpluses (Valuation) (Amendment) Regulations 1989* (amend SI 1987/412)
SI 1989/2387 Private Medical Insurance (Tax Relief) Regulations 1989
SI 1990/585 Occupational Pension Schemes (Additional Voluntary Contributions) (Amendment) Regulations 1990 (amend SI 1987/1749)
SI 1990/586 Retirement Benefits Schemes (Tax Relief on Contributions) (Disapplication of Earnings Cap) Regulations 1990 (lapsed)
SI 1990/626 IT (Purchased Life Annuities) (Amendment) Regulations 1990 (amend SI 1956/1230)
SI 1990/678 Personal Equity Plan (Amendment) Regulations 1990 (amend SI 1989/469)
SI 1990/1671 Movements of Capital (Required Information) Regulations 1990
SI 1990/2101 Retirement Benefit Schemes (Continuation of Rights of Members of Approved Schemes) Regulations 1990 (lapsed)
SI 1990/2231 IT (Building Societies) (Dividends and Interest) Regulations 1990 (revoked)
SI 1990/2232 IT (Deposit-takers) (Interest Payments) Regulations 1990 (revoked)
SI 1990/2361 Tax-exempt Special Savings Account Regulations 1990 (lapsed)
SI 1990/2546 Life Assurance (Apportionment of Receipts of Participating Funds) (Applicable Percentage) (Amendment) Order 1990 (amend SI 1990/1541)
SI 1991/512 IT (Building Societies) (Annual Payments) Regulations 1991 (repealed)
SI 1991/733 Personal Equity Plan (Amendment) Regulations 1991 (amend SI 1989/469)
SI 1991/889 Taxes (Interest Rate) (Amendment) Regulations 1991 (amend SI 1989/1297)
SI 1991/1614 Retirement Benefits Schemes (Restriction on Discretion to Approve) (Small Self-administered Schemes) Regulations 1991 (lapsed)
SI 1991/1997 Companies Act 1989 (Eligibility for Appointment as Company Auditor) (Consequential Amendments) Regulations 1991 (amend SI 1985/994)
SI 1991/2774 Personal Equity Plan (Amendment No 2) Regulations 1991 (amend SI 1989/469)
SI 1991/2808 IT (Purchased Life Annuities) (Amendment) Regulations 1991 (amend SI 1956/1230)
SI 1992/10 IT (Building Societies) (Audit Powers) Regulations 1992

Schemes) (Amendment) Regulations 1993 (amend SI 1990/2101)

SI 1993/3221 Retirement Benefits Schemes (Tax Relief on Contributions) (Disapplication of Earnings Cap) (Amendment) Regulations 1993 (amend SI 1990/586)

SI 1994/236 Distraint by Collectors (Fees, Costs and Charges) Regulations 1994

SI 1994/295 IT (Deposit-takers) (Interest Payments) (Amendment) Regulations 1994 (amend SI 1990/2232)

SI 1994/296 IT (Building Societies) (Dividends and Interest) (Amendment) Regulations 1994 (amend SI 1990/2231)

SI 1994/775 IT (Employments) (Amendment) Regulations 1994 (amend SI 1993/744)

SI 1994/777 IT (Car Benefits) (Replacement Accessories) Regulations 1994 (revoked)

SI 1994/778 IT (Replacement Cars) Regulations 1994 (revoked)

SI 1994/1212 IT (Employments) (Notional Payments) Regulations 1994

SI 1994/1307 Taxes (Interest Rate) (Amendment) Regulations 1994 (amend SI 1989/1297)

SI 1994/1479 IT (Definition of Unit Trust Scheme) (Amendment) Regulations 1994 (amend SI 1988/267)

SI 1994/1518 Private Medical Insurance (Disentitlement to Tax Relief and Approved Benefits) Regulations 1994 (lapsed)

SI 1994/1527 Private Medical Insurance (Tax Relief) (Amendment) Regulations 1994 (amend SI 1989/2387)

SI 1994/1567 Taxes (Interest Rate) (Amendment No 2) Regulations 1994 (amend SI 1989/1297)

SI 1994/1811 *Special Commissioners (Jurisdiction and Procedure) Regulations 1994* (revoked)

SI 1994/1812 *General Commissioners (Jurisdiction and Procedure) Regulations 1994* (revoked)

SI 1994/1813 General and Special Commissioners (Amendment of Enactments) Regulations 1994 (amend SI 1967/149, SI 1993/744)

SI 1994/2318 IT (Authorised Unit Trusts) (Interest Distributions) Regulations 1994

SI 1994/2656 Capital Gains Tax (Gilt-edged Securities) Order 1994

SI 1994/3036 Insurance Companies (Pension Business) (Transitional Provisions) (Amendment) Regulations 1994 (amend SI 1992/2326)

SI 1994/3226 Exchange Gains and Losses (Transitional Provisions) Regulations 1994

SI 1994/3227 Exchange Gains and Losses (Alternative Method of Calculation of Gain or Loss) Regulations 1994

SI 1994/3228 Exchange Gains and Losses (Deferral of Gains and Losses) Regulations 1994 (lapsed)

SI 1994/3229 Exchange Gains and Losses (Excess Gains and Losses) Regulations 1994 (lapsed)

SI 1994/3230 *Local Currency Elections Regulations 1994* (lapsed)

SI 1994/3231 Exchange Gains and Losses (Insurance Companies) Regulations 1994

SI 1994/3232 Exchange Gains and Losses (Debts of Varying Amounts) Regulations 1994 (insert FA 1993 s 136A)

SI 1994/3233 Currency Contracts and Options (Amendment of Enactments) Order 1994 (amends FA 1993 s 126, FA 1994 s 150)

SI 1994/3278 Overseas Life Assurance Fund (Amendment) Order 1994 (amends TA 1988 Sch 19AA)

SI 1995/171 Friendly Societies (Taxation of Transfers of Business) Regulations 1995 (revoked)

SI 1995/351 Lloyd's Underwriters (Tax) Regulations 1995

SI 1995/352 Lloyd's Underwriters (Tax) (1992–93 to 1996–97) Regulations 1995 (spent)

SI 1995/353 Lloyd's Underwriters (Special Reserve Fund) Regulations 1995

SI 1995/408 Exchange Gains and Losses (Transitional Provisions) (Amendment) Regulations 1995 (amend SI 1994/3226)

SI 1995/447 IT (Employments) (Amendment No 2) Regulations 1995 (amend SI 1993/744)

SI 1995/448 IT (Sub-contractors in the Construction Industry) (Amendment No 2) Regulations 1995 (amend SI 1993/743) (revoked)

SI 1995/853 IT (Employments) (Incapacity Benefit) Regulations 1995 (amend SI 1993/744)

SI 1995/917 *Profit-Related Pay (Shortfall Recovery) Regulation 1995* (lapsed)

SI 1995/1184 IT (Building Societies) (Dividends and Interest) (Amendment) Regulations 1995 (amend SI 1990/2231)

SI 1995/1185 Lloyd's Underwriters (Special Reserve Funds) (Amendment) Regulations 1995 (amend SI 1995/353)

SI 1995/1211 Life Assurance (Apportionment of Receipts of Participating Funds) (Applicable Percentage) (Amendment) Order 1995 (amend SI 1990/1541)
SI 1995/1212 IT (Interest Relief) (Housing Associations) (Amendment) Regulations 1995 (amend SI 1988/1347)
SI 1995/1213 IT (Interest Relief) (Amendment) Regulations 1995 (amend SI 1982/1236)
SI 1995/1223 IT (Employments) (Amendment No 3) Regulations 1995 (amend SI 1993/744)
SI 1995/1284 IT (Employments) (Amendment No 4) Regulations 1995 (amend SI 1993/744)
SI 1995/1324 IT (Manufactured Overseas Dividends) (Amendment) Regulations 1995 (amend SI 1993/2004)
SI 1995/1370 Deposit-takers (Interest Payments) (Discretionary or Accumulation Trusts) Regulations 1995
SI 1995/1539 Personal Equity Plan (Amendment) Regulations 1995 (amend SI 1989/469)
SI 1995/1551 Double Taxation Relief (Manufactured Overseas Dividends) (Amendment) Regulations 1995 (amend SI 1993/1957)
SI 1995/1730 Insurance Companies (Taxation of Reinsurance Business) Regulations 1995
SI 1995/1929 Tax-exempt Special Savings Account (Amendment) Regulations 1995 (amend SI 1990/2361)
SI 1995/1979 Venture Capital Trust Regulations 1995
SI 1995/2050 *IT (Dealers in Securities) (Tradepoint) Regulations 1995* (lapsed)
SI 1995/2052 IT (Manufactured Dividends) (Tradepoint) Regulations 1995 (revoked)
SI 1995/2151 Distraint by Collectors (Fees, Costs and Charges) (Amendment) Regulations 1995 (amend SI 1994/236)
SI 1995/2902 Taxation of Income from Land (Non-residents) Regulations 1995
SI 1995/2934 IT (Gilt-edged Securities) (Gross Payments of Interest) Regulations 1995 (lapsed)
SI 1995/3036 Manufactured Payments and Transfer of Securities (Tax Relief) Regulations 1995
SI 1995/3103 Retirement Benefits Schemes (Information Powers) Regulations 1995 (lapsed)
SI 1995/3134 Insurance Companies (Pension Business) (Transitional Provisions) (Amendment) Regulations 1995 (amend SI 1992/2326)
SI 1995/3192 *Retirement Age of General Commissioners Order 1995* (revoked)
SI 1995/3220 *Sale and Repurchase of Securities (Modification of Enactments) Regulations 1995* (revoked)
SI 1995/3224 Gilt-edged Securities (Periodic Accounting for Tax on Interest) Regulations 1995 (lapsed)
SI 1995/3225 Lloyd's Underwriters (Gilt-edged Securities) (Periodic Accounting for Tax on Interest) Regulations 1995 (lapsed)
SI 1995/3237 Insurance Companies (Overseas Life Assurance Business) (Compliance) Regulations 1995
SI 1995/3238 *Insurance Companies (Overseas Life Assurance Business) (Tax Credit) Regulations 1995* (lapsed)
SI 1995/3239 Tax-exempt Special Savings Account (Relevant European Institutions) Regulations 1995
SI 1995/3274 Vocational Training (Public Financial Assistance and Disentitlement to Tax Relief) (Amendment) Regulations 1995 (amend SI 1992/734 (lapsed))
SI 1995/3287 Personal Equity Plan (Amendment No 2) Regulations 1995 (amend SI 1989/469)
SI 1996/1 Insurance Companies (Pension Business) (Transitional Provisions) (Amendment) Regulations 1996 (amend SI 1992/2326)
SI 1996/223 IT (Building Societies) (Dividends and Interest) (Amendment) Regulations 1996 (amend SI 1990/2231)
SI 1996/673 Exchange Gains and Losses (Insurance Companies) (Amendment) Regulations 1996 (amend SI 1994/3231)
SI 1996/781 Lloyd's Underwriters (Tax) (Amendment) Regulations 1996 (amend SI 1995/351)
SI 1996/782 Lloyd's Underwriters (Tax) (1992–93 to 1996–97) (Amendment) Regulations 1996 (amend SI 1995/352 (spent))
SI 1996/783 Double Taxation Relief (Taxes on Income) (General) (Amendment) Regulations 1996 (amend SI 1970/488)
SI 1996/804 IT (Employments) (Amendment) Regulations 1996 (amend SI 1993/744)
SI 1996/805 Personal Pension Schemes (Deferred Annuity Purchase) (Acceptance of Contributions) Regulations 1996 (lapsed)

SI 1996/844 Tax-exempt Special Savings Account (Amendment) Regulations 1996 (amend SI 1990/2361)
SI 1996/846 Personal Equity Plan (Amendment) Regulations 1996 (amend SI 1989/469)
SI 1996/980 IT (Employments) (Amendment No 2) Regulations 1996 (amend SI 1993/744)
SI 1996/981 IT (Sub-contractors in the Construction Industry) (Amendment) Regulations 1996 (amend SI 1993/743) (revoked)
SI 1996/1014 Lloyd's Underwriters (Gilt-edged Securities) (Periodic Accounting for Tax on Interest) (Amendment) Regulations 1996 (amend SI 1995/3225)
SI 1996/1015 Gilt-edged Securities (Periodic Accounting for Tax on Interest) (Amendment) Regulations 1996 (amend SI 1995/3224)
SI 1996/1031 Capital Gains Tax (Gilt-edged Securities) Order 1996
SI 1996/1179 European Investment Bank (Designated International Organisation) Order 1996 (repealed)
SI 1996/1181 Gilt-edged Securities (Periodic Accounting for Tax on Interest) (Amendment No 2) Regulations 1996 (amend SI 1995/3224)
SI 1996/1182 Lloyd's Underwriters (Gilt-edged Securities) (Periodic Accounting for Tax on Interest) (Amendment No 2) Regulations 1996 (amend SI 1995/3225)
SI 1996/1184 Income Tax (Interest Relief) (Amendment) Regulations 1996 (amend SI 1982/1236)
SI 1996/1185 Vocational Training (Tax Relief) (Amendment) Regulations 1996 (amend SI 1992/746 (lapsed))
SI 1996/1229 Income Tax (Manufactured Overseas Dividends) (Amendment) Regulations 1996 (amend SI 1993/2004)
SI 1996/1311 Personal Pension Schemes (Tables of Rates of Annuities) Regulations 1996 (lapsed)
SI 1996/1312 Income Tax (Employments) (Amendment No 3) Regulations 1996 (amend SI 1993/744)
SI 1996/1323 Capital Allowances Act 1990, section 33A, (Appointed Day) Order 1996 (lapsed)
SI 1996/1347 Exchange Gains and Losses (Alternative Method of Calculation of Gain or Loss) (Amendment) Regulations 1996 (amend SI 1994/3227)
SI 1996/1348 Exchange Gains and Losses (Deferral of Gains and Losses) (Amendment) Regulations 1996 (amend SI 1994/3228)
SI 1996/1349 Exchange Gains and Losses (Transitional Provisions) (Amendment) Regulations 1996 (amend SI 1994/3226)
SI 1996/1355 Personal Equity Plan (Amendment No 2) Regulations 1996 (amend SI 1989/469)
SI 1996/1485 Exchange Gains and Losses (Insurance Companies) (Amendment No 2) Regulations 1996 (amend SI 1994/3231)
SI 1996/1582 Retirement Benefits Schemes (Restriction on Discretion to Approve) (Excepted Schemes) Regulations 1996 (lapsed)
SI 1996/1583 Capital Gains Tax (Pension Funds Pooling Schemes) Regulations 1996
SI 1996/1585 Income Tax (Pension Funds Pooling Schemes) Regulations 1996
SI 1996/1621 Insurance Companies (Taxation of Reinsurance Business) (Amendment) Regulations 1996 (amend SI 1995/1730)
SI 1996/1654 Income Tax (Payments on Account) Regulations 1996
SI 1996/1780 Income Tax (Paying and Collecting Agents) Regulations 1996 (lapsed)
SI 1996/1826 Manufactured Overseas Dividends (French Indemnity Payments) Regulations 1996
SI 1996/2381 Income Tax (Employments) (Amendment No 4) Regulations 1996 (amend SI 1993/744)
SI 1996/2396 Taxation of Benefits under Pilot Schemes (Earnings Top-up) Order 1996
SI 1996/2554 Income Tax (Employments) (Amendment No 5) Regulations 1996 (amend SI 1993/744)
SI 1996/2616 Income Tax (Interest Relief) (Housing Associations) (Amendment) Regulations 1996 (amend SI 1988/1347)
SI 1996/2631 Income Tax (Employments) (Amendment No 6) Regulations 1996 (amend SI 1993/744)
SI 1996/2642 Manufactured Overseas Dividends (French Indemnity Payments) (Amendment) Regulations 1996 (amend SI 1996/1826)
SI 1996/2643 Income Tax (Manufactured Overseas Dividends) (Amendment No 2) Regulations 1996 (amend SI 1993/2004)

SI 1997/1681 Taxes (Interest Rate) (Amendment) Regulations 1997 (amend SI 1989/1297)
SI 1997/1715 Open-ended Investment Companies (Tax) (Amendment) Regulations 1997 (amend SI 1997/1154)
SI 1997/1716 Personal Equity Plan (Amendment No 2) Regulations 1997 (amend SI 1989/469)
SI 1997/2388 Personal Pension Schemes (Establishment of Schemes) Order 1997 (amends TA 1988 s 632)
SI 1997/2491 Income Tax (Payments on Account) (Amendment) Regulations 1997 (amend SI 1996/1654)
SI 1997/2668 Building Societies Act 1997 (Commencement No 3) Order 1997 (see TA 1988 Sch 12(2))
SI 1997/2681 Lloyd's Underwriters (Partnerships) (Tax) 1997
SI 1997/2706 Income Tax (Manufactured Overseas Dividends) (Amendment No 2) Regulations 1997 (amend SI 1993/2004)
SI 1997/2707 Taxes (Interest Rate) (Amendment No 2) Regulations 1997 (amend SI 1989/1297)
SI 1997/2708 Finance Act 1989 Section 178(1) (Appointed Day) Order 1997 (not reproduced)
SI 1997/2781 Transfer of Functions (Insurance) Order 1997 (amends TA 1998 s 431(2))
SI 1997/2865 Insurance Companies (Pension Business) (Transitional Provisions) (Amendment) Regulations 1997 (amend SI 1992/2326)
SI 1997/2877 Friendly Societies (Modification of the Corporation Tax Acts) (Amendment No 2) Regulations 1997 (amend SI 1997/473)
SI 1998/311 Finance Act 1989 Section 178(1) (Appointed Day) Order 1998
SI 1998/354 Police Act 1997 (Commencement No 5 and Transitional Provisions) Order 1998 (see TA 1988 s 842A)
SI 1998/728 Retirement Benefits Schemes (Restriction on Discretion to Approve) (Small Self-administered Schemes) (Amendment) Regulations 1998 (amend SI 1991/1614)
SI 1998/729 Retirement Benefits Schemes (Restriction on Discretion to Approve) (Excepted Provisions) Regulations 1998 (lapsed)
SI 1998/1315 Retirement Benefits Schemes (Restriction on Discretion to Approve) (Small Self-administered Schemes) (Amendment No 2) Regulations 1998 (amend SI 1991/1614)
SI 1998/1513 Visiting Forces and Allied Headquarters (Income Tax and Capital Gains Tax) (Designation) Order (revoked)
SI 1998/1514 Visiting Forces (Income Tax and Capital Gains Tax) (Designation) Order (revoked)
SI 1998/1868 Gifts for Relief in Poor Countries (Designation) Order 1998
SI 1998/1869 *Personal Equity Plan (Amendment) Regulations 1998* (amend SI 1989/469)
SI 1998/1870 Individual Savings Account Regulations 1998
SI 1998/1871 Individual Savings Account (Insurance Companies) Regulations 1998 (lapsed)
SI 1998/1872 Insurance Companies (Overseas Life Assurance Business) (Compliance) (Amendment) Regulations 1998 (amend SI 1995/3237)
SI 1998/1891 Income Tax (Employments) (Notional Payments) (Amendment) Regulations 1998 (amend SI 1994/1212)
SI 1998/2484 Income Tax (Employments) (Amendment) Regulations 1998 (amend SI 1993/744)
SI 1998/2620 Finance Act 1995, Section 139(3), (Appointed Day) Order 1998
SI 1998/2622 *Income Tax (Sub-contractors in the Construction Industry) (Amendment) Regulations 1998 (amend SI 1993/743)* (revoked)
SI 1998/3081 Controlled Foreign Companies (Excluded Countries) Regulations 1998
SI 1998/3132 Civil Procedure Rules 1998 (Orders 53, 55, 77 and 91 only)
SI 1998/3173 Finance Act 1994, Section 199, (Appointed Day) Order 1998
SI 1998/3174 Individual Savings Account (Amendment) Regulations 1998 (amend SI 1998/1870 and SI 1998/1871)
SI 1998/3175 Corporation Tax (Instalment Payments) Regulations 1998
SI 1998/3176 Taxes (Interest Rate) (Amendment No 2) Regulations 1998 (amend SI 1989/1297)
SI 1998/3177 European Single Currency (Taxes) Regulations 1998
SI 1998/3178 Scotland Act 1998 (Commencement) Order 1998
SI 1999/70 Income Tax (Employments) (Amendment) Regulations 1999 (amend SI 1993/744)
SI 1999/358 Corporation Tax (Treatment of Unrelieved Surplus Advance Corporation Tax) Regulations 1999

SI 1999/3292 Special Commissioners (Jurisdiction and Procedure) (Amendment) Regulations 1999 (amend SI 1994/1811)
SI 1999/3293 General Commissioners (Jurisdiction and Procedure) (Amendment) Regulations 1999 (amend SI 1994/1812)
SI 1999/3308 Lloyd's Underwriters (Special Reserve Funds) Regulations 1999
SI 1999/3309 Welfare Reform and Pensions Act 1999 (Commencement No 1) Order 1999 (not reproduced)
SI 1999/3330 DTR (Taxes on Income) (Foreign Interest and Dividends) Regulations 1999
SI 1999/3420 Welfare Reform and Pensions Act 1999 (Commencement No 2) Order 1999
SI 2000/221 Civil Procedure (Amendment) Rules 2000 (amend SI 1998/3132)
SI 2000/288 Special Commissioners (Jurisdiction and Procedure) (Amendment) Regulations 2000 (amend SI 1994/1811)
SI 2000/600 Income Tax (Charge to Tax) (Payments out of Surplus Funds) (Relevant Rate) Order 2000 (lapsed)
SI 2000/629 Welfare Reform and Pensions Act 1999 (Commencement No 3) Order 2000 (not reproduced)
SI 2000/756 Films (Modification of the Definition of "British Film") Order 2000 (see Film Act 1985 Sch 1)
SI 2000/759 Charitable Deductions (Approved Schemes) (Amendment) Regulations 2000 (amend SI 1986/2211)
SI 2000/806 Income Tax (Indexation) Order 2000 (see TA 1988 ss 1, 257, 257A, 265(1))
SI 2000/807 Retirement Benefits Schemes (Indexation of Earnings Cap) Order 2000 (see TA 1988 s 590C)
SI 2000/808 Capital Gains Tax (Annual Exempt Amount) Order 2000 (see TCGA 1992 s 3)
SI 2000/809 Individual Savings Account (Amendment) Regulations 2000 (amend SI 1998/1870)
SI 2000/810 Income Tax (Cash Equivalents of Car Fuel Benefits) Order 2000 (amends TA 1988 s 158(2))
SI 2000/892 Corporation Tax (Instalment Payments) (Amendment) Regulations 2000 (amend SI 1998/3175)
SI 2000/893 Taxes (Interest Rate) (Amendment) Regulations 2000 (amend SI 1989/1297)
SI 2000/921 Income and Corporation Taxes Act 1988, Section 559(4A), Order 2000 (lapsed)
SI 2000/922 Finance Act 1995, Section 139(3), (Appointed Day) Order 2000
SI 2000/944 *Education (Student Loans) (Repayment) Regulations 2000* (revoked)
SI 2000/945 Income Tax (Electronic Communications) Regulations 2000 (revoked)
SI 2000/1047 Welfare Reform and Pensions Act 1999 (Commencement No 4) Order 2000 (not reproduced)
SI 2000/1085 Retirement Benefits Schemes (Sharing of Pensions on Divorce or Annulment) Regulations 2000 (lapsed)
SI 2000/1086 Retirement Benefits Schemes (Restriction on Discretion to Approve) (Small Self-administered Schemes) (Amendment) Regulations 2000 (amend SI 1991/1614)
SI 2000/1087 Retirement Benefits Schemes (Restriction on Discretion to Approve) (Excepted Provisions) Regulations 2000 (lapsed)
SI 2000/1088 Retirement Benefits Schemes (Restriction on Discretion to Approve) (Additional Voluntary Contributions) Regulations 2000 (amend SI 1993/3016)
SI 2000/1093 Finance Act 1999, Schedule 10, Paragraph 18, (First and Second Appointed Days) Order 2000
SI 2000/1116 Welfare Reform and Pensions Act 1999 (Commencement No 5) Order 2000 (not reproduced)
SI 2000/1151 Income Tax (Sub-contractors in the Construction Industry) (Amendment) Regulations 2000 (amend SI 1993/743) (revoked)
SI 2000/1152 Income Tax (Employments) (Amendment) Regulations 2000 (amend SI 1993/744)
SI 2000/1382 Welfare Reform and Pensions Act 1999 (Commencement No 7) Order 2000 (not reproduced)
SI 2000/1880 Income Tax (Sub-contractors in the Construction Industry) (Amendment No 2) Regulations 2000 (amend SI 1993/743) (revoked)
SI 2000/1973 Pollution Prevention and Control (England and Wales) Regulations 2000 (amend ICTA 1988 s 91A)
SI 2000/2004 Finance Act 1999, Section 59(3)(b), (Appointed Day) Order 2000
SI 2000/2074 Donations to Charity by Individuals (Appropriate Declarations) Regulations 2000

SI 2000/2075 Individual Savings Account (Insurance Companies) (Amendment) Regulations 2000 (amend SI 1998/1871)
SI 2000/2076 Individual Learning Accounts (Separate Employers Under the Crown) Regulations 2000
SI 2000/2079 Individual Savings Account (Amendment No 2) Regulations 2000 (amend SI 1998/1870)
SI 2000/2080 Income Tax (Benefits in Kind) (Exemption for Welfare Counselling) Regulations 2000
SI 2000/2081 Research and Development (Prescribed Activities) Regulations 2000 (revoked)
SI 2000/2082 Finance Act 2000, Section 108(3), (Appointed Day) Order 2000
SI 2000/2083 Charitable Deductions (Approved Schemes) (Amendment No 2) Regulations 2000
SI 2000/2089 Insurance Companies (Overseas Life Assurance Business) (Excluded Business) Regulations 2000
SI 2000/2090 Employee Share Ownership Plans (Partnership Shares—Notice of Effects on Benefits, Statutory Sick Pay and Statutory Maternity Pay) Regulations 2000
SI 2000/2104 *Insurance Companies (Overseas Life Assurance Business) (Compliance) (Amendment) Regulations 2000* (amend 1995/3237)
SI 2000/2129 Tonnage Tax (Training Requirement) Regulations 2000
SI 2000/2188 Overseas Life Assurance Fund (Amendment) Order 2000 (amends TA 1988 Sch 19AA)
SI 2000/2303 Tonnage Tax Regulations 2000
SI 2000/2314 Personal Pension Schemes (Restriction on Discretion to Approve) (Establishment of Schemes under Trusts) Regulations 2000 (lapsed)
SI 2000/2315 Personal Pension Schemes (Relief at Source) (Amendment) Regulations 2000 (amend SI 1988/1013)
SI 2000/2316 Personal Pension Schemes (Information Powers) Regulations 2000 (lapsed)
SI 2000/2317 Personal Pension Schemes (Establishment of Schemes) Regulations 2000 (amends TA 1988 s 632)
SI 2000/2318 Personal Pension Schemes (Concurrent Membership) Order 2000 (lapsed)
SI 2000/2550 Capital Gains Tax (Definition of Unit Trust Scheme) (Amendment) Regulations 2000 (amend SI 1988/266)
SI 2000/2551 Income Tax (Definition of Unit Trust Scheme) (Amendment) Regulations 2000 (amend SI 1988/267)
SI 2000/2710 Friendly Societies (Modification of the Corporation Tax Acts) (Amendment) Regulations 2000 (amend SI 1997/473)
SI 2000/2742 Income Tax (Sub-contractors in the Construction Industry and Employments) (Amendment) Regulations 2000 (amend SI 1993/743, 744) (revoked)
SI 2000/2875 Orders for the Delivery of Documents (Procedure) Regulations 2000
SI 2000/2958 Welfare Reform and Pensions Act 1999 (Commencement No 9, and Transitional and Savings Provisions) Order 2000 (not reproduced)
SI 2000/2996 Income Tax (Indexation) (No 2) Order 2000 (see TA 1988 ss 257, 257A)
SI 2000/3109 Personal Equity Plan (Amendment) Regulations 2000 (amend SI 1989/469)
SI 2000/3112 Individual Savings Account (Amendment No 3) Regulations 2000 (amend SI 1998/1870)
SI 2000/3158 Controlled Foreign Companies (Designer Rate Tax Provisions) Regulations 2000
SI 2000/3228 Corporation Tax (Simplified Arrangements for Group Relief) (Amendment) Regulations 2000 (amend SI 1999/2975)
SI 2000/3315 Exchange Gains and Losses (Miscellaneous Modifications) Regulations 2000
SI 2001/56 Income Tax (Electronic Communications) (Incentive Payments) Regulations 2001
SI 2001/117 Personal Pension Schemes (Restriction on Discretion to Approve) (Permitted Investments) Regulations 2001 (lapsed)
SI 2001/118 Personal Pension Schemes (Conversion of Retirement Benefits Schemes) Regulations 2001 (lapsed)
SI 2001/119 Personal Pension Schemes (Transfer Payments) Regulations 2001 (lapsed)
SI 2001/204 Taxes (Interest Rate) (Amendment No 1) Regulations 2001 (amend SI 1989/1297)
SI 2001/253 Finance Act 1989, Section 178(1), (Appointed Day) Order 2001
SI 2001/254 Taxes (Interest Rate) (Amendment No 2) Regulations 2001 (amend SI 1989/1297)

SI 2001/391 Investment Trusts (Approval of Accounting Methods for Creditor Relationships) Order 2001

SI 2001/403 IT (Manufactured Overseas Dividends) (Amendment) Regulations 2001 (amend SI 1993/2004)

SI 2001/404 IT (Building Societies) (Dividends and Interest) (Amendment) Regulations 2001 (amend SI 1990/2231)

SI 2001/405 IT (Interest Payments) (Information Powers) (Amendment) Regulations 2001 (revoked)

SI 2001/406 IT (Deposit-takers) (Interest Payments) (Amendment) Regulations 2001 (amend SI 1990/2232)

SI 2001/635 Income Tax (Cash Equivalents of Car Fuel Benefits) Order 2001 (amends TA 1988 s 158(2))

SI 2001/636 Capital Gains Tax (Annual Exempt Amount) Order 2001 (see TCGA 1992 s 3)

SI 2001/637 Retirement Benefits Schemes (Indexation of Earnings Cap) Order 2001 (see TA 1988 s 590C)

SI 2001/638 Income Tax (Indexation) Order 2001 (see TA 1988 ss 1, 265(1))

SI 2001/908 Individual Savings Account (Amendment) Regulations 2001 (amend SI 1998/1870)

SI 2001/923 Personal Equity Plan (Amendment) Regulations (amend SI 1989/469)

SI 2001/971 Education (Student Loans) (Repayment) (Amendment) Regulations 2001 (amend SI 2000/944)

SI 2001/1081 Income Tax (Electronic Communications) (Miscellaneous Amendments) Regulations (amend SI 2000/945 and SI 2001/56)

SI 2001/1122 Capital Gains Tax (Gilt-edged Securities) Order 2001

SI 2001/1123 Income Tax (Car Benefits) (Reduction of Value of Appropriate Percentage) Regulations 2001

SI 2001/1149 Postal Services Act 2000 (Consequential Modifications No 1) Order, SI 2001/1149 (amends TA 1988 ss 376, 481)

SI 2001/1156 Double Taxation Relief (Taxes on Income) (Underlying Tax on Dividends and Dual Resident Companies) Regulations 2001

SI 2001/1163 Double Taxation Relief (Surrender of Relievable Tax Within a Group) Regulations 2001

SI 2001/1304 *General Commissioners of Income Tax (Costs) Regulations 2001* (revoked)

SI 2001/1531 *Income Tax (Sub-contractors in the Construction Industry) (Amendment) Regulations 2001 (amend SI 1993/743)* (revoked)

SI 2001/1757 General Insurance Reserves (Tax) Regulations 2001

SI 2001/2541 Capital Allowances (Energy-saving Plant and Machinery) Order 2001

SI 2001/2724 Personal Portfolio Bonds (Tax) (Amendment) Regulations 2001 (amend SI 1999/1029)

SI 2001/2726 Overseas Insurers (Tax Representatives) (Amendment) Regulations 2001 (amend SI 1999/881)

SI 2001/3500 Transfer of Functions (Miscellaneous) Order 2001 (amends the Human Rights Act 1998)

SI 2001/3629 Financial Services and Markets Act 2000 (Consequential Amendments) (Taxes) Order 2001

SI 2001/3773 Income Tax (Indexation) (No 2) Order 2001

SI 2001/3777 Personal Equity Plan (Amendment No 2) Regulations 2001 (amend SI 1989/469)

SI 2001/3778 Individual Savings Account (Amendment No 2) Regulations 2001 (amend SI 1998/1870)

SI 2001/3799 Enterprise Management Incentives (Gross Asset Requirement) Order 2001 (amends FA 2000, Sch 14, para 16)

SI 2001/3860 Taxes (Interest Rate) (Amendment No 3) Regulations 2001

SI 2001/3873 Double Taxation Relief (Surrender of Relievable Tax Within a Group) (Amendment) Regulations 2001 (amend SI 2001/1163)

SI 2001/3973 Friendly Societies (Provisional Repayments for Exempt Business) (Amendment) Regulations 2001 (amend SI 1999/622)

SI 2001/3974 Individual Savings Account (Insurance Companies) (Amendment) Regulations 2001 (amend SI 1998/1871)

SI 2001/3975 Friendly Societies (Modification of the Corporation Tax Acts) (Amendment) Regulations 2001 (amend SI 1997/473)

SI 2001/4024 *Referrals to the Special Commissioners Regulations 2001* (revoked)

SI 2002/205 Income Tax (Exemption of Minor Benefits) Regulations 2002
SI 2002/653 Scottish Water (Transfer of Functions, etc) (Tax Provisions) Order 2002
SI 2002/680 Income Tax (Employments and Electronic Communications) (Miscellaneous Provisions) Regulations
SI 2002/1397 Secretaries of State for Education and Skills and for Work and Pensions Order 2002 (amends SI 1993/743 and SI 1993/744)
SI 2002/1409 Financial Services and Markets Act 2000 (Consequential Amendments) (Taxes) Order 2002
SI 2002/1596 Income Tax (Benefits in Kind) (Exemption for Employment Costs resulting from Disability) Regulations 2002
SI 2002/1818 Capital Allowances (Energy-saving Plant and Machinery) (Amendment) Order 2002 (amends SI 2001/2541)
SI 2002/1963 Controlled Foreign Companies (Excluded Countries) (Amendment) Regulations 2002 (amend SI 1998/3081)
SI 2002/1966 Relief for Community Amateur Sports Clubs (Designation) Order 2002
SI 2002/1967 Corporation Tax (Finance Leasing of Intangible Assets) Regulations 2002
SI 2002/1968 Income Tax (Prescribed Deposit-takers) Order 2002 (repealed)
SI 2002/1969 Exchange Gains and Losses (Transitional Provisions and Savings) Regulations 2002
SI 2002/1970 Exchange Gains and Losses (Bringing into Account Gains or Losses) Regulations 2002
SI 2002/1971 European Single Currency (Taxes) (Amendment) Regulations 2002 (amend SI 1998/3177)
SI 2002/1973 Open-ended Investment Companies (Tax) (Amendment) Regulations 2002 (amend SI 1997/1154)
SI 2002/1974 Individual Savings Account (Amendment No 2) Regulations 2002 (amend SI 1998/1870)
SI 2002/2058 Civil Procedure (Amendment) Rules 2002 (amend SI 1998/3132)
SI 2002/2225 *Income Tax (Sub-contractors in the Construction industry) (Amendment) Regulations 2002 (amend SI 1993/743)* (revoked)
SI 2002/2406 Controlled Foreign Companies (Excluded Countries) (Amendment No. 2) Regulations 2002 (amend SI 1998/3081)
SI 2002/2661 Venture Capital Trust (Exchange of Shares and Securities) Regulations 2002
SI 2002/2849 Capital Gains Tax (Gilt-edged Securities) Order 2002
SI 2002/2930 Income Tax (Indexation)(No2) Order 2002
SI 2002/2931 Income and Corporation Taxes Act 1988, Section 349B(3) Order 2002
SI 2002/2976 General Commissioners and Special Commissioners (Jurisdiction and Procedure) (Amendment) Regulations 2002
SI 2002/3047 Statutory Payment Schemes (Electronic Communications) Regulations 2002
SI 2002/3158 *Individual Savings Account (Amendment No 3) Regulations 2002* (amend SI 1998/1870)
SI 2003/23 Friendly Societies (Modification of the Corporation Tax Acts) (Amendment) Regulations 2003
SI 2003/88 Finance Act 2002, Section 57(3) and 4(*a*), (Appointed Day) Order 2003
SI 2003/96 Community Investment Tax Relief (Accreditation of Community Development Finance Institutions) Regulations 2003
SI 2003/282 Income and Corporation Taxes (Electronic Communications) Regulations 2003
SI 2003/536 *Income Tax (Sub-contractors in the Construction Industry and Employments) (Amendment) Regulations 2003 (amend SI 1993/743 and SI 1993/744)* (revoked)
SI 2003/843 *Retirement Benefits Schemes (Indexation of Earnings Cap) Order* 2003 (see TA 1988 s 590C)
SI 2003/1361 *Income Tax (Exemption of Minor Benefits) (Increase in Sums of Money) Order 2003* (amends ITEPA 2003)
SI 2003/1434 *Income Tax (Exemption of Minor Benefits) (Amendment) Regulations 2003* (amend SI 2002/205)
SI 2003/1652 *Income Tax (Professional Fees) Order 2003* (amends ITEPA 2003 s 343(2))
SI 2003/1744 *Capital Allowances (Energy-saving Plant and Machinery) (Amendment) Order 2003* (amends SI 2001/2541)
SI 2003/1745 *Charitable Deductions (Approved Schemes) (Amendment) Regulations 2003* (amend SI 1986/2211)
SI 2003/1828 *Insurance Companies (Taxation of Reinsurance Business) (Amendment) Regulations 2003* (amend SI 1995/1730)

SI 2003/1829 *Double Taxation Relief (Surrender of Relievable Tax Within a Group) (Amendment) Regulations 2003* (amend SI 2001/1163)
SI 2003/1830 Income Tax (Authorised Unit Trusts) (Interest Distributions) Regulations 2003
SI 2003/1831 *Open-ended Investment Companies (Tax) (Amendment) Regulations 2003* (amend SI 1997/1154)
SI 2003/1860 *Life Assurance (Apportionment and Receipts of Participating Funds)(Applicable Percentage) Order 2003* (revokes SI 1990/1541)
SI 2003/1861 *Corporation Tax (Treatment of Unrelieved Surplus Advance Corporation Tax) (Amendment) Regulations 2003* (amend SI 1999/358)
SI 2003/2066 Collective Investment Schemes (Miscellaneous Amendments) Regulations 2003 (amend SI 1989/469)
SI 2003/2076 Capital Allowances (Environmentally Beneficial Plant and Machinery) Order 2003
SI 2003/2082 Insurance Companies (Calculation of Profits: Policy Holders' Tax) Regulations 2003
SI 2003/2172 Finance Act 1995, Section 127(12) (Designated Transactions) Regulations 2003
SI 2003/2173 Finance Act 2003, Schedule 26 Paragraph 3(3) (Designated Transactions) Regulations 2003
SI 2003/2339 Taxation of Benefits under Government Pilot Schemes (Return to Work Credit and Employment Retention and Advancement Schemes) Order 2003
SI 2003/2494 Income Tax (Employments) (Amendment) Regulations 2003 (amend SI 1993/744)
SI 2003/2495 Income Tax (Incentive Payments for Voluntary Electronic Communication of PAYE Returns) Regulations 2003
SI 2003/2573 Insurance Companies (Taxation of Reinsurance Business) (Amendment No 2) Regulations 2003 (amend SI 1995/1730)
SI 2003/2581 Double Taxation Relief (Manufactured Overseas Dividends) (Revocation) Regulations 2003 (revoke SI 1993/1957)
SI 2003/2582 Income Tax (Manufactured Overseas Dividends) (Amendment) Regulations 2003 (amend SI 1993/2004)
SI 2003/2642 Insurance Companies (Taxation of Reinsurance Business) (Amendment No 3) Regulations 2003 (amend SI 1995/1730)
SI 2003/2682 Income Tax (Pay As You Earn) Regulations 2003
SI 2003/2714 Non-resident Insurance Companies Regulations 2003
SI 2003/2747 Individual Savings Account (Amendment) Regulations 2003 (amend SI 1998/1870)
SI 2003/2748 Personal Equity Plan (Amendment) Regulations 2003 (amend SI 1989/469)
SI 2003/3075 *Money Laundering Regulations 2003* (revoked)
SI 2003/3143 Income and Corporation Taxes (Electronic Certificates of Deduction of Tax and Tax Credit) Regulations 2003
SI 2003/3215 *Income Tax (Indexation) (No 2) Order 2003* (amend TA 1988)
SI 2003/3297 Reporting of Savings Income Information Regulations 2003
SI 2004/438 Capital Gains Tax (Gilt-edged Securities) Order 2004
SI 2004/439 Urban Regeneration Companies (Tax) (Designation) Order 2004
SI 2004/674 Recovery of Duties and Taxes etc Due in Other Member States (Corresponding UK Claims, Procedure and Supplementary) Regulations 2004
SI 2004/712 Research and Development (Prescribed Activities) Regulations 2004
SI 2004/851 IT (PAYE) (Amendment) Regulations 2004 (amend SI 2003/2682)
SI 2004/1075 Income Tax (Sub-contractors in the Construction Industry) (Amendment) Regulations 2004 (amend SI 1993/743) (revoked)
SI 2004/1175 *Education (Student Loans) (Repayment) (Amendment) Regulations 2004* (amend SI 2000/944)
SI 2004/1450 Child Trust Funds Regulations 2004
SI 2004/1676 *Personal Equity Plan (Amendment) Regulations 2004* (amend SI 1989/469)
SI 2004/1677 *Individual Savings Account (Amendment) Regulations 2004* (amend SI 1998/1870)
SI 2004/1819 Thalidomide Children's Trust (Application of Section 329AA of the Income and Corporation Taxes Act 1988) Order 2004
SI 2004/1863 Tax Avoidance Schemes (Prescribed Descriptions of Arrangements) Regulations 2004
SI 2004/1864 Tax Avoidance Schemes (Information) Regulations 2004 (revoked)

SI 2004/1865 Tax Avoidance Schemes (Promoters and Prescribed Circumstances) Regulations 2004
SI 2004/2093 *Capital Allowances (Energy-saving Plant and Machinery) (Amendment) Order 2004* (amends SI 2001/2541)
SI 2004/2094 *Capital Allowances (Environmentally Beneficial Plant and Machinery) (Amendment) Order 2004* (amends SI 2003/2076)
SI 2004/2199 Venture Capital Trust (Winding up and Mergers) Tax) Regulations 2004
SI 2004/2200 *Overseas Life Insurance Companies Regulations 2004* (revoked)
SI 2004/2201 *Finance Act 2002, Schedule 26, Parts 2 and 9 (Amendment) Order 2004* (amends FA 2002)
SI 2004/2255 *Tonnage Tax (Training Requirement) (Amendment) Regulations, SI 2004/2255* (amend SI 2000/2129)
SI 2004/2257 *Insurance Companies (Taxation of Reinsurance Business) (Amendment No 2) Regulations, SI 2004/2257* (amend SI 1995/1730)
SI 2004/2310 *Finance Act 2004, Sections 38 to 40 and 45 and Schedule 6 (Consequential Amendment of Enactments) Order 2004* (amending)
SI 2004/2422 Child Trust Funds Act 2004 (Commencement No 1) Order 2004
SI 2004/2429 *Tax Avoidance Schemes (Prescribed Descriptions of Arrangements) (Amendment) Regulations 2004* (amend SI 2004/1863)
SI 2004/2502 Corporation Tax (Notice of Coming within Charge—Information) Regulations 2004
SI 2004/2571 Finance Act 2004, Section 294 (Appointed Day) Order 2004
SI 2004/2572 Offshore Funds Regulations 2004
SI 2004/2613 *Tax Avoidance Schemes (Promoters, Prescribed Circumstances and Information) (Amendment) Regulations 2004*
SI 2004/2622 Exemption From Tax for Certain Interest Payments Regulations 2004
SI 2004/2664 *Energy-Saving Items (Deductions for Expenditure etc) Regulations 2004* (revoked)
SI 2004/2680 *Child Trust Funds (Insurance Companies) Regulations 2004* (lapsed)
SI 2004/3256 Loan Relationships and Derivative Contracts (Disregard and Bringing into Account of Profits and Losses) Regulations 2004
SI 2004/3259 *Exchange Gains and Losses (Bringing into Account Gains or Losses) (Amendment) Regulations 2004* (amend SI 2002/1970)
SI 2004/3260 *Insurance Companies (Reserves) (Tax) (Amendment) Regulations 2004* (amend SI 1996/2991)
SI 2004/3266 *Insurance Companies (Corporation Tax Acts) Order 2004* (amending)
SI 2004/3270 *Finance Act 2002, Schedule 26, Parts 2 and 9 (Amendment No 2) Order 2004*
SI 2004/3271 Loan Relationships and Derivative Contracts (Change of Accounting Practice) Regulations 2004
SI 2004/3272 *Overseas Insurers (Tax Representatives) (Amendment) Regulations 2004* (amend SI 1999/881)
SI 2004/3273 *Insurance Companies (Overseas Life Assurance Business) (Compliance) (Amendment) Regulations 2004* (amend SI 1995/3237)
SI 2004/3274 *Insurance Companies (Overseas Life Assurance Business) (Excluded Business) (Amendment) Regulations 2004* (amend SI 2000/2089)
SI 2004/3275 *Overseas Life Assurance Fund (Amendment) Order 2004* (amending)
SI 2004/3347 *Loan Relationships and Derivative Contracts (Change of Accounting Practice) (Amendment) Regulations 2004* (amend SI 2004/3271)
SI 2004/3369 Child Trust Funds Act 2004 (Commencement No 2) Order 2004
SI 2005/185 *Controlled Foreign Companies (Excluded Countries) Regulations 2005* (amend SI 1998/3081)
SI 2005/186 *Controlled Foreign Companies (Excluded Countries) (Amendment No 2) Regulations 2005* (amend SI 1998/3081)
SI 2005/191 Child Trust Funds (Non-tax Appeals)
SI 2005/276 Capital Gains Tax (Gilt-edged Securities) Order 2005
SI 2005/340 *General Commissioners (Jurisdiction and Procedure) (Amendment) Regulations 2005* (amend SI 1994/1812)
SI 2005/341 *Special Commissioners (Jurisdiction and Procedure) (Amendment) Regulations 2005* (amend SI 1994/1811)
SI 2005/409 Finance Act 1993, Section 86(2), (Single Payment Scheme) Order, (amends TCGA 1992 s 155)

SI 2005/644 Energy Act 2004 (Nuclear Decommissioning) (Exempt Activities and Further Conditions) Regulations 2005
SI 2005/646 *Finance Act 2002, Schedule 26, Parts 2 and 9 (Amendment) Order, SI 2005/646* (amends FA 2002)
SI 2005/695 Pensions Act 2004 (Commencement No 3, Transitional Provisions and Amendment) Order 2005
SI 2005/723 Retirement Benefits Schemes (Increase in Permitted Maximum in Transitional Cases) Order 2005
SI 2005/724 Charge to Income Tax by Reference to Enjoyment of Property Previously Owned Regulations 2005
SI 2005/990 Child Trust Funds (Appeals) Regulations 2005
SI 2005/1114 *Energy-Saving Items Regulations 2005* (revoked)
SI 2005/1133 Revenue and Customs (Inspections) Regulations 2005
SI 2005/1449 Tonnage Tax (Further Opportunity for Election) Order 2005
SI 2005/1479 *Recovery of Taxes etc Due in Other Member States (Amendment of Section 134 of the Finance Act 2002) Regulations 2005* (revoked)
SI 2005/1480 Tonnage Tax (Exception of Financial Year 2005) Order 2005
SI 2005/1538 Lloyd's Sourcebook (Amendment of the Finance Act 1993 and the Finance Act 1994) Order 2005
SI 2005/1539 *Reporting of Savings Income Information (Amendment) Regulations 2005* (amend SI 2003/3297)
SI 2005/1709 *Recovery of Duties and Taxes Etc Due in Other Member States (Corresponding UK Claims, Procedure and Supplementary) (Amendment) Regulations 2005* (amend SI 2004/674)
SI 2005/1869 Tax Avoidance Schemes (Information) (Amendment) Regulations 2005 (revoked)
SI 2005/1907 Pension Protection Fund (Tax) (2005–06) Regulations 2005
SI 2005/2005 *Friendly Societies (Modification of the Corporation Tax Acts) (Amendment) Regulations 2005* (amend SI 1997/473)
SI 2005/2012 *Loan Relationships and Derivative Contracts (Disregard and Bringing into Account of Profits and Losses) (Amendment) Regulations 2005* (amend SI 2004/3256)
SI 2005/2013 *Exchange Gains and Losses (Bringing into Account Gains or Losses) (Amendment) Regulations 2005* (amend SI 2002/1970)
SI 2005/2014 Friendly Societies (Modification of the Corporation Tax Acts) Regulations 2005
SI 2005/2017 Partnerships (Restrictions on Contributions to a Trade) Regulations 2005
SI 2005/2045 Income Tax (Construction Industry Scheme) Regulations 2005
SI 2005/2082 *Finance Act 2002, Schedule 26, Parts 2 and 9 (Amendment No 2) Order 2005*
SI 2005/2209 *Income Tax (Car Benefits) (Reduction of Value of Appropriate Percentage) (Amendment) Regulations 2005* (amend SI 2001/1123)
SI 2005/2295 *Tonnage Tax (Training Requirement) (Amendment) Regulations 2005* (amend SI 2000/2129)
SI 2005/2423 *Capital Allowances (Environmentally Beneficial Plant and Machinery) (Amendment) Order 2005* (amends SI 2003/2076)
SI 2005/2424 *Capital Allowances (Energy-saving Plant and Machinery) (Amendment) Order 2005* (amends SI 2001/2541)
SI 2005/2462 *Taxes (Interest Rate) (Amendment) Regulations 2005* (amend SI 1989/1297)
SI 2005/2561 *Individual Savings Account (Amendment No 2) Regulations 2005* (amend SI 1998/1870)
SI 2005/2562 *Personal Equity Plan (Amendment) Regulations 2005* (amend SI 1989/469)
SI 2005/2690 *Education (Student Loans) (Repayment) (Amendment) Regulations 2005* (amend SI 2000/944)
SI 2005/2691 *Income Tax (PAYE) (Amendment) Regulations 2005* (amend SI 2003/2682)
SI 2005/2790 *Donations to Charity by Individuals (Appropriate Declarations) (Amendment) Regulations 2005* (amend SI 2000/2074)
SI 2005/2899 *Exemption From Income Tax For Certain Interest and Royalty Payments (Amendment to Section 97(1) of the Finance Act 2004 and Section 757(2) of the Income Tax (Trading and Other Income) Act 2005) Order 2005* (amends FA 2004 and ITTOIA 2005)
SI 2005/2919 *Civil Partnership Act 2004 (Tax Credits, etc) (Consequential Amendments) Order 2005* (amends SI 2004/1450)
SI 2005/3289 *General Insurance Reserves (Tax) (Amendment) Regulations 2005* (amend SI 2001/1757)

SI 2006/212 Pension Schemes (Relevant Migrant Members) Regulations 2006
SI 2006/243 Income Tax (Pay As You Earn) (Amendment) Regulations 2006 (amend SI 2003/2682)
SI 2006/333 Tonnage Tax (Exception of Financial Year 2006) Order 2006
SI 2006/364 Registered Pension Schemes (Modification of the Rules of Existing Schemes) Regulations 2006
SI 2006/365 Registered Pension Schemes (Unauthorised Payments by Existing Schemes) Regulations 2006
SI 2006/497 Taxation of Judicial Pensions (Consequential Provisions) Order 2006
SI 2006/498 Registered Pension Schemes (Block Transfers) (Permitted Membership Period) Regulations 2006
SI 2006/499 Registered Pension Schemes (Transfer of Sums and Assets) Regulations 2006
SI 2006/567 Registered Pension Schemes (Provision of Information) Regulations 2006
SI 2006/568 Registered Pension Schemes (Prescribed Manner of Determining Amount of Annuities) Regulations 2006
SI 2006/569 Registered Pension Schemes (Splitting of Schemes) Regulations 2006
SI 2006/570 Registered Pension Schemes and Overseas Pension Schemes (Electronic Communication of Returns and Information) Regulations 2006
SI 2006/571 Registered Pension Schemes (Authorised Member Payments) (No 2) Regulations 2006
SI 2006/572 Taxation of Pension Schemes (Transitional Provisions) Order 2006
SI 2006/573 Pension Schemes (Transfers, Reorganisations and Winding Up) (Transitional Provisions) Order 2006
SI 2006/574 Registered Pension Schemes (Authorised Surplus Payments) Regulations 2006
SI 2006/575 Pension Protection Fund (Tax) Regulations 2006
SI 2006/614 Registered Pension Schemes (Authorised Payments—Arrears of Pension) Regulations 2006
SI 2006/643 Films (Definition of "British Film") Order 2006
SI 2006/777 *Income Tax (Pay As You Earn, etc), (Amendment) Regulations 2006* (amend SI 2003/2495 and SI 2003/2682)
SI 2006/843 Loan Relationships and Derivative Contracts (Disregard and Bringing into Account of Profits and Losses) Regulations 2006
SI 2006/871 Capital Gains Tax (Annual Exempt Amount) Order 2006 (amends TCGA 1992)
SI 2006/872 *Income Tax (Indexation) Order 2006* (amends TA 1988)
SI 2006/882 Income Tax (Exempt Amounts for Childcare Vouchers and for Employer Contracted Childcare) Order 2006
SI 2006/912 *Energy-Saving Items Regulations 2006* (revoked)
SI 2006/936 *Loan Relationships and Derivative Contracts (Disregard and Bringing into Account of Profits and Losses) (Amendment) Regulations 2006* (amend SI 2006/843)
SI 2006/959 *Income Tax (Trading and Other Income) Act 2005 (Consequential Amendments) Order 2006* (amending)
SI 2006/964 Authorised Investment Funds (Tax) Regulations 2006
SI 2006/981 *Unit Trust Schemes and Offshore Funds (Non-qualifying Investments Test) Order 2006* (amends FA 1996)
SI 2006/982 *Finance (No 2) Act 2005, Section 17(1), (Appointed Day) Order* 2006
SI 2006/1182 Investment Trusts and Venture Capital Trusts (Definition of Capital Profits, Gains or Losses) Order 2006
SI 2006/1465 Registered Pension Schemes (Authorised Reductions) Regulations 2006
SI 2006/1543 Tax Avoidance Schemes (Prescribed Descriptions of Arrangements) Regulations 2006
SI 2006/1639 Partnerships (Restrictions on Contributions to a Trade) Regulations 2006
SI 2006/1957 Registered Pension Schemes (Extension of Migrant Member Relief) Regulations 2006
SI 2006/1958 Pensions Schemes (Taxable Property Provisions) Regulations 2006
SI 2006/1959 Investment-regulated Pension Schemes (Exception of Tangible Moveable Property) Order 2006
SI 2006/1960 Pensions Schemes (Application of UK Provisions to Relevant Non-UK Schemes) (Amendment) Regulations 2006
SI 2006/1961 Registered Pension Schemes (Provision of Information) (Amendment) Regulations 2006
SI 2006/1962 Taxation of Pension Schemes (Transitional Provisions) (Amendment) Order 2006

SI 2006/1963 Taxation of Pension Schemes (Consequential Amendments) (No 2) Order 2006
SI 2006/2129 *Education Act 2005 (Commencement No 2 and Transitional Provisions and Savings) Order 2006*
SI 2006/2229 *Tonnage Tax (Training Requirement) (Amendment) Regulations*
SI 2006/2684 *Child Trust Funds (Amendment No 2) Regulations 2006*
SI 2006/2864 Real Estate Investment Trusts (Breach of Conditions) Regulations 2006
SI 2006/2865 Real Estate Investment Trusts (Financial Statements of Group Real Estate Investment Trusts) Regulations 2006
SI 2006/2866 Real Estate Investment Trusts (Joint Ventures) Regulations 2006 (revoked)
SI 2006/2867 Real Estate Investment Trusts (Assessment and Recovery of Tax) Regulations 2006
SI 2006/3170 Taxation of Chargeable Gains (Gilt-edged Securities) (No 2) Order 2006
SI 2006/3194 *Individual Savings Account (Amendment) Regulations 2006*
SI 2006/3195 *Child Trust Funds (Amendment No 3) Regulations 2006* (amend SI 2004/1450)
SI 2006/3222 *Real Estate Investment Trusts (Assessment and Recovery of Tax) (Amendment) Regulations 2006*
SI 2006/3236 *Loan Relationships and Derivative Contracts (Disregard and Bringing into Account of Profits and Losses) (Amendment) Regulations 2006*
SI 2006/3238 *Loan Relationships and Derivative Contracts (Change of Accounting Practice) (Amendment) Regulations 2006* (amend SI 2004/3271)
SI 2006/3239 *Authorised Investment Funds (Tax) (Amendment) Regulations 2006* (amend SI 2006/964)
SI 2006/3240 *Finance Act 2004, Section 77(1) and (7), (Appointed Day) Order 2006*
SI 2006/3241 *Income Tax (Indexation) (No 2) Order 2006*
SI 2006/3261 *Registered Pension Schemes (Enhanced Lifetime Allowance) (Amendment) Regulations 2006*
SI 2006/3262 Lloyd's Underwriters (Double Taxation Relief) (Corporate Members) Regulations 2006
SI 2006/3265 *Finance Act 2006, Section 53(2) (Films and Sound Recordings: Power to alter Dates) Order 2006*
SI 2006/3269 *Finance Act 2002, Schedule 26, (Parts 2 and 9) (Amendment) Order 2006*
SI 2006/3270 *Insurance Companies (Corporation Tax Acts) (Miscellaneous Amendments) Order 2006*
SI 2006/3271 Overseas Life Insurance Companies Regulations 2006
SI 2006/3273 *Lloyd's Sourcebook (Finance Act 1993 and Finance Act 1994) (Amendment) Order*
SI 2006/3281 Films (Certification) Regulations 2006
SI 2006/3286 Reporting of Savings Income Information (Amendment) Regulations
SI 2006/3288 *Exemption from Income Tax for Certain Interest and Royalty Payments (Amendment of Section 757(2) of the Income Tax (Trading and Other Income) Act 2005) Order*
SI 2006/3291 *CGT (Definition of Permanent Interest Bearing Share) Regulations 2006*
SI 2006/3296 Taxation of Securitisation Companies Regulations 2006
SI 2006/3387 *Insurance Companies (Corporation Tax Acts) (Amendment No 2) Order*
SI 2006/3389 Group Relief for Overseas Losses (Modification of the Corporation Tax Acts for Non-resident Insurance Companies) (No 2) Regulations 2006
SI 2006/3399 Finance Act 2006, Section 53(1) (Films and Sound Recordings) (Appointed Day) Order 2006
SI 2007/46 Finance Act 2004, Section 61(2), (Relevant Percentage) Order 2007
SI 2007/109 *Civil Partnership (Employee Share Ownership Plans) Order* (amending)
SI 2007/303 Capital Allowances (Leases of Background Plant or Machinery for a Building) Order 2007
SI 2007/304 Long Funding Leases (Elections) Regulations 2007
SI 2007/493 *Tax and Civil Partnerships Regulations 2007*
SI 2007/494 Registered Pension Schemes (Standard Lifetime and Annual Allowances) Order 2007
SI 2007/672 *Income Tax (Construction Industry Scheme) (Amendment) Regulations 2007*
SI 2007/678 Corporation Tax (Surrender of Terminal Losses on Films and Claims for Relief) Regulations 2007
SI 2007/683 *Authorised Investment Funds (Tax) (Amendment) Regulations 2007*
SI 2007/684 *Taxes (Interest Rate) (Amendment) Regulations 2007*
SI 2007/766 Transfer of the Northern Ireland Water Service (Tax) Regulations 2007

SI 2007/785 *NIC (Application of Part 7 of the Finance Act 2004) Regulations 2007* (modifying)
SI 2007/792 *Employee Share Schemes (Electronic Communication of Returns and Information) Regulations 2007*
SI 2007/793 *Registered Pension Schemes (Splitting of Schemes) (Amendment) Regulations 2007*
SI 2007/794 *Authorised Investment Funds (Tax) (Amendment No 2) Regulations 2007*
SI 2007/826 Registered Pension Schemes (Bridging Pensions) Regulations 2007
SI 2007/831 *Energy-Saving Items Regulations 2007* (revoked)
SI 2007/838 Registered Pension Schemes (Block Transfers) (Permitted Membership Period) (Amendment) Regulations 2007
SI 2007/849 *Income Tax (Qualifying Child Care) Regulations 2007* (amend ITEPA 2003)
SI 2007/850 Tonnage Tax (Exception of Financial Year 2007) Order 2007
SI 2007/881 *Orders for the Delivery of Documents (Procedure) (Amendment) Regulations 2007*
SI 2007/940 *Income Tax Act 2007 (Amendment) Order*
SI 2007/942 *CGT (Annual Exempt Amount) Order 2007*
SI 2007/943 *Income Tax (Indexation) Order 2007*
SI 2007/945 Business Premises Renovation Allowances Regulations 2007
SI 2007/948 *Loan Relationships and Derivative Contracts (Disregard and Bringing into Account of Profits and Losses) (Amendment) Regulations 2007*
SI 2007/949 *Finance Act 2005, Section 92 and Schedule 6, (Appointed Day) Order 2007*
SI 2007/950 *Loan Relationships and Derivative Contracts (Change of Accounting Practice) (Amendment) Regulations 2007*
SI 2007/1031 *Insurance Companies (Corporation Tax Acts) (Amendment) Order 2007*
SI 2007/1050 *Corporation Tax (Taxation of Films) (Transitional Provisions) Regulations 2007*
SI 2007/1077 *Income Tax (Pay as You Earn) (Amendment) Regulations 2007*
SI 2007/1081 *Finance Act 2006 (Section 94(5)) (PAYE: Retrospective Notional Payments — Appointment of Substituted Date) Order 2007*
SI 2007/1600 *Pension Schemes (Categories of Country and Requirements for Overseas Pension Schemes and Recognised Overseas Pension Schemes) (Amendment) Regulations 2007*
SI 2007/1616 *Finance Act 1994, Section 220 (Amendment) Regulations 2007*
SI 2007/1820 *Income Tax Act 2007 (Amendment) (No 2) Order 2007*
SI 2007/2069 *Income Tax (Pay as You Earn) (Amendment No 2) Regulations 2007*
SI 2007/2086 *Insurance Companies (Overseas Life Assurance Business) (Excluded Business) (Amendment) Regulations 2007*
SI 2007/2087 *Insurance Companies (Taxation of Reinsurance Business) (Amendment) Regulations 2007*
SI 2007/2088 *Insurance Companies (Overseas Life Assurance Business) (Compliance) (Amendment) Regulations 2007*
SI 2007/2090 *Income Tax (Exemption of Minor Benefits) (Amendment) Regulations 2007*
SI 2007/2119 *Individual Savings Account (Amendment) Regulations 2007*
SI 2007/2120 *Personal Equity Plan (Amendment) Regulations 2007*
SI 2007/2126 International Mutual Administrative Assistance in Tax Matters Order 2007
SI 2007/2134 *Friendly Societies (Modification of the Corporation Tax Acts) (Amendment) Regulations 2007*
SI 2007/2145 Insurance Companies (Tax Exempt Business) Regulations 2007
SI 2007/2153 Tax Avoidance Schemes (Information) (Amendment) Regulations 2007 (revoked)
SI 2007/2157 Money Laundering Regulations 2007 (revoked)
SI 2007/2165 *Capital Allowances (Energy-saving Plant and Machinery) (Amendment) Order 2007*
SI 2007/2166 *Capital Allowances (Environmentally Beneficial Plant and Machinery) (Amendment) Order 2007*
SI 2007/2296 *Income Tax (Pay As You Earn) (Amendment No 3) Regulations 2007*
SI 2007/2478 *Income Tax (Qualifying Child Care) (No 2) Regulations 2007*
SI 2007/2482 *Tonnage Tax (Training Requirement) (Amendment) Regulations 2007*
SI 2007/2483 Finance Act 2007 (Schedules 13 and 14) Order 2007
SI 2007/2484 *Sale and Repurchase of Securities (Amendment of Instruments) Order 2007*
SI 2007/2485 Sale and Repurchase of Securities (Modification of Schedule 13 to the Finance Act 2007) Regulations 2007

SI 2007/3543 *Civil Procedure (Amendment No 2) Rules 2007*
SI 2007/3612 *General Commissioners and Special Commissioners (Jurisdiction and Procedure) (Amendment) Regulations 2007*
SI 2008/219 *Serious Crime Act 2007 (Commencement No 1) Order 2008*
SI 2008/379 *Finance Act 2007 (Schedule 9) Order 2008*
SI 2008/381 *Insurance Business Transfer Schemes (Amendment of the Corporation Tax Acts) Order 2008*
SI 2008/403 Serious Crime Act 2007 (Disclosure of Information by Revenue and Customs) Order 2008
SI 2008/511 *Car Fuel Benefit Order 2008*
SI 2008/562 Income Tax (Purchased Life Annuities) Regulations 2008
SI 2008/568 Finance Act 2007, Schedule 24 (Commencement and Transitional Provisions) Order 2008
SI 2008/673 *Income Tax (Indexation) Order 2008*
SI 2008/704 *Individual Savings Account (Amendment) Regulations 2008*
SI 2008/705 *Authorised Investment Funds (Tax) (Amendment) Regulations 2008*
SI 2008/706 *Income Tax (Limits for Enterprise Management Incentives) Order 2008*
SI 2008/708 *CGT (Annual Exempt Amount) Order 2008*
SI 2008/709 *Income Tax (Indexation) (No 2) Order 2008*
SI 2008/720 *Registered Pension Schemes (Provision of Information) (Amendment) Regulations 2008*
SI 2008/740 *Income Tax (Construction Industry Scheme) (Amendment) Regulations 2008*
SI 2008/778 *Taxes (Interest Rate) (Amendment) Regulations 2008*
SI 2008/782 *Income Tax (Pay As You Earn) (Amendment) Regulations 2008*
SI 2008/836 *Income Tax (Professional Fees) Order 2008*
SI 2008/838 *Income Tax (Payments on Account) (Amendment) Regulations 2008*
SI 2008/948 *Companies Act 2006 (Consequential Amendments etc) Order 2008*
SI 2008/954 *Companies Act 2006 (Consequential Amendments) (Taxes and National Insurance) Order 2008*
SI 2008/1282 *Income Tax (Construction Industry Scheme) (Amendment No 2) Regulations 2008*
SI 2008/1464 (Taxation of Benefits under Government Pilot Schemes (Up-Front Childcare Fund) Order 2008
SI 2008/1481 *Income Tax (Purchased Life Annuities) (Amendment) Regulations 2008*
SI 2008/1520 Energy-Saving Items (Corporation Tax) Regulations 2008
SI 2008/1579 Corporation Tax (Implementation of the Mergers Directive) Regulations 2008
SI 2008/1588 Taxation of Chargeable Gains (Gilt-edged Securities) Order 2008
SI 2008/1783 *Films Co-Production Agreements (Amendment) Order 2008*
SI 2008/1878 *Finance Act 2006, Section 28 (Appointed Day) Order 2008*
SI 2008/1880 *Finance Act 2007, Section 50 (Appointed Day) Order 2008*
SI 2008/1905 *Insurance Companies (Corporation Tax Acts) (Amendment) Order 2008*
SI 2008/1906 *Insurance Companies (Calculation of Profits: Policy Holders' Tax) (Amendment) Regulations 2008*
SI 2008/1916 *Capital Allowances (Energy-saving Plant and Machinery) (Amendment) Order 2008*
SI 2008/1917 *Capital Allowances (Environmentally Beneficial Plant and Machinery) (Amendment) Order 2008*
SI 2008/1923 Insurance Companies (Taxation of Insurance Special Purpose Vehicles) Order 2008
SI 2008/1924 *Overseas Life Insurance Companies (Amendment) Regulations 2008*
SI 2008/1925 *Finance Act 2008, Section 30 (Appointed Day) Order 2008*
SI 2008/1926 Financing-Arrangement-Funded Transfers to Shareholders Regulations 2008
SI 2008/1928 *Finance Act 2008, Section 29 (Appointed Day) Order 2008*
SI 2008/1929 *Finance Act 2008, Section 28 (Appointed Day) Order 2008*
SI 2008/1930 *Finance Act 2008, Section 27 (Appointed Day) Order 2008*
SI 2008/1933 *Finance Act 2008, Section 26 (Appointed Day) Order 2008*
SI 2008/1934 *Individual Savings Account (Amendment No 2) Regulations 2008*
SI 2008/1936 Finance Act 2008 Section 135 (Disaster or Emergency) Order 2008
SI 2008/1937 *Friendly Societies (Modification of the Corporation Tax Acts) (Amendment) Regulations 2008*
SI 2008/1942 Friendly Societies (Transfers of Other Business) (Modification of the Corporation Tax Acts) Regulations 2008

Account of Profits and Losses) (Amendment) Regulations 2009
SI 2009/1890 *Companies Act 2006 (Consequential Amendments) (Taxes and National Insurance) Order 2009*
SI 2009/1916 Information Notice: Resolution of Disputes as to Privileged Communications Regulations 2009
SI 2009/1926 General Insurers' Technical Provisions (Appropriate Amount) (Tax) Regulations 2009
SI 2009/1989 *Taxation of Pension Schemes (Transitional Provisions) (Amendment No 2) Order 2009*
SI 2009/1994 *Individual Savings Account (Amendment No 2) Regulations 2009*
SI 2009/2029 *Income Tax (Pay As You Earn) (Amendment No 2) Regulations 2009*
SI 2009/2030 *Income Tax (Construction Industry Scheme) (Amendment) Regulations 2009*
SI 2009/2031 Special Annual Allowance Charge (Application to Members of Currently-Relieved Non-UK Pension Schemes) Order 2009
SI 2009/2032 *Taxes and Duties (Interest Rate) (Amendment) Regulations 2009*
SI 2009/2033 Tax Avoidance Schemes (Prescribed Descriptions of Arrangements) (Amendment) Regulations 2009
SI 2009/2034 Investment Trusts (Dividends) (Optional Treatment as Interest Distributions) Regulations 2009
SI 2009/2036 *Authorised Investment Funds (Tax) (Amendment) Regulations 2009*
SI 2009/2037 Corporation Tax (Land Remediation Relief) Order 2009
SI 2009/2039 Lloyd's Underwriters (Equalisation Reserves) (Tax) Regulations 2009 (revoked)
SI 2009/2050 *Income and Corporation Taxes (Electronic Certificates of Deduction of Tax and Tax Credit) (Amendment) Regulations 2009*
SI 2009/2192 International Movement of Capital (Required Information) Regulations 2009
SI 2009/2888 *Income Tax (Qualifying Child Care) (No 2) Regulations 2009*
SI 2009/2889 *Lloyd's Underwriters (Tax) (Amendment) Regulations 2009*
SI 2009/2971 Mutual Societies (Transfers of Business) (Tax) Regulations 2009
SI 2009/2998 Saving Gateway Accounts (No 2) Regulations 2009
SI 2009/3001 Offshore Funds (Tax) Regulations 2009
SI 2009/3024 Finance Act 2008, Section 128 and Part 2 of Schedule 43 (Appointed Day, Transitional Provision and Savings) Order 2009
SI 2009/3054 The Finance Act 2009, Section 96 and Schedule 48 (Appointed Day, Savings and Consequential Amendments) Order 2009
SI 2010/3055 Registered Pension Schemes (Modification of the Rules of Existing Schemes) Regulations 2009
SI 2009/3073 Taxes, etc (Fees for Payment by Telephone) Regulations 2009 (revoked)
SI 2009/3139 *Offshore Funds (Tax) (Amendment) Regulations 2009*
SI 2009/3173 Corporation Tax (Financing Costs and Income) Regulations 2009 (revoked)
SI 2009/3217 Corporation Tax (Tax Treatment of Financing Costs and Income) (Acceptable Financial Statements) Regulations 2009 (revoked)
SI 2009/3218 *Income and corporation taxes (electronic communications) (Amendment) Regulations 2009*
SI 2009/3227 Northern Rock Plc (Tax Consequences) Regulations 2009
SI 2009/3313 Corporation Tax (Exclusion from Short-Term Loan Relationships) Regulations 2009 (revoked)
SI 2009/3314 Distributions (Excluded Companies) Regulations 2009
SI 2009/3315 Real Estate Investment Trusts (Prescribed Arrangements) Regulations 2009
SI 2009/3332 Saving Gateway Accounts Act 2009 (commencement No 1) Order 2009
SI 2009/3333 Tax Credits (Excluded Companies) Regulations 2009
SI 2010/4 Employers' Duties (Implementation) Regulations 2010
SI 2010/5 Employers' Duties (Registration and Compliance) Regulations 2010
SI 2010/22 Transfer of Tribunal Functions Order 2010
SI 2010/40 *First-tier Tribunal and Upper Tribunal (Chambers) (Amendment) Order 2010* (revoked)
2010/41 The Tribunals, Courts and Enforcement Act 2007 (Miscellaneous Provisions) Order 2010
SI 2010/43 *Tribunal Procedure (Amendment) Rules 2010*
SI 2010/44 *Tribunal Procedure (Amendment No 2) Rules 2010*
SI 2010/86 Financial Services and Markets Act 2000 (Regulated Activities) (Amendment) Order 2010
SI 2010/157 *Enactment of Extra-Statutory Concessions Order 2010*

SI 2010/2743 *Tax Avoidance Schemes (Penalty) (Amendment) Regulations 2010*
SI 2010/2834 *Tax Avoidance Schemes (Prescribed Descriptions of Arrangements) (Amendment) Regulations 2010*
SI 2010/2879 *Income Tax (Indexation) Order 2010*
SI 2010/2901 *Taxation (International and Other Provisions) Act 2010 (Amendment) Order 2010*
SI 2010/2902 *Corporation Tax Act 2010 (Amendment) Order 2010*
SI 2010/2913 London Olympic Games and Paralympic Games Tax Regulations 2010
SI 2010/2928 The Tax Avoidance Schemes (Information) (Amendment) (No.2) Regulations 2010 (revoked)
SI 2010/2929 Treatment of Financing Costs and Income (Available Amount) Regulations 2010 (revoked)
SI 2010/2932 *Insurance Companies (Calculation of Profits: Policy Holders' Tax) (Amendment) Regulations 2010*
SI 2010/2938 *Finance Act 2010, Section 23 and Schedule 2 (High Income Excess Relief Charge) (Repeal) Order 2010*
SI 2010/2939 *Finance Act 2009, Schedule 35 (Special Annual Allowance Charge) (Cessation of Effect) Order 2010*
SI 2010/2942 *Income and Corporation Taxes (Electronic Communications) (Amendment) Regulations 2010*
SI 2010/2957 *ISA (Amendment No 2) Regs 2010*
SI 2010/3019 Finance Act 2010, Schedule 17 (Appointed Day) Order 2010
SI 2010/3025 Tax Treatment of Financing Costs and Income (Correction of Mismatches) Regs 2010 (revoked)
SI 2011/22 Dormant Bank and Building Society Accounts (Tax) regulations 2011
SI 2011/23 Finance Act 2008, Section 39(7) (Commencement) Order 2011
SI 2011/37 *Mutual Societies (Transfers of Business) (Tax) (Amendment) Regs 2011*
SI 2011/132 Finance (No 3) Act 2010, Schedule 11 (Appointed Day) Order 2011
SI 2011/171 Tax Avoidance Schemes (Information) (Amendment) Regs 2011 (revoked)
SI 2011/236 *Films Co-Production Agreements (Amendment) Order 2011* (revoked)
SI 2011/244 *Authorised Investment Funds (Tax) (Amendment) Regulations 2011*
SI 2011/301 *Registered Pension Schemes (Provision of Information) (Amendment) Regulations 2011*
SI 2011/302 *Registered Pension Schemes (Accounting and Assessment) (Amendment) Regulations 2011*
SI 2011/660 *Venture Capital Trust (Winding up and Mergers) (Tax) (Amendment) Regulations 2011*
SI 2011/662 Finance (No 3) Act 2010, Schedule 2 (Appointed Day) Order 2011
SI 2011/698 *Loan Relationships and Derivative Contracts (Disregard and Bringing into Account of Profits and Losses) (Amendment) Regulations 2011*
SI 2011/711 Taxes, etc (Fees for Payment by Internet) Regulations 2011 (revoked)
SI 2011/712 Qualifying Care Relief (Specified Social Care Schemes) Order 2011
SI 2011/976 Penalties, Offshore Income etc. (Designation of Territories) Order 2011
SI 2011/1079 International Mutual Administrative Assistance in Tax Matters Order 2011
SI 2011/1157 Skipton Fund Limited (Application of Sections 731, 733 and 734 of the Income Tax (Trading and Other Income) Act 2005) Order 2011
SI 2011/1211 *Offshore Funds (Tax) (Amendment) Regulations 2011*
SI 2011/1295 Taxation of Chargeable Gains (Gilt-edged Securities) Order 2011
SI 2011/1431 Corporation Tax (Implementation of the Mergers Directive) Regulations 2011
SI 2011/1502 Taxation of Equitable Life (Payments) Order 2011
SI 2011/1583 *Finance Act 2009 (Consequential Amendments) Order 2011*
SI 2011/1584 *Income Tax (Pay As You Earn) (Amendment) (No. 3) Regulations 2011*
SI 2011/1585 *Income Tax (Earnings and Pensions) Act 2003 (Section 684(3A)) Order 2011*
SI 2011/1502 Taxation of Equitable Life (Payments) Order 2011
SI 2011/1613 *The Undertakings for Collective Investment in Transferable Securities Regulations 2011*
SI 2011/1751 *Registered Pension Schemes (Miscellaneous Amendments) Regulations 2011*
SI 2011/1752 Registered Pension Schemes (Lifetime Allowance Transitional Protection) Regulations 2011
SI 2011/1782 *Taxation of Pension Schemes (Transitional Provisions) (Amendment) (No 2) Order 2011*
SI 2011/1783 Registered Pension Schemes (Relevant Income) Regulations 2011

SI 2012/1895 *Income Tax (Pay As You Earn) (Amendment No 2) Regulations 2012*
SI 2012/1898 Business Investment Relief Regulations 2012
SI 2012/1906 *Financial Services and Markets Act 2000 (Regulated Activities) (Amendment) Order 2012*
SI 2012/2933 Bank Levy: International Tax Enforcement Arrangements (Federal Republic of Germany) Order 2012
SI 2012/3008 Friendly Societies (Modifications of the Tax Acts) Regulations 2012
SI 2012/3009 Insurance Companies (Transitional Provisions) Regulations 2012
SI 2012/3024 Controlled Foreign Companies (Excluded Territories) Regulations 2012
SI 2012/3037 Car and Van Fuel Benefit Order 2012
SI 2012/3041 Controlled Foreign Companies (Excluded Banking Business Profits) Regulations 2012
SI 2012/3043 Authorised Investment Funds (Tax) (Amendment No. 3) Regulations 2012
SI 2012/3044 Insurance Companies and CFCs (Avoidance of Double Charge) Regulations 2012
SI 2012/3045 Taxation (International and Other Provisions) Act 2010 (Part 7) (Amendment) Regulations 2012
SI 2012/3047 Income Tax (Indexation) Order 2012
SI 2012/3070 Visiting Forces and International Military Headquarters (EU SOFA) (Tax Designation) Order 2012
SI 2012/3071 Visiting Forces and International Military Headquarters (NATO and PfP) (Tax Designation) Order 2012
SI 2013/5 Tonnage Tax (Training Requirement) (Amendment) Regulations 2013
SI 2013/13 Taxation of Chargeable Gains (Gilt-edged Securities) Order 2013
SI 2013/67 Finance Act 2009, Sections 101 and 102 (Machine Games Duty) (Appointed Day) Order 2013
SI 2013/157 Corporation Tax (Treatment of Unrelieved Surplus Advance Corporation Tax) (Amendment) Regulations 2013
SI 2013/234 *Enactment of Extra-Statutory Concessions Order 2013*
SI 2013/263 *Child Trust Funds (Amendment) Regulations 2013*
SI 2013/267 *Individual Savings Account (Amendment) Regulations 2013*
SI 2013/279 *Finance Act 2012, Schedule 38 (Tax Agents: Dishonest Conduct) (Appointed Day and Savings) Order 2013*
SI 2013/280 *Finance Act 2009, Section 101 (Tax Agents: Dishonest Conduct) (Appointed Day) Order 2013*
SI 2013/420 Profits from Patents (EEA Rights) Order 2013
SI 2013/460 Building Societies (Core Capital Deferred Shares) Regulations 2013
SI 2013/463 *Tax Law Rewrite Acts (Amendment) Order 2013*
SI 2013/464 *Capital Allowances (First-year Tax Credits) Order 2013*
SI 2013/472 Financial Services Act 2012 (Consequential Amendments and Transitional Provisions) Order 2013
SI 2013/477 *Tribunal Procedure (Amendment) Rules 2013*
SI 2013/489 Natural Resources Body for Wales (Tax Consequences) Order 2013
SI 2013/513 *Income Tax (Exempt Amount for Childcare Vouchers and for Employer Contracted Childcare) Order 2013*
SI 2013/521 *Income Tax (Pay As You Earn) (Amendment) Regulations 2013*
SI 2013/557 *Capital Gains Tax (Amendment) Regulations 2013*
SI 2013/587 *Finance Act 2012, Schedule 14 (Appointed Day) Order 2013*
SI 2013/605 *Income Tax (Removal of Ordinary Residence) Regulations 2013*
SI 2013/606 *Tribunal Procedure (Amendment No 2) Rules 2013*
SI 2013/620 *Income Tax (Construction Industry Scheme) (Amendment) Regulations 2013*
SI 2013/623 *Individual Savings Account (Amendment No 2) Regulations 2013*
SI 2013/661 *Offshore Funds (Tax) (Amendment) Regulations 2013*
SI 2013/662 *Capital Gains Tax (Annual Exempt Amount) Order 2013*
SI 2013/676 *Trusts (Capital and Income) Act 2013 (Commencement No 1) Order 2013*
SI 2013/744 *Finance Act 2012, Schedule 22 (Reduction of Supplementary Charge for Certain Oil Fields) (Appointed Day) Order 2013*
SI 2013/759 *Finance Act 1995, Section 55 (Appointed Date) Order 2013*
SI 2013/938 *Small Charitable Donations Regulations 2013*
SI 2013/1034 *Amendments to Schedule 6 to the Tribunals, Courts and Enforcement Act 2007 Order 2013*

SI 2013/2472 Finance Act 2009, Sections 101 and 102 (Annual Tax on Enveloped Dwellings) (Appointed Day) Order 2013
SI 2013/2556 Automatic Enrolment (Miscellaneous Amendments) Regulations 2013
SI 2013/2571 Annual Tax on Enveloped Dwellings Avoidance Schemes (Prescribed Descriptions of Arrangements) Regulations 2013
SI 2013/2592 Tax Avoidance Schemes (Information) (Amendment, etc) Regulations 2013
SI 2013/2595 Tax Avoidance Schemes (Prescribed Descriptions of Arrangements) (Amendment) Regulations 2013
SI 2013/2781 Loan Relationships and Derivative Contracts (Disregard and Bringing into Account of Profits and Losses) (Amendment) Regulations 2013
SI 2013/2796 Finance Act 2013, Schedule 2, Paragraph 31 (Enterprise Management Incentives) (Appointed Day) Order 2013
SI 2013/2819 *Unauthorised Unit Trusts (Tax) Regulations 2013*
SI 2013/2892 Tax Treatment of Financing Costs and Income (Excluded Schemes) Regulations 2013 (revoked)
SI 2013/2910 The Additionally-developed Oil Fields Order 2013
SI 2013/2983 Taxation of Chargeable Gains (Gilt-edged Securities) (No 2) Order 2013
SI 2013/2989 Income-related Benefits (Subsidy to Authorities) Amendment (No 2) Order 2013
SI 2013/2994 Authorised Investment Funds (Tax) (Amendment) (No 2) Regulations 2013
SI 2013/3033 Van Benefit and Car and Van Fuel Benefit Order 2013
SI 2013/3088 Income Tax (Indexation) Order 2013
SI 2013/3118 Capital Requirements (Country-by-Country Reporting) Regulations 2013
SI 2013/3209 Taxation of Regulatory Capital Securities Regulations 2013
SI 2013/3218 Corporation Tax Act 2009, Section 582 (Contract for Differences) (Amendment) Order 2013
SI 2014/211 Enactment of Extra-Statutory Concessions Order 2014
SI 2014/402 Income Tax (Earnings and Pensions) Act 2003 (Amendment to SAYE Option Schemes Contributions Limit) Order 2014
SI 2014/472 Income Tax (Pay As You Earn) and the Income Tax (Construction Industry Scheme) (Amendment) Regulations 2014
SI 2014/474 Income Tax (Pay As You Earn) (Amendment) Regulations 2014
SI 2014/489 Income and Corporation Taxes (Electronic Communications)(Amendment) Regulations 2014
SI 2014/496 Taxes (Interest Rate) (Amendment) Regulations 2014
SI 2014/506 Financial Services and Markets Act 2000 (Consumer Credit) (Miscellaneous Provisions) (No 2) Order 2014
SI 2014/514 Tribunal Procedure (Amendment) Rules 2014
SI 2014/518 Real Estate Investment Trust (Amendments to the Corporation Tax Act 2010 and Consequential Amendments) Regulations 2014
SI 2014/520 International Tax Compliance (Crown Dependencies and Gibraltar) Regulations 2014
SI 2014/584 Charitable Deductions (Approved Schemes) (Amendment) Regulations 2014
SI 2014/585 Unauthorised Unit Trusts (Tax) (Amendment) Regulations 2014
SI 2014/600 Tribunals, Courts and Enforcement Act 2007 (Consequential, Transitional and Saving Provision) Order 2014
SI 2014/631 Public Bodies (Abolition of the National Consumer Council and Transfer of the Office of Fair Trading's Functions in relation to Estate Agents etc) Order 2014
SI 2014/649 Child Trust Funds (Amendment) Regulations 2014
SI 2014/654 Individual Savings Account (Amendment) Regulations 2014
SI 2014/685 Investment Transactions (Tax) Regulations 2014
SI 2014/768 Tribunals, Courts and Enforcement Act 2007 (Commencement No 11) Order 2014
SI 2014/788 Police and Criminal Evidence Act 1984 (Application to Revenue and Customs) (Amendment) Order 2014 (revoked)
SI 2014/834 Public Bodies (Merger of the Director of Public Prosecutions and the Director of Revenue and Customs Prosecutions) Order 2014
SI 2014/852 Child Arrangements Order (Consequential Amendments to Subordinate Legislation) Order 2014
SI 2014/854 Annual Tax on Enveloped Dwellings (Indexation of Annual Chargeable Amounts) Order 2014
Investment Manager (Investment Transactions) Regulations 2014 (non-SI secondary legislation)

SI 2014/3133 Lloyd's Underwriters (Conversion of Partnerships to Underwriting through Successor Companies) (Tax) Regulations 2014
SI 2014/3183 Capital Allowances (Designated Assisted Areas) Order 2014
SI 2014/3187 Loan Relationships and Derivative Contracts (Change of Accounting Practice) (Amendment) Regulations 2014
SI 2014/3188 Loan Relationships and Derivative Contracts (Disregard and Bringing into Account of Profits and Losses) (Amendment) Regulations 2014
SI 2014/3226 Finance Act 2014, Section 12 (Appointed Day) Order 2014
SI 2014/3227 Income Tax (Recommended Medical Treatment) Regulations 2014
SI 2014/3237 Taxation (International and Other Provisions) Act 2010 (Amendment to Section 371RE) (Controlled Foreign Companies) Regulations 2014
SI 2014/3269 Finance Act 2009, Schedules 55 and 56 and Sections 101 and 102 (Stamp Duty Reserve Tax) (Appointed Days, Consequential and Finance Act 2009, Schedules 55 and 56 and Sections 101 and 102 (Stamp Duty Reserve Tax) (Appointed Days, Consequential and Transitional Provision) Order 2014
SI 2014/3273 Income Tax (Indexation) Order 2014
SI 2014/3294 Revenue Scotland and Tax Powers Act 2014 (Consequential Provisions and Modifications) Order 2014
SI 2014/3324 Finance Act 2009, Sections 101 and 102 (Remote Gambling Taxes) (Appointed Day) Order 2014
SI 2014/3325 Changes in Accounting Standards (Loan Relationships and Derivative Contracts) Regulations 2014
SI 2014/3327 Community Amateur Sports Clubs (Exemptions) Order 2014
SI 2014/3346 Finance Act 2009, Schedules 55 and 56 and Sections 101 and 102 (Stamp Duty Reserve Tax) (Appointed Days, Consequential and Transitional Provision) (Amendment) Order 2014
SI 2015/2 Income Tax (Pay As You Earn) (Amendment) Regulations 2015
SI 2015/11 Money Laundering (Amendment) Regulations 2015 (revoked)
SI 2015/60 Capital Allowances Act 2001 (Extension of first-year allowances) (Amendment) Order 2015
SI 2015/67 Social Security (Miscellaneous Amendments) Regulations 2015
SI 2015/80 Finance Act 2004 (Registered Pension Schemes and Annual Allowance Charge) (Amendment) Order 2015
SI 2015/86 Films (Definition of "British Film") Order 2015
SI 2015/118 Occupational Pension Schemes (Power to Amend Schemes to Reflect Abolition of Contracting-out) Regulations 2015
SI 2015/130 Promoters of Tax Avoidance Schemes (Prescribed Circumstances under Section 235) Regulations 2015
SI 2015/131 Finance Act 2014 (Schedule 34 Prescribed Matters) Regulations 2015
SI 2015/171 Income Tax (Pay As You Earn) (Amendment No 2) Regulations 2015
SI 2015/344 Bank Levy (Double Taxation Arrangements) (Netherlands) Regulations 2015
SI 2015/346 Income Tax (Qualifying Child Care) Regulations 2015
SI 2015/360 Finance Act 2014, Schedule 9 (Employment-related Securities etc.) (Consequential etc. Amendments) Regulations 2015
SI 2015/361 Venture Capital Trust (Winding up and Mergers) (Tax) (Amendment) Regulations 2015
SI 2015/411 Taxes (Interest Rate) (Amendment) Regulations 2015
SI 2015/429 Income Tax (Construction Industry Scheme) (Amendment) Regulations 2015
SI 2015/431 Independent Police Complaints Commission (Complaints and Misconduct) (Contractors) Regulations 2015
SI 2015/448 Childcare Payments (Eligibility) Regulations 2015
SI 2015/463 Unauthorised Unit Trusts (Tax) (Amendment) Regulations 2015
SI 2015/464 Annual Tax on Enveloped Dwellings Avoidance Schemes (Prescribed Descriptions of Arrangements) (Amendment) Regulations 2015
SI 2015/485 Authorised Investment Funds (Tax) (Amendment) Regulations 2015
SI 2015/522 Childcare Payments Regulations 2015
SI 2015/544 Life Insurance Qualifying Policies (Statement and Reporting Requirements) (Amendment) Regulations 2015
SI 2015/549 Finance Act 2014 (High Risk Promoters Prescribed Information) Regulations 2015
SI 2015/575 Solvency 2 Regulations 2015
SI 2015/578 Employment Allowance (Care and Support Workers) Regulations 2015

SI 2015/1607 Tonnage Tax (Training Requirement) (Amendment) (No 2) Regulations 2015 (revoked)
SI 2015/1641 Deregulation Act 2015 (Insolvency) (Consequential Amendments and Transitional and Savings Provisions) Order 2015
SI 2015/1667 Income Tax (Pay As You Earn) (Amendment No 3) Regulations 2015
SI 2015/1732 Deregulation Act 2015 (Commencement No 3 and Transitional and Saving Provisions) Order 2015
SI 2015/1783 Police and Criminal Evidence Act 1984 (Application to Revenue and Customs) Order 2015
SI 2015/1777 Taxes, etc. (Fees for Payment by Internet) (Amendment) Regulations 2015
SI 2015/1810 Scottish Rate of Income Tax (Consequential Amendments) Order 2015
SI 2015/1836 Finance Act 2015 (Paragraphs 10 to 12 of Schedule 6) Regulations 2015
SI 2015/1839 International Tax Compliance (Amendment) Regulations 2015
SI 2015/1886 Films Co-Production Agreements (Amendment) Order 2015
SI 2015/1790 Taxation of Chargeable Gains (Gilt-edged Securities) Order 2015
SI 2015/1948 Income Tax (Approved Expenses) Regulations 2015
SI 2015/1983 Lloyd's Underwriters (Transitional Equalisation Reserves) (Tax) Regulations 2015
SI 2015/1986 Enforcement by Deduction from Accounts (Prescribed Information) Regulations 2015
SI 2015/2000 Scotland Act 2012, Section 25 (Appointed Years) Order 2015
SI 2015/2002 Qualifying Private Placement Regulations 2015
SI 2015/2053 Unauthorised Unit Trusts (Tax) (Amendment No 2) Regulations 2015
SI 2015/2056 Taxation of Regulatory Capital Securities (Amendment) Regulations 2015
SI 2016/16 Individual Savings Account (Amendment) Regulations 2016
SI 2016/44 Enforcement by Deduction from Accounts (Imposition of Charges by Deposit-takers) Regulations 2016
SI 2016/74 Finance Act 2014, Schedule 9 (Consequential Amendment) Regulations 2016
SI 2016/99 Tax Avoidance Schemes (Prescribed Descriptions of Arrangements) (Amendment) Regulations 2016
SI 2016/208 Proceeds of Crime Act 2002 (Cash Searches: Code of Practice) Order 2016
SI 2016/209 Proceeds of Crime Act 2002 (Investigations: Code of Practice) (England and Wales and Northern Ireland) Order 2016
SI 2016/222 Proceeds of Crime Act 2002 (Investigative Powers of Prosecutors: Code of Practice) (England and Wales and Northern Ireland) Order 2016
SI 2016/237 Taxes (Base Erosion and Profit Shifting) (Country-by-Country Reporting) Regulations 2016
SI 2016/308 Registered Pension Schemes (Provision of Information) (Amendment) Regulations 2016
SI 2016/311 Occupational and Personal Pension Schemes (Automatic Enrolment) (Miscellaneous Amendments) Regulations 2016
SI 2016/333 Fees for Payment of Taxes, etc. by Credit Card Regulations 2016
SI 2016/364 Individual Savings Account (Amendment No 2) Regulations 2016
SI 2016/404 Income Tax (Construction Industry Scheme) (Amendment of Schedule 11 to the Finance Act 2004) Order 2016
WSI 2016/413 Social Services and Well-being (Wales) Act 2014 (Consequential Amendments) Regulations 2016
SI 2016/456 Finance Act 2015, Schedule 20 (Appointed Days) Order 2016
SI 2016/566 Banking Surcharge (Information) Regulations 2016
SI 2016/597 Lloyd's Underwriters (Roll-over Relief on Disposal of Assets of Ancillary Trust Fund) (Tax) Regulations 2016
SI 2016/719 Employers' Duties (Implementation) (Amendment) Regulations 2016
SI 2016/747 Income Tax (Pay As You Earn) (Amendment No 2) Regulations 2016
SI 2016/751 Capital Allowances (Designated Assisted Areas) Order 2016
SI 2016/771 Major Sporting Events (Income Tax Exemption) Regulations 2016
SI 2016/788 Civil Procedure (Amendment No 3) Rules 2016
SI 2016/819 Tonnage Tax (Training Requirement) (Amendment) Regulations 2016 (revoked)
SI 2016/874 Bank Levy (Amendment of Schedule 19 to the Finance Act 2011) Regulations 2016
SI 2016/881 Postal Services Act 2011 (Taxation) (Amendment) Regulations 2016
SI 2016/889 International Tax Compliance (Client Notification) Regulations 2016

Disclosure and Co-operation) Regulations 2017
SI 2017/338 Taxation of Northern Ireland Welfare Supplementary Payments Regulations 2017
SI 2017/345 Penalties Relating to Offshore Matters and Offshore Transfers (Additional Information) Regulations 2017
SI 2017/347 Employers' Duties (Implementation) (Amendment) Regulations 2017
SI 2017/351 Wales Act 2017 (Commencement No 1) Regulations 2017
SI 2017/355 Finance Act 2016, Section 113(1) to (4) (Commencement) Regulations 2017
SI 2017/364 Corporation Tax Act 2010 (Part 8C) (Amendment) Regulations 2017
SI 2017/377 Capital Gains Tax (Annual Exempt Amount) Order 2017
SI 2017/397 Registered Pension Schemes (Authorised Payments) (Amendment) Regulations 2017
SI 2017/398 Pension Schemes (Categories of Country and Requirements for Overseas Pension Schemes and Recognised Overseas Pension Schemes) (Amendments) Regulations 2017
SI 2017/399 Policing and Crime Act 2017 (Commencement No 1 and Transitional Provisions) Regulations 2017
SI 2017/414 Income Tax (Pay As You Earn) (Amendment) Regulations 2017
SI 2017/446 Scottish Infected Blood Support Scheme (Application of Sections 731, 733 and 734 of the Income Tax (Trading and Other Income) Act 2005) Order 2017
SI 2017/454 Corporation Tax (Treatment of Unrelieved Surplus Advance Corporation Tax) (Amendment) Regulations 2017
SI 2017/455 Scotland Act 2016 (Commencement No. 5) Regulations 2017
SI 2017/466 Individual Savings Account (Amendment No 2) Regulations 2017
SI 2017/468 Scotland Act 2016 (Income Tax Consequential Amendments) Regulations 2017
SI 2017/495 Enactment of Extra-Statutory Concessions Order 2017
SI 2017/497 Taxes (Base Erosion and Profit Shifting) (Country-by- Country Reporting) (Amendment) Regulations 2017
SI 2017/598 International Tax Compliance (Amendment) Regulations 2017
SI 2017/524 Crown Estate Transfer Scheme 2017
SI 2017/602 Scotland Act 2016 (Consequential and Saving Provisions) Regulations 2017
SI 2017/608 Scotland Act 2016 (Commencement No 6) Regulations 2017
SI 2017/614 Major Sporting Events (Income Tax Exemption) Regulations 2017
SI 2017/722 First-tier Tribunal and Upper Tribunal (Chambers) (Amendment) Order 2017
SI 2017/723 Tribunal Procedure (Amendment) Rules 2017
SI 2017/726 Policing and Crime Act 2017 (Commencement No 3 and Transitional and Saving Provisions) Regulations 2017
SI 2017/736 Police and Criminal Evidence Act 1984 (Application to Revenue and Customs) (Amendment) Order 2017
SI 2017/739 Criminal Finances Act 2017 (Commencement No 1) Regulations 2017
SI 2017/740 Capital Allowances Act 2001 (Cars Emissions) (Amendment) Order 2017
SI 2017/748 Child Trust Funds (Amendment No 2) Regulations 2017
SI 2017/752 Payment Services Regulations 2017
SI 2017/868 Employers' Duties (Miscellaneous Amendments) Regulations 2017
SI 2017/876 Facilitation of Tax Evasion Offences (Guidance About Prevention) Regulations 2017
SI 2017/882 Tonnage Tax (Training Requirement) (Amendment etc.) Regulations 2017
SI 2017/904 Infected Blood Schemes (Application of Sections 731, 733 and 734 of the Income Tax (Trading and Other Income) Act 2005) Order 2017
SI 2017/954 Tax Collection and Management (Wales) Act 2016 (Commencement No 1) Order 2017
SI 2017/970 Finance Act 2016, Section 166 (Appointed Day) Regulations 2017
SI 2017/988 Sections 106B, 106C and 106D of the Taxes Management Act 1970 (Specified Threshold Amount) Regulations 2017
SI 2017/989 Offshore Asset Moves Penalty (Specified Territories) (Amendment) Regulations 2017
SI 2017/991 Criminal Finances Act 2017 (Commencement No 2 and Transitional Provisions) Regulations 2017
SI 2017/1022 Tax Collection and Management (Administration) (Wales) Regulations 2017

1961/580

VISITING FORCES AND ALLIED HEADQUARTERS (INCOME TAX AND DEATH DUTIES) (DESIGNATION) ORDER 1961

Made by the Commissioners of Inland Revenue under FA 1960, s 73; now TA 1988 s 323

Made . . . .*24 March 1961*

1 Each of the countries specified in the First Schedule to this Order and each of the allied headquarters specified in the Second Schedule to this Order is hereby designated for the purposes of Section 73 of the Finance Act, 1960[1].

Note—[1] TA 1988 s 323.

2 This Order may be cited as the Visiting Forces and Allied Headquarters (Income Tax and Death Duties) (Designation) Order, 1961, and shall come into operation on the 30th day of March, 1961.

FIRST SCHEDULE

Article 1

Belgium, Canada, Denmark, France, Greece, Italy, Luxembourg, the Netherlands, Norway, Portugal, Turkey, and the United States of America.

SECOND SCHEDULE

Article 1

Channel Committee.
Channel Command.
Eastern Atlantic Area Command.
Supreme Headquarters Allied Powers Europe.
Allied Command Atlantic Headquarters.

1964/924

VISITING FORCES (INCOME TAX AND DEATH DUTIES) (DESIGNATION) ORDER 1964

Made under FA 1960, s 73; now TA 1988 s 323

Made . . . .*23 June 1964*

1 The Federal Republic of Germany is hereby designated for the purposes of section 73 of the Finance Act 1960[1].

Note—[1] TA 1988 s 323.

2 This Order may be cited as the Visiting Forces (Income Tax and Death Duties) (Designation) Order 1964, and shall come into operation on the 30th June 1964.

1967/149

CAPITAL GAINS TAX REGULATIONS 1967

Made by the Commissioners of Inland Revenue under FA 1965 Sch 10 para 2, now TMA 1970 s 57; see TA 1970 s 539(1), (3), (5) and TA 1988 Sch 30 para 21

Made . . . .*9 February 1967*

1 Citation and commencement

These Regulations may be cited as the Capital Gains Tax Regulations 1967, and shall come into operation on 16th February 1967.

2 Interpretation

(1) In the Regulations, unless the context otherwise requires—

"appeal" means an appeal against an assessment to capital gains tax or against a decision on a claim relating to capital gains tax;

"The Board" means the Commissioners of Inland Revenue;

"Commissioners" means (subject to Regulation 17) General Commissioners or Special Commissioners;

"third party" means a third or subsequent party joined under Regulation 8;

references to the Income Tax Management Act 1964[1] are references to that Act as applied in relation to capital gains tax by paragraph 1 of Schedule 10 to the Finance Act 1965[2];

references to Part III of the Finance Act 1965[2] include Schedules 6 to 10 to that Act and any other enactment to be construed as one with the said Part III;

subject to Regulation 15, other expressions have the same meaning as in Part III of the Finance Act 1965[2].

(2) The Interpretation Act 1889[3] shall apply to these Regulations as it applies to an Act of Parliament.

Note—[1] TMA 1970.
[2] TCGA 1992.
[3] Interpretation Act 1978.

Amendments—Definitions of "Commissioners" and "references to the Income Tax Management Act 1964" revoked by the Transfer of Tribunal Functions and Revenue and Customs Appeals Order, SI 2009/56 art 3, Sch 2 paras 1, 2 with effect from 1 April 2009.

3 Notices of appeals against assessments

. . .

Amendments—Revoked by FA 1969 Sch 21 Pt VIII.

4 Choice of appeal Commissioners

. . .

Amendments—Revoked by FA 1969 Sch 21 Pt VIII.

5 Assignment of appeals to General Commissioners

. . .

Amendments—Revoked by FA 1969 Sch 21 Pt VIII.

6 Representations in writing

. . .

Amendments—Revoked by the General and Special Commissioners (Amendment of Enactments) Regulations, SI 1994/1813 reg 2, Sch 1 para 27, Sch 2 with effect from 1 September 1994.

7 Representation of the inspector

. . .

Amendments—Revoked by the General and Special Commissioners (Amendment of Enactments) Regulations, SI 1994/1813 reg 2, Sch 1 para 27, Sch 2 with effect from 1 September 1994.

8 Joinder of third parties in appeals

(1) Where the market value of an asset on a particular date or the apportionment of any amount or value is a material question in an appeal any person whose liability to capital gains tax for any period may be affected by that market value or by the manner in which that amount or value is apportioned may apply under this Regulation to be joined as a party in the appeal.

(2) An application under this Regulation to be joined as a party in an appeal shall be made in writing to [an officer of Revenue and Customs][2] stating—

(*a*) the name and address of the applicant;
(*b*) the question which may affect his liability to capital gains tax;
(*c*) how his liability may be affected; and
(*d*) his contention with regard to that question.

(3) The [officer][2] shall send a copy of the application to the appellant and to any other party to the appeal.

[(4) If the application is received by the officer before the appeal has been notified to the tribunal, the officer shall, if satisfied that it is proper to join the applicant as a party in the appeal, join the applicant as a third party and give notice of the joinder to the appellant and any other party to the appeal.

(5) If the application is received by the officer after the appeal has been notified to the tribunal, or the officer is not satisfied that it is proper to join the applicant as a party in the appeal, the officer shall refer the application to the tribunal, which may at its discretion allow or refuse the application.][2]

(6) . . . [1]

Provided that an appeal shall not be so transferred unless the Commissioners to whom the application is made are satisfied that the balance of convenience to the parties is in favour of the transfer.

(7) At the hearing and on the determination of the appeal or of any question in the appeal a third party shall, so far as relates to the question in which he is interested, have the same rights as an appellant, including any right to require the statement of a case for the opinion of any Court.

(8) . . . [1]

(9) A person entitled under section 26(5) of the Finance Act 1965[3] (proceedings consequent on death) to be a party to an appeal shall, if he wishes to be made a party, apply to be joined under this Regulation.

Amendments—[1] Paras (6), (8) revoked by the General and Special Commissioners (Amendment of Enactments) Regulations, SI 1994/1813 reg 2, Sch 1 para 27, Sch 2 with effect from 1 September 1994.
[2] In paras (2), (3), words substituted, and paras (4), (5) substituted, by the Transfer of Tribunal Functions and Revenue and Customs Appeals Order, SI 2009/56 art 3, Sch 2 paras 1, 3 with effect from 1 April 2009.
[3] TCGA 1992.

9 Applications for determination of market value

(1) Where the market value of an asset on a particular date or the apportionment of any amount or value may affect the liability to capital gains tax for any period (and whether for the same or different periods) of two or more persons and is not (and has not been) a material question in an appeal already brought by any of them, any of those persons may apply to the [tribunal][1] to determine that market value or the manner in which that amount or value should be apportioned.

(2) An application under this Regulation shall be made by notice in writing sent to [an officer of Revenue and Customs][1] stating the question for determination and (to the best of the applicant's knowledge) the names and addresses of the other persons whose liability to capital gains tax may be affected by the question.

(3) . . . [1]

(4) The [officer][1] shall be a party to proceedings under this Regulation.

(5) . . . [1]

(6) Subject to paragraphs (1) to [(4)][1] above, these Regulations, Part III of the Finance Act 1965[2] and any enactment directly or indirectly applied by the said Part III shall, so far as they are applicable and with any necessary modifications, apply in relation to proceedings under this Regulation as they apply in relation to an appeal against an assessment to capital gains tax.

Amendments—[1] In paras (1),(2), (4) words substituted, paras (3), (5) revoked, and in para (6), reference substituted, by the Transfer of Tribunal Functions and Revenue and Customs Appeals Order, SI 2009/56 art 3, Sch 2 paras 1, 4 with effect from 1 April 2009.

[2] TMA 1970 s 47.

10 References of questions of value to other tribunals

(1)–(3) . . . [1,2]

Amendments—[1] Para (2) revoked by FA 1969 Sch 21 Pt VIII.

[2] Paras (1), (3) revoked by the General and Special Commissioners (Amendment of Enactments) Regulations, SI 1994/1813 reg 2, Sch 1 para 27, Sch 2 with effect from 1 September 1994.

11 Conclusive effect of a determination on appeal

(1) Where the market value of an asset on a particular date or the apportionment of any amount or value (being a market value or apportionment affecting or which may affect the liability to capital gains tax of two or more persons) is finally determined on an appeal that determination shall, subject to Regulation 14, be in all proceedings relating to capital gains tax conclusive between the Board or any officer of the Board and the following persons—

(*a*) parties to the appeal; and

(*b*) any person who was entitled to apply to be joined as a third party in the appeal, and had notice, in reasonable time for making such application, of the appeal and of the question in the appeal entitling him so to apply, not being a person who did so apply without undue delay and whose application was not allowed.

(2) For the purposes of these Regulations—

(*a*) the determination of an appeal or a question in an appeal shall be treated as final when the determination can no longer be varied by the tribunal making it or by the order of any court;

(*b*) the market value of an asset on a particular date or the apportionment of any amount or value shall be deemed to have been finally determined on an appeal notwithstanding that there was no dispute concerning that market value or apportionment if the market value or apportionment was a material question in the appeal and the appeal has been finally determined.

(3), (4) . . . [1]

Amendments—[1] Paras (3), (4) revoked by the General and Special Commissioners (Amendment of Enactments) Regulations, SI 1994/1813 reg 2, Sch 1 para 27, Sch 2 with effect from 1 September 1994.

12 Agreements in writing of market value or apportionment

(1) An agreement or notification which apart from this Regulation would have effect under section [54 of the Taxes Management Act 1970][1] (settlement of appeals by agreement or withdrawal) as if an appeal had been determined by [the tribunal][1] shall not have that effect in relation to any appeal in which a third party has been joined unless, at the time when such agreement is made or notification is given, the question in which the third party is interested has been finally determined on the appeal or disposed of by an agreement made in accordance with paragraph (2) below.

(2) Where the market value of an asset on a particular date or the apportionment of any amount or value may affect the liability to capital gains tax of two or more persons and is a material question in an appeal, then if the market value or apportionment is agreed in writing between [an][1] officer of the Board and all the parties to the appeal whose liability may be affected by it the agreement shall in all proceedings relating to the capital gains tax be conclusive between the Board or any officer of the Board and the following persons—

(*a*) parties to the agreement; and

(*b*) any person who was entitled, in respect of the question in the appeal to which the agreement relates, to apply to be joined as a third party in the appeal, and had notice of the appeal and of the question in the appeal not less than thirty days before the agreement was made, not being a person who did so apply before the agreement was made.

(3) A document purporting to be an agreement made in accordance with paragraph (2) above and produced from proper custody may be received in evidence in any proceedings relating to capital gains tax without further proof as such an agreement made by the persons by whom it purports to be signed.

Amendments—[1] In paras (1), (2), words substituted by the Transfer of Tribunal Functions and Revenue and Customs Appeals Order, SI 2009/56 art 3, Sch 2 paras 1, 5 with effect from 1 April 2009.

13 Persons affected by a determination or agreement in writing

(1) A determination or agreement which is by virtue of these Regulations conclusive against or in favour of any person shall to the same extent be conclusive against or in favour of his personal representatives and his trustee or assignee in bankruptcy or under a deed of arrangement.

(2) A determination or agreement relating to any settled property which is by virtue of these Regulations conclusive against or in favour of the trustees of the settlement shall to the same extent be conclusive against or in favour of any person becoming absolutely entitled to that property as against the trustees.

(3) A determination or agreement relating to an asset comprised in the estate of a deceased person, or in a testamentary disposition made by him, which is by virtue of these Regulations conclusive against or in favour of his personal representatives shall to the same extent be conclusive against or in favour of any person acquiring the asset as legatee.

(4) Where paragraph 20 of Schedule 7 to the Finance Act 1965[1] (disposals between husband and wife) or section 31(4) of that Act[2] (disposals of certain works of art, etc) applies in respect of the disposal of an asset, a determination or agreement relating to the asset which is by virtue of these Regulations conclusive against or in favour of the person making the disposal shall to the same extent be conclusive against or in favour of the person acquiring the asset.

Note—[1] TCGA 1992 s 58.
[2] TCGA 1992 s 258.

14 Fraud or wilful default

A determination or agreement shall not by virtue of these Regulations be conclusive in favour of any person if it is shown that any form of fraud or wilful default committed by or on behalf of that person procured or contributed to procure the determination or agreement.

15 Interpretation of certain expressions

For the purposes of these Regulations—

(*a*) The market value of an asset or the apportionment of any amount or value is a material question in an appeal notwithstanding that there is no dispute thereon between the appellant and the inspector if the adoption of a different market value or of a different apportionment might produce a different determination on the appeal.

(*b*) A person shall not be treated as being at any date a person whose liability to capital gains tax may be affected by the market value of an asset or by the apportionment of any amount or value paid, payable or ascertained in connection with an asset unless on or before that date, but since 6th April 1965, there has been (or is deemed to have been) a disposal or acquisition of the asset by that person, or by personal representatives from whom they may acquire the asset as legatee, or by a company or trustees whose chargeable gains may to any extent be treated as accruing to that person under section 13 (attribution of gains to members of nonresident companies), 86 (attribution of gains to settlors with interest in nonresident or dual resident settlements) or 87 (non-UK resident settlements: attribution of gains to beneficiaries) of the Taxation of Chargeable Gains Act 1992.][1]

(*c*) Personal representatives or trustees who are for the purposes of Part III of the Finance Act 1965[2] treated as a single and continuing body of persons shall be treated as a single person distinct from the persons who may from time to time be the personal representatives or trustees, and if the same persons are personal representatives or trustees in respect of more than one estate or settlement they shall be treated as a separate person in respect of each estate or settlement.

Amendments—[1] Para (*b*) substituted by the Capital Gains Tax (Amendment) Regulations 2013, SI 2013/557 with effect from 6 April 2013.
[2] TCGA 1992.

16 Notification of third parties

Where it appears to the inspector that a person is entitled to apply to be joined as a third party in an appeal the inspector may, and at that person's request shall, notify him of the appeal and disclose to him (so far as relevant to his interest in that appeal) the market value of any asset or the apportionment of any amount or value used in making the assessment or decision from which the appeal is brought.

17 Proceedings in Northern Ireland

. . .

Amendments—Revoked by the Transfer of Tribunal Functions and Revenue and Customs Appeals Order, SI 2009/56 art 3, Sch 2 paras 1, 6 with effect from 1 April 2009.

18 Service by post

Any notice or other document to be given, served, sent or delivered under these Regulations may be served by post.

1970/488

DOUBLE TAXATION RELIEF (TAXES ON INCOME) (GENERAL) REGULATIONS 1970

Made by the Commissioners of Inland Revenue under Income Tax Act 1952 s 351 and FA 1965 s 64, now TA 1988 s 791; see TA 1970 s 539 and TA 1988 Sch 30 para 21

Made . . . . *24 March 1970*

1—(1) These Regulations may be cited as the Double Taxation Relief (Taxes on Income) (General) Regulations 1970 and shall come into operation on 6th April 1970.

(2) The Interpretation Act 1889[1] shall apply to these Regulations as it applies to an Act of Parliament.

(3) In these Regulations "the Board" means the Commissioners of Inland Revenue; "year" means year of assessment.

(4) Except in relation to payments which are income of the year 1969–70 or an earlier year the Double Taxation Relief (Taxes on Income) (General) Regulations 1966 shall cease to have effect from 6th April 1970:

Provided that any notice, direction or claim given or made under Regulation 2, 9 or 11 of the said Regulations of 1966 (including any notice, direction or claim having effect as if so given or made) which was in force immediately before the coming into operation of these Regulations shall continue in force as if given or made under the corresponding provision of these Regulations and the following provisions of these Regulations shall apply accordingly.

Note—[1] Interpretation Act 1889.

2—(1) The following provisions of these Regulations shall have effect where, under arrangements having effect under section 497 of the Income and Corporation Taxes Act 1970[2], persons resident in the territory with the government of which the arrangements are made are entitled to exemption or partial relief from United Kingdom income tax in respect of any income from which deduction of tax is authorised or required by the Income Tax Acts.

(2) Any person who pays any such income (referred to in these Regulations as "the United Kingdom payer") to a person in the said territory who is beneficially entitled to the income (such person being referred to in these Regulations as "the non-resident") may be directed by a notice in writing given by or on behalf of the Board that in paying any such income specified in the notice to the non-resident he shall—

(*a*) not deduct tax, or

(*b*) not deduct tax at a higher rate than is specified in the notice, or

(*c*) deduct tax at a rate specified in the notice instead of at the [lower or basic][1] rate otherwise appropriate;

and where such notice is given, any income to which the notice refers, being income for a year for which the arrangements have effect, which the United Kingdom payer pays after the date of the notice to the non-resident named therein shall, subject to the following provisions of these regulations, be paid as directed in the notice:

Provided that income specified in a notice given under this paragraph shall not include distributions in respect of which income tax is chargeable under Schedule F.

Amendments—[1] Words substituted by the Double Taxation Relief (Taxes on Income) (General) (Amendment) Regulations, SI 1996/783 reg 2 with effect from 6 April 1996.

[2] TA 1988 s 788.

3 Where a notice given under Regulation 2(2) directs the United Kingdom payer to deduct tax at a rate specified in the notice, the provisions of the Income Tax Acts under which he would, but for the notice, have been chargeable with or liable to account for all or part of any tax deducted at the [lower or basic][1] rate shall apply as if those Acts required him to deduct tax at the rate so specified.

Amendments—[1] Words substituted by the Double Taxation Relief (Taxes on Income) (General) (Amendment) Regulations, SI 1996/783 reg 2 with effect from 6 April 1996.

4—(1) Where but for a notice given under Regulation 2(2) the United Kingdom payer would have been entitled to retain any income tax deductible on making any payment, there shall be made to him again the income tax otherwise payable by him for the relevant year an allowance equal to the amount of tax which, but for the notice, he would have been entitled to retain on making the payment but in compliance with the notice has not deducted.
(2) "The relevant year" means the year the [lower or basic][1] standard rate for which would (but for the notice) have determined the amount of the deduction authorised.

Amendments—[1] Words substituted by the Double Taxation Relief (Taxes on Income) (General) (Amendment) Regulations, SI 1996/783 reg 2 with effect from 6 April 1996.

5 The United Kingdom payer shall not, in respect of any payment, be charged with or liable to account for any tax which, but for a notice given under Regulation 2(2), he would have been required by the Income Tax Acts to deduct and account for on making the payment but in compliance with the notice has not deducted.

6 Where in compliance with a notice given under Regulation 2(2) a company makes the payment without deducting tax which, but for the notice, it would have been required to deduct in accordance with section 53 or 54 of the Income and Corporation Taxes Act 1970[1] the payment shall be treated for the purposes of section 248(4) of that Act[2] (which prohibits certain payments from being treated as charges on income for corporation tax) as if the company had deducted that tax in accordance with the said section 53 or 54 and had accounted for it under Part XI of that Act.

Note—[1] TA 1988 s 349.
[2] TA 1988 s 338(4).

7 Where, but for a notice given under Regulation 2(2), a person would have been chargeable with tax under section 53 of the Income and Corporation Taxes Act 1970[1] in respect of any such payment as is mentioned in subsection (1) thereof, the provisions of the Income Tax Acts relating to relief for losses shall apply as if the tax which he would have been so chargeable but in accordance with Regulation 5 is not so chargeable had been paid by him under an assessment under the said section 53.

Note—[1] TA 1988 s 349.

8 Any notice given under Regulation 2(2) may be expressed to become ineffective if certain specified events happen, or, whether so expressed or not, may be cancelled by a notice of cancellation given by or on behalf of the Board, and if to the knowledge of the United Kingdom payer any of those events happens or if such notice of cancellation is given, any payment made to the non-resident by the United Kingdom payer after the happening of that event becomes known to the United Kingdom payer or after the receipt of that notice, as the case may be, shall be subject to deduction of tax in accordance with the Income Tax Acts.

9 If it is discovered after a notice has been given under Regulation 2(2) that the non-resident is not entitled to exemption or partial relief from tax in respect of income referred to in the notice, any tax which, but for the notice, would have been deductible from any payment made to the non-resident by the United Kingdom payer but in compliance with the notice has not been so deducted—

(*a*) may be assessed on the non-resident under Case VI of Schedule D by an Inspector, or

(*b*) shall, if a direction to that effect is given by or on behalf of the Board, be deducted by the United Kingdom payer out of so much of the first payment made to the non-resident after the date of the direction as remains after the deduction of any tax deductible therefrom under the Income Tax Acts, and any balance which cannot be deducted out of the first such payment shall be deducted, subject to the same limitation, out of the next such payment, and so on until the whole of the tax (the amount of which shall be specified in the direction) has been deducted.

Any tax which the United Kingdom payer is required to deduct under paragraph (*b*) of this Regulation shall be accounted for as if it was tax deductible under section 53 of the Income and Corporation Taxes Act 1970[1] in respect of the payment from which it is deducted.

Note—[1] TA 1988 s 349.

10 A notice may be given under Regulation 2(2) where income is paid to a person authorised to receive that income on behalf of the non-resident, and in such a case the references in these Regulations to payment to the non-resident shall be treated as including references to payment to that person.

11 Regulations 2(2) and 8 shall not apply to payments in respect of coupons for any interest, but any such payments may, under arrangements approved by the Board, be made without deduction of tax or with tax deducted at a rate specified in the arrangements, if the non-resident or any person acting on his behalf makes a claim to the United Kingdom payer to that effect in such form as may be prescribed by the Board, and in the case of any payments so made Regulations 3 to 7 inclusive and Regulation 9 shall, with any necessary modifications, apply as if the claim were a notice given under Regulation 2(2).

1971/1035

MINERAL ROYALTIES (TAX) REGULATIONS 1971

Made by the Commissioners of Inland Revenue under FA 1970 s 29(6), now TA 1988 s 122(5); see TA 1988 Sch 30 para 21

Made . . . . *23 June 1971*
Coming into Operation . . . . *1 July 1971*

Commentary—*Simon's Taxes* **B5.616.**

1—(1) These Regulations may be cited as the Mineral Royalties (Tax) Regulations 1971, and shall come into operation on 1st July 1971.

(2) The Interpretation Act 1889[1] shall apply for the interpretation of these Regulations as it applies for the interpretation of an Act of Parliament.

(3) In these Regulations:—

the "principal section" means section 29 of the Finance Act 1970[2];

"agreement" means a mineral lease or agreement, as defined in the principal section;

"specified operations" means the winning and working, grading, washing, grinding and crushing of minerals, but in relation to any particular agreement, includes only such of those operations as are in fact authorised by the agreement;

"rights" includes liberties.

Note—[1] Interpretation Act 1978.
[2] TA 1988 s 122.

2 Subject to Regulation 3 below, where a payment is made on or after 6th April 1970 in respect of a sum receivable on or after that date under an agreement which relates both to the winning and working of minerals and to other matters, then, notwithstanding any allocation of the payment under the terms of the agreement, so much but no more of the payment is to be treated for the purposes of the principal section as mineral royalties as might reasonably have been expected to be provided for by the agreement if—

(*a*) it conferred only the right to carry out specified operations in relation to minerals in or under the land to which the agreement relates; and

(*b*) any buildings, structures, roads, shafts, adits or other works existing on the land at the time when the agreement was granted or made were not in existence.

Provided that no such payments are to be treated as mineral royalties unless minerals in or under the land are being or have been won and worked pursuant to rights conferred by or under the agreement, or there is reasonable prospect of their being so won and worked.

3 The whole of a payment under an agreement shall for the purposes of the principal section be treated as a mineral royalty if under Regulation 2 above nine-tenths or more of it would be so treated.

4 Nothing in these Regulations applies to any periodical payments such as are referred to in subsection (9)(*b*) of the principal section[1] (payments made under certain statutes in Northern Ireland).

Note—[1] TA 1988 s 122(2)(*b*).

1977/1143

FRIENDLY SOCIETIES (LIFE ASSURANCE PREMIUM RELIEF) REGULATIONS 1977

Made by the Chief Registrar of Friendly Societies under FA 1976 Sch 4 para 13, now TA 1988 Sch 14 para 3; see TA 1988 Sch 30 para 21

Made . . . . *7 July 1977*
Laid before Parliament . . . . *18 July 1977*
Coming into Operation . . . . *18 August 1977*

Commentary—*Simon's Taxes* **E1.1310.**

Cross references—See the Friendly Societies (Life Assurance Premium Relief) (Change of Rate) Regulations, SI 1980/1947.

1 Citation and Commencement

These Regulations may be cited as the Friendly Societies (Life Assurance Premium Relief) Regulations 1977, and shall come into operation on 18th August 1977.

2 Interpretation

(1) In these Regulations—

["friendly society", subject to paragraph (1A) of this regulation, means a friendly society, not being a collecting society, registered under the Friendly Societies Act 1974 and includes a Northern Ireland Friendly Society.][1]

"collecting society" has the meaning assigned by section 1 of the Industrial Assurance Act 1923 as amended by Schedule 6 to the Companies Act 1967;

["Northern Ireland Friendly Society" means a friendly society, not being a collecting society, which is registered in Northern Ireland for purposes corresponding to the Friendly Societies Act 1974.][1]

"friendly society contract" means a contract made by a friendly society with a member of the society in the course of its business in Great Britain, whether contained in the rules of the society or not;

"the prescribed scheme" means the scheme prescribed in Schedule 1 to these Regulations;

"an approved scheme" means a special scheme approved by the Chief Registrar of Friendly Societies in the circumstances provided for in regulation 7 of these Regulations;

"actuary" means an actuary having the qualifications which are prescribed by the Friendly Societies (Qualifications of Actuaries) Regulations 1968;

"net contribution" has the meaning assigned in paragraph 3 of Schedule 1 to these Regulations;

"gross contribution" means the contribution of the amount payable under the contract;

"parent" includes a stepfather or stepmother.

[(1A) References in these Regulations to a friendly society shall include references to a branch thereof registered under the Friendly Societies Act 1974.][1]

(2) The rules for the construction of Acts of Parliament contained in the Interpretation Act 1889[2] shall apply for the purposes of the interpretation of these Regulations.

Amendments—[1] In para (1) definition "friendly society" substituted, definition "Northern Ireland Friendly Society" inserted, and para (1A) inserted, by the Friendly Societies (Life Assurance Premium Relief) (Amendment) Regulations, SI 1978/1160 reg 2, with effect from 4 September 1978.

[2] Interpretation Act 1978.

3 Adoption of a scheme

(1) A friendly society may by resolution of its committee of management passed before 1st October 1978 adopt—

(*a*) the prescribed scheme, or

(*b*) an approved scheme

for the purpose of securing that in the case of friendly society contracts to which the scheme so adopted applies amounts equal to 171/2 per cent of the contributions payable are retained by or refunded to the persons paying the contributions.

(2) Where a friendly society has adopted any such scheme amounts equal to 17½ per cent of the contributions payable under contracts [made before 14th March 1984][1] to which the scheme applies shall be retained by or refunded to the persons paying the contributions as provided in the scheme so adopted.

(3) Written notice of a resolution adopting the prescribed or an approved scheme shall within fourteen days of the passing thereof be sent by the society to the Chief Registrar of Friendly Societies.

(4) Where a friendly society has resolved to adopt the prescribed or an approved scheme any right conferred by section 21 of the Friendly Societies Act 1974 on any person to receive a copy of the rules of the society shall be extended so as to include the right to receive a copy of the resolution and of the scheme adopted by the resolution.

Amendments—[1] Words in para (2) inserted by the Friendly Societies (Life Assurance Premium Relief) (Amendment) Regulations, SI 1984/323 reg 3(*a*), with effect from 14 March 1984.

4 Increase in contribution

(1) A resolution adopting the prescribed scheme may provide that in respect of any specified class of contract made by the society before 6th April 1979 to which the scheme applies under which the contribution does not exceed £4 every four weeks the contribution shall be increased with effect from that date to such sum as after deduction of 171/2 per cent thereof equals the amount expressed in the contract to be the contribution.

(2) Where such provision is made the resolution shall operate so as to effect the above mentioned increase in the contribution payable under every contract of a class to which the provision relates, and the prescribed scheme shall take effect accordingly.

5 Corresponding increase in sum assured

(1) Where an increase in contribution has been effected under regulation 4 the sum assured or guaranteed by the contract under which the increased contribution is payable shall be increased by an amount determined in accordance with rules which have been certified by an actuary to be fair in relation to the increased contribution payable and have been approved by the Chief Registrar of Friendly Societies.

(2) Where the sum assured or guaranteed by a contract is increased by virtue of the preceding paragraph the society shall on being requested in writing to do so by the person by whom the increased contribution is payable notify him in writing of the amount of the increase in the sum assured or guaranteed.

6—(1) Where a friendly society has adopted the prescribed scheme by a resolution making such provision as is referred to in regulation 4(1) the member insured under a contract of a class specified in the provision which was made before 6th April 1979 and under which the contribution exceeds £4 every four weeks may before that date irrevocably elect, in the form set out in Schedule 2 to these Regulations or in a form to the like effect, that the contribution payable under the contract under which he is insured shall be increased with effect from 6th April 1979 to such sum as is mentioned in regulation 4(1).

(2) Where such election has been made the increase in contribution shall be effective as from 6th April 1979 as if it had been effected under regulation 4(2), and regulation 5 shall apply in respect of an increase in contribution under this regulation as it applies in relation to an increase under regulation 4.

7 Approved schemes

The Chief Registrar of Friendly Societies may before 1st October 1978 approve a special scheme intended to be adopted by a friendly society for the purposes mentioned in regulation 3 if in his opinion in view of the manner in which the business of the society is conducted, or any other relevant matter, it is expedient that the special scheme should be adopted.

8 Notice to contribution payers

Every friendly society which carries on life or endowment business shall take all reasonable steps to ensure that every person who on 31st December 1978 is paying contributions under a friendly society contract which forms part of such business receives a notice in a form approved by the Chief Registrar of Friendly Societies setting out—

(*a*) the effect of these Regulations,

(*b*) whether the society has adopted the prescribed or an approved scheme, and

(*c*) the effect of the scheme which has been adopted;

and, as regards contracts made between 1st January 1979 and 5th April 1979, that such notice is received by the prospective contribution payer before the contract is made.

9 Amendment of rules

Notwithstanding anything contained in the rules of a friendly society which has adopted the prescribed scheme or an approved scheme, the committee of management of the society may by resolution passed before 6th April 1979 make amendments to the rules of the society in connection with the adoption by the society of any such scheme.

10 Modification of enactments

The enactments mentioned in Schedule 3 to these Regulations shall have effect subject to the adaptations and modifications set out in that Schedule.

SCHEDULE 1

PRESCRIBED SCHEME

Regulation 2

1 The scheme applies to every friendly society contract [made before 14th March 1984][2] assuring life or endowment benefits under which contributions are payable to a friendly society which has adopted the scheme in accordance with regulation 3.

2 Where the member is resident in the United Kingdom and entitled to relief under section 19 of the Income and Corporation Taxes Act 1970[3] the liability of the member in respect of any contribution [due and payable after 5th April 1979][1] under a contract to which the scheme relates shall be discharged by payment of the net contribution; and any payment made on account of such a contribution shall be deemed to have been made after deducting $17\frac{1}{2}$ per cent from an amount payable in respect of the gross contribution.

3 The net contribution shall be a sum equal to $82\frac{1}{2}$ per cent of the gross contribution, except that—

(*a*) where the gross contribution does not exceed £4 every four weeks and the said sum is not a multiple of one halfpenny, the said sum shall be rounded off to the nearer halfpenny, or, if the said sum is a multiple of one half of one halfpenny, to the nearer penny, and

(*b*) where the gross contribution exceeds £4 every four weeks and the said sum is not a multiple of one penny, the said sum shall be rounded off to the nearer penny, or, if the said sum is a multiple of one halfpenny, to the nearer even penny.

Amendments—[1] Words in para 2 substituted by the *Friendly Societies (Life Assurance Premium Relief) (Amendment) Regulations*, SI 1978/1160 reg 2, with effect from 4 September 1978.
[2] Words in para 1 inserted by the Friendly Societies (Life Assurance Premium Relief) (Amendment) Regulations, SI 1984/323 reg 3(*b*), with effect from 14 March 1984.
[3] TA 1988 s 266.

SCHEDULE 2

LIFE ASSURANCE PREMIUM RELIEF FORM OF ELECTION BY MEMBERS

Regulation 6

To: (Name of friendly society)

I (Name) of (Address)

irrevocably choose that as from 6th April 1979 the tax relief to which I shall be entitled in respect of the contributions paid by me in respect of the contract particulars of which are set out below shall take the form of an increase in the sum assured of an amount determined in accordance with rules approved by the Chief Registrar of Friendly Societies.

I understand that if I do not sign this form I shall be entitled to deduct and retain 17½ per cent of the contributions at present payable under the contract.

Signature of member

Date:

Particulars of Contract

Number, if any, and date of contract

Amount of contribution and interval at which payable

SCHEDULE 3

ADAPTATIONS AND MODIFICATIONS OF ENACTMENTS

Regulation 10

This Schedule contains incidental provisions and makes consequential adaptations and modifications to enactments relating to friendly societies.

1977/1144

INDUSTRIAL ASSURANCE (LIFE ASSURANCE PREMIUM RELIEF) REGULATIONS 1977

Made by the Industrial Assurance Commissioner under FA 1976 Sch 4 para 13, now TA 1988 Sch 14 para 3; see TA 1988 Sch 30 para 21

Made . . . . *7 July 1977*
Laid before Parliament . . . . *18 July 1977*
Coming into Operation . . . . *18 August 1977*

Cross references—See the Industrial Assurance (Life Assurance Premium Relief) (Change of Rate) Regulations, SI 1980/1948 reg 3 (amendment of a scheme adopted in accordance with these Regulations).

1 Citation and Commencement

These Regulations may be cited as the Industrial Assurance (Life Assurance Premium Relief) Regulations 1977, and shall come into operation on 18th August 1977.

2 Interpretation

(1) In these Regulations—

"industrial assurance company" and "collecting society" have the meanings assigned by section 1 of the Industrial Assurance Act 1923 as amended by Schedule 6 to the Companies Act 1967;

"industrial assurance contract" means a contract of assurance made by an industrial assurance company in the course of its industrial assurance business in Great Britain or a contract made by a collecting society with a member of the society in the course of its industrial assurance business in Great Britain, whether contained in the rules of the society or not;

"collecting society contract" means a contract, other than an industrial assurance contract, made by a collecting society with a member of the society in the course of business in Great Britain, whether contained in the rules of the society or not;

"the prescribed scheme" means the scheme prescribed in Schedule 1 to these Regulations;
"an approved scheme" means a special scheme approved by the Industrial Assurance Commissioner in the circumstances provided for in regulation 7 of these Regulations;
"actuary" means an actuary having the qualifications which are prescribed by the Friendly Societies (Qualifications of Actuaries) Regulations 1968;
"net premium" has the meaning assigned in paragraph 3 of Schedule 1 to these Regulations;
"gross premium" means the premium of the amount payable under the policy or contract;
"parent" includes a stepfather and a stepmother.

(2) The rules for the construction of Acts of Parliament contained in the Interpretation Act 1889[1] shall apply for the purposes of the interpretation of these Regulations.

Note—[1] Interpretation Act 1978.

3 Adoption of a scheme

(1) An industrial assurance company or collecting society may by resolution of its board of directors or, as the case may be, of its committee of management, passed before 1st October 1978, adopt—

(*a*) the prescribed scheme, or
(*b*) an approved scheme

for the purpose of securing that in the case of policies or contracts to which the scheme so adopted applies amounts equal to 17½ per cent of the premiums payable are retained by or refunded to the persons paying the premiums.

(2) Where an industrial assurance company or collecting society has adopted any such scheme amounts equal to 17½ per cent of the premiums payable under—

[(*a*) policies in respect of assurances made before 14th March 1984, or
(*b*) contracts made before that date, to which][1]

the scheme applies shall be retained by or refunded to the persons paying the premiums as provided in the scheme so adopted.

(3) Written notice of a resolution adopting the prescribed or an approved scheme shall within fourteen days of the passing thereof be sent by the industrial assurance company or collecting society to the Industrial Assurance Commissioner.

(4) Where a collecting society has resolved to adopt the prescribed or an approved scheme any right conferred by section 21 of the Friendly Societies Act 1974 or section 10(1) of the Industrial Assurance and Friendly Societies Act 1948 on any person to receive a copy of the rules of the society or of an amendment thereof shall be extended so as to include the right to receive a copy of the resolution and of the scheme adopted by the resolution.

Amendments—[1] Words in para (2) substituted by the Industrial Assurance (Life Assurance Premium Relief) (Amendment) Regulations, SI 1984/322 reg 3(*a*), with effect from 14 March 1984.

4 Increase in premium

(1) A resolution adopting the prescribed scheme may provide that in respect of any specified class of policy or contract issued or made by the company or society before 6th April 1979 to which the scheme applies under which the premium does not exceed £4 every four weeks the premium shall be increased with effect from that date to such sum as after deduction of 17½ per cent thereof equals the amount expressed in the policy or contract to be the premium.

(2) Where such provision is made the resolution shall operate so as to effect the above mentioned increase in the premium payable under every policy or contract of a class to which the provision relates, and the prescribed scheme shall take effect accordingly.

Cross references—See the Industrial Assurance (Life Assurance Premium Relief) (Change of Rate) Regulations, SI 1980/1948 regs 4, 5 (amendment of gross premium and corresponding amendment to sum assured).

5 Corresponding increase in sum assured

(1) Where an increase in premium has been effected under regulation 4 the sum assured or guaranteed by the policy or contract under which the increased premium is payable shall be increased by an amount determined in accordance with rules which have been certified by an actuary to be fair in relation to the increased premium payable and have been approved by the Industrial Assurance Commissioner.

(2) Where the sum assured or guaranteed by a policy or contract is increased by virtue of the preceding paragraph the company or society shall on being requested in writing to do so by the person by whom the increased premium is payable notify him in writing of the amount of the increase in the sum assured or guaranteed.

6—(1) Where an industrial assurance company or collecting society has adopted the prescribed scheme by a resolution making such provision as is referred to in regulation 4(1), the person insured under a policy or contract of a class specified in the provision which was issued or made before 6th August 1979 and under which the premium exceeds £4 every four weeks may before that date irrevocably elect, in the form set out in Schedule 2 to these Regulations or in a form to the like effect, that the premium under the contract under which he is insured shall be increased with effect from 6th April 1979 to such sum as is mentioned in regulation 4(1).

(2) Where such election has been made the increase in premium shall be effective as from 6th April 1979 as if it had been effected under regulation 4(2), and regulation 5 shall apply in respect of an increase in premium under this regulation as it applies in relation to an increase under regulation 4.

Cross references—See the Industrial Assurance (Life Assurance Premium Relief) (Change of Rate) Regulations, SI 1980/1948 reg 7 (amendment of gross premium and corresponding amendment to sum assured).

7 Approved schemes

The Industrial Assurance Commissioner may before 1st October 1978 approve a special scheme intended to be adopted by an industrial assurance company or collecting society for the purposes mentioned in regulation 3 if in his opinion, in view of the manner in which the business of the company or society is conducted, or any other relevant matter, it is expedient that the special scheme should be adopted.

Cross references—See the Industrial Assurance (Life Assurance Premium Relief) (Change of Rate) Regulations, SI 1980/1948 reg 8 (amendment of approved schemes).

8 Notice to premium payers

Every industrial assurance company and collecting society shall take all reasonable steps to ensure that every person who on 31st December 1978 is paying premiums under an industrial assurance or collecting society contract made by it receives a notice in a form approved by the Industrial Assurance Commissioner setting out—

(*a*) the effect of these Regulations,

(*b*) whether the company or society has adopted the prescribed or an approved scheme, and

(*c*) the effect of the scheme which has been adopted;

and, as regards contracts made between 1st January 1979 and 5th April 1979, that such notice is received by the prospective premium payer before the contract is made.

9 Amendment of rules

Notwithstanding anything contained in the rules of a collecting society which has adopted the prescribed scheme or an approved scheme, the committee of management of the society may by resolution passed before 6th April 1979 make amendments to the rules of the society in connection with the adoption by the society of any such scheme.

10 Modification of enactments

The enactments mentioned in Schedule 3 to these Regulations shall have effect subject to the adaptations and modifications set out in that Schedule.

SCHEDULE 1

PRESCRIBED SCHEME

Regulation 2

1 The scheme applies to every industrial assurance or collecting society contract [made before 14th March 1984][1] under which premiums are payable to an industrial assurance company or collecting society which has adopted the scheme in accordance with regulation 3.

Amendments—[1] Words in para 1 inserted by the Industrial Assurance (Life Assurance Premium Relief) (Amendment) Regulations, SI 1984/322 reg 3(*b*), with effect from 14 March 1984.

2 Where the person assured or member, as the case may be, is resident in the United Kingdom and entitled to relief under section 19 of the Income and Corporation Taxes Act 1970[2] the liability of that person or member in respect of any premium [due and payable after 5th April 1979][1] under a contract to which the scheme relates shall be discharged by payment of the net premium; and any payment made on account of such a premium shall be deemed to have been made after deducting 17½ per cent from an amount payable in respect of the gross premium.

Amendments—[1] Words in para 2 substituted by the Industrial Assurance (Life Assurance Premium Relief) (Amendment) Regulations, SI 1978/1161 reg 2, with effect from 4 September 1978.

[2] TA 1988 s 266.

3 The net premium shall be a sum equal to 82½ per cent of the gross premium, except that—

(*a*) in relation to an industrial assurance contract, where the said sum is not a multiple of one halfpenny, it shall be rounded off to the nearer halfpenny, or, if the said sum is a multiple of one half of one halfpenny, to the nearer penny; and

(*b*) in relation to a collecting society contract, where the said sum is not a multiple of one penny, it shall be rounded off to the nearer penny, or, if the said sum is a multiple of one halfpenny, to the nearer even penny.

SCHEDULE 2

LIFE ASSURANCE PREMIUM RELIEF

Regulation 6

Form of election by Policyholder

To: (Name of industrial assurance company or collecting society)

I (Name) of (Address)

irrevocably choose that as from 6th April 1979 the tax relief to which I shall be entitled in respect of the premiums paid by me in respect of the policy particulars of which are set out below shall take the form of an increase in the sum assured of an amount determined in accordance with rules approved by the Industrial Assurance Commissioner.

I understand that if I do not sign this form I shall be entitled to deduct and retain $17^1/_2$ per cent of the premium at present payable under the policy.

Date: Signature

Particulars of Policy

Number (if any) and date of policy

Amount of premium and interval at which payable

SCHEDULE 3

ADAPTATIONS AND MODIFICATIONS OF ENACTMENTS

Regulation 10

This Schedule contains incidental provisions and makes consequential adaptations and modifications to enactments relating to industrial assurance and friendly societies.

1978/1159

INCOME TAX (LIFE ASSURANCE PREMIUM RELIEF) REGULATIONS 1978

Made by the Commissioners of Inland Revenue under FA 1976 Sch 4 para 16 (as amended by FA 1978 Sch 3 para 10), now TA 1988 Sch 14 para 7; see TA 1988 Sch 30 para 21

Made . . . . *4 August 1978*

Coming into Operation . . . . *6 April 1979*

Commentary—*Simon's Taxes* **E1.1328**.

Cross references—See FA 2012 Sch 39 para 25 (time limit for claims).

1 Citation and commencement

These Regulations may be cited as the Income Tax (Life Assurance Premium Relief) Regulations 1978, and shall come into operation on 6th April 1979.

2 Interpretation

(1) In these Regulations unless the context otherwise requires—

"the Board" means the Commissioners of Inland Revenue;

"authorised officer" in relation to a life office means an official authorised for the purposes of these Regulations by resolution of the life office's Board, except that—

(*a*) in relation to a registered friendly society, it means an official so authorised by resolution of the society's committee of management, and

(*b*) in relation to underwriters falling within subsection (2)(*a*)(ii) of section 19 of the Income and Corporation Taxes Act 1970[3] it means the underwriting agent through whom their business is carried on;

"deficiency" means a deficiency recoverable under paragraph 5(*b*) of Schedule 4[4];

"financial year" in relation to a life office means a period for which the office makes up its accounts;

"four-weekly accounting period" means the period of 28 days commencing on 1 January in a calendar year, and each succeeding period throughout the year being a period of 28 days, except that a period including 29 February and the period commencing on 3 December shall be extended to 29 days;

"income tax month" means the period beginning on the 6th day of any calendar month and ending on the 5th day of the following calendar month; and in Regulations 6 and 7 below, in relation to an income tax month—

(*a*) "relevant calendar month" means a calendar month falling partly in the income tax month, and

(*b*) "component part" means the part falling within it of a relevant calendar month;

"industrial branch business" means [any such business carried on before 1st December 2001 as was][2] industrial assurance business as defined in section 1(2) of the Industrial Assurance Act 1923 or [Art 3(1) of the Industrial Assurance (Northern Ireland) Order 1979][1];
"insurance" includes a contract for a deferred annuity;
"life office" means any such body as is mentioned in section 19(*a*) of the Income and Corporation Taxes Act 1970[5] as amended by paragraph 3 of Schedule 4;
"net of deduction" means net of the deduction authorised by paragraph 5 of Schedule 4[6] (or by that paragraph as modified by Regulation 4 below);
"ordinary branch business" means life assurance business other than industrial branch business;
"Schedule 4" means Schedule 4 to the Finance Act 1976.

(2) The Interpretation Act 1889[7] shall apply for the interpretation of these Regulations as it applies for the interpretation of an Act of Parliament.

Amendments—[1] Words in the definition of "industrial branch business" in para (1) substituted by the Tax, Consumer Credit and Judicature (Northern Ireland Consequential Amendments) Order, SI 1979/1576 arts 1(2), 3, with effect from 3 January 1980.
[2] Words in the definition of "industrial branch business" in para (1) inserted by the Financial Services and Markets Act 2000 (Consequential Amendments) (Taxes) Order, SI 2001/3629 art 110 with effect from 1 December 2001, immediately after the coming into force of the Financial Services and Markets Act 2000 ss 411, 432(1), Sch 20 (and SI 2001/3629 Pts 1 and 2).
[3] TA 1988 s 266(2)(*a*)(ii).
[4] TA 1988 s 266(5)(*b*).
[5] TA 1988 266(2)(*a*).
[6] TA 1988 s 266(5).
[7] Interpretation Act 1978.

3 Information to be given to the life office

(1) A life office may at any time by notice in writing require an individual who pays or proposes to pay premiums net of deduction to furnish to the life office a statement under this Regulation.

(2) A statement under this Regulation shall be in such form and contain such particulars as the Board prescribe, and the particulars prescribed shall be such as are necessary for determining whether the person paying the premiums is or will be entitled to pay them net of deduction.

(3) Where an individual has been required to furnish a statement under this Regulation in relation to any insurance and has not furnished it then (until he does so)—

(*a*) if the statement was required before the first premium in respect of that insurance became due, he shall not be entitled to pay any premiums in respect of that insurance net of deduction, and

(*b*) in any other case, he shall not be entitled to pay net of deduction any premiums in respect of that insurance falling due more than 60 days after the date on which the notice requiring the statement was issued.

(4) If notwithstanding the furnishing of a statement under this Regulation in relation to any insurance the life office concerned is not satisfied that the premiums are properly payable net of deduction, and the person paying them does not agree to pay them without deduction, the life office shall notify the Board forthwith.

(5) Without prejudice to the generality of paragraph (1) above—

(*a*) a life office shall not accept payment of premiums net of deduction in respect of any insurance without first obtaining a statement under this Regulation in relation to that insurance, unless the particulars required in the statement are already in the possession of the life office [or the Board have by notice in writing to the life office dispensed with the requirement of this sub-paragraph in relation to that insurance][1] and

(*b*) where premiums in respect of any insurance are being paid net of deduction and it appears to the life office that they are no longer properly so payable, the life office shall require a statement under this Regulation unless the person paying the premiums agrees to pay them without deduction.

(6) Paragraph (5)(*a*) above shall not apply to insurances made before 1 September 1978 if the life office concerned has established to the satisfaction of the Board that on the basis of the information in the hands of the life office there is not a probability of more than one in ten that the amount claimed to be recoverable for any period under paragraph (5)(*b*) of Schedule 4 in respect of such insurances will exceed by more than 0·5 per cent the amount properly recoverable.

(7) Paragraphs (5)(*a*) and (6) above shall not apply to an insurance made before 6 April 1979 to which paragraph 11 of Schedule 4[2] applies.

Amendments—[1] Words in para (5)(*a*) inserted by the IT (Life Assurance Premium Relief) Regulations, SI 1979/346, with effect from 6 April 1979.
[2] TA 1988 Sch 14, para 2.

4 Rounding of sums payable by way of net premium

(1) This Regulation has effect for adjusting in certain cases the net amount payable by way of premium after the deduction authorised under paragraph 5 of Schedule 4[1], and in those cases the amount treated as deducted and retained under that paragraph shall also be adjusted accordingly.

(2) In the case of—

(*a*) an industrial assurance contract, as defined in any Regulations made under paragraph 13 of Schedule 4[2], or

(*b*) a friendly society contract, as defined in any such Regulations, in respect of which the premiums do not (before any deduction under paragraph 5 of Schedule 4[1]) exceed £4 every four weeks,

if the net amount payable is otherwise not a multiple of one new halfpenny it shall be adjusted and shall—

(i) where the premium is one to which a scheme adopted under Regulations made under paragraph 13 of Schedule 4[2] applies, be the amount payable in accordance with the scheme, and

(ii) in any other case be rounded to the nearer new halfpenny or, if it is a multiple of one half of one new halfpenny, to the nearer new penny.

(3) In the case of any insurance not included in paragraph (2)(*a*) or (*b*) above, if the net amount payable is otherwise not a multiple of one new penny it shall be rounded to the nearer new penny or, if it is a multiple of one new halfpenny, to the nearer even new penny.

Note—[1] TA 1988 s 266(5).
[2] TA 1988 Sch 14, para 3.

5 Deficiency claims: introductory

(1) Sums recoverable by a life office under paragraph 5(*b*) of Schedule 4[1] shall be recovered on a claim made to the Board for the purpose under these Regulations.

(2) A claim for any period allowed by these Regulations shall be a claim relating to the deficiency arising in respect of premiums received in that period, and accordingly references to premiums "for" a period are to premiums received in that period.

(3) Subject to paragraph (4) below a claim shall be for the claimant's financial year, and is referred to in these Regulations as an "annual claim".

(4) A claim may also be made in accordance with Regulation 6 or 8 below for a period shorter than the claimant's financial year, and is referred to in these Regulations as an "interim claim".

(5) A life office which carries on both industrial branch business and ordinary branch business may make annual and interim claims separately for business of each branch.

Note—[1] TA 1988 s 266(5)(*b*).

6 Interim claims in advance

(1) An interim claim for a period allowed by paragraphs (2) and (3) below may be made at any time within one month before the period for which it is made, and is referred to in these Regulations as an "interim claim in advance".

(2) The three kinds of period for which an interim claim in advance may be made are:—

(*a*) a calendar month, or

(*b*) an income tax month, or

(*c*) in the case of a claim relating to industrial branch business only, a four-weekly accounting period.

(3) Interim claims in advance made by one life office may not (except where a change is authorised by prior approval of the Board) be made for periods of different kinds: Provided that if the first claim made for industrial branch business (or the first such claim made after an authorised change) is a separate claim made for a four-weekly accounting period, this paragraph shall then apply separately in relation to industrial branch business and ordinary branch business.

(4) An interim claim in advance for a period shall be based on an estimate of the deficiency that will arise in respect of premiums for that period, and the estimate shall be certified by an authorised officer of the claimant as being the best estimate that can reasonably be made of the deficiency; and if the claim is for an income tax month the estimate shall show the part of the deficiency attributed to each component part of the month.

(5) If the Board are satisfied with the estimate they shall pay the estimated amount of the deficiency to the claimant before the end of the period for which the claim is made; if they are not so satisfied, they shall pay to the claimant before the end of the period such lesser amount if any as in their estimation will approximate to the deficiency.

7 Supplementary statements

(1) When a payment has been made to a life office under Regulation 6(5) above on an interim claim in advance, the life office shall deliver to the Board a supplementary statement under this Regulation, and (except where paragraph (5)(*b*) below applies) shall deliver the statement within two months after the end of the period for which the claim was made.

(2) The supplementary statement shall be a statement correcting (or confirming) the estimate of the deficiency given in accordance with Regulation 6(4) above, and shall—

(*a*) be based as far as possible on the amount of the premiums actually received in the period covered by the statement, and only as far as may be necessary on a revised estimate, and

(*b*) (subject to paragraph (5) below) be for the same period as the interim claim in advance;

and any estimate contained in the supplementary statement shall be certified by an authorised officer of the life office as the best estimate that can reasonably be made.

(3) If the supplementary statement shows a deficiency greater than the payment made under Regulation 6(5), the Board shall if satisfied with the statement pay the amount of the difference to the life office forthwith by way of supplementary payment on the claim; if the supplementary statement shows a deficiency less than the payment made under Regulation 6(5), the life office shall repay the amount of the difference to the Board with the statement.

(4) If in respect of an interim claim on which a payment has been made under Regulation 6(5) above a life office fails to deliver a supplementary statement within the time required by this Regulation, the amount of the payment shall immediately be recoverable by the Board in the same manner as tax charged by an assessment which has become final and conclusive.

(5) Where the interim claim in advance was for an income tax month the life office shall (instead of delivering a statement for that month) deliver a supplementary statement for each of the relevant calendar months, and the supplementary statement for a relevant calendar month shall—

(*a*) provide the information required by paragraph (2) above in respect of that month, and

(*b*) be delivered within two months and five days after the end of that month.

8 Interim claims in arrear

(1) An interim claim for a period allowed by paragraph (2) below may be made at any time within six months after the end of the period for which it is made.

(2) The period for which a claim may be made under this Regulation shall be one which—

(*a*) is not shorter than one calendar month, and

(*b*) falls wholly within the claimant's same financial year, and

(*c*) does not include any part of a period in respect of which a payment was made under Regulation 6(5) above (unless the payment in respect of that period or that part was recovered under Regulation 7(4) above).

(3) A claim under this Regulation may only be made to recover the deficiency arising in respect of premiums actually received and may not be based on an estimate.

(4) If the deficiency claimed is established to the Board's satisfaction, they shall pay the amount of the deficiency to the claimant; if they are not so satisfied they shall pay to the claimant any lesser amount established to their satisfaction.

9 Annual claims

(1) An annual claim for the claimant's financial year may, subject to paragraph (2) below, be made at any time within six years after the end of the financial year.

(2) Where in relation to any financial year a life office has received and not repaid any payment on a relevant interim claim, it shall within one year after the end of the financial year make an annual claim to establish the deficiency for that year.

In this Regulation "relevant interim claim" means, in relation to a financial year, an interim claim for a period falling wholly or partly within that year.

(3) An annual claim shall be a claim to establish and, so far as not already recovered, to recover the deficiency arising in respect of premiums actually received in the year and may not be based on an estimate.

(4) An annual claim required under paragraph (2) above shall bring into account payments made on relevant interim claims, and shall apportion as may be necessary any payment made on a relevant interim claim for any period falling partly in a different year; and for the purpose of this Regulation the "aggregate of the relevant interim payments" means the aggregate of the payments made (and not repaid) on relevant interim claims but excluding any part of a payment apportioned to a different year.

(5) Where the aggregate of the relevant interim payments shown by a claim exceeds the deficiency for the year shown by the claim, the life office shall repay the amount of the excess to the Board with the claim.

(6) If a life office fails to make an annual claim required under paragraph (2) above within the time limited by that paragraph, the Board may issue a notice to the life office showing the aggregate of the relevant interim payments for the year, and stating that the Board are not satisfied that the deficiency for the year exceeds a lower amount stated in the notice.

(7) If an annual claim is not delivered to the Board within two weeks after the issue of a notice under paragraph (6) above the amount of the difference between the aggregate and the lower amount stated in the notice shall immediately be recoverable by the Board in the same manner as tax charged by an assessment which has become final and conclusive.

(8) Where an annual claim has been made and the claimant subsequently discovers that an error or mistake has been made in the claim, the claimant may make a supplementary claim within the time allowed by paragraph (1) above.

Cross references—See FA 2012 Sch 39 para 25 (time limit for claims).

10 Deficiency claims: supplementary provisions

(1) Section 42 of the Taxes Management Act 1970 shall not apply to claims under these Regulations.

(2) No appeal shall lie from the Board's decision on an interim claim.

(3) An appeal [may be made against][1] the Board's decision on an annual claim, and the appeal shall be brought by giving written notice to the Board within 30 days of receipt of written notice of the decision.

(4) No payment or repayment made or other thing done on or in relation to an interim claim or a notice under Regulation 9(6) above shall prejudice the decision on an annual claim.

(5) Part V of the Taxes Management Act 1970 (appeals and other proceedings) shall apply to an appeal under paragraph (3) above, and on an appeal [that is notified to the tribunal, the tribunal][1] may vary the decision appealed against whether or not the variation is to the advantage of the appellant.

(6) All such payments and repayments shall be made as are necessary to give effect to the Board's decision on an annual claim, or to any variation of that decision on appeal.

(7) Claims and supplementary statements under these Regulations shall be in such form and contain such particulars as the Board prescribe and shall be signed by an authorised officer of the life office; and forms prescribed for annual claims may require a report to be given by the life office's auditor.

(8) Where for the purposes of an annual claim for a financial year it is necessary to apportion any payment made on an interim claim for a period falling partly within and partly outside that year, the apportionment shall be made in such manner as the Board prescribe.

Simon's Tax Cases—reg 10(6), *United Friendly Insurance plc v IRC* [1998] STC 621.

Amendments—[1] In paras (3), (5), words substituted by the Transfer of Tribunal Functions and Revenue and Customs Appeals Order, SI 2009/56 art 3, Sch 2 para 7 with effect from 1 April 2009.

11 Information from policyholders

The Board may by notice in writing require any person who has or had a policy of life insurance or contract for a deferred annuity with a life office or who pays or paid premiums under such a policy or contract to furnish them within such time as they may direct with such information (including copies of relevant documents) as they require for the purposes of section 19 of the Income and Corporation Taxes Act 1970 or of Schedule 4.[1]

Note—[1] TA 1988 s 266 and Sch 14.

12—(1) Every person to whom premiums are paid in respect of which a claim is made under these Regulations shall, whenever required to do so, make available for inspection by an authorised officer of the Board all such books, documents and other records in his possession or under his control containing information relating to—

(*a*) such premiums and the policies or contracts under which such premiums are paid, or

(*b*) the persons holding such policies or contracts or paying such premiums,

as may reasonably be required for determining whether the deficiency for which any claim is made under these Regulations is properly recoverable.

(2) Where records are maintained by computer the person required to make them available for inspection shall provide the officer making the inspection with all facilities necessary for obtaining information from them.

(3) Every statement made under Regulation 3 above shall be preserved by the life office to which it is made (or which is the insurer for the time being), in such manner as may be approved by the Board so as to be available for inspection under this Regulation, until three years after the termination of the insurance or contract to which it relates.

1980/1947

FRIENDLY SOCIETIES (LIFE ASSURANCE PREMIUM RELIEF) (CHANGE OF RATE) REGULATIONS 1980

Made by the Chief Registrar of Friendly Societies under FA 1976 Sch 4 para 13, now TA 1988 Sch 14 para 3; see TA 1988 Sch 30 para 21

Made . . . . *15 December 1980*

Laid before Parliament . . . . *29 December 1980*

Coming into Operation . . . . *20 January 1981*

Commentary—*Simon's Taxes* **E1.1310**.

Note—See FA 2012 Sch 39 Part 4: abolition of income tax relief for life assurance premiums under TA 1988 s 266.

1 Citation and commencement

These Regulations may be cited as the Friendly Societies (Life Assurance Premium Relief) (Change of Rate) Regulations 1980, and shall come into operation on 20th January 1981.

2 Interpretation

In these Regulations—

"the 1977 Regulations" means the Friendly Societies (Life Assurance Premium Relief) Regulations 1977;

"friendly society" means a friendly society, not being a collecting society, registered under the Friendly Societies Act 1974 or a branch so registered under that Act of a friendly society so registered;

"collecting society" [means a society which before 1st December 2001 was a collecting society within][1] the meaning assigned by section 1 of the Industrial Assurance Act 1923 as amended by Schedule 6 to the Companies Act 1967;

"the prescribed scheme" means the scheme prescribed in Schedule 1 to the Friendly Societies (Life Assurance Premium Relief) Regulations 1977;

"an approved scheme" means a special scheme approved by the Chief Registrar of Friendly Societies in the circumstances provided for in regulation 7 of the Friendly Societies (Life Assurance Premium Relief) Regulations 1977;

"gross contribution" means the contribution of the amount payable under the contract;

"actuary" means an actuary having the qualifications which are prescribed by the Friendly Societies (Qualifications of Actuaries) Regulations 1968;

"the authorised percentage" means the percentage for the time being in force under paragraph 5(*a*) of Schedule 4 to the Finance Act 1976;

"the effective date" means the date on which a change in the authorised percentage takes effect;

"parent" includes a stepfather and a stepmother.

["relevant authority" means—

(*a*) if the society is a PRA-authorised person within the meaning of section 2B of the Financial Services and Markets Act 2000, the Prudential Regulation Authority, and

(*b*) in any other case, the Financial Conduct Authority;][2]

Amendments—[1] Words in the definition of "collecting society" substituted by the Financial Services and Markets Act 2000 (Consequential Amendments) (Taxes) Order, SI 2001/3629 art 111 with effect from 1 December 2001, immediately after the coming into force of the Financial Services and Markets Act 2000 ss 411, 432(1), Sch 20 (and SI 2001/3629 Pts 1 and 2).
[2] Definition of "relevant authority" inserted by the Financial Services Act 2012 (Mutual Societies) Order, SI 2013/496 art 2(*c*), Sch 11, para 12(1), (2) with effect from 1 April 2013.

3 Amendment of a scheme

(1) Where a friendly society has adopted the prescribed scheme or an approved scheme in accordance with the provisions of the 1977 Regulations the society may, by resolution of its committee of management passed within eight months of the passing of any Act making a change in the authorised percentage, amend any such scheme so that amounts equal to the authorised percentage of the gross contributions due and payable on or after the effective date under contracts to which the scheme applies shall be retained by or refunded to the persons paying the contributions.

(2) Where a friendly society has amended any such scheme, amounts equal to the authorised percentage of the gross contributions payable under contracts to which the scheme applies shall be retained by or refunded to the persons paying the contributions as provided in the scheme so amended.

(3) Written notice of a resolution amending the prescribed scheme or an approved scheme shall within fourteen days of the passing thereof be sent by the society to the [relevant authority][1].

(4) Where a friendly society has resolved to amend the prescribed scheme or an approved scheme any right conferred by section 21 of the Friendly Societies Act 1974 on any person to receive a copy of the rules of the society shall be extended so as to include the right to receive a copy of the resolution and of the amended scheme adopted by the resolution.

Amendments—[1] In sub-para (3), words substituted by the Financial Services Act 2012 (Mutual Societies) Order, SI 2013/496 art 2(*c*), Sch 11, para 12(1), (3) with effect from 1 April 2013.

4 Amendment of gross contribution

(1) Where, by virtue of regulation 4 of the 1977 Regulations, a resolution adopting the prescribed scheme provided that the gross contribution was to be increased with effect from 6th April 1979 in respect of any specified class of contract, a resolution amending the prescribed scheme may also amend the gross contribution so that with effect from the effective date the gross contributions shall be amended to such sum as after deduction of the authorised percentage thereof equals the amount expressed in the contract to be the contribution.

(2) Where such an amendment is made, the resolution shall operate so as to effect the above mentioned amendment in the gross contribution payable under every contract of a class to which the provision relates, and the prescribed scheme as amended shall take effect accordingly.

[5 Corresponding amendment to sum assured

(1) This regulation applies if a gross contribution is amended under regulation 4.

(2) The friendly society may notify the [relevant authority][2] of a proposal to amend the sum assured or guaranteed by the contract by an amount determined in accordance with rules which have been certified by an actuary to be fair in relation to the gross contribution payable.

(3) The proposed amendment may be made at any time after the expiry of the period of 3 months beginning with the day on which the proposal is notified to the [relevant authority][2].][1]

Amendments—[1] This para substituted by FA 2012 s 227, Sch 39 para 26(5) with effect from 17 July 2012.
[2] In sub-paras (2), (3), words substituted by the Financial Services Act 2012 (Mutual Societies) Order, SI 2013/496 art 2(*c*), Sch 11, para 12(1), (3) with effect from 1 April 2013. Note that these amendments were purportedly made to the pre-FA 2012 version of this para. In the Publisher's view, the substitutions apply equally to the post-FA 2012 version and have been made accordingly.

6 Where the gross contribution is amended in accordance with these Regulations, the society shall, on being requested in writing after 5th April 1981 to do so by the person by whom the contribution is payable, notify him in writing of the amount of the effect of the amendment on the sum assured or guaranteed or of any other effect.

7 Where by virtue of regulation 6 of the 1977 Regulations a person insured under a contract irrevocably elected that the contribution under the contract under which he was insured should be increased with effect from 6th April 1979, the amendment to the gross contribution shall apply as from the effective date as if it had been effected under regulation 4(2), and regulations 5 and 6 shall apply in respect of an amended contribution under this regulation as they apply in relation to an amendment under regulation 4.

[8 Amendment of approved scheme

(1) This regulation applies if a friendly society adopted an approved scheme under regulation 7 of the 1977 Regulations.

(2) The friendly society may notify the [relevant authority][2] of a proposal to amend the approved scheme in consequence of any prospective change in the authorised percentage.

(3) The proposed amendment—

(*a*) may be made at any time after the expiry of the period of 3 months beginning with the day on which the proposal is notified to the [relevant authority][2], but

(*b*) must be made before 6 April 2015.][1]

Amendments—[1] This para substituted by FA 2012 s 227, Sch 39 para 26(5) with effect from 17 July 2012.
[2] In sub-paras (2), (3)(*a*), words substituted by the Financial Services Act 2012 (Mutual Societies) Order, SI 2013/496 art 2(*c*), Sch 11, para 12(1), (3) with effect from 1 April 2013. Note that these amendments were purportedly made to the pre-FA 2012 version of this para. In the Publisher's view, the substitutions apply equally to the post-FA 2012 version and have been made accordingly.

9 Notice or advertisement

Where a friendly society has, in accordance with the provisions of these Regulations, amended the prescribed scheme or an approved scheme adopted by it, as soon as is reasonably practicable it shall either:

(*a*) serve upon every person paying contributions to the society who is affected by the amendment a notice containing a statement setting out the effects thereof; or

(*b*) publish or cause to be published such notice by advertisement in one or more newspapers in general circulation in the area where the society carries on business.

10 Amendment of rules

Notwithstanding anything contained in the rules of a friendly society which has amended the prescribed scheme or an approved scheme, the committee of management of the society may, by resolution passed before the effective date, make amendments to the rules of the society in connection with the amendment by the society of any such scheme.

11 Modification of enactments

The enactments mentioned in the Schedule to these Regulations shall have effect subject to the adaptations and modifications set out in that Schedule.

SCHEDULE

ADAPTATIONS AND MODIFICATIONS OF ENACTMENTS

Regulation 11

This Schedule contains incidental provisions and makes consequential adaptations and modifications to enactments relating to friendly societies.

1980/1948

INDUSTRIAL ASSURANCE (LIFE ASSURANCE PREMIUM RELIEF) (CHANGE OF RATE) REGULATIONS 1980

Made by the Chief Registrar of Friendly Societies under FA 1976 Sch 4 para 13, now TA 1988 Sch 14 para 3; see TA 1988 Sch 30 para 21

Made . . . . *15 December 1980*

Laid before Parliament . . . . *29 December 1980*

Coming into Operation . . . .*20 January 1981*

Commentary—*Simon's Taxes* **E1.1310, E1.1323**.

Note—See FA 2012 Sch 39 Part 4: abolition of income tax relief for life assurance premiums under TA 1988 s 266.

1 Citation and commencement

These Regulations may be cited as the Industrial Assurance (Life Assurance Premium Relief) (Change of Rate) Regulations 1980, and shall come into operation on 20th January 1981.

2 Interpretation

In these Regulations—

"the 1977 Regulations" means the Industrial Assurance (Life Assurance Premium Relief) Regulations 1977;

"industrial assurance company" and "collecting society" have the meanings assigned by section 1 of the Industrial Assurance Act 1923 as amended by Schedule 6 to the Companies Act 1967;

"the prescribed scheme" means the scheme prescribed in Schedule 1 to the Industrial Assurance (Life Assurance Premium Relief) Regulations 1977;

"an approved scheme" means a special scheme approved by the Industrial Assurance Commissioner in the circumstances provided for in regulation 7 of the Industrial Assurance (Life Assurance Premium Relief) Regulations 1977;

"actuary" means an actuary having the qualifications which are prescribed by the Friendly Societies (Qualifications of Actuaries) Regulations 1968;

"net premium" has the meaning assigned in paragraph 3 of Schedule 1 to the Industrial Assurance (Life Assurance Premium Relief) Regulations 1977;

"gross premium" means the premium of the amount payable under the policy or contract;

"the authorised percentage" means the percentage for the time being in force under paragraph 5(*a*) of Schedule 4 to the Finance Act 1976;

"the effective date" means the date on which a change in the authorised percentage takes effect;

"amended net premium" shall be a sum equal to the gross premium less the authorised percentage, such sum to be rounded off in accordance with the principles set out in Schedule 1 of the 1977 Regulations;

"parent" includes a stepfather and a stepmother.

["relevant authority" means—

(a) if the industrial assurance company or collecting society is a PRA-authorised person within the meaning of section 2B of the Financial Services and Markets Act 2000, the Prudential Regulation Authority, and

(b) in any other case, the Financial Conduct Authority;][1]

Amendments—[1] Definition of "relevant authority" inserted by the Financial Services Act 2012 (Mutual Societies) Order, SI 2013/496 art 2(*c*), Sch 11, para 13(1), (2) with effect from 1 April 2013.

3 Amendment of a scheme

(1) Where an industrial assurance company or collecting society has adopted the prescribed scheme or an approved scheme in accordance with the provisions of the 1977 Regulations the company or society may, by resolution of its board of directors or, as the case may be, of its committee of management, passed within eight months of the passing of any Act making a change in the authorised percentage, amend any such scheme so that amounts equal to the authorised percentage of the gross premiums due and payable on or after the effective date under policies or contracts to which the scheme applies shall be retained by or refunded to the persons paying the premiums.

(2) Where an industrial assurance company or collecting society has amended any such scheme, amounts equal to the authorised percentage of the gross premiums payable under policies or contracts to which the scheme applies shall be retained by or refunded to the persons paying the premiums as provided in the scheme so amended.

(3) Written notice of a resolution amending the prescribed scheme or an approved scheme shall within fourteen days of the passing thereof be sent by the industrial assurance company or collecting society to the [relevant authority][2].[1]

(4) Where a collecting society has resolved to amend the prescribed scheme or an approved scheme any right conferred by section 21 of the Friendly Societies Act 1974 or section 10(1) of the Industrial Assurance and Friendly Societies Act 1948 on any person to receive a copy of the rules of the society or of an amendment thereof shall be extended so as to include the right to receive a copy of the resolution and of the amended scheme adopted by the resolution.

Amendments—[1] Reference to Industrial Assurance Commissioner to be construed as reference to Friendly Societies Commission, by virtue of the Friendly Societies Act 1992 (Transitional and Consequential Provisions) Regulations, SI 1995/710.

[2] In sub-para (3), words substituted by the Financial Services Act 2012 (Mutual Societies) Order, SI 2013/496 art 2(*c*), Sch 11, para 13(1), (3) with effect from 1 April 2013.

4 Amendment of gross premium

(1) Where, by virtue of regulation 4 of the 1977 Regulations, a resolution adopting the prescribed scheme provided that the gross premium was to be increased with effect from 6th April 1979 in respect of any specified class of policy or contract, a resolution amending the prescribed scheme may also amend the gross premium so that with effect from the effective date the gross premium shall be amended to such sum as after deduction of the authorised percentage thereof equals the amount expressed in the policy or contract to be the premium.

(2) Where such an amendment is made, the resolution shall operate so as to effect the above mentioned amendment in the gross premium payable under every policy or contract of a class to which the provision relates, and the prescribed scheme as amended shall take effect accordingly.

[5 Corresponding amendment to sum assured

(1) This regulation applies if a gross premium is amended under regulation 4.

(2) The industrial assurance company or collecting society may notify the [relevant authority][2] of a proposal to amend the sum assured or guaranteed by the policy or contract by an amount determined in accordance with rules which have been certified by an actuary to be fair in relation to the gross premium payable.

(3) The proposed amendment may be made at any time after the expiry of the period of 3 months beginning with the day on which the proposal is notified to the [relevant authority][2].][1]

Amendments—[1] This para substituted by FA 2012 s 227, Sch 39 para 27(5) with effect from 17 July 2012.

[2] In sub-paras (2), (3), words substituted by the Financial Services Act 2012 (Mutual Societies) Order, SI 2013/496 art 2(*c*), Sch 11, para 13(1), (3) with effect from 1 April 2013. Note that these amendments were purportedly made to the pre-FA 2012 version of this para. In the Publisher's view, the substitutions apply equally to the post-FA 2012 version and have been made accordingly.

6 Where the gross premium is amended in accordance with these Regulations, the industrial assurance company or collecting society shall, on being requested in writing after 5th April 1981 to do so by the person by whom the premium is payable, notify him in writing of the effect of the amendment on the sum assured or guaranteed or of any other effect.

7 Where by virtue of regulation 6 of the 1977 Regulations a person insured under a policy or contract irrevocably elected that the premium under the contract under which he was insured should be increased with effect from 6th April 1979, the amendment to the gross premium shall apply as from the effective date as if it had been effected under regulation 4(2), and regulations 5 and 6 shall apply in respect of an amended premium under this regulation as they apply in relation to an amendment under regulation 4.

Amendments—[1] Reference to Industrial Assurance Commissioner to be construed as reference to Friendly Societies Commission, by virtue of the Friendly Societies Act 1992 (Transitional and Consequential Provisions) Regulations, SI 1995/710.

[8 Amendment of approved schemes

(1) This regulation applies if an industrial assurance company or collecting society adopted an approved scheme under regulation 7 of the 1977 Regulations.

(2) The industrial assurance company or collecting society may notify the [relevant authority][2] of a proposal to amend the approved scheme in consequence of any prospective change in the authorised percentage.

(3) The proposed amendment—

(*a*) may be made at any time after the expiry of the period of 3 months beginning with the day on which the proposal is notified to the [relevant authority][2], but

(*b*) must be made before 6 April 2015.][2]

Amendments—[1] This para substituted by FA 2012 s 227, Sch 39 para 27(6) with effect from 17 July 2012.

In sub-paras (2), (3)(*a*), words substituted by the Financial Services Act 2012 (Mutual Societies) Order, SI 2013/496 art 2(*c*), Sch 11, para 13(1), (3) with effect from 1 April 2013. Note that these amendments were purportedly made to the pre-FA 2012 version of this para. In the Publisher's view, the substitutions apply equally to the post-FA 2012 version and have been made accordingly.

9 Notice or advertisement

Where an industrial assurance company or collecting society has, in accordance with the provisions of these regulations, amended the prescribed scheme or an approved scheme adopted by it, as soon as is reasonably practicable it shall either:

(*a*) serve upon every person paying premiums to the company or society who is affected by the amendment a notice containing a statement setting out the effects thereof; or

(*b*) publish or cause to be published such notice by advertisement in one or more newspapers in general circulation in the area where the company or society carries on business.

10 Amendment of rules

Notwithstanding anything contained in the rules of a collecting society which has amended the prescribed scheme or an approved scheme, the committee of management of the society may, by resolution passed before the effective date, make amendments to the rules of the society in connection with the amendment by the society of any such scheme.

11 Modifications of enactments

The enactments mentioned in the Schedule to these Regulations shall have effect subject to the adaptations and modifications set out in that Schedule.

SCHEDULE

ADAPTATIONS AND MODIFICATIONS OF ENACTMENTS

Regulation 11

This Schedule contains incidental provisions and makes consequential adaptations and modifications to enactments relating to friendly societies.

1981/233

CROWN PROCEEDINGS (NORTHERN IRELAND) ORDER 1981

Made by Order in Council under the Crown Proceedings Act 1947 s 53

Made . . . . *18 February 1981*

PART I

1 General

(1) This Order may be cited as the Crown Proceedings (Northern Ireland) Order 1981 and . . . shall come into operation on 19th March 1981.

(2) In this Order "the Act" means the Crown Proceedings Act 1947.

(5) This Order extends only to Northern Ireland.

Note—Words omitted are outside the scope of this work.

PART II

2 Extension of the Act to Northern Ireland

The provisions of the Act shall extend to Northern Ireland—

(*a*) in relation to Her Majesty's Government in the United Kingdom, with the additions, exceptions and modifications set out in Part III of this Order;

(*b*) in relation to Her Majesty's Government in Northern Ireland, with those additions, exceptions and modifications, but subject to the further additions, exceptions and modifications set out in Part IV of this Order.

PART III

3 Additions and exceptions to, and modifications of, the Act in its application to the Crown in right of both Her Majesty's government in the United Kingdom and (subject to Part IV) Her Majesty's government in Northern Ireland

For any reference to the commencement of the Act there shall be substituted a reference to 1st January 1950 (the date of coming into operation of the Northern Ireland (Crown Proceedings) Order 1949).

Regulations—Northern Ireland (Crown Proceedings) Order, SI 1949/1836.

8 In section 13, the words from "In this section" to the end shall be excepted.

10 In section 15(1) after "civil proceedings" there shall be inserted "by or".

11 For section 16 there shall be substituted the following section:

"16 Interpleader

The Crown may obtain relief by way of interpleader proceedings, and may be made a party to such proceedings, in the same manner in which a subject may obtain relief by way of such proceedings or be made a party thereto; and the provisions of Article 44 of the Judgments Enforcement (Northern Ireland) Order 1981 relating to interpleader proceedings shall, subject to the provisions of this Act, have effect accordingly.".

12—(1) For section 17(1) there shall be substituted the following subsection:

"(1) The Department of the Civil Service for Northern Ireland shall publish a list specifying the several departments of the Government of the United Kingdom which are authorised departments for the purposes of this Act in Northern Ireland, and the name and address for service of the person who is, or is acting for the purposes of this Act as, the solicitor in Northern Ireland for each such department, and may from time to time amend or vary the said list. The said list may in relation to any such department specify different solicitors for different types of proceedings.

Any document purporting to be a copy of a list published under this section and purporting to be printed under the superintendence or the authority of His Majesty's Stationery Office shall in any legal proceedings be received as evidence for the purpose of establishing what departments are authorised departments for the purposes of this Act, and what person is, or is acting for the purposes of this Act as, the solicitor in Northern Ireland for any such department.".

(2) After section 17(3) there shall be inserted the following subsection:

"(3A) Civil proceedings against the Crown may be instituted in Northern Ireland against the Attorney General if the alleged liability arises out of the performance of any function pursuant to an agency arrangement or the person instituting the proceedings has any reasonable doubt whether the alleged liability of the Crown arises in respect of His Majesty's Government in the United Kingdom or in respect of His Majesty's Government in Northern Ireland.".

13 In section 18 for "the Solicitor for the affairs of His Majesty's Treasury" there shall be substituted "the Crown Solicitor for Northern Ireland".

14 Section 19(1) shall be excepted.

15 In section 20(2) the words "or transfer" shall be excepted, for "transfer" where secondly occurring there shall be substituted "remittal" . . .

Note—Words omitted are outside the scope of this work.

17 In section 22 after "execution" there shall be inserted "and all enactments and Judgment Enforcement Rules relating to stay of enforcement of judgments".

18 For section 23(3) there shall be substituted the following subsection:

"(3) Notwithstanding anything in the preceding provisions of this section, the provisions of this Part of this Act shall not have effect with respect to any of the following proceedings brought by or against the Crown in right of His Majesty's Government in the United Kingdom, that is to say:

(*a*) proceedings brought by the Attorney General on the relation of some other person;

(*b*) proceedings by or against the Public Trustee;

(*c*) proceedings by or against the Land Purchase Trustee for Northern Ireland.".

19—(1) For section 24(1) there shall be substituted the following subsection:

"(1) Article 127 of the Judgments Enforcement (Northern Ireland) Order 1981 (which provides that a money judgment shall, subject to certain exceptions and to any contrary provision in the judgment, carry interest) shall apply to money judgments given against or in favour of the Crown.".

(2) Section 24(2) shall be excepted.

(3) In section 24(3) for the reference to section 3 of the Law Reform (Miscellaneous Provisions) Act 1934 there shall be substituted a reference to section 17 of the Law Reform (Miscellaneous Provisions) Act (Northern Ireland) 1937.

20 In section 25—

(*a*) in subsection (1) for "in any proceedings on the Crown side of the King's Bench Division" there shall be substituted "on any application for judicial review pursuant to section 18 of the Judicature (Northern Ireland) Act 1978";

(*b*) in subsection (4) for "no execution or attachment or process in the nature thereof shall be issued out of any court" there shall be substituted "no order or process in the nature of execution shall be made by or issued out of any court, and no enforcement order shall be made by the Enforcement of Judgments Office,".

21 For section 26(2) there shall be substituted the following subsections—

"(2) Without prejudice to the generality of subsection (1) above, the Judgments Enforcement (Northern Ireland) Order 1981, Judgment Enforcement Rules and rules of court shall, save as otherwise provided by any statutory provision within the meaning of that Order, apply to judgments given in favour of the Crown.

(2A) Articles 106 and 107 of that Order of 1981 (which relate respectively to limitation on arrest and imprisonment of debtors and to committal for default) shall apply to sums of money payable and debts due to the Crown.

(2B) Articles 115 and 125 of that Order of 1981 (which relate respectively to committal for contempt in certain cases of default and to the effect of imprisonment under Article 107 or 115) shall—

(*a*) have effect in relation to sums of money payable and debts due to the Crown; and

(*b*) have effect as if those provisions in terms applied to default in payment of any sum payable in respect of estate duty."

24 In section 35 in subsection (2)(*a*) after "Kingdom" there shall be inserted "or, in the case of county court rules, are not resident in Northern Ireland", and in subsection (2)(*d*), for "and for enabling any such proceedings to be put in proper cases into any special list which may be kept for the trial of short causes in which leave to defend is given under any such rule of court as aforesaid" there shall be substituted "or of any county court rule providing for process by default".

26—(1) In section 38(2) the following definitions shall be inserted at the appropriate points in alphabetical order—

"Agency arrangement" means an arrangement such as is mentioned in section 11 of the Northern Ireland Constitution Act 1973;

"Attorney General" means the Attorney General for Northern Ireland;

"County court" means a county court in Northern Ireland;

"County court rules" has the same meaning as in section 21(5) of the Interpretation Act (Northern Ireland) 1954;

"Department of Finance" means the Department of Finance for Northern Ireland;

"High Court" (except in a reference to that court as a prize court) means the High Court of Justice in Northern Ireland;

"Royal Courts of Justice" means those courts at Belfast;

"Rules of court" has the same meaning as in section 21(4) of the Interpretation Act (Northern Ireland) 1954.

(2) In section 38(2)—

(*a*) in the definition of "Civil proceedings" for "proceedings on the Crown side of the King's Bench Division" there shall be substituted "an application for judicial review pursuant to section 18 of the Judicature (Northern Ireland) Act 1978";

(*b*) at the end of the definition of "Order" there shall be inserted "or a dismiss by a county court";

(*c*) in the definition of "Statutory duty" for "Act of Parliament" there shall be substituted "enactment".

(3) At the end of section 38 there shall be added the following subsection:

"(7) Any reference (however expressed) in this Act to an enactment or an Act includes an enactment of the Irish Parliament, the Parliament of Northern Ireland or the Northern Ireland Assembly or an enactment contained in an Order in Council made under section 1(3) of the Northern Ireland (Temporary Provisions) Act 1972 or paragraph 1 of Schedule 1 to the Northern Ireland Act 1974.".

27—(1) In section 40(2), after "without prejudice to the general effect of the foregoing provision" there shall be inserted "but subject to the provisions of section 17(3A) and section 37(3) of this Act".

28 Part V and section 52 shall be excepted.

PART IV

29 Further additions and exceptions to, and modifications of, the Act in its application to the Crown in right of Her Majesty's government in Northern Ireland

The following provisions of the Act, that is to say,—

. . . , in section 17(5) the words "or an authorised Government department" and the words from "or in" onwards, section 26(2B)(*b*), . . . section 38(3) . . . and in Schedule 1, paragraph 2(1), the words from "including" onwards,

shall be excepted from the Act in its application to the Crown in right of Her Majesty's Government in Northern Ireland.

Note—Words omitted are outside the scope of this work.
For s 26(2B)(*b*) see Art 21.

30—(1) For any reference (except in section 17(3A), . . . or section 53 and except the second reference in section 32) to the Crown (including, except as aforesaid, any express reference which is to be construed as one to the Crown in right of Her Majesty's Government in the United Kingdom) there shall be substituted a reference to be construed as one to the Crown in right of Her Majesty's Government in Northern Ireland; for any reference which is to be construed as one to Her Majesty in right of Her Government in the United Kingdom there shall be substituted a reference to be construed as one to Her Majesty in right of Her Government in Northern Ireland; for any reference to a Government department there shall be substituted a reference to a Northern Ireland department; and for any reference which is to be construed as one to an officer, servant or agent of Her Majesty or an officer, servant or agent of the Crown or for any reference to a Minister of the Crown (except the references in sections 36 and 40(3) to the Secretary of State) there shall be substituted respectively a reference to be construed as one to an officer, servant or agent of Her Majesty's Government in Northern Ireland or a reference to the Head of a Northern Ireland department.

Note—Words omitted are outside the scope of this work.
For s 17(3A) see Art 12(2).

32 In section 17(1) the words "in Northern Ireland", where first occurring, shall be excepted.

Note—For s 17(1) see Art 12.

33 For section 23(3) there shall be substituted the following subsection—

"(3) Notwithstanding anything in the preceding provisions of this section, the provisions of this Part of this Act shall not have effect with respect to any of the following proceedings brought by or against the Crown in right of His Majesty's Government in Northern Ireland, that is to say—

(*a*) proceedings brought by the Attorney General on the relation of some other person;

(*b*) proceedings in respect of charities by or against the Attorney General;

(*c*) proceedings by or against the Department of Finance acting in pursuance of any enactment relating to charities;

(*d*) proceedings by or against the Registrar of Titles in Northern Ireland or any officers of the Land Registry of Northern Ireland or proceedings for compensation under section 71 of the Land Registration Act (Northern Ireland) 1970".

Note—For s 23(3) see Art 18.

1982/1236

INCOME TAX (INTEREST RELIEF) REGULATIONS 1982

Made by the Commissioners of Inland Revenue under FA 1982 s 29(3), now TA 1988 s 378; see TA 1988 Sch 30 para 21

Made . . . . *31 August 1982*
Laid before the House of Commons . . . . *1 September 1982*
Coming into Operation . . . . *1 October 1982*

Commentary—*Simon's Taxes* **A4.431–A4.433**.

1 Citation and commencement

These Regulations may be cited as the Income Tax (Interest Relief) Regulations 1982, and shall come into operation on 1st October 1982.

2 Interpretation

(1) In these Regulations unless the context otherwise requires—

"authorised officer" means the official registered by the Board as being authorised for the purposes of these Regulations by the lender;

"the Board" means the Commissioners of Inland Revenue;

"financial year" in relation to a lender means a period of 12 months or the period (not necessarily a period of 12 months) for which the lender makes up its accounts;

"lender" means a qualifying lender for the purposes of section 26;

"limited loan" means a loan to which either paragraph 5(1) or (2) or paragraph 24(3) of Schedule 1 to the Finance Act 1974[1] applies;

"a qualifying borrower" has the meaning given by Part III of Schedule 7[2] [which shall be deemed to include, for the application to them of sections 26 and 28 and Schedule 7[3] and these regulations those personal representatives and trustees to whom reference is made in Regulation 7A below, so long as they are all resident in the United Kingdom and in Regulation 7B below, so long as the conditions in that Regulation are fulfilled];

"relevant loan interest" has the meaning given by Part I of Schedule 7;[4]

"Schedule 7" means Schedule 7 to the Finance Act 1982;[5]

"section 26" means section 26 of the Finance Act 1982;[6]

"section 28" means section 28 of the Finance Act 1982;[7]

"tax year" means a period of 12 months ending on 5th April.

(2) In the application of these Regulations to Scotland—

(*a*) "a freehold or leasehold estate" means any interest in land; and

(*b*) any reference to a loan on the security of such an estate is a reference to a loan upon a heritable security within the meaning of section 9(8)(*a*) of the Conveyancing and Feudal Reform (Scotland) Act 1970.

Notes—[1] TA 1988 s 357(1) or s 365(3).
[2] TA 1988 s 376.
[3] TA 1988 ss 369–377.
[4] TA 1988 ss 370–373.
[5] TA 1988 ss 370–376.
[6] TA 1988 s 369.
[7] TA 1988 s 377.

Amendments—Words in the definition of "a qualifying borrower" in para (1) inserted by the IT (Interest Relief) (No 2) Regulations, SI 1983/311 reg 3, with effect from 15 March 1983.

3 Loans which the borrower may bring within the tax deduction scheme

(1) Loans the interest on which paid by a qualifying borrower is relevant loan interest are loans specified for the purposes of paragraph 7(1)(*a*) of Schedule 7 except—

(*a*) loans in respect of property which is used as the only or main residence of a dependent relative or former or separated spouse of his;

[(*b* loans the interest on which is eligible for relief under paragraph 4A of the Schedule 1 to the Finance Act 1974; or][1]

(*c*) loans to which the provisions of sub-paragraphs (*b*), (*c*) or (*d*) of the said paragraph 7(1) apply.

(2) . . .[2]

(3) Where the borrower is unable to provide the lender with the notice to which the said paragraph 7(1)(*a*) refers he may, if he considers that the interest payable on his loan is or will be relevant loan interest, apply to the Board for a notice under paragraph 7(1)(*b*) of Schedule 7 and the Board shall notify him of their decision on his application.

Notes—For FA 2982 Sch 7 para 7(1)(*a*), see now TA 1988 s 374(1)(*a*).
For FA 1974 Sch 2 para 4A see now TA 1988 s 356.

Amendments—[1] Para (1)(*b*) substituted by the IT (Interest Relief) (No 2) Regulations, SI 1983/311 reg 4, with effect from 15 March 1983.
[2] Para (2) revoked by the IT (Interest Relief) (Amendment) Regulations, SI 1995/1213 reg 3, with effect from 4 May 1995.

4 Loans made before tax year 1983–84 which the lender may bring within the tax deduction scheme

Loans of the following descriptions, not being loans to which the interest on which paragraph 2(3) of Schedule 7[1] applies, are specified for the purposes of paragraph 7(1)(*d*)[2] of Schedule 7—

(*a*) a loan secured on a freehold or leasehold estate in respect of property in relation to which the loan was granted in which the borrower (and in the case of joint borrowers each of them), or a dependent relative, or former or separated spouse of his, is residing at the time when the loan is made, or will so reside within 12 months of that time; being a loan

(i) which is not a limited loan (unless it is a limited loan in respect of which notice has been given to the Board under Regulation 7(1) before 1st December 1982);

(ii) in respect of which the lender has undertaken

(*a*) to inform the Board that it is a loan to which this Regulation applies together with the name and address of each borrower, and where known the Tax District to which he makes his return together with his tax reference; and

(*b*) to notify the borrower, not later than 30 days before the first payment of relevant loan interest falls due, that interest payable on the loan appears to be relevant loan interest; and

(iii) in respect of which the lender has not been notified that the interest is not relevant loan interest;

(*b*) a loan which is not a limited loan but otherwise qualifies for relief under the provisions of paragraph 24 of Schedule 1 to the Finance Act 1974[3].

Notes—[1] TA 1988 s 370(3).
[2] TA 1988 s 374(1)(*d*).
[3] TA 1988 s 365.

5 Commencement of tax deduction scheme before tax year 1983–84 in certain cases

. . .

6 Application of tax deduction scheme to home improvement loans

Where before 1st December in any year a lender notifies the Board that it wishes home improvement loans which it has made to which paragraph 4(1)(*b*) of Schedule 7[1] applies to be brought within the tax deduction scheme, the scheme shall begin to apply to relevant loan interest payable on such loans in the tax year beginning in the next following year; but in the case of home improvement loans to be made on or after the date of the lender's notice to the Board it shall begin to apply from the date specified in the notice.

Note—[1] TA 1988 s 372(1)(*b*).

7 Application of tax deduction scheme to limited loans

(1)

[(*a*) Subject to the provisions of sub-paragraph (*b*)—

(i) where before 1st October in any year a lender notifies the Board that it wishes limited loans which it has made to be brought within the tax deduction scheme, the scheme shall begin to apply in the tax year beginning in the next following year to the relevant loan interest payable on those loans in respect of which the Board has given notice as provided by paragraph 7(1)(*b*) of Schedule 7[3]; but in the case of limited loans which the lender makes on or after the date of the lender's notice the scheme shall begin to apply to the relevant loan interest payable on those loans after the date specified in the notice, not being a date earlier than 30 days after the date of that notice;

(ii) where at any time a lender notifies the Board of its wish to bring within the tax deduction scheme only those limited loans which it will make on or after the date of the lender's notice to the Board the scheme shall begin to apply to the relevant loan interest payable on those loans after the date specified in the notice, not being a date earlier than 30 days after the date of that notice].[1]

(*b*) within 30 days of the lender's giving such a notice the Board may notify the lender that the scheme shall not begin to apply in accordance with its notice and, where the Board so notifies the lender, the scheme shall begin to apply only on the date and to the loans which the Board has in writing authorised.

(2) Where a lender has not so notified the Board under paragraph (1)(*a*) the tax deduction scheme shall not begin to apply in the following circumstances—

(*a*) for the tax year 1983–84, in respect of interest on a loan which was a limited loan

(i) when the interest was last charged by the lender to the borrower's account in its records before February 1983, or

(ii) in the case of a loan made after January 1983, when the loan was made;

[(*b*) for any tax year after 5th April 1984 in respect of interest on a loan which was a limited loan

(i) when the interest was last charged by the lender to the borrower's account in its records at any time before March in the previous tax year, or

(ii) in the case of a loan made after the date when the qualifying lender last charged interest to borrowers' accounts in its records at any time before March in the previous tax year, when the loan was made.][2]

Amendments—[1] Para (1)(*a*) substituted by the IT (Interest Relief) (No 3) Regulations, SI 1985/1252 reg 3, with effect from 1 September 1985.

[2] Para (2)(*b*) substituted by the IT (Interest Relief) (No 2) Regulations, SI 1983/311 reg 5, with effect from 15 March 1983.

[3] TA 1988 s 374(1)(*b*).

7A [Application of tax deduction scheme to certain personal representatives and trustees

Interest which is paid and payable in the United Kingdom by persons as personal representatives of a deceased person or as trustees of a settlement made by his will the whole of which would have been eligible for relief under section 75 of the Finance Act 1972[1] (by virtue of paragraph 8 of Schedule 1 to the Finance Act 1974[2]), apart from section 26(1)[3] and paragraph 5 of Schedule 1 to the Finance Act 1974[4] is relevant loan interest within the meaning of Part I of Schedule 7[5] (but as if sub-paragraph (3) of paragraph 2 of that Schedule[6] were omitted) to which section 26(1)[7] applies.][8]

Note—[1] TA 1988 s 353.

[2] TA 1988 s 358.

[3] TA 1988 s 369(1).

[4] TA 1988 s 357.

[5] TA 1988 ss 370–373.

[6] TA 1988 s 370(3).

[7] TA 1988 s 369(1).

[8] This regulation inserted by the IT (Interest Relief) (No 2) Regulations, SI 1983/311 reg 6, with effect from 15 March 1983.

[7B In determining whether loan interest paid and payable by trustees to whom reference is made in section 24(4) of the Housing Subsidies Act 1967 (option mortgages) or Article 143(6) of the Housing (Northern Ireland) Order 1981 (option mortgages in Northern Ireland) is relevant loan interest, Schedule 7[2] shall have effect as if for sub-paragraph (3) of paragraph 2 there were substituted the words—

"(3) This sub-paragraph applies to interest payable by trustees which becomes due on or after 1st April 1983 and is payable on a loan—

(*a*) in respect of which there is in force on 31st March 1983 an option notice given under section 24(2) of the 1967 Act (option mortgages) or under Article 142(2) of the 1981 Order which has effect by virtue of section 24(4) of that Act or, as the case may be, by virtue of Article 143(6) of that Order; and (*b*) which relates to a dwelling in respect of which, at the time the interest is paid and on the assumption that one of those provisions continues to be applicable, the conditions in section 24(4) of the 1967 Act, or, as the case may be, Article 143(6) of the 1981 Order are fulfilled."][1]

Notes—[1] This regulation inserted by the IT (Interest Relief) (No 2) Regulations, SI 1983/311 reg 6, with effect from 15 March 1983.
[2] TA 1988 ss 370–376.

8 Variation of repayment terms of certain loans

(1) Expressions used in this Regulation have the same meaning as in section 28[1].

(2) Subject to the provisions of this Regulation the amount of each combined payment and the date on which it becomes due from a borrower, to whom a specified lender has given a notice under section 28(2)(*a*)[2] to vary the terms of repayment of the loan, shall be notified to the borrower by the lender.

(3) The notice under section 28(2)(*a*)[2] shall be in a form prescribed or authorised by the Board but shall not have effect unless—

(*a*) it contains a statement of the borrower's right under section 28(2)(*b*)[3] to give a counter notice; and

(*b*) there is a period of not less than 30 days between the giving of the notice and the due date for the first of the combined payments to which the notice relates.

(4) A borrower shall be entitled to give a counter notice under section 28(2)(*b*)[3] not later than 3 months after the due date for the first combined payment to which paragraph (2) above refers.

(5) On receipt of the borrower's counter notice under section 28(2)(*b*)[2] the lender shall give notice to the borrower of—

(*a*) the amount of the combined payments which will be due from him after taking account of the requirements of section 28(4)[4];

(*b*) the due date for the first such combined payment which shall be—

(i) where the borrower gives a counter notice under section 28(2)(*b*)[3] within 30 days of the lender's notice under section 28(2)(*a*)[2], the due date for the first combined payment to which paragraph (2) above refers; or

(ii) in any other case, a date not later than what apart from the borrower's counter notice, would have been the date of the second of his combined payments falling due after the date of that counter notice;

(*c*) an estimate of the total period which, assuming there is no change in the amount of the borrower's combined payments, will be required to satisfy the principal and the interest on the loan by means of those payments; and

(*d*) a statement of the borrower's right under section 28(4)[4] to make additional repayments of capital.

Notes—[1] TA 1988 s 377.
[2] TA 1988 s 377(2)(*a*).
[3] TA 1988 s 377(2)(*b*).
[4] TA 1988 s 377(4).

8A [Repayment claims by certain borrowers

(1) Where in a tax year a borrower has not been able to deduct the full amount of the sums deductible under the provisions of section 26(1)[2] from payments of relevant loan interest by reason of the circumstances described in paragraph 11 of Schedule 7,[3] he may make a claim to the Board for payment of a sum equal to the amount which he has not been able to deduct.

(2) Section 42 of the Taxes Management Act 1970 shall not apply to such a claim.

(3) The Board shall notify the borrower of its decision on the claim.][1]

Notes—[1] This regulation inserted by the IT (Interest Relief) (No 2) Regulations, SI 1983/311 reg 7, with effect from 15 March 1983.
[2] TA 1988 s 369(1).
[3] TA 1988 s 375(8).

[8B (1) This regulation applies in any case where an amount to which a borrower is not entitled is paid to him by the Board pursuant to a claim under regulation 8A.

(2) An officer of the Board may make such assessments as may in his judgment be required for recovering that amount from the borrower.

(3) [The Taxes Management Act 1970 shall apply to an assessment under paragraph (2) as if it were an assessment to income tax for the year of assessment for which the payment was made.][2]

(4) If in a case to which paragraph (1) applies, the borrower fraudulently or negligently makes any false statement or representation in connection with the making of a claim under regulation 8A, he shall be liable to a penalty not exceeding the amount referred to in that paragraph.

(5) If in a case to which paragraph (1) applies, the borrower is required to give notice under subsection (1) of section 375 of the Income and Corporation Taxes Act 1988, and there is any unreasonable delay in the giving of the notice, he shall be liable to a penalty not exceeding so much of the amount referred to in that paragraph as is attributable to that delay.][1]

Amendments—[1] This regulation inserted by the IT (Interest Relief) (Amendment) Regulations, SI 1995/1213 reg 4, with effect from 4 May 1995.

[2] Para (3) substituted by the IT (Interest Relief) (Amendment) Regulations, SI 1996/1184 reg 3, with effect in any case where an assessment is made on or after 20 May 1996 and is for the year 1996–97 or any subsequent year of assessment.

Para (3) is also substituted by the IT (Interest Relief) (Amendment) Regulations, SI 1996/1184 reg 4, with effect in any case where an assessment is made on or after 6 April 1988 and is for the year 1995–96 or any earlier year of assessment, as follows:

"(3) The Taxes Management Act 1970 shall apply to an assessment under paragraph (2) as if it were an assessment to income tax for the year of assessment for which the payment was made and as if the assessment were among those specified in section 55(1) of that Act (recovery of tax not postponed).".

9 Repayment claims by lenders: introductory

(1) Sums recoverable by a lender under section 26(7)[1] shall be recovered on a claim to the Board for the purpose under these Regulations.
(2) Subject to paragraph (3) a claim shall be for the lender's financial year, and is referred to in these Regulations as an "annual claim".
(3) A claim may also be made in accordance with Regulations 10 or 12 for a period shorter than the claimant's financial year and is referred to in these Regulations as an "interim claim".
(4) No payment in respect of sums recoverable on such a claim shall be made to a lender before 1st April 1983.

Note—[1] TA 1988 s 369(6).

10 Interim claims in advance

(1) An interim claim for a period allowed by paragraphs (2) and (3) may be made not later than 1 month, or such shorter period as the Board may allow, before the date to which paragraph (5) refers, and is referred to in these Regulations as an "interim claim in advance".
(2) The periods for which an interim claim in advance may be made are—
  (*a*) 1 calendar month; or
  (*b*) 3 calendar months.
(3) Interim claims in advance made by a lender may not (except where authorised by prior written approval of the Board) be made for different periods.
(4) An interim claim in advance for a period shall be based on an estimate of the amount deductible by borrowers in respect of payments of relevant loan interest to the lender falling due in that period, and the estimate shall be certified by an authorised officer of the lender as being the best estimate that can reasonably be made of the amount deductible.
(5) If the Board are satisfied with the estimate they shall pay a sum equal to the estimated amount deductible on the date prescribed in paragraph (6) or where it is not a working day the next following working day; if they are not so satisfied they shall pay the lender such lesser sum, if any, as in their estimation will approximate to the amount deductible.
(6) Subject to paragraph (7), the date referred to in paragraph (5) is—
  (*a*) in the case of a claim for 1 calendar month the 23rd of the month;
  (*b*) in the case of a claim for 3 calendar months the 15th of the second of those months.
(7) In the case of a claim for 1 calendar month, if the lender so claims and satisfies the condition in paragraph (8), the date referred to in paragraph (5) above is the 2nd, 9th or 15th instead of the 23rd of the month.
(8) The condition mentioned in paragraph (7) is that the lender's mean repayment date is closer to the date on which repayment is claimed than each of the other 3 dates and the lender's "mean repayment date" means—
  (*a*) the date which is found by multiplying the date of each day of the months of April to September in the previous year by the payments of interest due on that day, adding together the products so calculated for all the days of those 6 months, and dividing the total of those products by the total of all payments of interest due in those months; or
  (*b*) a date arrived at on some other basis which is authorised by the Board.

11 Supplementary statements

(1) When a payment has been made to a lender under Regulation 10(5) on an interim claim in advance, the lender shall deliver to the Board a supplementary statement under this Regulation and (except when paragraph (5) below applies) shall deliver the statement within 4 months after the end of the period for which the claim was made.
(2) The supplementary statement shall be a statement correcting (or confirming) the estimate of the amount deductible given in accordance with Regulation 10(4) above, and shall—

(*a*) be based as far as possible on the amount of relevant loan interest which actually fell due in the period covered by the statement, and only as far as may be necessary on a revised estimate; and

(*b*) be for the same period as the interim claim in advance;

and any estimate contained in the supplementary statement shall be certified by an authorised officer of the lender as the best estimate that can reasonably be made.

(3) If the supplementary statement shows that the amount deductible was greater than the payment made under Regulation 10(5) the Board shall, if satisfied with the statement, pay the amount of the difference to the lender by way of supplementary payment on the claim, but if the supplementary statement shows that the amount deductible was less than the payment made under Regulation 10(5) the lender shall repay the amount of the difference to the Board with the statement.

(4) If in respect of an interim claim on which a payment has been made under Regulation 10(5) a lender fails to deliver a supplementary statement within the time required by this Regulation, the amount of the payment shall immediately be recoverable by the Board in the same manner as tax charged by an assessment on the lender which has become final and conclusive.

(5) Where the lender debits interest in arrear to a borrower's account in its records and at intervals of more than a month the supplementary statement shall, if this date is later than the date in paragraph (1) above, be delivered not later than 5 months after the end of the month in which interest is so debited.

12 Interim claims in arrear

(1) An interim claim for a period allowed by paragraph (2) may be made by a lender within 6 months after the end of the period for which it is made.

(2) The period for which a claim may be made under this Regulation shall be one which—

(*a*) is not shorter than 1 calendar month;

(*b*) falls within the lender's same financial year; and

(*c*) does not include any part of a period in respect of which a payment was made under Regulation 10(5) (unless the payment in respect of the period or that part was recovered under Regulation 11(4)).

(3) A claim under this Regulation may not be based on an estimate but may only be made to recover the amount deductible in respect of interest which fell due in the period.

(4) If the amount claimed is established to the Board's satisfaction they shall pay the amount to the claimant; if they are not so satisfied they shall pay to the claimant any lesser amount established to their satisfaction.

13 Annual claims

(1) An annual claim for the lender's financial year may not be made at any time more than 6 years after the end of the financial year.

(2) Except where in relation to any financial year a lender repays all the payments made to it on relevant interim claims, it shall within 1 year after the end of the financial year make an annual claim to establish the amount deductible for that financial year.

In this Regulation "relevant interim claim" means, in relation to a financial year, an interim claim for a period falling wholly or partly within that financial year.

[(3) The annual claim may not be based on an estimate and shall, unless the lender makes an election under paragraph (4), include only the tax deducted from interest payments due from borrowers during the financial year to which the claim relates and paid not later than 4 months after the end of that year.][1]

(4) Where however a loan is secured on a freehold or leasehold estate in respect of property in relation to which the loan is made, the lender may in respect of any such loan elect to include in an annual claim the amount of tax deductible in respect of interest payments due from the borrower in the year, but always excluding the amounts of tax deductible in respect of interest written off as a bad debt in the accounts of the lender for the financial year to which the claim relates.

(5)

(*a*) Where in a tax year before the passing of the Act imposing tax for that year any deduction has been made in accordance with section 26[2] from a payment of interest at a rate in excess of that rate of tax ultimately so imposed, the lender may include in his annual claim the amount of the excess not recovered where—

(i) the loan has been repaid before the passing of the said Act, and

(ii) the lender has not been able to recover from the borrower the excess so deducted by the end of its financial year or within 6 months of the deduction whichever is the later.

(*b*) The amount included in respect of the excess shall be repaid to the lender by the Board as if it were an amount deductible from relevant loan interest in accordance with section 26[2] and the Board shall be entitled to recover from the borrower the amount so repaid in the same manner as tax charged by an assessment on the borrower which has become final and conclusive.

(6) An annual claim shall bring into account payments made on relevant interim claims, and shall apportion as may be necessary any payment made on such [a] claim for any period falling partly in a different financial year, and for the purpose of this Regulation the "aggregate of the relevant interim payments" means the aggregate of the payments made (and not repaid) on relevant interim claims but excluding any part of a payment relating to a different financial year.
(7) Where the aggregate of the relevant interim payments shown by an annual claim exceeds the amount deductible for the financial year shown on the claim, the lender shall repay the amount of the excess to the Board with the claim.
(8) If a lender fails to make an annual claim required under paragraph (2) within the time limited by that paragraph, the Board may issue a notice to the lender showing the aggregate of the relevant interim payments for the year, and stating that the Board are not satisfied that the amount due to the lender for the year exceeds the lower amount stated in the notice.
(9) If an annual claim is not delivered to the Board within 14 days after the issue of such a notice under paragraph (8) the amount of the difference between the aggregate and the lower amount stated in the notice shall immediately be recoverable by the Board in the same manner as tax charged by an assessment on the lender which has become final and conclusive.
(10) Where an annual claim has been made and the lender subsequently discovers that an error or mistake has been made in the claim the lender may make a supplementary annual claim within the time allowed in paragraph (1).

Notes—[1] Para (3) substituted by the IT (Interest Relief) (No 2) Regulations, SI 1983/311 reg 8, with effect from 15 March 1983.
[2] TA 1988 s 369.

14 Lender's claims: supplementary provisions

(1) Section 42 of the Taxes Management Act 1970 shall not apply to claims under these Regulations.
(2) No appeal shall lie from the Board's decision on an interim claim.
(3) An appeal [may be made against][1] the Board's decision on an annual claim, and the appeal shall be brought by giving written notice to the Board within 30 days of receipt of written notice of the decision.
(4) No payment or repayment made or other thing done on or in relation to an interim claim or a notice under Regulation 13(8) shall prejudice the decision on an annual claim.
(5) Part V of the Taxes Management Act 1970 (appeals and other proceedings) shall apply to an appeal under paragraph (3) above, and on an appeal [that is notified to the tribunal, the tribunal][1] may vary the decision appealed against whether or not the variation is to the advantage of the appellant.
(6) All such assessments, payments and repayments shall be made as are necessary to give effect to the Board's decision on an annual claim, or to any variation of that decision on appeal.
(7) Claims and supplementary statements under these Regulations shall be in such form and contain such particulars as the Board prescribe and shall be signed by an authorised officer of the lender; and forms prescribed for annual claims may require a report to be given by the lender's auditor.
(8) Where for the purposes of an annual claim for a financial year it is necessary to apportion any amount included in an interim claim for a period falling partly within and partly outside the financial year, the apportionment shall be made in such manner as the Board may prescribe.

Amendments—[1] In paras (3), (5), words substituted, by the Transfer of Tribunal Functions and Revenue and Customs Appeals Order, SI 2009/56 art 3, Sch 2 paras 9, 10 with effect from 1 April 2009.

15 Information to be provided to borrowers by lenders

A lender shall, at his request, provide the borrower with a certificate showing in respect of a tax year the amount of relevant loan interest due from and paid by the borrower and the amount of tax deducted from that interest.

16 Information to be provided to the Board

The Board may by notice in writing require any person who is a party to a loan agreement to which section 26 applies, or could in the opinion of the Board apply, to furnish them, within such time (not being less than 14 days) as may be provided by the notice, such information (including copies of any relevant documents or records) as they may reasonably require for the purposes of section 26 or Schedule 7.

17 Inspection of records

(1) Every person to whom payments of interest are made in respect of which a repayment claim is made by a lender under these Regulations shall, whenever required to do so, make available for inspection by an officer of the Board authorised for that purpose all such books, documents and other records in his possession or under his control containing information relating to—

(*a*) such interest and the terms of the loans (including relevant contracts or deeds) under which such interest is paid or,

(*b*) the persons holding such contracts or deeds or paying such interest

as may reasonably be required for determining whether the amount for which any such claim is made is properly recoverable.

(2) Where records are maintained by computer the person required to make them available for inspection shall provide the officer making the inspection with all facilities necessary for obtaining information from them.

(3)

(*a*) Every notice given to it by the borrower under paragraph 7(1)(*a*) of Schedule 7[1] shall be preserved by the lender to whom it is given and in such manner as may be approved by the Board, so as to be available for inspection under this Regulation, until two years after the termination of the loan or, if earlier, the date from which the interest ceases to be relevant loan interest;

(*b*) a copy of the notice shall on its written request be made available to the Board.

Note—[1] TA 1988 s 374(1)(*a*).

18 Application of penalty provisions of the Taxes Management Act 1970

(*Inserts words in second column of Table in TMA 1970 s 98.*)

19 Borrowers' appeals: supplementary provisions

(1) . . . [3]

(2) An appeal shall be brought by giving written notice to the Board within 30 days of the receipt by the borrower of the Board's decision or the notice as the case may be.

(3) Part V of the Taxes Management Act 1970 (appeals and other proceedings) shall apply to an appeal under this Regulation, and on an appeal [that is notified to the tribunal, the tribunal][3] may vary the decision or notice appealed from whether or not the variation is to the advantage of the appellant.

(4) All such . . . [2] payments or repayments shall be made by the inspector as are necessary to give effect to the Board's decision or notice or to any variation of that decision or notice on appeal.

(5), (6) . . . [2]

Amendments—[1] Word at end of para (1)(*b*) revoked and para (1)(*d*) and the preceding word "and" inserted by the IT (Interest Relief) (No 2) Regulations, SI 1983/311 reg 9, with effect from 15 March 1983.

[2] Word in para (4), and paras (5), (6), revoked by the IT (Interest Relief) (Amendment) Regulations, SI 1995/1213 reg 5, with effect from 4 May 1995.

[3] Para (1) revoked, and in para (3), words substituted, by the Transfer of Tribunal Functions and Revenue and Customs Appeals Order, SI 2009/56 art 3, Sch 2 paras 9, 11 with effect from 1 April 2009.

1984/2060

CAPITAL ALLOWANCES (VEHICLES FOR THE DISABLED) (SIMILAR PAYMENTS) ORDER 1984

Made by the Treasury under FA 1971 s 43(3) and FA 1980 s 64(12), now CAA 1990 ss 22(6)(*d*), 36(4)(*d*); see CAA 1990 s 163 [now CAA 2001 s 82(4)(*d*)]

Made . . . . *19 December 1984*

Coming into Operation . . . . *1 February 1985*

Commentary—*Simon's Taxes* **B3.332.**

1 This Order may be cited as the Capital Allowances (Vehicles for the Disabled) (Similar Payments) Order 1984 and shall come into operation on 1st February 1985.

2 In this Order—

"army inter-war pensioners" means former members of Her Majesty's military forces in receipt of a disability pension paid by the Secretary of State for Defence on account of disability attributable to injury sustained after 30th September 1921 but before 3rd September 1939.

3 The following payments are hereby specified as appearing to be of a similar kind to payments within paragraphs (*a*), (*b*) and (*c*) of subsection 3 of the said section 43 and of subsection 12 of the said section 64 for the purposes of the making of first-year allowances in respect of capital expenditure on the provision of mechanically propelled road vehicles, that is to say—

(1) mobility supplement paid under the Naval and Marine Pay and Pensions (Disablement Awards) Order 1984 or under the Naval and Marine Pay and Pensions (Disablement Awards) (No 2) Order 1984;

(2) mobility supplement paid under Queen's Regulations for the Royal Air Force; and

(3) supplementary allowance paid under Royal Warrant dated 30th December 1949 to army inter-war pensioners equivalent to the mobility supplement provided for by Article 26A of the Naval Military and Air Forces etc (Disablement and Death) Services Pensions Order 1983.

4 This Order has effect in relation to expenditure incurred on or after 21st November 1983.

1985/960

FILMS CO-PRODUCTION AGREEMENTS ORDER 1985

Made . . . . *25 June 1985*

Authority: Films Act 1985, Sch 1, para 4(5)

1 This Order may be cited as the Films Co-Production Agreements Order 1985 and shall come into operation on 22nd July 1985.

2 A film with respect to which the requirements of Schedule 1 to the Films Act 1985 as to the eligibility of a film for certification as a British film are not fulfilled shall be treated as a film with respect to which those requirements are fulfilled if the film was made in accordance with the respective agreements made between the Government of the United Kingdom and [the international organisations, authorities or][1] the Governments of the countries set out in the Schedule to this Order.

Amendments—[1] Words inserted by the Films Co-Production Agreements (Amendment) Order, SI 2011/236 art 2(*a*) with effect from 16 February 2011.

[SCHEDULE

Country/International Organisation/Authority	*Date of Agreement*	*Command Paper*
Australia	12th June 1990	Cm 1758
Brazil	28th September 2012	Cm 9075
Canada	12th September 1975	Cmnd 6380
	9th July 1985	Cmnd 9887
	5th July 1991	Cm 1807
China	20th April 2014	Cm 8877
France	8th November 1994	Cm 2992
India	5th December 2005	Cm 7123
Israel	3rd November 2010	Cm 7994
Jamaica	23rd April 2007	Cm 7168
Morocco	12th October 2009	Cm 7670
New Zealand	14th April 1993	Cm 2638
Palestine Liberation Organisation for the benefit of the Palestinian Authority	3rd November 2010	Cm 7995
South Africa	24th May 2006	Cm. 6866][1]

Amendments—[1] Schedule substituted by the Films Co-Production Agreements (Amendment) Order, SI 2015/1886 art 2 with effect from 12 November 2015.

1985/994

FILMS (CERTIFICATION) REGULATIONS 1985

Revocation—These Regulations revoked by the Films (Certification) Regulations, SI 2006/3281 with effect from 1 January 2007, subject to the following—

If an application falls to be determined by the Secretary of State in accordance with Schedule 1 to the Films Act 1985 as in force immediately before 1 April 2006 these Regulations shall continue to have effect to the application as if the Films (Certification) (Amendment) Regulations, SI 2006/3281 had not been made.

If an application falls to be determined by the Secretary of State in accordance with Schedule 1 to the Films Act 1985 as in force immediately before the commencement of SI 2006/3281, these Regulations shall continue to have effect to the application as if SI 2006/3281 had not been made.

1 *Citation and commencement*

These Regulations may be cited as the Films (Certification) Regulations 1985 and shall come into operation on 23rd July 1985.

2 *Interpretation*

In these Regulations—

"acquirer" in relation to a film, means any person who has acquired any description of rights in it;

"the Act" means the Films Act 1985[, as amended][1];

"co-production film" means a film which by virtue of any Order in Council made under paragraph [4(5)][3] of Schedule 1 to the Act is to be treated as if it were a British film for the purposes of Schedule 1 to the Act;

"group of companies" means a company and all other companies which are its subsidiaries within the meaning of section 736 of the Companies Act 1985;

. . . [2]

. . . [2]

Amendments—[1] Words inserted and substituted by the Films (Certification) (Amendment) Regulations, SI 1999/2224 regs 2, 3(*a*), (*b*) with effect from 27 August 1999.

[2] Definitions "Member State" and "television film" revoked by SI 1999/2224 regs 2, 3(*c*) with effect from 27 August 1999.

[3] In the definition of "co-production film", reference substituted by the Films (Certification) (Amendment) Regulations, SI 2006/642 regs 2, 3 with effect from 1 April 2006.

3 Applications

An application under paragraph 2(1) of Schedule 1 to the Act for the certification of a master negative, master tape or master disc of a film, other than a co-production film, as a qualifying film, qualifying tape or qualifying disc shall be made in writing to the Secretary of State and be [addressed to the Department of National Heritage][1].

Amendments—[1] Words substituted by the Transfer of Functions (National Heritage) Order, SI 1992/1311 Sch 2 with effect from 3 July 1992.

[4 Particulars

The application shall set out the particulars of the film described in Regulation 6 below.][1]

Amendments—[1] This regulation substituted by the Films (Certification) (Amendment) Regulations, SI 1999/2224 regs 2, 4 with effect from 27 August 1999.

5 Evidence

The application shall be accompanied by:

(a) a statutory declaration made by the applicant as to the truth of the particulars given in the application; and

[(b) a report to the Secretary of State prepared by a person referred to in (c) below:

[(i) verifying particulars E(v) and (vi);][2]

[(ii) verifying particulars EA, EB or EC; and][2]

[(iii) stating whether, in the opinion of that person, any point should be awarded under paragraphs 4A(4), 4B(4) or 4C(4) of Schedule 1 to the Act.][2]][1]

[(c) the persons referred to in regulation 5(b) are:

(i) an accountant who is a member of a body of accountants for the time being recognised for the purposes of section 389(1)(a) of the Companies Act 1985, or

(ii) a person authorised under section 389(1)(b) of that Act to be appointed as auditor of a company

and who in either case is not and was not at any time while the film was being made in partnership with, nor in the employment of the maker of the film or, where the maker is a company, is not and was not at any time while the film was being made—

(iii) an officer or servant of that company or, if that company is a member of a group of companies, of any other company in that group; or

(iv) in partnership with or in the employment of, any such officer or servant.][1]

Amendments—[1] Para (*b*) substituted, and para (*c*) inserted, by the Films (Certification) (Amendment) Regulations, SI 1999/2224 regs 2, 5 with effect from 27 August 1999.

[2] Para (*b*)(i), (ii), (iii) substituted for para (*b*)(i), (ii) by the Films (Certification) (Amendment) Regulations, SI 2006/642 regs 2, 4 with effect from 1 April 2006.

6 List of particulars

The particulars referred to in Regulation 4 above are as follows—

[A

(i) The title of the film or, in the case of a series of films or a part thereof, the title of the series or part,

(ii) whether the applicant for certification has incurred expenditure on the production or the acquisition of the master negative, master tape or master disc of the film,

(iii) if the applicant is not the maker of the film:

(a) the applicant's name and principal place of business, and

(b) if the applicant has incurred expenditure on the production of the master negative, master tape or master disc of the film, a brief description (including the amount) of that expenditure, and

(iv) the total playing time in minutes and seconds of the film, including credits and titles.][1]

B The following details about the maker . . . [3] *of the film—*

(i) in the case of an individual:

(a) his name and nationality, . . . [3]

(b) *the address of his principal place of business[, and]*[1]

[(c) the State in which he was ordinarily resident throughout the period during which the film was being made;][2]

(ii) *in the case of a partnership:*

(a) *the name of the partnership,*

(b) *the name and nationality of each partner,* . . . [3]

(c) *the address of the partnership's principal place of business; [and]*[2]

[(d) in respect of each partner, the State in which he was ordinarily resident throughout the period during which the film was being made;][2]

(iii) *in the case of a company:*

(a) *the name of the company,*

(b) *the address of the company's principal place of business,*

(c) *the address of the company's registered office throughout the time the film was made,*

(d) *the country under the laws of which the company was incorporated,* . . . [3]

(e) *the names and nationalities of its directors throughout the time the film was being made[, and]*[1]

[(f) the State in which the central management and control of the company's business was exercised throughout the period during which the film was being made.][2]

[BA Whether the individual, partnership or company referred to in B(i), (ii) or (iii) above undertook the arrangements necessary for the making of the film.][2]

[C The date on which production of the film began.

D The date on which production of the film was completed for the purposes of Schedule 1 to the Act.][1]

[DA If the applicant seeks treatment of a series of films as a single film in reliance upon paragraph 1(4) of Schedule 1 to the Act:

(i) *the number of parts in the series,*

(ii) *the combined playing time in minutes and seconds of those parts, including credits and titles, and*

(iii) *the reasons why the series constitutes a self-contained work or is a series of documentaries with a common theme.]*[1]

[E A statement showing:

(i) *whether the applicant seeks to rely on paragraphs 4A, 4B or 4C of Schedule 1 to the Act;*

(ii) *if the applicant seeks to rely on paragraph 4B of Schedule 1 to the Act, the reasons why the film should be considered to be a documentary;*

(iii) *if the application seeks to rely on paragraph 4C of Schedule 1 to the Act, the reasons why the film should be considered to be an animation;*

(iv) *the reasons why any point should be awarded under paragraphs 4A(3), 4B(3) or 4C(3) of Schedule 1 to the Act;*

(v) *the nationality and ordinary residence of all the persons mentioned in paragraphs 4A(5), 4B(5) or 4C(5) of Schedule 1 to the Act in relation to whom the applicant is applying for a point to be awarded;*

(vi) *the total expenditure on all the work carried out in the making of the film.]*[4]

[EA If the applicant seeks to rely on paragraph 4A of Schedule 1 to the Act, a statement showing:

(i) *the total number of days of principal photography and the number of days of principal photography carried out in the United Kingdom;*

(ii) *the total expenditure on visual effects and the expenditure on visual effects carried out in the United Kingdom;*

(iii) *the total expenditure on special effects and the expenditure on special effects carried out in the United Kingdom;*

(iv) *the total expenditure on performing and recording the original music score created for the film and the expenditure on performing and recording the original music score created for the film carried out in the United Kingdom;*

(v) *the total expenditure on audio post production and the expenditure on audio post production carried out in the United Kingdom;*

(vi) *the total expenditure on image processing and the expenditure on image processing carried out in the United Kingdom.]*[4]

[EB If the applicant seeks to rely on paragraph 4B of Schedule 1 to the Act (documentary), a statement showing:

(i) *the total expenditure on shooting and visual effects and the expenditure on shooting and visual effects carried out in the United Kingdom;*

(ii) *the total expenditure on research and development and the expenditure on research and development carried out in the United Kingdom;*

(iii) *the total expenditure on special effects and the expenditure on special effects carried out in the United Kingdom;*

(iv) the total expenditure on performing and recording the original music score created for the film and the expenditure on performing and recording the original music score created for the film carried out in the United Kingdom;

(v) the total expenditure on audio post production and the expenditure on audio post production carried out in the United Kingdom;

(vi) the total expenditure on image processing and the expenditure on image processing carried out in the United Kingdom.][4]

[EC If the applicant seeks to rely on paragraph 4C of Schedule 1 to the Act (animation), a statement showing:

(i) the total expenditure on shooting, visual design, layout and storyboarding and the expenditure on shooting, visual design, layout and storyboarding carried out in the United Kingdom;

(ii) the total expenditure on visual effects and the expenditure on visual effects carried out in the United Kingdom;

(iii) the total expenditure on special effects and the expenditure on special effects carried out in the United Kingdom;

(iv) the total expenditure on performing and recording the original music score created for the film and the expenditure on performing and recording the original music score created for the film carried out in the United Kingdom;

(v) the total expenditure on voice recording and audio post production and the expenditure on voice recording and audio post production carried out in the United Kingdom;

(vi) the total expenditure on image processing and the expenditure on image processing carried out in the United Kingdom.][4]

[F If any part of the film is derived from any other film ("the other film"):

(i) for each part of the film so derived and in respect of which:

(a) the maker of the other film is not the maker of the film, or

(b) the master negative, tape or disc of the other film is certified under paragraph 3(1) of Schedule 1 to the Act,

the playing time in minutes and seconds of that part;

(ii) the combined playing time in minutes and seconds of all of the parts referred to in (i) above; and

(iii) if the applicant seeks to rely upon paragraph 5(2) of Schedule 1 to the Act:

(a) a statement of the reasons why the film should be considered to be a documentary, and

(b) a statement of the reasons why the subject matter of the film makes it appropriate for paragraph 5(1) of Schedule 1 to the Act not to be applied.][1]

[G] , H . . . [5]

L . . . [3]

Amendments—[1] Paras A, C, D, E, F, and words in paras B, G (formerly para J), H (formerly para K) substituted, by the Films (Certification) (Amendment) Regulations, SI 1999/2224 regs 2, 6 with effect from 27 August 1999.

[2] Paras BA, DA, and words in para B, inserted by SI 1999/2224 regs 2, 6 with effect from 27 August 1999.

[3] Paras . . . I, L, and words in paras B, G (formerly para J), H (formerly para K) revoked, by SI 1999/2224 regs 2, 6 with effect from 27 August 1999.

[4] Paras E, EA, EB, EC substituted for para E by the Films (Certification) (Amendment) Regulations, SI 2006/642 regs 2, 5 with effect from 1 April 2006.

[5] Paras G, H revoked by SI 2006/642 regs 2, 6 with effect from 1 April 2006.

7 Statutory declarations

A statutory declaration under Regulation 5(a) above shall be deemed to have been made by the applicant if:

(a) in the case of an application by a partnership, it has been made on behalf of the partnership by one of the partners, or

(b) in the case of an application by a company, it has been made on behalf of the company by the Secretary or one of the directors of the company or by any person duly authorised by the company to make the declaration on its behalf.

8 [Transitional

If, following an election by the applicant pursuant to article 1(2) of the Films (Modification of the Definition of "British Film") Order 1999 ("the Order") the application falls to be determined by the Secretary of State in accordance with Schedule 1 to the Films Act 1985 as it stood before the commencement of the Order, these regulations shall apply to the application as if the Films (Certification) (Amendment) Regulations 1999 had not been made.][1]

Amendments—[1] This regulation inserted by the Films (Certification) (Amendment) (No 2) Regulations, SI 1999/2334 reg 2 with effect from 27 August 1999.

[9 If an application falls to be determined by the Secretary of State in accordance with Schedule 1 to the Act as in force immediately before the commencement of the Films (Definition of "British Film") Order 2006 these Regulations shall apply to the application as if the Film (Certification) (Amendment) Regulations 2006 had not been made.][1]

Amendments—[1] Regulation 9 inserted by the Films (Certification) (Amendment) Regulations, SI 2006/642 regs 2, 7 with effect from 1 April 2006.

1986/387

CAPITAL GAINS TAX (PARALLEL POOLING) REGULATIONS 1986

Made by the Treasury under FA 1985 Sch 19 para 21, now TCGA 1992 s 112; see TCGA 1992 Sch 11 para 29

Made . . . . *3 March 1986*

Laid before the House of Commons . . . . *4 March 1986*

Coming into Operation . . . . *1 April 1986*

Commentary—*Simon's Taxes* **C2.718**.

Cross references—See TCGA 1992 s 112(1) (these Regulations continue to have effect notwithstanding the repeal by TCGA 1992 Sch 12 of FA 1985 Sch 19 under para 21 of which these Regulations were made and for the purposes of the Interpretation Act 1978 para 21 is deemed not to have been revoked).

1 These Regulations may be cited as the Capital Gains Tax (Parallel Pooling) Regulations 1986 and shall come into operation on 1st April 1986.

2 In these Regulations unless the context otherwise requires—

"new holding" has the meaning given to it by paragraph 9(3) of Schedule 19 with the omission therefrom of the words "or sub-paragraph (2)";

"qualifying securities" are securities to which Regulation 3 applies;

"relevant securities" has the meaning given to it by section 88(9) of the Finance Act 1982;

"Schedule 6" means Schedule 6 to the Finance Act 1983;

"Schedule 19" means Schedule 19 to the Finance Act 1985;

"1982 holding" has the meaning given to it by paragraph 6 of Schedule 19;

"1983 holding" is a holding within the meaning of paragraph 3(3) of Schedule 6.

3 These Regulations shall have effect in relation to a disposal on or after 1st April 1985 of qualifying securities, within the meaning of Schedule 6—

(*a*) in respect of which an election under that Schedule had been made by a company and not revoked on or before 31st March 1987 or such further time as may be allowed by the Board under paragraph 20(1) of Schedule 19; and

(*b*) which, immediately before 1st April 1985, were regarded as indistinguishable parts of a single asset by virtue of paragraph 3 of Schedule 6;

and are designed to enable section 68 of, and Parts I to V of Schedule 19 to, the Finance Act 1985 to have full effect in relation to the qualifying securities concerned.

4 Of qualifying securities in each 1983 holding which is held by a company immediately before 1st April 1985 there shall be identified as at that time for the purposes of these Regulations—

(*a*) by reference to the provisions of Regulations 5, 6, 7 and 8, the 1982 holding and the new holding of such of those securities as are not relevant securities; and

(*b*) by reference to the provisions of Regulations 5, 6 and 9, the 1982 holding (and the securities not in the 1982 holding) of such of those securities as are relevant securities;

and, as modified by these Regulations, the relevant provisions of the said section 68 and Schedule 19 shall apply in relation to the 1982 holdings, the new holdings and the holdings of relevant securities.

5 For the purposes of these Regulations, or, as the case may be, the Schedule hereto, "A" to "H" shall be identified by reference to the circumstances obtaining in relation to each 1983 holding held by a company immediately before 1st April 1985 as follows—

(*a*) A is the number of qualifying securities in the 1983 holding.

(*b*) B is the amount of the unindexed pool of expenditure (within the meaning of paragraph 6 of Schedule 6) attributable to the 1983 holding.

(*c*) C is the amount of the indexed pool of expenditure attributable to the 1983 holding, computed on the assumption that an operative event within the meaning of paragraph 7(3) of Schedule 6 occurred immediately before 1st April 1985.

(*d*) D is the aggregate of—

(i) A; and

(ii) the number of securities which are of the same class as those to which paragraph (*a*) above refers, but which, because the conditions of paragraph 3(3)(*b*) of Schedule 6 are not fulfilled, do not form part of the 1983 holding.

(*e*) E is the aggregate of—

(i) B; and

(ii) the relevant allowable expenditure in relation to a disposal immediately before 1st April 1985 of the whole of the securities to which paragraph (*d*)(ii) above refers.

(*f*) F is the aggregate of the relevant allowable expenditure in relation to all disposals by the company made after March 1982 and before April 1985 of securities which are of the same class as those to which paragraph (*a*) above refers and which were acquired after 6th April 1965.

(*g*) G is—

(i) the number of securities of that same class which were held by the company immediately before 1st April 1982 and which comprise a holding within the meaning of Part II of Schedule 13 to the Finance Act 1982; or

(ii) where on or after 1st April 1982 there has been a reorganisation of share capital within the meaning of section 77(1) of the Capital Gains Tax Act 1979 the number of shares which (on the assumption that there had been no part disposal of original shares within the meaning of the provisions of that subsection) would comprise a new holding within the meaning of that section.

(*h*) H is the amount which would be the aggregate of the relevant allowable expenditure in relation to a disposal by the company immediately before 1st April 1985 of the whole of the securities to which paragraph (*g*) above refers.

6—(1) J is the number of qualifying securities in the 1982 holding, rounded to the nearest whole number and is given by the formula—

$$G \times \frac{E}{E+F}$$

(2) In relation to a disposal by the company of the whole of the 1982 holding on or after 1st April 1985, K is the relevant allowable expenditure, given by the formula—

$$H \times \frac{E}{E+F}$$

7 In respect of qualifying securities ("the securities")—

(*a*) the number of the securities which fall to be included in the new holding is given by the formula A – J;

(*b*) the relevant allowable expenditure in relation to a disposal by the company of all the securities referred to in paragraph (*a*) above immediately before 1st April 1985 is given by the formula B – K;

(*c*) the indexed pool of expenditure in relation to the securities referred to in paragraph (*a*) above for the purposes of paragraph 13(2) of Schedule 19 is given by the formula—

$$(B-K)\left(\frac{C}{B}+0.05\right)$$

8 In respect of the new holding ("the holding")—

(*a*) the number of securities in the holding is given by the formula D – J;

(*b*) the qualifying expenditure in relation to the holding is given by the formula E – K;

(*c*) the indexed pool of expenditure in relation to the holding is given by the aggregate of—

(i) the amount given by the formula

$$(B-K)\left(\frac{C}{B}+0.05\right)$$

(ii) the relevant allowable expenditure in relation to a disposal by the company immediately before 1st April 1985 of the whole of the securities to which Regulation 5(*d*)(ii) refers; and

(iii) any indexation allowance applicable to such a disposal on the assumption that the amendment of the Finance Act 1982 made by paragraphs 1 and 2 of Schedule 19 had always had effect.

9—(1) This Regulation applies to a holding of relevant securities ("relevant securities holding") which are qualifying securities comprised in a 1983 holding held by the company immediately before 1st April 1985 and, for the purposes of this Regulation, references to qualifying securities in Regulations 5 and 6 shall be treated as references to the relevant securities holding.

(2) In respect of the relevant securities holding—

(*a*) the number of relevant securities in the holding, not being relevant securities in the 1982 holding, is given by the formula A – J;

(*b*) the relevant securities in the holding to which paragraph (*a*) above refers shall be treated for the purposes of the Capital Gains Tax Act 1979 as having been acquired on 31st March 1984;

(*c*) the amount of the relevant allowable expenditure in relation to a disposal on or after 1st April 1985 of all the relevant securities in the holding to which paragraph (*a*) above refers is given by the formula

$$(B - K) \times \frac{C}{B}$$

and shall be apportioned rateably to the relevant securities.

10 The Schedule to these Regulations shall have effect only for providing an example of the operation of the Regulations and, in the event of any conflict between the provisions of the Schedule and the Regulations, the Regulations shall prevail.

SCHEDULE

INTRODUCTORY

In this Schedule—

Part I is a statement of facts which are to be assumed;

Part II is an application of the Regulations to qualifying securities which are not relevant securities;

Part III is an application of the Regulations to qualifying securities which are relevant securities.

PART I

1

QUALIFYING SECURITIES AND EXPENDITURE

PG plc held, acquired or disposed of qualifying securities as follows—

Date		Number of securities	Expenditure/proceeds
31st March 1982	holding	1,000	6,000
1st September 1982	purchased	2,000	12,000
1st March 1983	purchased	3,000	10,000
1st September 1983	rights	6,000	12,000
1st January 1985	sold	3,000	12,000
31st January 1985	purchased	3,000	10,000

2

RETAIL PRICES INDEX

The Retail Prices Index is assumed to be—

March 1982	100	*September 1984*	112
September 1983	107	*January 1985*	114
March 1984	110	*March 1985*	116

3

CALCULATION OF INDEXED POOL OF EXPENDITURE IN ACCORDANCE WITH SCHEDULE 6

	Securities	*Expenditure* *Excluded from pools* £	*Unindexed pool* £	*Indexed pool* £
31st March 1982	1,000		6,000	6,000
1st September 1983 indexed rise: $£6{,}000 \times \frac{107-100}{100}$				
= £6,000 × ·070				420
Additions to 1983 holding	2,000 *(Acquired 1st September 1982)*		12,000	12,000
Rights taken up	3,000	6,000		
	6,000	6,000	18,000	18,420
1st March 1984 indexed rise $£18{,}420 \times \frac{110-107}{107}$				
= £18,420 × ·028				516
Addition (including rights) to 1983 holding	6,000	6,000	10,000	10,000
	12,000	12,000	28,000	28,936
1st September 1984 indexed rise: $£28{,}936 \times \frac{112-110}{110}$				
= £28,936 × ·018				521
Expiry of 12 months following rights issue; expenditure no longer excluded		(12,000)	12,000	12,000
	12,000	—	40,000	41,457
1st January 1985 indexed rise: $£41{,}457 \times \frac{114-112}{112}$				
= £41,457 × ·018				746
	12,000		40,000	42,203
Disposal	3,000		10,000	10,551
	9,000		30,000	31,652

4

SECURITIES HELD LESS THAN ONE YEAR AT 31ST MARCH 1985

The 3,000 securities acquired on 31st January 1985 for £10,000 do not qualify for inclusion in the 1983 holding on 31st March 1985.

PART II

QUALIFYING SECURITIES WHICH ARE NOT RELEVANT SECURITIES

STEP 1—Regulation 5(*a*)–(*c*)

Index the indexed pool as if an operative event had occurred immediately before 1st April 1985

Indexed pool (see Part I.3, above)	£31,652
$£31{,}652 \times \dfrac{116 - 114}{114} = £31{,}652 \times \cdot 018$	570
	£32,222

Therefore—

A = 9,000

B = 30,000

C = 32,222

STEP 2—Regulation 5(*d*) and (*e*)

Number of securities not within 1983 holding (see Part I.4, above)	3,000
Relevant allowable expenditure	£10,000

Therefore—

D = 9,000 + 3,000 = 12,000

E = 30,000 + 10,000 = 40,000.

STEP 3—Regulation 5(*f*)

F = 10,000.

STEP 4—Regulation 5(*g*) and (*h*)

Number of securities held on 31st March 1982	1,000
Rights issue 1 for 1	1,000
	G = 2,000
Relevant allowable expenditure on securities	= £6,000
Relevant allowable expenditure on rights 1,000 @ £2 per share	= £2,000
	H = £8,000

STEP 5—Regulation 6

$$J = £2{,}000 \times \frac{40{,}000}{40{,}000 + 10{,}000} = 1{,}600$$

$$K = £8{,}000 \times \frac{40{,}000}{40{,}000 + 10{,}000} = £6{,}400$$

Therefore the 1982 holding comprises:

1,600 shares—relevant allowable expenditure £6,400.

Note: applying the above fraction to the separate components of H (step 4) £4,800 will qualify for indexation from March 1982 and £1,600 from September 1983 for the purposes of section 87 of, and paragraph 5 of Schedule 13 to, the Finance Act 1982.

STEP 6—Regulation 7

Number of securities in the 1983 holding forming part of new holding = 9,000 – 1,600 = 7,400

Relevant allowable expenditure on these securities = £30,000 – £6,400 = £23,600

Aggregate of relevant allowable expenditure and indexation allowance for the purposes of paragraph 13(2), Schedule 19 = 26,528

$$=(30{,}000-6{,}400)\left(\frac{32{,}222}{30{,}000}+0.05\right)$$

STEP 7—Regulation 8

Number of securities in new holding = 12,000 – 1,600 = 10,400

Qualifying expenditure = £40,000 – £6,400 = £33,600

Relevant allowable expenditure in relation to securities not included in 1983 holding = £10,000

Indexation allowance = £180

Indexed pool in relation to the new holding = £26,528 + £10,000 + £180 = £36,708

SUMMARY

1982 holding: 1,600 securities—relevant allowable expenditure £6,400 (of which £4,800 qualifies for indexation from March 1982 and £1,600 from September 1983).

New holding: 10,400 securities—qualifying expenditure £33,600 and indexed pool of expenditure £36,708.

PART III

QUALIFYING SECURITIES WHICH ARE RELEVANT SECURITIES

STEPS 1–5 as in Part II above.

STEP 6—Regulation 9

Number of relevant securities in 1983 holding not forming part of 1982 holding = 9,000 – 1,600 = 7,400

Relevant allowable expenditure

$$=(30{,}000-6{,}400)\times\frac{32{,}222}{30{,}000} = £25{,}348$$

Expenditure apportioned to securities

$$\frac{£25{,}348}{7{,}400} = £3.4254$$

Deemed date of acquisition of those securities—31st March 1984.

SUMMARY

1982 holding: 1,600 securities—relevant allowable expenditure £6,400 (of which £4,800 qualifies for indexation from March 1982 and £1,600 from September 1983).

Other relevant securities: 7,400 securities treated as acquired on 31st March 1984—relevant allowable expenditure £25,348.

3,000 securities treated as acquired on 31st January 1986—relevant allowable expenditure £10,000.

1986/2211

CHARITABLE DEDUCTIONS (APPROVED SCHEMES) REGULATIONS 1986

Made by the Treasury under FA 1986 s 28, now TA 1988 s 202(8)–(10); see TA 1988 Sch 30 para 21

Made . . . .*15 December 1986*

Laid before the House of Commons . . . .*16 December 1986*

Coming into Operation . . . .*8 January 1987*

1 Citation and commencement

These Regulations may be cited as the Charitable Deductions (Approved Schemes) Regulations 1986, and shall come into operation on 8th January 1987.

2 Interpretation

In these Regulations unless the context otherwise requires—

"approved agency" means a body approved as agent in accordance with Regulation 5;

"approved scheme" means a scheme approved in accordance with Regulation 3;

"employer" means a person paying emoluments;

"employee" means any person entitled to receive payments of emoluments;

"emoluments" means income to be taken into account in assessing liability to income tax under Schedule E, from payments of which income tax falls to be deducted by virtue of section 204[2] of the Taxes Act and regulations under that section;

"income tax month" means the period beginning on the 6th day of any calendar month and ending on the 5th day of the following calendar month;

"scheme" includes a kind of scheme;

. . .[1]

"year" means the period beginning on any 6th day of April and ending on the following 5th day of April.

Notes—[1] Definition of "supplement" revoked by the Charitable Deductions (Approved Schemes) (Amendment) Regulations, SI 2014/584 regs 2, 3 with effect from 6 April 2014.

[2] TA 1988 s 203.

3 Approval of schemes

The Board may grant approval of a scheme for the purposes of section 27 of the Finance Act 1986[4] if it is satisfied on an application by an approved agency that the scheme provides—

(*a*) for a contract between the approved agency and an employer to give effect to the scheme;

(*b*) that any employee to whom the employer pays emoluments on or after 6th April 1987 may . . .[2] request the employer, in such form as the Board may approve or prescribe, to withhold from such emoluments such sum as the employee may specify pursuant to the scheme to be paid (subject to the provisions of the scheme) either by way of gift to such charity or charities as the employee may specify or in exchange for vouchers which the employee may surrender by way of gift to the charity or charities of his choice;

(*c*) that under the scheme the employer is constituted the agent of the approved agency in holding moneys withheld from employees pursuant to the scheme;

(*d*) for any minimum sum which may be withheld pursuant to the scheme and for any limit which may be imposed on the number of charities which one employee may specify pursuant to the scheme;

(*e*) . . .[2]

(*f*) that no sum so withheld shall be due to the specified charity pursuant to a deed of covenant or, where the sum withheld is paid in exchange for vouchers, that the value of those vouchers shall not be due to the charity or charities to which they are surrendered pursuant to a deed of covenant;

(*g*) that the employer is to be bound to pay over to the approved agency sums withheld from employees pursuant to the scheme in any income tax month within 14 days of the end of that income tax month;

(*h*) that the approved agency will if so requested give written receipts to the employer in respect of sums paid over to it;

(*i*) that in no circumstances will sums duly withheld and paid over to the approved agency be returnable to the employer or to any employee;

(*j*) that the approved agency will, subject to any deduction in respect of its charges, pay sums paid to it by the employer pursuant to the scheme to the charities respectively specified by the employees or provide the employees with vouchers to be surrendered to the charities of their choice;

[(*ja*) that the approved agency will pay to the charities specified by the employees the sums paid to it by the employer pursuant to the scheme [before the expiry of the relevant period relating to such sums][3] set out in regulation 4A;][1]

(*k*) that the approved agency will if so requested by an employee at the end of any year give him a certificate of the amounts which the approved agency has paid to charities specified by him in respect of sums withheld from his emoluments in that year and of the maximum time elapsing in any period specified by the employee between the receipt of such sums from the employer and the payment to the charities of amounts in respect of such sums;

(*l*) that if for any reason it becomes impossible for the approved agency to pay any amount to a charity specified by an employee the approved agency shall pay that amount to such other charity as it may consider has objects similar to those of the charity specified by the employee, but so that it shall not in any circumstances appropriate that amount to its own funds; and that on so paying that amount to that other charity the approved agency will give notice to the employee that it has done so;

(*m*) that where an employee has been provided with a voucher by which payment may be made to a charity and that voucher has not been presented to the approved agency by way of payment within a time prescribed by the approved agency the approved agency will pay the amount represented by that voucher to such other charity as it sees fit, but so that it shall not in any circumstances appropriate that amount to its own funds; and that on so paying that amount to that other charity the approved agency will give notice to the employee that it has done so;

(*n*) for the method by which the approved agency's charges in relation to the operation of the scheme will be met and for the determining of the amount of such charges.

Amendments—[1] Para (*ja*) inserted by the Charitable Deductions (Approved Schemes) (Amendment) Regulations, SI 2000/759 reg 3 with effect from 6 April 2000.

[2] Words in para (*b*) and whole of para (*e*) revoked by the Charitable Deductions (Approved Schemes) (Amendment No 2) Regulations, SI 2000/2083 reg 4 with effect from 21 August 2000.

[3] In para (*ja*), words substituted by the Charitable Deductions (Approved Schemes) (Amendment) Regulations, SI 2014/584 regs 2, 4 with effect from 6 April 2014.

[4] TA 1988 s 202(1)–(7).

4 Applications by an approved agency in accordance with Regulation 3 shall be in such form as the Board may approve or prescribe.

[4A Period for payment by agencies to charities

(1) An approved agency shall, notwithstanding anything in the provisions of an approved scheme or in a contract entered into with the employer to give effect to an approved scheme, pay to the charities specified by the employees the sums paid to it by the employer pursuant to the scheme before the expiry of the relevant period in relation to such sums.

(2) The relevant period in relation to a sum referred to in paragraph (1), subject to paragraphs (3) and (4), is—

(*a*) the period of 35 days beginning on the day when the approved agency receives the sum described in paragraph (1) provided the approved agency is notified (on or before that day) of the identity of—

(i) the employee from whose emoluments the sum was withheld, and

(ii) the charity or charities specified by that employee;

(*b*) in any other case, the period of 60 days beginning on the day on which the approved agency receives—

(i) the sum described in paragraph (1) or, if later,

(ii) notification of the identity of the charity or charities specified by the employee from whose emoluments the sum was withheld.

(3) The receipt by an approved agency of a voucher provided to an employee by which payment may be made to a charity pursuant to an approved scheme shall be treated as a notification of the identity of a charity for the purposes of paragraph (2).

(4) Where—

(*a*) the relevant period in paragraph (2) (*a*) applies in relation to a sum, and

(*b*) the approved agency has made no payment pursuant to a scheme to the charity specified in relation to the sum within the 12 months period ending immediately before the receipt of that sum,

the approved agency may treat the relevant period specified by that paragraph as the period of 60 days beginning on the day when the sum is received.][1]

Amendments—[1] Regulation 4A substituted by the Charitable Deductions (Approved Schemes) (Amendment) Regulations, SI 2014/584 regs 2, 5 with effect from 6 April 2014.

5 Approval of agencies

The Board may grant approval as an agent for the purposes of section 27 of the Finance Act 1986[1] to any charity which the Board is satisfied is prepared and able to act as an approved agency in relation to approved schemes and to comply with the provisions of these Regulations.

Notes—[1] TA 1988 s 202(1)–(7), (11).

6 Applications by a charity for approval as an agent in accordance with Regulation 5 shall be in such form as the Board may approve or prescribe.

7 Withdrawal of approval of agencies

If at any time the Board is of opinion that an approved agency has ceased to be a charity or has failed to act properly in relation to an approved scheme or has failed to comply with these Regulations, it may give notice of withdrawal of approval to the approved agency and thereupon, from such date as the Board may specify in its notice, the agency shall cease to be approved and all schemes which have been approved on its application shall cease to be approved and all contracts to give effect to such schemes shall determine. When the Board gives such notice it shall inform every employer who has a contract with the approved agency to give effect to an approved scheme that it has so given notice.

8 Appeals

(1) Any person aggrieved by the Board's refusal to grant him approval as an agent in accordance with Regulation 5 or by the Board's withdrawal of such approval in accordance with Regulation 7 may [appeal][1], by notice in writing given to the Board within 30 days from the date on which he is notified of the Board's refusal or withdrawal of approval . . . [1].

(2) Any approved agency aggrieved by the Board's refusal to grant approval of a scheme in accordance with Regulation 3, may [appeal][1], by notice in writing given to the Board within 30 days from the date on which it is notified of the Board's refusal . . . [1].

Amendments—[1] In paras (1), (2) word inserted and words revoked, by the Transfer of Tribunal Functions and Revenue and Customs Appeals Order, SI 2009/56 art 3, Sch 2 paras 12, 22 with effect from 1 April 2009.

9 Information, returns and records

(1) Every approved agency shall, within 30 days of entering into a contract with an employer giving effect to an approved scheme, inform the Board, in such form as the Board may approve or prescribe, of the date of the contract and of the name and address of the employer.

(2) Where a contract giving effect to an approved scheme is terminated the approved agency shall, within 30 days, inform the Board of such termination.

[(3) An approved agency must inform the Board(a) in writing of its failure to make payment to a charity in accordance with regulation 4A no later than 7 days after the expiry of the relevant period applicable in relation to the sum concerned stating the amount of the sum and the reasons for failure to comply with that regulation.][1]

Amendments—[1] Para (3) substituted by the Charitable Deductions (Approved Schemes) (Amendment) Regulations, SI 2014/584 regs 2, 6 with effect from 6 April 2014.

10 On the ending of each year every approved agency shall, within 30 days of the end of such year or within such further time as the Board may allow, furnish a return to the Board, in such form as the Board may approve or prescribe, of the sums received from each employer with whom it has at any time within the year had a subsisting contract to give effect to an approved scheme, of the numbers of employees from whose emoluments such sums have been withheld, of the number of vouchers issued pursuant to any contract and the total values of such vouchers, of the amounts paid by it to each charity in relation to such approved schemes, and of its charges in relation to the operation of schemes.

11—(1) Every approved agency shall retain—

(*a*) records of approved schemes,

(*b*) records of contracts with employers until 3 years from the termination of each contract, [and] . . . [1]

(*c*) for not less than 3 years, records of sums received from employers, records of amounts paid to all charities specified by employees, and records of vouchers for charities issued by it to employees pursuant to approved schemes . . . [1]

(*d*) . . . [1]

(2) Every approved agency, when so required by notice served on it by the Board, shall within 30 days of such service produce for inspection by an officer of the Board all records required to be retained by it by paragraph (1) of this Regulation.

Amendments—[1] Word in para (1)(*b*) inserted, and para (1)(*d*) and preceding word revoked by the Charitable Deductions (Approved Schemes) (Amendment) Regulations, SI 2014/584 regs 2, 7 with effect from 6 April 2014.

12—(1) Every employer who has entered into a contract with an approved agency pursuant to an approved scheme shall retain—

(*a*) a copy of such contract until 3 years from the termination of the contract,
(*b*) all forms of request to deduct given by employees pursuant to the approved scheme until 3 years from the revocation or lapse of such request and,
(*c*) for not less than 3 years, records of all sums withheld from such employees pursuant to the approved scheme and evidence of all payments made to the approved agency pursuant to the approved scheme.

(2) Every employer who has entered into a contract with an approved agency pursuant to an approved scheme, when so required by notice served on him by the Board, shall within 30 days of such service produce for inspection by an officer of the Board all documents and records required to be retained by him pursuant to paragraph (1) of this Regulation.

13 Termination of contracts

If at any time an employer who has contracted to give effect to a scheme has without reasonable excuse failed in a significant respect to give effect to the scheme in accordance with his contract the approved agency shall forthwith give notice to the employer of termination of the contract.

14 Employee leaving employment

Where an employee who has requested his employer to withhold any sum pursuant to an approved scheme leaves his employment, the employer shall provide the employee with a statement, in such form as the Board may approve or prescribe, of the total amount so withheld from the employee's emoluments from that employment in the year in which the employee so leaves his employment.

15 Service by post

Any notice which is authorised or required to be given or served under these Regulations may be sent by post.

16 [Overpayment of supplement to be treated as unpaid tax

. . .[1]

Amendments—[1] This regulation revoked by the Statute Law (Repeals) Act 2013 s 1, Sch 1 Pt 10 with effect from 31 January 2013.

1987/530

INCOME TAX (ENTERTAINERS AND SPORTSMEN) REGULATIONS 1987

Made by the Treasury under FA 1986 Sch 11, now TA 1988 ss 555–558; see TA 1988 Sch 30 para 21

Made . . . .*26 March 1987*
Laid before the House of Commons . . . .*26 March 1987*
Coming into Force . . . . *1 May 1987*

Commentary—*Simon's Taxes* **E5.802–E5.807**.

1 Citation and commencement

These Regulations may be cited as the Income Tax (Entertainers and Sportsmen) Regulations 1987 and shall come into force on 1st May 1987.

2 Interpretation

(1) In these Regulations unless the context otherwise requires—

"associate" has the meaning given to it by section 303(3) of the Taxes Act;[1]

"Board" means Commissioners of Inland Revenue;

"control" shall be construed in accordance with section 302(2) to (6) of the Taxes Act;[2]

"entertainer" means any description of individuals (and whether performing alone or with others) who give performances in their character as entertainers or sportsmen in any kind of entertainment or sport; and "entertainment or sport" in this definition includes any activity of a physical kind, performed by such an individual, which is or may be made available to the public or any section of the public and whether for payment or not;

"Management Act" means the Taxes Management Act 1970;

a payment or transfer to which regulation 3 applies is described as "connected";

"relevant activity" has the meaning given to it by regulation 6;

["the relevant amount" means the amount of the personal allowance in section 35(1) of the Income Tax Act 2007 which applies for the tax year in which the payment or transfer is made;][1]

"Schedule 11" means Schedule 11 to the Finance Act 1986;[3]

"the Taxes Act" means the Income and Corporation Taxes Act 1970;

"the Tax Acts" has the meaning given to it by section 526(2) of the Taxes Act;[4]

"tax payment" has the meaning given to it by regulation 4;

"tax year" means year of assessment;

"value transferred" in relation to a transfer means the gross amount to which regulation 17(1) refers.

(2) Section 533 of the Taxes Act[5] (meaning of connected persons) applies for the purposes of these Regulations.

Notes—[1] TA 1988 s 417(3).
[2] TA 1988 s 416(2)–(6).
[3] TA 1988 ss 555–558.
[4] TA 1988 s 831(2).
[5] TA 1988 s 839.
[6] Definition of "the relevant amount" inserted by the Income Tax (Entertainers and Sportsmen) (Amendment) Regulations, SI 2012/1359 reg 2(1), (2) with effect in relation to a payment or transfer made on or after 1 July 2012.

3 Payments or transfers with prescribed connection

(1) This regulation applies for the purposes of and subject to the provisions of paragraph 2 of Schedule 11[1], the other provisions of that Schedule and these Regulations.

(2) Subject to paragraph (3) a payment or a transfer made for, in respect of, or which in any way derives either directly or indirectly from, the performance of a relevant activity, has a connection of a prescribed kind with the relevant activity.

(3) The following are descriptions of payments to which paragraph (2) shall not apply—

(*a*) a payment out of which a sum representing tax is or falls to be deducted under the Taxes Act apart from Schedule 11[2] or these Regulations;

(*b*)

(i) a payment (to which paragraph (ii) applies) made to a person who is resident . . . [3] in the United Kingdom, not being a person who is connected with or an associate of the entertainer concerned;

(ii) a payment to which paragraph (i) refers is a payment—

(*a*) which falls to be made for the provision of services ancillary to the performance of a relevant activity, and

(*b*) which is of an amount or value which does not exceed what would be reasonable for that provision between persons dealing with each other at arms' length;

(*c*) any payment made to an entertainer in respect of the proceeds of sale of records deriving from a sound recording made by the entertainer, being payments calculated by reference to those proceeds or payments on accounts of those proceeds.

Simon's Tax Cases—reg 3(2), *Agassi v Robinson (Inspector of Taxes)* [2004] STC 610.

Notes—[1] TA 1988 s 555(2)–(6).
[2] TA 1988 ss 555–558.
[3] In para (3)(*b*)(i), words "and ordinarily resident" revoked by the Income Tax (Removal of Ordinary Residence) Regulations, SI 2013/605 reg 3 with effect for the purposes of a person's liability to income tax for the tax year 2013–14 or any subsequent tax years.

4 Tax payments—rules for calculation

(1) Each of the sums mentioned in paragraph 2(2) and (3) of Schedule 11[1] ("tax payment") shall be calculated in accordance with the rules prescribed by this regulation.

(2) Except where it is otherwise provided by these Regulations or there is an arrangement to which this regulation refers, the tax payment shall be a proportion of the connected payment or of the value transferred by a connected transfer equal to the basic rate of income tax for the tax year in which the payment or transfer is made.

(3)

(*a*) Subject to sub-paragraph (*b*), where the connected payments and the value transferred by connected transfers for a tax year made to an entertainer, or to a person who is connected with him or who is an associate of his, do not together exceed [the relevant amount][4] the tax payment shall be a nil amount;

(*b*) connected payments and the value transferred by connected transfers made by any person who is connected with any other person by whom connected payments or connected transfers are made to the entertainer, or by any associate of such other person, shall together be treated as constituting a single connected payment in determining whether they exceed [the relevant amount][4].

(4) An arrangement to which paragraph (2) refers is an arrangement in writing between the Board and the person by whom the connected payment or connected transfer is made, the entertainer, or the recipient of the connected payment or connected transfer, made following a decision by the Board on an application to which regulation 5 refers, under which the tax payment is an amount which, as a proportion of the connected payment or value transferred by the connected transfer, is an amount less than the said basic rate ("reduced tax payment").

(5) The reduced tax payment may be arrived at by reference to a percentage of the connected payment or of the value transferred by a connected transfer or as a lump sum calculated without reference to any such percentage.

(6) In making an arrangement of the kind to which paragraph (2) refers the Board—

(*a*) shall, subject to sub-paragraph (*b*) and paragraph (7) below, at all times aim at securing that the tax payment shall be, as nearly as may be, the amount of the liability to tax of the entertainer or other person arising in relation to the connected payment or connected transfer under the Tax Acts, Schedule 11[2] and these Regulations, and

(*b*) may take into account the fact that the liability to the Board for tax has, in a manner satisfactory to them, been secured or otherwise provided for, whether by a guarantee (of whatever person) or other means.

(7) Where—

(*a*) a person makes a connected payment or connected transfer in relation to a relevant activity, and

(*b*) in respect of the same relevant activity that person has received a connected payment or connected transfer in respect of which the amount of the tax payment has been paid under these Regulations,

the person concerned shall not be required to deduct out of the connected payment or pay in respect of the connected transfer (to which sub-paragraph (a) refers) any sum to which paragraph 2 of Schedule 11[3] applies unless, and to the extent that, the tax payment which then falls to be made exceeds the amount of the tax payment to which sub-paragraph (b) refers.

Notes—[1] TA 1988 s 555(3).
[2] TA 1988 ss 555–558.
[3] TA 1988 s 555(2)–(6).
[4] In para (3), words substituted for amount "£1,000" (in each place), by the Income Tax (Entertainers and Sportsmen) (Amendment) Regulations, SI 2012/1359 reg 2(1), (3) with effect in relation to a payment or transfer made on or after 1 July 2012.

5 Reduced tax payment—application to be made to the Board

(1) Where a connected payment or connected transfer falls to be made subject to a tax payment to which regulation 4(2) refers the person by whom the connected payment or connected transfer is made, the entertainer, or recipient of the connected payment or connected transfer, may make an application in writing to the Board, not later than 30 days before the connected payment or connected transfer falls to be made, that it shall be subject instead to a reduced tax payment (within the meaning of regulation 4).

(2) Unless and until there is in force an arrangement under which such a reduced tax payment falls to be made regulation 4(2) shall at all times continue to apply to the connected payment or connected transfer.

6 Relevant activity

(1) Subject to this regulation, any activity performed in the United Kingdom by an entertainer (whether alone or involving others) of any of the descriptions in paragraph (2) is an activity of a prescribed description ("relevant activity") for the purposes of paragraph 1 of Schedule 11[1], that Schedule and these Regulations.

(2) A relevant activity to which paragraph (1) refers is an activity performed in the United Kingdom by an entertainer in his character as entertainer on or in connection with a commercial occasion or event and includes—

(*a*) any appearance of the entertainer by way of or in connection with the promotion of any such occasion or event;

(*b*) any participation by the entertainer in or for sound recording, films, videos, radio, television or other similar transmissions (whether live or recorded).

(3) A commercial occasion or event to which paragraph (2) refers includes any description of occasion or event—

(*a*) for which an entertainer (or other person) might receive or become entitled, for or by virtue of the entertainer's performance of the activity, to receive anything by way of cash or any other form of property; or

(*b*) which is designed to promote commercial sales or activity by advertising, the endorsement of goods or services, sponsorship, or other promotional means of any kind.

(4) For the purpose of this regulation—

"film" includes any record (with or without sound), however made, of a sequence or series of one or more visual images, which is a record capable of being used as a means of showing part or all of that sequence or series as a moving or still picture, and "record" in this definition includes video.

Simon's Tax Cases—reg 6(2), *Agassi v Robinson (Inspector of Taxes)* [2004] STC 610.
Notes—[1] TA 1988 s 555(1).

7 Persons other than entertainers receiving connected payments or transfers

(1) Any description of person in paragraph (2) is a person (not being the entertainer) to whom paragraph 7(1) of Schedule 11[1] refers.

(2) The descriptions of persons to whom paragraph (1) refers are—

(*a*) any person who is under the control of the entertainer;

(*b*) any person who is—

(i) not resident in the United Kingdom, and

(ii) not liable to tax by reason of residence, domicile, place of management or otherwise, in a territory outside the United Kingdom where the rate of tax charged on the profits or income of such a person is a rate exceeding 25 per cent;

(*c*)

(i) subject to paragraph (ii), any person in receipt (whether directly or indirectly) of a connected payment or value transferred by a connected transfer which is, is treated as, or falls to be included in the computation of, income arising under a settlement in relation to which the entertainer is a settlor;

(ii) for the purposes of paragraph (i)—

"income arising under a settlement" and "settlor" have the meanings given to them by section 454 of the Taxes Act[2], and

"settlement" has the meaning given to it by section 444(2) of the Taxes Act[3];

(*d*)

(i) any person to whom paragraph (2) of this regulation does not otherwise apply who receives any connected payment or connected transfer (whether directly or indirectly) at or in respect of a time when there is in force between that person and the entertainer concerned a contract or arrangement to which paragraph (ii) applies;

(ii) a contract or arrangement to which paragraph (i) refers is a contract or arrangement by or under which it is reasonable to suppose that the entertainer (or other person who is connected with or is an associate of the entertainer) is, will or may become, entitled to receive amounts, whether by way of cash or other value, not substantially less than the appropriate amount of profits or gains arising from the connected payment or connected transfer to which paragraph 8(1) of Schedule 11[4] applies.

Notes—[1] TA 1988 s 556(2).
[2] TA 1988 s 681.
[3] TA 1988 s 670.
[4] TA 1988 s 557(1).

8 Computation of profits arising from certain payments and transfers attributed to entertainer

(1) Subject to the provisions of these Regulations, the profits or gains (to which paragraph 7(2) of Schedule 11[1] refers) arising from the connected payment or connected transfer (to which paragraph 7(1) of that Schedule[2] refers) shall be computed in accordance with the provisions of the Taxes Act relating to the charging of profits or gains under Case I or II (as the case may be) of Schedule D, so that a just and reasonable amount of such a payment or value transferred by such a transfer is charged to tax as such profits or gains; and

(2) Notwithstanding any provision of the Taxes Act, in computing the said profits or gains such deductions of expenses incurred by any person (not being the entertainer) in relation to the payment or transfer concerned shall be made as are just and reasonable.

Notes—[1] TA 1988 s 556(3)(*a*).
[2] TA 1988 s 556(2).

9 Returns of information to be furnished by maker of connected payments or connected transfers

(1) A person who makes a connected payment or connected transfer shall, in accordance with this regulation, make a return to the Board of the connected payment or connected transfer which he makes and of any tax payment (including a nil amount) for which he is accountable to the Board.

(2) A return shall be made in the tax year for each successive period ending on 30th June, 30th September, 31st December and 5th April.

(3) The return for each period shall be made within 14 days after the end of the period.

(4) The Board may by notice in writing require any person who makes a connected payment or connected transfer, within such time as may be specified in the notice, to furnish to them particulars of such payments or transfers including—

(*a*) the dates and the amounts of each payment;
(*b*) the dates of and the value transferred by each transfer;
(*c*) a sufficient description to enable any asset or money's worth transferred to be identified;
(*d*) the business and private name and address of the person to whom each payment or transfer was made;
(*e*) the name and address of the entertainer concerned;
(*f*) the relevant activity to which the payment or transfer relates, including full particulars of all performances.

(5) The Management Act shall apply to a return to which this regulation relates as it applies to a return under the Taxes Acts.

10 Tax payments—due date

(1) A tax payment (including any reduced tax payment), whether any deduction out of a connected payment or provision in respect of a connected transfer has been made or not, shall be due at the time by which the return under regulation 9(1) is to be made ("the due date") and payment shall be made before, or at the time when, that return is made.

(2) A payment at any time so due shall be payable by the person who makes the connected payment or connected transfer concerned, without the making of any assessment in respect of it.

(3) Subject to the provisions of regulation 11, tax which has become due and payable under this regulation (whether or not it has been paid when the assessment is made) may be assessed on the person from whom it is due if that tax, or any part of it, is not paid on or before the due date.

11 Assessment of tax payments

(1) Assessments in respect of any tax due and payable in respect of any period to which regulation 9(2) refers may be made by the Board in relation to a tax year or to the period in question.

(2) Notwithstanding that an assessment under paragraph (1) may be said to relate to a period which is not a tax year—

(*a*) all the provisions of the Income Tax Acts as to the time within which an assessment may be made or the tax year to which an assessment relates shall apply to such an assessment, and

(*b*) the provisions of sections 36 and 37 of the Management Act as to the circumstances in which an assessment may be made out of time shall apply accordingly, but on the footing that the assessment relates to the tax year in which the period (to which regulation 9(2) refers) ends.

(3) Any tax which becomes due under an assessment made under paragraph (1)—

(*a*) shall be payable on or before whichever is earlier of the due date to which regulation 10(1) refers or the 14th day after the date of the notice of the assessment, and

(*b*) shall be treated for all the purposes of Parts VI and IX of the Management Act (including the purposes of section 69 of that Act) as tax with which the person assessed is charged by an assessment to income tax under Schedule D.

12 Tax liabilities and tax payments—supplementary

(1) Where under these Regulations there is accounted for and paid to the Board an amount of tax which is—

(*a*) in respect of a connected payment or connected transfer, or

(*b*) paid under an assessment made under regulation 11,

that amount shall, subject to this regulation, be treated as a payment of tax on account of the tax liability (of whatever person) in respect of the connected payment or connected transfer concerned.

(2) Where, in respect of a connected payment or connected transfer, there is a liability to tax under the Tax Acts as well as under Schedule 11[1] or these Regulations, the Board shall allocate any payment made to them to which paragraph (1) refers as is just and reasonable in discharge of some or all of those liabilities of the entertainer or other person concerned to whom these Regulations apply.

(3) Where—

(*a*) by virtue of paragraph 8 of Schedule 11[2] and these Regulations a connected payment or the value transferred by a connected transfer falls to be included in the amount of profits or gains to which paragraph 8(1)(*a*)[3] refers, and

(*b*) the amount of the connected payment or the value transferred (or an amount in respect of that value) is charged to tax under Schedule E

the amount charged under Schedule E (to which sub-paragraph (b) refers) shall be treated as expenditure which falls to be deducted in computing the profits or gains to which sub-paragraph (a) refers.

(4) Where a payment is a connected payment—

(*a*) which is, is treated as, or falls to be included in a computation of, income of the entertainer chargeable to tax by virtue of the provisions of Part XVI of the Taxes Act[4], or

(*b*) which is a receipt of a company which provides the services of the entertainer to perform the relevant activity, being a receipt which falls to be included in the computation of its profits which are chargeable to tax under Schedule D,

the charge under Schedule 11[1] shall have effect and the charges to which sub-paragraphs (a) and (b) refer shall be disregarded.

(5) A person making a connected payment or connected transfer in respect of which a tax payment has been made by virtue of these Regulations shall furnish the recipient with a certificate showing the gross amount of the payment or the value transferred, the amount of the tax payment, and the amount actually paid.

Notes—[1] TA 1988 ss 555–558.
[2] TA 1988 s 557.
[3] TA 1988 s 557(1)(*a*).
[4] TA 1988 Pt XV.

13 Claim that tax payment excessive to be made to Board

(1) Notwithstanding any other provision of these Regulations, where there has been made to a recipient a connected payment or connected transfer in respect of which a tax payment has been made, the entertainer or any person who, by virtue of Schedule 11[1] or these Regulations is, or is treated as, the person to whom (in relation to the connected payment or connected transfer) any tax liability arises may, by a claim in writing made to the Board, claim that the amount of the tax payment made is excessive.

(2) Subject to paragraph (3) the claim shall be treated as a claim made to an inspector to which section 42 of the Management Act applies.

(3) The claim shall be made not before, but within six years after, the end of the tax year in which the connected payment or connected transfer was made.

Notes—[1] TA 1988 ss 555–558.

14 Administration of tax—supplementary

(1) Nothing in these Regulations shall be taken to prejudice any powers conferred by or under the Tax Acts for the recovery of tax, penalties or interest by means of an assessment or otherwise.

(2) Subject to the provisions of these Regulations, the Management Act shall apply in relation to any tax assessable under these Regulations as if—

(*a*) an assessment of such tax was an assessment specified in section 55(1) (recovery of tax not postponed); and

(*b*) section 87 of that Act applied—

(i) with the insertion of the words "or the Income Tax (Entertainers and Sportsmen) Regulations 1987" after "Finance Act 1972" in subsection (1), and after "Schedule 20" in subsections (2)(*b*), (5) and (6),

(ii) with the insertion after "company" in subsection (5) of the words "or individual", and

(iii) with the insertion after "Schedules" in subsection (7) of the words "or those Regulations".

15 Modifications and adaptations of enactments in relation to trades etc

(1) In this regulation—

(*a*) "world-wide trade" means a trade of an entertainer which is a trade apart from Schedule 11[1] and these Regulations, and a "Schedule 11 trade" means a trade which is a separate trade of an entertainer only by virtue of Schedule 11[1] and these Regulations;

(*b*) "trade" includes profession or vocation.

(2) For the purposes of section 171 of the Taxes Act[2] (carry forward of losses) the world-wide trade and the Schedule 11 trade shall be treated as the same trade.

(3) For the purposes of section 174 of the Taxes Act[3] (carry back of terminal losses) a loss sustained for any relevant period under a Schedule 11 trade (to which otherwise that section would apply) shall not be a terminal loss except where the world-wide trade is permanently discontinued in that period, in which case such a loss in either trade shall be available under that section to be deducted or set off against profits or gains of those trades.

(4) For the purposes of section 30 of the Finance Act 1978[4] (losses in early years of trade) the world-wide trade and the Schedule 11 trade shall be treated as the same trade, but that section shall apply to any such loss of an entertainer only in the tax year in which the world-wide trade was first carried on and in the next 3 succeeding tax years.

Notes—[1] TA 1988 ss 555–558.
[2] TA 1988 s 385.
[3] TA 1988 ss 388, 389.
[4] TA 1988 ss 381–383.

16 Apportionment of payments, transfers etc

(1) The provisions of paragraph (2) are by way of supplementation of the provisions of section 127 of the Taxes Act[1].

(2) Where, in the case of any payment, value transferred or profits or gains to which Schedule 11[2] or these Regulations apply, it is necessary, in order to arrive at the appropriate amount of such payment, value or profits or gains for any tax year or other period, to make any apportionment, division or aggregation of any amounts or values, any such apportionment, division or aggregation, shall be made as is just and reasonable.

Notes—[1] TA 1988 s 72.
[2] TA 1988 ss 555–558.

17 Value of transfers—rules for calculation and grossing up

(1)

(*a*) The actual worth of what is transferred by a transfer to which paragraph 2(3) of Schedule 11[1] applies ("the net value") shall be treated as a net amount corresponding to a gross amount from which income tax at the basic rate has been deducted; and

(*b*) the said gross amount shall be treated as the value of what is transferred for the purposes of paragraph 2(4) of Schedule 11[2].

(2)

(*a*) The net value to which paragraph (1) refers shall be the cost of what is transferred, and

(*b*) the cost of what is transferred to which sub-paragraph (*a*) refers is the cost in or in connection with its provision (including its provision to the person who makes the transfer) or transfer, less so much of that cost which has been borne by the entertainer.

Notes—[1] TA 1988 s 555(3).
[2] TA 1988 s 555(4).

1988/266

CAPITAL GAINS TAX (DEFINITION OF UNIT TRUST SCHEME) REGULATIONS 1988

Made by the Treasury under CGTA 1979 s 92, now TCGA 1992 s 99; see TCGA 1992 Sch 11 para 29

Made . . . . *18 February 1988*
Laid before the House of Commons . . . . *18 February 1988*
Coming into Force . . . . *11 March 1988*

Commentary—*Simon's Taxes* **C2.803**.

1 Citation and commencement

These Regulations may be cited as the Capital Gains Tax (Definition of Unit Trust Scheme) Regulations 1988 and shall come into force on 11th March 1988.

2 Interpretation

In these Regulations unless the context otherwise requires—

"limited partnership" means a limited partnership registered under the Limited Partnerships Act 1907 and "general partner" and "limited partner" have the same meanings as in that Act;

"limited partnership scheme" means a unit trust scheme of the description specified in regulation 4;

["participant", in relation to a unit trust scheme, shall be construed in accordance with section 235 of the Financial Services and Markets Act 2000;][1]

"the principal Act" means the Capital Gains Tax Act 1979[2];

"scheme property" means, in relation to a unit trust scheme, property of any description, including money, which is held on trust for the participants in the scheme;

"unit trust scheme" means a scheme which, apart from these Regulations, is a unit trust scheme for the purposes of the principal Act.

Notes—[1] Definition of "participant" substituted by the Financial Services and Markets Act 2000 (Consequential Amendments) (Taxes) Order, SI 2001/3629 art 116 with effect from 1 December 2001, immediately after the coming into force of the Financial Services and Markets Act 2000 ss 411, 432(1), Sch 20 (and SI 2001/3629 Pts 1 and 2).
[2] TCGA 1992.

3 Exception of certain unit trust schemes from the principal Act

A unit trust scheme which is—

(*a*) a limited partnership scheme, or

(*b*) a profit sharing scheme which has been approved in accordance with Part I of Schedule 9 to the Finance Act 1978[1] [or

(*c*) an employee share ownership plan approved under Schedule 8 to the Finance Act 2000,][2]

shall be treated as not being a unit trust scheme for the purposes of the principal Act.

Notes—[1] TA 1988 Sch 9 Pt 1.
[2] Words inserted by the Capital Gains Tax (Definition of Unit Trust Scheme) (Amendment) Regulations, SI 2000/2550 reg 2 with effect from 11 October 2000.

4 Description of a limited partnership scheme

A unit trust scheme is a limited partnership scheme when the scheme property is held on trust for the general partners and the limited partners in a limited partnership.

1988/267

INCOME TAX (DEFINITION OF UNIT TRUST SCHEME) REGULATIONS 1988

Made by the Treasury under TA 1970 s 354A(7), now TA 1988 s 469(7); see TA 1988 Sch 30 para 21

Made . . . . *18 February 1988*
Laid before the House of Commons . . . . *18 February 1988*
Coming into Force . . . . *11 March 1988*

1 Citation and commencement

These Regulations may be cited as the Income Tax (Definition of Unit Trust Scheme) Regulations 1988 and shall come into force on 11th March 1988 and shall have effect in accordance with regulation 9.

2 Interpretation

(1) In these Regulations unless the context otherwise requires—

"charitable unit trust scheme" means a unit trust scheme of one of the descriptions specified in regulation 7;

"enterprise zone" has the same meaning as in section 74 of the Finance Act 1980;

"enterprise zone property scheme" means a unit trust scheme of the description specified in regulation 4;

"inspector" means any inspector of taxes;

"limited partnership" means a limited partnership registered under the Limited Partnerships Act 1907 and "general partner" and "limited partner" have the same meanings as in that Act;

"limited partnership scheme" means a unit trust scheme of the description specified in regulation 8;

["participant", in relation to a unit trust scheme, shall be construed in accordance with section 235 of the Financial Services and Markets Act 2000;][4]

"Schedule A" means the Schedule referred to as Schedule A in section 67(1) of the Taxes Act[1];

"Schedule D" means the Schedule referred to as Schedule D in section 108 of the Taxes Act[2];

"scheme property" means, in relation to a unit trust scheme, property of any description, including money, which is held on trust for the participants in the scheme;

"section 354A" means section 354A of the Taxes Act[3];

"tax year" means a year beginning with 6th April in any year and ending with 5th April in the following year;

"the Taxes Act" means the Income and Corporation Taxes Act 1970;

"trustee" means, in relation to a unit trust scheme, the person holding the scheme property on trust for the participants;

"unit trust scheme" means a scheme which, apart from these Regulations, is a unit trust scheme for the purposes of section 354A[3]

(2) The provisions of section 56 of the Finance Act 1985 shall have effect to determine when capital expenditure is to be taken to be incurred for the purposes of these Regulations.

Notes—[1] TA 1988 s 15(1).
[2] TA 1988 s 18.
[3] TA 1988 s 469.
[4] Definition of "participant" substituted by the Financial Services and Markets Act 2000 (Consequential Amendments) (Taxes) Order, SI 2001/3629 art 117 with effect from 1 December 2001, immediately after the coming into force of the Financial Services and Markets Act 2000 ss 411, 432(1), Sch 20 (and SI 2001/3629 Pts 1 and 2).

3 Exception of certain unit trust schemes from section 354A

Subject to the provisions of these Regulations, a unit trust scheme which is—

(*a*) an enterprise zone property scheme, or

(*b*) a charitable unit trust scheme, or

(*c*) a limited partnership scheme, or

(*d*) a profit sharing scheme which has been approved in accordance with Part I of Schedule 9 to the Finance Act 1978[2] [or

(*e*) an employee share ownership plan approved under Schedule 8 to the Finance Act 2000,]

shall be treated as not being a unit trust scheme for the purposes of section 354A[1].

Notes—[1] TA 1988 s 469.
[2] TA 1988 Sch 9 Pt 1.

Amendments—Words inserted by the Income Tax (Definition of Unit Trust Scheme) (Amendment) Regulations, SI 2000/2551 reg 2 with effect from 11 October 2000.

4 Description of an enterprise zone property scheme

(1) A unit trust scheme is an enterprise zone property scheme when it has the characteristics mentioned in paragraph (2) below.

(2) Those characteristics are—

(*a*) that, except as provided in paragraph (3)(*a*) below, the scheme property consists wholly of land (including any buildings or structures on that land)—

(i) the whole or substantially the whole of which, at the time when it became subject to the trusts of the scheme, was situated [or formerly situated][1] in one or more enterprise zones, and

(ii) any part of which not so situated [or formerly situated][1] was contiguous with land forming part of the scheme property which, at that time, was so situated [or formerly situated][1];

(*b*) that, except as provided in paragraph (3)(*b*) below, the contributions of the participants are expended on—
(i) the construction of, or the purchase of interests in, buildings or structures on that land,
(ii) the provision of machinery or plant which is an integral part of such buildings or structures,

as well as on the acquisition of, or of rights in or over, that land;

(*c*) that so much of the expenditure referred to in sub-paragraph (*b*) above as is not—
(i) expenditure on the acquisition of, or of rights in or over, the land itself, or
(ii) expenditure in relation to a building or structure, or to that part of a building or structure, which is not on land situated [or formerly situated][1] in an enterprise zone, or
(iii) expenditure on the provision of machinery or plant,

is expenditure in relation to which Chapter I of Part I of the Capital Allowances Act 1968 applies with the modifications specified in Schedule 13 to the Finance Act 1980[3];

(*d*) that the terms of the scheme secure that—
(i) the contributions of the participants are all to be made within the same tax year and no contributions can be made by participants in any subsequent tax year;
(ii) the capital expenditure referred to in sub-paragraph (*b*) above is to be incurred wholly in the tax year in which the participants make their contributions;
(iii) the nature of the rights and interests of all participants in the scheme is the same;
(iv) the rights and interests of the participants in the scheme cannot be purchased, or otherwise redeemed or cancelled, by the trustee in whole or in part except by way of distribution to the participants generally;
(v) in relation to any arrangements which are entered into after the making of these Regulations, the trustee is irrevocably authorised and obliged to undertake on behalf of the participants the responsibilities specified in regulation 5 and the duty once in every tax year to provide to the inspector in writing the information with respect to the preceding tax year concerning the participants in the scheme which is specified by regulation 6(2).

(3) A unit trust scheme is an enterprise zone property scheme notwithstanding that—
(*a*) the scheme property at any time consists also of—
(i) cash held temporarily by the trustee pending its expenditure as mentioned in paragraph (2)(*b*) above or sub-paragraph (*b*) below, or its distribution to the participants generally;
(ii) cash or other assets held by the trustee in connection with the management of the scheme property; or

(*b*) the contributions of the participants are expended for purposes incidental to, or arising out of, the expenditure referred to in paragraph (2)(*b*) above.

[(4) References in paragraph (2) of this Regulation to land formerly situated in an enterprise zone or in one or more enterprise zones are references to land on which buildings or structures were constructed where the expenditure on such construction was incurred, or was incurred under a contract entered into, at a time when the land was in an enterprise zone, being a time not more than ten years after the land was first included in an enterprise zone.][2]

Notes—[1] Words in para (2)(*a*)(i), (ii), (*c*)(ii) inserted by the IT (Definition of Unit Trust Scheme) (Amendment) Regulations, SI 1992/571 reg 3, with effect from 31 March 1992.
[2] Para (4) added by SI 1992/571 reg 3, with effect from 31 March 1992.
[3] CAA 1990 Pt 1.

5 Responsibilities of trustee of an enterprise zone property scheme

(1) The responsibilities of the trustee of an enterprise zone property scheme specified in this regulation are to negotiate and agree with the inspector on behalf of the participants—

(*a*) the amount of any expenditure referred to in regulation 4(2)(*b*) which is—
(i) capital expenditure of each of the participants for a chargeable period in relation to which Chapter I of Part I of the Capital Allowances Act 1968 applies, or applies with the modifications specified in Schedule 13 to the Finance Act 1980[1] and
(ii) capital expenditure of each of the participants on the provision of machinery or plant in respect of which a writing-down allowance is to be or may be made in accordance with section 44 of the Finance Act 1971[2];

(*b*) where, in relation to a building or structure which forms part of the scheme property, an event occurs which gives rise or may give rise to a balancing allowance or a balancing charge to or on each of the participants, the amount of any sale, insurance, salvage or compensation moneys within the meaning of section 86(1) of the Capital Allowances Act 1968[3] relevant to that event;

(c) the disposal value, calculated in accordance with section 44(6) of the Finance Act 1971[4] of any plant and machinery forming part of the scheme property which is or may be required to be brought into account by each of the participants for a chargeable period;

(d) the amount of any profits or gains arising for each accounting period of the scheme in respect of rents or receipts from the scheme property which are chargeable on the participants under Schedule A;

(e) the amount of any interest of money or other annual profits or gains from scheme property which are chargeable on the participants under Schedule D.

(2) The trustee of an enterprise zone property scheme shall also be responsible for providing within three months after the end of each accounting period of the scheme to each person who was a participant in the scheme at any time during that period, or to his personal representative as the case may be, a certificate showing in relation to that participant—

(a) the parts of amounts of capital expenditure incurred in that period, and agreed with the inspector in accordance with paragraph (1)(*a*)(i) and (ii) above, which are attributable to his interest in the scheme at the time when the expenditure in question was incurred;

(b) the parts of amounts of sale, insurance, salvage or compensation moneys in relation to events occurring in that period, and of the disposal values of plant and machinery agreed with the inspector in accordance with paragraph (1)(*b*) and (*c*) above, which are attributable to his interest in the scheme at the relevant time;

(c) the parts of amounts agreed with the inspector to be chargeable under Schedule A or Schedule D, as the case may be, in accordance with paragraph (1)(*d*) and (*e*) above which are attributable to his interest in the scheme for any period in the accounting period in question during which he held that interest.

Notes—[1] CAA 1990 Pt 1.
[2] CAA 1990 s 24.
[3] CAA 1990 s 154(1).
[4] CAA 1990 s 26(1), (2).

6 Provision of information by trustee of an enterprise zone property scheme

(1) The information concerning the participants in an enterprise zone property scheme which the trustee of the scheme shall once in every tax year provide to the inspector in writing with respect to the preceding tax year is that specified by paragraph (2) below.

(2) The information specified by this paragraph is—

(a) the name, address and tax office reference, and, if an individual resident in the United Kingdom at any time in the preceding tax year, the national insurance number, of each person who was a participant in the scheme at any time in that tax year;

(b) in respect of each such participant, the interest which he had in the scheme at any such time;

(c) a copy of any certificate referred to in regulation 5(2) which is supplied to a participant or his personal representative in relation to an accounting period of the scheme ending in, or at the same time as, the preceding tax year.

7 Descriptions of a charitable unit trust scheme

(1) A unit trust scheme is a charitable unit trust scheme if it is of one of the descriptions specified in paragraph (2) below.

(2) Those descriptions are—

(a) a common investment fund established under section 22 of the Charities Act 1960 or section 25 of the Charities Act (Northern Ireland) 1964;

[(aa) a common deposit fund established under section 22A of the Charities Act 1960;][1]

(b) an investment fund or a deposit fund within the meaning of the Scheme scheduled to the Church Funds Investment Measure 1958 or of the scheme contained in the First Schedule to the Methodist Church Funds Act 1960;

(c) a fund held by the Church of Scotland Trust under the provisions of section 15 of the Church of Scotland Trust Order 1932 [or under the provisions of the Church of Scotland (Properties and Investments) Order 1994][2];

[(ca) a fund held by the Church of Scotland General Trustees or the Church of Scotland Investors Trust under the provisions of the Church of Scotland (Properties and Investments) Order 1994;][2]

(d) a unit trust scheme under the terms of which—

(i) the scheme property is held by the trustee on trust for charitable purposes only, and

(ii) the participants are required to be bodies of persons established for charitable purposes only or trustees of trusts so established;

and the income of the participants in which is in either case applied to charitable purposes only.

Amendments—[1] Sub-para (2)(*aa*) inserted by the IT (Definition of Unit Trust Scheme) (Amendment No 2) Regulations, SI 1992/3133, with effect from 1 January 1993.

[2] Words in sub-para (2)(*c*) added and sub-para (2)(*ca*) inserted by the IT (Definition of Unit Trust Scheme) (Amendment) Regulations, SI 1994/1479 reg 2, with effect from 27 June 1994.

8 Description of a limited partnership scheme

A unit trust scheme is a limited partnership scheme when the scheme property is held on trust for the general partners and the limited partners in a limited partnership.

9 Effect of Regulations

These Regulations shall have effect in relation to distribution periods (within the meaning of section 354A[1]) beginning on or after 11th March 1988.

Notes—[1] TA 1988 s 469.

1988/1012

PERSONAL PENSION SCHEMES (MINIMUM CONTRIBUTIONS UNDER THE SOCIAL SECURITY ACT 1986) REGULATIONS 1988

Made by the Commissioners of Inland Revenue under TA 1988 s 649(4)

Made . . . . *9 June 1988*
Laid before the House of Commons . . . . *9 June 1988*
Coming into Force . . . . *1 July 1988*

1 Citation and commencement

These Regulations may be cited as the Personal Pension Schemes (Minimum Contributions under the Social Security Act 1986) Regulations 1988 and shall come into force on 1st July 1988.

2 Interpretation

In these Regulations unless the context otherwise requires—

"the Act" means the Income and Corporation Taxes Act 1988;

"the Board" means the Commissioners of Inland Revenue;

"tax week" means one of the successive periods in a tax year beginning with the first day of that year and every 7th day thereafter; the last day of a tax year (or, in the case of a tax year ending in a leap year, the last 2 days) to be treated accordingly as a separate tax week;

"tax year" means the 12 months beginning with 6th April in any year.

3 Recovery of any increase attributable to section 649 of the Act by the Secretary of State

. . .

Amendments—This regulation revoked by the Social Security Contributions (Transfer of Functions, etc) Act 1999 s 26(3), Sch 10 Pt II with effect from 1 April 1999, by virtue of the Social Security Contributions (Transfer of Functions, etc) Act 1999 (Commencement No 1 and Transitional Provisions) Order, SI 1999/527.

4, 5 Information

. . .

Amendments—These regulations revoked by the Social Security Contributions (Transfer of Functions, etc) Act 1999 s 26(3), Sch 10 Pt II with effect from 1 April 1999 by virtue of the Social Security Contributions (Transfer of Functions, etc) Act 1999 (Commencement No 1 and Transitional Provisions) Order, SI 1999/527.

6 Recovery of amounts representing basic rate tax

(1) The like provisions as are contained in section 30 of the Taxes Management Act 1970 (recovery of overpayment of tax, etc) shall apply in relation to the payment by the Secretary of State of an amount by way of minimum contributions which—

(*a*) he was not required to pay, or

(*b*) he was required to pay but which he paid to other persons than the trustees or managers of the personal pension scheme to whom he should have made the payment

as if an amount representing income tax at the basic rate on the amount paid had been income tax repaid to the person to, or in respect of, whom the amount was paid to which that person was not entitled.

(2) An assessment made by virtue of this regulation shall be made by the Board and, subject to the provisions of these Regulations, the like provisions as are contained in the Taxes Management Act 1970 shall apply as if the assessment were an assessment to tax for the year of assessment in respect of which the amount was paid.

7 Northern Ireland

In relation to Northern Ireland, these Regulations shall have effect as if—

(*a*) references to the Secretary of State were references to the Department of Health and Social Services for Northern Ireland; . . . [1]

(*b*) . . . [1]

Amendments—[1] Para (*b*) and the word "and" immediately preceding it revoked by the Social Security Contributions (Transfer of Functions, etc) (Northern Ireland) Order, SI 1999/671 art 24(3) Sch 9 Pt II, with effect from 1 April 1999 (by virtue of the Social Security Contributions (Transfer of Functions, etc) (1999 Order) (Commencement No 1 and Transitional Provisions) Order (Northern Ireland), SR 1999/149, art 2(*c*), Sch 2).

1988/1013

PERSONAL PENSION SCHEMES (RELIEF AT SOURCE) REGULATIONS 1988

Made by the Commissioners of Inland Revenue under TA 1988 s 639

Made . . . . *9 June 1988*
Laid before the House of Commons . . . . *9 June 1988*
Coming into Force . . . . *1 July 1988*

1 Citation and commencement

These Regulations may be cited as the Personal Pension Schemes (Relief at Source) Regulations 1988 and shall come into force on 1st July 1988.

2 Interpretation

(1) In these Regulations unless the context otherwise requires—

"arrangements" means approved personal pension arrangements within the meaning of section 630;

["basis year" shall be construed in accordance with section 646B;][1]

"the Board" means the Commissioners of Inland Revenue;

["earnings threshold" has the meaning given by section 630(1);][1]

["electronic signature" has the meaning given by section 7(2) of the Electronic Communications Act 2000;][1]

"net contribution" means a contribution from which an individual deducts an amount equal to income tax at the basic rate by virtue of section 639(3) and (4);

["net relevant earnings" means relevant earnings computed in accordance with section 646;][2]

["permitted maximum" has the meaning given by section 638(4);][2]

["qualifying post-cessation year" has the meaning given by section 646D(4) and (5);][2]

["relevant earnings" has the meaning given by section 644;][2]

"relevant superannuation scheme" means a scheme or arrangement as defined in section 645(3);

"retirement annuity contract or trust scheme" means a retirement annuity contract or trust scheme approved by the Board under Chapter III of Part XIV of the Act;

"scheme" means an approved personal pension scheme within the meaning of section 630;

"section" means a section of the Income and Corporation Taxes Act 1988;

"tax month" means a period beginning on the 6th day of any month and ending with the 5th day of the following month;

"year of assessment" means a year beginning with 6th April in any year and ending with 5th April in the following year.

(2) The Table below indexes other definitions in these Regulations—

Term defined	*Regulation*
annual claim	8
interim claim	8

Amendments—[1] Definitions of "basis year", "earnings threshold", "electronic signature" inserted by the Personal Pension Scheme (Relief at Source) (Amendment) Regulations, SI 2000/2315 reg 3 with effect for personal pension schemes after 5 April 2001.

[2] Definitions of "net relevant earnings", "permitted maximum", "qualifying post-cessation year", and "relevant earnings" substituted for the definitions of "net relevant Schedule E earnings" and "relevant Schedule E earnings" by, SI 2000/2315 reg 3 with effect for personal pension schemes after 5 April 2001.

3 Prescribed cases and conditions: introductory

Regulation 4 prescribes the cases in which, and regulations 5 to 7 the conditions subject to which, relief under section 639 shall be given in accordance with subsections (3) and (4) of that section.

4 Prescribed cases

The prescribed cases are cases where [an individual is eligible, by virtue of satisfying the provisions of section 632A of the Taxes Act, to make contributions for a year of assessment to the approved personal pension scheme concerned][1]

Amendments—[1] Words substituted by the Personal Pension Scheme (Relief at Source) (Amendment) Regulations, SI 2000/2315 reg 4 with effect for personal pension schemes after 5 April 2001.

5 Prescribed conditions

(1) The condition prescribed in this regulation is that an individual shall furnish . . . [1] to the scheme administrator before . . . [1] the time specified in paragraph (3) the particulars specified in paragraph (2).

(2) The particulars specified in this paragraph are—

(*a*) his full name and [permanent residential address including, where the address is in the United Kingdom, the postcode][1];

(*b*) his date of birth;

(*c*) his national insurance number[, unless aged under 16 or a citizen of a country outside the United Kingdom who is not resident in the United Kingdom,][1]

[(*d*) except where the scheme is an occupational pension scheme within the meaning of section 1 of the Pension Schemes Act 1993, the category of status specified in paragraph (2A) that is applicable in his case or, if more than one category is applicable, the one that is his principal source of income;][2]

[(*e*) in the circumstances specified in paragraph (2B), the requisite evidence, that is to say—

(i) a declaration specifying the year of assessment concerned, or an earlier year of assessment not being more than five years preceding that year, as the basis year for the purposes of section 646B (presumption of same level of relevant earnings etc for 5 years);

(ii) where the individual is an employee, the full names and addresses of all those employers who have paid, or will pay, net relevant earnings to him; and

(iii) the particulars specified in paragraph (2C) for the basis year.][2]

[(2A) The categories of status specified in this paragraph for the purposes of paragraph (2)(*d*) are as follows—

(*a*) employed, that is, a person chargeable to tax under Schedule E for the year of assessment concerned in respect of emoluments from an office or employment held by him;

(*b*) a person chargeable to tax under Schedule E for the year of assessment concerned in respect of a pension;

(*c*) self-employed, that is, a person chargeable to tax under Schedule D for the year of assessment concerned in respect of annual profits or gains arising or accruing from any trade, profession or vocation carried on by him;

(*d*) a child under the age of 16;

(*e*) other status not falling within any of sub-paragraphs (*a*) to (*d*) and, in relation to that status, specifying which of the following is applicable in his case or, if more than one, the most applicable—

(i) caring for one or more children aged under 16,

(ii) caring for a person aged 16 or over,

(iii) in full time education,

(iv) unemployed, or

(v) other.][3]

[(2B) The circumstances specified in this paragraph are where the total contributions to be made by the individual and, where he is an employee, his employer for the year of assessment concerned will exceed the earnings threshold, and the year of assessment either—

(*a*) is not a year already specified in a declaration under paragraph (2)(*e*)(i) as the basis year or is not one of the 5 years of assessment following that year, or

(*b*) is such a year but the total contributions to be made by the individual and, where he is an employee, his employer for that year will exceed the permitted maximum based on the net relevant earnings of the individual in the basis year specified in the declaration.][3]

[(2C) The particulars specified in this paragraph are—

(*a*) where the individual is an employee, one of the following—

(i) a copy of his payslip or Inland Revenue Form P60 showing relevant earnings for the basis year;

(ii) a declaration of his employer, signed by the employer or a person nominated by the employer, stipulating the amount of remuneration paid to the employee for the basis year or, where the basis year is the current year, an estimate of the amount of remuneration to be paid to the employee for that year;

(iii) a copy of the self-assessment included in the individual's income tax return for the basis year;

(iv) such other particulars of relevant earnings as may be required by notice in writing given by the Board;

(*b*) where the individual is self-employed, one of the following—

(i) a copy of the accounts for the basis year of the individual's trade, profession or vocation;

(ii) a copy of the income tax return for the basis year of the individual, or of the self-assessment included in that return, showing net relevant earnings of the individual;

(iii) such other particulars of relevant earnings as may be required by notice in writing given by the Board.][3]

[(2D) The reference in paragraph (2C)(*a*)(ii) to a declaration includes a declaration produced in electronic form and incorporating an electronic signature of the employer.][3]

[(3) The time specified in this paragraph is—

(*a*) in relation to the particulars specified in paragraph (2)(*a*) to (*d*), the time at which the individual first pays a net contribution;

(*b*) in relation to the particulars specified in paragraphs (2)(*e*) and (2C), immediately after the expiry of thirty days following the day on which the individual first pays a net contribution for the year of assessment concerned that, when aggregated with previous contributions made by him for that year, exceeds the earnings threshold or, as the case may be, the permitted maximum based on the net relevant earnings of the individual in the basis year.][2]

Amendments—[1] Words revoked in para (1), words substituted in para (2)(*a*), and words added in para (2)(*c*) by the Personal Pension Scheme (Relief at Source) (Amendment) Regulations, SI 2000/2315 regs 5, 6 with effect for personal pension schemes after 5 April 2001.

[2] Sub-paras (2)(*d*), (*e*), and para (3) substituted for paras (2)(*d*) to (*f*) by SI 2000/2315 regs 6, 8 with effect for personal pension schemes after 5 April 2001.

[3] Paras (2A)–(2D) inserted by SI 2000/2315 regs7 with effect for personal pension schemes after 5 April 2001.

6—(1) The condition prescribed in this regulation is that an individual shall furnish to the scheme administrator before . . . [1] the time specified in paragraph (3) the certificates specified in paragraph (2).

(2) The certificates specified in this paragraph are certificates which show—

(*a*) that, except where subsection (4) or subsection (5) of section 645 applies, the individual is not participating in a relevant superannuation scheme,

(*b*) whether or not the individual is paying contributions under other arrangements or under a retirement annuity contract or trust scheme;

(*c*) that the total contributions which the individual—

(i) is paying under any arrangements or scheme referred to in sub-paragraph (*b*), and

(ii) will pay under the arrangements to which the certificate relates

do not together exceed [the maximum amount permitted under section 640][1];

[(*d*) that the individual's eligibility to make contributions for the year of assessment concerned arises by virtue of section 632A(4) (actual net relevant earnings), the individual does not fulfil any of the conditions in section 632A(6) to (9), and his net relevant earnings do not fall within section 644(5).][2]

[(3) The time specified in this paragraph is—

(*a*) in relation to the certificate specified in paragraph (2)(*a*), (*b*) or (*c*)—

(i) the time at which the individual first pays a net contribution;

(ii) the time at which the individual makes a declaration in accordance with regulation 5(2)(*e*)(i) specifying a year of assessment as the basis year for the purposes of section 646B;

(*b*) in relation to the certificate specified in paragraph (2)(*d*), the time at which the individual first pays a net contribution, being a time when his eligibility to do so arises by virtue of section 632A(4) and he does not fulfil any of the conditions in section 632A(6) to (9).][2]

Amendments—[1] Words in para (1) revoked, and words in para (2)(*c*) substituted by the Personal Pension Scheme (Relief at Source) (Amendment) Regulations, SI 2000/2315 regs 9, 10 with effect for personal pension schemes after 5 April 2001.

[2] Paras (2)(*d*), (3) substituted by SI 2000/2315 regs 10, 11 with effect for personal pension schemes after 5 April 2001.

7—(1) The condition prescribed in this regulation is that on every occasion on which an individual furnishes particulars or a certificate (or both) in accordance with regulation 5 or 6 he shall furnish the declarations specified in paragraph (2).

(2) The declarations specified in this paragraph are declarations . . . [1] by the individual to the effect that—

(*a*) in relation to—

(i) the particulars specified in regulation 5(2), they are to the best of the knowledge and belief of the individual correct and complete;

(ii) a certificate specified in regulation 6(2), it is to the best of the knowledge and belief of the individual correct;

[(*b*) the individual will, not later than the date specified in paragraph (3), give notice to the administrator if an event occurs as a result of which the individual, having regard to section 632A(3) to (9), will no longer be eligible to make contributions.][1]

[(3) The date specified for the purposes of sub-paragraph (*b*) of paragraph (2) is the 5th April in the year of assessment in which the event referred to in that sub-paragraph occurs or the date that is 30 days following the occurrence of that event, whichever is the later.][2]

[(4) Certificates furnished under regulation 6, and declarations furnished under this regulation, if in writing, shall be signed by the maker of the certificates or declarations.][2]

[(5) Where particulars, certificates or declarations furnished by an individual under regulation 5 or 6 or this regulation are not in writing, the scheme administrator may—

(*a*) make a declaration in writing on behalf of the individual that the particulars or (as the case may be) the terms of the certificates or declarations so furnished are those recorded in the declaration, and

(*b*) send a copy of the declaration to the individual.][2]

[(6) Subject to any corrections notified by the individual to the scheme administrator within the period of 30 days following the date on which the copy of the declaration referred to in paragraph (5) was sent to the individual, and incorporated in a new declaration made by the scheme administrator, any such declaration shall take effect as from the date on which the copy of it was sent to the individual in accordance with that paragraph.][2]

[(7) Particulars, certificates or declarations furnished by an individual under regulation 5, 6 or this regulation shall be regarded as furnished in writing for the purposes of this regulation if they are furnished—

(*a*) by telephonic facsimile transmission, or

(*b*) by electronic communication containing an electronic signature of the individual.][2]

[(8) Declarations made by the scheme administrator under paragraph (5) of this regulation shall be regarded as made in writing if they are produced by electronic means; and the copy of a declaration to be sent to the individual in accordance with sub-paragraph (*b*) of that paragraph may be sent by telephonic facsimile transmission or by electronic communication.][2]

Amendments—[1] The word "signed" in para (2) revoked, and sub-para (*b*) substituted by the Personal Pension Scheme (Relief at Source) (Amendment) Regulations, SI 2000/2315 reg 12 with effect for personal pension schemes after 5 April 2001.

[2] Paras (3)–(8) added by SI 2000/2315 reg 13 with effect for personal pension schemes after 5 April 2001.

8 Claims: introductory

(1) Amounts recoverable by a scheme administrator under section 639(4)(*b*) shall be recovered on a claim made to the Board for the purpose of these Regulations.

(2) Subject to paragraph (3), a claim shall be for a year of assessment ("annual claim").

(3) A claim may also be made in accordance with regulation 9 for a tax month ("interim claim").

[(3A) No annual claim or interim claim may be made in respect of contributions made by an individual in a year of assessment that exceed the earnings threshold unless that year of assessment is—

(*a*) the basis year specified in a declaration under regulation 5(2)(*e*)(i),

(*b*) one of the 5 years of assessment following that year, or

(*c*) a qualifying post-cessation year.][1]

(4) Notwithstanding the provisions of any other enactment, the Board shall not be under an obligation to make any payment under regulation 9 or 10 earlier than the end of the month following the month in which the claim is received.

Amendments—[1] Para (3A) inserted by the Personal Pension Scheme (Relief at Source) (Amendment) Regulations, SI 2000/2315 reg 14 with effect for personal pension schemes after 5 April 2001.

9 Interim claims

(1) Subject to paragraph (3), an interim claim for a tax month may be made by a scheme administrator within 6 months after the end of the tax month for which it is made.

(2) A claim under this regulation may not be based on an estimate but may only be made to recover an amount deducted in respect of contributions paid in the tax month.

(3) An interim claim may not be made for the tax month ending 5th October or any subsequent month until the annual claim for the preceding year of assessment has been made by the scheme administrator and received by the Board.

(4) If the amount claimed is established to the Board's satisfaction they shall pay the amount to the claimant; if they are not so satisfied they shall pay to the claimant any lesser amount established to their satisfaction.

(5) Where a scheme administrator discovers that an amount paid to him under paragraph (4) was excessive he shall bring into account in the interim claim made by him next after the discovery (in this regulation referred to as "the subsequent claim") the amount of the excess; and if that amount exceeds the amount deducted in respect of the tax month for which the subsequent claim is made—

(*a*) the scheme administrator shall repay the amount of the excess to the Board with the claim; and

(*b*) if he fails so to do that amount shall immediately be recoverable by the Board in the same manner as tax charged by an assessment on the scheme administrator which has become final and conclusive.

10 Annual claims

(1) An annual claim for a year of assessment may, subject to paragraph (2), be made at any time within 6 years after the end of the year of assessment.

(2) Where in relation to any year of assessment a scheme administrator has received and not repaid in full any amount on an interim claim he shall within 6 months after the end of the year of assessment make an annual claim.

(3) A claim under this regulation—

(*a*) may not be based on an estimate but may only be made to recover an amount deducted in respect of contributions [paid in respect of][1] the year of assessment, and

(*b*) shall bring into account payments made in respect of the year of assessment; and for the purpose of this regulation "aggregate interim payments" means the aggregate of payments made (and not repaid) on interim claims.

(4) Where the aggregate of the interim payments shown by an annual claim exceeds the amount deducted for the year of assessment—

(*a*) the scheme administrator shall repay the amount of the excess to the Board with the claim; and

(*b*) if he fails so to do, that amount shall immediately be recoverable by the Board in the same manner as tax charged by an assessment on the scheme administrator which has become final and conclusive.

(5) If a scheme administrator fails to make an annual claim under paragraph (2) within the time limited by that paragraph, the Board may issue a notice to the scheme administrator showing the aggregate interim payments for the year, and stating that the Board are not satisfied that the amount due to the scheme administrator for the year of assessment exceeds the lower amount stated in the notice.

(6) If an annual claim is not delivered to the Board within 14 days after the issue of a notice under paragraph (5), the amount of the difference between the aggregate amount and the amount stated in the notice shall immediately be recoverable by the Board in the same manner as tax charged by an assessment on the scheme administrator which has become final and conclusive.

(7) Where an annual claim has been made and the scheme administrator subsequently discovers that an error or mistake has been made in the claim the scheme administrator may make a supplementary claim within the time limited by paragraph (1).

Amendments—[1] Words in para (3)(*a*) substituted by the Personal Pension Scheme (Relief at Source) (Amendment) Regulations, SI 2000/2315 reg 15 with effect for personal pension schemes after 5 April 2001.

11 Claims: supplementary provisions

(1) Section 42 of the Taxes Management Act 1970 (procedure for making claims) shall not apply to a claim under these Regulations.

(2) No appeal shall lie from the Board's decision on an interim claim.

(3) An appeal shall be to the Special Commissioners from the Board's decision on an annual claim, and the appeal shall be brought by giving written notice to the Board within 30 days of receipt of written notice of the decision.

(4) No payment made or other thing done on or in relation to an interim claim shall prejudice the decision on an annual claim.

(5) The like provisions as are contained in Part V of the Taxes Management Act 1970 (appeals and other proceedings) shall apply to an appeal under paragraph (3), and on an appeal the Special Commissioners may vary the decision appealed against whether or not the variation is to the advantage of the appellant.

(6) All such assessments, payments and repayments shall be made as are necessary to give effect to the Board's decision on an annual claim, or to any variation of that decision on appeal.

(7) Claims under these Regulations—

(*a*) shall contain such information and be in such form as the Board may prescribe (and forms prescribed for annual claims may require a report to be given by the scheme administrator's auditor);

(*b*) shall contain declarations to the effect that—

(i) sufficient records in respect of the scheme are maintained so as to enable the requirements of these Regulations to be satisfied, and

(ii) the information contained in the claim (including the declaration referred to in paragraph (i)) is correct; and

(*c*) shall be signed by the scheme administrator or by an authorised representative in the service of the scheme administrator.

12 Recovery on withdrawal of approval of schemes or of arrangements

Where a scheme administrator gives to the Board information in accordance with regulation 14(2) he shall at the time that he gives the information—

(*a*) pay to the Board the amount (if any) referred to in regulation 14(3)(*d*); and

(*b*) if he fails so to do, that amount shall immediately be recoverable by the Board in the same manner as tax charged by an assessment on the scheme administrator which has become final and conclusive.

13 Recovery of amounts by assessment

(1) The like provisions as are contained in section 30 of the Taxes Management Act 1970 (recovery of overpayment of tax, etc) shall apply in relation to the payment by the Board of an amount—

(*a*) paid under these Regulations to which a scheme administrator was not entitled, or

(*b*) recoverable from a scheme administrator under regulation 9(5), regulation 10(4) or (6) or regulation 12,

as if it had been income tax repaid to the scheme administrator to which he was not entitled.

(2) An assessment made by virtue of this regulation shall be made by the Board and, subject to the provisions of these Regulations, the like provisions as are contained in the Taxes Management Act 1970 shall apply as if the assessment were an assessment to tax for the year of assessment in respect of which the amount was paid or is recoverable.

14 Information

(1) The Board may by notice in writing require any person who is, or who at any time has been—

(*a*) a Scheme administrator to whom net contributions have been paid, or

(*b*) an individual who has paid such contributions,

to give to them within such time (not being less than 14 days) as may be provided in the notice such information and in such form as may be prescribed in the notice.

(2) If the Board by notice under section 650 withdraw their approval of a scheme, or of arrangements made in accordance with it and under which net contributions have been paid, the scheme administrator shall within 30 days give to the Board in relation to that scheme, or to those arrangements, the information prescribed in paragraph (3).

(3) The information prescribed in this paragraph is—

(*a*) the full name, address, national insurance number, and where known tax office reference of each individual who has paid net contributions after the date specified in the notice in relation to the scheme, or to the arrangements, as the case may be (in this regulation referred to as "the relevant contributions");

(*b*) the amount of the relief obtained under section 639(1) by means of the relevant contributions;

(*c*) the amount of such relief actually due; and

(*d*) the difference between the relief referred to in sub-paragraph (*b*) and that referred to in sub-paragraph (*c*).

(4) If an individual who has paid net contributions fails to comply with the requirements of regulations 5 to 7, the scheme administrator to whom such contributions have been made shall within 30 days give to the Board the information prescribed in paragraph (5).

(5) The information prescribed in this paragraph is—

(*a*) the full name, address, national insurance number, and where known tax office reference of the individual;

(*b*) the amount of relief obtained by him under section 639(1) by means of such contributions;

(*c*) the amount of such relief actually due; and

(*d*) the difference between the relief referred to in sub-paragraph (*b*) and that referred to in sub-paragraph (*c*).

15 Inspection of records

(1) Every scheme administrator to whom net contributions have been paid shall, whenever required so to do, make available for inspection by a person authorised by the Board for that purpose all books, documents and other records (including all particulars, certificates and declarations furnished under regulations 5 to 7) in his possession or under his control relating to—

(*a*) such contributions paid to him,

(*b*) the scheme and the arrangements made in accordance with it and under which the contributions were paid, and

(*c*) the individual who paid the contributions.

(2) Where records are maintained by computer the scheme administrator shall provide the person making the inspection with all facilities necessary to obtain information from them.

(3) Subject to paragraph (4), all books, documents and records referred to in paragraph (1), shall be preserved by the scheme administrator so as to be available for inspection under this regulation for a period of six years following the termination of the scheme, or of arrangements made in accordance with it, to which they relate.

(4) All particulars, certificates and declarations furnished under regulations 5 to 7 shall be so preserved for a period of six years following the date on which the individual to whom they relate ceased to make net contributions.

1989/1297

TAXES (INTEREST RATE) REGULATIONS 1989

Made by the Treasury under FA 1989 s 178

Made . . . . *27 July 1989*
Laid before the House of Commons . . . . *28 July 1989*
Coming into Force . . . . *18 August 1989*

Commentary—*Simon's Taxes* **A4.523, D1.1348, D1.1349; E4.632; I11.405, I11.532**.

1 Citation and commencement

These Regulations may be cited as the Taxes (Interest Rate) Regulations 1989 and shall come into force on 18th August 1989.

2 Interpretation

(1) In these Regulations unless the context otherwise requires—

["the 1998 Regulations" means the Corporation Tax (Instalment Payments Regulations 1998;][1]

"established rate" means—

(*a*) on the coming into force of these Regulations, 14 per cent per annum; and

(*b*) in relation to any date after the first reference date after the coming into force of these Regulations, the reference rate found on the immediately preceding reference date;

["operative date" means—

(*a*) the [twelfth][3] working day after the reference date, or

(*b*) where regulation 3ZA or 3BA applies—

(i) where the reference date is the first Tuesday, the day which is the Monday next following the first Tuesday, or

(ii) where the reference date is the second Tuesday, the day which is the Monday next following the second Tuesday;][2]

["reference date" means—

(*a*) the . . . [3] working day following the day on which the most recent meeting of the Monetary Policy Committee of the Bank of England took place, or

(*b*) where regulation 3ZA or 3BA applies—

(i) the day which is the Tuesday next following the day on which that meeting took place ("the first Tuesday"), and

(ii) the day which is the Tuesday ("the second Tuesday") occurring two weeks after the first Tuesday;][2]

"section 178" means section 178 of the Finance Act 1989;

"working day" means any day other than a non-business day within the meaning of section 92 of the Bills of Exchange Act 1882.

[(2) In these Regulations the reference rate found on a reference date is the official bank rate determined by the most recent meeting of the Monetary Policy Committee of the Bank of England.][3]

Amendments—[1] Words in para (1) inserted by the Taxes (Interest Rate) (Amendment No 2) Regulations, SI 1998/3176 reg 3 with effect for accounting periods ending on or after 1 July 1999 by virtue of the Finance Act 1994, Section 199 (Appointed Day) Order, SI 1998/3173 art 2.

[2] In para (1), definitions of "operative date" and "reference date" substituted by the Taxes and Duties (Interest Rate) (Amendment) Regulations, SI 2008/3234 reg 2 with effect from 7 January 2009.

[3] In definition of "operative date" word substituted, in definition of "reference date" word "second" revoked, and para (2) substituted, by the Taxes and Duties (Interest Rate) (Amendment) Regulations, SI 2009/2032 regs 2, 3 with effect from 12 August 2009.

2A [Applicable rate of interest equal to zero

In determining the rate of interest applicable under section 178 for any purposes mentioned in these Regulations, if the result is less than zero the rate shall be treated as zero for those purposes.][1,2]

Amendments—[1] This para inserted by the Taxes and Duties (Interest Rate) (Amendment) Regulations, SI 2008/3234 reg 2 with effect from 7 January 2009.

[2] This reg revoked by the Taxes and Duties (Interest Rate) (Amendment) Regulations, SI 2009/2032 regs 2, 4 with effect from 12 August 2009.

[3 [Applicable rates of interest on unpaid tax, tax repaid and repayment supplement]1

(1) For the purposes of—

(*a*) [section 86 (except where regulation 3AA(1)(*aa*) applies) and section 88][4] of the Taxes Management Act 1970,

[(aa) section 59C of the Taxes Management Act 1970, as it applies to any income tax or capital gains tax which has become payable in accordance with—

(i) section 55 of that Act, so far as it relates to an amendment or an assessment referred to in paragraphs (*a*) and (*b*) of subsection (1) of that section, or

(ii) section 59B of that Act,[7]

(*ab*) . . . [8]
(*b*) [section 118F of, and paragraph 6B of Schedule 3 to][2] the Income and Corporation Taxes Act 1988, . . .
[(*ba*) section 71(8A) of the Social Security Administration Act 1992 and section 69(8A) of the Social Security Administration (Northern Ireland) Act 1992, as they have effect in any case where the amount recoverable referred to in each of those sections is in respect of working families' tax credit or disabled person's tax credit, and paragraph 8 of Schedule 4 to the Tax Credits Act 1999;][5]
(*c*) paragraph 6(2)(*a*) of Schedule 1 to the Social Security Contributions and Benefits Act 1992, [. . . [6]
(*d*) section 15A of the Stamp Act 1891,] [3][; and][6]
[(*e*) sections 87 and 88 of the Finance Act 2003.][6]

the rate applicable under section 178 shall, subject to paragraph (2), be 8.5 per cent per annum.

(2) Where, on a reference date after 1st January 1997, the reference rate found on that date differs from the established rate, the rate applicable under section 178 for the purposes of the enactments referred to in paragraph (1) shall, on and after the next operative date, be the percentage per annum found by applying the formula specified in paragraph (3).

(3) The formula specified in this paragraph is—

$$RR + 2.5$$

where RR is the reference rate referred to in paragraph (2).][1]

Note—The rate of interest under this Regulation changes periodically in accordance with the specified formula. Changes are announced by HMRC press release. The rate applicable at any given time can be obtained from *Simon's Taxes*, Binder 1 and from *Simon's Weekly Tax Intelligence*.

Amendments—[1] This regulation substituted by the Taxes (Interest Rate) (Amendment No 4) Regulations, SI 1996/3187, with effect from 31 January 1997.

[2] Words in sub-para (1)(*b*) inserted by the Taxes (Interest Rate) (Amendment No 2) Regulations, SI 1997/2707 with effect from 9 December 1997.

[3] In para (1), word "and" in sub-para (*b*) revoked, word "and" in sub-para (*c*), and the whole of sub-para (*d*) inserted by the Taxes (Interest Rate) (Amendment No 3) Regulations, SI 1999/2538 reg 3 with effect from 1 October 1999.

[4] Words in para (1)(*a*) substituted by the Taxes (Interest Rate) (Amendment No 1) Regulations, SI 2001/204 reg 3, with effect from 6 March 2001.

[5] Para (1)(*ba*) inserted by the Taxes (Interest Rate) (Amendment No 2) Regulations, SI 2001/254 reg 3, with effect from 7 March 2001.

[6] In para (1), words in sub-para (*c*) revoked, word in sub-para (*d*) inserted, and sub-para (*e*) inserted, by the Taxes (Interest Rate) (Amendment) Regulations, SI 2005/2462 regs 2, 3 with effect from 26 September 2005.

[7] Para (1)(*aa*) repealed by the Finance Act 2009, Schedules 55 and 56 (Income Tax Self Assessment and Pension Schemes) (Appointed Days and Consequential and Savings Provisions) Order, SI 2011/702 art 16 with effect from 1 April 2011. This amendment has no effect in relation to a return or other document which is required to be made or delivered to HMRC or an amount of tax which is payable in relation to the tax year 2009–10 or any previous tax year (SI 2011/702 art 20).

[8] Para (1)(*ab*) revoked by the Finance Act 2009, Sections 101 to 103 (Income Tax Self Assessment) (Appointed Days and Transitional and Consequential Provisions) Order, SI 2011/701 art 10 with effect from 31 October 2011.

[3AA—(1) For the purposes of—
(*a*) sections 86A and 87 of the Taxes Management Act 1970,
[(*aa*) section 86 of the Taxes Management Act 1970 as it has effect in relation to accounting periods of companies ending before 1st October 1993 (interest on unpaid assessed corporation tax),][4]
(*b*) paragraph 3 of Schedule 16A to the Finance Act 1973,
(*c*) paragraphs 15 . . . [5]of Schedule 2, and paragraph 8 of Schedule 5, to the Oil Taxation Act 1975,
(d) paragraph 59 of Schedule 8 to the Development Land Tax Act 1976,[5]
(*e*) . . . [2]
(f) section 825 of, and paragraph 3 of Schedule 19A to, the Income and Corporation Taxes Act 1988,[5]

rate applicable under section 178 shall, [except where regulation 3AC applies and][3] subject to paragraph (2), [be—
(i) where paragraph (*aa*) above applies, 6.5 per cent per annum;
(ii) in all other cases, 6.25 per cent per annum.][4]

(2) Where, on a reference date after 1st January 1997, the reference rate found on that date differs from the established rate, the rate applicable under section 178 for the purposes of the enactments referred to in paragraph (1) shall, on and after the next operative date, be the percentage per annum found by applying the formula specified in paragraph (3) . . . [5].

[(3) The formula specified in this paragraph is—

$$RR + 2.5$$

where RR is the reference rate referred to in paragraph (2).][5]][1]

Note—The rate of interest under this Regulation changes periodically in accordance with the specified formula. Changes are announced by HMRC press release. The rate applicable at any given time can be obtained from *Simon's Taxes*, Binder 1 and from *Simon's Weekly Tax Intelligence*.

Amendments—[1] This regulation inserted by Taxes (Interest Rate) (Amendment No 4) Regulations, SI 1996/3187, with effect from 31 January 1997.

[2] Sub-para (1)(*e*) revoked by the Taxes (Interest Rate) (Amendment No 3) Regulations, SI 1999/2538 reg 4 with effect from 1 October 1999.

[3] Words inserted by Taxes (Interest Rate) (Amendment No 4) Regulations, SI 1999/2637 reg 4 with effect from 14 October 1999.

[4] Para (1)(*aa*) inserted and words at end of para (1) substituted by the Taxes (Interest Rate) (Amendment No 1) Regulations, SI 2001/204 reg 4, with effect from 6 March 2001.

[5] In para (1)(*c*), words revoked, para (1)(*d*), (*f*) revoked, in para (2), words revoked, and para (3) substituted, by the Taxes and Duties (Interest Rate) (Amendment) Regulations, SI 2009/2032 regs 2, 5 with effect from 12 August 2009.

[3AB—(1) For the purposes of—

(*a*) section 824 of the Income and Corporation Taxes Act 1988,

(*b*) paragraph 6(2)(*b*) of Schedule 1 to the Social Security Contributions and Benefits Act 1992, . . . [2]

(*c*) section 283 of the Taxation of Chargeable Gains Act 1992.

[(*d*) section 92 of the Finance Act 1986, . . . [3]

(*e*) section 110 of the Finance Act 1999,][2] [; and][3]

[(*f*) section 89 of the Finance Act 2003.][3]

the rate applicable under section 178 shall, subject to paragraph (2), be 4 per cent per annum.

(2) Where, on a reference date after 1st January 1997, the reference rate found on that date differs from the established rate, the rate applicable under section 178 for the purposes of the enactments referred to in paragraph (1) shall, on and after the next operative date, be the [higher of—

(*a*) 0.5% per annum, and

(*b*) the percentage per annum found by applying the formula specified in paragraph (3).][4]

[(3) The formula specified in this paragraph is—

$$RR - 1$$

where RR is the reference rate referred to in paragraph (2).][1]][1]

Note—The rate of interest under this Regulation changes periodically in accordance with the specified formula. Changes are announced by HMRC press release. The rate applicable at any given time can be obtained from *Simon's Taxes*, Binder 1 and from *Simon's Weekly Tax Intelligence*.

Amendments—[1] This regulation inserted by the Taxes (Interest Rate) (Amendment No 4) Regulations, SI 1996/3187, with effect from 31 January 1997.

[2] Word "and" in sub-para (1)(*b*) revoked, and sub-paras (1)(*d*), (*e*) inserted, by the Taxes (Interest Rate) (Amendment No 3) Regulations, SI 1999/2538 reg 5 with effect from 1 October 1999.

[3] In para (1), word in sub-para (*d*) revoked, word in sub-para (*e*) inserted, and sub-para (*f*) inserted, by the Taxes (Interest Rate) (Amendment) Regulations, SI 2005/2462 regs 2, 4 with effect from 26 September 2005.

[4] In para (2), words substituted, and para (3) substituted, by the Taxes and Duties (Interest Rate) (Amendment) Regulations, SI 2009/2032 regs 2, 7 with effect from 12 August 2009.

[3AC—(1) For the purposes of section 87 of the Taxes Management Act 1970 in so far as it relates to tax that becomes due and payable on or after 14th October 1999, the rate applicable under section 178 shall, subject to paragraph (2), be 7.5 per cent per annum.

(2) Where on a reference date after 14th October 1999 the reference rate found on that date differs from the established rate, the rate applicable under section 178 for the purposes mentioned in paragraph (1) shall, on and after the next operative date, be the percentage per annum found by applying the formula specified in paragraph (3).

(3) The formula specified in this paragraph is—

$$RR + 2.5$$

where RR is the reference rate referred to in paragraph (2).][1]

Amendments—[1] This regulation inserted by Taxes (Interest Rate) (Amendment No 4) Regulations, SI 1999/2637 reg 4 with effect from 14 October 1999.

[3A [Applicable rate of interest on overdue corporation tax

(1) For the purposes of section 87A of the Taxes Management Act 1970 the rate applicable under section 178 shall, [except where regulation 3ZA or 3ZB applies and][2] subject to paragraph(2), be 6.25 per cent per annum.

(2) Where, on a reference date after 1st October 1993, the reference rate found on that date differs from the established rate, the rate applicable under section 178 for the purposes of the enactment referred to in paragraph (1) shall, on and after the next operative date, be the percentage per annum found by applying the formula specified in paragraph (3) . . . [3]

[(3) The formula specified in this paragraph is—

$$RR + 2.5$$

where RR is the reference rate referred to in paragraph (2).][3]][1]

Note—The rate of interest under this Regulation changes periodically in accordance with the specified formula. Changes are announced by HMRC press release. The rate applicable at any given time can be obtained from *Simon's Taxes*, Binder 1 and from *Simon's Weekly Tax Intelligence*.

Amendments—[1] This regulation inserted by the Taxes (Interest Rate) (Amendment No 3) Regulations, SI 1993/2212 with effect from 1 October 1993.

[2] Words in para (1) inserted by the Taxes (Interest Rate) (Amendment No 2) Regulations, SI 1998/3176 reg 5 with effect for accounting periods ending on or after 1 July 1999 by virtue of FA 1994 s 199 (Appointed Day) Order, SI 1998/3173 art 2.

[3] In para (2), words revoked, and para (3) substituted, by the Taxes and Duties (Interest Rate) (Amendment) Regulations, SI 2009/2032 regs 2, 8 with effect from 12 August 2009.

[3AAA—(1) For the purposes of—

(*a*) paragraph 16 of Schedule 2 to the Oil Taxation Act 1975,

(*b*) paragraph 59 of Schedule 8 to the Development Land Tax Act 1976, and

(*c*) section 825 of, and paragraph 3 of Schedule 19A to, the Income and Corporation Taxes Act 1988,

the rate applicable under section 178 shall, subject to paragraph (3), be the percentage per annum found by applying the formula specified in paragraph (2), but if the result is not a multiple of one-quarter the result shall be rounded down to the nearest amount which is such a multiple.

(2) The formula specified for the purposes of paragraph (1) is—

$$((RR + 2.5) \times 80) / 100$$

where RR is the official bank rate determined at the meeting of the Monetary Policy Committee of the Bank of England which immediately preceded the coming into force of these Regulations.

(3) Where on a reference date after the coming into force of these Regulations, the reference rate found on that date differs from the established rate, the rate applicable under section 178 for the purposes of the enactments referred to in paragraph (1) shall, on and after the next operative date, be the higher of—

(*a*) 0.5% per annum, and

(*b*) the percentage per annum found by applying the formula specified in paragraph (4).

(4) The formula specified in this paragraph is—

$$RR - 1$$

where RR is the reference rate referred to in paragraph (3).][1]

Amendments—[1] Regulation inserted, by the Taxes and Duties (Interest Rate) (Amendment) Regulations, SI 2009/2032 regs 2, 6 with effect from 12 August 2009.

[3ZA—(1) For the purposes of section 87A of the Taxes Management Act 1970 in so far as it relates, by virtue of subsection (1A) of that section, to an amount or amounts treated as becoming due and payable in respect of the total liability of a large company for an accounting period ending on or after 1st July 1999 in accordance with regulation 5 of the 1998 Regulations, the rate applicable under section 178 shall, subject to paragraph (2), be 8.25 per cent per annum.

(2) Where on a reference date after 7th January 1999 the reference rate found on that date differs from the established rate, the rate applicable under section 178 for the purposes mentioned in paragraph (1) shall, on and after the next operative date and as respects the period specified in paragraph (3), be the percentage per annum found by applying the formula specified in paragraph (4).

(3) The period specified in this paragraph is any period falling between—

(*a*) the date on which the first instalment payment is treated as becoming due and payable for the accounting period concerned under regulation 5 of the 1998 Regulations, and

(*b*) the day following the expiry of nine months from the end of that accounting period,

during which any amount treated as becoming due and payable in accordance with regulation 5 of those Regulations for that accounting period remains unpaid.

(4) The formula specified in this paragraph is—

$$[RR + 1]$$

,[2]

where RR is the reference rate referred to in paragraph (2).][1]

Amendments—[1] This regulation inserted by the Taxes (Interest Rate) (Amendment No 2) Regulations, SI 1998/3176 reg 6 with effect for accounting periods ending on or after 1 July 1999 by virtue of FA 1994 s 199 (Appointed Day) Order, SI 1998/3173 art 2.

2 Formula substituted by the Taxes (Interest Rate) (Amendment) Regulations, SI 2000/893 reg 2(1), with effect as from 20 April 2000 in relation to interest running from before that day as well as to interest running from, or from after, that day.

[3ZB—(1) For the purposes of section 87A of the Taxes Management Act 1970 in so far as it relates to an unpaid amount in respect of the total liability of a company for an accounting period ending on or after 1st July 1999, other than an amount to which regulation 3ZA applies, the rate applicable under section 178 shall, subject to paragraph (2), be 8.5 per cent per annum.

(2) Where on a reference date after 7th January 1999 the reference rate found on that date differs from the established rate, the rate applicable under section 178 for the purposes mentioned in paragraph (1) shall, on and after the next operative date, be the percentage per annum found by applying the formula specified in paragraph (3).

(3) The formula specified in this paragraph is—

$$RR + 2.5$$

where RR is the reference rate referred to in paragraph (2).] [1]

Amendments—[1] This regulation inserted by the Taxes (Interest Rate) (Amendment No 2) Regulations, SI 1998/3176 reg 6 with effect for accounting periods ending on or after 1 July 1999 by virtue of FA 1994 s 199 (Appointed Day) Order, SI 1998/3173 art 2.

3B [Applicable rate of interest on tax overpaid

(1) For the purposes of section 826 of the Income and Corporation Taxes Act 1988 the rate applicable under section 178 shall, [except where regulation 3BA or 3BB applies and][2] subject to paragraph(2), be 3·25 per cent per annum.

(2) Where, on a reference date after 1st October 1993, the reference rate found on that date differs from the established rate, the rate applicable under section 178 for the purposes of the enactment referred to in paragraph (1) shall, on and after the next operative date, be the [higher of—

(*a*) 0.5% per annum, and

(*b*) the percentage per annum found by applying the formula specified in paragraph (3).][3]

[(3) The formula specified in this paragraph is—

$$RR - 1$$

where RR is the reference rate referred to in paragraph (2).][3]][1]

Note—The rate of interest under this Regulation changes periodically in accordance with the specified formula. Changes are announced by HMRC press release. The rate applicable at any given time can be obtained from *Simon's Taxes*, Binder 1 and from *Simon's Weekly Tax Intelligence*.

Amendments—[1] This regulation inserted by the Taxes (Interest Rate) (Amendment No 3) Regulations, SI 1993/2212 with effect from 1 October 1993.

2 Words in para (1) inserted by the Taxes (Interest Rate) (Amendment No 2) Regulations, SI 1998/3176 reg 5 with effect for accounting periods ending on or after 1 July 1999 by virtue of FA 1994 s 199 (Appointed Day) Order, SI 1998/3173 art 2.

3 In para (2), words substituted, and para (3) substituted, by the Taxes and Duties (Interest Rate) (Amendment) Regulations, SI 2009/2032 regs 2, 9 with effect from 12 August 2009.

[3BA—(1) For the purposes of section 826 of the Income and Corporation Taxes Act 1988 in so far as it relates to an amount paid by a company in respect of its total liability for an accounting period ending on or after 1st July 1999, being an amount falling within paragraph (*d*) of subsection (1) of that section (overpayment of instalment by large company under regulation 5 of the 1998 Regulations) or an amount falling within paragraph (*e*) of that subsection (payment by company other than large company prior to the day following the expiry of nine months from the end of the accounting period concerned), the rate applicable under section 178 shall, subject to paragraph (2), be 6 per cent per annum.

(2) Where on a reference date after 7th January 1999 the reference rate found on that date differs from the established rate, the rate applicable under section 178 for the purposes mentioned in paragraph (1) shall, on and after the next operative date and as respects the period specified in paragraph (3), be the [higher of—

(*a*) 0.5% per annum, and

(*b*) the percentage per annum found by applying the formula specified in paragraph (4).][2]

(3) The period specified in this paragraph is any period falling between—

(*a*) the date on which the first instalment payment is treated as becoming due and payable for the accounting period concerned under regulation 5 of the 1998 Regulations or, in the case of a company other than a large company, the date on which the first instalment payment would be so treated if the company were a large company, and

(*b*) the day following the expiry of nine months from the end of that accounting period,

during which there exists an amount paid by the company in respect of its total liability to which paragraph (1) applies.

(4) The formula specified in this paragraph is—

$$RR - 0.25$$

where RR is the reference rate referred to in paragraph (2).] [1]

Amendments—[1] This regulation inserted by the Taxes (Interest Rate) (Amendment No 2) Regulations, SI 1998/3176 reg 8 with effect for accounting periods ending after 30 June 1999 by virtue of FA 1994 s 199 (Appointed Day) Order, SI 1998/3173 art 2.

[2] In para (2), words substituted, by the Taxes and Duties (Interest Rate) (Amendment) Regulations, SI 2009/2032 regs 2, 10 with effect from 12 August 2009.

[3BB—(1) For the purposes of section 826 of the Income and Corporation Taxes Act 1988 in so far as it relates to an amount overpaid by a company in respect of its total liability for an accounting period ending on or after 1st July 1999, being an amount paid[, or which remains overpaid,][2] on or after the day following the expiry of nine months from the end of that period, the rate applicable under section 178 shall, subject to paragraph (2) [and on and after that day][2], be 5 per cent per annum.

(2) Where on a reference date after 7th January 1999 the reference rate found on that date differs from the established rate, the rate applicable under section 178 for the purposes mentioned in paragraph (1) shall, on and after the next operative date, be the [higher of—

(*a*) 0.5% per annum, and

(*b*) the percentage per annum found by applying the formula specified in paragraph (3).][3]

(3) The formula specified in this paragraph is—

$$RR - 1$$

where RR is the reference rate referred to in paragraph (2).][1]

Amendments—[1] This regulation inserted by the Taxes (Interest Rate) (Amendment No 2) Regulations, SI 1998/3176 reg 8 with effect for accounting periods ending on or after 1 July 1999 by virtue of FA 1994 s 199 (Appointed Day) Order, SI 1998/3173 art 2.

[2] Words in para (1) inserted by the Taxes (Interest Rate) (Amendment No 2) Regulations, SI 1999/1928 regs 1, 3 with effect from 28 July 1999.

[3] In para (2), words substituted, by the Taxes and Duties (Interest Rate) (Amendment) Regulations, SI 2009/2032 regs 2, 11 with effect from 12 August 2009.

4 . . .

Note—This regulation is reproduced in the IHT section of this publication.

5 [Applicable rate of official rate of interest

[(1) Subject to paragraph (2), the rate applicable under section 178 for the purposes of Chapter 7 of Part 3 of the Income Tax (Earnings and Pensions) Act 2003 ("Chapter 7") shall, [on and after 6th April 2017, be 2.50 per cent per annum][4] .][3]

(2) In relation to a loan outstanding for the whole or part of a year of assessment where—

(*a*) the loan was made in the currency of a country or territory specified in the Table below,

(*b*) the benefit of the loan is obtained by reason of the employment of a person who normally lives in that country or territory, and

(*c*) that person has lived in that country or territory at some time in the period of six years ending with that year,

the rate applicable under section 178 for the purposes of [Chapter 7][3] and the date on and after which that rate has effect shall be ascertained from the entries in the Table below relating to the country or territory concerned.

TABLE

Country or territory	*Date on and after which applicable rate has effect*	*Applicable rate*
Japan	6th June 1994	3·9 per cent per annum
Switzerland	[6th July 1994][2]	[5·5 per cent per annum][2]][1]

Notes—The rate of interest under this Regulation is subject to occasional changes made by statutory instruments. The rate applicable at any given time may be obtained from *Simon's Taxes*, Binder 1 and from *Simon's Weekly Tax Intelligence*.

TA 1988 s 160 has been replaced by ITEPA 2003 s 181.

Amendments—[1] This regulation substituted by the Taxes (Interest Rate) (Amendment) Regulations, SI 1994/1307.

[2] Words and percentage in Table substituted by SI 1994/1567.

[3] Para (1) substituted, and in para (2), words substituted for words "section 181", by the Taxes (Interest Rate) (Amendment) Regulations, SI 2009/199 reg 2 with effect from 1 March 2009.

[4] Words in para (1) substituted by the Taxes (Interest Rate) (Amendment) Regulations, SI 2017/305 reg 2 with effect from 6 April 2017.

6 Effect of change in applicable rate

Where the rate applicable under section 178 for the purpose of any of the enactments referred to in [these Regulations][1] changes on an operative date by virtue of these Regulations, that change shall have effect for periods beginning on or after the operative date in relation to interest running from before that date as well as from or from after that date.

Amendments—[1] Words substituted by the Taxes and Duties (Interest Rate) (Amendment) Regulations, SI 2009/2032 regs 2, 14 with effect from 12 August 2009.

1989/1299

INCOME TAX (STOCK LENDING) REGULATIONS 1989

Revocation—These Regulations revoked by the Stock Lending and Manufactured Payments (Revocations and Amendments) Regulations, SI 1997/987, reg 2, Sch 1, with effect from 1 July 1997 except in relation to any arrangement mentioned in TA 1988 s 129(1), (2) or (2A) (Stock lending) that is entered into before that date.

1989/2387

PRIVATE MEDICAL INSURANCE (TAX RELIEF) REGULATIONS 1989

Note—These Regulations lapsed on the repeal of the enabling power by F(No 2)A 1997 s 52, Sch 8, Pt II(2), with effect for the year 1997–98 and subsequent years of assessment, except in relation to the cases in which the relief that has been or may be given under FA 1989 s 54 in respect of any payment is unaffected by the provisions of F(No 2)A 1997 s 17(1).

1990/1671

MOVEMENTS OF CAPITAL (REQUIRED INFORMATION) REGULATIONS 1990

Made by the Commissioners of Inland Revenue under TA 1988 s 765A(2)

Made . . . . *10 August 1990*
Laid before the House of Commons . . . . *13 August 1990*
Coming into Force . . . . *3 September 1990*

Statement of Practice SP 2/92 para 23—Certain presumptions to apply to determine a company's residence in a member State.

Press releases etc—IR 9-2-94 (per EEA Agreement, these Regulations apply to movements of capital between persons resident in member States on or after 1 January 1994).

1 Citation and commencement

These Regulations may be cited as the Movements of Capital (Required Information) Regulations 1990 and shall come into force on 3rd September 1990.

2 Interpretation

In these Regulations unless the context otherwise requires—

"the Board" means the Commissioners of Inland Revenue;

"control" has, in relation to a body corporate, the meaning given by section 840 of the Income and Corporation Taxes Act 1988;

"the Directive" means the Directive of the Council of the European Communities dated 24th June 1988/88/361/EEC;

"the non-resident body corporate" means the body corporate which is not resident in the United Kingdom and created or issued shares or debentures, or the shares or debentures of which were transferred to any person, in the course of a relevant transaction;

"the principal section" means section 765A of the Income and Corporation Taxes Act 1988;

"relevant transaction" means a movement of capital which would be unlawful under section 765(1) of the Income and Corporation Taxes Act 1988 if Article 1 of the Directive did not apply to it;

"the resident body corporate" means the body corporate resident in the United Kingdom which has carried out a relevant transaction;

and any question whether a person is connected with another shall be determined in accordance with the like provisions as are contained in section 839(2) to (8) of the Income and Corporation Taxes Act 1988.

3 Information required for the purposes of the principal section

(1) This regulation specifies the information relating to a relevant transaction and the persons connected with it (in this regulation referred to as "the required information") which, subject to paragraph (5) below, is required to be given to the Board by the resident body corporate within six months of the carrying out of a relevant transaction.

(2) The required information so far as it relates to the resident body corporate is—
(*a*) its name;
(*b*) the nature of its trade or business;
(*c*) the tax office to which its accounts are submitted and its reference number there.
(3) The required information so far as it relates to the non-resident body corporate is—
(*a*) its name;
(*b*) the territory from the laws of which it derives its status as a body corporate;
(*c*) where the relevant transaction was causing or permitting the non-resident body corporate to issue shares, or to create and issue debentures, the member State in which the non-resident body corporate is claimed to have been resident for the purposes of the Directive at the time of that issue, or of that creation and issue, as the case may be, the grounds on which that claim is made and the facts which support it;
(*d*) the nature of its trade or business;
(*e*) the extent to which the resident body corporate has control over it and the means by which, or the powers by virtue of which, that control is exercisable—
(i) before the relevant transaction was carried out, and
(ii) after the relevant transaction was carried out.

(4) The required information so far as it relates to the relevant transaction is a full description of the transaction and of all steps taken in the course of the transaction and, without prejudice to the generality of that requirement, includes in particular—
(*a*) the date on which the transaction was carried out;
(*b*) the name of any person to whom shares or debentures were issued or transferred;
(*c*) where that person is a body corporate, the territory from the laws of which it derives that status;
(*d*) the member State in which that person is claimed to have been resident for the purposes of the Directive at the time of the issue or transfer, the grounds on which that claim is made and the facts which support it;
(*e*) whether, and if so in what way, any such person is connected with the resident body corporate;
(*f*) where the relevant transaction was causing or permitting the non-resident body corporate to issue shares—
(i) the class or category of those shares,
(ii) the dividend rights attaching to them, and
(iii) if the terms on which they were issued included provision for their redemption, the circumstances in which they can be redeemed;
(*g*) where the relevant transaction was causing or permitting the non-resident body corporate to create and issue debentures—
(i) the rate at which interest is payable on the amount secured by them,
(ii) any amount by which the issue price was less than the amount payable on their redemption, and
(iii) whether any amount payable in respect of the debentures is determined by reference to the movement of an index of prices, earnings or any other indicator of an economic nature published in the United Kingdom or elsewhere;
(*h*) where the relevant transaction was transferring shares or debentures, or causing or permitting shares or debentures to be transferred—
(i) the name of any body corporate making the transfer if that body corporate was not the resident body corporate,
(ii) the territory from the laws of which that body corporate derives that status,
(iii) the member State in which it is claimed to have been resident for the purposes of the Directive at the time of the transfer, the grounds on which that claim is made and the facts which support it;
(*i*) the consideration given for any issue or transfer of shares or debentures and, if that issue or transfer was not for full consideration in money or money's worth, the reason why full consideration was not given;
(*j*) the reason for the transaction and an estimate of the effect of that transaction on the liability to tax in the United Kingdom of the resident body corporate and of any company which would be deemed to be a member of the group of companies which includes the resident body corporate for the purposes of Chapter IV of Part X of the Income and Corporation Taxes Act 1988 if in section 413(3) of that Act the words "51 per cent subsidiary" were substituted for the words "75 per cent subsidiary".

(5) Where a resident body corporate has caused or permitted shares or debentures to be created, issued or transferred, or has transferred shares or debentures, and another resident body corporate has already given the required information relating to the creation, issue or transfer in question and the persons connected with it, the first mentioned resident body corporate is not required to give any information relating to those matters or those persons.

Statement of Practice SP 2/92 para 23—Certain presumptions to apply to determine a company's residence in a member State.

4 Notice to give further particulars—prescribed period

The period prescribed by this regulation within which the resident body corporate shall give to the Board such further particulars as the Board may require in accordance with subsection (2)(*b*) of the principal section is 60 days from the date of the notice given by the Board under that subsection.

1992/10

INCOME TAX (BUILDING SOCIETIES) (AUDIT POWERS) REGULATIONS 1992

Made by the Commissioners of Inland Revenue under TA 1988 ss 477A(1), (2), 482A

Made . . . . .8 *January 1992*
Laid before the House of Commons . . . . .9 *January 1992*
Coming into Force . . . . .30 *January 1992*

Revocation—These regulations revoked by the Income Tax (Deposit-takers and Building Societies) (Interest Payments) Regulations, SI 2008/2682 reg 20, Sch 3 with effect in relation to payments of interest made on or after 31 October 2008 and subject to savings in Sch 2.

1992/12

INCOME TAX (DEPOSIT-TAKERS) (AUDIT POWERS) REGULATIONS 1992

Made by the Commissioners of Inland Revenue under TA 1988 ss 482(11)(*aa*), (12), 482A

Made . . . . .8 *January 1992*
Laid before the House of Commons . . . . .9 *January 1992*
Coming into Force . . . . .30 *January 1992*

Revocation—These regulations revoked by the Income Tax (Deposit-takers and Building Societies) (Interest Payments) Regulations, SI 2008/2682 reg 20, Sch 3 with effect in relation to payments of interest made on or after 31 October 2008 and subject to savings in Sch 2.

1992/14

INCOME TAX (DEPOSIT-TAKERS) (NON-RESIDENTS) REGULATIONS 1992

Made by the Commissioners of Inland Revenue under TA 1988 s 482(11), (12)

Made . . . . .8 *January 1992*
Laid before the House of Commons . . . . .9 *January 1992*
Coming into Force . . . . .30 *January 1992*

Revocation—These regulations revoked by the Income Tax (Deposit-takers and Building Societies) (Interest Payments) Regulations, SI 2008/2682 reg 20, Sch 3 with effect in relation to payments of interest made on or after 31 October 2008 and subject to savings in Sch 2.

1992/15

INCOME TAX (INTEREST PAYMENTS) (INFORMATION POWERS) REGULATIONS 1992

Made by the Commissioners of Inland Revenue under TMA 1970 ss 17(5), (6), 18(3B), (3C)

Made . . . . .8 *January 1992*
Laid before the House of Commons . . . . .9 *January 1992*
Coming into Force . . . . .30 *January 1992*

Revocation—These Regulations revoked by the Reporting of Savings Income and Interest Payments (Data-gathering) Regulations, SI 2012/756 reg 3(*a*) with effect from 31 March 2012.

1992/42

TAXES (RELIEF FOR GIFTS) (DESIGNATED EDUCATIONAL ESTABLISHMENTS) REGULATIONS 1992

Made by the Secretary of State for Education and Science for England and the Secretaries of State for Scotland and Wales under TA 1988 s 84

Made . . . . .10 *January 1992*
Laid before the House of Commons . . . . .14 *January 1992*
Coming into Force . . . . .4 *February 1992*

1 These Regulations may be cited as the Taxes (Relief for Gifts) (Designated Educational Establishments) Regulations 1992 and shall come into force on 4th February 1992.

2—(1) In these Regulations—

"charity" has the same meaning as in section 506 of the Income and Corporation Taxes Act 1988 and a charity is an educational charity if the charitable purposes for which it is established are exclusively educational purposes;

["the Education Acts" has the meaning given in section 578 of the Education Act 1996;][1]

"the 1980 Act" means the Education (Scotland) Act 1980; and

"the 1989 Act" means the Self-Governing Schools etc (Scotland) Act 1989.

(2) Expressions used in these Regulations in relation to educational establishments in England and Wales have the same meaning as in the Education Acts . . .[1].

(3) Expressions used in these Regulations in relation to educational establishments in Scotland have the same meaning as in the 1980 Act or the 1989 Act.

Amendments—[1] In para (1) definition of "the Education Acts" inserted, and in para (2) words "1944 to 1992" revoked, by the Alternative Provision Academies and 16 to 19 Academies (Consequential Amendments to Subordinate Legislation) (England) Order, SI 2012/979 art 2, Schedule para 3(1), (2) with effect from 1 May 2012 in relation to England only.

3 The educational establishments and categories of educational establishments specified in the Schedule to these Regulations are hereby designated for the purposes of section 84 of the Income and Corporation Taxes Act 1988.

SCHEDULE

Regulation 3

PART I

SCHOOLS: ENGLAND AND WALES

1 Any school maintained by a [local authority][1].

Amendments—[1] Words substituted by the Local Education Authorities and Children's Services Authorities (Integration of Functions) (Local and Subordinate Legislation) Order SI 2010/1172 art 4, Sch 3 para 26(1), (2) with effect from 5 May 2010: see SI 2010/1172 art 2(1).

2 Any grant-maintained school.

3 Any special school not maintained by a [local authority][1].

Amendments—[1] Words substituted by the Local Education Authorities and Children's Services Authorities (Integration of Functions) (Local and Subordinate Legislation) Order SI 2010/1172 art 4, Sch 3 para 26(1), (2) with effect from 5 May 2010: see SI 2010/1172 art 2(1).

[**4** Any independent school, or any alternative provision Academy that is not an independent school, that—

(*a*) is on the register of independent schools in England; and

(*b*) is conducted by an educational charity.][1]

Amendments—[1] Para 4 substituted by the Alternative Provision Academies and 16 to 19 Academies (Consequential Amendments to Subordinate Legislation) (England) Order, SI 2012/979 art 2, Schedule para 3(1), (3)(*a*) with effect from 1 May 2012 in relation to England only. Para 4 previously read as follows—

> "**4** Any independent school registered pursuant to section 70 of the Education Act 1944 which is conducted by an educational charity.".

5 Any school maintained by the Service Children's Education Authority.

6 The European School established under Article 1 of the Statute of the European School, any school designated as a European School under Article 1 of the Protocol to that Statute and the European School established under article 1 of the Supplementary Protocol to that Statute.

7 Any nursery school recognised by the Secretary of State for the purpose of receiving grant under regulation 5 of the Direct Grant Schools Regulations 1959.

PART II

SCHOOLS: SCOTLAND

1 Any public school.

2 Any self-governing school.

3 Any grant-aided school.

4 Any independent school managed by an educational charity.

PART III

ESTABLISHMENTS OF FURTHER AND HIGHER EDUCATION: ENGLAND AND WALES

1 Any university.

2 [Any institution within the higher education sector (within the meaning of section 91(5) of the Further and Higher Education Act 1992) other than a university.][1]

Amendments—[1] This paragraph substituted by the Taxes (Relief for Gifts) (Designated Educational Establishments) (Amendment) Regulations, SI 1993/561, with effect from 1 April 1993.

3 . . .

Amendments—This paragraph revoked by the Taxes (Relief for Gifts) (Designated Educational Establishments) (Amendment) Regulations, SI 1993/561, with effect from 1 April 1993.

4 [Any institution of further or higher education (or both) maintained or assisted by a [local authority][2] or in receipt of grant under regulations made under section 100(1)(b) of the Education Act 1944.][1]

Amendments—[1] This paragraph substituted by the Taxes (Relief for Gifts) (Designated Educational Establishments) (Amendment) Regulations, SI 1993/561, with effect from 1 April 1993.

[2] Words substituted by the Local Education Authorities and Children's Services Authorities (Integration of Functions) (Local and Subordinate Legislation) Order SI 2010/1172 art 4, Sch 3 para 26(3) with effect from 5 May 2010: see SI 2010/1172 art 2(1).

5 [Any institution within the further education sector (within the meaning of section 91(3) of the Further and Higher Education Act 1992).][1]

Amendments—[1] This paragraph substituted by the Taxes (Relief for Gifts) (Designated Educational Establishments) (Amendment) Regulations, SI 1993/561, with effect from 1 April 1993.

[**5A** Any 16 to 19 Academy.][1]

Amendments—[1] Para 5A inserted by the Alternative Provision Academies and 16 to 19 Academies (Consequential Amendments to Subordinate Legislation) (England) Order, SI 2012/979 art 2, Schedule para 3(1), (3)(*b*) with effect from 1 May 2012 in relation to England only.

6–22 . . .

Amendments—Paras 6–22 revoked by the Taxes (Relief for Gifts) (Designated Educational Establishments) (Amendment) Regulations, SI 1993/561, with effect from 1 April 1993.

23 Any other establishment providing further or higher education (or both) which is conducted by an educational charity.

PART IV

ESTABLISHMENTS OF FURTHER AND HIGHER EDUCATION: SCOTLAND

1 Any university.

2 Any central institution, college of education or any institution established under section 77 of the 1980 Act.

3 Any establishment for the provision of further education under the management of—

(*a*) an education authority, or

(*b*) a company by virtue of section 65 of the 1989 Act.

4 Any other establishment for the provision of further or higher education (or both) managed by an educational charity.

1992/2326

INSURANCE COMPANIES (PENSION BUSINESS) (TRANSITIONAL PROVISIONS) REGULATIONS 1992

Made by the Commissioners of Inland Revenue under TA 1988 Sch 19AB paras 4, 5(4)

Made . . . . *29 September 1992*
Laid before the House of Commons . . . . *30 September 1992*
Coming into Force . . . . *2 October 1992*

Commentary—*Simon's Taxes* **D7.551.**

1 Citation and commencement

These Regulations may be cited as the Insurance Companies ([Pension][1] Business) (Transitional Provisions) Regulations 1992 and shall come into force on 2nd October 1992.

Amendments—[1] Word substituted by the Insurance Companies (Pension Business) (Transitional Provisions) (Amendment) Regulations, SI 1996/1 reg 3, with effect from 24 January 1996.

2 Interpretation

In these Regulations unless the context otherwise requires—

"accounting period" means any accounting period in relation to which Schedule 19AB has effect;

"the Board" means the Commissioners of Inland Revenue;

"the closing transitional date" shall be construed in accordance with regulation 3(2);

"the corresponding accounting period", in relation to a provisional repayment period, is the accounting period in which that provisional repayment period falls;

"insurance company" means a company to which Part II of the Insurance Companies Act 1982 applies;

"the Management Act" means the Taxes Management Act 1970;
"maximum reduced entitlement" has the meaning given by paragraph 4(6) of Schedule 19AB;
["notional repayment" shall be construed in accordance with paragraph 1A of Schedule 19AB (treated as inserted by regulation 6 of the Insurance Companies (Gilt-edged Securities) (Periodic Accounting for Tax on Interest) Regulations 1995 and, in relation to a notional repayment, "provisional repayment period" shall be construed in accordance with that paragraph of that Schedule;][1]
"the opening transitional date" shall be construed in accordance with regulation 3(1);
"paragraph 4" and "paragraph 5" mean, respectively, paragraph 4 and paragraph 5 of Schedule 19AB;
"provisional repayment" has the meaning given by paragraph 6(1) of Schedule 19AB and[, in relation to a provisional repayment,][1] "provisional repayment period" shall be construed in accordance with paragraph 1 of that Schedule;
"Schedule 19AB" means Schedule 19AB to the Taxes Act;
"the Taxes Act" means the Income and Corporation Taxes Act 1988.

Amendments—[1] Definition "notional repayment" and words in definition of "provisional repayment" inserted by the Insurance Companies (Pension Business) (Transitional Provisions) (Amendment) Regulations, SI 1996/1 reg 4, with effect from 24 January 1996.

3 Specification of "the opening transitional date" and "the closing transitional date"

(1) The date specified by these Regulations as "the opening transitional date" for the purpose of paragraph 4 is 2nd October 1992.

(2) The date specified by these Regulations as "the closing transitional date" for the purpose of paragraph 4 is 1st January 1999.

4 Reduction of provisional repayment by prescribed percentage

(1) This regulation prescribes the percentage by which the amount of any provisional repayment [or any notional repayment][4] to which an insurance company would otherwise be entitled under Schedule 19AB for any [of the accounting periods specified in paragraphs (2) to (5) (being accounting periods ending after the opening transitional date and before the closing transitional date) shall be reduced.][4]

[(2) The prescribed percentage is 7·5 per cent for an accounting period ending after 2nd October 1992 and before 1st January 1994.][1]

[(3) The prescribed percentage is 12·5 per cent for an accounting period ending after 31st December 1993 and before 1st January 1995.][2]

[(4) The prescribed percentage is 10 per cent for an accounting period ending after 31st December 1994 and before 1st January 1996.][3]

[(5) The prescribed percentage is 7·5 per cent for an accounting period ending after 31st December 1995 and before 1st January 1998.][5]

Amendments—[1] Para (2) substituted by the Insurance Companies (Pension Business) (Transitional Provisions) (Amendment) Regulations, SI 1993/3109.

[2] Para (3) substituted by the Insurance Companies (Pension Business) (Transitional Provisions) (Amendment) Regulations, SI 1994/3036 reg 2, with effect from 21 December 1994.

[3] Para (4) substituted (as substituted by SI 1994/3036 reg 2) by the Insurance Companies (Pension Business) (Transitional Provisions) (Amendment) Regulations, SI 1995/3134 reg 2, with effect from 31 December 1995.

[4] Words in para (1) inserted by the Insurance Companies (Pension Business) (Transitional Provisions) (Amendment) Regulations, SI 1996/1 reg 5, with effect from 24 January 1996 and the Insurance Companies (Pension Business) (Transitional Provisions) (Amendment) Regulations, SI 1997/2865 reg 3 with effect from 31 December 1997.

[5] Para (5) substituted by SI 1997/2865 reg 3(*b*), with effect from 31 December 1997.

5 Requirements to be specified in claim for provisional repayment

An insurance company claiming a provisional repayment [or a notional repayment][1] for a provisional repayment period falling within any accounting period [specified in regulation 4][2] shall specify in the claim—

(*a*) the maximum amount to which it could have been entitled by way of provisional repayment [or notional repayment][1] for that provisional repayment period apart from these Regulations;

(*b*) the maximum reduced entitlement for that provisional repayment period; and

(*c*) the amount of the provisional repayment [or the notional repayment][1] claimed for that provisional repayment period.

Amendments—[1] Words inserted by the Insurance Companies (Pension Business) (Transitional Provisions) (Amendment) Regulations, SI 1996/1 reg 6, with effect from 24 January 1996.

[2] Words substituted by the Insurance Companies (Pension Business) (Transitional Provisions) (Amendment) Regulations, SI 1997/2865 reg 4, with effect from 31 December 1997.

6 Interest where a provisional repayment exceeds the maximum reduced entitlement for a provisional repayment period

(1) [Where, in relation to a provisional repayment period falling within an accounting period specified in regulation 4, an insurance company claims, and is paid, by way of provisional repayment an amount in excess of the maximum reduced entitlement for that period][2], interest shall be charged for the period specified in paragraph (2) at the rate specified in paragraph (3).

(2) The period specified in this paragraph is a period beginning on the date on which the amount of the excess is paid to the company and ending on the first occurrence of any of the following—

(*a*) the date on which that amount is repaid to the Board;

(*b*) the date on which the company becomes entitled to that amount when effect is given to a claim such as is mentioned in section 7(6) of the Taxes Act, in section 42(5A) of the Management Act or in sub-paragraph (2) of paragraph 5, made in respect of the corresponding accounting period; [and][1]

(*c*) the date on which the company becomes entitled to that amount when the assessment to corporation tax for the corresponding accounting period becomes final and conclusive.

(3) The rate specified in this paragraph is the rate applicable under section 178 of the Finance Act 1989 for the purposes of section 87A of the Management Act.

(4) Interest charged by virtue of paragraph (1) shall be treated for the purposes of section 30 of the Management Act as if it were an amount of corporation tax which had been repaid and which ought not to have been repaid.

(5) In relation to an amount assessed to corporation tax under section 30 of the Management Act by virtue of these Regulations, section 87A of that Act shall apply with the modifications specified in paragraph (6).

(6) The modifications specified in this paragraph are that—

(*a*) the amount assessed to corporation tax under section 30 of the Management Act by virtue of these Regulations shall be taken to have become due and payable on the date on which that assessment was made; and

(*b*) the words "(in accordance with section 10 of the principal Act)" in subsection (1) shall accordingly be disregarded.

Amendments—[1] "and" substituted for "or" in para (2)(*b*) by the Insurance Companies (Pension Business) (Transitional Provisions) (Amendment) Regulations, SI 1993/3109.

[2] Words in para (1) substituted by the Insurance Companies (Pension Business) (Transitional Provisions) (Amendment) Regulations, SI 1997/2865 reg 5, with effect from 31 December 1997.

7 Claims during transitional application of pay and file provisions

A claim under sub-paragraph (2) of paragraph 5 shall be made at the time of the delivery of the return under section 11 of the Management Act for the accounting period to which the claim relates.

1992/2744

INCOME TAX (INSURANCE COMPANIES) (EXPENSES OF MANAGEMENT) REGULATIONS 1992

Note—These Regulations lapsed on the repeal of the enabling authority by SI 2001/3629, arts 13, 16(1), as from 1 December 2001.

1992/3066

CORPORATION TAX ACTS (PROVISIONS FOR PAYMENT OF TAX AND RETURNS) (APPOINTED DAYS) ORDER 1992

Made by the Treasury under F(No 2)A 1987 ss 82(1), 83, 85, 86(7), 88(7), 91(4), 95(2), (3), Sch 6 para 7, TA 1988 ss 8(3), 10(1)(a), 252(4), 419(1), (3), 584(10), 826(1), (8), (9), FA 1989 s 102(9), TCGA 1992 ss 137(5), 139(8), 180(1)(b), 189(6), 190(6)

Made . . . . 7 December 1992

1 This Order may be cited as the Corporation Tax Acts (Provisions for Payment of Tax and Returns) (Appointed Days) Order 1992.

2—(1) The day appointed for the purposes of the enactments specified in paragraph (2) of this article is 30th September 1993.

(2) The enactments specified in this paragraph are—

(*a*) sections 85, 86, 88 and 91 of, and paragraph 7 of Schedule 6 to, the Finance (No 2) Act 1987;

(*b*) sections 8(3), 10, 252(2) and (3), 419(1) and (3), 584(1), (2) and (5) to (10), and 826, of the Income and Corporation Taxes Act 1988;

(*c*) section 102 of the Finance Act 1989;

(*d*) sections 137(5), 139(8), 179, 189 and 190 of the Taxation of Chargeable Gains Act 1992.

3—(1) The day appointed for the purposes of the enactments specified in paragraph (2) of this article is 31st December 1993.
(2) The enactments specified in this paragraph are sections 82 and 83 of the Finance (No 2) Act 1987.

1992/3234

INCOME TAX (PRESCRIBED DEPOSIT-TAKERS) ORDER 1992

Amendment—This Order revoked by ITA 2007, s 1031, Sch 3 Pt 1, with effect for income tax purposes from 6 April 2007, and corporation tax purposes for accounting periods ending after 5 April 2007.

1993/743

INCOME TAX (SUB-CONTRACTORS IN THE CONSTRUCTION INDUSTRY) REGULATIONS 1993

Revocation—These regulations revoked by the Income Tax (Construction Industry Scheme) Regulations, SI 2005/2045 reg 60, Sch 2 with effect from 7 April 2007 (as notified in the London, Edinburgh and Belfast Gazettes, 9 March 2007).

1993/744

INCOME TAX (EMPLOYMENTS) REGULATIONS 1993

Amendment—These regulations are revoked by the Income Tax (Pay As You Earn) Regulations, SI 2003/2682 reg 220, Sch 2 with effect from 6 April 2004, subject to the transitional provisions in Sch 1 thereto.

1993/950

CAPITAL GAINS TAX (GILT-EDGED SECURITIES) ORDER 1993

Made by the Treasury under TCGA 1992 Sch 9 para 1

Made . . . . *30 March 1993*

1 This Order may be cited as the Capital Gains Tax (Gilt-edged Securities) Order 1993.

2 The following securities are hereby specified for the purposes of Schedule 9 to the Taxation of Chargeable Gains Act 1992—
8¾% Treasury Loan 1997 "D"
8¾% Treasury Loan 1997 "E"
4⅝% Index-Linked Treasury Stock 1998
7¼% Treasury Stock 1998
9% Conversion Stock 2000 "C"
9¾% Treasury Stock 2002 "C"
8% Treasury Stock 2003
10% Treasury Stock 2003 "B"
4⅜% Index-Linked Treasury Stock 2004
8½% Treasury Loan 2007 "A"
8½% Treasury Loan 2007 "B"
8% Treasury Stock 2009 "A"
9% Conversion Loan 2011 "B"
9% Treasury Stock 2012
9% Treasury Stock 2012 "A"
8¾% Treasury Stock 2017
8¾% Treasury Stock 2017 "A"
4⅛% Index-Linked Treasury Stock 2030.

1993/1957

DOUBLE TAXATION RELIEF (TAXES ON INCOME) (GENERAL) (MANUFACTURED OVERSEAS DIVIDENDS) REGULATIONS 1993

Amendment—These regulations revoked by the Double Taxation Relief (Manufactured Overseas Dividends) (Revocation) Regulations, SI 2003/2581 with effect from 1 November 2003.

1993/2004

INCOME TAX (MANUFACTURED OVERSEAS DIVIDENDS) REGULATIONS 1993

Made by the Treasury under TA 1988 Sch 23A paras 1(1), 4(6)–(8), 8

Made . . . . *9 August 1993*
Laid before the House of Commons . . . . *9 August 1993*
Coming into Force . . . . *1 October 1993*

Commentary—*Simon's Taxes* **D9.720–D9.728.**

Cross references—See TA 1988 s 737A(5) (sale of securities by a seller and repurchase by him or a connected person).

1 Citation and commencement

These Regulations may be cited as the Income Tax (Manufactured Overseas Dividends) Regulations 1993 and shall come into force on 1st October 1993.

2 Interpretation

[(1)] [3] In these Regulations unless the context otherwise requires—

. . . [2]

"approved United Kingdom collecting agent" means a person who is [a collecting agent . . . [3] and who is][2] resident in the United Kingdom or, if not so resident, is carrying on a trade in the United Kingdom through a [permanent establishment][5] and who [is approved by the Board for the purposes of these Regulations];[2]

"approved United Kingdom intermediary" means an overseas dividend manufacturer who is resident in the United Kingdom or, if not so resident, is carrying on a trade in the United Kingdom through a [permanent establishment][5] and who is [approved as an intermediary by the Board for the purposes of these Regulations][2]

"the Board" means the Commissioners of Inland Revenue;

["chargeable period" has the meaning given by regulation 2A;][1]

["collecting agent" means a person who, in the course of carrying on a trade in the United Kingdom, collects or secures payment of overseas dividends for another person or acts as custodian of any overseas securities;][4]

["foreign permanent establishment payment" means a payment made by a company in the course of a trade carried on through a permanent establishment in a territory outside the United Kingdom where section 18A of the Corporation Tax Act 2009 has effect in relation to the company for the accounting period in which the payment is made;

"foreign permanent establishment receipt" means a receipt by a company for the purposes of a trade carried on by the company through a permanent establishment in a territory outside the United Kingdom where section 18A of the Corporation Tax Act 2009 has effect in relation to the company for the accounting period in which the payment is received;][7]

. . . [5]

"gross amount of the manufactured overseas dividend" has the meaning given by paragraph 4(5)(*b*) of Schedule 23A;

["gross amount of the overseas dividend" has the meaning given by—

(*a*) section 589(4) of the Income Tax Act 2007 for income tax purposes, and

(*b*) section 813(3) of the Corporation Tax Act 2010 for corporation tax purposes;][6]

"the Income Tax Acts" has the meaning given by section 831(1)(*b*) of the Taxes Act;

"the Management Act" means the Taxes Management Act 1970;

"manufactured overseas dividend" shall be construed in accordance with paragraph 4(1) of Schedule 23A;

"overseas dividend", "overseas dividend manufacturer", "overseas securities", "overseas tax" and "overseas tax credit" have the meanings given by paragraph 1(1) of Schedule 23A;

"relevant withholding tax" has the meaning given by paragraph 4(5)(*a*) of Schedule 23A;

"Schedule 23A" means Schedule 23A to the Taxes Act;

"the Taxes Act" means the Income and Corporation Taxes Act 1988;

"the Tax Acts" has the meaning given by section 831(2) of the Taxes Act;

. . . [2]

["United Kingdom recipient" has the meaning given in section 918(5) and (5A) of the Income Tax Act 2007.][7]

[(2) References in regulations 3 to 11, 14 and 15 to manufactured overseas dividends do not include references to manufactured overseas dividends to which regulation 2B applies, and references in those regulations to overseas dividends do not include references to any overseas dividend of which a manufactured overseas dividend to which regulation 2B applies would be representative.][3]

[(3) In these Regulations references to a permanent establishment shall be read, in relation to accounting periods beginning before 1st January 2003, as references to a branch or agency.][5]

Amendments—[1] Definition of "chargeable period" substituted by the IT (Manufactured Overseas Dividends) (Amendment) Regulations, SI 1995/1324 reg 3, with effect from 7 June 1995.

[2] Definitions revoked, words in definitions of "approved United Kingdom collecting agent" and "approved United Kingdom intermediary" inserted or substituted by the IT (Manufactured Overseas Dividends) (Amendment) Regulations, SI 1996/1229 reg 3, with effect from 28 May 1996.

[3] Regulation renumbered as para (1), in definition of "approved United Kingdom collecting agent" words revoked and para (2) added, by the IT (Manufactured Overseas Dividends) (Amendment No 2) Regulations, SI 1996/2643 reg 3, with effect from 6 November 1996.

[4] Definition "collecting agent" substituted by the IT (Manufactured Overseas Dividends) (Amendment) Regulations, SI 2001/403 reg 2, with effect from 9 March 2001 (previously inserted by SI 1996/2643).

[5] Words in definition of "approved United Kingdom intermediary" substituted; definition of "the Double Taxation Regulations" revoked; definition of "United Kingdom recipient" substituted; and para (3) inserted; by the IT (Manufactured Overseas Dividends) (Amendment) Regulations, SI 2003/2582 regs 2, 3 with effect from 1 November 2003.

[6] Definition of "gross amount of the overseas dividend" inserted by the Income Tax (Manufactured Overseas Dividends) (Amendment) Regulations, SI 2010/925 regs 2, 3 with effect in relation to manufactured overseas dividends made or treated as made on or after 14 April 2010.

[7] Definitions of "foreign permanent establishment payment" and "foreign permanent establishment receipt" inserted, and definition of "United Kingdom recipient" substituted, by the Income Tax (Manufactured Overseas Dividends) (Amendment) Regulations, SI 2011/1787 regs 2, 3 with effect in relation to manufactured overseas dividends paid or treated as paid on or after 11 August 2011.

2A [Chargeable period

(1) In these Regulations "chargeable period"—

(*a*) as respects a company, means its accounting period for the purposes of corporation tax;

(*b*) as respects a person other than a company who [draws up accounts for any period ("the accounts period"), means][2] one of the periods specified in paragraph (2) below;

(*c*) as respects a person other than a company who [does not draw up accounts, means a year of assessment][2].

(2) The periods specified in this paragraph are—

(*a*) the period which begins at the beginning of the accounts period and ends at the expiration of 12 months from that date or, if earlier, at the end of the accounts period;

(*b*) any subsequent period which—

(i) begins at the end of the immediately preceding period, being a period specified in this paragraph, and

(ii) ends at the expiration of 12 months from that date or, if earlier, at the end of the accounts period.

(3) . . . [2]][1]

Amendments—[1] This regulation inserted by the IT (Manufactured Overseas Dividends) (Amendment) Regulations, SI 1995/1324 reg 4, with effect from 7 June 1995.

[2] Words in para (1)(*b*), (*c*) substituted and para (3) revoked by the IT (Manufactured Overseas Dividends) (Amendment) Regulations, SI 1997/988, regs 1, 3, with effect from 1 July 1997.

2B [Tax treatment of manufactured overseas dividends paid in connection with loan relationships

(1) For the purposes of the provisions of the Tax Acts relating to the charge to tax under Schedule D, paragraph 4(2) and (3) . . . [2] of Schedule 23A shall not apply to a manufactured overseas dividend paid in the circumstances prescribed in paragraph (2).

(2) The circumstances prescribed are where the manufactured overseas dividend is representative of an overseas dividend on an overseas security that represents a loan relationship.

(3) Where the payer of a manufactured overseas dividend to which paragraph (2) applies is neither a company nor carrying on a trade in circumstances where the manufactured overseas dividend is taken into account in computing the profits of that trade, the manufactured overseas dividend shall be treated, for the purposes of the provisions of the Tax Acts relating to the charge to tax under Schedule D and so far as the payer is concerned, as if the amount paid was an annual payment, within section 349(1) of the Taxes Act, but so that no amount is required to be deducted on account of income tax from the amount of the payment, or accounted for under section 350 of that Act.

(4) Where the recipient of a manufactured overseas dividend to which paragraph (2) applies is neither a company nor carrying on a trade in circumstances where the manufactured overseas dividend is taken into account in computing the profits of that trade, the manufactured overseas dividend shall be treated, for the purposes of the provisions of the Tax Acts relating to the charge to tax under Schedule D and so far as the recipient is concerned, as an overseas dividend of an amount equal to the amount of the manufactured overseas dividend received by him, but not so as to entitle the recipient to claim relief under Part XVIII of the Taxes Act in respect of any tax attributable to the manufactured overseas dividend received.

(5) For the purposes of paragraph (2), an overseas security shall be taken to represent a loan relationship if a company holding that security would have a loan relationship within the meaning of section 81 of the Finance Act 1996.

(6) References in paragraph (4) to the recipient of a manufactured overseas dividend include references to any person claiming title to the manufactured overseas dividend through or under the recipient.][1]

Simon's Tax Cases—*Chappell v R&C Comrs* [2014] UKUT 344 (TCC), [2015] STC 271; *Chappell v R&C Comrs* [2016] EWCA Civ 809, [2016] STC 1980.

Amendments—[1] This regulation inserted by the IT (Manufactured Overseas Dividends) (Amendment No 2) Regulations, SI 1996/2643 reg 4, with effect from 6 November 1996.

[2] Words in para (1) revoked by the Stock Lending and Manufactured Payments (Revocations and Amendments) Regulations, SI 1997/987, regs 1, 8, with effect from 1 July 1997.

3 Prescribed rates of relevant withholding tax

(1) Subject to [paragraphs (5) and (6)][2], the rate of relevant withholding tax which is prescribed in relation to any manufactured overseas dividend is the rate which is equal to the rate (or, if more than one, the highest rate) at which tax would have been payable (and not repayable) under the law of the overseas territory specified in paragraph (3) in respect of—

(*a*) an overseas dividend paid on the same date that the manufactured overseas dividend is paid to a person who is—

(i) resident in the United Kingdom and not carrying on a trade outside the United Kingdom through a [permanent establishment][1],

(ii) subject to tax under the law of the United Kingdom, and

(iii) not subject to a special relationship with any other person as respects any commercial or financial dealings,

in respect of the same kind of overseas securities as those in respect of which the manufactured overseas dividend was paid, and

(*b*) the overseas tax credit, if any, relating to that overseas dividend.

(2) The reference in paragraph (1) above to tax which would have been payable is a reference to tax which would have been eligible for relief either—

(*a*) pursuant to arrangements made with the government of the overseas territory specified in paragraph (3) which have effect by virtue of section 788 of the Taxes Act and relate to the overseas dividend concerned, or

(*b*) by virtue of other provisions of Part XVIII of the Taxes Act other than section 790(5)(*c*)(ii) of that Act.

(3) The overseas territory specified in this paragraph is the territory of the government or public or local authority which issued the securities in question or, where the securities were issued by any other body of persons not resident in the United Kingdom, the territory under whose law that tax would have been payable.

(4) . . .[1]

[(5) Where the recipient of the manufactured overseas dividend is a company, the reference in paragraph (1) to the highest rate is a reference to the highest rate that would have applied in relation to the overseas dividend specified in paragraph (1)(*a*) paid to a company which is within paragraphs (i) to (iii) of that paragraph.

(6) Where the manufactured overseas dividend—

(*a*) is paid to, or for the benefit of, a registered pension scheme (within the meaning given in Part 4 of the Finance Act 2004), or

(*b*) is linked solely to pension business for the purposes of section 438 of the Taxes Act at the time that the payment is made,

the reference in paragraph (1) to the highest rate is a reference to the rate that would have been suffered by the recipient in relation to the overseas dividend of which that manufactured overseas dividend is representative.][2]

Amendments—[1] Words in para (1)(*a*)(i) substituted, and para (4) revoked, by the IT (Manufactured Overseas Dividends) (Amendment) Regulations, SI 2003/2582 regs 2, 4 with effect from 1 November 2003.

[2] Words in para (1) substituted, and paras (5), (6) inserted, by the Income Tax (Manufactured Overseas Dividends) (Amendment) Regulations, SI 2007/2487 regs 2, 3 with effect in relation to manufactured overseas dividends made or treated as made on or after 1 October 2007: SI 2007/2487 reg 1.

4 Tax treatment of approved manufactured overseas dividends paid to approved United Kingdom intermediaries or approved United Kingdom collecting agents

(1) For the purposes of the provisions of the Tax Acts relating to the charge to tax under Schedule D other than paragraph 4(3) of Schedule 23A, [a manufactured overseas dividend][1] paid in the circumstances prescribed in paragraph (2)—

(*a*) shall not be treated as an annual payment pursuant to paragraph 4(2) of Schedule 23A;

(*b*) shall be paid without deduction of an amount on account of income tax;

(*c*) . . .[4].

[(2) The circumstances prescribed by this paragraph are where—

(*a*) a manufactured overseas dividend is paid to an approved United Kingdom intermediary or an approved United Kingdom collecting agent by an overseas dividend manufacturer who—

(i) is resident in the United Kingdom or, if not so resident, makes the payment in the course of a trade which he carries on through a [permanent establishment][3] in the United Kingdom, and

(ii) is not an approved United Kingdom intermediary; . . .[5]

(*b*) the manufactured overseas dividend is not representative of the overseas dividend received by the overseas dividend manufacturer][2][, and

(*c*) the receipt of the manufactured overseas dividend by the approved United Kingdom intermediary or approved United Kingdom collecting agent is not a foreign permanent establishment receipt.][5]

(3) Subject to paragraph (4), the approved United Kingdom intermediary or approved United Kingdom collecting agent referred to in paragraph (2) shall account for and pay an amount of tax in respect of the manufactured overseas dividend which he receives equal to that which the maker of the payment would have been required to account for and pay had paragraph 4(2) of Schedule 23A applied to the payment.

[(4) Paragraph (3) shall not apply where either paragraph (5) or (6) applies.][3]

[(5) This paragraph applies where the approved United Kingdom intermediary or approved United Kingdom collecting agent pays, in accordance with regulation 5, and without deduction of tax, a manufactured overseas dividend representative of the same overseas dividend as is represented by the manufactured overseas dividend received by him.][3]

[(6) This paragraph applies where the approved United Kingdom collecting agent is required to pay to an approved United Kingdom intermediary a manufactured overseas dividend representative of the same overseas dividend as is represented by the manufactured overseas dividend received by him and the approved United Kingdom intermediary—

(*a*) pays as mentioned in paragraph (5) the manufactured overseas dividend, and

(*b*) issues a notice to the approved United Kingdom collecting agent authorising him to make the payment without deduction of tax.][3]

Amendments—[1] Words substituted by the IT (Manufactured Overseas Dividends) (Amendment) Regulations, SI 1996/1229 reg 4, with effect from 28 May 1996.

[2] Para (2) substituted by the IT (Manufactured Overseas Dividends) (Amendment) Regulations, SI 1997/988, regs 1, 4, with effect from 1 July 1997.

[3] Words in para (2)(*a*)(i) substituted, and paras 4–6 substituted for para 4, by the IT (Manufactured Overseas Dividends) (Amendment) Regulations, SI 2003/2582 regs 2, 5 with effect from 1 November 2003.

[4] Para (1)(*c*) revoked by the Finance Act 2004, Sections 38 to 40 and 45 and Schedule 6 (Consequential Amendment of Enactments) Order, SI 2004/2310 art 2, Schedule para 73(1), (2) with effect from 28 September 2004. This amendment has effect for accounting periods beginning on or after 1 April 2004, subject to the transitional provisions set out in FA 2004 ss 43, 44.

[5] In para (2), word "and" at end of para (*a*) revoked, and para (*c*) and preceding word "and" inserted, by the Income Tax (Manufactured Overseas Dividends) (Amendment) Regulations, SI 2011/1787 regs 2, 4 with effect in relation to manufactured overseas dividends paid or treated as paid on or after 11 August 2011.

5 Tax treatment of approved manufactured overseas dividends paid to persons resident outside the United Kingdom

(1) [Subject to paragraph (1A),][2] for the purposes of the provisions of the Tax Acts relating to the charge to tax under Schedule D, [a manufactured overseas dividend][1] paid in [either of the circumstances prescribed by paragraphs (1B) and (2)][2] shall not be treated as an annual payment pursuant to paragraph 4(2) of Schedule 23A, and accordingly shall be paid without deduction of an amount on account of income tax.

[(1A) Where a manufactured overseas dividend is paid in the circumstances prescribed by paragraph (1B) by a person [who is not within the charge to corporation tax and][3] who is not an approved United Kingdom intermediary, the dividend shall be treated, for the purposes of the provisions of the Tax Acts relating to the charge to tax under Schedule D and so far as the payer is concerned, as if the amount paid was an annual payment, within section 349(1) of the Taxes Act, but so that no amount is required to be deducted on account of income tax from the amount of the payment, or accounted for under section 350 of that Act.][2]

[(1B) The circumstances prescribed by this paragraph are where—

(*a*) a manufactured overseas dividend is paid by a person who is resident in the United Kingdom, or, if not so resident, makes the payment in the course of a trade which he carries on through a permanent establishment in the United Kingdom;

(*b*) the payment is to or for the benefit of a person beneficially entitled to it who is not a United Kingdom recipient; and

(*c*) regulation 4(1) does not apply.][2]

(2) The circumstances prescribed by this paragraph are [where—

(*a*) a manufactured overseas dividend is paid by an approved United Kingdom intermediary who, if not resident in the United Kingdom, makes the payment in the course of a trade which he carries on through a permanent establishment in the United Kingdom; and;][2]

(*b*) the payment is made to another approved United Kingdom intermediary or to an approved United Kingdom collecting agent as part of a chain of payments where—

(i) each payment in the chain is a payment by an approved United Kingdom intermediary or an approved United Kingdom collecting agent of [a manufactured overseas dividend][1] representative of the same overseas dividend,

(ii) the maker of the last payment in the chain, if not resident in the United Kingdom, makes the payment in the course of a trade which he carries on through a [permanent establishment in the United Kingdom and makes the payment to or for the benefit of a person beneficially entitled to it who is not a United Kingdom recipient][2], . . . [4]

(iii) each recipient of payment in the chain[, apart from the last,][5] has issued a notice to the maker of the payment authorising him to make the payment without deduction of tax[, and

(iv) none of the payments are foreign permanent establishment payments.][4]

Amendments—[1] Words substituted by the IT (Manufactured Overseas Dividends) (Amendment) Regulations, SI 1996/1229 reg 4, with effect from 28 May 1996.

[2] Words in para (1) inserted and substituted, paras (1A), (1B) inserted, and words in para (2) substituted, by the IT (Manufactured Overseas Dividends) (Amendment) Regulations, SI 2003/2582 regs 2, 6 with effect from 1 November 2003.

[3] Words in para (1A) inserted by the Finance Act 2004, Sections 38 to 40 and 45 and Schedule 6 (Consequential Amendment of Enactments) Order, SI 2004/2310 art 2, Schedule para 73(1), (3) with effect from 28 September 2004. This amendment has effect for accounting periods beginning on or after 1 April 2004, subject to the transitional provisions set out in FA 2004 ss 43, 44.

[4] In para (2)(*b*), words "and" at end of sub-para (ii) revoked, and sub-para (iv) and preceding word "and" inserted, by the Income Tax (Manufactured Overseas Dividends) (Amendment) Regulations, SI 2011/1787 regs 2, 5 with effect in relation to manufactured overseas dividends paid or treated as paid on or after 11 August 2011.

[5] In para 2(b)(*iii*), words inserted by the Income Tax (Manufacturered Overseas Dividends) (Amendment No 2) Regulations, SI 2011/2503 regs 2, 3 with effect in relation to manufactured overseas dividends paid or treated as paid on or after 10 November 2011.

5A [Chains of payments where last payment made to, or for benefit of, registered pension scheme or is linked solely to pension business

(1) This regulation applies where—

(*a*) a person (the "original payer") pays a manufactured overseas dividend, and

(*b*) the payment is made to an approved United Kingdom intermediary or to an approved United Kingdom collecting agent as part of a chain of payments where conditions A to [E][2]are met.

(2) Condition A is that each payment in the chain, apart from the first, is a payment by an approved United Kingdom intermediary or an approved United Kingdom collecting agent of a manufactured overseas dividend representative of the same overseas dividend.

(3) Condition B is that the last payment in the chain—

(*a*) is made to, or for the benefit of, a registered pension scheme (within the meaning given in Part 4 of the Finance Act 2004), or

(*b*) is linked solely to pension business for the purposes of section 438 of the Taxes Act at the time that the payment is made.

(4) Condition C is that the last payment in the chain is made by a person who—

(*a*) is resident in the United Kingdom, or

(*b*) is not resident in the United Kingdom, but makes the payment in the course of a trade carried on through a permanent establishment.

(5) Condition D is that each recipient of payment in the chain[, apart from the last,][3] has issued a notice to the original payer to make the payment at the applicable rate of relevant withholding tax.

[(5A) Condition E is that none of the payments are foreign permanent establishment payments.][2]

(6) The applicable rate of relevant withholding tax for each payment in the chain [to an approved United Kingdom intermediary or to an approved United Kingdom collecting agent][3] shall be determined in accordance with paragraphs (7) and (8).

(7) If the last payment in the chain is made to, or for the benefit of, a registered pension scheme, the applicable rate shall be determined as if the person to whom the payment is made were the registered pension scheme to which the last payment in the chain is made.

(8) If the last payment in the chain is linked solely to pension business at the time that the payment is made, the applicable rate shall be determined as if the person to whom the payment is made were the person to whom the last payment in the chain is made.

(9) For the purposes of condition A (see paragraph (2)) it does not matter whether or not the first payment in the chain was made by an approved United Kingdom intermediary or an approved United Kingdom collecting agent.][1]

Amendments—[1] Regulation 5A inserted, by the Income Tax (Manufactured Overseas Dividends) (Amendment) Regulations, SI 2007/2487 regs 2, 4 with effect in relation to manufactured overseas dividends made or treated as made on or after 1 October 2007: SI 2007/2487 reg 1.

[2] In para (1)(*b*), "E" substituted for "D", and para (5A) inserted, by the Income Tax (Manufactured Overseas Dividends) (Amendment) Regulations, SI 2011/1787 regs 2, 6 with effect in relation to manufactured overseas dividends paid or treated as paid on or after 11 August 2011.

[3] In paras (5), (6), words inserted by the Income Tax (Manufactured Overseas Dividends) (Amendment No 2) Regulations, SI 2011/2503 regs 2, 4 with effect in relation to manufactured overseas dividends paid or treated as paid on or after 10 November 2011.

[5B Chains of payments involving central counterparties

(1) This regulation applies where—

(*a*) a person pays a manufactured overseas dividend, and

(*b*) the payment is made as part of a chain of payments ("a CCP chain"), which may form part of a chain of payments to which regulation 5(2) or 5A applies, where conditions A to C are met.

(2) Condition A is that each payment in the CCP chain is a payment of a manufactured overseas dividend representative of the same overseas dividend.

(3) Condition B is that each payment in the CCP chain is made—

(*a*) by or to a central counterparty,

(*b*) to a clearing member acting in the capacity as clearing member for another person where a corresponding payment is made by the clearing member to a central counterparty, or

(*c*) by a clearing member acting in the capacity as clearing member for another person where a corresponding payment is made to the clearing member by a central counterparty.

(4) Condition C is that a notice has been issued by or on behalf of the central counterparty to the first CCP payer and the final CCP recipient—

(*a*) confirming that conditions A and B are met, and

(*b*) either—

(i) stating names and registered addresses of the first CCP payer and the final CCP recipient, or

(ii) containing sufficient information to enable the parties to the CCP chain to meet their tax obligations in the United Kingdom with respect to the manufactured overseas dividend.

(5) For the purposes of Chapter 9 of Part 15 of the Income Tax Act 2007 and these Regulations—

(*a*) the first CCP payer is treated as required to pay to the final CCP recipient a manufactured overseas dividend representative of an overseas dividend on overseas securities paid under an arrangement for the transfer of securities,

(*b*) the payments in the CCP chain are disregarded, and

(*c*) a manufactured overseas dividend representative of the same overseas dividend is treated as paid by the first CCP payer to the final CCP recipient.

(6) In this regulation—

"central counterparty" means a recognised clearing house[", EEA central counterparty, third country central counterparty][2] or recognised investment exchange which carries on a business of providing a central counterparty clearing service in relation to arrangements for the transfer of overseas securities;

"central counterparty clearing service" means the service provided to parties to an arrangement for the transfer of overseas securities, or to a clearing member acting on behalf of either of those parties, where there are contracts between each of those parties, or a clearing member, and the central counterparty in place of, or as an alternative to, a contract directly between those parties;

"clearing member" means a party who provides clearing arrangements between a party to an arrangement for the transfer of overseas securities and a central counterparty;

["EEA central counterparty" has the meaning given by section 285(1)(*c*) of the Financial Services and Markets Act 2000;][2]

"final CCP recipient" means the party to whom the last payment in the CCP chain is made;

"first CCP payer" means the maker of the first payment in the CCP chain;

"recognised clearing house" has the meaning given by [section 285(1)(*b*)][2] of the Financial Services and Markets Act 2000;

"recognised investment exchange" means—

(*a*) a recognised investment exchange within the meaning of the Financial Services and Markets Act 2000 (see section 285),

(*b*) a regulated market within the meaning of Directive 2004/39/EC of the European Parliament and of the Council of 21 April 2004 on markets in financial instruments, or

(*c*) a multilateral trading facility within the meaning of that Directive.][1]

["third country central counterparty" has the meaning given by section 285(1)(d) of the Financial Services and Markets Act 2000.][2]

Amendments—[1] Reg 5B inserted by the Income Tax (Manufactured Overseas Dividends) (Amendment No 2) Regulations, SI 2011/2503 regs 2, 5 with effect in relation to manufactured overseas dividends paid or treated as paid on or after 10 November 2011.

[2] In para (6), in definition of "central counterparty", words inserted, in definition of "recognised clearing house", words substituted, and definitions of "EEA central counterparty" and "third country central counterparty" inserted by the Financial Services and Markets Act 2000 (Over the Counter Derivatives, Central Counterparties and Trade Repositories) Regulations, SI 2013/504 reg 31 with effect from 1 April 2013.

6 Retention and record of notices given under regulations [4 to 5B][3]

(1) A notice given under regulation 4[(6)(*b*)][1][, 5(2)(*b*)(iii), 5A(5) or 5B(4)][3] shall be in the form provided, or in a form authorised, by the Board.

(2) A recipient of such a notice—

(*a*) shall retain the notice for a period of six years and, whenever required to do so within that period, shall make it available for inspection by an officer of the Board, and

(*b*) if he receives more than one such notice during any chargeable period, shall in addition maintain a record showing—

(i) the date of each such notice received in that period, and

(ii) a description and the amount of the manufactured overseas dividend referred to in each such notice received in that period.

(3) A person who issues such a notice—

(*a*) shall retain a copy of it for a period of six years and, whenever required to do so within that period, shall make that copy available for inspection by an officer of the Board, and

(*b*) if he issues more than one such notice during any chargeable period, shall in addition maintain a record showing—

(i) the date of each such notice issued in that period, and

(ii) a description and the amount of the manufactured overseas dividend referred to in each such notice issued in that period.

(4) Any record required to be maintained by the recipient of a notice under paragraph (2)(*b*), or by the issuer of a notice under paragraph (3)(*b*), shall be retained by that person for a period of six years from the end of the chargeable period to which the record relates.

[(4A) In the case of a record retained under paragraph (2)(*b*) or (3)(*b*) which is in electronic form the person retaining it shall afford an officer of the Board such assistance and facilities as the officer may reasonably require in order to read the record.][2]

(5) Where the issuer of a notice fails to retain a copy of it for the period specified in paragraph (3)(*a*), or fails to maintain any such record as is specified in paragraph (3)(*b*) or to retain any such record for the period specified in paragraph (4), the Board may require that person to carry out, at his own expense, an audit of manufactured overseas dividends received by that person in order to ascertain the amount of tax, if any, liable to be deducted under paragraph 4(2) of Schedule 23A which was not deducted.

(6) The scope and method of the audit referred to in paragraph (5) shall be agreed between the Board and the issuer of the notice or, in the absence of agreement, determined by the Board, and the issuer of the notice shall account for and pay any tax which on the basis of the findings of the audit was liable to be deducted but which was not deducted from manufactured overseas dividends received by him.

Amendments—[1] Reference in para (1) substituted by the IT (Manufactured Overseas Dividends) (Amendment) Regulations, SI 2003/2582 regs 2, 7 with effect from 1 November 2003.

[2] Para (4A) inserted by the Income and Corporation Taxes (Electronic Certificates of Deduction of Tax and Tax Credit) Regulations, SI 2003/3143 reg 5(1), (2) with effect from 1 January 2004.

[3] In heading, reference substituted and in para (1), words substituted, by the Income Tax (Manufactured Overseas Dividends) (Amendment No 2) Regulations, SI 2011/2503 regs 2, 6 with effect in relation to manufactured overseas dividends paid or treated as paid on or after 10 November 2011.

6A [Reduction of tax payable under paragraph 4(3) of Schedule 23A

(1) Where, in a case to which paragraph 4(3) of Schedule 23A applies, overseas tax was charged on, or in respect of, the making of the manufactured overseas dividend received by the United Kingdom recipient, the amount of tax to be accounted for and paid under that provision shall, for the purposes of the provisions of the Tax Acts relating to the charge to tax under Schedule D, be taken as reduced in accordance with paragraph (2) or, as the case may be, paragraph (3).

(2) Where the amount specified in paragraph (4) exceeds the amount specified in paragraph (5), the amount of tax shall be reduced so as to equal the amount of the excess.

(3) Where the amount specified in paragraph (4) is equal to or less than the amount specified in paragraph (5), the amount of tax shall be reduced to nil.

(4) The amount specified in this paragraph is the amount of the manufactured overseas dividend received by the United Kingdom recipient.

(5) The amount specified in this paragraph is the amount which the United Kingdom recipient would have received by way of the overseas dividend of which the manufactured overseas dividend is representative, had the overseas dividend been paid to him.

(6) Relief claimed by the United Kingdom recipient under Part XVIII of the Taxes Act in a case to which paragraph (2) applies . . . [2] shall not exceed the aggregate of the amount of tax accounted for and paid by the United Kingdom recipient under paragraph 4(3) of Schedule 23A and the amount of overseas tax charged on, or in respect of, the making of the manufactured overseas dividend received by him.][1]

Amendments—[1] This regulation inserted by the IT (Manufactured Overseas Dividends) (Amendment No 2) Regulations, SI 1996/2643 reg 7, with effect from 6 November 1996.

[2] In para (6), words revoked by the Income Tax (Manufactured Overseas Dividends) (Amendment) Regulations, SI 2010/925 regs 2, 4 with effect in relation to manufactured overseas dividends made or treated as made on or after 14 April 2010.

7 Disapplication of paragraph 4(3) of Schedule 23A

(1) For the purposes of the provisions of the Tax Acts relating to the charge to tax under Schedule D, tax shall not be required to be accounted for and paid pursuant to paragraph 4(3) of Schedule 23A by a United Kingdom recipient of a manufactured overseas dividend which is received by him in any of the circumstances prescribed by paragraph (2).

(2) The circumstances prescribed by this paragraph are where the United Kingdom recipient—

[(*a*) pays, in accordance with regulation 5, and without deduction of tax, a manufactured overseas dividend representative of the same overseas dividend as is represented by the manufactured overseas dividend received by him, or;][3]

(*b*) . . . [3]

(*c*) is an approved United Kingdom collecting agent and the person beneficially entitled to the manufactured overseas dividend received by the approved United Kingdom collecting agent is not resident in the United Kingdom [and receipt of the manufactured overseas dividend by the person beneficially entitled to it would be otherwise than in the course of a trade carried on through a branch or agency in the United Kingdom][6], or

(*ca*) is an approved United Kingdom collecting agent and receipt of the manufactured overseas dividend by the person beneficially entitled to it would be a foreign permanent establishment receipt, or][6]

(*d*) is an approved United Kingdom collecting agent who is required to pay to an approved United Kingdom intermediary [a manufactured overseas dividend][1] representative of the same overseas dividend as is represented by [the manufactured overseas dividend][1] received by him, the approved United Kingdom intermediary is enabled or authorised as mentioned in sub-paragraph (*a*) above and issues a notice to the approved United Kingdom collecting agent authorising him to pay [the manufactured overseas dividend][1] without deduction of tax.

[or

(*e*) is an approved United Kingdom collecting agent or an approved United Kingdom intermediary in receipt of a manufactured overseas dividend who shows that the overseas dividend manufacturer concerned was entitled to payment of the overseas dividend of which the manufactured overseas dividend is representative either—

(i) as the holder of the overseas securities concerned, or

(ii) directly or indirectly from a person from whom he acquired those securities, or to whom he transferred them, and who was so entitled as the holder of those securities][2]

(3) A notice given under paragraph (2)(*d*) shall be in the form provided, or in a form authorised, by the Board.

(3A)–(3E) . . . [5]

(4) The United Kingdom recipient—

(*a*) shall maintain a record of all manufactured overseas dividends received by him in any chargeable period in the circumstances prescribed by paragraph (2), showing—

(i) a description and the amount of each such manufactured overseas dividend, and the date on which it was received, and

(ii) the total amount of all such manufactured overseas dividends received in that period;

(*b*) where he is an approved United Kingdom intermediary within sub-paragraph (*b*), or an approved United Kingdom collecting agent within sub-paragraph (*c*), of paragraph (2), shall in addition maintain a record of all manufactured overseas dividends paid by him as mentioned in sub-paragraph (*b*) or, as the case may be, sub-paragraph (*c*), of that paragraph in any chargeable period, showing—

(i) the name and address of the person beneficially entitled to each such payment,

(ii) a description and the amount of each such payment, and the date of the payment, and

(iii) the total amount of all such payments made in that period;

(*c*) shall retain any such record as is specified in sub-paragraph (*a*) or (*b*) of this paragraph for a period of six years from the end of the chargeable period to which the record relates, and shall make any such record available for inspection by an officer of the Board whenever required to do so during the period of retention;

(*d*) where he is an approved United Kingdom collecting agent within sub-paragraph (*d*) of paragraph (2), shall in addition—

(i) retain for a period of six years any notice received by him as mentioned in that sub-paragraph and, whenever required to do so, make it available for inspection by an officer of the Board, and

(ii) if he receives more than one such notice during any chargeable period, maintain a record showing the date of each such notice received in that period and a description and the amount of the manufactured overseas dividend referred to in each such notice, and retain the record for a period of six years from the end of the chargeable period to which the record relates.

[(4A) In the case of a record retained under paragraph (4) which is in electronic form the person retaining it shall afford an officer of the Board such assistance and facilities as the officer may reasonably require in order to read the record.][4]

(5) Where the United Kingdom recipient fails to maintain, or to retain for the requisite period, any such record as is referred to in paragraph (4), or fails to retain for the requisite period any such notice as is referred to in that paragraph, the Board may require that person to carry out, at his own expense, an audit of manufactured overseas dividends received by him in order to ascertain the amount of tax, if any, for which he was liable to account under paragraph 4(3) of Schedule 23A.

(6) The scope and method of the audit referred to in paragraph (5) shall be agreed between the Board and the United Kingdom recipient or, in the absence of agreement, shall be determined by the Board, and the United Kingdom recipient shall account for and pay any tax which on the basis of the findings of the audit he was liable under paragraph 4(3) of Schedule 23A to account for and pay.

Amendments—[1] Words substituted by the IT (Manufactured Overseas Dividends) (Amendment) Regulations, SI 1996/1229 reg 4, with effect from 28 May 1996.

[2] Para (2)(*e*) added by the IT (Manufactured Overseas Dividends) (Amendment) Regulations, SI 1996/2643 reg 8, with effect from 6 November 1996.

[3] In para (2), sub-para (*a*) substituted, and sub-para (*b*) revoked, by the IT (Manufactured Overseas Dividends) (Amendment) Regulations, SI 2003/2582 regs 2, 8 with effect from 1 November 2003.

[4] Para (4A) inserted by the Income and Corporation Taxes (Electronic Certificates of Deduction of Tax and Tax Credit) Regulations, SI 2003/3143 reg 5(1), (3) with effect from 1 January 2004.

[5] Paras (3A)–(3E) substituted for previous para (3A) by the Income Tax (Manufactured Overseas Dividends) (Amendment) Regulations, SI 2007/2487 regs 2, 5 with effect in relation to manufactured overseas dividends made or treated as made on or after 1 October 2007: SI 2007/2487 reg 1. Paras (3A)–(3E) subsequently revoked by the Income Tax (Manufactured Overseas Dividends) (Amendment) Regulations, SI 2009/2811 reg 2 with effect in relation to manufactured overseas dividends made or treated as made on or after 1.15 pm on 21 October 2009.

[6] Words in para (2)(*c*), and whole of para (2)(*ca*), inserted, by the Income Tax (Manufactured Overseas Dividends) (Amendment) Regulations, SI 2011/1787 regs 2, 7 with effect in relation to manufactured overseas dividends paid or treated as paid on or after 11 August 2011.

7A [Disapplication of paragraph 5 of Schedule 23A

. . .[1]

Amendments—[1] This regulation revoked by the Stock Lending and Manufactured Payments (Revocations and Amendments) Regulations, SI 1997/987, regs 1, 8, with effect from 1 July 1997 (previously inserted by the IT (Manufactured Overseas Dividends) (Amendment No 2) Regulations, SI 1996/2643 reg 9).

8 Tax treatment of manufactured overseas dividends to which regulations 4, 5 and 7 apply—further provision

For all purposes of the Tax Acts as they apply in relation to persons resident in the United Kingdom or to persons not so resident but carrying on a business through a [permanent establishment][1] in the United Kingdom, any manufactured overseas dividend to which regulation 4, 5 or 7 applies shall be treated in relation to the recipient, and all persons claiming title through or under him—

(*a*) as if it were an overseas dividend of an amount equal to the amount of the manufactured overseas dividend, or

(*b*) where paragraph (3) of regulation 4 applies and the amount of tax required under that paragraph in respect of the manufactured overseas dividend has been accounted for and paid, as if it were an overseas dividend of an amount equal to the gross amount of the manufactured overseas dividend, but paid after the withholding therefrom, on account of overseas tax, of the amount accounted for and paid; and the amount accounted for and paid shall accordingly be treated in relation to the recipient, and all persons claiming title through or under him, as an amount so withheld instead of an amount on account of income tax.

Amendments—[1] Words substituted by the IT (Manufactured Overseas Dividends) (Amendment) Regulations, SI 2003/2582 regs 2, 9 with effect from 1 November 2003.

9 Offsetting of tax by overseas dividend manufacturers

[(1) In the circumstances prescribed by paragraph (2) and subject to paragraph (4), a person who is an overseas dividend manufacturer in any chargeable period shall be entitled to set off the amounts specified in paragraph (1A) against the sums specified in paragraph (1B)][4]

[This is subject to regulation 9ZA.][6]

[(1A) The amounts specified in this paragraph are—

(*a*) amounts of overseas tax in respect of overseas dividends received by the overseas dividend manufacturer in the chargeable period [otherwise than as foreign permanent establishment receipts][7];

(*b*) amounts of overseas tax charged on, or in respect of, the making of manufactured overseas dividends so received by him [otherwise than as foreign permanent establishment receipts][7];

(*c*) amounts deducted under paragraph 4(2) of Schedule 23A from manufactured overseas dividends so received by him;

(*d*) amounts accounted for and paid under paragraph 4(3) of Schedule 23A in respect of manufactured overseas dividends so received by him;

(*e*) amounts accounted for and paid under regulation 4(3) in respect of manufactured overseas dividends so received by him.][4]

[(1B) The sums specified in this paragraph are sums due from the overseas dividend manufacturer on account of the amounts deducted by him under paragraph 4(2) of Schedule 23A from the manufactured overseas dividends paid by him in the chargeable period.][4]

(2) The circumstances prescribed by this paragraph are where—

(*a*) the overseas dividend manufacturer is an approved United Kingdom intermediary,

[(*aa*) . . .][1]

(*b*) the overseas dividends and manufactured overseas dividends referred to in [paragraph (1A)][4], if received by an overseas dividend manufacturer within sub-paragraph (*a*) of this paragraph who carries on a business in the ordinary course of which he receives overseas dividends and manufactured overseas dividends and pays manufactured overseas dividends, are such that a profit on the sale of the overseas securities to which those overseas dividends and manufactured overseas dividends relate would form part of the trading profits of that business,

(*c*) . . . [2]

(*d*) except in a case to which paragraph (3) applies, the overseas dividends or, as the case may be, the manufactured overseas dividends received by him, do not fall to be matched, in accordance with regulation 10(1), against manufactured overseas dividends paid by him in that period.

(3) This paragraph applies to a case where, under regulation 10(1), overseas dividends in respect of which overseas tax is payable received by the overseas dividend manufacturer in any chargeable period, and manufactured overseas dividends so received [on or in respect of the making of which overseas tax has been charged or][4] from which tax has been deducted or in respect of which tax falls to be accounted for and paid as mentioned in [paragraph (1A)][4] above, are matched against manufactured overseas dividends paid by him under deduction of tax in that period.

(4) Where paragraph (3) applies in respect of any chargeable period, the overseas dividend manufacturer shall be entitled to set off against each other—

(*a*) the tax [referred to in that paragraph that is] attributable to the matched overseas dividends and manufactured overseas dividends received, and

(*b*) the tax [referred to in that paragraph that is] attributable to the matched manufactured overseas dividends paid.

[(4A) Subject to paragraphs (4B) and (5), where overseas dividends or manufactured overseas dividends received by the overseas dividend manufacturer in any chargeable period fall to be matched, in accordance with regulation 10(1), against manufactured overseas dividends paid by him in that period, relief under Part XVIII of the Taxes Act may not be claimed by the overseas dividend manufacturer in respect of any tax referred to in paragraph (1A) that is attributable to those overseas dividends or manufactured overseas dividends received.][5]

[(4B) Where—

(*a*) overseas dividends or manufactured overseas dividends received by the overseas dividend manufacturer in any chargeable period fall to be matched, in accordance with regulation 10(1), against manufactured overseas dividends to which regulation 3(6), 5 or 5A applies that are paid by him in that period, and

(*b*) the gross amount of the overseas dividends or the manufactured overseas dividends is brought into account by the overseas dividend manufacturer as income for the purposes of income tax or corporation tax for that period,

relief under section 112 of the Taxation (International and Other Provisions) Act 2010 (deduction from income for foreign tax (instead of credit against UK tax)) shall be given to the overseas dividend manufacturer in respect of any tax referred to in paragraph (1A) that is attributable to those overseas dividends or manufactured overseas dividends received.][6]

[(4C) Subject to paragraph (5), where tax referred to in paragraph (1A) that is attributable to overseas dividends or manufactured overseas dividends received by the overseas dividend manufacturer in any chargeable period is set off, in accordance with this regulation, against tax referred to in paragraph (1B) that is attributable to manufactured overseas dividends paid by him in that period, relief under Part XVIII of the Taxes Act may not be claimed by the overseas dividend manufacturer in respect of any tax referred to in paragraph (1A) that is attributable to those overseas dividends or manufactured overseas dividends received.][5]

(5) Except in a case to which paragraph (3) applies, where in accordance with this regulation tax is set off by an overseas dividend manufacturer in any chargeable period and in relation to that period the sum of the overseas tax and amounts referred to in [paragraph (1A)][4] exceeds the total amount of the sums due as mentioned in [paragraph (1B)][4], relief under Part XVIII of the Taxes Act may be claimed by the overseas dividend manufacturer in respect of the amount of the excess.

(6) Where in accordance with this regulation tax is set off by an overseas dividend manufacturer in any chargeable period and in relation to that period the total amount of the sums due from the overseas dividend manufacturer as mentioned in [paragraph (1B)][4] exceeds the sum of the overseas tax and amounts referred to in [paragraph (1A)][4], the amount of the excess shall be payable to the Board.

(7) References to overseas tax in this regulation are references to the amount of such tax which is eligible for relief under Part XVIII of the Taxes Act either—

(*a*) pursuant to arrangements made with the government of the overseas territory specified in paragraph (8) which have effect by virtue of section 788 of the Taxes Act and relate to the overseas dividend [or manufactured overseas dividend] concerned, or

(*b*) by virtue of other provisions of Part XVIII of the Taxes Act other than section 790(5)(*c*)(ii) of that Act.

(8) The overseas territory specified [in this paragraph—

(*a*) so far as overseas dividends are concerned, is the territory of the government or public or local authority which issued the securities in question or, where the securities were issued by any other body of persons not resident in the United Kingdom, the territory under whose law that tax would have been payable;

(*b*) so far as manufactured overseas dividends are concerned, is the territory of the government by which tax is charged on, or in respect of, the making of the manufactured overseas dividend concerned.][4]

Amendments—[1] Para (2)(*aa*) inserted by the IT (Manufactured Overseas Dividends) (Amendment) Regulations, SI 1995/1324 reg 5(*a*), with effect from 7 June 1995, and revoked by the IT (Manufactured Overseas Dividends) (Amendment No 2) Regulations, SI 1996/2643 reg 10(*b*)(i), with effect from 6 November 1996.

[2] Para (2)(*c*) and the word "and" immediately following it revoked by the IT (Manufactured Overseas Dividends) (Amendment) Regulations, SI 1996/1229 reg 5, with effect from 28 May 1996.

[4] Paras (1), (1A), (1B) substituted for para (1) and words in paras (2)(*b*), (3), (4)(*a*), (*b*), (5), (6), (7)(A), (8) substituted or inserted by the IT (Manufactured Overseas Dividends) (Amendment No 2) Regulations, SI 1996/2643 reg 10, with effect from 6 November 1996.

[5] Paras (4A), (4C) substituted for para (4A) by the IT (Manufactured Overseas Dividends) (Amendment) Regulations, SI 1997/988, regs 1, 6, with effect from 1 July 1997.

[6] In para (1), words inserted, para (4B) substituted, by the Income Tax (Manufactured Overseas Dividends) (Amendment) Regulations, SI 2010/925 regs 2, 5 with effect in relation to manufactured overseas dividends made or treated as made on or after 14 April 2010.

[7] In para (1A)(*a*), (*b*) words inserted by the Income Tax (Manufactured Overseas Dividends) (Amendment) Regulations, SI 2011/1787 regs 2, 8 with effect in relation to manufactured overseas dividends paid or treated as paid on or after 11 August 2011.

9ZA [Entitlement to offsetting

(1) There shall be no entitlement to set off under regulation 9(1) in relation to overseas dividends or manufactured overseas dividends received by an overseas dividend manufacturer in any chargeable period if—

(*a*) the overseas dividends or the manufactured overseas dividends do not fall to be matched, in accordance with regulation 10(1), against manufactured overseas dividends paid by the overseas dividend manufacturer in that period, and

(*b*) the gross amount of the overseas dividends or manufactured overseas dividends is not brought into account in accordance with generally accepted accounting practice by the overseas dividend manufacturer as income for the purposes of income tax or corporation tax for that period.

This is subject to paragraph (2).

(2) Paragraph (1) does not apply if the overseas dividend manufacturer elects to bring into account the gross amount of the overseas dividends or manufactured overseas dividends received in any chargeable period as income for the purpose of calculating his liability to income tax or corporation tax for that period.

(3) An election under paragraph (2)—

(*a*) must be made in writing to Her Majesty's Revenue and Customs,

(*b*) applies in relation to overseas dividends and manufactured overseas dividends received in the chargeable period in which the election is made and in subsequent periods, and

(*c*) may be revoked by notice in writing to Her Majesty's Revenue and Customs with effect from the chargeable period in which the notice is given.][1]

Amendments—[1] Para inserted by the Income Tax (Manufactured Overseas Dividends) (Amendment) Regulations, SI 2010/925 regs 2, 6 with effect in relation to manufactured overseas dividends made or treated as made on or after 14 April 2010.

9A [Offsetting of tax by overseas dividend manufacturers who are not United Kingdom intermediaries

(1) An overseas dividend manufacturer who is not an approved United Kingdom intermediary shall be entitled to set off in any chargeable period amounts of overseas tax in respect of overseas dividends received by him in that chargeable period [otherwise than as a foreign permanent

establishment receipt][5] against sums due from him on account of the amounts deducted by him under paragraph 4(2) of Schedule 23A from manufactured overseas dividends paid by him in that chargeable period that are representatives of those overseas dividends.
(2) Where overseas tax referred to in paragraph (1) is set off against sums referred to in that paragraph, relief under Part XVIII of the Taxes Act may not be claimed by the overseas dividend manufacturer in respect of that overseas tax.
[(2A) This paragraph applies where an overseas dividend manufacturer who is not an approved United Kingdom intermediary receives in any chargeable period overseas dividends or manufactured overseas dividends and pays in that period manufactured overseas dividends to which [regulation 3(6), 5 or 5A][3] applies that are representative of those overseas dividends or manufactured overseas dividends received.][2]
[(2B) Where paragraph (2A) applies—
(*a*) relief under section 811 of the Taxes Act shall be given to the overseas dividend manufacturer in respect of any tax referred to in regulation 9(1A) that is attributable to the overseas dividends or manufactured overseas dividends received by him; and
(*b*) no other relief under Part 18 of the Taxes Act may be claimed by him in respect of any such tax.][2]
[(2C) But paragraph (2B) only applies to a case where the gross amount of the overseas dividends or, as the case may be, the manufactured overseas dividends received by the overseas dividend manufacturer in any chargeable period is brought into account as income for the purposes of income tax or corporation tax for that period.][4]
(3) References in this regulation to overseas tax shall be construed in accordance with regulation 9(7).][1]

Amendments—[1] This regulation inserted by the IT (Manufactured Overseas Dividends) (Amendment) Regulations, SI 1997/988, regs 1, 7, with effect from 1 July 1997.
[2] Paras 2A, 2B inserted by the IT (Manufactured Overseas Dividends) (Amendment) Regulations, SI 2003/2582 regs 2, 10 with effect from 1 November 2003.
[3] Words in para (2A) substituted for words "regulation 5" by the Income Tax (Manufactured Overseas Dividends) (Amendment) Regulations, SI 2007/2487 regs 2, 7 with effect in relation to manufactured overseas dividends made or treated as made on or after 1 October 2007: SI 2007/2487 reg 1.
[4] Para (2C) inserted by the Income Tax (Manufactured Overseas Dividends) (Amendment) Regulations, SI 2010/925 regs 2, 7 with effect in relation to manufactured overseas dividends made or treated as made on or after 14 April 2010.
[5] Words in para (1) inserted by the Income Tax (Manufactured Overseas Dividends) (Amendment) Regulations, SI 2011/1787 regs 2, 9 with effect in relation to manufactured overseas dividends paid or treated as paid on or after 11 August 2011.

10 Matching of dividends and manufactured overseas dividends

(1) For the purpose of paragraphs (2)(*d*) and (3) of regulation 9, overseas dividends paid on overseas securities of a particular kind in respect of a particular dividend date which are received in any chargeable period by an overseas dividend manufacturer, and manufactured overseas dividends representative of those overseas dividends which are received by him in that period—
(*a*) shall be matched against manufactured overseas dividends representative of those overseas dividends which are paid by him in that period in accordance with the following order of priority—
(i) manufactured overseas dividends received without deduction of tax [other than manufactured overseas dividends in respect of which tax falls to be accounted for and paid under paragraph 4(3) of Schedule 23A or regulation 4(3)][1]
(ii) overseas dividends received; and
(iii) manufactured overseas dividends received [to which tax referred to in regulation [9(1A)][3] is attributable][2]; and
(*b*) shall first be matched against manufactured overseas dividends paid without deduction of tax under paragraph 4(2) of Schedule 23A [by virtue of [regulation 3(6), 5 or 5A][5]][4],
and the balance, if any, shall be matched against manufactured overseas dividends paid by him from which tax has been deducted under paragraph 4(2) of Schedule 23A.
[(1A) But the following cannot be matched under paragraph (1)—
(*a*) overseas dividends received as foreign permanent establishment receipts,
(*b*) manufactured overseas dividends received as foreign permanent establishment receipts, and
(*c*) manufactured overseas dividends paid as foreign permanent establishment payments.][6]
(2)–(4) [7]

Amendments—[1] Words in para (1)(*a*) (i) substituted by the IT (Manufactured Overseas Dividends) (Amendment) Regulations, SI 1995/1324 reg 6, with effect from 7 June 1995.
[2] Words in para (1)(*a*)(iii), and paras (2), (3), substituted, and words in para (4)(*a*) inserted, by the IT (Manufactured Overseas Dividends) (Amendment No 2) Regulations, SI 1996/2643 reg 11, with effect from 6 November 1996.
[3] Figures in para (1)(*a*)(iii) substituted for "9(3)" by the IT (Manufactured Overseas Dividends) (Amendment) Regulations, SI 1997/988, regs 1, 8, with effect from 1 July 1997.
[4] Words in para (1) substituted, and words in paras (2)–(4) inserted and substituted, by the IT (Manufactured Overseas Dividends) (Amendment) Regulations, SI 2003/2582 regs 2, 11 with effect from 1 November 2003.

[5] Words in para (1)(*b*) substituted for words "regulation 5" by the Income Tax (Manufactured Overseas Dividends) (Amendment) Regulations, SI 2007/2487 regs 2, 7 with effect in relation to manufactured overseas dividends made or treated as made on or after 1 October 2007: SI 2007/2487 reg 1.

[6] Para (1A) inserted by the Income Tax (Manufactured Overseas Dividends) (Amendment) Regulations, SI 2011/1787 regs 2, 10 with effect in relation to manufactured overseas dividends paid or treated as paid on or after 11 August 2011.

[7] Paras (2)–(4) revoked by the Income Tax (Manufactured Overseas Dividends) (Amendment No 2) Regulations, SI 2011/2503 regs 2, 7 with effect in relation to manufactured overseas dividends paid or treated as paid on or after 10 November 2011.

11 Accounting for tax payable under paragraph 4(2) and (3) of Schedule 23A and these Regulations

(1) Within 30 days of the end of a chargeable period—

(*a*) an overseas dividend manufacturer shall pay to the Board all amounts which he was liable to deduct under paragraph 4(2) of Schedule 23A on account of income tax from manufactured overseas dividends paid by him in that period;

(*b*) an overseas dividend manufacturer who is an approved United Kingdom intermediary shall pay to the Board the amount of any excess payable under regulation 9(6) attributable to that period;

(*c*) a United Kingdom recipient shall pay to the Board all amounts of tax for which he was liable to account under paragraph 4(3) of Schedule 23A in respect of manufactured overseas dividends received by him in that period;

(*d*) an approved United Kingdom intermediary or an approved United Kingdom collecting agent shall pay to the Board all amounts of tax for which he was liable to account under regulation 4(3) in respect of . . . [1] manufactured overseas dividends received by him in that period.

(2) Within [30][2] days of the end of a chargeable period—

(*a*) an overseas dividend manufacturer shall make a return to the Board or an inspector, in such form as the Board may prescribe, showing—

(i) the amounts which he was liable to deduct under paragraph 4(2) of Schedule 23A on account of income tax from . . . [1] manufactured overseas dividends paid by him in that period,

(ii) . . . [1], and

(iii) the amount of any excess payable under regulation 9(6) attributable to that period;

(*b*) a United Kingdom recipient shall make a return to the Board or an inspector, in such form as the Board may prescribe, showing the amounts of tax for which he was liable to account under paragraph 4(3) of Schedule 23A in respect of manufactured overseas dividends received by him in that period;

(*c*) an approved United Kingdom intermediary or an approved United Kingdom collecting agent shall make a return to the Board or an inspector, in such form as the Board may prescribe, showing the amounts of tax for which he was liable to account under regulation 4(3) in respect of . . . [1] manufactured overseas dividends received by him in that period.

(3) Any amount referred to in paragraph (1) shall be due at the end of the period of 30 days specified in that paragraph and shall be payable without the making of any assessment but may be assessed on the overseas dividend manufacturer or, as the case may be, the United Kingdom recipient, approved United Kingdom intermediary or approved United Kingdom collecting agent (whether or not it has been paid when the assessment is made) if it is not paid in full on or before that date.

(4) In any case where—

(*a*) it appears to the inspector that there is—

(i) a manufactured overseas dividend paid, or an overseas dividend or a manufactured overseas dividend received, by an overseas dividend manufacturer in a chargeable period, or

(ii) an overseas dividend or a manufactured overseas dividend received by a United Kingdom recipient, an approved United Kingdom intermediary or an approved United Kingdom collecting agent in a chargeable period,

which ought to have been but which has not been included in a return under paragraph (2) relating to that period, or

(*b*) the inspector is dissatisfied with any return under paragraph (2),

the inspector may make an assessment to the best of his judgment on the overseas dividend manufacturer or, as the case may be, the United Kingdom recipient, approved United Kingdom intermediary or approved United Kingdom collecting agent.

(5) Any income tax due under an assessment made by virtue of paragraph (4) shall be treated for the purposes of interest on unpaid tax as having been payable at the end of the period of 30 days specified in paragraph (1).

(6) Any amount for which an approved United Kingdom intermediary is liable to account under regulation 6(6), and any amount for which a United Kingdom recipient is liable to account under regulation 7(6), in respect of manufactured overseas dividends received by them in a chargeable period, shall be due at the end of the period of 30 days from the end of that period, and shall be

payable without the making of any assessment but may be assessed on the approved United Kingdom intermediary or, as the case may be, the United Kingdom recipient (whether or not it has been paid when the assessment is made) if it is not paid in full on or before that date.

(7) The like provisions as are contained in the Income Tax Acts with respect to the time within which an assessment may be made, so far as they refer or relate to the year of assessment for which an assessment is made, or the year to which an assessment relates, shall have effect in relation to an assessment under this regulation notwithstanding that, under this regulation, the assessment may be said to relate to a period which is not a year of assessment; and the like provisions as are contained in section 36 of the Management Act as to the circumstances in which an assessment may be made out of time shall have effect accordingly on the footing that any such assessment relates to the year of assessment in which the period in question ends.

(8) Income tax assessed on a person under this regulation shall be due at the end of the period of 30 days after the issue of the notice of assessment (unless due earlier under paragraph (3) or (6)).

(9) Any tax assessable under any one or more of the provisions of this regulation may be included in one assessment if the tax so included is all due on the same date.

(10) Section 31 and Part V of the Management Act shall apply to an appeal against any assessment to tax under this regulation.

(11) Subsections (1), (7) and (8) of section 87 of the Management Act shall apply to tax assessable under this regulation as they apply to tax assessable in accordance with Schedules 13 and 16 to the Taxes Act, and accordingly those subsections shall have effect as if references to those schedules included references to this regulation.

(12) Section 98 of the Management Act shall apply in relation to a return under paragraph (2) with the modification specified in paragraph (13).

(13) At the end of the second column of the Table in section 98 of the Management Act there shall be inserted—

"Regulation 11(2) of the Income Tax (Manufactured Overseas Dividends) Regulations 1993".

Amendments—[1] Words revoked by the IT (Manufactured Overseas Dividends) (Amendment) (Regulations, SI 1996/1229 reg 6, with effect from 28 May 1996.

[2] Figure in para (2) substituted by the IT (Manufactured Overseas Dividends) (Amendment) Regulations, SI 1997/988, regs 9, with effect in relation to chargeable periods ending on or after 1 July 1997.

12 Tax treatment of manufactured overseas dividends representative of foreign dividends

[(1) This regulation applies to a case where a manufactured overseas dividend is paid to a collecting agent in circumstances where, had it been the overseas dividend of which it is representative, it would have been—

(*a*) a foreign dividend (as defined in section 18(3D) of the Taxes Act, or

(*b*) interest on a quoted Eurobond (as defined by section 124 of that Act) held in a recognised clearing system.][2]

(2) Where this regulation applies—

(*a*) . . . [3] deduction of an amount determined by reference to the gross amount of the manufactured overseas dividend shall be made by the . . . [2] collecting agent from the manufactured overseas dividend on account of income tax similar to the deduction that would, in the case of the overseas dividend of which the manufactured overseas dividend is representative, have been made under [Chapter VIIA of Part IV of the Taxes Act][1]; and

[(*b*) the provisions of that Chapter relating to collecting agents shall apply in relation to amounts falling to be deducted under sub-paragraph (*a*) as if references in that Chapter to relevant dividends, or the proceeds of sale or other realisation of coupons for relevant dividends, included references to manufactured overseas dividends to which this regulation applies or, as the case may be, the proceeds of sale or other realisation of manufactured overseas dividends to which this regulation applies.][1]

(3) . . . [3]

Amendments—[1] Words in sub-para (2)(*a*), and sub-para (2)(*b*), substituted by the IT (Manufactured Overseas Dividends) (Amendment) Regulations, SI 1996/1229 reg 7(*b*), with effect from 28 May 1996.

[2] Para (1) substituted by the IT (Manufactured Overseas Dividends) (Amendment No 2) Regulations, SI 1996/2643 reg 12, with effect from 6 November 1996.

[3] Words in sub-para (2)(*a*) and para (3) revoked by the Income Tax (Manufactured Overseas Dividends) (Amendment No 2) Regulations, SI 1997/2706, with effect from 9 December 1997. Para (3) is rendered obsolete by the Income Tax (Paying and Collecting Agents) (Amendment) Regulations, SI 1997/2705 which come into force on the same day and amend the Income Tax (Paying and Collecting Agents) Regulations, SI 1996/1780.

13 Further provision relating to manufactured overseas dividends representative of foreign dividends

. . .

Amendments—This regulation revoked by the IT (Manufactured Overseas Dividends) (Amendment No 2) Regulations, SI 1996/2643 reg 13, with effect from 6 November 1996.

14 Records to be kept in respect of certain manufactured overseas dividends paid without deduction of tax

(1) An overseas dividend manufacturer or an approved United Kingdom collecting agent shall maintain a record in respect of any manufactured overseas dividend paid by him to which this regulation applies showing—

(*a*) the date of payment and the amount of the manufactured overseas dividend,

[(*b*) the name of the person to whom payment was made,][1]

[(*ba*) his grounds for believing that the payment should be made without deduction of tax, and][1]

(*c*) particulars of the overseas securities and the overseas dividend on those securities to which the manufactured overseas dividend relates.

[(2) This regulation applies to any manufactured overseas dividend which an overseas dividend manufacturer or an approved United Kingdom collecting agent, by virtue of regulation 5(1B), pays without deduction of tax.][1]

[(3) An overseas dividend manufacturer or an approved United Kingdom collecting agent—

(*a*) shall retain for a period of six years—

(i) any record required to be maintained by him under paragraph (1), and

(ii) any evidence relevant to his grounds for believing that the payment should be made without deduction of tax; and

(*b*) whenever required to do so within that period, shall make any such record or evidence available for inspection by an officer of the Board.][1]

[(3A) In the case of evidence or a record retained under paragraph (3) which is in electronic form the person retaining it shall afford an officer of the Board such assistance and facilities as the officer may reasonably require in order to read the record or certificate.][2]

(4) Where an overseas dividend manufacturer or an approved United Kingdom collecting agent fails to maintain, or to retain for the requisite period, any such record, or fails to retain any such [evidence][1] for the requisite period, the Board may require that person to carry out, at his own expense, an audit of manufactured overseas dividends paid by him in order to ascertain the amount of tax, if any, liable to be deducted under paragraph 4(2) of Schedule 23A which was not deducted.

(5) The scope and method of the audit referred to in paragraph (4) shall be agreed between the Board and the person concerned or, in the absence of agreement, shall be determined by the Board.

Amendments—[1] Sub-paras (1)(*b*), (*ba*) substituted for sub para (1)(*b*); paras (2), (3) substituted; and word in sub-para (4) substituted; by the IT (Manufactured Overseas Dividends) (Amendment) Regulations, SI 2003/2582 regs 2, 12 with effect from 1 November 2003.

[2] Para (3A) inserted by the Income and Corporation Taxes (Electronic Certificates of Deduction of Tax and Tax Credit) Regulations, SI 2003/3143 reg 5(1), (4) with effect from 1 January 2004.

15 Issue of vouchers in respect of manufactured overseas dividends paid under deduction of tax

(1) Subject to [paragraph (3)][2], where an overseas dividend manufacturer makes a payment of a manufactured overseas dividend from which an amount is deducted by him under paragraph 4(2) of Schedule 23A . . . [1] he shall furnish the recipient of the payment with a voucher showing the details specified in paragraph (4).

(2) . . . [2]

(3) Where the overseas dividend manufacturer is an approved United Kingdom intermediary, he shall not be required to furnish the recipient of a payment with the voucher referred to in paragraph (1) unless the recipient requests such a voucher.

(4) The details specified in this paragraph are that the voucher shall show—

(*a*) the gross amount of the payment,

(*b*) the amount deducted or, where more than one amount has been deducted, each such amount separately, and

(*c*) the actual amount paid.

(5) An approved United Kingdom collecting agent, where requested to do so by the person beneficially entitled to a manufactured overseas dividend in respect of which tax has been paid or is due to be paid by the approved United Kingdom collecting agent under paragraph 4(3) of Schedule 23A or regulation 4(3), shall furnish that person with a voucher showing—

(*a*) the gross amount of the manufactured overseas dividend received by him,

(*b*) the amount of tax paid or due to be paid by him in respect of the manufactured overseas dividend, and

(*c*) the actual amount paid.

Amendments—[1] Words in para (2) revoked by the IT (Manufactured Overseas Dividends) (Amendment No 2) Regulations, SI 1996/2643 reg 14, with effect from 6 November 1996.

[2] In para (1), words substituted, and para (2) revoked, by the Income Tax (Manufactured Overseas Dividends) (Amendment No 2) Regulations, SI 2011/2503 regs 2, 8 with effect in relation to manufactured overseas dividends paid or treated as paid on or after 10 November 2011.

16 . . . [Modifications of section 21 of the Management Act in relation to overseas dividend manufacturers][1]

Amendments—[1] This regulation revoked by the Stock Lending and Manufactured Payments (Revocations and Amendments) Regulation, SI 1997/987, reg 8(1), (4), (5), with effect in relation to (*a*) transactions entered into on or after 1 July 1997 in respect of which information may be obtained under TMA 1970 s 21, and (*b*) payments made on or after that date (whether under transactions entered into before, or under transactions entered into on or after, that date) in respect of which information may be obtained under that section.

1993/3016

RETIREMENT BENEFITS SCHEMES (RESTRICTION ON DISCRETION TO APPROVE) (ADDITIONAL VOLUNTARY CONTRIBUTIONS) REGULATIONS 1993

Revocation—These Regulations lapse by virtue of the coming into force of FA 2004 Part 4 (ss 149–284) with effect from 6 April 2006.

1994/236

DISTRAINT BY COLLECTORS (FEES, COSTS AND CHARGES) REGULATIONS 1994

Made by the Treasury under TMA 1970 s 61(6)

Made . . . . *3 February 1994*
Laid before the House of Commons . . . . *4 February 1994*
Coming into Force . . . . *1 March 1994*

Commentary—*Simon's Taxes* **A1.712**.

1 Citation and commencement

These Regulations may be cited as the Distraint by Collectors (Fees, Costs and Charges) Regulations 1994 and shall come into force on 1st March 1994.

2 Interpretation

In these Regulations—

"close possession" means physical possession by the distrainor or a person acting on his behalf of the goods and chattels distrained;

"walking possession" means possession in accordance with an agreement between the distrainor and the distrainee whereby, in consideration of the distrainor not remaining in close possession, the distrainee undertakes not to dispose of the goods distrained or any part thereof, or permit their removal by any person not authorised by the distrainor to remove them.

3 Ascertainment of fees, costs and charges

The fees chargeable on or in connection with the levying of distress and the costs and charges recoverable where distress has been levied shall be those specified in the Schedule to these Regulations, but subject to any provision of that Schedule.

4 Deduction of fees, costs and charges by the collector

The fees, costs and charges specified in the Schedule to these Regulations shall be deducted by the collector from the sums received on or in connection with the levying of distress or where distress has been levied.

5 Disputes as to fees, costs and charges

(1) In the case of dispute as to any fees chargeable, or costs and charges recoverable under the Schedule to these Regulations, the amount of those fees, costs and charges shall be taxed.

(2) Such a taxation shall be carried out by the district judge of the county court for the district in which the distress is or is intended to be levied, and he may give such directions as to the costs of the taxation as he thinks fit.

(3) In the application of paragraph (2) to Northern Ireland, there shall be substituted for the words "by the district judge of the county court for the district in which the distress is or is intended to be levied" the words "by the Master (Taxing Office)".

SCHEDULE

Regulation 3

Action taken	*Fees, Costs and Charges*
On or in connection with the levying of distress	*Fees*
For making a visit to premises with a view to levying distress (whether the levy is made or not).	[A sum not exceeding £12·50][1].
Levying distress where the total sum charged is £100 or less.	£12·50.
Levying distress where the total sum charged is more than £100.12	½ per cent on the first £100 of the amount to be recovered; 4 per cent on the next £400; 2½ per cent on the next £1,500; 1 per cent on the next £8,000; ¼ per cent on any additional sum.
Where distress has been levied	*Costs and Charges*
1 Taking possession	
Where close possession is taken.	£4·50 for the day of levy only.
Where walking possession is taken.	45p per day, payable for the day the distress is levied and up to 14 days thereafter.
2 Removal and storage of goods	The reasonable costs and charges of removal and storage.
3 Appraisement	The reasonable fees, charges and expenses of the person appraising.
4 Sale	
[Where the sale is held on the auctioneer's premises, for the auctioneer's commission (to include all out-of-pocket expenses other than charges for advertising, removal and storage).	15 per cent on the sum realised plus the reasonable costs of advertising, removal and storage.
Where the sale is held on the debtor's premises, for the auctioneer's commission (not to include out-of-pocket expenses or charges for advertising).	7½ per cent on the sum realised plus out-of-pocket expenses actually and reasonably incurred and the reasonable costs of advertising.][1]

1 In any case where close possession is taken, an individual left in possession must provide his own board.

2 For the purpose of calculating any percentage fees, costs and charges, a fraction of £1 is to be reckoned as £1, but any fraction of a penny in the total amount so calculated is to be disregarded.

3 In addition to any amount authorised by this Schedule in respect of the supply of goods or services on which value added tax is chargeable there may be added a sum equivalent to value added tax at the appropriate rate on that amount.

Amendments—[1] Words substituted by the Distraint by Collectors (Fees, Costs and Charges) (Amendment) Regulations, SI 1995/2151 reg 2, with effect from 8 September 1995.

[2] These regulations revoked, to the extent that they apply to England and Wales only, by the Tribunals, Courts and Enforcement Act 2007 (Consequential, Transitional and Saving Provision) Order, SI 2014/600 art 7, Schedule Pt 2 with effect from 6 April 2014.

1994/777

INCOME TAX (CAR BENEFITS) (REPLACEMENT ACCESSORIES) REGULATIONS 1994

Amendments—These Regulations revoked by ITEPA 2003 s 724, Sch 8 with effect, for income tax purposes, from 2003–04; and for corporation tax purposes, for accounting periods ending after 5 April 2003. For transitional provisions and savings see ITEPA 2003 s 723, Sch 7.

1994/778

INCOME TAX (REPLACEMENT CARS) REGULATIONS 1994

Amendment—These Regulations revoked by ITEPA 2003 s 724, Sch 8 with effect, for income tax purposes, from 2003–04; and for corporation tax purposes, for accounting periods ending after 5 April 2003. For transitional provisions and savings see ITEPA 2003 s 723, Sch 7.

1994/1212

INCOME TAX (EMPLOYMENTS) (NOTIONAL PAYMENTS) REGULATIONS 1994

Made by the Commissioners of Inland Revenue under TA 1988 s 203

Made . . . . *4 May 1994*
Laid before the House of Commons . . . . *4 May 1994*
Coming into Force . . . . *25 May 1994*

Amendment—These regulations are revoked by the Income Tax (Pay As You Earn) Regulations, SI 2003/2682 reg 220, Sch 2 with effect from 6 April 2004, subject to transitional provisions contained in Sch 1 thereto.

1994/1811

SPECIAL COMMISSIONERS (JURISDICTION AND PROCEDURE) REGULATIONS 1994

Revocation—These Regulations revoked by the Transfer of Tribunal Functions and Revenue and Customs Appeals Order, SI 2009/56 art 3, Sch 2 para 187(*e*) with effect from 1 April 2009.

1994/1812

GENERAL COMMISSIONERS (JURISDICTION AND PROCEDURE) REGULATIONS 1994

Made by the Lord Chancellor under TMA 1970 ss 46A, 56B

Made . . . . *6 July 1994*
Laid before Parliament . . . . *14 July 1994*
Coming into Force . . . . *1 September 1994*

Revocation—These Regulations revoked by the Transfer of Tribunal Functions and Revenue and Customs Appeals Order, SI 2009/56 art 3, Sch 2 para 187(*f*) with effect from 1 April 2009, subject to transitional and savings provisions in Sch 3 para 11.

1994/2318

INCOME TAX (AUTHORISED UNIT TRUSTS) (INTEREST DISTRIBUTIONS) REGULATIONS 1994

Amendment—These regulations are revoked by the IT (Authorised Unit Trusts) (Interest Distributions) Regulations, SI 2003/1830 reg 11 with effect for interest distributions made after 15 October 2002.

1994/2656

CAPITAL GAINS TAX (GILT-EDGED SECURITIES) ORDER 1994

Made by the Treasury under TCGA 1992 Sch 9, para 1

Made . . . . *11 October 1994*

1 This Order may be cited as the Capital Gains Tax (Gilt-edged Securities) Order 1994.

2 The following securities are hereby specified for the purposes of Schedule 9 to the Taxation of Chargeable Gains Act 1992—

7% Treasury Convertible Stock 1997
7¼% Treasury Stock 1998 "A"
7¼% Treasury Stock 1998 "B"
6% Treasury Stock 1999
Floating Rate Treasury Stock 1999

7% Treasury Stock 2001
7% Treasury Stock 2001 "A"
8% Treasury Stock 2003 "A"
6¾% Treasury Stock 2004
6¾% Treasury Stock 2004 "A"
7¼% Treasury Stock 2006
8½% Treasury Loan 2007 "C"
9% Treasury Loan 2008 "D"
6¼% Treasury Stock 2010
9% Conversion Loan 2011 "C"
9% Conversion Loan 2011 "D"
8% Treasury Stock 2013.

1994/3226

EXCHANGE GAINS AND LOSSES (TRANSITIONAL PROVISIONS) REGULATIONS 1994

Made by the Treasury under FA 1993 ss 164(14), 165(4), (5), 167(1), (4)–(6), Sch 16

Made . . . .*15 December 1994*
Laid before the House of Commons . . . .*16 December 1994*
Coming into Force . . . .*23 March 1995*

Commentary—*Simon's Taxes.*
Modification—See the Exchange Gains and Losses (Transitional Provisions and Savings) Regulations, SI 2002/1969 (SI 1994/3226, as modified by SI 2002/1969, to continue to have effect notwithstanding the repeal of FA 1993 ss 164(14), 165(4)–(6), 167(1), (4)–(6), Sch 16 by FA 2002 ss 79(1)(*b*), 141, Sch 40 Pt 3(10) with effect for accounting periods beginning after 30 September 2002).

PART I
INTRODUCTORY PROVISIONS

1 Citation, commencement and interpretation

(1) These Regulations may be cited as the Exchange Gains and Losses (Transitional Provisions) Regulations 1994.
(2) These Regulations shall come into force on 23rd March 1995.
(3) In these Regulations, subject to any contrary intention—
(*a*) "the 1992 Act" means the Taxation of Chargeable Gains Act 1992;
(*b*) "the 1993 Act" means the Finance Act 1993;
[(*ba*) "discounted debt" has the same meaning as "relevant discounted security" as that term is defined for the purposes of Schedule 13 to the Finance Act 1996 by paragraphs 3 and 14(1) of that Schedule;][1]
(*c*) any reference to Chapter II is a reference to Chapter II of Part II of the 1993 Act;
(*d*) any reference to a particular section is a reference to that section of that Act;
(*e*) any reference to an exchange gain or loss is a reference to an exchange gain or loss of a trade or part of a trade or a non-trading exchange gain or loss;
(*f*) any reference to an exchange difference is a reference to any gain or loss which is attributable to fluctuations in currency exchange rates;
[(*g*) "a regulation 6(3) asset" means an existing asset the basic valuation of which was determined for the purposes of Chapter II in accordance with regulation 6(3) of these Regulations;][2]
(*h*) "the regulation 2(2) provisions" means the provisions specified in regulation 2(2) [; and
(*i*) "the relevant accounting period", in relation to a company, means the company's first accounting period to begin on or after 1st October 2002.][2]

(4) In determining for the purposes of these Regulations whether any gain or loss or other amount has or has not been taken into account for the purposes of corporation tax in computing a company's profits and gains (or the profits and gains of a trade) for an accounting period, or would have been or would not have been so taken into account if the company had been within the charge to corporation tax at the time the gain or loss accrued, there shall be disregarded, subject to any contrary intention, any insufficiency of profits or gains for that period.
(5) In computing the chargeable profits for an accounting period of a controlled foreign company as respects which—
(*a*) a direction under section 747 of the Income and Corporation Taxes Act 1988 has been given for the company's accounting period which includes the day preceding the day on which these Regulations come into force, or

(*b*) it can reasonably be assumed that such a direction would have been given for that accounting period but for the fact that the company pursues, within the meaning of Part I of Schedule 25 to that Act, an acceptable distribution policy,

it shall be assumed for the purposes of these Regulations (if it would not otherwise be so assumed) that the company is resident in the United Kingdom for the period as respects which the computation is being made for any other period (whether earlier or later than the period referred to in paragraph (a) or (b) above), and any gain or loss or other amount which is, or has been, taken into account in computing the company's chargeable profits for any period (or which would have been so taken into account if such a computation had been made) shall be treated for those purposes as being, or having been, taken into account for the purposes of corporation tax in computing the company's profits and gains for that period.

Amendments—[1] Definition of "discounted debt" inserted by the Exchange Gains and Losses (Transitional Provisions) (Amendment) Regulations, SI 1996/1349 reg 3, with effect from 30 June 1996.

[2] Sub-para (3)(*g*) substituted, and sub-para (3)(*i*) inserted by the Exchange Gains and Losses (Transitional Provisions and Savings) Regulations, SI 2002/1969 regs 2, 3 with effect for accounting periods beginning after 30 September 2002.

2 Interaction with other Exchange Gains and Losses provisions

(1) Subject to any provision to the contrary, in any case where a calculation falls to be made in relation to an existing asset, liability or contract in accordance with any of these Regulations and at the same time or in relation to the same event a calculation also falls to be made in relation to that asset, liability or contract in accordance with any of the provisions specified in paragraph (2) below, then the calculation to be made in accordance with these Regulations shall be made first and shall have effect for the purposes of the calculation falling to be made in accordance with any of those provisions.

(2) The provisions referred to above are the following—

[1]

The Exchange Gains and Losses (Alternative Method of Calculation of Gain or Loss) Regulations 1994;

. . . [1]

Amendments—[1] Words revoked by the Exchange Gains and Losses (Transitional Provisions and Savings) Regulations, SI 2002/1969 regs 2, 4 with effect for accounting periods beginning after 30 September 2002.

PART II
MISCELLANEOUS TRANSITIONAL PROVISIONS

3–6 . . .

Amendment—Regulations 3–6 revoked by the Exchange Gains and Losses (Transitional Provisions and Savings) Regulations, SI 2002/1969 regs 2, 5 with effect for accounting periods beginning after 30 September 2002.

PART III
PRE-COMMENCEMENT GAINS AND LOSSES: CASE I ASSETS AND LIABILITIES AND CAPITAL ASSETS

7 Interpretation

(1) For the purposes of any computation required to be made for the purposes of regulation 10 or 11 below, an amount which is a gain shall be taken to be a positive figure and an amount which is a loss shall be taken to be a negative figure, but for the purposes of regulations 12 and 13 all amounts shall be taken to be positive.

(2) In this Part—

"attributed gain", in relation to any asset or liability, means a gain which is attributed to the asset or liability under regulation 8(3) or 9(2) below;

"attributed loss", in relation to any asset or liability, means a loss which is attributed to the asset or liability under regulation 8(3) or 9(2) below;

"current period" has the meaning given by regulation 10 below;

"the cumulative gain" has the meaning given by regulation 10 below;

"the cumulative loss" has the meaning given by regulation 10 below;

"the cumulative taxed gain" has the meaning given by regulation 11 below;

"the cumulative taxed loss" has the meaning given by regulation 11 below;

["the final accounting period", in relation to a company, means the company's accounting period preceding the relevant accounting period;][1]

. . . [1]

Amendment—[1] In sub-para (2), definition of "the final accounting period" inserted, and words revoked, by the Exchange Gains and Losses (Transitional Provisions and Savings) Regulations, SI 2002/1969 regs 2, 6 with effect for accounting periods beginning after 30 September 2002.

8 Attributed gains and losses: trade assets and liabilities

(1) Paragraph (3) below applies in relation to an existing asset held by a qualifying company—

(*a*) if a profit or loss would have accrued to the company if it had disposed of the asset immediately before the company's commencement day for a consideration equal to the asset's basic valuation; and

(*b*) that profit or loss would have been taken into account in computing for the purposes of corporation tax the profits and gains of a trade carried on by the company for the accounting period which includes the day immediately before the company's commencement day.

(2) Paragraph (3) below applies in relation to an existing liability owed by a qualifying company—

(*a*) if a profit or loss would have accrued to the company—

(i) in a case falling within section 153(2)(*a*), if the liability had been satisfied in full by the company immediately before the company's commencement day, or

(ii) in a case falling within section 153(2)(*c*) or (*d*), if the right to settlement or the share or shares in question (as the case may be) had been acquired by the company immediately before the company's commencement day for a consideration equal to the consideration for the company becoming subject to the liability, and

(*b*) that profit or loss (if it had accrued) would have been taken into account in computing for the purposes of corporation tax the profits and gains of a trade carried on by the company for the accounting period ending immediately before the company's commencement day.

(3) The amount of any such profit or loss as is mentioned in paragraph (1) or (2) above reduced in accordance with paragraph (4) below if applicable, shall be attributed to the asset or liability (as the case may be) and—

(*a*) in the case of a profit shall be attributed as a gain, and

(*b*) in the case of a loss shall be attributed as a loss.

(4) In any case where unrealised exchange differences which have accrued in respect of the asset or liability are taken into account for the purposes of corporation tax for the accounting period ending immediately before the company's commencement day or any earlier accounting period, the amount of the profit or loss referred to in paragraph (3) above shall be reduced by an amount equal to the amount of those differences.

(5) Section 159 applies for the purposes of this regulation as modified by regulation 6 [of these Regulations][1].

Amendment—[1] Words in sub-para (5) substituted by the Exchange Gains and Losses (Transitional Provisions and Savings) Regulations, SI 2002/1969 regs 2, 7 with effect for accounting periods beginning after 30 September 2002.

9 Attributed gains and losses: regulation 6(3) assets

(1) This regulation applies in relation to any regulation 6(3) asset held by a qualifying company a disposal of which by that company immediately before its commencement day at the asset's market value at that time would have given rise to a chargeable gain or allowable loss, but does not apply in any case where any such disposal of the asset by the company would fall within section 116(10)(*b*) of the 1992 Act.

(2) Subject to paragraph (3) below, an amount equal to any chargeable gain or allowable loss (as the case may be) which would have accrued to the company had it disposed of the asset as mentioned in paragraph (1) above shall be attributed to the asset and—

(*a*) if a chargeable gain would have accrued, it shall be attributed as a gain, and

(*b*) if an allowable loss would have accrued, it shall be attributed as a loss.

(3) In any case where—

(*a*) the asset was held by a company which at any time before its commencement day was not resident in the United Kingdom, and

(*b*) if the asset had been disposed of at that time and a gain had accrued to the company on that disposal, it would not have been included in the company's chargeable profits by virtue of section 10(3) of the 1992 Act,

then for the purposes of paragraph (1) above the company shall be deemed to have acquired the asset, at market value, on the first day on which any gain which would have accrued to the company if the asset had been disposed of on that day (assuming that the disposal gave rise to a gain and disregarding any allowable losses which might be available for deduction under section 8(1) of, or Schedule 7A to, the 1992 Act) would have been included in the company's chargeable profits for the purposes of corporation tax (whether because the company became resident or the asset became situated in the United Kingdom on that day or for any other reason).

(4) In any case where the company referred to in paragraph (1) above acquired the asset on a no gain/no loss disposal, then the reference in paragraph (3) above to a company includes the company from which it acquired the asset, and if that company also acquired the asset on such a disposal, to the company from which it acquired the asset, and so on for a series of such disposals.

(5) The disposal referred to in paragraph (1) above shall be taken not to be a no gain/no loss disposal, and for the purposes of this regulation a disposal is a no gain/no loss disposal if, by virtue of any enactment specified in section 35(3)(*d*) of the 1992 Act, neither a gain nor a loss accrues to the person making the disposal.

(6) In any case where section 176 of the 1992 Act would have applied in relation to the disposal referred to in paragraph (1) above if that disposal had actually taken place, that section shall apply for the calculation of any allowable loss for the purposes of that paragraph.

(7) Any expression used in this regulation which is not defined in Chapter II shall have the same meaning as in the 1992 Act.

10 The cumulative gain and the cumulative loss

(1) Subject to regulation 15, in the case of any existing asset or liability held or owed by a company as respects which an initial exchange gain or loss accrues to the company for an accrual period ("the current period"), there shall be calculated the aggregate amount of initial exchange gains and losses which have accrued as respects the asset or liability in question for all earlier accrual periods and for the current period, and that aggregate amount—

(*a*) if positive, shall be the cumulative gain for that asset or liability for the current period, and

(*b*) if negative, shall be the cumulative loss for that asset or liability for the current period,

but in cases where that aggregate amount is zero there shall be either a cumulative gain or a cumulative loss equal to zero for the period, according to whether there was a cumulative gain or a cumulative loss of any amount (including zero) for the accrual period immediately preceding the current period.

(2) For the purposes of paragraph (1) above, the amount of any initial exchange gain or loss shall be determined disregarding the following provisions of this Part and the regulation 2(2) provisions.

[(3) Where—

(*a*) the asset held or the liability owed by the company consists of a discounted debt, and

(*b*) the company did not cease on 31st March 1996 to be entitled to the asset or (as the case may be) subject to the liability,

it shall be regarded, for the purposes of paragraph (1) above the section 158 (translation times and accrual periods), as ceasing on that date to be entitled or subject, and references in this regulation and in regulations 11 and 12 to accrual periods (including references to an accrual period as the current period) shall, as respects that asset or liability, be construed accordingly.][1]

Amendments—[1] Para (3) added by the Exchange Gains and Losses (Transitional Provisions) (Amendment) Regulations, SI 1996/1349 reg 5, with effect from 30 June 1996.

11 The cumulative taxed gain and the cumulative taxed loss

(1) In the case of any asset or liability to which regulation 10 applies, there shall be calculated the aggregate amount of the initial exchange gains and losses which have accrued to the company as respects the asset or liability for accrual periods earlier than the current period, and—

(*a*) if that aggregate amount is positive it shall be the cumulative taxed gain for that asset or liability for the current period,

(*b*) if it is negative it shall be the cumulative taxed loss for that asset or liability for the current period, and

(*c*) if that aggregate amount is zero or, by virtue of regulation 12, there is no aggregate amount, there shall be taken to be a cumulative taxed loss equal to zero for the period.

(2) For the purposes of paragraph (1) above—

(*a*) the question whether any initial exchange gain or loss has accrued for any period other than the current period shall be determined in accordance with this Part but as if the regulation 2(2) provisions had never come into force; and

(*b*) there shall be disregarded any gain or loss which accrued for an accrual period other than the current period unless—

(i) it has been taken into account in computing the profits or gains of the company holding or owing the asset or liability for the purposes of corporation tax for accounting periods ending before the beginning of the current period, or

(ii) it would have been so taken into account if the regulation 2(2) provisions had never come into force; or

(iii) it is equal to zero.

12 Assets and liabilities as respects which there is an attributed gain or loss

(1) Subject to regulation 15, in relation to an asset or liability held or owed by a company as respects which—

(*a*) there is an attributed gain, E, or an attributed loss, F, and

(*b*) an initial exchange gain or loss ("the actual gain or loss") accrues to the company for the current period,

Table A or Table B below (as appropriate) shall apply and in any case falling within the first column of that Table, the actual gain or loss shall be deemed not to accrue but, subject to any conditions specified in the second column, the gain or loss specified in relation thereto in the third column shall be deemed to accrue and shall be an initial exchange gain or loss (as the case may be) accruing in the place of the actual gain or loss.

(2) For the purposes of paragraph (1)(*b*) above, the question whether any initial exchange gain or loss has accrued shall be determined disregarding this Part and the regulation 2(2) provisions.

TABLE A
IF THERE IS AN ATTRIBUTED GAIN E

Case for the current period	Condition	Deemed gain or loss
1 Cumulative loss B and no cumulative taxed gain or loss	B is greater than E	Loss equal to B–E
2 Cumulative loss B and a cumulative taxed loss C	(i) B is not greater than E and C is greater than zero	(i) Gain equal to C
	(ii) B is greater than E and C is less than (B – E)	(ii) Loss equal to (B – E) – C
	(iii) B is greater than E and C is greater than (B – E)	(iii) Gain equal to C – (B – E)
3 Cumulative loss B and a cumulative taxed gain D	(i) B is greater than E	(i) Loss equal to (B – E) + D
	(ii) B is not greater than E	(ii) Loss equal to D
4 Cumulative gain A and a cumulative taxed gain D	(i) A is greater than D	(i) Gain equal to A – D
	(ii) D is greater than A	(ii) Loss equal to D – A
5 Cumulative gain A and a cumulative taxed loss C		Gain equal to C + A

TABLE B
IF THERE IS AN ATTRIBUTED LOSS F

Case for the current period	Condition	Deemed gain or loss
1 Cumulative gain A and no cumulative taxed gain or loss	A is greater than F	Gain equal to A – F
2 Cumulative gain A and a cumulative taxed gain D	(i) A is not greater than F	(i) Loss equal to D
	(ii) A is greater than F and D is less than (A – F)	(ii) Gain equal to (A – F) – D
	(iii) A is greater than F and D is greater than (A – F)	(iii) Loss equal to D – (A – F)
3 Cumulative gain A and a cumulative taxed loss C	(i) A is greater than F	(i) Gain equal to (A – F) + C
	(ii) A is not greater than F and C is greater than zero	(ii) Gain equal to C
4 Cumulative loss B and a cumulative taxed loss C	(i) B is greater than C	(i) Loss equal to B – C
	(ii) C is greater than B	(ii) Gain equal to C – B
5 Cumulative loss B and a cumulative taxed gain D		Loss equal to B + D

13 Gains and losses on disposal of assets and liabilities

(1) Subject to regulations [14 and 14A][1], paragraph (2) or (3) below applies where—

(*a*) an accrual period ends as respects an existing asset or liability held or owed by a company which is the last accrual period as respects that asset or liability, and

(*b*) there is as respects the asset or liability an attributed gain or loss.

[(1A) For the purposes of paragraph (1)(*a*) above, the final accounting period shall be treated as the last accrual period as respects any asset or liability held or owed by the company immediately after the end of the final accounting period.][1]

(2) If there is an attributed gain, E, as respects the asset or liability, then—

(*a*) if there is a cumulative gain, A, as respects the asset or liability for the last period, an amount equal to E shall be deemed to be a relevant gain, accruing to the company as respects that asset or liability immediately [after the end of the final accounting period][1];

(*b*) if there is a cumulative loss, B, as respects the asset or liability for the last period, and E exceeds B, an amount equal to the excess shall be deemed to be a relevant gain, accruing to the company as respects that asset or liability immediately [after the end of the final accounting period][1]; and

(*c*) if there is neither a cumulative loss nor a cumulative gain as respects the asset or liability for the last period, an amount equal to E shall be deemed to be a relevant gain, accruing to the company as respects that asset or liability immediately [after the end of the final accounting period][1].

(3) If there is an attributed loss, F, as respects the asset or liability, then—

(*a*) if there is a cumulative loss, B, as respects the asset or liability for the last period, an amount equal to F shall be deemed to be a relevant loss, accruing to the company as respects that asset or liability immediately [after the end of the final accounting period][1];

(*b*) if there is a cumulative gain, A, as respects the asset or liability for the last period, and F exceeds A, an amount equal to the excess shall be deemed to be a relevant loss, accruing to the company as respects that asset or liability immediately [after the end of the final accounting period][1]; and

(*c*) if there is neither a cumulative loss nor a cumulative gain as respects the asset or liability for the last period, an amount equal to F shall be deemed to be a relevant loss, accruing to the company as respects that asset or liability immediately [after the end of the final accounting period][1].

[(4) In paragraphs (2) and (3) above, a relevant gain or loss in relation to a regulation 6(3) asset is a chargeable gain or an allowable loss.][1]

[(4A) In relation to any asset other than a regulation 6(3) asset or any liability, an amount equal to the amount of any relevant gain or loss that is deemed to accrue to the company under paragraph (2) or (3) above shall be treated for the purposes of Chapter 2 of Part 4 of the Finance Act 1996 (according to whether it is a relevant gain or loss)—

(*a*) as a credit in respect of a loan relationship of the company, or

(*b*) as a debit in respect of a loan relationship of the company,

which falls to be brought into account under section 82(2) of that Act.][1]

(5)–(8) . . .[1]

Amendments—[1] Words in sub-paras (1), (2), (3) substituted, sub-para (1A) inserted, sub-paras (4), (4A) substituted for para (4), and sub-paras (5)–(8) revoked, by the Exchange Gains and Losses (Transitional Provisions and Savings) Regulations, SI 2002/1969 regs 2, 8 with effect for accounting periods beginning after 30 September 2002.

14 [Elections to defer bringing into account relevant gains and losses deemed to accrue immediately after the end of the final accounting period

(1) In any case where, apart from this regulation, relevant gains or losses would accrue to a company immediately after the end of the final accounting period by virtue of regulation 13, the company may elect, by notice to the inspector within two years of the end of the final accounting period, that this regulation shall apply as respects—

(*a*) subject to paragraph (3) below, all relevant gains or losses to which paragraph (4) of regulation 13 would apply;

(*b*) all relevant gains or losses to which paragraph (4A) of that regulation would apply; or

(*c*) both.

An election under this paragraph shall be irrevocable.

(2) Where an election is made under paragraph (1) above, every gain or loss to which this regulation applies shall be treated as accruing only when the asset or liability to which the gain or loss relates ceases to be held or owed by the company.

(3) No election may be made under paragraph (1) above as respects relevant gains or losses to which regulation 13(4) would apply if an election under regulation 14A is made as regards such losses.][1]

Amendments—[1] Regulations 14, 14A and 14B substituted for regulation 14 as originally enacted by the Exchange Gains and Losses (Transitional Provisions and Savings) Regulations, SI 2002/1969 regs 2, 9 with effect for accounting periods beginning after 30 September 2002.

14A [Elections to treat losses deemed to accrue immediately after the end of the final accounting period as debits in respect of loan relationships

(1) In any case where—

(*a*) apart from this regulation, relevant losses would accrue to a company as respects regulation 6(3) assets immediately after the end of the final accounting period by virtue of regulation 13; and

(*b*) if relevant gains would accrue as respects such assets at that time by virtue of that regulation, such losses would exceed them,

the company may elect, by notice to the inspector within two years of the end of the final accounting period, that this regulation shall apply as respects such losses or, in a case where sub-paragraph (b) applies, such losses to the extent that they exceed the relevant gains.

An election under this paragraph shall be irrevocable.

(2) Where an election is made under paragraph (1) above, an amount equal to the amount of the losses to which this regulation applies shall be treated for the purposes of Chapter 2 of Part 4 of the Finance Act 1996 as a debit in respect of a loan relationship of the company for the new accounting period and not falling to be brought into account under section 82(2) of that Act.][1]

Amendments—[1] Regulations 14, 14A and 14B substituted for regulation 14 as originally enacted by the Exchange Gains and Losses (Transitional Provisions and Savings) Regulations, SI 2002/1969 regs 2, 9 with effect for accounting periods beginning after 30 September 2002.

14B [Treatment of losses available to be carried forward at the end of the final accounting period as a result of an election made under regulation 14(5) or 16(1)

(1) This regulation apples where, as a result of an election made under regulation 14(5) or 16(1) of these Regulations, an amount of available losses ("the relevant amount") was available at the end of the final accounting period to be carried forward and, apart from this regulation, to be set against a company's exchange gains.

(2) Where this regulation applies an amount equal to the relevant amount shall be treated for the purposes of Chapter 2 of Part 4 of the Finance Act 1996 as a debit in respect of a loan relationship of the company for the new accounting period and not falling to be brought into account under section 82(2) of that Act.][1]

Amendments—[1] Regulations 14, 14A and 14B substituted for regulation 14 as originally enacted by the Exchange Gains and Losses (Transitional Provisions and Savings) Regulations, SI 2002/1969 regs 2, 9 with effect for accounting periods beginning after 30 September 2002.

15 Elections to treat pre-commencement day gains and losses as accruing after commencement day over 6 year period

. . .

Amendment—Regulations 15, 16 revoked by the Exchange Gains and Losses (Transitional Provisions and Savings) Regulations, SI 2002/1969 regs 2, 10 with effect for accounting periods beginning after 30 September 2002.

16 Set off of certain pre-commencement losses against exchange gains

. . .

Amendment—Regulations 15, 16 revoked by the Exchange Gains and Losses (Transitional Provisions and Savings) Regulations, SI 2002/1969 regs 2, 10 with effect for accounting periods beginning after 30 September 2002.

PART IV
PRE-COMMENCEMENT GAINS AND LOSSES: DEBTS OF FIXED AMOUNTS

. . .

Amendment—Pt IV (regs 17–22) revoked by the Exchange Gains and Losses (Transitional Provisions and Savings) Regulations, SI 2002/1969 regs 2, 11 with effect for accounting periods beginning after 30 September 2002.

1994/3227

EXCHANGE GAINS AND LOSSES (ALTERNATIVE METHOD OF CALCULATION OF GAIN OR LOSS) REGULATIONS 1994

Made by the Treasury under FA 1993 ss 164(14), 167(1), (4)–(6), Sch 15

Made . . . . 15 December 1994

Laid before the House of Commons . . . . 16 December 1994

Coming into Force . . . . 23 March 1995

Commentary—*Simon's Taxes.*

Modification—See the Exchange Gains and Losses (Transitional Provisions and Savings) Regulations, SI 2002/1969 (SI 1994/3227, as modified by SI 2002/1969, to continue to have effect notwithstanding the repeal of FA 1993 ss 164(14), 167(1), (4)–(6), Sch 15 by FA 2002 ss 79, 141, Sch 40 Pt 3(10) with effect for accounting periods beginning after 30 September 2002).

GENERAL

1 Citation, commencement and interpretation

(1) These Regulations may be cited as the Exchange Gains and Losses (Alternative Method of Calculation of Gain or Loss) Regulations 1994.

(2) These Regulations shall come into force on 23rd March 1995.

(3) In these Regulations "the 1993 Act" means the Finance Act 1993.

ASSETS ETC HELD IN EXEMPT CIRCUMSTANCES

2 Reduction in exchange gains and losses

. . .

Amendment—Regulations 2, 3 revoked by the Exchange Gains and Losses (Transitional Provisions and Savings) Regulations, SI 2002/1969 regs 12, 13 with effect for accounting periods beginning after 30 September 2002.

UNREMITTABLE INCOME

3 Reduction in exchange gains and losses

. . .

Amendment—Regulations 2, 3 revoked by the Exchange Gains and Losses (Transitional Provisions and Savings) Regulations, SI 2002/1969 regs 12, 13 with effect for accounting periods beginning after 30 September 2002.

MATCHING

4 Interpretation

(1) This regulation has effect for the interpretation of regulations 5 to 11.

(2) In those regulations—

"the Taxes Act" means the Income and Corporation Taxes Act 1988;

"the 1992 Act" means the Taxation of Chargeable Gains Act 1992;

"accounts", in relation to a company, means the accounts of the company prepared in accordance with normal accountancy practice being either—

(i) the annual accounts of the company prepared in accordance with Part VII of the Companies Act 1985 or

(ii) if the company is not required to prepare such accounts, the accounts which it is required to keep under the law of its home State or, if it is not so required to keep accounts, such of its accounts as most closely correspond to accounts which it would have been required to prepare if the provisions of that Part applied to the company;

"a local currency election" means an election under the Local Currency Elections Regulations 1994;

"chargeable gain" has the same meaning as it has for the purposes of the 1992 Act;

"a liability" means—

(*a*) a liability falling within section 153(2)(*a*) of the 1993 Act, or

(*b*) in relation to a currency contract held by a company, the duty of the company under that contract to pay in exchange for one currency an amount of a second currency;

["qualifying asset" shall be construed in accordance with subsection (1) of section 153 of the 1993 Act, read with subsections (3) and (4) of that section][1]

and in relation to a currency contract references to initial exchange gains or losses shall be construed as references to initial exchange gains or losses accruing as regards the second currency.

(3) For the purposes of this regulation and regulations 5 to 11, any reference to an asset being matched in part only shall include a reference to any asset matched in accordance with an election under regulation 10(2)(*c*).

(4) A liability is matched by an asset at any time only to the extent that the value of the liability at that time is matched by the value of the asset at that time and, subject to that, if the election concerned is made under regulation 10(2)(*c*) so that the asset is matched in part only, the liability shall be taken to be matched only to a corresponding extent.

(5) The value of a company's asset or liability at any time shall be taken to be the value attributed to the asset or liability as at that time by the company for the purposes of its accounts for the accounting period which includes that time (expressed in the currency in which those accounts are prepared).

(6) Any reference to the disposal of an asset and to the time of the disposal of an asset shall be construed as a reference to any event which is a disposal for the purposes of the 1992 Act and the time at which the disposal occurs for the purposes of that Act, and for the purposes of the foregoing, any reference to a disposal includes a part disposal.

Modifications—Para (2) modified by the Exchange Gains and Losses (Miscellaneous Modifications) Regulations, SI 2000/3315 regs 6, 8 with effect for any accounting period of a company beginning after 31 December 1999 for which FA 2000 ss 105, 106 have effect. Para (2) as modified reads as follows—

(2) In those regulations—

"the Taxes Act" means the Income and Corporation Taxes Act 1988;

"the 1992 Act" means the Taxation of Chargeable Gains Act 1992;

"accounts", in relation to a company, means the accounts of the company prepared in accordance with normal accountancy practice being either—

(i) the annual accounts of the company prepared in accordance with Part VII of the Companies Act 1985 or

(ii) if the company is not required to prepare such accounts, the accounts which it is required to keep under the law of its home State or, if it is not so required to keep accounts, such of its accounts as most closely correspond to accounts which it would have been required to prepare if the provisions of that Part applied to the company;

["branch" shall be construed in accordance with section 93(7) of the 1993 Act;]

. . .

"chargeable gain" has the same meaning as it has for the purposes of the 1992 Act;

"a liability" means—

(*a*) a liability falling within section 153(2)(*a*) of the 1993 Act, or

(*b*) in relation to a currency contract held by a company, the duty of the company under that contract to pay in exchange for one currency an amount of a second currency;

"qualifying asset" shall be construed in accordance with subsection (1) of section 153 of the 1993 Act, read with subsections (3) and (4) of that section

["the relevant foreign currency" has the meaning given by section 93(7) of the 1993 Act.]

and in relation to a currency contract references to initial exchange gains or losses shall be construed as references to initial exchange gains or losses accruing as regards the second currency."

Amendments—[1] Definition of "qualifying asset" added by the Exchange Gains and Losses (Alternative Method of Calculation of Gain or Loss) (Amendment) Regulations, SI 1996/1347 regs 2, 3, with effect from 30 June 1996.

5 Gains and losses accruing as regards matched liabilities to be found by the alternative method of calculation

(1) This regulation applies in any case where—

(*a*) a liability is owed by a company, and

(*b*) the liability is eligible to be matched with an asset on a day which falls within an accrual period for that liability, and

(*c*) an election made under regulation 10 is in effect for that day matching the liability (wholly or in part) with an eligible asset held by the company;

and in this regulation "the current period" means that accrual period.

(2) In any case where this regulation applies, then, subject to [paragraphs (3) and (3A)][1] below—

(*a*) the amount of the initial exchange gain or initial exchange loss which, apart from this regulation, would accrue to the company for the current period as respects the liability shall be found in accordance with the alternative method of calculation, and

(*b*) the accrued amount for each day in that period during which the liability and asset are matched shall—

(i) if the whole of the liability is matched, be reduced to nil, or

(ii) if only a proportion of the liability is matched, be reduced by a corresponding proportion.

(3) If in any case where this regulation applies—

(*a*) at any time during the current period there is a major change in the extent to which the liability is matched, and

(*b*) there is a significant change in the rate of exchange relevant to the computation of the accrued amounts during the current period, and

(*c*) that time is not (disregarding this regulation) a translation time as respects the liability,

then[, subject to paragraph (3A) below,] the initial exchange gain or loss as respects the liability for the current period shall be calculated, in accordance with paragraph (2) above, as if that time were a translation time (but not so as to create more than one accrual period) so that separate calculations are made for different parts of the period.

[(3A) If in a case where this regulation applies—

(*a*) only a proportion of a liability owed by the company is matched with an asset, not being an asset that is a ship or an aircraft, or

(*b*) another liability owed by the company is eligible to be matched with that asset at the time the election is made, but is not matched, and

(*c*) an exchange loss in relation to—

(i) the whole of the liability referred to in sub-paragraph (*a*) or (*b*), or

(ii) a proportion of that liability, being in the case of the liability referred to in sub-paragraph (*a*), a greater proportion than the proportion matched,

is shown in the company's accounts for the period which is or includes the current period, in the reserves,

the amount of the initial exchange loss as respects that liability for the current period, calculated in accordance with this regulation, shall be reduced by the amount by which the exchange loss shown in the reserves and relating to that liability exceeds the exchange loss relating to the proportion (if any) of the liability that was matched.][1]

(4) A liability (not being a duty under a currency contract) is eligible to be matched with an asset if—

(*a*) the liability does not represent either—

(i) a duty to settle under a debt in respect of goods or services supplied to the company in the ordinary course of its trade, or

(ii) accrued interest, and

(*b*) the nominal currency of the liability is such that borrowing in that currency could reasonably be expected to eliminate or substantially reduce the economic risk of holding the asset which is attributable to fluctuations in exchange rates.

Where the asset is matched in part only, references in this paragraph to the asset are to the part matched.

(5) In the case of a liability which is a duty under a currency contract, the liability is eligible to be matched with an asset if the second currency to which it relates is such that the company could by entering into that contract reasonably expect to eliminate or substantially reduce the economic risk of holding the asset which is attributable to fluctuations in exchange rates.
Where the asset is matched in part only, references in this paragraph to the asset are to the part matched.

(6) An asset held by a company is an eligible asset at any time if at that time—

(*a*) it is shares in a company which is not resident in the United Kingdom, but this sub-paragraph only applies if at the time the election is made the company is an associated company of the company making the election; or

(*b*) it is shares in a company which—

(i) is resident in the United Kingdom, and

(ii) has made a local currency election and is entitled, by virtue of that election, to have the basic profits and losses of a trade, or part of a trade, which it carries on in the United Kingdom computed in a currency other than sterling, and

(iii) is a 90 per cent subsidiary (within the meaning of paragraph (7) below) of the company making the election; or

(*c*) it is a debt on a security which under the terms of issue can be converted into or exchanged for shares falling within sub-paragraph (*a*) or (*b*) above [and which is not a qualifying asset]; or

(*d*) it is the company's net investment in a branch outside the United Kingdom through which the company carries on a trade or part of a trade and the company has made a local currency election and is entitled, by virtue of that election, to have the basic profits and losses of that trade or that part computed in a currency other than sterling; or

(*e*) it is a ship or an aircraft.

(7) For the purposes of paragraph (6) above—

(*a*) "shares" includes stock but does not include any asset which is a qualifying asset, . . . [1]

[(*aa*) all shares in the same company shall constitute a single asset,

(*ab*) all debts on a security issued by the same company shall constitute a single asset, and][1]

(*b*) a company is a 90 per cent subsidiary of another company if it is a 90 per cent subsidiary of that other within the meaning of section 838 of the Taxes Act or would be if "directly or indirectly" were substituted for "directly" in subsection (1)(*c*) of that section.

(8) An asset held by a company is also an eligible asset at any time (whether or not it also falls within any provision of paragraph (6)) if at that time—

(*a*) a gain accruing on the disposal of the asset by a person resident in the United Kingdom would be a chargeable gain, and

(*b*) the asset—

(i) is not a qualifying asset, and

(ii) is held by a branch of the company outside the United Kingdom through which the company carries on a trade or part of a trade and the company is not entitled to have the basic profits and losses of that trade or that part computed in a currency other than sterling by virtue of a local currency election.

(9) For the purposes of paragraphs (6) and (8) above—

(*a*) a company is an associated company of another if that other directly controls 20 per cent or more of the voting power in the company;

(*b*) the net investment of a company in a branch is the value of the assets of that branch less the liabilities of the branch and any other liabilities owed by the company for the purposes of the trade or part trade carried on through the branch.

Modifications—This regulation modified by the Exchange Gains and Losses (Miscellaneous Modifications) Regulations, SI 2000/3315 regs 6, 8 with effect for any accounting period of a company beginning after 31 December 1999 for which FA 2000 ss 105, 106 have effect. Paras (6), (6A), (8), (9) as modified read as follows—

"(6) An asset held by a company [which prepares its accounts as a whole in sterling] is an eligible asset at any time if at that time—

(*a*) it is shares in a company which is not resident in the United Kingdom, but this sub-paragraph only applies if at the time the election is made the company is an associated company of the company making the election; or

(*b*) it is shares in a company which—

(i) is resident in the United Kingdom, and

[(ii) is a company to which section 93 of the 1993 Act applies by virtue of its accounts as a whole being prepared in a currency other than sterling in accordance with normal accounting practice, and]

(iii) is a 90 per cent subsidiary (within the meaning of paragraph (7) below) of the company making the election; or

(*c*) it is a debt on a security which under the terms of issue can be converted into or exchanged for shares falling within sub-paragraph (*a*) or (*b*) above [and which is not a qualifying asset]; or (*d*) it is the company's net investment [in a branch through which the company carries on a business or part of a business and, by virtue of section 93 of the 1993 Act, the profits and losses of that business or that part are to be computed and expressed in a currency other than sterling]; or

(*e*) it is a ship or an aircraft.

(6A) An asset held by a company which prepares its accounts as a whole in a currency other than sterling is an eligible asset at any time if at that time—

(*a*) it is shares which—

(i) are denominated in a currency other than the relevant foreign currency for the company making the election, and

(ii) are in a company that is not resident in the United Kingdom and is, at the time the election is made, an associated company of the company making the election; or

(*b*) it is shares in a company which—

(i) is resident in the United Kingdom, and

(ii) prepares its accounts as a whole either in sterling or in a currency other than sterling which is not the relevant foreign currency for the company making the election, and

(iii) is a 90 per cent. subsidiary (within the meaning of paragraph (7) below) of the company making the election; or

(*c*) it is a debt on a security which under the terms of issue can be converted into or exchanged for shares falling within sub-paragraph (*a*) or (*b*) above and which is not a qualifying asset; or

(*d*) it is the company's net investment in a branch through which the company carries on a business or part of a business and, by virtue of section 93 of the 1993 Act, the profits and losses of that business or that part are to be computed and expressed in a currency other than the relevant foreign currency for the company; or

(*e*) it is a ship or an aircraft.".

"(8) An asset held by a company is also an eligible asset at any time (whether or not it also falls within any provision of paragraph (6)) if at that time—

(*a*) a gain accruing on the disposal of the asset by a person resident in the United Kingdom would be a chargeable gain, and

[(*b*) the asset is not a qualifying asset, and

(*c*) the asset is held by a branch of the company outside the United Kingdom through which the company carries on a business or part of a business, and

(i) where the company prepares its accounts as a whole in sterling, the profits and losses of that business or that part are not to be computed and expressed in a currency other than sterling by virtue of section 93 of the 1993 Act, or

(ii) where the company prepares its accounts as a whole in a currency other than sterling, the profits and losses of that business or that part are not to be computed and expressed in a currency other than the relevant foreign currency for the company by virtue of that section.]

(9) For the purposes of paragraphs [(6), (6A) and (8)] above—

(*a*) a company is an associated company of another if that other directly controls 20 per cent or more of the voting power in the company;

(*b*) the net investment of a company in a branch is the value of the assets of that branch less the liabilities of the branch and any other liabilities owed by the company for the purposes of the [business] or part [business] carried on through the branch.".

Amendments—[1] Words in para (2) substituted, words in paras (3), (6)(*c*), and paras (3A), (7)(*aa*), (*ab*), inserted, and at the end of para (7)(*a*) word revoked, by the Exchange Gains and Losses (Alternative Method of Calculation of Gain or Loss) (Amendment) Regulations, SI 1996/1347 regs 2, 4, with effect as respects accrual periods ending on or after 30 June 1996.

6 Controlled foreign companies

(1) Where an accounting period of a controlled foreign company is or includes an accrual period, then, for the purposes of computing in accordance with Schedule 24 to the Taxes Act the company's chargeable profits for that accounting period, an election for matching may be made by a company resident in the United Kingdom which has, or jointly by companies resident in the United Kingdom which together have, a majority interest in the foreign company, notwithstanding that in such a case the company owing any liability or acquiring or holding any asset will not be the company making the election.

(2) Paragraph 4(3) and (4) of that Schedule shall apply for the purposes of determining whether one or more companies has a majority interest in another company and, for that purpose, the relevant accounting period is the accounting period referred to in paragraph (1) above.

7 Deemed gains and losses on disposal of matched assets

(1) [Paragraphs (3) to (5) below apply in any case where a disposal of an asset is deemed by virtue of paragraph (1A) below to have been made by a company immediately before the first day of its first accounting period to begin on or after 1st October 2002][1] ("the disposal time") and at any time before the disposal time it was (to any extent) a matched asset for the purposes of an election for matching made by the company ("the relevant election").

[(1A) For the purposes of paragraph (1) above, any asset held by the company at the beginning of the first day of its first accounting period to begin on or after 1st October 2002 shall be deemed to have been disposed of by the company immediately before that first day.][1]

(2) . . . [1]

(3) There shall be found as respects the liability or liabilities matched with the asset for each accrual period for which the relevant election has had effect—

(*a*) the amount of the initial exchange gain (if any) calculated in accordance with the preceding regulations, and

(*b*) the amount of the initial exchange gain which would have accrued if the relevant election had not had effect;

and the excess of the amount found under sub-paragraph (b) over that found under sub-paragraph (a), or if no amount is found under sub-paragraph (a) the amount found under sub-paragraph (b), for each period is referred to below as the amount by which the initial exchange gain for the period has been reduced.

(4) There shall be found as respects the liability or liabilities matched with the asset for each accrual period for which the relevant election has had effect—

(*a*) the amount of the initial exchange loss (if any) calculated in accordance with the preceding regulations, and

(*b*) the amount of the initial exchange loss which would have accrued if the relevant election had not had effect;

and the excess of the amount found under sub-paragraph (b) over that found under sub-paragraph (a), or if no amount is found under sub-paragraph (a) the amount found under sub-paragraph (b), for each period is referred to below as the amount by which the initial exchange loss for the period has been reduced.

(5) There shall be found—

(*a*) the aggregate of the amounts by which the initial exchange gains accruing as respects the liability for accrual periods for which the relevant election has effect have been reduced, and

(*b*) the aggregate of the amounts by which the initial exchange losses accruing as respects the liability for accrual periods for which the relevant election has effect have been reduced.

(6)–(8) . . . [1]

Amendments—[1] Words in para (1) substituted, para (1A) inserted, paras (2), (6)–(8) revoked, by the Exchange Gains and Losses (Transitional Provisions and Savings) Regulations, SI 2002/1969 regs 12, 14 with effect for accounting periods beginning after 30 September 2002.

8 Deferral etc of deemed gains and losses in certain cases

. . .

Amendment—Regulations 8, 9 revoked by the Exchange Gains and Losses (Transitional Provisions and Savings) Regulations, SI 2002/1969 regs 12, 15 with effect for accounting periods beginning after 30 September 2002.

9 Transactions to which section 116 or 127 of the 1992 Act applies

. . .

Amendment—Regulations 8, 9 revoked by the Exchange Gains and Losses (Transitional Provisions and Savings) Regulations, SI 2002/1969 regs 12, 15 with effect for accounting periods beginning after 30 September 2002.

10 Elections for matching

(1) Subject to the provisions of these Regulations, an election under this regulation—

(*a*) may be made by notice given to the inspector by the company which owes the liability to be matched by the election,

(*b*) shall have effect as from the day on which it is made, and

(*c*) shall be irrevocable.

(2) An election for matching must identify—

(*a*) . . . ;[1]

(*b*) the asset to be matched;

(*c*) if the liability [to be matched by the election][1] is not being matched with the whole of the asset either—

(i) a fixed percentage of the asset which is to be available for matching; or

(ii) the value of the whole asset as at the time the election is made and a specific amount which is to be available for matching; or

(iii) a proportion or part of the asset which is to be available for matching where the value of the proportion or part is to be determined by reference to a formula or other method of calculation specified in the election and may vary from time to time in accordance with that formula or other method of calculation;

(*d*) . . . ;[1]

(*e*) the provision of these Regulations by virtue of which the asset is an eligible asset.

(3) An election under paragraph (2)(*c*)(i) or (ii) above may be varied by a subsequent election under this regulation so as to increase the percentage or amount which is specified in the election.

(4) An election to match a liability with an asset falling within regulation 5(6)(*a*), (*b*), (*c*) or (*d*) or 5(8), shall not have effect for any accrual period for which an initial exchange gain accrues as respects the liability unless—

(*a*) any exchange difference arising in relation to the asset, and (*b*) at least part of any exchange difference arising in relation to the liability,

are shown, in the company's accounts for the period which is or includes the accrual period in which those differences arise, in the reserves, and if only part of the exchange differences relating to the liability are shown in the reserves, the election shall have effect for that period only to that part. Where the liability or asset (or both) are matched in part only, references in this paragraph to the liability or asset are to the part matched.

(5) An election shall not cease to have effect at any time by reason only that the liability [matched by][1] the election ceased at that time to match the asset to which the election refers either at all or to the same extent to which it matched it at the time the election was made (either by reason of its ceasing to be owed by the company or because it is reduced or its value changes), but where [in any such case at any time after the election is made or, in the case of an election to which regulation 11(2) applies, has effect, the company is subject to another eligible liability][1] which might have been [matched by][1] the election if the election had been made at that time, the election shall continue to have effect in relation to that other liability.

This paragraph shall apply with the necessary modifications in relation to any such other liability as it applies in relation to the liability originally [matched by][1] the election.

(6) In any case where the asset to which the election refers was original shares as defined by section 126 of the 1992 Act and by reason of a reorganisation (as so defined) the asset ceased at any time to match the liability [matched by][1] the election, then if the whole or any part of the new holding (as so defined) might have been specified in the election if the election had been made at the time of the reorganisation, the election shall not cease to have effect but shall continue to have effect in relation to the new holding or part as the case may be.

(7) Any question as to which liability is matched with which asset shall be determined on a just and reasonable basis.

Modifications—This regulation modified by the Exchange Gains and Losses (Miscellaneous Modifications) Regulations, SI 2000/3315 regs 6, 8 with effect for any accounting period of a company beginning after 31 December 1999 for which FA 2000 ss 105, 106 have effect. Para (4) as modified reads as follows—

"(4) An election to match a liability with an asset falling within regulation 5(6)(*a*), (*b*), (*c*) or (*d*) [or 5(6A)(*a*), (*b*), (*c*) or (*d*)] or 5(8), shall not have effect for any accrual period for which an initial exchange gain accrues as respects the liability unless—

(*a*) any exchange difference arising in relation to the asset, and

(*b*) at least part of any exchange difference arising in relation to the liability,

are shown, in the company's accounts for the period which is or includes the accrual period in which those differences arise, in the reserves, and if only part of the exchange differences relating to the liability are shown in the reserves, the election shall have effect for that period only to that part.".

Amendments—[1] Para (2)(*a*), (*d*) revoked, words in para (2)(*c*) inserted and words in paras (5), (6) substituted, by the Exchange Gains and Losses (Alternative Method of Calculation of Gain or Loss) (Amendment) Regulations, SI 1996/1347 regs 2, 5, with effect from 30 June 1996.

11 Effectiveness of elections

(1) An election which does not comply with regulation 10(2) shall be of no effect.

[(1A) Notwithstanding the following provisions of this regulation, an election made under regulation 10 or this regulation—

(*a*) shall have effect only in relation to accounting periods beginning before 1st October 2002, and

(*b*) an election which specifies a day as the day from which the election is to have effect must specify a day that falls within an accounting period beginning before 1st October 2002.][2]

(2) Notwithstanding regulation 10(1) above, if an election—

(*a*) specifies as an eligible asset an asset which the company acquired not more than 92 days before the day on which the election is made, and

(*b*) specifies the date of acquisition as the date as from which the election is to have effect,

the election shall have effect, so far as it relates to that asset and any liability to be matched with that asset, as from that date.

(3) Notwithstanding regulation 10(1) above, an election under regulation 10(3) may specify a day not more than 92 days earlier than the day on which the election is made as the date as from which the election is to have effect, and in such a case the election shall have effect as from that date.

(4) Notwithstanding regulation 10(1) above, if an election specifies an asset as an eligible asset which the company held on its commencement day and the election is made before the expiry—

(*a*) of the period of 183 days beginning with 23rd March 1995, or

(*b*) of the period of 92 days beginning with the company's commencement day,

whichever is the later, and the election specifies the company's commencement day as the date as from which the election is to have effect, the election shall have effect, so far as it relates to that asset and any liability to be matched with that asset, as from that specified day.

(5) Notwithstanding regulation 10(1) above, an election expressed to be made under this paragraph and made—

(*a*) in pursuance of regulation 6 above in relation to a controlled foreign company as respects which a direction under section 747 of the Taxes Act is given on or after 23rd March 1995 for an accounting period of the company [or, where the direction is given on or after 1st April 1996, no earlier accounting period of that company is an ADP exempt period][1], whenever beginning, (and a direction under that section has not been given with respect to an earlier accounting period of that company), and

(*b*) before the expiry of the period of 92 days beginning with the date of that direction,

shall have effect from the latest of the following days, that is to say, the first day of the first accounting period as respects which the direction has effect, the first day of the first accounting period beginning on or after 23rd March 1995, and the day on which the asset in question is acquired by the company.

[(6) In paragraph (5) above "ADP exempt period" means an accounting period of the company—

(*a*) which begins on or after 28th November 1995, and

(*b*) in respect of which the company has pursued, within the meaning of Part I of Schedule 25 to the Taxes Act, an acceptable distribution policy.][1]

Amendments—[1] Words in para 5(*a*) inserted and para (6) added by the Exchange Gains and Losses (Alternative Method of Calculation of Gain and Loss) (Amendment) Regulations, SI 1996/1347 regs 2, 6, with effect from 30 June 1996.

[2] Para (1A) substituted by the Exchange Gains and Losses (Transitional Provisions and Savings) Regulations, SI 2002/1969 regs 12, 16 with effect for accounting periods beginning after 30 September 2002.

TRANSACTIONS NOT AT ARM'S LENGTH

12 Disregard of regulations 2 and 4 to 11

. . .

Amendment—Regulation 12 revoked by the Exchange Gains and Losses (Transitional Provisions and Savings) Regulations, SI 2002/1969 regs 12, 17 with effect for accounting periods beginning after 30 September 2002.

1994/3228

EXCHANGE GAINS AND LOSSES (DEFERRAL OF GAINS AND LOSSES) REGULATIONS 1994

Note—These regulations lapsed on the repeal of the enabling authority by FA 2002, ss 79(1)(*b*), (3), 141, Sch 40, Pt 3(10), with effect from 1 October 2002.

1994/3229

EXCHANGE GAINS AND LOSSES (EXCESS GAINS AND LOSSES) REGULATIONS 1994

Note—These regulations lapsed on the repeal of the enabling authority by FA 2002, ss 79(1)(*b*), (3), 141, Sch 40, Pt 3(10), with effect from 1 October 2002.

1994/3230

LOCAL CURRENCY ELECTIONS REGULATIONS 1994

Revocation—These Regulations lapsed on the substitution of the enabling authority by FA 2000 s 105(1) with effect for accounting periods beginning on or after 1 January 2000 and ending on or after 1 March 2000.

1994/3231

EXCHANGE GAINS AND LOSSES (INSURANCE COMPANIES) REGULATIONS 1994

Made by the Treasury under FA 1993 ss 167(1), 168(2)–(5)

Made . . . . *15 December 1994*
Laid before the House of Commons . . . . *16 December 1994*
Coming into Force . . . . *23 March 1995*

Modification—See the Exchange Gains and Losses (Transitional Provisions and Savings) Regulations, SI 2002/1969 (SI 1994/3231 as modified by SI 2002/1969 to continue to have effect, notwithstanding the repeal, with effect for accounting periods beginning after 30 September 2002, of FA 1993 ss 167(1), 168(2)–(5) by FA 2002 ss 79(1)(*b*), 141, Sch 40 Pt 3(10)).

1—(1) These Regulations may be cited as the Exchange Gains and Losses (Insurance Companies) Regulations 1994.

(2) These Regulations shall come into force on 23rd March 1995.

[(3) In these Regulations unless the context otherwise requires—

"basic valuation" shall be construed in accordance with section 159(1) of the 1993 Act;

["the final accounting period", in relation to a company, means the company's accounting period preceding the first accounting period to begin on or after 1st October 2002;][2]

"loan relationship" shall be construed in accordance with the Corporation Tax Acts, except that a relationship shall not be a loan relationship where the profits or gains chargeable to tax under Case III of Schedule D which arise from the relationship are confined to interest;

"new holding" and "original shares" have the meanings given by section 126(1) of the 1992 Act;

"regulation 7 asset" shall be construed in accordance with regulation 7(1);

"the Taxes Act" means the Income and Corporation Taxes Act 1988;

"the 1992 Act" means the Taxation of Chargeable Gains Act 1992;

"the 1993 Act" means the Finance Act 1993.][1]

Amendments—[1] Para (3) substituted by the Exchange Gains and Losses (Insurance Companies) (Amendment) Regulations, SI 1996/673 regs 1, 3.

[2] Definition of "the final accounting period" inserted by the Exchange Gains and Losses (Transitional Provisions and Savings) Regulations, SI 2002/1969 regs 18, 19 with effect for accounting periods beginning after 30 September 2002.

2–5A. . .

Amendment—Regulations 2–5A revoked by the Exchange Gains and Losses (Transitional Provisions and Savings) Regulations, SI 2002/1969 regs 18, 20 with effect for accounting periods beginning after 30 September 2002.

6 . . .

Amendments—Regulation 6 revoked by the Exchange Gains and Losses (Insurance Companies) (Amendment) Regulations, SI 1996/673 regs 1(3), 5, with effect for accounting periods ending after 31 March 1996.

[7—[(1) An asset specified by this regulation is referred to in regulations 7A and 8 to 12 as a "regulation 7 asset".][4]

(2) An asset is specified by this regulation if it is an asset which, at the time of its disposal—

(*a*) represents a loan relationship of a company;

(*b*) is an asset to which paragraph (3), (4), (5) or (6) below applies; and

(*c*) is held in exempt circumstances.

(3) This paragraph applies to an asset if—

(*a*) the settlement currency of a debt to which it relates is a currency other than sterling; and

(*b*) that debt is not a debt on a security.

(4) This paragraph applies to an asset if the debt to which it relates is a debt on a security and is in a foreign currency.

(5) This paragraph applies to an asset if it is comprised in a relevant holding and is denominated in a currency other than sterling.

(6) This paragraph applies to an asset if—

(*a*) it is a qualifying corporate bond,

(*b*) it would not, apart from this paragraph, be a regulation 7 asset,

(*c*) it constitutes a new holding, and

(*d*) the original shares, in relation to the new holding, consisted of a regulation 7 asset by virtue of paragraph (3), (4) or (5) above.

(7) For the purposes of paragraph (4) above a debt is a debt in a foreign currency if it is—

(*a*) a debt expressed in a currency other than sterling;

(*b*) a debt the amount of which in sterling falls at any time to be determined by reference to the value at that time of a currency other than sterling; or

(*c*) subject to paragraph (8) below, a debt as respects which provision is made for its conversion into, or redemption in, a currency other than sterling.

(8) A debt is not a debt in a foreign currency for the purposes of paragraph (4) above by reason only that provision is made for its redemption on payment of an amount in a currency other than sterling equal, at the rate prevailing at the date of redemption, to a specified amount in sterling.

(9) For the purposes of paragraph (5) above an asset is comprised in a relevant holding if it consists of—

(*a*) a unit in a unit trust scheme, or

(*b*) a relevant interest in an offshore fund[, or][2]

[(*c*) a share in an open-ended investment company][2]

to which section 212 of the 1992 Act does not apply or would not apply if the asset were an asset of the company's [long-term insurance][3] fund.

(10) For the purposes of paragraph (5) above—

(*a*) a unit in a unit trust scheme, or

(*b*) a right (other than a share in a company) which constitutes a relevant interest in an offshore fund,

shall be taken to be denominated in a currency other than sterling if the price at which it may be acquired from, or disposed of to, persons concerned in the management of the trust or fund is fixed by those persons in a currency other than sterling.

(11) For the purposes of paragraph (5) above shares constituting a relevant interest in an offshore fund shall be taken to be denominated in a currency other than sterling if their nominal value is expressed in such a currency [; and shares of a given class in an open-ended investment company shall be taken to be denominated in a currency other than sterling if the price at which they may be acquired from, or disposed of to, the company or its authorised corporate director is fixed by the company or director in a currency other than sterling, or (as the case may be) the price or prices at which they are quoted in The Stock Exchange Daily Official List is in a currency other than sterling][2].

(12) The reference in paragraph (2)(*c*) above to exempt circumstances shall be construed in accordance with paragraph 3 of Schedule 17 to the 1993 Act, but as if references in that paragraph to a currency were references to the debt to which the relationship relates.

(13) In this regulation—

"debt on a security" shall be construed in accordance with section 132 of the 1992 Act;

"[long-term insurance][3] fund" has the meaning given by section 431(2) of the Taxes Act;

["open-ended investment company" and "authorised corporate director" in relation to such a company have the meanings given by subsection (10) of section 468 of the Taxes Act, read with subsections (11) to (18) of that section, as those sub-sections are added in relation to open-ended investment companies by regulation 10(4) of the Open-ended Investment Companies (Tax) Regulations 1997; and accordingly references in subsections (11) to (16) of that section to "the Tax Acts" shall be construed as if they included references to these Regulations;][2]

"qualifying corporate bond" has the same meaning as in the 1992 Act;

"relevant interest in an offshore fund" has the meaning given by section 212(5) of the 1992 Act;

"security" includes a debenture that is deemed to be a security for the purposes of section 251 of the 1992 Act by virtue of subsection (6) of that section;

"unit trust scheme" shall be construed in accordance with section 99 of the 1992 Act.][1]

Amendments—[1] This regulation inserted by the Exchange Gains and Losses (Insurance Companies) (Amendment) Regulations, SI 1996/673 regs 1(2), 4, with effect for disposals made after 31 March 1996.

[2] Para (9)(*c*) (and word "or" preceding it), words in para (11) and definitions of "open-ended investment company" and "authorised corporate director" in para (13) inserted by the Exchange Gains and Losses (Insurance Companies) (Amendment) Regulations, SI 1997/1155, with effect in relation to disposals taking place on or after 28 April 1997.

[3] Words substituted in paras (9), (13) by the Financial Services and Markets Act 2000 (Consequential Amendments) (Taxes) Order, SI 2001/3629 art 138 with effect from 1 December 2001, immediately after the coming into force of the Financial Services and Markets Act 2000 ss 411, 432(1), Sch 20 (and SI 2001/3629 Pts 1 and 2).

[4] Para (1) substituted by the Exchange Gains and Losses (Transitional Provisions and Savings) Regulations, SI 2002/1969 regs 18, 21 with effect for accounting periods beginning after 30 September 2002.

[7A—(1) An asset shall be deemed to have been disposed of by an insurance company immediately before its first accounting period to begin on or after 1st October 2002 where—

(*a*) the asset was a regulation 7 asset at the time of its deemed disposal, and

(*b*) at that time, the insurance company had made no election under regulation 8A of these Regulations.

(2) Subject to regulation 7B, any chargeable gain or allowable loss accruing on the deemed disposal under paragraph (1) above of an asset shall be brought into account as if it had accrued immediately after the end of the final accounting period.][1]

Amendments—[1] Regulations 7A, 7B inserted by the Exchange Gains and Losses (Transitional Provisions and Savings) Regulations, SI 2002/1969 regs 18, 22 with effect for accounting periods beginning after 30 September 2002.

[7B In any case where, apart from this regulation, chargeable gains or allowable losses would accrue to an insurance company immediately after the end of the final accounting period by virtue of regulation 7A—

(*a*) the insurance company may elect, by notice to the inspector within two years of the end of the final accounting period, that this regulation shall apply as respects all such gains or losses, and

(*b*) where such an election is made, every such gain or loss to which this regulation applies shall be treated as accruing only when the asset or liability to which the gain or loss relates ceases to be held or owed by the insurance company.][1]

Amendments—[1] Regulations 7A, 7B inserted by the Exchange Gains and Losses (Transitional Provisions and Savings) Regulations, SI 2002/1969 regs 18, 22 with effect for accounting periods beginning after 30 September 2002.

[8—(1) The amount of the chargeable gain accruing on the [the deemed disposal under regulation 7A(1) of an asset] shall, subject to paragraphs (5) and (6) below and to [regulations [9][3] to 12][2], be computed by ascertaining the amount specified in paragraph (3) below ("the first amount") and the amount specified in paragraph (4) below ("the second amount").

(2) Where the second amount exceeds the first amount the excess shall be a chargeable gain; where the first amount exceeds the second amount the excess shall be an allowable loss; and where the first amount and the second amount are equal there shall be neither a chargeable gain nor an allowable loss.

(3) The first amount is the basic valuation of the asset translated into sterling at the time immediately after the company becomes entitled to the asset.
(4) The second amount is the basic valuation of the asset translated into sterling at the time immediately before the company ceases to be entitled to the asset.
(5) Where any profit on the sale of a regulation 7 asset would be treated wholly as a receipt falling to be brought into account in computing profits or gains charged under Case I of Schedule D, neither a chargeable gain nor an allowable loss shall be treated as arising.
(6) Where any profit on the sale of a regulation 7 asset would be treated partly as a receipt falling to be brought into account in computing profits or gains charged under Case I of Schedule D, any chargeable gain or allowable loss accruing by virtue of this regulation shall be reduced on a just and reasonable basis.
(7) Any translation into sterling required by this regulation shall be made by reference to the London closing rate.
(8) The provisions of Chapters III and IV of Part II of the 1992 Act shall not apply to any computation required by this regulation.
(9) All regulation 7 assets which are the subject of the computation required by this regulation shall be treated as relevant securities within the meaning given by subsection (1) of section 108 of the 1992 Act; and that section shall apply accordingly.
(10) Nothing in this regulation shall be taken as preventing any gain or loss which is deemed to accrue by virtue of section 116(10)(*b*) of the 1992 Act from being brought into charge to tax.][1]

Amendments—[1] This regulation inserted by the Exchange Gains and Losses (Insurance Companies) (Amendment) Regulations, SI 1996/673 regs 1(2), 4, with effect for disposals made after 31 March 1996.
[2] Words substituted by the Exchange Gains and Losses (Insurance Companies) (Amendment No 2) Regulations, SI 1996/1485 regs 2,4, with effect from 30 June 1996.
[3] Words in para (1) substituted by the Exchange Gains and Losses (Transitional Provisions and Savings) Regulations, SI 2002/1969 regs 18, 23 with effect for accounting periods beginning after 30 September 2002.

8A . . .

Amendment—Regulation 8A revoked by the Exchange Gains and Losses (Transitional Provisions and Savings) Regulations, SI 2002/1969 regs 18, 24 with effect for accounting periods beginning after 30 September 2002.

[**9**—(1) This regulation applies in any case where—
(*a*) an insurance company has acquired a regulation 7 asset, and
(*b*) the asset was held by the company immediately before 1st April 1996.
(2) Regulation 8 shall apply on the [deemed disposal under regulation 7A(1) of the asset][2] with the modification that the first amount shall be the basic valuation of the asset translated into sterling by reference to the London closing rate on 1st April 1996.][1]

Amendments—[1] This regulation inserted by the Exchange Gains and Losses (Insurance Companies) (Amendment) Regulations, SI 1996/673 regs 1(2), 4, with effect for disposals made after 31 March 1996.
[2] Words in para (2) substituted by the Exchange Gains and Losses (Transitional Provisions and Savings) Regulations, SI 2002/1969 regs 18, 25 with effect for accounting periods beginning after 30 September 2002.

[**10**—(1) This regulation applies in any case where, for the purposes of sections 126 to 131 of the 1992 Act—
(*a*) a regulation 7 asset constitutes the original shares, and
(*b*) another regulation 7 asset constitutes the new holding.
(2) Regulation 8 shall apply on the disposal of the new holding with the modifications specified in paragraphs (3) and (4) below.
(3) The modification specified in this paragraph is that the first amount shall be the aggregate of—
(*a*) the basic valuation of the original shares translated into sterling at the time immediately after the company became entitled to the original shares, and
(*b*) the basic valuation of the new holding translated into sterling at the time immediately after the company became entitled to the new holding.
(4) The modification specified in this paragraph is that the second amount shall be the aggregate of—
(*a*) the basic valuation of the original shares translated into sterling at the time immediately before the company became entitled to the new holding, and
(*b*) the basic valuation of the new holding translated into sterling at the time immediately before the company ceased to be entitled to the new holding.][1]

Amendments—[1] This regulation inserted by the Exchange Gains and Losses (Insurance Companies) (Amendment) Regulations, SI 1996/673 regs 1(2), 4, with effect for disposals made after 31 March 1996.

[**11**—(1) This regulation applies in any case where—
(*a*) an asset is a regulation 7 asset by virtue of paragraph (5) of that regulation, and
(*b*) the asset has at any time after 31st March 1996 and during the company's period of ownership been an asset which did not represent a loan relationship.

(2) Regulation 8 shall apply on the [deemed disposal under regulation 7A(1) of the asset][2] with the modification that the first amount shall be the basic valuation of the asset translated into sterling at the beginning of the accounting period in which the asset first became a regulation 7 asset by virtue of paragraph (5) of that regulation.][1]

Amendments—[1] This regulation inserted by the Exchange Gains and Losses (Insurance Companies) (Amendment) Regulations, SI 1996/673 regs 1(2), 4, with effect for disposals made after 31 March 1996.

[2] Words in para (2) substituted by the Exchange Gains and Losses (Transitional Provisions and Savings) Regulations, SI 2002/1969 regs 18, 26 with effect for accounting periods beginning after 30 September 2002.

[12—(1) This regulation applies in any case where an asset is a regulation 7 asset by virtue of paragraph (6) of that regulation.

(2) Regulation 8 shall apply on the [deemed disposal under regulation 7A(1) of the asset][2] with the modifications that—

(*a*) the first amount shall be the basic valuation of the original shares in relation to the asset translated into sterling at the time immediately after the company became entitled to the original shares, and

(*b*) the second amount shall be the basic valuation of the original shares in relation to the asset translated into sterling at the time immediately before the company ceased to be entitled to the original shares.][1]

Amendments—[1] This regulation inserted by the Exchange Gains and Losses (Insurance Companies) (Amendment) Regulations, SI 1996/673 regs 1(2), 4, with effect for disposals made after 31 March 1996.

[2] Words in para (2) substituted by the Exchange Gains and Losses (Transitional Provisions and Savings) Regulations, SI 2002/1969 regs 18, 27 with effect for accounting periods beginning after 30 September 2002.

1995/351

LLOYD'S UNDERWRITERS (TAX) REGULATIONS 1995

Made by the Commissioners of Inland Revenue under FA 1993 ss 179(2), 179A(3)(b), 182(1), (4), (5), 184(1), (3), FA 1994 ss 227(2), 229, 230(1), (3)

Made . . . . *15 February 1995*

Laid before the House of Commons . . . . *16 February 1995*

Coming into Force . . . . *9 March 1995*

Commentary—*Simon's Taxes* **E5.613, E5.614, E5.619, E5.619A, E5.624, E5.642.**

PRELIMINARY

1 Citation, commencement and effect

These Regulations may be cited as the Lloyd's Underwriters (Tax) Regulations 1995 and shall come into force on 9th March 1995, but except as otherwise provided shall have effect—

(*a*) in their application to members who are individuals, with respect to the year 1992–93 and subsequent years of assessment;

(*b*) in their application to corporate members, with respect to the underwriting year 1994 and subsequent underwriting years.

2 Interpretation

(1) In these Regulations unless the context otherwise requires—

"ancillary trust fund" in relation to a member who is an individual has the meaning given by section 184(1) of the Finance Act 1993 and in relation to a corporate member has the meaning given by section 230(1) of the Finance Act 1994;

"the Board" means the Commissioners of Inland Revenue;

"Chapter III" means Chapter III of Part II of the Finance Act 1993 and "Chapter V" means Chapter V of Part IV of the Finance Act 1994;

"inspector" includes any officer of the Board;

"Management Act" means the Taxes Management Act 1970;

"managing agent" in relation to a member who is an individual has the meaning given by section 184(1) of the Finance Act 1993 as extended by regulation 3, and in relation to a corporate member has the meaning given by section 230(1) of the Finance Act 1994 as extended by that regulation;

"member" means a member of Lloyd's who is an individual or, as the case may be, a corporate member and who is or has been an underwriting member;

"quota share contract" in relation to a member who is an individual has the meaning given by section 178(4) of the Finance Act 1993 and in relation to a corporate member has the meaning given by section 225(4) of the Finance Act 1994;

"Schedule 19" and "Schedule 20" mean respectively Schedule 19 and Schedule 20 to the Finance Act 1993;

"the Taxes Act" means the Income and Corporation Taxes Act 1988;

"section 179" and "section 179A" mean respectively, section 179 and section 179A of the Finance Act 1993;

["tax credit" means a tax credit under section 231 of the Taxes Act;][1]

"underwriting business" in relation to a member who is an individual has the meaning given by section 184(1) of the Finance Act 1993 and in relation to a corporate member has the meaning given by section 230(1) of the Finance Act 1994.

(2) For the purposes of these Regulations an underwriting year and a year of assessment shall be deemed to correspond to each other if the underwriting year ends in the year of assessment.

(3) References in these Regulations to the profits or losses of the underwriting business of a member who is an individual are references to profits or losses of that business within Chapter III, and references to the profits or losses of a corporate member's underwriting business are references to the profits or losses of that business within Chapter V.

Amendments—[1] Definition of "tax credit" in sub-para (1) inserted by the Lloyd's Underwriters (Tax) (Amendment) Regulations, SI 1996/781 regs 1, 3 with effect from 5 April 1996.

3 Managing agents

Amendment—Regulations 3, 7, 8 revoked by the Lloyd's Underwriters (Tax) Regulations, SI 2005/3338 reg 18.
SI 2005/3338 came into force on 27 December 2005, and has effect—

(a) in its application to members who are individuals, for the year 2006–07 (including any actions taken before 6 April 2006, in relation to the year 2006–07) and subsequent years of assessment; and

(b) in its application to corporate members, for accounting periods ending after 31 December 2005 (but not in relation to profits and losses arising to corporate members which are mentioned in FA 1994 s 220(2) and are declared in 2005).

ASSESSMENT AND COLLECTION OF TAX

4 Assessment and collection—general

Subject to regulations 5 to 8 below and regulations 6 to 12, 14 and 15 of the Lloyd's Underwriters (Tax) (1992–93 to 1996–97) Regulations 1995, the like provisions as are contained in the Management Act and the Tax Acts relating to the assessment and collection of tax shall have effect in relation to tax charged in accordance with section 171 of the Finance Act 1993 or, as the case may be, section 219 of the Finance Act 1994.

5 Amount payable under stop-loss insurance—individual member

(1) This regulation applies where—

(*a*) any insurance money payable to a member under a stop-loss insurance in respect of a loss in his underwriting business, or any amount payable to a member out of the High Level Stop Loss Fund in respect of such a loss, falls to be treated by virtue of section 178(2) of the Finance Act 1993 as a trading receipt in computing the profits arising from the business for the year of assessment which corresponds to the underwriting year in which the loss arose or, as respects an amount payable in respect of a loss declared in the underwriting year 1997 or a subsequent underwriting year, the underwriting year in which the loss was declared;

(*b*) the amount so treated operates to reduce or extinguish the amount of the loss sustained by the member in his underwriting business for that year of assessment;

(*c*) section 178(3) of the Finance Act 1993 does not apply as respects the payment of that amount; and

(*d*) the inspector is precluded—

(i) by section 34 of the Management Act from making an assessment under section 29(3)(*c*) of that Act or, as respects the year 1996–97 and subsequent years of assessment, section 29(1)(*c*) of that Act, in respect of the whole or any part of that amount, or

(ii) by section 30(5) of the Management Act from making an assessment under that section in respect of the whole or any part of that amount.

(2) An assessment under section 29(3)(*c*) or, as the case may be, section 29(1)(*c*) or 30 of the Management Act in respect of the whole or any part of that amount shall not be out of time if made before the end of the underwriting year following the underwriting year in which the amount was received.

6 Amount payable under stop-loss insurance—corporate member

(1) This regulation applies where—

(*a*) any insurance money is payable to a corporate member under a stop-loss insurance in respect of a loss in its underwriting business, and the insurance money or, as the case may be, the apportioned part of the insurance money falls to be treated by virtue of section 225(2) of the Finance Act 1994 as a trading receipt in computing the profits arising from the business for an accounting period;

(*b*) the amount so treated operates to reduce or extinguish the amount of the loss sustained by the corporate member in its underwriting business for that accounting period;

(*c*) section 225(3) of the Finance Act 1994 does not apply as respects the payment of the insurance money; and

(*d*) the inspector is precluded—

(i) by section 34 of the Management Act from making an assessment under section 29(3)(*c*) of that Act or, as respects an accounting period ending on or after such day as is appointed under section 199(3) of the Finance Act 1994 section 29(1)(*c*) of the Management Act, in respect of the whole or any part of the amount so treated, or

(ii) by section 30(5) of the Management Act from making an assessment under that section in respect of the whole or any part of that amount.

(2) An assessment under section 29(3)(*c*) or, as the case may be, section 29(1)(*c*) or 30 of the Management Act in respect of the whole or any part of that amount shall not be out of time if made before the end of the underwriting year following the underwriting year in which the amount was received.

7 Non-delivery of return—reasonable excuse

Amendment—Regulations 3, 7, 8 revoked by the Lloyd's Underwriters (Tax) Regulations, SI 2005/3338 reg 18. SI 2005/3338 came into force on 27 December 2005, and has effect—

(a) in its application to members who are individuals, for the year 2006–07 (including any actions taken before 6 April 2006, in relation to the year 2006–07) and subsequent years of assessment; and

(b) in its application to corporate members, for accounting periods ending after 31 December 2005 (but not in relation to profits and losses arising to corporate members which are mentioned in FA 1994 s 220(2) and are declared in 2005).

7A [Payment of income tax—taxed income and tax credits

The like provisions as are contained in sections 59A and 59B of the Management Act shall have effect for the year 1996–97 and subsequent years of assessment in relation to tax which—

(*a*) is charged on income in accordance with section 171 of the Finance Act 1993, being income falling within section 172(1)(*c*) of that Act, and

(*b*) either—

(i) was paid by way of deduction at source, or

(ii) is represented by a tax credit,

as if references to income tax deducted or treated as deducted from any income or treated as paid on any income in respect of a year of assessment were references to income tax deducted or treated as deducted or paid in respect of the underwriting year corresponding to that year of assessment.][1]

Amendments—[1] This regulation inserted by the Lloyd's Underwriters (Tax) (Amendment) Regulations, SI 1996/781 regs 1, 4 with effect from 5 April 1996.

[7B The like provisions as are contained in section 824 of the Taxes Act shall have effect for the year 1996–97 and subsequent years of assessment in relation to—

(*a*) any repayment of tax which was paid by way of deduction at source in respect of income charged to tax in accordance with section 171, and falling within section 172(1)(*c*), of the Finance Act 1993, and

(*b*) any payment of the whole or part of a tax credit (to which section 824 of the Taxes Act applies by virtue of subsection (2) of that section) in respect of such income,

as if the reference in subsection (3)(b) of that section to the year of assessment for which the tax was charged was a reference to the year of assessment for which the tax was assessed on the member concerned.][1]

Amendments—[1] This regulation inserted by the Lloyd's Underwriters (Tax) (Amendment) Regulations, SI 1996/781 regs 1, 4 with effect from 5 April 1996.

[7C [Year of assessment to which taxed income and tax credits attributable

The like provision as is contained in paragraph (*a*) of section 835(6) of the Taxes Act (total income) shall have effect for the year 1994–95 and subsequent years of assessment as if it provided that income falling within that paragraph and within section 172(1)(*c*) of the Finance Act 1993 should be deemed to be income of the year of assessment corresponding to the underwriting year in which it was received by the member concerned, and not income of the year of assessment referred to in that paragraph.][1]

Amendments—[1] This regulation inserted by the Lloyd's Underwriters (Tax) (Amendment) Regulations, SI 1996/781 regs 1, 4 with effect from 5 April 1996.

8 *Determinations and notices of determinations*

Amendment—Regulations 3, 7, 8 revoked by the Lloyd's Underwriters (Tax) Regulations, SI 2005/3338 reg 18.
SI 2005/3338 came into force on 27 December 2005, and has effect—

(a) in its application to members who are individuals, for the year 2006–07 (including any actions taken before 6 April 2006, in relation to the year 2006–07) and subsequent years of assessment; and

(b) in its application to corporate members, for accounting periods ending after 31 December 2005 (but not in relation to profits and losses arising to corporate members which are mentioned in FA 1994 s 220(2) and are declared in 2005).

CESSATION OF MEMBER'S UNDERWRITING BUSINESS

9 Cessation of individual member's underwriting business—final year of assessment

(1) Where a member who is an individual ceases to carry on his underwriting business, whether by reason of death or otherwise, the member's final year of assessment shall, in the cases specified in paragraphs (2) to (5) below and subject to subsection (3) of section 179, be ascertained in accordance with the provisions of those paragraphs.

(2) In any case where a letter is issued by the Membership Department of Lloyd's to the member or his agent inviting an application for the repayment of the member's deposit, the member's final year of assessment shall be not later than the year of assessment in which falls the date which is 180 days after the date of issue of the letter.

(3) In any case where the member's deposit at Lloyd's is paid over to a person other than the member or his personal representatives or assigns, the member's final year of assessment shall be that which corresponds to the underwriting year in which his deposit is so paid over or, where paragraph (2) above applies and the year of assessment specified in that paragraph is earlier, that earlier year of assessment.

(4) In any case where the member or another person is released from any arrangement entered into by the member or that person in order to satisfy the requirement on the part of the member to provide a deposit at Lloyd's, the member's final year of assessment shall, except in a case to which paragraph (5) below applies, be that which corresponds to the underwriting year in which the release occurs.

(5) In any case where the member's deposit at Lloyd's is extinguished or released before the last open year of account of any syndicate of which he is a member is closed, the member's final year of assessment shall be either—

(*a*) the year of assessment next following the year of assessment which corresponds to the underwriting year in which the last open year of account of any syndicate of which he is a member is closed or, if later,

(*b*) the year of assessment which corresponds to the underwriting year in which he ceases to be a member of Lloyd's under the rules or practice of Lloyd's.

(6) This regulation has effect in relation to any member—

(*a*) whose deposit at Lloyd's is paid over to him or another person or, as the case may be, released or extinguished, on or after 1st January 1993, and

(*b*) in whose case the last open year of account of any syndicate of which he was a member is closed on or after that date.

(7) For the purposes of this regulation, the last open year of account of a syndicate of which a person is a member shall be regarded as having closed either—

(*a*) when the member is treated under the rules or practice of Lloyd's as having been discharged of all his liabilities in relation to that syndicate, whether by the syndicate closing its accounts or by the member or his personal representatives or assigns entering into a quota share contract, or

(*b*) in a case where the member enters, or his personal representatives or assigns enter, into a quota share contract before the end of the closing year of the syndicate, at the end of the underwriting year in which the contract is made.

10 Cessation of individual member's underwriting business by reason of death on or after 6th April 1994—date of cessation of business

(1) For the purposes of the Income Tax Acts, where a member ceases to carry on his underwriting business by reason of his death, the business shall, in the cases specified in paragraphs (2) to (5) below, be treated as continuing until the date specified in those paragraphs in relation to the appropriate case.

(2) In any case where a letter is issued by the Membership Department of Lloyd's to the member's agent, or his personal representatives or assigns, inviting an application for the repayment of the member's deposit, the member's business shall be treated as continuing until the date which is 180 days after the date of issue of the letter.

(3) In any case where the member's deposit at Lloyd's is paid over to a person other than the member's personal representatives or assigns, the member's business shall be treated as continuing until his deposit is so paid over or, where paragraph (2) above applies and the date specified in that paragraph occurs earlier, that earlier date.

(4) In any case where the member's personal representatives are, or another person is, released from any arrangement entered into by the member or that person in order to satisfy the requirement on the part of the member to provide a deposit at Lloyd's, the member's business shall, except in a case to which paragraph (5) below applies, be treated as continuing until the date on which the release occurs.

(5) In any case where the member's deposit at Lloyd's is extinguished or released before the last open year of account of any syndicate of which he was a member is closed, the member's business shall be treated as continuing until either—

(*a*) the end of the year of assessment next following the year of assessment which corresponds to the underwriting year in which the last open year of account of any syndicate of which he was a member is closed or, if later,

(*b*) the end of the year of assessment which corresponds to the underwriting year in which he ceased to be a member of Lloyd's under the rules or practice of Lloyd's.

(6) For the purposes of paragraph (5) above, the last open year of account of a syndicate of which a person was a member shall be regarded as having closed either—

(*a*) when the member is treated under the rules or practice of Lloyd's as having been discharged of all his liabilities in relation to that syndicate, whether by the syndicate closing its accounts or by the member or his personal representatives entering into a quota share contract, or

(*b*) in a case where the member enters, or his personal representatives enter, into a quota share contract before the end of the closing year of the syndicate, at the end of the underwriting year in which the contract is made.

(7) This regulation has effect in relation to any member whose death occurs on or after 6th April 1994.

11 Profits and losses arising after death of member before 6th April 1994

For the purposes of the provisions of Chapter III other than Schedule 20, where—

(*a*) the death of a member occurred before 6th April 1994;

(*b*) the member's deposit at Lloyd's, if paid over to him or his personal representatives or assigns, was not paid over prior to 1st January 1993; and

(*c*) income arises to, or expenses are incurred or paid by, his personal representatives after his death from the carrying on by them of the member's underwriting business in circumstances where the income or expenses would have been taken into account, by virtue of those provisions, in computing the profits or losses arising to the member from his underwriting business had they arisen or been incurred or paid prior to his death,

the income and expenses shall be regarded as arising to, or incurred or paid by, the member and are accordingly to be taken into account in computing profits or losses arising to the member from his underwriting business for the purposes of those provisions.

12 Cessation of individual member's underwriting business by reason of death on or after 6th April 1994—profits or losses arising after death

For the purposes of the provisions of Chapter III other than Schedule 20, where—

(*a*) the death of a member occurs on or after 6th April 1994; and

(*b*) income arises to, or expenses are incurred or paid by, his personal representatives after his death from the carrying on by them of the member's underwriting business in circumstances where the income or expenses would have been taken into account, by virtue of those provisions, in computing the profits or losses arising to the member from his underwriting business had they arisen or been incurred or paid prior to his death,

the profits or losses arising to the personal representatives from the income and expenses shall be computed as if references in those provisions to profits and losses arising to the member from his underwriting business included references to the profits and losses arising to the personal representatives.

13 Cessation of individual member's underwriting business—claim for relief where business commenced before 1st January 1972

(1) This regulation applies where—

(*a*) a member who is an individual has ceased to be a member of Lloyd's under the rules or practice of Lloyd's or, if earlier, has given notice of resignation of membership under the rules or practice of Lloyd's which has not been withdrawn; and

(*b*) the member's underwriting business as an underwriting member of Lloyd's commenced before 1st January 1972.

(2) The member may claim that—

(*a*) for the last year of assessment in which profits or losses of his underwriting business arising directly from his membership of one or more syndicates, or from assets forming part of a premiums trust fund of one or more syndicates, being profits or losses declared in the underwriting year following the closing year, fall to be included by virtue of the provisions of Chapter III, he shall be charged to tax in respect of those profits on the amount of the actual profits of the period beginning on 6th April and ending on 31st December in that underwriting year (but subject to any deduction or set-off to which he may be entitled under section 385 of the Taxes Act); and

(*b*) for the year of assessment immediately preceding that referred to in subparagraph (*a*) above, there shall be deducted in computing profits arising as mentioned in that sub-paragraph an amount equal to the lesser of—

(i) the amount of those profits, and

(ii) the amount of the profits of his underwriting business for the underwriting year 1972.

(3) For the purposes only of determining the last year of assessment under paragraph (2) above in any case where the member enters into a quota share contract in relation to a syndicate before the end of the closing year of the syndicate, any loss declared by that syndicate following the making of the contract shall be treated as if it were a declared profit.

(4) A member may not make more than one claim under paragraph (2) above.

14 Cessation of individual member's underwriting business—terminal loss relief

(1) This regulation applies where a member ceases to carry on his underwriting business, whether by reason of death or otherwise, and either—

(*a*) his deposit at Lloyd's is paid over to him or his personal representatives or assigns on or after 1st January 1993, or

(*b*) the last open year of account of any syndicate of which he is a member is closed after 31st December 1992.

(2) Notwithstanding section 179 or section 179A, or regulation 9 or 10 of these Regulations, the date on which the member's underwriting business is permanently discontinued for the purposes of section 388 of the Taxes Act (carry-back of terminal losses) shall be deemed to be the 5th April in the last year of assessment in which profits or losses of that business which arise directly from his membership of one or more syndicates, or from assets forming part of a [premium][1] trust fund, fall to be included by virtue of the provisions of Chapter III.

(3) No claim may be made by a member under section 388 of the Taxes Act until—

(*a*) he has ceased to be a member under the rules or practice of Lloyd's or, if earlier,

(*b*) he has given (and not withdrawn) notice of resignation of membership under the rules or practice of Lloyd's.

(4) A member may not make more than one claim under section 388 of the Taxes Act in respect of the same underwriting business.

(5) For the purposes of paragraph (1)(*b*) above, the last open year of account of a syndicate of which a person is a member shall be regarded as having closed either—

(*a*) when the member is treated under the rules or practice of Lloyd's as having been discharged of all his liabilities in relation to that syndicate, whether by the syndicate closing its accounts or by the member or his personal representatives or assigns entering into a quota share contract; or

(*b*) in a case where the member enters, or his personal representatives or assigns enter, into a quota share contract before the end of the closing year of the syndicate, at the end of the underwriting year in which the contract is made.

(6) For the purposes only of determining the last year of assessment under paragraph (2) above in any case where the member enters into a quota share contract in relation to a syndicate before the end of the closing year of the syndicate, any loss declared by that syndicate following the making of the contract shall be treated as if it were a declared profit.

Amendments—[1] Word in para (2) substituted by the Financial Services and Markets Act 2000 (Consequential Amendments) (Taxes) Order, SI 2001/3629 art 139 with effect from 1 December 2001, immediately after the coming into force of the Financial Services and Markets Act 2000 ss 411, 432(1), Sch 20 (and SI 2001/3629 Pts 1 and 2).

15 Cessation of individual member's underwriting business by reason of death—winding up of old-style special reserve fund

(1) In any case where—

(*a*) a member ceases to carry on his underwriting business by reason of his death;

(*b*) the member's final year of assessment, ascertained in accordance with the provisions of Chapter III and these Regulations, is the year 1992–93 or any subsequent year of assessment; and

(*c*) prior to his death no new-style fund had been set up in relation to the member;

subsection (4) of section 175 of the Finance Act 1993 (winding-up of old-style fund) shall apply as if paragraph (b) of that subsection was omitted.

(2) In paragraph (1) above, "new-style fund" and "old-style fund" have the meanings given by paragraph 12(1) of Schedule 20.

16 Cessation of corporate member's underwriting business—final underwriting year

(1) Where a corporate member ceases to carry on its underwriting business, whether by reason of being wound up or otherwise, its final underwriting year shall, in the cases specified in paragraphs (2) to (5) below, be ascertained in accordance with the provisions of those paragraphs.

(2) In any case where a letter is issued by the Membership Department of Lloyd's to the corporate member or its agent inviting an application for the repayment of the corporate member's deposit, the corporate member's final underwriting year shall be not later than the underwriting year in which falls the date which is 180 days after the date of issue of the letter.

(3) In any case where the corporate member's deposit at Lloyd's is paid over to a person other than the corporate member, its final underwriting year shall be the underwriting year in which its deposit is so paid over or, where paragraph (2) above applies and the underwriting year specified in that paragraph is earlier, that earlier underwriting year.

(4) In any case where the corporate member or another person is released from any arrangement entered into by the corporate member or that person in order to satisfy the requirement on the part of the corporate member to provide a deposit at Lloyd's, the corporate member's final underwriting year shall, except in a case to which paragraph (5) below applies, be the underwriting year in which the release occurs.

(5) In any case where the corporate member's deposit at Lloyd's is extinguished or released before the last open year of account of any syndicate of which it is a member is closed, the corporate member's final underwriting year shall be either—

(*a*) the underwriting year next following the underwriting year in which the last open year of account of any syndicate of which it was a member is closed or, if later,

(*b*) the underwriting year in which the corporate member ceases to be a member of Lloyd's under the rules or practice of Lloyd's.

(6) For the purposes of this regulation, the last open year of account of a syndicate of which a person is a corporate member shall be regarded as having closed when the member is treated under the rules or practice of Lloyd's as having been discharged of all its liabilities in relation to that syndicate, whether by the syndicate closing its accounts or by the member entering into a quota share contract.

SUPPLEMENTAL

17 Revocations

(1) The Lloyd's Underwriters (Tax) Regulations 1974, the Lloyd's Underwriters (Tax) (No 2) Regulations 1974 and the Lloyd's Underwriters (Schedule 19A to the Income and Corporation Taxes Act 1988) Regulations 1990 are hereby revoked.

(2) A claim made under regulation 21 of the Lloyd's Underwriters (Tax) Regulations 1974 which was valid for the purposes of that regulation immediately before the coming into force of these Regulations but which had not been finally determined at that time ("a pending claim") shall have effect as if made under regulation 13 of these Regulations, and accordingly references in that regulation to a claim shall be construed as including references to a pending claim.

1995/352

LLOYD'S UNDERWRITERS (TAX) (1992–93 TO 1996–97) REGULATIONS 1995

Note—These Regulations are now spent.

1995/353

LLOYD'S UNDERWRITERS (SPECIAL RESERVE FUNDS) REGULATIONS 1995

Made by the Commissioners of Inland Revenue under FA 1993 ss 182(1)(c), (4), 184(1), (3), Sch 20 paras 3(2), 4(8), 5(10), 6(1), (3), 11(5)

Made . . . .*15 February 1995*
Laid before the House of Commons . . . .*16 February 1995*
Coming into Force . . . .*9 March 1995*

Commentary—*Simon's Taxes* **E5.645.**

1 Citation, commencement and effect

These Regulations may be cited as the Lloyd's Underwriters (Special Reserve Funds) Regulations 1995, shall come into force on 9th March 1995 and, except as otherwise provided by these Regulations, shall have effect for the year 1992–93 and subsequent years of assessment.

2 Interpretation

In these Regulations "Schedule 20" means Schedule 20 to the Finance Act 1993.

3 Syndicate profit or loss—modification of definition—running-off syndicates

. . .

Note—Reg 3 amends FA 1993 Sch 20, para 1(2).

4 Cash calls—running-off syndicates—modification of paragraph 4 of Schedule 20

. . .

Note—Reg 4 amends FA 1993 Sch 20, para 4.

5 Payments into or out of special reserve fund—prescribed periods

(1) The period prescribed for the purposes of paragraph 3(1) of Schedule 20 is the period which begins on 1st January in the calendar year in which the profits and losses comprising the syndicate profit made by the member for the underwriting year concerned are declared and ends on 31st October in that calendar year or, if earlier, on the date on which payment is made to or on behalf of the member of an amount representing any part of the syndicate profit made by the member for that underwriting year.

(2) The period prescribed for the purposes of any payments required by paragraph 4(1) of Schedule 20—

(*a*) where the accounts of the syndicate have remained open beyond the end of the closing year and the cash call concerned is made—

(i) in respect of an underwriting year determined by reference to paragraph 1(2)(*c*) [of Schedule 20][1], and

(ii) in a calendar year ("the relevant calendar year") after the end of the closing year,

is the period which begins on 1st January in the relevant calendar year and ends on the date which is 90 days after the date on which the cash call is made on the member;

(*b*) in any other case, is the period which begins on 1st January in the calendar year next but one preceding the underwriting year which is the closing year for the syndicate concerned and ends on the earlier of the following dates, namely—

(i) the date which is 90 days after the date on which the cash call concerned is made on the member, and

(ii) the date which is 90 days after the end of the closing year.

(3) The period prescribed for the purposes of any payments required by paragraph 4(2) of Schedule 20 is the period which begins on 1st January in the calendar year in which the profits and losses comprising the syndicate profit or loss of the member for the underwriting year concerned are declared and ends on the earlier of the following dates, namely—

(*a*) 31st October in that calendar year;

(*b*) where there is a syndicate profit made by the member for the underwriting year concerned, the date on which payment is made to or on behalf of the member of an amount representing any part of that profit.

(4) The period prescribed for the purposes of any payment required by paragraph 4(3) of Schedule 20 is the period of 90 days following the date on which the stop-loss payment is made to the member in respect of his syndicate loss.

(5) The period prescribed for the purposes of any payments required by paragraph 4(6) of Schedule 20 is the period of 90 days following the date on which the whole or part of the stop-loss payment made to the member is repaid by him.

(6) The period prescribed for the purposes of any payments required by paragraph 5(1) of Schedule 20 is the period which begins on 1st January in the calendar year in which the profits and losses comprising the syndicate loss sustained by the member for the underwriting year concerned are declared and ends on 31st October in that calendar year.

(7) The period prescribed for the purposes of any payment required by paragraph 5(4) of Schedule 20 is the period of 90 days following the date on which the stop-loss payment is made to the member in respect of his syndicate loss.

(8) The period prescribed for the purposes of any payments required by paragraph 5(7) of Schedule 20 is the period of 90 days following the date on which the whole or part of the stop-loss payment made to the member is repaid by him.

(9) The period prescribed for the purposes of any payments required by paragraph 6(2) of Schedule 20 is the period of 90 days following the last day of the underwriting year in respect of which the valuation giving rise to the payments is made.

Amendments—[1] Words in para (2) substituted by the Lloyd's Underwriters (Special Reserve Funds) (Amendment) Regulations, SI 1995/1185 reg 3 with effect from 23 May 1995.

6 Valuation of special reserve fund

(1) Paragraph (2) below prescribes the manner in which the value of a member's special reserve fund as at the end of an underwriting year shall be determined, and paragraph (3) below prescribes the matters which, in addition to the value of the fund, are to be stated by the fund manager in his report to the member of the value of the fund.

(2) The value of the fund shall be determined so as to be in accordance with—

(*a*) the market value of the assets of the fund, and

(*b*) the rules of Lloyd's relating to the method of valuation of the fund.

(3) The matters prescribed are—

(*a*) the amount of any payment made in the underwriting year to which the valuation relates under any of the paragraphs of Schedule 20 specified in paragraph (4) below, and

(*b*) the date on which each such payment was made.

(4) The paragraphs specified are paragraphs 3(1), 4(1), (2), (3) and (6), 5(1), (4) and (7), 6(2) and 7(1).

(5) This regulation shall have effect for the underwriting year 1994 and subsequent underwriting years.

[7 Cessation of underwriting business—modifications of Part I of Schedule 20

(1) For the purposes of the Income Tax Acts and these Regulations—

(*a*) references in paragraphs 1, 3 to 6, 8 and 10 of Schedule 20 to a member, other than references relating to a member's special reserve fund, shall be construed, in the circumstances specified in paragraph (2) below and unless the context otherwise requires, as including references to the member's personal representatives;

(*b*) references in those paragraphs to a member's special reserve fund shall be construed, in the circumstances specified in paragraph (2) below and unless the context otherwise requires, as including references to income arising after the death of the member from assets of the fund and retained by the trustees, and profits arising from the investment of that income.

(2) The circumstances specified in this paragraph are where—

(*a*) the member dies on or after 6th April 1994, and

(*b*) the member's personal representatives carry on his underwriting business after his death.

(3) This regulation shall have effect—

(*a*) in its application to paragraphs 1, 3 to 6 and 8 of Schedule 20, for the year 1994–95 and subsequent years of assessment;

(*b*) in its application to paragraph 10 of Schedule 20, for the year 1997–98 and subsequent years of assessment.]

Amendments—This regulation substituted together with reg 7A for reg 7 as originally enacted by the Lloyd's Underwriters (Special Reserve Funds) (Amendment) Regulations, SI 1995/1185 reg 4 with effect from 23 May 1995.

[7A—(1) Paragraph 9 of Schedule 20 (tax exemption for profits arising from assets of fund) shall apply with the modifications specified in paragraphs (2) and (3) below.

(2) In sub-paragraph (1) after the words "special reserve fund" there shall be inserted the words "or arising after the death of the member from the investment of income retained by the trustees".
(3) In sub-paragraphs (2) and (3) after the words "special reserve fund" in both places where they occur there shall be inserted the words "or arising after the death of the member as mentioned in sub-paragraph (1) above".
(4) This regulation shall have effect for the year 1994–95 and subsequent years of assessment.][1]

Amendments—[1] This regulation substituted together with reg 7 for reg 7 as originally enacted by the Lloyd's Underwriters (Special Reserve Funds) (Amendment) Regulations, SI 1995/1185 reg 4 with effect from 23 May 1995.

1995/917

PROFIT-RELATED PAY (SHORTFALL RECOVERY) REGULATIONS 1995

Note—These Regulations lapsed on the repeal of the enabling authority by FA 1997 ss 61(2), 113, Sch 18 Pt VI(3), with effect in relation to any payment made by reference to a profit period beginning on or after 1 January 2000.

1995/1370

DEPOSIT-TAKERS (INTEREST PAYMENTS) (DISCRETIONARY OR ACCUMULATION TRUSTS) REGULATIONS 1995

Revocation—These Regulations revoked by ITA 2007 s 1031, Sch 3 Pt1, with effect for income tax purposes from 6 April 2007, and for corporation tax purposes for accounting periods ending after 5 April 2007.

1995/1730

INSURANCE COMPANIES (TAXATION OF REINSURANCE BUSINESS) REGULATIONS 1995

Made by the Commissioners of Inland Revenue under TA 1988, ss 431C(1), 439A, 442A(2)–(6), FA 1995 Sch 8, para 58

Made . . . . *7 July 1995*
Laid before the House of Commons . . . . *7 July 1995*
Coming into Force . . . . *28 July 1995*

Commentary—*Simon's Taxes* **D7.515, D7.542.**

1 Citation, commencement and effect

These Regulations may be cited as the Insurance Companies (Taxation of Reinsurance Business) Regulations 1995, shall come into force on 28th July 1995, and shall have effect with respect to accounting periods beginning on or after 1st January 1995.

2 Interpretation

In these Regulations unless the context otherwise requires—

"accounting period" means an accounting period of a cedant company during which a reinsurance arrangement is in force;

"basic life assurance and general annuity business" has the meaning given by section 431F of the Taxes Act;

"the Board" means the Commissioners of Inland Revenue;[4]

["deposit-back arrangement" has the meaning given to "deposit back arrangements" by section 431(2) of the Taxes Act;][4]

["EEA Agreement" and "EEA State" have the meanings given in Schedule 1 to the Interpretation Act 1978;][3]

["expense risk" means the risk that the amount of expenses attributable to a policy or contract over its duration is greater than the amount expected by the cedant company when it entered into the policy or contract;][1]

. . .[5]

["insurance business transfer scheme" has the meaning given by section 431(2) of the Taxes Act;][1]

["internal linked fund" has the meaning given by section 431(2) of the Taxes Act;][3]

"investment return" means the investment return to be treated as accruing to a cedant company in respect of a policy pursuant to subsection (1) of section 442A in an accounting period;

"linked assets" has the meaning given by section 432ZA(1) of the Taxes Act, and "non-linked assets" means assets other than linked assets;

"linked business" means business which comprises the effecting and carrying out by an insurance company of policies where benefits provided for under each policy are to be determined by reference to the value of linked assets;

"morbidity risk" in relation to a policy means the risk that the person whose life is insured by the policy will suffer any sickness, accident or infirmity;

"mortality risk" in relation to a policy means the risk that the person whose life is insured by the policy will die;

"periodical return" has the meaning given by section 431(2) of the Taxes Act;

"policy" includes an annuity contract;

["the Prudential Sourcebook (Insurers)" has the meaning given by section 431(2) of the Taxes Act;][2]

"reinsurance arrangement" means a reinsurance arrangement to which section 442A applies;

"relevant profits" has the meaning given by section 88(3) of the Finance Act 1989;

"section 431C", "section [431G[3]]" and "section 442A" mean respectively section 431C, section [431G][3] and section 442A of the Taxes Act;

"90% subsidiary" means a body corporate 90 per cent or more of whose ordinary share capital is owned directly or indirectly by another body corporate;

"the Taxes Act" means the Income and Corporation Taxes Act 1988.

Amendments—[1] Definitions of "expense risk" and "insurance business transfer scheme" inserted by the Insurance Companies (Taxation of Reinsurance Business) (Amendment No 2) Regulations, SI 2003/2573 regs 2, 3(*a*), (*b*) with effect for periods of account beginning after 31 October 2003: SI 2003/2573 reg 1(2).

[2] Definition of "the Prudential Sourcebook (Insurers)" inserted by SI 2003/2573 regs 2, 3(*c*) with effect for periods of account beginning after 31 December 2000: SI 2003/2573 reg 1(3).

[3] Definitions " 'EEA Agreement' and 'EEA State' ", "internal linked fund", and reference in definition of "section 431G", substituted, by the Insurance Companies (Taxation of Reinsurance Business) (Amendment) Regulations, SI 2007/2087 regs 2, 3 with effect for periods of account beginning on or after 1 January 2007 and ending on or after 13 August 2007: SI 2007/2087 reg 1(1), (2).

[4] Definition of "the Board" revoked, and definition of "deposit-back arrangement" substituted, by the Insurance Companies (Taxation of Reinsurance Business) (Amendment) Regulations, SI 2008/1944 regs 2, 3 with effect in relation to accounting periods beginning on or after 1 January 2008.

[5] Definition of "inspector" revoked by the Insurance Companies (Taxation of Reinsurance Business) (Amendment) (No 2) Regulations, SI 2008/2670 regs 2, 3 with effect from 29 October 2008.

3 Calculation of investment return in sole accounting period

(1) Where the period during which a reinsurance arrangement is in force falls wholly within a single accounting period, the amount of the investment return in that accounting period ("I") shall be calculated in accordance with the formula—

$$I = (C - P) \times R$$

where—

[C is the aggregate of—

(*a*) so much of any amount payable by the reinsurer to the cedant company during that accounting period as a result of the death, illness, or infirmity of, or accident to, any person as does not exceed the amount which would have been paid by the reinsurer if the policy had been surrendered immediately before the death, illness, or infirmity of, or accident to, that person, and

(*b*) other amounts paid by the reinsurer to the cedant company during that accounting period, being sums paid by way of commission or as a result of the surrender in whole or in part of the rights under the policy or otherwise, but excluding any sum which forms part of the relevant profits of the cedant company or is paid by way of commission that has been [charged to tax . . . [4]][3]][1];

P is the aggregate of the sums paid by the cedant company to the reinsurer during that accounting period by way of premium [or otherwise, or treated as paid where that company makes a payment to another person, and in pursuance of any arrangements that other person or a person connected with it (within the meaning of section 839 of the Taxes Act 1988) puts the reinsurer in funds][2]; and

R is the percentage rate of return prescribed by paragraph (2) below.

(2) The percentage rate of return prescribed is 100 per cent.

Commentary—*Simon's Taxes* **D7.544**.

Amendments—[1] Words substituted by the Insurance Companies (Taxation of Reinsurance Business) (Amendment) Regulation, SI 1996/1621 regs 2, 3, with effect with respect to accounting periods beginning on or after 1 January 1995.

[2] Words in the definition of P in para (1) inserted by the Insurance Companies (Taxation of Reinsurance Business) (Amendment No 2) Regulations, SI 2004/2257 regs 2, 3 with effect from 15 September 2004.

[3] Words in the definition of C in para (1) substituted by the Finance Act 2004, Sections 38 to 40 and 45 and Schedule 6 (Consequential Amendment of Enactments) Order, SI 2004/2310 art 2, Schedule para 74(1), (2) with effect from 28 September 2004. This amendment has effect for accounting periods beginning on or after 1 April 2004, subject to the transitional provisions set out in FA 2004 ss 43, 44.

[4] In para (1), in the definition of "C", in para (*b*) words revoked, by the Insurance Companies (Taxation of Reinsurance Business) (Amendment) Regulations, SI 2008/1944 regs 2, 4 with effect in relation to accounting periods beginning on or after 1 January 2008.

4 Calculation of investment return in first accounting period

Where the period during which a reinsurance arrangement is in force falls within more than one accounting period, the amount of the investment return in the first accounting period ("I1") shall be calculated in accordance with the formula—

$$I_1 = (P - C) \times R$$

where—

P is the aggregate of the sums paid by the cedant company to the reinsurer during that accounting period by way of premium or otherwise[, or treated as paid where that company makes a payment to another person, and in pursuance of any arrangements that other person or a person connected with it (within the meaning of section 839 of the Taxes Act 1988) puts the reinsurer in funds][2] . . . [2];

C is the aggregate of the sums paid by the reinsurer to the cedant company during that accounting period by way of commission or as a result of the surrender in part of the rights under the policy or otherwise [(but excluding any such sums paid by way of a loan or otherwise creating a debt such as is mentioned in paragraph [9(3)][3](*a*)(i) of Appendix 9.4 of the Prudential Sourcebook (Insurers))][1]; and

R is the percentage rate of return prescribed by regulation 7(2);

but where [C is greater than P][1], taking the amount to be zero.

Commentary—*Simon's Taxes* **D7.544**.

Amendments—[1] Words inserted and substituted by the Insurance Companies (Taxation of Reinsurance Business) (Amendment No 2) Regulations, SI 2003/2573 regs 2, 4 with effect for periods of account beginning after 31 December 2000: SI 2003/2573 reg 1(3).

[2] Words in definition of P (which were inserted by SI 2003/2573) revoked, and words inserted, by the Insurance Companies (Taxation of Reinsurance Business) (Amendment No 2) Regulations, SI 2004/2257 regs 2, 4 with effect for accounting periods beginning on or after 1 January 2003: SI 2004/2257 reg 1(2).

However, notwithstanding SI 2004/2257 reg 1(2), no amount shall be treated as an amount of investment return given by this regulation for an accounting period ending before 1 January 2004 if that amount arises solely by virtue of the amendment made to this regulation by SI 2004/2257 reg 4(3) (ie the insertion of words in the definition of P): SI 2004/2257 reg 1(3).

[3] Reference in definition of C substituted, by the Insurance Companies (Taxation of Reinsurance Business) (Amendment) Regulations, SI 2007/2087 regs 2, 4(*a*) with effect for periods of account ending on or after 31 January 2005: SI 2007/2087 reg 1(1), (3).

5 Calculation of investment return in second and subsequent accounting periods other than final accounting period

(1) Where the period during which a reinsurance arrangement is in force falls within more than one accounting period, the amount of the investment return in the second or any subsequent accounting period other than the final accounting period ("In") shall be calculated in accordance with the formula—

$$I_n = ((P_n - C_n) + I_{n-1}) \times R$$

where—

P_n is the aggregate of the sums paid by the cedant company to the reinsurer during that accounting period and earlier accounting periods by way of premium or otherwise[, or treated as paid where that company makes a payment to another person, and in pursuance of any arrangements that other person or a person connected with it (within the meaning of section 839 of the Taxes Act 1988) puts the reinsurer in funds][4] . . . [4];

C_n is the aggregate of the sums paid by the reinsurer to the cedant company during that accounting period and earlier accounting periods by way of commission or as a result of the surrender in part of the rights under the policy or otherwise [(but excluding any such sums paid by way of a loan or otherwise creating a debt such as is mentioned in paragraph [9(3)][5] (*a*)(i) of Appendix 9.4 of the Prudential Sourcebook (Insurers))][3];

I_{n-1} is the aggregate amount of the net investment return in previous accounting periods, that is to say, net of tax [at the appropriate rate or rates prescribed][1] by paragraph (2) below; and

R is the percentage rate of return prescribed by regulation 7(4) or (6), as the case may be;

but where [((Pn – Cn) + In–1)][3] is less than zero, taking the amount to be zero.

[(2) The rates prescribed by this paragraph are—

(*a*) as respects an accounting period ending before the financial year 1996, the rate applicable in accordance with section 88(1) of the Finance Act 1989;

(*b*) as respects an accounting period commencing in or after the financial year 1996 [and ending before the financial year 2003][2], the rate applicable in accordance with section 88A(1) of the Finance Act 1989;

(*c*) as respects an accounting period part of which falls in the financial year 1995 ("the 1995 part") and part in the financial year 1996 ("the 1996 part"), the rate applicable in accordance with section 88(1) of the Finance Act 1989 in relation to the proportion of the amount of the investment return attributable to the 1995 part, and the rate applicable in accordance with section 88A(1) of that Act in relation to the proportion of the amount of the investment return attributable to the 1996 part.][1]

[(*d*) as respects an accounting period commencing in or after the financial year 2003, the rate applicable in accordance with section 88(1) of the Finance Act 1989;][2]

[(*e*) as respects an accounting period part of which falls in the financial year 2002 ("the 2002 part") and part in the financial year 2003 ("the 2003 part"), the rate applicable in accordance with section 88A(1) of the Finance Act 1989 in relation to the proportion of the amount of the investment return attributable to the 2002 part, and the rate applicable in accordance with section 88(1) of that Act in relation to the proportion of the amount of the investment return attributable to the 2003 part.][2]

Commentary—*Simon's Taxes* **D7.544**.

Cross references—Insurance Companies (Taxation of Reinsurance Business) (Amendment No 2) Regulations, SI 2004/2257 reg 1(4) (for the purposes of computing In-1 in SI 1995/1730 reg 5 in respect of an amount of investment return to which SI 2004/2257 reg 1(3) applies (see note 4 below), the rate of tax prescribed by virtue of para (2) above shall be treated as nil).

Amendments—[1] Words in para (1), and para (2), substituted by the Insurance Companies (Taxation of Reinsurance Business) (Amendment) Regulations, SI 1996/1621 regs 2,4, with effect with respect to accounting periods beginning on or after 1 January 1995.

[2] Words in sub-para (2)(*b*) inserted, and sub-paras (2)(*d*), (*e*) inserted, by the Insurance Companies (Taxation of Reinsurance Business) (Amendment) Regulations, SI 2003/1828 regs 1(2), 3 with effect for accounting periods ending in the financial year 2003, and subsequent financial years.

[3] Words inserted and substituted by the Insurance Companies (Taxation of Reinsurance Business) (Amendment No 2) Regulations, SI 2003/2573 with effect for periods of account beginning after 31 December 2000: SI 2003/2573 reg 1(3).

[4] In para (1), words in definition of Pn (which were inserted by SI 2003/2573) revoked, and words inserted, by the Insurance Companies (Taxation of Reinsurance Business) (Amendment No 2) Regulations, SI 2004/2257 regs 2, 4 with effect for accounting periods beginning on or after 1 January 2003: SI 2004/2257 reg 1(2). However, notwithstanding SI 2004/2257 reg 1(2), no amount shall be treated as an amount of investment return given by SI 1995/1730 reg 4 for an accounting period ending before 1 January 2004 if that amount arises solely by virtue of the amendment made to that regulation by SI 2004/2257 reg 4(3) (ie the insertion of words in the definition of P): SI 2004/2257 reg 1(3).

[5] In para (1), reference in definition of Cn substituted, by the Insurance Companies (Taxation of Reinsurance Business) (Amendment) Regulations, SI 2007/2087 regs 2, 4(*b*) with effect for periods of account ending on or after 31 January 2005: SI 2007/2087 reg 1(1), (3).

6 Calculation of investment return in final accounting period

(1) Where the period during which a reinsurance arrangement is in force falls within more than one accounting period, the amount of the investment return in the final accounting period is the amount by which the profit over the whole period during which the policy and the reinsurance arrangement was in force ("the whole period") exceeds the aggregate of the amounts of the investment returns [treated as accruing][1] in earlier accounting periods.

(2) For the purposes of paragraph (1) above, the profit over the whole period is the amount by which the aggregate of the amounts specified in paragraph (3) below exceeds the aggregate of all amounts paid to the reinsurer by way of premiums in respect of the policy.

(3) The amounts specified in this paragraph are—

(*a*) any amount payable by the reinsurer to the cedant company as a result of the maturity of the policy concerned;

(*b*) so much of any amount payable by the reinsurer as a result of the death, illness, or infirmity of, or accident to, any person as does not exceed the amount which would have been paid by the reinsurer if the policy had been surrendered immediately before the death, illness, infirmity or accident;

(*c*) any amount payable by the reinsurer as a result of the surrender in whole of the rights conferred by the policy;

(*d*) any amount payable by the reinsurer as a result of the surrender in part of the rights conferred by the policy;

(*e*) any amount not falling within any of sub-paragraphs (*a*) to (*d*) above which is payable by the reinsurer to the cedant company in respect of the policy, other than an amount which—

(i) forms part of the relevant profits of the cedant company, or

(ii) is paid by way of commission that has been [charged to tax . . .[3]][2].

[(4) For the purposes of paragraph (1) above, the aggregate of the amounts of the investment returns treated as accruing in earlier accounting periods are the amounts treated as accruing in those accounting periods but—

(*a*) prior to any setting off permitted by regulation 7A(2)(*c*), calculated in accordance with regulations 4 and 5 as if in regulation 7(7) the formula were—

(X × 100)/Y; and

(*b*) in any case falling within paragraph (10)(*b*)(iii) of regulation 7, adjusted by such an amount as [is][4] just and reasonable in the circumstances after taking into account the factor specified in paragraph (12)(*d*) of that regulation.][1]

Commentary—*Simon's Taxes* **D7.544.**

Amendments—[1] Words inserted, and para (4) inserted, by the Insurance Companies (Taxation of Reinsurance Business) (Amendment No 2) Regulations, SI 2003/2573 regs 2, 6 with effect for periods of account beginning after 31 December 2000: SI 2003/2573 reg 1(3).

[2] Words in para (3)(*e*)(ii) substituted by the Finance Act 2004, Sections 38 to 40 and 45 and Schedule 6 (Consequential Amendment of Enactments) Order, SI 2004/2310 art 2, Schedule para 74(1), (3) with effect from 28 September 2004. This amendment has effect for accounting periods beginning on or after 1 April 2004, subject to the transitional provisions set out in FA 2004 ss 43, 44.

[3] In para (3)(*e*)(ii), words revoked, by the Insurance Companies (Taxation of Reinsurance Business) (Amendment) Regulations, SI 2008/1944 regs 2, 5 with effect in relation to accounting periods beginning on or after 1 January 2008.

[4] In para (4)(*b*), word substituted by the Insurance Companies (Taxation of Reinsurance Business) (Amendment) (No 2) Regulations, SI 2008/2670 regs 2, 4 with effect from 29 October 2008.

7 Prescribed percentage rates of return for the purposes of regulations 4 and 5

(1) Where the period during which a reinsurance arrangement is in force falls within more than one accounting period, the percentage rate of return—

(*a*) in relation to the first accounting period, is the rate prescribed by paragraph (2) below;

(*b*) in relation to any subsequent accounting period other than the final accounting period or an accounting period falling within paragraph (6) below, is the rate prescribed by paragraph (4) below.

(2) The rate prescribed by this paragraph is the rate ("R") found by the formula—

$$\frac{R = (D - E) \times F}{G}$$

where—

D is such percentage rate as is specified in any of paragraphs (7) to (10) below and is applicable to the reinsurance arrangement concerned and, if more than such rate is so applicable, is the first applicable rate specified in the order of those paragraphs;

E is the percentage rate which results from applying the formula specified in paragraph (3) below;

F is the number of days in the first accounting period falling after the date prescribed by regulation 8(2); and

G is the number of days in that accounting period;

. . . [2]

(3) The formula specified in this paragraph is—

$$\frac{A}{P - C}$$

where—

A is the amount of any payment made by the reinsurer to the cedant company which forms part of the relevant profits of that company for the first accounting period, other than a payment which falls to be taken into account under these Regulations in calculating the investment return to be treated as accruing to that company in that accounting period; and

P and C have the meanings given by regulation 4.

(4) The rate prescribed by this paragraph is the rate ("R") found by the formula—

$$R = (D - H)$$

where—

D has the meaning given by paragraph (2) above; and

H is the percentage rate which results from applying the formula specified in paragraph (5) below;

. . . [2]

(5) The formula specified in this paragraph is—

$$\frac{B}{(P_n - C_n) + I^{n-1}}$$

Where—

B is the amount of any payment made by the reinsurer to the cedant company which forms part of the relevant profits of that company for the subsequent accounting period concerned, other than a payment which falls to be taken into account under these Regulations in calculating the investment return to be treated as accruing to that company in that accounting period; and

Pn, Cn and In–1 have the meanings given by regulation 5(1).

(6) In any case where a subsequent accounting period other than the final accounting period is less than 12 months in duration, the percentage rate of return prescribed in relation to that accounting period is the rate ("R") found by the formula—

$$R = \frac{J \times K}{365}$$

where—

J is the rate prescribed by paragraph (4) above, and

K is the number of days in that accounting period.

(7) In any case where—

(*a*) assets by reference to the value of which benefits payable under the reinsurance arrangement concerned are to be determined are held by the reinsurer in an internal linked fund, or by another company in an internal linked fund, or

(*b*) such assets are held directly by the reinsurer, that is to say, without being appropriated to an internal linked fund,

the percentage rate of return specified is the rate, expressed as a rate per annum, which is found by the formula—

$$\left(\frac{X \times 100}{Y}\right) \times \textit{the relevant fraction}$$

where—

X is the amount of investment income arising from those assets for the accounting period concerned, increased by the amount of any increase in the value of those assets which is identified in the records of the reinsurer or (as the case may be) the other company, or reduced by the amount of any reduction in the value of those assets which is so identified; and

Y is the mean of the value of those assets at the beginning and end of the accounting period concerned, as identified in those records;

. . . [2]

[(7A) For the purposes of paragraph (7) above, *the Relevant Fraction is*—

(*a*) in a case where, in finding X, the amount of investment income is increased by the amount of an increase in the value of the assets mentioned in sub-paragraphs (a) and (b) of that paragraph—

$$\frac{(X - X1)}{X}$$

(*b*) in a case where, in finding X, the amount of investment income is decreased by the amount of a reduction in the value of those assets and, after being so decreased, is not less than zero—

$$\frac{(X2 - X1)}{X2}\ ; or$$

(*c*) in a case where X is an amount that is less than zero—

[

$$1 + \left\{0.5 \times \left(\frac{X1}{X2}\right)\right\}$$

][3]

where—

X is the same as for the purposes of that paragraph;

*X*1 is the amount included in the amount of investment income used in finding X which represents dividends and other distributions that are not chargeable to corporation tax by virtue of section 208 of the Taxes Act (which provides that dividends and other distributions of a company resident in the United Kingdom are not generally so chargeable); and

*X*2 is the amount of investment income before it is decreased by the amount of any reduction in the value of the assets mentioned in sub-paragraphs (*a*) and (*b*) of that paragraph.][2]

(8) In any case where—

(*a*) there is in force a deposit-back arrangement as part of the reinsurance arrangement, and

(*b*) the calculation of the rate of return on the deposit is capable of being expressed as a percentage rate per annum, the percentage rate of return specified is such of the calculated rates of return on the deposit as is applicable to a period which includes any part of the accounting period concerned and is capable of being expressed not later than six months after the end of that accounting period and, if there is more than one such rate of return, is the average of those rates for periods beginning with the period which includes the date of commencement of the accounting period and ending with the period which includes the date of the end of the accounting period.

(9) In any case where the policy being reinsured provides for a percentage rate of return which is fixed or is capable of being determined for the accounting period concerned not later than six months after the end of that period, the percentage rate of return specified is that percentage rate plus 1 per cent.

(10) In any case not falling within paragraph (7), (8) or (9) above, the percentage rate of return specified is either—

[(*a*) the rate found by expressing the amount of the expected income from non-linked assets for the accounting period concerned as a percentage of the value of the total non-linked assets (other than assets not providing income) as identified in the relevant part of the periodical return of the cedant company specified in paragraph (11) below; or][2]

(*b*) where—

(i) that periodical return contains no relevant part, or

(ii) the cedant company is not required to make a periodical return, or

(iii) the cedant company shows that in the circumstances the calculation specified in sub-paragraph (*a*) above would not produce a reasonable result,

such rate as [is][5] just and reasonable in the circumstances after taking into account the factors specified in paragraph (12) below.

(11) The periodical return specified in this paragraph is the periodical return for the period of account immediately preceding the period of account in which the accounting period concerned falls, and "the relevant part" of that return means—

(*a*) in the case of a cedant company [which is resident][4] in the United Kingdom, the part which shows the expected income from non-linked assets in respect of the whole of the company's [long-term][1] business;

(*b*) in the case of a cedant company which is an overseas life insurance company—

(i) the part which shows the expected income from non-linked assets of the company's [long-term insurance][1] fund relating exclusively to business carried on through a [permanent establishment][4] in the United Kingdom or, if there is no such part,

(ii) the part which shows the expected income from non-linked assets of the company's [long-term insurance][1] fund relating exclusively to business carried on through [permanent establishments][4] in the United Kingdom and EEA States taken together.

(12) The factors specified in this paragraph are—

(*a*) the nature of the policy concerned;

(*b*) the rate of interest assumed by the cedant company in determining the valuation of its liabilities in respect of the policy for the purposes of its periodical return;

(*c*) any undertaking by the cedant company with respect to—

(i) the nature of the assets in which the premiums it receives will be invested, or

(ii) the rate of return which it is offering or has offered on that or any similar policy[;

(*d*) the extent to which the reinsurer is in receipt of dividends and other distributions which—

(i) arise from assets held by the reinsurer which may reasonably be regarded as related to the reinsurance arrangement in question; and

(ii) are not chargeable to corporation tax by virtue of section 208 of the Taxes Act.][2]

(13), (14) . . .[5]

Commentary—*Simon's Taxes* **D7.544**.

Amendments—[1] Words in para (11) substituted by the Financial Services and Markets Act 2000 (Consequential Amendments) (Taxes) Order, SI 2001/3629 art 140 with effect from 1 December 2001, immediately after the coming into force of the Financial Services and Markets Act 2000 ss 411, 432(1), Sch 20 (and SI 2001/3629 Pts 1 and 2).

[2] Words in paras (2), (4), (7) revoked, formula in para (7) substituted, para (7A) inserted, sub-para (10)(*a*) substituted, and sub-para (12)(*d*) and words in para (13) inserted, by the Insurance Companies (Taxation of Reinsurance Business) (Amendment No 2) Regulations, SI 2003/2573 regs 2, 7 with effect for periods of account beginning after 31 December 2000: SI 2003/2573 reg 1(3).

[3] Formula in sub-para (7A)(*c*) substituted by the Insurance Companies (Taxation of Reinsurance Business) (Amendment No 3) Regulations, SI 2003/2642 with effect for periods of account beginning after 31 December 2000.

[4] In para (11), in sub-paras (*a*), (*b*)(i), (ii), words substituted by the Insurance Companies (Taxation of Reinsurance Business) (Amendment) Regulations, SI 2008/1944 regs 2, 6 with effect in relation to accounting periods beginning on or after 1 January 2008.

[5] In para (10), word substituted and paras (13), (14) revoked, by the Insurance Companies (Taxation of Reinsurance Business) (Amendment) (No 2) Regulations, SI 2008/2670 regs 2, 5 with effect from 29 October 2008.

7A [Treatment of amounts of investment return which are less than zero

(1) This regulation applies where the amount of investment return on a policy or contract, as calculated in accordance with regulation 3, 4 or 5, is less than zero ("the negative amount").

(2) The negative amount may be set off in the following order against the following amounts—

(*a*) first, the amount of any income (other than any investment return which is treated under these Regulations as accruing) which—

(i) accrues in the same accounting period as that in which the negative amount is treated as accruing; and

(ii) is referable to basic life assurance and general annuity business and is charged to tax under Case VI of Schedule D;

(*b*) secondly, the amount of any investment return which—

(i) is treated under these Regulations as accruing in the same accounting period as that in which the negative amount is treated as accruing; and

(ii) is more than zero; and

(*c*) thirdly, the amount of any investment return which is treated under these Regulations as accruing—

(i) in an accounting period subsequent to that in which the negative amount is treated as accruing; and

(ii) in respect of the same policy or contract as that in respect of which the negative amount is treated as accruing;

and is more than zero.

(3) Any setting off under paragraph (2)(*c*) above shall, so far as possible, reduce amounts accruing in an earlier accounting period before reducing amounts accruing in a later one.

(4) Except as is provided for by paragraph (2) above, the negative amount shall be treated for the purposes of section 396 of the Taxes Act as if it were zero.][1]

[(5) Where section 442A of the Taxes Act applies to the life or endowment business carried on by friendly societies subject to the modification prescribed by regulation 19 of the Friendly Societies (Modification of the Corporation Tax Acts) Regulations 2005, this regulation shall have effect as if the reference in paragraph (2)(*a*)(ii) above to basic life assurance and general annuity business were a reference to taxable basic life assurance and general annuity business (within the meaning given by section 431(2) of the Taxes Act as modified by regulation 6 of those regulations).][2]

Commentary—*Simon's Taxes* **D7.544**.

Amendments—[1] This regulation inserted by the Insurance Companies (Taxation of Reinsurance Business) (Amendment No 2) Regulations, SI 2003/2573 regs 2, 8 with effect for periods of account beginning after 31 December 2000: SI 2003/2573 reg 1(3).

[2] Para (5) inserted by the Insurance Companies (Taxation of Reinsurance Business) (Amendment) Regulations, SI 2007/2087 regs 2, 5 with effect for periods of account beginning on or after 1 January 2007 and ending on or after 13 August 2007: SI 2007/2087 reg 1(1), (2).

8 Ascertainment of investment return—prescribed dates of payments made under reinsurance arrangements

(1) For the purposes of ascertaining the investment return in each accounting period, the payments specified in paragraphs (2) to (6) below shall be treated as paid on the dates prescribed by those paragraphs in relation to the payment concerned.

(2) In any case where under the reinsurance arrangement a premium or any other amount is payable to the reinsurer within 30 days of the date on which the first premium is paid to the reinsurer, the date prescribed as the date on which that premium or other amount is to be treated as paid is the date on which the first premium is paid.

(3) In any case where under the reinsurance arrangement commission or any other amount is payable by the reinsurer in respect of the policy concerned at the same time as the first premium is paid to the reinsurer or within 30 days of the date on which the first premium is paid to the reinsurer, the date prescribed as the date on which that commission or other amount is to be treated as paid is the date on which the first premium is paid.

(4) In any case where under the reinsurance arrangement—

(*a*) a premium other than the first premium or a premium falling within paragraph (2) above, or any other amount not being an amount falling within paragraph (2) above, is paid to the reinsurer before the end of the accounting period in which the first premium is paid, or

(*b*) commission or any other amount, not being commission or an amount falling within paragraph (3) above, is paid by the reinsurer to the cedant company before the end of that accounting period,

the date prescribed as the date on which that premium or other amount is to be treated as paid to the reinsurer, or that commission or other amount is to be treated as paid by the reinsurer, is the first day of the next accounting period.

(5) The dates prescribed as the dates on which any premium or any other amount paid to the reinsurer under the reinsurance arrangement, other than a premium or amount falling within paragraph (2) or (4)(*a*) above, is to be treated as paid are the following—

(*a*) as to one half of the amount of the premium or other amount, the date on which the premium or other amount is paid;

(*b*) as to the other half, the first day of the accounting period next following that in which the premium or other amount is paid.

(6) The dates prescribed as the dates on which any commission or any other amount paid by the reinsurer under the reinsurance arrangement, not being commission or an amount falling within paragraph (3) or (4)(*b*) above, is to be treated as paid are the following—

(*a*) as to one half of the commission or other amount, the date on which the commission or other amount is paid;

(*b*) as to the other half, the first day of the accounting period next following that in which the commission or other amount is paid.

Commentary—*Simon's Taxes* **D7.544**.

9 Exclusion of certain reinsurance arrangements from section 442A

(1) There shall be excluded from the operation of section 442A any reinsurance arrangement in respect of a policy which falls within any of the descriptions prescribed by paragraphs (2) to [(4)][2] below.

(2) The description prescribed by this paragraph is of any reinsurance arrangement where—

(*a*) both the cedant company and the reinsurer are insurance companies which are either resident in the United Kingdom or, as respects the reinsurance arrangement or, as the case may be, the business to which the reinsurance is attributable, are within the charge to corporation tax by virtue of section 11 of the Taxes Act;

(*b*) the cedant company is a 90% subsidiary of the reinsurer, or the reinsurer is a 90% subsidiary of the cedant company, or each is a 90% subsidiary of another body corporate; and

(*c*) the reinsurer is not a company which is charged to tax under Case I of Schedule D [by virtue of section 431G(3)(*a*) of the Taxes Act][3].

(3) The description prescribed by this paragraph is of any reinsurance arrangement where—

(*a*) the reinsurer is a company which in the relevant period is chargeable to tax under the laws of the territory in which it is domiciled or resident in respect of amounts to which the reinsurance arrangement gives rise;

(*b*) the head office of the reinsurer is in an EEA State;

(*c*) the charge to tax in the relevant period is such a charge made otherwise than by reference to profits as (by disallowing their deduction in computing the amount chargeable) to require sums payable and other liabilities arising under reinsurance arrangements to be treated as sums or liabilities falling to be met out of amounts subject to tax in the hands of the reinsurer;

(*d*) the rate of tax fixed for the purposes of that charge in relation to the amounts subject to tax in the hands of the reinsurer (not being amounts arising or accruing in respect of investments that are of a particular description for which a special relief or exemption is generally available) has in the relevant period been at least 20 per cent;

(*e*) none of the obligations of the reinsurer under the reinsurance arrangement to pay any sum or meet any other liability, other than obligations in respect of mortality risk or morbidity risk, has itself been the subject of a reinsurance arrangement;

(*f*) no deposit-back arrangements are in force in respect of the reinsurance arrangement; and

(*g*) the reinsurer is not subject in the relevant period to a restriction in the amount of the expenses which may be deducted in computing its liability to tax, where the restriction is calculated by reference to the amount of its profits.

(4) The description prescribed by this paragraph is of any reinsurance arrangement under which—

(*a*)

[(i) the mortality risk or the morbidity risk (but no other risk other than the expense risk) is being reinsured, or both the mortality risk and the morbidity risk (but no other risk other than the expense risk) are being reinsured, and][1]

(ii) no payment by way of surrender value is capable of being made by the reinsurer to the cedant company; or

(*b*) either—

(i) no profit such as is referred to in regulation 6(2) is capable of arising; or

(ii) such profit is capable of arising only as a result of the death, illness or infirmity of, or accident to, a person or the lapsing of the policy.

(4A) . . . [2]

(5) In paragraph (3) above, "the relevant period" means a period for which the reinsurer draws up accounts and which ends in or at the end of an accounting period of the cedant company or, if there is more than one such period ending in or at the end of the same accounting period, the period which is the first to end.

(6) For the purposes of paragraph (4) above, the fact that a premium payable by the cedant company under the reinsurance arrangement is calculated so as to reflect a guarantee by that company under the terms of the policy that it will issue a different policy at a future date shall not be taken to mean that risks other than mortality risk or morbidity risk are being reinsured under the reinsurance arrangement.

Commentary—*Simon's Taxes* **D7.543**.

Amendments—[1] Reference in para (1) substituted, sub-para (4)(*a*)(i) substituted, and para (4A) inserted, by the Insurance Companies (Taxation of Reinsurance Business) (Amendment No 2) Regulations, SI 2003/2573 regs 2, 9 with effect for periods of account beginning after 31 October 2003: SI 2003/2573 reg 1(2).

[2] Reference in para (1) substituted, and para (4A) revoked, by the Insurance Companies (Taxation of Reinsurance Business) (Amendment No 2) Regulations, SI 2004/2257 regs 2, 5 with effect for accounting periods beginning on or after 1 November 2003: SI 2004/2257 reg 1(2).

However, notwithstanding SI 2004/2257 reg 1(2), no amount shall be treated as an amount of investment return given by SI 1995/1730 reg 4 for an accounting period ending before 1 January 2004 if that amount arises solely by virtue of the amendment made to that regulation by SI 2004/2257 reg 4(3) (ie the insertion of words in the definition of P): SI 2004/2257 reg 1(3).

[3] In para (2)(*c*), words inserted by the Insurance Companies (Taxation of Reinsurance Business) (Amendment) Regulations, SI 2008/1944 regs 2, 7 with effect in relation to accounting periods beginning on or after 1 January 2008.

10 [Exclusion of policy and contract from section 442A

(1)] [1] There shall be excluded from the operation of section 442A—

[(*a*) any policy which evidences a contract of long-term insurance which is neither—

(i) a qualifying contract of insurance, nor

(ii) a reinsurance contract; and][1]

(*b*) any annuity contract under which—

(i) payment of the annuity is to commence not later than 12 months after the date of the contract, and

(ii) no surrender value is capable of being produced.

[(2) In paragraph (1)(*a*) above, "contract of long-term insurance" means any contract which falls within Part 2 of Schedule 1 to the Financial Services and Markets Act 2000 (Regulated Activities) Order 2001 and "qualifying contract of insurance" has the meaning given by article 3(1) of that Order.][1]

Commentary—*Simon's Taxes* **D7.543**.

Amendments—[1] Para (1) renumbered as such, sub-para (1)(*a*) substituted, and para (2) inserted, by the Financial Services and Markets Act 2000 (Consequential Amendments) (Taxes) Order, SI 2002/1409 art 4 with effect from 2 July 2002.

11 Exclusion of certain business from section 431C

There shall be excluded from section 431C any reinsurance business where—

(*a*) in relation to the reinsurance arrangement—

(i) the cedant company is a 90% subsidiary of the reinsurer, or the reinsurer is a 90% subsidiary of the cedant company, or each is a 90% subsidiary of another body corporate,

(ii) the cedant company is either resident in the United Kingdom or is an overseas life insurance company which, as respects the reinsurance arrangement or, as the case may be, the business being reinsured, is within the charge to corporation tax by virtue of section 11 of the Taxes Act, and

(iii) the business being reinsured is basic life assurance and general annuity business in the hands of the cedant company; or

(*b*) . . . [4]

(*c*) the business—

(i) is the reinsurance of the business of a company which is not resident in the United Kingdom,

(ii) is not business [which is overseas life assurance business within the meaning given by section 431D(1)][3] of the Taxes Act[, being business for which the policy or contract concerned was made on or after 1st November 1994][1] [and before the first accounting period of the company to begin on or after 1st January 2007][5], and

(iii) is linked business where the linked assets concerned consist wholly or substantially of land in the United Kingdom [or

[(*d*) the business is business in relation to which an election under regulation 11A has been made.][4]][2]

Commentary—*Simon's Taxes* **D7.5125, D7.5131.**

Simons Tax Cases—*Royal London Mutual Insurance Society Ltd v Barrett (Insp of Taxes)* [2002] STC(SCD) 61.

Amendments—[1] Words inserted by the Insurance Companies (Taxation of Reinsurance Business) (Amendment) Regulations, SI 1996/1621 regs 2, 5(*a*), with effect with respect to accounting periods ending on or after 15 July 1996.

[2] Para (*d*) and the word "or" preceding it, added by the Insurance Companies (Taxation of Reinsurance Business) (Amendment) Regulations, SI 1996/1621 regs 2, 5(*b*) with effect with respect to accounting periods beginning on or after 1 January 1995.

[3] In sub-paras (*b*), (*c*)(ii), words substituted by the Insurance Companies (Taxation of Reinsurance Business) (Amendment) Regulations, SI 2003/1828 regs 1(3), 4 with effect for any policy or contract for any life assurance business made after 21 August 2000.

4 Para (*b*) revoked, and para (*d*) substituted, by the Insurance Companies (Taxation of Reinsurance Business) (Amendment No 2) Regulations, SI 2003/2573 regs 2, 10 with effect for periods of account beginning after 31 October 2003: SI 2003/2573 reg 1(2).

5 Words in para (*c*)(ii) inserted by the Insurance Companies (Taxation of Reinsurance Business) (Amendment) Regulations, SI 2007/2087 regs 2, 6 with effect for periods of account beginning on or after 1 January 2007 and ending on or after 13 August 2007: SI 2007/2087 reg 1(1), (2).

11A [Election for certain business to be excluded from section 431C

(1) A company may make an election under this regulation in relation to—

- (*a*) any period of account beginning on or after 1st November 2003; and
- (*b*) any of its reinsurance business which is business of the kind specified in paragraph (2), (3) or (4) below.

(2) The business specified in this paragraph is business—

- (*a*) which is of any of the descriptions specified in section 431D(1)(*b*) of the Taxes Act [(as it has effect before the substitution made by paragraph 9(2) of Schedule 7 to the Finance Act 2007)][2], being business for which the policy or contract concerned was made on or after 1st November 1994; and
- (*b*) the contract for which was made before the beginning of the company's first period of account to begin on or after 1st November 2003.

(3) The business specified by this paragraph is business the contract for which—

- (*a*) was effected by a company resident in the United Kingdom at or through a branch or agency outside the United Kingdom where none, or no significant part, of the reinsurance business carried on relates to life assurance business with policy holders or annuitants residing in the United Kingdom; and
- (*b*) was made before 1st November 1994.

(4) The business specified by this paragraph is business the contract for which was made after the beginning of the company's first period of account to begin on or after 1st November 2003 and replaces—

- (*a*) a contract made before the beginning of the company's first period of account to begin on or after 1st November 2003 such as is mentioned in paragraph (2) above;
- (*b*) a contract made before 1st November 1994 such as is mentioned in paragraph (3) above; or
- (*c*) a contract that replaced a contract such as is mentioned in sub-paragraph (*a*) or (*b*).

(5) For the purposes of paragraph (4) above, a contract replaces a contract if it results in—

- (*a*) no significant difference in the type of business being reinsured; and
- (*b*) no significant variation in the terms on which that business is reinsured.

(6) For the purposes of paragraph (5) above, where more than one contract replaces a contract—

- (*a*) there is no significant difference in the type of business being reinsured if the replacement contracts, when taken together, do not result in such a difference; and
- (*b*) there is no significant variation in the terms on which business is reinsured if the replacement contracts, when taken together, do not result in such a variation.

(7) Where there is a relevant transfer from one person ("the transferor") to another ("the transferee") and the transferor makes an election under this regulation in relation to that business, the transferee is to be treated for the purposes of these Regulations as making the election.

(8) In paragraph (7) above, "a relevant transfer" means a transfer of reinsurance business that is effected by—

- (*a*) novation; or
- (*b*) an insurance business transfer scheme.

(9) A company may revoke an election under this regulation with effect for any period of account in relation to which it would have effect.

(10) A revocation under paragraph (9) above must be in respect of all elections under this regulation which a company has made or is treated as having made.][1]

[(11) An election made by a company under this regulation ceases to have effect at the end of the accounting period immediately preceding the first accounting period of the company which begins on or after 1st January 2007.][2]

Commentary—*Simon's Taxes* **D7.5125, D7.5131.**

Amendments—[1] This regulation inserted by the Insurance Companies (Taxation of Reinsurance Business) (Amendment No 2) Regulations, SI 2003/2573 regs 2, 11 with effect for periods of account beginning after 31 October 2003: SI 2003/2573 reg 1(2).

2 Words in para (2)(*a*), and para (11), inserted, by the Insurance Companies (Taxation of Reinsurance Business) (Amendment) Regulations, SI 2007/2087 regs 2, 7 with effect for periods of account beginning on or after 1 January 2007 and ending on or after 13 August 2007: SI 2007/2087 reg 1(1), (2).

12 [Exclusion of certain reinsurance business from subsection (3) of section 431G]

There shall be excluded from [subsection (3) of section 431G][1] any reinsurance business carried on by a company ("the reinsurer") whose reinsurance business is limited to arrangements where—

- (*a*) the cedant company is a 90% subsidiary of the reinsurer, or the reinsurer is a 90% subsidiary of the cedant company, or each is a 90% subsidiary of another body corporate, and
- (*b*) the cedant company either—

(i) is resident in the United Kingdom, or

(ii) is not so resident but, as respects all the business reinsured with the reinsurer, is within the charge to corporation tax by virtue of section 11 of the Taxes Act.

Commentary—*Simon's Taxes* **D7.516.**

Amendments—[1] Words in first sentence, and cross-heading, substituted, by the Insurance Companies (Taxation of Reinsurance Business) (Amendment) Regulations, SI 2007/2087 regs 2, 8 with effect for periods of account beginning on or after 1 January 2007 and ending on or after 13 August 2007: SI 2007/2087 reg 1(1), (2).

13 [Transfers of reinsurance arrangements effected by novation or insurance business transfer schemes

(1) Where a transfer of a reinsurance arrangement from one insurance company ("the transferor") to another ("the transferee") is effected by novation or an insurance business transfer scheme, these Regulations shall apply in relation to the reinsurance arrangement concerned as follows.

(2) Regulation 3 shall not apply.

[(3) For the purposes of regulations 4 to 7—

(*a*) if there is no accounting period of the transferor ending on the day of the transfer, an accounting period of the transferor shall be treated as ending on that day;

(*b*) an accounting period of the transferor which ends (or is treated as ending) on the day of the transfer shall not be treated as the final accounting period during which the reinsurance arrangement concerned is in force;

(*c*) if there is no accounting period of the transferee beginning on, or immediately after, the day of the transfer an accounting period of the transferee shall be treated as beginning immediately after that day; and

(*d*) an accounting period of the transferee which begins on, or immediately after, (or is treated as beginning immediately after) the day of the transfer shall not be treated as the first accounting period during which the reinsurance arrangement concerned is in force.][4]

(4) For the purposes of regulation 5, 6 and 9, the references in regulations 5(1), 6(3) and 9(6) respectively to the cedant company shall be treated as including (as well as the transferee)—

(*a*) the transferor; and

(*b*) any insurance company from which the reinsurance arrangement concerned was transferred on an earlier transfer effected by novation or an insurance business transfer scheme.

(5) For the purposes of regulation 5, the reference in paragraph (1) of that regulation to previous accounting periods shall be treated as including (as well as the previous accounting periods of the transferee)—

(*a*) previous accounting periods of the transferor; and

(*b*) previous accounting periods of any insurance company from which the reinsurance arrangement concerned was transferred on an earlier transfer effected by novation or an insurance business transfer scheme.

(6) For the purposes of regulation 6, the reference in paragraph (1) of that regulation to the amounts of the investment returns in earlier accounting periods shall be treated as including (as well as the amounts of the investment returns in earlier accounting periods of the transferee)—

(*a*) the amounts of the investment returns in earlier accounting periods of the transferor; and

(*b*) the amounts of the investment returns in earlier accounting periods of any insurance company from which the reinsurance arrangement concerned was transferred on an earlier transfer effected by novation or an insurance business transfer scheme.

[(6A) For the purposes of regulation 7A, any negative amount that is available before the transfer to be set off by the transferor in accordance with paragraph (2)(*c*) of that regulation shall be treated as if it had accrued in an earlier accounting period of the transferee.][2]

(7) The following questions shall be determined in respect of the transferor as the cedant company before the transfer and then, as a separate matter, in respect of the transferee as the cedant company after the transfer—

(*a*) whether the reinsurance arrangement concerned falls within the description prescribed by regulation 9(2);

(*b*) whether, in relation to the reinsurance arrangement concerned, any of the circumstances set out in regulations 11(*a*) and 12 exist.

(8) . . .[3].][1]

Commentary—*Simon's Taxes* **D7.544**.

Amendments—[1] This regulation inserted by the Insurance Companies (Taxation of Reinsurance Business) (Amendment) Regulations, SI 2003/1828 regs 1(4), 5 with effect for transfers of reinsurance arrangements taking place after 31 December 2002.

[2] Para (6A) inserted by the Insurance Companies (Taxation of Reinsurance Business) (Amendment No 2) Regulations, SI 2003/2573 regs 2, 12(1), (2) with effect for transfers of reinsurance arrangements taking place after 31 December 2002: SI 2003/2573 reg 1(4).

[3] Para (8) revoked by the Insurance Companies (Taxation of Reinsurance Business) (Amendment No 2) Regulations, SI 2003/2573 regs 2, 12(1), (3) with effect for periods of account beginning after 31 October 2003: SI 2003/2573 reg 1(2).

[4] Para (3) substituted by the Insurance Companies (Taxation of Reinsurance Business) (Amendment) Regulations, SI 2008/1944 regs 2, 8 with effect in relation to accounting periods beginning on or after 1 January 2008.

1995/1979

VENTURE CAPITAL TRUST REGULATIONS 1995

Made by the Treasury under FA 1995 s 73(1)–(4)

Made . . . . .26 *July 1995*
Laid before the House of Commons . . . . .26 *July 1995*
Coming into Force . . . . .16 *August 1995*

Commentary—*Simon's Taxes* **Division E3.2.**

PART I
INTRODUCTORY

1 Citation and commencement

These Regulations may be cited as the Venture Capital Trust Regulations 1995 and shall come into force on 16th August 1995.

2 Interpretation

(1) In these Regulations unless the context otherwise requires—

"accounting date" has the meaning given by section 834(1) [of the Income and Corporation Taxes Act 1988][2];

["accounting period" shall be construed in accordance with section 12 of the Income and Corporation Taxes Act 1988;][2]

"the Board" means the Commissioners [for Her Majesty's Revenue and Customs][2];

["director" means a person appointed as a director of the trust company;][2]

"eligible shares" has the meaning given by [section 273(1)][2];

. . . [1]

"full approval" means approval in pursuance of [section 274][2];

["investor" means a person—

(*a*) who holds or has held shares in a company which is or has been a trust company, or

(*b*) for whom a nominee holds or has held shares in a company which is or has been a trust company;

. . . [2]

"period of account" has the meaning given by section [989][2];

. . . [1]

"provisional approval" means approval in pursuance of [section 275(2)][2];

"qualifying holding" shall be construed in accordance with [Chapter 4 of Part 6][2];

"trust company" means a venture capital trust within the meaning given by section [259(1)][2];

["VCT approval" has the meaning it has in section 259(2);][2]

"year" means a year beginning with 6th April in any year and ending with 5th April in the following year.

[(2) In these Regulations, a reference to a "section" or "Part" without more is a reference to a section or Part of the Income Tax Act 2007.][2]

Amendments—[1] Definitions of "enduring declaration" and "permitted maximum" in para (1) revoked by the Venture Capital Trusts (Amendment) Regulations, SI 1999/819 reg 3 with effect for distributions made by a venture capital trust after 5 April 1999.

[2] The following amendments are made by the Venture Capital Trust (Amendment) Regulations, SI 2008/1893 regs 2, 3, with effect from 1 September 2008.

In para (1)—

– in definition of "accounting date" words inserted
– in definitions of "the Board", "eligible shares", "full approval", "period of account", "provisional approval", "qualifying holding", "trust company", words substituted;
– definition of "the Management Act" revoked;
– definitions of "accounting period", "director", and "VCT approval" inserted.

Para (2) substituted.

[3] Definition of "investor" substituted by the Venture Capital Trust (Amendment) Regulations, SI 2014/1929 reg 2(1), (2) with effect from 12 August 2014.

PART II
APPROVAL OF A COMPANY FOR PURPOSES OF [PART 6][1]

Amendments—[1] Words in heading substituted by the Venture Capital Trust (Amendment) Regulations, SI 2008/1893 regs 2, 4 with effect from 1 September 2008.

3 Applications for approval

(1) A company making an application for approval as a venture capital trust for the purposes of [Part 6][1] shall apply to the Board in writing.

(2) The application shall be either for full approval or for provisional approval.

(3) An application for full approval shall contain a declaration—

(*a*) that the conditions for full approval were fulfilled in relation to the most recent complete accounting period of the company;

(*b*) that to the best of the company's knowledge and belief, the conditions for full approval will also be fulfilled in relation to the accounting period of the company which is current when the application for full approval is made; and

(*c*) that to the best of the company's knowledge and belief, the particulars given in the application are true and correct.

(4) An application for provisional approval shall contain a declaration that to the best of the company's knowledge and belief—

(*a*) the conditions for full approval will be fulfilled within the periods specified in [section 275(3)][1]; and

(*b*) the particulars given in the application are true and correct.

(5) An application for approval for the purposes of [Part 6][1] shall be signed by the secretary or by a director of the company.

Amendments—[1] In paras (1), (5), words substituted, and in para (4)(*a*), words substituted, by the Venture Capital Trust (Amendment) Regulations, SI 2008/1893 regs 2, 5 with effect from 1 September 2008.

4 Approval of a company

(1) The Board's approval of a company as a trust company for the purposes of [Part 6][1] shall be given to the company by notice in writing.

(2) The notice shall specify—

(*a*) the date on which the Board's approval is given, and

(*b*) the date from which the approval shall have effect.

(3) A notice giving provisional approval may include conditions designed to ensure that the company will fulfil the conditions specified in [section 274][1].

(4) The company may appeal . . . [2] against the inclusion of any of the conditions mentioned in paragraph (3) above.

Amendments—[1] In paras (1), (4), words substituted by the Venture Capital Trust (Amendment) Regulations, SI 2008/1893 regs 2, 6 with effect from 1 September 2008.

[2] In para (4), words revoked by the Transfer of Tribunal Functions and Revenue and Customs Appeals Order, SI 2009/56 art 3, Sch 2 paras 23, 24 with effect from 1 April 2009.

5 Refusal of approval of a company

(1) The Board's refusal of approval of a company as a trust company for the purposes of [Part 6][1] shall be given to the company by notice in writing.

(2) The notice shall specify—

(*a*) the date on which the Board's refusal of approval is given, and

(*b*) the reasons for the Board's refusal of approval.

(3) The company may appeal . . . [2] against the refusal of approval.

Amendments—[1] In para (1), words substituted by the Venture Capital Trust (Amendment) Regulations, SI 2008/1893 regs 2, 7 with effect from 1 September 2008.

[2] In para (3), words revoked by the Transfer of Tribunal Functions and Revenue and Customs Appeals Order, SI 2009/56 art 3, Sch 2 paras 23, 25 with effect from 1 April 2009.

6 Withdrawal of approval of a company

(1) The Board's withdrawal of approval of a company as a trust company for the purposes of [Part 6][1] shall be given to the company by notice in writing.

(2) The notice shall specify—

(*a*) the date from which the Board's withdrawal of approval shall have effect, and

(*b*) the reasons for the Board's withdrawal of approval.

(3) The company may appeal . . . [2] against the withdrawal of approval.

Amendments—[1] In para (1) words substituted by the Venture Capital Trust (Amendment) Regulations, SI 2008/1893 regs 2, 8 with effect from 1 September 2008.

[2] In para (3), words revoked by the Transfer of Tribunal Functions and Revenue and Customs Appeals Order, SI 2009/56 art 3, Sch 2 paras 23, 26 with effect from 1 April 2009.

7 Appeals to the [tribunal]

(1) This regulation applies where a company appeals . . . [1] pursuant to regulation 4(4), 5(3) or 6(3).

(2) The appeal shall be made by notice in writing given to the Board before the end of the period of 30 days beginning with the day on which the notice of provisional approval, refusal of approval or withdrawal of approval, as the case may be, was given to the company.

(3) Subject to paragraph (4) below, the [tribunal shall, on an appeal notified to it,][1] confirm the notice unless they are satisfied that the notice ought to be quashed.

(4) Where the appeal is against the inclusion of any of the conditions mentioned in regulation 4(3), the [tribunal][1] may vary any of those conditions.

(5) If the [tribunal allows][1] an appeal against a refusal of approval, [the tribunal][1] shall specify the date from which the approval is to have effect.

Amendments—[1] In cross-heading word substituted, in para (1), words revoked, in para (3) words substituted and words revoked, in para (4), word substituted, and in para (5), words substituted, by the Transfer of Tribunal Functions and Revenue and Customs Appeals Order, SI 2009/56 art 3, Sch 2 paras 23, 27 with effect from 1 April 2009.

8 [Notification of breach of conditions for approval

(1) Where a trust company has been given full approval and—

(*a*) any condition specified in section 274 has ceased to be met or is broken, or

(*b*) the company considers that it is likely that any such condition will cease to be met or will be broken,

the company shall as soon as reasonably possible give notice in writing to the Board of that fact.

(2) Where a trust company has been given provisional approval and—

(*a*) either—

(i) any condition specified in section 274 has not been met in relation to the period specified in section 275(3) in respect of that condition, or

(ii) the company considers that it is likely that any such condition will not be met in relation to the period so specified;

(*b*) any condition included in a notice giving provisional approval and given under regulation 4(3) has not been met or has been broken, or the company considers that it is likely that any such condition will not be met or will be broken; or

(*c*) after meeting the conditions specified in section 274 within the periods specified in section 275(3) any condition has ceased to be met, or the company considers that it is likely that any such condition will cease to be met or will be broken;

the company shall as soon as reasonably possible give notice in writing to the Board of that fact.

(3) A notice required under this regulation to be given by a company must—

(*a*) specify the circumstances that caused or are likely to cause any condition to cease to be met or to be broken or not met,

(*b*) so far as possible, state the extent to which any condition—

(i) has ceased or will cease to be met, or

(ii) has been or will be broken or not met, and

(*c*) where the company considers that any condition is likely to cease to be met or to be broken or not met by or on a date occurring after the date of the notice, specify (if possible) that future date.

(4) A notice required under this regulation must be signed by the secretary or a director of the company.

(5) Paragraph (6) below applies if a company has given notice under this regulation in respect of circumstances that are likely to cause any condition to cease to be met or to be broken or not met ("the notified circumstances").

(6) If this paragraph applies, no further notice under this regulation is required in relation to the notified circumstances where any condition ceases to be met or is broken or not met in, or as a result of, the notified circumstances.

(7) Paragraph (6) above does not prevent a company giving a further notice under this regulation in respect of the notified circumstances for the purpose of enabling an application under regulation 8A(1) to be made.][1]

Amendments—[1] Regulations 8–8J substituted for previous reg 8, by the Venture Capital Trust (Amendment) Regulations, SI 2008/1893 regs 2, 9 with effect from 1 September 2008.

8A [Breach of conditions for VCT approval: applications for approval to continue

(1) If a trust company has not met or is likely not to meet the conditions for its VCT approval to continue in force in, or as a result of, the circumstances notified under regulation 8 it may apply in writing to the Board for a determination that the Board will not exercise their power conferred by section 281(1) to withdraw the company's VCT approval.

This is subject to paragraph (3) below.

(2) An application under paragraph (1) above—

(*a*) may only be made by being included in or with a notice under regulation 8;

(*b*) must specify the measures, if any, the company has taken or intends to take to rectify or avoid the failure or likely failure to meet the conditions for its VCT approval to continue in force; and

(*c*) must specify—

(i) the date on which the failure to meet the conditions for its VCT approval to continue in force was rectified, or

(ii) the date by which it expects to meet the conditions for its VCT approval to continue in force where the conditions are not met at the time of the application or will cease to be met after the time of the application.

(3) In a case where a company considers that it is likely not to meet the conditions for its VCT approval to continue in force, an application under paragraph (1) above may only be made if the likely failure to meet the conditions is expected to arise or occur within the period of 90 days commencing on the date on which notice under regulation 8 is given by the company.][1]

Amendments—[1] Regulations 8–8J substituted for previous reg 8, by the Venture Capital Trust (Amendment) Regulations, SI 2008/1893 regs 2, 9 with effect from 1 September 2008.

8B [Rectifying a breach of a condition required to be met throughout a period

(1) This regulation applies where—

(*a*) a condition for a trust company's VCT approval to continue in force must be met throughout, or satisfied at all times during, a relevant period,

(*b*) the condition has not been so met or satisfied, and

(*c*) after the failure to so meet or satisfy the condition, the circumstances of the company become such that were they to exist, or had they existed, throughout the relevant period, the condition would be or would have been, so met or satisfied.

(2) The failure to meet or satisfy the condition is to be treated for the purposes of this Part of these Regulations as having been rectified on the date when the circumstances of the company became such as are mentioned in paragraph (1)(*c*) above.

(3) In this regulation a reference to "a relevant period", in relation to a condition, means—

(a) where the company has been given full approval, the relevant period as defined by section 274(2) in relation to the condition,

(b) where the company has been given provisional approval, the relevant period as defined by section 275(3) in relation to the condition, or

(c) where the condition is included in a notice giving provisional approval and given under regulation 4(3), the period specified in the notice in relation to the condition.][1]

Amendments—[1] Regulations 8–8J substituted for previous reg 8, by the Venture Capital Trust (Amendment) Regulations, SI 2008/1893 regs 2, 9 with effect from 1 September 2008.

8C [Determination of applications: breach of conditions rectified at time of application

(1) This regulation applies where—

(*a*) an application under regulation 8A(1) is in respect of the trust company's failure to meet the conditions for its VCT approval to continue in force, and

(*b*) the failure has been rectified at the date of the application.

(2) Where this regulation applies, the Board shall determine that they will not exercise their power under section 281(1) (power to withdraw VCT approval of a company) if the Board are satisfied that—

(*a*) the failure was as a result of circumstances outside the control of the company,

(*b*) those circumstances prevented the company from meeting the conditions for its VCT approval to continue in force,

(*c*) the company took all reasonable measures to continue to meet the conditions for its VCT approval to continue in force, and

(*d*) the failure was—

(i) rectified by the company as soon as reasonably possible after the circumstances causing the failure arose, or

(ii) rectified notwithstanding that no measures could be taken by the company to rectify it.

This is subject to regulation 8E (circumstances within the control of the company: investment managers).][1]

Amendments—[1] Regulations 8–8J substituted for previous reg 8, by the Venture Capital Trust (Amendment) Regulations, SI 2008/1893 regs 2, 9 with effect from 1 September 2008.

8D [Determination of applications: breach of conditions not rectified at time of application

(1) This regulation applies where—

(*a*) an application under regulation 8A(1) is in respect of the trust company's failure to meet the conditions for its VCT approval to continue in force, and

(*b*) the failure has not been rectified at the date of the application or the failure is likely to occur after the date of the application.

(2) Where this regulation applies, the Board shall determine that they will not exercise their power under section 281(1) (power to withdraw VCT approval of a company) if the they are satisfied that—

(*a*) the failure is or will be as a result of circumstances outside the control of the company,

(*b*) those circumstances prevent or will prevent the company from meeting the conditions for its VCT approval to continue,

(*c*) the company took and will take all reasonable measures to rectify or avoid the failure to meet the conditions for its VCT approval to continue, and

(*d*) either—

(i) measures were taken or will be taken to rectify or avoid the failure as soon as possible and in any event within a reasonable period from the date of the application, or

(ii) where no measures to rectify or avoid the failure can be taken, the failure will nevertheless become rectified or be avoided within a reasonable period from the date of the application.

This is subject to regulation 8E.][1]

Amendments—[1] Regulations 8–8J substituted for previous reg 8, by the Venture Capital Trust (Amendment) Regulations, SI 2008/1893 regs 2, 9 with effect from 1 September 2008.

8E [Circumstances within the control of the company: investment managers

(1) For the purposes of regulations 8C and 8D, circumstances within the control of any investment manager of a company are to be treated as being within the control of the company.

(2) In paragraph (1) above "investment manager", in relation to a company, means a person appointed by, or acting for or on behalf of, the company who—

(*a*) manages investments in an account or portfolio on a discretionary basis under the terms of an agreement with the company which confers discretionary management of those investments on that person, or

(*b*) manages investments in an account or portfolio without exercising any discretion in relation to those investments under the terms of an agreement with the company.][1]

Amendments—[1] Regulations 8–8J substituted for previous reg 8, by the Venture Capital Trust (Amendment) Regulations, SI 2008/1893 regs 2, 9 with effect from 1 September 2008.

8F [Determinations: supplemental provisions

(1) A determination under regulation 8C(2) or 8D(2) shall be given by notice in writing to the company which applied for it.

(2) Where the Board make a determination under regulation 8D(2), the determination shall have effect for the period of 90 days commencing on the date on which they give notice to the company of it.

(3) A company given notice of a determination under regulation 8D(2) must give written notice to the Board when the failure or likely failure has been rectified or avoided.

(4) A notice under paragraph (3) above must—

(*a*) confirm that the failure or likely failure has been rectified or avoided,

(*b*) specify the date on which the failure or likely failure was rectified or avoided, and

(*c*) be given within 14 days of the date on which the failure or likely failure is rectified or avoided.][1]

Amendments—[1] Regulations 8–8J substituted for previous reg 8, by the Venture Capital Trust (Amendment) Regulations, SI 2008/1893 regs 2, 9 with effect from 1 September 2008.

8G [Determination in force: further circumstances causing breach of conditions

(1) This regulation applies where—

(*a*) the Board have made a determination under regulation 8D(2), and

(*b*) during the period in which that determination has effect further circumstances arise or occur which—

(i) have caused, cause or are likely to cause the company to fail to meet or to cease to meet any condition (including a condition imposed under regulation 4(3)) for its VCT approval to continue in force, or

(ii) in relation to a condition to which the determination relates, have caused, cause or are likely to cause that condition to be broken further or to increase the extent of the failure to meet the condition by the company.

(2) In relation to the further circumstances referred to in paragraph (1)(*b*) above, the company—

(*a*) must give notice in accordance with regulation 8, and

(*b*) may make an application in accordance with regulation 8A(1).][1]

Amendments—[1] Regulations 8–8J substituted for previous reg 8, by the Venture Capital Trust (Amendment) Regulations, SI 2008/1893 regs 2, 9 with effect from 1 September 2008.

8H [Further determinations in respect of same application

After the expiry of a determination made under regulation 8D(2), the Board may make a further determination under that regulation in respect of the same application if—

(*a*) the company requests in writing that a further determination be made in respect of that application,

(*b*) a return made in accordance with regulation 8I accompanies the request for the further determination, and

(*c*) the Board continue to be satisfied in relation to the matters specified in regulation 8D(2).][1]

Amendments—[1] Regulations 8–8J substituted for previous reg 8, by the Venture Capital Trust (Amendment) Regulations, SI 2008/1893 regs 2, 9 with effect from 1 September 2008.

8I [Monitoring of breach of conditions: returns

(1) If a company requests under regulation 8H that a further determination be made in respect of an application under regulation 8A(1) a return must be made by the company in accordance with this regulation and must be included in or with that request.

(2) A return under this regulation must be made—

(*a*) in relation to a first request under regulation 8H, in respect of the period from the date of the application under regulation 8A(1) to the date on which the first determination under regulation 8D(2) ceases to have effect, and

(*b*) in relation to a subsequent request under regulation 8H, in respect of the period commencing on the day after the end of the period to which the last return under this regulation relates and ending on the date on which the most recent determination under regulation 8D(2) ceases to have effect.

This is subject to paragraph (5) below.

(3) The return must—

(*a*) so far as is possible, state the extent to which the conditions for the company's VCT approval to continue in force—

(i) have ceased or will cease to be met, or

(ii) have been or will be broken or not met,

(*b*) specify what measures, if any, have been taken during that period to rectify or avoid the failure, or the likely failure, to meet the conditions for the company's VCT approval to continue in force,

(*c*) specify any alterations to the measures specified in the application made under regulation 8A(1), or in the last return under this regulation if later, that the company intends to take to rectify or avoid the failure, or likely failure, to meet the conditions for its VCT approval to continue,

(*d*) specify the date by which the company expects to meet the conditions for its VCT approval to continue, and

(*e*) be signed by the secretary or a director of the company.

(4) A return under this regulation must be made within 7 days after the date on which the period to which it relates ends.

(5) If more than one determination of the Board is in effect at the same time in relation to the same company, the Board may direct that one return applicable to those determinations is made in relation to a specified period.

(6) A return under this regulation shall be in such form as the Board may specify or authorise.][1]

Amendments—[1] Regulations 8–8J substituted for previous reg 8, by the Venture Capital Trust (Amendment) Regulations, SI 2008/1893 regs 2, 9 with effect from 1 September 2008.

8J [Withdrawal of VCT approval where determination has been made

(1) A determination under regulation 8C(2) or 8D(2) shall not prevent the Board from exercising their power under section 281(1) to withdraw the company's VCT approval where they have grounds for doing so in relation to other circumstances not the subject of an application under regulation 8A(1) to which the determination relates.

(2) A determination under regulation 8D(2) shall not prevent the Board from exercising their power under section 281(1) to withdraw the company's VCT approval where the failure or likely failure to which the determination relates has not been rectified or avoided within a reasonable period from the date of the application to which the determination relates.][1]

Amendments—[1] Regulations 8–8J substituted for previous reg 8, by the Venture Capital Trust (Amendment) Regulations, SI 2008/1893 regs 2, 9 with effect from 1 September 2008.

PART III
RELIEF FROM INCOME TAX
CHAPTER I
RELIEF IN RESPECT OF INVESTMENTS IN TRUST COMPANIES

9 Certificate to be given to investor

(1) If an ["investor (who is an individual)][2] to whom [(or to whose nominee)][2] eligible shares have been issued so requires, a trust company shall, within 30 days, give him a certificate containing the particulars specified in paragraph (2) below and certifying as specified in paragraph (3) below.

(2) The particulars specified are—

(*a*) the name of the investor,

(*b*) his permanent address including postcode,

(*c*) the date on which the eligible shares were issued to him [(or to his nominee)][2],

(*d*) the amount payable in respect of those shares and the date on which that amount will be payable, and

(*e*) the amount paid in respect of those shares and the date on which that amount was paid.

(3) The certificate shall certify—

(*a*) that eligible shares have been issued to the investor [(or to his nominee)][2],

(*b*) that to the best of the trust company's knowledge and belief the shares were both subscribed for and issued as mentioned in [section 261(3)][1], and

(c) that to the best of the trust company's knowledge and belief the shares were not issued in a case where the investor is not entitled to relief under [Chapter 2 of Part 6][1] because the case is one to which [section 264][1] applies.

(4) The trust company shall keep a record of the information contained in any certificate given under this regulation.

Amendments—[1] In para (3)(*b*), (*c*), words substituted by the Venture Capital Trust (Amendment) Regulations, SI 2008/1893 regs 2, 10 with effect from 1 September 2008.

[2] In para (1), words substituted for word "individual" and words inserted, and in paras (2)(*c*), (3)(*a*), words inserted by the Venture Capital Trust (Amendment) Regulations, SI 2014/1929 reg 2(1), (3) with effect from 12 August 2014.

[CHAPTER II

RELIEF IN RESPECT OF DISTRIBUTIONS BY TRUST COMPANIES][1]1

Amendments—[1] Part III Chapter II (regs 10–21) revoked by the Venture Capital Trusts (Amendment) Regulations, SI 1999/819 reg 4 with effect for distributions made by a venture capital trust after 5 April 1999.

21A [Return containing particulars of amounts subscribed for eligible shares

(1) A company which at any time in the period specified in paragraph (2) below ("the specified period") is a trust company, shall deliver to the Board, in respect of the specified period and within the time limit specified in paragraph (3) below, a return containing, in respect of each amount subscribed by any investor for eligible shares in the specified period, the particulars specified in paragraph (4) below.

(2) The specified period is—

(*a*) a year, or

(*b*) a period beginning on the 6th April and ending on the day on which that company ceased to be approved as a trust company,

whichever is the shorter.

(3) The time limit specified is—

(*a*) six months after the end of the year, or

(*b*) six months after the day on which the company ceased to be approved as a trust company,

whichever is the earlier.

(4) The particulars specified are—

(*a*) the full name of the investor,

(*b*) his permanent residential address, including postcode,

(*c*) his date of birth,

(*d*) if he has one, his national insurance number,

(*e*) the amount paid in respect of eligible shares subscribed for in that period, and

(*f*) the date on which that amount was paid.

(5) A return under this regulation shall be in such form as the Board may prescribe or authorise.][1]

Amendments—[1] This regulation inserted by the Venture Capital Trusts (Amendment) Regulations, SI 1999/819 reg 5 with effect for distributions made by a venture capital trust after 5 April 1999.

PART IV

RETURN OF PARTICULARS OF INVESTMENTS, KEEPING OF RECORDS AND PROVISION OF INFORMATION

22 Return containing particulars of investments

(1) A company which is, or has been, a trust company shall deliver to the Board, in respect of the period specified in paragraph (2) below ("the specified period"), and within the time limit specified in paragraph (3) below, a return containing the particulars specified in paragraph (4) [and regulation 22A][3] below, the certificate specified in paragraph (5) below and the declaration specified in paragraph (6) below.

(2) The specified period is—

(*a*) an accounting period of a trust company,

(*b*) a period beginning on the date from which the Board's approval of a company for the purposes of [Part 6][2] has effect and ending on an accounting date of the company, or

(*c*) a period beginning at the commencement of an accounting period of a company and ending on the day on which that company ceased to be approved for the purposes of [Part 6][2],

whichever is the shortest.

(3) The time limit specified is—

(*a*) twelve months after the end of the accounting period of the trust company, or

(*b*) twelve months after the day on which the company ceased to be approved for the purposes of [Part 6][2],

whichever is the [earlier][4].

(4) The particulars specified are—

(*a*) in respect of each investment held by the company at the beginning of the specified period, the value of that investment computed in accordance with subsections (5) and (11) of [section 278][2];

(*b*) in respect of any new investment made by the company during the specified period—

(i) the date on which that investment was made, and

(ii) the value of that investment together with any revaluation of investments, computed in accordance with subsections (5) and (11) of [section 278][2], which is required as a result of the making of that investment;

(*c*) in relation to each investment, whether or not it is a qualifying holding; *[and]*[1]

(*d*) in relation to each qualifying holding—

(i) the name of the company in which the investment has been made, and

(ii) the address of that company's registered or principal office; [*and*[3]

(*e*) in respect of each disposal of an investment by the company during the specified period—

(i) the name of the company in which the investment was held,

(ii) the address of that company's registered or principal office,

(iii) the date of the disposal, *and*[3]

(iv) the value, immediately after the disposal, computed in accordance with subsections (5) and (11) of [section 278][2], of the remainder of any holding of investments from which the disposal was made][1][, and

(v) the value at which the investment was disposed of;][3]

(*f*) in respect of each fund manager of the company during the specified period—

(i) the name and address of its registered or principal office, and

(ii) its Financial Services Register reference number;

(*g*) where a new investment was made during the specified period—

(i) immediately before the relevant holding was issued, the value of the relevant company's gross assets, or if it was a parent company, the value of the group assets,

(ii) the total investment in the relevant company at the investment date (within the meaning given by section 280B(3A)), less the value of the new investment,

(iii) a description of each qualifying activity, whether carried on by the relevant company or one of the companies mentioned in section 291(7) and (8), for the purposes of which, at the time the relevant holding was issued, the money raised was intended to be used,

(iv) when the relevant holding was issued, the relevant company's full-time equivalent employee number, or if it was a parent company, the sum of the full-time equivalent employee number for it and each of its qualifying subsidiaries, and

(v) whether or not the relevant company received a non-statutory opinion from Her Majesty's Revenue and Customs on the eligibility of that investment as a qualifying holding, and if it did—

(aa) whether that opinion indicated that the investment would or would not be likely to be eligible as such, and

(ab) the date of that opinion;

(*h*) where a new investment was made during the specified period, but after the end of the initial investing period of the relevant company—

(i) under which of conditions A, B or C of section 280C the investment was made, and

(ii) the date of the relevant first commercial sale made by the relevant company; and

(*i*) where a new investment was made during the specified period and the relevant company was a knowledge-intensive company on the date the investment was made—

(i) whether or not the total investment in the relevant company at the investment date exceeded the amount specified in section 280B(2)(*b*)(ii),

(ii) whether or not the investment was made after the period specified in section 280C(3)(b), and

(iii) whether or not the full-time equivalent employee number provided further to sub-paragraph (*g*)(iv) exceeded the number specified in section 297A(3A)(*b*) at the time the relevant holding was issued.

(4A) Expressions used in Chapter 4 of Part 6 which are also used in sub-paragraphs (*g*), (*h*) and (*i*) of paragraph (4) have the same meaning in those sub-paragraphs as they do in that Chapter.][3]

(5) The certificate specified is—

(*a*) where the trust company has been given full approval or has been given provisional approval three years or more before the beginning of the specified period, that the trust company satisfied all the conditions in [section 274][2] throughout the specified period; or

(*b*) where the trust company has been given provisional approval less than three years before the beginning of the specified period, that the trust company satisfied all the conditions of [section 274][2] and any other conditions attached to the provisional approval throughout the specified period; or

(c) that the company has ceased to be approved for the purposes of [Part 6][2].

(6) The declaration specified, is a declaration that the particulars contained in the return are, to the best of the company's knowledge and belief, true and correct.

(7) The declaration specified in paragraph (6) above shall be signed by the secretary or by a director of the company.

(8) A return under this regulation shall be in such form as the Board may specify or authorise.

Amendments—[1] In reg 22(4), word "and" immediately following sub-para (c) revoked, and sub-para (e) inserted, by the Venture Capital Trusts (Amendment) Regulations, SI 1999/819 reg 6 with effect for distributions made by a venture capital trust after 5 April 1999.

[2] In paras (2)(b), (c), (3)(b), (4)(a), (b)(ii), (e)(iv), (5)(a), (b), (c), words substituted, by the Venture Capital Trust (Amendment) Regulations, SI 2008/1893 regs 2, 11 with effect from 1 September 2008.

[3] The following amendments made by the Venture Capital Trust (Amendment) Regulations, SI 2016/1192 regs 2, 3 with effect for each specified period ending on or after 31 December 2016. "Specified period" has the meaning given in para (2): SI 2016/1192 reg 1(3)—

- in para (1), words inserted;
- in para (3), word substituted for word "shorter"; and
- in para (4)(d)(ii), (e)(iii), word "and" at the end repealed, para (4)(e)(v), (f)–(i) and preceding word inserted, and para (4A) inserted.

[22A Particulars to be returned in respect of relevant investments, raised money and derived money relating to the traceable period

(1) Where condition one or condition two applies, the return required by regulation 22(1) must also contain the particulars specified in paragraphs (4) and (5).

(2) Condition one is that on the last day of the specified period—

(a) the company held a relevant investment, and

(b) that relevant investment would not have been capable of being regarded as comprised in the company's qualifying holdings on that day unless it had been acquired using raised money or derived money.

(3) Condition two is that—

(a) on the last day of the specified period the company held derived money,

(b) on that day, the company maintained information identifying derived money or relevant investments acquired using raised money or derived money, and

(c) the purpose or one of the main purposes of maintaining that information was to be able to make any future relevant investment which would not be capable of being comprised in the company's qualifying holdings unless it was made using derived money.

(4) The particulars specified are—

(a) for each relevant investment held at any time during the specified period which the company acquired using raised money or derived money—

(i) where the investment was acquired using raised money, the date or dates the company raised the money used to acquire that investment,

(ii) where the investment was acquired using derived money, the date or dates the company raised the money from which that money derived,

(iii) the name, company registration number and address of the registered or principal office of the company in which the relevant investment was made, and

(iv) if held on the last day of the specified period, the value of the relevant investment on that day; or

(b) a statement by the company that it did not hold any such relevant investments during the specified period.

(5) The particulars specified are—

(a) for derived money held by the company on the last day of the specified period—

(i) the amount of that money, and

(ii) the date or dates the company raised the money from which that money derived; or

(b) a statement by the company that it did not hold any such money on that date.

(6) In this regulation—

"derived money" means money, including money in the company's possession or a sum owed to it over which it has account-holder's rights, which is derived from the investment by the company of raised money, and section 285(5) and (6) has effect for interpreting "account-holder's rights";

"raised money" means money raised by the issue during the traceable period of shares in or securities of the company;

"a relevant investment" means shares in or securities of another company which are held by the company;

"the specified period" has the meaning given in regulation 22(2);

"the traceable period" means the period beginning on 6th April 1995 and ending on 5th April 2008.][1]

Amendments—[1] Regulation 22A inserted by the Venture Capital Trust (Amendment) Regulations, SI 2016/1192 regs 2, 4 with effect for each specified period ending on or after 31 December 2016. "Specified period" has the meaning given in reg 22(2): SI 2016/1192 reg 1(3).

23 Records to be kept by trust company

(1) A company which is or has been a trust company shall at all times during the relevant period keep sufficient accounts, records and other information to enable the requirements of [Part 6][1] and these Regulations to be satisfied.

(2) In paragraph (1) above, the "relevant period" means—

(*a*) in the case of a company which has ceased to be approved for the purposes of [Part 6][1], the period of [ten][2] years from the date on which the company ceased to be so approved, and

(*b*) in any other case, the period of [ten][2] years from the end of the period of account or the year to which the accounts, records and information relate, whichever is the longer.

Amendments—[1] In paras (1), (2)(*a*), words substituted by the Venture Capital Trust (Amendment) Regulations, SI 2008/1893 regs 2, 12 with effect from 1 September 2008.

[2] In para (2)(*a*), (*b*), word substituted for word "six" by the Venture Capital Trust (Amendment) Regulations, SI 2016/1192 regs 2, 5 with effect for each specified period ending on or after 31 December 2016. "Specified period" has the meaning given in reg 22(2): SI 2016/1192 reg 1(3).

24 Information to be provided to the Board

[(1) The Board may by notice require—

(*a*) any company which is or has been a trust company,

(*b*) any investor, or

(*c*) any nominee for an investor,

within such period as may be specified in the notice, to furnish them with such information as they may reasonably require for the purposes of Part 6 or these Regulations.][1]

(2) The period specified in a notice given under paragraph (1) above shall be not less than 14 days.

Amendments—[1] Paragraph 1 substituted by the Venture Capital Trust (Amendment) Regulations, SI 2014/1929 reg 2(1), (4) with effect from 12 August 2014.

25 Inspection of records by officer of the Board

[(1) The Board may by notice require—

(*a*) any company which is or has been a trust company,

(*b*) any investor, or

(*c*) any nominee for an investor,

within such period as may be specified in the notice, to make available for inspection by an officer of the Board authorised for that purpose such accounts, records and other information as are in that person's possession or under that person's control as the Board may reasonably require for the purposes of Part 6 or these Regulations.][1]

(2) The period specified in a notice given under paragraph (1) above shall be not less than 14 days.

(3) Where records are maintained by computer the person required to make them available for inspection shall provide the officer making the inspection with all the facilities necessary for obtaining information from them.

Amendments—[1] Paragraph 1 substituted by the Venture Capital Trust (Amendment) Regulations, SI 2014/1929 reg 2(1), (5) with effect from 12 August 2014.

1995/2050

INCOME TAX (DEALERS IN SECURITIES) (TRADEPOINT) REGULATIONS 1995

Note—These Regulations lapsed on the repeal of TA 1988 s 732 by FA 2008 s 66(1) with effect in relation to cases where the purchase by the first buyer (within the meaning of TA 1988 s 731(2)) is made on or after 1 April 2008.

1995/2052

INCOME TAX (MANUFACTURED DIVIDENDS) (TRADEPOINT) REGULATIONS 1995

Revocation—These Regulations revoked by the Stock Lending and Manufactured Payments (Revocations and Amendments) Regulations, SI 1997/987, reg 6, with effect from 1 July 1997 except in relation to any payment of a manufactured dividend to which these Regulations apply that is made before that date.

1995/2902

TAXATION OF INCOME FROM LAND (NON-RESIDENTS) REGULATIONS 1995

Made by the Commissioners of Inland Revenue under TA 1988 s 42A

Made . . . . *10 November 1995*

Laid before the House of Commons . . . . *10 November 1995*

Coming into Force . . . . *1 December 1995*

Modification—ITA 2007 s 1034, Sch 2 para 169 (references to payments to be made to the Board, in respect of tax that is or may become chargeable as the income from a business of a non-resident (as defined in these regulations), from 6 April 2007, to be read as references to income tax to be paid to the Commissioners for Her Majesty's Revenue and Customs in respect of non-resident landlord income (as defined in ITA 2007 section 971(2)).

ITA 2007 Sch 2 para 169 (modification of these regulations in relation to any references to payments to be made to the Board in respect of tax that is or may become chargeable as the income from a business of a non-resident. On and after 6 April 2007 those references are to be read as references to income tax to be paid to the Commissioners for HMRC in respect of non-resident landlord income (as defined in ITA 2007 S 971(2))).

PRELIMINARY

1 Citation, commencement and effect

(1) These Regulations may be cited as the Taxation of Income from Land (Non-residents) Regulations 1995 and shall come into force on 1st December 1995.

(2) These Regulations shall have effect with respect to any payment made on or after 6th April 1996 which—

(*a*) constitutes income of a Schedule A business carried on by a non-resident, and

(*b*) either—

(i) is made by a person falling within subsection (2)(*a*) of section 42A who is a prescribed person in respect of the non-resident, or

(ii) is received by an agent who is a prescribed person in respect of the non-resident or by another person at the direction of that agent.

2 Interpretation

In these Regulations unless the context otherwise requires—

"agent" means a person falling within subsection (2)(*b*) of section 42A;

"annual period" means the period commencing on 1st April and ending on the following 31st March;

"the Board" means the Commissioners of Inland Revenue;

"deductible expense" means an expense which is deductible under the Tax Acts in computing the profits or gains of a non-resident's Schedule A business;

"Management Act" means the Taxes Management Act 1970;

"non-resident" means a person who has his usual place of abode outside the United Kingdom;

"notice" means notice in writing;

"prescribed person" means a person prescribed by regulation 3;

"professional trustee" means a person who carries on, or is employed by, a business which consists of or includes the management of trusts, and who acts as trustee in the course of that business or employment;

"quarter" means—

(*a*) the period from 6th April 1996 to 30th June 1996;

(*b*) any subsequent period of 3 months ending with the last day of September, December, March or June;

"section 42A" means section 42A of the Taxes Act;

"Schedule A business" shall be construed in accordance with subsection (8)(*a*) of section 42A;

"Taxes Act" means the Income and Corporation Taxes Act 1988;

"year" means year of assessment.

PRESCRIBED PERSONS

3 Prescribed persons for the purposes of section 42A

(1) In any case where a person falling within subsection 2(*a*) or (*b*) of section 42A is issued with a notice by the Board stating that he is a prescribed person for the purposes of subsection (1) of that section in respect of the Schedule A business of a non-resident, or a part of that business, that person is prescribed for the purposes of subsection (1) of that section in respect of that business or, as the case may be, the part referred to in the notice.

(2) Except where it relates to a part of a non-resident's Schedule A business, a notice under paragraph (1) above need not specify the name of the non-resident concerned or describe his Schedule A business.

(3) In any case where—

(*a*) no notice has been issued by the Board under paragraph (1) above in respect of a non-resident's Schedule A business, or there is a part of his business in respect of which no notice has been issued under that paragraph; and

(*b*) a person whose usual place of abode is in the United Kingdom—

(i) is an agent in respect of that business or that part,

(ii) has power to receive income in respect of that business or that part or has control over the direction of that income, and

(iii) is not an excluded person,

that person is, subject to paragraph (4) below, prescribed for the purposes of subsection (1) of section 42A in respect of that business or, as the case may be, that part.

(4) Where in a case falling within paragraph (3) above there is more than one person to whom sub-paragraph (*b*) of that paragraph applies as respects the same business or the same part of a business, the person who is the elected agent or, if there is no elected agent, the last agent is the person prescribed for the purposes of subsection (1) of section 42A in respect of that business or, as the case may be, that part.

(5) In any case where—

(*a*) no notice has been issued by the Board under paragraph (1) above in respect of a non-resident's Schedule A business, or there is a part of his business in respect of which no notice has been issued under that paragraph;

(*b*) there is no person to whom paragraph (3)(*b*) above applies in respect of that business or that part; and

(*c*) a person whose usual place of abode is in the United Kingdom—

(i) is a tenant of premises owned by the non-resident in connection with that business or that part, and

(ii) is liable to pay to the non-resident in respect of his occupation of those premises sums exceeding in the aggregate £5,200 per annum or, where he occupies the premises for less than one year, the proportionate amount of that sum which is determined by the duration of his occupation,

that person is prescribed for the purposes of subsection (1) of section 42A in respect of that business or, as the case may be, that part.

4 Interpretation of regulation 3

(1) In regulation 3—

(*a*) "excluded person" means an agent whose activity on behalf of the non-resident in connection with the management or administration of his Schedule A business or part thereof (as the case may be) is confined to the provision of legal advice or legal services;

(*b*) "elected agent" means the agent who is elected jointly by the last agent and himself to assume the responsibilities of a prescribed person for the purposes of subsection (1) of section 42A in relation to the Schedule A business or part thereof (as the case may be);

(*c*) "last agent" means the agent by whom sums constituting income from the non-resident's Schedule A business or part thereof (as the case may be) are paid directly to the non-resident or to an agent whose usual place of abode is outside the United Kingdom or to a person who is not an agent.

(2) An election shall be made by notice to the Board signed by the last agent and the person to be elected, and any such notice shall state—

(*a*) the name and address of the agent elected, and

(*b*) the date from which the election has effect, not being a date earlier than the first day of the quarter in which the election is made.

(3) An election may be revoked by notice to the Board given by either of the agents who made the election, and any such revocation shall have effect—

(*a*) from the first day of the quarter next following the date on which the notice is received by the Board, or

(*b*) after the expiry of 30 days following the date on which the notice is received by the Board,

whichever is the later to occur.

5 Partnerships

In any case where a liability to make any payment to the Board under these Regulations arises from amounts payable or things done in the course of a business carried on by any persons in partnership, that partnership as such shall be treated for the purposes of these Regulations as a person falling within subsection (2)(*a*) or (*b*) (as the case may be) of section 42A.

6 Multiple branches

(1) In any case where an agent—

(*a*) is a prescribed person by virtue of regulation 3 in respect of the Schedule A business, or part thereof, of more than one non-resident,

(*b*) acts on behalf of those non-residents through branches of his business in circumstances where the average number of non-residents in each branch at the relevant time is not less than five, and

(*c*) is a person approved by the Board for the purposes of this regulation,

that person shall be treated for the purposes of these Regulations as if in respect of each branch he were a separate and distinct person.

(2) An application for approval under paragraph (1) above shall be made to the Board in a form provided or authorised by the Board which shall contain—

(*a*) such information as is necessary to identify the branches concerned,

(*b*) the number of non-residents in each branch, and

(*c*) a declaration by the prescribed person that he does not act on behalf of any non-residents other than those whose business is managed by the branches so identified.

(3) An approval under paragraph (1) above shall, unless revoked or withdrawn, have effect for the quarter following that in which it is given and for any subsequent quarter.

(4) An approval may be revoked by the prescribed person by notice to the Board and, subject to paragraph (5) below, such revocation shall have effect for the quarter following that in which it is given and for any subsequent quarter.

(5) Notwithstanding the revocation of approval under paragraph (4) above, a further application for approval may be made by the prescribed person in accordance with paragraph (2) above at any time following the revocation; and paragraph (3) above shall apply accordingly in relation to an approval given in response to that application.

(6) The Board may, by notice to the prescribed person, refuse approval where they have reason to believe that—

(*a*) the average number of non-residents in each branch is less than five at the relevant time, or

(*b*) there is likely to be a failure on the part of the prescribed person to comply with the obligations imposed on him under these Regulations in relation to any branch, or

(*c*) the declaration given by the prescribed person pursuant to paragraph (2)(*c*) above is incorrect.

(7) The Board may, by notice to the prescribed person, withdraw approval where they have reason to believe that—

(*a*) the average number of non-residents in each branch was at the relevant time, or has since become, less than five, or

(*b*) there has been a failure on the part of the prescribed person to comply with the obligations imposed on him under these Regulations in relation to any branch, or

(*c*) the declaration given by the prescribed person pursuant to paragraph (2)(*c*) above was, or has become, incorrect.

(8) The prescribed person may appeal against a notice under paragraph (6) above refusing approval, or a notice under paragraph (7) above withdrawing approval, by notice to the Board within 30 days of the date of issue of the notice of refusal or, as the case may be, the notice of withdrawal.

(9) The appeal shall be to the General Commissioners except that the prescribed person may elect (in accordance with section 46(1) of the Management Act) to appeal to the Special Commissioners.[1]

(10) [The tribunal shall, on an appeal notified to it,][1] confirm the notice of refusal or withdrawal unless . . .[1] satisfied that it ought to be quashed.

(11) In this regulation—

(*a*) references to branches of an agent's business are references to the units (of whatever kind) into which the agent has divided his business;

(*b*) references to "the relevant time" are references to the time at which an application for approval is made by the prescribed person.

Amendments—[1] Para (9) revoked, in para (10), words substituted and words revoked, by the Transfer of Tribunal Functions and Revenue and Customs Appeals Order, SI 2009/56 art 3, Sch 2 paras 23, 28 with effect from 1 April 2009.

7 Registration by prescribed persons

(1) The person prescribed by paragraph (2) below shall, within the period of 30 days following the date specified in paragraph (3) below, register with the Board the following details—

(*a*) his name and address, and

(*b*) his tax office reference, if he has one.

(2) The person prescribed by this paragraph is any person who is—

(*a*) an agent in respect of the Schedule A business, or part thereof, of a non-resident, and

(*b*) a person prescribed by regulation 3 in respect of that business or that part.

(3) The date specified in this paragraph is the date on which the agent became a person prescribed by regulation 3 in respect of that business or that part.

8 Payment and recovery of tax Calculation of payment of tax by person falling within subsection (2)(a) of section 42A

(1) A person falling within subsection (2)(*a*) of section 42A who is a prescribed person in respect of the Schedule A business, or part thereof, of a non-resident shall calculate for each quarter the amount of any payment to be made to the Board in respect of tax which is or may become chargeable on the income from that business or that part.

(2) The amount of the payment to be calculated by that person is the amount of tax at the basic rate on the aggregate of all income which falls to be treated as a receipt of that business or that part, other than income specified in paragraph (3) below, and which either—

(*a*) was paid by him in the quarter to the non-resident, or

(*b*) was paid by him in the quarter to a person other than the non-resident, not being a payment which he can reasonably be satisfied is a deductible expense.

(3) The income specified in this paragraph is any income which—

(*a*) is attributable to a branch of the non-resident in the United Kingdom, and

(*b*) is chargeable to corporation tax.

9 Calculation of payment of tax by agent

(1) An agent who is a prescribed person in respect of the Schedule A business, or part thereof, of a non-resident shall calculate for each quarter the amount of any payment to be made to the Board in respect of tax which is or may become chargeable on the income from that business or that part.

(2) The amount of the payment to be calculated is the amount of tax at the basic rate on the amount which results after deducting from the income specified in paragraph (3) below—

(*a*) the expenses specified in paragraph (4) below, and

(*b*) any excess amount of expenses falling to be deducted from that income in accordance with paragraph (5) below.

(3) The income specified is all income which falls to be treated as a receipt of that business or that part, other than income specified in regulation 8(3), and which either—

(*a*) was received by the prescribed person in the quarter concerned, or

(*b*) was income which it was in his power to receive or over whose direction he had control but which was paid at his direction to another person in that quarter without being received by him.

(4) The expenses specified are all amounts paid in the quarter by the prescribed person or by another person at his direction that he can reasonably be satisfied are deductible under the Tax Acts in computing the profits or gains of that business or that part.

(5) Where in any quarter in an annual period the expenses specified in paragraph (4) above exceed the income specified in paragraph (3) above—

(*a*) the amount of the excess shall first be deducted from the income specified in paragraph (3) above for previous quarters in that annual period, taking later quarters before earlier quarters, and

(*b*) any balance remaining of that amount shall be carried forward and deducted from the income specified in paragraph (3) above for subsequent quarters, including quarters after the end of that annual period, taking earlier quarters before later quarters.

(6) Where an amount paid by a prescribed person in a previous quarter becomes repayable as a result of an excess amount being deducted from income pursuant to paragraph (5)(*a*) above, the amount repayable—

(*a*) shall first be set off by the prescribed person against payments due under this regulation in respect of other non-residents in respect of whose Schedule A business or part thereof he is a prescribed person for the quarter in which the excess amount arises, and

(*b*) any balance remaining shall, on a claim being made to the Board by the prescribed person, be repaid to him.

(7) A claim under paragraph (6)(*b*) above ("a repayment claim") shall be made in a quarterly return under regulation 10.

(8) An appeal . . . [1] from the Board's decision on a repayment claim . . . [1] shall be brought by giving notice to the Board within 30 days of receipt of notice of the decision.

(9) All such assessments, payments and repayments shall be made as are necessary to give effect to the Board's decision on a repayment claim or to any variation of that decision on appeal.

Amendments—[1] In para (8), words revoked, by the Transfer of Tribunal Functions and Revenue and Customs Appeals Order, SI 2009/56 art 3, Sch 2 paras 23, 29 with effect from 1 April 2009.

10 Accounting for tax—quarterly returns

(1) In the circumstances specified in paragraph (2) below and within 30 days after the end of a quarter, a prescribed person shall make a return to the Board, in such form as the Board may prescribe, containing the information specified in paragraph (3) below and the declaration specified in paragraph (4) below.

(2) The circumstances specified are where—

(*a*) an amount is payable by the prescribed person in respect of the quarter, calculated in accordance with regulation 8 or 9 as the case may be, or
(*b*) a repayment of tax is due under regulation 9(6)(*b*), or
(*c*) the Board have issued a notice to the prescribed person requiring a return to be made in respect of that quarter.

(3) The information specified is—
(*a*) the name and address of the prescribed person;
(*b*) where the prescribed person is a person falling within subsection (2)(*a*) of section 42A, the aggregate of the amounts payable by him for that quarter, calculated in accordance with regulation 8, in respect of all non-residents in respect of whose Schedule A businesses (or parts thereof) he is a prescribed person;
(*c*) where the prescribed person is an agent, the aggregate of the amounts payable by him for that quarter, calculated in accordance with regulation 9, in respect of all non-residents in respect of whose Schedule A businesses (or part thereof) he is a prescribed person, after set off of any amounts repayable pursuant to paragraph (6)(*a*) of that regulation; and
(*d*) a claim for repayment of an amount pursuant to regulation 9(6)(*b*), where appropriate.

(4) The declaration specified is a declaration by the prescribed person that the particulars given in the return are to the best of his knowledge correct and complete.

(5) The aggregate amount referred to in paragraph (3)(*b*) or (*c*) above shall be due at the time by which the return under paragraph (1) above is to be made, and that amount so due—
(*a*) shall be payable by the prescribed person without the making of an assessment, and
(*b*) may be assessed on the prescribed person (whether or not it has been paid when the assessment is made) if it, or any part of it, is not paid on or before the due date.

(6) The amount so due shall carry interest at the rate applicable under section 178 of the Finance Act 1989 to section 87 of the Management Act from the date when the amount becomes due until payment.

(7) Where an amount paid by a prescribed person in a previous quarter is repaid pursuant to a claim under regulation 9(6)(*b*), the repayment shall not affect interest under paragraph (6) above on the amount repaid for such time as is specified in paragraph (8) below but, subject to that, paragraph (6) above shall apply as if any such amount which is repaid had never become payable.

(8) The time for which interest is not affected is—
(*a*) any time before the expiration of the period of 30 days from the end of the quarter in which the excess of expenses giving rise to the repayment arose, unless the return for that quarter is made earlier in that period; and
(*b*) if that return is made earlier in that period, any time ending before the date on which the return is made.

(9) If it appears to the Board that there is an amount which ought to have been but has not been included in a quarterly return as payable to the Board, or if the Board are dissatisfied with any quarterly return, they may make an assessment on the prescribed person to the best of their judgment in respect of that amount.

(10) The like provisions as are contained in paragraph 10 of Schedule 16 to the Taxes Act (assessments and due date of tax) shall have effect in relation to an assessment under paragraph (9) above as if—
(*a*) for references to an assessment under that Schedule there were substituted references to an assessment under paragraph (9) above;
(*b*) the references to paragraphs 4(1) and 9 of that Schedule were omitted;
(*c*) sub-paragraph (5) were omitted.

(11) Any income tax due under an assessment made by virtue of paragraph (9) above shall carry interest at the rate applicable under section 178 of the Finance Act 1989 to section 87 of the Management Act from the date when the tax becomes due until payment; and for that purpose the tax shall be treated as having become due at the time when it would have become due if a correct return had been made.

11 Annual returns

(1) Not later than the 5th July following the end of an annual period, a prescribed person, other than a person specified in paragraph (3) below, shall make a return to the Board for that period—
(*a*) in respect of the non-resident or, if more than one, each non-resident separately, in respect of whose Schedule A business (or part thereof) he was a prescribed person at any time falling within that period, and
(*b*) containing the information specified in paragraph (4) below and the declaration specified in paragraph (5) below.

(2) A return under paragraph (1) above shall be in such form as the Board may prescribe.

(3) The person specified is any tenant who, as a result of a notice given by the Board under regulation 17(5)(*b*), was not obligated to make payments to the Board in respect of any payments made to a non-resident in that period.

(4) The information specified is—

(*a*) the name of the non-resident;

(*b*) where the non-resident is—

(i) an individual, or

(ii) a trustee other than a corporate or a professional trustee,

the principal residential address of the non-resident;

(*c*) where the non-resident is a company, the address of its registered office or its principal place of business;

(*d*) where the non-resident is a professional trustee, the address of his employment or principal place of business;

(*e*) where the prescribed person is an agent, the amount of income which, before deduction of any expenses, fell to be taken into account in the annual period in calculating under regulation 9 amounts of tax payable by him in respect of the Schedule A business (or part thereof) of the non-resident, or which would have fallen so to be taken into account if the non-resident had not been an approved person for the purposes of regulation 17 in that period;

(*f*) where the prescribed person is a person falling within subsection (2)(*a*) of section 42A, the aggregate of the following amounts of income—

(i) the amount of income which fell to be taken into account in the annual period in calculating under regulation 8 amounts of tax payable by him in respect of the Schedule A business (or part thereof) of the non-resident, or which would have fallen so to be taken into account if the non-resident had not been an approved person for the purposes of regulation 17 in that period, and

(ii) the amount of income which did not fall so to be taken into account because it was paid to a person other than the non-resident in circumstances where the prescribed person could reasonably be satisfied that the amount of the payment was a deductible expense;

(*g*) except where the non-resident is an approved person for the purposes of regulation 17, the aggregate of—

(i) all amounts paid during the annual period on behalf of the non-resident by or at the direction of the prescribed person which the prescribed person could reasonably be satisfied constituted deductible expenses, and

(ii) amounts carried forward to that period from a previous period pursuant to regulation 9(5)(*b*);

(*h*) the aggregate of the amounts specified as payable to the Board in quarterly returns made by the prescribed person for the annual period;

(*j*) the reference number relating to an approval by the Board of the non-resident under regulation 17.

(5) The declaration specified is a declaration by the prescribed person that the particulars given in the return are to the best of his knowledge correct and complete.

12 Certificate of tax liability

(1) Not later than the 5th July following the end of an annual period, a prescribed person who is liable under these Regulations to make any payments to the Board for any quarter falling within that period in respect of tax chargeable on the income of a non-resident, shall provide the non-resident with a certificate which shall include the particulars specified in paragraph (2) below and the declaration specified in paragraph (3) below.

(2) The particulars specified are—

(*a*) the name of the non-resident;

(*b*) where the non-resident is—

(i) an individual, or

(ii) a trustee other than a corporate or a professional trustee,

the principal residential address of the non-resident;

(*c*) where the non-resident is a company, the address of its registered office or its principal place of business;

(*d*) where the non-resident is a professional trustee, the address of his employment or principal place of business;

(*e*) the name and address of the prescribed person;

(*f*) the annual period to which the certificate relates;

(*g*) the aggregate amount of the liability referred to in paragraph (1) above for all quarters falling within the annual period.

(3) The declaration specified is a declaration by the prescribed person that the certificate is to the best of his knowledge correct and complete.

PROVISION OF INFORMATION AND INSPECTION AND KEEPING OF RECORDS

13 Information to be provided to the Board by prescribed persons

The Board may by notice require a prescribed person to furnish them, within such time (not being less than 14 days) as may be provided by the notice, such information as they may reasonably require to satisfy themselves that the prescribed person has complied with the requirements of these Regulations.

14 Inspection of records by officer of the Board

(1) The Board may by notice require a prescribed person, within such time (not being less than 14 days) as may be provided by the notice, to make available for inspection by an officer of the Board authorised for that purpose all such books, documents and other records in his possession or under his control as they may reasonably require to satisfy themselves that the prescribed person has complied with the requirements of these Regulations.

(2) Where a document or other record is maintained by computer, the prescribed person shall provide the officer making the inspection with all the facilities necessary for obtaining information from that document or other record.

15 Keeping of records

A prescribed person shall at all times maintain and retain sufficient records to enable an officer of the Board to satisfy himself on inspection of those records that the prescribed person has complied with the requirements of these Regulations.

16 Use of information

(1) Subject to paragraph (2) below, information obtained by the Board under regulation 13 or 14—

(*a*) shall not be used for the purpose of ascertaining the tax liability (if any) of any person other than—

(i) a person whose usual place of abode is outside the United Kingdom, or

(ii) a person falling within subsection (2)(*a*) of section 42A, or

(iii) an agent.

(2) Paragraph (1) above shall not be construed as preventing any disclosure of information within section 182(5) of the Finance Act 1989.

GROSS PAYMENT OF PROPERTY INCOME

17 Application for gross payment of property income

(1) A non-resident may apply to the Board for the obligation imposed under these Regulations to make payments to the Board not to apply in relation to payments falling to be treated as receipts of a Schedule A business carried on by him.

(2) An application under paragraph (1) above shall be made on a form provided by the Board and shall contain the information specified in paragraph (3) below and the undertakings specified in paragraph (4) below.

(3) The information specified is—

(*a*) the name of the applicant;

(*b*) the date of the application;

(*c*) where the applicant is—

(i) an individual, or

(ii) a trustee other than a corporate or a professional trustee,

the principal residential address of the applicant;

(*d*) where the applicant is a company, the address of its registered office or its principal place of business, and the names and principal residential addresses of its directors;

(*e*) where the applicant is a professional trustee, the address of his employment or principal place of business;

(*f*) the applicant's national insurance number, if he has one;

(*g*) the applicant's United Kingdom tax office reference, if he has one;

(*h*) the name and address of the prescribed person or, if more than one, each of the prescribed persons by or through whom payments falling to be treated as receipts of the applicant's Schedule A business are made;

(*j*) a statement that—

(i) the applicant has complied with all obligations imposed on him by or under the Tax Acts or the Management Act prior to the date of the application; or

(ii) the applicant has not had any obligations imposed on him by or under the Tax Acts or the Management Act prior to the date of the application; or

(iii) he does not expect to be liable to pay any amount by way of United Kingdom income tax for the year in which the application is made.

(4) The undertakings specified are that—

(*a*) where the applicant makes a statement falling within paragraph (3)(*j*)(iii) above, he will notify the Board in writing if he becomes liable to pay any such amount;

(*b*) the applicant will fully comply with all obligations imposed on him by or under the Tax Acts or the Management Act;

(*c*) the applicant will inform the Board if his usual place of abode ceases to be outside the United Kingdom.

(5) Where the Board approve an application under paragraph (1) above, they shall give—

(*a*) notice of the approval to the non-resident, and

(*b*) notice to the prescribed person or, if more than one, each prescribed person, specifying the date from which the obligations referred to in paragraph (1) above shall cease to apply in relation to payments falling to be treated as receipts of the applicant's Schedule A business and made on or after that date.

(6) The Board may, by notice to the applicant, refuse an application under paragraph (1) above where—

(*a*) they are not satisfied that the statement contained in the application and falling within paragraph (3)(*j*)(i), (ii) or (iii) above, as the case may be, is correct; or

(*b*) they are not satisfied that the applicant will comply with the undertakings contained in the application.

(7) The applicant may appeal against the Board's refusal of his application under paragraph (6) above by giving notice to the Board within 90 days of receipt of the notice of refusal.

(8) . . . [1]

(9) [The tribunal shall, on an appeal notified to it,][1] confirm the notice refusing approval unless . . . [1] satisfied that the notice ought to be quashed.

Amendments—[1] Para (8) revoked, in para (9), words substituted and words revoked, by the Transfer of Tribunal Functions and Revenue and Customs Appeals Order, SI 2009/56 art 3, Sch 2 paras 23, 30 with effect from 1 April 2009.

18 Review of approval under regulation 17—furnishing of information

Where the Board have approved an application under regulation 17, they may by notice require the non-resident by whom the application was made to furnish them, within such time (not being less than 42 days) as may be provided by the notice, such information as they may reasonably require to enable them to review the approval.

19 Withdrawal of approval under regulation 17

(1) An approval of an application under regulation 17 may be withdrawn by the Board by notice to the non-resident by whom the application was made specifying—

(*a*) the reasons for the withdrawal, and

(*b*) the date from which the withdrawal of approval shall take effect.

(2) The Board may withdraw their approval of an application where—

(*a*) they cease to be satisfied that the statement contained in the application and falling within regulation 17(3)(*j*)(i), (ii) or (iii), as the case may be, is correct; or

(*b*) they cease to be satisfied that the non-resident will comply with the undertakings contained in the application; or

(*c*) the non-resident fails to furnish information to the Board in accordance with regulation 18.

(3) Where the Board withdraw their approval of an application under paragraph (1) above, they shall give notice to the prescribed person or, if more than one, each prescribed person, specifying the date from which the obligations imposed under these Regulations to make payments to the Board shall apply in relation to payments falling to be treated as receipts of the applicant's Schedule A business and made on or after that date.

(4) A non-resident may appeal against the Board's withdrawal of approval under paragraph (1) above by giving notice to the Board within 90 days of the date of issue of the notice withdrawing approval.

(5) . . . [1]

(6) [The tribunal shall, on an appeal notified to it,][1] confirm the notice withdrawing approval unless . . . [1] satisfied that the notice ought to be quashed.

Amendments—[1] Para (5) revoked, in para (6), words substituted and words revoked, by the Transfer of Tribunal Functions and Revenue and Customs Appeals Order, SI 2009/56 art 3, Sch 2 paras 23, 31 with effect from 1 April 2009.

PROVISIONS RELATING TO SELF-ASSESSMENT

20 Self-assessment—payments on account

Section 59A of the Management Act (payments on account of income tax) ("section 59A") shall have effect in relation to payments to be made to the Board by virtue of section 42A in respect of any tax as if any reference in section 59A to income tax deducted at source included a reference to such payments.

21 Self-assessment—consequential provisions

(1) A non-resident may set off against either of the amounts specified in paragraph (2) below the aggregate amount of the payments which—

(*a*) were liable to be made to the Board under these Regulations for each quarter ending in a year by any person who is a prescribed person in respect of the Schedule A business (or part thereof) carried on by the non-resident in that year, and (*b*) were retained by the prescribed person out of sums due from him to the non-resident in order to meet that liability.

(2) The amounts specified are—

(*a*) the amount in which the non-resident is chargeable to income tax for the year in question, and

(*b*) the amount of the first payment on account of his liability to income tax for that year.

(3) Where pursuant to paragraph (1) above an amount is set off against the amount specified in paragraph (2)(*a*) above, section 59A (as modified by regulation 20) shall have effect as if the reference in subsection (1) of that section to the amount which is the assessed amount were a reference to that assessed amount reduced by the amount set off.

(4) Where pursuant to paragraph (1) above an amount is set off against the amount specified in paragraph (2)(*b*) above, section 59A (as so modified) shall have effect as if the reference in subsection (2) of that section to the first payment on account were a reference to the amount of that payment reduced by the amount set off.

(5) In any case where—

(*a*) by virtue of regulation 17 the obligations imposed under these Regulations to make payments to the Board do not apply in any year in relation to payments falling to be treated as receipts of a Schedule A business carried on by a non-resident in that year, and

(*b*) those obligations applied to such payments in the immediately preceding year,

subsection (1) of section 59A (as so modified) shall have effect as if those obligations did not apply in the immediately preceding year.

1995/3036

MANUFACTURED PAYMENTS AND TRANSFER OF SECURITIES (TAX RELIEF) REGULATIONS 1995

Made by the Treasury under TA 1988 s 730A(7), 737D(1)

Made . . . . *28 November 1995*
Laid before the House of Commons . . . . *28 November 1995*
Coming into Force . . . . *2 January 1996*

1 Citation, commencement and effect

(1) These Regulations may be cited as the Manufactured Payments and Transfer of Securities (Tax Relief) Regulations 1995 and shall come into force on 2nd January 1996.

(2) These Regulations have effect in relation to—

(*a*) any manufactured payment made on or after 2nd January 1996, and

(*b*) any payment of interest deemed to be made on or after that date under an agreement to sell securities entered into on or after 1st May 1995.

2 Interpretation

In these Regulations—

"manufactured payment" has the meaning given by section 737D(2) of the Taxes Act;

"the Taxes Act" means the Income and Corporation Taxes Act 1988.

3 Tax relief for manufactured payments

(1) Any manufactured payment made to a person for the benefit of—

(*a*) [a pension scheme][2] referred to in section [186(1) of the Finance Act 2004][2], or

(*b*) any fund referred to in section [613(4)(*a*) or 614(2), (3) or (4) of the Taxes Act,][2]

shall be treated as comprised in income of that person that is eligible for relief from tax by virtue of that section.

(2) Any manufactured payment made to an insurance company shall be treated, to the extent of so much of the payment as is referable to the company's pension business [or individual savings account business within the meaning of regulation 3 of the Individual Savings Account (Insurance Companies) Regulations 1998][1], as comprised in income of that company that is eligible for relief from tax by virtue of section 438 of the Taxes Act.

Amendments—[1] Words inserted in para 2 by the Individual Savings Account (Insurance Companies) Regulations, SI 1998/1871, with effect from 6 April 1999. Note that SI 1998/1871 lapsed on the repeal of the enabling authority by FA 2007 ss 38(1), 114, Sch 7 paras 2, 55, Sch 27 Pt 2(7), for periods of account of insurance companies beginning on or after 1 January 2007.

[2] Words in para (1) substituted by the Taxation of Pension Schemes (Consequential Amendments) Order, SI 2006/745 art 22(1), (2) with effect from 6 April 2006.

4 Tax relief for deemed payments of interest

(1) Where, pursuant to section 730A(2) of the Taxes Act (treatment of price differential on sale and repurchase of securities), a payment of interest is deemed to be made to a person in circumstances where, if it were actually made, it would be received by that person for the benefit of—

(*a*) [a pension scheme][2] specified in section [186(1) of the Finance Act 2004][2], or

(*b*) any fund referred to in section [613(4)(*a*) or 614(2), (3) or (4) of the Taxes Act,][2]

the amount of the payment shall be treated as comprised in income that is eligible for relief from tax by virtue of that section.

(2) Where, pursuant to section 730A(2) of the Taxes Act, a payment of interest is deemed to be made to an insurance company, it shall be treated, to the extent of so much of the deemed payment as is referable to the company's pension business [or individual savings account business within the meaning of regulation 3 of the Individual Savings Account (Insurance Companies) Regulations 1998][1], as comprised in income that is eligible for relief from tax by virtue of section 438 of the Taxes Act.

Amendments—[1] Words inserted in para 2 by the Individual Savings Account (Insurance Companies) Regulations, SI 1998/1871, with effect from 6 April 1999.

[2] Words in para (1) substituted by the Taxation of Pension Schemes (Consequential Amendments) Order, SI 2006/745 art 22(1), (3) with effect from 6 April 2006.

1995/3103

RETIREMENT BENEFITS SCHEMES (INFORMATION POWERS) REGULATIONS 1995

Note—These Regulations lapse by virtue of the coming into force of FA 2004 Part 4 (ss 149–284) with effect from 6 April 2006.

1995/3192

RETIREMENT AGE OF GENERAL COMMISSIONERS ORDER 1995

Revocation—These Regulations revoked by the Transfer of Tribunal Functions and Revenue and Customs Appeals Order, SI 2009/56 art 3, Sch 2 para 187(*h*) with effect from 1 April 2009.

1995/3220

SALE AND REPURCHASE OF SECURITIES (MODIFICATION OF ENACTMENTS) REGULATIONS 1995

Made by the Treasury under TA 1988 s 737E(1), (2), (4)

Made . . . . *6 December 1995*

Laid before the House of Commons . . . . *11 December 1995*

Coming into Force . . . . *2 January 1996*

Commentary—*Simon's Taxes* **D9.2.**

Revocation—These Regulations revoked by the Sale and Repurchase of Securities (Amendment of Instruments) Order, SI 2007/2484 art 5 with effect in relation to arrangements that come into force on or after 1 October 2007: SI 2007/2484 art 1(1).

1995/3237

INSURANCE COMPANIES (OVERSEAS LIFE ASSURANCE BUSINESS) (COMPLIANCE) REGULATIONS 1995

Made by the Commissioners of Inland Revenue under TA 1988, s 431E and FA 1995 Sch 8, para 58

Made . . . . *12 December 1995*

Laid before the House of Commons . . . . *12 December 1995*

Coming into Force . . . . *2 January 1996*

Commentary—*Simon's Taxes* **D7.5137.**

ARRANGEMENT OF REGULATIONS

Preliminary

PRELIMINARY

1 Citation, commencement and effect

These Regulations may be cited as the Insurance Companies (Overseas Life Assurance Business) (Compliance) Regulations 1995, shall come into force on 2nd January 1996, and shall have effect in relation to accounting periods beginning on or after 1st November 1994.

2 Interpretation

(1) In these Regulations unless the context otherwise requires—

"basic life assurance and general annuity business" has the meaning given by section 431F;

["beneficiary" has the meaning given by regulation 2 of the Excluded Business Regulations;][3]

"the Board" means the Commissioners [for Her Majesty's Revenue and Customs][8];

"branch" includes agency;

["child trust fund business" has the meaning given by section 431BA;][7]

["company tax return" has the meaning given by paragraph 3 of Schedule 18 to the Finance Act 1998;][1]

. . . [9]

["excepted business" means pension business, individual savings account business, child trust fund business, life reinsurance business and long-term business which is not life assurance business;][7]

["excluded business" means business which is excluded from section 431D (as amended by section 108 of the Finance Act 2000 and from time to time) by the Excluded Business Regulations;][3]

["the Excluded Business Regulations" means the Insurance Companies (Overseas Life Assurance Business) (Excluded Business) Regulations 2000;][3]

["the first [long-term][5] insurance Directive" means Council Directive 79/267 of 5th March 1979;][1]

["individual savings account business" has the meaning given by section 431BB;][7]

"life reinsurance business" has the meaning given by section 431C;

"pension business" has the meaning given by section 431B;

"policy holder" includes annuitant;

["relevant business" means—

(*a*) in the case of an overseas life insurance company, life assurance business carried on through a permanent establishment in the United Kingdom which is not excepted business, and

(*b*) in any other case, life assurance business which is not excepted business;][7]

"relevant policy" means any policy or contract . . . [7] which has at any time been treated as relating to overseas life assurance business[, or any policy or contract for business to which regulation 5(3) applies;][1]

"relevant record" means—

(*a*) any certificate, declaration, undertaking or other document which in these Regulations is either prescribed or specified, or

(*b*) any other document relating to a relevant policy;

. . . [3]

["the Solvency 2 Directive" means Directive 2009/138/EC of the European Parliament and of the Council of 25 November 2009 on the taking-up and pursuit of the business of Insurance and Reinsurance (Solvency II);][9]

[["term assurance business" means life assurance business in relation to which the policy or contract, or the underlying policy, is one which—

(*a*) is for a specified term; and

(*b*) is not capable of acquiring a surrender value that exceeds the amount of premiums paid;][3]

"the third [long-term][5] insurance Directive" means Council Directive 92/96 of 10th November 1992;][1]

. . . [7]

(2) Subject to paragraph (3) below, in any case where the obligations under any policy or contract of the body that issued, entered into or effected it ("the original insurer") are at any time the obligations of another body ("the transferee") to whom there has been a transfer of the whole or any part of a business previously carried on by the original insurer, any reference to an insurance company (however expressed) shall, unless the context otherwise requires, include the transferee.

(3) Paragraph (2) above does not apply to regulations 5 to [7A][2], . . . [7] or 21 to 23.

(4) In these Regulations any reference to a particular provision, without more, is a reference to that provision of the Income and Corporation Taxes Act 1988.

[(5) Save where otherwise indicated, any reference in these Regulations to any of the provisions of section 431D is a reference to that provision as it had effect prior to the amendment of that section by section 108 of the Finance Act 2000.][4]

Commentary—*Simon's Taxes* **D7.5137.**

Modifications—Overseas Life Insurance Companies Regulations, SI 2006/3271 reg 42 (modification of this para in relation to an overseas life insurance company, with effect for periods of account ending on or after 31 December 2006).

Amendments—[1] Definitions of "company tax return", "the first long term insurance Directive", "term assurance business" and "the third long term insurance Directive", and words in definition of "relevant policy" inserted, by the Insurance Companies

(Overseas Life Assurance Business) (Compliance) (Amendment) Regulations, SI 1999/2839, reg 3(1)–(4), with effect from 8 November 1999.

2 Reference in para (3) substituted by the Insurance Companies (Overseas Life Assurance Business) (Compliance) (Amendment) Regulations, SI 2000/2104 reg 3(1), (3) with effect for policies or contracts made by, or, as the case may be, transferred to, an insurance company after 7 November 1999.

3 Definitions of "beneficiary" and "term assurance business" substituted, definitions of "excluded business" and "the Excluded Business Regulations" inserted and definition of "settlor" revoked by SI 2000/2104 reg 3(1), (2), with effect for policies or contracts made by, or, as the case may be, transferred to, an insurance company after 21 August 2000.

4 Para (5) inserted by SI 2000/2104 reg 3(1), (4) with effect from 23 August 2000.

5 Words in para (1) substituted by the Financial Services and Markets Act 2000 (Consequential Amendments) (Taxes) Order, SI 2001/3629 art 142(*a*) with effect from 1 December 2001, immediately after the coming into force of the Financial Services and Markets Act 2000 ss 411, 432(1), Sch 20 (and SI 2001/3629 Pts 1 and 2).

7 In para (1) definitions of "child trust fund business", and "excepted business" inserted; definitions of "individual savings account business", and "relevant business" substituted; words in definition of "relevant policy", whole of definition of "underlying policy", and words in para (3), revoked; by the Insurance Companies (Overseas Life Assurance Business) (Compliance) (Amendment) Regulations, SI 2007/2088 regs 2, 3 with effect for accounting periods beginning on or after 1 January 2007 and ending on or after 13 August 2007: SI 2007/2088 reg 1.

8 In para (1), in definition of "the Board", words substituted for words "of Inland Revenue", by the Insurance Companies (Overseas Life Assurance Business) (Compliance) (Amendment) Regulations, SI 2008/2627 reg 2(1), (2) with effect in relation to policies or contracts assigned on or after 27 October 2008.

9 In para (2), definition of "the Consolidated Life Assurance Directive" revoked and definition of "the Solvency 2 Directive" inserted by the Solvency 2 Regulations, SI 2015/575 reg 60, Sch 2 para 5(1), (2) with effect from 1 January 2016.

3 Meaning of specified event

. . .

Amendments—This regulation revoked by the Insurance Companies (Overseas Life Assurance Business) (Compliance) (Amendment) Regulations, SI 1999/2839, reg 4, with effect from 8 November 1999.

3A [Exclusion of business of friendly society which is exempt from tax

These Regulations do not apply to any business of a friendly society the profits arising from which are exempt from income tax and corporation tax under section 460(1).][1]

Amendments—[1] This regulation inserted by the Insurance Companies (Overseas Life Assurance Business) (Compliance) (Amendment) Regulations, SI 1997/481, with effect from 19 March 1997 in relation to accounting periods beginning after 31 October 1994.

3B [Exclusion of tax exempt life assurance business

These Regulations do not apply to any business of an insurance company the profits arising from which are exempt from corporation tax by virtue of section 460(11) or (12) of the Income and Corporation Taxes Act 1988.][1]

Amendments—[1] This regulation inserted by the Insurance Companies (Overseas Life Assurance Business) (Compliance) (Amendment) Regulations, SI 2007/2088 regs 2, 4 with effect for accounting periods beginning on or after 1 January 2007 and ending on or after 13 August 2007: SI 2007/2088 reg 1.

4 Business which is overseas life assurance business General

In the circumstances prescribed in regulations 5 to [8][1], any issue as to whether business is overseas life assurance business shall be determined by reference to the matter prescribed in those regulations.

Amendments—[1] Reference substituted by the Insurance Companies (Overseas Life Assurance Business) (Compliance) (Amendment) Regulations, SI 2007/2088 regs 2, 5 with effect for accounting periods beginning on or after 1 January 2007 and ending on or after 13 August 2007: SI 2007/2088 reg 1.

5 Business other than reinsurance business effected by a company resident in the United Kingdom outside the United Kingdom

(1) This regulation applies in circumstances where—

(*a*) an insurance company has entered into relevant business which is not reinsurance business,

(*b*) that business is with a policy holder not residing in the United Kingdom,

(*c*) the policy or contract for that business was effected by an insurance company resident in the United Kingdom at or through a [permanent establishment][6] outside the United Kingdom, . . .[1]

(*d*) the policy or contract was made on or after 1st January 1996 [and

(*e*) to the best of the company's knowledge and belief the policy or contract is not [for excluded business][3].][1]

[(1A) This regulation also applies in circumstances where—

(*a*) on or after 8th November 1999 business is transferred to an insurance company in accordance with an authorisation granted outside the United Kingdom for the purposes of—

(i) Article 31a.2 of the first [long-term][4] insurance Directive, or

(ii) Article 11 of the third [long-term][4] insurance Directive,

(*b*) that business is with a policy holder not residing in the United Kingdom,

(*c*) that business is, immediately after the transfer, carried on by an insurance company resident in the United Kingdom at or through a [permanent establishment][6] outside the United Kingdom, and (*d*) to the best of the company's knowledge and belief the policy or contract [is not for excluded business][3].][1]

[(1B) This regulation also applies in circumstances where—

(*a*) on or after 19th December 2002 business is transferred to an insurance company in accordance with an authorisation granted outside the United Kingdom for the purposes of [Article 39 or 167 of the Solvency 2 Directive][7],

(*b*) that business is with a policy holder not residing in the United Kingdom,

(*c*) that business is, immediately after the transfer, carried on by an insurance company resident in the United Kingdom at or through a [permanent establishment][6] outside the United Kingdom, and

(*d*) to the best of the company's knowledge and belief the policy or contract is not for excluded business.][5]

[(2) Except in relation to business to which paragraph (3) below applies, the business referred to in paragraphs (1) [to (1B)][5] above shall be overseas life assurance business.

(3) This paragraph applies to business—

(*a*) which is not term assurance business, and

(*b*) for which the policy or contract is one—

(i) in respect of which the insurance company completes the certificate prescribed in paragraph (4) below, or

(ii) which falls within a class of policies or contracts in respect of which the company completes the certificate prescribed in paragraph (4A) below.

(4) The certificate prescribed is a certificate—

(*a*) showing the date on which it is given,

(*b*) stating the territory in which the [permanent establishment][6] is situated, and

(*c*) identifying the policy or contract by stating the name of the policy holder and any unique identifying designation given to the policy or contract.][1]

[(4A) The certificate prescribed is a certificate—

(*a*) stating the territory in which the [permanent establishment][6] is situated,

(*b*) setting out the unique characteristics of a class of policies or contracts which is not being treated by the insurance company as relating to overseas life assurance business, and

(*c*) confirming that any policy or contract within the class is capable of being identified readily in the books and records of the company by virtue of a unique identifying designation given to policies or contracts within that class.][1]

(5) A certificate under this regulation shall be given by an employee of the insurance company, and shall show the name of that employee and his position within the company.

(6) Paragraph (7) below applies in any case where—

(*a*) policies or contracts for business to which [paragraph (2) above][2] applies were effected at or through a particular [permanent establishment][6] outside the United Kingdom [or, where paragraph (1A) [or (1B)][5] above applies, transferred to an insurance company so as to be carried on at or through a particular [permanent establishment][6] outside the United Kingdom,][1], and

(*b*) those policies or contracts were effected by[, or transferred to,][1] an insurance company within the same accounting period.

[(7) The insurance company may combine a certificate under paragraph (3)(*b*)(i) above with another certificate under paragraph (3)(*b*)(i) above in a single document.][1]

(8) The insurance company shall complete the certificate prescribed in this regulation [before the date on which it makes its company tax return for the accounting period in which the policy or contract was made or, where paragraph (1A) [or (1B)][5] above applies, transferred.][2]

Commentary—*Simon's Taxes* **D7.5137.**

Amendments—[1] In para (1)(*d*) word "and" revoked, paras (1)(*e*), (1A), (4), and words in para (6) inserted, and paras (2)–(4), (7) substituted, by the Insurance Companies (Overseas Life Assurance Business) (Compliance) (Amendment) Regulations, SI 1999/2839, reg 5(1)–(5), (7) with effect in relation to accounting periods ending on or after 31 December 1999, or where an insurance company so elects by written notice given to an officer of the Board on or before 31 December 1999, the first accounting period beginning on or after 1 October 1999 and ending after 31 December 1999 and subsequent accounting periods.

[2] In paras (6), (8) words substituted by SI 1999/2839, reg 5(1), (6), (8) with effect in relation to accounting periods ending on or after 31 December 1999, or where an insurance company so elects by written notice given to an officer of the Board on or before 31 December 1999, the first accounting period beginning on or after 1 October 1999 and ending after 31 December 1999 and subsequent accounting periods.

[3] Words in paras (1)(*e*), (1A)(*d*) substituted by the Insurance Companies (Overseas Life Assurance Business) (Compliance) (Amendment) Regulations, SI 2000/2104 reg 4 with effect for policies or contracts made by, or, as the case may be, transferred to, an insurance company after 21 August 2000.

[4] Words in sub-para (1A)(*a*) substituted by the Financial Services and Markets Act 2000 (Consequential Amendments) (Taxes) Order, SI 2001/3629 art 142(*b*) with effect from 1 December 2001, immediately after the coming into force of the Financial Services and Markets Act 2000 ss 411, 432(1), Sch 20 (and SI 2001/3629 Pts 1 and 2).

5 Para (1B) and words in paras (6)(*a*), (8) inserted, and words in para (2) substituted, by the Insurance Companies (Overseas Life Assurance Business) (Compliance) (Amendment) Regulations, SI 2004/3273 regs 2, 4 with effect from 31 December 2004.

6 Words substituted by the Insurance Companies (Overseas Life Assurance Business) (Compliance) (Amendment) Regulations, SI 2007/2088 regs 2, 6(*a*) with effect for accounting periods beginning on or after 1 January 2007 and ending on or after 13 August 2007: SI 2007/2088 reg 1.

7 In para (1B)(*a*), words substituted for words "Article 14 or 53(2) of the Consolidated Life Assurance Directive" by the Solvency 2 Regulations, SI 2015/575 reg 60, Sch 2 para 5(1), (3)(*a*) with effect from 1 January 2016.

6 Business other than reinsurance business effected either by a company resident in the United Kingdom otherwise than outside the United Kingdom or by an overseas life insurance company—policies or contracts made before 1st January 1996

(1) This regulation applies in circumstances where—

(*a*) an insurance company has entered into relevant business which is not reinsurance business,

(*b*) that business is with a policy holder not residing in the United Kingdom,

(*c*) the policy or contract for that business was effected either by an insurance company resident in the United Kingdom otherwise than at or through a branch outside the United Kingdom, or by an overseas life insurance company, and

(*d*) the policy or contract was made before 1st January 1996.

(2) The business shall be overseas life assurance business where the insurance company completes—

(*a*) the certificate prescribed in paragraph (3) below, and

(*b*) the declaration prescribed—

(i) in a case where the policy holder is an individual, in paragraph (4) below, or

(ii) in a case where the policy holder is not an individual, in paragraph (5) below.

(3) The certificate prescribed is a certificate—

(*a*) stating that to the best of the company's knowledge and belief the policy holder was not residing in the United Kingdom on the date the policy or contract was made, and

(*b*) specifying the territory in which to the best of the company's knowledge and belief the policy holder was residing on that date.

(4) The declaration prescribed is a declaration that to the best of the company's knowledge and belief—

(*a*) the policy or contract is not one to which section 431D(2) applies, and

(*b*) where the policy or contract is one to which section 431D(2) does not apply solely by virtue of section 431D(5), that the conditions specified in section 431D(5) are fulfilled.

(5) The declaration prescribed is a declaration that to the best of the company's knowledge and belief—

(*a*) the policy or contract is one to which subsection (5) of section 431D applies and that the conditions specified in that subsection are fulfilled, or

(*b*) the policy or contract is one to which subsection (7) of section 431D applies and that the conditions specified in that subsection are fulfilled.

(6) A certificate or declaration under this regulation shall be given by an employee of the insurance company, and shall show the name of that employee and his position within the company.

(7) The insurance company shall complete any certificate or declaration prescribed in this regulation either within six months following the end of the insurance company's accounting period in which the policy or contract was made, or by 1st March 1996, whichever is the later.

7 Business other than reinsurance business effected either by a company resident in the United Kingdom otherwise than outside the United Kingdom or by an overseas life insurance company—policies or contracts made on or after 1st January 1996

(1) This regulation applies in circumstances where—

(*a*) an insurance company has entered into relevant business which is [neither reinsurance business nor term assurance business][1];

(*b*) that business is with a policy holder [who is an individual not residing in the United Kingdom and either—

(i) is a British citizen, or

(ii) is a person in respect of whose business the company has treated this regulation as applying,][1];

(*c*) the policy or contract for that business was effected either by an insurance company resident in the United Kingdom otherwise than at or through a [permanent establishment][5] outside the United Kingdom, or by an overseas life insurance company, and

(*d*) the policy or contract was made on or after 1st January 1996.

[(1A) This regulation also applies where—

(*a*) on or after 8th November 1999 relevant business which is neither reinsurance business nor term assurance business is transferred to an insurance company in accordance with an authorisation granted outside the United Kingdom for the purposes of—

(i) Article 31a.2 of the first [long-term][3] insurance Directive, or

(ii) Article 11 of the third [long-term][2] insurance Directive, (*b*) that business has not been treated by the transferor as relating to overseas life assurance business,

(*c*) that business is with a policy holder who is an individual not residing in the United Kingdom and either—

(i) is a British citizen, or

(ii) is a person in respect of whose business with the company has treated this regulation as applying, and

(*d*) that business is, immediately after the transfer, carried on by an insurance company resident in the United Kingdom otherwise than at or through a branch outside the United Kingdom, or by an overseas life insurance company.][1]

[(1B) This regulation also applies in circumstances where—

(*a*) on or after 19th December 2002 business is transferred to an insurance company in accordance with an authorisation granted outside the United Kingdom for the purposes of Article 14 or 53(2) of [Article 39 or 167 of the Solvency 2 Directive][6],

(*b*) that business has not been treated by the transferor as relating to overseas life assurance business;

(*c*) that business is with a policy holder who is an individual not residing in the United Kingdom and either—

(i) is a British citizen, or

(ii) is a person in respect of whose business the company has treated this regulation as applying, and

(*d*) that business is, immediately after the transfer, carried on by an insurance company resident in the United Kingdom otherwise than at or through a [permanent establishment][6] outside the United Kingdom, or by an overseas life insurance company.][4]

(2) The business shall be overseas life assurance business where the insurance company obtains—

(*a*) the document prescribed in paragraph (3) below from the policy holder, and

(*b*) in any case where [the business is of a description falling within the circumstances set out in regulation 5 of the Excluded Business Regulations][2] and the policy or contract is held otherwise than by the trustees of the trust, the certificate prescribed in paragraph (8) below from the trustees of the trust.

(3) The document prescribed is a document containing—

(*a*) the certificate prescribed in paragraph (4) below,

[(*b*) the declaration prescribed in paragraph (5) below, and][1]

(*c*) the undertaking prescribed in paragraph (7) below.

(4) The certificate prescribed is a certificate—

(*a*) stating that the policy holder was not residing in the United Kingdom on the date the policy or contract was made [or, where paragraph (1A) [or (1B)][4] above applies, transferred][1], and

(*b*) specifying the territory in which the policy holder was residing on that date.

[(5) The declaration prescribed is a declaration that the policy or contract is not for excluded business.][2]

(6) . . . [1]

(7) The undertaking prescribed is an undertaking that the policy holder will notify the company if—

(*a*) the policy holder begins residing in the United Kingdom, or

(*b*) the rights conferred by the policy or contract come to be held subject to a trust, or

(*c*) the declaration prescribed in paragraph (5) [above][1] ceases to be true.

[(8) The certificate prescribed is a certificate stating that the circumstances are as set out in paragraph (1)(*b*) or (*c*), as the case may be, of regulation 5 of the Excluded Business Regulations.][2]

(9) The insurance company shall obtain the document prescribed in paragraph (3) above and, in any case where [the business is of a description falling within the circumstances set out in regulation 5 of the Excluded Business Regulations][2] and the policy or contract is held otherwise than by the trustees of the trust, the certificate prescribed in paragraph (8) above, [before the date on which it makes its company tax return for the accounting period in which the policy or contract was made or, where paragraph (1A) above applies, transferred.][1]

Commentary—*Simon's Taxes* **D7.5137.**

Amendments—[1] Words in paras (1)(*a*), (*b*), (7)(*c*), (9), and para (3)(*b*) substituted, para (1A) and words in para (4)(*a*) inserted and para (6) revoked by the Insurance Companies (Overseas Life Assurance Business) (Compliance) (Amendment) Regulations, SI 1999/2839, reg 6, with effect for policies or contracts made by or, as the case may be, transferred to, an insurance company after 7 November 1999.

[2] Words in paras (2)(*b*), (9) and whole of paras (5), (8) substituted by the Insurance Companies (Overseas Life Assurance Business) (Compliance) (Amendment) Regulations, SI 2000/2104 reg 5 with effect for policies or contracts made by, or, as the case may be, transferred to, an insurance company after 21 August 2000.

[3] Words in sub-para (1A)(*a*) substituted by the Financial Services and Markets Act 2000 (Consequential Amendments) (Taxes) Order, SI 2001/3629 art 142(*c*) with effect from 1 December 2001, immediately after the coming into force of the Financial Services and Markets Act 2000 ss 411, 432(1), Sch 20 (and SI 2001/3629 Pts 1 and 2).

[4] Para (1B) inserted, and words in para (4) inserted, by the Insurance Companies (Overseas Life Assurance Business) (Compliance) (Amendment) Regulations, SI 2004/3273 regs 2, 5 with effect from 31 December 2004.

5 Words substituted by the Insurance Companies (Overseas Life Assurance Business) (Compliance) (Amendment) Regulations, SI 2007/2088 regs 2, 6(*b*) with effect for accounting periods beginning on or after 1 January 2007 and ending on or after 13 August 2007: SI 2007/2088 reg 1.

6 In para (1B)(*a*), words substituted for words "Article 14 or 53(2) of the Consolidated Life Assurance Directive" by the Solvency 2 Regulations, SI 2015/575 reg 60, Sch 2 para 5(1), (3)(*b*) with effect from 1 January 2016.

7A [Business other than reinsurance business effected either by a company resident in the United Kingdom otherwise than outside the United Kingdom or by an overseas life insurance company—policy holder not within regulation 7

(1) This regulation applies in circumstances where—

(*a*) an insurance company has entered into relevant business which is neither reinsurance business nor term assurance business,

(*b*) that business is with a policy holder not residing in the United Kingdom who either—

(i) is not an individual, or

(ii) if an individual, is not one falling within regulation 7(1)(*b*)(i) or (ii),

(*c*) the policy or contract for that business was effected either by an insurance company resident in the United Kingdom otherwise than at or through a [permanent establishment][6] outside the United Kingdom, or by an overseas life insurance company, and

(*d*) the policy or contract was made on or after 8th November 1999.

(2) This regulation also applies where—

(*a*) on or after 8th November 1999 relevant business which is neither reinsurance business nor term assurance business is transferred to an insurance company in accordance with an authorisation granted outside the United Kingdom for the purposes of—

(i) Article 31a.2 of the first [long-term][4] insurance Directive, or

(ii) Article 11 of the third [long-term][4] insurance Directive,

(*b*) that business has not been treated by the transferor as relating to overseas life assurance business,

(*c*) that business is with a policy holder not residing in the United Kingdom who either—

(i) is not an individual, or

(ii) if an individual, is not one falling within regulation 7(1)(*b*)(i) or (ii), and

(*d*) that business is, immediately after the transfer, carried on by an insurance company resident in the United Kingdom otherwise than at or through a branch outside the United Kingdom, or by an overseas life insurance company.

[(2A) This regulation also applies in circumstances where—

(*a*) on or after 19th December 2002 relevant business which is neither reinsurance business nor term assurance business is transferred to an insurance company in accordance with an authorisation granted outside the United Kingdom for the purposes of [Article 39 or 167 of the Solvency 2 Directive][7],

(*b*) that business has not been treated by the transferor as relating to overseas life assurance business;

(*c*) that business is with a policy holder not residing in the United Kingdom who—

(i) is not an individual, or

(ii) if an individual is not one falling within regulation 7(1)(*b*)(i) or (ii), and

(*d*) that business is, immediately after the transfer, carried on by an insurance company resident in the United Kingdom otherwise than at or through a [permanent establishment][6] outside the United Kingdom, or by an overseas life insurance company.][5]

[(3) The business shall be overseas life assurance business where the insurance company completes the certificate prescribed in paragraph (4) or (5) below.][2]

(4) The certificate prescribed is a certificate—

(*a*) showing the date on which it is given,

(*b*) stating the name of the policy holder,

(*c*) stating any unique identifying designation given to the policy or contract,

(*d*) stating the territory which, to the best of the company's knowledge and belief, is the territory in which the policy holder resides,

(*e*) stating that the company has no knowledge of any information making it reasonable for the company to assume that the policy holder was residing in the United Kingdom at the time the policy or contract was made or, where paragraph (2) [or (2A)][5] above applies, transferred,

(*f*) stating that to the best of the company's knowledge and belief the policy or contract is not[for excluded business][2],

(*g*) . . . [2]

(*h*) where the company makes the statement mentioned in sub-paragraph [(*f*)][2] above, stating that the company is in possession of information enabling it to make that statement, and stating the nature of that information.

[(5) The certificate prescribed is a certificate—

(*a*) showing the date on which it is given,

(*b*) stating the name of the policy holder,

(*c*) stating any unique identifying designation given to the policy or contract, and
(*d*) stating that to the best of the company's knowledge and belief the policy or contract is for business of a description falling within regulation 7(*b*) of the Excluded Business Regulations.][3]

(6) A certificate under this regulation shall be given by an employee of the insurance company, and shall show the name of that employee and his position within the company.

(7) Paragraph (8) below applies in any case where policies or contracts for business to which this regulation applies were effected by, or where paragraph (2) [or (2A)][5] above applies, transferred to, an insurance company within the same accounting period.

(8) The insurance company may—
(*a*) combine a certificate under paragraph (4) above with another certificate under paragraph (4) above in a single document, or
(*b*) combine a certificate under paragraph (5) above with another certificate under paragraph (5) above in [a single document,][3]

but a certificate under paragraph (4) above shall not be combined with a certificate under paragraph (5) above in a single document.

(9) The insurance company shall complete the certificate prescribed in this regulation before the date on which it makes its company tax return for the accounting period in which the policy or contract was made or, where paragraph (2) [or (2A)][5] above applies, transferred.][1]

Amendments—[1] This regulation inserted by the Insurance Companies (Overseas Life Assurance Business) (Compliance) (Amendment) Regulations, SI 1999/2839, reg 7, with effect in relation to policies or contracts made by or, as the case may be, transferred to, an insurance company after 7 November 1999.

[2] Para (3) and words in para (4)(*f*), (*h*) substituted and para (4)(*g*) revoked by the Insurance Companies (Overseas Life Assurance Business) (Compliance) (Amendment) Regulations, SI 2000/2104 reg 6 with effect for policies or contracts made by, or, as the case may be, transferred to, an insurance company after 21 August 2000.

[3] Para (5) and words in para (8)(*b*) substituted by SI 2000/2104 reg 6(1), (4), (5) with effect from 23 August 2000.

[4] Words in sub-para (2)(*a*) substituted by the Financial Services and Markets Act 2000 (Consequential Amendments) (Taxes) Order, SI 2001/3629 art 142(*d*) with effect from 1 December 2001, immediately after the coming into force of the Financial Services and Markets Act 2000 ss 411, 432(1), Sch 20 (and SI 2001/3629 Pts 1 and 2).

[5] Para (2A) and words in paras (4)(*e*), (7), (9) inserted by the Insurance Companies (Overseas Life Assurance Business) (Compliance) (Amendment) Regulations, SI 2004/3273 regs 2, 6 with effect from 31 December 2004.

[6] Words substituted by the Insurance Companies (Overseas Life Assurance Business) (Compliance) (Amendment) Regulations, SI 2007/2088 regs 2, 6(*c*) with effect for accounting periods beginning on or after 1 January 2007 and ending on or after 13 August 2007: SI 2007/2088 reg 1.

[7] In para (2A)(*a*), words substituted for words "Article 14 or 53(2) of the Consolidated Life Assurance Directive" by the Solvency 2 Regulations, SI 2015/575 reg 60, Sch 2 para 5(1), (3)(*c*) with effect from 1 January 2016.

8 Certain business other than reinsurance business where the company comes into possession of additional information

(1) This regulation applies in circumstances where—
(*a*) an insurance company has entered into relevant business which is [neither reinsurance business nor term assurance business][1],
[(*b*) that business was entered into by the insurance company with a policy holder referred to in regulation 7(1)(*b*);][1]
(*c*) the policy or contract for that business was effected either by an insurance company resident in the United Kingdom otherwise than at or through a [permanent establishment][5] outside the United Kingdom, or by an overseas life insurance company, and
(*d*) the insurance company comes to be in possession of information making it reasonable for the company to assume [either—
(i) that there has been a change in the identity of the policy holder and the new policy holder is a person referred to in regulation 7(1)(*b*), or
(ii) that the policy holder (being a person referred to in regulation 7(1)(*b*)) has ceased to be beneficially entitled to the rights conferred by the policy or contract.][1]

[(1A) This regulation also applies in circumstances where—
(*a*) on or after 8th November 1999 relevant business which is neither reinsurance business nor term assurance business is transferred to an insurance company in accordance with an authorisation granted outside the United Kingdom for the purposes of—
(i) Article 31a.2 of the first [long-term][3] insurance Directive, or
(ii) Article 11 of the third [long-term][3] insurance Directive,
(*b*) that business was entered into with a policy holder referred to in regulation 7(1)(*b*),
(*c*) that business is, immediately after the transfer, carried on by an insurance company resident in the United Kingdom otherwise than at or through a branch outside the United Kingdom, or by an overseas life insurance company, and
(*d*) the insurance company to whom the business is transferred comes to be in possession of information making it reasonable for the company to assume either—
(i) that there has been a change in the identity of the policy holder and the new policy holder is a person referred to in regulation 7(1)(*b*), or

(ii) that the policy holder (being a person referred to in regulation 7(1)(*b*)) has ceased to be beneficially entitled to the rights conferred by the policy or contract.][1]

[(1B) This regulation also applies in circumstances where—

(*a*) on or after 19th December 2002 relevant business which is neither reinsurance business nor term assurance business is transferred to an insurance company in accordance with an authorisation granted outside the United Kingdom for the purposes of [Article 39 or 167 of the Solvency 2 Directive][6],

(*b*) that business was entered into with a policy holder referred to in regulation 7(1)(*b*);

(*c*) that business is, immediately after the transfer, carried on by an insurance company resident in the United Kingdom otherwise than at or through a [permanent establishment][5] outside the United Kingdom, or by an overseas life insurance company, and

(*d*) the insurance company to whom the business is transferred comes to be in possession of information making it reasonable for the company to assume either—

(i) that there has been a change in the identity of the policy holder and the new policy holder is a person referred to in regulation 7(1)(*b*), or

(ii) that the policy holder (being a person referred to in regulation 7(1)(*b*)) has ceased to be entitled to the rights conferred by the policy or contract.][4]

(2) The business shall continue to be overseas life assurance business where the insurance company obtains—

(*a*) the document prescribed in paragraph (3) below from the policy holder, and

(*b*) in any case where [the business is of a description falling within the circumstances set out in regulation 5 of the Excluded Business Regulations][2], the certificate prescribed in paragraph (8) below from the trustees of the trust.

(3) The document prescribed is a document containing—

(*a*) the certificate prescribed in paragraph (4) below,

[(*b*) the declaration prescribed in paragraph (5) below, and]

(*c*) the undertaking prescribed in paragraph (7) below.

(4) The certificate prescribed is a certificate—

(*a*) stating that the policy holder was not residing in the United Kingdom—

(i) in a case where it is reasonable for the company to assume that there has been a change in the identity of the policy holder, on the date he became the policy holder, or

(ii) in a case where it is reasonable for the company to assume that the policy holder has ceased to be beneficially entitled to the rights conferred by the policy or contract, on the date on which he ceased to be beneficially entitled to those rights, and

(*b*) specifying the territory in which the policy holder was residing on that date.

[(5) The declaration prescribed is a declaration that the policy or contract is not for excluded business.][2]

(6) . . . [1]

(7) The undertaking prescribed is an undertaking that the policy holder will notify the company if—

(*a*) the policy holder begins residing in the United Kingdom, or

(*b*) the rights conferred by the policy or contract come to be held subject to a trust, or

(*c*) the declaration prescribed in paragraph (5) [above][1] ceases to be true.

[(8) The certificate prescribed is a certificate stating that the circumstances are as set out in regulation 5(1)(*b*) or (*c*) of the Excluded Business Regulations.][2]

(9) The insurance company shall obtain the document prescribed in paragraph (3) above and, in any case where [the business is of a description falling within the circumstances set out in regulation 5 of the Excluded Business Regulations][2] applies, the certificate prescribed in paragraph (8) above, [before the date on which the insurance company makes its company tax return for the accounting period in which][1]the insurance company comes to be in possession of information making it reasonable for the company to assume that there has been a change in the identity of the policy holder or that the policy holder has ceased to be beneficially entitled to the rights conferred by the policy or contract, as the case may be.

Commentary—*Simon's Taxes* **D7.5137.**

Amendments—[1] Words in paras (1), (7)(*c*), (9), and para (3)(*b*) substituted, para (1A) inserted and para (6) revoked, by the Insurance Companies (Overseas Life Assurance Business) (Compliance) (Amendment) Regulations, SI 1999/2839, reg 8, with effect in any case where the date on which the insurance company comes to be in possession of information making it reasonable for the company to assume that there has been a change in the identity of the policy holder, or the policy holder ceased to be beneficially entitled to the rights conferred by the policy or contract, falls after 8 November 1999.

[2] Words in paras (2)(*b*), (9) and whole of paras (5), (8) substituted by the Insurance Companies (Overseas Life Assurance Business) (Compliance) (Amendment) Regulations, SI 2000/2104 reg 7 with effect for policies or contracts made by, or, as the case may be, transferred to, an insurance company after 21 August 2000.

[3] Words in sub-para (1A)(*a*) substituted by the Financial Services and Markets Act 2000 (Consequential Amendments) (Taxes) Order, SI 2001/3629 art 142(*e*) with effect from 1 December 2001, immediately after the coming into force of the Financial Services and Markets Act 2000 ss 411, 432(1), Sch 20 (and SI 2001/3629 Pts 1 and 2).

[4] Para (1B) inserted by the Insurance Companies (Overseas Life Assurance Business) (Compliance) (Amendment) Regulations, SI 2004/3273 regs 2, 7 with effect from 31 December 2004.

[5] Words substituted by the Insurance Companies (Overseas Life Assurance Business) (Compliance) (Amendment) Regulations, SI 2007/2088 regs 2, 6(*d*) with effect for accounting periods beginning on or after 1 January 2007 and ending on or after 13 August 2007: SI 2007/2088 reg 1.

[6] In para (1B)(*a*), words substituted for words "Article 14 or 53(2) of the Consolidated Life Assurance Directive" by the Solvency 2 Regulations, SI 2015/575 reg 60, Sch 2 para 5(1), (3)(*d*) with effect from 1 January 2016.

9 Reinsurance of business effected by a company resident in the United Kingdom outside the United Kingdom

. . .

Amendments—This regulation repealed by the Insurance Companies (Overseas Life Assurance Business) (Compliance) (Amendment) Regulations, SI 2007/2088 regs 2, 7(*a*) with effect for accounting periods beginning on or after 1 January 2007 and ending on or after 13 August 2007: SI 2007/2088 reg 1.

10 Reinsurance of business effected either by a company resident in the United Kingdom otherwise than outside the United Kingdom or by an overseas life insurance company

. . .

Amendments—This regulation repealed by the Insurance Companies (Overseas Life Assurance Business) (Compliance) (Amendment) Regulations, SI 2007/2088 regs 2, 7(*b*) with effect for accounting periods beginning on or after 1 January 2007 and ending on or after 13 August 2007: SI 2007/2088 reg 1.

10A [Reinsurance of business effected either by a company resident in the United Kingdom otherwise than outside the United Kingdom or by an overseas life insurance company—policy holder not within regulation 7

. . .

Amendments—This regulation repealed by the Insurance Companies (Overseas Life Assurance Business) (Compliance) (Amendment) Regulations, SI 2007/2088 regs 2, 7(*c*) with effect for accounting periods beginning on or after 1 January 2007 and ending on or after 13 August 2007: SI 2007/2088 reg 1.

11 Certain reinsurance business where the company comes into possession of additional information

. . .

Amendments—This regulation repealed by the Insurance Companies (Overseas Life Assurance Business) (Compliance) (Amendment) Regulations, SI 2007/2088 regs 2, 7(*a*) with effect for accounting periods beginning on or after 1 January 2007 and ending on or after 13 August 2007: SI 2007/2088 reg 1.

TERRITORIES IN WHICH POLICY HOLDERS RESIDING

12 General

In the circumstances prescribed in regulations 13 to [14A][1], any issue as to whether a policy holder is residing in the United Kingdom or in some other territory shall be determined by reference to the matters prescribed in those regulations.

Amendments—[1] Reference substituted by the Insurance Companies (Overseas Life Assurance Business) (Compliance) (Amendment) Regulations, SI 2007/2088 regs 2, 8 with effect for accounting periods beginning on or after 1 January 2007 and ending on or after 13 August 2007: SI 2007/2088 reg 1.

13 Business other than reinsurance business effected by a company resident in the United Kingdom outside the United Kingdom

(1) This regulation applies in circumstances where—

(*a*) an insurance company has entered into relevant business which is not reinsurance business, and

(*b*) the policy or contract for that business was effected by an insurance company resident in the United Kingdom at or through a [permanent establishment][7] outside the United Kingdom.

[(1A) This regulation also applies where—

(*a*) on or after 8th November 1999 relevant business which is not reinsurance business is transferred to an insurance company in accordance with an authorisation granted outside the United Kingdom for the purposes of—

(i) Article 31a.2 of the first [long-term][5] insurance Directive, or

(ii) Article 11 of the third [long-term][5] insurance Directive, and

(*b*) that business is, immediately after the transfer, carried on by an insurance company resident in the United Kingdom at or through a branch outside the United Kingdom.][1]

[(1B) This regulation also applies in circumstances where—

(*a*) on or after 19th December 2002 relevant business which is neither reinsurance business nor term assurance business is transferred to an insurance company in accordance with an authorisation granted outside the United Kingdom for the purposes of [Article 39 or 167 of the Solvency 2 Directive][9], and

(*c*) that business is, immediately after the transfer, carried on by an insurance company resident in the United Kingdom at or through a [permanent establishment][7] or agency outside the United Kingdom.][6]

(2) Subject to paragraph (3) below, the territory in which the policy holder was residing at the time the policy or contract was made [or, where paragraph (1A) applies, transferred][1] shall be the territory in which the [permanent establishment][7] was situated.
(3) Where, at the time the policy or contract was made [or transferred][3] or at any time within [eighteen][2] months thereafter, the company was in possession of information making it reasonable for the company to assume that the policy holder was residing in the United Kingdom at the time the policy or contract was made [or transferred][3] or at any time within [twelve][2] months thereafter, the territory in which the policy holder was residing at the time the policy or contract was made [or transferred][3] shall be the United Kingdom.
(4) Where, pursuant to paragraph (2) or (3) above, a policy holder has been treated as residing in a particular territory at the time the policy or contract was made [or transferred][1], the territory in which the policy holder is residing at any time thereafter shall, subject to paragraph (5) below, be that same territory.
(5) Subject to paragraph (3) above, where at any time after the policy or contract was made [or transferred][1] the company comes to be in possession of information making it reasonable for the company to assume that the policy holder, [being neither—

- (*a*) the person with whom the policy or contract was originally effected, nor
- (*b*) a person to whom the rights conferred by the policy or contract have been assigned in circumstances where the assignment did not constitute a chargeable event within the meaning of [section 484 of the Income Tax (Trading and Other Income) Act 2005][8], nor
- (*c*) a personal representative in whom those rights have been vested by operation of law][4],

was residing in the United Kingdom at the time he became the policy holder or at any time thereafter, the territory in which the policy holder is residing shall, from the date on which it is reasonable for the company so to assume, be the United Kingdom.

Note—The numbering in para (1B) above appears erroneous. This appears to be a drafting error. In addition, SI 2004/3273 purports to make a further amendment to this regulation. This also appears to be a drafting error, as the text to be substituted does not appear in this regulation.

Amendments—[1] Para (1A), and words in para (2), (4), (5), inserted, by the Insurance Companies (Overseas Life Assurance Business) (Compliance) (Amendment) Regulations, SI 1999/2839, reg 13(1)–(3), (5), (6)(*a*), with effect from 8 November 1999.

[2] Words in para (3) substituted by SI 1999/2839, reg 13(1), (4)(*a*), (*b*), with effect in relation to policies or contracts made by or, as the case may be, transferred to, an insurance company on or after 8 November 1999.

[3] Words in para (3) inserted by SI 1999/2839, reg 13(1), (4)(*c*), with effect in relation to policies or contracts made by or, as the case may be, transferred to, an insurance company on or after 8 November 1999.

[4] Words in para (5) substituted by SI 1999/2839, reg 13(1), (6)(*b*), with effect from 8 November 1999.

[5] Words in sub-para (1A)(*a*) substituted by the Financial Services and Markets Act 2000 (Consequential Amendments) (Taxes) Order, SI 2001/3629 art 142(*f*) with effect from 1 December 2001, immediately after the coming into force of the Financial Services and Markets Act 2000 ss 411, 432(1), Sch 20 (and SI 2001/3629 Pts 1 and 2).

[6] Para (1B) inserted by the Insurance Companies (Overseas Life Assurance Business) (Compliance) (Amendment) Regulations, SI 2004/3273 regs 2, 8 with effect from 31 December 2004.

[7] Words substituted by the Insurance Companies (Overseas Life Assurance Business) (Compliance) (Amendment) Regulations, SI 2007/2088 regs 2, 9(*a*) with effect for accounting periods beginning on or after 1 January 2007 and ending on or after 13 August 2007: SI 2007/2088 reg 1.

[8] In para (5)(*b*), words substituted for words "section 540, 542 or 545" by the Insurance Companies (Overseas Life Assurance Business) (Compliance) (Amendment) Regulations, SI 2008/2627 reg 2(1), (3)(*a*) with effect in relation to policies or contracts assigned on or after 27 October 2008.

[9] In para (1B)(*a*), words substituted for words "Article 14 or 53(2) of the Consolidated Life Assurance Directive" by the Solvency 2 Regulations, SI 2015/575 reg 60, Sch 2 para 5(1), (3)(*e*) with effect from 1 January 2016.

14 Business other than reinsurance business effected either by a company resident in the United Kingdom otherwise than outside the United Kingdom or by an overseas life insurance company

(1) This regulation applies in circumstances where—

- (*a*) an insurance company has entered into relevant business which is not reinsurance business, and
- (*b*) the policy or contract for that business was effected either by an insurance company resident in the United Kingdom otherwise than at or through a [permanent establishment][8] outside the United Kingdom, or by an overseas life insurance company [and
- (*c*) that business is with a policy holder referred to in regulation 7(1)(*b*).][1]

[(1A) This regulation also applies in circumstances where—

- (*a*) on or after 8th November 1999 relevant business which is not reinsurance business is transferred to an insurance company in accordance with an authorisation granted outside the United Kingdom for the purposes of—
  - (i) Article 31a.2 of the first [long-term][6] insurance Directive, or
  - (ii) Article 11 of the third [long-term][6] insurance Directive,
- (*b*) that business has not been treated by the transferor as relating to overseas life assurance business,

(*c*) that business is, immediately after the transfer, carried on either by an insurance company resident in the United Kingdom otherwise than at or through a branch outside the United Kingdom, or by an overseas life insurance company, and

(*d*) that business is with a policy holder referred to in regulation 7(1)(*b*).][1]

[(1B) This regulation also applies in circumstances where—

(*a*) on or after 19th December 2002 business is transferred to an insurance company in accordance with an authorisation granted outside the United Kingdom for the purposes of [Article 39 or 167 of the Solvency 2 Directive][10],

(*b*) that business has not been treated by the transferor as relating to overseas life assurance business,

(*c*) that business is, immediately after the transfer, carried on by an insurance company resident in the United Kingdom at or through a [permanent establishment][8] outside the United Kingdom, or by an overseas life insurance company; and

(*d*) that business is with a policy holder referred to in regulation 7(1)(*b*).][7]

(2) Subject to [paragraphs (3) and (3A)][5] below, the territory in which the policy holder was residing at the time the policy or contract was made [or, where paragraph (1A) [or (1B)][7] applies, transferred][1] shall be the territory specified in the certificate prescribed in regulation 6(3) or, as the case may be, 7(4).

(3) Where, at the time the policy or contract was made [or transferred][3] or at any time within [eighteen][2] months thereafter, the company was in possession of information making it reasonable for the company to assume that the policy holder was residing in the United Kingdom at the time the policy or contract was made [or transferred][3] or at any time within [twelve][2] months thereafter, the territory in which the policy holder was residing at the time the policy or contract was made [or transferred][3] shall be the United Kingdom.

[(3A) Subject to paragraph (3) above, where the policy is for term assurance business, the territory in which the policy holder was residing at the time the policy was made or transferred shall be the territory in which, to the best of the company's knowledge or belief, the policy holder was residing at the time the policy was made or transferred.][5]

(4) Where, pursuant to paragraph (2)[, (3) or (3A)][5]above, a policy holder has been treated as residing in a particular territory at the time the policy or contract was made [or transferred][1], the territory in which the policy holder is residing at any time thereafter shall, subject to paragraph (5) below, be that same territory.

(5) Subject to paragraph (3) above, where at any time after the policy or contract was made [or transferred][1] the company comes to be in possession of information making it reasonable for the company to assume that the policy holder, [being neither—

(*a*) the person with whom the policy or contract was originally effected, nor

(*b*) any person to whom the rights conferred by the policy or contract have been assigned in circumstances where the assignment did not constitute a chargeable event within the meaning of [section 484 of the Income Tax (Trading and Other Income) Act 2005][9], nor

(*c*) a personal representative in whom those rights have been vested by operation of law][4],

was residing in the United Kingdom at the time he became the policy holder or at any time thereafter, the territory in which the policy holder is residing shall, from the date on which it is reasonable for the company so to assume, be the United Kingdom.

Amendments—[1] Para (1)(*c*) and word "and" preceding it, para (1A), and words in paras (2), (4), (5) inserted, by the Insurance Companies (Overseas Life Assurance Business) (Compliance) (Amendment) Regulations, SI 1999/2839, reg 14(1)–(4), (6), (7)(*a*), with effect from 8 November 1999.

[2] Words in para (3) substituted by SI 1999/2839, reg 14(1), (5)(*a*), (*b*), with effect in relation to policies or contracts made by or, as the case may be, transferred to, an insurance company on or after 8 November 1999.

[3] Words in para (3) inserted by SI 1999/2839, reg 14(1), (5)(*c*), with effect in relation to policies or contracts made by or, as the case may be, transferred to, an insurance company on or after 8 November 1999.

[4] Words in para (5) substituted by SI 1999/2839, reg 14(1), (7)(*b*), with effect from 8 November 1999.

[5] Words in paras (2), (4) substituted and para (3A) inserted by the Insurance Companies (Overseas Life Assurance Business) (Compliance) (Amendment) Regulations, SI 2000/2104 reg 13 with effect for policies or contracts made by, or, as the case may be, transferred to, an insurance company after 21 August 2000.

[6] Words in sub-para (1A)(*a*) substituted by the Financial Services and Markets Act 2000 (Consequential Amendments) (Taxes) Order, SI 2001/3629 art 142(*g*) with effect from 1 December 2001, immediately after the coming into force of the Financial Services and Markets Act 2000 ss 411, 432(1), Sch 20 (and SI 2001/3629 Pts 1 and 2).

[7] Para (1B) and words in para (2) inserted by the Insurance Companies (Overseas Life Assurance Business) (Compliance) (Amendment) Regulations, SI 2004/3273 regs 2, 9 with effect from 31 December 2004.

[8] Words substituted by the Insurance Companies (Overseas Life Assurance Business) (Compliance) (Amendment) Regulations, SI 2007/2088 regs 2, 9(*b*) with effect for accounting periods beginning on or after 1 January 2007 and ending on or after 13 August 2007: SI 2007/2088 reg 1.

[9] In para (5)(*b*), words substituted by the Insurance Companies (Overseas Life Assurance Business) (Compliance) (Amendment) Regulations, SI 2008/2627 reg 2(1), (3)(*b*) with effect in relation to policies or contracts assigned on or after 27 October 2008.

[10] In para (1B)(*a*), words substituted for words "Article 14 or 53(2) of the Consolidated Life Assurance Directive" by the Solvency 2 Regulations, SI 2015/575 reg 60, Sch 2 para 5(1), (3)(*f*) with effect from 1 January 2016.

14A [Business other than reinsurance business effected either by a company resident in the United Kingdom otherwise than outside the United Kingdom or by an overseas life insurance company—policy holder not within regulation 7

(1) This regulation applies in circumstances where—

(*a*) an insurance company has entered into relevant business which is not reinsurance business,

(*b*) that business is with a policy holder not residing in the United Kingdom who either—

(i) is not an individual, or

(ii) if an individual, is not one falling within regulation 7(1)(*b*)(i) or (ii),

(*c*) the policy or contract for that business was effected either by an insurance company resident in the United Kingdom otherwise than at or through a [permanent establishment][5] outside the United Kingdom, or by an overseas life insurance company, and

(*d*) the policy or contract was made on or after 8th November 1999.

(2) This regulation also applies where—

(*a*) on or after 8th November 1999 relevant business which is not reinsurance business is transferred to an insurance company in accordance with an authorisation granted outside the United Kingdom for the purposes of—

(i) Article 31a.2 of the first [long-term][3] insurance Directive, or

(ii) Article 11 of the third [long-term][3] insurance Directive,

(*b*) that business has not been treated by the transferor as relating to overseas life assurance business,

(*c*) that business is with a policy holder not residing in the United Kingdom who either—

(i) is not an individual, or

(ii) if an individual, is not one falling within regulation 7(1)(*b*)(i) or (ii), and

(*d*) that business is, immediately after the transfer, carried on by an insurance company resident in the United Kingdom otherwise than at or through a branch outside the United Kingdom, or by an overseas life insurance company.

[(2A) This regulation also applies in circumstances where—

(*a*) on or after 19th December 2002 relevant business which is neither reinsurance business nor term assurance business is transferred to an insurance company in accordance with an authorisation granted outside the United Kingdom for the purposes of [Article 39 or 167 of the Solvency 2 Directive][7],

(*b*) that business has not been treated by the transferor as relating to overseas life assurance business;

(*c*) that business is with a policy holder not residing in the United Kingdom who—

(i) is not an individual, or

(ii) if an individual is not one falling within regulation 7(1)(*b*)(i) or (ii), and

(*d*) that business is, immediately after the transfer carried on by an insurance company resident in the United Kingdom otherwise than at or through a [permanent establishment][5] outside the United Kingdom, or by an overseas life insurance company.][4]

(3) Subject to[paragraphs (4), (4A) and (4B) below][2], the territory in which the policy holder was residing at the time the policy or contract was made or, where paragraph (2) [or paragraph (2A)][4] above applies, transferred shall be the territory specified in the certificate prescribed in [regulation 7A(4) above][2] or, as the case may be, paragraph (5) of that regulation.

(4) Where, at the time the policy or contract was made or transferred or at any time within eighteen months thereafter, the company was in possession of information making it reasonable for the company to assume that the policy holder was residing in the United Kingdom at the time the policy or contract was made or transferred or at any time within twelve months thereafter, the territory in which the policy holder was residing at the time the policy or contract was made or transferred shall be the United Kingdom.

[(4A) Subject to paragraph (4) above, where the policy is for term assurance business, the territory in which the policy holder was residing at the time the policy was made or transferred shall be the territory in which, to the best of the company's knowledge or belief, the policy holder was residing at the time the policy was made or transferred.

(4B) Where the policy or contract is for business of a description falling within regulation 7(*b*) of the Excluded Business Regulations, the territory in which the policy holder was residing at the time the policy or contract was made or transferred shall be the territory under the law of which the scheme mentioned in that regulation is established.][2]

(5) Where, pursuant to paragraph (3)[, (4), (4A) or (4B)][2] above, a policy holder has been treated as residing in a particular territory at the time the policy or contract was made or transferred, the territory in which the policy holder is residing at any time thereafter shall, subject to paragraph (6) below, be that same territory.

(6) Subject to paragraph (4) above, where at any time after the policy or contract was made or transferred the company comes to be in possession of information making it reasonable for the company to assume that the policy holder, being neither—

(*a*) the person with whom the policy or contract was originally effected, nor (*b*) a person to whom the rights conferred by the policy or contract have been assigned in circumstances where the assignment did not constitute a chargeable event within the meaning of [section 484 of the Income Tax (Trading and Other Income) Act 2005][6], nor

(*c*) a personal representative in whom those rights have been vested by operation of law,

was residing in the United Kingdom at the time he became the policy holder or at any time thereafter, the territory in which the policy holder is residing shall, from the date on which it is reasonable for the company so to assume, be the United Kingdom.][1]

Amendments—[1] This regulation inserted by the Insurance Companies (Overseas Life Assurance Business) (Compliance) (Amendment) Regulations, SI 1999/2839, reg 15, with effect in relation to policies or contracts made by or, as the case may be, transferred to, an insurance company on or after 8 November 1999.

[2] Words in paras (3), (5) substituted and paras (4A), (4B) inserted by the Insurance Companies (Overseas Life Assurance Business) (Compliance) (Amendment) Regulations, SI 2000/2104 reg 14 with effect for policies or contracts made by, or, as the case may be, transferred to, an insurance company after 21 August 2000.

[3] Words in sub-para (2)(*a*) substituted by the Financial Services and Markets Act 2000 (Consequential Amendments) (Taxes) Order, SI 2001/3629 art 142(*h*) with effect from 1 December 2001, immediately after the coming into force of the Financial Services and Markets Act 2000 ss 411, 432(1), Sch 20 (and SI 2001/3629 Pts 1 and 2).

[4] Para (2A) and words in para (3) inserted by the Insurance Companies (Overseas Life Assurance Business) (Compliance) (Amendment) Regulations, SI 2004/3273 regs 2, 10 with effect from 31 December 2004.

[5] Words substituted by the Insurance Companies (Overseas Life Assurance Business) (Compliance) (Amendment) Regulations, SI 2007/2088 regs 2, 9(*c*) with effect for accounting periods beginning on or after 1 January 2007 and ending on or after 13 August 2007: SI 2007/2088 reg 1.

[6] In para (6)(*b*), words substituted by the Insurance Companies (Overseas Life Assurance Business) (Compliance) (Amendment) Regulations, SI 2008/2627 reg 2(1), (3)(*c*) with effect in relation to policies or contracts assigned on or after 27 October 2008.

[7] In para (2A)(*a*), words substituted for words "Article 14 or 53(2) of the Consolidated Life Assurance Directive" by the Solvency 2 Regulations, SI 2015/575 reg 60, Sch 2 para 5(1), (3)(*g*) with effect from 1 January 2016.

15 Reinsurance business effected by a company resident in the United Kingdom outside the United Kingdom

. . .

Amendments—This regulation repealed by the Insurance Companies (Overseas Life Assurance Business) (Compliance) (Amendment) Regulations, SI 2007/2088 regs 2, 10(*a*) with effect for accounting periods beginning on or after 1 January 2007 and ending on or after 13 August 2007: SI 2007/2088 reg 1.

16 Reinsurance business effected either by a company resident in the United Kingdom otherwise than outside the United Kingdom or by an overseas life insurance company

. . .

Amendments—This regulation repealed by the Insurance Companies (Overseas Life Assurance Business) (Compliance) (Amendment) Regulations, SI 2007/2088 regs 2, 10(*b*) with effect for accounting periods beginning on or after 1 January 2007 and ending on or after 13 August 2007: SI 2007/2088 reg 1.

16A [Reinsurance business effected either by a company resident in the United Kingdom otherwise than outside the United Kingdom or by an overseas life insurance company—policy holder not within regulation 7

. . .

Amendments—This regulation repealed by the Insurance Companies (Overseas Life Assurance Business) (Compliance) (Amendment) Regulations, SI 2007/2088 regs 2, 10(*c*) with effect for accounting periods beginning on or after 1 January 2007 and ending on or after 13 August 2007: SI 2007/2088 reg 1.

CERTIFICATES TO BE OBTAINED ON THE HAPPENING OF SPECIFIED EVENTS

17 Business other than reinsurance business effected either by a company resident in the United Kingdom otherwise than outside the United Kingdom or by an overseas life insurance company

. . .

Amendments—This regulation revoked by the Insurance Companies (Overseas Life Assurance Business) (Compliance) (Amendment) Regulations, SI 1999/2839, reg 4, with effect in relation to specified events occurring after 7 November 1999.

SANCTIONS

18 Reclassification of policy or contract from date when it was effected

(1) Subject to paragraph (2) below, this regulation applies in any case where an insurance company—

(*a*) treats a policy or contract as relating to overseas life assurance business—

(i) in the circumstances prescribed in regulation 6(1) where the insurance company has not completed the certificate prescribed in regulation 6(3) or one of the declarations prescribed in paragraphs (4) and (5) of regulation 6 within the period limited in regulation 6(7), or

(ii) in the circumstances prescribed in regulation 7(1) where the insurance company has not obtained the document prescribed in regulation 7(3) or, in any case where section 431D(5)[, or where the business is of a description falling within the circumstances set out in regulation 5 of the Excluded Business Regulations,][3] applies and the policy or contract is held otherwise than by the trustees of the trust, the certificate prescribed in regulation 7(8) within the period limited in regulation 7(9), or

[(iii) in the circumstances prescribed in regulation [7A(1)][4] where the insurance company has not completed the certificate prescribed in regulation 7A(4) or (5) within the period limited in regulation 7A(9), or][1]

(*aa*) . . . [5]

(*b*) . . . [5]

(*ba*) . . . [5]

(*c*) treats a policy or contract as relating to overseas life assurance business in the circumstances prescribed in regulation 13(3)[, 14(3) or 14A(4)][2], or

(*d*) . . . [5]

(*e*) treats a [policy or contract][5] as relating to overseas life assurance business in circumstances where the insurance company, at the time the policy or contract was made [or transferred][1] . . . [5], was in possession of information making it reasonable for the insurance company to assume [that—

[(i)] [5] any of the requirements of section 431D (other than those relating to where the policy holder is residing) was not fulfilled (notwithstanding its possession of any certificate, declaration or other document), or

[(ii)] [5] the business was excluded business.][3]

(2) This regulation shall not apply in any case specified in sub-paragraph [(aa), (b), (ba), (d) or (e)][2] of paragraph (1) above where the insurance company is a company to which section 439A applies.[5]

[(3) The company shall treat the policy or contract as relating to basic life assurance and general annuity business from the date the policy or contract was made or transferred.][5]

(4) All necessary adjustments, whether by way of assessment [self-assessment,][1] or otherwise, shall be made to give effect to paragraph (3) above; and any such assessment may be made without limits on time.

Commentary—*Simon's Taxes* **D7.5137.**

Amendments—[1] Para 1(*a*)(iii), (*aa*), (*ba*), and words in para (1)(*e*), (3)(*a*), (4), inserted, by the Insurance Companies (Overseas Life Assurance Business) (Compliance) (Amendment) Regulations, SI 1999/2839, reg 19(1)–(4), (7), (9), (10), with effect from 8 November 1999.

[2] Words substituted by SI 1999/2839, reg 19(5), (6), (8), with effect from 8 November 1999.

[3] Words in para (1)(*a*)(ii) inserted and words in para (1)(*e*) substituted by the Insurance Companies (Overseas Life Assurance Business) (Compliance) (Amendment) Regulations, SI 2000/2104 reg 17(1), (2)(*a*), (3) with effect for policies or contracts made by, or, as the case may be, transferred to, an insurance company after 21 August 2000.

[4] Words in para (1)(*a*)(iii) substituted by SI 2000/2104 reg 17(1), (2)(*b*) with effect from 23 August 2000.

[5] Para (1)(*aa*), (*b*), (*ba*), (*d*), words in para (1)(*e*), and whole of para (2), revoked; words in para (1)(*e*), and whole of para (3), substituted; para (1)(*e*)(i), (ii) renumbered as such; by the Insurance Companies (Overseas Life Assurance Business) (Compliance) (Amendment) Regulations, SI 2007/2088 regs 2, 11 with effect for accounting periods beginning on or after 1 January 2007 and ending on or after 13 August 2007: SI 2007/2088 reg 1.

18A [Reclassification of policy or contract as relating to overseas life assurance business from date when it was made or transferred

(1) This regulation applies in any case where an insurance company—

(*a*) does not treat a policy or contract as relating to overseas life assurance business in the circumstances prescribed in regulation 5(1)[, (1A) or (1B)][3], and

(*b*) has not completed the certificate prescribed in regulation 5(4) [or (4A)][2] within the period limited in regulation 5(8).

(2) The company shall treat the policy or contract as relating to overseas life assurance business from the date the policy or contract was made or transferred.

(3) All necessary adjustments, whether by way of assessment or otherwise, shall be made to give effect to paragraph (2).][1]

Amendments—[1] This regulation inserted by the Insurance Companies (Overseas Life Assurance Business) (Compliance) (Amendment) Regulations, SI 1999/2839, reg 20, with effect from 8 November 1999.

[2] Words in para (1)(*b*) substituted by the Insurance Companies (Overseas Life Assurance Business) (Compliance) (Amendment) Regulations, SI 2000/2104 reg 18 with effect for cases occurring after 7 November 1999.

[3] Words in para (1)(*a*) substituted by the Insurance Companies (Overseas Life Assurance Business) (Compliance) (Amendment) Regulations, SI 2004/3273 regs 2, 11 with effect from 31 December 2004.

19 Reclassification of policy or contract from date after it was effected

(1) Subject to paragraph (2) below, this regulation applies in any case where an insurance company—

(*a*) treats a policy or contract as relating to overseas life assurance business in the circumstances prescribed in regulation 8(1) where the insurance company has not obtained the document prescribed in regulation 8(3) or, in any case where section 431D(5) applies[, or the business is of a description falling within the circumstances set out in regulation 5 of the Excluded Business Regulations,][3] the certificate prescribed in regulation 8(8) within the period limited in regulation 8(9), or

(*b*) . . . [4]

(*c*) treats a policy or contract as relating to overseas life assurance business in the circumstances prescribed in regulation 13(5)[, 14(5) or 14A(6)][1], or

(*d*) . . . [4]

(*e*) treats a [policy or contract][4] as relating to overseas life assurance business in circumstances where the insurance company, at any time after the policy or contract was made [or transferred][1] . . . [4], was in possession of information making it reasonable for the insurance company to assume [that—

[(i)] [4] any of the requirements of section 431D (other than those relating to where the policy holder is residing) was not fulfilled (notwithstanding its possession of any certificate, declaration or other document), or

[(ii)] [4] the business was excluded business.][3]

(2) . . . [4]

[(3) Subject to paragraphs (3A) and (3B) below, the company shall treat the policy or contract as relating to basic life assurance and general annuity business from the end of the accounting period in which the relevant date falls.][4]

[(3A) Paragraph (3) above shall not apply where—

(*a*) the case concerned falls within paragraph (1)(*e*) above,

(*b*) section 431D(7) applied to the policy or contract when it was made or transferred, or the underlying policy when it was made,

(*c*) the case falls within paragraph (1)(*e*) above by reason of the fact that, at some time that is—

(i) more than three years after the date on which the policy or contract was made or transferred, or the underlying policy was made, but

(ii) is not earlier than 8th November 1999,

the number of persons for or in respect of whom benefits were to be provided under the policy or contract, or the underlying policy, and who were not relevant overseas employees within the meaning of section 431D(8), became a not insignificant number ('the relevant number') for the purposes of section 431D(7), and

(*d*) the relevant number has at no time exceeded the number which is equal to twenty per cent of the total number of persons for or in respect of whom benefits are to be provided under the policy or contract or the underlying policy.][1]

[(3B) Paragraph (3) above shall not apply where—

(*a*) the case concerned falls within paragraph (1)(*e*) above,

(*b*) the policy or contract fell within the description set out in regulation 7(*c*) of the Excluded Business Regulations when it was made or transferred, or the underlying policy fell within that description when it was made,

(*c*) the case falls within paragraph (1)(*e*) above by reason of the fact that, at some time that is more than three years after the date on which the policy or contract was made or transferred, or the underlying policy was made, the number of persons for or in respect of whom benefits were to be provided under the policy or contract, or the underlying policy, and who were not relevant overseas employees within the meaning of regulation 2 of the Excluded Business Regulations, became a not insignificant number ('the relevant number') for the purposes of regulation 7(*c*) of those Regulations, and

(*d*) the relevant number has at no time exceeded the number which is equal to twenty per cent of the total number of persons for or in respect of whom benefits are to be provided under the policy or contract or the underlying policy.][3]

(4) All necessary adjustments, whether by way of assessment or otherwise, shall be made to give effect to paragraph (3) above; and any such assessment may be made without limits on time.

(5) In paragraph (3) above "the relevant date" means—

(*a*) in any case specified in sub-paragraph (*a*) or (*b*) of paragraph (1) above, the last day by which the insurance company should have obtained any certificate, document or undertaking mentioned in either of those sub-paragraphs, or

(*b*) in any case specified in sub-paragraph (*c*) or (*d*) of paragraph (1) above, the date when it became reasonable for the company to assume as mentioned in regulation 13(5)[, 14(5), 15(5) or 16(5)][2] as the case may be, or

(*c*) in any case specified in sub-paragraph (*e*) of paragraph (1) above, the date when it became reasonable for the insurance company to assume as mentioned in that sub-paragraph.

Commentary—*Simon's Taxes* **D7.5137.**

Amendments—[1] In para (1)(*c*), (*d*) words substituted, and words in para (1)(*e*), (3) and whole of para (3A) inserted, by the Insurance Companies (Overseas Life Assurance Business) (Compliance) (Amendment) Regulations, SI 1999/2839, reg 21, with effect in relation to accounting periods ending on or after 31 December 1999, or where an insurance company so elects by written notice given to an officer of the Board on or before 31 December 1999, the first accounting period beginning on or after 1 October 1999 and ending after 31 December 1999 and subsequent accounting periods.

2 Words in para (5)(*b*) substituted by the Insurance Companies (Overseas Life Assurance Business) (Compliance) (Amendment) Regulations, SI 2000/2104 reg 19(1), (6) with effect for—

(a) accounting periods ending on or after 31st December 1999; or

(b) where an insurance company has so elected by written notice given to an officer of the Board on or before 31 December 1999, the first accounting period beginning on or after 1 October 1999 and ending after 31 December 1999 and subsequent accounting periods.

3 Words in para (1)(*a*) and whole of para (3A) inserted and words in paras (1)(*e*), (3) substituted by SI 2000/2104 reg 19(1)–(5) with effect for policies or contracts made by, or, as the case may be, transferred to, an insurance company after 21 August 2000.

4 Paras (1)(*b*), (*d*), words in para (1)(*e*), and whole of para (2), repealed; words in para (1)(*e*), substituted; para (1)(*e*)(i), (ii) renumbered as such; and para (3) substituted; by the Insurance Companies (Overseas Life Assurance Business) (Compliance) (Amendment) Regulations, SI 2007/2088 regs 2, 12 with effect for accounting periods beginning on or after 1 January 2007 and ending on or after 13 August 2007: SI 2007/2088 reg 1.

20 Charge to tax where no certificate under regulation 17

. . .

Amendments—This regulation revoked by the Insurance Companies (Overseas Life Assurance Business) (Compliance) (Amendment) Regulations, SI 1999/2839, reg 4, with effect in relation to specified events occurring after 7 November 1999.

KEEPING AND INSPECTION OF RECORDS AND PROVISION OF INFORMATION

21 Records to be kept and transfers of records

(1) A company (including any transferee) shall at all times keep sufficient records in respect of each relevant policy to enable the requirements of these Regulations to be satisfied.

(2) Without prejudice to the generality of paragraph (1) above, any relevant record shall be preserved by the company, in such manner as may be approved by the Board, so as to be available for inspection under regulation 23 for a period of six years after the termination of the policy or contract.

(3) In any case where the obligations under any policy or contract of the body that issued, entered into or effected it ("the original insurer") are at any time the obligations of another body (in this regulation and in regulations 22 and 23 referred to as the "transferee") to whom there has been a transfer of the whole or any part of a business previously carried on by the original insurer, the original insurer shall deliver any relevant record to the transferee within the period of three months after the transfer.

(4) Paragraph (3) above has effect in relation to transfers on or after 1st January 1996.

Commentary—*Simon's Taxes* **D7.5137.**

22 Information to be provided to the Board

An officer of the Board authorised for the purposes of this regulation may by notice require any company which has at any time effected a relevant policy or any transferee, within such time as may be provided by the notice (not being less than 30 days), to furnish him with such information relating to any relevant policy as he may reasonably require for the purposes of these Regulations.

Commentary—*Simon's Taxes* **D7.5137.**

23 Inspection of records

(1) An officer of the Board authorised for the purposes of this regulation may by notice require any company which has at any time effected a relevant policy or any transferee, within such time as may be provided in the notice (not being less than 30 days), to make available for inspection by him such books, documents and other records as are in the company's possession or under the company's control containing such information relating to any relevant policy as he may reasonably require for the purposes of these Regulations.

(2) The officer to whom the books, documents and other records are made available shall be entitled to take copies, or make extracts from, any book, document or record made available to him by virtue of paragraph (1) above.

Commentary—*Simon's Taxes* **D7.5137.**

1995/3238

INSURANCE COMPANIES (OVERSEAS LIFE ASSURANCE BUSINESS) (TAX CREDIT) REGULATIONS 1995

Note—These Regulations lapsed following the repeal of TA 1988 s 414A(3)–(5) by F(No 2)A 1997 ss 34, 52, Sch 4 para 28, Sch 8 Part II(10) with effect in relation to distributions made on or after 6 April 1999.

1995/3239

TAX-EXEMPT SPECIAL SAVINGS ACCOUNT (RELEVANT EUROPEAN INSTITUTIONS) REGULATIONS 1995

Made by the Commissioners of Inland Revenue under TA 1988 s 326C(1), (1A), 326D

Made . . . . *12 December 1995*
Laid before the House of Commons . . . . *12 December 1995*
Coming into Force . . . . *2 January 1996*

PART I
GENERAL

1 Citation and commencement

These Regulations may be cited as the Tax-exempt Special Savings Account (Relevant European Institutions) Regulations 1995 and shall come into force on 2nd January 1996.

2 Interpretation

In these Regulations—

"the Board" means the Commissioners of Inland Revenue;

"notice" means notice in writing and "notify" shall be construed accordingly;

"the principal Regulations" means the Tax-exempt Special Savings Account Regulations 1990;

"a relevant European institution" has the meaning given by section 326A(10) of the Taxes Act:

"the Taxes Act" means the Income and Corporation Taxes Act 1988;

and in Part III of these Regulations "regulation" means a regulation of the principal Regulations.

PART II
TAX REPRESENTATIVES

3 Accounts held with relevant European institutions

(1) An account held with a relevant European institution shall not be a tax-exempt special savings account at the time it is opened, or shall cease to be a tax-exempt special savings account at a given time, unless at the time concerned one of the following three requirements is fulfilled.

(2) The first requirement is that—

(*a*) a person who falls within subsection (5) of section 326D of the Taxes Act is appointed by the institution to be responsible for securing the discharge of the duties prescribed by regulation 4 which fall to be discharged by the institution, and

(*b*) his identity and the fact of his appointment have been notified to the Board by the institution.

(3) The second requirement is that there are other arrangements with the Board for a person other than the institution to secure the discharge of such duties.

(4) The third requirement is that there are other arrangements with the Board designed to secure the discharge of such duties.

4 Prescribed duties of tax representatives

The duties prescribed by this regulation are those that fall to be discharged by a society or institution under the principal Regulations.

5 Termination of appointment

The appointment of a person in pursuance of the first requirement mentioned in regulation 3(2) shall be treated as terminated in circumstances where—

(*a*) the Board have reason to believe that the person concerned—

(i) has failed to secure the discharge of any of the duties prescribed by regulation 4 or

(ii) does not have adequate resources to discharge those duties; and

(*b*) the Board have notified the institution and that person that they propose to treat his appointment as having terminated with effect from the date specified in the notice.

6 Powers and liabilities of tax representative

Where, in accordance with the first requirement mentioned in regulation 3(2), a person is at any time appointed to be responsible for securing the discharge of duties the person concerned—

(*a*) shall be entitled to act on the institution's behalf for any of the purposes of the provisions relating to the duties;

(*b*) shall secure (where appropriate by acting on the institution's behalf) the institution's compliance with and discharge of the duties;

(*c*) shall be personally liable in respect of any failure of the institution to comply with or discharge any such duty as if the duties imposed on the institution were imposed jointly and severally on the institution and the person concerned.

7 Effect of section 326B(3) of the Taxes Act

Section 326B(3) of the Taxes Act shall have effect as if the reference to subsection (1) included a reference to this Part of these Regulations.

PART III

AMENDMENTS TO THE PRINCIPAL REGULATIONS

8–11 (*Amend* the Tax-exempt Special Savings Account Regulations 1990, SI 1990/2361, regs 2(1), 5, 11, 16.)

1996/805

PERSONAL PENSION SCHEMES (DEFERRED ANNUITY PURCHASE) (ACCEPTANCE OF CONTRIBUTIONS) REGULATIONS 1996

Note—These Regulations lapse by virtue of the coming into force of FA 2004 Part 4 (ss 149–284) with effect from 6 April 2006.

1996/1031

CAPITAL GAINS TAX (GILT-EDGED SECURITIES) ORDER 1996

Made by the Treasury under TCGA 1992 Sch 9 para 1

Made 3 April 1996

1 This Order may be cited as the Capital Gains Tax (Gilt-edged Securities) Order 1996.

2 The following securities are hereby specified for the purposes of Schedule 9 to the Taxation of Chargeable Gains Act 1992—

8% Treasury Stock 2000
8% Treasury Stock 2000 "A"
8½% Treasury Stock 2005
7½% Treasury Stock 2006
8% Treasury Stock 2015
8% Treasury Stock 2015 "A".

1996/1179

EUROPEAN INVESTMENT BANK (DESIGNATED INTERNATIONAL ORGANISATION) ORDER 1996

Amendment—This Order revoked by ITA 2007, s 1031, Sch 3 Pt 1, with effect for income tax purposes from 6 April 2007, and corporation tax purposes for accounting periods ending after 5 April 2007.

1996/1311

PERSONAL PENSION SCHEMES (TABLES OF RATES OF ANNUITIES) REGULATIONS 1996

Note—These Regulations lapse by virtue of the coming into force of FA 2004 Part 4 (ss 149–284) with effect from 6 April 2006.

1996/1582

RETIREMENT BENEFITS SCHEMES (RESTRICTION ON DISCRETION TO APPROVE) (EXCEPTED SCHEMES) REGULATIONS 1996

Note—These Regulations lapse by virtue of the coming into force of FA 2004 Part 4 (ss 149–284) with effect from 6 April 2006.

1996/1583

CAPITAL GAINS TAX (PENSION FUNDS POOLING SCHEMES) REGULATIONS 1996

Made by the Treasury under TCGA 1992 s 99(3)

Made . . . . *19 June 1996*
Laid before the House of Commons . . . . *19 June 1996*

Coming into Force ....*11 July 1996*

1 These Regulations may be cited as the Capital Gains Tax (Pension Funds Pooling Schemes) Regulations 1996 and shall come into force on 11th July 1996.

2 In these Regulations—

"pension funds pooling scheme" means a unit trust scheme of the description specified in regulation 4 of the Income Tax (Pension Funds Pooling Schemes) Regulations 1996;

"unit trust scheme" has the meaning given by section [237(1) of the Financial Services and Markets Act 2000][1].

3 A unit trust scheme which is a pension funds pooling scheme shall be treated as not being a unit trust scheme for the purposes of the Taxation of Chargeable Gains Act 1992.

Amendments—[1] Words in definition of "unit trust scheme" substituted by the Financial Services and Markets Act 2000 (Consequential Amendments) (Taxes) Order, SI 2001/3629 art 143 with effect from 1 December 2001, immediately after the coming into force of the Financial Services and Markets Act 2000 ss 411, 432(1), Sch 20 (and SI 2001/3629 Pts 1 and 2).

1996/1585

INCOME TAX (PENSION FUNDS POOLING SCHEMES) REGULATIONS 1996

Made by the Treasury under TA 1988 s 469(7), (8)

Made ....*19 June 1996*
Laid before the House of Commons ....*19 June 1996*
Coming into Force ....*11 July 1996*

1 Citation and commencement

These Regulations may be cited as the Income Tax (Pension Funds Pooling Schemes) Regulations 1996 and shall come into force on 11th July 1996.

2 Interpretation

(1) In these Regulations unless the context otherwise requires—

"address" in relation to any person means—

(*a*) where that person is an individual, the address of his principal place of business or, if he has none, his principal residential address;

(*b*) where that person is a company, the address of its registered or principal office;

"the Board" means the Commissioners of Inland Revenue;

"cancellation event" means an occasion when the rights and interests of a participant in the scheme property of a unit trust scheme are wholly redeemed, or otherwise wholly purchased or wholly cancelled, by the trustee of that scheme, other than an occasion when the rights and interests of the participant in the scheme property become the rights and interests of its successor in the scheme property;

"descendant" in relation to a former participant in a unit trust scheme ("the relevant participant") means the participant for the time being in the scheme which is either the successor of the relevant participant or the successor of another former participant in the scheme which, at the time it so participated, was part of the line of succession of participants that commenced with the relevant participant;

["employee" and "employer" have the meaning given in section 279(1) of the Finance Act 2004);][2]

"notice" means notice in writing;

["recognised overseas pension scheme" has the meaning given in section 150(8) of the 2004 Act;][2]

"pension funds pooling scheme" means a unit trust scheme of the description specified in regulation 4;

["pension scheme" has the meaning given by section 150(1) of the 2004 Act;][2]

["registered pension scheme" in section 150(2) of the 2004 Act, (for the purpose of these Regulations), must also be an "occupational pension scheme" within the meaning of section 150(5) of that Act;][2]

"relevant period" in relation to a unit trust scheme means a period which—

(*a*) commences when the trustee of the scheme first incurs expenditure in respect of which an allowance under the 1990 Act is to be, or may be, made, or next incurs such expenditure after the end of a relevant period, and

(*b*) ends when it is first the case that the trustee of the scheme has disposed of all interests in respect of which such expenditure is incurred, unless immediately after that time the scheme incurs further expenditure in respect of which an allowance under the 1990 Act is to be, or may be, made;

. . . [2]

. . . [2]

"scheme property" in relation to a unit trust scheme means property of any description, including money, which is held on trust for the participants in the scheme;

"section 469" means section 469 of the Taxes Act;

"sponsor" in relation to a pension funds scheme means any person who established the scheme or who for the time being has authority to vary the terms of, or to terminate, the scheme, or to appoint or replace a manager of the scheme;

"successor" in relation to a former participant in a unit trust scheme means the participant which—

(*a*) was not a participant in the scheme immediately before the time when that former participant ceased to participate in the scheme, and

(*b*) immediately after that time became entitled to all the rights and interests in the scheme property to which that former participant was entitled immediately before ceasing so to participate;

"tax year" means a year beginning on 6th April and ending on 5th April in the following calendar year;

"Taxes Act" means the Income and Corporation Taxes Act 1988;

"trustee" in relation to a unit trust scheme means the person or persons for the time being holding the scheme property on trust for the participants in that scheme;

"units" and "unit trust scheme" have the meanings given by section [237 of the Financial Services and Markets Act 2000][1];

"1990 Act" means the Capital Allowances Act 1990;

"1992 Act" means the Taxation of Chargeable Gains Act 1992.

["2004 Act" means the Finance Act 2004.][2]

(2) . . . [2]

(3) References in these Regulations to a superannuation fund are references to a superannuation fund which either—

(*a*) falls within subsection (6) of section 615 of the Taxes Act, or

(*b*) is before the Board in order for them to decide whether the superannuation fund falls within that subsection.

(4) References in these Regulations to [a registered pension scheme][2], a superannuation fund or [a recognised overseas pension scheme][3] as a participant in a unit trust scheme, are references to the appropriate person or persons specified in paragraph (5) who is or are for the time being a participant or participants in the unit trust scheme [and, for the purposes of this paragraph, "participant" shall be construed in accordance with section 235 of the Financial Services and Markets Act 2000][1].

(5) The persons specified are—

(*a*) in the case of [a registered pension scheme][2] set up under trust or a superannuation fund, the trustees of that scheme or fund;

(*b*) in the case of [a registered pension scheme][2] not set up under trust, the sponsor of that scheme;

(*c*) in the case of [a recognised overseas pension scheme][3], the persons who are for the time being parties to the arrangements constituting that scheme, other than an employee in his capacity as a beneficiary of the scheme.

(6) The like provisions as are contained in section 159(2) to (8) of the 1990 Act shall have effect to determine when capital expenditure is to be taken to be incurred for the purposes of these Regulations.

Amendments—[1] In para (1), words in definition of "units" and "unit trust scheme", and words in para (4) substituted by the Financial Services and Markets Act 2000 (Consequential Amendments) (Taxes) Order, SI 2001/3629 art 145 with effect from 1 December 2001, immediately after the coming into force of the Financial Services and Markets Act 2000 ss 411, 432(1), Sch 20 (and SI 2001/3629 Pts 1 and 2).

[2] In para (1), definitions substituted, revoked and inserted, para (2) revoked, and words in paras (4), (5) substituted, by the Taxation of Pension Schemes (Consequential Amendments) Order, SI 2006/745 art 23(1), (2) with effect from 6 April 2006.

[3] Words in paras (4), (5)(*c*) substituted by SI 2006/745 art 23(1), (3) with effect from 6 April 2006.

3 Exception of pension funds pooling scheme from section 469

A unit trust scheme which is a pension funds pooling scheme shall be treated as not being a unit trust scheme for the purposes of section 469.

4 Description of a pension funds pooling scheme

(1) Subject to paragraph (2), a unit trust scheme is a pension funds pooling scheme at any time if at that time it has the characteristics specified in paragraph (3).

(2) [Subject to paragraph (2A),][3] a unit trust scheme which at any time in a tax year, or at the end of a tax year, ceases to have the characteristics specified in paragraph (3) is not a pension funds pooling scheme as regards that year.

[(2A) Paragraph (2) does not apply if the unit trust scheme ceases to have the characteristics specified in paragraph (3) solely because it is wound up.][3]

(3) The characteristics specified in this paragraph are that—

(*a*) subject to regulation 9(10) and (11), each participant in the scheme is—

(i) [a registered pension scheme][2], or

(ii) a superannuation fund, or

(iii) [a recognised overseas pension scheme][1];

(*b*) each participant in the scheme has been approved by the Board in accordance with regulation 7 as eligible to participate in the scheme and, subject to regulation 9(10) and (11), that approval has not subsequently been revoked or withdrawn under regulation 7(8) or (9);

(*c*) all the participants in the scheme are jointly absolutely entitled as against the trustee of that scheme, within the meaning of section 60 of the 1992 Act, to the scheme property;

(*d*) subject to paragraph (4), the scheme property consists of any or all of the following—

(i) land;

(ii) buildings or structures on land;

(iii) shares, stock or other investments which are the subject of transactions falling within subsection (12) of section 127 of the Finance Act 1995 (read with subsection (13) of that section);

(iv) investments comprising futures contracts or options contracts relating to land (including contracts falling within subsection (13) of that section);

(*e*) except as provided in paragraph (5), the contributions of the participants are expended on any or all of the following—

(i) the acquisition of, or of rights in or over, land, or the management or development of that land;

(ii) the acquisition or construction of, or the purchase of interests in, buildings or structures on land, or the management or development of those buildings or structures;

(iii) the provision of machinery or plant which is an integral part of those buildings or structures, or the management, alteration or improvement of that machinery or plant;

(iv) the making of any investments falling within sub-paragraph (*d*)(iii) or (iv) above, or the management of those investments;

(*f*) where expenditure falling within sub-paragraph (*e*) is expenditure in respect of which an allowance under the 1990 Act is to be, or may be, made, the terms of the scheme secure that the conditions specified in regulation 5 (read with regulation 6) are satisfied;

(*g*) the terms of the scheme secure that no participant has rights or interests in any part of the scheme property that are different in nature from the rights or interests which any other participant has in that part of the scheme property;

(*h*) the terms of the scheme secure that, in relation to any arrangements which are entered into on or after the date of coming into force of these Regulations—

(i) a participant is obliged to give to the trustee of the scheme, in the situation described, and within the period of time specified, in paragraph (1) of regulation 8, the notification specified in that regulation;

(ii) the trustee of the scheme is irrevocably authorised and obliged to undertake on behalf of the participants the responsibilities specified in regulation 10 and the duties specified in regulations 9 and 11;

(*j*) the trustee of the scheme has given notice to the Board electing for the scheme to be treated, pursuant to these Regulations, the Capital Gains Tax (Pension Funds Pooling Schemes) Regulations 1996, and the Stamp Duty and Stamp Duty Reserve Tax (Pension Funds Pooling Schemes) Regulations 1996, as not being a unit trust scheme for the purposes specified in each of the Regulations.

(4) A unit trust scheme is a pension funds pooling scheme notwithstanding that the scheme property at any time consists wholly or partly of—

(*a*) cash held temporarily by the trustee that is subsequently expended as mentioned in sub-paragraph (*e*) of paragraph (3), or for purposes incidental to, or arising out of, any of the expenditure referred to in that sub-paragraph,

(*b*) cash held temporarily by the trustee that is subsequently expended in making payment to a participant or former participant in the scheme following the redemption, purchase or cancellation of any of the rights or interests of that participant or former participant in the scheme property.

(*c*) cash held temporarily by the trustee that is subsequently expended by way of distribution to the participants generally,

(*d*) cash held temporarily by the trustee that is subsequently expended on the management of the scheme, or the management or development of the scheme property,

(*e*) cash held temporarily by the trustee that is subsequently expended on the acquisition or maintenance of assets falling within sub-paragraph (*f*) below, or

(*f*) other assets held by the trustee in connection with the management of the scheme, or the management or development of the scheme property.

(5) A unit trust scheme is a pension funds pooling scheme notwithstanding that the contributions of the participants are expended—

(*a*) for purposes incidental to, or arising out of, the expenditure referred to in paragraph (3)(*e*),

(*b*) for any of the purposes mentioned in sub-paragraphs (*a*) to (*e*) of paragraph (4), or

(*c*) on the acquisition or maintenance of assets falling within sub-paragraph (*f*) of that paragraph.

(6) In this regulation—

"management" includes insurance, repair and maintenance;

"development" includes alteration or improvement.

Amendments—[1] Words in para (3)(*a*)(iii) substituted, by the Taxation of Pension Schemes (Consequential Amendments) Order, SI 2006/745 art 23(1), (3) with effect from 6 April 2006.

[2] Words in para (3)(*a*)(i) substituted by SI 2006/745 art 23(1), (4) with effect from 6 April 2006.

[3] Words in para (2) inserted, and para (2A) inserted, by the Income Tax (Pension Funds Pooling Schemes) (Amendment) Regulations, SI 2006/1162 with effect from 16 May 2006.

5 Expenditure qualifying for capital allowances—specification of conditions

(1) The conditions specified for the purposes of regulation 4(3)(*f*) are those set out in paragraphs (2) to (6).

(2) The first condition is that each participant in the scheme in a relevant period is either—

(*a*) an enduring participant, or

(*b*) a participant that is a descendant of a former participant in the scheme which was a participant at the commencement of that period.

(3) The second condition is that, during a relevant period, no participant in the scheme is the successor of more than one former participant which ceased to participate in the scheme—

(*a*) immediately before the commencement of that period, or

(*b*) at the time of the commencement of that period, or

(*c*) at any subsequent time before the end of that period.

(4) The third condition is that during a relevant period—

(*a*) an enduring participant's share of the scheme property remains the same as it was at the commencement of that period, and

(*b*) the share of a participant which is a descendant of a former participant which was participant at the commencement of the relevant period remains the same as the share of that former participant was at the commencement of that period,

until such time as a cancellation event occurs, or, if earlier, the rights and interests in the scheme property of the participant concerned become the rights and interests in the scheme property of its successor.

(5) The fourth condition is that, immediately after the occurrence of a cancellation event during a relevant period, the ratio that the shares of the scheme property belonging to the participants at that time bear to each other is the same as the ratio that the shares of the scheme property belonging to those participants bore to each other immediately before the occurrence of that event.

(6) The fifth condition is that, following the occurrence of a cancellation event during a relevant period, every participant's share of the scheme property remains the same as it was immediately after the occurrence of that event or, where a participant is a descendant of a former participant which was a participant immediately after the occurrence of that event, the same as the share of that former participant was at that time, until that period ends or, if earlier, a further cancellation event occurs or the rights and interests in the scheme property of the participant concerned become the rights and interests in the scheme property of its successor.

(7) In this regulation "enduring participant" in relation to a relevant period means a participant which has been a participant since the commencement of that period.

6 Expenditure qualifying for capital allowances—provisions supplementary to regulation 5

(1) Where the rights and interests of a participant in the scheme property become the rights and interests of its successor in the scheme property at the time when a relevant period commences or a cancellation event occurs during a relevant period, those rights and interests shall be treated, for the purposes of regulation 5, as having become the rights and interests of the successor before the commencement of the relevant period or (as the case may be) the occurrence of the cancellation event.

(2) Where the rights and interests of a participant in the scheme property become the rights and interests of its successor in the scheme property at the time when a relevant period ends, those rights and interests shall be treated, for the purposes of regulation 5, as having become the rights and interests of the successor after the end of that period.

(3) Where contributions by participants in the scheme are made at the time when—

(*a*) a relevant period commences, or

(*b*) a cancellation event occurs during a relevant period, or

(*c*) a relevant period ends,

those contributions shall be treated, for the purposes of regulation 5, as having been made before the commencement of the relevant period or the occurrence of the cancellation event, or after the end of the relevant period (as the case may be).

(4) Where during a relevant period the rights and interests of a participant in the scheme property become the rights and interests of its successor in the scheme property at the same time as the trustee of the scheme makes a disposal of any interest or rights in or over an asset which, immediately before that disposal was made, formed part of the scheme property, the disposal shall be treated, for the purposes of regulation 5, as having been made after the participant's rights and interests in the scheme property have become the successor's rights and interests in the scheme property.

(5) Where, as a result of a business reorganisation, amalgamation or other form of reconstruction, a merger of participants occurs, that is, the whole of the rights and interests of two or more participants in the scheme property become the whole of the rights and interests of a single participant in the scheme property, then for the purposes of regulation 5—

(*a*) where the merger occurs at the time when a relevant period commences, it shall be treated as having occurred before that time;

(*b*) where the merger occurs at the time when a relevant period ends, it shall be treated as having occurred after that time;

(*c*) where the merger occurs during a relevant period, it shall be treated as never having occurred.

(6) Where, as a result of a business reorganisation, fragmentation or other form of reconstruction, a demerger relating to participants occurs, that is, the whole of the rights and interests of a single participant in the scheme property ("the demerging participant") become the whole of the rights and interests of two or more participants in the scheme property ("the replacement participants"), then for the purposes of regulation 5—

(*a*) where the demerger occurs at the time when a relevant period commences or a cancellation event occurs during a relevant period, it shall be treated as having occurred before that time;

(*b*) where the demerger occurs at the time when a relevant period ends, it shall be treated as having occurred after that time;

(*c*) where the demerger occurs during a relevant period, the demerging participant shall be treated as having been comprised of participants whose successors are the replacement participants.

(7) For the purposes of paragraph (6)(*c*), where one of the replacement participants is the demerging participant, that participant shall be treated as if, in its capacity as a replacement participant, it were a separate and distinct participant from the demerging participant.

(8) In paragraph (4) "disposal" shall be construed in accordance with the provisions of Chapter II of Part II of the 1992 Act relating to disposals of assets.

(9) Where during a relevant period of a unit trust scheme it first occurs that the scheme has the characteristics specified in regulation 4(3), that period shall be treated, for the purposes of regulation 5 and this regulation, as having commenced at the time of that first occurrence.

7 Approval of participants

(1) An application for approval of a scheme or fund as eligible to participate in a pension funds pooling scheme shall be made in writing by the trustee of that pension funds pooling scheme to the Board and shall contain the information specified in paragraph (2) or, as the case may be, in paragraph (3) . . . [1].

(2) As regards [a registered pension scheme][1] or a superannuation fund, the information is—

(*a*) the full title of the scheme or fund;

(*b*) the Board's reference number relating to the scheme or fund.

(3) As regards [a recognised overseas pension scheme][1], the information is—

(*a*) the full title of the scheme;

(*b*) where the scheme is established under trust, the names and addresses of the sponsors and trustees of the scheme;

(*c*) where the scheme is not established under trust, the names and addresses of the sponsors and managers of the scheme;

(*d*) the names and addresses of any employers who contribute to, but are not sponsors of, the scheme;

(*e*) where the arrangements constituting the scheme are made between two or more persons, details of any undertakings or promises made between any of those persons that are, or are likely to be, relevant to the custodianship of any rights or interests of that scheme in the pension funds pooling scheme, and the name and address of each of those persons;

[(*f*) either—

(i) evidence demonstrating that the scheme fulfils the requirements set out in regulations 2 and 3 of the Pension Schemes (Categories of Country and Requirements for Overseas Pension Schemes and Recognised Overseas Pension Schemes) Regulations 2006; or

(ii) in respect of information which has already been provided in accordance with section 169 of the Finance Act 2004 (recognised transfers) to an officer of Her Majesty's Revenue and Customs, notification of any reference used by an officer of Her Majesty's Revenue and Customs in respect of that information;][1]

(*h*) –(*o*) . . . [1]

(4) . . . [1]

(5) Where the Board determine to approve a scheme or fund pursuant to an application under paragraph (1), they shall give notice of the approval to the trustee of the pension funds pooling scheme.

(6) Approval may be given by the Board in full where they are satisfied that the scheme or fund is eligible to participate in the pension funds pooling scheme, or may be given on a provisional basis—

(*a*) in the case of a scheme falling within paragraph (3), pending the Board's consideration of information received by them pursuant to that paragraph, or

[(*b*) in the case of a superannuation fund which is before the Board for the purposes referred to in regulation 2(3)(*b*).][1]

(7) On receipt of a notice of approval, the trustee of the pension funds pooling scheme may admit the scheme or fund which is the subject of the notice to be a participant in the pension funds pooling scheme.

(8) The Board shall, by notice to the trustee, either convert to full approval or revoke an approval given on a provisional basis and, where the approval is revoked, the notice shall state the reason why it is considered by the Board that the participant is not eligible to participate in the pension funds pooling scheme.

(9) The Board may, by notice to the trustee, withdraw approval of a participant where they are satisfied that a participant is not eligible to participate in the pension funds pooling scheme, and the notice shall state the reason why it is considered by the Board that the participant is not so eligible.

(10) In this regulation references to a pension funds pooling scheme include references to any arrangements which, although not constituting such a scheme at the time an application for approval is made under paragraph (1), have been entered into with the intention that they will constitute such a scheme, and references to the trustee of a pension funds pooling scheme shall be construed accordingly.

Amendments—[1] Words in para (1) revoked; words in para (3) substituted; para (3)(*f*) substituted for para (3)(*f*), (*g*); paras (3)(*h*)–(*o*), (4) revoked; and para (6)(*b*) substituted; by the Taxation of Pension Schemes (Consequential Amendments) Order, SI 2006/745 art 23(1), (5) with effect from 6 April 2006.

8 Notification by participant of non-eligibility

(1) On becoming aware that, by reason of a change in its circumstances or otherwise, it is not, or may not be, eligible to participate in a pension funds pooling scheme, a participant shall notify the trustee of the scheme in writing of that fact within seven days after its becoming so aware.

(2) A notification under paragraph (1)—

(*a*) shall state the reason why the participant considers that it is not, or may not be, so eligible, and

(*b*) shall be accompanied by a copy of any document in the participant's possession that confirms or suggests that it is not, or may not be, so eligible.

9 Duties of trustee of a pension funds pooling scheme—participants ceasing to be eligible to participate

(1) On receiving a notification by a participant in accordance with regulation 8(1), the trustee of a pension funds pooling scheme shall, within 14 days after the date of receipt of the notification, give notice to the Board that a notification has been received by him.

(2) A notice under paragraph (1) shall state the full title of the participant concerned and, in the case of a notification received from a participant which is [a registered pension scheme][2] or a superannuation fund, the Board's reference number relating to that participant.

(3) A notice under paragraph (1) shall be accompanied by—

(*a*) a copy of the notification received from the participant, and

(*b*) a copy of the information provided by the participant to the trustee in accordance with regulation 8(2)(*b*), together with a translation of that information into English where the document in which the information is comprised is in a language other than English.

(4) Where, as a result of receiving any information, other than information provided in accordance with regulation 8(1), the trustee of a pension funds pooling scheme has reason to believe that—

(*a*) in the case of a participant which is [a registered pension scheme][2] or a superannuation fund, the participant is not eligible to participate in the scheme, or

(*b*) in the case of a participant which is [a recognised overseas pension scheme][1], the Board would be likely, were they to be in possession of the information received by the trustee, to have reason to revoke or withdraw their approval of the participant under regulation 7(8) or (9),

the trustee shall, within 14 days after the date of receipt of that information, give notice to the Board containing the information specified in paragraph (5).

(5) The information specified in this paragraph is—

(*a*) the full title of the participant,

(*b*) in the case of a participant which is [a registered pension scheme][2] or a superannuation fund, the Board's reference number relating to the scheme or fund concerned,

(*c*) details of the information received by the trustee;

(*d*) a statement setting out the reasons for the trustee's belief that—

(i) in the case of a participant which is [a registered pension scheme][2] or a superannuation fund, the participant is not eligible to participate in the scheme, or

(ii) in the case of a participant which is [a recognised overseas pension scheme][1], the Board would be likely to have reason to revoke or withdraw their approval of the participant.

(6) A notice under paragraph (4) above shall be accompanied by a copy of any document in the trustee's possession that contains information in support of his belief as mentioned in paragraph (5)(*d*), together with a translation of that information into English where the document is in a language other than English.

(7) Where a notice is given by the trustee under paragraph (1) or (4) in relation to a participant which is [a recognised overseas pension scheme][1], an officer of the Board may, for the purpose of ascertaining whether or not the participant is eligible to participate in the scheme, by notice require the trustee to furnish him, within such time (not being less than 21 days) as may be provided by the notice, such information relating to the participant as is specified in regulation 7(3) . . . [2].

(8) On receiving a notice given by the Board revoking or withdrawing approval under regulation 7(8) or (9), the trustee of the scheme shall forthwith give notice to the participant concerned that every unit in the scheme held by the participant, or by a nominee on its behalf, will be sold or cancelled by the trustee within 28 days after the date on which the notice given by the Board was received by the trustee.

(9) A notice given by the trustee under paragraph (8) shall state the reason why the participant is not eligible to participate in the scheme.

(10) Where all the units referred to in paragraph (8) are sold or cancelled by the trustee within the period of 28 days referred to in that paragraph, the unit trust scheme shall not cease to have the characteristics specified in regulation 4(3)(*a*) and (*b*).

(11) Where any of the units referred to in paragraph (8) are not sold or cancelled by the trustee within the period of 28 days referred to in that paragraph, the unit trust scheme shall be regarded as ceasing to satisfy the characteristics specified in regulation 4(3)(*a*) and (*b*) with effect from the date on which the notice given by the Board under regulation 7(8) or (9) was received by the trustee.

(12) References in this regulation to a participant which is [a registered pension scheme][2] or a superannuation fund include references to a participant which is no longer [a registered pension scheme][2] or a superannuation fund but which was such a scheme or fund at the time when notice of approval was given by the Board to the trustee in accordance with regulation 7(5).

Amendments—[1] Words in paras (4)(*b*), (5)(*d*)(ii), (7) substituted, by the Taxation of Pension Schemes (Consequential Amendments) Order, SI 2006/745 art 23(1), (3) with effect from 6 April 2006.

[2] Words in paras (2), (4), (5), (12) substituted, and words in para (7) revoked, by SI 2006/745 art 23(1), (6) with effect from 6 April 2006.

10 Responsibilities of trustee of a pension funds pooling scheme

(1) The trustee of a pension funds pooling scheme shall be responsible for negotiating and agreeing with an officer of the Board on behalf of the participants the matters specified in paragraph (2).

(2) The matters specified in this paragraph are—

(*a*)

(i) a method of calculating the amount of any income arising from the scheme property in each accounting period of the scheme, and of attributing to each participant the appropriate allocation of that amount;

(ii) the amount of any income arising from the scheme property in each accounting period of the scheme, and the amount of that income that is attributable to each participant;

(*b*) the amount of any profits or gains arising in each accounting period of the scheme in respect of rents or receipts from the scheme property in that period that are attributable to each of those participants in the scheme which are chargeable on such profits or gains under Schedule A;

(*c*) the amount of any interest of money or other annual profits or gains from the scheme property arising in each accounting period of the scheme that are attributable to each of those participants in the scheme which are chargeable on such interest or other annual profits or gains under Schedule D;

(*d*) the amount of any dividends or other distributions from the scheme property arising in each accounting period of the scheme that are attributable to each of those participants in the scheme which are chargeable on such dividends or other distributions under Schedule F;

(*e*)

(i) where in an accounting period an event occurs that gives rise, or may give rise, to a balancing allowance or a balancing charge under the 1990 Act to or on those participants which were participants immediately before or immediately after that event, a method of computing the amount of the balancing allowance or charge attributable to each of those participants;

(ii) the amount of the balancing allowance or charge referred to in paragraph (*i*) of this sub-paragraph that is attributable to each of the participants concerned;

(*f*) in relation to expenditure to which regulation 4(3)(*f*) applies, the amount of any such expenditure incurred in each accounting period of the scheme which is—
(i) capital expenditure for a chargeable period in relation to which Part I of the 1990 Act applies, or
(ii) capital expenditure on the provision of machinery or plant in respect of which a writing-down allowance is to be, or may be, made in accordance with sections 24 to 26 of the 1990 Act;

(*g*) the amount of the expenditure calculated in accordance with sub-paragraph (*f*) for an accounting period that is attributable to each participant;

(*h*) where, in relation to a building or structure which forms part of the scheme property, an event occurs in an accounting period which gives rise, or may give rise, to a balancing allowance or a balancing charge under the 1990 Act to or on each of the participants which were participants immediately before or immediately after that event, the amount of any sale, insurance, salvage or compensation moneys within the meaning of section 156 of the 1990 Act which are relevant to that event;

(*j*) the disposal value, calculated in accordance with section 26 of the 1990 Act, of any plant and machinery forming part of the scheme property which is or may be required to be brought into account for a chargeable period;

(*k*) the form of the certificate referred to in paragraph (3).

(3) The trustee of a pension funds pooling scheme shall also be responsible for providing within three months after the end of each accounting period of the scheme to each participant in the scheme in that period, a certificate in relation to that participant showing the information specified in paragraph (4).

(4) The information specified in this paragraph is—

(*a*) the amount of the income agreed with the officer of the Board under paragraph (2)(*a*)(ii) which is attributable to that participant for the accounting period concerned;

(*b*) the amount (if any) agreed with the officer of the Board under paragraph (2)(*b*) to be chargeable under Schedule A which is attributable to that participant for the accounting period concerned;

(*c*) the amount (if any) agreed with the officer of the Board under paragraph (2)(*c*) to be chargeable under Schedule D which is attributable to that participant for the accounting period concerned;

(*d*) the amount (if any) agreed with the officer of the Board under paragraph (2)(*d*) to be chargeable under Schedule F which is attributable to that participant for the accounting period concerned;

(*e*) where in the accounting period concerned an event occurs that gives rise to a balancing allowance or a balancing charge under the 1990 Act, the amount (if any) of that allowance or charge agreed with the officer of the Board under paragraph (2)(*e*)(ii) which is attributable to that participant for that period;

(*f*) the amount (if any) of the expenditure agreed with the officer of the Board under paragraph (2)(*g*) which is attributable to that participant for the accounting period concerned;

(*g*) where applicable, the parts of amounts of sale, insurance, salvage or compensation moneys in relation to events occurring in the accounting period concerned, and of the disposal values of plant and machinery agreed with the officer of the Board under paragraph (2)(*h*) and (*j*), which are attributable to that participant for that period.

(5) In this regulation any reference to a participant in the scheme in relation to an accounting period includes a reference to a participant which, although not a participant throughout that period, was a participant at some time during that period.

11 Duties of trustee of a pension funds pooling scheme—annual provision of information

(1) Where, at the end of a tax year, a unit trust scheme has the characteristics specified in regulation 4(3), the trustee of that scheme shall, within three months after the end of that year ("the relevant year"), provide to an officer of the Board, in a form authorised, or in the form provided, by the Board—

(*a*) the information concerning each participant in the scheme specified in paragraph (2), or, as the case may be, paragraph (3), and

(*b*) a declaration made by the trustee and signed by him or, if the trustee is a company, signed by the company secretary or other person authorised by the company for that purpose, that the information so provided is correct to the best of the declarant's knowledge and belief.

(2) As regards a participant in the relevant year which is [a registered pension scheme][2] or a superannuation fund, the information is—

(*a*) the full title of the scheme or fund;

(*b*) the Board's reference number relating to the scheme or fund;

(*c*) a copy of any certificate referred to in regulation 10(3) which was supplied by the trustee to the participant in respect of any accounting period of the scheme ending in or at the end of the relevant year;

(*d*) where the trustee has in the relevant year received a notice given by the Board under regulation 7(8) or (9) revoking or withdrawing approval in relation to that participant—

(i) a copy of the notice given to the participant by the trustee under regulation 9(8);

(ii) the date or dates (if any), whether during the relevant year or subsequently but prior to the making of the declaration under paragraph (1)(*b*), on which units held by the participant, or by a nominee on its behalf, at the time the notice given by the Board was received by the trustee, were sold or cancelled;

(iii) if applicable, the date on which the participant ceased to participate in the scheme;

(*e*) where the trustee has not, whether in the relevant year or subsequently but prior to the making of the declaration under paragraph (1)(*b*), received a notice given by the Board under regulation 7(8) or (9) revoking or withdrawing approval in relation to that participant, confirmation that the participant had not at any time in that year received notification from the Board that it was not [a registered pension scheme][2] or, as the case may be, a superannuation fund.

(3) As regards a participant in the relevant year which is [a recognised overseas pension scheme][1], the information is—

(*a*) the full title of the scheme;

(*b*) details of any matters falling within sub-paragraphs (*b*) to [(*f*)][3] of regulation 7(3) which, by reason of changes to those matters having occurred in the relevant year, differ from—

(i) the details of those matters which were included in the trustee's application under regulation 7(1) in respect of the participant, or

(ii) (if applicable) the details of those matters which were most recently provided in accordance with this sub-paragraph in respect of the participant in relation to tax years ending before the relevant year;

(*c*) the like information as is specified in paragraph (2)(*c*);

(*d*) if applicable, the like information as is specified in paragraph (2)(*d*).

(4) As regards a participant in the relevant year which is [a recognised overseas pension scheme][1], an officer of the Board may, at any time after the form referred to in paragraph (1) has been provided to him by the trustee of the scheme, by notice require the trustee to furnish him, within such time (not being less than 21 days) as may be provided by the notice, with a statement in writing setting out details of matters—

(*a*) falling within sub-paragraphs (*b*) to [(*f*)][3] of regulation 7(3) with respect to that scheme, and

(*b*) subsisting at any time during the relevant year.

(5) In this regulation any reference to a participant in the relevant year which is [a registered pension scheme][2] or a superannuation fund or [a recognised overseas pension scheme][1] (as the case may be)—

(*a*) includes a reference to a participant which, although not a participant throughout that year, was a participant at some time during that year, and

(*b*) includes a reference to a participant which is no longer [a registered pension scheme][2] or a superannuation fund or [a recognised overseas pension scheme][1] but which was such a scheme or fund at the time when notice of approval was given by the Board to the trustee of the scheme in accordance with regulation 7(5).

Amendments—[1] Words in paras (3), (4), (5) substituted, by the Taxation of Pension Schemes (Consequential Amendments) Order, SI 2006/745 art 23(1), (3) with effect from 6 April 2006.

[2] Words in paras (2), (5) substituted by SI 2006/745 art 23(1), (6)(*a*) with effect from 6 April 2006.

[3] Words in paras (3)(*b*), (4)(*a*) substituted by SI 2006/745 art 23(1), (7) with effect from 6 April 2006.

1996/1654

INCOME TAX (PAYMENTS ON ACCOUNT) REGULATIONS 1996

Made by the Commissioners of Inland Revenue under TMA 1970 s 59A(1)

Made . . . .*26 June 1996*

Laid before the House of Commons . . . .*26 June 1996*

Coming into Force . . . .*17 July 1996*

Commentary—*Simon's Taxes* **E1.251.**

1—(1) These Regulations may be cited as the Income Tax (Payments on Account) Regulations 1996 and shall come into force on 17th July 1996.

(2) Regulation 3 shall have effect as respects the year 1996–97 and subsequent years of assessment.

(3) Regulation 4 shall have effect as respects the year 1997–98 and subsequent years of assessment.

2 In these Regulations "subsection (1)" means subsection (1) of section 59A of the Taxes Management Act 1970.

3 The prescribed amount for the purposes of paragraph (*c*) of subsection (1) is the amount of [£1,000][1].

Amendment—[1] Figure substituted for figure £500 by the Income Tax (Payments on Account) (Amendment) Regulations, SI 2008/838 reg 2 with effect from 6 April 2009, for the year 2009–10 and subsequent years of assessment.

4 The prescribed proportion for the purposes of paragraph (*d*) of subsection (1), that is to say, the proportion which the relevant amount as mentioned in paragraph (*c*) of subsection (1) bears to the assessed amount as mentioned in paragraph (*b*) of subsection (1), is the proportion of one to [five][1].

Amendments—[1] Amount in regulation 4 substituted by the Income Tax (Payments on Account) (Amendment) Regulations, SI 1997/2491 with effect from 7 November 1997.

1996/1826

MANUFACTURED OVERSEAS DIVIDENDS (FRENCH INDEMNITY PAYMENTS) REGULATIONS 1996

Made by the Treasury under TA 1988 Sch 23A paras 1(1), 8

Made . . . .*12 July 1996*
Laid before the House of Commons . . . .*15 July 1996*
Coming into Force . . . .*1 August 1996*

Commentary—*Simon's Taxes* **D9.729.**

1 Citation and commencement

These Regulations may be cited as the Manufactured Overseas Dividends (French Indemnity Payments) Regulations 1996 and shall come into force on 1st August 1996.

2 Interpretation

(1) In these Regulations—

"French equities" means shares of any company resident in France;

"French indemnity payment" means a payment, representative of a dividend on French equities, that a party to a transaction for the sale of those equities is required, under the rules of the Society of French Stock Exchanges, to make to the other party to that transaction;

"manufactured overseas dividend" shall be construed in accordance with paragraph 4(1) of Schedule 23A;

"Schedule 23A" means Schedule 23A to the Taxes Act;

"the Tax Acts" has the meaning given by section 831(2) of the Taxes Act;

"the Taxes Act" means the Income and Corporation Taxes Act 1988.

(2) References in these Regulations to "the dividend concerned" are references to the dividend of which a French indemnity payment is representative.

[(3) For the purposes of the Income Tax Acts references in these Regulations to "the sale and repurchase of French equities" include an arrangement which—

(*a*) involves the sale of French equities and the subsequent purchase of French equities, and

(*b*) is a repo.

(4) In paragraph (3) "repo" shall be construed in accordance with section 569 of the Income Tax Act 2007 (read, if appropriate, with the modifications made by the Sale and Repurchase of Securities (Modification of Enactments) Regulations 2007).

(5) For the purposes of the Corporation Tax Acts references in these Regulations to "the sale and repurchase of French equities" include an arrangement which—

(*a*) involves the sale of French equities and the subsequent purchase of French equities, and

(*b*) is a debtor repo, a debtor quasi-repo, a creditor repo or a creditor quasi-repo.

(6) In paragraph (5) "debtor repo", "debtor quasi-repo", "creditor repo" and "creditor quasi-repo" shall be construed in accordance with Schedule 13 to the Finance Act 2007 (read, if appropriate, with the modifications made by the Sale and Repurchase of Securities (Modification of Schedule 13 to the Finance Act 2007) Regulations 2007).][1]

Cross reference—FA 2007 Sch 13 para 14(6) (an arrangement is in force from the time when the securities are initially sold until the earlier of the time when the relevant repurchase takes place, and the time when it becomes apparent that that repurchase will not take place).

Amendments—[1] Paras (3)–(6) substituted for previous para (3) by the Sale and Repurchase of Securities (Amendment of Instruments) Order, SI 2007/2484 art 2 with effect in relation to arrangements that come into force on or after 1 October 2007: SI 2007/2484 art 1(1). FA 2007 Sch 13 para 14(6) applies for the purpose of determining the times at which an arrangement is in force: SI 2007/2484 art 1(2).

3 Tax treatment of French indemnity payments

(1) This regulation applies where a person makes or receives a payment of a manufactured overseas dividend that is a French indemnity payment, other than a payment which arises from an arrangement for the sale and repurchase of French equities.

(2) For the purposes of the Tax Acts—

(*a*) [paragraph 4][1] of Schedule 23A shall not apply in relation to the indemnity payment, but where the maker of the payment receives the dividend concerned, he (and no other person) shall be chargeable to tax in respect of that dividend;

(*b*) subject to paragraph (3)—

(i) relief by way of deduction in computing profits or gains, or deduction or set off against income or total profits, shall not be given under any provision of the Tax Acts in respect of the indemnity payment to the maker of the payment, and

(ii) the indemnity payment shall not be chargeable to tax.

(3) For the purposes of the Tax Acts and the Taxation of Chargeable Gains Act 1992 the amount paid or payable in respect of the sale of the French equities to which the dividend concerned relates shall, as respects both the seller and the purchaser of those equities, be taken as reduced by the amount of the indemnity payment.

(4) Any entitlement to relief under Part XVIII of the Taxes Act (double taxation relief) in respect of the indemnity payment shall be extinguished.

Amendments—[1] Words in para (2)(*a*) substituted by the Manufactured Overseas Dividends (French Indemnity Payments) (Amendment) Regulations, SI 1996/2642 reg 2, with effect from 6 November 1996.

4—(1) This regulation applies where a person makes or receives a payment of a manufactured overseas dividend that is a French indemnity payment arising from an arrangement for the sale and repurchase of French equities.

(2) For the purposes of the Tax Acts—

(*a*) [paragraph 4][1] of Schedule 23A shall not apply in relation to the indemnity payment, but where the maker of the payment receives the dividend concerned, he (and no other person) shall be chargeable to tax in respect of that dividend;

(*b*) the indemnity payment shall be treated as an annual payment, within section 349(1) of the Taxes Act, but so that no amount is required to be deducted on account of income tax from the amount of the payment, or accounted for under section 350 of that Act;

(*c*) in relation to a recipient of the indemnity payment, or a person claiming title to it through or under him, who is resident in the United Kingdom or, if not so resident, is carrying on business through a branch or agency in the United Kingdom, the payment shall be treated as if it were an overseas dividend of an amount equal to the amount of the payment, but without prejudice to paragraph (3).

(3) Any entitlement to relief under Part XVIII of the Taxes Act in respect of the indemnity payment shall be extinguished.

Amendments—[1] Words in para (2)(*a*) substituted by the Manufactured Overseas Dividends (French Indemnity Payments) (Amendment) Regulations, SI 1996/2642 reg 2, with effect from 6 November 1996.

1996/2396

TAXATION OF BENEFITS UNDER PILOT SCHEMES (EARNINGS TOP-UP) ORDER 1996

Made by the Treasury under FA 1996 s 151(1)(a), (2), (5), (7)

Made . . . . *13 September 1996*

Laid before the House of Commons . . . . *16 September 1996*

Coming into Force . . . . *8 October 1996*

1 Citation, commencement and effect

(1) This Order may be cited as the Taxation of Benefits under Pilot Schemes (Earnings Top-up) Order 1996 and shall come into force on 8th October 1996.

(2) This Order shall have effect in relation to amounts of Earnings Top-up payable on or after 8th October 1996.

2 Interpretation

In this Order—

"benefit" shall be construed in accordance with section 151(6) of the Finance Act 1996;

"Earnings Top-up" means the benefit payable under that name by virtue of a Government pilot scheme;

"Government pilot scheme" has the meaning given by subsections (3) and (4) of section 151 of the Finance Act 1996.

3 Exemption of Earnings Top-up from income tax

The Income Tax Acts shall have effect in relation to any amount of Earnings Top-up as if it were wholly exempt from income tax and, accordingly, to be disregarded in computing the amount of any receipts brought into account for income tax purposes.

1996/2991

INSURANCE COMPANIES (RESERVES) (TAX) REGULATIONS 1996

Made by the Treasury under TA 1988 ss 444BA(10), 444BB(1), (3), (4), (5), 444BC, 444BD(1), (4), (5)

Made 27 .... November 1996
Laid before the House of Commons .... 28 November 1996
Coming into Force .... 23 December 1996

Revocation—These Regulations revoked by the Lloyd's Underwriters (Transitional Equalisation Reserves) (Tax) Regulations, SI 2015/1983 reg 5(*a*) with effect from 1 January 2016.

PART I
GENERAL

1 *Citation, commencement and effect*

These Regulations may be cited as the Insurance Companies (Reserves) (Tax) Regulations 1996, shall come into force on 23rd December 1996, and shall have effect for accounting periods of insurance companies ending on or after that day.[1]

Amendments—[1] These Regulations revoked by the Lloyd's Underwriters (Transitional Equalisation Reserves) (Tax) Regulations, SI 2015/1983 reg 5(*a*) with effect from 1 January 2016.

2 *Interpretation*

(1) In these Regulations unless the context otherwise requires—

"the Board" means the [Commissioners for Her Majesty's Revenue and Customs][5];

. . . [5]

["company tax return" has the meaning given by paragraph 3(1) of Schedule 18 to the Finance Act 1998;][2]

"credit insurance business" has the meaning given by subsection (7) of section 444BD;

"credit insurance equalisation reserve" means a reserve which is an equivalent reserve for the purposes of section 444BD by virtue of subsection (3) of that section;

"double taxation relief" has the meaning given by subsection (6) of section 444BB;

["EEA firm" means an EEA firm of the kind mentioned in paragraph 5(d) [or *(da)*][5] of Schedule 3 to the Financial Services and Markets Act 2000;][1]

"equivalent reserve" shall be construed in accordance with section 444BD;

["equalisation reserve rules" means the rules in [Chapter 1.4 of INSPRU][5] made by the Financial Services Authority under the Financial Services and Markets Act 2000;][3]

["INSPRU" means the Prudential Sourcebook for Insurers made by the Financial Services Authority under the Financial Services and Markets Act 2000][5]

. . . [2]

. . . [5]

. . . [5]

["paragraph 58 method of accounting on a non-annual basis" means the method of accounting on a non-annual basis described in paragraph 58 of Schedule 3 to the Large and Medium-sized Companies and Groups (Accounts and Reports) Regulations 2008;][5]

"return period" means the period covered in a document prepared by an insurance company for the purposes of section [9.3 of the Prudential Sourcebook (Insurers)][2];

. . . [2]

"section 444BA", "section 444BB", "section 444BC" and "section 444BD" means sections 444BA, 444BB, 444BC and 444BD respectively of the Taxes Act;

"the Taxes Act" means the Income and Corporation Taxes Act 1988;

["Treaty firm" means a firm which has permission under paragraph 4 of Schedule 4 to the Financial Services and Markets Act 2000 (as a result of qualifying for authorisation under paragraph 2 of that Schedule) to effect or carry out contracts of insurance in the United Kingdom and, in this definition, "contract of insurance" has the meaning given by Article 3(1) of the Financial Services and Markets Act 2000 (Regulated Activities) Order 2001;][1]

. . . [2]

(2) In these Regulations "statutory accounts", in relation to a company, means—

(*a*) *the annual accounts of the company prepared in accordance with [Part 15 of the Companies Act 2006][4], or*

(*b*) *if the company is not required to prepare such accounts, the accounts which it is required to keep under the law of its home state or, if it is not so required to keep accounts, such of its accounts as most closely correspond to accounts which it would have been required to prepare if the provisions of that Part applied to the company.*

(3) For the purposes of these Regulations a return period and an accounting period are related if any day falls within both the return period and the accounting period.[6]

Amendments—[1] Definition of "EEA firm" substituted for definition of "EC company", and definition of "Treaty firm" inserted, by the Financial Services and Markets Act 2000 (Consequential Amendments) (Taxes) Order, SI 2001/3629 art 147(1), (3), (9) with effect from 1 December 2001, immediately after the coming into force of the Financial Services and Markets Act 2000 ss 411, 432(1), Sch 20 (and SI 2001/3629 Pts 1 and 2).

[2] Definition of "company tax return" and "equalisation reserve rules" inserted, definition of "the Management Act", "section 34A regulations, and "the 1982 Act" revoked, and words in the definition of "return period" substituted, by SI 2001/3629 art 147(1), (2), (4)–(8), (10), (11) with effect for periods of account ending after 30 November 2001.

[3] Definition of "equalisation reserve rules" substituted by the Insurance Companies (Reserves) (Tax) (Amendment) Regulations, SI 2004/3260 with effect in respect of accounting periods of insurance companies ending on or after 31 December 2004.

[4] Words in para (2)(*a*) substituted by the Companies Act 2006 (Consequential Amendments) (Taxes and National Insurance) Order, SI 2008/954 art 46 with effect from 6 April 2008.

[5] In para (2), in definition of "the Board" words substituted, definition of "branch" revoked, in definition of "EEA firm" words inserted, in definition of "equalisation reserve rules" words substituted, definitions of "paragraph 52 method of accounting on a non-annual basis" and "the Prudential Sourcebook (Insurers)" revoked, definition of "INSPRU" and "paragraph 58 method of accounting on a non-annual basis" inserted, by the Insurance Companies (Reserves) (Tax) (Amendment) Regulations, SI 2008/2679 regs 2, 3 with effect in relation to accounting periods beginning on or after 6 April 2008 and ending on or after 30 October 2008.

[6] These Regulations revoked by the Lloyd's Underwriters (Transitional Equalisation Reserves) (Tax) Regulations, SI 2015/1983 reg 5(*a*) with effect from 1 January 2016.

3 *Differing treatments of reserves*

(1) This regulation applies in any case where for any accounting period—

(*a*) *an insurance company maintains any reserve to which these Regulations apply, and*

(*b*) *the amount of that reserve for the purposes of the Tax Acts is different from the amount of that reserve as maintained for regulatory purposes.*

(2) A separate computation of the amount of the reserve for the purposes of the Tax Acts and of the amount of the reserve as maintained for regulatory purposes shall be made for each accounting period until, in any later accounting period, the two computations produce the same opening balance for the reserve.

(3) For the purposes of this regulation a reserve is maintained by a company for regulatory purposes if it is maintained—

(*a*) *by virtue of [equalisation reserves rules]*[1]*, or*

(*b*) *for the purposes of the company's statutory accounts, or*

(*c*) *for the purposes of any credit insurance business in accordance with requirements specified in subsection (3) of section 444BD.*[2]

Amendments—[1] Words in sub-para (3)(*a*) substituted by the Financial Services and Markets Act 2000 (Consequential Amendments) (Taxes) Order, SI 2001/3629 art 151 with effect for periods of account ending after 30 November 2001.

[2] These Regulations revoked by the Lloyd's Underwriters (Transitional Equalisation Reserves) (Tax) Regulations, SI 2015/1983 reg 5(*a*) with effect from 1 January 2016.

PART II
EQUALISATION RESERVES, ETC

OVERALL SCOPE

4 *Scope of this Part*

(1) Subject to paragraph (2), this Part of these Regulations applies to—

(*a*) *any equalisation reserve which an insurance company is required to maintain by virtue of [equalisation reserves rules]*[1]*, and*

(*b*) *any reserve which is an equivalent reserve by virtue of subsection (2) of section 444BD.*

(2) This part of these Regulations does not apply to any credit insurance equalisation reserve.[2]

Amendments—[1] Words in sub-para (1)(*a*) substituted by the Financial Services and Markets Act 2000 (Consequential Amendments) (Taxes) Order, SI 2001/3629 art 151 with effect for periods of account ending after 30 November 2001.

[2] These Regulations revoked by the Lloyd's Underwriters (Transitional Equalisation Reserves) (Tax) Regulations, SI 2015/1983 reg 5(*a*) with effect from 1 January 2016.

ACCOUNTING ON A NON-ANNUAL BASIS

5 *Non-annual accounts: tax returns prepared on an annual basis*

. . .

Amendments—This regulation revoked by the Insurance Companies (Reserves) (Tax) (Amendment) Regulations, SI 2008/2679 regs 2, 4 with effect in relation to accounting periods beginning on or after 6 April 2008 and ending on or after 30 October 2008.

These Regulations revoked by the Lloyd's Underwriters (Transitional Equalisation Reserves) (Tax) Regulations, SI 2015/1983 reg 5(*a*) with effect from 1 January 2016.

GENERAL PROVISIONS

6 *Companies carrying on mutual business and business other than mutual business*

(1) This regulation applies in any case where an insurance company which, in accordance with [equalisation reserves rules][1], is required to make transfers into or out of an equalisation reserve in respect of any business carried on by that company for any accounting period, is carrying on both mutual business and business other than mutual business for the whole or any part of that period.

(2) Paragraphs (*a*) and (*b*) of subsection (2) of section 444BA shall be modified so as to provide that, for the purposes of corporation tax, the amounts of the net premiums earned, the net premiums written and the net claims incurred which, in accordance with [equalisation reserves rules][1], are used for the purpose of computing the amounts transferred into or out of the equalisation reserve or the amount of the maximum reserve in relation to the equalisation reserve for the accounting period in question, shall be restricted to the amounts attributed to business other than mutual business.

(3) For the purposes of corporation tax, the modifications specified in paragraph (2) shall be made before subsections (4) to (6) of section 444BA are applied.

(4) In paragraph (2) "net premiums earned", "net premiums written", "net claims incurred" and "maximum reserve" have the meanings given by [equalisation reserves rules][1], [2]

Amendments—[1] Words in paras (1), (2) and (4) substituted by the Financial Services and Markets Act 2000 (Consequential Amendments) (Taxes) Order, SI 2001/3629 art 151 with effect for periods of account ending after 30 November 2001.

[2] These Regulations revoked by the Lloyd's Underwriters (Transitional Equalisation Reserves) (Tax) Regulations, SI 2015/1983 reg 5(*a*) with effect from 1 January 2016.

7 *[EEA firms and Treaty firms]*

(1) This regulation applies in any case where for any accounting period—

(*a*) *an equivalent reserve is maintained, otherwise than by virtue of [equalisation reserves rules][3], by an [EEA firm or a Treaty firm][1] carrying on business in the United Kingdom through a [permanent establishment][5], and*

(*b*) *the three conditions specified in paragraphs (2) to (4) are satisfied.*

(2) The first condition is that the [permanent establishment][5] in the United Kingdom has submitted, together with its [company tax return][2], a balance sheet ("the [permanent establishment][5] balance sheet") in respect of the trade of the [permanent establishment][5].

(3) The second condition is that the [permanent establishment][5] balance sheet includes as a liability an amount in respect of an equalisation reserve which is equal to the amount which it would have been required to include as a liability in respect of an equalisation reserve maintained by virtue of [equalisation reserves rules][3] if the [permanent establishment][5] had been subject to such [rules][4].

(4) The third condition is that a balance sheet drawn up on the same day as the [permanent establishment][5] balance sheet for the purposes of the company's statutory accounts ("the company balance sheet"), either—

(*a*) *includes as a liability an amount in respect of an equalisation reserve equal to or greater than the amount in respect of the equalisation reserve included in the [permanent establishment][5] balance sheet, or*

(*b*) *in a case where the amount in respect of the equalisation reserve included in the [permanent establishment][5] balance sheet exceeds the amount in respect of the equalisation reserve included in the company balance sheet, shows the amount of the excess in the company balance sheet otherwise than as funds belonging to, or available for distribution either immediately or prospectively to, the proprietors of the company.*

(5) For the purpose of calculating the amount of the excess referred to in paragraph (4), any amount in the company balance sheet denominated in a currency other than sterling is to be translated into sterling at the London closing exchange rate on the last day of the accounting period in question.

(6) Section 444BA shall have effect, subject to the modification specified in paragraph (7), in relation to the equalisation reserve included in the [permanent establishment][5] balance sheet as it has effect in relation to equalisation reserves maintained by virtue of [equalisation reserves rules][3].

(7) Section 444BA shall be modified so as to provide in addition that in any case where, after the conditions specified in paragraphs (2) to (4) have been satisfied in an earlier accounting period, any of those conditions ceases to be satisfied in a later accounting period, then, for the purposes of the Tax Acts—

(*a*) *any balance which exists in the reserve at the end of the later accounting period shall be deemed to have been transferred out of the reserve immediately before the end of that accounting period;*

(*b*) *that transfer shall be deemed to be a transfer in respect of that company's business for that accounting period; and*

(*c*) *the amount of the reserve shall thereupon be deemed to be nil.*[6]

Amendments—[1] Cross-heading and words in sub-para (1)(*a*) substituted by the Financial Services and Markets Act 2000 (Consequential Amendments) (Taxes) Order, SI 2001/3629 art 149(1), (2) with effect from 1 December 2001, immediately after the coming into force of the Financial Services and Markets Act 2000 ss 411, 432(1), Sch 20 (and SI 2001/3629 Pts 1 and 2).

[2] Words in para (2) substituted by SI 2001/3629 art 149(3) with effect for periods of account ending after 30 November 2001.

[3] Words in paras (1)(*a*), (3) and (6) substituted by the Financial Services and Markets Act 2000 (Consequential Amendments) (Taxes) Order, SI 2001/3629 art 151 with effect for periods of account ending after 30 November 2001.

[4] Word in para (3) substituted by the Financial Services and Markets Act 2000 (Consequential Amendments) (Taxes) Order, SI 2002/1409 art 5 with effect from 2 July 2002.

[5] Words substituted throughout this regulation, by the Insurance Companies (Reserves) (Tax) (Amendment) Regulations, SI 2008/2679 regs 2, 5 with effect in relation to accounting periods beginning on or after 6 April 2008 and ending on or after 30 October 2008.

[6] These Regulations revoked by the Lloyd's Underwriters (Transitional Equalisation Reserves) (Tax) Regulations, SI 2015/1983 reg 5(*a*) with effect from 1 January 2016.

8 Certain insurance business carried on outside the United Kingdom

(1) [Subject to regulation 8B][1] this regulation applies in any case where for any accounting period—

(*a*) *an equivalent reserve is maintained, otherwise than by virtue of [equalisation reserves rules]*[3]*, in respect of any insurance business* . . .[2] *which is carried on outside the United Kingdom by a company resident in the United Kingdom, and*

(*b*) *the condition specified in paragraph (2) is satisfied.*

(2) The condition is that the company prepares statutory accounts in which the balance sheet includes as a liability an amount in respect of an equalisation reserve which is equal to the amount which it would have been required to include as a liability in respect of an equalisation reserve maintained by virtue of [equalisation reserves rules][3] if the company had been subject to such [rules][4].

(3) For the purpose of calculating the amount of the liability referred to in paragraph (2), any amount in the company balance sheet denominated in a currency other than sterling is to be translated into sterling at the London closing exchange rate on the last day of the accounting period in question.

(4) Section 444BA shall have effect, subject to the modification specified in paragraph (5), in relation to the equalisation reserve included in the statutory accounts as it has effect in relation to equalisation reserves maintained by virtue of [equalisation reserves rules][3].

(5) Section 444BA shall be modified so as to provide in addition that in any case where, after the condition specified in paragraph (2) has been satisfied in an earlier accounting period, that condition ceases to be satisfied in a later accounting period, then, for the purposes of the Tax Acts—

(*a*) *any balance which exists in the reserve at the end of the later accounting period shall be deemed to have been transferred out of the reserve immediately before the end of that accounting period;*

(*b*) *that transfer shall be deemed to be a transfer in respect of that company's business for that accounting period; and*

(*c*) *the amount of the reserve shall thereupon be deemed to be nil.*

[*(6)* In paragraph (1)(*a*) "insurance business" means business which consists of the effecting or carrying out of contracts of insurance and, for the purposes of this definition, "contract of insurance" has the meaning given by Article 3(1) of the Financial Services and Markets Act 2000 (Regulated Activities) Order 2001.][2, 5]

Modification—Group Relief for Overseas Losses (Modification of the Corporation Tax Acts for Non-resident Insurance Companies) (No 2) Regulations 2006, SI 2006/3389, reg 12 (modification of reg 8 in relation to an EEA general insurer). Note that SI 2006/3389 is revoked by SI 2008/2646 reg 5 with effect for accounting periods beginning on or after 28 October 2008.

Group Relief for Overseas Losses (Modification of the Corporation Tax Acts for Non-resident Insurance Companies) Regulations, SI 2008/2646 regs 2, 4 (modification of reg 8 so as to apply to EEA general insurers. This modification has effect for accounting periods beginning on or after 28 October 2008.).

Amendments—[1] Words inserted by the Non-resident Companies (General Insurance Business) Regulations, SI 1999/1408 reg 7(2) with effect from 10 June 1999.

[2] Words in sub-para (1)(*a*) revoked, and para (6) added, by the Financial Services and Markets Act 2000 (Consequential Amendments) (Taxes) Order, SI 2001/3629 art 150 with effect from 1 December 2001, immediately after the coming into force of the Financial Services and Markets Act 2000 ss 411, 432(1), Sch 20 (and SI 2001/3629 Pts 1 and 2).

[3] Words in paras (1)(*a*), (2) and (4) substituted by the Financial Services and Markets Act 2000 (Consequential Amendments) (Taxes) Order, SI 2001/3629 art 151 with effect for periods of account ending after 30 November 2001.

[4] Word in para (2) substituted by the Financial Services and Markets Act 2000 (Consequential Amendments) (Taxes) Order, SI 2002/1409 art 5 with effect from 2 July 2002.

[5] These Regulations revoked by the Lloyd's Underwriters (Transitional Equalisation Reserves) (Tax) Regulations, SI 2015/1983 reg 5(*a*) with effect from 1 January 2016.

8A [Certain insurance business carried on outside the United Kingdom by a controlled foreign company—non-annual accounts but returns prepared on an annual basis

(1) Subject to regulation 8B, this regulation applies in any case where—

(*a*) *paragraphs (1) and (2) of regulation 8 apply in respect of an accounting period of a [CFC (within the meaning of Part 9A of the Taxation (International and Other Provisions) Act 2010)]*[4]*, [and]*[3]

(*b*) *the statutory accounts drawn up by the [CFC]*[4] *for that period use a [paragraph 58]*[3] *method of accounting on a non-annual basis* . . .[3]

(*c*) . . .[3]

(2) Paragraph (3) of regulation 8 shall apply in relation to this regulation as it applies in relation to that regulation.

(3) Section 444BA shall have effect, subject to the modifications specified in paragraph (5) of regulation 8 and in paragraph (4) of this regulation, in relation to the equalisation reserve included in the statutory accounts as it has effect in relation to equalisation reserves maintained by virtue of [equalisation reserves rules][2].

(4) The operation of paragraphs (*a*) and (*b*) of subsection (2) of section 444BA shall be modified so as to provide that, for the purposes of the Tax Acts, the amounts which are transferred into or out of the equalisation reserve in respect of the [CFC's][4] business for the accounting period in question shall be the amounts which would have been transferred into or out of the equalisation reserve if [the CFC][4] had been required to maintain an equalisation reserve by reference to accounts prepared on an accident year basis.

(5) . . . [3]

[(6) For the purposes of paragraph (4), accounts are prepared on an accident year basis where the accounts and statements required to be deposited with the Financial Services Authority pursuant to Chapter 9 of IPRU(INS) are prepared using Forms 21, 22 and 23 prescribed by the Accounts and Statements Rules contained in that Chapter.][3]

[(7) For the purposes of paragraph (6), "IPRU(INS)" means the Interim Prudential Sourcebook for Insurers made by the Financial Services Authority under the Financial Services and Markets Act 2000.][3]][1], [5]

Amendments—[1] Reg 8A inserted by the Non-resident Companies (General Insurance Business) Regulations, SI 1999/1408 reg 7(3) with effect from 10 June 1999.

[2] Words in para (3) substituted by the Financial Services and Markets Act 2000 (Consequential Amendments) (Taxes) Order, SI 2001/3629 art 151 with effect for periods of account ending after 30 November 2001.

[3] In para (1)(*a*), word inserted, in para (1)(*b*), words substituted and word revoked, paras (1)(*c*), (5) revoked, para (6) substituted, and para (7) inserted, by the Insurance Companies (Reserves) (Tax) (Amendment) Regulations, SI 2008/2679 regs 2, 6 with effect in relation to accounting periods beginning on or after 6 April 2008 and ending on or after 30 October 2008.

[4] In sub-para (1)(*a*), (*b*), words substituted for words "controlled foreign company"; and in sub-para (4), words substituted for words "controlled foreign company's" and "the company", by FA 2012 s 180, Sch 20 paras 46, 47 with effect in relation to accounting periods of CFCs beginning on or after 1 January 2013. This is subject to savings in FA 2012 Sch 20 para 50(9) which provides, broadly, that the amendments in question will not take effect until an accounting period under the new CFC rules in TIOPA 2010 Part 9A begins.

[5] These Regulations revoked by the Lloyd's Underwriters (Transitional Equalisation Reserves) (Tax) Regulations, SI 2015/1983 reg 5(*a*) with effect from 1 January 2016.

8B [Disapplication of regulations 8 and 8A where controlled foreign company prepares non-annual accounts and final replacement of the technical provision does not take place in conformity with the Companies Act

Regulations 8 and 8A shall not apply in any case where for an accounting period a [CFC (within the meaning of Part 9A of the Taxation (International and Other Provisions) Act 2010)][3]

- (*a*) *draws up its statutory accounts for that period using a [paragraph 58][2] method of accounting on a non-annual basis, and*
- (*b*) *the final replacement of the technical provision, as described in sub-paragraph (4) of that paragraph does not take place on or before the end of the year referred to in that sub-paragraph as the third year following the underwriting year.]*[1], [4]

Amendments—[1] Reg 8B inserted by the Non-resident Companies (General Insurance Business) Regulations, SI 1999/1408 reg 7(2) with effect from 10 June 1999.

[2] In para (*a*), words substituted by the Insurance Companies (Reserves) (Tax) (Amendment) Regulations, SI 2008/2679 regs 2, 7 with effect in relation to accounting periods beginning on or after 6 April 2008 and ending on or after 30 October 2008.

[3] Words substituted for words "controlled foreign company" by FA 2012 s 180, Sch 20 paras 46, 48 with effect in relation to accounting periods of CFCs beginning on or after 1 January 2013. This is subject to savings in FA 2012 Sch 20 para 50(9) which provides, broadly, that the amendments in question will not take effect until an accounting period under the new CFC rules in TIOPA 2010 Part 9A begins.

[4] These Regulations revoked by the Lloyd's Underwriters (Transitional Equalisation Reserves) (Tax) Regulations, SI 2015/1983 reg 5(*a*) with effect from 1 January 2016.

9 United Kingdom branches of companies not resident in the United Kingdom which maintain equalisation reserves by virtue of [equalisation reserves rules]

(1) If the three conditions prescribed in paragraphs (2) to (4) below are satisfied, section 444BA shall have effect in the case of an equalisation reserve maintained by an insurance company which—

- (*a*) *is not resident in the United Kingdom, and*
- (*b*) *carries on business in the United Kingdom through a [permanent establishment]*[2].

(2) The first condition is that the [permanent establishment][2] in the United Kingdom has submitted, together with its [company tax return][2], a balance sheet ("the [permanent establishment][2] balance sheet") in respect of the trade of the [permanent establishment][2].

(3) The second condition is that the [permanent establishment][2] balance sheet includes as a liability an amount in respect of an equalisation reserve maintained by virtue of [equalisation reserves rules][1].

(4) The third condition is that a balance sheet drawn up on the same day as the [permanent establishment][2] balance sheet for the purposes of the company's statutory accounts ("the company balance sheet"), either—

- (*a*) *includes as a liability an amount in respect of an equalisation reserve equal to or greater than the amount in respect of the equalisation reserve included in the [permanent establishment]*[2] *balance sheet, or*
- (*b*) *in a case where the amount in respect of the equalisation reserve included in the [permanent establishment]*[2] *balance sheet exceeds the amount in respect of the equalisation reserve*

included in the company balance sheet, shows the amount of the excess in the company balance sheet otherwise than as funds belonging to, or available for distribution either immediately or prospectively to, the proprietors of the company.

(5) For the purpose of calculating the amount of the excess referred to in paragraph (4), any amount in the company balance sheet denominated in a currency other than sterling is to be translated into sterling at the London closing exchange rate on the last day of the accounting period in question.

(6) Where, after the conditions prescribed in paragraphs (2) to (4) have been satisfied in an earlier accounting period, any of those conditions ceases to be satisfied in a later accounting period, then, for the purposes of the Tax Acts—

(*a*) *any balance which exists in the reserve at the end of the later accounting period shall be deemed to have been transferred out of the reserve immediately before the end of that accounting period;*

(*b*) *that transfer shall be deemed to be a transfer in respect of that company's business for that accounting period; and*

(*c*) *the amount of the reserve shall thereupon be deemed to be nil.*[3]

Amendments—[1] Words in cross-heading and para (3) substituted by the Financial Services and Markets Act 2000 (Consequential Amendments) (Taxes) Order, SI 2001/3629 art 151 with effect for periods of account ending after 30 November 2001.

[2] Words substituted throughout this regulation, and in para (2), words substituted, by the Insurance Companies (Reserves) (Tax) (Amendment) Regulations, SI 2008/2679 regs 2, 8 with effect in relation to accounting periods beginning on or after 6 April 2008 and ending on or after 30 October 2008.

[3] These Regulations revoked by the Lloyd's Underwriters (Transitional Equalisation Reserves) (Tax) Regulations, SI 2015/1983 reg 5(*a*) with effect from 1 January 2016.

10 Double taxation relief

(1) This regulation applies in any case where an insurance company which, in accordance with [equalisation reserves rules][1], is required to make transfers into or out of an equalisation reserve in respect of any business carried on by that company for any accounting period, is carrying on any business by reference to which double taxation relief is afforded in respect of any income or gains.

(2) Paragraphs (*a*) and (*b*) of subsection (2) of section 444BA shall be modified so as—

(*a*) *to require that the amounts which, in accordance with [equalisation reserves rules][1], are transferred into or out of the equalisation reserve in respect of the company's business for the accounting period in question shall be apportioned amongst each [permanent establishment][2] outside the United Kingdom through which the company carries on business and business which is not carried on through [permanent establishments][2] outside the United Kingdom; and*

(*b*) *to provide that only those amounts which, pursuant to sub-paragraph (a), are apportioned to* each [permanent establishment][2] outside the United Kingdom through which the company carries on business shall be brought into account for the purposes of computing the profits or losses by reference to which double taxation relief is afforded.

(3) The apportionment of each transfer into the equalisation reserve which is required by this regulation shall be made in accordance with the formula—

$$\frac{A \times B}{C}$$

where—

A is the amount which, in accordance with [equalisation reserves rules][1], is transferred into the equalisation reserve in respect of the company's business for the accounting period in question;

B is the amount of net premiums written by reference to which A is calculated that is attributable to business carried on through the [permanent establishment][2] outside the United Kingdom for the accounting period in question; and

C is the amount of net premiums written by reference to which A is calculated for the accounting period in question.

(4) In paragraph (3) "net premiums written" means gross premiums written net of reinsurance premiums payable under reinsurance ceded.

(5) The apportionment of each transfer out of the equalisation reserve which is required by this regulation shall be made in accordance with the formula—

$$\frac{D \times E}{F}$$

where—

D is the amount which, in accordance with [equalisation reserves rules][1], is transferred out of the equalisation reserve in respect of the company's business for the accounting period in question;

E is the amount of claims attributable to business carried on through the [permanent establishment][2] outside the United Kingdom that is to be taken into account in determining whether, by comparison with premiums, any transfer out of the equalisation reserve needs to be made for the period in question; and

F is the amount of claims to be taken into account in determining whether, by comparison with premiums, any transfer out of the equalisation reserve needs to be made for the period in question.

(6) Paragraph (7) applies where—

(*a*) *an insurance company carries on business through one or more branches outside the United Kingdom,*

(*b*) *an amount is transferred into an equalisation reserve in respect of the business of that company for any accounting period, and*

(*c*) *the company has made an election for the purposes of subsection (4) of section 444BA so that there is an unrelieved transfer in relation to that accounting period.*

(7) The company—

(*a*) *shall apportion the amount transferred into the equalisation reserve in accordance with paragraph (3) without having regard to the existence of the unrelieved transfer, and*

(*b*) *may then set the amount of the unrelieved transfer, or any part of that amount, against the amount transferred into the equalisation reserve for that accounting period (and the action of the company under this sub-paragraph is called "the allocation" in paragraph (8)).*

(8) The allocation may be made—

(*a*) *in such amounts, and*

(*b*) *in relation to such of the apportioned amounts transferred into the equalisation reserve pursuant to paragraph (7)(a)* (and whether in relation to business carried on in the United Kingdom or in relation to business which the company carries on through a [permanent establishment][2] outside the United Kingdom),

as the company thinks fit.

(9) Paragraph (10) applies where—

(*a*) *an insurance company carries on business through one or more branches outside the United Kingdom,*

(*b*) *an amount is transferred out of an equalisation reserve in respect of the business of that company for any accounting period, and*

(*c*) *the accounting period is one to which any amount representing one or more unrelieved transfers has been carried forward under subsection (4) of section 444BA.*

(10) The company—

(*a*) *shall ascertain the amount to which the rule mentioned in subsection (2)(b)* of section 444BA applies by virtue of the operation of subsection (5) of that section (in this paragraph and in paragraph (11) referred to as "the ascertained amount"), and

(*b*) *shall then apportion the ascertained amount.*

(11) Paragraph (5) shall apply for the purposes of the apportionment of the ascertained amount as it applies for the purposes of the apportionment of each transfer out of the equalisation reserve which is required by this regulation, with the modification that in the formula set out in that paragraph D shall be the ascertained amount.

(12) In paragraphs (6), (7) and (9) "unrelieved transfer" shall be construed in accordance with subsection (4) of section 444BA.[3]

Amendments—[1] Words in para (1), (2)(*a*), (3) and (5) substituted by the Financial Services and Markets Act 2000 (Consequential Amendments) (Taxes) Order, SI 2001/3629 art 151 with effect for periods of account ending after 30 November 2001.

[2] Words substituted throughout this regulation, and in para (2)(*a*), words substituted, by the Insurance Companies (Reserves) (Tax) (Amendment) Regulations, SI 2008/2679 regs 2, 9 with effect in relation to accounting periods beginning on or after 6 April 2008 and ending on or after 30 October 2008.

[3] These Regulations revoked by the Lloyd's Underwriters (Transitional Equalisation Reserves) (Tax) Regulations, SI 2015/1983 reg 5(*a*) with effect from 1 January 2016.

PART III
RESERVES MAINTAINED FOR THE PURPOSES OF CREDIT INSURANCE BUSINESS

11 Scope of this Part

This Part of these Regulations applies to any credit insurance equalisation reserve.[1]

Amendments—[1] These Regulations revoked by the Lloyd's Underwriters (Transitional Equalisation Reserves) (Tax) Regulations, SI 2015/1983 reg 5(*a*) with effect from 1 January 2016.

12 Application of section 444BA

Where for any accounting period an insurance company maintains a credit insurance equalisation reserve, section 444BA shall have effect in relation to that reserve as it has effect in relation to equalisation reserves maintained by virtue of [equalisation reserves rules][1], [2]

Amendments—[1] Words substituted by the Financial Services and Markets Act 2000 (Consequential Amendments) (Taxes) Order, SI 2001/3629 art 151 with effect for periods of account ending after 30 November 2001.

[2] These Regulations revoked by the Lloyd's Underwriters (Transitional Equalisation Reserves) (Tax) Regulations, SI 2015/1983 reg 5(*a*) with effect from 1 January 2016.

13 Transitional provision

(1) This regulation applies in any case where an insurance company was required, pursuant to regulations 76 to 78 of, and Schedule 14 to, the Insurance Companies Regulations 1994, to maintain a credit insurance equalisation reserve.

(2) Paragraph 2(2) of Schedule 2 to the Insurance Companies (Reserves) Regulations 1996 shall be disregarded for the purposes of the Tax Acts in determining how much is required, on any occasion, to be transferred into the credit insurance equalisation reserve.[1]

Amendments—[1] These Regulations revoked by the Lloyd's Underwriters (Transitional Equalisation Reserves) (Tax) Regulations, SI 2015/1983 reg 5(*a*) with effect from 1 January 2016.

14 Application of provisions contained in Part II of these Regulations

Subject to regulation 13, regulations . . . [1] 6, 9 and 10 shall have effect in relation to any credit insurance equalisation reserve as they have effect in relation to any reserve to which Part II of these Regulations applies.[2]

Amendments—[1] Figure revoked by the Insurance Companies (Reserves) (Tax) (Amendment) Regulations, SI 2008/2679 regs 2, 10 with effect in relation to accounting periods beginning on or after 6 April 2008 and ending on or after 30 October 2008.

[2] These Regulations revoked by the Lloyd's Underwriters (Transitional Equalisation Reserves) (Tax) Regulations, SI 2015/1983 reg 5(*a*) with effect from 1 January 2016.

1997/57

ELECTRONIC LODGEMENT OF TAX RETURNS ORDER 1997

Made by the Treasury under TMA 1970 Sch 3A para 2(1)

Made . . . . *15 January 1997*
Laid before the House of Commons . . . . *16 January 1997*
Coming into Force . . . . *1 March 1997*

1 This Order may be cited as the Electronic Lodgement of Tax Returns Order 1997, shall come into force on 1st March 1997 and shall have effect for the year 1996–97 and subsequent years of assessment.

2—(1) The provisions set out in paragraph (2) are, by virtue of paragraph 2(1)(*b*) of Schedule 3A to the Taxes Management Act 1970, specified for the purposes of that Schedule.

(2) The provisions are—

(*a*) section 8 of the Taxes Management Act 1970 (personal return);
(*b*) section 8A of that Act (trustee's return);
(*c*) section 12AA of that Act (partnership return).

3 The day appointed pursuant to paragraph 2(1)(*c*) of Schedule 3A to the Taxes Management Act 1970 in relation to notices requiring returns to be delivered or made under the provisions specified by article 2 is 1st March 1997.

1997/168

INTERNATIONAL ORGANISATIONS (MISCELLANEOUS EXEMPTIONS) ORDER 1997

Made by the Treasury under TA 1988 s 582A(1)

Made . . . . *27 January 1997*

Commentary—*Simon's Taxes* **D1.240.**

1 This Order may be cited as the International Organisations (Miscellaneous Exemptions) Order 1997.

2 The following international organisations are designated for the purposes of subsections (2) and (4) to (6) of section 582A and subsection (4) of section 118B of the Income and Corporation Taxes Act 1988—

Asian Development Bank
European Bank for Reconstruction and Development

International Bank for Reconstruction and Development
International Development Association
Multilateral Investment Guarantee Agency.

3 The following international organisations are designated for the purposes of subsection (5) of section 582A and subsection (4) of section 118B of the Income and Corporation Taxes Act 1988—
African Development Bank
European Investment Bank
Inter-American Development Bank.

4 The International Organisations (Miscellaneous Exemptions) Order 1991 and the International Organisations (Miscellaneous Exemptions) Order 1992 are hereby revoked.

1997/265

LIFE ASSURANCE AND OTHER POLICIES (KEEPING OF INFORMATION AND DUTIES OF INSURERS) REGULATIONS 1997

Made by the Commissioners of Inland Revenue under TA 1988, s 552(4A)(b), (4B), (4C)

Made . . . . *10 February 1997*
Laid before the House of Commons . . . . *10 February 1997*
Coming into Force . . . . *1 April 1997*

1 Citation and commencement

These Regulations may be cited as the Life Assurance and Other Policies (Keeping of Information and Duties of Insurers) Regulations 1997 and shall come into force on 1st April 1997.

2 Interpretation

(1) In these Regulations unless the context otherwise requires—
"the Board" means the Commissioners [for Her Majesty's Revenue and Customs][2];
"relevant records", in respect of a policy or contract, means the books, documents and records specified in regulation 3;
"Schedule 15" means Schedule 15 to the Taxes Act;
"section 552" means section 552 of the Taxes Act [and a reference to that section without more includes, where necessary, a reference to section 552ZA of the Taxes Act;][1]
"the Taxes Act" means the Income and Corporation Taxes Act 1988.

(2) For the purposes of these Regulations, an "insurer"—
(*a*) in a case where the obligations under any policy or contract of the body that issued, entered into or effected it ("the original insurer") are at any time the obligations of another body ("the transferee") to whom there has been a transfer of the whole or any part of a business previously carried on by the original insurer, means the transferee, and
(*b*) in any other case, means the body by or with whom the policy or contract was issued, entered into or effected.

(3) For the purposes of these Regulations and in relation to an insurer, a policy or contract is a relevant policy or contract [if—
(*a*) on][3] the happening of a chargeable event within the meaning of [Chapter 9 of Part 4 of the Income Tax (Trading and Other Income) Act 2005][2] in relation to the policy or contract, the insurer is under the duty to deliver a certificate pursuant to section 552; and, for the purposes of this paragraph, [the words "unless satisfied that no gain is to be treated as arising by reason of the event" in subsection (1)(*a*) shall be disregarded][1] [or
(*b*) it is a qualifying policy.][3]

(4) For the purposes of these Regulations and in respect of any policy or contract, any reference to books, documents and records includes books, documents and records (including material prepared for the purposes of advertising or publicity) which contain information—
(*a*) relating to the terms of the policy or contract, or
(*b*) required for the purposes of a certificate to be delivered under section 552.

Amendments—[1] Definition of "section 552" in para (1) amended, and words in para (3) substituted by the Life Assurance and Other Policies (Keeping of Information and Duties of Insurers) (Amendment) Regulations, SI 2002/444 reg 3 with effect from 6 April 2002.

[2] In paras (1), (3), words substituted by the Life Assurance and Other Policies (Keeping of Information and Duties of Insurers) (Amendment) Regulations, SI 2008/2628 reg 2 with effect from 27 October 2008.

[3] Para (3)(a) designated as such, and para (3)(b) inserted by the Life Insurance Qualifying Policies (Statement and Reporting Requirements) Regulations, SI 2013/1820 reg 6(1), (2) with effect from 12 August 2013.

3 Keeping of records—general

An insurer shall, in respect of each relevant policy or contract, keep sufficient books, documents and records to enable the Board—

(*a*) to ascertain the terms of the policy or contract,

(*b*) to ascertain whether there has been or is likely to be any contravention of the requirements of section 552, . . . [1]

(*c*) to verify any certificate delivered under that section,

[(*d*) to ascertain whether there has been or is likely to be any contravention of the requirements of the regulations made under section 552ZB(1), and

(*e*) to verify any information provided to an officer of Revenue and Customs as required by the regulations made under section 552ZB(1).][1]

Amendments—[1] In para (*b*) word "and" revoked, and paras (*d*), (*e*) inserted by the Life Insurance Qualifying Policies (Statement and Reporting Requirements) Regulations, SI 2013/1820 reg 6(1), (3) with effect from 12 August 2013.

4 Period for which records to be kept

(1) Subject to paragraph (2), an insurer shall, in respect of each relevant policy or contract, keep the relevant records for a period of three years after the termination of the policy or contract.

(2) In any case where—

(*a*) a relevant policy is connected with another policy for the purposes of paragraph 13 or 14 of Schedule 15, or

(*b*) in relation to a relevant policy under which a single premium only is payable, liability for that payment is discharged in accordance with paragraph 15(2) of Schedule 15, or

(*c*) a relevant policy is issued in substitution for, or on the maturity of and in consequence of an option conferred by, another policy,

an insurer shall, in respect of each policy, keep the relevant records for a period of three years after the termination of the final policy which is in force.

5 Transfers of records

(1) This regulation applies in any case where the obligations under any policy or contract of the body that issued, entered into or effected it ("the original insurer") are at any time the obligations of another body ("the transferee") to whom there has been a transfer of the whole or any part of a business previously carried on by the original insurer.

(2) The original insurer shall, in respect of that policy or contract, deliver the relevant records to the transferee within the period of three months after the transfer.

(3) This regulation has effect in relation to transfers on or after 1st April 1997.

6—(1) This regulation applies in any case where each of the three conditions specified in paragraphs (2) to (4) is fulfilled.

(2) The first condition is that one policy (the "new policy") is issued in substitution for another policy (the "old policy").

(3) The second condition is that the new policy is issued in substitution for an old policy issued by an insurance company (the "old insurer") which was resident outside the United Kingdom at the time the old policy was issued.

(4) The third condition is that the new policy is issued by an insurance company (the "new insurer") pursuant to arrangements made between the old insurer and the new insurer for the issue of policies in substitution for ones held by persons becoming resident in the United Kingdom.

(5) The new insurer shall, in respect of the old policy, obtain the relevant records from the old insurer within the period of three months after the issue of the new policy.

(6) This regulation has effect in relation to any new policy where the insurance for that new policy is made, and that new policy is issued, on or after 1st April 1997.

7—(1) This regulation applies in any case where each of the conditions specified in paragraphs (2) and (3) is fulfilled.

(2) The first condition is that one policy ("the new policy") is issued in substitution for, or on the maturity of and in consequence of an option conferred by, another policy ("the old policy").

(3) The second condition is that, at the time the new policy is issued, the insurance company issuing the new policy ("the new insurer") and the insurance company which issued the old policy ("the old insurer") are both members of a group of companies.

(4) For the purposes of paragraph (3) two companies are members of a group of companies if one is the 51 per cent subsidiary of the other or both are 51 per cent subsidiaries of a third company.

(5) The original insurer shall, in respect of the old policy, deliver the relevant records to the new insurer within the period of three months beginning with the date on which the new policy was substituted for the old policy or, as the case may be, the date of the exercise of the option on the maturity of the old policy.

(6) This regulation has effect in relation to any new policy where the insurance for that new policy is made, and that new policy is issued, on or after 1st April 1997.

8 Information to be provided to the Board

(1) The Board may by notice require any person to whom premiums under any policy are or have at any time been payable, within such period as may be specified in the notice, to furnish them with such information as they may reasonably require to enable them—

(*a*) to ascertain whether there has been or is likely to be any contravention of the requirements of section 552, and

(*b*) to verify any certificate delivered under that section.

(2) The period specified in a notice given under paragraph (1) shall be a period of not less than 14 days beginning with the date on which the notice is given.

9 Inspection of records by officer of the Board

(1) The Board may by notice require any person to whom premiums under any policy are or have at any time been payable, to make available for inspection by an officer of the Board authorised for that purpose, at such time as that officer may reasonably require, all such books, documents and records as are in that person's possession or under that person's control and are such as may be required by the Board under regulation 8 [or required by regulation 3(*d*) and (*e*)][1].

(2) The time specified in a notice given under paragraph (1) shall not fall within the period of 14 days beginning with the date on which the notice is given.

Amendments—[1] Words in para (1) inserted by the Life Insurance Qualifying Policies (Statement and Reporting Requirements) Regulations, SI 2013/1820 reg 6(1), (4) with effect from 12 August 2013.

1997/405

LLOYD'S UNDERWRITERS (DOUBLE TAXATION RELIEF) REGULATIONS 1997

Made by the Commissioners of Inland Revenue under FA 1993 s 182(1)

Made . . . . *21 February 1997*

Laid before the House of Commons . . . . *21 February 1997*

Coming into Force . . . . *14 March 1997*

Commentary—*Simon's Taxes* **E5.651.**

1 Citation, commencement and effect

(1) These Regulations may be cited as the Lloyd's Underwriters (Double Taxation Relief) Regulations 1997 and shall come into force on 14th March 1997.

(2) These Regulations shall have effect for the year 1996–97 and subsequent years of assessment.

2 Interpretation

(1) In these Regulations—

"Canadian tax" means the appropriate income tax or income taxes imposed by the Government of Canada;

"final year of assessment" shall be construed in accordance with section 179(2);

"foreign tax" means tax chargeable under the law of a territory outside the United Kingdom;

"member" means a member of Lloyd's who is an individual and who is or has been an underwriting member;

"Part XVIII" means Part XVIII of the Taxes Act;

"the Taxes Act" means the Income and Corporation Taxes Act 1988;

"United States tax" means the appropriate Federal income tax or Federal income taxes of the United States of America imposed by the Internal Revenue Code.

(2) For the purposes of these Regulations an underwriting year and a year of assessment shall be deemed to correspond to each other if the underwriting year ends in the year of assessment.

(3) References to a section, without more, are references to that section of the Finance Act 1993.

3 Pooled foreign tax

(1) For the purposes of Part XVIII foreign tax paid in respect of profits or losses arising from a member's underwriting business in a year of assessment shall be taken into account in accordance with paragraph (2).

(2) Foreign tax paid as mentioned in paragraph (1) shall be taken into account by reference to the aggregate amount of such amounts of foreign tax as are paid (whether or not under the law of more than one territory outside the United Kingdom) in respect of income that is taken into account in computing the profits or losses of the member's underwriting business; and accordingly the provisions of Part XVIII shall apply as if—

(*a*) references, however expressed, to tax paid under the law of a territory outside the United Kingdom were references to that aggregate amount paid as a single payment in respect of a single source of income, and (*b*) references to United Kingdom tax chargeable in respect of any income were references to United Kingdom tax chargeable in respect of the total profits of the member's underwriting business.

4 Allocation of foreign tax to United Kingdom years of assessment—syndicate profits

(1) For the purposes of regulation 3, foreign tax referred to in that regulation that is paid in respect of income specified in paragraph (2), other than foreign tax to which regulation 6 or 7 applies, shall be allocated to the year of assessment specified in paragraph (3).

(2) The income specified is the income that is taken into account in computing the profits or losses of the member's underwriting business falling within section 172(1)(*a*) or (*b*).

(3) The year of assessment specified is the same year of assessment as the year of assessment to which, by virtue of section 172, the profits or losses referred to in paragraph (2) relate.

5 Allocation of foreign tax to United Kingdom years of assessment—non-syndicate profits

(1) For the purposes of regulation 3, foreign tax referred to in that regulation that is paid in respect of income specified in paragraph (2), other than foreign tax to which regulation 6 or 7 applies, shall be allocated to the year of assessment specified in paragraph (3).

(2) The income specified is the income that is taken into account in computing the profits or losses of the member's underwriting business falling within section 172(1)(*c*).

(3) The year of assessment specified is the same year of assessment as the year of assessment to which, by virtue of section 172, the profits or losses referred to in paragraph (2) relate.

6 Allocation of foreign tax to United Kingdom years of assessment—United States tax

(1) This regulation applies to foreign tax that is United States tax paid by Lloyd's in accordance with a United States tax return rendered by them for a calendar year in respect of income that is taken into account in computing the profits or losses of the member's underwriting business.

(2) For the purposes of regulation 3 and subject to paragraph (3), United States tax paid as mentioned in paragraph (1) shall be allocated to the year of assessment next but one following the year of assessment to which the underwriting year for which the return is made corresponds.

(3) Where the member's final year of assessment is the year 1996–97, United States tax paid as mentioned in paragraph (1) which under paragraph (2) would have been eligible for relief in a later year of assessment had not the member's final year of assessment been the year 1996–97 and which has not been used for relief in an earlier year of assessment, shall be allocated to the year 1996–97.

7 Allocation of foreign tax to United Kingdom years of assessment—Canadian tax

(1) This regulation applies to foreign tax that is Canadian tax paid by Lloyd's in accordance with a Canadian tax return rendered by them for a calendar year in respect of income that is taken into account in computing the profits or losses of the member's underwriting business.

(2) For the purposes of regulation 3 and subject to paragraph (3), Canadian tax paid as mentioned in paragraph (1) shall be allocated to the year of assessment next following the year of assessment to which the underwriting year for which the return is made corresponds.

(3) Where the member's final year of assessment is the year 1996–97, Canadian tax paid as mentioned in paragraph (1) which under paragraph (2) would have been eligible for relief in a later year of assessment had not the member's final year of assessment been the year 1996–97 and which has not been used for relief in an earlier year of assessment, shall be allocated to the year 1996–97.

8 Allocation of foreign tax to United Kingdom years of assessment—additional payments of foreign tax

(1) Where—

(*a*) payment of foreign tax ("the primary payment") is made for an underwriting year in respect of income that falls to be taken into account in computing the profits or losses of a member's underwriting business, and

(*b*) payment of an additional amount of foreign tax in respect of that income is subsequently required,

then, notwithstanding anything in regulations 4 to 7 but subject to paragraph (2), the additional amount paid shall, for the purposes of regulation 3, be treated as foreign tax paid for the underwriting year in which it was paid and not as foreign tax paid for the underwriting year for which the primary payment was made.

(2) Where the underwriting year in which the additional amount of foreign tax is paid is an underwriting year that is subsequent to the underwriting year corresponding to the member's final year of assessment, the additional amount paid shall, for the purposes of regulation 3, be treated as foreign tax paid for the underwriting year corresponding to the member's final year of assessment.

9 Refunds of foreign tax

(1) Where—

(*a*) income that is taken into account in computing the profits or losses of a member's underwriting business is treated as reduced by foreign tax under section 811 of the Taxes Act, and (*b*) an amount of that foreign tax is subsequently repaid to the member,

the amount repaid shall be treated as a payment received as mentioned in section 172(1)(c).

(2) Subject to paragraph (3), where—

(*a*) relief for foreign tax is given by way of credit against United Kingdom tax on profits arising from a member's underwriting business, and

(*b*) an amount of that foreign tax is subsequently repaid to the member,

the amount of United Kingdom tax charged on the profits arising from the member's underwriting business for the relevant year of assessment shall be treated as increased by the amount repaid.

(3) Where—

(*a*) relief by way of credit against United Kingdom tax on profits arising from a member's underwriting business is claimed for an amount of foreign tax,

(*b*) relief is given in respect of part only of the amount of the foreign tax claimed, and

(*c*) an amount of the foreign tax claimed is subsequently repaid to the member,

the amount of United Kingdom tax charged on the profits arising from the member's underwriting business for the relevant year of assessment shall be treated as increased by the amount (if any) which is equal to so much of the amount received as exceeds the amount of the foreign tax in respect of which relief was not given.

(4) In paragraphs (2) and (3) "the relevant year of assessment"—

(*a*) where the underwriting year in which the repayment of foreign tax was received is an underwriting year subsequent to the underwriting year corresponding to the member's final year of assessment, means the member's final year of assessment;

(*b*) in any other case, means the year of assessment corresponding to the underwriting year in which the repayment of foreign tax was received.

1997/473

FRIENDLY SOCIETIES (MODIFICATION OF THE CORPORATION TAX ACTS) REGULATIONS 1997

Revocation—These regulations revoked by the Friendly Societies (Modification of the Corporation Tax Acts) Regulations, SI 2005/2014 reg 46, Schedule with effect from 12 August 2005. The revocation has effect in relation to accounting periods beginning on or after 1 January 2005.

1997/992

MANUFACTURED INTEREST (TAX) REGULATIONS 1997

Made by the Treasury under TA 1988 Sch 23A paras 1(1), 8(1), (2)–(4)

Made . . . . *20 March 1997*
Laid before the House of Commons . . . . *20 March 1997*
Coming into Force . . . . *1 July 1997*

Revocation—These Regulations revoked by the Manufactured Interest (Tax) Regulations, SI 2007/2488 reg 3 with effect in relation to payments of manufactured interest made or treated as made on or after 1 October 2007: SI 2007/2488 reg 1(1).

1997/993

MANUFACTURED DIVIDENDS (TAX) REGULATIONS 1997

Made by the Treasury under TA 1988 Sch 23A paras 1(1), 2(3)–(5), 8(1), (2)–(4)

Made . . . . *20 March 1997*
Laid before the House of Commons . . . . *20 March 1997*
Coming into Force . . . . *1 July 1997*

Commentary—*Simon's Taxes* **D9.702.**

1 Citation and commencement

These Regulations may be cited as the Manufactured Dividends (Tax) Regulations 1997 and shall come into force on 1st July 1997.

2 Interpretation

(1) In these Regulations unless the context otherwise requires—

"the Board" means the Commissioners of Inland Revenue;

"chargeable period" has the meaning given by regulation 3;

"dividend" means a dividend on United Kingdom equities, not being a foreign income dividend within Chapter VA of Part VI of the Taxes Act;

"the Management Act" means the Taxes Management Act 1970;

"manufactured dividend" shall be construed in accordance with paragraph 2(1) of Schedule 23A;

"relevant period" means—

(*a*) each complete quarter falling within a chargeable period, that is to say, each of the periods of three months ending with 31st March, 30th June, 30th September or 31st December which falls within that period;

(*b*) each part of the chargeable period which is not a complete quarter and ends on the first (or only), or begins immediately after the last (or only), of those dates which falls within the chargeable period;

(*c*) if none of those dates falls within a chargeable period which is an accounting period, the whole chargeable period;

"the Taxes Act" means the Income and Corporation Taxes Act 1988.

(2) References in these Regulations to a "creditable amount" in respect of a dividend or manufactured dividend received in any period—

[(*za*) are references to such amount in respect of a dividend or manufactured dividend other than a dividend or manufactured dividend that is paid on or after 6th April 1999, and either][1]

(*a*) are references to the tax credit in respect of that dividend or manufactured dividend, not being an amount of tax credit to which paragraph (3) applies, or

(*b*) where the recipient of the dividend or manufactured dividend is a company that is not resident in the United Kingdom and the dividend or manufactured dividend is attributable to a branch or agency through which the company trades in the United Kingdom, are references to an amount of tax equal to the amount of advance corporation tax payable in respect of that dividend or manufactured dividend, or (as the case may be) the amount of advance corporation tax that would have been payable in respect of that dividend or manufactured dividend if—

(i) the person by whom the dividend or manufactured dividend was paid were a company resident in the United Kingdom, and

(ii) the manufactured dividend were a distribution by that company.

(3) This paragraph applies to the amount of tax credit in respect of a distribution which—

(*a*) . . . [2]

(*b*) is a distribution in respect of which that company has claimed or may claim the payment of a tax credit under section 438(4) or 441A(7).

(4) References in these Regulations to a section or Schedule, without more, are references to that section of, or that Schedule to, the Taxes Act.

Amendments—[1] Para (2)(*za*) inserted by the Manufactured Dividends (Tax) Amendment Regulations, SI 1999/621 reg 2, with effect from 30 March 1999.

[2] Para (3)(*a*) revoked by the Overseas Life Insurance Companies Regulations, SI 2006/3271 reg 43, Sch Pt 1 with effect in relation to periods of account ending on or after 31 December 2006.

3 Chargeable period

(1) In these Regulations "chargeable period" means—

(*a*) as respects a company, its accounting period;

(*b*) as respects a person other than a company who draws up accounts for any period ("the accounts period"), one of the periods specified in paragraph (2);

(*c*) as respects a person other than a company who does not draw up accounts, a year of assessment.

(2) The periods specified in this paragraph are—

(*a*) the period which begins at the beginning of the accounts period and ends at the expiration of 12 months from that date or, if earlier, at the end of the accounts period;

(*b*) any subsequent period which—

(i) begins at the end of the immediately preceding period, being a period specified in this paragraph, and

(ii) ends at the expiration of 12 months from that date or, if earlier, at the end of the accounts period.

4 Accountability for tax

(1) Where—

(*a*) a manufactured dividend is paid by any person other than a company resident in the United Kingdom, and

(*b*) the payment is one in relation to which either the dividend manufacturer or the recipient of the payment is a person to whom paragraph (2) below applies ("the appropriate person"),

the appropriate person shall be liable to account to the Board, to the extent and in the manner specified in these Regulations, for tax as mentioned in paragraph 2(3) of Schedule 23A.

(2) Subject to regulation 5, the appropriate person is—

(*a*) where paragraph 2(5) of Schedule 23A applies in relation to the manufactured dividend, the dividend manufacturer;

(*b*) where sub-paragraph (*a*) above does not apply in relation to the manufactured dividend and either of the conditions specified in paragraph (3) below applies, the recipient of the payment.

(3) The conditions specified in this paragraph are—

(*a*) that the recipient is a person resident in the United Kingdom;

(*b*) that the recipient is a company that is not so resident but carries on a trade in the United Kingdom through a branch or agency, and the manufactured dividend is attributable to the carrying on of that trade through that branch or agency.

5 Liability for tax where the manufacturer receives the dividend of which the manufactured dividend is representative

(1) Regulation 4(2)(*b*) shall not apply in any case where the recipient of the manufactured dividend shows that—

(*a*) the dividend manufacturer was entitled to payment of the dividend of which the manufactured dividend is representative either—

(i) as the holder of the securities concerned, or

(ii) directly or indirectly from a person from whom he acquired those securities, or to whom he transferred them, and who was so entitled as the holder of those securities, and

(*b*) the aggregate of the amount of the dividend received by the dividend manufacturer and any amount paid to him in respect of a tax credit in relation to that dividend ("the aggregate amount") does not exceed the amount of the dividend.

(2) Where paragraph (1) applies, the dividend manufacturer concerned shall be liable for tax, in respect of the manufactured dividend paid by him, in an amount equal to the amount (if any) of a tax credit in respect of the dividend received by him which, assuming him to have made a claim under arrangements having effect by virtue of section 788, the dividend manufacturer is entitled to have paid to him in respect of the dividend received by him.

(3) The amount of tax for which the dividend manufacturer is liable shall be set against the amount of the tax credit to which, on the assumption made in paragraph (2), he is entitled as mentioned in that paragraph.

(4) Where paragraph (1) does not apply by reason only of the fact that sub-paragraph (*b*) of that paragraph does not apply, the amount of tax for which the recipient of the manufactured dividend shall be liable to account under paragraph 2(3) of Schedule 23A shall be reduced to an amount equal to the amount by which the aggregate amount exceeds the amount of the dividend.

6 Accounting for tax by recipients that are United Kingdom resident companies

(1) This regulation applies in any case where a recipient of a manufactured dividend—

(*a*) is liable under regulation 4 to account to the Board for any tax in respect of that manufactured dividend, and

(*b*) is a company resident in the United Kingdom.

(2) Paragraphs 1 to 3, 8 and 10 of Schedule 13 (collection of advance corporation tax) and, on or after the appointed day referred to in section 137(2) of the Finance Act 1996, paragraph 7A of that Schedule, shall apply in relation to the amount of tax for which the company is liable to account in respect of that manufactured dividend as if—

(*a*) paragraph 1 of that Schedule required a return under that paragraph to include in addition manufactured dividends received by the company in each of its accounting periods and the tax for which it is liable to account in respect of those manufactured dividends;

(*b*) paragraph 2(1) of that Schedule required a return for any return period to include in addition the amount of any manufactured dividends received by the company in that period, and the amount of tax for which it is liable to account in respect of those manufactured dividends;

(*c*) references in paragraph 3 of that Schedule to franked payments and advance corporation tax in respect of such payments included references to manufactured dividends required to be included in a return under that Schedule by virtue of this regulation and tax for which the company is liable to account in respect of those manufactured dividends;

(*d*) paragraph 8 of that Schedule included a reference to a manufactured dividend included in a return under that Schedule by virtue of this regulation;

(*e*) paragraph 10 of that Schedule included a reference to tax for which the company is liable to account in respect of manufactured dividends received in any accounting period.

7 Accounting for tax by persons other than United Kingdom resident companies

(1) This regulation applies in any case where the payer or recipient of a manufactured dividend ("the relevant person")—

(*a*) is liable under regulation 4 to account to the Board for any tax in respect of that manufactured dividend, and (*b*) is not a company resident in the United Kingdom.

(2) The relevant person shall be liable to account in respect of any relevant period for an amount of tax equal to the sum of the following—

(*a*) the amount (if any) by which for that period the aggregate amount of tax for which he is accountable in respect of manufactured dividends paid by him exceeds the aggregate amount of creditable amounts in respect of dividends and manufactured dividends received by him, and

(*b*) the amount (if any) for that period of the aggregate amount of tax for which he is accountable in respect of manufactured dividends received by him.

(3) Tax for which the relevant person is accountable under paragraph (2)—

(*a*) shall be due not later than 14 days after the end of the relevant period concerned, and

(*b*) shall be payable without the making of an assessment.

(4) Tax due under paragraph (3) shall, whether or not an assessment is made under paragraph (10) of this regulation or under regulation 8(4), carry interest at the rate applicable under section 178 of the Finance Act 1989 to section 87 of the Management Act from the end of the period of 14 days referred to in that paragraph until payment.

(5) Where the aggregate amount of creditable amounts in respect of dividends and manufactured dividends received by the relevant person in a relevant period exceeds the aggregate amount of tax for which he is accountable in respect of manufactured dividends paid by him in that period, the amount of the excess may be carried forward to any subsequent relevant period falling within the same chargeable period for the purposes of offsetting, pursuant to paragraph (2)(*a*), that excess amount against the aggregate amount of tax for which he is accountable in respect of manufactured dividends paid by him in respect of that subsequent relevant period.

(6) Where—

(*a*) the aggregate amount of tax for which the relevant person is accountable in respect of manufactured dividends paid by him in a relevant period ("the first period") exceeds the aggregate amount of creditable amounts in respect of dividends and manufactured dividends received by him in that period, and

(*b*) in any subsequent relevant period falling within the same chargeable period there is an excess of the aggregate amount of creditable amounts in respect of dividends and manufactured dividends received by him over the aggregate amount of tax for which he is accountable in respect of manufactured dividends paid by him,

that excess amount may be set off, for the purposes of paragraph (2)(a), against the aggregate amount of tax for which the relevant person is accountable in respect of manufactured dividends paid by him in the first period, and a repayment of tax shall be made accordingly.

(7) Where—

(*a*) the relevant person is a company that is not resident in the United Kingdom, and

(*b*) the aggregate amount of creditable amounts in respect of dividends and manufactured dividends received by him in a chargeable period exceeds the aggregate amount of tax for which the company is accountable in respect of manufactured dividends paid by him in that period,

the amount of that excess may be carried forward so as to be regarded, for the purposes of paragraph (2), as a creditable amount in respect of dividends or manufactured dividends received by him in the first relevant period of the next chargeable period.

(8) Where—

(*a*) the relevant person was under an obligation to make a return under regulation 20 of the Income Tax (Dividend Manufacturing) Regulations 1992 in respect of the return period ending 30th June 1997, and

(*b*) surplus tax credits received by the relevant person fell to be carried forward on that date to its next accounting period under paragraph (10)(*a*) of that regulation or would have fallen so to be carried forward if its accounting period had ended on that date, references in these Regulations to creditable amounts shall, as respects the relevant period commencing 1st July 1997, be taken as including references to those surplus tax credits.

(9) The same creditable amount shall not be taken into account both under this regulation and under any other provision of the Tax Acts.

(10) Tax which has become due from a person under paragraph (3) may be assessed on that person (whether or not it has been paid when the assessment is made) if that tax, or any part of it, is not paid on or before the due date.

8 Returns by persons other than United Kingdom resident companies

(1) This regulation applies in any case where under regulation 7 the relevant person is liable to account for an amount of tax in respect of any relevant period falling within a chargeable period.

(2) The relevant person shall, within 30 days from the end of the chargeable period, make a return for that period to the Board.

(3) A return under paragraph (2) shall show—

(*a*) the aggregate amount of the manufactured dividends received by the relevant person in the chargeable period in respect of which he is liable to account for tax under regulation 7,
(*b*) the aggregate amount of the manufactured dividends paid by the relevant person in the chargeable period in respect of which he is liable to account for tax under regulation 7,
(*c*) the aggregate amount of creditable amounts in respect of dividends and manufactured dividends received by the relevant person in the chargeable period,
(*d*) the amount of creditable amounts brought forward from the previous chargeable period under regulation 7(7);
(*e*) the amount of creditable amounts carried forward to the next chargeable period under regulation 7(7);
(*f*) the aggregate amount of tax for which he is liable to account under regulation 7 for the chargeable period which is the subject of the return.

(4) If it appears to an officer of the Board that there is a manufactured dividend which ought to have been and has not been included in a return under paragraph (2), or if he is otherwise dissatisfied with any such return, he may make an assessment on the relevant person to the best of his judgment.
(5) Section 98 of the Management Act ("section 98") shall apply in relation to a return under paragraph (2) with the modification specified in paragraph (6).
(6) At the end of the second column of the Table in section 98 there shall be added—
"Regulation 8(2) of the Manufactured Dividends (Tax) Regulations 1997."

9 Set off of tax by companies not resident in the United Kingdom

(1) Subject to the modification specified in paragraph (2), the provisions of section 239 other than subsection (7) of that section, section 246(5) and section 797(4) shall apply in relation to the aggregate amount of tax for which a company that is not resident in the United Kingdom is liable in accordance with regulation 7(2)(*a*) to account for all relevant periods falling within any chargeable period in respect of manufactured dividends paid by it, as if that tax were advance corporation tax paid by the company in respect of distributions made by it in that chargeable period.
(2) Subsection (3) of section 239 shall apply as if the reference in that subsection to any of the company's accounting periods beginning in the six years preceding the accounting period concerned were a reference to any of the company's accounting periods ending on or after 1st July 1997 and beginning in the six years preceding that accounting period.

1997/1154

OPEN-ENDED INVESTMENT COMPANIES (TAX) REGULATIONS 1997

Made by the Treasury under TA 1995 s 152

Made . . . . 3 *April 1997*
Laid before the House of Commons . . . . 7 *April 1997*
Coming into Force . . . . 28 *April 1997*

Amendment—These regulations revoked by the Authorised Investment Funds (Tax) Regulations, SI 2006/964 reg 111.
SI 2006/964 came into force on 1 April 2006, with effect—
(a) for the purposes of income tax—
(i) for the tax year 2006–07 and subsequent tax years, and
(ii) for distributions made on or after 6 April 2006;
(b) for the purposes of corporation tax—
(i) on income, for accounting periods beginning on or after 1 April 2006,
(ii) on chargeable gains, in relation to disposals made on or after 1 April 2006, and
(iii) for distributions made on or after 1 April 2006; and
(c) for the purposes of capital gains tax, in relation to disposals made on or after 6 April 2006.

1997/1158

INCOME TAX (SCHEDULE 22 TO THE FINANCE ACT 1995) (PRESCRIBED AMOUNTS) REGULATIONS 1997

Made by the Commissioners of Inland Revenue under FA 1995 Sch 22 paras 1(3), 2(4)(b), 3(3), 5(4)(b), 6(3), 7(3), 9(3)(a), 10(3)

Made . . . . 3 *April 1997*
Laid before the House of Commons . . . . 4 *April 1997*
Coming into Force . . . . 25 *April 1997*

Commentary—*Simon's Taxes* **B4.107.**

1 Citation and commencement

These Regulations may be cited as the Income Tax (Schedule 22 to the Finance Act 1995) (Prescribed Amounts) Regulations 1997 and shall come into force on 25th April 1997.

2 Interpretation

(1) In these Regulations "appropriate period" means—

(*a*) where paragraph 1(3) applies, "the transitional period" within the meaning given by paragraph 1(4);

(*b*) where paragraph 3(3) applies so as to modify paragraph 1(3), "the transitional overlap period" within the meaning given by paragraph 3(4);

(*c*) where paragraph 6(3) applies so as to modify paragraph 1(3), the years of assessment 1995–96 and 1996–97;

(*d*) where paragraph 7(3) applies so as to modify paragraph 1(3), "the transitional overlap period" within the meaning given by paragraph 7(4).

(2) References in these Regulations to a paragraph are to that paragraph of Schedule 22 to the Finance Act 1995.

3 Amounts prescribed under paragraph 1(3)—persons other than partners

As respects a trade, profession or vocation carried on by any person (other than in partnership)—

(*a*) the amount prescribed for the purposes of paragraph 1(3)(*a*) and of that provision as applied by paragraphs 3(3), 6(3) and 7(3) is £10,000;

(*b*) the amount prescribed for the purposes of paragraph 1(3)(*c*) and of that provision as applied by paragraphs 3(3), 6(3) and 7(3) is £50,000.

4 Amount prescribed under paragraph 1(3)(a)—persons in partnership

As respects a trade, profession or vocation carried on by persons in partnership, the amount prescribed for the purposes of paragraph 1(3)(*a*) and of that provision as applied by paragraphs 3(3), 6(3) and 7(3)—

(*a*) where the maximum number of partners comprising the partnership in the appropriate period does not exceed 20, is the amount determined by the formula—

£7,500 × A

where A is the maximum number of partners comprising the partnership in the appropriate period;

(*b*) where the maximum number of partners comprising the partnership in the appropriate period exceeds 20, is the amount determined by the formula—

£150,000 + (£1,000 × B)

where B is the number by which the maximum number of partners comprising the partnership in the appropriate period exceeds 20.

5 Amount prescribed under paragraph 1(3)(c)—persons in partnership

As respects a trade, profession or vocation carried on by persons in partnership, the amount prescribed for the purposes of paragraph 1(3)(*c*) and of that provision as applied by paragraphs 3(3), 6(3) and 7(3) is the amount determined by the formula—

£50,000 × C

where C is the maximum number of partners comprising the partnership in the appropriate period.

6 Amount prescribed under paragraph 2(4)(b)

The amount prescribed for the purposes of paragraph 2(4)(*b*) is £15,000.

7 Amount prescribed under paragraph 5(4)(b)

The amount prescribed for the purposes of paragraph 5(4)(*b*) is £7,500.

8 Amount prescribed under paragraph 9(3)(a)

The amount prescribed for the purposes of paragraph 9(3)(*a*) and of that provision as applied by paragraph 10(3) is £7,500.

1997/2681

LLOYD'S UNDERWRITERS (PARTNERSHIPS) (TAX) REGULATIONS 1997

Made by the Commissioners of Inland Revenue under FA 1993 s 182(1) and FA 1994 s 229

Made . . . . *7 November 1997*

Laid before the House of Commons . . . . *10 November 1997*

Coming into force 1 December 1997

Note—The title of these regulations has been amended by the Lloyd's Underwriters (Scottish Limited Partnerships) (Tax) (Amendment) Regulations, SI 2006/111 regs 2, 3 with effect from 14 February 2006. This amendment has effect with respect to accounting periods of Lloyd's partnerships ending on or after that date.

Commentary—*Simon's Taxes* **E5.601.**

PRELIMINARY

1 Citation, commencement and effect

These Regulations may be cited as the Lloyd's Underwriters (. . . [1] Partnerships) (Tax) Regulations 1997, shall come into force on 1st December 1997 and shall have effect with respect to accounting periods of Lloyd's Scottish limited partnerships ending on or after that date.

Amendments—[1] Words revoked by the Lloyd's Underwriters (Scottish Limited Partnerships) (Tax) (Amendment) Regulations, SI 2006/111 regs 2, 3 with effect from 14 February 2006. This amendment has effect with respect to accounting periods of Lloyd's partnerships ending on or after that date.

2 Interpretation

(1) In these Regulations unless the context otherwise requires—

"accounting period" in relation to a Lloyd's . . . [1] partnership has the meaning given by regulation 6(2);

"corporate member" has the meaning given by section 230(1) of the Finance Act 1994;

["Lloyd's partnership" means—

(*a*) a Lloyd's Scottish limited partnership, or

(*b*) a limited liability partnership formed under the law of any part of the United Kingdom which is a member of Lloyd's.][2]

"Lloyd's Scottish limited partnership" means a limited partnership formed under the laws of Scotland which is a member of Lloyd's;

"member" means a member of Lloyd's who is or has been an underwriting member;

"the Taxes Act" means the Income and Corporation Taxes Act 1988.

(2) For the purposes of these Regulations an underwriting year and a year of assessment shall be deemed to correspond to each other if the underwriting year ends in the year of assessment.

Amendments—[1] Words revoked by the Lloyd's Underwriters (Scottish Limited Partnerships) (Tax) (Amendment) Regulations, SI 2006/111 regs 2, 4 with effect from 14 February 2006. This amendment has effect with respect to accounting periods of Lloyd's partnerships ending on or after that date.

[2] Definition of "Lloyd's partnership" inserted by SI 2006/111 regs 2, 5 with effect from 14 February 2006. This amendment has effect with respect to accounting periods of Lloyd's partnerships ending on or after that date.

PROVISIONS RELATING TO BOTH INDIVIDUAL AND CORPORATE PARTNERS IN A LLOYD'S . . . PARTNERSHIP

Amendments—Words revoked by the Lloyd's Underwriters (Scottish Limited Partnerships) (Tax) (Amendment) Regulations, SI 2006/111 regs 2, 4 with effect from 14 February 2006. These amendments have effect with respect to accounting periods of Lloyd's partnerships ending on or after that date.

3 Operation of partnership assessment rules

(1) Where [section 849 of the Income Tax (Trading and Other Income) Act 2005][2] applies in relation to a Lloyd's . . . [1] partnership—

(*a*) the provisions of Chapter III of Part II of the Finance Act 1993 shall apply, subject to the amendments made by these Regulations, as if the partnership were a member who is an individual;

(*b*) the Lloyd's Underwriters (Tax) Regulations 1995 shall have effect in relation to that partnership—

(i) as if it were a member who is an individual, and

(ii) with the omission of regulations 9 to 17;

[(*ba*) the Lloyd's Underwriters (Tax) Regulations 2005 shall have effect in relation to the partnership as if it were a member who is an individual.][2]

(*c*) the Lloyd's Underwriters (Double Taxation Relief) Regulations 1997 shall have effect in relation to that partnership as if it were a member who is an individual.

(2) Where section 114(1) of the Taxes Act applies in relation to a Lloyd's . . . [1] partnership—

(*a*) the provisions of Chapter V of Part IV of the Finance Act 1994 shall apply, subject to the amendments made by these Regulations, as if the partnership were a member which is a corporate member;

(*b*) the Lloyd's Underwriters (Tax) Regulations 1995 shall have effect in relation to that partnership—

(i) as if it were a member which is a corporate member, and

(ii) with the omission of regulations 9 to 17[; and

(*c*) the Lloyd's Underwriters (Tax) Regulations 2005 shall have effect in relation to the partnership as if it were a member which is a corporate member.][3]

Amendments—[1] Words revoked by the Lloyd's Underwriters (Scottish Limited Partnerships) (Tax) (Amendment) Regulations, SI 2006/111 regs 2, 4 with effect from 14 February 2006. These amendments have effect with respect to accounting periods of Lloyd's partnerships ending on or after that date.

[2] In para (1), words substituted, and sub-para (*ba*) inserted by SI 2006/111 regs 2, 6 with effect from 14 February 2006. These amendments have effect with respect to accounting periods of Lloyd's partnerships ending on or after that date.

[3] Para (2)(*c*) inserted by SI 2006/111 regs 2, 7 with effect from 14 February 2006. This amendment has effect with respect to accounting periods of Lloyd's partnerships ending on or after that date.

4 Disapplication of cessation provisions

(1) Sections 179 and 179A of the Finance Act 1993 shall not apply in relation to a Lloyd's . . . [1] partnership which, by virtue of regulation 3(1), is treated as a member who is an individual.

(2) Section 227 of the Finance Act 1994 shall not apply in relation to a Lloyd's . . . [1] partnership which, by virtue of regulation 3(2), is treated as a member which is a corporate member.

Amendments—[1] Words revoked by the Lloyd's Underwriters (Scottish Limited Partnerships) (Tax) (Amendment) Regulations, SI 2006/111 regs 2, 4 with effect from 14 February 2006. These amendments have effect with respect to accounting periods of Lloyd's partnerships ending on or after that date.

5 Ancillary trust funds relating to a Lloyd's . . . partnership

(1) An ancillary trust fund set up in relation to a Lloyd's . . . [1] partnership shall be regarded as an ancillary trust fund of that partnership, irrespective of whether the fund is established by the partnership itself or by one or more of the partners in the partnership; and, subject to the modification specified in paragraph (2), section 176 of the Finance Act 1993 and section 223 of the Finance Act 1994 shall apply accordingly.

(2) Subsections (3) and (4) of section 176 of the Finance Act 1993 shall be omitted.

(3) In paragraph (1) "ancillary trust fund"—

(*a*) where regulation 3(1) applies, has the meaning given by section 184(1) of the Finance Act 1993;

(*b*) where regulation 3(2) applies, has the meaning given by section 230(1) of the Finance Act 1994.

Amendments—[1] Words revoked by the Lloyd's Underwriters (Scottish Limited Partnerships) (Tax) (Amendment) Regulations, SI 2006/111 regs 2, 4 with effect from 14 February 2006. These amendments have effect with respect to accounting periods of Lloyd's partnerships ending on or after that date.

PROVISIONS RELATING TO INDIVIDUAL PARTNERS IN A LLOYD'S . . . PARTNERSHIP

Amendments—Words revoked by the Lloyd's Underwriters (Scottish Limited Partnerships) (Tax) (Amendment) Regulations, SI 2006/111 regs 2, 4 with effect from 14 February 2006. These amendments have effect with respect to accounting periods of Lloyd's partnerships ending on or after that date.

6 Basis of assessment

(1) Where regulation 3(1) applies in relation to a Lloyd's . . . [1] partnership—

(*a*) [Chapter 15 of Part 2 of the Income Tax (Trading and Other Income) Act 2005][2] shall not apply in relation to that partnership;

(*b*) section 172 of the Finance Act 1993 shall apply in relation to that partnership as if—

(i) in each of paragraphs (*a*) and (*b*) of subsection (1) of that section for the reference to the corresponding underwriting year there were substituted a reference to the accounting period ending in the corresponding underwriting year;

(ii) in paragraph (*c*) of that subsection for the reference to profits or losses derived from payments made or received in the corresponding underwriting year there were substituted a reference to profits or losses attributable to the accounting period ending in the corresponding underwriting year.

(2) In paragraph (1)(*b*)(i) and (ii) "accounting period" in relation to a Lloyd's . . . [1] partnership means the period—

(*a*) beginning on the 1st January in each year, or the date on which the partnership was formed (if later in that year), and

(*b*) ending on—

(i) the 31st December in that year, or the date when the partnership is terminated (if earlier), or

(ii) where the partnership was formed later than 1st January in that year, the 31st December in the following year, or the date when the partnership is terminated (if earlier).

Amendments—[1] Words revoked by the Lloyd's Underwriters (Scottish Limited Partnerships) (Tax) (Amendment) Regulations, SI 2006/111 regs 2, 4 with effect from 14 February 2006. These amendments have effect with respect to accounting periods of Lloyd's partnerships ending on or after that date.

[2] Words in para (1)(*a*) substituted by SI 2006/111 regs 2, 8 with effect from 14 February 2006. This amendment has effect with respect to accounting periods of Lloyd's partnerships ending on or after that date.

7 Disapplication of section 175 of the Finance Act 1993 (special reserve funds)

(1) Section 175 of, and Schedule 20 to, the Finance Act 1993 shall not apply in relation to a Lloyd's . . . [1] partnership which, by virtue of regulation 3(1), is treated as a member who is an individual.

(2) Paragraph (1) shall not prevent the setting up of a special reserve fund in relation to an individual who is both a member of Lloyd's and a partner in a Lloyd's . . . [1] partnership, but in such a case the special reserve fund shall take account only of the underwriting business carried on by that person as a member.

Amendments—[1] Words revoked by the Lloyd's Underwriters (Scottish Limited Partnerships) (Tax) (Amendment) Regulations, SI 2006/111 regs 2, 4 with effect from 14 February 2006. These amendments have effect with respect to accounting periods of Lloyd's partnerships ending on or after that date.

8 Disapplication of section 180 of the Finance Act 1993 (underwriting profits to be earned income)

Section 180 of the Finance Act 1993 shall not apply in relation to the profits arising to an individual as a partner in a Lloyd's Scottish limited partnership.

9 Death of partner

(1) This regulation applies where—

(*a*) regulation 3(1) applies in relation to a Lloyd's . . . [1] partnership, and

(*b*) an individual who is a partner in the partnership dies.

(2) The carrying on of the deceased partner's partnership business by his personal representatives shall not be treated for the purposes of the Income Tax Acts as a change in the persons engaged in the carrying on of that business.

(3) The deceased partner's partnership business shall be treated for the purposes of the Income Tax Acts as continuing until either—

(*a*) any security provided by him in relation to that business is released or repaid by Lloyd's to his personal representatives, or

(*b*) his interest in the partnership is assigned by his personal representatives.

Amendments—[1] Words revoked by the Lloyd's Underwriters (Scottish Limited Partnerships) (Tax) (Amendment) Regulations, SI 2006/111 regs 2, 4 with effect from 14 February 2006. This amendment has effect with respect to accounting periods of Lloyd's partnerships ending on or after that date.

10 Terminal loss relief

(1) This regulation applies where—

(*a*) regulation 3(1) applies in relation to a Lloyd's . . . [1] partnership, and

(*b*) an individual who is a partner in the partnership ceases to carry on his partnership business, whether by reason of death or otherwise.

(2) The date on which the individual's partnership business is permanently discontinued for the purposes of section 388 of the Taxes Act (carry-back of terminal losses) ("section 388") shall be deemed to be the 5th April in the last year of assessment in which his share of the profits or losses of that business arising from the partnership's membership of one or more syndicates, or from assets forming part of a premiums trust fund, fall to be included in a [calculation under Part 9 of the Income Tax (Trading and Other Income) Act 2005][2].

(3) A partner may not make more than one claim under section 388 in respect of the same partnership business.

Amendments—[1] Words revoked by the Lloyd's Underwriters (Scottish Limited Partnerships) (Tax) (Amendment) Regulations, SI 2006/111 regs 2, 4 with effect from 14 February 2006. This amendment has effect with respect to accounting periods of Lloyd's partnerships ending on or after that date.

[2] Words substituted by SI 2006/111 regs 2, 9 with effect from 14 February 2006. This amendment has effect with respect to accounting periods of Lloyd's partnerships ending on or after that date.

1998/311

FINANCE ACT 1989, SECTION 178(1) (APPOINTED DAY) ORDER 1998

Made by the Treasury under FA 1989 s 178(7)

Made . . . . *12 February 1998*

1 This Order may be cited as the Finance Act 1989, section 178(1), (Appointed Day) Order 1998.

2 The day appointed for sections 59C and 103A of the Taxes Management Act 1970 for periods beginning on or after which section 178(1) of the Finance Act 1989 shall have effect is 9th March 1998.

1998/729

RETIREMENT BENEFITS SCHEMES (RESTRICTION ON DISCRETION TO APPROVE) (EXCEPTED PROVISIONS) REGULATIONS 1998

Revocation—These Regulations lapse by virtue of the coming into force of FA 2004 Part 4 (ss 149–284) with effect from 6 April 2006.

1998/1513

VISITING FORCES AND ALLIED HEADQUARTERS (INCOME TAX AND CAPITAL GAINS TAX) (DESIGNATION) ORDER 1998

Made . . . . *24 June 1998*
Coming into force . . . . *24 June 1998*

Revocation—This Order revoked by the Visiting Forces and International Military Headquarters (NATO and PfP) (Tax Designation) Order, SI 2012/3071 art 2, Sch 1, with effect from 13 December 2012.

1998/1514

VISITING FORCES (INCOME TAX AND CAPITAL GAINS TAX) (DESIGNATION) ORDER 1998

Made . . . . *24 June 1998*
Coming into force in relation to each country specified in article 2, the date determined in accordance with . . . . *article 1(2)*

Revocation—This Order revoked by the Visiting Forces and International Military Headquarters (NATO and PfP) (Tax Designation) Order, SI 2012/3071 art 2, Sch 1, with effect from 13 December 2012.

1998/1868

GIFTS FOR RELIEF IN POOR COUNTRIES (DESIGNATION) ORDER 1998

Made by the Treasury under FA 1998 s 47(8) and 48(9)

Made . . . . *31 July 1998*
Laid before the House of Commons . . . . *31 July 1998*
Coming into force . . . . *21 August 1998*

Commentary—*Simon's Taxes* **D1.317**.
Press releases etc—HMT 31-7-98 (eighty countries eligible for Millennium Gift Aid).

1 This Order may be cited as the Gifts for Relief in Poor Countries (Designation) Order 1998 and shall come into force on 21st August 1998

2 The descriptions of countries specified for the purposes of sections 47 and 48 of the Finance Act 1998 are—

(*a*) the countries included in the lists of countries which are eligible for lending by the International Development Association ("the Association"), and by the Association and the International Bank for Reconstruction and Development ("the Bank"), published by the Association and the Bank (under the name of The World Bank) in Appendix 5 to The World Bank Annual Report 1997, under the headings "Countries eligible for IDA funds only" and "Countries eligible for a blend of IBRD and IDA funds", and (*b*) any further countries included in those lists as published in The World Bank Annual Reports issued between the date on which this Order is made and 31st December 2000.

Commentary—*Simon's Taxes* **D1.317; E1.804**.

Press releases etc—IR 31-7-98 (Eighty countries eligible for Millennium Gift Aid announced).

1998/1870

INDIVIDUAL SAVINGS ACCOUNT REGULATIONS 1998

Made by the Treasury under TA 1988 ss 333, 333A and 333B, TCGA 1992 s 151 and FA 1998 ss 75 and 76(3)

Made . . . . *31 July 1998*

Laid before the House of Commons . . . . *31 July 1998*

Coming into force In accordance with . . . . *regulation 1*

Commentary—*Simon's Taxes* **Division E3.3**.

ARRANGEMENT OF REGULATIONS

1	Citation and commencement
2	Interpretation
2A	Meaning of account investor
2B	Meaning of junior ISA account
2C	Meaning of "registered contact" etc
2D	Regulations that do not apply to junior ISA accounts
2E	Contracts entered into by or on behalf of a child who is 16 or over
2F	Special provision in respect of Looked After Children
3	Introductory
4	General conditions for accounts and subscriptions to accounts
4ZA	Subscriptions to an account other than a junior ISA account
4ZB	Subscriptions to a junior ISA account
4ZC	Inalienability of a junior ISA account
4ZD	Permitted withdrawals from a junior ISA account
4ZE	Permitted withdrawals from a junior ISA account where the named child is terminally ill
4A	Repair of certain incompatible accounts and excess subscriptions
4AA	Application of the repair provisions to Lifetime ISAs
4B	Closure of cash account prior to the opening of the same type of account to be disregarded once
4C	Removal of insurance components at 6th April 2005
4D	Removal of maxi-accounts, mini-accounts and TESSA only accounts at 6th April 2008
5	*Transfers from matured tax-exempt special savings accounts* (repealed)
5A	*Treatment of sums held in accounts managed by Icesave Bank* (revoked)
5B	*Treatment of certain sums held in accounts managed by Keydata Investment Services Limited* (revoked)
5C	Treatment of certain sums held in dormant accounts
5D	Subscriptions disregarded for the purposes of the subscription limits in regulations 4ZA and 4ZB
5DA	Defaulted cash account subscription
5DAA	Defaulted Lifetime ISA subscription
5DB	Defaulted investment subscription
5DC	Default event in respect of cash account
5DD	Defaulted investment payment
5DDA	Additional permitted subscription to an account other than a junior ISA account
5DDB	Flexible account
5DDC	Additional permitted subscription of cash to an account other than a junior ISA on closure of Help to Buy ISA
5DE	Additional permitted subscription to a junior ISA account
5DF	Information required by regulation 5D
5DFA	Declarations required by regulation 5D
5DFB	Notices required by regulation 5D
5DG	Single regulation 5D subscription
5DH	Default event or default investment payment occurring in the period beginning on 6th April 2011 and ending on 7th August 2012

1 Citation and commencement

These Regulations may be cited as the Individual Savings Account Regulations 1998 and shall come into force for the purposes of—

(*a*) applications under regulations 12 and 13 relating to the year 1999–00, to subscribe to an account in that year,

(*b*) applications under regulation 14 to be approved as an account manager to manage accounts in the year 1999–00 and subsequent years, and

(*c*) regulations 16 to 18 and 20, so far as they relate to applications referred to in paragraph (*b*),

on 1st October 1998, and for all other purposes on 6th April 1999.

2 Interpretation

(1) In these Regulations unless the context otherwise requires—

(*a*) "account", except in the case of—

(i) an account with a deposit-taker, or

(ii) . . . [12]

(iii) a share or deposit account with a building society, or

(iv) a deposit account with [a person falling within][3] [section 991(2) of the Income Tax Act 2007][24]

shall be construed in accordance with [regulation 4(1) and, where appropriate, regulation 2B(*b*)][17] [and shall include a personal equity plan treated on and from the 6th April 2008 as a stocks and shares account][12];

an "account investment" is an investment under the account which is a qualifying investment for a stocks and shares component[, a cash component[an innovative finance component or a Lifetime ISA component][36], as the case may be, within the meaning of regulation 7, 8[, 8ZA][36] or 8A][33];

[an "account investor" has the meaning given in regulation 2A;][17]

an "account manager" is a person who fulfils the conditions of these Regulations and is approved by the Board for the purposes of these Regulations as an account manager;

[. . . [27]

. . . [26]][13]

"approved profit sharing scheme" has the same meaning as in Chapter IV of Part V of the Taxes Act;

["article 36H agreement" is to be construed in accordance with article 36H(4) of the Regulated Activities Order 2001 and is an agreement entered into by an account investor as lender with a borrower with the facilitation of an operator and for the purposes of regulation 8A(2) includes such an agreement notwithstanding that, after it is entered into, the operator assumes the rights of the lender under it;][33]

an "assurance undertaking" means [a direct life insurance undertaking within the meaning of Article 2 of Directive 2009/138/EC of the European Parliament and of the Council of 25 November 2009 on the taking-up and pursuit of the business of Insurance and Reinsurance (Solvency II)][30];

["bank" has the meaning given by section 991(2) to (5) of the Income Tax Act 2007;][24]

["the Board" means the Commissioners for Her Majesty's Revenue and Customs;][8]

["borrower" is to be construed in accordance with article 36H(9) of the Regulated Activities Order 2001;][33]

"building society" means a building society within the meaning of the Building Societies Act 1986, or the Irish Building Societies Act 1989;

["building society bonus", except in regulation 22(1)(*a*)(i), excludes any bonus, distribution of funds or the conferring of rights in relation to shares—

(*a*) in connection with an amalgamation, transfer of engagements or transfer of business of a building society, and

(*b*) mentioned in section 96 or 100 of the Building Societies Act 1986,

and "payment under a building society bonus scheme" shall be construed accordingly;][11]

["business day" means any day except—

(*a*) a Saturday, Sunday, Good Friday or Christmas Day;

(*b*) a bank holiday under the Banking and Financial Dealings Act 1971;][17]

["ceasing to be subject to the plan", in relation to plan shares under [a Schedule 2][26] SIP, shall be construed in accordance with the SIP code (see section 488(3) of ITEPA 2003);][13]

["charity" has the meaning given in paragraph 1(1) of Schedule 6 to the Finance Act 2010;][34]

["child" means an individual under 18;][17]

["child trust fund" has the meaning given by section 1 of the Child Trust Funds Act 2004;][18]

["collective investment scheme" has the meaning in section 235 of FISMA 2000;][15]

"company", except in regulation 7(4), means any body corporate having a share capital other than—

(i) an open-ended investment company, within the meaning given by section [236 of the Financial Services and Markets Act 2000][3], [or][29]

[(ii) a UK UCITS, recognised UCITS or non-UCITS retail scheme[;][29]][15]

(iii) . . . [29]

(iv) . . . [29]

["credit union" means a society registered as a credit union under the Industrial and Provident Societies Act 1965 or the Credit Unions (Northern Ireland) Order 1985;][9]

["debenture" includes any instrument creating or acknowledging indebtedness within the meaning of article 77(1) and (2) of the Regulated Activities Order 2001 but with the omission of the words "such of the following as do not fall within article 78;][34]

["CTA 2010" means the Corporation Tax Act 2010;][18]
["current year payments" has the meaning given in regulation 10A(3);][36]
["deceased's account" is an account which the deceased held with an account manager at the date of the deceased's death;][28]
"deposit-taker" has the meaning given by [section 853 of ITA 2007][13];
["the Director of Savings" has the same meaning as in the National Debt Act 1972;][1]
["dormant account" means a cash account which is a "relevant dormant account" within the meaning given in section 39(2) of the Finance Act 2008, omitting the words—

(a) "is to be, or"; and

(b) "will apply, or" (in both places they appear);][16]

["EEA Agreement" means the agreement on the European Economic Area signed at Oporto on 2nd May 1992, together with the Protocol adjusting that Agreement signed at Brussels on 17th March 1993, as modified or supplemented from time to time;
"EEA State", in relation to any time, means a state which at that time is a member State, or any other state which at that time is a party to the EEA Agreement;][21]
["eligible child" means a child—

(*a*) born—

(i) on or after 3rd January 2011; or

(ii) before the time mentioned in paragraph (i) but who is not an "eligible child" within the meaning given in the Child Trust Funds Act 2004; and

(*b*) who, at the time when the application to open an account pursuant to a junior ISA application described in regulation 12A is made, is—

(i) resident . . . [19] in the United Kingdom;

(ii) a person who has general earnings from overseas Crown employment subject to United Kingdom tax within the meaning given by section 28 of ITEPA 2003;

(iii) married to, or in a civil partnership with, a person mentioned in paragraph (ii); or

(iv) a dependant of a person mentioned in paragraph (ii);][17]

["eligible conveyancer" has the meaning given in paragraph 7 of the Schedule;][36]
["European institution" means an EEA firm of the kind mentioned in [paragraph 5(*a*) to (*d*), (*f*) and (*h*)][23] of Schedule 3 to the Financial Services and Markets Act 2000 which is an authorised person for the purposes of that Act as a result of qualifying for authorisation under paragraph 12[(1) to (4) and (7)][23] of that Schedule;][3]
["FISMA 2000" means the Financial Services and Markets Act 2000;][15]
["51% subsidiary" and "75% subsidiary" have the same meanings as they do in section 1154 of CTA 2010;][18]
["first subscription", in any year, means the first subscription into an account in that year which is not a subscription made in accordance with regulation 5D;][31]
["flexible account" has the meaning given in regulation 5DDB;][32]
"gains", except in regulations 22(1)(*a*)(ii) to (v) and 35(6), means "chargeable gains" within the meaning of the Taxation of Chargeable Gains Act 1992;
"gilt-edged securities" has the meaning given by [paragraphs 1 and 1A][1] of Schedule 9 to the Taxation of Chargeable Gains Act 1992;
["government bonus" has the meaning given in the Schedule;][36]
. . . [13]
an "incorporated friendly society" means a society incorporated under the Friendly Societies Act 1992;
. . . [29]
["innovative finance account" has the meaning given in regulation 4(1ZA);][33]
["interim permission" is to be construed in accordance with Chapter 4 of Part 8 of the Financial Services and Markets Act 2000 (Regulated Activities) (Amendment) (No 2) Order 2013;][33]
["investment trust" means an investment trust within the meaning of section 1158 of the Corporation Tax Act 2010][35]
["ITA 2007" means the Income Tax Act 2007;
"ITEPA 2003" means the Income Tax (Earnings and Pensions) Act 2003;
"ITTOIA 2005" means the Income Tax (Trading and Other Income) Act 2005;][13]
. . . [3]
["junior ISA account" has the meaning given in regulation 2B;][17]
["lender" is to be construed in accordance with article 36H(9) of the Regulated Activities Order 2001;][33]
"Looked After Child" has the meaning given in regulation 2F (special provision in respect of Looked After Children);][18]
["Lifetime ISA" has the meaning given in regulation 4(1ZB);
"Lifetime ISA payment limit" has the meaning given in regulation 4ZA(1A);
"Lifetime ISA qualifying individual" has the meaning given in regulation 10A;][36]

"the Management Act" means the Taxes Management Act 1970;
"market value" shall be construed in accordance with section 272 of The Taxation of Chargeable Gains Act 1992;
["named child" means a child who holds an account opened pursuant to a junior ISA application described in regulation 12A;][17]
"notice", except in [regulations 9 and 36][1], means notice in writing and "notify" shall be construed accordingly;
["parental responsibility" means—
(*a*) parental responsibility within the meaning of the Children Act 1989 or the Children (Northern Ireland) Order 1995, or
(*b*) parental responsibilities within the meaning of the Children (Scotland) Act 1995;][17]
["operator" means a person who has permission (other than an interim permission) under Part 4A of FISMA 2000 to carry on the regulated activity specified in article 36H(1) of the Regulated Activities Order 2001;][33]
["outstanding principal balance" means, in respect of a qualifying investment for an innovative finance component, the amount in respect of the investment owing to the account investor at any time;][34]
["participant", in relation to [a Schedule 2][26] SIP, shall be construed in accordance with the SIP code (see section 488(3) of ITEPA 2003);
"plan shares", in relation to [a Schedule 2][26] SIP, shall be construed in accordance with the SIP code (see section 488(3) of ITEPA 2003) except that—
(*a*) paragraph 87(6) of Schedule 2 to ITEPA 2003 (meaning of the word "shares" in the context of company reconstructions) shall not apply, and
(*b*) in paragraph 88(2) of that Schedule (treatment of shares acquired under rights issue) the words "or securities or rights" shall be treated as omitted;][13]
["qualifying addition" has the meaning given in the Schedule;][36]
"qualifying distribution" has the same meaning as in [section 1136 of the Corporation Tax Act 2010][17];
["qualifying investments for an innovative finance component" has the meaning given in regulation 8A;][33]
"recognised stock exchange" has the same meaning as in [section 1005 of ITA 2007][17];
a "registered friendly society" has the meaning given by the Friendly Societies Act 1992, and includes any society that by virtue of section 96(2) of that Act is to be treated as a registered friendly society;
["Regulated Activities Order 2001" means the Financial Services and Markets Act 2000 (Regulated Activities) Order 2001;][33]
"release date" has the meaning given by section 187(2) of the Taxes Act;
"relevant authorised person" has the same meaning as in [section 697(2)(*b*) of ITTOIA 2005][13];
. . . [24]
["replacement subscription" has the meaning given in regulation 5DDB;][32]
["responsible person" means a person who is the responsible person in respect of the management of a junior ISA account in accordance with regulation 2C(4);][17]
. . .
"security", except in regulations [7(2)(*c*) to][1] [(*cc*) and (8)(*b*), 8(2)(*f*)][14] and 34(3), means any loan stock or similar security of a company whether secured or unsecured[, and in regulation 7(2)(*cc*) has the same meaning but with the omission of the words "of a company"][14];
["the Stakeholder Products Regulations" means the Financial Services and Markets Act 2000 (Stakeholder Products) Regulations 2004;][7]
"tax" where neither income tax nor capital gains tax is specified means either of those taxes;
"tax credit" means a tax credit under section 231 of the Taxes Act;
"the Taxes Act" means the Income and Corporation Taxes Act 1988;
. . . [12]
["transferable security" has the meaning given in section 102A(3) of FISMA 2000;][34]
"year" means a year of assessment, and "the year 1999–00" means the year of assessment beginning on 6th April 1999;

(*b*) ["authorised fund" means—
(i) an authorised unit trust, or
(ii) an open-ended investment company . . . [13];][3]
"authorised unit trust" means a unit trust scheme in the case of which an authorisation order made by the Financial Services Authority under section [243 of the Financial Services and Markets Act 2000][3] is in force;
[a "Chapter 5 UCITS" means a UCITS complying with Chapter 5 of the Collective Investment schemes sourcebook;][13, 15]
["the Collective Investment Schemes Sourcebook" means the sourcebook of that name made by the Financial Services Authority under the Financial Services and Markets Act 2000;][4]

["depositary interest" means the rights of the person mentioned in paragraph (*b*), under a certificate or other record (whether or not in the form of a document) acknowledging—

(*a*) that a person holds relevant investments or evidence of the right to them, and

(*b*) that another person is entitled to rights in or in relation to those or identical relevant investments, including the right to receive such investments, or evidence of the right to them or the proceeds from such investments, from the person mentioned in paragraph (*a*),

where "relevant investments" means investments which are exclusively qualifying investments for a stocks and shares component falling within any of regulation 7(2)(a) to (h), and the rights mentioned in paragraph (*b*) are exclusively rights in or in relation to relevant investments;][2]

. . . [13]

["insolvency event" means the procedures listed in the definition of "insolvency event" in regulation 19(15) of the Payment Services Regulations 2009;][17]

["non-UCITS retail scheme"—

(*a*) has the meaning in the . . . [13] Collective Investment Schemes Sourcebook (that is, a scheme to which, or to whose authorised fund manager and depositary, [COLL 5.1, 5.4 and 5.6][15] apply),

(*b*) includes a "recognised scheme" by virtue of section . . . [20] 272 of the Financial Services and Markets Act 2000, which would fall within paragraph (*a*) of this definition if it were an authorised fund, and

(*c*) includes a sub-fund of an umbrella which the terms of the scheme identify as a sub-fund which would fall within paragraph (*a*) or (*b*) of this definition if it were itself an authorised fund or a recognised scheme.

In this definition, expressions defined in the Glossary forming part of the Financial Services Authority Handbook have those defined meanings;][10]

["open-ended investment company" means a company incorporated in the United Kingdom to which section 236 of the Financial Services and Markets Act 2000 applies;][13]

["qualifying units in or shares of a non-UCITS retail scheme" means that—

(*a*) the instrument constituting the scheme secures that redemption of the units or shares in question shall take place no less frequently than bi-monthly (see Rule 6.2.16(6) of the . . . [13] Collective Investment Schemes Sourcebook omitting the words "Except where (7) applies, and", read with Rule 6.3.4(1), whether or not those Rules apply to the scheme), and

(*b*) a provision for suspension of dealings in exceptional conditions in accordance with Rule 7.2 of that Sourcebook (or any foreign procedure which is a direct foreign equivalent of that Rule) shall not be treated as a provision contrary to paragraph (*a*) of this definition;][10]

["recognised UCITS" means—

(*a*) a collective investment scheme constituted in an EEA State, which is a "recognised scheme" under section 264 of FISMA 2000, and complies with the requirements to be a "UCITS scheme" for the purposes of the Collective Investment Schemes Sourcebook (see in particular COLL 1.2.2); or

(*b*) a part of a recognised UCITS mentioned in paragraph (a) of this definition, which would be a sub-fund of an umbrella scheme which is a recognised UCITS;][15]

["Schedule 2 SIP" shall be construed in accordance with the SIP code (see section 488(3) of ITEPA 2003);][26]

["Schedule 3 SAYE option scheme" shall be construed in accordance with the SAYE code (see section 516(3) of ITEPA 2003);][27]

. . . [4]

. . . [13]

. . . [15]

["UK UCITS" means—

(*a*) a collective investment scheme authorised under section 31(1)(*a*) of FISMA 2000, which complies with the requirements to be a "UCITS scheme" for the purposes of the Collective Investment Schemes Sourcebook (see in particular COLL 1.2.2); or

(*b*) a part of a UK UCITS mentioned in paragraph (*a*) of this definition which would be a sub-fund of an umbrella scheme which is a UK UCITS;][15]

["umbrella scheme" means an authorised fund which according to the terms of the scheme is an umbrella scheme belonging to the category under that name established by the Financial Services Authority, and

(i) in the case of an authorised fund which is an authorised unit trust, references to a part of an umbrella scheme shall be construed in accordance with subsection (8) of section 468 of the Taxes Act, [and sub-paragraphs (6) and (7) of regulation 7 of the Authorised Investment Funds (Tax) Regulations 2006 shall apply for the purposes of these Regulations as they apply for the purposes of those Regulations, and][13]

(ii) in the case of an authorised fund which is an open-ended investment company, references to a part of an umbrella scheme shall be construed in accordance with subsection (18) of section 468 of the Taxes Act as that subsection is added in relation to open-ended investment companies by regulation 10(4) of the 1997 Regulations, and, in relation to a part of an umbrella scheme, references to investments of the company shall be construed in accordance with [subsection (4) of section 468A of the Taxes Act, and sub-paragraphs (2) and (3) of regulation 7 of the Authorised Investment Funds (Tax) Regulations 2006 shall apply for the purposes of these Regulations as they apply for the purposes of those Regulations;][13]

["unit holder" means a person entitled to a share of the investments subject to the trusts of a unit trust scheme;

"unit trust scheme" has the meaning given by section 237 of the Financial Services and Markets Act 2000;][13]

"units", in relation to an authorised unit trust, means the rights or interests (however described) of the unit holders in that authorised unit trust and, in relation to a part of an umbrella scheme, means the rights or interests for the time being of the unit holders in that part;

"units in, or shares of, a . . . [4] [UK UCITS or recognised][15] UCITS" means the rights or interests (however described) of the holders of the units or shares in that . . . [4] [UK UCITS or recognised][15] UCITS;

. . . [13]

[(1A) In these Regulations—

(*a*) a "bulk transfer of accounts" occurs where two or more accounts are transferred by an account manager ("the transferor") to another account manager ("the transferee")—

[(i) pursuant to an agreement made between the transferor and the transferee where the transfers are not made pursuant to requests made by a person who is the account investor or registered contact in relation to the accounts transferred; or

(ii) pursuant to an insurance business transfer scheme or a banking business transfer scheme under Part 7 (Control of Business Transfers) of the Financial Services and Markets Act 2000;][22]

(*b*) a "group transfer of accounts" occurs where a bulk transfer of accounts is made between account managers that are members of the same group of companies when the transfer occurs;

(*c*) two companies are members of the same group of companies if—

(i) one is a 75% subsidiary of the other, or

(ii) both are 75% subsidiaries of a third company.][18]

(2) The Table below indexes other definitions in these Regulations—

Term defined	*Regulation*
Account	4(1)
[Cash account	[4(1A)(*a*) and (*c*)][17]][12]
Component	[4(1A)(*b*) and (*c*)][17]
The disqualifying circumstances	17(1)
Interim claim	25
. . . [12]	. . . [12]
. . . [12]	. . . [12]
. . . [17]	. . . [17]
Qualifying circumstances	14(1)
Qualifying individual	10
Qualifying investments for a stock and shares component	7
Qualifying investments for a cash component	8
[Qualifying investments for a Lifetime ISA component	8ZA][36]
. . . [7]	. . . [7]
Qualifying securities	7(2)(*b*)
[Registered contact	2C][17]

Term defined	*Regulation*
[Stocks and shares account	[4(1A)(*a*) and (*b*)][17]][12]
...[17]	...[17]
[Subscription limit – junior ISA account][25]	[4ZB][17]
[Subscription limit – other accounts][25]	[4ZA][17]
[12] . . .	[12] . . .

Amendments—[1] Words in para (1)(*a*) amended by the Individual Savings Account (Amendment) Regulations, SI 1998/3174 reg 3(2) with effect from 6 April 1999.

[2] Definition of "depositary interest" inserted by the Individual Savings Account (Amendment No 3) Regulations, SI 2000/3112 reg 3 with effect from 13 December 2000.

[3] In sub-para (1)(*a*), words in the definition of "account" and "company" substituted, definition of "European institution" substituted, and definition of "long term business" revoked; in sub-para (1)(*b*), definition of "authorised fund" inserted, words in definition of "authorised unit trust"; definition of "umbrella scheme" substituted for definitions of "umbrella scheme" and "umbrella company", by the Financial Services and Markets Act 2000 (Consequential Amendments) (Taxes) Order, SI 2001/3629 art 169 with effect from 1 December 2001, immediately after the coming into force of the Financial Services and Markets Act 2000 ss 411, 432(1), Sch 20 (and SI 2001/3629 Pts 1 and 2).

[4] Definitions of "a Chapter 5 UCITS" and "the Collective Investment Schemes Sourcebook" inserted, and words in definition of "relevant UCITS" and "units in, or shares of, a relevant UCITS" revoked, by the Individual Savings Account (Amendment) Regulations, SI 2003/2747 regs 1(1), (2), 2, 3 with effect from 17 November 2003.

[5] In para (2), words in definition of "UCITS" substituted by the Collective Investment Schemes (Miscellaneous Amendments) Regulations, SI 2003/2066 reg 13(4) with effect from 13 February 2004.

[7] In para (1)(*a*), definition of "the Stakeholder Products Regulations" inserted; and in para (2), definition of "qualifying investments for an insurance component" revoked; by the ISA (Amendment No 2) Regulations, SI 2004/2996 regs 2, 3(*a*), (*c*), 4 with effect from 6 April 2005.

[8] In para (1)(*a*), definition of "the Board" substituted by the ISA (Amendment No 2) Regulations, SI 2005/2561 regs 2, 3 with effect from 6 October 2005.

[9] In para (1)(*a*), definition of "credit union" inserted by the ISA (Amendment No 3) Regulations, SI 2005/3350 regs 2, 3 with effect from 27 December 2005.

[10] In para (1)(*b*), definitions of "non-UCITS retail scheme" and "qualifying units in or shares of a non-UCITS retail scheme" inserted; by SI 2005/3350 regs 2, 4 with effect from 27 December 2005.

[11] In para (1)(*a*), definition of "building society bonus" inserted by the ISA (Amendment) Regulations, SI 2006/3194 regs 2, 3 with effect from 1 January 2007.

[12] In para (1)(*a*), in the definition of "account" para (ii) and following word "or" revoked, and words inserted, and definition of "tax-exempt special savings account" revoked; in para (2) words in Table substituted, and entries in Table revoked and inserted, by the Individual Savings Account (Amendment) Regulations, SI 2007/2119 regs 2–4 with effect from 6 April 2008.

[13] In para (1)(*a*), definitions of "approved SAYE option scheme" and "approved SIP", substituted; definitions of "ceasing to be subject to the plan", "ITA 2007", ITEPA 2003", ITTOIA 2005", "participant" and "plan shares" inserted; words in definitions of "deposit-taker", "relevant authorised person" substituted; definitions of "income tax quarter" and "savings-related share option scheme" revoked; in para (1)(*b*) words in definitions of "authorised fund", "non-UCITS retail scheme" and "qualifying units in or shares of a non-UCITS retail scheme" revoked; definitions of "Chapter 5 UCITS", "open-ended investment company", "unit holder" and "unit trust scheme" substituted; definitions of "the first condition", "the second condition", "fund of funds scheme", "money market scheme", "the New Collective Investment Schemes Sourcebook", "securities scheme", "the 1997 Regulations" and "warrant scheme" revoked; words in definition of "umbrella scheme" substituted; by the Individual Savings Account (Amendment) Regulations, SI 2008/704 regs 2, 3 with effect from 6 April 2008 immediately after the ISA (Amendment) Regulations, SI 2007/2119 come into force.

[14] In para (1)(*a*) in the definition of "security", words substituted and words inserted at the end, by the Individual Savings Account (Amendment No 3) Regulations, SI 2008/3025 regs 2, 3 with effect from 16 December 2008.

[15] In para (1)(*a*), in definition of "company", para (ii) substituted, in para (1)(*b*), definitions of "Chapter 5 UCITS" and "UCITS" revoked, in definition of "non-UCITS retail scheme", words substituted for words "Sections 5.1, 5.4 and 5.6 of that Sourcebook", definition of a "relevant UCITS" substituted, in definition of "units in, or shares of, a UCITS", words inserted, definitions of "collective investment scheme", "FISMA 2000" and "UK UCITS" inserted, by the Individual Savings Account (Amendment No 2) Regulations, SI 2009/1994 regs 2, 3 with effect from 8 October 2008.

[16] In para (1)(*a*), definition of "dormant account" inserted by the Dormant Bank and Building Society Accounts (Tax) Regulations, SI 2011/22 reg 9(1), (2) with effect from 1 February 2011.

[17] In para (1)(*a*), in definition of "account", words substituted; definition of "account investor" substituted ; definitions of "business day", "child", "eligible child", "junior ISA account", "named child", "parental responsibility" and "responsible person" inserted; in definition of "qualifying distribution" words substituted; and in definition of "recognised stock exchange", words substituted; in para (1)(b), definition of "insolvency event" inserted and in Table in para (2), in entries relating to "Cash account", "component", "Stocks and shares account", words substituted, entries for "Overall subscription limit" and "Subscription limits" revoked and entry for "Registered contact" and references, inserted, by the Individual Savings Account (Amendment No 2) Regulations SI 2011/1780 regs 3, 4, 5 with effect from 1 November 2011.

[18] In para (1)(*a*), definitions of "child trust fund", "CTA 2010" and "Looked After Child" inserted, in definition of "company" words substituted, definition of "51% subsidiary" and "75% subsidiary" substituted, and para (1A) inserted, by the Individual Savings Account (Amendment) (No 2) Regulations, SI 2012/1871 regs 4–6, with effect generally from 8 August 2012, but subject to the following—

– insertion of definition of "child trust fund": with effect from 1 November 2011;

– substitution of words in definition of "company", insertion of definition of "CTA 2010" and substitution of definition of "51% subsidiary" and "75% subsidiary": with effect from 9 November 2011, in so far as these amendments relate to the amendments made by SI 2012/1871 regs 6, 16(*b*), (*c*), (*d*), 18(*a*), (*b*), 19 below.

19 In para (1)(*a*), in definition of "eligible child", in para (*b*)(i) words "and ordinarily resident" revoked by the Income Tax (Removal of Ordinary Residence) Regulations, SI 2013/605 reg 4(1), (2) with effect for the purposes of a person's liability to income tax for the tax year 2013–14 or any subsequent tax years.

20 In para (1)(*b*), in definition of "non-UCITS retail scheme", para (*b*), words "270 or" revoked by the Alternative Investment Fund Managers Regulations, SI 2013/1773 reg 81, Sch 2 para 4 with effect from 22 July 2013.

21 In para (1)(*a*) definitions of "EEA Agreement" and "EEA State" substituted by the Individual Savings Account (Amendment No 3) Regulations, SI 2013/1743 regs 2, 3(*a*) with effect from 5 August 2013.

22 In para (1A)(*a*), sub-paras (i), (ii) substituted by the Individual Savings Account (Amendment No 3) Regulations, SI 2013/1743 regs 2, 3(*b*) with effect from 5 March 2013.

23 In para (1)(*a*) in definition of "European institution" words substituted, and words inserted, by the Individual Savings Account (Amendment) Regulations, SI 2014/654 regs 2, 3(*c*) with effect from 15 August 2013.

24 In para (1)(*a*), in definition of "account", in para (iv) words substituted, definition of "bank" inserted, and definition of "relevant European institution" revoked, by the Individual Savings Account (Amendment) Regulations, SI 2014/654 regs 2, 3(*a*), (*b*), (*d*), (*e*) with effect from 6 April 2014.

25 In para (2), in table, words substituted by the Individual Savings Account (Amendment No 2) Regulations, SI 2014/1450 regs 2, 3 with effect from 1 July 2014.

26 In para (1)(*a*), definition of "approved SIP" revoked, in definitions of "ceasing to be subject to the plan", "participant" and "plan shares" for "an approved", words substituted, and definition of "Schedule 2 SIP" inserted, by FA 2014 s 51, Sch 8 paras 84, 85. These amendments are treated as having come into force on 6 April 2014.

27 In para (1)(*a*), definition of "approved SAYE option scheme" revoked, and definition of "Schedule 3 SAYE option scheme" inserted, by FA 2014 s 51, Sch 8 paras 143, 144. These amendments are treated as having come into force on 6 April 2014.

28 In para (1)(*a*), definition of "deceased's account" inserted by the Individual Savings Account (Amendment No 2) Regulations, SI 2015/869 regs 2, 3 with effect from 6 April 2015.

29 In para (1)(*a*), in definition of "company", word at the end of sub-para (i) revoked, semicolon substituted for comma at the end of sub-para (ii), sub-paras (iii), (iv) revoked and definition of "industrial and provident society" revoked by the Individual Savings Account (Amendment No 4) Regulations, SI 2015/1370 regs 2, 3 with effect from 1 July 2015.

30 In para (1), in definition of "assurance undertaking", words substituted by the Solvency 2 Regulations, SI 2015/575 reg 60, Sch 2 para 8 with effect from 1 January 2016.

31 In para (1), definition of "first subscription" inserted by the Individual Savings Account (Amendment) Regulations, SI 2016/16 regs 2, 3(1) with effect from 1 February 2016.

32 In para (1)(*a*), definitions of "flexible account" and "replacement subscription" inserted by the Individual Savings Account (Amendment) Regulations, SI 2016/16 regs 2, 3(2), (3) with effect from 6 April 2016.

33 In para (1)(*a*), words in definition of "account investment" substituted, and definitions of "article 36H agreement", "borrower", "interim permission", "innovative finance account", "lender", "operator", "qualifying investments for an innovative finance component" and "Regulated Activities Order 2001" inserted by the Individual Savings Account (Amendment No 2) Regulations, SI 2016/364 regs 2, 3 with effect from 6 April 2016.

34 In para (1)(*a*), definition of "outstanding principal balance" substituted, and definitions of "charity", "debenture" and "transferable security" inserted, by the Individual Savings Account (Amendment No 3) Regulations, SI 2016/977 regs 2, 3 with effect from 1 November 2016.

35 In para (1)(*a*), definition of "investment trust" substituted by the Individual Savings Account (Amendment) Regulations, SI 2017/186 regs 2, 3 with effect from 6 April 2017.

36 In para (1)(*a*), in definition of "account investment", words substituted and words inserted, definitions of "current year payments", "eligible conveyancer", "government bonus", "Lifetime ISA", "Lifetime ISA payment limit", "Lifetime ISA qualifying individual", and "qualifying addition" inserted, and in para (2), in Table, entry relating to Qualifying investments for a Lifetime ISA component" inserted, by the Individual Savings Account (Amendment No 2) Regulations, SI 2017/466 regs 2, 3 with effect from 6 April 2017.

2A [Meaning of account investor

(1) This regulation makes provision for the meaning of "account investor" in these Regulations.

(2) In relation to an account that is not a junior ISA account [nor a Lifetime ISA][3], "account investor" means an individual who subscribes to an account and who is a qualifying individual within the meaning of regulation 10.

(3) In relation to a junior ISA account, "account investor" has different meanings in relation to the application of the regulations specified in paragraphs (4) and (5) as provided for in those paragraphs.

(4) For the purposes of the application of regulations 5C, [5D to 5DC, 5DF,][2] 6(3), 7, 8, 9 (other than regulation 9(3)(*b*)(iii) and (6)), 21A(1) (other than its first occurrence therein), 21A(2) and (3), 22, 24, 28, 31, 34, 35 (other than regulation 35(10)) and 36, "account investor" means the named child in relation to the account in question.

(5) For the purposes of the application of regulations 4, 9(6), 15, 17, 19, 20, 21A(7), 35(10) and its first occurrence in regulation 21A(1), "account investor" means the registered contact in relation to the account in question.

[(6) In relation to a Lifetime ISA, "account investor" means an individual who—

(a) makes, or has made, a qualifying addition to a Lifetime ISA, and

(b) at the time of each qualifying addition by the individual into the Lifetime ISA, is a Lifetime ISA qualifying individual.][3]][1]

Amendments—[1] Regs 2A–2E inserted by the Individual Savings Account (Amendment No 2) Regulations, SI 2011/1780 regs 2, 6 with effect from 1 November 2011.

2 Words in para (4) inserted by the Individual Savings Account (Amendment) (No 2) Regulations, SI 2012/1871 regs 4, 7 with effect from 8 August 2012.

[3] In para (2), words inserted, and para (6) inserted, by the Individual Savings Account (Amendment No 2) Regulations, SI 2017/466 regs 2, 4 with effect from 6 April 2017.

Prospective amendments—In para (2)(*b*), in definition of "insolvency event", words "regulation 23(18) of the Payment Services Regulations 2017" to be substituted for words "regulation 19(15) of the Payment Services Regulations 2009" by the Payment Services Regulations, SI 2017/752 reg 156, Sch 8 para 7 with effect from 13 January 2018.

2B [Meaning of junior ISA account

In these Regulations—

(*a*) an account opened pursuant to a junior ISA application described in regulation 12A is a junior ISA account at any time when it is held by a child;

(*b*) references to "account" shall be construed as including a reference to an account that is a junior ISA account except where the context otherwise requires; and

(*c*) references to an account held by a child are references to an account in respect of which the child is the beneficial owner of the account investments under that account.][1]

Amendments—[1] Regs 2A–2E inserted by the Individual Savings Account (Amendment No 2) Regulations, SI 2011/1780 regs 2, 6 with effect from 1 November 2011.

2C [Meaning of "registered contact" etc

(1) In these Regulations "registered contact" means the person who may give instructions in respect of the management of a junior ISA account to the person who is the account manager in relation to that account.

(2) The person who may give instructions in respect of the management of a junior ISA account to the account manager of that account is—

(*a*) the named child who holds the account if the application to open the account in accordance with regulation 12A was made by that child,

(*b*) the named child who holds the account if—

(i) the child has attained the age of 16 years,

(ii) paragraph (3) does not apply in relation to the child, and

(iii) the child has assumed responsibility for the management of the account in accordance with paragraph (6), or

(*c*) in any other case, the responsible person in relation to the account.

(3) [For the purposes of paragraph (2)(*b*)(ii) this paragraph applies in relation to the child—

(*a*) if the child is resident in England and Wales and lacks capacity in relation to the management of the junior ISA account under section 2(1) of the Mental Capacity Act 2005;][2]

(*b*) [if the child is resident in Scotland, the child is suffering mental disorder within the meaning given by][2] section 328 of the Mental Health (Care and Treatment) (Scotland) Act 2003;

(*c*) [if the child is resident in Northern Ireland, the child is suffering mental disorder within the meaning given by][2] Article 3 of the Mental Health (Northern Ireland) Order 1986.

(4) A person is the responsible person in relation to a junior ISA account if—

(*a*) that person—

(i) makes the application to open the account in question in accordance with regulation 12A; or

(ii) assumes responsibility for the management of the account in accordance with paragraph (6); and

(*b*) that person has parental responsibility in relation to the named child who holds the account at the time when that person—

(i) makes the application described in sub-paragraph (*a*)(i); or

(ii) assumes responsibility for the management of the account as described in sub-paragraph (*a*)(ii).

(5) A person ceases to be the person who may give instructions in respect of the management of a junior ISA account to the person who is the account manager in relation to that account when another person assumes responsibility for the management of the account in accordance with paragraph (6).

(6) A person assumes responsibility for the management of a junior ISA account if—

(*a*) the person makes an application to assume responsibility for the management of the account in accordance with paragraph (7), and

(*b*) the account manager of the account in question accepts the application.

(7) An application by a person ("the applicant") to assume responsibility for the management of a junior ISA account must—

(*a*) be made to the account manager of the account in question;

(*b*) contain—

(i) the applicant's full name,

(ii) the applicant's address (including postcode),

(iii) the named child's full name and date of birth,

(iv) the named child's address (including postcode),

(v) the named child's national insurance number if the child is over 16 and has been issued with a national insurance number, and

(vi) the authorisation specified in paragraph (8);

(*c*) contain a declaration by the applicant that the applicant—

(i) is 16 years of age or over,

(ii) is the named child who holds the account in question or has parental responsibility in relation to the named child who holds the account in question, and

(iii) is to be the registered contact for the account.

(8) The authorisation specified by this paragraph is authority given by the applicant to the account manager (on behalf of the named child who holds the account where appropriate)—

(*a*) to hold the subscriptions, account investments, interest, dividends and any other rights or proceeds in respect of those investments and cash;

(*b*) to make on behalf of the named child any claims to relief from tax in respect of account investments; and

(*c*) to make a record in writing in accordance with paragraph (11) where that paragraph requires the account manager to do so.

(9) An account manager must not accept an application to assume responsibility for the management of a junior ISA account if—

(*a*) except in the circumstances specified in paragraph (10), the person who is the registered contact in relation to the account at the time when the application is made does not consent to the applicant assuming responsibility for the management of the account; or

(*b*) the account manager has reason to believe that the applicant has given untrue information in the application.

(10) The circumstances specified in this paragraph are—

(*a*) the death of the most recent registered contact,

(*b*) the incapacity of the registered contact,

(*c*) where the registered contact cannot be contacted,

(*d*) the bringing to an end of a Court order under which the registered contact is a responsible person,

(*e*) where the applicant is the named child who holds the account and is aged 16 or over,

(*f*) where, under an adoption order, the applicant is the adopter of the named child who holds the account,

(*g*) where a Court so orders,

(*h*) where the applicant has been appointed to be a guardian or special guardian of the named child who holds the account.

(11) Where the application to assume responsibility for the management of a junior ISA account is not in writing or the account manager operates a record system under which all original written applications are not retained—

(*a*) the account manager must, immediately after receiving the application, record, in writing, on behalf of the applicant the declaration required by paragraph (7)(*c*) and the authorisation required by paragraphs (7)(*b*)(vi) and (8);

(*b*) the account manager must notify the applicant of the contents of the written record within 5 business days of making it; and

(*c*) the written record (as amended by any corrections notified to the account manager by the applicant within 30 days of the notification mentioned in sub-paragraph (*b*)) shall be treated as the applicant's declaration required by paragraph (7)(*c*) and authorisation required by paragraphs (7)(*b*)(vi) and (8).][1]

Amendments—[1] Regs 2A–2E inserted by the Individual Savings Account (Amendment No 2) Regulations, SI 2011/1780 regs 2, 6 with effect from 1 November 2011.

[2] In para (3), words substituted, and in sub-paras (*b*), (*c*) words substituted, by the Individual Savings Account (Amendment) Regulations, SI 2014/654 regs 2, 4 with effect from 6 April 2014.

2D [Regulations that do not apply to junior ISA accounts

Regulations 4(6)(fa), 4ZA, 4A, [4AA,][7] 4B, . . . [3] . . . [7] [5DDA,][4] [5DDB,][6] [5DDC,][5] [5DI to 5DM,][2] 7(2)(*h*), [8ZA, 8A, 10 to 12, 12B,][7] 21, . . . [3] and 30, do not apply to a junior ISA account.][1]

Amendments—[1] Regs 2A–2E inserted by the Individual Savings Account (Amendment No 2) Regulations, SI 2011/1780 regs 2, 6 with effect from 1 November 2011.

[2] Words inserted by the Individual Savings Account (Amendment) (No 2) Regulations, SI 2012/1871 regs 4, 8 with effect from 8 August 2012.

[3] Words revoked by the Individual Savings Account (Amendment No 2) Regulations, SI 2014/1450 regs 2, 4 with effect from 1 July 2014.

[4] Words inserted by the Individual Savings Account (Amendment No 2) Regulations, SI 2015/869 regs 2, 4 with effect from 6 April 2015.

[5] Reference inserted by the Individual Savings Account (Amendment) Regulations, SI 2016/16 regs 2, 4(*b*) with effect from 1 February 2016.

6 Reference inserted by the Individual Savings Account (Amendment) Regulations, SI 2016/16 regs 2, 4(*a*) with effect from 6 April 2016.

7 Reference inserted and revoked, and references substituted, by the Individual Savings Account (Amendment No 2) Regulations, SI 2017/466 regs 2, 5 with effect from 6 April 2017.

2E [Contracts entered into by or on behalf of a child who is 16 or over

Where, by virtue of the opening of an account pursuant to a junior ISA application described in regulation 12A, a contract is entered into by a child who is—

(*a*) aged 16 or over; and

(*b*) the child who—

(i) holds the account, or

(ii) has parental responsibility in relation to the child who holds the account,

the contract has effect as if the child who opened the account had been 18 or over when the contract was entered into.][1]

Amendments—[1] Regs 2A–2E inserted by the Individual Savings Account (Amendment No 2) Regulations, SI 2011/1780 regs 2, 6 with effect from 1 November 2011.

[2F Special provision in respect of Looked After Children

(1) A child is a Looked After Child where, after 2nd January 2011, there is a continuous period of at least 12 months during which paragraph (2) applies in relation to the child.

(2) This paragraph applies in relation to a child where the child is—

(*a*) looked after by a local authority within the meaning of section 22(1) of the Children Act 1989 (general duty of local authority in relation to children looked after by them);

[(*ab*) looked after by a local authority within the meaning of section 74 of the Social Services and Well-being (Wales) Act 2014;][3]

(*b*) provided with accommodation by an authority by virtue of article 21 of the Children (Northern Ireland) Order 1995 (provision of accommodation for children: general);

(*c*) the subject of an order made under article 50(1)(*a*) of the Children (Northern Ireland) Order 1995 (care orders and supervision orders);

(*d*) provided with accommodation by a local authority by virtue of section 25 of the Children (Scotland) Act 1995 (provision of accommodation for children, etc);

(*e*) the subject of a supervision requirement made under section 70(1) of the Children (Scotland) Act 1995 (disposal of referral by children's hearing: supervision requirements, including residence in secure accommodation);

[(*ea*) the subject of a compulsory supervision order within section 83 of the Children's Hearings (Scotland) Act 2011 ("the 2011 Act") (meaning of compulsory supervision order);

(*eb*) the subject of an interim compulsory supervision order within section 86 of the 2011 Act (meaning of interim compulsory supervision order);][2]

(*f*) the subject of a permanence order made under section 80 of the Adoption and Children (Scotland) Act 2007 (permanence orders); or

(*g*) treated as if the child were subject to an order described in sub-paragraph (*f*) by virtue of article 13(1) of the Adoption and Children (Scotland) Act 2007 (Commencement No 4, Transitional and Savings) Order 2009.

(3) In relation to a Looked After Child, regulations 2C(4)(*b*) (meaning of "registered contact" etc) and 12A(4)(*b*)(i) (conditions for application to open an account that is a junior ISA account) must be construed as if the Share Foundation has parental responsibility in respect of that child.

(4) In relation to an application to assume responsibility for the management of a junior ISA account by the Share Foundation, regulation 2C(7)(*c*) must be construed as requiring a declaration that—

(*a*) the applicant is the Share Foundation;

(*b*) the application is in relation to a Looked After Child; and

(*c*) the Share Foundation is to be the registered contact for the account.

(5) Where an application to assume responsibility for the management of a junior ISA account is made in relation to which the registered contact is the Share Foundation, regulation 2C(9)(*a*) must be construed as referring only to sub-paragraphs (*e*) and (*g*) of paragraph (10).

(6) Where the registered contact in relation to a junior ISA account is the Share Foundation, any reference in these Regulations to the residence of the registered contact must be construed as meaning a reference to the registered offices of the Share Foundation.

(7) In this regulation "the Share Foundation" means the company limited by guarantee (number 4500923) and charity registered with the Charity Commission of England and Wales (number 1108068) as "The Share Foundation".".[1]

Amendments—[1] Reg 2F inserted by the Individual Savings Account (Amendment) (No 2) Regulations, SI 2012/1871 regs 4, 9 with effect from 8 August 2012.

2 Para (2)(*ea*), (*eb*) inserted by the Individual Savings Account (Amendment No 3) Regulations, SI 2013/1743 regs 2, 4 with effect from 24 June 2013.

3 Para (2)(*ab*) inserted by the Individual Savings Account (Amendment) Regulations, SI 2017/186 regs 2, 4 with effect from 6 April 2017.

3 Introductory

These Regulations provide for the setting up of plans in the form of an account, by account managers approved by the Board, under which individuals may make certain investments, for the conditions under which they may invest and under which those accounts are to operate, for relief from tax in respect of account investments and generally for the administration of tax in relation to such accounts.

4 General conditions for accounts and subscriptions to accounts

[(1) An account is a scheme of investment, to which a subscription may be made, [which is an innovative finance account [or a Lifetime ISA][14] or in respect of which—][12]

(*a*) the conditions and requirements contained in paragraphs (1A) and (5) to (8) are fulfilled; and[2]

(*b*) either—

(i) the conditions contained in paragraph (1B) are fulfilled, or

(ii) at the time when the subscription to the account is made, the account is a junior ISA account.][7]

[(1ZA) An innovative finance account is an account in respect of which—

(*a*) the conditions in paragraphs (1A)(*a*) and (*ca*); [(1B)(*ba*) and (*c*), *d*(i) and (*e*)][14]; (5); (6)(*a*), (*e*) and (*g*) are fulfilled;

(*b*) in relation to cash held in an account, the conditions in paragraphs (6)(*f*) and (*fa*) and (7) are fulfilled; and

(*c*) the application to open the account is made in accordance with regulation 12.][12]

[(1ZB) A Lifetime ISA is an account in respect of which—

(*a*) the conditions in paragraphs (1A)(*a*) and (*cb*), (1B)(*bb*), (*c*), (*d*)(ii), (*e*) and (*f*) and (5) to (10) are fulfilled; and

(*b*) the application to open the account is made in accordance with regulation 12B.][14]

[(1A) The conditions in this paragraph are—

(*a*) the account is set up as a stocks and shares account[, a cash account[, an innovative finance account or a Lifetime ISA", and][14]][12];

(*b*) a stocks and shares account is made up of a single stocks and shares component only;

(*c*) a cash account is made up of a single cash component only;

[(*ca*) an innovative finance account is made up of a single innovative finance component only;][12]

[(*cb*) a Lifetime ISA is made up of a single Lifetime ISA component only;][14]

(*d*) the application to open the account is made in accordance with regulation 12 or 12A.

(1B) The conditions in this paragraph are—

(*a*) [except for a subscription made in accordance with regulation 5D(2)(*a*)(i),(iv) or (v),][11] a qualifying individual who is 16 or over may only subscribe to a single cash account that is not a junior ISA account in a particular year;

(*b*) [except for a subscription made in accordance with regulation 5D(2)(*a*)(iv),][11] a qualifying individual who is 18 or over may only subscribe to a single stocks and shares account that is not a junior ISA account in a particular year;

[(*ba*) except for a subscription made in accordance with regulation 5D(2)(*a*)(iv), a qualifying individual who is 18 or over may only subscribe to a single innovative finance account in a particular year;][12]

[(*bb*) a Lifetime ISA qualifying individual may only make a qualifying addition to a single Lifetime ISA in a particular year;][14]

(*c*) it is an account to which only one qualifying individual subscribes [or, in the case of a Lifetime ISA, to which only one Lifetime ISA qualifying individual makes a qualifying addition][14];

[(d) subject to regulations 5DDA(2)(*e*) and 7(2)(*h*), it is—

(i) an account that is not a Lifetime ISA account to which the qualifying individual subscribes only by payment to the account manager of a sum or sums of the individual's cash, or

(ii) a Lifetime ISA to which the Lifetime ISA qualifying individual makes qualifying additions only by—

(*aa*) payment to the account manager of a sum or sums of the individual's cash; or

(*bb*) a transfer of qualifying investments for a Lifetime ISA component from another account of the account investor;][14]

(*e*) the subscriptions made by the qualifying individual to accounts (ignoring transfers and payments from account managers to the individual) do not in the aggregate in any year exceed the subscription [limit][8] in regulation 4ZA(1) . . . [8][and.][7]

(*f*) in the case of a Lifetime ISA the current year payments made by a Lifetime ISA qualifying individual do not in aggregate in any year exceed the Lifetime ISA payment limit in regulation 4ZA(1A).][14]

(2) ...[7]

(3) ...[7]

(4) . . . [2, 6]

(5) An account must at all times be managed in accordance with these Regulations by an account manager and under terms agreed in a recorded form between the account manager and the account investor.

(6) Apart from other requirements of these Regulations the terms agreed to which paragraph (5) refers shall [secure[7]]—

[(*a*) that the account investments shall be in the beneficial ownership of—

(i) in the case of an account that is not a junior ISA account, the account investor; or

(ii) in the case of a junior ISA account, the named child;][7]

(*b*) that, except in relation to qualifying investments for a cash component within regulation 8(2)(*a*), (*b*) or (*e*) [and qualifying investments for an innovative finance component][12], and subject to regulation 15—

(i) [in relation to an account that is not a junior ISA account,][7] the title to all account investments shall be vested in the account manager or his nominee or jointly in one of them and the account investor,

[(ia) in relation to an account that is a junior ISA account, title to all investments shall be vested in the account manager or his nominee or jointly in one of them and either one of the registered contact or named child to the account in question as the account manager considers appropriate,][7] and

(ii) where a share certificate or other document evidencing title to an account investment is issued, it shall be held by the account manager or as he may direct;

(*c*) that, in relation to a stocks and shares component, [qualifying investments for an innovative finance component][13][, a Lifetime ISA component][14][and qualifying investments falling within sub-paragraph (*h*) of regulation 8(2)][9], the account manager shall, if the account investor so elects, arrange for the account investor to receive a copy of the annual report and accounts issued to investors by every company, unit trust, open-ended investment company or other entity in which he has account investments;

(*d*) that, in relation to a stocks and shares component, [qualifying investments for an innovative finance component][13][, a Lifetime ISA component][14] [and qualifying investments falling within sub-paragraph (*h*) of regulation 8(2)][9], the account manager shall be under an obligation (subject to any provisions made under any enactment and if the account investor so elects) to arrange for the account investor to be able—

(i) to attend any meetings of investors in companies, unit trusts, open-ended investment companies and other entities in which he has account investments,

(ii) to vote, and

(iii) to receive, in addition to the documents referred to in sub-paragraph (*c*), any other information issued to investors in such companies, unit trusts, open-ended investment companies and other entities;

(*e*) that the account manager shall satisfy himself that any person to whom he delegates any of his functions or responsibilities under the terms agreed with the account investor is competent to carry out those functions or responsibilities;

(*f*) that [on the instructions of the account investor ("the transfer instructions") and within such time as is stipulated by the account investor in the transfer instructions[1]]—

(i) an account, with all rights and obligations of the parties to it, or

(ii) such parts thereof as may be agreed between the account investor and the account manager, [shall][1] be transferred to another account manager subject to and in accordance with [regulation 21 or 21B][7] [and, where it applies, regulation 21A][5];

(*fa*) that on the instructions, subject to regulation 9(3)(*b*), of the account investor ("the withdrawal instructions") and within such time as is stipulated by the account investor in the withdrawal instructions, account investments, interest, dividends, rights or other proceeds in respect of such investments or any cash shall be transferred or paid to him [or, where paragraph 6(12) of the Schedule applies, an eligible conveyancer][14];][1]

(*g*) that the account manager shall notify the account investor if by reason of any failure to satisfy the provisions of these Regulations an account is or will become no longer exempt from tax by virtue of regulation 22(1).

[(7) The time stipulated in the transfer instructions or withdrawal instructions shall be subject to any reasonable business period of the account manager required for the practical implementation of the instructions, but such period—

(*a*) must not exceed 30 days; and

(*b*) must be consistent with regulation 21A where it applies.][5]

[Where the account is a Lifetime ISA and an amount is being withdrawn for the purpose of a first-time residential purchase by the account investor under paragraph 6 of the Schedule, the period of 30 days referred to in sub-paragraph (a) runs from the date on which the account manager receives the information from the account investor's conveyancer in accordance with paragraph 8(2) and (3) of the Schedule.][14]

[(8) Where an account holds units in or shares of a UK UCITS, recognised UCITS or non-UCITS retail scheme, and dealings in the units or shares are suspended in accordance with Rule 7.2 of the Collective Investment Schemes Sourcebook (COLL 7.2), or any direct foreign equivalent of that Rule, the business period in paragraph (7) may be extended to 7 days after the end of such suspension.][4]

[(9) A Lifetime ISA opened in accordance with regulation 12B is to be treated as such an account notwithstanding that the account investor reaches 50 years of age or over and that no further qualifying addition can be made to the account.

(10) A Lifetime ISA in relation to which an account manager has received notification of closure within 30 days after the latest applicable cancellation period start date for the purposes of the Conduct of Business Sourcebook (published by the Financial Conduct Authority under FISMA 2000) is to be treated for all purposes of these Regulations as never having been such an account.

(11) Where a Lifetime ISA is opened ("the new account") on a transfer from another such account ("the original account") of the account investor, the latest applicable cancellation period start date for the original account is to be treated for the purposes of paragraph (10) as the latest applicable cancellation start date for the new account.

(12) If during the year 2017–18 after the opening of a Lifetime ISA a withdrawal is made other than in any of the circumstances specified in paragraph (13) or described in paragraph 11 of the Schedule the account is to be treated for all purposes of these Regulations as never having been such an account.

(13) The circumstances specified in this paragraph are where—

(*a*) the withdrawal is by way of a transfer to another Lifetime ISA in accordance with regulation 21;

(*b*) the account investor is suffering from a terminal illness (within the meaning of paragraph 4(2) of the Schedule); or

(*c*) the withdrawal is made at a time after the account investor's death.][14]

Commentary—*Simon's Taxes* **E3.307, E3.309, E3.310**.

Amendments—[1] In para 6(*f*), words substituted; and para 6(*fa*) inserted by the ISA (Amendment No 2) Regulations, SI 2002/1974 regs 1–3 with effect from 1 October 2002. The amendments apply to all accounts, whether set up before or after that date.

[2] Paras (1)(*a*)–(*h*), (4) substituted by the Individual Savings Account (Amendment) Regulations, SI 2007/2119 regs 2, 5, 6 with effect from 6 April 2008.

[4] Para (8) inserted by the Individual Savings Account (Amendment No 2) Regulations, SI 2009/1994 regs 2, 4 with effect from 8 October 2008.

[5] In para (6)(*f*), words inserted, and para (7) substituted, by the Individual Savings Account (Amendment No 2) Regulations, SI 2010/2957 regs 2, 3 with effect from 6 April 2011.

[6] Paras (2), (3) substituted and para (4) revoked, by the Individual Savings Account (Amendment) Regulations, SI 2011/782 regs 3–5 with effect for the tax year 2011–2012 and all subsequent tax years.

[7] Para (1) substituted, paras (1A), (1B) inserted, paras (2) and (3) revoked, in para (6) word substituted, para 6 (*a*) substituted, in para 6 (*b*) (I) words inserted, para 6(*b*)(*ia*) inserted and in para 6(*f*) words substituted, by the Individual Savings Account (Amendment No 2) Regulations, SI 2011/1780 regs 2, 7 with effect from 1 November 2011.

[8] In para (1B)(*e*), word substituted and words revoked, by the Individual Savings Account (Amendment No 2) Regulations, SI 2014/1450 regs 2, 5(*a*) with effect from 1 July 2014.

[9] In paras (6)(*c*), (*d*), words substituted by the Individual Savings Account (Amendment No 2) Regulations, SI 2014/1450 regs 2, 5(*b*) with effect in respect of investments purchased or made on or after 1 July 2014.

[10] In para (1B)(*d*), words inserted by the Individual Savings Account (Amendment No 2) Regulations, SI 2015/869 regs 2, 5 with effect from 6 April 2015.

[11] In para (1B)(*a*), (*b*), words inserted by the Individual Savings Account (Amendment) Regulations, SI 2016/16 regs 2, 5 with effect from 1 February 2016.

[12] In paras (1), (1A)(*a*), words substituted, paras (1ZA), (1A)(*ca*), (1B)(*ba*), (9)–(13) inserted, and in para (6)(*b*), (7), words inserted, by the Individual Savings Account (Amendment No 2) Regulations, SI 2016/364 regs 2, 5 with effect from 6 April 2016.

[13] In para (6)(*c*), (*d*), words inserted by the Individual Savings Account (Amendment No 3) Regulations, SI 2016/977 regs 2, 4 with effect from 1 November 2016.

[14] The following amendments made by the Individual Savings Account (Amendment No 2) Regulations, SI 2017/466 regs 2, 6 with effect from 6 April 2017—

- in paras (1), (1B)(*c*), (6)(*c*), (*d*), (*fa*), words inserted;
- in paras (1ZA), (1A), words substituted;
- paras (1ZB), (1A)(*cb*), (1B)(*bb*), (*f*) and preceding word inserted; and
- para (1B)(*d*) substituted.

4ZA [Subscriptions to an account other than a junior ISA account

(1) The overall subscription limit for any qualifying individual for any year (that is the aggregate of the qualifying individual's subscriptions to all accounts that are not junior ISA accounts in that year) is [£20,000.][3]

(*a*) . . . [2]

(*b*) . . . [2]

[(1A) The overall Lifetime ISA payment limit in respect of current year payments for any Lifetime ISA qualifying individual for any year is £4,000.][4]

(2) [2] . . .

(3) A qualifying individual may not subscribe to an account that was a junior ISA account while it was held by the qualifying individual as the named child for the account unless the account manager of that account has been provided with—

(*a*) the qualifying individual's national insurance information specified by paragraph (4);

(*b*) a declaration specified by paragraph (5);

(*c*) the authorisation specified by paragraph (6); and

(*d*) if the account manager of the account requires, an authorisation specified by paragraph (7).

(4) The national insurance information specified by this paragraph is—

(*a*) the qualifying individual's national insurance number; or

(*b*) a declaration by the qualifying individual that the qualifying individual does not have a national insurance number.

(5) The declaration specified by this paragraph is a declaration by the qualifying individual that, if the qualifying individual were making an application to open an account pursuant to regulation 12, would be in accordance with paragraph (3)(*c*) to (*f*) of that regulation.

(6) The authorisation specified by this paragraph is an authorisation by the qualifying individual that, if the qualifying individual were making an application to open an account pursuant to regulation 12, would be in accordance with paragraphs (4)(*e*) and (4A)(*c*) of that regulation.

(7) The authorisation specified by this paragraph is an authorisation by the qualifying individual that, if the qualifying individual were making an application to open an account pursuant to regulation 12, would be in accordance with paragraphs (4)(*e*) and (4A)(*a*) and (*b*) of that regulation.

(8) Regulation 12(7), (9) and (10) apply in relation to the declaration specified by paragraph (5) and authorisations specified by paragraphs (6) and (7) as if they were made in relation to an application made by the qualifying individual to open an account pursuant to regulation 12.

(9) For the purposes of paragraphs (5) to (8)—

(*a*) references in regulation 12 to "the applicant" are references to the qualifying individual making the declaration specified by paragraph (5) or giving an authorisation specified in paragraphs (6) and (7);

(*b*) references in regulation 12(3)(*c*) to (*f*) to "the year in which paragraph (2) refers" (the first year to which the application to open the account relates) are references to the year in which the declaration specified by paragraph (5) is made by the qualifying individual.][1]

Amendments—[1] Regs 4ZA–4ZE inserted by the Individual Savings Account (Amendment No 2) Regulations, SI 2011/1780 regs 2, 8 with effect from 1 November 2011.

[2] Para (1)(*a*), (*b*) revoked, and para (2) revoked, by the Individual Savings Account (Amendment No 2) Regulations, SI 2014/1450 regs 2, 6 with effect from 1 July 2014.

[3] In para (1), figure substituted by the Individual Savings Account (Amendment) Regulations, SI 2017 regs 2, 5 with effect from 6 April 2017. Figure was previously £15,240.

[4] Para (1A) inserted by the Individual Savings Account (Amendment No 2) Regulations, SI 2017/466 regs 2, 7 with effect from 6 April 2017.

4ZB [Subscriptions to a junior ISA account

(1) Any person may subscribe to a junior ISA account provided the overall amount subscribed by that person and any other person for any year in respect of the same named child does not exceed [£4,080][2].

(2) An amount paid to a junior ISA account in excess of the amount mentioned in paragraph (1) is not an amount subscribed to a junior ISA account and must not be held in that account.

(3) A single subscription for an amount equal to the amount mentioned in paragraph (1) or any number of smaller amounts that, when aggregated, do not exceed the amount mentioned in paragraph (1), may be made in respect of the same named child—

(*a*) to a cash account held by that child,

(*b*) to a stocks and shares account held by that child, or

(*c*) in any proportion between such accounts.

(4) No subscription may be made to a cash account that is a junior ISA account held by a named child where—

(*a*) the balance in the account is less than one penny; and

(*b*) that child holds another cash account opened pursuant to a junior ISA application described in regulation 12A after the time when the account mentioned in sub-paragraph (*a*) was opened.

(5) No subscription may be made to a stocks and shares account that is a junior ISA account held by a named child where—

(*a*) the balance in the account is less than one penny; and

(*b*) that child holds another stocks and shares account opened pursuant to a junior ISA application described in regulation 12A after the time when the account mentioned in sub-paragraph (a) was opened.][1]

Amendments—[1] Regs 4ZA–4ZE inserted by the Individual Savings Account (Amendment No 2) Regulations, SI 2011/1780 regs 2, 8 with effect from 1 November 2011.

[2] Figure in para (1) substituted by the Individual Savings Account (Amendment) Regulations, SI 2017/186 regs 2, 6 with effect from 6 April 2017. Figure was previously £4,080.

[4ZC Inalienability of a junior ISA account

(1) Any assignment of, or agreement to assign, investments under a junior ISA account, and any charge on or agreement to charge any such investments, is void.

(2) On the bankruptcy of the named child holding a junior ISA account, the entitlement to investments under it does not pass to any trustee or other person acting on behalf of the child's creditors.

(3) "Assignment" includes assignation; and "assign" is to be construed accordingly.

(4) "Charge on or agreement to charge" includes a right in security over or an agreement to create a right in security over.

(5) "Bankruptcy", in relation to a named child, includes the sequestration of the child's estate.

(6) Paragraph (1) shall not render void anything done to vest title to an account investment as required by regulation 4(6)(*b*)(ia) or 15(*a*) by virtue of—

(*a*) a transfer of an account in accordance with regulation 21B; or

(*b*) a change of registered contact in relation to a junior ISA account.][1]

Amendments—[1] Regs 4ZA–4ZE inserted by the Individual Savings Account (Amendment No 2) Regulations, SI 2011/1780 regs 2, 8 with effect from 1 November 2011.

4ZD [Permitted withdrawals from a junior ISA account

Withdrawals from a junior ISA account may only be made—

(*a*) by the account manager, to settle any management charges and other incidental expenses, which are due by or under the management agreement,

(*b*) in accordance with regulation 4ZE, or

(*c*) where the account manager is satisfied that the named child who held the account has died.][1]

Amendments—[1] Regs 4ZA–4ZE inserted by the Individual Savings Account (Amendment No 2) Regulations, SI 2011/1780 regs 2, 8 with effect from 1 November 2011.

4ZE Permitted withdrawals from a junior ISA account where the named child is terminally ill

(1) A registered contact may make a claim to the Board for withdrawals from a junior ISA account to be permitted in accordance with this regulation.

(2) The claim shall be—

(*a*) made in a manner prescribed by the Board, which shall include the giving of any consent necessary for the verification or consideration of the claim, and

(*b*) accepted in either of the following cases:

[Case 1

The named child holding the account:

(i) in England and Wales or Scotland, falls within either section 72(5) of the Social Security Contributions and Benefits Act 1992 (special rules for terminally ill person's entitlement to care component of disability living allowance) or section 82(4) of the Welfare Reform Act 2012 (terminal illness); or

(ii) in Northern Ireland, falls within section 72(5) of the Social Security Contributions and Benefits (Northern Ireland) Act 1992 (the care component).][2]

Case 2

Evidence that the named child holding the account is terminally ill has been supplied to the satisfaction of the Board.

(3) The Board shall issue a letter to the registered contact authorising withdrawals from the account under this regulation [. . .][2].

(4) Once a claim has been accepted, withdrawals of any amount (including the proceeds from a policy of life insurance and an amount sufficient to close the account) may be made by the registered contact at any time (but this does not include the transfer of a policy of life insurance otherwise than in accordance with regulation 21B).

(5) Where account investments are withdrawn in a form other than sterling currency, the named child shall be treated as having sold the account investments in question, and as having reacquired them in his personal capacity, for a consideration equal to their market value at the time of their withdrawal.

(6) In this regulation, "terminally ill" has the meaning:

[(*a*) for England and Wales and Scotland][2] in section 66(2)(*a*) of the Social Security Contributions and Benefits Act 1992 [or section 82(4) of the Welfare Reform Act 2012 (terminal illness); or

(*b*) for Northern Ireland, section 72(5) of the Social Security Contributions and Benefits (Northern Ireland) Act 1992 (the care component)][2].][1]

Amendments—[1] Regs 4ZA–4ZE inserted by the Individual Savings Account (Amendment No 2) Regulations, SI 2011/1780 regs 2, 8 with effect from 1 November 2011.

[2] In para (2)(*b*) Case 1 substituted, in para (3) words revoked and in para (6) words inserted, by the Individual Savings Account (Amendment) Regulations, SI 2014/654 regs 2, 7 with effect from 6 April 2014.

4A [[Repair of certain incompatible account and excess subscriptions – accounts other than junior ISA accounts]

(1) An invalid account is "eligible for repair" if, in relation to the year in which the subscriptions to the account were made ("the relevant year"), it satisfies—

[(*a*) both the First and Second Conditions below, or

(*b*) the Third Condition.

First Condition

The account is invalid because a subscription to the account causes the account investor to breach the conditions in [regulation 4(1B)(*a*)[, (*b*) or (*ba*)][5]][3] (which, taken together, allow an individual to subscribe to a single cash account[, a single stocks and shares account and a single innovative finance account][5], in a particular year) and for no other reason.

Second Condition

The account is (disregarding any account exempt from tax under regulation 4B) the earliest account in the relevant year, the subscriptions to which caused the account investor to breach the conditions in regulation [regulation 4(1B)(*a*)[, (*b*) or (*ba*)][5]]][3] as the case may be (that is, it was first subscribed to earlier in that year than any other such account).

Third Condition

The account is invalid because a subscription to the account breaches the overall subscription limit in [regulation [4ZA(1)][4]][3], and for no other reason.][2]

(2) In this regulation—

(*a*) where an account investor subscribes to a particular account in more than one year, each year's subscriptions shall be treated as a separate account for the purposes of this regulation, and regulation 4B (except for determining when an account is closed) only;

(*b*) "date of discovery" means the date on which an officer of the Board gives a notice ("notice of discovery") to the account manager or account investor that the account is invalid, and (if appropriate) directions under paragraph (5) below;

(*c*) . . . [2]

(*d*) "valid account" means an account which (apart from under this regulation) is exempt from tax under regulation 22(1);

(*e*) "invalid account" means a scheme of investment which is not exempt from tax under these Regulations but which (if so exempt) would be an account within the meaning in [regulation 4(1A)(a)][3] and, in relation to an invalid account, references to an account [and component][2] have corresponding meanings; and

(*f*) (for the avoidance of doubt) "repair" of an account is without prejudice to loss of, and accounting to the Board for, any relief from tax given for the period up to the date of discovery.

(3) An invalid account which is eligible for repair shall be treated as—

(*a*) exempt from tax under this regulation (as if under regulation 22), and

(*b*) complying with the conditions of regulation [regulation 4(1B)(*a*)[, (*b*) or (*ba*)][5]], or 4ZA(1) . . . [4]][3], as the case may be,

as from the date of discovery, to the extent of the relevant proportion mentioned in paragraph (4)(*b*).

[(4)

(*a*) Calculate the extent to which the subscriptions made (and counting towards the subscription [limit][4]) during the relevant year—

(i) to that account, any other account which is eligible for repair, and any valid account (but ignoring subscriptions to any closed account within the meaning in regulation 4B)) do not exceed,

(ii) the subscriptions [limit][4] in [regulation 4ZA(1)][3] . . . [4], and][2]

(*b*) an officer of the Board shall apportion that result between the accounts mentioned in sub-paragraph (*a*)(i), and the amount apportioned to the account mentioned in paragraph (3) is the relevant proportion.

(5) The account manager must comply within 30 days with any directions in the notice of discovery which—

(*a*) make the apportionment under paragraph (4)(*b*) and identify the account and component from which excess subscriptions or allocations (if any) are to be removed;

(*b*) direct the removal of subscriptions and proceeds representing them from an account; or

(*c*) direct the removal of subscriptions and proceeds representing them from a component.][1]

[(6) For the purposes of this regulation, a subscription to an account that is a junior ISA account shall be disregarded.][3].

[(7) This regulation is subject to regulation 4AA.][6]

Commentary—*Simon's Taxes* **E3.312**.

Amendments—[1] This regulation inserted by the Individual Savings Account (Amendment No 3) Regulations, SI 2002/3158 regs 1(2)(*a*), 3 with effect where a notice of discovery is given after 7 January 2003, and in relation to subscriptions to accounts made after 5 April 2001.

[2] Para (1)(*a*), (*b*) and the Four Conditions substituted, para (2)(*c*) revoked, words in paras (2)(*e*), (3)(*b*) substituted, and whole of para (4)(*a*) substituted, by the Individual Savings Account (Amendment) Regulations, SI 2007/2119 regs 2, 7 with effect from 6 April 2008.

[3] Heading substituted; in para (1), words in First, Second and Third Conditions substituted; in paras (2)(*e*), (3)(*b*), (4)(*a*)(*ii*) words substituted; and para (6) inserted; by the Individual Savings Account (Amendment No 2) Regulations, SI 2011/1780 regs 2, 9 with effect from 1 November 2011.

[4] In para (1), reference substituted, in para (3)(*b*), words revoked, and in para (4), word substituted in both places and words revoked, by the Individual Savings Account (Amendment No 2) Regulations, SI 2014/1450 regs 2, 8 with effect from 1 July 2014.

[5] In para (1), words in First and Second Conditions substituted, and words in para (3)(*b*) substituted, by the Individual Savings Account (Amendment No 2) Regulations, SI 2016/364 regs 2, 6 with effect from 6 April 2016.

[6] Para (7) inserted by the Individual Savings Account (Amendment No 2) Regulations, SI 2017/466 regs 2, 8 with effect from 6 April 2017.

[4AA Application of the repair provisions to Lifetime ISAs

(1) The following modifications to regulation 4A apply where one or more of the accounts to which the investor subscribes in the relevant year is a Lifetime ISA.

(2) Where an investor has made current year payments in excess of the Lifetime ISA payment limit in regulation 4ZA(1A) to a single Lifetime ISA, an officer of the Board may direct the removal of the excess and proceeds representing the excess, whether or not the overall subscription limit in regulation 4ZA(1) has been exceeded.

(3) Where an investor has exceeded the overall subscription limit in regulation 4ZA(1), but has not exceeded the Lifetime ISA payment limit in regulation 4ZA(1A), the excess shall be removed from the accounts which are not Lifetime ISAs.

(4) Where an investor has made current year payments or a payment described in regulation 10A(4)(*c*) to more than one Lifetime ISA, only one account will be a valid account which is eligible for the payment of a government bonus.][1]

Amendments—[1] Regulation 4AA inserted by the Individual Savings Account (Amendment No 2) Regulations, SI 2017/466 regs 2, 9 with effect from 6 April 2017.

4B [Closure of [cash] account [that is not a junior ISA account] prior to the opening of the same type of account to be disregarded once

(1) Where—

(*a*) an account investor, within the same year—

(i) subscribes to a [cash][2] account,

(ii) then closes it ("the closed account"), and

(iii) subsequently first subscribes to another [cash account][2], and

(*b*) the closed account was (apart from under this regulation) exempt from tax under regulation 22(1),

the earliest account in that year to fall within the terms of sub-paragraph (a)(iii) (the "first later account") shall be eligible for the relief in paragraph (2).

(2) The first later account shall be treated, as from the date of the first subscription to it mentioned in paragraph (1)(*a*)(iii) [as complying with the conditions of [regulation 4(1B)(*a*)][3]][2] in the same manner as the closed account.

(3) In this regulation, an account is closed where—

(*a*) the account investor withdraws from the account all account investments, other proceeds in respect of such investments and cash, representing subscriptions to the account (and closure shall be treated as occurring at the date of such withdrawal), and

(*b*) no further subscriptions to the account are made during the remainder of the year, after such withdrawal.

[(4) This regulation does not apply to a subscription to an account made in accordance with regulation 5D.][4]][1]

Commentary—*Simon's Taxes* **E3.312**.

Amendments—[1] This regulation inserted by the Individual Savings Account (Amendment No 3) Regulations, SI 2002/3158 regs 1(2)(*b*), 4 with effect for subscriptions to accounts after 5 April 2003.

[2] Words in cross-heading, and in paras (1)(*a*)(i), (iii), (2) substituted by the Individual Savings Account (Amendment) Regulations, SI 2007/2119 regs 2, 8 with effect from 6 April 2008.

[3] In heading, words relating to junior ISAs inserted, and in para (2) words substituted, by the Individual Savings Account (Amendment No 2) Regulations, SI 2011/1870 regs 2, 10 with effect from 1 November 2011.

[4] Para (4) inserted by the Individual Savings Account (Amendment) Regulations, SI 2016/16 regs 2, 6 with effect from 1 February 2016.

4C Removal of insurance components at 6th April 2005

Amendments—Regulation 4C revoked by the Individual Savings Account (Amendment No 2) Regulations, SI 2014/1450 regs 2, 9 with effect from 1 July 2014.

4D Removal of maxi-accounts, mini-accounts and TESSA only accounts at 6th April 2008

Amendments—Regulation 4D revoked by the Individual Savings Account (Amendment No 2) Regulations, SI 2014/1450 regs 2, 10 with effect from 1 July 2014.

5 Transfers from matured tax-exempt special savings accounts

Amendments—This regulation revoked by the Individual Savings Account (Amendment) Regulations, SI 2007/2119 regs 2, 10 with effect from 6 April 2008.

5A [[Treatment of sums held in accounts managed by Icesave Bank

Amendments—Reg 5A revoked by the Individual Savings Account (Amendment No 2) Regulations, SI 2011/1780 regs 2, 11 with effect from 1 November 2011.

5B *Treatment of certain sums held in accounts managed by Keydata Investment Services Limited*

Amendments—Reg 5B revoked by the Individual Savings Account (Amendment) (No 2) Regulations, SI 2012/1871 regs 4, 10 with effect from 8 August 2012.

5C [Treatment of certain sums held in dormant accounts

(1) Regulations 30 and 31 (information by account managers) shall not apply to a dormant account, while section 1 or 2 of the Dormant Bank and Building Society Accounts Act 2008 ("the 2008 Act") applies in relation to that account.

(2) Where, following a repayment claim, the balance of a dormant account is paid—

(*a*) back into the account (in a case where the original cash account can be reinstated with the same account manager, the same account investor and number), or

(*b*) into another cash account in the same account investor's name, with the same account manager (in any other case),

the payment into the account shall not count towards the subscription [limit][2] in [regulation 4ZA(1)][2]

(3) In this regulation, "repayment claim" means a repayment claim mentioned in section 5(6) of the 2008 Act, and other terms used in this regulation and that Act have the same meaning in this regulation as in that Act.][1]

Amendments[1] Reg 5C inserted by the Dormant Bank and Building Society Accounts (Tax) Regulations, SI 2011/22 reg 9(1), (3) with effect from 1 February 2011.

[2] In para (2), word substituted for words "limits", and words substituted for words "regulation 4ZA(2)", by the Individual Savings Account (Amendment No 2) Regulations, SI 2014/1450 regs 2, 11 with effect from 1 July 2014.

[5D Subscriptions disregarded for the purposes of the subscription limits in regulations [4ZA(1)][6] and 4ZB

(1) A subscription to an account made in accordance with this regulation must be disregarded for the purposes of the subscription limits in regulations [4ZA(1)][6] (subscriptions to an account other than a junior ISA account) and 4ZB (subscriptions to a junior ISA account).

(2) A subscription to an account held by an account investor is made in accordance with this regulation if—

(*a*) the subscription is—

(i) a defaulted cash account subscription;

[(ia) a defaulted Lifetime ISA subscription;

(ib) a returned withdrawal from a Lifetime ISA following failure of a purchase to complete under paragraph 10(1) of the Schedule;][6]

(ii) a defaulted investment subscription; . . . [2]

[(iia) a replacement subscription;][5]

(iii) permitted in accordance with regulation 5DE; [. . . [4]

(iv) permitted in accordance with regulation 5DDA; [or][4]][2]

[(v) permitted in accordance with regulation 5DDC; and][4]

(*b*) the account manager of the account to which the subscription is made is provided with the information specified in regulation 5DF as relevant to the subscription[;][1]

[(*c*) in a case within sub-paragraph (a)(iv)—

(i) the account manager of the account to which the subscription is made is provided with the declarations required by regulation 5DFA as relevant to the subscription;

(ii) the notices specified in regulation 5DFB(1) and (3) are given, as relevant to the subscription; and

(iii) the information and declarations required by regulation 5DFC(2) are provided.

[(3) A subscription to an account held by an account investor is made in accordance with this regulation if it comprises a transfer provided for by regulation 20A of the Child Trust Funds Regulations 2004[; and][3]][2]

(*d*) in a case within paragraph (2)(*a*)(ib) the account manager of the Lifetime ISA to which the subscription is made is provided with the information specified in paragraph 9(3)(b) of the Schedule.][6]

Press releases etc—HMRC Guidance Note, 10 September 2012: Guidance on ISA reinstatement and payments outside the annual ISA subscription limit.

Amendments—[1] Regs 5D–5DM inserted by the Individual Savings Account (Amendment) (No 2) Regulations, SI 2012/1871 regs 4, 11 with effect from 8 August 2012.

[2] In para (2), word in para (*a*)(ii) revoked, and paras (*a*)(iv), (*c*) inserted by the Individual Savings Account (Amendment No 2) Regulations, SI 2015/869 regs 2, 6 with effect from 6 April 2015.

[3] Para (3) inserted by the Individual Savings Account (Amendment No 3) Regulations, SI 2015/941 regs 2, 3 with effect from 6 April 2015.
[4] In para (2), word at end of sub-para (*a*)(iii) revoked, at end of sub-para (*a*)(iv) word substituted, and sub-para (*a*)(v) inserted, by the Individual Savings Account (Amendment) Regulations, SI 2016/16 regs 2, 7(*b*)–(*d*) with effect from 1 February 2016.
[5] Para (2)(*a*)(iia) inserted by the Individual Savings Account (Amendment) Regulations, SI 2016/16 regs 2, 7(*a*) with effect from 6 April 2016.
[6] In heading and para (1), reference substituted, and para (2)(*a*)(ia), (ib), (*d*) and preceding word inserted, by the Individual Savings Account (Amendment No 2) Regulations, SI 2017/466 regs 2, 10 with effect from 6 April 2017.

[5DA Defaulted cash account subscription

A subscription is a defaulted cash account subscription if—

(*a*) it is made to an account (which may be a stocks and shares account[, a cash account, an innovative finance account or a Lifetime ISA][2]) held by an account investor who held a cash account ("defaulted cash account") in respect of which a default event occurred no more than 180 days before the subscription is made; and

(*b*) it does not exceed the amount held in the defaulted cash account immediately before the default event occurred (including interest accrued but not paid at that time).][1]

Press releases etc—HMRC Guidance Note, 10 September 2012: Guidance on ISA reinstatement and payments outside the annual ISA subscription limit.

Amendments—[1] Regs 5D–5DM inserted by the Individual Savings Account (Amendment) (No 2) Regulations, SI 2012/1871 regs 4, 11 with effect from 8 August 2012.
[2] In para (*a*), words substituted by the Individual Savings Account (Amendment No 2) Regulations, SI 2017/466 regs 2, 11 with effect from 6 April 2017.

[5DAA Defaulted Lifetime ISA subscription

A subscription is a defaulted Lifetime ISA subscription if—

(*a*) it is made to a Lifetime ISA held by the account investor who held the Lifetime ISA in respect of which a defaulted investment payment has been made no more than 180 days before the subscription is made; and

(*b*) it does not exceed the defaulted investment payment.][1]

Amendments—[1] Regulation 5DAA inserted by the Individual Savings Account (Amendment No 2) Regulations, SI 2017/466 regs 2, 12 with effect from 6 April 2017.

[5DB Defaulted investment subscription

A subscription is a defaulted investment subscription if—

(*a*) it is made to [an account][2] held by the account investor who held the account in respect of which a defaulted investment payment has been made no more than 180 days before the subscription is made; and

(*b*) it does not exceed the amount of the defaulted investment payment.][1]

Press releases etc—HMRC Guidance Note, 10 September 2012: Guidance on ISA reinstatement and payments outside the annual ISA subscription limit.

Amendments—[1] Regs 5D–5DM inserted by the Individual Savings Account (Amendment) (No 2) Regulations, SI 2012/1871 regs 4, 11 with effect from 8 August 2012.
[2] In para (*a*), words substituted by the Individual Savings Account (Amendment No 2) Regulations, SI 2014/1450 regs 2, 12 with effect from 1 July 2014.

[5DC Default event in respect of cash account

A default event in respect of a cash account held by an account investor occurs where the account manager of that account is determined to be unable or likely to be unable to satisfy claims against the account manager in accordance with the rules of the scheme for compensation established pursuant to section 213 of the Financial Services and Markets Act 2000.][1]

Press releases etc—HMRC Guidance Note, 10 September 2012: Guidance on ISA reinstatement and payments outside the annual ISA subscription limit.

Amendments—[1] Regs 5D–5DM inserted by the Individual Savings Account (Amendment) (No 2) Regulations, SI 2012/1871 regs 4, 11 with effect from 8 August 2012.

[5DD Defaulted investment payment

[A defaulted investment payment occurs where a payment is made (otherwise than by accretion to an account) by way of compensation in respect of poor performance, loss (in whole or in part), depreciation or risk of depreciation of an investment ("defaulted investment")—

(*a*) described in regulation 7, held in a stocks and shares account (whether or not the defaulted investment continues to be held in the account at the time of the payment); . . . [3]

(*b*) described in regulation 8A, held in an innovative finance account (whether or not the defaulted investment continues to be held in the account at the time of the payment); or.][2]][1]

(*c*) described in regulation 7 or 8, held in a Lifetime ISA (whether or not the defaulted investment continues to be held in the account at the time of the payment).][3]

Press releases etc—HMRC Guidance Note, 10 September 2012: Guidance on ISA reinstatement and payments outside the annual ISA subscription limit.

Amendments—[1] Regs 5D–5DM inserted by the Individual Savings Account (Amendment) (No 2) Regulations, SI 2012/1871 regs 4, 11 with effect from 8 August 2012.

2 Text of regulation 5DD substituted by the Individual Savings Account (Amendment No 2) Regulations, SI 2016/364 regs 2, 7 with effect from 6 April 2016.

3 In para (*a*), word revoked, and para (*c*) and preceding word inserted, by the Individual Savings Account (Amendment No 2) Regulations, SI 2017/466 regs 2, 13 with effect from 6 April 2017.

[5DDA Additional permitted subscription to an account other than a junior ISA account

(1) A subscription to an account other than a junior ISA account is permitted by this regulation if—

(*a*) it is made in the circumstances described in paragraph (2); and

(*b*) the amount of the subscription, or the aggregate of a number of such subscriptions, does not exceed in value the amount determined in accordance with paragraph (3).

(2) The circumstances are—

(*a*) an account investor dies on or after 3 December 2014 leaving a surviving spouse or civil partner (S);

(*b*) subject to paragraph (6), a subscription is made by S to an account or accounts managed by a single account manager or, in a case within sub-paragraph (*e*), the deceased's account manager;

(*c*) the subscription is within the permitted period;

(*d*) S and the deceased were living together at the date of the deceased's death; and

(*e*) where the subscription comprises non-cash assets—

(i) the deceased held an account either comprising or including non-cash assets at the date of the deceased's death;

(ii) S inherits all or part of those assets;

(iii) S makes a subscription comprising those assets or any part therof; . . . [3]

(iv) throughout the period beginning with the day on which the deceased's account manager was notified of the deceased's death and ending immediately before the subscription is made, title to those assets is vested in the deceased's account manager, that manager's nominee or jointly in one of them and another[; and][3]

[(v) in the case of an innovative finance account, paragraph (iv) shall apply but with the words from "title to" to "and another." being substituted by "those assets remain under the management of the deceased's account manager.][3]

(3) The amount is—

(*a*) where the deceased held a single account with a single account manager, then the value of that account at the date of the deceased's death; or

(*b*) where the deceased held more than one account with a single account manager, then the combined value of those accounts at the date of the deceased's death;

but does not include any sums the deceased held in a junior ISA account.

[(3A) In respect of an innovative finance account, for the purposes of paragraph (3), the value of the account at the date of the deceased's death is the combined value of the outstanding principal balance under those [qualifying investments for an innovative finance component][4] in respect of which payments are due to be made to the account manager of the account investor and cash deposited by the account investor under regulations 6(4) to (6).][3]

[(3B) For the purposes of paragraph (3) the value of a Lifetime ISA at the date of the deceased's death includes any government bonus that has accrued to the date of death but has not been paid.][5]

(4) In this regulation, the permitted period means—

(*a*) in the case of a subscription comprising non-cash assets made in accordance with paragraph (2), the period beginning with distribution to S by the deceased's estate of the non-cash assets and ending no more than 180 days thereafter;

(*b*) in the case any other subscription under this regulation, the period beginning with the date of the deceased's death and ending either—

(i) no more than 3 years thereafter; or

(ii) no more than 180 days after administration of the estate is complete;

whichever is the later.

(5) Where the deceased died in the period beginning with 3 December 2014 and ending on 5 April 2015—

(*a*) for the purposes of paragraph (4)(*a*), distribution to S by the deceased's estate of non-cash assets is treated as occurring on either 6th April 2015, or, the actual date of distribution, whichever is the later; and

(*b*) for the purposes of paragraph(4)(*b*), the deceased is treated as dying on 6 April 2015.

(6) The requirement in paragraph (2)(*b*) is deemed as met where the Board authorises an account manager to accept a subscription from S.

(7) The following regulations do not apply to a subscription permitted by this regulation—

(*a*), (*b*) . . . [2]

(*c*) 6(3);

(*d*)–(*f*) . . . [2]

(8)–(10) . . . [2]

(11) In this regulation—

(*a*) "inherits" in paragraph (2)(*e*)(ii) includes inherits under a will trust or as a result of a deed of variation;

(*b*) "non-cash assets" means—

(i) those investments specified in regulation 7, other than those in paragraph (2)(*j*); and

(ii) those investments specified in regulation 8(2)(*f*), (*h*), (*p*) or (*q*); and

[(iii) the right to exercise the rights of the lender in respect of the outstanding principal balance under an article 36H agreement; and][3]

[(iv) those investments specified in regulation 8A(2)(*ca*); and][4]

(*c*) the value of a subscription comprising non-cash assets made pursuant to paragraph (2) is the value of the assets at the date of the subscription.][1]

1 Regulation 5DDA inserted by the Individual Savings Account (Amendment No 2) Regulations, SI 2015/869 regs 2, 7 with effect from 6 April 2015.

2 Paras (7)(*a*), (*b*), (*d*)–(*f*), (8)–(10) revoked by the Individual Savings Account (Amendment) Regulations, SI 2016/16 regs 2, 8 with effect from 6 April 2016.

3 In para (2)(*e*), at the end of sub-para (iii), word revoked, at the end of sub-para (iv), words substituted for full stop, and sub-para (v) inserted, and paras (3A), (11)(*b*)(iii) inserted by the Individual Savings Account (Amendment No 2) Regulations, SI 2016/364 regs 2, 8 with effect from 6 April 2016.

4 In para (3A), words substituted for words "article 36H agreements", and para (11)(*b*)(iv) inserted, by the Individual Savings Account (Amendment No 3) Regulations, SI 2016/977 regs 2, 5 with effect from 1 November 2016.

5 Para (3B) inserted by the Individual Savings Account (Amendment No 2) Regulations, SI 2017/466 regs 2, 14 with effect from 6 April 2017.

[5DDB Flexible account

(1) The terms and conditions of an account (other than a junior ISA account [or a Lifetime ISA][3]) ("flexible account") may provide for an account investor to be able to replace (in whole or part) a cash amount withdrawn by the account investor in any year by a replacement subscription of a cash amount [or qualifying investments for a stocks and shares component within regulation 7(2)(*h*)][2] ("replacement subscription") made in that year.

(2) Subject to regulation [4(1B)(*a*), (*b*)[, (*ba*) and (*bb*)[3]][2], a replacement subscription in respect of a subscription counting towards the limit in regulation 4ZA(1) may be made into any account of the account investor.

(3) Any other replacement subscription may be made only to the account from which the withdrawal of a cash amount it is replacing was made.

(4) Any withdrawal of a cash amount in any year is to be deemed to be made first out of a current year's subscription.

(5) Any replacement subscription is to be deemed to be a replacement first of any withdrawal of a cash amount made out of a previous years' subscription.

(6) On any transfer under regulation 21 of the whole of previous years' subscriptions, the right of the account investor under paragraph (1) in relation to an account transferred is to cease in respect of a withdrawal of a cash amount from the account made before the transfer.

(7) Paragraph (6) does not apply where an account is transferred in a bulk transfer of accounts.

(8) For the purposes of this regulation-

"current year's subscription" means (other than a subscription made in accordance with regulation 5D)-

(*a*) a subscription made to the account by the account investor in the year in which a replacement subscription is made;

(*b*) a subscription made to any other account by the account investor in the year in which a replacement subscription is made and transferred to the account; and

(*c*) the qualifying investments and other proceeds (including income) representing the subscriptions in sub-paragraphs (*a*) and (*b*) of this definition;

"previous years' subscription" means-

(*a*) a subscription made to the account (or any other account or former personal equity plan) in any earlier year or years;

(*b*) any replacement subscription of a withdrawal of a cash amount made out of that subscription; and

(*c*) the qualifying investments and other proceeds (including income) representing the subscriptions in sub-paragraphs (*a*) and (*b*) of this definition.][1]

Amendments—1 Reg 5DDB inserted by the Individual Savings Account (Amendment) Regulations, SI 2016/16 regs 2, 10 with effect from 6 April 2016.

2 Words in para (1) inserted, and words in para (2) substituted, by the Individual Savings Account (Amendment No 2) Regulations, SI 2016/364 regs 2, 9 with effect from 6 April 2016.

3 Words in para (1) inserted, and words in para (2) substituted, by the Individual Savings Account (Amendment No 2) Regulations, SI 2017/466 regs 2, 15 with effect from 6 April 2017.

[5DDC Additional permitted subscription of cash to an account other than a junior ISA on closure of Help to Buy ISA

(1) A subscription of cash to an account, other than a junior ISA account, is permitted by this regulation if—

(*a*) it is made in the circumstances described in paragraph (2); and

(*b*) the amount of the subscription does not exceed in value the amount determined in accordance with paragraph (3).

(2) The circumstances are—

(*a*) the account investor has closed their Help to Buy ISA;

(*b*) the account investor has provided to the account manager evidence in accordance with the terms and conditions of the Help to Buy ISA of a failure of a completion of a purchase of a home;

(*c*) the subscription is within the permitted period described in paragraph (4).

(3) The amount is an amount up to that which the account investor withdrew from the Help to Buy ISA at the time of closure.

(4) In this regulation, the permitted period means the period of no more than 12 months beginning with the date of closure of the Help to Buy ISA.

(5) Only one subscription may be made under paragraph (1) in the circumstances of paragraph (2), even if the subscription made is less than the full amount which could have been made in accordance with paragraph (3).

(6) In this regulation "Help to Buy ISA" means a cash account (or an element of one) which is managed and held in accordance with these Regulations and scheme rules from time to time made by the Treasury in order to help an individual who is eligible under those rules to purchase a home.][1]

Amendments—[1] Reg 5DDC inserted by the Individual Savings Account (Amendment) Regulations, SI 2016/16 regs 2, 10 with effect from 1 February 2016.

[5DE Additional permitted subscription to a junior ISA account

A subscription is permitted by this regulation if it is made to a junior ISA account that is a cash account but would have been a defaulted investment subscription if it had been made to a stocks and shares account.][1]

Press releases etc—HMRC Guidance Note, 10 September 2012: Guidance on ISA reinstatement and payments outside the annual ISA subscription limit.

Amendments—[1] Regs 5D–5DM inserted by the Individual Savings Account (Amendment) (No 2) Regulations, SI 2012/1871 regs 4, 11 with effect from 8 August 2012.

[5DF Information required by regulation 5D

(1) The information specified by this regulation is—

(*a*) in relation to a defaulted cash account subscription—

(i) [evidence of][3] the amount held in the defaulted cash account to which the subscription relates immediately before the default event occurred (including interest accrued but not paid at that time);

[(ia) in the case of a flexible account, in the year in which the default event occurred and before such event, evidence of the amount (if any) of cash withdrawn from the account which was not replaced by a replacement subscription;][4]

(ii) the current year's subscription made to that account; and

(iii) the date on which the first subscription (if any) was made to that account, in the year in which the defaulted cash subscription is made;

(*b*) in relation to a defaulted investment subscription[, defaulted Lifetime ISA subscription][5] or a subscription permitted by regulation 5DE—

(i) evidence of the amount of the defaulted investment payment to which the subscription relates and the date it was paid;

(ii) details of the defaulted investment in respect of which the defaulted investment payment was made;

(iii) the full name and address (including postcode) of the account manager of the stocks and shares account[, innovative finance account or Lifetime ISA][5] in which the defaulted investment was held;

(iv) the full name and address (including postcode) of the maker of the defaulted investment payment[;][2]

[(*c*) in relation to a subscription permitted by regulation 5DDA—

(i) the deceased's full name;

(ii) the full address of the deceased's permanent residence at the date of death;

(iii) the deceased's National Insurance number, if known;

(iv) the deceased's date of birth and date of death; and

(v) the date of S's marriage or civil partnership to the deceased;

(*d*) in relation to a subscription permitted by regulation 5DDA and made with an account manager other than the deceased's account manager, the name and address of the deceased's account manager.

(1A) The requirements in sub-paragraph (1)(*c*) are met where the information is provided on the first instance a subscription permitted by regulation 5DDA is made to an account.][2]

(2) In this regulation—

"current year's subscription" in relation to a defaulted cash account means—

(*a*) subscriptions [(other than a subscription to the account made in accordance with regulation 5D)][3] made to the account in the year in which the defaulted cash account subscription is made, but before the default event; ande

(*b*) subscriptions made to any other account held by the account investor in the year in which the defaulted cash account subscription is made and transferred to the account before the subscription is made.][1]

Press releases etc—HMRC Guidance Note, 10 September 2012: Guidance on ISA reinstatement and payments outside the annual ISA subscription limit.

Amendments—[1] Regs 5D–5DM inserted by the Individual Savings Account (Amendment) (No 2) Regulations, SI 2012/1871 regs 4, 11 with effect from 8 August 2012.

[2] In para (1)(*b*), (iv) semicolon substituted for full stop, and paras (1)(*c*), (*d*), (1A) inserted by the Individual Savings Account (Amendment No 2) Regulations, SI 2015/869 regs 2, 8 with effect from 6 April 2015.

[3] Words in paras (1)(*a*), (2)(*a*) inserted by the Individual Savings Account (Amendment) Regulations, SI 2016/16 regs 2, 11(*a*), (*c*) with effect from 1 February 2016.

[4] Para (1)(*a*)(ia) inserted by the Individual Savings Account (Amendment) Regulations, SI 2016/16 regs 2, 11(*b*) with effect from 6 April 2016.

[5] Words in para (1)(*b*) inserted, and words in para (1)(*b*)(iii) substituted, by the Individual Savings Account (Amendment No 2) Regulations, SI 2017/466 regs 2, 16 with effect from 6 April 2017.

[5DFA Declarations required by regulation 5D

(1) The declarations in regulation 5D(2)(*c*) required by S in relation to a subscription permitted by regulation 5DDA are—

(*a*) in all cases, those specified in paragraph (2);

(*b*) in a case where the subscription is made with the deceased's account manager (A), those specified in paragraph (3); and

(*c*) in a case where the subscription is being made with an account manager other than the deceased's account manager (B), those specified in paragraph (4).

(2) The declarations specified in this paragraph are—

(*a*) that S is the surviving spouse or civil partner of the deceased;

(*b*) that S and the deceased were living together so as to meet the requirements specified in section 1011 of the Income Tax Act 2007, at the date of the deceased's death; and

(*c*) that the subscription is being made under regulation 5DDA.

(3) The declarations specified in this paragraph are that the subscription is being made—

(*a*) in the case of a subscription of non-cash assets made in accordance with paragraph (2) of that regulation—

(i) in the period beginning with distribution to S by the deceased's estate of those assets and ending no more than 180 days thereafter; or

(ii) in the case of the deceased's death occurring in the period beginning with 3rd December 2014 and ending with 5th April 2015, no later than 2nd October 2015;

whichever is the later; and

(*b*) in the case of any other subscription under that regulation, in the period beginning with the date of the deceased's death and ending—

(i) no more than 3 years thereafter, or in the case of the deceased's death occurring in the period beginning with 3rd December 2014 and ending with 5th April 2015, no later than 5th April 2018; or

(ii) no more than 180 days after administration of the estate is complete.

(4) The declarations specified in this paragraph are—

(*a*) that the subscription is being made by a payment of cash;

(*b*) that, in the permitted period, S has not made, with A, any subscription permitted by regulation 5DDA in respect of the amount determined in accordance with paragraph (3) of that regulation; and

(*c*) that the subscription is being made in the period beginning with the date of the deceased's death and ending—

(i) no more than 3 years thereafter, or in the case of the deceased's death occurring in the period beginning with 3rd December 2014 and ending with 5th April 2015, no later than 5th April 2018; or

(ii) no more than 180 days after administration of the estate is complete.

(5) The requirements in sub-paragraphs (2)(*a*), (*b*) and (4)(*b*) are met where the information is provided on the first instance a subscription permitted by regulation 5DDA in respect of an amount determined in accordance with paragraph (3) of that regulation is made to an account.][1]

Amendments—[1] Regulations 5DFA–5DFD inserted by the Individual Savings Account (Amendment No 2) Regulations, SI 2015/869 regs 2, 9 with effect from 6 April 2015.

[5DFB Notices required by regulation 5D

(1) Where an account manager (B) has—

(*a*) been notified by S that S wishes to make a subscription under regulation 5DDA; or

(*b*) received an application from S to make such a subscription;

that account manager shall, within the period of 30 days beginning with the day on which the notification or application is received, give to the deceased's account manager (A) a notice containing the information specified in paragraph (2).

(2) The information specified in this paragraph is—

(i) the name and address of the deceased;

(ii) the deceased's date of birth and date of death;

(iii) the deceased's National Insurance number, if known;

(iv) S's name and address;

(v) a statement that B has either received an application from S to make a subscription under regulation 5DDA or been notified that S wishes to make such a subscription; and

(vi) a statement that B has, subject to relevant checks, accepted that application or, where B has been notified that S wishes to make such a subscription, that B will accept such an application subject to relevant checks.

(3) Where A receives from B a notice under paragraph (1), A shall, within the period of 30 days beginning with the day on which that notification is received, give B a notice containing—

(i) the deceased's full name;

(ii) the full address of the deceased's permanent residence at the date of death;

(iii) the deceased's date of birth and date of death;

(iv) the deceased's National Insurance number, if known;

(v) the amount determined in accordance with paragraph (3) of regulation 5DDA;

(vi) a declaration that, in the permitted period, S has not made to an account held by A, any subscription permitted by regulation 5DDA in respect of the amount determined in accordance with paragraph (3) of that regulation;

(vii) an undertaking that, other than in the case of an authorisation given under paragraph (6) of regulation 5DDA, A will not accept a subscription made by S in respect of the amount determined in accordance with paragraph (3) of that regulation; and

(viii) an undertaking that, other than in the case of an authorisation given under paragraph (6) of regulation 5DDA, A will not provide the information and declarations in this paragraph to another account manager in respect of the amount determined in accordance with paragraph (3) of that regulation.

(4) In this regulation relevant checks means checks by B in relation to the information and declarations provided by S pursuant to regulations 5DF and 5DFA.][1]

Amendments—[1] Regulations 5DFA–5DFD inserted by the Individual Savings Account (Amendment No 2) Regulations, SI 2015/869 regs 2, 9 with effect from 6 April 2015.

[5DFC (1) Where the deceased's account manager receives a request from S made in accordance with paragraph (2), that account manager shall, within the period of 30 days beginning with the day on which the request is received, provide to S a statement of the amount determined in accordance with paragraph (3) of regulation 5DDA.

(2) The request shall contain the information required by regulation 5DF(1)(*c*) and the declarations required by regulation 5DFA(1)(*a*) and (*b*).][1]

Amendments—[1] Regulations 5DFA–5DFD inserted by the Individual Savings Account (Amendment No 2) Regulations, SI 2015/869 regs 2, 9 with effect from 6 April 2015.

[5DFD Regulation 12(7) to (11), (12) and (13) applies in relation to any information or declaration required under regulations 5DF(1)(*c*) and 5DFA as it applies to any application to open an account.][1]

Amendments—[1] Regulations 5DFA–5DFD inserted by the Individual Savings Account (Amendment No 2) Regulations, SI 2015/869 regs 2, 9 with effect from 6 April 2015.

[5DG Single regulation 5D subscription

Only one defaulted cash account subscription, defaulted investment subscription[, defaulted Lifetime ISA subscription][2] or subscription permitted by regulation 5DE may be made in respect of a defaulted cash account or a defaulted investment payment as the case may be even if the subscription made is an amount less than that which could have been made by way of such subscription in accordance with regulation 5D.][1]

Press releases etc—HMRC Guidance Note, 10 September 2012: Guidance on ISA reinstatement and payments outside the annual ISA subscription limit.

Amendments—[1] Regs 5D–5DM inserted by the Individual Savings Account (Amendment) (No 2) Regulations, SI 2012/1871 regs 4, 11 with effect from 8 August 2012.

[2] Words inserted by the Individual Savings Account (Amendment No 2) Regulations, SI 2017/466 regs 2, 17 with effect from 6 April 2017.

[5DH Default event or default investment payment occurring in the period beginning on 6th April 2011 and ending on 7th August 2012

Anything occurring in the period commencing on 6th April 2011 and ending on 7th August 2012 that, if it had occurred after that period, would have been—

(i) a default event in respect of a cash account within regulation 5DC, or

(ii) a defaulted investment payment within regulation 5DD,

shall be treated as occurring on 8th August 2012 for the purposes of regulations 5D to 5DG.][1]

Press releases etc—HMRC Guidance Note, 10 September 2012: Guidance on ISA reinstatement and payments outside the annual ISA subscription limit.

Amendments—[1] Regs 5D–5DM inserted by the Individual Savings Account (Amendment) (No 2) Regulations, SI 2012/1871 regs 4, 11 with effect from 8 August 2012.

[5DI Special provision in respect of Lehman Brothers investments and Keydata investments

(1) Regulations 5DJ to 5DM make special provision in respect of an investment that is a Lehman Brothers investment or a Keydata investment.

(2) An investment is a Lehman Brothers investment if—

(*a*) the investment was a qualifying investment held by an account investor in a stocks and shares account on 15th September 2008;

(*b*) Lehman Brothers Holdings Inc. acted as the sole counterparty underwriting the investment on that day; and

(*c*) the investment was not sold or otherwise disposed of on that day so as to cause it to cease to be a qualifying investment of the account on that day or any other day.

(3) An investment is a Keydata investment if—

(*a*) the investment was a qualifying investment held by an account investor in a stocks and shares account on 8th June 2009;

(*b*) Keydata Investment Services Limited (Keydata) on that day—

(i) was the account manager of the account, or

(ii) administered the account for another account manager; and

(*c*) the investment was not sold or otherwise disposed of on that day so as to cause it to cease to be a qualifying investment of the account on that day or any other day.][1]

Press releases etc—HMRC Guidance Note, 10 September 2012: Guidance on ISA reinstatement and payments outside the annual ISA subscription limit.

Amendments—[1] Regs 5D–5DM inserted by the Individual Savings Account (Amendment) (No 2) Regulations, SI 2012/1871 regs 4, 11 with effect from 8 August 2012.

[5DJ Special application of regulations 5DB, 5DD, 5DF and 5DH in respect of a Lehman Brothers investment

In respect of a Lehman Brothers investment—

(*a*) regulation 5D shall apply as if after paragraph (2) there is added—

"(3) No defaulted investment subscription may be made in respect of a defaulted investment payment made or treated as made on 8th August 2012 other than a single defaulted investment payment treated as made by virtue of regulation 5DL(2).";

(*b*) regulation 5DB shall apply as if paragraph (*b*) provided that a defaulted investment subscription must not exceed the amount of the defaulted investment payment determined in accordance with regulation 5DL;

(*c*) regulation 5DD is subject to regulation 5DL(2);

(*d*) regulation 5DF(1)(*b*) shall apply as if the information specified by it is—

(i) the information specified in paragraphs (i)-(iv) of that regulation;

(ii) the value of the defaulted investment at the opening of trading on the London Stock Exchange on 15th September 2008;

(iii) the date and amount of any earlier defaulted investment subscriptions in respect of the Lehman Brothers investment in question made before the making of the defaulted investment subscription;

(iv) the name and address (including postcode) of the account manager to whom any subscription referred to in sub-paragraph (iii) of this paragraph was made;

(*e*) regulation 5DH—

(i) shall apply as if the period mentioned in that regulation were the period commencing on 16th September 2008 and ending on 7th August 2012;

(ii) is subject to regulation 5DL(2).][1]

Press releases etc—HMRC Guidance Note, 10 September 2012: Guidance on ISA reinstatement and payments outside the annual ISA subscription limit.

Amendments—[1] Regs 5D–5DM inserted by the Individual Savings Account (Amendment) (No 2) Regulations, SI 2012/1871 regs 4, 11 with effect from 8 August 2012.

[5DK Deemed defaulted investment payment in respect of a Lehman Brothers investment

A defaulted investment payment shall be treated as made on 8th August 2012 in respect of a Lehman Brothers investment to the account investor who held it.][1]

Press releases etc—HMRC Guidance Note, 10 September 2012: Guidance on ISA reinstatement and payments outside the annual ISA subscription limit.

Amendments—[1] Regs 5D–5DM inserted by the Individual Savings Account (Amendment) (No 2) Regulations, SI 2012/1871 regs 4, 11 with effect from 8 August 2012.

[5DL Specified amount for the purposes of a defaulted investment subscription in respect of a Lehman Brothers investment

(1) This regulation determines the amount which a defaulted investment subscription must not exceed for the purposes of regulation 5DB(*b*) in relation to a defaulted investment payment made or treated as made in respect of a Lehman Brothers investment.

(2) Where one or more defaulted investment payments in respect of a Lehman Brothers investment are made on 8th August 2012 or are treated as made on that day by virtue of regulations 5DH or 5DK, they shall be treated as if they comprised a single defaulted investment payment made on that day of an amount which is the greater of—

(*a*) the value of the investment at the opening of trading on the London Stock Exchange on 15th September 2008; or

(*b*) the total of the payments made or treated as made by virtue of regulation 5DH on 8th August 2012.

(3) Where a defaulted investment payment in respect of a Lehman Brothers investment is made after 8th August 2012, its amount for the purposes of regulation 5DB(*b*) is the greater of—

(*a*) the amount determined by the formula $A - B$ where—

(i) "A" is the total of the single defaulted investment payment treated as made on 8th August 2012 in respect of the investment by virtue of paragraph (2) and all defaulted investment payments made in respect of it in the period commencing immediately after that day and ending immediately after the defaulted investment payment in question;

(ii) "B" is the total of all defaulted investment subscriptions made in respect of the Lehman Brothers investment before the subscription in question; or

(*b*) the amount determined by the formula $C - D$ where—

(i) "C" is the value of the investment at the opening of trading on the London Stock Exchange on 15th September 2008;

(ii) "D" is the total of all defaulted investment subscriptions made in respect of the Lehman Brothers investment before the subscription in question.][1]

Press releases etc—HMRC Guidance Note, 10 September 2012: Guidance on ISA reinstatement and payments outside the annual ISA subscription limit.

Amendments—[1] Regs 5D–5DM inserted by the Individual Savings Account (Amendment) (No 2) Regulations, SI 2012/1871 regs 4, 11 with effect from 8 August 2012.

[5DM Special application of regulations 5DJ to 5DL in respect of a Keydata investment

In respect of a Keydata investment—

(*a*) regulations 5DJ to 5DL shall apply as if—

(i) a reference to a Lehman Brothers investment were a reference to a Keydata investment;

(ii) the reference in regulation 5DJ(*e*)(i) to 16th September 2008 were a reference to 9th June 2009;

(*b*) regulation 5DJ(*d*)(ii) shall apply as if the information it requires is the amount for which the Keydata investment in question was acquired;

(*c*) regulation 5DL(2)(*a*) shall apply as if it referred to the amount of subscriptions made to the account (or any other account or personal equity plan) and other proceeds (including income) representing those subscriptions used to purchase the investment;

(*d*) regulation 5DL(3)(*a*)(i) shall apply as if element "A" is the amount described in regulation 5DL(2)(a) as construed in accordance with paragraph (*c*) of this regulation;

(*e*) regulation 5DL(3)(*b*)(i) shall apply as if element "C" is the total of the single defaulted investment payment treated as made on 8th August 2012 in respect of the investment by virtue of regulation 5DL(2) and all defaulted investment payments made in respect of it in the period commencing immediately after that day and ending immediately after the defaulted investment payment in question.][1]

Press releases etc—HMRC Guidance Note, 10 September 2012: Guidance on ISA reinstatement and payments outside the annual ISA subscription limit.

Amendments—[1] Regs 5D–5DM inserted by the Individual Savings Account (Amendment) (No 2) Regulations, SI 2012/1871 regs 4, 11 with effect from 8 August 2012.

[5E Subscriptions made by account investors issued with certificates by Royal Bank of Scotland Group disregarded for the purposes of regulations 4ZA and 31(3)(*c*)(ii)

(1) A subscription to an account made in accordance with this regulation on or before 5th April 2013 must be disregarded for the purposes of—

(*a*) the subscription [limit][2] in regulation 4ZA (subscriptions to an account other than a junior ISA account); and

(*b*) regulation 31(3)(*c*)(ii) (returns of information by account manager).

(2) A subscription to an account is made in accordance with this regulation if—

(*a*) it is made to a cash account held by an account investor;

(*b*) a withdrawal was made during the relevant period from a cash account held by the account investor with the account manager holding the cash account to which the subscription is made;

(*c*) the account manager of the account to which the subscription is made holds the certificate issued to the account investor in accordance with paragraph (3) (or a copy of it);

(*d*) the subscription does not exceed the amount determined in accordance with paragraph (4); and

(*e*) no earlier subscription in accordance with this regulation has been made to an account held by the account investor with the account manager holding the cash account to which the subscription in question is made.

(3) A certificate is issued to an account investor in accordance with this paragraph if—

(*a*) it is issued to the account investor by a RBSG bank;

(*b*) it contains the name and address (including postcode) of the account investor;

(*c*) it identifies the period in respect of which the delay certified in accordance with sub-paragraph (*d*) occurred; and

(*d*) it certifies—

(i) that the account investor held with a RBSG bank a banking facility (other than an account opened in accordance with regulation 12), in respect of which the updating of the records of deposits made to and payments from the facility was delayed during the relevant period; or

(ii) that a deposit, payment or other transfer of money to the account investor was delayed in the relevant period by reason of the delay described in paragraph (i).

(4) The amount referred to in paragraph (2)(*d*) is the total of all withdrawals made in the relevant period from any cash account held with the account manager holding the cash account to which the subscription in question is made.

(5) In this regulation—

(*a*) a bank is a "RBSG bank" if it is—

(i) The Royal Bank of Scotland plc, a company incorporated in Scotland (Company Number 090312);

(ii) National Westminster Bank plc, a company incorporated in England and Wales (Company Number 00929027);

(iii) Ulster Bank, Limited, a company incorporated in Northern Ireland (Company Number R0000733);

(*b*) the "relevant period" is 19th June to 6th July 2012 (but to 22nd July 2012 where the bank in paragraph (3)(d) is Ulster Bank, Limited).][1]

Amendments—[1] Regulation 5E inserted by the Individual Savings Account (Amendment No 2) Regulations, SI 2013/623 reg 2(1), (2) with effect from 5 April 2013.

[2] In para (1)(*a*), word substituted by the Individual Savings Account (Amendment No 2) Regulations, SI 2014/1450 regs 2, 13 with effect from 1 July 2014.

6 General investment rules

(1) [Subject to paragraph (1ZB), all transactions][9] by way of purchase by an account manager of investments under an account shall be made—

[(*a*) in the case of an authorised fund which is a dual priced unit trust, at the manager's price for the sale of the relevant class of units within the meaning of, and complying with the requirements of,[rules 6.3.5 and 6.3.5B of the Collective Investment schemes sourcebook][7];][2]

[(*b*) in the case of an authorised fund which is a single priced unit trust or an open-ended investment company, at the price of a unit or share within the meaning of, and complying with the requirements of, [rules 6.3.5 and 6.3.5A of the Collective Investment schemes sourcebook][7]; and][2]

(*c*) in the case of all other account investments, at the price for which those investments might reasonably be expected to be purchased in the open market.

[(1ZA) In paragraph (1)(*a*) and (*b*)—

. . . [3]

"a dual priced unit trust" means an authorised unit trust in respect of which the manager gives different prices for buying and selling units at the same time;

"a single priced unit trust" means an authorised unit trust in respect of which the manager gives the same price for buying and selling units at the same time.][2]

[(1ZB) Where an investment is made of a kind described in regulation 8A(2)(*a*), the amount of the payments made pursuant to the article 36H agreement must be such as might reasonably be expected to be made under such an agreement entered into in the open market."][9]

(2) All other transactions by way of sale or otherwise . . . [10] in investments under an account shall be made at the price for which those investments might reasonably be expected to be sold or otherwise transacted, as the case may be, in the open market.

[(2A) Where the right to exercise the rights of the lender under an article 36H agreement is sold or otherwise transacted, that sale or transaction must be made at a price for which the investment might reasonably be expected to be sold or otherwise transacted, as the case may be, in the open market.][9]

(3) Investments, or rights in respect of investments, may not at any time—

(*a*) be purchased or made otherwise than out of cash which an account manager holds under an account [and component][6], for which those investments or rights are qualifying investments; or

(*b*) be purchased from—

(i) an account investor, or

(ii) the spouse [or civil partner][5] of an account investor,

so as to become account investments under an account to which the account investor subscribes or has subscribed.

(4) Subject to paragraphs (5) and (6), [cash subscriptions and other cash][8] held by an account manager under an account shall be held only in sterling and be deposited in—

(i) an account with a deposit-taker [(including for this purpose a credit union)][4], or a deposit account or a share account with a building society, or

(ii) in the case where the account manager is [the Director of Savings][1], an account with [the Director of Savings][1],

which is designated as an ISA account for the purposes of these Regulations only.

(5) An account manager who is a European institution, a relevant authorised person or an assurance undertaking may hold [cash subscriptions and other cash][8] held under an account in the currency of the EEA State in which he has his principal place of business and may deposit such cash in an account, which is designated as mentioned in paragraph (4), with any person authorised under the law of that State to accept deposits.

(6) Cash by way of dividends, interest, distributions, and other rights or proceeds [(including any government bonus)][11] in respect of qualifying investments for any [account][6] shall at all times be recorded and accounted for separately from that for any other [account][6], and may be invested only—

(*a*) in qualifying investments for the [appropriate][6] component; or

(*b*) by way of cash deposit in accordance with paragraphs (4) and (5).

Commentary—*Simon's Taxes* **E3.310**.

Amendments—[1] Words in para (4)(ii) substituted by the Individual Savings Account (Amendment) Regulations, SI 1998/3174 reg 4 with effect from 6 April 1999.

[2] Paras (1)(*a*), (*b*) substituted, and para (1ZA) inserted, by the Financial Services and Markets Act 2000 (Consequential Amendments) (Taxes) Order, SI 2001/3629 art 171 with effect from 1 December 2001, immediately after the coming into force of the Financial Services and Markets Act 2000 ss 411, 432(1), Sch 20 (and SI 2001/3629 Pts 1 and 2).

[3] In para (1ZA), definition of "the Collective Investment Schemes Sourcebook" revoked by the Individual Savings Account (Amendment) Regulations, SI 2003/2747 regs 1(1), (2), 2, 4 with effect from 17 November 2003.

[4] Words in para (4) inserted by the ISA (Amendment No 3) Regulations, SI 2005/3350 regs 2, 5 with effect from 27 December 2005.

[5] Words in para (3)(*b*)(ii) inserted by Tax and Civil Partnership (No 2) Regulations, SI 2005/3230 reg 10(1), (2), with effect from 5 December 2005 (reg 1).

[6] Words in paras (3)(*a*), (6) substituted by the Individual Savings Account (Amendment) Regulations, SI 2007/2119 regs 2, 11 with effect from 6 April 2008.

[7] Words in para (1)(*a*), (*b*) substituted by the Individual Savings Account (Amendment) Regulations, SI 2008/704 regs 2, 5 with effect from 6 April 2008.

[8] In paras (4), (5) words substituted by the Individual Savings Account (Amendment No 2) Regulations, SI 2011/1780 regs 2, 14 with effect from 1 November 2011.

[9] In para (1), words substituted, and paras (1ZA), (2A) inserted by the Individual Savings Account (Amendment No 2) Regulations, SI 2016/364 regs 2, 11 with effect from 6 April 2016.

[10] In para (2), words "by an account manager" revoked by the Individual Savings Account (Amendment No 3) Regulations, SI 2016/977 regs 2, 6 with effect from 1 November 2016.

[11] In para (6), words inserted by the Individual Savings Account (Amendment No 2) Regulations, SI 2017/466 regs 2, 18 with effect from 6 April 2017.

7 Qualifying investments for a stocks and shares component

(1) This regulation specifies the kind of investments ("qualifying investments for a stocks and shares component") which may be purchased, made or held under a stocks and shares component, and in this regulation and regulations 31 and 34, "shares" without more includes stock.

(2) Qualifying investments for a stocks and shares component to which paragraph (1) refers are—

(*a*) shares, not being shares in an investment trust[—

(i) issued by a company wherever incorporated, [and][24]

(ii) subject to paragraph (3), [either officially listed on a recognised stock exchange or, in the European Economic Area, admitted to trading on a recognised stock exchange][22][.][24] . . .[24]][12]

(iii) . . .[24]

(*b*) securities ("qualifying securities")—

(i) issued by a company wherever incorporated, [and][27]

[(ii) where the securities in question satisfy at least one of the conditions specified in paragraph (5)[.][27]][24]

(*iii*) . . .[27]

[(*c*) gilt-edged securities . . .[24];

(*ca*) any securities issued by or on behalf of a government of any EEA State . . .[24];

[(*cb*) any securities which, in relation to a security mentioned in sub-paragraph (*ca*), would be a strip of that security if "strip" had the same meaning as in section 47 of the Finance Act 1942, with the omission of the words "issued under the National Loans Act 1968"][24]

[(*cc*) securities issued by a multilateral institution, contributions to which may be reported as official development assistance, listed in Part I of Annex 2 to the DAC Statistical Reporting Directive (approved by the Development Assistance Committee of the Organisation for Economic Co-operation and Development), where the securities satisfy the [condition][24] in [paragraph][24] (5)(*b*) . . .[24];][18]

(*d*) shares in an investment trust, . . .[23] . . .[27];

(*e*) . . .[17]

(*f*) units in, or shares of, a [UK UCITS or recognised UCITS][19] . . .[24];

[(*g*) qualifying units in or shares of a non-UCITS retail scheme . . .[24];][13]

(*h*) subject to the conditions specified in paragraph (10)[—

(i) shares which the qualifying individual has exercised the right to acquire in accordance with the provisions of a [[a Schedule 3][26] SAYE option scheme][17],

(ii) shares which have been appropriated to the qualifying individual in accordance with the provisions of an approved profit sharing scheme, or

(iii) plan shares of [a Schedule 3][25] [SIP][17] which cease to be subject to the plan but have remained in the beneficial ownership of the participant,][4]

and such shares shall be treated as fulfilling the condition as to payment of cash in [regulation 4(1B)(*d*)][20];

[(*ha*) a depositary interest;][5]

(*j*) cash deposited in accordance with regulation 6(4) to (6) . . .[24];

[(*k*) investments which—

(i) were held under a stocks and shares component [or a personal equity plan][16] on 28th November 2001,

(ii) on that date were admitted to trading on a recognised stock exchange in an EEA State and were not listed by a competent authority in an EEA State for the purposes of Council Directive 2001/34,

(iii) since that date have not ceased to be so admitted and have not become so listed,

(iv) do not fall within any of the other sub-paragraphs of this paragraph, and

(v) are not investments which, having fallen within any of those sub-paragraphs, have ceased so to fall on or after that date.][7]

[(*l*) investments which—

(i) were held under the stocks and shares component [or a personal equity plan][16] on 6th April 2004; and

(ii) immediately before that date, fell within sub-paragraphs (*e*), (*f*) or (*g*), or sub-paragraph (*ha*) so far as the relevant investments (within the meaning in the definition of "depositary interest") fell within any of those sub-paragraphs.][10]

[(*m*) units in a relevant collective investment scheme specified as a stakeholder product by regulation 5 of the Stakeholder Products Regulations . . .[24];][11]

[(*n*) policies of life insurance falling within regulation 9, issued in respect of an insurance made on or after 6th April 2005 . . .[24];][11]

(*o*) . . .[24]

[(*p*) in the case of a personal equity plan which is treated on and from 6th April 2008 as a stocks and shares account, investments which, immediately before that date, were qualifying investments for the plan under regulation 6(2)(*m*) of the Personal Equity Plan Regulations 1989[.][24]][16]

[(*q*) core capital deferred shares within the meaning of regulation 2 of the Building Societies (Core Capital Deferred Shares) Regulations 2013, provided that such shares are listed on the official list of a recognised stock exchange.][24]

(3) [An investment in shares fulfils the conditions as to official listing and admission to trading in paragraph (2)(a)][23] if—

(*a*) in pursuance of a public offer, the account manager applies for the allotment or allocation to him of shares in a company . . . [23] which are due to be admitted to such listing [or admitted to such trading][22] within 30 days of the allocation or allotment, and which, when admitted to such listing [or trading][22], would be qualifying investments for a stocks and shares component, and

(*b*) the shares are not allotted or allocated to the account manager in the circumstances specified in paragraph (4).

(4) The circumstances specified in this paragraph are where—

(*a*) the allotment or allocation of the shares was connected with the allotment or allocation of—

(i) shares in the company or trust of a different class, or

(ii) rights to shares in the company or trust of a different class, or

(iii) shares or rights to shares in another company or trust, or

[(iv) units in or shares in, or rights to units in or shares in, an authorised fund or a part of an umbrella scheme [, or][8]][6]

(vi) securities or rights to securities of the company or trust, or of another company or trust,

to the account manager, the account investor or any other person; and

(*b*) the terms on which the first-mentioned shares in this paragraph were offered were significantly more favourable to the account manager or account investor than they would have been if their allotment or allocation had not been connected as described in sub-paragraph (*a*).

(5) The conditions specified in this paragraph are—

(*a*) that the shares in the company issuing the securities are listed on the official list of a recognised stock exchange;

(*b*) that the securities are so listed;

(*c*) that the company issuing the securities is a [75%][21] subsidiary of a company whose shares are so listed[;][27]

[(*d*) that the shares in the company issuing the securities are admitted to trading on a recognised stock exchange in the European Economic Area;

(*e*) that the securities are so admitted to trading;

(*f*) that the company issuing the securities is a 75% subsidiary of a company whose shares are so admitted to trading.][27]

(6) . . . [24]

(7) . . . [17]

(8) . . . [27]

(9) . . . [17]

(10) The conditions specified in this paragraph are—

(*a*) in relation to shares which the individual has exercised his right to acquire in accordance with the provisions of [[a Schedule 2][25] SAYE option scheme][17], that the shares are transferred to the account manager or his nominee before the expiry of the period of 90 days following the exercise of that right;

(*b*) in relation to shares appropriated to the individual in accordance with the provisions of an approved profit-sharing scheme, that the shares are transferred to the account manager or his nominee before the expiry of the period of 90 days following the date when the individual directed the trustees to transfer the ownership of the shares to him or, if earlier, the release date in relation to the shares;

[(*ba*) in relation to plan shares mentioned in paragraph (2)(*h*)(iii), that the shares are transferred to the account manager or his nominee before the expiry of the period of 90 days following the date when the plan shares ceased to be subject to the plan;][4]

(*c*) that the aggregate market value at the date of transfer of any shares transferred to the account manager or his nominee in accordance with sub-paragraphs [(*a*), (*b*) or (*ba*)][4] in any year, and the individual's cash subscriptions in that year [to that account, do not together exceed the overall subscription limit in [regulation 4ZA(1)][24] in that year, reduced by the subscriptions by the individual in that year to a cash account][16].

(11) In paragraph (4)(*a*), "company" means any body corporate having a share capital.

(12) . . . [24]

[(13) The references to "shares" in paragraphs (2)(*h*) and (10) shall include references to a depositary interest where the relevant investments in question (referred to in paragraphs (*a*) and (*b*) of the definition of "depositary interest") are shares falling within both paragraphs (2)(*h*) and (10).][5]

(14) . . . [24]

(15) . . . [24]

[(16) In this regulation, references, in relation to qualifying investments, to the value, are to be construed in accordance with regulation 6(2), but deducting the incidental costs that would be incurred by a disposal and, in the case of a policy of life insurance, omitting any benefits payable in the event of the death of the account investor.][24]

(17) . . .[24]

Commentary—*Simon's Taxes* **E3.315**.

Amendments—[1] Para (2)(*c*) substituted and para 2(*ca*) inserted by the Individual Savings Account (Amendment) Regulations, SI 1998/3174 reg 5(2) with effect from 6 April 1999.

[2] Words in para (8) substituted by SI 1998/3174 reg 5(3) with effect from 6 April 1999.

[4] Words in para (2)(*h*) and (10)(*c*) substituted and para (10)(*ba*) inserted by the Individual Savings Account (Amendment No 2) Regulations, SI 2000/2079 reg 4 with effect from 21 August 2000.

[5] Para (2)(*ha*) inserted and para (13) inserted by the Individual Savings Account (Amendment No 3) Regulations, SI 2000/3112 reg 4 with effect from 13 December 2000.

[6] Sub-paras (2)(*e*), (*g*) and para (9) substituted, in para(4), sub-para (*a*)(iv) substituted for sub-paras (*a*)(iv) and (*a*)(v), words in sub-para (8) substituted, by the Financial Services and Markets Act 2000 (Consequential Amendments) (Taxes) Order, SI 2001/3629 art 172 with effect from 1 December 2001, immediately after the coming into force of the Financial Services and Markets Act 2000 ss 411, 432(1), Sch 20 (and SI 2001/3629 Pts 1 and 2).

[7] Sub-para (2)(*k*) inserted by the Individual Savings Account (Amendment No 2) Regulations, SI 2001/3778 art 3 with effect from 19 December 2001.

[8] Word in para (4)(*a*) substituted for by the Financial Services and Markets Act 2000 (Consequential Amendments) (Taxes) Order, SI 2002/1409 art 7 with effect from 2 July 2002.

[10] Words in sub-paras (2)(*e*), (*g*) substituted, and sub-para (2)(*l*) inserted, by the Individual Savings Account (Amendment) Regulations, SI 2003/2747 regs 1(1), (3), 2, 5(*a*), (*b*), (*d*) with effect from 6 April 2004.

[11] Para (2)(*m*), (*n*) inserted; and words in para (10) revoked, by the ISA (Amendment No 2) Regulations, SI 2004/2996 regs 2, 7–11 with effect from 6 April 2005.

[12] Words in para (2)(*a*) substituted, by the ISA (Amendment No 2) Regulations, SI 2005/2561 regs 2, 5 with effect from 6 October 2005.

[13] In para (2), sub-para (*c*) revoked; words in sub-para (*e*) substituted; and sub-para (*g*) substituted for sub-paras (*g*), (*ga*); by the ISA (Amendment No 3) Regulations, SI 2005/3350 regs 2, 6 with effect from 27 December 2005.

[16] Words in para (2)(*k*)(i), (*l*)(i) substituted, para (2)(*p*) inserted and words in para (10)(*c*) substituted, by the Individual Savings Account (Amendment) Regulations, SI 2007/2119 regs 2, 12, 13 with effect from 6 April 2008.

[17] Words in paras (2)(*b*)(iii), (*h*)(i), (iii), (8), (10)(*a*) substituted, paras (2)(e), (7), (9) revoked, by the Individual Savings Account (Amendment) Regulations, SI 2008/704 regs 2, 6 with effect from 6 April 2008 immediately after the ISA (Amendment) Regulations, SI 2007/2119 come into force.

[18] Para (2)(*cc*) inserted by the Individual Savings Account (Amendment No 3) Regulations, SI 2008/3025 regs 2, 4 with effect from 16 December 2008.

[19] In para (2)(*f*) words substituted by the Individual Savings Account (Amendment No 2) Regulations, SI 2009/1994 regs 2, 6 with effect from 8 October 2008.

[20] In para (2)(*h*), words substituted, by the Individual Savings Account (Amendment No 2) Regulations, SI 2011/1780 regs 2, 15 with effect from 1 November 2011.

[21] In paras (5)(*c*), (8), words substituted by the Individual Savings Account (Amendment) (No 2) Regulations, SI 2012/1871 regs 4, 12 with effect from 8 August 2012.

[22] In para (2)(a)(ii), words substituted for words , and in para (3) words inserted, by the Individual Savings Account (Amendment No 3) Regulations, SI 2013/1743 regs 2, 5 with effect from 5 August 2013.

[23] In paraa (2)(*d*), (3)(*a*), words revoked, and in para (3) words substituted, by the Individual Savings Account (Amendment) Regulations, SI 2014/654 regs 2, 8 with effect from 6 April 2014.

[24] The following changes made by the Individual Savings Account (Amendment No 2) Regulations, SI 2014/1450 regs 2, 14 with effect from 1 July 2014—

- in para (2)(*a*)(i), at the end, word inserted;
- in para (2)(*a*)(ii), at the end, full stop substituted for comma and word revoked;
- para (2)(*a*)(iii) revoked;
- para (2)(*b*)(ii), (*cb*) substituted;
- in para (2)(*c*), (*ca*), (*f*), (*g*), (*j*), (*m*),(*n*), words revoked;
- in para (2)(*cc*), words substituted, and words revoked;
- para (2)(*o*) revoked; note that this amendment only has effect in respect of investments purchased or made on or after 1 July 2014;
- at end of para (2)(*p*), semi-colon substituted for full stop, and sub-para (*q*) inserted;
- para (6) revoked;
- in para (8)(*b*), full stop substituted for comma and words revoked;
- in para (10)(*c*), words substituted;
- paras (12), (14), (15), (17) revoked; and
- para (16) substituted.

[25] In para (2)(*h*)(iii), words substituted by FA 2014 s 51, Sch 8 paras 84, 86. This amendment is treated as having come into force on 6 April 2014.

[26] In paras (2)(*h*)(i), (10)(*a*), words substituted by FA 2014 s 51, Sch 8 paras 143, 145. These amendments are treated as having come into force on 6 April 2014.

[27] In para (2)(*b*), word at the end of sub-para (i) inserted, at the end of sub-para (ii), full stop substituted for word "and", paras (2)(*b*)(iii), (8) revoked, in sub-para (2)(*d*), words ", in circumstances where the trust satisfies the conditions specified in paragraph (8)" revoked, semicolon at the end of para (5)(*c*) substituted for full stop, and para (5)(*d*)–(*f*) inserted by the Individual Savings Account (Amendment No 4) Regulations, SI 2015/1370 regs 2, 4 with effect from 1 July 2015.

8 Qualifying investments for a cash component

(1) This regulation specifies the kind of investments ("qualifying investments for a cash component") which may be purchased, made or held under a cash component.

(2) Qualifying investments for a cash component to which paragraph (1) refers are, subject to paragraph (3)—

[(*a*) cash deposited in a deposit account with—

(i) a building society,

(ii) a credit union,

[(iii) a bank, other than of a type at paragraph (*a*), (*d*) or (*e*) of section 991(2) of the ITA 2007,[9], . . .

(iv) . . . [9]][7]

(*b*) cash deposited in a share account with a building society;

(*c*), (*d*) . . . [6]

[(*e*) such investment deposits with the National Savings Bank which, according to the terms and conditions subject to which they are made, are expressly permitted to be held under a cash component of an account;

(*f*) any securities issued under the National Loans Act 1968—

(i) for the purpose of or in connection with raising money under the auspices of the Director of Savings within the meaning of section 11(1)(*a*) of the National Debt Act 1972, and

(ii) other than national savings certificates, premium savings bonds, national savings stamps and national savings gift tokens, which, according to the terms and conditions subject to which they are issued and purchased, are expressly permitted to be held under a cash component of an account.][1]

(*g*) . . . [10]

[(*h*) a depositary interest (with the references in that definition to a stocks and shares component and to regulation 7(2)(*a*) to (*h*) being replaced with references to a cash component and to regulation [8(2)(*a*) to (*f*)][10])][2]

[(*j*) a deposit account specified as a stakeholder product by regulation 4 of the Stakeholder Products Regulations;][3]

(*k*)–(*m*) . . . [10]

[(*n*) arrangements falling within section 47 of the Finance Act 2005 (alternative finance arrangements) under which the person referred to in that section as Y is a financial institution;][5]

[(*o*) arrangements falling within section 49 of that Act[;][1]][5]

[(*p*) a short-term money market fund which meets the conditions in COLL section 5.9.3.R;

(*q*) a money market fund which meets the conditions in COLL section 5.9.5R.][11]

[(3) A deposit account or share account which is a qualifying investment for a cash component falling within sub-paragraphs (*a*) or (*b*) of paragraph (2) respectively ("Account A") must not be connected with any other account falling within the descriptions in those sub-paragraphs ("Account B"), held by the account investor or any other person.

(4) For the purposes of paragraph (3), Account A is connected with Account B if all of the following circumstances apply—

(*a*) either of the accounts was opened with reference to the other, or with a view to enabling the other to be opened on particular terms, or with a view to facilitating the opening of the other on particular terms,

(*b*) the terms on which Account A was opened would have been significantly less favourable to the holder if Account B had not been opened, and

(*c*) Account B is not a tax exempt account.

(5) The following are tax exempt accounts for the purposes of paragraph (4)—

(*a*) an account opened (or treated as opened) in accordance with regulation 12 or 12A;

(*b*) a child trust fund.][8]

Commentary—*Simon's Taxes* **E3.316.**

Amendments—[1] Para (2) (*e*) substituted and para 2(*f*) inserted by the Individual Savings Account (Amendment) Regulations, SI 1998/3174 reg 6 with effect from 6 April 1999.

[2] Sub-para (2)(*h*) inserted by the Individual Savings Account (Amendment) Regulations, SI 2003/2747 regs 1(1), (2), 2, 7 with effect from 17 November 2003.

[3] Paras (2)(*j*)–(*m*) inserted by the ISA (Amendment No 2) Regulations, SI 2004/2996 regs 2, 12 with effect from 6 April 2005.

[5] In para (2), sub-paras (*n*), (*o*) inserted, by the ISA (Amendment No 3) Regulations, SI 2005/3350 regs 2, 9 with effect from 27 December 2005.

[6] Para (2)(*c*), (*d*) revoked, by the Individual Savings Account (Amendment) Regulations, SI 2008/704 regs 2, 7 with effect from 6 April 2008 immediately after the ISA (Amendment) Regulations, SI 2007/2119 come into force.

[7] Para (2)(*a*) substituted by the Individual Savings Account (Amendment No 2) Regulations, SI 2008/1934 regs 2, 4 with effect in relation to events occurring on and after 13 September 2007.

[8] Paras (3)–(5) substituted for previous para (3), by the Individual Savings Account (Amendment) (No 2) Regulations, SI 2012/1871 regs 4, 13 with effect from 1 November 2011.

9 Para (2)(*a*)(iii) substituted, and para (2)(*a*)(iv) and preceding word revoked, by the Individual Savings Account (Amendment) Regulations, SI 2014/654 regs 2, 9 with effect from 6 April 2014.

10 Paras (2)(*g*), (*k*), (*l*), (*m*) revoked, and in para (2)(*h*), words substituted, by the Individual Savings Account (Amendment No 2) Regulations, SI 2014/1450 regs 2, 15(*a*), (*b*). These amendments only have effect in respect of investments purchased or made on or after 1 July 2014.

11 In para (2)(*o*), semi-colon substituted for full stop, and paras (2)(*p*), (*q*) inserted, by the Individual Savings Account (Amendment No 2) Regulations, SI 2014/1450 regs 2, 15(*c*) with effect from 1 July 2014.

[8ZA Qualifying investments for a Lifetime ISA component

The kind of investments ("qualifying investments for a Lifetime ISA component") which may be purchased, made or held under a Lifetime ISA are—

(*a*) qualifying investments for a stocks and shares component; and

(*b*) qualifying investments for a cash component.][1]

Amendments—[1] Regulation 8ZA inserted by the Individual Savings Account (Amendment No 2) Regulations, SI 2017/466 regs 2, 19 with effect from 6 April 2017.

[8A Qualifying investments for an innovative finance component

(1) This regulation specifies the kind of investments ("qualifying investments for an innovative finance component") which may be purchased, made or held under an innovative finance account.

(2) Qualifying investments for an innovative finance component to which paragraph (1) refers are—

(*a*) payments by a borrower made under an article 36H agreement where the conditions in paragraph (3) are met;

(*b*) payments by an assignee for the right to exercise the rights of the lender under an article 36H agreement where the conditions in paragraph (3)(*c*) and (*d*) are met;

(*c*) payments by a novatee in respect of the novation of an article 36H agreement where the conditions in paragraph (3)(*c*) and (*d*) are met;

[(*ca*) debentures where the conditions in paragraph (4) are met;][2]

(*d*) cash deposited in accordance with regulation 6(4) to (6); and

(*e*) payments by way of compensation in respect of a matter described in regulation 5DD in relation to an investment specified in this regulation.

(3) The conditions in this paragraph are—

(*a*) the payment is a payment of interest or capital or both;

(*b*) the payment is made to the account manager of the account investor;

(*c*) the article 36H agreement is made on genuine commercial terms; and

(*d*) the article 36H agreement is not part of a scheme or arrangement the main purpose, or one of the main purposes, of which is the avoidance of tax.][1]

[(4) The conditions in this paragraph are—

(*a*) the debenture is a transferable security issued by a company or a charity;

(*b*) the investment in the debenture is facilitated by a person carrying on an activity of the kind specified in article 25 of the Regulated Activities Order 2001 through an electronic system operated by that person in an EEA State for such purpose;

(*c*) that person or another, acting under an arrangement with that person or at that person's direction, in respect of the investment, treats the account investor as its client and undertakes on behalf of the account investor to—

(i) receive payments in respect of the debenture;

(ii) make payments, when due, in respect of the debenture to the account investor; and

(iii) exercise, or facilitate the exercise of, rights in respect of the debenture;

(*d*) the investment in the debenture is not part of a scheme or arrangement the main purpose, or one of the main purposes, of which is the avoidance of tax;

(*e*) the debenture is not made available to the account investor by reason of their or of another's status, whether past, present or prospective, as an employee, director, partner, trustee or the holder of any office;

(*f*) the account investor is not connected with the issuer of the debenture, and for this purpose "connected" has the meaning given in section 170 of ITA 2007 with the omission of the reference to "in period A" in sub-section (7);

(*g*) the debenture must not be connected with any other investment held outside an account by the account investor or any other person, and for this purpose an investment is to be treated as connected with another if—

(i) either was made with reference to the other or with a view to enabling the other to be made on particular terms;

(ii) the terms on which either investment was made would have been significantly less favourable if the other investment had not been made; and

(*h*) the investment in the debenture is made on genuine commercial terms.][2]

Amendments—[1] Regulation 8A inserted by the Individual Savings Account (Amendment No 2) Regulations, SI 2016/364 regs 2, 12 with effect from 6 April 2016.

[2] Paras (2)(*ca*), (4) inserted by the Individual Savings Account (Amendment No 3) Regulations, SI 2016/977 regs 2, 7 with effect from 1 November 2016.

9 [Insurance policies]
[(1) Policies referred to in regulation 7(2)(*n*) or (o) . . . [8] must, subject to compliance with [paragraphs (4) to (9) as appropriate][7], satisfy the conditions specified in paragraph (3).][5]
[(2) In paragraph (1) "policies" includes rights under a linked long-term contract specified as a stakeholder product by regulation 6 of the Stakeholder Products Regulations.][5]
(3) The conditions specified in this paragraph are that—
(*a*) the insurance is on the life of the account investor only;
(*b*) the terms and conditions of the policy provide—
(i) that the policy may only be owned or held as a qualifying investment for . . . [5] an account which satisfies the provisions of these Regulations;
(ii) [in the case of a policy that is held under an account that is not a junior ISA account,][7] that the policy shall automatically terminate if [it comes to the notice of the account manager, in any manner, that either of the events specified in paragraph (8) has occurred in relation to the policy][1];
[(iia) in the case of a policy that is held under an account that is a junior ISA account, that the policy shall automatically terminate if it comes to the notice of the account manager, in any manner, that the event specified in paragraph (8A) has occurred in relation to the policy;][7]
[(iii) subject to paragraph (3B), for an express prohibition of any transfer, assignment or (in Scotland) assignation of the policy to the account investor who holds the account under which the policy is held or, in the case of a policy held under an account that is a junior ISA account, the registered contact or named child in relation to that account;][7]
(iv) . . [7]
[(*c*) the policy evidences or secures a contract of insurance which—
(i) falls within paragraph I or III of Part II of Schedule 1 to the Financial Services and Markets Act 2000 (Regulated Activities) Order 2001, or
(ii) would fall within either of those paragraphs if the insurer was a company with permission under Part 4 of the Financial Services and Markets Act 2000 to effect or carry out contracts of insurance;][4]
(*d*) the policy is not—
(i) a contract to pay an annuity on human life, or
(ii) a personal portfolio bond within the meaning given by [[section 516 of ITTOIA 2005][6], or][3]
(iii) a contract, the effecting and carrying out of which constitutes "pension business" within the meaning given by section 431B(1) of the Taxes Act; and
(*e*) after the first payment in respect of a premium in relation to the policy has been made, there is no contractual obligation on any person to make any other such payment.
[(3A) In paragraphs (3)(*b*)(iii) and (3B), "policy" includes—
(*a*) the rights conferred by a policy; and
(*b*) any share or interest in the rights conferred by a policy.
(3B) The prohibition required by paragraph (3)(*b*)(iii) must not prohibit—
(*a*) the cash proceeds from the termination of the policy or a partial surrender of the policy ownership—
(i) being paid to the account investor where the policy is held under an account that is not a junior ISA account;
(ii) being withdrawn in accordance with regulation 4ZD (permitted withdrawals from a junior ISA account) and (4ZE) (permitted withdrawals from a junior ISA account where the named child is terminally ill);
(*b*) the transfer of title to the policy so that it is vested as required from time to time by regulations 4(6)(*b*)(i) and (ia) (general conditions for accounts) and 15(*a*) (special provisions relating to insurer-managers) by virtue of—
(i) a transfer of an account in accordance with regulations 21 or 21B;
(ii) a change of registered contact in relation to a junior ISA account; or
(iii) an account ceasing to be a junior ISA account upon the named child in relation to the account attaining 18 years;
(*c*) the vesting of the policy in the personal representatives of the account investor.][7]
(4) A policy . . . [5] must not be connected with any other policy ("the linked policy"), held by the account investor or any other person, and for this purpose a policy is connected with another if—
(*a*) either policy was issued in respect of an insurance made with the reference to the other, or with a view to enabling the other to be made on particular terms, or with a view to facilitating the making of the other on particular terms, and
(*b*) the terms on which the first-mentioned policy in this paragraph was issued would have been significantly less favourable to the holder if the linked policy had not been issued.

(5) References to "the linked policy" in paragraph (4) shall include a contract of insurance, and references to the issuing of the linked policy shall include the making of such a contract.

(6) No sum may at any time, at or after the making of the insurance, be lent to or at the direction of the account investor or by arrangement with the insurer for the time being responsible for the obligations under the policy.

[(7) Where [any of the events specified in paragraphs (8) or (8A)][7] occurs in relation to a policy, the policy shall nevertheless be treated, for the purposes of these Regulations, [excepting paragraphs (3)(*b*)(ii) and (iia), (8) and (8A)][7] and regulation 36, as if it had satisfied the conditions in paragraph (3)(*b*)(i) during the period—

(*a*) commencing at the time at which the specified event occurred, and

(*b*) ending immediately before—

(i) the end of the [final insurance year in relation to the policy, within the meaning given by section 499 of ITTOIA 2005][6], or

(ii) the time at which the specified event came to the notice of the account manager, whichever first occurs (the "termination event").

(8) The events specified in this paragraph are—

(*a*) that the policy has ceased to be one in respect of which the conditions in paragraph (3)(*b*)(i) are satisfied: and

(*b*) that those conditions were not satisfied in relation to the policy at the date on which the insurance was made.

[(8A) The event specified in this paragraph is that—

(*a*) the policy has ceased to be one in respect of which the conditions in paragraph (3)(*b*)(i) are satisfied or those conditions were not satisfied in relation to the policy at the date on which the insurance was made; and

(*b*) the breach or non-compliance cannot be remedied in accordance with regulation 21C or has not been remedied within a reasonable time.][7]

(9) Where—

(*a*) it comes to the notice of the account manager, in any manner, that an event specified in [paragraph (8) or (8A)][7] has occurred in relation to a policy, and

(*b*) the account manager is not the insurer for the time being responsible for the obligations under the policy or, where the policy is not still in existence, the person who was the last such insurer, the account manager shall, within 30 days of the event coming to his notice, give notice to that insurer, specifying the event mentioned in sub-paragraph (*a*), and the termination event.][2]

Commentary—*Simon's Taxes* **D7.5127**; **E3.317**.

Amendments—[1] Words in para (3)(*b*)(ii) substituted by the Individual Savings Account (Amendment) Regulations, SI 1998/3174 reg 7(2) with effect from 6 April 1999.

[2] Para (7) substituted and paras (8), (9) inserted by SI 1998/3174 reg 7(3) with effect from 6 April 1999.

[3] Words in para (3)(*d*)(ii) substituted by the Individual Savings Account (Amendment) Regulations, SI 2001/908 reg 4 with effect from 6 April 2001.

[4] Sub-para (3)(*c*) substituted by the Financial Services and Markets Act 2000 (Consequential Amendments) (Taxes) Order, SI 2001/3629 art 174 with effect from 1 December 2001, immediately after the coming into force of the Financial Services and Markets Act 2000 ss 411, 432(1), Sch 20 (and SI 2001/3629 Pts 1 and 2).

[5] Heading and paras (1), (2) substituted, and words in paras (3), (4) revoked, by the ISA (Amendment No 2) Regulations, SI 2004/2996 regs 2, 13 with effect from 6 April 2005.

[6] Words in paras (3)(*d*)(ii), (7)(*b*)(i) substituted, by the Individual Savings Account (Amendment) Regulations, SI 2008/704 regs 2, 8 with effect from 6 April 2008 immediately after the ISA (Amendment) Regulations, SI 2007/2119 come into force.

[7] In paras (1), (7), (9), words substituted; words at beginning of para (3)(*b*)(ii) and para (3)(*b*)(*iia*) inserted; para (3)(*b*)(*iii*) substituted, para (3)(*b*)(*iv*) revoked; paras (3A), (3B), (8A) inserted; by the Individual Savings Account (Amendment No 2) Regulations, SI 2011/1780 regs 2, 16 with effect from 1 November 2011.

[8] In para (1), words revoked by the Individual Savings Account (Amendment No 2) Regulations, SI 2014/1450 regs 2, 16 with effect from 1 July 2014.

10 Qualifying individuals who may invest under an account [that is not a junior ISA account][6] [nor a Lifetime ISA][11]

[(1) This regulation specifies the description of individual ("qualifying individual") who may invest under an account [that is not a junior ISA account][6] [nor a Lifetime ISA][11].

(2) A qualifying individual to whom paragraph (1) refers is an individual—

[(*a*) who, in the case of a cash account, is 16 years of age or over and, in the case of a stocks and shares account [or innovative finance account][10], is 18 years of age or over;

(*b*) who, [except for a subscription made in accordance with regulation [5D(2)(*a*)(iia) or (iv)][10],][9] in the case of a stocks and shares account, has not subscribed, and will not subscribe, to any other stocks and shares account, in the year in which the subscription is made;

(*c*) who, [except for a subscription made in accordance with regulation [5D(2)(*a*)(i), (iia), (iv) or (v)][10],][9] in the case of a cash account, has not subscribed, and will not subscribe, to any other cash account, in the year in which the subscription is made;

[(*cza*) who, except for a subscription made in accordance with regulation 5D(2)(*a*)(iia) or (iv), in the case of an innovative finance account, has not subscribed and will not subscribe, to any other innovative finance account, in the year in which the subscription is made;][10]

(*ca*) who has not exceeded the appropriate overall subscription limit in [regulation 4ZA(1)][6] . . . [8] in that year;][3]

(*d*)

(i) who is resident . . . [7] in the United Kingdom, or

[(ii) who, though not resident in the United Kingdom, has general earnings from overseas Crown employment subject to United Kingdom tax within the meaning given by section 28 of ITEPA 2003][4][, or

(iii) who, though not resident in the United Kingdom, is married [or in a civil partnership with][2] to a person mentioned in paragraph (ii)][1][; or][9]

[(iv) who, where the terms and conditions of an account allow for it, though not resident in the United Kingdom, makes a subscription to the account in accordance with regulation 5D.][9]

[(3) For the purposes of paragraph (2)(*b*) and (*c*), a subscription to a junior ISA account shall be disregarded.][6]

Commentary—*Simon's Taxes* **D7.5127**; **E3.305**.

Amendments—[1] In para (2), words in sub-para (*a*) inserted, and sub-para (*d*)(iii) added, by the Individual Savings Account (Amendment) Regulations, SI 2001/908 reg 5 with effect from 6 April 2001.

[2] Words in para (2)(*d*)(iii) inserted by Tax and Civil Partnership (No 2) Regulations, SI 2005/3230 reg 10(1), (3), with effect from 5 December 2005 (reg 1).

[3] Para (2)(*a*)–(*ca*) substituted for previous para (2)(*a*)–(*c*) by the Individual Savings Account (Amendment) Regulations, SI 2007/2119 regs 2, 14 with effect from 6 April 2008.

[4] Para (2)(*d*)(ii) substituted, by the Individual Savings Account (Amendment) Regulations, SI 2008/704 regs 2, 9 with effect from 6 April 2008 immediately after the ISA (Amendment) Regulations, SI 2007/2119 come into force.

[6] In heading, words inserted, para (1) substituted, in para (2)(*ca*), words substituted, and para (3) inserted, by the Individual Savings Account (Amendment No 2) Regulations, SI 2011/1780 regs 2, 17 with effect from 1 November 2011.

[7] In para (2)(*d*)(i), words revoked by the Income Tax (Removal of Ordinary Residence) Regulations, SI 2013/605 reg 4(1), (3) with effect for the purposes of a person's liability to income tax for the tax year 2013–14 or any subsequent tax years.

[8] In para (2)(*ca*), words revoked by the Individual Savings Account (Amendment No 2) Regulations, SI 2014/1450 regs 2, 17 with effect from 1 July 2014.

[9] In para (2), words in sub-paras (*b*), (*c*) inserted, and sub-para (*d*)(iv) and preceding word "or" inserted, by the Individual Savings Account (Amendment) Regulations, SI 2016/16 regs 2, 12 with effect from 1 February 2016.

[10] In para (2), words in sub-para (*a*) inserted, words in sub-paras (*b*), (*c*) substituted, and sub-para (*cza*) inserted by the Individual Savings Account (Amendment No 2) Regulations, SI 2016/364 regs 2, 13 with effect from 6 April 2016.

[11] In heading and para 1, words inserted by the Individual Savings Account (Amendment No 2) Regulations, SI 2017/466 regs 2, 20 with effect from 6 April 2017.

[10A Lifetime ISA qualifying individuals who may invest under a Lifetime ISA

(1) This regulation specifies the description of individual ("Lifetime ISA qualifying individual") who may invest under a Lifetime ISA.

(2) A Lifetime ISA qualifying individual to whom paragraph (1) refers is an individual who—

(*a*) is 18 years of age or over;

(*b*) in relation to a current year payment is under 50 years of age;

(*c*) in relation to a current year payment or a payment under paragraph (4)(*c*), has not made, and will not make, any such payment to any other Lifetime ISA in the year in which the payment is made;

(*d*) has not exceeded the overall subscription limit in regulation 4ZA(1) in that year;

(*e*) has not exceeded the overall Lifetime ISA payment limit in regulation 4ZA(1A) in that year; and

(*f*) in relation to a current year payment or a payment under paragraph (4)(*c*), is resident in the United Kingdom or, if not so resident—

(i) is a person who has general earnings from overseas Crown employment subject to United Kingdom tax within the meaning given by section 28 of ITEPA 2003, or

(ii) is married to or in a civil partnership with a person mentioned in paragraph (i).

(3) Subject to paragraph (4), the following are current year payments—

(*a*) a subscription of money;

(*b*) a subscription of shares to which regulation 7(2)(*h*) applies;

(*c*) a subscription to which regulation 5D applies;

(*d*) an additional permitted subscription in accordance with regulation 5DDA;

(*e*) a replacement subscription in accordance with regulation 5DDB;

(*f*) an additional permitted subscription on closure of a Help to Buy ISA in accordance with regulation 5DDC; and

(*g*) a transfer of qualifying investments for a Lifetime ISA component from an account which is not a Lifetime ISA.

(4) The following are not current year payments—

(*a*) a defaulted Lifetime ISA subscription under regulation 5D(2)(*a*)(ia);

(*b*) a returned withdrawal under regulation 5D(2)(*a*)(ib); and

(*c*) the first or only transfer from a Help to Buy ISA (as described in regulation 5DDC(6)) to a Lifetime ISA in the year 2017–18 in an amount not exceeding the balance on the Help to Buy ISA as at 5th April 2017 plus accrued interest.][1]

Amendments—[1] Regulation 10A inserted by the Individual Savings Account (Amendment No 2) Regulations, SI 2017/466 regs 2, 21 with effect from 6 April 2017.

11 Account investor ceasing to qualify

Notwithstanding any other provision of these Regulations an account investor who, after subscribing [or making a qualifying addition][1] to an account, at any time ceases to fulfil the conditions of regulation 10(2)(*d*) [or 10A(2)(*f*), as the case may be,][1] may retain the benefits of the account (including the right to any relief or exemption due under the account) subsisting at that time but, so long as he fails to fulfil those conditions, shall not be entitled to subscribe further [or make a qualifying addition][1] to such an account.

Amendments—[1] Words inserted by the Individual Savings Account (Amendment No 2) Regulations, SI 2017/466 regs 2, 22 with effect from 6 April 2017.

12 [Conditions for application to open an account that is not a junior ISA account [or a Lifetime ISA][16]]

(1) An application by an individual to [open][9] an account in the year in which he first subscribes to that account, and in the year following a year in which that individual has not subscribed to the account, must be made to an account manager in a statement and, subject to paragraph (5), must fulfil the conditions specified in paragraphs (2), (3) and (4).

(2) An application must specify the first year to which the application relates.

(3) An application [must contain][9] a declaration by the applicant that—

[(*a*) his application is to [open][9] a stocks and shares account[, cash account or innovative finance account][15], as the case may be;][6]

(*b*) the declaration shall have effect for the year to which paragraph (2) refers, and each successive year following that year, in which the applicant subscribes to the account;

(*c*) all cash subscriptions made, and to be made, to the account are the applicant's cash;

[(*d*) in the case of a stocks and shares account, the applicant[, except for a subscription made in accordance with regulation [5D(2)(*a*)(iia) or (iv)[15]][14]]—

(i) has not subscribed, and will not subscribe, to any other stocks and shares account, in the year to which paragraph (2) refers, and

(ii) will not subscribe to any other stocks and shares account, in each successive year following that year, in which the declaration has effect;

(*e*) in the case of a cash account, the applicant[, except for a subscription made in accordance with regulation [5D(2)(*a*)(i), (iia), (iv) or (v)[15]][14]]—

(i) has not subscribed, and will not subscribe, to any other cash account, in the year to which paragraph (2) refers, and

(ii) will not subscribe to any other cash account, in each successive year following that year, in which the declaration has effect;

(*ea*) that the applicant has not subscribed, and will not subscribe, more than the . . . [13] overall subscription limit in [regulation 4ZA(1)][9] (aggregating subscriptions to all accounts)—

(i) in the year to which paragraph (2) refers, and

(ii) in each successive year following that year, in which the declaration has effect;

(*eb*) . . . [13]

[(*f*) the applicant is 16 years of age or over, and [except in relation to a subscription made in accordance with regulation 5D into an account opened solely to receive such a subscription[14]]—

(i) is resident . . . [11] in the United Kingdom, or

[(ii) is a person who has general earnings from overseas Crown employment subject to United Kingdom tax within the meaning given by section 28 of ITEPA 2003,][7]

(iii) is married to [or in a civil partnership with][4] a person mentioned in paragraph (ii),

and will inform the account manager if he ceases to be so resident . . . [11], or to perform such duties, or to be married to [or in a civil partnership with][4] a person who performs such duties, as the case may be;][1]

[(*fa*) in the case of an innovative finance account, except for a subscription made in accordance with regulation 5D(2)(*a*), (iia) or (iv), the applicant—

(i) has not subscribed, and will not subscribe, to any other innovative finance account, in the year to which paragraph (2) refers, and

(ii) will not subscribe to any other innovative finance account, in each successive year following that year in which the declaration has effect;][15]

(*g*) ...[9]

(4) An application must contain—

(*a*) the applicant's full name,
(*b*) the address of his permanent residence, including postcode,
(*c*) his national insurance number, or confirmation that he does not have one, ...[9]
(*d*) his date of birth[,
(e) the authorisation specified in paragraph (4A)][9];

[(4A) The authorisation specified by this paragraph is authority given by the applicant to the account manager—

(*a*) to hold the subscriptions, account investments, interest, dividends and any other rights or proceeds in respect of those investments and cash;
(*b*) to make on behalf of the applicant any claims to relief from tax in respect of account investments; and
(*c*) to make a record in writing in accordance with paragraph (7) where that paragraph requires the account manager to do so.][9]

(5) . . .[6]

(6) An account manager may not accept as an account investor any individual if he has reason to believe that—

(*a*) he is not or might not be a qualifying individual, or
(*b*) he has given untrue information in his application.

[(7) Where an application is not in writing or the manager operates a record system under which all original written applications are not retained—

(*a*) the account manager must, immediately after receiving the application, record in writing on behalf of the applicant, the declaration required by paragraph (3) and authorisation required by paragraphs (4)(*e*) and (4A);
(*b*) the account manager must notify the applicant of the contents of the written record within 5 business days of making it; and
(*c*) the written record (as amended by any corrections notified to the account manager by the applicant within 30 days of the notification mentioned in sub-paragraph (*b*)) shall be treated as the applicant's declaration required by paragraph (3) and authorisation required by paragraphs (4)(*e*) and (4A).][9]

(7A) ...[9]

(8) Section 95 of the Management Act shall have effect as if—

(*a*) the statement and declarations to which paragraphs (1), (3) and (7) refer were a statement or declarations, as the case may be, within the meaning of subsection (1)(*b*), and
(*b*) there were substituted for subsection (3) the following words—

"(3) The relevant years of assessment for the purposes of this section are the year of assessment in respect of which any claim to relief or exemption from tax in connection with which the statement or declarations are relevant, is made, the next following, and any preceding year of assessment."

[(9) An application furnished by an individual under this regulation . . .[2] shall be regarded as in writing if it is furnished—

(*a*) by telephonic facsimile transmission containing the signature of the individual, or
(*b*) by electronic communication containing an electronic signature of the individual.][1]

[(10) Where an account manager is required by paragraph (7) to make a record in writing—

(*a*) a record shall be regarded as being a written record if it is produced by electronic means;
(*b*) the notification of the contents of the record by the account manager to the applicant required by paragraph (7)(*b*) may be sent to the applicant by telephonic facsimile transmission or by electronic communication.][9]

[(11) In this regulation—

["electronic communication" includes any communication conveyed by means of an electronic communications network.][3]

"electronic signature" has the meaning given by section 7(2) of the Electronic Communications Act 2000.][1]

[(11A) In paragraph (3), references to subscriptions to an account do not include subscriptions to an account that is a junior ISA account.][9]

[(12) An application may be made on an individual's behalf—

(*a*) if the individual is resident in England and Wales—
  (i) pursuant to an order under section 16(2)(*a*) of the Mental Capacity Act 2005; or
  (ii) by a deputy appointed under section 16(2)(*b*) of that Act; or
(*b*) if the individual is resident in Scotland or Northern Ireland and is suffering from mental disorder, by a parent, guardian, spouse, civil partner, son or daughter of the individual.][12]

[(13) In paragraph (12) "mental disorder" has the meaning given by . . .[12] in Scotland, [section 328 of the Mental Health (Care and Treatment) (Scotland) Act 2003][5] or, in Northern Ireland Article 3 of the Mental Health (Northern Ireland) Order 1986.][2]

[(14) This regulation does not apply to a Lifetime ISA.][16]

Commentary—*Simon's Taxes* **E3.306**.

Amendments—[1] Para (3)(*f*) substituted, and paras (9)–(11) added, by the Individual Savings Account (Amendment) Regulations, SI 2001/908 reg 6 with effect from 6 April 2001.

[2] Words in paras (9), (10) revoked, and para (11) inserted, by the Individual Savings Account (Amendment No 3) Regulations, SI 2002/3158 reg 5 with effect from 8 January 2003.

[3] In para (11), definition of "electronic communication" substituted by the Communications Act 2003 (Consequential Amendments) Order, SI 2003/2155 art 3(2), Schedule 1 para 24 with effect from 17 September 2003.

[4] Words in para (3) inserted by the Tax and Civil Partnership Regulations, SI 2005/3230 reg 10(1), (4), with effect from 5 December 2005 (reg 1).

[5] Words in para (13) substituted by the Mental Health (Care and Treatment) (Scotland) Act 2003 (Consequential Provisions) Order, SI 2005/2078 art 15, Sch 2 para 19 with effect from 5 October 2005. This amendment is also made by the Mental Health (Care and Treatment) (Scotland) Act 2003 (Modification of Subordinate Legislation) Order, SSI 2005/445 art 2, Schedule para 28 with effect from 5 October 2005.

[6] Para (3)(*a*), (*d*)–(*ea*) substituted, and para (5) revoked, by the Individual Savings Account (Amendment) Regulations, SI 2007/2119 regs 2, 15, 16 with effect from 6 April 2008.

[7] Para (3)(*f*)(ii) substituted, words in para (3)(*g*)(iv) substituted, and words in para (10) substituted and revoked, by the Individual Savings Account (Amendment) Regulations, SI 2008/704 regs 2, 10 with effect from 6 April 2008 immediately after the ISA (Amendment) Regulations, SI 2007/2119 come into force.

[8] Paras (7), (7A) substituted by the Individual Savings Account (Amendment No 2) Regulations, SI 2009/1994 regs 2, 7 with effect from 8 October 2008.

[9] Heading substituted; in para (1), word substituted; in para (3), in opening words, words substituted; in sub-paras (*a*), (*ea*), words substituted; sub-para (*g*) revoked; in para (4), word revoked and sub-para (*e*) inserted; para (4A) inserted; para (7) substituted, para (7A) revoked; para (10) substituted; and para (11A) inserted; by the Individual Savings Account (Amendment No 2) Regulations, SI 2011/1780 regs 2, 18 with effect from 1 November 2011.

[10] In para (1), words revoked, by the Individual Savings Account (Amendment) (No 2) Regulations, SI 2012/1871 regs 4, 14 with effect from 8 August 2012.

[11] In para (3)(*f*), in both places, words revoked by the Income Tax (Removal of Ordinary Residence) Regulations, SI 2013/605 reg 4(1), (4) with effect for the purposes of a person's liability to income tax for the tax year 2013–14 or any subsequent tax years.

[12] Para (12) substituted and in para (13) words revoked by the Individual Savings Account (Amendment) Regulations, SI 2014/654 regs 2, 10 with effect from 6 April 2014.

[13] In para (3)(*ea*), word revoked, and para (3)(*eb*) revoked, by the Individual Savings Account (Amendment No 2) Regulations, SI 2014/1450 regs 2, 18 with effect from 1 July 2014.

[14] In para (3), words in sub-paras (*d*), (*e*), (*f*) inserted by the Individual Savings Account (Amendment) Regulations, SI 2016/16 regs 2, 13 with effect from 1 February 2016.

[15] In para (3)(*a*), (*d*), (*e*), words substituted, and para (3)(*h*) inserted by the Individual Savings Account (Amendment No 2) Regulations, SI 2016/364 regs 2, 14 with effect from 6 April 2016. **Publisher's note**: SI 2016/364 reg 14(*d*) inserted para (3)(*f*). This has been corrected by SI 2017/186, regs 2, 8 to read para (3)(*fa*) and the amendment has been made accordingly.

[16] In heading, words inserted, and para (14) inserted, by the Individual Savings Account (Amendment No 2) Regulations, SI 2017/466 regs 2, 23 with effect from 6 April 2017.

12A [Conditions for application to open an account that is a junior ISA account

(1) An application ("junior ISA application") to open a junior ISA account with an account manager may only be made if the account will be held by an eligible child immediately following the opening of the account [or by the holder of a junior ISA account arising from a transfer provided for by regulation 20A of the Child Trust Funds Regulations 2004, or if the application is preliminary to such a transfer][3].

(2) [A][3] child may hold—

(*a*) only one account set up as a cash account; and

(*b*) only one account set up as a stocks and shares account.

(3) For the purposes of paragraphs (2) and (7), an account holding an amount of less than one penny shall be disregarded.

[(3A) Except in the case of an account that will be held by an eligible child as mentioned in paragraph (1), the word "eligible" in paragraphs (4), (6), (7)(*g*), (*h*) and (*i*) and (8) must be disregarded.][3]

(4) A junior ISA application may be made by a person who—

(*a*) is over 16, and

(*b*) in relation to the junior ISA account to be opened pursuant to the application is—

(i) a person who has parental responsibility in relation to the eligible child who will hold the account; or

(ii) the eligible child who will hold the account.

(5) A junior ISA application must be made to an account manager in a statement and must fulfil the conditions specified in paragraphs (6), (7) and (8).

(6) A junior ISA application must specify the eligible child as being the beneficial owner of the account investments under that account.

(7) A junior ISA application must contain a declaration by the applicant that—

(*a*) the application is made to open a junior ISA account;

(*b*) the information provided in accordance with paragraph (8) is true;

(*c*) the child who will hold the account opened pursuant to the application is not an "eligible child" within the meaning given in the Child Trust Funds Act 2004 ["(but this is not required if the person who will hold the account is already the holder of a junior ISA account arising from a transfer mentioned in paragraph (1), or if the application is preliminary to such a transfer)]³;

(*d*) the child who will hold the account opened pursuant to the application is—

(i) resident . . . ² in the United Kingdom [(but this is not required if the application is preliminary to a transfer mentioned in paragraph (1))]³,

(ii) a person who has general earnings from overseas Crown employment subject to United Kingdom tax within the meaning given by section 28 of ITEPA 2003,

(iii) married to or in a civil partnership with a person mentioned in paragraph (ii), or

(iv) a dependant of a person mentioned in paragraph (ii);

(*e*) the applicant is the person who, upon the opening of the account, will be the registered contact in relation to the account;

(*f*) the application is to open a stocks and shares account or cash account, as the case may be;

(*g*) in the case of a stocks and shares account, the applicant—

(i) has not subscribed, and will not subscribe, to any other stocks and shares account that is a junior ISA account held by the same eligible child, and

(ii) is not aware of any other stocks and shares account held by the eligible child that is a junior ISA account;

(*h*) in the case of a cash account, the applicant—

(i) has not subscribed, and will not subscribe, to any other cash account that is a junior ISA account held by the same eligible child, and

(ii) is not aware of any other cash account held by the eligible child that is a junior ISA account;

(*i*) as far as the applicant is aware, the applicant has not subscribed amounts to the account (or any other account) that, when aggregated with other subscriptions, exceed the overall subscription limit in regulation 4ZB(1) (subscriptions to accounts opened in accordance with this regulation) in relation to the eligible child who will hold the account in the year in which the junior ISA application is made; and

(*j*) the applicant will not knowingly subscribe amounts to the account that, when aggregated with other subscriptions, exceed the overall subscription limit in regulation 4ZB(1) applicable from time to time (subscriptions to accounts opened in accordance with this regulation) in each successive year following the year in which the junior ISA application is made.

(8) A junior ISA application must contain—

(*a*) the applicant's full name,

(*b*) the address of the applicant's permanent residence, including postcode,

(*c*) the full name of the eligible child,

(*d*) the date of birth of the eligible child,

(*e*) where the applicant is not the eligible child, the address of the eligible child's permanent residence, including postcode,

(*f*) the eligible child's national insurance number if the child—

(i) is 16 or over, and

(ii) has been issued with a national insurance number,

(*g*) the authorisation specified in paragraph (9).

(9) The authorisation specified by this paragraph is authority given by the applicant to the account manager (on behalf of the child who holds the account where appropriate)—

(*a*) to hold the subscriptions, account investments, interest, dividends and any other rights or proceeds in respect of those investments and cash;

(*b*) to make on behalf of the child any claim to relief from tax in respect of account investments; and

(*c*) to make a record in writing in accordance with paragraph (11) where that paragraph requires the account manager to do so.

(10) An account manager must not accept a junior ISA application if the account manager has reason to believe that the applicant has given untrue information in the application.

(11) Where the junior ISA application is not in writing, or the account manager operates a record system under which all original written applications are not retained—

(*a*) the account manager must, immediately after receiving the application, record in writing on behalf of the applicant, the declaration required by paragraph (7) and authorisation required by paragraphs (8)(*g*) and (9);

(*b*) the account manager must notify the applicant of the contents of the written record within 5 business days of making it; and (*c*) the written record (as amended by any corrections notified to the account manager by the applicant within 30 days of the notification mentioned in sub-paragraph (b)) shall be treated as the applicant's declaration required by paragraph (7) and authorisation required by paragraphs (8)(*g*) and (9).

(12) An application furnished by an applicant under this regulation shall be regarded as in writing if it is furnished—

(*a*) by telephonic facsimile transmission containing the signature of the applicant, or

(*b*) by electronic communication containing an electronic signature of the applicant.

(13) Where an account manager is required by paragraph (11) to make a record in writing—

(*a*) a record shall be regarded as being a written record if it is produced by electronic means;

(*b*) the notification of the contents of the record by the account manager to the applicant required by paragraph (11)(*b*) may be sent to the applicant by telephonic facsimile transmission or by electronic communication.

(14) In this regulation—

"electronic communication" includes any communication conveyed by means of an electronic communications network;

"electronic signature" has the meaning given by section 7(2) of the Electronic Communications Act 2000.][1]

Amendments—[1] Reg 12A inserted by the Individual Savings Account (Amendment No 2) Regulations, SI 2011/1780 regs 2, 19 with effect from 1 November 2011.

[2] In para (7)(*d*)(i), words revoked by the Income Tax (Removal of Ordinary Residence) Regulations, SI 2013/605 reg 4(1), (5) with effect for the purposes of a person's liability to income tax for the tax year 2013–14 or any subsequent tax years.

[3] In paras (1), (7)(*c*), (*d*)(i), words inserted, in para (2), words substituted, and para (3A) inserted by the Individual Savings Account (Amendment No 3) Regulations, SI 2015/941 regs 2, 4 with effect from 6 April 2015.

[12B Conditions for application to open an account that is a Lifetime ISA

(1) An application by an individual to open a Lifetime ISA must be made to an account manager in the year in which the applicant first makes a payment to that account and must fulfil the conditions specified in paragraph (2).

(2) The application must state that it is an application to open a Lifetime ISA and—

(*a*) specify the first year to which the application relates;

(*b*) contain the information and authorisation specified in paragraph (3); and

(*c*) contain a declaration by the applicant in accordance with paragraph (4).

(3) The application must contain—

(*a*) the applicant's full name;

(*b*) the address and postcode of the applicant's permanent residence;

(*c*) the applicant's national insurance number;

(*d*) the applicant's date of birth; and

(*e*) the authorisation specified in paragraph (7).

(4) The application must contain a declaration by the applicant that—

(*a*) all subscriptions of money made, and to be made, to the account are or will be the applicant's money;

(*b*) in the first year and in any subsequent year to which the application relates, the applicant has not—

(i) in relation to a qualifying addition made into the account, made and will not make, any such addition to any other Lifetime ISA,

(ii) exceeded, and will not exceed, the overall subscription limit in regulation 4ZA(1), and

(iii) made, and will not make, current year payments that exceed the overall Lifetime ISA payment limit in regulation 4ZA(1A);

(*c*) the applicant is 18 years of age or over;

(*d*) except where paragraph (5) applies, the applicant is under 40 years of age, and

(i) is resident in the United Kingdom, or

(ii) is a person who has general earnings from overseas Crown employment subject to United Kingdom tax within the meaning given by section 28 of ITEPA 2003, or

(iii) is married to or in a civil partnership with a person mentioned in sub-paragraph (ii); and

(*e*) the applicant will inform the account manager if any of the circumstances under sub-paragraph (*d*)(i) to (iii) changes.

(5) This paragraph applies where the Lifetime ISA is being opened to receive—

(*a*) a transfer of current year's subscriptions or previous years' subscriptions from another Lifetime ISA (within the meaning of regulation 21(1)), or

(*b*) a payment in accordance with regulation 5D(2)(*a*)(ia) or (ib).

(6) A declaration under paragraph (4) shall have effect for each year in which the applicant makes a payment to the account to which the declaration relates except that after the account has been opened the reference to 40 in paragraph (4)(*d*) is deemed to be 50.

(7) The authorisation specified by this paragraph is authority given by the applicant to the account manager—

(*a*) to hold the payments, account investments, interest, dividends and any other rights or proceeds (including any government bonus) in respect of those investments and cash;
(*b*) to make on behalf of the applicant any claims to relief from tax in respect of account investments;
(*c*) to submit any government bonus claims to the Board on the applicant's behalf;
(*d*) to withhold and deduct from a balance in the account and pay to the Board—
(i) any charges due to the Board from the account manager on withdrawals from the account; and
(ii) any amount wrongly paid by way of government bonus accountable to the Board by the account manager under paragraph 12 of the Schedule; and
(*e*) to make a record in writing in accordance with paragraph (9)(*a*) where that paragraph requires the account manager to do so.

(8) An account manager may not accept as an account investor any individual if the account manager has reason to believe that—
(*a*) the individual is not, or might not be, a Lifetime ISA qualifying individual;
(*b*) the individual has given untrue information in an application; or
(*c*) subject to the exceptions described in paragraph (5), the individual is 40 years of age or over.

(9) Where an application is not in writing, or the account manager operates a record system under which all original written applications are not retained—
(*a*) the account manager must, immediately after receiving the application, record in writing on behalf of the applicant, the declaration required by paragraph (2)(*c*) and the authorisation required by paragraph (3)(*e*);
(*b*) the account manager must notify the applicant of the contents of the written record within 5 business days of making it; and
(*c*) the written record, as amended by any corrections notified to the account manager by the applicant within 30 days of the notification mentioned in sub-paragraph (*b*), shall be treated as the applicant's declaration required by paragraph (2)(*c*) and the authorisation required by paragraph (3)(*e*).

(10) For the purposes of paragraph (9), "in writing" and "written record" have the same meanings as in regulation 12A(12) to (14).

(11) The application may be made on an individual's behalf—
(*a*) if the individual is resident in England and Wales—
(i) pursuant to an order under section 16(2)(*a*) of the Mental Capacity Act 2005; or
(ii) by a deputy appointed under section 16(2)(*b*) of that Act; or
(*b*) if the individual is resident in Scotland or Northern Ireland and is suffering from mental disorder, by a parent, guardian, spouse, civil partner, son or daughter of the individual.

(12) In paragraph (11)(*b*) "mental disorder" has the meaning given by, in Scotland section 328 of the Mental Health (Care and Treatment) (Scotland) Act 2003 or, in Northern Ireland, Article 3 of the Mental Health (Northern Ireland) Order 1986.][1]

Amendments—[1] Regulation 12B inserted by the Individual Savings Account (Amendment No 2) Regulations, SI 2017/466 regs 2, 24 with effect from 6 April 2017.

13 Application by curator bonis

. . .[1]

Amendments—[1] Regulation 13 revoked by the Individual Savings Account (Amendment No 3) Regulations, SI 2002/3158 reg 6 with effect from 8 January 2003.

14 Account manager—qualifications and Board's approval

(1) This regulation specifies the circumstances ("qualifying circumstances") in which a person may be approved by the Board as an account manager.

(2) The qualifying circumstances to which paragraph (1) refers are the following—
(*a*) the person must make an application to the Board for approval in a form prescribed by the Board;
[(*aa*) if the person intends to be an account manager in relation to a junior ISA account, the person must undertake to the Board to—
(i) publicise (and update where appropriate) statements of the minimum amount which may be subscribed to a junior ISA account on a single occasion, and the permitted means of payment of subscriptions; and
(ii) inform persons proposing to make a subscription to a junior ISA account (other than the named child) that the subscription is a gift to the child;][6]
(*b*) an account manager must be—
(i) an authorised person within the meaning of [section 31(1)(*a*) or (*c*) of, or Schedule 5 to, the Financial Services and Markets Act 2000 who has permission [(other than an interim permission)][9] to carry on one or more of the activities specified in Articles 14, 21, 25,

[36H, 37, 39G][9], 40, 45, [51ZA, 51ZC, 51ZE][10] and 53 and, in so far as it applies to any of those activities, Article 64 of the Financial Services and Markets Act 2000 (Regulated Activities) Order 2001 but excluding any person falling within paragraph (iv) below][2]; or

(ii) a European institution which [carries on one or more of those activities][2]; or

[(iia) in the case of a credit union, an authorised person within the meaning of [FISMA 2000][7], who has permission to carry on one or more of the activities specified in Article 5 of the Financial Services And Markets Act 2000 (Regulated Activities) Order 2001;][4]

(iii) . . . [3] [the Director of Savings][1], a building society [or a person falling within section 991(2)(*b*) or (*c*) or (3)(*c*) of ITA 2007 (bank or credit union)][8]; or

(iv) . . . [3] an insurance company, within the meaning given by section 431(2) of the Taxes Act, an incorporated friendly society, or a registered friendly society; or

(v) [any][3] assurance undertaking which does not fall within paragraph (iv) above;

(*c*) an account manager must not be prevented from acting as such by [any requirement imposed under [sections 42 and 43][6] of the Financial Services and Markets Act 2000, or by any prohibition imposed by or under any rules made by the Financial Services Authority under that Act][2]; and

(*d*) an account manager who—

(i) is a European institution or a relevant authorised person and who does not have a branch or business establishment in the United Kingdom, or has such a branch or business establishment but does not intend to carry out all his functions as an account manager at that branch or business establishment, or

(ii) falls within sub-paragraph (*b*)(v),

must fulfil one of the three requirements specified in regulation 16.

(3) The terms of the Board's approval may—

(*a*) approve a person to set up and administer [cash accounts only, or stocks and shares accounts only, [or innovative finance accounts only, [or Lifetime ISAs only,][11] or any combination of such accounts][9]][5]; and

(*b*) include conditions designed to ensure that the provisions of these Regulations are satisfied.

Commentary—*Simon's Taxes* **E3.321, E3.322**.

Amendments—[1] Words in para (2)(*b*)(iii) substituted by the Individual Savings Account (Amendment) Regulations, SI 1998/3174 reg 8 with effect from 6 April 1999.

[2] Words in sub-paras (2)(*b*), (*c*) substituted by the Financial Services and Markets Act 2000 (Consequential Amendments) (Taxes) Order, SI 2001/3629 art 175 with effect from 1 December 2001, immediately after the coming into force of the Financial Services and Markets Act 2000 ss 411, 432(1), Sch 20 (and SI 2001/3629 Pts 1 and 2).

[3] Words in paras (2)(*b*), (3)(*a*) revoked, and words in para (2)(*b*)(v) substituted, by the ISA (Amendment No 2) Regulations, SI 2004/2996 regs 2, 14 with effect from 6 April 2005.

[4] Para (2)(*b*)(iia) inserted by the ISA (Amendment No 3) Regulations, SI 2005/3350 regs 2, 10 with effect from 27 December 2005.

[5] Words in para (3)(*a*) substituted by the Individual Savings Account (Amendment) Regulations, SI 2007/2119 regs 2, 17 with effect from 6 April 2008.

[6] Para (2)(*aa*) inserted, and in para (2)(*c*), words substituted, by the Individual Savings Account (Amendment No 2) Regulations, SI 2011/1780 regs 2, 20 with effect from 1 November 2011.

[7] In para (2)(*b*)(iia), words substituted by the Financial Services Act 2012 (Consequential Amendments and Transitional Provisions) (No 3) Order, SI 2013/1765 art 3 with effect from 1 September 2013.

[8] Words in para (2)(*b*)(iii) substituted by the Individual Savings Account (Amendment) Regulations, SI 2014/654 regs 2, 11 with effect from 6 April 2014.

[9] Words in para (2)(*b*)(i) inserted and reference substituted, and reference in para (3)(*a*) substituted by the Individual Savings Account (Amendment No 2) Regulations, SI 2016/364 regs 2, 15 with effect from 6 April 2016.

[10] In para (2)(*b*)(i), reference substituted by the Individual Savings Account (Amendment) Regulations, SI 2017/186 regs 2, 7 with effect from 6 April 2017.

[11] In para (3)(*a*), words inserted by the Individual Savings Account (Amendment No 2) Regulations, SI 2017/466 regs 2, 25 with effect from 6 April 2017.

15 Special requirements relating to insurer-managers

If and so long as a person falling within regulation 14(2)(*b*)(iv) or (v) acts as account manager of an account, and the account investments include a policy of life insurance—

(*a*) the title to all such policies shall be vested in the account investor; and

(*b*) where a policy document or other document evidencing title to such policies of life insurance is issued, it shall be held by the account investor.

16 Account manager—appointment of tax representative

(1) This regulation specifies the requirements mentioned in regulation 14(2)(*d*).

(2) The first requirement specified in this regulation is that—

(*a*) a person who falls within [section 698(2)(*b*) of ITTOIA 2005][1] is for the time being appointed by the account manager to be responsible for securing the discharge of the duties prescribed by paragraph (5) which fall to be discharged by the account manager, and (*b*) his identity and the fact of his appointment have been notified to the Board by the account manager.

(3) The second requirement specified in this regulation is that there are for the time being other arrangements with the Board for a person other than the account manager to secure the discharge of such duties.

(4) The third requirement specified in this regulation is that there are for the time being other arrangements with the Board designed to secure the discharge of such duties.

(5) The duties prescribed by this paragraph are those that fall to be discharged by an account manager under these Regulations.

(6) The appointment of a person in pursuance of the first requirement shall be treated as terminated in circumstances where—

(*a*) the Board have reason to believe that the person concerned—

(i) has failed to secure the discharge of any of the duties prescribed by paragraph (5), or

(ii) does not have adequate resources to discharge those duties, and

(*b*) the Board have notified the account manager and that person that they propose to treat his appointment as having terminated with effect from the date specified in the notice.

(7) Where, in accordance with the first requirement, a person is at any time responsible for securing the discharge of duties, the person concerned—

(*a*) shall be entitled to act on the account manager's behalf for any of the purposes of the provisions relating to the duties;

(*b*) shall secure (where appropriate by acting on the account manager's behalf) the account manager's compliance with and discharge of the duties; and

(*c*) shall be personally liable in respect of any failure of the account manager to comply with or discharge any such duty as if the duties imposed on the account manager were imposed jointly and severally on the account manager and the person concerned.

Commentary—*Simon's Taxes* **E3.322**.

Amendments—[1] Words in para (2)(*a*) substituted by the Individual Savings Account (Amendment) Regulations, SI 2008/704 regs 2, 11 with effect from 6 April 2008 immediately after the ISA (Amendment) Regulations, SI 2007/2119 come into force.

17 Account manager—withdrawal by Board of approval

(1) This regulation specifies the circumstances ("the disqualifying circumstances") in which the Board may by notice withdraw their approval of a person as an account manager in relation to an account.

(2) The disqualifying circumstances to which paragraph (1) refers are that the Board have reason to believe—

(*a*) that any provision of these Regulations is not or at any time has not been satisfied in respect of an account managed by the account manager; or

(*b*) that a person to whom they have given approval to act as an account manager is not qualified so to act.

(3) The notice to which paragraph (1) refers—

(*a*) may withdraw an approval in part, that is, in respect of particular types of accounts specified in the notice;

(*b*) shall specify the date from which the Board's approval is withdrawn; and

(*c*) shall specify the disqualifying circumstances.

[(4) On receiving the notice referred to in paragraph (1), subject to any appeal in accordance with regulation 18, the account manager shall notify the person who is the account investor in relation to the account held with the account manager of the right to transfer the account under regulations 21 or 21B (as appropriate), and the provision made by regulation 20(3).][1]

Commentary—*Simon's Taxes* **E3.323**.

Amendments—[1] Para (4) inserted by the Individual Savings Account (Amendment No 2) Regulations, SI 2011/1780 regs 2, 21with effect from 1 November 2011.

18 Account manager—appeal against withdrawal of Board's approval

(1) An account manager to whom notice of withdrawal of approval has been given under regulation 17 may appeal against the withdrawal by notice given to the Board within 30 days after the date of the notice of withdrawal.

(2) . . . [1]

(3) The like provisions as are contained in Part V of the Management Act (appeals and other proceedings) shall apply to an appeal and the [tribunal, on an appeal notified to it, shall][1] confirm the notice unless . . . [1] satisfied that the notice ought to be quashed.

Commentary—*Simon's Taxes* **E3.323**.

Amendments—[1] Para (2) revoked, in para (3), words substituted and words revoked, by the Transfer of Tribunal Functions and Revenue and Customs Appeals Order, SI 2009/56 art 3, Sch 2 paras 45, 46 with effect from 1 April 2009.

[19 Account manager's intention to make a bulk transfer of accounts or to cease to act as an account manager

(1) An account manager must give notice to the Board if the account manager—

(*a*) intends to cease to act as an account manager; or

(*b*) intends to make a bulk transfer of accounts.

(2) An account manager must give notice to a person who is the account investor in relation to an account held with the account manager if the account manager—

(*a*) intends to cease to act as an account manager; or

(*b*) intends that the account will be one of the accounts transferred in a bulk transfer of accounts.

(3) The notices described in paragraphs (1) and (2) must—

(*a*) specify whether the account manager—

(i) intends to cease to act as an account manager; or

(ii) intends to make a bulk transfer of accounts;

(*b*) where the notice specifies an intention to cease to act as an account manager,—

(i) specify the day on or after which the account manager intends to cease to act as an account manager; and

(ii) be given no less than 30 days before that day;

(*c*) where the notice specifies an intention to make a bulk transfer of accounts,—

(i) specify the day on or after which the account manager intends to make the first transfer in the bulk transfer of accounts;

(ii) be given no less than 30 days before that day; and

(iii) advise the name and address of the person to whom the account manager intends to transfer accounts.

(4) The notice described in paragraph (2) must also—

(*a*) identify the account to which it relates;

(*b*) advise the account investor that the account may be transferred in accordance with regulation 21 or 21B otherwise than in a bulk transfer of accounts if sufficient instructions are provided to enable the account manager to do so;

(*c*) advise the day by which the account manager must receive sufficient instructions for the account to be transferred otherwise than in a bulk transfer of accounts.

(5) Where an account manager intends to make a bulk transfer of accounts in consequence of an intention to cease to act as an account manager, such intention may be specified in the same notice to the Board or an account investor (as appropriate) provided the requirements of paragraphs (3) and (4) are met.][1]

Amendments—[1] Reg 19 substituted by the Individual Savings Account (Amendment) (No 2) Regulations, SI 2012/1871 regs 4, 15 with effect from 8 August 2012.

20 Account manager ceasing to qualify

[(1) A person shall cease to qualify as an account manager and shall notify the Board within 30 days of the relevant event in sub-paragraphs (*a*) to (*e*), of that relevant event, where—

(*a*) the person no longer fulfils the conditions of regulation 14;

(*b*) there is an insolvency event in relation to the account manager;

[(*ba*) a debt relief order is made in respect of the person (under Part 7A of the Insolvency Act 1986) or;][5]

(*c*) an application has been made for a bank insolvency order or a bank administration order;

(*d*) in the case of a building society, a person falling within section 991 of ITA 2007 or a credit union—

(i) it ceases to be a building society or to fall within section 991 of ITA 2007 or to be a credit union, as the case may be;

(ii) its directors have made a proposal under Part 1 of the Insolvency Act 1986 for a composition in satisfaction of its debts or a scheme of arrangement of its affairs; or

(iii) a receiver or manager of its property has been appointed; or

(*e*) in the case of a European institution, a relevant authorised person or an assurance undertaking which falls within regulation 14(2)(*b*)(iv) and (v), action corresponding to any described in sub-paragraphs (*b*) to (*d*) has been taken by or in relation to the institution, person or undertaking under the law of an EEA State.][4]

(2) On giving the notice referred to in paragraph (1), the person shall also notify the account investor of his right to transfer the account under regulation 21 [or 21B (as appropriate)][4], and the notice shall inform the account investor of his rights under paragraph (3).

(3) Where the account investor—

(*a*) receives a notice under paragraph (2), or [regulation 17(4) or 19][4], and

(*b*) within 30 days of the sending of the notice to him, transfers the account to another account manager pursuant to regulation 21 [or 21B (as appropriate)][4],

the period between the transferor ceasing to act or qualify as an account manager, and the transfer to the transferee, shall be ignored in determining whether the account has at all times been managed by an account manager.

Commentary—*Simon's Taxes* **E3.323**.

Modifications—In so far as this reg applies in relation to liquidation and administration, it applies as if reference to "administration" includes a reference to a bank administration under Part 3 of the Banking Act 2009 (Banking Act 2009 (Parts 2 and 3 Consequential Amendments) Order, SI 2009/317 art 3, Schedule).

In so far as this reg applies in relation to liquidation and administration, it applies as if reference to the provisions of the Insolvency Act 1986 and the Insolvency (Northern Ireland) Order 1989, in the context of bank insolvency or bank administration, shall be read to include those provisions as applied and modified by the Banking Act ss 103, 145 (Banking Act 2009 (Parts 2 and 3 Consequential Amendments) Order, SI 2009/317 art 3, Schedule).

Amendments—[1] Words in sub-para (1)(*d*) substituted by the Financial Services and Markets Act 2000 (Consequential Amendments) (Taxes) Order, SI 2001/3629 art 176 with effect from 1 December 2001, immediately after the coming into force of the Financial Services and Markets Act 2000 ss 411, 432(1), Sch 20 (and SI 2001/3629 Pts 1 and 2).

[2] Words in para (1)(*d*)(iii) substituted by the Enterprise Act 2002 (Insolvency) Order, SI 2003/2096 art 5, Schedule para 73 with effect from 15 September 2003. However, this amendment does not apply in any case where a petition for an administration order was presented before that date.

[3] Words in para (1)(*b*) inserted by the Enterprise Act 2002 (Disqualification from Office: General) Order, SI 2006/1722 art 2(2) Sch 2 para 12 with effect from 29 June 2006.

[4] Para (1) substituted; in paras (2), (3)(*b*), words inserted, in para (3)(*a*) words substituted; by the Individual Savings Account (Amendment No 2) Regulations, SI 2011/1780 regs 2, 23 with effect from 1 November 2011.

[5] Para (1)(*ba*) inserted by the Tribunals, Courts and Enforcement Act 2007 (Consequential Amendments) Order, SI 2012/2404 art 3(3), Sch 3 para 11 with effect in relation to a debt relief order the application for which is made on or after 1 October 2012.

21 [Transfers relating accounts other than junior ISA accounts]

[(1) [In this regulation, in relation to a transfer of an account that is not a junior ISA account[3]]—

"the current year's subscriptions" means—

(*a*) subscriptions made to the account by the account investor in the year in which the transfer takes place, but before the transfer,

(*b*) subscriptions made to any other account by the account investor in the year in which the transfer takes place and transferred to the account before the transfer, and

(*c*) the qualifying investments and other proceeds (including [income and any government bonus)][11] representing the subscriptions in sub-paragraphs (*a*) and (*b*) of this definition;

"the previous years' subscriptions" means—

(*a*) subscriptions made to the account (or any other account or former personal equity plan) in any earlier year or years, and

(*b*) the qualifying investments and other proceeds (including [income and any government bonus)][11] representing those subscriptions.

["subscriptions" includes all payments made into a Lifetime ISA.][11]

(2) Any transfer relating to an account or part of an account shall be made—

(*a*) directly between one account manager ("the transferor") and another account manager ("the transferee"), or

(*b*) where the same person is account manager before and after the transfer, solely by that manager (who shall maintain the records of both transferor and transferee required by this regulation).

(3) The current year's subscriptions may only be transferred as a whole (with or without the whole or part of any previous years' subscriptions).

(4) [The][7] current year's subscriptions and the previous years' subscriptions may only be transferred to—

(*a*) a stocks and shares account (if the account investor is 18 years of age or over), . . . [10]

(*b*) a cash account, [. . . [1]

(*c*) an innovative finance account (if the account investor is 18 years of age or over),][10]

belonging to the same account investor[, or

(*d*) a Lifetime ISA (if the account investor is 18 or over).][11]

(4A) . . . [7]

[(4B) Where the current year's subscriptions (with or without other subscriptions) are transferred under paragraph (4), the subscriptions in sub-paragraphs (*a*) and (*b*) in the definition of "the current year's subscriptions" in paragraph (1) shall be treated, for all purposes . . . [8]), as if they had been made to the account held with the transferee.][7]

(4C) Where the current year's subscriptions (with or without other subscriptions) are transferred from—

(*a*) a cash account to a cash account, . . . [10]

(*b*) a stocks and shares account to a stocks and shares account, [. . . [11]

(*c*) an innovative finance account to an innovative finance account,][10] [or

(*d*) a Lifetime ISA to a Lifetime ISA,][11]

the subscriptions transferred, and no other subscriptions, shall be treated as the same account, for the purpose of making any remaining permitted subscriptions [or qualifying additions][11] in that year.

[(4CA) [Regulations 12(1) and 12B(1) do][11] not prevent the current year's subscriptions and the previous years' subscriptions being transferred to an account that was held immediately before the transfer but to which no subscription has been made in the year in which the transfer occurs or the year immediately before that year.][4]

(4D) The account investor shall[, subject to paragraph (4DA),][4] make a fresh application under regulation [12 or 12B, as the case may be,][11] (with any necessary modifications to reflect that it is made on a transfer) to the transferee.

[(4DA) Paragraph (4D) does not apply where—

(*a*) an account is transferred in a bulk transfer of accounts;

(*b*) a cash account (whether or not in a bulk transfer of accounts) is transferred to a cash account held with the transferee immediately before the time when the transfer is made;

(*c*) a stocks and shares account (whether or not in a bulk transfer of accounts) is transferred to a stocks and shares account held with the transferee immediately before the time when the transfer is made; . . . [7]

[(*ca*) an innovative finance account (whether or not in a bulk transfer of accounts) is transferred to an innovative finance account held with the transferee immediately before the time when the transfer is made;][10]

[(*cb*) a Lifetime ISA (whether or not in a bulk transfer of accounts) is transferred to a Lifetime ISA held with the transferee immediately before the time when the transfer is made;][11]

(*d*) a cash account is transferred (otherwise than in a bulk transfer of accounts) to [a Lifetime ISA,][11] a stocks and shares account [or an innovative finance account][10] held with the transferee immediately before the time when the transfer is made . . . [10]

[(*e*) a stocks and shares account is transferred (otherwise than in a bulk transfer of accounts) to [a Lifetime ISA,][11] a cash account [or an innovative finance account][10] held with the transferee immediately before the time when the transfer is made . . . [10][; or][7]

(*f*) an innovative finance account is transferred (otherwise than in a bulk transfer of accounts) [a Lifetime ISA,][11] to a cash account or a stocks and shares account held with the transferee immediately before the time when the transfer is made.][10]

(4DB) Where an account is transferred in a bulk transfer of accounts that is not also a transfer described in paragraph [(4DA)(*b*), (*c*) or (*ca*)][10], a subscription to the account after the transfer may only be made if—

(*a*) the subscription is made after the account investor has, during the period of time determined in accordance with paragraph (4DC), made an application to the transferee in relation to the account in accordance with regulation 12 (with any necessary modifications where appropriate to reflect that the account has been transferred in a bulk transfer of accounts);

(*b*) the subscription is made in the year immediately following a year in which a subscription has been made to the account other than a subscription permitted by virtue of paragraph (4DE); or

(*c*) the subscription is permitted by virtue of paragraph (4DE).

[This paragraph does not apply to a Lifetime ISA.][11]

(4DC) The period of time referred to in paragraph (4DB)(*a*) is the period—

(*a*) starting at the beginning of the year immediately preceding the year in which the subscription is made, and

(*b*) ending immediately before the subscription is made.

[(4DCA) In the case of a Lifetime ISA, where the account is transferred in a bulk transfer of accounts which is not a transfer described in paragraph (4DA)(*cb*) a payment by the account investor to the account after the transfer may only be made (unless permitted by paragraph (4DE)) after the account investor has made an application to the transferee in relation to the account in accordance with regulation 12B (with any necessary modifications where appropriate to reflect the fact that the account has been transferred in a bulk transfer of accounts).][11]

(4DD) For the purposes of paragraphs (4DB) and (4DE), the current year's subscriptions and the previous years' subscriptions transferred are not subscriptions to the account.

(4DE) A subscription to an account is permitted by this paragraph if—

(*a*) the account has been transferred to the transferee [in a bulk transfer of accounts pursuant to a scheme described in regulation 2(1A)(*a*)(ii) or][6] in a group transfer of accounts;

(*b*) the most recent application in accordance with regulation 12 [or 12B][11] relating to the transferred account made before its transfer is available to the transferee; and

(*c*) [except in relation to a Lifetime ISA,][11] the subscription is made—

(i) in the year in which the account is transferred (provided a subscription has been made to the account in that year before the account was transferred); or

(ii) in a year immediately following a year in which a subscription has been made to the transferred account (including a subscription made before the transfer).

(4DF) For the purposes of paragraph (4DE)(*b*), an application in accordance with regulation 12 [or 12B][11] as described in that paragraph is available to a transferee if—

(*a*) paragraph (4DG) or (4DH) applies; and

(*b*) [except in relation to a Lifetime ISA,][11] the transferor has advised the transferee whether a subscription has been made to the transferred account in the year immediately preceding the year in which the transfer takes place.

(4DG) This paragraph applies where the application described in paragraph (4DE)(*b*) (or a copy of it) is held by the transferee.

(4DH) This paragraph applies where—

(*a*) the application described in paragraph (4DE)(*b*) (or a copy of it) is held by the transferor; and

(*b*) the transferee can require the transferor to make it available to the transferee for any purpose necessary to ensure the transferee's compliance with these regulations.

(4DI) An account transferred in accordance with this regulation in a bulk transfer of accounts is an account opened in accordance with regulation 12 for the purposes of these Regulations whether or not an application in accordance with regulation 12 [or 12B][11] as described in paragraph (4DB)(*a*) [or (4DCA), as the case requires,][11] is made.][4]

(4E) This regulation shall also apply where an account is transferred in consequence of an account manager ("the transferor") ceasing to act or to qualify as an account manager.][1]

[(5) Where an account is transferred, the transferor must, subject to paragraph (5B), give to the transferee a notice containing the information specified in paragraph (6) before the relevant time specified in paragraph (5A).

(5A) The relevant time specified in this paragraph is—

(*a*) in the case of an account transferred in a bulk transfer of accounts, the time of the transfer;

(*b*) in any other case, the expiry of 30 days after the day of the transfer.

(5B) Paragraph (5) does not apply where a transferor provides information to a transferee in accordance with regulation 21A(2)(*b*)(ii).][5]

(6) The information specified in this paragraph is—

(*a*) as regards the account investor—

(i) his full name,

(ii) the address of his permanent residence, including postcode,

(iii) his date of birth, and

(iv) if he has one, his national insurance number, and

(*b*) as regards an account [or any part of an account][1] transferred pursuant to paragraph (2)—

(i) whether the account is a [cash account[, stocks and shares account[, an innovative finance account or a Lifetime ISA][11]][10],][1]

(ii) the date of the transfer,

(iii) the total amount of cash subscribed to the account during the period from the beginning of the year in which the transfer takes place to the date of the transfer . . . [1][,disregarding a subscription made in accordance with regulation 5D (except for a replacement subscription), less, in the case of a flexible account, the amount of any cash withdrawn from it during that period and if the result is in the negative, the amount to be reported is nil][9],

[(iv) the date on which the first subscription (if any) was made to the account, in the year in which the transfer takes place,][1] [and][7]

(v) the amount of any dividends on account investments which are payable to, but have not been received by, the transferor at the date of the transfer[.][7]

(vi) . . . [7]

[(*ba*) where the transfer is as described in regulation 10A(4)(*c*), that the amount being transferred is in respect of a Help to Buy ISA and is as described in that regulation (and in this case paragraph (6)(*b*)(i) and (iii) to (v) is not to apply).]

(*c*) . . . [1]

[(*d*) as regards an account or any part of an account transferred pursuant to paragraph (2) which is a Lifetime ISA—

(i) the date on which that Lifetime ISA was first opened and for the purposes of a payment made in accordance with regulation 5D(2)(*a*)(ia) or (ib), a Lifetime ISA opened for the purpose of receiving the payment is to be treated as being the same Lifetime ISA from which the money the subject of the payment originated;

(ii) the date of the first qualifying addition to the account in the year of transfer;

(iii) the amount of any government bonus that has accrued, but not been claimed, at the date of the transfer,

(iv) the number allocated to the account by the transferor;

(v) any government bonus already paid within the current year;

(vi) the total amount of qualifying additions to the Lifetime ISA during the period from the beginning of the year in which the transfer takes place to the date of transfer, with separate entries for a Help to Buy transfer under regulation 10A(4)(*c*) and any other qualifying additions;

(vii) details of qualifying additions to the Lifetime ISA for which a claim has not been made with separate entries for a Help to Buy transfer under regulation 10A(4)(*c*) and any other qualifying additions;

(viii) confirmation of whether or not there has been a withdrawal for a first-time residential purchase, for which information required under paragraph 9 of the Schedule and expected by the transferor has not been received;

(ix) if there has been such a withdrawal, an undertaking to pass on to the transferee any such information received without delay.][11]

[(6A) Where a Lifetime ISA is transferred, the transferee must before the time of the transfer give to the transferor a notice stating whether or not the account to which the investments are being transferred is a Lifetime ISA.

(6B) A Lifetime ISA of an account investor to which another Lifetime ISA of the account investor ("the original") is transferred in accordance with this regulation is a successor to the original.][11]

(7) . . .[2]

Commentary—*Simon's Taxes* **E3.325.**

Amendments—[1] Heading substituted, paras (1)–(4E) substituted, words in para (6)(*b*) inserted and substituted, and para (6)(*c*) and preceding word "and" revoked, by the Individual Savings Account (Amendment) Regulations, SI 2007/2119 regs 2, 18 with effect from 6 April 2008.

[2] Para (7) revoked, by the Individual Savings Account (Amendment No 2) Regulations, SI 2009/1994 regs 2, 8 with effect from 8 October 2008.

[3] Heading substituted, and in para (1) words substituted, by the Individual Savings Account (Amendment No 2) Regulations, SI 2011/1780 regs 2, 24 with effect from 1 November 2011.

[4] Paras (4CA), (4DA)–(4DI) inserted, and words in para (4D) inserted, by the Individual Savings Account (Amendment) (No 2) Regulations, SI 2012/1871 regs 4, 16(*b*)–(*d*) with effect from 9 November 2011.

[5] Paras (5)–(5B) substituted for previous para (5), by the Individual Savings Account (Amendment) (No 2) Regulations, SI 2012/1871 regs 4, 16(*a*), (*e*) with effect from 8 August 2012.

[6] In para (4DE)(*a*), words inserted by the Individual Savings Account (Amendment No 3) Regulations, SI 2013/1743 regs 2, 6 with effect from 5 March 2013.

[7] The following amendments made by the Individual Savings Account (Amendment No 2) Regulations, SI 2014/1450 regs 2, 19 with effect from 1 July 2014—

- in para (4), words revoked, and word substituted;
- para (4A) revoked;
- para (4B) substituted;
- in para (4DA)(*c*), word revoked;
- para (4DA)(*e*) inserted;
- in para (6)(*b*), in sub-para (iv) word inserted, in sub-para (v) full stop substituted for ", and", and sub-para (vi) revoked.

[8] In para (4B), words revoked by the Individual Savings Account (Amendment No 3) Regulations, SI 2015/941 regs 2, 5 with effect from 6 April 2015.

[9] Words in para (6)(*b*)(iii) inserted by the Individual Savings Account (Amendment) Regulations, SI 2016/16 regs 2, 14 with effect from 1 February 2016.

[10] The following amendments made by the Individual Savings Account (Amendment No 2) Regulations, SI 2016/364 regs 2, 16 with effect from 6 April 2016—

- in para (4), word at the end of sub-para (*a*) revoked, and sub-para (*c*) and preceding word inserted;
- in para (4C), word at the end of sub-para (*a*) revoked, and sub-para (*c*) and preceding word inserted;
- in para (4DA), sub-para (*ca*) inserted, and sub-para (*f*) and preceding word inserted; in sub-paras (*d*), (*e*), words inserted, word at the end of sub-para (*d*) revoked, and full stop at the end of sub-para (*e*) revoked;
- in para (4DB), reference substituted; and
- in para (6)(*b*)(i), words substituted.

[11] The following amendments made by the Individual Savings Account (Amendment No 2) Regulations, SI 2017/466 regs 2, 26 with effect from 6 April 2017—

- in para (1), in definitions of "the current year's subscriptions", para (*c*) and "the previous years' subscriptions", para (*b*), words substituted, and definition of "subscriptions" inserted;
- in paras (4)(*b*), (4C)(*b*), words revoked, paras (4)(*d*), (4C)(*d*) inserted, and in para (4C), words inserted;
- in paras (4CA), (4D), (6)(*b*)(i), words substituted;
- in paras (4DA)(*d*)–(*f*), (4DB), (4DE), (4DE)(*c*), (4DF), (4DF)(*b*), (4DI), words inserted; and
- paras (4DA)(*cb*), (4DCA), (5)(*ba*), (*d*), (6A), (6B) inserted.

21A [Further requirements relating to transfers between cash accounts

(1) This regulation applies where an account investor, through the agency of an account manager ("the transferee"), gives instructions ("transfer instructions") to an account manager with whom the account investor holds a cash account ("the transferor") for that account or part of that account to be transferred, subject to and in accordance with [regulations 21 or 21B, to a cash account held by the account investor with the transferee.][2]

(2) Where this regulation applies—

(*a*) the transferee shall, within 5 business days beginning on the instruction day, send to the transferor—

(i) the transfer instructions; and

(ii) a notice specifying that the transferee consents to the transfer ("the consent notice");

(*b*) the transferor shall, within 5 business days beginning on the day that the transferor receives the transfer instructions and the consent notice,—

(i) transfer to the transferee the subscriptions specified in the transfer instructions; and

(ii) send to the transferee a notice containing the information specified in paragraph (3); and

(*c*) the transferee shall ensure that the subscriptions specified in the transfer instructions are transferred to a cash account [held by the account investor][2] with the transferee within 3 business days beginning on the day that the transferee receives the subscriptions and the notice referred to in sub-paragraph (*b*)(ii).

(3) The information specified in this paragraph is—

(*a*) as regards the account investor—

(i) the full name of the account investor,

(ii) the address of the account investor's permanent residence, including postcode,

(iii) the date of birth of the account investor, and

(iv) the national insurance number of the account investor (if any), . . . [2]

(*b*) as regards the cash account or any part of the cash account—

(i) the date of the transfer,

(ii) the total amount of cash subscribed to the account during the period from the beginning of the year in which the transfer takes place to the date of the transfer[, disregarding a subscription made in accordance with regulation 5D (except for a replacement subscription), less, in the case of a flexible account, the amount of any cash withdrawn from it during that period and if the result is in the negative, the amount to be reported is nil][4],

[(iii) in relation to the transfer of an account that is not a junior ISA account, the date on which the first subscription (if any) was made to the account in the year in which the transfer takes place,

(iiia) in relation to the transfer of an account that is a junior ISA account, the date on which the subscription described in paragraph (3A) was made (if appropriate), and][3]

(iv) the reference number or other means used by the transferor to identify the account belonging to the account investor in respect of which the transfer is made[, and

(*c*) in relation to an account that is a junior ISA account—

(i) the full name of the registered contact,

(ii) the address of the registered contact's permanent residence, including postcode][2].

[(3A) The subscription referred to in paragraph (3)(*b*)(iiia) is the first subscription to the account provided the subscription is made in the same year as the transfer.][3]

(4) For the purposes of paragraph (2)(*a*) and (*b*), the transfer instructions and the notices (as appropriate) shall be treated as sent if they are—

(*a*) posted to, or left at, the proper address of the transferor or the transferee (as appropriate); or

(*b*) transmitted by electronic communication.

(5) For the purposes of paragraph (2)(*b*), where the transferor receives the transfer instructions and consent notice on different days, they must both be treated as received on the latest of those days.

(6) For the purposes of paragraph (2)(*c*), where the transferee receives subscriptions specified in the transfer instructions and the notice described in paragraph (2)(*b*) on different days, they must all be treated as received on the latest of those days.

(7) In this regulation—

. . . [2]

"electronic communication" includes any communication conveyed by means of an electronic communications network;

"instruction day" means—

(*a*) the day stipulated by the account investor for the transferee to begin the transfer process, or

(*b*) if no day is stipulated, the day that the transfer instructions are received by the transferee;

"subscriptions" means the current year's subscriptions and the previous years' subscriptions as described in regulation 21(1).

(8) For the purposes of this regulation—

(*a*) a document is "posted" if it is sent pre-paid by a postal service which seeks to deliver documents by post within the United Kingdom no later than the next business day in all or the majority of cases, and to deliver by post outside the United Kingdom within such a period as is reasonable in all the circumstances; and

(*b*) the "proper address" to which a document is to be sent is any current address provided by the transferor or transferee as an address for service of such documents, but if no current address is provided then it shall be the address of its registered or principal office in the United Kingdom.][1]

Commentary—*Simon's Taxes* **E3.325**.

Amendments—[1] Reg 21A inserted by the Individual Savings Account (Amendment No 2) Regulations, SI 2010/2957 regs 2, 5 with effect in relation to instructions given on or after 4 January 2011 for a cash account or part of a cash account held by an account investor with an account manager to be transferred, subject to and in accordance with reg 21 of these Regulations, to a cash account belonging to the account investor which is held with another account manager (SI 2010/2957 reg 1(3)).

[2] In paras (1), (2)(*c*), words substituted, in para (3)(*a*) word revoked, para (3)(*c*) and preceding word "and" inserted, and in para (7) definition of "business day" revoked, by the Individual Savings Account (Amendment No 2) Regulations, SI 2011/1780 regs 2, 25 with effect from 1 November 2011.

[3] Para (3)(*b*)(iii), (iiia) substituted for previous para (3)(*b*)(iii), and para (3A) inserted, by the Individual Savings Account (Amendment) (No 2) Regulations, SI 2012/1871 regs 4, 17 with effect from 8 August 2012.

[4] Words in para (3)(*b*)(ii) inserted by the Individual Savings Account (Amendment) Regulations, SI 2016/16 regs 2, 15 with effect from 1 February 2016.

21B [Transfers relating to junior ISA accounts

(1) This regulation only applies to an account that is a junior ISA account.

(2) In this regulation, in relation to a transfer—

"the current year's subscriptions" means—

(*a*) subscriptions made to the account in the year in which the transfer takes place, but before the transfer;

(*b*) subscriptions made in the year in which the transfer takes place to any other account held by the named child and transferred to the account before the transfer, and

(*c*) the qualifying investments and other proceeds (including income) representing the subscriptions in sub-paragraphs (*a*) and (*b*) of this definition;

"the previous years' subscriptions" means—

(*a*) subscriptions made to the account (or any other account) in any earlier year or years, and

(*b*) the qualifying investments and other proceeds (including income) representing those subscriptions.

[(2A) Anything transferred to the account as part of the transfer mentioned in regulation 12A(1) is treated as previous years' subscriptions for the purposes of this regulation.][5]

(3) Any transfer relating to an account or part of an account shall be made—

(*a*) directly between one account manager ("the transferor") and another account manager ("the transferee"), or

(*b*) where the same person is account manager before and after the transfer, solely by that manager (who shall maintain the records of both transferor and transferee required by this regulation).

(4) The current year's subscriptions may only be transferred as a whole (with or without the whole or part of any previous years' subscriptions).

(5) In the case of a cash account—

(*a*) all or part of the previous years' subscriptions and, if current year's subscriptions are to be transferred, all of the current year's subscriptions made to the cash account, may be transferred to a junior ISA account that is a stocks and shares account belonging to the same named child, or

(*b*) all of the subscriptions made to the cash account ("old cash account") that are held in the account immediately before the transfer may be transferred to a junior ISA account that is a cash account ("new cash account") belonging to the same named child (and, for the avoidance of doubt, no transfer may be made to a new cash account if the transfer does not comprise all of the subscriptions held in the old cash account immediately before the transfer).

(6) In the case of a stocks and shares account—

(*a*) all or part of the previous years' subscriptions and, if current year's subscriptions are to be transferred, all of the current year's subscriptions made to the stocks and shares account, may be transferred to a junior ISA account that is a cash account belonging to the same named child, or

(*b*) all of the subscriptions made to the stocks and shares account ("old stocks and shares account") that are held in the account immediately before the transfer may be transferred to a junior ISA account that is a stocks and shares account ("new stocks and shares account") belonging to the same named child (and, for the avoidance of doubt, no transfer may be made to a new stocks and shares account if the transfer does not comprise all of the subscriptions held in the old stocks and shares account immediately before the transfer).

(7) Where current year's subscriptions are transferred from a junior ISA account to another junior ISA account, the current year's subscriptions transferred shall count towards the overall subscription limit for the child holding the account for that year.

(8) The registered contact shall[, subject to paragraph (8A),][2] make a fresh application under regulation 12A (with any necessary modifications to reflect that it is made on a transfer) to the transferee.

[(8A) Paragraph (8) does not apply where an account is transferred in a bulk transfer of accounts.

(8B)–(8G) . . . [5]

(8H) An account transferred in accordance with this regulation in a bulk transfer of accounts is a junior ISA account opened pursuant to an application in accordance with regulation 12A for the purposes of these Regulations whether or not an application in accordance with regulation 12A . . . [5] is made.][2]

(9) This regulation shall also apply where an account is transferred in consequence of an account manager ("the transferor") ceasing to act or qualify as an account manager.

[(10) Where an account is transferred, the transferor must, subject to paragraph (10B), give to the transferee a notice containing the information specified in paragraph (11) before the relevant time specified in paragraph (10A).

(10A) The relevant time specified in this paragraph is—

(*a*) in the case of an account transferred in a bulk transfer of accounts, the time of the transfer;

(*b*) in any other case, the expiry of 30 days after the day of the transfer.

(10B) Paragraph (10) does not apply where a transferor provides information to a transferee in accordance with regulation 21A(2)(*b*)(ii).][3]

(11) The information specified in this paragraph is—

(*a*) as regards the named child who holds the account transferred—

(i) the full name of the child,

(ii) the address (including postcode) of the permanent residence of the child,

(iii) the date of birth of the child,

(iv) the national insurance number of the child (if any) [(otherwise, any unique reference number he may have had as mentioned in the Child Trust Funds Regulations 2004)][5]; and

(*b*) as regards an account from which the transfer is made—

(i) whether the account is a cash account or stocks and shares account,

(ii) the date of the transfer,

(iii) the total amount of cash subscribed to the account during the period from the beginning of the year in which the transfer takes place to the date of the transfer,

[(iv) the date on which the subscription described in paragraph (12) was made (if appropriate), and][3]

(v) the amount of any dividends on account investments which are payable to, but have not been received by, the transferor at the date of the transfer,

(vi) the full name of the person who is the registered contact in relation to the account, and

(vii) the address of the registered contact's permanent residence, including postcode.

[(12) The subscription referred to in paragraph (11)(*b*)(iv) is the first subscription to the account provided the subscription is made in the same year as the transfer.][3]][1]

Amendments—[1] Regs 21B, 21C inserted by the Individual Savings Account (Amendment No 2) Regulations, SI 2011/1780 regs 2, 26 with effect from 1 November 2011.

[2] In para (8), words inserted, and paras (8A)–(8H) inserted, by the Individual Savings Account (Amendment) (No 2) Regulations, SI 2012/1871 regs 4, 18(*a*), (*b*) with effect from 9 November 2011.

[3] Paras (10)–(10B) substituted for previous para (10), para (11)(*b*)(iv) substituted, and para (12) inserted, by the Individual Savings Account (Amendment) (No 2) Regulations, SI 2012/1871 regs 4, 18(*c*)–(*e*) with effect from 8 August 2012.

[4] In para (8D)(*a*), words inserted by the Individual Savings Account (Amendment No 3) Regulations, SI 2013/1743 regs 2, 7 with effect from 5 March 2013.

[5] Para (2A) inserted, paras (8B)–(8G) revoked, words in para (8H) revoked, and words in para (11)(*a*)(iv) inserted, by the Individual Savings Account (Amendment No 3) Regulations, SI 2015/941 regs 2, 6, 7 with effect from 6 April 2015.

21C [Repair of invalid junior ISA accounts

(1) It is an overriding requirement to be satisfied in relation to a junior ISA account that the account manager and registered contact, as the case may be, take any steps necessary to remedy any breach of these Regulations.

(2) Where a breach is remedied as mentioned in paragraph (1), the account shall, to the extent of that breach, be treated as having been a valid account at all times.][1]

[1] Regs 21B, 21C inserted by the Individual Savings Account (Amendment No 2) Regulations, SI 2011/1780 regs 2, 26 with effect from 1 November 2011.

22 Exemption from tax of account income and gains

(1) Subject to these Regulations—

(*a*) no tax shall be chargeable on the account manager or his nominee or on the account investor—

(i) in respect of interest, dividends, distributions or gains in respect of account investments [([including any government bonus, but excluding][8] any building society bonus)][4], or

[(ia) in respect of alternative finance return paid by a financial institution in accordance with Part 10A of ITA 2007, or][3, 6] (ib) in respect of a payment under a building society bonus scheme, so far as the payment is calculated by reference to account investments (and if paid directly by the society into the account, the payment shall not count towards the subscription [limit][7] in [regulations [4ZA(1) and 4ZB(1)][7]][6]; or][4]

(ii) on any annual profits or gains treated [under Part 12 of ITA 2007 (accrued income profits)][5] as having been received by any of them in respect of account investments, or

[(iii) on an offshore income gain to which a disposal by any of them of an account investment would otherwise give rise to a charge to tax under regulation 17 of the Offshore Funds (Tax) Regulations 2009, or][6]

[(iv) on a profit on the disposal of a deeply discounted security within the meaning given by section 430 of ITTOIA 2005,][5]

(v) in respect of gains treated [under Chapter 9 of Part 4 of ITTOIA 2005][5] as arising in connection with a policy of life insurance which is an account investment . . . [2];

(*b*) losses in respect of account investments shall be disregarded for the purposes of capital gains tax;

[(*ba*) any gain or loss accruing on and attributable to a payment within paragraph (ib) of sub-paragraph (*a*) shall not be a chargeable gain or allowable loss for capital gains tax purposes;][4]

[(*c*) a deficiency arising in a tax year and falling within section 539(1) of ITTOIA 2005, so far as it relates to an account investment, shall not be allowable as a deduction from the total income of the account investor;][5]

(*d*) relief in respect of tax shall be given in the manner and to the extent provided by these Regulations; ...[6]

(*e*) [in relation to an account that is not a junior ISA account,][6] interest on a cash deposit which is an account investment held under a cash component shall not[, except for the purposes of [section 629 of ITTOIA 2005][5],][1] be regarded as income for any income tax purposes[;

(*f*) in relation to a junior ISA account, income arising from account investments shall not be regarded as income for any income tax purposes (including section 629 of ITTOIA 2005)][6].

(2) An account investor who, after [the opening of][6] an account, at any time ceases to be resident in the United Kingdom, shall be treated as if he were resident in the United Kingdom for the purposes of determining his entitlement to, or to payment of, tax credits in respect of qualifying distributions, so far as they relate to account investments under an account held by him.

[(3) A reference to "interest" in this regulation includes a reference to any bonus and to a dividend paid or credited in respect of a share account with a building society.][6]

Amendments—[1] Words inserted in para (1)(*e*) by the Individual Savings Account (Amendment) Regulations, SI 2001/908 reg 8 with effect from 6 April 2001.

[2] Words in para (1) revoked by the ISA (Amendment No 2) Regulations, SI 2004/2996 regs 2, 15 with effect from 6 April 2005.

[3] Para (1)(*a*)(ia) inserted by the ISA (Amendment No 3) Regulations, SI 2005/3350 regs 2, 11 with effect from 27 December 2005.

[4] Words in para (1)(*a*)(i); and para (1)(*a*)(ib) and preceding word "or", and para (1)(*ba*), inserted by the ISA (Amendment) Regulations, SI 2006/3194 regs 2, 4, 5 with effect from 1 January 2007.

[5] Words in para (1)(*a*)(ii), (v), (*e*) whole of para (1)(*a*)(iv), (*c*), substituted by the Individual Savings Account (Amendment) Regulations, SI 2008/704 regs 2, 11 with effect from 6 April 2008 immediately after the ISA (Amendment) Regulations, SI 2007/2119 come into force.

[6] Para (1)(*a*)(ia) substituted; in paras (1)(*a*)(ib), (2) words substituted; para (1)(*a*)(iii) substituted; word "and" immediately preceding para (1)(*e*) revoked; in para (1)(*e*), words inserted; para (1)(*f*) inserted; and para (3) inserted; by the Individual Savings Account (Amendment No 2) Regulations, SI 2011/1780 regs 2, 27 with effect from 1 November 2011.

[7] In para (1)(*a*)(ib), word substituted, and references substituted, by the Individual Savings Account (Amendment No 2) Regulations, SI 2014/1450 regs 2, 20 with effect from 1 July 2014.

[8] In para (1)(*a*)(i), words substituted by the Individual Savings Account (Amendment No 2) Regulations, SI 2017/466 regs 2, 27 with effect from 6 April 2017.

23 [Interest on cash deposits held under a stocks and shares component of an account that is not a junior ISA account]

Amendments—Regulation 23 revoked by the Individual Savings Account (Amendment No 2) Regulations, SI 2014/1450 regs 2, 21 with effect from 1 July 2014.

24 Tax liabilities and reliefs—account manager to act on behalf of account investor

(1) An account manager may under these Regulations make claims, conduct appeals and agree on behalf of the account investor liabilities for and reliefs from tax in respect of an account.

(2) Claims shall be made to the Board in accordance with the provisions of regulations 25 and 26.

(3) Where any relief or exemption from tax previously given in respect of an account has by virtue of these Regulations become excessive, in computing the relief due on any claim there shall be deducted (so that amounts equal to that excess are set-off or repaid to the Board, as the case may be) notwithstanding that those amounts have been invested—

(*a*) any amount repaid in respect of income tax or paid in respect of a tax credit; [and][2]

(*b*) . . . [2]

(*c*) any other amount due to the Board by an account manager in respect of any tax liability in respect of account investments under an account including (but without prejudice to the making of an assessment under the provisions of that Schedule) any amount falling due in respect of a liability under [Chapter 9 of Part 15 of ITA 2007][1].

(4) Any amount deducted under paragraph (3) shall be treated as an amount of income tax deducted at source and not repayable within the meaning and for the purposes of section 95(2)(*a*) of the Management Act.

Commentary—*Simon's Taxes* **E3.326**.

Amendments—[1] Words in para (3)(*c*) substituted by the Individual Savings Account (Amendment) Regulations, SI 2008/704 regs 2, 13 with effect from 6 April 2008 immediately after the ISA (Amendment) Regulations, SI 2007/2119 come into force.

[2] In para (3)(*a*), word inserted, and para (3)(*b*) revoked, by the Individual Savings Account (Amendment No 2) Regulations, SI 2014/1450 regs 2, 23 with effect from 1 July 2014.

25 Repayments in respect of tax to account manager—interim claims

(1) Notwithstanding the provisions of any other enactment, the Board shall not be under an obligation to make any repayment in respect of tax under these Regulations earlier than the end of the month following the month in which the claim for the repayment is received.

(2) A claim for repayment in respect of tax which is not an annual claim ("interim claim") may be made only for a period of a month (or a number of months not exceeding six) beginning on the 6th day of the month and ending on the 5th day of the relevant following month.

(3) No claim for repayment may be made for the month ending 5th October or any subsequent month until the annual return under regulation 26(2) due in respect of an account for the preceding year has been duly made by the account manager and received by the Board.

(4) Where, on the occasion of a claim, there is due to the Board an amount in respect of tax, that amount shall be recoverable by the Board in the same manner as tax charged by an assessment on the account manager which has become final and conclusive.

(5) This regulation and regulation 26 shall not apply to any repayment in respect of tax on [policies of life insurance falling within regulation 9][2], or on distributions and other rights or proceeds in respect of [such policies][2] [except in so far as [a return is required in respect of][3] any gain treated as arising in accordance with regulation 36(3)(*a*) or (*b*)][1].

Commentary—*Simon's Taxes* **E3.326**.

Amendments—[1] Words in para (5) inserted by the Individual Savings Account (Amendment) Regulations, SI 1998/3174 reg 9 with effect from 6 April 1999.

[2] Words in para (5) substituted by the ISA (Amendment No 2) Regulations, SI 2004/2996 regs 2, 17 with effect from 6 April 2005.

[3] In para (5), words substituted by the Individual Savings Account (Amendment No 2) Regulations, SI 2014/1450 regs 2, 23 with effect from 1 July 2014.

26 Repayments in respect of tax to account manager—annual returns and annual claims

(1) An annual claim is a claim for repayment in respect of tax for a year and may not be made at any time more than six years after the end of the year.

(2) An account manager shall within six months after the end of the year make a return of all income, . . . [2] [and any gain treated as arising in accordance with regulation 36(3)(*a*) or (*b*)][1], and in addition an annual claim to establish the total of repayments due under an account for that year . . . [2].

(3) Where the aggregate of the repayments in respect of interim claims for the year shown by an annual claim exceeds the amount repayable for the year shown on the claim, the account manager shall repay the amount of the excess to the Board with the claim.

(4) If an account manager fails to make the return and the annual claim required under this regulation within the time limited, the Board may issue a notice to the account manager showing the aggregate of payments in respect of the interim claims for the year, and stating that the Board are not satisfied that the amount due to the account manager for that year exceeds the lower amount stated in the notice.

(5) If a return and an annual claim are not delivered to the Board within 14 days after the issue of such a notice under paragraph (4) the amount of the difference between the aggregate and the lower amount stated in the notice shall immediately be recoverable by the Board in the same manner as tax charged by an assessment on the account manager which has become final and conclusive.

(6) Where a return and an annual claim have been made and the account manager subsequently discovers that an error or mistake has been made in the return or claim the account manager may make a supplementary return or annual claim within the time allowed in paragraph (1).

Commentary—*Simon's Taxes* **E3.326**.

Amendments—[1] Words in para (2) inserted by the Individual Savings Account (Amendment) Regulations, SI 1998/3174 reg 10 with effect from 6 April 1999.

[2] In para (2), words revoked by the Individual Savings Account (Amendment No 2) Regulations, SI 2014/1450 regs 2, 24 with effect from 1 July 2014.

27 Account manager's returns and claims—supplementary provisions

(1) Section 42 of the Management Act shall not apply to claims under these Regulations.

(2) No appeal shall lie from the Board's decision on an interim claim.

(3) An appeal . . . [1] from the Board's decision on an annual claim . . . [1] shall be brought by giving notice to the Board within 30 days of receipt of notice of the decision.

(4) No payment or repayment made or other thing done on or in relation to an interim claim or a notice under regulation 26(4) shall prejudice the decision on an annual claim.

(5) The like provisions as are contained in Part V of the Management Act (appeals and other proceedings) shall apply to an appeal under paragraph (3) above, and [on an appeal that is notified to the tribunal, the tribunal][1] may vary the decision appealed against whether or not the variation is to the advantage of the appellant.

(6) All such assessments, payments and repayments shall be made as are necessary to give effect to the Board's decision on an annual claim or to any variation of that decision on appeal.

(7) Returns and claims under these Regulations shall be in such form and contain such particulars as the Board prescribe and, subject to regulation 31(1) and (2), shall be signed by the account manager, and forms prescribed for annual claims may require a report to be given by a person qualified for appointment as auditor of a company.

Commentary—*Simon's Taxes* **E3.326**.

Amendments—[1] In para (3), words revoked, and in para (5), words substituted, by the Transfer of Tribunal Functions and Revenue and Customs Appeals Order, SI 2009/56 art 3, Sch 2 paras 45, 47 with effect from 1 April 2009.

28 Assessments for withdrawing relief and recovering tax

(1) Where—

(*a*) any relief or exemption from tax given in respect of income or gains under an account is found not to be due or to be excessive, or

(*b*) the full amount of tax in respect of the income or gains under an account has not otherwise been fully accounted for and paid to the Board by or on behalf of the account investor,

an assessment to tax may be made by the Board in the amount or further amount which in their opinion ought to be charged.

(2) An assessment to which paragraph (1) refers may be made on the account manager or on the account investor.

(3) If the assessment is made to recover tax in respect of income (including any amount in respect of a tax credit) under an account it shall be made under [Chapter 8 of Part 5 of ITTOIA 2005][1].

Commentary—*Simon's Taxes* **E3.337**.

Amendments—[1] In para (3), words substituted by the Individual Savings Account (Amendment No 2) Regulations, SI 2011/1780 regs 2, 29 with effect from 1 November 2011.

29 Records to be kept by account manager

[(1)] An account manager shall at all times keep sufficient records in respect of an account to enable the requirements of these Regulations to be satisfied.

[(2) Where an account is transferred by an account manager ("the transferor") to another account manager ("the transferee") in a group transfer of accounts, any records (or copies of records) kept by the transferor in respect of the account at the time when it is transferred shall be treated for the purposes of this regulation as kept by the transferee for so long as sub-paragraphs (*a*), (*b*) and (*c*) of paragraph (3) apply.

(3) For the purposes of paragraph (2)—

(*a*) this sub-paragraph applies if the records described in paragraph (2) are kept by the transferor;

(*b*) this sub-paragraph applies if the transferor and transferee are members of the same group of companies; and

(*c*) this sub-paragraph applies if the transferee can require the transferor to make the records available to the transferee for any purpose necessary to ensure the transferee's compliance with these regulations.][1]

Commentary—*Simon's Taxes* **E3.330**.

Amendments—[1] Para (1) numbered as such, and paras (2), (3) inserted, by the Individual Savings Account (Amendment) (No 2) Regulations, SI 2012/1871 regs 4, 19 with effect from 9 November 2011.

30 Information to be given to account investor by account manager [in relation to an account that is not a junior ISA account]

(1) . . . [1]

(2) An account manager who makes a payment to an account investor out of or in respect of which tax, or a sum representing tax, has been deducted shall, if the account investor so requests in writing, furnish the account investor with a statement in writing showing the gross amount of the payment, the amount deducted and the amount actually paid.

(3) On the transfer to an account investor of an account investment, subject to regulation 9(3)(*b*), the account manager shall provide for the account investor details in writing of the market value on the date of transfer.

Commentary—*Simon's Taxes* **E3.331**.

Amendments—Words in heading inserted by the Individual Savings Account (Amendment No 2) Regulations, SI 2011/1780 regs 2, 30 with effect from 1 November 2011.

1 Para (1) revoked by the Individual Savings Account (Amendment No 2) Regulations, SI 2013/623 reg 2(1), (3) with effect from 5 April 2013.

31 Returns of information by account manager

(1) An account manager shall within 60 days after the end of each year (beginning with the year 1999–00) in which he acts as an account manager, and after ceasing to act or to qualify as an account manager, deliver to the Board a return for that year, or for the part of that year in which he so acted or qualified, which contains the information specified in [paragraphs (3), (4), (5), (7) and (7A)][8], and is accompanied by a certificate as to the contents of the return, in the form prescribed by the Board, signed by the account manager or on his behalf.

[(1A) For the purposes of a Lifetime ISA in relation to paragraphs (3) and (10), paragraph (1B) applies instead of paragraph (1).

(1B) An account manager of a Lifetime ISA must, within 14 days after the end of each year in which the account manager acts as an account manager, and after ceasing to act or qualify as an account manager, deliver to the Board a return for the year or part of a year in which the account manager so acted or was qualified, in a form or manner prescribed by the Board, which contains the information specified in the sub-paragraphs referred to in paragraph (9).][19]

(2) . . . [6]

(3) The information specified in this paragraph is information relating to each account, in respect of which he acted as account manager, in the year or the part of the year for which the return is made, other than accounts transferred to another account manager under Regulation 21(2) in that year or part of a year, as to—

(*a*) as regards the account investor—

(i) his full name,

(ii) the address of his permanent residence, including postcode,

(iii) his date of birth, and

(iv) if he has one, his national insurance number [(otherwise, any unique reference number he may have had as mentioned in the Child Trust Funds Regulations 2004)][13];

(*b*) as regards each such account—

(i) the number allocated to the account by the account manager, and

(ii) [in relation to a cash account or stocks and shares account,][17] the market value of the account investments held under [the][5] component of the account, . . . [10] the value of each account investment being determined either as at 5th April in that year, or any other valuation date in that year, not falling earlier than 5th October, and

(*c*) as regards each such [account][5] . . . [15]—

(i) whether the account is a [cash account[, a stocks and shares account or an innovative finance account][17]][5],

[(ia) whether the account was a junior ISA account at any time in the year or part of the year for which the return is made,][8]

[(ib) whether the account is a flexible account,][15]

[(ii) [subject to [paragraphs (3A) and (3AB)(*a*)][9],][8] the total amount[, disregarding a subscription made in accordance with regulation 5D,][15] subscribed to the account, in the year or the part of the year for which the return is made;][5]

[(iia) in place of the provision in paragraph (ii) in the case of a flexible account, in the year or part of the year for which the return is made, disregarding a subscription made in accordance with regulation 5D (except for a replacement subscription), the total amount subscribed to the account less the amount of any cash withdrawn from it and if the result is in the negative, the amount to be reported is nil,][16]

(iii) [subject to [paragraphs (3AB)(*b*) and (3B)][9],][8] the date on which the first subscription[, if any,][15] (being either cash, . . . [2] or shares pursuant to regulation 7(2)(*h*)) was made to the account, in the year or the part of the year for which the return is made, ...[8]

(iv) the aggregate market value at the date of transfer of any shares transferred to the account manager or his nominee in accordance with regulation 7(2)(*h*) in the year or the part of the year for which the return is made [. . . [12] [and][15]

(v) [subject to paragraph (3C),][8] the date when any such [cash][5] account was closed, where that occurred during the year or the part of the year for which the return was made][2][.][15]

(vi) . . . [15][; and

(*d*) in relation to an innovative finance account comprising investments of the kind [specified at regulation 8A(2)(*a*) or 8A(2)(*ca*)][18], the aggregate of the amounts set out at sub-paragraphs (i) and (ii)—

(i) the outstanding principal balance as at 5th April in that year, or the date on which an account manager ceases to act or qualify as an account manager, under those [qualifying investments for an innovative finance component in respect of which payments are due to be made][18]; and

(ii) the amount of cash held in the account as at 5th April in that year, or the date on which an account manager ceases to act or qualify as an account manager;][17]

[(3A) Where a subscription is made to an account that ceases to be a junior ISA account in the year or part of the year for which the return is made, the return must show, as separate amounts, the total amount of cash subscribed to the account at times—

(*a*) when the account is a junior ISA account; and

(*b*) when the account is not a junior ISA account.

[(3AB) Where a defaulted cash account subscription in accordance with regulation 5D (subscriptions disregarded for the purposes of the subscription limits in regulations 4ZA and 4ZB) is made to an account in the year or part of the year for which a return required by this regulation is made—

(*a*) the amount of subscriptions reported to an account manager in accordance with regulation 5DF(1)(*a*)(ii) (current year's subscriptions made to the defaulted cash account) must be included as part of the total amount of cash subscribed to the account required by paragraph (3)(*c*)(ii);

(*b*) paragraph (3)(*c*)(iii) must be construed as requiring (in addition to the information specified in that paragraph) the date reported to the account manager in accordance with regulation 5DF(1)(*a*)(iii).][9]

(3B) In relation to an account that is a junior ISA account, the information described in paragraph (3)(*c*)(iii) shall only be provided in the return for the year or part of the year in which the application to open the account in accordance with regulation 12A is made.

(3C) The information provided in accordance with paragraph (3)(*c*)(v) must not include information relating to an account that was a junior ISA account immediately before it was closed.][8]

(4) [Subject to paragraph (5), the][3] information specified in this paragraph is—

(*a*) the respective market values at the end of the year or the part of the year for which the return is made of account investments held under stocks and shares components, by him or a nominee for him on behalf of account investors, under all the accounts in respect of which he acted as account manager in that year or part, with separate values for—

(i) shares, not being shares in an investment trust or in a [UK UCITS, recognised UCITS or non-UCITS retail scheme],[7] [officially listed on a recognised stock exchange][10],

[(ia) such shares admitted to trading on a recognised stock exchange in an EEA State,][10]

(ii) qualifying securities [listed on the official list of a recognised stock exchange][14],

[(iiaa) qualifying securities admitted to trading on a recognised stock exchange in an EEA State,][14]

[(iia) government securities falling within regulation 7(2)(*c*), (*ca*) or (*cb*);][4]

(iii) shares in investment trusts,

[(iv) units in an authorised unit trust,][6]

(v) units in, or shares of, a [recognised UCITS, or non-UCITS retail scheme (constituted outside the United Kingdom)][7],

[(vi) shares in an open-ended investment company,][6]

[(via) the surrender value of life insurance policies . . . [11],][6]

(vii) cash, including cash represented in share accounts with building societies,

with depositary interests being included in the paragraph to which their relevant investments (referred to in paragraphs (a) and (b) of the definition of "depositary interest") relate][1];

[(*aa*) the information specified in sub-paragraph (*a*) in respect of any such account investments (excluding cash (including cash represented in share accounts with building societies)) that are held under Lifetime ISA components;][19]

[(*b*) the respective market values at the end of the year or the part of the year for which the return is made of account investments held under cash components, by him or a nominee for him on behalf of account investors, under all the accounts in respect of which he acted as account manager in that year or part, with separate values for—

(i) cash, including cash represented in share accounts with building societies, [and][11]

[(ii) investments other than those specified in paragraph (i); and][11, 6]

[(*ba*) the information specified in sub-paragraph (*b*), in respect of any such account investments that are held under Lifetime ISA components;][19]

(*c*) the aggregate market value at that date of all such account investments held by him or his nominee[; and][17]

[(*d*) the amount at the end of the year or part of the year for which the return is made of account investments held under innovative finance components, by him or a nominee for him on behalf of account investors, under all the accounts in respect of which he acted as account manager in that year or part of a year, with separate values for—

(i) cash, and

(ii) the outstanding principal balance under those article 36H agreements in respect of which payments are due to be made to the account manager[, and][17]

(iii) the outstanding principal balance under those investments specified in regulation 8A(2)(*ca*) in respect of which payments are due to be made.][18]

(5) [Paragraph (4) shall apply to policies of life insurance falling within regulation 9][3] with the omission of the words "by him or a nominee for him on behalf of account investors," with references to the market value of account investments, in the case of policies of life insurance, being replaced with references to the surrender value of such policies, and as if separate valuations were required of such policies . . . [3].

(6) . . . [6]

(7) [The information specified in this paragraph is information relating to all accounts to which subscriptions were made in the year or part of the year, in respect of which he was acting as account manager immediately before the end of the year or part of the year for which the return is made, or in the case of an account that was closed during the year, in respect of which he was acting as manager at the date the account was closed, as to[6]]—

(*a*) the total number of accounts to which subscriptions were made, with separate figures for—

[(i) cash accounts holding policies of life insurance falling within regulation 9,

(ii) all cash accounts,

(iii) stocks and shares accounts holding policies of life insurance falling within regulation 9, and

(iv) all stocks and shares accounts,][5]

[(v) accounts receiving subscriptions made in accordance with regulation 5D(2)(*a*)(iv); and][15]

[(vi) all innovative finance accounts; and][17]

(*b*) the total amount of . . . [15] subscriptions made in the [year or part of the year][6][, disregarding a subscription made in accordance with regulation 5D,][15]—

(i) to stocks and shares components of accounts;

(ii) to cash components of accounts; . . . [3]

[(iia) in respect of subscriptions made in accordance with regulation 5(D)(2)(*a*)(iv);][15]

[(iib) to innovative finance components of accounts;][17]

[(iii) invested in policies (within the meaning in regulation 9(1)) under stocks and shares components; and][4]

[(iv) invested in policies (within that meaning) under cash components.][4]

[[In relation to this paragraph (7), in the case][17] of a flexible account, in the year or part of the year for which the return is made, there is to be disregarded, in respect of each account, a subscription made in accordance with regulation 5D (except for a replacement subscription) and there is to be deducted from the total amount subscribed the amount of any cash withdrawn from the account and if the result is in the negative, the amount to be reported is nil.][16]

[(7A) The information specified in this paragraph is information relating to all accounts in respect of which the account manager was acting as account manager immediately before the end of the year or part of the year for which the return is made that were junior ISA accounts at the end of the period covered by the return (whether or not a subscription was made to the account during that period) with separate figures for cash accounts and stocks and shares accounts.][8]

(8) No claim for repayment, or repayment, may be made under regulations 25 and 26 until the returns which have become due under this regulation have been duly made by the account manager and received by the Board.

[(9) Paragraphs (3) (except as provided in paragraph (10)) and (3A), (3B), (3C), (7) and (7A) do not apply to a Lifetime ISA.

(10) The following provisions of paragraph (3) apply to a Lifetime ISA—

(*a*) sub-paragraph (*a*) with the omission of "if he has one" and the words in parentheses;

(*b*) sub-paragraph (*b*) with the substitution of "a Lifetime ISA" for " a cash account or stocks and shares account";

(*c*) sub-paragraph (*c*)(ii) with the substitution of "paragraph (3AB)(*a*)" for "paragraphs (3A) and (3AB)(*a*)"; and

(*d*) sub-paragraph (*c*)(iv).][19]

Commentary—*Simon's Taxes* **E3.327–E3.329**.

Amendments—[1] Words in para (4)(*a*) added by the Individual Savings Account (Amendment No 3) Regulations, SI 2000/3112 reg 5 with effect from 13 December 2000.

[2] Words in para (3)(*c*) revoked, and para (3)(*c*)(v) inserted, by the Individual Savings Account (Amendment No 3) Regulations, SI 2002/3158 reg 7 with effect from 6 April 2003.

[3] Words in paras (4), (5) substituted, words in para (5) revoked, and para (7)(*b*)(iii) and word preceding revoked, by the ISA (Amendment No 2) Regulations, SI 2004/2996 regs 2, 18, 19 with effect from 6 April 2005.

4 Paras (4)(*a*)(iia), (7)(*b*)(iii), (iv) inserted, and para (4)(*b*)(ii) revoked, by the Individual Savings Account (Amendment No 2) Regulations, SI 2005/2561 regs 2, 7 with effect from 6 October 2005.

5 Words in para (3)(*b*)(ii), (*c*) substituted, whole of paras (3)(*c*)(ii), (7)(*a*)(i)–(iv) substituted, by the Individual Savings Account (Amendment) Regulations, SI 2007/2119 regs 2, 20, 21 with effect from 6 April 2008.

6 Words in para (7) substituted, paras (2), (6) revoked, paras (4)(*a*)(iv), (vi), (vi)*a*), (4)(*b*) substituted, by the Individual Savings Account (Amendment) Regulations, SI 2008/704 regs 2, 14 with effect from 6 April 2008 immediately after the ISA (Amendment) Regulations, SI 2007/2119 come into force.

7 In para (4)(*a*)(i), (v) words substituted, by the Individual Savings Account (Amendment No 2) Regulations, SI 2009/1994 regs 2, 9 with effect from 8 October 2008.

8 In para (1), words substituted; para (3)(*c*)(ia) inserted; in paras (3)(*c*)(ii), (iii) words inserted; word "and" immediately preceding para (3)(*c*)(iv) revoked; in para (3)(*c*)(v) words inserted; and paras (3A), (3B), (3C), (7A) inserted; by the Individual Savings Account (Amendment No 2) Regulations, SI 2011/1780 regs 2, 31 with effect from 1 November 2011.

9 In para (3)(*c*)(ii), (iii), words substituted, and para (3AB) inserted, by the Individual Savings Account (Amendment) (No 2) Regulations, SI 2012/1871 regs 4, 20 with effect from 8 August 2012.

10 In para (3)(*b*)(ii) words revoked, words inserted in para (4)(*a*)(i), and para (4)(*a*)(ia) inserted, by the Individual Savings Account (Amendment) Regulations, SI 2014/654 regs 2, 12 with effect from 6 April 2014.

11 In para (4)(*a*)(via), words revoked, in para (4)(*b*), word "and" inserted at end of sub-para (i), and sub-para (ii) substituted for previous sub-paras (ii), (iii), by the Individual Savings Account (Amendment No 2) Regulations, SI 2014/1450 regs 2, 25 with effect from 1 July 2014.

12 In para (3)(*c*)(iv), word revoked, and in para (3)(*c*)(v), comma substituted for full stop by the Individual Savings Account (Amendment No 2) Regulations, SI 2015/869 regs 2, 10 with effect from 6 April 2015.

13 In para (3)(*a*)(iv), words inserted by the Individual Savings Account (Amendment No 3) Regulations, SI 2015/941 regs 2, 7 with effect from 6 April 2015.

14 In para (4)(*a*)(ii), words inserted, and para (4)(*a*)(iiaa) inserted by the Individual Savings Account (Amendment No 4) Regulations, SI 2015/1370 regs 2, 5 with effect from 1 July 2015.

15 In para (3)(*c*), words revoked, substituted and inserted, and in para (7), words inserted and revoked, by the Individual Savings Account (Amendment) Regulations, SI 2016/16 regs 2, 15 with effect from 1 February 2016.

16 Para (3)(*c*)(iia) inserted, and words following para (7)(*b*)(iv) inserted, by the Individual Savings Account (Amendment) Regulations, SI 2016/16 regs 2, 16(1)(*d*), (2)(*c*) with effect from 6 April 2016.

17 The following amendments made by the Individual Savings Account (Amendment No 2) Regulations, SI 2016/364 regs 2, 17 with effect from 6 April 2016—

- in para (3), in sub-para (*b*)(ii), words inserted, in sub-para (*c*)(i), words substituted, and sub-para (*d*) and preceding word inserted;
- in para (4), words in sub-para (*c*) substituted, and sub-para (*d*) and preceding word inserted; and
- in para (7), sub-paras (*a*)(vi), (*b*)(iib) inserted, and words at the end substituted.

18 In para (3)(*d*), words substituted for words "specified at regulation 8A(2)(*a*)" and words "article 36H agreements in respect of which payments are due to be made to the account manager", in para (4)(*d*)(ii), words substituted for full stop, and para (4)(*d*)(iii) inserted, by the Individual Savings Account (Amendment No 3) Regulations, SI 2016/977 regs 2, 8 with effect from 1 November 2016.

19 Paras (1A), (1B) (4)(*aa*), (*ba*), (9), (10) inserted by the Individual Savings Account (Amendment No 2) Regulations, SI 2017/466 regs 2, 28 with effect from 6 April 2017.

32 [Information to be provided to the Board

Amendments—Reg 32 revoked by the Individual Savings Account (Amendment No 2) Regulations, SI 2011/1780 regs 2, 32 with effect from 1 November 2011.

33 [Inspection of records by officer of the Board

Amendments—Reg 33 revoked by the Individual Savings Account (Amendment No 2) Regulations, SI 2011/1780 regs 2, 32 with effect from 1 November 2011.

34 Capital gains tax—adaptation of enactments

(1) For the purposes of capital gains tax on the occasion when the title to account investments is transferred from an account manager to an account investor there shall be deemed to be a disposal and reacquisition by the account investor of those investments for a consideration equal to their market value at the date of the transfer.

(2) Sections 104 to 114 of the Taxation of Chargeable Gains Act 1992 shall apply for the purposes of pooling and identifying account investments as if—

(*a*) in section 106A after subsection (11) there were added—

"(12) This section and sections 104, 110, 110A and 114—

(*a*) shall apply separately in relation to any securities which are held by a person as account investments so long as they are so held, and

(*b*) shall apply in relation to any such securities which became account investments by being transferred or renounced to an account manager or to a nominee for an account manager in the circumstances specified in regulation 7(2)(*h*) and [(10)(*a*), (*b*) or (*ba*)][1] as if they had been account investments—

(i) in the case of securities acquired by that person in accordance with the provisions of a savings-related share option scheme, which were transferred in the circumstances specified in regulation [7(2)(*h*)(i)][1] and (10)(*a*), from the date of their acquisition by him, or

(ii) in the case of securities appropriated to that person in accordance with the provisions of an approved profit sharing scheme, which were transferred in the circumstances specified in regulation [7(2)(*h*)(ii)][1] and (10)(*b*), from the date when he directed the trustees to transfer the ownership of the securities to him or, if earlier, the release date in relation to those securities, [or

(iii) in the case of securities which were plan shares of [a Schedule 2][4] [SIP][3] before being transferred in the circumstances specified in regulation 7(2)(*h*)(iii) and (10)(*ba*), from the date when the securities ceased to be subject to the plan, and][1]

(*c*) while applying separately to any such securities, shall have effect as if that person held them in a capacity other than that in which he holds any other securities of the same class whether under another such account or otherwise.

(13) In this section—

(*a*) "account", "account investment" and "account manager" have the same meanings as in the Individual Savings Account Regulations 1998 and "regulation" means a regulation of those Regulations;

(*b*) "approved profit sharing scheme" has the same meaning as in Chapter IV of Part V of the Taxes Act and "savings-related share option scheme" has the meaning given by paragraph 1 of Schedule 9 to that Act.";

[(*c*) "[Schedule 2][4] SIP" and "ceased to be subject to the plan" shall be construed in accordance with the SIP code (see section 488(3) of ITEPA 2003); and

(*d*) "plan shares", in relation to [a Schedule 2][4] SIP, shall be construed in accordance with the SIP code (see section 488(3) of ITEPA 2003) except that—

(i) paragraph 87(6) of Schedule 2 to ITEPA 2003 (meaning of the word "shares" in the context of company reconstructions) shall not apply, and

(ii) in paragraph 88(2) of that Schedule (treatment of shares acquired under rights issue) the words "or securities or rights" shall be treated as omitted.][3]

(*b*) in section 110A after subsection (5) there were added—

"(6) Where part of a section 104 holding is treated by section 106A(12)(*b*)(ii) as having been account investments since a particular date—

(*a*) an operative event shall be regarded as having occurred for the purposes of this section immediately before that date, consisting of the disposal of the part of that section 104 holding which is so treated, and

(*b*) this section shall apply in relation to the occurrence of that operative event as it would have applied if it had always applied separately in relation to the part of that section 104 holding which is so treated."

(3) Section 106A of the Taxation of Chargeable Gains Act 1992 shall apply for the purposes of identifying securities within the meaning of that section which are eligible to become account investments as if—

(*a*) in subsection (4), there were added at the beginning the words "Subject to subsection (14) below";

(*b*) in subsection (6), the words "subsections (4) and (5) above" were replaced with the words "subsections (4), (5) and (14)"; and

(*c*) after subsections (12) and (13), as added by paragraph (2), there were added—

"(14) Where a person disposes of securities and securities of the same class which were eligible for transfer to an account under regulation 7(2)(*h*) were—

(*a*) held by him immediately before that disposal, or

(*b*) acquired by him on the same day as that disposal, or

(*c*) acquired by him within the period of thirty days after that disposal,

and those securities were acquired in the circumstances specified in that regulation, he shall be treated as having first disposed of any securities of that class held or acquired by him which were not so eligible."

(4) Sections 127 to 131 of the Taxation of Chargeable Gains Act 1992 shall not apply [in relation to qualifying investments falling within any of sub-paragraphs (*a*), (*b*), (*d*), (*e*), (*f*), (*g*) and (*h*) of regulation 7(2)][2] which are held under an account if there is by virtue of any allotment for payment as is mentioned in section 126(2) of that Act a reorganisation affecting those shares or securities.

Amendments—[1] In the provisions treated as added to section 106A, words in sub-s (12)(*b*) substituted by the Individual Savings Account (Amendment No 2) Regulations, SI 2000/2079 reg 5 with effect from 21 August 2000.

[2] Words in para (4) substituted by the Financial Services and Markets Act 2000 (Consequential Amendments) (Taxes) Order, SI 2001/3629 art 178 with effect from 1 December 2001, immediately after the coming into force of the Financial Services and Markets Act 2000 ss 411, 432(1), Sch 20 (and SI 2001/3629 Pts 1 and 2).

[3] In the provisions treated as added to s 106A, words in sub-s (12)(*b*)(iii) and whole of sub-s (13)(*c*), (*d*), substituted, by the Individual Savings Account (Amendment) Regulations, SI 2008/704 regs 2, 15 with effect from 6 April 2008 immediately after the ISA (Amendment) Regulations, SI 2007/2119 come into force.

[4] In para (2)(*a*), in the inserted sub-ss (12)(*b*)(iii), (13)(*c*), (13)(*d*), words substituted by FA 2014 s 51, Sch 8 paras 84, 87. This amendment is treated as having come into force on 6 April 2014.

35 Administration of tax in relation to accounts—supplementary

(1) Nothing in these Regulations shall be taken to prejudice any powers conferred or duties imposed by or under any enactment in relation to the making of returns of income or gains, or for the recovery of tax, penalties or interest by means of an assessment or otherwise.

(2) Notwithstanding the provisions of these Regulations an account manager shall not be released from obligations under these Regulations in relation to an account except under conditions agreed in writing with and notified to that person by the Board.

(3) The like provisions as are contained in the Management Act shall apply to any assessment under these Regulations as if it were an assessment to tax for the year in which, apart from these Regulations, the account investor would have been liable (by reason of his ownership of the investments).

(4) In the application of the like provisions as are contained in section 86 of the Management Act by virtue of paragraph (3) in relation to any sums due and payable by virtue of an assessment made on an account manager under these Regulations, the relevant date—

(*a*) is the 1st January in the year for which the account investor would have been liable where the account manager has made an interim claim for a period falling within that year; and

(*b*) in any other case, is the later of the following dates, that is to say—

(i) the 1st January in that year; or

(ii) the date of the making of the repayment by the Board following receipt of the annual claim for that year.

(5) The like provisions as are contained in section 97(1) of the Management Act shall apply as if—

(*a*) there were inserted after the words "[section 95][3] above" the words "or the Individual Savings Account Regulations 1998", and

[(5A) Paragraphs (3) to (5) do not apply to an assessment made or deemed to be made under the Schedule.][4]

(*b*) there were inserted after the words "that they were" the words "or have become".

[(6) If—

(*a*) a chargeable event, within the meaning given by [Chapter 9 of Part 4 of ITTOIA 2005][3], has happened in relation to a policy of life insurance which is an account investment . . . [2]; and

(*b*) the body by whom the policy was issued is satisfied that no gain is to be treated as chargeable to tax on the happening of the event by virtue of regulation 22(1)(*a*)(v),

the body shall not be obliged to deliver the certificates mentioned in section 552(1) of that Act. This paragraph does not prevent the operation of section 552(1) in a case to which regulation 36(1) applies.][1].

[(7) A termination of a policy of insurance pursuant to regulation 9(3)(*b*)(ii) shall be treated as the surrender of all rights under the policy for the purposes of section 484(1)(*a*)(i) of ITTOIA 2005.][3]

(8) Where there are in force relevant insurances within the meaning given by section 552A of the Taxes Act then, so far as they consist of policies of life insurance which are account investments . . . [2], they shall be disregarded in calculating the amount or value of gross premiums, for the purposes of subsection (4)(*b*) of that section.

(9) Any form prescribed by the Board for the purposes of these Regulations shall provide for a declaration that all the particulars given in the form are correctly stated to the best of the knowledge and belief of the person concerned.

[(9A) Paragraph (9) does not apply to any form prescribed under regulation 31(1B) or the Schedule.][4]

(10) No obligation as to secrecy imposed by statute or otherwise shall preclude the Board from disclosing to an account manager or account investor that any provision of these Regulations has not been satisfied or that relief has been given or claimed in respect of investments under an account.

Commentary—*Simon's Taxes* **E3.337**.

Amendments—[1] Para (6) substituted by the Individual Savings Account (Amendment) Regulations, SI 2002/453 regs 3, 4 with effect from 6 April 2002 for the tax year 2002–03 and subsequent tax years.

[2] Words in paras (6)(*a*), (8) revoked by the ISA (Amendment No 2) Regulations, SI 2004/2996 regs 2, 20, 21 with effect from 6 April 2005.

[3] Words in paras (5)(*a*), (6)(*a*) and whole of para (7), substituted, by the Individual Savings Account (Amendment) Regulations, SI 2008/704 regs 2, 16 with effect from 6 April 2008 immediately after the ISA (Amendment) Regulations, SI 2007/2119 come into force.

[4] Paras (5A), (9A) inserted by the Individual Savings Account (Amendment No 2) Regulations, SI 2017/466 regs 2, 29 with effect from 6 April 2017.

36 [Application of the provisions of Chapter II of Part XIII of the Taxes Act [and of Chapter 9 of Part 4 of ITTOIA 2005] to policies where an investor ceases to be or was not entitled to relief from tax

(1) This paragraph applies to a case where—

(*a*) an event specified in regulation 9(8) has occurred in relation to a policy of life insurance, and (*b*) a termination event within the meaning given by regulation 9(7) occurs in relation to that policy.

(2) Where—

(*a*) there is a case to which paragraph (1) applies, and

(*b*) a chargeable event in relation to the policy, [falling within section 484(1) of ITTOIA 2005][4], has occurred prior to the time at which the termination event mentioned in paragraph (1)(*b*) occurs,

the account investor shall cease to be, and shall be treated as not having been, entitled to relief from tax under regulation 22(1)(a)(v), in respect of gains treated as arising on the occurrence of any chargeable event mentioned in sub-paragraph (b).

(3) The provisions of Chapter II of Part XIII of the Taxes Act [and of Chapter 9 of Part 4 of ITTOIA 2005][4] shall apply, in a case to which paragraph (1) applies, to—

(*a*) the termination event mentioned in paragraph (1)(*b*), and

(*b*) any chargeable event mentioned in paragraph (2)(*b*),

with the modifications provided for in regulation 35(7) and paragraphs (4) to (7) of this regulation, and the account investor and the account manager shall account to the Board in accordance with this regulation for tax from which relief under regulation 22(1)(a)(v) has been given on the basis that the account investor was so entitled, or in circumstances such that the account investor was not so entitled.

[(4) Section 530 of ITTOIA 2005 does not apply to a gain in a case in which paragraph (1) applies.][4]

(5) Relief under [section 535 of ITTOIA 2005][4] shall be computed as if paragraph (4) had not been enacted.

[(6) In section 552 of the Taxes Act—

(*a*) in subsection (1)(*b*) for the words "policy holder" there shall be substituted "account investor";

(*b*) *in subsection (3)*—

(i) . . . [5]

(ii) for the words "the name and address of the appropriate policy holder" there shall be substituted "the name and address of the account investor";

(iii) . . . [5]

(*c*) in subsection (5)—

(i) for the words "the appropriate policy holder" there shall be substituted "the account investor";

(ii) sub-paragraph (*b*)(ii) shall be omitted;

(iii) paragraph (*c*) shall be omitted;

(iv) in paragraph (*d*) the words "except where paragraph (c) above applies," shall be omitted; and

(v) paragraph (*f*) shall be omitted;

(*d*) in subsection (6)—

(i) paragraph (*b*) shall be omitted;

(ii) for paragraph (*c*) there shall be substituted—

"(*c*) if the event is a death, the period of three months beginning with the receipt of written notification of the death;";

(iii) after paragraph (c) there shall be inserted—

"(*d*) [if the event is—

(i) a termination event, or

(ii) a chargeable event preceding such a termination event (as mentioned in regulation 36(2) of the Individual Savings Account Regulations 1998), the period of three months beginning with the date on which the insurer received notice under regulation 9(9)(*b*) of those Regulations or, if earlier, actual notice of the termination event.[3]]";

(*e*) in subsection (7)—

(i) . . . [5]

(ii) paragraph (*b*) shall be omitted;

(iii) for paragraph (*c*) there shall be substituted—

"(*c*) if the event is a death, the period of three months beginning with the receipt of written notification of the death;";

(iv) after paragraph (*c*) there shall be inserted—

"(*ca*) [if the event is—

(i) a termination event, or

(ii) a chargeable event preceding such a termination event (as mentioned in regulation 36(2) of the Individual Savings Account Regulations 1998), the period of three months beginning with the date on which the insurer received notice under regulation 9(9)(*b*) of those Regulations or, if earlier, actual notice of the termination event.]";[3]

and

(v) in paragraph (*d*) for the words "paragraph (*c*)" there shall be substituted "paragraph (*c*) or (*ca*)";

(*f*) in subsection (8)—

(i) in paragraph (*b*) for "policy holder" there shall be substituted "account investor in respect";

(*ii*) [5]

(*g*) . . . [4]

(*h*) in subsection 10—

(i) before the definition of "amount" there shall be inserted—

"account investor" has the same meaning as in the Individual Savings Account Regulations 1998;

(ii) the definition of "appropriate policy holder" shall be omitted; [and][5]

(iii), (iv). . . [5];

(v) after the definition of "section 546 excess" there shall be inserted—

"termination event" has the same meaning as in the Individual Savings Account Regulations 1998;"; . . . [5]

(*i*) . . . [5]

[(6A) In section 552ZA of the Taxes Act—

(*a*) in subsection (2)(b) the words "or an assignment" shall be omitted; and

(*b*) subsections (3) and (4) shall be omitted.][2]

(7) . . . [2]

(8) The account manager shall account for and pay income tax at the [basic rate][5] in force for the year of assessment in which the termination event, or the chargeable event mentioned in paragraph (2)(*b*), occurred, as the case may be, and any amount so payable—

(*a*) may be set off against any repayment in respect of tax due under regulation 25 or regulation 26 and, subject thereto

(*b*) shall be treated as an amount of tax due not later than 6 months after the end of the year in which the event specified in regulation 9(8) came to the notice of the account manager, and

(*c*) shall be payable without the making of an assessment.

(9) Where tax is charged in accordance with paragraph (3)(*a*) or (*b*)—

(*a*) an assessment to income tax at the [basic rate][5] [determined in pursuance of section 6(2) of ITA 2007][6] in force for the relevant year of assessment may be made on the account manager or on the account investor, and

[(*b*) an assessment to income tax may be made on the account investor at the higher rate and additional rate (determined in pursuance of section 6(2) of ITA 2007) for that year of assessment as appropriate to the account investor's income tax liability calculated in accordance with section 23 of ITA 2007,][6]

[not more than 4 years after the end of][6] that year of assessment, and regulation 28 shall not apply.][1]

Commentary—*Simon's Taxes* **E3.338**.

Amendments—[1] This regulation inserted by the Individual Savings Account (Amendment) Regulations, SI 1998/3174 reg 12 with effect from 6 April 1999.

[2] Para (6) substituted, para (6A) inserted, and para (7) revoked, by the Individual Savings Account (Amendment) Regulations, SI 2002/453 regs 3, 5 with effect from 6 April 2002 for the tax year 2002–03 and subsequent tax years.

[3] Words in para (6) substituted by the Individual Savings Account (Amendment No. 3) Regulations, SI 2002/3158 reg 8 with effect from 8 January 2003.

[4] Words in cross-heading and paras (2)(*b*), (5) substituted, words in para (3) inserted, and para (4) substituted, by the Individual Savings Account (Amendment) Regulations, SI 2008/704 regs 2, 17 with effect from 6 April 2008 immediately after the ISA (Amendment) Regulations, SI 2007/2119 come into force.

[5] In para (6), sub-paras (*b*)(i), (iii), (*e*)(i), (*f*)(ii), (*g*) revoked, in sub-para (*h*)(ii) word "and" inserted, sub-para (*h*)(iii), (iv) revoked, sub-para (*i*) and preceding word "and" revoked, and in paras (8), (9)(*a*), words substituted for words "lower rate", by the Individual Savings Account (Amendment No 2) Regulations, SI 2008/1934 regs 2, 6 with effect in relation to events occurring on and after 13 September 2007.

[6] In para (9)(*a*), words inserted, para (9)(*b*) substituted, and in para (9)(*c*), words substituted, by the Individual Savings Account (Amendment No 2) Regulations, SI 2011/1780 regs 2, 33 with effect from 1 November 2011.

[37 The Schedule makes further provision for Lifetime ISA.][1]

[1] Regulation 37 inserted by the Individual Savings Account (Amendment No 2) Regulations, SI 2017/466 regs 2, 30 with effect from 6 April 2017.

SIs

[SCHEDULE
LIFETIME ISA FURTHER PROVISION]

[1] Scgedule inserted by the Individual Savings Account (Amendment No 2) Regulations, SI 2017/466 regs 2, 31 with effect from 6 April 2017.

[Interpretation

1 (1) In this Schedule—

"claim period" has the meaning given in sub-paragraphs (2) and (3);

"government bonus" is an amount equal to 25% of the aggregate of qualifying additions made to a Lifetime ISA in a relevant period;

"qualifying addition" means a current year payment or a payment under regulation 10A (4)(*c*) which is made into a Lifetime ISA;

"relevant period" means the year 2017–2018 and any subsequent year;

"Schedule 1" means Schedule 1 to the Savings (Government Contributions) Act 2017;

"withdrawal charge" has the meaning given in paragraph 9(4) of Schedule 1.

(2) "Claim period" means—

(*a*) for the year 2017–18, except where sub-paragraph (3) applies, that year, and

(*b*) for the year 2018–19 and subsequent years, a month,

or such period as the Board may specify from time to time pursuant to paragraph 2(1).

(3) Where an account manager during the year 2017–18 is notified of a death or determination in accordance with paragraph 4(2) of a terminal illness of an account investor, "claim period" means—

(*a*) the period beginning with the date of the opening of the account, or, where there has been a transfer, the date of the original opening of the transferred account, and ending at the end of the month in which such notification is received, and

(*b*) in the case of a continuing terminal illness of the account investor, each month subsequent to the period determined under sub-paragraph (*a*), in which a qualifying addition has been made to the account.

(4) For the purposes of sub-paragraphs (2) and (3) "month" is a period beginning on the 6th of one month and ending on the 5th of the following month.][1]

[1] Schedule inserted by the Individual Savings Account (Amendment No 2) Regulations, SI 2017/466 regs 2, 31 with effect from 6 April 2017.

[Government bonus claim

2 (1) The Board may from time to time specify—

(*a*) the information to be included in a claim for a government bonus;

(*b*) the periods to which such a claim is to relate; and

(*c*) the form or manner in which such a claim is to be made.

(2) A government bonus is only payable if a claim for it is made in accordance with this Schedule.

(3) The person who must make a claim for a government bonus for qualifying additions made to the Lifetime ISA in a claim period is—

(*a*) subject to sub-paragraph (*b*), the person who is, or was, the account manager of a Lifetime ISA at the end of a claim period or on closure of a Lifetime ISA;

(*b*) where a Lifetime ISA is transferred to another such account of the account investor during a claim period, the account manager of the account at the end of the period.

(4) The claim is to be made within 14 days beginning with the day after the end of a claim period.

(5) The Board (subject to checking and if necessary correcting the amount of the claim) must pay the account manager any government bonus amount that is due—

(*a*) where the claim is made by the due date, within 14 days beginning with the day after the due date for the claim; and

(*b*) where the claim is made later than the due date, within 14 days beginning with the day after the due date for a claim for the claim period in which the late claim is made.

(6) Any government bonus payment which on being made is not paid into a Lifetime ISA of the account investor must be treated as a withdrawal.

(7) Where a claim has been made and the account manager becomes aware within six years after the end of the claim period that—

(*a*) anything which should have been included in the claim has not been included,

(*b*) anything which should not have been included in the claim has been included, or

(*c*) any other error has occurred in the claim,

the account manager must correct the error without delay.

(8) If the account manager corrects a claim, such assessments, adjustments, payments or repayments of government bonus as are necessary for achieving the objective mentioned in sub-paragraph (9) must be made.
(9) The objective is that the entitlement (or otherwise) of the account investor to a government bonus should be the same as it would have been if a correct claim had been delivered.
(10) The Board may enquire into a claim and return if—

(*a*) they have reasonable grounds for believing that an error has occurred in the claim, and

(*b*) they give notice to the account manager of their intention to do so no later than 12 months after the date on which the claim is made.

(11) Otherwise than where an account manager is notified of a death or determination in accordance with paragraph 4(2) of a terminal illness of an account investor, no claim for a government bonus arising in respect of the year 2017–18 may be made before the end of that year.][1]

[1] Schedule inserted by the Individual Savings Account (Amendment No 2) Regulations, SI 2017/466 regs 2, 31 with effect from 6 April 2017.

[Rejection of government bonus claim

3 (1) The Board must notify the account manager of a rejection of any claim for a government bonus together with reasons for the decision—

(*a*) where the claim is made by the due date, within 14 days beginning with the day after the due date for the claim, and

(*b*) where the claim is made later than the due date, within 14 days beginning with the day after receipt of the claim.

(2) The account manager on receipt of such notification must notify the account investor within 14 days beginning with the day after the day of receipt.
(3) An account investor may within 90 days beginning with the day after receipt of a notification under sub-paragraph (2) apply to the Board for payment of a government bonus which has been refused.
(4) Paragraph 16 (appeals) applies, in relation to an account manager, to a notification under sub-paragraph (1), and, in relation to an account investor, to a decision in respect of an application under sub-paragraph (3).
(5) The effect of any notification or decision is not suspended by the making of an application or an appeal.][1]

[1] Schedule inserted by the Individual Savings Account (Amendment No 2) Regulations, SI 2017/466 regs 2, 31 with effect from 6 April 2017.

[Specified age; terminal illness; transfer to another Lifetime ISA—no withdrawal charge

4 (1) For the purposes of paragraph 7(1)(*a*) of Schedule 1 (withdrawals not triggering a charge-specified age) the specified age is 60.
(2) For the purposes of paragraph 7(5)(*c*) of Schedule 1 (withdrawals not triggering a charge-terminal illness) an account investor is to be considered as suffering from a terminal illness if the account manager of the account investor's Lifetime ISA has received written evidence from a registered medical practitioner that the account investor is expected to live for less than one year.
(3) For the purposes of paragraph 7(5)(*d*) of Schedule 1 (withdrawals not triggering a charge-transfer to another Lifetime ISA), a withdrawal by way of transfer from one Lifetime ISA of the account investor to another such account of the investor must be made in accordance with regulation 21.][1]

[1] Schedule inserted by the Individual Savings Account (Amendment No 2) Regulations, SI 2017/466 regs 2, 31 with effect from 6 April 2017.

[Specified percentage for withdrawal charge

5 For the purposes of paragraph 8(2) of Schedule 1 (charge when unlisted withdrawal made) the specified percentage is 25%.][1]

[1] Schedule inserted by the Individual Savings Account (Amendment No 2) Regulations, SI 2017/466 regs 2, 31 with effect from 6 April 2017.

[First-time residential purchase

6 (1) For the purposes of paragraph 7(5)(*a*) and (*b*) of Schedule 1 (withdrawals not triggering a charge) the provisions in sub-paragraphs (2) to (14) apply.
(2) The withdrawal must only be used by the account investor towards defraying the purchase price for the acquisition by the account investor as a first-time buyer of a residential property.
(3) The purchase price must not exceed £450,000.
(4) The account investor must be purchasing as sole owner or as joint owner with another individual who may already own the property.
(5) The purchase must be of a legal interest in land situated in the United Kingdom with a view to the account investor becoming a residential property owner.

(6) The purchase must be—

(*a*) funded by a loan that will be secured by a charge over the land by way of—

(i) a legal mortgage (if land in England and Wales),

(ii) a heritable security (if land in Scotland), or

(iii) a legal charge, mortgage by conveyance, demise, assignment or sub-demise (if land in Northern Ireland); or

(*b*) made under the terms of a regulated home purchase plan.

(7) Except in the circumstances specified in paragraph (8) the charge under paragraph (6)(*a*) must not be by way of a Buy to Let Mortgage.

(8) The circumstances specified in this paragraph are where the account investor is an individual described in regulation 10A(2)(*f*)(i) or (ii) who is unable to occupy the land as their only or main residence at the time of the acquisition but intends, in the future, to so occupy such land.

(9) The account investor must—

(*a*) on completion of the purchase occupy the land as their only or main residence; or

(*b*) in consequence of the land comprising a residential property in the process of being constructed or adapted for use as a dwelling, on completion of the purchase must intend it to be their only or main residence and must occupy it as such on its becoming suitable for such use; or

(*c*) in consequence of the account investor being an individual described in regulation 10A(2)(*f*)(i) or (ii), be unable to so occupy the land but must intend to do so in the future.

(10) The withdrawal and, where there is more than one withdrawal made for the purposes of the purchase, the aggregate of them, must not exceed the purchase price on completion of the purchase.

(11) The account investor's Lifetime ISA from which the withdrawal is made must have been open for at least 12 months after the date of the first payment into it and, for this purpose, a Lifetime ISA opened in the circumstances provided for in regulation 12B(5) is to be treated as being the same Lifetime ISA as the one from which the moneys transferred or paid into the account originated.

(12) The amount of the withdrawal must be passed directly by the account manager to the account investor's conveyancer, who must be an eligible conveyancer.

(13) The account investor must—

(*a*) provide to their conveyancer the information specified in paragraph 8(1) together with the declaration specified in paragraph 8(3); and

(*b*) procure that the conveyancer provide the information set out in paragraph (8)(2) to their account manager together with the declaration specified in paragraph 8(3).

(14) Where the account manager has received all of the information specified in paragraph (13)(*b*) and has no reason to believe that the information and declarations are not true and complete, the account manager must transfer the amount of the withdrawal to the account investor's conveyancer within the period stipulated under regulation 4(7).][1]

1 Schedule inserted by the Individual Savings Account (Amendment No 2) Regulations, SI 2017/466 regs 2, 31 with effect from 6 April 2017.

[Definitions for the purposes of paragraph 6

7 The following definitions apply for the purposes of paragraph 6—

"Buy to Let Mortgage" means a loan made to one or more borrowers to be secured by a mortgage over a residential property that is—

(*a*) either—

(i) let at the date the mortgage is granted, or

(ii) intended by the borrower or borrowers to be let either at that time or in the future, and

(*b*) marketed as being intended for such purpose;

"eligible conveyancer" means—

(*a*) in England and Wales, a conveyancer within the meaning of rule 217A of the Land Registration Rules 2003;

(*b*) in Scotland, a solicitor or advocate within the meaning of section 65 of the Solicitors (Scotland) Act 1980, or a conveyancing practitioner as defined in section 23 of the Law Reform (Miscellaneous Provisions) (Scotland) Act 1990; or

(*c*) in Northern Ireland, a person enrolled as a solicitor of the Court of Judicature of Northern Ireland pursuant to the Solicitors (Northern Ireland) Order 1976;

"first-time buyer" means an account investor who is not, and never has been, a residential property owner;

"a legal interest in land" includes land which will be acquired under the terms of a regulated home purchase plan;

"purchase price" means—

(*a*) in connection with the acquisition of any legal interest in land in circumstances other than those described in paragraph (*b*), (*c*) or (*d*), the value of the consideration required to be paid, and which is paid, by the purchaser under the sale and purchase agreement entered into in connection with the acquisition of that interest in land; or

(*b*) in connection with the acquisition of any legal interest in land under the terms of a regulated home purchase plan, the value of the consideration required to be paid, and which is paid, to the original seller for the interest in that land; or

(*c*) in connection with the acquisition of a legal interest in land by an individual who as a result of the acquisition becomes a joint owner of the land with another individual who previously owned the land, the market value of the whole of the land as determined at the time of the acquisition; or

(*d*) in connection with the acquisition of a leasehold legal interest in land under a shared ownership arrangement—

(i) the value determined in accordance with paragraph (*a*), or

(ii) the value of the premium required to be paid, and which is paid, by the purchaser under the sale and purchase agreement entered into in connection with the acquisition of that interest, divided by the fraction representing the share of the property to be acquired on completion by the purchaser in return for the premium (howsoever described in the sale and purchase agreement or the lease);

"regulated home purchase plan" means a home purchase plan that is a regulated home purchase plan within the meaning of article 63F of the Regulated Activities Order 2001;

"residential property owner" means an individual who owns as sole or joint owner an interest in residential property (including a legal interest in land acquired under the terms of a regulated home purchase plan or a shared ownership arrangement) which is—

(*a*) in England or Wales—

(i) freehold;

(ii) leasehold, where the lease was originally granted for a term certain exceeding 21 years; or

(iii) commonhold;

(*b*) in Scotland, registered or recorded, or would be capable of being registered or recorded, as a right of absolute ownership in the Land Register of Scotland or General Register of Sasines in Scotland, as applicable;

(*c*) in Northern Ireland—

(i) freehold; or

(ii) leasehold, where the lease was originally granted for a term certain exceeding 21 years; or

(*d*) an equivalent interest in land to the legal interests in land listed in paragraphs (*a*) to (*c*) under the laws of any jurisdiction outside the United Kingdom;

"residential property" means a legal interest in land which comprises a building that is used or suitable for use as a dwelling, or is in the process of being constructed or adapted for such use; and

"shared ownership arrangement" means an arrangement whereby a purchaser acquires from a housing association, local authority or other person a leasehold legal interest in a property which is specified in the sale and purchase agreement and the lease to be comprised of—

(*a*) a share for which the purchaser is required to pay a premium on completion, and

(*b*) a separate share in respect of which the purchaser is required to pay a periodic rent over the term of the lease.][1]

1 Schedule inserted by the Individual Savings Account (Amendment No 2) Regulations, SI 2017/466 regs 2, 31 with effect from 6 April 2017.

[Specified information for the purposes of paragraph 6

8 (1) The information to be provided by the account investor to their conveyancer under this sub-paragraph is—

(*a*) the amount of the withdrawal;

(*b*) the full name and address details (including postcode) of the account manager and the account number of the Lifetime ISA to which the withdrawal relates;

(*c*) a declaration that the account investor is a first-time buyer;

(*d*) the full address details of the residential property;

(*e*) the purchase price of the residential property;

(*f*) a declaration that the withdrawal will only be used towards defraying the purchase price for the acquisition of the residential property;

(*g*) a declaration that the account investor—

(i) is not also claiming a bonus under a Help to Buy ISA (within the meaning of regulation 5DDC(6)); and

(ii) has not received payment of such a bonus unless its full amount has been repaid to the scheme administrator of the Help to Buy ISA in accordance with applicable scheme rules;

(*h*) if known, the name and address of the seller's conveyancer for the acquisition to whom the amount of the withdrawal should be paid by the account investor's conveyancer; and

(*i*) a declaration that the provisions of paragraph 6(2) to (13) have been, or will on completion of the purchase, be complied with or, in the case of occupation under paragraph 6(9)(*b*), when that will take place.

(2) The information to be provided by the account investor's conveyancer to the account investor's account manager under this sub-paragraph is—

(*a*) a declaration that they are an eligible conveyancer;

(*b*) a declaration that they have received the information under sub-paragraph (1) and sub-paragraph (3) relative to the account investor;

(*c*) the purchase price of the residential property in question;

(*d*) a declaration that the funds withdrawn from the Lifetime ISA will only be released towards defraying the purchase price for the acquisition of the residential property;

(*e*) the account details where the withdrawal should be transferred; and

(*f*) the conveyancer's unique conveyancer registration number with the appropriate professional body.

(3) Information provided under sub-paragraphs (1) and (2) must be accompanied by a declaration made by the individual providing it that it is true and complete to the best of the individual's knowledge and belief.][1]

[1] Schedule inserted by the Individual Savings Account (Amendment No 2) Regulations, SI 2017/466 regs 2, 31 with effect from 6 April 2017.

[Information from conveyancer

9 (1) Within 10 business days after either of the events listed in sub-paragraph (2) the account investor must procure that the conveyancer provides the information referred to in sub-paragraph (3) to the account investor's account manager of the Lifetime ISA from which the withdrawal for the acquisition was made.

(2) The events referred to in sub-paragraph (1) are—

(*a*) the purchase of the residential property being completed;

(*b*) the purchase not completing within 90 days of the date of receipt of the withdrawal by the conveyancer or, if earlier, the withdrawal of the account investor or the seller from the sale and purchase of the residential property.

(3) The information referred to in sub-paragraph (1) is—

(*a*) in the case of a purchase completing—

(i) the date of completion of the purchase;

(ii) the account number of the Lifetime ISA from which the withdrawal was made; and

(iii) the conveyancer's unique conveyancer reference number with the appropriate professional body.

(*b*) in the case of a purchase not completing,—

(i) a declaration that the purchase of the residential property in question has not completed;

(ii) the amount of the withdrawal that is being returned and, if it is not the full amount, an account of any shortfall;

(iii) the name and address of the account investor;

(iv) the account number of the Lifetime ISA from which the withdrawal was made;

(v) the conveyancer's unique conveyancer registration number with the appropriate professional body; and

(*c*) in either of the events listed in sub-paragraph (2), a declaration, to the best of the individual's knowledge and belief, as to whether any of the requirements of paragraph 6(2) to (13) has not been complied with or any information provided under paragraph 8 is not true or complete.][1]

[1] Schedule inserted by the Individual Savings Account (Amendment No 2) Regulations, SI 2017/466 regs 2, 31 with effect from 6 April 2017.

[Purchase failure

10 (1) Where a purchase fails to complete, the account investor must procure that the conveyancer, within 10 business days of either of the events listed in paragraph 9(2)(b), must return the full amount of the account investor's withdrawal for the purchase to the account manager, to be held for the account investor in a Lifetime ISA.
(2) If there is a shortfall in the amount returned to the account manager, that amount is to be treated for the purposes of paragraph 7(4) of Schedule 1 as a withdrawal to which paragraph 8(6) of that Schedule applies.
(3) Where a person accountable under this paragraph is notified by the Board that an amount is due from them under it, that amount shall be treated for the purposes of Part 6 of the Management Act (collection and recovery) as if it were tax charged in an assessment and due and payable.
(4) The time limits in sections 34, 36 and 40 of the Management Act, as they apply to assessments, apply to amounts payable under sub-paragraph (3).
(5) Paragraph 16 (appeals) applies to any notification under this paragraph.
(6) The effect of any notification is suspended by an appeal under paragraph 16 until the appeal is determined or withdrawn.][1]

1 Schedule inserted by the Individual Savings Account (Amendment No 2) Regulations, SI 2017/466 regs 2, 31 with effect from 6 April 2017.

[Amounts not treated as withdrawals

11 For the purposes of paragraphs 7(2) and 11(*b*) of Schedule 1, withdrawals, removals or losses from a Lifetime ISA do not count for the application of a withdrawal charge if they are in respect of—

(*a*) a payment (including a government bonus) to an invalid account under regulation 4A or 4AA;
(*b*) excess payments and their proceeds described in regulation 4AA;
(*c*) any fees or charges properly levied or charged in respect of the management by the account manager of a Lifetime ISA and account investments in accordance with their terms and conditions;
(*d*) a default event under regulation 5DC or in respect of an act or omission or circumstance not attributable to the account investor; or
(*e*) an amount recouped in accordance with paragraph 12.][1]

1 Schedule inserted by the Individual Savings Account (Amendment No 2) Regulations, SI 2017/466 regs 2, 31 with effect from 6 April 2017.

[Recoupment of government bonus payment

12 (1) Where an amount has been wrongly paid by way of government bonus, the amount must be accounted for to the Board by—

(*a*) the account manager of the Lifetime ISA (to the extent that assets relating to the account, or directly or indirectly representing the amount, are in the account manager's possession or control);
(*b*) the person who is the account investor (to the extent that the amount has been made or credited to the account investor); and
(*c*) any person in whom the amount, or any property directly or indirectly representing any of it, is vested (whether beneficially or otherwise);

and the persons under (*a*), (*b*) and (*c*) shall be jointly and severally liable for the repayment of the amount (subject to the limitation applying under sub-paragraphs (*a*) and (*b*)).
(2) Where a person accountable under this paragraph is notified by the Board that an amount is due from them that amount shall be treated for the purposes of Part 6 of the Management Act as if it were tax charged in an assessment and due and payable.
(3) The time limits in sections 34, 36 and 40 of the Management Act, as they apply to assessments, apply to amounts payable under this paragraph.
(4) Paragraph 16 (appeals) applies to any notification under this paragraph.
(5) The effect of sub-paragraph (2) is suspended by an appeal under paragraph 16 until the appeal is determined or withdrawn.][1]

1 Schedule inserted by the Individual Savings Account (Amendment No 2) Regulations, SI 2017/466 regs 2, 31 with effect from 6 April 2017.

[Withdrawals: information returns

13 (1) For the purposes of paragraph 9(1)(*a*) of Schedule 1, within 14 days after the end of a claim period, a person who is or was an account manager of a Lifetime ISA during that period must submit to the Board returns of information relating to the Lifetime ISA in respect of that period.
(2) The Board may from time to time specify—

(*a*) the information to be included in a return;
(*b*) the form of a return;
(*c*) the form or manner in which a return is to be submitted; and
(*d*) the period to which a return must relate.

(3) Where a return has been made and the account manager becomes aware within four years after the end of the claim period that—

(*a*) anything which should have been included in the return has not been so included,
(*b*) anything which should not have been included in the return has been so included, or
(*c*) any other error has occurred in the return,

the account manager must correct the error without delay.

(4) The Board may enquire into a return if the Board has reasonable grounds for believing that an error has occurred in the return and give notice to the account manager of the Board's intention to do so no later than 12 months after the date on which the return is made.

(5) Sub-paragraph (1) is not to apply for 2017–18 to an account manager for an account which has been transferred to another account before the end of the claim period.][1]

1 Schedule inserted by the Individual Savings Account (Amendment No 2) Regulations, SI 2017/466 regs 2, 31 with effect from 6 April 2017.

[Payment to the Board of withdrawal charges

14 (1) For the purpose of paragraph 9(1)(*e*) of Schedule 1, an account manager liable under paragraph 8(3)(*b*) of that Schedule must pay to the Board within 14 days after the end of each claim period the amounts due in respect of the period.

(2) Where a person accountable under paragraph 8 of Schedule 1 is notified by the Board that an amount is due from them, that amount shall be treated for the purposes of Part 6 of the Management Act as if it were tax charged in an assessment and due and payable.

(3) The time limits in sections 34, 36 and 40 of the Management Act, as they apply to assessments, apply to amounts payable under sub-paragraph (2).

(4) An account investor may apply to the Board where a withdrawal charge has been wrongly made (including, without limitation, in circumstances not attributable to the account investor where paragraphs 4(2) or (3) would otherwise apply) for a refund of the amount of the withdrawal charge.

(5) An application under sub-paragraph (4) must be made within 4 years after the making of the withdrawal charge.

(6) If an application is made, the Board must make any necessary repayment of the charge.

(7) Paragraph 16 (appeals) applies to any decision of the Board in relation to a notification under sub-paragraph (2) or an application under sub-paragraph (4).

(8) The effect of any notification under sub-paragraph (2) is suspended by the making of an appeal under paragraph 16 until the appeal is determined or withdrawn.

(9) The effect of any decision in relation to an application under sub-paragraph (4) is not suspended by the making of an appeal in relation to such an application.

(10) A transfer from a Lifetime ISA to an account other than another Lifetime ISA of the account investor is to be treated as a withdrawal.][1]

1 Schedule inserted by the Individual Savings Account (Amendment No 2) Regulations, SI 2017/466 regs 2, 31 with effect from 6 April 2017.

[Payments and interest

15 (1) Any amount which is payable by virtue of an assessment made, or treated as made, under this Schedule is payable on the day following the end of the period of 30 days beginning with the day on which the notice of assessment is given.

(2) Sections 101 and 103 of the Finance Act 2009 apply for late payment interest on any amount that is payable to the Board under this Schedule which amount payable for this purpose is to be treated as income tax.

(3) Sections 102 and 103 of that Act apply for repayment interest on any amount that is payable by the Board under this Schedule which amount payable is to be treated as a repayment of an overpayment of income tax.][1]

1 Schedule inserted by the Individual Savings Account (Amendment No 2) Regulations, SI 2017/466 regs 2, 31 with effect from 6 April 2017.

[Appeals

16 (1) This paragraph applies to a review or appeal in respect of a decision made or notification given by the Board under any of paragraphs 3 (rejection of government bonus claim), 10 (purchase failure), 12 (recoupment of government bonus), 14 (withdrawal charges) and 15(1) (payments and interest).

(2) Notice of an appeal must be given to the Board within 30 days after the date on which notice of the decision or other notification was given.

(3) Notice of an appeal must—

(*a*) specify the grounds of appeal;

(*b*) be given in writing;

(*c*) contain sufficient information to identify the appellant and the decision against which the appeal is being made; and

(*d*) be signed, or authenticated in another way approved by the Board, by or on behalf of the appellant.

(4) Sections 49, 49A to 49I and 54 of the Management Act apply in relation to proceedings for a review and appeal.

(5) The following provisions apply where a person is appealing to the Tribunal.

(6) The Tribunal must either—

(*a*) dismiss the appeal, or

(*b*) quash the whole or part of the decision to which the appeal relates.

(7) The Tribunal may act as mentioned in sub-paragraph (6)(*b*) only to the extent that it is satisfied that the decision was wrong on one or more of the following grounds—

(*a*) that the decision was based, wholly or partly, on an error of fact;

(*b*) that the decision was wrong in law.

(8) If the Tribunal quashes the whole or part of a decision, it may either—

(*a*) refer the matter back to the Board with a direction to reconsider and make a new decision in accordance with its ruling, or

(*b*) substitute its own decision for that of the Board.

(9) The Tribunal may not direct the Board to take any action which they would not otherwise have the power to take in relation to the decision.

(10) A decision of the Tribunal made by virtue of this section has the same effect as, and may be enforced in the same manner as, a decision of the Board.

(11) In this paragraph "the Tribunal" means the First-tier Tribunal, or when determined by or under Tribunal Procedure Rules, the Upper Tribunal.][1]

[1] Schedule inserted by the Individual Savings Account (Amendment No 2) Regulations, SI 2017/466 regs 2, 31 with effect from 6 April 2017.

[Information to be given by account manager to account investor

17 If the account investor so requests in writing, an account manager who makes a payment to an account investor out of an account from which a withdrawal charge has been deducted must, within 30 days beginning with the day after the day of receipt of the request, furnish the account investor with a statement in writing showing—

(*a*) the gross amount of the payment,

(*b*) the amount deducted, and

(*c*) the amount actually paid.][1]

[1] Schedule inserted by the Individual Savings Account (Amendment No 2) Regulations, SI 2017/466 regs 2, 31 with effect from 6 April 2017.

[Extensions

18 The Board may authorise an extension to any period of time provided for under this Schedule.][1]

[1] Schedule inserted by the Individual Savings Account (Amendment No 2) Regulations, SI 2017/466 regs 2, 31 with effect from 6 April 2017.

1998/1871

INDIVIDUAL SAVINGS ACCOUNT (INSURANCE COMPANIES) REGULATIONS 1998

Revocation—These Regulations lapsed on the repeal of the enabling authority by FA 2007 ss 38(1), 114, Sch 7 paras 2, 55, Sch 27 Pt 2(7), for periods of account of insurance companies beginning on or after 1 January 2007, subject to transitional provisions in Sch 7 Pt 2 thereto.

1998/2620

FINANCE ACT 1995, SECTION 139(3), (APPOINTED DAY) ORDER 1998

Made by the Treasury under FA 1995 s 139(3) and FA 1998 Sch 8 para 7

Made . . . . *23 October 1998*

Commentary—*Simon's Taxes* **E5.501, E5.502**.

1 This Order may be cited as the Finance Act 1995, Section 139(3), (Appointed Day) Order 1998.

2 The day appointed for the purposes of sub-paragraphs (2) and (3)(*b*) of paragraph 3 of Schedule 27 to the Finance Act 1995 is 23rd November 1998.

3 The day appointed for the purposes of paragraphs 1, 2, 3(1) and 4 to 7 of Schedule 27 to the Finance Act 1995 is 1st August 1999.

4 Certificates under section 561 of the Income and Corporation Taxes Act 1988 which have been issued or renewed before the date on which this Order is made, for periods ending on or after the day appointed in paragraph 3 of this Order, shall cease to have effect at the end of the day preceding that appointed day.

1998/3081

CONTROLLED FOREIGN COMPANIES (EXCLUDED COUNTRIES) REGULATIONS 1998

Made by the Commissioners of Inland Revenue under TA 1988 s 748(1)(e) and TA 1988 s (1A)

Made . . . .*9 December 1998*
Laid before the House of Commons . . . .*10 December 1998*
Coming into force . . . .*31 December 1998*

Commentary—*Simon's Taxes* **D4.362**.

Press releases etc—IR 5-10-93 (non-statutory excluded countries list for accounting periods ending before 1 July 1999).

1 Citation, commencement and effect

(1) These Regulations may be cited as the Controlled Foreign Companies (Excluded Countries) Regulations 1998, shall come into force on 31st December 1998, and shall have effect with respect to any appropriate accounting period of a relevant company.

(2) In this regulation—

"appropriate accounting period" means an accounting period ending on or after the day to be appointed under section 199 of the Finance Act 1994 (corporation tax self-assessment);

"relevant company" means a company resident in the United Kingdom that had a relevant interest in a controlled foreign company at any time during an accounting period of the controlled foreign company ending in an appropriate accounting period of the relevant company;

"relevant interest" shall be construed in accordance with section 752A of the Taxes Act.

Note—The day appointed for the purpose of "appropriate accounting period" in reg 1 is 1 July 1999 by virtue of FA 1994 s 199 (Appointed Day) Order SI 1998/3173 art 2.

2 Interpretation

(1) In these Regulations unless the context otherwise requires—

"controlled foreign company" shall be construed in accordance with section 747(2) of the Taxes Act;

"gains" in relation to a controlled foreign company means any gains of that company other than a gain accruing to the company on a disposal of an asset which, on the assumption that the company was within the charge to corporation tax, would have fallen to be treated as a chargeable gain and would not have been taken into account as a receipt in computing the company's income or profits or gains or losses for the purposes of the Income Tax Acts;

"insurance company" means a company carrying on [the business of effecting or carrying out contracts which fall within Part I or II of Schedule 1 to the Financial Services and Markets Act 2000 (Regulated Activities) Order 2001][1];

"Schedule 1" and "Schedule 2" mean Schedule 1 and Schedule 2 respectively to these Regulations;

"section 748(1)(*e*)" means section 748(1)(*e*) of the Taxes Act;

"the Taxes Act" means the Income and Corporation Taxes Act 1988.

(2) For the purposes of these Regulations a company is resident in a territory if—

(*a*) by reason of the law of that territory relating to domicile, residence or place of management, the company is liable to tax in that territory, or

(*b*) if there is either no such law or such law does not apply to the company, the company is [incorporated in that territory and liable to tax in that territory on its profits;][2]

and references in these Regulations to the territory of residence of a company shall be construed accordingly.

(3) For the purposes of these Regulations a controlled foreign company is resident in a territory, within the meaning of paragraph (2), in an accounting period only if it is so resident throughout that accounting period.

(4) References in these Regulations to a branch or agency of a controlled foreign company are references to a branch or agency situated in a territory other than the territory of residence of the controlled foreign company.

Amendments—[1] In para (1), words in definition of "insurance company" substituted by the Financial Services and Markets Act 2000 (Consequential Amendments) (Taxes) Order, SI 2001/3629 art 180 with effect from 1 December 2001, immediately after the coming into force of the Financial Services and Markets Act 2000 ss 411, 432(1), Sch 20 (and SI 2001/3629 Pts 1 and 2).

[2] Words in para (2)(*b*) substituted by the Controlled Foreign Companies (Excluded Countries) (Amendment) Regulations, SI 2005/185 regs 2, 3 with effect from 31 March 2005. This amendment has effect in relation to accounting periods of companies resident outside the United Kingdom beginning on or after 3 December 2004.

However, where an accounting period of a company resident outside the United Kingdom—

(a) would, without amendment, have ended on or after 2 December 2004; but

(b) is amended on or after that date so as end before that date

an accounting period of the company shall, for the purposes of these regulations, be treated as having ended on that date: SI 2005/185 reg 6.

3 Limitation on apportionment of chargeable profits of a controlled foreign company—specified territories

The territory in which a controlled foreign company is required to be resident as respects an accounting period for the purposes of section 748(1)(*e*) is—

(*a*) as respects an accounting period beginning before 9th July 1998, any territory specified in Part I or in Part II of Schedule 1;

(*b*) as respects an accounting period beginning on or after that date, any territory specified in Part I or in Part II of Schedule 2.

4 Limitation on apportionment of chargeable profits of a controlled foreign company—conditions to be satisfied

[(A1) Paragraph (A2) specifies the condition which is required to be satisfied as respects an accounting period by a controlled foreign company, wherever it is resident in that accounting period.][1]

[(A2) The condition specified in this paragraph is that, during the accounting period, the company has not been involved in a scheme or arrangement the purpose, or one of the main purposes, of which is to achieve a reduction in United Kingdom tax.

In this paragraph—

"arrangement" means an arrangement of any kind, whether in writing or not; and

"United Kingdom tax" means corporation tax or any tax chargeable as if it were corporation tax.][1]

(1) Paragraph (2) specifies the condition which is required to be satisfied as respects an accounting period, for the purposes of section 748(1)(*e*), by a controlled foreign company which is resident in a territory specified in Part I of Schedule 1 or, as the case may be, in Part I of Schedule 2, in that accounting period.

(2) The condition specified is that the requirement with respect to the controlled foreign company's income and gains specified in regulation 5 is satisfied by the controlled foreign company in relation to that accounting period.

(3) Paragraph (4) specifies the conditions which are required to be satisfied as respects an accounting period, for the purposes of section 748(1)(*e*), by a controlled foreign company which is resident in a territory specified in column 1 of Part II of Schedule 1 or, as the case may be, in column 1 of Part II of Schedule 2, in that accounting period.

(4) The conditions specified in this paragraph are that the controlled foreign company—

(*a*) satisfies the requirement with respect to its income and gains specified in regulation 5 in relation to that accounting period, and

(*b*) at no time during that accounting period—

(i) is entitled to any tax exemption, tax reduction or other benefit, or

(ii) falls within any condition,

specified in column 2 of Part II of Schedule 1 or, as the case may be, in column 2 of Part II of Schedule 2, opposite the specification of the territory in which the controlled foreign company is resident.

Amendments—[1] Paras (A1), (A2) inserted by the Controlled Foreign Companies (Excluded Countries) (Amendment No 2) Regulations, SI 2005/186 reg 2 with effect from 31 March 2005. This amendment has effect in relation to accounting periods of companies resident outside the United Kingdom beginning on or after that date.

However, where an accounting period of a company resident outside the United Kingdom—

(a) would, without amendment, have ended on or after 31 March 2005, but

(b) is amended on or after that date so as to end before that date,

an accounting period of the company shall, for the purposes of these regulations, be treated as having ended on that date: SI 2005/186 reg 3.

5 Income and gains requirement

(1) The requirement with respect to the income and gains of a controlled foreign company as respects an accounting period is that the amount of its non-local source income arising in that accounting period does not exceed whichever is the greater of—

(*a*) £50,000 or, where that accounting period is less than twelve months in duration, that amount proportionately reduced, and

(*b*) an amount equal to ten per cent of its commercially quantified income arising in that accounting period.

(2) In paragraphs (1) and (3) "commercially quantified income" means the amount of profits of the controlled foreign company before tax, determined in accordance with generally accepted accounting standards other than an equity basis of accounting, [subject to the qualifications in paragraphs (2A) and (2C)][1].

[(2A) In computing a controlled foreign company's commercially quantified income capital profits and losses shall be disregarded.][1]

[(2B) Paragraph (2C) applies if a controlled foreign company—

(*a*) has invested, whether directly or indirectly, in an entity which is not a company, but is engaged in economic activity;

(*b*) is capable of exercising control over the entity; and

(*c*) the entity receives, whether directly or indirectly, at least 50 per cent. of its commercially quantified income, computed in accordance with paragraphs (2) and (2A) above from bodies which are associated or connected with the company, the reference to paragraph (2C) in paragraph (2) being disregarded for this purpose.][1]

[(2C) Where this paragraph applies, that part of the income and gains of the entity mentioned in paragraph (2B)(*a*), which bears to the whole the same proportion as the extent of control, determined in accordance with regulation 7(1A) below, bears to the whole ("the controller's share"), shall be treated, for the purposes of these Regulations, as the income and gains of the controlled foreign company by which the entity is controlled (if not already included in that income or those gains).][1]

(3) Subject to [paragraphs (3A) to (4) (special rules about connected persons and about banks and insurance companies)][1], for the purposes of paragraph (1) the amount of a controlled foreign company's non-local source income arising in an accounting period is the aggregate of the following amounts, namely—

(*a*) the gross amount of income consisting of distributions recognised as income in computing the commercially quantified income of that company for that period from the profits of companies not resident in the territory of residence of that company, other than branch or agency income;

(*b*) the gross amount of income and gains recognised as income in computing the commercially quantified income of that company for that period and deriving from loans to, or deposits with, persons not resident in the territory of residence of that company, or branches or agencies situated outside that territory of companies resident in that territory, other than branch or agency income and gains;

(*c*) the gross amount of income and gains recognised as income in computing the commercially quantified income of that company for that period in relation to royalties payable by persons not resident in the territory of residence of that company, or by branches or agencies situated outside that territory of companies resident in that territory, other than branch or agency income and gains;

(*d*) the gross amount of income and gains recognised as income in computing the commercially quantified income of that company for that period in relation to premiums and rents payable in respect of property situated outside the territory of residence of that company by persons not resident in that territory, or by branches situated outside that territory of companies resident in that territory, other than branch or agency income and gains;

(*e*) the amount of any branch or agency income and gains recognised as income in computing the commercially quantified income of that company for that period, calculated in accordance with regulation 6;

(*f*) the gross amount of any income not falling within any of sub-paragraphs (*a*) to (*e*) above that is recognised as income in computing the commercially quantified income of that company for that period and does not constitute income which either—

(i) is treated under the laws of the territory of residence of that company as accruing or arising in, or derived from, that territory, or

(ii) where there are no laws of that territory treating that income as accruing or arising in, or derived from, that territory or another territory, would be treated as accruing or arising in, or derived from, that territory if there were such laws in force in that territory and those laws were identical to the laws of the United Kingdom treating income as accruing or arising in, or derived from, a territory for the purposes of the Corporation Tax Acts, and which

(iii) in either case is within that territory's charge to tax.

[(3A) Where a controlled foreign company—

(*a*) has entered into one or more transactions with one or more connected or associated persons;

(*b*) the value to the company of that transaction, or the aggregate value to the company of all of those transactions, exceeds fifty per cent. of the commercially quantified income of the company; and

(*c*) the income and gains arising to, or the expenditure incurred by, the connected or associated person as a result of that transaction is taken into account—

(i) in computing the company's profits for tax purposes in the territory in which resides but not in computing its chargeable profits, or

(ii) in computing the company's chargeable profits, but not in computing its profits for tax purposes in the territory in which it resides; paragraph (3B) applies.][1]

[(3B) If this paragraph applies—

(*a*) the income and gains to which paragraph (3A)(c) applies shall be treated as non- local source income of the controlled foreign company; and

(*b*) an amount equal to which paragraph (3A)(c) applies shall be treated as non-local source income (and accordingly added to the amounts produced by sub-paragraphs (a) to (f) of paragraph (3) for the purpose of computing the amount of non-local source income).][1]

(4) Where—

(*a*) the controlled foreign company concerned is an institution carrying on the business of banking, or an assurance company, and

(*b*) income of that company falling within any of sub-paragraphs (*a*) to (*d*) of paragraph (3)—

(i) is an integral part of income arising or accruing to the company from the trade of banking or insurance carried on by the company, being income which, if the company were resident in the United Kingdom, would be income arising to the company from a trade for the purposes of the Corporation Tax Acts, and

(ii) is within the charge to tax of the territory of residence of that company,

the aggregate amount of that income shall be disregarded in computing the aggregate amount of the company's non-local source income.

Amendments—[1] Words in paras (2), (3) substituted, and paras (2A)–(2C), (3A), (3B) inserted, by the Controlled Foreign Companies (Excluded Countries) (Amendment) Regulations, SI 2005/185 regs 2, 4 with effect from 31 March 2005. This amendment has effect in relation to accounting periods of companies resident outside the United Kingdom beginning on or after 3 December 2004.

However, where an accounting period of a company resident outside the United Kingdom—

(a) would, without amendment, have ended on or after 2 December 2004; but

(b) is amended on or after that date so as to end before that date,

an accounting period of the company shall, for the purposes of these regulations, be treated as having ended on that date: SI 2005/185 reg 6.

6 Branch or agency income and gains

(1) The amount of any branch or agency income and gains as mentioned in regulation 5(3)(*e*) is—

(*a*) where the conditions specified in paragraph (2) are satisfied with respect to the branch or agency for the accounting period concerned, the amount (being not more than 10 per cent of the net amount of the profits of that branch or agency for that period) by reference to which the condition specified in sub-paragraph (*d*) of that paragraph is satisfied by that branch or agency;

(*b*) where the conditions specified in paragraph (2) are not satisfied with respect to the branch or agency for the accounting period concerned, the net amount or, where paragraph (3) applies, the gross amount of the branch or agency income and gains for that accounting period.

(2) The conditions specified in this paragraph are that—

(*a*) the branch or agency is situated in a territory specified in Part I or in Part II of Schedule 1 or, as the case may be, in Part I or in Part II of Schedule 2, and where the territory is one specified in Part II of Schedule 1 or in Part II of Schedule 2, at no time during the accounting period—

(i) is entitled to any tax exemption, tax reduction or other benefit, or

(ii) falls within any condition,

specified in column 2 of that Part opposite the specification of that territory;

(*b*) the profits of the branch or agency are within the charge to tax of that territory;

(*c*) the profits attributed to the branch or agency for tax purposes in that territory are those which it might be expected to make if it were a distinct and separate enterprise from the company of which it is a branch or agency, engaged in the same or similar activities under the same or similar conditions and dealing wholly independently with the company of which it is a branch or agency;

(*d*) not more than 10 per cent of the net amount of the profits of the branch or agency for the accounting period would, on the assumption that the branch or agency was not a branch or agency of the controlled foreign company but a separate controlled foreign company, be attributable to the aggregate of the gross amounts of any income and gains falling within any of sub-paragraphs (*a*) to (*d*) of regulation 5(3) and arising outside the territory in which the branch or agency is situated;

(*e*) amounts falling to be deducted in computing the taxable profits of the branch or agency, being amounts which are paid to, or are in respect of costs incurred by, the head office of the company of which it is a branch or agency, either—

(i) are liable to tax, or are disallowed as an expense, in the territory of residence of that company, or

(ii) where that company is liable to tax in its territory of residence in respect of the whole of its profits wherever arising, are not allowed as a deduction in computing the taxable profits of that company except where the amount in question is paid by that company to another person.

(3) This paragraph applies to a case where the net amount of the income and gains referred to in paragraph (1) in the accounting period concerned does not exceed an amount which would be equal to the aggregate of the gross amounts of any income and gains falling within any of sub-paragraphs (*a*) to (*d*) of regulation 5(3) in that period if branch or agency income and gains fell within those sub-paragraphs.

7 Interpretation of regulations 5 and 6

(1) In regulation 5(2) "capital profits or losses" means profits or losses arising in relation to chargeable assets.

[(1A) For the purposes of regulation 5(2B) a company ("C") is capable of exercising control over another entity—

(*a*) where C is entitled to a share of more than one half of the assets, or more than one half of the income of the entity; or

(*b*) where, if the entity were a company and C were resident in the United Kingdom, C would be treated as having control of it for the purposes of Chapter 4 of Part 17 of the Taxes Act (tax avoidance: controlled foreign companies).][2]

(2) In regulations 5(3) and 6 references to "branch or agency income" or to "branch or agency income and gains" are references to income and gains that—

(*a*) arise in or are derived from any branch or agency of a controlled foreign company, and

(*b*) fall within sub-paragraph (*e*) of regulation 5(3) in the accounting period concerned.

(3) In regulation 5(3)—

(*a*) the reference to "the gross amount" of any income in sub-paragraphs (*a*) and (*f*) are references to the amount of that income before deduction of expenses or reserves;

(*b*) the reference to "the gross amount" of any income and gains in sub-paragraph (*b*) is a reference to the amount of that income and those gains found—

(i) after excluding any gain or loss arising on any loan or deposit referred to in that sub-paragraph which is offset by a loss or gain on a contract ancillary to that loan or deposit which [is a derivative contract][1], and

(ii) after deducting any exchange losses attributable to the loans or deposits referred to in that sub-paragraph to the extent that those losses have not already been excluded by virtue of paragraph (i) above, but

(iii) before deducting other expenses or reserves;

(*c*) the references to "the gross amount" of any income and gains in sub-paragraphs (*c*) and (*d*) are references to the amount of that income and those gains found after deducting any exchange losses attributable to the royalties, premiums or rents referred to in those sub-paragraphs but before deducting other expenses or reserves;

and the references to "the gross amounts" in regulation 6(2)(d) and (3) shall be construed accordingly.

(4) In regulation 5(3) references to persons not resident in the territory of residence of a controlled foreign company do not include references to a company not so resident in circumstances where—

(*a*) the branch or agency of the company is situated in that territory, and

(*b*) the transaction giving rise to the income and gains in question of the controlled foreign company is made with that branch or agency.

(5) In regulation 6(1)(*b*) the reference to the gross amount of income and gains is a reference to the amount of that income or of those gains before deduction of expenses or reserves.

(6) In regulation 6(1)(*b*) the reference to "the net amount" of the branch or agency income and gains, and in regulation 6(2)(*d*) the reference to "the net amount" of the profits of the branch or agency concerned, are references to the amount of that income, or of those profits, after deduction of expenses but before tax, as determined in accordance with a generally accepted method of accounting for profits of branches or profits of agencies of companies.

(7) In paragraph (1) of this regulation a "chargeable asset" is any asset in the case of which one of the following conditions is satisfied, that is to say—

(*a*) a gain accruing to the company on a disposal of that asset on or after the date of coming into force of these Regulations would, on the assumption that the company was within the charge to corporation tax, have fallen to be treated in relation to the company as a chargeable gain and would not have been taken into account as a receipt in computing the company's income or profits or gains or losses for the purposes of the Income Tax Acts;

(*b*) a chargeable gain or allowable loss would, on the assumption mentioned in sub-paragraph (*a*), be deemed to have accrued to the company on any disposal of that asset on or after the date mentioned in that sub-paragraph.

(8) . . . [1]

Amendments—[1] In para 3(*b*)(i), words substituted for the words "would be a qualifying contract if the company were a qualifying company", and para (8) revoked, by the Controlled Foreign Companies (Excluded Countries) (Amendment) Regulations, SI 2002/1963 with effect for accounting periods beginning after 30 September 2002.

[2] Para (1A) inserted by the Controlled Foreign Companies (Excluded Countries) (Amendment) Regulations, SI 2005/185 regs 2, 5 with effect from 31 March 2005. This amendment has effect in relation to accounting periods of companies resident outside the United Kingdom beginning on or after 3 December 2004.

However, where an accounting period of a company resident outside the United Kingdom—

(a) would, without amendment, have ended on or after 2 December 2004; but

(b) is amended on or after that date so as to end before that date,

an accounting period of the company shall, for the purposes of these regulations, be treated as having ended on that date: SI 2005/185 reg 6.

SCHEDULE 1

ACCOUNTING PERIODS BEGINNING BEFORE 9TH JULY 1998

Regulations 3, 4 and 6(2)(a)

PART I

SPECIFIED TERRITORIES

Australia	Germany	Papua New Guinea
Austria	Ghana	Poland
Bangladesh	Honduras	Romania
Bolivia	Hungary	Senegal
Botswana	Iceland	Sierra Leone
Brazil	India	Slovak Republic
Canada	Indonesia	Solomon Islands
Colombia	Ivory Coast	South Africa
Czech Republic	Japan	Spain
Denmark	Korea, Republic of	Swaziland
Dominican Republic	Lesotho	Sweden
Falkland Islands	Malawi	Trinidad and Tobago
Fiji	Mexico	Turkey
Finland	New Zealand	Zambia
France	Nigeria	Zimbabwe
Gambia	Norway	

PART II

SPECIFIED TERRITORIES WITH QUALIFICATIONS

Argentina	Companies obtaining exemption from tax on income from transactions, activities or operations carried on in, or from goods located in, tax free areas in accordance with Law 19640 of 16th May 1972.
Belgium	**1** Companies which are regarded as Foreign Sales Corporations in section 922(*a*) of the United States Internal Revenue Code 1954 and which accordingly qualify for reduced Belgian taxation. **2** Companies approved under Royal Decree No 187 of 30th December 1982 as Co-ordination Centres.
Brunei	Companies qualifying as "pioneer companies" under the Investment Incentives Enactment 1975.

Bulgaria	Any company obtaining a tax benefit under Article 111 of Decree 56 of 9th January 1989 (Free Zone legislation).
Chile	Companies obtaining exemption from tax under Law 16,441 of 1st March 1966 on income from property located in the Department of Isla da Pascua or from activities developed in that Department.
China	Companies deriving income in or from the Hong Kong Special Administrative Region and submitting tax returns to the authorities of that Region.
Egypt	Companies which do not fall within the scope of Article 111, Book 2 of Law 157 of 1981 because they do not operate in Egypt.
Faroe Islands	Companies deriving interest from Faroese financial institutions from which tax is deducted at source under Law 4 of 26th March 1953.
Greece	**1** Companies whose profits are exempt from tax under Article 6(2)(*c*) of Law 3843/1958 (profits from the operation of ships under the Greek flag).
	2 Companies having profits exempt from company income tax by virtue of Article 25 of Law 25/1975 or by virtue of Law 89/1967 (profits from shipping and associated activities).
Ireland	**1** Companies obtaining relief or exemption from tax under Chapters 1 and 2 of Part 14 of the Taxes Consolidation Act 1997.
	2 Holding companies having income exempted from tax under section 44 in Chapter 3 of Part 3 of the Taxes Consolidation Act 1997.
Italy	Companies benefiting from paragraphs 12 to 14 of Article 11 of Law 413 of 30th December 1991 (Trieste Free Zone Financial and Insurance Centre).
Kenya	Companies having income exempted from tax under paragraph 11 of Schedule 1 to the Income Tax Act 1973.
Luxembourg	**1** Companies obtaining any special tax benefit under the Law of 31st July 1929, the decree of 17th December 1938 or the Grand Ducal Regulation of 29th July 1977 (holding companies).
	2 Any reinsurance company established in Luxembourg requiring authorisation under Article 92 of the Law of 6th December 1991.
Malaysia	**1** Companies exempt from tax in accordance with section 54A of the Income Tax Act 1967 (shipping).
	2 Companies subject to tax at 5 per cent in accordance with sections 60A and 60B of the Income Tax Act 1967 (inward reinsurance and offshore insurance).
	3 Companies deriving dividends from a company or companies deriving income from one or more of the activities referred to in paragraphs 1 and 2 above.
	4 Companies obtaining a tax benefit under the Offshore Companies Act (Island of Labuan) 1990.
Malta	**1** Companies entitled to exemption or relief from tax under section 11(2) of the Income Tax Act 1948.
	2 Companies obtaining exemption from tax under section 86 of the Merchant Shipping Act 1973.
	3 Companies obtaining exemption or relief from tax under section 30 of the Malta International Business Activities Act 1988.
	4 Companies obtaining exemption or relief from tax under section 18 of the Malta Freeports Act 1989.
Morocco	Companies receiving a tax benefit under Law 58-90 of 1992 (offshore financial centres).
Netherlands	Companies which are regarded as Foreign Sales Corporations under section 922(*a*) of the United States Internal Revenue Code 1954.
Pakistan	Companies deriving royalties, commissions or fees which are exempt from tax under paragraph 139 in Part I of the second Schedule to the Income Tax Ordinance 1979.
Philippines	**1** Companies authorised under Presidential Decree 1034 of 30th September 1976, or under Presidential Decree 1035 of 30th September 1976, to operate an offshore Banking Unit or a Foreign Currency Deposit Unit as defined in those Decrees.
	2 Companies receiving interest on deposits with a Foreign Currency Deposit Unit, or other interest subject to the reduced rates of tax under section 27(D) of the National Internal Revenue Code 1997.

Portugal	Companies obtaining tax benefits under Decree Law 502/85 of 30th December 1985, Articles 41 and 51(*g*) of the Tax Benefits statute (EBF) approved by Decree Law 215/90 of 31st August 1989 (free zone in Madeira), or Decree Law 501/85 of 28th December 1985 as implemented by Decree Law 63/87 of 5th February 1987 (free zone in the Azores).	
Puerto Rico	**1** Companies obtaining a tax benefit under section 2(*o*) of the Industrial Incentive Act 1978 (designated service industries).	
	2 Companies obtaining a tax benefit under section 25 of the International Banking Centre Regulatory Act 1989 (International Banking Entities).	
Singapore	**1** Any company obtaining tax concessions under Ministry of Finance Regulations pursuant to section 43A, and sections 43C to 43J, of the Income Tax Act.	
	2 Companies obtaining exemption from tax on the income of a shipping enterprise in accordance with section 13A of the Income Tax Act.	
	3 Companies obtaining relief from tax in accordance with sections 45 to 55 (international trade incentives), and sections 75 to 84 (warehouse and service incentives), of the Economic Expansion Incentives (Relief from Income Tax) Act.	
	4 Companies deriving dividends from a company or companies deriving income from one or more of the activities falling within paragraphs 1 to 3 above.	
Sri Lanka	Companies obtaining relief or exemption from income tax under any of the following provisions of the Inland Revenue Act 1979—	
	(*a*)	section 8(*c*)(iv) (foreign currency banking units);
	(*b*)	sections 10(*d*) and 15(*b*) (income derived from approved bank accounts);
	(*c*)	section 10(*e*) (interest of newly resident companies);
	(*d*)	section 15(*cc*) (services rendered outside Sri Lanka);
	(*e*)	section 15(*p*) (re-export of approved products).
Tanzania	Companies relieved or exempted from income tax under section 15(1) or (1A) of the Income Tax Act 1973.	
Thailand	Companies obtaining a tax benefit under Royal Decree 280 of 22nd September 1992 (offshore banking units).	
Tunisia	Companies obtaining exemption from, or reduction of, tax under Law 76-63 of 12th July 1976 (financial and banking institutions dealing with non-residents).	
United States	Domestic International Sales Corporations as defined in section 992(*a*) of the Internal Revenue Code 1954.	

SCHEDULE 2
ACCOUNTING PERIODS BEGINNING ON OR AFTER 9TH JULY 1998

Regulations 3, 4 and 6(2)(a)

PART I
SPECIFIED TERRITORIES

Australia
Austria
Bangladesh
Bolivia
Botswana
Brazil
Bulgaria
Canada
Colombia
Czech Republic
Denmark
Dominican Republic
Falkland Islands
Gambia
Germany
Ghana
Honduras
Iceland
India
Indonesia
Ivory Coast
Japan
Korea, Republic of
Lesotho
Malawi
Mexico
Papua New Guinea
Poland
Romania
Senegal
Sierra Leone
Slovak Republic
Solomon Islands
South Africa
Swaziland
Sweden
Trinidad and Tobago
Turkey

Fiji	New Zealand	Zambia
Finland	Nigeria	Zimbabwe
France	Norway	

PART II
SPECIFIED TERRITORIES WITH QUALIFICATIONS

Argentina Companies obtaining exemption from tax on income from transactions, activities or operations carried on in, or from goods located in, tax free areas in accordance with Law 19640 of 16th May 1972.

Belgium **1** Companies which are regarded as Foreign Sales Corporations in section 922(*a*) of the United States Internal Revenue Code 1954 and which accordingly qualify for reduced Belgian taxation.

2 Companies approved under Royal Decree No 187 of 30th December 1982 as Co-ordination Centres.

Brunei Companies qualifying as "pioneer companies" under the Investment Incentives Enactment 1975.

Chile Companies obtaining exemption from tax under Law 16,441 of 1st March 1966 on income from property located in the Department of Isla da Pascua or from activities developed in that Department.

China **1** Companies deriving income in or from the Hong Kong Special Administrative Region and submitting tax returns to the authorities of that Region.

2 From 20th December 1999, companies deriving income in or from the Macao Special Administrative Region and submitting tax returns to the authorities of that Region.

Egypt Companies which do not fall within the scope of Article 111, Book 2 of Law 157 of 1981 because they do not operate in Egypt.

Faroe Islands Companies deriving interest from Faroese financial institutions from which tax is deducted at source under Law 4 of 26th March 1953.

Greece **1** Companies whose profits are exempt from tax under Article 6(2)(*c*) of Law 3843/1958 (profits from the operation of ships under the Greek flag).

2 Companies having profits exempt from company income tax by virtue of Article 25 of Law 25/1975 or by virtue of Law 89/1967 (profits from shipping and associated activities).

Hungary Companies benefiting from the reduced rate of tax for extra-territorial companies under section 19(2) of Act LXXXI of 1996 on Corporate Tax and Dividend Tax.

. . . [1]

Italy Companies benefiting from paragraphs 12 to 14 of Article 11 of Law 413 of 30th December 1991 (Trieste Free Zone Financial and Insurance Centre).

Kenya Companies having income exempted from tax under paragraph 11 of Schedule 1 to the Income Tax Act 1973.

Luxembourg **1** Companies obtaining any special tax benefit under the Law of 31st July 1929, the decree of 17th December 1938 or the Grand Ducal Regulation of 29th July 1977 (holding companies).

2 Any reinsurance company established in Luxembourg requiring authorisation under Article 92 of the law of 6th December 1991.

Malaysia **1** Companies exempt from tax in accordance with section 54A of the Income Tax Act 1967 (shipping).

2 Companies subject to tax at 5 per cent in accordance with sections 60A and 60B of the Income Tax Act 1967 (inward reinsurance and offshore insurance).

3 Companies deriving dividends from a company or companies deriving income from one or more of the activities referred to in paragraphs 1 and 2 above.

4 Companies obtaining a tax benefit under the Offshore Companies Act (Island of Labuan) 1990.

Malta **1** Companies entitled to exemption or relief from tax at the discretion of the Minister responsible for finance under section 12(2) of the Income Tax Act 1948.

2 Companies obtaining exemption from tax under section 86 of the Merchant Shipping Act 1973.

3 Companies obtaining exemption or relief from tax under section 30 of the Malta International Business Activities Act 1988 or section 30 of the Malta Financial Services Centre Act 1988.

4 Companies obtaining exemption or relief from tax under section 18 of the Malta Freeports Act 1989.

Morocco Companies receiving a tax benefit under Law 58-90 of 1992 (offshore financial centres).

Netherlands **1** Companies which are regarded as Foreign Sales Corporations under section 922(*a*) of the United States Internal Revenue Code 1954.

2 A company ("the first company") receiving interest, rents or royalties in an accounting period directly or indirectly from a Dutch company ("the second company") which is connected with the first company within the meaning of section 839 of the Taxes Act, in circumstances where—

(*a*) the second company does not satisfy the income and gains requirement in regulation 5 as respects its accounting period in which the interest, rents or royalties were paid, and

(*b*) the aggregate of the non-local source income of the first company in its accounting period in question and the interest, rents and royalties received by it from the second company in that period exceeds whichever is the greater of—

(i) £50,000 or, where that period is less than twelve months in duration, that amount proportionately reduced, and

(ii) an amount equal to ten per cent of its commercially quantified income arising in that period.

Pakistan Companies deriving royalties, commissions or fees which are exempt from tax under paragraph 139 in Part I of the second Schedule to the Income Tax Ordinance 1979.

Philippines **1** Companies authorised under Presidential Decree 1034 of 30th September 1976, or under Presidential Decree 1035 of 30th September 1976, to operate an offshore Banking Unit or a Foreign Currency Deposit Unit as defined in those Decrees.

2 Companies receiving interest on deposits with a Foreign Currency Deposit Unit, or other interest subject to the reduced rates of tax under section 27(D) of the National Internal Revenue Code 1997.

Portugal Companies obtaining tax benefits under Decree Law 502/85 of 30th December 1985, Articles 41 and 51(*g*) of the Tax Benefits statute (EBF) approved by Decree Law 215/90 of 31st August 1989 (free zone in Madeira), or Decree Law 501/85 of 28th December 1985 as implemented by Decree Law 63/87 of 5th February 1987 (free zone in the Azores).

Puerto Rico **1** Companies obtaining a tax benefit under section 2(*o*) of the Industrial Incentive Act 1978 (designated service industries).

2 Companies obtaining a tax benefit under section 25 of the International Banking Centre Regulatory Act 1989 (International Banking Entities).

Singapore **1** Any company obtaining tax concessions under Ministry of Finance Regulations pursuant to section 43A, and sections 43C to 43K, of the Income Tax Act.

2 Companies obtaining exemption from tax on the income of a shipping enterprise in accordance with section 13A of the Income Tax Act.

3 Companies obtaining relief from tax in accordance with sections 45 to 55 (international trade incentives), and sections 75 to 84 (warehouse and service incentives), of the Economic Expansion Incentives (Relief from Income Tax) Act.

4 Companies deriving dividends from a company or companies deriving income from one or more of the activities falling within paragraphs 1 to 3 above.

Spain **1** Companies which are registered in the official register of the Canary Islands Special Zone (Zona Especial Canaria) established under Law 19/1994 and which benefit from the special low tax rate applied to such companies.

2 Companies benefiting from the alternative taxation regime for co-ordination centres established by the provincial governments of the Basque Country under laws pursuant to Norma Foral 3/1996 of 26th June 1996, Norma Foral 7/1996 of 4th July 1996, and Norma Foral 24/1996 of 5th July 1996.

Sri Lanka Companies obtaining relief or exemption from income tax under any of the following provisions of the Inland Revenue Act 1979—

(*a*) section 8(*c*)(iv) (foreign currency banking units);

(*b*) sections 10(*d*) and 15(*b*) (income derived from approved bank accounts);
(*c*) section 10(*e*) (interest of newly resident companies);
(*d*) section 15(*cc*) (services rendered outside Sri Lanka);
(*e*) section 15(*p*) (re-export of approved products).

Tanzania Companies relieved or exempted from income tax under section 15(1) or (1A) of the Income Tax Act 1973.

Thailand Companies obtaining a tax benefit under Royal Decree 280 of 22nd September 1992 (offshore banking units).

Tunisia Companies obtaining exemption from, or reduction of, tax under Law 76-63 of 12th July 1976 (financial and banking institutions dealing with non-residents).

United States Domestic International Sales Corporations as defined in section 992(*a*) of the Internal Revenue Code 1954.

Amendments—[1] Entry in respect of Ireland revoked by the Controlled Foreign Companies (Excluded Countries) (Amendment No. 2) Regulations, SI 2002/2406 with effect for accounting periods beginning after 10 October 2002.

1998/3132

CIVIL PROCEDURE RULES 1998

Made . . . . *10 December 1998*
Laid before Parliament . . . . *17 December 1998*
Coming into force . . . . *26 April 1999*

Note—These rules superseded the Rules of the Supreme Court (Revision), SI 1965/1776, with effect from 26 April 1999.

[PART 54
[JUDICIAL REVIEW AND STATUTORY REVIEW][2]][1]

Amendments—[1] This Part inserted by the Civil Procedure (Amendment No 4) Rules, SI 2000/2092, r 22, Schedule with effect from 2 October 2000 except in relation to an application for permission to make an application for judicial review in accordance with RSC Order 53 before that date.
[2] Part heading substituted by the Civil Procedure (Amendment) Rules, SI 2003/364 r 3 with effect from 1 April 2003 (by virtue of SI 2003/754).

54.1 Scope and interpretation

(1) [This Section of this Part][2] contains rules about judicial review.
(2) [In this Section[2]]—
(*a*) a "claim for judicial review" means a claim to review the lawfulness of—
(i) an enactment; or
(ii) a decision, action or failure to act in relation to the exercise of a public function.
(*b*)–(*d*) . . . [3]
(*e*) "the judicial review procedure" means the Part 8 procedure as modified by [this Section][2];
(*f*) "interested party" means any person (other than the claimant and defendant) who is directly affected by the claim; and
(*g*) "court" means the High Court, unless otherwise stated.

(Rule 8.1(6)(*b*) provides that a rule or practice direction may, in relation to a specified type of proceedings, disapply or modify any of the rules set out in Part 8 as they apply to those proceedings)][1]

Amendments—[1] Rule inserted as stated in note at the start of this Part, see above.
[2] Words substituted by the Civil Procedure (Amendment) Rules, SI 2003/364 r 5(*a*), (*b*) with effect from 1 April 2003 (by virtue of SI 2003/754).
[3] Para (2)(*b*)–(*d*) revoked by the Civil Procedure (Amendment No 5) Rules, SI 2003/3361 r 12 with effect from 1 May 2004.

[54.1A Who may exercise the powers of the High Court

(1) [A court officer assigned to the Administrative Court office who is—
(*a*) a barrister; or
(*b*) a solicitor,

may exercise the jurisdiction of the High Court with regard to the matters set out in paragraph (2) with the consent of the President of the Queen's Bench Division.
(2) The matters referred to in paragraph (1) are—
(*a*) any matter incidental to any proceedings in the High Court;
(*b*) any other matter where there is no substantial dispute between the parties; and
(*c*) the dismissal of an appeal or application where a party has failed to comply with any order, rule or practice direction.
(3) A court officer may not decide an application for—

(*a*) permission to bring judicial review proceedings;
(*b*) an injunction;
(*c*) a stay of any proceedings, other than a temporary stay of any order or decision of the lower court over a period when the High Court is not sitting or cannot conveniently be convened, unless the parties seek a stay by consent.

(4) Decisions of a court officer may be made without a hearing.

(5) A party may request any decision of a court officer to be reviewed by a judge of the High Court.

(6) At the request of a party, a hearing will be held to reconsider a decision of a court officer, made without a hearing.

(7) A request under paragraph (5) or (6) must be filed within 7 days after the party is served with notice of the decision.][1]

Amendments—[1] Rule 54.1A inserted by the Civil Procedure (Amendment No 2) Rules, SI 2012/2008 rr 2, 9(*b*) with effect from 1 October 2012.

54.2 [When this [Section][2] must be used

The judicial review procedure must be used in a claim for judicial review where the claimant is seeking—

(*a*) a mandatory order;
(*b*) a prohibiting order;
(*c*) a quashing order; or
(*d*) an injunction under section 30 of the [Senior Courts Act 1981][3] (restraining a person from acting in any office in which he is not entitled to act).][1]

Amendments—[1] Rule inserted as stated in note at the start of this Part, see above.
[2] Word in heading substituted by the Civil Procedure (Amendment) Rules, SI 2003/364 r 5(*c*) with effect from 1 April 2003 (by virtue of SI 2003/754).
[3] In para (*d*), words substituted by the Constitutional Reform Act 2005 s 59(5), Sch 11 para 1(2) with effect from 1 October 2009 (by virtue of SI 2009/1604).

54.3 [When this [Section][3] may be used

(1) The judicial review procedure may be used in a claim for judicial review where the claimant is seeking—

(*a*) a declaration; or
(*b*) an injunction.

(Section 31(2) of the [Senior Courts Act 1981][2] sets out the circumstances in which the court may grant a declaration or injunction in a claim for judicial review)

(Where the claimant is seeking a declaration or injunction in addition to one of the remedies listed in rule 54.2, the judicial review procedure must be used)

(2) A claim for judicial review may include a claim for damages[, restitution or the recovery of a sum due][4] but may not seek [such a remedy][4] alone.

(Section 31(4) of the [Senior Courts Act 1981][2] sets out the circumstances in which the court may award damages[, restitution or the recovery of a sum due][4] on a claim for judicial review)][1]

Amendments—Word in heading substituted by the Civil Procedure (Amendment) Rules, SI 2003/364 r 5(*c*) with effect from 1 April 2003 (by virtue of SI 2003/754).
[1] Rule inserted as stated in note at the start of this Part, see above.
[2] Words in paras (1), (2) substituted by the Constitutional Reform Act 2005 s 59(5), Sch 11 para 1(2) with effect from 1 October 2009 (by virtue of SI 2009/1604 art 2(*d*)).
[3] Word in heading substituted by the Civil Procedure (Amendment) Rules, SI 2003/364 r 5(*c*) with effect from 1 April 2003 (by virtue of SI 2003/754).
[4] In para (2), words inserted and substituted, and in words following para (2), words inserted by the Civil Procedure (Amendment No 5) Rules, SI 2003/3361 r 13 with effect from 1 May 2004.

54.4 [Permission required

The court's permission to proceed is required in a claim for judicial review whether started under this [Section][2] or transferred to the Administrative Court.][1]

Amendments—[1] Rule inserted as stated in note at the start of this Part, see above.
[2] Word substituted by the Civil Procedure (Amendment) Rules, SI 2003/364 r 5(*d*) with effect from 1 April 2003 (by virtue of SI 2003/754).

54.5 [Time limit for filing claim form

[(A1) In this rule—

"the planning acts" has the same meaning as in section 336 of the Town and Country Planning Act 1990;

["decision governed by the Public Contracts Regulations 2015" means any decision the legality of which is or may be affected by a duty owed to an economic operator by virtue of regulations 89 or 90 of those Regulations (and for this purpose it does not matter that the claimant is not an economic operator); and][3]

"economic operator" has the same meaning as in [regulation 2(1) of the Public Contracts Regulations 2015][3].][2]

(1) The claim form must be filed—

(*a*) promptly; and

(*b*) in any event not later than 3 months after the grounds to make the claim first arose.

(2) The time [limits][2] in this rule may not be extended by agreement between the parties.

(3) This rule does not apply when any other enactment specifies a shorter time limit for making the claim for judicial review.][1]

[(4) Paragraph (1) does not apply in the cases specified in paragraphs (5) and (6).

(5) Where the application for judicial review relates to a decision made by the Secretary of State or local planning authority under the planning acts, the claim form must be filed not later than six weeks after the grounds to make the claim first arose.

(6) Where the application for judicial review relates to a decision governed by [the Public Contracts Regulations 2015][3], the claim form must be filed within the time within which an economic operator would have been required by [regulation 92(2)][4] of those Regulations (and disregarding the rest of that regulation) to start any proceedings under those Regulations in respect of that decision.][2]

Amendments—[1] Rule inserted as stated in note at the start of this Part, see above.

[2] Para A1 inserted, in para (2), word substituted, and paras (4)–(6) inserted by the Civil Procedure (Amendment No 4) Rules, SI 2013/1412 r 4(*a*) with effect from 1 July 2013. This amendment does not apply to to an application for judicial review where the grounds arose before 1 July 2013 (SI 2013/1412 r 5(2).

[3] In para (A1), definition of "decision governed by the Public Contracts Regulations 2006" substituted, in definition of "economic operator", words substituted for words "regulation 4 of the Public Contracts Regulations 2006", and in para (6), words substituted for words "the Public Contracts Regulations 2006", by the Public Contracts Regulations, SI 2015/102 reg 116, Sch 6 para 11 with effect from 26 February 2015. This amendment does not extend to Scotland: SI 2015/102 reg 1(7). Definition of "decision governed by the Public Contracts Regulations 2006" previously read as follows—

"decision governed by the Public Contracts Regulations 2006" means any decision the legality of which is or may be affected by a duty owed to an economic operator by virtue of regulation 47A of those Regulations (and for this purpose it does not matter that the claimant is not an economic operator);".

[4] In para (6), words substituted by the Civil Procedure (Amendment No 3) Rules, SI 2016/788 r 11 with effect from 3 October 2016.

54.6 [Claim form

(1) In addition to the matters set out in rule 8.2 (contents of the claim form) the claimant must also state—

(*a*) the name and address of any person he considers to be an interested party;

(*b*) that he is requesting permission to proceed with a claim for judicial review; . . . [3]

(*c*) any remedy (including any interim remedy) he is claiming[; and

(Part 25 sets out how to apply for an interim remedy)

[(*d*) where appropriate, the grounds on which it is contended that the claim is an Aarhus Convention claim.

(Rules 45.41 to 45.44 make provision about costs in Aarhus Convention claims.)][3]

(2) The claim form must be accompanied by the documents required by [Practice Direction 54A][2].][1]

Amendments—[1] Rule inserted as stated in note at the start of this Part, see above.

[2] In para (2), words substituted by the Civil Procedure (Amendment No 2) Rules, SI 2009/3390 rule 29(*b*) with effect from 6 April 2010.

[3] In para (1)(*b*), word revoked, in para (1)(*c*), word inserted, and para (1)(*d*) inserted by the Civil Procedure (Amendment) Rules, SI 2013/262 r 18 with effect from 1 April 2013.

54.7 [Service of claim form

The claim form must be served on—

(*a*) the defendant; and

(*b*) unless the court otherwise directs, any person the claimant considers to be an interested party, within 7 days after the date of issue.]

Amendments—[1] Rule inserted as stated in note at the start of this Part, see above.

[54.7A (1) [This rule applies where an application is made, following refusal by the Upper Tribunal of permission to appeal against a decision of the First Tier Tribunal, for judicial review—

(*a*) of the decision of the Upper Tribunal refusing permission to appeal; or

(*b*) which relates to the decision of the First Tier Tribunal which was the subject of the application for permission to appeal.

(2) Where this rule applies—

(*a*) the application may not include any other claim, whether against the Upper Tribunal or not; and

(*b*) any such other claim must be the subject of a separate application.

(3) The claim form and the supporting documents required by paragraph (4) must be filed no later than 16 days after the date on which notice of the Upper Tribunal's decision was sent to the applicant.

(4) The supporting documents are—

(*a*) the decision of the Upper Tribunal to which the application relates, and any document giving reasons for the decision;

(*b*) the grounds of appeal to the Upper Tribunal and any documents which were sent with them;
(*c*) the decision of the First Tier Tribunal, the application to that Tribunal for permission to appeal and its reasons for refusing permission; and
(*d*) any other documents essential to the claim.

(5) The claim form and supporting documents must be served on the Upper Tribunal and any other interested party no later than 7 days after the date of issue.

(6) The Upper Tribunal and any person served with the claim form who wishes to take part in the proceedings for judicial review must, no later than 21 days after service of the claim form, file and serve on the applicant and any other party an acknowledgment of service in the relevant practice form.

(7) The court will give permission to proceed only if it considers—
(*a*) that there is an arguable case, which has a reasonable prospect of success, that both the decision of the Upper Tribunal refusing permission to appeal and the decision of the First Tier Tribunal against which permission to appeal was sought are wrong in law; and
(*b*) that either—
(i) the claim raises an important point of principle or practice; or
(ii) there is some other compelling reason to hear it.

(8) If the application for permission is refused on paper without an oral hearing, rule 54.12(3) (request for reconsideration at a hearing) does not apply.

(9) If permission to apply for judicial review is granted—
(*a*) If permission to apply for judicial review is granted
(*b*) if no request for a hearing is made within that period, the court will make a final order quashing the refusal of permission without a further hearing.

(10) The power to make a final order under paragraph (9)(*b*) may be exercised by the Master of the Crown Office or a Master of the Administrative Court.][1]

Amendments—[1] Rule 54.7A inserted by the Civil Procedure (Amendment No 2) Rules, SI 2012/2008 rr 2, 9(*c*) with effect from 1 October 2012.

54.8 [Acknowledgement of service

(1) Any person served with the claim form who wishes to take part in the judicial review must file an acknowledgement of service in the relevant practice form in accordance with the following provisions of this rule.

(2) Any acknowledgement of service must be—
(*a*) filed not more than 21 days after service of the claim form; and
(*b*) served on—
(i) the claimant; and
[(ia) where the person filing it intends to contest the application for permission on the basis that it is highly likely that the outcome for the claimant would not have been substantially different if the conduct complained of had not occurred, set out a summary of the grounds for doing so; and][2]
(ii) subject to any direction under rule 54.7(*b*), any other person named in the claim form,

as soon as practicable and, in any event, not later than 7 days after it is filed.

(3) The time limits under this rule may not be extended by agreement between the parties.

(4) The acknowledgement of service—
(*a*) must—
(i) where the person filing it intends to contest the claim, set out a summary of his grounds for doing so; and
(ii) state the name and address of any person the person filing it considers to be an interested party; and
(*b*) may include or be accompanied by an application for directions.

(5) Rule 10.3(2) does not apply.][1]

[(Section 31(3C) of the Senior Courts Act 1981 requires the court, where it is asked to do so by the defendant, to consider whether the outcome for the claimant would have been substantially different if the conduct complained of had not occurred.)][3]

Amendments—[1] Rule inserted as stated in note at the start of this Part, see above.
[2] Para (4)(*a*)(ai) inserted, and words following para (5) inserted, by the Civil Procedure (Amendment No 2) Rules, SI 2015/670 rr 4, 7, 8 with effect from 13 April 2015, being the date on which CJA 2015 s 84 comes into force (by virtue of SI 2015/778): see SI 2015/670 r 2(4)). This amendment does not apply to an application for judicial review where the claim form was filed before 13 April 2015: see SI 2015/670 r 12(2).

54.9 [Failure to file acknowledgement of service

(1) Where a person served with the claim form has failed to file an acknowledgement of service in accordance with rule 54.8, he—
(*a*) may not take part in a hearing to decide whether permission should be given unless the court allows him to do so; but

(*b*) provided he complies with rule 54.14 or any other direction of the court regarding the filing and service of—

(i) detailed grounds for contesting the claim or supporting it on additional grounds; and

(ii) any written evidence,

may take part in the hearing of the judicial review.

(2) Where that person takes part in the hearing of the judicial review, the court may take his failure to file an acknowledgement of service into account when deciding what order to make about costs.

(3) Rule 8.4 does not apply.][1]

Amendments—[1] Rule inserted as stated in note at the start of this Part, see above.

54.10 [Permission given

(1) Where permission to proceed is given the court may also give directions.

[(2) Directions under paragraph (1) may include—

(*a*) a stay of proceedings to which the claim relates;

(*b*) directions requiring the proceedings to be heard by a Divisional Court.][2]][1]

Amendments—[1] Rule inserted as stated in note at the start of this Part, see above.

[2] Para (2) substituted by the Civil Procedure (Amendment No 3) Rules SI 2010/2577 r 3 with effect from 20 October 2010: see SI 2010/2577 r 1(2).

54.11 [Service of order giving or refusing permission

The court will serve—

(*a*) the order giving or refusing permission; and

[(*ai*) any certificate (if not included in the order) that permission has been granted for reasons of exceptional public interest in accordance with section 31(3F) of the Senior Courts Act 1981; and][3]

(*b*) any directions,

on—

(i) the claimant;

(ii) the defendant; and

(iii) any other person who filed an acknowledgement of service.][1]

Amendments—[1] Rule inserted as stated in note at the start of this Part, see above.

[2] Para (*ai*) inserted by the Civil Procedure (Amendment No 2) Rules, SI 2015/670 rr 4, 9 with effect from 13 April 2015, being the date on which CJA 2015 s 84 comes into force (by virtue of SI 2015/778): see SI 2015/670 r 2(4)). This amendment does not apply to an application for judicial review where the claim form was filed before 13 April 2015: see SI 2015/670 r 12(2).

[54.11A Permission decision where court requires a hearing

(1) This rule applies where the court wishes to hear submissions on—

(*a*) whether it is highly likely that the outcome for the claimant would not have been substantially different if the conduct complained of had not occurred; and if so

(*b*) whether there are reasons of exceptional public interest which make it nevertheless appropriate to give permission.

(2) The court may direct a hearing to determine whether to give permission.

(3) The claimant, defendant and any other person who has filed an acknowledgment of service must be given at least 2 days' notice of the hearing date.

(4) The court may give directions requiring the proceedings to be heard by a Divisional Court.

(5) The court must give its reasons for giving or refusing permission.][1]

Amendments—[1] Rule 54.11A inserted by the Civil Procedure (Amendment No 2) Rules, SI 2015/670 rr 4, 10 with effect from 13 April 2015, being the date on which CJA 2015 s 84 comes into force (by virtue of SI 2015/778): see SI 2015/670 r 2(4)). This amendment does not apply to an application for judicial review where the claim form was filed before 13 April 2015: see SI 2015/670 r 12(2).

54.12 [Permission decision without a hearing

(1) This rule applies where the court, without a hearing—

(*a*) refuses permission to proceed; or

(*b*) gives permission to proceed—

(i) subject to conditions; or

(ii) on certain grounds only.

(2) The court will serve its reasons for making the decision when it serves the order giving or refusing permission in accordance with rule 54.11.

(3) [Subject to paragraph (7), the][3] claimant may not appeal but may request the decision to be reconsidered at a hearing.

(4) A request under paragraph (3) must be filed within 7 days after service of the reasons under paragraph (2).

(5) The claimant, defendant and any other person who has filed an acknowledgement of service will be given at least 2 days' notice of the hearing date.][1]

[(6) The court may give directions requiring the proceedings to be heard by a Divisional Court.][2]

[(7) Where the court refuses permission to proceed and records the fact that the application is totally without merit in accordance with rule 23.12, the claimant may not request that decision to be reconsidered at a hearing.][3]

Amendments—[1] Rule inserted as stated in note at the start of this Part, see above.
[2] Para (6) inserted by the Civil Procedure (Amendment No 3) Rules SI 2010/2577 r 4 with effect from 20 October 2010: see SI 2010/2577 r 1(2).
[3] In para (3), words substituted, and para (7) inserted by the Civil Procedure (Amendment No 4) Rules, SI 2013/1412 r 4(*b*) with effect from 1 July 2013. This amendment does not apply to to an application for judicial review where the claim form was filed before 1 July 2013 (SI 2013/1412 r 5(1)).

54.13 [Defendant etc may not apply to set aside

Neither the defendant nor any other person served with the claim form may apply to set aside an order giving permission to proceed.][1]

Amendments—[1] Rule inserted as stated in note at the start of this Part, see above.

54.14 [Response

(1) A defendant and any other person saved with the claim form who wishes to contest the claim or support it on additional grounds must file and serve—
(*a*) detailed grounds for contesting the claim or supporting it on additional grounds; and
(*b*) any written evidence,
within 35 days after service of the order giving permission.
(2) The following rules do not apply—
(*a*) rule 8.5(3) and 8.5(4) (defendant to file and serve written evidence at the same time as acknowledgement of service); and
(*b*) rule 8.5(5) and 8.5(6) (claimant to file and serve any reply within 14 days).][1]

Amendments—[1] Rule inserted as stated in note at the start of this Part, see above.

54.15 [Where claimant seeks to rely on additional grounds

The court's permission is required if a claimant seeks to rely on grounds other than those for which he has been given permission to proceed.][1]

Amendments—[1] Rule inserted as stated in note at the start of this Part, see above.

54.16 [Evidence

(1) Rule 8.6[(1)][2] does not apply.
(2) No written evidence may be relied on unless—
(*a*) it has been served in accordance with any—
(i) rule under this [Section][3]; or
(ii) direction of the court; or
(*b*) the court gives permission.][1]

Amendments—[1] Rule inserted as stated in note at the start of this Part, see above.
[2] Figure inserted by the Civil Procedure (Amendment) Rules, SI 2002/2058 r 21 with effect from 2 December 2002.
[3] Word substituted by the Civil Procedure (Amendment) Rules, SI 2003/364 r 5(*d*) with effect from 1 April 2003 (by virtue of SI 2003/754).

54.17 [Court's powers to hear any person

(1) Any person may apply for permission—
(*a*) to file evidence; or
(*b*) make representations at the hearing of the judicial review.
(2) An application under paragraph (1) should be made promptly.][1]

Amendments—[1] Rule inserted as stated in note at the start of this Part, see above.

54.18 [Judicial review may be decided without a hearing

The court may decide the claim for judicial review without a hearing where all the parties agree.][1]

Amendments—[1] Rule inserted as stated in note at the start of this Part, see above.

54.19 [Court's powers in respect of quashing orders

(1) This rule applies where the court makes a quashing order in respect of the decision to which the claim relates.
[(2) The court may—
(*a*)
(i) remit the matter to the decision-maker; and
(ii) direct it to reconsider the matter and reach a decision in accordance with the judgment of the court; or
(*b*) in so far as any enactment permits, substitute its own decision for the decision to which the claim relates.
(Section 31 of the Supreme Court Act 1981 enables the High Court, subject to certain conditions, to substitute its own decision for the decision in question.)][2]
(3) . . . [2]][1]

Amendments—[1] Rule inserted as stated in note at the start of this Part, see above.

[2] Para (2) substituted, and para (3) revoked, by the Civil Procedure (Amendment No 2) Rules, SI 2007/3543 r 7(*b*), (*c*) with effect from 6 April 2008 (SI 2007/3543 r 1(*b*)).

54.20 [Transfer

The court may—

(*a*) order a claim to continue as if it had not been started under this [Section][2]; and

(*b*) where it does so, give directions about the future management of the claim.

(Part 30 (transfer) applies to transfers to and from the Administrative Court)][1]

Amendments—[1] Rule inserted as stated in note at the start of this Part, see above.

[2] Word substituted by the Civil Procedure (Amendment) Rules, SI 2003/364 r 5(*e*) with effect from 1 April 2003 (by virtue of SI 2003/754).

(Section II of this Part is not relevant to this work, and has therefore been omitted)

1998/3173

FINANCE ACT 1994, SECTION 199, (APPOINTED DAY) ORDER 1998

Made by the Treasury under FA 1994 s 199(3)

Made . . . . *17 December 1998*

Commentary—*Simon's Taxes* **D1.1301**.

1 This Order may be cited as the Finance Act 1994, Section 199, (Appointed Day) Order 1998.

2 The day appointed for the purposes of Chapter III of Part IV of the Finance Act 1994 (corporation tax self-assessment) is 1st July 1999.

1998/3175

CORPORATION TAX (INSTALMENT PAYMENTS) REGULATIONS 1998

Made by the Treasury under TMA 1970 ss 59DA(8) and 59E, TA 1988 s 826A and FA 1998 s 30

Made . . . . *17 December 1998*

Laid before the House of Commons . . . . *17 December 1998*

Coming into force . . . . *7 January 1999*

Commentary—*Simon's Taxes* **D1.1328**.

Cross-reference—FA 2011 s 7 (increase in rate of supplementary charge – application of these regulations in transitional period where a company has an accounting period beginning before 24 March 2011 and ending on or after that date).

Press releases etc—IR Tax Bulletin April 2001 p 831 (discussion of some practical issues regarding quarterly interest payments and group payment arrangements).

1 Citation, commencement and effect

(1) These Regulations may be cited as the Corporation Tax (Instalment Payments) Regulations 1998 and shall come into force on 7th January 1999.

(2) These Regulations have effect in relation to accounting periods of companies ending on or after 1st July 1999.

2 [Interpretation

(1) In these Regulations—

"accounting period" shall be construed in accordance with Chapter 2 of Part 2 of CTA 2009;

"applicable accounting period" means any accounting period for which bank levy is chargeable in respect of the chargeable period determined in accordance with—

(*a*) paragraph 50 of Schedule 19 where bank levy is charged in relation to a relevant group; or

(*b*) paragraph 51 of that Schedule where bank levy is charged in relation to a relevant entity;

"large company" has the meaning given by regulation 3;

"Schedule 18" means Schedule 18 to the Finance Act 1998;

"Schedule 19" means Schedule 19 to the Finance Act 2011;

"the bank levy" means the tax charged in accordance with Schedule 19;

"the chargeable period" has the meaning given by paragraph 4 or paragraph 5 of Schedule 19 (as the case may be);

"the relevant entity" has the meaning given by paragraph 5 of Schedule 19;

"the relevant group" has the meaning given by paragraph 4 of Schedule 19;

"the responsible member" has the meaning given by paragraph 54 of Schedule 19;

"the Management Act" means the Taxes Management Act 1970; and

"the Taxes Act" means the Income and Corporation Taxes Act 1988.

(2) References in these Regulations to profits of a company in any accounting period are references to the company's augmented profits within the meaning given by section [279G][2] of CTA 2010.

(3) References in these Regulations to the total liability of a company for an accounting period are references to the amount of tax payable for that period by the company as calculated in accordance with paragraph 8(1) of Schedule 18.][1]

Amendments—[1] Reg 2 substituted by the Corporation Tax (Instalment Payments) (Amendment) Regulations, SI 2011/1785 regs 2, 3 with effect in relation to accounting periods ending on or after 1 January 2011.

[2] In para (2), reference substituted for "32" by the Corporation Tax (Instalment Payments) (Amendment) Regulations, SI 2014/2409 reg 2(1), (2) with effect in relation to accounting periods ending on or after 1 April 2015. Note that the commencement provision in SI 2014/2409 reg 1(2) originally read " accounting periods *beginning* on or after 1 April 2015". F(No 2)A 2015 s 39(1) corrected this error; the correction is treated as always having had effect. Consequently, for the purposes of the application of para (2), CTA 2010 ss 279F, 279G (definitions of "related 51% group company " and "augmented profits") have effect in relation to accounting periods beginning before, and ending on or after, 1 April 2015, and FA 2014 Sch 1 para 22 is to be disregarded (F(No 2)A 2015 s 39(2)).

3 Large companies

[(1) Subject to the following paragraphs in this regulation, a large company is a company whose profits in any accounting period exceed £1,500,000.][4]

[(1A) In relation to any applicable accounting period an entity which is the relevant entity or the responsible member for the purposes of Schedule 19 is a large company for that period for the purposes of these Regulations.][3]

(2) A company is not a large company as respects an accounting period if the amount of its total liability for that period does not exceed [£10,000][1] or, where the accounting period is less than twelve months, that amount proportionately reduced.

[This paragraph does not apply if a company is the relevant entity or the responsible member.][3]

(3) A company is not a large company as respects an accounting period if—

(*a*) its profits for that accounting period do not exceed £10,000,000, and

(*b*) apart from this paragraph, it was not a large company in the twelve months preceding that accounting period.

[This paragraph does not apply if a company is the relevant entity or the responsible member.][3]

[(3A) Any question whether a company is, or is not, a large company as respects an accounting period beginning on or after 17th April 2002 shall, so far as not falling to be determined by reference to the company's total liability, be determined as it would have been determined apart from [sections 330 (supplementary charge in respect of ring fence trades) and 331 (meaning of "financing costs" etc) of CTA 2010][3].][2]

(4) . . . [3]

[(5) If a company has one or more related 51% group companies in an accounting period—

(*a*) the amount specified in paragraph (1) is substituted by the following amount—

$$\frac{£1,500,000}{(1+N)}$$

where N is the number of related 51% group companies, and

(*b*) the amount specified in paragraph (3)(*a*) is substituted by the following amount—

$$\frac{£10,000,000}{(1+N)}$$

where N is the number of those related 51% group companies.

(5A) The number of related 51% group companies in paragraph (5) is determined by reference to the number of such companies existing at the end of the immediately preceding accounting period of the company or, if there is no immediately preceding accounting period or the immediately preceding accounting period did not end on the day before the accounting period concerned commenced, by reference to the number existing at the commencement of the accounting period concerned.

(5B) In paragraphs (5) and (5A) "related 51% group company" has the same meaning as in section 279F of CTA 2010.][4]

(6) For the purposes of paragraph (3)(*b*) a company shall be treated as not being a large company in the period of twelve months preceding the accounting period in question in either of the following circumstances—

(*a*) during any part of the period of twelve months it either did not exist or did not have an accounting period;

(*b*) a relevant accounting period of the company either falls within or ends in that period of twelve months.

(7) In paragraph (6) "relevant accounting period" means an accounting period as respects which, by virtue of the provisions of this regulation other than paragraph (3), the company was not a large company.

[(8) For the purposes of this regulation for an accounting period of less than 12 months the amounts in paragraphs (1) and (3)(*a*) and the amounts of £1,500,000 and £10,000,000 in paragraph (5) are proportionately reduced.][4]

Cross-reference—FA 2011 s 7 (increase in rate of supplementary charge – application of these regulations in transitional period where a company has an accounting period beginning before 24 March 2011 and ending on or after that date).

Amendments—[1] Sum in para (2) substituted by the Corporation Tax (Instalment Payments) (Amendment) Regulations, SI 2000/892 reg 2, with effect for accounting periods ending on or after 1 July 2000.

[2] Para (3A) inserted by FA 2002 s 92(5)–(7).

[3] Para (1A) inserted, in paras (2), (3) words inserted, in para (3A) words substituted, and para (4) revoked, by the Corporation Tax (Instalment Payments) (Amendment) Regulations, SI 2011/1785 regs 2, 4 with effect in relation to accounting periods ending on or after 1 January 2011.

[4] Paras (1), (8) substituted, and paras (5)–(5B) substituted for previous para (5), by the Corporation Tax (Instalment Payments) (Amendment) Regulations, SI 2014/2409 reg 2(1), (3) with effect in relation to accounting periods ending on or after 1 April 2015. Note that the commencement provision in SI 2014/2409 reg 1(2) originally read " accounting periods *beginning* on or after 1 April 2015". F(No 2)A 2015 s 39(1) corrected this error; the correction is treated as always having had effect. Consequently, for the purposes of the application of para (5B), CTA 2010 ss 279F, 279G (definitions of "related 51% group company " and "augmented profits") have effect in relation to accounting periods beginning before, and ending on or after, 1 April 2015 and FA 2014 Sch 1 para 22 is to be disregarded (F(No 2)A 2015 s 39(2)).

4 Instalment payments—transitional provision

(1) In relation to an accounting period of a large company ending on or after 1st July 1999 but before 1st July 2000—

(*a*) an amount equal to 60 per cent of the company's total liability for that period shall be treated as becoming due and payable in accordance with regulation 5;

(*b*) the balance of the company's total liability for that period shall be payable in accordance with section 59D(1) of the Management Act, that is, on the day following the expiry of nine months from the end of the accounting period ("the due and payable date").

(2) In relation to an accounting period of a large company ending on or after 1st July 2000 but before 1st July 2001—

(*a*) an amount equal to 72 per cent of the company's total liability for that period shall be treated as becoming due and payable in accordance with regulation 5;

(*b*) the balance of the company's total liability for that period shall be payable on the due and payable date.

(3) In relation to an accounting period of a large company ending on or after 1st July 2001 but before 1st July 2002—

(*a*) an amount equal to 88 per cent of the company's total liability for that period shall be treated as becoming due and payable in accordance with regulation 5;

(*b*) the balance of the company's total liability for that period shall be payable on the due and payable date.

Cross-reference—FA 2011 s 7 (increase in rate of supplementary charge – application of these regulations in transitional period where a company has an accounting period beginning before 24 March 2011 and ending on or after that date).

4A [Instalment payments—transitional provisions: the bank levy (applicable accounting periods ending on or before 19th July 2011 where company becomes a large company by virtue of regulation 3(1A))

(1) This regulation applies if—

(*a*) an entity ("E") is the relevant entity or the responsible member in relation to an applicable accounting period ("the period") which ended on or before 19th July 2011;

(*b*) E is a large company for the purposes of these Regulations only by virtue of regulation 3(1A); and

(*c*) accordingly, E would not otherwise be liable to make instalment payments in relation to the period.

(2) The total liability of E for the period shall be treated as becoming due and payable in accordance with regulation 5, but this is subject to paragraphs (3) to (5).

(3) An instalment payment which apart from this regulation would be treated as becoming due and payable on a date falling before 11th August 2011 shall be treated as not being due and payable.

(4) If there is no instalment payment which is treated as becoming due and payable on a date falling on or after 11th August 2011, the total liability of E shall be treated as becoming due and payable on 18th August 2011.

(5) If in relation to the period there is an instalment payment which is treated as becoming due and payable on a date falling on or after 11th August 2011, the amount of that instalment payment, or the amount of the first of those instalment payments, shall be increased by the adjustment amount.

(6) In paragraph (5) the adjustment amount is the aggregate of the amounts of the instalment payments which would have been treated as being due and payable, on a date falling before 11th August 2011, determined on the basis that—

(*a*) the provisions of Schedule 19 had effect on the date on which each instalment payment would have been treated as becoming due and payable; and

(*b*) paragraph (3) does not apply in relation to each instalment payment.][1]

Amendments—[1] Paras (4A)–(4D) inserted by the Corporation Tax (Instalment Payments) (Amendment) Regulations, SI 2011/1785 regs 2, 5 with effect in relation to accounting periods ending on or after 1 January 2011.

4B [Instalment payments—transitional provisions: the bank levy (applicable accounting periods ending on or before 19th July 2011 where company is a large company otherwise than by virtue of regulation 3(1A))

(1) This regulation applies if—

(a) an entity ("E") is the relevant entity or the responsible member in relation to an applicable accounting period ("the period") which ended on or before 19th July 2011; and

(b) E is a large company for the purposes of these Regulations otherwise than by virtue of regulation 3(1A).

(2) The total liability of E for the period shall be treated as becoming due and payable in accordance with regulation 5, but this is subject to paragraphs (3) to (5).

(3) An instalment payment which apart from this regulation would be treated as becoming due and payable on a date falling before 11 August 2011 shall be treated as not being due and payable to the extent that it includes an amount in respect of the bank levy.

(4) If, apart from paragraph (5), in relation to the period there is an instalment payment, or more than one instalment payment, which is treated as becoming due and payable on a date falling or after 11th August 2011, the amount of that instalment payment, or the amount of the first of those instalment payments, shall be increased by the adjustment amount.

(5) If, apart from this paragraph, in relation to the period there is no instalment payment which is treated as becoming due and payable on a date falling on or after 11th August 2011, a further instalment payment of an amount equal to the adjustment amount shall be treated as becoming due and payable on 18th August 2011.

(6) For the purposes of paragraphs (4) and (5) the adjustment amount is the difference between—

(a) the aggregate amount of the instalment payments which were treated as becoming due and payable before 11th August 2011, determined on the basis that the total liability of E did not include any liability to the bank levy; and

(b) the aggregate amount of those instalment payments including E's liability to the bank levy determined on the basis that paragraph (3) does not apply in relation to those instalment payments.][1]

Amendments—[1] Paras (4A)–(4D) inserted by the Corporation Tax (Instalment Payments) (Amendment) Regulations, SI 2011/1785 regs 2, 5 with effect in relation to accounting periods ending on or after 1 January 2011.

4C [Instalment payments—transitional provisions: the bank levy (applicable accounting periods beginning on or before 19th July 2011 and ending after that date where company is a large company by virtue of regulation 3(1A))

(1) This regulation applies if—

(a) an entity ("E") is the relevant entity or the responsible member in relation to an applicable accounting period ("the period") which began on or before 19th July 2011 and ends after that date;

(b) E is a large company for the purposes of these Regulations only by virtue of regulation 3(1A); and

(c) accordingly, E would not otherwise be liable to make instalment payments in relation to the period.

(2) The total liability of E for the period shall be treated as becoming due and payable in accordance with regulation 5, but this is subject to paragraphs (3) and (4).

(3) An instalment payment which apart from this regulation would be treated as becoming due and payable on a date falling before 11th August 2011 shall be treated as not being due and payable.

(4) The amount of the first instalment payment which is treated as becoming due and payable on a date falling on or after 11th August 2011 shall be increased by the adjustment amount.

(5) In paragraph (4) the adjustment amount is the aggregate of the amounts of instalment payments which would have been treated as becoming due and payable before 11th August 2011, determined on the basis that—

(a) the provisions of Schedule 19 had effect at the date on which each instalment payment would have been treated as becoming due and payable; and

(b) paragraph (3) does not apply in relation to each instalment.][1]

Amendments—[1] Paras (4A)–(4D) inserted by the Corporation Tax (Instalment Payments) (Amendment) Regulations, SI 2011/1785 regs 2, 5 with effect in relation to accounting periods ending on or after 1 January 2011.

4D [Instalment payments—transitional provisions: the bank levy (applicable accounting periods beginning on or before 19th July 2011 but ending after that date where company is a large company otherwise than by virtue of regulation 3(1A))

(1) This regulation applies if—

(a) an entity ("E") is the relevant entity or the responsible member in relation to an applicable accounting period ("the period") which began on or before 19th July 2011 and ends after that date; and

(b) E is a large company for the purposes of these Regulations otherwise than by virtue of regulation 3(1A).

(2) The total liability of E for the period shall be treated as becoming due and payable in accordance with regulation 5, but this is subject to paragraphs (3) and (4).

(3) An instalment payment which apart from this regulation would be treated as becoming due and payable on a date falling before 11 August 2011 shall be treated as not being due and payable to the extent that it includes an amount in respect of the bank levy.

(4) In relation to the period, the amount of the first instalment payment which is treated as becoming due and payable on a date falling on or after 11th August 2011 shall be increased by the adjustment amount.

(5) For the purposes of paragraph (4) the adjustment amount is the difference between—

(a) the aggregate amount of the instalment payments which were treated as becoming due and payable on a date falling before 11th August 2011, determined on the basis that the total liability of E did not include any liability to the bank levy; and

(b) the aggregate amount of those instalment payments including E's liability to the bank levy determined on the basis that paragraph (3) does not apply in relation to those instalment payments.][1]

Amendments—[1] Paras (4A)–(4D) inserted by the Corporation Tax (Instalment Payments) (Amendment) Regulations, SI 2011/1785 regs 2, 5 with effect in relation to accounting periods ending on or after 1 January 2011.

5 Instalment payments—principal provision

(1) Save as regards any amount falling within regulation 4(1)(*b*), (2)(*b*)[, (3)(*b*) or regulation 5A][1], amounts in respect of the total liability of a large company for an accounting period shall be treated as becoming due and payable as follows.

(2) Subject to paragraph (4), the amount of the company's total liability for that period or, as the case may be, the specified percentage amount shall be treated as becoming due and payable in instalments (not exceeding four) on the dates specified in paragraph (3).

(3) The first instalment payment shall be treated as becoming due and payable on the date which is six months and thirteen days from the start of the accounting period.

The final instalment payment shall be treated as becoming due and payable on the date which is three months and fourteen days from the end of the accounting period.

An additional instalment payment or additional instalment payments shall, where the length of the accounting period so allows, each be treated as becoming due and payable on the date which is three months after the date of the immediately preceding instalment payment.

(4) Where the length of the accounting period is such that the date which is three months and fourteen days from the end of the accounting period falls earlier than the date which is six months and thirteen days from the start of the accounting period, the amount of the company's total liability for that period or, as the case may be, the specified percentage amount shall be treated as becoming due and payable on the date which is three months and fourteen days from the end of the accounting period.

(5) Where in accordance with paragraph (2) amounts in respect of the amount of the company's total liability for an accounting period or in respect of the specified percentage amount are treated as becoming due and payable in instalments, the amount treated as becoming due and payable on any instalment payment date shall be calculated in accordance with paragraphs (6) to (8) and by reference to the formula—

$$3 \times \frac{CTI}{n}$$

where—

CTI is the amount of the company's total liability for that accounting period or the specified percentage amount [less any amounts falling within regulation 5A(1)][1], and

n is the number of whole months falling within that accounting period plus the appropriate decimal.

(6) The amount treated as becoming due and payable on the first instalment payment date is the smaller of CTI and the amount resulting from the formula specified in paragraph (5).

(7) The amount treated as becoming due and payable on each subsequent instalment payment date other than the final instalment payment date is the smaller of—

(*a*) the balance of the company's total liability for that accounting period or of the specified percentage amount carried forward from the immediately preceding instalment payment date, and

(*b*) the amount resulting from the formula specified in paragraph (5).

(8) The amount treated as becoming due and payable on the final instalment payment date is the balance of the company's total liability for that accounting period or of the specified percentage amount carried forward from the immediately preceding instalment payment date.

(9) In this regulation—

"the appropriate decimal" is a decimal, calculated to two places rounded arithmetically where necessary, representing the number of days in the accounting period falling outside the whole months falling within that period and corresponding to the fraction of which the numerator is the number of those days and the denominator is 30;

"the specified percentage amount" means an amount equal to the percentage specified in regulation 4(1)(*a*), (2)(*a*) or (3)(*a*), as the case may be.

Cross-reference—FA 2011 s 7 (increase in rate of supplementary charge – application of these regulations in transitional period where a company has an accounting period beginning before 24 March 2011 and ending on or after that date).

Amendments—[1] In para (1), words substituted for the words, and words in para (5) inserted, by the Corporation Tax (Instalment Payments) (Amendment) Regulations, SI 2005/889 regs 2, 3 with effect from 13 April 2005 (the commencement date). These amendments—

(a) have effect in relation to accounting periods of companies ending on or after 1 July 2005, but

(b) do not affect any amount which is treated as becoming due and payable, by virtue of SI 1998/3175 as they had effect before the coming into force of SI 2005/889, before the commencement date: SI 2005/889 reg 1.

5A [Instalment payments—ring fence profits and adjusted ring fence profits

(1) This regulation applies to amounts in respect of the liability to corporation tax and supplementary charge in relation to the ring fence profits and adjusted ring fence profits of a large company for an accounting period ("the ring fence amount").

(2) The ring fence amount shall be treated as becoming due and payable in instalments (not exceeding three) on the dates specified in paragraph (3).

(3) The first instalment payment shall be treated, subject to paragraph (4), as being due and payable on the date which is six months and 13 days from the start of the accounting period.

The final instalment payment shall be treated as being due and payable on the date which is 14 days from the end of the accounting period.

An additional instalment payment shall, where the length of the accounting period so allows, be treated as becoming due and payable on the date which is three months after the date of the first instalment payment.

(4) Where the length of the accounting period is such that the date which is 14 days from the end of the accounting period falls earlier than the date which is six months and 13 days from the start of the accounting period, the ring fence amount shall be treated as becoming due and payable on the date which is 14 days from the end of the accounting period.

(5) Where in accordance with paragraph (2) ring fence amounts are treated as becoming due and payable in instalments, the amount treated as becoming due and payable on any instalment payment date shall be calculated in accordance with paragraphs (6) to (8) and by reference to the formula—

(*a*) in relation to an accounting period of a large company ending on or after 1st July 2005 but before 1st July 2006, 3 × RFA / n, and

(*b*) thereafter, 4 × RFA / n

where—

RFA is the ring fence amount, and

n is the number of whole months falling within that accounting period plus the appropriate decimal.

(6) The amount treated as becoming due and payable on the first instalment payment date is the smaller of RFA and the amount resulting from the formula in paragraph (5).

(7) The amount treated as becoming due and payable on any subsequent instalment payment date other than the final instalment payment date is the smaller of—

(*a*) the balance of the company's ring fence amount for that accounting period carried forward from the immediately preceding instalment payment date, and

(*b*) the amount resulting from the formula specified in paragraph (5).

(8) The amount treated as becoming due and payable on the final instalment payment date is the balance of the company's ring fence amount for that accounting period carried forward from the immediately preceding instalment payment date.

(9) In this regulation—

"adjusted ring fence profits" has the meaning given in [330(2) of CTA 2010][2];

"the appropriate decimal" is a decimal, calculated to two places rounded arithmetically where necessary, representing the number of days in the accounting period falling outside the whole months falling within that period and corresponding to the fraction of which the numerator is the number of those days and the denominator is 30;

"ring fence profits" has the meaning given in [276 of CTA 2010][2];

"supplementary charge" means the charge imposed by [330(1) of CTA 2010][2].][1]

Cross-reference—FA 2011 s 7 (increase in rate of supplementary charge – application of these regulations in transitional period where a company has an accounting period beginning before 24 March 2011 and ending on or after that date).

Amendments—[1] Paragraph 5A inserted by the Corporation Tax (Instalment Payments) (Amendment) Regulations, SI 2005/889 regs 2, 4 with effect from 13 April 2005 (the commencement date). These amendments—

(a) have effect in relation to accounting periods of companies ending on or after 1 July 2005, but

(b) do not affect any amount which is treated as becoming due and payable, by virtue of SI 1998/3175 as they had effect before the coming into force of SI 2005/889, before the commencement date: SI 2005/889 reg 1.

[2] In para (9), in definitions of "adjusted ring fence profits", "ring fence profits" and "supplementary charge", words substituted,. by the Corporation Tax (Instalment Payments) (Amendment) Regulations, SI 2011/1785 regs 2, 6 with effect in relation to accounting periods ending on or after 1 January 2011.

5B [Instalment payments—the bank levy—anti-avoidance

(1) Paragraphs (3) and (4) apply if on or after 31st March 2011 there is a relevant amendment—

(a) in relation to the accounting period of an entity (E) which is the chargeable member; or

(b) in relation to the accounting periods of E and any other chargeable member; and

as a consequence of the relevant amendment there is no chargeable member which meets, or would meet, the requirements of paragraph 54(3) or (5) of Schedule 19 (meaning of the responsible member) at the end of the chargeable period.

(2) In relation to E and, where relevant, any other chargeable member a relevant amendment is an alteration to—

(a) the ending of an accounting period, as a result of an event referred to in section 10 (end of accounting period) or section 12 (companies being wound up) of CTA 2009; or

(b) the commencement of an accounting period, as a result of an event referred to in section 9 (beginning of an accounting period) or section 12(5) of CTA 2009;

the main purpose, or one of the main purposes, of which is to obtain a tax advantage.

(3) Where this paragraph applies for the purposes of ascertaining the dates on which instalment payments are treated as becoming due and payable in accordance with regulation 5(3), the applicable accounting period of the entity that is the responsible member in relation to the chargeable period is to be treated as beginning and ending on the dates on which the chargeable period begins and ends ("the assumption").

(4) Where paragraph (3) applies, the assumption will apply in relation to any applicable accounting periods that relate to a subsequent chargeable period where there is no chargeable member which meets the requirements of paragraph 54(3) or (5) of Schedule 19.

(5) In this regulation—

"tax advantage" has the same meaning as in section 1139 of CTA 2010; and

"the chargeable member" has the meaning given by paragraph 54(2) of Schedule 19.][1]

Amendments—[1] Reg 5B inserted by the Corporation Tax (Instalment Payments) (Amendment) Regulations, SI 2011/1785 regs 2, 7 with effect in relation to accounting periods ending on or after 1 January 2011.

6 Repayment of amounts in respect of a large company's total liability for an accounting period

(1) This regulation applies where a large company—

(*a*) has paid an amount or amounts by way of instalments in respect of its total liability for an accounting period in accordance with regulation [4A, 4B, 4C, 4D, 5, 5A or 5B (as the case may be)][2], and

(*b*) subsequently has grounds for believing that, by reason of a change in the circumstances of the company since the payment or payments were made—

(i) the amount of its total liability for that period is likely to be less than previously calculated, and

(ii) the aggregate amount so paid exceeds the aggregate amount ("the revised aggregate amount") that would have been treated as becoming due and payable by the relevant date having regard to the revised calculation of that liability.

(2) The company may, by notice given to an officer of [Revenue and Customs][2], make a claim to an officer of [Revenue and Customs][2] for the repayment of so much of the aggregate amount so paid as in the company's view exceeds the revised aggregate amount.

(3) The notice under paragraph (2) must state—

(*a*) the amount which the company considers should be repaid, and

(*b*) the grounds referred to in paragraph (1)(*b*).

(4) If the company has appealed against an amendment of an assessment, or an assessment, in respect of the amount of its total liability for the accounting period concerned, and the appeal has not been finally determined, it may apply to the [tribunal][1] to whom the appeal stands referred for a determination of the amount which should be repaid to the company pending determination of the amount of its total liability for that accounting period.

[(5) Any claim under paragraph (2) or application under paragraph (4) is to be subject to the relevant provisions of Part 5 of the Taxes Management Act 1970 (see, in particular, section 48(2)(*b*) of that Act).][1]

(6) If the company makes an application under section 55(3) or (4) of the Management Act (application to postpone payment pending determination of appeal), that application may be combined with an application under paragraph (4).

(7) In paragraph (1)(*b*) "the relevant date" means the date on which a claim under paragraph (2) is made.

(8) Section 59DA of the Management Act (claim for repayment in advance of liability being established) shall not apply in any case where this regulation applies.

Cross-reference—FA 2011 s 7 (increase in rate of supplementary charge – application of these regulations in transitional period where a company has an accounting period beginning before 24 March 2011 and ending on or after that date).

FA 2012 Sch 34 para 12(6) (references in para (1)(*a*) to regs 4A, 4B, 4C, 4D, 5, 5A or 5B are to be read as including a reference to FA 2012 Sch 34 para 12(1)–(5)).

FA 2013 s 200(11) (references in para (1)(*a*) to regs 4A, 4B, 4C, 4D, 5, 5A or 5B are to be read as including a reference to FA 2013 s 200(6)–(10)).

FA 2015 s 76(10)(*a*) (references in para (1)(*a*) to regs 4A, 4B, 4C, 4D, 5, 5A or 5B are to be read as including a reference to FA 2015 s 76(5)–(9)).

F(No 2)A 2015 Sch 2 para 1(8) (references in para (1)(*a*) to regs 4A, 4B, 4C, 4D, 5, 5A or 5B are to be read as including a reference to F(No 2)A 2015 Sch 2 para 1(4)–(7)).

F(No 2)A 2015 Sch 3 paras 14(9), 16(9) (references in para (1)(*a*) to regs 4A, 4B, 4C, 4D, 5, 5A or 5B are to be read as including a reference to F(No 2)A 2015 Sch 1 para 14(5)–(8)).

Amendments—[1] In para (4), word substituted, and para (5) substituted, by the Transfer of Tribunal Functions and Revenue and Customs Appeals Order, SI 2009/56 art 3, Sch 2 paras 48, 49 with effect from 1 April 2009.

[2] In para (1)(*a*), words substituted, and in para (2), words substituted in both places, by the Corporation Tax (Instalment Payments) (Amendment) Regulations, SI 2011/1785 regs 2, 8 with effect in relation to accounting periods ending on or after 1 January 2011.

6A [Allocation of payments

(1) This regulation applies where—

- (a) an entity (E) is either—
  - (i) the relevant entity; or
  - (ii) the responsible member; and
- (b) there has been an underpayment of E's total liability for an applicable accounting period.

(2) Any payment made by E in respect of that applicable accounting period shall be treated—

- (a) as a payment in respect of any amount of the bank levy which is unpaid for the applicable accounting period; and
- (b) to the extent that the payment exceeds the unpaid amount of the bank levy, as a payment in respect of corporation tax other than the bank levy for the applicable accounting period.

(3) Whether there has been an underpayment of E's total liability shall be ascertained in accordance with the provisions of Schedule 18.".

Amendments—[1] Reg 6A inserted by the Corporation Tax (Instalment Payments) (Amendment) Regulations, SI 2011/1785 regs 2, 9 with effect in relation to accounting periods ending on or after 1 January 2011.

7 Interest on unpaid amounts of a large company's total liability for an accounting period

(1) Section 87A of the Management Act shall apply in relation to any unpaid amount in respect of the total liability of a large company for an accounting period, with the modifications specified in paragraphs (2) to (5).

(2) After subsection (1) there shall be inserted the following subsection—

"(1A) An amount or amounts treated as becoming due and payable in respect of the total liability of a large company for an accounting period in accordance with regulation [4A, 4B, 4C, 4D, 5, 5A or 5B (as the case may be)][1] of the Corporation Tax (Instalment Payments) Regulations 1998 shall carry interest at the rate applicable under section 178 of the Finance Act 1989 from the date or dates specified in [the regulation in question][1] as the date or dates when that amount or those amounts are treated as becoming due and payable until payment."

(3) In subsection (2)—

- (*a*) for the words "Subsection (1) above applies" there shall be substituted "Subsections (1) and (1A) above apply";
- (*b*) for the words "that subsection" there shall be substituted "those subsections".

(4) In subsection (3) there shall be added at the end the words ", and the reference in subsection (1A) above to the date or dates when an amount or amounts are treated as becoming due and payable in respect of the total liability of a large company for an accounting period is a reference to the date or dates when that amount or those amounts are treated as having become due and payable by the company".

(5) After subsection (9) there shall be added—

"(10) In subsections (1A) and (3) above "large company" has the meaning given by regulation 3 of the Corporation Tax (Instalment Payments) Regulations 1998."

Cross-reference—FA 2011 s 7 (increase in rate of supplementary charge – application of these regulations in transitional period where a company has an accounting period beginning before 24 March 2011 and ending on or after that date).

FA 2012 Sch 34 para 12(6) (references in para (2) to regs 4A, 4B, 4C, 4D, 5, 5A or 5B are to be read as including a reference to FA 2012 Sch 34 para 12(1)–(5)).
FA 2013 s 200(11) (references in para (2) to regs 4A, 4B, 4C, 4D, 5, 5A or 5B are to be read as including a reference to FA 2013 s 200(6)–(10), and reference "the regulation in question" is to be read accordingly).
FA 2015 s 76(10)(*a*) (references in para (2) to regs 4A, 4B, 4C, 4D, 5, 5A or 5B are to be read as including a reference to FA 2015 s 76(5)–(9)), and reference to "the regulation in question" is to be read accordingly).
F(No 2)A 2015 Sch 2 para 1(8) (references in para (2) to regs 4A, 4B, 4C, 4D, 5, 5A or 5B are to be read as including a reference to F(No 2)A 2015 Sch 2 para 1(4)–(7), and reference to "that regulation" is to be read accordingly).
F(No 2)A 2015 Sch 3 paras 14(9), 16(9) (references in para (2) to regs 4A, 4B, 4C, 4D, 5, 5A or 5B are to be read as including a reference to F(No 2)A 2015 Sch 1 para 14(5)–(8), and reference to "the regulation in question" is to be read accordingly).

Amendments—[1] In para (2), words substituted by the Corporation Tax (Instalment Payments) (Amendment) Regulations, SI 2011/1785 regs 2, 10 with effect in relation to accounting periods ending on or after 1 January 2011.

8 Interest on overpaid amounts of a company's total liability for an accounting period

(1) Section 826 of the Taxes Act shall apply in relation to—

(*a*) an amount or amounts paid by a large company in accordance with regulation [4A, 4B, 4C, 4D, 5, 5A or 5B,][2] in respect of its total liability for an accounting period, and

(*b*) an amount or amounts paid by a company that is not a large company in an accounting period in respect of its total liability for that accounting period, where the payment is made prior to the day following the expiry of nine months from the end of that accounting period,

with the modifications specified in paragraphs (2) and (3).

(2) In subsection (1)—

(*a*) after paragraph (*c*) there shall be inserted "[or

[(*ca*)] [2] the total amount paid by a large company (as defined in regulation 3 of the Corporation Tax (Instalment Payment) Regulations 1998) up to a point in time in respect of its total liability for an accounting period in accordance with regulation [4A, 4B, 4C, 4D, 5, 5A or 5B][2] of those Regulations exceeds the amount that is treated as having become due and payable by the company for that period at that time in accordance with that regulation, or

[(*cb*)] [2]an amount paid by a company that is not a large company in an accounting period in respect of the amount of its total liability for that period is paid prior to the day following the expiry of nine months from the end of that period ('the normal due date'),";

(*b*) for the words "the repayment or payment shall" there shall be substituted the words "or, in a case to which paragraph [(*ca*)][2] above applies, until the date on which the excess amount arising as mentioned in that paragraph is extinguished or, in a case to which paragraph [(*cb*)][2] above applies, until the normal due date, the repayment or payment or excess amount shall".

(3) After subsections (3) there shall be inserted—

"[(3ZA)] [2] In relation to an excess amount in respect of a company's total liability arising as mentioned in subsection [(1)(*ca*)][2] above, the material date is the date on which the first instalment payment for the accounting period concerned is treated as becoming due as mentioned in regulation [4A, 4B, 4C, 4D, 5(3), 5A(3) or 5B(3)][2] of the Corporation Tax (Instalment Payments) Regulations 1998 or, if later, the date on which the excess amount arises.

[(3ZB)] [2] In relation to a case falling within subsection [(1)(*cb*)][2] above—

(*a*) if the payment for the accounting period concerned was made on or before the date which, if the company had been a large company, would have been the date on which the first instalment payment for that accounting period would have been treated as becoming due as mentioned in regulation 5(3) [or 5A(3)][2] of the Regulations referred to in subsection [(3ZA)][2] above, the material date is that date, or

(*b*) if the payment for the accounting period concerned was made later than the date referred to in paragraph (*a*) above, the material date is the date on which that payment was made."

Cross-reference—FA 2011 s 7 (increase in rate of supplementary charge – application of these regulations in transitional period where a company has an accounting period beginning before 24 March 2011 and ending on or after that date).
FA 2012 Sch 34 para 12(6) (references in paras (1)(*a*), (2)(*a*) to regs 4A, 4B, 4C, 4D, 5, 5A or 5B are to be read as including a reference to FA 2012 Sch 34 para 12(1)–(5)).
FA 2013 s 200(11) (references in para (1)(*a*), (2)(*a*) to regs 4A, 4B, 4C, 4D, 5, 5A or 5B are to be read as including a reference to FA 2013 s 200(6)–(10); and reference to "that regulation" is to be read accordingly).
FA 2015 s 76(10)(*a*) (references in paras (1)(*a*), (2)(*a*) to regs 4A, 4B, 4C, 4D, 5, 5A or 5B are to be read as including a reference to FA 2015 s 76(5)–(9)), and reference to "that regulation" is to be read accordingly).
F(No 2)A 2015 Sch 2 para 1(8) (references in paras (1)(*a*), (2)(*a*) to regs 4A, 4B, 4C, 4D, 5, 5A or 5B are to be read as including a reference to F(No 2)A 2015 Sch 2 para 1(4)–(7), and reference to "that regulation" is to be read accordingly).

F(No 2)A 2015 Sch 3 paras 14(9), 16(9) (references in para (1)(*a*), (2)(*a*) to regs 4A, 4B, 4C, 4D, 5, 5A or 5B are to be read as including a reference to F(No 2)A 2015 Sch 1 para 14(5)–(8), and reference to "that regulation" is to be read accordingly).

Amendments—[1] Words inserted by the Corporation Tax (Instalment Payments) (Amendment) Regulations, SI 2005/889 regs 2, 7 with effect from 13 April 2005 (the commencement date). These amendments—

(a) have effect in relation to accounting periods of companies ending on or after 1 July 2005, but

(b) do not affect any amount which is treated as becoming due and payable, by virtue of SI 1998/3175 as they had effect before the coming into force of SI 2005/889, before the commencement date: SI 2005/889 reg 1.

[2] In para (1), words substituted, in para (2)(*a*), the inserted para (*d*) renumbered as para (*ca*), words substituted, and para (*e*) renumbered as para (*cb*), in para (2)(*b*), "(ca)" substituted for "(d)" and "(cb)" substituted for "(e)", in para (3), the inserted sub-s (3A) renumbered as sub-s (3ZA) and in that sub-s "(1)(ca)" substituted for "(1)(d)" and words substituted for words "5(3) or 5A(3)", and the inserted sub-s (3B) renumbered as sub-s (3ZB) and in that sub-s "(1)(cb)" substituted for "(1)(e)" and "(3ZA)" substituted for "(3A)", by the Corporation Tax (Instalment Payments) (Amendment) Regulations, SI 2011/1785 regs 2, 11 with effect in relation to accounting periods ending on or after 1 January 2011.

9 [Consequential amendment of Chapter 4 of Part 22 of CTA 2010

(1) Chapter 4 of Part 22 of CTA 2010 (surrender of tax refund within a group) applies with the modifications specified in paragraphs (2) to (5) in any case where a tax refund is due to be made to the surrendering company in respect of an amount paid in respect of its total liability for an accounting period and—

(a) either the surrendering company or the recipient company referred to in that Chapter is a large company as respects that accounting period; or

(b) both the surrendering company and the recipient company referred to in that Chapter are large companies as respects that accounting period.

(2) In section 963 (power to surrender tax refund), after subsection (2) insert—

"(2A) If, and to the extent that, the tax refund surrendered is within subsection (4)(c) and is of an amount paid in respect of the surrendering company's bank levy liability for the accounting period, the requirement in subsection (2)(b) is to be read as a requirement that the surrendering company and the recipient company are both entities which are jointly and severally liable for the surrendering company's bank levy liability for that period in accordance with paragraph 53 of Schedule 19 to the Finance Act 2011.

(2B) In subsection (2A) the reference to the surrendering company's bank levy liability for the accounting period is to any liability within paragraph 53(8) of that Schedule which the company has for that accounting period.".

(3) In subsection (4) of that section—

(a) omit the "or" at the end of paragraph (a); and

(b) after paragraph (b) insert—

", or

(c) the repayment in whole or in part of any amount paid by way of an instalment under the Corporation Tax (Instalment Payments) Regulations 1998 in respect of the company's total liability for the period (within the meaning of regulation 2(3)).".

(4) In section 964 (effects of surrender of tax refund), in subsection (6), after "refund" insert "other than a refund of instalment corporation tax".

(5) After that subsection insert—

"(6A) For the purpose of this Chapter "the relevant date", in relation to a refund of instalment corporation tax, means—

(a) in so far as the refund falls to be treated in accordance with subsections (6C) to (6E) as consisting of a repayment of the whole or any part of a payment made on or before the earliest due date, that date, and

(b) in so far as the refund falls to be treated in accordance with those subsections as consisting of the repayment of the whole or any part of a payment made after the earliest due date, the date on which the payment was made.

(6B) For the purposes of subsection (6A), the earliest due date, in relation to a refund of instalment corporation tax, is—

(a) where the surrendering company is a large company for the relevant accounting period, the earliest date on which any amount is treated as having become due and payable by that company under regulation 4A, 4B, 4C, 4D, 5, 5A or 5B of the Corporation Tax (Instalment Payments) Regulations 1998 in respect of that company's total liability for that period, and

(b) where the surrendering company is not a large company for that accounting period, the date that would have been the earliest due date under paragraph (a) had it been a large company for that period.

(6C) For the purposes of subsection (6A), at the same time as giving notice under section 963(2) in the case of any refund of instalment corporation tax relating to any accounting period, the surrendering company must also give notice to an officer of Revenue and Customs identifying the extent to which it requires the refund to be treated as consisting of amounts comprised in any payment or payments made for that period.

(6D) Where, in a case to which subsection (6C) applies, an officer of Revenue and Customs notifies the surrendering company that the amount of the refund of instalment corporation tax relating to the accounting period is less than the aggregate of the amounts identified under that subsection, the company must, no later than 30 days after the notification, give a revised notice under that subsection to the officer of Revenue and Customs.

(6E) Where in a case to which subsection (6D) applies—

(a) a notification has been given to the surrendering company under that subsection, and

(b) the surrendering company does not give a revised notice in accordance with the requirements of that subsection,

the same consequences follow as if a notice had not been given in accordance with section 963(2) in relation to the refund.

(6F) In this section—

(a) references to a refund of instalment corporation tax are references to any refund of tax for any accounting period which falls in relation to that accounting period within paragraph (c) of the definition of "tax refund" in section 963(4),

(b) "large company" has the same meaning as in regulation 3 of the Corporation Tax (Instalment Payments) Regulations 1998, and

(c) references to the total liability of a company for an accounting period are to be construed in accordance with regulation 2(3) of those Regulations.".

Cross-reference—FA 2012 Sch 34 para 12(6) (references in para (5) to regs 4A, 4B, 4C, 4D, 5, 5A or 5B are to be read as including a reference to FA 2012 Sch 34 para 12(1)–(5)).

FA 2012 Sch 34 para 12(6)(*b*) (reference in para (3) to the Instalment Payment Regulations is to be read as including a reference to FA 2012 Sch 34 para 12(1)–(5)).

FA 2013 s 200(11) (references in para (5) to regs 4A, 4B, 4C, 4D, 5, 5A or 5B are to be read as including a reference to FA 2013 s 200(6)–(10); reference in para (3) to the Corporation Tax (Instalment Payments) Regulations, SI 1998/3175 is to be read as including a reference to FA 2013 s 200(6)–(10)).

FA 2015 s 76(10)(*a*), (*b*) (references in para (5) to regs 4A, 4B, 4C, 4D, 5, 5A or 5B are to be read as including a reference to FA 2015 s 76(5)–(9)), and reference in para (3) to "those regulations" is to be read accordingly.

F(No 2)A 2015 Sch 2 para 1(8) (references in para (5) to regs 4A, 4B, 4C, 4D, 5, 5A or 5B are to be read as including a reference to F(No 2)A 2015 Sch 2 para 1(4)–(7), and reference in para (3) to "those regulations" is also to be read as including a reference to F(No 2)A 2015 para 1(4)–(7)).

F(No 2)A 2015 Sch 1 paras 14(9), 16(9) (references in para (5) to regs 4A, 4B, 4C, 4D, 5, 5A or 5B are to be read as including a reference to F(No 2)A 2015 Sch 1 para 14(5)–(8), and reference in para (3) to "those regulation" is to be read as including a reference to F(No 2)A 2015 para 1(5)–(8)).

Amendments—Reg 9 substituted by the Corporation Tax (Instalment Payments) (Amendment) Regulations, SI 2011/1785 regs 2, 12 with effect in relation to accounting periods ending on or after 1 January 2011.

9A [Entity not liable to the bank levy

(1) This regulation applies where—

(a) a relevant entity (E) has made a payment for an accounting period which includes an amount in respect of the bank levy for the chargeable period; but

(b) another member of the relevant group (OM) is the responsible member for that chargeable period.

(2) Where this regulation applies—

(a) no repayment of the amount paid by E in respect of the bank levy shall be made to or be due to E;

(b) E shall not be entitled, as a result of the payment of the amount in respect of the bank levy, to set off or otherwise treat as discharged any liability to corporation tax or to any other tax or duty for any period;

(c) the amount of the payment made by E in respect of the bank levy for the chargeable period shall be treated as if it were a payment made by OM, on the date on which the payment was made by E; and

(d) if OM does not have an applicable accounting period which is the same as the chargeable period,

(i) the payment made by E shall be treated as a payment of an amount of the bank levy due and payable in respect of the earliest instalment payment in relation to the earliest applicable accounting period of OM for the chargeable period; and

(ii) the balance, if any, shall be treated as a payment of the bank levy due and payable in respect of OM's next instalment payment in relation to the earliest applicable accounting period and so on in relation to that applicable accounting period and any subsequent applicable accounting period.

(3) In paragraph (2)(d) the reference to an applicable accounting period being the same as the chargeable period shall be construed in accordance with paragraph 54 of Schedule 19.][1]

Amendments—[1] Reg 9A inserted by the Corporation Tax (Instalment Payments) (Amendment) Regulations, SI 2011/1785 regs 2, 13 with effect in relation to accounting periods ending on or after 1 January 2011.

10 Information to be provided to the [HMRC]

(1) [HMRC][1] may, at any time following the relevant date, by notice require any company to furnish them, within such time (not being less than thirty days) as may be provided by the notice—

(*a*) such information relating to the computation of any amount paid in respect of the company's total liability for an accounting period in accordance with regulation [4A, 4B, 4C, 4D, 5, 5A or 5B, as the case may be,][1] as they may reasonably require for ascertaining whether the amount of the payment was consistent with the quality and quantity of the information available to the company, at the time the payment was due, regarding its total liability for that period;

(*b*) such information as they may reasonably require for ascertaining the reasons for non-payment by the company at any time in accordance with regulation [4A, 4B, 4C, 4D, 5, 5A or 5B, as the case may be,][1] of any amount in respect of the company's total liability for an accounting period;

(*c*) such information as they may reasonably require for ascertaining whether a claim for repayment of an amount under regulation 6(2) was properly made.

(2) In paragraph (1) "the relevant date" means the date specified in paragraph 14(1) of Schedule 18 as the filing date for the company tax return for the accounting period concerned.

Cross-reference—FA 2011 s 7 (increase in rate of supplementary charge – application of these regulations in transitional period where a company has an accounting period beginning before 24 March 2011 and ending on or after that date).

FA 2012 Sch 34 para 12(6) (references in para (1) to regs 4A, 4B, 4C, 4D, 5, 5A or 5B are to be read as including a reference to FA 2012 Sch 34 para 12(1)–(5)).

FA 2013 s 200(11) (references in para (1) to regs 4A, 4B, 4C, 4D, 5, 5A or 5B are to be read as including a reference to FA 2013 s 200(6)–(10).

FA 2015 s 76(10)(*a*) (references in para (1) to regs 4A, 4B, 4C, 4D, 5, 5A or 5B are to be read as including a reference to FA 2015 s 76(5)–(9)).

F(No 2)A 2015 Sch 2 para 1(8) (references in para (1) to regs 4A, 4B, 4C, 4D, 5, 5A or 5B are to be read as including a reference to F(No 2)A 2015 Sch 2 para 1(4)–(7)).

F(No 2)A 2015 Sch 3 paras 14(9), 16(9) (references in para (1) to regs 4A, 4B, 4C, 4D, 5, 5A or 5B are to be read as including a reference to F(No 2)A 2015 Sch 1 para 14(5)–(8).

Press releases etc—IR 8-6-99 (the Revenue will only use their information powers contained in this regulation where there are indications that a company may have deliberately or recklessly failed to comply with its payment obligations, or fraudulently or negligently made a claim for repayment).

Amendments—[1] In heading, para (1), words substituted, by the Corporation Tax (Instalment Payments) (Amendment) Regulations, SI 2011/1785 regs 2, 14 with effect in relation to accounting periods ending on or after 1 January 2011.

10A [Additional information to be provided to HMRC where the large company is an entity which is responsible for the payment of the bank levy

(1) This regulation applies if the relevant entity or the responsible member ("E") makes an instalment payment which includes an amount in respect of the bank levy.

(2) Subject to paragraph (4), E must provide written notice (a "quantification notice") identifying the amount of the instalment payment which is in respect of the bank levy.

(3) A quantification notice must be given to an officer of Revenue and Customs on or before the date on which payment is made.

(4) Where E is a member of a group payment arrangement under section 59F of the Management Act (arrangements for paying tax on behalf of group members), but E is not the member which is responsible for discharging the liability of the group under that arrangement—

(a) E shall provide the quantification notice to the member (M) which, in accordance with the group payment arrangement, is responsible for discharging the liability of all the members of the group; and

(b) accordingly M shall be responsible for providing the quantification notice to the officer of Revenue and Customs as required by paragraphs (2) and (3) and for the purposes of paragraph (5).

(5) The requirement to provide a quantification notice under this regulation shall be treated as a requirement to comply with an information notice for the purposes of Part 7 of Schedule 36 to the Finance Act 2008 (information and inspection powers).][1]

Amendments—[1] Reg 10A inserted by the Corporation Tax (Instalment Payments) (Amendment) Regulations, SI 2011/1785 regs 2, 15 with effect in relation to accounting periods ending on or after 1 January 2011.

11 Production of records

(1) [HMRC][1] may, at any time following the relevant date, by notice require a company to produce, within such time (not being less than thirty days) as may be provided by the notice—

(*a*) all such books, documents and other records in its possession or power relating to the computation of any amount paid in respect of the company's total liability for an accounting period in accordance with regulation [4A, 4B, 4C, 4D, 5, 5A or 5B (as the case may be)][1] as they may reasonably require for ascertaining whether the amount of the payment was consistent with the quality and quantity of the information available to the company, at the time the payment was due, regarding its total liability for that period;

(*b*) all such books, documents and other records in its possession or power as they may reasonably require for ascertaining the reasons for non-payment by the company at any time in accordance with regulation [4A, 4B, 4C, 4D, 5, 5A or 5B (as the case may be)][1] of any amount in respect of the company's total liability for an accounting period;

(*c*) all such books, documents and other records in its possession or power as they may reasonably require for ascertaining whether a claim for repayment of an amount under regulation 6(2) was properly made.

(2) In complying with a notice under paragraph (1) copies of books, documents and other records may be produced instead of originals, but—

(*a*) the copies must be photographic or other facsimiles, and

(*b*) an officer of [Revenue and Customs][1] may require the original to be made available for inspection in accordance with regulation 12.

(3) In paragraph (1) "the relevant date" has the same meaning as in regulation 10.

Cross-reference—FA 2011 s 7 (increase in rate of supplementary charge – application of these regulations in transitional period where a company has an accounting period beginning before 24 March 2011 and ending on or after that date).

FA 2012 Sch 34 para 12(6) (references in para (1) to regs 4A, 4B, 4C, 4D, 5, 5A or 5B are to be read as including a reference to FA 2012 Sch 34 para 12(1)–(5)).

FA 2013 s 200(11) (references in para (1) to regs 4A, 4B, 4C, 4D, 5, 5A or 5B are to be read as including a reference to FA 2013 s 200(6)–(10).

FA 2015 s 76(10)(*a*) (references in para (1) to regs 4A, 4B, 4C, 4D, 5, 5A or 5B are to be read as including a reference to FA 2015 s 76(5)–(9)).

F(No 2)A 2015 Sch 2 para 1(8) (references in para (1) to regs 4A, 4B, 4C, 4D, 5, 5A or 5B are to be read as including a reference to F(No 2)A 2015 Sch 2 para 1(4)–(7)).

F(No 2)A 2015 Sch 3 paras 14(9), 16(9) (references in para (1) to regs 4A, 4B, 4C, 4D, 5, 5A or 5B are to be read as including a reference to F(No 2)A 2015 Sch 1 para 14(5)–(8).

Press releases etc—IR 8-6-99 (the Revenue will only use their information powers contained in this regulation where there are indications that a company may have deliberately or recklessly failed to comply with its payment obligations, or fraudulently or negligently made a claim for repayment).

Amendments—[1] In paras (1), (2)(*b*) words substituted by the Corporation Tax (Instalment Payments) (Amendment) Regulations, SI 2011/1785 regs 2, 16 with effect in relation to accounting periods ending on or after 1 January 2011.

12 Inspection of records

(1) An officer [of Revenue and Customs][2] authorised to do so may, at any time following the relevant date, require a company [by notice][1] to make available for inspection, at such time as that officer may reasonably require, all such books, documents and other records in its possession or power as could be required to be produced by notice . . . [2] under regulation 11.

(2) Where records are maintained by computer the officer making the inspection shall be provided by the company with all the facilities necessary for obtaining information from them.

(3) In paragraph (1) "the relevant date" has the same meaning as in regulation 10.

Cross-reference—FA 2011 s 7 (increase in rate of supplementary charge – application of these regulations in transitional period where a company has an accounting period beginning before 24 March 2011 and ending on or after that date).

Press releases etc—IR 8-6-99 (the Revenue will only use their information powers contained in this regulation where there are indications that a company may have deliberately or recklessly failed to comply with its payment obligations, or fraudulently or negligently made a claim for repayment).

Amendments—[1] Words in para (1) inserted by the Corporation Tax (Instalment Payments) (Amendment) Regulations, SI 1999/1929 regs 1, 4 with effect for accounting periods ending after 30 June 1999.

[2] In para (1), words substituted and words revoked by the Corporation Tax (Instalment Payments) (Amendment) Regulations, SI 2011/1785 regs 2, 17 with effect in relation to accounting periods ending on or after 1 January 2011.

13 Penalty for unpaid tax

The circumstances prescribed for the purposes of section 59E(4) of the Management Act (penalty not exceeding twice the amount of interest charged by virtue of regulation 7 on any unpaid amount in respect of the total liability of a company for an accounting period) are where—

(*a*) the company, or a person acting on its behalf, deliberately or recklessly fails to pay the amount in question in accordance with regulation [4A, 4B, 4C, 4D, 5, 5A or 5B (as the case may be)][1];

(*b*) the company, or a person acting on its behalf, fraudulently or negligently makes a claim for repayment of an amount under regulation 6(2).

Cross-reference—FA 2011 s 7 (increase in rate of supplementary charge – application of these regulations in transitional period where a company has an accounting period beginning before 24 March 2011 and ending on or after that date).

FA 2012 Sch 34 para 12(6) (references to regs 4A, 4B, 4C, 4D, 5, 5A or 5B are to be read as including a reference to FA 2012 Sch 34 para 12(1)–(5)).

FA 2013 s 200(11) (references to regs 4A, 4B, 4C, 4D, 5, 5A or 5B are to be read as including a reference to FA 2013 s 200(6)–(10).

FA 2015 s 76(10)(*a*) (references to regs 4A, 4B, 4C, 4D, 5, 5A or 5B are to be read as including a reference to FA 2015 s 76(5)–(9)).

F(No 2)A 2015 Sch 2 para 1(8) (references to regs 4A, 4B, 4C, 4D, 5, 5A or 5B are to be read as including a reference to F(No 2)A 2015 Sch 2 para 1(4)–(7)).

F(No 2)A 2015 Sch 3 paras 14(9), 16(9) (references to regs 4A, 4B, 4C, 4D, 5, 5A or 5B are to be read as including a reference to F(No 2)A 2015 Sch 1 para 14(5)–(8).

Press releases etc—IR 8-6-99 (the Revenue will seek a penalty under TMA 1970 s 59E(4) in only the most serious cases involving flagrant abuse of the regulations).

Amendments—[1] In para (*a*), words substituted by the Corporation Tax (Instalment Payments) (Amendment) Regulations, SI 2011/1785 regs 2, 18 with effect in relation to accounting periods ending on or after 1 January 2011.

14 Anti-avoidance provision

. . .

Amendments—Reg 14 revoked by the Corporation Tax (Instalment Payments) (Amendment) Regulations, SI 2011/1785 regs 2, 19(*a*) with effect in relation to accounting periods ending on or after 1 January 2011.

15 Insurance companies and friendly societies—supplementary provision

. . .

Amendments—Reg 15 revoked by the Corporation Tax (Instalment Payments) (Amendment) Regulations, SI 2011/1785 regs 2, 19(*b*) with effect in relation to accounting periods ending on or after 1 January 2011.

1998/3177

EUROPEAN SINGLE CURRENCY (TAXES) REGULATIONS 1998

Made by the Treasury under FA 1993 ss 93(1) and (6), 94(1), (2), (3) and (11) and 95(1), (2) and (3) and FA 1998 s 163

Made . . . . *17 December 1998*

Laid before the House of Commons . . . . *17 December 1998*

Coming into force . . . . *1 January 1999*

ARRANGEMENT OF REGULATIONS

PART I
INTRODUCTORY

1 Citation and commencement

These Regulations may be cited as the European Single Currency (Taxes) Regulations 1998 and shall come into force on 1st January 1999.

Commentary—*Simon's Taxes* **D4.206**.

Press releases etc—HMRC press release, 17 December 1998. Preparing British business for the euro—European Single Currency (Taxes) Regulations.

2 Interpretation

(1) In these Regulations unless the context otherwise requires—

"commodity or financial futures" has the meaning given by subsection (2)(*a*) of section 143 of the 1992 Act, and references in these Regulations to commodity or financial futures include references to a commodity or financial futures contract referred to in subsection (7)(*a*) or (*b*);

"debt", other than a debt on a security, includes a debt owed by a bank which is not in sterling and which is represented by a sum standing to the credit of a person in an account in the bank;

"derivative" means any commodity or financial futures or an option;

"ecu" shall be construed in accordance with section 95(5) of the Finance Act 1993;

"euro" means the single currency adopted or proposed to be adopted as its currency by a member State in accordance with the Treaty establishing the European Community;

"euroconversion" has the meaning given by regulation 3;

. . .

"member State" means a member State other than the United Kingdom;

"participating member State" means a member State that adopts the euro as its currency;

. . .

"reconventioning" in relation to a relevant asset means a change, consequent on simple redenomination, in the terms of the asset as a result of which the new terms become aligned to the prevailing terms of equivalent marketable relevant assets denominated in euro;

"relevant asset" means a debt (whether or not a debt on a security), [an option], or any commodity or financial futures;

"renominalisation" in relation to a relevant asset means a change, consequent on simple redenomination, in the minimum nominal amount in which the asset can be held or traded to a new round amount;

"security" has the meaning given by section 132(3)(*b*) of the 1992 Act;

"simple redenomination" means the conversion of the currency in which an asset, liability, contract or instrument is expressed from the currency of a participating member State into euro, and any rounding of the resulting amount to the nearest euro cent;

"the Taxes Act" means the Income and Corporation Taxes Act 1988;

"the 1992 Act" means the Taxation of Chargeable Gains Act 1992.

(2) In these Regulations references to an option, without more, are references to an option to which section 144 or 144A of the 1992 Act applies.

Commentary—*Simon's Taxes* **C1.307**.

Amendments—Definitions of "long-term capital asset" and "long-term capital liability", and "qualifying contract" revoked, and in definition of "relevant asset" words substituted, by the European Single Currency (Taxes) (Amendment) Regulations, SI 2002/1971 with effect for accounting periods beginning after 30 September 2002.

3 Definition of euroconversion

(1) "Euroconversion" means—

(*a*) in relation to any currency, or an amount expressed in any currency, of a participating member State, the conversion or restating of that currency or that amount into euro and any rounding of the resulting amount within a euro;

(*b*) in relation to any asset, liability, contract or instrument—

(i) the simple redenomination of that asset, liability, contract or instrument, or

(ii) in the case of a relevant asset, the simple redenomination of that asset accompanied by either or both of renominalisation and reconventioning, or

(iii) the substitution (whether by way of exchange, conversion, replacement or otherwise) for the asset, liability, contract or instrument of an equivalent replacement asset, liability, contract or instrument.

(2) An equivalent replacement asset, liability, contract or instrument means an asset, liability, contract or instrument whose amount, terms and conditions are identical to what is reasonable to assume would be the amount, terms and conditions of the original asset, liability, contract or instrument were it to undergo a simple redenomination, or (in the case of a relevant asset) a simple redenomination accompanied by either or both of renominalisation and reconventioning.

(3) For the purposes of paragraphs (1) and (2) a simple redenomination is accompanied (in the case of a relevant asset) by renominalisation or reconventioning if either—

(*a*) the renominalisation or reconventioning is effected simultaneously, or

(*b*) it is effected within a period of time following the simple redenomination which is such as to enable it reasonably to be inferred that the renominalisation or reconventioning is associated with the simple redenomination.

Commentary—*Simon's Taxes* **D6.211**.

PART II
DEDUCTIBILITY OF COSTS OF EUROCONVERSION OF SHARES AND OTHER SECURITIES

4 Interpretation

References in this Part of these Regulations to a euroconversion in relation to shares and other securities of a company ("the original shares and other securities") are references to a euroconversion that is effected solely by the issue of shares and other securities in replacement of the original shares and other securities.

5 Trading companies

Costs incurred in respect of a euroconversion of its shares or other securities by a company carrying on a trade shall be deductible in computing the amount of its profits chargeable to corporation tax under Case I of Schedule D as if those costs constituted money wholly and exclusively laid out or expended for the purposes of the trade within section 74(1)(*a*) of the Taxes Act.

6 Investment companies and insurance companies—deemed expenses of management

(1) Costs which—

(*a*) are incurred by an investment company or a company carrying on life assurance business in respect of a euroconversion of its shares or other securities, and

(*b*) except where the costs are referable to life assurance business of a company whose profits in relation to that business are charged to tax [under the I minus E basis][2], are not deductible under regulation 5,

[shall be treated in accordance with paragraph (1A)][1].

[(1A) If the company—

(*a*) is a company with investment business, the costs shall be treated as expenses of management deductible under section 75 to the extent they otherwise would not be, or

(*b*) is one in relation to which section 76 applies, the costs shall be treated for the purposes of that section as expenses payable which fall to be brought into account at Step 1 in subsection (7) of that section to the extent that they otherwise would not be.][1]

(2), (3) . . . [1]

(4) In this regulation—

"investment company" [and "company with investment business" have the meanings][1] given by section 130 of the Taxes Act;

"life assurance business" shall be construed in accordance with section 431(2) of the Taxes Act.

Commentary—*Simon's Taxes* **D4.206, D7.307**.

Amendments—[1] Words in paras (1), (4) substituted, para (1A) inserted, and paras (2), (3) revoked, by the Finance Act 2004, Sections 38 to 40 and 45 and Schedule 6 (Consequential Amendment of Enactments) Order, SI 2004/2310 art 2, Schedule para 77 with effect from 28 September 2004. These amendments have effect for accounting periods beginning on or after 1 April 2004, subject to the transitional provisions set out in FA 2004 ss 43, 44.

[2] Words in para (1)(*b*) substituted by the European Single Currency (Taxes) (Amendment) Regulations, SI 2008/2647 reg 2 with effect from 28 October 2008.

PART III

EXCHANGE GAINS AND LOSSES, INTEREST RATE AND CURRENCY CONTRACTS AND OPTIONS, DEBT CONTRACTS AND OPTIONS, AND RELEVANT DISCOUNTED SECURITIES

7–11 Deferral of unrealised gains

. . .

Amendment—Regulations 7–11 revoked by the European Single Currency (Taxes) (Amendment) Regulations, SI 2002/1971 regs 1, 2, 4 with effect for accounting periods beginning after 30 September 2002.

12 Exchange or conversion of relevant discounted securities

(1) A euroconversion of relevant discounted securities that is effected solely by means of an exchange or conversion of those securities shall be treated as not constituting either—

(*a*) a transfer of those securities within the meaning of paragraph 4 of Schedule 13 to the Finance Act 1996 ("Schedule 13"), or

(*b*) a conversion of those securities for the purposes of paragraph 5 of Schedule 13.

(2) The relevant discounted securities ("the new securities") resulting from the exchange or conversion referred to in paragraph (1) shall be deemed for the purposes of Schedule 13 to have been acquired for the amount resulting from the formula—

$$A - B$$

Where—

A is the amount equal to the acquisition cost of the relevant discounted securities replaced by the new securities, and

B is the amount of any cash payment received by a person in respect of the euroconversion, to the extent that that amount does not exceed A.

(3) Where a cash payment is received by a person in respect of relevant discounted securities as a result of a euroconversion of those securities which—

(*a*) involves a simple redenomination of those securities, accompanied by either or both of renominalisation and reconventioning as a consequence of that simple redenomination, and

(*b*) is effected otherwise than by means of—

(i) a transfer of those securities, or

(ii) an exchange or conversion of those securities,

those securities shall be deemed for the purposes of Schedule 13 to have been acquired for the amount resulting from the formula—

$$C - D$$

where—

C is the amount equal to the acquisition cost of the relevant discounted securities, and—

D is the amount of the cash payment received, to the extent that that amount does not exceed C.

(4) Where—

(*a*) the amount of the cash payment referred to in the description of B in paragraph (2) exceeds the amount referred to in the description of A in that paragraph, or

(*b*) the amount of the cash payment referred to in the description of D in paragraph (3) exceeds the amount referred to in the description of C in that paragraph,

an amount equal to the excess in either case shall constitute a profit realised by a person from the discount on a relevant discounted security for the purposes of paragraph 1 of Schedule 13 (charge to tax on realised profit comprised in discount).

(5) In this regulation "relevant discounted security" has the meaning given by paragraph 3 of Schedule 13.

PART IV
AGREEMENTS FOR SALE AND REPURCHASE OF SECURITIES

13 Interpretation

In this Part of these Regulations—

"capital payment" means any payment on the euroconversion of securities other than any interest, dividend or other annual payment payable in respect of the securities;

"original owner" and "interim holder" shall be construed in accordance with section 730A(1) of the Taxes Act;

"transferor" shall be construed in accordance with sections 727A(1) and 737A(1) of the Taxes Act.

Commentary—*Simon's Taxes* **D9.1001**.

14 Replacement of securities in a euroconversion

(1) This regulation applies in a case where—

(*a*) there is an agreement for the sale of securities, and

(*b*) there is a euroconversion of the securities to which the agreement relates ("the old securities"), effected wholly or in part by the issue of new securities to replace them.

(2) The new securities which replace the old securities shall be regarded for the purposes of sections 727A(1), 730A(1) and 737A(1) of the Taxes Act, and section 263A(1) of the 1992 Act, as similar securities in relation to the old securities.

(3) In paragraph (2) the reference to similar securities shall be construed in accordance with section 727A(4), 730B(4) or 737B(6), as the case may be.

[(4) The new securities which replace the old securities shall be regarded as similar securities for the purposes of paragraphs 2 and 7 of Schedule 13 to the Finance Act 2007.

(5) In paragraph (4) the reference to similar securities shall be construed in accordance with paragraph 14(4) of Schedule 13 to the Finance Act 2007.][1]

Commentary—*Simon's Taxes* **D9.1002**.

Cross reference—FA 2007 Sch 13 para 14(6) (an arrangement is in force from the time when the securities are initially sold until the earlier of the time when the relevant repurchase takes place, and the time when it becomes apparent that that repurchase will not take place).

Amendments—[1] Paras (4), (5) inserted by the Sale and Repurchase of Securities (Amendment of Instruments) Order, SI 2007/2484 art 3(1), (2) with effect in relation to arrangements that come into force on or after 1 October 2007: SI 2007/2484 art 1(1). FA 2007 Sch 13 para 14(6) applies for the purpose of determining the times at which an arrangement is in force: SI 2007/2484 art 1(2).

15 Payment or benefit received by interim holder on euroconversion

(1) This regulation applies in a case where—

(*a*) there is an arrangement for the sale and repurchase of securities to which section 263A(1) of the 1992 Act applies,

(*b*) a capital payment, but for the arrangement, would be received by the original owner on the euroconversion of those securities,

(*c*) the interim holder is not required under the arrangement to pay to the original owner an amount representative of that capital payment, and an amount representative of that capital payment is not required under the arrangement to be taken into account in computing the repurchase price of the securities, and

(*d*) the amount of the capital payment would not exceed 500 euros.

(2) The interim holder shall not be regarded, for the purposes of section 263A of the 1992 Act, as receiving a benefit under subsection (3)(*b*) of that section equal to the amount of the capital payment.

Commentary—*Simon's Taxes* **D9.1001, D9.1035**.

16 Payment deemed to be made by interim holder on euroconversion

(1) This regulation applies in a case where—

(*a*) there is an arrangement for the sale and repurchase of securities to which section 730A(1) of the Taxes Act, or section 263A(1) of the 1992 Act, applies, or to which section 730A(1) of the Taxes Act would apply if the sale price and the repurchase price were different,

(*b*) there is a euroconversion of those securities prior to their being repurchased, and (*c*) it is reasonable to assume that an amount that is representative of a capital payment in respect of the euroconversion is taken into account in computing the repurchase price of those securities.

(2) The amount referred to in paragraph (1)(*c*) shall be treated as if it were a separate representative payment in respect of the euroconversion made by the interim holder to the person required or entitled under the arrangement to repurchase the securities.

(3) The repurchase price of the securities shall be treated, for the purposes of section 730A of the Taxes Act and the 1992 Act, as increased by an amount equal to the amount of the separate payment treated as made by paragraph (2).

Commentary—*Simon's Taxes* **D9.1035**.

17 Renominalisation resulting in new minimum denomination in which securities can be held or traded

(1) This regulation applies in a case where—

(*a*) there is an arrangement for the sale and repurchase of securities to which section 730A(1) or 737A(1) of the Taxes Act, or section 263A(1) of the 1992 Act, applies, or to which section 730A(1) of the Taxes Act would apply if the sale price and the repurchase price were different,

(*b*) there is a euroconversion of those securities prior to their being repurchased,

(*c*) the aggregate nominal value (expressed in euros) of the securities sold, or of securities issued to replace them in a euroconversion is, as a result of renominalisation, not a whole multiple of the new minimum denomination in which those securities can be traded at the time of repurchase under the arrangement,

(*d*) securities the aggregate nominal value of which is equal to the largest whole multiple of the new minimum denomination which does not exceed the aggregate nominal value referred to in sub-paragraph (*c*) are required under the arrangement to be sold back to the original owner or the transferor or a person connected with him, and

(*e*) the interim holder is required under the arrangement to pay to the original owner or transferor, or person connected with him, an amount which either—

(i) is equal to the amount of what would, but for the arrangement, have been the proceeds of disposal of the remainder of the securities on the renominalisation received by the original owner, or

(ii) is equal to the value, at the time of the repurchase of securities pursuant to the arrangement, of the remainder if the remainder could still be held at that time though not traded.

(2) Where this regulation applies, the requirement for payment of the amount specified in paragraph (1)(*e*) is to be regarded for the purposes of sections 727A, 730A and 737A of the Taxes Act, and section 263A of the 1992 Act, as equivalent to a requirement on the original owner, transferor or person connected with him to repurchase the remainder of the securities.

(3) The value referred to in paragraph (1)(*e*)(ii) is the appropriate proportion (based on nominal value) of the market value of the minimum amount of the original securities that, at the time of the repurchase of the securities pursuant to the arrangement, could be traded.

(4) Where the amount calculated in accordance with sub-paragraph (*e*) of paragraph (1) does not exceed 500 euros, and the arrangement does not require payment of a sum equal to this amount, this regulation shall have effect as if the amount calculated in accordance with that sub-paragraph were nil and the requirement specified in that sub-paragraph were satisfied.

(5) Where, in a case to which paragraph (1)(*a*) to (*d*) applies—

(*a*) no amount is paid as mentioned in paragraph (1)(*e*) by the interim holder to the original owner, transferor or person connected with him in respect of securities that, as a result of the renominalisation, could not be traded, but

(*b*) it is reasonable to assume that an amount that is representative of an amount that could have been paid as mentioned in sub-paragraph (*a*) was taken into account in computing the repurchase price of the securities,

that amount shall be treated as if it were a separate payment made by the interim holder to the original owner, transferor or person connected with him that is representative of a capital payment on the euroconversion of the securities, and the repurchase price of the securities shall be treated as increased by an amount equal to the amount of that separate payment so treated as made.

Commentary—*Simon's Taxes* **D9.1035**.

18 Payment made or deemed to be made by interim holder in respect of euroconversion—chargeable gains consequences

(1) This regulation applies in a case where—

(*a*) there is an arrangement for the sale and repurchase of securities to which section 263A(1) of the 1992 Act applies, and (*b*) as a result of a euroconversion of those securities, a payment representative of a capital payment is made, or treated under regulation 16(2) or 17(5) as made ("deemed payment"), by the interim holder to the original owner or the transferor or a person connected with him.

(2) The payment or deemed payment shall be treated, for the purposes of the 1992 Act—

(*a*) where the original owner and the repurchaser are the same person, as a capital payment received by the original owner in respect of the euroconversion of the securities concerned on such date as, on a just and reasonable view, may be inferred from the terms of the arrangement to be the date when the original owner would, but for the arrangement, have received a capital payment in respect of which the payment or deemed payment is made;

(*b*) where the original owner and the repurchaser are not the same person and so far as concerns persons other than the interim holder, as reducing the repurchase price; and

(*c*) as deductible by the interim holder in computing any capital gain arising—

(i) on a disposal of the securities received by the interim holder under the arrangement, or

(ii) where there has been an exchange of those securities as a result of the euroconversion, on a disposal of the securities received by the interim holder in exchange for the original securities received by him under the arrangement.

19 Euroconversion—loan relationships consequences

. . .

Cross reference—FA 2007 Sch 13 para 14(6) (an arrangement is in force from the time when the securities are initially sold until the earlier of the time when the relevant repurchase takes place, and the time when it becomes apparent that that repurchase will not take place).

Amendments—Regulation 19 revoked by the Sale and Repurchase of Securities (Amendment of Instruments) Order, SI 2007/2484 art 3(1), (3) with effect in relation to arrangements that come into force on or after 1 October 2007: SI 2007/2484 art 1(1). FA 2007 Sch 13 para 14(6) applies for the purpose of determining the times at which an arrangement is in force: SI 2007/2484 art 1(2).

PART V
STOCK LENDING ARRANGEMENTS

Commentary—*Simon's Taxes* **C1.414C**.

20 Interpretation

In this Part of these Regulations—

"capital payment" means any payment on the euroconversion of securities other than any interest, dividend or other annual payment payable in respect of the securities;

"stock lending arrangement", "borrower" and "lender" have the meanings given by section 263B(1) of the 1992 Act.

Commentary—*Simon's Taxes* **C1.414C**.

21 Deemed capital payment

(1) This regulation applies in a case where—

(*a*) there is a stock lending arrangement in relation to securities,

(*b*) a capital payment resulting from the euroconversion of those securities would, but for the arrangement, be received by the lender, and

(*c*) the stock lending arrangement does not include a requirement for the borrower to make a payment to the lender that is representative of the capital payment referred to in sub-paragraph (*b*).

(2) Subject to paragraph (3), the lender shall be treated, for all purposes of the Taxes Acts, as having received a capital payment in respect of the euroconversion of the securities concerned—

(*a*) on such date as it is reasonable to assume would have been, but for the arrangement, the first date on which the lender could have received the payment mentioned in paragraph (1)(*b*), and

(*b*) in an amount equal to the amount of the payment he could have received.

(3) Paragraph (2) shall not apply where the amount of the capital payment that the lender could have received is less than 500 euros.

Commentary—*Simon's Taxes* **C1.414A, C1.414C, D9.601**.

22 Renominalisation resulting in new minimum amount in which securities can be held or traded

(1) This regulation applies in a case where—

(*a*) there is a stock lending arrangement in relation to securities,

(*b*) there is a euroconversion of those securities prior to their being transferred back to the lender under the arrangement,

(*c*) the aggregate nominal value (expressed in euros) of the securities transferred to the borrower under the arrangement, or of the securities issued to replace them in the euroconversion, is, as a result of renominalisation, not a whole multiple of the new minimum denomination in which those securities can be traded at the time of the transfer of securities back to the lender under the arrangement, (*d*) securities the aggregate nominal value of which is equal to the largest whole multiple of the new minimum denomination which does not exceed the aggregate nominal value referred to in sub-paragraph (*c*) are transferred back to the lender pursuant to the arrangement, and

(*e*) the borrower is required under the arrangement to pay to the lender an amount which either—

(i) is equal to the amount of what would, but for the arrangement, have been the proceeds of disposal of the remainder of the securities on the renominalisation received by the lender, or

(ii) is equal to the value, at the time of the transfer of securities back to the lender under the arrangement, of the remainder of the securities if the remainder could still be held at that time though not traded.

(2) Where this regulation applies, the requirement for payment of the amount specified in paragraph (1)(*e*) is to be regarded for the purposes of section 263B of the 1992 Act as a requirement on the part of the borrower to transfer the remainder of the securities back to the lender.

(3) The value referred to in paragraph (1)(*e*)(ii) is the appropriate proportion (based on nominal value) of the market value of the minimum amount of the original securities that, at the time of the transfer back of securities to the lender under the arrangement, could be traded.

(4) Where the value, or proceeds of disposal, of the remainder of the securities referred to in sub-paragraph (*e*) of paragraph (1) does not exceed 500 euros, and the arrangement does not require payment of a sum equal to this amount, this regulation shall have effect as if the amount calculated in accordance with that sub-paragraph were nil and the requirement specified in that sub-paragraph were satisfied.

Commentary—*Simon's Taxes* **C1.414A, C1.414C, D9.601.**

23 Payment made by borrower to lender in respect of euroconversion—chargeable gains consequences

(1) This regulation applies in a case where—

(*a*) there is a stock lending arrangement in relation to securities, and

(*b*) a payment representative of a capital payment resulting from a euroconversion of those securities is made by the borrower to the lender.

(2) The representative payment shall be treated, for all purposes of the Taxes Acts—

(*a*) as a capital payment received by the lender in respect of the euroconversion of the securities concerned on such date as it is reasonable to assume would have been, but for the arrangement, the first date on which the lender could have received the capital payment, and

(*b*) as deductible by the borrower in computing any capital gain arising—

(i) on a disposal of the securities received by the borrower under the arrangement, or

(ii) where the euroconversion is effected by means of an exchange of securities, on a disposal of the securities received by the borrower in exchange for the original securities received by him under the arrangement.

Commentary—*Simon's Taxes* **C1.414A, C1.414C, D9.601.**

PART VI

REPURCHASES AND STOCK LENDING—STAMP DUTY AND STAMP DUTY RESERVE TAX

24–30 *[Not reproduced. See Orange Tax Handbook Stamp Taxes section.]*

PART VII

ACCRUED INCOME SCHEME

31 Interpretation

In this Part of these Regulations—

"the accrued amount" has the meaning given by section 713(4) of the Taxes Act;

"the accrued income provisions" means sections 710 to 728 of the Taxes Act;

"interest period" shall be construed in accordance with section 711(3) and (4) of the Taxes Act except that, where securities are issued on an exchange of securities to which regulation 32 (exchange of securities resulting from euroconversion) applies, paragraph (*a*) of section 711(3) of that Act (commencement of interest period) shall have effect for the purposes of regulation 33 as if the reference in that paragraph to the day following that on which securities are issued were a reference to the day on which they are issued;

"the rebate amount" has the meaning given by section 713(5) of the Taxes Act;

"securities" has the meaning given by section 710(2) to (4) of the Taxes Act;

"transfer" in relation to a transfer of securities has the meaning given by subsection (5), read with subsection (13), of section 710 of the Taxes Act.

32 Disapplication of accrued income provisions in respect of an exchange or conversion of securities resulting from a euroconversion

An exchange or conversion of securities that arises solely as a result of actions to effect a euroconversion of those securities shall not constitute, or be treated as, a transfer of those securities for the purposes of the accrued income provisions.

Commentary—*Simon's Taxes* **D9.427**.

33 Disapplication of variable interest rate provision in certain circumstances

(1) This regulation applies in a case where, solely to provide for actions reasonably required to effect a euroconversion of a security—

(*a*) there may be a change in the rate of interest carried by the security in relation to the interest period in which the euroconversion occurs, or

(*b*) there may be a change in the rate of interest carried by the security in relation to subsequent periods but, throughout the subsequent periods, the new rate of interest falls within one, and one only, of the categories specified in paragraphs (*a*) to (*c*) of section 717(2) of the Taxes Act, or

(*c*) there may be a change in the rate of interest as mentioned in sub-paragraph (*a*) and a change in the rate of interest as mentioned in sub-paragraph (*b*).

(2) The provision for change in the rate of interest referred to in paragraph (1)(*a*) or (*b*) shall not cause the security concerned to be one to which section 717 of the Taxes Act applies.

Commentary—*Simon's Taxes* **D9.426, D9.427**.

34 Calculation of accrued amount or rebate amount in the event of a euroconversion of securities

(1) This regulation applies in a case where—

(*a*) there is a transfer of securities at any time in an interest period, and

(*b*) at any time in that interest period there is a euroconversion of the securities transferred in that period.

(2) The accrued amount or, as the case may be, the rebate amount arising in respect of the transferred securities on the transfer shall be such amount as is just and reasonable.

Commentary—*Simon's Taxes* **D9.413, D9.427**.

35 Treatment of capital sum receivable on euroconversion of securities

(1) This regulation applies in a case where—

(*a*) otherwise than as a result of a transfer of securities that is not an exchange or conversion of securities to which regulation 32 applies, a person becomes entitled in an interest period to a capital sum in connection with a euroconversion of securities, and

(*b*) any part of that sum is, on a just and reasonable view—

(i) attributable to a reduction in the interest payable on those securities, or

(ii) by way of compensation for a deferral of the interest payable on those securities.

(2) The person entitled to a capital sum in an interest period as mentioned in paragraph (1)(*a*) shall be regarded as entitled in that interest period to a sum on the securities, for the purposes of section 713(2)(*a*) or (3)(*a*), in an amount equal to the part of the sum referred to in paragraph (1)(*b*).

Commentary—*Simon's Taxes* **D9.427**.

PART VIII
CHARGEABLE GAINS

36 Equation of holding of non-sterling currency with new euro holding on euroconversion

A euroconversion of currency ("the original currency") shall not be treated for the purposes of the 1992 Act as involving any disposal of the original currency or any acquisition of the new euro holding or any part of it, but the original currency (taken as a single asset) and the new euro holding (taken as a single asset) shall be treated for those purposes as the same asset acquired as the original currency was acquired.

Commentary—*Simon's Taxes* **C1.301**.

37 Equation of debt (other than a debt on a security) on euroconversion

A euroconversion of a debt other than a debt on a security ("the original debt") shall not be treated for the purposes of the 1992 Act as involving any disposal of that debt by the creditor or any acquisition by him of a new debt or any part of it, but the original debt and the new debt shall be treated for those purposes (to the extent that they are not already so treated) as the same asset acquired as the original asset was acquired.

Commentary—*Simon's Taxes* **C1.308**.

38 Derivatives over assets the subject of euroconversion

(1) This regulation applies where—

(*a*) a derivative represents rights or obligations in respect of any asset or liability or other amount ("the underlying asset"), (*b*) there is a euroconversion of the underlying asset,

(*c*) a transaction is entered into in relation to that derivative that would, but for this regulation, result in a disposal for the purposes of the 1992 Act of the derivative ("the original derivative") and the acquisition of a new derivative,

(*d*) the terms of the new derivative differ from the terms of the original derivative only to the extent necessary to reflect the euroconversion of the underlying asset, and

(*e*) no party to the transaction receives any consideration in respect of the original derivative other than the new derivative.

(2) The transaction described at paragraph (1)(*c*) shall not be treated for the purposes of the 1992 Act as involving any disposal of the original derivative or any acquisition of the new derivative, but the original derivative and the new derivative shall be treated for those purposes as the same asset acquired as the original derivative was acquired.

Commentary—*Simon's Taxes* **C1.307**.

39 Cash payments received on euroconversion of securities

Chapter II of Part IV of the 1992 Act shall have effect as if after section 133 of that Act (premiums on conversion of securities) there were inserted the following section—(*inserts* TCGA 1992 s 133A).

PART IX
CONTROLLED FOREIGN COMPANIES

40 Replacement of currency used in accounts of controlled foreign company by euro

(1) This regulation applies in a case where, as a result of the adoption of the euro by a participating member State, the currency used in the accounts of a controlled foreign company for the first relevant accounting period of the company is to be replaced by the euro.

(2) Section 747A(2) of the Taxes Act shall have effect as if it provided that—

(*a*) where the currency used in the accounts of the controlled foreign company for the first relevant accounting period was the ecu, the chargeable profits for any subsequent accounting period ending on or after 1st January 1999 should be computed and expressed in the euro;

(*b*) where the currency used in the accounts of the controlled foreign company for the first relevant accounting period was a currency other than the ecu—

(i) the chargeable profits for any subsequent accounting period in which, or in any part of which, the currency continues to exist as a legal sub-unit of the euro should be computed and expressed in either the currency so used or the euro;

(ii) the chargeable profits for any accounting period beginning after the end of the latest accounting period referred to in paragraph (i) should be computed and expressed in the euro.

PART X
AMENDMENTS TO THE LOCAL CURRENCY ELECTIONS REGULATIONS

Amendments—This Part (regs 41–47) revoked by the Exchange Gains and Losses (Miscellaneous Modifications) Regulations, SI 2000/3315 reg 10 to the extent that it is not previously revoked with effect for any accounting period of a company beginning after 31 December 1999 for which FA 2000 ss 105, 106 have effect.

1998/3178

SCOTLAND ACT 1998 (COMMENCEMENT) ORDER 1998

Made by the Secretary of State for Scotland under the Scotland Act 1998 ss 115(2), 126(1) and 130

Made . . . . 16 December 1998

1 Citation and interpretation

(1) This Order may be cited as the Scotland Act 1998 (Commencement) Order 1998.

(2) In this Order, "the Act" means the Scotland Act 1998.

2 Appointed days

(1) All the provisions of the Act, so far as not then in force, shall come into force on 1st July 1999, except the provisions specified in Schedule 5 to this Order.

(2) The provisions of the Act, specified in column 1 of any of the Schedules to this Order and the subject matter of which is described in column 2 of that Schedule shall, so far as not then in force, come into force on the day appointed in relation to that Schedule in the Table below but, where a particular purpose is specified in relation to any provision in column 3 of that Schedule, that provision shall come into force on that day only for that purpose.

TABLE

Schedule	*Appointed day*

1	25th January 1999
2	1st April 1999
3	6th May 1999
4	20th May 1999
5	1st April 2000

3 Principal Appointed Day

The principal appointed day is 1st July 1999.

SCHEDULE 3

Article 2(2)

PROVISIONS OF THE ACT WHICH COME INTO FORCE ON 6TH MAY 1999

Column 1	*Column 2*	*Column 3*
Provisions of the Act	*Subject matter*	*Purpose*
. . .		
Part IV	The tax-varying power	

NOTE—

Provisions outside the scope of this work have been omitted. Scotland Act 1998 Part 4 (ss 73–80) was repealed by the Scotland Act 2012 s 25(1), (2) with effect from 1 July 2012.

Tax year 2016–17 is appointed as the first tax year for which a Scottish rate resolution made by the Scottish Parliament under Scotland Act 1998 s 80C (power to set Scottish rate for Scottish taxpayers) is to have effect).

1999/358

CORPORATION TAX (TREATMENT OF UNRELIEVED SURPLUS ADVANCE CORPORATION TAX) REGULATIONS 1999

Made by the Treasury under FA 1998 s 32

Made . . . .*15 February 1999*

Laid before the House of Commons . . . .*16 February 1999*

Coming into force . . . .*9 March 1999*

Press releases etc—IR 16–2–99 (regulations for relief of past surplus ACT).

HMRC Manuals—Company Taxation Manual CTM18260–18700 (unrelieved surplus ACT, including definition of a group and examples).

1 Citation and commencement

These Regulations may be cited as the Corporation Tax (Treatment of Unrelieved Surplus Advance Corporation Tax) Regulations 1999 and shall come into force on 9th March 1999.

2 Introductory

(1) These Regulations make provision for and in connection with enabling unrelieved surplus ACT that a company has as at 6th April 1999 to be set against its liability to corporation tax on profits charged to corporation tax for an accounting period beginning on or after that date, other than an accounting period that is subsequent to the company's final accounting period.

(2) In paragraph (1) the reference to unrelieved surplus ACT of a company includes, where the company is a member of a group at any time in an accounting period to which that paragraph applies, a reference to unrelieved surplus ACT that another company, which is a member of the same group at any time in that accounting period, has as at 6th April 1999.

3 Interpretation

(1) In these Regulations unless the context otherwise requires—

["abnormal dividend" has the meaning given by regulation 6A;][1]

"accounting period" shall be construed in accordance with regulation 2(1);

"ACT" means advance corporation tax;

"the Board" means the Commissioners of Inland Revenue;[1]

["company" in regulation 6A means a company referred to in section 733 (company liable to counteraction of corporation tax advantage) of the Corporation Tax Act 2010;

"the CTA" means the Corporation Tax Act 2010][1]

"distribution" has the meaning given by section 832(1);

["exempt ABGH distribution" means a distribution which—

(*a*) is a distribution for the purposes of the Corporation Tax Acts only because it falls within paragraph A, B, G or H in section 1000(1) of CTA 2010; and

(*b*) is exempt for the purposes of Part 9A of CTA 2009 (company distributions);][2]

"final accounting period" shall be construed in accordance with regulations 4 and 5;

"franked distribution" means the sum of the amount or value of a relevant distribution and such proportion of that amount or value as corresponds to the rate of shadow ACT specified in regulation 11(9), and references in these Regulations to any accounting period in which a franked distribution is made are references to the accounting period in which the relevant distribution in question is made;

. . . [2]

"group" has the meaning given by regulation 6;

"notification" means notification in writing;

"parent company" in relation to a group shall be construed in accordance with regulation 6(1) to (7); and "immediate parent company" shall be construed in accordance with regulation 6(8);

["qualifying investment income" means an exempt ABGH distribution of a company grossed up by ten-ninths;][2]

"relevant distribution" means a distribution made on or after 6th April 1999;

"shadow ACT" means a notional amount of ACT treated as paid by a company in respect of a relevant distribution and computed in accordance with regulation 11;

"straddling accounting period" means an accounting period beginning before, and ending on or after, 6th April 1999, and includes a separate accounting period mentioned in sections 245(2), 245A(2) and 245B(2);

"surplus [qualifying][2] investment income"—

(*a*) as respects an accounting period beginning on or after 6th April 1999, has the meaning given by regulation 11(13);

(*b*) as respects an accounting period beginning before that date, has the meaning given by section 238(1A);

"surplus shadow ACT" means the excess amount of shadow ACT over the total amount of shadow ACT set against a company's liability to corporation tax for an accounting period in accordance with regulation 12(1);

"the Taxes Act" means the Income and Corporation Taxes Act 1988;

"unrelieved surplus ACT" means the ACT (if any) which, apart from sub-paragraph (3) of paragraph 12 of Schedule 3 to the Finance Act 1998 but otherwise in accordance with that paragraph, would be treated by virtue of section 239(4) as paid in respect of distributions made by a company in the first accounting period of the company to begin on or after 6th April 1999.

(2) References in these Regulations to the profits of a company charged to corporation tax for any accounting period are references to the amount of the company's profits for that period on which corporation tax falls finally to be borne.

(3) References in these Regulations, however expressed, to a company's liability to corporation tax for an accounting period include references to a company's liability in respect of any sums chargeable on the company for that period under section 747(4)(*a*) (controlled foreign companies).

(4) For the purposes only of these Regulations, a straddling accounting period shall be treated as if—

(*a*) it were composed of two accounting periods, the one ending on 5th April 1999 and the other beginning on 6th April 1999;

(*b*) there were apportioned to each of those accounting periods the proportionate part of the profits of the company charged to corporation tax for the straddling accounting period.

(5) References in these Regulations to an accounting period beginning on or after 6th April 1999 include references to—

(*a*) an accounting period deemed by virtue of paragraph (4) of this regulation to begin on 6th April 1999, and

(*b*) a separate accounting period referred to in regulations 16(2) and 17(2) that begins on or after that date.

(6) References in these Regulations, other than the reference in paragraph (4)(*b*) above, to a requirement for profits charged to corporation tax for an accounting period to be apportioned between two separate parts of that accounting period are references to a requirement for those profits to be apportioned either—

(*a*) on a time basis, or

(*b*) where that basis would be unjust and unreasonable, on such basis as would be just and reasonable.

(7) In these Regulations any reference to a particular provision, without more, is a reference to that provision of the Taxes Act.

Amendments—[1] In para (1), definitions of "abnormal dividend", "company" and "the CTA" inserted, definition of "the Board" revoked, and definition of "franked investment income" substituted, by the Corporation Tax (Treatment of Unrelieved Surplus Advance Corporation Tax) (Amendment) Regulations, SI 2010/669 regs 2, 3 with effect from 1 April 2010.

[2] In para (1), definitions of "exempt ABGH distribution" and "qualifying investment income" inserted, definition of "franked investment income" revoked, and in definition of "surplus franked investment income", word substituted, by the Corporation

Tax (Treatment of Unrelieved Surplus Advance Corporation Tax) (Amendment) Regulations, SI 2017/454 regs 2, 3 with effect for company distributions made in an accounting period commencing on or after 6 April 2016, subject to transitional provisions for accounting periods straddling that date (SI 2017/454 reg 1(3)).

4 Definition of final accounting period—company not a member of a group

(1) For the purpose of regulation 2(1) and subject to paragraphs (3) to (5) of this regulation and to regulation 5(10), where a company is not a member of a group at any time in the relevant accounting period, the final accounting period of that company is the accounting period beginning in the period of twelve months immediately following the end of the relevant accounting period or, if there is more than one accounting period beginning in that period of twelve months, the latest accounting period beginning in that period.

(2) In paragraph (1) "the relevant accounting period" is the first accounting period of the company after which no amount of unrelieved surplus ACT is available to be set against the company's liability to corporation tax in accordance with these Regulations.

(3) Paragraph (1) shall not apply where, at any time in the first of its accounting periods to begin on or after 6th April 1999, the company notifies [an officer of Revenue and Customs][1] that it will not seek or, as the case may be, will cease to seek recovery of unrelieved surplus ACT in respect of that accounting period or any subsequent accounting period.

(4) Where, otherwise than in a case to which paragraph (3) applies, the company notifies [an officer of Revenue and Customs][1] at any time in an accounting period that it wishes that accounting period to be its final accounting period and that it will not seek recovery of unrelieved surplus ACT in respect of any subsequent accounting period, the final accounting period of that company is, subject to paragraph (5), the accounting period in which the notification is made.

(5) Where—

(*a*) there is an amount of surplus shadow ACT in respect of an accounting period of the company beginning in the period of twelve months ("the relevant period") immediately following the end of the accounting period in which the company notifies [an officer of Revenue and Customs][1] as mentioned in paragraph (4) or, if there is more than one such accounting period, the latest accounting period beginning in the relevant period, and

(*b*) that amount or any part of it falls to be carried back in accordance with regulation 12(7) to the accounting period in which that notification is made,

the final accounting period shall be the accounting period or, as the case may be, the latest accounting period beginning in the relevant period from which an amount of surplus shadow ACT falls to be carried back as mentioned in sub-paragraph (b) of this paragraph, and not the accounting period in which the notification is made.

Amendments—[1] Words substituted by the Corporation Tax (Treatment of Unrelieved Surplus Advance Corporation Tax) (Amendment) Regulations, SI 2010/669 regs 2, 6 with effect from 1 April 2010.

5 Definition of final accounting period—company a member of a group

(1) For the purpose of regulation 2 and subject to paragraphs (3) to (10), where a company is a member of a group at any time in the relevant accounting period, the final accounting period of that company in its capacity as a member of that group is the accounting period beginning in the period of twelve months immediately following the end of the relevant accounting period or, if there is more than one accounting period beginning in that period of twelve months, the latest accounting period beginning in that period.

(2) In paragraph (1) "the relevant accounting period" is the first accounting period of the company after which no amount of unrelieved surplus ACT belonging to the company or any other company which is a member of the group at any time in that accounting period is available to be set against any liability to corporation tax in accordance with these Regulations; and for this purpose unrelieved surplus ACT belonging to another company that is a member of the group at any time in that accounting period shall be regarded as so available until the end of that other company's accounting period.

(3) Paragraph (1) shall not apply where—

(*a*) the company is a member of the group as at 6th April 1999, and

(*b*) at any time in the first accounting period of the parent company of the group to begin on or after that date, the parent company notifies [an officer of Revenue and Customs][1] on behalf of the group that the group will not seek or, as the case may be, will cease to seek recovery of unrelieved surplus ACT in respect of any accounting period of any member of the group that begins on or after that date.

(4) A notification made in accordance with paragraph (3) shall, subject to paragraph (9), be binding on each company that was a member of the group as at 6th April 1999.

(5) Where, otherwise than in a case to which paragraph (3) applies, at any time in an accounting period of the parent company of the group the parent company notifies [an officer of Revenue and Customs][1] on behalf of the group that the group wishes the accounting period of any member of the group in which the notification is made to be the final accounting period of that member and that it will not seek recovery of amounts of unrelieved surplus ACT available to that member in respect of

any subsequent accounting period, the final accounting period of that member and the final accounting period of the parent company is, subject to paragraphs (7) to (10), the accounting period of the parent company in which the notification by the parent company is made.

(6) A notification made in accordance with paragraph (5) shall, subject to paragraph (10), be binding on each company that was a member of the group when the notification was made or that subsequently becomes a member of the group prior to the end of the parent company's final accounting period.

(7) Where paragraph (5) applies and the accounting period of a company in the group other than the parent company that would otherwise be its final accounting period in accordance with that paragraph begins before the end of, but ends after, the accounting period of the parent company in which the notification by the parent company is made, the accounting period of the company concerned shall be treated as if the part ending with the last day of the parent company's accounting period, and the part after, were two separate accounting periods; and the part ending with the last day of the parent company's accounting period shall, subject to paragraph (10), be treated as the company's final accounting period for the purposes of this regulation.

(8) Where—

(*a*) there is an amount of surplus shadow ACT in respect of an accounting period of any company that is a member of the group beginning in the period of twelve months ("the relevant period") immediately following the end of the accounting period of the company in which the parent company notifies [an officer of Revenue and Customs][1] as mentioned in paragraph (5), and

(*b*) all or any part of that surplus amount falls to be carried back under regulation 12 or 13 to an accounting period of a company that is a member of the group ending before the relevant period of the company referred to in sub-paragraph (*a*),

the final accounting period of any company that is a member of the group at any time in the relevant period shall, subject to paragraph (10), be the accounting period or, if more than one, the latest accounting period beginning in the relevant period from which an amount of surplus shadow ACT falls to be carried back as mentioned in sub-paragraph (b) of this paragraph, and not the accounting period referred to in paragraph (5).

(9) Where in an accounting period ("the material period") subsequent to the accounting period in which the parent company notifies [an officer of Revenue and Customs][1] as mentioned in paragraph (3), a company which has an amount of unrelieved surplus ACT becomes a member of the group, these Regulations shall apply in relation to the material period (but not earlier accounting periods) as if no notification had been made in accordance with that paragraph, but not so as to entitle any company to whom that notification, when made, applied to seek recovery of any amount of unrelieved surplus ACT.

(10) Where in an accounting period ("the material period") subsequent to the final accounting period as determined in accordance with paragraph (1), (5), (7) or (8), a company which has an amount of unrelieved surplus ACT becomes a member of the group, these Regulations shall apply in relation to the material period (but not earlier accounting periods) as if the final accounting period had not yet been determined in accordance with any of those paragraphs, but not so as to entitle a company whose final accounting period had previously been determined in accordance with those provisions to seek recovery of any amount of unrelieved surplus ACT.

(11) Where—

(*a*) a company is a member of two or more groups,

(*b*) its final accounting period as a member of one or more, but not all, of the groups concerned has been determined in accordance with the previous provisions of this regulation, and

(*c*) at least one of those determinations is as a result of a notification made by a parent company in accordance with paragraph (5) of this regulation,

these Regulations shall have effect in relation to the group or groups in respect of which the final accounting period of the company has not been determined as if the total amount of its unrelieved surplus ACT had been set against its liability to corporation tax in accordance with regulation 14.

Amendments—[1] Words substituted by the Corporation Tax (Treatment of Unrelieved Surplus Advance Corporation Tax) (Amendment) Regulations, SI 2010/669 regs 2, 6 with effect from 1 April 2010.

6 Definition of group

(1) In these Regulations "group" means a company resident in [an EEA state][1] ("the parent company") which has one or more 51 per cent subsidiaries together with that or those subsidiaries.

(2) For the purposes of paragraph (1)—

(*a*) "51 per cent subsidiary" means a 51 per cent subsidiary that is a company resident in the United Kingdom;

(*b*) a company is not the parent company within a group if—

(i) it has no 51 per cent subsidiary but is itself a 51 per cent subsidiary of another company, or

(ii) it and its 51 per cent subsidiaries are all members of another group;

(*c*) the question whether a company is a 51 per cent subsidiary of the parent company shall be determined, subject to paragraph (3), in accordance with section 838, except that the parent company shall be treated as not being the owner—

(i) of any share capital which it owns directly in a company if a profit on the sale of the shares would be treated as a trading receipt of its trade; or

(ii) of any share capital which it owns indirectly, and which is owned directly by a body corporate for which a profit on the sale of the shares would be treated as a trading receipt of its trade; or

(iii) of any share capital which it owns directly or indirectly in a body corporate not resident in the United Kingdom.

(3) Where a company would otherwise not be a 51 per cent subsidiary, but—

(*a*) persons, whether company members or not, enjoy extraordinary rights or powers under the articles of association or under any other document regulating the company, and

(*b*) because of that fact, ownership of the ordinary share capital (for the purposes of the definition of "51 per cent subsidiary" in section 838(1)(*a*)) may not be an appropriate test of whether a company is a 51 per cent subsidiary of the parent company,

then in considering whether a company is a 51 per cent subsidiary of the parent company for the purposes of paragraph (1), holdings of all kinds of share capital, including preference shares, or of any particular category of share capital, or voting power or any other kind of special power may be taken into account instead of ordinary share capital.

(4) Notwithstanding that, apart from this paragraph, a company ("the subsidiary company") would at any time be a 51 per cent subsidiary of the parent company for the purposes of this regulation, the subsidiary company shall not be treated at that time as a 51 per cent subsidiary for those purposes—

(*a*) if arrangements are in existence by virtue of which any person has or could obtain, or any persons together have or could obtain, control of the subsidiary company but not of the parent company; and

(*b*) unless the following conditions are also fulfilled, namely—

(i) that the parent company is beneficially entitled to more than 50 per cent of any profits available for distribution to equity holders of the subsidiary company; and

(ii) that the parent company would be beneficially entitled to more than 50 per cent of any assets of the subsidiary company available for distribution to its equity holders on a winding up.

(5) In paragraph (4)—

"arrangements" means arrangements of any kind, whether in writing or not, other than arrangements whose sole or main purpose is to reduce the amount of surplus shadow ACT available to be utilised by a company other than the subsidiary company in accordance with regulation 13;

"control" has the meaning given by section 840.

(6) Where by virtue of any enactment a Minister of the Crown or Northern Ireland department has power to give directions to a statutory body as to the disposal of assets belonging to, or to a subsidiary of, that body, the existence of that power shall not be regarded as constituting (or as having at any time constituted) an arrangement within the meaning of paragraph (4)(*a*).

(7) The provisions of Schedule 18 shall apply for the purposes of paragraph (4)(*b*) as if—

(*a*) for any reference to section 413(7) to (9) there were substituted a reference to paragraph (4)(*b*);

(*b*) paragraph 7(1) of that Schedule were omitted and for any reference to "the relevant accounting period" there were substituted a reference to the accounting period current at the time in question.

(8) For the purposes of these Regulations, a company ("A") is the "immediate parent company" of another company ("B") if, disregarding any other company of which B is a 51 per cent subsidiary by virtue of section 838 and this regulation, A would be the parent company of B by virtue of section 838 and this regulation.

Commentary—*Simon's Taxes* **A1.574**.

Press releases etc—HMRC Tax Information and Impact Note "Shadow Advance Corporation Tax", 8 November 2012.

Amendments—[1] In para (1), words substituted for words "the United Kingdom' by the Corporation Tax (Treatment of Unrelieved Surplus Advance Corporation Tax) (Amendment) Regulations, SI 2013/157 reg 2(1) with effect in relation to distributions made on or after 11 March 2013.

6A [Abnormal dividends: general

(1) In regulation 10A an abnormal dividend has been received by a company where section 740 (abnormal dividends: general) of the CTA as modified by paragraph (2) has been applied to it.

(2) For the purposes of regulation 10A, an amount received by way of dividend in subsection (1) of section 740 of the CTA shall, for the avoidance of doubt, be interpreted as being in connection with—

(*a*) the purchase of securities where the purchase is followed by the sale of the same or other securities,

(*b*) the sale of securities where the sale is followed by the purchase of the same or other securities,
(*c*) the distribution, transfer or realisation of assets of a company, or
(*d*) the application of such assets in discharge of liabilities.][1]

Amendments—[1] Reg 6A inserted by the Corporation Tax (Treatment of Unrelieved Surplus Advance Corporation Tax) (Amendment) Regulations, SI 2010/669 regs 2, 4 with effect from 1 April 2010.

7 Restriction on [qualifying] investment income—replacement of income

Where a company takes any action the effect of which is that income consisting of interest to which a company is or will be entitled becomes or is replaced by income consisting of a distribution, and the main purpose of that action is to reduce the amount of shadow ACT which it would be treated as having paid under regulation 11 for an accounting period, the income consisting of the distribution shall not be regarded for the purposes of these Regulations as [qualifying][1] investment income.

Amendments—[1] Word substituted in text and in heading by the Corporation Tax (Treatment of Unrelieved Surplus Advance Corporation Tax) (Amendment) Regulations, SI 2017/454 regs 2, 4 with effect for company distributions made in an accounting period commencing on or after 6 April 2016, subject to transitional provisions for accounting periods straddling that date (SI 2017/454 reg 1(3)).

8 Restriction on [qualifying] investment income—arrangements to pass on value of [qualifying] investment income

(1) This regulation applies in any case where—
(*a*) a person ("A") who is a company is entitled to [qualifying][1] investment income;
(*b*) arrangements subsist such that another person ("B") obtains, whether directly or indirectly, a payment representing any of the value of that [qualifying][1] investment income, in excess of the payment that would have been made in the circumstances specified in paragraph (2);
(*c*) the arrangements (whether or not made directly between A and B) were entered into for an unallowable purpose, and
(*d*) neither A nor B is a company whose final accounting period has been determined in accordance with regulation 4 or 5.

(2) The circumstances specified in this paragraph are where—
(*a*) the payment representing any of the value of that [qualifying][1] investment income was made under a transaction between persons at arm's length both of whom were companies;
(*b*) neither company was or had been at any time a member of a group, and
(*c*) neither company was entitled to an amount of unrelieved surplus ACT as at 6th April 1999.

(3) This regulation does not apply if and to the extent that any provision of the Tax Acts has the effect of cancelling or reducing the tax advantage which would otherwise be obtained by virtue of the arrangements.

(4) Where this regulation applies, the [qualifying][1] investment income referred to in paragraph (1) shall not be regarded for the purposes of these Regulations as [qualifying][1] investment income.

(5) For the purposes of this regulation, the question whether any arrangements were entered into for an "unallowable purpose" shall be determined in accordance with paragraphs (6) and (7).

(6) Arrangements are entered into for an unallowable purpose if the purposes for which A is a party to the arrangements include the purpose of reducing the amount of shadow ACT treated as paid, in accordance with regulation 11, on relevant distributions made—
(*a*) by A, or
(*b*) where A is a member of a group, by any other company which is a member of that group, at any time in, or after the end of, the accounting period in which the arrangements are entered into.

(7) In determining for the purposes of paragraph (6) whether a company could have used [qualifying][1] investment income for the purpose of reducing shadow ACT, the company shall be taken to use its actual [qualifying][1] investment income for that purpose before using the [qualifying][1] investment income in question.

(8) In this regulation—
"arrangements" means arrangements of any kind, whether in writing or not (and includes a series of arrangements, whether or not between the same parties);
"tax advantage" has the same meaning as in Chapter I of Part XVII of the Taxes Act.

Amendments—[1] Word substituted in text and in heading by the Corporation Tax (Treatment of Unrelieved Surplus Advance Corporation Tax) (Amendment) Regulations, SI 2017/454 regs 2, 4 with effect for company distributions made in an accounting period commencing on or after 6 April 2016, subject to transitional provisions for accounting periods straddling that date (SI 2017/454 reg 1(3)).

9 Restriction on [qualifying] investment income—dealers

(1) Where a dealer receives—
(*a*) a distribution which is made by a company resident in the United Kingdom ("a UK distribution"), or any payment which is representative of a UK distribution, and
(*b*) the distribution or, as the case may be, the payment is taken into account in computing the profits of the dealer which are chargeable to tax in accordance with the provisions of the Taxes Act applicable to Case I or II of Schedule D,

the distribution or payment shall not be regarded for the purposes of these Regulations as [qualifying][1] investment income.

(2) In paragraph (1) "dealer" means a person who is a dealer in relation to a distribution within the meaning of section 95(2).

Amendments—[1] Word substituted in text and in heading by the Corporation Tax (Treatment of Unrelieved Surplus Advance Corporation Tax) (Amendment) Regulations, SI 2017/454 regs 2, 4 with effect for company distributions made in an accounting period commencing on or after 6 April 2016, subject to transitional provisions for accounting periods straddling that date (SI 2017/454 reg 1(3)).

10 Restriction on [qualifying] investment income—intra-group distributions

(1) A distribution received by a company which is a member of a group from another company within the group, or from another company in the circumstances specified in paragraph (2) or (3) shall, subject to paragraph (4), not be regarded for the purposes of these Regulations as [qualifying][1] investment income.

(2) The circumstances specified in this paragraph are where the company making the distribution in question is not a member of the group at the time the distribution is received but arrangements in place at that time are such as to give rise to a reasonable expectation that the company will join or, as the case may be, rejoin the group.

(3) The circumstances specified in this paragraph are where the distribution in question was made by reference to the shareholdings existing at a time when both the company making the distribution and the company owning the shares at that time were members of the same group.

(4) Where the distribution is a relevant distribution and the company making the relevant distribution has elected as mentioned in regulation 11(3)(*b*), paragraph (1) of this regulation shall not apply to so much of the franked distribution in respect of which that election is made.

Amendments—[1] Word substituted in text and in heading by the Corporation Tax (Treatment of Unrelieved Surplus Advance Corporation Tax) (Amendment) Regulations, SI 2017/454 regs 2, 4 with effect for company distributions made in an accounting period commencing on or after 6 April 2016, subject to transitional provisions for accounting periods straddling that date (SI 2017/454 reg 1(3)).

10A [Restriction on [qualifying] investment income—abnormal dividends

(1) For the purposes of these Regulations an abnormal dividend shall not be regarded as [qualifying][2] investment income where it has been received by—

(*a*) company (R1) from company (P1) where P1 and R1 are not members of a group, or

(*b*) company (R2) from company (P2) where P2 and R2 are members of the same group.

(2) Sub-paragraph (*b*) of paragraph (1) shall apply notwithstanding that company P2 has made an election under regulation 11(3)(*b*).][1]

Amendments—[1] Reg 10A inserted by the Corporation Tax (Treatment of Unrelieved Surplus Advance Corporation Tax) (Amendment) Regulations, SI 2010/669 regs 2, 5 with effect from 1 April 2010.

[2] Word substituted in text and in heading by the Corporation Tax (Treatment of Unrelieved Surplus Advance Corporation Tax) (Amendment) Regulations, SI 2017/454 regs 2, 4 with effect for company distributions made in an accounting period commencing on or after 6 April 2016, subject to transitional provisions for accounting periods straddling that date (SI 2017/454 reg 1(3)).

11 Computation of shadow ACT

(1) Where a company resident in the United Kingdom makes a relevant distribution, other than a relevant distribution to which paragraph (2) applies, shadow ACT shall, for the purposes of determining the amount of unrelieved surplus ACT that may be set against a company's liability to corporation tax for an accounting period in accordance with regulation 14, be treated as having been paid by the company in accordance with the provisions of this regulation.

(2) This paragraph applies to a relevant distribution—

(*a*) which is a manufactured dividend to which paragraph 2(2) of Schedule 23A applies, or

(*b*) which is made, otherwise than in the circumstances specified in paragraph (3), by a company that is a member of a group to another company within the group.

(3) The circumstances specified in this paragraph are where the company making the distribution—

(*a*) has received, in the accounting period in which the distribution is made, [qualifying investment income][1] of an amount sufficient to ensure that the amount of shadow ACT that, apart from paragraph (2)(*b*), would be treated as having been paid in respect of that distribution would have been less than it would have been had the company not received that amount of [qualifying investment income][1];

(*b*) has elected in its tax return for the accounting period in which the distribution is made, or in an amendment to that tax return, that an amount of the franked distribution equal to the whole or a stated amount of that [qualifying investment income][1] (multiplied by nine-eighths) should not be excluded in computing its shadow ACT for that period; and

(*c*) has informed the company receiving the distribution that sub-paragraphs (*a*) and (*b*) of this paragraph apply in relation to the distribution, and of the amount of the distribution to which the election under sub-paragraph (*b*) applies.

(4) An election to which paragraph (3)(*b*) refers—

(*a*) shall be made not later than two years after the end of the accounting period in which the distribution is made, and
(*b*) shall be irrevocable.

(5) Where a relevant distribution to which paragraph (1) applies does not fall within an accounting period of the company making the distribution, it shall be treated, for all purposes of these Regulations, as falling within an accounting period that—
(*a*) begins—
(i) on the same date as the date on which the accounting period of the company's immediate parent company in which the distribution falls begins or, if later
(ii) on the date immediately following the end of the last accounting period of the company making the distribution that precedes the date on which the distribution is made, and
(*b*) ends—
(i) on the same date as the date on which the accounting period of the company's immediate parent company in which the distribution falls ends or, if earlier
(ii) on the date immediately before the beginning of an accounting period of the company making the distribution.

(6) For the purposes of paragraph (5), where the distribution referred to in that paragraph is made at a time when there is no accounting period of the company's immediate parent company, that paragraph shall have effect as if for the references to the accounting period of the company's immediate parent company there were substituted references to the accounting period of the immediate parent company of the company's immediate parent company (and so on until the accounting period of an immediate parent company in which the distribution falls is found).

(7) Where a company ceases to be a member of a group, shadow ACT shall be computed in accordance with paragraph (1) in relation to the accounting period of the company in which it ceases to be a member of the group as if the part ending on the date on which the company ceases to be member of the group, and the part after, were two separate accounting periods.

(8) Where there is a change of ownership of a company and the change—
(*a*) is not such as to cause the company to cease to be a member of a group, but
(*b*) occurs in circumstances where either regulation 16 or regulation 17 applies,

shadow ACT shall be computed in accordance with paragraph (1) in relation to the accounting period of the company in which the change occurs as if the part ending with the change, and the part after, were two separate accounting periods.

(9) Subject to paragraphs (10) to (12), for the financial year 1999 and any subsequent financial year, shadow ACT shall be treated as having been paid at the rate of 25 per cent on an amount equal to the amount or value of the relevant distribution.

(10) Where in any accounting period a company receives [qualifying investment income][1], subject to regulation 22(1), shadow ACT shall not be treated as having been paid by the company in respect of relevant distributions made by it in that period unless the amount of franked distributions made by it in that period exceeds the aggregate of—
(*a*) nine-eighths of the amount of [qualifying investment income][1] consisting of distributions made to the company in that period, and
(*b*) the amount of any surplus of [qualifying investment income][1] carried forward from the previous accounting period in accordance with paragraph (12).

(11) If in an accounting period there is such an excess, shadow ACT shall be treated as having been paid on an amount which, when the shadow ACT treated as having been paid thereon is added to it, is equal to the excess.

(12) Where a company has a surplus of [qualifying][1] investment income in any accounting period, the surplus shall be carried forward to the next accounting period for the purposes of paragraphs (3), (10) and (13).

[(13) A company has a surplus of qualifying investment income in an accounting period for the purposes of paragraph (12) if an amount equal to—
(*a*) the aggregate of nine-eighths of the qualifying investment income consisting of distributions made to the company in that period; and
(*b*) the surplus of qualifying investment income carried forward from the previous accounting period in accordance with paragraph (12),

exceeds the amount of the franked distributions made by it in that period; and the amount of that excess is to be regarded as the amount of the surplus of qualifying investment income for the purposes of paragraph (12).][1]

(14) In the application of paragraphs (12) and (13) to a straddling accounting period of a company, or to the case where an accounting period of a company ends on 5th April 1999 and its next accounting period begins on 6th April 1999—
(*a*) there shall be ascertained the amount of surplus [qualifying][1] investment income in the accounting period ending or, in the case of a straddling accounting period, deemed by virtue of regulation 3(4) to end, on 5th April 1999;

(*b*) that amount shall be treated as carried forward to the accounting period beginning or, in the case of a straddling accounting period, deemed by virtue of regulation 3(4) to begin, on 6th April 1999 and shall be treated as mentioned in paragraph (10).

Amendments—[1] In paras (3), (10), words substituted, in paras (12), (14)(*a*), word substituted, and para (13) substituted, by the Corporation Tax (Treatment of Unrelieved Surplus Advance Corporation Tax) (Amendment) Regulations, SI 2017/454 regs 2, 5 with effect for company distributions made in an accounting period commencing on or after 6 April 2016, subject to transitional provisions for accounting periods straddling that date (SI 2017/454 reg 1(3)).

12 Utilisation of shadow ACT

(1) Shadow ACT which a company is treated as having paid in accordance with regulation 11 in respect of any relevant distribution made by it in an accounting period shall, for the purposes mentioned in regulation 11(1) and in accordance with the provisions of this regulation, be set against the company's liability to corporation tax on any profits charged to corporation tax for that accounting period, but not so as to reduce the amount of that liability.

(2) Subject to paragraph (7)(*b*), shadow ACT shall be utilised as mentioned in paragraph (1) before any amount of unrelieved surplus ACT is set against a company's liability to corporation tax in accordance with regulation 14.

(3) The amount of shadow ACT to be set against a company's liability for any accounting period under paragraph (1)—

(*a*) shall not exceed the amount of shadow ACT that would have been treated as paid (apart from regulation 11(10) to (12)) in respect of a relevant distribution made at the end of that period of an amount which, together with the shadow ACT treated as paid in respect of it, is equal to the company's profits charged to corporation tax for that period;

(*b*) shall be computed, where applicable, by reference to the like provisions with respect to separate accounting periods on a change of ownership of a company that are contained in regulations 16 and 17 for the purposes of computing the amount of unrelieved surplus ACT to be set against the company's liability for an accounting period.

(4) Where an amount of credit for foreign tax falls to be allowed in accordance with section 797 against corporation tax attributable to any income or chargeable gain ("the relevant income or gain"), then—

(*a*) paragraph (3) shall have effect only in relation to so much of the company's profits chargeable to corporation tax for the relevant accounting period as does not include the relevant income or gain;

(*b*) in so far as the company's liability to corporation tax for the relevant accounting period relates to the relevant income or gain, it shall be taken to be reduced by the amount of the credit for foreign tax attributable to that income or gain, as determined in accordance with subsections (2) and (3) of section 797; and

(*c*) the amount of shadow ACT which may be set against that liability, so far as it relates to the relevant income or gain, shall not exceed whichever is the lower of the limits specified in paragraph (5).

(5) The limits specified in this paragraph are—

(*a*) the limit which would apply under paragraph (3) if the amount of the relevant income or gain, determined in accordance with subsection (3) of section 797, were the company's only income or gain for the relevant accounting period; and

(*b*) the amount of corporation tax for which, after taking account of the reduction mentioned in paragraph (4)(*b*), the company is liable in respect of that income or gain.

(6) In paragraph (4) "the relevant accounting period" shall be construed in accordance with subsection (2) of section 797.

(7) Where in respect of any accounting period of a company ("the principal period") there is an amount of surplus shadow ACT, that amount shall be treated as if it were shadow ACT which the company is treated as having paid in respect of relevant distributions made by it in any of its accounting periods beginning on or after 6th April 1999 and in the six years preceding the principal period, but so that that amount—

(*a*) is set, so far as possible, against the company's liability for a more recent accounting period before a more remote one,

(*b*) does not cause the amount of shadow ACT specified in paragraph (3)(*a*) as respects an accounting period of the company to be exceeded,

(*c*) where the company is a member of a group, is not set against the liability of another company in the group for an accounting period, and

(*d*) except in relation to the period beginning twenty four months before the end of the principal period and ending the day before the commencement of the principal period, does not displace any amount of unrelieved surplus ACT that, by virtue of regulation 14, is set against the company's liability for an accounting period.

(8) For the purposes of paragraph (7)—

(a) the reference to any of the company's accounting periods beginning on or after 6th April 1999 includes a reference to a separate accounting period mentioned in regulations 16 and 17 beginning on or after that date;

(b) where an accounting period begins before, but ends during, the period of twenty four months referred to in sub-paragraph (d) of that paragraph, the amount of unrelieved surplus ACT falling to be displaced as mentioned in that sub-paragraph shall be proportionately reduced by reference to the part of that accounting period that falls outside the period of twenty four months.

(9) Subject to regulation 13 (intra-group allocation of shadow ACT), where in respect of any accounting period of a company there is an amount of surplus shadow ACT which has not been dealt with under paragraph (7), that amount shall be treated for the purposes of this regulation (including any further application of this paragraph) as if it were shadow ACT which the company is treated as having paid in the next accounting period.

13 Intra-group allocation of surplus shadow ACT

(1) Where in respect of any accounting period of a company that is a member of a group at any time in that accounting period, there is an amount of surplus shadow ACT that has not been utilised as mentioned in regulation 12(7), the whole or part of that amount shall, for the purposes mentioned in regulation 11(1) and in accordance with the provisions of this regulation, be allocated by the parent company to another company, or other companies, that are members of the group ("the potential recipients").

(2) Where an amount of surplus shadow ACT is allocated to another company in the group under paragraph (1), that amount shall be set against the balance (if any) of that company's liability to corporation tax on any profits charged to corporation tax for an accounting period to which that amount is attributed in accordance with paragraph (8), that remains after the amount of that company's shadow ACT in respect of its own distributions for that period (together with the amount of any surplus shadow ACT treated as belonging to that company under paragraph (6)) has been set against that liability in accordance with regulation 12(1), but not so as to reduce the amount of that liability or so as to exceed the capacity of that company to utilise that amount.

(3) No company that is a member of a group at any time in an accounting period shall be entitled to set an amount of unrelieved surplus ACT against its liability to corporation tax for that accounting period in accordance with regulation 14 until all surplus shadow ACT of that company for that period has been allocated under paragraph (1).

(4) Where the amount of surplus shadow ACT referred to in paragraph (1) is insufficient in relation to the capacity of all the potential recipients fully to utilise surplus shadow ACT, the parent company in the group shall determine the recipients to whom that amount shall be allocated under that paragraph, and the proportion of that amount to be allocated to each of those recipients in accordance with the capacity of each of those recipients to utilise that amount.

(5) Where the amount referred to in paragraph (1) exceeds the amount which could be utilised by all the potential recipients—

(a) so much of that amount as is able to be utilised by the potential recipients shall be allocated to them by the parent company under that paragraph in accordance with the capacity of each of the potential recipients to utilise that amount, and

(b) the balance shall, subject to paragraph (6), be retained by the company in which the amount arose and shall be treated by that company (in accordance with regulation 12(9)) as if it were shadow ACT which the company is treated as having paid in the next accounting period.

(6) Where, in a case to which paragraph (1) applies, the company concerned ceases to be a member of the group, otherwise than by reason of a transaction or arrangements between that company or that company's immediate parent company (or the latter company's immediate parent company and so on) and another person who is not connected with that company within the meaning of section 839, the amount of surplus shadow ACT shall be treated for the purposes of this regulation as belonging to the immediate parent company of that company at the time it ceases to be a member of the group or, where the immediate parent company ceases to be a member of the group at the same time as that company, as belonging to the next immediate parent company (and so on as necessary until an immediate parent company is found who has not ceased to be a member of the group at the same time as that company).

(7) An amount of surplus shadow ACT allocated to a company under paragraph (1) may subsequently be reallocated at any time under that paragraph, but not so as to reduce the amount allocated to a company to an amount below its capacity to utilise surplus shadow ACT after the time limit for amending that company's tax return has expired.

(8) Where the whole or part of an amount of surplus shadow ACT is allocated to a company under paragraph (1), it shall be attributed to a relevant accounting period, or relevant accounting periods, of that company in the following order—

(a) an accounting period beginning and ending on the same dates as, or otherwise contained within, the accounting period of the company whose surplus shadow ACT is allocated ("the transferring company's accounting period");

(*b*) an accounting period beginning before, but ending in, the transferring company's accounting period;

(*c*) an accounting period beginning in, but ending after, the end of the transferring company's accounting period;

(*d*) any further period (whether the whole or part of an accounting period) beginning twenty four months or less prior to the end of the transferring company's accounting period.

(9) In paragraph (8) "relevant accounting period" means an accounting period in which both the transferring company and the company receiving the amount were at some time members of the group.

(10) Where the further period referred to in paragraph (8)(*d*) is a part of an accounting period, the capacity of the company to utilise the amount attributed to that further period shall be proportionately reduced by reference to the part of its accounting period which falls outside that further period.

(11) Where in accordance with paragraph (8) amounts of surplus shadow ACT in respect of accounting periods of two or more companies are attributed to a relevant accounting period, or relevant accounting periods, of a company, the parent company in the group shall determine the order of priority in which those amounts are attributed, and the order of priority so determined shall apply on any subsequent reallocation of those amounts.

(12) Where a company is a member of more than one group and there is an allocation to that company under paragraph (1) of an amount of surplus shadow ACT by the parent company of more than one group, the order of priority in which allocations are attributed to an accounting period, or accounting periods, of that company in accordance with paragraph (8) shall be determined by reference to the date on which an allocation is made (an earlier allocation having priority over a later allocation).

(13) Where in accordance with paragraph (8) an amount falls to be attributed to an accounting period which is either the first or the last accounting period in which both the transferring company and the company receiving the amount were members of the group, then for the purpose of determining the amount to be attributed to that accounting period—

(*a*) the capacity of the company receiving the amount to utilise the amount to be attributed to that accounting period—

(i) shall be proportionately reduced by reference to the part of that period during which the transferring company and the company receiving the amount were not both members of the group, and

(ii) shall be further reduced by any prior attribution to that period by reason of the allocation to the company receiving the amount of the surplus shadow ACT of another company, and

(*b*) the amount shall be treated as attributable to a separate accounting period comprising the part of that accounting period during which both the transferring company and the company receiving the amount were members of the group.

(14) Where in accordance with paragraph (8) an amount is attributed to a relevant accounting period referred to in sub-paragraph (*b*) or (*d*) of that paragraph, that amount—

(*a*) shall displace any amount of unrelieved surplus ACT that, by virtue of regulation 14, was set against the company's liability to corporation tax on any profits charged to corporation tax for that accounting period, but

(*b*) shall not displace any amount of surplus shadow ACT that, in accordance with regulation 12, has previously been set against that company's liability for corporation tax for that accounting period or (as the case may be) has been treated as shadow ACT which that company is treated as having paid in respect of any relevant distributions made by the company in that accounting period.

(15) Where the parent company fails to allocate an amount of surplus shadow ACT in accordance with this regulation—

(*a*) that amount may be allocated in accordance with this regulation by [an officer of Revenue and Customs][1];

(*b*) if that amount is subsequently allocated by the parent company in accordance with this regulation, any allocation by [an officer of Revenue and Customs][1] under sub-paragraph (*a*) shall be treated as if it had not been made.

Amendments—[1] Words substituted by the Corporation Tax (Treatment of Unrelieved Surplus Advance Corporation Tax) (Amendment) Regulations, SI 2010/669 regs 2, 6 with effect from 1 April 2010.

14 Set-off of unrelieved surplus ACT against liability to corporation tax

(1) Subject to paragraphs (2) to (4), a company's unrelieved surplus ACT shall be set against its liability to corporation tax on any profits charged to corporation tax for an accounting period beginning on or after 6th April 1999, and shall accordingly discharge a corresponding amount of that liability.

(2) Unrelieved surplus ACT shall not be set against a company's liability to corporation tax for an accounting period under paragraph (1) to the extent that it can be set against the company's liability to corporation tax for an earlier accounting period.

(3) Where section 116(2) applies in relation to a company which is a member of a partnership, no unrelieved surplus advance corporation tax may be set against its liability to corporation tax on its share in the profits of the relevant accounting period of the partnership.
(4) The amount of unrelieved surplus ACT to be set against a company's liability for an accounting period under paragraph (1) shall not exceed the amount calculated in accordance with the formula—

$$A - B$$

where—

A is the amount of the company's capacity to utilise unrelieved surplus ACT calculated in accordance with regulation 12, and

B is the amount of any shadow ACT attributed to that period in accordance with regulations 12 and 13.

(5) References to "the relevant accounting period" in paragraph (3) shall be construed in accordance with section 116(3).

15 Restriction on set-off of company's unrelieved surplus ACT against subsidiary company's liability to corporation tax

(1) Subject to paragraph (2) and regulation 17, unrelieved surplus ACT consisting of ACT which a subsidiary is treated as having paid by virtue of section 240(2) shall be set off against the subsidiary's liability to corporation tax for an accounting period in accordance with regulation 14 before unrelieved surplus ACT consisting of ACT paid in respect of any distribution made by the subsidiary.
(2) No unrelieved surplus ACT consisting of ACT which a subsidiary is treated as having paid by virtue of section 240(2) shall be set against the subsidiary's liability to corporation tax in accordance with regulation 14 for any accounting period in which, or in any part of which, it was not a subsidiary of the surrendering company, unless throughout that period or part both companies were subsidiaries of a third company.
(3) In this regulation "surrendering company" and "subsidiary" have the same meanings as in section 240.

16 Calculation of unrelieved surplus ACT on change of ownership of company

(1) This regulation applies where—

(*a*) within any period of three years there is both a change in the ownership of a company and, either earlier or later in that period, or at the same time, a major change in the nature or conduct of a trade or business carried on by the company; or

(*b*) at any time after the scale of the activities in a trade or business carried on by a company has become small or negligible, and before any considerable revival of the trade or business, there is a change in the ownership of the company.

(2) Regulation 14 shall apply in relation to an accounting period in which the change of ownership occurs as if the part ending with the change of ownership, and the part after, were two separate accounting periods; and for that purpose the profits of the company charged to corporation tax for the accounting period shall be apportioned between those parts.
(3) No unrelieved surplus ACT of the company shall be set off against the company's liability to corporation tax on any profits charged to corporation tax for an accounting period ending after the change of ownership; and for this purpose an accounting period in which the change of ownership occurs shall be treated as if the part ending with the change of ownership, and the part after, were two separate accounting periods.
(4) Paragraph (3) applies to unrelieved surplus ACT consisting of ACT which a subsidiary is treated as having paid by virtue of section 240(2) as it applies to unrelieved surplus ACT consisting of ACT paid in respect of any distribution made by the subsidiary.
(5) Sections 768(8) and (9) and 769 shall apply for the purposes of this regulation as if in subsection (3) of section 769 the reference to the benefit of the losses were a reference to the benefit of unrelieved surplus ACT.
(6) In paragraph (1) "a major change in the nature or conduct of a trade or business" includes—

(*a*) a major change in the type of property dealt in, or services or facilities provided, in the trade or business;

(*b*) a major change in customers, outlets or markets of the trade or business;

(*c*) a change whereby the company ceases to be a trading company and becomes an investment company or vice versa; or

(*d*) where the company is an investment company, a major change in the nature of the investments held by the company;

and this paragraph applies even if the change is the result of a gradual process which began outside the period of three years mentioned in paragraph (1).
(7) In this regulation—

"trading company" means a company whose business consists wholly or mainly in the carrying on of a trade or trades;

"investment company" means a company (other than a holding company) whose business consists wholly or mainly in the making of investments and the principal part of whose income is derived therefrom;

"holding company" means a company whose business consists wholly or mainly in the holding of shares or securities of companies which are its 90 per cent subsidiaries and which are trading companies;

"90 per cent subsidiary" has the meaning given by section 838.

17 Restriction on application of regulation 15 on change of ownership of company

(1) This regulation applies where—

(*a*) there is a change in the ownership of a company ("the relevant company"),

(*b*) there is an amount of unrelieved surplus ACT which the relevant company, as a subsidiary company, is treated as having paid by virtue of section 240(2), and

(*c*) within the period of six years beginning three years before the change, there is a major change in the nature or conduct of a trade or business of the company which is for the purposes of regulation 15 the surrendering company in relation to that amount.

(2) The amount of unrelieved surplus ACT referred to in paragraph (1)(*b*) shall not be set off in accordance with regulation 14 against the relevant company's liability to corporation tax on profits charged to corporation tax for an accounting period ending after the change of ownership; and for this purpose an accounting period in which the change of ownership occurs shall be treated as if the part ending with the change of ownership, and the part after, were two separate accounting periods.

(3) Paragraphs (5) to (7) of regulation 16 shall apply for the purposes of this regulation as they apply for the purposes of that regulation and as if the reference in paragraph (6) of regulation 16 to the period of three years mentioned in paragraph (1) of that regulation were a reference to the period mentioned in paragraph (1)(*c*) of this regulation.

18 Restriction on set-off under regulation 14 where asset transferred after change of ownership of company

(1) This regulation applies where—

(*a*) there is a change in the ownership of a company ("the relevant company"),

(*b*) after the change the relevant company acquires an asset from another company in circumstances such that section 171(1) of the Taxation of Chargeable Gains Act 1992 applies to the acquisition, and

(*c*) a chargeable gain accrues to the relevant company on the disposal of the asset within the period of three years beginning with the change of ownership.

(2) For the purposes of paragraph (1)(*c*) an asset acquired by the relevant company as mentioned in paragraph (1)(*b*) shall be treated as the same as an asset owned at a later time by that company if the value of the second asset is derived in whole or in part from the first asset, and in particular where the second asset is a freehold, and the first asset was a leasehold and the lessee has acquired the reversion.

(3) In relation to the accounting period in which the chargeable gain accrues to the relevant company ("the relevant period"), regulation 14 shall have effect as if the limit imposed by paragraph (4) of that regulation on the amount of unrelieved surplus ACT to be set against the relevant company's liability to corporation tax were reduced by an amount equal to 20 per cent of the amount of the chargeable gain.

(4) Paragraph (5) of regulation 16 shall apply for the purposes of this regulation as it applies for the purposes of that regulation.

19 Recovery of unrelieved surplus ACT wrongly set off

If [an officer of Revenue and Customs][1] discovers that any set off of unrelieved surplus ACT of a company by virtue of regulation 14 ought not to have been made, or has become excessive, the officer may make any such assessments as may in his judgment be required for recovering any tax that ought to have been paid and generally for securing that the resulting liability to tax (including interest on unpaid tax) of the company is what it would have been if only such set off had been made as ought to have been made.

Amendments—[1] Words substituted by the Corporation Tax (Treatment of Unrelieved Surplus Advance Corporation Tax) (Amendment) Regulations, SI 2010/669 regs 2, 6 with effect from 1 April 2010.

20 Set off of unrelieved surplus ACT against liability to corporation tax on profits of a controlled foreign company apportioned to a company

(1) In any case where—

(*a*) an amount of chargeable profits ("Chapter IV profits") of a controlled foreign company is apportioned to a company resident in the United Kingdom under the provisions of Chapter IV of Part XVII of the Taxes Act, and (*b*) the company to whom the amount is apportioned has an amount of surplus shadow ACT, calculated in accordance with regulation 12 and (where applicable) regulation 13, available to be set against the company's liability to corporation tax for the appropriate accounting period (including, by virtue of regulation 3(3), its liability to tax under section 747(4)(*a*) for that period),

then so much of that amount as does not exceed the relevant maximum shall be set against the company's liability to tax under that section in respect of the Chapter IV profits.

(2) So much of any unrelieved surplus ACT of the company as does not exceed the relevant amount may be set against the company's liability to tax in respect of the Chapter IV profits.

(3) Where—

(*a*) the whole of the amount of the company's surplus shadow ACT has not been set off against the company's liability to tax as mentioned in paragraph (1), and

(*b*) the company is a member of a group,

the part of that amount that has not been so utilised may be allocated by the parent company to any other company in the group to whom an amount of Chapter IV profits has been apportioned, and the provisions of this regulation shall apply accordingly to that other company.

(4) In this regulation—

(*a*) "the appropriate accounting period" has the same meaning as in paragraph 1 of Schedule 26;

(*b*) "the relevant amount" is the amount (if any) which is the difference between the amount of the relevant maximum and the amount of surplus shadow ACT set against the company's liability in respect of the Chapter IV profits in accordance with paragraph (1);

(*c*) "the relevant maximum" is the amount calculated in accordance with the formula—

$$C - D$$

where—

C is the amount of shadow ACT that would have been treated as paid (apart from regulation 11(10) to (12)) in respect of a relevant distribution made at the end of the company's appropriate accounting period of an amount which, together with the shadow ACT treated as paid in respect of it, is equal to the amount calculated in accordance with the formula specified in paragraph (5), and

D is the portion of the controlled foreign company's creditable tax (if any) which is apportioned to the company for that accounting period as mentioned in section 747(4)(*a*).

(5) The formula specified in this paragraph is—

$$E - F$$

where—

E is the amount of the Chapter IV profits on which the company is chargeable to corporation tax for the appropriate accounting period, and

F is the total of any relevant allowances which are to be regarded, by virtue of paragraph 1(5) of Schedule 26, as having been allowed as a deduction against the company's profits together with any such additional amount as would fall to be so regarded if a claim under paragraph 1(1) of Schedule 26 were made in respect of all relevant allowances that are available under that paragraph.

21 Displacement of unrelieved surplus ACT—consequential provision

(1) Where, with respect to an accounting period of a company ("the affected company") that is a member of a group at any time in that accounting period—

(*a*) an amount of unrelieved surplus ACT is displaced under regulation 12(7)(*d*) or 13(8)(*b*) or (*d*), and

(*b*) as a consequence the affected company is assessed to, or an amendment of its self-assessment is made in respect of, an amount of corporation tax for that accounting period,

then, if the whole of that amount of corporation tax is not paid by the affected company within six months from the date determined under paragraph (2), any other company that is a member of the group at any time in that accounting period may, at any time within two years from that date, be assessed and charged (in the name of the affected company) to the whole or, as the case may be, the unpaid part of that amount; and a company paying any amount of corporation tax under this paragraph shall be entitled to recover from the affected company a sum equal to the aggregate of the amount paid and any interest paid by the company under section 87A of the Taxes Management Act 1970 on that amount.

(2) The date referred to in paragraph (1) is whichever is the later of—

(*a*) the date when the amount of corporation tax became due and payable by the affected company or, as the case may be, the date when that amount is treated as having become due and payable under the Corporation Tax (Instalment Payments) Regulations 1998; and
(*b*) the date when an amendment of the affected company's self-assessment was made.

22 Life assurance companies

(1) [So much of the policy holder's [qualifying][2] investment income from investments of a company's [long-term business][2] as is referable to its][1] life assurance business—

(*a*) shall not be used (for the purposes of computing the amount of shadow ACT which the company is treated as having paid for an accounting period under regulation 11(10)) to frank relevant distributions made by the company in that period;
(*b*) shall be disregarded in determining whether the company has a surplus of [qualifying][1] investment income as mentioned in regulation 11(13), or the amount of the surplus.

(2) For the purposes of regulations 12 to 14, the profits charged to corporation tax for any accounting period of a company carrying on life assurance business shall be reduced by deducting the policy holders' share of [the qualifying investment income][2].

[(3) In this regulation—

"life assurance business" [has the meaning given by section 56 of the Finance Act 2012

"long-term business" has the meaning given by section 63(1) of the Finance Act 2012;

"policy holders' share of the qualifying investment income" is the amount given by the formula—

$$(1 - RP) \times Q$$

where—

"RP" is the relevant proportion set out in section 105(4) of the Finance Act 2012; and

"Q" is the qualifying investment income,

but where the formula gives an amount of less than zero, the policy holders' share of the qualifying investment income is to be treated as zero.][2]

Commentary—*Simon's Taxes* **D7.5213**.

Amendments—[1] Words in para (1) substituted, and words in para (2) inserted by the Corporation Tax (Treatment of Unrelieved Surplus Advance Corporation Tax) (Amendment) Regulations, SI 2003/1861 with effect for distributions made after 8 April 2003 in accounting periods beginning before, as well as accounting periods ending on or after, 7 August 2003.

[2] In paras (1), (2), words substituted, and para (3) substituted, by the Corporation Tax (Treatment of Unrelieved Surplus Advance Corporation Tax) (Amendment) Regulations, SI 2017/454 regs 2, 6 with effect for company distributions made in an accounting period commencing on or after 6 April 2016, subject to transitional provisions for accounting periods straddling that date (SI 2017/454 reg 1(3)).

23 Cancellation of tax advantage

. . .

Amendments—Reg 23 revoked by the Corporation Tax (Treatment of Unrelieved Surplus Advance Corporation Tax) (Amendment) Regulations, SI 2010/669 regs 2, 7 with effect from 1 April 2010.

1999/498

INSURANCE COMPANIES (CAPITAL REDEMPTION BUSINESS) (MODIFICATION OF THE CORPORATION TAX ACTS) REGULATIONS 1999

Made by the Treasury under TA 1988 s 458A

Made . . . . *1 March 1999*
Laid before the House of Commons . . . . *2 March 1999*
Coming into force . . . . *23 March 1999*

1 Citation, commencement and effect

These Regulations may be cited as the Insurance Companies (Capital Redemption Business) (Modification of the Corporation Tax Acts) Regulations 1999, shall come into force on 23rd March 1999 and shall have effect with respect to accounting periods of insurance companies ending on or after 1st July 1999.

2 Interpretation

In these Regulations—

"capital redemption business" means any capital redemption business within the meaning of section 458 of the Taxes Act, other than business referred to in subsection (4) of that section;

"the life assurance provisions of the Corporation Tax Acts" shall be construed in accordance with section 458A(4) of the Taxes Act;

"the Taxes Act" means the Income and Corporation Taxes Act 1988.

3 Application of life assurance provisions of the Corporation Tax Acts to capital redemption business

The life assurance provisions of the Corporation Tax Acts specified in regulations 4 to 16 shall have effect in relation to any insurance company carrying on capital redemption business—

(*a*) as if the company's capital redemption business were life assurance business; and

(*b*) as respects its capital redemption business, with the modifications provided for in those regulations.

Commentary—*Simon's Taxes* **D7.5172.**

4 Modifications of section 76 of the Taxes Act

. . .

Amendment—Regulation 4 revoked by the Finance Act 2004, Sections 38 to 40 and 45 and Schedule 6 (Consequential Amendment of Enactments) Order, SI 2004/2310 art 2, Schedule para 78 with effect from 28 September 2004. This revocation has effect for accounting periods beginning on or after 1 April 2004, subject to the transitional provisions set out in FA 2004 ss 43, 44.

5 Modifications of section 431 of the Taxes Act

(1) Section 431 of the Taxes Act shall be modified as follows.

(2) In subsection (2)—

(*a*) after the definition of "basic life assurance and general annuity business" there shall be inserted the following definition—

"'capital redemption business' has the same meaning as in section 458;";

(*b*) in the definition of "life assurance business" there shall be added at the end the words "and capital redemption business".

Commentary—*Simon's Taxes* **D7.5172.**

6 Modification of section 431B of the Taxes Act

(1) Section 431B of the Taxes Act shall be modified as follows.

(2) In subsection (1) after the words "life assurance business" there shall be inserted the words ", other than its capital redemption business,".

Commentary—*Simon's Taxes* **D7.5172.**

7 Modification of section 458 of the Taxes Act

(1) Section 458 of the Taxes Act shall be modified as follows.

(2) Subsections (1) and (2) shall be omitted.

8 Modification of Schedule 19AC to the Taxes Act

. . .

Amendments—This regulation revoked by the Overseas Life Insurance Regulations, SI 2006/3271 reg 43, Sch Pt 1 with effect in relation to periods of account ending on or after 31 December 2006.

9 Modification of section 44 of the Finance Act 1989

(1) Section 44 of the Finance Act 1989 shall be modified as follows.

(2) After subsection (12) there shall be inserted the following subsection—

" (12A) In subsection (12) above 'life assurance business' has the same meaning as in Chapter I of Part XII of the Taxes Act 1988."

10 Modification of section 82 of the Finance Act 1989

(1) Section 82 of the Finance Act 1989 shall be modified as follows.

(2) After subsection (8) there shall be added the following subsection—

" In(9)this section and in sections 83, 83AA(*d*), 85, 86, 88, 88A(*e*) and 89, and in paragraph 1A(1) of Schedule 8A(*f*), 'life assurance business' has the same meaning as in Chapter I of Part XII of the Taxes Act 1988."

11 Modification of section 213 of the Taxation of Chargeable Gains Act 1992

(1) Section 213 of the Taxation of Chargeable Gains Act 1992shall be modified as follows.

(2) In subsection (1A) for the words from "which" to the end there shall be substituted the words "which are referable to basic life assurance and general annuity business".

12 Modification of section 214 of the Taxation of Chargeable Gains Act 1992

(1) Section 214 of the Taxation of Chargeable Gains Act 1992 shall be modified as follows.

(2) In subsection (1)(*c*) (definition of "relevant linked liabilities") after the words "general annuity business" there shall be inserted the words ", other than capital redemption business,".

13 Modification of section 65 of the Finance (No 2) Act 1992

(1) Section 65 of the Finance (No 2) Act 1992 shall be modified as follows.

(2) In subsection (3)(*b*) there shall be added at the end the words "and capital redemption business".

14 Modification of Schedule 18 to the Finance Act 1994

(1) Schedule 18 to the Finance Act 1994 shall be modified as follows.

(2) In paragraph 1A(1) the words "or capital redemption business" shall be omitted.

15 Modifications of Schedule 11 to the Finance Act 1996

(1) Schedule 11 to the Finance Act 1996 shall be modified as follows.

(2) In paragraph 1(1)(*a*) and (2) the words "or capital redemption business", in both places where they occur, shall be omitted.

(3) In paragraph 2—

(*a*) for sub-paragraph (1) there shall be substituted the following paragraph—

"(1) Where an insurance company carries on basic life assurance and general annuity business, a separate computation, using only the non-trading credits and non-trading debits referable to that business, shall be made for the purposes of this Chapter in relation to that business.";

(*b*) in sub-paragraph (3) for the words from "Where" to "capital redemption business," there shall be substituted the words "Where an insurance company carries on life assurance business or any category of life assurance business,".

(4) In paragraph 4—

(*a*) in sub-paragraph (1) for the words from "paragraph 2 above" to "capital redemption business," there shall be substituted the words "paragraph 2 above for basic life assurance and general annuity business,";

(*b*) in sub-paragraph (2)(*a*) for the words "the relevant category of business" there shall be substituted the words "basic life assurance and general annuity business";

(*c*) in sub-paragraph (7) for the words "the relevant category of business" there shall be substituted the words "its basic life assurance and general annuity business";

(*d*) in sub-paragraph (10) for the words "the relevant category of business" there shall be substituted the words "basic life assurance and general annuity business";

(*e*) in sub-paragraph (16) the definition of "the relevant category of business" and the word "and" immediately preceding it shall be omitted.

(5) In paragraph 6—

(*a*) the definition of "capital redemption business" shall be omitted;

(*b*) in the definition of "life assurance business" after the words "annuity business" there shall be inserted the words "or capital redemption business".

16 Modification of paragraph 19 of Schedule 12 to the Finance Act 1997

(1) Paragraph 19 of Schedule 12 to the Finance Act 1997 shall be modified as follows.

(2) After sub-paragraph (4) there shall be added the following sub-paragraph—

"(5) In this paragraph 'life assurance business' has the same meaning as in Chapter I of Part XII of the Taxes Act 1988."

1999/564

FINANCE ACT 1993, SECTION 86(2), (FISH QUOTA) ORDER 1999

Made by the Treasury under FA 1993 s 86(2)

Made . . . . .3 March 1999
Laid before the House of Commons . . . . .8 March 1999
Coming into force . . . . .29 March 1999

Commentary—*Simon's Taxes* **C3.301–C3.303**.

1—(1) This Order may be cited as the Finance Act 1993, Section 86(2), (Fish Quota) Order 1999 and shall come into force on 29 March 1999.

(2) This Order shall have effect—

(*a*) in a case where the old assets (but not the new assets) referred to in section 152(1) are fish quota, where the disposal of the old assets takes place on or after the day on which this Order comes into force;

(*b*) in a case where the new assets (but not the old assets) referred to in section 152(1) are fish quota, where the acquisition of the new assets takes place on or after the day on which this Order comes into force; and

(*c*) in a case where both the old assets and the new assets referred to in section 152(1) are fish quota, where both the disposal of the old assets and the acquisition of the new assets take place on or after the day on which this Order comes into force.

2 In this Order, "section 152(1)" and "section 155" mean section 152(1) and 155 of the Taxation of Chargeable Gains Act 1992, respectively.

3 (*inserts* TCGA 1992 s 155 Class 7).

1999/619

FINANCE ACT 1998, SECTION 37, (APPOINTED DAY) ORDER 1999

Made by the Treasury under FA 1998 s 37(3)

Made . . . .*9 March 1999*

Commentary—*Simon's Taxes* **D9.902.**

1 This Order may be cited as the Finance Act 1998, Section 37, (Appointed Day) Order 1999.

2 The day appointed for the purposes of section 37 of the Finance Act 1998 (abolition of periodic accounting of tax on interest on gilt-edged securities) is 1st April 1999.

1999/622

FRIENDLY SOCIETIES (PROVISIONAL REPAYMENTS FOR EXEMPT BUSINESS) REGULATIONS 1999

Revocation—These Regulations lapsed on the repeal of FA 1993 s 121, by FA 2001 s 110, Sch 33 Pt 2(12), with effect in relation to income tax borne by deduction from payments received after 30 September 2001.

1999/623

INSURANCE COMPANIES (GILT-EDGED SECURITIES) (PERIODIC ACCOUNTING FOR TAX ON INTEREST) REGULATIONS 1999

Revocation—These Regulations lapsed following the repeal of TA 1988 s 51B in relation to payments of interest falling due on or after 1 April 1999, as from 1 April 2000.

1999/624

FRIENDLY SOCIETIES (GILT-EDGED SECURITIES) (PERIODIC ACCOUNTING FOR TAX ON INTEREST) REGULATIONS 1999

Revocation—These Regulations lapsed following the repeal of TA 1988 s 51B and FA 1993 s 121, effective partly in relation to payments of interest falling due on or after 1 April 1999 and fully in relation to income tax borne by deduction from payments received after 30 September 2001.

1999/881

OVERSEAS INSURERS (TAX REPRESENTATIVES) REGULATIONS 1999

Made by the Commissioners of Inland Revenue under TA 1988 s 552A

Made . . . .*18 March 1999*
Laid before the House of Commons . . . .*18 March 1999*
Coming into force . . . .*6 April 1999*

1 Citation and commencement

These Regulations may be cited as the Overseas Insurers (Tax Representatives) Regulations 1999 and shall come into force on 6th April 1999.

2 Interpretation

In these Regulations—

"the Board" means the Commissioners [for Her Majesty's Revenue and Customs][2];

. . . [2]

["EEA state" has the meaning given in Schedule 1 to the Interpretation Act 1978;][2] and

["ITTOIA 2005" means the Income Tax (Trading and Other Income) Act 2005;][2]

"the Management Act" means the Taxes Management Act 1970;

["notice" means notice given either in writing or in such form and by such means of electronic communications as may be approved by directions given by the Board, and 'notify' and 'notification' shall be construed accordingly;][1]

"the relevant duties" has the meaning given for the purposes of section 552B by subsection (2) of that section;

. . .[1];

"the Taxes Act" means the Income and Corporation Taxes Act [1988, and a reference to a numbered section, without more, is a reference to the section of the Taxes Act bearing that number.][1]

Amendments—[1] Definition of "notice" substituted, definitions of "section 552A" and "section 552B" revoked, and definition of "the Taxes Act" amended, by the Overseas Insurers (Tax Representatives) (Amendment) Regulations, SI 2002/443 regs 3, 4 with effect from 6 April 2002 in respect of chargeable events occurring after 5 April 2002.

[2] In definition of "the Board" words substituted, definition of "EEA Agreement" revoked, definition of "EEA State" substituted, and definition of "ITTOIA 2005" inserted, by the Overseas Insurers (Tax Representatives) (Amendment) Regulations, SI 2008/2626 regs 2, 3 with effect from 27 October 2008.

3 Designated day

The day specified for the purpose of the definition of "the designated day" in subsection (12) of section 552A is 6th April 1999.

4 Nomination of tax representative by overseas insurer

(1) A nomination to the Board of a tax representative by an overseas insurer must be in writing and must contain the following information—

(*a*) the full name or title under which the overseas insurer is registered in the country in which his principal place of business is situated and the address in that country of that principal place of business;

(*b*) the business address of any branch or agency which the overseas insurer has in the United Kingdom;

(*c*) the name of the person nominated and—

(i) if he is an individual, the address of that person's fixed place of residence in the United Kingdom, or

(ii) if he is not an individual, the address of his business establishment in the United Kingdom;

(*d*) the consent of the person nominated that he is willing to secure that the relevant duties are discharged by or on behalf of the overseas insurer signed—

(i) if he is an individual, by that individual, or

(ii) if he is not an individual, by the proper officer of the company as defined for the purposes of section 108 of the Management Act by subsection (3) of that section in the case of a company and by any partner who is an individual in the case of a partnership;

(*e*) the [office of Her Majesty's Revenue and Customs][1] to which, and the tax reference under which, the person nominated submits tax returns.

(2) A nomination which does not contain the information required by paragraph (1) is invalid.

Amendments—[1] Words in para (1)(*e*) substituted by the Overseas Insurers (Tax Representatives) (Amendment) Regulations, SI 2008/2626 regs 2, 3 with effect from 27 October 2008.

5 Board's decision on nomination

(1) Within the period of thirty days after receipt of a nomination the Board must give notice to the overseas insurer and the person nominated that they—

(*a*) approve the person nominated by the overseas insurer as his tax representative; or

(*b*) refuse to approve the person nominated by the overseas insurer as his tax representative on one or more of the grounds specified in sub-paragraphs (*a*), (*b*) and (*c*) of paragraph (4); or

(*c*) require the overseas insurer or the person nominated or both of them to supply within the period of thirty days after the date of the notice such further information as may be reasonably required before the Board can be satisfied that the person nominated is a fit and proper person to be a tax representative.

(2) A notice under sub-paragraph (*c*) of paragraph (1) must specify the information that the Board require.

(3) Where the overseas insurer or the person nominated, or both of them, supplies information pursuant to a notice under sub-paragraph (*c*) of paragraph (1), the Board must within the period of thirty days after receiving the information—

(*a*) give notice to the overseas insurer and the person nominated—

(i) that they approve the person nominated, or

(ii) that they refuse to approve the person nominated, stating on which of the grounds specified in sub-paragraphs (*a*), (*b*) and (*c*) of paragraph (4) they rely, or

(*b*) give a further notice under sub-paragraph (*c*) of paragraph (1).

(4) The grounds on which the Board may refuse to approve the person nominated by the overseas insurer as his tax representative are that—

(*a*) he does not satisfy the requirements of subsection (7) of section 552A;

(*b*) they have reason to believe that he cannot or will not secure that the relevant duties are properly discharged by or on behalf of the overseas insurer;

(*c*) information which was specified by a notice given under sub-paragraph (*c*) of paragraph (1) has not been supplied.

(5) If at any time there is a change in the information required by regulation 4, or in the further information required by paragraph (1)(*c*) of this regulation, the overseas insurer must notify the Board of that change.

(6) Where the Board have refused to approve the person nominated, and subject to paragraph (5) of regulation 13, the overseas insurer must nominate another person to be his tax representative within the period of three months after the date of the notice of that refusal.

(7) Where the overseas insurer nominates another person in accordance with paragraph (6) that nomination must contain the information required by regulation 4 and paragraphs (1) to (4) of this regulation apply to that nomination in the same way that they applied to the original nomination.

(8) Where the Board approve the person nominated the date of his appointment is the date on which notice was given under paragraph (1) or (3).

6 Termination by the Board of appointment of person nominated

(1) The Board may at any time give notice to both the overseas insurer and the person nominated that they have decided to withdraw the approval which they have given to the person nominated on the grounds that—

- (*a*) he no longer satisfies the requirements of subsection (7) of section 552A; or
- (*b*) they have reason to believe that he cannot or will not secure that the relevant duties are properly discharged by or on behalf of the overseas insurer; or
- (*c*) they have reason to believe that he has failed to secure that relevant duties have been properly discharged by or on behalf of the overseas insurer.

(2) Where the Board have given notice of their decision to withdraw their approval under paragraph (1) of a person nominated—

- (*a*) that person continues to be the tax representative of the overseas insurer until they give notice of their approval of the nomination of another person or themselves appoint another person in his place;
- (*b*) subject to paragraph (5) of regulation 13, the overseas insurer must nominate another person to be his tax representative within the period of three months after the date on which the Board gave notice of their decision; and
- (*c*) any such nomination must contain the information required by regulation 4 and the Board must give their decision on that nomination in accordance with regulation 5.

7 Termination by overseas insurer of appointment of person nominated

(1) The overseas insurer may at any time after the Board have approved the person nominated by him as his tax representative give notice to the Board that he no longer wishes that person to be his tax representative.

(2) Where notice is given by the overseas insurer under paragraph (1), the appointment of the person nominated continues until such time as the Board approve the nomination of another person in his place.

(3) At the same time as the Board give notice of their decision approving the nomination of another person they must give notice to the person originally nominated that his appointment ceased on the date of that notice.

8 Termination by person nominated of his appointment

(1) The person nominated may at any time after the Board have approved him as the tax representative of the overseas insurer give notice to the Board and to the overseas insurer that he no longer wishes to be the overseas insurer's tax representative and in that event the overseas insurer must nominate another person to be his tax representative within the period of three months after the date of that notice.

(2) Where the overseas insurer nominates another person in accordance with paragraph (1), that nomination must contain the information required by regulation 4 and the Board must give their decision on that nomination in accordance with regulation 5.

(3) At the same time as the Board give notice of their decision approving the nomination of another person they must give notice to the person originally nominated that his appointment ceased on the date of that notice.

9 Termination of appointment on bankruptcy or death or on dissolution or winding-up of a company or partnership

(1) Where the person nominated by an overseas insurer is an individual who becomes bankrupt, or in Scotland his estate is sequestrated, or makes any arrangement or composition with his creditors generally or dies, or is a company or a partnership which is dissolved or wound up, the appointment of that person ceases and the overseas insurer must nominate another person to be his tax representative within the period of three months after the event in question.

(2) Any such nomination must contain the information required by regulation 4 and the Board must give their decision on that nomination in accordance with regulation 5.

10 Appointment by the Board of an overseas insurer's tax representative

(1) In circumstances where the overseas insurer has failed—

(*a*) to nominate a person to be his tax representative in accordance with subsection (6) of section 552A; or

(*b*) following the refusal of the Board to approve a person nominated by him, to nominate another person to be his tax representative in accordance with paragraph (6) of regulation 5; or

(*c*) following the withdrawal by the Board of their approval of a person nominated, to nominate another person to be his tax representative in accordance with paragraph (2)(*b*) of regulation 6; or

(*d*) following the notification by a person nominated under paragraph (1) of regulation 8 that he no longer wishes to be the overseas insurer's tax representative or on the occurrence of one of the events described in paragraph (1) of regulation 9, to nominate another person in accordance with the paragraph in question; or

(*e*) following the giving of a notice by the Board in accordance with paragraph (3) of regulation 11, to nominate a person to be his tax representative in accordance with paragraph (4) of that regulation; or

(*f*) following—

(i) the refusal of the Board to agree to release him from the requirement that there be a tax representative, or

(ii) the disclosure to the Board of information with respect to relevant insurances ceasing to be a criminal offence under the law of the EEA [state][2] in which he is resident, or

(iii) notification by him to the Board that the total amount or value of gross premiums paid under relevant insurances is £1 million or more, or

(iv) the giving of a notice by the Board of their intention to withdraw from their agreement to release him from the requirement that there be a tax representative,

to nominate a person to be his tax representative in accordance with paragraph (9) of regulation 12; or

(*g*) to notify the Board that the total amount or value of gross premiums paid under relevant insurances is £1 million or more; or

(*h*) following the termination of the appointment of a person appointed under this paragraph, to nominate another person in accordance with paragraph (4) of this regulation;

the Board may appoint a person who satisfies the description in paragraph (2) to be the overseas insurer's tax representative.

(2) A person appointed by the Board to be the tax representative of an overseas insurer must be a person who has a significant business or economic connection with the overseas insurer and may in particular (but without prejudice to the generality of the preceding words) be—

(*a*) a company which is connected with the overseas insurer within the meaning of section 839 . . .[1] (connected persons); or

(*b*) the branch or agency in the United Kingdom of any such company.

(3) The Board must give notice of their decision to the person appointed under this regulation and to the overseas insurer and, subject to paragraph (6) of regulation 13, the date of the appointment is the date of the notice.

(4) The Board may at any time terminate the appointment of the person appointed by them as the tax representative of an overseas insurer by giving notice to the person appointed and to the overseas insurer and in that event the overseas insurer must nominate another person to be his tax representative within the period of three months after the date of that notice.

(5) The overseas insurer may at any time nominate a person to be his tax representative in place of the person appointed by the Board and, if the Board approve the nomination of that person, at the same time as the Board give notice of their decision approving the nomination they must give notice to the person appointed by them that his appointment ceased on the date of the notice.

(6) Where the overseas insurer nominates another person in accordance with paragraph (4) or (5), that nomination must contain the information required by regulation 4 and the Board must give their decision on that nomination in accordance with regulation 5.

Amendments—[1] Words in para (2)(*a*) revoked by the Overseas Insurers (Tax Representatives) (Amendment) Regulations, SI 2002/443 regs 3, 5 with effect from 6 April 2002 in respect of chargeable events occurring after 5 April 2002.

[2] Word in para (1)(*f*)(ii) substituted by the Overseas Insurers (Tax Representatives) (Amendment) Regulations, SI 2008/2626 regs 2, 5 with effect from 27 October 2008.

11 Other arrangements

(1) An overseas insurer may make other arrangements with the Board for the purpose of securing the discharge by him or on his behalf of the relevant duties.

(2) Where such arrangements have been made with the Board by the overseas insurer, section 552A is to be regarded as never having applied to the overseas insurer so long as those arrangements remain in force.

(3) If the Board have reason to believe that any arrangements which have been made do not secure the discharge by the overseas insurer or on his behalf of the relevant duties, they may give notice to the overseas insurer that those arrangements are no longer in force with effect from the date of the notice.

(4) Where notice is given by the Board in accordance with paragraph (3)—

(*a*) subject to paragraph (5) of regulation 13, the overseas insurer must nominate a person to be his tax representative within the period of three months after the date of the notice;

(*b*) that nomination must contain the information required by regulation 4; and

(*c*) the Board must give their decision on that nomination in accordance with regulation 5.

12 Release of overseas insurer from requirement to nominate a tax representative

(1) The Board may agree to release an overseas insurer to whom section 552A applies from the requirement that there must be a tax representative where—

(*a*) the overseas insurer is resident in an EEA [state][1] and the disclosure by him to the Board of information with respect to holders of relevant insurances is a criminal offence under the law of that [state][1] and was such an offence on 17th March 1998; or

(*b*) subject to the condition specified in paragraph (2), at any time after section 552A first applies to the overseas insurer the total amount or value of the gross premiums paid under the relevant insurances referred to in paragraph (*b*) of subsection (4) of that section is nil or a negligible amount; or

(*c*) subject to paragraph (5), the overseas insurer enters into an undertaking—

(i) in relation to relevant insurances referred to in paragraph (3), in the terms set out in Part II of the Schedule;

(ii) in relation to relevant insurances referred to in paragraph (4), in the terms set out in Part III of the Schedule.

(2) The condition specified in this paragraph is that the overseas insurer gives notice of the fact to the Board forthwith if, at any time following the agreement to release the overseas insurer from the requirement that there must be a tax representative, the total amount or value of the gross premiums paid under the relevant insurances referred to in paragraph (*b*) of subsection (4) of section 552A is £1 million or more.

(3) The relevant insurances referred to in this paragraph are—

(*a*) policies of life insurance issued in respect of insurances made before 6th April 2000;

(*b*) contracts for life annuities made before 6th April 2000;

(*c*) capital redemption policies where the contract was effected before 6th April 2000.

(4) The relevant insurances referred to in this paragraph are—

(*a*) policies of life insurance issued in respect of insurances made on or after 6th April 2000;

(*b*) contracts for life annuities made on or after 6th April 2000;

(*c*) capital redemption policies where the contract was effected on or after 6th April 2000.

(5) The Board may at any time give notice to the overseas insurer of their decision to withdraw from their agreement to release him from the requirement that there be a tax representative where that agreement has been given in the circumstances described in sub-paragraph (*c*) of paragraph (1).

(6) An application by an overseas insurer to be released from the requirement that there must be a tax representative must be by notice to the Board specifying which of the circumstances described in sub-paragraphs (*a*), (*b*) and (*c*) of paragraph (1) apply to his case and the Board must, within the period of thirty days after the receipt of the notice of any such application, give notice to the overseas insurer that they—

(*a*) agree to release him from the requirement that there be a tax representative, or

(*b*) refuse to agree to release him from that requirement, or

(*c*) require him to supply within the period of thirty days after the date of that notice such information as may be reasonably required before they can be satisfied that he comes within the relevant circumstances.

(7) A notice under sub-paragraph (*c*) of paragraph (6) must specify the information which the Board require.

(8) Where the overseas insurer supplies information pursuant to a notice under sub-paragraph (*c*) of paragraph (6), the Board must within the period of thirty days after receiving the information—

(*a*) give notice to the insurer that they agree or refuse to agree to release him from the requirement that there be a tax representative, or

(*b*) give a further notice under sub-paragraph (*c*) of paragraph (6).

(9) Where—

(*a*) the Board give notice that they refuse to agree to release the overseas insurer from the requirement that there be a tax representative, or

(*b*) it ceases to be a criminal offence under the law of the EEA [state][1] in which the overseas insurer is resident for him to disclose to the Board information with respect to the holders of relevant insurances, or (*c*) the overseas insurer gives notice to the Board in accordance with the condition in paragraph (2) that the total amount or value of the gross premiums paid under relevant insurances is £1 million or more, or

(*d*) the Board give notice to the overseas insurer of their decision to withdraw from their agreement to release him from the requirement that there be a tax representative,

and subject to paragraph (5) of regulation 13, the overseas insurer must nominate a person to be his tax representative within the period of three months after the date of the notice or the date when disclosure to the Board ceased to be criminal offence, as the case may be.

(10) Where the overseas insurer nominates a person to be his tax representative in accordance with paragraph (9), that nomination must contain the information required by regulation 4 and the Board must give their decision in accordance with regulation 5.

Note—The Overseas Insurers (Tax Representatives) (Amendment) Regulations, SI 2002/443 reg 10 provides that for the purposes of para (1)(*c*) above, an undertaking given by an overseas insurer before the coming into force of those Regulations, which complied with the terms of SI 1999/881 Schedule Pts II and III as then in force, shall have effect as if it were an undertaking in the terms required by the Schedule as amended by SI 2002/443. Accordingly, any agreement by the Board to release the insurer under para (1)(*c*) above given before the coming into force of SI 2002/443 shall continue to have effect until the Board give notice of their decision to withdraw from it. SI 2002/443 has effect from 6 April 2002 in respect of chargeable events occurring after 5 April 2002.

Amendments—[1] Words in paras (1)(*a*), (9)(*b*) substituted by the Overseas Insurers (Tax Representatives) (Amendment) Regulations, SI 2008/2626 regs 2, 6 with effect from 27 October 2008.

13 Appeals against decisions of the Board

(1) An overseas insurer to whom notice has been given of a decision of the Board—

(*a*) refusing to approve a person nominated by him as his tax representative,

(*b*) withdrawing their approval of a person nominated by him as his tax representative,

(*c*) appointing a person to be his tax representative,

(*d*) that arrangements made under regulation 11 are no longer in force,

(*e*) refusing to agree to release him from the requirement that there be a tax representative, or

(*f*) to withdraw from their agreement to release him from the requirement that there be a tax representative,

may appeal against the decision contained in that notice by notice given to the Board within the period of thirty days after the date of the notice of the decision in question.

(2) A person to whom notice has been given of a decision of the Board appointing him to be the tax representative of an overseas insurer under regulation 10 may appeal against the decision contained in that notice within the period of thirty days after the date of the notice of that decision.

(3) . . .

(4) The like provisions as are contained in Part V of the Management Act (appeals and other proceedings) . . . [1] apply to an appeal under this regulation and the Special Commissioners must on appeal to them confirm the decision contained in the notice unless . . . [1] satisfied that it ought to be quashed.

(5) Where an overseas insurer appeals against a decision of the Board referred to in sub-paragraph (*a*), (*b*), (*d*), (*e*) or (*f*) of paragraph (1), and the decision of the Board is confirmed on appeal, the period of three months within which he must nominate another person, or a person, as his tax representative does not begin until such time as there is no possibility of a further appeal against that decision.

(6) Where an overseas insurer appeals against a decision of the Board appointing a person to be his tax representative, or the person appointed by the Board to be the tax representative of an overseas insurer appeals against the decision of the Board appointing him, and the decision of the Board is confirmed on appeal, the date of the appointment of that person is the first date on which there is no possibility of a further appeal against that decision.

(7) Where an overseas insurer appeals against a decision of the Board referred to in sub-paragraph (*a*) of paragraph (1) and the decision of the Board is quashed on appeal, the date of the appointment of the person nominated as the tax representative of the overseas insurer is the first date on which there is no possibility of a further appeal against the decision quashing the decision of the Board.

Amendments—[1] Para (3) revoked, in para (4), words revoked and words substituted, by the Transfer of Tribunal Functions and Revenue and Customs Appeals Order, SI 2009/56 art 3, Sch 2 paras 57, 58 with effect from 1 April 2009.

SCHEDULE

Regulation 12(1)(c)

PART I

INTERPRETATION

1 In this Schedule—

"basic rate limit" has the meaning given by [section 20(2) of the Income Tax Act 2007][2];

. . .

"gain" means a gain which is treated as arising in connection with a policy or contract under [Chapter 9 of Part 4 of ITTOIA 2005] . . . [1];

. . . [2]

. . . [2]

["tax year" has the meaning given by section 4(2) of the Income Tax Act 2007.][2]

Amendments—[1] In the definition of "gain", words revoked by the Overseas Insurers (Tax Representatives) (Amendment) Regulations, SI 2002/443 regs 3, 6 with effect from 6 April 2002 in respect of chargeable events occurring after 5 April 2002.

[2] In definition of "basic rate limit", words substituted, definitions of "financial year", "inspector" and "year of assessment" revoked, in definition of "gain" words substituted, and definition of "tax year" inserted, by the Overseas Insurers (Tax Representatives) (Amendment) Regulations, SI 2008/2626 regs 2, 7(1), (2) with effect from 27 October 2008.

2 . . .

Amendments—Paragraph revoked by the Overseas Insurers (Tax Representatives) (Amendment) Regulations, SI 2008/2626 regs 2, 7(1), (3) with effect from 27 October 2008.

PART II

UNDERTAKING BY OVERSEAS INSURER—PRE 6TH APRIL 2000 INSURANCES

3 The terms of the undertaking referred to in regulation 12(1)(*c*)(i) are that the overseas insurer undertakes, within three months after the end of each [tax year][1], . . . [1] to supply to the [Board][1] the information referred to in paragraph 6 about relevant events occurring in that [tax year][1] . . . [1] in connection with a policy or contract held by a policy holder where to the best of the overseas insurer's information and belief the policy holder was resident in the United Kingdom immediately before the relevant event occurred.

Amendments—[1] Words substituted and revoked by the Overseas Insurers (Tax Representatives) (Amendment) Regulations, SI 2008/2626 regs 2, 7(1), (4) with effect from 27 October 2008.

4 For the purposes of this undertaking a relevant event is a chargeable event within the meaning of [Chapter 9 of Part 4 of ITTOIA 2005][2]

(*a*) in respect of which an insurer is under an obligation to deliver a certificate under [section 552 (as read with section 552ZA)][1];

(*b*) which occurs three months or more after section 552A first applies to the overseas insurer;

(*c*) which is the last such event to occur in relation to the policy or contract;

[(*d*) by reason of which the aggregate sum payable, or other benefits to be conferred, by the overseas insurer exceeds twice the basic rate limit for the tax year in which it occurs.][2]

Amendments—[1] In sub-para (*a*), words substituted by the Overseas Insurers (Tax Representatives) (Amendment) Regulations, SI 2002/443 regs 3, 7 with effect from 6 April 2002 in respect of chargeable events occurring after 5 April 2002.

[2] Words in opening sentence, and whole of sub-para (*d*), substituted, by the Overseas Insurers (Tax Representatives) (Amendment) Regulations, SI 2008/2626 regs 2, 7(1), (5) with effect from 27 October 2008.

5 In determining whether the aggregate sum payable, or other benefits to be conferred, by reason of a relevant event exceeds twice the basic rate limit for [the tax year in which it occurs][1], . . . [1] all sums payable and benefits to be conferred are to be taken into account which are payable or to be conferred by reason of relevant events occurring in [that tax year][1] . . . [1] in connection with policies or contracts—

(*a*) under which immediately before the relevant event in question the same insurer has obligations, and

(*b*) which are held by the same policy holder.

Amendments—[1] Words substituted and revoked by the Overseas Insurers (Tax Representatives) (Amendment) Regulations, SI 2008/2626 regs 2, 7(1), (6) with effect from 27 October 2008.

6 The information referred to in this paragraph is—

(*a*) the name and address of the policy holder;

(*b*) any unique identifying designation given to the policy or contract in connection with which a relevant event has occurred;

(*c*) the date and nature of each such relevant event;

(*d*) the aggregate of the sums payable, or other benefits to be conferred, as a result of all such relevant events.

PART III

UNDERTAKING BY OVERSEAS INSURER—POST 5TH APRIL 2000 INSURANCES

7 The terms of the undertaking referred to in regulation 12(1)(*c*)(ii) are that the overseas insurer undertakes—

(*a*) within three months after a relevant event occurs in connection with a policy or contract, to deliver to the policy holder a certificate containing the information referred to in paragraph 10; and

(*b*) within three months after the end of each [tax year][1] . . . [1] in which such a certificate is delivered, and in the circumstances described in paragraph 9, to supply to the [Board][1] a copy of that certificate;

where to the best of the overseas insurer's information and belief the policy holder was resident in the United Kingdom immediately before the relevant event occurred.

Amendments—[1] Words substituted and revoked by the Overseas Insurers (Tax Representatives) (Amendment) Regulations, SI 2008/2626 regs 2, 7(1), (7) with effect from 27 October 2008.

[**8** For the purpose of this undertaking a relevant event is a chargeable event within the meaning of Chapter 9 of Part 4 of ITTOIA 2005 in respect of which an insurer is under an obligation to deliver a certificate under section 552.][1]

Amendments—[1] Paras 8, 8A substituted for previous para 8 by the Overseas Insurers (Tax Representatives) (Amendment) Regulations, SI 2008/2626 regs 2, 7(1), (8) with effect from 27 October 2008.

[**8A** For the purposes of this Part of this Schedule, in the determination of the amount of a gain in connection with a policy or contract, no account is to be taken of the effect of section 541A of ITTOIA 2005.][1]

Amendments—[1] Paras 8, 8A substituted for previous para 8 by the Overseas Insurers (Tax Representatives) (Amendment) Regulations, SI 2008/2626 regs 2, 7(1), (8) with effect from 27 October 2008.

9 The circumstances described in this paragraph are where the aggregate amount of connected gains [in the tax year][1] exceeds one half of the basic rate limit for [that tax year][1] and, for the purposes of this paragraph, a gain is connected with another gain where—

(*a*) both gains arise in connection with policies or contracts containing obligations which, immediately before the relevant event in question, were obligations of the same overseas insurer;

(*b*) the policy holder of those policies and contracts is the same; and

[(*c*) both gains arise in the same tax year.][1]

Amendments—[1] Words substituted by the Overseas Insurers (Tax Representatives) (Amendment) Regulations, SI 2008/2626 regs 2, 7(1), (9) with effect from 27 October 2008.

10 The information referred to in this paragraph is—

(*a*) the name and address of the policy holder;

(*b*) any unique identifying designation given to the policy or contract in connection with which the relevant event has occurred;

(*c*) the date and nature of the relevant event;

(*d*) the amount of the gain;

(*e*) the number of years relevant for computing the appropriate fraction of the gain for the purposes of section [536, apart from section 536(7), of ITTOIA 2005][1];

(*f*) whether the policy holder is to be treated as having paid income tax at the basic . . . [1] rate on the amount of the gain in accordance with section [530, apart from section 528, of ITTOIA 2005][1].

Amendments—[1] Words substituted and revoked by the Overseas Insurers (Tax Representatives) (Amendment) Regulations, SI 2008/2626 regs 2, 7(1), (10) with effect from 27 October 2008.

1999/1029

PERSONAL PORTFOLIO BONDS (TAX) REGULATIONS 1999

Made by the Treasury under TA 1988 s 553C

Made . . . . *30 March 1999*
Laid before the House of Commons . . . . *30 March 1999*
Coming into force . . . . *6 April 1999*

1 Citation, commencement and effect

(1) These Regulations may be cited as the Personal Portfolio Bonds (Tax) Regulations 1999 and shall come into force on 6th April 1999.

(2) These Regulations shall have effect, in relation to personal portfolio bonds, with respect to any year ending on or after 6th April 2000.

2 Interpretation

(1) In these Regulations unless the context otherwise requires—

"building society" means a building society within the meaning of the Building Societies Act 1986, or the Irish Building Societies Act 1989;

"collective investment scheme" has the meaning given by section [235 of the Financial Services and Markets Act 2000][1], and "interest" in relation to a collective investment scheme means the beneficial entitlement (however described) of a participant (within the meaning of that section);

"company" has the meaning given by section 832(1) and (2) of the Taxes Act;

"insurance company" means [an undertaking carrying on the business of effecting or carrying out contracts of insurance and, for the purposes of this definition, "contract of insurance" has the meaning given by Article 3(1) of the Financial Services and Markets Act 2000 (Regulated Activities) Order 2001][1];

"internal linked fund" has the meaning given by [section 11.1 of the Prudential Sourcebook (Insurers) and in this definition "the Prudential Sourcebook (Insurers)" means the Interim Prudential Sourcebook for Insurers made by the Financial Services Authority under the Financial Services and Markets Act 2000][2];

"market value" shall be construed in accordance with section 272 of the Taxation of Chargeable Gains Act 1992;

"personal portfolio bond" has the meaning given by regulation 4, subject to regulation 3;

"policy holder", except in regulation 4(1), includes a holder of a life annuity contract;

"recognised stock exchange" has the meaning given by section 841 of the Taxes Act;

"security" has the same meaning as in section 132(3)(*b*) of the Taxation of Chargeable Gains Act 1992;

"share" includes stock;

"the Taxes Act" means the Income and Corporation Taxes Act 1988;

"unit trust scheme" has the meaning given by subsection (6) of section 468 of the Taxes Act;

"warrant" has the same meaning as in [paragraph 14 of Schedule 2 to the Financial Services and Markets Act 2000][1];

"year" in relation to a personal portfolio bond means a year as defined in section 546(4) of the Taxes Act, and "the final year" has the meaning given by that section.

(2) In these Regulations references to the premium paid, or the amount of the premium paid, include—

(*a*) references to lump sum, or any other, consideration,

(*b*) where more than one amount is payable by way of premium in respect of the policy or contract, references to the aggregate of the premiums paid, and

(*c*) references to the market value at the date of transfer of any property other than cash transferred to the insurance company in satisfaction of any premium.

(3) In these Regulations references to a section, without more, are to that section of the Taxes Act.

Amendments—[1] In para (1) words in the definition of "collective investment scheme", "insurance company" and "warrant" substituted by the Financial Services and Markets Act 2000 (Consequential Amendments) (Taxes) Order, SI 2001/3629 arts 183, 184(1), (2), (4), (5) with effect from 1 December 2001, immediately after the coming into force of the Financial Services and Markets Act 2000 ss 411, 432(1), Sch 20 (and SI 2001/3629 Pts 1 and 2).

[2] In para (1) words in the definition of "internal linked fund" substituted by SI 2001/3629 arts 183, 184(3), (6) with effect for periods of account ending after 30 November 2001.

3 Policies or contracts issued or made before 17th March 1998 which are the subject of special exclusions from being personal portfolio bonds

(1) A policy or contract is not a personal portfolio bond if it is a policy or contract—

(*a*) which, in the case of a policy, was issued in respect of an insurance made before 17th March 1998 and, in the case of a contract, was made before 17th March 1998,

(*b*) whose terms are not varied on or after 16th July 1998 so as to increase the benefits secured or to extend the term of the policy or contract (any exercise of rights conferred by the policy or contract being regarded for this purpose as a variation), and

(*c*) which is a policy or contract to which either paragraph (2) or paragraph (3) applies.

(2) This paragraph applies to a policy or contract under whose terms the benefits have at no time during its existence been capable of being determined either in whole or in part by reference to any index other than those referred to in regulation 4(7), or to any property other than—

(*a*) shares or securities listed on a recognised stock exchange;

(*b*) shares or securities of a company which are dealt in on the Unlisted Securities Market or the Alternative Investment Market, and which satisfy the conditions specified in paragraph (4); and

(*c*) property described in regulation 4(3) and (4).

(3) This paragraph applies to a policy or contract—

(*a*) under whose terms the benefits were at some time during its existence capable of being determined either in whole or in part by reference to property other than that referred to in paragraph (2)(*a*), (*b*) and (*c*), or by reference to an index other than those referred to in regulation 4(7), but at no time during its existence have been so determined, and

(*b*) whose terms are varied before the end of the first year, in relation to that policy or contract, which commences on or after 6th April 1999, subject to paragraph (5), so that the only property that may be selected as mentioned in regulation 4(1) consists of property referred to in paragraph (2)(*a*), (*b*) and (*c*), and the only index that may be so selected consists of an index referred to in regulation 4(7).

(4) The conditions specified in this paragraph are that—

(*a*) any holding of shares or securities of a company, by reference to which any benefits under the policy or contract are or have been capable of being determined during any period, does not at any time during that period exceed 10 per cent. of the issued share capital of the company concerned; and

(*b*) the amount invested in any shares or securities of a single company to which this condition applies does not at any time exceed 10 per cent. of the premium paid in respect of the policy or contract (and "amount invested" includes the market value at the date of transfer of any property other than cash transferred to the insurance company in satisfaction of any premium).

(5) In a case where—

(*a*) the policy holder was not resident in the United Kingdom on 17th March 1998, and

(*b*) after that date, the policy holder is at any time resident in the United Kingdom,

paragraph (3)(b) shall apply with the modification that, for the year mentioned in that sub-paragraph, there is substituted a reference to whichever is the later of that year, and the first year, in relation to that policy or contract, which commences after the time mentioned in sub-paragraph (b) of this paragraph or, where there is more than one such time, the earliest such time.

(6) Any reference in paragraphs (2) and (3) to the period of existence of a policy or contract, or to a period in paragraph (4), or to a time during either such period, shall be construed ignoring any such period or time before 6th April 1994, but shall include any other such period or time (whether before or after the coming into force of these Regulations).

(7) Any reference in paragraphs (2)(*a*) and (*b*) and (4) to shares or securities, or to a holding of shares or securities, includes a reference to any option, warrant or other right to acquire shares or securities.

4 Definition of personal portfolio bond (applying to all policies or contracts whenever issued or made)

(1) Subject to paragraph (2) and regulation 3, "personal portfolio bond" means a policy of life insurance, contract for a life annuity or capital redemption policy under whose terms—

(*a*) some or all of the benefits are determined by reference to the value of, or the income from, property of any description (whether or not specified in the policy or contract) or fluctuations in, or in an index of, the value of property of any description (whether or not so specified); and

(*b*) some or all of the property, or such an index, may be selected by, or by a person acting on behalf of, the holder of the policy or contract or a person connected with him (or the holder of the policy or contract and a person connected with him).

(2) A policy or contract is not a personal portfolio bond if—

(*a*) the only property which may be selected as mentioned in paragraph (1)(*b*) is of the description prescribed by either or both of paragraphs (3) and (4), and

(*b*) the only index which may be selected as mentioned in paragraph (1)(*b*) is of the description prescribed by paragraph (7).

(3) The description prescribed by this paragraph is of property which the insurance company has appropriated to an internal linked fund, where the property satisfies the condition specified in paragraph (5).

(4) The description prescribed by this paragraph is of property consisting of any of the following—

(*a*) units in an authorised unit trust within the meaning of subsection (6) of section 468, read with subsections (7) to (9) of that section,

(*b*) shares in an investment trust within the meaning of section 842,

(*c*) shares in an open-ended investment company within the meaning of section [236 of the Financial Services and Markets Act 2000][1]

(*d*) cash, including cash deposited in a deposit account or share account with a building society, or in a bank account or similar account, except where the acquisition of the cash was made wholly or partly for the purpose of realising a gain from the disposal of it,

(*e*) policies or contracts to which Chapter II of Part XIII of the Taxes Act applies, which satisfy the conditions specified in paragraph (6), and

(*f*) an interest in a collective investment scheme which is constituted by—

(i) a company, not being an open-ended investment company, which is resident outside the United Kingdom,

(ii) a unit trust scheme the trustees of which are not resident in the United Kingdom, or

(iii) any arrangements which do not fall within paragraph (i) or (ii), which take effect by virtue of the law of a territory outside the United Kingdom and which, under that law, create rights in the nature of co-ownership (without restricting that expression to its meaning in the law of any part of the United Kingdom), where the property concerned satisfies, or further satisfies, as the case may be, the condition specified in paragraph (5).

(5) The condition specified in this paragraph is that, at the time when the property is available to be selected, the opportunity to select property of the same description as the first-mentioned property is available to, or to persons acting on behalf of, all the policy holders of the insurance company concerned or one, or more than one, class of policy holders of that insurance company, as mentioned in paragraph (8)(*a*) to (*c*).

(6) The conditions specified in this paragraph are that neither—

(*a*) the policy or contract, nor

(*b*) any property by reference to which the value of any benefits under the policy or contract is or has been directly or indirectly capable of being determined, nor

(*c*) any property which, in relation to the policy or contract, or the premium paid in respect thereof, is "derived property" within the meaning of section 660A(10) of the Taxes Act,

is a personal portfolio bond.

(7) The description prescribed by this paragraph is of indices consisting of any of the following—

(*a*) the retail prices index,

(*b*) any similar general index of prices which is published by the government of any foreign state, or by an agent of such a government, or

(*c*) any published index of prices of shares listed on a recognised stock exchange,

in circumstances where, at the time when the index is available to be selected, the opportunity to select the same index is available to, or to persons acting on behalf of, all the policy holders of the insurance company concerned or one, or more than one, class of policy holders of that insurance company, as mentioned in paragraph (8)(a) to (c).

(8) In paragraphs (5) and (7) a "class" of policy holders means a number of policy holders to whom the opportunity is given to select property or an index as mentioned in paragraphs (5) and (7) in circumstances where—

(*a*) that opportunity is clearly identified in marketing or other promotional literature published by the insurance company concerned to members of the public, or members of the public who are intending investors, as available generally to any person falling within its terms,

(*b*) the class and the opportunity are not limited to connected persons, and

(*c*) the composition of the class (which means the inclusion in or exclusion from the class of any person, or the ability of that person to take the opportunity, if he so chooses) is determined by the insurance company alone.

Amendments—[1] Words in sub-para (4)(*c*) substituted by the Financial Services and Markets Act 2000 (Consequential Amendments) (Taxes) Order, SI 2001/3629 arts 183, 185 with effect from 1 December 2001, immediately after the coming into force of the Financial Services and Markets Act 2000 ss 411, 432(1), Sch 20 (and SI 2001/3629 Pts 1 and 2).

5 Personal portfolio bonds-computation of gain

(1) This regulation makes provision for amounts to be treated as gains arising in connection with a personal portfolio bond in any year ending on or after 6th April 2000 other than the final year (a "relevant year") for the purposes of charging those gains to tax in accordance with the provisions of Chapter II of Part XIII of the Taxes Act applied (with modifications) by regulation 6.

[(2) There shall be treated as a gain arising in a relevant year the amount calculated in accordance with the formula—

$$0.15 \times (A + B - C)$$

Here—

A is the amount of the premium paid in respect of the personal portfolio bond;

B is the sum of the amounts found by applying the formula at the end of each of the previous years during which the personal portfolio bond was in existence in succession starting with the first such year; and

C is the amount calculated in accordance with the formula in paragraph (2A).][1]

[(2A) **C** is the amount calculated in accordance with the formula—

$$R - G$$

(*a*) at the end of the year immediately preceding the relevant year if the calculation produces an excess; and

(*b*) at the end of any earlier year during the existence of the bond when the calculation produces an excess; and

(*c*) adding together all the amounts produced by sub-paragraphs (*a*) and (*b*).

Here—

R is the reckonable aggregate value mentioned in section 546(2); and

G is the allowable aggregate amount referred to in section 546(3).][1]

[(2B) For the purposes of the computation of **C**—

(*a*) section 546(1)(*a*) shall be read as if the words "or assignment" and "assigned for money or money's worth, or" and sub-paragraph (ii) and the word "; or" preceding it were omitted;

(*b*) section 546(6) shall be disregarded; and

(*c*) sections 546B to 546D shall be disregarded.][1]

(3) The gain calculated in accordance with paragraph (2) shall be treated as arising at the end of the relevant year [concerned.

This is subject to paragraphs (4) and (4A).][1]

(4) The references—

(*a*) in paragraph (3) to the end of a relevant year, and

(*b*) in paragraph (2), in the definition of "B", to the end of any previous year,

shall each be construed as a reference to the time immediately before any gain treated as arising in connection with the same policy or contract at the end of that year under section 541, 543 or 545, on the occurrence of such an excess as is mentioned in section 540(1)(a)(v), 542(1)(c) or 545(1)(d).

[(4A) For the purposes of paragraphs (2) to (3), any gain treated as arising under section 546C shall be treated as arising immediately after the gain calculated in accordance with paragraph (2).][1]

(5) Where the terms of a policy or contract, to which regulation 3(3) applies as modified by regulation 3(5), are varied, within the alternative period permitted by regulation 3(5), (that is, the first year which commences after the time mentioned in regulation 3(5)(*b*) falls later than the year mentioned in regulation 3(3)(*b*)), no gain shall be treated as arising under paragraph (2) at the end of the first year, in relation to the policy or contract, which ends after the time mentioned in regulation 3(5)(*b*).

Amendments—[1] Paras (2), (2A) and (2B) substituted for para (2), words in para (3) substituted, and para (4A) inserted, by the Personal Portfolio Bonds (Tax) Regulations, SI 2001/2724 regs 2, 3 with effect for gains treated as arising after 16 August 2001.

6 Application of Chapter II of Part XIII of the Taxes Act

(1) The gain treated as arising in accordance with regulation 5(2) shall be treated, for the purposes of section 547 and paragraph (2) (other than sub-paragraph (*b*) of that paragraph), as arising on the happening of a chargeable event, which takes place at the time given by regulation 5(3) and (4).

(2) The provisions of Chapter II of Part XIII of the Taxes Act (other than section 553C) shall, so far as concerns policies or contracts that are also personal portfolio bonds, apply, subject to the omissions and modifications specified in paragraphs (3) to (8), both in relation to—

(*a*) the gain treated as arising on the happening of a chargeable event in accordance with regulation 5(2) and paragraph (1), and

(*b*) other gains treated as arising in accordance with that Chapter.

(3) In section 547 (method of charging gain to tax)—

(*a*) in subsection (1) after "[545 or 546C]"[1] there shall be inserted the words "or regulations 5(2) and 6(1) of the Personal Portfolio Bonds (Tax) Regulations 1999";

(*b*) in each of subsections (5A) and (7) after "[543 or 546C(7)(*b*)]"[1] there shall be inserted the words "or regulations 5(2) and 6(1) of the Personal Portfolio Bonds (Tax) Regulations 1999".

(4) In each of paragraphs (*a*), (*b*) and (*c*) of section 541(1), after sub-paragraph (ii) there shall be added—

"and

(iii) the total amount treated under regulation 5 of the Personal Portfolio Bonds (Tax) Regulations 1999 as a gain arising in a relevant year in relation to the policy, prior to the happening of the chargeable event;"

(5) In each of paragraphs (*a*) and (*b*) of section 543(1), after sub-paragraph (ii) there shall be added—

"and

(iii) the total amount treated under regulation 5 of the Personal Portfolio Bonds (Tax) Regulations 1999 as a gain arising in a relevant year in relation to the contract, prior to the happening of the chargeable event;"

(6) Section 550 (relief where gain charged at a higher rate) shall be omitted.

[(7) In section 552—

(*a*) in subsection (1)—

(i) in paragraph (*a*) the words "unless satisfied that no gain is to be treated as arising by reason of the event," shall be omitted;

(ii) in paragraph (*b*), for "paragraph (*a*) or (*b*) of subsection (2)" there shall be substituted "subsection (2)";

(*b*) for subsection (2) there shall be substituted—

"(2) For the purposes of this section the condition is that the amount of the gain, or the aggregate amount of the gain and any other gains connected with it, exceeds one half of the basic rate limit for the relevant year of assessment."

(*c*) in subsection (5)—

(i) for paragraph (*b*) there shall be substituted—

"(*b*) the nature of the chargeable event and the date on which it is treated as having happened;"

(ii) paragraph (*c*) shall be omitted;

(iii) for paragraph (*d*) there shall be substituted—

"(*d*) the amount of the gain treated as arising in accordance with regulations 5(2) and 6(1) of the Personal Portfolio Bonds (Tax) Regulations 1999;"

(iv) in paragraph (*f*)(ii) the words ", except in a case where paragraph (*c*) above applies," shall be omitted;

(*d*) for subsection (6) there shall be substituted—

"(6) For the purposes of subsection (1)(*a*) above, the relevant three month period is the period of three months beginning with the time given by regulation 5(3), (4) and (4A) of the Personal Portfolio Bonds (Tax) Regulations 1999."

(*e*) for subsection (7) there shall be substituted—

"(7) For the purposes of subsection (1)(*b*) above, the relevant three month period is whichever of the following periods ends later—

(*a*) the period of three months following the end of the year of assessment or, where the policy holder is a company, the financial year, in which the event happened; or

(*b*) if a certificate under subsection (1)(*b*) would not be required in respect of the event apart from the happening of another event, and that other event is a death or an assignment, the period of three months beginning with receipt of written notification of the death or the assignment."

(*f*) for subsection (9) there shall be substituted—

"(9) For the purposes of this section, the year of assessment or financial year to which a gain is attributable is the year in which the gain, treated as arising under regulations 5(2) and 6(1) of the Personal Portfolio Bonds (Tax) Regulations 1999, is treated as arising in accordance with regulation 5(3), (4) and (4A) of those Regulations."

(*g*) in subsection (10)—

(i) for the definition of "appropriate policy holder" there shall be substituted—

" "appropriate policy holder" means the person who is the policy holder immediately before the happening of the event;" and

(ii) the definition of "section 546 excess" shall be omitted; and

(*h*) each of the references to a chargeable event shall be taken to include a reference to the chargeable event treated as occurring by reason of paragraph (1).][2]

[(7A) In section 552ZA subsection (3) shall be omitted.][2]

(8) In section 553—

(*a*) in each of subsections (3) and (6) after "section [541 or 546C(7)(*b*)]"[1] there shall be inserted the words "or regulations 5(2) and 6(1) of the Personal Portfolio Bonds (Tax) Regulations 1999"; and

(*b*) in subsection (10) after "[545 or 546C(7)(*a*)]"[1] there shall be inserted the words "or, in relation to a gain treated as arising in relation to a policy under regulations 5(2) and 6(1) of the Personal Portfolio Bonds (Tax) Regulations 1999, the same meaning as in section 553C(4)(*b*)."

Amendments—[1] Words in paras (3), (8) substituted by the Personal Portfolio Bonds (Tax) (Amendment) Regulations, SI 2001/2724 regs 2, 4 with effect for gains treated as arising after 16 August 2001.

[2] Paras (7), (7A) substituted for para (7) by the Personal Portfolio Bonds (Tax) (Amendment) Regulations, SI 2002/455 with effect from 6 April 2002, as respects gains treated as arising after 5 April 2002.

1999/1408

NON-RESIDENT COMPANIES (GENERAL INSURANCE BUSINESS) REGULATIONS 1999

Made by the Treasury under TA 1988 ss 444BB(5), 444BD(1), (4), (5), 755B(5) and 755C

Made . . . . *20 May 1999*
Laid before the House of Commons . . . . *20 May 1999*
Coming into force . . . . *10 June 1999*

Commentary—*Simon's Taxes* **D4.330**.

1 Citation, commencement and effect

(1) These Regulations may be cited as the Non-resident Companies (General Insurance Business) Regulations 1999 and shall come into force on 10th June 1999.

(2) These Regulations have effect with respect to any appropriate accounting period of a relevant company.

2 Interpretation

(1) In these Regulations unless the context otherwise requires—

"appropriate accounting period" means an accounting period ending on or after 1st July 1999;

"controlled foreign company" shall be construed in accordance with section 747(2);

"general insurance business" has the meaning given by section 755B(6);

"non-resident company" means a company resident outside the United Kingdom;

"relevant company" means a company resident in the United Kingdom that had a relevant interest in a non-resident company at any time during an accounting period of the non-resident company ending in an appropriate accounting period of the relevant company;

"relevant interest" shall be construed in accordance with section 752A on the assumption that the non-resident company is a controlled foreign company;

"the Taxes Act" means the Income and Corporation Taxes Act 1988.

(2) In these Regulations references to a particular provision, without more, are references to that provision of the Taxes Act.

3 Modifications of Chapter IV of Part XVII of the Taxes Act

Chapter IV of Part XVII of the Taxes Act shall have effect with the modifications prescribed in regulations 4 to 6 in any case where a non-resident company—

(*a*) carries on general insurance business, and

(*b*) draws up accounts relating to that business using a method falling within subsection (2) of section 755B.

4 After section 754A there shall be inserted—

"Returns where it is not established whether a non-resident company carrying on general insurance business is a controlled foreign company

754AA (1) This section applies where—

(*a*) if an apportionment were made in accordance with section 747 of the chargeable profits for an accounting period of a company resident outside the United Kingdom ('the non-resident company'), a company resident in the United Kingdom ('the UK company') would be chargeable to tax by virtue of subsection (5) of that section with reference to the whole or a part of the non-resident company's chargeable profits for that accounting period ('the relevant accounting period');

(*b*) the non-resident company carries on general insurance business within the meaning given by section 755B(6) and draws up accounts relating to that business using a method falling within section 755B(2);

(*c*) the UK company delivers a company tax return for the accounting period in which the relevant accounting period of the non-resident company ends; and

(*d*) at the time when the UK company delivers the company tax return for that accounting period, it is not established whether in the relevant accounting period the non-resident company is subject to a lower level of taxation in the territory in which it is resident so as to constitute a controlled foreign company.

(2) Prior to delivering its company tax return for the accounting period mentioned in paragraph (1)(*c*), the UK company shall consider whether or not the non-resident company is likely, in the relevant accounting period, to be subject to a lower level of taxation in the territory in which it is resident so as to constitute a controlled foreign company.

(3) If the UK company is of the opinion that in the relevant accounting period the non-resident company is likely to be subject to a lower level of taxation in the territory in which it is resident so as to constitute a controlled foreign company, the UK company shall make the company tax return on the basis that the relevant accounting period is an accounting period of a company which is a controlled foreign company.

(4) If the UK company is of the opinion that in the relevant accounting period the non-resident company is not likely to be subject to a lower level of taxation in the territory in which it is resident so as to constitute a controlled foreign company, the UK company shall make the company tax return on the basis that the relevant accounting period is an accounting period of a company which is not a controlled foreign company.

(5) In any case where—

(*a*) the UK company makes the company tax return on the basis mentioned in subsection (3) above, but

(b) it becomes established that in the relevant accounting period the non-resident company is not subject to a lower level of taxation in the territory in which it is resident,

the UK company shall amend the company tax return on the basis that the relevant accounting period is an accounting period of a company which is not a controlled foreign company.

(6) In any case where—

(a) the UK company makes the company tax return on the basis mentioned in subsection (4) above, but

(b) it becomes established that in the relevant accounting period the non-resident company is subject to a lower level of taxation in the territory in which it is resident,

the UK company shall amend the company tax return on the basis that the relevant accounting period is an accounting period of a company which is a controlled foreign company.

(7) Any amendment required to be made to the company tax return by virtue of subsection (5) or (6) above shall be made by the UK company before the expiration of the period commencing immediately following the close of the underwriting year and ending on the date which is eighteen months plus thirty days thereafter.

(8) Subject to subsection (9) below, an amendment of a company tax return in accordance with subsection (7) above is subject to, and must be in accordance with, the other provisions of the Corporation Tax Acts as they apply for the purposes of this Chapter.

(9) The time limits otherwise applicable to amendment of a company tax return do not apply to an amendment of a company tax return in accordance with subsection (7) above.

(10) A company which fails to make an amendment required by subsection (6) above in accordance with subsection (7) above shall be liable to a tax-related penalty under paragraph 20 of Schedule 18 to the Finance Act 1998 (penalty, not exceeding amount of tax understated, for incorrect or uncorrected return).

(11) In subsection (7) above 'the close of the underwriting year' means—

(a) the date on which final replacement of the technical provision, as described in [sub-paragraph (4) of paragraph 58 of Schedule 3 to the Large and Medium-sized Companies and Groups (Accounts and Reports) Regulations 2008][1], takes place, or

(b) where there is no final replacement of the technical provision in the three years following the underwriting year, the date referred to in section 755B(4), that is, the end of the third year following the underwriting year."

Amendments—[1] Words in (11)(*a*) substituted by the Companies Act 2006 (Consequential Amendments) (Taxes and National Insurance) Order, SI 2008/954 art 47 with effect for periods of account beginning on or after 6 April 2008.

5—(1) Section 755B shall be modified as follows.

(2) After subsection (4) there shall be inserted—

"(4A) Where in accordance with subsection (4) above the technical provision is treated as finally replaced by a provision for estimated claims outstanding ('the deemed provision'), the amount of the deemed provision which may be deducted from the chargeable profits of the controlled foreign company for the accounting period concerned shall not exceed the amount that, on the assumptions in Schedule 24, would have been deductible from those profits if the deemed provision had been an actual provision as mentioned in subsection (2)(*a*) above."

6— . . .

Amendments—Reg 6 revoked by the Non-resident Companies (General Insurance Business) (Amendment) Regulations, SI 2008/2643 reg 2, with effect in relation to accounting periods of relevant companies ending on or after 28 October 2008.

7 Amendments to the Insurance Companies (Reserves) (Tax) Regulations 1996

(1) The Insurance Companies (Reserves) (Tax) Regulations 1996 shall be amended as follows.

(2) (*amends* SI 1996/2991 reg 8(1)).

(3) (*inserts* SI 1996/2991 regs 8A, 8B).

1999/1964

RETIREMENT BENEFITS SCHEMES (RESTRICTION ON DISCRETION TO APPROVE) (ADDITIONAL VOLUNTARY CONTRIBUTIONS) (AMENDMENT) REGULATIONS 1999

Note—These Regulations lapse by virtue of the coming into force of FA 2004 Part 4 (ss 149–284) with effect from 6 April 2006.

1999/2118

GIFTS FOR RELIEF IN POOR COUNTRIES (DESIGNATION OF KOSOVO) ORDER 1999

Made by the Treasury under FA 1998 s 48(9) and FA 1999 s 56(8)

Made . . . . .27 *July 1999*
Laid before the House of Commons . . . . .27 *July 1999*
Coming into force . . . . .21 *August 1999*

Commentary—*Simon's Taxes* **E1.804**.

1 This Order may be cited as the Gifts for Relief in Poor Countries (Designation of Kosovo) Order 1999 and shall come into force on 21st August 1999, but shall have effect in relation to gifts made on or after 6th April 1999.

2 This Order designates Kosovo (in the Federation of Yugoslavia) as a territory for the purposes of paragraph (*c*) of section 48(2) of the Finance Act 1998.

1999/2155

INCOME TAX (EMPLOYMENTS) (AMENDMENT NO 3) REGULATIONS 1999

Made by the Commissioners of Inland Revenue under TA 1988 s 203

Made . . . . .29 *July 1999*
Laid before the House of Commons . . . . .29 *July 1999*
Coming into force . . . . .19 *August 1999*

Amendment—These regulations revoked by the Income Tax (Pay As You Earn) Regulations, SI 2003/2682 reg 220, Sch 2 with effect from 6 April 2004, subject to transitional provisions contained in Sch 1 thereto.

1999/2156

FINANCE ACT 1995, SECTION 139(3), (APPOINTED DAY) ORDER 1999

Made by the Treasury under FA 1995 s 139(3), Sch 29 Part VIII(21).

Made . . . . .29 *July 1999*

Commentary—*Simon's Taxes* **E5.501**.

1 This Order may be cited as the Finance Act 1995, Section 139(3), (Appointed Day) Order 1999.

2 The day appointed for the purposes of the repeals effected by Part VIII(21) of Schedule 29 to the Finance Act 1995—

(*a*) in or of subsections (1), and (3) to (6) of section 561 of the Income and Corporation Taxes Act 1988, and

(*b*) of section 28 of the Finance Act 1988,

is 6th August 1999.

1999/2975

CORPORATION TAX (SIMPLIFIED ARRANGEMENTS FOR GROUP RELIEF) REGULATIONS 1999

Made by the Treasury under FA 1998 Sch 18 para 77.

Made . . . . .1 *November 1999*
Laid before the House of Commons . . . . .2 *November 1999*
Coming into force . . . . .23 *November 1999*

Commentary—*Simon's Taxes* **D2.213**.

1 Citation and commencement

These Regulations may be cited as the Corporation Tax (Simplified Arrangements for Group Relief) Regulations 1999 and shall come into force on 23rd November 1999.

2 Introductory

These Regulations make provision for arrangements for the surrendering and claiming of group relief in relation to any accounting period of a claimant company ending on or after 1st July 1999.

3 Interpretation

(1) In these Regulations unless the context otherwise requires—

"the arrangements" means the arrangements made by these Regulations as mentioned in regulation 2;

"authorised company" has the meaning given by regulation 4;

"authorising companies" has the meaning given by regulation 5;

"the Board" means the Commissioners of Inland Revenue;

"claimant company" has the meaning given by section 402(1);

"consortium company" has the meaning given by section 406(1)(*b*);

"group of companies" means a collection of companies such that every pair of companies within that collection comprises companies that are members of the same group of companies within the meaning of section 413(3)(*a*);

"group relief" has the meaning given by subsection (1) of section 402, read with subsection (2) of that section (group claim) and subsection (3) of that section and section 406 (consortium claim);

"insolvency practitioner" in relation to a company means a liquidator, provisional liquidator, administrator, administrative receiver, or a supervisor of a voluntary arrangement under Part I of the Insolvency Act 1986;

"the Management Act" means the Taxes Management Act 1970;

"member of the consortium" shall be construed in accordance with section 413(6);

"Schedule 18" means Schedule 18 to the Finance Act 1998;

"three month date" shall be construed in accordance with regulation 7(1).

(2) In these Regulations references to a section, without more, are to that section of the Income and Corporation Taxes Act 1988.

Modifications—So far as these Regulations apply in relation to liquidation and administration, they apply as if references to "liquidator" include a reference to a bank liquidator, references to "provisional liquidator" include a reference to a provisional bank liquidator, under Part 2 of the 2009 Act; references to "administrator" include a reference to a bank administrator, references to "provisional liquidator" include a reference to a provisional bank administrator under Part 3 of the 2009 Act; references to a person acting as an "insolvency practitioner" (as defined in section 388 of the Insolvency Act 1986) include a person acting as a bank liquidator or bank administrator, references to the provisions of the Insolvency Act 1986 and the Insolvency (Northern Ireland) Order 1989, in the context of bank insolvency or bank administration, shall be read to include those provisions as applied and modified by the Banking Act 2009 ss 103, 145, under Parts 2 and 3 of the 2009 Act (Banking Act 2009 (Parts 2 and 3 Consequential Amendments) Order, SI 2009/317 art 3, Schedule).

4 Authorised company

A company is an "authorised company" for the purposes of these Regulations if—

(*a*) it is authorised by companies within regulation 5 to act on their behalf in relation to the arrangements, and

(*b*) it is a member of the same group of companies as that referred to in regulation 5(1)(*a*).

5 Authorising company

(1) In these Regulations an "authorising company" means a company which for the time being—

(*a*) is a member of a group of companies, or

(*b*) is a consortium company in circumstances where a company falling within sub-paragraph (*a*) is a member of the consortium concerned, and

(*c*) in either case satisfies one of the conditions specified in paragraph (2).

(2) Those conditions are that the company—

(*a*) is one of the companies named in the application made by the authorised company in accordance with regulation 6;

(*b*) following the making of that application, is treated for the purposes of these Regulations, by agreement between the company, the authorised company and the Board, as if it had been one of the companies named in that application.

6 Application by authorised company

(1) An application by the authorised company on behalf of itself and the authorising companies to enter into the arrangements must be made in writing to an officer of the Board.

(2) The application must specify—

(*a*) the name and the tax office reference of the authorised company,

(*b*) the names and the tax office references of the authorising companies, and

(*c*) details relating to the authorised company and each of the authorising companies that are sufficient to demonstrate that the company concerned is a member of the group of companies or, as the case may be, a consortium company.

(3) The application must contain a statement by the authorised company and the authorising companies that they agree to be covered by the arrangements and to be bound by claims, surrenders and withdrawals made under the arrangements.

(4) The application must be accompanied—

(*a*) by a specimen copy of the statement referred to in regulation 10(2) that the authorised company proposes to use for the purpose of making and withdrawing surrenders and claims on behalf of itself and the authorising companies;

(*b*) in the case of a company which is a consortium company, by an agreement, signed by each member of the consortium and the consortium company, consenting to the authorised company acting on their behalf in relation to the arrangements.

(5) The application must be signed on behalf of each of the companies concerned by a person referred to in section 108(1) of the Management Act as a person through whom that company may act.

(6) The application must be sent to the tax office dealing with the tax affairs of the authorised company.

7 Matters consequential to the making of an application

(1) Except where paragraph (2), (3) or (4) applies and subject to regulation 9, the authorised company may enter into the arrangements on behalf of itself and the authorising companies at any time on or after the date ("the three month date") that is three months after the date on which the application is delivered to the tax office in accordance with regulation 6(6).

(2) An officer of the Board may, prior to the three month date, accept the application and permit the authorised company to enter into the arrangements on behalf of itself and the authorising companies with effect from the date notified to the authorised company by the officer of the Board.

(3) An officer of the Board may, prior to the three month date, accept the application and permit the authorised company to enter into the arrangements with effect from the date notified to the company by the officer of the Board, but exclude from the arrangements any of the authorising companies on the grounds that he has reason to believe that that company—

(*a*) has failed to comply with its obligations under the Corporation Tax Acts in relation to any accounting period (whether an accounting period ending before, or on or after, 1st July 1999), or

(*b*) is a company in relation to which a person is acting as an insolvency practitioner.

(4) An officer of the Board may, prior to the three month date, refuse the application on the grounds that—

(*a*) he has reason to believe that one or more of the companies named in the application is not a member of a group of companies, or is not a consortium company in circumstances where a company which is a member of that group is a member of the consortium concerned,

(*b*) he has reason to believe that one or more of the companies named in the application has failed to comply with its obligations under the Corporation Tax Acts in relation to any accounting period (whether an accounting period ending before, or on or after, 1st July 1999),

(*c*) the case is not one in which all, or substantially all, of the companies named in the application deliver their company tax returns to the same tax office, or

(*d*) the specimen copy of the statement referred to in regulation 6(4)(*a*) is not adequate for the purpose of enabling an officer of the Board to deal with claims for group relief.

(5) Where following the making of an application by an authorised company under regulation 6 a company is treated by agreement in accordance with regulation 5(2)(*b*) as if it had been one of the companies named in the application, the authorised company may enter into the arrangements on behalf of that company from the date of the agreement.

Modifications—So far as these Regulations apply in relation to liquidation and administration, they apply as if references to a person acting as an "insolvency practitioner" (as defined in section 388 of the Insolvency Act 1986) include a person acting as a bank liquidator or bank administrator under Parts 2 and 3 of the Banking Act 2009 (Banking Act 2009 (Parts 2 and 3 Consequential Amendments) Order, SI 2009/317 art 3, Schedule).

8 Change in members of consortium

(1) Where following the making of an application under regulation 6 there is a change in the members of the consortium referred to in paragraph (4)(*b*) of that regulation, as from the date of the change the authorised company may not act in accordance with the provisions of regulation 10 in relation to the consortium company concerned unless it takes the action specified in paragraph (2).

(2) The action specified in this paragraph is that the company must ensure that a new agreement, signed by the consortium company concerned and each company that is a member of the consortium immediately after the change, consenting to the authorised company acting on their behalf in relation to the arrangements, is sent to the tax office referred to in regulation 6(6).

(3) Where in accordance with paragraph (2) a new agreement is entered into and sent to the tax office, that agreement is effective for the purposes of the arrangements as from the date on which acceptance of the agreement is notified by an officer of the Board to the authorised company.

9 Exclusion of company from the arrangements

An officer of the Board may, at any time on or after the three month date or, if earlier, the date on which an application under regulation 6 was accepted, exclude from the arrangements a company named, or treated under regulation 5(2)(*b*) as named, in that application, on the grounds that he has reason to believe that that company—

(*a*) is not an authorising company at that time by reason of the company not falling within regulation 5(1)(*a*) or (*b*);

(*b*) has failed to comply with its obligations under the Corporation Tax Acts in relation to any accounting period (whether an accounting period ending before, or on or after, 1st July 1999); or

(*c*) is a company in relation to which a person is acting as an insolvency practitioner.

Modifications—So far as these Regulations apply in relation to liquidation and administration, they apply as if references to a person acting as an "insolvency practitioner" (as defined in section 388 of the Insolvency Act 1986) include a person acting as a bank liquidator or bank administrator under Parts 2 and 3 of the Banking Act 2009 (Banking Act 2009 (Parts 2 and 3 Consequential Amendments) Order, SI 2009/317 art 3, Schedule).

9A [Group relief claims under the arrangements not accompanied by copy of notice of consent to surrender

(1) Where an application by an authorised company is accepted by an officer of the Board under regulation 7, any of the authorising companies may make a claim for group relief in accordance with the following provisions of this regulation.

(2) A claim may be made without being accompanied by the copy of the notice of consent required under paragraph 70(4) of Schedule 18 if the authorised company gives authority for the claim being so made.

(3) The authority given by the authorised company must—

(*a*) be included in the company tax return of the authorising company for the accounting period for which the claim is made,

(*b*) be included in that return as originally made, and

(*c*) be signed on behalf of the authorised company by a person referred to in section 108(1) of the Management Act as a person through whom that company may act.][1]

Amendments—[1] Regulation 9A inserted by the Corporation Tax (Simplified Arrangements for Group Relief) (Amendment) Regulations, SI 2000/3228, reg 2 with effect from 29 December 2000.

10 Group relief claims and surrenders under the arrangements

(1) Where an application by an authorised company is accepted by an officer of the Board under regulation 7, the authorised company may act in accordance with the following provisions of this regulation in relation to itself and to any of the authorising companies, other than a company excluded from the arrangements in accordance with regulation 7(3) or 9.

(2) The authorised company may from time to time furnish to an officer of the Board on behalf of itself and the authorising companies a statement in writing, in the form provided, or in a form authorised, by the Board, containing information necessary for the amendment in accordance with the provisions of Part VIII of Schedule 18 of the company tax returns of itself and the authorising companies for the purpose of making and withdrawing claims and surrenders of group relief.

(3) Where a statement is furnished to an officer of the Board as mentioned in paragraph (2)—

(*a*) the provisions of Part VIII of Schedule 18, other than paragraph 70(4) (claim for group relief ineffective unless accompanied by copy of notice of consent to surrender) and paragraph 71(4) (notice of withdrawal of consent to surrender ineffective unless accompanied by notice of consent of claimant company to withdrawal), shall apply in relation to the authorised company as if references to the claimant company and the surrendering company included references to the authorised company;

(*b*) amendments made in accordance with the provisions of Part VIII of Schedule 18 to the company tax returns of the authorising companies in reliance on the information contained in the statement shall have effect for the purposes of the Corporation Tax Acts as if the amendments had been made by those companies.

(4) Without prejudice to the generality of paragraph (2), the information to be contained in the statement must include in particular—

(*a*) as regards the amount claimed, the same information as is specified in paragraph 68 of Schedule 18,

(*b*) as regards the amount surrendered, the same information as is specified in paragraph 71(1) of Schedule 18,

(*c*) where applicable, details showing the effect of the claim on each company's self-assessment included in its company tax return, and

(*d*) where applicable, details showing which of the company tax returns of the companies concerned are returns into which an enquiry is in progress under Part IV of Schedule 18.

(5) A statement provided under paragraph (2) that does not contain information that is sufficient for the amendment of the company tax returns of the authorised company and the authorising companies in accordance with the provisions of Part VIII of Schedule 18 is ineffective.

(6) An authorising company remains liable, in accordance with the provisions of Schedule 18, for any incorrect claim or incorrect company tax return arising from a statement provided by the authorised company under paragraph (2).

11 Termination of arrangements and exclusion of applicant company from arrangements
(1) Either the Board or the authorised company may at any time give notice in writing to the other terminating the arrangements with effect from the date of issue of the notice.
(2) The authorised company may at any time give notice in writing to the Board excluding an authorising company from the arrangements with effect from the date of issue of the notice.

1999/3308

LLOYD'S UNDERWRITERS (SPECIAL RESERVE FUNDS) REGULATIONS 1999

Made by the Commissioners of Inland Revenue under FA 1993 s 182(1)(b), (c)

Made . . . . *9 December 1999*
Laid before the House of Commons . . . . *10 December 1999*
Coming into force . . . . *31 December 1999*

1 Citation, commencement and effect
(1) These Regulations may be cited as the Lloyd's Underwriters (Special Reserve Funds) Regulations 1999.
(2) These Regulations shall come into force on 31st December 1999, but except for regulation 3 shall have effect—
(*a*) for the year 2000–01 and subsequent years of assessment, and
(*b*) in relation to payments and transfers of assets made on or after 1st January 2000.

2 Interpretation
In these Regulations "Schedule 20" means Schedule 20 to the Finance Act 1993.

3–5 Amendments to and modifications of Schedule 20
(*Amend FA 1993, Sch 20, paras 6(2), 8(1), 10(4).*)

6—(1) Paragraph 11 of Schedule 20 is modified as follows.
(2) In sub-paragraph (2)—
(*a*) for the words "any payment which is" there shall be substituted the words "the aggregate of any payments which are";
(*b*) after the word "above" there shall be inserted the words "(except where they are also made under paragraph 6(2) above)";
(*c*) in paragraph (*a*) at the beginning there shall be inserted the words "subject to sub-paragraph (2A) below,";
(*d*) in paragraph (*b*) after the words "being a" there shall be inserted the word "single".
(3) After sub-paragraph (2) the following sub-paragraph shall be inserted—
"(2A) Where the member ceases to carry on his underwriting business by reason of his death, any payment falling within sub-paragraph (2) above shall be treated, for the purposes of sections 59C and 86 of the Management Act, as if made immediately after the commencement of his final year of assessment.".
(4) In sub-paragraph (3)—
(*a*) in paragraph (*b*) after the word "paragraph" there shall be inserted "3(1),";
(*b*) the word "and" which immediately follows paragraph (*b*) shall be omitted;
(*c*) at the end the following paragraphs shall be added—
"(*d*) as increased by an amount equal to any profits, and reduced by an amount equal to any losses, arising to the trustees from assets after the end of that year (excluding any gains or losses on assets whose transfer is treated as an acquisition by sub-paragraph (4)(*a*) or (*b*) below); and
(*e*) as increased by the aggregate amount of any payments made—
(i) by the trustees to the member or his personal representatives or assigns,
(ii) out of his special reserve fund under paragraph 7(1) above (except where they are also made under paragraph 6(2) above), or otherwise than out of his special reserve fund, and
(iii) before the end of that year,
and for this purpose the amount of any payment which is made by way of the transfer of an asset shall be taken to be the market value of the asset at the date of the transfer and 'market value' shall be construed in accordance with section 272 of the Taxation of Chargeable Gains Act 1992."
(5) In sub-paragraph (4)—
(*a*) after the word "above" there shall be inserted the words "or otherwise than out of his special reserve fund";

(*b*) for the words from ", to be" to the end there shall be substituted—

"—

(*a*) in a case where the asset was held by the trustees at the end of the penultimate underwriting year, as an acquisition of the asset by the member or his personal representatives or assigns at the end of that year for a consideration equal to its market value at that time;

(*b*) in a case where the asset was acquired by the trustees after the end of the penultimate underwriting year, as an acquisition of the asset by the member or his personal representatives or assigns, at the date on which, and for the consideration for which, the asset was acquired by the trustees; and

(*c*) in a case where the asset was both acquired by the trustees and transferred by them to the member or his personal representatives or assigns before the end of the penultimate underwriting year, as an acquisition of the asset by the member or his personal representatives or assigns at the date of the transfer and for a consideration equal to its market value at that time.".

1999/3330

DOUBLE TAXATION RELIEF (TAXES ON INCOME) (FOREIGN INTEREST AND DIVIDENDS) REGULATIONS 1999

Made by the Commissioners of Inland Revenue under the Income and Corporation Taxes Act 1988, s 798B(4)

Made . . . . *13 December 1999*
Laid before the House of Commons . . . . *13 December 1999*
Coming into force . . . . *3 January 2000*

1 Citation and commencement

These Regulations may be cited as the Double Taxation Relief (Taxes on Income) (Foreign Interest and Dividends) Regulations 1999 and shall come into force on 3rd January 2000.

2 Interpretation

(1) In these Regulations unless the context otherwise requires—

"the cost of acquiring the asset", in relation to a foreign dividend, means—

(*a*) the cost of acquiring the right to the dividend (if any), and

(*b*) the cost of acquiring the stocks, funds, shares or securities (if any) out of which, or in respect of which, the dividend is paid;

"interbank market" means the market that exists between banks in a particular place for the purpose of borrowing and lending funds and dealing in currencies, and "the relevant interbank market" means the interbank market which is most appropriate in relation to a loan having regard to all the terms on which it was made;

"interest period", in relation to a loan, means—

(*a*) any period specified in the loan agreement as a period for which interest is to be calculated, or, as the case may be, selected in accordance with that agreement by one of the parties thereto, beginning either on the date on which the loan was first made or on the expiry of the preceding interest period; or

(*b*) where no such period is specified in the loan agreement, but interest is to be calculated under that agreement by reference to a period of at least 360 days, and is payable on two or more specified dates within that period, any period beginning immediately after one and ending on the next of those dates; or

(*c*) in any other case, any period not exceeding one year which is appropriate in the circumstances of the loan;

"loan agreement" means, in relation to a loan, any agreement in pursuance of which the loan is made;

"qualifying taxpayer" has the meaning given by section 798(4) and (5);

"the specified circumstances" means circumstances in which—

(*a*) section 798 applies, and

(*b*) the amount of the qualifying taxpayer's financial expenditure in relation to the earning of the foreign interest or foreign dividends in question is not readily ascertainable;

"subsection (3)" means subsection (3) of section 798B.

(2) References in these Regulations to a particular section, without more, are to that section of the Income and Corporation Taxes Act 1988.

3 Determination of the sum which it is just and reasonable to attribute to the earning of foreign interest or foreign dividends—matters to be taken into account

(1) This regulation specifies, for the purpose of supplementing subsection (3), matters to be taken into account in determining such sum as it is just and reasonable to attribute to the earning of foreign interest or foreign dividends, in the specified circumstances.

(2) Subject to paragraph (6), in relation to a loan there shall be taken into account (whether or not the interest rate payable is determined by reference to rates at which deposits are offered in an interbank market) the interbank bid rates, determined in accordance with regulation 4, which at any time are most appropriate in the circumstances of the loan, having regard to—

(*a*) the amount of principal outstanding on the loan during each interest period,

(*b*) the currency in which the loan is denominated, and

(*c*) the length of each interest period.

(3) In relation to foreign interest other than loan interest, paragraph (2), regulation 4 and the definitions of "interbank market", "the relevant interbank market" and "interest period" shall apply, with the modifications that—

(*a*) references to the loan, or to the loan agreement, are replaced with references to the obligations, under which the right to interest arises;

(*b*) the reference to the date on which the loan was first made is replaced with a reference to the date on which any of those obligations first came into existence; and

(*c*) the reference to principal outstanding is replaced with a reference to any amount other than interest which is owing (whether or not yet due and payable) by the payer of the foreign interest to the qualifying taxpayer.

(4) In relation to foreign dividends, paragraph (2), regulation 4 and the definitions of "interbank market" and "the relevant interbank market" shall apply as if—

(*a*) so much of the cost of acquiring the asset as has not been repaid to the qualifying taxpayer represented a loan from the payee of the dividend to the payer thereof and the dividend represented interest on that loan;

(*b*) the date on which any of the cost of acquiring the asset was first expended by the qualifying taxpayer were the date on which that loan was made; and

(*c*) the interest periods were periods of one year, beginning either—

(i) on the date on which the loan is treated as made by sub-paragraph (*b*), or

(ii) on the expiry of the preceding interest period,

except in a case where the loan so treated as made subsists for less than a year, where the interest period shall be equal to the period for which the loan so treated as made subsists.

(5) Where, in relation to a loan it would be impracticable to establish the interbank bid rates, there shall be taken into account such amount as would, when deducted from the foreign interest payable on the loan in the interest period, provide the lender with a margin no greater than would be usual in the case of loans of that description.

(6) Where a qualifying taxpayer establishes to the satisfaction of the inspector that, in relation to all loans, obligations and assets referred to in this regulation ("arrangements") made or held by him, on which foreign interest or foreign dividends arose in any chargeable period, the sums attributable under paragraphs (2) to (5) would be greater than the total amount of the expenditure incurred in financing those arrangements, there shall be taken into account the best estimate of such total expenditure, and in determining that figure, regard is to be had to the cost to the qualifying taxpayer of obtaining funds for such financing, to the terms on which the arrangements were made and to any other relevant matters.

4 Determination of interbank bid rates of interest

The interbank bid rates referred to in regulation 3(2) shall be taken to be the average of the bids that would be made in relation to each interest period applicable to the loan in the relevant interbank market on terms corresponding to the terms of the loan.

5 Revocation

(1) (*Revokes the Double Taxation Relief (Taxes on Income) (Foreign Loan Interest) Regulations, SI 1988/88.*)

(2) Anything whatsoever begun under any regulation revoked by these Regulations may be continued under these Regulations as if begun under these Regulations.

SIs

2000/600

INCOME TAX (CHARGE TO TAX) (PAYMENTS OUT OF SURPLUS FUNDS) (RELEVANT RATE) ORDER 2000

Note—These Regulations lapse by virtue of the coming into force of FA 2004 Part 4 (ss 149–284) with effect from 6 April 2006.

2000/921

INCOME AND CORPORATION TAXES ACT 1988, SECTION 559(4A), ORDER 2000

Revocation—These Regulations lapse by virtue of the coming into force of FA 2004 Part 4 (ss 149–284) with effect from 6 April 2006.

2000/922

FINANCE ACT 1995, SECTION 139(3), (APPOINTED DAY) ORDER 2000

Made by the Treasury under FA 1995 s 139(3)

Made . . . . *30 March 2000*

Commentary—*Simon's Taxes* **E5.528.**

1 This Order may be cited as the Finance Act 1995, Section 139(3), (Appointed Day) Order 2000.

2 The day appointed for the purposes of section 139(1) of the Finance Act 1995 is 6th April 2000.

2000/944

EDUCATION (STUDENT LOANS) (REPAYMENT) REGULATIONS 2000

Revocation—Revoked by the Education (Student Loans) (Repayment) Regulations, SI 2009/470 reg 2(1), Schedule, with effect from 6 April 2009.

2000/945

INCOME TAX (ELECTRONIC COMMUNICATIONS) REGULATIONS 2000

Amendments—These Regulations revoked by the Income and Corporation Taxes (Electronic Communications) Regulations, SI 2003/282 reg 11 with effect from 5 March 2003.

2000/1085

RETIREMENT BENEFITS SCHEMES (SHARING OF PENSIONS ON [THE DISSOLUTION OR ANNULMENT OF A MARRIAGE OR CIVIL PARTNERSHIP]) REGULATIONS 2000

Revocation—These Regulations lapse by virtue of the coming into force of FA 2004 Part 4 (ss 149–284) with effect from 6 April 2006.

2000/1087

RETIREMENT BENEFITS SCHEMES (RESTRICTION ON DISCRETION TO APPROVE) (EXCEPTED PROVISIONS) REGULATIONS 2000

Revocation—These Regulations lapse by virtue of the coming into force of FA 2004 Part 4 (ss 149–284) with effect from 6 April 2006.

2000/1093

FINANCE ACT 1999, SCHEDULE 10, PARAGRAPH 18, (FIRST AND SECOND APPOINTED DAYS) ORDER 2000

Made by the Treasury under FA 1999 Sch 10 para 18(1)

Made . . . . *18 April 2000*

Commentary—*Simon's Taxes* **E7.105.**

Press releases—IR 19-4-2000: Pension sharing on divorce to begin 1 December 2000.

1 This Order may be cited as the Finance Act 1999, Schedule 10, Paragraph 18, (First and Second Appointed Days) Order 2000.

2 For the purposes of paragraph 18 of Schedule 10 to the Finance Act 1999—

(*a*) the day appointed as "the first appointed day" is 10th May 2000;

(*b*) the day appointed as "the second appointed day" is 1st December 2000.

2000/2004

FINANCE ACT 1999, SECTION 59(3)(B), (APPOINTED DAY) ORDER 2000

Made by the Treasury under FA 1999 s 59(3)(b)

Made . . . .*25 July 2000*

1 This Order may be cited as the Finance Act 1999, Section 59(3)(*b*) (Appointed Day) Order 2000.

2 The day appointed for the purposes of section 59(2) and (3)(*b*) of the Finance Act 1999 is 1st September 2000.

2000/2074

DONATIONS TO CHARITY BY INDIVIDUALS (APPROPRIATE DECLARATIONS) REGULATIONS 2000

Made by the Commissioners of Inland Revenue under FA 1990 s 25(3), (3A) FA 1999 ss 132(1)(a), (2)(a), (8), (9), (10), 133(1) and (2) and FA 2000 s 39(10)

Made . . . .*28 July 2000*

Laid before the House of Commons . . . .*31 July 2000*

Coming into force . . . .*21 August 2000*

Commentary—*Simon's Taxes* **E1.804.**

1 Citation, commencement and effect

(1) These Regulations may be cited as the Donations to Charity by Individuals (Appropriate Declarations) Regulations 2000 and shall come into force on 21st August 2000.

(2) These Regulations shall have effect in relation to—

(*a*) gifts made on or after 6th April 2000 [and on or before 5th April 2017][3] which are not covenanted payments; and

(*b*) covenanted payments falling to be made on or after [6th April 2000][2].

2 Interpretation

In these Regulations—

"appropriate declaration" has the same meaning as in section 25(1)(*c*) of the Finance Act 1990;

["the Commissioners" means the Commissioners for Her Majesty's Revenue and Customs;][2]

"donor" has the same meaning as in section 25(1) of the Finance Act 1990;

["electronic communications" includes any communications conveyed by means of an electronic communications network.][1]

Amendments—[1] Definition of "electronic communications" substituted by the Communications Act 2003 (Consequential Amendments) Order, SI 2003/2155 art 3(1), Schedule para 23(1)(*c*), (2) with effect from 17 September 2003.

[2] Definition of "the Commissioners" substituted for that of "the Board" by the Donations to Charity by Individuals (Appropriate Declarations) (Amendment) Regulations, SI 2005/2790 regs 2, 3 with effect from 1 November 2005.

[3] In para (2)(*a*), words inserted, and in para (2)(*b*), words substituted for words "that date", by the Donations to Charity (Gift Aid Declarations) Regulations, SI 2016/1195 reg 3 with effect in relation to gifts made on or after 6 April 2017. Any declaration given before 6 April 2017 which is capable of covering charitable donations made on or after that date, continues to have effect (SI 2016/1195 reg 3(2), (3)).

3 Manner in which an appropriate declaration may be given

An appropriate declaration may be given by a donor to a charity—

(*a*) in writing; [or

(*b*) orally;

including the use of written or oral methods of electronic communications, as the case may be.][1]

Amendments—[1] Words substituted by the Donations to Charity by Individuals (Appropriate Declarations) (Amendment) Regulations, SI 2005/2790 regs 2, 4 with effect from 1 November 2005.

4 [Giving appropriate declarations

(1) An appropriate declaration must—

(*a*) contain the name and home address of the donor,

(*b*) name the charity (or be made in circumstances where the charity is identified),

(*c*) identify the gift or gifts to which the declaration relates, and (*d*) confirm that the identified gift or gifts are to be qualifying donations for the purposes of section 25 of the Finance Act 1990 (Donations to charity by individuals).

(2) The explanation of section 25(8) of the Finance Act 1990 referred to in regulation 5(2)(*b*) or (4)(*b*), as the case may be, must be given to the donor in order for an appropriate declaration to have effect (subject to regulation 6).][1]

Amendments—[1] Regulations 4–7 substituted by the Donations to Charity by Individuals (Appropriate Declarations) (Amendment) Regulations, SI 2005/2790 regs 2, 5 with effect from 1 November 2005.

5 [Recording and audit of appropriate declarations

(1) A charity must either—

(*a*) maintain an auditable record of appropriate declarations given to it, or

(*b*) comply with paragraphs (4) to (6) in relation to each declaration.

This is subject to paragraph (3).

(2) An auditable record is a record of evidence—

(*a*) of appropriate declarations and the making of them, and

(*b*) that (whether or not separate from the declaration) statements explaining the effect of section 25(8) of the Finance Act 1990 were given to donors at the time the declarations were made,

in a form, and to a standard, which can be inspected and audited by the Commissioners.

(3) If the Commissioners notify the charity that the record, or the records relating to particular declarations or classes of declarations, do not meet with their satisfaction, the charity must comply with paragraphs (4) to (6) in relation to the declarations in question.

(4) Where paragraph (1)(*b*) or (3) applies, the charity shall in each case send the donor a statement in writing ("written statement") containing—

(*a*) the information required by regulation 4(1)(*a*) to (*d*),

(*b*) an explanation of the effect of section 25(8) of the Finance Act 1990,

(*c*) the date on which the charity sends the statement to the donor, and

(*d*) a statement that the donor is entitled to cancel his declaration by giving notice in writing to the charity not later than 30 days following the date in sub-paragraph (*c*).

(5) Where paragraph (4) applies, the donor is entitled to cancel the declaration by giving notice of cancellation to the charity in accordance with paragraph (4)(*d*).

(6) The charity shall maintain an auditable record of—

(*a*) written statements, and

(*b*) any cancellation notices,

in a form, and to a standard, which can be inspected and audited by the Commissioners.

(7) Where a donor who has given an appropriate declaration to a charity notifies the charity of any change to his name or home address, the charity must keep a record of those changes with the declaration.][1]

Amendments—[1] Regulations 4–7 substituted by the Donations to Charity by Individuals (Appropriate Declarations) (Amendment) Regulations, SI 2005/2790 regs 2, 5 with effect from 1 November 2005.

6 [Prescribed circumstances in which appropriate declarations are deemed never to have had effect

An appropriate declaration shall be treated for the purposes of the Taxes Acts as never having had effect where—

(*a*) the charity has not sent the written statement to the donor in a case where it is required to do so by regulation 5(4);

(*b*) the donor cancels the declaration by giving notice in accordance with regulation 5(5); or

(*c*) the Commissioners notify the charity that the records relating to that declaration under regulation 5(6) do not meet with their satisfaction.][1]

Amendments—[1] Regulations 4–7 substituted by the Donations to Charity by Individuals (Appropriate Declarations) (Amendment) Regulations, SI 2005/2790 regs 2, 5 with effect from 1 November 2005.

7 [Prescribed circumstances in which appropriate declarations cease to have effect

An appropriate declaration shall cease to have effect for the purposes of the Taxes Acts where—

(*a*) the donor notifies the charity of the cancellation of his declaration (other than in accordance with regulation 5(5)), and

(*b*) the cancellation takes effect from (or after) the date of its receipt by the charity.][1]

Amendments—[1] Regulations 4–7 substituted by the Donations to Charity by Individuals (Appropriate Declarations) (Amendment) Regulations, SI 2005/2790 regs 2, 5 with effect from 1 November 2005.

2000/2076

INDIVIDUAL LEARNING ACCOUNTS (SEPARATE EMPLOYERS UNDER THE CROWN) REGULATIONS 2000

Made by the Treasury under ICTA 1988 s 200G(3)

Made . . . .*28 July 2000*
Laid before the House of Commons . . . .*31 July 2000*
Coming into force . . . .*21 August 2000*

1 These Regulations may be cited as the Individual Learning Accounts (Separate Employers under the Crown) Regulations 2000 and shall come into force on 21st August 2000.

2—(1) For the purposes of section 200G of the Income and Corporation Taxes Act 1988, Crown servants mentioned in paragraphs (2) and (3) shall be treated as holding office or employment in accordance with those paragraphs.

(2) Any Crown servant who is in—

(*a*) employment under or for the purposes of a Government department,

(*b*) service as a member of staff of the Scottish Administration, or holds an office in that Administration which is not a ministerial office,

(*c*) service as a member of the staff of the National Assembly for Wales,

(*d*) employment under or for the purposes of a Northern Ireland department, or

(*e*) service as a member of staff of the Northern Ireland Assembly, shall be treated as holding office or employment under the organisation concerned.

(3) Service as a member of—

(*a*) the Royal Navy and Royal Marines,

(*b*) the Military Forces of the Crown, or

(*c*) the Regular Air Force,

shall be treated as employment of the organisation concerned (and each of those organisations shall be treated as an entity for the purposes of these Regulations).

2000/2080

INCOME TAX (BENEFITS IN KIND) (EXEMPTION FOR WELFARE COUNSELLING) REGULATIONS 2000

Made by the Treasury under TA 1988 s 155ZB

Made . . . .*28 July 2000*
Laid before the House of Commons . . . .*31 July 2000*
Coming into force . . . .*21 August 2000*

1 These Regulations may be cited as the Income Tax (Benefits in Kind) (Exemption for Welfare Counselling) Regulations 2000 and shall come into force on 21st August 2000.

2—(1) There shall be exempted from section 154 of the Income and Corporation Taxes Act 1988 a benefit consisting of welfare counselling that is made available to an employer's employees generally on similar terms.

(2) In paragraph (1) "welfare counselling" means counselling of any kind other than—

(*a*) medical treatment of any kind, or

(*b*) advice specified in paragraph (3).

(3) The advice specified in this paragraph is advice on finance (other than on debt problems), advice on tax, or on leisure or recreation, and legal advice.

HMRC Manuals—Employment Income Manual EIM21845 (exemption for welfare counselling).

2000/2081

RESEARCH AND DEVELOPMENT (PRESCRIBED ACTIVITIES) REGULATIONS 2000

Note—These regulations revoked by the Research and Development (Prescribed Activities) Regulations, SI 2004/712, with effect from 1 April 2004.

2000/2082

FINANCE ACT 2000, SECTION 108(3), (APPOINTED DAY) ORDER 2000

Made by the Treasury under FA 2000 s 108(3)

Made . . . .*28 July 2000*

Commentary—*Simon's Taxes* **D7.539.**

1 This Order may be cited as the Finance Act 2000, Section 108(3), (Appointed Day) Order 2000.

2 The day appointed for the purposes of section 108(3) of the Finance Act 2000 is 22nd August 2000.

2000/2089

INSURANCE COMPANIES (OVERSEAS LIFE ASSURANCE BUSINESS) (EXCLUDED BUSINESS) REGULATIONS 2000

Made by the Commissioners of Inland Revenue under TA 1988 s 431D

Made . . . . *1 August 2000*
Laid before the House of Commons . . . . *1 August 2000*
Coming into force . . . . *22 August 2000*

Commentary—*Simon's Taxes* **D7.539.**

1 Citation, commencement and effect

(1) These Regulations may be cited as the Insurance Companies (Overseas Life Assurance Business) (Excluded Business) Regulations 2000 and shall come into force on 22nd August 2000.

(2) These Regulations shall have effect in relation to policies or contracts made by an insurance company on or after 22nd August 2000.

2 Interpretation

(1) In these Regulations—

"beneficiary" means any person who is, or will or may become, entitled to any benefit under a trust, including—

(*a*) any person who may become so entitled on the exercise of a discretion; and

(*b*) a settlor who has an interest in the trust property for the purpose of [sections 624 to 627 of the Income Tax (Trading and Other Income) Act 2005][2];

"the Board" means the Commissioners of Inland Revenue;

"charity" means a person or body of persons established for charitable purposes only;

"collective investment scheme" has the meaning given by section [235 of the Financial Services and Markets Act 2000][1];

"discretionary trust" means any trust under which—

(*a*) the income arising to the trustees is to be accumulated and no person other than the trustees is entitled to that income before it is distributed; or

(*b*) the beneficiaries may become entitled to a benefit on the exercise of a discretion (whether or not the trustees have power to accumulate income) and no person is entitled to any benefit before the exercise of that discretion;

"holding company" means a company whose assets all, or all but an insignificant part, consist of shares in companies which, for the purposes of the Tax Acts, are deemed to be its 51 per cent subsidiaries by virtue of section 838;

"investment company" means any company whose business consists wholly or mainly in the making of investments and the principal part of whose income is derived therefrom, but excludes any holding company or collective investment scheme;

"relevant overseas employees" means persons who are not residing in the United Kingdom and are—

(*a*) employees of a policy holder or annuitant; or

(*b*) employees of a person connected with a policy holder or annuitant; or

(*c*) employees in respect of whose employment there is established a superannuation fund to which section 615(3) applies;

and, for the purpose of paragraph (b), whether a person is connected with a policy holder or annuitant shall be determined in accordance with section 839;

"relevant former employees" means—

(*a*) former employees of a policy holder or annuitant; or

(*b*) former employees of a person connected with a policy holder or annuitant; or

(*c*) former employees in respect of whose employment there is established a superannuation fund to which section 615(3) applies;

and, for the purpose of paragraph (b), whether a person is connected with a policy holder or annuitant shall be determined in accordance with section 839;

"settlor" means the person, or each of the persons, by whom the trust was directly or indirectly created, and for this purpose a person shall, in particular, be regarded as having created a trust if he provided or undertook to provide funds directly or indirectly for the purposes of the trust, or made with any other person a reciprocal arrangement for that other person to create the trust;

"term assurance business" means life assurance business in relation to which the policy or contract, or the underlying policy, is one which—

(*a*) is for a specified term; and

(*b*) is not capable of acquiring a surrender value that exceeds the amount of premiums paid.

(2) In these Regulations any reference to a particular provision, without more, is a reference to that provision of the Income and Corporation Taxes Act 1988.

Amendments—[1] In para (1), words in definition of "collective investment scheme" substituted by the Financial Services and Markets Act 2000 (Consequential Amendments) (Taxes) Order, SI 2001/3629 art 187 with effect from 1 December 2001, immediately after the coming into force of the Financial Services and Markets Act 2000 ss 411, 432(1), Sch 20 (and SI 2001/3629 Pts 1 and 2).

[2] In para (1), in definition of "beneficiary", words in para (*b*) substituted by the Insurance Companies (Overseas Life Assurance Business) (Excluded Business) (Amendment) Regulations, SI 2008/2625 regs 2, 3 with effect from 27 October 2008.

3 [Life assurance business prescribed for the purposes of section 431D(1A)(d)

(1) Subject to paragraph (2), life assurance business is prescribed for the purposes of section 431D(1A)(*d*) (meaning of "overseas life assurance business") if it is of a description—

(*a*) that does not fall within any of the circumstances set out in regulations 4 to 7; or

(*b*) that falls within the circumstances set out in regulation 9.

(2) Where a policy or contract for business is owned by two or more policy holders or annuitants who do not hold the policy or contract as trustees of the same trust, the business is prescribed for the purposes of section 431D(1A)(*d*) where, if any of the policy holders or annuitants were the only policy holder or annuitant, paragraph (1) would so prescribe it.][1]

Commentary—*Simon's Taxes* **D7.5131.**

Amendments—[1] This regulation substituted by the Insurance Companies (Overseas Life Assurance Business) (Excluded Business) (Amendment) Regulations, SI 2007/2086 regs 2, 3(1) with effect for accounting periods beginning on or after 13 August 2007 (SI 2007/2086 reg 1(1), (2)).

4 [Circumstances where business not prescribed for the purposes of section 431D(1A)(d)][1]

The circumstances set out in this regulation are where—

(*a*) the business is with a policy holder or annuitant who—

(i) is not a company, or

(ii) is a company which holds the policy or contract for the business in a fiduciary or representative capacity;

(*b*) the rights conferred by the policy or contract for the business are not held subject to a trust; and

(*c*) not less than 65 per cent of any benefit under the policy or contract for the business is payable to—

(i) persons residing outside the United Kingdom; and

(ii) charities.

Commentary—*Simon's Taxes* **D7.5131.**

Amendments—[1] Heading to regs 4–7 substituted by virtue of the Insurance Companies (Overseas Life Assurance Business) (Excluded Business) (Amendment) Regulations, SI 2007/2086 regs 2, 3(2) with effect for accounting periods beginning on or after 13 August 2007 (SI 2007/2086 reg 1(1), (2)).

5—(1) The circumstances set out in this paragraph are where—

(*a*) the rights conferred by the policy or contract for the business are held subject to a trust;

(*b*) in the case of a discretionary trust, each beneficiary is either an individual not residing in the United Kingdom or a charity; and

(*c*) in the case of a non-discretionary trust, beneficiaries who are—

(i) not residing in the United Kingdom, or

(ii) charities,

have an interest in not less than 65 per cent of the capital of the trust;

(2) For the purposes of paragraph (1)(*b*), an individual who, as a trustee of any trust, is a beneficiary under the trust referred to in paragraph (1)(*a*) shall not be regarded as an individual.

Commentary—*Simon's Taxes* **D7.5131.**

6—(1) The circumstances set out in this paragraph are where—

(*a*) the business is with a policy holder or annuitant which—

(i) is a company, and

(ii) does not hold the policy or contract for the business in a fiduciary or representative capacity;

(*b*) in a case where the company is an investment company which is not controlled, or is not treated as controlled, by the trustees of any trust, the company is not controlled, or is not treated as controlled, by persons residing in the United Kingdom; and

(*c*) in a case where the company is an investment company which is controlled, or is treated as controlled, by the trustees of any trust, the business would, if the trustees were the policy holders or the annuitants, be of a description falling within the circumstances set out in regulation 5.

(2) For the purposes of paragraph (1)(*b*), whether a company is not controlled, or is not treated as controlled, by persons residing in the United Kingdom shall be determined in accordance with section 416 but as if in subsection (6) of that section the words "five or fewer participators" read "persons residing in the United Kingdom".

(3) For the purposes of paragraph (1)(*c*), whether a company is controlled, or is treated as controlled, by the trustees of any trust shall be determined in accordance with section 416 but as if in subsection (6) of that section the words "five or fewer participators" read "the trustees of any trust".

Commentary—*Simon's Taxes* **D7.5131.**

7 The circumstances set out in this regulation are where—

(*a*) the business is term assurance business; or

[(*b*) the policy or the contract for the business is held for the purposes of, or in connection with, a scheme which is for the time being a [recognised overseas pension scheme within the meaning given by section 150(8) of the Finance Act 2004][3];][2]

(*c*) the policy or contract for the business is held solely to provide benefits for or in respect of—

(i) persons all, or all but an insignificant number, of whom are relevant overseas employees or relevant former employees, or

(ii) spouses, widows, widowers, [civil partners, surviving civil partners,][1] children or dependants of such persons.

Commentary—*Simon's Taxes* **D7.5131.**

Amendments—[1] Words in para (*c*)(ii) inserted by Tax and Civil Partnership (No 2) Regulations, SI 2005/3230 reg 12, with effect from 5 December 2005 (reg 1).

[2] Para (*b*) substituted by the Insurance Companies (Overseas Life Assurance Business) (Excluded Business) (Amendment) Regulations, SI 2007/2086 regs 2, 4 with effect in relation to policies or contracts made by an insurance company on or after 13 August 2007 (SI 2007/2086 reg 1(1), (3)).

[3] Words in para (*b*) substituted by the Insurance Companies (Overseas Life Assurance Business) (Excluded Business) (Amendment No 2) Regulations, SI 2007/3445 reg 2(1), (2) with effect in relation to policies or contracts made by an insurance company on or after 28 December 2007: SI 2007/3445 reg 1(1), (2).

8 Trustees residing in the United Kingdom

(1) A trustee who is a policy holder or annuitant residing in the United Kingdom shall be treated for the purposes of section 431D as not so residing where the policy or contract for the business is held for the purposes set out in regulation 7(*b*) or (*c*).

(2) Nothing in [Chapter 9 of Part 4 of the Income Tax (Trading and Other Income) Act 2005][1] shall apply to a policy or contract which—

(*a*) constitutes overseas life assurance business by virtue of paragraph (1), and

(*b*) is held for the purposes set out in regulation 7(*b*).

Amendments—[1] In para (2), words substituted by the Insurance Companies (Overseas Life Assurance Business) (Excluded Business) (Amendment) Regulations, SI 2008/2625 regs 2, 4 with effect from 27 October 2008.

9 [Circumstances where business prescribed for the purposes of section 431D(1A)(d)

(1) The circumstances set out in this regulation are where the benefits provided for under the policy or contract for the business are determined by reference to the value of assets consisting of or including land in the United Kingdom.

(2) In paragraph (1), "land" includes buildings and other structures, land covered with water and any estate, interest, easement, servitude, right or licence in or over land.][1]

Amendments—[1] This regulation inserted by the Insurance Companies (Overseas Life Assurance Business) (Excluded Business) (Amendment) Regulations, SI 2007/2086 regs 2, 5 with effect for accounting periods beginning on or after 13 August 2007 (SI 2007/2086 reg 1(1), (2)).

2000/2090

EMPLOYEE SHARE OWNERSHIP PLANS (PARTNERSHIP SHARES—NOTICE OF EFFECTS ON BENEFITS, STATUTORY SICK PAY AND STATUTORY MATERNITY PAY) REGULATIONS 2000

Made by the Commissioners of Inland Revenue under FA 2000 s 47, Sch 8 para 38

Made . . . . *1 August 2000*

Laid before the House of Commons . . . . *1 August 2000*

Coming into force . . . . *22 August 2000*

Commentary—*Simon's Taxes* **E4.501.**

1 Citation and commencement

These Regulations may be cited as the Employee Share Ownership Plans (Partnership Shares—Notice of Effects on Benefits, Statutory Sick Pay and Statutory Maternity Pay) Regulations 2000 and shall come into force on 4th August 2000.

2 Prescribed form of notice of effect of deductions from salary on entitlement to social security benefit

The form of notice prescribed under paragraph 38 of Schedule 8 to the Finance Act 2000 (employee share ownership plans—notice of possible effect of deductions on benefit entitlement) to be included in a partnership share agreement under the rules of the employee share plan is set out below.

Notice Deductions from your pay to buy partnership shares under this agreement may affect your entitlement to or the level of, some contributory social security benefits, statutory maternity pay and statutory sick pay.

They may also have a similar effect in respect of some contributory social security benefits paid to your [spouse or civil partner][1].

With this agreement you should have been given information on the effect of deductions from your pay to buy partnership shares on entitlement to social security benefits, statutory sick pay and statutory maternity pay. The effect is particularly significant if your earnings are brought below the lower earnings limit for National Insurance purposes, and is explained in the information—it is therefore important that you read it. If you have not been given a copy, ask your employer for it. Otherwise a copy may be obtained from any office of the Inland Revenue, the Department of Social Security, or, in Northern Ireland, the Department for Social Development. You should take the information you have been given into account in deciding whether to buy partnership shares.

Amendments—[1] Words substituted by the Civil Partnership (Employee Share Ownership Plans) Order, SI 2007/109 art 2 with effect from 13 February 2007.

2000/2129

TONNAGE TAX (TRAINING REQUIREMENT) REGULATIONS 2000

Made by the Secretary of State for the Environment, Transport and the Regions under FA 2000 Sch 22 paras 24, 27 to 33, 34(2) and 36

Made . . . . .3 *August 2000*
Laid before Parliament . . . . .9 *August 2000*
Coming into force . . . . .31 *August 2000*

1 Citation and commencement

These Regulations may be cited as the Tonnage Tax (Training Requirement) Regulations 2000 and shall come into force on 31st August 2000.

2 Interpretation

In these Regulations—

"the Act" means the Finance Act 2000;

["approved training" means any of the following referred to in the STCW Convention:

(a) in relation to an able seafarer deck, the training referred to in paragraph 2.3.3.2 of Regulation II/5;

(b) in relation to an able seafarer engine, the training referred to in paragraph 2.3.3.2 of Regulation III/5;

(c) in relation to an electro-technical rating, the training referred to in paragraph 2.2.2.2 of Regulation III/7;][2]

"back-up officer" means a master or a deck or engineer officer required for the purpose of enabling a ship to be operated on an indefinite basis, allowing for leave, in addition to the officers required by the safe manning document;

"base rate" means the interest rate set by the Bank of England which is used as the basis for other banks' rates;

"British citizen" means a person who is a British citizen within the meaning of the British Nationality Act 1981;

"British citizen from the Channel Islands or Isle of Man" means a person who holds British citizenship by virtue of the fact that he, a parent or grandparent was born, adopted, naturalised or registered in one of those islands, and neither he nor any parent or grandparent was born, adopted, naturalised or registered in the United Kingdom, and he has never been ordinarily resident in the United Kingdom for five years;

"Chamber of Shipping" means the trade association for the United Kingdom shipping industry, incorporated under that name as a company limited by guarantee;

"conversion training" means training of at least ten months' duration for a merchant navy rating, a person formerly employed in Her Majesty's Navy or a skipper or crew member of a fishing vessel, which leads to a first certificate of competency;

["EEA Agreement" and "EEA State" have the meaning given in Schedule 1 to the Interpretation Act 1978;][1]

"effective officer complement" means the class comprising the relevant officers and back-up officers for a ship, and is calculated in accordance with regulation 4;
"eligible officer trainee" has the meaning given by regulation 7;
["eligible rating trainee" has the meaning given by regulation 7;][2]
"first certificate of competency" means any of the following certificates referred to in the STCW Convention—
(*a*) the appropriate certificate for an officer in charge of a navigational watch referred to in Regulation II/1.1, II/3.1 or II/3.3,
(*b*) the appropriate certificate for an officer in charge of an engineering watch referred to in Regulation III/1.1;
[(*c*) the appropriate certificate for an electro-technical officer serving on a seagoing ship powered by main propulsion machinery of 750kW or more referred to in paragraphs 1 and 2 of Regulation III/6.][2]
"IMO number" means the number assigned to the ship in accordance with Resolution A.600(15) of 19th November 1987 of the International Maritime Organization;
"Maritime Training Trust" means the body of that name which has been set up by the Chamber of Shipping, the National Union of Marine, Aviation and Shipping Transport Officers (NUMAST) and the National Union of Rail, Maritime and Transport Workers (RMT) to hold and allocate monies contributed by organisations for the purpose of promoting the training of seafarers;
"Merchant Navy Training Board" means the body of that name which is recognised by the Secretary of State under section 2 of the Employment and Training Act 1973 as a national training organisation for maintaining and enhancing skills in the shipping industry;
"nationality groups" means the following groups—
(*a*) British citizens,
(*b*) nationals of EEA States other than the United Kingdom, and
(*c*) people who do not fall within paragraph (*a*) or (*b*);
"Ratings Task Force" means the ad hoc group of that name comprising representatives from industry, trade unions and government and chaired by the Chamber of Shipping;
"relevant course" means a course which leads to a first certificate of competency;
"relevant four month period" means a period of four months commencing 1st October, 1st February or 1st June;
"relevant officer" means a master or a deck or engineer officer [or an electro- technical officer][2];
"safe manning document" means a document described as such or as a safe manning certificate and issued, in the case of a United Kingdom ship, by the Secretary of State, and in the case of any other ship, by or on behalf of the government of the State whose flag the ship is entitled to fly;
["the STCW Convention" means the International Convention on Standards of Training, Certification and Watchkeeping for Seafarers, 1978, as amended;][2]
"United Kingdom ship" means a ship registered in the United Kingdom under Part II of the Merchant Shipping Act 1995; and
"year" means a twelve month period beginning on 1 October.

Amendments—[1] Definition of "EEA Agreement and EEA State" substituted by the Tonnage Tax (Training Requirement) (Amendment) (No 2) Regulations, SI 2013/2245 reg 3(1), (2) with effect for the purposes of calculating the payments in lieu of training in respect of a relevant four-month period falling after 30 September 2013. "A relevant four-month period" means a period of four months commencing on 1 February, 1 June or 1 October in any year (SI 2013/2245 reg 1(2)).

[2] Definitions of "approved training" and "elegible rating trainee inserted, in definition of "first certificate of competency", para (*c*) inserted, in definition of "relevant officer", words inserted, and definition of "the STCW Convention" substituted by the Tonnage Tax (Training Requirement) (Amendment) Regulations, SI 2015/788 reg 2(1), (2) with effect from 1 October 2015.

3 The minimum training obligation

The minimum obligations of a tonnage tax company as regards the training of seafarers shall be calculated as set out in regulations 4 and 5.

4—(1) Subject to the provisions of this regulation—
(*a*) for every 15 posts in the effective officer complement for the qualifying ships operated by the company during a year, and
(*b*) in any case where there are less than 15 posts in that effective officer complement,
a tonnage tax company shall during that year provide the first year of training on a relevant course for not less than one eligible officer trainee.

(2) Where a safe manning document is required to be carried on board a qualifying ship, the number of posts in the effective officer complement shall be calculated by adding the number of relevant officers required by the safe manning document for the ship and the number of back-up officers required for that ship.

(3) Where a safe manning document is not required to be carried on board a qualifying ship, the number of posts in the effective officer complement shall be deemed to be three.

(4) Where the number of posts in the effective officer complement is more than 15 but is not a multiple of 15, the calculation of the number of eligible officer trainees for whom training is to be provided under paragraph (1) is as follows—

(*a*) divide the number of posts in the effective officer complement by 15,

(*b*) if the resulting number involves a fraction of less than a half, round it down to the nearest whole number, and

(*c*) if the resulting number involves a fraction of a half or more, round it up to the nearest whole number.

(5) For the purposes of paragraph (2) and regulation 8(4)(*b*)(iv)(*bb*), the number of back-up officers required for a ship shall be calculated by reference to the ratio of leave to work for officers on that ship, but shall not in any event be less than 50% of the number of relevant officers required by the safe manning document for that ship.

(6) In addition to the training provided under paragraph (1) during a year, the company shall during that year provide training on a relevant course for not less than the same number of eligible officer trainees as the number referred to in paragraph (7).

[(7) The number referred to in paragraph (6) is the total number of eligible officer trainees who, in a previous year when the company was a tonnage tax company—

(*a*) started a relevant course which continues in the year in question; but this shall not include any eligible officer trainee who started a relevant course more than two years before the year in question, or

(*b*) would have started a relevant course which would have continued in the year in question, if the company had provided the first year of training for the minimum number of eligible officer trainees for whom such training was required under paragraph (1); and for these purposes such a course shall be deemed to continue for three years.][1]

[(7A) A tonnage tax company may satisfy the requirement for providing the first year of training for an eligible officer trainee, other than a conversion trainee, by providing approved training for three eligible rating trainees.][2]

(8) Where the training provided for an eligible officer trainee consists of conversion training, the trainee shall count as half a trainee for the purposes of paragraphs (1) and (6).

Amendments—[1] Para (7) substituted by the Tonnage Tax (Training Requirement) (Amendment) Regulations, SI 2003/2320 reg 3 with effect from 1 October 2003.

[2] Para (7A) inserted by the Tonnage Tax (Training Requirement) (Amendment) Regulations, SI 2015/788 reg 2(1), (3) with effect from 1 October 2015.

5 The Board of directors of a tonnage tax company shall each year review the feasibility of adopting the options agreed by the Ratings Task Force for the training of ratings.

6 Where a company is a member of a tonnage tax group, references in regulations 3, 4 and 5 to "tonnage tax company" and "company" shall be treated as references to "tonnage tax group" and "group" respectively.

[7 Meaning of "eligible officer trainee" and "eligible rating trainee"

For the purposes of these Regulations a person who is—

(*a*) a national of an EEA State, or a British citizen from the Channel Islands or Isle of Man, and

(*b*) ordinarily resident in the United Kingdom.

is an "eligible officer trainee" if that person is on a relevant course and an "eligible rating trainee" if that person is undergoing relevant training.][1]

Amendments—[1] Regulation 7 substituted by the Tonnage Tax (Training Requirement) (Amendment) Regulations, SI 2015/788 reg 2(1), (4) with effect from 1 October 2015.

8 The training commitment

(1) Except where paragraph (2) applies, a tonnage tax company shall annually produce a training commitment in respect of the coming year.

(2) Where a company is a member of a tonnage tax group, the tonnage tax group shall annually produce a training commitment in respect of the coming year.

(3) The tonnage tax company in paragraph (1), or the tonnage tax group in paragraph (2), shall submit the training commitment to the Secretary of State for approval.

(4) The training commitment submitted to the Secretary of State shall contain the following information—

(*a*) either—

(i) the total numbers of relevant officers and of ratings, and the breakdowns of these numbers in terms of nationality groups, employed in each ship which the company or group expects to operate as a qualifying ship during the coming year, or

(ii) the total numbers of relevant officers and of ratings, and the breakdowns of these numbers in terms of nationality groups, employed in all ships which the company or group expects to operate as qualifying ships during the coming year;

(*b*) in respect of each ship which the company or group expects to operate as a qualifying ship during the coming year—
  (i) the name of the ship,
  (ii) the IMO number, if assigned,
  (iii) the State or territory in which the ship is registered, or if it is not registered in any State or territory, the State whose flag the ship is entitled to fly,
  (iv) where a safe manning document is required to be carried on board the ship—
    (*aa*) the number of relevant officers required by that document, and
    (*bb*) the figure, calculated by reference to the number of back-up officers required for a ship, by which the number referred to in sub-paragraph (*aa*) is to be multiplied to obtain the number of posts in the effective officer complement, and
  (v) the number of posts in the effective officer complement;

(*c*) [the total number of eligible officer trainees and the total number of eligible rating trainees][1] for whom the company or group expects to provide the first year of training [on relevant courses or undergoing approved training][1] during the coming year;

(*d*) details of the company's or group's proposals to meet the minimum training obligation by making payments in lieu of training, and the reasons for meeting the obligation in this way;

(*e*) details of the company's or group's proposals for adopting the options agreed by the Ratings Task Force for the training of ratings or, where applicable, reasons for not adopting those options; and

(*f*) the number of ratings who the company or group expects to be involved in the adoption of any options referred to in paragraph (*e*).

(5) In addition to the information required under paragraph (4), the training commitment submitted to the Secretary of State shall contain an undertaking by the company or group—

(*a*) to comply with the minimum training obligation;

(*b*) to exercise best endeavours to provide the training referred to in regulation [4(1), (6) and (7A),][1] and to make payments in lieu of training where such training is not provided;

(*c*) to make payments in lieu of training, in any case where—
  (i) a qualifying ship is operated by the company or group in addition to those which were expected to be operated, but
  (ii) it is not practicable to train the additional trainees required to meet the minimum training obligation; and

(*d*) to comply with the requirements of regulation 12 and with any direction to the company or group under regulation 19.

Amendments—[1] In para (4)(*c*), words substituted for words "the total number of eligible officer trainees" and "on approved courses", and in para (5)(*b*), words substituted for words "4(1) and (6)," by the Tonnage Tax (Training Requirement) (Amendment) Regulations, SI 2015/788 reg 2(1), (5) with effect from 1 October 2015.

9 When considering whether to approve a training commitment, the Secretary of State may consult the Merchant Navy Training Board or the Maritime Training Trust or both.

10—(1) Where the Secretary of State is minded not to approve a training commitment, he shall notify the company or group and shall invite representations.

(2) If the Secretary of State and the company or group are unable to reach agreement on the contents of the training commitment by the end of the period of 30 days beginning with the date of the Secretary of State's notification, the Secretary of State may set the training commitment for the year.

(3) On the application of the company or group concerned, made after consultation with the Maritime Training Trust, the Secretary of State may vary the training commitment set by him under paragraph (2).

11—(1) On the application of the company or group concerned, the Secretary of State may adjust a training commitment (to any extent) to take account of changed circumstances.

(2) Such an application shall contain the following information—

(*a*) details of the changed circumstances, and

(*b*) reasons why the training commitment should be adjusted.

(3) When considering an application for adjustment, the Secretary of State may consult the Merchant Navy Training Board or the Maritime Training Trust or both.

12 "End of period adjustments"

(1) A tonnage tax company or tonnage tax group shall make a return (known as an "end of period adjustment") within 30 days after the end of each relevant four month period.

(2) The return shall be made to the Secretary of State and to the Maritime Training Trust.

(3) The return shall contain the following information—

(*a*) [the total number of eligible officer trainees and the total number of eligible rating trainees][1] for whom training on a relevant course has been provided, determined as at the first day of each month in the relevant four month period;

(*b*) where there is an increase in the total number of qualifying ships operated by the company or group, compared with the training commitment, which occurs during the relevant four month period and relates to a period of not less than one month, details of—

(i) the additional ships, and

(ii) any consequent increase in [the total number of eligible officer trainees and the total number of eligible rating trainees][1] for whom training should have been provided in order to meet the minimum training obligation of the company or group referred to in regulation 3; and

(*c*) details of the payments made or proposed to be made in lieu of training in respect of the relevant four month period.

Amendments—[1] In para (3)(*a*), (*b*)(ii) words substituted for words "the total number of eligible officer trainees" by the Tonnage Tax (Training Requirement) (Amendment) Regulations, SI 2015/788 reg 2(1), (6) with effect from 1 October 2015.

13 Payments in lieu of training

Where a company or group is unable to provide the training required by regulation 4(1) or (6), it may propose in its training commitment to meet the minimum training obligation by making payments in lieu of training.

14 A company or group shall make payments in lieu of training—

(*a*) where its training commitment provides for such payments, or

(*b*) where training is not provided in accordance with its training commitment.

15—(1) The payments in lieu of training shall be calculated in respect of each relevant four month period as follows—

(*a*) in respect of each eligible officer trainee for whom training is required to be provided under regulation 4(1) or (6), calculate the number of months in that period during which—

(i) the training commitment of the company or group provided for payment in lieu of training, or

(ii) the company or group did not provide training in accordance with its training commitment,

or both sub-paragraphs (i) and (ii) applied; and

(*b*) multiply that number of months by [£1,259][1], and the total is the amount of the payments in lieu of training which is due for that period.

(2) For the purposes of the calculation in paragraph (1)(*a*), any surplus (as compared with the requirements in regulation 4(1) and (6)) in the number of months when training is provided during the relevant four month period shall be offset against any shortfall (as compared with those requirements) in that period.

Amendments—[1] Figure in para (1)(*b*) substituted for previous figure "£1,236" by the Tonnage Tax (Training Requirement) (Amendment) Regulations, SI 2017/822 reg 3(1), (2) with effect for the purposes of calculating the payments in lieu of training in respect of a relevant four-month period falling after 30 September 2017. A "relevant four-month period" means a period of four months commencing on 1 February, 1 June or 1 October in any year (SI 2016/819 reg 2(2)).

16 The payments in lieu of training shall be made to the Maritime Training Trust, and shall become due 30 days after the end of each relevant four month period.

17 If in any case there is a failure in relation to a company or group to comply with the requirements of Part IV of Schedule 22 to the Act with respect to—

(*a*) the submission of training commitments, or

(*b*) the making of returns or provision of information,

the Secretary of State may determine to the best of his information and belief the amount of the payments in lieu of training to be made by the company or group.

18—(1) A payment in lieu of training that has become due but is unpaid—

(*a*) is a debt to the Maritime Training Trust, and

(*b*) carries interest at an annual rate equivalent to base rate plus two per cent per annum.

(2) The costs or expenses of any legal or other proceedings for recovering the debt or interest shall be recoverable, and carry interest, in the same way as the debt.

19 Directions to provide information

The Secretary of State may direct any person to provide such information as the Secretary of State may reasonably require for the purposes of ascertaining—

(*a*) what the minimum training obligation of a company or group should be,

(*b*) whether the proposals in a training commitment are adequate to meet the minimum training obligation of a company or group, or

(*c*) whether a company or group has complied with its training commitment.

20 Audits

The Secretary of State may appoint one or more persons to carry out on his behalf an audit of the accounts or other records—

(*a*) of a qualifying single company, or

(*b*) of the qualifying companies in a group,

for the purpose of checking that any return or information provided to the Secretary of State is correct.

21 Higher rate of payment in case of failure to meet training requirement

(1) Subject to paragraph (3), a company or group is to be treated as failing to meet its training commitment in any year where it fails to provide training on a relevant course for at least 50% of the total number of eligible officer trainees [(or the equivalent number of posts where the training commitment is satisfied by training ratings under regulation 4(7))][2] for whom the company or group proposed to provide such training in its training commitment.

(2) Subject to paragraph (3)—

(*a*) if a company fails to meet its training commitment in a particular year, the basic rate of any payments in lieu of training that fall to be made by the company in the following year shall be increased by 50%;

(*b*) if a group fails to meet its training commitment in a particular year, the basic rate of any payments in lieu of training that fall to be made by any member of the group in the following year shall be increased by 50%; and

(*c*) if a company or group fails to meet its training commitment in two or more successive years, the basic rate of any payments in lieu of training shall be increased by 100% in the third and subsequent years.

(3) The higher rate shall not be payable where the Secretary of State is satisfied that there are mitigating circumstances for the company's or group's failure to meet the training commitment.

(4) For the purposes of paragraph (2), "the basic rate" is [£1,172][1] per eligible officer trainee per month.

Amendments—[1] Figure in para (4) substituted for previous figure "£1,151" by the Tonnage Tax (Training Requirement) (Amendment) Regulations, SI 2017/822 reg 3(1), (3) with effect for the purposes of calculating the payments in lieu of training in respect of a relevant four-month period falling after 30 September 2017. A "relevant four-month period" means a period of four months commencing on 1 February, 1 June or 1 October in any year (SI 2016/819 reg 2(2)).

[2] In para (1), words inserted by the Tonnage Tax (Training Requirement) (Amendment) Regulations, SI 2015/788 reg 2(1), (7) with effect from 1 October 2015.

22 Certificate of non-compliance

(1) The Secretary of State may issue a certificate of non-compliance in respect of a single company if—

(*a*) the company fails to meet its training commitment for successive periods amounting to not less than two years, or

(*b*) the company, or any of its officers, commits an offence under Schedule 22 to the Act.

(2) The Secretary of State may issue a certificate of non-compliance in respect of a group if—

(*a*) the group fails to meet its training commitment for successive periods amounting to not less than two years, or

(*b*) a member of the group, or an officer of a member, commits an offence under Schedule 22 to the Act.

(3) The Secretary of State shall issue a certificate of non-compliance if any circumstances referred to in paragraph (1) or (2) arise, unless the Secretary of State is satisfied that there are good reasons why a certificate should not be issued.

23—(1) A company or group in respect of which a certificate of non-compliance has been issued may apply to the Secretary of State to cancel the certificate.

(2) Any such application shall contain information showing that—

(*a*) the training commitment has been complied with for at least one year since the period in relation to which the certificate was issued, and

(*b*) the company or group has made arrangements to ensure that its training commitment for the current and future years will be complied with.

24 When considering an application to cancel a certificate of non-compliance, the Secretary of State may consult the Merchant Navy Training Board or the Maritime Training Trust or both.

25 Disclosure of information

For the purposes of paragraph 34(2) of Schedule 22 to the Act, the following persons are prescribed persons involved in the training of seafarers—

(*a*) the Merchant Navy Training Board, and

(*b*) the Maritime Training Trust.

2000/2303

TONNAGE TAX REGULATIONS 2000

Made by the Commissioners of Inland Revenue under FA 2000 Sch 22 paras 47, 85(3), 112(7), 113(4), 130–136

Made . . . . *24 August 2000*
Laid before the House of Commons . . . . *25 August 2000*
Coming into force . . . . *31 August 2000*

Statement of Practice SP 4/00—General operation of the tonnage tax regime.

1 Citation and commencement

These Regulations may be cited as the Tonnage Tax Regulations 2000 and shall come into force on 31st August 2000.

2 Interpretation

(1) In these Regulations—

"corporate partner" means a company which carries on activities in partnership;
"the 1990 Act" means the Capital Allowances Act 1990;
"the paragraph 85(2)(*a*) amount", in relation to an asset, means the amount determined under paragraph 85(2)(*a*) of Schedule 22 for that asset, subject to regulation 8(2)(*a*), and "the paragraph 112(2) amount" and "the paragraph 113(2) amount" shall have corresponding meanings;
"qualifying expenditure" has the meaning in paragraph 135 of Schedule 22;
"Schedule 22" means Schedule 22 to the Finance Act 2000;
"Schedule 28AA" means Schedule 28AA to the Taxes Act;
"the 75% limit" has the meaning given in paragraph 37(4) of Schedule 22;
"the Taxes Act" means the Income and Corporation Taxes Act 1988.

(2) In these Regulations, the following expressions have the same meaning as in Schedule 22—

"bareboat charter terms"
"company"
"core qualifying activities"
"group" (and "member" of a group)
"leaving tonnage tax"
"operating (a ship)"
"qualifying company"
"qualifying ship"
"relevant shipping profits"
"ship"
"ship-related activities"
"subject to tonnage tax"
"tonnage tax company"
"tonnage tax group" (and "member" of such a group)
"tonnage tax profits"
"tonnage tax trade".

(3) References in regulation 3(3)(*a*) to (*j*) and (4) to a qualifying ship operated by a company, where the company is a member of a tonnage tax group, include references to a qualifying ship operated by another qualifying company in the same tonnage tax group.

(4) For the purposes of the definition of "arm's length provision" (regulation 3(3)(*a*)(ii)), where any provision is made or imposed as between a company's tonnage tax trade and other activities carried on by it, the assumptions in paragraph 59(1)(*a*) to (*c*) of Schedule 22 and paragraph 1(3) of Schedule 28AA shall apply.

3 Qualifying secondary activities

(1) The descriptions of activity to be regarded as qualifying secondary activities shall be determined in accordance with the following paragraphs.

(2) A tonnage tax company's qualifying secondary activities means its ship-related activities, other than commercial activities which form part of the operation of a port carried on for profit, that—

(*a*) have a substantial connection with the company's core qualifying activities or, where the company is a member of a tonnage tax group, the core qualifying activities of another qualifying company in that group,
(*b*) fall within the descriptions in paragraph (3) or (4), and
(*c*) in the case of paragraph (3) are carried on at any level and in the case of paragraph (4) are carried on at the permitted level.

(3) The descriptions in this paragraph are—

(*a*) the carriage of passengers or cargo otherwise than on board a qualifying ship operated by the company, where—

(i) there is a single contract with the customer for a journey which includes a voyage on the qualifying ship, and

(ii) the transport for the remainder of the journey is purchased or obtained by the company by provision ("arm's length provision") which would have been made as between independent enterprises;

(*b*) administrative and insurance services which are directly related to the carriage of passengers or cargo, including under a contract described in sub-paragraph (*a*)(i);

(*c*) the embarkation and disembarkation of passengers on a qualifying ship operated by the company, and the provision of relevant facilities by the company;

(*d*) the provision of excursions for passengers of a qualifying ship operated by the company, where any cabin for the passenger remains available for his exclusive use;

(*e*) the provision of holidays, sold to the customer under a single contract, where—

(i) part of the holiday is a voyage on a qualifying ship operated by the company, and the remaining part is land-based ("the land-based part"),

(ii) the land-based part is purchased or obtained by the company by arm's length provision, and

(iii) the cost to the company of the land-based part in accordance with paragraph (ii) is less than one half of the price paid by the customer under the single contract;

(*f*) sales and facilities which are normally provided to customers by seagoing passenger ships, including—

(i) the provision of food or drink,

(ii) entertainment, but not betting or gambling (see paragraph (4)(*b*)(i)),

(iii) the sale of alcoholic beverages, perfume and tobacco, but not luxury goods (see paragraph (4)(*b*)(ii)),

(iv) the exchange of amounts of different currencies for personal expenditure;

(*g*) the loading and unloading of cargo carried on a qualifying ship operated by the company, and the provision by the company of facilities used exclusively for those purposes;

(*h*) the consolidation or breaking of cargo carried on a qualifying ship operated by the company, immediately before or after the voyage, where the activity is not haulage-related;

(*i*) the temporary placement of cargo carried on a qualifying ship operated by the company, on or at the dockside, where the activity is not part of a long-term storage operation;

(*j*) the rental or provision to customers of containers for goods to be carried on a qualifying ship operated by the company;

(*k*) activities carried on by the company in relation to a qualifying ship operated by another qualifying company in the same tonnage tax group, which would be core qualifying activities of the first-mentioned company if carried on in relation to a qualifying ship operated by that company.

(4) The descriptions and permitted levels in this paragraph are—

(*a*) services which, if carried out in relation to qualifying ships operated by the company, would be core qualifying activities of the company or activities of the company which would fall within the descriptions in paragraph (3), but only to the level where—

(i) the relevant staff and assets are needed by the company to carry out the company's main function, and the services are undertaken to make full use of those staff and assets, and

(ii) the services are minimal compared to the main function;

(*b*) (i) betting or gambling facilities normally offered to customers by seagoing passenger ships for entertainment, and

(ii) the sale to passengers on seagoing ships of luxury goods of a kind normally offered to such passengers,

but only to the level where the turnover from those activities is negligible compared to the turnover from the company's core qualifying activities.

(5) In paragraph (4)(*a*) "the company's main function" means the company's core qualifying activities and those of its activities which fall within the descriptions in paragraph (3).

4 Plant and machinery other than expensive motor cars and long-life assets—writing-down basis

(1) This regulation applies to any asset mentioned in paragraph 85(2) of Schedule 22, where the provisions of Part II of the 1990 Act would have applied to the asset on the footing that the company had not been subject to tonnage tax ("the tax condition"), other than—

(*a*) a motor car, to which the provisions of section 34 of the 1990 Act (expensive motor cars) would have effect on that condition, or

(*b*) a long-life asset, where Chapter IVA of Part II of the 1990 Act would have applied to the capital expenditure incurred on the provision of the asset, on that condition.

(2) The written down value of the paragraph 85(2)(*a*) amount for the asset shall be determined by multiplying that amount by the percentage given by the table in paragraph (3).

(3) That table is as follows—

Length of qualifying holding period for the asset	*Percentage of the paragraph 85(2)(a) amount which is qualifying expenditure under Part II of the 1990 Act*
Less than or equal to 1 year	75
1 year and one day to 2 years	55
2 years and one day to 3 years	40
3 years and one day to 4 years	30
4 years and one day to 5 years	25
5 years and one day to 6 years	15
6 years and one day to 7 years	12
7 years and one day to 8 years	10
8 years and one day to 9 years	5
More than 9 years	Nil

(4) References in this regulation and regulations 5 and 6 to the qualifying holding period for an asset are references to the period between—

(*a*) the date on which the expenditure represented by the paragraph 85(2)(*a*) amount, or the part thereof, was incurred, and

(*b*) the date on which the company leaves tonnage tax.

5 Expensive motor cars—writing-down basis

(1) This regulation applies to motor cars described in regulation 4(1)(*a*).

(2) The written down value of the paragraph 85(2)(*a*) amount for the motor car shall be determined in accordance with the following provisions—

Rule 1

The paragraph 85(2)(*a*) amount for the motor car shall be reduced by £3,000 for each complete year in the qualifying holding period, subject to Rule 2.

Rule 2

Rule 1 shall cease to apply at the end of the complete year where the paragraph 85(2)(*a*) amount is first reduced below £12,000, and Rule 3 shall thereafter apply to that amount as reduced at the end of that year ("the reduced amount").

Rule 3

The table in regulation 4(3) shall apply to the reduced amount, in relation to any subsequent period in the qualifying holding period, as if for the date mentioned in regulation 4(4)(*a*) there were substituted a reference to the end of the year mentioned in Rule 2.

6 Long-life assets—writing-down basis

(1) This regulation applies to long-life assets described in regulation 4(1)(*b*).

(2) The written down value of the paragraph 85(2)(*a*) amount for the asset shall be determined by multiplying that amount by the percentage given by the table in paragraph (3).

(3) That table is as follows—

Length of qualifying holding period for the asset	*Percentage of the paragraph 85(2)(a) amount which is qualifying expenditure under Part II of the 1990 Act*
Less than or equal to 1 year	94
From 1 year and one day to 2 years	88
From 2 years and one day to 3 years	83
From 3 years and one day to 4 years	78
From 4 years and one day to 5 years	73
From 5 years and one day to 6 years	69
From 6 years and one day to 7 years	65
From 7 years and one day to 8 years	61
From 8 years and one day to 9 years	57
From 9 years and one day to 10 years	54
From 10 years and one day to 11 years	51
From 11 years and one day to 13 years	47
From 13 years and one day to 16 years	40

Length of qualifying holding period for the asset	*Percentage of the paragraph 85(2)(a) amount which is qualifying expenditure under Part II of the 1990 Act*
From 16 years and one day to 19 years	33
From 19 years and one day to 22 years	27
From 22 years and one day to 25 years	23
From 25 years and one day to 30 years	18
From 30 years and one day to 35 years	13
From 35 years and one day to 40 years	10
From 40 years and one day to 45 years	7
From 45 years and one day to 50 years	5
From 50 years and one day to 60 years	3
From 60 years and one day to 70 years	2
More than 70 years	Nil

7 Plant and machinery used for the purposes of the company's offshore activities—writing-down basis

(1) This regulation applies to any asset mentioned in paragraph 110(2)(*a*) of Schedule 22, where—

(*a*) the provisions of Part II of the 1990 Act apply to the asset by virtue of paragraph 110(2) of Schedule 22, and

(*b*) the paragraph 112(2) amount or the paragraph 113(2) amount for the asset, as the case may be ("the relevant amount"), falls to be written down under paragraph 112(6) or 113(3) of Schedule 22.

(2) The written down value of the relevant amount shall be determined by applying regulation 4, 5 or 6, as the case may be, as if—

(*a*) the tax condition were omitted,

(*b*) for references to the paragraph 85(2)(*a*) amount there were substituted references to the relevant amount, and

(*c*) for regulation 4(4)(*a*) and (*b*) there were substituted a reference to the period mentioned in paragraph 112(6) or 113(3) of Schedule 22, as the case may be.

8 Adjustments to be made for capital allowance purposes to the amount of qualifying expenditure for assets where a corporate partner leaves tonnage tax

(1) This regulation applies where—

(*a*) a corporate partner leaves tonnage tax,

(*b*) an asset has been used by the corporate partner for the purposes of tonnage tax activities which it carries on as a member of a partnership, and

(*c*) as at the beginning of the partnership chargeable period in which the corporate partner leaves tonnage tax (the beginning of which period is referred to in this regulation as "the relevant time") the asset—

(i) was partnership property of the partnership concerned, or

(ii) would have been so treated by regulation 9(2), or by section 65 of the 1990 Act if the corporate partner had not been subject to tonnage tax,

and applies to the corporate partner and all the other members of the partnership.

In this paragraph "the partnership chargeable period" means the accounting period or period of account used by the partnership in its partnership computation under section 114(1) of the Taxes Act or section 111(2) of that Act, as the case may be.

(2) In relation to any asset mentioned in paragraph (1)(*b*) and (*c*)—

(*a*) there shall be determined the amount for that asset which is referred to in paragraph 85(2)(*a*) of Schedule 22 (which amount is referred to in this regulation as "the paragraph 85(2)(*a*) amount" for the asset), on the assumptions—

(i) that the corporate partner left tonnage tax at the relevant time, and

(ii) (where it is not otherwise the case) that the asset was held by the corporate partner at that time; and

(*b*) where the asset is counted in a calculation under paragraphs (3) to (7) of this regulation, it shall not be counted again in any determination under paragraph 85(1) of Schedule 22 on the same occasion of the corporate partner leaving tonnage tax.

(3) In the following paragraphs of this regulation—

"unrelieved qualifying expenditure", in relation to an asset, means the balance of qualifying expenditure attributable to that asset that would otherwise have been carried forward under Part II of the 1990 Act, including postponed allowances attributable to that asset; and "postponed allowances" means qualifying expenditure which is unrelieved by virtue of notice having been given under—

(*a*) section 30(1) of the 1990 Act (postponement or reduction of first allowances), or

(*b*) section 31(3) of that Act (postponement of writing-down allowance in respect of expenditure in single ship pool).

(4) The unrelieved qualifying expenditure for any asset mentioned in paragraph (1)(*b*) and (*c*), so far as it is not represented by postponed allowances, that would otherwise have been carried forward as at the relevant time, shall be adjusted to the amount resulting from the calculation in paragraph (5) or (6), as the case may be.

(5) Except in the case described in paragraph (6), the calculation is—

$$(A\% \times B) + ((100\% - A\%) \times C)$$

where—

A equals the corporate partner's share (expressed as a percentage) in the partnership property of the partnership concerned at the relevant time, subject to paragraph (8);

B equals the written down value of the paragraph 85(2)(*a*) amount for the asset calculated by applying regulation 4, 5 or 6, as the case may be—

(*a*) as if for regulation 4(4)(*b*), there were substituted a reference to the relevant time; and

(*b*) on the assumptions contained in paragraph (2)(*a*) where applicable;

C equals the unrelieved qualifying expenditure for the asset, so far as it is not represented by postponed allowances, as at the relevant time.

(6) In a case where all the members of the partnership other than the corporate partner are—

(*a*) persons who (within the meaning in section 161 of the 1990 Act) are not within the charge to tax in the United Kingdom on the profits of the trade carried on in the partnership in question, or

(*b*) companies which are subject to tonnage tax,

the calculation is of B, which has the same meaning as in paragraph (5).

(7) The unrelieved qualifying expenditure for any asset mentioned in paragraph (1)(*b*) and (*c*), so far as it is represented by postponed allowances, that would otherwise have been carried forward as at the relevant time (the amount of which is referred to as "D" in this paragraph), shall be reduced to the percentage of D which is represented by the following calculation—

$$(100\% - A\%) \times D$$

where A has the same meaning as in paragraph (5).

(8) Where the share of the corporate partner in the partnership property (expressed as a proportion of the whole) varied during the period—

(*a*) beginning on the last to occur of—

(i) the date on which the corporate partner became a member of the partnership concerned,

(ii) the date on which the corporate partner entered tonnage tax, or

(iii) the date six years before the relevant time, and

(*b*) ending at the relevant time,

the calculation of A in paragraphs (5) and (7) shall be made according to the average of the corporate partner's interest in the property of the relevant partnership during that period, and any necessary apportionment on a daily basis shall be made.

(9) A payment made by a corporate partner to another corporate partner in the same partnership which is compensation for any adjustment carried out under paragraphs (4) to (7)—

(*a*) shall not be taken into account in computing profits or losses of either company for corporation tax purposes, and

(*b*) shall not for any of the purposes of the Corporation Tax Acts, (within the meaning in section 831(1)(*a*) of the Taxes Act) be regarded as a distribution or a charge on income.

9 Corporate partners—modifications of the requirements for being a qualifying company (with supplementary provision relating to finance leases)

(1) Paragraphs (1) to (3), (5) and (6) of this regulation prescribe modifications to the requirements for determining whether—

(*a*) a corporate partner operates qualifying ships within the meaning in paragraphs 16(1)(*b*) and 18(1) to (4) of Schedule 22, and

(*b*) those ships are strategically and commercially managed in the United Kingdom within the meaning in paragraph 16(1)(*c*) of Schedule 22.

(2) Where—

(*a*) a qualifying ship is owned by, or (other than by a charter described in paragraph (3)) chartered to, one or more of the members of a partnership but is not partnership property, and (*b*) activities of the partnership business which, if carried on by a tonnage tax company, would be tonnage tax activities, are carried on in relation to the ship,

the ship shall be treated as if it were owned by, or chartered to, all the partners, as the case may be, and as if everything done by or to any of the partners in relation to it had been done by or to all the partners.

(3) Any charter of a ship from one or more members of the partnership to the other partners, or to the partnership, for use in the tonnage tax activities carried on in that partnership, shall be treated for the purposes of paragraph 18(4) of Schedule 22 as a charter to a person who is not a third party.

(4) A finance lease (within the meaning in section 82A of the 1990 Act) of a qualifying ship where the lessee is one or more members of a partnership which includes a tonnage tax company as a member, or is such a partnership, and the ship is used in the tonnage tax activities which the tonnage tax company carries on as a member of the partnership, shall be treated for the purposes of Part X of Schedule 22 as if—

(*a*) the qualifying ship were provided (within the meaning in paragraph 89(1) of Schedule 22) to the tonnage tax company;

(*b*) the tonnage tax company were the "lessee" for the purposes of paragraphs 98 and 99 of Schedule 22; and

(*c*) the references in paragraph 92 of Schedule 22 to the ship being owned by a tonnage tax company included references to the ship being owned by one or more of the partners, or by the partnership.

(5) Paragraph 16(1)(*c*) of Schedule 22 shall be modified as if, in relation to activities carried on by a corporate partner in a partnership, the reference to those ships were replaced with a reference to the requisite proportion of those ships.

(6) In paragraph (5) "the requisite proportion of those ships" means a proportion of those ships such that—

$$\frac{E}{F} \text{ is not less than G}$$

where—

E equals the aggregate net tonnage of all the qualifying ships which are—

(*a*) operated by the partners of the partnership concerned, in their capacity as such partners, and

(*b*) strategically and commercially managed in the United Kingdom;

F equals the aggregate net tonnage of all the qualifying ships which are operated by the partners of the partnership concerned, in their capacity as such partners; and

G equals the share of the corporate partner, expressed as a fraction, in the partnership property of the partnership concerned.

10 Rules for calculating the tonnage tax profits and relevant shipping profits of a corporate partner

(1) Paragraph (2) applies to any corporate partner which is a tonnage tax company (but only in relation to the share of profits or losses which such a partner derives from the activities carried on in the partnership concerned).

(2) Section 114 of the Taxes Act shall apply to the profits and losses of the partnership as if the partnership were a tonnage tax company, for the purpose of calculating—

(*a*) the tonnage tax profits, and

(*b*) the relevant shipping profits (or such of the corresponding losses as fall within paragraph 3(2) of Schedule 22),

of any corporate partner to whom this paragraph applies (but not the share of profits or losses of any other partner).

(3) Where a ship falls to be counted as operated by a partnership in a calculation under paragraph (2)(*a*) carried out in relation to a corporate partner, it shall not be counted again in any computation of the tonnage tax profits of that corporate partner, and the same provision shall apply as between a calculation under paragraph (2)(*b*) and the relevant shipping profits (or relevant corresponding losses) of a corporate partner.

11 Ships chartered to partners—further provision relating to chartering in

(1) Where a corporate partner carries on activities in partnership which include the operation of a qualifying ship, the calculation whether the 75% limit is exceeded by—

(*a*) that corporate partner (if it is a single company), or

(*b*) a group of which that corporate partner is a member, so far as the calculation relates to the corporate partner,

shall be made in accordance with this regulation.

(2) The calculation is as follows—

Step One

Find out the aggregate net tonnage of the qualifying ships that are operated by the members of the partnership concerned, in their capacity as such partners.

Step Two

Find out the proportion, in percentage terms, of the result of Step One which represents tonnage of ships which are chartered to the partners, or to the partnership, otherwise than on bareboat charter terms ("chartered in"), ignoring any such charters which are from another qualifying member of any group of which the corporate partner is also a member.

Step Three

Determine the corporate partner's share of the results of Steps One and Two according to the interests of the partners in the partnership property in the accounting period in question, expressed as a figure of net tonnage and the percentage of it which is chartered in.

Step Four

Follow Steps One to Three for each partnership of which the corporate partner is a member and aggregate the results, to arrive at a total figure of net tonnage and the percentage of it which is chartered in.

Step Five

Aggregate the results of Step Four with the results of the calculation for the purposes of paragraph 37(1)(*a*) or (*b*) of Schedule 22, as the case may be, in relation to any ships other than those which the corporate partner operates as a member of a partnership.

Step Six

Apply paragraph 37(1)(*a*) or (*b*) of Schedule 22, as the case may be, to the results of Step Five.

(3) Where the interests of the partners in the partnership property, expressed as a proportion of the whole, vary in the course of an accounting period, the interest of a corporate partner for that period shall be calculated according to the average interest of that partner during that period.

12 Chargeable gains—use of assets by partnerships which include corporate partners

Where—

(*a*) an asset has been used wholly and exclusively for the purposes of activities of a partnership which are (or would be, if the partnership were a tonnage tax company) tonnage tax activities;

(*b*) throughout the period of use of the asset as mentioned in sub-paragraph (*a*), there was a corporate partner member of the partnership which was also a tonnage tax company; and

(*c*) the asset is disposed of by that corporate partner, or by another member of a group of which that corporate partner is a member,

references in paragraph 65(1) and (3) of Schedule 22 to a tonnage tax asset, or to any time at which or period during which an asset was a tonnage tax asset, shall respectively include references to the asset and period mentioned in this regulation, and references to a period during which an asset was not a tonnage tax asset shall be construed accordingly.

13 Transactions not at arm's length between a partnership (where a corporate partner is a tonnage tax company) and another partner

(1) Where a corporate partner which is a tonnage tax company ("the relevant company") carries on tonnage tax activities in partnership, paragraph 58 of Schedule 22 shall apply to provision made or imposed as between—

(*a*) the partnership, and

(*b*) another partner,

if the condition in paragraph (2) is satisfied, and in that event on the assumptions in paragraph (3).

(2) The condition is that the relevant company (in addition to the partner referred to in paragraph (1)(*b*)) is a major participant in the partnership's enterprise, within the meaning of that expression in paragraph 4(7) of Schedule 28AA.

(3) The assumptions are that the partnership—

(*a*) is a tonnage tax company, and

(*b*) is regarded for the purposes of paragraph 58(1)(*a*) of Schedule 22 as carrying on the tonnage tax trade of the relevant company, so far as that trade consists of activities carried on by the relevant company in the partnership in question.

2000/2314

PERSONAL PENSION SCHEMES (RESTRICTION ON DISCRETION TO APPROVE) (ESTABLISHMENT OF SCHEMES UNDER TRUSTS) REGULATIONS 2000

Revocation—These Regulations lapse by virtue of the coming into force of FA 2004 Part 4 (ss 149–284) with effect from 6 April 2006.

2000/2316

PERSONAL PENSION SCHEMES (INFORMATION POWERS) REGULATIONS 2000

Revocation—These Regulations lapse by virtue of the coming into force of FA 2004 Part 4 (ss 149–284) with effect from 6 April 2006.

2000/2318

PERSONAL PENSION SCHEMES (CONCURRENT MEMBERSHIP) ORDER 2000

Revocation—These Regulations lapse by virtue of the coming into force of FA 2004 Part 4 (ss 149–284) with effect from 6 April 2006.

2000/2875

ORDERS FOR THE DELIVERY OF DOCUMENTS (PROCEDURE) REGULATIONS 2000

Made . . . . *23 October 2000*
Laid before Parliament . . . . *23 October 2000*
Coming into force . . . . *13 November 2000*

Commentary—*Simon's Taxes* **A4.151.**

The Commissioners of Inland Revenue, in exercise of the powers conferred on them by paragraphs 2(2), 3(2), 6, 7(1) and (2), 10 and 11(*a*) of Schedule 1AA to the Taxes Management Act 1970, hereby make the following Regulations:

1 Citation and commencement

These Regulations may be cited as the Orders for the Delivery of Documents (Procedure) Regulations 2000 and shall come into force on 13th November 2000.

2 Interpretation

In these Regulations—

"the appropriate judicial authority" has the meaning given by section 20D(1) of the Management Act;

["the Commissioners" means the Commissioners for Her Majesty's Revenue and Customs;][1]

. . . [1]

"the court" has the meaning given by paragraph 9(2) of Schedule 1AA to the Management Act;

"items subject to legal privilege" has the meaning given by paragraph 5(2) of Schedule 1AA to the Management Act;

"the Management Act" means the Taxes Management Act 1970;

"notice of application" means the notice of intention to apply for an order to which a person is entitled under paragraph 3(1) of Schedule 1AA to the Management Act;

"order" means an order under section 20BA of the Management Act;

"working day" means any day other than a Saturday, Sunday or public holiday.

Amendments—[1] Definition of "the Board" revoked, and definition of "the Commissioners" inserted by the Orders for the Delivery of Documents (Procedure) (Amendment) Regulations, SI 2005/1131 regs 2, 3 with effect from 18 April 2005.

3 [Approval of decision to apply for an order

Before the hearing of an application for an order, an officer of Her Majesty's Revenue and Customs who is a member of the Senior Civil Service in the Criminal Investigation Directorate must approve in writing the decision to apply for that order.][1]

Amendments—[1] Regulation substituted by the Orders for the Delivery of Documents (Procedure) (Amendment) Regulations, SI 2007/881 reg 2 with effect from 9 April 2007.

4 Notice of application

(1) Notice of application must be given in writing and must contain the following details—

(*a*) the date, time and place of the hearing of the application;

(*b*) the specifications or descriptions of documents which are the subject of the application;

(*c*) a description of the suspected offence to which the application relates; and

(*d*) the name of the person suspected of committing, having committed or being about to commit the suspected offence.

(2) Notice of application must be given to the person entitled to it not less than five working days before the hearing of the application.

5 Notice of an order, or notice of application, treated as having been given

(1) Where notice of an order, or notice of application, is delivered to a person, or left at his proper address, notice shall be treated as having been given to that person on the day on which it is delivered or left or, where that day is not a working day, on the next working day.

(2) Where notice of application, or notice of an order, is sent to a person's proper address by facsimile transmission or other similar means which produce a document containing a text of the communication, notice shall be treated as given when the text is received in a legible form.

(3) For the purposes of this regulation, a person's proper address is—

(*a*) the usual or last known place of residence, or the place of business or employment, of that person; or

(*b*) in the case of a company, the address of the company's registered office; or

(*c*) in the case of a liquidator of a company, the liquidator's address for the purposes of the liquidation.

6 Complying with an order

(1) A person complies with an order by producing the documents specified or described in the order to the officer of the Board specified in the order within—

(*a*) the period mentioned in section 20BA(2) of the Management Act; or

(*b*) such further period, if any, as is agreed with that officer.

(2) For the purposes of paragraph (1), documents are produced to [an officer of Revenue and Customs][1] if they are either—

(*a*) delivered to the officer; or

(*b*) left for the officer at an address specified in the relevant order.

(3) Where documents are sent to [an officer of Revenue and Customs][1] at the address specified in the relevant order by post, they shall be treated, unless the contrary is proved, as having been produced to the officer—

(*a*) if first class post is used, on the second working day after posting;

(*b*) if second class post is used, on the fourth working day after posting.

Commentary—*Simon's Taxes* **A6.315.**

Note—It appears that the substitution made by SI 2005/1131 reg 5 (see note 1 below) ought also to apply to the words "officer of the Board" in para (1) above).

Amendments—[1] Words substituted by the Orders for the Delivery of Documents (Procedure) (Amendment) Regulations, SI 2005/1131 regs 2, 5 with effect from 18 April 2005.

7 Resolution of disputes as to legal privilege

(1) This regulation applies where there is a dispute between [the Commissioners][1] and a person against whom an order has been made as to whether a document, or part of a document, is an item subject to legal privilege.

(2) The person against whom an order has been made may apply to the appropriate judicial authority to resolve the dispute.

(3) All the documents to which an application under paragraph (2) relates must be lodged in the court at the same time as the application is made and shall be held by the court until the appropriate judicial authority resolves the dispute.

(4) The court shall give [the Commissioners][1] notice of an application made under paragraph (2) not less than five working days before the hearing of the application, and [the Commissioners][1] shall be entitled to appear and be heard at that hearing in addition to the person making the application.

(5) On the hearing of an application made under paragraph (2), the appropriate judicial authority shall—

(*a*) resolve the dispute by confirming whether the document, or part of the document, is or is not an item subject to legal privilege; and

(*b*) order the costs of the application to be met by [the Commissioners][1] except where it holds that no document, or no part of any document, to which the application relates is an item subject to legal privilege.

(6) Where a person makes an application under paragraph (2) within the period mentioned in regulation 6(1), he shall be treated as having complied with the order in relation to the documents to which the application relates until the appropriate judicial authority resolves the dispute.

(7) A dispute may be resolved at any time by [the Commissioners][1] and the person against whom an order has been made reaching an agreement, whether in writing or otherwise, and, for all purposes, the consequences of such an agreement shall be the same as those which would have ensued if, at the time when the agreement was reached, the appropriate judicial authority had resolved the dispute.

Commentary—*Simon's Taxes* **A6.315.**

Amendments—[1] Words substituted by the Orders for the Delivery of Documents (Procedure) (Amendment) Regulations, SI 2005/1131 regs 2, 6 with effect from 18 April 2005.

2000/3158

CONTROLLED FOREIGN COMPANIES (DESIGNER RATE TAX PROVISIONS) REGULATIONS 2000

Made by the Commissioners of Inland Revenue under TA 1988 s 750A(2) to (4)

Made . . . . . 29 November 2000

Laid before the House of Commons . . . . . 29 November 2000

Coming into force . . . . . 20 December 2000

Commentary—*Simon's Taxes* **D4.307.**

1 Citation, commencement and effect

(1) These Regulations may be cited as the Controlled Foreign Companies (Designer Rate Tax Provisions) Regulations 2000 and shall come into force on 20th December 2000.

(2) These Regulations have effect in relation to any accounting period of a company resident outside the United Kingdom which begins on or after 6th October 1999.

2 Interpretation

In these Regulations "the Board" means the Commissioners of Inland Revenue.

3 Specified designer rate tax provisions

For the purposes of section 750A(1) of the Income and Corporation Taxes Act 1988 (deemed lower level of taxation—designer rate tax provisions) the following provisions are specified, being provisions which appear to the Board to be designed to enable companies to exercise significant control over the amount of tax which they pay—

(*a*) the provisions contained in Part XVIIA (international bodies) of the Income Tax (Guernsey) Law, 1975;

(*b*) Article 123B (international business companies) of the Income Tax (Jersey) Law 1961;

(*c*) the provisions contained in Part 1 (International Companies) of the Isle of Man International Business Act 1994, and the provisions contained in Part 3 (Miscellaneous and Supplemental) of that Act so far as relating to Part 1 of that Act;

(*d*) section 41 (rates for qualifying companies) of the Gibraltar Income Tax Ordinance.

2000/3315

EXCHANGE GAINS AND LOSSES (MISCELLANEOUS MODIFICATIONS) REGULATIONS 2000

Made by the Treasury under FA 1993 ss 164(14), 167(1), (4)–(6) and Schs 15, 16 and FA 1998 s 63

Made . . . . . 18 December 2000

Laid before the House of Commons . . . . . 19 December 2000

Coming into force . . . . . 9 January 2001

Modifications—See the Exchange Gains and Losses (Transitional Provisions and Savings) Regulations, SI 2002/1969 (SI 2000/3315, as modified by SI 2002/1969 to continue to have effect notwithstanding the repeal, with effect for accounting periods beginning after 30 September 2002, of FA 1993 ss 164(14), 167(1), (4)–(6), Schs 15, 16 by FA 2002 ss 79(1)(*b*), 141, Sch 40 Pt 3(10)).

1 Citation, commencement and effect

(1) These Regulations may be cited as the Exchange Gains and Losses (Miscellaneous Modifications) Regulations 2000 and shall come into force on 9th January 2001.

(2) Regulations 2 to 10 shall have effect in relation to any accounting period of a company beginning on or after 1st January 2000 for which sections 105 and 106 of the Finance Act 2000 have effect.

2–5 Modification of the Exchange Gains and Losses (Transitional Provisions) Regulations 1994

(*Modified* the Exchange Gains and Losses (Transitional Provisions) Regulations, SI 1994/3226 regs 17, 18, 22; *repealed by* the Exchange Gains and Losses (Transitional Provisions and Savings) Regulations, SI 2002/1969 regs 28, 29 with effect for accounting periods beginning after 30 September 2002.)

6–9 Modification of the Exchange Gains and Losses (Alternative Method of Calculation of Gain or Loss) Regulations 1994

(*Modify* Exchange Gains and Losses (Alternative Method of Calculation of Gain or Loss) Regulations, SI 1994/3226 regs 4, 5, 10.)

10 Revocation of the European Single Currency (Taxes) Regulations 1998

Part X of the European Single Currency (Taxes) Regulations 1998 is revoked to the extent that it is not previously revoked.

11 Modification of the effect of section 146 of the Finance Act 1993

. . .

Amendment—Regulation 11 repealed by the Exchange Gains and Losses (Transitional Provisions and Savings) Regulations, SI 2002/1969 regs 28, 30 with effect for accounting periods beginning after 30 September 2002.

2001/56

INCOME TAX (ELECTRONIC COMMUNICATIONS) (INCENTIVE PAYMENTS) REGULATIONS 2001

Made by the Commissioners of Inland Revenue under FA 2000 s 143(1) and Sch 38

Made . . . . *11 January 2001*

Laid before the House of Commons . . . . *11 January 2001*

Coming into force . . . . *1 February 2001*

Commentary—*Simon's Taxes* **E1.206, E1.250.**

1 Citation, commencement and effect

(1) These Regulations may be cited as the Income Tax (Electronic Communications) (Incentive Payments) Regulations 2001 and shall come into force on 1st February 2001.

(2) Nothing in these Regulations affects the operation of the Electronic Lodgement of Tax Returns Order 1997 or the Income Tax (Electronic Communications) Regulations 2000.

2 Interpretation

In these Regulations—

"the Board" means the Commissioners of Inland Revenue;

"employer" means any person paying emoluments;

"Employments Regulations" means the Income Tax (Employments) Regulations 1993;

"incentive payment" means a payment by way of an incentive to use electronic communications for the delivery of information under regulation 3, 4 or 5;

"the Management Act" means the Taxes Management Act 1970;

"tax credit" means working families' tax credit or, as the case may be, disabled person's tax credit.

3 Incentive payment—return under sections 8 and 9 of the Management Act

(1) The Board shall make an incentive payment in the amount of £10 to any individual who—

(*a*) makes and delivers a return under sections 8 and 9 of the Management Act for a year of assessment using electronic communications, and

(*b*) satisfies the conditions specified in any direction given by the Board under paragraph (2).

(2) The Board may give a direction specifying any or all of the following conditions—

(*a*) a condition that the year of assessment for which the return is to be made and delivered is one specified in the direction,

(*b*) a condition specifying the form of electronic communication by which the return is to be delivered,

(*c*) a condition that the individual by whom the return is to be made and delivered is one who is authorised to use the form of electronic communication specified in the direction,

(*d*) a condition that where the individual by whom the return is made and delivered becomes liable to pay an amount by way of income tax for the year of assessment concerned, the payment or, if more than one, at least one of the payments, made by him in meeting that liability is made using one of the forms of electronic payment specified in the direction,

(*e*) a condition that the return is made and delivered using the form of electronic communication specified in the direction,

(*f*) a condition that the return is made and delivered by the individual on or before the day mentioned in section 8(1A) of the Management Act,

(*g*) a condition that any amount payable by way of income tax by the individual for the year of assessment concerned is paid in accordance with the provisions for payment of income tax contained in sections 59A and 59B of the Management Act.

(3) Where an officer of the Board considers that the individual has failed to satisfy one or more of the conditions specified in the direction, he may give notice to the individual that the conditions are not met or, where the incentive payment has already been authorised or made, notice withdrawing the incentive payment.

(4) Where prior to the giving of a notice under paragraph (3) an incentive payment has already been made to the individual, an officer of the Board may recover the amount of the incentive payment in accordance with paragraph (5).

(5) For the purposes of paragraph (4), subsections (1), (4), (5) and (6) of section 30 of the Management Act (recovery of overpayment of tax, etc) and section 30A of that Act (assessing procedure) shall apply as if the amount of the incentive payment to be recovered were an amount of income tax repaid to that individual which ought not to have been repaid to him.

(6) The Board may give a direction relating to appeals against notices under paragraph (3) and appeals against assessments made in pursuance of paragraph (5).

4 Incentive payment—return under regulation 43 of the Employments Regulations

(1) The Board [shall][1] make an incentive payment in the amount of £50 to any employer who—

(a) renders a return under regulation 43 of the Employments Regulations for a year of assessment using electronic communications, and

(b) satisfies the conditions specified in any direction given by the Board under paragraph (2).

(2) The Board may give a direction specifying any or all of the following conditions—

(a) a condition that the year of assessment for which the return is to be rendered is one specified in the direction;

(b) a condition specifying the form of electronic communication by which the return is to be rendered,

(c) a condition that the employer by whom the return is to be rendered is one who is authorised to use the form of electronic communication specified in the direction,

(d) a condition that at least one of the payments made by the employer under regulation 40 or 41 of the Employments Regulations in the year of assessment concerned is made using one of the forms of electronic payment specified in the direction,

(e) a condition that the return is rendered by the employer, or by an agent of the employer authorised to render the return, using the form of electronic communication specified in the direction,

(f) a condition that, where the return is rendered by the employer's agent on the employer's behalf—

(i) the employer has registered online to use the form of electronic communication specified in the direction,

(ii) the employer has used that form of electronic communication to notify the Board of his agent's name and address, and

(iii) his agent is authorised by him to render the return on his behalf and to use that form of electronic communication,

(g) a condition that the return is rendered not later than the end of the period mentioned in regulation 43(1) of the Employments Regulations,

(h) a condition that each of the payments required to be made by the employer under regulation 40 or 41 for the year of assessment concerned is made not later than the end of the period mentioned in regulation 40(1) or, as the case may be, regulation 41(1).

(3) Where an officer of the Board considers that the employer has failed to satisfy one or more of the conditions specified in the direction, he may give notice to the employer that the conditions are not met or, where the incentive payment has already been authorised or made, notice withdrawing the incentive payment.

(4) Where prior to the giving of a notice under paragraph (3) an incentive payment has already been made to the employer, an officer of the Board may recover the amount of the incentive payment in accordance with paragraph (5).

(5) For the purposes of paragraph (4), subsections (1), (4), (5) and (6) of section 30 of the Management Act and section 30A of that Act shall apply as if the amount of the incentive payment to be recovered were an amount of income tax repaid to a person which ought not to have been repaid to him.

(6) The Board may give a direction relating to appeals against notices under paragraph (3) and appeals against assessments made in pursuance of paragraph (5).

Amendments—[1] Word substituted by the Income Tax (Electronic Communications) (Miscellaneous Amendments) Regulations, SI 2001/1081 reg 22 with effect from 9 April 2001.

5 Incentive payment—return of payments of tax credit

(1) The Board shall make an incentive payment in the amount of £50 to any employer who—

(a) pays tax credit to one or more of his employees during a year of assessment,

(b) in accordance with regulation 6(7) of the Tax Credits (Payment by Employers) Regulations 1999 records on the certificate contained in a return under regulation 43 of the Employments Regulations the total tax credit paid to his employees for that year,

(c) renders that return using electronic communications, and

(d) satisfies the conditions specified in any direction given by the Board under paragraph (2).

(2) The Board may give a direction specifying any or all of the following conditions—

(*a*) a condition that the year of assessment for which the return is to be rendered is one specified in the direction,

(*b*) a condition specifying the form of electronic communication by which the return is to be rendered,

(*c*) a condition that the employer by whom the return is to be rendered is one who is authorised to use the form of electronic communication specified in the direction,

(*d*) a condition that the employer satisfies each of the conditions specified in a direction made under regulation 4(2) of these Regulations,

(*e*) a condition that the employer has paid tax credit in the year of assessment concerned in accordance with regulation 6 of the Tax Credits (Payment by Employers) Regulations 1999 (obligation to pay tax credit on paying emoluments to employees entitled to tax credit).

(3) Where an officer of the Board considers that the employer has failed to satisfy one or more of the conditions specified in the direction, he may give notice to the employer that the conditions are not met or, where the incentive payment has already been authorised or made, notice withdrawing the incentive payment.

(4) Where prior to the giving of a notice under paragraph (3) an incentive payment has already been made to the employer, an officer of the Board may recover the amount of the incentive payment in accordance with paragraph (5).

(5) For the purposes of paragraph (4), subsections (1), (4), (5) and (6) of section 30 of the Management Act and section 30A of that Act shall apply as if the amount of the incentive payment to be recovered were an amount of income tax repaid to a person which ought not to have been repaid to him.

(6) The Board may give a direction relating to appeals against notices under paragraph (3) and appeals against assessments made in pursuance of paragraph (5).

2001/117

PERSONAL PENSION SCHEMES (RESTRICTION ON DISCRETION TO APPROVE) (PERMITTED INVESTMENTS) REGULATIONS 2001

Revocation—These Regulations lapse by virtue of the coming into force of FA 2004 Part 4 (ss 149–284) with effect from 6 April 2006.

2001/118

PERSONAL PENSION SCHEMES (CONVERSION OF RETIREMENT BENEFITS SCHEMES) REGULATIONS 2001

Revocation—These Regulations lapse by virtue of the coming into force of FA 2004 Part 4 (ss 149–284) with effect from 6 April 2006.

2001/119

PERSONAL PENSION SCHEMES (TRANSFER PAYMENTS) REGULATIONS 2001

Revocation—These Regulations lapse by virtue of the coming into force of FA 2004 Part 4 (ss 149–284) with effect from 6 April 2006.

2001/253

FINANCE ACT 1989, SECTION 178(1), (APPOINTED DAY) ORDER 2001

Made by the Treasury under FA 1989 s 178(7)

Made . . . . *1 February 2001*

1 This Order may be cited as the Finance Act 1989, section 178(1), (Appointed Day) Order 2001.

2—(1) The day appointed for the enactments specified in paragraph (2) for periods beginning on or after which section 178(1) of the Finance Act 1989 shall have effect is 7th March 2001.

(2) The enactments specified are—

(*a*) section 71(8A) of the Social Security Administration Act 1992;

(*b*) section 69(8A) of the Social Security Administration (Northern Ireland) Act 1992;

(*c*) paragraph 8 of Schedule 4 to the Tax Credits Act 1999.

2001/391

INVESTMENT TRUSTS (APPROVAL OF ACCOUNTING METHODS FOR CREDITOR RELATIONSHIPS) ORDER 2001

Made by the Treasury under FA 1996 Sch 10 paras 1, 9(1)

Made ....*14 February 2001*
Laid before the House of Commons ....*14 February 2001*
Coming into force ....*7 March 2001*

1 Citation, commencement and effect

This Order may be cited as the Investment Trusts (Approval of Accounting Methods for Creditor Relationships) Order 2001 and shall come into force on 7th March 2001, but shall have effect in relation to accounting periods of investment trusts ending after 31st March 1996.

2 Interpretation

(1) In this Order—
"Chapter II" means Chapter II of Part IV of the Finance Act 1996;
"creditor relationship" has the same meaning as in section 103(1);
"investment trust" has the meaning given by section 842 of the Taxes Act;
"statutory accounts" shall be construed in accordance with section 86(8);
"the Taxes Act" means the Income and Corporation Taxes Act 1988.

(2) References in this Order to a section, or a Schedule, without more, are references to that section of, or that Schedule to, the Finance Act 1996.

3 Approval of the use of accounting methods

The accounting methods that are approved for use for the creditor relationships of investment trusts for the purposes of paragraph 1 of Schedule 10 are—
(*a*) the method ("the main method") contained in a Statement of Recommended Practice issued by the Association of Investment Trust Companies bearing the date December 1995 ("the Statement"), as modified by article 4 of this Order;
(*b*) the method contained in the Statement as varied by a Guidance Note issued by that Association on 8th January 1997 ("the simple method"), and as modified by article 4.

4 Modifications of the main method and the simple method

(1) The main method and the simple method shall be modified as follows.

(2) For paragraph R604 in the Statement there shall be substituted the following paragraph—

"**R604** An ITC shall be under an obligation—
(*a*) to make proper provision for allocating payments under a creditor relationship to accounting periods (and that expression has the same meaning as in sub-section (3) of section 85 of the Finance Act 1996, on the assumption that the words 'loan relationship' in that sub-section were replaced with the words 'creditor relationship'), and
(*b*) not to make any provision (other than provision comprised in authorised arrangements for bad debt, within the meaning in section 85(5)(*a*) of the Finance Act 1996) that gives debits by reference to the valuation at different times of any asset representing a creditor relationship (within the meaning in section 103(1) of the Finance Act 1996)."

(3) Paragraph R606 in the Statement shall be omitted.

(4) In this Order, "the modified main method" and "the modified simple method" mean the main method, and the simple method, as so modified, respectively.

5 Purposes for which accounting methods are approved

(1) his article has effect for the purpose of determining which of the accounting methods approved under article 3 is to be used as respects the creditor relationships of an investment trust.

(2) The same method shall be used as respects all creditor relationships of an investment trust for any single accounting period.

(3) The modified main method shall be used for any accounting period where—
(*a*) the investment trust uses the main method or the modified main method for the purposes of its statutory accounts for that accounting period;
(*b*) the investment trust has in an earlier accounting period (not being an accounting period described in paragraph (4)) used the modified main method as an authorised accounting method for the purposes of Chapter II; or
(*c*) the investment trust has, at any time during the accounting period referred to in the words preceding sub-paragraph (*a*), held—
(i) a relevant discounted security within the meaning of Schedule 13; or

(ii) a security to which section 717 of the Taxes Act applies.

(4) The accounting period described in this paragraph is one—

(*a*) which ended before the coming into force of this Order; and

(*b*) during which the investment trust did not at any time hold any of the securities referred to in paragraph (3)(*c*)(i) or (ii).

2001/544

FINANCIAL SERVICES AND MARKETS ACT 2000 (REGULATED ACTIVITIES) ORDER 2001

Approved by both Houses of Parliament

Made . . . . 26th February 2001

Laid before Parliament . . . . 27th February 2001

Coming into force in accordance with article 2

The Treasury, in exercise of the powers conferred on them by sections 22(1) and (5), 426 and 428(3) of, and paragraph 25 of Schedule 2 to, the Financial Services and Markets Act 2000, hereby make the following Order:

PART I
GENERAL

1 Citation

This Order may be cited as the Financial Services and Markets Act 2000 (Regulated Activities) Order 2001.

2 Commencement

(1) Except as provided by paragraph (2), this Order comes into force on the day on which section 19 of the Act comes into force.

(2) This Order comes into force—

(a) for the purposes of articles 59, 60 and 87 (funeral plan contracts) on 1st January 2002; and

(b) for the purposes of articles 61 to 63, 88, 90 and 91 (regulated mortgage contracts) [on such a day as the Treasury may specify]][1].

[(3) Any day specified under paragraph (2)(b) must be caused to be notified in the London, Edinburgh and Belfast Gazettes published not later than one week before that day.][1]

Amendments—[1] In para (2)(b), words substituted, and para (3) inserted, by SI 2002/1777 art 2(1), (2) with effect from 30 August 2002.

PART 2
SPECIFIED ACTIVITIES

[CHAPTER 6A

CREDIT BROKING]

[The Activity]

[36A Credit broking]

[(1) Each of the following is a specified kind of activity—

(a) effecting an introduction of an individual or relevant recipient of credit who wishes to enter into a credit agreement to a person ("P") with a view to P entering into by way of business as lender a regulated credit agreement (or an agreement which would be a regulated credit agreement but for any of the relevant provisions);

(b) effecting an introduction of an individual or relevant recipient of credit who wishes to enter into a consumer hire agreement to a person ("P") with a view to P entering into by way of business as owner a regulated consumer hire agreement or an agreement which would be a regulated consumer hire agreement but for article 60O (exempt agreements: exemptions relating to the nature of the agreement) or 60Q (exempt agreements: exemptions relating to the nature of the hirer);

(c) effecting an introduction of an individual or relevant recipient of credit who wishes to enter into a credit agreement or consumer hire agreement (as the case may be) to a person who carries on an activity of the kind specified in sub-paragraph (a) or (b) by way of business;

(d) presenting or offering an agreement which would (if entered into) be a regulated credit agreement (or an agreement which would be a regulated credit agreement but for any of the relevant provisions);

(e) assisting an individual or relevant recipient of credit by undertaking preparatory work with a view to that person entering into a regulated credit agreement (or an agreement which would be a regulated credit agreement but for any of the relevant provisions);

(f) entering into a regulated credit agreement (or an agreement which would be a regulated credit agreement but for any of the relevant provisions) on behalf of a lender.

(2) Paragraph (1) does not apply in so far as the activity is an activity of the kind specified by article 36H (operating an electronic system in relation to lending).

(3) For the purposes of paragraph (1) it is immaterial whether the credit agreement or consumer hire agreement is subject to the law of a country outside the United Kingdom.

(4) For the purposes of this article, the "relevant provisions" are the following provisions—

(a) article 60C (exempt agreements: exemptions relating to the nature of the agreement);

(b) article 60D (exempt agreements: exemptions relating to the purchase of land for non-residential purposes);

(c) article 60E (exempt agreements: exemptions relating to the nature of the lender)[, except for paragraph (5) of that article][2];

(d) article 60G (exempt agreements: exemptions relating to the total charge for credit);

(e) article 60H (exempt agreements: exemptions relating to the nature of the borrower).][1]

Amendments—[1] Reg 36A inserted by SI 2013/1881 arts 2, 4 with effect for certain purposes from 26 July 2013 and for remaining purposes from 1 April 2014.

[2] In para (4)(c), words inserted by SI 2014/1448 art 2 with effect from 27 June 2014.

[CHAPTER 6B

OPERATING AN ELECTRONIC SYSTEM IN RELATION TO LENDING]

[The Activity]

[36H Operating an electronic system in relation to lending]

[(1) Where the [conditions in paragraphs (2), (2A) and (2C) are][2] satisfied, operating an electronic system which enables the operator ("A") to facilitate persons ("B" and "C") becoming the lender and borrower under an article 36H agreement is a specified kind of activity.

(2) The condition [in this paragraph][2] is that the system operated by A is capable of determining which agreements should be made available to each of B and C (whether in accordance with general instructions provided to A by B or C or otherwise).

[(2A) The condition in this paragraph is that A, or another person ("X") acting under an arrangement with A or at A's direction, undertakes to—

(a) receive payments in respect of [either interest or capital or both][3] due under the article 36H agreement from C, and

(b) make payments in respect of [either interest or capital or both][3] due under the article 36H agreement to B.

(2B) For the purposes of paragraph (2A)—

(a) an agreement by A to appoint X to perform the activities in that paragraph is to be treated as an undertaking by A within the meaning of that paragraph;

(b) it is immaterial that—

(i) payments may be subject to conditions;

(ii) A, or X, may be entitled to retain a portion or the entirety of any payment received from C.

(2C) The condition in this paragraph is that A, or another person ("X") acting under an arrangement with A or at A's direction, undertakes to perform, or A undertakes to appoint or direct another person to perform either or both of the following activities—

(a) taking steps to procure the payment of a debt under the article 36H agreement;

(b) exercising or enforcing rights under the article 36H agreement on behalf of B.][2]

[(2D) Where A carries on an activity of the kind specified in paragraph (1), it is a specified kind of activity for A to operate an electronic system where—

(a) that system enables A to facilitate a person ("B") assuming the rights of the lender under an article 36H agreement by assignment or operation of law, and

(b) the conditions in paragraphs (2), (2A) and (2C) are satisfied where C is the borrower under the agreement in sub-paragraph (a).][3]

(3) The following are specified kinds of activities if carried on by A in the course of, or in connection with, the carrying on by A of the activity specified by paragraph (1) [or (2D)][3]—

(a) presenting or offering article 36H agreements to [either B or C][3] with a view to B becoming the lender under the article 36H agreement [or][3] C becoming the borrower under the article 36H agreement,

(b) furnishing information relevant to the financial standing of a person ("Y") with a view to assisting in the determination as to whether another person should—

(i) enter into, as the lender, an article 36H agreement with Y, or

(ii) assume the rights of the lender under an article 36H agreement under which Y is the borrower,

(c) taking steps to procure the payment of a debt due under an article 36H agreement,

(d) [taking steps to perform duties, or exercise or enforce][3] rights under an article 36H agreement on behalf of the lender,

(e) [taking steps with a view to][3] ascertaining whether a credit information agency (within the meaning given by article 89A(6)) holds information relevant to the financial standing of an individual or relevant person,

(f) [taking steps with a view to][3] ascertaining the contents of such information,

(g) [taking steps with a view to][3] securing the correction of, the omission of anything from, or the making of any other kind of modification of, such information, . . .[3]

(h) [taking steps with a view to][3] securing that a credit information agency which holds such information—

(i) stops holding the information, or

(ii) does not provide it to any other person[, or

(i) giving advice in relation to the taking of any of the steps in sub-paragraphs (e) to (h)][3].

[(4) An "article 36H agreement" is an agreement by which one person provides another person with credit and in relation to which—

(a) the condition in paragraph (4A) is satisfied, and

(b) the condition in either paragraph (5) or (6) is satisfied, or was satisfied at the time the agreement was entered into.

(4A) The condition in this paragraph is that A does not provide credit, assume the rights (by assignment or operation of law) of a person who provided credit, or receive credit under the agreement.][3]

(5) The condition in this paragraph is that the lender is an individual or relevant person.

(6) The condition in this paragraph is that the borrower is an individual or relevant person and—

(a) the lender provides the borrower with credit less than or equal to £25,000, or

(b) the agreement is not entered into by the borrower wholly or predominantly for the purposes of a business carried on, or intended to be carried on, by the borrower.

(7) Paragraphs (5) and (6) of article 60C (exempt agreements: exemptions relating to the nature of the agreement) apply for the purposes of paragraph (6)(b).

(8) It is immaterial for the purposes of this article whether the lender is carrying on a regulated activity.]

[(9) In this article—

"assignment", in relation to Scotland, means assignation;

"borrower" means a person who receives credit under an article 36H agreement or a person to whom the rights and duties of a borrower under such an agreement have passed by assignment or operation of law;

"credit" has the meaning given by article 60L;

"lender" means—

(a) a person providing credit under an article 36H agreement, or

(b) a person who by assignment or operation of law has assumed the rights of a person who provided credit under such an agreement;

"relevant person" means—

(a) a partnership consisting of two or three persons not all of whom are bodies corporate, or

(b) an unincorporated body of persons which does not consist entirely of bodies corporate and is not a partnership.][3]

[(10) For the purposes of the application of section 22(1) of the Act (regulated activities) to an activity of a kind specified by this article, article 88D (credit agreement), and article 73 (investments: general) in so far as it relates to that article, [have][3] effect as if the reference to a credit agreement in article 88D includes a reference to an article 36H agreement.][4]][1]

Amendments—[1] Reg 36H inserted by SI 2013/1881 arts 2, 4 with effect for certain purposes from 26 July 2013 and remaining purposes from 1 April 2014.

[2] In para (1) words substituted, in para (2) words inserted, paras (2A)–(2C) inserted, by SI 2014/366 art 2(1), (9) with effect for certain purposes from 14 February 2014 and for remaining purposes from 1 April 2014.

[3] In paras (2A)(a), (b), (10) words substituted, para (2D) inserted, in para (3) words inserted, substituted and revoked, paras (4), (4A), (9) substituted, by SI 2016/392 art 2(1), (5) with effect from 17 March 2016.

[4] Para (10) inserted by SI 2014/366 art 2(1), (9)(d) with effect for certain purposes from 14 February 2014, and for remaining purposes from 1 April 2014.

2001/1122

CAPITAL GAINS TAX (GILT-EDGED SECURITIES) ORDER 2001

Made by the Treasury under TCGA 1992 Sch 9, para 1

Made . . . . *22 March 2001*

1 This Order may be cited as the Capital Gains Tax (Gilt-edged Securities) Order 2001.

2 The following securities are hereby specified for the purposes of Schedule 9 to the Taxation of Chargeable Gains Act 1992—

FLOATING RATE TREASURY STOCK 2001

7%	Treasury Stock 2002
6½%	Treasury Stock 2003
5%	Treasury Stock 2004
7¼%	Treasury Stock 2007
5¾%	Treasury Stock 2009
8%	Treasury Stock 2021
6%	Treasury Stock 2028
4¼%	Treasury Stock 2032.

2001/1123

INCOME TAX (CAR BENEFITS) (REDUCTION OF VALUE OF APPROPRIATE PERCENTAGE) REGULATIONS 2001

Made by the Treasury under TA 1988 Sch 6, paras 5E, 8

Made . . . . *21 March 2001*
Laid before the House of Commons . . . . *22 March 2001*
Coming into force . . . . *12 April 2001*

Amendment—These regulations revoked by the Income Tax (Car Benefits) (Reduction of Value of Appropriate Percentage) (Amendment) Regulations, SI 2010/695, reg 3, with effect from 6 April 2011.

2001/1156

DOUBLE TAXATION RELIEF (TAXES ON INCOME) (UNDERLYING TAX ON DIVIDENDS AND DUAL RESIDENT COMPANIES) REGULATIONS 2001

Made by the Treasury under TA 1988 s 801(2A)(b)

Made . . . . *26 March 2001*
Laid before the House of Commons . . . . *26 March 2001*
Coming into force . . . . *31 March 2001*

1 Citation, commencement and application

(1) These Regulations may be cited as the Double Taxation Relief (Taxes on Income) (Underlying Tax on Dividends and Dual Resident Companies) Regulations 2001.

(2) These Regulations shall come into force on 31st March 2001 and shall apply in relation to any claim for an allowance by way of credit made on or after that date in respect of a dividend paid by an overseas company to a company resident in the United Kingdom, unless the dividend was paid before that date.

2 Interpretation

In these Regulations—

"the Act" means the Income and Corporation Taxes Act 1988, and a reference to a numbered section is a reference to the section of the Act which is so numbered;

"dual resident company" means a company which is liable, by reason of its domicile, residence or place of management or of incorporation, or other similar criterion, to tax in two or more territories;

"overseas company" has the meaning given in section 801(1) (dividends paid between related companies—relief for UK and third country taxes); and

"third company" means the company referred to as such in section 801(2).

3 Additional cases prescribed for the purposes of section 801(2) of the Act

(1) The cases specified in paragraphs (2) and (3) are prescribed for the purposes of section 801(2) (cases where the overseas company receives a dividend from a related third company and in respect of which relief allowable for underlying tax is subject to a restriction under section 799(1)(*b*)).

(2) The case specified in this paragraph is that the overseas company is a dual resident company as respects an accounting period and, although resident in the same territory as the third company—

(*a*) it is treated for the purposes of Chapter IV of Part XVII of the Act (tax avoidance—controlled foreign companies) as resident in a different territory; or

(*b*) it would be so treated in accordance with paragraphs (*a*) to (*c*) of subsection (3) of section 749 (residence of controlled foreign companies) if that subsection applied to it.

(3) The case specified in this paragraph is that the third company is a dual resident company as respects an accounting period and although resident in the same territory as the overseas company—

(*a*) it is treated for the purposes of Chapter IV of Part XVII of the Act as resident in a different territory; or

(*b*) it would be so treated in accordance with paragraphs (*a*) to (*c*) of subsection (3) of section 749 if that subsection applied to it.

2001/1163

DOUBLE TAXATION RELIEF (SURRENDER OF RELIEVABLE TAX WITHIN A GROUP) REGULATIONS 2001

Made by the Commissioners of Inland Revenue under TA 1988 s 806H

Made . . . .*23 March 2001*
Laid before the House of Commons . . . .*26 March 2001*
Coming into force . . . .*31 March 2001*

1 Citation, commencement and effect

(1) These Regulations may be cited as the Double Taxation Relief (Surrender of Relievable Tax Within a Group) Regulations 2001 and shall come into force on 31st March 2001.

(2) These Regulations shall have effect in relation to any claim made on or after 31st March 2001 for the surrender of an amount of EUFT arising in respect of a dividend falling within section 806A(2) that is paid by a company resident outside the United Kingdom to a company resident in the United Kingdom, unless the dividend was paid before that date.

2 Interpretation

(1) In these Regulations—

"EUFT" means eligible unrelieved foreign tax;

"group" shall be construed in accordance with subsection (3)(*a*) of section 413, read with subsections (4), (5) and (7) of that section;

"the Taxes Act" means the Income and Corporation Taxes Act 1988.

(2) In these Regulations the following expressions have the meanings given by section 413(2)—

"claimant company";

"company";

"group relief";

"surrendering company".

(3) In these Regulations references to a section, without more, are to that section of the Taxes Act.

3 Introductory

These Regulations make provision for, and in connection with, allowing a company which is a member of a group to surrender an amount of EUFT arising to it in an accounting period to another company which is a member of the same group.

4 Amount of EUFT available for surrender

(1) Subject to paragraph (2), the amount of EUFT arising in an accounting period in the cases set out in sections 806A and 806B that may be surrendered by the surrendering company to a claimant company must not exceed the amount (if any) that remains ("the remaining amount") after the surrendering company has fully utilised in accordance with the relevant provisions of sections 806D to 806G the EUFT arising in that accounting period.

(2) For the purposes of paragraph (1), where the surrendering company chooses not to utilise section 806D(4)(*c*) or (5)(*c*) (carry back provision), the remaining amount shall be computed in accordance with that paragraph as if the surrendering company had in fact fully utilised that provision.

(3) Where the surrendering company carries on life assurance business, the policy holders' share of the amount of EUFT attributable to BLAGAB may not be surrendered to another company in the group.

(4) Where—

(*a*) an amount of EUFT is surrendered to a claimant company, and

(*b*) the claimant company carries on life assurance business,

the amount surrendered may not be set against the policy holders' share of the corporation tax attributable [by virtue of section 797(1)][1] to any single dividend referable [by virtue of section 432A][1] to the claimant company's BLAGAB.

(5) In this regulation—

. . . [1];

"BLAGAB" means basic life assurance and general annuity business [within the meaning given by section 431F][1];

["the policy holders' share of the amount of EUFT attributable to BLAGAB" means the relevant fraction of—

(*a*) where all of the company's long-term business within the meaning given by section 431(2) is BLAGAB, the whole of the amount of EUFT;

(*b*) in any other case, so much of the amount of EUFT as is attributable to BLAGAB by virtue of section 804B(3) or (4);

"the policy holders' share of the corporation tax attributable to any single dividend referable to the claimant company's BLAGAB" means the relevant fraction of that tax;

"the relevant fraction" means the fraction arrived at by dividing—

(*a*) the policy holders' share of the company's relevant profits for the relevant accounting period, by

(*b*) the company's BLAGAB profits for that period, and, for the purposes of this definition, "the policy holders' share of the company's relevant profits" shall be construed in accordance with sections 88(3) and 89 of the Finance Act 1989 and "the company's BLAGAB profits" shall be construed in accordance with [section 431(2YB) of the Income and Corporation Taxes Act 1988][2];][1]

"the relevant provisions of sections 806D to 806G" means all provisions of those sections other than section 806D(4)(*b*) and (5)(*b*) (carry forward provision);

"single dividend" has the meaning given by section 806E(6).

Amendments—[1] Words in paras (4), (5) inserted, in para (5), definitions substituted, and definition of attributable repealed, by the Double Taxation Relief (Surrender of Relievable Tax Within a Group) (Amendment) Regulations, SI 2003/1829 with effect for distributions made after 8 April 2003 in accounting periods ending after 6 August 2003.

[2] In para (5), words in definition of "the relevant fraction" substituted by the Double Taxation Relief (Surrender of Relievable Tax Within a Group) (Amendment) Regulations, SI 2008/2681 reg 2 with effect in relation to accounting periods beginning on or after 1 January 2008 and ending after 30 October 2008.

5 Claiming of EUFT

(1) The claimant company may claim the whole or part of the amount of EUFT available for surrender in accordance with regulation 4.

(2) The amount of EUFT claimed by the claimant company may be utilised by the claimant company in accordance with the provisions of sections 806D to 806G.

6 Accounting periods of surrendering company and claimant company

(1) The surrendering company and the claimant company must be members of the same group throughout the accounting period of the surrendering company in which the amount of EUFT available for surrender arises.

(2) Where the accounting period of the surrendering company in which the amount of EUFT available for surrender arises and the accounting period of the claimant company are not coterminous—

(*a*) the amount of EUFT arising in that accounting period of the surrendering company which is surrendered to the claimant company in accordance with regulations 4 and 5 shall be treated as if it arose on a dividend received by the claimant company, and

(*b*) that dividend shall be treated as arising in that one of the claimant company's accounting periods in which falls the last day of the accounting period of the surrendering company in which the amount of EUFT surrendered arises.

7 Calculation of Schedule D Case V income when EUFT claimed

An amount of EUFT that is utilised by the claimant company in accordance with the provisions of sections 806D to 806G shall not be taken into account as underlying tax under section 795(2)(*b*) in computing the amount of income of the claimant company.

8 Form of claim and withdrawal of claim

(1) The like provisions as those contained in Part VIII of Schedule 18 to the Finance Act 1998 ("Schedule 18") and listed below shall have effect, with necessary modifications, in relation to claims for amounts of EUFT available for surrender as they have effect in relation to claims for group relief.

(2) Those provisions of Schedule 18 are paragraphs 67, 68, 70(1), (3) and (4), 71, 72(1) and (4), 73, 75, 75A and 76.

9 Time limit for claims

(1) A claim for the whole or part of the amount of EUFT available for surrender in an accounting period of the surrendering company may only be made or withdrawn before the expiration of—

(*a*) six years after the expiration of that accounting period or, if later,

(*b*) one year after the end of the accounting period in which the foreign tax in question is paid.

(2) The time limits otherwise applicable to amendment of a company tax return under the Corporation Tax Acts do not apply to an amendment to the extent that it makes or withdraws a claim for the surrender of an amount of EUFT in accordance with these Regulations within the time allowed under paragraph (1).

10 Miscellaneous provisions

(1) The like provisions as those contained in Chapter IV of Part X of the Taxes Act ("Chapter IV") and listed below shall have effect, with necessary modifications, in relation to claims for amounts of EUFT available for surrender as they have effect in relation to claims for group relief.

(2) Those provisions of Chapter IV are sections 402(1), (2), (5) and (6), . . .[1] 410(1), (4) and (5) to (7) and 411(1).

Amendments—[1] Figure revoked by the Double Taxation Relief (Surrender of Relievable Tax Within a Group) (Amendment) Regulations, SI 2001/3873 with effect from 5 December 2001.

2001/1304

GENERAL COMMISSIONERS OF INCOME TAX (COSTS) REGULATIONS 2001

Revocation—These Regulations revoked by the Transfer of Tribunal Functions and Revenue and Customs Appeals Order, SI 2009/56 art 3, Sch 2 para 187(*m*) with effect from 1 April 2009, subject to transitional and savings provisions in Sch 3 para 11.

2001/1757

GENERAL INSURANCE RESERVES (TAX) REGULATIONS 2001

Made by the Commissioners of Inland Revenue under FA 2000 s 107.

Made . . . . *8 May 2001*

Laid before the House of Commons . . . . *8 May 2001*

Coming into force . . . . *29 May 2001*

1 Citation, commencement and effect

These Regulations may be cited as the General Insurance Reserves (Tax) Regulations 2001 and shall come into force on 29th May 2001, and shall have effect for periods of account of general insurers—

(*a*) beginning on or after 1 January 2001, and

(*b*) ending on or after 29th May 2001.

2 Interpretation

(1) In these Regulations unless the context otherwise requires—

"controlled foreign company" has the meaning in Chapter IV of Part XVII of the Income and Corporation Taxes Act 1988 ("the Taxes Act");

["corporate general insurer" means a general insurer which is a company;][1]

"Schedule 9A" means Schedule 9A to the Companies Act 1985;

"section 107" means section 107 of the Finance Act 2000;

other references to a section, without more, are to that section of the Taxes Act; and

"statutory accounts", in relation to a company other than an underwriting member, has the meaning given by section 86(8)(*a*) and (*c*) to (*e*) of the Finance Act 1996.

(2) References to a company being connected with another company shall be construed in accordance with section 839(5) to (7).

[(3) In these Regulations a reference to a numbered Rule is a reference to the Rule in regulation 3 bearing that number.][1]

Amendments—[1] In para (1), definition of "corporate general insurer" inserted, and para (3) inserted, by the General Insurance Reserves (Tax) (Amendment) Regulations, SI 2003/2862 regs 3, 4 with effect from 5 December 2003.

3 Recalculation of technical provisions for the purposes of section 107

(1) This regulation and regulation 4 apply for determining for the purposes of section 107 whether an amount representing the whole or part of the technical provisions made and taken into account in computing for tax purposes the profits of a general insurer other than an underwriting member (see regulation 7(2)) for a period of account was excessive or insufficient, and the amount of the excess or deficiency.

(2) In the following provisions of this regulation and regulation 4—

"the balance sheet date" means the end of the earlier period of account (as the latter expression is defined in paragraph (3));

"the recalculation date" means the end of the later period of account (as the latter expression is defined in paragraph (3));

["relevant transaction" means any disposal or acquisition (in whole or in part) of the rights or liabilities of—

(*a*) a corporate general insurer under a contract of insurance; or

(*b*) a reinsurer under a contract of reinsurance;][1]

and

"taken into account" means taken into account in computing for tax purposes the profits of the general insurer's trade for the relevant period of account;

and expressions which are used in Schedule 9A have the same meanings as in that Schedule.

(3) As at the end of each period of account which begins on or after 1 January 2001 (and the period which is relevant to the calculation in question is referred to as "the later period of account"), recalculate the provisions for claims outstanding made and taken into account for each earlier period of account which—

(*a*) began on or after 1 January 2000[1], . . .

(*b*) . . .

separately for each such period (and the earlier period which is relevant to the calculation in question is referred to as "the earlier period of account"). The recalculation shall be made in accordance with the following rules.

Amendments—[1] In para (2), definition of "relevant transaction" inserted; sub-para (3)(*b*) and word preceding it revoked; in Rule 2.1, para (*a*) substituted, and words in para (*b*) substituted; words in Rule 3.1 substituted; Rules 4.1–4.1C substituted for Rule 4.1; words in Rules 4.2, 5.4, 8.1 inserted; in Rule 5.4, para (*b*)(i), (ii) revoked; Rules 8A.1–8A.5, 9.1A, 9.1B inserted; words in Rule 9 substituted; by the General Insurance Reserves (Tax) (Amendment) Regulations, SI 2003/2862 regs 3, 5 with effect from 5 December 2003. In Rule 8A.3(*b*) words inserted, and words in Rule 9.3 substituted, by the General Insurance Reserves (Tax) (Amendment) Regulations, SI 2005/3289 regs 2, 3 with effect from 21 December 2005.

Rule 1

1.1. Subject to regulation 5, the calculation under Rules 2 to 9 shall be carried out in sterling, and the sterling discount rate in paragraph (*a*) of Rule 5.4. shall apply.

Rule 2

2.1. Find out the amount of the provisions for claims outstanding made and taken into account for the earlier period of account which—

[(*a*) where the earlier period of account is the general insurer's first period of account which began on or after 1st January 2000, were provisions made and taken into account for that period, and][1]

(*b*) in any other case, [were provisions][1] made and taken into account for that period for liabilities which (according to their treatment in the statutory accounts of the general insurer) arose in respect of that period.

2.2. The result of this Rule is referred to as "the original provisions for the earlier period of account".

Amendments—[1] In Rule 2.1, para (*a*) substituted, and words in para (*b*) substituted by the General Insurance Reserves (Tax) (Amendment) Regulations, SI 2003/2862 regs 3, 5 with effect from 5 December 2003.

Rule 3

3.1. In relation to the original provisions for the earlier period of account, find out (subject to Rule 4) the cost of settling the liabilities to which the provisions relate, including the amount of—

(*a*) claims paid (gross amount, less reinsurer's share), between the balance sheet date and the recalculation date, (calculated in accordance with Note 4 on the profit and loss account format in section B of Chapter I of Part I of Schedule 9A, but as if the references to the addition and deduction of provisions for claims were omitted),

(*b*) bonuses and rebates (if any), net of reinsurance (calculated in accordance with Note 5 on that profit and loss account format),

(*c*) premiums (if any) paid, or treated as paid, between the balance sheet date and the recalculation date, under a reinsurance to close contract[, qualifying contract or relevant transaction][1], and

(*d*) provisions (if any) for claims outstanding, net of reinsurance, which are carried forward as at the recalculation date (calculated in accordance with paragraphs 43 and 47 of Schedule 9A), and which are taken into account for the later period of account.

3.2. Any such payment, bonus, rebate, deemed payment or provision is referred to in Rule 5 (except in paragraph (*a*) of Rule 5.2.) as a "liability".

Amendments—[1] Words in Rule 3.1 substituted by the General Insurance Reserves (Tax) (Amendment) Regulations, SI 2003/2862 regs 3, 5 with effect from 5 December 2003.

Rule 4

[4.1 This Rule applies where either Rule 4.1A or 4.1B is satisfied.][1]

[4.1A This Rule is satisfied if—

(*a*) on or after 1st January 2004 a corporate general insurer enters into a qualifying contract, other than a reinsurance to close contract, with another person ("the reinsurer") and—

(i) the corporate general insurer and the reinsurer are connected companies; or

(ii) the qualifying contract is, or forms part of, a transaction, as a result of which a company connected with the corporate general insurer ("the connected company") directly or indirectly agrees to meet a liability of the corporate general insurer or any further liability representing that liability, through any number of such agreements ("the replacement agreements"); and

(*b*) Rule 4.1C applies.][1]

[4.1B This Rule is satisfied if—

(*a*) on or after 1st January 2004, as a result of—

(i) a relevant transaction between a corporate general insurer and a company with which it is connected ("a connected company"), or

(ii) a series of transactions having the same effect as a relevant transaction between a corporate general insurer and a connected company,

the connected company directly or indirectly replaces the corporate general insurer as a party to a contract of insurance including by way of novation; and

(*b*) Rule 4.1C applies.][1]

[4.1C This Rule applies if the person assuming the liabilities—

(*a*) is not within the charge to corporation tax in respect of income arising from the qualifying contract or the relevant replacement agreement, assuming there were such income; and

(*b*) is not a controlled foreign company in relation to which—

(i) an apportionment under section 747(3) falls to be made regarding, or

(ii) section 748(1)(a) applies to,

the accounting period in which the qualifying contract is made.

This is subject to the following qualification.

This Rule applies only to the extent that the qualifying contract reinsures liabilities represented in technical provisions which the corporate general insurer has previously taken into account.

In this Rule "the person assuming the liabilities" means, as the case requires, the reinsurer referred to in Rule 4.1A(*a*) or the connected company referred to in Rule 4.1A(*a*)(ii).][1]

4.2. Where, or to the extent that, this Rule applies, the qualifying contract [or the relevant transaction][1] shall be ignored for the purposes of Rule 3, and accordingly—

(*a*) premiums paid under that contract [or that transaction][1] shall be ignored for the purposes of paragraph (*c*) of Rule 3.1, and

(*b*) the claims paid, bonuses and rebates and provisions for claims for the purposes of paragraphs (*a*), (*b*) and (*d*) of Rule 3.1. shall be calculated without deduction for reinsurance, so that each such liability shall be calculated gross.

Amendments—[1] Rules 4.1–4.1C substituted for Rule 4.1; words in Rule 4.2; by the General Insurance Reserves (Tax) (Amendment) Regulations, SI 2003/2862 regs 3, 5 with effect from 5 December 2003.

Rule 5

5.1. Discount the amount of each liability as defined in Rule 3 to the present value of the liability as at the balance sheet date, by the application of a discount factor, reflecting the time value of money between the balance sheet date and the date of payment of the liability (the period between those dates being referred to as "the discount period"), subject to Rule 5.2.

5.2. The discount period for any liability shall not extend later than 10 years after—

(*a*) the date on which the corresponding liability to which the provisions relate (as referred to in Rule 3.1. in the words preceding paragraph (*a*)) arose (within the meaning in paragraph (*b*) of Rule 2.1.), or

(*b*) the end of the general insurer's first period of account which began on or after 1 January 2000,

whichever is the later.

5.3. It shall be assumed for the purposes of this calculation that the provisions mentioned in paragraph (*d*) of Rule 3.1. were a single payment made by the general insurer on the recalculation date.

5.4. The discount rate for the whole of the discount period to be used in calculating the discount factor shall be determined as follows—

(*a*) in a case where the sterling discount rate is to apply (see Rule 1), the discount rate shall be found from the formula—

(A – 2.3 per cent), or nil per cent, whichever is the greater;

(*b*) in a case [where the calculations under these Regulations are carried out in Australian dollars, Canadian dollars, euro, Japanese yen, Swiss francs or United States dollars ("the relevant foreign currency")][1], the discount rate shall be found from the formula—

(A – 2.3 per cent) + (B – C), or nil per cent, whichever is the greater.

5.5. In this Rule—

A is the average of the gross redemption yields, expressed as a percentage, applicable to 5–year British Government Stocks as compiled by the Financial Times, the Institute of Actuaries and the Faculty of Actuaries, which were compiled for each of the first five business days beginning with the day on which the balance sheet date fell or, if that day was not a business day, the first business day thereafter;

B is the London Interbank Offered Rate, in the market which exists between banks in London for the purpose of borrowing and lending funds and dealing in currencies, at which deposits for a term of 12 months were offered in the relevant foreign currency on the day on which the balance sheet date fell (or if that day was not a business day, the first business day thereafter) as determined by the British Banking Association; and

C has the same meaning as B, but with the word "sterling" substituted for the words "the relevant foreign currency".

5.6. The discount shall in principle be computed separately for each liability, save that statistical methods may be used where they may be expected to give approximately the same result as individual calculations.

5.7. Aggregate the discounted liabilities and the result is referred to as "the recalculated provisions" for the earlier period of account.

Amendments—[1] Words in Rule 5.4; in Rule 5.4, para (*b*)(i), (ii) revoked by the General Insurance Reserves (Tax) (Amendment) Regulations, SI 2003/2862 regs 3, 5 with effect from 5 December 2003.

Rule 6

6.1. Compare the difference between—

(*a*) the original provisions for the earlier period of account, and

(*b*) the recalculated provisions for the earlier period of account,

with a margin for error of 5 per cent of the recalculated provisions for the earlier period of account.

Rule 7

7.1. If the amount of the difference does not exceed the margin for error, the difference is assumed to be nil, for the purposes of that period's recalculation.

7.2. If the amount of the difference exceeds the margin for error, deduct the margin for error from the difference, for the purposes of that period's recalculation.

7.3. The result of Rule 7 represents the cumulative excess or deficiency found from the recalculation under this regulation—

(*a*) in the later period of account, and

(*b*) in any periods of account which fell between the earlier period of account and the later period of account ("intervening periods"),

in relation to the same earlier period of account.

Rule 8

8.1. Compare—

(*a*) the result of Rule 7, with

(*b*) the aggregate excess or deficiency found by combining the results of the recalculation under this regulation in any intervening periods in relation to [the same earlier period of account[1]]—

(i) . . . [1]

(ii) . . . [1]

and find out the adjustment (if any) to the amount mentioned in paragraph (b) above which is necessary to make it equal the amount mentioned in paragraph (a) above. If the adjustment is an excess, that is the amount of the excess referred to in section 107(2). If the adjustment is a deficiency, that is [subject to Rule 8A][1] the amount of the deficiency referred to in section 107(3).

8.2. Where there has been no intervening period (as mentioned in paragraph (*b*) of Rule 7.3.), or the result of paragraph (*b*) of Rule 8.1. is neither an excess nor a deficiency, the result of Rule 7 shall be the amount of the excess referred to in section 107(2), or the amount of the deficiency referred to in section 107(3), as the case may be.

Amendments—[1] Words in Rule 8.1 inserted by the General Insurance Reserves (Tax) (Amendment) Regulations, SI 2003/2862 regs 3, 5 with effect from 5 December 2003.

[Rule 8A

8A.1 This Rule applies if, in respect of the provisions made for the earlier period of account—

(*a*) an election has been made under section 107(4) for the earlier period of account in question, and

(*b*) the result of applying Rule 8 is a deficiency.][1]

[8A.2 Where Rule 8A.1 applies, apply Rules 6 to 8 but, in carrying out the calculation made at the end of the later period of account, add to the amount of the original provisions—

(*a*) the amount of any losses set off, under section 393 of the Taxes Act (losses other than terminal losses of a trade) against the trading income of the company's general insurance business for the period of account for which an election under section 107(4) was made in respect of the provisions for the earlier period of account; and

(*b*) any amount which remains to be set off against the profits of the company's general insurance business for the period of account for which an election under section 107(4) was made in respect of the provisions for the earlier period of account under—

(i) section 393A of the Taxes Act (trading losses: set off against the profits of the same or an earlier accounting period);

(ii) Chapter 4 of Part 10 of the Taxes Act (group relief);

(iii) section 83 of, and Schedule 8 to the Finance Act 1996 (non-trading deficit on loan relationships);

(iv) paragraph 35 of Schedule 29 to the Finance Act 2002 (non-trading losses on intangible fixed assets); and

(v) other charges on the income of the company;

after treating any other profits of the general insurer for the earlier period as being reduced in priority to the profits of its general insurance business.

This is subject to the following qualifications.][1]

[8A.3 The qualifications referred to in Rule 8A.2 are that—

(*a*) the total amount added in accordance with it to the provisions for all earlier periods of account taken together shall not exceed the sum of the amounts found under paragraphs (a) and (b) of that Rule; and

(*b*) the adjustment made under that Rule shall not exceed the amount of the technical provisions for the earlier period of account [for which an election under section 107(4) was made in respect of the provision for the earlier period][2].][1]

[8A.4 Compare the result of applying Rule 8A.2 with that found before applying it.

If both the amounts are deficiencies, for the purposes only of Rule 9 the smaller deficiency is the amount referred to in section 107(3).

If the result of applying Rule 8A.2 is an excess—

(*a*) it is disregarded for the purposes of section 107(2); and

(*b*) the deficiency produced by Rule 8 is disregarded for the purposes of section 107(3).][1]

[8A.5 If any amount mentioned in Rule 8A.2 is amended in accordance with any provision of the Taxes Act, the adjustment made under that Rule shall be amended accordingly.][1]

Amendments—[1] Rules 8A.1–8A.5, inserted by the General Insurance Reserves (Tax) (Amendment) Regulations, SI 2003/2862 regs 3, 5 with effect from 5 December 2003.

[2] In para (3), words in Rule 8A.3(*b*) inserted by the General Insurance Reserves (Tax) (Amendment) Regulations, SI 2005/3289 regs 2, 3 with effect from 21 December 2005.

Rule 9

9.1. Interest shall be calculated on the amount of the result of Rule 8, [at the rate or rates specified in respect of the period mentioned below][1] in Regulation 3ZA(1) of the Taxes (Interest Rate) Regulations 1989—

(*a*) but as if there were deducted [from the amount of such interest][1] corporation tax at the rate fixed for companies generally (within the meaning in section 13(1) of the Taxes Act) for the later period of account, and

(*b*) save that the rate of interest is a compound rate, with annual rests,

from the date when corporation tax for the earlier period of account became due and payable [until the stop date][1].

[9.1A Interest shall be calculated on the amount of the result of Rule 8 or 8A (as the case requires) in respect of the period—

(*a*) beginning with the stop date, and

(*b*) ending with the date when corporation tax for the later period of account becomes due and payable at the rate specified in regulation 3ZA(1) of the Taxes (Interest Rate) Regulations 1989,

but as if there were deducted from the amount of such interest corporation tax at the rate fixed for companies generally (within the meaning of section 13(1) of the Taxes Act) for the later period of account.][1]

[9.1B In Rules 9.1 and 9.1A the "stop date" is the earlier of—

(*a*) the date when corporation tax for the later period of account becomes due and payable; and

(*b*) the tenth anniversary of the date on which corporation tax for the earlier period of account became due and payable.

Subsection (1) of section 59D of the Taxes Management Act 1970 (day when corporation tax due and payable) applies for the purposes of this Rule and Rules 9.1 and 9.1A as it applies for the purposes of that section but as if the references in that subsection to an accounting period were to a period of account.][1]

9.2. Where the later period of account falls in more than one financial year, the rates of corporation tax for those financial years shall be apportioned to the later period of account on a daily basis.

9.3. The amount of interest so calculated is the amount to be treated as a receipt or an expense, as the case may be, in accordance with section 107, and is the amount of a receipt or expense, as the case may be, referred to, or to be taken into account in a computation of profits and losses under, [sections 92 to 92C][2] of the Finance Act 1993, in a case where those sections apply.

Amendments—[1] Words in Rule 9 substituted; by the General Insurance Reserves (Tax) (Amendment) Regulations, SI 2003/2862 regs 3, 5 with effect from 5 December 2003.

[2] Words in Rule 9.3 substituted, by the General Insurance Reserves (Tax) (Amendment) Regulations, SI 2005/3289 regs 2, 3 with effect from 21 December 2005.

Rule 10

10.1 No amount representing provisions for unearned premiums or provisions for unexpired risks shall be determined as excessive or insufficient for the purposes of section 107.

4 Provisions supplementing regulation 3

(1) Paragraph (2) applies where a general insurer ("the transferor") transfers the whole or part of its general business to another body ("the transferee") by—

[(*a*) a transfer effected under a scheme falling within section 105 of the Financial Services and Markets Act 2000, including an excluded scheme falling within Case 2, 3 or 4 of subsection (3) of that section, or][1]

[(*ab*) a scheme which would be an insurance business transfer scheme but for section 105(1)(b) of the Financial Services and Markets Act 2000;][2]

[(*b*) a transfer in accordance with an authorisation granted outside the United Kingdom for the purposes of Article 12 of Council Directive 92/49/EC on the co-ordination of the laws, regulations and administrative provisions relating to direct insurance other than life assurance and amending Directives 73/329/EEC and 88/357/EEC,][2]

on or after the date on which these Regulations come into force.

[(1A) Paragraph (2) also applies where, as a result of—

(*a*) a relevant transaction effected after 5th December 2003 between a corporate general insurer and another company—

(i) with which it is connected, and

(ii) which is within the charge to corporation tax in respect of that transaction, or

(*b*) a series of transactions having the same effect as a relevant transaction effected after 5th December 2003 between two companies which—

(i) have been connected with each other at any time in the course of that series of transactions, and

(ii) are within the charge to corporation tax in respect of the relevant transaction,

one of those companies directly or indirectly replaces the other as the insurer under a contract of insurance, or as the reinsurer under a contract of reinsurance, including (in either case) by way of novation.][2]

(2) Where this paragraph applies, the transferor and the transferee shall be treated for the purposes of section 107 and regulation 3 as if—

(*a*) technical provisions made and taken into account by the transferor, so far as they relate to the general business transferred, had been made and taken into account by the transferee, . . . [2]

[(*ab*) an election made under section 107(4) by the transferor had been made by the transferee; and][2]

(*b*) any other act or thing mentioned in Rules 1 to 9 in regulation 3(3) and regulation 5 which was done to or by the transferor, so far as it relates to the general business transferred, had been done to or by the transferee.

[(2A) In paragraph (2)(*a*) "technical provisions made and taken into account by the transferor" means, in relation to a period of account in which a transfer of business occurs, the technical provisions which would have been made and taken into account had the transferor's period of account ended immediately before the transfer.

The time at which the technical provisions are treated as made and taken into account by this paragraph shall be treated as the end of a period of account for the purposes of regulation 3(3) (and an election under section 107(4) may accordingly be made in respect of that period).][2]

(3) Where Rule 4 in regulation 3(3) would apply but for the condition in [Rule 4.1C][2] not being satisfied, in a case falling within [Rule 4.1A(*a*)(i)][2] the reinsurer, and in a case falling within [Rule 4.1A(*a*)(ii)][2] the connected company (and the relevant person is referred to as "the transferee"), and [the corporate general insurer][2], shall be treated for the purposes of section 107 and regulation 3 as if—

(*a*) technical provisions made and taken into account by the [corporate][2] general insurer, so far as they relate to the liabilities reinsured, had been made and taken into account by the transferee,

(*b*) premiums paid under the contract were ignored, and

(*c*) any other act or thing mentioned in [Rules 1 to 10][2] in regulation 3(3) and regulation 5 which was done to or by the [corporate][2] general insurer, so far as it relates to the liabilities reinsured, had been done to or by the transferee.

Amendments—[1] Sub-para (1)(*a*) substituted by the Financial Services and Markets Act 2000 (Consequential Amendments) (Taxes) Order, SI 2001/3629 art 193(1)(*a*) with effect from 1 December 2001, immediately after the coming into force of the Financial Services and Markets Act 2000 ss 411, 432(1), Sch 20 (and SI 2001/3629 Pts 1 and 2). The amendment has effect for any transfer under a scheme falling within the Financial Services and Markets Act 2000 s 105, including an excluded scheme falling within Case 2, 3 or 4 of the Financial Services and Markets Act 2000 s 105(3).

[2] Para (1)(*ab*), (*b*) substituted for para (1)(*b*); word in para (2)(*a*) revoked; paras (1A), (2)(*ab*), (2A) inserted; and words in para (3) substituted; by the General Insurance Reserves (Tax) (Amendment) Regulations, SI 2003/2862 regs 3, 6 with effect from 5 December 2003.

5 [Currency accounting and relevant discount rate

(1) Subject to paragraph (3), in respect of a general insurer's business to which section 92B of the Finance Act 1993 applies, any calculation required under these Regulations shall be made in the functional currency.

(2) Subject to paragraph (3), in respect of a general insurer's business to which section 92C of the Finance Act 1993 applies, any calculation required under these Regulations shall be made in the accounts currency.

(3) In respect of any foreign operation, so much of any calculation required under these Regulations as relates to that operation shall be made in the currency in which the activities of the foreign operation are conducted.

(4) Where paragraph (3) applies any amount of interest calculated in accordance with these Regulations to be treated as a receipt or expense under Rule 9.3 shall be translated into the currency in which profits or losses are required to be computed under sections 92 to 92C of the Finance Act 1993 by reference to the appropriate exchange rate.

(5) If the currency determined by paragraphs (1) to (3) to be used in calculations under these Regulations is one of the currencies mentioned in paragraph (b) of Rule 5.4, the discount rate to be applied to those calculations shall be found in accordance with the formula in that paragraph, and in any other case shall be found in accordance with the formula in paragraph (*a*) of Rule 5.4.

(6) In this regulation—

"accounts currency" has the meaning given in section 92C(1) and (2) of the Finance Act 1993;

"appropriate exchange rate" has the meaning given in section 92D(2) of the Finance Act 1993;

"foreign operation" means—

(*a*) in the case of a general insurer not resident in the United Kingdom, its permanent establishment in the United Kingdom, and

(*b*) in any other case, an entity that is a subsidiary, associate, joint venture or branch of a general insurer the activities of which are conducted in a currency other than the functional currency;

"functional currency" has the meaning given in section 92E(3) of the Finance Act 1993.][1]

Amendments—[1] This regulation substituted by the General Insurance Reserves (Tax) (Amendment) Regulations, SI 2005/3289 regs 2, 4(1) with effect from 21 December 2005.

If an election was made before 31 December 2003 under para (1) as it stood immediately before the substitution of this regulation made by the General Insurance Reserves (Tax) (Amendment) Regulations, SI 2003/2862, the currency chosen under para (5) as it stood before that substitution may continue to be used as it might have been had the substitution made by SI 2005/3289 para 4(1) not occurred: SI 2005/3289 reg 4(2).

Also, the currency determined by this regulation as it stood immediately before the substitution made by SI 2005/3289 para 4(1) to be used in calculations in respect of part of a general insurer's business may continue to be used in relation to that part of the general insurer's business as it might have been had the substitution not occurred: SI 2005/3289 reg 4(3).

6 Excluded descriptions of general insurer

[(1)] [2] The descriptions of general insurer which are excluded from the operation of section 107(1) to (4) are—

(*a*) a company which [is in][2] insolvent liquidation (within the meaning in section 214(6) of the Insolvency Act 1986 ("the Act") or Article 178(6) of the Insolvency (Northern Ireland) Order 1989 ("the Order")), where the exclusion takes effect from the date on which it goes into liquidation (within the meaning in section 247(2) of the Act or Article 6(2) of the Order);

(*b*) a company in relation to which an administration order has been made under . . . [1] Article 21 of the Order [or a company which is in administration within the meaning of Schedule B1 to the Act][1];

(*c*) a company in respect of which a provisional liquidator [is][2] appointed under section 135 of the Act or Article 115 of the Order; and

(*d*) a company in respect of which a relevant arrangement or compromise (within the meaning in section 74(2) of the Taxes Act) [is in force][2].

[This is subject to the following qualification.][2]

[(2) A general insurer is not excluded from the operation of section 107 by virtue of paragraph (1)(*c*) or (*d*) unless—

(*a*) it is insolvent at the time the provisional liquidator is appointed or the relevant arrangement or compromise comes into force; or

(*b*) in a case falling within paragraph (1)(*d*), it would be insolvent but for the relevant arrangement or compromise coming into force.][2]

Amendments—[1] In para (1)(*b*), words revoked and words inserted by the Enterprise Act 2002 (Insolvency) Order, SI 2003/2096 art 5, Schedule para 78 with effect from 15 September 2003. However, this amendment does not apply in any case where a petition for an administration order was presented before 15 September 2003: SI 2003/2096 art 6.

[2] Para (1) numbered as such, words in sub-paras (*a*), (*c*), (*d*) thereof substituted, and words inserted; and para (2) inserted, by the General Insurance Reserves (Tax) (Amendment) Regulations, SI 2003/2862 regs 3, 8 with effect from 5 December 2003.

7 "Technical provisions" in relation to an underwriting member

(1) "Technical provisions" in relation to an underwriting member and the premium paid or treated as paid by him under a reinsurance to close contract means—

(*a*) where the member is a continuing member, that is, a member not only of the syndicate as a member of which he pays, or is treated as paying, the premium ("the reinsured syndicate") but also of the syndicate as a member of which he receives or is treated as receiving it or part of it ("the reinsurer syndicate"), so much of the premium as equals—

(i) the amount of the premium which he pays or is treated as paying, or

(ii) the amount of the premium which he receives or is treated as receiving,

whichever is the lesser (subject to sub-paragraph (b)); and

(*b*) where the member is not entitled to participate in the underwriting business of the reinsurer syndicate, or his entitlement to participate in either of the reinsured syndicate or the reinsurer syndicate is less than 4 per cent of the whole, none of the premium.

(2) Regulations 3 to 5 shall apply to—

(*a*) any premium or part of a premium treated as "technical provisions" by paragraph (1)(*a*), with the modifications to regulation 3(3) contained in paragraphs (3) to [(5)][1], and

(*b*) any provisions or part of provisions treated as "technical provisions" by paragraph (8), with the modifications contained in paragraphs (3), (4), (5)(*c*) . . . [1] and (7).

(3) In regulation 3(3) in the words preceding sub-paragraph (*a*), for the reference to provisions for claims outstanding there shall be substituted a reference to technical provisions.

(4) In Rule 2—

(*a*) for the reference to provisions for claims outstanding, there shall be substituted a reference to technical provisions, and

(*b*) for paragraph (*b*) of Rule 2.1. there shall be substituted—

"(*b*) in any other case, [were provisions][1] for liabilities arising directly from the underwriting member's membership of one or more syndicates, whose closing year was the year immediately preceding the earlier period of account, but excluding liabilities which the member acquired by means of a reinsurance to close contract, the premium for which was treated as a technical provision for the same member for that preceding year.".

(5) In Rule 3—

(*a*) in paragraph (*a*) "claims paid" shall be construed as a reference to claims paid by the member in consequence of his membership of the reinsurer syndicate or of any further syndicate which, directly or indirectly, reinsures the liabilities to which the provisions relate under any further reinsurance to close contracts;

(*b*) where any claim, bonus, rebate or premium was paid by the member as a member of the reinsurer syndicate, the payment shall be treated for the purposes of Rules 3 and 5 as made one year later than the date of the actual payment; and

(*c*) in Rule 3.1.(*d*) for the reference to provisions for claims outstanding, there shall be substituted a reference to provisions made for the unpaid liabilities of the reinsurer syndicate where it is an open syndicate.

(6) . . . [1]

(7) The modification contained in this paragraph is the modification to Rule 3 in paragraph (5)(*b*) omitting the words "as a member of the reinsurer syndicate".

(8) "Technical provisions" in relation to an underwriting member and the provisions made for the unpaid liabilities of an open syndicate of which he is a member means—

(*a*) where the member's entitlement to participate in the underwriting business of the open syndicate is equal to or more than 4 per cent of the whole, the share of those provisions which corresponds to his proportionate entitlement; and

(*b*) in any other case, none of the provisions.

(9) In determining a member's entitlement to participate in the business of a syndicate, or share of a premium, for the purposes of paragraphs (1) and (8), there shall be attributed to a member which is a company any entitlement to participate in the relevant syndicate of any company which is connected with the member.

(10) In a case falling within the provisions of both paragraphs (1) and (9), where—

(*a*) there is a change in the entitlement of a company to participate, as between the reinsured syndicate and the reinsurer syndicate, such that,

(*b*) the reinsurance to close contract has the same financial effect as if a liability were transferred from that company to a company connected with it,

the provisions of [sub-paragraphs (a), (ab) and (b) of regulation 4(2)][1] shall to that extent apply as if there were a transfer of business between those companies.

(11) A syndicate's managing agent (within the meaning in Chapter III of Part II of the Finance Act 1993) shall, on request from a member or former member of the syndicate, provide the member with the information which he needs, and which is within the agent's possession or power, to make a recalculation under regulation 3 (as applied by paragraph (2)) in relation to his proportionate entitlement in the syndicate.

Amendments—[1] References in para (2) substituted and revoked; words in paras (4)(*b*), (10) substituted; para (6) revoked; by the General Insurance Reserves (Tax) (Amendment) Regulations, SI 2003/2862 regs 3, 9 with effect from 5 December 2003.

8 Elections under section 107(4), or paragraph 4(2) of Schedule 24 to the Taxes Act

[(1) An election by a general insurer for the purposes of section 107(4) or for the purposes of paragraph 4(2) of Schedule 24 to the Taxes Act may be made or withdrawn at any time up to whichever is the last of the following dates—

(*a*) the first anniversary of the filing date for the company tax return of the company making the election for the period of account in respect of which the election is made;

(*b*) if notice of enquiry is given into that return, 30 days after the enquiry is completed;

(*c*) if, after such an enquiry, the Board amend the return under paragraph 34(2) of Schedule 18 to the Finance Act 1998, 30 days after the notice of the amendment is issued; and

(*d*) if an appeal is brought against such an amendment, 30 days after the date on which the appeal is finally determined.][1]

[(1A) Paragraph (1) applies to an underwriting member other than a body corporate with the substitution for paragraphs (*a*) to (*c*) of—

"(*a*) the first anniversary of 31st January next following the end of the year of assessment in which falls the end of the period of account in respect of which the election is made;

(*b*) if notice of enquiry is given into the underwriting member's tax return for that year of assessment, 30 days after the enquiry is completed;

(*c*) if after such an enquiry the Board amend the return under section 28A of the Taxes Management Act 1970, 30 days after the amendment of the return;".][1]

(2) Where a general insurer delivers a tax return based wholly or partly on accounts drawn up using the method described in paragraph 52 of Schedule 9A (which provides for a technical provision to be made in the accounts which is later replaced by a provision for estimated claims outstanding) the period in [paragraph (1)(*a*)][1] is extended until two years from the date on which the provision was replaced.

(3) Where a general insurer which is a controlled foreign company draws up accounts using a method falling within section 755B(2), the period of twenty months mentioned in paragraph 4(2) of Schedule 24 to the Taxes Act (elections by a United Kingdom resident company or companies) shall be extended until two years immediately following the close of the underwriting year (within the meaning in section 754AA(11)).

[(4) An election under section 107(4) by a controlled foreign company may be communicated, on its behalf, by the person or persons resident in the United Kingdom by whom it is controlled to the Board.][1]

[(5) An election under section 107(4) shall be made in writing and shall specify—

(*a*) the period of account in respect of which the election is made;

(*b*) the earlier period or periods of account to which the technical provisions in question relate;

(*c*) the amount of technical provisions being disclaimed in respect of each such period; and

(*d*) the currency in which the technical provisions being disclaimed are expressed.][1]

Amendments—[1] Paras (1), (1A) substituted for para (1), words in para (2) substituted, and paras (4), (5) inserted; by the General Insurance Reserves (Tax) (Amendment) Regulations, SI 2003/2862 regs 3,10 with effect from 5 December 2003.

9 Generally

For the purposes of any computation under these Regulations any necessary apportionments shall be made and the method of apportionment adopted shall, subject to the express provisions of these Regulations, be just and reasonable.

10 [Modification: companies subject to these Regulations on or after 5th December 2003

(1) Paragraph (2) applies to a company if any of the following Cases applies.

Case 1

The company is one to which these Regulations first apply on or after 5th December 2003 by reason of its becoming—

(*a*) a controlled foreign company on or after that date; or

(*b*) subject to corporation tax for the first time on of after that date.

Case 2

The company, already being subject to corporation tax in respect of its general insurance business, is charged to tax under Case I of Schedule D in respect of that business for the first time for a period of account beginning on or after 5th December 2003.

Case 3

The company is a controlled foreign company and the first period of account in respect of which—

(*a*) an apportionment falls to be made under section 747(3), or

(*b*) section 748(1)(*a*) applies,

is a period of account ending on or after 5th December 2003.

Case 4

The company is one to which these Regulations apply on 5th December 2003 by reason only of the amendments made by regulation 8 of the General Insurance Reserves (Tax) (Amendment) Regulations 2003 to regulation 6 of these Regulations.

(2) In the case of a company to which this paragraph applies, regulations 2 to 9 of these Regulations shall apply as if references to the first earlier period of account were to the period of account preceding that during which the company first becomes subject to these Regulations and references to original technical provisions shall be construed accordingly.

(3) If paragraph (2) applies, an election may be made under section 107(4) in respect of the original technical provisions of the period of account preceding that during which the company in question first becomes subject to these Regulations.][1]

Modification—Group Relief for Overseas Losses (Modification of the Corporation Tax Acts for Non-resident Insurance Companies) (No 2) Regulations 2006, SI 2006/3389, reg 11 (modification of reg 10 in relation to an EEA general insurer). Note that SI 2006/3389 is revoked by SI 2008/2646 reg 5 with effect for accounting periods beginning on or after 28 October 2008.

Amendments—[1] This regulation inserted by the General Insurance Reserves (Tax) (Amendment) Regulations, SI 2003/2862 regs 3,11 with effect from 5 December 2003.

2001/2541

CAPITAL ALLOWANCES (ENERGY-SAVING PLANT AND MACHINERY) ORDER 2001

Made by the Treasury under CAA 2001 ss 45A(3), (4), 45B(1), 45C(2)(b), (3)(b) and 180A(2)

Made . . . . *16 July 2001*

Laid before the House of Commons . . . . *16 July 2001*

Coming into force . . . . *7 August 2001*

1 Citation and commencement

This Order may be cited as the Capital Allowances (Energy-saving Plant and Machinery) Order 2001 and shall come into force on 7th August 2001.

2 Interpretation

In this Order—

"Capital Allowances Act" means the Capital Allowances Act 2001;

["Energy Technology Criteria List" means the list dated [7 September][2] and issued by the Secretary of State for [Business, Energy and Industrial Strategy][2] on [7 September][2];][1]

["Energy Technology Product List" means the list dated [7 September][2] and issued by the Secretary of State for [Business, Energy and Industrial Strategy][2] on [7 September][2].][1]

Amendments—[1] Definitions of "Energy Technology Criteria List" and "Energy Technology Product List" substituted by the Capital Allowances (Energy-saving Plant and Machinery) (Amendment) Order, SI 2011/2221 arts 2, 3 with effect from 1 October 2011.

[2] In definitions of "Energy Technology Criteria List" and "Energy Technology Product List", dates substituted, and words substituted for words "Energy and Climate Change", by the Capital Allowances (Energy-saving Plant and Machinery) (Amendment) Order, SI 2015/1508 art 2 with effect from 6 October 2016. Substituted dates were previously 2 July 2015.

3 Description of energy-saving plant and machinery

(1) Plant or machinery is energy-saving plant or machinery for the purposes of section 45A of the Capital Allowances Act (expenditure on energy-saving plant or machinery) if—

(*a*) it falls within a technology class specified in the Energy Technology Criteria List,

(*b*) it meets the energy-saving criteria set out in that List, and

(*c*) [subject to [paragraphs (3)[", (4) and (5)][8]][2]][1] in the case of plant or machinery falling within any of the technology classes specified in paragraph (2), it is of a type that—

(i) is specified in, and has not been removed from, the Energy Technology Product List, or

(ii) has been accepted for inclusion in the Energy Technology Product List.

(2) The technology classes specified for the purposes of paragraph (1)(*c*) are—

(*a*) boilers,
(*b*) motors and drives,
(*c*) refrigeration,
(*d*) . . . [4]
[(*e*) heat pumps,][1]
[(*f*) radiant and warm air heaters,][1]
[(*g*) compressed air equipment,][1]
[(*h*) solar thermal systems.][1]
[(*i*) automatic monitoring and targeting equipment.][2]
[(*j*) air-to-air energy recovery equipment;][3]
(*k*) . . . [6]
[(*l*) heating, ventilation and air conditioning [equipment;][5]][3]
[(*m*) uninterruptible power supplies;][5]
[(*n*) high speed hand air dryers][7]

[(3) In the case of solar thermal systems either the solar thermal system or the solar collector included in the system must be of a type within paragraph (i) or (ii) of article 3(1)(*c*).][1]
[(4) In the case of automatic monitoring and targeting equipment, automatic monitoring and targeting systems need not be of a type within paragraph (i) or (ii) of article 3(1)(*c*).][8]
[(5) In the case of heat pumps, air source split and multi split (including variable refrigerant flow) heat pumps need not be of a type within paragraph (i) or (ii) of article 3(1)(*c*).][8]

Amendments—[1] Words in para (1)(*c*) inserted, and paras (2)(*e*)–(*h*), (3) inserted, by the Capital Allowances (Energy-saving Plant and Machinery) (Amendment) Order, SI 2002/1818 regs 2, 4 with effect from 5 August 2002.
[2] In para (1)(*c*), words substituted for the words "paragraph (3)", and paras (2)(*i*) and (4) inserted, by the Capital Allowances (Energy-saving Plant and Machinery) (Amendment) Order, SI 2003/1744 arts 2, 4 with effect from 5 August 2003.
[3] Para (3)(*j*)–(*l*) inserted by the Capital Allowances (Energy-saving Plant and Machinery) (Amendment) Order, SI 2004/2093 art 2(1), (3) with effect from 26 August 2004.
[4] Para (2)(*d*) revoked by the Capital Allowances (Energy-saving Plant and Machinery) (Amendment) Order, SI 2006/2233, art 2(1), (3), with effect from 7 September 2006.
[5] In para (2)(*l*), words substituted for words "zone controls.", and para (2)(*m*) inserted, by the Capital Allowances (Energy-saving Plant and Machinery) (Amendment) Order, SI 2009/1863 arts 2, 4 with effect from 4 August 2009.
[6] Para (2)(*k*) (compact heat exchangers) revoked by the Capital Allowances (Energy-saving Plant and Machinery) (Amendment) Order, SI 2010/2286 arts 2, 4 with effect from 8 October 2010.
[7] Para (2)(*n*) (high-speed hand air dryers) inserted by the Capital Allowances (Energy-saving Plant and Machinery) (Amendment) Order, SI 2011/2221 arts 2, 4 with effect from 1 October 2011.
[8] In para (1)(*c*), words substituted for words "and (4)", para (4) substituted, and para (5) inserted by the Capital Allowances (Energy-saving Plant and Machinery) (Amendment) Order, SI 2014/2541 arts 2, 4 with effect from 7 August 2014.

4 Certification of energy-saving plant and machinery

[(1) In the case of plant or machinery falling within the technology class "Combined Heat and Power" specified in the Energy Technology Criteria List no section 45A allowance may be made unless a relevant certificate of energy efficiency is in force with respect to that plant or machinery.][1]
(2) In paragraph (1) "section 45A allowance" and "relevant certificate of energy efficiency" have the meanings given by section 45B of the Capital Allowances Act.

Amendments—[1] Para (1) substituted by the Capital Allowances (Energy-saving Plant and Machinery) (Amendment) Order, SI 2011/2221 arts 2, 5 with effect from 1 October 2011.

5 Energy-saving components of plant or machinery

Where one or more components of certain plant or machinery (but not all of that plant or machinery)—

[(*a*) meets the conditions set out in sub-paragraphs (*a*) to (*c*) of article 3(1), and][1]
[(*b*) falls within any of the technology classes specified in sub-paragraphs (a) to (*c*), (*f*), (*g*), (*j*)[,][2] (*l*) [and (*m*)][2] of article 3(2),][1]

the amount specified in respect of each such component for the purposes of section 45C of the Capital Allowances Act is the amount specified in the Energy Technology Product List in relation to that component.

Amendments—[1] Sub-paras (*a*), (*b*) substituted by the Capital Allowances (Energy-saving Plant and Machinery) (Amendment) Order, SI 2005/2424 arts 2, 4 with effect from 22 September 2005.
[2] In sub-para (*b*), comma substituted for word "and", and words inserted, by the Capital Allowances (Energy-saving Plant and Machinery) (Amendment) Order, SI 2009/1863 arts 2, 5 with effect from 4 August 2009.

6 Energy services providers

The class of plant or machinery specified for the purposes of section 180A(2) of the Capital Allowances Act is the technology class "Combined Heat and Power" specified in the Energy Technology Criteria List.

Commentary—*Simon's Taxes* **B3.324**.

2001/3973

FRIENDLY SOCIETIES (PROVISIONAL REPAYMENTS FOR EXEMPT BUSINESS) (AMENDMENT) REGULATIONS 2001

Made by the Treasury under FA 1993 s 121, FA 2001 s 87(3), (4)

Made . . . . *11 December 2001*
Laid before the House of Commons . . . . *11 December 2001*
Coming into force . . . . *1 January 2002*

1 Citation, commencement and effect

These Regulations may be cited as the Friendly Societies (Provisional Repayments for Exempt Business) (Amendment) Regulations 2001 and shall come into force on 1st January 2002, and shall have effect in relation to accounting periods of friendly societies beginning on or after 1st January 2002.

2 Interpretation

In these Regulations—

"the principal Regulations" means the Friendly Societies (Provisional Repayments for Exempt Business) Regulations 1999;

"Schedule 19AB" means Schedule 19AB to the Income and Corporation Taxes Act 1988.

3 Amendments to the principal Regulations and further modifications to Schedule 19AB

(*amends* SI 1999/622 reg 2).

4 (*amends* SI 1999/622 reg 3(1)).

5 (*omits* SI 1999/622 reg 3(3)).

6 (*amends* TA 1988 Sch 19AB para 1(1) as substituted by SI 1999/622 reg 4(2)).

7 (*amends* TA 1988 Sch 19AB para 1(5)–(5E) as substituted by SI 1999/622 reg 5(2)).

8 (*omits* SI 1999/622 regs 6, 7).

9 (*amends* SI 1999/622 reg 8).

10 (*amends* SI 1999/622 reg 9).

11 (*amends* SI 1999/622 reg 10).

12 (*amends* SI 1999/622 reg 12).

13 In the heading to Schedule 19AB for the words "pension business—payments on account of tax credits and deducted tax" there shall be substituted the words "tax exempt business—payments on account of tax credits".

14 The Schedule to these Regulations sets out the text of Schedule 19AB as applied by the principal Regulations and these Regulations.

SCHEDULE

Regulation 14

"SCHEDULE 19AB TAX EXEMPT BUSINESS—PAYMENTS ON ACCOUNT OF TAX CREDITS

Entitlement to certain payments on account

1—

(1) A friendly society carrying on both tax exempt business and business other than tax exempt business shall for each provisional repayment period in an accounting period be entitled on a claim made in that behalf to a payment (in this Schedule referred to as a 'provisional repayment') of an amount equal to—

(*a*) –(*b*) . . .

(*c*) as respects any distribution made on or after 6 April 1999 and before 6 April 2004 that—

(i) is received by the society in that provisional repayment period, and

(ii) is referable to its tax exempt business,

(iii)

the appropriate portion of any tax credit in respect of that distribution.

(2) For the purposes of this paragraph, a 'provisional repayment period' of a society—

(*a*) shall begin whenever—

(i) the society begins, at a time when it is carrying on only tax exempt business, to carry on business other than tax exempt business;

(ii) the society begins, at a time when it is carrying on only business other than tax exempt business, to carry on tax exempt business;

(iii) an accounting period of the society begins at a time when the society is carrying on both tax exempt business and business other than tax exempt business; or

(iv) a provisional repayment period of the society ends, at a time when the society is carrying on both tax exempt business and business other than tax exempt business; and

(*b*) shall end on the first occurrence of either of the following—

(i) the expiration of three months from the beginning of the provisional repayment period; or

(ii) the end of an accounting period of the society.

(3) . . .

(4) The provisional fraction for the purposes of this paragraph for an accounting period which begins before 6 April 2004 shall be such fraction as the society may reasonably estimate, being a fraction which is not likely to be greater than the relevant fraction for its tax exempt business which would be determined in accordance with subsections (5) to (9B) of section 432A for that accounting period.

(5) . . .

(5A) In sub-paragraph (1)(*c*) above 'the appropriate portion' means—

(*a*) where the distribution in question is income arising from assets linked to tax exempt basic life assurance and general annuity business or to tax exempt class IV business the profits of which are exempt from tax by virtue of section 460(1) ('section 460(1) exempt business'), the whole;

(*b*) where the distribution in question is income arising from assets of the society's overseas life assurance fund, the fraction whose numerator is the mean of the opening and closing liabilities to policyholders in respect of the society's tax exempt overseas life assurance business and whose denominator is the opening and closing liabilities to policyholders in respect of the whole of the society's overseas life assurance business;

(*c*) if and to the extent that the distribution in question is income arising from assets of the society's long term business fund but, on the assumption that section 460(1) exempt business were a separate category of business within section 432A, is not referable to a category of business by virtue of subsection (3) or (4) of that section, the provisional fraction;

(*d*) except as provided by paragraph (*a*), (*b*) or (*c*) above, none.

(5B) . . .

(5C) In determining the provisional fraction for the purposes of sub-paragraph (5A)(*c*) above, tax exempt basic life assurance and general annuity business and section 460(1) exempt business shall be taken to be a single category for the purposes of section 432A(5).

(5D) In sub-paragraph (5A) above references to assets of the society's long term business fund—

(*a*) as respects societies to which regulation 13(1) of the Friendly Societies (Modification of the Corporation Tax Acts) Regulations 1997 applies, shall be construed in accordance with the definition in subsection (11) of section 432A, read with subsections (12) to (14) of that section, as those subsections are added by regulation 13(5) of those Regulations;

(*b*) as respects other societies, shall be construed in accordance with the definitions of 'long term business' (as substituted by regulation 6(4) of those Regulations) and 'long term business fund' in section 431(2).

(5E) In sub-paragraphs (5A) and (5C) above—

'tax exempt basic life assurance and general annuity business' shall be construed in accordance with the definition inserted in section 431(2) by regulation 6(2) of the Friendly Societies (Modification of the Corporation Tax Acts) Regulations 1997;

'tax exempt class IV business' shall be construed in accordance with the definition inserted in section 431(2) by regulation 7(2) of those Regulations;

'tax exempt overseas life assurance business' shall be construed in accordance with section 441(4D).

(6) Paragraphs 57 to 60 of Schedule 18 to the Finance Act 1998 (general provisions as to procedure on claims and elections) do not apply to a claim for a provisional repayment.

(6A) A claim for a provisional repayment shall be in such form as the Board may determine and the form of claim shall provide for a declaration to the effect that all the particulars given in the form are correctly stated to the best of the knowledge and belief of the person making the claim.

(7) A provisional repayment for a provisional repayment period shall be regarded as a payment on account of the amounts (if any) which the society would, apart from this Schedule, be entitled to be paid in respect of its tax exempt business for the accounting period in which that provisional repayment period falls, in respect of—

(*a*) . . .

(*b*) tax credits in respect of distributions received by the society in that accounting period and referable to its tax exempt business,

on a claim such as is mentioned in paragraph 9(3) of Schedule 18 to the Finance Act 1998 in respect of that accounting period.

(8)–(11) . . .

2

Repayment, with interest, of excessive provisional repayments

3—

(1) In any case where—

(*a*) a friendly society's self-assessment for an accounting period becomes final, and

(*b*) the aggregate amount of the provisional repayments made to the society for that accounting period exceeds the appropriate amount,

the excess, together with the amount of any relevant interest, shall be treated for the purposes of paragraph 52 of Schedule 18 to the Finance Act 1998 as if it were an amount of corporation tax for that accounting period which had been repaid to the friendly society and which ought not to have been so repaid.

(1A) For the purposes of sub-paragraph (1)(*b*) above, the appropriate amount for an accounting period of a society is the amount (if any) which, on the assumption in sub-paragraph (1B) below and disregarding any provisional repayments, the society would be entitled to be paid when its self-assessment for the period becomes final, in respect of its tax exempt business for that accounting period on a claim such as is mentioned in paragraph 9(3) of Schedule 18 to the Finance Act 1998 in respect of—

(*a*) . . .

(*b*) tax credits in respect of distributions received by the society in that accounting period and referable to its tax exempt business.

(1B) The assumption is that no payments have been made to the society in respect of—

(*a*) . . .

(*b*) tax credits such as are mentioned in paragraph (*b*) of sub-paragraph (1A) above,

before the society's self-assessment for the accounting period in question becomes final.

(1C) . . .

(1D) Paragraph 53 of Schedule 18 to the Finance Act 1998 (time limit for recovery of excessive repayments etc) does not apply to an assessment under paragraph 52 of that Schedule made by virtue of this paragraph.

But such an assessment is not out of time under paragraph 46 of that Schedule (general six year time limit for assessments) if it is made not later than the end of the accounting period following that in which the self-assessment mentioned in sub-paragraph (1)(*a*) above becomes final.

(2) In this paragraph, 'relevant interest' means interest—

(*a*) in so much of the excess referred to in sub-paragraph (1) above as is or was from time to time outstanding,

(*b*) for any period for which it is or was so outstanding, and

(*c*) at the rate applicable under section 178 of the Finance Act 1989 for the purposes of section 87A of the Management Act (interest on overdue corporation tax).

(3) In the application of section 87A of the Management Act in relation to an amount assessed to corporation tax under paragraph 52 of Schedule 18 to the Finance Act 1998 by virtue of this paragraph—

(*a*) the amount so assessed shall be taken to have become due and payable on the date on which that assessment was made; and (*b*) the words '(in accordance with section 59D of this Act)' in subsection (1) shall accordingly be disregarded.

(4) In determining the amount of any relevant interest, any question whether the excess mentioned in sub-paragraph (1) above (in the following provisions of this paragraph referred to as 'the principal') or any part of it is or was 'outstanding' at any time shall be determined in accordance with sub-paragraphs (5) to (8) below.

(5) So much of the principal as does not exceed the amount of the last provisional repayment made to the society for the accounting period in question shall be taken to have become outstanding on the date on which that provisional repayment was made.

(6) So much (if any) of the principal as—

(*a*) exceeds the amount of the provisional repayment referred to in sub-paragraph (5) above, but

(*b*) does not exceed the amount of the preceding provisional repayment for that accounting period,

shall be taken to have become outstanding on the date on which that preceding provisional repayment was made; and so on with any remaining portion of the principal and any preceding provisional repayments for that accounting period.

(7) So much (if any) of the principal as has become outstanding as mentioned in sub-paragraph (5) or (6) above and has at any time neither been repaid to the Board nor been assessed to corporation tax under paragraph 52 of Schedule 18 to the Finance Act 1998 by virtue of this paragraph shall be taken to remain outstanding at that time (and an amount shall accordingly be taken to cease being outstanding only when it is repaid to the Board or when it is so assessed).

(8) For the purposes of sub-paragraph (7) above, any repayment made by the society in respect of an amount paid to it in respect of—

(*a*) . . .

(*b*) tax credits such as are mentioned in paragraph (*b*) of sub-paragraph (1A) above,

shall be treated as a repayment in respect of the principal, taking an earlier such repayment by the society before a later.

(9) In this paragraph 'self-assessment' means an assessment included in a company tax return and includes a reference to such an assessment as amended.

4–5

. . .

6 Interpretation

(1) In this Schedule—

'provisional fraction' shall be construed in accordance with paragraph 1(4) above;

'provisional repayment' means a provisional repayment under paragraph 1 above;

'provisional repayment period' shall be construed in accordance with paragraph 1 above;

'tax exempt business' means any business of a friendly society the profits arising from which are exempt from income tax and corporation tax under section 460(1).

(2) Any reference in this Schedule to a provisional repayment for an accounting period is a reference to a provisional repayment for a provisional repayment period falling within that accounting period.

(3)–(6) . . . "

2001/3974

INDIVIDUAL SAVINGS ACCOUNT (INSURANCE COMPANIES) (AMENDMENT) REGULATIONS 2001

Made by the Treasury under TA 1988 s 333B, FA 2001 s 87(3), (4)

Made . . . .*11 December 2001*
Laid before the House of Commons . . . .*11 December 2001*
Coming into force . . . .*1 January 2002*

1 Citation, commencement and effect

These Regulations may be cited as the Individual Savings Account (Insurance Companies) (Amendment) Regulations 2001 and shall come into force on 1st January 2002, and shall have effect in relation to accounting periods of insurance companies beginning on or after 1st January 2002.

2 Interpretation

In these Regulations—

"the principal Regulations" means the Individual Savings Account (Insurance Companies) Regulations 1998;
"regulation" means a regulation of the principal regulations;
"Schedule 19AB" means Schedule 19AB to the Income and Corporation Taxes Act 1988.

3, 4 Amendments to the principal Regulations
(*amend* SI 1998/1871 regs 20, 21)

5 The Schedule to these Regulations sets out the text of Schedule 19AB as applied by the principal Regulations and these Regulations.

SCHEDULE

Regulation 5

"SCHEDULE 19AB INDIVIDUAL SAVINGS ACCOUNT BUSINESS—PAYMENTS ON ACCOUNT OF TAX CREDITS

1 Entitlement to certain payments on account
(1) An insurance company carrying on individual savings account business shall for each provisional repayment period in an accounting period be entitled on a claim made in that behalf to a payment (in this Schedule referred to as a 'provisional repayment') of an amount equal to—
(*a*) . . .
(*b*) the appropriate portion of any tax credit in respect of a distribution received by the company in that provisional repayment period and referable to its individual savings account business,
or of such lesser amount as may be specified in the claim.
(2) For the purposes of this paragraph, a 'provisional repayment period' of a company—
(*a*) shall begin whenever—
(i) the company begins to carry on individual savings account business;
(ii) an accounting period of the company begins, at a time when the company is carrying on such business; or
(iii) a provisional repayment period of the company ends, at a time when the company is carrying on such business; and
(*b*) shall end on the first occurrence of either of the following—
(i) the expiration of three months from the beginning of the provisional repayment period; or
(ii) the end of an accounting period of the company.
(3)–(4) . . .
(4A) The provisional fraction for the purposes of this paragraph for a relevant accounting period shall be such fraction as the company may reasonably estimate, being a fraction which is not likely to be greater than the relevant fraction for its individual savings account business which would be determined in accordance with subsections (5) to (9B) of section 432A for that accounting period.
(4B) In sub-paragraph (4A) above 'relevant accounting period' means—
(*a*) the accounting period in which 6th April 1999 falls, or
(*b*) any succeeding accounting period which begins before 6th April 2004.
(5) In sub-paragraph (1) above 'the appropriate portion' means—
(*a*) in the case of an insurance company carrying on individual savings account business and no other category of long term business, the whole; and
(*b*) in the case of an insurance company carrying on more than one category of long term business—
(i) where the distribution in question is income arising from an asset linked to individual savings account business, the whole; and
(ii) if and to the extent that the distribution in question is income which is not referable to a category of business by virtue of subsection (3) or (4) of section 432A, the provisional fraction; and
(iii) except as provided by sub-paragraph (i) or (ii) above, none.
(6) Paragraphs 57 to 60 of Schedule 18 to the Finance Act 1998 (general provisions as to procedure on claims and elections) do not apply to a claim for a provisional repayment.
(6A) A claim for a provisional repayment shall be in such form as the Board may determine and the form of claim shall provide for a declaration to the effect that all the particulars given in form are correctly stated to the best of the knowledge and belief of the person making the claim.
(7) A provisional repayment for a provisional repayment period shall be regarded as a payment on account of the amounts (if any) which the company would, apart from this Schedule, be entitled to be paid in respect of its individual savings account business for the accounting period in which that provisional repayment period falls, in respect of—
(*a*) . . .

(*b*) tax credits in respect of distributions received by the company in that accounting period and referable to its individual savings account business,

on a claim such as is mentioned in paragraph 9(3) of Schedule 18 to the Finance Act 1998 in respect of that accounting period.

(8)–(11) . . .

2 . . .

3—(1) In any case where—

(*a*) an insurance company's self-assessment for an accounting period becomes final, and

(*b*) the aggregate amount of the provisional repayments made to the company for that accounting period exceeds the appropriate amount,

the excess, together with the amount of any relevant interest, shall be treated for the purposes of paragraph 52 of Schedule 18 to the Finance Act 1998 as if it were an amount of corporation tax for that accounting period which had been repaid to the insurance company and which ought not to have been so repaid.

(1A) For the purposes of sub-paragraph (1)(*b*) above, the appropriate amount for an accounting period of a company is the amount (if any) which, on the assumption in sub-paragraph (1B) below and disregarding any provisional repayments, the company would be entitled to be paid, when its self-assessment for the period becomes final, in respect of its individual savings account business for that accounting period on a claim such as is mentioned in paragraph 9(3) of Schedule 18 to the Finance Act 1998 in respect of—

(*a*) . . .

(*b*) tax credits in respect of distributions received by the company in that accounting period and referable to its individual savings account business.

(1B) The assumption is that no payments have been made to the company in respect of—

(*a*) . . .

(*b*) tax credits such as are mentioned in paragraph (*b*) of sub-paragraph (1A) above,

before the company's self-assessment for the accounting period in question becomes final.

(1C) . . .

(1D) Paragraph 53 of Schedule 18 to the Finance Act 1998 (time limit for recovery of excessive repayments etc) does not apply to an assessment under paragraph 52 of that Schedule made by virtue of this paragraph.

But such an assessment is not out of time under paragraph 46 of that Schedule (general six year time limit for assessments) if it is made not later than the end of the accounting period following that in which the self-assessment mentioned in sub-paragraph (1)(*a*) above becomes final.

(2) In this paragraph, 'relevant interest' means interest—

(*a*) on so much of the excess referred to in sub-paragraph (1) above as is or was from time to time outstanding,

(*b*) for any period for which it is or was so outstanding, and

(*c*) at the rate applicable under section 178 of the Finance Act 1989 for the purposes of section 87A of the Management Act (interest on overdue corporation tax).

(3) In the application of section 87A of the Management Act in relation to an amount assessed to corporation tax under paragraph 52 of Schedule 18 to the Finance Act 1998 by virtue of this paragraph—

(*a*) the amount so assessed shall be taken to have become due and payable on the date on which that assessment was made; and

(*b*) the words '(in accordance with section 59D of this Act)' in subsection (1) shall accordingly be disregarded.

(4) In determining the amount of any relevant interest, any question whether the excess mentioned in sub-paragraph (1) above (in the following provisions of this paragraph referred to as 'the principal') or any part of it is or was 'outstanding' at any time shall be determined in accordance with sub-paragraphs (5) to (8) below.

(5) So much of the principal as does not exceed the amount of the last provisional repayment made to the company for the accounting period in question shall be taken to have become outstanding on the date on which that provisional repayment was made.

(6) So much (if any) of the principal as—

(*a*) exceeds the amount of the provisional repayment referred to in sub-paragraph (5) above, but

(*b*) does not exceed the amount of the preceding provisional repayment for that accounting period,

shall be taken to have become outstanding on the date on which that preceding provisional repayment was made; and so on with any remaining portion of the principal and any preceding provisional repayments for that accounting period.

(7) So much (if any) of the principal as has become outstanding as mentioned in sub-paragraph (5) or (6) above and has at any time neither been repaid to the Board nor been assessed to corporation tax under paragraph 52 of Schedule 18 to the Finance Act 1998 by virtue of this paragraph shall be taken to remain outstanding at that time (and an amount shall accordingly be taken to cease being outstanding only when it is repaid to the Board or when it is so assessed).
(8) For the purposes of sub-paragraph (7) above, any repayment made by the company in respect of an amount paid to it in respect of—

(*a*) . . .

(*b*) tax credits such as are mentioned in paragraph (*b*) of sub-paragraph (1A) above,

shall be treated as a repayment in respect of the principal, taking an earlier such repayment by the company before a later.
(9) In this paragraph 'self-assessment' means an assessment included in a company tax return and includes a reference to such an assessment as amended.

4–5 . . .

6 Interpretation
(1) In this Schedule—

'provisional fraction' shall be construed in accordance with paragraph 1(4A) above;

'provisional repayment' means a provisional repayment under paragraph 1 above;

'provisional repayment period' shall be construed in accordance with paragraph 1 above.

(2) Any reference in this Schedule to a provisional repayment for an accounting period is a reference to a provisional repayment for a provisional repayment period falling within that accounting period.
(3)–(6) . . . "

2001/4024

REFERRALS TO THE SPECIAL COMMISSIONERS REGULATIONS 2001

Revocation—These Regulations revoked by the Transfer of Tribunal Functions and Revenue and Customs Appeals Order, SI 2009/56 art 3, Sch 2 para 187(*o*) with effect from 1 April 2009.

2002/205

INCOME TAX (EXEMPTION OF MINOR BENEFITS) REGULATIONS 2002

Made by the Treasury under TA 1988 s 155ZB

Made . . . . *4 February 2002*
Laid before the House of Commons . . . . *5 February 2002*
Coming into force . . . . *6 April 2002*

1 Citation, commencement and effect

(1) These Regulations may be cited as the Income Tax (Exemption of Minor Benefits) Regulations 2002 and shall come into force on 6th April 2002.
(2) These Regulations have effect for the year 2002–03 and subsequent years of assessment.

2 Interpretation

In these Regulations—

"bus" and "minibus" mean a bus, or a minibus, by means of which is provided a works bus service to which [section 242 of ITEPA][1] applies;

. . .[3]

"employment" includes an office and related expressions have a corresponding meaning;

["health screening" means an assessment to identify employees who might be at a particular risk of ill health;][2]

["ITEPA" means the Income Tax (Earnings and Pensions) Act 2003;][1]

["medical check-up" means a physical examination of an employee by a health professional which is limited to determining that employee's state of health;][2]

. . .[1]

"working day", in relation to an employee, means a day on which his attendance at a workplace is necessary in the performance of the duties of the employment;

"workplace", in relation to an employee, means a place at which his attendance is necessary in the performance of the duties of the employment.

Amendments—[1] Words in definition of "bus" and "minibus" substituted, definition of "ITEPA" inserted, and the definition of "the Taxes Act" revoked, by the IT (Exemption of Minor Benefits) (Amendment) Regulations, SI 2003/1434 reg 2 with effect from 25 June 2003.

[2] Definitions of "health screening" and "medical check-up" inserted by the Income Tax (Exemption of Minor Benefits) (Amendment) Regulations, SI 2007/2090 reg 2(1), (2) with effect from the tax year 2007–08: SI 2007/2090 reg 1(2). Note that SI 2007/2090 is revoked by the Income Tax (Exemption of Minor Benefits) (Revocation) Regulations, SI 2009/695 reg 2 with

effect from 6 April 2009. However, SI 2007/2090 shall continue to have effect until the exemption which it provides is re-enacted (with or without modifications) by amendment of ITEPA 2003.

3 Definition of "cycle" repealed by the Income Tax (Exemption of Minor Benefits) (Amendment) Regulations, SI 2012/1808 reg 2(*a*) with effect for the tax year 2013–14 and subsequent tax years.

3 Exemption in respect of the provision of qualifying meals

[(1) There is no charge to tax under Chapter 10 of Part 3 of ITEPA in respect of the provision for employees of qualifying meals.][1]

(2) . . . [1]

(3) . . . [2]

Amendments—[1] Para (1) substituted, and para (2) revoked, by the IT (Exemption of Minor Benefits) (Amendment) Regulations, SI 2003/1434 reg 3 with effect from 25 June 2003.

2 Reg 3 repealed by the Income Tax (Exemption of Minor Benefits) (Amendment) Regulations, SI 2012/1808 reg 2(*b*) with effect for the tax year 2013–14 and subsequent tax years.

4 Exemption in respect of the provision of bus or minibus

(1) There is no charge to tax under [Chapter 10 of Part 3 of ITEPA][1] in respect of the provision for employees of a bus, or a minibus, for conveying employees of one or more employers on relevant journeys.

(2) For the purposes of this regulation, a "relevant journey", in relation to an employee, is a journey which—

(*a*) is a single journey of a distance of not more than 10 miles;

(*b*) is between his workplace and shops or other amenities; and

(*c*) is made on a working day.

Amendments—[1] Words in para (1) substituted by the IT (Exemption of Minor Benefits) (Amendment) Regulations, SI 2003/1434 reg 3 with effect from 25 June 2003.

5 [Exemption in respect of the provision of pensions advice

(1) There is no charge to tax under Chapter 10 of Part 3 of ITEPA in respect of the provision to an employee, on behalf of an employer, of pension information and advice.

(2) The exemption conferred by paragraph (1) applies only if the cash equivalent of the benefit of provision of pension information and advice to an employee does not exceed £150 in total in a year of assessment.][1, 2]

Amendments—[1] Regulations 5, 6 inserted by the Income Tax (Exemption of Minor Benefits) (Amendment) Regulations, SI 2004/3087 with effect from 14 December 2004. This regulation has effect from 2005–06.

2 Regulation 5 revoked by F(No 2)A 2017 s 3(3) with effect for the tax year 2017–18 and subsequent tax years.

6 [Exemption in respect of the provision of recreational facilities and subsidised meals to third parties

(1) Where there is no charge to tax under—

(*a*) section 261 of ITEPA (exemption of recreational benefits), or

(*b*) section 317 of ITEPA (subsidised meals) in respect of the provision of recreational facilities or subsidised meals to employees, paragraph (2) applies.

(2) If this paragraph applies, the provision of the facilities or meals referred to in paragraph (1) to other persons who work on the premises of the employer in question shall be exempt notwithstanding that the conditions set out in section 261 or section 317 respectively of ITEPA may not be satisfied in respect of those persons.][1]

Amendments—[1] Regulations 5, 6 inserted by the Income Tax (Exemption of Minor Benefits) (Amendment) Regulations, SI 2004/3087 with effect from 14 December 2004. This regulation has effect from 2005–06.

7 [Exemption in respect of the provision of health screening and medical check-ups

(1) There is no charge to tax under Chapter 10 of Part 3 (taxable benefits: residual liability to charge) of ITEPA in respect of the provision to an employee, on behalf of an employer, of one health screening and one medical check-up each year.

(2) In order for this regulation to apply—

(*a*) *health screenings must be available to all employees, and*

(*b*) *medical check-ups must be available to either—*

(i) *all employees, or*

(ii) *those employees who have been identified in a health screening as requiring a medical check-up.]*[1]

Amendments—[1] This regulation inserted by the Income Tax (Exemption of Minor Benefits) (Amendment) Regulations, SI 2007/2090 reg 2(1), (3) with effect from the tax year 2007–08: SI 2007/2090 reg 1(2). Note that SI 2007/2090 is revoked by the Income Tax (Exemption of Minor Benefits) (Revocation) Regulations, SI 2009/695 reg 2 with effect from 6 April 2009. SI 2007/2090 continued to have effect until the exemption which it provided was enacted by amendment of ITEPA 2003. See ITEPA 2003 s 320B as inserted by FA 2009 s 55 with effect for the tax year 2009–10 and subsequent tax years.

2002/653

SCOTTISH WATER (TRANSFER OF FUNCTIONS, ETC) (TAX PROVISIONS) ORDER 2002

Made by the Treasury under the Scotland Act 1998 ss 104(1), 112(1), (5), 126(1)

Made . . . .*11 March 2002*
Laid before Parliament . . . .*11 March 2002*
Coming into force . . . .*1 April 2002*

1 Citation and commencement

This Order may be cited as the Scottish Water (Transfer of Functions, etc) (Tax Provisions) Order 2002 and shall come into force on 1st April 2002.

2 Interpretation

In this Order—

"the Corporation Tax Acts" has the meaning given by section 831(1)(*a*) of the Taxes Act;

"the new water and sewerage authorities" means the bodies established by section 62(1) of the Local Government etc. (Scotland) Act 1994, that is, the East of Scotland Water Authority, the West of Scotland Water Authority and the North of Scotland Water Authority;

"Scottish Water" means the body corporate known as Scottish Water and established by section 20 of, and Schedule 3 to, the Water Industry (Scotland) Act 2002;

"the Taxes Act" means the Income and Corporation Taxes Act 1988.

3 Tax Provisions consequential on the transfer of functions etc to Scottish Water

Articles 4 to 7 make provision in consequence of the transfer on 1st April 2002 of the functions, property and liabilities of the new water and sewerage authorities to Scottish Water by virtue of sections 21 and 22 of the Water Industry (Scotland) Act 2002.

4 Corporation tax—general

(1) For all purposes of the Corporation Tax Acts in relation to accounting periods beginning on or after 1st April 2002—

(*a*) Scottish Water shall be treated as if it were the same person as each of the new water and sewerage authorities, and

(*b*) the new water and sewerage authorities shall be treated as if together they were the same person as Scottish Water.

(2) For the purposes of section 393 of the Taxes Act (losses other than terminal losses) the new water and sewerage authorities shall be treated as if, before 1st April 2002, they had together carried on a single trade.

(3) Section 400 of the Taxes Act (write-off of government investment) shall not apply with regard to any debt transferred to Scottish Water by virtue of section 22 of the Water Industry (Scotland) Act 2002.

(4) For the purposes of section 400 of the Taxes Act the new water and sewerage authorities shall be treated as if, before 1st April 2002, they had together carried on a single trade.

(5) For the purposes of corporation tax on chargeable gains—

(*a*) Scottish Water shall be treated as having acquired all assets transferred from the new water and sewerage authorities by virtue of section 22 of the Water Industry (Scotland) Act 2002 at the time when they were acquired by the new water and sewerage authorities, and

(*b*) on any disposal of any of those assets by Scottish Water, any expenditure incurred by a new water and sewerage authority which would, if the disposal had been made by that authority, have been allowable by virtue of section 38 of the Taxation of Chargeable Gains Act 1992 in computing the chargeable gain or allowable loss on the disposal of the asset shall be treated as though it had been incurred by Scottish Water.

5 Transfer arrangements

The existence or exercise of the powers of the Scottish Ministers under the Water Industry (Scotland) Act 2002 shall not be regarded as constituting or creating arrangements within the meaning of section 410 of the Taxes Act (arrangements for transfer of company to another group or consortium).

6 Tax-free benefits

Nothing in this Order or Part 3 of the Water Industry (Scotland) Act 2002, and nothing done under this Order or that Part, shall be regarded as a scheme or arrangement for the purposes of section 30 of the Taxation of Chargeable Gains Act 1992 (tax-free benefits).

7 Stamp Duty

No transfer from the new water and sewerage authorities to Scottish Water effected by virtue of the Water Industry (Scotland) Act 2002 shall give rise to any liability to stamp duty.

2002/680

INCOME TAX (EMPLOYMENTS AND ELECTRONIC COMMUNICATIONS) (MISCELLANEOUS PROVISIONS) REGULATIONS 2002

Made by the Commissioners of Inland Revenue under TA 1988 s 203(10) and FA 1999 s 132

Made . . . .*13 March 2002*
Laid before the House of Commons . . . .*13 March 2002*
Coming into force . . . .*8 April 2002*

1 Citation, commencement and interpretation

(1) These Regulations may be cited as the Income Tax (Employments and Electronic Communications) (Miscellaneous Provisions) Regulations 2002 and shall come into force on 8th April 2002.

(2) In these Regulations "the Board" means the Commissioners of Inland Revenue.

2 Notices given by the Board under regulation 34 of the Education (Student Loans) (Repayment) Regulations 2000

(1) Any notice to be given by the Board under regulation 34 of the Education (Student Loans) (Repayment) Regulations 2000 (notices to employers by the Board to deduct repayments from emoluments) ("regulation 34") may be given, either to the employer or a person acting on his behalf, in such form and by such means of electronic communications as are for the time being approved by directions issued by the Board if the employer—

(*a*) has given his consent to the delivery of documents by the Board by that means; and
(*b*) has not notified the Board that that consent has been withdrawn.

(2) If it is recorded on an official computer system that a notice under regulation 34 has been given to any person by an approved means of electronic communications, it shall be presumed, unless the contrary is proved, that a notice—

(*a*) was given by that means;
(*b*) was given to the person recorded on that system as the recipient;
(*c*) was given at the time recorded on that system as the time of delivery; and
(*d*) contained the information recorded on that system in respect of that notice.

(3) A document certified by an officer of the Board to be a printed-out version of a notice, given by means of electronic communications in accordance with paragraph (1), which is recorded on an official computer system as at a particular date shall be presumed unless the contrary is proved—

(*a*) to have been recorded on an official computer system at that date;
(*b*) to constitute the entirety of the electronic communication so recorded.

(4) A document purporting to be such a certificate as is mentioned in paragraph (3) shall be presumed to be such a certificate unless the contrary is proved.

(5) For the purposes of this regulation "employer" and "official computer system" have the same meanings as they have in the Income Tax (Employments) Regulations 1993.

3–8 *(amended SI 1993/744; revoked by SI 2003/2682, subject to transitional provisions contained in Sch 1 thereto)*

2002/1596

INCOME TAX (BENEFITS IN KIND) (EXEMPTION FOR EMPLOYMENT COSTS RESULTING FROM DISABILITY) REGULATIONS 2002

Made by the Treasury under TA 1988 s 155ZB

Made . . . .*18 June 2002*
Laid before the House of Commons . . . .*18 June 2002*
Coming into force . . . .*9 July 2002*

1 These Regulations may be cited as the Income Tax (Benefits in Kind) (Exemption for Employment Costs resulting from Disability) Regulations 2002 and shall come into force on 9th July 2002.

2 In these Regulations—

(*a*) "the Access to Work programme" means the programme known by that name and provided in pursuance of arrangements made by or on behalf of the Secretary of State under section 2 of the Employment and Training Act 1973, in Scotland, made under section 2(3) of the Enterprise and New Towns (Scotland) Act 1990 or, in Northern Ireland, made by or on behalf of the Department of Employment and Learning under section 1 of the Employment and Training (Northern Ireland) Act 1950; and (*b*) any reference to a section, without more, is to that section of the Income and Corporation Taxes Act 1988.

3 There shall be exempted from section 154 any benefit which satisfies each of the following conditions.

Condition 1

The benefit is provided to a disabled employee.

Condition 2

The main purpose of providing the benefit is to enable the employee to perform the duties of his employment.

Condition 3

The benefit consists in the provision of a hearing aid or other equipment, services or facilities, excepting any excluded benefit within the meaning in section 155ZA and Regulations made under that section.

Condition 4

The benefit is provided under, or within the terms of the provisions of, the Disability Discrimination Act 1995, the Access to Work programme, or any other statutory provision or arrangements, whether or not the employer has any legal duty to provide the benefit.

Condition 5

The benefit is made available to the employer's employees generally on similar terms (which include terms identical to Conditions 1 to 4).

2002/1966

RELIEF FOR COMMUNITY AMATEUR SPORTS CLUBS (DESIGNATION) ORDER 2002

Made . . . . *25 July 2002*
Laid before the House of Commons . . . . *25 July 2002*
Coming into force . . . . *15 August 2002*

1 This Order may be cited as the Relief for Community Amateur Sports Clubs (Designation) Order 2002 and shall come into force on 15th August 2002.

2 A sport is designated as an eligible sport for the purposes of Schedule 18 to the Finance Act 2002 where that sport appears on the list maintained by the National Sports Councils of activities recognised by them.

3 "The National Sports Councils" means UK Sport, Sport England, Sport Scotland, the Sports Council of Wales and the Sports Council of Northern Ireland.

2002/1967

CT (FINANCE LEASING OF INTANGIBLE ASSETS) REGULATIONS 2002

Made . . . . *25 July 2002*
Laid before the House of Commons . . . . *25 July 2002*
Coming into force . . . . *15 August 2002*

1 Citation, commencement and effect

These Regulations may be cited as the Corporation Tax (Finance Leasing of Intangible Assets) Regulations 2002, shall come into force on 15th August 2002, and shall have effect from 1st April 2002.

2 Interpretation

In these Regulations—

"financial asset" shall be construed in accordance with paragraph 75 of Schedule 29;

"finance lease", "finance lessor" and "finance lessee" shall be construed in accordance with paragraph 104(4) and (5) of Schedule 29;

"Schedule 29" means Schedule 29 to the Finance Act 2002 (gains and losses of a company from intangible fixed assets).

3 Application of Schedule 29

Schedule 29 shall apply in relation to a company that is the finance lessor of an intangible asset that is the subject of a finance lease as if, notwithstanding that the asset is accounted for by the finance lessor as a financial asset, it were an intangible fixed asset of the lessor and not a financial asset.

4 References in Schedule 29 to capitalised expenditure on an intangible fixed asset shall accordingly be taken as including references to any amount accounted for by the finance lessor as a financial asset as a consequence of the finance lease of the asset, except that—

(*a*) no election may be made under paragraph 10 of Schedule 29 (election for writing down on fixed rate basis) in respect of that amount,

(*b*) that amount is not to be treated as capitalised expenditure for the purposes of paragraph 39(1)(*b*) of Schedule 29 (roll-over relief in case of realisation and reinvestment—conditions to be met in relation to expenditure on other assets), and

(*c*) accordingly any amount treated by paragraph 57(2) of Schedule 29 (roll-over relief on reinvestment—acquisition of group company treated as equivalent to acquisition of underlying assets) as expenditure on acquiring the financial asset is not to be treated as capitalised expenditure for the purposes of paragraph 39(1)(*b*) of that Schedule.

5 Intangible fixed asset becoming financial asset — consequentials

Where an asset formerly recognised by the lessor for accounting purposes as an intangible fixed asset becomes subject to a finance lease (and accordingly comes to be accounted for as a financial asset)—

(*a*) a realisation of the intangible fixed asset shall be treated, for the purposes of Part 4 of Schedule 29 (realisation of intangible fixed assets), as having occurred on the commencement of the finance lease,

(*b*) the accounting value of the financial asset so created shall be recognised as realisation proceeds of the intangible fixed asset for the purposes of that Part, and

(*c*) that amount shall not be taken into account in determining the accounting value of the financial asset immediately after the realisation for the purposes of paragraph 22(2) of that Schedule (apportionment in case of part realisation).

6 Financial assets excluded from Schedule 29

(1) Assets partially excluded from Schedule 29 by virtue of paragraphs 78 to 81 (assets excluded except as regards royalties) shall be entirely excluded from that Schedule as regards the finance lessor if they are subject to a finance lease and are accounted for by the lessor as financial assets. Accordingly in relation to such assets—

(*a*) Schedule 29 applies only to royalties recognised for accounting purposes prior to the asset becoming subject to the finance lease, or after it ceases to be subject to the finance lease,

(*b*) to the extent that such royalties are brought into account for tax purposes under Schedule 29, they shall not be brought into account for tax purposes again, and

(*c*) to the extent that such royalties are brought into account for tax purposes otherwise than under Schedule 29, they shall not be brought into account for tax purposes under that Schedule.

(2) Except for the purposes of regulation 5, an asset shall be excluded from Schedule 29 if it is used by the finance lessee for the purposes of a trade or business in respect of which he is within the charge to income tax.

(3) Nothing in these Regulations shall be read as enabling Schedule 29 to apply to existing assets excluded from the application of that Schedule by paragraph 118 of that Schedule.

(4) An asset shall count as an existing asset in the hands of the finance lessor for the purposes of paragraph 118 of Schedule 29 if the finance lessee—

(*a*) is a company for whom the asset was the whole or part of an existing asset, or

(*b*) is a person who is a related party in relation to such a company.

(5) References in paragraph (1) to royalties being brought into account for tax purposes include references to royalties which would have been so brought into account if the person concerned had been within the charge to corporation tax.

(6) In paragraph (4)(*b*) "related party" shall be construed in accordance with paragraph 95, read with paragraphs 96 to 101, of Schedule 29.

2002/1968

INCOME TAX (PRESCRIBED DEPOSIT-TAKERS) ORDER 2002

Amendment—This Order revoked by ITA 2007, s 1031, Sch 3 Pt 1, with effect for income tax purposes from 6 April 2007, and corporation tax purposes for accounting periods ending after 5 April 2007.

2002/1969

EXCHANGE GAINS AND LOSSES (TRANSITIONAL PROVISIONS AND SAVINGS) REGULATIONS 2002

Made . . . . *25 July 2002*

Laid before the House of Commons . . . . *25 July 2002*
Coming into force . . . . *1 October 2002*

PART 1
INTRODUCTION

1 Citation, commencement and effect

(1) These Regulations may be cited as the Exchange Gains and Losses (Transitional Provisions and Savings) Regulations 2002 and shall come into force on 1st October 2002.
(2) These Regulations have effect in relation to accounting periods beginning on or after 1st October 2002.

PART 2
SAVING OF THE EXCHANGE GAINS AND LOSSES (TRANSITIONAL PROVISIONS) REGULATIONS 1994 WITH MODIFICATIONS

2 Introduction

The Exchange Gains and Losses (Transitional Provisions) Regulations 1994 are modified in accordance with regulations 3 to 11 below and, as modified, continue to have effect (notwithstanding the repeal of sections 164(14), 165(4) to (6) and 167(1) and (4) to (6) of, and Schedule 16 to, the Finance Act 1993 by sections 79(1)(*b*) and 141 of, and Part 3(10) of Schedule 40 to, the Finance Act 2002).

3 Modification of regulation 1

In regulation 1(3)—

(*a*) for sub-paragraph (*g*) substitute—

" (*g*) "a regulation 6(3) asset" means an existing asset the basic valuation of which was determined for the purposes of Chapter II in accordance with regulation 6(3) of these Regulations;";

(*b*) at the end of sub-paragraph (*h*) add "; and

(i) "the relevant accounting period", in relation to a company, means the company's first accounting period to begin on or after 1st October 2002.".

4 Modification of regulation 2

In regulation 2(2)—

(*a*) omit "Sections 136, 137 and 139 to 141 of the 1993 Act;";
(*b*) omit "The Exchange Gains and Losses (Deferral of Gains and Losses) Regulations 1994.".

5 Omission of regulations 3 to 6

Omit regulations 3 to 6.

6 Modification of regulation 7

In regulation 7(2)—

(*a*) after the definition of "the cumulative taxed loss" insert—

" "the final accounting period", in relation to a company, means the company's accounting period preceding the relevant accounting period;";

(*b*) omit the words from "and any reference" to the end.

7 Modification of regulation 8

In regulation 8(5) for "above" substitute "of these Regulations".

8 Modification of regulation 13

(1) Modify regulation 13 as follows.
(2) In paragraph (1) for "14(1) and 15(1)" substitute "14 and 14A".
(3) After paragraph (1) insert—

"(1A) For the purposes of paragraph (1)(*a*) above, the final accounting period shall be treated as the last accrual period as respects any asset or liability held or owed by the company immediately after the end of the final accounting period.".

(4) In paragraphs (2)(*a*), (*b*) and (*c*) and (3)(*a*), (*b*) and (*c*) for "before the end of the last accrual period" substitute "after the end of the final accounting period".
(5) For paragraph (4) substitute—

"(4) In paragraphs (2) and (3) above, a relevant gain or loss in relation to a regulation 6(3) asset is a chargeable gain or an allowable loss. (4A) In relation to any asset other than a regulation 6(3) asset or any liability, an amount equal to the amount of any relevant gain or loss that is deemed to accrue to the company under paragraph (2) or (3) above shall be treated for the purposes of Chapter 2 of Part 4 of the Finance Act 1996 (according to whether it is a relevant gain or loss)—

(*a*) as a credit in respect of a loan relationship of the company, or (*b*) as a debit in respect of a loan relationship of the company,

which falls to be brought into account under section 82(2) of that Act.".

(6) Omit paragraphs (5) to (8).

9 Substitution of regulation 14

For regulation 14 substitute—

"Elections to defer bringing into account relevant gains and losses deemed to accrue immediately after the end of the final accounting period

14 (1) In any case where, apart from this regulation, relevant gains or losses would accrue to a company immediately after the end of the final accounting period by virtue of regulation 13, the company may elect, by notice to the inspector within two years of the end of the final accounting period, that this regulation shall apply as respects—

(*a*) subject to paragraph (3) below, all relevant gains or losses to which paragraph (4) of regulation 13 would apply;

(*b*) all relevant gains or losses to which paragraph (4A) of that regulation would apply; or

(*c*) both.

An election under this paragraph shall be irrevocable.

(2) Where an election is made under paragraph (1) above, every gain or loss to which this regulation applies shall be treated as accruing only when the asset or liability to which the gain or loss relates ceases to be held or owed by the company.

(3) No election may be made under paragraph (1) above as respects relevant gains or losses to which regulation 13(4) would apply if an election under regulation 14A is made as regards such losses.

Elections to treat losses deemed to accrue immediately after the end of the final accounting period as debits in respect of loan relationships

14A (1) In any case where—

(*a*) apart from this regulation, relevant losses would accrue to a company as respects regulation 6(3) assets immediately after the end of the final accounting period by virtue of regulation 13; and

(*b*) if relevant gains would accrue as respects such assets at that time by virtue of that regulation, such losses would exceed them,

the company may elect, by notice to the inspector within two years of the end of the final accounting period, that this regulation shall apply as respects such losses or, in a case where sub-paragraph (b) applies, such losses to the extent that they exceed the relevant gains.

An election under this paragraph shall be irrevocable.

(2) Where an election is made under paragraph (1) above, an amount equal to the amount of the losses to which this regulation applies shall be treated for the purposes of Chapter 2 of Part 4 of the Finance Act 1996 as a debit in respect of a loan relationship of the company for the new accounting period and not falling to be brought into account under section 82(2) of that Act.

Treatment of losses available to be carried forward at the end of the final accounting period as a result of an election made under regulation 14(5) or 16(1)

14B (1) This regulation apples where, as a result of an election made under regulation 14(5) or 16(1) of these Regulations, an amount of available losses ("the relevant amount") was available at the end of the final accounting period to be carried forward and, apart from this regulation, to be set against a company's exchange gains.

(2) Where this regulation applies an amount equal to the relevant amount shall be treated for the purposes of Chapter 2 of Part 4 of the Finance Act 1996 as a debit in respect of a loan relationship of the company for the new accounting period and not falling to be brought into account under section 82(2) of that Act.".

10 Omission of regulation 15 and 16

Omit regulations 15 and 16.

11 Omission of Part 4

Omit the whole of Part 4.

PART 3
SAVING OF THE EXCHANGE GAINS AND LOSSES (ALTERNATIVE METHOD OF CALCULATION) REGULATIONS 1994 WITH MODIFICATIONS

12 Introduction

The Exchange Gains and Losses (Alternative Method of Calculation) Regulations 1994 are modified in accordance with regulations 13 to 17 below and, as modified, continue to have effect (notwithstanding the repeal of sections 164(14) and 167(1) and (4) to (6) of, and Schedule 15 to, the Finance Act 1993 by sections 79(1)(*b*) and 141 of, and Part 3(10) of Schedule 40 to, the Finance Act 2002).

13 Omission of regulations 2 and 3

Omit regulations 2 and 3.

14 Modification of regulation 7

(1) Modify regulation 7 as follows.

(2) In paragraph (1) for the words from "Subject to" to "by a company at any time" substitute "Paragraphs (3) to (5) below apply in any case where a disposal of an asset is deemed by virtue of paragraph (1A) below to have been made by a company immediately before the first day of its first accounting period to begin on or after 1st October 2002".

(3) After paragraph (1) insert—

"(1A) For the purposes of paragraph (1) above, any asset held by the company at the beginning of the first day of its first accounting period to begin on or after 1st October 2002 shall be deemed to have been disposed of by the company immediately before that first day.".

(4) Omit paragraph (2).

(5) Omit paragraphs (6) to (8).

15 Omission of regulations 8 and 9

Omit regulations 8 and 9.

16 Modification of regulation 11

In regulation 11 after paragraph (1) insert—

"(1A) Notwithstanding the following provisions of this regulation, an election made under regulation 10 or this regulation—

(*a*) shall have effect only in relation to accounting periods beginning before 1st October 2002, and

(*b*) an election which specifies a day as the day from which the election is to have effect must specify a day that falls within an accounting period beginning before 1st October 2002.".

17 Omission of regulation 12

Omit regulation 12.

PART 4
SAVING OF THE EXCHANGE GAINS AND LOSSES (INSURANCE COMPANIES) REGULATIONS 1994 WITH MODIFICATIONS

18 Introduction

The Exchange Gains and Losses (Insurance Companies) Regulations 1994 are modified in accordance with regulations 19 to 27 below and, as modified, continue to have effect (notwithstanding the repeal of sections 167(1) and 168(2) to (5) of the Finance Act 1993 by sections 79(1)(*b*) and 141 of, and Part 3(10) of Schedule 40 to, the Finance Act 2002).

19 Modification of regulation 1

In regulation 1 after the definition of "basic valuation" insert—

" "the final accounting period", in relation to a company, means the company's accounting period preceding the first accounting period to begin on or after 1st October 2002;".

20 Omission of regulations 2 to 5A

Omit regulations 2 to 5A.

21 Modification of regulation 7

In regulation 7 for paragraph (1) substitute—

"(1) An asset specified by this regulation is referred to in regulations 7A and 8 to 12 as a "regulation 7 asset".".

22 Insertion of regulations 7A and 7B

After regulation 7 insert—

"**7A** (1) An asset shall be deemed to have been disposed of by an insurance company immediately before its first accounting period to begin on or after 1st October 2002 where—

(*a*) the asset was a regulation 7 asset at the time of its deemed disposal, and

(*b*) at that time, the insurance company had made no election under regulation 8A of these Regulations.

(2) Subject to paragraph 7B, any chargeable gain or allowable loss accruing on the deemed disposal under paragraph (1) above of an asset shall be brought into account as if it had accrued immediately after the end of the final accounting period.

7B In any case where, apart from this regulation, chargeable gains or allowable losses would accrue to an insurance company immediately after the end of the final accounting period by virtue of regulation 7A—

(*a*) the insurance company may elect, by notice to the inspector within two years of the end of the final accounting period, that this regulation shall apply as respects all such gains or losses, and

(*b*) where such an election is made, every such gain or loss to which this regulation applies shall be treated as accruing only when the asset or liability to which the gain or loss relates ceases to be held or owed by the insurance company.".

23 Modification of regulation 8

In regulation 8(1)—

(*a*) for "disposal of a regulation 7 asset" substitute "the deemed disposal under regulation 7A(1) of an asset";

(*b*) for "8A" substitute "9".

24 Omission of regulation 8A

Omit regulation 8A.

25 Modification of regulation 9

In regulation 9(2) for "disposal of the asset" substitute "deemed disposal under regulation 7A(1) of the asset".

26 Modification of regulation 11

In regulation 11(2) for "disposal of the asset" substitute "deemed disposal under regulation 7A(1) of the asset".

27 Modification of regulation 12

In regulation 12(2) for "disposal of the asset" substitute "deemed disposal under regulation 7A(1) of the asset".

PART 5
SAVING OF THE EXCHANGE GAINS AND LOSSES (MISCELLANEOUS MODIFICATIONS) REGULATIONS 2000 WITH MODIFICATIONS

28 Introduction

The Exchange Gains and Losses (Miscellaneous Modifications) Regulations 2000(a) are modified in accordance with regulations 29 and 30 below and, as modified, continue to have effect (notwithstanding the repeal of sections 164(14), 167(1) and (4) to (6) of, and Schedules 15 and 16 to, the Finance Act 1993 by sections 79(1)(*b*) and 141 of, and Part 3(10) of Schedule 40 to, the Finance Act 2002).

29 Omission of regulations 2 to 5

Omit regulations 2 to 5.

30 Omission of regulation 11

Omit regulation 11.

2002/1970

EXCHANGE GAINS AND LOSSES (BRINGING INTO ACCOUNT GAINS OR LOSSES) REGULATIONS 2002

Made . . . . *25 July 2002*

Laid before the House of Commons . . . . *25 July 2002*

Coming into force . . . . *1 October 2002*

1 Citation, commencement and effect

(1) These Regulations may be cited as the Exchange Gains and Losses (Bringing into Account Gains or Losses) Regulations 2002 and shall come into force on 1st October 2002 immediately after the Exchange Gains and Losses (Transitional Provisions and Savings) Regulations 2002.

(2) These Regulations have effect in relation to accounting periods beginning on or after 1st October 2002.

2 Interpretation

(1) In these Regulations—

"Chapter 2" means Chapter 2 of Part 4 of the Finance Act 1996;

"chargeable gain" and "allowable loss" have the same meaning as they have for the purposes of the 1992 Act;

["foreign business asset" means, in relation to a company, an asset of an operation of the company which for accounting purposes is a foreign operation consisting of a branch;][1]

[" no gain/no loss disposal" means a disposal on which, by virtue of any of the no gain/no loss provisions (within the meaning of section 288(3A) of the 1992 Act), neither a gain nor a loss accrues;][2]

"original shares" and "new holding" have the same meaning as in section 127 of the 1992 Act or (as the case may be) that section as applied by virtue of any enactment relating to chargeable gains;

"paragraph 16" means paragraph 16 of Schedule 26 to the Finance Act 2002;

"section 84A" means section 84A of the Finance Act 1996;

["statement of recognised gains and losses and statement of changes in equity" mean the statements mentioned in subsection (3) of section 84A or sub-paragraph (3) of paragraph 16;][1]

"the 1992 Act" means the Taxation of Chargeable Gains Act 1992;

"the 1994 Regulations" means the Exchange Gains and Losses (Alternative Method of Calculation of Gain or Loss) Regulations 1994;

["the Disregard Regulations" means the Loan Relationships and Derivative Contracts (Disregard and Bringing into Account of Profits and Losses) Regulations 2004.][1]

[(1A) For the purposes of these Regulations a relevant transaction to which section 116(10) of the 1992 Act applies shall be treated as a disposal.][2]

(2) In these Regulations—

(*a*) any reference to a disposal of an asset shall be construed as a reference to any event which is or is treated as a disposal for the purposes of the 1992 Act; and

(*b*) any reference to the time of the disposal of an asset shall be construed as a reference to the time at which the disposal occurs for the purposes of that Act,

and, for the purposes of this paragraph, any reference to a disposal includes a part disposal.

[(2A) In these Regulations any reference to the amount or value of the consideration for the disposal of the asset is a reference to any amount treated as disposal consideration by any provision of the 1992 Act.]

(3) In these Regulations—

(*a*) any reference to an asset which is a ship or aircraft includes a reference to a contract—

(i) to which section 67 of the Capital Allowances Act 2001 applies; and

(ii) which relates to plant or machinery which is a ship or aircraft; and

(*b*) any reference to a disposal of an asset which is a ship or aircraft by a person includes a reference to the case where a person ceases to be entitled to the benefit of such a contract and does not then in fact become the owner of the plant or the machinery to which the contract relates.

Amendments—[1] In para (1), definition of "foreign business asset" substituted, and definitions of "statement of recognised gains and losses and statement of changes in equity" and "the Disregard Regulations" inserted, by the Exchange Gains and Losses (Bringing into Account Gains or Losses) (Amendment) Regulations, SI 2004/3259 regs 2, 3 with effect in relation to accounting periods beginning on or after 1 January 2005.

[2] Definition substituted and paras (1A), (2A) inserted, by the Exchange Gains and Losses (Bringing into Account Gains or Losses) (Amendment) Regulations, SI 2010/809, regs 2, 3, with effect in relation to a disposal of an asset made on or after 6 April 2010, subject to savings in regs 13, 14(4). Definition previously read as follows:

""a no gain/no loss disposal" means a disposal on which neither a gain nor a loss accrues by virtue of any of the following provisions of the 1992 Act—

(*a*) section 139;
(*b*) section 140A;
(*c*) section 171;
(*d*) section 215; and
(*e*) section 216;"

3 Prescribed circumstances in which regulation 4 applies

(1) Regulation 4 applies in [any][1] of the circumstances prescribed by paragraphs [(1A),][1] (2) and (3) below.

[(1A) The circumstances prescribed by this paragraph are that—

(*a*) there is a disposal of an asset by a company in an accounting period beginning on or after 1st January 2005; and

(*b*) in relation to a liability representing a loan relationship [of the company][2] or [an obligation under][2] a derivative contract of the company, an exchange gain or loss arose to the company which—

(i) was recognised in the company's statement of recognised gains and losses or statement of changes in equity and was set off by or against an amount which represents the whole or part of an exchange gain or loss arising in relation to the asset, or

(ii) was prescribed by regulation 3 or 4 of the Disregard Regulations.][1]

(2) The circumstances prescribed by this paragraph are where there is a disposal of an asset by a company and—

(*a*) any exchange gain or loss arose to the company in relation to the asset in an accounting period beginning on or after 1st October 2002 [but before 1st January 2005][1]; and

(*b*) in accordance with generally accepted accounting practice an amount representing the whole or part of an exchange loss or gain which arises to the company in relation to a liability representing a loan relationship of the company or an obligation under a derivative contract—

(i) was carried to or sustained by the reserve mentioned in subsection (5) of section 84A or sub-paragraph (4) of paragraph 16; and

(ii) was set off by or against an amount which represents the whole or part of an exchange gain or loss arising in relation to the asset and falls within subsection (6) of section 84A or sub-paragraph (5) of paragraph 16.

(3) The circumstances prescribed by this paragraph are where there is a disposal of an asset by a company and there is in relation to the asset any of the following—

(*a*) a deemed disposal under regulation 7(1A) of the 1994 Regulations (as modified by the Exchange Gains and Losses (Transitional Provisions and Savings) Regulations 2002);

(*b*) a deferred gain or loss under regulation 8 of the 1994 Regulations in relation to which paragraph (3) or (4) of that regulation did not apply immediately before the relevant day;

(*c*) a deferred gain or loss under regulation 9 of the 1994 Regulations in relation to which paragraph (3)(*a*) or (*b*) or paragraph (4)(*a*) or (*b*) of that regulation, as the case may be, did not apply immediately before the relevant day.

(4) In paragraph (3)(*b*) and (*c*) above "the relevant day" means the first day of the company's first accounting period to begin on or after 1st October 2002.

[(5) In this regulation an obligation under a derivative contract is the obligation of the company to pay in exchange for one currency an amount in a second currency.][2]

Amendments—[1] Word in para (1) substituted, and reference inserted; para (1A) inserted; and words in para (2)(*a*) inserted; by the Exchange Gains and Losses (Bringing into Account Gains or Losses) (Amendment) Regulations, SI 2004/3259 regs 2, 4 with effect in relation to accounting periods beginning on or after 1 January 2005.

[2] Words in para (1A) inserted, and para (5) inserted, by the Exchange Gains and Losses (Bringing into Account Gains or Losses) (Amendment) Regulations, SI 2005/2013 regs 2, 3 with effect from 11 August 2005.

4 [General rule for bringing amounts into account

(1) For the purposes of the 1992 Act, the amount or value of the consideration for the disposal of the asset shall be—

(*a*) increased by the amount of any net gain, and

(*b*) subject to paragraph (2) below, reduced by the amount of any net loss.

This is subject to [paragraphs (4) and (5)][2] below and regulations 6 and 8.

(2) If the amount of any net loss exceeds the amount or value of the consideration that would be brought into account but for the application of this regulation, the amount of the excess of the net loss shall be treated as consideration for the acquisition of the asset for the purposes of section 38(1)(*a*) of the 1992 Act.

(3) If section 42 of the 1992 Act applies, this regulation shall not apply to determine the amount or value of the consideration for the disposal referred to as "A" in that section in apportioning the sums attributable to the asset.

(4) Paragraph (1) above does not apply if, immediately before the disposal, the asset is a foreign business asset other than shares not held on trading account.

[(5) Paragraph (1) does not apply so far as the net gain or net loss falls to be brought into account apart from this regulation or regulation 6.][2]][1]

Amendments—[1] Reg 4 substituted by the Exchange Gains and Losses (Bringing into Account Gains or Losses) (Amendment) Regulations, SI 2010/809, regs 2, 4, with effect in relation to a disposal of an asset made on or after 6 April 2010, subject to savings in regs 13, 14(4). Reg 4 previously read as follows:

"**4 General rule for bringing amounts into account**

(1) For the purposes of the 1992 Act, there shall be brought into account for the accounting period in which the disposal of the asset occurs—

(*a*) as a chargeable gain accruing to the company at the time of the disposal, the amount of any net gain; or

(*b*) as an allowable loss accruing to the company at the time of the disposal, the amount of any net loss.

(2) Paragraph (1) above does not have effect if the asset disposed of—

(*a*) is a foreign business asset immediately before its disposal; or

(*b*) consists of shares or an asset related to shares on the disposal of which no chargeable gain is treated as accruing by virtue of Part 1 of Schedule 7AC to the 1992 Act.

(3) Paragraph (1) above is subject to regulations 6 and 8."

2 In para (1), words substituted for words "paragraph (4)", and para (5) inserted, by the Exchange Gains and Losses (Bringing into Account Gains or Losses) (Amendment) Regulations, SI 2015/1960 reg 2(1), (2) with effect in relation to accounting periods beginning on or after 1 January 2016.

5 Calculation of the amount of any net gain or net loss for the purposes of regulation 4

(1) The amount of any net gain or net loss referred to in regulation 4(1) shall be calculated in accordance with this regulation.

[(1A) The net gain or net loss must be calculated in the company's relevant currency at the time of the disposal of the asset.][2]

(2) . . . [1] The amount of any net gain or loss shall be calculated by finding the aggregate of the amounts representing exchange gains or losses which accrued in relation to liabilities matched with the asset disposed of during the period in which the asset was held by the company disposing of it.

[(2A) Where section 9C of the Corporation Tax Act 2010 (chargeable gains and losses of companies) applies in relation to the asset disposed of, in determining the amounts representing accrued exchange gains or losses—

(*a*) exchange gains and losses must be calculated in the relevant currency of the company for the period in which the gains or losses arose,

(*b*) if there is a change in the company's relevant currency before the asset is disposed of, the amount of any accrued exchange gains or losses must be translated (or if it has previously been translated under this paragraph, further translated) into the relevant currency of the company immediately following the change by reference to the spot rate of exchange for the day of the change, and

(*c*) if sub-paragraph (*b*) applies as a result of more than one change in the company's relevant currency, it is to be applied in relation to each change in the order the changes were made (with the earliest first).][2]

(3) The aggregate referred to in paragraph (2) above shall be found in any manner that is just and reasonable having regard to—

(*a*) the effect of regulation 6 in the accounting period in which the disposal occurs or in any earlier accounting period; and

(*b*) the way in which such an aggregate was found for any earlier accounting period in accordance with this regulation.

(4) Notwithstanding that a loss accruing to a company on the disposal of the asset is not deductible except from a chargeable gain of the kind mentioned in section 18(3) of the 1992 Act, where the aggregate referred to in paragraph (2) would be an amount of net gain for the purposes of regulation 4(1) in relation to that disposal, the amount of such a loss may be deducted from the aggregate.[1]

[(5) Subject to paragraph (6), for the purposes of this regulation and regulation 8, a company's relevant currency at any time is its functional currency at that time.

(6) If at any time—

(*a*) a company is a UK resident investment company, and

(*b*) the company has a designated currency which is different from its functional currency,

the company's relevant currency at that time is that designated currency.

(7) In this regulation—

"designated currency" means the currency a company elects as its designated currency under section 9A of the Corporation Tax Act 2010;

"functional currency" has the same meaning as in section 17(4) of that Act;

"investment company" has the meaning given by section 17(3A) of that Act.][2]

Amendments—[1] In para (2), words "Subject to paragraph (4) below", and para (4), repealed, by the Exchange Gains and Losses (Bringing into Account Gains or Losses) (Amendment) Regulations, SI 2010/809, regs 2, 5, with effect in relation to a disposal of an asset made on or after 6 April 2010, subject to savings in regs 13, 14(4).

2 Paras (1A), (2A), (5)–(7) inserted by the Exchange Gains and Losses (Bringing into Account Gains or Losses) (Amendment) Regulations, SI 2013 1843 reg 2(1), (2) with effect in relation to a disposal of an asset made on or after 1st September 2013.

6 Assets representing certain loan relationships and ships or aircraft

(1) This paragraph applies [to an accounting period beginning on or after 1st January 2005][1] where the asset disposed of—

(*a*) represents a loan relationship of the company . . . [1], or

(*b*) is a ship or aircraft.

[(2) Where paragraph (1) above applies, the amount of any net gain or net loss referred to in regulation 4 shall not be brought into account under that regulation but instead, for the purposes of Part 5 of the Corporation Tax Act 2009, shall be brought into account for the accounting period in which the disposal of the asset occurs as a credit or a debit (according to whether it is an amount of net gain or net loss) in respect of the loan relationships of the company.][2]

(3), (4) . . . [1]

Amendments—[1] Words in para (1) inserted, words in para (1)(*a*) revoked, and paras (3), (4) revoked, by the Exchange Gains and Losses (Bringing into Account Gains or Losses) (Amendment) Regulations, SI 2004/3259 regs 3, 5 with effect in relation to accounting periods beginning on or after 1 January 2005.

[2] Para (2) substituted by the Exchange Gains and Losses (Bringing into Account Gains or Losses) (Amendment) Regulations, SI 2010/809, regs 2, 6, with effect in relation to a disposal of an asset made on or after 6 April 2010, subject to savings in regs 13, 14(4). Para (2) previously read as follows:

"(2) Where paragraph (1) applies, the amount to be brought into account under regulation 4(1) shall not be brought into account, for the purposes of the 1992 Act, as a chargeable gain or allowable loss but instead, for the purposes of Chapter 2, as a credit or a debit (according to whether it is an amount of net gain or net loss) in respect of the loan relationships of the company."

7 Regulations 5 and 6—supplementary

(1) This regulation has effect for the purposes of regulations 5 and 6.

(2) References to the asset disposed of include references to any predecessor asset which was—

(*a*) original shares; or

(*b*) "the old asset" construed in accordance with section 116 of the 1992 Act.

(3) References to the company disposing of the asset include references to any predecessor company which was "the disposing company" for the purposes of regulation 8 of the 1994 Regulations [and these Regulations][3].

(4) In respect of any time falling within an accounting period beginning before 1st October 2002 a liability [or obligation][2] is matched with an asset to the extent that it is matched in accordance with an election under regulation 10 of the 1994 Regulations.

(5) In respect of any time falling within an accounting period beginning on or after 1st October 2002 [but before 1st January 2005][1]

(*a*) a liability [or obligation][2] is fully matched with an asset where an amount representing the whole of an exchange gain or loss arising in relation to the liability is treated as mentioned in subsection (5) of section 84A or sub-paragraph (4) of paragraph 16; and

(*b*) where the amount treated as mentioned in that subsection or that sub-paragraph represents only part of an exchange gain or loss, the liability shall be treated as being matched only to the corresponding extent.

[(5A) In respect of any time falling within an accounting period beginning on or after 1st January 2005—

(*a*) a liability [or obligation][2] is fully matched with an asset if—

(i) an amount representing the whole of an exchange gain or loss arising in relation to the liability [or obligation][2] is recognised in the company's statement of recognised gains and losses or statement of changes in equity, and

(ii) the whole of an exchange gain or loss arising in relation to the asset is also so recognised, or

(iii) it is matched with that asset in accordance with regulation 3 or 4 of the Disregard Regulations; and

(*b*) a liability [or obligation][2] is partly matched with an asset if—

(i) an amount representing part of an exchange gain or loss arising in relation to the liability [or obligation][2] is recognised in the company's statement of recognised gains and losses or statement of changes in equity, and

(ii) part of an exchange gain or loss arising in relation to the asset is also so recognised, or

(iii) an amount representing part of an exchange gain or loss arising in relation to the liability [or obligation][2] is matched with that asset in accordance with regulation 3 or 4 of the Disregard Regulations.][1]

(6) Where in any accounting period beginning on or after 1st October 2002 [but before 1st January 2005][1]

(*a*) a company holds more than one asset in relation to which there are amounts falling within subsection (6) of section 84A or sub-paragraph (5) of paragraph 16; and

(*b*) the assets are denominated and the liabilities are expressed in the same currency,

the extent to which an asset is matched shall be determined in accordance with the rules set out in paragraph (7) below.

(7) The following rules shall apply in relation to—

(*a*) any disposal of an asset occurring before the relevant disposal;

(*b*) any asset held at the time of the relevant disposal.

Rule 1

Liabilities [or obligations][2] are to be regarded as having been matched to the greatest possible extent with assets which—

(*a*) represent loan relationships of the company . . . [1]; or

(*b*) are ships or aircraft.

Rule 2

Subject to Rule 1, liabilities [or obligations][2] are to be regarded as having been matched to the greatest possible extent with assets (other than foreign business assets) on the disposal of which a chargeable gain accrues or would accrue.

Rule 3

Subject to Rules 1 and 2, liabilities [or obligations][2] are to be regarded as having been matched with assets—

(*a*) on the disposal of which no chargeable gain is treated as accruing by virtue of Part 1 of Schedule 7AC to the 1992 Act;

(*b*) on a disposal of which no chargeable gain would be treated as accruing by virtue of that Part if the disposal were made on a date falling more than twelve months after the date of the relevant disposal but excluding assets which—

(i) are actually disposed of on a date falling less than twelve months after the date of the relevant disposal, and

(ii) have been held for less than twelve months at the date of the actual disposal; or

(*c*) which are foreign business assets held at the time of the relevant disposal.

[(8) For the purposes of paragraph (6), the currency in which a liability [or obligation][2] is expressed is to be treated as the currency in which an asset is denominated if—

(*a*) borrowing in that currency, or

(*b*) the entering into a derivative contract whose underlying subject matter is that currency,

could reasonably be expected to eliminate or substantially reduce the economic risk of holding the asset which is attributable to fluctuations in exchange rates.][1]

(9) In paragraph (7) above, "the relevant disposal" means the disposal referred to in regulation 4.

Amendments—[1] Words in paras (5), (6) inserted, para (5A) inserted, words in para (7) Rule 1 revoked, and para (8) substituted, by the Exchange Gains and Losses (Bringing into Account Gains or Losses) (Amendment) Regulations, SI 2004/3259 regs 2, 6 with effect in relation to accounting periods beginning on or after 1 January 2005.

[2] Words inserted by the Exchange Gains and Losses (Bringing into Account Gains or Losses) (Amendment) Regulations, SI 2005/2013 regs 2, 4 with effect from 11 August 2005.

[3] Words in para (3) inserted by the Exchange Gains and Losses (Bringing into Account Gains or Losses) (Amendment) Regulations, SI 2010/809, regs 2, 7, with effect in relation to a disposal of an asset made on or after 6 April 2010, subject to savings in regs 13, 14(4).

8 No gain/no loss disposals

(1) This regulation applies where the disposal of the asset is a no gain/no loss disposal.

[(2) Where this regulation applies, regulation 4 shall not apply to bring into account the net gain or net loss on the occasion of the no gain/no loss disposal but shall instead apply to bring that net gain or net loss into account on the first relevant disposal of the asset.][1]

[(2A) Where section 9C of the Corporation Tax Act 2010 applies in relation to the asset on or before the first relevant disposal, for the purposes of determining the net gain or net loss to be brought into account on the first relevant disposal of the asset—

(*a*) where the relevant currency of the company disposing of the asset is different from the relevant currency of the company acquiring the asset, the net gain or net loss must be translated into the relevant currency of the company acquiring the asset at the time of the no gain/no loss disposal by reference to the spot rate of exchange at that time,

(*b*) if there is a change in the acquiring company's relevant currency before the asset is disposed of, the amount of the net gain or net loss must be translated (or if it has previously been translated under this paragraph, further translated) into the relevant currency of the company immediately following the change by reference to the spot rate of exchange for the day of the change,

(*c*) if sub-paragraph (*b*) applies as a result of more than one change in the company's relevant currency, it is to be applied in relation to each change in the order the changes were made (with the earliest first), and

(*d*) sub-paragraphs (*a*) and (*b*) apply in relation to each no gain/no loss disposal of the asset before the first relevant disposal of the asset.][2]

(3) In [this regulation][2] above, in relation to the disposal of an asset which is a no gain/no loss disposal, "the first relevant disposal" means the first subsequent disposal of that asset which is not a no gain/no loss disposal.

Cross reference—See the Exchange Gains and Losses (Bringing into Account Gains or Losses) (Amendment) Regulations, SI 2010/809, reg 14.

Amendments—[1] Para (2) substituted, and "(*b*)" in para (3) revoked, by the Exchange Gains and Losses (Bringing into Account Gains or Losses) (Amendment) Regulations, SI 2010/809, regs 2, 8, with effect in relation to a disposal of an asset made on or after 6 April 2010, subject to savings in regs 13, 14(4). Para (2) previously read as follows:

"(2) Where this regulation applies, the amount to be brought into account under regulation 4(1) as a chargeable gain or allowable loss—

(*a*) shall not be brought into account for the accounting period in which the disposal of the asset occurs, but instead

(*b*) for the purposes of the 1992 Act, shall be brought into account as a chargeable gain or allowable loss, as the case may be, by the company making the first relevant disposal of the asset for the accounting period in which the first relevant disposal occurs."

2 Para (2A) inserted, and in para (3), words substituted for words "paragraph (2) above" by the Exchange Gains and Losses (Bringing into Account Gains or Losses) (Amendment) Regulations, SI 2013 1843 reg 2(1), (3) with effect in relation to a disposal of an asset made on or after 1st September 2013.

9 Cases where there is no disposal of the asset by virtue of section 116(10) of the 1992 Act

(1) This regulation applies in the circumstances prescribed by paragraph (2) below.

(2) The circumstances prescribed by this paragraph are where the circumstances prescribed by [regulation 3(1A) and (2)][1] would exist but for there being no disposal of the asset for the purposes of the 1992 Act by virtue of section 116(10) of that Act ("section 116(10)").

(3) Where this regulation applies, the amount which, but for section 116(10), would be brought into account under regulation 4(1) as a chargeable gain or allowable loss shall be found and paragraph (4) below shall apply.

(4) Where this paragraph applies—

(*a*) *if the amount found under paragraph (3) above would be brought into account as a chargeable gain, the market value of the asset shall, for the purposes of paragraph* (*a*) of section 116(10), be increased by an amount equal to that amount;

(*b*) *if the amount found under paragraph (3) above would be brought into account as an allowable loss—*

(i) *the market value of the asset shall, for the purposes of paragraph* (*a*) of section 116(10), be reduced by an amount equal to that amount; and

(ii) *if that amount exceeds the amount of the market value, an allowable loss equal in amount to the excess shall be treated as accruing on the subsequent disposal of the new asset (within the meaning of section 116(4) of the 1992 Act).*[2]

Amendments—[1] In para (2), reference substituted by the Exchange Gains and Losses (Bringing into Account Gains or Losses) (Amendment) Regulations, SI 2004/3259 regs 2, 7 with effect in relation to accounting periods beginning on or after 1 January 2005.

2 Reg 9 revoked by the Exchange Gains and Losses (Bringing into Account Gains or Losses) (Amendment) Regulations, SI 2010/809, regs 2, 9, with effect in relation to a disposal of an asset made on or after 6 April 2010, subject to savings in regs 13, 14(4).

10 Cases where, but for section 116, section 127 of the 1992 Act would apply in relation to assets as regards which paragraph (2)(a), but not paragraph (2)(b), of regulation 8 has had effect

(1) This regulation applies in the circumstances prescribed by paragraph (2) below.

(2) The circumstances prescribed by this paragraph are where, but for section 116 of the 1992 Act, section 127 of that Act would apply in relation to a transaction involving original shares which are or include an asset as regards which paragraph (2)(*a*), but not paragraph (2)(*b*), of regulation 8 has had effect.

(3) Where this regulation applies, regulation 9(4) shall apply to the amount which, by virtue of regulation 8(2)(*a*), is not brought into account as a chargeable gain or an allowable loss for the accounting period in which the disposal of the asset occurs in the same way as it applies to an amount found under regulation 9(3).[1]

Amendments—[1] Reg 10 revoked by the Exchange Gains and Losses (Bringing into Account Gains or Losses) (Amendment) Regulations, SI 2010/809, regs 2, 10, with effect in relation to a disposal of an asset made on or after 6 April 2010, subject to savings in regs 13, 14(4).

11 Cases where there is no disposal of the asset by virtue of section 127 of the 1992 Act

(1) This regulation applies in the circumstances prescribed by paragraph (2) below.

(2) The circumstances prescribed by this paragraph are where the circumstances prescribed by [regulation 3(1A) and (2)][1] would exist but for there being no disposal of the asset for the purposes of the 1992 Act by virtue of section 127 of that Act ("section 127").

(3) Where this regulation applies, the amount which, but for section 127, would be brought into account under regulation 4(1) as a chargeable gain or allowable loss shall be found and paragraph (4) below shall apply.

(4) Where this paragraph applies—

(*a*) *if the amount found under paragraph (3) above would be brought into account as a chargeable gain, in computing the amount of any chargeable gain or allowable loss accruing on the subsequent disposal of the new holding, the consideration received on that disposal shall be increased by an amount equal to that amount;*

(*b*) *if the amount found under paragraph (3) above would be brought into account as an allowable loss—*

(i) *in computing the amount of any chargeable gain or allowable loss accruing on the subsequent disposal of the new holding, the consideration received on that disposal shall be reduced by an amount equal to that amount; and*

(ii) *if that amount exceeds the amount of the consideration, an allowable loss equal in amount to the excess shall be treated as accruing on that disposal.*[2]

Amendments—[1] In para (2), reference substituted by the Exchange Gains and Losses (Bringing into Account Gains or Losses) (Amendment) Regulations, SI 2004/3259 regs 2, 8 with effect in relation to accounting periods beginning on or after 1 January 2005.

[2] Reg 11 revoked by the Exchange Gains and Losses (Bringing into Account Gains or Losses) (Amendment) Regulations, SI 2010/809, regs 2, 11, with effect in relation to a disposal of an asset made on or after 6 April 2010, subject to savings in regs 13, 14(4).

12 Cases where section 127 of the 1992 Act applies in relation to assets as regards which paragraph (2)(a), but not paragraph (2)(b), of regulation 8 has had effect

(1) This regulation applies in the circumstances prescribed by paragraph (2) below.

(2) The circumstances prescribed by this paragraph are where section 127 of the 1992 Act applies in relation to a transaction involving original shares which are or include an asset as regards which paragraph (2)(*a*), but not paragraph (2)(*b*), of regulation 8 has had effect.

(3) Where this regulation applies, regulation 11(4) shall apply to the amount which, by virtue of regulation 8(2)(*a*), has not been brought into account as a chargeable gain or an allowable loss for the accounting period in which the disposal of the asset occurs in the same way as it applies to an amount found under regulation 11(3).[1]

Amendments—[1] Reg 12 revoked by the Exchange Gains and Losses (Bringing into Account Gains or Losses) (Amendment) Regulations, SI 2010/809, regs 2, 12, with effect in relation to a disposal of an asset made on or after 6 April 2010, subject to savings in regs 13, 14(4).

13 [Cases where matched assets represent loan relationships]

(1) [Subject to paragraph (3A),][3] this regulation applies in the circumstances prescribed by [paragraphs (2)[, (2A) and (2B)][2]][1] below.

(2) The circumstances prescribed by this paragraph are where there is a disposal of an asset by a company and the asset disposed of represents a loan relationship of the company in relation to which exchange gains or losses have fallen within subsection (4) of section 84A.

[(2A) The circumstances prescribed by this paragraph are where there is a disposal of an asset in an accounting period beginning on or after 1st January 2005 representing a loan relationship in relation to which exchange gains or losses were recognised in the company's statement of recognised gains and losses or statement of changes in equity.][1]

[(2B) The circumstances prescribed by this paragraph are where there is a disposal of an asset representing a loan relationship in relation to which amounts have fallen within regulation 12A of the Loan Relationships and Derivative Contracts (Disregard and Bringing into Account of Profits and Losses) Regulations 2004.][2]

(3) Where this regulation applies, an amount equal to the amount of any net gain or net loss shall be brought into account, for the purposes of Chapter 2, as a credit or a debit (according to whether it is an amount of net gain or net loss) in respect of the loan relationship for the accounting period in which the disposal occurs.

[(3A) This regulation does not apply so far as the net gain or net loss falls to be brought into account apart from this regulation.][3]

(4) For the purposes of this regulation, the amount of any net gain or net loss shall be calculated by finding the aggregate of the amounts representing the exchange gains and losses which fell within [paragraphs (2) and (2A)][1] [and amounts within paragraph (2B)][2].

Amendments—[1] Heading substituted, references in paras (1), (4) substituted, and para (2A) inserted, by the Exchange Gains and Losses (Bringing into Account Gains or Losses) (Amendment) Regulations, SI 2004/3259 regs 2, 9 with effect in relation to accounting periods beginning on or after 1 January 2005.

[2] In paras (1), (4) words inserted, and para (2B) inserted, by the Changes in Accounting Standards (Loan Relationships and Derivative Contracts) Regulations, SI 2014/3325 reg 2 with effect from 31 December 2014. Note that if, in consequence of a relevant change in accounting policy, a company adopts a relevant accounting change for a period of account beginning on or after 1 October 2012, these amendments have effect in relation to the accounting period which coincides with that period and subsequent accounting periods (SI 2014/3325 reg 1(2)).

[3] In para (1) words inserted, and para (3A) inserted, by the Exchange Gains and Losses (Bringing into Account Gains or Losses) (Amendment) Regulations, SI 2015/1960 reg 2(1), (3) with effect in relation to accounting periods beginning on or after 1 January 2016.

14 [Cases where there are no matching assets

. . .

Amendment—This regulation (which was inserted by SI 2004/3259 regs 2, 10) revoked by the Exchange Gains and Losses (Bringing into Account Gains or Losses) (Amendment) Regulations, SI 2005/2013 regs 2, 5 with effect from 11 August 2005.

2002/2661

VENTURE CAPITAL TRUST (EXCHANGE OF SHARES AND SECURITIES) REGULATIONS 2002

Made by the Treasury under TA 1988 s 842AA(5AD), Sch 28B para 11B

Made ....*22 October 2002*
Laid before the House of Commons ....*23 October 2002*
Coming into force ....*13 November 2002*

1 Citation, commencement and effect

(1) These Regulations may be cited as the Venture Capital Trust (Exchange of Shares and Securities) Regulations 2002 and shall come into force on 13th November 2002.

(2) These Regulations have effect in relation to exchanges of shares or securities occurring on or after 21st March 2000.

2 Interpretation

(1) In these Regulations unless the context otherwise requires—

"earn-out right" has the meaning in section 138A(1) of the 1992 Act (references to "debentures" being read as references to "securities" as defined below);

the "issue" of any shares or securities has the meaning in section 135 of the 1992 Act, except for a security consisting in a liability in respect of an unsecured loan where it has effect as a reference to the making of the loan;

"market value" shall be construed in accordance with sections 272 and 273 of the 1992 Act;

"a monetary right" means a right under an agreement to receive a monetary amount at a future time in respect of shares or securities, whether or not the amount is ascertainable at the date of the agreement;

"original shares or securities" has the meaning in paragraph 11B(2) of Schedule 28B;

"recognised stock exchange" has the meaning given by section 841;

"Schedule 28B" means Schedule 28B to the Taxes Act;

"securities" has the meaning given by section 842AA(12);

"the 1992 Act" means the Taxation of Chargeable Gains Act 1992;

"the Taxes Act" means the Income and Corporation Taxes Act 1988;

"venture capital trust" has the meaning given by section 842AA(1).

(2) References in these Regulations (except regulation 5(1)(*a*), (*b*) and (*d*)) to an exchange of shares or securities shall be construed in accordance with paragraph 11B(2) of Schedule 28B, and "exchanged" has a corresponding meaning.

(3) For the purposes of these Regulations, old shares and new shares are matching shares in relation to each other if the old shares are the shares for which the new shares are exchanged under the arrangements, and the same provision shall apply, with any necessary modifications, as between old securities and new securities, and old securities and new shares.

(4) References in these Regulations to a section, without more, are to that section of the Taxes Act.

3 Scope of Regulations

These Regulations apply to any exchange of shares or securities held by a venture capital trust—

(*a*) which falls within the terms of paragraph 11B(1)(*a*) to (*c*) of Schedule 28B,

(*b*) which falls within one of the cases described in regulations 4 to 6, and

(*c*) where the trust company receives, in respect of the old shares or old securities, new shares or new securities, with or without other consideration.

4 Exchange of shares or securities for those in the same company

(1) The case described in this regulation is an exchange of shares or securities where—

(*a*) persons are, whether for payment or not, issued shares in or securities of a company in respect of and in proportion to (or as nearly as may be in proportion to) their holdings of shares in or securities of the company or of any class of shares in or securities of the company,

(*b*) the person in question is a venture capital trust,

(*c*) the new shares are issued in respect of old shares or old securities, and the new securities are issued solely in respect of old securities,

(*d*) immediately after the exchange, the old shares and old securities are cancelled or otherwise extinguished, and

(*e*) the exchange is not an exchange of convertibles for shares to which paragraph 10D of Schedule 28B applies.

(2) In paragraph (1) and regulation 7—

(*a*) expressions have the same meanings as in section 126(2) of the 1992 Act;

(*b*) the shares or securities issued to the trust company are referred to as the "new shares" and the "new securities" respectively, and the trust company's former holding mentioned in paragraph (1)(*a*) is referred to, separately and as the case may be, as the "old shares" and the "old securities" respectively.

5 Exchange of shares or securities for those in another company

(1) The case described in this regulation is where—

(*a*) a company ("company B") issues shares or securities to a person in exchange for the shares in or securities of another company ("company A"),

(*b*) either—

(i) in consequence of the exchange, company B will hold more than 50% of the ordinary share capital of company A, or

(ii) company B issues the shares or securities in exchange for shares in or securities of company A as the result of a general offer made to members of company A or any class of them (with or without exceptions for persons connected with company B), and made in the first instance on a condition such that if it were satisfied company B would have control of company A,

(*c*) the person in question is a venture capital trust,

(*d*) the new shares are issued in exchange for old shares or old securities, and the new securities are issued solely in exchange for old securities, and

(*e*) the arrangements under which the exchange takes place are not arrangements to which paragraph 10C of Schedule 28B (acquisitions for restructuring purpose) applies.

(2) In paragraph (1)(*a*), (*b*) and (*d*) and regulation 8—

(*a*) expressions (other than "securities") have the same meanings as in section 135 of the 1992 Act;

(*b*) the shares in or securities of company B issued to the trust company are referred to as the "new shares" and the "new securities" respectively, and the shares in or securities of company A held by the trust company and mentioned in paragraph (1)(*a*) are referred to as the "old shares" and the "old securities" respectively.

6 Scheme of reconstruction involving issue of shares or securities

(1) The case described in this regulation is where—

(*a*) an arrangement between a company ("company A") and—

(i) the persons holding shares in or securities of the company, or

(ii) where there are different classes of shares in or securities of the company, the persons holding any class of those shares or securities,

is entered into for the purposes of, or in connection with, a scheme of reconstruction,

(*b*) under the arrangement—

(i) another company ("company B") issues shares or securities to those persons in respect of and in proportion to (or as nearly as may be in proportion to) their original holding, but

(ii) the shares in or securities of company A comprised in their original holding are either retained by those persons or cancelled, redeemed or otherwise extinguished,

(*c*) the person in question is a venture capital trust, and

(*d*) the new shares are issued in respect of old shares or old securities, and the new securities are issued solely in respect of old securities.

(2) In paragraph (1) and regulation 9—

(*a*) expressions (other than "securities") have the same meanings as in section 136(1) and (3) to (5) of the 1992 Act (references to "debentures" in those provisions being read as references to "securities" as defined above);

(*b*) the shares in or securities of company B issued to the trust company are referred to as the "new shares" and the "new securities" respectively, and the trust company's original holding in company A is referred to, separately and as the case may be, as the "old shares" and the "old securities" respectively.

7 Provision where there is an exchange of shares or securities in the same company

(1) In relation to any case described in regulation 4 the following paragraphs have effect.

(2) For the purposes of subsection (2)(*b*) to (*d*) of section 842AA, the aggregate value of the new shares and new securities shall be determined, immediately after the exchange and until such time as those shares or securities fall to be revalued in accordance with subsection (5) of that section, in accordance with the following formula:

$$Nv = Ov \times \frac{Nmv}{Nmv + c}$$

where—

Nv is the aggregate value of the new shares and new securities to be determined in accordance with this paragraph,

Ov is the aggregate value of the old shares and old securities when last valued in accordance with subsection (5) of section 842AA ("historic values",

Nmv is the aggregate market value, immediately after the exchange, of the new shares and new securities,

C is the aggregate market value, immediately after the exchange, of—

(i) any monetary amount,

(ii) any monetary right (without any discount for postponement of the right to receive the payment or any part of it), and

(iii) any other consideration or receipt (except the new shares and new securities),

received by the venture capital trust as consideration for, or in respect of, the old shares or old securities, and

"immediately after the exchange" in this regulation means immediately after the events mentioned in regulation 4(1)(d).

(3) For the purposes of subsection (2)(*b*) to (*d*) of section 842AA, where the venture capital trust retains original shares or securities in the company which are not included in the exchange of old shares or old securities for new shares or new securities, such original shares or securities shall, immediately after the exchange, continue to be valued at their value, or apportioned value, as the case may be, when last valued before the exchange in accordance with subsection (5) of section 842AA, until such time as they fall to be revalued in accordance with that subsection.

(4) For the purposes of paragraph 10B of Schedule 28B the like provisions as are contained in paragraphs (2) and (3) shall apply (substituting references to valuations in accordance with paragraph 10B for references to valuations in accordance with subsection (5) of section 842AA).

(5) Where the company in which the venture capital trust holds the old shares or old securities is deemed to satisfy the requirements of paragraph 2 of Schedule 28B (unquoted company) by virtue of sub-paragraph (6) of that paragraph for a period of five years after ceasing to be to be an unquoted company, the company shall be deemed to satisfy those requirements in relation to the new shares or new securities for the same five year period.

(6) Subject to paragraph (7), where the old shares or old securities are shares or securities in relation to which the requirements of paragraphs 6 and 8 of Schedule 28B were (or were deemed to be) satisfied to any extent immediately before the exchange, those requirements shall be deemed, at all times after that time, to be satisfied to the same extent in relation to the matching new shares or new securities.

(7) Where there is a time following the exchange when (apart from the exchange) the requirements of paragraph 6 of Schedule 28B would have ceased under—

(*a*) sub-paragraph (2) of that paragraph, or

(*b*) this paragraph,

to be satisfied in relation to the old shares or old securities, those requirements shall cease at that time to be satisfied in relation to the matching new shares or new securities.

(8) For the purposes of paragraph 7 of Schedule 28B any new shares or new securities shall be deemed—

(*a*) to have been issued at the time when the matching old shares or old securities were issued (or, as the case may be, were deemed to have been issued), and

(*b*) by virtue of that issue, to have raised the same amount of money as was raised (or, as the case may be, was deemed to be raised) by virtue of the issue of the matching old shares or old securities.

(9) In determining whether the requirements of paragraph 9 of Schedule 28B are satisfied in relation to the company at any time in the period for giving effect to the exchange, the exchange shall be disregarded.

(10) The reference in paragraph (9) to the period for giving effect to the exchange is to the period which—

(*a*) begins on the day when a shareholder disposes of, redeems or otherwise ceases to possess shares or securities in consequence of the exchange or, where there is more than one exchange of shares or securities involved in a company reorganisation, the exchanges, and is the first shareholder to do so, and

(*b*) ends on the earlier of—

(i) the date when the last of the shares or securities to be issued in consequence of the exchange or exchanges is issued, and

(ii) the day six months after the date in sub-paragraph (*a*) (or such later date as the Board may by notice in writing allow).

8 Provision where exchange of shares or securities for those in another company

(1) In relation to a case described in regulation 5, the following paragraphs have effect.

(2) For the purposes of subsection (2)(*b*) to (*d*) of section 842AA, the aggregate value of the new shares and new securities issued to the venture capital trust shall be determined, immediately after the exchange and until such time as those shares or securities fall to be revalued in accordance with subsection (5) of that section, in accordance with the formula in regulation 7(2) (substituting references to the period for giving effect to the exchange for references to the events mentioned in regulation 4(1)(*d*)).

(3) For the purposes of paragraph 10B of Schedule 28B, the like provisions as are contained in paragraph (2) shall apply (substituting references to valuations in accordance with paragraph 10B for references to valuations in accordance with subsection (5) of section 842AA).

(4) The new shares and new securities held by the venture capital trust shall be treated, during the period for giving effect to the exchange, as meeting the requirements of Schedule 28B.

(5) The requirements of and arrangements referred to in paragraph 9 of Schedule 28B, to the extent that they are incidental to the exchange, shall be disregarded before and during that period.

(6) The new shares and new securities shall be treated at all times following the end of the period for giving effect to the exchange as having met the requirements of paragraphs 6 and 7 of Schedule 28B.

(7) Where, immediately after the end of the period for giving effect to the exchange, any of the new shares or new securities are found not to meet the requirements of paragraph 2 of Schedule 28B, or of that paragraph and any other paragraphs of that Schedule (other than paragraph 6 or 7), those shares or securities shall be treated as meeting those requirements until the end of the period specified in paragraph (8) or the disposal by the venture capital trust of those shares or securities, whichever is the earlier to occur.

(8) The period specified is the period that—

(*a*) begins on the date when new shares or new securities are first issued to the venture capital trust or, if later, on the date on which all the new shares or new securities issued to the venture capital trust become fully tradeable, and

(*b*) ends immediately before the second anniversary of that date.

(9) Where, immediately after the end of the period for giving effect to the exchange, any of the new shares or new securities are found not to meet the requirements of any paragraph of Schedule 28B other than paragraph 2, 6 or 7, those shares or securities shall be treated as meeting those requirements until the end of the period—

(*a*) beginning on the date when new shares or new securities are first issued to the venture capital trust ("the first issue date"), and

(*b*) ending on the earlier of—

(i) the disposal by the venture capital trust of those shares or securities, or

(ii) subject to paragraph (10), in the case of shares, the day 3 years after the first issue date and, in the case of securities, the day 5 years after the first issue date.

(10) Where, in a case falling within the terms of paragraph (9)(*b*)(ii), before the relevant date there mentioned, the new shares or new securities become marketed to the general public (within the meaning of paragraph 2(3) of Schedule 28B), there shall be substituted for that date the second anniversary of the date on which the new shares or new securities became so marketed or, if later, the second anniversary of the date on which those shares or securities became fully tradeable.

(11) References in this regulation to the period for giving effect to the exchange are references to the period which—

(*a*) begins when a shareholder or holder of securities ceases to possess shares in or securities of company A in consequence of the exchange, and is the first shareholder or holder of securities to do so, and

(*b*) ends when the last of the shares in or securities of company B to be issued in consequence of the exchange (excluding shares or securities issued in pursuance of an earn-out right) is issued.

(12) Shares or securities become fully tradeable for the purposes of this regulation and regulation 9 when, in circumstances where they are offered for issue to the shareholders or holders of securities of company A, they cease to be subject to—

(*a*) rules of the recognised stock exchange (or other exchange) governing the offer that prohibit or restrict the disposal of the shares or securities to any other person, and

(*b*) conditions prohibiting or restricting the disposal of the shares or securities to any other person that are contained in any contract entered into by any of the following persons—

(i) company B, or a company disposing of the shares or securities,

(ii) the person or persons sponsoring, underwriting or organising the offer, and

(iii) the venture capital trust in question.

9 Provision where scheme of reconstruction involving issue of shares or securities

(1) In relation to a case described in regulation 6 the following paragraphs have effect as regards—

(*a*) any shares in or securities of company A that are retained by the venture capital trust after the scheme of reconstruction, whether old shares or old securities or original shares or securities, not included in the scheme of reconstruction (the "company A shares or securities"), and

(*b*) the shares in or securities of company B issued to the venture capital trust as mentioned in regulation 6(2)(*b*) (the "new shares" and the "new securities" respectively).

(2) For the purposes of subsection (2)(*b*) to (*d*) of section 842AA, the aggregate value of the new shares and new securities and any company A shares or securities shall be determined, immediately after the reorganisation period and until such time as those shares or securities fall to be revalued in accordance with subsection (5) of that section, in accordance with the formula in regulation 7(2) but where—

Nv is the aggregate value of the new shares and new securities, and of the company A shares or securities, to be determined in accordance with that paragraph,

Nmv is the aggregate market value, immediately after the reorganisation period, of the new shares and new securities and the company A shares or securities, and

any reference to events mentioned in regulation 4(1)(d) is replaced with a reference to the reorganisation period.

(3) For the purposes of paragraph 10B of Schedule 28B, the like provisions as are contained in paragraph (2) shall apply (substituting references to valuations in accordance with paragraph 10B for references to valuations in accordance with subsection (5) of section 842AA).

(4) The new shares and new securities held by the venture capital trust shall be treated, during the reorganisation period, as meeting the requirements of Schedule 28B.

(5) The requirements of and arrangements referred to in paragraph 9 of Schedule 28B, to the extent that they are incidental to the scheme of reconstruction, shall be disregarded before and during the reorganisation period.

(6) The new shares or new securities held by the venture capital trust shall be treated at all times following the date on which they were issued to the trust company as having met the requirements of paragraphs 6 and 7 of Schedule 28B.

(7) Where, immediately after the date on which the new shares or new securities were issued to the venture capital trust, those shares or securities are found not to meet the requirements of paragraph 2 of that Schedule, or of that paragraph and any other paragraph of that Schedule excepting paragraph 6 or 7, those shares or securities shall be treated as meeting those requirements until the end of the period specified in paragraph (8) or the disposal by the venture capital trust of those shares or securities, whichever is the earlier to occur.

(8) The period specified is the period that—

(*a*) begins on the date on which the new shares or new securities were issued to the venture capital trust or, if later, on the date on which all those shares or securities become fully tradeable, and

(*b*) ends immediately before the second anniversary of that date.

(9) Where, immediately after the date on which the new shares or new securities were issued to the venture capital trust, those shares or securities are found not to meet the requirements of any paragraph of Schedule 28B other than paragraph 2, 6 or 7, those shares or securities shall be treated as meeting the requirements of that Schedule until the end of the period—

(*a*) beginning on the date when new shares or new securities are first issued to the venture capital trust ("the first issue date"), and

(*b*) ending on the earlier of—

(i) the disposal by the venture capital trust of those shares or securities, or

(ii) subject to paragraph (10), in the case of shares, the day 3 years after the first issue date and, in the case of securities, the day 5 years after the first issue date.

(10) Where, in a case falling within the terms of paragraph (9)(*b*)(ii), before the relevant date there mentioned, the new shares or new securities become marketed to the general public (within the meaning of paragraph 2(3) of Schedule 28B), there shall be substituted for that date the second anniversary of the date on which the new shares or new securities became so marketed or, if later, the second anniversary of the date on which those shares or securities became fully tradeable.

(11) In this regulation references to the reorganisation period are to the period which—

(*a*) begins when a shareholder or holder of securities receives shares in or securities of company B in consequence of the scheme of reconstruction, and is the first person to do so, and

(*b*) ends when the last of the shares in or securities of company B to be issued in consequence of the scheme of reconstruction (excluding shares or securities issued in pursuance of an earn-out right) is issued.

10 Earn-outs

(1) Where, in a case described in either regulation 5 or 6—

(*a*) shares in or securities of company B ("earn-out shares or securities") are issued to a venture capital trust in pursuance of an earn-out right, which was conferred on the trust company in exchange for old shares or old securities, and

(*b*) the requirements of regulation 5(1)(*d*) or 6(1)(*d*), as the case may be, would be satisfied if the earn-out right were treated as replaced by the earn-out shares or securities that are issued in pursuance of it—

(i) regulation 8(4) to (12) or regulation 9(4) to (11), as the case may be, shall apply to the earn-out shares and securities as they apply to new shares and new securities; and

(ii) the trust company may elect to recalculate the formula in regulation 7(2) (as applied by regulation 8(2) or (3) or 9(2) or (3)).

(2) The recalculation shall be made—

(*a*) including the earn-out shares and securities in the calculation of Nv and Nmv (but at their market value immediately after they were issued), and

(*b*) omitting the earn-out right from the calculation of C.

(3) An election under this regulation in respect of any right—

(*a*) must be made, by a notice given to an officer of the Board, within the period of one year from the end of the accounting period in which the relevant earn-out shares and securities are issued, and

(*b*) shall be irrevocable.

11 Apportionment

(1) For the purposes of these Regulations (and of subsection (2)(*b*) to (*d*) of section 842AA and paragraph 10B of Schedule 28B), where it is necessary to apportion any value between the new shares or new securities issued to the venture capital trust (or one or more classes thereof), such apportionment shall be carried out—

(*a*) in the first instance, having regard to the historic values of any old shares or old securities in relation to which the new shares or new securities are matching shares or securities,

(*b*) otherwise according to such method as is just and reasonable, and

(*c*) in any event, with a view to securing that the requirements of section 842AA(2)(*b*) to (*d*), or paragraph 10B of Schedule 28B, as the case may be, do not cease to be met.

(2) In the application of paragraph (1) to regulation 9, references to new shares and new securities shall be construed as extending to company A shares or securities (as defined in that regulation) with any necessary modifications.

2002/2849

CAPITAL GAINS TAX (GILT-EDGED SECURITIES) ORDER 2002

Made by the Treasury under TCGA 1992 Sch 9

Made . . . . 18 November 2002

1 This Order may be cited as the Capital Gains Tax (Gilt-edged Securities) Order 2002.

2 The following securities are hereby specified for the purposes of Schedule 9 to the Taxation of Chargeable Gains Act 1992—

5% Treasury Stock 2008
5% Treasury Stock 2012
5% Treasury Stock 2014
5% Treasury Stock 2025
2% Index-linked Treasury Stock 2035.

2002/3047

STATUTORY PAYMENT SCHEMES (ELECTRONIC COMMUNICATIONS) REGULATIONS 2002

Made by the Commissioners of Inland Revenue under FA 1999 ss 132 and 133(2)

Made . . . . 11 December 2002
Laid before the House of Commons . . . . 11 December 2002
Coming into force . . . . 1 January 2003

PART 1
INTRODUCTION

1 Citation, commencement and interpretation

(1) These Regulations may be cited as the Statutory Payment Schemes (Electronic Communications) Regulations 2002 and shall come into force on 1st January 2003.

(2) In these Regulations—

"the Board" means the Commissioners of Inland Revenue;

"official computer system" means a computer system maintained by or on behalf of the Board—

(*a*) to send or receive information or payments; or

(*b*) to process or store information; and

"the statutory payments" means statutory maternity pay, [statutory paternity pay][1][, statutory shared parental pay][2] and statutory adoption pay.

(3) References in these Regulations to information and to the delivery of information shall be construed in accordance with section 132(8) of the Finance Act 1999.

Amendments—[1] In para (2), words substituted and inserted by the Statutory Payment Schemes (Electronic Communications) (Amendment) Regulations, SI 2015/125 reg 2 with effect from 5 April 2015..

2 Scope of these Regulations

These Regulations apply to—

(*a*) the delivery of information to or by the Board, the delivery of which is required or authorised in connection with the statutory payments; and

(*b*) the making or recovery of any of the statutory payments or of any other sum in connection with those payments.

PART 2
ELECTRONIC COMMUNICATIONS—GENERAL PROVISIONS

3 Restrictions on the use of electronic communications

(1) The Board may use electronic communications in connection with the matters referred to in regulation 2.

(2) A person other than the Board may only use electronic communications in connection with the matters referred to in regulation 2 if the conditions specified in paragraphs (3) to (6) are satisfied.

(3) The first condition is that the person is for the time being permitted to use electronic communications by an authorisation given by means of a direction of the Board.

(4) The second condition is that the person uses—

(*a*) an approved method for authenticating the identity of the sender of the communication;

(*b*) an approved method of electronic communications; and

(*c*) an approved method for authenticating any information delivered by means of electronic communications.

(5) The third condition is that any information or payment sent by means of electronic communications is in a form approved for the purposes of these Regulations.

(6) The fourth condition is that the person maintains such records in written or electronic form as may be specified in a general or specific direction given by the Board.

(7) In this regulation "approved" means approved for the purposes of these Regulations and for the time being by means of a general or specific direction of the Board.

Use of intermediaries

4 The Board may use intermediaries in connection with—

(*a*) the delivery of information about any statutory payment by means of electronic communications;

(*b*) the making or recovery of any statutory payment by those means; and

(*c*) the authentication or security of anything transmitted by any such means,

and may require other persons to use intermediaries in connection with those matters.

PART 3
ELECTRONIC COMMUNICATIONS — EVIDENTIAL PROVISIONS

5 Effect of delivering information by means of electronic communications

(1) Information to which these Regulations apply, and which is delivered by means of electronic communications, shall be treated as having been delivered, in the manner or form required by or under any provision of the Social Security Acts, section 7 or 8 of the Employment Act 2002 or Article 8 or 9 of the Employment (Northern Ireland) Order 2002 if, but only if, all the conditions specified by—

(*a*) these Regulations, and

(*b*) any specific or general direction given by the Board,

are satisfied.

(2) Information delivered by means of electronic communications shall be treated as having been delivered on the day on which the last of the conditions imposed as mentioned in paragraph (1) is satisfied.

This is subject to the following qualification.

(3) The Board may by a general or specific direction provide for information to be treated as delivered upon a different date (whether earlier or later) (than that given by paragraph (2).

(4) In paragraph (1) "the Social Security Acts" means the Social Security Contributions and Benefits Act 1992, the Social Security Administration Act 1992, the Social Security Contributions and Benefits (Northern Ireland) Act 1992 and the Social Security Administration (Northern Ireland) Act 1992.

6 Proof of identity of sender or recipient of information

If it is necessary to prove, for any purpose, the identity of—

(*a*) the sender of any information delivered by means of electronic communications to an official computer system, or

(*b*) the recipient of any information delivered by means of electronic communications from an official computer system,

the sender or recipient (as the case may be) shall be presumed to be the person recorded as such on an official computer system unless the contrary is proved.

7 Proof of delivery of information and payments

(1) If it is necessary to prove, for any purpose, that the use of electronic communications has resulted in the making of any payment to or by the Board, or the delivery of any information to or by them, this shall be presumed, unless the contrary is proved—

(*a*) in the case of information delivered or a payment made to the Board, if the making of the payment, or the delivery of the information, has been recorded on an official computer system;

(*b*) in the case of information delivered, or payment made, by the Board, if the despatch of that payment or information has been recorded on an official computer system, and

(*c*) not to be the case if it has not been so recorded.

(2) If it is necessary to prove, for any purpose, when any information or payment sent by electronic communications has been received, the time of receipt shall be presumed to be that recorded on an official computer system unless the contrary is proved.

8 Proof of content of information

If it is necessary to prove, for any purpose the content of any information sent by means of electronic communications, the content shall be presumed to be that recorded on an official computer system unless the contrary is proved.

9 Certificates as to official records

A document certified by an officer of the Board to be a printed-out version of any electronic communication recorded on an official computer system as at a particular date shall be presumed, unless the contrary is proved—

(*a*) to have been recorded on an official computer system at that date; and

(*b*) to constitute the entirety of the electronic communication so recorded.

10 Presumption as to certificates

A document purporting to be a certificate issued by an officer of the Board under regulation 9 shall be presumed to be such a certificate unless the contrary is proved.

2003/96

COMMUNITY INVESTMENT TAX RELIEF (ACCREDITATION OF COMMUNITY DEVELOPMENT FINANCE INSTITUTIONS) REGULATIONS 2003

Made by the Treasury under FA 2002 Sch 16 paras 4(2)(b), (4), (5), (6) and 5

Made .... *23 January 2003*
Laid before Parliament .... *23 January 2003*
Coming into force .... *13 February 2003*

PART 1
INTRODUCTORY

1 Citation and commencement

These Regulations may be cited as the Community Investment Tax Relief (Accreditation of Community Development Finance Institutions) Regulations 2003 and shall come into force on 13th February 2003.

2 Interpretation

In these Regulations—

"accreditation" means accreditation as a community development finance institution;

. . .[1]

"CDFI" means a body accredited as a community development finance institution under [Chapter 2 of Part 7 of the Income Tax Act 2007][1];

. . .[2]

["the five year period" means the period of five years beginning with the day the investment is made;][1]

. . .[1]

["the first investment" in relation to an investment made in a CDFI means the first investment made in the CDFI in its current period of accreditation;][22]

["investment"—

(*a*) in relation to an individual, shall be construed in accordance with section 336 of the Income Tax Act 2007; and

(*b*) in relation to a company, has the meaning given in [section 221 of the Corporation Tax Act 2010][2];][1]

"investment fund" has the meaning given in regulation 9;

"notice" means notice in writing;

"qualifying enterprise" has the meaning given in regulation 10;

["qualifying investment"—

(*a*) in relation to an investment made by an individual, means an investment in respect of which the individual is eligible under section 334 of the Income Tax Act 2007 for community investment tax relief; and

(*b*) in relation to an investment made by a company, has the meaning given in [section 225 of the Corporation Tax Act 2010][2].

"relevant investment" has the meaning given in regulation 11;

"residential property" has the meaning given in Annex D of the Material Concerning the Accreditation of Community Development Finance Institutions published by the Secretary of State;

"retail community development finance institution" shall be construed in accordance with [section 340(6)(*b*), (7) and (8) of the Income Tax Act 2007][1];

"the Small Business Service" means the entity so named being an executive agency of the Department of Trade and Industry;

["tax relief certificate" means a certificate issued by the CDFI in respect of the investment which is in the form specified by the Commissioners for Her Majesty's Revenue and Customs;][1]

Amendments—[1] Words in definitions of "CDFI" and "retail community development finance institution" substituted, definitions of "the board", "the Investment Director" and "the Small Business Service" revoked, definition of "the Director of Enterprise Environment" inserted, definitions of "the five year period", "investment", "qualifying investment" and "tax relief certificate" substituted, by the Community Investment Tax Relief (Accreditation of Community Development Finance Institutions) (Amendment) Regulations, SI 2008/383 arts 2, 3 with effect from 11 March: SI 2008/383 art 1.

[2] Definition of "the Director of Enterprise Environment" revoked, definition of "the first investment" inserted, and in definitions of "investment" and "qualifying investment", words substituted by the Community Investment Tax Relief (Accreditation of Community Development Finance Institutions) (Amendment) Regulations, SI 2013/417 regs 4, 5 with effect from 1 April 2013.

PART 2
APPLICATION AND CRITERIA FOR ACCREDITATION

3 Criteria for accreditation

For the purposes of [section 340(2)(*b*) of the Income Tax Act 2007][1] the criteria to be satisfied for accreditation are specified in Part 2 (Application and Criteria for Accreditation) of the Material Concerning the Accreditation of Community Development Finance Institutions published by the Secretary of State.

Amendments—[1] Words substituted by the Community Investment Tax Relief (Accreditation of Community Development Finance Institutions) (Amendment) Regulations, SI 2008/383 arts 2, 4 with effect from 11 March: SI 2008/383 art 1.

4 Notification of accreditation or refusal

The Secretary of State must give notice to a body of the grant of an accreditation specifying the date of the grant of accreditation and the date on which the period of accreditation begins.

5 The Secretary of State must give notice to a body of a refusal to grant accreditation specifying the date of the refusal and the reasons for the refusal.

PART 3
TERMS AND CONDITIONS OF ACCREDITATION

6 An accreditation is subject to the terms set out in this Part.

7 Publication of details

(1) It is a term of accreditation that the CDFI agrees to the publication of the information specified in paragraph (2) in a list which the Secretary of State may publish from time to time.

(2) The information specified for the purpose of paragraph (1) is—

(*a*) the name of the CDFI;

(*b*) the business address of the CDFI;

(*c*) the name of an individual who may be contacted at the CDFI;

(*d*) the date the CDFI was granted accreditation; and

(*e*) an outline of the aims and business operations of the CDFI.

(3) The CDFI must give notice to the Secretary of State of—

(*a*) any change to the information specified in subparagraphs (a) to (d) of paragraph (2), and

(*b*) any material change to the information specified in subparagraph (e) of paragraph (2),

within 30 days of the relevant change.

(4) The CDFI is liable to a penalty of £100 payable to the [Department for Business, Energy and Industrial Strategy][2] for each failure to notify a change to the specified information in accordance with paragraph (3) unless the [Secretary of State][1] is satisfied that the CDFI had a reasonable excuse for failing to notify the change.

Amendments—[1] In para (4), words substituted by the Community Investment Tax Relief (Accreditation of Community Development Finance Institutions) (Amendment) Regulations, SI 2013/417 regs 4, 12(*a*) with effect from 1st April 2013.

[2] In para (4), words substituted by the Secretaries of State for Business, Energy and Industrial Strategy, for International Trade and for Exiting the European Union and the Transfer of Functions (Education and Skills) Order, SI 2019/992 art 14, Schedule para 27(*a*) with effect from 9 November 2016.

[8 [General CDFI investment terms

(1) It is a term of accreditation that—

(*a*) on or before the first anniversary of [the date the first investment was made in the CDFI][2], at least 25% of the amount of the investment fund is invested in relevant investments in qualifying enterprises;

(*b*) on or before the second anniversary of [the date the first investment was made in the CDFI][2], at least 50% of the amount of the investment fund is invested in relevant investments in qualifying enterprises;

(*c*) on or before the third anniversary of [the date the first investment was made in the CDFI][2] at least 75% of the amount of the investment fund is invested in relevant investments in qualifying enterprises; and

(*d*) at the end of each year ending on a subsequent anniversary of [the date the first investment was made in the CDFI][2], an average of at least 75% of the amount of the investment fund has been invested in relevant investments in qualifying enterprises.

(2) For the purpose of paragraph (1)(*d*), the average percentage of the investment fund invested in relevant investments in qualifying enterprises is to be found on the last day of the year in question by calculating—

(*a*) the average of the percentages so invested as at close of business on each day of that year, or

(*b*) the average of the percentages so invested as at close of business on the relevant dates.

(3) "The relevant dates", in relation to a year, means—

(*a*) a date falling within the first three months of the year,

(*b*) a date falling within the second three months of the year,

(*c*) a date falling within the third three months of the year, and

(*d*) a date falling within the final three months of the year,

(4) A date falling within any of the time periods specified in paragraph (3)(*b*), (*c*) and (*d*) must be at least 87 days but not more than 95 days after the preceding date.

(5) If the percentage of the investment fund invested in relevant investments in qualifying enterprises at close of business on any day exceeds 100% of the investment fund, the excess shall be disregarded.][1]

Amendments—[1] Regulation substituted by the Community Investment Tax Relief (Accreditation of Community Development Finance Institutions) (Amendment) Regulations, SI 2008/383 arts 2, 6 with effect from 11 March: SI 2008/383 art 1.

[2] In para (1)(*a*), words substituted for words "the date the CDFI was first granted accreditation ("the accreditation date")", and in paras (1)(*b*), (*c*), (*d*), words substituted for words "the accreditation date" by the Community Investment Tax Relief (Accreditation of Community Development Finance Institutions) (Amendment) Regulations, SI 2013/417 regs 4, 6 with effect in relation to a CDFI whose current accreditation period starts on or after 1st April 2013.

9 Meaning of the "investment fund"

(1) The amount of the investment fund at a given date ("the relevant date") is the sum of—

$$A - (B + C)$$

Here—

A is the amount of qualifying investments and investments by other CDFIs in the CDFI made on or before the relevant date and held continuously since the investment was made until the relevant date, but does not include any qualifying investments or investments by other CDFIs in the CDFI made at any time during the three months prior to the relevant date;
B is any amount payable by the CDFI at the relevant date or at any time during the three months following the relevant date to repay, redeem or buy-back the capital element of any qualifying investment;
C is the amount of any investment made by the CDFI from the investment fund which has been written-off in accordance with generally accepted accounting practice.

(2) For the purpose of paragraph (1) where a qualifying investment is a loan which authorises the CDFI to draw down amounts of the loan over a period of time, the amount of the qualifying investment is the amount drawn down at the relevant date.

10 Meaning of "qualifying enterprise"

(1) For the purposes of these Regulations an enterprise is a qualifying enterprise if—
(*a*) the enterprise is a small or medium-sized enterprise;
(*b*) the CDFI can demonstrate that at the time the investment in the enterprise was made the enterprise was unable to obtain finance from other sources; and
(*c*) the enterprise falls within one of the following Cases.

Case 1

The enterprise is located in a geographic area identified in Annex A of the Material Concerning the Accreditation of Community Development Finance Institutions published by the Secretary of State.

Case 2

The enterprise is located in an area which the CDFI, by reference to Government-recognised measures of disadvantage relating to—
(i) income;
(ii) employment;
(iii) health, deprivation and disability;
(iv) education, skills and training;
(v) geographical access to services, and
(vi) housing,
can demonstrate has a level of disadvantage comparable to those identified in Annex A of the Material Concerning the Accreditation of Community Development Finance Institutions published by the Secretary of State.

Case 3

The enterprise is owned and operated by, or intended to serve, individuals recognised as being disadvantaged on account of their ethnicity, gender, age, disability or other similar defining characteristic.

[(2) For the purpose of paragraph (1)(*a*), a "small or medium-sized enterprise" means a micro, small or medium-sized enterprise as defined in Commission Recommendation 2003/361/EC of 6th May 2003 ("the Recommendation", references to the Annex being references to the Annex to the Recommendation), subject to the qualification set out in paragraph (3).

(3) If a company ("C") is a micro, small or medium-sized enterprise, disregarding any partner enterprise or linked enterprise, and, taken alone, it would satisfy the employee limit and a least one of the financial limits, but—
(*a*) the number of employees, annual turnover or annual balance sheet total (as the case may be) of a partner enterprise or linked enterprise to which it is related has been taken into account in determining whether the employee limit or the financial limits have been exceeded, and
(*b*) a partner enterprise or linked enterprise to which C is related would, disregarding the number of employees, and the annual turnover and balance sheet totals of C, exceed the employee limit or both of the financial limits,
Article 4(2) of the Annex shall be disregarded in determining whether C is a small or medium-sized enterprise for an accounting period in which it exceeds the employee or financial limits.

(4) For the purpose of paragraph (3), references to the employee limit and the financial limits are to the limits respectively on the number of employees, and the annual turnover and balance sheet totals, contained in Article 2(1) of the Annex.][1]

Amendments—[1] Paras (2)–(4) substituted for previous para (2) by the Community Investment Tax Relief (Accreditation of Community Development Finance Institutions) (Amendment) Regulations, SI 2008/383 arts 2, 9 with effect from 11 March 2008: SI 2008/383 art 1.

11 Meaning of "relevant investment"

(1) Subject to paragraph (4), for the purposes of these Regulations a relevant investment is an investment made by the CDFI in an enterprise where—
(*a*) it makes a loan (whether secured or unsecured) to the enterprise, or
(*b*) an issue of securities of or shares in the enterprise, for which the CDFI has subscribed, is made to the CDFI.

(2) For the purposes of paragraph (1)(a)—

(*a*) the CDFI does not make a loan to an enterprise where—

(i) the enterprise uses overdraft facilities provided by the CDFI, or

(ii) the CDFI subscribes for or otherwise acquires securities of the enterprise;

(*b*) where the loan agreement authorises the enterprise to draw down amounts of the loan over a period of time the loan is treated as made at the time when the first amount is drawn down.

(3) For the purpose of these Regulations where a relevant investment is a loan within paragraph (2)(*b*) the amount of the relevant investment is the amount drawn down at a given date.

(4) The investments specified in Schedule 1 are not relevant investments.

12 Limits on qualifying investments

(1) The CDFI must give notice to the [Secretary of State][1] at least one month before entering into any arrangements or commitments with the aim of increasing qualifying investments in the CDFI to more than 125% of the amount stated in its application for accreditation ("the 125% limit).

(2) The [Secretary of State][1] may approve the increase by notice to the CDFI.

(3) Where—

(*a*) the CDFI fails to give notice in accordance with paragraph (1), or

(*b*) the [Secretary of State][1] does not approve the increase in accordance with paragraph (2),

the [Secretary of State][1] may treat all or some of the investments made by the CDFI after the date on which the qualifying investments exceed the 125% limit as not being relevant investments for the purposes of regulation 8 up to an amount equal to the amount by which the qualifying investments exceed the 125% limit.

Amendments—[1] In para (4), words substituted by the Community Investment Tax Relief (Accreditation of Community Development Finance Institutions) (Amendment) Regulations, SI 2013/417 regs 4, 12(*b*) with effect from 1st April 2013.

12A Notice of first investment in a CDFI

(1) A CDFI must notify the Secretary of State in writing of the date the first investment is made in the CDFI, no later than three months after that date.

(2) A CDFI that does not comply with paragraph (1) is liable to a penalty of £500 payable to the [Department for Business, Energy and Industrial Strategy][2].

(3) But paragraph (2) does not apply if in the opinion of the Secretary of State the CDFI had a reasonable excuse for failing to comply with paragraph (1).][1]

Amendments—[1] Regulation 12A inserted by the Community Investment Tax Relief (Accreditation of Community Development Finance Institutions) (Amendment) Regulations, SI 2013/417 regs 4, 7 with effect in relation to a CDFI whose current accreditation period starts on or after 1st April 2013.

[2] In para (2), words substituted by the Secretaries of State for Business, Energy and Industrial Strategy, for International Trade and for Exiting the European Union and the Transfer of Functions (Education and Skills) Order, SI 2019/992 art 14, Schedule para 27(*b*) with effect from 9 November 2016.

13 Reporting requirements

(1) The CDFI must make an annual report to the [Department for Business, Energy and Industrial Strategy][3]

(*a*) within three months of each anniversary of [the date the first investment was made in the CDFI][1], or

(*b*) subject to paragraph (2), on such other date coincident with the CDFI's reporting cycle and agreed with the [Department for Business, Innovation and Skills][1].

(2) The first annual report made by the CDFI must be made no later than 18 months after [the date the first investment was made in the CDFI][1].

(3) The annual report shall be in the form provided by the Secretary of State for this purpose.

(4) Subject to paragraph (5), the CDFI is liable to a penalty of £500 payable to the [Department for Business, Energy and Industrial Strategy][2] where the annual report is not made within three months of date on which it was due under paragraph (1).

(5) Paragraph (4) does not apply if in the opinion of the [Secretary of State][3] the CDFI had reasonable excuse for failing to make an annual return.

Amendments—[1] In paras (1)(*a*), (2), words substituted by the Community Investment Tax Relief (Accreditation of Community Development Finance Institutions) (Amendment) Regulations, SI 2013/417 regs 4, 8 with effect in relation to a CDFI whose current accreditation period starts on or after 1st April 2013.

[2] In para (5), words substituted by the Community Investment Tax Relief (Accreditation of Community Development Finance Institutions) (Amendment) Regulations, SI 2013/417 regs 4, 12(*c*) with effect from 1st April 2013.

[3] In paras (1), (4), words substituted by the Secretaries of State for Business, Energy and Industrial Strategy, for International Trade and for Exiting the European Union and the Transfer of Functions (Education and Skills) Order, SI 2019/992 art 14, Schedule para 27(*c*) with effect from 9 November 2016.

14 Tax relief certificate

(1) Subject to paragraph (2), the CDFI must issue a tax relief certificate to the investor or its nominee within 30 days of receiving an investment from an individual or a company.

(2) Where the investment is received before the grant of accreditation but an application for accreditation is made before 6th April 2003, the CDFI must issue a tax relief certificate within 30 days of the grant of accreditation.

PART 4
GENERAL PROVISIONS

15 Withdrawal of accreditation

(1) The Secretary of State must withdraw the CDFI's accreditation—

(*a*) [subject to regulations 15A to 15E,][1] with effect from the time of the failure, where the CDFI fails to satisfy the terms of regulation 8;

(*b*) subject to paragraph (2), where the CDFI makes a direct or indirect investment in residential property from the investment fund; and

(*c*) subject to paragraph (3), where the CDFI fails to make an annual report within 12 months of the date on which it was due under paragraph (1) of regulation 13.

(2) Paragraph (1)(*b*) does not apply where—

(*a*) the CDFI can demonstrate that to the best of its knowledge and belief it had not invested in residential property, and

(*b*) the CDFI divested itself of the investment within three months of—

(i) the date it discovered that the investment was in residential property, or

(ii) the date of receipt of a notice from the [Department for Business, Energy and Industrial Strategy][3] that the investment is in residential property,

whichever is the earlier.

(3) Paragraph (1)(*c*) does not apply if in the opinion of the [Secretary of State][2] the CDFI had reasonable excuse for failing to make an annual return.

(4) A withdrawal of an accreditation must be given by notice by the Secretary of State specifying the date from which accreditation is withdrawn and the reasons for the withdrawal.

(5) The CDFI must within 30 days of receiving notice under paragraph (4) of withdrawal of accreditation give notice to each of the investors to which it has issued a tax relief certificate in respect of investments made within the specified period stating that accreditation has been withdrawn and specifying the date from which accreditation is withdrawn.

(6) For the purpose of paragraph (5) "specified period" means the five years immediately preceding the date from which accreditation is withdrawn.

Amendments—[1] Words substituted by the Community Investment Tax Relief (Accreditation of Community Development Finance Institutions) (Amendment) Regulations, SI 2008/383 arts 2, 7 with effect from 11 March: SI 2008/383 art 1.

[2] In para (3), words substituted by the Community Investment Tax Relief (Accreditation of Community Development Finance Institutions) (Amendment) Regulations, SI 2013/417 regs 4, 12(*d*) with effect from 1st April 2013.

[3] In para (2)(*b*)(ii), words substituted by the Secretaries of State for Business, Energy and Industrial Strategy, for International Trade and for Exiting the European Union and the Transfer of Functions (Education and Skills) Order, SI 2019/992 art 14, Schedule para 27(*d*) with effect from 9 November 2016.

15A Applications relating to failures to satisfy the conditions of regulation 8

(1) This regulation applies where after the end of a year ending upon the anniversary of [the date the first investment was made in the CDFI][2] a CDFI becomes aware of a failure to satisfy the conditions of regulation 8 in respect of that year.

(2) Where this regulation applies, the CDFI may apply in writing to the Secretary of State within 3 months after the end of that year for a determination that the accreditation shall not be withdrawn notwithstanding the failure to satisfy the conditions of regulation 8.

(3) An application under this regulation must specify—

(*a*) the circumstances that have led to the failure to satisfy the conditions of regulation 8, and

(*b*) the measures taken by the CDFI to avoid the failure.

(4) Where the failure relates to a condition specified in regulation 8(1)(*a*), (*b*) or (*c*), the application must state—

(*a*) the maximum percentage of the investment fund that was suitably invested during that year, and

(*b*) the maximum percentage that would have been so invested had it not been for the circumstances that led to the failure.

(5) Where the failure relates to the condition specified in regulation 8(1)(*d*), the application must state—

(*a*) the average percentage of the investment fund suitably invested as calculated in accordance with regulation 8(2), and

(*b*) the average percentage of the investment fund that would have been suitably invested as calculated in accordance with regulation 8(2) had it not been for the circumstances that led to the failure.][1]

Amendments—[1] Regulations 15A–15E inserted by the Community Investment Tax Relief (Accreditation of Community Development Finance Institutions) (Amendment) Regulations, SI 2008/383 arts 2, 8 with effect from 11 March 2008: SI 2008/383 art 1.

[2] In para (1), words substituted for words "the date that the CDFI was first granted accreditation" by the Community Investment Tax Relief (Accreditation of Community Development Finance Institutions) (Amendment) Regulations, SI 2013/417 regs 4, 9 with effect in relation to a CDFI whose current accreditation period starts on or after 1st April 2013.

15B [Applications relating to anticipated failures to satisfy conditions of regulation 8

(1) This regulation applies where during a year ending upon the anniversary of [the date the first investment was made in a CDFI][2] the CDFI anticipates likely failure to satisfy the conditions of regulation 8 in respect of that year.

(2) Where this regulation applies the CDFI may apply in writing to the Secretary of State for a decision that, should the anticipated likely failure occur at the end of the year as a result of the circumstances specified in the application, the Secretary of State will determine after the end of the year in respect of which the application relates, that accreditation will not be withdrawn.

(3) An application under this regulation must specify—

(*a*) the circumstances that are anticipated will lead to the failure to satisfy the conditions of regulation 8, and

(*b*) any measures that have been taken or that will be taken by the CDFI in that year—

(i) to avoid that failure, and

(ii) to ensure that the maximum amount of the investment fund that is possible in all the circumstances will be suitably invested.

(4) Where the failure relates to a condition specified in regulation 8(1)(*a*), (*b*), or (*c*) the application must state—

(*a*) the maximum percentage of the investment fund suitably invested at the time the application under this regulation is submitted to the Secretary of State,

(*b*) the maximum percentage of the investment fund that would have been so invested had it not been for the circumstances that are anticipated to lead to the failure, and

(*c*) as far as possible, the maximum possible percentage of the investment fund that the CDFI anticipates will be so invested as a result of the measures taken under paragraph (3)(*b*).

(5) Where the anticipated failure relates to a condition specified in regulation 8(1)(d), the application must state—

(*a*) the average percentage of the investment fund suitably invested as calculated in accordance with regulation 8(2)(*a*) for each day of that year before the day on which the application is submitted to the Secretary of State, and

(*b*) as far as possible the average percentage of the investment fund that will be suitably invested on the final day of that year as calculated in accordance with regulation 8(2)(*a*) or (*b*) further to the measures taken under paragraph (3)(*b*).

(6) Where a CDFI submits an application under this regulation further to which the Secretary of State decides under regulation 15D that after the end of the year to which the application relates accreditation will not be withdrawn and the CDFI thereafter anticipates that it will fail—

(*a*) to take the measures as specified in the application, or

(*b*) to ensure that the maximum or average amount of the investment fund as specified in the application will be suitably invested,

it may make a further application under this paragraph (2) in respect of that anticipated failure and this regulation will apply to that failure as it would apply to an application in respect of an anticipated failure to satisfy the conditions of regulation 8.][1]

Amendments—[1] Regulations 15A–15E inserted by the Community Investment Tax Relief (Accreditation of Community Development Finance Institutions) (Amendment) Regulations, SI 2008/383 arts 2, 8 with effect from 11 March: SI 2008/383 art 1.

[2] In para (1), words substituted for words "the date a CDFI was first granted accreditation" by the Community Investment Tax Relief (Accreditation of Community Development Finance Institutions) (Amendment) Regulations, SI 2013/417 regs 4, 10 with effect in relation to a CDFI whose current accreditation period starts on or after 1st April 2013.

15C [Applications under regulation 15A: failures that have occurred

(1) This regulation applies where an application under regulation 15A has been made in respect of a failure to meet the conditions of regulation 8.

(2) Where the Secretary of State is satisfied that—

(*a*) the failure to satisfy the conditions of regulation 8 was as a result of the circumstances specified in the application,

(*b*) those circumstances were outside the control of the CDFI and, where applicable, any person connected with it, and

(*c*) the CDFI acted reasonably in its attempts to avoid failing to satisfy the conditions of regulation 8 and to minimise the extent of failure,

the Secretary of State must determine that accreditation shall not be withdrawn and shall notify the CDFI of the determination.

(3) Where the Secretary of State does not have sufficient information to make a determination under this regulation he may ask the CDFI to supply further information prior to making a determination.][1]

Amendments—[1] Regulations 15A–15E inserted by the Community Investment Tax Relief (Accreditation of Community Development Finance Institutions) (Amendment) Regulations, SI 2008/383 arts 2, 8 with effect from 11 March 2008: SI 2008/383 art 1.

15D [Applications under regulation 15B: anticipated failures

(1) This regulation applies where an application under regulation 15B has been made in respect of an anticipated failure to meet the conditions of regulation 8.

(2) Where the Secretary of State is satisfied that—

(*a*) the anticipated failure to satisfy the conditions of regulation 8 arises from the circumstances specified in the application,

(*b*) those circumstances are outside the control of the CDFI and, where applicable, any person connected with it, and

(*c*) the measures specified in the application that have been taken or that will be taken to prevent failure or to minimise the extent of failure are reasonable in all the circumstances,

he must, subject to paragraphs (4) and (5), decide that where such measures as are specified in the application are taken by the CDFI but the CDFI thereafter fails to meet the conditions of regulation 8 as a result of the circumstances specified in the application the accreditation shall not be withdrawn after the end of that year if failure occurs as a result of those circumstances.

(3) The Secretary of State must notify the CDFI of his decision made under paragraph (2).

(4) Where the Secretary of State does not have sufficient information to make a decision under this regulation he may request the CDFI to provide more information prior to making a decision.

(5) Where the Secretary of State decides under paragraph (2) that accreditation will not be withdrawn after the end of the year to which the application relates and the CDFI—

(*a*) becomes aware that the measures specified in the application will not prevent the failure or minimise the extent of failure, or

(*b*) becomes unable to implement such measures,

the CDFI may submit a further application under regulation 15B in respect of the same circumstances specifying further measures that will be taken to avoid or minimise the extent of failure.

(6) Where the Secretary of State notifies the CDFI under paragraph (3) that accreditation may be withdrawn the CDFI may submit a further application under regulation 15B.][1]

Amendments—[1] Regulations 15A–15E inserted by the Community Investment Tax Relief (Accreditation of Community Development Finance Institutions) (Amendment) Regulations, SI 2008/383 arts 2, 8 with effect from 11 March 2008: SI 2008/383 art 1.

15E [Regulations 15A to 15D: supplementary

(1) Where a CDFI has submitted an application under regulation 15B but the Secretary of State does not make a decision under regulation 15D before the end of the year in question and the CDFI thereafter fails to satisfy the conditions of regulation 8 for that year it must submit an application under regulation 15A.

(2) Where the Secretary of State has received one or more applications under regulation 15B upon which no decision has yet been made, the Secretary of State must not make a decision that accreditation will not be withdrawn until he is satisfied that it should not be withdrawn in respect of each and every application.

(3) A determination under regulation 15C not to withdraw accreditation and a decision under regulation 15D that accreditation may not be withdrawn shall not prevent the Secretary of State from withdrawing accreditation where he has grounds for doing so as a result of other circumstances which are not the subject of an application under regulation 15A or 15B.

(4) For the purposes of regulations 15A and 15B "suitably invested" means invested in relevant investments in qualifying enterprises.

(5) For the purposes of regulations 15C and 15D—

(*a*) a person who acts on behalf of a CDFI to manage its investment is treated as a CDFI, and

(*b*) section 993 of the Income Tax Act 2007 shall apply for determining whether a person is connected with a CDFI.][1]

Amendments—[1] Regulations 15A–15E inserted by the Community Investment Tax Relief (Accreditation of Community Development Finance Institutions) (Amendment) Regulations, SI 2008/383 arts 2, 8 with effect from 11 March 2008: SI 2008/383 art 1.

16 Appeals against refusal to grant accreditation or withdrawal of accreditation

(1) An appeal to the Special Commissioners may be brought against a refusal to grant accreditation or a withdrawal of accreditation.

(2) Notice of an appeal under this regulation must be given—

(*a*) in writing,

(*b*) within 30 days of the date of the notification of the refusal under regulation 5 or the withdrawal under regulation 15(4), and

(*c*) to the [Secretary of State][2].

(3) The notice of appeal must require the [Secretary of State][2] to transmit to the [tribunal[1]]—

(*a*) in an appeal against a refusal to grant accreditation, the application for accreditation, together with any information or particulars provided by the body to the Secretary of State in support of the application, or (*b*) in an appeal against a withdrawal of accreditation, the notice under regulation 15(4) together with any information or particulars prepared by the [Department for Business, Energy and Industrial Strategy][3] leading to the issue of that notice.

(4) The [tribunal][1] may allow the appeal and—

(*a*) in an appeal against a refusal to grant accreditation, direct that the Secretary of State accredit the body within 14 days of its decision, or

(*b*) in an appeal against a withdrawal of accreditation, direct that the withdrawal was ineffective.

[(5) Notwithstanding the provisions of sections 11 and 13 of the Tribunals, Courts and Enforcement Act 2007, the decision of the tribunal shall be final.][1]

Amendments—[1] In para (1), words revoked, in paras (3), (4), words substituted, and para (5) substituted, by the Transfer of Tribunal Functions and Revenue and Customs Appeals Order, SI 2009/56 art 3, Sch 2 para 83 with effect from 1 April 2009.

[3] In paras (2)(*c*), (3), words substituted by the Community Investment Tax Relief (Accreditation of Community Development Finance Institutions) (Amendment) Regulations, SI 2013/417 regs 4, 12(*e*) with effect from 1st April 2013.

[2] In para (3)(*b*), words substituted by the Secretaries of State for Business, Energy and Industrial Strategy, for International Trade and for Exiting the European Union and the Transfer of Functions (Education and Skills) Order, SI 2019/992 art 14, Schedule para 27(*e*) with effect from 9 November 2016.

SCHEDULE 1

Regulation 11(4)

INVESTMENTS WHICH ARE NOT RELEVANT INVESTMENTS

1 General Investments

Any investment which benefits directly or indirectly from the security offered by a Phoenix Fund guarantee or by any similar publicly-funded underwriting or guarantee arrangement.

2—(1) Any loan to a profit-distributing enterprise—

(*a*) which is not made on terms that are equivalent to those offered by conventional sources of finance, or

(*b*) as a consequence of which, and for so long as, the total amount of loans to that enterprise exceeds £100,000 ("the £100,000 limit").

(2) Where the £100,000 limit is exceeded—

(*a*) by two or more loans made on the same day, or

(*b*) in any other circumstances where it is not possible to establish which loan caused the limit to be exceeded,

the [Secretary of State][1] shall determine which of those loans shall not constitute relevant investments so that the amount of relevant investments in the enterprise approximates to but does not exceed the £100,000 limit.

Amendments—[1] In sub-para (2), words substituted by the Community Investment Tax Relief (Accreditation of Community Development Finance Institutions) (Amendment) Regulations, SI 2013/417 regs 4, 12(*f*) with effect from 1st April 2013.

3—(1) Any loan to a profit-distributing enterprise which is not made at market rates or above, or, where interest is not charged on loans the fee structure is not at an equivalent level.

(2) In paragraph (1) "market rate" means the European Commission's Hurdle Rate, which is the Reference Rate (as published at ec.europa.eu/competition/state_aid/legislation/reference_rates.html) plus four percentage points, or more.

[**3A** Any equity investment in a profit-distributing enterprise.][1]

Amendments—[1] Para inserted by the Community Investment Tax Relief (Accreditation of Community Development Finance Institutions) (Amendment) Regulations, SI 2008/383 arts 2, 11 with effect from 11 March 2008: SI 2008/383 art 1.

4—(1) Any loan to . . . [1] a non-profit-distributing enterprise for the purposes of undertaking community projects as a consequence of which, and for so long as, the total amount invested in that enterprise exceeds £250,000 ("the £250,000 limit").

(2) For the purpose of paragraph (1) "community projects" means—

(*a*) public sector projects,

(*b*) projects which benefit charities and other non-profit distributing bodies which are engaged entirely in public functions, non-competitive and non-commercial activity, or

(*c*) projects which are commercial in the sense that there is remuneration for the service provider and competition for their supply, but which are small-scale and purely local in nature.

(3) Where the £250,000 limit is exceeded—

(*a*) by two or more loans . . . [1] made on the same day, or

(*b*) in any other circumstances where it is not possible to establish which loan . . . [1] caused the limit to be exceeded,

the [Secretary of State][2] [shall determine which of those loans shall not][1] constitute relevant investments so that the amount of relevant investments in the enterprise approximates to but does not exceed the £250,000 limit.

Amendments—[1] In sub-paras (1), (3)(*a*), (*b*) words revoked, and in sub-para (3), words substituted by the Community Investment Tax Relief (Accreditation of Community Development Finance Institutions) (Amendment) Regulations, SI 2013/417 regs 4, 11(1), (2) with effect in relation to investments made in a CDFI on or after 1st April 2013.

[2] In sub-para (3), words substituted by the Community Investment Tax Relief (Accreditation of Community Development Finance Institutions) (Amendment) Regulations, SI 2013/417 regs 4, 12(*f*) with effect from 1st April 2013.

5 Any investment in an enterprise as a consequence of which, and for so long as, the total amount invested by the CDFI in that enterprise exceeds 20% of the amount of the investment fund at—

(*a*) for the first year following accreditation, the date the investment is made by the CDFI, and

(*b*) thereafter, the immediately preceding anniversary of the accreditation date.

6—(1) Any investment in an enterprise within Case 2 of regulation 10 as a consequence of which, and for so long as—

(*a*) the total amount invested out of the investment fund by the CDFI in enterprises in Case 2 exceeds the amount invested in enterprises within Cases 1 and 3; or

(*b*) the number of investments out of the investment fund by the CDFI in enterprises in Case 2 exceeds the number of investments in enterprises within Cases 1 and 3.

(2) For the purposes of paragraph (1) an investment in an enterprise which is within both Case 2 and Case 3 shall be treated as being only within Case 3.

7 Property investments, which are not relevant investments

Any investment which funds directly or indirectly the acquisition, construction or development of residential property.

8—(1) Any investment which funds directly or indirectly the acquisition, construction or development of non-residential property where, on the next anniversary of the date on which the CDFI was granted accreditation, in consequence of that investment—

(*a*) the total amount of investment within Case 1 below exceeds the amount of relevant investments other than those in Case 1, or

(*b*) the total amount of investment within Case 2 below exceeds one half of the relevant investments within Case 1.

Case 1

1.1 Investment in a non profit-distributing enterprise, the main activity of which is to hold and invest in or to develop non-residential property.

1.2 Investment in a development trust or other social enterprise for the purpose of investment in or development of non-residential property, whether owned by the trust or by others.

Case 2

2.1 Investment in a profit-distributing enterprise, the main activity of which is holding land with the aim of benefiting from capital appreciation of that land, or with the aim of receiving income through the exploitation of an interest in it.

2.2 Investment in a profit-distributing enterprise, the main activity of which is non-residential property development.

(2) For the purposes of paragraph (1) where a investment is a loan which authorises the CDFI to draw down amounts of the loan over a period of time, the amount of the investment is the amount drawn down at the relevant date.

9 Investments by retail community investment finance institutions

Where the CDFI has been accredited as a retail community investment finance institution, any investment in another CDFI or in any other body whose objective is to provide finance for enterprises in or for disadvantaged communities where, as a consequence of that investment, and for so long as, for more than three months the total amount invested in such bodies exceeds 10% of the amount of the investment fund at—

[(*a*) for the first year following the date the first investment is made in the CDFI, the date the investment is made by that CDFI, and][1]

(*b*) thereafter, the immediately preceding anniversary of the [date the first investment is made in the CDFI][1].

Amendments—[1] Sub-para (*a*) substituted, and in sub-para (*b*), words substituted for words "accreditation date" by the Community Investment Tax Relief (Accreditation of Community Development Finance Institutions) (Amendment) Regulations, SI 2013/417 regs 4, 11(1), (3) with effect in relation to a CDFI whose current accreditation period starts on or after 1st April 2013.

10 Any investment by a retail community investment finance institution in a body other than a CDFI whose objective is to provide finance for enterprises in or for disadvantaged communities as a consequence of which, and for so long as, the total amount of investment in such enterprises exceeds £250,000.

11 Investments by wholesale CDFIs

(1) Any investment made by a wholesale CDFI in an enterprise where as a consequence of which, and for so long as, the total amount of investment in that enterprise exceeds—

(*a*) 20% of the amount of the investment fund at—

[(i) for the first year following the date the first investment is made in the CDFI, the date the investment is made by that CDFI, and][1]

(ii) thereafter, the immediately preceding anniversary of [date the first investment is made in the CDFI][1], or

(*b*) £2,500,000

whichever is the lesser amount.

(2) Any investment made by a wholesale CDFI in a body other than a CDFI whose objective is to provide finance for enterprises in or for disadvantaged communities as a consequence of which, and for so long as, the total amount invested in that body exceeds £250,000.

(3) A "wholesale CDFI" means a CDFI which is not accredited as a retail community investment finance institution.

Commentary—*Simon's Taxes* **A1.586.**

Amendments—[1] Sub-para (1)(*a*)(i) substituted, and in sub-para (1)(*a*)(ii), words substituted for words "accreditation date" by the Community Investment Tax Relief (Accreditation of Community Development Finance Institutions) (Amendment) Regulations, SI 2013/417 regs 4, 11(1), (4) with effect in relation to a CDFI whose current accreditation period starts on or after 1st April 2013.

2003/282

INCOME AND CORPORATION TAXES (ELECTRONIC COMMUNICATIONS) REGULATIONS 2003

Made by the Commissioners of Inland Revenue under FA 1999 ss 132, and 133(2)

Made . . . . *12 February 2003*

Laid before the House of Commons . . . . *12 February 2003*

Coming into force . . . . *5 March 2003*

Commentary—*Simon's Taxes* **D1.1313.**

PART 1
INTRODUCTION

1 Citation, commencement and interpretation

(1) These Regulations may be cited as the Income and Corporation Taxes (Electronic Communications) Regulations 2003 and shall come into force on 5th March 2003.

(2) In these Regulations—

"the Board" means the Commissioners of Inland Revenue;

"the Management Act" means the Taxes Management Act 1970;

"official computer system" means a computer system maintained by or on behalf of the Board—

(*a*) to send or receive information or payments, or

(*b*) to process or store information; . . . [2]

["secure mailbox" means a facility or feature which—

(*a*) forms part of an official computer system, and

(*b*) can be accessed by an individual permitted to use electronic communications by an authorisation given by means of a direction by the Board; and][2]

"the Taxes Act" means the Income and Corporation Taxes Act 1988.

[(2A) The provision these Regulations make for company tax returns relates to Schedule 18 to the Finance Act 1998 (corporation tax—company tax returns, etc), consequently where they refer to—

(*a*) "company tax return", it has the meaning in paragraph 3 of that Schedule,

(*b*) "return period", it means the period for which a company tax return is required under paragraph 5 of that Schedule,

(*c*) "amendment", it has the meaning in paragraph 15 of that Schedule, and

(*d*) "filing date", it has the meaning in paragraph 14 of that Schedule (but it has the meaning in paragraph 35(2) when in connection with a company tax return for an "outstanding period" in paragraph 35(1)).

(2B) The "extra time" in connection with the filing date mentioned in regulation 3(8)(*c*) refers to a stage—

(*a*) for which there is an excuse for late delivery of the company tax return under paragraph 19 of Schedule 18 to the Finance Act 1998 (delivery of accounts to registrar of companies in time); or,

(*b*) arising under section 117(2) of that Act in conjunction with section 118(2) of the Management Act (further time allowed by the Board, reasonable excuse for being late, etc).][1]

(3) References in these Regulations to information and to the delivery of information shall be construed in accordance with section 132(8) of the Finance Act 1999.
[Such references shall be construed in accordance with section 135(8) of the Finance Act 2002 (mandatory e-filing) when in connection with a company tax return.][1]

Amendments—[1] Paras (2A), (2B) and words in para (3) inserted, by the Income and Corporation Taxes (Electronic Communications) (Amendment) Regulations, SI 2009/3218 reg 2, Sch paras 1, 2, with effect from 1 January 2010.
[2] Word "and" at end of definition of "official computer system" revoked, and definition of "secure mailbox" inserted, by the Income and Corporation Taxes (Electronic Communications)(Amendment) Regulations, SI 2014/489 regs 2, 3 with effect from 27 March 2014.

2 Scope of these Regulations

(1) These Regulations apply to—

(*a*) the delivery of information, to or by the Board, the delivery of which is authorised or required by or under—

(i) any provision of section 8, 8A, [8B,][4] 9, [9ZA, 9ZB,][4] 9A, 9B, 9C, 9D, 12AA, [12AAA,][4] 12AB, [12ABA, 12ABB,][4] 12AC, 12AD, 12AE, [28A, 28B, 28C, 30B, 59C,][4] [59DA, 59E or 100][4] of the Management Act,

(ii) Schedule 1A to the Management Act,

[(iia) the Lloyd's Underwriters (Tax) Regulations 2005,][1]

(iii) section . . . [3] 36 of the Finance Act 1998, . . . [4]

(iv) Schedule 18 to the Finance Act 1998 [(and in connection with which they also make specific provision for mandatory e-filing of company tax returns as mentioned in regulation 1(3))][2][,][4]

(*b*) the making of any payment or repayment of tax or other sums in connection with the operation of those provisions[, or the making of any payment in connection with the operation of section 87A of the Management Act (interest on overdue corporation tax etc), and they apply in such a way that the corporation tax-related payments in regulation 3(2C) are subject to the mandatory electronic payment envisaged by section 204 of the Finance Act 2003][2].

[(v) paragraph 13 of Schedule 24 to the Finance Act 2007,

(vi) paragraph 1 or 46 of Schedule 36 to the Finance Act 2008, or

(vii) paragraph 17A, 17B or 18 of Schedule 55, or paragraph 11 of Schedule 56, to the Finance Act 2009; and][4]

(2) Nothing in these Regulations affects the operation of the Electronic Lodgement of Tax Returns Order 1997.

Amendments—[1] Para (1)(*a*)(iia) inserted by the Lloyd's Underwriters (Tax) Regulations, SI 2005/3338 reg 15 with effect from 27 December 2005.
SI 2005/3338 has effect—

(a) in its application to members who are individuals, for the year 2006–07 (including any actions taken before 6 April 2006, in relation to the year 2006–07) and subsequent years of assessment; and

(b) in its application to corporate members, for accounting periods ending after 31 December 2005 (but not in relation to profits and losses arising to corporate members which are mentioned in FA 1994 s 220(2) and are declared in 2005): SI 2005/3338 reg 1.

[2] Words in para (1)(*a*)(iv), and (1)(*b*) inserted by the Income and Corporation Taxes (Electronic Communications) (Amendment) Regulations, SI 2009/3218 reg 2, Sch paras 3, 4, with effect from 1 January 2010.
[3] Words in para (1)(*a*)(iii) revoked by the Statute Law (Repeals) Act 2013 s 1, Sch 1 Pt 10 with effect from 31 January 2013.
[4] In para (1)(*a*)(i), references inserted and substituted, in para (1)(*a*)(iii), word revoked, in para (1)(*a*)(iv), word substituted, and para (1)(*a*)(v)–(vii) inserted, by the Income and Corporation Taxes (Electronic Communications)(Amendment) Regulations, SI 2014/489 regs 2, 4 with effect from 27 March 2014.

PART 2
ELECTRONIC COMMUNICATIONS —GENERAL PROVISIONS

3 [Use of electronic communications]

(1) The Board may only use electronic communications in connection with the matters referred to in regulation 2(1) if—

(*a*) the recipient has indicated that he consents to the Board using electronic communications in connection with those matters; and

(*b*) the Board have not been informed that that consent has been withdrawn.

[(1ZA) The Board may specify by specific or general direction the manner in which consent may be provided and withdrawn, including the time from which consent and withdrawal of consent is to take effect.][3]

[(1A) [Paragraphs (1) and (1ZA) do][3] not apply to a company tax return delivered by, or a corporation tax-related payment made by, electronic communications under paragraphs (2A) to (2C).][1]

(2) A person other than the Board may only use electronic communications in connection with the matters referred to in regulation 2(1) if the conditions specified in paragraphs (3) to (6) are satisfied.

[(2A) Such a person must use electronic communications to deliver a company tax return, and in doing so need only satisfy the second to fourth of those conditions.

This paragraph only applies to a company tax return delivered on 1 April 2011 or later, relating to a return period ending on 1 April 2010 or later.

It does not apply to an amendment to such a company tax return.

(2B) The payer must use electronic communications to make the corporation tax-related payments in paragraph (2C), and in doing so need only satisfy the second and third of those conditions (excluding those in paragraphs (4)(*a*) (authenticating identity) and (4)(*c*) (authenticating information)).

This paragraph only applies to payments made on 1 April 2011 or later.

The Board need not accept such payments tendered in breach of this paragraph.

(2C) Paragraph (2B) applies to payment of each of the following—

(*a*) any amount of corporation tax that must be calculated as payable under paragraph 8 of Schedule 18 to the Finance Act 1998 (calculation of corporation tax payable);

(*b*) any amount treated as such under regulation 5 or 5A of the Corporation Tax (Instalment Payments) Regulations 1998;

(*c*) any interest payable on overdue corporation tax etc under section 87A of the Management Act and regulation 7 of those Regulations;

(*d*) a flat-rate penalty for failing to deliver a company tax return by the filing date under paragraph 17 of that Schedule;

(*e*) a tax-related penalty for failing to deliver a company tax return for an accounting period under paragraph 18 of that Schedule.][1]

(3) The first condition is that the person is for the time being permitted to use electronic communications for the purpose in question by an authorisation given by means of a direction of the Board.

(4) The second condition is that the person uses—

(*a*) an approved method for authenticating the identity of the sender of the communication;

(*b*) an approved method of electronic communications; and

(*c*) an approved method for authenticating any information delivered by means of electronic communications.

(5) The third condition is that any information or payment sent by means of electronic communications is in a form approved for the purpose of these Regulations[, and Extensible Business Reporting Language (XBRL), Inline XBRL and other electronic data handling techniques are among the forms that may be so approved][1].

Here "form" includes the manner in which the information is presented.

(6) The fourth condition is that the person maintains such records in written or electronic form as may be specified in a general or specific direction of the Board.

(7) In this regulation "approved" means approved, for the purposes of these Regulations and for the time being, by means of a general or specific direction of the Board.

[(8) The conditions mentioned in paragraph (2A) (company tax returns) are to be taken to be satisfied in connection with that paragraph only where the Board is satisfied about one or more of the following—

(*a*) there are no contraventions or failures to comply;

(*b*) the accumulated contraventions or failures to comply do not undermine the purpose of that paragraph (delivery of company tax returns by approved electronic means);

(*c*) at least one of the contraventions or failures to comply was necessary in order to deliver the company tax return by the filing date or within any extra time arising, despite genuine efforts not to undermine that purpose.

(9) The consequences of contravening or failing to comply with paragraph (2A) (company tax returns) are—

(*a*) that the Board must accept delivery of the return, but only if satisfied about paragraph (8)(*b*) or (8)(*c*), or about both; otherwise,

(*b*) the Board must disregard the return and treat it as not having been delivered.

(10) Electronic communications need not be used to deliver a company tax return while the company required to deliver it by the notice under paragraph 3(1) of Schedule 18 to the Finance Act 1998 is—

(*a*) the subject of a winding-up order,

(*b*) having its affairs, business and property managed by an administrator, or

(*c*) in administrative receivership.

The expressions "winding-up order", "administrator" and "in administrative receivership" each has the same meaning here as it does in section 81 of the Value Added Tax Act 1994 (insolvency procedures, etc).

[(10A) Electronic communications need not be used to deliver a company tax return while the company required to deliver it by the notice mentioned in paragraph (10)—

(*a*) has a liquidator appointed for the purposes of a creditors' voluntary winding up (within sections 90 and 100 of the Insolvency Act 1986 or Articles 76 and 86 of the Insolvency (Northern Ireland) Order 1989);

(*b*) has a liquidator provisionally appointed by a court (within section 135 of that Act or Article 115 of that Order);
(*c*) has a supervisor carrying out functions in relation to a company voluntary arrangement (within section 7(2) of or Schedule A1, paragraph 39(2) to that Act or Article 20(2) of or Schedule A1, paragraph 49(2) to that Order);
(*d*) has a compromise or arrangement in effect (within Part 26 of the Companies Act 2006); or
(*e*) is a limited liability partnership, and
(i) has a liquidator appointed, or
(ii) is the subject of a winding up order by the court,
(within section 1273(4)(a) of the Corporation Tax Act 2009).][2]

(11) Paragraph (2A) (company tax returns) does not apply to the use of electronic communications in a way incompatible with the beliefs of a religious society or order of which—
(*a*) all the company's directors (and, if there is one, the company's secretary) are practising members, or
(*b*) all the individuals in the unincorporated association are such members.][1]

[(12) The exceptions created by paragraphs (10) to (11) also apply in circumstances corresponding to those listed or described there but governed by the law of a place outside the United Kingdom.][2]

Revenue Directions—These directions apply in relation to the delivery of information and the making of payments by or on behalf of a company in relation to the application of the Corporation Tax Acts and of Schedule 18 to the Finance Act 1998.

General

1 Authorisation to use electronic communications – Regulation 3(2) & (3)

The Commissioners for Her Majesty's Revenue & Customs (HMRC) hereby direct that a company, or the agent for a company, that is or may be required to deliver information in response to a notice under paragraph 3 of Schedule 18 to the Finance Act 1998, or to pay corporation tax or any associated interest or penalties, is authorised to do so using electronic communications.

2 Authenticating identity of Sender – Regulation 3(4)(*a*)

The Commissioners for Her Majesty's Revenue & Customs hereby direct that the methods approved by them for authenticating the identity of the person sending information to HMRC by electronic communications are the use of a User ID and password, or a digital certificate where available. These must be set up as part of the HMRC or Business Link website registration process and Government Gateway verification process, in accordance with the Terms and Conditions for Online Services set out on the HMRC website (online.inlandrevenue.gov.uk/application?namespace=re&=privacyStatement.jsp&=link.termsAndConditions or successor web address).

3 Method of Electronic Communications – Regulation 3(4)(*b*)

The Commissioners for Her Majesty's Revenue & Customs hereby direct that the method of electronic communications approved by them for the delivery of information to HMRC is the Internet ("online delivery").

Company tax returns under paragraph 3 of Schedule 18 to the Finance Act 1998.

4 Method of Electronic Communications – Regulation 3(4)(*b*)

The Commissioners for Her Majesty's Revenue & Customs hereby direct that a company that is, or may be, required to deliver a company tax return in response to a notice under paragraph 3 of Schedule 18 to the Finance Act 1998, or its agent, is authorised to do so online. The Commissioners further direct that a company that wishes to amend its company tax return for any period, or its agent, is authorised to do so online.

5 Authenticating Company Tax Returns – Regulation 3(4)(*c*) and 3(6)

The Commissioners for Her Majesty's Revenue & Customs hereby direct that the method approved by them for authenticating a company tax return delivered by means of electronic communications is as follows:

Companies delivering their own company tax returns

Completion of a declaration in the return to confirm that the return is correct and complete to the best of the knowledge and belief of the person delivering it.

Agents delivering such returns on behalf of companies

(1) Completion of a declaration in the return to confirm that the return is correct and complete to the best of the knowledge and belief of the person delivering it; and
(2) Completion of the following procedure before the company tax return is sent:
(a) the making by the agent of a copy (electronic or paper) of the information, and
(b) the confirmation to the agent, by the proper officer or other person authorised to act for the company in this regard, that the information is correct and complete to the best of the knowledge and belief of that person.

The confirmation mentioned in paragraph (2)(b) must be in writing, but may be given in electronic or non-electronic form.

6 Form of Electronic Communications – Regulation 3(5)

The Commissioners for Her Majesty's Revenue & Customs hereby direct that the form approved by them in which the company tax return is to be delivered by means of electronic communications is as follows:

Compulsory electronic company tax returns to which regulation 3(2A) applies

Where a company must use electronic communications to deliver its company tax return in accordance with regulation 3(2A), the whole company tax return must be delivered online either where the company meets the relevant criteria*, using, and in accordance with the guidance for, the filing product provided by HMRC for the purpose on its website, or using other software** that produces a company tax return meeting the following requirements:

(a) The information required by the specified return form must be provided in Extensible Mark-up Language (XML) format. The "specified return form" means the version of HMRC's Form CT600 and related supplementary pages relevant to the period to which the return relates.

(b) Where other software is used, or where a company using the HMRC filing product chooses not to use the integrated accounts template, the company's individual accounts required to be prepared under Chapter 4 of Part 15 of the Companies Act 2006, or under the Building Societies Act 1986, or the Friendly and Industrial and Provident Societies Act 1968, or the Friendly Societies Act 1992, or the Insurance Accounts Directive (Miscellaneous Insurance Undertakings) Regulations 2008 ("the Companies Act etc") must be delivered in iXBRL*** format.

(c) In the case of a parent company that chooses or is required to prepare group accounts under Chapter 4 of Part 15 of the Companies Act 2006 as well as individual accounts, the company may instead deliver consolidated accounts in iXBRL format, provided that those accounts provide the same information about the company as would be provided by individual accounts of the company.

(d) Companies not required to prepare individual accounts under the Companies Act etc may deliver the accounts required by the Notice to deliver a company tax return in iXBRL format.

(e) An overseas company resident in the UK must deliver the accounts required by the notice to deliver a Company Tax Return in iXBRL format.

(f) A company not resident in the UK but carrying on a trade in the UK through a permanent establishment, branch or agency in the UK must deliver any trading and profit and loss account and any balance sheet of the UK establishment, branch or agency required to be delivered as part of its company tax return in iXBRL format.

(g) Where other software is used, or where a company using the HMRC filing product chooses not to use the integrated computations template, computations showing the derivation of the entries in the company tax return from the accounts must be delivered in iXBRL format.

(h) Accounts and computations delivered in iXBRL format must be delivered as separate iXBRL instance documents within the overall return.

(i) Other information, accounts, statements, reports, claims or correspondence included as part of the return must be sent as Portable Document Format (PDF) files.

(j) All parts of the company tax return, including any PDF documents, must be proper and complete and the content must be viewable by HMRC officers using appropriate software.

* The "relevant criteria" are those set out in the guidance for use of the HMRC product on the HMRC website at the time the electronic communications are used.

** Commercial products that have been successfully tested by HMRC to demonstrate that they can produce a company tax return in the required form are listed on the HMRC website.

*** "iXBRL" is Inline Extensible Business Reporting Language, a specification published by XBRL International Inc for embedding Extensible Business Reporting Language (XBRL) fragments into Hypertext Mark-up Language (XHTML) documents such that the fragments can be extracted to form a complete XBRL document.

Voluntary electronic company tax returns to which regulation 3(2A) does not apply, and amendments to any company tax return

Where a company that does not have to do so chooses to use electronic communications to deliver its company tax return, the whole return must be delivered online using either HMRC's own filing product or other software that produces a company tax return in the form set out, at the time of, and for the purposes of, the delivery of such a return or amendment in the Terms and Conditions for Online Services on the HMRC website (online.inlandrevenue.gov.uk/application?namespace=re&=privacyStatement.jsp&=link.termsAndConditions). All parts of the company tax return, including any PDF documents, must be proper and complete and the content must be viewable by HMRC officers using appropriate software.

7 Accuracy and Completeness – Regulation 10(3)

The Commissioners for Her Majesty's Revenue & Customs hereby direct that the standards of accuracy and completeness for the delivery of a company tax return to which regulation 3(2A) applies are as follows: The specified XBRL taxonomies must be correctly applied:

– For accounts, the extracted XBRL must conform to the UK Common Data taxonomy and either the UK GAAP taxonomy or the UK IFRS taxonomy published by XBRL UK (http://www.xbrl.org.uk/techguidance/taxonomies.html) applicable to the period covered by the return.

– For tax computations, the extracted XBRL must conform to the HMRC tax computation taxonomy published by HMRC on its website (www.hmrc.gov.uk/ebu/ct_techpack/index.htm) applicable to the period covered by the return.

iXBRL accounts and tax computations must include XBRL fragments which can be extracted in respect of all specified information included in those accounts and computations.

"Specified information" means items within the minimum set of XBRL tags within the taxonomy applicable to the period covered by the return, as defined in the CT Online Technical Pack for Software Developers on the HMRC website.

The information required by the specified return form must conform to the relevant CT600 XML Schema and CT600 Schematron schema published within the Corporation Tax Online: Internet Service Technical Pack for Software Developers on the HMRC website (www.hmrc.gov.uk/ebu/ct_techpack/index.htm).

Mandatory electronic payments under Regulation 3(2B) – Regulations 3(4) and 3(5)

8 The Commissioners for Her Majesty's Revenue & Customs hereby direct that the methods and forms of electronic communication approved for the purposes of making payments under regulation 3(2B) are the services known as: Direct Debit; BACS direct credit; CHAPS; debit and credit card over the Internet ("BillPay") or telephone; Paymaster; Bank Giro; and Alliance and Leicester Commercial Bank.

Other communications within the scope of the Income and Corporation Taxes (Electronic Communications) Regulations 2003

9 The Commissioners for Her Majesty's Revenue & Customs hereby direct that

– companies and their agents may use telephonic facsimile for other communications to which the Regulations apply, and
– companies and their agents who are members of the Shared Workspace online service may also use that facility for such communications.

General

10 The following items mentioned above form part of this Direction, so far as relevant to it:

– The Terms and Conditions for Online Services
– The guidance for the filing product provided by HMRC
– The specified XBRL taxonomies
– The CT Online Technical Pack for Software Developers
– The CT600 XML Schema and Schematron schema

Revocation

11 The following direction is revoked:

Date: 4 March 2003. Description: Directions under regulation 3 of the Income and Corporation Tax (Electronic Communications) Regulations 2003

Commencement

12 These directions have effect from 11 January 2010.

Amendments—[1] Paras (1A), (2A)–(2C), words in para (5) and paras (8)–(11) inserted, and cross-heading substituted, by the Income and Corporation Taxes (Electronic Communications) (Amendment) Regulations, SI 2009/3218 reg 2, Sch paras 5–9, with effect from 1 January 2010.

[2] Paras (10A), (12) inserted by the Income and Corporation Taxes (Electronic Communications) (Amendment) Regulations, SI 2010/2942 reg 2 with effect from 4 January 2011.

[3] Para (1)(*za*) inserted, and words in para (1A) substituted, by the Income and Corporation Taxes (Electronic Communications)(Amendment) Regulations, SI 2014/489 regs 2, 5, (6) with effect from 27 March 2014.

3A [Corporation tax-related payments by cheque

(1) Paragraph (2) applies instead of section 70A of the Management Act to each of the corporation tax-related payments in regulation 3(2C) tendered by cheque, but only if the Board receives that cheque on 1 April 2011 or later and that cheque is paid on its first presentation by the Board to the banker on whom it is drawn.

(2) The payment is to be treated as made on the second business day after the day on which the Board received that cheque.

(3) For these purposes, a "business day" is any day except—

(*a*) Saturday, Sunday, Good Friday or Christmas Day;
(*b*) a bank holiday under the Banking and Financial Dealings Act 1971;
(*c*) a day appointed by Royal proclamation as a public fast or thanksgiving day;
(*d*) a day declared by an order under section 2 of the Banking and Financial Dealings Act 1971 to be a non-business day.][1]

Amendments—[1] Reg 3A inserted by the Income and Corporation Taxes (Electronic Communications) (Amendment) Regulations, SI 2009/3218, reg 2, Sch para 10, with effect from 1 January 2010.

4 Use of intermediaries

The Board may use intermediaries in connection with—

(*a*) the delivery of information or the making of payments or repayments by means of electronic communications in connection with the matters referred to in regulation 2(1), and
(*b*) the authentication or security of anything transmitted by such means,

and may require other persons to use intermediaries in connection with those matters.

PART 3
ELECTRONIC COMMUNICATIONS—EVIDENTIAL PROVISIONS

5 Effect of delivering information by means of electronic communications

(1) Information to which these Regulations apply, and which is delivered by means of electronic communications, shall be treated as having been delivered, in the manner or form required by any provision of the Taxes Act[, the relevant Finance Acts][2] or the Management Act if, but only if, all the conditions imposed by—

(*a*) these Regulations,
(*b*) any other applicable enactment (except to the extent that the condition thereby imposed is incompatible with these Regulations), and
(*c*) any specific or general direction given by the Board,

are satisfied [or, but only in the case of the conditions mentioned in regulation 3(2A) (electronic delivery of company tax returns), are taken to be satisfied under regulation 3(8)][1].

(2) Information delivered by means of electronic communications shall be treated as having been delivered on the day on which the last of the conditions imposed as mentioned in paragraph (1) is satisfied.

This is subject to paragraphs (3) and (4).

(3) The Board may by a general or specific direction provide for information to be treated as delivered upon a different date (whether earlier or later) than that given by paragraph (2).

(4) Information shall not be taken to have been delivered to an official computer system by means of electronic communications unless it is accepted by the system to which it is delivered.
[(5) For the purposes of this Part, information which is delivered by means of electronic communications includes information delivered to a secure mailbox.
(6) For the purposes of paragraph (1) "the relevant Finance Acts" means the Finance Act 2007, the Finance Act 2008 or the Finance Act 2009.][2]

Amendments—[1] Words inserted at the end of para (1) by the Income and Corporation Taxes (Electronic Communications) (Amendment) Regulations, SI 2009/3218, reg 2, Sch para 11, with effect from 1 January 2010.
[2] In para (1), words inserted, and paras (5), (6) inserted, by the Income and Corporation Taxes (Electronic Communications)(Amendment) Regulations, SI 2014/489 regs 2, (7) with effect from 27 March 2014.

6 Proof of content

(1) A document certified by an officer of the Board to be a printed-out version of any information delivered by means of electronic communications under these Regulations on any occasion shall be evidence, unless the contrary is proved, that that information—

(*a*) was delivered by means of electronic communications on that occasion; and
(*b*) constitutes the entirety of what was delivered on that occasion.

(2) A document purporting to be a certificate given in accordance with paragraph (1) shall be presumed to be such a certificate unless the contrary is proved.

7 Proof of sender or recipient

The identity of—

(*a*) the sender of any information delivered to an official computer system by means of electronic communications under these Regulations, or
(*b*) the recipient of any information delivered by means of electronic communications from an official computer system,

shall be presumed, unless the contrary is proved, to be the person recorded as such on an official computer system.

8 Information delivered electronically on another's behalf

Any information delivered by an approved method of electronic communications on behalf of any person shall be deemed to have been delivered by him unless he proves that it was delivered without his knowledge or connivance.

9 Proof of delivery of information and payments

(1) The use of an authorised method of electronic communications shall be presumed, unless the contrary is proved, to have resulted in the making of a payment or the delivery of information—

(*a*) in the case of information falling to be delivered, or a payment falling to be made, to the Board, if the making of the payment or the delivery of the information has been recorded on an official computer system; and
(*b*) in the case of information falling to be delivered, or a payment falling to be made, by the Board, if the despatch of that payment or information has been recorded on an official computer system.

(2) The use of an authorised method of electronic communications shall be presumed, unless the contrary is proved, not to have resulted in the making of a payment, or the delivery of information—

(*a*) in the case of information falling to be delivered, or a payment falling to be made, to the Board, if the making of the payment or the delivery of the information has not been recorded on an official computer system; and
(*b*) in the case of information falling to be delivered, or a payment falling to be made, by the Board, if the despatch of that payment or information has not been recorded on an official computer system.

(3) The time of receipt of any information or payment sent by an authorised means of electronic communications shall be presumed, unless the contrary is proved, to be that recorded on an official computer system.

10 Use of unauthorised means of electronic communications

(1) Paragraph (2) applies to information which is required to be delivered to the Board in connection with the matters mentioned in regulation 2(1).
(2) The use of a means of electronic communications, for the purpose of delivering any information to which this paragraph applies, shall be conclusively presumed not to have resulted in the delivery of that information, unless—

(*a*) that means of electronic communications is for the time being approved for delivery of information of that kind; and
(*b*) the sender is approved[, if necessary,][1] for the use of that means of electronic communications in relation to information of that kind.

[(3) A company tax return delivered under regulation 3(2A) by means of electronic communications must meet standards of accuracy and completeness set by a specific or general direction given by the Board.
The Board may treat failure to meet those standards as failure to deliver that return.][1]

Revenue Directions—See under reg 3 for Directions issued by HMRC which also apply to reg 10.
Amendments—[1] Words in para (2)(*b*), and whole of para (3), inserted, by the Income and Corporation Taxes (Electronic Communications) (Amendment) Regulations, SI 2009/3218, reg 2, Sch paras 12, 13, with effect from 1 January 2010.

PART 4
REVOCATIONS

11 Revocation and saving
(1) There are revoked—
(*a*) the Income Tax (Electronic Communications) Regulations 2000; and
(*b*) Part 2 of the Income Tax (Electronic Communications) (Miscellaneous Amendments) Regulations 2001 and, in regulation 1(2) of those Regulations, the definition of "the Electronic Communications Regulations".
(2) Notwithstanding the revocations in paragraph (1), any direction given by the Board under the provisions revoked, to the extent that it could be given under these Regulations, shall continue to have effect as if given under these Regulations.
Commentary—*Simon's Taxes* **A4.165.**

2003/1830

INCOME TAX (AUTHORISED UNIT TRUSTS) (INTEREST DISTRIBUTIONS) REGULATIONS 2003

Made by the Commissioners of Inland Revenue under TA 1988 s 468PB

Made . . . . *16 July 2003*
Laid before the House of Commons . . . . *17 July 2003*
Coming into force . . . . *7 August 2003*

1 Citation, commencement and effect
(1) These Regulations may be cited as the Income Tax (Authorised Unit Trusts) (Interest Distributions) Regulations 2003 and shall come into force on 7th August 2003.
(2) These Regulations have effect in relation to interest distributions made on or after 16th October 2002.

2 Interpretation
In these Regulations—
"authorised unit trust" and "unit holder" have the meanings given by section 468(6) of the Taxes Act;
"the Board" means the Commissioners of Inland Revenue; "interest distribution" has the meaning given by section 468L(3) of the Taxes Act; "the Taxes Act" means the Income and Corporation Taxes Act 1988 and references to a section number without more are references to a section of that Act; "the Tax Acts" has the meaning given by section 831(2) of the Taxes Act; "unit trust scheme" has the meaning given by section 469(7) of the Taxes Act.
Modification—See the Open-ended Investment Companies (Tax) Regulations, SI 1997/1154 reg 28(1)–(3) (modification of this regulation in its application to open-ended investment companies).

3 Modification of sections 468M(1)(a), 468O and 468P in relation to interest distributions made to or received under a trust
Except in a case to which regulation 7 applies, section 468M(1)(a), section 468O and section 468P shall apply in relation to an interest distribution made to or received under a trust (other than a unit trust scheme) with the modifications specified in regulations 4, 5 and 6.

4 In section 468M(1)(a) after the word "company" insert the words "except where the company is the trustee of the trust to which or under which the interest distribution is made or received,".

5 In section 468O for subsection (1) substitute the following subsection—
"(1) For the purposes of section 468M, the residence condition is fulfilled with respect to a unit holder in the case of an interest distribution made to or received under a trust if there is a valid declaration made by the trustees of that trust that—
(*a*) the trustees are not resident in the United Kingdom, and
(*b*) each beneficiary of the trust is either not ordinarily resident or, in the case of a beneficiary which is a company, not resident in the United Kingdom.
(1ZA) In subsection (1) and in section 468P, references to a beneficiary are references to any person who is known to the trustees of the trust to be either—
(*a*) a person who is, or will or may become, entitled to any income of the trust, whether in the form of income or not, or

(*b*) a person to whom any such income may be paid, or for whose benefit any such income may be applied, whether in the form of income or not, in the exercise of a discretion by them.".

Modification—See the Open-ended Investment Companies (Tax) Regulations, SI 1997/1154 reg 28(1), (2), (4) (modification of this regulation in its application to open-ended investment companies).

6 In section 468P—

(*a*) in subsection (1)(*c*) for the words "subsections (2) or (3)" substitute the words "subsection (2)";

(*b*) for subsection (2) substitute the following subsection—

"(2) A declaration made as mentioned in section 468O(1) must contain—

(*a*) the names and principal residential addresses of the trustees of the trust or, in the case of a trustee which is a company, the name of the company and the address of its registered or principal office;

(*b*) the names and principal residential addresses of the beneficiaries of the trust or, in the case of a beneficiary which is a company, the name of the company and the address of its registered or principal office; and

(*c*) an undertaking that the trustees of the trust will notify the trustees of the authorised unit trust in question if—

(i) they become resident in the United Kingdom,

(ii) any beneficiary of the trust named in the declaration becomes ordinarily resident or, in the case of a company, resident in the United Kingdom, or

(iii) any person who becomes a beneficiary of the trust after the making of the declaration either is at the time of becoming a beneficiary, or subsequently becomes, ordinarily resident or, in the case of a company, resident in the United Kingdom.";

(*c*) omit subsection (3);

(*d*) in subsection (5)(a) for the words "the person in question" substitute the words "the trustees of the trust have become resident in the United Kingdom, or any beneficiary of the trust";

(*e*) in subsection (5)(b) for the words "the person in question" substitute the words "the trustees of the trust are or may be resident in the United Kingdom, or any beneficiary of the trust".

Modification—See the Open-ended Investment Companies (Tax) Regulations, SI 1997/1154 reg 28(1), (2), (5) (modification of this regulation in its application to open-ended investment companies).

7 Modification of section 468O in cases where an interest distribution made to or received under a trust is income of a person other than the trustees

(1) This regulation applies in any case where the whole of an interest distribution made to or received under a trust (other than a unit trust scheme) is, or falls to be treated as, or under any provision of the Tax Acts is deemed to be, the income of a person other than the trustees of that trust.

(2) Where this regulation applies, sections 468M, 468O and 468PA shall apply as if references to a unit holder in those sections were references to the person referred to in paragraph (1).

Modification—See the Open-ended Investment Companies (Tax) Regulations, SI 1997/1154 reg 28(1), (2), (6) (modification of this regulation in its application to open-ended investment companies).

8 Information to be provided to the Board—interest distributions made without deduction of tax

The Board may by notice require the trustees of an authorised unit trust, within such time (not being less than 14 days) as may be provided by the notice, to supply them with such information (including copies of any relevant books, documents or other records) as they may reasonably require for the purpose of determining whether, having regard to section 468M, section 468O and section 468P, interest distributions were properly made by that authorised unit trust without deduction of tax.

Modification—See the Open-ended Investment Companies (Tax) Regulations, SI 1997/1154 reg 28(1), (2), (7) (modification of this regulation in its application to open-ended investment companies).

9 Inspection of records

The trustees of an authorised unit trust shall, whenever required to do so, make available for inspection by an officer of the Board authorised for that purpose, at such time as that officer may reasonably require, all such copies of books, documents or other records in their possession or under their control as may be required by the Board under regulation 8.

Modification—See the Open-ended Investment Companies (Tax) Regulations, SI 1997/1154 reg 28(1), (2), (8) (modification of this regulation in its application to open-ended investment companies).

10 Use of information

(1) Subject to paragraph (3), information obtained by the Board under regulation 8 or 9 shall not be used for the purpose of ascertaining the tax liability (if any) of any person other than the persons specified in paragraph (2) and shall otherwise be used only for the purposes of these Regulations.

(2) The persons specified in this paragraph are—

(*a*) the trustees of the authorised unit trust in question;
(*b*) a unit holder beneficially entitled to an interest distribution made without deduction of tax to whom the information obtained relates;
(*c*) where an interest distribution is made to or received under a trust without deduction of tax and sub-paragraph (d) does not apply, the trustees of that trust and any beneficiary of the trust to whom the information obtained relates; and
(*d*) where the whole of an interest distribution made to or received under a trust without deduction of tax is, or falls to be treated as, or under any provision of the Tax Acts is deemed to be, the income of a person other than the trustees of that trust, that person in so far as the information obtained relates to him.

(3) Paragraph (1) shall not be construed as preventing any disclosure of information within section 182(5) of the Finance Act 1989.

(4) In paragraph (2)(*c*), "any beneficiary of the trust" means—
(*a*) any person who is, or will or may become, entitled to any income of the trust, whether in the form of income or not, and
(*b*) any person to whom any such income may be paid, or for whose benefit any such income may be applied, whether in the form of income or not, in the exercise of a discretion by the trustees of the trust.

Modification—See the Open-ended Investment Companies (Tax) Regulations, SI 1997/1154 reg 28(1), (2), (9) (modification of this regulation in its application to open-ended investment companies).

11 Revocation

The Income Tax (Authorised Unit Trusts) (Interest Distributions) Regulations 1994 are revoked.

2003/2076

CAPITAL ALLOWANCES (ENVIRONMENTALLY BENEFICIAL PLANT AND MACHINERY) ORDER 2003

Made by the Treasury under CAA 2001 ss 45H(3), (4), 45J(3)(b)

Made . . . . *11 August 2003*
Laid before the House of Commons . . . . *11 August 2003*
Coming into force . . . . *1 September 2003*

1 Citation and commencement

This Order may be cited as the Capital Allowances (Environmentally Beneficial Plant and Machinery) Order 2003 and shall come into force on 1st September 2003.

2 Interpretation

In this Order—

"the Capital Allowances Act" means the Capital Allowances Act 2001;

["the Water Technology Criteria List" means the list dated [June 2016][2] and issued by the Secretary of State for the Environment, Food and Rural Affairs on [6 July 2016][2];][1]

["the Water Technology Product List" means the list dated [June 2016][2] and issued by the Secretary of State for the Environment, Food and Rural Affairs on [6 July 2016][2].][1]

Notes—The Water Technology Criteria List and the Water Technology Product List are available at www.defra.gov.uk and www.gov.uk/government/publications/water-efficient-enhanced-capital-allowances.

Amendments—[1] Definitions of "the Water Technology Criteria List" and "the Water Technology Product List" substituted by the Capital Allowances (Environmentally Beneficial Plant and Machinery) (Amendment) Order, SI 2009/1864 art 2 with effect from 4 August 2009.

[2] Dates substituted by the Capital Allowances (Environmentally Beneficial Plant and Machinery) (Amendment) (No 2) Order, SI 2016/952 arts 2, 3 with effect from 6 October 2016. Those dates were previously 28 June 2015 and 7 July 2015 respectively.

3 Description of environmentally beneficial plant and machinery

(1) Plant or machinery is environmentally beneficial plant or machinery for the purposes of section 45H of the Capital Allowances Act (expenditure on environmentally beneficial plant or machinery) if—
(*a*) it falls within a technology class specified in the Water Technology Criteria List,
(*b*) it meets the environmental criteria set out in that List, and
(*c*) in the case of plant or machinery falling within any of the technology classes specified in paragraph (2), it is of a type that—
(i) is specified in, and has not been removed from, the Water Technology Product List, or
(ii) has been accepted for inclusion in the Water Technology Product List.

[(2) The technology classes specified for the purposes of paragraph (1)(*c*) are—
(*a*) flow controllers;
(*b*) leakage detection equipment;
[(*c*) meters and monitoring equipment;

(*d*) efficient taps;
(*e*) efficient toilets;][4]
(*f*) rainwater harvesting equipment;
[(*g*) water reuse systems;][4]
(*h*) cleaning in place equipment;
(*i*) efficient showers.
[(*j*) efficient washing machines;
(*k*) small scale slurry and sludge dewatering equipment.][2]
[(*l*) vehicle wash waste reclaim units;][3]
[(*m*) water efficient industrial cleaning equipment;
(*n*) water management equipment for mechanical seals;][4]][1]
[(*o*) greywater recovery and reuse equipment.][5]

Amendments—[1] Para (2) substituted by the Capital Allowances (Environmentally Beneficial Plant and Machinery) (Amendment) Order, SI 2005/2423 arts 2, 4 with effect from 22 September 2005.
[2] Sub-paras (*j*), (*k*) inserted by the Capital Allowances (Environmentally Beneficial Plant and Machinery) (Amendment) Order, SI 2006/2235, arts 2(1), 3, with effect from 7 September 2006.
[3] Sub-para (*l*) inserted by the Capital Allowances (Environmentally Beneficial Plant and Machinery) (Amendment) Order, SI 2007/2166 art 2(1), (3) with effect from 16 August 2007.
[4] Para (2)(*c*)–(*e*), (*g*), (*m*), (*n*) substituted, by the Capital Allowances (Environmentally Beneficial Plant and Machinery) (Amendment) Order, SI 2008/1917 art 2(1), (3) with effect from 11 August 2008.
[5] Sub-para (2)(*o*) inserted by the Capital Allowances (Environmentally Beneficial Plant and Machinery) (Amendment) Order, SI 2013/1762 arts 2, 4 with effect from 7 August 2013.

4 Environmentally beneficial components of plant or machinery

Where one or more components of certain plant or machinery (but not all of that plant or machinery)—

(*a*) meets the conditions set out in article 3(1)(a) to (c), and
(*b*) falls within any of the technology classes specified in article 3(2)(a) to (c),

the amount specified in respect of each such component for the purposes of section 45J of the Capital Allowances Act is the amount specified in the Water Technology Product List in relation to that component.

5 [Certification of environmentally beneficial plant and machinery

(1) In a case in which paragraph (2) applies, no section 45H allowance may be made unless a relevant certificate of environmental benefit is in force.

[(2) This paragraph applies in the case of expenditure on—

(*a*) efficient membrane filtration systems for the treatment of wastewater for recovery and reuse; and
(*b*) efficient wastewater recovery and reuse systems, falling within the technology class "water reuse systems" specified in the Water Technology Criteria List][2]

(3)In paragraph (1), "section 45H allowance" has the meaning given by section 45I(1) of the Capital Allowances Act, and "relevant certificate of environmental benefit" means a certificate of environmental benefit, as defined in subsection (2) of section 45I of the Capital Allowances Act, and which has been issued in accordance with subsection (3) of that section.][1]

Amendments—[1] This regulation inserted by the Capital Allowances (Environmentally Beneficial Plant and Machinery) (Amendment) Order, SI 2005/2423 arts 2, 5 with effect from 22 September 2005.
[2] Para (2) substituted, by the Capital Allowances (Environmentally Beneficial Plant and Machinery) (Amendment) Order, SI 2008/1917 art 2(1), (4) with effect from 11 August 2008.

2003/2082

INSURANCE COMPANIES (CALCULATION OF PROFITS: POLICY HOLDERS' TAX) REGULATIONS 2003

Made by the Treasury under FA 1989 s 82A

Made . . . . *11 August 2003*
Laid before the House of Commons . . . . *11 August 2003*
Coming into force . . . . *1 September 2003*

1 Citation, commencement and effect

(1) These Regulations may be cited as the Insurance Companies (Calculation of Profits: Policy Holders' Tax) Regulations 2003 and shall come into force on 1st September 2003.

(2) These Regulations have effect in relation to periods of account beginning on or after 1st January 2003 and ending on or after these Regulations come into force.

2 Calculation of Profits: Policy Holders' Tax

Tax expended on behalf of policy holders or annuitants is allowed as a deduction in calculating the profits for a period of account to the extent permitted by—

(*a*) subject to regulation 5, the basis of deduction specified in regulation 3 [or 3A][1]; and
(*b*) regulation 5.

Amendments—[1] Words inserted in para (*a*) by the Insurance Companies (Calculation of Profits: Policy Holders' Tax) (Amendment) Regulations, SI 2010/2932 regs 2, 3 with effect in relation to periods of account ending on or after 31 December 2010.

3 For the purpose of regulation 2 the basis of deduction is—
(*a*) the basis used in the company's latest company tax return to determine the amount of tax expended on behalf of policy holders or annuitants allowed as a deduction in calculating the profits for that accounting period; or
(*b*) where the company has no latest company tax return—
(i) where the company was the transferee of life assurance business under an insurance business transfer scheme, the basis used in the latest company tax return of the transferor company to determine the amount of tax expended on behalf of policy holders or annuitants allowed as a deduction in calculating the profits for that accounting period; or
(ii) in any other case, the basis the company would have used to determine the amount of tax expended on behalf of policy holders or annuitants allowed as a deduction in calculating the profits for an accounting period had it been required to deliver a company tax return for an accounting period beginning before 1st January 2003.

[This regulation does not apply for a period of account in which there has been a substantial change in the business of the company, except to the extent permitted by regulation 3A(2)(a), or for any subsequent period of account.][1]

Commentary—*Simon's Taxes* **D7.5186.**

Amendments—[1] Words inserted by the Insurance Companies (Calculation of Profits: Policy Holders' Tax) (Amendment) Regulations, SI 2010/2932 regs 2, 4 with effect in relation to periods of account ending on or after 31 December 2010.

[3A Basis of deduction following a substantial change in the business of a company

(1) This regulation applies for the purposes of regulation 2 where there has been a substantial change in the long-term business of a company.

(2) Where the change occurred or occurs on or before 31st December 2010—
(*a*) in the first period of account ending on or after 31st December 2010 the basis of deduction is either—
(i) the basis specified in regulation 3; or
(ii) such other basis to determine the amount of tax expended on behalf of policy holders or annuitants as is just and reasonable; and
(*b*) for any subsequent period of account, the basis of deduction is such basis to determine the amount of tax expended on behalf of policy holders or annuitants as is just and reasonable.

(3) Where the change occurs in a period of account beginning on or after 1st January 2011, the basis of deduction to be used in relation to the period of account in which the change occurs and in relation to each subsequent period of account shall be such basis to determine the amount of tax expended on behalf of policy holders or annuitants as is just and reasonable.

(4) For the purpose of determining whether a substantial change in the long-term business of a company has occurred in relation to—
(*a*) the first period of account ending on or after 31st December 2010, the long-term business of the company as at the end of the last day of that period of account is to be compared with the long-term business of the company as at the end of the last day of the first period of account to which these regulations applied; and
(*b*) a period of account beginning on or after 1st January 2011, the long-term business of the company as at the end of the last day of the period of account in which the substantial change occurs is to be compared with the long-term business of the company as at the end of the last day of the immediately preceding period of account.

(5) For the purposes of this regulation, a basis to determine the amount of tax expended on behalf of policy holders and annuitants is just and reasonable if it takes account of and is consistent with—
(*a*) the long-term business activities of the company; and
(*b*) the structure of the long-term insurance fund.

(6) In this regulation "a substantial change in the long-term business of a company" includes but is not limited to—
(*a*) an insurance business transfer scheme;
(*b*) the commencement of a new category of long-term business;
(*c*) ceasing to write a category of long-term business; or
(*d*) a change in the structure of the long-term insurance fund.][1]

Amendments—[1] Reg 3A inserted by the Insurance Companies (Calculation of Profits: Policy Holders' Tax) (Amendment) Regulations, SI 2010/2932 regs 2, 5 with effect in relation to periods of account ending on or after 31 December 2010.

[4 Interpretation of regulations 3 and 3A

(1) In regulation 3 "the latest company tax return" means the company tax return for the latest preceding accounting period of the company or the transferor company for which such a return has been delivered before the day on which these Regulations come into force.

(2) In regulations 3 and 3A "an insurance business transfer scheme" means a scheme falling within section 105 of the Financial Services and Markets Act 2000, including an excluded scheme falling within Case 2, 3, 4 or 5 of subsection (3) of that section.

(3) In regulation 3A—

"long-term business"; and

"long-term insurance fund"

have the meanings given by section 431(2) of the Income and Corporation Taxes Act 1988.][1]

Amendments—[1] This reg substituted by the Insurance Companies (Calculation of Profits: Policy Holders' Tax) (Amendment) Regulations, SI 2010/2932 regs 2, 6 with effect in relation to periods of account ending on or after 31 December 2010.

5 A deduction for tax expended on behalf of policy holders or annuitants but not brought into account shall be allowed but only where such an amount has been included in any value deemed to be brought into account by virtue of section 83(2B) of the Finance Act 1989.

2003/2172

FINANCE ACT 1995, SECTION 127(12) (DESIGNATED TRANSACTIONS) REGULATIONS 2003

Made by the Treasury under FA 1995 s 127(12)(c)

Made . . . . . . 21 August 2003
Laid before the House of Commons . . . . . . 22 August 2003
Coming into force . . . . . . 12 September 2003

1 Citation and commencement

These Regulations may be cited as the Finance Act 1995, Section 127(12) (Designated Transactions) Regulations 2003 and shall come into force on 12th September 2003.

2 Designated transaction

(1) In this regulation "section 127(12)" means section 127(12) of the Finance Act 1995 (meaning of "investment transaction" for the purposes of determining whether person capable of being the UK representative of a non-resident taxpayer).

(2) For the purposes of section 127(12) a transaction falling within paragraph (3) is designated.

(3) A transaction falls within this paragraph if it is a contract, not otherwise falling within section 127(12), whose terms—

(*a*) provide that—

(i) after setting off their obligations to each other under the contract, a cash payment is to be made by one party to the other in respect of the excess, if any, or

(ii) each party is liable to make to the other party one or more cash payments in respect of that party's obligations to the other under the contract, and

(*b*) do not provide for the delivery of any property other than currency.

This is subject to the following qualification.

(4) A transaction does not fall within paragraph (3) if it is—

(*a*) a contract which relates to land;

(*b*) a contract of insurance; or

(*c*) a contract effected in the course of capital redemption business within the meaning of section 458 of the Income and Corporation Taxes Act 1988.

2003/2173

FINANCE ACT 2003, SCHEDULE 26, PARAGRAPH 3(3) (DESIGNATED TRANSACTIONS) REGULATIONS 2003

Made by the Treasury under FA 2003 Sch 26 para 3(3)(c)

Made . . . . . . 21 August 2003
Laid before the House of Commons . . . . . . 22 August 2003
Coming into force . . . . . . 12 September 2003

1 Citation and commencement

These Regulations may be cited as the Finance Act 2003, Schedule 26 Paragraph 3(3) (Designated Transactions) Regulations 2003 and shall come into force on 12th September 2003.

2 Designated transaction

(1) In these Regulations "paragraph 3(3)" means paragraph 3(3) of Schedule 26 to the Finance Act 2003 (meaning of "investment transaction" for the purposes of determining whether a person is an agent of independent status in respect of investment transactions).

(2) For the purposes of paragraph 3(3) a transaction falling within paragraph (3) is designated.

(3) A transaction falls within this paragraph if it is a contract, not otherwise falling within paragraph 3(3), whose terms—

(*a*) provide that—

(i) after setting off their obligations to each other under the contract, a cash payment is to be made by one party to the other in respect of the excess, if any, or

(ii) each party is liable to make to the other party one or more cash payments in respect of that party's obligations to the other under the contract, and

(*b*) do not provide for the delivery of any property other than currency.

This is subject to the following qualification.

(4) A transaction does not fall within paragraph (3) if it is—

(*a*) a contract which relates to land;

(*b*) a contract of insurance; or

(*c*) a contract effected in the course of capital redemption business within the meaning of section 458 of the Income and Corporation Taxes Act 1988.

2003/2339

TAXATION OF BENEFITS UNDER GOVERNMENT PILOT SCHEMES (RETURN TO WORK CREDIT AND EMPLOYMENT RETENTION AND ADVANCEMENT SCHEMES) ORDER 2003

Made by the Treasury under FA 1996 s 151(1)(a), (2), (5) and (7)

Made . . . . *10 September 2003*
Laid before the House of Commons . . . . *10 September 2003*
Coming into force . . . . *1 October 2003*

Commentary—*Simon's Taxes* **E4.328.**

1 Citation and commencement

This Order may be cited as the Taxation of Benefits under Government Pilot Schemes (Return to Work Credit and Employment Retention and Advancement Schemes) Order 2003 and shall come into force on 1st October 2003.

2 Interpretation

In this Order—

"benefit" has the meaning given by subsection (6) of section 151 of the Finance Act 1996;

"Employment Retention and Advancement Scheme payment" means a payment of benefit under the Government pilot scheme known as the Employment Retention and Advancement Scheme;

"Government pilot scheme" has the meaning given by subsections (3) and (4) of section 151 of the Finance Act 1996; and

"Return to Work Credit payment" means a payment of benefit under the Government pilot scheme known as the Return to Work Credit Scheme.

3 Exemptions from income tax

The Income Tax Acts shall have effect in relation to any amount of an Employment Retention and Advancement Scheme payment, and any amount of a Return to Work Credit Scheme payment, as if that amount were wholly exempt from income tax and accordingly to be disregarded in computing the amount of any receipts brought into account for income tax purposes.

2003/2495

INCOME TAX (INCENTIVE PAYMENTS FOR VOLUNTARY ELECTRONIC COMMUNICATION OF PAYE RETURNS) REGULATIONS 2003

Made by the Commissioners of Inland Revenue under FA 2000 s 143(1), Sch 38

Made . . . . *29 September 2003*
Laid before the House of Commons . . . . *29 September 2003*
Coming into force . . . . *20 October 2003*

1 Citation, commencement and interpretation

(1) These Regulations may be cited as the Income Tax (Incentive Payments for Voluntary Electronic Communication of PAYE Returns) Regulations 2003 and shall come into force on 20th October 2003.

(2) In these Regulations—

"approved" means approved by means of a general or specific direction of the Board;

"the Board" means the Commissioners of Inland Revenue;

"direction" means a direction given by the Board;

["employee" has the meaning given in section 4 of ITEPA 2003, and cognate expressions shall be construed accordingly;][1]

"incentive payment" has the meaning given in Schedule 38;

["ITEPA 2003" means the Income Tax (Earnings and Pensions) Act 2003;][1]

"the Management Act" means the Taxes Management Act 1970;

["the PAYE Regulations" means the Income Tax (Pay As You Earn) Regulations 2003;][1]

"Schedule 38" means Schedule 38 to the Finance Act 2000;

"the specified date" means, in relation to a year of assessment, such date in the immediately preceding year of assessment as is announced annually by means of a direction given by the Board not later than 30th November of that preceding year; and

references to the delivery of information have the same meaning as they have in section 132 of the Finance Act 1999.

(3) In these Regulations "a small employer" is a person treated as paying PAYE income to 49 or fewer recipients at the specified date.

A person is treated as paying PAYE income to a recipient at the specified date if at that date—

(*a*) he is required by the [PAYE Regulations or by][2] [paragraph 6 of Schedule 4 to the Social Security (Contributions) Regulations 2001 . . . [2]][1] to prepare or maintain a deductions working sheet in respect of the recipient; and

(*b*) he has not delivered, sent or transmitted to the inspector a statement required by regulation 23 of the PAYE Regulations for the recipient.

Amendments—[1] In para (2), definitions of "employee" and "ITEPA 2003" inserted, and definition of "the PAYE regulations" substituted, and words in para (3) substituted, by the Income Tax (Incentive Payments for Voluntary Electronic Communication of PAYE Returns) (Amendment) Regulations, SI 2005/826 regs 2, 3 with effect from 8 April 2005.

[2] Words in para (3)(*a*) substituted and revoked by the Income Tax (Pay As You Earn, etc), (Amendment) Regulations, SI 2006/777 reg 6 with effect for 2007–08 and subsequent tax years.

2 Construction of references to numbers of employees

(1) If an election has been made under [regulation 98][1] of the PAYE Regulations (multiple employers) and—

(*a*) no notice under [regulation 99 of those Regulations][1] (elections for improper purposes) has been given, or

(*b*) any notice under [that regulation][1] has been withdrawn,

paragraph (2) applies.

(2) Where this paragraph applies, a reference in these Regulations to a number of recipients shall be construed as a reference to the number of such employees treated as employed in a separate undertaking by virtue of [regulation 98][1] of the PAYE Regulations.

Amendments—[1] Words substituted by the Income Tax (Incentive Payments for Voluntary Electronic Communication of PAYE Returns) (Amendment) Regulations, SI 2005/826 regs 2, 4 with effect from 8 April 2005.

3 Scope

(1) These Regulations apply to the persons specified in paragraph (2) who deliver, or cause to be delivered, the return and supporting information required under [regulation 73][1] of the PAYE Regulations by an approved method of electronic communications if—

(*a*) the return and that information are delivered in respect of a year of assessment specified in paragraph (3); and

(*b*) the return satisfies the conditions mentioned in regulation 4(1)(*b*).

(2) The persons specified in this paragraph are those who—

(*a*) are small employers on the specified date; or

(*b*) not being small employers on that date, are treated as making payments of PAYE income for the first time after that date.

(3) The years of assessment specified in this paragraph are 2004–05 to 2008–09.

Amendments—[1] Words in para (1) substituted by the Income Tax (Incentive Payments for Voluntary Electronic Communication of PAYE Returns) (Amendment) Regulations, SI 2005/826 regs 2, 5 with effect from 8 April 2005.

4 Incentive payment—return under [regulation 73] of the PAYE Regulations

(1) The Board shall make an incentive payment in the amount prescribed in paragraph (3) to a person specified in regulation 3(2) for the year of assessment in question, if—

(*a*) he delivers, or causes to be delivered, a return under [regulation 73][1] of the PAYE Regulations for that year of assessment by an approved method of electronic communications; and (*b*) the return satisfies the conditions as to accuracy and completeness specified in any direction given by the Board.

This is subject to [paragraphs (2) and (2A)][2].

(2) An incentive payment shall not be made in respect of a return which contains only information supplied in accordance with any of the provisions and arrangements mentioned in [regulation 141][1] of the PAYE Regulations.

[(2A) An incentive payment shall not be made where a small employer—

(*a*) has been established,

(*b*) employs employees, or

(*c*) makes payments of PAYE income (within the meaning of section 683 of ITEPA 2003), wholly or mainly for an impermissible purpose.][2]

[(2B) For the purpose of paragraph (2A)—

(*a*) a small employer is "established" where—

(i) persons enter into partnership, within the meaning of section 4 of the Partnership Act 1894, in accordance with the principles set out in section 2 of that Act,

(ii) a limited partnership is registered in accordance with the Limited Partnerships Act 1907,

(iii) a limited liability partnership is incorporated in accordance with section 2 of the Limited Liability Partnerships Act 2000 . . . [3],

(iv) a company is incorporated under . . . [3] the Companies Act [2006][3] . . . [3], or

(v) an unincorporated association, or a body corporate, not falling within the previous paragraphs, is created,

and it is intended at the time of incorporation, formation or creation that it should be a small employer;

(*b*) a small employer is established for an impermissible purpose if it is established for the purpose of—

(i) obtaining an advantage in relation to income tax, corporation tax or national insurance contributions;

(ii) obtaining an incentive under these Regulations; or

(iii) avoiding an obligation to file a return by means of electronic communications under any enactment relating to income tax, corporation tax or national insurance.][2]

[(2C) For the purposes of paragraph (2B)(*b*)(i) "advantage"—

(*a*) in relation to income tax and corporation tax, has the meaning given by section 318 of the Finance Act 2004 (interpretation for the purposes of Part 7: tax avoidance schemes); and

(*b*) in relation to national insurance, has the meaning which would be given by that section were national insurance a tax to which it applied.][2]

(3) The amounts prescribed are those shown in the Table 1 for the relevant year of assessment.

TABLE 1
AMOUNTS OF INCENTIVE PAYMENT

Year of assessment	*Amount of incentive payment*
2004–05	£250
2005–06	£250
2006–07	£150
2007–08	£100
2008–09	£75

[(3A) If an officer of the Board considers that, by virtue of paragraph (2A), a person will not be entitled to an incentive payment for a year of assessment, he may give notice to that effect to that person.][2]

(4) Where an officer of the Board considers that a person, who has claimed to be entitled to an incentive under these Regulations—

(*a*) does not satisfy one or more of the requirements of these Regulations or the directions made under them, or

(*b*) is not entitled to an incentive payment by virtue of paragraph [(2) or (2A)][2],

the officer shall give notice to that person that the conditions are not met or, where the incentive payment has already been authorised or made, notice withdrawing the incentive payment.

(5) Where, prior to the giving of a notice under paragraph (4), an incentive payment has already been made to the person referred to in that paragraph, an office of the Board may recover the amount of the incentive payment in accordance with paragraph (6).

(6) For the purpose of paragraph (5), subsections (1), (4), (5) and (6) of section 30 and section 30A of the Management Act (recovery of overpayment of tax, etc and assessing procedure) shall apply as if the amount to be recovered were an amount of income tax repaid to a person which ought not to have been repaid to him.

Amendments—[1] Words in Heading and paras (1), (2) substituted by the Income Tax (Incentive Payments for Voluntary Electronic Communication of PAYE Returns) (Amendment) Regulations, SI 2005/826 regs 2, 6(1)–(3)(*a*), (4) with effect from 8 April 2005.

[2] Words in para (1) substituted, paras (2A)–(2C), (3A) inserted, and reference in para (4)(*b*) substituted, by SI 2005/826 regs 2, 6(1), (3)(*b*), (5)–(7) with effect from 19 March 2005. These amendments have effect—

(a) if the obligation to maintain a deductions working sheet under any of the provisions listed below arises for the first time in relation to 2004–05 after the coming into force of SI 2005/826, in relation to any return delivered in respect of that year; and

(b) except as provided by sub-paragraph (*a*), in relation to any return delivered in respect of 2005–06 to 2008–09.

The provisions referred to above are—

(a) the Social Security (Contributions) Regulations, SI 2001/1004 Sch 4 para 6;

(b) the Working Tax Credit (Payment by Employers) Regulations, SI 2002/2172 reg 6(6); and

(c) the Income Tax (Pay As You Earn) Regulations, SI 2003/2682 reg 66: SI 2005/826 reg 1.

[3] In sub-para (2B), in para (*a*)(iii), words repealed, and in para (*a*)(iv), year substituted, and words repealed, by the Companies Act 2006 (Consequential Amendments) (Taxes and National Insurance) Order, SI 2009/1890 art 3(7), (8) with effect from 1 October 2009.

4A [Descriptions of incentives

(1) Any incentive under these Regulations shall take the form of—

(*a*) in the case of a person, from whom a sum of any of the descriptions mentioned in paragraph (3) has become due to the Board, a reduction in the person's liability for that sum;

(*b*) in the case of a person in respect of whom an account is maintained by the Board, not falling within sub-paragraph (*a*), a credit to that account; or

(*c*) in any other case, or at the request of a person who would be entitled to a credit to his account as mentioned in sub-paragraph (*b*), a payment by the Board.

(2) Where the amount of an incentive due to a person falling within paragraph (1)(*a*) exceeds the amount of his liability, the excess shall be credited to any account maintained in respect of that person by the Board, or, if that person so requests, paid to him by the Board

(3) The sums referred to in paragraph (1) are those which a person is liable to pay to a collector of inland revenue in pursuance of an obligation as an employer, contractor or a sub-contractor.

(4) If an incentive is given as mentioned in paragraph (1)(*a*) or (*b*) an officer of the Board shall notify the person entitled to the incentive of the form it has taken.][1]

Commentary—*Simon's Taxes* **E4.11153**.

Amendments—[1] Paragraph 4A inserted by the Income Tax (Incentive Payments for Voluntary Electronic Communication of PAYE Returns) (Amendment) Regulations, SI 2005/826 regs 2, 7 with effect from 8 April 2005.

5 Notice of non-entitlement to incentive payment

If, during the year of assessment 2003–04, an officer of the Board considers that a person—

(*a*) is not a small employer in respect of the year of assessment 2004–05; but

(*b*) is treated as paying PAYE income to less than 250 employees at the specified date in respect of that year;

the officer shall give notice to that person that he is not entitled to an incentive payment under these Regulations for the year of assessment 2004–05.

6 Appeals

(1) An appeal lies[, subject to paragraph (1A)][1] against a decision made by an officer of the Board under [regulation 4(3A) or (4)][1] or 5 and may be brought—

(*a*) by notice [in writing][1] to an officer of the Board; and

(*b*) within 30 days of the issue of the officer's notice under that regulation.

[(1A) A person may not appeal against a decision under regulation 4(4)(*b*) where he has already appealed unsuccessfully against a notice given under regulation 4(3A) in respect of the same year of assessment.][1]

(2) An appeal may be brought against an officer's notice under [regulation 4(3A) or (4)][1] on the grounds that the recipient of the notice—

(*a*) has satisfied all the requirements of these Regulations and the directions made under them so far as they apply to him; and

(*b*) is not precluded from receiving an incentive payment by virtue of [regulation 4(2) or (2A)][1].

(3) The recipient of an officer's notice under regulation 5 may appeal against it on the grounds that he is entitled to an incentive payment for the year of assessment 2004–05.

[(4) Section 31A(5) of the Management Act applies to an appeal under these Regulations as it applies to an appeal under section 31 of that Act.][2]

Amendments—[1] Words in para (1) inserted, words in paras (1), (2) substituted, and para (1A) inserted, by the Income Tax (Incentive Payments for Voluntary Electronic Communication of PAYE Returns) (Amendment) Regulations, SI 2005/826 regs 2, 8 with effect from 19 March 2005. These amendments have effect—

(a) if the obligation to maintain a deductions working sheet under any of the provisions listed below arises for the first time in relation to 2004–05 after the coming into force of SI 2005/826, in relation to any return delivered in respect of that year; and

(b) except as provided by sub-paragraph (a), in relation to any return delivered in respect of 2005–06 to 2008–09.

The provisions referred to above are—

(a) the Social Security (Contributions) Regulations, SI 2001/1004 Sch 4 para 6;

(b) the Working Tax Credit (Payment by Employers) Regulations, SI 2002/2172 reg 6(6); and

(c) the Income Tax (Pay As You Earn) Regulations, SI 2003/2682 reg 66: SI 2005/826 reg 1.

2 Para (4) substituted for previous paras (4)–(7) by the Transfer of Tribunal Functions and Revenue and Customs Appeals Order, SI 2009/56 art 3, Sch 2 para 91 with effect from 1 April 2009.

SIs

2003/2682

INCOME TAX (PAY AS YOU EARN) REGULATIONS 2003

Made by the Commissioners of Inland Revenue under ITEPA 2003 ss 684, 685(4), 692, 704, 705, 706, 707, 708 and 710; TMA 1970 ss 59A(10), 59B(8), 98A and 113(1); FA 1999 ss 132 and 133(2); FA 2002 s 136 and FA 2003 ss 145(4) and 205.

Made . . . . *21 October 2003*
Laid before Parliament . . . . *30 October 2003*
Coming into force . . . . *6 April 2004*

ARRANGEMENT OF REGULATIONS

PART 1
INTRODUCTION
Citation and commencement

Interpretation

Application to payers and payees

PART 2
CODES
Determination of code

Appeals and amendment

PART 3
DEDUCTION AND REPAYMENT OF TAX

CHAPTER 1
DEDUCTION AND REPAYMENT

Deduction and repayment by reference to employee's code

The cumulative basis

CHAPTER 3A
BENEFITS IN KIND

CHAPTER 4
MISCELLANEOUS

PART 4
PAYMENTS, RETURNS AND INFORMATION

CHAPTER 1
PAYMENT OF TAX AND ASSOCIATED RETURNS

Real time returns

PART 1
INTRODUCTION

1 Citation and commencement

These Regulations may be cited as The Income Tax (Pay As You Earn) Regulations 2003 and shall come into force on 6th April 2004.

Commentary—*Simon's Taxes* **E4.1101.**
Cross-references—See ITEPA 2003 Pt 2 Ch 10 (workers' services provided to public sector through intermediaries).

2 Interpretation

(1) In these Regulations, unless the context otherwise requires—

"additional pay" means the appropriate amount, established from an employee's code (where it is a K code not used on the cumulative basis) and the tax tables, to be added to the relevant payments made to an employee in order to determine the taxable payments;

["additional rate" in relation to the charging of income tax for any tax year, means the rate of income tax determined under section 6(2) of ITA[, except where the employee is a Scottish taxpayer where it means [any Scottish additional rate of income tax set by a Scottish rate resolution of the Scottish Parliament under section 80C of the Scotland Act 1998][15]][14];][5]

"agency" has the meaning given in section 44 of ITEPA;

["agency worker" means a worker who is treated by section 44 of ITEPA(f) as holding an employment with the agency for income tax purposes;][13]

"approved method of electronic communications" has the meaning given in regulation 189;

"basic rate", in relation to the charging of income tax for any tax year, means the rate of income tax [set by a Scottish rate resolution of the Scottish Parliament under section 80C of the Scotland Act 1998][15], [except where the employee is a Scottish taxpayer where it means the Scottish basic rate of income tax determined under section 6A of that Act][14];

"Board of Inland Revenue" means the Commissioners of Inland Revenue (as to which see in particular the Inland Revenue Regulation Act 1890);
["the client" has the meaning given in section 44 of ITEPA, and cognate expressions shall be construed accordingly;][13]
["closed tax year" means any tax year preceding the current year, and cognate expressions shall be construed accordingly;][1]
"code" and related expressions have the meanings given in regulation 7;
["combined amount" means an amount which includes tax due under these regulations and one or more of the following—

(*a*) earnings-related contributions due under the SSC Regulations;
(*b*) amounts due under the Income Tax (Construction Industry Scheme) Regulations 2005;
(*c*) payments of repayments of student loans due under the Student Loan Regulations;][2]
[(*d*) apprenticeship levy due under these Regulations;][15]

"cumulative basis" means the basis of deduction or repayment of tax provided for in regulation 23;
"deductions working sheet" means—

(*a*) any form of record in which are to be kept the matters required by these Regulations in connection with an employee's relevant payments and tax;
(*b*) . . . [9]

"earnings" has the meaning given in sections 62 and 721(7) of ITEPA;
"electronic communications" has the meaning given in regulation 189;
"employee's code" has the meaning given in regulation 8(1);
"employer reference" means the combination of letters, numbers or both used by the Inland Revenue to identify an employer for the purposes of these Regulations;
"employer's PAYE reference", in relation to an employer, means the combination of the employer's employer reference and the Inland Revenue office number;
"employment", subject to regulations 10 to 12, has the meaning given in sections 4 and 5 of ITEPA; and "employer" and "employee" have corresponding meanings;
"excluded business expenses" has the meaning given in regulation 5;
["employment intermediary" has the meaning given in section 716B(2) of ITEPA;][13]
"family" and "family or household", in relation to a person, have the meanings given in section 721(4) and (5) of ITEPA;
"free pay" means the appropriate amount, established from an employee's code (where not used on the cumulative basis) and the tax tables, to be subtracted from relevant payments to arrive at taxable payments (and accordingly represents an appropriate part of reliefs allowable against those payments);
"general earnings" has the meaning given in section 7(3) of ITEPA;
"higher rate", in relation to the charging of income tax for any tax year, means the rate of income tax determined under [section 6(2) of ITA, except where the employee is a Scottish taxpayer where it means [any Scottish higher rate of income tax set by a Scottish rate resolution of the Scottish Parliament under section 80C of the Scotland Act 1998][15]][14];
["HMRC" means Her Majesty's Revenue and Customs;][1]
"ICTA" means the Income and Corporation Taxes Act 1988;
"Inland Revenue" means any officer of the Board of Inland Revenue;
"Inland Revenue office", in relation to an employer, means the office of the Inland Revenue from which codes are normally issued to the employer;
"Inland Revenue office number" means the number which identifies an employer's Inland Revenue office;
["ITA" means the Income Tax Act 2007;][2]
"ITEPA" means the Income Tax (Earnings and Pensions) Act 2003;
["large employer" has the meaning given in regulation 198A;][4]
["lower earnings limit" means the lower earnings limit for Class 1 contributions for the purposes of section 5(1) of the Social Security Contributions and Benefits Act 1992;][7]
"national insurance number" means the national insurance number allocated within the meaning of regulation 9 of the Social Security (Crediting and Treatment of Contributions, and National Insurance Numbers) Regulations 2001;
"net PAYE income" has the meaning given in regulation 3;
"non-cumulative basis" means the basis of deduction of tax provided for in regulation 27;
["non-Real Time Information employer" means an employer other than one within regulation 2A;][6]
["non-Real Time Information pension payer" means a pension payer other than one within regulation 2B;][6]
["notice" means as follows and "notify" must be read accordingly—

(*a*) notice in writing, or in a form authorised (in relation to the case in question) by directions under section 118 of the Finance Act 1998 (which allows certain claims etc to be made by telephone)

[(*b*) for the purposes of regulation 17 (notice to employee of code) and regulation 19 (amendment of code) notice—

(i) by an approved method of electronic communications;

(ii) in writing (other than a notice falling within sub-paragraph (i)); or

(iii) by telephone;][11]][5]

"notional payment" has the meaning given in section 710(2)(*a*) of ITEPA;

"objects" means gives a notice of objection to the Inland Revenue;

"official computer system" has the meaning given in regulation 189;

"other payee" means a person receiving relevant payments in a capacity other than employee, agency worker or pensioner;

"other payer" means a person making relevant payments in a capacity other than employer, agency or pension payer;

["overriding limit" means the limit on the amount of tax to be deducted from a relevant payment and is an amount equal to 50% of the amount of the relevant payment;][12]

"PAYE income" has the meaning given in section 683 of ITEPA;

"PAYE pension income" has the meaning given in section 683(3) of ITEPA;

"PAYE threshold" must be determined in accordance with regulation 9;

"payee" means an employee, agency worker, pensioner or other payee;

"payer" means an employer, agency, pension payer or other payer;

"pension" means a pension, annuity or other payments of PAYE pension income;

"pensioner" means a person receiving PAYE pension income;

"pension payer" means a person making payments of PAYE pension income;

"PSA" means a PAYE settlement agreement made in accordance with regulation 105;

"qualifying general earnings", in relation to a PSA, has the meaning given in regulation 106;

["qualifying payment" means a payment which becomes retrospective employment income as a relevant payment (including a notional payment);][1]

["Real Time Information employer" has the meaning given in regulation 2A;][6]

["Real Time Information pension payer" has the meaning given in regulation 2B;][6]

. . . [10]

"relevant payments" has the meaning given in regulation 4;

"relevant pension payments" has the meaning given in regulation 6;

["the relevant time", in relation to retrospective employment income, has the meaning given by section 710(7) of ITEPA, as modified by subsection (7A) of that section, but subject to section 94(5)(*c*) of the Finance Act 2006;][1]

"reliefs from income tax" includes allowances and deductions;

["retrospective contributions regulations" has the meaning given by regulation 1(2) of the SSC Regulations;][1]

["retrospective employment income" means payments which are retrospectively treated as payments of employment income by virtue of a retrospective tax provision;][1]

["retrospective tax provision" means a provision of the Income Tax Acts charging to income tax amounts of employment income paid before the enactment containing the provision was passed;][1]

["Scottish taxpayer" has the same meaning as in section 989 of ITA (the definitions);][14]

["seconded expatriate" means an employee meeting one of the following descriptions—

(*a*) an employee in section 689 of ITEPA (employee of non-UK employer); or

(*b*) an employee in a branch of an employer where—

(i) these Regulations would not apply to that employer but for that branch,

(ii) the employer seconded the employee to that branch, and

(iii) the employee was not employed in the United Kingdom immediately before the secondment;][7]

["specified date" for the purposes of Chapter 3 of Part 10, has the meaning given in regulation 198A;][4]

["SSC Regulations" means the Social Security (Contributions) Regulations 2001;][1]

. . . [2]

["Student Loan Regulations" means the Education (Student Loans) (Repayment) Regulations 2009 or, in Northern Ireland, the Education (Student Loans) (Repayment) Regulations (Northern Ireland) 2009;][7]

"taxable payments" means relevant payments reduced by free pay or, as the case may be, increased by additional pay (where the employee's code is not used on the cumulative basis);

"tax month" means the period beginning on the 6th day of a calendar month and ending on the 5th day of the following calendar month;

"tax not deducted because of the overriding limit" means any tax—

(*a*) which is due at the relevant date in accordance with the appropriate tax tables in respect of any taxable payments or total taxable payments to date, but

(*b*) which has not been deducted because of the overriding limit;

"tax period" means—

(*a*) tax quarter, if . . . [8] regulation 70 (quarterly tax periods) applies, or

(*b*) tax month, in every other case;

"tax quarter" means any of the following (inclusive) periods—

6th April to 5th July,

6th July to 5th October,

6th October to 5th January, and

6th January to 5th April;

"tax tables" means the tax tables prepared by the Board of Inland Revenue under section 685 of ITEPA;

"tax week" means 6th April to 12th April (inclusive) and each successive period of 7 days, except that the final tax week in a tax year ("Week 53") is just the last day of the tax year (or last 2 days in a leap year);

"tax year" means a year for which any Act provides for income tax to be charged;

"TMA" means the Taxes Management Act 1970;

"total additional pay to date" means the appropriate amount, established from an employee's code (where it is a K code to be used on the cumulative basis) and the tax tables, to be added to the total payments to date in order to determine the total taxable payments to date;

"total free pay to date", in relation to any date, means the appropriate amount, established from an employee's code (where used on the cumulative basis) and the tax tables, to be subtracted from total payments to date to arrive at total taxable payments to date (and accordingly represents an appropriate part of reliefs allowable against those payments);

"total net tax deducted", in relation to the relevant payments made to an employee during any period, means the total tax deducted from those payments plus any tax accounted for in accordance with regulation 62(5) (notional payments), less any tax repaid to the employee;

"total payments to date", in relation to any date, means the sum of all relevant payments made by the employer to the employee from the beginning of the tax year up to and including that date;

"total tax to date" means the tax due at any date in accordance with the appropriate tax tables in respect of any total taxable payments to date;

"total taxable payments to date" means total payments to date reduced by total free pay to date or, as the case may be, increased by total additional pay to date (where the employee's code is used on the cumulative basis);

"trade dispute" has the meaning given in section 35(1) of the Jobseekers Act 1995 or, in Northern Ireland, in article 2(2) of the Jobseekers (Northern Ireland) Order 1995;

["tribunal" means the First-tier Tribunal or, where determined by or under Tribunal Procedure Rules, the Upper Tribunal;][3].

["United Kingdom continental shelf" means the area designated under section 1(7) of the Continental Shelf Act 1964.][13]

(2) References in these Regulations to income tax in respect of PAYE income (however expressed) are references to income tax in respect of that income if reasonable assumptions are, when necessary, made about other income.

Commentary—*Simon's Taxes* **E4.1103**.

Derivation—The Income Tax (Employments) Regulations, SI 1993/744 reg 2(1); ITEPA 2003 ss 4, 5, 7(3), 62, 683, 684(7B), 720(2), 721(4), (5), (7).

Notes—A definition of "Scottish rate" was to have been inserted by SI 2015/1667 with effect in relation to the 2016–17 tax year and subsequent tax years. However, that definition was revoked by the Income Tax (Pay As You Earn) (Amendment No 4) Regulations, SI 2015/1927 regs 2, 3 with effect from 14 December 2015 (ie before the definition had come into effect). That definition would have read: " "Scottish rate" means the rate set by the Scottish Parliament for the tax year under Chapter 2 of Part 4A of the Scotland Act 1998 (taxation);".

Modifications—See the Income Tax (PAYE) Regulations, SI 2003/2682 reg 150 (modification of this regulation in its application to payments of taxable jobseeker's allowance made to a claimant).

SI 2003/2682 reg 174 (modification of this regulation in its application to payments of taxable incapacity benefit).

Press releases etc—See HMRC TIIN "Legislative changes resulting from the introduction of the Scottish rate of income tax", published at Budget 2014 (19 March 2014), see *SWTI 2014, Budget Issue* (27 March 2014).

Amendments—[1] Definitions of "closed tax year", "HMRC", "qualifying payment", "the relevant time", retrospective contributions regulations", "retrospective employment income", "retrospective tax provision" and "SSC Regulations" inserted, by the Income Tax (Pay as You Earn) (Amendment) Regulations, SI 2007/1077 regs 2, 3 with effect from 6 April 2007.

[2] Definitions of "combined amount", "ITA" and former definition of "Student Loan Regulations" inserted, and definition of "starting rate" revoked, by the Income Tax (Pay As You Earn) (Amendment) Regulations, SI 2008/782 regs 2, 3 with effect from 6 April 2008.

3 Definition of "tribunal" inserted by the Transfer of Tribunal Functions and Revenue and Customs Appeals Order, SI 2009/56 art 3, Sch 2 paras 92, 93 with effect from 1 April 2009.

4 Definitions of "large employer" and "specified date" substituted by the Income Tax (Pay As You Earn) (Amendment) Regulations, SI 2010/668, regs 2, 15, with effect in relation to the tax year 2011–12 and subsequent tax years.

5 Definition of "additional rate" inserted and definition of "notice" substituted, by the Income Tax (Pay As You Earn) (Amendment) Regulations, SI 2011/729 regs 2, 3 with effect from 6 April 2011.

6 Definitions of "non-Real Time Information employer", "non-Real Time Information pension payer", "Real Time Information employer", and "Real Time Information pension payer" inserted, by the Income Tax (Pay As You Earn) (Amendment) Regulations, SI 2012/822 regs 2, 3 with effect from 6 April 2012.

7 Definitions of "lower earnings limit" and "seconded expatriate" inserted and definition of "Student Loan Regulations" substituted by the Income Tax (Pay As You Earn) (Amendment) Regulations, SI 2012/822 regs 2, 60 with effect from 6 April 2012.

8 In definition of "tax period", in para (a), words revoked by the Income Tax (Pay As You Earn) (Amendment) Regulations, SI 2013/521 regs 2, 6 with effect from 6 April 2014.

9 In definition of "deductions working sheet", para (b) revoked by the Income Tax (Pay As You Earn) and the Income Tax (Construction Industry Scheme) (Amendment) Regulations, SI 2014/472 regs 2, 3 with effect from 6 April 2014.

10 Definition of "reckonable date" revoked by the Finance Act 2009, Sections 101 and 102 (Interest on Late Payments and Repayments), Appointed Days and Consequential Provisions Order, SI 2014/992 art 9(1), (2) with effect in relation to payments due and payable in respect of the tax year 2014–15 and subsequent tax years.

11 In definition of "notice", para (*b*) substituted by the Income Tax (Pay As You Earn) (Amendment) Regulations, SI 2015/2 reg 2(1), (2) with effect from 29 January 2015.

12 Definition of "overriding limit" substituted by the Income Tax (Pay As You Earn) (Amendment No 4) Regulations, SI 2014/2689 regs 2, 3 with effect from 6 April 2015.

13 Definition of "agency worker" substituted, and definitions of "the client", "employment intermediary" and "United Kingdom continental shelf" inserted by the Income Tax (Pay As You Earn) (Amendment No 2) Regulations, SI 2015/170 reg 2(1), (2) with effect in relation to tax quarters beginning on or after 6 April 2015.

14 In definition of "additional rate", words inserted, definition of "Scottish taxpayer" inserted, and in definitions of "basic rate" and "higher rate", words substituted by the Income Tax (Pay As You Earn) (Amendment No 3) Regulations, SI 2015/1667 regs 2, 3 with effect in relation to the 2016–17 tax year (as appointed under the Scotland Act 2012 s 25(5) by SI 2015/2000 art 3) and subsequent tax years.

15 In definitions of "additional rate", "basic rate" and "higher rate", words substituted, and in definition of "combined amount", words inserted, by the Income Tax (Pay As You Earn) (Amendment) Regulations, SI 2017/414 reg 2(1), (2) with effect from 6 April 2017.

2A [Real Time Information employers

(1) The following are Real Time Information employers—

(*a*) an employer who has entered into an agreement with HMRC to comply with the provisions of these Regulations which are expressed as relating to Real Time Information employers,

(*b*) an employer within paragraph (2),

(*c*) . . . [2] and

(*d*) on and after 6th October 2013, all employers[, except employers within paragraph (3)][2].

(2) An employer is within this paragraph if the employer has been given a general or specific direction by the Commissioners for Her Majesty's Revenue and Customs before 6th October 2013 to deliver to HMRC returns under regulation 67B (real time returns of information about relevant payments).

[(3) An employer is within this paragraph if the employer—

(*a*) has an existing special arrangement under regulation 141 (direct collection and special arrangements), and

(*b*) has not been given a direction under paragraph (2) by the Commissioners for Her Majesty's Revenue and Customs.][2]][1]

Amendments—[1] Regs 2A, 2B inserted by the Income Tax (Pay As You Earn) (Amendment) Regulations, SI 2012/822 regs 2, 4 with effect from 6 April 2012.

2 In para (1), sub-para (*c*) revoked and words in sub-para (*d*) inserted, and para (3) inserted, by the Income Tax (Pay As You Earn) (Amendment) Regulations, SI 2013/521 regs 2, 14 with effect from 6 April 2013 in relation to the tax year 2013–14 and subsequent tax years.

2B [Real Time Information pension payers

(1) The following are Real Time Information pension payers—

(*a*) a pension payer who has entered into an agreement with HMRC to comply with the provisions of these Regulations which are expressed as relating to Real Time Information pension payers or Real Time Information employers,

(*b*) a pension payer within paragraph (2),

(*c*) on and after 6th April 2013, pension payers to whom regulation 67D (exceptions to regulation 67B) applies, and

(*d*) on and after 6th October 2013, all pension payers.[2]

(2) A pension payer is within this paragraph if the pension payer has been given a general or specific direction by the Commissioners for Her Majesty's Revenue and Customs before 6th October 2013 to deliver to HMRC returns under regulation 67B (real time returns of information about relevant payments).][1]

Amendments—[1] Regs 2A, 2B inserted by the Income Tax (Pay As You Earn) (Amendment) Regulations, SI 2012/822 regs 2, 4 with effect from 6 April 2012.

[2] Para (1)(*c*) revoked by the Income Tax (Pay As You Earn) (Amendment) Regulations, SI 2013/521 regs 2, 15 with effect from 6 April 2013 in relation to the tax year 2013–14 and subsequent tax years.

3 Net PAYE income

(1) "Net PAYE income" means PAYE income less any—

(*a*) allowable pension contributions, and

(*b*) allowable donations to charity.

(2) In paragraph (1)—

["allowable pension contributions" means any contribution under a registered pension scheme which is withheld from the payment of PAYE income which is allowed to be deducted from employment income by the sponsoring employer under section 193(2) of the Finance Act 2004 (relief under net pay arrangements);][1]

["registered pension scheme" and "sponsoring employer" have the meanings given by section 150(2) and (6) respectively, of the Finance Act 2004.][1]

"allowable donations to charity" means any donation which is withheld from the payment of PAYE income and for which a deduction must be allowed under section 713 of ITEPA (donations to charity: payroll deduction scheme).

Commentary—*Simon's Taxes* **E4.1110**.

Derivation—The Income Tax (Employments) Regulations, SI 1993/744 reg 2(1).

Amendments—[1] Definitions substituted for the definition of "allowable pension contributions" by the Taxation of Pension Schemes (Consequential Amendments) Order, SI 2006/745 art 27(1), (2) with effect from 6 April 2006.

4 Relevant payments

(1) In these Regulations, any reference (however expressed) to relevant payments means payments of, or on account of, net PAYE income, except payments of, or on account of,—

(*a*) PAYE social security income, except in so far as it is provided for in Part 8,

(*b*) United Kingdom social security pensions,

(*c*) excluded relocation expenses,

(*d*) . . . [1]

(*e*) excluded pecuniary liabilities, and

(*f*) excluded notional payments.

(2) In paragraph (1)—

. . . [1]

"excluded notional payments" means notional payments which an employer is treated as making by section 694 or 695 of ITEPA (non-cash vouchers and credit tokens) as a result of an employee using a non-cash voucher or credit token on behalf of the employer, except where the voucher or token is used as, or as part of, any scheme or arrangement the purpose, or one of the main purposes, of which is—

(*a*) to provide the employee with money or an asset, or

(*b*) to avoid the making of a relevant payment;

"excluded pecuniary liabilities" means payments made to a person other than an employee to meet the employee's liability to that other person, but which are not made—

(*a*) in fulfilment (in whole or in part) of the employee's right to a sum of money, nor

(*b*) as, or as part of, any scheme or arrangement the purpose, or one of the main purposes, of which is to avoid the making of a relevant payment;

"excluded relocation expenses" means payments in respect of removal expenses, as defined by section 272 of ITEPA (removal benefits and expenses to which section 271 applies), if, and to the extent that, they are payments of net PAYE income;

"PAYE social security income" has the meaning given in section 683(5) of ITEPA;

"United Kingdom social security pensions" means income which is taxable income in accordance with section 578 of ITEPA (UK social security pensions).

Commentary—*Simon's Taxes* **E4.1110.**

Derivation—The Income Tax (Employments) Regulations, SI 1993/744 reg 2(3).

Amendments—[1] Para (1)(*d*) revoked, and in para (2), definition of "excluded business expenses" revoked, by the Income Tax (Pay As You Earn) (Amendment No 4) Regulations, SI 2015/1927 regs 2, 4 with effect in relation to relevant payments made in the tax year 2016–17.

5 *Excluded business expenses*

Amendments—Reg 5 revoked by the Income Tax (Pay As You Earn) (Amendment No 4) Regulations, SI 2015/1927 regs 2, 5 with effect in relation to relevant payments made in the tax year 2016–17.

6 Relevant pension payments

In these Regulations, any reference (however expressed) to relevant pension payments means relevant payments in respect of PAYE pension income.

Derivation—The Income Tax (Employments) Regulations, SI 1993/744 reg 2(1).

7 Meaning of "code" etc

(1) In these Regulations, "code" means—

(*a*) a combination of letters, numbers or both for use in accordance with the tax tables to establish free pay, additional pay, total free pay to date or total additional pay to date;

(*b*) any of the special codes (whether expressed in words or represented by a combination of letters, numbers or both) for use in accordance with the tax tables or otherwise.

(2) "K code" means a code which gives rise to additional pay or total additional pay to date.

[(2A) "S code" means a code which effects deductions of tax at the rates [set by a Scottish rate resolution of the Scottish Parliament under section 80C of the Scotland Act 1998][4].][3]

(3) The special codes are—

(*a*) the basic rate code, which effects deductions of tax wholly at the basic rate;

(*b*) the higher rate code, which effects deductions of tax wholly at the higher rate;

[(*ba*) the additional rate code, which effects deductions of tax wholly at the additional rate;][2]

(*c*) the nil tax code, which requires no deductions of tax;

[(*ca*) the 0T code, which without allowing for personal allowances, effects deductions of tax at the basic rate, higher rate and additional rate so that during the tax year the amounts subject to deductions at the rate or rates concerned are in accordance with section 10 of ITA (income charged at the basic, higher and additional rates: individuals);][2]

[(*d*) the emergency code, which, after allowing for the personal allowance, effects deductions of tax at—

[(i) the basic rate, or

(ii) the basic and higher rates, or

(iii) the basic, higher and additional rates

so that during the tax year the amounts subject to deductions at the rate or rates concerned are in accordance with section 10 of ITA (income charged at the basic, higher and additional rates: individuals);][2]

(*e*) the emergency IB codes which, after allowing for the personal allowance and the blind person's allowance, effect deductions at the basic rate, so that during the tax year the amounts subject to deductions at that rate are in accordance with section 10 of ITA.][1]

[(4) In paragraph (3)—

"blind person's allowance" means an allowance claimed under either section 265 of ICTA (blind person's allowance) or section 38 of ITA (blind person's allowance);

"personal allowance" means an allowance claimed under either section 257(1) of ICTA (personal allowance) or section 35 of ITA (personal allowances for those aged under 65).][1]

Commentary—*Simon's Taxes* **E4.1131, E4.1133.**

Derivation—The Income Tax (Employments) Regulations, SI 1993/744 regs 2(1), 9, 29(2), (3), 30(2), (3), 32, 84(7), 98C(1), (3), (4).

Press releases etc—See HMRC TIIN "Legislative changes resulting from the introduction of the Scottish rate of income tax", published at Budget 2014 (19 March 2014), see *SWTI 2014, Budget Issue* (27 March 2014).

Amendments—[1] Para (3)(*d*), (*e*) substituted, and para (4) inserted, by the Income Tax (Pay As You Earn) (Amendment) Regulations, SI 2008/782 regs 2, 4 with effect from 6 April 2008.

[2] In para (3), sub-paras (*ba*), (*ca*) inserted, and in sub-para (*d*) words substituted, by the Income Tax (Pay As You Earn) (Amendment) Regulations, SI 2011/729 regs 2, 4 with effect from 6 April 2011.

[3] Para (2A) inserted by the Income Tax (Pay As You Earn) (Amendment No 3) Regulations, SI 2015/1667 regs 2, 4 with effect in relation to the 2016–17 tax year (appointed by the Treasury under the Scotland Act 2012 s 25(5) by virtue of SI 2015/2000) and subsequent tax years.

[4] In para (2A), words substituted by the Income Tax (Pay As You Earn) (Amendment) Regulations, SI 2017/414 reg 2(1), (3) with effect from 6 April 2017.

8 Employee's code

(1) An employee's code is the code—

(*a*) issued to an employer for use in respect of the employee for a tax year,

(*b*) applied by these Regulations for use by an employer in respect of the employee, or

(*c*) issued to an employee in accordance with regulation 142 (direct collection).

(2) A code is issued to an employer if it is contained in a document that is sent—

(*a*) to the employer, or

(*b*) to a person acting on behalf of the employer,

by the Inland Revenue, and any code so issued is received by the employer for the purposes of these Regulations.

Commentary—*Simon's Taxes* **E4.1131.**

Derivation—The Income Tax (Employments) Regulations, SI 1993/744 regs 2(1), 6(4), 13(6), 104(1).

9 PAYE threshold

(1) The rules set out in Table 1 apply in order to determine whether a relevant payment made by an employer to an employee is a relevant payment which exceeds the PAYE threshold.

(2) Rules 1 to 5 apply if the employer normally pays the employee at regular intervals.

(3) If the employer does not normally pay the employee at regular intervals—

(*a*) rule 6 applies to determine whether a relevant payment made less than a week since the previous relevant payment exceeds the PAYE threshold, and (*b*) rule 7 applies to determine whether any other relevant payment exceeds the PAYE threshold.

TABLE 1
DETERMINATION OF PAYE THRESHOLD

Employee's payment interval	*Rule to determine whether relevant payment exceeds PAYE threshold*
1 Weekly	1 If the sum of the relevant payment and any other relevant payments made earlier in the same tax week is more than the weekly PAYE threshold.
2 Monthly	2 If the sum of the relevant payment and any other relevant payments made earlier in the same tax month is more than the monthly PAYE threshold.
3 Regular intervals which are multiples of a week	3 If the sum of the relevant payment and any other relevant payments made earlier in the same interval is more than the corresponding multiple of the weekly PAYE threshold.
4 Regular intervals, longer than a week, which are fractions or multiples of a month	4 If the sum of the relevant payment and any other relevant payments made earlier in the same interval is more than the corresponding fraction or multiple of the monthly PAYE threshold.
5 Regular intervals, longer than a week, which are not within rules 1 to 4	5 If the sum of the relevant payment and any other relevant payments made earlier in the same interval is more than the corresponding proportion of the weekly PAYE threshold.
6 Intervals shorter than a week, whether regular or irregular	6 If the sum of the relevant payment and any other relevant payments made earlier in the same tax week is more than the weekly PAYE threshold.
7 Irregular intervals longer than a week	7 If the relevant payment is more than the corresponding proportion of the weekly PAYE threshold since—
	(*a*) any previous relevant payment in the tax year, or
	(*b*) if none, the start of the employment or the start of the tax year (whichever is later).

(4) Regulations 24 and 30 (employee not paid weekly or monthly)—
- (*a*) apply for the purpose of establishing an employee's normal payment interval, but
- (*b*) must otherwise be ignored for the purpose of determining whether a relevant payment exceeds the PAYE threshold.

(5) If an employee has more than one normal payment interval in respect of payments made by the same employer, the rules must be applied on the basis of the shorter or shortest of those intervals.
(6) If an employee's normal payment interval is longer than a year, the rules must be applied as if the normal payment interval were a year.
(7) "Weekly PAYE threshold" means 1/52 of the personal allowance specified in section 257(1) of ICTA, rounded to the nearest pound.
(8) "Monthly PAYE threshold" means 1/12 of the personal allowance specified in section 257(1) of ICTA, rounded to the nearest pound.
(9) The "corresponding proportion of the weekly PAYE threshold" is established by dividing the number of days in the payment interval by 7, and multiplying the result by the weekly PAYE threshold.

Commentary—*Simon's Taxes* **E4.1106.**
Derivation—The Income Tax (Employments) Regulations, SI 1993/744 regs 18, 28(1), (2).

APPLICATION TO PAYERS AND PAYEES

10 Application to agencies and agency workers
(1) For the purposes of these Regulations—
- (*a*) agencies are treated as employers; and
- (*b*) agency workers are treated as employees.

(2) For the purposes of the regulations listed in paragraph (3), an agency ceases to employ an agency worker at the earlier of—
- (*a*) the end of the relationship between the agency and agency worker, or
- (*b*) the end of a period of 3 months during which the agency makes no relevant payments to the agency worker,

and not each time the agency worker stops providing services to a client of the agency.
(3) The regulations are—

regulation 36	Cessation of employment: Form P45
regulation 37	PAYE income paid after employment ceased
regulation 46(6)	Employer to ignore code relating to employment which has ceased
regulation 51(5) to (7)	effects of employment ceasing on Form P45 procedure
regulation 94(3) to (7)	Information to former employees of other earnings.

(4) The following regulations do not apply to agencies or agency workers in their capacity as such—

. . .[1]	. . .[1]
. . .[1]	. . .[1]
regulation 91	termination awards: information to be provided
regulation 92	termination awards: return if award changes
regulation 93	termination awards: return if more than one employer
regulation 96	termination awards: information to employees
Part 6	PAYE settlement agreements
regulation 167	jobseeker's allowance paid by employer
regulation 168	regulation 167 cases: application of other regulations.

Commentary—*Simon's Taxes* **E4.1188.**

Derivation—The Income Tax (Employments) Regulations, SI 1993/744 reg 2(1).

Amendments—[1] In para (4), references to regulations 34 and 35 revoked by the Income Tax (Pay As You Earn) (Amendment) Regulations, SI 2013/521 regs 2, 7 with effect from 6 April 2014.

11 Application to pension payers and pensioners

(1) For the purposes of these Regulations—

(*a*) pension payers are treated as employers;

(*b*) pensioners are treated as employees; and

(*c*) a pensioner's "employment" with a pension payer starts when the pension starts and ends when the pension ends.

(2) The following regulations do not apply to pension payers or pensioners in their capacity as such—

regulation 25	cumulative basis: subsidiary PAYE income of employee paid weekly or at greater intervals
. . .[1]	. . .[1]
. . .[1]	. . .[1]
regulation 38	death of employee (other than pensioner)
Chapter 2 of Part 3	new employees (other than pensioners): Forms P45 and P46
regulation 63	repayment during unpaid leave
regulation 64	trade disputes
regulation 65	repayment if no longer employed
regulation 71	modification of [regulations 67G and 68][1] in case of trade dispute
regulation 75	additional return in case of trade dispute
regulations 85 to 89	employers: annual return of other earnings
regulation 90	quarterly return if car becomes available or unavailable
regulation 91	termination awards: information to be provided
regulation 92	termination awards: return if award changes
regulation 93	termination awards: return if more than one employer
regulation 94	employers: information to employees of other earnings
regulation 95	third parties: information to employees of other earnings
regulation 96	termination awards: information to employees
regulation 100	tips: special arrangements
regulation 102(1)	succession to a business etc: employees (other than pensioners)

regulation 104	succession to a business: trade disputes
Part 6	PAYE settlement agreements
Chapter 3 of Part 7	holiday pay funds
regulation 151	obtaining the claimant's Form P45
regulation 167	jobseeker's allowance paid by employer
regulation 168	regulation 167 cases: application of other regulations.

Commentary—*Simon's Taxes* **E4.1103.**

Derivation—The Income Tax (Employments) Regulations, SI 1993/744 reg 2(1).

Amendments—[1] In para (2), in entry relating to reg 71, words substituted by the Income Tax (Pay As You Earn) (Amendment) Regulations, SI 2012/822 regs 2, 5 with effect from 6 April 2012.

[2] In para (2), references to regulations 34 and 35 revoked by the Income Tax (Pay As You Earn) (Amendment) Regulations, SI 2013/521 regs 2, 7 with effect from 6 April 2014.

12 Application to other payers and payees

(1) For the purposes of these Regulations—

(*a*) other payers are treated as employers;

(*b*) other payees are treated as employees; and

(*c*) an other payee's "employment" with an other payer starts when relevant payments start and ends when relevant payments end.

(2) The following regulations do not apply to other payers or other payees in their capacity as such—

. . . [1]	. . . [1]
[1]	[1]
regulation 85 to 88	Employers: annual return of other earnings
regulation 90	Quarterly return if car becomes available or unavailable
regulation 91	Termination awards: information to be provided
regulation 92	Termination awards: return if award changes
regulation 93	Termination awards: return if more than one employer
regulation 94	Employers: information to employees of other earnings
regulation 95	third parties: information to employees of other earnings
regulation 96	Termination awards: information to employees
Part 6	PAYE settlement agreements
regulation 134	Interpretation of Chapter 3 (holiday pay funds)
regulation 167	Jobseeker's allowance paid by employer
regulation 168	Regulation 167 cases: application of other regulations.

(3) Paragraph (2) is subject to regulation 91(9) (termination awards: former employers and employees).

(4) The following regulation does not apply to other payees in their capacity as such—

regulation 64	trade disputes.

Amendments—[1] In para (2), references to regulations 34 and 35 revoked by the Income Tax (Pay As You Earn) (Amendment) Regulations, SI 2013/521 regs 2, 7 with effect from 6 April 2014.

PART 2
CODES

Commentary—*Simon's Taxes* **E4.1103.**

Derivation—The Income Tax (Employments) Regulations, SI 1993/744 reg 2(1).

Cross references—See the Income Tax (PAYE) Regulations, SI 2003/2682 reg 123 (this Part does not apply to relevant payments made by the Ministry of Defence to members of the reserve forces specified in SI 2003/2682 reg 122).

SI 2003/2682 reg 135 (this Part does not apply to holiday pay).

SI 2003/2682 reg 168 (subject to SI 2003/2682 reg 168(3), this Part applies to the taxable jobseeker's allowance paid to a Part 8 Chapter 2 (of SI 2003/2682) claimant by the employer on behalf of the Department under SI 2003/2682 reg 167, as if it were a relevant payment from the employment).

DETERMINATION OF CODE

13 Determination of code by Inland Revenue

The Inland Revenue must determine the code for use by an employer in respect of an employee for a tax year.

Commentary—*Simon's Taxes* **E4.1132.**
Derivation—The Income Tax (Employments) Regulations, SI 1993/744 reg 7(1).

14 Matters relevant to determination of code

(1) If the Inland Revenue determine a code under this regulation, they must have regard to the following matters so far as known to them—

(*a*) the reliefs from income tax to which the employee is entitled for the tax year in which the code is determined, so far as the employee's title to those reliefs has been established at the time of the determination;

(*b*) any PAYE income of the employee (other than the relevant payments in relation to which the code is being determined);

(*c*) any tax overpaid for any previous tax year which has not been repaid;

(*d*) any tax remaining unpaid for any previous tax year which is not otherwise recovered;

(*e*) any tax repaid to the employee in excess of the amount properly due to the employee which may be recovered as if it were unpaid tax under section 30(1) of TMA (recovery of overpayment of tax etc) and which is not otherwise recovered;

(*f*) unless the employee objects, any other income of the employee which is not PAYE income; and

(*g*) such other adjustments as may be necessary to secure that, so far as possible, the tax in respect of the employee's income in relation to which the code is determined will be deducted from the relevant payments made during that tax year.

(2) If the Inland Revenue determine the code before the beginning of the tax year for which it is determined, the Inland Revenue—

(*a*) must have regard to any expected change in the amount of any relief referred to in paragraph (1)(*a*), but

(*b*) may disregard any such relief if they are not satisfied that the employee will be entitled to it for the tax year for which the code is determined.

(3) Paragraphs (1)(*c*) and (*d*) are subject to regulations 186 and 187 (recovery and repayment: adjustment of employee's code).

Commentary—*Simon's Taxes* **E4.1132.**
Derivation—The Income Tax (Employments) Regulations, SI 1993/744 reg 7(1), (2).
Modifications—See the Income Tax (PAYE) Regulations, SI 2003/2682 reg 150 (modification of this regulation in its application to payments of taxable jobseeker's allowance made to a claimant).

[14A Determination of code in respect of recovery of relevant debts

(1) HMRC may determine a code so as to effect recovery of all or part of a relevant debt within the meaning of section 684 of ITEPA (sums owed to HMRC).

(2) A determination in reliance on paragraph (1) does not prevent recovery by other means (whether or not under a provision of TMA) of all or any part of a relevant debt that is not recovered by deduction in accordance with the code (whether or not it was at any stage expected to be recovered by deduction).

(3) Sums deducted or to be deducted as a result of a determination made in reliance on paragraph (1) are to be treated, for the purposes of employers' obligations and enforcement, in the same way as amounts of tax which the employer is liable to pay under provisions of these Regulations (so, for example, regulation 84 applies for the purposes of recovery).

(4) Sums deducted as a result of a determination made in reliance on paragraph (1) are to be treated for the purposes of interest on the relevant debt as having been paid on the first day of the tax year in respect of which the determination is made.][1]

Amendments—[1] Reg 14A inserted by the Income Tax (Pay As You Earn) (Amendment) (No. 3) Regulations, SI 2011/1584 reg 2(2) with effect from 6 April 2012.

[14B Determination of code in respect of high income child benefit charge

HMRC may determine a code, if and to the extent that the payee does not object, to secure that—

(*a*) income tax payable for a tax year by the payee by virtue of section 681B of ITEPA (high income child benefit charge) is deducted from PAYE income of the payee paid during that year, and

(*b*) repayments are made in a tax year in respect of any amounts overpaid on account of income tax under that section for that tax year.][1]

Amendments—[1] Reg 14B inserted by the Income Tax (Pay As You Earn) (Amendment) Regulations, SI 2013/521 regs 2, 3 with effect from 6 April 2013 in relation to the tax year 2013–14 and subsequent tax years.

[14C Determination of code in respect of recovery of tax credit debts

(1) HMRC may determine a code, if and to the extent that the payee does not object, to effect the recovery of all or part of a tax credit debt.

(2) Sums deducted or to be deducted as a result of a determination made in reliance on paragraph (1) are to be treated, for the purposes of employers' obligations and enforcement, in the same way as amounts of tax which the employer is liable to pay under provisions of these Regulations (so, for example, regulation 84 applies for the purposes of recovery).

(3) Sums deducted as a result of a determination made in reliance on paragraph (1) are to be treated for the purposes of interest on the tax credit debt as having been paid on the first day of the tax year in respect of which the determination is made.

(4) In this regulation "tax credit debt" means child tax credit or working tax credit that the payee is liable to repay to the Commissioners under or by virtue of an enactment.][1]

Amendments—[1] Regulations 14C, 14D inserted by the Income Tax (Pay As You Earn) (Amendment No 4) Regulations, SI 2014/2689 regs 2, 4 with effect in relation to codes determined for use by an employer in respect of an employee for the tax year 2015–16 and subsequent tax years.

[14D Recovery of debts: overall limit

(1) This regulation applies where HMRC determines a code under, or by reference to, one or both of the following provisions—

(*a*) regulation 14A(1) (determination of code in respect of recovery of relevant debts); or

(*b*) regulation 14C(1) (determination of code in respect of recovery of tax credit debts).

(2) Column 2 of Table 1A sets out the total amount of debt that may be recovered from an employee ("E") under a code to which this regulation applies, by reference to the expected amount of PAYE income of E in the tax year for which that code is determined.

TABLE 1A
TOTAL AMOUNT OF DEBT THAT MAY BE RECOVERED

1 The expected amount of PAYE income of E in the tax year for which the code is determined	*2 The total amount of debt that may be recovered from E in that tax year*
Less than £30,000	No more than £3,000
£30,000 or more but less than £40,000	No more than £5,000
£40,000 or more but less than £50,000	No more than £7,000
£50,000 or more but less than £60,000	No more than £9,000
£60,000 or more but less than £70,000	No more than £11,000
£70,000 or more but less than £80,000	No more than £13,000
£80,000 or more but less than £90,000	No more than £15,000
£90,000 or more	No more than £17,000.

(3) In this regulation the "total amount of debt" means the sum recovered or to be recovered by virtue of a code determined under, or by reference to, one or both of regulations 14A(1) or 14C(1).][1]

Amendments—[1] Regulations 14C, 14D inserted by the Income Tax (Pay As You Earn) (Amendment No 4) Regulations, SI 2014/2689 regs 2, 4 with effect in relation to codes determined for use by an employer in respect of an employee for the tax year 2015–16 and subsequent tax years.

15 Flat rate codes

[(A1) HMRC may determine that the code for use by an employer in respect of an employee for a tax year is the additional rate code, if they have reason to believe that the employee will be chargeable at the additional rate on all or a substantial part of the employee's relevant payments.][2]

(1) The Inland Revenue may determine that the code for use by an employer in respect of an employee for a tax year is the higher rate code, if they have reason to believe that the employee will be chargeable at the higher rate on all or a substantial part of the employee's relevant payments.

(2) The Inland Revenue may determine that the code for use by an employer in respect of an employee for a tax year is the basic rate code, if they have reason to believe that the employee will be chargeable at the basic rate on all or a substantial part of the employee's relevant payments.

(3) The Inland Revenue may determine that the code for use by an employer in respect of an employee for a tax year is the nil tax code, if—

(*a*) the employee's PAYE income will be taken into account as taxable income other than PAYE income in any assessment,

(*b*) the Inland Revenue are not satisfied that the employee's income will be chargeable, or

(*c*) the Inland Revenue have reason to believe that the employee will be entitled to a deduction under Chapter 6 of Part 5 of ITEPA (deductions from seafarers' earnings) in respect of the employee's PAYE income or so much of it as remains after any deductions under [sections 188 to 195 of the Finance Act 2004 (members' contributions).][1]

(4) References in this regulation to an employee's relevant payments, PAYE income and income are references to the payments or income in respect of which the employee's code is being determined for the purposes of the employment in question.

Commentary—*Simon's Taxes* **E4.1131.**

Derivation—The Income Tax (Employments) Regulations, SI 1993/744 reg 9(1), (2).

Modifications—See the Income Tax (PAYE) Regulations, SI 2003/2682 reg 150 (modification of this regulation in its application to payments of taxable jobseeker's allowance made to a claimant).

SI 2003/2682 reg 174 (modification of this regulation in its application to payments of taxable incapacity benefit).

Cross references—See the Income Tax (PAYE) Regulations, SI 2003/2682 reg 34 (this regulation does not apply to cases where SI 2003/2682 regs 34, 35 apply).

Amendments—[1] Words in para (3)(*c*) substituted by the Taxation of Pension Schemes (Consequential Amendments) Order, SI 2006/745 art 27(1), (3) with effect from 6 April 2006.

[2] Para (A1) inserted by the Income Tax (Pay As You Earn) (Amendment) Regulations, SI 2011/729 regs 2, 5 with effect from 6 April 2011.

16 Continued application of employee's code

(1) If the Inland Revenue determine that the code for use by an employer in respect of an employee for a tax year remains the same as at the previous 5th April, the Inland Revenue need not issue a code to the employer.

(2) If for any tax year the employer does not receive a code for an employee who was in that employer's employment on the previous 5th April, the code which applied on that date is treated as having been issued by the Inland Revenue for the tax year in question.

Commentary—*Simon's Taxes* **E4.1136.**

Derivation—The Income Tax (Employments) Regulations, SI 1993/744 reg 8(1), (2).

Modifications—See the Income Tax (PAYE) Regulations, SI 2003/2682 reg 150 (modification of this regulation in its application to payments of taxable jobseeker's allowance made to a claimant).

SI 2003/2682 reg 174 (modification of this regulation in its application to payments of taxable incapacity benefit).

Cross references—See the Income Tax (PAYE) Regulations, SI 2003/2682 reg 34 (this regulation does not apply to cases where SI 2003/2682 regs 34, 35 apply).

17 Notice to employee of code

(1) The Inland Revenue must give notice to an employee of the code which they have determined for use in respect of that employee for any tax year.

(2) But notice need not be given if—

(*a*) the code for use in respect of the employee remains the same as at the previous 5th April; . . .

[(*b*) the change in the code is solely because of an alteration or proposed alteration—

(i) in the rates of any of the personal reliefs allowable under Chapters 2 (personal allowance etc.) and 3 (tax reductions etc.) of Part 3 of the Income Tax Act 2007; or

(ii) in the tax tables;

(*c*) the employee's PAYE income is not chargeable to tax; or

(*d*) the employee does not have a liability to tax in respect of any PAYE income.][1]

Commentary—*Simon's Taxes* **E4.1136.**

Derivation—The Income Tax (Employments) Regulations, SI 1993/744 reg 10.

Modifications—See the Income Tax (PAYE) Regulations, SI 2003/2682 reg 150 (modification of this regulation in its application to payments of taxable jobseeker's allowance made to a claimant).

SI 2003/2682 reg 174 (modification of this regulation in its application to payments of taxable incapacity benefit).

Amendments—[1] In para (2) word "or" at end of sub-para (*a*) revoked, and sub-paras (*b*)–(*d*) substituted for previous sub-para (*b*), by the Income Tax (Pay As You Earn) (Amendment) Regulations, SI 2015/2 reg 2(1), (3) with effect from 29 January 2015.

APPEALS AND AMENDMENT

18 Objections and appeals against employee's code

(1) An employee who objects to the determination of a code must state the grounds of objection.

(2) On receiving the notice of objection the Inland Revenue may amend the determination of the code by agreement with the employee.

(3) If the Inland Revenue and employee do not reach agreement, the employee may appeal . . . [1] against the determination of the code by giving notice to the Inland Revenue.

(4) [On an appeal that is notified to the tribunal, the tribunal][1] must determine the code in accordance with these Regulations.

(5) For the purposes of paragraph 3(1)(a) of Schedule 3 to TMA (rules for assigning proceedings to General Commissioners), the relevant place for an appeal under this regulation is—

(a) the place where the employment is situated, or

(b) if there is no such place, the place where the employee lives.[1]

Commentary—*Simon's Taxes* **E4.1137.**

Derivation—The Income Tax (Employments) Regulations, SI 1993/744 reg 11(1), (2), (3), (5).

Modifications—SI 2003/2682 reg 150 (modification of this regulation in its application to payments of taxable jobseeker's allowance made to a claimant).

SI 2003/2682 reg 174 (modification of this regulation in its application to payments of taxable incapacity benefit).

Cross references—See the Income Tax (PAYE) Regulations, SI 2003/2682 reg 19(5) (this regulation applies in relation to an amended code as it does to the original code).

SI 2003/2682 reg 19(6) (this regulation also applies if the Revenue do not agree that circumstances have changed (as provided for in SI 2003/2682 reg 19), and so refuse to amend the code in accordance with SI 2003/2682 reg 19(2)).

SI 2003/2682 reg 50 (procedure in Form P46 cases where code treated as issued by the Revenue: this does not apply for the purposes of this regulation).

Amendments—[1] In para (3), words revoked, in para (4), words substituted, and para (5) revoked, by the Transfer of Tribunal Functions and Revenue and Customs Appeals Order, SI 2009/56 art 3, Sch 2 paras 92, 94 with effect from 1 April 2009.

19 Amendment of code

(1) Paragraph (2) applies if the code for use by an employer in respect of an employee is found to be inappropriate because the actual circumstances are different from the circumstances by reference to which it was determined, whether by the Inland Revenue or the [tribunal][1].

(2) The Inland Revenue may, and if required by the employee must, amend the code by reference to the actual circumstances.

(3) The Inland Revenue must give notice of the amended code to the employee by the date on which the notice under regulation 20(1) is issued to the employer.

[(4) But notice need not be given—

(*a*) if the change in the code is because of an alteration or a proposed alteration—

(i) in the rates of any of the personal reliefs allowable under Chapters 2 (personal allowance etc.) and 3 (tax reductions etc.) of Part 3 of the Income Tax Act 2007; or

(ii) in the tax tables; or

(*b*) if as a consequence of any change to the code—

(i) the employee's PAYE income is not chargeable to tax; or

(ii) the employee does not have a liability to tax in respect of any PAYE income.][2]

(5) Regulation 18 (objections and appeals) applies in relation to the amended code as it applies in relation to the original code.

(6) Regulation 18 also applies if the Inland Revenue do not agree that the circumstances have changed and so refuse to amend the code in accordance with paragraph (2).

Commentary—*Simon's Taxes* **E4.1136.**

Derivation—The Income Tax (Employments) Regulations, SI 1993/744 reg 12.

Modifications—See the Income Tax (PAYE) Regulations, SI 2003/2682 reg 150 (modification of this regulation in its application to payments of taxable jobseeker's allowance made to a claimant).

SI 2003/2682 reg 174 (modification of this regulation in its application to payments of taxable incapacity benefit).

Amendments—[1] In para (1), word substituted by the Transfer of Tribunal Functions and Revenue and Customs Appeals Order, SI 2009/56 art 3, Sch 2 paras 92, 95 with effect from 1 April 2009.

[2] Para (4) substituted by the Income Tax (Pay As You Earn) (Amendment) Regulations, SI 2015/2 reg 2(1), (4) with effect from 29 January 2015.

20 Notice to employer of amended code

(1) If the code for use by an employer in respect of an employee is amended after notice of it has been issued to the employer, the Inland Revenue must issue the amended code to the employer.

(2) An amended code is issued to an employer if it is contained in a document that is sent to the employer or a person acting on behalf of the employer by the Inland Revenue, and any code so issued is received by the employer for the purposes of these Regulations.

(3) On making any subsequent relevant payment to the employee, the employer must deduct or repay tax by reference to the amended code.

(4) Paragraphs (5) and (6) apply if there is a change or proposed change in the rates of any of the personal reliefs allowable under sections 257 and 257A of ICTA (personal allowance and married couple's allowance).

(5) If the change or proposed change relates to the current tax year, the Inland Revenue may give notice requiring the employer, with effect from the date specified in the notice, to amend specified codes as directed.

(6) If the change relates to the following tax year, the Inland Revenue may give notice requiring the employer to carry forward to the following tax year specified codes of the current tax year and adjust them as directed in the notice.

(7) A code which has—

(*a*) been amended by virtue of paragraph (5) in respect of the current tax year, or

(*b*) been carried forward to the following tax year and adjusted by virtue of paragraph (6),

is treated as having been determined and issued by the Inland Revenue as the employee's code for that tax year.

(8) A notice under paragraphs (5) and (6) may be issued to the employer or to a person acting on behalf of the employer.

Commentary—*Simon's Taxes* **E4.1136.**

Derivation—The Income Tax (Employments) Regulations, SI 1993/744 regs 8(5), 13(1), (2), (4), 6).

Modifications—See the Income Tax (PAYE) Regulations, SI 2003/2682 reg 150 (modification of this regulation in its application to payments of taxable jobseeker's allowance made to a claimant).

SI 2003/2682 reg 174 (modification of this regulation in its application to payments of taxable incapacity benefit).

PART 3
DEDUCTION AND REPAYMENT OF TAX

Cross references—See the Income Tax (PAYE) Regulations, SI 2003/2682 reg 123 (this Part does not apply to relevant payments made by the Ministry of Defence to members of the reserve forces specified in SI 2003/2682 reg 122).
SI 2003/2682 reg 135 (this Part does not apply to holiday pay).
SI 2003/2682 reg 168 (subject to SI 2003/2682 reg 168(3), this Part applies to the taxable jobseeker's allowance paid to a Part 8 Chapter 2 (of SI 2003/2682) claimant by the employer on behalf of the Department under SI 2003/2682 reg 167, as if it were a relevant payment from the employment).

CHAPTER 1
DEDUCTION AND REPAYMENT

DEDUCTION AND REPAYMENT BY REFERENCE TO EMPLOYEE'S CODE

21 Deduction and repayment of tax by reference to employee's code

(1) On making a relevant payment to an employee during a tax year, an employer must deduct or repay tax in accordance with these Regulations by reference to the employee's code, if the employer has one for the employee.
(2) The employer must deduct or repay tax by reference to the employee's code, even if the code is the subject of an objection or appeal.

Commentary—*Simon's Taxes* **E4.1102, E4.1140.**
Derivation—The Income Tax (Employments) Regulations, SI 1993/744 reg 6(1)–(3).
Modifications—See the Income Tax (PAYE) Regulations, SI 2003/2682 reg 150 (modification of this regulation in its application to payments of taxable jobseeker's allowance made to a claimant).
SI 2003/2682 reg 174 (modification of this regulation in its application to payments of taxable incapacity benefit).
Cross references—See the Income Tax (PAYE) Regulations, SI 2003/2682 reg 34 (this regulation does not apply to cases where SI 2003/2682 regs 34, 35 apply).
SI 2003/2682 reg 37 (PAYE income paid after employment ceased: this regulation not to apply)

THE CUMULATIVE BASIS

22 The cumulative basis

An employer must deduct or repay tax on the cumulative basis, unless these Regulations provide otherwise.

Commentary—*Simon's Taxes* **E4.1146.**
Derivation—The Income Tax (Employments) Regulations, SI 1993/744 reg 14(1).
Modifications—See the Income Tax (PAYE) Regulations, SI 2003/2682 reg 174 (modification of this regulation in its application to payments of taxable incapacity benefit).
Cross references—See the Income Tax (PAYE) Regulations, SI 2003/2682 reg 26(2) (if SI 2003/2682 reg 26 applies, then this regulation does not apply).
SI 2003/2682 reg 32 (if an employee's code is the higher rate code, the employer must deduct tax at the higher rate, and this regulation and SI 2003/2682 reg 26 do not apply).
SI 2003/2682 reg 33 (application of this regulation in the case of a nil tax code).
SI 2003/2682 reg 34 (this regulation does not apply to cases where SI 2003/2682 regs 34, 35 apply).
SI 2003/2682 reg 37 (PAYE income paid after employment ceased: this regulation not to apply)

23 Cumulative basis: deduction and repayment

(1) This regulation provides for deductions and repayments on the basis of total payments to date (the cumulative basis).
(2) In this regulation—
(*a*) TT is the total tax to date relating to an employee;
(*b*) UT is any tax not deducted because of the overriding limit when the last relevant payment was made to the employee, and is nil if the payment in question is the first relevant payment to the employee in any tax year;
(*c*) PT is the previous total tax to date relating to the employee, and is nil if the payment in question is the first relevant payment to the employee in any tax year.
(3) The employer must, before making any relevant payment to the employee, calculate TT.
(4) If TT + UT exceeds PT, the employer must deduct the excess from the relevant payment on making the payment.
(5) But . . . [1] the deduction is not to exceed the overriding limit, subject to 62(6) (notional payments).
(6) If TT + UT is less than PT, the employer must repay the difference to the employee on making the payment, subject to regulations 25(4) (extra payment made before main payment) and 64 (trade disputes).
(7) If TT + UT equals PT, the employer must neither deduct nor repay tax when making the payment.
(8) "Previous total tax to date" means the total tax to date corresponding to the employee's total payments to date and the employee's code—
(*a*) at the date of the last preceding relevant payment, or

(*b*) if later, at the date on which the employer complied with this regulation as if a relevant payment had been made.

(9) But—

(*a*) if the employee's code is an amended code, and

(*b*) the employee's previous code was not used on the cumulative basis,

"previous total tax to date" means the total net tax deducted by the employer.

(10) Paragraphs (2)(*c*), (8) and (9) are subject to regulations 43(9) and (10), 52(11) and (12), 53(4) and 61(4) (which modify the meaning of previous total tax to date in certain circumstances).

Commentary—*Simon's Taxes* **E4.1146.**

Derivation—The Income Tax (Employments) Regulations, SI 1993/744 regs 2(1), 14, 15.

Modifications—See the Income Tax (PAYE) Regulations, SI 2003/2682 reg 174 (modification of this regulation in its application to payments of taxable incapacity benefit).

Cross references—See the Income Tax (PAYE) Regulations, SI 2003/2682 reg 34 (this regulation does not apply to cases where SI 2003/2682 regs 34, 35 apply).

SI 2003/2682 reg 37 (PAYE income paid after employment ceased: this regulation not to apply)

Amendments—[1] In para (5), words "if the employee's code is a K code," revoked by the Income Tax (Pay As You Earn) (Amendment No 4) Regulations, SI 2014/2689 regs 2, 5 with effect from 6 April 2015.

24 Cumulative basis: employee not paid weekly or monthly

(1) This regulation applies if—

(*a*) an employer normally makes main relevant payments to an employee at regular intervals which are longer than a week, other than monthly, and

(*b*) the employee's code is used on the cumulative basis.

(2) The first main relevant payment in a tax year is treated for the purposes of calculating the deduction or repayment of tax as having been made at the end the period which—

(*a*) starts on the first day of the tax year, and

(*b*) finishes at the end of the employee's normal regular payment interval.

(3) Subsequent main relevant payments in the tax year are treated for the purposes of calculating the deduction or repayment of tax as having been made at the end of the period which—

(*a*) starts the day after the date on which the previous main relevant payment is treated as having been made (by paragraph (2) or this paragraph), and

(*b*) finishes at the end of the employee's normal regular payment interval or the last day of the tax year (if earlier).

(4) If the employee's main relevant payments are normally made at regular intervals which are longer than a year, any such payment in a tax year is treated, for the purposes of calculating the deduction or repayment of tax, as made on the last day of that tax year.

(5) But, in every case, the employer must record the actual date of every payment in the deductions working sheet.

(6) This regulation does not apply if the payment falls within regulation 31(1) (payments in short payment periods).

Commentary—*Simon's Taxes* **E4.1142.**

Derivation—The Income Tax (Employments) Regulations, SI 1993/744 reg 18.

Modifications—See the Income Tax (PAYE) Regulations, SI 2003/2682 reg 174 (modification of this regulation in its application to payments of taxable incapacity benefit).

Cross references—See the Income Tax (PAYE) Regulations, SI 2003/2682 reg 34 (this regulation does not apply to cases where SI 2003/2682 regs 34, 35 apply).

25 Cumulative basis: subsidiary PAYE income of employee paid weekly or at greater intervals

(1) This regulation applies if—

(*a*) an employee's main relevant payments are normally made at regular intervals of a week or more,

(*b*) the employee's code is used on the cumulative basis, and

(*c*) the employer makes a payment in respect of overtime or other extra earnings (the "extra payment").

(2) For the purposes of calculating the deduction or repayment of tax, the extra payment is treated as made on the same date as that on which the main relevant payment in the payment period is due to be paid or is due to be treated as paid by regulation 24 (employee not paid weekly or monthly).

(3) But paragraph (4) applies if the extra payment is actually made before the date on which the main relevant payment in the payment period is due to be paid (disregarding the effects of regulation 24).

(4) A repayment which would (but for this paragraph) be due under regulation 23(6) on making the extra payment must not be paid to the employee, but must instead be added to the previous total tax (as defined by regulation 23(8)) on making the next relevant payment.

(5) This regulation does not apply if the extra payment is made in a short payment period (but regulation 31 applies instead if that period contains an extra pay day).

(6) "Payment period"—

(*a*) in the case of an employee normally paid weekly, means a tax week,

(*b*) in the case of an employee normally paid monthly, means a tax month, (*c*) in the case of an employee normally paid at other regular intervals, has the meaning given in paragraph (7).

(7) In the case mentioned in paragraph (6)(*c*)—

(*a*) the first payment period in a tax year starts on 6th April and finishes at the end of the employee's normal regular payment interval, and

(*b*) subsequent payment periods in the tax year start the day after the end of the previous payment period and finish—

(i) at the end of the employee's normal regular payment interval, or

(ii) on 5th April (if earlier).

(8) "Short payment period" means the last payment period in a tax year if, because of paragraph (7)(*b*)(ii), it is shorter than the previous payment periods.

(9) "Extra pay day" has the meaning given in regulation 31(4).

Commentary—*Simon's Taxes* **E4.1147.**

Derivation—The Income Tax (Employments) Regulations, SI 1993/744 reg 19.

Modifications—See the Income Tax (PAYE) Regulations, SI 2003/2682 reg 174 (modification of this regulation in its application to payments of taxable incapacity benefit).

Cross references—See the Income Tax (PAYE) Regulations, SI 2003/2682 reg 11 (this regulation not to apply to pension payers or pensioners in their capacity as such).

SI 2003/2682 reg 34 (this regulation does not apply to cases where SI 2003/2682 regs 34, 35 apply).

THE NON-CUMULATIVE BASIS

26 The non-cumulative basis

(1) An employer must deduct tax in accordance with regulation 27 (the non-cumulative basis) from any relevant payment made to an employee if—

(*a*) the Inland Revenue direct, or

(*b*) these Regulations provide,

that the non-cumulative basis is to apply.

(2) If this regulation applies then regulation 22 (cumulative basis) does not apply.

Commentary—*Simon's Taxes* **E4.1136.**

Derivation—The Income Tax (Employments) Regulations, SI 1993/744 reg 17(1), (2).

Modifications—See the Income Tax (PAYE) Regulations, SI 2003/2682 reg 174 (modification of this regulation in its application to payments of taxable incapacity benefit).

Cross references—SI 2003/2682 reg 32 (if an employee's code is the higher rate code, the employer must deduct tax at the higher rate, and this regulation and SI 2003/2682 reg 22 do not apply).

SI 2003/2682 reg 34 (this regulation does not apply to cases where SI 2003/2682 regs 34, 35 apply).

SI 2003/2682 reg 37 (PAYE income paid after employment ceased: this regulation not to apply)

27 Non-cumulative basis: general rule for deductions

(1) On making a relevant payment, the employer must deduct the amount of tax which would have been deductible in accordance with the appropriate tax tables, by reference to the employee's code, if the payment had been made on the first day of the tax year.

(2) This is subject to—

regulation 28	Modification of general rule
regulation 29	Aggregation of payments.

Commentary—*Simon's Taxes* **E4.1136, E4.1151, E4.1153.**

Derivation—The Income Tax (Employments) Regulations, SI 1993/744 reg 17(2).

Modifications—See the Income Tax (PAYE) Regulations, SI 2003/2682 reg 174 (modification of this regulation in its application to payments of taxable incapacity benefit).

Cross references—See the Income Tax (PAYE) Regulations, SI 2003/2682 reg 34 (this regulation does not apply to cases where SI 2003/2682 regs 34, 35 apply).

SI 2003/2682 reg 37 (PAYE income paid after employment ceased: this regulation not to apply)

28 Non-cumulative basis: modification of general rule

(1) Paragraphs (2) to (5) modify the general rule in regulation 27(1) (the non-cumulative basis) in certain circumstances.

(2) If regulation 30 (employee not paid weekly or monthly) applies to the employee's main relevant payments, the employer must deduct from a relevant payment the amount of tax which would have been deductible, by reference to the employee's code, if the payment (whether or not it is a main relevant payment) had been made on the date given by that regulation.

(3) If the employer does not normally make relevant payments to the employee at regular intervals, the employer must deduct from a relevant payment the amount of tax which would have been deductible, by reference to the employee's code—

(*a*) if the payment is the first payment in the tax year, on the date it is made, or (*b*) in any other case, on the date found by counting forward *x* days starting on 5th April, where *x* is the number of days found by starting with the date of the previous relevant payment and counting forward to the date of the payment in question.

(4) But if two or more relevant payments are made in the same tax week, the employer must deduct from the second or subsequent relevant payment the amount of tax which (subject to regulation 29(5)) would have been deductible, by reference to the employee's code, if that payment were made at the date given by paragraph (3) for the first payment.

(5) . . . [1] The deduction is not to exceed the overriding limit, subject to regulation 62(6) (notional payments).

Derivation—The Income Tax (Employments) Regulations, SI 1993/744 regs 14(2), 17(2), 18.

Modifications—See the Income Tax (PAYE) Regulations, SI 2003/2682 reg 174 (modification of this regulation in its application to payments of taxable incapacity benefit).

Cross references—See the Income Tax (PAYE) Regulations, SI 2003/2682 reg 34 (this regulation does not apply to cases where SI 2003/2682 regs 34, 35 apply).

Amendments—[1] In para (5), words "if the employee's code is a K code," revoked by the Income Tax (Pay As You Earn) (Amendment No 4) Regulations, SI 2014/2689 regs 2, 5 with effect from 6 April 2015.

29 Non-cumulative basis: aggregation of payments

(1) Paragraph (2) applies if—

(*a*) relevant payments are normally made to an employee at regular intervals of a week or more, and

(*b*) the employee's code is used on the non-cumulative basis.

(2) If the relevant payment is the second or subsequent relevant payment made to the employee during the payment period (as defined by regulation 25(6)), the amount of tax to be deducted must be—

(*a*) calculated by reference to the aggregate of the relevant payments made to the employee during the payment period (as defined by regulation 25(6)),

(*b*) increased by any tax not deducted because of the overriding limit when the previous relevant payment in that payment period was made to the employee, and

(*c*) reduced by the amount of tax calculated when the employer made the previous relevant payment in that payment period.

(3) But, for the purposes of the aggregate, any effects of regulation 30(2) (regular payments treated as made at later date) must be disregarded.

(4) Paragraph (5) applies if relevant payments to an employee—

(*a*) are normally made at regular intervals of less than a week, or

(*b*) are made at irregular intervals of less than a week.

(5) If the relevant payment is the second or subsequent relevant payment made to the employee during a tax week, the amount of tax to be deducted must be—

(*a*) calculated by reference to the aggregate of the relevant payments made to the employee in the tax week,

(*b*) increased by any tax not deducted because of the overriding limit when the previous relevant payment in that tax week was made to the employee, and

(*c*) reduced by the amount of tax calculated when the employer made the previous relevant payment in that tax week.

Commentary—*Simon's Taxes* **E4.1151.**

Derivation—The Income Tax (Employments) Regulations, SI 1993/744 regs 14(2), 21.

Modifications—See the Income Tax (PAYE) Regulations, SI 2003/2682 reg 174 (modification of this regulation in its application to payments of taxable incapacity benefit).

Cross references—See the Income Tax (PAYE) Regulations, SI 2003/2682 reg 34 (this regulation does not apply to cases where SI 2003/2682 regs 34, 35 apply).

30 Non-cumulative basis: employee not paid weekly or monthly

(1) This regulation applies if—

(*a*) an employer normally makes main relevant payments to an employee at regular intervals which are longer than a week, other than monthly, and

(*b*) the employee's code is used on the non-cumulative basis.

(2) Each main relevant payment in a tax year is treated for the purposes of calculating the deduction of tax as having been made at the end the period which—

(*a*) starts on 6th April, and

(*b*) finishes at the end of the employee's regular payment interval.

(3) If the employee's main relevant payments are normally made at regular intervals which are longer than a year, any such payment in a tax year is treated, for the purposes of calculating the deduction of tax, as made on 5th April in that tax year.

(4) But, in every case, the employer must record the actual date of every payment in the deductions working sheet.

Derivation—The Income Tax (Employments) Regulations, SI 1993/744 reg 18.

Modifications—See the Income Tax (PAYE) Regulations, SI 2003/2682 reg 174 (modification of this regulation in its application to payments of taxable incapacity benefit).

Cross references—See the Income Tax (PAYE) Regulations, SI 2003/2682 reg 34 (this regulation does not apply to cases where SI 2003/2682 regs 34, 35 apply).

31 Payments in short payment periods

(1) An employer must deduct tax on the non-cumulative basis from any relevant payment made to an employee in a short payment period which includes an extra pay day, even if the employee's code is normally used on the cumulative basis.

(2) Paragraph (1) does not apply if the employee's code is the basic rate code.

(3) If—

(*a*) the employee's total payments to date do not exceed the employee's total free pay to date, and

(*b*) the employee's code is normally used on the cumulative basis,

the employer must not deduct any tax from relevant payments made in a short payment period which includes an extra pay day.

(4) "Extra pay day" means the last day in a tax year on which a main relevant payment is due to be made to an employee if—

(*a*) the employee's main relevant payments are normally made weekly or at greater intervals which results in the number of pay days varying from tax year to tax year (solely because of the number of days in a calendar year), and

(*b*) the day falls in a short payment period.

(5) "Short payment period" has the meaning given in regulation 25(8).

Commentary—*Simon's Taxes* **E4.1152.**

Derivation—The Income Tax (Employments) Regulations, SI 1993/744 reg 17(1).

Modifications—See the Income Tax (PAYE) Regulations, SI 2003/2682 reg 174 (modification of this regulation in its application to payments of taxable incapacity benefit).

Cross references—See the Income Tax (PAYE) Regulations, SI 2003/2682 reg 24(6) (SI 2003/2682 reg 24 not to apply where a payment falls within para (1) above).

SI 2003/2682 reg 34 (this regulation does not apply to cases where SI 2003/2682 regs 34, 35 apply).

HIGHER RATE AND NIL TAX CODES

32 [Higher rate, additional rate and nil tax codes][1]

If an employee's code is the higher rate code the employer must deduct tax at the higher rate, and regulations 22 and 26 (cumulative and non-cumulative basis) do not apply.

Commentary—*Simon's Taxes* **E4.1153.**

Derivation—The Income Tax (Employments) Regulations, SI 1993/744 reg 16(1), (2).

Cross references—See the Income Tax (PAYE) Regulations, SI 2003/2682 reg 34 (this regulation does not apply to cases where SI 2003/2682 regs 34, 35 apply).

Amendment—[1] Italic cross-heading substituted by the Income Tax (Pay As You Earn) (Amendment) Regulations, SI 2011/729 regs 2, 6 with effect from 6 April 2011.

32A [Additional rate code: deductions

If the employee's code is the additional rate code the employer must deduct tax at the additional rate and regulations 22 and 26 (cumulative and non-cumulative basis) do not apply.][1]

Amendments—[1] Reg 32A inserted by the Income Tax (Pay As You Earn) (Amendment) Regulations, SI 2011/729 regs 2, 7 with effect from 6 April 2011.

33 Nil tax code: no deductions or repayments

(1) If an employee's code is the nil tax code the employer must not deduct or repay any tax, and so regulation 22 (cumulative basis) does not apply.

(2) But—

(*a*) if the nil tax code is an amended code, and

(*b*) the Inland Revenue so direct,

regulation 22 applies to the next relevant payment the employer makes in the same tax year, and the employer must make any repayment of tax due.

Commentary—*Simon's Taxes* **E4.1153.**

Derivation—The Income Tax (Employments) Regulations, SI 1993/744 reg 16(1), (3).

Modifications—See the Income Tax (PAYE) Regulations, SI 2003/2682 reg 174 (modification of this regulation in its application to payments of taxable incapacity benefit).

Cross references—See the Income Tax (PAYE) Regulations, SI 2003/2682 reg 34 (this regulation does not apply to cases where SI 2003/2682 regs 34, 35 apply).

SIMPLIFIED DEDUCTION SCHEME

34 Simplified deduction scheme for personal employees

. . .

Amendments—Regs 34, 35 revoked by the Income Tax (Pay As You Earn) (Amendment) Regulations, SI 2013/521 regs 2, 5 with effect from 6 April 2014.

35 Simplified deduction schemes: records

. . .

Amendments—Regs 34, 35 revoked by the Income Tax (Pay As You Earn) (Amendment) Regulations, SI 2013/521 regs 2, 5 with effect from 6 April 2014.

CESSATION OF EMPLOYMENT

36 Cessation of employment: Form P45

(1) On ceasing to employ an employee in respect of whom a code has been issued, the employer must complete Form P45.

[(1A) If Part 3 of Form P45 is not available—

(*a*) the employer is not required to complete that Part of the Form, and

(*b*) where the employer does not complete that Part, any requirement, however expressed, in these Regulations which relates only to Part 3 does not apply.][3]

(2) The employer must then—

(*a*) send Part 1 of that form to the Inland Revenue [if the employer is one to whom paragraph (2A) applies][2], and

(*b*) provide Parts 1A, 2 and 3 to the employee,

on the day on which the employment ceases or, if that is not practicable, without unreasonable delay.

[(2A) This paragraph applies to—

(*a*) non-Real Time Information employers, and

(*b*) Real Time Information employers to whom HMRC has given a notice requiring the employer to send to HMRC Form P45 or Form P46 on the commencement of a new employee's employment.][2]

(3) Retirement on pension is not a cessation of employment for the purposes of this regulation if the PAYE pension income is paid by the same employer after retirement.

(4) The information listed in column 1 of Table 2 must, subject to the conditions set out in column 2, be provided in the various Parts of Form P45 as indicated in columns 3 to 5.

TABLE 2
INFORMATION WHICH MUST BE PROVIDED IN FORM P45

1 *Information to be provided*	*2* *Conditions*	*3–5* *Form P45 Part*		
		1	*1A*	*2, 3*
1 the employer's PAYE reference		yes	yes	yes
2 the employee's national insurance number	if known	yes	yes	yes
3 the employee's name		yes	yes	yes
[3A	the employee's date of birth	yes	no	no
3B	the employee's sex	yes	no	no][1]
4 the date on which the employment ceased		yes	yes	yes
5 the employee's code or, if more than one, the latest code, issued by the Inland Revenue for the tax year during which the employment ceased		yes	yes	yes
6 whether the employee's code is used on the cumulative basis		yes	yes	yes
7 the tax week or month in which the last relevant payment was made to the employee or, in a case falling within regulation 24, was treated as having been made	if the employee's code is used on the cumulative basis	yes	yes	yes
8 the total payments to date and the corresponding total net tax deducted	if the employee's code is used on the cumulative basis	yes	yes	yes
9 the total payments to date relating to the employment in question and the corresponding total net tax deducted	if the employee's code is used on the cumulative basis, and if different from the information supplied under item 8	yes	yes	no

1 *Information to be provided*	*2* *Conditions*	*3–5* *Form P45 Part*		
10 the total payments to date relating to the employment in question and the corresponding total net tax deducted	if the employee's code is not used on the cumulative basis	yes	yes	no
11 the number used by the employer to identify the employee	if any	yes	no	no
12 the department or branch in which the employee was employed	if any	yes	no	no
13 the employee's address	if known	yes	no	no
14 the employer's name		yes	yes	no
15 the employer's address		yes	yes	no
16 the date the Form is completed		yes	yes	no

(5) This regulation is subject to regulations 38, 39 and 180 (death of employee etc).

Commentary—*Simon's Taxes* **E4.1166.**

Derivation—The Income Tax (Employments) Regulations, SI 1993/744 reg 23(1)–(3).

Modifications—See the Income Tax (PAYE) Regulations, SI 2003/2682 reg 174 (modification of this regulation in its application to payments of taxable incapacity benefit).

Cross references—See the Income Tax (PAYE) Regulations, SI 2003/2682 reg 10 (when an agency is treated as ceasing to employ an agency worker).

SI 2003/2682 reg 34 (this regulation does not apply to cases where SI 2003/2682 regs 34, 35 apply).

Amendments—[1] In para (4), in the Table, entries for items 3A, 3B inserted by the Income Tax (Pay As You Earn) (Amendment No 4) Regulations, SI 2007/2969 regs 2, 3 with effect from 6 April 2009.

[2] In para (2)(*a*), words inserted, and para (2A) inserted, by the Income Tax (Pay As You Earn) (Amendment) Regulations, SI 2012/822 regs 2, 6 with effect from 6 April 2012.

[3] Para (1A) inserted by the Income Tax (Pay As You Earn) (Amendment) Regulations, SI 2013/521 regs 2, 16 with effect from 6 April 2013 in relation to the tax year 2013–14 and subsequent tax years.

36A [Income subject to retrospective tax provision—information to employee

(1) This regulation applies if—

(*a*) a payment is made to an employee;

(*b*) the employment in connection with which it was paid ceases;

(*c*) the payment becomes a qualifying payment after the cessation of the employment;

(*d*) the tax year in which the payment was actually made is not closed, and

(*e*) the amount of the qualifying payment was not included in Form P45.

(2) If this regulation applies the person who made the payment must provide to the employee, without unreasonable delay after the relevant time, details of—

(*a*) the date on which the qualifying payment was actually made;

(*b*) the amount of the qualifying payment; and

(*c*) the amount of tax deducted under regulation 62(4) or (5).][1]

Amendments—[1] Regulation inserted by the Income Tax (Pay as You Earn) (Amendment) Regulations, SI 2007/1077 regs 2, 4 with effect from 6 April 2007.

37 PAYE income paid after employment ceased

(1) This regulation applies if a relevant payment is made to an employee after the employment has ceased—

(*a*) by the former employer in respect of the former employment, or

(*b*) by any other person in respect of an obligation of the former employer,

and the payment has not been included in Form P45.

[(1A) But this regulation does not apply if regulation 37A applies.][1]

[(2) [The][4] person making the payment must deduct tax on the non-cumulative basis using the 0T Code.[3]

(2A) . . . [3, 4]

(2B) . . . [3, 4]

(3) But—

(*a*) the payment does not affect the cessation of employment, and

(*b*) the provisions listed in paragraph (4) do not apply.

(4) The provisions are—

regulation 21	Deduction and repayment of tax by reference to employee's code
regulations 22 and 23	Cumulative basis

. . . [2]	. . . [2]
Chapters 2 and 3 of this Part	new employees and new pensioners: Forms P45 and P46.

(5) The person making the payment must record the following information in a deductions working sheet (which the person must prepare for the purpose if one has not already been prepared for that tax year).

(6) The information is—

(*a*) the date of the payment,

(*b*) the amount of the relevant payment, and

(*c*) the amount of tax deducted on making the payment, or to be deducted or accounted for under regulation 62(4) or (5) (notional payments).

(7) The person making the payment must also notify the employee of the information mentioned in paragraph (6) without unreasonable delay.

Commentary—*Simon's Taxes* **E4.1167.**

Derivation—The Income Tax (Employments) Regulations, SI 1993/744 reg 24; the Income Tax (Employments) (Notional Payments) Payments, SI 1994/1212 reg 13(1).

Cross references—See the Income Tax (PAYE) Regulations, SI 2003/2682 reg 10 (when an agency is treated as ceasing to employ an agency worker).

Amendments—[1] Paragraph (1A) inserted by the Income Tax (Pay as You Earn) (Amendment) Regulations, SI 2007/1077 regs 2, 5 with effect from 6 April 2007.

[2] In para (4), words revoked by the Income Tax (Pay As You Earn) (Amendment) Regulations, SI 2011/729 regs 2, 8 with effect from 6 April 2011.

[3] Paras (2)–(2B) substituted for previous para (2), by the Income Tax (Pay As You Earn) (Amendment) (No 2) Regulations, SI 2011/1054 reg 3 with effect from 6 April 2011.

[4] Words in para (2) substituted and paras (2A), (2B) revoked, by the Income Tax (Pay As You Earn) (Amendment) Regulations, SI 2012/822 regs 2, 65 with effect from 6 April 2012.

37A [Income paid after cessation of employment subsequently becoming subject to PAYE

(1) This regulation applies if—

(*a*) a payment has been made, after the cessation of the employment, to a former employee—

(i) by the former employer, or

(ii) by any other person in respect of an obligation of the former employer;

(*b*) that payment becomes a qualifying payment after the employment ceased; and

(*c*) the amount of the qualifying payment has not been included in Form P45.

(2) Where a qualifying payment has been made in a closed year, the employer must deduct tax, from any other payment made to the former employee in the tax period at the relevant time—

(*a*) in accordance with the last code used for the tax year in which the qualifying payment was made, or

(*b*) if the employer has not been notified of a code for that tax year, at the [additional][2] rate of tax applicable for that year.

(3) Where a qualifying payment has been made in an open year, the employer must deduct tax from any other payment made to the former employee—

(*a*) in accordance with the code in force in the final tax period in which the employee was employed, or

(*b*) if the employer has not been notified of a code, at the [additional][2] rate of tax applicable for that year.

(4) Neither the making of the qualifying payment, nor its subsequently becoming taxable, affect the cessation of the employment, and the provisions listed in regulation 37(4) do not apply in relation that payment.

(5) The employer must record the following information in a deductions working sheet for the tax year in which that payment was made.

If a deductions working sheet has not already been prepared for that tax year, the employer must prepare one.

(6) The information is—

(*a*) the date on which the qualifying payment was actually made;

(*b*) the amount of that payment; and

(*c*) the amount of tax to be deducted or accounted for under regulation 62(4) or (5) (notional payments).

(7) The employer must also notify the employee of the information listed in paragraph (6) without unreasonable delay after the relevant time.][1]

Amendments—[1] Regulation inserted by the Income Tax (Pay as You Earn) (Amendment) Regulations, SI 2007/1077 regs 2, 6 with effect from 6 April 2007.

[2] In paras (2)(*b*), (3)(*b*), word substituted by the Income Tax (Pay As You Earn) (Amendment) Regulations, SI 2011/729 regs 2, 9 with effect from 6 April 2011.

38 Death of employee

[(A1) This regulation applies to—

(*a*) non-Real Time Information employers, and

(*b*) Real Time Information employers to whom HMRC has given a notice requiring the employer to send to HMRC Form P45 or Form P46 on the commencement of a new employee's employment.][1]

(1) On the death of an employee (other than a pensioner) in respect of whom a code has been issued by the Inland Revenue, the employer must—

(*a*) complete Form P45 indicating in Part 1 that the employee has died, and

(*b*) send it to the Inland Revenue.

(2) The employer must comply with paragraph (1)—

(*a*) on the day on which the employer learns of the employee's death, or

(*b*) if that is not practicable, without unreasonable delay.

(3) The employer must, on making a relevant payment after learning of the employee's death but before completing Form P45, deduct or repay tax as if the deceased employee were still alive and employed by the employer at the date of the payment.

(4) Regulation 37(2) to (6) applies to any relevant payment which—

(*a*) is made in respect of the employee's employment after the date of the employee's death, and

(*b*) is not included in Form P45.

Commentary—*Simon's Taxes* **E4.1168.**

Derivation—The Income Tax (Employments) Regulations, SI 1993/744 reg 27.

Cross references—See the Income Tax (PAYE) Regulations, SI 2003/2682 reg 11 (this regulation not to apply to pension payers or pensioners in their capacity as such).

Amendments—[1] Para (A1) inserted by the Income Tax (Pay As You Earn) (Amendment) Regulations, SI 2012/822 regs 2, 7 with effect from 6 April 2012.

39 Death of pensioner

[(A1) This regulation applies to—

(*a*) non-Real Time Information pension payers, and

(*b*) Real Time Information pension payers to whom HMRC has given a notice requiring the pension payer to send to HMRC Form P45 or Form P46(Pen) on the commencement of a new pensioner's pension.][1]

(1) On the death of a pensioner in respect of whom a code has been issued by the Inland Revenue, the pension payer must—

(*a*) complete Form P45 indicating in Part 1 that the pensioner has died, and

(*b*) send it to the Inland Revenue.

(2) The pension payer must comply with paragraph (1)—

(*a*) on the day on which the pension payer learns of the pensioner's death, or

(*b*) if that is not practicable, without unreasonable delay.

(3) Paragraph (4) applies if the pension payer makes any relevant pension payments after the date of the pensioner's death—

(*a*) before completing Form P45, or

(*b*) after completing Form P45 but during the tax year in which the pensioner died.

(4) The pension payer must, on making any such payment, deduct or repay tax as if the deceased pensioner were still alive and in receipt of a pension at the date of the payment.

(5) Regulation 37(2) to (6) applies to any relevant pension payment which—

(*a*) is made in a tax year following the tax year in which the pensioner died, and

(*b*) is not included in Form P45.

Commentary—*Simon's Taxes* **E4.1168.**

Derivation—The Income Tax (Employments) Regulations, SI 1993/744 reg 27.

Amendments—[1] Para (A1) inserted by the Income Tax (Pay As You Earn) (Amendment) Regulations, SI 2012/822 regs 2, 8 with effect from 6 April 2012.

EMPLOYEE'S DUTY TO PROVIDE FORM P45

40 Duty of employee to give new employer Form P45

(1) An employee who has Parts 2 and 3 of Form P45 must give them to the new employer on commencing a new employment.

(2) If an employee receives Parts 2 and 3 of Form P45 after commencing a new employment, the employee must immediately give them to the new employer.

(3) [But paragraphs (4) and (6) apply][1] if an employee objects to the disclosure of the total payments to date to the new employer.

(4) [If the employer is a non-Real Time Information employer or a Real Time Information employer to whom HMRC has given a notice requiring the employer to send to HMRC Form P45 or Form P46 on the commencement of a new employee's employment, the][1] employee may, instead of complying with paragraph (1) or (2), send Parts 2 and 3 of Form P45 to the Inland Revenue before commencing the new employment or as soon as the employee receives Form P45 (as the case may be).

(5) The Inland Revenue—

(*a*) must then issue a code in respect of the employee to the new employer, and
(*b*) may direct that the non-cumulative basis is to apply to all relevant payments which the new employer makes to the employee.

[(6) If the employer is a Real Time Information employer, the employee need not comply with paragraphs (1) and (2).][1]

Commentary—*Simon's Taxes* **E4.1166, E4.1170.**

Derivation—The Income Tax (Employments) Regulations, SI 1993/744 reg 25(1), (11).

Amendments—[1] In paras (3), (4), words substituted, and para (6) inserted, by the Income Tax (Pay As You Earn) (Amendment) Regulations, SI 2012/822 regs 2, 9 with effect from 6 April 2012.

40A [Duty of employee to assist with completion of new employee fields in returns under regulations 67B and 67D

(1) An employee who commences employment with a Real Time Information employer must provide the information required to allow the employer to complete the new employee fields in the first return required by regulation 67B (real time returns of information about relevant payments) or 67D (exceptions to regulation 67B) which includes information in respect of the employee.
(2) The employer must verify the information given under paragraph (1) before making that return.
(3) In this regulation, "the new employee fields" means the information required under paragraphs 36 to 44 of Schedule A1.][1]

Amendments—[1] Reg 40A inserted by the Income Tax (Pay As You Earn) (Amendment) Regulations, SI 2012/822 regs 2, 10 with effect from 6 April 2012.

CHAPTER 2

NEW EMPLOYEES (OTHER THAN PENSIONERS): FORMS P45 AND P46

Cross references—See the Income Tax (PAYE) Regulations, SI 2003/2682 reg 11 (this Chapter not to apply to pension payers or pensioners in their capacity as such).
SI 2003/2682 reg 37 (PAYE income paid after employment ceased: this Chapter not to apply)

41 Scope of Chapter 2

This Chapter sets out the procedure to be followed for deductions and repayments (Form P45 and P46 procedure) in cases to which Chapter 3 (new pensioners: Forms P45 and P46) does not apply (see regulation 54).

42 Procedure if employer receives Form P45

(1) This regulation applies—
(*a*) if an employee gives Parts 2 and 3 of Form P45 to the employer on commencing employment, and
(*b*) in the circumstances mentioned in regulation 51(2) (late presentation of Form P45: before employer required to send Form P46).
(2) The new employer must prepare a deductions working sheet and record on it the following information shown in Parts 2 and 3 of Form P45—
(*a*) the employee's name,
(*b*) the employee's national insurance number.
(3) If Parts 2 and 3 of Form P45 show that the earlier employment ended in the current tax year, the new employer must comply with regulation 43.
(4) If—
(*a*) Parts 2 and 3 of Form P45 show that the earlier employment ended in the previous tax year, and
(*b*) the new employment commences on or before 24th May,
the new employer must comply with regulation 44.
(5) If—
(*a*) Parts 2 and 3 of Form P45 show that the employment ended in the previous tax year, and
(*b*) the employment commences after 24th May,
the new employer must comply with regulation 45.
(6) If Parts 2 and 3 of Form P45 show that the employment ended in any earlier tax year, the new employer must comply with regulation 45.
[(6A) Paragraphs (7) and (8) apply if the employer is either—
(*a*) a non-Real Time Information employer, or
(*b*) a Real Time Information employer to whom HMRC has given a notice requiring the employer to send to HMRC Form P45 or Form P46 on the commencement of a new employee's employment.][2]
(7) In all cases the new employer must then insert in Part 3 of Form P45—
(*a*) the employer's employer reference,
(*b*) the date on which the new employment commenced,
(*c*) any number used to identify the employee,

(*d*) the employee's code in use by the employer if different from the code shown in Parts 2 and 3 of Form P45,
(*e*) any figure recorded in accordance with paragraph (5)(*c*) or (6)(*c*) of regulation 43 (Form P45 for current tax year), if different from the total tax to date shown on Parts 2 and 3 of Form P45,
(*f*) the employee's address,
(*g*) the employee's date of birth, . . .[1]
[(*ga*) the employee's sex,][1]
(*h*) the employee's job title or description,
(*i*) the employer's name, and
(*j*) the employer's address.

(8) The employer must then send Part 3 of Form P45 to the employer's Inland Revenue office.

Commentary—*Simon's Taxes* **E4.1170.**

Derivation—The Income Tax (Employments) Regulations, SI 1993/744 reg 25(1)–(3), (8), 34(2).

Cross references—See the Income Tax (PAYE) Regulations, SI 2003/2682 reg 34 (this regulation does not apply to cases where SI 2003/2682 regs 34, 35 apply).

Amendments—[1] In para (7), words revoked, and sub-para (*ga*) inserted, by the Income Tax (Pay As You Earn) (Amendment No 4) Regulations, SI 2007/2969 regs 2, 4 with effect from 6 April 2009.

[2] Para (6A) inserted by the Income Tax (Pay As You Earn) (Amendment) Regulations, SI 2012/822 regs 2, 11 with effect from 6 April 2012.

43 Form P45 for current tax year

(1) The new employer must record in the deductions working sheet the code shown in Parts 2 and 3 of Form P45 as the employee's code.

(2) Paragraphs (3) to (10) apply if Parts 2 and 3 of Form P45 show that the cumulative basis was used.

(3) The employer must record in the deductions working sheet the total payments to date (if any) shown in Parts 2 and 3 of Form P45.

(4) The employer must record in the deductions working sheet the following additional information, or keep such records as enable its production.

(5) If the code shown in Parts 2 and 3 of Form P45 is a K code, the additional information is—
(*a*) the total additional pay to date,
(*b*) the total taxable payments to date, and
(*c*) the lower of the total tax to date as at the week or month shown in Parts 2 and 3 of Form P45 and the total net tax deducted shown in it.

(6) In any other case, the additional information is—
(*a*) the total free pay to date,
(*b*) the total taxable payments to date, and
(*c*) the corresponding total tax to date as at the week or month shown in Parts 2 and 3 of Form P45.

(7) The amounts required by paragraphs (5)(*a*) and (*b*) and (6)(*a*) and (*b*) must be arrived at by the employer by reference to the information shown in Parts 2 and 3 of Form P45.

(8) On making any relevant payment to the employee, the employer must deduct or repay tax by reference to the employee's code on the cumulative basis.

(9) For the purposes of—
(*a*) paragraph (8), and
(*b*) item 8 of Table 2 in regulation 36(4) (Form P45), and
(*c*) regulation 55(4)(*f*) [(Form P46(Pen))][1],

the total payments to date recorded in the deductions working sheet in accordance with paragraph (3), and the figure recorded in accordance with paragraph (5)(c) or (6)(c) must be treated as if they were relevant payments made to the employee by, and tax deducted by, the new employer.

(10) For the purposes of regulation 23(8) (cumulative basis: meaning of previous total tax to date) the figure recorded in accordance with paragraph (5)(*c*) or (6)(*c*) must be treated as the previous total tax to date when the employer next makes a relevant payment to the employee.

(11) If Parts 2 and 3 of Form P45 show that the non-cumulative basis has been used, on making any relevant payment to the employee the employer must, subject to regulation 32 (higher rate code: deductions), deduct or repay tax by reference to the employee's code on the non-cumulative basis.

(12) The receipt by the employer of Parts 2 and 3 of Form P45 is treated as the issue by the Inland Revenue of the code shown in Parts 2 and 3 of Form P45 as the code for use in respect of the employee.

Commentary—*Simon's Taxes* **E4.1170.**

Derivation—The Income Tax (Employments) Regulations, SI 1993/744 regs 25(3), (4), (5), (7), (9), 27(1), 34(2).

Cross references—See the Income Tax (PAYE) Regulations, SI 2003/2682 reg 34 (this regulation does not apply to cases where SI 2003/2682 regs 34, 35 apply).

Amendments—[1] In para (7), words substituted by the Income Tax (Pay As You Earn) (Amendment No 4) Regulations, SI 2007/2969 regs 2, 5 with effect from 6 April 2009.

44 Form P45 for previous tax year: employment starting on or before 24th May

(1) The new employer must—

(*a*) record in the deductions working sheet the code shown in Parts 2 and 3 of Form P45 as the employee's code, and

(*b*) deduct or repay tax by reference to that code on the cumulative basis, subject to regulation 32 (higher rate code: deductions).

(2) The receipt by the employer of Parts 2 and 3 of Form P45 is treated as the issue by the Inland Revenue of the code shown in Parts 2 and 3 of Form P45 as the code for use in respect of the employee.

Commentary—*Simon's Taxes* **E4.1170.**

Derivation—The Income Tax (Employments) Regulations, SI 1993/744 reg 25(8), (9).

Cross references—See the Income Tax (PAYE) Regulations, SI 2003/2682 reg 34 (this regulation does not apply to cases where SI 2003/2682 regs 34, 35 apply).

45 Other Forms P45

(1) The new employer must—

(*a*) record in the deductions working sheet the emergency code as the employee's code, and

(*b*) deduct tax from each relevant payment using the emergency code on the non-cumulative basis.

(2) The emergency code is treated as having been issued to the employer by the Inland Revenue as the code for use in respect of the employee.

Commentary—*Simon's Taxes* **E4.1170.**

Derivation—The Income Tax (Employments) Regulations, SI 1993/744 regs 25(8), 32.

Cross references—See the Income Tax (PAYE) Regulations, SI 2003/2682 reg 34 (this regulation does not apply to cases where SI 2003/2682 regs 34, 35 apply).

45A [Application of regulations 46 to 49E: Real Time Information employers and non-Real Time Information employers

(1) Regulations 46 to 49 (procedure where no Form P45) apply in relation to—

(*a*) non-Real Time Information employers, and

(*b*) Real Time Information employers to whom HMRC has given a notice requiring the employer to send to HMRC Form P45 or Form P46 on the commencement of a new employee's employment.

(2) Regulations 49A to 49E (procedure where employee fails to assist with completion of new employee fields or no Form P45) apply in relation to Real Time Information employers other than those within paragraph (1)(*b*).][1]

Amendments—[1] Reg 45A inserted by the Income Tax (Pay As You Earn) (Amendment) Regulations, SI 2012/822 regs 2, 12 with effect from 6 April 2012.

46 Form P46 where employer does not receive Form P45 and code not known

(1) This regulation applies if—

(*a*) an employee commences employment without giving the employer Parts 2 and 3 of Form P45, and

(*b*) a code in respect of the employee has not otherwise been issued to the employer.

[(1A) The employee must provide the following information in Form P46.

(1B) The information is—

(*a*) the employee's national insurance number (if known),

(*b*) the employee's full name,

(*c*) the employee's sex,

(*d*) the employee's date of birth, and

(*e*) the employee's full address including postcode.

[A seconded expatriate who is a national of an EEA state (see section 56(3)(*za*) of ITA) . . . [5] must provide confirmation of this as additional information.][2]][1]

(1C) . . . [5]

(2) The employee must indicate in Form P46 which . . . [1] of the following statements [applies][1]

Statement A: that the employment referred to in paragraph (1)(a) is the employee's first employment since the preceding 6th April, and the employee has not since that date received—

(*a*) jobseeker's allowance[, incapacity benefit or employment and support allowance][6] which is subject to income tax, or

(*b*) a retirement pension or an occupational pension;

Statement B: that the employee is not receiving a retirement pension or an occupational pension and since the preceding 6th April—

(*a*) has had another employment, but is not now in receipt of employment income from it, or

(*b*) has received jobseeker's allowance[, incapacity benefit or employment and support allowance][6] which is subject to income tax, but payment of that allowance or benefit has ceased;

Statement C: that the employee either has another employment (which is continuing) or is in receipt of a retirement pension or an occupational pension.

[A seconded expatriate must indicate instead which of the following statements applies—

Statement A: the employee intends to live in the United Kingdom for [183 days or more][6];

Statement B: the employee intends to live in the United Kingdom for less than [183 days][6];

Statement C: the employee will work both inside and outside the United Kingdom, but will live outside.][2]][1]

[(2A) A Form P46 must be—

(*a*) signed by the employee; or

(*b*) delivered by the employer by an approved method of electronic communications after he has complied with paragraph (2B).

(2B) To the extent that the information contained in it relates to the employee, the employer must verify the content of a Form P46 before it is delivered.

(2C) If, despite the requirements of paragraphs (2) to (2B), a Form P46 is sent or delivered to an officer of Revenue and Customs without the requirements of those paragraphs being satisfied, the employer must deduct tax [on the non-cumulative basis using code 0T][3] from the employee's earnings.][1]

[(3) The employer must provide the following information in the Form P46—

(*a*) the date on which the employment started;

(*b*) the employee's works payroll number and the department or branch (if any) in which the employee is employed;

(*c*) the title of the job;

(*d*) the employer's PAYE reference;

(*e*) the employer's name;

(*f*) the employer's full address, including the postcode; and

(*g*) the tax code used in relation to the employee's earnings.][1]

(4) The employer must keep the Form P46 until required to send it to the Inland Revenue in accordance with regulations 47 to 49.

(5) Before sending the Form P46, the employer must indicate in the Form which code is being used in respect of the employee and whether it is being used on the non-cumulative basis.

(6) For the purposes of paragraph (1)(*b*), the employer must ignore any code issued to the employer in respect of an employee's earlier employment which has ceased.

(7) This regulation ceases to apply in the circumstances mentioned in regulation [51(2)(*a*)][4] (late presentation of Form P45: before employer required to send Form P46).

Commentary—*Simon's Taxes* **E4.1171.**

Derivation—The Income Tax (Employments) Regulations, SI 1993/744 regs 28(1), (1A), (1B), (4), 29, 30.

Cross references—See the Income Tax (PAYE) Regulations, SI 2003/2682 reg 10 (when an agency is treated as ceasing to employ an agency worker for the purposes of para (6) above).

SI 2003/2682 reg 50 (procedure in Form P46 cases where code treated as issued by the Revenue: this does not apply for the purposes of this regulation).

Amendments—[1] Paras (1A), (1B), (2A)–(2C) inserted; words in para (2), para (3) inserted by the Income Tax (PAYE) (Amendment) Regulations, SI 2005/2691 regs 2, 3 with effect from 6 April 2006.

[2] Words in paras (1B), (2) inserted, by the Income Tax (PAYE) (Amendment) Regulations, SI 2009/588 regs 2, 3(1)–(3) with effect from 6 April 2009.

[3] In para (2C), words substituted by the Income Tax (Pay As You Earn) (Amendment) Regulations, SI 2011/729 regs 2, 10 with effect from 6 April 2011.

[4] In para (7), reference substituted by the Income Tax (Pay As You Earn) (Amendment) Regulations, SI 2012/822 regs 2, 13 with effect from 6 April 2012.

[5] Words in para (1B) and the whole of para (1C) revoked by the Income Tax (Pay As You Earn) Regulations, SI 2012/822 regs 2, 61, 66 with effect from 6 April 2012.

[6] In para (2), in para (*a*) of first Statement A and para (*b*) of first Statement B, words substituted for words "or incapacity benefit", in the second Statement A, words substituted for words "more than 6 months", and in the second Statement B, words substituted for words "6 months", by the Income Tax (Pay As You Earn) (Amendment) Regulations, SI 2013/521 regs 2, 17 with effect from 6 April 2013 in relation to the tax year 2013–14 and subsequent tax years.

47 [Procedure in Form P46 cases: (a) seconded expatriate is national of EEA state or Commonwealth citizen, or (b) employee is not seconded expatriate and Statement A applies]

[(1) This regulation applies in the case of an employee [(not a seconded expatriate)][3] who indicates that Statement A applies.

[It also applies to a seconded expatriate who confirms being a national of an EEA state . . . [4] (see regulation 46(1B)).][3]][1]

(2) On making the first relevant payment which [equals or exceeds the lower earnings limit][2] to the employee, the employer must—

[(*a*) send the Form P46 to Her Majesty's Revenue and Customs,][2]

(*b*) prepare a deductions working sheet and enter the total payments to date, and

(*c*) deduct tax on the cumulative basis using the emergency code.

[(2A) To comply with paragraph (2)(*a*)—

(*a*) the employer must send the Form P46 to Her Majesty's Revenue and Customs even if the employee has not provided all of the information required by regulation 46, and

(*b*) the employer must provide any of the information required by regulation 46(1B) that the employee has not provided.][2]

(3) On making any subsequent relevant payment before the Inland Revenue issue a code for use in respect of the employee, the employer must continue to deduct or repay tax on the cumulative basis using the emergency code.

(4) . . . [4]

Commentary—*Simon's Taxes* **E4.1153, E4.1171.**

Derivation—The Income Tax (Employments) Regulations, SI 1993/744 regs 28(1), (1A), 29.

Cross references—See the Income Tax (PAYE) Regulations, SI 2003/2682 reg 50 (procedure in Form P46 cases where code treated as issued by the Revenue: this does not apply for the purposes of this regulation).

Amendments—[1] Para (1) substituted by the Income Tax (PAYE) (Amendment) Regulations, SI 2005/2691 regs 2, 4 with effect from 6 April 2006.

[2] In para (2), words substituted, sub-para (*a*) substituted, and para (2A) inserted, by the Income Tax (Pay As You Earn) (Amendment No 4) Regulations, SI 2007/2969 regs 2, 6 with effect from 6 April 2008.

[3] Heading substituted, and in para (1) words inserted, by the Income Tax (PAYE) (Amendment) Regulations, SI 2009/588 regs 2, 3(4), (5) with effect from 6 April 2009.

[4] Words in para (1) and the whole of para (4) revoked, by the Income Tax (Pay As You Earn) (Amendment) Regulations, SI 2012/822 regs 2, 62, 67 with effect from 6 April 2012.

48 [Procedure in Form P46 cases: (a) Statement B applies (not seconded expatriate), or (b) Statement B or C applies (seconded expatriate)]

(1) This regulation applies in the case of an employee [(not a seconded expatriate)][3] who indicates in the Form P46 that . . . [1] Statement B applies.

[It also applies in the case of a seconded expatriate who indicates in the Form P46 that Statement B or C applies.][3]

(2) On making the first relevant payment which [equals or exceeds the lower earnings limit][2] to the employee, the employer must—

[(*a*) send the P46 to Her Majesty's Revenue and Customs,][2]

(*b*) prepare a deductions working sheet and enter the total payments to date, and

(*c*) deduct tax on the non-cumulative basis using the emergency code.

[(2A) To comply with paragraph (2)(*a*)—

(*a*) the employer must send the Form P46 to Her Majesty's Revenue and Customs even if the employee has not provided all of the information required by regulation 46, and

(*b*) the employer must provide any of the information required by regulation 46(1B) that the employee has not provided.][2]

(3) On making any subsequent relevant payment before the employee's code is issued, the employer must continue to deduct or repay tax on the non-cumulative basis using the emergency code.

(4) . . . [4]

Commentary—*Simon's Taxes* **E4.1153, E4.1171.**

Derivation—The Income Tax (Employments) Regulations, SI 1993/744 regs 28(1), (1A), 30(1)–(3).

Cross references—See the Income Tax (PAYE) Regulations, SI 2003/2682 reg 50 (procedure in Form P46 cases where code treated as issued by the Revenue: this does not apply for the purposes of this regulation).

Amendments—[1] In para (1), word revoked by the Income Tax (PAYE) (Amendment) Regulations, SI 2005/2691 regs 2, 5 with effect from 6 April 2006.

[2] In para (2), words substituted, sub-para (*a*) substituted, and para (2A) inserted, by the Income Tax (Pay As You Earn) (Amendment No 4) Regulations, SI 2007/2969 regs 2, 7 with effect from 6 April 2008.

[3] Heading substituted, and in para (1) words inserted, by the Income Tax (PAYE) (Amendment) Regulations, SI 2009/588 regs 2, 3(6), (7) with effect from 6 April 2009.

[4] Para (4) revoked by the Income Tax (Pay As You Earn) (Amendment) Regulations, SI 2012/822 regs 2, 62 with effect from 6 April 2012.

49 [Procedure in Form P46 cases: (a) Statement C applies (not seconded expatriate), or (b) Statement A applies (seconded expatriate) . . .][3]

(1) This regulation applies in any case which is not dealt with by regulation 47 or 48 which concerns an employee to whom regulation 46(1) applies.

(2) On making the first relevant payment to the employee, the employer must—

[(*a*) send the Form P46 to Her Majesty's Revenue and Customs,][1]

(*b*) prepare a deductions working sheet and enter both the total payments to date and the total tax to date before the first payment as nil,

(*c*) deduct tax on the cumulative basis using the basic rate code.

[(2A) To comply with paragraph (2)(*a*)—

(*a*) the employer must send the Form P46 to Her Majesty's Revenue and Customs even if the employee has not provided all of the information required by regulation 46, and

(*b*) the employer must provide any of the information required by regulation 46(1B) that the employee has not provided.][1]

(3) On making any subsequent relevant payment before the employee's code is issued, the employer must continue to deduct tax on the cumulative basis using the basic rate code.

[(4) In the case of a seconded expatriate, the emergency code must be used instead of the basic rate code mentioned in paragraphs (2)(*c*) and (3) (see also regulation 7(3) about the codes).][2]

Commentary—*Simon's Taxes* **E4.1171.**

Derivation—The Income Tax (Employments) Regulations, SI 1993/744 regs 28(1), (1A), 31(1), (2), (4).

Cross references—See the Income Tax (PAYE) Regulations, SI 2003/2682 reg 50 (procedure in Form P46 cases where code treated as issued by the Revenue: this does not apply for the purposes of this regulation).

Amendments—[1] Para (2)(*a*) substituted, and para (2A) inserted, by the Income Tax (Pay As You Earn) (Amendment No 4) Regulations, SI 2007/2969 regs 2, 8 with effect from 6 April 2008.

[2] Heading substituted, and para (4) inserted, by the Income Tax (PAYE) (Amendment) Regulations, SI 2009/588 regs 2, 3(8), (8) with effect from 6 April 2009.

[3] In heading, words revoked by the Income Tax (Pay As You Earn) (Amendment) Regulations, SI 2011/729 regs 2, 11 with effect from 6 April 2011.

49A [Procedure where employee fails to assist with completion of new employee fields in returns under regulations 67B and 67D

(1) If, despite the requirements of regulation 40A(1) and (2) (duty of employee to assist with completion of new employee fields in returns under regulations 67B and 67D) and regulations 67B (real time returns of information about relevant payments) and 67D (exceptions to regulation 67B), a return is sent to HMRC under those regulations without the new employee fields being completed in respect of the employee, the employer must deduct tax on the non-cumulative basis using code 0T.

(2) In paragraph (1), "the new employee fields" has the same meaning as in regulation 40A.][1]

Amendments—[1] Regs 49A–49E inserted by the Income Tax (Pay As You Earn) (Amendment) Regulations, SI 2012/822 regs 2, 14 with effect from 6 April 2012.

49B [Procedure where no Form P45 and code not known: application of regulations 49C to 49E

(1) Regulations 49C to 49E (procedure where no Form P45) apply if—

(*a*) regulation 49A does not apply,

(*b*) an employee commences employment without giving the employer Parts 2 and 3 of Form P45 and the circumstances mentioned in regulation 51(2)(*b*) (late presentation of Form P45) do not apply, and

(*c*) a code in respect of the employee has not otherwise been issued to the employer.

(2) For the purposes of paragraph (1)(*c*), the employer must ignore any code issued to the employer in respect of an employee's earlier employment which has ceased.][1]

Amendments—[1] Regs 49A–49E inserted by the Income Tax (Pay As You Earn) (Amendment) Regulations, SI 2012/822 regs 2, 14 with effect from 6 April 2012.

49C [Procedure where no Form P45 and: (a) employee is not a seconded expatriate and paragraph 41(a) of Schedule A1 applies; or (b) seconded expatriate is national of EEA state

(1) This regulation applies where—

(*a*) the employee is not a seconded expatriate and has indicated in accordance with regulation 40A(1) (duty of employee to assist with completion of new employee fields in returns under regulations 67B and 67D) that the statement in paragraph 41(*a*) of Schedule A1 (real time returns) is correct, or

(*b*) the employee is a seconded expatriate and has confirmed in accordance with regulation 40A(1) being a national of an EEA state.

(2) On making the first relevant payment which equals or exceeds the lower earnings limit to the employee, the employer must—

(*a*) prepare a deductions working sheet and enter the total payments to date, and

(*b*) deduct tax on the cumulative basis using the emergency code.

(3) On making any subsequent relevant payment before HMRC issue a code for use in respect of the employee, the employer must continue to deduct or repay tax on the cumulative basis using the emergency code.][1]

Amendments—[1] Regs 49A–49E inserted by the Income Tax (Pay As You Earn) (Amendment) Regulations, SI 2012/822 regs 2, 14 with effect from 6 April 2012.

49D [Procedure where no Form P45 and: (a) employee is not a seconded expatriate and paragraph 41(b) of Schedule A1 applies; or (b) employee is a seconded expatriate and paragraph 43(b) or 43(c) of Schedule A1 applies

(1) This regulation applies where—

(*a*) the employee is not a seconded expatriate and has indicated in accordance with regulation 40A(1) that the statement in paragraph 41(*b*) of Schedule A1 is correct, or

(*b*) the employee is a seconded expatriate to whom regulation 49C does not apply and has indicated in accordance with regulation 40A(1) that the statement in paragraph 43(*b*) or 43(*c*) of Schedule A1 is correct.

(2) On making the first relevant payment which equals or exceeds the lower earnings limit to the employee, the employer must—

(*a*) prepare a deductions working sheet and enter the total payments to date, and

(*b*) deduct tax on the non-cumulative basis using the emergency code.

(3) On making any subsequent relevant payment before the employee's code is issued, the employer must continue to deduct or repay tax on the non-cumulative basis using the emergency code.][1]

Amendments—[1] Regs 49A–49E inserted by the Income Tax (Pay As You Earn) (Amendment) Regulations, SI 2012/822 regs 2, 14 with effect from 6 April 2012.

49E [Procedure where no Form P45 and: (a) employee is a not seconded expatriate and paragraph 41(c) of Schedule A1 applies; or (b) employee is a seconded expatriate and paragraph 43(a) of Schedule A1 applies

(1) This regulation applies in any case which is not dealt with by regulation 49C or 49D.

(2) On making the first relevant payment to the employee, the employer must—

(*a*) prepare a deductions working sheet and enter both the total payments to date and the total tax to date before the first payment as nil,

(*b*) deduct tax on the cumulative basis using the basic rate code.

(3) On making any subsequent relevant payment before the employee's code is issued, the employer must continue to deduct tax on the cumulative basis using the basic rate code.

(4) In the case of a seconded expatriate, the emergency code must be used instead of the basic rate code mentioned in paragraphs (2)(*b*) and (3).][1]

Amendments—[1] Regs 49A–49E inserted by the Income Tax (Pay As You Earn) (Amendment) Regulations, SI 2012/822 regs 2, 14 with effect from 6 April 2012.

50 [No Form P45: code treated as issued by HMRC]

(1) [Code 0T, the][1] emergency code or the basic rate code used by the employer in accordance with regulations [46][1] to [49E][1] is treated, for the purposes of Parts 2 to 4 (codes; deduction and repayment of tax; payments, returns and information) as having been issued by the Inland Revenue as the code for use in respect of the employee.

(2) This does not apply for the purposes of regulation 18 (objections and appeals) and regulations 46 to [49E][1] and 51 to 53 (. . . [1]late presentation of Form P45).

Commentary—*Simon's Taxes* **E4.1172.**

Derivation—The Income Tax (Employments) Regulations, SI 1993/744 reg 32

Amendments—[1] Heading substituted, and words substituted and revoked, by the Income Tax (Pay As You Earn) (Amendment) Regulations, SI 2012/822 regs 2, 15, 16 with effect from 6 April 2012.

50A [Procedure in cases of retrospective earnings: code treated as issued by HMRC

(1) If—

(*a*) as a result of a retrospective tax provision, a qualifying payment was made in a year (whether open or closed) to a person, and

(*b*) a code has never been issued to the employer in respect of employment with whom that qualifying payment was made,

paragraph (2) applies.

(2) Where this paragraph applies the higher rate code applicable to the year in which the qualifying payment was made is treated, for the purposes of Parts 2 to 4 (codes, deduction and repayment of tax, payments, information and returns) as having been issued by HMRC as the code for use in respect of the employee in relation to that year.

(3) Paragraph (2) does not apply for the purposes of regulation 18 (objections and appeals) and regulations 46 to [49E][2] and 51 to 53 (Form P46 procedure and late presentation of Form P45).][1]

Amendment—[1] Regulation inserted by the Income Tax (Pay as You Earn) (Amendment) Regulations, SI 2007/1077 regs 2, 7 with effect from 6 April 2007.

[2] In para (3), reference substituted by the Income Tax (Pay As You Earn) (Amendment) Regulations, SI 2012/822 regs 2, 17 with effect from 6 April 2012.

51 Late presentation of Form P45

(1) This regulation applies if an employee gives Parts 2 and 3 of Form P45 to the employer after commencing employment.

[(2) If the employee gives Parts 2 and 3 of Form P45 to the employer before, as the case may be—

(*a*) the employer is required to send Form P46 to HMRC under regulations 47 to 49, or

(*b*) the employer is required to send the first return in relation to the employee under regulation 67B (real time returns of information about relevant payments) or 67D (exceptions to regulation 67B) to HMRC,

regulation 42 (procedure if employer receives Form P45) applies.][1]

(3) If the employee gives Parts 2 and 3 of Form P45 to the employer—

[(*a*) after, as the case may be—

(i) Form P46 is required to have been sent to HMRC, or

(ii) the employer is required to send the first return in relation to the employee under regulation 67B or 67D to HMRC,

but][1]

(*b*) before the employee's code has been issued to the employer,

this regulation and regulation 52 (late presentation of Form P45: employer's duties) apply.

(4) If the employee gives Parts 2 and 3 of Form P45 to the employer after the employee's code has been issued to the employer, they must be destroyed.

(5) If Parts 2 and 3 of Form P45 show that the employment ended in the current tax year then, unless the employer has already ceased to employ the employee—

(*a*) the code shown in Parts 2 and 3 of Form P45 is treated as having been issued by the Inland Revenue to the employer on the day the employee gives them to the employer, and

(*b*) the employer must comply with regulation 52.

(6) If Parts 2 and 3 of Form P45 show that the employment ended in the previous tax year and the employee gives them to the employer on or before 24th May then, unless the employer has already ceased to employ the employee—

(*a*) the code shown in Parts 2 and 3 of Form P45 is treated as having been issued by the Inland Revenue to the employer on the day the employee gives them to the employer,

(*b*) the employer must deduct or repay tax by reference to that code using the cumulative basis, subject to regulation 32 (higher rate code: deductions), and

(*c*) the employer must comply with paragraphs (2) and (3) of regulation 52.

(7) Parts 2 and 3 of Form P45 must be destroyed—

(*a*) if they show that the employment ended in the previous tax year and the employee gives them to the employer after 24th May, or

(*b*) if they show that the employment ended in an earlier tax year.

Commentary—*Simon's Taxes* **E4.1171**.

Derivation—The Income Tax (Employments) Regulations, SI 1993/744 reg 34(1)–(3).

Cross references—See the Income Tax (PAYE) Regulations, SI 2003/2682 reg 10 (when an agency is treated as ceasing to employ an agency worker for the purposes of para (5)–(7) above).

SI 2003/2682 reg 50 (procedure in Form P46 cases where code treated as issued by the Revenue: this does not apply for the purposes of this regulation).

Amendments—[1] Paras (2), (3)(*a*) substituted by the Income Tax (Pay As You Earn) (Amendment) Regulations, SI 2012/822 regs 2, 18 with effect from 6 April 2012.

52 Late presentation of Form P45: employer's duties

(1) This regulation applies in the circumstances mentioned in regulation 51(5); and paragraphs (2) and (3) of this regulation also apply in the circumstances mentioned in regulation 51(6).

[(1A) Paragraphs (2) and (3) apply if the employer is either—

(*a*) a non-Real Time Information employer, or

(*b*) a Real Time Information employer to whom HMRC has given a notice requiring the employer to send to HMRC Form P45 or Form P46 on the commencement of a new employee's employment.][2]

(2) The employer must insert in Part 3 of Form P45—

(*a*) the employer's employer reference,

(*b*) the date on which the new employment commenced,

(*c*) any number used to identify the employee,

(*d*) the employee's code in use by the employer if different from the code shown in Parts 2 and 3 of Form P45,

(*e*) if Parts 2 and 3 of the Form P45 show that the cumulative basis has been used, the figure (if any) recorded in accordance with paragraph (7)(*c*) or (8)(*c*) if different from the total tax to date shown on Parts 2 and 3 of Form P45,

(*f*) the employee's address,

(*g*) the employee's date of birth, . . . [1]

[(*ga*) the employee's sex,][1]

(*h*) the employee's job title or description,

(*i*) the employer's name, and

(*j*) the employer's address.

(3) The employer must then send Part 3 of Form P45 to the employer's Inland Revenue office.

(4) The employer must prepare a deductions working sheet (unless the employer has already prepared one) in accordance with the following information shown in Parts 2 and 3 of Form P45—

(*a*) the employee's name,

(*b*) the employee's national insurance number, and

(*c*) the employee's code.

(5) The employer must record in the deductions working sheet the sum of—

(*a*) the total payments to date (if any) shown in Parts 2 and 3 of Form P45, and

(*b*) the relevant payments which have been made by the employer since the employment commenced which have not already been recorded in the deductions working sheet.

(6) If Parts 2 and 3 of Form P45 show that the cumulative basis has been used, the employer must also record the following additional information in the deductions working sheet, or keep such records as enable its production.

(7) If the code shown in Parts 2 and 3 of Form P45 is a K code, the additional information is—

(*a*) the total additional pay to date,

(*b*) the total taxable payments to date, and

(*c*) the lower of the total tax to date as at the week or month shown in Parts 2 and 3 of Form P45 or the total net tax deducted shown in it.

(8) In any other case, the additional information is—

(*a*) the total free pay to date,

(*b*) the total taxable payments to date, and

(*c*) the corresponding total tax to date as at the week or month shown in Parts 2 and 3 of Form P45.

(9) The employer must ascertain the amounts required by paragraphs (7)(*a*) and (*b*) and (8)(*a*) and (*b*) by reference solely to the information shown in Parts 2 and 3 of Form P45.

(10) If Parts 2 and 3 of Form P45 show that the cumulative basis has been used, the employer, on making any subsequent relevant payment to the employee, must deduct or repay tax by reference to the code shown in Parts 2 and 3 of Form P45 on the cumulative basis.

(11) For the purposes of—

(*a*) paragraph (10), and

(*b*) item 8 of Table 2 in regulation 36(4) (Form P45), and

(*c*) regulation 55(4)(*f*) [(Form P46(Pen))][1],

the total payments to date recorded in the deductions working sheet in accordance with paragraph (5) and the figure recorded in accordance with paragraph (7)(c) or (8)(c) must be treated as if they were relevant payments made to the employee by, and tax deducted by, the new employer.

(12) For the purposes of regulation 23(8) (cumulative basis: meaning of previous total tax to date), the figure recorded in accordance with paragraph (7)(*c*) or (8)(*c*) must be added to any actual previous total tax to date, and the total treated as the previous total tax to date when the employer next makes a relevant payment to the employee.

(13) If Parts 2 and 3 of Form P45 show that the non-cumulative basis has been used, on making any relevant payment to the employee, the employer must, subject to regulation 32 (higher rate code: deductions), deduct tax by reference to the code shown in Parts 2 and 3 of Form P45 on the non-cumulative basis.

Commentary—*Simon's Taxes* **E4.1171.**

Derivation—The Income Tax (Employments) Regulations, SI 1993/744 regs 25(2), (3), (4), (5), (7), 34(2), (3).

Cross references—See the Income Tax (PAYE) Regulations, SI 2003/2682 reg 50 (procedure in Form P46 cases where code treated as issued by the Revenue: this does not apply for the purposes of this regulation).

Amendments—[1] In para (2)(*g*), words revoked, para (2)(*ga*) inserted, and in para (11) words substituted, by the Income Tax (Pay As You Earn) (Amendment No 4) Regulations, SI 2007/2969 regs 2, 9 with effect from 6 April 2009.

[2] Para (1A) inserted by the Income Tax (Pay As You Earn) (Amendment) Regulations, SI 2012/822 regs 2, 19 with effect from 6 April 2012.

53 [No Form P45: subsequent procedure on issue of employee's code]

(1) On making any relevant payment to an employee falling within regulation 47 to [49E (procedure where no Form P45)][2] after the Inland Revenue have issued a code to the employer for use in respect of the employee, the employer must deduct or repay tax by reference to that code.

(2) For the purposes of paragraph (1) and regulation 66 (deductions working sheets)—

(*a*) any total payments to date notified to the employer by the Inland Revenue are treated as if they represented relevant payments made by the employer; and

(*b*) the total net tax deducted before the first payment made in accordance with this regulation is taken to be the sum of—

(i) the total net tax deducted, if any, notified to the employer by the Inland Revenue, and

(ii) any tax which the employer was liable to deduct from the employee's relevant payments under regulation 47, 48[, 49, 49C, 49D or 49E][2].

(3) For the purposes of—

(*a*) item 8 of Table 2 in regulation 36(4) (Form P45), and

(*b*) regulation 55(4)(*f*) [(Form P46(Pen))][1],

any total payments to date and total net tax deducted which are notified to the employer by the Inland Revenue must be treated as if they were relevant payments made to the employee by, and tax deducted by, the employer.

(4) If the employee's previous code was used on the cumulative basis, any amount notified to the employer under paragraph (2)(*b*)(i) must be added to the previous total tax to date for the purposes of regulation 23(8) (cumulative basis: meaning of previous total tax to date).

Derivation—The Income Tax (Employments) Regulations, SI 1993/744 reg 33.

Cross references—See the Income Tax (PAYE) Regulations, SI 2003/2682 reg 50 (procedure in Form P46 cases where code treated as issued by the Revenue: this does not apply for the purposes of this regulation).

Amendments—[1] In para (3), words substituted by the Income Tax (Pay As You Earn) (Amendment No 4) Regulations, SI 2007/2969 regs 2, 10 with effect from 6 April 2009.

[2] Heading substituted, and in paras (1), (2)(*b*)(ii) words substituted, by the Income Tax (Pay As You Earn) (Amendment) Regulations, SI 2012/822 regs 2, 20, 21 with effect from 6 April 2012.

CHAPTER 3

[NEW PENSIONERS: FORMS P45 AND P46(PEN)]

Cross references—See the Income Tax (PAYE) Regulations, SI 2003/2682 reg 37 (PAYE income paid after employment ceased: this Chapter not to apply).

Amendment—Heading substituted for previous heading "New Pensioners: Forms P45 and P46", by the Income Tax (Pay As You Earn) (Amendment No 4) Regulations, SI 2007/2969 regs 2, 11 with effect from 6 April 2009.

54 Scope of Chapter 3

This Chapter applies (instead of Chapter 2) when a pension starts and either—

(*a*) the pensioner will be continuing in employment and will be receiving relevant pension payments in addition to relevant payments from their employer, or

(*b*) the pensioner will not be receiving relevant payments other than relevant pension payments.][1]

Commentary—*Simon's Taxes* **E4.1175.**

Amendments—[1] Reg 54 substituted by the Income Tax (Pay As You Earn) (Amendment) Regulations, SI 2011/729 regs 2, 12 with effect from 6 April 2011.

54ZA [Application of this Chapter to Real Time Information pension payers

(1) Any requirement in this Chapter to complete (howsoever expressed) and send to HMRC Part 3 of Form P45 or Form P46(Pen) applies only to—

(*a*) non-Real Time Information pension payers, and

(*b*) Real Time Information pension payers to whom HMRC has given a notice requiring the pension payer to send to HMRC Form P45 or Form P46(Pen) on the commencement of a new pensioner's pension.

(2) Paragraph (1) is without prejudice to the requirement in regulation 55(3)(*b*) (PAYE pension income paid by former employer) to complete and give Form P46(Pen) to the pensioner.][1]

Amendments—[1] Reg 54ZA inserted by the Income Tax (Pay As You Earn) (Amendment) Regulations, SI 2012/822 regs 2, 22 with effect from 6 April 2012.

[54A [Relevant pension payments and relevant payments being received by a pensioner

(1) This regulation applies if the pensioner begins to receive relevant pension payments whilst continuing to receive relevant payments from their employer.

(2) On making relevant pension payments to the pensioner, the pension payer must deduct tax on the non-cumulative basis using the 0T tax code.

(3) The pension payer must send to HMRC the following information in the Form P46(Pen)—

(*a*) the pensioner's national insurance number, if known,

(*b*) the pensioner's full name,

(*c*) the pensioner's sex,

(*d*) the pensioner's date of birth,

(*e*) the pensioner's full address including postcode,

(*f*) the date upon which the pension payments started,

(*g*) the pensioner's work payroll number and the department or branch (if any) in which the pensioner is employed,

(*h*) confirmation that the recipient of the relevant payments is a pensioner,

(*i*) the pension payer's PAYE reference,

(*j*) the pension payer's name,

(*k*) the pension payer's full address including postcode, and

(*l*) the tax code used in relation to the pension.

(4) Before sending the Form P46(Pen), the pension payer must indicate in the form that code 0T is being used on a non-cumulative basis in respect of the pension.][1]

Commentary—*Simon's Taxes* **E4.1175.**

Amendments—[1] Regs 54A, 54B inserted by the Income Tax (Pay As You Earn) (Amendment) Regulations, SI 2011/729 regs 2, 13 with effect from 6 April 2011.

54B [[Procedure in regulation 54A cases: code treated as issued by HMRC]

(1) The 0T code used by the pension payer in accordance with regulation 54A is treated, for the purposes of Parts 2 to 4 (codes; deduction and repayment of tax; payments, returns and information), as having been issued by HMRC as the code for use in respect of the pensioner.

(2) This does not apply for the purposes of regulation 18 (objections and appeals) and regulations 58, 60 and 61 . . . [2] late presentation of Form P45 etc).][1]

Commentary—*Simon's Taxes* **E4.1175.**

Amendments—[1] Regs 54A, 54B inserted by the Income Tax (Pay As You Earn) (Amendment) Regulations, SI 2011/729 regs 2, 13 with effect from 6 April 2011.

[2] Heading substituted, and words in para (2) revoked, by the Income Tax (Pay As You Earn) (Amendment) Regulations, SI 2012/822 regs 2, 23, 24 with effect from 6 April 2012.

55 PAYE pension income paid by former employer

(1) This regulation applies if the pension payer was, immediately before the pensioner's retirement, the pensioner's employer and so, in accordance with regulation 36(3), no Form P45 was completed.

(2) On making relevant pension payments to the pensioner, the pension payer must deduct tax on the non-cumulative basis, subject to regulation 32 (higher rate code: deductions), for the remainder of the tax year in which the pension starts or until directed otherwise by the Inland Revenue.

(3) Within 14 days after the pensioner's retirement, the pension payer must prepare a [Form P46(Pen)][1] and—

(*a*) send it to the Inland Revenue, and

(*b*) give [a copy of the information][1] to the pensioner.

(4) The [Form P46(Pen)][1] must contain the following information—

(*a*) the pensioner's name,

(*b*) the pensioner's address, . . . [1]

[(*ba*) the pensioner's date of birth,

(*bb*) the pensioner's sex,][1]

(*c*) the pensioner's national insurance number, if known,

(*d*) the pension payer's PAYE reference,

(*e*) the date of retirement,

(*f*) the total payments to date at the date of retirement,

(*g*) the total payments to date relating to the employment in question at the date of retirement,

(*h*) the total net tax deducted corresponding to the total payments to date relating to the employment in question,

(*i*) the amount of pension payable [annually][1],

(*j*) any number used to identify the pensioner,

(*k*) whether the pensioner's code is use on the cumulative basis,

(*l*) the pension payer's name, and

(*m*) the pension payer's address.

(5) Paragraph (4) is subject to regulation 212 (modifications for electronic version of [Form P46(Pen)][1] . . . [1]).

Commentary—*Simon's Taxes* **E4.1175.**

Derivation—The Income Tax (Employments) Regulations, SI 1993/744 regs 17, 26(1), (1A), (2).

Modification—See the Income Tax (PAYE) Regulations, SI 2003/2682 reg 212 (modification of this regulation where pensioner's retirement statement delivered by an approved method of electronic communications).

Cross references—See the Income Tax (PAYE) Regulations, SI 2003/2682 reg 34 (this regulation does not apply to cases where SI 2003/2682 regs 34, 35 apply).

Amendments—[1] In paras (3), (3)(*b*), (4), (4)(*i*), (5), words substituted, in paras (4)(*b*), (5), words revoked and para (4)(*ba*), (*bb*) inserted, by the Income Tax (Pay As You Earn) (Amendment No 4) Regulations, SI 2007/2969 regs 2, 12 with effect from 6 April 2009.

56 PAYE pension income paid by other pension payer

(1) This regulation applies if the pensioner gives Parts 2 and 3 of Form P45 to the pension payer when a pension starts.

(2) The pension payer must insert in Part 3 of Form P45—

(*a*) the pensioner's address,

(*b*) any number used to identify the pensioner, . . . [1]

(*c*) the date on which the pension started.

(*d*) the pensioner's date of birth, and

(*e*) the pensioner's sex.][1]

(3) The pension payer must then send Part 3 of Form P45 to the pension payer's Inland Revenue office.

(4) The receipt by the pension payer of Parts 2 and 3 of Form P45 under paragraph (1) is treated as the issue by the Inland Revenue of the code shown in Parts 2 and 3 of Form P45 as the code for use in respect of the pensioner.

(5) On making relevant pension payments to the pensioner, the pension payer must, subject to regulation 32 (higher rate code: deductions), deduct or repay tax—

(*a*) on the non-cumulative basis, for the remainder of the tax year to which Parts 2 and 3 of Form P45 relate;

(*b*) on the cumulative basis, for subsequent tax years.

(6) Paragraph (5) applies until the pension payer is directed otherwise by the Inland Revenue.

Commentary—*Simon's Taxes* **E4.1176.**

Derivation—The Income Tax (Employments) Regulations, SI 1993/744 regs 17(1), 25(2), 26(3).

Amendments—[1] In para (2) word "and" at the end of sub-para (*b*) revoked, and sub-paras (*d*), (*e*) inserted, by the Income Tax (Pay As You Earn) (Amendment No 4) Regulations, SI 2007/2969 regs 2, 13 with effect from 6 April 2009.

57 [Information to be provided in Form P46(Pen) if code not known: non UK residents]

(1) This regulation applies if a pension payer pays a pension, which does not arise wholly from an employment carried on abroad, to a pensioner—

(*a*) who is not resident in the United Kingdom,

(*b*) who has not given Parts 2 and 3 of Form P45 to the pension payer, and

(*c*) in respect of whom a code has not otherwise been issued by the Inland Revenue.

(2) On making the first payment which exceeds the PAYE threshold, the pension payer must send to the Inland Revenue the following information in [Form P46(Pen)][2].

[(3) The information is—

(*a*) the pensioner's national insurance number (if known),

(*b*) the pensioner's full name,

(*c*) the pensioner's sex,

(*d*) the pensioner's date of birth,

(*e*) the pensioner's full address including postcode,

(*f*) date upon which payment of the pension started,

(*g*) the pensioner's works payroll number and the department or branch (if any),

(*h*) the fact that the recipient is a pensioner,

(*i*) the pension payer's PAYE reference,

(*j*) the pension payer's name,

(*k*) the pension payer's full address, including the postcode.][1]

(4) For the purposes of paragraph (1)(*c*), the pension payer must ignore any code issued to the pension payer in respect of a previous pension of the pensioner which has ended.

Commentary—*Simon's Taxes* **E4.1135, E4.1177.**

Derivation—The Income Tax (Employments) Regulations, SI 1993/744 reg 28(4), (5), (5A), (5B).

Amendments—[1] Para (3) substituted by the Income Tax (PAYE) (Amendment) Regulations, SI 2005/2691 regs 2, 7 with effect from 6 April 2006.

[2] Heading substituted, and in para (2) words substituted f, by the Income Tax (Pay As You Earn) (Amendment No 4) Regulations, SI 2007/2969 regs 2, 14 with effect from 6 April 2009.

58 [Procedure if no Form P45 and code not known: UK pensioners]

(1) This regulation applies if—

(*a*) a pension payer starts to make relevant pension payments to a pensioner,

(*b*) the pensioner is resident in the United Kingdom,

(*c*) the pensioner does not give to the pension payer Parts 2 and 3 of Form P45, and

(*d*) a code in respect of the pensioner has not otherwise been issued to the pension payer.

[(1A) This regulation does not apply where the relevant pension payment is a relevant lump sum payment.][3]

(2) On making any relevant pension payments to the pensioner before the Inland Revenue issue a code for use in respect of the pensioner, the pension payer must deduct tax on the non-cumulative basis applying the emergency code.

(3) The pension payer must send the Inland Revenue the following information in [Form P46(Pen)][2].

[(4) The information is—

(*a*) the pensioner's national insurance number (if known),

(*b*) the pensioner's full name,

(*c*) the pensioner's sex,

(*d*) the pensioner's date of birth,

(*e*) the pensioner's full address including postcode,

(*f*) date upon which payment of the pension started,

(*g*) the pensioner's works payroll number and the department or branch (if any),

(*h*) the fact that the recipient is a pensioner,

(*i*) the pension payer's PAYE reference,

(*j*) the pension payer's name,

(*k*) the pension payer's full address, including the postcode, and

(*l*) the tax code used in relation to the pension.][1]

(5) The pension payer must also indicate in the Form that the emergency code is being used on the non-cumulative basis.

(6) For the purposes of paragraph (1)(*d*), the pension payer must ignore any code issued to the pension payer in respect of a previous pension of the pensioner which has ended.

[(7) In this regulation, and in regulation 58A (procedure if no Form P45 and code not known where payment is a relevant lump sum payment), a "relevant lump sum payment" is—

(*a*) a payment of taxable pension income under section 636B or 636C of ITEPA, or treated as such a payment, and

(*b*) which is made at a time when the pension payer is not making any other payments of PAYE pension income to the pensioner under the same registered pension scheme.][3]

Commentary—*Simon's Taxes* **E4.1176.**

Derivation—The Income Tax (Employments) Regulations, SI 1993/744 regs 28(1), (1A), (1B), (4), 31(1), (3), (4).

Amendments—[1] Para (4) substituted by the Income Tax (PAYE) (Amendment) Regulations, SI 2005/2691 regs 2, 8 with effect from 6 April 2006.

[2] In para (3) words substituted by the Income Tax (Pay As You Earn) (Amendment No 4) Regulations, SI 2007/2969 regs 2, 15 with effect from 6 April 2009.

[3] Paras (1A), (7) inserted by the Income Tax (Pay As You Earn) (Amendment) Regulations, SI 2013/521 regs 2, 12 with effect from 6 April 2013 in relation to the tax year 2013–14 and subsequent tax years.

Heading substituted by the Income Tax (Pay As You Earn) (Amendment) Regulations, SI 2012/822 regs 2, 25 with effect from 6 April 2012.

[58A Procedure if no Form P45 and code not known where payment is a relevant lump sum payment

(1) This regulation applies if—

(*a*) a pension payer makes a payment of a relevant lump sum payment,

(*b*) the pensioner is resident in the United Kingdom,

(*c*) the pensioner does not give to the pension payer Parts 2 and 3 of Form P45, and

(*d*) a code in respect of the pensioner has not otherwise been issued to the pension payer.

(2) On making a relevant lump sum payment to the pensioner before HMRC issue a code for use in respect of the pensioner, the pension payer must deduct tax using the basic rate code on the non-cumulative basis.

(3) Where the pension payer is one to whom paragraph (6) applies on the day on which the relevant lump sum payment is made, or if that is not practicable, without unreasonable delay, the pension payer must complete Form P45 and provide—

(*a*) Part 1 of Form P45 to HMRC, and

(*b*) Parts 1A, 2 and 3 to the pensioner.

(4) Where paragraph (6) does not apply, on the day on which the relevant lump sum payment is made, or if that is not practicable, without unreasonable delay, the pension payer must complete and provide Parts 1A, 2 and 3 of Form P45 to the pensioner.

(5) The information listed in rows 1 to 6, and 10 to 16 of column 1 of Table 2 to regulation 36 must, subject to the conditions set out in column 2, be provided in the various Parts of Form P45 as indicated in columns 3 to 5, as if—

(*a*) references to "employer" were to "pension payer", and

(*b*) references to "employee" were to "pensioner.

(6) This paragraph applies to—

(*a*) a pension payer who is a non-Real Time Information pension payer, and

(*b*) a Real Time Information pension payer to whom HMRC has given a notice requiring the pension payer to send to HMRC Form P45.][1]

Amendments—[1] Reg 58A inserted by the Income Tax (Pay As You Earn) (Amendment) Regulations, SI 2013/521 regs 2, 13 with effect from 6 April 2013 in relation to the tax year 2013–14 and subsequent tax years.

59 UK resident pensioner's code treated as issued by Inland Revenue

(1) The emergency code used by the pension payer in accordance with regulation 58 is treated, for the purposes of Parts 2 to 4 (codes; deduction and repayment of tax; payments, returns and information) as having been issued by the Inland Revenue as the code for use in respect of the pensioner.

(2) This does not apply for the purposes of regulation 18 (objections and appeals) and regulations 58, 60 and 61 . . . [1] late presentation of Form P45 etc).

Derivation—The Income Tax (Employments) Regulations, SI 1993/744 reg 32.

Amendments—[1] Words revoked by the Income Tax (Pay As You Earn) (Amendment) Regulations, SI 2012/822 regs 2, 26 with effect from 6 April 2012.

60 Late presentation of Form P45

(1) Paragraphs (2) to (6) apply if the pensioner gives Parts 2 and 3 of Form P45 to the pension payer after the pension has started but before a code has been issued.

(2) The pension payer must insert in Part 3 of Form P45—

(*a*) the pensioner's address,

(*b*) any number used to identify the pensioner, and

(*c*) the date on which the pension started.

(3) The pension payer must then send Part 3 of Form P45 to the pension payer's Inland Revenue office.

(4) The receipt by the pension payer of Parts 2 and 3 of Form P45 under paragraph (1) is treated, except for the purposes of paragraph (1), as the issue by the Inland Revenue of the code shown in that Form as the pensioner's code.

(5) On making relevant pension payments to the pensioner, the pension payer must, subject to regulation 32 (higher rate code: deductions), deduct or repay tax—

(*a*) on the non-cumulative basis, for the remainder of the tax year to which Parts 2 and 3 of Form P45 relate;

(*b*) on the cumulative basis, for subsequent tax years.

(6) Paragraph (5) applies until the pension payer is directed otherwise by the Inland Revenue.

(7) If Parts 2 and 3 of Form P45 are given to the pension payer after the pension has started and after a code has been issued by the Inland Revenue, they must be destroyed.

Commentary—*Simon's Taxes* **E4.1176.**

Derivation—The Income Tax (Employments) Regulations, SI 1993/744 regs 25(2), (5), 34(1), (2), (3).

61 Subsequent procedure on issue of UK resident pensioner's code

(1) On making any relevant pension payment to a pensioner falling within regulation 58 after the Inland Revenue have issued a code to the pension payer for use in respect of the pensioner, the pension payer must deduct or repay tax by reference to that code.

(2) For the purposes of paragraph (1) and regulation 66 (deductions working sheets)—

(*a*) any total payments to date notified to the pension payer by the Inland Revenue are treated as if they represented relevant pension payments made by pension payer; and

(*b*) the total net tax deducted before the first payment made in accordance with this regulation is taken to be the sum of—

(i) the total net tax deducted, if any, notified to the pension payer by the Inland Revenue, and

(ii) any tax which the pension payer was liable to deduct from the pensioner's relevant pension payments under regulation 58.

(3) For the purposes of—

(*a*) item 8 of Table 2 in regulation 36(4) (Form P45), and

(*b*) regulation 55(4)(*f*) [(P46(Pen))][1],

any total payments to date and total net tax deducted which are which are notified to the employer by the Inland Revenue must be treated as if they were relevant pension payments made to the pensioner by, and tax deducted by, the pension payer.

(4) If the pensioner's previous code was used on the cumulative basis, any amount notified to the pension payer under paragraph (2)(*b*)(i) must be added to the previous total tax to date for the purposes of regulation 23(8) (meaning of previous total tax to date).

Commentary—*Simon's Taxes* **E4.1176.**

Derivation—The Income Tax (Employments) Regulations, SI 1993/744 reg 33.

Amendments—[1] In para (3)(*b*), words substituted by the Income Tax (Pay As You Earn) (Amendment No 4) Regulations, SI 2007/2969 regs 2, 17 with effect from 6 April 2009.

[CHAPTER 3A

BENEFITS IN KIND]

Amendments—Chapter 3A (regs 61A–61M) inserted by the Income Tax (Pay As You Earn) (Amendment No 4) Regulations, SI 2015/1927 regs 2, 6 with effect in relation to specified benefits (as defined in reg 61A) provided on or after 6 April 2016.

[61A Interpretation

In this Chapter—

"authorised employer" has the meaning given by regulation 61C;

"main relevant payment" means the relevant payment normally made to the specified employee at regular intervals of a week or more;

"making good payment" means the payment referred to in regulation 61E(2) or 61G(2)(*b*);

["specified benefit" means any benefit treated as earnings under any of the following provisions of Part 3 of ITEPA (employment income: earnings and benefits etc. treated as earnings)—

(*a*) section 87 (non-cash vouchers) except where section 694 (non-cash vouchers: treated as payments of PAYE income) of ITEPA applies,

(*b*) section 94 (credit-tokens) except where section 695 (credit-tokens: treated as payments of PAYE income) of ITEPA applies,

(*c*) section 120 (car),

(*d*) section 149 (car fuel),

(*e*) section 154,

(*f*) section 160,

(*g*) section 203 (employment-related benefit);][2]

"specified employee" means an employee to whom an authorised employer provides a specified benefit;

"Taxable Amount of the Benefit" has the meaning given in regulation 61D(1).][1]

Amendments—[1] Chapter 3A (regs 61A–61M) inserted by the Income Tax (Pay As You Earn) (Amendment No 4) Regulations, SI 2015/1927 regs 2, 6 with effect in relation to specified benefits (as defined in reg 61A) provided on or after 6 April 2016.

[2] Definition of "specified benefit" substituted by the Income Tax (Pay As You Earn) (Amendment No 3) Regulations, SI 2016/1137 regs 2, 3 with effect for the tax year 2017–18 and subsequent tax years.

[61B PAYE: benefits in kind

(1) This Chapter applies where during a tax year an authorised employer provides a specified benefit to a specified employee.

(2) Where this Chapter applies—

(*a*) the specified benefit is to be treated as a payment of PAYE income for the purposes of these Regulations; and (*b*) any reference (howsoever expressed) in these Regulations to relevant payment includes an amount in respect of the provision of a specified benefit, such amount to be determined in accordance with regulations 61D, 61H, 61I, 61J, [61K, 61L and 61LA][2], as the case may be;

but this is subject to paragraph (3).

(3) An amount determined in accordance with regulation 61D, 61H, 61I, 61J, [61K, 61L or 61LA][2], as the case may be, is not to be included as a relevant payment for the purpose of calculating whether the deduction of tax would exceed the overriding limit.][1]

Amendments—[1] Chapter 3A (regs 61A–61M) inserted by the Income Tax (Pay As You Earn) (Amendment No 4) Regulations, SI 2015/1927 regs 2, 6 with effect in relation to specified benefits (as defined in reg 61A) provided on or after 6 April 2016.
[2] In paras (2)(*b*), (3), words substituted by the Income Tax (Pay As You Earn) (Amendment No 3) Regulations, SI 2016/1137 regs 2, 4 with effect for the tax year 2017–18 and subsequent tax years.

[61C Authorised employer

(1) An employer is an authorised employer in respect of a specified employee for a tax year for the purposes of this Chapter if—

(*a*) HMRC has authorised that employer to make—

(i) deductions of income tax in respect of the provision of a specified benefit from payments which that employer actually makes of, or on account of, PAYE income of that employee; or

(ii) repayments of such income tax; and

(*b*) such authorisation has not been withdrawn.

(2) An employer will be authorised by HMRC if the conditions set out in paragraph (3) are met.

(3) The conditions are that—

(*a*) before the start of the tax year the employer has made an application for authorisation in respect of one or more specified employees to HMRC; and

(*b*) such an application identifies the specified benefit or benefits that will be provided to the specified employees.

(4) But in cases falling within paragraph (5), an employer may make an application for authorisation in respect of one or more specified employees during a tax year.

(5) The cases are that—

(*a*) a specified benefit or benefits is to be provided to the specified employees referred to in the application for the first time during the tax year;

(*b*) a specified benefit or benefits is to be provided to an employee upon commencement of employment and the employer is already an authorised employer for the purposes of this Chapter; or

(*c*) the application made before the start of the tax year contained an error.

(6) If during the tax year an authorised employer notifies HMRC that the application for authorisation is withdrawn in respect of the specified employees identified in the notification, then the employer will cease to be an authorised employer in respect of those specified employees from the end of the tax year in which that notice is given.

(7) But in cases falling within paragraph (8), where an authorised employer notifies HMRC the application for authorisation is withdrawn in respect of the specified employees identified in the notification, then the employer will cease to be an authorised employer in respect of those employees from the date that the notification is received by HMRC.

(8) The cases are—

(*a*) the relevant payment actually made to the specified employee named in the withdrawal notification will be insufficient to enable the authorised employer to deduct the full amount of tax due in respect of the relevant payment;

(*b*) that during the tax year the authorised employer stops providing a specified benefit or benefits to the specified employees identified in the withdrawal notification and the Revised Taxable Amount of the Benefit provided is nil; or

(*c*) the application made before the start of the year contained an error.

(9) Any application or notice must be made to HMRC using an approved method of electronic communication unless the employer is one to whom regulation 67D applies.

(10) For the purposes of this regulation, "Revised Taxable Amount of the Benefit" means the result of the calculation at step 3 of regulation 61I(2), as applied by regulation 61J(2).][1]

Amendments—[1] Chapter 3A (regs 61A–61M) inserted by the Income Tax (Pay As You Earn) (Amendment No 4) Regulations, SI 2015/1927 regs 2, 6 with effect in relation to specified benefits (as defined in reg 61A) provided on or after 6 April 2016.

[61D Deduction and repayments of tax: general rule

(1) Where this Chapter applies an authorised employer must take the following steps—

Step 1

Before making the first main relevant payment to a specified employee in a tax year, the cash equivalent of the specified benefit or benefits to be provided in that tax year must be determined in accordance with regulation 61E, 61F or 61G (methods of calculating the cash equivalent of specified benefits), as the case may be.

Step 2
Determine the number of main relevant payments to be made to the specified employee in that tax year.
Step 3
Divide the amount obtained from step 1 by the number obtained from step 2.
The resulting amount is the Taxable Amount of the Benefit.
Step 4
Add the Taxable Amount of the Benefit to the first main relevant payment.
Step 5
Deduct or repay tax on the amount obtained at step 4 in accordance with these Regulations by reference to the employee's code if the employer has one for the employee, even if the code is the subject of an objection or appeal.
(2) On making any subsequent main relevant payment in the tax year the authorised employer must add the Taxable Amount of the Benefit to that payment and apply step 5 of paragraph (1) to that amount.
(3) This regulation is subject to regulations 61H, 61I, 61J, [61K, 61L and 61LA][2] (modifications to the general rule).][1]

Amendments—[1] Chapter 3A (regs 61A–61M) inserted by the Income Tax (Pay As You Earn) (Amendment No 4) Regulations, SI 2015/1927 regs 2, 6 with effect in relation to specified benefits (as defined in reg 61A) provided on or after 6 April 2016.
[2] In para (3), words substituted by the Income Tax (Pay As You Earn) (Amendment No 3) Regulations, SI 2016/1137 regs 2, 5 with effect for the tax year 2017–18 and subsequent tax years.

[61E Method of calculating the cash equivalent of the benefit of a car or van
(1) Where the specified benefit is the provision of a car or a van the cash equivalent of that benefit is calculated in accordance with section 121 or 155 of ITEPA (cash equivalent of the benefit), as the case may be.
(2) For the purposes of paragraph (1), the authorised employer may take into account payments that the specified employee is required to make in the tax year as a condition of the car or van being available for that employee's private use.][1]

Amendments—[1] Chapter 3A (regs 61A–61M) inserted by the Income Tax (Pay As You Earn) (Amendment No 4) Regulations, SI 2015/1927 regs 2, 6 with effect in relation to specified benefits (as defined in reg 61A) provided on or after 6 April 2016.

[61F Method of calculating the cash equivalent of the benefit of fuel
(1) Where the specified benefit is the provisions of car fuel or van fuel the cash equivalent of that benefit is calculated in accordance with section 150 or 161 of ITEPA (car fuel and van fuel: cash equivalent), as the case may be.
(2) For the purposes of paragraph (1), the authorised employer may take into account payments that the specified employee is required to make during the tax year in connection with the provision of fuel for that employee's private use.][1]

Amendments—[1] Chapter 3A (regs 61A–61M) inserted by the Income Tax (Pay As You Earn) (Amendment No 4) Regulations, SI 2015/1927 regs 2, 6 with effect in relation to specified benefits (as defined in reg 61A) provided on or after 6 April 2016.

[61G Method of calculating the cash equivalent of [non-cash vouchers, credit-tokens and][2] employment-related benefits
(1) Where the specified benefit is [a non-cash voucher, credit-token or][2] any employment-related benefit the cash equivalent of the specified benefit is to be calculated in accordance with [sections 87, 94 or][2] 203 of ITEPA (cash equivalent of benefit treated as earnings).
(2) For the purposes of paragraph (1), the authorised employer may make reasonable assumptions about—
(*a*) the cost of a specified benefit to be incurred in a tax year where the cost is not known at the start of the tax year; and
(*b*) payments that a specified employee is expected to make in the tax year to make good any part of the cost incurred in providing the benefit to that employee.][1]

Amendments—[1] Chapter 3A (regs 61A–61M) inserted by the Income Tax (Pay As You Earn) (Amendment No 4) Regulations, SI 2015/1927 regs 2, 6 with effect in relation to specified benefits (as defined in reg 61A) provided on or after 6 April 2016.
[2] In heading, words inserted, and in para (1), words inserted and substituted, by the Income Tax (Pay As You Earn) (Amendment No 3) Regulations, SI 2016/1137 regs 2, 6, 7 with effect for the tax year 2017–18 and subsequent tax years.

[61H Modification of the general rule: cessation of employment but continuing benefit
(1) This regulation applies instead of regulation 61D(2) if during a tax year the employment of a specified employee ceases but the authorised employer continues to provide the specified benefit to that employee.
(2) Before the employment ceases the authorised employer must take the following steps—
Step 1
Determine at that time the number of remaining main relevant payments to be made in the employment.
Step 2

If the cost to the authorised employer of the specified benefit has changed, redetermine the cash equivalent in accordance with regulations 61E, 61F or 61G, as the case may be, otherwise the cash equivalent of the specified benefit is that previously determined for the tax year under step 1 of regulation 61D(1).
The result is the revised cash equivalent of the specified benefit provided during the employment.
Step 3
Calculate the taxable amount of the benefit provided to date by—
(*a*) determining the number of main relevant payments that have been made to date, then
(*b*) multiplying that number by the Taxable Amount of the Benefit obtained under step 3 of regulation 61D(1).
Step 4
Subtract the taxable amount of the benefit provided to date (the amount obtained from step 3) from the revised cash equivalent of the benefit provided during the employment (the amount obtained from step 2).
Step 5
Divide the amount obtained from step 4 by the number obtained at step 1.
The result is the Adjusted Taxable Amount of the Benefit.
Step 6
Add the Adjusted Taxable Amount of the Benefit to either—
(*a*) the next main relevant payment, where that is the only main relevant payment remaining in the employment; or
(*b*) each of the remaining main relevant payments, where the number of remaining main relevant payment determined under step 1 of paragraph (2) is more than one,
and apply step 5 of regulation 61D(1) to that amount or amounts, as the case may be.][1]

Amendments—[1] Chapter 3A (regs 61A–61M) inserted by the Income Tax (Pay As You Earn) (Amendment No 4) Regulations, SI 2015/1927 regs 2, 6 with effect in relation to specified benefits (as defined in reg 61A) provided on or after 6 April 2016.

[61I Modification of the general rule: in-year adjustments: change to the benefit during the year with effect from the date of the change

(1) This regulation applies instead of regulation 61D(2) if during a tax year there is a change to the specified benefit provided to a specified employee and, for the purposes of calculating the cash equivalent of that benefit under ITEPA, that change has effect from the date the revised benefit is provided to the employee.
(2) Subject to paragraph (4), the authorised employer must take the following steps—
Step 1
Before making the next main relevant payment after the change to the specified benefit has taken effect, calculate the revised cash equivalent of the specified benefit by—
(*a*) determining the cash equivalent of the specified benefit that has been provided in the tax year accordance with sections [sections 87, 94][2] 121, 150, 155, 161 or 203 of ITEPA, as the case may be, then
(*b*) determining the cash equivalent of the specified benefit, that will be provided for the remainder of the tax year, in accordance with regulation 61E, 61F or 61G, as the case may be, and
(*c*) adding these numbers together.
Step 2
Calculate the taxable amount of the benefit provided to date by—
(*a*) determining the number of main relevant payments that have been made to date, then
(*b*) multiplying that number by the Taxable Amount of the Benefit determined under step 3 of regulation 61D(1).
Step 3
Subtract the taxable amount of the benefit provided to date (the amount obtained from step 2) from the revised cash equivalent of the specified benefit (the amount obtained from step 1).
Step 4
Determine the number of remaining main relevant payments to be made in the tax year.
Step 5
Divide the amount obtained from step 3 by the number obtained at step 4.
The result, where the amount is a positive value, is the Increased Taxable Amount of the Benefit.
The result, where the amount is a negative value, is the Reduced Taxable Amount of the Benefit.
Step 6
Add the Increased Taxable Amount of the Benefit to, or subtract the Reduced Taxable Amount of the Benefit from, the next main relevant payment and apply step 5 of regulation 61D(1) to that amount.
(3) On making any subsequent main relevant payment in that year, the employer must add the Increased Taxable Amount of the Benefit to, or subtract the Reduced Taxable Amount of the Benefit from, that payment and apply step 5 of regulation 61D(1) to that amount.

(4) Where the change to the specified benefit occurs in the final tax month of a tax year and the authorised employer is not able to take the steps set out in paragraph (2) before the final main relevant payment for that year is made that employer must—

(*a*) comply with steps 1 to 5 of paragraph (2) before the first main relevant payment of the next tax year ("tax year 2") is made;

(*b*) add the Increased Taxable Amount of the Benefit to, or subtract the Reduced Taxable Amount of the Benefit from, the first main relevant payment to be made in tax year 2; and

(*c*) apply step 5 of regulation 61D(1) to that amount.][1]

Amendments—[1] Chapter 3A (regs 61A–61M) inserted by the Income Tax (Pay As You Earn) (Amendment No 4) Regulations, SI 2015/1927 regs 2, 6 with effect in relation to specified benefits (as defined in reg 61A) provided on or after 6 April 2016.

[2] In para (2), Step 1(*a*), words inserted by the Income Tax (Pay As You Earn) (Amendment No 3) Regulations, SI 2016/1137 regs 2, 8 with effect for the tax year 2017–18 and subsequent tax years.

[61J Modification of the general rule: in-year adjustments: change to the benefit during the year with effect from the start of tax year and other changes

(1) This regulation applies if during a tax year:

(*a*) there is a change to the specified benefit provided to a specified employee and, for the purposes of calculating the cash equivalent of that benefit under ITEPA, that change has effect from the start of the tax year;

(*b*) the employer becomes aware that the cash equivalent of the specified benefit determined at the start of the year in accordance with regulation 61E, 61F or 61G (method of calculating the cash equivalent) is no longer accurate;

(*c*) the employer will stop providing a specified benefit during the tax year; or

(*d*) there is a change to the number of main relevant payments used to determine the Taxable Amount of the Benefit where the specified employee is paid at irregular intervals.

(2) Where this regulation applies, regulation 61D(2) no longer applies and regulation 61I applies but with the modification in paragraph (3).

(3) For the purposes of calculating the revised cash equivalent of the specified benefit, step 1 of regulation 61I(2) is modified as follows—

Step 1

In cases where regulation 61J(1)(*a*), (*b*) or (*c*) applies, redetermine the cash equivalent of the specified benefit in accordance with regulations 61E, 61F or 61G, as the case may be. In cases where regulation 61J(1)(*d*) applies, use the cash equivalent of the benefit determined at the start of the year under step 1 of regulation 61D(1).

(4) Any references in regulation 61I(2) to the revised cash equivalent of the benefit or to the amount obtained under step 1 of 61I(2) are to be read in accordance with paragraph (3).][1]

Amendments—[1] Chapter 3A (regs 61A–61M) inserted by the Income Tax (Pay As You Earn) (Amendment No 4) Regulations, SI 2015/1927 regs 2, 6 with effect in relation to specified benefits (as defined in reg 61A) provided on or after 6 April 2016.

[61K Modification of the general rule: making good

(1) This regulation applies instead of regulation 61D(2) where immediately before the authorised employer makes the final main relevant payment of the tax year the specified employee has not made any or all of the making good payment.

(2) The authorised employer must—

(*a*) ascertain the difference between:

(i) the amount of the making good payment that has been taken into account when determining the cash equivalent of the specified benefit at the start of the tax year; and

(ii) the amount the specified employee has actually paid at that time;

(*b*) add the amount obtained under sub-paragraph (a) to the final main relevant payment, and

(*c*) apply step 5 of regulation 61D(1) to that amount.

(3) Where this regulation applies the authorised employer may not take into account making good payments for the purposes of calculating the cash equivalent of the same specified benefit provided to the same specified employee in the following tax year.][1]

Amendments—[1] Chapter 3A (regs 61A–61M) inserted by the Income Tax (Pay As You Earn) (Amendment No 4) Regulations, SI 2015/1927 regs 2, 6 with effect in relation to specified benefits (as defined in reg 61A) provided on or after 6 April 2016.

[61L Modification of the general rule: failure to make good fuel benefit

(1) This regulation applies if the specified employee has not made the payment referred to in regulation 61F(2) before 1st June following the end of the tax year ("tax year 1") in which the specified benefit of car fuel or van fuel was provided.

(2) Before making the first main relevant payment after 1st June following the end of tax year 1 ("the first main relevant payment in tax year 2") the authorised employer must take the following steps—

Step 1

Redetermine the cash equivalent of the specified benefit of car fuel or van fuel received in tax year 1 in accordance with section 150 or 161 of ITEPA on the basis that Condition A in section 151 or 162 of ITEPA (car fuel and van fuel: nil cash equivalent), as the case may be, has not been met.

The result is the Outstanding Taxable Amount of the Fuel Benefit for Tax Year 1.

Step 2
Add the Outstanding Taxable Amount of the Fuel Benefit for Tax Year 1 to the first main relevant payment in tax year 2 and apply step 5 of regulation 61D(1) to that amount.

(3) Where this regulation applies and the authorised employer is continuing to provide the specified benefit of car fuel or van fuel in tax year 2, the employer must make an in-year adjustment for that year, in accordance with regulation 61J(1)(*b*), and redetermine the cash equivalent of the specified benefit without taking into account payments the employee is required to make, in connection with the private use of fuel, as referred to in regulation 61F(2).][1]

Amendments—[1] Chapter 3A (regs 61A–61M) inserted by the Income Tax (Pay As You Earn) (Amendment No 4) Regulations, SI 2015/1927 regs 2, 6 with effect in relation to specified benefits (as defined in reg 61A) provided on or after 6 April 2016.

[61LA Modification of the general rule: failure to make good benefit of credit-token

(1) This regulation applies where the specified benefit is a credit-token and the specified employee has not made all of the making good payments referred to in regulation 61G(2)(*b*) before 1st June following the end of the tax year ("tax year 1") in which the credit-token was used.

(2) Before making the first main relevant payment after 1st June in the following tax year ("the first main relevant payment in tax year 2") the authorised employer must take the following steps—

Step 1
Calculate the outstanding taxable amount of the benefit of the credit-token used in tax year 1 by—

(*a*) determining the cash equivalent of the benefit of the credit-token used in that tax year in accordance with section 94 ITEPA;

(*b*) subtracting from that amount the cash equivalent of the benefit of the credit-token used as determined under step 1 of regulation 61I(2) as modified by regulation 61J(3) during that tax year.

Step 2
Add the amount obtained from step 1 to the first main relevant payment in tax year 2 and apply step 5 of regulation 61D(1) to that amount.

(3) Where this regulation applies regulation 61G(2)(*b*) does not apply in respect of credit-tokens used in tax year 2.][1]

Amendments—[1] Regulation 61LA inserted by the Income Tax (Pay As You Earn) (Amendment No 3) Regulations, SI 2016/1137 regs 2, 9 with effect for the tax year 2017–18 and subsequent tax years.

[61M Information to specified employees

(1) Before 1st June following the end of the tax year in which the specified benefits have been provided, an authorised employer must provide a statement to every specified employee identifying—

(*a*) every specified benefit provided to that employee during that tax year; and

(*b*) the cash equivalent of the specified benefit provided during that tax year treated as a payment of PAYE income under this Chapter.

(2) In this regulation—

(*a*) "authorised employer" includes an employer who ceased to be an authorised employer during or after the tax year; and

(*b*) "specified employee" includes an employee who was a specified employee for only part of the tax year.][1]

Amendments—[1] Chapter 3A (regs 61A–61M) inserted by the Income Tax (Pay As You Earn) (Amendment No 4) Regulations, SI 2015/1927 regs 2, 6 with effect in relation to specified benefits (as defined in reg 61A) provided on or after 6 April 2016.

CHAPTER 4

MISCELLANEOUS

62 Deductions in respect of notional payments

(1) This regulation applies if an employer makes a relevant payment which is a notional payment [(including a notional payment arising by virtue of a retrospective tax provision)][1] to an employee.

(2) The employer must, so far as possible, deduct tax required to be deducted in respect of a notional payment in accordance with any of [the provisions listed in paragraph (3)][1] from any relevant payment or payments which the employer actually makes to the employee at the same time as the notional payment.

(3) [The provisions are—][1]

regulations 22 to 25	cumulative basis
regulations 26 to 31	non-cumulative basis
regulation 32	higher rate code: deductions
. . . [2]	. . . [2]
regulation 37	PAYE income paid after employment ceased.

[paragraphs (2) and (3) of regulation 37A	Income paid after cessation of employment becoming subject to PAYE.][1]

(4) If the employer cannot deduct the full amount of tax as required by paragraph (2) from another relevant payment made at the same time as the notional payment, the employer must, so far as possible, deduct the tax from any payment or payments which the employer makes later in the same tax period.

(5) If the relevant payments actually made are insufficient to enable the employer to deduct the full amount of tax due in respect of notional payments, the employer must account to the Board of Inland Revenue for any amount which the employer is unable to deduct.

(6) Regulations 23(5) and 28(5) (deductions on cumulative or non-cumulative basis not to exceed the overriding limit) do not apply to the extent that the tax to be deducted is in respect of a notional payment.

Commentary—*Simon's Taxes* **E4.1145.**

Derivation—The Income Tax (Employments) Regulations, SI 1993/744 regs 6(1), 14(2), 24(2).

Amendments—[1] Words in para (1) inserted, words in paras (2), (3) substituted, and table entry inserted, by the Income Tax (Pay as You Earn) (Amendment) Regulations, SI 2007/1007 regs 2, 8 with effect from 6 April 2007.

[2] In para (3), reference to regulation 34 revoked by the Income Tax (Pay As You Earn) (Amendment) Regulations, SI 2013/521 regs 2, 8 with effect from 6 April 2014.

63 Repayment during unpaid leave

(1) This regulation applies if—

(*a*) an employee is not entitled to receive any relevant payments on a normal pay day because of absence from work,

(*b*) the cumulative basis would have been used in relation to a payment made on that day,

(*c*) the employee does not fall within regulation 64(1) (absence from work due to participation in trade dispute), and

(*d*) the employee, or the employee's authorised representative, makes an application in person to the employer.

(2) The employer must—

(*a*) comply with regulation 23 (cumulative basis: deduction and repayment) and accordingly repay any tax due to the employee, and

(*b*) comply with regulation 66(4) to (6) (completion of deductions working sheet),

as if the pay day were one on which relevant payments of nil had been made.

Commentary—*Simon's Taxes* **E4.1161.**

Derivation—The Income Tax (Employments) Regulations, SI 1993/744 reg 35.

Cross references—See the Income Tax (PAYE) Regulations, SI 2003/2682 reg 11 (this regulation not to apply to pension payers or pensioners in their capacity as such).

64 Trade disputes

(1) This regulation applies if an employee—

(*a*) is absent from work because of a trade dispute at the employee's place of work, and

(*b*) is participating or directly interested in the trade dispute.

(2) The employer must—

(*a*) on making any relevant payment, calculate the amount of tax to be deducted or repaid, and

(*b*) comply with paragraphs (5) to (8).

(3) If no relevant payments are to be made on the normal pay day but the employee's code would be used on the cumulative basis if a relevant payment were made on that day, the employer must—

(*a*) calculate, in accordance with regulation 23 (cumulative basis: deduction and repayment) whether any tax is due to be repaid on that day as if it were a day on which relevant payments of nil had been paid, and

(*b*) comply with paragraphs (5) to (8).

(4) Paragraphs (2) and (3) are subject to paragraphs (9) and (10).

(5) The employer—

(*a*) must not repay any tax due to be repaid until the end of the employee's strike action, but

(*b*) must deduct any tax due to be deducted, less any repayment for the tax year which has not been made.

(6) The amount of any repayment—

(*a*) made at the end of the employee's strike action under paragraph (5)(*a*), or

(*b*) set against tax due to be deducted under paragraph (5)(*b*),

must be reduced by any amount previously set off in accordance with paragraph (5)(b).

(7) If the absence of an employee extends beyond the end of the tax year, the employer must—

(*a*) before 1st June following the end of the tax year, give notice to the employee of the amount of any repayment of tax for the tax year in question calculated in accordance with paragraph (2) which has not been set off against any tax due to be deducted under paragraph (5)(*b*); and (*b*) complete the certificate which must be given under regulation 67 (Form P60) and the return which must be sent under regulation 73 (Form P35 and P14) as if that tax had been repaid to the employee.

(8) If the employer has not made any repayment of tax withheld under paragraph (5) within 42 days after the end of the employee's strike action, the employer must instead immediately pay the tax not repaid to the Inland Revenue, and regulation 69(2) (receipt where requested) applies to that payment.

(9) An employee from whom a repayment of tax has been withheld in accordance with paragraph (5) may request a benefit officer to certify that—

(*a*) section 14 of the Jobseekers Act 1995, or

(*b*) in Northern Ireland, article 16 of the Jobseekers (Northern Ireland) Order 1995,

(no allowance to those involved in trade dispute) does not disqualify the employee from receiving jobseeker's allowance, whether or not the employee is in fact entitled to receive jobseeker's allowance.

(10) If a benefit officer certifies in accordance with paragraph (9), the employer must make such repayment to the employee as may be due.

(11) In this regulation—

"benefit officer" means the appropriate officer—

(*a*) of the Department for Work and Pensions or,

(*b*) in Northern Ireland, of the Department for Social Development;

"end of the employee's strike action" means any of the following—

(*a*) the employee is no longer absent from work because of the trade dispute,

(*b*) the employer ceases to employ the employee,

(*c*) the employee has become genuinely employed elsewhere in the occupation which the employee usually follows,

(*d*) the employee has become regularly engaged in some other occupation, or

(*e*) the employee dies;

"jobseeker's allowance" has the same meaning as in regulation 148;

"place of work" has the meaning given in section 14(4) of the Jobseekers Act 1995 or, in Northern Ireland, in article 16(4) of the Jobseekers (Northern Ireland) Order 1995.

Commentary—*Simon's Taxes* **E4.1161.**

Derivation—The Income Tax (Employments) Regulations, SI 1993/744 reg 36.

Cross references—See the Income Tax (PAYE) Regulations, SI 2003/2682 reg 11 (this regulation not to apply to pension payers or pensioners in their capacity as such).

SI 2003/2682 reg 12 (this regulation not to apply to other payees in their capacity as such).

65 Repayment if no longer employed

(1) This regulation applies if, in a tax year, a person ("P")—

(*a*) was employed,

(*b*) is no longer employed, and

(*c*) applies for a repayment of tax.

(2) P must give the Inland Revenue—

(*a*) . . . [1]

(*b*) either certificate A or B, depending on P's circumstances, and

(*c*) such evidence of P's unemployment as the Inland Revenue may require.

(3) Certificate A is one which certifies that P is unemployed and, to the best of P's knowledge and belief, P—

(*a*) will not be a claimant during the period starting with the date on which the application is made and ending at the end of the tax year, and

(*b*) will not be employed during that period.

(4) Certificate B is one which certifies that P is unemployed and is not a claimant when the application is made.

(5) On receiving P's application, the Inland Revenue must make any repayment of tax which is appropriate, having regard to P's employee's code and the following information.

(6) If P gives certificate A the information is—

(*a*) the total payments to date and the corresponding total tax to date as at the week or month shown in Parts 2 and 3 of Form P45 (or, if lower, the total net tax deducted shown in it),

(*b*) any other relevant payments received by P in the tax year to date, and

(*c*) any other payments P will receive in the tax year.

(7) If P does not give certificate A the information is—

(*a*) the total payments to date and the corresponding total tax to date as at the week or month shown in Parts 2 and 3 of Form P45 (or, if lower, the total net tax deducted shown in it), and

(*b*) any other relevant payments received by P in the tax year to date.

(8) For the purposes of this regulation, "claimant" means a person who is—

(*a*) a claimant as defined by regulation 148 (jobseeker's allowance), or

(*b*) a claimant in receipt of taxable benefit as defined by regulation 173 (incapacity benefit).

Commentary—*Simon's Taxes* **E4.1162.**

Derivation—The Income Tax (Employments) Regulations, SI 1993/744 reg 37.

Cross references—See the Income Tax (PAYE) Regulations, SI 2003/2682 reg 11 (this regulation not to apply to pension payers or pensioners in their capacity as such).

Amendments—[1] Para (2)(*a*) revoked by the Income Tax (Pay As You Earn) (Amendment) Regulations, SI 2016/329 regs 2, 3 with effect from 6 April 2016.

66 Deductions working sheets

(1) Paragraph (2) applies if a code has been issued to an employer in respect of an employee.

(2) The employer must, on making a relevant payment to the employee, prepare a deductions working sheet (unless the employer has already done so).

(3) The employer must record in the deductions working sheet—

- (*a*) the employee's name,
- (*b*) the employee's national insurance number, if known,
- (*c*) the employee's code, and
- (*d*) the tax year to which the deductions working sheet relates.

(4) The employer must record in the deductions working sheet in respect of every relevant payment which the employer makes to the employee—

- (*a*) the date of the payment,
- (*b*) the amount of the payment, and
- (*c*) the amount of tax, if any, deducted or repaid on making the payment, or to be deducted or accounted for under regulation 62(4) or (5) (notional payments).

[(4A) For the purposes of paragraphs (4)(*a*) and (6)(*a*), (*b*), (*c*), and (*e*)(i), a relevant payment—

- (*a*) which comprises an amount of retrospective employment income, and
- (b) which was actually paid during a tax year which is not closed,

shall be treated, for the purpose of computing the amount of tax to be deducted, as paid at the earlier of the relevant time and the end of the last tax period in which the former employee was employed.][1]

(5) If the employee's code is used on the cumulative basis, the employer must, in respect of every relevant payment which the employer makes to the employee, either—

- (*a*) record the following information in the deductions working sheet, or
- (*b*) keep such records as enable its production.

(6) The information is—

- (*a*) the total payments to date in relation to the date of payment,
- (*b*) the total free pay to date or, as the case may be, the total additional pay to date, in relation to that date,
- (*c*) the total taxable payments to date in relation to that date,
- (*d*) the corresponding total tax to date,
- [(*e*) the tax due to be deducted at that date (subject to the overriding limit),
- (*ea*) the overriding limit, if any, in relation to the payment,
- (*eb*) the amount of any tax not deducted at that date because of the overriding limit, and][2]
- (*f*) any amount of tax which is not to be repaid because of regulation 64 (trade disputes).

(7) If the employee's code is not used on the cumulative basis, the employer must, in respect of every relevant payment which the employer makes to the employee, either—

- (*a*) record the following information in the deductions working sheet, or
- (*b*) keep such records as enable its production.

(8) The information is—

- (*a*) the free pay, or, as the case may be, the additional pay for the employee's code,
- (*b*) the taxable payments, and
- (*c*) . . . [2] the tax due to be deducted and the overriding limit.

[(9) Nothing in this regulation applies to a closed tax year (see regulation 66A).][1]

Commentary—*Simon's Taxes* **E4.1141.**

Derivation—The Income Tax (Employments) Regulations, SI 1993/744 regs 17(3), (4), 38, (4); the Income Tax (Employments) (Notional Payments) Regulations, SI 1994/1212 reg 13(1), (2).

Modifications—See the Income Tax (PAYE) Regulations, SI 2003/2682 reg 174 (modification of this regulation in its application to payments of taxable incapacity benefit).

Cross references—See the Income Tax (PAYE) Regulations, SI 2003/2682 reg 34 (this regulation does not apply to cases where SI 2003/2682 regs 34, 35 apply).

Amendments—[1] Paragraphs (4A), (9) inserted by the Income Tax (Pay as You Earn) (Amendment) Regulations, SI 2007/1007 regs 2, 9 with effect from 6 April 2007.

[2] In para (6), sub-paras (*e*)–(*eb*) substituted for previous sub-para (*e*), and in para (8)(*c*) words revoked, by the Income Tax (Pay As You Earn) (Amendment No 4) Regulations, SI 2014/2689 regs 2, 6 with effect from 6 April 2015.

66A [Deduction working sheets: retrospective employment income in closed tax year

(1) Paragraph (2) applies if—

- (*a*) a code has been issued to an employer in respect of an employee for a tax year which has subsequently become a closed tax year ("the relevant tax year"); and
- (*b*) after the end of that tax year a payment made during it to that employee becomes a qualifying payment.

(2) The employer must at the relevant time—

(*a*) in a case where there was a deductions working sheet for the employee for the relevant tax year, revise it to reflect the effect of the retrospective tax provision on the total PAYE income including the retrospective employment income for that year; and

(*b*) in a case where there was no deductions working sheet for the employee for the relevant year, produce one showing that effect on that income for that year.

(3) In a case falling within paragraph (2)(*b*) the employer must record in the deductions working sheet—

(*a*) the employee's name,

(*b*) the employee's national insurance number, if known,

(*c*) the employee's final code for the relevant tax year, and

(*d*) details of the relevant tax year.

(4) The employer must record in the deductions working sheet in respect of every qualifying payment—

(*a*) the date on which the payment is made,

(*b*) the amount of the payment, and

(*c*) the amount of tax, if any, to be deducted or accounted for under regulation 62(4) or (5) (notional payments).

(5) Despite paragraph (4)(*a*), in completing the deductions working sheet, the amount of any retrospective employment income shall be treated, for the purpose of computing the amount of tax to be deducted, as if it were paid in the final tax period, in which the employee was employed, in the relevant tax year.][1]

Amendments—[1] Regulation inserted by the Income Tax (Pay as You Earn) (Amendment) Regulations, SI 2007/1007 regs 2, 10 with effect from 6 April 2007.

67 Information to employees about payments and tax deducted (Form P60)

(1) Before 1st June following the end of the tax year, an employer must give a certificate (Form P60) to every employee—

(*a*) who was in the employer's employment on the last day of the tax year, and

(*b*) from whose relevant payments the employer was required to deduct tax at any time during that tax year.

(2) The certificate must show—

(*a*) the tax year to which it relates,

(*b*) the employer's PAYE reference,

(*c*) the employee's name,

(*d*) the employee's national insurance number, if known,

(*e*) any number used by the employer to identify the employee,

(*f*) the total amount of the relevant payments made by the employer to the employee during the tax year in respect of the employment in question,

(*g*) the total net tax deducted in relation to those payments, subject to regulation 64(7)(*b*) (trade disputes),

(*h*) the employee's code,

(*i*) the employer's name, and

(*j*) the employer's address.

(3) In the case of an employee taken into employment after the beginning of the tax year, the certificate must also show—

(*a*) any amounts required by regulation 43(9), 52(11), 53(3) or 61(3) to be treated as relevant payments made by the employer to the employee during the tax year,

(*b*) any amounts treated as tax deducted by the employer at the end of the tax year by any of those regulations,

(*c*) the sum of the figures given under sub-paragraph (*a*) of this paragraph and paragraph (2)(*f*),

(*d*) the sum of the figures given under sub-paragraph (*b*) of this paragraph and paragraph (2)(*g*).

Commentary—*Simon's Taxes* **E4.11121.**

Derivation—The Income Tax (Employments) Regulations, SI 1993/744 reg 39.

67A [Revised information to employees about payments and tax deducted (Form P 60)

(1) This regulation applies where—

(*a*) an enactment containing a retrospective tax provision applicable to a closed tax year is passed; and

(*b*) in consequence of the passing of that enactment an employee's employment income in that closed tax year is increased.

(2) Before 1st January next following the passing of the enactment—

(*a*) if the employer has previously given the employee a certificate (Form P60), the employer must give the employee a revised certificate (Form P60); and

(*b*) if the employer has not previously given the employee such a certificate, the employer must give the employee a copy of the revised form P14 completed in accordance with regulation 73A (amended return of relevant payments (Forms P14 and P35(RL)).

(3) Paragraphs (2) and (3) of regulation 67 apply, in a case falling within paragraph (2)(a), for the purposes of this regulation as they apply for the purposes of that regulation, save that—

(*a*) sub-paragraph (f) of paragraph (2) shall have effect as if for "the total amount" there were substituted "the revised total amount"; and

(*b*) sub-paragraph (g) of that paragraph shall have effect as if for "total net tax" there were substituted "the revised total amount of net tax";

with references to revised amounts being construed as references to the amounts of relevant payments and net tax deducted computed after the application of the retrospective tax provision.

(4) Where a revised certificate is given under this regulation—

(*a*) the employer must endorse it to show that it supersedes an earlier certificate; and

(*b*) the employee must not use the certificate which it supersedes.][1]

Amendments—[1] Regulation inserted by the Income Tax (Pay as You Earn) (Amendment) Regulations, SI 2007/1007 regs 2, 11 with effect from 6 April 2007.

PART 4
PAYMENTS, RETURNS AND INFORMATION

Modifications—See the Income Tax (PAYE) Regulations, SI 2003/2682 reg 174 (modification of this regulation in its application to payments of taxable incapacity benefit).

Cross references—See the Income Tax (PAYE) Regulations, SI 2003/2682 reg 168 (subject to SI 2003/2682 reg 168(3), this Part applies to the taxable jobseeker's allowance paid to a Part 8 Chapter 2 (of SI 2003/2682) claimant by the employer on behalf of the Department under SI 2003/2682 reg 167, as if it were a relevant payment from the employment).

CHAPTER 1
PAYMENT OF TAX AND ASSOCIATED RETURNS
[REAL TIME RETURNS

67B Real time returns of information about relevant payments

(1) [Subject to [paragraph (1A)][4],][3] On or before making a relevant payment to an employee, a Real Time Information employer must deliver to HMRC the information specified in Schedule A1 in accordance with this regulation unless the employer is not required by regulation 66 (deductions working sheets) to maintain a deductions working sheet for any employees.

[(1A) But a Real Time Information employer—

(*a*) which for the tax year 2014–15 meets Conditions A and B, or

(*b*) which for the tax year 2015–16 meets Conditions A and C,

may instead for that tax year deliver to HMRC the information specified in Schedule A1 (real time returns) in respect of all relevant payments made to an employee in a tax month on or before making the last relevant payment in that month.

(1B) Condition A is that, at 5th April 2014, the Real Time Information employer is one to whom HMRC has issued an employer's PAYE reference.

(1C) Condition B is that, at 6th April 2014, the Real Time Information employer employs no more than 9 employees.

(1D) Condition C is that, at 6th April 2015, the Real Time Information employer employs no more than 9 employees.][4]

(2) The information must be included in a return.

(3) Subject to paragraph (4), if relevant payments are made to more than one employee at the same time, the return under paragraph (2) must include the information required by Schedule A1 in respect of each employee to whom a relevant payment is made at that time.

(4) If relevant payments are made to more than one employee at the same time but the employer operates more than one payroll, the employer must make a return in respect of each payroll.

(5) The return is to be made using an approved method of electronic communications.

(6) . . . [2]

(7) . . . [2]][1]

Commentary—*Simon's Taxes* **E4.11114.**

Cross-references—Income Tax (Pay As You Earn) (Amendment) Regulations, SI 2012/822 regs 53–57 (transitional provisions on introduction of real time information).

Definitions—"Relevant payments": see reg 4 above.

Amendments—[1] Regs 67B–67H inserted by the Income Tax (Pay As You Earn) (Amendment) Regulations, SI 2012/822 regs 2, 27 with effect from 6 April 2012.

[2] Paras (6), (7) revoked by the Income Tax (Pay As You Earn) (Amendment) Regulations, SI 2013/521 regs 2, 18 with effect from 6 April 2013 in relation to the tax year 2013–14 and subsequent tax years.

[3] Words in para (1) inserted, by the Income Tax (Pay As You Earn) (Amendment No 2) Regulations, SI 2013/2300 reg 2 with effect from 6 October 2013. These amendments have effect in relation to relevant payments made in the period beginning on 6 October 2013 and ending on 5 April 2014.

[4] In para (1), words substituted for words "paragraphs (1A) and (1B)", and paras (1A)-(1D) substituted for paras (1A), (1B), by the Income Tax (Pay As You Earn) and the Income Tax (Construction Industry Scheme) (Amendment) Regulations, SI 2014/472 regs 2, 4 with effect from 6 April 2014.

[67BA Employees in respect of whom employer is not required to maintain deductions working sheets

(1) This regulation applies if an employer makes a relevant payment to an employee in respect of whom the employer is not required by regulation 66 (deductions working sheets) to maintain a deductions working sheet.

(2) The employer need not deliver the information required by regulation 67B(1) on or before making the payment.

(3) The employer must deliver that information no later than the end of the period of 7 days starting with the day following the day on which the payment is made.][1]

Commentary—*Simon's Taxes* **E4.11114.**

Amendments—[1] Regs 67BA–67BC inserted by the Income Tax (Pay As You Earn) (Amendment) Regulations, SI 2013/521 regs 2, 19 with effect from 6 April 2013 in relation to the tax year 2013–14 and subsequent tax years.

[67BB Employees paid in specified circumstances

(1) This regulation applies if an employer makes a payment to an employee and all of the circumstances in paragraph (2) apply.

(2) The circumstances are that—

(*a*) the payment includes an amount which is a relevant payment for work undertaken by the employee on—

(i) the day the payment is made, or

(ii) provided that the payment is made before the employee leaves the place of work at the end of the employee's period of work, the day before the payment is made,

(*b*) in respect of the work mentioned in sub-paragraph (a), it was not reasonably practicable for the employer to calculate the payment due before the completion of the work, and

(*c*) it is not reasonably practicable for the employer to deliver the information required by regulation 67B(1) on making the payment.

(3) The employer need not deliver the information required by regulation 67B(1) on or before making the payment.

(4) The employer must deliver that information no later than the end of the period of 7 days starting with the day following the day on which the payment is made.][1]

Commentary—*Simon's Taxes* **E4.11114.**

Amendments—[1] Regs 67BA–67BC inserted by the Income Tax (Pay As You Earn) (Amendment) Regulations, SI 2013/521 regs 2, 19 with effect from 6 April 2013 in relation to the tax year 2013–14 and subsequent tax years.

[67BC Regulations 67BA and 67BB: supplementary

Where regulation 67BA or 67BB applies, the information required by regulation 67B(1) in respect of the relevant payment may be included in a return with the information for any other relevant payment.][1]

Commentary—*Simon's Taxes* **E4.11114.**

Amendments—[1] Regs 67BA–67BC inserted by the Income Tax (Pay As You Earn) (Amendment) Regulations, SI 2013/521 regs 2, 19 with effect from 6 April 2013 in relation to the tax year 2013–14 and subsequent tax years.

67C [Modification of the requirements of regulation 67B: notional payments

(1) This regulation applies if an employer makes a relevant payment which is a notional payment (including a notional payment arising by virtue of a retrospective tax provision) to an employee.

[(2) If the employer is unable to comply with the requirements in regulation 67B(1) to deliver the information required by that regulation on or before making the relevant payment, the employer must instead deliver the information as soon as reasonably practicable after the payment is made and in any event no later than 14 days after the end of the tax month in which the payment is made.][2]][1]

Commentary—*Simon's Taxes* **E4.11114A.**

Amendments—[1] Regs 67B–67H inserted by the Income Tax (Pay As You Earn) (Amendment) Regulations, SI 2012/822 regs 2, 27 with effect from 6 April 2012.

[2] Para (2) substituted by the Income Tax (Pay As You Earn) (Amendment) Regulations, SI 2013/521 regs 2, 20 with effect from 6 April 2013 in relation to the tax year 2013–14 and subsequent tax years.

[67CA Notifications of relevant payments to and by providers of certain electronic payment methods

(1) A Real Time Information employer who makes a relevant payment using an approved method of electronic communications which falls to be included in a return under regulation 67B must—

(a) generate a reference under paragraph (3) and include it in that return,

(b) notify the service provider that the payment is a relevant payment, and

(c) generate a sub-reference under paragraph (3) in respect of the relevant payment and notify the service provider of that sub-reference.

(2) A service provider who receives a notification under paragraph (1)(b) must notify HMRC of the information it holds that is required for generating a reference under paragraph (3) in relation to the relevant payment.

(3) A reference and sub-reference under this paragraph is to be generated using the method specified by the Commissioners for Her Majesty's Revenue and Customs in a direction.

(4) In paragraphs (1) and (2), "service provider" means the provider of the approved method of electronic communications using which the payment is made.

(5) For the purposes of paragraphs (1) and (4), an "approved method of electronic communications" is any method of electronic communications which has been approved for the purposes of regulation 199 (large employers required to make specified payments electronically).

(6) A direction under paragraph (3) may also—

(a) specify circumstances in which paragraphs (1) and (2) are not to apply, and

(b) specify the form and manner of the notifications required by paragraphs (1)(b) and (c) and (2).][1]

Commentary—*Simon's Taxes* **E4.1103A, E4.11114A.**

HMRC Directions—Direction under regulation 67CA of the Income Tax (Pay As You Earn) Regulations 2003

Notifications of relevant payments to and by providers of certain electronic payment methods

The Commissioners for Her Majesty's Revenue and Customs make the following direction under regulation 67CA of the Income Tax (Pay As You Earn) Regulations 2003 (S.I. 2003/2682):

Effect

1. This direction has effect in relation to relevant payments made on and after 1st September 2012.

Circumstances in which regulation 67CA(1) and (2) of the Regulations does not apply

2. Regulation 67CA(1) and (2) of the Regulations does not apply if:

(a) a relevant payment is made using an approved method of electronic communications other than Bacs Direct Credit, or

(b) a relevant payment is made using Bacs Direct Credit but it is not made under the unique service user number allocated under the Bacs system solely for the use of the employer making the relevant payment.

Method of generating a reference in respect of a relevant payment

3. The reference required by regulation 67CA(1)(a) and (3) of the Regulations must be generated by entering into SHA 256 algorithm software the following information in the order given:

(a) the sub-reference generated under paragraph 5,

(b) the originator's bank sort code,

(c) the recipient's bank sort code,

(d) the amount of the payment the service provider is instructed to make in respect of the relevant payment.

Form of a notification to a service provider of a relevant payment

4. The notification required by regulation 67CA(1)(b) of the Regulations must take the form of a "/".

Method of generating a sub-reference in respect of a relevant payment

5. The sub-reference required by regulation 67CA(1)(c) and (3) of the Regulations must take the form of:

(a) the "/" required by paragraph 4, followed by

(b) a random three character string formed from the following characters:

(i) upper case A - Z,

(ii) 0-9,

(iii) full stop,

(iv) hyphen, and

(v) "/".

Manner of notification to a service provider

6. The combined notification and sub-reference described in paragraph 5 must be notified to the service provider in the place in the service provider's payment instruction indicated by the service provider.

Interpretation

7. In this direction:

"approved method of electronic communications" means any method of electronic communications which has been approved for the purposes of regulation 199 of the Regulations,

"relevant payment" has the meaning given in regulation 4 of the Regulations,

"service provider" has the meaning given in regulation 67CA(4) of the Regulations,

"SHA 256 algorithm software" has the meaning given by the National Institute of Standards and Technology in Federal Information Processing Standards Publication Secure Hash Standard (SHS) [Information Technology Laboratory, National Institute of Standards and Technology, Gaithersburg, MD 20899-8900, United States of America, October 2008, FIPS PUB 180-3], and

"the Regulations" means the Income Tax (Pay As You Earn) Regulations 2003.

Amendments—[1] Reg 67CA inserted by the Income Tax (Pay As You Earn) (Amendment No 2) Regulations, SI 2012/1895 reg 2 with effect in relation to relevant payments made on and after 1 September 2012. "Relevant payments" has the meaning given in reg 4 of these Regulations (SI 2012/1895 reg 1(3)).

67D [Exceptions to regulation 67B

(1) This regulation applies to—

(*a*) an individual who is a practising member of a religious society or order whose beliefs are incompatible with the use of electronic communications,

(*b*) a partnership, if all the partners fall within sub-paragraph (*a*),

(*c*) a company, if all the directors and the company secretary fall within sub-paragraph (*a*), . . . [2]

(*d*) a care and support employer[, and

(*e*) an employer to whom a direction has been given under paragraph (11)][2] [,

but this is subject to paragraph (2B).][3]

(2) A Real Time Information employer to whom this regulation applies may proceed in accordance this regulation instead of regulation 67B.

[(2A) Before 6th April 2014, a Real Time Information employer to whom this regulation applies may proceed as if the employer were a non-Real Time Information employer and the provisions of these Regulations apply accordingly to such an employer.][2]
[(2B) This regulation does not apply if a Real Time Information employer within paragraph (1) makes a return using an approved method of electronic communications.][3]
(3) [On and after 6th April 2014, a][2] Real Time Information employer must deliver to HMRC the information specified in Schedule A1 in respect of each employee to whom relevant payments are made in a tax [quarter][3] unless the employer is not required by regulation 66 (deductions working sheets) to maintain a deductions working sheet for any employees and, for the purposes of this regulation, references in Schedule A1 to a relevant payment shall be read as if they were references to all the relevant payments made to the employee in the tax [quarter][3].
(4) The information must be included in a return.
(5) The return required under paragraph (4) must be delivered within 14 days after the end of the tax [quarter][3] the return relates to.
(6) If relevant payments have been made to more than one employee in the tax [quarter][3], the return under paragraph (4) must include the information required by Schedule A1 in respect of each employee to whom a relevant payment has been made.
(7) . . . [2]
(8) . . . [2]
(9) In paragraph (1)(*c*), "company" means a body corporate or unincorporated association but does not include a partnership.
(10) In paragraph (1)(*d*), "a care and support employer" means an individual ("the employer") who employs a person to provide domestic or personal services at or from the employer's home where—

(*a*) the services are provided to the employer or a member of the employer's family,
(*b*) the recipient of the services has a physical or mental disability, or is elderly or infirm, and
(*c*) it is the employer who delivers the return (and not some other person on the employer's behalf).

[(11) Where the Commissioners for Her Majesty's Revenue and Customs are satisfied that—

(*a*) it is not reasonably practicable for an employer to make a return using an approved method of electronic communication, and
(*b*) it is the employer who delivers the return (and not some other person on the employer's behalf)

they may make a direction specifying that the employer is not required to make a return using an approved method of electronic communication.][2]][1]

Commentary—*Simon's Taxes* **E4.11114A.**

Cross-references—Income Tax (Pay As You Earn) (Amendment) Regulations, SI 2012/822 regs 53–57 (transitional provisions on introduction of real time information).

Amendments—[1] Regs 67B–67H inserted by the Income Tax (Pay As You Earn) (Amendment) Regulations, SI 2012/822 regs 2, 27 with effect from 6 April 2012.

[2] In para (1), word "and" in sub-para (*c*) revoked, para (*e*) and preceding word "and" inserted, paras (2A), (11) inserted; in para (3) words substituted for word "A"; and paras (7), (8) revoked; by the Income Tax (Pay As You Earn) (Amendment) Regulations, SI 2013/521 regs 2, 21 with effect from 6 April 2013 in relation to the tax year 2013–14 and subsequent tax years.

[3] In para (1)(*e*), words inserted, whole of para (2B) inserted, and in paras (3), (5), (6) word substituted for word "month", by the Income Tax (Pay As You Earn) and the Income Tax (Construction Industry Scheme) (Amendment) Regulations, SI 2014/472 regs 2, 5 with effect from 6 April 2014.

67E [Returns under regulations 67B and 67D: amendments

(1) This regulation applies where [there is an inaccuracy in a return][3] made under regulation 67B (real time returns of information about relevant payments) or 67D (exceptions to regulation 67B)[, whether careless or deliberate,][3] and paragraph (2), (3) or (4) applies.
(2) This paragraph applies where the [inaccuracy][3] relates to the information given in the return in respect of an employee under paragraph 16 or 17 of Schedule A1 (real time returns).
(3) This paragraph applies where the [inaccuracy][3] was the omission of details of a relevant payment to an employee.
(4) This paragraph applies where the [inaccuracy][3] arises because, as a result of a retrospective tax provision, the total amount of the relevant payments made by an employer to an employee increases for any tax year in which the employer was a Real Time Information employer.
[(5) Where an employer becomes aware of an inaccuracy in a return submitted under regulation 67B or 67D, the employer must provide the correct information in the next return for the tax year in question.][3]
(6) But if the information has not been corrected before 20th April following the end of the tax year in question, the employer must make a return under this paragraph.
(7) A return under paragraph (6)—

(*a*) must include the following—

(i) the information specified in paragraphs 2 to 4, 8 to [13, 15 and 22A][2] of Schedule A1,
(ii) . . . [2]

(iii) the value of the adjustment to the information given under paragraphs 16 or 17 of Schedule A1 in the final return under regulation 67B or 67D containing information in respect of the employee in the tax year in question,

[(iv) the tax code used by the employer in respect of the employee in the tax year in question and,][2]

(v) if paragraph (8) applies, the information specified in paragraphs 36 to [43][2] of Schedule A1,

(*b*) must be made as soon as reasonably practicable after the [employer becomes aware of the inaccuracy][3], and

(*c*) must be made by an approved method of electronic communications.

(8) This paragraph applies if—

(*a*) the [inaccuracy][3] is within paragraph (3),

(*b*) the relevant payment was the first relevant payment to the employee in the employment, and

(*c*) the information specified in paragraphs 36 to [43][2] of Schedule A1 has not otherwise been provided.

(9) In the application of paragraphs (6) and (7) to cases within paragraph (3), if no information was given in any returns under regulation 67B or 67D in respect of the employee in the tax year, the value of the adjustments required must be calculated as if there was a final return containing information for the employee in the year and the figure requiring adjustment was zero.

(10) Paragraph (7)(c) does not apply if the employer is one to whom regulation 67D applies.][1]

Commentary—*Simon's Taxes* **E4.11114C.**

Amendments—[1] Regs 67B–67H inserted by the Income Tax (Pay As You Earn) (Amendment) Regulations, SI 2012/822 regs 2, 27 with effect from 6 April 2012.

[2] In para (7), in sub-para (*a*)(i) words substituted for words "13 and 15", sub-para (*a*)(ii) revoked, sub-para (*a*)(iv) substituted, and in sub-paras (*a*)(v), (*c*) figure substituted for figure "44", by the Income Tax (Pay As You Earn) (Amendment) Regulations, SI 2013/521 regs 2, 22 with effect from 6 April 2013 in relation to the tax year 2013–14 and subsequent tax years.

[3] In para (1), words substituted for words "an employer discovers an error in a return", and words inserted, in paras (2), (3), (4), (8)(*a*), word substituted for word "error", para (5) substituted, and in para (7)(*b*), words substituted for words "discovery of the error", by the Income Tax (Pay As You Earn) and the Income Tax (Construction Industry Scheme) (Amendment) Regulations, SI 2014/472 regs 2, 6 with effect from 6 April 2014.

[67EA Failure to make a return under regulation 67B or 67D

(1) This regulation applies where an employer does not make a return as required by regulation 67B (real time returns of information about relevant payments) or 67D (exceptions to regulation 67B).

(2) The employer must provide the information in the next return made under regulation 67B or 67D for the tax year in question.

(3) If the information has not been provided before 20th April following the end of the tax year in question, the employer must make a return under this paragraph.

(4) A return under paragraph (3) must—

(a) include the information specified in Schedule A1,

(b) be made as soon as reasonably practicable after the discovery of the failure to make the return, and

(c) be made using an approved method of electronic communications.

(5) If a return under paragraph (3) is not made before 20th May following the end of the tax year in question section 98A of TMA 1970 (special penalties in case of certain returns) will apply to the return[, but this paragraph does not apply to a return in respect of the tax year 2014–15 or a subsequent tax year][2].][1]

Commentary—*Simon's Taxes* **E4.11114CA.**

Amendments—[1] Reg 67EA inserted by the Income Tax (Pay As You Earn) (Amendment) Regulations, SI 2013/521 regs 2, 23 with effect from 6 April 2013 in relation to the tax year 2013–14 and subsequent tax years

[2] Word in para (5) inserted by the Finance Act 2009, Schedule 55 (Penalties for failure to make returns) (Appointed Days and Consequential Provision) Order, SI 2014/2395 art 3.

67F [Additional information about payments

(1) A Real Time Information employer may send to HMRC a notification if—

(*a*) for a tax period, the employer was not required to make any returns in accordance with regulation 67B or 67D because no relevant payments were made during the tax period, or

(*b*) the employer has sent the final return under regulation 67B or 67D that the employer expects to make—

(i) in the circumstances described in paragraph 5 of Schedule A1 (real time returns), or

(ii) for the tax year.

(2) A notification under paragraph (1)(*b*) must—

(*a*) . . . [3]

(*b*) be sent within 14 days of the end of final tax period of the tax year,

[(*c*) the notification is under paragraph (1)(*b*)(i), include the date on which the PAYE scheme ceased.][2]

(3) A notification under this regulation must—

(*a*) state—

(i) the tax year to which it relates,

(ii) the employer's HMRC office number,

(iii) the employer's PAYE reference, and

(iv) the employer's accounts office reference, and

(*b*) be sent using an approved method of electronic communications unless the employer is one to whom regulation 67D applies.

[(4) This regulation applies in addition to the provisions set out in regulation 147D (duty to report amount of apprenticeship levy to be paid).][4]][1]

Commentary—*Simon's Taxes* **E4.11114D.**

Amendments—[1] Regs 67B–67H inserted by the Income Tax (Pay As You Earn) (Amendment) Regulations, SI 2012/822 regs 2, 27 with effect from 6 April 2012.

[2] Para (2)(*c*) inserted by the Income Tax (Pay As You Earn) (Amendment) Regulations, SI 2013/521 regs 2, 24 with effect from 6 April 2013 in relation to the tax year 2013–14 and subsequent tax years. Publisher's Note: it is submitted that the word "if" has erroneously been omitted from the beginning of the inserted para (2)(*c*).

[3] Para (2)(*a*) revoked by the Income Tax (Pay As You Earn) (Amendment) Regulations, SI 2015/2 reg 2(1), (5) with effect in relation to returns filed on or after 6 March 2015.

[4] Para (4) inserted by the Income Tax (Pay As You Earn) (Amendment) Regulations, SI 2017/414 reg 2(1), (4) with effect from 6 April 2017.

[PAYMENT AND RECOVERY OF TAX BY EMPLOYER

67G Payments to and recoveries from HMRC for each tax period by Real Time Information employers

(1) For each tax period, a Real Time Information employer must pay to, or may recover from, HMRC the amount arrived at under the formula in paragraph (4).

(2) If the amount arrived at under the formula in paragraph (4) is a positive amount, the employer must pay the excess to HMRC.

(3) If the amount arrived at under the formula in paragraph (4) is a negative amount, the employer may recover that amount either—

(*a*) by deducting it from the amount which the employer is liable to pay under paragraph (2) for a later period in the tax year, or

(*b*) from the Commissioners for Her Majesty's Revenue and Customs.

[(3A) Where a return for a tax period contains a correction under regulation 67E(5) (returns under regulations 67B and 67D: amendments)) and paragraph (3) of this regulation applies, the negative amount is treated as having been paid to HMRC—

(*a*) 17 days after the end of the tax period in respect of which that return is delivered, where payment is made using an approved method of electronic communications, or

(*b*) 14 days after the end of the tax period in respect of which that return is delivered, in any other case.][3]

(4) The formula in this paragraph is A–B, where—

A is the sum total of the relevant amounts for each of the employer's employees, and

B is amount A for the previous tax period in the tax year, if any.

(5) For the purposes of paragraph (4), a "relevant amount" is the amount shown under paragraph 17 of Schedule A1 (real time returns) for an employee in the most recent return made in the tax year by the employer under regulation 67B (real time returns of information about relevant payments) or 67D (exceptions to regulation 67B) which contains information about that employee.

[(5A) If the employer makes a return under regulation 67EA(3) (failure to make a return under regulation 67B or 67D) a "relevant amount" for the purposes of paragraph (4) is the amount shown under paragraph 17 of Schedule A1 (real time returns) for an employee in that return for the tax year to which that return relates.][2]

(6) In paragraph (5) "the most recent return" means the return which, as at the end of the tax period, contains the most up to date information under paragraph 17 of Schedule A1 about the employee.

(7) This regulation is subject to regulations 67H (payments to and recoveries from HMRC for each tax period by Real Time Information employers: returns under regulation 67E(6)), 71 (modification of regulations 67G and 68 in case of trade dispute) and 75B (certificates under regulation 75A: excess payments).][1]

Commentary—*Simon's Taxes* **E4.11114F.**

Amendments—[1] Regs 67B–67H inserted by the Income Tax (Pay As You Earn) (Amendment) Regulations, SI 2012/822 regs 2, 27 with effect from 6 April 2012.

[2] Para (5A) inserted by the Income Tax (Pay As You Earn) (Amendment) Regulations, SI 2013/521 regs 2, 25 with effect from 6 April 2013 in relation to the tax year 2013–14 and subsequent tax years.

[3] Para (3A) inserted by the Income Tax (Pay As You Earn) (Amendment No 2) Regulations, SI 2014/1017 reg 2(*a*) with effect in relation to amounts due and payable for the tax year 2014–15 and subsequent tax years.

67H [Payments to and recoveries from HMRC for each tax period by Real Time Information employers: returns under regulation 67E(6)

(1) This regulation applies if, during any tax period, an employer makes a return under regulation 67E(6) (returns under regulations 67B and 67D: amendments) other than by virtue of regulation 67E(4).

[(2) If the return shows an adjustment under regulation 67E(7)(a)(iii) and the value of the adjustment is a positive amount, that amount is an amount due to be paid to HMRC for the final tax period of the tax year the return relates to.][2]

(3) [If the return shows such an adjustment and the value of the adjustment is a negative amount, that amount is an amount due to be repaid to the employer for the final tax period of the tax year the return relates to and][2] the employer may recover that amount—

(*a*) by setting it off against the amount the employer is liable to pay under regulation 67G for the tax period the return was made in, or

(*b*) from the Commissioners for Her Majesty's Revenue and Customs.][1]

[(4) Where the value of the adjustment is a negative amount, that amount is treated as having been paid to HMRC—

(*a*) 17 days after the end of the final tax period of the tax year the return relates to, if payment is made using an approved method of electronic communications, or

(*b*) 14 days after the end of the final tax period of the tax year the return relates to, in any other case.][3]

Commentary—*Simon's Taxes* **E4.11114F, E4.11114G.**

Amendments—[1] Regs 67B–67H inserted by the Income Tax (Pay As You Earn) (Amendment) Regulations, SI 2012/822 regs 2, 27 with effect from 6 April 2012.

[2] Para (2) substituted, and in para (3) words substituted for words "if the value of the adjustment required by paragraph (2) is a negative amount", by the Income Tax (Pay As You Earn) (Amendment) Regulations, SI 2013/521 regs 2, 26 with effect from 6 April 2013 in relation to the tax year 2013–14 and subsequent tax years.

[3] Para (4) inserted by the Income Tax (Pay As You Earn) (Amendment No 2) Regulations, SI 2014/1017 reg 2(*b*) with effect in relation to amounts due and payable for the tax year 2014–15 and subsequent tax years.

[Penalties under Schedule 55 to the Finance Act 2009

67I Penalty: failure to comply with regulation 67B or 67D

(1) For the purposes of paragraph 6C of Schedule 55 to the Finance Act 2009 (amount of penalty: real time information for PAYE), a Real Time Information employer which fails to deliver a return falling within item 4 in the Table in paragraph 1 of that Schedule in accordance with—

(*a*) regulation 67B (real time returns of information about relevant payments);

(*b*) regulation 67BA (employees in respect of whom employer is not required to maintain a deductions working sheet);

(*c*) regulation 67BB (employees paid in specific circumstances);

(*d*) regulation 67C (modification of the requirements of regulation 67B: notional payments); or

(*e*) regulation 67D (exceptions to regulation 67B) as the case may be, is liable to a penalty of the amount set out in paragraph (2).

(2) Where a Real Time Information employer fails to deliver such a return and the number of persons employed in the period to which the return relates is—

(*a*) no more than 9, the penalty is £100;

(*b*) at least 10 but no more than 49, the penalty is £200;

(*c*) at least 50 but no more than 249, the penalty is £300; and

(*d*) at least 250, the penalty is £400.][1]

Commentary—*Simon's Taxes* **E4.11119, A4.554**

Definitions—"Real time information employer", "large existing real time information employer", "small existing real time information employer", "new real time information employer": see SI 2014/2396 reg 1(3).

"Relevant payments": see reg 4.

Press releases etc—HMRC press release, 9 September 2014: HMRC delays PAYE late filing penalties for small employers (see *SWTI 2014, Issue 37*).

Amendments—[1] Regs 67I–67K inserted by the Income Tax (Pay As You Earn) (Amendment No 3) Regulations, SI 2014/2396 reg 2 with effect in relation to a failure to deliver a return to HMRC in relation to relevant payments made—

– on or after 6 October 2014, where the employer is a large existing real time information employer; and

– on or after 6 March 2015 where—

(a) the employer is a small existing real time information employer; or

(b) a person becomes a new real time information employer after 6 October 2014.

[67J Penalty: initial period

For the purposes of paragraph 6C(3), (4) and (5) of Schedule 55 to the Finance Act 2009 (initial period), the duration of the initial period is thirty days.][1]

Commentary—*Simon's Taxes* **E4.11119, A4.554**

Amendments—[1] Regs 67I–67K inserted by the Income Tax (Pay As You Earn) (Amendment No 3) Regulations, SI 2014/2396 reg 2 with effect in relation to a failure to deliver a return to HMRC in relation to relevant payments made—

– on or after 6 October 2014, where the employer is a large existing real time information employer; and

– on or after 6 March 2015 where—

(a) the employer is a small existing real time information employer; or

(b) a person becomes a new real time information employer after 6 October 2014.

[67K Penalty: first failure to deliver a return in a tax year

(1) Paragraph 6C(4) of Schedule 55 to the Finance Act 2009 (unpenalised default) does not apply to any failure to deliver a return falling within item 4 in the Table in paragraph 1 of that Schedule in accordance with regulation 67B, regulation 67BA, regulation 67BB, regulation 67C or regulation 67D, as the case may be,—

(*a*) by a small existing Real Time Information employer or a new Real Time Information employer in the period 6 March 2015 to 5 April 2015; or

(*b*) for any tax year for which a Real Time Information employer operates an annual PAYE Scheme.

(2) For the purposes of paragraph (1)(*a*)—

(*a*) an employer is a small existing Real Time Information employer if at 6th October 2014 that employer employed no more than 49 employees; and

(*b*) an employer is a new Real Time Information employer if it is issued with an employer's PAYE reference after 6th October 2014.

(3) For the purposes of paragraph (1)(*b*), a Real Time Information employer operates an annual PAYE Scheme for a tax year if for that year—

(*a*) all the employees are paid annually;

(*b*) all the employees are paid on the same date; and

(*c*) the Real Time Information employer is only required under regulation 69 (due date and receipts for payment of tax) to pay HMRC annually.][1]

Commentary—*Simon's Taxes* **E4.11119, A4.554**

Definitions—"Real time information employer", "large existing real time information employer", "small existing real time information employer", "new real time information employer": see SI 2014/2396 reg 1(3).

"Relevant payments": see reg 4.

Amendments—[1] Regs 67I–67K inserted by the Income Tax (Pay As You Earn) (Amendment No 3) Regulations, SI 2014/2396 reg 2 with effect in relation to a failure to deliver a return to HMRC in relation to relevant payments made—

– on or after 6 October 2014, where the employer is a large existing real time information employer; and

– on or after 6 March 2015 where—

(a) the employer is a small existing real time information employer; or

(b) a person becomes a new real time information employer after 6 October 2014.

68 [Periodic payments to and recoveries from HMRC: non-Real Time Information employers]

(1) This regulation applies to determine how much [a non-Real Time Information employer][2] must pay or can recover for a tax period.

(2) If A exceeds B, the employer must pay the excess to the Inland Revenue.

(3) But if B exceeds A, the employer may recover the excess either—

(*a*) by deducting it from the amount which the employer is liable to pay under paragraph (2) for a later tax period in the tax year, or

(*b*) from the Board of Inland Revenue.

(4) In this Regulation—

A is—

(*a*) the total amount of tax which the employer was liable to deduct from relevant payments made by the employer in the tax period, plus

(*b*) the total amount of tax for which the employer was liable to account in respect of notional payments made [or treated by virtue of a retrospective tax provision as made,][1] by the employer in that period under regulation 62(5) (notional payments);

B is the total amount which the employer was liable to repay in the tax period.

(5) Paragraphs (2) and (3) are subject to regulation 71 (modification in case of trade disputes).

(6) Paragraph (2) is also subject to regulation 78(11) (entitlement to set off excess payments).

[(7) In the application of paragraph (4) to notional payments arising by reason of the coming into force of the Finance Act 2006, the reference to section 710(7A)(*a*) of ITEPA 2003 shall be modified as mentioned in section 94(5)(*c*) of the Finance Act 2006.][1]

Commentary—*Simon's Taxes* **E4.11115.**

Derivation—The Income Tax (Employments) Regulations, SI 1993/744 regs 40, 41(1), (2), 42(6); the Income Tax (Employments) (Notional Payments) Regulations, SI 1994/1212 reg 13(5), (6).

Modifications—See the Income Tax (PAYE) Regulations, SI 2003/2682 reg 71 (modification of this regulation in case of trade dispute).

SI 2003/2682 reg 174 (modification of this regulation in its application to payments of taxable incapacity benefit).

SI 2003/2682 Sch 1 para 15 (for the purposes of giving effect to any enactment or instrument which refers to an amount which is, or would in certain circumstances be, payable to the collector, para (2) above has effect as if that paragraph required payment of the amount to which it refers to the collector).

Amendments—[1] Words in para (4), and whole of para (7), inserted, by the Income Tax (Pay as You Earn) (Amendment) Regulations, SI 2007/1077 regs 2, 12 with effect from 6 April 2007.

[2] Cross heading which formerly preceded reg 68 omitted, heading substituted, and words in para (1) substituted by the Income Tax (Pay As You Earn) (Amendment) Regulations, SI 2012/822 regs 2, 27, 28, 29 with effect from 6 April 2012.

69 Due date and receipts for payment of tax

(1) An employer must pay amounts due under regulation [67G(2)[, as adjusted by regulation 67H(2) where appropriate,][3] or][2] 68(2)—

(*a*) within 17 days after the end of the tax period, where payment is made by an approved method of electronic communications, or

(*b*) within 14 days after the end of the tax period, in any other case.

[(1A) In paragraph (1), the reference to amounts due under regulation 67G(2) includes any amount the employer was liable to deduct from employees during the tax period whether or not that amount was included in any return under regulation 67B (real time returns of information about relevant payments) or 67D (exceptions to regulation 67B).][4]

(2) The Inland Revenue must give a receipt to the employer for the total amount paid under regulation [67G(2)[, as adjusted by regulation 67H(2) where appropriate,][3] or][2] 68(2) if asked.

(3) But no separate receipt for tax only need be given if a receipt is given for the total amount of tax and any earnings-related contributions (as defined by regulation 1(2) of [the SSC Regulations][1]) paid at the same time.

[(4) In paragraph (1) "the tax period", in relation to an amount of retrospective employment income, means the tax period immediately following the relevant time.][1]

Commentary—*Simon's Taxes* **E4.11115, E4.11154.**

Derivation—The Income Tax (Employments) Regulations, SI 1993/744 regs 2(1), 40(1), 41(1), 42(1).

Modifications—See the Income Tax (PAYE) Regulations, SI 2003/2682 reg 174 (modification of this regulation in its application to payments of taxable incapacity benefit).

SI 2003/2682 Sch 1 para 18 (modification of this regulation in so far as the provisions apply in relation to tax periods ending before 6 April 2004).

Cross references—See the Income Tax (PAYE) Regulations, SI 2003/2682 reg 219 (for the purposes of this regulation, if payment to the Revenue is made by cheque, and cheque paid on its first presentation to the banker on whom drawn, the payment is treated as made on day cheque received by the Revenue).

Amendments—[1] Words in para (3) substituted, and para (4) inserted, by the Income Tax (Pay as You Earn) (Amendment) Regulations, SI 2007/1077 regs 2, 13 with effect from 6 April 2007.

[2] Words in paras (1), (2) inserted by the Income Tax (Pay As You Earn) (Amendment) Regulations, SI 2012/822 regs 2, 30 with effect from 6 April 2012.

[3] In paras (1), (2), words inserted by the Income Tax (Pay As You Earn) (Amendment) Regulations, SI 2013/521 regs 2, 27 with effect from 6 April 2013 in relation to the tax year 2013–14 and subsequent tax years.

[4] Para (1A) inserted by the Income Tax (Pay As You Earn) (Amendment No 2) Regulations, SI 2014/1017 reg 2(*c*) with effect in relation to amounts due and payable for the tax year 2014–15 and subsequent tax years.

[69A Circumstances in which payment of a lesser amount is to be treated as payment in full for the purposes of paragraph 6(2) of Schedule 56 to the Finance Act 2009

(1) A payment that is less than the full amount due under regulation 67G(2) (payments to and recoveries from HMRC for each tax period), as adjusted by regulation 67H (payments due and recoveries from HMRC for each tax period: returns under regulation 67E(6)) where appropriate, will for the purposes of paragraph 6(2) of Schedule 56 to the Finance Act 2009 (amount of penalty: PAYE and CIS) be treated as payment of the full amount if the difference between the full amount and the amount paid is no more than £100 ("the tolerance"), but this is subject to paragraphs (2) and (3).

(2) Paragraph (1) does not apply where—

(*a*) the payment relates to a return which is correcting information given in a return filed in respect of a relevant payment made in an earlier tax month, and

(*b*) the return is delivered after 19th April following the end of the tax year in question.

(3) If the total sum paid by the employer to HMRC for the tax period includes not only the amount due under regulation 67G(2), as adjusted by regulation 67H where appropriate, but also one or more of—

(*a*) any earnings-related contributions (as defined by regulation 1(2) of the SSC Regulations 2001),

(*b*) any payment under regulation 7(1) of the Income Tax (Construction Industry Scheme) Regulations 2005, or

(*c*) any repayment due under the Student Loans Regulations,

the tolerance is applied to the total sum paid to HMRC for the tax period to which the payments relate.][1]

Amendments—[1] Regulation 69A inserted by the Income Tax (Pay As You Earn) and the Income Tax (Construction Industry Scheme) (Amendment) Regulations, SI 2014/472 regs 2, 7 with effect in relation to a payment made in relation to the tax year 2014–15 and subsequent tax years.

70 Quarterly tax periods

(1) This regulation applies, so that the tax period is a tax quarter, if an employer—

(*a*) has reasonable grounds for believing that the average monthly amount will be less than £1,500, and

(*b*) chooses to pay tax quarterly.

[(1A) But this regulation does not apply, so that the tax period remains a month, in respect of amounts of retrospective employment income.][2]

(2) "The average monthly amount" is the average, for tax months falling within the current tax year, of the amounts found by the formula—

$$[(P + N + L + S) - (SP + CD)]^{1}$$

(3) In paragraph (2)—

P is the amount which would be payable to the Inland Revenue under regulation [67G[, as adjusted by regulation 67H(2) where appropriate,][7] or][5] 68 [but disregarding any amount payable in respect of retrospective employment income][2] . . . [1];

N is the amount which would be payable to the Inland Revenue under the SSCBA and the SSC Regulations disregarding—

(*a*) any amount of secondary Class 1 contributions in respect of which liability has been transferred to the employed earner by an election made jointly by the employed earner and the secondary contributor for the purposes of paragraph 3B(1) of Schedule 1 to the SSCBA (transfer of liability to be borne by earner); . . . [1]

[(*aa*) any amount payable under retrospective contributions regulations (see paragraph 1(2) of Schedule 4 to the SSC Regulations) in respect of retrospective earnings (within the meaning of those Regulations);][2]

(*b*) . . . [1]

L is the amount which would be payable to the Inland Revenue under regulation [54(1) or, in Northern Ireland, 49(1)][6] of the Student Loans Regulations (payment of repayments deducted to the Inland Revenue) disregarding—

(*a*) the reduction referred to in paragraph (3) of [those regulations][6], . . . [1]

(*b*) . . . [1]

S is the amount which would be payable by the employer to the Inland Revenue under sections 559 and 559A of ICTA (deduction on account of tax etc from payments to certain sub-contractors) and regulation 8 of the Income Tax (Sub-contractors in the Construction Industry) Regulations 1993 . . . [1];

. . . [1]

SP is the amount which would be payable by the employer to employees by way of statutory sick pay, statutory maternity pay, [statutory paternity pay][7][, statutory shared parental pay][7] and statutory adoption pay under the SSCBA; and

CD is—

(*a*) if the employer is a company, the amount which others would deduct from payments to it, in its position as a sub-contractor, under section 559 of ICTA (deduction on account of tax etc from payments to certain sub-contractors);

(*b*) in any other case, nil.

(4) In this regulation—

"employed earner" has the same meaning as in the SSCBA;

"SSCBA" means the Social Security Contributions and Benefits Act 1992 or, in Northern Ireland, the Social Security Contribution and Benefits (Northern Ireland) Act 1992;

. . . [3]

. . . [1]

Commentary—*Simon's Taxes* **E4.1115**.

Derivation—The Income Tax (Employments) Regulations, SI 1993/744 regs 2(1), 41(1), (3).

Modifications—See the Income Tax (PAYE) Regulations, SI 2003/2682 reg 174 (modification of this regulation in its application to payments of taxable incapacity benefit).

Amendments—[1] Formula in para (2) substituted, words in para (3) revoked, and definitions of "WTC adjustment" and "WTC Regulations" in para (4) revoked, by the Income Tax (PAYE, etc), (Amendment) Regulations, SI 2006/777 regs 2, 3 with effect from 6 April 2006.

[2] In para (3), words in definition of "P", and sub-para (*aa*) in definition of "N", inserted, by the Income Tax (Pay as You Earn) (Amendment) Regulations, SI 2007/1077 regs 2, 14 with effect from 6 April 2007.

[3] In para (4), definitions of "SSC Regulations" and "Student Loan Regulations" revoked, by the Income Tax (Pay As You Earn) (Amendment) Regulations, SI 2008/782 regs 2, 5 with effect from 6 April 2008.

[4] In para (3), in the value for "SP", words substituted for words "statutory paternity pay" by the Income Tax (Pay As You Earn) (Amendment No 2) Regulations, SI 2010/2496 regs 2, 3 with effect from 14 November 2010.

[5] In para (3), in definition of "P", words inserted by the Income Tax (Pay As You Earn) (Amendment) Regulations, SI 2012/822 regs 2, 31 with effect from 6 April 2012.

[6] In para (3), in definition of "L", words substituted by the Income Tax (Pay As You Earn) (Amendment) Regulations, SI 2012/822 regs 2, 63 with effect from 6 April 2012.

[7] In para (3), words inserted by the Income Tax (Pay As You Earn) (Amendment) Regulations, SI 2013/521 regs 2, 28 with effect from 6 April 2013 in relation to the tax year 2013–14 and subsequent tax years.

[8] In para (3), words substituted and inserted by the Statutory Payment Schemes (Electronic Communications) (Amendment) Regulations, SI 2015/125 reg 3 with effect from 5 April 2015..

71 Modification of [regulations 67G and 68] in case of trade dispute

(1) This regulation modifies the amount payable or recoverable by an employer under [regulations 67G and 68][1] in cases where regulation 64 (trade disputes) applies—

(*a*) by providing for the amount which would otherwise be payable by the employer for a tax period to be reduced by an amount of repayments ("R") that cannot be made to employees in the tax period, and

(*b*) by providing—

(i) for amounts which would otherwise be payable in later tax periods to be increased, or

(ii) for amounts which would otherwise be recoverable in later tax periods to be reduced,

by a total of R.

(2) This regulation applies for consecutive tax periods—

(*a*) starting with the first tax period at the end of which there is an amount calculated as due to be repaid but which is required to be withheld by regulation 64(5) (tax to be withheld during strike action), and

(*b*) ending with the next tax period at the end of which no amount is required to be withheld by that regulation.

(3) Column 3 of Table 3 shows the amount payable under regulation [67G(2)[, as adjusted by regulation 67H(2) where appropriate,][2] or, as the case may be,][1] 68(2) in the cases set out in column 2 for the first and subsequent tax periods.

TABLE 3

MODIFIED AMOUNT PAYABLE UNDER REGULATION [67G or,] 68

1 Tax period	*2 Case*	*3 Amount payable*
First tax period	if B equals or exceeds A	nil
First tax period	any other case	A – B, reduced by P (or by so much of P as reduces the amount payable to nil)
Subsequent tax periods	if B equals or exceeds (A + Q)	nil
Subsequent tax periods	any other case	(A + Q) – B, reduced by P (or by so much of P as reduces the amount payable to nil).

(4) The amount (if any) recoverable under regulation [67G[, as adjusted by regulation 67H(2) where appropriate,][2] or, as the case may be,][1] 68(3) must be reduced to the extent that it includes amounts—

(*a*) for which reduction was made under paragraph (3) in an earlier tax period, or

(*b*) which are otherwise being recovered.

(5) In this regulation—

A is—

(*a*) the total amount of tax which the employer was liable to deduct from relevant payments made by the employer in the tax period, plus

(*b*) the total amount of tax for which the employer was liable to account in respect of notional payments made by the employer in that period under regulation 62(5) (notional payments);

B is the total amount which the employer is liable to repay in the tax period, not including any amounts—

(*a*) for which a reduction was made under paragraph (3) in an earlier tax period; or

(*b*) which are being recovered under paragraph (4);

P is the total of amounts calculated as due to be repaid in the tax period but required to be withheld during that tax period by regulation 64(5);

Q is the total of amounts—

(*a*) which, because of regulation 64(5)(*b*), are set off against tax due to be deducted in the tax period, and

(*b*) which also, under paragraph (3), have reduced the amount payable in an earlier tax period.

Commentary—*Simon's Taxes* **E4.11115.**

Derivation—The Income Tax (Employments) Regulations, SI 1993/744 regs 40(2), 41(2), 42(6); the Income Tax (Employments) (Notional Payments) Regulations, SI 1994/1212 reg 13(5), (6).

Cross references—See the Income Tax (PAYE) Regulations, SI 2003/2682 reg 11 (this regulation not to apply to pension payers or pensioners in their capacity as such).

Amendments—[1] Words in heading substituted, words in para (1) substituted, and words in paras (3), (4) inserted, by the Income Tax (Pay As You Earn) (Amendment) Regulations, SI 2012/822 regs 2, 32, 33 with effect from 6 April 2012.

[2] In paras (3), (4), words inserted by the Income Tax (Pay As You Earn) (Amendment) Regulations, SI 2013/521 regs 2, 29 with effect from 6 April 2013 in relation to the tax year 2013–14 and subsequent tax years.

72 Recovery from employee of tax not deducted by employer

(1) This regulation applies if—

(*a*) it appears to the Inland Revenue that the deductible amount exceeds the amount actually deducted, and

(*b*) condition A or B is met.

(2) In this regulation [and regulations 72A and 72B][1]

"the deductible amount" is the amount which an employer was liable to deduct from relevant payments made to an employee in a tax period;

"the amount actually deducted" is the amount actually deducted by the employer from relevant payments made to that employee during that tax period;

"the excess" means the amount by which the deductible amount exceeds the amount actually deducted.

(3) Condition A is that the employer satisfies the Inland Revenue—

(*a*) that the employer took reasonable care to comply with these Regulations, and

(*b*) that the failure to deduct the excess was due to an error made in good faith.

(4) Condition B is that the Inland Revenue are of the opinion that the employee has received relevant payments knowing that the employer wilfully failed to deduct the amount of tax which should have been deducted from those payments.

(5) The Inland Revenue may direct that the employer is not liable to pay the excess to the Inland Revenue.

[(5A) Any direction under paragraph (5) must be made by notice ("the direction notice"), stating the date the notice was issued, to—

(*a*) the employer and the employee if condition A is met;

(*b*) the employee if condition B is met.][1]

[(5B) A notice need not be issued to the employee under paragraph (5A)(*a*) if neither the Inland Revenue nor the employer are aware of the employee's address or last known address.][1]

(6) If a direction is made, the excess must not be added under regulation 185(5) or 188(3)(*a*) (adjustments to total net tax deducted for self-assessments and other assessments) in relation to the employee.

(7) If condition B is met, tax payable by an employee as a result of a direction carries interest, as if it were unpaid tax due from an employer, in accordance with [section 101 of the Finance Act 2009][2]).

(8) . . . [2]

Commentary—*Simon's Taxes* **E4.11117.**

Derivation—The Income Tax (Employments) Regulations, SI 1993/744 regs 42(2), (3), (4), 101(6), 101A(2); the Income Tax (Employments) Regulations, SI 1994/1212 reg 13(7).

Modifications—See the Income Tax (PAYE) Regulations, SI 2003/2682 reg 174 (modification of this regulation in its application to payments of taxable incapacity benefit).

Cross references—See the Income Tax (PAYE) Regulations, SI 2003/2682 reg 218(3), (4) (a certificate of the Inland Revenue that, to the best of their knowledge and belief, any amount of interest payable under para (7) above has not been paid by an employer or employee, is sufficient evidence that the amount mentioned in the certificate is unpaid and due to the Crown).

SI 2003/2682 reg 219 (for the purposes of this regulation, if payment to the Revenue is made by cheque, and cheque paid on its first presentation to the banker on whom drawn, the payment is treated as made on day cheque received by the Revenue).

Amendments—[1] Words in para (2) inserted, and paras (5A), (5B) inserted, by the IT (PAYE) (Amendment) Regulations, SI 2004/851 regs 2, 3 with effect from 12 April 2004.

[2] Words in para (7) substituted, and para (8) revoked by the Finance Act 2009, Sections 101 and 102 (Interest on Late Payments and Repayments), Appointed Days and Consequential Provisions Order, SI 2014/992 art 9(1), (3) with effect in relation to payments due and payable in respect of the tax year 2014–15 and subsequent tax years.

72A [Employer's request for a direction and appeal against refusal

(1) In relation to condition A in regulation 72(3), the employer may by notice to the Inland Revenue ("the notice of request") request that the Inland Revenue make a direction under regulation 72(5).

(2) The notice of request must—

(*a*) state—

(i) how the employer took reasonable care to comply with these Regulations; and

(ii) how the error resulting in the failure to deduct the excess occurred;

(*b*) specify the relevant payments to which the request relates;

(*c*) specify the employee or employees to whom those relevant payments were made; and

(*d*) state the excess in relation to each employee.

(3) The Inland Revenue may refuse the employer's request under paragraph (1) by notice to the employer ("the refusal notice") stating—

(*a*) the grounds for the refusal, and

(*b*) the date on which the refusal notice was issued.

(4) The employer may appeal against the refusal notice—

(*a*) by notice to the Inland Revenue,

(*b*) within 30 days of the issue of the refusal notice,

(*c*) specifying the grounds of the appeal.

(5) For the purpose of paragraph (4) the grounds of appeal are that—

(*a*) the employer did take reasonable care to comply with these Regulations, and
(*b*) the failure to deduct the excess was due to an error made in good faith.

(6) If on appeal under paragraph (4) [that is notified to the tribunal][2] it appears to the [tribunal][2] that the refusal notice should not have been issued [the tribunal][2] may direct that the Inland Revenue make a direction under regulation 72(5) in an amount the [tribunal determines][2] is the excess for one or more tax periods falling within the relevant tax year.][1]

Commentary—*Simon's Taxes* **E4.11117**.

Amendments—[1] Regulations 72A–72D inserted by the IT (PAYE) (Amendment) Regulations, SI 2004/851 regs 2, 4 with effect from 12 April 2004.

[2] In para (6), words inserted, words substituted by the Transfer of Tribunal Functions and Revenue and Customs Appeals Order, SI 2009/56 art 3, Sch 2 paras 92, 96 with effect from 1 April 2009.

72B [Employee's appeal against a direction notice where condition A is met

(1) An employee may appeal against a direction notice under regulation 72(5A)(*a*)—
(*a*) by notice to the Inland Revenue,
(*b*) within 30 days of the issue of the direction notice,
(*c*) specifying the grounds of the appeal

(2) For the purpose of paragraph (1) the grounds of appeal are that—
(*a*) the employer did not act in good faith,
(*b*) the employer did not take reasonable care, or
(*c*) the excess is incorrect.

(3) On an appeal under paragraph (1) [that is notified to the tribunal, the tribunal][2] may—
(*a*) if it appears . . . [2] that the direction notice should not have been made, set aside the direction notice; or
(*b*) if it appears . . . [2] that the excess specified in the direction notice is incorrect, increase or reduce the excess specified in the notice accordingly.][1]

Commentary—*Simon's Taxes* **E4.11117.**

Amendments—[1] Regulations 72A–72D inserted by the IT (PAYE) (Amendment) Regulations, SI 2004/851 regs 2, 4 with effect from 12 April 2004.

[2] In para (3), words substituted, and words revoked in both places, by the Transfer of Tribunal Functions and Revenue and Customs Appeals Order, SI 2009/56 art 3, Sch 2 paras 92, 97 with effect from 1 April 2009.

72C [Employee's appeal against a direction notice where condition B is met

(1) An employee may appeal against a direction notice under regulation 72(5A)(*b*)—
(*a*) by notice to the Inland Revenue,
(*b*) within 30 days of the issue of the direction notice,
(*c*) specifying the grounds of the appeal.

(2) For the purpose of paragraph (1) the grounds of appeal are that—
(*a*) the employee did not receive the payments knowing that the employer wilfully failed to deduct the amount of tax which should have been deducted from those payments, or
(*b*) the excess is incorrect.

(3) On an appeal under paragraph (1) [that is notified to the tribunal, the tribunal][2] may—
(*a*) if it appears . . . [1] that the direction notice should not have been made, set aside the direction notice; or
(*b*) if it appears . . . [1] that the excess specified in the direction notice is incorrect, increase or reduce the excess specified in the notice accordingly.][1]

Commentary—*Simon's Taxes* **E4.11117**.

Amendments—[1] Regulations 72A–72D inserted by the IT (PAYE) (Amendment) Regulations, SI 2004/851 regs 2, 4 with effect from 12 April 2004.

[2] In para (3), words substituted for words, and words revoked in both places, by the Transfer of Tribunal Functions and Revenue and Customs Appeals Order, SI 2009/56 art 3, Sch 2 paras 92, 98 with effect from 1 April 2009.

72D [Appeals: supplementary provisions

(1) This regulation applies to appeals under regulations 72A(4), 72B, [72C, 72G and 81A][2].

(2), (3) . . . [3]

(4) [This paragraph applies if][3] in respect of the same error by an employer in relation to condition A in regulation 72(3)—
(*a*) more than one employee is appealing under regulation 72B; or
(*b*) there is an appeal by an employer under regulation 72A(4) and by an employee under regulation 72B

. . . [3].

(5)–(7) . . . [3]

[(8) Where paragraph (4) applies or the appeal is material to the liability to tax of the employer and the employee, all the persons concerned are entitled to be parties to the appeal.][3]

(9) . . . [31]

Commentary—*Simon's Taxes* **E4.11117**.

Amendments—[1] Regulations 72A–72D inserted by the IT (PAYE) (Amendment) Regulations, SI 2004/851 regs 2, 4 with effect from 12 April 2004.

2 Words in para (1) substituted by the Income Tax (Pay As You Earn) (Amendment) Regulations, SI 2008/782 regs 2, 6 with effect from 6 April 2008.

3 Paras (2), (3), (5)–(7), (9) revoked, in para (4), words substituted and words revoked, and para (8) substituted, by the Transfer of Tribunal Functions and Revenue and Customs Appeals Order, SI 2009/56 art 3, Sch 2 paras 92, 99 with effect from 1 April 2009.

72E [Conditions where regulation 72F applies

(1) Regulation 72F applies where—

(*a*) [one or more employees have][2] received a relevant payment;

(*b*) it appears to HMRC that an amount intended to represent tax on the payment—

[(i) is likely to have been self-assessed by one or more of the employees, or][2]

(ii) has not been self-assessed, but has been paid under section 59A TMA (payments on account of income tax), section 559A of ICTA (treatment of sums deducted under s 559 (sub-contractors)) or section 62 of the Finance Act 2004 (treatment of sums deducted (sub-contractors));

(*c*) any of conditions A, B and C is met;

(*d*) a trigger event has occurred; and

(*e*) a trigger event did not occur before 6th April 2008.

(2) Condition A is that it appears to HMRC that the amount which the employer was liable to deduct—

(*a*) from the relevant payment; or

(*b*) in the case of a notional payment, from other relevant payments,

exceeds the amount actually deducted.

(3) Condition B is that it appears to HMRC that the amount for which the employer was required to account under regulation 62(5) (notional payments) in respect of the relevant payment exceeds the amount actually accounted for.

(4) Condition C is that—

(*a*) tax on the relevant payment was included in a determination under regulation 80 (determination of unpaid tax and appeal against determination); and

(*b*) the full amount of the determination is not paid within 30 days from the date on which the determination became final and conclusive.

(5) The following are trigger events—

(*a*) HMRC serve notice of a determination under regulation 80 that includes tax on the relevant payment;

(*b*) HMRC receive a return under section 8 of TMA (personal return) which includes a self-assessment which includes tax on the relevant payment as tax treated as deducted;

(*c*) HMRC receive—

(i) an amended return under section 9ZA of TMA (amendment of personal or trustee return by taxpayer), or

(ii) a claim under section 33 of TMA (error or mistake),

which includes tax on the relevant payment as tax treated as deducted;

(*d*) HMRC receive a letter of offer.

(6) In paragraph (5)—

"letter of offer" means an offer in writing by the employer to agree an amount in settlement of the employer's liability to pay an amount that includes tax on the relevant payment;

"tax treated as deducted" has the meaning given by regulation 185(6).

(7) For the purposes of this regulation tax is self-assessed if—

(*a*) it is included in a return under section 8 of TMA which includes a self-assessment; and

(*b*) ignoring any relevant credit, the tax is or would be assessed as payable by way of income tax.

(8) In paragraph (7), "relevant credit" means—

(*a*) a payment made under section 59A of TMA (payments on account of income tax) or 59B (payment of income tax and capital gains tax); or

(*b*) tax deducted at source or tax treated as deducted (within the meaning given by regulation 185(6)).][1]

Amendments—[1] Regulations 72E–72G inserted by the Income Tax (Pay As You Earn) (Amendment) Regulations, SI 2008/782 regs 2, 7 with effect from 6 April 2008.

2 In para (1)(*a*), words substituted for words "an employee has", and para (1)(*b*)(i) substituted, by the Income Tax (Pay As You Earn) and the Income Tax (Construction Industry Scheme) (Amendment) Regulations, SI 2014/472 regs 2, 8 with effect from 6 April 2014.

72F [Recovery from employee of tax that has been self-assessed etc

(1) Where this regulation applies, HMRC may direct that the employer is not liable to pay an amount of tax to them.

(2) The direction may be in respect of one or more amounts that appear to HMRC to fall within regulation 72E(1)(*b*)(i) and (ii).

(3) A direction must be made by notice to both the employer and the employee, stating—

(*a*) the date the notice was issued;

[(*b*) the—

(i) amount (or amounts) within regulation 72E(1)(b) to which it relates, or

(ii) employment in respect of which the relevant payment within regulation 72E(1)(*a*) was received and in respect of which the amount within regulation 72E(1)(*b*)(i) is likely to have been self-assessed, and][2]

(*c*) which of conditions A, B and C in regulation 72E have been met.

(4) A direction may be combined with one or more other directions relating to the same employer and may be made by issuing one notice to the employer, but each employee must be issued with a separate notice.

(5) A notice need not be issued to the employee if neither HMRC nor the employer are aware of the employee's address or last known address.

(6) The amount specified in a notice to the employee must not be added under regulation 185(5) or 188(3)(*a*) (adjustments to total net tax deducted for self-assessments and other assessments) in relation to the employee.][1]

Amendments—[1] Regulations 72E–72G inserted by the Income Tax (Pay As You Earn) (Amendment) Regulations, SI 2008/782 regs 2, 7 with effect from 6 April 2008.

[2] Para (3)(*b*) substituted by the Income Tax (Pay As You Earn) and the Income Tax (Construction Industry Scheme) (Amendment) Regulations, SI 2014/472 regs 2, 9 with effect from 6 April 2014.

72G [Employee's appeal against a direction notice

(1) An employee may appeal against a direction notice under regulation 72F—

(*a*) by notice to HMRC,

(*b*) within 30 days of the issue of the direction notice,

(*c*) specifying the grounds of the appeal.

(2) For the purposes of paragraph (1) the grounds of appeal are that—

(*a*) the employee did not receive a relevant payment;

(*b*) the amount specified in the notice is incorrect, because all or part of it did not fall within regulation 72E(1)(*b*)(i) or (ii);

(*c*) no trigger event within regulation 72E(5) occurred; or

(*d*) a trigger event within regulation 72E(5) occurred before 6th April 2008.

(3) On an appeal under paragraph (1) [that is notified to the tribunal, the tribunal][2] may—

(*a*) if it appears . . . [2] that the direction should not have been made, set aside the direction; or

(*b*) if it appears . . . [2] that the amount specified in the notice is incorrect, increase or reduce the amount accordingly.][1]

Amendments—[1] Regulations 72E–72G inserted by the Income Tax (Pay As You Earn) (Amendment) Regulations, SI 2008/782 regs 2, 7 with effect from 6 April 2008.

[2] In para (3), words substituted for words and words revoked in both places, by the Transfer of Tribunal Functions and Revenue and Customs Appeals Order, SI 2009/56 art 3, Sch 2 paras 92, 100 with effect from 1 April 2009.

ANNUAL RETURNS OF RELEVANT PAYMENTS AND TAX

72H [Application of regulations 73 to 75

Regulations 73 to 75 apply to—

(*a*) non-Real Time Information employers,

(*b*) Real Time Information employers in relation to tax years in which they were, for the whole of the tax year, non-Real Time Information employers, and

(*c*) Real Time Information employers to whom HMRC has given a notice requiring a return under regulation 73 in respect of a tax year.][1]

Amendments—[1] Reg 72H inserted by the Income Tax (Pay As You Earn) (Amendment) Regulations, SI 2012/822 regs 2, 34 with effect from 6 April 2012.

73 Annual return of relevant payments liable to deduction of tax (Forms P35 and P14)

(1) Before 20th May following the end of a tax year, an employer must deliver to the Inland Revenue a return containing the following information.

(2) The information is—

(*a*) the tax year to which the return relates,

(*b*) the total amount of the relevant payments made by the employer during the tax year to all employees in respect of whom the employer was required at any time during that year to prepare or maintain deductions working sheets, and

(*c*) the total net tax deducted in relation to those payments.

(3) The return must be supported by the following information in respect of each of the employees mentioned in paragraph (2)(*b*).

(4) The supporting information is—

(*a*) the employee's name,

(*b*) the employee's address, if known,

(*c*) either—

(i) the employee's national insurance number, or

(ii) if that number is not known, the employee's date of birth, if known, and sex, (*d*) the employee's code,

(*e*) the tax year to which the return relates,

(*f*) the total amount of the relevant payments made by the employer to the employee during that tax year, and

(*g*) the total net tax deducted in relation to those payments.

(5) Paragraphs (2)(*c*) and (4)(*g*) are subject to regulation 64(7) (trade disputes).

(6) If an employee was taken into employment after the beginning of the tax year, the employer must also provide the total amounts of—

(*a*) any amounts required by regulation 43(9), 52(11), 53(3) or 61(3) to be treated as relevant payments made by the employer to the employee during the tax year,

(*b*) any amounts treated as tax deducted by the employer by any of those regulations,

(*c*) the sum of the figures given under sub-paragraph (*a*) of this paragraph and paragraph (4)(*f*),

(*d*) the sum of the figures given under sub-paragraph (*b*) of this paragraph and paragraph (4)(*g*).

(7) The return must include—

(*a*) a statement and declaration containing a list of all deductions working sheets which the employer was required to prepare or maintain at any time during that tax year; and

(*b*) a certificate showing—

(i) the total net tax deducted or the total net tax repaid in the case of each employee, and

(ii) the total net tax deducted or repaid in respect of all the employees,

during that tax year.

(8) The statement and declaration and the certificate must be—

(*a*) signed by the employer, or

(*b*) if the employer is a body corporate, signed either by the secretary or by a director.

(9) Paragraph (8) is subject to regulation 211(5) (authentication in approved manner if return sent electronically).

(10) Section 98A of TMA (special penalties in case of certain returns) applies to paragraph (1).

Commentary—*Simon's Taxes* **E4.11121, E4.11122.**

Derivation—The Income Tax (Employments) Regulations, SI 1993/744 reg 43(1)–(1B), (2)–(7), (12).

Modifications—See the Income Tax (PAYE) Regulations, SI 2003/2682 reg 174 (modification of this regulation in its application to payments of taxable incapacity benefit).

73A [Amended returns of relevant payments and tax (Forms P14 and P35(RL))

(1) This regulation applies where, as a result of a retrospective tax provision, the total amount of the relevant payments made by an employer to employees increases for any closed tax year.

(2) Where this regulation applies, before 20th May following the end of the tax year in which the enactment containing the retrospective tax provision is passed, the employer must deliver to HMRC a return containing the following information.

(3) The information is—

(*a*) the tax year to which the return relates,

(*b*) the revised total amounts of the relevant payments made, or treated as made, during the tax year to all employees in respect of whom the employer was required, or has subsequently become required, to prepare or maintain deductions working sheets for any time during that year,

(*c*) the total net tax deducted in respect of those payments.

(4) The return must be supported by the same information in respect of each of the employees mentioned in paragraph (3)(*b*) as is required by regulation 73(3) to support a return under that regulation.

(5) The return must include—

(*a*) a statement and declaration containing a list of all deductions working sheets which the employer was required to prepare or maintain at any time during that year, and

(*b*) a certificate showing—

(i) the total original net tax deducted or repaid in the case of each employee,

(ii) the revised total net tax deducted or repaid in the case of each employee;

(iii) the total original net tax deducted or repaid in respect of all the employees,

(iv) the revised total net tax deducted or repaid in respect of all the employees, and

(v) the difference between the figures given in paragraphs (iii) and (iv) above.

(6) The statement and declaration and the certificate must be—

(*a*) signed by the employer, or

(*b*) if the employer is a body corporate, signed either by the secretary or by a director.

(7) Section 98A of TMA (special penalties in case of certain returns) applies to a return under paragraph (2).][1]

1 Regulation inserted, by the Income Tax (Pay as You Earn) (Amendment) Regulations, SI 2007/1077 regs 2, 15 with effect from 6 April 2007.

74 Annual return of relevant payments not liable to deduction of tax (Form P38A)

(1) Before 20th May following the end of a tax year, an employer must deliver a return to the Inland Revenue in respect of every relevant employee.

(2) The return must contain the following information—

(*a*) the employee's name,

(*b*) the employee's address, if known,

(*c*) the employee's national insurance number, if known,

(*d*) the employee's job title or description,

(*e*) the tax year to which the return relates,

(*f*) the dates during which the employee was employed in the tax year, and

(*g*) the total amount of the relevant payments made by the employer to the employee during the tax year.

(3) A "relevant employee" is one—

(*a*) to whom relevant payments exceeding the PAYE threshold were made at any time during the tax year,

(*b*) who was employed for more than a week, or

(*c*) who was paid more than £100 during the tax year.

(4) But the following are not relevant employees—

(*a*) an employee included on a return under regulation 73 (Forms P35 and P14),

(*b*) an employee who has indicated that statement A or statement B [applies][1] on Form P46 (see regulation 46), and to whom the employer has not made relevant payments exceeding the PAYE threshold at any time during that tax year.

Commentary—*Simon's Taxes* **E4.11123.**

Derivation—The Income Tax (Employments) Regulations, SI 1993/744 reg 44.

Modifications—See the Income Tax (PAYE) Regulations, SI 2003/2682 reg 174 (modification of this regulation in its application to payments of taxable incapacity benefit).

Amendments—[1] Words in para (4)(*b*) substituted by the Income Tax (PAYE) (Amendment) Regulations, SI 2005/2691 regs 2, 9 with effect from 6 April 2006.

75 Additional return in case of trade dispute

(1) An employer must immediately deliver an additional return to the Inland Revenue on each occasion that—

(*a*) the employer has not made any repayment of tax withheld under regulation 64(5) (trade disputes) within 42 days after the end of the employee's strike action, and

(*b*) a return has been made under regulation 73 which, in accordance with regulation 64(7)(*b*), treats that tax as if it were repaid.

(2) The return must contain the following information—

(*a*) the tax year to which it relates,

(*b*) such information as the Board of Inland Revenue may require for identifying each of the employees in question, and

(*c*) the amount of tax not repaid to each of those employees.

(3) The return must be accompanied by a statement containing the following information—

(*a*) a list of all employees in respect of whom the additional return is made,

(*b*) the amount of tax not repaid to each of those employees,

(*c*) the total tax not repaid by the employer to those employees for that tax year.

Commentary—*Simon's Taxes* **E4.11127.**

Derivation—The Income Tax (Employments) Regulations, SI 1993/744 reg 45.

Cross references—See the Income Tax (PAYE) Regulations, SI 2003/2682 reg 11 (this regulation not to apply to pension payers or pensioners in their capacity as such).

FAILURE TO ACCOUNT FOR DEDUCTIBLE TAX

75A [Power of HMRC to issue a notice and certificate in cases where regulation 67B or 67D returns are not made, etc

(1) This regulation applies if, 17 days or more after the end of a tax period, condition A or B or C is met.

(2) Condition A is that a Real Time Information employer—

(*a*) has not paid to HMRC any tax for that tax period,

(*b*) has not made any returns under regulation 67B (real time returns of information about relevant payments) or 67D (exceptions to regulation 67B) in respect of the tax period, and

(*c*) has not sent HMRC a notification under regulation 67F(1)(*a*) (additional information about payments),

and HMRC are not satisfied that no relevant payments have been made in the tax period.

(3) Condition B is that—

(*a*) a Real Time Information employer has paid an amount of tax for that tax period, whether or not the amount is the amount due under regulation 67G (payments to and recoveries from HMRC for each tax period by Real Time Information employers) [as adjusted by regulation 67H(2) where appropriate,][2] but

(*b*) HMRC are not satisfied, after seeking the employer's explanation, that the amount due under regulation 67G[, as adjusted by regulation 67H(2) where appropriate][2] is the amount which would have been due had any tax returned under regulation 67B or 67D as deducted from each of the employer's employees during the period been the amount that the employer was liable to deduct.

(4) Condition C is that a Real Time Information employer has not paid to HMRC the amount of tax due under regulation 67G[, as adjusted by regulation 67H(2) where appropriate][2].

(5) HMRC, on consideration of the matters specified in paragraph (6), may—

(*a*) specify to the best of their judgment, the amount of tax, or a combined amount, they consider the employer is liable to pay, and

(*b*) serve notice on the employer requiring payment of that amount within 7 days of the issue of the notice ("the notice period").

(6) The matters specified in this paragraph are—

(*a*) the employer's record of past payments, whether of tax or combined amounts,

(*b*) any returns made by the employer under regulation 67B or 67D in respect of the tax period,

(*c*) any returns made by the employer under regulation 67B or 67D in respect of earlier tax periods,

(*d*) any returns made by the employer under regulation 67E(6),

(*e*) any returns made by the employer under regulation 73 (annual return of relevant payments liable to deduction of tax (Forms P35 and P14)) in relation to previous tax years.

(7) If the notice extends to two or more consecutive tax periods in a tax year, this regulation has effect as if they were the latest period specified in the notice.

(8) If, during the notice period, the employer—

(*a*) claims that the amount paid in respect of the tax period specified in the notice represents the full amount of tax the employer was liable to deduct from each of the employer's employees during the period, but

(*b*) does not satisfy HMRC that this is the case,

the employer may require HMRC to inspect the employer's PAYE records as if the employer had been required to produce those records under Schedule 36 to the Finance Act 2008 (information and inspection powers).

(9) If there is an inspection by virtue of paragraph (8), the notice given by HMRC under paragraph (5) must be disregarded.

(10) If the amount specified in the notice, or any part of it, is not paid during the notice period—

(*a*) the amount unpaid is treated as an amount of tax or as including an amount of tax which the employer was liable to pay for that tax period under regulation 67G[, where appropriate][2], and

(*b*) HMRC may prepare a certificate showing how much of that amount remains unpaid.

(11) Regulation 218 deals with the use of certificates as evidence that sums are due and unpaid.][1]

Amendments—[1] Regs 75A, 75B inserted by the Income Tax (Pay As You Earn) (Amendment) Regulations, SI 2012/822 regs 2, 35 with effect from 6 April 2012.

[2] In paras (3), (4), (10)(*a*), words inserted by the Income Tax (Pay As You Earn) (Amendment) Regulations, SI 2013/521 regs 2, 30 with effect from 6 April 2013 in relation to the tax year 2013–14 and subsequent tax years.

75B [Certificates under [regulation] 75A: excess payments

(1) This regulation applies if, as a consequence of paying a certified amount of tax under regulation 75A in relation to the tax year, the total amount of tax paid to HMRC for the tax year under these Regulations by an employer exceeds the amount which would have been paid had it not been necessary for HMRC to prepare the certificate.

(2) The employer is entitled to set off the excess tax against any amount which the employer is liable to pay under regulation 67G[, as adjusted by regulation 67H(2) where appropriate,][2] for any subsequent tax period or, if the tax year in question has ended, the excess of tax paid may be repaid.][1]

Amendments—[1] Regs 75A, 75B inserted by the Income Tax (Pay As You Earn) (Amendment) Regulations, SI 2012/822 regs 2, 35 with effect from 6 April 2012.

[2] In heading, word substituted for word "regulations", and in para (2) words inserted, by the Income Tax (Pay As You Earn) (Amendment) Regulations, SI 2013/521 regs 2, 31 with effect from 6 April 2013 in relation to the tax year 2013–14 and subsequent tax years.

76 Certificate if tax in regulation 73 return is unpaid

(1) Paragraph (2) applies if an employer—

(*a*) delivers a return under regulation 73 showing an amount of total net tax deducted by the employer for a tax year, and

(*b*) does not pay that amount to the Inland Revenue before 20th April following the end of the tax year.

(2) The Inland Revenue may prepare a certificate showing how much of that amount remains unpaid.
(3) Regulation 218 deals with the use of certificates as evidence that sums are due and unpaid.

Commentary—*Simon's Taxes* **E4.11116.**

Derivation—The Income Tax (Employments) Regulations, SI 1993/744 reg 43(8).

Modifications—See the Income Tax (PAYE) Regulations, SI 2003/2682 reg 174 (modification of this regulation in its application to payments of taxable incapacity benefit).

Cross references—See the Income Tax (PAYE) Regulations, SI 2003/2682 reg 218(1), (2) (a certificate of the Inland Revenue that, to the best of their knowledge and belief, any amount shown in a certificate under this regulation has not been paid by an employer, is sufficient evidence that the amount mentioned in the certificate is unpaid and due to the Crown).

77 Return and certificate if tax may be unpaid: amounts due under regulation 68]

(1) This regulation applies if, 17 days or more after the end of a tax period, condition A or B is met.
(2) Condition A is that—
- (*a*) an employer has not paid any tax under regulation 68 for that tax period, and
- (*b*) the Inland Revenue are unaware of the amount (if any) which the employer is liable to pay.

(3) Condition B is that—
- (*a*) an employer has paid an amount of tax under regulation 68 for that period, but
- (*b*) the Inland Revenue are not satisfied that it is the full amount which the employer is liable to pay for that period.

(4) The Inland Revenue may give notice to the employer requiring the employer within 14 days of the issue of the notice to deliver a return showing the amount of tax which the employer is liable to pay under regulation 68 in respect of the tax period.
(5) If the notice extends to two or more consecutive tax periods in a tax year, this regulation has effect as if they were one tax period.
(6) On receiving a return made by the employer under paragraph (4), the Inland Revenue may prepare a certificate showing the amount of tax which the employer is liable to pay for the tax period and how much (if any) of that amount remains unpaid.
(7) Regulation 218 deals with the use of certificates as evidence that sums are due and unpaid.

Commentary—*Simon's Taxes* **E4.11116.**

Derivation—The Income Tax (Employments) Regulations, SI 1993/744 reg 47(1)–(5).

Modifications—See the Income Tax (PAYE) Regulations, SI 2003/2682 Sch 1 para 18 (modification of this regulation in so far as the provisions apply in relation to tax periods ending before 6 April 2004).

Cross references—See the Income Tax (PAYE) Regulations, SI 2003/2682 reg 218(1), (2) (a certificate of the Inland Revenue that, to the best of their knowledge and belief, any amount shown in a certificate under para (6) above has not been paid by an employer, is sufficient evidence that the amount mentioned in the certificate is unpaid and due to the Crown).

Amendments—Words in heading inserted by the Income Tax (Pay As You Earn) (Amendment) Regulations, SI 2012/822 regs 2, 36 with effect from 6 April 2012.

78 Notice and certificate if tax may be unpaid[: amounts due under regulation 68][3]

(1) This regulation applies if, 17 days or more after the end of a tax period, condition A or B is met.
(2) Condition A is that—
- (*a*) an employer has not paid any tax under regulation 68 for that tax period, and
- (*b*) [HMRC][1] have reason to believe that the employer is liable to pay an amount of tax.

(3) Condition B is that—
- (*a*) an employer has paid an amount of tax under regulation 68 for that tax period, but
- (*b*) [HMRC][1] are not satisfied, after seeking the employer's explanation, that it is the full amount which the employer is liable to pay for that period.

(4) [HMRC][1], on consideration of the employer's record of past payments [whether of tax or of combined amounts][1], may—
- (*a*) specify, to the best of their judgment, the amount of tax [or a combined amount][1] which they consider the employer is liable to pay, and
- (*b*) serve notice on the employer requiring payment of that amount within 7 days of the issue of the notice ("the notice period").

(5) If the notice extends to two or more consecutive tax periods in a tax year, this regulation has effect as if they were the latest tax period specified in the notice.
(6) If, during the notice period, the employer—
- (*a*) claims that any payment made in respect of the tax period specified in the notice is [or includes][1] the full amount [of tax][1] the employer is liable to pay, but
- (*b*) does not satisfy [HMRC][1] that this is the case,

the employer may require [HMRC][1] to inspect the employer's PAYE records as if the employer had been required to produce those records [under Schedule 36 to the Finance Act 2008 (information and inspection powers)][2].
(7) If there is an inspection by virtue of paragraph (6) . . . [2] the notice given by [HMRC][1] under paragraph (4) must be disregarded.
(8) If the amount . . . [1] specified in the notice, or any part of it, is not paid during the notice period—
- (*a*) the amount unpaid is treated as an amount of tax [or as including an amount of tax][1] which the employer was liable to pay for that tax period under regulation 68, and

(*b*) [HMRC][1] may prepare a certificate showing how much of that [amount][1] remains unpaid.

(9) But paragraph (8) does not apply if during the notice period—

(*a*) the employer pays the full amount of tax which the employer is liable to pay under regulation 68 for that tax period, or

(*b*) the employer satisfies [HMRC][1] that no amount, or no further amount, is due for that tax period.

(10) Paragraph (11) applies if the employer pays an amount [of tax, whether separately or as part of a combined amount, which is][1] certified under this regulation [and][1] which exceeds the amount the employer would have been liable to pay in respect of that tax period apart from this regulation.

(11) The employer is entitled to set off the excess [tax][1] against any amount which the employer is liable to pay under regulation 68 for any subsequent tax period in the tax year.

(12) Paragraph (13) applies if the employer—

(*a*) delivers the return required by regulation 73(1) after the end of the tax year, and

(*b*) pays the total net tax which the employer is liable to pay.

(13) Any excess of tax paid, and not otherwise recovered by set-off in accordance with this regulation, must be repaid.

(14) Regulation 218 deals with the use of certificates as evidence that sums are due and unpaid.

Commentary—*Simon's Taxes* **E4.11116.**

Derivation—The Income Tax (Employments) Regulations, SI 1993/744 reg 48(1)–(7), (11), (12).

Modifications—See the Income Tax (PAYE) Regulations, SI 2003/2682 Sch 1 para 18 (modification of this regulation in so far as the provisions apply in relation to tax periods ending before 6 April 2004).

Cross references—See the Income Tax (PAYE) Regulations, SI 2003/2682 reg 218(1), (2) (a certificate of the Inland Revenue that, to the best of their knowledge and belief, any amount shown in a certificate under para (8) above has not been paid by an employer, is sufficient evidence that the amount mentioned in the certificate is unpaid and due to the Crown).

SI 2003/2682 reg 219 (for the purposes of this regulation, if payment to the Revenue is made by cheque, and cheque paid on its first presentation to the banker on whom drawn, the payment is treated as made on day cheque received by the Revenue).

Amendments—[1] References to HMRC substituted throughout, words in paras (4), (6), (10), (11) inserted, words in para (8) revoked, inserted and substituted, by the Income Tax (Pay As You Earn) (Amendment) Regulations, SI 2008/782 regs 2, 8 with effect from 6 April 2008.

[2] In para (6), words substituted, and in para (7), words revoked, by the Income Tax (PAYE) (Amendment) Regulations, SI 2009/588 regs 2, 4 with effect from 1 April 2009.

[3] Words in heading inserted by the Income Tax (Pay As You Earn) (Amendment) Regulations, SI 2012/822 regs 2, 37 with effect from 6 April 2012.

79 Certificate after inspection of PAYE records

(1) This regulation applies if there is an inspection of an employer's PAYE records under [Schedule 36 to the Finance Act 2008 (information and inspection powers)][1].

(2) The Inland Revenue may, by reference to the information obtained from the inspection, prepare a certificate showing—

(*a*) the amount of tax which it appears that the employer is liable to pay for the tax years or tax periods covered by the inspection; and

(*b*) any amount of that tax which remains unpaid.

(3) Regulation 218 deals with the use of certificates as evidence that sums are due and unpaid.

Commentary—*Simon's Taxes* **E4.11116.**

Derivation—The Income Tax (Employments) Regulations, SI 1993/744 reg 55(8).

Simon's Tax Cases—*Bulley v Hemmer Investments Ltd* [2010] STC 1779.

Modifications—See the Income Tax (PAYE) Regulations, SI 2003/2682 reg 174 (modification of this regulation in its application to payments of taxable incapacity benefit).

Cross references—See the Income Tax (PAYE) Regulations, SI 2003/2682 reg 218(1), (2) (a certificate of the Inland Revenue that, to the best of their knowledge and belief, any amount shown in a certificate under this regulation has not been paid by an employer, is sufficient evidence that the amount mentioned in the certificate is unpaid and due to the Crown).

Amendments—[1] In para (1), words substituted by the Income Tax (PAYE) (Amendment) Regulations, SI 2009/588 regs 2, 5 with effect from 1 April 2009.

80 Determination of unpaid tax and appeal against determination

(1) This regulation applies if it appears to [HMRC][1] that there may be tax payable for a tax year under regulation [67G[, as adjusted by regulation 67H(2) where appropriate,][5] or][4] 68 by an employer which has neither been—

(*a*) paid to [HMRC][1], nor

(*b*) certified by [HMRC][1] under regulation [75A,][4] 76, 77, 78 or 79.

[(1A) In paragraph (1), the reference to tax payable for a tax year under regulation 67G includes a reference to any amount the employer was liable to deduct from employees during the tax year whether or not that amount was included in any return under regulation 67B (real time returns of information about relevant payments) or 67D (exceptions to regulation 67B).][4]

(2) [HMRC][1] may determine the amount of that tax to the best of their judgment, and serve notice of their determination on the employer.

(3) A determination under this regulation must not include tax in respect of which a direction under regulation 72(5) has been made; and directions under that regulation do not apply to tax determined under this regulation.

[(3A) A determination under this regulation must not include tax in respect of which a direction under regulation 72F has been made.][1]

(4) A determination under this regulation may—

(*a*) cover the tax payable by the employer under regulation [67G or[, as adjusted by regulation 67H(2) where appropriate,][5]][4] 68 for any one or more tax periods in a tax year, and

(*b*) extend to the whole of that tax, or to such part of it as is payable in respect of—

(i) a class or classes of employees specified in the notice of determination (without naming the individual employees), or

(ii) one or more named employees specified in the notice.

(5) A determination under this regulation is subject to Parts 4, 5[, 5A][3] . . . [2] and 6 of TMA (assessment, appeals, collection and recovery) as if—

(*a*) the determination were an assessment, and

(*b*) the amount of tax determined were income tax charged on the employer,

and those Parts of that Act apply accordingly with any necessary modifications.

(6) . . . [2]

Commentary—*Simon's Taxes* **E4.11116.**

Derivation—The Income Tax (Employments) Regulations, SI 1993/744 reg 49(1)–(4), (7), (8).

Cross references—See the Income Tax (PAYE) Regulations, SI 2003/2682 Sch 1 para 20 (this regulation does not apply in relation to unpaid tax in respect of a tax year ending on or before 5 April 1992).

Amendments—[1] References to HMRC substituted throughout, and para (3A) inserted, by the Income Tax (Pay As You Earn) (Amendment) Regulations, SI 2008/782 regs 2, 9 with effect from 6 April 2008.

[2] Words in para (5), and whole of para (6), revoked, by the Transfer of Tribunal Functions and Revenue and Customs Appeals Order, SI 2009/56 art 3, Sch 2 paras 92, 101 with effect from 1 April 2009.

[3] Reference in para (5) inserted by the Income Tax (Pay As You Earn) (Amendment) Regulations, SI 2010/668, regs 2, 3, with effect in relation to the tax year 2010–11 and subsequent tax years.

[4] Words in paras (1), (4), and whole of para (1A), inserted, by the Income Tax (Pay As You Earn) (Amendment) Regulations, SI 2012/822 regs 2, 38 with effect from 6 April 2012.

[5] In paras (1), (4)(*a*), words inserted by the Income Tax (Pay As You Earn) (Amendment) Regulations, SI 2013/521 regs 2, 32 with effect from 6 April 2013 in relation to the tax year 2013–14 and subsequent tax years.

81 Employee liability if tax unpaid after regulation 80 determination

(1) This regulation applies if—

(*a*) any part of the tax determined under regulation 80 is not paid within 30 days from the date on which the determination became final and conclusive, and

(*b*) condition A or B is met in relation to an employee.

(2) Condition A is that the Inland Revenue are of the opinion that the employee in respect of whose relevant payments the determination was made has received those payments knowing that the employer has wilfully failed to deduct the amount of tax which should have been deducted from those payments.

(3) Condition B is that the unpaid tax represents an amount for which the employer was required to account under regulation 62(5) (notional payments) in relation to a notional payment to the employee.

(4) The Inland Revenue may direct that the employer is not liable to pay the amount of tax which appears to them should have been but was not—

(*a*) deducted on making those relevant payments, or

(*b*) accounted for under regulation 62(5).

[(4A) If condition A or B is met, any direction under paragraph (4) must be made by notice ("the direction notice") to the employee stating the date the notice was issued.][1]

(5) If a direction is made, the amount of tax must not be added under regulation 185(5) or 188(3)(*a*) (adjustments for self-assessments and other assessments) in relation to the employee.

(6) Tax payable by an employee as a result of a direction carries interest, as if it were unpaid tax due from an employer, in accordance with [section 101 of the Finance Act 2009][2].

(7) . . . [2]

Commentary—*Simon's Taxes* **E4.11117.**

Derivation—The Income Tax (Employments) Regulations, SI 1993/744 reg 49(5), (6), 101(6), 101A(2); the Income Tax (Employments) (Notional Payments) Regulations, SI 1994/1212 reg 13(7).

Cross references—See the Income Tax (PAYE) Regulations, SI 2003/2682 reg 218(3), (4) (a certificate of the Inland Revenue that, to the best of their knowledge and belief, any amount of interest payable under para (6) above has not been paid by an employer or employee, is sufficient evidence that the amount mentioned in the certificate is unpaid and due to the Crown).

Amendments—[1] Para (4A) inserted by the IT (PAYE) (Amendment) Regulations, SI 2004/851 regs 2, 5 with effect from 12 April 2004.

[2] Words in para (6) substituted, and para (7) revoked by the Finance Act 2009, Sections 101 and 102 (Interest on Late Payments and Repayments), Appointed Days and Consequential Provisions Order, SI 2014/992 art 9(1), (4) with effect in relation to payments due and payable in respect of the tax year 2014–15 and subsequent tax years.

81A [Employee's appeal against direction notice

(1) An employee may appeal against a direction notice under regulation 81(4A)—

(*a*) by notice to the Inland Revenue,

(*b*) within 30 days of the issue of the direction notice,

(*c*) specifying the grounds of the appeal.

(2) For the purpose of paragraph (1) the grounds of appeal are that—

(*a*) in relation to condition A in regulation 81, the employee did not receive the payments knowing that the employer wilfully failed to deduct the amount of tax which should have been deducted from those payments,

(*b*) in relation to condition B in regulation 81, the relevant payment was not a notional payment, or

(*c*) the excess is incorrect.

(3) On an appeal under paragraph (1) [that is notified to the tribunal, the tribunal][2] may—

(*a*) if it appears . . . [2] that the direction notice should not have been made, set aside the notice; or

(*b*) if it appears . . . [2] that the amount of tax specified in the direction notice is incorrect, increase or reduce the amount specified in the notice accordingly.

(4) Regulation 72D applies to appeals under this regulation.][1]

Commentary—*Simon's Taxes* **E4.11117**.

Amendments—[1] This regulation inserted by the IT (PAYE) (Amendment) Regulations, SI 2004/851 regs 2, 6 with effect from 12 April 2004.

[2] In para (3), words substituted for words and words revoked in both places, by the Transfer of Tribunal Functions and Revenue and Customs Appeals Order, SI 2009/56 art 3, Sch 2 paras 92, 102 with effect from 1 April 2009.

INTEREST

82 Interest on tax overdue

Amendments—Regulations 82, 83 revoked by the Finance Act 2009, Sections 101 and 102 (Interest on Late Payments and Repayments), Appointed Days and Consequential Provisions Order, SI 2014/992 art 9(1), (4) with effect in relation to payments due and payable in respect of the tax year 2014–15 and subsequent tax years.

83 Interest on tax overpaid

. . .

Amendments—Regulations 82, 83 revoked by the Finance Act 2009, Sections 101 and 102 (Interest on Late Payments and Repayments), Appointed Days and Consequential Provisions Order, SI 2014/992 art 9(1), (4) with effect in relation to payments due and payable in respect of the tax year 2014–15 and subsequent tax years.

RECOVERY

84 Recovery of tax and interest

(1) In this regulation, "the unpaid amount" means any amount of tax or interest which—

(*a*) an employer is liable to pay under regulation [75A(10),][2] 76(2), 77(6), 78(8)[or 79(2)(*b*)][3];

(*b*) an employee is liable to pay under regulation 72(7) or regulation 81(6).

(2) Part 6 of TMA (collection and recovery) applies to the recovery of the unpaid amount [or combined amount and any interest on it][1] as if it were income tax charged on the employer or employee (as the case may be) but with the modification indicated in paragraph (3).

(3) Summary proceedings for the recovery of the unpaid amount may be brought in England and Wales or Northern Ireland at any time before the end of the period which applies for the purposes of the regulation in question, as shown in Table 4.

TABLE 4

PERIOD FOR SUMMARY PROCEEDINGS FOR THE RECOVERY OF UNPAID AMOUNT

1 Regulation	*2 Period*
Regulation 76(2)	(*a*) 12 months after the date by which the statement specified in regulation 73(7) must be delivered, or
	(*b*) if that statement is delivered after that date, 12 months after its delivery.
Regulations [75A(10),][2] 77(6) [and][3], 78(8) . . . [3]	(*a*) 12 months after the date on which the unpaid amount [or combined amount and any interest on it][1] became payable, or
	(*b*) if a return has been required under regulation 77, 12 months after the date of the delivery of that return to the Inland Revenue.
Regulation 79(2)(*b*)	12 months after the date of the certificate.
Regulations 72(7) and 81(6)	12 months after the date on which the unpaid amount became payable.

(4) Proceedings against an employer may be brought for the recovery of the unpaid amount [or combined amount and any interest on it][1] without distinguishing the amounts which the employer is liable to pay in respect of each employee and without specifying the employees in question.

(5) The unpaid amount [or combined amount and any interest on it][1] is one cause of action or one matter of complaint for the purposes of proceedings under sections 65, 66 and 67 of TMA (magistrates' courts, county courts and inferior courts in Scotland).

(6) But paragraphs (4) and (5) do not prevent the bringing of separate proceedings for the recovery of each of the amounts which the employer is liable to pay for any tax period in respect of each of the employees.

Commentary—*Simon's Taxes* **E4.11118.**
Derivation—The Income Tax (Employments) Regulations, SI 1993/744 regs 43(9), 47(6), 48(6), 52(3), 54(1)–(5), 55(9).
Simon's Tax Cases—*Bulley v Hemmer Investments Ltd* [2010] STC 1779.
Modifications—See the Income Tax (PAYE) Regulations, SI 2003/2682 reg 174 (modification of this regulation in its application to payments of taxable incapacity benefit).
Amendments—[1] Words in paras (2)–(4) inserted, by the Income Tax (Pay As You Earn) (Amendment) Regulations, SI 2008/782 regs 2, 11 with effect from 6 April 2008.
[2] Words in paras (1)(*a*) and in Table 4 in para , (3) inserted by the Income Tax (Pay As You Earn) (Amendment) Regulations, SI 2012/822 regs 2, 40 with effect from 6 April 2012.
[3] Words in para (1)(*a*) substituted, and in para (3), in Table 4, column 1, words inserted and revoked, by the Finance Act 2009, Sections 101 and 102 (Interest on Late Payments and Repayments), Appointed Days and Consequential Provisions Order, SI 2014/992 art 9(1), (6) with effect in relation to payments due and payable in respect of the tax year 2014–15 and subsequent tax years.

[Continental shelf workers: provisions relating to certificates

84A Application for certificate

(1) An employer who meets the conditions in paragraph (2) may apply to HMRC for the issue of a UKCS continental shelf workers certificate.
(2) The conditions are that—
(*a*) the employer supplies or intends to supply a continental shelf worker for whom the oil field licensee is the relevant person;
(*b*) the employer has or intends to have a contractual relationship under which the employer acts, directly or indirectly, as an agent of the oil field licensee in connection with these Regulations; and
(*c*) the employer or an associated company has not had a certificate cancelled previously for a failure to comply with their obligations under regulation 84B.
(3) An application under this regulation must be made in writing and must include—
(*a*) the name and address of the employer and employer's PAYE reference;
(*b*) the name and address of a person in the United Kingdom who is authorised to accept service on behalf of the employer;
(*c*) confirmation that the employer understands and intends to comply with their obligations contained in regulation 84B; and
(*d*) the name, address, and employer's PAYE reference of any associated company which is a current or former holder of a UKCS continental shelf workers certificate.
(4) When the employer makes the first application under this regulation, the employer may also comply with the obligation under regulation 84B(*e*) by including those details (if known) in the application.
(5) An application made under this regulation may be combined with an application made under regulation 114A of the SSC Regulations.
(6) Upon receipt of an application under this regulation, an officer of Revenue and Customs may, if they are satisfied the conditions in paragraph (2) are met, issue a UKCS continental shelf workers certificate.
(7) A UKCS continental shelf workers certificate must include—
(*a*) the name of the UKCS continental shelf workers certificate holder;
(*b*) the employer's PAYE reference of the UKCS continental shelf workers certificate holder; and
(*c*) the date on which the certificate is issued.
(8) A UKCS continental shelf workers certificate may be issued to—
(*a*) the person authorised to accept service on behalf of the employer;
(*b*) the employer; or
(*c*) both the person authorised to accept service on behalf of the employer and the employer.
(9) A certificate may be combined with a certificate issued under regulation 114A of the SSC Regulations.
(10) Where an employer ceases to meet the conditions in paragraph (2) or to comply with its obligations under regulation 84B, or regulation 114B of the SSC Regulations, an officer of Revenue and Customs may, by notice in writing to the person authorised to accept service on behalf of the employer, cancel the UKCS continental shelf workers certificate from the date specified in the notice of cancellation.
(11) The date specified in paragraph (10) may not be earlier than 10 working days after the date of the notice.
(12) A notice under paragraph (10) may be combined with a notice under regulation 114A of the SSC Regulations.
(13) In this regulation "associated company" means any company within the meaning of section 449 of the Corporation Tax Act 2010.][1]

Amendments—[1] Regulations 84A–84D inserted by the Income Tax (Pay As You Earn) (Amendment) Regulations, SI 2014/474 reg 2 with effect from 6 April 2014.

[84B UKCS continental shelf workers certificate holder: obligations

(1) A UKCS continental shelf workers certificate holder must—

(*a*) make such deductions, returns and repayments as are required of a relevant person;

(*b*) keep written records of—

(i) the name, date of birth, and national insurance number of the continental shelf workers supplied;

(ii) the name, registered office and oil field licence number of the oil field licensee to whom each of the workers were supplied;

(iii) the offshore installation to which each of the workers were supplied; and

(iv) the dates between which the workers worked on the offshore installation;

(*c*) keep the records required by sub-paragraph (*b*) for a period of 6 years from the end of the tax year to which they relate;

(*d*) where an officer of Revenue and Customs requires them in writing to do so, provide copies of the records required by sub-paragraph (*b*) to HMRC within 30 days of the date of the request; and

(*e*) before supplying the oil field licensee with continental shelf workers for the first time, inform HMRC in writing of the details of the oil field licensee including name, business address, and oil field licence number of the oil field licensee.

(2) In this regulation "offshore installation" means a structure which is, is to be, or has been, put to a relevant use while in water but a structure is not an offshore installation if—

(*a*) it has permanently ceased to be put to a relevant use,

(*b*) it is not, and is not to be, put to any other relevant use, and

(*c*) since permanently ceasing to be put to a relevant use, it has been put to a use which is not a relevant use.

(3) In paragraph (2) a use is a relevant use if it is—

(*a*) for the purposes of exploiting mineral resources,

(*b*) for the purposes of exploration with a view to exploiting mineral resources,

(*c*) for the storage of gas in or under the shore or the bed of any waters,

(*d*) for the recovery of gas so stored,

(*e*) for the conveyance of things by means of a pipe,

(*f*) mainly for the provision of accommodation for individuals who work on or from a structure which is, is to be, or has been put to any of the above uses while in the water,

(*g*) for the purposes of decommissioning any structure which has been used for or in connection with any of the relevant uses above.

(4) For the purposes of paragraphs (3) and (4) a structure is put to use while in water if it is put to use while—

(i) standing in any waters,

(ii) stationed (by whatever means) in any waters, or

(iii) standing on the foreshore or other land intermittently covered with water.

(5) For the purposes of paragraphs (2), (3) and (4) a "structure" includes a ship or other vessel except where it is used wholly or mainly—

(a) for the transport of supplies;

(b) as a safety vessel;

(c) for a combination of (*a*) and (*b*); or

(d) for the laying of cables.][1]

Amendments—[1] Regulations 84A–84D inserted by the Income Tax (Pay As You Earn) (Amendment) Regulations, SI 2014/474 reg 2 with effect from 6 April 2014.

[84C UKCS oil field licensee certificate

(1) Where a UKCS continental shelf workers certificate holder has notified HMRC that the employer intends to supply continental shelf workers to an oil field licensee an officer of Revenue and Customs must issue a UKCS oil field licensee certificate to the oil field licensee.

(2) The UKCS oil field licensee certificate must include—

(*a*) the name of the oil field licensee;

(*b*) the registered office of that oil field licensee;

(*c*) the oil field licence number;

(*d*) the name of the UKCS continental shelf workers certificate holder;

(*e*) the date on which it is issued; and

(*f*) a description of the continental shelf workers to whom it applies.

(3) Where a UKCS oil field licensee certificate is in force the holder of that certificate is not liable to make deductions in respect of any continental shelf worker of a description set out in the certificate.

(4) If a UKCS continental shelf workers certificate is cancelled by an officer of Revenue and Customs that officer must also, by notice in writing, cancel the UKCS oil field licensee certificate.

(5) A notice under paragraph (4) must—

(*a*) be sent on the same day as the notice cancelling the UKCS continental shelf workers certificate;

(*b*) specify the date of cancellation of the UKCS oil field licensee certificate; and

(*c*) notify the oil field licensee that it is liable to meet its obligations as a relevant person.

(6) The date of cancellation of the UKCS oil field licensee certificate must be the same date as that specified in the UKCS continental shelf workers certificate cancellation notice.

(7) In this regulation "UKCS oil field licensee certificate" means a certificate issued under paragraph (1).][1]

Amendments—[1] Regulations 84A–84D inserted by the Income Tax (Pay As You Earn) (Amendment) Regulations, SI 2014/474 reg 2 with effect from 6 April 2014.

[84D Interpretation of regulations 84A to 114C

In regulations 84A to 84C—

"oil field licensee" means the holder of a licence under Part 1 of the Petroleum Act 1998 in respect of the area in which the duties of the continental shelf worker's employment are performed;

"UKCS continental shelf workers certificate" means a certificate issued under regulation 84A.][1]

Amendments—[1] Regulations 84A–84D inserted by the Income Tax (Pay As You Earn) (Amendment) Regulations, SI 2014/474 reg 2 with effect from 6 April 2014.

[Employment Intermediaries: return of information relating to agency workers for whom they have not operated PAYE

84E Specified employment intermediaries

An employment intermediary is a specified employment intermediary if at any time during a tax quarter—

(*a*) the employment intermediary is an agency;

(*b*) more than one individual provides services to a client under or in consequence of a contract between the employment intermediary and one or more clients;

(*c*) those services are not provided exclusively on the United Kingdom continental shelf; and

(*d*) the employment intermediary makes one or more payments in respect of, or connected with, the services provided by one or more individuals that—

(i) is required by regulation 67B to be included in a return delivered to HMRC by the employment intermediary when the payment is made but has not been ("a reporting failure"); or

(ii) is not required by regulation 67B to be included in a return delivered to HMRC by the employment intermediary when the payment is made because the individual is not an employee or treated as an employee under regulation 10 ("no reporting requirement").][1]

Amendments—[1] Regulations 84E–84H and preceding crosshead inserted by the Income Tax (Pay As You Earn) (Amendment No 2) Regulations, SI 2015/170 reg 2(1), (3) with effect in relation to tax quarters beginning on or after 6 April 2015.

[84F Returns by specified employment intermediaries

(1) A specified employment intermediary must, for each tax quarter, provide to HMRC the information specified in regulation 84G no later than the end of the tax month following that quarter.

(2) The information must be included in a return in a form prescribed by HMRC and include a declaration that the information provided in the return is correct and complete to the best of the knowledge and belief of the person completing it.

(3) The return is to be made using an approved method of electronic communication.

(4) The return may be amended until the end of the tax month following the tax quarter after the tax quarter to which the return relates.

(5) Where a return is made in relation to a tax quarter, the specified employment intermediary shall continue to provide a return to HMRC in relation to every subsequent tax quarter until either—

(*a*) regulation 84E(*b*) to 84E(*d*) has not been satisfied for 4 consecutive tax quarters in respect of the specified intermediary; or

(*b*) the specified employment intermediary notifies HMRC that it is no longer an employment intermediary.][1]

Amendments—[1] Regulations 84E–84H and preceding crosshead inserted by the Income Tax (Pay As You Earn) (Amendment No 2) Regulations, SI 2015/170 reg 2(1), (3) with effect in relation to tax quarters beginning on or after 6 April 2015.

[84G Specified information

The specified information is—

(*a*) in respect of the specified employment intermediary making the return its—

(i) name;

(ii) address;

(iii) postcode;

(iv) employer's PAYE reference number where it is required to have one;

(*b*) in respect of each individual providing the services referred to in regulation 84E—

(i) the individual's—

(*aa*) name;

(*bb*) address;

(*cc*) postcode;

(*dd*) national insurance number (if the individual has one) or gender and date of birth (where the individual does not have a national insurance number);

(*ee*) Unique Taxpayer Reference issued by HMRC (if self-employed or a member of a partnership);

(ii) the date on which the individual began providing the services referred to in regulation 84E;

(iii) the date (if any) on which the individual stopped providing the services referred to in regulation 84E; and

(*c*) where a payment is made to an individual in respect of, or in connection with, the services referred to in regulation 84E, but that payment is not included in a return delivered to HMRC under regulation 67B at the time the payment was made because there is no reporting requirement or there is a reporting failure—

(i) the full name (or if a partnership the name under which they trade) and address of the person receiving the payment made by the specified employment intermediary (if not the same as in 84G(*b*)(i)(aa) and (bb));

(ii) the total of the payments made by the specified employment intermediary to the person in the tax quarter;

(iii) the reason why the specified employment intermediary has not deducted income tax from those payments;

(iv) where the reason for the non deduction given in (iii) is that the payments made are to a limited company the full name of the company and company registration number of that company; and

(v) whether the payments included amounts in respect of Value Added Tax.][1]

Amendments—[1] Regulations 84E–84H and preceding crosshead inserted by the Income Tax (Pay As You Earn) (Amendment No 2) Regulations, SI 2015/170 reg 2(1), (3) with effect in relation to tax quarters beginning on or after 6 April 2015.

[84H Retention of records

(1) A specified employment intermediary must keep and preserve non-PAYE records which are not required to be sent to HMRC under any other provision of these Regulations for not less than three years after the end of the tax year to which they relate.

(2) The duty under paragraph (1) to keep and preserve non-PAYE records may be discharged by preserving them in any form or by any means.

(3) In this regulation "non-PAYE records" means information, records and documents which evidence the specified information.][1]

Amendments—[1] Regulations 84E–84H and preceding crosshead inserted by the Income Tax (Pay As You Earn) (Amendment No 2) Regulations, SI 2015/170 reg 2(1), (3) with effect in relation to tax quarters beginning on or after 6 April 2015.

CHAPTER 2

OTHER RETURNS AND INFORMATION

RETURNS INVOLVING PAYE INCOME OTHER THAN PAYMENTS

85 Employers: annual return of other earnings ([Form P11D][1])

(1) Before 7th July following the end of a tax year, the employer must provide the Inland Revenue—

(*a*) with the information listed in regulation 86 for each employee, and

(*b*) with the additional information listed in regulation 87 for each employee whose employment is subject to the benefits code.

(2) At the same time and in the same manner as the employer provides that information, the employer must also provide a declaration stating that—

(*a*) all information required to be provided has been provided, and

(*b*) the information is complete and accurate to the best of the employer's knowledge and belief.

(3) For the purposes of this regulation an employment is "subject to the benefits code" if, for the purposes of the benefits code in ITEPA, it is a taxable employment under Part 2 of ITEPA (as defined by section 66(3) of ITEPA) . . . [1].

[(4) But this regulation does not apply in relation to a benefit provided in a tax year which has been treated as a payment of PAYE income under Chapter 3A of the Regulations.][2].

Commentary—*Simon's Taxes* **E4.11124.**

Derivation—The Income Tax (Employments) Regulations, SI 1993/744 reg 46(1), (7A), (7B).

Cross references—See the Income Tax (PAYE) Regulations, SI 2003/2682 reg 11 (this regulation not to apply to pension payers or pensioners in their capacity as such).

SI 2003/2682 reg 12 (this regulation not to apply to other payers or other payees in their capacity as such).

Amendments—[1] In heading, words substituted , and in para 3, words revoked, by the Income Tax (Pay As You Earn) (Amendment No 4) Regulations, SI 2015/1927 regs 2, 7(*a*), (*b*) with effect in relation to any returns and information provided for the tax year 2016–17 and subsequent tax years.

[2] Para (4) inserted by the Income Tax (Pay As You Earn) (Amendment No 4) Regulations, SI 2015/1927 regs 2, 7(*c*) with effect in relation to specified benefits (as defined in reg 61A) provided on or after 6 April 2016.

86 Information employer must provide for each employee

(1) Particulars of the following information must be provided in the case of each employee—

(*a*) any earnings which the employee receives from the employer or related third party otherwise than in money, including the amount of those earnings;

(*b*) any payments made on behalf of the employee by the employer or related third party and not repaid, including the amounts;

(*c*) any non-cash voucher provided by the employer or related third party by reason of which the employee is treated by section 87(1) of ITEPA (benefit of non-cash voucher treated as earnings) as receiving earnings in that tax year, including the amount of those earnings;

(*d*) any use of a credit-token provided by the employer or related third party by reason of which the employee is treated by section 94(1) of ITEPA (benefit of credit-token treated as earnings) as receiving earnings in that tax year, including the amount of those earnings;

(*e*) the due amount in respect of any notional payment where that amount is treated by section 222 of ITEPA (payments on account of tax where deduction not possible) as earnings of the employee received in that tax year;

(*f*) any living accommodation which has been provided for the employee or a member of the employee's family or household by the employer or related third party, including the amount that is treated as earnings for that tax year by section 102 of ITEPA (benefit of living accommodation treated as earnings);

(*g*) any earnings consisting of the amount by which the value of the exemption under subsection (2) of section 287 of ITEPA (limit on exemption of removal expenses and removal benefits) exceeds the limit specified in subsection (1) of that section and having effect in relation to the employee.

(2) Particulars of removal expenses and removal benefits to which section 271 of ITEPA (limited exemption of removal benefits and expenses) applies are required—

(*a*) only under paragraph (1)(*g*), and

(*b*) only to the extent that they exceed the limit in section 287(1) of ITEPA which applies to the change of residence of the employee in question.

(3) In the case of any earnings relating to business entertainment, as defined by section 577 of ICTA, the employer must also inform the Inland Revenue whether the amount of the earnings has been or will be disallowed as a deduction or inclusion as mentioned in section 577(1)(*a*) of that Act in any tax computation relating to the trade, business, profession or vocation of the employer.

(4) "Related third party" means a person making payments or providing benefits to an employee, if the making or provision of the payments or benefits by that person has been arranged, guaranteed or in any way facilitated by the employer.

Commentary—*Simon's Taxes* **E4.11124.**

Derivation—The Income Tax (Employments) Regulations, SI 1993/744 reg 46(1), (2), (4), (5), (7), (8).

Cross references—See the Income Tax (PAYE) Regulations, SI 2003/2682 reg 11 (this regulation not to apply to pension payers or pensioners in their capacity as such).

SI 2003/2682 reg 12 (this regulation not to apply to other payers or other payees in their capacity as such).

87 Information employer must also provide for benefits code employees

(1) Particulars of the following information must also be provided in the case of each employee whose employment is subject to the benefits code—

(*a*) . . . [1]

(*b*) any sums put by the employer or related third party at the disposal of the employee by reason of the employment and paid away by the employee;

(*c*) any benefits provided by the employer or related third party for the employee such as give rise to any amount treated by Chapters 6 to 10 of Part 3, and section 223, of ITEPA (cars and vans, loans, shares, other benefits and payments on account of director's tax) as earnings of the employee received in that tax year, including the amount of those earnings.

[(*d*) any mileage allowance payments which are not approved mileage allowance payments;

(*e*) any passenger payments which are not approved passenger payments.][2]

(2) Particulars are not required under paragraph (1) of removal expenses and removal benefits to which section 271 of ITEPA (limited exemption of removal benefits and expenses) applies (as to which see regulation 86(2)).

(3) In the case of any earnings relating to business entertainment, as defined by section 577 of ICTA, the employer must also inform the Inland Revenue whether the amount of the earnings has been or will be disallowed as a deduction or inclusion as mentioned in section 577(1)(*a*) of that Act in any tax computation relating to the trade, business, profession or vocation of the employer.

(4) [In this regulation—][3]

[“approved mileage allowance payments” are mileage allowance payments that are approved in accordance with section 229(3) of ITEPA;

“approved passenger payments” are passenger payments that are approved in accordance with section 233(4) of ITEPA;

“mileage allowance payments” have the meaning given by section 229(2) of ITEPA;

“passenger payments” have the meaning given by section 233(3) of ITEPA.][2]

“[related][3] *third party” has the meaning given in regulation 86(4).*

(5) Regulation 85(3) (meaning of employment “subject to benefits code”) applies for the purposes of this regulation.

Commentary—*Simon's Taxes* **E4.11124.**

Derivation—The Income Tax (Employments) Regulations, SI 1993/744 reg 46(1), (3), (4), (5), (7), (8).

Cross references—See the Income Tax (PAYE) Regulations, SI 2003/2682 reg 11 (this regulation not to apply to pension payers or pensioners in their capacity as such).

SI 2003/2682 reg 12 (this regulation not to apply to other payers or other payees in their capacity as such).

Amendments—[1] Para (1)(*a*) revoked by the Income Tax (Pay As You Earn) (Amendment No 4) Regulations, SI 2015/1927 regs 2, 8 with effect in relation to any returns and information provided for the tax year 2016–17 and subsequent tax years.

[2] Para (1)(*d*), (*e*) inserted, and in para (4), entries for “approved mileage allowance payments”, “approved passenger payments”, “mileage allowance payments” and “passenger payments” inserted by the Income Tax (Pay As You Earn) (Amendment No 2) Regulations, SI 2016/747 reg 2 with effect from 8 August 2016.

[3] In para (4), words inserted, and word substituted, by the Income Tax (Pay As You Earn) (Amendment No 3) Regulations, SI 2016/1137 regs 2, 10 with effect for the tax year 2017–18 and subsequent tax years.

88 Annual return of other earnings: amounts

(1) Paragraph (2) applies if an employer is required by regulations 85 to 87 to provide an amount which is or is treated as earnings.

(2) The employer must make all deductions and other adjustments which the employer is able to show, by reference to information in the employer's possession or otherwise available to the employer, are authorised or required by Part 3 of ITEPA (earnings and benefits etc treated as earnings).

Commentary—*Simon's Taxes* **E4.11124.**

Derivation—The Income Tax (Employments) Regulations, SI 1993/744 reg 46(6).

Cross references—See the Income Tax (PAYE) Regulations, SI 2003/2682 reg 11 (this regulation not to apply to pension payers or pensioners in their capacity as such).

SI 2003/2682 reg 12 (this regulation not to apply to other payers or other payees in their capacity as such).

89 Annual return of other earnings: exclusion for notional payments

The employer is not required to provide particulars in the return under regulation 85 of any notional payment which is a relevant payment made by the employer to the employee (as particulars of it may be required under regulation 73 or 74 (annual returns of relevant payments)).

Commentary—*Simon's Taxes* **E4.11124.**

Derivation—The Income Tax (Employments) Regulations, SI 1993/744 reg 46(7).

Cross references—See the Income Tax (PAYE) Regulations, SI 2003/2682 reg 11 (this regulation not to apply to pension payers or pensioners in their capacity as such).

90 Quarterly return if a car becomes available or unavailable (Form P46 (Car))

(1) This regulation applies if—

(*a*) section 120 of ITEPA (benefit of car treated as earnings) treats the benefit of a car as giving rise to an amount as earnings of an employee received in a tax year, and

(*b*) one or more of the following occurs in a tax quarter—

(i) the car becomes available;

(ii) the car becomes unavailable;

(iii) the car is available and the employee's employment becomes subject to the benefits code (as defined by regulation 85(3)).

[(1A) This regulation does not apply if—

(*a*)the reason a car becomes available or unavailable is that one is replaced with another; or

(*b*) Chapter 3A of these Regulations applies.][2]

(2) The employer must provide [HMRC][1] with the following information in respect of the employee not later than 28 days after the end of the tax quarter.

(3) The information is—

(*a*) the employee's name,

(*b*) the employee's national insurance number, if known,

(*c*) details of the car in question,

(*d*) the interim sum determined at step 4 of section 121(1) of ITEPA (method of calculating cash equivalent of benefit of a car),

(*e*) any capital sum contributed by the employee to expenditure on the provision of the car or on any qualifying accessory which is taken into account in so determining the interim sum in respect of the car, (*f*) any amount which, as a condition of the car being available for the employee's private use, the employee is required to pay in the tax year concerned for that use (whether by way of deduction from relevant payments or otherwise),

(*g*) whether any fuel is provided for private use.

(4) In this regulation—

"available" and "unavailable" are to be read in accordance with sections 116(1) and 143(2) of ITEPA (meaning of when car is available and unavailable to employee);

"qualifying accessory" has the meaning given in section 125 of ITEPA (meaning of accessory etc).

Commentary—*Simon's Taxes* **E4.11126.**

Derivation—The Income Tax (Employments) Regulations, SI 1993/744 reg 46A.

Cross references—See the Income Tax (PAYE) Regulations, SI 2003/2682 reg 11 (this regulation not to apply to pension payers or pensioners in their capacity as such).

SI 2003/2682 reg 12 (this regulation not to apply to other payers or other payees in their capacity as such).

Amendments—[1] Para (1A) inserted, and in para (2) words substituted, by the Income Tax (PAYE) (Amendment) Regulations, SI 2009/588 regs 2, 9 with effect from 6 April 2009. Note, the Publisher considers that the intention was to substitute word "HMRC" for words "the Inland Revenue" and para (2) above has been amended accordingly.

[2] Para (1A) substituted by the Income Tax (Pay As You Earn) (Amendment No 4) Regulations, SI 2015/1927 regs 2, 9 with effect in relation to specified benefits (as defined in reg 61A) provided on or after 6 April 2016.

91 Termination awards: information to be provided

(1) Before 7th July following the end of the tax year, an employer must, in respect of each employee who received a termination award, provide the Inland Revenue with the information specified in paragraph (3) relating to that award.

(2) "Termination award" means an award consisting of payments combined with other benefits, or consisting solely of other benefits—

(*a*) which were awarded in that tax year in connection with the termination of the employee's employment with the employer, or any change in the duties of or earnings from that employment,

(*b*) which when provided (whether in that or a subsequent tax year) would constitute payments and other benefits received to which Chapter 3 of Part 6 of ITEPA applies (payments and benefits on termination of employment etc), and

(*c*) the total amount of which is estimated by the employer to exceed £30,000, when aggregated with other payments and other benefits provided or to be provided (whether in that or a subsequent tax year) in respect of the same person as mentioned in section 404(1) of ITEPA (aggregation of payments in respect of other related employments).

(3) The information to be provided is—

(*a*) the total amount of the payments and other benefits awarded;

(*b*) the total amount of the payments made in that tax year in connection with the award;

(*c*) details of the non-cash benefits provided in that tax year in connection with the award, other than benefits previously contained in a return for that tax year under regulation 85, and the total amount of their amounts calculated in accordance with section 415(2) of ITEPA (valuation of benefits);

(*d*) the estimated total number of the tax years in which payments and non-cash benefits are to be provided in connection with the award and, if the duration of any of those payments and non-cash benefits is capable of being reduced in certain circumstances, details of those circumstances;

(*e*) the estimated total amount of the payments to be made in subsequent tax years in connection with the award;

(*f*) a description of each of the other benefits to be provided in subsequent tax years in connection with the award, and the terms of their provision.

(4) In calculating the cash equivalents of non-cash benefits for the purposes of this regulation, the employer must make all deductions and other adjustments which the employer is able to show, by reference to information in the employer's possession or otherwise available to the employer, are authorised or required by any of the provisions of the benefits code as applied by section 415 of ITEPA.

(5) In calculating the total amount of payments and other benefits for the purposes of paragraphs (2)(*c*) and (3)(*a*), the employer—

(*a*) must have regard to the provisions of Chapter 3 of Part 6 of ITEPA,

(*b*) must take into account the matters referred to in paragraph (3)(*d*),(*e*) and (*f*), and

(*c*) in valuing the amount of non-cash benefits for future tax years in connection with the award, must assume that the provisions of ITEPA relating to those benefits will remain unchanged with respect to those years.

(6) Information required to be provided by an employer in accordance with paragraphs (1) and (3) may be provided after the termination award is made but before the end of the tax year in which it is made.

(7) If information is provided in accordance with paragraph (6), paragraph (3)(*b*) and (*c*) have effect, so far as concerns the providing of information relating to the tax year, as if they required the amounts and benefits there specified to be estimated by the employer as accurately as possible.
(8) This regulation is subject to regulation 93 (return if more than one employer).
(9) In this regulation and regulations 92, 93 and 96 (further provisions about termination awards)—
"employee" includes a former employee; and
"employer" includes a former employer.

Commentary—*Simon's Taxes* **E4.11125.**
Derivation—The Income Tax (Employments) Regulations, SI 1993/744 reg 46ZA(1)–(4), (10)–(12).
Cross references—See the Income Tax (PAYE) Regulations, SI 2003/2682 reg 10 (this regulation not to apply to agencies or agency workers in their capacity as such).
SI 2003/2682 reg 11 (this regulation not to apply to pension payers or pensioners in their capacity as such).
SI 2003/2682 reg 12 (this regulation not to apply to other payers or other payees in their capacity as such).

92 Termination awards: return if award changes

(1) Paragraph (3) applies if—
(*a*) information has not been provided by the employer under regulation 91(1) solely because either—
(i) the total amount of payments and other benefits awarded in the tax year in respect of the employee is estimated in accordance with regulation 91(2)(*c*) not to exceed £30,000, or
(ii) the award made in the tax year consisted of payments only, and
(*b*) there is a change in the award in a subsequent tax year.
(2) "Change in the award" means—
(*a*) that there is a change in—
(i) the amount of the payments awarded, or
(ii) the nature and amounts of the other benefits awarded,
so that the total amount of those payments and other benefits is estimated in accordance with regulation 91(2)(c) to exceed £30,000; or
(*b*) that the nature of the award is changed so that it consists—
(i) of payments combined with other benefits, or
(ii) solely of other benefits,
estimated in accordance with regulation 91(2)(c) to exceed £30,000.
(3) The employer must, before 7th July following the tax year in which the change in the award occurred, provide the Inland Revenue with the information specified in regulation 91(3) with respect to those payments and other benefits.
(4) Paragraph (5) applies if, after the employer has provided information in accordance with regulation 91(1) or paragraph (3) above, there is a material change—
(*a*) in the amount of the payments awarded, or
(*b*) in the nature and amounts of the other benefits awarded,
in relation to the employee.
(5) The employer must, before 7th July following the end of the tax year in which the material change occurred, give details of the material change to the Inland Revenue.
(6) For the avoidance of doubt, an employer is not required to provide details under this regulation of a change which arises solely because of amendments to the provisions of ITEPA which relate to non-cash benefits.
(7) This regulation is subject to regulation 93 (return if more than one employer).

Commentary—*Simon's Taxes* **E4.11125.**
Derivation—The Income Tax (Employments) Regulations, SI 1993/744 reg 46ZA(5), (6), (9), (10).
Cross references—See the Income Tax (PAYE) Regulations, SI 2003/2682 reg 10 (this regulation not to apply to agencies or agency workers in their capacity as such).
SI 2003/2682 reg 11 (this regulation not to apply to pension payers or pensioners in their capacity as such).
SI 2003/2682 reg 12 (this regulation not to apply to other payers or other payees in their capacity as such).

93 Termination awards: return if more than one employer

(1) This regulation applies if the payments and other benefits aggregated in accordance with regulation 91(2)(*c*) include amounts in respect of different employments with more than one employer.
(2) The person who must provide information to the Inland Revenue under regulation 91 or 92, or to the employee under regulation 96, is the employer providing the greatest amount of payments and other benefits so aggregated.

Commentary—*Simon's Taxes* **E4.11125.**
Derivation—The Income Tax (Employments) Regulations, SI 1993/744 reg 46ZA(10).
Cross references—See the Income Tax (PAYE) Regulations, SI 2003/2682 reg 10 (this regulation not to apply to agencies or agency workers in their capacity as such).
SI 2003/2682 reg 11 (this regulation not to apply to pension payers or pensioners in their capacity as such).
SI 2003/2682 reg 12 (this regulation not to apply to other payers or other payees in their capacity as such).

INFORMATION TO BE GIVEN TO EMPLOYEES

94 Employers: information to employees of other earnings ([Form P11D][1])

(1) Before 7th July following the end of a tax year, the employer must give a statement to every current employee in respect of whom particulars are to be provided under regulation 85(1) by the employer for that tax year.

(2) The statement must contain the particulars provided under regulations 86 and 87 in so far as they relate to the employee.

(3) If a person who was a current employee ceases to be an employee at any time before 7th July following the end of the tax year, the statement is given to the employee if it is sent or delivered to, or left at, that person's usual or last known address.

(4) A former employee in respect of whom particulars are to be provided under regulation 85(1) by the employer for a tax year may by notice require the employer to give the statement specified in paragraph (2) to that former employee—

(*a*) before 7th July following the end of the tax year, or

(*b*) within 30 days of receiving the notice,

whichever is the later.

(5) The notice may be given to the employer at any time up to 3 years after the end of the tax year.

(6) A former employee who has received a statement from the employer under paragraph (4) in respect of a tax year may not require a further statement from the employer under that paragraph in respect of the same tax year.

(7) In this regulation—

"current employee" means a person who was an employee on 5th April in the tax year to which the particulars provided under regulation 85(1) relate;

"former employee" means a person who was an employee during a part of the tax year to which the particulars provided under regulation 85(1) relate, but who was no longer an employee on 5th April in that tax year.

Commentary—*Simon's Taxes* **E4.11124.**

Derivation—The Income Tax (Employments) Regulations, SI 1993/744 reg 46AA.

Cross references—See the Income Tax (PAYE) Regulations, SI 2003/2682 reg 10 (when an agency is treated as ceasing to employ an agency worker for the purposes of paras (3)–(7) above).

SI 2003/2682 reg 11 (this regulation not to apply to pension payers or pensioners in their capacity as such).

SI 2003/2682 reg 12 (this regulation not to apply to other payers or other payees in their capacity as such).

Amendments—[1] In heading, words substituted by the Income Tax (Pay As You Earn) (Amendment No 4) Regulations, SI 2015/1927 regs 2, 10 with effect in relation to any returns and information provided for the tax year 2016–17 and subsequent tax years.

95 Third parties: information to employees of other earnings

(1) This regulation applies if a person ("the third party") has, in a tax year—

(*a*) made any unrelated payments to, or on behalf of, another person's employee, or

(*b*) provided any unrelated benefits to, or in respect of, another person's employee.

(2) Before 7th July following the end of the tax year, the third party must give the employee a statement containing such of the particulars specified by regulations 86 and 87 as relate to the unrelated payments or unrelated benefits.

(3) A benefit or payment is "unrelated" if—

(*a*) the employee's employer is not required to provide particulars about it under regulation 85(1), and

(*b*) the third party would have been required to provide particulars about it under regulation 85(1) had the third party been the employee's employer.

Commentary—*Simon's Taxes* **E4.11124.**

Derivation—The Income Tax (Employments) Regulations, SI 1993/744 reg 46AB.

Cross references—See the Income Tax (PAYE) Regulations, SI 2003/2682 reg 11 (this regulation not to apply to pension payers or pensioners in their capacity as such).

SI 2003/2682 reg 12 (this regulation not to apply to other payers or other payees in their capacity as such).

96 Termination awards: information to employees

(1) This regulation applies if an employer is required to provide the information specified in regulation 91(3) to the Inland Revenue by—

(*a*) regulation 91(1) (termination award), or

(*b*) regulation 92(3) (change in termination award).

(2) The employer must also give a copy of that information to the employee before 7th July following the end of the tax year.

(3) A copy of the information is given to the employee if it is sent or delivered to, or left at, the employee's usual or last known address.

(4) As to the person who is the employer in cases where there is more than one employer, see regulation 93.

Commentary—*Simon's Taxes* **E4.11125.**

Derivation—The Income Tax (Employments) Regulations, SI 1993/744 reg 46ZA(7), (8), (10).

Cross references—See the Income Tax (PAYE) Regulations, SI 2003/2682 reg 10 (this regulation not to apply to agencies or agency workers in their capacity as such).
SI 2003/2682 reg 11 (this regulation not to apply to pension payers or pensioners in their capacity as such).
SI 2003/2682 reg 12 (this regulation not to apply to other payers or other payees in their capacity as such).

CHAPTER 3

PAYE RECORDS

97 [Retention by employer of PAYE records

(1) An employer must keep and preserve for not less than three years after the end of the tax year to which they relate all PAYE records which are not required to be sent to HMRC by other provisions in these Regulations.

(2) The duty under paragraph (1) to keep and preserve PAYE records may be discharged by preserving them in any form or by any means.

(3) "PAYE records" means the following documents and records—

(*a*) all wages sheets, deductions working sheets, documents completed under regulation 46 (Form P46)[, information provided under regulation 40A(1) (duty of employee to assist with completion of new employee fields in returns under regulations 67B and 67D)][2] and other documents and records relating to—

(i) the calculation of the PAYE income of the employees,

(ii) relevant payments to the employees, or

(iii) the deduction of tax from, or accounting for tax in respect of, such payments, and

(*b*) all documents relating to any information which an employer is required to provide to HMRC under regulation 85 ([Form P11D][3]).][1]

Commentary—*Simon's Taxes* **A6.704, A6.705.**

Amendments—[1] This regulation substituted by the Income Tax (PAYE) (Amendment) Regulations, SI 2009/588 regs 2, 6 with effect from 1 April 2009.

[2] Words in para (3)(*a*) inserted by the Income Tax (Pay As You Earn) (Amendment) Regulations, SI 2012/822 regs 2, 41 with effect from 6 April 2012.

[3] In para (3)(*b*), words substituted by the Income Tax (Pay As You Earn) (Amendment No 4) Regulations, SI 2015/1927 regs 2, 11 with effect in relation to any returns and information provided for the tax year 2016–17 and subsequent tax years.

[CHAPTER 3A

CERTAIN DEBTS OF COMPANIES UNDER CHAPTER 7 OF PART 2 OF ITEPA (AGENCIES)

97ZA Interpretation of Chapter 3A

In this Chapter—

"company" includes a limited liability partnership;

"HMRC" means Her Majesty's Revenue and Customs;

"director" has the meaning given by section 67 of ITEPA;

"personal liability notice" has the meaning given by regulation 97ZB(2);

"relevant PAYE debt", in relation to a company, means—

(*a*) any amount that the company is to deduct, or account for, in accordance with these Regulations by virtue of—

(i) section 44(4) to (6) of ITEPA (persons providing fraudulent documents), or

(ii) section 46A of that Act (anti-avoidance), and

(*b*) any interest or penalty, in respect of an amount within paragraph (*a*), for which the company is liable;

"the relevant date", in relation to a relevant PAYE debt, means—

(*a*) in a case where the relevant PAYE debt is to be deducted or accounted for, or arises, by virtue of subsections (4) to (6) of section 44 of ITEPA, the date on which the fraudulent document was provided as mentioned in subsection (4) of that section, or

(*b*) in a case where the relevant PAYE debt is to be deducted or accounted for, or arises, by virtue of section 46A of ITEPA, the date the arrangements mentioned in subsection (1)(*b*) of that section were entered into;

"the specified amount" has the meaning given by regulation 97ZB(2)(*a*).][1]

Amendments—[1] This Chapter (regs 97ZA–97ZF) inserted by FA 2014 s 17(1) with effect in relation to relevant PAYE debts that are to be deducted, accounted for or paid on or after 6 April 2014. This amendment is to be treated as having been made by the Commissioners for HMRC in exercise of the power conferred by ITEPA 2003 s 688(2A): FA 2014 s 17(5)).

[97ZB Liability of directors for relevant PAYE debts

(1) This regulation applies in relation to an amount of relevant PAYE debt of a company if the company does not deduct, account for or (as the case may be) pay that amount by the time by which the company is required to do so.

(2) HMRC may serve a notice (a "personal liability notice") on any person who was, on the relevant date, a director of the company—

(*a*) specifying the amount of relevant PAYE debt in relation to which this regulation applies ("the specified amount"), and

(*b*) requiring the director to pay to HMRC—

(i) the specified amount, and

(ii) specified interest on that amount.

(3) The interest specified in the personal liability notice—

(*a*) is to be at the rate applicable under section 178 of the Finance Act 1989 for the purposes of section 86 of TMA, and

(*b*) is to run from the date the notice is served.

(4) A director who is served with a personal liability notice is liable to pay to HMRC the specified amount and the interest specified in the notice within 30 days beginning with the day the notice is served.

(5) If HMRC serve personal liability notices on more than one director of the company in respect of the same amount of relevant PAYE debt, the directors are jointly and severally liable to pay to HMRC the specified amount and the interest specified in the notices.][1]

Amendments—[1] This Chapter (regs 97ZA–97ZF) inserted by FA 2014 s 17(1) with effect in relation to relevant PAYE debts that are to be deducted, accounted for or paid on or after 6 April 2014. This amendment is to be treated as having been made by the Commissioners for HMRC in exercise of the power conferred by ITEPA 2003 s 688(2A): FA 2014 s 17(5)).

[97ZC Appeals in relation to personal liability notices

(1) A person who is served with a personal liability notice in relation to an amount of relevant PAYE debt of a company may appeal against the notice.

(2) A notice of appeal must—

(*a*) be given to HMRC within 30 days beginning with the day the personal liability notice is served, and

(*b*) specify the grounds of the appeal.

(3) The grounds of appeal are —

(*a*) that all or part of the specified amount does not represent an amount of relevant PAYE debt, of the company, to which regulation 97ZB applies, or

(*b*) that the person was not a director of the company on the relevant date.

(4) But a person may not appeal on the ground mentioned in paragraph (3)(*a*) if it has already been determined, on an appeal by the company, that—

(*a*) the specified amount is a relevant PAYE debt of the company, and

(*b*) the company did not deduct, account for, or (as the case may be) pay the debt by the time by which the company was required to do so.

(5) Subject to paragraph (6), on an appeal that is notified to the tribunal, the tribunal is to uphold or quash the personal liability notice.

(6) In a case in which the ground of appeal mentioned in paragraph (3)(*a*) is raised, the tribunal may also reduce or increase the specified amount so that it does represent an amount of relevant PAYE debt, of the company, to which regulation 97ZB applies.][1]

Amendments—[1] This Chapter (regs 97ZA–97ZF) inserted by FA 2014 s 17(1) with effect in relation to relevant PAYE debts that are to be deducted, accounted for or paid on or after 6 April 2014. This amendment is to be treated as having been made by the Commissioners for HMRC in exercise of the power conferred by ITEPA 2003 s 688(2A): FA 2014 s 17(5)).

[97ZD Withdrawal of personal liability notices

(1) A personal liability notice is withdrawn if the tribunal quashes it.

(2) An officer of Revenue and Customs may withdraw a personal liability notice if the officer considers it appropriate to do so.

(3) If a personal liability notice is withdrawn, HMRC must give notice of that fact to the person upon whom the notice was served.][1]

Amendments—[1] This Chapter (regs 97ZA–97ZF) inserted by FA 2014 s 17(1) with effect in relation to relevant PAYE debts that are to be deducted, accounted for or paid on or after 6 April 2014. This amendment is to be treated as having been made by the Commissioners for HMRC in exercise of the power conferred by ITEPA 2003 s 688(2A): FA 2014 s 17(5)).

[97ZE Recovery of sums due under personal liability notice: application of Part 6 of TMA

(1) For the purposes of this Chapter, Part 6 of TMA (collection and recovery) applies as if—

(*a*) the personal liability notice were an assessment, and

(*b*) the specified amount, and any interest on that amount under regulation 97ZB(2)(*b*)(ii), were income tax charged on the director upon whom the notice is served,

and that Part of that Act applies with the modification in paragraph (2) and any other necessary modifications.

(2) Summary proceedings for the recovery of the specified amount, and any interest on that amount under regulation 97ZB(2)(*b*)(ii), may be brought in England and Wales or Northern Ireland at any time before the end of the period of 12 months beginning with the day after the day on which personal liability notice is served.][1]

Amendments—[1] This Chapter (regs 97ZA–97ZF) inserted by FA 2014 s 17(1) with effect in relation to relevant PAYE debts that are to be deducted, accounted for or paid on or after 6 April 2014. This amendment is to be treated as having been made by the Commissioners for HMRC in exercise of the power conferred by ITEPA 2003 s 688(2A): FA 2014 s 17(5)).

[97ZF Repayment of surplus amounts

(1) This regulation applies if—

(*a*) one or more personal liability notices are served in respect of an amount of relevant PAYE debt of a company, and

(*b*) the amounts paid to HMRC (whether by directors upon whom notices are served or the company) exceed the aggregate of the specified amount and any interest on it under regulation 97ZB(2)(*b*)(ii).

(2) HMRC is to repay the difference on a just and equitable basis and without unreasonable delay.

(3) HMRC is to pay interest on any sum repaid.

(4) The interest—

(*a*) is to be at the rate applicable under section 178 of the Finance Act 1989 for the purposes of section 824 of ICTA, and

(*b*) is to run from the date the amounts paid to HMRC come to exceed the aggregate mentioned in subsection (1)(*b*).][1]

Amendments—[1] This Chapter (regs 97ZA–97ZF) inserted by FA 2014 s 17(1) with effect in relation to relevant PAYE debts that are to be deducted, accounted for or paid on or after 6 April 2014. This amendment is to be treated as having been made by the Commissioners for HMRC in exercise of the power conferred by ITEPA 2003 s 688(2A): FA 2014 s 17(5)).

[CHAPTER 3B

CERTAIN DEBTS OF COMPANIES UNDER SECTION 339A OF ITEPA (TRAVEL EXPENSES OF WORKERS PROVIDING SERVICES THROUGH EMPLOYMENT INTERMEDIARIES)

97ZG Interpretation of Chapter 3B: "relevant PAYE debt" and "relevant date"

(1) In this Chapter "relevant PAYE debt", in relation to a company means an amount within any of paragraphs (2) to (5).

(2) An amount within this paragraph is an amount that the company is to account for in accordance with these Regulations by virtue of section 339A(7) to (9) of ITEPA (persons providing fraudulent documents).

(3) An amount within this paragraph is an amount which a company is to deduct and pay in accordance with these Regulations by virtue of section 339A of ITEPA in circumstances where—

(*a*) the company is an employment intermediary,

(*b*) on the basis that section 339A of ITEPA does not apply by virtue of subsection (3) of that section the company has not deducted and paid the amount, but

(*c*) the company has not been provided by any other person with evidence from which it would be reasonable in all the circumstances to conclude that subsection (3) of that section applied (and the mere assertion by a person that the manner in which the worker provided the services was not subject to (or to the right of) supervision, direction or control by any person is not such evidence).

(4) An amount within this paragraph is an amount that the company is to deduct and pay in accordance with these Regulations by virtue of section 339A of ITEPA in a case where subsection (4) of that section applies (services provided under arrangements made by intermediaries).

(5) An amount within this paragraph is any interest or penalty in respect of an amount within any of paragraphs (2) to (4) for which the company is liable.

(6) In this Chapter "the relevant date" in relation to a relevant PAYE debt means the date on which the first payment is due on which PAYE is not accounted for.][1]

Amendments—[1] Chapter 3B (regs 97ZG–97ZM) inserted by FA 2016 s 14(4) with effect in relation to relevant PAYE debts that are to be deducted, accounted for or paid on or after 6 April 2016. This amendment is to be treated as having been made by the Commissioners for HMRC in exercise of the power conferred by ITEPA 2003 s 688B (FA 2016 s 14(5)).

[97ZH Interpretation of Chapter 3B: general

In this Chapter—

"company" includes a limited liability partnership;

"director" has the meaning given by section 67 of ITEPA;

"personal liability notice" has the meaning given by regulation 97ZI(2);

"the specified amount" has the meaning given by regulation 97ZI(2)(*a*).][1]

Amendments—[1] Chapter 3B (regs 97ZG–97ZM) inserted by FA 2016 s 14(4) with effect in relation to relevant PAYE debts that are to be deducted, accounted for or paid on or after 6 April 2016. This amendment is to be treated as having been made by the Commissioners for HMRC in exercise of the power conferred by ITEPA 2003 s 688B (FA 2016 s 14(5)).

[97ZI Liability of directors for relevant PAYE debts

(1) This regulation applies in relation to an amount of relevant PAYE debt of a company if the company does not deduct that amount by the time by which the company is required to do so.

(2) HMRC may serve a notice (a "personal liability notice") on any person who was, on the relevant date, a director of the company—

(*a*) specifying the amount of relevant PAYE debt in relation to which this regulation applies ("the specified amount"), and

(*b*) requiring the director to pay to HMRC—

(i) the specified amount, and

(ii) specified interest on that amount.

(3) The interest specified in the personal liability notice—

(*a*) is to be at the rate applicable under section 178 of the Finance Act 1989 for the purposes of section 86 of TMA, and

(*b*) is to run from the date the notice is served.

(4) A director who is served with a personal liability notice is liable to pay to HMRC the specified amount and the interest specified in the notice within 30 days beginning with the day the notice is served.

(5) If HMRC serve personal liability notices on more than one director of the company in respect of the same amount of relevant PAYE debt, the directors are jointly and severally liable to pay to HMRC the specified amount and the interest specified in the notices.[1]

Amendments—[1] Chapter 3B (regs 97ZG–97ZM) inserted by FA 2016 s 14(4) with effect in relation to relevant PAYE debts that are to be deducted, accounted for or paid on or after 6 April 2016. This amendment is to be treated as having been made by the Commissioners for HMRC in exercise of the power conferred by ITEPA 2003 s 688B (FA 2016 s 14(5)).

[97ZJ Appeals in relation to personal liability notices

(1) A person who is served with a personal liability notice in relation to an amount of relevant PAYE debt of a company may appeal against the notice.

(2) A notice of appeal must—

(*a*) be given to HMRC within 30 days beginning with the day the personal liability notice is served, and

(*b*) specify the grounds of the appeal.

(3) The grounds of appeal are—

(*a*) that all or part of the specified amount does not represent an amount of relevant PAYE debt, of the company, to which regulation 97ZI applies, or

(*b*) that the person was not a director of the company on the relevant date.

(4) But a person may not appeal on the ground mentioned in paragraph (3)(*a*) if it has already been determined, on an appeal by the company, that—

(*a*) the specified amount is a relevant PAYE debt of the company, and

(*b*) the company did not deduct, account for, or (as the case may be) pay the debt by the time by which the company was required to do so.

(5) Subject to paragraph (6), on an appeal that is notified to the tribunal, the tribunal is to uphold or quash the personal liability notice.

(6) In a case in which the ground of appeal mentioned in paragraph (3)(*a*) is raised, the tribunal may also reduce or increase the specified amount so that it does represent an amount of relevant PAYE debt, of the company, to which regulation 97ZI applies.][1]

Amendments—[1] This Chapter (regs 97ZG–97ZM) inserted by FA 2016 s 14(4) with effect in relation to relevant PAYE debts that are to be deducted, accounted for or paid on or after 6 April 2016. This amendment is to be treated as having been made by the Commissioners for HMRC in exercise of the power conferred by ITEPA 2003 s 688B: FA 2016 s 14(5).

[97ZK Withdrawal of personal liability notices

(1) A personal liability notice is withdrawn if the tribunal quashes it.

(2) An officer of Revenue and Customs may withdraw a personal liability notice if the officer considers it appropriate to do so.

(3) If a personal liability notice is withdrawn, HMRC must give notice of that fact to the person upon whom the notice was served.][1]

Amendments—[1] Chapter 3B (regs 97ZG–97ZM) inserted by FA 2016 s 14(4) with effect in relation to relevant PAYE debts that are to be deducted, accounted for or paid on or after 6 April 2016. This amendment is to be treated as having been made by the Commissioners for HMRC in exercise of the power conferred by ITEPA 2003 s 688B (FA 2016 s 14(5)).

[97ZL Recovery of sums due under personal liability notice: application of Part 6 of TMA

(1) For the purposes of this Chapter, Part 6 of TMA (collection and recovery) applies as if—

(*a*) the personal liability notice were an assessment, and

(*b*) the specified amount, and any interest on that amount under regulation 97ZI(2)(*b*)(ii), were income tax charged on the director upon whom the notice is served,

and that Part of that Act applies with the modification in paragraph (2) and any other necessary modifications.

(2) Summary proceedings for the recovery of the specified amount, and any interest on that amount under regulation 97ZI(2)(*b*)(ii), may be brought in England and Wales or Northern Ireland at any time before the end of the period of 12 months beginning with the day after the day on which the personal liability notice is served.[1]

Amendments—[1] Chapter 3B (regs 97ZG–97ZM) inserted by FA 2016 s 14(4) with effect in relation to relevant PAYE debts that are to be deducted, accounted for or paid on or after 6 April 2016. This amendment is to be treated as having been made by the Commissioners for HMRC in exercise of the power conferred by ITEPA 2003 s 688B (FA 2016 s 14(5)).

[97ZM Repayment of surplus amounts

(1) This regulation applies if—

(*a*) one or more personal liability notices are served in respect of an amount of relevant PAYE debt of a company, and

(*b*) the amounts paid to HMRC (whether by directors upon whom notices are served or the company) exceed the aggregate of the specified amount and any interest on it under regulation 97ZI(2)(*b*)(ii).

(2) HMRC is to repay the difference on a just and equitable basis and without unreasonable delay.

(3) HMRC is to pay interest on any sum repaid.

(4) The interest—

(*a*) is to be at the rate applicable under section 178 of the Finance Act 1989 for the purposes of section 824 of ICTA, and

(*b*) is to run from the date the amounts paid to HMRC come to exceed the aggregate mentioned in subsection (1)(*b*).][1]

Amendments—[1] Chapter 3B (regs 97ZG–97ZM) inserted by FA 2016 s 14(4) with effect in relation to relevant PAYE debts that are to be deducted, accounted for or paid on or after 6 April 2016. This amendment is to be treated as having been made by the Commissioners for HMRC in exercise of the power conferred by ITEPA 2003 s 688B (FA 2016 s 14(5)).

[CHAPTER 4

DEBTS OF MANAGED SERVICE COS][1]1

Amendments—[1] This Chapter (regs 97A–97L) inserted by the Income Tax (Pay as You Earn) (Amendment No 2) Regulations, SI 2007/2069 reg 2 with effect from 6 August 2007 (SI 2007/2069 reg 1).

[97A Interpretation of Chapter 4

(1) In this Chapter—

"HM Revenue and Customs" means Her Majesty's Revenue and Customs;

"lower amount" means the amount mentioned in regulation 97C(5);

"managed service company" has the meaning given by section 61B of ITEPA;

"paragraph (*b*) associate" means a person who—

(*a*) is within section 688A(2)(*d*), and

(*b*) is within that provision by virtue of a connection with a person who is within section 688A(2)(*b*);

"paragraph (*c*) associate" means a person who—

(*a*) is within section 688A(2)(*d*), and

(*b*) is within that provision by virtue of a connection with a person who is within section 688A(2)(*c*);

"qualifying period" means a tax period beginning on or after 6th August 2007;

["relevant apprenticeship levy debt" means a debt specified in regulation 97B][2].

"relevant PAYE debt" means a debt specified in regulation 97B;

"specified amount" means the amount mentioned in regulation 97C(1)(*b*);

"transfer notice" means the notice mentioned in regulation 97C(4);

"transferee" means the person mentioned in regulation 97C(4).

(2) In this Chapter references to section 688A, however expressed, are references to section 688A of ITEPA.][1]

Amendments—[1] This Chapter (regs 97A–97L) inserted by the Income Tax (Pay as You Earn) (Amendment No 2) Regulations, SI 2007/2069 reg 2 with effect from 6 August 2007 (SI 2007/2069 reg 1).

[2] Definition of "relevant apprenticeship levy debt" inserted by the Income Tax (Pay As You Earn) (Amendment) Regulations, SI 2017/414 reg 2(1), (5) with effect from 6 April 2017.

[97B Relevant PAYE [and apprenticeship levy][3] debts of managed service companies

[(1) A managed service company has a relevant PAYE debt or a relevant apprenticeship levy debt if a managed service company must pay an amount of tax or apprenticeship levy for a qualifying period, and—

(*a*) in the case of a relevant PAYE debt one of conditions A to E is met, and

(*b*) in the case of a relevant apprenticeship levy debt one of conditions F or G is met.][3]

(2) Condition A is met if—

(*a*) an amount of tax for a qualifying period has been determined in accordance with regulation 80 (determination of unpaid tax and appeal against determination), and

(*b*) any part of the tax determined has not been paid within 14 days from the date on which the determination became final and conclusive.

[(2A) Condition A2 is met if—

(*a*) HMRC serve a notice on an employer under regulation 75A(5) (power of HMRC to issue a notice and certificate in cases where regulation 67B or 67D returns are not made, etc) requiring payment of the amount of tax they consider the employer is liable to pay, and

(*b*) any part of that amount remains unpaid at the end of a period of 14 days beginning with the date on which the notice is prepared.][2]

(3) Condition B is met if—

(*a*) an employer delivers a return under regulation 73 (annual return of relevant payments) for the tax year 2007–08, or any later tax year, showing an amount of total net tax deducted by the employer for that tax year,

(*b*) HM Revenue and Customs prepare a certificate under regulation 76 (certificate if tax in regulation 73 return is unpaid) showing how much of that amount remains unpaid, and

(*c*) any part of that amount remains unpaid at the end of a period of 14 days beginning with the date on which the certificate is prepared.

(4) Condition C is met if—

(*a*) HM Revenue and Customs prepare a certificate under regulation 77(6) (return and certificate if tax may be unpaid) showing an amount of tax which the employer is liable to pay for a qualifying period, and

(*b*) any part of that amount remains unpaid at the end of a period of 14 days beginning with the date on which the certificate is prepared.

(5) Condition D is met if—

(*a*) HM Revenue and Customs serve notice on an employer under regulation 78(4) (notice and certificate if tax may be unpaid) requiring payment of the amount of tax which they consider the employer is liable to pay, and

(*b*) any part of that amount remains unpaid at the end of a period of 14 days beginning with the date on which the notice is prepared.

(6) Condition E is met if—

(*a*) HM Revenue and Customs prepare a certificate under regulation 79(2) (certificate after inspection of PAYE records) showing an amount of tax which it appears that the employer is liable to pay for a qualifying period,

(*b*) HM Revenue and Customs make a written demand for payment of that amount of tax, and

(*c*) any part of that amount remains unpaid at the end of a period of 14 days beginning with the date on which the written demand for payment is made.

[(7) Condition F is met if—

(*a*) an amount of apprenticeship levy for a qualifying period has been assessed in accordance with regulation 147L (assessment of unpaid apprenticeship levy), and

(*b*) any part of the apprenticeship levy assessed has not been paid within 14 days beginning with the date on which the assessment is served.

(8) Condition G is met if—

(*a*) an employer delivers a return under regulation 147D (duty to report the amount of apprenticeship levy to be paid), showing an amount of apprenticeship levy payable by the employer for the tax year,

(*b*) HM Revenue and Customs assesses the amount of apprenticeship levy under regulation 147L showing how much of that amount remains unpaid, and

(*c*) any part of that amount remains unpaid at the end of a period of 14 days beginning with the date on which the assessment is served.][3]][1]

Amendments—[1] This Chapter (regs 97A–97L) inserted by the Income Tax (Pay as You Earn) (Amendment No 2) Regulations, SI 2007/2069 reg 2 with effect from 6 August 2007 (SI 2007/2069 reg 1).

[2] Para (2A) inserted by the Income Tax (Pay As You Earn) (Amendment) Regulations, SI 2012/822 regs 2, 42 with effect from 6 April 2012.

[3] In heading, words inserted, para (1) substituted, and paras (6), (7) inserted, by the Income Tax (Pay As You Earn) (Amendment) Regulations, SI 2017/414 reg 2(1), (6) with effect from 6 April 2017.

[97C Transfer of debt of managed service company

(1) This regulation applies if—

(*a*) a managed service company has a relevant PAYE debt [or a relevant apprenticeship levy debt][2], and

(*b*) an officer of Revenue and Customs is of the opinion that the relevant PAYE debt [or the relevant apprenticeship levy debt][2] or a part of the relevant PAYE debt [or part of the relevant apprenticeship levy debt][2] (the "specified amount") is irrecoverable from the managed service company within a reasonable period.

(2) HM Revenue and Customs may make a direction authorising the recovery of the specified amount from the persons specified in section 688A(2) (managed service companies: recovery from other persons).

(3) Upon the making of a direction under paragraph (2), the persons specified in section 688A(2) become jointly and severally liable for the relevant PAYE debt [or the relevant apprenticeship levy debt][2], but subject to what follows.

(4) HM Revenue and Customs may not recover the specified amount from any person in accordance with a direction made under paragraph (2) until they have served a notice (a "transfer notice") on the person in question (the "transferee").

(5) If an officer of Revenue and Customs is of the opinion that it is appropriate to do so, HM Revenue and Customs may accept an amount less than the specified amount (the "lower amount") from a transferee; but this acceptance shall not prejudice the recovery of the specified amount from any other transferee.

(6) HM Revenue and Customs may not serve a transfer notice on a person mentioned in section 688A(2)(*c*), or on a paragraph (*c*) associate, if the relevant PAYE debt is incurred before 6th January 2008.

(7) HM Revenue and Customs may not serve a transfer notice on a person mentioned in section 688A(2)(*c*), or on a paragraph (*c*) associate, unless an officer of Revenue and Customs certifies that, in his opinion, it is impracticable to recover the specified amount from persons mentioned in paragraphs (*a*) and (*b*) of section 688A(2) and from paragraph (*b*) associates.

(8) In determining, for the purposes of paragraph (7), whether it is impracticable to recover the specified amount from persons mentioned in paragraphs (*a*) and (*b*) of section 688A(2) and from paragraph (*b*) associates, the officer of Revenue and Customs may have regard to all managed service companies in relation to which a person is a person mentioned in paragraph (*a*) or (*b*) of section 688A(2) or a paragraph (*b*) associate.

(9) In determining which of the persons mentioned in section 688A(2)(*c*) and which of the paragraph (*c*) associates are to be served with transfer notices and the amount of those notices, HM Revenue and Customs must have regard to the degree and extent to which those persons are persons who (directly or indirectly) have encouraged or been actively involved in the provision by the managed service company of the services of the individual mentioned in that provision.][1]

Amendments—[1] This Chapter (regs 97A–97L) inserted by the Income Tax (Pay as You Earn) (Amendment No 2) Regulations, SI 2007/2069 reg 2 with effect from 6 August 2007 (SI 2007/2069 reg 1).

[2] In paras (1)(*a*), (*b*), (3), words inserted by the Income Tax (Pay As You Earn) (Amendment) Regulations, SI 2017/414 reg 2(1), (7) with effect from 6 April 2017.

[97D Time limits for issue of transfer notices

(1) A transfer notice must be served before the end of the period determined in accordance with this regulation.

(2) Paragraphs [(3) to (7B)][2] apply if the transfer notice is served on a person mentioned in paragraph (*a*) or (*b*) of section 688A(2) or on a paragraph (*b*) associate.

(3) In a case in which condition A in regulation 97B is met, the transfer notice must be served before the end of a period of 12 months beginning with the date on which the determination became final and conclusive.

[(3A) In a case in which condition A2 in regulation 97B is met, the transfer notice must be served before the end of a period of 12 months beginning with the date on which HMRC serve notice to the employer under regulation 75A(5).][3]

(4) In a case in which condition B in regulation 97B is met, the transfer notice must be served before the end of a period of 12 months beginning with the date on which HM Revenue and Customs received the return delivered under regulation 73.

(5) In a case in which condition C in regulation 97B is met, the transfer notice must be served before the end of a period of 12 months beginning with the date on which HM Revenue and Customs prepare the certificate under regulation 77(6).

(6) In a case in which condition D in regulation 97B is met, the transfer notice must be served before the end of a period of 12 months beginning with the date on which HM Revenue and Customs serve notice to the employer under regulation 78(4).

(7) In a case in which condition E in regulation 97B is met, the transfer notice must be served before the end of a period of 12 months beginning with the date on which HM Revenue and Customs carry out the inspection of the employer's PAYE records.

[(7A) In a case in which condition F in regulation 97B is met, the transfer notice must be served before the end of a period of 12 months beginning with the date on which the assessment became final and conclusive.

(7B) In a case in which condition G in regulation 97B is met, the transfer notice must be served before the end of a period of 12 months beginning with the date on which HM Revenue and Customs serves the assessment under regulation 147L.][4]

(8) If the transfer notice is served on a person mentioned in paragraph (*c*) of section 688A(2) or on a paragraph (*c*) associate, the transfer notice must be served before the end of a period of [three months][2] beginning with the date on which the officer of Revenue and Customs certifies the matters specified in regulation 97C(7).][1]

Amendments—[1] This Chapter (regs 97A–97L) inserted by the Income Tax (Pay as You Earn) (Amendment No 2) Regulations, SI 2007/2069 reg 2 with effect from 6 August 2007 (SI 2007/2069 reg 1).

[2] Words in para (8) substituted by the Income Tax (Pay As You Earn) (Amendment No 3) Regulations, SI 2007/2296 reg 2 with effect from 6 August 2007: SI 2007/2296 reg 1.

[3] Para (3A) inserted by the Income Tax (Pay As You Earn) (Amendment) Regulations, SI 2012/822 regs 2, 43 with effect from 6 April 2012.

[4] In para (2), words substituted, and paras (7A), (7B) inserted, by the Income Tax (Pay As You Earn) (Amendment) Regulations, SI 2017/414 reg 2(1), (8) with effect from 6 April 2017.

[97E Contents of transfer notice

(1) A transfer notice must contain the following information—

(*a*) the name of the managed service company to which the relevant PAYE debt [or the relevant apprenticeship levy debt][2] relates;

(*b*) the address of the managed service company to which the relevant PAYE debt [or the relevant apprenticeship levy debt][2] relates;

(*c*) the amount of the relevant PAYE debt [or the relevant apprenticeship levy debt][2];

(*d*) the tax periods to which the relevant PAYE debt [or the relevant apprenticeship levy debt][2] relates;

(*e*) if the tax periods to which the relevant PAYE debt [or the relevant apprenticeship levy debt][2] relates are comprised in more than one tax year, the apportionment of the relevant PAYE debt [or the relevant apprenticeship levy debt][2] among those tax years;

(*f*) which of the [conditions A to G][2] specified in regulation 97B is met;

(*g*) the transferee's name;

(*h*) the transferee's address;

(*j*) whether the transferee is a person mentioned in paragraph (*a*), (*b*) or (*c*) of section 688A, a paragraph (*b*) associate or a paragraph (*c*) associate;

(*k*) if the transferee is a person mentioned in paragraph (*c*) of section 688A or a paragraph (*c*) associate—

(i) the date on which the officer of Revenue and Customs certified the matters specified in regulation 97C(7), and

(ii) the names of the persons from whom it has been impracticable to recover the specified amount;

(*l*) the specified amount;

(*m*) the tax periods to which the specified amount relates;

(*n*) if the tax periods to which the specified amount relates are comprised in more than one tax year, the apportionment of the specified amount among those tax years;

(*o*) the address to which payment must be sent;

(*p*) the address to which an appeal must be sent.

(2) The transfer notice may specify the lower amount if HM Revenue and Customs are prepared to accept the lower amount from the transferee.

(3) The transfer notice must also contain a statement, made by the officer of Revenue and Customs serving the notice, that in his opinion the specified amount is irrecoverable from the managed service company within a reasonable period.][1]

Amendments—[1] This Chapter (regs 97A–97L) inserted by the Income Tax (Pay as You Earn) (Amendment No 2) Regulations, SI 2007/2069 reg 2 with effect from 6 August 2007 (SI 2007/2069 reg 1).

[2] In para (1)(*a*)–(*e*), words inserted, and in para (1)(*f*), words substituted, by the Income Tax (Pay As You Earn) (Amendment) Regulations, SI 2017/414 reg 2(1), (9) with effect from 6 April 2017.

[97F Payment of the specified amount

(1) If a transfer notice is served, the transferee must pay the specified amount to HM Revenue and Customs at the address specified in the transfer notice.

(2) The transferee must pay the specified amount within 30 days beginning with the date on which the transfer notice is served (the "specified period").

(3) If a transfer notice is served on a person mentioned in paragraph (*a*) or (*b*) of section 688A(2), or on a paragraph (*b*) associate, the specified amount carries interest from the reckonable date until the date on which payment is made.

(4) If a transfer notice is served on a person mentioned in paragraph (*c*) of section 688A(2), or on a paragraph (*c*) associate, the specified amount carries interest from the day following the expiry of the specified period until the date on which payment is made.][1]

Amendments—[1] This Chapter (regs 97A–97L) inserted by the Income Tax (Pay as You Earn) (Amendment No 2) Regulations, SI 2007/2069 reg 2 with effect from 6 August 2007 (SI 2007/2069 reg 1).

[97G Appeals

(1) A transferee may appeal against the transfer notice.

(2) A notice of appeal must—

(*a*) be given to HM Revenue and Customs at the address specified in the transfer notice within 30 days beginning with the date on which the transfer notice was served, and

(*b*) specify the grounds of the appeal.

(3) The grounds of appeal are any of the following—

(*a*) that the relevant PAYE debt (or part of the relevant PAYE debt) [or the relevant apprenticeship levy debt (or part of the relevant apprenticeship levy debt)][3] is not due from the managed service company to HM Revenue and Customs;

(*b*) that the specified amount does not relate to a company which is a managed service company;
(*c*) that the specified amount is not irrecoverable from the managed service company within a reasonable period;
(*d*) that the transferee is not a person mentioned in section 688A(2);
(*e*) that the transferee was not a person mentioned in section 688A(2) during the tax periods to which the specified amount relates;
(*f*) that the transferee was not a person mentioned in section 688A(2) during some part of the tax periods to which the specified amount relates;
(*g*) that the transfer notice was not served before the end of the period specified in regulation 97D;
(*h*) that the transfer notice does not satisfy the requirements specified in regulation 97E;
(*j*) in the case of a transferee mentioned in section 688A(2)(*c*) or of a paragraph (*c*) associate, that it is not impracticable to recover the specified amount from persons mentioned in paragraphs (*a*) and (*b*) of section 688A(2) or from paragraph (*b*) associates;
(*k*) in the case of a transferee mentioned in section 688A(2)(*c*) or of a paragraph (*c*) associate, that the amount specified in the transfer notice does not have regard to the degree and extent to which the transferee is a person who (directly or indirectly) has encouraged or been actively involved in the provision by the managed service company of the services of the individual mentioned in that provision.

(4) Paragraph (3)(*a*) is subject to regulation 97H(4).

(5) . . . [2]][1]

Amendments—[1] This Chapter (regs 97A–97L) inserted by the Income Tax (Pay as You Earn) (Amendment No 2) Regulations, SI 2007/2069 reg 2 with effect from 6 August 2007 (SI 2007/2069 reg 1).

[2] Para (5) revoked by the Transfer of Tribunal Functions and Revenue and Customs Appeals Order, SI 2009/56 art 3, Sch 2 paras 92, 103 with effect from 1 April 2009.

[3] In para (3)(*a*), words inserted by the Income Tax (Pay As You Earn) (Amendment) Regulations, SI 2017/414 reg 2(1), (10) with effect from 6 April 2017.

[97H Procedure on appeals

(1) On an appeal [that is notified to the tribunal, the tribunal][2] shall uphold or quash the transfer notice.

(2) The general rule in paragraph (1) is subject to the following qualifications.

(3) In the case of the ground of appeal specified in regulation 97G(3)(*a*), the [tribunal][2] shall investigate the matter and shall—
(*a*) uphold the amount of the relevant PAYE debt [or the relevant apprenticeship levy debt][3] specified in the transfer notice, or
(*b*) reduce or increase the amount of the relevant PAYE debt [or the relevant apprenticeship levy debt][3] specified in the transfer notice to such amount as in [the tribunal's opinion][2] is just and reasonable.

(4) If the [tribunal determines][2] the amount of the relevant PAYE debt [or the relevant apprenticeship levy debt][3] of a managed service company under paragraph (3), that amount is conclusive as to the amount of that relevant PAYE debt in any later appeal relating to that debt.

(5) In the case of the ground of appeal specified in regulation 97G(3)(*f*), the [tribunal][2] may reduce the amount specified in the transfer notice to an amount determined in accordance with the equation—

$$RA = \frac{P}{TP} \times AS$$

(6) In paragraph (5)—

RA means the reduced amount;

P means the number of days in the tax periods specified in the transfer notice during which the transferee was a person mentioned in section 688A(2);

TP means the number of days in the tax periods specified in the transfer notice;

AS means the amount specified in the transfer notice.

(7) In the case of the ground of appeal specified in regulation 97G(3)(*k*), the [tribunal][2] may reduce the amount specified in the transfer notice to such amount as in [the tribunal's opinion][2] is just and reasonable.][1]

Amendments—[1] This Chapter (regs 97A–97L) inserted by the Income Tax (Pay as You Earn) (Amendment No 2) Regulations, SI 2007/2069 reg 2 with effect from 6 August 2007 (SI 2007/2069 reg 1).

[2] In paras (1), (3), (4), (5), (7), words substituted by the Transfer of Tribunal Functions and Revenue and Customs Appeals Order, SI 2009/56 art 3, Sch 2 paras 92, 104 with effect from 1 April 2009.

[3] In paras (3)(*a*), (*b*), (4), words inserted by the Income Tax (Pay As You Earn) (Amendment) Regulations, SI 2017/414 reg 2(1), (11) with effect from 6 April 2017.

[97J Withdrawal of transfer notices

(1) A transfer notice shall be withdrawn if the [tribunal quashes][2] it.

(2) A transfer notice may be withdrawn if, in the opinion of an officer of Revenue and Customs, it is appropriate to do so.
(3) If a transfer notice is withdrawn, HM Revenue and Customs must give written notice of that fact to the transferee.][1]

Amendments—[1] This Chapter (regs 97A–97L) inserted by the Income Tax (Pay as You Earn) (Amendment No 2) Regulations, SI 2007/2069 reg 2 with effect from 6 August 2007 (SI 2007/2069 reg 1).
[2] In para (1), words substituted by the Transfer of Tribunal Functions and Revenue and Customs Appeals Order, SI 2009/56 art 3, Sch 2 paras 92, 105 with effect from 1 April 2009.

[97K Application of Part 6 of TMA

(1) For the purposes of this Chapter, Part 6 of TMA (collection and recovery) applies as if—
(*a*) the transfer notice were an assessment, and
(*b*) the amount specified in the transfer notice, and any interest payable on that amount under paragraph (3) or (4) of regulation 97F, were income tax charged on the transferee;
and that Part of that Act applies with the modification specified in paragraph (2) and any other necessary modifications.
(2) Summary proceedings for the recovery of the specified amount may be brought in England and Wales or Northern Ireland at any time before the end of a period of 12 months beginning immediately after the expiry of the period mentioned in regulation 97F(2).
(3) The specified amount is one cause of action or one matter of complaint for the purposes of proceedings under sections 65, 66 and 67 of TMA (magistrates' courts, county courts and inferior courts in Scotland).
(4) But paragraph (3) does not prevent the bringing of separate proceedings for the recovery of each of the amounts which the transferee is liable to pay for any tax period.][1]

Amendments—[1] This Chapter (regs 97A–97L) inserted by the Income Tax (Pay as You Earn) (Amendment No 2) Regulations, SI 2007/2069 reg 2 with effect from 6 August 2007 (SI 2007/2069 reg 1).

[97L Repayment of surplus amounts

(1) This regulation applies if the amounts paid to HM Revenue and Customs in respect of a relevant PAYE debt [or a relevant apprenticeship levy debt][2] exceed the specified amount.
(2) HM Revenue and Customs shall repay the difference on a just and equitable basis and without unreasonable delay.
(3) Interest on any sum repaid shall be paid in accordance with [section 102 of the Finance Act 2009 (repayment interest on sums to be paid by HMRC)][2].][1]

Amendments—[1] This Chapter (regs 97A–97L) inserted by the Income Tax (Pay as You Earn) (Amendment No 2) Regulations, SI 2007/2069 reg 2 with effect from 6 August 2007 (SI 2007/2069 reg 1).
[2] In para (1), words inserted, and in para (3), words substituted, by the Income Tax (Pay As You Earn) (Amendment) Regulations, SI 2017/414 reg 2(1), (12) with effect from 6 April 2017.

[PART 4A

SECURITY FOR PAYMENT OF PAYE

97M Interpretation

In this Part—
"a further notice" has the meaning given in regulation 97U(3); and
"PGS" has the meaning given in regulation 97S(1).][1]

Amendments—[1] Part 4A (regs 97M–97X) inserted by the Income Tax (Pay As You Earn) (Amendment) Regulations, SI 2012/822 regs 2, 58 with effect from 6 April 2012.

[97N Requirement for security

(1) In circumstances where an officer of Revenue and Customs considers it necessary for the protection of the revenue, the officer may require a person described in regulation 97P(1) (persons from whom security can be required) to give security or further security for the payment of amounts in respect of which an employer described in regulation 97O (employers) is or may be accountable to HMRC under regulation 67G[, as adjusted by regulation 67H(2) where appropriate][2], 68 or 80 (payments to HMRC and determination of unpaid amounts).
(2) Paragraph (1) does not apply to any amount which the employer is required to pay to HMRC that relates to income to which Part 8 (social security benefits) applies.][1]

Amendments—[1] Part 4A (regs 97M–97X) inserted by the Income Tax (Pay As You Earn) (Amendment) Regulations, SI 2012/822 regs 2, 58 with effect from 6 April 2012.
[2] Words in para (1) inserted by the Income Tax (Pay As You Earn) (Amendment) Regulations, SI 2013/521 regs 2, 34 with effect from 6 April 2013 in relation to the tax year 2013–14 and subsequent tax years.

[97O Employers

(1) The employer is any employer other than—
(*a*) the Crown,
(*b*) an employer to whom paragraph (2) applies,
(*c*) . . .[2] *and*
(*d*) a care and support employer within the meaning given by regulation 206(4) (employers).

(2) This paragraph applies to employers who at the relevant time could not be liable to a penalty under Schedule 56 to the Finance Act 2009 by virtue of paragraph 10 of that Schedule (suspension of penalty for failure to make payments on time during currency of agreement for deferred payment).
(3) In paragraph (2), the relevant time is a time at which, but for paragraph (1)(*b*), the officer would require security.][1]

Amendments—[1] Part 4A (regs 97M–97X) inserted by the Income Tax (Pay As You Earn) (Amendment) Regulations, SI 2012/822 regs 2, 58 with effect from 6 April 2012.
[2] Para (1)(*c*) revoked by the Income Tax (Pay As You Earn) (Amendment) Regulations, SI 2013/521 regs 2, 9 with effect from 6 April 2014.

[97P Persons from whom security can be required

(1) The persons are—
(*a*) the employer,
(*b*) any of the following in relation to the employer—
(i) a director,
(ii) a company secretary,
(iii) any other similar officer, or
(iv) any person purporting to act in such a capacity, and
(*c*) in a case where the employer is a limited liability partnership, a member of the limited liability partnership.
(2) An officer of Revenue and Customs may require—
(*a*) a person to give security or further security of a specified value in respect of the employer, or
(*b*) more than one person to give security or further security of a specified value in respect of the employer, and where the officer does so those persons shall be jointly and severally liable to give that security or further security.][1]

Amendments—[1] Part 4A (regs 97M–97X) inserted by the Income Tax (Pay As You Earn) (Amendment) Regulations, SI 2012/822 regs 2, 58 with effect from 6 April 2012.

[97Q Notice of requirement

(1) An officer of Revenue and Customs must give notice of a requirement for security to each person from whom security is required and the notice must specify—
(*a*) the value of security to be given,
(*b*) the manner in which security is to be given,
(*c*) the date on or before which security is to be given, and
(*d*) the period of time for which security is required.
(2) The notice must include, or be accompanied by, an explanation of—
(*a*) the employer's right to make a request under paragraph 10(1) of Schedule 56 to the Finance Act 2009, and
(*b*) the effect of regulation 97R(2) and (3) (date on which security is due).
(3) In a case which falls within regulation 97P(2)(*b*), the notice must include, or be accompanied by, the names of each other person from whom security is required.
(4) The notice may contain such other information as the officer considers necessary.
(5) A person shall not be treated as having been required to provide security unless HMRC comply with this regulation and regulation 97R(1).][1]

Amendments—[1] Part 4A (regs 97M–97X) inserted by the Income Tax (Pay As You Earn) (Amendment) Regulations, SI 2012/822 regs 2, 58 with effect from 6 April 2012.

[97R Date on which security is due

(1) The date specified under regulation 97Q(1)(*c*) (notice of requirement) may not be earlier than the 30th day after the day on which the notice is given.
(2) If, before the date specified under regulation 97Q(1)(*c*), the employer makes a request under paragraph 10(1) of Schedule 56 to the Finance Act 2009, the requirement to give security on or before that date does not apply.
(3) In a case which falls within paragraph (2), if HMRC does not agree to the employer's request, security is to be given on or before the 30th day after the day on which HMRC notifies the employer of that decision.][1]

Amendments—[1] Part 4A (regs 97M–97X) inserted by the Income Tax (Pay As You Earn) (Amendment) Regulations, SI 2012/822 regs 2, 58 with effect from 6 April 2012.

[97S Application for reduction in the value of security held

(1) A person who has given security ("PGS") may apply to an officer of Revenue and Customs for a reduction in the value of security held by HMRC if—
(*a*) PGS' circumstances have changed since the day the security was given because—
(i) of hardship, or
(ii) PGS has ceased to be a person mentioned in regulation 97P(1) (person from whom security can be required), or

(*b*) since the day the security was given there has been a significant reduction in the number of employees of the employer to whom the security relates or that employer has ceased to be an employer.

(2) Where regulation 97P(2)(*b*) applies, a person who has not contributed to the value of the security given may not make an application under paragraph (1).][1]

Amendments—[1] Part 4A (regs 97M–97X) inserted by the Income Tax (Pay As You Earn) (Amendment) Regulations, SI 2012/822 regs 2, 58 with effect from 6 April 2012.

[97T Outcome of application for reduction in the value of security held

(1) If an application under regulation 97S(1) (application for reduction in the value of security held) is successful, the officer must inform PGS of the reduced value of security that is still required or, where that value is nil, that the requirement for security has been cancelled.

(2) HMRC may make such arrangements as they think fit to ensure the necessary reduction in the value of security held.][1]

Amendments—[1] Part 4A (regs 97M–97X) inserted by the Income Tax (Pay As You Earn) (Amendment) Regulations, SI 2012/822 regs 2, 58 with effect from 6 April 2012.

[97U Outcome of application for reduction in the value of security held: further provision

(1) This regulation applies—

(*a*) in cases which fall within regulation 97P(2)(*b*), and

(*b*) where PGS' application is made under regulation 97S(1)(*a*).

(2) As a consequence of arrangements made under regulation 97T(2) (outcome of application for reduction in the value of security held), an officer of Revenue and Customs may require any other person who was given notice under regulation 97Q (notice of requirement) in relation to the security ("the original security"), or any other person mentioned in regulation 97P(1), to provide security in substitution for the original security.

(3) Where an officer of Revenue and Customs acts in reliance on paragraph (2), the officer must give notice ("a further notice").

(4) Regulation 97Q and regulation 97R (date on which security is due) apply in relation to a further notice.

(5) Subject to paragraph (6), regulation 97V(1) (appeals) applies in relation to a further notice.

(6) A person who is given a further notice and who was also given notice under regulation 97Q in relation to the original security may only appeal on the grounds the person is not a person mentioned in regulation 97P(1).][1]

Amendments—[1] Part 4A (regs 97M–97X) inserted by the Income Tax (Pay As You Earn) (Amendment) Regulations, SI 2012/822 regs 2, 58 with effect from 6 April 2012.

[97V Appeals

(1) A person who is given notice under regulation 97Q may appeal against the notice or any requirement in it.

(2) PGS may appeal against—

(*a*) the rejection by an officer of Revenue and Customs of an application under regulation 97S(1), and

(*b*) a smaller reduction in the value of security held than PGS applied for.

(3) Notice of an appeal under this regulation must be given—

(*a*) before the end of the period of 30 days beginning with—

(i) in the case of an appeal under paragraph (1), the day after the day on which the notice was given, and

(ii) in the case of an appeal under paragraph (2), the day after the day on which PGS was notified of the outcome of the application, and

(*b*) to the officer of Revenue and Customs by whom the notice was given or the decision on the application was made, as the case may be.

(4) Notice of an appeal under this regulation must state the grounds of appeal.

(5) On an appeal under paragraph (1) that is notified to the tribunal, the tribunal may—

(*a*) confirm the requirements in the notice,

(*b*) vary the requirements in the notice, or

(*c*) set aside the notice.

(6) On an appeal under paragraph (2) that is notified to the tribunal, the tribunal may—

(*a*) confirm the decision on the application, or

(*b*) vary the decision on the application.

(7) On the final determination of an appeal under this regulation—

(*a*) subject to any alternative determination by a tribunal or court, any security to be given is due on the 30th day after the day on which the determination is made, or

(*b*) HMRC may make such arrangements as it sees fit to ensure the necessary reduction in the value of security held.

(8) An appeal under this regulation is subject to the provisions of Part 5 of TMA (appeals and other proceedings) apart from—

(*a*) section 46D,
(*b*) section 47B,
(*c*) section 50(6) to (9), and
(*d*) sections 54A to 57.][1]

Amendments—[1] Part 4A (regs 97M–97X) inserted by the Income Tax (Pay As You Earn) (Amendment) Regulations, SI 2012/822 regs 2, 58 with effect from 6 April 2012.

[97W Appeals: further provision for cases which fall within regulation 97R(2)

In a case which falls within regulation 97R(2) (date on which security is due), if the request mentioned in that provision is made before an appeal under regulation 97V(1) (appeals), regulation 97V(3)(*a*)(i) applies as if the words "the day after the day on which the notice was given" were "the day after the day on which HMRC notifies the employer of its decision".][1]

Amendments—[1] Part 4A (regs 97M–97X) inserted by the Income Tax (Pay As You Earn) (Amendment) Regulations, SI 2012/822 regs 2, 58 with effect from 6 April 2012.

[97X Offence

(1) For the purposes of section 684(4A) of ITEPA (PAYE regulations—security for payment of PAYE: offence)—

(*a*) in relation to a requirement for security under a notice under regulation 97Q (notice of requirement) the period specified is the period which starts with the day the notice is given and ends with—
(i) the first day after the date specified under regulation 97Q(1)(*c*), or
(ii) in a case which falls within regulation 97R(2), the first day after the date determined under regulation 97R(3),

(*b*) in relation to a requirement for security under a further notice the period specified is the period which starts with the day the further notice is given and ends with—
(i) the first day after the date specified under regulation 97Q(1)(*c*) as it applies in relation to the further notice, or
(ii) in a case which falls within regulation 97R(2), the first day after the date determined under regulation 97R(3) as it applies in relation to the further notice, and

(*c*) in relation to a requirement for security to which regulation 97V(7)(*a*) applies the period specified is the period which starts with the day the determination is made and ends with the first day after—
(i) the day the tribunal or court determines to be the day that the security is to be given, or
(ii) the day determined in accordance with that regulation,

as the case may be.][1]

Amendments—[1] Part 4A (regs 97M–97X) inserted by the Income Tax (Pay As You Earn) (Amendment) Regulations, SI 2012/822 regs 2, 58 with effect from 6 April 2012.

PART 5
EMPLOYERS

SPECIAL ARRANGEMENTS

98 Multiple PAYE schemes

(1) An employer may elect, for the purposes of these Regulations, to be treated as different employers in relation to different groups of employees.

(2) Where the employer makes an election, these Regulations apply as if—
(*a*) in respect of each group the employer were a different employer;
(*b*) each group constituted all of the employer's employees;
(*c*) each group were employed in a separate undertaking from the others; and
(*d*) an employee who has moved from one group to another has left one employment and started employment with a new employer.

(3) While an election is in force, an employer must allocate any new employees to one of the groups.

(4) An election must be made by notice to the Inland Revenue containing—
(*a*) such information as may be necessary to identify the groups of employees, and
(*b*) a certificate that each employee falls into one of the groups.

(5) An employer must, subject to paragraph (6), make an election before the beginning of the tax year for which it is to have effect.

(6) An employer who acquires the whole or a part of any business of another employer may, within 90 days of the acquisition, elect—
(*a*) to be treated as a different employer in relation to the acquired employees, or two or more different employers in relation to groups of the acquired employees, whether or not an election is already in force in respect of the existing employees, or
(*b*) to add some or all of the acquired employees to existing groups of employees in respect of whom an election is already in force,

and such an election has effect for the tax year in which the acquisition takes place.

(7) In paragraph (6)—

"business" includes any trade, concern or undertaking;

"acquired employee" means an employee who was employed in the acquired business.

(8) An election continues in effect until revoked by a notice given to the Inland Revenue.

(9) A notice of revocation must be given before the beginning of the tax year for which the election is to be revoked, but the revocation of an election does not prevent the making of a new election for that or a later tax year.

(10) An election which has not yet come into effect may be revoked at any time before the beginning of the tax year for which it is to have effect.

(11) This regulation is subject to regulation 99.

Commentary—*Simon's Taxes* **E4.11113.**

Derivation—The Income Tax (Employments) Regulations, SI 1993/744 reg 3.

Modifications—See the Income Tax (PAYE) Regulations, SI 2003/2682 reg 150 (modification of this regulation in its application to payments of taxable jobseeker's allowance made to a claimant).

SI 2003/2682 reg 174 (modification of this regulation in its application to payments of taxable incapacity benefit).

99 Multiple PAYE schemes: election made for improper purpose ineffective

(1) An election made under regulation 98 must be disregarded if the Inland Revenue—

(*a*) issue a notice to the employer stating that it appears to them that the election is made wholly or mainly for an improper purpose ("an improper purpose notice"), and

(*b*) issue the improper purpose notice within 60 days of the making of the election.

(2) An election is made for an "improper purpose" if it is made for the purpose of—

(*a*) avoiding the requirement imposed by regulation 199 (large employers required to make specified payments electronically),

(*b*) . . . [2]

(*c*) . . . [1]

(3) An employer may appeal against an improper purpose notice by giving notice to the Inland Revenue within 30 days of the issue of the improper purpose notice.

(4) The grounds of appeal are—

(*a*) that the election was not made wholly or mainly for an improper purpose, or

(*b*) that the improper purpose notice was not issued within 60 days of the election.

(5) If the appeal is successful the improper purpose notice must be withdrawn.

(6) Regulation 217 (appeals: supplementary provisions) applies to appeals under this regulation.

Commentary—*Simon's Taxes* **E4.11113.**

Cross reference—See the Income Tax (PAYE) Regulations, SI 2003/2682 reg 217 (TMA 1970 ss 31A(5), (6), 31B and 31D apply to an appeal under para (3) above as they apply to an appeal under TMA 1970 s 31).

Amendment—[1] Para (2)(*c*) revoked by the Income Tax (Pay as You Earn) (Amendment) Regulations, SI 2010/668 regs 2, 16(*a*), (*b*) with effect from 6 April 2010.

[2] Para (2)(*b*) revoked by the Income Tax (Pay As You Earn) (Amendment) Regulations, SI 2010/668, regs 2, 16(*c*), with effect in relation to the tax year 2011–12 and subsequent tax years.

100 Tips: special arrangements

(1) This regulation applies if an organised arrangement exists for tips to be shared among employees by a person ("T") who is not the principal employer.

(2) On becoming aware of the existence of an arrangement, the principal employer must notify the Inland Revenue about the arrangement giving T's name, if known.

(3) For the purposes of these Regulations—

(*a*) every payment made to an employee by way of the employee's share of tips by T (including the retention by T of T's own share if T is also an employee) is regarded as a relevant payment by T; and

(*b*) to the extent of any such payment, T is regarded as the employer.

(4) But if in any case the Inland Revenue are satisfied that T has failed to comply with any of the requirements of these Regulations and they so direct, then—

(*a*) any tips paid to T through the principal employer for sharing among the employees are to be dealt with in accordance with paragraph (5), and

(*b*) any other tips may be taken into account by the Inland Revenue under regulation 14(1)(*b*) in determining the code for each employee.

(5) If this paragraph applies—

(*a*) the principal employer is treated as the employer for the purposes of these Regulations in relation to the tips;

(*b*) T must, before the principal employer pays any tips to T, give the principal employer such particulars of every payment by way of the sharing of tips to be made to an employee as may be necessary to enable the principal employer to comply with these Regulations;

(*c*) the principal employer must, on making any payment of tips to T, deduct or repay tax in accordance with these Regulations in respect of the amount of such tips to be paid to each employee, and notify T of each amount so deducted or repaid.

(6) Paragraph (2) does not apply if the arrangement came into existence before 6th April 2004.

(7) In this regulation—

"the principal employer" means the person under whose general control and management the employees work;

"tips" means gratuities and service charges.

Commentary—*Simon's Taxes* **E4.1114**.

Derivation—The Income Tax (Employments) Regulations, SI 1993/744 reg 5.

Cross references—See the Income Tax (PAYE) Regulations, SI 2003/2682 reg 11 (this regulation not to apply to pension payers or pensioners in their capacity as such).

DEATH OF EMPLOYER AND SUCCESSION

101 Death of employer

(1) This regulation applies if an employer dies.

(2) Anything which the employer would have been liable to do under these Regulations must be done by the employer's personal representatives.

(3) But if the employer made payments on behalf of another person ("the principal"), anything which the employer would have been liable to do under these Regulations in respect of or in connection with those payments must be done by the principal.

Commentary—*Simon's Taxes* **E4.11111**.

Derivation—The Income Tax (Employments) Regulations, SI 1993/744 reg 79.

102 Succession to a business etc

(1) This regulation applies if there is a change in an employee's employer while the employee remains in employment in the same business.

(2) This regulation also applies if there is a change in the pension payer who pays a pension to a pensioner.

(3) The change is not to be treated as a cessation of employment for the purposes of regulation 36 (cessation of employment: Form P45).

(4) The new employer is, in relation to any matter arising after the change, liable to do anything which the former employer would have been liable to do under these Regulations if the change had not taken place.

(5) Paragraph (4) is subject to paragraphs (6) and (7) and regulation 104 (succession to a business: trade disputes).

(6) The new employer is not liable for the payment of any tax which was deductible from relevant payments made to the employee—

(*a*) before the change took place, unless those payments were made by the new employer, or

(*b*) by the former employer after the change took place.

(7) The new employer is not liable for the payment of any tax which was to be deducted or accounted for in accordance with regulation 62(4) or (5) (notional payments) in respect of notional payments made to the employee—

(*a*) before the change took place, unless those payments were made by the new employer, or

(*b*) by the former employer after the change took place.

(8) The former employer must give the new employer any particulars which the new employer needs in order to comply with this regulation.

(9) In paragraph (1), "business" includes any trade, concern or undertaking.

Commentary—*Simon's Taxes* **E4.11112**.

Derivation—The Income Tax (Employments) Regulations, SI 1993/744 reg 80(1)–(3), (5).

Modifications—See the Income Tax (PAYE) Regulations, SI 2003/2682 reg 150 (modification of this regulation in its application to payments of taxable jobseeker's allowance made to a claimant).

SI 2003/2682 reg 174 (modification of this regulation in its application to payments of taxable incapacity benefit).

Cross references—See the Income Tax (PAYE) Regulations, SI 2003/2682 reg 11 (para (1) above not to apply to pension payers or pensioners in their capacity as such).

103 Death and succession

(1) Regulation 101 (death of employer) does not affect the operation of regulation 102 (succession to a business etc) for the purposes of which the deceased employer's personal representative or the principal may also be the new employer.

(2) But paragraph (3) applies where a person ("P") is both the new employer and also the deceased employer's personal representative or the principal.

(3) Paragraphs (6) and (7) of regulation 102 (new employer not liable for certain payments of tax) do not apply to P in P's capacity as personal representative or principal.

(4) "Principal" has the same meaning as in regulation 101.

Commentary—*Simon's Taxes* **E4.11112**.

104 Succession to a business: trade disputes

(1) This regulation applies if a trade dispute began, but did not end, before a change to which regulation 102 (succession to a business etc) applies took place.

(2) The former employer must comply with regulations 64(8) (trade disputes: payments to Revenue) and 75 (additional return in case of trade dispute) as though the time limit of 42 days ran out on the date on which the change took place.
(3) The new employer is liable to repay, in accordance with regulation 64, any tax that was withheld in the tax year in which the change took place by the former employer.
(4) The new employer may recover from the Board of Inland Revenue an amount repayable under paragraph (3), as if it were an amount recoverable under regulation [67G(3)(*b*)[, as adjusted by regulation 67H(2) where appropriate,][2] (payments to and recoveries from HMRC for each tax period by Real Time Information employers) or, as the case may be,][1] 68(3)(*b*) (periodic payments to and recoveries from Revenue).
(5) But any amount recovered under paragraph (4) must be ignored when determining how much the new employer must pay or can recover under regulation [67G or][1] 68.

Commentary—*Simon's Taxes* **E4.11112**.
Derivation—The Income Tax (Employments) Regulations, SI 1993/744 reg 80(4).
Cross references—See the Income Tax (PAYE) Regulations, SI 2003/2682 reg 11 (this regulation not to apply to pension payers or pensioners in their capacity as such).
Amendments—[1] Words in paras (4), (5) inserted by the Income Tax (Pay As You Earn) (Amendment) Regulations, SI 2012/822 regs 2, 44 with effect from 6 April 2012.
[2] Words in para (4) inserted by the Income Tax (Pay As You Earn) (Amendment) Regulations, SI 2013/521 regs 2, 35 with effect from 6 April 2013 in relation to the tax year 2013–14 and subsequent tax years.

PART 6
PAYE SETTLEMENT AGREEMENTS

Cross references—SI 2003/2682 reg 12 (this Part not to apply to other payers or other payees in their capacity as such).

MAKING AND EFFECT OF PSA

105 Inland Revenue and employer may make PSA

(1) The Inland Revenue and an employer may agree that paragraph (2) applies in respect of income tax on qualifying general earnings of the employer's employees for a tax year.
(2) In relation to qualifying general earnings included in the agreement, the employer is—
  (*a*) accountable to the Board of Inland Revenue in accordance with the terms of the agreement and this Part, and
  (*b*) not accountable in accordance with the rest of these Regulations.
(3) Such an agreement is referred to as a PAYE settlement agreement ("PSA").

Commentary—*Simon's Taxes* **E4.11110**.
Derivation—The Income Tax (Employments) Regulations, SI 1993/744 reg 80A(1), (2).

106 Qualifying general earnings

(1) Qualifying general earnings are those general earnings which meet conditions A and B.
(2) Condition A is that the general earnings consist of—
  (*a*) taxable benefits provided or made available by reason of employments with the employer, or
  (*b*) expenses paid to persons holding those employments.
(3) Condition B is that the employer and the Inland Revenue agree that the general earnings are—
  (*a*) minor, as regards the amount of the sums paid or the type of benefit provided or made available,
  (*b*) irregular, as regards the frequency in which, or the times at which, the sums are paid or the benefit is provided or made available,
  (*c*) paid in circumstances where deduction of tax by reference to the tax tables is impracticable, or
  (*d*) in the case of a benefit provided or made available, shared between employees so that apportionment of the benefit between the employees is impracticable.
(4) "Taxable benefit", in relation to an employee, means any benefit provided or made available, other than in the form of a payment of money, to the employee or to a person who is a member of the employee's family or household.
(5) General earnings to which regulation 112(2)(*a*) or (*b*) (pre-agreement general earnings etc) apply are not qualifying general earnings.

Commentary—*Simon's Taxes* **E4.11110**.
Derivation—The Income Tax (Employments) Regulations, SI 1993/744 reg 80A(3), (4).

107 Effect of PSA

(1) Qualifying general earnings included in the PSA are treated as excluded from an employee's income for the purposes of determining the amount of the employee's liability to income tax for the tax year to which the PSA relates.
(2) But this does not affect—
  (*a*) the chargeability of those qualifying general earnings to income tax, or
  (*b*) the employer's liability under the PSA to account for income tax in respect of those qualifying general earnings.

(3) Sums in respect of income tax for which an employer is accountable to the Board of Inland Revenue under a PSA are not to be treated, for the purposes of these Regulations, as tax deducted from relevant payments.

(4) An employee has no right to be treated as having paid tax in respect of sums for which the employer is accountable under a PSA, and accordingly is not entitled to claim or receive any refund of tax paid by the employer under the PSA.

(5) An employee must, subject to paragraph (6), be treated as relieved from any obligations under the Income Tax Acts—

(*a*) to keep records containing information relating to qualifying general earnings included in a PSA, or

(*b*) to deliver returns in respect of those qualifying general earnings.

(6) Paragraph (5) does not apply for the purposes of the obligations imposed on the employer under regulation 117 (inspection of PSA records).

(7) Qualifying general earnings comprised in a PSA are not to be included—

(*a*) in a return by the employer under regulation [67B, 67D, 67E,][1] 73, 74, or 75 (returns of relevant payments and tax deducted), nor

(*b*) in particulars provided by the employer under regulation 85 (annual return of other earnings ([Form P11D][2]).

Commentary—*Simon's Taxes* **E4.11110**.

Derivation—The Income Tax (Employments) Regulations, SI 1993/744 regs 80A(5), 80E.

Amendments—[1] Words in para (7)(*a*) inserted by the Income Tax (Pay As You Earn) (Amendment) Regulations, SI 2012/822 regs 2, 45 with effect from 6 April 2012.

[2] In para (7)(*b*), words substituted by the Income Tax (Pay As You Earn) (Amendment No 4) Regulations, SI 2015/1927 regs 2, 12 with effect in relation to any returns and information provided for the tax year 2016–17 and subsequent tax years.

PAYMENT OF TAX UNDER PSA

108 Calculation of tax payable under PSA

(1) A PSA must provide for the sums in respect of income tax for which an employer is to be accountable to the Board of Inland Revenue under the PSA—

(*a*) to be computed in accordance with the factors specified in paragraph (2), and

(*b*) to be comprised of the amounts specified in paragraph (3).

(2) The factors are—

(*a*) in the case of qualifying general earnings comprising sums paid in respect of expenses, the estimated aggregate amount of such payments on which income tax is chargeable, reduced by such amount (if any) as would have been deductible if the qualifying general earnings had not been included in the PSA;

(*b*) in the case of qualifying general earnings comprising benefits provided or made available, the estimated aggregate amount of the cash equivalents and other amounts on which income tax is chargeable, reduced by such amount (if any) as would have been deductible if the qualifying general earnings had not been included in the PSA;

(*c*) the total number of employees in receipt of qualifying general earnings comprised in the PSA;

[(*d*) the number of those employees respectively chargeable to income tax—

(i) at only the basic rate for the tax year to which the PSA relates, and

(ii) at both the basic rate and the higher rate for that tax year;][1] [and

(iii) at the basic, higher and additional rates for that tax year;][2]

(*e*) such other matters as are agreed by [HMRC][1] and the employer to be relevant in relation to the qualifying general earnings comprised in the PSA.

(3) The amounts specified for the purposes of paragraph (1)(*b*) are—

(*a*) an amount equal to income tax on the aggregate of the amounts computed in accordance with paragraph (2)(*a*) and (*b*), calculated so as to take account of the factor specified in paragraph (2)(*d*); and

(*b*) a further amount reflecting an estimate of the income tax on the benefit to the employees of having no tax liability on the qualifying general earnings included in the PSA.

Commentary—*Simon's Taxes* **E4.11110**.

Derivation—The Income Tax (Employments) Regulations, SI 1993/744 reg 80F(1)–(3).

Amendments—[1] In para (2), whole of sub-para (*d*), and reference to HMRC in sub-para (*e*), substituted, by the Income Tax (Pay As You Earn) (Amendment) Regulations, SI 2008/782 regs 2, 12 with effect from 6 April 2008.

[2] Para (2)(*d*)(iii) and preceding word "and" inserted , by the Income Tax (Pay As You Earn) (Amendment) Regulations, SI 2011/729 regs 2, 14 with effect from 6 April 2011.

109 Payment of tax and recovery proceedings

(1) The employer must pay to the Inland Revenue by the due date the aggregate amount for which the employer is accountable to the Board of Inland Revenue under a PSA.

(2) "The due date" means 19th October following the end of the tax year to which the PSA relates.

(3) Part 6 of TMA (collection and recovery) applies to the recovery of the aggregate amount or any part of it ("the amount of tax") as if it were income tax charged on the employer.

(4) But summary proceedings for the recovery of the amount of tax may be brought in England, Wales or Northern Ireland at any time before the expiry of 12 months beginning with the due date.
(5) Proceedings may be brought for the recovery of the amount of tax without distinguishing the amounts which the employer is liable to pay in respect of each employee under the PSA and without specifying the employees in question.
(6) The amount of tax is one cause of action or one matter of complaint for the purposes of proceedings under sections 65, 66 and 67 of TMA (magistrates' courts, county courts and inferior courts in Scotland).

Commentary—*Simon's Taxes* **E4.11110**.
Derivation—The Income Tax (Employments) Regulations, SI 1993/744 reg 80G.

110 Formal determination of tax payable by the employer

(1) This regulation applies if it appears to the Inland Revenue that there may be an amount payable under regulation 109(1) for any tax year which has not been paid by the due date (as defined by regulation 109(2)).
(2) The Inland Revenue may determine the amount payable to the best of their judgment.
(3) If a determination is made, the Inland Revenue must serve notice of it on the employer.
(4) A determination under this regulation is subject to Parts 4, 5[, 5A][2] and 6 of TMA (assessment, appeals, collection and recovery) as if—
(*a*) the determination were an assessment, and
(*b*) the amount determined were income tax charged on the employer,
and those Parts of TMA apply accordingly with any necessary modifications.
(5) . . . [1]

Commentary—*Simon's Taxes* **E4.11110**.
Derivation—The Income Tax (Employments) Regulations, SI 1993/744 reg 80H.
Amendments—[1] Para (5) revoked by the Transfer of Tribunal Functions and Revenue and Customs Appeals Order, SI 2009/56 art 3, Sch 2 paras 92, 106 with effect from 1 April 2009.
[2] Reference in para (4) inserted by the Income Tax (Pay As You Earn) (Amendment) Regulations, SI 2010/668, regs 2, 3, with effect in relation to the tax year 2010–11 and subsequent tax years.

FORM AND COMMENCEMENT OF PSA

Statement of Practice—See Statement of Practice 5/96 PAYE Settlement Agreements.

111 Form of PSA

(1) A PSA must be—
(*a*) in writing, and
(*b*) signed and dated by the employer and the Inland Revenue.
(2) A PSA must incorporate, whether by specification or indirect reference—
(*a*) the qualifying general earnings included in the PSA,
(*b*) the method of calculation, determined in accordance with regulation 108, of the amount of income tax for which the employer is to be accountable in respect of those qualifying general earnings, and
(*c*) the due date by which, in accordance with regulation 109, income tax in respect of those qualifying general earnings is due and payable.

Commentary—*Simon's Taxes* **E4.11110**.
Derivation—The Income Tax (Employments) Regulations, SI 1993/744 reg 80B.

112 Commencement of PSA

(1) A PSA may be entered into at any time before 6th July following the end of the tax year for which it is to have effect ("the year in question").
(2) A PSA entered into after the beginning of the year in question cannot apply to—
(*a*) general earnings which, when the PSA is entered into, have been, or should have been, paid earlier in the year in question under deduction of tax in accordance with Part 3, or
(*b*) general earnings consisting of benefits which, when the PSA is entered into, are or were reflected in the employee's code for the year in question in accordance with Part 2.

Commentary—*Simon's Taxes* **E4.11110**.
Derivation—The Income Tax (Employments) Regulations, SI 1993/744 reg 80C.

VARIATION AND CANCELLATION OF PSA

113 Variation of PSA

(1) The Inland Revenue and the employer may, by agreement and consistently with the provisions of this Part, vary the terms of a PSA entered into by them.
(2) The agreement must be—
(*a*) in writing, and
(*b*) signed and dated by the employer and by the Inland Revenue.
(3) The last date for variation of a PSA is 6th July following the end of the tax year to which it relates.

Commentary—*Simon's Taxes* **E4.11110**.

Derivation—The Income Tax (Employments) Regulations, SI 1993/744 reg 80D.

114 Cancellation of PSA

(1) The Inland Revenue may cancel a PSA if the employer has seriously or persistently failed—
- (*a*) to account to the Board of Inland Revenue for sums for which the employer is accountable under the PSA, or otherwise to comply with the terms of the PSA,
- (*b*) to produce records in accordance with regulation 117 (inspection of PSA records),
- (*c*) to deduct, or account for, tax in accordance with Parts 3 and 4 (deduction and repayment of tax; payments, returns and information), or
- (*d*) to deliver returns in accordance with Parts 3 and 4.

(2) Cancellation must be effected by notice to the employer.
(3) A cancellation comes into effect from the date of the notice.
(4) If a PSA is cancelled, this Part does not apply to general earnings—
- (*a*) to which the cancelled PSA related, and
- (*b*) which are paid, or (as the case may be) provided or made available, after the employer receives notice of the cancellation.

Commentary—*Simon's Taxes* **E4.11110**.
Derivation—The Income Tax (Employments) Regulations, SI 1993/744 reg 80M.

INTEREST

115 Interest on unpaid tax

(1) This regulation applies if an employer has not paid to the Inland Revenue by the due date (as defined by regulation 109(2)) the full amount for which the employer is liable under this Part.
(2) The unpaid amount carries interest at the prescribed rate from the due date until payment ("the interest period").
(3) Paragraph (2) applies even if the due date is a non-business day as defined by section 92 of the Bills of Exchange Act 1882.
(4) Any change made to the prescribed rate during the interest period applies to the unpaid amount from the date of the change.
(5) Interest is recoverable as if it were an amount payable under the PSA.
(6) "The prescribed rate" means the rate applicable under section 178 of the Finance Act 1989 for the purposes of section 86 of TMA.

Commentary—*Simon's Taxes* **E4.11110**.
Derivation—The Income Tax (Employments) Regulations, SI 1993/744 reg 80J(1), (2), (5), (7), (8).
Cross references—See the Income Tax (PAYE) Regulations, SI 2003/2682 reg 218(3), (4) (a certificate of the Inland Revenue that, to the best of their knowledge and belief, any amount of interest payable under this regulation has not been paid by an employer or employee, is sufficient evidence that the amount mentioned in the certificate is unpaid and due to the Crown).
SI 2003/2682 reg 219 (for the purposes of this regulation, if payment to the Revenue is made by cheque, and cheque paid on its first presentation to the banker on whom drawn, the payment is treated as made on day cheque received by the Revenue).

116 Interest on overpaid tax

(1) This regulation applies if tax in respect of the tax year to which a PSA relates is repaid to the employer after the due date (as defined by regulation 109(2)).
(2) The tax repaid carries interest at the prescribed rate from the later of—
- (*a*) the due date, and
- (*b*) the date on which the tax was paid,

until the order for the repayment is issued ("the interest period").
(3) Any change made to the prescribed rate during the interest period applies to the tax repaid from the date of the change.
(4) "The prescribed rate" means the rate applicable under section 178 of the Finance Act 1989 for the purposes of section 824 of ICTA.

Commentary—*Simon's Taxes* **E4.11110**.
Derivation—The Income Tax (Employments) Regulations, SI 1993/744 reg 80K(1), (2).
Cross references—See the Income Tax (PAYE) Regulations, SI 2003/2682 reg 219 (for the purposes of this regulation, if payment to the Revenue is made by cheque, and cheque paid on its first presentation to the banker on whom drawn, the payment is treated as made on day cheque received by the Revenue).

RECORDS

117 Inspection of PSA records

(1) An authorised officer may require an employer who has entered into a PSA to produce all PSA records, or such PSA records as may be specified by the authorised officer, for inspection—
- (*a*) at the prescribed place, and
- (*b*) at such time as that officer may reasonably require.

(2) "PSA records" means all books, documents and other records relating to—
- (*a*) the qualifying general earnings comprised in the PSA,
- (*b*) the calculation of amounts for which the employer is accountable to the Board of Inland Revenue in accordance with the PSA, and
- (*c*) the payment of those amounts to the Inland Revenue.

(3) "The prescribed place" means such place in the United Kingdom as the employer and the authorised officer may agree upon, or in the absence of agreement—

(*a*) the place in the United Kingdom at which the PSA records are normally kept, or

(*b*) if there is no such place, the employer's principal place of business in the United Kingdom.

(4) The authorised officer may—

(*a*) take copies of, or make extracts from, any records produced for inspection in accordance with paragraph (1);

(*b*) remove any records so produced if the officer considers it necessary to do so, at a reasonable time and for a reasonable period.

(5) If any record is removed in accordance with paragraph (4)(*b*), the authorised officer must provide—

(*a*) a receipt for the record, and

(*b*) a copy of the record, free of charge, to the person by whom it was produced or caused to be produced, within 7 days of that person requesting a copy, if the record is reasonably required for the proper conduct of a business.

(6) If a lien is claimed on a record produced in accordance with paragraph (1), the removal of the document under paragraph (4)(*b*) is not to be regarded as breaking the lien.

(7) If records are maintained by computer, the person required to make them available for inspection must provide the authorised officer with all facilities necessary for obtaining information from them.

(8) An employer must keep PSA records for not less than 3 years after the end of the most recent tax year to which they relate.

Commentary—*Simon's Taxes* **E4.11110**.

Derivation—The Income Tax (Employments) Regulations, SI 1993/744 reg 80N.

PART 7
SPECIAL CASES

CHAPTER 1

COUNCILLORS' ALLOWANCES

118 Interpretation of Chapter 1

(1) In this Chapter—

"allowances" means—

(*a*) payments by way of attendance allowance within section 173(1) or 175(1) of the Local Government Act 1972,

(*b*) payments within regulations made under section 18(1) of the Local Government and Housing Act 1989,

(*c*) payments within regulations made under section 100(1)(*a*) or (*c*) of the Local Government Act 2000,

(*d*) payments by way of attendance allowance within section 47(1) of the Local Government (Scotland) Act 1973, or

(*e*) payments within regulation 3(1), 4(1) or 5(1) of the Local Government (Payments to Councillors) Regulations (Northern Ireland) 1999;

"councillor" means a person entitled to receive any allowances;

"local council" means the local authority, council, joint authority or joint committee paying allowances.

(2) For the purposes of paragraph (1)—

"council" and "joint committee" are to be read in accordance with section 148(1) of the Local Government Act (Northern Ireland) 1972; and

"local authority" in England and Wales has the meaning given in section 270(1) of the Local Government Act 1972, and in Scotland has the meaning given in section 235(1) of the Local Government (Scotland) Act 1973.

Commentary—*Simon's Taxes* **E4.1185**.

Derivation—The Income Tax (Employments) Regulations, SI 1993/744 reg 56.

119 Councillor's option to have tax deducted at basic rate

(1) A councillor may, by notice to the Inland Revenue, opt to have income tax deducted from allowances at the basic rate in force at the time of payment of the allowances (the "basic rate option").

(2) On receiving any such notice the Inland Revenue must give notice to the local council of the councillor's exercise of the basic rate option.

(3) On receiving a notice under paragraph (2), the local council must, when making any payment of allowances to the councillor, deduct income tax at the basic rate in force at the time of that payment on the non-cumulative basis.

(4) Paragraph (5) applies if—

(*a*) a councillor has exercised the basic rate option, and

(*b*) the Inland Revenue consider that the councillor may incur deductible expenses.

(5) The Inland Revenue may direct the local council to disregard an appropriate amount of the allowances in calculating the tax to be deducted.

(6) In paragraph (4)(*b*), "deductible expenses" means expenses of a kind which would be deductible under sections 336 to 338 of ITEPA (expenses incurred wholly, exclusively and necessarily in performance of duties, and travel expenses).

Commentary—*Simon's Taxes* **E4.1185**.

Derivation—The Income Tax (Employments) Regulations, SI 1993/744 reg 57(1), (3)–(5).

120 Particulars that local council must record

(1) This regulation applies if the Inland Revenue have given notice to the local council of the exercise by a councillor of the basic rate option.

(2) The local council must record, in a deductions working sheet (which it must prepare for the purpose unless it has already prepared one) the following particulars about every payment of allowances which it makes to the councillor.

(3) The particulars are—

(*a*) the councillor's name,

(*b*) the councillor's national insurance number, if known,

(*c*) the date of the payment,

(*d*) the amount of the allowances,

(*e*) where regulation 119(5) applies, the net amount of the allowances from which tax has been deducted, and

(*f*) the amount of tax deducted from the allowances.

Commentary—*Simon's Taxes* **E4.1185**.

Derivation—The Income Tax (Employments) Regulations, SI 1993/744 reg 57(6), (7).

121 Regulations apply as if basic rate option were issue of code

If a councillor exercises the basic rate option, these Regulations apply as if the Inland Revenue had issued the basic rate code in respect of the allowances.

Commentary—*Simon's Taxes* **E4.1185**.

CHAPTER 2

RESERVE FORCES' PAY

122 Interpretation of Chapter 2

(1) In this Chapter—

"the Ministry" means the Ministry of Defence;

"reserve forces" means the forces specified in paragraph (2);

"reserve pay" means relevant payments made by the Ministry to members of the reserve forces[, excluding such payments made on 6 April 2009 or later][1];

"reservist" means any person in receipt of reserve pay, but does not include a person who is not resident in the United Kingdom and is serving outside the United Kingdom.

(2) The forces specified in this paragraph are—

(*a*) the Royal Naval Reserve (including Queen Alexandra's Royal Naval Nursing Service Reserve),

(*b*) the Royal Marines Reserve,

(*c*) the Territorial Army,

(*d*) the Royal Auxiliary Air Force,

(*e*) the University Air Squadron, and

(*f*) Officers, Adult Instructors and Adult Warrant Officers of the Sea Cadet Corps, Army Cadet Force, Air Training Corps or Combined Cadet Force.

Commentary—*Simon's Taxes* **E4.1181**.

Derivation—The Income Tax (Employments) Regulations, SI 1993/744 reg 59.

Amendments—[1] In para (1), in meaning for "reserve pay", words inserted by the Income Tax (PAYE) (Amendment) Regulations, SI 2009/588 regs 2, 10 with effect from 6 April 2009.

123 Application of other Parts

(1) Parts 2 (codes) and 3 (deduction and repayment of tax) do not apply to reserve pay.

(2) The rest of these Regulations apply as if the Inland Revenue had issued the basic rate code in respect of reserve pay.

Commentary—*Simon's Taxes* **E4.1181**.

Derivation—The Income Tax (Employments) Regulations, SI 1993/744 reg 60.

124 Deduction of tax

(1) On making any payment of reserve pay to a reservist during a tax year, the Ministry must deduct income tax at the basic rate in force when the payment is made.

(2) But the Ministry must not deduct income tax if—

(*a*) it has received notice from the Inland Revenue of a determination for that tax year under this Chapter that tax is not to be deducted from reserve pay, and

(*b*) it has not received notice of any amendment of that determination.

(3) This regulation applies even if an objection or appeal has been made under this Chapter.

Commentary—*Simon's Taxes* **E4.1181**.

Derivation—The Income Tax (Employments) Regulations, SI 1993/744 reg 61(1), (2), (4).

125 Determination by Inland Revenue

(1) The Inland Revenue may make a determination that tax is not to be deducted from reserve pay if the Inland Revenue are satisfied that the reservist will not be liable to income tax on the full amount of the reserve pay in a tax year.

(2) For the purpose of making a determination, it must be assumed—

(*a*) that any reliefs from income tax to which the reservist is entitled are allowable primarily against the reservist's PAYE income from other sources, and

(*b*) unless the reservist objects, that the balance (if any) of such reliefs is next allowable against the reservist's income other than PAYE income.

(3) The Inland Revenue may make a determination before, or at any time during, the tax year.

(4) On making a determination the Inland Revenue must notify the reservist and the Ministry.

Commentary—*Simon's Taxes* **E4.1181**.

Derivation—The Income Tax (Employments) Regulations, SI 1993/744 reg 62.

126 Objection against deduction of tax

(1) A reservist who objects to tax being deducted in accordance with regulation 124 (deduction at basic rate) must state the grounds of objection.

(2) On receiving the notice of objection, the Inland Revenue must make a determination whether income tax at the basic rate is to be deducted from the reserve pay.

(3) Regulation 125(2) (assumptions) applies for the purpose of making the determination.

(4) The Inland Revenue must notify the reservist of the determination.

(5) The Inland Revenue may amend the determination by agreement with the reservist.

(6) If the Inland Revenue and the reservist do not reach agreement, the reservist may appeal against the determination by giving notice to the Inland Revenue.

(7) . . . [1]

Amendments—[1] Para (7) revoked by the Transfer of Tribunal Functions and Revenue and Customs Appeals Order, SI 2009/56 art 3, Sch 2 paras 92, 107 with effect from 1 April 2009.

Commentary—*Simon's Taxes* **E4.1181**.

Derivation—The Income Tax (Employments) Regulations, SI 1993/744 reg 63(1)–(4).

127 Appeal to [the tribunal]

(1) On [an appeal that is notified to the tribunal, the tribunal][1] must determine whether income tax at the basic rate is to be deducted from the reserve pay.

(2) Regulation 125(2) (assumptions) applies for the purpose of making the determination.

(3) If, on appeal, the [tribunal determines][1] that tax is not to be deducted from the reserve pay, the Inland Revenue must give notice of the determination to the Ministry.

(4) . . . [1]

Commentary—*Simon's Taxes* **E4.1181**.

Derivation—The Income Tax (Employments) Regulations, SI 1993/744 reg 63(5)–(7), (9).

Amendments—[1] In heading, paras (1), (3), words substituted and para (4) revoked, by the Transfer of Tribunal Functions and Revenue and Customs Appeals Order, SI 2009/56 art 3, Sch 2 paras 92, 107 with effect from 1 April 2009.

128 Amended determinations

(1) This regulation applies if a determination by the Inland Revenue or the [tribunal][1] under regulation 125, 126 or 127 is found to be inappropriate because the actual circumstances are different from the circumstances by reference to which it was made.

(2) The Inland Revenue must amend the determination.

(3) The Inland Revenue must give notice of the amended determination to the reservist and the Ministry.

(4) Regulations 126 and 127 apply in relation to an amended determination as they apply in relation to a determination under regulation 126(2).

Commentary—*Simon's Taxes* **E4.1181**.

Derivation—The Income Tax (Employments) Regulations, SI 1993/744 reg 64.

Amendments—[1] In para (1), word substituted by the Transfer of Tribunal Functions and Revenue and Customs Appeals Order, SI 2009/56 art 3, Sch 2 paras 92, 109 with effect from 1 April 2009.

129 Certificate of tax deducted

(1) On making any payment of reserve pay from which tax is deducted, the Ministry may, and if the reservist so requires must, give the reservist a certificate showing the following particulars.

(2) The particulars are—

(*a*) the reservist's name,

(*b*) the reservist's national insurance number, if known,

(*c*) the date of the payment,
(*d*) the amount of the payment, and
(*e*) the amount of tax deducted.

Commentary—*Simon's Taxes* **E4.1181**.
Derivation—The Income Tax (Employments) Regulations, SI 1993/744 reg 65.

130 Repayment to reservist during tax year

(1) The Ministry must not repay tax in respect of reserve pay to a reservist.
(2) If a reservist applies for a repayment of tax deducted from reserve pay, the Inland Revenue may make such repayment at any time during the tax year as may be appropriate.
(3) In deciding what is appropriate the Inland Revenue must have regard to—
(*a*) the reserve pay of the reservist for the period from the beginning of the tax year up to and including the date of the application,
(*b*) the amount of tax deducted from the reserve pay as evidenced by certificates of pay and tax supplied under regulation 129,
(*c*) any reliefs from income tax to which the reservist is entitled, and
(*d*) the reservist's other PAYE income for the tax year and, unless the reservist objects, the reservist's income for the tax year from all other sources, and liability to tax on that income, as estimated by the Inland Revenue.

Commentary—*Simon's Taxes* **E4.1181**.
Derivation—The Income Tax (Employments) Regulations, SI 1993/744 reg 66.

131 Particulars that Ministry must record

(1) The Ministry must record, in a deductions working sheet, the following particulars about every payment of reserve pay made to a reservist.
(2) The particulars are—
(*a*) the reservist's name,
(*b*) the reservist's national insurance number, if known,
(*c*) the tax year to which the deductions working sheet relates,
(*d*) the date of the payment,
(*e*) the amount of the payment, and
(*f*) the amount of tax (if any) deducted on making the payment.

Commentary—*Simon's Taxes* **E4.1181**.
Derivation—The Income Tax (Employments) Regulations, SI 1993/744 reg 67.

132 End of year certificate

(1) The Ministry must give an end of year certificate to a reservist in respect of whom the Ministry was required to prepare or maintain a deductions working sheet.
(2) The certificate must be given before 1st June following the end of the tax year to which it relates.
(3) The certificate must show—
(*a*) the tax year to which it relates,
(*b*) the reservist's name,
(*c*) the reservist's national insurance number, if known,
(*d*) the total amount of reserve pay paid by the Ministry to the reservist during the tax year,
(*e*) the total tax deducted from the reserve pay,
(*f*) the force in which the reservist was serving, and
(*g*) the reservist's service number.

Commentary—*Simon's Taxes* **E4.1181**.
Derivation—The Income Tax (Employments) Regulations, SI 1993/744 reg 68.

133 Other PAYE income of reservist

Nothing in this Chapter affects the application of these Regulations to any other PAYE income of a reservist.

Commentary—*Simon's Taxes* **E4.1181**.
Derivation—The Income Tax (Employments) Regulations, SI 1993/744 reg 70.

[CHAPTER 2A

SOCIAL SECURITY LUMP SUMS][1] 1

Amendments—[1] This Chapter inserted by the Income Tax (PAYE) (Amendment) Regulations, SI 2006/243 with effect from 6 April 2006.

[133A Interpretation of Chapter 2A

(1) In this Chapter—
"the Act" means the Finance (No 2) Act 2005 and a reference (without more) to a numbered provision is a reference to the provision of the Act bearing that number;
["basic rate", in relation to the charging of income tax for any tax year, means the rate of income tax determined under section 6(2) of ITA;][2]
"the Department" means—

(*a*) in Great Britain, the Department for Work and Pensions; and

(*b*) in Northern Ireland, the Department for Social Development;

["higher rate", in relation to the charging of income tax for any tax year, means the rate of income tax determined under section 6(2) of ITA;][2]

"lump sum" means a social security pension lump sum as defined in section 9 of the Act;

"the recipient" means a person who has become entitled to a lump sum.][1]

Amendments—[1] This Chapter inserted by the Income Tax (PAYE) (Amendment) Regulations, SI 2006/243 with effect from 6 April 2006.

[2] Definitions of "basic rate" and "higher rate" inserted by the Income Tax (Pay As You Earn) (Amendment No 3) Regulations, SI 2015/1667 regs 2, 5 with effect in relation to the tax year 2016–17 (appointed by the Treasury under the Scotland Act 2012 s 25(5) by virtue of SI 2015/2000) and subsequent tax years.

[133B Application of other Parts

(1) Parts 2 (codes) and 3 (deduction and repayment of tax) do not apply to lump sums.

(2) The rest of these Regulations apply as if Her Majesty's Revenue and Customs had issued a code in respect of a social security pension lump sum at either—

(*a*) the rate notified to the Department by the recipient pursuant to regulation 133D, or

(*b*) the basic rate, if the recipient has not notified the Department of a rate.][1]

Amendments—[1] This Chapter inserted by the Income Tax (PAYE) (Amendment) Regulations, SI 2006/243 with effect from 6 April 2006.

[133C Determination of Rate of Deduction

(1) On making any payment of a lump sum to a recipient during a tax year, the Department must deduct income tax at the marginal rate calculated in accordance with sub-paragraph (2).

(2) For the purposes of this chapter the marginal rate is either—

(*a*) the rate notified to the Department by the recipient in accordance with regulation 133D, or

(*b*) in default of any such notification, the basic rate.][1]

Amendments—[1] This Chapter inserted by the Income Tax (PAYE) (Amendment) Regulations, SI 2006/243 with effect from 6 April 2006.

[133D Notification by Recipient of Notice of Tax Rate

(1) The recipient shall notify the Department that he considers the nil tax code should be applied to the lump sum or that one of the following rates should be used—

(*a*) . . . [2]

(*b*) the basic rate, or

(*c*) the higher rate,

in accordance with section 7(5) of the Act.

(2) Notification shall be in the form, and made within the period, specified by the Department.][1]

Amendments—[1] This Chapter inserted by the Income Tax (PAYE) (Amendment) Regulations, SI 2006/243 with effect from 6 April 2006.

[2] Para (1)(*a*) revoked by the Income Tax (Pay As You Earn) (Amendment) Regulations, SI 2008/782 regs 2, 13 with effect from 6 April 2008.

[133E Certificate of tax deducted

(1) On making any payment of a lump sum from which tax is deducted, the Department may and if the recipient so requires, must, give the recipient an award notification showing the following particulars.

(2) The particulars are—

(*a*) the recipient's name,

(*b*) the recipient's national insurance number, if known,

(*c*) the date of the payment,

(*d*) the amount of the payment, and

(*e*) the amount of tax deducted.][1]

Amendments—[1] This Chapter inserted by the Income Tax (PAYE) (Amendment) Regulations, SI 2006/243 with effect from 6 April 2006.

[133F Repayment to recipient during tax year

The Department may repay tax deducted from a lump sum to a recipient at any time during the tax year in which it was paid, if it appears to the Department that the incorrect rate of income tax was applied to the payment due to an administrative error by the Department.][1]

Amendments—[1] This Chapter inserted by the Income Tax (PAYE) (Amendment) Regulations, SI 2006/243 with effect from 6 April 2006.

[133G Records and notices

(1) The Department must record, in a deductions working sheet, the following particulars about any payment of a lump sum.

(2) The particulars are—

(*a*) the recipient's name,

(*b*) the recipient's national insurance number, if known,

(*c*) the amount of the payment,
(*c*) the date of the payment,
(*d*) the amount of tax (if any) deducted from the payment,
(*e*) the tax rate (if any) notified by the recipient to the Department, and
(*f*) the amount of any repayment made to the recipient in respect of the lump sum.

(3) The Department shall notify an officer of Revenue and Customs when a lump sum payment is made.

(4) The notification referred to in sub-paragraph (3) shall contain the following information—
(*a*) the recipient's name and address,
(*b*) the recipient's national insurance number, if known,
(*c*) the date of the payment, and
(*d*) the recipient's date of birth.

(5) The Department shall administer a separate PAYE scheme for the lump sum payments.][1]

Amendments—[1] This Chapter inserted by the Income Tax (PAYE) (Amendment) Regulations, SI 2006/243 with effect from 6 April 2006.

[133H Other PAYE income of recipient

Nothing in this Chapter affects the application of these Regulations to any other PAYE income of a recipient.][1]

Amendments—[1] This Chapter inserted by the Income Tax (PAYE) (Amendment) Regulations, SI 2006/243 with effect from 6 April 2006.

CHAPTER 3

HOLIDAY PAY FUNDS

Cross references—See the Income Tax (PAYE) Regulations, SI 2003/2682 reg 11 (this Chapter not to apply to pension payers or pensioners in their capacity as such).

134 Interpretation of Chapter 3

In this Chapter—

"fund" means a person who pays holiday pay—
(*a*) to an individual who is not employed by the person, or
(*b*) in respect of such an individual who has died;

"holiday pay" means—
(*a*) any payment received by an individual in exchange for a voucher, stamp or similar document purchased by a person who employs (or employed) that individual for any holiday period, or
(*b*) if such an individual has died, any payment received by a person claiming in respect of that individual's right to such a payment;

"recipient" means a person who is paid holiday pay.

Commentary—*Simon's Taxes* **E4.1115**.
Derivation—The Income Tax (Employments) Regulations, SI 1993/744 reg 71.
Cross references—SI 2003/2682 reg 12 (this regulation not to apply to other payers or other payees in their capacity as such).

135 Application of other Parts

(1) Parts 2 (codes) and 3 (deduction and repayment of tax) do not apply to holiday pay.

(2) The rest of these Regulations apply as if the Inland Revenue had issued the basic rate code in respect of holiday pay.

Commentary—*Simon's Taxes* **E4.1115**.
Derivation—The Income Tax (Employments) Regulations, SI 1993/744 reg 72.

136 Deduction of tax

On making any payment of holiday pay to a recipient, a fund must deduct income tax at the basic rate in force at the time the payment is made.

Commentary—*Simon's Taxes* **E4.1115**.
Derivation—The Income Tax (Employments) Regulations, SI 1993/744 reg 73.

137 Certificate of tax deducted

(1) On making any payment of holiday pay, a fund must give the recipient a certificate showing the following particulars.

(2) The particulars are—
(*a*) the recipient's name,
(*b*) the recipient's national insurance number, if known,
(*c*) the tax year in which the payment is made,
(*d*) the date of the payment,
(*e*) the amount of the payment, and
(*f*) the amount of tax deducted on making the payment.

Commentary—*Simon's Taxes* **E4.1115**.

Derivation—The Income Tax (Employments) Regulations, SI 1993/744 reg 74.

138 Repayment to recipient during tax year

(1) A fund must not repay tax deducted from a payment of holiday pay to a recipient.

(2) If a recipient applies for a repayment of tax deducted from holiday pay, the Inland Revenue may make such repayment at any time during the tax year as may be appropriate.

(3) In deciding what is appropriate the Inland Revenue must have regard to—

(*a*) the holiday pay of the recipient for the period from the beginning of the tax year up to and including the date of the application,

(*b*) the amount of tax deducted from the holiday pay as evidenced by certificates supplied under regulation 137,

(*c*) any entitlement of the recipient to relief from income tax, and

(*d*) the recipient's other PAYE income for the tax year and, unless the recipient objects, the recipient's income for the tax year from all other sources, and liability to tax on that income, as estimated by the Inland Revenue.

Commentary—*Simon's Taxes* **E4.1115**.

Derivation—The Income Tax (Employments) Regulations, SI 1993/744 reg 75.

139 Particulars that fund must record

(1) A fund must record, in a deductions working sheet, the following particulars about every payment of holiday pay made to a recipient.

(2) The particulars are—

(*a*) the recipient's name,

(*b*) the recipient's national insurance number, if known,

(*c*) the tax year to which the deductions working sheet relates,

(*d*) the date of the payment,

(*e*) the amount of the payment, and

(*f*) the amount of tax (if any) deducted on making the payment.

Commentary—*Simon's Taxes* **E4.1115**.

Derivation—The Income Tax (Employments) Regulations, SI 1993/744 reg 76.

140 Other PAYE income of recipient

Nothing in this Chapter affects the application of these Regulations to any other PAYE income of a recipient.

Commentary—*Simon's Taxes* **E4.1115**.

Derivation—The Income Tax (Employments) Regulations, SI 1993/744 reg 78.

CHAPTER 4

DIRECT COLLECTION AND SPECIAL ARRANGEMENTS

141 Direct collection and special arrangements

(1) In—

(*a*) cases of casual employment, and

[(*b*) any other case in which HMRC are of the opinion that deduction of tax by reference to the tax tables is impracticable,

the direct collection procedure in regulation 142 applies to any PAYE income, unless HMRC makes special arrangements for the collection of tax in respect of that PAYE income.][1]

(2) A special arrangement does not apply to PAYE income of an employer's employees if—

(*a*) the arrangement has not been agreed with the employer, and

(*b*) the employer does not proceed in accordance with the arrangement.

Commentary—*Simon's Taxes* **E4.1144**.

Derivation—The Income Tax (Employments) Regulations, SI 1993/744 reg 102.

Modifications—See the Income Tax (PAYE) Regulations, SI 2003/2682 reg 174 (modification of this regulation in its application to payments of taxable incapacity benefit).

Amendments—[1] In para (1), sub-para (*b*) and subsequent words substituted by the Income Tax (Pay As You Earn) and the Income Tax (Construction Industry Scheme) (Amendment) Regulations, SI 2014/472 regs 2, 10 with effect from 6 April 2014.

[142 Direct collection: employee to report payments

(1) On receiving a relevant payment—

(*a*) an employee (E) must proceed in accordance with paragraph (3) or paragraph (4), as the case may be, and

(*b*) regulations 143 to 147A (direct collection) apply to E,

unless E objects to the application of the direct collection procedure.

(2) E may, within 30 days beginning with the date of receipt of written notification from HMRC that the direct collection procedure applies, object by written notice to HMRC to that procedure.

(3) E must deliver the information specified in Schedule A1 as if E were a Real Time Information employer for the purposes of regulations 67B (real time information returns of information about relevant payments), 67E (returns under regulations 67B and 67D: amendments), 67EA (failure to make a return under regulation 67B or 67D) and 67F (additional information about payments) and references to "an employer making a relevant payment" are to be read as if they were references to "the employee receiving a relevant payment".

(4) But if E—

(*a*) is an individual who is a practising member of a religious society or order whose beliefs are incompatible with the use of electronic communications, or

(*b*) has been given a direction under paragraph (5),

E may instead proceed as if E were a Real Time Information employer to whom regulations 67D (exceptions to regulation 67B), 67E (returns under regulations 67B and 67D: amendments), 67EA (failure to make a return under regulation 67B or 67D) and 67F (additional information about payments) apply with the modification referred to in paragraph (3).

(5) Where the Commissioners for Her Majesty's Revenue are satisfied that—

(*a*) it is not reasonably practicable for E to make a return using an approved form of electronic communication, and

(*b*) it is E who delivers the return (and not some other person on E's behalf),

they may make a direction specifying that E is not required to make a return using an approved method of electronic communication.][1]

Commentary—*Simon's Taxes* **E4.1144.**

Amendments—[1] Regulation 142 substituted by the Income Tax (Pay As You Earn) and the Income Tax (Construction Industry Scheme) (Amendment) Regulations, SI 2014/472 regs 2, 11 with effect from 6 April 2014.

143 Direct collection: employee to keep records

(1) Whenever the employee receives any relevant payment during the tax year, the employee must record in [a deductions][1] working sheet—

(*a*) the amount of the payment,

(*b*) the date on which it was received, and

(*c*) the total payments to date.

(2) In addition, the employee must record in [that deductions][1] working sheet in relation to the last date in a tax quarter on which the employee receives a relevant payment—

(*a*) the total free pay to date or, as the case may be, the total additional pay to date in relation to that date according to the employee's code, and

(*b*) the corresponding total tax to date.

(3) If the employee does not receive any relevant payments in a tax quarter, the last day of the quarter must be used for the purposes of paragraph (2).

(4) If the employee receives relevant payments in more than one capacity, no account is to be taken for the purposes of this regulation and regulations 144 to 147 of the relevant payments received by the employee in any capacity other than that mentioned in [that deductions][1] working sheet.

(5) In this regulation . . . [2], "total payments to date" means, in relation to any date, the sum of all relevant payments received by the employee from the beginning of the tax year up to and including that date, irrespective of the person or persons from whom it was received.

Commentary—*Simon's Taxes* **E4.1144.**

Derivation—The Income Tax (Employments) Regulations, SI 1993/744 reg 104(2), (14), (15).

Amendments—[1] In paras (1), (2), (4) words substituted for words "the deductions" by the Income Tax (Pay As You Earn) and the Income Tax (Construction Industry Scheme) (Amendment) Regulations, SI 2014/472 regs 2, 12 with effect from 6 April 2014.

[2] In para (5), words "and regulation 146" revoked by the Income Tax (Pay As You Earn) and the Income Tax (Construction Industry Scheme) (Amendment) Regulations, SI 2014/472 regs 2, 13 with effect from 6 April 2015.

144 Direct collection: payment

(1) In this regulation—

["the current total tax" means the amount required to be recorded at paragraph 17 of Schedule A1 (real time returns) in the most recent return which the employee is required to make in the tax year, or where the employee is required to make a return under regulation 67EA(3) (failure to make a return under regulation 67B), the amount required to be recorded at paragraph 17 of Schedule A1 for the tax year to which that return relates;][1]

"the previous total tax" means the total tax to date (if any) required to be recorded for the previous tax quarter in the tax year.

(2) If, in relation to any tax quarter, the current total tax exceeds the previous total tax, the employee must pay the excess to the Inland Revenue, within 14 days after the end of the tax quarter.

(3) But if, in relation to any tax quarter, the previous total tax exceeds the current total tax, the employee may recover the excess—

(*a*) by deducting it from the amount payable under paragraph (2) for a later quarter in the tax year, or

(*b*) from the Board of Inland Revenue.

(4) . . . [2] The amount payable under paragraph (2) is not to exceed the overriding limit in relation to the relevant payments which the employee has received in that tax quarter.
(5) Any amount which is not payable because of the application of paragraph (4) must be added to the current total tax for the purpose of the calculation in paragraph (2) or (3) for the next tax quarter (if any) of that tax year.

Commentary—*Simon's Taxes* **E4.1144**.
Derivation—The Income Tax (Employments) Regulations, SI 1993/744 reg 104(2), (3).
Amendments—[1] In para (1), definition of "the current total tax" substituted by the Income Tax (Pay As You Earn) and the Income Tax (Construction Industry Scheme) (Amendment) Regulations, SI 2014/472 regs 2, 14 with effect from 6 April 2014.
[2] In para (4), words "if the employee's code is a K code," revoked by the Income Tax (Pay As You Earn) (Amendment No 4) Regulations, SI 2014/2689 regs 2, 5 with effect from 6 April 2015.

145 Direct collection: return when relevant payments cease

Amendments—Regulation 145 revoked by the Income Tax (Pay As You Earn) and the Income Tax (Construction Industry Scheme) (Amendment) Regulations, SI 2014/472 regs 2, 15 with effect from 6 April 2014.

146 Direct collection: end of year return

Amendments—Regulation 146 revoked by the Income Tax (Pay As You Earn) and the Income Tax (Construction Industry Scheme) (Amendment) Regulations, SI 2014/472 regs 2, 16 with effect from 6 April 2015.

147 Direct collection: failure to pay

(1) This regulation applies if, within 14 days after the end of any tax quarter—
- (*a*) the employee has not paid any tax for that quarter, and the Inland Revenue are unaware of the amount, if any, which the employee is liable to pay for that quarter, or
- (*b*) the employee has paid an amount of tax for that quarter, but the Inland Revenue are not satisfied that it is the full amount which the employee is liable to pay for that quarter.

(2) The Inland Revenue may give notice to the employee requiring the employee, within 14 days of the issue of the notice, to deliver a return showing the amount of tax which the employee is liable to pay under regulation 144(2) in respect of the tax quarter in question.
(3) If such a notice is given, regulations 77, 84 and 218(5) and (6) (which relate to the certification and recovery of tax unpaid by an employer) apply with the necessary modifications for the purposes of ascertaining, certifying and recovering the tax payable by the employee as if it were tax which the employee was liable to deduct from relevant payments paid by the employee.

Commentary—*Simon's Taxes* **E4.1144**.
Derivation—The Income Tax (Employments) Regulations, SI 1993/744 reg 104(5), (6).

[147A Circumstances in which payment of a lesser amount is to be treated as payment in full for the purposes of paragraph 6(2) of Schedule 56 to the Finance Act 2009

(1) A payment that is less than the full amount due under regulation 67G(2) (payments to and recoveries from HMRC for each tax period), as adjusted by regulation 67H (payments due and recoveries from HMRC for each tax period: returns under regulation 67E(6)) where appropriate, will for the purposes of paragraph 6(2) of Schedule 56 to the Finance Act 2009 (amount of penalty: PAYE and CIS) be treated as payment of the full amount if the difference between the full amount and the amount paid is no more than £100 ("the tolerance"), but this is subject to paragraphs (2) and (3).
(2) Paragraph (1) does not apply where—
- (*a*) the payment relates to a return which corrects information given in a return filed in respect of a relevant payment made in an earlier tax month, and
- (*b*) the return is delivered after 19th April following the end of the tax year in question.

(3) If the total sum paid by the employer to HMRC for the tax period includes not only the amount due under regulation 67G(2), as adjusted by regulation 67H where appropriate, but also one or more of—
- (*a*) any earnings-related contributions (as defined by regulation 1(2) of the SSC Regulations 2001),
- (*b*) any payment under regulation 7(1) of the Income Tax (Construction Industry Scheme) Regulations 2005, or
- (*c*) any repayment due under the Student Loans Regulations,

the tolerance is applied to the total sum paid to HMRC for the tax period to which the payments relate.][1]

Amendments—[1] Regulation 147A inserted by the Income Tax (Pay As You Earn) and the Income Tax (Construction Industry Scheme) (Amendment) Regulations, SI 2014/472 regs 2, 17 with effect in relation to a payment made in relation to the tax year 2014–15 and subsequent tax years.

[PART 7A
APPRENTICESHIP LEVY]

Amendments—Part 7A (regs 147B–147N) inserted by the Income Tax (Pay As You Earn) (Amendment) Regulations, SI 2017/414 reg 3 with effect from 6 April 2017.

[147B Interpretation of Part 7A

In this Part—

"monthly pay bill" means the total amount of earnings paid by a person in a tax month on which Class 1 secondary contributions are payable but for the condition in section 6(1)(b) of the Contributions and Benefits Act (liability for Class 1 contributions).][1]

Amendments—[1] Part 7A (regs 147B–147N) inserted by the Income Tax (Pay As You Earn) (Amendment) Regulations, SI 2017/414 reg 3 with effect from 6 April 2017.

[147C Due date for payment of apprenticeship levy

(1) A person must pay the amount of apprenticeship levy due under this Part within—

(*a*) 17 days after the end of the tax month, where the payment is made by an approved method of electronic communications, or

(*b*) 14 days after the end of the tax month, in any other case.

(2) The person must pay the apprenticeship levy mentioned in paragraph (1) at the same time as the amount of tax and any earnings-related contributions due and in accordance with Part 4 and Chapter 1 of these Regulations (payment, returns and information).

(3) In this regulation, "earnings-related contributions" means any contributions other than Class 1A and 1B contributions payable under the Contributions and Benefits Act in respect of earnings paid to or for the benefit of an earner in respect of employed earners employment.][1]

Amendments—[1] Part 7A (regs 147B–147N) inserted by the Income Tax (Pay As You Earn) (Amendment) Regulations, SI 2017/414 reg 3 with effect from 6 April 2017.

[147D Duty to report amount of apprenticeship levy to be paid

(1) Subject to paragraph (2) this regulation applies where—

(a) a person's pay bill in the tax year preceding the year in which the apprenticeship levy liability falls to be reported was over £3 million, or

(b) a person considers that their pay bill will be over £3 million in the current tax year.

(2) In the case of a member of a company unit or charities unit this regulation applies where—

(a) the total amount of the pay bill for the company unit or the charities unit in the tax year preceding the year in which the apprenticeship levy liability falls to be reported was over £3 million, or

(b)

(i) the annual entitlement to levy allowance has been determined for each member of the company unit or charities unit in the current tax year in accordance with sections 101 or 102 of the Finance Act 2016, and

(ii) a member considers that their annual pay bill will be over £T where T is an amount equal to the levy allowance determined for that member divided by 0.005.

(3) A Real Time Information employer must inform HMRC of their apprenticeship levy liability after deducting any amount of levy allowance to which they are entitled for the tax month from it.

(4) The information must be given in a return.

(5) The return mentioned under paragraph (4) must be sent within 14 days after the end of the tax month.

(6) A return under this regulation must—

(a) state—

(i) the tax year to which it relates,

(ii) the employer's HMRC office number,

(iii) the employer's PAYE reference to which the return of the apprenticeship levy relates,

(iv) the employer's accounts office reference,

(v) the amount of annual levy allowance the employer is allocating to the employer's PAYE reference,

(vi) the amount of apprenticeship levy due to date which the employer has calculated, and

(vii) the tax month to which it relates, and

(b) be sent using an approved method of electronic communications unless the employer is one to whom regulation 67D applies.

(7) This regulation applies in addition to the provisions set out in regulation 67F (additional information about payments).][1]

Amendments—[1] Part 7A (regs 147B–147N) inserted by the Income Tax (Pay As You Earn) (Amendment) Regulations, SI 2017/414 reg 3 with effect from 6 April 2017.

[147E Calculation of monthly levy allowance

(1) This regulation applies where the monthly levy allowance falls to be calculated by a person.

(2) Subject to regulations 147F and 147G, the monthly levy allowance is an amount equal to—

N / P

where—*N* is the levy allowance for the tax year, and

P is twelve.

(3) Subject to regulations 147F and 147G, the monthly cumulative levy allowance is an amount equal to the monthly levy allowance aggregated in accordance with the tax month within the tax year as shown in the table below.

Table 1

Relevant month in the tax year	*Monthly cumulative levy allowance*
Month 1	£1,250
Month 2	£2,500
Month 3	£3,750
Month 4	£5,000
Month 5	£6,250
Month 6	£7,500
Month 7	£8,750
Month 8	£10,000
Month 9	£11,250
Month 10	£12,500
Month 11	£13,750
Month 12	£15,000][1]

Amendments—[1] Part 7A (regs 147B–147N) inserted by the Income Tax (Pay As You Earn) (Amendment) Regulations, SI 2017/414 reg 3 with effect from 6 April 2017.

[147F Apportionment of levy allowance between employer's PAYE references

(1) This regulation applies where a person has more than one employer's PAYE reference in respect of its employees.

(2) The person may elect to apportion their annual entitlement of levy allowance amongst the employer's PAYE references mentioned in paragraph (1) in accordance with the proportions they choose.

(3) The monthly levy allowance for each employer's PAYE reference is an amount equal to one twelfth of the annual apportioned entitlement for that reference.

(4) The person must notify HM Revenue and Customs of the election mentioned in paragraph (2) with their first return of the apprenticeship levy.][1]

Amendments—[1] Part 7A (regs 147B–147N) inserted by the Income Tax (Pay As You Earn) (Amendment) Regulations, SI 2017/414 reg 3 with effect from 6 April 2017.

[147G Apportionment of levy allowance between employer's PAYE references: members of a company unit or charities unit

(1) This regulation applies where—

(*a*) members of a company unit or charities unit ("the relevant members") have determined what amount of levy allowance each of them is entitled to for the tax year, and

(*b*) at least one of the relevant members mentioned in sub-paragraph (1)(a) has more than one employer's PAYE reference.

(2) The relevant members may elect to apportion their share of levy allowance amongst their respective employer's PAYE references in accordance with the proportions they choose.

(3) The relevant members must—

(*a*) make the election mentioned in sub-paragraph (2) at the beginning of the tax year, and

(*b*) notify HMRC of the election made with their first return of the apprenticeship levy.][1]

Amendments—[1] Part 7A (regs 147B–147N) inserted by the Income Tax (Pay As You Earn) (Amendment) Regulations, SI 2017/414 reg 3 with effect from 6 April 2017.

[147H Calculation of monthly apprenticeship levy for the first month of the tax year

A person must calculate the amount of their apprenticeship levy for the first month of the tax year in accordance with the following steps.

Step 1

Multiply the amount of the monthly pay bill by 0.5%.

Step 2

Deduct the monthly levy allowance for the first month as mentioned in Table 1 from the amount obtained from step 1.

If the resulting amount is positive, that amount is the apprenticeship levy payable for the first month of the tax year.

If the resulting amount is negative or zero, there will be no apprenticeship levy payable for the first month of the tax year.][1]

Amendments—[1] Part 7A (regs 147B–147N) inserted by the Income Tax (Pay As You Earn) (Amendment) Regulations, SI 2017/414 reg 3 with effect from 6 April 2017.

[147I Calculation of monthly apprenticeship levy for subsequent months of the tax year

(1) A person must calculate the amount of apprenticeship levy for any month following the first month of the tax year (the relevant month) in accordance with the following steps.

Step 1

Determine the cumulative amount of the monthly pay bill for the relevant months of the tax year.

Step 2

Multiply the amount obtained from step 1 by 0.5%.

Step 3

Determine the amount of the monthly cumulative levy allowance for the relevant month in accordance with Table 1.

Step 4

Deduct the amount obtained from step 3 from the amount obtained from step 2.

If the resulting amount is negative, that amount is to be treated as zero for the purpose of the calculation mentioned in step 6.

If the resulting amount is a positive amount, that amount is to be used in the calculation mentioned in step 6.

Step 5

Determine the amount of the cumulative apprenticeship levy paid up to the month preceding the relevant month and reduce that amount by any credit gained in the preceding month.

Step 6

Deduct the amount obtained from step 5 from the amount obtained from step 4.

If the resulting amount is a positive amount, that amount is the apprenticeship levy due to be paid for the relevant month.

If the resulting amount is negative, that amount is the credit gained in the relevant month.

(2) In this regulation, "credit" means any amount which is negative which can be used by a person to reduce the combined amount in the relevant month.][1]

Amendments—[1] Part 7A (regs 147B–147N) inserted by the Income Tax (Pay As You Earn) (Amendment) Regulations, SI 2017/414 reg 3 with effect from 6 April 2017.

[147J Recovery of overpaid apprenticeship levy by an employer

(1) This regulation applies where a person has overpaid apprenticeship levy in a tax year.

(2) The person must set off any overpaid apprenticeship levy against any amount which that person is liable to pay under these Regulations before making a claim to HMRC for a refund of the overpaid levy.][1]

Amendments—[1] Part 7A (regs 147B–147N) inserted by the Income Tax (Pay As You Earn) (Amendment) Regulations, SI 2017/414 reg 3 with effect from 6 April 2017.

[147K Liability to pay and duty to make a return of apprenticeship levy: Continental shelf workers certificate holders

(1) This regulation applies to persons specified in certificates in force under section 120(4) of the Social Security Contributions and Benefits Act 1992 (employment at sea: continental shelf operations).

(2) The person specified in paragraph (3) must—

(*a*) pay apprenticeship levy under regulation 147C, and

(*b*) make a return of apprenticeship levy under regulation 147D.

(3) The person referred to paragraph (2) is a UKCS continental shelf workers certificate holder who has obligations under regulation 114B of the SSC Regulations (UKCS continental shelf workers certificate holder: obligations and responsibilities) to make deductions, returns and repayments as are required by a secondary contributor.

(4) In this regulation a UKCS continental shelf workers certificate holder means a holder of a certificate issued under regulation 114A of the SSC Regulations (application for certificate).][1]

Amendments—[1] Part 7A (regs 147B–147N) inserted by the Income Tax (Pay As You Earn) (Amendment) Regulations, SI 2017/414 reg 3 with effect from 6 April 2017.

[147L Assessment of unpaid apprenticeship levy

(1) This regulation applies if it appears to HMRC that there may be apprenticeship levy payable for a tax year under regulations 147E, 147H or 147I (calculation of apprenticeship levy) by an employer which has not been—

(*a*) paid to HMRC under regulation 147C, and

(*b*) reported on a return under regulation 147D.

(2) HMRC may assess the amount of apprenticeship levy which to the best of their judgement is due, and serve notice of their assessment on the employer.

(3) An assessment under this regulation may—

(*a*) cover the apprenticeship levy payable by the employer under regulation 147E, 147H or 147I for any one or more tax periods in a tax year, and

(*b*) extend to the whole of the apprenticeship levy, or such part of it as is payable in respect of—

(i) a class or classes of employees specified in the notice of assessment (without naming the individual employees), or

(ii) one or more named employees specified in the notice.

(4) Section 30A of the TMA (assessing procedure) applies in relation to an assessment under this regulation as it applies in relation to an assessment to income tax.

(5) Any amount of apprenticeship levy which is payable by virtue of an assessment made under this regulation shall be payable on the day following the end of the period of 30 days beginning with the day on which the notice of assessment is served.][1]

Amendments—[1] Part 7A (regs 147B–147N) inserted by the Income Tax (Pay As You Earn) (Amendment) Regulations, SI 2017/414 reg 3 with effect from 6 April 2017.

[147M Recovery of overpayment of apprenticeship levy by HMRC

(1) Where an amount of apprenticeship levy has been repaid to any person which ought not to have been repaid to that person, that amount may be assessed and recovered as if it were unpaid apprenticeship levy.

(2) An assessment under this regulation shall not be out of time under section 108 of the Finance Act 2016 (time limits for assessment) if it is made before the end of the year of assessment following that in which the amount assessed was repaid.

(3) In this regulation any reference to an amount repaid includes a reference to an amount allowed by way of a set-off.][2]

Amendments—[1] Part 7A (regs 147B–147N) inserted by the Income Tax (Pay As You Earn) (Amendment) Regulations, SI 2017/414 reg 3 with effect from 6 April 2017.

[147N Retention by employer of apprenticeship levy records

(1) An employer must keep and preserve for not less than three years after the end of the tax year to which they relate all apprenticeship levy records which are not required to be sent to HMRC under regulation 147D.

(2) The duty under paragraph (1) to preserve apprenticeship levy records may be discharged by preserving them in any form or by any means.

(3) In this regulation, "apprenticeship levy records" means documents relating to the calculation of the amount of apprenticeship levy payable by the employer.][1]

Amendments—[1] Part 7A (regs 147B–147N) inserted by the Income Tax (Pay As You Earn) (Amendment) Regulations, SI 2017/414 reg 3 with effect from 6 April 2017.

PART 8
SOCIAL SECURITY BENEFITS

CHAPTER 1

JOBSEEKER'S ALLOWANCE: NORMAL CASES

Commentary—*Simon's Taxes* **E4.11101.**

Cross references—See the Income Tax (PAYE) Regulations, SI 2003/2682 reg 165 (except for SI 2003/2682 reg 148, this Chapter does not apply to claimants under Pt 8 Chapter 2 (jobseekers' allowance: special cases).

148 Interpretation of Chapters 1 and 2

In Chapters 1 and 2—

"award" means an award of a jobseeker's allowance;

"claim" means a claim for a jobseeker's allowance;

"claimant" means a person who has made a claim, or who is treated for the purposes of the JSA Regulations as having made a claim;

"Chapter 2 claimant" means—

(*a*) a claimant who is entitled to a jobseeker's allowance by virtue of regulation 17 of the JSA Regulations (laid off and short time workers); or

[(*b*) a claimant who is a share fisherman—

(i) where the JSA Regulations apply, as defined in regulation 156 of those Regulations; and

(ii) where the Jobseeker's Allowance Regulations 2013 apply, as defined in regulation 67 of those Regulations;][1]

"Department" means the Department for Work and Pensions or, in Northern Ireland, the Department for Social Development;

"JSA Regulations" means the Jobseeker's Allowance Regulations 1996 or, in Northern Ireland, the Jobseeker's Allowance Regulations (Northern Ireland) 1996;

"jobseeker's allowance" means benefit payable under—

(*a*) the Jobseekers Act 1995, or

(*b*) in Northern Ireland, the Jobseekers (Northern Ireland) Order 1995;

"taxable jobseeker's allowance" means any amount of jobseeker's allowance which is chargeable to income tax under Chapter 2 of Part 10 of ITEPA (tax on social security income).

Commentary—*Simon's Taxes* **E4.11101.**

Derivation—The Income Tax (Employments) Regulations, SI 1993/744 regs 81, 83(1), 94.

Amendments—[1] In entry for "Chapter 2 claimant", para (*b*) substituted by the Universal Credit (Consequential, Supplementary, Incidental and Miscellaneous Provisions) Regulations, SI 2013/630 reg 83 with effect from 29 April 2013.

Prospective amendments—In entry for "Chapter 2 claimant", in para (*b*)(ii), words "or Jobseeker's Allowance Regulations (Northern Ireland) 2016" to be inserted after words "Jobseeker's Allowance Regulations 2013" by the Universal Credit (Consequential, Supplementary, Incidental and Miscellaneous Provisions) Regulations (Northern Ireland), NISR 2016/236 art 59 with effect from a date to be appointed.

149 Scope of Chapter 1

This Chapter applies to claimants who are not Chapter 2 claimants.

Commentary—*Simon's Taxes* **E4.11101.**

150 Application of other regulations

(1) The following regulations apply to payments of taxable jobseeker's allowance made to a claimant with the modifications mentioned in paragraphs (2) and (3)—

Regulation 2	interpretation
Regulation 14	matters relevant to determination of code
Regulation 15	flat rate codes
Regulation 16	continued application of employee's code
Regulation 17	notice to employee of code
Regulation 18	objections and appeals against employee's code
Regulation 19	amendment of code
Regulation 20	notice to employer of amended code
Regulation 21	deduction and repayment of tax by reference to employee's code
Regulation 97	[retention by employer of PAYE records][1]
Regulation 98	multiple PAYE schemes
Regulation 102	succession to a business etc
[Regulation 185	adjusting total net tax deducted for purposes of sections 59A(1), 59B(1) and 59BA(2) TMA][2]
Regulation 188	assessments other than self-assessments
Regulation 211	how information must or may be delivered by employers
Regulation 214	how information must be provided by employees
Regulation 216	service by post.

(2) In the application of those regulations, the expressions listed in column 1 of Table 5 have the meanings shown in column 2 of the table.

TABLE 5
MEANING OF EXPRESSIONS IN APPLICATION OF OTHER REGULATIONS

1 Expression	*2 Meaning for purposes of this Chapter*
Employee	claimant
Employer	Department
Employment	award
Relevant payments	taxable jobseeker's allowance.

(3) In the application of regulations 20 and 21, any reference to the deduction or repayment of tax must be read as a reference to the tax calculation which the Department is required to make at the end of the tax year or on the cessation of an award (by virtue of regulations 157(2)(*a*) and 158(2) respectively).

Commentary—*Simon's Taxes* **E4.11101.**

Derivation—The Income Tax (Employments) Regulations, SI 1993/744 regs 82, 83(3).

Amendments—[1] In para (1), in table, words substituted by the Income Tax (PAYE) (Amendment) Regulations, SI 2009/588 regs 2, 7 with effect from 1 April 2009.

[2] In para (1), in table, entry for "regulation 185" substituted by the Income Tax (Pay As You Earn) (Amendment) Regulations, SI 2017/414 reg 4 with effect from 6 April 2017.

151 Obtaining the claimant's Form P45

(1) A claimant who has Parts 2 and 3 of Form P45 must deliver them to the Department on making a claim for a jobseeker's allowance which includes taxable jobseeker's allowance.
(2) If, on making a claim, the claimant declares that the claimant's last employer did not provide Parts 2 and 3 of Form P45, the Department may require the employer to deliver them to a specified office of the Department.

Commentary—*Simon's Taxes* **E4.11101.**
Derivation—The Income Tax (Employments) Regulations, SI 1993/744 regs 84(1), (2), (8).
Cross references—See the Income Tax (PAYE) Regulations, SI 2003/2682 reg 11 (this regulation not to apply to pension payers or pensioners in their capacity as such).

152 Deductions working sheet for claimants awarded taxable jobseeker's allowance

(1) The Department must prepare a deductions working sheet in respect of each claimant whose award includes taxable jobseeker's allowance.
(2) If the Department obtains Parts 2 and 3 of Form P45 relating to the claimant, it must immediately prepare the deductions working sheet using the information shown in Parts 2 and 3 of Form P45 in accordance with regulation 153.
(3) If the Department does not obtain Parts 2 and 3 of Form P45 relating to the claimant, it must prepare the deductions working sheet in accordance with regulation 154.

Commentary—*Simon's Taxes* **E4.11101.**
Derivation—The Income Tax (Employments) Regulations, SI 1993/744 reg 84(3), (7).

153 Form P45: deductions working sheet and return

(1) If Parts 2 and 3 of Form P45 relate to the current tax year, the Department must record in the deductions working sheet the total payments to date shown in Parts 2 and 3 of Form P45.
(2) If Parts 2 and 3 of Form P45 relate to the current tax year and show that the cumulative basis has been used, the Department must also—
- (*a*) record the following information from Parts 2 and 3 of Form P45 in the deductions working sheet, or
- (*b*) keep such records as enable production of the information.

(3) If the code shown in Parts 2 and 3 of Form P45 is a K code, the information is—
- (*a*) the total additional pay to date,
- (*b*) the total taxable payments to date, and
- (*c*) the lower of the total tax to date as at the week or month shown in Parts 2 and 3 of Form P45 or the total net tax deducted shown in them.

(4) In any other case the information is—
- (*a*) the total free pay to date,
- (*b*) the total taxable payments to date, and
- (*c*) the corresponding total tax to date as at the week or month shown in Parts 2 and 3 of Form P45.

(5) Paragraph (6) applies if—
- (*a*) the claim is made by 24th May in a tax year, and
- (*b*) Parts 2 and 3 of Form P45 show that the last relevant payment was made in the preceding tax year.

(6) The Department must complete the deductions working sheet but without recording the total payments to date or total net tax deducted (if any) shown in Parts 2 and 3 of Form P45.
(7) In cases falling within paragraphs (1) and (5), the code shown in Parts 2 and 3 of Form P45 must be treated as the claimant's code for the purposes of these Regulations.
(8) If, in a case not falling within paragraph (5), Parts 2 and 3 of Form P45 show that the last relevant payment was made in a tax year preceding that in which the claim was made, the Department—
- (*a*) must complete the deductions working sheet but without recording the total payments to date or total net tax deducted (if any) shown in Parts 2 and 3 of Form P45, and
- (*b*) must record the emergency code as the claimant's code.

(9) The Department must supply the information recorded under this regulation to the Inland Revenue together with such further information as may be required for the purposes of these Regulations.

Commentary—*Simon's Taxes* **E4.11101.**
Derivation—The Income Tax (Employments) Regulations, SI 1993/744 reg 84(3), (5)–(7).

154 No Form P45: deductions working sheet and return

(1) In a case falling within regulation 152(3) (no Form P45), the Department must—
- (*a*) prepare the deductions working sheet within 14 days of the award of a taxable jobseeker's allowance, and
- (*b*) record the emergency code as the claimant's code.

(2) The Department must also deliver a return to the Inland Revenue, giving—
- (*a*) the claimant's name,
- (*b*) the claimant's national insurance number,

(*c*) the claimant's date of birth, if known,
(*d*) the date on which the claim was made, and
(*e*) the reference number of the benefit office submitting the return.

(3) But the return need not be delivered if the claimant certifies that the claimant—
(*a*) is undergoing a course of full-time education and has not had regular employment since the previous 6th April, or
(*b*) has not had regular employment since finishing full-time education.

Commentary—*Simon's Taxes* **E4.11101.**
Derivation—The Income Tax (Employments) Regulations, SI 1993/744 reg 84(7), (9), (10).

155 Claimant's code etc to be used for calculations

(1) This regulation applies if, in respect of a claimant, the Department receives notification from the Inland Revenue of—
(*a*) a code or amended code,
(*b*) total payments to date, or
(*c*) total net tax deducted.

(2) The Department must record that notification in substitution for any previous record and use it for the purpose of all calculations required under this Chapter.

Commentary—*Simon's Taxes* **E4.11101.**
Derivation—The Income Tax (Employments) Regulations, SI 1993/744 reg 85(2).

156 Recording the amount of taxable jobseeker's allowance

Whenever a payment of jobseeker's allowance is made, the Department must record the taxable jobseeker's allowance included in the payment.

Commentary—*Simon's Taxes* **E4.11101.**
Derivation—The Income Tax (Employments) Regulations, SI 1993/744 reg 87.

157 Obligations at end of tax year

(1) This regulation applies in respect of each award which includes taxable jobseeker's allowance and which continues beyond the end of a tax year.

(2) Before 1st June following the end of the tax year, the Department must—
(*a*) make a tax calculation in accordance with regulation 161 if the claimant's code is used on the cumulative basis;
(*b*) subject to paragraph (3), issue a certificate to the claimant; and
(*c*) deliver a return to the Inland Revenue.

(3) The Department need not issue the certificate if—
(*a*) no taxable jobseeker's allowance has been paid, and
(*b*) a tax calculation in accordance with regulation 161 is not required.

(4) The certificate must show—
(*a*) the tax year to which it relates,
(*b*) the total jobseeker's allowance for the tax year excluding any amounts previously notified under regulation 159(2) or 160(2),
(*c*) the taxable jobseeker's allowance included in the total jobseeker's allowance,
(*d*) the claimant's code,
(*e*) the claimant's national insurance number,
(*f*) the claimant's name,
(*g*) the claimant's address, if known,
(*h*) any previous relevant payments and any tax deducted from those relevant payments which the Department was required to take into account under regulation 161,
(*i*) any total payments to date recorded by the Department in accordance with regulation 153(1) plus the total taxable jobseeker's allowance for the tax year, and the corresponding total net tax deducted, and
(*j*) the amount of tax refunded by the Department.

(5) The return must show—
(*a*) the particulars specified in paragraph (4), and
(*b*) if a calculation is required under regulation 161, any amount of tax outstanding.

Commentary—*Simon's Taxes* **E4.11101.**
Derivation—The Income Tax (Employments) Regulations, SI 1993/744 reg 88(1), (2), (4), (5).

158 When an award ceases

(1) For the purposes of these Regulations an award ceases when entitlement to a jobseeker's allowance ceases.

(2) When an award of a taxable jobseeker's allowance ceases the Department must make a tax calculation in accordance with regulation 161 if the claimant's code is used on the cumulative basis.

(3) The relevant date for the purposes of that calculation is the date on which the award ceases.

(4) The date on which the award ceases is the last day for which benefit was paid and was not recoverable, except that if the last day is 4th or 5th April the date is the preceding 3rd April.

(5) But the Department need not amend a tax calculation solely because the date used for the purposes of the calculation is subsequently shown to be incorrect.

Commentary—*Simon's Taxes* **E4.11101.**

Derivation—The Income Tax (Employments) Regulations, SI 1993/744 regs 89, 91(4).

159 Cessation of award: Form P45U

(1) When an award of a taxable jobseeker's allowance ceases the Department must immediately complete Form P45U.

(2) The Department must then—

(*a*) send Part 1 of Form P45U to the Inland Revenue, and

(*b*) provide Part 1A of Form P45U and Parts 2 and 3 of Form P45 to the claimant.

(3) The information listed in column 1 of Table 6 must, subject to the conditions set out in column 2, be provided in Parts 1 and 1A of Form P45U and Parts 2 and 3 of Form P45 as indicated in columns 3 to 5.

TABLE 6
INFORMATION WHICH MUST BE PROVIDED IN FORM P45U

1	*2*	*3*	*4*	*5*
Information to be provided	*Conditions*	*FormP45U*		*Form P45*
		Part 1	*Part 1A*	*Parts 2 & 3*
1 the tax reference as shown in the deductions working sheet		yes	yes	yes
2 claimant's national insurance number		yes	yes	yes
3 claimant's name		yes	yes	yes
4 the date on which the award ceased		yes	yes	yes
5 the claimant's code or, if more than one, the latest code for the tax year during which the award ceased		yes	yes	yes
6 whether the claimant's code is used on the cumulative basis		yes	yes	yes
7 the tax week or month in which the award ceased	if the claimant's code is used on the cumulative basis	yes	yes	yes
8 the total payments to date (including taxable jobseeker's allowance) at the date the award ceased, and the corresponding total net tax deducted	if the claimant's code is used on the cumulative basis	yes	yes	yes
9 the taxable jobseeker's allowance paid during the tax year by virtue of the award in question	if the claimant's code is used on the cumulative basis, and if different from the information supplied under item 8	yes	yes	no
10 the taxable jobseeker's allowance paid during the tax year by virtue of the award in question	if the claimant's code is not used on the cumulative basis	yes	yes	no
11 any amount of tax outstanding	if the claimant's code is used on the cumulative basis	yes	no	no
12 whether the claimant was self-employed immediately before the claim was made		yes	no	no

1	2	3	4	5
Information to be provided	*Conditions*	*FormP45U*		*Form P45*
		Part 1	*Part 1A*	*Parts 2 & 3*
13 whether the claimant is receiving a pension by reason of a former employment		yes	no	no
14 the claimant's address	if known	yes	no	no
15 the address of the benefit officer		yes	yes	no
16 the date the form is completed		yes	yes	no

(4) The Department must also give notice to the claimant of—

(*a*) the total jobseeker's allowance for the tax year excluding any sums previously notified under this regulation or regulation 160, 171 or 172, and

(*b*) the taxable jobseeker's allowance included in that total.

(5) Expressions used in Parts 2 and 3 of Form P45 have the following meanings—

(*a*) "employee" means "claimant",

(*b*) "leaving date" means "date the award ceased", and

(*c*) "pay" means "jobseeker's allowance".

(6) Regulation 163 (death of claimant) modifies the requirements of this regulation if an award of taxable jobseeker's allowance has ceased on the death of the claimant.

Commentary—*Simon's Taxes* **E4.11101.**
Derivation—The Income Tax (Employments) Regulations, SI 1993/744 reg 89(2).

160 Notification of taxable jobseeker's allowance adjustment

(1) Paragraph (2) applies if—

(*a*) after a certificate under regulation 157(2)(*b*) has been issued (or would have been issued but for regulation 157(3)), or

(*b*) after a notice has been issued under regulation 159(4) or this regulation,

further taxable jobseeker's allowance is paid to, or taxable jobseeker's allowance overpaid is recovered from, the claimant.

(2) The Department must—

(*a*) give notice to the claimant of the revised figure of total jobseeker's allowance and the taxable jobseeker's allowance included in that revised figure in accordance with the relevant regulation, and

(*b*) notify the Inland Revenue of the sums paid or refunded.

Commentary—*Simon's Taxes* **E4.11101.**
Derivation—The Income Tax (Employments) Regulations, SI 1993/744 regs 88(3), 90.

161 Tax calculation

(1) This regulation applies, subject to regulation 162, if the Department is required by regulation 157 or 158 to make a tax calculation.

(2) The Department must calculate in respect of the claimant as at the relevant date—

(*a*) the total payments to date, and

(*b*) the claimant's total tax.

(3) If the recorded tax exceeds the claimant's total tax, the Department must repay the excess to the claimant.

(4) But if the recorded tax is less than the claimant's total tax—;

(*a*) the difference is tax outstanding for the purposes of regulation 157(5)(*b*) or item 11 of Table 6 in regulation 159(3), and

(*b*) the Department must treat the claimant's code as issued by the Inland Revenue on the non-cumulative basis from the relevant date.

(5) In this regulation—

["claimant's total tax" means the lesser of—

(*a*) 50% of the claimant's total payments to date, and

(*b*) the tax due in accordance with the appropriate tax tables in respect of the claimant's total taxable payments to date at the relevant date;][1]

"recorded tax" means the total tax to date or (as the case may be) the total net tax deducted which was recorded in accordance with regulation 153(3) or (4) when the claim was made;

"relevant date" means—

(*a*) the end of the tax year, if the calculation is required by regulation 157;

(*b*) the date used for the purposes of the calculation, if the calculation is required by regulation 158;

"total payments to date" means any payments to date recorded by the Department in accordance with regulation 153(1), plus the total taxable jobseeker's allowance.

Commentary—*Simon's Taxes* **E4.11101.**

Derivation—The Income Tax (Employments) Regulations, SI 1993/744 reg 91(1)–(3).

Cross references—See the Income Tax (PAYE) Regulations, SI 2003/2682 reg 162 (cases where a tax calculation under this regulation is not required).

Amendments—[1] In para (5), definition of "claimant's total tax" substituted by the Income Tax (Pay As You Earn) (Amendment No 4) Regulations, SI 2014/2689 regs 2, 7 with effect from 6 April 2015.

162 No tax calculation required in certain cases

(1) A tax calculation under regulation 161 is not required in any of the following cases—

(*a*) if the claimant does not give the Department Parts 2 and 3 of Form P45, and does not certify in accordance with regulation 154(3) (students etc);

(*b*) if the claimant gives the Department Parts 2 and 3 of Form P45, but they do not relate to the claimant's last employment or award before the present award, whichever is later;

(*c*) if the claimant is in receipt of a pension in respect of a former employment;

(*d*) if it appears to the Department on the occasion of a claim that a previous award should have been treated as having ceased in accordance with regulation 158 (when an award ceases); or

(*e*) if the claimant's code is a nil tax code, basic rate code or higher rate code.

(2) Those cases are treated as if the Inland Revenue had made a direction that the claimant's code must be used on the non-cumulative basis.

(3) Those cases are subject to a notification from the Inland Revenue under regulation 155 that revised particulars are to be substituted and used.

Commentary—*Simon's Taxes* **E4.11101.**

Derivation—The Income Tax (Employments) Regulations, SI 1993/744 reg 91(4), (5).

163 Death of claimant

(1) On being informed of the death of a claimant whose award included taxable jobseeker's allowance, the Department must send the Inland Revenue the completed Form P45U indicating in Part 1 that the claimant has died.

(2) If the Department knows the name and address of the claimant's personal representative, the Department must send the notice referred to in regulation 159(4) to the personal representative.

(3) But if the Department has not been notified of the name and address of the claimant's personal representative within 30 days of the claimant's death, the Department is not required—

(*a*) to make a tax calculation under regulation 161, nor

(*b*) to issue the notice under regulation 159(4).

Commentary—*Simon's Taxes* **E4.11101.**

Derivation—The Income Tax (Employments) Regulations, SI 1993/744 reg 92.

164 Finance

(1) The Board of Inland Revenue must advance monies to the National Insurance Funds of Great Britain and Northern Ireland at intervals to be agreed with the Department for use in making repayments of income tax under these Regulations.

(2) The Department must provide the Board with a quarterly statement of receipts and payments.

Commentary—*Simon's Taxes* **E4.11101.**

Derivation—The Income Tax (Employments) Regulations, SI 1993/744 reg 93.

CHAPTER 2

JOBSEEKER'S ALLOWANCE: SPECIAL CASES

165 Scope of Chapter 2

(1) This Chapter applies only to Chapter 2 claimants (as defined by regulation 148).

(2) Except for regulation 148 (interpretation), Chapter 1 does not apply to Chapter 2 claimants.

Commentary—*Simon's Taxes* **E4.11101.**

166 Jobseeker's allowance paid directly to claimant

(1) This regulation applies if the Department makes a payment of taxable jobseeker's allowance directly to a Chapter 2 claimant.

(2) The Department must—

(*a*) record the amount, and

(*b*) pay the full sum without any deduction or repayment of income tax.

Commentary—*Simon's Taxes* **E4.11101.**

Derivation—The Income Tax (Employments) Regulations, SI 1993/744 reg 95.

167 Jobseeker's allowance paid by employer

(1) If—

(*a*) a jobseeker's allowance is paid to a Chapter 2 claimant by the claimant's employer on behalf of the Department, and

(*b*) the employer calculates the jobseeker's allowance payable by reference to instructions supplied by the Department,

the employer must also calculate the taxable jobseeker's allowance in accordance with those instructions.

(2) If—

(*a*) a jobseeker's allowance is paid to a Chapter 2 claimant by the claimant's employer on behalf of the Department, and

(*b*) paragraph (1)(*b*) does not apply,

the Department must notify the employer of the amount of jobseeker's allowance and of taxable jobseeker's allowance.

(3) If the employer has undertaken to pay a jobseeker's allowance on behalf of the Department, the Department must pay the full amount to the employer without any deduction on account of income tax.

Commentary—*Simon's Taxes* **E4.11101.**

Derivation—The Income Tax (Employments) Regulations, SI 1993/744 reg 96(1)–(3).

Cross references—See the Income Tax (PAYE) Regulations, SI 2003/2682 reg 10 (this regulation not to apply to agencies or agency workers in their capacity as such).

SI 2003/2682 reg 11 (this regulation not to apply to pension payers or pensioners in their capacity as such).

SI 2003/2682 reg 12 (this regulation not to apply to other payers or other payees in their capacity as such).

168 Regulation 167 cases: application of other regulations

(1) Parts 2 to 4 (codes; deduction and repayment of tax; payments, returns and information) apply to the taxable jobseeker's allowance paid to a Chapter 2 claimant by the employer on behalf of the Department under regulation 167, as if it were a relevant payment from the employment.

(2) But this is subject to paragraph (3), which applies in any case in which it appears to the Inland Revenue that deduction of tax from the taxable jobseeker's allowance paid by the employer on behalf of the Department by reference to the tax tables is impracticable.

(3) The Inland Revenue may make such other arrangements as are appropriate for the collection of tax in respect of taxable jobseeker's allowance.

(4) Regulations 170 to 172 (information to be supplied etc) do not apply if—

(*a*) the Chapter 2 claimant's employer has been paying the jobseeker's allowance in accordance with regulation 167, and

(*b*) the employer provides the information in question.

Commentary—*Simon's Taxes* **E4.11101.**

Derivation—The Income Tax (Employments) Regulations, SI 1993/744 reg 96(4), (5).

Cross references—See the Income Tax (PAYE) Regulations, SI 2003/2682 reg 10 (this regulation not to apply to agencies or agency workers in their capacity as such).

SI 2003/2682 reg 11 (this regulation not to apply to pension payers or pensioners in their capacity as such).

SI 2003/2682 reg 12 (this regulation not to apply to other payers or other payees in their capacity as such).

169 When a Chapter 2 award ceases

For the purposes of this Chapter, an award ceases when entitlement to a jobseeker's allowance which depends on regulation 17 or 156 of the JSA Regulations ceases.

Commentary—*Simon's Taxes* **E4.11101.**

Derivation—The Income Tax (Employments) Regulations, SI 1993/744 reg 97(1).

170 Information to be supplied at end of tax year

(1) This regulation applies in respect of an award of taxable jobseeker's allowance which continues beyond the end of a tax year.

(2) Before 1st June following the end of the tax year, the Department must give notice to the Inland Revenue and the Chapter 2 claimant of—

(*a*) the total jobseeker's allowance, and

(*b*) the taxable jobseeker's allowance,

paid in respect of the award during that tax year.

Commentary—*Simon's Taxes* **E4.11101.**

Derivation—The Income Tax (Employments) Regulations, SI 1993/744 reg 97(2).

Cross references—See the Income Tax (PAYE) Regulations, SI 2003/2682 reg 168 (cases where this regulation does not apply).

171 Information to be supplied when an award of taxable jobseeker's allowance ceases

(1) When an award of taxable jobseeker's allowance ceases, the Department must give notice to the Inland Revenue and, except where the Chapter 2 claimant has died, the claimant, of—

(*a*) the total jobseeker's allowance, and

(*b*) the taxable jobseeker's allowance,

paid in respect of the award, showing the amounts appropriate to the award for the tax year in which it ceased.

(2) If the Department has been notified of the name and address of a deceased claimant's personal representative within 30 days of the claimant's death, the Department must send the notice to the personal representative.

Commentary—*Simon's Taxes* **E4.11101.**

Derivation—The Income Tax (Employments) Regulations, SI 1993/744 reg 97(2).

Cross references—See the Income Tax (PAYE) Regulations, SI 2003/2682 reg 168 (cases where this regulation does not apply).

172 Adjustments of taxable jobseeker's allowance

(1) Paragraph (2) applies if, after the issue of a notice under regulation 170 or 171(1)—

(*a*) further taxable jobseeker's allowance is paid to the Chapter 2 claimant, or

(*b*) taxable jobseeker's allowance overpaid is recovered from the Chapter 2 claimant.

(2) The Department must—

(*a*) notify the Chapter 2 claimant of the revised figure of total jobseeker's allowance and the taxable jobseeker's allowance included in that revised figure, and

(*b*) notify the Inland Revenue of any adjustment to the figure of taxable jobseeker's allowance,

showing the amounts appropriate to each tax year.

Commentary—*Simon's Taxes* **E4.11101.**

Derivation—The Income Tax (Employments) Regulations, SI 1993/744 reg 98.

Cross references—See the Income Tax (PAYE) Regulations, SI 2003/2682 reg 168 (cases where this regulation does not apply).

CHAPTER 3

INCAPACITY BENEFIT

173 Interpretation of Chapter 3

In this Chapter—

"award" means an award of incapacity benefit;

"claim" means a claim for incapacity benefit;

"claimant" means a person who has made a claim;

"Department" means the Department for Work and Pensions or, in Northern Ireland, the Department for Social Development;

"incapacity benefit" means short-term incapacity benefit or long-term incapacity benefit payable under—

(*a*) sections 30A(1), 30A(5), 40 or 41 of the Social Security Contributions and Benefits Act 1992, or

(*b*) in Northern Ireland, section 30A(1), 30A(5), 40 or 41 of the Social Security Contributions and Benefits (Northern Ireland) Act 1992;

"single-income claimant" means a claimant who, for a tax year—

(*a*) is not entitled to receive any relevant payments in addition to the payments of taxable incapacity benefit, or

(*b*) is so entitled but has failed to provide any details relating to those payments when making the claim,

and who is not a self-employed earner as defined by section 2 of the Social Security Contributions and Benefits Act 1992 or, in Northern Ireland, section 2 of the Social Security Contributions and Benefits (Northern Ireland) Act 1992;

"taxable incapacity benefit" means any amount of incapacity benefit which is chargeable to income tax under Chapter 2 of Part 10 of ITEPA (tax on social security income).

Commentary—*Simon's Taxes* **E4.11102.**

Derivation—The Income Tax (Employments) Regulations, SI 1993/744 regs 81, 98A, 98C.

174 Application of other regulations

(1) The following regulations apply, subject to this Chapter, to payments of taxable incapacity benefit with the modifications mentioned in paragraphs (2) to (4)—

Regulation 2	Interpretation
Regulation 15	flat rate codes
Regulation 16	Continued application of employee's code
Regulation 17	notice to employee of code
Regulation 18	Objections and appeals against employee's code
Regulation 19	Amendment of code
Regulation 20	notice to employer of amended code
Regulation 21	Deduction and repayment of tax by reference to employee's code
Regulations 22 to 25	Cumulative basis
Regulations 26 to 31	non-cumulative basis
Regulation 33	nil tax code: no deductions or repayments
Regulation 36	Cessation of employment: Form P45
Regulation 66	Deductions working sheets

Regulation 67	Information to employees about payments and tax deducted
Regulation 68	periodic payments to and recoveries from the Revenue
Regulation 69	due date and receipts for payments of tax
Regulation 70	Quarterly tax periods
Regulation 72	Recovery from employee of tax not deducted by employer
Regulation 73	annual return of relevant payments liable to deduction of tax
Regulation 74	annual return of relevant payments not liable to deduction of tax
Regulation 76	Certificate if tax in regulation 73 return is unpaid
Regulation 79	Certificate after inspection of PAYE records
Regulation 84	Recovery of tax and interest
Regulation 97	[retention by employer of PAYE records][1]
Regulation 98	multiple PAYE schemes
Regulation 102	Succession to a business etc
Regulation 141	direct collection and special arrangements
Regulation 185	Adjusting total net tax deducted for purposes of sections 59A(1) and 59B(1) TMA
Regulation 188	Assessments other than self-assessments
Regulation 211	how information must or may be delivered by employers
Regulation 216	service by post
Regulation 218	Certificate that sum due
Regulation 219	Payment by cheque.

(2) In the application of those regulations, the expressions listed in column 1 of Table 7 have the meanings shown in column 2 of the table.

TABLE 7
MEANING OF EXPRESSIONS IN APPLICATION OF OTHER REGULATIONS

1 Expression	*2 Meaning for purposes of this Chapter*
Employee	Claimant
Employer	Department
Employment	Award
Relevant payments	taxable incapacity benefit.

(3) In regulation 15 (flat rate codes)—

(*a*) omit paragraph (1);

(*b*) omit paragraph (3)(*a*); and

(*c*) for paragraph (3)(*c*) substitute—

"(*c*) the Inland Revenue consider that the code which would otherwise be the claimant's code would result in too much tax being deducted for the tax year in question."

(4) In regulation 21(1) (deduction and repayment of tax by reference to employee's code), for "in accordance with these Regulations" substitute "in accordance with Chapter 3 of Part 8".

Commentary—*Simon's Taxes* **E4.11102.**

Derivation—The Income Tax (Employments) Regulations, SI 1993/744 regs 82, 98B, 98G(1).

Amendments—[1] In para (1), in table, words substituted by the Income Tax (PAYE) (Amendment) Regulations, SI 2009/588 regs 2, 7 with effect from 1 April 2009.

175 Emergency IB code to be used before claimant's code issued

(1) Paragraph (2) applies if the Department makes a payment of taxable incapacity benefit during a tax year to a single-income claimant before a code has been issued by the Inland Revenue for that year in respect of that award.

(2) The Department must—

(*a*) deduct tax using an emergency IB code on the non-cumulative basis, and

(*b*) keep records in a deductions working sheet which it must prepare for the purpose.

(3) The use of an emergency IB code under this regulation is treated as the issue of a code for the purposes of regulations 21, 36 and 180.

Commentary—*Simon's Taxes* **E4.11102.**
Derivation—The Income Tax (Employments) Regulations, SI 1993/744 reg 98C(1).

176 Return in respect of all claimants to taxable incapacity benefit

(1) When the Department first makes a payment of taxable incapacity benefit to a claimant it must immediately deliver a return to the Inland Revenue containing the following information.
(2) The information is—
(*a*) the claimant's name,
(*b*) the claimant's address,
(*c*) the claimant's date of birth, if known,
(*d*) the claimant's national insurance number,
(*e*) the date on which the claimant's entitlement to taxable incapacity benefit began,
(*f*) the weekly rate of taxable incapacity benefit being paid to the claimant,
(*g*) if a code is being used for the payment, that code and whether it is used on the non-cumulative basis,
(*h*) if the payment was preceded by payment of incapacity benefit which was not taxable, the date that benefit was first paid, and
(*i*) the claimant's tax reference, if known.

Commentary—*Simon's Taxes* **E4.11102.**
Derivation—The Income Tax (Employments) Regulations, SI 1993/744 reg 98D(1), (2).

177 Further return required in certain cases

(1) On making a subsequent payment of taxable incapacity benefit to the claimant, the Department must deliver a further return in accordance with regulation 176 as if that subsequent payment were the first payment, if conditions A and B are met.
(2) Condition A is that the Inland Revenue have previously determined the claimant's code in relation to the payments of incapacity benefit to be a nil tax code.
(3) Condition B is that the subsequent payment is the first payment to be made at a different rate from the rate subsisting at the time of that determination.
(4) In addition to providing the information listed in regulation 176(2), the Department must indicate in the further return that the weekly rate of taxable incapacity benefit being paid to the claimant represents a revised amount.

Commentary—*Simon's Taxes* **E4.11102.**
Derivation—The Income Tax (Employments) Regulations, SI 1993/744 reg 98D(3).

178 Delivery of Form P45 to Department

(1) This regulation applies if a single-income claimant—
(*a*) has Parts 2 and 3 of Form P45, and
(*b*) has not made, and does not intend to make, a claim for repayment of tax.
(2) The claimant must deliver Parts 2 and 3 of Form P45 when making a claim, and the Department must immediately send them to the Inland Revenue office.

Commentary—*Simon's Taxes* **E4.11102.**
Derivation—The Income Tax (Employments) Regulations, SI 1993/744 reg 98E(1).

179 Determination of claimant's code by Inland Revenue

(1) On receiving a return under regulation 176 relating to a single-income claimant, the Inland Revenue must determine the code for the claimant.
(2) The Inland Revenue may determine the code for a claimant who is not a single-income claimant if they consider that it would be impractical to collect tax arising on the claimant's taxable incapacity benefit by other means.
(3) In determining the code for a claimant under this regulation, regulation 14(1) (matters to which Revenue must have regard in determining an employee's code) does not apply.
(4) If the Inland Revenue are satisfied the claimant is entitled, for the tax year for which the code is determined, to any of the following reliefs from income tax, they must have regard to that relief in determining the code for the claimant under this regulation.
(5) The reliefs are—
(*a*) personal allowance (section 257(1) of ICTA),
(*b*) married couple's allowance (section 257A of ICTA), and
(*c*) blind person's allowance (section 265(1) of ICTA).
(6) If the Inland Revenue determine the code for a claimant before the beginning of the tax year for which it is determined, the Inland Revenue—
(*a*) must have regard to any expected change in the amounts of those reliefs, but
(*b*) may disregard any of those reliefs if they are not satisfied that the claimant will be entitled to it for the tax year for which it is determined.

Commentary—*Simon's Taxes* **E4.11102.**
Derivation—The Income Tax (Employments) Regulations, SI 1993/744 reg 98F(1)–(4).

180 Death of claimant

(1) On the death of a claimant in respect of whom a code has been issued by the Inland Revenue, the Department must—

(*a*) complete Form P45 indicating in Part 1 that the claimant has died, and

(*b*) send it to the Inland Revenue.

(2) The Department must comply with paragraph (1)—

(*a*) on the day on which it learns of the claimant's death, or

(*b*) if that is not practicable, without unreasonable delay.

(3) Paragraph (4) applies if the Department makes any payment of taxable incapacity benefit after the date of the claimant's death—

(*a*) before completing Form P45, or

(*b*) after completing Form P45 but during the tax year in which the claimant died.

(4) The Department must, on making the payment, deduct or repay tax as if the deceased claimant were still alive and the award had not ceased at the date of payment.

(5) Regulation 37(2) to (6) (PAYE income paid after employment ceased) applies to any payment of taxable incapacity benefit which—

(*a*) is made in a tax year following the tax year in which the claimant died, and

(*b*) is not included in Form P45.

Commentary—*Simon's Taxes* **E4.11102.**

Derivation—The Income Tax (Employments) Regulations, SI 1993/744 regs 27, 98B.

CHAPTER 4

INCOME SUPPORT

181 Interpretation of Chapter 4

In this Chapter—

"award" means an award of income support;

"claim" means a claim for income support;

"claimant" means a person who has made a claim;

"Department" means the Department for Work and Pensions or, in Northern Ireland, the Department for Social Development;

"income support" means benefit payable under—

(*a*) section 124 of the Social Security Contributions and Benefits Act 1992, or

(*b*) in Northern Ireland, section 123 of the Social Security Contributions and Benefits (Northern Ireland) Act 1992;

"taxable income support" means any amount of income support which is chargeable to income tax under Chapter 2 of Part 10 of ITEPA (tax on social security income).

182 Recording the amount of taxable income support

Whenever the Department makes a payment of taxable income support it must—

(*a*) record the amount, and

(*b*) pay the full sum without any deduction or repayment of income tax.

183 Information to be supplied when an award of taxable income support ceases

(1) This regulation applies when an award of taxable income support ceases.

(2) The Department must give notice to the Inland Revenue and, except where the claimant has died, the claimant of—

(*a*) the total income support, and

(*b*) the taxable income support,

paid in respect of the award showing the amounts appropriate to each tax year.

(3) If the Department has been notified of the name and address of a deceased claimant's personal representative within 30 days of the claimant's death, the Department must send the notice to the personal representative.

184 Adjustments of taxable income support

(1) Paragraph (2) applies if, after the issue of a notice under regulation 183(2)—

(*a*) further taxable income support is paid to the claimant, or

(*b*) taxable income support overpaid is recovered from the claimant.

(2) The Department must—

(*a*) notify the claimant of the revised figure of total income support and the taxable income support included in that revised figure, and

(*b*) notify the Inland Revenue of any adjustment to the figure of taxable income support,

showing the amounts appropriate to each tax year.

[CHAPTER 5

EMPLOYMENT AND SUPPORT ALLOWANCE][1]1

Amendments—[1] Chapter 5 (ss 184A–184S) inserted by the Income Tax (Pay As You Earn) (Amendment) (No 2) Regulations, SI 2008/2601 regs 2, 3 with effect from 27 October 2008.

184A [Interpretation of Chapter 5

In this Chapter—

"award" means an award of employment and support allowance;

"claim" means a claim for employment and support allowance;

"claimant" means a person who has made a claim;

"Department" means the Department for Work and Pensions or, in Northern Ireland, the Department for Social Development;

"employment and support allowance" means benefit payable under—

(*a*) the Welfare Reform Act 2007, or

(*b*) in Northern Ireland, the Welfare Reform Act (Northern Ireland) 2007;

"taxable employment and support allowance" means any amount of employment and support allowance which is chargeable to income tax under Chapter 2 of Part 10 of ITEPA (tax on social security income).][1]

Amendments—[1] Chapter 5 (ss 184A–184S) inserted by the Income Tax (Pay As You Earn) (Amendment) (No 2) Regulations, SI 2008/2601 regs 2, 3 with effect from 27 October 2008.

184B [Application of other regulations

(1) The following regulations apply to payments of employment and support allowance made to a claimant with the modifications mentioned in paragraphs (2) to [(5)][5]

regulation 2	interpretation
regulation 14	matters relevant to determination of code
regulation 15	flat rate codes
regulation 16	continued application of employee's code
regulation 17	notice to employee of code
regulation 18	objections and appeals against employee's code
regulation 19	amendment of code
regulation 20	notice to employer of amended code
regulation 21	deduction and repayment of tax by reference to employee's code
regulation 97	[retention by employer of PAYE records][2]
regulation 98	multiple PAYE schemes
regulation 102	succession to a business etc
[regulation 185	adjusting total net tax deducted for purposes of sections 59A(1), 59B(1) and 59BA(2) TMA][7]
[regulation 205	mandatory use of electronic communications][6]
[regulation 206	employers . . .[6]
regulation 207	specified information
regulation 208	*e-filing notice and appeals*[4]
regulation 209	standards of accuracy and completeness
regulation 210	penalty for failing to deliver . . .[6] specified information
regulation 210B	penalty: form P45 (Part 1 or Part 3), P46 or P46(Pen)
regulation 210C	appeals and interest][3]
regulation 211	how information must or may be delivered by employers
regulation 214	how information must be provided by employees
regulation 216	service by post.

(2) In the application of those regulations, the expressions listed in column 1 of Table 7A have the meanings shown in column 2 of the table.

Table 7A
Meaning of expressions in application of other regulations

1. Expression	*2. Meaning for purposes of this Chapter*
Employee	claimant
[Employer . . . [6]][3]	Department
Employment	award
Relevant payments	taxable employment and support allowance

(3) In the application of regulations 20 (notice to employer of amended code) and 21 (deduction and repayment of tax by reference to employee's code), any reference to the deduction or repayment of tax shall be read as a reference to the tax calculation which the Department is required to make at the end of the tax year or on the cessation of an award (by virtue of regulation 184I(2)(*a*) and 184K(2).
(4) In the application of regulation 207 (specified information) the reference to specified information shall be read as including references to—
(*a*) the return and accompanying information required by regulations 184G (return in respect of all claimants to taxable employment and support allowance) and 184J (annual return),
(*b*) Part 1 of Form P45ESA, and
(*c*) the information required under regulation 184E(9).][1]
[(5) In the application of regulation [210AA][6] (penalty for failing to deliver specified information)—
(*a*) where the specified information is the return and accompanying information required by regulation 184J (annual return) the penalty will be determined in accordance with regulation 210A, and
(*b*) where the specified information is 184G (return in respect of all claimants to taxable employment and support allowance), Part 1 of Form P45ESA or the information required under regulation 184E(9) the penalty will be determined in accordance with [regulations 210B and 210BA][6].][5]

Amendments—[1] Chapter 5 (ss 184A–184S) inserted by the Income Tax (Pay As You Earn) (Amendment) (No 2) Regulations, SI 2008/2601 regs 2, 3 with effect from 27 October 2008.
[2] In para (1), in table, words substituted by the Income Tax (PAYE) (Amendment) Regulations, SI 2009/588 regs 2, 7 with effect from 1 April 2009.
[3] In para (1), in table, entries substituted, and in para (2), in table, words substituted, by the Income Tax (Pay As You Earn) (Amendment No 2) Regulations, SI 2009/2029 regs 2, 3 with effect in relation to the tax year 2009–10 and subsequent tax years.
[4] Entry for reg 208 revoked by the Income Tax (Pay as You Earn) (Amendment) Regulations, SI 2010/668 regs 2, 17(*b*)(iii) with effect only in relation to the tax year 2010–11 and subsequent tax years.
[5] Reference in para (1) substituted, entry relating to reg 210B revoked, and para (5) inserted, by the Income Tax (Pay as You Earn) (Amendment) Regulations, SI 2010/668 regs 2, 17(1)(*a*), (*b*)(v), (*d*) with effect from 6 April 2010.
[6] In para (1), entry for "regulation 205" substituted for previous entries for regs 205A–205B; in entry for reg 206 words substituted, and in entry relating to reg 210, words, revoked, in para (2), in Table 7A words revoked, and in inserted para (5), words substituted by the Income Tax (Pay As You Earn) (Amendment) Regulations, SI 2010/668, regs 2, 17(*b*)(i), (ii), (iv), (*c*), (*e*), with effect in relation to the tax year 2011–12 and subsequent tax years.
[7] In para (1), entry for "regulation 85" substituted by the Income Tax (Pay As You Earn) (Amendment) Regulations, SI 2017/414 reg 5 with effect from 6 April 2017.

184C [Obtaining the claimant's Form P45

(1) A claimant who has Parts 2 and 3 of Form P45 must deliver them to the Department on making a claim for employment and support allowance which includes taxable employment and support allowance.
(2) If on making a claim, the claimant declares that the claimant's last employer did not provide Parts 2 and 3 of Form P45, the Department may require the employer to deliver them to a specified officer of the Department.][1]

Amendments—[1] Chapter 5 (ss 184A–184S) inserted by the Income Tax (Pay As You Earn) (Amendment) (No 2) Regulations, SI 2008/2601 regs 2, 3 with effect from 27 October 2008.

184D [Deductions working sheet for claimants awarded taxable employment and support allowance

(1) The Department must prepare a deductions working sheet in respect of each claimant whose award includes taxable employment and support allowance.
(2) If the Department obtains Parts 2 and 3 of Form P45 relating to the claimant, it must immediately prepare the deductions working sheet using the information shown in Parts 2 and 3 of Form P45 in accordance with regulation 184E.
(3) If the Department does not obtain Parts 2 and 3 of Form P45 relating to the claimant, it must prepare the deductions working sheet in accordance with regulation 184F.][1]

Amendments—[1] Chapter 5 (ss 184A–184S) inserted by the Income Tax (Pay As You Earn) (Amendment) (No 2) Regulations, SI 2008/2601 regs 2, 3 with effect from 27 October 2008.

184E [Form P45: deductions working sheet and return

(1) If Parts 2 and 3 of Form P45 relate to the current tax year, the Department must record in the deductions working sheet the total payments to date shown in Parts 2 and 3 of Form P45.

(2) If Parts 2 and 3 of Form P45 relate to the current tax year and show that the cumulative basis has been used, the Department must also—

(*a*) record the following information from Parts 2 and 3 of Form P45 in the deductions working sheet, or

(*b*) keep such records as enable production of the information.

(3) If the code shown in Parts 2 and 3 of Form P45 is a K code, the information is—

(*a*) the code show,

(*b*) the total additional pay to date,

(*c*) the total taxable payments to date, and

(*d*) the lower of the total tax to date as at the week or month shown in Parts 2 and 3 of Form P45 or the total net tax deducted shown in them.

(4) In any other case, the information is—

(*a*) the code shown,

(*b*) the total free pay to date,

(*c*) the total taxable payments to date, and

(*d*) the corresponding total tax to date as at the week or month shown in Parts 2 and 3 of Form P45.

(5) Paragraph (6) applies if—

(*a*) the claim is made by 24th May in a tax year, and

(*b*) Parts 2 and 3 of Form P45 show that the last relevant payment was made in the preceding tax year.

(6) The Department must complete the deductions working sheet but without recording the total payments to date or total net tax deducted (if any) shown in Parts 2 and 3 of Form P45.

(7) In cases falling within paragraphs (1) and (6), the code shown in Parts 2 and 3 of Form P45 must be treated as the claimant's code for the purposes of these Regulations.

(8) If, in a case not falling within paragraph (6), Parts 2 and 3 of Form P45 show that the last relevant payment was made in a tax year preceding that in which the claim was made, the Department—

(*a*) must complete the deductions working sheet but without recording the total payments to date or total net tax deducted (if any) shown in parts 2 and 3 of Form P45, and

(*b*) must record the emergency code as the claimant's code.

(9) The Department must supply the information recorded under this regulation to HMRC together with such further information as may be required for the purposes of these Regulations.][1]

Amendments—[1] Chapter 5 (ss 184A–184S) inserted by the Income Tax (Pay As You Earn) (Amendment) (No 2) Regulations, SI 2008/2601 regs 2, 3 with effect from 27 October 2008.

184F [No Form P45: deductions working sheet and return

In a case falling within regulation 184D(3) (no Form P45), the Department must—

(*a*) prepare the deductions working sheet within 14 days of the award of a taxable employment and support allowance, and

(*b*) record the emergency code as the claimant's code.][1]

Amendments—[1] Chapter 5 (ss 184A–184S) inserted by the Income Tax (Pay As You Earn) (Amendment) (No 2) Regulations, SI 2008/2601 regs 2, 3 with effect from 27 October 2008.

184G [Return in respect of all claimants to taxable employment and support allowance

(1) When the Department first makes a payment of taxable employment and support allowance to a claimant it must deliver a return to HMRC containing the following information.

(2) The information is—

(*a*) the claimant's name,

(*b*) the claimant's address,

(*c*) the claimant's date of birth, if known,

(*d*) the claimant's national insurance number,

(*e*) the date on which the claimant's entitlement to taxable employment and support allowance began,

(*f*) the weekly rate of taxable employment and support allowance being paid to the claimant,

(*g*) if the payment was preceded by a payment of employment and support allowance which was not taxable, the date that benefit was first paid, and

(*h*) the claimant's tax reference, if known.

(3) But the return need not be delivered if the claimant certifies that the claimant—

(*a*) is undergoing a course of full-time education and has not had regular employment since the previous 6th April, or

(*b*) has not had regular employment since finishing full-time education.][1]

Amendments—[1] Chapter 5 (ss 184A–184S) inserted by the Income Tax (Pay As You Earn) (Amendment) (No 2) Regulations, SI 2008/2601 regs 2, 3 with effect from 27 October 2008.

184H [Further return required in certain cases

(1) On making a subsequent payment of taxable employment and support allowance to the claimant, the Department must deliver a further return in accordance with regulation 184G as if that subsequent payment were the first payment, if the condition set out in paragraph (2) is met.

(2) The condition is that the subsequent payment is the first payment to be made at a different rate from the rate subsisting at the time of that determination.

(3) In addition to providing the information listed in regulation 184G(2), the Department must indicate in the further return that the weekly rate of taxable employment and support allowance being paid to the claimant represents a revised amount.][1]

Amendments—[1] Chapter 5 (ss 184A–184S) inserted by the Income Tax (Pay As You Earn) (Amendment) (No 2) Regulations, SI 2008/2601 regs 2, 3 with effect from 27 October 2008.

184I [Obligations at the end of the year

(1) This regulation applies in respect of each award which includes taxable employment and support allowance and which continues beyond the end of a tax year.

(2) Before 1st June following the end of the tax year the Department must—

(*a*) make a tax calculation in accordance with regulation 184N if the claimant's code is used on the cumulative basis; and

(*b*) subject to paragraph (3), issue a certificate to the claimant.

(3) The Department need not issue a certificate if—

(*a*) no taxable employment and support allowance has been paid, and

(*b*) a tax calculation in accordance with regulation 184N is not required.

(4) The certificate must show—

(*a*) the tax year to which it relates,

(*b*) the total employment and support allowance for the tax year excluding any amounts previously notified under regulations 184L(4) and 184Q(2)(a),

(*c*) the taxable employment and support allowance included in the total employment and support allowance,

(*d*) the claimant's code,

(*e*) the claimant's national insurance number,

(*f*) the claimant's address (if known),

(*h*) any previous relevant payments and any tax deducted from those relevant payments which the Department was required to take into account under regulation 184N,

(*i*) any total payments to date recorded by the Department in accordance with regulation 184E(1) plus the total taxable employment and support allowance for the tax year, and the corresponding total net tax deducted, and

(*j*) the amount of tax refunded by the Department.][1]

Amendments—[1] Chapter 5 (ss 184A–184S) inserted by the Income Tax (Pay As You Earn) (Amendment) (No 2) Regulations, SI 2008/2601 regs 2, 3 with effect from 27 October 2008.
Note that there appears to be no sub-para (4)(*g*).

184J [Annual return

(1) This regulation applies in respect of each award which includes taxable employment and support allowance.

(2) Before 1st June following the end of the tax year, the Department must deliver a return to HMRC.

(3) The return must show—

(*a*) the particulars specified in regulation 184I(4), and

(*b*) if a calculation is required under regulation 184N any amount of tax outstanding.][1]

Amendments—[1] Chapter 5 (ss 184A–184S) inserted by the Income Tax (Pay As You Earn) (Amendment) (No 2) Regulations, SI 2008/2601 regs 2, 3 with effect from 27 October 2008.

184K [When an award ceases

(1) For the purposes of these Regulations an award ceases when entitlement to an employment and support allowance ceases.

(2) When an award of a taxable employment and support allowance ceases, the Department must make a tax calculation in accordance with regulation 184N.

(3) The relevant date for the purposes of that calculation is the date on which the award ceases.

(4) The date on which the award ceases is the last day for which benefit was paid and was not recoverable, except that if the last day is 4th or 5th April the date is the preceding 3rd April.

(5) But the Department need not amend a tax calculation solely because the date used for the purposes of the calculation is subsequently shown to be incorrect.][1]

Amendments—[1] Chapter 5 (ss 184A–184S) inserted by the Income Tax (Pay As You Earn) (Amendment) (No 2) Regulations, SI 2008/2601 regs 2, 3 with effect from 27 October 2008.

184L [Cessation of award: Form P45ESA

(1) When an award of a taxable employment and support allowance ceases, the Department must immediately complete Form P45ESA.

(2) The Department must then—

(*a*) send Part 1 of Form P45ESA to HMRC; and

(*b*) provide Part 1A of P45ESA and Parts 2 and 3 of Form P45 to the claimant.

(3) The information listed in column 1 of Table 7B must, subject to the conditions set out in column 2, be provided in Parts 1 and 1A of Form P45ESA and Parts 2 and 3 of Form P45 as indicated in columns 3 to 5.

Table 7B
Information which must be provided in Form P45ESA

1	*2*	*3*	*4*	*5*
Information to be provided	*Conditions*	*Form P45ESA*	*Form P45ESA*	*Form P45*
		Part 1	*Part 1A*	*Parts 2 and 3*
1. the tax reference as shown in the deductions working sheet		yes	yes	yes
2. claimant's national insurance number		yes	yes	yes
3. claimant's name		yes	yes	yes
4. the date on which the award ceased		yes	yes	yes
5. the claimant's code or, if more than one, the latest code for the tax year during which the award ceased		yes	yes	yes
6. whether the claimant's code is used on the cumulative basis		yes	yes	yes
7. the tax week or month in which the award ceased	if the claimant's code is used on the cumulative basis	yes	yes	yes
8. the total payments to date (including taxable employment and support allowance) at the date the award ceased, and the corresponding total net tax deducted	if the claimant's code is used on the cumulative basis	yes	yes	yes
9. the taxable employment and support allowance paid during the tax year by virtue of the award in question	if the claimant's code is used on the cumulative basis, and if different from the information supplied under item 8	yes	yes	no
10. the taxable employment and support allowance paid during the tax year in question by virtue of the award in question	if the claimant's code is not used on the cumulative basis	yes	yes	no
11. any amount of tax outstanding	if the claimant's code is used on the cumulative basis	yes	no	no
12. whether the claimant was self-employed immediately before the claim was made.		yes	no	no
13. whether the claimant is receiving a pension by reason of a former employment.		yes	no	no

1	*2*	*3*	*4*	*5*
Information to be provided	*Conditions*	*Form P45ESA*	*Form P45ESA*	*Form P45*
		Part 1	*Part 1A*	*Parts 2 and 3*
14. the claimant's address	if known	yes	no	no
15. the address of the benefit office		yes	yes	no
16. the date the form is completed		yes	yes	no

(4) The Department must also give notice to the claimant of—

(*a*) the total employment and support allowance for the tax year excluding any sums previously notified under this regulation and regulation 184Q(2)(a), and

(*b*) the taxable employment and support allowance included in that total.

(5) Expressions used in Parts 2 and 3 of Form P45 have the following meanings—

(*a*) "employee" means "claimant";

(*b*) "leaving date" means "date the award ceased"; and

(*c*) "pay" means "employment and support allowance".

(6) Regulation 184M (death of claimant) modifies the requirements of this regulation if an award of taxable employment and support allowance has ceased on the death of the claimant.

(7) If Form P45ESA has not come into use when the award of taxable employment and support allowance ceases, the Department must complete form P45U and any references to form P45ESA in these regulations shall be read as a reference to form P45U.][1]

Amendments—[1] Chapter 5 (ss 184A–184S) inserted by the Income Tax (Pay As You Earn) (Amendment) (No 2) Regulations, SI 2008/2601 regs 2, 3 with effect from 27 October 2008.

184M [Death of claimant

(1) On being informed of the death of a claimant whose award included taxable employment and support allowance, the Department must send HMRC the completed Form P45ESA indicating in Part 1 that the claimant has died.

(2) If the Department knows the name and address of the claimant's personal representative the Department must send the notice referred to in regulation 184L(4) to the personal representative.

(3) But if the Department has not been notified of the name and address of the claimant's personal representative within 30 days of the claimant's death, the Department is not required—

(*a*) to make a tax calculation under regulation 184N, nor

(*b*) to issue the notice under regulation 184L(4).][1]

Amendments—[1] Chapter 5 (ss 184A–184S) inserted by the Income Tax (Pay As You Earn) (Amendment) (No 2) Regulations, SI 2008/2601 regs 2, 3 with effect from 27 October 2008.

184N [Tax calculation

(1) This regulation applies, subject to regulation 184O, if the Department is required by regulation 184I or 184K to make a tax calculation.

(2) The Department must calculate in respect of the claimant as at the relevant date—

(*a*) the total payments to date, and

(*b*) the claimant's total tax.

(3) If the recorded tax exceeds the claimant's total tax, the Department must repay the excess to the claimant.

(4) But if the recorded tax is less than the claimant's total tax—

(*a*) the difference is tax outstanding for the purposes of regulation 184J(3)(*b*) or item 11 of table 7B in regulation 184L(3), and

(*b*) the Department must treat the claimant's code as issued by HMRC on the non-cumulative basis from the relevant date.

(5) In this regulation—

"claimant's total tax" means—

(*a*) if the claimant's code is a K code, the lesser of—

(i) 50% of the claimant's total payments to date, and

(ii) the tax due in accordance with the appropriate tax tables in respect of the claimant's total taxable payments to date at the relevant date,

(*b*) in any other case, the tax due in accordance with the appropriate tax tables in respect of the claimant's total taxable payments to date at the relevant date;

"recorded tax" means the total tax to date or (as the case may be) the total net tax deducted which was recorded in accordance with regulation 184E(3) or (4) when the claim was made;

"relevant date" means—

(*a*) the end of the tax year, if the calculation is required by regulation 184I, (*b*) the date used for the purposes of the calculation, if the calculation is required by regulation 184K;

"total payments to date" means any payments to date recorded by the Department in accordance with regulation 184E(1) plus the total taxable employment and support allowance.][1]

Amendments—[1] Chapter 5 (ss 184A–184S) inserted by the Income Tax (Pay As You Earn) (Amendment) (No 2) Regulations, SI 2008/2601 regs 2, 3 with effect from 27 October 2008.

184O [No tax calculation required in certain cases

(1) A tax calculation made under regulation 184N is not required in any of the following cases—

(*a*) if the claimant does not give the Department Parts 2 and 3 of form P45 and does not certify in accordance with regulation 184G(3) (students etc),

(*b*) if the claimant gives the Department Parts 2 and 3 of Form P45 but they do not relate to the claimant's last employment or award before the present award, whichever is the later,

(*c*) if the claimant is in receipt of a pension in respect of a former employment,

(*d*) if it appears to the Department on the occasion of a claim that a previous award should have been treated as having ceased in accordance with regulation 184K (when an award ceases), or

(*e*) if the claimant's code is a nil tax code, basic rate code or higher rate code.

(2) Those cases are treated as if HMRC had made a direction that the claimant's code must be used on the non-cumulative basis.

(3) Those cases are subject to a notification from HMRC under regulation 184P that revised particulars are to be substituted and used.][1]

Amendments—[1] Chapter 5 (ss 184A–184S) inserted by the Income Tax (Pay As You Earn) (Amendment) (No 2) Regulations, SI 2008/2601 regs 2, 3 with effect from 27 October 2008.

184P [Claimant's code etc to be used for calculations

(1) This regulation applies if, in respect of a claimant, the Department receives notification from HMRC of—

(*a*) a code or amended code,

(*b*) total payments to date, or

(*c*) total net tax deducted.

(2) The Department must record that notification in substitution for any previous record and use it for the purpose of all calculations required under this Chapter.][1]

Amendments—[1] Chapter 5 (ss 184A–184S) inserted by the Income Tax (Pay As You Earn) (Amendment) (No 2) Regulations, SI 2008/2601 regs 2, 3 with effect from 27 October 2008.

184Q [Notification of taxable employment and support allowance

(1) Paragraph (2) applies if—

(*a*) after a certificate under regulation 184I(2)(*b*) has been issued (or would have been issued but for regulation 184I(3)), or

(*b*) after a notice has been issued under regulation 184L(4) or this regulation,

further taxable employment and support allowance is paid to, or taxable employment and support allowance overpaid is recovered from, the claimant.

(2) The Department must—

(*a*) give notice to the claimant of the revised figure of total employment and support allowance and the taxable employment and support allowance included in that revised figure in accordance with the relevant regulation, and

(*b*) notify HMRC of the sums paid or refunded.][1]

Amendments—[1] Chapter 5 (ss 184A–184S) inserted by the Income Tax (Pay As You Earn) (Amendment) (No 2) Regulations, SI 2008/2601 regs 2, 3 with effect from 27 October 2008.

184R [Recording the amount of taxable employment and support allowance

Whenever a payment of employment and support allowance is made, the Department must record the taxable employment and support allowance included in the payment.][1]

Amendments—[1] Chapter 5 (ss 184A–184S) inserted by the Income Tax (Pay As You Earn) (Amendment) (No 2) Regulations, SI 2008/2601 regs 2, 3 with effect from 27 October 2008.

184S [Finance

(1) HMRC must advance monies to the National Funds of Great Britain and Northern Ireland at intervals to be agreed with the Department for use in making repayments of income tax under these Regulations.

(2) The Department must provide HMRC with a quarterly statement of receipts and payments made under this Chapter.][1]

Amendments—[1] Chapter 5 (ss 184A–184S) inserted by the Income Tax (Pay As You Earn) (Amendment) (No 2) Regulations, SI 2008/2601 regs 2, 3 with effect from 27 October 2008.

PART 9
ASSESSMENT AND SELF-ASSESSMENT

185 Adjusting total net tax deducted for purposes of sections [59A(1), 59B(1) and 59BA(2)][2] TMA

(1) This regulation applies for the purpose of determining—

(*a*) the excess mentioned in section 59A(1) of TMA (payments on account of income tax: income tax assessed exceeds amount deducted at source), . . .[2]

(*b*) the difference mentioned in section 59B(1) of TMA (payments of income tax and capital gains tax: difference between tax contained in self-assessment and aggregate of payments on account or deducted [at source), and][2]

[(*c*) the difference mentioned in section 59BA(2) of TMA (payments of income tax and capital gains tax: difference between tax contained in simple assessment and aggregate of payments on account or deducted at source).][2]

(2) For those purposes, the amount of income tax deducted at source under these Regulations is the total net tax deducted during the relevant tax year ("A") after making any additions or subtractions required by paragraphs (3) to (5).

(3) Subtract from A any repayments of A which are made before the taxpayer's return and self-assessment is made under section 8 or 8A of TMA (personal return and trustee's return).

(4) Add to A any overpayment of tax from a previous tax year, to the extent that it was taken into account in determining the taxpayer's code for the relevant tax year.

(5) Add to A any tax treated as deducted, other than any direction tax, but—

(*a*) only if there would be an amount payable by the taxpayer under section 59B(1) of TMA on the assumption that there are no payments on account and no addition to A under this paragraph, and then

(*b*) only to a maximum of that amount.

(6) In this regulation—

"direction tax" means any amount of tax which is the subject of a direction made under [regulation 72(5), regulation 72F][1] or regulation 81(4) in relation to the taxpayer in respect of one or more tax periods falling within the relevant tax year;

"relevant tax year" means—

(*a*) in relation to section 59A(1) of TMA, the immediately preceding year referred to in that subsection;

(*b*) in relation to section 59B(1) of TMA, the tax year for which the self-assessment referred to in that subsection is made;

[(*c*) in relation to section 59BA(2) of TMA the tax year for which the simple assessment referred to in that subsection is made;][2]

"tax treated as deducted" means any tax which in relation to relevant payments made by an employer to the taxpayer in the relevant tax year—

(*a*) the employer was liable to deduct from payments but failed to do so, or

(*b*) the employer was liable to account for in accordance with regulation 62(5) (notional payments) but failed to do so;

"the taxpayer" means the person referred to in section 59A(1) of TMA [or the person whose simple assessment is referred to in section 59BA(2) of TMA][2] or the person whose self-assessment is referred to in section 59B(1) of TMA (as the case may be).

Commentary—*Simon's Taxes* **E4.11131.**

Derivation—The Income Tax (Employments) Regulations, SI 1993/744 regs 101(4)–(6), 101A(1), (2), (4); the Income Tax (Employments) (Notional Payments) Regulations, SI 1994/1212 reg 13(1).

Modifications—See the Income Tax (PAYE) Regulations, SI 2003/2682 reg 150 (modification of this regulation in its application to payments of taxable jobseeker's allowance made to a claimant).

SI 2003/2682 reg 174 (modification of this regulation in its application to payments of taxable incapacity benefit).

Amendments—[1] In para (6), words in definition of "direction tax" substituted by the Income Tax (Pay As You Earn) (Amendment) Regulations, SI 2008/782 regs 2, 14 with effect from 6 April 2008.

[2] The following amendments made by the Income Tax (Pay As You Earn) (Amendment) Regulations, SI 2017/414 reg 6 with effect from 6 April 2017—

- in heading and para (1)(*b*), words substituted;
- in para (1)(*a*), words revoked;
- para (1)(*c*) inserted; and
- in para (6), in definition of "relevant tax year", sub-para (*c*) inserted, and in definition of "the taxpayer", words inserted.

186 Recovery: adjustment of employee's code

(1) This regulation applies if, on the assumption mentioned in paragraph (2), the difference for a tax year mentioned in section 59B(1) of TMA (difference between tax contained in a self-assessment and aggregate of payments on account) would be payable by the taxpayer.

(2) The assumption is that, in respect of the tax year, nothing will be deducted at source under these Regulations in a subsequent tax year.

(3) The Inland Revenue must have regard to the difference in determining a taxpayer's code for a subsequent tax year under regulation 14 (matters relevant to determination of code) if—

(*a*) it is less than [£3,000][2], and

(*b*) the return for the tax year is—

(i) delivered by an approved method of electronic communications before 31st December following the end of the tax year, or

(ii) delivered by any other method before [1st November][1] following the end of the tax year.

(4) In a case not falling within paragraph (3)(*b*)(i), the Inland Revenue may have regard to the difference in determining a taxpayer's code for a subsequent tax year under regulation 14 if—

(*a*) it is less than [£3,000][2], and

(*b*) the return for the tax year is delivered on or after [1st November][1] following the end of the tax year and the code is determined before 31st December.

(5) But the Inland Revenue must not have regard to the difference if the taxpayer objects at the time the return is delivered or subsequently.

Commentary—*Simon's Taxes* **E4.11132.**

Derivation—The Income Tax (Employments) Regulations, SI 1993/744 reg 101A(3).

Amendments—[1] In paras (3)(*b*)(ii), (4)(*b*) words substituted by the Income Tax (Pay As You Earn) (Amendment No 4) Regulations, SI 2007/2969 regs 2, 18 with effect from 6 April 2008.

[2] In paras (3)(*a*), (4)(*a*) amount substituted by the Income Tax (Pay As You Earn) (Amendment) (No. 3) Regulations, SI 2011/1584 reg 2(3) with effect from 6 April 2012.

187 Repayment: adjustment of employee's code

(1) This regulation applies if the difference for a tax year mentioned in section 59B(1) of TMA (difference between tax contained in a self-assessment and aggregate of payments on account) is payable to the taxpayer.

(2) The Inland Revenue may have regard to the difference in determining the employee's code for a subsequent tax year under regulation 14 (matters relevant to determination of code).

(3) But the Inland Revenue must not have regard to the difference if the taxpayer objects at the time the return is delivered or subsequently.

Commentary—*Simon's Taxes* **E4.11132.**

188 Assessments other than self-assessments

(1) In this regulation, "assessment" means an assessment other than one under section 9 of TMA (self-assessment).

(2) The tax payable by the employee is—

$$A - (B - C)$$

where

A is the tax payable under the assessment;

B is the total net tax deducted in relation to the employee's relevant payments during the tax year for which the assessment is made, adjusted as required by paragraph (3); and

C is so much, if any, of B as is subsequently repaid.

(3) For the purpose of determining the tax payable by the employee, and subject to paragraphs (4) and (5)—

(*a*) add to B any tax which—

(i) the employer was liable to deduct from relevant payments but failed to do so, or

(ii) the employer was liable to account for in accordance with regulation 62(5) (notional payments) but failed to do so;

(*b*) make any necessary adjustment to B in respect of any tax overpaid or remaining unpaid for any tax year; and

(*c*) make any necessary adjustment to B in respect of any amount to be recovered as if it were unpaid tax under section 30(1) of TMA (recovery of overpayment of tax etc) to the extent that—

(i) [HMRC][1] took that amount into account in determining the employee's code, and

(ii) the total net tax deducted was in consequence greater than it would otherwise have been.

(4) No direction tax is to be included in calculating the amount of tax referred to in paragraph (3)(*a*).

(5) If a direction is made after the making of the assessment, the amount (if any) shown in the notice of assessment as a deduction from, or a credit against, the tax payable under the assessment is to be taken as reduced by so much of the direction tax as was included in calculating the amount of tax referred to in paragraph (3)(*a*).

(6) Instead of requiring payment by the employee, [HMRC][1] may take the tax payable by the employee into account in determining the employee's code for a subsequent tax year.

(7) In this regulation—

"direction" means a direction made under [regulation 72(5), regulation 72F][1] or 81(4) in relation to the employee in respect of one or more tax periods falling within the tax year in question;

"direction tax" means any amount of tax which is the subject of a direction;

"tax payable under the assessment" means the amount of tax shown in the assessment as payable without regard to any amount shown in the notice of assessment as a deduction from, or a credit against, the amount of tax payable.

Commentary—*Simon's Taxes* **E4.11133.**

Derivation—The Income Tax (Employments) Regulations, SI 1993/744 reg 101(2)–(4), (6), (7); the Income Tax (Employments) (Notional Payments) Regulations, SI 1994/1212 reg 13(1).

Modifications—See the Income Tax (PAYE) Regulations, SI 2003/2682 reg 150 (modification of this regulation in its application to payments of taxable jobseeker's allowance made to a claimant).

SI 2003/2682 reg 174 (modification of this regulation in its application to payments of taxable incapacity benefit).

SI 2003/2682 Sch 1 para 25 (overpayments and underpayments of tax: tax years before the tax year ending 5 April 2002: modification of this regulation).

Amendments—[1] References to HMRC substituted throughout, and in para (7), words in definition of "direction" substituted, by the Income Tax (Pay As You Earn) (Amendment) Regulations, SI 2008/782 regs 2, 15 with effect from 6 April 2008.

PART 10
COMMUNICATIONS

CHAPTER 1
ELECTRONIC COMMUNICATIONS: INTERPRETATION

189 Meaning of electronic communications etc

In these Regulations—

"approved method of electronic communications", in relation to the delivery of information or the making of a payment in accordance with a provision of these Regulations, means a method of electronic communications which has been approved, by specific or general directions issued by the Board of Inland Revenue, for the delivery of information of that kind or the making of a payment of that kind under that provision;

"electronic communications" has the meaning given in section 132(10) of the Finance Act 1999;

"official computer system" means a computer system maintained by or on behalf of the Board of Inland Revenue or an officer of the Board.

Commentary—*Simon's Taxes* **E4.11150.**

Derivation—The Income Tax (Employments) Regulations, SI 1993/744 reg 2(1).

HMRC Directions—The following directions (dated 13 March 2012) were published on the HMRC website on 19 March 2012—

HMRC directions for approved methods of electronic communications from April 2012

Directions under regulations 189 and 205(2) of the Income Tax (Pay As You Earn) Regulations 2003 (SI 2003/2682) and regulation 1(2) of the Social Security (Contributions) Regulations 2001 (SI 2001/1004) and Approval under regulation 211(5) of the Income Tax (Pay As You Earn) Regulations 2003 (SI 2003/2682) and 80(3A) of the Social Security (Contributions) Regulations 2001 (SI 2001/1004).

Interpretation

In these directions and this approval—

'EDI' means the Electronic Data Interchange;

'PAYE Regulations' means the Income Tax (Pay As You Earn) Regulations 2003 (S.I. 2003/2682);

'Contributions Regulations' means the Social Security (Contributions) Regulations 2001 (S.I. 2001/1004).

Directions

The Commissioners for Her Majesty's Revenue and Customs (HMRC) give the following directions about approved methods of electronic communications for the delivery of information and the making of payments and approve the specified manner of authentication of employers' annual returns delivered electronically.

The directions and approval have effect from 6 April 2012.

Approved methods of electronic communications for delivery of information by employers or persons acting on behalf of employers to HMRC

1. The methods of electronic communications approved for the delivery of the information listed in column 1 of the table by an employer or a person acting on behalf of an employer are:

(a) the internet services provided through PAYE Online for Employers and PAYE Online for Agents, where indicated in column 2, and

(b) the EDI services provided through PAYE Online for Employers and PAYE Online for Agents, where indicated in column 3.

1.	2.	3.
Description of the kind of information to be delivered	Internet	EDI
PAYE Regulations[1]		
Simplified deductions scheme: deductions working sheet. Form P12 (regulation 35).	Yes	No
Simplified deductions scheme: annual return of deductions working sheets. Form P37 (regulation 35).	Yes	No
Cessation of employment. Form P45, Part 1 (regulation 36).	Yes	Yes
Death of employee. Form P45, Part 1 (regulation 38).	Yes	Yes
Death of pensioner. Form P45, Part 1 (regulation 39).	Yes	Yes
Procedure if new employer receives Form P45. Form P45, Part 3 (regulation 42).	Yes	Yes
Information to be provided if code not known. Form P46 (regulations 47, 48 and 49).	Yes	Yes
Late presentation of Form P45. Form P45, Part 3 (regulation 52).	Yes	Yes
Information on retirement. Form P46 (Pen) (regulation 55).	Yes	Yes
Procedure if new pension payer receives Form P45. Form P45, Part 3 (regulation 56).	Yes	Yes
Information to be provided if code not known (non-UK resident pensioners). Form P46 (Pen) (regulation 57).	Yes	Yes
Information to be provided if code not known (UK resident pensioners). Form P46 (Pen) (regulation 58).	Yes	Yes
Late presentation of Form P45. Form P45, Part 3 (regulation 60).	Yes	Yes
Annual return of relevant payments liable to deduction of tax. Forms P35 and P14 (regulation 73).	Yes	Yes
Annual return of relevant payments not liable to deduction of tax. Form P38A (regulation 74).	Yes	Yes
Employers: annual return of other PAYE income: benefits code employee. Form P11D (regulation 85).	Yes	Yes
Quarterly return of cars becoming available or unavailable. Form P46 (Car) (regulation 90).	Yes	Yes
Contributions Regulations		
Return by employer of Class 1A National Insurance contributions. Form P11D(b) (regulation 80(1)).	Yes	Yes
Return by employer at end of year. Forms P35 and P14 (paragraph 22 of Schedule 4)	Yes	Yes

[1]Regulation 211 permits electronic delivery of certain information. This direction approves the methods of electronic communications for delivery of that information.

Approved methods of electronic communications for mandatory electronic filing of specified information

2. The methods of electronic communications approved for the delivery of specified information, by an employer or a person acting on behalf of an employer, in accordance with regulation 205 of the PAYE Regulations (and, in accordance with paragraph 22 of Schedule 4 and regulation 90N(1) of the Contributions Regulations) are the internet services and the EDI services provided through PAYE Online for Employers and PAYE Online for Agents.

Approved methods of electronic communications for delivery of information by HMRC to employers or persons acting on behalf of employers

3. The methods of electronic communications approved for delivery of the information listed in column 1 of the table by HMRC to an employer or a person acting on behalf of an employer are:

(a) the internet services provided through PAYE Online for Employers and PAYE Online for Agents, where indicated in column 2, and

(b) the EDI services provided through PAYE Online for Employers and PAYE Online for Agents, where indicated in column 3.

1.	2.	3.
Description of the kind of information to be delivered	Internet	EDI
PAYE Regulations[2]		
Issue of code to employer or agent. Form P6 or P9 (regulations 8 and 20).	Yes	Yes

1.	2.	3.
Description of the kind of information to be delivered	Internet	EDI
Notice to employer to amend codes. Form P7X or P9X (regulation 20).	Yes	Yes
Notice to employer of payments and total net tax deducted. Form P6 (regulation 53).	Yes	Yes
Notice to pension payer of payments and total net tax deducted. Form P6 (regulation 61).	Yes	Yes

[2] Regulation 213 permits electronic delivery of certain information. This direction approves the methods of electronic communications for delivery of that information.

Approved method of authentication of the return required by regulation 73 (annual return of relevant payments liable to deduction of tax, Forms P35 and P14) of the PAYE Regulations and regulation 80 (Return by employer) of the Contributions Regulations where the return is delivered electronically

4. The method approved for authenticating a return required by regulation 73 of the PAYE Regulations or regulation 80 of the Contributions Regulations and delivered by a method of electronic communications is the completion of any certificate or declaration contained in the electronic return or form and, where the sender is acting on behalf of an employer, completion of the following procedure before the information is sent:

(a) the sender must make a copy of the information before it is sent, and

(b) the employer must confirm to the sender that the information is complete and accurate to the best of his knowledge and belief.

Approved methods of electronic communications for the making of a payment

5. The methods of electronic communications approved for the making of payments required by the PAYE Regulations and the Contributions Regulations are the services known as Direct Debit, BACS Direct Credit (including telephone and internet banking), CHAPS, debit and credit card over the internet ('BillPay'), Government Banking Service (formerly known as Paymaster), Bank Giro and payments made through the Post Office.

190 Specified date

. . .

Amendment—Regs 190 and 191 revoked by the Income Tax (Pay As You Earn) (Amendment) Regulations, SI 2010/668, regs 2, 4, with effect in relation to the tax year 2011–12 and subsequent tax years.

191 Large and medium sized employers

. . .

Amendments—Regs 190 and 191 revoked by the Income Tax (Pay As You Earn) (Amendment) Regulations, SI 2010/668, regs 2, 4, with effect in relation to the tax year 2011–12 and subsequent tax years.

CHAPTER 2
ELECTRONIC COMMUNICATIONS: GENERAL

192 Whether information has been delivered electronically

For the purpose of these Regulations, information is taken to have been delivered to an official computer system by an approved method of electronic communications only if it is accepted by that official computer system.

Commentary—*Simon's Taxes* **E4.11151.**

Derivation—The Income Tax (Employments) Regulations, SI 1993/744 reg 2A.

193 Proof of content of electronic delivery

(1) A document certified by the Inland Revenue to be a printed-out version of any information delivered by an approved method of electronic communications is evidence, unless the contrary is proved, that the information—

(*a*) was delivered by an approved method of electronic communications on that occasion, and

(*b*) constitutes everything which was delivered on that occasion.

(2) A document which purports to be a certificate given in accordance with paragraph (1) is presumed to be such a certificate unless the contrary is proved.

Commentary—*Simon's Taxes* **E4.11151.**

Derivation—The Income Tax (Employments) Regulations, SI 1993/744 reg 2B.

194 Proof of identity of person sending or receiving electronic delivery

The identity of—

(*a*) the person sending any information delivered by an approved method of electronic communications to the Inland Revenue, or

(*b*) the person receiving any information delivered by an approved method of electronic communications by the Inland Revenue, is presumed, unless the contrary is proved, to be the person recorded as such on an official computer system.

Commentary—*Simon's Taxes* **E4.11151.**
Derivation—The Income Tax (Employments) Regulations, SI 1993/744 reg 2C.

195 Information sent electronically on behalf of a person

(1) Any information delivered by an approved method of electronic communications—

(*a*) to the Inland Revenue, or

(*b*) to an official computer system,

on behalf of a person is taken to have been delivered by that person.

(2) But this does not apply if the person proves that the information was delivered without the person's knowledge or connivance.

Commentary—*Simon's Taxes* **E4.11151.**
Derivation—The Income Tax (Employments) Regulations, SI 1993/744 reg 46ZB.

196 Proof of delivery of information sent electronically

(1) The use of an approved method of electronic communications is presumed, unless the contrary is proved, to have resulted in the delivery of information—

(*a*) to the Inland Revenue, if the delivery of the information has been recorded on an official computer system;

(*b*) by the Inland Revenue, if the despatch of the information has been recorded on an official computer system.

(2) The use of an approved method of electronic communications is presumed, unless the contrary is proved, not to have resulted in the delivery of information—

(*a*) to the Inland Revenue, if the delivery of the information has not been recorded on an official computer system;

(*b*) by the Inland Revenue, if the despatch of the information has not been recorded on an official computer system.

(3) The time of receipt or despatch of any information delivered by an approved method of electronic communications is presumed, unless the contrary is proved, to be the time recorded on an official computer system.

Commentary—*Simon's Taxes* **E4.11151.**
Derivation—The Income Tax (Employments) Regulations, SI 1993/744 reg 2D.

197 Proof of payment sent electronically

(1) The use of a method of electronic communications is presumed, unless the contrary is proved, to have resulted in the making of a payment—

(*a*) to the Inland Revenue, if the making of the payment has been recorded on an official computer system;

(*b*) by the Inland Revenue, if the despatch of the payment has been recorded on an official computer system.

(2) The use of a method of electronic communications is presumed, unless the contrary is proved, not to have resulted in the making of a payment—

(*a*) to the Inland Revenue, if the making of the payment has not been recorded on an official computer system;

(*b*) by the Inland Revenue, if the despatch of the payment has not been recorded on an official computer system.

(3) The time of receipt or despatch of any payment sent by a method of electronic communications is presumed, unless the contrary is proved, to be the time recorded on an official computer system.

(4) In this regulation, "the Inland Revenue" means the Board of Inland Revenue or any officer of the Board.

Commentary—*Simon's Taxes* **E4.11151.**
Derivation—The Income Tax (Employments) Regulations, SI 1993/744 reg 2D.

198 Use of unauthorised method of electronic communications

(1) This regulation applies to information which is required to be delivered to the Board of Inland Revenue or to the Inland Revenue under a provision of these Regulations.

(2) The use of a method of electronic communications for the purpose of delivering such information is conclusively presumed not to have resulted in the delivery of that information, unless that method of electronic communications is for the time being approved for delivery of information of that kind under that provision.

Commentary—*Simon's Taxes* **E4.11151.**
Derivation—The Income Tax (Employments) Regulations, SI 1993/744 reg 2E.

CHAPTER 3

ELECTRONIC PAYMENT BY LARGE EMPLOYERS

198A [Large employers

(1) "Large employer" means an employer treated as paying PAYE income to 250 or more employees at the specified date.

(2) An employer is treated as paying PAYE income to an employee at the specified date if the employer—

(*a*) is required at that date by these Regulations to prepare or maintain a deductions working sheet in respect of that employee, and

(*b*) has not sent to HMRC Part 1 of Form P45 in respect of that employee [or, as the case may be, has not indicated in a return under regulation 67B or 67D that the employee's employment has ceased][3].

[(3) The specified date for a particular tax year is 31st October in the preceding tax year.][2]][1]

Amendments—[1] Reg 198A inserted by the Income Tax (Pay As You Earn) (Amendment) Regulations, SI 2010/668, regs 2, 5, with effect in relation to the tax year 2011–12 and subsequent tax years.

[2] Para (3) substituted by the Income Tax (Pay As You Earn) (Amendment) Regulations, SI 2011/729 regs 2, 15 with effect from 6 April 2011.

[3] Words in para (2)(*b*) inserted by the Income Tax (Pay As You Earn) (Amendment) Regulations, SI 2012/822 regs 2, 46 with effect from 6 April 2012.

199 Large employers required to make specified payments electronically

(1) A large employer . . . [2] must use an approved method of electronic communications to make specified payments.

[(2) "Specified payments", in this regulation, means payments of tax under regulation [67G (payments to and recoveries from HMRC: Real Time Information employers)[", as adjusted by regulation 67H(2) where appropriate,][4] or 68 (periodic payments to and recoveries from HMRC: non-Real Time Information employers)][3].][2]

(3) The Board of Inland Revenue may give specific or general directions—

(*a*) suspending, for any period during which the use of an approved method of electronic communications for the making of specified payments is impossible or impractical, any requirement imposed by these Regulations relating to the use of such methods,

(*b*) substituting alternative requirements for the suspended ones, and

(*c*) making any provision that is necessary in consequence of the imposition of the substituted requirements.

[(4) This regulation does not apply to a payment of tax in respect of retrospective employment income for a closed year.][1]

[(5) A specified payment is not treated as received in full by HMRC on or before the date by which that specified payment is required in accordance with regulation 69 unless it is made in a manner which secures (in a case where the specified payment is made otherwise than in cash) that, on or before that date, all transactions can be completed which need to be completed before the whole amount of the specified payment becomes available to the Commissioners for Her Majesty's Revenue and Customs.][2]

Commentary—*Simon's Taxes* **E4.11154.**

Derivation—The Income Tax (Employments) Regulations, SI 1993/744 reg 42A(1), (2), (5).

Amendments—[1] Paragraph (4) inserted by the Income Tax (Pay as You Earn) (Amendment) Regulations, SI 2007/1077 regs 2, 17 with effect from 6 April 2007.

[2] Words in para (1) revoked, para (2) substituted, and para (5) inserted, by the Income Tax (Pay As You Earn) (Amendment) Regulations, SI 2010/668, regs 2, 6, with effect in relation to the tax year 2010–11 and subsequent tax years.

[3] Words in para (2) substituted by the Income Tax (Pay As You Earn) (Amendment) Regulations, SI 2012/822 regs 2, 47 with effect from 6 April 2012.

[4] Words in para (2) inserted by the Income Tax (Pay As You Earn) (Amendment) Regulations, SI 2013/521 regs 2, 36 with effect from 6 April 2013 in relation to the tax year 2013–14 and subsequent tax years.

200 E-payment notices and appeal

. . .

Amendment—Regs 200–202 revoked by the Income Tax (Pay As You Earn) (Amendment) Regulations, SI 2010/668, regs 2, 7, with effect in relation to the tax year 2010–11 and subsequent tax years.

201 Employer in default if specified payment not received by applicable due date

. . .

Amendment—Regs 200–202 revoked by the Income Tax (Pay As You Earn) (Amendment) Regulations, SI 2010/668, regs 2, 7, with effect in relation to the tax year 2010–11 and subsequent tax years.

202 Default notice and appeal

. . .

Amendment—Regs 200–202 revoked by the Income Tax (Pay As You Earn) (Amendment) Regulations, SI 2010/668, regs 2, 7, with effect in relation to the tax year 2010–11 and subsequent tax years.

203 Default surcharge

. . .

(1) An employer in default in respect of any specified payment to whom—

(a) *a default notice under regulation 202, and*

(b) *a surcharge notice under regulation 204,*

have been issued, is liable to a surcharge.

(2) The surcharge is the sum of the surcharges, calculated in accordance with paragraph (3), in respect of each default relating to the tax year in which were made the relevant payments to which the specified payment referred to in paragraph (1) relates.

(3) The surcharge in respect of each default is the specified percentage of (A – B).

(4) In paragraph (3)—

(a) *A is the total amount of tax due for the tax year in which the relevant payments to which the specified payment relates were made;*

(b) *B is the total of the amounts deducted from A under—*

(i) . . . [1]

(ii) *regulations 4, 5 and 6 of the Statutory Maternity Pay (Compensation of Employers) and Miscellaneous Amendment Regulations 1994,*

(iii) *regulations 3 and 5 of the Statutory Paternity Pay and Statutory Adoption Pay (Administration) Regulations 2002, and*

(iv) *regulation 44B of the Income Tax (Sub-contractors in the Construction Industry) Regulations 1993;*

(c) *the specified percentage is determined by reference to the number of the default during a surcharge period in accordance with Table 8.*

TABLE 8
SPECIFIED PERCENTAGE FOR EACH DEFAULT IN A SURCHARGE PERIOD

1 Default number (within a surcharge period)	*2 Specified percentage*
1st	0%
2nd	0%
3rd	0.17%
4th	0.17%
5th	0.17%
6th	0.33%
7th	0.33%
8th	0.33%
9th	0.58%
10th	0.58%
11th	0.58%
12th and subsequent defaults	0.83%

(5) A surcharge period is a period which—

(a) *begins on the day following the date by which payment is required in accordance with regulation 69 for the first specified payment in respect of which the employer is in default, and*

(b) *ends at the end of a tax year in relation to which the employer has not been in default in respect of any specified payment.*

(6) A surcharge payable under this regulation is payable 30 days after the issue of the surcharge notice.

(7) Section 102 of TMA (mitigation of penalties) applies to a surcharge payable under this regulation as if it were a penalty.

[(8) Section 108 of the Finance Act 2009 (suspension of penalties during currency of agreement for deferred payment) applies to a surcharge payable under this regulation with the following modifications—

(a) *in the Table in subsection (5), insert at the end—*

"Specified payments within the meaning of regulation 199 of the Income Tax (Pay As You Earn) Regulations 2003	Surcharge under regulation 203 of the Income Tax (Pay As You Earn) Regulations 2003."

, and

(b) *omit subsections (7), (8), (9) and (11).]*[2], [3]

Commentary—*Simon's Taxes* **E4.11154.**
Derivation—The Income Tax (Employments) Regulations, SI 1993/744 reg 42B(9), (10), (16), (17).
Amendments—[1] Para (4)(*b*)(i) revoked by the Income Tax (PAYE, etc), (Amendment) Regulations, SI 2006/777 regs 2, 5 with effect from 6 April 2006.
[2] Para (8) inserted by the Income Tax (Pay As You Earn) (Amendment No 2) Regulations, SI 2009/2029 regs 2, 4 with effect in relation to deferred payment agreements made on or after 13 August 2009.
[3] Regs 203, 204 revoked by the Finance Act 2009, Schedule 56 (Appointed Day and Consequential Provisions) Order, SI 2010/466 art 4 with effect from 6 April 2010, however, these regs will continue to have effect for surcharges that arise in respect of late payments of tax where the tax was chargeable in respect of a tax period ending on or before 5 April 2010 (see SI 2010/466 art 4(3)).

204 Surcharge notice and appeal

(1) The Inland Revenue must issue a surcharge notice to an employer who has been in default on three or more occasions during a surcharge period and consequently will be liable to a surcharge under regulation 203.
(2) The surcharge notice must show the total surcharge liability for the tax year.
(3) The surcharge notice must be issued within 6 years of—
(*a*) *the end of the tax year, or*
(*b*) *if earlier, the date on which the employer delivered a return in accordance with regulation 73 (annual return of relevant payments liable to deduction of tax (Forms P35 and P14)).*
(4) An employer may appeal against a surcharge notice by giving notice to the Inland Revenue within 30 days of the issue of the surcharge notice.
(5) The grounds of appeal are—
(*a*) *that the number of defaults stated in the notice is incorrect, or*
(*b*) *that the amount of the surcharge is incorrect.*
(6) But paragraph (5)(*a*) does not apply in respect of a disputed default which has already been the subject of an appeal under regulation 202, following which the default notice was not withdrawn.
(7) Parts 4, 5 and 6 of TMA (assessment, appeals, collection and recovery) apply to the surcharge notice as if it were an assessment and the amount of the surcharge was tax charged by the assessment, subject to paragraphs (4), (5) and (8).
(8) On an appeal section 50(6) to (8) of TMA (procedure) do not apply, but the [tribunal][1] may—
(*a*) *if it appears . . .* [1] *that no surcharge has been incurred, set the surcharge notice aside,*
(*b*) *if the amount of the total surcharge liability appears . . .* [1] *to be correct, confirm the surcharge notice, or*
(*c*) *if the amount of the total surcharge liability appears . . .* [1] *to be incorrect, increase or reduce it to the correct amount.*
(9) Regulation 217(3) (appeals: supplementary provisions) applies to appeals under this regulation.[2]

Commentary—*Simon's Taxes* **E4.11154.**
Derivation—The Income Tax (Employments) Regulations, SI 1993/744 reg 42B(11), (12), (13), (14), (15).
Amendments—[1] In para (8), word substituted and words revoked in each place, by the Transfer of Tribunal Functions and Revenue and Customs Appeals Order, SI 2009/56 art 3, Sch 2 paras 92, 110 with effect from 1 April 2009.
[2] Regs 203, 204 revoked by the Finance Act 2009, Schedule 56 (Appointed Day and Consequential Provisions) Order, SI 2010/466 art 4 with effect from 6 April 2010, however, these regs will continue to have effect for surcharges that arise in respect of late payments of tax where the tax was chargeable in respect of a tax period ending on or before 5 April 2010 (see SI 2010/466 art 4(3)).

CHAPTER 4

MANDATORY USE OF ELECTRONIC COMMUNICATIONS[: SPECIFIED INFORMATION]

Amendments—Words in heading inserted by the Income Tax (Pay As You Earn) (Amendment) Regulations, SI 2012/822 regs 2, 48 with effect from 6 April 2012.

205 [Mandatory use of electronic communications

(1) An employer (as to which see regulation 206) must deliver specified information by an approved method of electronic communications to HMRC.
(2) The Commissioners for Her Majesty's Revenue and Customs may make a general or specific direction requiring an employer to deliver specified information by a particular approved method of electronic communications.
(3) Specified information may be delivered by a person on behalf of an employer.
(4) This regulation does not apply to specified information which relates to payments of tax due under a retrospective tax provision for a closed year.
(5) References in this Chapter to information and to the delivery of information must be construed in accordance with section 135(8) of the Finance Act 2002 (mandatory e-filing).][1]

HMRC Directions—The following directions (dated 13 March 2012) were published on the HMRC website on 19 March 2012—

HMRC directions for approved methods of electronic communications from April 2012

Directions under regulations 189 and 205(2) of the Income Tax (Pay As You Earn) Regulations 2003 (SI 2003/2682) and regulation 1(2) of the Social Security (Contributions) Regulations 2001 (SI 2001/1004) and Approval under regulation 211(5) of the Income Tax (Pay As You Earn) Regulations 2003 (SI 2003/2682) and 80(3A) of the Social Security (Contributions) Regulations 2001 (SI 2001/1004)

Interpretation

In these directions and this approval—

'EDI' means the Electronic Data Interchange;

'PAYE Regulations' means the Income Tax (Pay As You Earn) Regulations 2003 (S.I. 2003/2682);

'Contributions Regulations' means the Social Security (Contributions) Regulations 2001 (S.I. 2001/1004).

Directions

The Commissioners for Her Majesty's Revenue and Customs (HMRC) give the following directions about approved methods of electronic communications for the delivery of information and the making of payments and approve the specified manner of authentication of employers' annual returns delivered electronically.

The directions and approval have effect from 6 April 2012.

Approved methods of electronic communications for delivery of information by employers or persons acting on behalf of employers to HMRC

1. The methods of electronic communications approved for the delivery of the information listed in column 1 of the table by an employer or a person acting on behalf of an employer are:

(a) the internet services provided through PAYE Online for Employers and PAYE Online for Agents, where indicated in column 2, and

(b) the EDI services provided through PAYE Online for Employers and PAYE Online for Agents, where indicated in column 3.

1.	2.	3.
Description of the kind of information to be delivered	Internet	EDI
PAYE Regulations[1]		
Simplified deductions scheme: deductions working sheet. Form P12 (regulation 35).	Yes	No
Simplified deductions scheme: annual return of deductions working sheets. Form P37 (regulation 35).	Yes	No
Cessation of employment. Form P45, Part 1 (regulation 36).	Yes	Yes
Death of employee. Form P45, Part 1 (regulation 38).	Yes	Yes
Death of pensioner. Form P45, Part 1 (regulation 39).	Yes	Yes
Procedure if new employer receives Form P45. Form P45, Part 3 (regulation 42).	Yes	Yes
Information to be provided if code not known. Form P46 (regulations 47, 48 and 49).	Yes	Yes
Late presentation of Form P45. Form P45, Part 3 (regulation 52).	Yes	Yes
Information on retirement. Form P46 (Pen) (regulation 55).	Yes	Yes
Procedure if new pension payer receives Form P45. Form P45, Part 3 (regulation 56).	Yes	Yes
Information to be provided if code not known (non-UK resident pensioners). Form P46 (Pen) (regulation 57).	Yes	Yes
Information to be provided if code not known (UK resident pensioners). Form P46 (Pen) (regulation 58).	Yes	Yes
Late presentation of Form P45. Form P45, Part 3 (regulation 60).	Yes	Yes
Annual return of relevant payments liable to deduction of tax. Forms P35 and P14 (regulation 73).	Yes	Yes
Annual return of relevant payments not liable to deduction of tax. Form P38A (regulation 74).	Yes	Yes
Employers: annual return of other PAYE income: benefits code employee. Form P11D (regulation 85).	Yes	Yes
Quarterly return of cars becoming available or unavailable. Form P46 (Car) (regulation 90).	Yes	Yes
Contributions Regulations		

1.	2.	3.
Description of the kind of information to be delivered	Internet	EDI
Return by employer of Class 1A National Insurance contributions. Form P11D(b) (regulation 80(1)).	Yes	Yes
Return by employer at end of year. Forms P35 and P14 (paragraph 22 of Schedule 4)	Yes	Yes

[1]Regulation 211 permits electronic delivery of certain information. This direction approves the methods of electronic communications for delivery of that information.

Approved methods of electronic communications for mandatory electronic filing of specified information

2. The methods of electronic communications approved for the delivery of specified information, by an employer or a person acting on behalf of an employer, in accordance with regulation 205 of the PAYE Regulations (and, in accordance with paragraph 22 of Schedule 4 and regulation 90N(1) of the Contributions Regulations) are the internet services and the EDI services provided through PAYE Online for Employers and PAYE Online for Agents.

Approved methods of electronic communications for delivery of information by HMRC to employers or persons acting on behalf of employers

3. The methods of electronic communications approved for delivery of the information listed in column 1 of the table by HMRC to an employer or a person acting on behalf of an employer are:

(a) the internet services provided through PAYE Online for Employers and PAYE Online for Agents, where indicated in column 2, and

(b) the EDI services provided through PAYE Online for Employers and PAYE Online for Agents, where indicated in column 3.

1.	2.	3.
Description of the kind of information to be delivered	Internet	EDI
PAYE Regulations[2]		
Issue of code to employer or agent. Form P6 or P9 (regulations 8 and 20).	Yes	Yes
Notice to employer to amend codes. Form P7X or P9X (regulation 20).	Yes	Yes
Notice to employer of payments and total net tax deducted. Form P6 (regulation 53).	Yes	Yes
Notice to pension payer of payments and total net tax deducted. Form P6 (regulation 61).	Yes	Yes

[2] Regulation 213 permits electronic delivery of certain information. This direction approves the methods of electronic communications for delivery of that information.

Approved method of authentication of the return required by regulation 73 (annual return of relevant payments liable to deduction of tax, Forms P35 and P14) of the PAYE Regulations and regulation 80 (Return by employer) of the Contributions Regulations where the return is delivered electronically

4. The method approved for authenticating a return required by regulation 73 of the PAYE Regulations or regulation 80 of the Contributions Regulations and delivered by a method of electronic communications is the completion of any certificate or declaration contained in the electronic return or form and, where the sender is acting on behalf of an employer, completion of the following procedure before the information is sent:

(a) the sender must make a copy of the information before it is sent, and

(b) the employer must confirm to the sender that the information is complete and accurate to the best of his knowledge and belief.

Approved methods of electronic communications for the making of a payment

5. The methods of electronic communications approved for the making of payments required by the PAYE Regulations and the Contributions Regulations are the services known as Direct Debit, BACS Direct Credit (including telephone and internet banking), CHAPS, debit and credit card over the internet ('BillPay'), Government Banking Service (formerly known as Paymaster), Bank Giro and payments made through the Post Office.

Amendments—[1] Reg 205 substituted for previous regs 205–205B by the Income Tax (Pay As You Earn) (Amendment) Regulations, SI 2010/668, regs 2, 8, with effect in relation to the tax year 2011–12 and subsequent tax years.

206 [Employers]

(1) . . . [2]

[(2) [For the purposes of this Chapter, the following shall not be regarded as employers—][2]

(*a*) an individual who is a practising member of a religious society or order whose beliefs are incompatible with the use of electronic communications;

(*b*) a partnership, if all the partners fall within sub-paragraph (a);
(*c*) a company, if all the directors and company secretary fall within sub-paragraph (a);
(*d*) . . . [3]
(*e*) a care and support employer[, and
(*f*) an employer to whom a direction has been given under regulation 67D (exceptions to regulation 67B) or regulation 142 (direct collection: employee to report payments)][4]][1]

(3) In paragraph (2)(*c*), "company" means a body corporate or unincorporated association but does not include a partnership.

[(4) In paragraph (2)(*e*), "a care and support employer" means an individual ("the employer") who employs a person to provide domestic or personal services at or from the employer's home where—
(*a*) the services are provided to the employer or a member of the employer's family;
(*b*) the recipient of the services has a physical or mental disability, or is elderly or infirm;
(*c*) the employer has not received an incentive payment in respect of any of the last 3 tax years; and
(*d*) it is the employer who delivers the [specified information][2] (and not some other person on the employer's behalf).

(5) In this regulation an "incentive payment" means an incentive payment received under the Income Tax (Incentive Payments for Voluntary Electronic Communication of PAYE Returns) Regulations 2003.][1]

Commentary—*Simon's Taxes* **E4.11152.**

Derivation—The Income Tax (Employments) Regulations, SI 1993/744 reg 46ZD(1)–(4).

Amendments—[1] Para (2) substituted and paras (4), (5) inserted, by the Income Tax (Pay As You Earn) (Amendment No 2) Regulations, SI 2009/2029 regs 2, 6, 7 with effect in relation to the tax year 2009–10 and subsequent tax years. These amendments shall not have effect for the tax year 2009–10 in relation to an employer who—
(a) is not a specified employer,
(b) ceases paying PAYE income during the tax year 2009–10, and
(c) submits the return and accompanying information, required by regulation 73, before 6 April 2010 (SI 2009/2029 reg 1(4), (5)).

[2] Heading substituted, para (1) revoked, words in paras (2), (4)(*d*), substituted by the Income Tax (Pay As You Earn) (Amendment) Regulations, SI 2010/668, regs 2, 9, with effect in relation to the tax year 2011–12 and subsequent tax years.

[3] Para (2)(*d*) revoked by the Income Tax (Pay As You Earn) (Amendment) Regulations, SI 2013/521 regs 2, 10 with effect from 6 April 2014.

[4] Para (2)(*f*) and preceding word "and" inserted by the Income Tax (Pay As You Earn) and the Income Tax (Construction Industry Scheme) (Amendment) Regulations, SI 2014/472 regs 2, 18 with effect from 6 April 2014.

206A [Relevant annual return

. . .

Amendments—Reg 206A revoked by the Income Tax (Pay As You Earn) (Amendment) Regulations, SI 2010/668, regs 2, 12(1)(*a*), with effect in relation to the tax year 2011–12 and subsequent tax years.

207 Specified information

[(1) In this Chapter, "specified information" means—
(*a*) Part 1 of Form P45;
(*b*) Part 3 of Form P45;
(*c*) Form P46;
(*d*) Form P46(Pen);
[(*e*) the return and accompanying information required by regulation 73 (annual return of relevant payments liable to deduction of tax (Forms P35 and P14)).][2]][1]

(2) . . . [3]

Commentary—*Simon's Taxes* **E4.11152.**

Derivation—The Income Tax (Employments) Regulations, SI 1993/744 reg 46ZE(1), (2).

Amendments—[1] Para (1) substituted by the Income Tax (Pay As You Earn) (Amendment No 4) Regulations, SI 2007/2969 regs 2, 19 with effect from 6 April 2009.

[2] Para (1)(*e*) inserted by the Income Tax (Pay As You Earn) (Amendment) Regulations, SI 2010/668, regs 2, 10, with effect in relation to the tax year 2011–12 and subsequent tax years.

[3] Para (2) revoked by the Income Tax (Pay As You Earn) and the Income Tax (Construction Industry Scheme) (Amendment) Regulations, SI 2014/472 regs 2, 19 with effect from 6 April 2014.

208 E-filing notice and appeals

. . .

Amendments—Reg 208 revoked by the Income Tax (Pay As You Earn) (Amendment) Regulations, SI 2010/668, regs 2, 12(1)(*b*), with effect in relation to the tax year 2010–11 and subsequent tax years.

[209 Standards of accuracy and completeness

(1) Any . . . [2] specified information delivered by a method of electronic communications must meet the standards of accuracy and completeness set by specific or general directions given by the Commissioners for Her Majesty's Revenue and Customs.

(2) Any . . . [2] specified information which fails to meet those standards must be treated as not having been delivered.][1]

Commentary—*Simon's Taxes* **E4.11152.**

Amendments—[1] Regulation substituted by the Income Tax (Pay As You Earn) (Amendment No 2) Regulations, SI 2009/2029 regs 2, 11 with effect in relation to the tax year 2009–10 and subsequent tax years. This amendment shall not have effect for the tax year 2009–10 in relation to an employer who—

(a) is not a specified employer,

(b) ceases paying PAYE income during the tax year 2009–10, and

(c) submits the return and accompanying information, required by regulation 73, before 6 April 2010 (SI 2009/2029 reg 1(4), (5)).

[2] Words in both places revoked by the Income Tax (Pay As You Earn) (Amendment) Regulations, SI 2010/668, regs 2, 12(2), with effect in relation to the tax year 2011–12 and subsequent tax years.

210 [[Penalty for failing to deliver . . . specified information]

[(1) An employer who fails to deliver specified information or any part of it in accordance with regulation 205 is liable to a penalty.

(2) Where the specified information is the return and accompanying information required by regulation 73 (annual return of relevant payments liable to deduction of tax (Forms P35 and P14) the penalty will be determined in accordance with regulation 210AA.][3]

(3) The penalty must be determined in accordance with [regulations 210B and 210BA][3] in all other cases.

(4) Regulation 210C applies irrespective of how the penalty falls to be determined.[1], [2]

Commentary—*Simon's Taxes* **E4.11152.**

Amendments—[1] Regulations 210–210C substituted for previous reg 210 by the Income Tax (Pay As You Earn) (Amendment No 4) Regulations, SI 2007/2969 regs 2, 20 with effect from 6 April 2009.

[2] Heading to reg 210 substituted by the Income Tax (Pay As You Earn) (Amendment No 2) Regulations, SI 2009/2029 regs 2, 12, 13 with effect in relation to the tax year 2009–10 and subsequent tax years. This amendment shall not have effect for the tax year 2009–10 in relation to an employer who—

(a) is not a specified employer,

(b) ceases paying PAYE income during the tax year 2009–10, and

(c) submits the return and accompanying information, required by regulation 73, before 6 April 2010 (SI 2009/2029 reg 1(4), (5)).

[3] In heading, words revoked, paras (1), (2) substituted for previous paras (A1)–(2), and in para (3) words substituted, by the Income Tax (Pay As You Earn) (Amendment) Regulations, SI 2010/668, regs 2, 11, with effect in relation to the tax year 2011–12 and subsequent tax years.

210A [Penalty: relevant annual return for the tax year ending 5th April 2010

. . .

Amendments—Reg 210A revoked by the Income Tax (Pay As You Earn) (Amendment) Regulations, SI 2010/668, regs 2, 12, with effect in relation to the tax year 2011–12 and subsequent tax years.

210AA [[Penalty: forms P35 and P14]

Table 9ZA sets out the penalty for the tax year ending 5th April 2011 and subsequent years, depending on the number of employees for whom particulars should have been included with the [specified information][2].

TABLE 9ZA
PENALTIES: TAX YEARS ENDING 5TH APRIL 2011 AND SUBSEQUENT YEARS

1 Number of employees for whom particulars should have been included with the [specified information][2]	*2 Penalty*
1–5	£100
6–49	£300
50–249	£600
250–399	£900
400–499	£1200
500–599	£1500
600–699	£1800
700–799	£2100
800–899	£2400
900–999	£2700
1000 or more	£3000][1]

Amendments—[1] Regulations 210A, 210AA substituted for previous reg 210A by the Income Tax (Pay As You Earn) (Amendment No 2) Regulations, SI 2009/2029 regs 2, 14 with effect in relation to the tax year 2009–10 and subsequent tax years. This amendment shall not have effect for the tax year 2009–10 in relation to an employer who—

(a) is not a specified employer,

(b) ceases paying PAYE income during the tax year 2009–10, and

(c) submits the return and accompanying information, required by regulation 73, before 6 April 2010 (SI 2009/2029 reg 1(4), (5)).

2 Heading substituted for previous heading and words substituted, by the Income Tax (Pay As You Earn) (Amendment) Regulations, SI 2010/668, regs 2, 11, with effect in relation to the tax year 2011–12 and subsequent tax years.

210B [[Penalty: form P45 (Part 1 or Part 3), P46 or P46 (Pen); tax years ending 5th April 2012 and 5th April 2013]

[(1) This regulation applies for the tax years ending 5th April 2012 and 5th April 2013 (the "relevant period").][2]

(2) Table 9A sets out the penalties for the relevant period depending on the number of items of specified information the employer has failed to deliver in each tax quarter falling within that period.

TABLE 9A
[PENALTIES: TAX YEARS ENDING 5TH APRIL 2012 AND 5TH APRIL 2013]

1 Number of items of specified information the employer has failed to deliver in the tax quarter	*2 Penalty*
[1–2][2]	Nil
[3–49][2]	£100
50–149	£300
150–299	£600
300–399	£900
400–499	£1,200
500–599	£1,500
600–699	£1,800
700–799	£2,100
800–899	£2,400
900–999	£2,700
1000 or more	£3,000

(3) Each of the types of specified information mentioned in sub-paragraphs (*a*) to (*d*) of regulation 207(1) counts as a separate item of specified information for this purpose.

(4) An item of specified information counts even if it relates to the same employee as one or more other items.][1]

Commentary—*Simon's Taxes* **E4.11152.**

Amendments—[1] Regulations 210–210C substituted for previous reg 210 by the Income Tax (Pay As You Earn) (Amendment No 4) Regulations, SI 2007/2969 regs 2, 20 with effect from 6 April 2009.

2 Heading substituted, para (1) substituted, Table 9A heading substituted, and in first column of that table, first entry substituted for previous entry "1–5" and second entry substituted, by the Income Tax (Pay As You Earn) (Amendment) Regulations, SI 2010/668, regs 2, 11, with effect in relation to the tax year 2011–12 and subsequent tax years.

210BA [Penalty: form P45 (Part 1 or Part 3), P46 or P46(Pen); tax years ending 5th April 2014 and subsequent years

(1) Table 9AA sets out penalties depending on the number of items of specified information the employer has failed to deliver in each tax quarter falling within the tax year ending 5th April 2014 and subsequent years.

TABLE 9AA
PENALTIES: TAX YEAR ENDING 5TH APRIL 2014 AND SUBSEQUENT YEARS

1 Number of items of specified information the employer has failed to deliver in the tax quarter	*2 Penalty*
1–49	£100
50–149	£300
150–299	£600
300–399	£900
400–499	£1,200
500–599	£1,500
600–699	£1,800
700–799	£2,100
800–899	£2,400
900–999	£2,700

1000+	£3,000

(2) Each of the types of specified information mentioned in sub-paragraphs (*a*) to (*d*) of regulation 207(1) counts as a separate item of specified information for this purpose.

(3) An item of specified information counts even if it relates to the same employee as one or more other items.][1]

Amendments—[1] Reg 210BA inserted by the Income Tax (Pay As You Earn) (Amendment) Regulations, SI 2010/668 reg 7 with effect in relation to the tax year 2011–12 and subsequent tax years.

210C [Appeals and interest

(1) An employer is not liable to a penalty if the employer had a reasonable excuse for failing to comply with regulation 205 . . . [3] which had not ceased at the time the . . . [3] specified information was delivered.

(2) A notice of appeal against a determination under section 100 of TMA of a penalty can only be on the grounds that—

(*a*) . . . [3]

[(*aa*) the employer is not regarded as an employer the purposes of this Chapter][2]

(*b*) the employer did comply with regulation 205 . . . [3],

(*c*) the amount of the penalty is incorrect, or

(*d*) paragraph (1) applies.

(3) . . . [3]

(4) Section 103A of TMA (interest on penalties) applies to this penalty.][1]

Commentary—*Simon's Taxes* **E4.11152.**

Amendments—[1] Regulations 210–210C substituted for previous reg 210 by the Income Tax (Pay As You Earn) (Amendment No 4) Regulations, SI 2007/2969 regs 2, 20 with effect from 6 April 2009.

[2] In para (2) words inserted, by the Income Tax (Pay As You Earn) (Amendment No 2) Regulations, SI 2009/2029 regs 2, 15 with effect in relation to the tax year 2009–10 and subsequent tax years. This amendment shall not have effect for the tax year 2009–10 in relation to an employer who—

(a) is not a specified employer,

(b) ceases paying PAYE income during the tax year 2009–10, and

(c) submits the return and accompanying information, required by regulation 73, before 6 April 2010 (SI 2009/2029 reg 1(4), (5)).

[3] Words in both places, in para (1) words, and paras (2)(*a*), (3), revoked, by the Income Tax (Pay As You Earn) (Amendment) Regulations, SI 2010/668, regs 2, 12(3), with effect in relation to the tax year 2011–12 and subsequent tax years.

[CHAPTER 4A

MANDATORY USE OF ELECTRONIC COMMUNICATIONS: REAL TIME RETURNS OF INFORMATION ABOUT RELEVANT PAYMENTS OF TAX AND ASSOCIATED MATTERS

210D Application of Chapter 4 to real time returns of information about relevant payments of tax and associated matters

Regulation 205(3) applies to the delivery of the following as if they were specified information within the meaning given by regulation 207—

(*a*) returns under regulation 67B (real time returns of information about relevant payments),

(*b*) returns under regulation 67E(6) (returns under regulation 67B and 67D: amendments), unless the employer is one to whom regulation 67D (exceptions to regulation 67B) applies, and

(*c*) notifications under regulation 67F (additional information about payments) unless the employer is one to whom regulation 67D applies.][1]

Amendments—[1] Chapter 4A inserted by the Income Tax (Pay As You Earn) (Amendment) Regulations, SI 2012/822 regs 2, 49 with effect from 6 April 2012.

CHAPTER 5

METHODS OF PROVIDING INFORMATION ETC

211 How information must or may be delivered by employers

(1) Table 10 applies to determine how employers must or may comply with the requirements of the regulations listed in column 1.

(2) The requirements of the regulation must be complied with in a document or format provided or approved by the Board of Inland Revenue if so indicated in column 4.

(3) Where appropriate, the relevant form number is listed in column 3.

(4) Instead of sending a document to the Inland Revenue, the requirements of the regulation may be complied with by an employer arranging for the information it would contain to be delivered to the Inland Revenue by an approved method of electronic communications if so indicated in column 5.

TABLE 10
REGULATIONS WHICH REQUIRE APPROVED DOCUMENT OR FORMAT, AND WHICH PERMIT ELECTRONIC DELIVERY

1 *Regulation*	2 *Description of information*	3 *Form number*	4 *Approved document or format*	5 *Electronic communications*
. . . [6]	. . . [6]	. . . [6]	. . . [6]	. . . [6]
. . . [6]	. . . [6]	. . . [6]	. . . [6]	. . . [6]
36(1), (2)(*a*)	cessation of employment	Form P45, Part 1	yes	yes
36(1), (2)(*b*)	cessation of employment	Form P45, Parts 1A, 2, 3	yes	[not applicable][8]
38(1)	death of employee	Form P45, Part 1	yes	yes
39(1)	death of pensioner	Form P45, Part 1	yes	yes
42(8)	procedure if new employer receives Form P45	Form P45, Part 3	yes	yes
46(4), 47(2)(*a*) 48(2)(*a*) 49(2)(*a*)	information to be provided if code not known	Form P46	yes	yes
52(3)	late presentation of Form P45	Form P45, Part 3	yes	yes
[55(3)(a)	information on retirement	P46(Pen)	yes	yes][3]
55(3)(*a*)	retirement statement	Form P160	no	yes
56(3)	procedure if new pension payer receives Form P45	Form P45, Part 3	yes	yes
57(2)	information to be provided if code not known (non-UK resident pensioners)	[Form P46(Pen)][3]	yes	yes
58(3)	information to be provided if code not known (UK resident pensioners)	[Form P46(Pen)][3]	yes	yes
60(3)	late presentation of Form P45	Form P45, Part 3	yes	yes
67(1)	information to employees about payments and tax deducted	Form P60	yes	[not applicable][5]
73	annual return of relevant payments liable to deduction of tax	Forms P35 and P14	yes	yes
[73A	annual return of relevant payments by virtue of a retrospective tax provision	Form P35 (RL)	yes	no][1]
74	annual return of relevant payments not liable to deduction of tax	Form P38A	yes	yes
77(4)	return of tax for which employer is liable under regulation 68	Form P100	yes	no
. . .	. . .	. . .	. . .	. . . [7]
85(1)(*a*) and (*b*)	employers: annual return of other PAYE income: benefits code employee	Form P11D	yes	yes
85(2)	employers: annual return of other PAYE income: declaration	Form P11D(*b*)	yes	yes
90(2)	quarterly return of cars becoming available or unavailable	Form P46 (car)	yes	yes
[98(4)	multiple PAYE schemes	Form P350	yes	yes][8]
129(1)	reserve forces' pay: certificate of tax deducted	Form P59	yes	no

1 Regulation	*2* Description of information	*3* Form number	*4* Approved document or format	*5* Electronic communications
132(1)	reserve forces' pay: end of year certificate	Form P60	yes	[not applicable][5]
137(1)	holiday pay funds: certificate of tax deducted	Form P403	yes	No
152(2)	deductions working sheet for claimants awarded taxable JSA	Form PB8	yes	No
153(9)	Department's return for claimant who delivers Form P45	Forms PB3 and P45 Part 3	yes	No
154(2)	Department's return for claimant who does not deliver Form P45	Form PB3	yes	No
157(2)(*b*)	claimant's end of year certificate	Form P60U	yes	[not applicable][5]
157(2)(*c*)	Department's end of year return	Form P14U	yes	No
159(2)	cessation of award of JSA	Form P45U	yes	No
160(2)(*b*)	Department's notification of taxable JSA adjustment	Form P180	yes	No
164(2)	Department's quarterly statement to Board of receipts and payments in respect of taxable JSA	—	yes	No
[184D	deductions working sheet for claimants awarded taxable ESA	Form PB8	yes	no
184E(9)	Department's return for claimant who delivers form P45	Forms PB8 and P45 Part 3	yes	yes
[184G(1)][5]	Department's return for claimant who does not deliver form P45	Form PB3	yes	yes
184I(2)(*b*)	claimant's end of year certificate	Form P60ESA	yes	[not applicable][5]
184J(2)	Department's end of year return	Form P14U	yes	yes
184L(1)	cessation of award of ESA	Form P45ESA	yes	yes
184Q(2)(*b*)	Department's notification of taxable ESA adjustment	Form P180	yes	no
184S(2)	Department's quarterly statement to HMRC of receipts and payments in respect of taxable ESA		yes	no][2]

(5) If an employer delivers electronically the return required by regulation 73 (annual return of relevant payments liable to deduction of tax (Forms P35 and P14)), the statement and declaration and the certificate must, instead of being signed as required by regulation 73(8), be authenticated by or on behalf of the employer in such manner as may be approved by the Board of Inland Revenue.

[(6) For the purposes of this regulation "ESA" means employment and support allowance.][2]

Commentary—*Simon's Taxes* **E4.11150, E4.11151.**

HMRC Directions—The following directions (dated 13 March 2012) were published on the HMRC website on 19 March 2012—

HMRC directions for approved methods of electronic communications from April 2012

Directions under regulations 189 and 205(2) of the Income Tax (Pay As You Earn) Regulations 2003 (SI 2003/2682) and regulation 1(2) of the Social Security (Contributions) Regulations 2001 (SI 2001/1004) and Approval under regulation 211(5) of the Income Tax (Pay As You Earn) Regulations 2003 (SI 2003/2682) and 80(3A) of the Social Security (Contributions) Regulations 2001 (SI 2001/1004)

Interpretation

In these directions and this approval—

'EDI' means the Electronic Data Interchange;

'PAYE Regulations' means the Income Tax (Pay As You Earn) Regulations 2003 (S.I. 2003/2682);

'Contributions Regulations' means the Social Security (Contributions) Regulations 2001 (S.I. 2001/1004).

Directions

The Commissioners for Her Majesty's Revenue and Customs (HMRC) give the following directions about approved methods of electronic communications for the delivery of information and the making of payments and approve the specified manner of authentication of employers' annual returns delivered electronically.

The directions and approval have effect from 6 April 2012.

Approved methods of electronic communications for delivery of information by employers or persons acting on behalf of employers to HMRC

1. The methods of electronic communications approved for the delivery of the information listed in column 1 of the table by an employer or a person acting on behalf of an employer are:

(a) the internet services provided through PAYE Online for Employers and PAYE Online for Agents, where indicated in column 2, and

(b) the EDI services provided through PAYE Online for Employers and PAYE Online for Agents, where indicated in column 3.

1. Description of the kind of information to be delivered	2. Internet	3. EDI
PAYE Regulations[1]		
Simplified deductions scheme: deductions working sheet. Form P12 (regulation 35).	Yes	No
Simplified deductions scheme: annual return of deductions working sheets. Form P37 (regulation 35).	Yes	No
Cessation of employment. Form P45, Part 1 (regulation 36).	Yes	Yes
Death of employee. Form P45, Part 1 (regulation 38).	Yes	Yes
Death of pensioner. Form P45, Part 1 (regulation 39).	Yes	Yes
Procedure if new employer receives Form P45. Form P45, Part 3 (regulation 42).	Yes	Yes
Information to be provided if code not known. Form P46 (regulations 47, 48 and 49).	Yes	Yes
Late presentation of Form P45. Form P45, Part 3 (regulation 52).	Yes	Yes
Information on retirement. Form P46 (Pen) (regulation 55).	Yes	Yes
Procedure if new pension payer receives Form P45. Form P45, Part 3 (regulation 56).	Yes	Yes
Information to be provided if code not known (non-UK resident pensioners). Form P46 (Pen) (regulation 57).	Yes	Yes
Information to be provided if code not known (UK resident pensioners). Form P46 (Pen) (regulation 58).	Yes	Yes
Late presentation of Form P45. Form P45, Part 3 (regulation 60).	Yes	Yes
Annual return of relevant payments liable to deduction of tax. Forms P35 and P14 (regulation 73).	Yes	Yes
Annual return of relevant payments not liable to deduction of tax. Form P38A (regulation 74).	Yes	Yes
Employers: annual return of other PAYE income: benefits code employee. Form P11D (regulation 85).	Yes	Yes
Quarterly return of cars becoming available or unavailable. Form P46 (Car) (regulation 90).	Yes	Yes
Contributions Regulations		
Return by employer of Class 1A National Insurance contributions. Form P11D(b) (regulation 80(1)).	Yes	Yes
Return by employer at end of year. Forms P35 and P14 (paragraph 22 of Schedule 4)	Yes	Yes

[1]Regulation 211 permits electronic delivery of certain information. This direction approves the methods of electronic communications for delivery of that information.

Approved methods of electronic communications for mandatory electronic filing of specified information

2. The methods of electronic communications approved for the delivery of specified information, by an employer or a person acting on behalf of an employer, in accordance with regulation 205 of the PAYE Regulations (and, in accordance with paragraph 22 of Schedule 4 and regulation 90N(1) of the Contributions Regulations) are the internet services and the EDI services provided through PAYE Online for Employers and PAYE Online for Agents.

Approved methods of electronic communications for delivery of information by HMRC to employers or persons acting on behalf of employers

3. The methods of electronic communications approved for delivery of the information listed in column 1 of the table by HMRC to an employer or a person acting on behalf of an employer are:

(a) the internet services provided through PAYE Online for Employers and PAYE Online for Agents, where indicated in column 2, and

(b) the EDI services provided through PAYE Online for Employers and PAYE Online for Agents, where indicated in column 3.

1.	2.	3.
Description of the kind of information to be delivered	Internet	EDI
PAYE Regulations[2]		
Issue of code to employer or agent. Form P6 or P9 (regulations 8 and 20).	Yes	Yes
Notice to employer to amend codes. Form P7X or P9X (regulation 20).	Yes	Yes
Notice to employer of payments and total net tax deducted. Form P6 (regulation 53).	Yes	Yes
Notice to pension payer of payments and total net tax deducted. Form P6 (regulation 61).	Yes	Yes

[2] Regulation 213 permits electronic delivery of certain information. This direction approves the methods of electronic communications for delivery of that information.

Approved method of authentication of the return required by regulation 73 (annual return of relevant payments liable to deduction of tax, Forms P35 and P14) of the PAYE Regulations and regulation 80 (Return by employer) of the Contributions Regulations where the return is delivered electronically

4. The method approved for authenticating a return required by regulation 73 of the PAYE Regulations or regulation 80 of the Contributions Regulations and delivered by a method of electronic communications is the completion of any certificate or declaration contained in the electronic return or form and, where the sender is acting on behalf of an employer, completion of the following procedure before the information is sent:

(a) the sender must make a copy of the information before it is sent, and

(b) the employer must confirm to the sender that the information is complete and accurate to the best of his knowledge and belief.

Approved methods of electronic communications for the making of a payment

5. The methods of electronic communications approved for the making of payments required by the PAYE Regulations and the Contributions Regulations are the services known as Direct Debit, BACS Direct Credit (including telephone and internet banking), CHAPS, debit and credit card over the internet ('BillPay'), Government Banking Service (formerly known as Paymaster), Bank Giro and payments made through the Post Office.

Derivation—The Income Tax (Employments) Regulations, SI 1993/744 regs 20(2), (3), 23(1), (3), 25(2), 26(1A), (4), 27(1), 28(1A), (5A), 29(1), 30(1), 39(2), 43(1), (1C), (3B), (4), 44(2), 46(1), (1A), (7A), (7B), 46A(1), 47(2), 65(1), 68(2), 74(1), 84(3), 88(4), (5), 89(2), 90, 93(2).

Modifications—See the Income Tax (PAYE) Regulations, SI 2003/2682 reg 150 (modification of this regulation in its application to payments of taxable jobseeker's allowance made to a claimant).

SI 2003/2682 reg 174 (modification of this regulation in its application to payments of taxable incapacity benefit).

Amendments—[1] Entry in Table 10 inserted by the Income Tax (Pay as You Earn) (Amendment) Regulations, SI 2007/1077 regs 2, 19 with effect from 6 April 2007.

[2] Entries in Table 10, and whole of para (6), inserted, by the Income Tax (Pay As You Earn) (Amendment) (No 2) Regulations, SI 2008/2601 regs 2, 4 with effect from 27 October 2008.

[3] In para (4), in Table 10, entry relating to reg 55(3)(*a*) substituted, and in column 3 of entries relating to regs 57(2) and 58(3) words substituted for words "Form P46", by the Income Tax (Pay As You Earn) (Amendment No 4) Regulations, SI 2007/2969 regs 2, 21 with effect from 6 April 2009.

[4] Word "yes" previously substituted for word "no" by the Income Tax (Pay as You Earn) (Amendment) Regulations, SI 2010/668 regs 2, 13 with effect only in relation to the tax year 2010–11 and subsequent tax years.

[5] In the entries relating to regs 67(1), 132(1), 157(2)(*b*) and 184I(2)(*b*), words substituted for word "yes", and in entry for reg 184G(1) reference corrected, by the Income Tax (Pay As You Earn) Regulations, SI 2012/822 regs 2, 68 with effect from 6 April 2012.

[6] In Table 10, references to reg 35 revoked by the Income Tax (Pay As You Earn) (Amendment) Regulations, SI 2013/521 regs 2, 11 with effect from 6 April 2014.

[7] In Table 10, entry relating to reg 85(1)(*a*) revoked by the Income Tax (Pay As You Earn) (Amendment No 4) Regulations, SI 2015/1927 regs 2, 13 with effect in relation to any returns and information provided for the tax year 2016–17 and subsequent tax years.

[8] In Table 10, in entry relating to reg 36(1) and 36(2)(*b*) words substituted, and entry relating to reg 98(4) inserted, by the Income Tax (Pay As You Earn) (Amendment) Regulations, SI 2016/329 regs 2, 4 with effect from 6 April 2016.

212 [Modifications for electronic version of Form P46(Pen)]

(1) This regulation applies if instead of sending to the Inland Revenue [Form P46(Pen)][1] a pension payer delivers the information it would contain to the Inland Revenue by an approved method of electronic communications (as permitted by regulation 211).

(2) For sub-paragraphs (*a*) to (*m*) of regulation 55(4) (information to be provided in [Form P46(Pen)][1]) substitute—

"(*a*) the pension payer's PAYE reference,

(*b*) the pensioner's name,

(*c*) the date of retirement,

(*d*) the date on which the pension started,

(*e*) the pensioner's code immediately before retirement and whether it was being used on the cumulative basis,

(*f*) if the pensioner's code immediately before retirement was used on the cumulative basis—

(i) the tax week or tax month in which the last relevant payment before retirement was made to the pensioner or, in a case falling within regulation 24, was treated as having been made,

(ii) the total payments to date at the date of retirement,

(iii) the total net tax deducted,

(*g*) any number used to identify the pensioner,

(*h*) the tax code in use for the pensioner, and whether it is being used on the cumulative basis,

(*i*) the pensioner's address, . . . [1]

(*j*) the pensioner's sex,

(*k*) the pensioner's national insurance number, if known,

(*l*) the pensioner's date of birth, . . . [1]

(*m*) the amount of pension payable annually."

Commentary—*Simon's Taxes* **E4.1175.**
Derivation—The Income Tax (Employments) Regulations, SI 1993/744 reg 26(2).
Amendments—[1] Heading substituted, in paras (1), (2) words substituted, and in para (2)(*i*), (*l*) words revoked, by the Income Tax (Pay As You Earn) (Amendment No 4) Regulations, SI 2007/2969 regs 2, 22 with effect from 6 April 2009.

213 How information may be delivered by Inland Revenue

(1) Table 11 applies to determine how the Inland Revenue may comply with requirements of the regulations listed in column 1.

(2) Instead of sending a document to the employer or (where relevant) the employer's agent, the requirements of the regulation may be complied with by the Inland Revenue arranging for the information it would contain to be delivered to the employer or (where relevant) the employer's agent by an approved method of electronic communications if so indicated in column 4.

(3) The relevant form number is listed in column 3.

TABLE 11
REGULATIONS WHICH PERMIT ELECTRONIC DELIVERY BY INLAND REVENUE

1 *Regulation*	*2* *Description of information*	*3* *Form number*	*4* *Electronic communications*
8(2), 20(2)	issue of code to employer or agent	Form P6 or P9	Yes
20(5), (6)	notice to employer to amend codes	Form P7X or P9X	Yes
53(2)	notice to employer of payments and total net tax deducted	Form P6	Yes
61(2)	notice to pension payer of payments and total net tax deducted	Form P6	Yes
[97Q(1), 97U(3)	notice of requirement for security	notice of requirement	yes][4]
[199(1)	*e-payment notice*	*MP(L)(Band 1)*	*yes*[2]
206(1)	*e-filing notice*	*MP(L)(Band 1)*	*yes]*[1]

(4) But the Inland Revenue may only deliver information by an approved method of electronic communications if the employer or employer's agent (as the case may be) has consented to delivery of information in that way, and the Inland Revenue have not been notified that the consent has been withdrawn.

[(5) References in paragraphs (2) and (4) to—

(*a*) an employer include, in relation to regulations 97Q(1) (notice of requirement) and 97U(3) (outcome of application for reduction in the value of security held: further provision), any person to whom a notice under those regulations is given, and

(*b*) an employer's agent are to a person acting on behalf of the employer.][4]

Commentary—*Simon's Taxes* **E4.11151.**

Derivation—The Income Tax (Employments) Regulations, SI 1993/744 regs 6(4), 13(6), 33.

Amendments—[1] In para (3), in Table 11, entries inserted by the Income Tax (Pay As You Earn) (Amendment No 4) Regulations, SI 2007/2969 regs 2, 23 with effect from 6 April 2008.

[2] Entry in table relating to reg 199(1) revoked by the Income Tax (Pay as You Earn) (Amendment) Regulations, SI 2010/668 regs 2, 14(*a*) with effect only in relation to the tax year 2010–11 and subsequent tax years.

[3] Entry in table relating to reg 206(1) revoked by the Income Tax (Pay As You Earn) (Amendment) Regulations, SI 2010/668, regs 2, 14(*b*), with effect in relation to the tax year 2011–12 and subsequent tax years.

[4] Entry in table relating to regs 97Q(1), 97U(3) inserted, and para (5) substituted, by the Income Tax (Pay As You Earn) (Amendment) Regulations, SI 2012/822 regs 2, 59 with effect from 6 April 2012.

214 How information must be provided by employees

(1) An employee must comply with the requirements of the regulations listed in column 1 of Table 12 in a document or format provided or approved by the Board of Inland Revenue.

(2) Where appropriate, the relevant form number is listed in column 3 of the Table.

TABLE 12
REGULATIONS WHICH REQUIRE EMPLOYEE TO USE APPROVED DOCUMENT OR FORMAT

1	2	*3*
Regulation	*Subject*	*Form number*
46(2)	Form P46 where employer does not receive Form P45 and code not known	Form P46
145(1)	direct collection: return when relevant payments cease	—
146(1)	direct collection: end of year return	Form P14
147(2)	direct collection: return of unpaid tax	—
154(3)	claimant's certificate of full-time education	Form P187
[184G(3)	claimant's certificate of full-time education	Form P187][1]

Commentary—*Simon's Taxes* **E4.11151.**

Derivation—The Income Tax (Employments) Regulations, SI 1993/744 regs 29(1), 30(1), 84(10), 104(6), (9), (11).

Modifications—See the Income Tax (PAYE) Regulations, SI 2003/2682 reg 150 (modification of this regulation in its application to payments of taxable jobseeker's allowance made to a claimant).

Amendments—[1] Entry in Table 12 inserted by the Income Tax (Pay As You Earn) (Amendment) (No 2) Regulations, SI 2008/2601 regs 2, 5 with effect from 27 October 2008.

215 [Meaning of Form P45, P46 and P46(Pen)]

In these Regulations—

"Form P45" means the form provided or approved for use in accordance with regulations 36 (cessation of employment: Form P45), 38 (death of employee) or 39 (death of pensioner);

"Parts 2 and 3 of Form P45" means—

(*a*) the Parts 2 and 3 of the Form P45 provided to the employee or claimant (as the case may be) in accordance with regulation 36, . . .[1]

(*b*) the Parts 2 and 3 of the Form P45 provided to the claimant in accordance with regulation 159 (cessation of award: Form P45U); [or][1]

[(*c*) the Parts 2 and 3 of the Form P45 provided to the claimant in accordance with regulation 184L (cessation of award: Form P45ESA);][1]

["Form P45ESA" means the form required to be completed in accordance with regulation 184L;][1]

"Form P45U" means the form required to be completed in accordance with [regulation 159 or 184L][1];

["Form P46" means the form provided or approved for use in accordance with regulation 46 (form P46 where employer does not receive P45 and code not known);][2]

["Form P46(Pen)" means the form provided or approved for use in accordance with regulation 55(3)(*a*), 57(2) or 58(3).][2]

Commentary—*Simon's Taxes* **E4.1166, E4.1171.**

Derivation—The Income Tax (Employments) Regulations, SI 1993/744 regs 23(1)–(3), 89(2).

Amendments—[1] In definition "Parts 2 and 3 of Form P45", word "or" at end of para (a) revoked, para (c) and preceding word "or" inserted, definition "Form P45ESA" inserted, and words in definition "Form P45U" substituted, by the Income Tax (Pay As You Earn) (Amendment) (No 2) Regulations, SI 2008/2601 regs 2, 6 with effect from 27 October 2008.

[2] Heading substituted, definition of "Form P46" substituted, and definition of "Form P46(Pen)" inserted, by the Income Tax (Pay As You Earn) (Amendment No 4) Regulations, SI 2007/2969 regs 2, 24 with effect from 6 April 2009.

216 Service by post

Any notice or deductions working sheet which is authorised or required to be given, served or issued under these Regulations may be sent by post.

Derivation—The Income Tax (Employments) Regulations, SI 1993/744 reg 109.

Modifications—See the Income Tax (PAYE) Regulations, SI 2003/2682 reg 150 (modification of this regulation in its application to payments of taxable jobseeker's allowance made to a claimant).

SI 2003/2682 reg 174 (modification of this regulation in its application to payments of taxable incapacity benefit).

PART 11
SUPPLEMENTARY PROVISIONS
MISCELLANEOUS APPEALS

217 Appeals: supplementary provisions

(1) The following provisions of TMA apply to appeals under the regulations listed in paragraph (2) as they apply to an appeal under section 31 of TMA—

Section 31A(5) . . . [1]	notice of appeal
. . . [1]	. . . [1]
. . . [1]	. . . [1]

(2) The regulations are—

Regulation 99(3)	appeal against improper purpose notice
Regulation 200(3)	appeal against e-payment notice
Regulation 202(2)	appeal against default notice
Regulation 208(2)	appeal against e-filing notice.

(3), (4) . . . [1]

Commentary—*Simon's Taxes* **E4.11155.**

Derivation—The Income Tax (Employments) Regulations, SI 1993/744 reg 46ZH(1), (3), (4).

Amendments—[1] Words in para (1), entries for section 31B and section 31D, and paras (3), (4), revoked, by the Transfer of Tribunal Functions and Revenue and Customs Appeals Order, SI 2009/56 art 3, Sch 2 paras 92, 111 with effect from 1 April 2009.

CERTIFICATE THAT SUM DUE AND PAYMENT BY CHEQUE

218 Certificate that sum due

(1) A certificate of [HMRC][1] that, to the best of their knowledge and belief, any amount shown in a certificate under the regulations listed in paragraph (2) has not been paid by an employer, is sufficient evidence that the amount mentioned in the certificate is unpaid and due to the Crown.

(2) The regulations are—

[regulation 75A(10)	unpaid amounts from regulation 75A specification][3]
Regulation 76	unpaid amounts in regulation 73 return (Form P35)
Regulation 77(6)	unpaid amounts in regulation 77 return
Regulation 78(8)	unpaid amounts from regulation 78 specification
Regulation 79	unpaid amounts following inspection under [Schedule 36 to the Finance Act 2008][2].

[(2A) HMRC may prepare a certificate showing the whole or any part of a combined amount which includes tax without specifying the components of the combined amount.

Paragraph (1) shall apply with any necessary modifications to the certificate.][1]

(3) A certificate of [HMRC][1] that, to the best of their knowledge and belief, any amount of interest payable under the regulations listed in paragraph (4) has not been paid by an employer or employee is sufficient evidence that the amount mentioned in the certificate is unpaid and due to the Crown.

(4) The regulations are—

Regulation 72(7)	interest consequential on regulation 72 direction
Regulation 81(6)	interest consequential on regulation 81 direction
. . . [4]	. . . [4]
Regulation 115	interest on tax overdue under PSA.

[(4A) HMRC may prepare a certificate showing the total amount of interest payable in respect of the whole or any part of the combined amount without specifying which components of the combined amount the interest relates to.

Paragraph (3) shall apply with any necessary modifications to the certificate.][1]

(5) The production of—

(*a*) the return made by the employer under paragraph (4) of regulation 77 (return and certificate if tax unpaid), and

(*b*) the certificate of [HMRC][1] under paragraph (6) of that regulation,

is sufficient evidence that the amount shown in the certificate is the amount of tax which the employer is liable to pay to [HMRC][1] in respect of the tax period in question under that regulation.

(6) A document which purports to be a certificate under [this regulation][1], or regulation 77(6), is treated as such a certificate until the contrary is proved.

Derivation—The Income Tax (Employments) Regulations, SI 1993/744 regs 42(8), (9), 43(10), (11), 47(7), (8), 48(6), (9), (10), 49(9), (10), 51(4), (5), 54(6), (7), 55(8), (10), (11), 80J(3), (4).

Modifications—See the Income Tax (PAYE) Regulations, SI 2003/2682 reg 174 (modification of this regulation in its application to payments of taxable incapacity benefit).

Amendments—[1] References to HMRC substituted throughout, paras (2A), (4A) inserted, and words in para (6) substituted by the Income Tax (Pay As You Earn) (Amendment) Regulations, SI 2008/782 regs 2, 16 with effect from 6 April 2008.

[2] In para (2), in table, words substituted by the Income Tax (PAYE) (Amendment) Regulations, SI 2009/588 regs 2, 8 with effect from 1 April 2009.

[3] In para (2), in table, entry relating to reg 75A(10) inserted by the Income Tax (Pay As You Earn) (Amendment) Regulations, SI 2012/822 regs 2, 50 with effect from 6 April 2012.

[4] In para (4), in table, entry relating to reg 82 revoked by the Finance Act 2009, Sections 101 and 102 (Interest on Late Payments and Repayments), Appointed Days and Consequential Provisions Order, SI 2014/992 art 9(1), (7) with effect in relation to payments due and payable in respect of the tax year 2014–15 and subsequent tax years.

219 Payment by cheque

(1) For the purposes of the following provisions, if—

(*a*) any payment to the Inland Revenue is made by cheque, and

(*b*) the cheque is paid on its first presentation to the banker on whom it is drawn,

the payment is treated as made on the day on which the cheque was received by the Inland Revenue.

(2) The provisions are—

Regulation 69	due date and receipts for payments of tax
Regulation 72	recovery from employee of tax not deducted by employer
[regulation 75A	notice and certificate in cases where regulation 67B or 67D returns are not made][1]
Regulation 78	notice and certificate if tax may be unpaid
. . . [2]	. . . [2]
. . . [2]	. . . [2]
Regulation 115	interest on tax due under PSA
Regulation 116	interest due on tax overpaid under PSA.

Commentary—*Simon's Taxes* **E4.11115.**

Derivation—The Income Tax (Employments) Regulations, SI 1993/744 regs 42(7A), 48(7A), 52(4), 80J(6), 80K(3).

Modifications—See the Income Tax (PAYE) Regulations, SI 2003/2682 reg 174 (modification of this regulation in its application to payments of taxable incapacity benefit).

SI 2003/2682 Sch 1 para 23 (modification of this regulation in relation to interest on overpaid tax: provisions applying to tax years from 1992–93 to 1995–96).

Amendments—[1] In para (2), in table, entry relating to reg 75A inserted by the Income Tax (Pay As You Earn) (Amendment) Regulations, SI 2012/822 regs 2, 51 with effect from 6 April 2012.

[2] In para (2), in table, entries relating to regs 82 and 83(2)(*b*) revoked by the Finance Act 2009, Sections 101 and 102 (Interest on Late Payments and Repayments), Appointed Days and Consequential Provisions Order, SI 2014/992 art 9(1), (8) with effect in relation to payments due and payable in respect of the tax year 2014–15 and subsequent tax years.

TRANSITIONAL PROVISIONS, SAVINGS AND REVOCATIONS

220 Transitional provisions, savings and revocations

(1) Schedule 1 (transitional provisions and savings) has effect.

(2) The regulations listed in column 1 of Schedule 2 are revoked to the extent specified in column 3 of that Schedule.

(3) Paragraph (2) is subject to Schedule 1.

[SCHEDULE A1

REAL TIME RETURNS

Regulations 67B and 67D

1 The information specified in this Schedule is as follows.][1]

Cross-references—Income Tax (Pay As You Earn) (Amendment) Regulations, SI 2012/822 regs 53–57 (transitional provisions on introduction of real time information).

Social Security (Contributions) (Amendment and Application of Schedule 38 to the Finance Act 2012) Regulations, SI 2013/622 regs 29–32 (transitional arrangements in relation to information requirements under real time information).

Amendments—[1] Schedule A1 inserted by the Income Tax (Pay As You Earn) (Amendment) Regulations, SI 2012/822 regs 2, 52, Schedule with effect from 6 April 2012.

[Information about the employer

2 The employer's HMRC office number.

3 The employer's PAYE reference.

4 The employer's accounts office reference.

5 If applicable, an indication that this is the final return under regulation 67B (real time returns of information about relevant payments) or 67D (exceptions to regulation 67B) that the employer expects to make because this PAYE scheme has ceased [(and, in that case, the date of cessation),][1] unless that information will be included in a notification under regulation 67F (additional information about payments).

Amendments—[1] Words inserted by the Income Tax (Pay As You Earn) (Amendment) Regulations, SI 2013/521 regs 2, 37(*a*) with effect from 6 April 2013 in relation to the tax year 2013–14 and subsequent tax years.

6 If applicable, an indication that this is the final return under regulation 67B or 67D that the employer expects to make for the tax year, unless that information will be included in a notification under regulation 67F.

7

Amendments—Para 7 revoked by the Income Tax (Pay As You Earn) (Amendment) Regulations, SI 2015/2 reg 2(1), (6) with effect in relation to returns filed on or after 6 March 2015.

[Information about the employee

8 The employee's name.

9 The employee's date of birth.

10 The employee's current gender.

11 If known, the employee's national insurance number.

12 If the employee's national insurance is not known, the employee's address.

13 The number used by the employer to identify the employee [in this employment][1].

Amendments—[1] Words substituted for words ", if any" by the Income Tax (Pay As You Earn) (Amendment) Regulations, SI 2013/521 regs 2, 37(*c*) with effect from 6 April 2013 in relation to the tax year 2013–14 and subsequent tax years.

14 If the number used by the employer to identify the employee is different to that shown on the previous return for the employee (if any), an indication of that and the number shown on the previous return.][1]

Amendments—[1] Schedule A1 inserted by the Income Tax (Pay As You Earn) (Amendment) Regulations, SI 2012/822 regs 2, 52, Schedule with effect from 6 April 2012.

[14A If applicable, an indication that the payment to which the return relates is a payment to any one of—

(*a*) a body corporate,

(*b*) a trustee of a trust of which the employee is a beneficiary,

(*c*) if the employee has died, the employee's personal representative.][1]

Amendments—[1] Paras 14A, 14B inserted by the Income Tax (Pay As You Earn) (Amendment) Regulations, SI 2013/521 regs 2, 37(*d*) with effect from 6 April 2013 in relation to the tax year 2013–14 and subsequent tax years.

[14B Where the return relates to a payment within paragraph 14A, the information required by paragraphs 8 to 12 need not be provided.][1]

Amendments—[1] Paras 14A, 14B inserted by the Income Tax (Pay As You Earn) (Amendment) Regulations, SI 2013/521 regs 2, 37(*d*) with effect from 6 April 2013 in relation to the tax year 2013–14 and subsequent tax years.

[Information about payments to the employee, etc

15 The tax year to which the return relates.

16 The total payments to date in this employment.

17 The total net tax deducted in relation to those payments.

18 The employee's pay frequency or an indication that payments are made to the employee on an irregular basis.

19 The date of the payment the return relates to.

20 The tax week number or tax month number in which the payment is made.

21 An indication of which of the following bands the number of normal hours worked each week by the employee falls into—

(*a*) up to 15.99,
[(*b*) 16 to 23.99,
(*ba*) 24 to 29.99,][1]
(*c*) 30 or more,

or an indication that none of the bands is applicable.

Amendments—[1] Sub-paras (*b*), (*ba*) substituted for previous para (*b*) by the Income Tax (Pay As You Earn) and the Income Tax (Construction Industry Scheme) (Amendment) Regulations, SI 2014/472 regs 2, 20 with effect from 6 April 2014.

22 The value of the payment the return relates to.

[22A If applicable, an indication that comprised within the payment is—

(*a*) a pension and if so—
(i) the amount of the pension.
(ii) an indication of whether it is an occupational pension, and
(iii) an indication of whether the pension is being paid because the pensioner is a bereaved spouse or civil partner,

(*b*) a trivial commutation lump sum, within the meaning given by paragraph 7 or 7A of Schedule 29 to the Finance Act 2004 and, if so, the amount of that lump sum,

(*c*) a lump sum that falls within regulation 11 (de minimis rule for pension schemes) or 12 (payments by larger pension schemes) of the Registered Pension Schemes (Authorised Payments) Regulations 2009 and, if so, the amount of that lump sum,

(*d*) a lump sum that falls within regulation 11A (payments by schemes which are not public service pension schemes or occupational pension schemes) of those Regulations and, if so, the amount of that lump sum.][1]

Amendments—[1] Para 22A inserted by the Income Tax (Pay As You Earn) (Amendment) Regulations, SI 2013/521 regs 2, 37(*e*) with effect from 6 April 2013 in relation to the tax year 2013–14 and subsequent tax years.

[22B If applicable, an indication that comprised within the payment is an amount treated as a payment of PAYE income under regulation 61B (PAYE: benefits in kind) and, if so, the amount of the specified benefit in respect of which tax has been deducted.][1]

Amendments—[1] Para 22B inserted by the Income Tax (Pay As You Earn) (Amendment No 4) Regulations, SI 2015/1927 regs 2, 14(*a*) with effect in relation to specified benefits (as defined in reg 61A) provided on or after 6 April 2016.

[22C (1) If applicable, an indication that comprised within the payment is an amount in respect of a reportable payment and the amount of that reportable payment.

(2) For the purposes of sub-paragraph (1) a "reportable payment" is—

(*a*) a payment of an uncrystallised funds pension lump sum,
(*b*) a lifetime annuity under a flexible annuity contract, or
(*c*) a payment made out of—
(i) a fund referred to in section 227G(2), (4) or (5) of the Finance Act 2004,
(ii) an arrangement referred to in section 227G(3) of the Finance Act 2004, or
(iii) a scheme pension referred to in section 227G(9) of the Finance Act 2004.

(3) For the purposes of sub-paragraph (2)—

(*a*) "flexible annuity contract" has the meaning given by section 227G(8) of the Finance Act 2004, and
(*b*) "uncrystallised funds pension lump sum" has the meaning given by paragraph 4A of Schedule 29 to the Finance Act 2004.][1]

Amendments—[1] Paras 22C, 22D inserted by the Income Tax (Pay As You Earn) (Amendment) Regulations, SI 2016/329 regs 2, 5 with effect from 6 April 2016.

[22D If applicable, an indication that comprised within the payment is a lump sum to which section 636A(4ZA) of ITEPA applies and the amount of that lump sum.][1]

Amendments—[1] Paras 22C, 22D inserted by the Income Tax (Pay As You Earn) (Amendment) Regulations, SI 2016/329 regs 2, 5 with effect from 6 April 2016.

23 The tax code operated on the payment the return relates to.

24 If applicable, an indication that the employee's tax code is being operated on a non-cumulative basis.

25 The total net tax deducted from the payment the return relates to.

26 The value of any amount comprised within the payment made to the employee which falls to be reported under regulation 85 (employees: annual return of other earnings ([Form P11D][1]) and in respect of which tax has been deducted.

Amendments—[1] Words substituted by the Income Tax (Pay As You Earn) (Amendment No 4) Regulations, SI 2015/1927 regs 2, 14(*b*) with effect in relation to any returns and information provided for the tax year 2016–17 and subsequent tax years.

[26A The value of the amounts referred to in paragraph 26 in the tax year to date.][1]

Amendments—[1] Para 26A inserted by the Income Tax (Pay As You Earn) (Amendment) Regulations, SI 2013/521 regs 2, 37(*f*) with effect from 6 April 2013 in relation to the tax year 2013–14 and subsequent tax years.

27 [If the employer is required by regulation 67CA(1)(*a*) (notifications of relevant payments to and by providers of certain electronic payment methods) to include a reference in the return, the][1] value of any amount which is not subject to tax or national insurance paid to the employee at the same time as the payment.

Amendments—[1] Words substituted for word "the" by the Income Tax (Pay As You Earn) (Amendment) Regulations, SI 2013/521 regs 2, 37(*g*) with effect from 6 April 2013 in relation to the tax year 2013–14 and subsequent tax years.

28 [If the employer is required by regulation 67CA(1)(*a*) to include a reference in the return, the][1] value of any deductions made from the payment which do not otherwise fall to be reported under this Schedule.

Amendments—[1] Words substituted for word "the" by the Income Tax (Pay As You Earn) (Amendment) Regulations, SI 2013/521 regs 2, 37(*h*) with effect from 6 April 2013 in relation to the tax year 2013–14 and subsequent tax years.

29 The value of the payment after allowable pension contributions within the meaning given by regulation 3(2) (net PAYE income) and the deduction of tax, national insurance and deductions due under the Student Loan Regulations.

30 The value, if any, of allowable pension contributions within the meaning given by regulation 3(2) deducted from the payment of PAYE income comprising the payment.

[30A The value of the contributions referred to in paragraph 30 in the tax year to date.][1]

Amendments—[1] Para 30A inserted by the Income Tax (Pay As You Earn) (Amendment) Regulations, SI 2013/521 regs 2, 37(*I*) with effect from 6 April 2013 in relation to the tax year 2013–14 and subsequent tax years.

31 The value, if any, of employee pension contributions other than allowable pension contributions within the meaning given by regulation 3(2) deducted from the payment.

[31A The value of the contributions referred to in paragraph 31 in the tax year to date.][1]

Amendments—[1] Para 31A inserted by the Income Tax (Pay As You Earn) (Amendment) Regulations, SI 2013/521 regs 2, 37(*j*) with effect from 6 April 2013 in relation to the tax year 2013–14 and subsequent tax years.

32 The value of any earnings for the purposes of the Social Security Contributions and Benefits Act 1992 comprised within the total payment which are included in the gross earnings from the employment for the purpose of calculating liability to Class 1 contributions under that Act but in respect of which tax is not deducted under these Regulations, excluding allowable pension contributions.

33 In paragraphs 15 to 31, "payment" means the relevant payment the information being given in accordance with this Schedule relates to.

34 In paragraph 32, "total payment" means the relevant payment the information being given in accordance with this Schedule relates to plus any other amount paid to the employee at the same time as the relevant payment.

[34A If applicable, an indication that during the period since the employer last made a return under regulation 67B or 67D containing information about the employee—

(*a*) regulation 64 (trade disputes) has at any time applied in relation to the employee, or (*b*) the employee has been absent from the employment without pay.][2]][1]

Amendments—[1] Schedule A1 inserted by the Income Tax (Pay As You Earn) (Amendment) Regulations, SI 2012/822 regs 2, 52, Schedule with effect from 6 April 2012.

[2] Para 34A inserted by the Income Tax (Pay As You Earn) (Amendment) Regulations, SI 2013/521 regs 2, 37(*k*) with effect from 6 April 2013 in relation to the tax year 2013–14 and subsequent tax years.

[Information on the commencement of employment

35 If the return is the first return in respect of the employee in this employment the information required by paragraphs 36 to 44.

36 The date on which the employment commenced or will commence.

37 The employee's address.

38 If known, the employee's passport number.

39 An indication of which of the statements in paragraph 41 applies to the employee.

40 If the employee is a seconded expatriate, the information required by paragraph 42 and an indication of which of the statements in paragraph 43 applies to the employee.

41 The statements in this paragraph are—

(*a*) the employment is the employee's first employment since the preceding 6th April, and the employee has not since that date received—

(i) jobseeker's allowance[, incapacity benefit or employment and support allowance][1] which is subject to income tax, or

(ii) a retirement pension or an occupational pension,

(*b*) the employee is not receiving a retirement pension or an occupational pension and since the preceding 6th April—

(i) has had another employment, but is not now in receipt of employment income from it, or

(ii) has received jobseeker's allowance[, incapacity benefit or employment and support allowance][1] which is subject to income tax, but payment of that allowance or benefit has ceased,

(*c*) the employee either has another employment (which is continuing) or is in receipt of a retirement pension or an occupational pension.

Amendments—[1] In sub-paras (*a*)(i), (*b*)(ii), words substituted for words "or incapacity benefit" by the Income Tax (Pay As You Earn) (Amendment) Regulations, SI 2013/521 regs 2, 37(*l*) with effect from 6 April 2013 in relation to the tax year 2013–14 and subsequent tax years.

42 An indication of whether the employee is a seconded expatriate who is a national of an EEA state.

43 The statements in this paragraph are—

(*a*) the employee intends to live in the United Kingdom for [183 days][1] or more,

(*b*) the employee intends to live in the United Kingdom for less than [183 days][1], or

(*c*) the employee will work both inside and outside the United Kingdom, but will live outside.

Amendments—[1] In sub-paras (*a*), (*b*), words substituted for words "six months" by the Income Tax (Pay As You Earn) (Amendment) Regulations, SI 2013/521 regs 2, 37(*m*) with effect from 6 April 2013 in relation to the tax year 2013–14 and subsequent tax years.

44

Amendments—Para 44 revoked by the Income Tax (Pay As You Earn) (Amendment) Regulations, SI 2013/521 regs 2, 37(*n*) with effect from 6 April 2013 in relation to the tax year 2013–14 and subsequent tax years.

[Information on the cessation of employment

45 If the employment has ceased, the date of cessation.

46 If applicable, an indication that the payment to which the details under this Schedule relate was made after cessation of the employment.][1]

Amendments—[1] Schedule A1 inserted by the Income Tax (Pay As You Earn) (Amendment) Regulations, SI 2012/822 regs 2, 52, Schedule with effect from 6 April 2012.

SCHEDULE 1

TRANSITIONAL PROVISIONS AND SAVINGS

Regulation 220

PART 1

GENERAL PROVISIONS

Continuity of the law

1 The revocation of provisions and their making in a rewritten form in these Regulations does not affect the continuity of the law.

2 Paragraph 1 does not apply to any change in the law made by these Regulations.

3 Anything which—

(*a*) has been done, or has effect as if done, under or for the purposes of a provision of the revoked Regulations, and

(*b*) is in force or effective immediately before the commencement of these Regulations,

has effect after that commencement as if done under or for the purposes of the corresponding provision of these Regulations.

4 Any reference (express or implied) in these Regulations or any document made under these Regulations to—

(*a*) a provision of these Regulations, or

(*b*) things done or falling to be done under or for the purposes of a provision of these Regulations,

is to be read as including, in relation to times, circumstances or purposes in relation to which any corresponding provision of the revoked Regulations had effect, a reference to the provision of the revoked Regulations or to things done or falling to be done under or for the purposes of the provision of the revoked Regulations.

5 Any reference (express or implied) in these Regulations to relevant payments, relevant payments exceeding the PAYE threshold or similar concepts created by these Regulations is to be read as including, in relation to times, circumstances or purposes in relation to which any corresponding concept of the revoked Regulations had effect, a reference to the concept of the revoked Regulations.

6 Any reference (express or implied) in these Regulations to—

(*a*) a provision of ITEPA, or

(*b*) things done or falling to be done under or for the purposes of a provision of ITEPA,

is to be read as including, in relation to times, circumstances or purposes in relation to which any corresponding provision repealed by ITEPA had effect, a reference to the repealed provision or to things done or falling to be done under or for the purposes of the repealed provision.

7 Any reference (express or implied) in these Regulations to general earnings, PAYE income or similar concepts created by ITEPA is to be read as including, in relation to times, circumstances or purposes in relation to which any corresponding concept which has been superseded by ITEPA had effect, a reference to the superseded concept.

8 Paragraphs 4, 5, 6 and 7 apply only in so far as the context permits.

9 Paragraph 5 is without prejudice to the generality of paragraph 4 and paragraph 7 is without prejudice to the generality of paragraph 6.

10 These Regulations have effect in relation to tax liable, under the Income Tax (Employments) Regulations 1993 or section 710 of ITEPA, to be deducted or accounted for in respect of payments made before 6th April 2004 as if the tax had been liable to be deducted or accounted for under these Regulations.

11 Paragraph 10 is without prejudice to the generality of paragraphs 1 to 9.

12 Paragraphs 1 to 11 have effect instead of paragraph (*b*) of section 17(2) of the Interpretation Act 1978.

General saving for old savings

13—(1) The revocation by these Regulations of a provision previously revoked subject to savings does not affect the continued operation of those savings.

(2) The revocation by these Regulations of a saving on the previous revocation of a provision does not affect the operation of the saving in so far as it is not specifically reproduced in these Regulations but remains capable of having effect.

Interpretation

14 In this Part of this Schedule, "the revoked Regulations" means the Regulations which are revoked by these Regulations.

PART 2
SPECIFIC PROVISIONS

Modification of reference to payment to the Inland Revenue in regulation 68(2)

15 For the purposes of giving effect to any enactment or instrument which refers to an amount which is, or would in certain circumstances be, payable to the collector, paragraph (2) of regulation 68 has effect as if that paragraph required payment of the amount to which it refers to the collector.

Derivation—The Income Tax (Employments) Regulations, SI 1993/744 regs 40(1), 41(1).

FPCS information for the tax year ending 5th April 2002: employees not covered by regulation 46(1) of 1993 Regulations

16—(1) This paragraph applies to a person (a "former FPCS employee")—

(*a*) who was employed by an employer during a part of the tax year ending 5th April 2002, but who was no longer employed by that employer on 5th April 2002, and

(*b*) in respect of whom the employer—

(i) has provided information to the Inland Revenue under the FPCS arrangement for the tax year ending 5th April 2002, or

(ii) has delivered information by an approved method of electronic communications to an official computer system under the FPCS arrangement for the tax year ending 5th April 2002, but

(*c*) in respect of whom no particulars were required to be provided by the employer under regulation 46(1) of the 1993 Regulations for the tax year ending 5th April 2002.

(2) The former FPCS employee may by notice require the employer to give a statement to the former FPCS employee containing—

(*a*) particulars of the amount of the taxable profit, if any, for the tax year ending 5th April 2002 in respect of car allowances and motor mileage allowances paid to the former FPCS employee in the tax year ending 5th April 2002 for business travel, calculated by reference to the FPCS arrangement, or

(*b*) particulars of the total amount of the car allowances and motor mileage allowances paid to the former FPCS employee in the tax year ending 5th April 2002 for business travel, and the total amount of miles covered by the former FPCS employee in the tax year ending 5th April 2002 in the course of business travel for which the motor mileage allowances were paid.

(3) The former FPCS employee may give the notice to the employer at any time before 6th April 2005.

(4) The employer must give the statement to the former FPCS employee within 30 days of receiving the notice.

(5) A former FPCS employee who has received the statement from the employer may not require a further statement from the employer in respect of the tax year ending 5th April 2002.

(6) In this paragraph—

"business travel" has the meaning given by section 168(5)(*c*) of ICTA as that definition had effect for the tax year ending 5th April 2002 by virtue of regulation 46AA(6) of the 1993 Regulations;

"the FPCS arrangement" means the arrangement known as the Fixed Profit Car Scheme made between the employer and the Inland Revenue for providing information in respect of payments of car allowances and motor mileage allowances made to employees for business travel.

(7) The reference in sub-paragraph (1)(*b*)(ii) to the delivery of information by an approved method of electronic communications to an official computer system includes, in relation to information which was delivered before the commencement of these Regulations, a reference to the delivery of information to an official computer system within the meaning of regulation 2(1) of the 1993 Regulations by a means of electronic communications approved for the purposes of regulation 46AA(3) of those Regulations.

Derivation—The Income Tax (Employments) Regulations, SI 1993/744 reg 46AA(3), (4), (5), (6).

FPCS information for the tax year ending 5th April 2002: employees covered by regulation 46(1) of 1993 Regulations

17—(1) This paragraph applies to a former employee who would be a former FPCS employee were it not for the fact that the employer was required under regulation 46(1) of the 1993 Regulations to provide particulars in respect of the former employee for the tax year ending 5th April 2002.

(2) If the former employee gives notice to the employer under paragraph (4) of regulation 94 requiring a statement relating to the tax year ending 5th April 2002, the statement must contain (in addition to the particulars mentioned in paragraph (2) of that regulation)—

(*a*) particulars of the amount of the taxable profit, if any, for the tax year ending 5th April 2002 in respect of car allowances and motor mileage allowances paid to the former employee in the tax year ending 5th April 2002 for business travel, calculated by reference to the FPCS arrangement, or

(*b*) particulars of the total amount of the car allowances and motor mileage allowances paid to the former employee in the tax year ending 5th April 2002 for business travel, and the total amount of miles covered by the former employee in the tax year ending 5th April 2002 in the course of business travel for which the motor mileage allowances were paid.

(3) "Former employee" has the same meaning as in regulation 94(7).

(4) Expressions used in this paragraph which are defined in paragraph 16 have the same meaning in this paragraph as in that paragraph.

Derivation—The Income Tax (Employments) Regulations, SI 1993/744 reg 46AA(3), (4), (6).

Due date for payments of tax in respect of tax periods ending before 6th April 2004

18—(1) The following provisions have effect with the following modifications in so far as the provisions apply in relation to tax periods ending before 6th April 2004.

(2) For sub-paragraphs (*a*) and (*b*) of regulation 69(1) (due date for payments of tax) substitute "within 14 days after the end of the tax period".

(3) In regulation 77(1) (return and certificate if tax may be unpaid) for "17 days" substitute "14 days".

(4) In regulation 78(1) (notice and certificate if tax may be unpaid) for "17 days" substitute "14 days".

Derivation—The Income Tax (Employments) Regulations, SI 1993/744 regs 40(1), 41(1), 47(1), 48(1).

Interest on unpaid tax: disapplication of regulation 82 for tax years before the tax year ending 5th April 1993

19 Regulation 82 (interest on tax overdue) does not apply in relation to unpaid tax in respect of a tax year ending on or before 5th April 1992.

Derivation—The Income Tax (Employments) Regulations, SI 1993/744 reg 51(1).

Interest on unpaid tax: provisions applying to tax years before the tax year ending 5th April 1993

20—(1) This paragraph applies if the Inland Revenue make a determination under regulation 80 (determination of unpaid tax) which relates to tax payable for a tax year ending on or before 5th April 1992.

(2) This paragraph also applies if—

(*a*) the inspector, at any time after 19th April 1988, made a determination under regulation 49 of the 1993 Regulations (determination of tax payable by employer),

(*b*) the determination relates to tax payable for a tax year ending on or before 5th April 1992, and

(*c*) tax remains payable pursuant to the determination immediately before the commencement of these Regulations.

(3) The tax payable pursuant to the determination carries interest at the prescribed rate from the relevant start date until payment ("the interest period").

(4) Sub-paragraph (3) applies even if the relevant start date is a non-business day as defined by section 92 of the Bills of Exchange Act 1882.

(5) Any change made to the prescribed rate during the interest period applies to the tax payable pursuant to the determination from the date of change.

(6) Regulation 84 (recovery of tax and interest) applies to an amount of interest which an employer is liable to pay under this paragraph as if it were the unpaid amount for the purposes of that regulation.

(7) Paragraphs (3) and (6) of regulation 218 (certificate of interest due) apply in relation to an amount which an employer is liable to pay under this paragraph as if this paragraph were a regulation included among those listed in paragraph (4) of that regulation.

(8) Regulation 219 (payment by cheque) applies for determining when a payment is made for the purposes of this paragraph as if this paragraph were included among the provisions listed in paragraph (2) of that regulation.

(9) In this paragraph—

"inspector" means an inspector of taxes;

"the prescribed rate" means the rate applicable under section 178 of the Finance Act 1989 for the purposes of section 86 of TMA;

"the relevant start date" means—

(*a*) in a case where the determination relates to tax payable for a tax year ending on or before 5th April 1988, 19th April 1988, and

(*b*) in a case where the determination relates to tax payable for a tax year ending after 5th April 1988 but on or before 5th April 1992, the 14th day after the end of the tax year to which the determination relates.

Derivation—The Income Tax (Employments) Regulations, SI 1993/744 regs 2(1), 50(1)–(3), 52(1)–(4), 54(1), (2), (6), (7).

Interest on tax overdue: application of regulation 82 to tax years from 1992–93 to 2003–04

21—(1) Regulation 82 (interest on tax overdue) has effect with the following modifications where the tax year in respect of which tax is unpaid is—

(*a*) the tax year ending 5th April 1993, or

(*b*) a tax year ending after 5th April 1993 but on or before 5th April 2004.

(2) In paragraph (1) for "the total net tax payable in respect of a tax year" substitute "the total net tax deductible by him in respect of all of his employees during a tax year".

(3) In paragraph (4) for "a direction made under [regulation 72(5), 72F][1] or 81(4)" substitute "a direction made under regulation 42(2) or (3) or 49(5) of the 1993 Regulations or regulation 72(5) or 81(4) of these Regulations".

(4) Omit paragraph (6).

(5) For paragraph (8) substitute—

"(8) The "reckonable date" means 14 days after the end of the tax year."

(6) After that paragraph insert—

"(9) "The 1993 Regulations" means the Income Tax (Employments) Regulations 1993."

Derivation—The Income Tax (Employments) Regulations, SI 1993/744 reg 51(1)–(3).

Amendments—[1] Words in sub-para (3) substituted by the Income Tax (Pay As You Earn) (Amendment) Regulations, SI 2008/782 regs 2, 17 with effect from 6 April 2008.

Interest on overpaid tax: disapplication of regulation 83 for tax years before the tax year ending 5th April 1997

22 Regulation 83 (interest on overpaid tax) does not apply to tax which was paid by an employer in respect of a tax year ending on or before 5th April 1996.

Derivation—The Income Tax (Employments) Regulations, SI 1993/744 reg 53A(1).

Interest on overpaid tax: provisions applying to tax years from 1992–93 to 1995–96

23—(1) This paragraph applies in relation to tax which—

(*a*) was paid by an employer in respect of the tax year ending 5th April 1993 or in respect of a tax year ending after 5th April 1993 but on or before 5th April 1996, and

(*b*) is repaid to the employer after the end of the tax year in respect of which the tax was paid.

(2) If the late repayment condition is met, the tax repaid carries interest at the prescribed rate from the relevant time until the order for the repayment is issued ("the interest period").

(3) The late repayment condition is that the tax is repaid—

(*a*) after the end of the tax year following the tax year in respect of which the tax was paid, and

(*b*) after the end of the tax year in which the tax was paid.

(4) Any change made to the prescribed rate during the interest period applies to the tax repaid from the date of change.

(5) Regulation 219 (payment by cheque) applies for determining when a payment is made for the purposes of this paragraph as if this paragraph were included among the provisions listed in paragraph (2) of that regulation.

(6) In this paragraph—

"the prescribed rate" means the rate applicable under section 178 of the Finance Act 1989 for the purposes of section 824 of ICTA;

"the relevant time" means—

(*a*) in a case where the tax was paid more than twelve months after the end of the tax year in respect of which the payment was made, the end of the tax year in which that tax was paid, and

(*b*) in any other case, the end of the tax year after the tax year in respect of which the payment was made.

Derivation—The Income Tax (Employments) Regulations, SI 1993/744 reg 53(1)–(5).

Overpayments and underpayments of tax: tax years before the tax year ending 5th April 1997

24—(1) Despite the revocations made by these Regulations, regulation 101 of the 1993 Regulations (repayment of overpayments and recovery of underpayments) continues to apply in relation to an assessment for a tax year ending on or before 5th April 1996, but with the modifications mentioned in sub-paragraph (2).

(2) The modifications are—

(*a*) the references in paragraphs (1) and (2) of regulation 101 to the appropriate code for a subsequent year are to be read as references to the employee's code for a subsequent tax year;

(*b*) the references in paragraphs (1) and (2) of that regulation to the inspector and to the collector are to be read as references to the Inland Revenue;

(*c*) the reference in paragraph (6) of that regulation to a direction made by the collector under regulation 42(2) of the 1993 Regulations in relation to the employee and in respect of one or more income tax periods falling within the year is to be read as including a reference to a direction under regulation 72(5) of these Regulations in relation to that employee in respect of one or more tax periods falling within the tax year;

(*d*) the reference in that paragraph to a direction made by the Board under regulation 42(3) of the 1993 Regulations in relation to the employee and in respect of one or more income tax periods falling within the year is to be read as including a reference to a direction under regulation 72(5) of these Regulations in relation to that employee in respect of one or more tax periods falling within the tax year;

(*e*) the reference in that paragraph to a direction made by the Board under regulation 49(5) of the 1993 Regulations in relation to the employee and in respect of one or more income tax periods falling within the year is to be read as including a reference to a direction under regulation 81(4) of these Regulations in relation to that employee in respect of one or more tax periods falling within the tax year.

(3) Any tax which is payable to the Inland Revenue under regulation 101(2) as it continues to have effect by virtue of this paragraph is payable within 14 days of the date on which the Inland Revenue first makes application for its payment.

Derivation—The Income Tax (Employments) Regulations, SI 1993/744 reg 105(2).

Overpayments and underpayments of tax: tax years before the tax year ending 5th April 2002

25—(1) Regulation 188 (assessments other than self-assessments)—

(*a*) does not apply in relation to an assessment for a tax year ending on or before 5th April 1996, and

(*b*) has effect in particular with the following modification in relation to an assessment, other than one under section 9 of TMA, for a tax year beginning on or after 6th April 1996 and ending on or before 5th April 2001.

(2) In paragraph (3), after sub-paragraph (*a*) insert—

"(*aa*) make any necessary adjustment to B in respect of any shortfall in deductions made in accordance with the Income Tax (Employments) Regulations 1993 from the employee, where—

(i) payments of profit-related pay have been made to the employee in accordance with a profit-related pay scheme registered under Chapter 3 of Part 5 of ICTA,

(ii) in consequence of the relief given by that Chapter less tax has been deducted from those payments than would have been deducted if the scheme had not been registered, and

(iii) the registration of the scheme has subsequently been cancelled with effect from a time before that relevant for the purposes of the relief;".

Derivation—The Income Tax (Employments) Regulations, SI 1993/744 reg 101(3), (4).

Attribution of repayments: tax years before the tax year ending 5th April 1997

26—(1) Despite the revocations made by these Regulations, regulations 106 to 108 of the 1993 Regulations (attribution of repayments) continue to apply in relation to a repayment to which section 824(5) of ICTA applies for a tax year ending on or before 5th April 1996, but with the modification mentioned in sub-paragraph (2).

(2) The modification is that the reference to the collector in regulation 107(3) is to be read as including a reference to the Inland Revenue.

Certificate that sum due: certificate of the collector

27—(1) A certificate of the collector that any amount shown in a certificate under the regulations listed in paragraph (2) of regulation 218 has not been paid by an employer to the collector or, to the best of the collector's knowledge and belief, to any other collector or to any person acting on the collector's behalf or on behalf of another collector is sufficient evidence that the amount mentioned in the collector's certificate is unpaid and due to the Crown.
(2) A certificate of the collector that any amount of interest payable under the regulations listed in paragraph (4) of regulation 218 has not been paid by an employer or employee to the collector or, to the best of the collector's knowledge and belief, to any other collector or to any person acting on the collector's behalf or on behalf of another collector is sufficient evidence that the amount mentioned in the certificate is unpaid and due to the Crown.
(3) A document which purports to be a certificate of the collector under sub-paragraph (1) or (2) is treated as such a certificate until the contrary is proved.

Interpretation

28—In this Part of this Schedule—

"the 1993 Regulations" means the Income Tax (Employments) Regulations 1993;
"collector" means a collector of taxes.

Derivation—The Income Tax (Employments) Regulations, SI 1993/744 reg 2(1).

SCHEDULE 2
REVOCATIONS
Regulation 220

1 Regulations revoked	*2 Reference*	*3 Extent of revocation*
The Income Tax (Employments) Regulations 1993	SI 1993/744	The whole Regulations.
The Income Tax (Employments) (Amendment) Regulations 1993	SI 1993/2276	The whole Regulations.
The Income Tax (Employments) (Amendment) Regulations 1994	SI 1994/775	The whole Regulations.
The Income Tax (Employments) (Notional Payments) Regulations 1994	SI 1994/1212	The whole Regulations.
The Income Tax (Employments) (Amendment) Regulations 1995	SI 1995/216	The whole Regulations.
The Income Tax (Employments) (Amendment No 2) Regulations 1995	SI 1995/447	The whole Regulations.
The Income Tax (Employments) (Incapacity Benefit) Regulations 1995	SI 1995/853	The whole Regulations.
The Income Tax (Employments) (Amendment No 3) Regulations 1995	SI 1995/1223	The whole Regulations.
The Income Tax (Employments) (Amendment No 4) Regulations 1995	SI 1995/1284	The whole Regulations.
The Income Tax (Employments) (Amendment) Regulations 1996	SI 1996/804	The whole Regulations.
The Income Tax (Employments) (Amendment No 2) Regulations 1996	SI 1996/980	The whole Regulations.
The Income Tax (Employments) (Amendment No 3) Regulations 1996	SI 1996/1312	The whole Regulations.
The Income Tax (Employments) (Amendment No 4) Regulations 1996	SI 1996/2381	The whole Regulations.
The Income Tax (Employments) (Amendment No 5) Regulations 1996	SI 1996/2554	The whole Regulations.
The Income Tax (Employments) (Amendment No 6) Regulations 1996	SI 1996/2631	The whole Regulations.
The Income Tax (Employments) (Amendment) Regulations 1997	SI 1997/214	The whole Regulations.

1 Regulations revoked	*2 Reference*	*3 Extent of revocation*
The Income Tax (Employments) (Notional Payments) (Amendment) Regulations 1998	SI 1998/1891	The whole Regulations.
The Income Tax (Employments) (Amendment) Regulations 1998	SI 1998/2484	The whole Regulations.
The Income Tax (Employments) (Amendment) Regulations 1999	SI 1999/70	The whole Regulations.
The Income Tax (Employments) (Amendment No 2) Regulations 1999	SI 1999/824	The whole Regulations.
The Income Tax (Employments) (Amendment No 3) Regulations 1999	SI 1999/2155	The whole Regulations.
The Income Tax (Employments) (Amendment) Regulations 2000	SI 2000/1152	The whole Regulations.
The Income Tax (Sub-contractors in the Construction Industry and Employments) (Amendment) Regulations 2000	SI 2000/2742	Regulation 3.
The Income Tax (Electronic Communications) (Miscellaneous Amendments) Regulations 2001	SI 2001/1081	In regulation 1(2), the definition of "the Employments Regulations". Regulations 7 to 21.
The Income Tax (Employments and Electronic Communications) (Miscellaneous Provisions) Regulations 2002	SI 2002/680	Regulations 3 to 8.
The Income Tax (Sub-contractors in the Construction Industry and Employments) (Amendment) Regulations 2003	SI 2003/536	In regulation 1(2), the definition of "the Employments Regulations". Regulation 9.
The Income Tax (Employments) (Amendment) Regulations 2003	SI 2003/2494	The whole Regulations.

2003/2714

NON-RESIDENT INSURANCE COMPANIES REGULATIONS 2003

Made by the Inland Revenue under TA 1988 s 11AA(5) and FA 2003 s 149(6)

Made . . . . .22 *October 2003*
Laid before the House of Commons . . . . .23 *October 2003*
Coming into force . . . . .13 *November 2003*

1 These Regulations may be cited as the Non-resident Insurance Companies Regulations 2003, shall come into force on 13th November 2003, and have effect in relation to accounting periods of non-resident insurance companies beginning on or after 1st January 2003.

2 In these Regulations—

"non-resident insurance company" means an insurance company that is not resident in the United Kingdom; and for this purpose "insurance company" has the meaning given by section 431(2) of the Income and Corporation Taxes Act 1988.

3—(1) In applying subsection (2) of section 11AA of the Income and Corporation Taxes Act 1988 in relation to a non-resident insurance company, it shall be assumed that the permanent establishment has assets such that its free assets would be not less than they would be in the circumstances specified in that subsection.

(2) "Free assets" means the amount by which—

(*a*) the value of the assets of the permanent establishment, exceeds

(*b*) the aggregate of the permanent establishment's loan capital and technical provisions; and for this purpose, the reinsurers' share of technical provisions is not to be included in determining the assets of the permanent establishment.

(3) "Value" means the amount that, at the time at which the value falls to be determined, the non-resident insurance company would obtain from an independent person for the transfer of all the company's rights in respect of the asset.

(4) "Technical provision" means each of the following—

(*a*) provision for unearned premiums;

(*b*) long term business provision;

(*c*) claims outstanding;

(*d*) provision for bonuses and rebates;

(*e*) provision for unexpired risks;

(*f*) technical provisions for linked liabilities;

(*g*) deposits received from reinsurers; and in the case of the items listed in sub-paragraphs (*a*) to (*f*), the amount to be brought into account is the amount by which the gross amount exceeds the reinsurance amount. In this paragraph expressions also used in [Schedule 3 to the Large and Medium-sized Companies and Groups (Accounts and Reports) Regulations 2008][1] have the same meaning as in that Schedule.

Amendments—[1] Words in para (4)(g) substituted by the Companies Act 2006 (Consequential Amendments) (Taxes and National Insurance) Order, SI 2008/954 art 52 with effect for periods of account beginning on or after 6 April 2008.

4—(1) In accordance with the separate enterprise principle, profits from assets attributable, by virtue of regulation 3, to the permanent establishment of a non-resident insurance company are attributed to that establishment.

(2) "The separate enterprise principle" means the principle in subsection (2) of section 11AA of the Income and Corporation Taxes Act 1988 (read with subsection (3) of that section).

2003/3075

MONEY LAUNDERING REGULATIONS 2003

Made by the Treasury under the European Communities Act 1972 s 2(2) and the Financial Services and Markets Act 2000 ss 168(4)(b), 402(1)(b), 417(1) and 428(3)

Revocation—These Regulations revoked by the Money Laundering Regulations, SI 2007/2157, reg 1(3) with effect from 15 December 2007: SI 2007/2157 reg 1(1).

2003/3143

INCOME AND CORPORATION TAXES (ELECTRONIC CERTIFICATES OF DEDUCTION OF TAX AND TAX CREDIT) REGULATIONS 2003

Made by the Commissioners of Inland Revenue under FA 1999 s 132

Made . . . . *4 December 2003*
Laid before the House of Commons . . . . *5 December 2003*
Coming into force . . . . *1 January 2004*

1 Citation, commencement and interpretation

(1) These Regulations may be cited as the Income and Corporation Taxes (Electronic Certificates of Deduction of Tax and Tax Credit) Regulations 2003 and shall come into force on 1st January 2004.
(2) In these Regulations references to the delivery of a document include that document being made available to a person in circumstances where—
(*a*) the sender and that person have agreed to his having access to the document on a website,
(*b*) the document is a document to which the agreement relates; and
(*c*) the person is notified in a manner for the time being agreed for the purpose between him and the sender of—
(i) the placing of the document on the website;
(ii) the address of the website; and
(iii) the place on the website at which, and the manner in which, the document may be accessed. Here "document" means anything authorised to be delivered by means of electronic communications under these Regulations.
(3) In these Regulations—
"electronic communications" has the meaning given by section 132(10) of the Finance Act 1999;
"the sender" means—
(*a*) in relation to a statement to which regulation 2 applies, the company making the qualifying distribution, or a person acting on its behalf;
(*b*) in relation to a statement to which regulation 3 applies, the person under the duty to furnish the certificate, or another person acting on his behalf; and
(*c*) in relation to statement, notice, certificate or voucher to which regulation 4 applies, the person required or authorised, under the relevant provision mentioned in paragraph (2) of that regulation, to deliver that statement, notice, certificate or voucher, or another person acting on his behalf; and "the Taxes Act" means the Income and Corporation Taxes Act 1988.

2 Delivering information electronically about distributions, dividends, interest payments and associated tax credits

(1) A statement under section 234(1) or 234A(2) [or (3)][1] of the Taxes Act (information relating to distributions, dividends, interest payments and associated tax credits) by a company making a qualifying distribution may be delivered by means of electronic communications if the following conditions are satisfied.
(2) The first condition is that the sender has indicated to the proposed recipient that it intends to use electronic communications for the purposes of delivering statements under those sections.
(3) The second condition is that the proposed recipient has consented to information being delivered by the sender by means of electronic communications, and that consent has not been withdrawn.
(4) The third condition is that the statement is delivered in an electronic format—
(*a*) in which the statement may be stored;
(*b*) which permits a paper copy of the information contained in the statement to be printed; and
(*c*) which is designed to prevent alteration of the contents.

Amendments—[1] Words inserted by the Income and Corporation Taxes (Electronic Certificates of Deduction of Tax and Tax Credit) (Amendment) Regulations, SI 2009/2050 reg 2 with effect from 1 September 2009.

3 Delivering information electronically about deduction of tax

(1) A statement under section 352 of the Taxes Act (certificates of deduction of tax) may be delivered by means of electronic communications if the following conditions are satisfied.
(2) The first condition is that the sender has indicated to the proposed recipient that he intends to use electronic communications to furnish statements under section 352.
(3) The second condition is that the proposed recipient has consented to information being delivered by the sender by means of electronic communications, and that consent has not been withdrawn.
(4) The third condition is that the statement is delivered in an electronic format—
(*a*) in which the statement may be stored;
(*b*) which permits a paper copy of the information contained in the statement to be printed; and
(*c*) which is designed to prevent alteration of the contents.

4 Sending information electronically about manufactured dividends

(1) A statement, notice, certificate or voucher required or authorised to be delivered under the provisions listed in paragraph (2) may be delivered by means of electronic communications if the conditions specified in paragraphs (3) to (5) are satisfied.
(2) The provisions referred to in paragraph (1) are—

(*a*) paragraphs 2(6) and 3(8) of Schedule 23A to the Taxes Act (information about manufactured dividends); and

(*b*) regulations 4(4)(*c*), 5(2)(*b*)(iii), 7(2)(*d*), 10(3)(*b*) and (4)(*b*) and 15(1) and (5) of the Income Tax (Manufactured Overseas Dividends) Regulations 1993.

(3) The first condition is that the sender has indicated to the proposed recipient that he intends to use electronic communications to deliver documents of that type.

(4) The second condition is that the proposed recipient has consented to information being delivered by the sender by means of electronic communications, and that consent has not subsequently been withdrawn.

(5) The third condition is that the document in question is delivered in an electronic format—

(*a*) in which it may be stored;

(*b*) which permits a paper copy of the information contained in it to be printed; and

(*c*) which is designed to prevent alteration of its contents.

5 Amendments of the Income Tax (Manufactured Overseas Dividends) Regulations 1993
(*amends the Income Tax (Manufactured Overseas Dividends) Regulations, SI 1993/1957*).

2003/3297

REPORTING OF SAVINGS INCOME INFORMATION REGULATIONS 2003

Made by the Treasury under FA 2003 s 199

Made . . . . *16 December 2003*
Laid before the House of Commons . . . . *17 December 2003*
Coming into force in accordance with . . . . *regulation 1(2)*

PART 1
INTRODUCTORY PROVISIONS

1 Citation and commencement

(1) These Regulations may be cited as the Reporting of Savings Income Information Regulations 2003.

(2) These Regulations shall come into force on such date, being not earlier than 1st January 2005, as is determined by the Treasury and specified by notices in the London, Edinburgh and Belfast Gazettes.

2 Interpretation

(1) In these Regulations—

["the Savings Directive" means Council Directive 2003/48/EC of 3rd June 2003 ("the Directive of 2003") on the taxation of savings income in the form of interest payments, as amended by Council Directive 2004/66/EC, and a reference, without more, to a numbered Article is a reference to the Article of the Directive of 2003, as so amended, which bears that number;][1]

"the Securities Directive" means Directive 2001/34/EC of 28th May 2001 on the admission of securities to official stock exchange listing and on information to be published on those securities as amended;

"the UCITS Directive" means [Council Directive 2009/65/EC of 13th July 2009] [2]on the co-ordination of laws, regulations and administrative provisions relating to undertakings for collective investment in transferable securities as amended.

(2) In these Regulations—

"agent" means paying agent or receiving agent as appropriate;

["arrangements" means agreements or arrangements made with a territory being a dependent or associated territory of a member State in relation to the automatic exchange of information or, during the transitional period defined in Article 10 of the Savings Directive, the application of a withholding tax referred to in paragraph 2(ii) of Article 17 of the Savings Directive;][1]

["country" includes a territory;][1]

["economic operator" is a paying agent established in another member State or in a territory (construed in accordance with the Savings Directive or the arrangements with the territory, as appropriate) with which arrangements have been made;][1]

"money debt" is a debt arising from a transaction for the lending of money and which falls to be, or may be, settled—

(*a*) by the payment of money; or

(*b*) by the transfer of a right to settlement under a debt which is itself a money debt,

subject to the qualification in regulation 17;

["paying agent", unless the context otherwise requires, has the meaning given in regulation 3;][1]

["a prescribed territory" means another member State, Aruba, the British Virgin Islands, Gibraltar, Guernsey, the Isle of Man, Jersey, Montserrat or the Netherlands Antilles;][1]

"receiving agent" has the meaning given in regulation 6;
"relevant payee" has the meaning given in regulation 7;
"resident" and "residence" shall be construed in accordance with regulation 9;
"residual entity" has the meaning given in regulation 4;
["Revenue and Customs", except in the expression "an officer of Revenue and Customs", means Her Majesty's Revenue and Customs (see section 4 of the Commissioners for Revenue and Customs Act 2005);][1]
"savings income" has the meaning given in regulation 8;
"third country" means a territory other than a member State;
"UCITS" means an undertaking for collective investment in transferable securities within the UCITS Directive.

(3) For the purposes of these Regulations a person makes savings income payments to another person if the person—

(*a*) makes payments of savings income to another person, or
(*b*) secures the payment of savings income for the other person.

Amendments—[1] In para (1), definition of "the Savings Directive" substituted; and in para (2), definition of "arrangements", "country" and "Revenue and Customs" inserted, and definitions of "economic operator", "paying agent" and "a prescribed territory" substituted; by the Reporting of Savings Income Information (Amendment) Regulations, SI 2005/1539 regs 2, 3, with effect on a date notified in the London, Edinburgh and Belfast Gazettes (1 July 2005; see London Gazette, 14 June 2005).
[2] In para (1), in definition of "the UCITS Directive", words substituted by the Undertakings for Collective Investment in Transferable Securities Regulations, SI 2011/1613 reg 16, Schedule para 4 with effect from 1 July 2011.

3 Meaning of paying agent

A paying agent is a person who—

(*a*) is established in the United Kingdom;
(*b*) makes savings income payments in the course of his business or profession; and
(*c*) makes those payments—
  (i) for the immediate benefit of a relevant payee; or
  (ii) to a residual entity established in a prescribed territory.

Here a "person" includes any officer in any public office or in any government department and any savings income payments made by such a person will be treated as if the payment were made in the course of that person's business or profession.

4 Meaning of residual entity

(1) Subject to paragraph (2) a residual entity is an entity established in a member State [or in a territory with respect to which arrangements have been made][1] other than an entity—

(*a*) which is a legal person;
(*b*) the profits of which are taxed under the general arrangements for business taxation; or
(*c*) which is a UCITS authorised in accordance with the UCITS Directive [or an equivalent undertaking for collective investment established in a territory with which arrangements have been made][1].

(2) In paragraph (1)(*a*) a legal person excludes—

(*a*) in Finland, avoin yhtiö (Ay) and kommandiittiyhtiö (Ky)/ öppet bolag and kommanditbolag; and
(*b*) in Sweden, handelsbolag (HB) and kommanditbolag (KB).

(3) A paying agent shall regard an entity as a residual entity unless the paying agent has reason to believe, on the basis of official evidence produced by the entity to the paying agent, that sub-paragraph (*a*), (*b*) or (*c*) of paragraph (1) applies.

[An entity which presents to the paying agent or economic operator a certificate—

(*a*) issued by the member State in which that entity is established in accordance with Article 4(3), or
(*b*) issued by the territory with which arrangements have been made in which that entity is established in accordance with provisions which are equivalent to Article 4(3),

shall, for the purposes of this regulation, be treated as if it were a UCITS authorised in accordance with the UCITS Directive or an equivalent undertaking for collective investment established in the territory with which arrangements have been made (as the case may be).][1]

Amendments—[1] Words in para (1) inserted, and words in sub-s (3) substituted, by the Reporting of Savings Income Information (Amendment) Regulations, SI 2005/1539 regs 2, 4 with effect on a date to be notified in the London, Edinburgh and Belfast Gazettes (1 July 2005; see London Gazette, 14 June 2005).

5 Election by an entity to be treated as a UCITS

(1) An entity established in the United Kingdom may obtain a certificate to the effect that it is to be treated as a UCITS authorised in accordance with the UCITS Directive for the purposes of the Savings Directive in accordance with this regulation.

(2) A notice requesting the issue of a certificate shall be given to [Revenue and Customs][1] by or on behalf of the entity.

(3) The notice shall include the following information—

(*a*) the name and address of the entity;

(*b*) where the notice is given on behalf of the entity, the name, address and position of the person giving notice;

(*c*) a statement that—

(i) the entity is established in the United Kingdom;

(ii) the entity is not a legal person;

(iii) the entity's profits are not taxed under the general arrangements for business taxation;

(iv) the entity is not a UCITS authorised in accordance with the UCITS Directive; and

(v) the entity elects to be treated as if it were a UCITS authorised in accordance with the UCITS Directive for the purposes of the Savings Directive; and

(*d*) a signed and dated declaration by the person giving notice to the effect that it is to the best of his knowledge correct and complete.

(4) [Revenue and Customs][1] will issue a certificate to that entity confirming that it is to be treated as if it were a UCITS authorised in accordance with the UCITS Directive for the purposes of the Savings Directive and that certificate shall have effect from the date specified in that certificate.

Amendments—[1] Words in paras (2), (4) substituted by the Reporting of Savings Income Information (Amendment) Regulations, SI 2005/1539 regs 2, 5 with effect on a date to be notified in the London, Edinburgh and Belfast Gazettes (1 July 2005; see the London Gazette, 14 June 2005).

6 Meaning of receiving agent

A receiving agent is an entity—

(*a*) which is a residual entity;

(*b*) which is established in the United Kingdom; and

(*c*) to which a savings income payment is made for the benefit of a relevant payee by a person established in a member State [or in a territory with which arrangements have been made][1] in the course of his business or profession.

Amendments—[1] Words in para (c) inserted by the Reporting of Savings Income Information (Amendment) Regulations, SI 2005/1539 regs 2, 6 with effect on a date to be notified in the London, Edinburgh and Belfast Gazettes (1 July 2005; see the London Gazette, 14 June 2005).

7 Meaning of relevant payee

(1) The agent shall regard a person as a relevant payee if he is an individual—

(*a*) resident in a prescribed territory; and

(*b*) who has received a savings income payment or for whom a savings income payment has been secured,

unless he provides evidence to the agent that the payment is not received or secured for his own benefit because of one of the reasons listed in paragraph (2).

(2) The reasons referred to in paragraph (1) are that the individual—

(*a*) is acting as [a paying agent][1] or an economic operator;

(*b*) acts on behalf of a residual entity;

(*c*) acts on behalf of an entity—

(i) which is a legal person;

(ii) the profits of which are taxed under the general arrangements for business taxation;

(iii) which is a UCITS authorised in accordance with the UCITS [Directive, or an equivalent undertaking for collective investment established in a territory with which arrangements have been made;][1]

(iv) which is treated as being a UCITS [authorised][1] in accordance with the UCITS Directive for the purposes of the Savings Directive by virtue of Article 4(3); . . .[1]

[(v) which is treated as being an equivalent undertaking for collective investment established in a territory with which arrangements have been made for the purposes of those arrangements by virtue of provisions which are equivalent to Article 4(3); or][1]

(*d*) acts on behalf of another individual for whose benefit the payment is received or secured.

(3) An individual who provides evidence that he is acting on behalf of a residual entity must in addition provide the name and address of that residual entity to the agent.

(4) An individual who provides evidence that he acts on behalf of another individual must in addition provide the agent with the name and address, and where appropriate the tax identification number or date and place of birth, of that individual. The individual providing the evidence must obtain and verify this information in accordance with regulation 9.

(5) If the agent has information which suggests that the individual who receives a savings income payment or for whom a savings income payment is secured may not be the relevant payee for the reason referred to in paragraph (2)(*d*), then paragraph (6) applies.

(6) The agent must take reasonable steps to establish who is the relevant payee and if the agent is unable to identify the relevant payee, he shall treat the individual who receives a savings income payment or for whom a savings income payment is secured as the relevant payee.

Amendments—[1] Words in para (2) substituted and inserted by the Reporting of Savings Income Information (Amendment) Regulations, SI 2005/1539 regs 2, 7 with effect on a date to be notified in the London, Edinburgh and Belfast Gazettes (1 July 2005; see the London Gazette, 14 June 2005).

8 Meaning of savings income

(1) Subject to paragraphs (3) to (6) and (8) savings income is—

(*a*) interest;

(*b*) interest accrued or capitalised at the sale, refund or redemption of a money debt;

(*c*) income distributed by a collective investment fund which is derived directly or indirectly, via other collective investment funds or residual entities, from interest;

(*d*) income realised upon the sale, refund or redemption of shares or units in a collective investment fund if that fund invests directly or indirectly, via other collective investment funds or residual entities, more than 40% of its assets in money debts.

(2) In paragraph (1) "interest"—

(*a*) includes—

(i) prizes attaching to money debts (including premium bonds);

(ii) premiums and discounts derived from money debts;

(iii) any dividend derived from shares (including permanent interest bearing shares) in a building society; . . . [1]

(iv) any share interest paid by a registered industrial and provident society; and

[(v) any share interest paid by a credit union registered under the Credit Unions (Northern Ireland) Order 1985; and][1]

(*b*) excludes—

(i) any interest which is not related to a money debt; and

(ii) penalty charges for late payment.

(3) In respect of savings income described in paragraph (1)(*b*), where an agent has no information concerning the amount of interest which is accrued or capitalised at the sale, refund or redemption of a money debt the total amount of the proceeds of the sale, redemption or refund is savings income.

(4) In respect of savings income described in paragraphs (1)(*c*), where an agent has no information concerning the proportion of income which derives from interest the total amount of the income is savings income.

(5) In respect of savings income described in paragraphs (1)(*c*) and (*d*), subject to paragraph (9)—

(*a*) where a collective investment fund established in the United Kingdom has invested 15% or less of its assets directly or indirectly, via other collective investment funds or residual entities, in money debts there is no savings income;

(*b*) where a collective investment fund—

(i) is established in another member State which has derogated from paragraphs (1)(*c*) and (*d*) of Article 6 in accordance with Article 6(6); and

(ii) the collective investment fund has invested 15% or less of its assets in money debts in accordance with the law of that member State in the application of that derogation,

there is no savings income.

[(*c*) where a collective investment fund—

(i) is established in a territory with which arrangements have been made which has made provisions equivalent to the derogation in the first sentence of Article 6(6); and

(ii) the collective investment fund has invested 15% or less of its assets in money debts in accordance with the law of that territory in the application of those provisions,

there is no savings income][1]

(6) In respect of savings income described in paragraph (1)(*d*)—

(*a*) where an agent has no information concerning the percentage of assets invested in money debts or in shares or units in collective investment funds, that percentage shall be considered to be more than 40%;

(*b*) where the agent cannot determine the amount of income realised by the relevant payee, the income shall be deemed to correspond to the proceeds of the sale, refund or redemption of the shares or units.

(7) From 1st January 2011 paragraphs (1)(*d*) and (6)(*a*) shall have the effect with the substitution of "25%" for "40%".

(8) Subject to paragraph (9)—

(*a*) where a residual entity established in the United Kingdom invests 15% or less of its assets directly or indirectly, via collective investment funds or other residual entities, in money debts there is no savings income;

(*b*) where a residual entity—

(i) is established in another member State which has derogated from [paragraph 4 of Article 6][1] in accordance with Article 6(6); and

(ii) the residual entity has invested 15% or less of its assets in money debts in accordance with the law of that member State in the application of that derogation,

there is no savings income.

[(*c*) where a residual entity—

(i) is established in a territory with which arrangements have been made which has made provisions equivalent to the derogation in the second sentence of Article 6(6); and

(ii) the residual entity has invested 15% or less of its assets in money debts in accordance with the law of that territory in the application of those provisions,

there is no savings income][1]

(9) In the application of paragraphs (5) and (8), where the agent cannot ascertain whether or not the collective investment fund or residual entity, as appropriate, has invested 15% or less of its assets in money debts in accordance with those provisions, there is savings income.

(10) The percentages referred to in this regulation shall be determined by reference to the investment policy as laid down in the fund rules or instruments of incorporation of the collective investment fund or residual entity concerned and, failing which, by reference to the actual composition of the assets of the collective investment fund or residual entity.

(11) In this regulation a collective investment fund is—

(*a*) a UCITS authorised in accordance with the UCITS Directive [or an equivalent undertaking for collective investment established in a territory with which arrangements have been made][1];

(*b*) an entity which is treated as being a UCITS authorised in accordance with the UCITS Directive for the purposes of the Savings Directive by virtue of Article 4(3); or

[(*ba*) an entity which is treated as being an equivalent undertaking for collective investment established in a territory with which arrangements have been made for the purposes of those arrangements by virtue of provisions which are equivalent to Article 4(3); or][1]

[(*c*) an undertaking for collective investment which is not established in the Community or in a territory with which arrangements have been made.][1]

This is subject to the following qualification.

If a collective investment fund provides arrangements for separate pooling of the contributions of the participants and the profits or income out of which payments are to be made to them and under which participants are entitled to exchange rights in one pool for rights in another, each separate pool shall be treated as a separate collective investment fund.

(12) In this regulation—

"building society" means a building society within the meaning of the Building Societies Act 1986;

"permanent interest bearing shares" has the meaning given in section 117(11) of the Taxation of Chargeable Gains Act 1992;

"registered industrial and provident society" has the meaning given in section 486(12) of the Income and Corporation Taxes Act 1988 as extended by section 486(9) of that Act; and

"share interest" has the meaning given in section 486(12) of the Income and Corporation Taxes Act 1988.

Amendments—[1] In para (2), word revoked, and sub-para (a)(v) and preceding word inserted; paras (5)(c), (8)(c), (11)(ba) inserted; words in para (8)(b) substituted; words in para (11)(a) inserted; and para (11)(c) substituted; by the Reporting of Savings Income Information (Amendment) Regulations, SI 2005/1539 regs 2, 8 with effect on a date to be notified in the London, Edinburgh and Belfast Gazettes (1 July 2005; see the London Gazette, 14 June 2005).

PART 2
INFORMATION TO BE OBTAINED, VERIFIED AND REPORTED

9 Identity and residence of relevant payees

(1) Where—

(*a*) a paying agent makes a savings income payment to an individual whom he believes to be a relevant payee, or

(*b*) a receiving agent receives or secures a savings income payment for an individual whom he believes to be a relevant payee,

the agent must establish the identity and country of residence of that individual in accordance with this regulation.

(2) Subject to the conditions set out in this regulation, for the purposes of this regulation the country of residence means the country where the individual has his permanent address.

(3) Where contractual relations between the agent and the individual are entered into before 1st January 2004 the agent must verify the name, address and country of residence of the individual by using the information at its disposal, including information obtained pursuant to the Money Laundering Regulations 1993 and the Money Laundering Regulations 2001.

(4) Where contractual relations between the agent and the individual are entered into, or transactions are carried out in the absence of contractual relations, on or after 1st January 2004, the agent shall obtain and verify—

[(*a*) the name and address of the individual, and

(i) where the individual is resident for tax purposes in a member State, the tax identification number (if any) allocated by that member State but if it is not available the individual's date and place of birth,

(ii) where the individual is resident for tax purposes other than in a member State, the individual's date and place of birth,

in accordance with paragraphs (5) and (7);][1]

(*b*) the country of residence of the individual in accordance with paragraphs (8) and (9).

(5) The information in paragraph (4)(*a*) shall be verified by the presentation by the individual of his passport or official identity card to the agent.

(6) If the address does not appear on that passport or official identity card, it shall be verified by the presentation by the individual of any other documentary proof of identity to the agent.

(7) If the tax identification number [is not required or if it is and it][1] is not mentioned on the passport, official identity card or any other documentary proof of identity presented by the individual, the agent shall instead verify the individual's date and place of birth on the basis of his passport or official identity card.

(8) Subject to paragraph (9), the country of residence of the individual shall be determined on the basis of his address verified in accordance with paragraphs (5) and (6).

[(9) Where an individual presents a passport or official identity card issued by a member State and declares himself to be resident in a third country—][1]

(*a*) . . . [1] the agent shall establish the country of residence by means of a certificate of residence for tax purposes issued by the competent authority of the third country which the individual claims to be his country of residence;

(*b*) if the individual fails to present such a certificate, the member State that issued the passport or other official identity document shall be considered to be the country of residence.

(10) The individual may present a certified copy of any of the documents referred to in this regulation.

Here "certified copy" means a copy certified or otherwise authenticated in such manner as would make it admissible in evidence in proceedings before a court.

(11) In this regulation—

"competent authority" means the competent authority for the purposes of bilateral or multilateral tax conventions or, failing that, such other authority as is competent to issue certificates of residence for tax purposes;

"other documentary proof of identity" includes certificates of residence for tax purposes.

Amendments—[1] Para (4)(*a*) substituted; words in para (7) inserted; and words in para (9) substituted and revoked; by the Reporting of Savings Income Information (Amendment) Regulations, SI 2005/1539 regs 2, 9 with effect on a date to be notified in the London, Edinburgh and Belfast Gazettes (1 July 2005; see the London Gazette, 14 June 2005).

10 Information to be reported to [Revenue and Customs] by paying agents making payments to relevant payees

(1) When a paying agent makes a savings income payment for the immediate benefit of a relevant payee the information prescribed by paragraph (2) must be reported by the paying agent to [Revenue and Customs][1] in accordance with regulations 14 and 15.

(2) The information prescribed is—

(*a*) the name and address of the paying agent;

(*b*) the name, address and country of residence of the relevant payee established in accordance with regulation 9;

(*c*) where contractual relations between the relevant payee and the paying agent were entered into, or transactions are carried out in the absence of contractual relations, on or after 1st January 2004, the tax identification number . . . [2], or if it is not available, the relevant payee's date and place of birth, established in accordance with regulation 9;

(*d*) the account number of the relevant payee or, where there is none, identification of the money debt or other instrument giving rise to the savings income;

(*e*) the amount and category of the savings income payments made to the relevant payee in accordance with regulation 13 and the currency in which they were paid.

Amendments—[1] Words in the Heading and para (1) substituted by the Reporting of Savings Income Information (Amendment) Regulations, SI 2005/1539 regs 2, 10 with effect on a date to be notified in the London, Edinburgh and Belfast Gazettes (1 July 2005; see the London Gazette, 14 June 2005).

[2] Words in para (2)(*c*) revoked by the Reporting of Savings Income and Interest Payments (Data-gathering) Regulations, SI 2012/756 reg 2(1), (2) with effect from 1 April 2012.

11 Information to be reported to [Revenue and Customs] by paying agents making payments to residual entities

(1) When a paying agent makes a savings income payment to a residual entity established in a prescribed territory the information prescribed by paragraph (2) must be reported by the paying agent to [Revenue and Customs][1] in accordance with regulations 14 and 15.

(2) The information prescribed is—

(*a*) the name and address of the paying agent;

(*b*) the name and address of the residual entity (including the territory in which it is established); and

(*c*) the total amount and category of the savings income payments made to the residual entity in accordance with regulation 13 and the currency in which they were paid.

Amendments—[1] Words in the Heading and para (1) substituted by the Reporting of Savings Income Information (Amendment) Regulations, SI 2005/1539 regs 2, 11 with effect on a date to be notified in the London, Edinburgh and Belfast Gazettes (1 July 2005; see the London Gazette, 14 June 2005).

12 Information to be reported to [Revenue and Customs] by receiving agents

(1) When a receiving agent receives or secures savings income the information prescribed by paragraph (2), in respect of each relevant payee the savings income is attributable to, must be reported by the receiving agent to [Revenue and Customs][1] in accordance with regulations 14 and 15.

(2) The information prescribed is—

(*a*) a statement that the savings income has been received or secured by the receiving agent in his capacity as such;

(*b*) the name and address of the receiving agent;

(*c*) the name, address and country of residence of the relevant payee established in accordance with regulation 9;

(*d*) where contractual relations between the relevant payee and the receiving agent were entered into, or transactions are carried out in the absence of contractual relations, on or after 1st January 2004, the tax identification number . . . [2], or if it is not available, the relevant payee's date and place of birth, established in accordance with regulation 9;

(*e*) the account number of the relevant payee or, where there is none, identification of the money debt or other instrument giving rise to the savings income;

(*f*) the amount and category of the savings income received or secured by the receiving agent in accordance with regulation 13 and the currency in which it was paid.

Amendments—[1] Words in the Heading and para (1) substituted by the Reporting of Savings Income Information (Amendment) Regulations, SI 2005/1539 regs 2, 12 with effect on a date to be notified in the London, Edinburgh and Belfast Gazettes (1 July 2005; see the London Gazette, 14 June 2005).

[2] Words in para (2)(*d*) revoked by the Reporting of Savings Income and Interest Payments (Data-gathering) Regulations, SI 2012/756 reg 2(1), (2) with effect from 1 April 2012.

13 The amount of savings income to be reported to [Revenue and Customs]

(1) The information concerning the savings income prescribed by paragraph (2) must be reported by the agent to [Revenue and Customs][1].

(2) The agent shall identify under which of the following three categories he is reporting the savings income and where the savings income is of the type prescribed by—

(*a*) regulation 8(1)(*a*), report the amount of savings income;

(*b*) sub-paragraph (*b*) or (*d*) of regulation 8(1), report either the amount of savings income or the full amount of the proceeds from the sale, redemption or refund;

(*c*) regulation 8(1)(*c*), report either the amount of savings income or the full amount of the distribution.

(3) Where the agent has reported savings income under sub-paragraph (*a*) or (*c*) of paragraph (2) no further report of the same savings income is required under sub-paragraph (*b*) of that paragraph.

Amendments—[1] Words in the Heading and para (1) substituted by the Reporting of Savings Income Information (Amendment) Regulations, SI 2005/1539 regs 2, 13 with effect on a date to be notified in the London, Edinburgh and Belfast Gazettes (1 July 2005; see the London Gazette, 14 June 2005).

PART 3
REPORTING THE INFORMATION

14 Paying and receiving agents to notify [Revenue and Customs] of reportable payments

(1) An agent who must report information to [Revenue and Customs][1] in accordance with these Regulations must notify [Revenue and Customs][1] in writing that he needs to make a report within 14 days of the end of the tax year in which—

(*a*) in the case of a paying agent, the savings income payment was made, or

(*b*) in the case of a receiving agent, the savings income was secured or received,

unless the agent has already received a notice under regulation 15 from [Revenue and Customs][1] in respect of that tax year.

(2) An agent who fails to comply with paragraph (1) is liable to a penalty not exceeding £3000 determined in accordance with section 100 of the Taxes Management Act 1970.

(3) Sections 100A, 100B, 102, 103(4) and 118(2) of the Taxes Management Act 1970 apply to a penalty determined in accordance with paragraph (2).

Amendments—[1] Words in the Heading and para (1) substituted by the Reporting of Savings Income Information (Amendment) Regulations, SI 2005/1539 regs 2, 14 with effect on a date to be notified in the London, Edinburgh and Belfast Gazettes (1 July 2005; see the London Gazette, 14 June 2005).

15 Reports by paying and receiving agents to [Revenue and Customs]

(1) [Revenue and Customs][1] must send a notice to—

(*a*) an agent who has notified [Revenue and Customs][1] in accordance with regulation 14(1);

(*b*) any person [Revenue and Customs][1] considers should have notified it in accordance with regulation 14(1) but has not done so; and

(*c*) any person who has notified [Revenue and Customs][1] in accordance with regulation 14(1) in respect of a previous tax year, unless—

(i) the person has informed [Revenue and Customs][1]; or

(ii) an officer of [Revenue and Customs][1] has reasonable grounds to believe,

that he is no longer an agent.

(2) The notice must specify—

(*a*) the information prescribed by these Regulations which must be reported;

(*b*) the tax year in respect of which the report must be made and that the report must be in respect of all savings income payments for that tax year;

(*c*) the form in which the report must be made;

(*d*) the address to which the report must be delivered; and

(*e*) the date by which the report must be delivered which shall be a date no earlier than 30 days after the date of the notice.

(3) For the report for the tax year in which the commencement date falls, the reference to the tax year in paragraph (2)(*b*) means the period beginning on the commencement date and ending at the end of the tax year in which the commencement date falls.

Here "commencement date" is the date specified in the notices under regulation 1(2).

(4) The notice may be combined with a notice issued under [paragraph 1 of Schedule 23 to the Finance Act 2011 (data-gathering powers).][2]

(5) The agent or person, as appropriate, must make and deliver the report in accordance with the requirements specified in the notice.

(6) Paragraph (5) applies regardless of whether any savings income is reportable in accordance with these Regulations.

Amendments—[1] In the Heading and para (1), words substituted by the Reporting of Savings Income Information (Amendment) Regulations, SI 2005/1539 regs 2, 15 with effect on a date to be notified in the London, Edinburgh and Belfast Gazettes (1 July 2005; see the London Gazette, 14 June 2005).

[2] Words in para (4) substituted by the Reporting of Savings Income and Interest Payments (Data-gathering) Regulations, SI 2012/756 reg 2(1), (3) with effect from 1 April 2012.

PART 4
AUDIT

16 Audit and related issues

(1) An officer of [Revenue and Customs][1] may by notice require an agent, or a person who appears to [that officer][1] to be an agent, to furnish them within such time, not being less than 14 days, as may be provided by the notice, such information (including copies of any relevant books, documents or other records) as they may reasonably require for the purposes of determining whether information contained in a report under these Regulations by that agent or person, as appropriate, was correct and complete.

(2) An agent or person, as appropriate, required to make and deliver a report under these Regulations shall, whenever required to do so within the period specified in paragraph (4)(*c*), make available for inspection by [an officer of Revenue and Customs][1], at such time as that officer may reasonably require, all such copies of books, documents or other records in his possession or under his control as may be required by [an officer of Revenue and Customs][1] under paragraph (1).

(3) An agent or person, as appropriate, required to make and deliver a report under these Regulations shall retain, for the period specified in paragraph (4), all such books, documents and other records copies of which he may be required to make available for inspection under paragraph (2). These documents include copies of the documents presented by relevant payees in accordance with regulation 9.

(4) The period specified is—

(*a*) in relation to information concerning the identity and country of residence of a relevant payee the period of two years beginning immediately after the end of the tax year in which transactions between the relevant payee and paying agent cease;

(*b*) in relation to the official evidence referred to in regulation 4(3) the period of two years beginning immediately after the end of the tax year in which transactions between the [entity][1] and paying agent cease; and (*c*) in relation to information concerning savings income the period of two years beginning immediately after the end of the tax year to which the notice referred to in regulation 15(1) relates.

(5) Paragraphs (3) and (4) are without prejudice to the following provisions—

[(i) regulations 8(5) and 14(6) of the Income Tax (Deposit-takers and Building Societies) (Interest Payments) Regulations 2008][2]

(ii), (iii) . . . [2]

(iv) regulation 9 of the Income Tax (Authorised Unit Trusts) (Interest Distributions) Regulations 2003 including that regulation as modified by regulation 28(8) of the Open-ended Investment Companies (Tax) Regulations 1997.

(6) Subject to paragraph (7), information obtained by [Revenue and Customs][1] under this Regulation—

(*a*) shall not be used for the purpose of ascertaining the tax liability (if any) of any person other than—

(i) a person beneficially entitled to a payment to whom the information obtained relates, and

(ii) the person by whom the payment was made or received; and

(*b*) shall otherwise be used only for the purposes of—

(i) these Regulations, unless the notice issued under regulation 15(1) is combined with a notice under section 17 or 18, or both of those sections, of the Taxes Management Act 1970, in which case only for the purposes of these Regulations and with whichever of those sections the notice was combined,

(ii) the provisions of [Chapter 2 of Part 15 of the Income Tax Act 2007][2] relating to the deduction of tax from payments by building societies and deposit-takers,

[(iii) the Income Tax (Deposit-takers and Building Societies) (Interest Payments) Regulations 2008, and][2]

(iv) . . . [2]

(v) the Income Tax (Authorised Unit Trusts) (Interest Distributions) Regulations 2003 including these Regulations as modified by the Open-ended Investment Companies (Tax) Regulations 1997.

(7) Paragraph (6) shall not be construed as preventing any disclosure of information under section 182(5) of the Finance Act 1989.

Amendments—[1] Words in paras (1), (2), (4)(b), (6) substituted by the Reporting of Savings Income Information (Amendment) Regulations, SI 2005/1539 regs 2, 16 with effect on a date to be notified in the London, Edinburgh and Belfast Gazettes (1 July 2005; see the London Gazette, 14 June 2005).

[2] In para (5), sub-para (i) substituted and sub-paras (ii), (iii) revoked, in para (6)(b), words in sub-para (ii) substituted, sub-para (iii) substituted and sub-para (iv) revoked, by the Income Tax (Deposit-takers and Building Societies) (Interest Payments) Regulations, SI 2008/2682 reg 20, Sch 1 with effect in relation to payments of interest made on or after 31 October 2008.

PART 5
TRANSITIONAL PROVISIONS

17 Transitional provisions—negotiable debt securities

(1) Until 31st December 2010 negotiable debt securities to which paragraph (2) applies shall not be considered to be money debts.

(2) This paragraph applies to negotiable debt securities—

(*a*) which were first issued before 1st March 2001; or

(*b*) for which the original prospectus was approved before that date by—

(i) the competent authority within the meaning of the Securities Directive; or

(ii) the responsible authorities in third countries,

provided that no further issues of such negotiable debt securities are made on or after 1st March 2002.

(3) Where a further issue is made on or after 1st March 2002 of negotiable debt securities described in paragraphs (2)(*a*) and (*b*) issued by a Government or a related entity acting as a public authority or whose role is recognised by an international treaty, as defined in the Schedule, the entire issue of such security, consisting of the original issue and any further issue, shall be considered a money debt.

(4) If a further issue is made on or after 1st March 2002 of a negotiable debt security described in paragraphs (2)(*a*) and (*b*) issued by a person not referred to in paragraph (3), such further issue shall be considered a money debt.

(5) Where an agent cannot ascertain whether paragraphs (2) to (4) apply the entire issue of the negotiable debt security shall be considered a money debt.

(6) A negotiable debt security is a security that can be transferred from one creditor to another without the approval of the debtor.

SCHEDULE

NEGOTIABLE DEBT SECURITIES: ENTITIES REFERRED TO IN REGULATION 17(3)

Regulation 17(3)

For the purposes of regulation 17(3), an entity is "a related entity acting as a public authority or whose role is recognised by an international treaty" if it is listed in Table 1 or Table 2 below or it is situate in a third country and meets the following criteria—

(*a*) the entity is clearly considered to be a public entity according to the national criteria;

(*b*) such public entity is a non-market producer which administers and finances a group of activities, principally providing non-market goods and services, intended for the benefit of the community and which are effectively controlled by general government;

(*c*) such public entity is a large and regular issuer of debt; and

(*d*) the State concerned is able to guarantee that such public entity will not exercise early redemption in the event of gross-up clauses.

Entities within the European Union

TABLE 1

Member State	*Entity*
Belgium	Vlaams Gewest (Flemish Region)
	Région wallonne (Walloon Region)
	Région bruxelloise/Brussels Gewest (Brussels Region)
	Communauté française (French Community)
	Vlaamse Gemeenschap (Flemish Community)
	Deutschsprachige Gemeinschaft (German-speaking Community)
[Bulgaria	Общините (municipalities) Социалноосгурителни Фондове (Social Security Funds)][2]
France	La Caisse d'amortissement de la dette sociale (CADES) (Social Debt Redemption Fund)
	L'Agence française de développement (AFD) (French Development Agency)
	Réseau Ferré de France (RFF) (French Rail Network)
	Caisse Nationale des Autoroutes (CNA) (National Motorways Fund)
	Assistance publique Hôpitaux de Paris (APHP) (Paris Hospitals Public Assistance)
	Charbonnages de France (CDF) (French Coal Board)
	Entreprise minière et chimique (EMC) (Mining and Chemicals Company)
Greece	Οργαυισμος Τηλεπικοινωνιων Ελλαδος
	National Telecommunications Organisation)
	Οργαυισμος Σιδηροδρομων Ελλαδος
	(National Railways Organisation)
	ΔημοσιαΕπιχειρηση Ηλεκτρισμου
	(Public Electricity Company)
Italy	Regions
	Provinces
	Miunicipalities
[Latvia	Pašvaldibas (Local governments)][1]
[Poland	Gminy (Communes)
	Powiaty (Provinces)
	Województwa (Districts)
	Zwiazki gmin (Associations of Communes)
	Zwiazki powiatów (Associations of Provinces)
	Zwiazki województw (Associations of Districts)
	Miasto Stoleczne Warszawa (Capital City of Warsaw)

Member State	*Entity*
	Agencja Restrukturyzacji I Modernizacji Rolnictwa (Agency for Reconstruction and Modernisation of Agriculture)
	Agencja Nieruchomosci Rolnych (Agricultural Property Agency)][1]
[Romania	autorităţile administraiei publice locale (local public administration authorities)][2]
Portugal	Região Autónoma de Madeira (Autonomous Region of Madeira)
	Região Autónoma dos Açores (Autonomous Region of Azores)
	Municipalities
[Slovakia	Mestá a Obce (Municipalities)
	Zeleznice Slovenskej republiky (Slovak Railway Company)
	Štátny Fond Cestného Hospodártsva (State Road Management Fund)
	Slovenské Elektrárne (Slovak Power Plants)
	Vodohospodárska výstavba (Water Economy Building Company)][1]
Spain	Xunta de Galicia (Regional Executive of [Galicia][1])
	Junta de Andalucía (Regional Executive of Andalusia)
	Junta de Extremadura (Regional Executive of Extremadura)
	Junta de Castilla-La Mancha (Regional Executive of Castilla-La Mancha)
	Junta de Castilla-León (Regional Executive of Castilla-León)
	Gobierno Foral de Navarra (Regional Government of Navarre)
	Govern de les Illes Balears (Government of the Balearic Islands)
	Generalitat de Catalunya (Autonomous Government of Catalonia)
	Generalitat de Valencia (Autonomous Government of Valencia)
	Diputación General de Aragón (Regional Council of Aragon)
	Gobierno de las Islas Canarias (Government of the Canary Islands)
	Gobierno de Murcia (Government of Murcia)
	Gobierno de Madrid (Government of Madrid)
	Gobierno de la Comunidad Autónoma del País Vasco/Euzkadi (Government of the Autonomous Community of the Basque Country)
	Diputación Foral de Guipúzcoa (Regional Council of Guipúzcoa)
	Diputación Foral de Vizcaya/Bizkaia (Regional Council of Vizcaya)
	Diputación Foral de Alava (Regional Council of Alava)
	Ayuntamiento de Madrid (City Council of Madrid)
	Ayuntamiento de Barcelona (City Council of Barcelona)
	Cabildo Insular de Gran Canaria (Island Council of Gran Canaria)
	Cabildo Insular de Tenerife (Island Council of Tenerife)
	Instituto de Crédito Oficial (Public Credit Institution)
	Instituto Catalán de Finanzas (Finance Institution of Catalonia)
	Instituto Valenciano de Finanzas (Finance Institution of Valencia

Amendments—[1] Entries inserted, and word in the entry for Spain substituted, by the Reporting of Savings Income Information (Amendment) Regulations, SI 2005/1539 regs 2, 17(a)–(c) with effect on a date to be notified in the London, Edinburgh and Belfast Gazettes (1 July 2005; see the London Gazette, 14 June 2005).

[2] Entries inserted by the Reporting of Savings Income Information (Amendment) Regulations, SI 2006/3286 reg 2 with effect from 1 January 2007.

TABLE 2

International entities

European Bank for Reconstruction and Development
European Investment Bank
Asian Development Bank

African Development Bank
World Bank/IBRD/IMF
International Finance Corporation
Inter-American Development Bank
Council of Europe Social Development Fund
Euratom
European Community
Corporación Andina de Fomento (CAF) (Andean Development Corporation)
Eurofima
European Coal and Steel Community
Nordic Investment Bank
Caribbean Development Bank

Note: The provisions of regulation 17 are without prejudice to any international obligations that member States [or territories with which arrangements have been made][1] may have entered into with respect to the international entities listed in Table 2.

Amendments—[1] Words in the Note inserted by the Reporting of Savings Income Information (Amendment) Regulations, SI 2005/1539 regs 2, 17(d) with effect on a date to be notified in the London, Edinburgh and Belfast Gazettes (1 July 2005; see the London Gazette, 14 June 2005).

2004/438

CAPITAL GAINS TAX (GILT-EDGED SECURITIES) ORDER 2004

Made by the Treasury under TCGA 1992 Sch 9 para 1

Made . . . . *23 February 2004*

1 This Order may be cited as the Capital Gains Tax (Gilt-edged Securities) Order 2004.

2 The following securities are hereby specified for the purposes of Schedule 9 to the Taxation of Chargeable Gains Act 1992—

4½% Treasury Stock 2007;
4% Treasury Stock 2009;
4¾% Treasury Stock 2015.

2004/439

URBAN REGENERATION COMPANIES (TAX) (DESIGNATION) ORDER 2004

Made by the Treasury under TA 1988 s 79B(5), and according to the criteria listed in s 79B(7)

Made . . . . *23 February 2004*
Coming into force . . . . *24 February 2004*

1 Citation, commencement and effect

(1) This Order may be cited as the Urban Regeneration Companies (Tax) (Designation) Order 2004 and shall come into force on 24th February 2004.
(2) Article 2 takes effect on 1st April 2003.
(3) Article 3 takes effect on 8th April 2003.
(4) Article 4 takes effect on 17th July 2003.
(5) Article 5 takes effect on 2nd December 2003.

2 Designation of urban regeneration companies taking effect on 1st April 2003

For the purposes of section 79B of the Income and Corporation Taxes Act 1988 the following companies limited by guarantee are designated as urban regeneration companies—

(*a*) Bradford City Centre Urban Regeneration Company Limited;
(*b*) Camborne Pool Redruth Urban Regeneration Company Limited;
(*c*) Corby Urban Regeneration Company Limited;
(*d*) Hull Urban Regeneration Company Limited;
(*e*) Leicester Regeneration Company Limited;
(*f*) Liverpool Vision;
(*g*) New East Manchester Limited;
(*h*) Newport Urban Regeneration Company Limited;
(*i*) Sheffield City Centre Urban Regeneration Company Limited;
(*j*) Sunderland ARC Limited;

(*k*) Swindon Urban Regeneration Company Limited; and
(*l*) Tees Valley Urban Regeneration Company Limited.

3 Designation of urban regeneration companies taking effect on 8th April 2003
For the purposes of section 79B of the Income and Corporation Taxes Act 1988 the following companies limited by guarantee are designated as urban regeneration companies—
(*a*) Derby Cityscape Limited;
(*b*) Sandwell Regeneration Company Limited; and
(*c*) Furness West Cumbria New Vision Urban Regeneration Company Limited.

4 Designation of urban regeneration company taking effect on 17th July 2003
For the purposes of section 79B of the Income and Corporation Taxes Act 1988 Ilex Urban Regeneration Company Limited, a company limited by guarantee, is designated as an urban regeneration company.

5 Designation of urban regeneration company taking effect on 2nd December 2003
For the purposes of section 79B of the Income and Corporation Taxes Act 1988 Walsall Regeneration Company Limited, a company limited by guarantee, is designated as an urban regeneration company.

Commentary—*Simon's Taxes* **B2.450.**

2004/674

RECOVERY OF DUTIES AND TAXES ETC DUE IN OTHER MEMBER STATES (CORRESPONDING UK CLAIMS, PROCEDURE AND SUPPLEMENTARY) REGULATIONS 2004

Made by the Treasury under FA 2002 Sch 39 para 3(1),(2),(3) and the Commissioners of Customs and Excise and the Commissioners of Inland Revenue, under FA 2002 Sch 39 paras 2(2) and 3(4)

Made . . . . *9 March 2004*
Laid before the House of Commons . . . . *10 March 2004*
Coming into force . . . . *1 April 2004*

Amendments—

These regulations revoked by the MARD Regulations, SI 2011/2931 reg 18, Schedule with effect from 1 January 2012.

2004/712

RESEARCH AND DEVELOPMENT (PRESCRIBED ACTIVITIES) REGULATIONS 2004

Made by the Treasury under TA 1988 s 837A(3)

Made . . . . *11 March 2004*
Laid before the House of Commons . . . . *11 March 2004*
Coming into force . . . . *1 April 2004*

1 Citation, commencement and effect
(1) These Regulations may be cited as the Research and Development (Prescribed Activities) Regulations 2004, come into force on 1st April 2004, and subject to paragraphs (2) to (9) have effect—
(*a*) for the purposes of corporation tax, for accounting periods ending on or after 1st April 2004, and
(*b*) for the purposes of income tax and capital gains tax, in relation to the year 2004–05 and subsequent years of assessment.
(2) These Regulations have effect in relation to shares issued on or after 6th April 2004 in relation to Chapter 3 of Part 7 of the Income and Corporation Taxes Act 1988 (enterprise investment scheme).
(3) Nothing in these Regulations affects the operation of the following provisions in relation to shares issued before 6th April 2004—
(*a*) Chapter 3 of Part 7 of the Income and Corporation Taxes Act 1988 (enterprise investment scheme);
(*b*) sections 573 and 574 of that Act (relief for losses on unlisted shares in trading companies); and

(*c*) Schedule 5B to the Taxation of Chargeable Gains Act 1992 (enterprise investment scheme: re-investment).

(4) These Regulations have effect for the purpose of determining whether shares or securities issued on or after 6th April 2004 are, for the purposes of section 842AA of the Income and Corporation Taxes Act 1988 (venture capital trusts), to be regarded as comprised in a company's qualifying holdings.

(5) Nothing in these Regulations affects the operation of Schedule 28B to the Income and Corporation Taxes Act 1988 as it has effect for the purpose of determining whether shares or securities issued before 6th April 2004 are, for the purposes of section 842AA of the Income and Corporation Taxes Act 1988, to be regarded as comprised in a company's qualifying holdings.

(6) These Regulations have effect in relation to shares issued on or after 6th April 2004 in relation to Schedule 15 to the Finance Act 2000 (corporate venturing scheme).

(7) Nothing in these Regulations affects the operation of the Schedule specified in paragraph (6) in relation to shares issued before 6th April 2004.

(8) In relation to—

(*a*) Chapter 9 of Part 7 of the Income Tax (Earnings and Pensions) Act 2003 (enterprise management incentives), and

(*b*) Part 4 of Schedule 7D to the Taxation of Chargeable Gains Act 1992 (enterprise management incentives), these Regulations have effect in relation to share options granted on or after 6th April 2004.

(9) Nothing in these Regulations affects the operation of the provisions specified in paragraph (8) in relation to share options granted before 6th April 2004.

2 Activities prescribed as research and development

For the purposes of section 837A of the Income and Corporation Taxes Act 1988—

(*a*) activities that fall to be treated as research and development in accordance with the "Guidelines on the Meaning of Research and Development for Tax Purposes" issued by the Secretary of State for Trade and Industry on 5 March 2004, are research and development; and

(*b*) activities that do not fall to be treated as such in accordance with those guidelines are not research and development.

3 Revocation of the Research and Development (Prescribed Activities) Regulations 2000

The Research and Development (Prescribed Activities) Regulations 2000 are revoked.

Commentary—*Simon's Taxes* **B3.702, B3.703; D1.401.**

2004/1450

CHILD TRUST FUNDS REGULATIONS 2004

Made by the Treasury, in exercise of the powers conferred upon them by the Child Trust Funds Act 2004 ss 3(1) to (5) and (7), 5(1), (4) and (5), 6, 7, 8(1), 9(2) and (10)(b), 11(1), 12(2), 13, 15, 16, 23(1) and 28(1) to (4)

Made . . . . *27 May 2004*

Laid before Parliament . . . . *27 May 2004*

Coming into force in accordance with . . . . *regulation 1*

PART 1

INTRODUCTORY

1 Citation and commencement

These Regulations may be cited as the Child Trust Funds Regulations 2004 and shall come into force for the purposes of—

(*a*) issuing vouchers (see regulation 3),

(*b*) completing account-opening formalities (see regulation 5),

(*c*) applications under regulation 13 to open an account with effect from the appointed day,

(*d*) applications under regulation 14 to be approved as an account provider to manage accounts from the appointed day,

(*e*) regulation 17, so far as it relates to applications referred to in paragraph (*d*), . . . [1]

(*f*) . . . [1]

on 1st January 2005, and for all other purposes on the appointed day.

Amendments—[1] Para (*f*) and preceding word "and" revoked by the Child Trust Funds (Amendment) Regulations, SI 2013/263 reg 2(1), (4)(a) with effect from 16 March 2013.

2 Interpretation

(1) In these Regulations—

(*a*) the following expressions have the meanings given in the Child Trust Funds Act 2004 ("the Act")—

"child"

"child trust fund"

"eligible child"

"Inland Revenue"

"Inland Revenue contributions" (see section 11(2) of the Act),

"parental responsibility" (see section 3(9) of the Act);

"relevant person" (see section 15(2) of the Act),

["relevant social security benefit" (see section 9(6) of the Act)][5]

"responsible person" . . . [13] (see section 3(8) of the Act),

["tax year" (see section 9(6) of the Act)][5]

["the income threshold" (see section 9(6) of the Act)][5]

["the relevant income" (see section 9(6) of the Act)][5]

"the person entitled to child benefit in respect of the child" (see section 2(1)(*a*), (4) and (6) of the Act);

(*b*) except where the context otherwise requires—

"account" means a scheme of investment which (except in regulation 22(1)) qualifies as a child trust fund, other than in the cases of—

(i) an account with a deposit-taker,

(ii) a share or deposit account with a building society, or

(iii) a deposit account with a person falling within [section 991(2) of the Income Tax Act 2007][10], or a [credit union][6];

an "account investment" is an investment under the account which is a qualifying investment for an account within the meaning of regulation 12;

an "account provider" is a person who fulfils the conditions of these Regulations and is approved by the Board for the purpose of these Regulations as an account provider;

["adoption order" has the meaning in section 46(1) of the Adoption and Children Act 2002 or section 28 of the Adoption and Children (Scotland) Act 2007 or of "Adoption Order" in Article 2(2) of the Adoption (Northern Ireland) Order 1987, as the case may be, and includes any corresponding order under the Adoption (Scotland) Act 1978, and any order of a court in the Isle of Man or any of the Channel Islands which, under section 108 of the Adoption and Children Act 2002, is declared to correspond to an adoption order made under that Act;][6]

"appointed day" means the day appointed under section 27 of the Act, for the purposes of sections 8 and 9 of the Act;

"assurance undertaking" [means a direct life insurance undertaking within the meaning of Article 2 of Directive 2009/138/EC of the European Parliament and of the Council of 25 November 2009 on the taking-up and pursuit of the business of Insurance and Reinsurance (Solvency II)][14];

["Bank of England base rate" means the rate announced from time to time by the Monetary Policy Committee of the Bank of England as the official dealing rate, being the rate at which the Bank is willing to enter into transactions for providing short-term liquidity in the money markets;][1]

["the Board" means the Commissioners for Her Majesty's Revenue and Customs;][3]

"building society" means a building society within the meaning of the Building Societies Act 1986, or the Irish Building Societies Act 1989;

["building society bonus", except in regulation 24(*a*)(i), excludes any bonus, distribution of funds or the conferring of rights in relation to shares—

(*a*) in connection with an amalgamation, transfer of engagements or transfer of business of a building society, and

(*b*) mentioned in section 96 or 100 of the Building Societies Act 1986,

and "payment under a building society bonus scheme" shall be construed accordingly;][4]

"company", except in regulation 12(4)(*a*), means any body corporate having a share capital other than—

(i) an open-ended investment company, within the meaning given by section 236 of the Financial Services and Markets Act 2000,[or][13]

(ii) a UCITS[.][13]

(iii) . . . [13]

(iv) . . . [13]

["credit union" means a society registered as a credit union under the Industrial and Provident Societies Act 1965 or the Credit Unions (Northern Ireland) Order 1985;][2]

"deposit-taker" has the meaning given by [section 853 (as extended under section 854) of ITA 2007[6]];

"the Director of Savings" has the same meaning as in the National Debt Act 1972;

"the Distance Marketing Directive" means Directive 2002/65/EC of the European Parliament and of the Council of 23rd September 2002, and includes any provisions by which an EEA State or the United Kingdom has transposed the Directive or has corresponding obligations in its domestic law, and "distance contract" has the meaning in that Directive;

"electronic communications" includes any communications by means of a telecommunication system (within the meaning in the Telecommunications Act 1984);

["EEA Agreement" means the Agreement on the European Economic Area signed at Oporto on 2nd May 1992, together with the Protocol adjusting that Agreement signed at Brussels on 17th March 1993, as modified or supplemented from time to time;]

"EEA State"[in relation to any time, means a state which at that time is a member State, or any other state which at that time is a party to the EEA Agreement;][9]

"European institution" means an EEA firm of the kind mentioned in [paragraph 5(*a*) to (*d*), (*f*) and (*h*)][10] of Schedule 3 to the Financial Services and Markets Act 2000 which is an authorised person for the purposes of that Act as a result of qualifying for authorisation under paragraph 12[(1) to (4) and (7)][1] of that Schedule;

"51 per cent. subsidiary" and "75 per cent. subsidiary" have the meanings given by section 838 of the Taxes Act;

["FISMA 2000" means the Financial Services and Markets Act 2000;][6]

"gains", except in regulations 22(1) to (3), 24(a)(ii), (iii) and (v), 37(5) and 38, means "chargeable gains" within the meaning in the 1992 Act;

"gilt-edged securities" has the meaning given by paragraphs 1 and 1A of Schedule 9 to the 1992 Act;

["guardian" means a guardian of a child within the meaning in section 5 of the Children Act 1989, section 7 of the Children (Scotland) Act 1995 or Article 2(2) of the Children (Northern Ireland) Order 1995, as the case may be;][6]

"incorporated friendly society" means a society incorporated under the Friendly Societies Act 1992;

. . .[11]

["investment trust" means an investment trust within the meaning of section 1158 of the Corporation Tax Act 2010;][15]

"investments under the account" has the same meaning as investments under a child trust fund in the Act; "investment trust" has the meaning given by section 842 of the Taxes Act, and references to the "eligible rental income" of an investment trust have the same meaning as in that section;

["ITA 2007" means the Income Tax Act 2007;][6]

["ITTOIA 2005" means the Income Tax (Trading and Other Income) Act 2005;][6]

"the Management Act" means the Taxes Management Act 1970;

"market value" shall be construed in accordance with section 272 of the 1992 Act;

[6]

"the 1992 Act" means the Taxation of Chargeable Gains Act 1992;

["non-UCITS retail scheme"—

(*a*) has the meaning in the . . . [6] Collective Investment Schemes Sourcebook (that is, a scheme to which, or to whose authorised fund manager and depositary, Sections 5.1, 5.4 and 5.6 of that Sourcebook apply),

(*b*) includes a "recognised scheme" by virtue of section . . .[8] 272 of the Financial Services and Markets Act 2000, which would fall within paragraph (*a*) of this definition if it were an authorised fund, and

(*c*) includes a sub-fund of an umbrella which the terms of the scheme identify as a sub-fund which would fall within paragraph (*a*) or (*b*) of this definition if it were itself an authorised fund or a recognised scheme.

In this definition, expressions defined in the Glossary forming part of the Financial Services Authority Handbook have those defined meanings;][3]

"notice", except in regulations 12(12) and 37(6)(*a*), means notice in writing;

["qualifying units in or shares of a non-UCITS retail scheme" means that—

(*a*) the instrument constituting the scheme secures that redemption of the units or shares in question shall take place no less frequently than bi-monthly (see Rule 6.2.16(6) of the . . . [6] Collective Investment Schemes Sourcebook omitting the words "Except where (7) applies, and", read with Rule 6.3.4(1), whether or not those Rules apply to the scheme), and

(*b*) a provision for suspension of dealings in exceptional conditions in accordance with Rule 7.2 of that Sourcebook (or any foreign procedure which is a direct foreign equivalent of that Rule) shall not be treated as a provision contrary to paragraph (*a*) of this definition;][3]

"recognised stock exchange" has the same meaning as in [section 1005 of ITA 2007;][8]

["registered contact" means the person who has the authority to manage the child trust fund by virtue of section 3(6) of the Act;][14]

"registered friendly society" has the meaning given by the Friendly Societies Act 1992 and includes any society that by virtue of section 96(2) of that Act is to be treated as a registered friendly society;

. . .[13]

["relevant authorised person" means a firm mentioned in section 697(2)(b) of ITTOIA 2005;][6]

. . .[6]

"security", means any loan stock or similar security of a company whether secured or unsecured;

["special guardian" has the meaning in section 14A of the Children Act 1989;][6]

"subscriptions" has the meaning in section 12(1) of the Act (but excluding Inland Revenue contributions and income or gains arising from investments under the account);

"tax" where neither income tax nor capital gains tax is specified means either of those taxes;

"the Taxes Act" means the Income and Corporation Taxes Act 1988;

"year", except in the expression "subscription year" in regulations 9, 21(5)(*b*) and 32(2)(*b*)(iv), means a year of assessment (within the meaning in section 832(1) of the Taxes Act, or section 288(1) of the 1992 Act, as the case may be);

(*c*) "authorised fund" means—

(i) an authorised unit trust, or

(ii) an open-ended investment company . . .[6] in the case of which an authorisation order made by the Financial Services Authority under regulation 14 of the Open-Ended Investment Companies Regulations 2001 is in force;

"authorised unit trust" means a unit trust scheme in the case of which an authorisation order made by the Financial Services Authority under section 243 of the Financial Services and Markets Act 2000 is in force;

"the Collective Investment Schemes Sourcebook" means the sourcebook of that name made by the Financial Services Authority under the Financial Services and Markets Act 2000;

"depositary interest" means the rights of the person mentioned in paragraph (ii), under a certificate or other record (whether or not in the form of a document) acknowledging—

(i) that a person holds relevant investments or evidence of the right to them; and

(ii) that another person is entitled to rights in or in relation to those or identical relevant investments, including the right to receive such investments, or evidence of the right to them or the proceeds from such investments, from the person mentioned in paragraph (*i*), where "relevant investments" means investments which are exclusively qualifying investments for an account falling within regulation 12(2)(*a*) to (*i*), and the rights mentioned in paragraph (ii) are exclusively rights in or in relation to relevant investments;

["insolvency event" means the procedures listed in the definition of "insolvency event" in regulation 19(15) of the Payment Services Regulations 2009;][6]

. . .[6]

"open-ended investment company" [means a company to which section 236 of FISMA 2000 applies][6], and "shares" in relation to an open-ended investment company, includes shares of any class and of any denomination of a given class and, in relation to a part of an umbrella company, means shares in the company which confer for the time being rights in that part;

["recognised UCITS" means—

(*a*) a collective investment scheme constituted in an EEA State, which is a "recognised scheme" under section 264 of FISMA 2000, and complies with the requirements to be a "UCITS scheme" for the purposes of the Collective Investment Schemes Sourcebook (see in particular COLL 1.2.2), or

(*b*) a part of a recognised UCITS mentioned in paragraph (*a*) of this definition, which would be a sub-fund of an umbrella scheme which is a recognised UCITS;][6]

. . .[6]

. . .[6]

. . .[6]

["UK UCITS" means—

(*a*) a collective investment scheme authorised under section 31(1)(a) of FISMA 2000, which complies with the requirements to be a "UCITS scheme" for the purposes of the Collective Investment Schemes Sourcebook (see in particular COLL 1.2.2), or

(*b*) a part of a UK UCITS mentioned in paragraph (*a*) of this definition which would be a sub-fund of an umbrella scheme which is a UK UCITS;][6]

"umbrella scheme" means an authorised fund which according to the terms of the scheme is an umbrella scheme belonging to the category under that name established by the Financial Services Authority, and

(i) in the case of an authorised fund which is an authorised unit trust, references to a part of an umbrella scheme shall be construed in accordance with subsection (8) of section 468 of the Taxes Act, [and paragraphs (6) and (7) of regulation 7 of the Authorised Investment Funds (Tax) Regulations 2006 shall apply for the purposes of these Regulations as they apply for the purposes of those Regulations][6], and

(ii) in the case of an authorised fund which is an open-ended investment company, references to a part of an umbrella scheme shall be construed in accordance with [subsection (4) of section 468A of the Taxes Act, and paragraphs (2) and (3) of regulation 7 of the Authorised Investment Funds (Tax) Regulations 2006 shall apply for the purposes of these Regulations as they apply for the purposes of those Regulations][6];

"units", in relation to an authorised unit trust, means the rights or interests (however described) of the unit holders in that unit trust and, in relation to a part of an umbrella scheme, means the rights or interests for the time being of the unit holders in that part;

[units in, or shares of, a UK UCITS or recognised UCITS" means the rights (however described) of the holders of the units or shares in that UK UCITS or recognised UCITS;][6]

. . .[6]

[(1A) In these Regulations—

(*a*)a "bulk transfer of accounts" occurs where two or more accounts are transferred, without a break in the management of the accounts, by an account provider ("the transferor") direct to another account provider ("the transferee")—

(i) pursuant to an agreement made between the transferor and the transferee where the transfers are not made pursuant to requests made by the person who is the registered contact in relation to the accounts transferred; or

(ii) pursuant to an insurance business transfer scheme or a banking business transfer scheme under Part 7 (Control of Business Transfers) of FISMA 2000;

(*b*) . . .[12]

(*c*) . . .[12]

(2) The table below indexes other definitions in these Regulations:

Term defined	*Regulation*
"the applicant"	5
"the commencement date"	7(8)
"description" of an account	4
"the disqualifying circumstances"	16
. . .[7]	. . .[7]
. . .[7]	. . .[7]
"initial contribution"	7(1)
"interim tax claim"	26(2)
"local authority"	[33A(6)][15]
"looked after child"	[33A(6)][15]
"management agreement"	5
"the named child"	5 and 8(1)
"qualifying circumstances"	14
"qualifying investments for an account"	12
. . .[13]	. . .[13]
. . .[7]	. . .[7]
"special contribution"	7(1)
"subscription year"	9(2)
"supplementary contribution"	7(5)
the "termination event"	12(12)
"the transfer instructions"	8(2)(*h*)
"the internal transfer instructions"	8(2)(*i*)

Amendments—[1] In para (1)(b), definition of "Bank of England base rate" inserted by the Child Trust Funds (Amendment) Regulations, SI 2004/2676 regs 2, 3 with effect from 6 April 2005 (by virtue of SI 2004/3369).

[2] In para (1)(b), definition of "credit union" inserted by the Child Trust Funds (Amendment No 2) Regulations, SI 2005/909 regs 2, 3 with effect from 6 April 2005.

[3] In para (1)(b), definition of "the Board" substituted; and definitions of "non-UCITS retail scheme" and "qualifying units in or shares of a non-UCITS retail scheme" inserted; by the Child Trust Funds (Amendment No 3) Regulations, SI 2005/3349 regs 2, 3 with effect from 27 December 2005.

[4] In para (1)(b), definition of "building society bonus" inserted by the Child Trust Funds (Amendment No 3) Regulations, SI 2006/3195 regs 2, 3 with effect from 1 January 2007.

5 In para (1)(*a*), definitions inserted by the Child Trust Funds (Amendment) Regulations, SI 2009/475 regs 2, 3 with effect where the child benefit commencement date for the child (first day for which child benefit was paid in respect of the child) is on or after 6 April 2008.

6 Amendments made by the Child Trust Funds (Amendment) Regulations, SI 2010/582 regs 2, 3 with effect from 6 April 2010.

7 In para (2), in the table, entries relating to "first return period", "fortnightly period" and "second return period" revoked by the Child Trust Funds (Amendment) Regulations, SI 2013/263 reg 2(1), (4)(*b*) with effect from 16 March 2013.

8 In para (1)(*b*), in definition of "non-UCITS retail scheme", para (*b*), words "270 or" revoked by the Alternative Investment Fund Managers Regulations, SI 2013/1773 reg 81, Sch 2 para 18 with effect from 22 July 2013.

9 In para (1)(*b*), definitions of "EEA Agreement" and "EEA State" substituted, in definition of "recognised stock exchange", words substituted, and para (1A) inserted by the Child Trust Funds (Amendment No 2) Regulations, SI 2013/1744 regs 2–4 with effect from 5 August 2013.

10 In para (1)(*b*), in definition of "account", words substituted, and in definition of "European institution", words substituted and words inserted, by the Child Trust Funds (Amendment) Regulations 2014, SI 2014/1450 regs 2, 3 with effect from 6 April 2014.

11 In para (1)(*b*), in definition of "company", in para (iii) words substituted, and in para (iv), words substituted, definition of "industrial and provident society" revoked, and definition of "registered society" inserted, by the Co-operative and Community Benefit Societies and Credit Unions Act 2010 (Consequential Amendments) Regulations, SI 2014/1815 reg 2, Sch para 13 with effect from 1 August 2014.

12 Para (1A)(*b*), (*c*) revoked by the Child Trust Funds (Amendment No 2) Regulations, SI 2015/876 regs 2, 3 with effect from 6 April 2015.

13 In para (1)(*a*), in definition of "responsible person", words ", in relation to a child under 16" revoked, in para (1)(*b*), in definition of "company", in sub-para (i), word inserted, at the end of sub-para (ii), semi-colon substituted for comma, and sub-paras (iii), (iv) revoked, definition of "registered contact" inserted, definition of "registered society" revoked, and in para (2), in table, entry for "registered contact" revoked by the Child Trust Funds (Amendment No 3) Regulations, SI 2015/1371 regs 2–4 with effect from 1 July 2015.

14 In para (1)(*b*), in definition of "assurance undertaking", words substituted for words "has the meaning in Article 2 of the Council Directive of 5th November 2002 concerning life assurance (2002/83/EC)" by the Solvency 2 Regulations, SI 2015/575 reg 60, Sch 2 para 18 with effect from 1 January 2016.

15 In para (1)(*b*), definition of "investment trust" substituted, and in para (2) ref substituted for ref "33(1)" in both places, by the Child Trust Funds (Amendment) Regulations, SI 2017/185 regs 2, 3 with effect from 6 April 2017. Definition previously read as follows—

""investment trust" refers to a company that is such a trust for the purposes of the Corporation Tax Acts, or would be such a trust but for section 1158(3) of the Corporation Tax Act 2010;".

Prospective amendments—In para (1)(*c*), in definition of "insolvency event", words "regulation 23(18) of the Payment Services Regulations 2017" to be substituted for words "regulation 19(15) of the Payment Services Regulations 2009" by the Payment Services Regulations, SI 2017/752 reg 156, Sch 8 para 9 with effect from 13 January 2018.

3 Vouchers

(1) The voucher to be issued under section 5(1) of the Act shall contain the following particulars—

(*a*) the full name of the child,

(*b*) his date of birth,

(*c*) his unique reference number,

(*d*) the [short expiry date][2] of the voucher, and

(*e*) the amount of the initial contribution (see regulation 7(1)), and a statement that the voucher cannot be exchanged for money.

(2) The voucher shall be sent to the person who is entitled to child benefit in respect of the child (or, in the case of a child who is an eligible child because of section 2(3) of the Act, to a responsible person in relation to the child) by post.

(3) The expiry date . . . [1] shall be whichever is the earlier of—

(*a*) the date 12 months from the date of issue of the voucher, or

(*b*) where the child is over 17 years of age, the date on which he will attain the age of 18 years.

[(4) But for references in these Regulations to the short expiry date of the voucher paragraph (3) applies with "60 days" instead of "12 months".][2]

Amendments—1 Words in para (3) revoked by the Child Trust Funds (Amendment) Regulations, SI 2006/199 regs 2, 3 with effect from 7 February 2006.

2 Words in para (1)(*d*) substituted, and para (4) inserted, by the Child Trust Funds (Amendment No 3) Regulations, SI 2011/2447 regs 2, 3 with effect in relation to vouchers issued on or after 1 January 2012.

4 Descriptions of accounts

(1) An account may be of either of the following descriptions—

Stakeholder account

Where the account meets the characteristics and conditions in the Schedule to these Regulations.

Non-stakeholder account

Where any of those characteristics or conditions is not met.

(2) Accounts opened by the Inland Revenue (see regulation 6) must be stakeholder accounts.

5 Opening of account by responsible person or the child

(1) For the purposes of these Regulations, subject to [paragraphs (1A) and (2)][1], an account is opened for a child ("the named child") with an account provider on the date the last of the following conditions is satisfied (in any order), where "the applicant" means—

(*a*) if the named child is 16 or over, the child; and

(*b*) in any other case, a responsible person in relation to the named child—

Condition 1

The applicant gives the voucher relating to the named child to the account provider [not later than 7 days after its [short expiry date][3] [or, where the account provider has chosen to open accounts without sight of the relevant voucher, the applicant gives the following information to the account provider:

(*a*) the [short expiry date][3] of the voucher,

(*b*) the amount of the initial contribution as specified on the voucher, and

(*c*) where the date of birth shown on the voucher differs from the actual date of birth of the child (see regulation 13(5)(*c*)), the date of birth shown on the voucher][2]][1].

Condition 2

The applicant enters into an agreement with the account provider (the "management agreement") for the management of the account (see regulation 8(1) and (2)), which includes the application and declaration required by regulation 13.

Condition 3

Where that application is not in writing the applicant has agreed, or is treated as having agreed, the contents of the copy of the declaration required by regulation 13(3).

Condition 4

(*a*) In any case where the management agreement is a distance contract, the agreement must be an initial service agreement for the purposes of the Distance Marketing Directive, and contain the instructions required by regulation 8(1)(*f*), and

(*b*) in every case where there is any right to cancel (or automatic cancellation of) the management agreement, the period during which it may be exercised or occur has expired without that right being exercised or cancellation occurring.

[(1A) The application to open the account must be made, and Condition 2 satisfied, not later than the [short expiry date][3] of the voucher.][1]

(2) An account must satisfy the requirements that—

(*a*) no subscription to the account is accepted by the account provider until the account has been opened in accordance with paragraph (1); and

(*b*) where the account is so opened before the appointed day, it shall not be treated as open for the purpose of accepting subscriptions until the appointed day.

Amendments—[1] Words in para (1) substituted and inserted, and para (1A) inserted, by the Child Trust Funds (Amendment) Regulations, SI 2006/199 regs 2, 4 with effect from 7 February 2006.

[2] Words in para (1), condition 1, inserted by the Child Trust Funds (Amendment No 2) Regulations, SI 2009/694 regs 2, 3 with effect in relation to—

(a) applications to open an account made before 6 April 2009 where the account has not been opened before that date; and

(b) applications to open an account made on or after 6 April 2009 (SI 2009/694 reg 1(2)).

[3] In Condition 1 in para (1) and in para (1A), words substituted by the Child Trust Funds (Amendment No 3) Regulations, SI 2011/2447 regs 2, 4 with effect in relation to vouchers issued on or after 1 January 2012.

6 Opening of account by Inland Revenue—(Revenue allocated accounts)

(1) The Board shall apply to open an account for a child to whom section 6 of the Act applies, by forwarding to an account provider the particulars which would be required for a voucher (see regulation 3), but omitting paragraph (1)(*d*) of that regulation.

(2) The account provider shall immediately open a stakeholder account in the name of the child, which shall have the same effect as if a responsible person for the child (or the child if aged 16 or over) had entered into the account provider's standard management agreement for the stakeholder account in question, including the terms mentioned in Condition 2 of regulation 5(1) (but treating the reference to the application and declaration required by regulation 13 as a reference to the authorisation required by regulation 13(4)) and regulation 8(1)(*f*).

(3) The Inland Revenue shall maintain (and update from time to time) a list of account providers who have agreed to accept Revenue allocated accounts under this regulation, in the order of the date of their agreement, and the account provider shall be selected in rotation from the current list.

(4) Where the account provider offers two or more types of stakeholder account[—

(*a*) the account provider shall select the type or types to be used for the purposes of this regulation (subject to sub-paragraph (*b*)),

(*b*) any type selected must be offered to the general public at the time of opening a Revenue allocated account of that type, and

(*c*) if more than one type has been selected, the account to be opened shall be chosen by the account provider in rotation between the selected types of accounts.][2]

[(5) The Inland Revenue shall write to the person who is entitled to child benefit in respect of the child (or, in the case of a child who is an eligible child because of section 2(3) of the Act, to a responsible person in relation to the child) to inform them of the opening of the account and particulars of it.][1]

Amendments—[1] Para (5) inserted by the Child Trust Funds (Amendment) Regulations, SI 2004/2676 regs 2, 4 with effect from 6 April 2005 (by virtue of SI 2004/3369).

[2] Words in para (4) substituted by the Child Trust Funds (Amendment No 3) Regulations, SI 2005/3349 regs 2, 4 with effect from 27 December 2005.

7 Government contributions

(1) The amounts of the contribution for the purposes of section 8(1) of the Act are set out in paragraphs (2) to [(4B)][4], (the amounts set out in paragraphs [(2), (4)(*a*) and (4A)][4] to be known as the "initial contribution", and the amounts set out in paragraphs [(3), (4)(b) and (4B)][4] as the "special contribution").

(2) Where the child is an eligible child on the appointed day by virtue of section 2(1)(*a*) of the Act (by reason of a child benefit award), and—

(i) was born after 31st August 2002 but before 6th April 2003, the amount is £277,
(ii) was born between 6th April 2003 and 5th April 2004, the amount is £268, and
(iii) was born between 6th April 2004 and the day preceding the appointed day, the amount is £256.

(3) [Subject to paragraphs (4A) and (4B), where][4] the child is an eligible child on the appointed day by virtue of section 2(1)(*b*) of the Act (by reason of being a child in the care of a local authority at that date) and—

(i) was born after 31st August 2002 but before 6th April 2003, the amount is £554,
(ii) was born between 6th April 2003 and 5th April 2004, the amount is £536, and
(iii) was born between 6th April 2004 and the day preceding the appointed day, the amount is £512.

(4) Where the child [becomes an eligible child][1] on or after the appointed day and—

(*a*) is first an eligible child by virtue of section 2(1)(*a*) of the Act, the amount is £250, and
(*b*) is first an eligible child by virtue of section 2(1)(*b*) of the Act, the amount is £500.

[(4A) Where a child—

(*a*) is first an eligible child by virtue of section 2(1)(a) of the Act, and
(*b*) the commencement date for the child (see paragraph (8)) is after the relevant 2010 date (see paragraph (10E)),

the amount is £50.

(4B) Where a child—

(*a*) is first an eligible child by virtue of section 2(1)(*b*) of the Act, and
(*b*) either—
(i) is born on or after the relevant 2010 date, or
(ii) is first in the United Kingdom (other than temporarily) on or after the relevant 2010 date, or
(iii) becomes an eligible child on or after 3 months (less one day) after the relevant 2010 date,

the amount is £100.][4]

(5) The amounts of the supplementary contribution for the purposes of section 9(2) of the Act (to be known as the "supplementary contribution") are set out in paragraphs (6) and (7).

(6) Where the child is an eligible child on the appointed day (and is a child to whom section 9 of the Act applies), the amount—

(*a*) if the commencement date was after 31st August 2002 but before 6th April 2003, is £266,
(*b*) if the commencement date was between 6th April 2003 and 5th April 2004, is £258,
(*c*) if the commencement date was between 6th April 2004 and the appointed day, is £250.

(7) [Subject to paragraph (7A), where][4] the child becomes an eligible child after the appointed day (and is a child to whom section 9 of the Act applies), the amount is £250.

[(7A) Where the child is one to whom section 9 of the Act applies, and the commencement date for the child is after the relevant 2010 date, the amount is £50.][4]

(8) The "commencement date", in relation to a child, means the first day for which child benefit was paid (under a decision mentioned in section 2(6) of the Act) in respect of the child, except that—

(*a*) where entitlement to child benefit is wholly excluded by a directly applicable Community provision, it means the date on which that exclusion took effect, . . .
(*b*) . . . [4]

[(9) The Inland Revenue shall, following final determination of entitlement to child tax credit, write to the person who is entitled to child benefit in respect of the child (or, in the case of a child who is an eligible child because of section 2(3) of the Act, to a responsible person in relation to the child) to inform them that the supplementary contribution is being paid into the child's account.][1]

[(10) A further contribution under section 10 of the Act of £50 is due for any child where—

(*a*) the commencement date (for child benefit: see paragraph (8)) in relation to that child is after 5th April 2005, and
(*b*) income support or income-based jobseeker's allowance was paid for that commencement date to a person whose applicable amount included an amount in respect of the child.][2]

[(10A) A further contribution under section 10 of the Act of £50 is due for any child if—

(*a*) an account is held by the child,

(*b*) the child was first an eligible child by virtue of section 2(1)(*a*) of the Act,
(*c*) section 9 of the Act does not apply to the child,
(*d*) a contribution is not, and has not been, due for the child under paragraph (10),
(*e*) the child is an eligible child on the day identified under the provisions of paragraph (10B) or (10C) as the case may be, and
(*f*) the condition in paragraph (10B) or (10C) is satisfied in relation to the child.

(10B) The condition in this paragraph is that it has been determined in accordance with the provision made by and by virtue of sections 18 to 21 of the Tax Credits Act 2002—
(*a*) that a person was, or persons were, entitled to child tax credit in respect of the child for any day falling—
(i) after the commencement date, but
(ii) not later than three months immediately preceding the expiry date of the voucher for the child (see regulation 3), and
(*b*) that either the relevant income of the person or persons for the tax year in which that day fell does not exceed the income threshold or the person, or either of those persons, was entitled to a relevant social security benefit for that day,

and that determination has not been overturned.

(10C) The condition in this paragraph is that income support, or income-based jobseeker's allowance, was paid for any day falling—
(*a*) after the commencement date, but
(*b*) not later than one month immediately preceding the expiry date of the voucher for the child (see regulation 3),

to a person whose applicable amount included an amount in respect of the child.][3]

[(10D) Her Majesty's Revenue and Customs must inform the account provider holding the child's account where an amount is payable to the account under paragraph (10) or (10A).

(10E) In this regulation, "the relevant 2010 date" means—
(*a*) 2nd August 2010; or
(*b*) if later, the day on which regulation 3 of the Child Trust Funds (Amendment No 3) Regulations 2010 came into force.][4]

[(11) On receipt of the further contribution [mentioned in paragraph (10) or (10A)][3] from the Inland Revenue the account provider must credit the account held by the child with the amount of the payment.][2]

Amendments—[1] Words in para (4) substituted, and para (9) inserted, by the Child Trust Funds (Amendment) Regulations, SI 2004/2676 regs 2, 5 with effect from 6 April 2005 (by virtue of SI 2004/3369).

[2] Paras (10), (11) inserted by the Child Trust Funds (Amendment) Regulations, SI 2005/383 regs 2, 3 with effect from 6 April 2005.

[3] Paras (10A)–(10C), and words in para (11), inserted, by the Child Trust Funds (Amendment) Regulations, SI 2009/475 regs 2, 4 with effect where the child benefit commencement date for the child (first day for which child benefit was paid in respect of the child) is on or after 6 April 2008.

[4] The following amendments made by the Child Trust Funds (Amendment No 3) Regulations, SI 2010/1894 regs 2, 3 with effect from 2 August 2010—
- In para (1), "(4B)" substituted for "(4)", "(2), (4)(*a*) and (4A)" substituted for "(2) and (4)(*a*)", and "(3), (4)(*b*) and (4B)" substituted for "(3) and (4)(*b*)".
- In paras (4), (7), words substituted.
- Paras (4A), (4B), (7A), (10D), (10E) inserted.
- In para (8) sub-para (*b*) and preceding word "and" revoked.
- In paras (10), (10A)(4) figure substituted. Note that this amendment has effect where the commencement date for the child (within the meaning of para (8) above, as amended by SI 2010/1894 reg 3(7)) is after 2 August 2010 (see SI 2010/1894 reg 1(4)).

[7A Age 7 payments

. . .

Amendments—This regulation revoked by the Child Trust Funds (Amendment No 3) Regulations, SI 2010/1894 regs 2, 4 with effect from 1 August 2010.

7B [Yearly disability payments

(1) A further contribution under section 10 of the Act is due for any eligible child who is entitled in [the year 2009/10 or 2010/11][2] to a disability living allowance, in accordance with paragraphs (2) to (4).

(2) Where it has been determined that the child is entitled to the care component of a disability living allowance at the highest weekly rate (see section 72(4)(*a*) of either the Social Security Contributions and Benefits Act 1992 or the Social Security Contributions and Benefits (Northern Ireland) Act 1992), at any time in the year (whether it is paid or not), the contribution payable for the year shall be £200.

(3) In any other case where it has been determined that the child is entitled to a disability living allowance at any time in the year (whether it is paid or not), the contribution payable for the year shall be £100.

(4) This regulation shall apply until 5th April 2018.[2]

(5) Her Majesty's Revenue and Customs must inform the account provider holding the child's account where an amount is payable to that account under this regulation.
(6) On receipt of each further contribution from Her Majesty's Revenue and Customs, the account provider must credit the child's account with the amount of the payment.][1]

Amendments—[1] Reg 7B inserted by the Child Trust Funds (Amendment No 2) Regulations, SI 2010/836 regs 2, 3 with effect where a child falls within the terms of this regulation for a year of assessment commencing on or after 6 April 2009.
[2] In para (1), words substituted, and para (4) revoked, by the Child Trust Funds (Amendment No 3) Regulations, SI 2010/1894 regs 2, 5 with effect from 1 August 2010.

PART 2
OTHER REQUIREMENTS TO BE SATISFIED IN RELATION TO ACCOUNTS

8 General requirements for accounts

(1) An account must satisfy the requirements that—
- (*a*) it is the account for a single child ("the named child");
- (*b*) the named child is or has been an eligible child;
- (*c*) no child may hold more than one account;
- (*d*) . . . [3]
- (*e*) the account must at all times be managed in accordance with these Regulations by an account provider and, subject to regulation 6(2), under terms agreed and recorded in a management agreement made between the account provider and the registered contact (on behalf of the named child where appropriate); and
- (*f*) the management agreement must include instructions to the provider as to the manner in which Inland Revenue contributions and any subscriptions made are to be invested under the account.

(2) Apart from other requirements of these Regulations the terms so agreed shall include the conditions that—
- (*a*) the account investments shall be in the beneficial ownership of the named child;
- (*b*) the title to all account investments, except those falling within regulation 12(2)(*k*), (*l*) or (*m*) , shall be vested in the account provider or his nominee, subject to sub-paragraph (*f*);
- (*c*) where a share certificate or other document evidencing title to an account investment is issued, it shall be held by the account provider or as he may direct, subject to sub-paragraph (*f*);
- (*d*) in relation to qualifying investments falling within regulation 12(2)(*a*), (*b*) and (*f*) to (*j*), the account provider shall, if the registered contact so elects (and subject to any charge for the arrangement), arrange for the registered contact to receive a copy of the annual report and accounts issued to investors by every company, unit trust, open-ended investment company or other entity in which account investments are held;
- (*e*) in relation to qualifying investments falling within regulation 12(2)(*a*), (*b*) and (*f*) to (*j*), the account provider shall, if the registered contact so elects (subject to any charge for the arrangement, and to any provisions made under any enactment), be under an obligation to arrange for the registered contact to be able—
  - (i) to attend any meetings of investors in companies, unit trusts, open-ended investment companies and other entities in which account investments are held,
  - (ii) to vote, and
  - (iii) to receive, in addition to the documents referred to in sub-paragraph (*d*), any other information issued to investors in such companies, unit trusts, open-ended investment companies and other entities;
- (*f*) if and so long as a person falling within regulation 14(2)(*d*)(iv) acts as account provider of an account, and the account investments include a policy of life insurance—
  - (i) the title to all such policies shall be vested in the registered contact, and
  - (ii) where a policy document or other document evidencing title to such policies of life insurance is issued, it shall be held by the registered contact;
- (*g*) the account provider shall satisfy himself that any person to whom he delegates any of his functions or responsibilities under the management agreement is competent to carry out those functions or responsibilities;
- (*h*) on the instructions of the registered contact ("the transfer instructions") and within such time as is stipulated by the registered contact in the transfer instructions, the whole of an account, with all rights and obligations of the parties to it, shall be transferred free of expense (except any incidental expenses) to another account provider subject to and in accordance with regulation 21;
- [(*ha*) where the account is or has been transferred to the account provider by a transfer under regulation 21, that no charges or expenses are due in respect of that transfer, except in accordance with sub-paragraph (*h*);][1]
- [(*hb*) any transfer under regulation 20A shall be free of expense (except any incidental expenses);][2]

(*i*) where the account provider offers accounts of another description or type, on the instructions of the registered contact ("the internal transfer instructions") and within such time as is stipulated by the registered contact in the internal transfer instructions, the account shall become (free of expense, except any incidental expenses) an account of that other description or type (any necessary change in the investments being made accordingly); and

(*j*) the account provider shall notify the registered contact if by reason of any failure to satisfy the provisions of these Regulations an account is or will become no longer exempt from tax by virtue of regulation 24.

(3) Where the transfer instructions or internal transfer instructions, or any new management agreement entered into by the registered contact with the account provider (or a new account provider) under regulation 8(1)(*e*), is a distance contract, the transfer or internal transfer shall only take effect once those contracts satisfy Condition 4 in regulation 5(1).

(4) The time stipulated in transfer instructions or internal transfer instructions shall be subject to any reasonable business period (not exceeding 30 days) of the account provider required for the practical implementation of the instructions.

(5) In this regulation, "incidental expenses" means stamp duty and other dealing costs of disposing of or acquiring investments.

Amendments—[1] Para (2)(*ha*) inserted by the Child Trust Funds (Amendment) Regulations, SI 2004/2676 regs 2, 6 with effect from 6 April 2005 (by virtue of SI 2004/3369).

[2] Para (2)(*hb*) inserted by the Child Trust Funds (Amendment No 2) Regulations, SI 2015/876 regs 2, 4 with effect from 6 April 2015.

[3] Para (1)(*d*) revoked by the Child Trust Funds (Amendment No 3) Regulations, SI 2015/1371 regs 2, 5 with effect from 1 July 2015.

9 Annual limit on subscriptions

(1) Any person (including the child) may make subscriptions to a child's account, subject to paragraphs (2) and (3).

(2) Subscriptions to an account made during any subscription year, that is—

(*a*) the period beginning with the day on which the account is opened (or if opened before the appointed day, opened for the purpose of accepting subscriptions under regulation 5(2)(*b*)), and ending immediately before the child's next birthday, and

(*b*) any succeeding period of twelve months, shall not in aggregate exceed the sum of [£4,128][1].

(3) Where the aggregate of subscriptions in any year falls short of [£4,128][1] or is nil, there shall be no addition to the amount for any succeeding year.

Amendments—[1] In paras (2), (4), figure substituted by the Child Trust Funds Regulations, SI 2017/185 regs 2, 3 with effect from 6 April 2017. Figure was previously £4,080.

10 Statements for an account

[(1) The account provider must produce a statement for the account—

(*a*) subject to paragraphs (6) and (7), annually ("an annual statement"), and

(*b*) where an account is transferred . . . [3] under regulation [20A or][3] 21, as at the transfer date ("a transfer statement").

(2) References in paragraphs (2A)(*b*), (3), (4), (5), (6) and (8) to a statement (without more) shall be construed as references to any statement required to be produced in accordance with this regulation.

(2A) The account provider must produce an annual statement at a date (a "relevant date") not later than 12 months from the latest of—

(*a*) the date of the opening of the account;

(*b*) the date at which the most recent statement was produced; and

(*c*) the last date at which, but for paragraph (6), a previous annual statement would have had to have been produced.][2]

(3) [A statement required to be produced in accordance with this regulation][2] shall be sent—

(*a*) where the named child is the registered contact, to the child,

(*b*) where a responsible person is the registered contact, to the named child care of the registered contact,

[(*c*) where a person has been appointed by the Treasury or the Secretary of State by virtue of section 3(10) of the Act, to that person on behalf of the child, and][4]

(*d*) in any other case, to the named child, within 30 days of the [date specified in paragraph (3A)][2].

[(3A) The date specified in this paragraph is—

(*a*) in relation to an annual statement, the relevant date;

(*b*) in relation to a transfer statement, the transfer date; or

(*c*) where paragraph (7) applies, the later of the relevant date in relation to the annual statement requested and the date that the request is received by the account provider.][2]

(4) Statements shall include the following information—

(*a*) the full name of the child;

(*b*) his address;

(*c*) his date of birth;

(*d*) his unique reference number;
(*e*) the description of the account (see regulation 4);
(*f*) the name of the registered contact (if any);
(*g*) the [relevant date][2];
[(*h*) the total market value of the investments under the account at the date at which the most recent statement was produced (if any);][2]
(*i*) the amount of any Government contributions [(see regulation 7) received by the account provider][1], during the period between—
[(i) the date at which the most recent statement was produced, or the opening of the account (whichever is the later), and][2]
(ii) the [relevant date][2];
(*j*) the aggregate amount of subscriptions (if any) received during the period in sub-paragraph (*i*);
(*k*) the total amount of deductions (including management charges) made during the period in sub-paragraph (*i*);
(*l*) the total market value of the investments under the account at the [relevant date][2];
(*m*) the number or amount, description and market value of each of the investments under the account at the [relevant date][2];
(*n*) the basis used in calculating the market value of each investment under the account (together with a statement of any change from a basis used in the previous statement); and
(*o*) the exchange rate used where any investment is, or is denominated in, a currency other than sterling.

[(5) As an alternative to the information in paragraph (4)(*k*), the statement may include, in relation to any management charges or other incidental expenses deducted from the account during the period in paragraph (4)(*i*)—
(*a*) the rate, expressed as an annual percentage rate, at which, and the period in relation to which, such deductions were made, or
(*b*) where such deductions were made in relation to different periods at different rates—
(i) each rate, expressed as an annual percentage rate, at which those deductions were made; and
(ii) the period in relation to which they were made at that rate.][1]

[(6) Where, in relation to an annual statement, at a relevant date—
(*a*) the aggregate market value of the account investments held under the account is less than £300, or
(*b*) no subscriptions under regulation 9 have been made to the account during the relevant period,
then, subject to paragraph (7), the account provider need only produce the annual statement if it would be the first statement to be produced following the child's fourth, tenth or fifteenth birthday.

(7) Paragraph (6) shall not apply where any potential recipient of an annual statement (see paragraph (3)) requests such a statement.

(8) "The relevant period" means the period—
(*a*) beginning on the latest of—
(i) the date of the opening of the account;
(ii) the date at which the most recent statement was produced; and
(iii) the last date as at which, but for paragraph (6), an annual statement would have had to have been produced; and
(*b*) ending on the relevant date.][2]

Amendments—[1] Words in para (4)(i) substituted, and para (5) inserted, by the Child Trust Funds (Amendment) Regulations, SI 2004/2676 regs 2, 7 with effect from 6 April 2005 (by virtue of SI 2004/3369).

[2] Paras (1), (2), (2A) substituted for previous paras (1), (2), in paras (3), (4)(*g*), (*i*)(ii), (*l*), (*m*), words substituted, para (3A) inserted, para (4)(*h*), (*i*)(i) substituted, and paras (6), (7), (8) inserted, by the Child Trust Funds (Amendment No 2) Regulations, SI 2011/992 reg 2 with effect from 20 April 2011.

[3] In para (1)(*b*), words revoked and inserted by the Child Trust Funds (Amendment No 2) Regulations, SI 2015/876 regs 2, 5 with effect from 6 April 2015.

[4] Para (3)(*c*) substituted by the Child Trust Funds (Amendment No 2) Regulations, SI 2017/748 regs 2, 3 with effect from 1 October 2017. Para (3)(*c*) previously read as follows—

"(*c*) where the Official Solicitor or Accountant of Court has been appointed under section 3(10) of the Act, to the Official Solicitor or Accountant of Court, on behalf of the child, and".

11 General investment rules

(1) All transactions by way of purchase by an account provider of investments under an account shall be made—
(*a*) in the case of an authorised fund which is a dual priced unit trust, at the [maximum sale price of a unit of the relevant class at the relevant valuation point][3] within the meaning of, and complying with the requirements of, [rules 6.3.5 and 6.3.5B][3] of the Collective Investment Schemes Sourcebook;

(*b*) in the case of an authorised fund which is a single priced unit trust or an open-ended investment company, at the price of a unit [of the relevant class at the relevant valuation point][3] within the meaning of, and complying with the requirements of, [rules 6.3.5 and 6.3.5A][3] of the Collective Investment Schemes Sourcebook; and

(*c*) in the case of all other account investments, at the price for which those investments might reasonably be expected to be purchased in the open market.

(2) In paragraph (1)—

"a dual priced unit trust" means an authorised unit trust in respect of which the manager gives different prices for buying and selling units at the same time;

"a single priced unit trust" means an authorised unit trust in respect of which the manager gives the same price for buying and selling units at the same time.

(3) All other transactions by way of sale or otherwise by an account provider in investments under an account shall be made at the price for which those investments might reasonably be expected to be sold or otherwise transacted, as the case may be, in the open market.

(4) Investments, or rights in respect of investments, may not at any time—

(*a*) be purchased or made otherwise than out of cash which an account provider holds under an account at that time; or

(*b*) be purchased from—

(i) the named child, or

(ii) the spouse [or civil partner][2] of the named child, so as to become account investments under the account.

(5) Subject to paragraph (6), contributions, subscriptions and any other cash held by an account provider under an account shall be held only in sterling and be deposited in an account with a deposit-taker [(including for this purpose a credit union)][1], or a deposit account or a share account with a building society, which is designated as a CTF account for the purposes of these Regulations only.

(6) An account provider who is a European institution, a relevant authorised person or an assurance undertaking may hold an account investor's cash subscription and other cash held under an account in the currency of the EEA State in which he has his principal place of business and may deposit such cash in an account, which is designated as mentioned in paragraph (5), with any person authorised under the law of that State to accept deposits.

Amendments—[1] Words in para (5) inserted by the Child Trust Funds (Amendment No 2) Regulations, SI 2005/909 regs 2, 4 with effect from 6 April 2005.

[2] Words in para (4)(b)(ii) inserted by the Civil Partnership Act 2004 (Tax Credits, etc) (Consequential Amendments) Order, SI 2005/2919 art 15 with effect from 5 December 2005.

[3] Amendments made by the Child Trust Funds (Amendment) Regulations, SI 2010/582 regs 2, 4 with effect from 6 April 2010.

12 Qualifying investments for an account

(1) This regulation specifies the kind of investments ("qualifying investments for an account") which may be purchased, made or held under an account.

(2) Qualifying investments for an account to which paragraph (1) refers are—

(*a*) shares, not being shares in an investment trust, issued by a company wherever incorporated and [either officially listed on a recognised stock exchange or, in the European Economic Area, admitted to trading on a recognised stock exchange (see paragraph (3))][4];

(*b*) securities—

(i) issued by a company wherever incorporated, [and][2]

(ii) which satisfy at least one of the conditions specified in paragraph (5) . . . [2]

(iii) in the case of securities of an investment trust, purchased or acquired by the account provider in circumstances where the investment trust satisfies the condition specified in paragraph (6);

(*c*) gilt-edged securities;

(*d*) any securities issued by or on behalf of a government of any EEA State;

(*e*) any securities which, in relation to a security mentioned in sub-paragraph (*d*), would be a strip of that security if "strip" had the same meaning as in section 47 of the Finance Act 1942, with the omission of the words "issued under the National Loans Act 1968";

(*f*) shares in an investment trust . . . [6] . . . [2];

(*g*) . . . [2]

(*h*) . . . [2]

(*i*) [units in, or shares of, a UK UCITS or recognised UCITS;][2]

(*j*) a depositary interest;

(*k*) cash deposited in a deposit account with a building society, or a person falling within [section 991 of ITA 2007 (including for this purpose a credit union)][2], subject to paragraph (8);

(*l*) cash deposited in a share account with a building society, subject to paragraph (8);

(*m*) policies of life insurance which satisfy the conditions specified in paragraphs (9) and (10);

(*n*) any securities issued under the National Loans Act 1968—

(i) for the purpose of or in connection with raising money under the auspices of the Director of Savings within the meaning of section 11(1)(*a*) of the National Debt Act 1972, and

(ii) other than national savings certificates, premium savings bonds, national savings stamps and national savings gift tokens,

which, according to the terms and conditions subject to which they are issued and purchased, are expressly permitted to be held under an account.

[(*o*) arrangements falling within section 47 of the Finance Act 2005 (alternative finance arrangements) under which the person referred to in that section as Y is a financial institution;][2]

[(*p*) arrangements falling within section 49 of that Act;][2]

[(*q*) qualifying units in or shares of a non-UCITS retail scheme[; and][5]][2]

[(*r*) core capital deferred shares within the meaning of regulation 2 of the Building Societies (Core Capital Deferred Shares) Regulations 2013, provided that such shares are listed on the official list of a recognised stock exchange.][5]

(3) [An investment in shares fulfils the conditions as to official listing and admission to trading in paragraph (2)(*a*),][6] if—

(*a*) in pursuance of a public offer, the account provider applies for the allotment or allocation to him of shares in a company . . . [6] which are due to be admitted to such listing [or admitted to such trading][4] within 30 days of the allocation or allotment, and which, when admitted to such listing [or trading][4], would be qualifying investments for an account, and

(*b*) the shares are not allotted or allocated to the account provider in the circumstances specified in paragraph (4).

(4) The circumstances specified in this paragraph are where—

(*a*) the allotment or allocation of the shares was connected with the allotment or allocation of—

(i) shares in the company or investment trust of a different class, or

(ii) rights to shares in the company or investment trust of a different class, or

(iii) shares or rights to shares in another company or investment trust, or

(iv) units in or shares in, or rights to units in or shares in, an authorised fund or a part of an umbrella scheme, or

(v) securities or rights to securities of the company or investment trust, or of another company or investment trust, to the account provider, the registered contact or any other person; and

(*b*) the terms on which the first-mentioned shares in this paragraph were offered were significantly more favourable to the account provider or the named child than they would have been if their allotment or allocation had not been connected as described in sub-paragraph (*a*).

(5) The conditions specified in this paragraph are—

(*a*) that the shares in the company issuing the securities are listed on the official list of a recognised stock exchange;

(*b*) that the securities are so listed;

(*c*) that the company issuing the securities is a 75 per cent. subsidiary of a company whose shares are so listed[;][8]

[(*d*) that the shares in the company issuing the securities are admitted to trading on a recognised stock exchange in the European Economic Area;

(*e*) that the securities are so admitted to trading;

(*f*) that the company issuing the securities is a 75 per cent. subsidiary of a company whose shares are so admitted to trading.][8]

(6) . . . [2]

(7) In paragraph (4)(*a*), "company" means any body corporate having a share capital.

[(8) A deposit account or share account which is a qualifying investment for an account falling within paragraph (2)(k) or (l) must not be connected with any other investment, held by the named child or any other person.

(8A) For the purposes of paragraph (8), a deposit account or share account described in that paragraph, is connected with another investment if—

(*a*) either was opened or acquired with reference to the other, or with a view to enabling the other to be opened or acquired on particular terms, or with a view to facilitating the opening or acquisition of the other on particular terms,

(*b*) the terms on which the deposit account or share account was opened would have been significantly less favourable to the holder if the other investment had not been held, and

(*c*) the other investment is not a tax exempt investment.

(8B) The following are tax exempt investments for the purposes of paragraph (8A)—

(*a*) an account investment held under a child trust fund;

(*b*) an account investment within the meaning given in the Individual Savings Account Regulations 1998(c) held under an account opened (or treated as opened) in accordance with regulation 12 or 12A of those regulations.][3]

(9) The conditions specified in this paragraph are that—

(*a*) the insurance is on the life of the named child only;

(*b*) the terms and conditions of the policy provide—

(i) that the policy may only be owned or held as a qualifying investment for an account which satisfies the provisions of these Regulations;

(ii) that the policy shall automatically terminate if it comes to the notice of the account provider, in any manner, that the event specified in paragraph (11) has occurred in relation to the policy;

(iii) for an express prohibition of any payment of the proceeds from the termination of the policy or a partial surrender of the rights conferred by the policy, to the named child (while he is still a child) [except in accordance with regulation 18A (terminal illness)][1]; and

(iv) that the policy, the rights conferred by the policy and any share or interest in the policy or rights respectively, shall not be capable of assignment or (in Scotland) assignation, other than that they may be vested in the named child's personal representatives, and that the title to the policy may be transferred to a new account provider subject to and in accordance with regulations 8(2)(*f*) and 21;

(*c*) the policy evidences or secures a contract of insurance which—

(i) falls within paragraph 1 or 3 of Part 2 of Schedule 1 to the Financial Services and Markets Act 2000 (Regulated Activities) Order 2001, or

(ii) would fall within either of those paragraphs if the insurer were a company with permission under Part 4 of the Financial Services and Markets Act 2000 to effect or carry out contracts of insurance;

(*d*) the policy is not—

(i) a contract to pay an annuity on human life,

(ii) a personal portfolio bond within the meaning given by regulation 2(1) of the Personal Portfolio Bonds (Tax) Regulations 1999, or

(iii) a contract, the effecting and carrying out of which constitutes "pension business" within the meaning given by section 431B(1) of the Taxes Act; and

(*e*) after the first payment in respect of a premium in relation to the policy has been made, there is no contractual obligation on any person to make any other such payment.

(10) The condition specified in this paragraph is that no sum may at any time, at or after the making of the insurance, be lent to or at the direction of the named child or registered contact by or by arrangement with the insurer for the time being responsible for the obligations under the policy.

(11) The event specified in this paragraph is that—

(*a*) there has been a breach of any of the conditions in paragraph (9) or (10), or any of those conditions was not satisfied at the date on which the insurance was made; and

(*b*) the breach or non-compliance cannot be remedied in accordance with regulation 23, or (in any other case), has not been remedied within a reasonable time.

(12) Where the event specified in paragraph (11) occurs in relation to a policy, the policy shall nevertheless be treated, for the purposes of these Regulations, excepting paragraphs (9)(*b*)(ii) and (11), and regulations 37(6) and 38, as if it had satisfied the conditions in paragraphs (9) and (10) during the period—

(*a*) commencing at the time when that specified event occurred, and

(*b*) ending immediately before—

[(i) the end of the final insurance year in relation to the policy, within the meaning given by section 499 of ITTOIA 2005, or][2]

(ii) the time at which that specified event came to the notice of the account provider, whichever first occurs (the "termination event").

Amendments—[1] Words in para (9)(*b*)(iii) inserted by the Child Trust Funds (Amendment) Regulations, SI 2004/2676 regs 2, 8 with effect from 6 April 2005 (by virtue of SI 2004/3369).

[2] Paras (2)(*o*)–(*q*) inserted by the Child Trust Funds (Amendment No 3) Regulations, SI 2005/3349 regs 2, 5 with effect from 27 December 2005.

[3] Amendments made by the Child Trust Funds (Amendment) Regulations, SI 2010/582 regs 2, 5 with effect from 6 April 2010.

[4] Paras (8)–(8B) substituted for previous para (8), by the Child Trust Funds (Amendment) Regulations, SI 2012/1870 reg 2 with effect from 8 August 2012.

[5] In para (2)(*a*), words substituted, and para (3), (3)(*a*) words inserted by the Child Trust Funds (Amendment No 2) Regulations, SI 2013/1744 regs 2, 5 with effect from 5 August 2013.

[6] In para (2)(*q*), word substituted, and para (2)(*r*) inserted by the Child Trust Funds (Amendment) (No 2) Regulations, SI 2014/263 regs 2, 4 with effect from 1 July 2014.

[7] In paras (2)(*f*), (3)(*a*), words revoked, and in para (3), words substituted by the Child Trust Funds (Amendment) Regulations, SI 2014/1453 regs 2, 5 with effect from 6 April 2014.

[8] In para (5)(*c*), semi-colon substituted for full stop, and para (5)(*d*)–(*f*) inserted by the Child Trust Funds (Amendment No 3) Regulations, SI 2015/1371 regs 2, 6 with effect from 1 July 2015.

13 Conditions for application by responsible person or the child to open an account (and changes to an account)

(1) An application by a responsible person in relation to a child or the child if 16 or over, as the case may be, ("the applicant") to open an account for the child with an account provider must be made to the account provider in a statement which must satisfy the conditions specified in paragraphs (2) to (6).

(2) An application must specify the description of account applied for.

(3) An application must incorporate a declaration by the applicant that he—

(*a*) is aged 16 years of age or over,

(*b*) is—

(i) (where the child is under 16) a responsible person in relation to the named child (that is, that he has parental responsibility [or, in Scotland, parental responsibilities][1] in relation to the child), or

(ii) the child if 16 or over, and

(*c*) is to be the registered contact for the account; and where the application is not in writing, must authorise the account provider to record the terms of the declaration in a written declaration made on behalf of the applicant.

(4) The applicant must authorise the account provider (on behalf of the named child where appropriate)—

(*a*) to hold the child's Inland Revenue contributions, subscriptions, account investments, interest, dividends and any other rights or proceeds in respect of those investments and cash, and

(*b*) to make on his behalf any claims to relief from tax in respect of account investments, and the authority must continue until a further application and declaration is made in accordance with paragraph (10).

(5) An application must contain—

(*a*) the applicant's full name,

(*b*) his address, including postcode,

(*c*) the named child's full name [and date of birth][1],

(*d*) his address, including postcode, and

(*e*) the child's unique reference number on the voucher.

(6) There may be only one declaration and authorisation under paragraphs (3) to (5) in force for an account at any time.

(7) Except in the case—

(*a*) of the death or incapacity of the registered contact,

(*b*) where the registered contact cannot be contacted,

(*c*) of the bringing to an end of a Court order, under which he is a responsible person for the named child,

(*d*) of the named child attaining the age of 16 years,

[(*da*) where the new registered contact has been appointed to be a guardian or special guardian of the named child,

(*db*) where the new registered contact is the adopter of the named child under an adoption order,][3]

[(*e*) where a person is appointed by the Treasury or the Secretary of State by virtue of section 3(10) of the Act, or][5]

(*f*) where a Court so orders,

any change in the identity of the registered contact shall require confirmation by the current registered contact that his declaration and authorisation under paragraphs (3)(*c*) and (4) is cancelled[, and in the cases in sub-paragraphs (*a*) to (*f*) it shall be treated as automatically cancelled][3].

(8) An account provider must decline to accept an application if he has reason to believe that—

(*a*) the voucher has expired, or is not or might not be genuine, or

(*b*) the applicant has given untrue information in his application.

(9) Where the application is not in writing, the account provider shall make the written declaration referred to in paragraph (3), and notify the applicant of its contents, and such declaration shall take effect from the date on which the applicant agrees the contents (subject to any corrections), and if he neither agrees or disagrees with the contents within 30 days, he shall be treated as having agreed them.

(10) Where—

(*a*) there is a change in the identity of the registered contact, the new registered contact, or

(*b*) an account has been opened by the Inland Revenue under regulation 6 (Revenue allocated accounts) [and—

(i) a responsible person in relation to the child subsequently applies to the account provider to be the registered contact for the account, or

(ii) the child, if the child is 16 or over and has elected to manage the account, subsequently applies to the account provider to be the registered contact for the account,

that individual must make the application or declaration required by paragraphs (3) to (5) but as if for regulation 13(3)(b) there were substituted—

"(*b*) is—

(i) a responsible person in relation to the named child (that is, that he has parental responsibility or, in Scotland, parental responsibilities in relation to the child), or

(ii) the child, where the child is 16 or over and has elected to manage the account."][4]

[(11) Where the new registered contact is [the person appointed by the Treasury or the Secretary of State by virtue of section 3(10) of the Act, that person][5] shall make the declaration and authorisation required by paragraphs (3)(*c*) and (4) [and shall be treated as a party to the existing management agreement for the account in question][2].][1]

Amendments—[1] Words in paras (3), (5) inserted, and para (11) inserted, by the Child Trust Funds (Amendment) Regulations, SI 2004/2676 regs 2, 9 with effect from 6 April 2005 (by virtue of SI 2004/3369).

[2] Words in para (11) inserted by the Child Trust Funds (Amendment No 2) Regulations, SI 2004/3382 regs 2, 3 with effect from 6 April 2005.

[3] Amendments made by the Child Trust Funds (Amendment) Regulations, SI 2010/582 regs 2, 6 with effect from 6 April 2010.

[4] In para (10)(*b*), words substituted for words "and a responsible person in relation to the child (or the child, if 16 or over) subsequently applies to the account provider to be the registered contact for the account, he shall make the application and declaration required by paragraphs (3) to (5)." by the Child Trust Funds (Amendment No 3) Regulations, SI 2015/1371 regs 2, 7 with effect from 1 July 2015.

[5] Para (7)(*e*) substituted, and in para (11), words substituted for words "the Official Solicitor or the Accountant of Court, he", by the Child Trust Funds (Amendment No 2) Regulations, SI 2017/748 regs 2, 4 with effect from 1 October 2017. Para (7)(*e*) previously read as follows—

"(*e*) where the Official Solicitor or Accountant of Court is appointed under section 3(10) of the Act, or".

14 Account provider – qualifications and Board's approval

(1) This regulation specifies the circumstances ("qualifying circumstances") in which a person may be approved by the Board as an account provider.

(2) The qualifying circumstances are the following—

(*a*) the person must make an application to the Board for approval in a form specified by the Board;

(*b*) the person must undertake with the Board—

(i) to either offer stakeholder accounts to the general public (whether or not accounts of another description are offered), or to fulfil the requirements in paragraph (3),

(ii) to accept vouchers from any responsible person or the child if 16 or over (subject to [paragraph (iia) and][2] regulation 13(8)),

[(iia) in the case of a credit union, to accept vouchers from any responsible person or the child if 16 or over, if the child to which the voucher relates is a member, or fulfils or is treated as fulfilling a qualification for admission to membership, of the credit union (subject to regulation 13(8)),][2]

(iii) where the person accepts Revenue allocated accounts, to allow instructions for their management to be made or given by post (whether or not other methods are allowed),

(iv) to publicise (and up-date where appropriate) statements of the minimum amount which may be subscribed to an account on a single occasion, and the permitted means of payment of subscriptions,

(v) to inform persons proposing to make subscriptions to an account (other than the named child) that the subscription is a gift to the child,

(vi) to publicise (and up-date where appropriate) statements of the extent to which social, environmental or ethical decisions are taken into account in selecting, retaining or realising investments,

(vii) that a child's unique reference number shall only be used for the purposes of the child's account (and of fulfilling the requirements of these Regulations with regard to that account), and

(viii) that whether there is an initial contribution or special contribution to an account, whether there is a supplementary contribution to the account, and whether the account is a Revenue allocated account is information held for the purposes mentioned in paragraph (vii) only, and shall not be used for other purposes (including marketing other products);

(*c*) . . . [5]

(*d*) an account provider must be—

(i) an authorised person within the meaning of section 31(1)(*a*) or (*c*) of, or Schedule 5 to, the Financial Services and Markets Act 2000, who has permission to carry on one or more of the activities specified in Articles 14, 21, 25, 37, 40, 45, [51ZA, 51ZC, 51ZE][7], 53 and (in so far as it applies to any of those activities) 64 of the Financial Services and Markets Act 2000 (Regulated Activities) Order 2001, but excluding any person falling within paragraph (iv) below;

[[(iia)] [3] in the case of a credit union, an authorised person within the meaning of [FISMA 2000][6], who has permission to carry on one or more of the activities specified in Article 5 of the Financial Services and Markets Act 2000 (Regulated Activities) Order 2001;][2]

(ii) a European institution which carries on one or more of those activities;

(iii) a building society, [or a person falling within section 991 of ITA 2007 (including for this purpose a credit union)][4]; or

(iv) an insurance company within the meaning given by section 431(2) of the Taxes Act, an incorporated friendly society or a registered friendly society, or any other assurance undertaking;

(*e*) an account provider must not be prevented from acting as such by any [limitation or requirement imposed under section 42 or 43 of FISMA 2000, or by any prohibition or prohibition order in or made under that Act][4]; and

(*f*) an account provider who—

(i) is a European institution or a relevant authorised person and who does not have a branch or business establishment in the United Kingdom, or has such a branch or business establishment but does not intend to carry out all his functions as an account provider at that branch or business establishment, or

(ii) falls within the expression "any other assurance undertaking" in sub-paragraph (*d*)(iv),

must fulfil one of the three requirements specified in regulation 15.

(3) The requirements in this paragraph are that the person provides to any potential applicant for a child trust fund ([before commencement of completion of][1] any application under regulation 13)—

(*a*) a statement that a stakeholder account is available from a named alternative account provider who offers it on the terms in paragraph (2)(*b*)(*i*) (omitting the words from ", or to" to the end);

(*b*) a detailed description of that stakeholder account; and

(*c*) sufficient information (according to the method of communication used, and including documentation where appropriate) to put the potential applicant in the position to make an application to that alternative account provider, complying with regulation 13.

(4) The terms of the Board's approval may include conditions designed to ensure that the provisions of these Regulations are satisfied.

Amendments—[1] Words in para (3) substituted by the Child Trust Funds (Amendment) Regulations, SI 2004/2676 regs 2, 10 with effect from 6 April 2005 (by virtue of SI 2004/3369).

[2] Words in para (2)(b)(i) inserted, and paras (2)(b)(ii) and (2)(d)(ia) inserted, by the Child Trust Funds (Amendment No 2) Regulations, SI 2005/909 regs 2, 6–8 with effect from 6 April 2005.

[3] Para (2)(d)(iia) numbered as such by the Child Trust Funds (Amendment No 3) Regulations, SI 2005/3349 regs 2, 6 with effect from 27 December 2005.

[4] Amendments made by the Child Trust Funds (Amendment) Regulations, SI 2010/582 regs 2, 7 with effect from 6 April 2010.

[5] Para (2)(*c*) revoked by the Child Trust Funds (Amendment) Regulations, SI 2013/263 reg 2(1), (4)(*c*) with effect from 16 March 2013.

[6] In para (2)(*d*)(iia), words substituted for words by the Financial Services Act 2012 (Consequential Amendments and Transitional Provisions) (No 3) Order, SI 2013/1765 art 8 with effect from 1 September 2013.

[7] In para (2)(*d*)(i), words substituted by the Child Trust Funds Regulations, SI 2017/185 regs 2, 5 with effect from 6 April 2017.

15 Account provider—appointment of tax representative

(1) This regulation specifies the requirements mentioned in regulation 14(2)(*f*).

(2) The first requirement specified in this regulation is that—

(*a*) a person who falls within [section 698(2)(b) of ITTOIA 2005][1] is for the time being appointed by the account provider to be responsible for securing the discharge of the duties prescribed by paragraph (5) which fall to be discharged by the account provider, and

(*b*) his identity and the fact of his appointment have been notified to the Board by the account provider.

(3) The second requirement specified in this regulation is that there are for the time being other arrangements with the Board for a person other than the account provider to secure the discharge of such duties.

(4) The third requirement specified in this regulation is that there are for the time being other arrangements with the Board designed to secure the discharge of such duties.

(5) The duties prescribed by this paragraph are those that fall to be discharged by an account provider under these Regulations.

(6) The appointment of a person in pursuance of the first requirement shall be treated as terminated in circumstances where—

(*a*) the Board have reason to believe that the person concerned—

(i) has failed to secure the discharge of any of the duties prescribed by paragraph (5), or
(ii) does not have adequate resources to discharge those duties, and

(*b*) the Board have notified the account provider and that person that they propose to treat his appointment as having terminated with effect from the date specified in the notice.

(7) Where, in accordance with the first requirement, a person is at any time responsible for securing the discharge of duties, the person concerned—

(*a*) shall be entitled to act on the account provider's behalf for any of the purposes of the provisions relating to the duties;

(*b*) shall secure (where appropriate by acting on the account provider's behalf) the account provider's compliance with and discharge of the duties; and

(*c*) shall be personally liable in respect of any failure of the account provider to comply with or discharge any such duty as if the duties imposed on the account provider were imposed jointly and severally on the account provider and the person concerned.

Amendments—[1] Amendments made by the Child Trust Funds (Amendment) Regulations, SI 2010/582 regs 2, 8 with effect from 6 April 2010.

16 Account provider—withdrawal by Board of approval

(1) This regulation specifies the circumstances ("the disqualifying circumstances") in which the Board may by notice withdraw their approval of a person as an account provider in relation to an account.

(2) The disqualifying circumstances are that the Board have reason to believe—

(*a*) that any provision of the Act or these Regulations, or any term of an undertaking given in accordance with regulation 14(2)(*b*) or condition under regulation 14(4), is not or at any time has not been satisfied, either in respect of an account managed by the account provider or otherwise; or

(*b*) that a person to whom they have given approval to act as an account provider is not qualified so to act.

[(2A) Where paragraph (2B) applies, a term of an undertaking given in accordance with regulation 14(2)(b) shall not be taken as not satisfied only by reason that the person to whom the Board's approval as an account provider has been given does not accept vouchers.

(2B) This paragraph applies where—

(*a*) a person does not accept any voucher after a day specified by that person; and

(*b*) no less than 30 days before the specified day, notice in writing is given to the Board of the person's intention not to accept vouchers after that day.][2]

(3) The notice to which paragraph (1) refers shall specify—

(*a*) the date from which the Board's approval is withdrawn; and

(*b*) the disqualifying circumstances.

[(4) On receiving the notice referred to in paragraph (1), subject to any appeal under section 22(1)(b) of the Act, the account provider shall notify the registered contact (or, if there is no registered contact, the named child) of the right to transfer the account under regulation 21, and of his or her rights under regulation 20(3).][1]

Amendments—[1] Amendments made by the Child Trust Funds (Amendment) Regulations, SI 2010/582 regs 2, 9 with effect from 6 April 2010.

[2] Paras (2A), (2B) inserted by the Child Trust Funds (Amendment No 4) Regulations, SI 2010/2599 regs 2, 3 with effect from 16 November 2010.

17 Account provider—appeal against non-approval or withdrawal of Board's approval

A person who has been notified of a decision by the Board not to approve that person as an account provider, or an account provider to whom notice of withdrawal of approval has been given under regulation 16, may appeal against the decision by notice given to the Board within 30 days after the date of the notification or notice.

18 Permitted withdrawals from an account

Withdrawals from an account before the date on which the named child attains the age of 18 years may only be made—

(*a*) by the account provider, to settle any management charges and other incidental expenses, which are due by or under the management agreement, or

[(*ab*) in accordance with regulation 18A, or][1]

(*b*) where the account provider is satisfied that the named child has died under that age.

Amendments—[1] Para (*ab*) inserted by the Child Trust Funds (Amendment) Regulations, SI 2004/2676 regs 2, 11 with effect from 6 April 2005 (by virtue of SI 2004/3369).

18A [Permitted withdrawals from an account where the child is terminally ill

(1) A person with parental responsibility (or, in Scotland, parental responsibilities) for the named child (including a local authority, but excluding a person under 16), or the named child if 16 or over, may make a claim to the Board, for withdrawals from an account to be permitted in accordance with this regulation.

(2) The claim shall be—

(*a*) made in a manner prescribed by the Board, which shall include the giving of any consent necessary for the verification or consideration of the claim, and

(*b*) accepted in either of the following cases:

[Case 1

The child—

(i) in England and Wales or Scotland falls within either section 72(5) of the Social Security Contributions and Benefits Act 1992 (special rules for terminally ill person's entitlement to care component of disability living allowance) or section 82(4) of the Welfare Reform Act 2012 (terminal illness); or

(ii) in Northern Ireland, falls within section 72(5) of the Social Security Contributions and Benefits (Northern Ireland) Act 1992 (the care component).][2]

Case 2

Evidence that the named child is terminally ill has been supplied to the satisfaction of the Board.

(3) The Board shall issue a letter to the claimant authorising withdrawals from the account under this regulation . . . [2]

(4) Once a claim has been accepted, withdrawals may be made by the registered contact (on behalf of the named child, where he is not the child) at any time—

(*a*) provided that, immediately following any withdrawal, a balance sufficient to keep the account open is maintained in the account, and

(*b*) excepting any transfer of a policy of life insurance (as opposed to the proceeds from such a policy).

(5) Where account investments are withdrawn in a form other than sterling currency, regulation 36(1)(*b*) shall apply (with any necessary modifications) to any such investment immediately before it is withdrawn.

(6) In this regulation, "terminally ill" has the meaning.

[(*a*) for England, Wales and Scotland, in section 66(2)(*a*) of the Social Security Contributions and Benefits Act 1992 or in section 82(4) of the Welfare Reform Act 2012 (terminal illness); or

(*b*) for Northern Ireland, in section 72(5) of the Social Security Contributions and Benefits (Northern Ireland) Act 1992 (the care component)][2]][1]

Amendments—[1] Paragraph 18A inserted by the Child Trust Funds (Amendment) Regulations, SI 2004/2676 regs 2, 12 with effect from 6 April 2005 (by virtue of SI 2004/3369).

[2] In para 2, Case 1 substituted, in para (3), words revoked, para (6)(*a*) created and words inserted, and para (6)(*b*) and preceding word inserted by the Child Trust Funds (Amendment) Regulations, SI 2014/1453 regs 2, 6 with effect from 6 April 2014.

[19 Account provider's intention to make a bulk transfer of accounts or to cease to act as an account provider

(1) An account provider must give notice to the Board if the account provider—

(*a*) intends to cease to act as an account provider; or

(*b*) intends to make a bulk transfer of accounts.

(2) An account provider must give notice to the person who is the registered contact (or, if there is no registered contact, the named child) if the account provider—

(*a*) intends to cease to act as an account provider; or

(*b*) intends that the account will be one of the accounts transferred in a bulk transfer of accounts.

(3) The notices described in paragraphs (1) and (2) must—

(*a*) specify whether the account provider—

(i) intends to cease to act as an account provider; or

(ii) intends to make a bulk transfer of accounts;

(*b*) where the notice specifies an intention to cease to act as an account provider—

(i) specify the day on or after which the account provider intends to cease to act as an account provider; and

(ii) be given no less than 30 days before that day;

(*c*) where the notice specifies an intention to make a bulk transfer of accounts—

(i) specify the day on or after which the account provider intends to make the first transfer in the bulk transfer of accounts;

(ii) be given no less than 30 days before that day; and

(iii) advise the name and address of the person to whom the account provider intends to transfer accounts.

(4) The notice described in paragraph (2) must also—

(*a*) identify the account to which it relates;

(*b*) in the case of a notice under paragraph (2)(*a*), advise the registered contact of the right to transfer the account under regulation 21 and of his rights under regulation 20(3);

(*c*) in the case of a notice under paragraph (2)(*b*)

(i) advise the registered contact that the account may be transferred otherwise than in a bulk transfer of accounts, such that regulation 21 applies, if sufficient instructions are provided to enable the account provider to do so; and

(ii) advise the day by which the account provider must receive sufficient instructions for the account to be transferred otherwise than in a bulk transfer of accounts.

(5) Where an account provider intends to make a bulk transfer of accounts in consequence of an intention to cease to act as an account provider, such intention may be specified in a single notice to the Board or to a registered contact (or, if there is no registered contact, the named child) (as appropriate, respectively) provided the requirements of paragraphs (3), (4)(*a*) and (*c*) are met.][1]

Amendments—[1] Regulations 19, 19A substituted for previous reg 19 by the Child Trust Funds (Amendment No 2) Regulations, SI 2013/1744 regs 2, 6 with effect from 5 August 2013.

[19A Account provider ceasing to act (or ceasing to accept Revenue allocated accounts)

A person shall give notice to the Board of his intention to cease to accept further Revenue allocated accounts under regulation 6, not less than 30 days before he so ceases.][1]

Amendments—[1] Regulations 19, 19A substituted for previous reg 19 by the Child Trust Funds (Amendment No 2) Regulations, SI 2013/1744 regs 2, 6 with effect from 5 August 2013.

20 Account provider ceasing to qualify

(1) A person shall cease to qualify as an account provider and shall notify the Board within 30 days of the relevant event in sub-paragraphs (*a*) to (*f*), of that relevant event, where—

(*a*) the person no longer fulfils the conditions of regulation 14;

[(*b*) there is an insolvency event in relation to the account provider;

[(*ba*) a debt relief order is made in respect of the person (under Part 7A of the Insolvency Act 1986);][2]

(*c*) an application has been made for a bank insolvency order or a bank administration order;][1]

(*d*) . . . [1]

(*e*) in the case of a building society, a person falling within [section 991 of ITA 2007 or a credit union][1]

(i) it ceases to be a building society or to fall within [section 991 of ITA 2007 or to be a credit union][1], as the case may be;

(ii) its directors have made a proposal under Part 1 of the Insolvency Act 1986 for a composition in satisfaction of its debts or a scheme of arrangement of its affairs; or

(iii) a receiver or manager of its property has been appointed; or

(*f*) in the case of a European institution, a relevant authorised person or an assurance undertaking which falls within regulation 14(2)(*d*)(iv), action corresponding to any described in sub-paragraph (*b*) to (*e*) has been taken by or in relation to the institution, person or undertaking under the law of an EEA State.

(2) On giving the notice referred to in paragraph (1), the person shall also notify the registered contact (or, if there is no registered contact, the named child) of the right to transfer the account under regulation 21, and the notice shall inform the recipient of the rights under paragraph (3).

(3) Where a registered contact—

(*a*) receives a notice under paragraph (2), or regulation [16(4) or][1] [19(2)(*a*)][3], and

(*b*) within 30 days of the sending of the notice, transfers the account to another account provider pursuant to regulation 21,

the period between the transferor ceasing to act or qualify as an account provider, and the transfer to the transferee, shall be ignored in determining whether the account has at all times been managed by an account provider.

Amendments—[1] Amendments made by the Child Trust Funds (Amendment) Regulations, SI 2010/582 regs 2, 10 with effect from 6 April 2010.

[2] Para (1)(*ba*) inserted by the Tribunals, Courts and Enforcement Act 2007 (Consequential Amendments) Order, SI 2012/2404 art 3(3), Sch 3 para 34 with effect in relation to a debt relief order the application for which is made on or after 1 October 2012.

[3] In para (3)(*a*), reference substituted by the Child Trust Funds (Amendment No 2) Regulations, SI 2013/1744 regs 2, 7 with effect from 5 August 2013.

[20A Transfers to other accounts for children

(1) An account provider must at the request of the registered contact—

(*a*) transfer all the investments under the child trust fund, or an amount representing their value in cash, to a protected child account that is provided by a person chosen by the registered contact, and

(*b*) when all the investments have been transferred, close the child trust fund.

(2) An account is only a protected child account for the purposes of section 7A(2) of the Act if it satisfies the condition of being a junior ISA account within regulation 2B of the Individual Savings Account Regulations 1998.][1]

Amendments—[1] Regulation 20A inserted by the Child Trust Funds (Amendment No 2) Regulations, SI 2015/876 regs 2, 6 with effect from 6 April 2015.

21 Transfer of accounts . . . [5]

(1) Where—

(*a*) arrangements are made by a registered contact to transfer the whole of the investments under an account from one account provider ("the transferor") to another account provider ("the transferee"), . . . [4]

(*b*) the whole of the investments under an account are so transferred in consequence of an account provider ("the transferor") ceasing to act or to qualify as an account provider, the transfer shall be treated as a transfer of the account[, . . . [5]

[(*ba*) there is a transfer under regulation 20A to a protected child account, or][5]

(*c*) an account is transferred in a bulk transfer of accounts . . . [5],][4]

(2) The account and its description under regulation 4 shall not be affected for the purposes of these Regulations by reason of the transfer [in paragraph (1)(*a*), (*b*) or (*c*)][5], save that, where the registered contact specifies in accordance with paragraph (3)(*a*) an account of a different description, the account shall, on the transfer, become an account of that other description.

(3) The registered contact shall make—

(*a*) the application required by regulation 13(2) (modified as if the words "applied for" were replaced with "[following the transfer[1]]"), and

(*b*) the application and declaration required by regulation 13(3) to (5),

to the transferee [but (in the case mentioned in subparagraph (b)) as if for regulation 13(3)(b) there were substituted—

"(*b*) is—

(i) a responsible person in relation to the named child (that is, that he has parental responsibility or, in Scotland, parental responsibilities in relation to the child, or

(ii) the child, where the child is 16 or over and has elected to manage the account."][6]

[(3A) Paragraph (3) does not apply where an account is transferred [under regulation 20A or][5] in a bulk transfer of accounts.

(3B)–(3F) . . . [5]

(3G) An account transferred in accordance with this regulation in a bulk transfer of accounts is an account opened pursuant to an application in accordance with regulation 13 for the purposes of these Regulations . . . [5].][4]

[[(3H)][4] Where a registered contact applies in accordance with paragraph (3) to a potential transferee for a transfer under this regulation, specifying a stakeholder account offered by the transferee, the transferee shall not decline to accept that application (or the transfer in consequence of it) except where—

(*a*) the transferee has reason to believe that the registered contact has given untrue information in his application;

(*b*) the transferee demonstrates to the satisfaction of the Board that acceptance of transfers, or a class of transfers, during a particular period would jeopardise his ability to prevent any of the matters mentioned in regulation 16(2)(*a*); or

(*c*) the transferor does not give the transferee the notice in accordance with paragraph (4).][1]

(4) The transferor shall on the date of the transfer give the transferee a notice containing the information specified in paragraph (5) . . . [7]

[(4A) In relation to paragraph (1)(*ba*), the account provider shall on the date of the transfer give the person providing the protected child account a notice containing the information specified in paragraph (5)(*a*) and (*b*)(i), (ii) and (iv) . . . [7].][5]

(5) The information specified in this paragraph is—

(*a*) as regards the named child—

(i) his full name,

(ii) his date of birth,

(iii) his unique reference number;

(*b*) as regards the account—

(i) the description of the account,

(ii) the date of the transfer,

(iii) the total amount subscribed to the account during the period from the beginning of the subscription year in which the transfer takes place to the date of the transfer,

(iv) any amount which has been claimed from the Board under regulations [26 or 27][3] and which has not been paid at the date of the transfer[, and

(v) the total amount subscribed to the account during the previous subscription year, where that subscription year ended later than the 5th April preceding the date of the transfer.][2]

(*c*) the full name and address, including postcode, of the registered contact who has made the transfer arrangements.

(6) . . . [7]

Amendments—[1] Words in para (3)(a) substituted, and para (3A) inserted, by the Child Trust Funds (Amendment) Regulations, SI 2004/2676 regs 2, 13 with effect from 6 April 2005 (by virtue of SI 2004/3369).

[2] Amendments made by the Child Trust Funds (Amendment) Regulations, SI 2010/582 regs 2, 11 with effect from 6 April 2010.

[3] In para (5)(*b*)(iv), words substituted for words "26, 27 or 30" by the Child Trust Funds (Amendment) Regulations, SI 2013/263 reg 2(1), (4)(*d*) with effect from 16 March 2013.

[4] In para (1)(*a*), word "or" revoked, para(1)(*c*) and preceding word inserted, para (3A) renumbered as para (3H), and paras (3A)–(3G) inserted by the Child Trust Funds (Amendment No 2) Regulations, SI 2013/1744 regs 2, 8 with effect from 5 August 2013.

[5] Words in heading, paras (1)(*c*), (3G) revoked, word in para (1)(*b*) revoked, and paras (3B)–(3F) revoked; paras (1)(*bc*), (4A) inserted, and words in paras (2), (3A) inserted by the Child Trust Funds (Amendment No 2) Regulations, SI 2015/876 regs 2, 7, 8 with effect from 6 April 2015.

[6] In para (3)(*b*), words inserted by the Child Trust Funds (Amendment No 3) Regulations, SI 2015/1371 regs 2, 8 with effect from 1 July 2015.

[7] In paras (4), (4A), words revoked, and para (6) revoked by the Child Trust Funds Regulations, SI 2017/185 regs 2, 6 with effect from 6 April 2017.

22 Recoupment of Inland Revenue contributions to void accounts (and other accounts)

(1) Where—

(*a*) the named child has never been an eligible child (see regulation 8(1)(*b*)), or

(*b*) there is a breach of regulation 8(1)(*c*) in relation to an account, the account is void, and the persons mentioned in paragraph (3) shall account to the Inland Revenue for Inland Revenue contributions paid in respect of the account, together with income and gains which have arisen in consequence of the crediting of any of those payments to the account.

(2) Where—

(*a*) the condition in section 9(5) of the Act [or regulation 7(10B) or 7A(4)][2] was satisfied in relation to a child, but the determination under sections 18 to 21 of the Tax Credits Act 2002 has been overturned, or

(*b*) the condition in section 9(8) of the Act was satisfied in relation to a child, but it has subsequently been determined that payment of the relevant benefit or tax credit mentioned in that subsection should not have been made, or that the applicable amount or tax credit should not have included an amount or credit in respect of the child, [or

(*c*) the requirements of regulation 7(10) were[, or the condition in regulation 7(10C)[, 7A(5) or 7B(1)][3] was,][2] satisfied in relation to a child, but it has subsequently been determined that payment of the relevant benefit mentioned in [the relevant provision][2] should not have been made, or that the applicable amount should not have included an amount in respect of that child,][1]

the persons mentioned in paragraph (3) shall account to the Inland Revenue for any supplementary contribution[, or further contribution, as the case may be,][1] paid in respect of the account, together with income and gains which have arisen in consequence of the crediting of any such payment to the account.

(3) The persons mentioned in paragraphs (1) and (2) are—

(*a*) the account provider (to the extent that he has assets in his possession or control),

(*b*) the registered contact,

(*c*) the named child, and

(*d*) any person in whom the Inland Revenue contributions, income or gains, or any property directly or indirectly representing any of them, is vested (whether beneficially or otherwise)

and they shall be jointly and severally liable.

(4) Where a person accountable under this regulation is notified by the Inland Revenue that an amount is due from him under it, that amount shall be treated for the purposes of Part 6 of the Management Act (collection and recovery) as if it were tax charged in an assessment on that person, and due and payable.

Amendments—[1] Para (2)(*c*) and words in para (2) inserted by the Child Trust Funds (Amendment) Regulations, SI 2005/383 regs 2, 4 with effect from 6 April 2005.

[2] In para (2)(*a*) words inserted, and in para (2)(*c*) words inserted and substituted, by the Child Trust Funds (Amendment) Regulations, SI 2009/475 regs 2, 6 with effect from 6 April 2009.

[3] Words in para (2)(*c*) substituted by the Child Trust Funds (Amendment No 2) Regulations, SI 2010/836, regs 2, 4, with effect where a child falls within the terms of reg 7B for a year of assessment commencing on or after 6 April 2009.

23 "Repair" of invalid accounts

(1) Except in the case of a breach of regulation 8(1)(*b*) or (*c*) (where no repair of an account is possible), it is an overriding requirement to be satisfied in relation to an account that the account provider and registered contact, as the case may be, take any steps necessary to remedy any breach of these Regulations.

(2) Where a breach is remedied as mentioned in paragraph (1), the account shall, to the extent of that breach, be treated as having been a valid account at all times, except for determining whether there has been a breach of these Regulations for the purposes of section 20 of the Act (penalties).

PART 3
TAX AND ADMINISTRATION OF ACCOUNTS

24 Exemption from tax of account income and gains

Subject to compliance with these Regulations (and in particular regulation 9)—

(*a*) no tax shall be chargeable on the account provider or his nominee, or on the named child or registered contact (on his behalf)—

(i) in respect of interest, dividends, distributions or gains in respect of account investments [(excluding any building society bonus)][2],

[(ia) in respect of alternative finance return or profit share return paid by a financial institution (within the meanings in Chapter 5 of Part 2 of the Finance Act 2005);][1]

[(ib) in respect of a payment under a building society bonus scheme, so far as the payment is calculated by reference to account investments (and if paid directly by the society into the account, the payment shall not count towards the subscription limit in regulation 9);][2]

(ii) on any annual profits or gains treated [under Part 12 of ITA 2007][3] as having been received by any of them in respect of account investments,

(iii) on an offshore income gain to which a disposal made by any of them of an account investment gives rise, which is treated by section 761(1) of the Taxes Act as constituting profits or gains,

[(iv) on a profit on the disposal of a deeply discounted security within the meaning given by section 430 of ITTOIA 2005;]ee

(v) in respect of gains treated [under Chapter 9 of Part 4 of ITTOIA 2005][3] as arising in connection with a policy of life insurance which is an account investment;

(*b*) losses accruing on any disposal of account investments shall be disregarded for the purposes of capital gains tax;

[(*ba*) any gain or loss accruing on and attributable to a payment within paragraph (ib) of sub-paragraph (*a*) shall not be a chargeable gain or allowable loss for capital gains tax purposes;][2]

(*c*) [section 935 of ITA 2007][3] shall apply with the following modifications—

(i) for references to a plan manager, substitute references to an account provider,

(ii) for references to a plan, substitute references to an account, and

(iii) for the reference to [Chapter 3 of Part 6 of ITTOIA 2005][1], substitute a reference to the Act;

(*d*) [a deficiency arising in a tax year and falling within section 539(1) of ITTOIA 2005][3], so far as it relates to a policy of life insurance which is an account investment, shall not be allowable as a deduction from the total income of the named child;

(*e*) relief in respect of tax shall be given in the manner and to the extent provided by these Regulations; and

(*f*) income arising from account investments shall not be regarded as income for any income tax purposes (including [section 629 of ITTOIA 2005][1]).

Amendments—[1] Para (a)(ia) inserted; and words in paras (c)(iii), (f) substituted; by the Child Trust Funds (Amendment No 3) Regulations, SI 2005/3349 regs 2, 7 with effect from 27 December 2005.

[2] Words in para (a)(i), and paras (a)(ib) and (ba), inserted, by the Child Trust Funds (Amendment No 3) Regulations, SI 2006/3195 regs 2, 4, 5 with effect from 1 January 2007.

[3] Amendments made by the Child Trust Funds (Amendment) Regulations, SI 2010/582 regs 2, 12 with effect from 6 April 2010.

25 Tax liabilities and reliefs—account provider to act on behalf of the named child

(1) An account provider may under these Regulations make tax claims, conduct appeals and agree on behalf of the named child (or of the registered contact in respect of the child) liabilities for and reliefs from tax in respect of an account.

(2) Tax claims shall be made to the Board in accordance with the provisions of regulations 26 and 27.

(3) Where any relief or exemption from tax previously given in respect of an account has by virtue of these Regulations become excessive, in computing the relief due on any claim there shall be deducted (so that amounts equal to that excess are set-off or repaid to the Board, as the case may be) notwithstanding that those amounts have been invested, any other amount of tax due to the Board by the account provider in respect of any tax liability in respect of account investments under an account including (but without prejudice to the making of an assessment under that Schedule) any amount falling due in respect of a liability under [Chapter 9 of Part 15 of ITA 2007][1].

Amendments—[1] Amendments made by the Child Trust Funds (Amendment) Regulations, SI 2010/582 regs 2, 13 with effect from 6 April 2010.

26 Repayments in respect of tax to account provider—interim tax claims

(1) Notwithstanding the provisions of any other enactment, the Board shall not be under an obligation to make any repayment in respect of tax under these Regulations earlier than the end of the month following the month in which the claim for the repayment is received.

(2) A claim for repayment in respect of tax which is not an annual claim ("interim tax claim") may be made only for a period of a month (or a number of months not exceeding six) beginning on the 6th day of the month and ending on the 5th day of the relevant following month.
(3) No claim for repayment may be made for the month ending 5th October or any subsequent month in a year until the annual claim due under regulation 27(2) in respect of an account for the preceding year has been duly made by the account provider and received by the Board.
(4) Where, on the occasion of a claim, there is due to the Board an amount in respect of tax, that amount shall be recoverable by the Board in the same manner as tax charged by an assessment on the account provider which has become final and conclusive.
(5) This regulation and regulation 27 shall not apply to any repayment in respect of tax on account investments falling within regulation 12(2)(*m*) (life insurance), or on distributions and other rights or proceeds in respect of those investments.

27 Repayments in respect of tax to account provider—annual tax claims

(1) An annual tax claim is a claim for repayment in respect of tax for a year and may not be made at any time more than six years after the end of the year.
(2) Where the account provider—

(*a*) has made at least one interim tax claim during a year, or

(*b*) wishes to reclaim tax, or there is due to the Board an amount in respect of tax, following the end of the year,

the account provider shall within six months after the end of the year make an annual tax claim to establish the total of tax repayments due under an account for that year.
(3) Where the aggregate of the repayments in respect of interim tax claims for the year shown by an annual tax claim exceeds the amount of tax repayable for the year shown on the claim, the account provider shall repay the amount of the excess to the Board with the claim.
(4) If an account provider fails to make the annual tax claim required under paragraph (2)(*a*) within the time limited, the Board may issue a notice to the account provider showing the aggregate of payments in respect of the interim tax claims for the year, and stating that the Board are not satisfied that the amount due to the account provider for that year exceeds the lower amount stated in the notice.
(5) If an annual tax claim is not delivered to the Board within 14 days after the issue of a notice under paragraph (4) the amount of the difference between the aggregate and the lower amount stated in the notice shall immediately become recoverable by the Board in the same manner as tax charged by an assessment on the account provider which has become final and conclusive.
(6) Where an annual tax claim has been made and the account provider subsequently discovers that an error or mistake has been made in the claim the account provider may make a supplementary annual claim within the time allowed in paragraph (1).

28 Account provider's tax claims—supplementary provisions

(1) Section 42 of the Management Act shall not apply to tax claims under these Regulations.
(2) No appeal shall lie from the Board's decision on an interim tax claim.
(3) An appeal . . .[1] from the Board's decision on an annual tax claim . . .[1] shall be brought by giving notice to the Board within 30 days of receipt of notice of the decision.
(4) No payment or repayment made or other thing done on or in relation to an interim tax claim or a notice under regulation 27(4) shall prejudice the decision on an annual tax claim.
(5) The provisions contained in Part 5 of the Management Act (appeals and other proceedings) shall apply to an appeal under paragraph (3) above [and, on an appeal that is notified to the tribunal, the tribunal][1] may vary the decision appealed against whether or not the variation is to the advantage of the appellant.
(6) All such assessments, payments and repayments shall be made as necessary to give effect to the Board's decision on an annual tax claim or to any variation of that decision on appeal.
(7) Claims under these Regulations shall be in such form and contain such particulars as the Board prescribe and, subject to regulation 32(1), shall be signed by the account provider, and forms prescribed for annual claims may require a report to be given by a person qualified for appointment as auditor of a company.

Amendments—[1] In para (3), words revoked, and in para (5), words substituted, by the Transfer of Tribunal Functions and Revenue and Customs Appeals Order, SI 2009/56 art 3, Sch 2 para 127 with effect from 1 April 2009.

29 Assessments for withdrawing relief and recovering tax

(1) Where—

(*a*) any relief or exemption from tax given in respect of income or gains under an account is found not to be due or to be excessive, or

(*b*) the full amount of tax in respect of the income or gains under an account has not otherwise been fully accounted for and paid to the Board on behalf of the named child, an assessment to tax may be made by the Board in the amount or further amount which in their opinion ought to be charged.

(2) An assessment to which paragraph (1) refers may be made on the account provider or on the registered contact (in respect of the child where the child is under the age of 16).

(3) If the assessment is made to recover tax in respect of income under an account it shall be made under Case VI of Schedule D.

(4) . . . [1]

Amendments—[1] Para (4) revoked by the Child Trust Funds, Registered Pension Schemes and Stamp Duty Reserve Tax (Consequential Amendments) Regulations, SI 2012/886 reg 2 with effect from 6 April 2012.

30 Fortnightly claim and financial returns

Amendments—Reg 30 revoked by the Child Trust Funds (Amendment) Regulations, SI 2013/263 reg 2(1), (3) with effect from 16 March 2013, in respect of what would otherwise be fortnightly and initial return periods within reg 30(1) of these regulations beginning on or after that day.

31 Records to be kept by account provider

(1) An account provider shall at all times keep sufficient records in respect of an account to enable the requirements of these Regulations to be satisfied.

(2) In particular, an account provider shall produce (when required to do so by an officer of the Board) any—

(*a*) application made under regulation 13(1) or (10),

(*b*) voucher given to him,

(*c*) annual statement issued by him, and

(*d*) transfer notice given to him under regulation 21(4),

or electronic copies, within the period of 3 years from when it was made, issued or given (notwithstanding any transfer of the account under regulation [20A or][1] 21).

(3), (4) . . . [1]

Amendments—[1] In para (2), words inserted, and paras(3), (4) revoked by the Child Trust Funds (Amendment No 2) Regulations, SI 2015/876 regs 2, 9 with effect from 6 April 2015.

32 Returns of information by account provider

(1) An account provider shall within 60 days after the end of each year in which he acts as an account provider, and after ceasing to act or to qualify as an account provider, deliver by means of electronic communications to the Board a return for that year, or for the part of that year in which he so acted or qualified, in a form specified by the Board, which contains the information specified in paragraph (2).

(2) The information specified in this paragraph is information relating to each account in respect of which he acted as account provider, in the year or the part of the year for which the return is made, other than accounts transferred . . . [3] under regulation [20A or][3] 21 in that year or part of a year, as to—

(*a*) as regards the named child—

(i), (ii) . . . [1]

(iii) his unique reference number;

(*b*) as regards each such account—

(i) whether or not the account is a stakeholder account,

(ii) whether or not there is a registered contact for the account,

(iii) the aggregate market value of the account investments held under the account, subject to paragraph (3), the value of each account investment being determined either as at 5th April in that year, or any other valuation date not falling earlier than 5th October in that year, and

(iv) the total amount of cash subscribed to the account, in the subscription year ending during the year or the part of the year for which the return is made.

[(2A) Where, during the year or part of the year, the named child reaches the age of 18 years or dies, there shall be substituted for paragraph (2)(*b*)(iii)—

"(iii the aggregate market value of the account investments held under the account immediately before the relevant event mentioned in paragraph (2A),"][2]

(3) The reference in paragraph (2)(*b*)(iii) to market value shall be construed—

(*a*) in the case of policies of life insurance, as a reference to their surrender value, and

(*b*) as referring to separate values for—

(*i*) cash falling within regulation 12(2)(*k*) or (*l*), and

(ii) policies of life insurance and all other account investments.

(4) No claim for repayment, or repayment, may be made under regulations 26 and 27 until the returns which have become due under this regulation have been duly made by the account provider and received by the Board.

Amendments—[1] Para (2)(a)(i), (ii) revoked by the Child Trust Funds (Amendment No 2) Regulations, SI 2005/909 regs 2, 9 with effect from 6 April 2005.

[2] Amendments made by the Child Trust Funds (Amendment) Regulations, SI 2010/582 regs 2, 14 with effect from 6 April 2010.

[3] In para (2), words inserted and revoked by the Child Trust Funds (Amendment No 2) Regulations, SI 2015/876 regs 2, 10 with effect from 6 April 2015.

33 Information about "looked after children" from Local Authorities

Amendments—Reg 33 revoked by the Child Trust Funds (Amendment) Regulations, SI 2011/781 regs 2, 3 with effect from 7 April 2011.

33A [[The person appointed by the Treasury or the Secretary of State by virtue of section 3(10) of the Act] to be the person who has the authority to manage an account

[(1) The person appointed by the Treasury or the Secretary of State by virtue of section 3(10) of the Act is to be the person who has the authority to manage a child's account for the purposes of section 3(6)(b) of the Act where the circumstances specified in paragraph (2) apply.][9]

(2) The circumstances specified are where—

[(*za*)except in a case of a person who was a looked after child or a looked after and accommodated child on 30th September 2017, there is a continuous period of at least twelve months during which the circumstances under sub-paragraphs (*a*) and (*b*) apply,

(*zb*) in a case of a person who was a looked after child or a looked after and accommodated child on 30th September 2017, the circumstances under subparagraphs (*a*) and (*b*) apply,][9]

(*a*) [a child][9] is looked after (in Scotland, looked after and accommodated) by the local authority, and

(*b*) at least one of the following conditions is satisfied.

Condition 1

There is no person, or no person other than the local authority, who has parental responsibility (in Scotland, parental responsibilities) for the child.

Condition 2

It is part of the care plan for the child that—

(*a*) the child will live indefinitely away from home (or his former home), and

(*b*) the child will not have face to face contact with any parent having parental responsibility (in Scotland, parental responsibilities) for the child.

Condition 3

An order has been made under section 34(4) of the Children Act 1989 or Article 53(4) of the Children (Northern Ireland) Order 1995, authorising the local authority to refuse to allow contact between the child and any person with parental responsibility [(or, in Scotland, a compulsory supervision order or an interim compulsory supervision order is in force and contains a direction regulating contact to the effect that the child has no contact with a person who has parental responsibilities in relation to that child)][6], and there is no other individual with parental responsibility (in Scotland, parental responsibilities) for the child to act as registered contact.

[In this Condition—

(*a*) "compulsory supervision order" has the meaning given by section 83 of the Children's Hearings (Scotland) Act 2011;

(*b*) "interim compulsory supervision order" has the meaning given by section 86 of that Act; and

(*c*) "contact direction" means a measure mentioned in section 83(2)(*g*) of that Act and contained within a compulsory supervision order or an interim compulsory supervision order.][6]

Condition 4

The Court of Protection has—

(*a*) appointed a [deputy][3] for a person with parental responsibility for the child, or

[(*b*) determined that such a person lacks capacity within the meaning of the Mental Capacity Act 2005 (c 9) to manage the child's property and affairs][3],

and there is no other individual with parental responsibility for the child to act as registered contact.

In Scotland, in this Condition for—

(*a*) "Court of Protection" substitute "Sheriff",

(*b*) "[deputy[2]]" substitute "guardian appointed under section 58 of the Adults with Incapacity (Scotland) Act 2000",

(*c*) the reference to a [person lacking capacity][3], substitute "incapable for the purposes of the Adults with Incapacity (Scotland) Act 2000," and

(*d*) "parental responsibility" substitute "parental responsibilities".

Condition 5

The child has been lost or abandoned, and there is no prospect for the foreseeable future of reunification of the child with a parent having parental responsibility (in Scotland, parental responsibilities) for the child.

In this Condition, "lost or abandoned"—

(*a*) in England . . .[8], has the meaning in section 20(1)(*b*) of the Children Act 1989;

[(*ab*) in Wales, has the meaning in section 76 of the Social Services and Well-being (Wales) Act 2014;][8]

(*b*) in Northern Ireland, has the meaning in Article 21(1)(*b*) of the Children (Northern Ireland) Order 1995; and (*c*) in Scotland, has the meaning in section 25(1)(*b*) of the Children (Scotland) Act 1995.

[*Condition 6*

In England and Wales, an adoption agency or local authority has been authorised to place the child for adoption under section 19, or by a placement order under section 21, of the Adoption and Children Act 2002, or in Northern Ireland, an Order has been made under Article 17 or 18 of the Adoption (Northern Ireland) Order 1987 to free the child for adoption.][2]

[(2A) The information specified in this paragraph is—

(*a*) the name, address and unique identifier of the local authority making the return;

(*b*) the name of the local authority officer responsible for the return;

(*c*) the full name, sex and date of birth of the child;

(*d*) the full name and address of the child's mother, if known by the local authority (or failing that the full name and address of the child's father, if known), unless the local authority considers the child's situation to be particularly sensitive;

(*e*) any information that the local authority has about whether the child is or may be a person subject to immigration control within the meaning of section 115(9) of the Immigration and Asylum Act 1999, and the nature of that information;

(*f*) a correspondence address for the child; and

(*g*) if known by the local authority, the child's unique reference number as stated on the voucher issued under section 5(1) of the Child Trust Funds Act 2004 (if any).][4, 9]

[(2B) The unique identifier of a local authority as referred to in paragraph (2A)(a) is the number allocated to the local authority by the Board for the purpose of these Regulations.][5, 9]

(3) Where—

[(*a*) the local authority delivers to the Board a return under this regulation in respect of any child, and][4]

(*b*) the Board (subject to checking and if necessary correcting the contents of the form) delivers it to the Official Solicitor (where the child is in England and Wales or Northern Ireland) or the Accountant of Court (where the child is in Scotland),

the Official Solicitor or Accountant of Court, as the case may be, shall be the person who has the authority to manage the child's account for the purposes of section 3(6)(b) of the Act.[9]

(4) The [person appointed by the Treasury or the Secretary of State by virtue of section 3(10) of the Act][9] shall cease to be the person who has the authority to manage the child's account (and shall be discharged from the duties of registered contact) where—

(*a*) the child [is 16 or over and has elected to manage the account][7],

(*b*) in any case where the child is . . . [7] still looked after (in Scotland, looked after and accommodated) by a local authority—

(i) the local authority confirms to the [person appointed by the Treasury or the Secretary of State by virtue of section 3(10) of the Act][9] that there is a named responsible person in relation to the child, who is able to be the registered contact for the child's account, and that none of the Conditions in paragraph (2) applies, and

(ii) the [person appointed by the Treasury or the Secretary of State by virtue of section 3(10) of the Act][9] cancels his declaration and authorisation in accordance with regulation 13(7) and is replaced as registered contact by that responsible person, in accordance with regulation 13(10), or

(*c*) in any case where the child . . . [7] is not looked after (in Scotland, looked after and accommodated) by a local authority—

(i) a responsible person for the child provides evidence to the satisfaction of the [person appointed by the Treasury or the Secretary of State by virtue of section 3(10) of the Act][9], as the case may be, that he has parental responsibility for the child, and

(ii) the [person appointed by the Treasury or the Secretary of State by virtue of section 3(10) of the Act][9] cancels his declaration and authorisation in accordance with regulation 13(7) and is replaced as registered contact by that responsible person, in accordance with regulation 13(10).

(5) A local authority shall, for the purposes of paragraph (4), confirm to the Official Solicitor or Accountant of Court, as the case may be—

(*a*) whether the child is still looked after (in Scotland, looked after and accommodated) by the authority, and

(*b*) the identity of the person or persons who had parental responsibility for the child at the date when he ceased to be looked after (in Scotland, looked after and accommodated) by the authority (or, at the option of the authority, any later date).[9]

[(6) In this regulation—

"local authority" includes an authority within the meaning of the Children (Northern Ireland) Order 1995;

"looked after and accommodated child", in Scotland, means a child who is—

(*a*) both looked after, and provided with or placed in accommodation, by a local authority within the meaning of those expressions in Part 2 of the Children (Scotland) Act 1995, or (*b*) accommodated by a local authority under section 22 of that Act,

and related expressions shall be construed accordingly;

"looked after child"—

(*a*) in England . . . [8], has the meaning given in section 22(1) of the Children Act 1989, extended to include a child accommodated by a local authority under section 17 of that Act, . . . [8]

[(*ab*) in Wales means looked after by a local authority within the meaning of section 74 of the Social Services and Well-being (Wales) Act 2014; and][8]

(*b*) in Northern Ireland, means a child accommodated under Part 4 of the Children (Northern Ireland) Order 1995,

and related expressions shall be construed accordingly;

"return period" means a period—

(*a*) beginning on 7th April 2011 and ending on 6th May 2011, and

(*b*) each succeeding period of one month.][4], [9]

[(7) Where the appointment of a person ("original appointee") by the Treasury or the Secretary of State by virtue of section 3(10) of the Act ceases, the original appointee must provide any information held by that person in connection with the management of a child trust fund to the new person (if any) appointed instead.][9]][1]

Amendments—[1] Regulation 33A inserted by the Child Trust Funds (Amendment No 2) Regulations, SI 2004/3382 regs 2, 5 with effect from 6 April 2005.

[2] In para (2), Condition 6 inserted by the Child Trust Funds (Amendment No 2) Regulations, SI 2006/2684 regs 2, 5, with effect from 31 October 2006.

[3] In para (2), in condition 4, word in sub-para (a) and whole of sub-para (b) substituted, and in the modifications of condition 4 for Scotland words in sub-paras (b), (c) substituted by the Mental Capacity Act 2005 (Transitional and Consequential Provisions) Order, SI 2007/1898 art 6, Sch 1 para 33 with effect from 1 October 2007.

[4] Para (2A) inserted, and paras (3)(*a*), (6) substituted, by the Child Trust Funds (Amendment) Regulations, SI 2011/781 regs 2, 4 with effect from 7 April 2011.

[5] Para (2B) inserted by the Child Trust Funds (Amendment No 3) Regulations, SI 2011/2447 regs 2, 6 with effect from 1 November 2011.

[6] In para (2), in Condition 3, words substituted and words inserted by the Children's Hearings (Scotland) Act 2011 (Consequential and Transitional Provisions and Savings) Order, SI 2013/1465 art 17, Sch 1 para 21 with effect from 24 June 2013.

[7] In para (1)(*a*)(ii), figure substituted; in para (4)(*a*), words substituted; and in para (4)(*c*), (*b*), wordsrevoked, by the Child Trust Funds (Amendment No 3) Regulations, SI 2015/1371 regs 2, 9 with effect from 1 July 2015—

[8] In para (2), Condition 5, words in sub-para (*a*) revoked, para (2)(*ab*) inserted, in para (6), in definition of "looked after child", words in sub-para (*a*) revoked, and para (6)(*ab*) inserted, by the Child Trust Funds Regulations, SI 2017/185 regs 2, 7 with effect from 6 April 2017.

[9] The following amendments made by the Child Trust Funds (Amendment No 2) Regulations, SI 2017/748 regs 2, 5 with effect from 1 October 2017—

- in heading, words substituted for words "The Official Solicitor or Accountant of Court";
- para (1) substituted;
- para (2)(*za*), (*zb*) inserted, and in para (2)(*a*), words substituted for words "the child";
- paras (2A), (2B), (3), (5) revoked, and in sub-para (6), definition of "return period" revoked;
- in para 4, words substituted for words "Official Solicitor or Accountant of Court" in each place; and
- para (7) inserted.

Para (1) previously read as follows—

"(1) Every local authority shall be under a duty to—

(*a*) identify any child who—

(i) is born after 31st August 2002 and before 3rd January 2011;

(ii) is under 18 years of age at the end of the return period, and

(iii) during the return period falls within the circumstances specified in paragraph (2) for the first time since the child became looked after (in Scotland, looked after and accommodated) by the local authority; and

(*b*) deliver to the Board, within 10 days of the end of each return period and by means of electronic communications, a return for that period in a form specified by the Board containing the information specified in paragraph (2A) for each child identified under sub-paragraph (*a*).".

34 *Information to be provided to the Board*

Amendments—Regs 34, 35 revoked by the Child Trust Funds (Amendment) Regulations, SI 2010/582 regs 2, 16 with effect from 6 April 2010.

35 *Inspection of records by officer of the Board*

Amendments—Regs 34, 35 revoked by the Child Trust Funds (Amendment) Regulations, SI 2010/582 regs 2, 16 with effect from 6 April 2010.

36 Capital gains tax—adaptation of enactments

(1) For the purposes of capital gains tax—

(*a*) any assets held by a named child as account investments shall be regarded as held by the child in a separate capacity from that in which he holds any other assets of the same description; and

(*b*) the named child shall be treated as having sold all the account investments, and as having reacquired them in his personal capacity, for a consideration equal to their market value, immediately before he attains the age of 18 years (and ceases to be a child).

(2) Sections 127 to 131 of the 1992 Act shall not apply in relation to qualifying investments falling within any of sub-paragraphs (*a*), (*b*), and (*f*) to (*i*) of regulation 12(2) which are held under an account if there is by virtue of any allotment for payment as is mentioned in section 126(2) of that Act a reorganisation affecting those assets.

37 Administration of tax in relation to accounts—supplementary

(1) Nothing in these Regulations shall be taken to prejudice any powers conferred or duties imposed by or under any enactment in relation to the making of returns of income or gains, or for the recovery of tax, penalties or interest by means of an assessment or otherwise.

(2) Notwithstanding the provisions of these Regulations an account provider shall not be released from obligations under these Regulations in relation to an account except under conditions agreed in writing with and notified to that person by the Board.

(3) The provisions contained in the Management Act shall apply to any assessment under these Regulations as if it were an assessment to tax for the year in which, apart from these Regulations, the named child would have been liable (by reason of his ownership of the investments).

(4) No obligation as to secrecy imposed by statute or otherwise shall preclude the Board from disclosing to an account provider or registered contact that any provision of these Regulations has not been satisfied or that relief has been given or claimed in respect of investments under an account.

(5) If—

(*a*) a chargeable event, within the meaning given by [Chapter 9 of Part 4 of ITTOIA 2005][1], has happened in relation to a policy of life insurance which is an account investment, and

(*b*) the body by whom the policy was issued is satisfied that no gain is to be treated as chargeable to tax on the happening of the event by virtue of regulation 24(*a*)(v), the body shall not be obliged to deliver the certificates mentioned in section 552(1) of [the Taxes Act][1].

This paragraph does not prevent the operation of section 552(1) in a case to which regulation 38(1) applies.

(6) Where—

(*a*) it comes to the notice of the account provider, in any manner, that the event specified in regulation 12(11) has occurred in relation to a policy, and

(*b*) the account provider is not the insurer for the time being responsible for the obligations under the policy or, where the policy is not still in existence, the person who was the last such insurer, the account provider shall, within 30 days of the event coming to his notice give notice to that insurer, specifying the event mentioned in sub-paragraph (*a*) and the termination event.

Amendments[1] Amendments made by the Child Trust Funds (Amendment) Regulations, SI 2010/582 regs 2, 17 with effect from 6 April 2010.

38 Application of the provisions of Chapter 2 of Part 13 of the Taxes Act [and of Chapter 9 of Part 4 of ITTOIA 2005] to policies

(1) This paragraph applies to a case where—

(*a*) the event specified in regulation 12(11) has occurred in relation to a policy of life insurance, and

(*b*) a termination event within the meaning in regulation 12(12) occurs in relation to that policy.

(2) Where—

(*a*) there is a case to which paragraph (1) applies, and

(*b*) a chargeable event in relation to the policy, within the meaning given by section 540 of the Taxes Act, has occurred prior to the time at which the termination event mentioned in paragraph (1)(*b*) occurs, the named child shall cease to be, and shall be treated as not having been, entitled to relief from tax under regulation 24(*a*)(*v*), in respect of gains treated as arising on the occurrence of any chargeable event mentioned in sub-paragraph (*b*).

(3) The provisions of Chapter 2 of Part 13 of the Taxes Act shall apply, in a case to which paragraph (1) applies, to—

(*a*) the termination event mentioned in paragraph (1)(*b*), and

(*b*) any chargeable event mentioned in paragraph (2)(*b*), with the modifications provided for in paragraphs (4) to (8) of this regulation, and the registered contact and the account provider shall account to the Board in accordance with this regulation for tax from which relief under regulation 24 has been given on the basis that the named child was so entitled, or in circumstances such that the named child was not so entitled.

(4) A termination of a policy of insurance pursuant to regulation 12(9)(*b*)(ii) shall be treated as the surrender [of all rights under the policy for the purposes of section 484(1)(*a*)(i) of ITTOIA 2005][1].

[(5) Section 530 of ITTOIA 2005 does not apply to a gain in a case to which paragraph (1) applies.][1]

(6) Relief under section 550 of the Taxes Act shall be computed as if paragraph (5) had not been enacted.

(7) In section 552 of the Taxes Act—

(*a*) in subsection (1)(*b*) for "policy holder" substitute "named child";

(*b*) in subsection (3)—

(i) omit "(or, where the appropriate policy holder is a company, the corresponding financial year)";

(ii) for "the name and address of the appropriate policy holder" substitute "the name and address of the named child";

(iii) omit "and the corresponding financial year,";

(*c*) in subsection (5)—

(i) for "the appropriate policy holder" substitute "the named child";

(ii) omit sub-paragraph (*b*)(ii);

(iii) omit paragraph (*c*);

(iv) in paragraph (*d*) omit "except where paragraph (*c*) above applies,";

(v) omit paragraph (*f*);

(*d*) in subsection (6)—

(i) omit paragraph (*b*);

(ii) for paragraph (*c*) substitute—

"(*c*) if the event is a death, the period of three months beginning with the receipt of written notification of the death;";

(iii) after paragraph (*c*) insert—

"(*d*) if the event is—

(*i*) a termination event, or

(ii) a chargeable event preceding a termination event (as mentioned in regulation 38(2) of the Child Trust Funds Regulations 2004), the period of three months beginning with the date on which the insurer received notice under regulation 37(6) of those Regulations or, if earlier, actual notice of the termination event.";

(*e*) in subsection (7)—

(i) in paragraph (*a*) omit ", or, where the policy holder is a company, the financial year,";

(ii) omit paragraph (*b*);

(iii) for paragraph (*c*) substitute—

"(*c*) if the event is a death, the period of three months beginning with the receipt of written notification of the death;";

(iv) after paragraph (*c*) insert—

"(*ca*) if the event is—

(i) a termination event, or

(ii) a chargeable event preceding such a termination event (as mentioned in regulation 38(2) of the Child Trust Funds Regulations 2004, the period of three months beginning with the date on which the insurer received notice under regulation 37(6) of those Regulations or, if earlier, actual notice of the termination event."; and

(v) in paragraph (*d*) after "paragraph (*c*)" insert "or (*ca*)";

(*f*) in subsection (8)—

(i) in paragraph (*b*) for "policy holder" substitute "named child in respect";

(ii) in paragraph (*c*) omit the words from "or" to the end;

(*g*) in subsection (9) omit "or financial year" in each place where they occur;

(*h*) in subsection (10)—

(i) before the definition of "amount" insert—

"named child" has the same meaning as in the Child Trust Funds Regulations 2004;";

(ii) omit the definitions of "appropriate policy holder" and "financial year";

(iii) for the definition of "the relevant year of assessment" substitute—

"the relevant year of assessment", in the case of any gain, means the year of assessment to which the gain is attributable;"; and

(iv) after the definition of "section 546 excess" insert— " "termination event" has the same meaning as in the Child Trust Funds Regulations 2004;"; and

(v) omit subsection (11).

(8) In section 552ZA of the Taxes Act—

(*a*) in subsection (2)(*b*) omit the words "or an assignment"; and

(*b*) omit subsections (3) and (4).

(9) The account provider shall account for and pay income tax at the [basic][1] rate in force for the year in which the termination event, or the chargeable event mentioned in paragraph (2)(*b*) occurred, as the case may be, and any amount so payable—

(*a*) may be set off against any repayment in respect of tax due under regulation 26 or 27 and subject thereto,

(*b*) shall be treated as an amount of tax due not later than 6 months after the end of the year in which the event specified in regulation 12(11) came to the notice of the account provider, and

(*c*) shall be payable without the making of an assessment.

(10) Where tax is charged in accordance with paragraph (3)(*a*) or (*b*)—

(*a*) an assessment to income tax at the [basic][1] rate in force for the relevant year may be made on the account provider or on the registered contact (on behalf of the named child), and

(*b*) an assessment to income tax at the higher rate within the meaning of [section 10(3) of ITA 2007][1], for that year, may be made on the registered contact (on behalf of the named child) within five years after the 31st January next following that year, and regulation 29 shall not apply.

Amendments[1] Amendments made to cross-heading and regulation by the Child Trust Funds (Amendment) Regulations, SI 2010/582 regs 2, 18 with effect from 6 April 2010.

SCHEDULE

STAKEHOLDER ACCOUNTS

Description of stakeholder account

1 An account is a stakeholder account where it has the characteristics and complies with the conditions set out in paragraph 2.

Characteristics of stakeholder account etc

2—(1) A stakeholder account must have the characteristics set out in sub-paragraph (2) and must comply with the conditions set out in sub-paragraphs (3) to (5).

(2) The characteristics of a stakeholder account are—

(*a*) the account does not directly hold investments of any of the following kinds

(i) those referred to in regulation 12(2)(*f*) (shares in an investment trust);

(ii) securities of an investment trust;

(iii) rights in with-profits endowment policies;

(iv) rights, under a contract of insurance, in a with-profits fund;

(v) units or shares in a relevant collective investment scheme unless it is a requirement of that scheme that the purchase and sale price of those units or shares shall, at any given time, not differ from each other and that the price must be made available to the public on a daily basis;

(vi) rights under a contract of insurance which are expressed as shares in funds held by the insurer unless it is a requirement of the contract of insurance that the purchase and sale price of those shares shall, at any given time, not differ from each other and that the price must be made available to the public on a daily basis;

[(via) shares referred to in regulation 12(2)(a) (shares issued by a company wherever incorporated and officially listed on a recognised stock exchange [or, in the European Economic Area, admitted to trading on a recognised stock exchange][4]);][1]

(vii) depositary interests, where the investments concerned are investments of any of the kinds listed above in this paragraph;

(*b*) [the requirement is fulfilled that][1] the account provider, and any relevant person, must ensure that, subject to the other provisions of this paragraph, the account has exposure to equities . . . [1];

[(*ba*) interest accrues on investments referred to in regulation 12(2)(*k*) and (*l*) (cash deposited in a deposit account or in a share account) on a daily basis at a rate that is not less than the Bank of England base rate minus 1 per cent per annum[, except where cash is held temporarily on deposit in the course of dealing in investments under the account][3];][1]

[(*baa*) when the Bank of England base rate increases, the interest rate on investments referred to in regulation 12(2)(*k*) and (*l*) (cash deposited in a deposit account or in a share account) must be raised within one month of the date of that increase;][2]

[(*bb*) in relation to qualifying investments which are securities (other than in an investment trust) or a depositary interest where the relevant investments (within the meaning in that definition) are such securities, the requirement is fulfilled that—

(i) the securities fall within regulation 12(2)(*c*)[, (*d*) or (*e*)][2], or

(ii) where the securities fall within regulation 12(2)(*b*) . . . [2] or (*n*), the contract under which the securities are or have been acquired, or any other transaction entered into by the registered contact or any other person, has the effect that the named child is not exposed, or not exposed to a significant extent, to the risk of loss from fluctuations in the value of the securities exceeding 20% of the capital consideration paid or payable for the acquisition of those securities, during the period when the securities in question are held in the account.][1]

(*c*) [the requirement is fulfilled that][1] the account provider and any relevant person . . . [1] have regard to—

(i) the need for diversification of investments of the account, in so far as is appropriate to the circumstances of the account; and

(ii) the suitability for the purposes of the account of any investment, investment strategy or investment option proposed[.][6]

(*d*) . . . [6]

(3) The account provider must permit payment of subscriptions to the account by—

(*a*) cheque;

(*b*) direct debit;

(*c*) standing order;

(*d*) direct credit (other than standing order).

[For the purposes of this sub-paragraph, those means of payment do not include payments by cash, credit card or debit card or any combination including a payment by cash, credit card or debit card.][1]

(4) The minimum amount which may be subscribed to the account on a single occasion is £10 except where the account provider permits a smaller amount.

(5) Deductions from the account may only be made in the circumstances, and to the extent, set out in paragraph 3.

(6) In this paragraph—

"equities" means shares issued by a company wherever incorporated and officially listed on a recognised stock exchange [or, in the European Economic Area, admitted to trading on a recognised stock exchange][4];

"insurer" means—

(*a*) a person who has permission under Part 4 of the Financial Services and Markets Act 2000 to effect or carry out contracts of insurance, or

(*b*) an EEA firm of the kind mentioned in paragraph 5(*d*) of Schedule 3 to that Act, which has permission under paragraph 15 of that Schedule (as a result of qualifying for authorisation under paragraph 12 of that Schedule) to effect or carry out contracts of insurance;

. . . [6]

"relevant collective investment scheme" means an authorised unit trust scheme, an authorised open-ended investment company or a recognised scheme, as the case may be, as defined in section 237(3) of the Financial Services and Markets Act 2000;

"relevant person" means any person to whom the account provider has delegated any of his functions or responsibilities under the management agreement; and "with-profits fund" means a fund maintained by an insurer in respect of a particular part of its long-term business for which—

(*a*) separate accounting records are maintained by the insurer in respect of all income and expenditure relating to that part of its business; and

(*b*) the benefits payable in respect of policies allocated to that fund are determined partly by reference to a discretion exercisable by any person.

(7) In this paragraph, the definitions of "contract of insurance" and "insurer" must be read with—

(*a*) section 22 of the Financial Services and Markets Act 2000,

(*b*) any relevant order made under that section, and

(*c*) Schedule 2 to that Act.

Amendments—[1] Sub-paras (2)(a)(via), (*ba*), (*bb*) inserted, words in sub-paras (2)(*b*), (*c*) inserted and words therein repealed, and words in sub-para (3) inserted, by the Child Trust Funds (Amendment) Regulations, SI 2004/2676 regs 2, 15(*a*)–(*e*) with effect from 6 April 2005 (by virtue of SI 2004/3369).

[2] Sub-para (2)(*baa*) inserted, words in sub-para (2)(*bb*)(i) substituted, and reference in sub-para (2)(*bb*)(ii) revoked, by the Child Trust Funds (Amendment No 2) Regulations, SI 2004/3382 regs 2, 6 with effect from 6 April 2005.

[3] Words in sub-para (2)(*ba*) inserted, by the Child Trust Funds (Amendment No 2) Regulations, SI 2006/2684 regs 2, 6, with effect from 31 October 2006.

[4] In sub-paras (2)(*a*)(via), (6), words inserted by the Child Trust Funds (Amendment No 2) Regulations, SI 2013/1744 regs 2, 10 with effect from 5 August 2013.

[5] In sub-para (6), in definition of "lifestyling", figure substituted by the Child Trust Funds (Amendment No 2) Regulations, SI 2015/876 regs 2, 11 with effect from 6 April 2015.

[6] In sub-para (2)(*c*)(ii), word substituted, sub-para (2)(*d*) revoked, and in sub-para (6), definition of "lifestyling" revoked, by the Child Trust Funds Regulations, SI 2017/185 regs 2, 8 with effect from 6 April 2017.

3 Stakeholder accounts—charges etc

(1) Deductions from a stakeholder account may only be made to the extent set out in this paragraph.

(2) Subject to sub-paragraph (5), charges for the management of, and other expenses in connection with, a stakeholder account may be recovered from the account to the extent that they do not exceed whichever is the greater of—

(*a*) 3/730 per cent of the value of the child's rights in the account for each day on which the account is held; or

(*b*) 3/730 per cent of the value of the investments under the account for each day on which the account is held.

(3) For the purposes of sub-paragraph (2)—

(*a*) the frequency, which must be daily, weekly or monthly, with which rights or investments are to be valued; and

(*b*) where valuation is to take place weekly or monthly, the day of the week or, as the case may be, the date in the month on which it is to take place, must be specified in advance in writing by the account provider to the registered contact, and the specification may not be amended during the period of 12 months after the date on which it is made.

(4) When calculating the value of a child's rights or of investments for the purposes of sub-paragraph (2) where the account provider has specified under sub-paragraph (3) that they are to be valued weekly or monthly—

(*a*) where they are to be valued weekly, they are to be valued on such day of the week ("the specified day") as has been so specified by the account provider (except that, where that day is not a working day, the rights are to be valued on the next working day), and the value of the rights on each subsequent day prior to the next specified day is to be taken to be the value of the rights on the previous specified day; and

(*b*) where they are to be valued monthly, they are to be so valued on such date in each month ("the specified date") as has been so specified by the account provider (except that, where that date is not a working day, the rights are to be valued on the next working day), and the value of the rights on each subsequent day prior to the next specified date is to be taken to be the value of the rights on the previous specified date.

(5) The following charges and expenses may be deducted in full from the account and are not subject to and do not count towards the limit provided for in sub-paragraph (2)—

(*a*) any stamp duty, stamp duty reserve tax, [value added tax][1] or other charges [(including any dilution levy)][1] incurred by the account provider directly or indirectly in the sale or purchase of investments held under the account;

[(*aa*) where any amount of tax is paid or anticipated to be payable in respect of income received or capital gains realised by the account provider in respect of investments held for the purposes of the account, the amount so deducted or anticipated;][1]

(*b*) any charges or expenses incurred by the account provider directly or indirectly in complying with an order of the court or any other requirements imposed by law; and

(*c*) expenses incurred by the account provider in complying with its obligations under regulation 8(2)(*d*) and (*e*).

(6) Valuations for the purpose of sub-paragraph (2) shall be after the deduction of any charges or expenses properly deducted from the account under sub-paragraph (5).

Amendments—[1] Words in sub-para (5)(a) inserted, and sub-para (5)(aa) inserted, by the Child Trust Funds (Amendment) Regulations, SI 2004/2676 regs 2, 15(f), (g) with effect from 6 April 2005 (by virtue of SI 2004/3369).

2004/1819

THALIDOMIDE CHILDREN'S TRUST (APPLICATION OF SECTION 329AA OF THE INCOME AND CORPORATION TAXES ACT 1988) ORDER 2004

Made by the Treasury under TA 1988 s 329AB(3)

Made . . . . 14 *July 2004*
Laid before the House of Commons . . . . 15 *July 2004*
Coming into force . . . . 5 *August 2004*

1 Citation, commencement and interpretation

(1) This Order may be cited as the Thalidomide Children's Trust (Application of Section 329AA of the Income and Corporation Taxes Act 1988) Order 2004 and shall come into force on 5th August 2004.

(2) In this Order "the Thalidomide Children's Trust" means the Trust established by that name by a declaration of trust made on the 10th August 1973 by Sir Henry Gordon Willmer, Arthur Halsall Walton and Sir Donald Macleod Douglas.

2 Modified application of section 329AA of the Income and Corporation Taxes Act 1988

(1) Section 329AA of the Income and Corporation Taxes Act 1988 (personal injury damages in the form of periodical payments) applies to periodical payments by the Thalidomide Children's Trust as it applies to payments to which subsection (1) of that section applies, but subject to the following modifications.

(2) In subsection (1)—

(*a*) after "Where" insert "the Thalidomide Children's Trust makes periodical payments to a beneficiary of that Trust"; and

(*b*) omit paragraphs (*a*) and (*b*).

(3) In subsection (2)—

(*a*) for paragraph (*a*) substitute—

"(*a*) the person ("A") entitled to the payments made by the Thalidomide Children's Trust;";

(*b*) in paragraphs (*b*) and (*c*) for "whether in pursuance of the agreement or order or otherwise" substitute "whether under the terms of the Thalidomide Children's Trust or otherwise".

(4) In subsection (3) omit ", if the agreement or order mentioned in that subsection or a subsequent agreement so provides,".

(5) For subsection (5) substitute—

"(5) In this section "the Thalidomide Children's Trust" means the Trust established by that name by a declaration of trust made on the 10th August 1973 by Sir Henry Gordon Willmer, Arthur Halsall Walton and Sir Donald Macleod Douglas.".

(6) Omit subsections (6) to (8).

2004/1863

TAX AVOIDANCE SCHEMES (PRESCRIBED DESCRIPTIONS OF ARRANGEMENTS) REGULATIONS 2004

Made by the Treasury under FA 2004 s 306(1)(a), (b)

Made . . . . *22 July 2004*
Laid before the House of Commons . . . . *22 July 2004*
Coming into force . . . . *1 August 2004*

Amendment—These regulations revoked by the Tax Avoidance Schemes (Prescribed Descriptions of Arrangements) Regulations, SI 2006/1543 reg 18 with effect from 1 August 2006.

However, SI 2006/1543 does not have effect—

(a) for the purposes of FA 2004 s 308(1), if the relevant date (as defined by FA 2004 s 308(2)) falls before 1 August 2006;

(b) for the purposes of FA 2004 s 308(3), if the date on which the promoter first becomes aware of any transaction forming part of notifiable arrangements falls before 1 August 2006;

(c) for the purposes of FA 2004 ss 309(1), 310, if the date on which any transaction forming part of notifiable arrangements is entered into falls before 1 August 2006.

2004/1864

TAX AVOIDANCE SCHEMES (INFORMATION) REGULATIONS 2004

Made by the Treasury under FA 1999 s 132, FA 2002 s 135, FA 2004 ss 308(1), (3), 309(1), 310, 312, 313(1), (3), (4)(g), 317(2), 318(1)

Made . . . . *22 July 2004*
Laid before the House of Commons . . . . *22 July 2004*
Coming into force . . . . *1 August 2004*

Revocation—These Regulations revoked by the Tax Avoidance Schemes (Information) Regulations, SI 2012/1836 reg 3, Schedule, with effect from 1 September 2012.

Note—Anything begun under or for the purpose of these Regulations shall be construed under or, as the case may be, for the purpose of the corresponding provision of the Tax Avoidance Schemes (Information) Regulations, SI 2012/1836. Where any document refers to a provision of these Regulations, such reference shall, unless the context otherwise requires, be construed as a reference to the corresponding provision of SI 2012/1836 (SI 2012/1836 reg 3(2), (3)).

2 Interpretation

In the Regulations—

"the Act" means the Finance Act 2004, and a reference to a numbered section (without more) is a reference to the section of the Act which is so numbered;

"the Arrangements Regulations" means the Tax Avoidance Schemes (Prescribed Descriptions of Arrangements) [Regulations 2006][2];

["the IHT Arrangements Regulations" means the Inheritance Tax Avoidance Schemes (Prescribed Descriptions of Arrangements) Regulations 2011;][3]
["the SDLT Arrangements Regulations" means the Stamp Duty Land Tax Avoidance Schemes (Prescribed Descriptions of Arrangements) Regulations 2005;][1]
"corporation tax" shall be construed in accordance with section 318(1);
"employment" has the same meaning as it has for the purposes of the employment income Parts of the Income Tax (Earnings and Pensions) Act 2003 (see section 4 of that Act) and includes offices to which the provisions of those Parts that are expressed to apply to employments apply equally (see section 5 of that Act); and "employee" and "employer" have corresponding meanings;
"notifiable arrangements" has the meaning given by section 306(1);
"notifiable proposal" has the meaning given by section 306(2);
"promoter" has the meaning given by section 307;
"the prescribed taxes" means capital gains tax, corporation tax[, income tax[, inheritance tax][3] and stamp duty land tax][1];
"the relevant date" has the meaning given by section 308(2).

Revocation—These Regulations revoked by the Tax Avoidance Schemes (Information) Regulations, SI 2012/1836 reg 3, Schedule, with effect from 1 September 2012.

Amendments—[1] Definition of "the SDLT Arrangements Regulations" inserted, and words in the definition of "the prescribed taxes" substituted, by the Tax Avoidance Schemes (Information) (Amendment) Regulations, SI 2005/1869 regs 2, 3 with effect from 1 August 2005.

However, these amendments do not have effect in respect of proposals or arrangements (as the case may be) which are notifiable by virtue of the Stamp Duty Land Tax Avoidance Schemes (Prescribed Descriptions of Arrangements) Regulations, SI 2005/1868—

(a) for the purposes of FA 2004 s 308(1), if the relevant date in relation to a proposal falls before 1 August 2005;
(b) for the purposes of FA 2004 s 308(3), if the date on which the promoter first becomes aware of any transaction forming part of the arrangements falls before that date;
(c) for the purposes of FA 2004 s 309 or 310, the date on which any transaction forming part of the arrangements is entered into falls before that date: SI 2005/1869 reg 1.

[2] Words in the definition of "the Arrangements Regulations" substituted for the words "Regulations 2004" by the Tax Avoidance Schemes (Information) (Amendment) Regulations, SI 2006/1544 regs 2, 3 with effect from 1 August 2006.

[3] Definition of "the IHT Arrangements Regulations", and words in definition of "the prescribed taxes", inserted, by the Tax Avoidance Schemes (Information) (Amendment) Regulations, SI 2011/171 regs 2, 3 with effect from 6 April 2011.

3 Prescribed information in respect of notifiable proposals and arrangements

(1) The information which must be provided to the Board by a promoter under section 308(1) in respect of a notifiable proposal is sufficient information as might reasonably be expected to enable an officer of the Board to comprehend the manner in which the proposal is intended to operate, including—

(*a*) the promoter's name and address;
(*b*) details of the provision of the Arrangements Regulations[, the IHT Arrangements Regulations][2] [or the SDLT Arrangement Regulations][1] by virtue of which the proposal is notifiable;
(*c*) a summary of the proposal and the name (if any) by which it is known;
(*d*) information explaining each element of the proposed arrangements (including the way in which they are structured) from which the tax advantage expected to be obtained under those arrangements arises; and
(*e*) the statutory provisions, relating to any of the prescribed taxes, on which that tax advantage is based.

(2) The information which must be provided to the Board by a promoter under section 308(3) in respect of notifiable arrangements is sufficient information as might reasonably be expected to enable an officer of the Board to comprehend the manner in which the arrangements are intended to operate, including—

(*a*) the promoter's name and address;
(*b*) details of the provision of the Arrangements Regulations[, the IHT Arrangements Regulations][2] [or the SDLT Arrangement Regulations][1] by virtue of which the arrangements are notifiable;
(*c*) a summary of the arrangements and the name (if any) by which they are known;
(*d*) information explaining each element of the arrangements (including the way in which they are structured) from which the tax advantage expected to be obtained under the arrangements arises; and
(*e*) the statutory provisions, relating to any of the prescribed taxes, on which that tax advantage is based.

(3) The information which must be provided to the Board by a client under section 309 (duty of person dealing with promoter outside the United Kingdom) in respect of notifiable arrangements is sufficient information as might reasonably be expected to enable an officer of the Board to comprehend the manner in which the arrangements are intended to operate, including—

(*a*) the client's name and address;

(*b*) the name and address of the promoter;

(*c*) details of the provision of the Arrangements Regulations[, the IHT Arrangements Regulations][2] [or the SDLT Arrangement Regulations][1] by virtue of which the arrangements are notifiable;

(*d*) a summary of the arrangements, and the name (if any) by which they are known;

(*e*) information explaining each element of the arrangements (including the way in which they are structured) from which the tax advantage expected to be obtained under the arrangements arises; and

(*f*) the statutory provisions, relating to any of the prescribed taxes, on which that tax advantage is based.

(4) The information which must be provided to the Board by a person obliged to do so by section 310 (duty of parties to notifiable arrangements not involving promoter) is sufficient information as might reasonably be expected to enable an officer of the Board to comprehend the manner in which the arrangements of which that transaction forms part are intended to operate, including—

(*a*) the name and address of the person entering into the transaction;

(*b*) details of the provision of the Arrangements Regulations[, the IHT Arrangements Regulations][2] [or the SDLT Arrangement Regulations][1] by virtue of which the arrangements are notifiable;

(*c*) a summary of the arrangements and the name (if any) by which they are known;

(*d*) information explaining each element of the arrangements (including the way in which they are structured) from which the tax advantage expected to be obtained under the arrangements arises; and

(*e*) the statutory provisions, relating to any of the prescribed taxes, on which that tax advantage is based.

[(5) If, but for this paragraph—

(*a*) a person would be obliged to provide information in relation to two or more notifiable arrangements,

(*b*) those arrangements are substantially the same (whether they relate to the same parties or different parties), and

(*c*) he has already provided information under paragraph (4) in relation to any of the other arrangements, he need not provide further information under paragraph (4).][1]

Commentary—*Simon's Taxes* **A7.230, A7.232.**

Revocation—These Regulations revoked by the Tax Avoidance Schemes (Information) Regulations, SI 2012/1836 reg 3, Schedule, with effect from 1 September 2012.

Amendments—[1] Words inserted, and para (5) inserted, by the Tax Avoidance Schemes (Information) (Amendment) Regulations, SI 2005/1869 regs 2, 4 with effect from 1 August 2005.

However, these amendments do not have effect in respect of proposals or arrangements (as the case may be) which are notifiable by virtue of the Stamp Duty Land Tax Avoidance Schemes (Prescribed Descriptions of Arrangements) Regulations, SI 2005/1868—

(a) for the purposes of FA 2004 s 308(1), if the relevant date in relation to a proposal falls before 1 August 2005;

(b) for the purposes of FA 2004 s 308(3), if the date on which the promoter first becomes aware of any transaction forming part of the arrangements falls before that date;

(c) for the purposes of FA 2004 s 309 or 310, the date on which any transaction forming part of the arrangements is entered into falls before that date: SI 2005/1869 reg 1.

[2] In paras (1)(*b*), (2)(*b*), (3)(*c*), (4)(*b*), words inserted by the Tax Avoidance Schemes (Information) (Amendment) Regulations, SI 2011/171 regs 2, 4 with effect from 6 April 2011.

4 [Time for providing information under section 308, 308A, 309 or 310]

(1) The period or time (as the case may be) [within which—

(*a*) the prescribed information under section 308, 309 or 310, and

(*b*) the information or documents which will support or explain the prescribed information under section 308A,][4]

must be provided to the Board is found in accordance with the following paragraphs of this regulation.

[(1A) Where a proposal or arrangements (not being otherwise notifiable) is or are treated as notifiable by virtue of an order under section 306A(1), the prescribed period is the period of 10 days beginning on the day after that on which the order is made.][4]

(2) In the case of a notification under section 308(1), the prescribed period is the period of 5 days beginning with the day after the relevant date.

(3) In the case of a notification under section 308(3), the prescribed period is the period of 5 days beginning with the day after that on which the promoter first becomes aware of any transaction forming part of arrangements to which that subsection applies.

[(3A) Neither paragraph (2) nor (3) applies in a case falling within paragraph (1A) or (3B).

(3B) In the case of a requirement to provide specified information about, or documents relating to, the notifiable proposal or arrangements which arises by virtue of an order under section 308A(2), the prescribed period is the period of 10 days beginning on the day after that on which the order is made.][4]

(4) In the case of a notification under section 309(1), the prescribed period is the period of 5 days beginning with the day after that on which the client enters into the first transaction forming part of notifiable arrangements to which that subsection applies.

(5) In the case of a notification under section 310 the prescribed time is any time [during the period of 30 days beginning with the day after that on which the person enters into the first transaction forming part of the notifiable arrangements.][3]

[This is subject to [paragraph (5A)][2].][1]

(5ZA) . . . [2]

[(5A) In the case of a notification under section 310 which arises by virtue of the application of regulation 6 of the Tax Avoidance Schemes (Promoters and Prescribed Circumstances) Regulations 2004 (persons not to be treated as promoters: legal professional privilege), the prescribed time is any time during the period of 5 days beginning with the day after [that on][4] which the person enters into the first transaction forming part of the notifiable arrangements.][1]

(6) In reckoning any period under this regulation or regulation 5 any day which is a non-business day within the meaning of section 92 of the Bills of Exchange Act 1882 shall be disregarded.

(7) Where paragraph (2), (3) or (4) applies, if the prescribed period referred to in that paragraph would otherwise end before 30th September 2004, it shall instead end upon that date.

(8) This regulation is subject to regulations 5 (statutory clearances) and 6 (transitional provisions).

Commentary—*Simon's Taxes* **A7.213, A7.231**.

Revocation—These Regulations revoked by the Tax Avoidance Schemes (Information) Regulations, SI 2012/1836 reg 3, Schedule, with effect from 1 September 2012.

Amendments—[1] Words in para (5) inserted, and para (5A) inserted, by the Tax Avoidance Schemes (Promoters, Prescribed Circumstances and Information) (Amendment) Regulations, SI 2004/2613 reg 3 with effect from 14 October 2004. However, in any case where the latest time at which a person would by virtue of para (5A) above, be required to provide information to the Board under FA 2004 s 310 would be earlier than 19 November 2004, the latest time at which that information shall be required to be provided shall instead be 19 November 2004: SI 2004/2613 reg 1.

[2] Words in para (5) substituted, and para (5ZA) revoked, by the Tax Avoidance Schemes (Information) (Amendment) Regulations, SI 2010/410, regs 2, 3, with effect from 1 April 2010.

[3] Words in para (5) substituted by the Tax Avoidance Schemes (Information) (Amendment) Regulations, SI 2006/1544 regs 2, 4 with effect from 1 August 2006.

[4] Heading, and words in paras (1), (5ZA), (5A), substituted, and paras (1A), (3A) inserted, by the Tax Avoidance Schemes (Information) (Amendment) Regulations, SI 2007/2153 regs 2, 3 with effect from 1 September 2007: SI 2007/2153 reg 1.

5 Statutory clearances

(1) If—

(*a*) a promoter must provide information under subsection (1) of section 308;

(*b*) the relevant date by reference to which he must provide that information is that referred to in subsection (2)(*a*) of that section; and

(*c*) he reasonably expects to make an application on behalf of a client under any of the provisions listed in paragraph (3) ("a clearance application");

the prescribed period is that beginning with the day after the relevant date and ending with the applicable date.

(2) The applicable date is—

(*a*) the date on which the first transaction occurs in pursuance of the arrangements, or

(*b*) if the promoter ceases to hold the reasonable expectation referred to in paragraph (1)(*c*) 5 days after he ceases to hold it.

(3) The provisions are—

(*a*) sections 215, 225, 444A and 707 of the Income and Corporation Taxes Act 1988; and

(*b*) sections 138, 139, 140B and 140D of the Taxation of Chargeable Gains Act 1992.

Commentary—*Simon's Taxes* **A7.231**.

Revocation—These Regulations revoked by the Tax Avoidance Schemes (Information) Regulations, SI 2012/1836 reg 3, Schedule, with effect from 1 September 2012.

6 Time for providing information under section 308, 309 or 310: transitional provisions

. . .

Revocation—These Regulations revoked by the Tax Avoidance Schemes (Information) Regulations, SI 2012/1836 reg 3, Schedule, with effect from 1 September 2012.

Amendment—This regulation revoked by the Tax Avoidance Schemes (Information) (Amendment) Regulations, SI 2006/1544 regs 2, 5 with effect from 1 August 2006.

[7 [Prescribed information under sections 312 and 312A]

For the purposes of sections 312(2) and (5) (duty of promoter to notify client of number) and 312A(2) (duty of client to notify parties of number) the prescribed information is—

(*a*) the name and address of the promoter;

(*b*) the name, or a brief description of the notifiable arrangements or proposal;

(*c*) the reference number (or if more than one, any one reference number) allocated under the provisions of section 311; and
(*d*) the date that the reference number was—
(i) sent by the promoter to the client; or (as the case may be)
(ii) sent to any other person by the client under section 312A(2).][1]

Commentary—*Simon's Taxes* **A7.233**.
Revocation—These Regulations revoked by the Tax Avoidance Schemes (Information) Regulations, SI 2012/1836 reg 3, Schedule, with effect from 1 September 2012.
Amendments—Regulation heading substituted by the Tax Avoidance Schemes (Information) (Amendment) Regulations, SI 2008/1947 regs 2, 3 with effect from 1 November 2008.

[1] This regulation substituted by the Tax Avoidance Schemes (Information) (Amendment) Regulations, SI 2009/611 regs 2, 3 with effect in relation to duties under FA 2004 ss 312 or 312A which arise on or after 1 April 2009.

7A [Time for providing information under 312A
In the case of a notification under section 312A the prescribed period is the period of 30 days beginning with—
(*a*) the day on which the client first becomes aware of any transaction forming part of notifiable arrangements or proposed notifiable arrangements; or, if later,
(*b*) the day on which the prescribed information is notified to the client by the promoter under section 312.][1]

Revocation—These Regulations revoked by the Tax Avoidance Schemes (Information) Regulations, SI 2012/1836 reg 3, Schedule, with effect from 1 September 2012.
Amendments—[1] Regulations 7A, 7B inserted by the Tax Avoidance Schemes (Information) (Amendment) Regulations, SI 2008/1947 regs 2, 4 with effect from 1 November 2008.

7B [Exemption from duty under section 312A
The duty of a client to notify other persons under section 312A does not apply to an employer of an employee where the employee by reason of employment receives or expects to receive a tax advantage in respect of income tax or capital gains tax as a result of notifiable arrangements or proposed notifiable arrangements.][1]

Revocation—These Regulations revoked by the Tax Avoidance Schemes (Information) Regulations, SI 2012/1836 reg 3, Schedule, with effect from 1 September 2012.
Amendments—[1] Regulations 7A, 7B inserted by the Tax Avoidance Schemes (Information) (Amendment) Regulations, SI 2008/1947 regs 2, 4 with effect from 1 November 2008.

[8 Prescribed information under section 313: timing and manner of delivery
(1) For the purposes of section 313(1) (duty of parties to notifiable arrangements to notify HMRC of number etc) the prescribed information is that specified in whichever of paragraphs (4)[, (5) or (5A)][2] is applicable.
(2) For the purposes of section 313(3)(*a*) (cases in which the prescribed information is to be included in returns) the prescribed cases are those specified at paragraphs (6) to [(8A)][3].
(3) For the purposes of section 313(3)(*b*) (cases in which the prescribed information is to be provided separately)—
(*a*) the prescribed cases are those specified at paragraphs (10) to [(14A)][2]; and
(*b*) the prescribed times are those specified at paragraph (15).
(4) In the cases prescribed at paragraphs (6) to [(8A)][3] the prescribed information is—
(*a*) the reference number allocated by HMRC under section 311 to the notifiable arrangements or proposed notifiable arrangements; and
(*b*) the year of assessment, tax year or accounting period (as the case may be) in which, or the date on which, the person providing the information expects a tax advantage to be obtained.
(5) In the cases prescribed at paragraphs (10) to (14) the prescribed information is—
(*a*) the name and address of the person providing it;
(*b*) any National Insurance number, tax reference number, PAYE reference number or other personal identifier allocated by HMRC to the person to whom the information relates;
(*c*) the reference number allocated to the scheme by HMRC under section 311 to the notifiable arrangements or proposed notifiable arrangements;
(*d*) the year of assessment, tax year or accounting period (as the case may be) in which, or the date on which, the person providing the information or, in the case of paragraph (10), an employee of that person, expects to obtain a tax advantage by virtue of the notifiable arrangements;
(*e*) the name of the person providing the declaration as to the accuracy and completeness of the notification; and
(*f*) the capacity in which the person mentioned in sub-paragraph (*e*) is acting.
[(5A) In the case prescribed at paragraph (14A) the prescribed information is—
(*a*) the name and address of the purchaser;
(*b*) the reference number (or, if more than one, any one reference number) allocated under the provisions of section 311;
(*c*) the address of the property forming the subject of the arrangements ("the property");

(*d*) the title number of the property (if any is allocated);
(*e*) the unique transaction reference number(if a land transaction return has been submitted to HMRC at the time the prescribed information is provided);
(*f*) the market value of the property, taking into account all chargeable interests in the property held by the same person or connected persons;
(*g*) the effective date of the first land transaction which forms part of the arrangements;
(*h*) the name of the person providing the declaration as to the accuracy and completeness of the notification; and
(i) the capacity in which that person is acting.][2]

(6) Subject to paragraphs (10), (12) and (13), in the case of a person who—
(*a*) expects an advantage to arise in respect of his liability to pay, entitlement to a repayment of, or to a deferment of his liability to pay, income tax or capital gains tax as a result of notifiable arrangements; and
(*b*) is required to make a return to HMRC by a notice under section 8 or 8A of the Taxes Management Act 1970 (income tax and capital gains tax: personal return and trustee's return), in respect of income tax or capital gains tax,

the prescribed information shall be included in the return under that section which relates to the year of assessment in which the person first enters into a transaction forming part of the notifiable arrangements and in the return for each subsequent year of assessment until the advantage ceases to apply to that person.

This paragraph does not apply if the advantage arises in respect of a partner's share of partnership profits or gains.

(7) Subject to paragraphs (10), (12) and (13), in the case of a company which—
(*a*) expects a tax advantage to arise in respect of its liability to pay, entitlement to a repayment of, or to a deferment of its liability to pay, corporation tax as a result of notifiable arrangements; and
(*b*) is required to make a return to HMRC by a notice under paragraph 3 of Schedule 18 to the Finance Act 1998 (company tax return), in respect of corporation tax,

the prescribed information shall be notified to HMRC in the return under that paragraph covering the period in which the company first enters into a transaction forming part of the notifiable arrangements and in the return covering each subsequent period until the tax advantage ceases to apply to the company.

This paragraph does not apply if the advantage arises in respect of a partner's share of partnership profits or gains.

(8) Subject to paragraphs (10) to (13) [and (14A)][2], in the case of a partnership—
(*a*) which expects an advantage to arise in respect of a partner's liability to pay, entitlement to a repayment of, or to a deferment of the partner's liability to pay any of the prescribed taxes in respect of partnership profits or gains as a result of notifiable arrangements; and
(*b*) in respect of which a return is required to be made to the Board by virtue of a notice under section 12AA of the Taxes Management Act 1970 (partnership return) in respect of any of the prescribed taxes,

the prescribed information shall be included in the returns specified in paragraph (9) covering the period in which the partnership first enters into a transaction forming part of the notifiable arrangements and in the returns covering each subsequent period until the tax advantage ceases to apply to the partner in question.

[(8A) Subject to paragraphs (11A), (12) and (13) in the case of a person who—
(*a*) is a party to notifiable arrangements which are prescribed by the Inheritance Tax Avoidance Schemes (Prescribed Descriptions of Arrangements) Regulations 2011; and
(*b*) is required to make a return to HMRC under section 216 of the Inheritance Tax Act 1984 in respect of a transaction forming part of the notifiable arrangements,

the prescribed information shall be notified to HMRC in the return under that section.][3]

(9) The returns referred to in paragraph (8) are—
(*a*) the partnership's return under section 12AA of the Taxes Management Act 1970; and
(*b*) the return under section 8 or 8A of that Act, or under paragraph 3 of Schedule 18 to the Finance Act 1998, of the partner in respect of whom an advantage is expected.

(10) In the case of a person who is the employer of an employee, by reason of whose employment a tax advantage is expected to arise to any person in respect of income tax, corporation tax or capital gains tax as a result of notifiable arrangements—
(*a*) paragraphs (6) to (8) shall not apply; and
(*b*) the prescribed information shall be provided separately to HMRC in such form and manner as they may specify by the time in paragraph (15).

(11) In the case of a person who would be obliged to comply with a duty under paragraphs (6) to (8), but is not required, in respect of a year of assessment, accounting period or tax year—

(*a*) in the case of notifiable arrangements to which paragraph (6) applies, to make a return under either of the provisions mentioned in paragraph (6)(*b*);
(*b*) in the case of notifiable arrangements to which paragraph (7) applies, to make a return under the provision referred to in paragraph (7)(b); or
(*c*) in the case of notifiable arrangements to which paragraph (8) applies, to make a return under any of the provisions in paragraph (9);

the person must provide the information specified in paragraph (5) separately to HMRC in such form and manner as they may specify by the time in paragraph (15).

[(11A) In the case of a person who—
(*a*) is a party to notifiable arrangements which are prescribed by the Inheritance Tax Avoidance Schemes (Prescribed Descriptions of Arrangements) Regulations 2011; and
(*b*) is not required to make a return to HMRC under section 216 of the Inheritance Tax Act 1984 in respect of a transaction forming part of the notifiable arrangements within a period of 12 months of the end of the month in which the first transaction forming part of the arrangements is entered into,

the prescribed information shall be provided separately to HMRC in such form and manner as they may specify.][3]

(12) In a case of a person who is obliged to comply with a duty under paragraphs (6) to [(8A)][3] and—
(*a*) the relevant return is not delivered by the filing date; or
(*b*) the relevant return is delivered by the filing date but does not include the prescribed information;

paragraphs (6) to [(8A)][3] shall not apply and the prescribed information shall be provided separately to HMRC in such form and manner as they may specify by the time in paragraph (15).

(13) In a case where—
(*a*) a person is required to provide information relating to more than one reference number;
(*b*) the information is included in a return under paragraphs (6) to [(8A)][3]; and
(*c*) the number of reference numbers in relation to which information is required exceeds the number of spaces allocated to the information on the return form;

the information relating to so many of the reference numbers as exceeds the number of allocated spaces shall be provided separately to HMRC in such form and manner as they may specify by the time in paragraph (15).

(14) In addition to the duty under any other paragraph above, in a case where the arrangements give rise to a claim submitted separately from the return under—
(*a*) section 261B of the Taxation of Chargeable Gains Act 1992 (treating trade loss etc as CGT loss); or
(*b*) Part 4 of the Income Tax Act 2007 (loss relief);

the prescribed information shall be provided separately to HMRC in such form and manner as they may specify at the time in paragraph (15).

[(14A) In a case where a purchaser expects an advantage to arise in respect of his liability to pay, entitlement to a repayment of, or to a deferment of his liability to pay stamp duty land tax as a result of notifiable arrangements the prescribed information shall be provided separately to HMRC in such form and manner as they may specify by the time in paragraph (15).

(14B) If paragraph 14A applies in relation to a land transaction entered into as purchaser by or on behalf of a partnership notification of the prescribed information by or in relation to the responsible partners may instead be done by or in relation to a representative partner or partners.][2]

(15) The prescribed times for providing information separately under paragraphs (10) to [(14A)][2] are—
(*a*) in the case of paragraph (10), any time during the period ending on the date on which—
 (i) the return under regulation 73 of the Income Tax (Pay As You Earn) Regulations 2003 is or would be due in respect of the tax year in which the employer first enters into a transaction forming part of the notifiable arrangements; and
 (ii) the return for each subsequent year is or would be due until an advantage ceases to apply to any person;
(*b*) in the case of paragraph (11)—
 (i) for sub-paragraph (*a*), any time during the period ending on 31st January next following the end of the year of assessment in question;
 (ii) for sub-paragraph (*b*), any time during the period ending on the date defined as the filing date for the purposes of paragraph 14 of Schedule 18 to the Finance Act 1998 in respect of the period of account in question;
 (iii) for sub-paragraph (*c*), any time during the period ending on the earliest date by which the person in question could be required to file a return under section 12AA of the Taxes Management Act 1970, determined in accordance with whichever of subsections (4) and (5) of that section is applicable;

[(*ba*) in the case of paragraph (11A), any time during the period of 12 months of the end of the month in which the first transaction forming part of the arrangement is entered into.][3]

(*c*) in the case of paragraphs (12) and (13), any time during the period ending on the filing date for the relevant return;

(*d*) in the case of paragraph (14), the time that the claim is made;

[(*e*) in the case of paragraph (14A) no later than 30 days following the later of—

(i) the effective date of the first land transaction which forms part of the arrangements; or

(ii) the receipt of the reference number allocated under the provisions of section 311.][2]

(16) For the purposes of paragraph (15)(*c*) "the filing date" is whichever date in paragraph (i) to (iii) of paragraph (15)(*b*) applies to the relevant return.

[(16A) In paragraphs (5A), (14A), (14B) and (15), expressions which are used in Part 4 of the Finance Act 2003 have the same meaning as in that Part.][2]

(17) . . . [2]][1]

Commentary—*Simon's Taxes* **A7.233**.

Revocation—These Regulations revoked by the Tax Avoidance Schemes (Information) Regulations, SI 2012/1836 reg 3, Schedule, with effect from 1 September 2012.

Amendments—[1] This regulation substituted by the Tax Avoidance Schemes (Information) (Amendment) Regulations, SI 2009/611 regs 2, 4 with effect in relation to—

(a) reference numbers notified to a person under FA 2004 ss 311, 312 or 312A on or after 1 April 2009, where that person has a duty under FA 2004 s 313; and

(b) claims under either of the provisions mentioned in para (14) of the substituted reg 8 above, made on or after 1 April 2009 (SI 2009/611 reg 1(3)).

[2] Words in paras (1), 3)(*a*), (15) substituted, words in para (8), and paras (5A), (14A), (14B), (16A) inserted, and para (17) revoked, by the Tax Avoidance Schemes (Information) (Amendment) Regulations, SI 2010/410, regs 2, 3, with effect from 1 April 2010.

[3] In paras (2), (4), (12), (13)(*b*), reference substituted for reference "(8)", and paras (8A), (11A) and (15)(*b*) inserted, by the Tax Avoidance Schemes (Information) (Amendment) Regulations, SI 2011/171 regs 2, 5 with effect from 6 April 2011.

8ZA [Prescribed information under section 313ZA: information and timing

(1) For the purposes of section 313ZA(3) (duty of promoter to provide client lists)—

(*a*) the prescribed period is 30 days;

(*b*) the prescribed information is—

(i) any reference number allocated by HMRC under section 311 to the arrangements (or to a proposal for them) to which the information provided relates;

(ii) the name and address of each client in relation to whom the relevant date occurs in the relevant period in relation to which the information is being provided;

(ii) the promoter's name and address; and

(iv) the end date of the relevant period in relation to which the information is being provided.

(*c*) in sub-paragraph (*b*)(ii) the address of the client is the address to which the promoter has sent or would have sent the prescribed information under section 312.

(2) For the purposes of section 313ZA(4) the relevant period is each calendar quarter.][1]

Revocation—These Regulations revoked by the Tax Avoidance Schemes (Information) Regulations, SI 2012/1836 reg 3, Schedule, with effect from 1 September 2012.

Amendments—[1] Reg 8ZA inserted by the Tax Avoidance Schemes (Information) (Amendment) (No 2) Regulations, SI 2010/2928 regs 2, 3 with effect from 1 January 2011.

8A [Time for providing information under section 313A and 313B

(1) In the case of a requirement under or by virtue of section 313A(1), the prescribed period is the period of 10 days beginning on the day after that on which the notice is issued.

(2) In the case of a requirement under or by virtue of section 313B(1), the prescribed period is the period of 14 days beginning on the day after that on which the order is made.][1]

Revocation—These Regulations revoked by the Tax Avoidance Schemes (Information) Regulations, SI 2012/1836 reg 3, Schedule, with effect from 1 September 2012.

Amendments—[1] This reg inserted by the Tax Avoidance Schemes (Information) (Amendment) Regulations, SI 2007/2153 regs 2, 4 with effect from 1 September 2007: SI 2007/2153 reg 1.

8B [Higher rate of penalty following a failure to comply with an order under section 306A or 314A

(1) For the purposes of section 98C(2A) of the Taxes Management Act 1970 (higher rate of penalty after the making of an order under section 306A) the prescribed period is the period of 10 days beginning on the date on which the order is made.

(2) For the purposes of section 98C(2B) of the Taxes Management Act 1970 (higher rate of penalty after the making of an order under section 314A) the prescribed period is the period of 10 days beginning on the date on which the order is made.][1]

Revocation—These Regulations revoked by the Tax Avoidance Schemes (Information) Regulations, SI 2012/1836 reg 3, Schedule, with effect from 1 September 2012.

Amendments—[1] This reg substituted by the Tax Avoidance Schemes (Information) (Amendment) (No 2) Regulations, SI 2010/2928 regs 2, 4 with effect from 1 January 2011.

8C [Prescribed information under section 313C: information and timing

(1) For the purposes of section 313C(1) (information provided to introducers) the prescribed information is—

(*a*) P's name and address; and

(*b*) the name and address of each person who has provided P with any information relating to the proposal.

(2) For the purposes of section 313C(3)(a) the prescribed period is 10 days.][1]

Revocation—These Regulations revoked by the Tax Avoidance Schemes (Information) Regulations, SI 2012/1836 reg 3, Schedule, with effect from 1 September 2012.

Amendments—[1] This reg inserted by the Tax Avoidance Schemes (Information) (Amendment) (No 2) Regulations, SI 2010/2928 regs 2, 5 with effect from 1 January 2011.

9 Exemption from liability for penalty

For the purposes of section 313(4)(*g*) (exemption from liability to penalty under other provisions about returns in respect of duty to notify Board of reference number for notifiable arrangements) section 98A(4) of the Taxes Management Act 1970 is prescribed.

Revocation—These Regulations revoked by the Tax Avoidance Schemes (Information) Regulations, SI 2012/1836 reg 3, Schedule, with effect from 1 September 2012.

10 Electronic delivery of information

(1) Information required to be delivered to the Board or to any other person by virtue of these Regulations may be delivered in such form and by such means of electronic communications as are for the time being authorised for that purpose.

(2) The use of a particular means of electronic communications is authorised for the purposes of paragraph (1) only if—

(*a*) it is authorised by directions given by the Board under section 132(5) of the Finance Act 1999 (voluntary filing by electronic means of returns and other documents); and

(*b*) the user complies with any conditions imposed by the Board under that section.

(3) Nothing in this regulation prevents the delivery of information by electronic communications if the information is contained in a return which is—

(*a*) authorised to be delivered electronically by virtue of regulations under section 132 of the Finance Act 1999; or

(*b*) required to be so delivered by virtue of regulations under section 135 of the Finance Act 2002 (mandatory e-filing).

Revocation—These Regulations revoked by the Tax Avoidance Schemes (Information) Regulations, SI 2012/1836 reg 3, Schedule, with effect from 1 September 2012.

2004/1865

TAX AVOIDANCE SCHEMES (PROMOTERS AND PRESCRIBED CIRCUMSTANCES) REGULATIONS 2004

Made by the Commissioners of Inland Revenue under FA 2004 ss 307(5), 318(1)

Made . . . . *22 July 2004*
Laid before the House of Commons . . . . *22 July 2004*
Coming into force . . . . *1 August 2004*

Note—National Insurance Contributions (Application of Part 7 of the Finance Act 2004) Regulations, SI 2012/1868 reg 27(1) (these Regulations apply to notifiable contribution arrangements and notifiable contribution proposals as they apply to income tax with the modifications noted below, and any reference in these Regulations to FA 2004 ss 306–313C and s 314A shall be construed as a reference to the corresponding provision of SI 2012/1868).

1 Citation, commencement and interpretation

(1) These Regulations may be cited as the Tax Avoidance Schemes (Promoters and Prescribed Circumstances) Regulations 2004 and shall come into force on 1st August 2004.

(2) In these Regulations—

"notifiable arrangements" has the meaning given by section 306(1);

"notifiable proposal" has the meaning given by section 306(2); and

except where the context otherwise requires a reference to a numbered section (without more) is a reference to the section of the Finance Act 2004 which is so numbered.

(3) For the purposes of these Regulations section 839 of the Income and Corporation Taxes Act 1988 applies to determine whether persons are connected.

Modification—National Insurance Contributions (Application of Part 7 of the Finance Act 2004) Regulations, SI 2012/1868 reg 27(2) (modification of this reg in relation to NIC avoidance schemes and proposals).

2 Persons not to be treated as promoters—groups

(1) A person is not to be treated as a promoter where—

(*a*) the person carrying on the relevant business referred to in section 307(1) is a company ("company A"); and

(*b*) on the date specified in paragraph (2) the other person (or each of the other persons) to whom company A provides services in connection with a notifiable proposal or notifiable arrangements is a company which is a member of the same group as company A.

(2) The date specified by this paragraph is—

(*a*) in relation to a notifiable proposal, the relevant date within the meaning given by section 308(2);

(*b*) in relation to notifiable arrangements, the date mentioned in section 308(3).

(3) For the purposes of this regulation two companies are members of the same group if they would, by virtue of the provisions of section 170 of the Taxation of Chargeable Gains Act 1992, be members of the same group for the purposes of sections 171 to 181 of that Act if section 170 were modified as follows—

(*a*) for each of the references to a 75 per cent subsidiary there were substituted a reference to a 51 per cent subsidiary;

(*b*) subsection (3)(*b*) and subsections (6) to (8) were omitted.

Commentary—*Simon's Taxes* **A7.210**.

3 Persons not to be treated as promoters—employees

(1) A person is not to be treated as a promoter in relation to a notifiable proposal or notifiable arrangements where he is an employee of an employer who is—

(*a*) a promoter in relation to the proposal or the arrangements; or

(*b*) a person who—

(i) is to enter into any transaction forming part of the proposed arrangements; or

(ii) enters into any transaction forming part of the arrangements.

(2) In this regulation "employee" and "employer" have the same meanings as they have for the purposes of the employment income Parts of the Income Tax (Earnings and Pensions) Act 2003 (see section 4 of that Act) and—

(*a*) "employee" includes an office holder to whom the provisions of those Parts that are expressed to apply to employments apply equally (see section 5 of that Act); and

(*b*) "employer" includes a person under whom an office holder holds office and to whom those provisions similarly apply.

(3) For the purposes of this regulation an employee of a person who is connected with another person ("A") shall be treated as an employee of A.

[(4) This regulation does not apply where, but for this paragraph, it would result in a duty under section 309 falling on any person.][1]

Commentary—*Simon's Taxes* **A7.210**.

Amendments—[1] Para (4) inserted by the Tax Avoidance Schemes (Promoters and Prescribed Circumstances) (Amendment) Regulations, SI 2015/945 regs 2, 3 with effect from 17 April 2015.

4 Persons not to be treated as promoters under section 307(1)(a)(i) or (b)(i)

(1) A person is not to be treated as a promoter under section 307(1)(*a*)(i) or (*b*)(i) where paragraph (2), (3) or (4) applies.

(2) This paragraph applies where, in the course of providing tax advice, a person is not responsible for the design of any element of the proposed arrangements or arrangements (including the way in which they are structured) from which the tax advantage expected to be obtained arises.

(3) This paragraph applies where—

(*a*) a person, in the course of a business that is a relevant business for the purposes of section 307 by virtue of subsection (2)(*a*) of that section, is to any extent responsible for the design of the proposed arrangements or arrangements; but

(*b*) does not provide tax advice in the course of carrying out his responsibilities in relation to the proposed arrangements or arrangements.

(4) This paragraph applies where a person—

(*a*) is not responsible for the design of all the elements of the proposed arrangements or arrangements (including the way in which they are structured) from which the tax advantage expected to be obtained arises; and

(*b*) could not reasonably be expected to have—

(i) sufficient information as would enable him to know whether or not the proposal is a notifiable proposal or the arrangements are notifiable arrangements; or

(ii) sufficient information as would enable him to comply with section 308(1) or (3).

Commentary—*Simon's Taxes* **A7.210, A7.228**.

Modification—National Insurance Contributions (Application of Part 7 of the Finance Act 2004) Regulations, SI 2012/1868 reg 27(3) (modification of this reg in relation to NIC avoidance schemes and proposals).

5 Persons not to be treated as promoters under section 307(1)(b)(ii)

Amendments—Regulation 5 revoked by the Tax Avoidance Schemes (Promoters and Prescribed Circumstances) (Amendment) Regulations, SI 2015/945 regs 2, 4 with effect from 17 April 2015.

6 [Persons not to be treated as promoters: legal professional privilege

A person is not to be treated as a promoter in relation to a notifiable proposal or notifiable arrangements where his involvement with the proposal or arrangements is such that he is not required to provide all of the information prescribed in [regulation 4(1) of the Tax Avoidance Schemes (Information) Regulations 2012][2] by virtue of section 314 (legal professional privilege).][1]

Commentary—*Simon's Taxes* **A7.210, A7.213**.

Modification—National Insurance Contributions (Application of Part 7 of the Finance Act 2004) Regulations, SI 2012/1868 reg 27(4) (modification of this reg in relation to NIC avoidance schemes and proposals).

Amendments—[1] Regulation 6 inserted by the Tax Avoidance Schemes (Promoters, Prescribed Circumstances and Information) (Amendment) Regulations, SI 2004/2613 reg 2 with effect from 14 October 2004. However, in any case where the latest time at which a person would by virtue of SI 2004/1864 reg 4(5A), be required to provide information to the Board under FA 2004 s 310 would be earlier than 19 November 2004, the latest time at which that information shall be required to be provided shall instead be 19 November 2004: SI 2004/2613 reg 1.

[2] Words substituted for words "paragraph (1) or (2) (as the case may be) of regulation 3 of the Tax Avoidance Schemes (Information) Regulations 2004", by the Tax Avoidance Schemes (Information) Regulations, SI 2012/1836 reg 18 with effect from 1 September 2012.

2004/2199

VENTURE CAPITAL TRUST (WINDING UP AND MERGERS) (TAX) REGULATIONS 2004

Made by the Treasury under FA 2002 Sch 33 paras 2–5, 7–9, 11 and 16

Made . . . . *27 August 2004*
Laid . . . . *27 August 2004*
Coming into force . . . . *17 September 2004*

1 Citation, commencement and effect

(1) These Regulations may be cited as the Venture Capital Trust (Winding up and Mergers) (Tax) Regulations 2004 and shall come into force on 17th September 2004.

(2) These Regulations have effect as follows—

(*a*) regulations 3 to 8 have effect in relation to any VCT-in-liquidation whose winding-up commences on or after 17th April 2002;

(*b*) regulations 9 to 13 have effect in relation to any merger where the transactions for effecting the merger take place on or after 17th April 2002; and

(*c*) regulation 14 has effect in relation to shares issued on or after 6th April 2004.

2 Interpretation

[(1) In these Regulations, references to provisions of an Act or to Parts of an Act are to provisions or Parts of the Income Tax Act 2007 unless otherwise stated.

(2) In these Regulations—

"the Commissioners" means the Commissioners for Her Majesty's Revenue and Customs;

"market value" shall be construed in accordance with sections 272 and 273 of the Taxation of Chargeable Gains Act 1992;

"the 1992 Act" means the Taxation of Chargeable Gains Act 1992;

"prescribed winding-up period", in relation to a VCT-in-liquidation, means the period—

(*a*) beginning on the commencement of the company's winding-up, and

(*b*) ending on the earliest of—

(i) the end of the company's winding-up;

(ii) the company's ceasing to be wound up;

(iii) the dissolution of the company;

(iv) the third anniversary of the commencement of the winding-up;

"qualifying holdings" shall be construed in accordance with Chapter 4 of Part 6;

"securities", except in regulation 12, has the same meaning as in section 285(2);

"statement of affairs" means a statement as to the affairs of a company, in the form prescribed under and complying with section 99 or 131 of the Insolvency Act 1986;

"the 15% test" means the 15% holding limit condition specified in the table in section 274(2) and as provided for in sections 275 to 279;

"the 70% tests" means the conditions specified in the last two entries in the table in section 274(2) and as provided for in sections 275, 278, 280 and 280A;

"the 30% test" means the condition which was specified in the table at section 274(2) and as provided for in sections 275, 278 and 280, ignoring the amendments made to section 274(2) by paragraph 2(2)(*b*) and (*c*) of Schedule 2 to the Finance (No 3) Act 2010.

(3) In regulations 9 to 14 and in this paragraph—

a "section 323(1) merger" means a merger described in section 323(1);

a "section 323(2) merger" means a merger described in section 323(2);

"share for business transfer" means an issue of shares as mentioned in section 323(1)(*b*)(ii) or 323(2)(*b*)(ii), as the case may be;

"share for share exchange" means an exchange of shares as mentioned in section 323(1)(*b*)(i) or 323(2)(*b*)(i), as the case may be;

"shares issued to effect the merger" means—

(*a*) in the case of a section 323(1) merger, shares in the successor company issued as mentioned in section 323(1); and

(*b*) in the case of a section 323(2) merger, shares in the successor company issued as mentioned in section 323(2);

"shares issued for new consideration" means shares in the successor company issued in the period during which the merger takes place for a consideration other than as mentioned in section 323(1)(*b*) or 323(2)(*b*).

(4) Section 319(3) (references in sections 314 to 318 to things done by a VCT-in-liquidation to include things done by the liquidator of a VCT-in-liquidation) shall apply for the purposes of regulations 3 to 8 as it applies to Chapter 5 of Part 6.][1]

(5) References to a resolution passed, or petition presented, to wind up a company (or other references to insolvency procedure) shall, where the winding up is wholly or partly other than under the law of England and Wales, include references to the corresponding local equivalents.

Amendments—[1] Paras (1)–(4) substituted by the Venture Capital Trust (Winding up and Mergers) (Tax) (Amendment) Regulations, SI 2011/660 regs 2, 3 with effect from 6 April 2011.

3 Winding up of Venture Capital Trusts

(1) Regulations 4 to 8 apply, subject to paragraphs (2) and (3), in the case of a VCT-in-liquidation—

(*a*) whose VCT approval has had effect for the continuous period of 3 years immediately preceding the commencement of its winding up, or

(*b*) which is being wound up by the court under section 122(1) of the Insolvency Act 1986 (other than under paragraph (*a*) of that provision) or under any corresponding local equivalent,

and which has given notice to the [Commissioners][1] that a resolution has been passed, or a petition presented, to wind up the company, pursuant to regulation 8(1) of the Venture Capital Trust Regulations 1995.

(2) Where a company—

(*a*) on or after 6th April 2004 and before 6th April 2006, makes an issue of shares falling within the circumstances in [section 280(1)(*a*) and (*b*)][1] (that is, whether or not the company makes a further issue as mentioned in paragraph (*c*) of that provision), and

(*b*) has not made an issue of shares falling within those circumstances, before 6th April 2004, the period in paragraph (1)(*a*) shall be 5 years.

(3) Paragraph (1) shall not apply to any VCT-in-liquidation which is, or has at any time been, a merging company (other than a successor company).

Amendments—[1] In para (2)(*a*), words substituted by the Venture Capital Trust (Winding up and Mergers) (Tax) (Amendment) Regulations, SI 2011/660 regs 2, 4 with effect in relation to any VCT in liquidation whose winding-up commences on or after 6 April 2011.

[2] In para (1), word substituted by the Venture Capital Trust (Winding up and Mergers) (Tax) (Amendment) Regulations, SI 2011/660 regs 2, 13 with effect from 6 April 2011.

4 For the purposes of [section 268][1], the commencement of the winding up shall not affect the status of the VCT-in-liquidation as a venture capital trust.

Amendments—[1] Words substituted by the Venture Capital Trust (Winding up and Mergers) (Tax) (Amendment) Regulations, SI 2011/660 regs 2, 5 with effect in relation to any VCT in liquidation whose winding-up commences on or after 6 April 2011.

5 Section 100(1) of the 1992 Act (read with section 16(2) of that Act as regards losses) shall have effect as if a VCT-in-liquidation that would not otherwise be a venture capital trust were treated as a venture capital trust, during its prescribed winding-up period, in relation to gains and losses accruing on the disposal of assets acquired by the trust company before the commencement of its winding up.

6—(1) Sections 151A (excepting subsection (3)) and 151B of the 1992 Act shall have effect as follows.

(2) During the VCT-in-liquidation's prescribed winding-up period those provisions shall have effect as if–

(*a*) the conditions in [section 274][1] were fulfilled, and

(*b*) the VCT-in-liquidation, if not otherwise a venture capital trust, were so treated.

(3) At the end of the prescribed winding-up period, if—

(*a*) the VCT-in-liquidation is still in existence, and

(*b*) the conditions in [section 274][1] are not fulfilled immediately following the end of that period,

VCT approval shall be treated, for the purposes of sections 151A(1) and 151B(6) and (7), as having been withdrawn from the VCT-in-liquidation immediately following the end of that period.

Amendments—[1] In paras (2)(*a*), (3)(*b*), words substituted by the Venture Capital Trust (Winding up and Mergers) (Tax) (Amendment) Regulations, SI 2011/660 regs 2, 6 with effect in relation to any VCT in liquidation whose winding-up commences on or after 6 April 2011.

7—(1) Paragraph 3(1) of Schedule 5C to the 1992 Act ("paragraph 3(1)") shall have effect as if—

(*a*) the VCT-in-liquidation, if not otherwise a venture capital trust, were so treated during its prescribed winding-up period;

(*b*) during its prescribed winding-up period, paragraph (*f*) of paragraph 3(1) were omitted;

(*c*) in paragraph (*g*) of paragraph 3(1), for "(*f*)" there were substituted "(*e*)"; and

(*d*) there were added at the end of paragraph 3(1)—

"or

(*h*) a VCT-in-liquidation—

(i) to which regulation 7 of the Venture Capital Trust (Winding up and Mergers) (Tax) Regulations 2004 applies, and

(ii) in which those shares are shares,

is still in existence immediately following the end of its prescribed winding-up period (within the meaning in those Regulations).".

(2) Paragraph 3(6) of that Schedule shall be modified as if for "(*f*)" there were substituted "(*h*)".

(3) Paragraph 5(1) of that Schedule shall be modified as if for paragraph (*d*) there were substituted—

"(*d*) to the person who holds the shares in question immediately following the end of the company's prescribed winding-up period (within the meaning in the Venture Capital Trust (Winding up and Mergers) (Tax) Regulations 2004),".

8 Transfer of investments in specie from a VCT-in-liquidation to a venture capital trust

(1) This regulation applies where –

(*a*) a VCT-in-liquidation has made all reasonable endeavours to sell shares or securities comprised in its qualifying holdings at, or as near as may be to, their market value, but has been unable to do so;

(*b*) the VCT-in-liquidation, during its prescribed winding-up period, transfers the shares or securities to a venture capital trust by way of a bargain made at arm's length, or for a consideration not less than their market value; and

(*c*) the value of all shares or securities transferred under this regulation by the VCT-in-liquidation to venture capital trusts during its prescribed winding-up period does not exceed 7.5% of the aggregate value of the investments of the VCT-in-liquidation at the commencement of its winding up.

(2) For the purposes of paragraph (1)(*c*) the value of investments (including shares or securities) shall be taken to be—

(*a*) those used in the VCT-in-liquidation's statement of affairs, or

(*b*) where sub-paragraph (*a*) does not provide a value for the investment, its market value at the commencement of the winding up.

(3) Where the requirements of any of [sections 286(2)(*b*), 287, 293, 294, 297 and 331(2) and (3)][1] were satisfied (or deemed to be satisfied) to any extent or for any period in relation to the investment when held by the VCT-in-liquidation (whether before or after the commencement of its winding up), they shall be treated as satisfied to the same extent or for the same period in relation to the investment when held by the venture capital trust.

Amendments—[1] In para (3), words substituted by the Venture Capital Trust (Winding up and Mergers) (Tax) (Amendment) Regulations, SI 2011/660 regs 2, 7 with effect in relation to any VCT in liquidation whose winding-up commences on or after 6 April 2011.

9 Mergers of Venture Capital Trusts

(1) Regulations 11 to 13 shall apply to a merger of two or more companies, each of which was a venture capital trust immediately before the merger begins to be effected, in any case where, before the transactions for effecting the merger take place, the [Commissioners][3] have notified their approval of the merger, subject to paragraph (2).

(2) In the case of a [section 323(2) merger][2], the approval of the merger (and the application of regulations 11 to 13) shall be conditional on the successor company having VCT approval, and on the VCT approval having taken effect, at any relevant time for the purposes of those regulations (excepting regulation 13(4)(*a*)).

(3) The [Commissioners][3] shall not approve the merger unless, on the application of a merging company or a successor company, the [Commissioners][3] are satisfied that—

(*a*) the merger is effected for bona fide commercial reasons and is not part of a scheme or arrangement the main purpose of which, or one of the main purposes of which, is the avoidance of tax;

(*b*) in the case of a [section 323(2) merger][2], that the shares issued to effect the merger will be issued only at times when there are no issued shares in the successor company, other than subscriber shares, such shares as may be required to obtain a trading certificate under [section 761 of the Companies Act 2006][1] and shares previously issued to effect the merger;

(*c*) where there is a share for share exchange, more than 50% of the issued share capital, immediately before the transactions for effecting the merger, of—

(i) each of the other merging companies (in a [section 323(1) merger][2]), or

(ii) each of the merging companies (in a [section 323(2) merger][2]), (or shares representing them) will be exchanged for shares issued to effect the merger;

(*d*) where any consideration other than shares in the successor company is offered to—

(i) all or any members of another merging company (in a [section 323(1) merger][2]), or

(ii) all or any members of a merging company (in a [section 323(2) merger][2]), in exchange for their holdings in that company, the amount or value of such consideration does not exceed 10% of the aggregate amount or value of consideration offered to the members of that company;

(*e*) where there is a share for business transfer, the shares are issued in respect of and in proportion to (or as nearly as may be in proportion to) the holdings of the persons to whom they are issued in the other merging company or companies (in a [section 323(1) merger][2]) or merging companies (in a [section 323(2) merger][2]);

(*f*) where there is a transfer of part of the business of a merging company to the successor company as mentioned in [section 323(1)(*b*)(ii) or section 323(2)(*b*)(ii)][2], the market value of the part not so transferred is merely incidental in comparison with the market value of the part so transferred; and

(*g*) the money raised by any shares issued for new consideration (or any assets directly or indirectly derived from that money) to be used for the purpose of the successor company purchasing its own shares, or those of any of the merging companies, shall not exceed the least of A, B and C,

where:

A equals 20% of the amount of money raised by the shares issued for new consideration (or of the aggregate of those amounts if there has been more than one such share issue);

B equals 5% of the aggregate of all amounts subscribed for eligible shares issued before the merger in—

(i) the successor company, and

(ii) the merging companies, or other merging companies, as the case may be; and

C equals £3,000,000.

Amendments—[1] Words in para (3)(*b*) substituted by the Companies Act 2006 (Consequential Amendments) (Taxes and National Insurance) Order, SI 2008/954 art 54 with effect from 6 April 2008.

[2] Words substituted by the Venture Capital Trust (Winding up and Mergers) (Tax) (Amendment) Regulations, SI 2011/660 regs 2, 8 with effect in relation to any merger where the transactions bringing the merger into effect take place on or after 6 April 2011.

[3] In para (1), (3), word substituted by the Venture Capital Trust (Winding up and Mergers) (Tax) (Amendment) Regulations, SI 2011/660 regs 2, 13 with effect from 6 April 2011.

10 Procedure for [Commissioners]' approval

(1) Any application under regulation 9(3) shall be in writing and shall contain particulars of the transactions in connection with the merger that are to be effected and the [Commissioners][2] may, within 30 days of the receipt of the application or of any further particulars previously required under this paragraph, by notice require the applicant to furnish further particulars for the purposes of enabling the [Commissioners][2] to make their decision; and if any such notice is not complied with within 30 days or such longer period as the [Commissioners][2] may allow, the [Commissioners][2] need not proceed further on the application.

(2) The [Commissioners][2] shall notify their decision to the applicant within 30 days of receiving the application or, if they give a notice under paragraph (1), within 30 days of the notice being complied with.

(3) If the [Commissioners][2] notify the applicant that they are not satisfied as mentioned in regulation 9(3) or do not notify their decision to the applicant within the time required by paragraph (2), the applicant may within 30 days of the notification or of that time require the [Commissioners][2] to transmit the application, together with any notice given and further particulars furnished under paragraph (1), to the [tribunal][1], and in that event any notification of approval by the [tribunal][1] shall have effect for the purposes of these Regulations as if it were a notification of approval by the [Commissioners][2].

(4) If any particulars provided under this regulation do not fully and accurately disclose all facts and circumstances (including any change in circumstances) material for the decision of the [Commissioners][2] or the [tribunal][1] then, unless the applicant shows that the information in question was not in his possession or power, any resulting notification of approval by the [Commissioners][2] or [tribunal][1] shall be void.

(5) The [Commissioners][2] may supply to any joint applicant—

(*a*) any information relating to the application, to a decision made on the application or to any change in circumstances relevant to the application or a decision; and

(*b*) any communication made or received relating to the application, decision or any change in circumstances.

Amendments—[1] In para (3), word substituted for words in both places, and in para (4), word substituted, by the Transfer of Tribunal Functions and Revenue and Customs Appeals Order, SI 2009/56 art 3, Sch 2 para 128 with effect from 1 April 2009.
[2] Word substituted for word in each place by the Venture Capital Trust (Winding up and Mergers) (Tax) (Amendment) Regulations, SI 2011/660 regs 2, 13 with effect from 6 April 2011.

11 An individual shall not be entitled to claim relief under [Chapter 2 of Part 6][1] in respect of any shares issued to him to effect the merger by the successor company, and they shall be disregarded in determining whether the permitted maximum for the purposes of [that Chapter][1] has been exceeded (but this regulation does not extend to shares issued for new consideration).

Amendments—[1] Words substituted by the Venture Capital Trust (Winding up and Mergers) (Tax) (Amendment) Regulations, SI 2011/660 regs 2, 9 with effect in relation to any merger where the transactions bringing the merger into effect take place on or after 6 April 2011.

12—(1) Where there has been a merger, the [70% tests][1], the 30% test and (subject to regulation 13(6)) the 15% test, and the requirements of [section 274(2)][1] and [Chapter 4 of Part 6][1], shall apply to the successor company–

(*a*) as if the property of the merging companies were vested in the successor company (transfers between a merging company and the successor company being disregarded accordingly),

(*b*) disregarding, in the hands of the successor company, any assets that consist in rights against, or in shares or securities of, another company which is a merging company, and

(*c*) disregarding, in the hands of the successor company, the use of any money which, in the hands of another company which is a merging company, would have been disregarded under [section 280(2)][1], for the same periods as are mentioned in that provision.

(2) Section 171(2)(*cc*) of the Taxation of Chargeable Gains Act 1992 shall not apply to a disposal following a merger, where the disposal is—

(*a*) by a merging company to the successor company, and

(*b*) of an asset held by the merging company immediately before, or in the period during which, the merger takes place.

Amendments—[1] Words in para (1) substituted by the Venture Capital Trust (Winding up and Mergers) (Tax) (Amendment) Regulations, SI 2011/660 regs 2, 10 with effect in relation to any merger where the transactions bringing the merger into effect take place on or after 6 April 2011.

13—(1) Where there has been a merger, the following paragraphs apply.

(2) The relevant shares issued to effect the merger are referred to as the "new shares" and—

(*a*) in the case of a share for share exchange, the corresponding shares for which they were exchanged, and

(*b*) in the case of a share for business transfer, the corresponding shares in respect of which they were issued,

are referred to as the "old shares".

(3) For the purposes of [Chapter 2 of Part 6][1], and of Schedule 5C to the 1992 Act—

(*a*) any share for share exchange or share for business transfer shall not be treated as a disposal of the old shares, or as a chargeable event for the purposes of Schedule 5C to the 1992 Act,

(*b*) any other act (including the giving of relief under [Chapter 2 of Part 6][1], or under paragraph 2 of Schedule 5C to the 1992 Act) carried out, or failure to act, in relation to the old shares shall be treated as carried out, or omitted, in relation to the corresponding new shares, and

(*c*) references to the company in which the old shares were held shall be read as references to the successor company.

(4) For the purposes of sections 151A and 151B of the 1992 Act, where the successor company—

(*a*) was not a venture capital trust at the time when shares issued to effect the merger were acquired, but

(*b*) is a venture capital trust at the time of a subsequent disposal of those shares, it shall be treated as a venture capital trust at and from the former time.

(5) Where the requirements of [Chapter 4 of Part 6 (except section 296(1) and (2))][1] were satisfied (or deemed to be satisfied) to any extent or for any period, in relation to an investment when held by a merging company immediately before the merger, they shall be treated as satisfied to the same extent or for the same period, in relation to the investment when held by the successor company, as if the successor company and the other company were the same company.

(6) For the purposes of [section 296(1) and (2)][1] and the 15% test—

(*a*) the period during which the merger takes place shall be disregarded, and

(*b*) if, as a result of the merger, the requirements of [that section][1] or that test, as the case may be, would not be met immediately after the merger, those requirements shall be treated as met for a further period of one year.

(7) For the purposes of [section 274(2)][1] the value of investments in the hands of the successor company immediately after the merger shall be their value when last valued before the merger, [in accordance with that section][1], unless there has been a transaction (other than the merger) whereby those investments would fall to be so revalued.

(8) For the purposes of [section 289][1] the like provisions as are contained in paragraph (7) shall apply (substituting references to valuations in accordance with [section 289][1] for references to valuations in accordance with [section 278(1) to (3)][1]).

(9) Where—

(*a*) a merging company, other than a successor company, obtained VCT approval in exercise of the power conferred by [section 275(1) to (3)][1] (provisional approval), and

(*b*) the approval is withdrawn following the merger, [section 281][1] shall apply to the withdrawal of approval with the modifications that, in [subsection (2)][1] the words "Subject to [subsections (3) and (4)][1]," and [subsections (3) and (4)][1], are omitted.

[(10) Section 281(1)(*f*) applies to a successor company except—

(*a*) it does not apply in relation to new shares issued on or after 6th April 2014 which correspond to old shares that were issued before that date, and

(*b*) in relation to new shares issued on or after 6th April 2014 which correspond to old shares that were issued on or after that date—

(i) those new shares are treated as having been issued at the same time as those old shares, and

(ii) the amount of the successor company's share capital and share premium in respect of those new shares is treated as the amount of share capital and share premium of the merging company in respect of those old shares.][2]

Amendments—[1] Words in paras (3), (5)–(9) substituted by the Venture Capital Trust (Winding up and Mergers) (Tax) (Amendment) Regulations, SI 2011/660 regs 2, 11 with effect in relation to any merger where the transactions bringing the merger into effect take place on or after 6 April 2011.

[2] Para (10) inserted by the Venture Capital Trust (Winding up and Mergers) (Tax) (Amendment) Regulations, SI 2015/361 reg 2 with effect in relation to new shares issued on or after 6th April 2014. "New shares" has the same meaning as in this regulation: SI 2015/361 reg 1(3).

14 [Limiting the operation of section 280]

(1) [Section 280(2)][1] shall apply to a further issue of shares (in the circumstances mentioned in subsection [(1)][1] of that section) conditionally on the money being raised by that further issue for the purposes of investment (that is, for the purpose of the trust company acquiring additional investments which fulfil the [70% tests][1] and the 30% test).

(2) The condition mentioned in paragraph (1) shall be treated (in particular) as not fulfilled if—

(*a*) any of the money raised by the further issue (or any assets directly or indirectly derived from that money) is used for the purpose of the trust company purchasing any of its own shares, and

(*b*) either—

(i) the [Commissioners][2] are of the opinion that the shares being purchased are not insignificant in relation to the issued ordinary share capital of the company, or

(ii) the purchase is made as the result of a general offer to members (with or without exceptions for persons connected with the trust company).

(3) Where the further issue of shares is of shares issued for new consideration, paragraph (1) shall be treated (in particular) as not fulfilled if—

(*a*) any of the money raised by the further issue (or any assets directly or indirectly derived from that money) is used for the purpose of the successor company purchasing shares in any of the merging companies, or the other merging companies, as the case may be, and

(*b*) the money so used exceeds the least of A, B and C in regulation 9(3)(*g*).

(4) Where any of the money raised by the further issue (or any assets directly or indirectly derived from that money) is used for a purpose other than as mentioned in paragraph (1), [section 280(2)][1] shall be treated as not having applied to the further issue from the time immediately before that use of the money or other assets.

(5) Where, in consequence of paragraph (4), the [70% tests][1] and the 30% test fall to be applied immediately before the use of money mentioned in that paragraph, the trust company's investments for the purposes of [section 274][1] shall be treated as including any money raised by that further issue (or assets directly or indirectly derived from that money).

Commentary—*Simon's Taxes* **D8.207, D8.211, D8.212.**

Amendments—[1] Heading and words in paras (1), (4), (5) substituted by the Venture Capital Trust (Winding up and Mergers) (Tax) (Amendment) Regulations, SI 2011/660 regs 2, 12 with effect in relation to shares issued on or after 6 April 2011.

[2] Word substituted by the Venture Capital Trust (Winding up and Mergers) (Tax) (Amendment) Regulations, SI 2011/660 regs 2, 13 with effect from 6 April 2011.

2004/2200

OVERSEAS LIFE INSURANCE COMPANIES REGULATIONS 2004

Amendments—These Regulations revoked by the Overseas Life Insurance Companies Regulations, SI 2006/3271 reg 43, Sch Pt 2 with effect in relation to periods of account ending on or after 31 December 2006.

2004/2422

CHILD TRUST FUNDS ACT 2004 (COMMENCEMENT NO 1) ORDER 2004

Made by The Treasury under Child Trust Funds Act 2004 s 27

Made . . . . *16 September 2004*

1 Citation and interpretation

(1) This Order may be cited as the Child Trust Funds Act 2004 (Commencement No 1) Order 2004.

(2) In this Order—

"account" means an account which (from the appointed day) is capable of being a child trust fund (within the meaning in the Act);

"the Act" means the Child Trust Funds Act 2004;

"the appointed day" means the day appointed under section 27 of the Act for the purposes of sections 8 and 9 of the Act.

2 Commencement of certain provisions of the Act

The following provisions of the Act shall come into force on 1st January 2005 for the purposes mentioned in relation to each provision:

Provision	*Purposes*
Section 1(3) of the Act	All purposes
Section 3(1) and (3) of the Act	All purposes (save that an account may only be a child trust fund from the appointed day)
Section 3(2), (4) to (9) and (12) of the Act	To allow accounts to be opened, and contracts with an account provider for their management to be signed, save that the account is only to be: (*a*) a child trust fund, or (*b*) subscribed to and operated, from the appointed day.
Section 5(1) and (2) of the Act	To ensure an orderly introduction of accounts, by issuing some vouchers before the appointed day.
Section 5(3) to (5) of the Act	Where a voucher has been issued before the appointed day under section 5(1) of the Act, to allow accounts to be opened, save that the account is only to be: (*a*) a child trust fund, or (*b*) subscribed to and operated, from that day.
Section 15(1), (2)(*a*) and (3) of the Act	So far as those provisions relate to the persons referred to in section 15(2)(*a*) of the Act
Section 17 of the Act	All purposes
Section 18 of the Act	All purposes
Section 20(1) (except paragraphs (*b*) and (*c*)), (2) to (6), (7) (except paragraph (*c*)), (8) and (9) of the Act	All purposes (except for the purposes of sections 6, 7, 9, 10 or 13 of the Act)
Section 21 of the Act	For the purposes of the provisions of section 20 of the Act which are commenced by this Order
Section 22(1) and (6) of the Act	All purposes
Section 23(1) to (3) of the Act	For the purposes of section 22(1) and (6) of the Act
Section 24(1) (except paragraph (*c*)), (2) and (3) of the Act	For the purposes of section 22(1) and (6) of the Act

Section 24(5) to (7) of the Act	All purposes

2004/2502

CORPORATION TAX (NOTICE OF COMING WITHIN CHARGE—INFORMATION) REGULATIONS 2004

Made . . . . 22 September 2004
Laid before the House of Commons . . . . 22 September 2004
Coming into force . . . . 13 October 2004

The Commissioners of Inland Revenue, in exercise of the powers conferred upon them by section 55(2)(*c*), (3) and (5) of the Finance Act 2004, make the following Regulations:

1 Citation, commencement and interpretation

(1) These Regulations may be cited as the Corporation Tax (Notice of Coming within Charge—Information) Regulations 2004 and shall come into force on 13th October 2004.

(2) In these Regulations—

"the section" means section 55 of the Finance Act 2004; and

a reference, without more, to a numbered subsection is a reference to the subsection of the section which is so numbered.

2 Information prescribed for the purposes of section 55(2)(c) of the Finance Act 2004

(1) For the purposes of subsection (2)(*c*) the information specified in the following paragraphs of this regulation is prescribed.

(2) In the case of the company's accounting period falling within either paragraph (*a*) or (*b*) of subsection (1), the prescribed information is the date on which that accounting period commenced (within the meaning of section 12(2) of the Income and Corporation Taxes Act 1988), together with the information in paragraph (3).

(3) The information to be given in respect of any company to which the section applies is—

(*a*) the company's name and its registered number;
(*b*) the address of the company's registered office;
(*c*) the address of the company's principal place of business;
(*d*) the nature of the business being carried on by the company;
(*e*) the date to which the company intends to prepare accounts;
(*f*) the full name and home address of each of the directors of the company;
(*g*) if the company has taken over any business, including any trade, profession or vocation formerly carried on by another—
  (i) the name and address of that former business; and
  (ii) the name and address of the person from whom the business was acquired;
(*h*) if the company is deemed, by virtue of section 413(3) of the Income and Corporation Taxes Act 1988, to be a member of a group of companies for the purposes of Chapter 4 of Part 10 of that Act, the name of the parent company and the address of its registered office; and
(*i*) in the case of a company which, at the time it gives notice under the section, has been obliged to comply with the requirements of the Income Tax (Pay as You Earn) Regulations 2003, the date on which that obligation first arose.

2004/2572

OFFSHORE FUNDS REGULATIONS 2004

Made . . . . 30 September 2004
Laid before the House of Commons . . . . 1 October 2004
Coming into force . . . . 22 October 2004

Made by the Treasury under TA 1988 s 758(7) and (8), Sch 27 para 21, Sch 28 para 9 and FA 2004 s 145(2)(b)

1 Citation, commencement and effect

(1) These Regulations may be cited as the Offshore Funds Regulations 2004 and shall come into force on 22nd October 2004.

(2) These Regulations have effect in relation to account periods ending on or after 22nd July 2004.

2 Interpretation

In these Regulations—

"class of interest" has the meaning given by section 756C of ICTA 1988;

"ICTA 1988" means the Income and Corporation Taxes Act 1988;
"main fund" has the meaning given by section 756C(1) of ICTA 1988;
"umbrella fund" has the meaning given by section 756B(1) of ICTA 1988; and
references to a part of a fund are references to a part of an umbrella fund which is regarded as a separate offshore fund by virtue of section 756B(2) of ICTA 1988.

3 Section 758 of ICTA 1988

(1) Section 758 of ICTA 1988 applies to—

(*a*) a part of an umbrella fund which is regarded as a separate offshore fund by virtue of section 756B(2) of that Act, and

(*b*) a class of interest, within a main fund, which is regarded as separate offshore fund by virtue of section 756C(1) of that Act,

subject to the following modifications.

(2) For subsection (1)(*b*) substitute—

"(*b*) the umbrella fund or main fund makes a distribution to—

(i) a holder of units in a part of that fund which is regarded as a separate offshore fund by virtue of section 756B(2); or

(ii) a holder of a class of interest in an offshore fund which is regarded as a separate offshore fund by virtue of section 756C(1); for a period which begins before the date of his acquisition of those units or that interest;".

(3) After subsection (1) insert—

"(1A) In this section in the case of—

(*a*) an umbrella fund, part of which is regarded as a separate offshore fund by virtue of section 756B(2), or

(*b*) a main fund, a class of interest in which is regarded as a separate offshore fund by virtue of section 756C(1),

references to the equalisation arrangements or to the equalisation account of the offshore fund shall be construed respectively as references to the equalisation arrangements of, or to the equalisation account maintained by, the umbrella fund or the main fund in respect of the separate offshore fund in question.".

(4) For subsection (2)(*a*) substitute—

"(*a*) his acquisition is by way of subscription for, or allotment of new shares, units or other classes of interest issued or created—

(i) by an umbrella fund;

(ii) in a fund which is regarded as a separate offshore fund by virtue of section 756B(2);

(iii) by a main fund; or

(iv) in a class of interest which is regarded as a separate offshore fund by virtue of section 756C(1);".

4 Modification of Schedule 27 to ICTA 1988

(1) Schedule 27 to ICTA 1988 (distributing funds) applies to—

(*a*) a part of a fund which is regarded as a separate offshore fund by virtue of section 756B(2) of that Act, and

(*b*) a class of interest, within a main fund, which is regarded as a separate offshore fund by virtue of section 756C(1) of that Act,

subject to the following modifications.

(2) In paragraph 1 (requirements as to distributions)—

(*a*) after sub-paragraph (2) add—

"(2A) In the case of a class of interest which is regarded as a separate offshore fund the reference in sub-paragraph (2)(*b*) to the amount of the gross income shall be a reference to the amount of the gross income of the main fund (as defined in section 756C(1)).";

(*b*) after sub-paragraph (3) add—

"(3A) In the case of a part of a fund or a class of interest which is regarded as a separate offshore fund, the accounts referred to in sub-paragraph (3) shall be the accounts of the umbrella fund or the main fund, of which the part of the fund, or the class of interest forms part.";

and

(*c*) after sub-paragraph (6) add—

"(7) In sub-paragraph (6) references to—

(*a*) the offshore fund do not include—

(i) parts of an umbrella fund which are regarded as separate offshore funds by virtue of sections 756B(2); or

(ii) classes of interest which are regarded as separate offshore funds by virtue of section 756C(1); or

(*b*) the making of distributions, in relation to a part of an umbrella fund or to a class of interest in a main fund, are references to distributions made (as the case may be) by—

(i) the umbrella fund to persons having an interest in part of that fund which is regarded as a separate offshore fund by virtue of section 756B(2); and

(ii) the main fund to a person having an interest of that class which is regarded as a separate offshore fund by virtue of section 756C(1).".

(3) In paragraph 2 (funds operating equalisation arrangements) after sub-paragraph (2) add—

"(2A) In this paragraph in the case of—

(*a*) an umbrella fund, part of which is regarded as a separate offshore fund by virtue of section 756B(2), or

(*b*) a main fund, a class of interest in which is regarded as a separate offshore fund by virtue of section 756C(1),

references to the equalisation arrangements or to the equalisation account of the offshore fund shall be construed respectively as references to the equalisation arrangements of, or to the equalisation account maintained by, the umbrella fund or the main fund in respect of the separate offshore fund in question.

(2B) In this paragraph references to making a distribution, in relation to a part of an umbrella fund or to a class of interest in a main fund, is a reference to a distribution made (as the case may be) by—

(*a*) the umbrella fund to persons having an interest in part of that fund which is regarded as a separate offshore fund by virtue of section 756B(2); and

(*b*) the main fund to a person having an interest of that class which is regarded as a separate offshore fund by virtue of section 756C(1).".

(4) After paragraph 4(3) insert—

"(3A) For the purposes of sub-paragraph (3), in determining the relevant amount of expenditure attributable to—

(*a*) each part of a fund which is regarded as a separate offshore fund by virtue of section 756B(2), or

(*b*) each class of interest which is regarded as a separate offshore fund by virtue of section 756C(1),

any expenditure shall be apportioned in such manner as is just and reasonable.".

(5) At the end of paragraph 5 (United Kingdom equivalent profits) add—

"(6) In sub-paragraph (5) references to the offshore fund do not include—

(*a*) a part of a fund, within an umbrella fund, where that part is regarded as a separate offshore fund by virtue of section 756B(2); or

(*b*) a class of interest, within a main fund which is regarded as a separate offshore fund by virtue of section 756C(1).

(7) For the purposes of sub-paragraph (5) if an offshore fund has within it—

(*a*) any part which is regarded as a separate offshore fund by virtue of section 756B(2); or

(*b*) any class of interest which is regarded as a separate offshore fund by virtue of section 756C(1), the relevant amount of income attributable to each part, or each class of interest, within the fund, shall be apportioned between them in such manner as is just and reasonable.".

(6) At the end of paragraph 11 (offshore funds with wholly-owned subsidiaries) add—

"(5) In sub-paragraphs (1) to (2) references to the offshore fund do not include a class of interest which is regarded as a separate offshore fund by virtue of section 756C(1).

(6) In the case of a class of interest, references to the offshore fund in sub-paragraphs (1), (2) and (4)(*b*) shall be to the main fund.

(7) For the purposes of sub-paragraph (4) if—

(*a*) there are parts of an umbrella fund which are regarded as separate offshore funds by virtue of section 756B(2); or

(*b*) there are classes of interest in a main fund which are regarded as separate offshore funds by virtue of section 756C(1), the receipts and expenditure shall be apportioned in such manner as is just and reasonable.".

(7) In paragraph 15 (application for certification) for sub-paragraph (1)(*b*) substitute—

"(*b*) the application is accompanied by—

(i) the accounts of the fund for, or for a period which includes, the account period to which the application relates; or

(ii) in the case of—

(*aa*) part of an umbrella fund, or

(*bb*) a class of interest in a main fund,

which is regarded as a separate offshore fund, the accounts of the umbrella fund or the main fund (as the case may be) for, or for a period which includes, the account period to which the application relates; and".

5 Modification of Schedule 28 to ICTA 1988

(1) Schedule 28 to ICTA 1988 (computation of offshore income gains) applies to—

(*a*) a part of a fund which is regarded as a separate offshore fund by virtue of section 756B(2) of that Act, and

(*b*) a class of interest, within a main fund, which is regarded as a separate offshore fund by virtue of section 756C(1) of that Act,

subject to the following modifications.

(2) At the end of paragraph 6 add—

"(7) In this paragraph in the case of—

(*a*) an umbrella fund, part of which is regarded as a separate offshore fund by virtue of section 756B(2), or

(*b*) a main fund, a class of interest in which is regarded as a separate offshore fund by virtue of section 756C(1),

references to the equalisation account of the offshore fund shall be construed as references to the equalisation account maintained by the umbrella fund or the main fund in respect of the separate offshore fund in question.".

6 Modification of Schedule 26 to the Finance Act 2004: new funds within existing umbrella funds

(1) This regulation applies to an umbrella fund established on or before 22nd July 2004 and which has not made an election under paragraph 1(3) or paragraph 2(3) of Schedule 26 to the Finance Act 2004 (elections in respect of computation of UK equivalent profits from creditor relationships and derivative contracts).

(2) Paragraph (3) applies to a part of a fund which—

(*a*) is regarded as a separate offshore fund by virtue of section 756B(2) of ICTA 1988; and

(*b*) is established after 22nd July 2004.

(3) In relation to a part of a fund to which this paragraph applies, the repeals contained in paragraph 1(2) or 2(2) of Schedule 26 to the Finance Act 2004 (as the case requires) shall be disregarded, and accordingly—

(*a*) paragraph 3 of Schedule 10 to the Finance Act 1996, (assumptions to be made in relation to creditor relationships for the purposes of Schedule 27 to ICTA 1988), or

(*b*) paragraph 35 of Schedule 26 to the Finance Act 2002 (assumptions to be made in relation to derivative contracts for those purposes),

(as the case requires) shall apply in relation to that part of the umbrella fund as they would have applied had those repeals not been enacted.

7 Modification of Schedule 26 to the Finance Act 2004: new classes of interest within existing main funds

(1) This regulation applies in relation to a main fund established on or before 22nd July 2004 and which has not made an election under paragraph 1(3) or paragraph 2(3) of Schedule 26 to the Finance Act 2004.

(2) Paragraph (3) applies to a class of interest within a main fund which—

(*a*) is regarded as a separate offshore fund by virtue of section 756C(1) of ICTA 1988; and

(*b*) is established after 22nd July 2004.

(3) In relation to a class of interest to which this paragraph applies, the repeals contained in paragraph 1(2) or 2(2) of Schedule 26 to the Finance Act 2004 (as the case requires) shall be disregarded, and accordingly—

(*a*) paragraph 3 of Schedule 10 to the Finance Act 1996, (assumptions to be made in relation to creditor relationships for the purposes of Schedule 27 to ICTA 1988), or

(*b*) paragraph 35 of Schedule 26 to the Finance Act 2002 (assumptions to be made for the purposes of the Schedule in relation to derivative contracts for those purposes),

(as the case requires) shall apply in relation to that class of interest as they would have applied but for those repeals.

2004/2622

EXEMPTION FROM TAX FOR CERTAIN INTEREST PAYMENTS REGULATIONS 2004

Made . . . . *8 October 2004*
Laid before the House of Commons . . . . *11 October 2004*
Coming into force . . . . *1 November 2004*

The Board, in exercise of the powers conferred upon them by section 100 of the Finance Act 2004 hereby make the following Regulations:

1 Citation and commencement

These Regulations may be cited as the Exemption From Tax For Certain Interest Payments Regulations 2004 and shall come into force on 1st November 2004.

2 Interpretation

In these Regulations—

"the Act" means the Finance Act 2004;

"the Board" means the Commissioners of Inland Revenue;

"a company in Condition 1" means a company in Condition 1 in section 98(2) of the Act;

"a company in Condition 2" means a company in Condition 2 in section 98(3) of the Act;

"an exemption notice" is a notice issued by the Board under section 98(5) of the Act;

3 Request for and issue of an exemption notice and notification of refusal

(1) An exemption notice may be issued only on the request of an officer of a company in Condition 2 or its appointed agent.

(2) On receipt of a request under paragraph (1) the Board must determine whether to issue an exemption notice within three months of receipt of the request and the certificate.

(3) An exemption notice must be given to the person requesting the issue of the notice and the company in Condition 1.

(4) The Board must notify in writing the person requesting the issue of the notice of a refusal to issue a notice specifying the date of the refusal and the reasons for the refusal.

4 Information to be provided in the certificate

(1) A person requesting the issue of an exemption notice must provide a certificate certifying that Conditions 1 to 3 in section 98 of the Act are satisfied and that section 104 of the Act (anti-avoidance) does not apply.

(2) For the purposes of paragraph (1), the certificate must provide—

(*a*) proof of the residence for tax purposes of the company in Condition 2 and, where necessary, the existence of a permanent establishment;

(*b*) information as to the beneficial entitlement of the company in Condition 2 to the income in respect of which the payment is made;

(*c*) details of the United Kingdom corporation tax or tax corresponding to that tax to which the company in Condition 2 is subject;

(*d*) information establishing that the company in Condition 1 and the company in Condition 2 are 25% associates within section 99(4) of the Act; and

(*e*) a copy of the loan agreement or other document providing the legal justification for the interest payment.

5 Special relationship

If section 103 of the Act (special relationship) applies or may apply to a payment of interest, an exemption notice may specify—

(*a*) the amount of the payment, or

(*b*) the method to be used for determining the amount of the payment

in relation to which the notice has effect.

6 Requirements where Conditions for exemption cease to be satisfied

(1) If the person who has requested the issue of an exemption notice becomes aware that any of Conditions 1 to 3 in section 98 of the Act has ceased to be satisfied he must as soon as possible notify the Board and the company in Condition 1.

(2) If the company in Condition 1 becomes aware that any of Conditions 1 to 3 in section 98 of the Act has ceased to be satisfied it must as soon as possible notify the Board.

(3) An exemption notice becomes ineffective if the company in Condition 1—

(*a*) receives notice under paragraph (1), or

(*b*) becomes aware that any of Conditions 1 to 3 in section 98 of the Act has ceased to be satisfied.

7 Cancellation of exemption notice

If—

(*a*) the Board receives notice under regulation 6,

(*b*) it appears to the Board that any of Conditions 1 to 3 in section 98 of the Act has ceased to be satisfied, or

(*c*) it appears to the Board that section 104 of the Act (anti-avoidance) applies,

the Board may cancel the exemption notice by notice in writing to the person who requested the issue of the exemption notice and the company in Condition 1.

8 Recovery of tax not deducted

(1) If after an exemption notice has been issued, it is discovered that any of Conditions 1 to 3 in section 98 of the Act was not satisfied in the case of a payment of interest and tax deductible from the payment has not been deducted, that tax may be recovered—

(*a*) by assessment on the company in Condition 2 under Case VI of Schedule D, or

(*b*) if a direction to that effect is given by the Board, by deduction from subsequent payments by the company in Condition 1.

(2) Any tax deducted in accordance with paragraph (1)(*b*) shall be treated as tax deductible under section 349 of the Income and Corporation Taxes Act 1988 in respect of the payment from which it is deducted.

9 Appeals against refusal to issue an exemption notice or cancellation of an exemption notice

(1) An officer of a company in Condition 2 or its appointed agent may appeal . . . [1] against a refusal to issue an exemption notice or the cancellation of an exemption notice.

(2) An appeal under this regulation must be by notice in writing to the Board within 30 days of the date of notification of the refusal under regulation 3 or the cancellation under regulation 7.

(3) The grounds of appeal are

(*a*) that Conditions 1 to 3 in section 98 of the Act are satisfied, and

(*b*) section 104 of the Act (anti-avoidance) does not apply.

(4) [If, on its being notified to the tribunal, the tribunal allows the appeal it may also][1]

(*a*) in an appeal against a refusal to issue an exemption notice, direct that the Board issue an exemption notice within 14 days of its decision, or

(*b*) in an appeal against the cancellation of an exemption notice, direct that the cancellation was ineffective.

[(5) Notwithstanding the provisions of sections 11 and 13 of the Tribunals, Courts and Enforcement Act 2007, the decision of the tribunal shall be final.][1]

Amendments—[1] In para (1), words revoked, in para (4), words substituted, and para (5) substituted, by the Transfer of Tribunal Functions and Revenue and Customs Appeals Order, SI 2009/56 art 3, Sch 2 para 130 with effect from 1 April 2009.

2004/2664

ENERGY-SAVING ITEMS (DEDUCTIONS FOR EXPENDITURE ETC) REGULATIONS 2004

Revocation—Regulations revoked by the Energy-Saving Items Regulations, SI 2007/831 reg 5, Sch, with effect in relation to expenditure incurred on or after 6 April 2007.

2004/2680

CHILD TRUST FUNDS (INSURANCE COMPANIES) REGULATIONS 2004

Made by the Treasury under TA 1988 s 333B as extended by Child Trust Funds Act 2004 s 14(1)

Revocation—These Regulations lapsed on the repeal of the enabling authority by FA 2007 ss 38(1), 114, Sch 7 paras 2, 4, Sch 27 Pt 2(7), with effect for periods of account of insurance companies beginning on or after 1 January 2007.

2004/3256

LOAN RELATIONSHIPS AND DERIVATIVE CONTRACTS (DISREGARD AND BRINGING INTO ACCOUNT OF PROFITS AND LOSSES) REGULATIONS 2004

Made by the Treasury under FA 1996 ss 84A(3A), 85B(3)(*a*) and 85B(5)(*b*) and FA 2002 Sch 26 paras 16(3A), 17C(1) and 17C(3)(*b*)

Made . . . . *9 December 2004*

Laid before the House of Commons . . . . *10 December 2004*

Coming into force . . . . *1 January 2005*

Commentary—*Simon's Taxes* **D1.7104**.

Press releases etc—HMRC Brief 10/08, 26-2-08 (detailed guidance on changes to the tax rules on "forex matching").

1 Citation, commencement and effect

(1) These Regulations may be cited as the Loan Relationships and Derivative Contracts (Disregard and Bringing into Account of Profits and Losses) Regulations 2004 and shall come into force on 1st January 2005.

(2) These Regulations have effect in relation to periods of account beginning on or after 1st January 2005.

2 Interpretation

(1) In these Regulations—

. . .[5]

["CTA 2009" means the Corporation Tax Act 2009;

"CTA 2010 means the Corporation Tax Act 2010;][6]

["deferred shares" has the same meaning as in the Building Societies Act 1986;][4]

"derivative contract" has the same meaning as in [Part 7 of CTA 2009][6];

["exchange gain or loss" has the same meaning as in [section 475 of CTA 2009][6];][1]

. . .[7]

["fair value profit or loss" means the profit or loss brought into account in relation to a derivative contract or an asset or liability representing a loan relationship where for the period in question—

(*a*) the derivative contract or asset or liability representing a loan relationship is measured at fair value, or

(*b*) the derivative contract or asset or liability representing a loan relationship is a hedged item in a designated fair value hedge and the carrying value of the hedged item is adjusted for changes in fair value attributable to the hedged risk;][7]

["loan relationship" has the same meaning as in [section 302 of CTA 2009][6];][1]

["[a section 614 or 615 credit or debit[6]]" means the credit or debit to be brought into account in accordance with [section 614 or 615 of CTA 2009][6];][1]

["a prior period adjustment credit or debit" means so much of any credit or debit as represents a prior period adjustment taken into account by virtue of [section 597(1)(*b*) of CTA 2009][6] as a result of a change of accounting basis;][1]

["regulatory capital security" has the meaning given in regulation 2 of the Taxation of Regulatory Capital Securities Regulations 2013;][5]

"underlying subject matter" has the same meaning as in [Part 7 of CTA 2009][6].

(2) In these Regulations—

"for accounting purposes" means for the purposes of accounts drawn up in accordance with generally accepted accounting practice;

"generally accepted accounting practice" has the meaning given in [section 1127 of CTA 2010][6]; and

"amortised cost"[, "consolidated accounts"], "designated", "effective hedge", "effective interest method", ["fair value hedge",][6] "firm commitment", "forecast transaction", "foreign operation[, fair value, items of other comprehensive income][7]" and "net investment in a foreign operation" have the same meaning as for accounting purposes.

(3) In these Regulations any reference to an asset which is a ship or aircraft includes a reference to a contract—

(*a*) to which section 67 of the Capital Allowances Act 2001 applies; and

(*b*) which relates to plant or machinery which is a ship or aircraft.

[(3A) For the purposes of these Regulations, a liability representing a loan relationship or a derivative contract is treated as matched with shares, ships or aircraft from the date that, and to the extent that, either condition 1 or 2 of regulations 3(3) or 4(3) are satisfied.][3]

(4) In these Regulations—

(*a*) any reference to a hedging instrument includes a reference to part of an instrument; and

(*b*) any reference to a hedged item includes a reference to part of a hedged item.

(5) For the purposes of these Regulations, a company has a hedging relationship between a derivative contract or a liability representing a loan relationship on the one hand ("the hedging instrument") and an asset, liability, receipt or expense on the other ("the hedged item") if and to the extent that—

(*a*) the hedging instrument and the hedged item are designated by the company as a hedge; or

(*b*) in any other case the hedging instrument is intended to act as a hedge of—

(i) the exposure to changes in fair value of a hedged item which is a recognised asset or liability or an unrecognised firm commitment or an identified portion of such an asset, liability or commitment that is attributable to a particular risk and could affect profit or loss of the company;

(ii) the exposure to variability in cash flows that is attributable to a particular risk associated with a hedged item that is a recognised asset or liability or a forecast transaction and could affect profit or loss of the company; or

(iii) a net investment in a foreign operation of the company.

[(6) For the purposes of regulations 3 to 5, where an asset referred to is shares in a company, the asset comprises all the shares held in that company whenever acquired.][2]

Amendments—[1] In para (1), definition of "exchange gain or loss" substituted, and definitions inserted, by the Loan Relationships and Derivative Contracts (Disregard and Bringing into Account of Profits and Losses) (Amendment) Regulations, SI 2005/2012 regs 2, 3 with effect from 11 August 2005. These amendments have effect in relation to periods of account beginning on or after 1 January 2005 and ending after SI 2005/2012 comes into force (ie 11 August 2005).

[2] Words in para (2), and whole of para (6), inserted, by the Loan Relationships and Derivative Contracts (Disregard and Bringing into Account of Profits and Losses) (Amendment No 2) Regulations, SI 2007/3431 reg 2(1), (2) with effect in relation to accounting periods beginning on or after 1 January 2008: SI 2007/3431 reg 1(2).

[3] Para (3A) inserted by the Loan Relationships and Derivative Contracts (Disregard and Bringing into Account of Profits and Losses) (Amendment No 2) Regulations, SI 2011/2912 regs 2, 3 with effect from 11.45am on 6 December 2011. This amendment has effect in relation to shares, ships or aircraft which are matched on or after that date in accordance with regs 3 or 4 of these Regulations.

[4] In para (1), definitions of "Additional Tier 1 instrument" and "deferred shares" inserted by the Loan Relationships and Derivative Contracts (Disregard and Bringing into Account of Profits and Losses) (Amendment) Regulations, SI 2013/2781 reg 2(1), (2) with effect in relation to loan relationships and derivative contracts entered into on or after 21 November 2013.

[5] In para (1), definition of "Additional Tier 1 instrument" revoked, and definition of "regulatory capital security" inserted, by the Taxation of Regulatory Capital Securities Regulations, SI 2013/3209 reg 10(1), (2) with effect as follows—

- for income tax purposes, for payments made on or after 1 January 2014;
- for capital gains tax purposes, in relation to disposals made on or after 1 January 2014; and
- for corporation tax purposes, for accounting periods beginning on or after 1 January 2014 (subject to transitional provisions).

[6] The following amendments made by the Loan Relationships and Derivative Contracts (Disregard and Bringing into Account of Profits and Losses) (Amendment) Regulations, SI 2014/3188 regs 2, 8(1), (2) with effect from 31 December 2014—

(a) in para (1)—
- definitions of "CTA 2009" and "CTA 2010" inserted;
- in definitions of "derivative contract", "exchange gain or loss", "loan relationship", "a paragraph 50A credit or debit", "a prior period adjustment credit or debit" and "underlying subject matter", words substituted;

(b) in para (2)—
- in definition of "generally accepted accounting practice" words substituted; and
- words inserted.

[7] In para (1), definition of "fair value accounting" revoked, and definition of "fair value profit or loss" substituted, and words in para (2) inserted, by the Loan Relationships and Derivative Contracts (Disregard and Bringing into Account of Profits and Losses) (Amendment) Regulations, SI 2015/1961 regs 2, 3 with effect in relation to accounting periods beginning on or after 1 January 2016. Definition of "fair value accounting" previously read as follows—

" "fair value accounting" has the meaning given in section 313 of CTA 2009;".

Definition of "fair value profit or loss" previously read as follows—

" "fair value profit or loss" means the profit or loss brought into account in relation to a derivative contract or an asset or liability representing a loan relationship where for the period in question fair value accounting is used, and where fair value accounting is used in relation to only part of a contract it means the profit or loss brought into account in relation to that part;".

3 Exchange gains or losses arising from liabilities or assets hedging shares etc

(1) For the purposes of [section 328(4) of CTA 2009][10] there is prescribed an exchange gain or loss arising to a company in an accounting period in relation to a liability representing a loan relationship of the company which is matched with the whole or part of any shares, ships or aircraft.

[(1ZA) But where the matched shares, ships or aircraft are matched after the company became party to the loan relationship, paragraph (1) only applies to a just and reasonable proportion of any exchange gain or loss having regard to—

(a) the fraction of the accounting period for which the shares, ships or aircraft are matched with the loan relationship,

(b) the fraction of the accounting period for which the company was party to the loan relationship, and

(c) fluctuations in exchange rates during the accounting period.][6]

(1A) . . .[9]

(2) This regulation does not apply if movements in the fair value[, or profits or losses arising on the disposal,][1] of any shares, ships or aircraft which are an asset falling within regulation 3(1) are brought into account by the company in computing, for the purposes of corporation tax, the profits of a trade carried on by it which consists of or includes dealing in shares, ships or aircraft.

(3) [Shares, ships or aircraft are matched to the greatest possible extent with—

(*a*) the liability representing the loan relationship designated as a hedge if condition 1 is satisfied;

(*b*) subject to paragraph (*a*), the liability representing the loan relationship referred to in condition 2 if that condition is satisfied;][1]

SIs

. . . [1]

Condition [1][1]

The condition is that ...[6] the shares, ships or aircraft are a hedged item under a designated hedge of exchange rate risk in which the liability is the hedging instrument.

Condition [2][1]

The condition is that the currency in which the liability is expressed is such that the company [intends][1], by entering into [[or][5] continuing to be subject to][1] that liability, . . . [1] to eliminate or substantially reduce the economic risk of holding the asset, or part of the asset, which is attributable to fluctuations in exchange rates.

(4) If [condition 2][1] applies, a liability is matched with an asset only to the extent that the carrying value of the liability . . . .[4] does not exceed the unmatched carrying value of the asset at [the relevant time][4].

(5) For the purposes of [section 328(4) of CTA 2009][10] there is prescribed an exchange gain or loss arising to a company in an accounting period in relation to an asset representing a loan relationship of the company which is matched with the whole or part [of—

(*a*) any share capital of the company,

(*b*) in relation to a building society, any deferred shares issued by the building society to the extent that they are accounted for as equity instruments in accordance with generally accepted accounting practice, or

(*c*) [a regulatory capital security][8] issued by the company to the extent that it is accounted for as an equity instrument in accordance with generally accepted accounting practice.][7]

(6) An asset is matched with share capital [in particular where][3] for the accounting period of the company immediately preceding the first accounting period to which these Regulations apply—

(*a*) exchange gains and losses on the asset were taken to a reserve; and

(*b*) set off there against exchange gains and losses on the share capital.

(7) In this regulation—

"carrying value" means, in relation to a liability, the value as shown in the company's accounts of that liability; and

"unmatched carrying value" means, in relation to an asset, an amount equal to the [relevant value][2] to the extent that that amount has not previously been matched in accordance with this regulation or regulation 4.

Commentary—*Simon's Taxes* **D1.732.**

Amendments—[1] This regulation amended by the Loan Relationships and Derivative Contracts (Disregard and Bringing into Account of Profits and Losses) (Amendment) Regulations, SI 2005/2012 regs 2, 4 with effect from 11 August 2005. These amendments have effect in relation to periods of account beginning on or after 1 January 2005 and ending after SI 2005/2012 comes into force (ie 11 August 2005).

[2] In para (7), words in the definition of "unmatched carrying value" substituted by the Loan Relationships and Derivative Contracts (Disregard and Bringing into Account of Profits and Losses) (Amendment No 2) Regulations, SI 2005/3374 regs 2, 3 with effect from 29 December 2005. This amendment has effect in relation to periods of account beginning on or after 1 January 2005 and ending after SI 2005/3374 comes into force (ie 29 December 2005).

[3] Words in para (6) substituted by SI 2005/3374 regs 2, 4 with effect from 29 December 2005. This amendment has effect in relation to periods of account beginning on or after 1 January 2005 and ending after SI 2005/3374 comes into force (ie 29 December 2005).

[4] In para (4) words repealed and words substituted by the Loan Relationships and Derivative Contracts (Disregard and Bringing into Account of Profits and Losses) (Amendment No 2) Regulations, SI 2007/3431 reg 2(1), (3) with effect in relation to accounting periods beginning on or after 1 January 2008: SI 2007/3431 reg 1(2).

[5] In para (3), in Condition 2, word substituted by the Loan Relationships and Derivative Contracts (Disregard and Bringing into Account of Profits and Losses) (Amendment) Regulations, SI 2011/698 regs 2, 3 with effect in relation to accounting periods beginning on or after 1 April 2011.

[6] Para (1ZA) inserted and in para (3) in Condition 1, words revoked, by the Loan Relationships and Derivative Contracts (Disregard and Bringing into Account of Profits and Losses) (Amendment No 2) Regulations, SI 2011/2912 regs 2, 4 with effect from 11.45am on 6 December 2011. These amendments have effect in relation to shares, ships or aircraft which are matched on or after that date in accordance with regs 3 or 4 of these Regulations.

[7] In para (5), words substituted for words "of any share capital of the company", by the Loan Relationships and Derivative Contracts (Disregard and Bringing into Account of Profits and Losses) (Amendment) Regulations, SI 2013/2781 reg 2(1), (3) with effect in relation to loan relationships and derivative contracts entered into on or after 21 November 2013.

[8] In para (5)(*c*), words substituted for words "any Additional Tier 1 instrument", by the Taxation of Regulatory Capital Securities Regulations, SI 2013/3209 reg 10(1), (3) with effect as follows—

- for income tax purposes, for payments made on or after 1 January 2014;
- for capital gains tax purposes, in relation to disposals made on or after 1 January 2014; and
- for corporation tax purposes, for accounting periods beginning on or after 1 January 2014 (subject to transitional provisions).

Note that the substituted text began with the word "any", although SI 2013/3209 reg 10(3) treated the substituted text as if it had begun with the word "an".

[9] Para (1A) revoked by the Loan Relationships and Derivative Contracts (Disregard and Bringing into Account of Profits and Losses) (Amendment) Regulations, SI 2014/3188 regs 2, 3 with effect in relation to accounting periods beginning on or after 1 January 2015. An accounting period beginning before and ending on or after 1 January 2015 is to be treated for the purposes this amendment as if so much of the period as falls before that date, and so much of the period as falls on or after that date, were separate accounting periods (SI 2014/3188 reg 1(3)). Para (1A) previously read as follows—

"(1A) For the purposes of paragraph (1) a liability representing a loan relationship does not include any liability representing a relationship within section 100(1) of the Finance Act 1996.".

10 In paras (1), (5), words substituted for words "section 84A(3A) of the Finance Act 1996" by the Loan Relationships and Derivative Contracts (Disregard and Bringing into Account of Profits and Losses) (Amendment) Regulations, SI 2014/3188 regs 2, 8(1), (3) with effect from 31 December 2014.

4 Exchange gains or losses arising from derivative contracts hedging shares etc

(1) For the purposes of [section 606(4) and 598(1)(*a*) of CTA 2009][9] there is prescribed an exchange gain or loss arising to a company in an accounting period in relation to a derivative contract of the company which is matched with the whole or part of any shares, ships or aircraft.

[(1A) But where the matched shares, ships or aircraft are matched after the company became party to the derivative contract, paragraph (1) only applies to a just and reasonable proportion of any exchange gain or loss having regard to—

the fraction of the accounting period for which the shares, ships or aircraft are matched with the derivative contract,

the fraction of the accounting period for which the company was party to the derivative contract, and

fluctuations in exchange rates during the period.][6]

(2) This regulation does not apply if movements in the fair value[, or profits or losses arising on the disposal,][1] of any shares, ships or aircraft which are an asset falling within regulation 4(1) are brought into account by the company in computing, for the purposes of corporation tax, the profits of a trade carried on by it which consists of or includes dealing in shares, ships or aircraft.

(3) [Shares, ships or aircraft are matched to the greatest possible extent with—

(*a*) the derivative contract designated as a hedge if condition 1 is satisfied;

(*b*) subject to paragraph (*a*), the derivative contract referred to in condition 2 if that condition is satisfied.][1]

. . .[1]

Condition [1][1]

The condition is that ...[6] the shares, ships or aircraft are a hedged item under a designated hedge of exchange rate risk in which the derivative contract is the hedging instrument.

Condition [2][1]

The condition is that the underlying subject matter of the derivative contract is such that the company [intends][1], by entering into [[or][5] continuing to be party to][1] that contract, . . .[1] to eliminate or substantially reduce the economic risk of holding the asset, or part of the asset, which is attributable to fluctuations in exchange rates.

(4) If [condition 2][1] applies, a derivative contract is matched with an asset only to the extent that the [value of the obligation under][1] the derivative contract . . .[4] does not exceed the unmatched carrying value of the asset at [the relevant time][4].

[(4A) For the purposes of [section 606(4) of CTA 2009][9] there is prescribed an exchange gain or loss arising to a company in an accounting period in relation to a derivative contract of the company which is matched with the whole or part [of—

(*a*) any share capital of the company,

(*b*) in relation to a building society, any deferred shares issued by the building society to the extent that they are accounted for as equity instruments in accordance with generally accepted accounting practice, or

(*c*) [a regulatory capital security][8] issued by the company to the extent that it is accounted for as an equity instrument in accordance with generally accepted accounting practice.][7]][3]

[(4B) A derivative contract is matched with share capital in particular where for the accounting period of the company immediately preceding the first accounting period beginning on or after 1st January 2005—

(*a*) exchange gains and losses on the derivative contract were taken to a reserve; and

(*b*) set off there against exchange gains and losses on the share capital.][3]

(5) In this regulation—

. . .[1]

"unmatched carrying value" means, in relation to an asset, an amount equal to the [relevant value][2] to the extent that that amount has not previously been matched in accordance with this regulation or regulation 3.

["the value of the obligation under the derivative contract" means the value of the obligation of the company to pay in exchange for one currency an amount of a second currency and includes any notional obligation to pay an amount of currency in respect of a contract for differences.][1]

Commentary—*Simon's Taxes* **D1.854, D1.855.**

Amendments—[1] This regulation amended by the Loan Relationships and Derivative Contracts (Disregard and Bringing into Account of Profits and Losses) (Amendment) Regulations, SI 2005/2012 regs 2, 5 with effect from 11 August 2005. These amendments have effect in relation to periods of account beginning on or after 1 January 2005 and ending after SI 2005/2012 comes into force (ie 11 August 2005).

2 In para (5), words in the definition of "unmatched carrying value" substituted by the Loan Relationships and Derivative Contracts (Disregard and Bringing into Account of Profits and Losses) (Amendment No 2) Regulations, SI 2005/3374 regs 2, 3 with effect from 29 December 2005. This amendment has effect in relation to periods of account beginning on or after 1 January 2005 and ending after SI 2005/3374 comes into force (ie 29 December 2005).

3 Paras (4A), (4B) inserted by SI 2005/3374 regs 2, 5 with effect from 29 December 2005. This amendment has effect in relation to periods of account beginning on or after 1 January 2005 and ending after SI 2005/3374 comes into force (ie 29 December 2005).

4 In para (4) words repealed and words substituted by the Loan Relationships and Derivative Contracts (Disregard and Bringing into Account of Profits and Losses) (Amendment No 2) Regulations, SI 2007/3431 reg 2(1), (4) with effect in relation to accounting periods beginning on or after 1 January 2008: SI 2007/3431 reg 1(2).

5 In para (3), in Condition 2, word substituted by the Loan Relationships and Derivative Contracts (Disregard and Bringing into Account of Profits and Losses) (Amendment) Regulations, SI 2011/698 regs 2, 4 with effect in relation to accounting periods beginning on or after 1 April 2011.

6 Para (1A) inserted and in para (3) in Condition 1, words revoked, by the Loan Relationships and Derivative Contracts (Disregard and Bringing into Account of Profits and Losses) (Amendment No 2) Regulations, SI 2011/2912 regs 2, 5 with effect from 11.45am on 6 December 2011. These amendments have effect in relation to shares, ships or aircraft which are matched on or after that date in accordance with regs 3 or 4 of these Regulations.

7 In para (4A), words substituted for words "of any share capital of the company", by the Loan Relationships and Derivative Contracts (Disregard and Bringing into Account of Profits and Losses) (Amendment) Regulations, SI 2013/2781 reg 2(1), (3) with effect in relation to loan relationships and derivative contracts entered into on or after 21 November 2013.

8 In para (4A)(*c*), words substituted for words "any Additional Tier 1 instrument", by the Taxation of Regulatory Capital Securities Regulations, SI 2013/3209 reg 10(1), (3) with effect as follows—

– for income tax purposes, for payments made on or after 1 January 2014;
– for capital gains tax purposes, in relation to disposals made on or after 1 January 2014; and
– for corporation tax purposes, for accounting periods beginning on or after 1 January 2014 (subject to transitional provisions).

Note that the substituted text began with the word "any", although SI 2013/3209 reg 10(3) treated the substituted text as if it had begun with the word "an".

9 In para (1) words substituted for words "paragraph 16(3A) and 17C(1)(*a*) of Schedule 26 to the Finance Act 2002", and in para (4A) words substituted for words "paragraph 16(3A) of Schedule 26 to the Finance Act 2002", by the Loan Relationships and Derivative Contracts (Disregard and Bringing into Account of Profits and Losses) (Amendment) Regulations, SI 2014/3188 regs 2, 8(1), (4), (5) with effect from 31 December 2014.

4A [Relevant value

(1) For the purposes of regulations 3(7) and 4(5), "relevant value" means—

(*a*) in relation to shares held by the company in another company ("Company A"), where the company elects, the higher of—
  (i) the net asset value underlying the shares in Company A, and
  (ii) the value shown in the accounts of the company; and

(*b*) in any other case, the value shown in the accounts of the company.

(2) In paragraph (1)(*a*)(i) the net asset value underlying the shares in Company A is an amount equal to—

(*a*) the value of the assets, less
(*b*) the value of the liabilities

of Company A and any direct or indirect subsidiary of Company A denominated in the relevant currency.

This is subject to paragraph (6).

(3) The value of assets and liabilities referred to in paragraph (2) is the value at the relevant time shown in—

(*a*) a balance sheet of Company A, or
(*b*) where Company A has a direct or indirect subsidiary, a notional consolidated balance sheet of Company A prepared in the relevant currency.

(4) For the purposes of paragraph (3) in determining whether an asset or liability would be recognised in the balance sheet or notional consolidated balance sheet and, if so recognised the value that would be accorded to it, regard shall be had to the accounting treatment of the asset or liability—

(*a*) in any consolidated accounts prepared by the company, or
(*b*) where the company does not prepare consolidated accounts, in any consolidated accounts prepared by a company that directly or indirectly controls the company.

(5) Nothing in paragraphs (3) or (4) shall prevent an asset or liability, which might be eliminated in the preparation of any consolidated accounts, from being taken into account in paragraph (2).

(6) If the company does not directly hold the entire issued share capital in Company A, the net asset value underlying the shares in Company A shall be reduced by such amount as is just and reasonable having regard to—

(*a*) the proportion of the issued shares held by the company, and
(*b*) where there is more than one class of share, the rights attached to the shares held by the company.

[(7) An election under paragraph (1)—

(*a*) must be made by the company by notice in writing to an officer of Revenue and Customs, and
(*b*) must specify the review period.

(7A) An election—

(*a*) applies to all the shareholdings held by the company which are matched in accordance with regulation 3(3)(*b*) or 4(3)(*b*), and

(*b*) has effect from a date specified in the notice which must be later than the date the notice is given.

(7B) An election may be amended or revoked by notice in writing to an officer of Revenue and Customs—

(*a*) before the election has effect, or

(*b*) with effect from a date specified in the notice which must be—

(i) later than the date the notice is given, and

(ii) at least 12 months after the election was made.

(7C) Where the date specified in a notice under paragraph (7) or (7B) is not the first day of an accounting period so much of the period as falls before that date and so much of the period as falls on or after that date are treated as separate accounting periods.][3]

(8)–(8B) . . . [3]

[(9)] [2]In this regulation—

"relevant currency" means the currency which, as a result of exchange rate fluctuations, gives rise to the economic risk referred to in regulations 3(3) and 4(3);

"control" has the meaning given in [section 1124 of CTA 2010][4].][1]

Amendments—[1] Regulations 4A–4C substituted for previous para 4A by the Loan Relationships and Derivative Contracts (Disregard and Bringing into Account of Profits and Losses) (Amendment No 2) Regulations, SI 2007/3431 reg 2(1), (5) with effect in relation to accounting periods beginning on or after 1 January 2008: SI 2007/3431 reg 1(2).

[2] Para (9) numbered as such (para (9) was previously numbered as a second para (6)), by the Loan Relationships and Derivative Contracts (Disregard and Bringing into Account of Profits and Losses) (Amendment) Regulations, SI 2011/698 regs 2, 5 with effect in relation to accounting periods beginning on or after 1 April 2011.

[3] Paras (7)–(7C) substituted for previous para (7), and paras (8)–(8B) revoked, by the Loan Relationships and Derivative Contracts (Disregard and Bringing into Account of Profits and Losses) (Amendment) Regulations, SI 2014/3188 regs 2, 4 with effect in relation to accounting periods beginning on or after 1 January 2015. An accounting period beginning before and ending on or after 1 January 2015 is to be treated for the purposes this amendment as if so much of the period as falls before that date, and so much of the period as falls on or after that date, were separate accounting periods (SI 2014/3188 reg 1(3)). Para (7) previously read as follows—

"(7) An election under paragraph (1)—

(a) is irrevocable,

(b) applies to all the shareholdings held by the company which are matched in accordance with regulation 3(3)(*b*) or 4(3)(*b*),

(c) has effect from the beginning of the accounting period in which the election is made,

(d) must be made in writing to Her Majesty's Revenue and Customs within the time limit specified in paragraph (8), and

(e) must specify the review period.

This is subject to paragraph (8A).".

Paras (8)–(8B) previously read as follows—

"(8) The time limit for making an election is—

(a) in relation to shares held on and before the start of the first accounting period beginning on or after 1st January 2008, the later of—

(i) 31st March 2008, and

(ii) 30 days from the start of that accounting period; and

(b) in any other case, within 30 days of shares being matched in accordance with regulation 3(3)(*b*) or 4(3)(*b*).

(8A) Where a company has made an election before 1st April 2011 and has specified a review period of 92 days or less, it may amend that election to increase the length of the review period specified.

(8B) An amendment to an election must be made by 1st June 2011 by notice in writing to Her Majesty's Revenue and Customs.".

[4] In para (9), in definition of "control", words substituted for words "section 840 of the Income and Corporation Taxes Act 1988" by the Loan Relationships and Derivative Contracts (Disregard and Bringing into Account of Profits and Losses) (Amendment) Regulations, SI 2014/3188 regs 2, 8(1), (6) with effect from 31 December 2014.

4B [Relevant time

(1) For the purposes of regulations 3(4), 4(4) and 4A(3) "relevant time" is determined as follows.

(2) In a case within regulation 4A(1)(*a*) (relevant value determined by net asset value) the relevant time is the start of each review period in an accounting period.

(3) In a case within regulation 4A(1)(*b*) (relevant value determined by accounts value), the relevant time is the time when the liability or contract is entered into or, if later, when the asset is acquired.][1]

Amendments—[1] Regulations 4A–4C substituted for previous para 4A by the Loan Relationships and Derivative Contracts (Disregard and Bringing into Account of Profits and Losses) (Amendment No 2) Regulations, SI 2007/3431 reg 2(1), (5) with effect in relation to accounting periods beginning on or after 1 January 2008: SI 2007/3431 reg 1(2).

4C [Review period

(1) For the purposes of [regulations 4A(7)(*b*)][2] and 4B(2), a review period is a period, or one of a series of successive periods, of a length specified by a company making an election in accordance with regulation 4A(1)(*a*).

This is subject to the provisions of this regulation.

(2) A review period, or where more than one in an accounting period the first review period in that accounting period, begins on the first day of the accounting period or, if later, the date that a liability or derivative contract first becomes matched with shares in accordance with regulation 3(3)(*b*) or 4(3)(*b*).

(3) A review period, or where more than one in an accounting period the last review period in that accounting period, must end on the last day of the accounting period.

(4) If a company has matched shares in accordance with regulation 3(3)(*b*) or 4(3)(*b*) ("the first asset"), the first review period in relation to shares which are subsequently matched—

(*a*) begins when the subsequent matching occurs, and

(*b*) ends at the same time as the review period which is current in relation to the first asset when the subsequent matching occurs.

(5) If during a review period ("the current period") there is a significant variation in the net asset value underlying shares which have been matched in accordance with regulation 3(3)(*b*) or 4(3)(*b*), there shall be a new review period in relation to those shares which—

(*a*) begins on the day that any variation in the net asset value becomes a significant variation, and

(*b*) ends at the same time as the current period.

(6) In paragraph (5) "significant variation" means an increase or decrease of 10% or more in the net asset value underlying the matched shares.

(7) In this regulation the net asset value underlying shares shall be determined in accordance with regulation 4A(2).][1]

Commentary—*Simon's Taxes* **D1.854, D1.855.**

Amendments—[1] Reg 4C substituted by the Loan Relationships and Derivative Contracts (Disregard and Bringing into Account of Profits and Losses) (Amendment) Regulations, SI 2011/698 regs 2, 6 with effect in relation to accounting periods beginning on or after 1 April 2011.

[2] In para (1), words substituted for words "regulations 4A(7)(*e*)" by the Loan Relationships and Derivative Contracts (Disregard and Bringing into Account of Profits and Losses) (Amendment) Regulations, SI 2014/3188 regs 2, 5 with effect in relation to accounting periods beginning on or after 1 January 2015. An accounting period beginning before and ending on or after 1 January 2015 is to be treated for the purposes this amendment as if so much of the period as falls before that date, and so much of the period as falls on or after that date, were separate accounting periods (SI 2014/3188 reg 1(3)).

5 Regulations 3 and 4: supplementary

(1) Where in any accounting period—

(*a*) a company holds more than one asset in relation to which there are amounts of exchange gains and losses falling within regulations 3 or 4; and

(*b*) the currency—

(i) in which the assets are denominated and the liability [mentioned in regulation 3(1)][1] expressed; or

(ii) which is the underlying subject matter of the derivative contract [mentioned in regulation 4(1)][1],

is the same currency, . . . [1] [the extent to which an asset is matched is determined in accordance with the following rules][1].

[*Rule 1*

Liabilities and contracts are regarded as matched to the greatest possible extent with assets which are ships or aircraft.][1]

Rule 2

Subject to Rule 1, liabilities and contracts are regarded as matched to the greatest possible extent with assets on the disposal of which a chargeable gain would accrue [if the disposal were made on a date falling more than 12 months after the date of acquisition of the asset][1].

Rule 3

Subject to Rules 1 and 2, liabilities [and contracts][1] are regarded as matched with assets on a disposal of which no chargeable gain would be treated as accruing by virtue of Part 1 of Schedule 7AC to the Taxation of Chargeable Gains Act 1992 . . . [1]

(2) If—

(*a*) part only of a liability falling within the [condition 2][2] in regulation 3, or

(*b*) part only of a contract falling within the [condition 2][2] in regulation 4,

could reasonably be expected to eliminate or substantially reduce the economic risk of holding the asset which is attributable to fluctuations in exchange rates, the liability or contract is to be treated as being matched with a corresponding amount of value of an asset.

(3) For the purposes of paragraph (1), a currency in which a liability is expressed or which is the underlying subject matter of a derivative contract, is to be treated, if it is not the case, as the same currency in which an asset is denominated if—

(*a*) borrowing in that currency, or

(*b*) the obligation to deliver that currency,

could reasonably be expected to eliminate or substantially reduce the economic risk of holding the asset, or part of the asset, which is attributable to fluctuations in exchange rates.

(4) Where regulation 3 or [section 328(3) of CTA 2009][3] applies to a company in an accounting period in relation to a liability representing a loan relationship there is prescribed, for the purposes of regulation 3 or [section 328(4)][3] of that Act, an exchange gain or loss treated by virtue of [section 192(1) of the Taxation (International and Other Provisions) Act 2010][3] as arising in that accounting period to another company in relation to the same loan relationship.

Commentary—*Simon's Taxes* **D1.733, D1.849, D1.854.**

Amendments—[1] This regulation amended by the Loan Relationships and Derivative Contracts (Disregard and Bringing into Account of Profits and Losses) (Amendment) Regulations, SI 2005/2012 regs 2, 6 with effect from 11 August 2005. These amendments have effect in relation to periods of account beginning on or after 1 January 2005 and ending after SI 2005/2012 comes into force (ie 11 August 2005).

[2] Words in para (2)(a), (b) substituted by the Loan Relationships and Derivative Contracts (Disregard and Bringing into Account of Profits and Losses) (Amendment) Regulations, SI 2007/948 regs 2, 4 with effect from 11 April 2007. This amendment has effect in relation to periods of account ending on or after 11 April 2007.

[3] In para (4), words substituted for words "section 84A(3) of the Finance Act 1996", "section 84A(3A)" and "paragraph 6D(2) of Schedule 28AA to the Taxes Act 1988", by the Loan Relationships and Derivative Contracts (Disregard and Bringing into Account of Profits and Losses) (Amendment) Regulations, SI 2014/3188 regs 2, 8(1), (7) with effect from 31 December 2014.

[5A Net investment hedge of foreign operations

(1) For the purposes of sections 328(4) and 606(4) of CTA 2009 there is prescribed an exchange gain or loss arising to a company in an accounting period in relation to a liability representing a loan relationship or derivative contract of the company where—

(a) the loan relationship or derivative contract is a designated hedge of a net investment in a foreign operation of the company, and

(b) amounts representing exchange gains or losses in respect of the loan relationship or derivative contract have, in accordance with generally accepted accounting practice, been recognised in the company's accounts as items of other comprehensive income.

(2) In determining what amounts fall within paragraph (1)(b) at any time in an accounting period, it is to be assumed that the accounting policy applied in drawing up the company's accounts for the period was also applied in previous accounting periods.

(3) But if the company's accounts for the period are, in accordance with generally accepted accounting practice, drawn up on an assumption as to the accounting policy in previous accounting periods which differs from that mentioned in paragraph (2), that different assumption applies in determining what amounts fall within paragraph (1)(b) at the time in question.][1]

Amendments—[1] Reg 5A inserted by the Loan Relationships and Derivative Contracts (Disregard and Bringing into Account of Profits and Losses) (Amendment) Regulations, SI 2015/1961 regs 2, 4 with effect in relation to accounting periods beginning on or after 1 January 2016.

[6 Application of regulations 7, 8 and 9 in relation to derivative contracts where fair value accounting applies

(1) Regulation 7, 8 or 9 apply in relation to a derivative contract (which satisfies the conditions in regulation 7(1)(*a*), 8(1)(*a*) or 9(1), as the case may be) if—

(*a*) an election under regulation 6A has effect in relation to the contract,

(*b*) the contract or part of the contract is a designated fair value hedge,

(*c*) the hedged item is a loan relationship in relation to which the company uses fair value accounting, or

(*d*) the contract forms part of an arrangement the main purpose, or one of the main purposes, of which is to obtain a tax advantage in relation to that contract that would not arise if regulation 7, 8 or 9 applies.

(2) In paragraph (1)(*d*)—

"arrangement" includes any agreement, understanding, scheme, transaction or series of transactions (whether or not legally enforceable);

"tax advantage" has the meaning given in section 1139 of CTA 2010.][1]

Amendments—[1] Regs 6, 6A substituted for previous reg 6 by the Loan Relationships and Derivative Contracts (Disregard and Bringing into Account of Profits and Losses) (Amendment) Regulations, SI 2014/3188 regs 2, 6 with effect in relation to periods of account beginning on or after 1 January 2015. Reg 6 previously read as follows—

"6 Rules about fair value profits and losses

(1) Regulations 7, 7A, 8 and 9 contain specific rules about excluding fair value profits and losses for the purposes of Schedule 26 to the Finance Act 2002.

(2) For the purposes of regulations 7, 7A, 8 and 9 it is immaterial that the hedging relationship is not an effective hedge for accounting purposes.

(3) Except where an election has been made under paragraph (3A) a company may elect that—

(a) regulation 7 shall not apply to its currency contracts which satisfy the conditions contained in regulation 7(1); and

(b) regulation 8 shall not apply to its commodity contracts or debt contracts which satisfy the conditions contained in that regulation.

(3A) A company may elect that regulation 9A shall apply and—

(a) regulation 7 shall not apply, to its currency contracts which satisfy the conditions contained in regulation 7(1), and

(b) regulation 8 shall not apply, to its commodity or debt contracts which satisfy the conditions contained in regulation 8(1).

(4) Any election made under paragraph (3) or (3A) shall apply

(a) all of the currency contracts entered into by the company which satisfy the conditions contained in regulation 7(1); and

(b) all of the commodity contracts or debt contracts entered into by the company which satisfy the conditions contained in regulation 8(1).

(5) Subject to paragraph (5A) and except where an election has been made under paragraph (5B) a company may elect that regulation 9 shall not apply to its interest rate contracts which satisfy the conditions contained in that regulation but that regulation 9A shall apply and any election under this regulation shall apply to all of the interest rate contracts entered into by the company which satisfy the conditions contained in regulation 9(1).

(5A) An election under paragraph (5) has no effect in relation to interest rate contracts—

(a) where—

(i) the contract or a portion of the contract ("the hedging instrument") is designated as a hedge in respect of any risks arising in respect of an asset, liability, receipt or expense ("the hedged item");

(ii) fair value profits or losses arising on the hedged item or in relation to any of the risks,in relation to which the contract was intended to act as a hedge, arising in respect of the hedged item, or any portion of the hedged item, are not brought into account for the purposes of corporation tax for that period; and

(iii) fair value profits or losses arising on the hedging instrument are not recognised in the company's statement of recognised gains and losses or statement of changes in equity;

(b) where the hedged item is a loan relationship to which section 87(1) of the Finance Act 1996 applies, or

(c) where the hedged item is a regulatory capital security in relation to which the company uses fair value accounting.

(5B) Subject to paragraph (5C), a company may elect that regulation 9 shall not apply to its interest rate contracts which satisfy the conditions contained in that regulation but that regulation 9A shall apply, and any election under this regulation shall apply to all of the interest rate contracts entered into by the company which satisfy the conditions contained in regulation 9(1).

(5C) An election under paragraph (5B) has no effect in relation to interest rate contracts—

(a) where the conditions in paragraph (5A)(*a*) are met;

(b) where the hedged item is an asset representing a loan relationship—

(i) to which section 87(1) of the Finance Act 1996 applies, and

(ii) in relation to which the company uses fair value accounting, or

(c) where the hedged item is a regulatory capital security in relation to which the company uses fair value accounting.

(6) Subject to paragraph (6A) and (7), an election under paragraph (3) or (5) shall be made before—

(a) 1st October 2005 in the case of an election under paragraph (3), or

(b) 31st March 2006 in the case of an election under paragraph (5),

and has effect for that accounting period and all subsequent accounting periods unless, in the case of an election under paragraph (3), revoked.

(6A) In any case where a company—

(a) does not use fair value accounting in relation to its derivative contracts for an accounting period beginning on or after 1st January 2005, and

(b) begins to use fair value accounting in a subsequent accounting period ("the subsequent period") in relation to contracts to which regulations 7 or 8, or regulation 9 apply and to which it is a party at the start of that period, an election under paragraph (3), (3A), (5) or (5B) shall be made before the start of the subsequent period.

This paragraph does not apply to cases within paragraph (7).

(7) In any case where a company is not a party to any contracts to which regulations 7 or 8, or regulation 9 apply immediately before the start of the company's first accounting period to which the Regulations apply, an election under paragraph (3), (3A), (5) or (5A) shall be made within 90 days of the company entering into its first contract to which regulation 7 or 8, or regulation 9 applies, as the case may be or, if later, 31st March 2006.

(7A) An election under paragraph (3A) or (5B)—

(a) must be made before the later of—

(i) 1st April 2007; and
(ii) the date determined by paragraph (6A) or (7) as the date before which an election must be made;

(b) must be made in writing to Her Majesty's Revenue and Customs;
(c) is irrevocable; and
(d) applies in relation to accounting periods beginning on or after 1st January 2006.

(7B) An election—

(a) under paragraph (3A) revokes any previous election under paragraph (3);
(b) under paragraph (5B) revokes any previous election under paragraph (5).

(8) A company may revoke an election under paragraph (3) with effect from the date on which notice is given of it, but contracts entered into before that date shall not be affected.

(9) An election under paragraph (3) shall be made, and may be revoked by company which made it, by notice in writing to Her Majesty's Revenue and Customs.

(9A) An election under paragraph (5) shall be made in writing to Her Majesty's Revenue and Customs and is irrevocable except where revoked by an election made under paragraph (5B).

(10) If—

(a) a company ("the electing company") makes an election under paragraph (3), (3A), (5) or (5B) in relation to its contracts;
(b) any other company which is a party to a derivative contract to which the election applies is a member of the same group of companies as the electing company; and
(c) that other company has not made an election under paragraph (3), (3A), (5) or (5B) in relation to the contract, as the case may be,

then the other company is to be treated as if it had made the election but only in relation to that contract.

(11) Paragraph (10) does not apply if the electing company, or the other company, entered into the contract in the ordinary course of a banking business or a business as a securities house.

(12) If a contract to which regulation 7, 8 or 9 applies is transferred by a company in circumstances to which paragraph 28 of Schedule 26 to the Finance Act 2002 would apply but for paragraph 30 of that Schedule—

(a) paragraph 30 shall not apply (and accordingly paragraph 28 shall apply) and paragraph 50A(3B) of that Schedule shall be modified in accordance with paragraph (12A); and
(b) the transferee company is to be treated as not having made the election under paragraph (3), (3A), (5) or (5B) as the case may be ("the relevant election") in relation to that contract, if it has made a relevant election in relation to all of its contracts.

(12A) The modification to paragraph 50A(3B) of Schedule 26 to the Finance Act is as follows—

(a) in paragraph (*a*) delete "and";
(b) after paragraph (*b*) insert—

", and

(*c*) regulations 7, 8 and 9 of the Loan Relationships and Derivative Contracts (Disregard and Bringing into Account of Profits and Losses) Regulations 2004.".

(13) If a company ("the electing company") makes an election under paragraph (3), (3A), (5) or (5B) in relation to its contracts—

(a) a contract to which the election applies is transferred to another company ("the transferee company") in circumstances to which paragraph 28 of Schedule 26 to the Finance Act 2002 applies, or
(b) would apply but for paragraph 30 of that Schedule,

and the transferee company has not made an election under paragraph (3), (3A), (5) or (5B) in relation to the contract as the case may be, then the transferee company is to be treated as if it had made the election but only in relation to that contract.

(14) In this Regulation—

"group of companies" shall be construed in accordance with section 170 of the Taxation of Chargeable Gains Act 1992; and

"securities house" means a person—

(a) who is authorised for the purposes of the Financial Services and Markets Act 2000; and
(b) whose business consists wholly or mainly of dealing as a principal in financial instruments within the meaning of section 349(5) and (6) of the Taxes Act 1988.".

[6A Election to apply regulations 7, 8 or 9

(1) An election for the purposes of regulation 6(1)(*a*) must be made by a company by notice in writing to an officer of Revenue and Customs and applies regulations 7, 8 and 9 unless the notice states which of those regulations apply to the company's derivative contracts.

(2) The election has effect—

(*a*) in the case of a new adopter where the election is made on or before the later of the dates set out in paragraph (3), in relation to derivative contracts held in the first relevant period and any subsequent period, and (*b*) in any other case, in relation to derivative contracts entered into on or after a date specified in the election which must be later than the date the election is made, and in the case of a new adopter cannot be before two years after the end of the first relevant period.

(3) The dates referred to in paragraph (2)(*a*) are—

(*a*) the date six months after the start of the first relevant period,

(*b*) the date six months after the date the company first enters into a relevant derivative contract [which the company measures at fair value][2], and

(*c*) in the case of a company which is not a qualifying company for the purposes of Schedule 46 to the Finance Act 2009, the date 12 months after the end of the first relevant period.

(4) An election may be amended or revoked by notice in writing to an officer of Revenue and Customs—

(*a*) in the case of an election made by a new adopter within paragraph (2)(*a*), before the later of the applicable dates set out in paragraph (3), or

(*b*) [either][2]—

(i) before the election has effect, or

(ii) after the election has effect, in relation to derivative contracts entered into on or after a date specified in the notice which must be later than the date the notice is given, and in the case of a new adopter cannot be before two years after the end of the first relevant period.

(5) For the purposes of this regulation—

(*a*) a "new adopter" is a company which [measures a relevant derivative contract at fair value for the first time on or after 1st January 2015][2],

(*b*) "the first relevant period" is the first accounting period in which a company [measures a relevant derivative contract at fair value][2],

(*c*) a "relevant derivative contract" is a derivative contract which satisfies the conditions in regulation 7(1)(*a*), 8(1)(*a*) or 9(1).][1]

Amendments—[1] Regs 6, 6A substituted for previous reg 6 by the Loan Relationships and Derivative Contracts (Disregard and Bringing into Account of Profits and Losses) (Amendment) Regulations, SI 2014/3188 regs 2, 6 with effect in relation to periods of account beginning on or after 1 January 2015.

[2] In para (3)(*b*) words substituted for words "in relation to which the company uses fair value accounting", in para (4)(*b*) words substituted for words "in any other case", and in para (5) words in sub-paras (*a*), (*b*) substituted, by the Loan Relationships and Derivative Contracts (Disregard and Bringing into Account of Profits and Losses) (Amendment) Regulations, SI 2015/1961 regs 2, 5 with effect in relation to accounting periods beginning on or after 1 January 2016. Para (5)(*a*), (*b*) previously read as follows—

"(*a*) a "new adopter" is a company which adopts fair value accounting for the first time on or after 1 January 2015 in relation to a relevant derivative contract,

"(*b*) "the first relevant period" is the first accounting period in which a company uses fair value accounting in relation to a relevant derivative contract,".

[6B Effect of elections on group member replacing another as party to derivative contract: regulations 7 and 8

(1) This regulation applies if—

(*a*) one company replaces another as party to a derivative contract in relation to which regulation 7 or 8 applies, in circumstances in which section 625 of CTA 2009 applies or would apply but for section 628 of that Act,

(*b*) the transferee (within the meaning of section 625 of CTA 2009) meets the conditions in regulation 7(1)(*a*)(i) and (ii) or 8(1)(*a*)(i) and (ii), as the case may be, in relation to the contract, and

(*c*) the hedged item in relation to the derivative contract remains the same before and after the change of party.

(2) Where this regulation applies—

(*a*) section 628 applies (and accordingly section 625 does not apply),

(*b*) regulation 7 or 8, as the case may be, applies in respect of the contract in relation to the transferee, and

(*c*) regulation 10(9) applies.][1]

Amendments—[1] Regs 6B–6D substituted for previous reg 6B by the Loan Relationships and Derivative Contracts (Disregard and Bringing into Account of Profits and Losses) (Amendment) Regulations, SI 2015/1961 regs 2, 6 with effect in relation to accounting periods beginning on or after 1 January 2016. Reg 6B previously read as follows—

"6B Effect of elections on transfers within groups

(1) If a derivative contract, in relation to which regulation 7, 8 or 9 applies, is transferred by a company in circumstances in which section 625 of CTA 2009 would apply but for section 628 of that Act—

(a) section 628 does not apply (and accordingly section 625 applies),

(b) regulation 7, 8 or 9, as the case may be, applies for the purposes of determining the carrying value of the contract for the purposes of section 702 of CTA 2009 as those regulations apply for the purposes of determining the debits and credits to be brought into account under Part 7 of that Act, and

(c) regulation 7, 8 or 9, as the case may be, applies in respect of that contract in relation to the transferee.

(2) If a derivative contract, in relation to which no election under regulation 6A has effect, is transferred by a company in circumstances in which section 625 of CTA 2009 applies or would apply but for section 628 of that Act, any election made by the transferee company under regulation 6A has no effect in relation to that contract.".

[6C Effect of elections on transfers within groups: regulation 9

(1) This regulation applies if—

(*a*) one company replaces another as party to a derivative contract in relation to which regulation 9 applies, in circumstances in which section 625 of CTA 2009 applies or would apply but for section 628 of that Act,

(*b*) the transferee (within the meaning of section 625 of CTA 2009) meets the conditions in regulation 9(1)(*a*) and (*b*) in relation to the contract, and

(*c*) the hedged item in relation to the derivative contract is the same before and after the change of party.

(2) Where this regulation applies—

(*a*) section 628 does not apply (and accordingly section 625 applies),

(*b*) regulation 9 applies for the purposes of determining the carrying value of the contract for the purposes of section 702 of CTA 2009 as that regulation applies for the purposes of determining the debits and credits to be brought into account under Part 7 of that Act, and

(*c*) regulation 9 applies in respect of the contract in relation to the transferee.][1]

Amendments—[1] Regs 6B–6D substituted for previous reg 6B by the Loan Relationships and Derivative Contracts (Disregard and Bringing into Account of Profits and Losses) (Amendment) Regulations, SI 2015/1961 regs 2, 6 with effect in relation to accounting periods beginning on or after 1 January 2016.

[6D Transfers within groups where no election under regulation 6A

(1) This regulation applies if—

(*a*) one company replaces another as party to a derivative contract in relation to which no election under regulation 6A has effect in circumstances in which section 625 of CTA 2009 applies or would apply but for section 628 of that Act,

(*b*) the transferee (within the meaning of section 625 of CTA 2009) meets the conditions in regulation 7(1)(*a*)(i) and (ii), 8(1)(*a*)(i) and (ii) or 9(1)(*a*) and (*b*), as the case may be, in relation to the contract, and

(*c*) the hedged item in relation to the derivative contract is the same before and after the change of party.

(2) Where this regulation applies, any election made by the transferee under regulation 6A has no effect in relation to the contract.][1]

Amendments—[1] Regs 6B–6D substituted for previous reg 6B by the Loan Relationships and Derivative Contracts (Disregard and Bringing into Account of Profits and Losses) (Amendment) Regulations, SI 2015/1961 regs 2, 6 with effect in relation to accounting periods beginning on or after 1 January 2016.

7 Fair value profits or losses arising from derivative contracts which are currency contracts

[(1) For the purposes of [section 598(1)(*a*) of CTA 2009][3] there is prescribed in relation to a derivative contract whose underlying subject matter consists wholly of currency—

(*a*) all credits and debits representing the whole or part of a company's fair value profit or loss in an accounting period if—

(i) there is a hedging relationship between the contract or part of the contract and a forecast transaction or a firm commitment ("the hedged item") of the company; and

(ii) the hedged item is not one [for which fair value profits or losses are brought into account for the purposes of corporation tax][2];

(*b*) a company's [section 614 or 615 credit or debit][4] in relation to such a contract, if for the accounting period in which the [section 614 or 615 credit or debit][4] falls to be brought into account sub-paragraph (*a*) applies to the contract; and

(*c*) a company's prior period adjustment credit or debit in relation to such a contract, if for the accounting period in which the prior period adjustment credit or debit falls to be brought into account sub-paragraph (*a*) applies to the contract, and the credits and debits mentioned in sub-paragraphs (*a*) to (*c*) together make up the regulation 7 fair value profits or losses.][1]

(2) . . . [1]

(3) Where there is a hedging relationship between part of a currency contract and a hedged item, the part of the [regulation 7][1] fair value profit or loss that is prescribed is the part which bears to the whole the proportion which the value of that part of the contract which is in the hedging relationship bears to the value of the whole of the contract.

(4) . . . [5]

[(5) Where regulation 4 applies to a contract to which this regulation applies, nothing in this regulation or regulation 10 is to require any exchange gains or losses in relation to that contract to be brought into account.][5]

Commentary—*Simon's Taxes* **D1.848.**

Amendments—[1] Para (1) substituted, para (2) revoked, and words in para (3) inserted, by the Loan Relationships and Derivative Contracts (Disregard and Bringing into Account of Profits and Losses) (Amendment) Regulations, SI 2005/2012 regs 2, 8 with effect from 11 August 2005. These amendments have effect in relation to periods of account beginning on or after 1 January 2005 and ending after SI 2005/2012 comes into force (ie 11 August 2005).

[2] Words in para (1)(*a*) substituted by the Loan Relationships and Derivative Contracts (Disregard and Bringing into Account of Profits and Losses) (Amendment No 2) Regulations, SI 2005/3374 regs 2, 8 with effect from 29 December 2005. This amendment has effect in relation to periods of account beginning on or after 1 January 2005 and ending after SI 2005/3374 comes into force (ie 29 December 2005).

[3] In para (1), words substituted for words "paragraph 17C(1)(*a*) of Schedule 26 to the Finance Act 2002" by the Loan Relationships and Derivative Contracts (Disregard and Bringing into Account of Profits and Losses) (Amendment) Regulations, SI 2014/3188 regs 2, 8(1), (8)(*a*) with effect from 31 December 2014.

[4] In para (1) words substituted for words "paragraph 50A credit or debit", and in para (4) words substituted for words "paragraph 16(3) of Schedule 26 to the Finance Act 2002", by the Loan Relationships and Derivative Contracts (Disregard and Bringing into Account of Profits and Losses) (Amendment) Regulations, SI 2014/3188 regs 2, 8(9), (10) with effect from 31 December 2014. Note that transitional provisions apply in relation to any company which at any time before the start of the first period of account beginning on or after 1 January 2015 uses fair value accounting in relation to a derivative contract which satisfies the conditions in reg 7(1)(*a*), 8(1)(*a*) or 9(1) (SI 2014/3188 reg 9)..

[5] Para (4) revoked, and para (5) inserted, by the Loan Relationships and Derivative Contracts (Disregard and Bringing into Account of Profits and Losses) (Amendment) Regulations, SI 2015/1961 regs 2, 7 with effect in relation to accounting periods beginning on or after 1 January 2016. Para (4) previously read as follows—

"(4) section 606(3) of CTA 2009 does not apply to any regulation 7 fair value profit or loss.".

7A [Exchange gains or losses arising from derivative contracts hedging anticipated or future proceeds from certain issues of shares

(1) For the purposes of section 598(1)(*a*) of the Corporation Tax Act 2009, an exchange gain or loss arising to a company is an excluded amount in an accounting period in relation to a derivative contract if—

(*a*) the underlying subject matter of the contract consists wholly of currency; and

(*b*) there is a relevant hedging relationship within the meaning of paragraph (2).

(2) There is a relevant hedging relationship between a derivative contract (or part of a derivative contract) and the anticipated or future proceeds of an announced or proposed rights issue or open offer of shares ("relevant share issue") if, and to the extent that—

(*a*) the contract (or part of the contract) is intended to hedge the economic risk to future capital raised under the relevant share issue ("the hedged item"); and

(*b*) the economic risk is attributable to fluctuations in exchange rates between the currency in which the relevant share issue is denominated and the company's functional currency.

(3) If there is a hedging relationship between part of a currency contract and a hedged item, the part of the fair value profit or loss that is an excluded amount is the part which bears to the whole the proportion which the value of that part of the contract which is in the hedging relationship bears to the value of the whole contract.

(4) Paragraph (1) shall not apply to a derivative contract which is entered into with a person ("person A") to whom the company is connected unless—

(*a*) a person who is connected to the company enters into a derivative contract with a person who is not connected with the company; and

(*b*) that contract confers rights or imposes liabilities which are equivalent to those of A under the contract which A entered with the company.

(5) Section 466 of the Corporation Tax Act 2009 (companies connected for an accounting period) applies for the purposes of paragraph (4).

(6) A derivative contract to which this regulation applies may act as a hedge of the anticipated or future proceeds from a relevant share issue only to the extent that the value of the obligation under the derivative contract (within the meaning of regulation 4(5)) does not exceed the anticipated or future proceeds from the relevant share issue which, but for the derivative contract, would not be hedged.

(7) Subsections (3) and (4) of section 606 of the Corporation Tax Act 2009 do not apply to any exchange gain or loss which is an excluded amount by virtue of paragraph (1).

(8) In this regulation—

(*a*) "functional currency", in relation to a company, means the currency of the primary economic environment in which the company operates; and

(*b*) "rights issue or open offer of shares" means an offer or invitation to existing shareholders to subscribe for or purchase further shares in proportion to (or as nearly as may be in proportion to) their current holdings.][1]

Amendments—[1] Reg 7A inserted by the Loan Relationships and Derivative Contracts (Disregard and Bringing into Account of Profits and Losses) (Amendment) Regulations, SI 2009/1886 regs 3, 5 with effect in relation to derivative contracts—

(a) entered into on or after 1 January 2009 and which formed part of a relevant hedging relationship up to and including 10 March 2009; or
(b) entered into on or after 10 March 2009.

8 Profits or losses arising from derivative contracts which are commodity contracts or debt contracts

[(1) For the purposes of [section 598(1)(*a*) of CTA 2009][3] there is prescribed in relation to a commodity contract or debt contract—

(*a*) all credits and debits representing the whole or part of a company's fair value profit or loss arising in an accounting period if—

(i) there is a hedging relationship between the contract or part of the contract and a forecast transaction or a firm commitment ("the hedged item") of the company; and

(ii) the hedged item is not one [for which fair value profits or losses are brought into account for the purposes of corporation tax][2];

(*b*) a company's [section 614 or 615 credit or debit][4], if for the accounting period in which the [section 614 or 615 credit or debit][4] falls to be brought into account, sub-paragraph (*a*) applies to the contract; and

(*c*) a company's prior period adjustment credit or debit, if for the accounting period in which the prior period adjustment credit or debit falls to be brought into account, sub-paragraph (*a*) applies to the contract,

and the credits and debits mentioned in sub-paragraphs (a) to (c) together make up the regulation 8 fair value profits or losses.][1]

(2) In this regulation—

"a commodity contract" means a derivative contract whose underlying subject matter is commodities unless the contract is an interest rate contract within the meaning of regulation 9(4); and

"a debt contract" means a derivative contract whose underlying subject matter is an asset or liability representing a loan relationship unless the contract is an interest rate contract within the meaning of regulation 9(4).

(3) Where there is a hedging relationship between part of a commodity contract or part of a debt contract as the case may be and a hedged item, the part of the [regulation 8][1] fair value profit or loss that is prescribed is the part which bears to the whole the proportion which the value of that part of the contract which is in the hedging relationship bears to the value of the whole of the contract.

Commentary—*Simon's Taxes* **D1.849.**

Amendments—[1] Para (1) substituted and words in para (3) inserted by the Loan Relationships and Derivative Contracts (Disregard and Bringing into Account of Profits and Losses) (Amendment) Regulations, SI 2005/2012 regs 2, 9 with effect from 11 August 2005. These amendments have effect in relation to periods of account beginning on or after 1 January 2005 and ending after SI 2005/2012 comes into force (ie 11 August 2005).

[2] Words in para (1)(a)(ii) substituted by the Loan Relationships and Derivative Contracts (Disregard and Bringing into Account of Profits and Losses) (Amendment No 2) Regulations, SI 2005/3374 regs 2, 8 with effect from 29 December 2005. This amendment has effect in relation to periods of account beginning on or after 1 January 2005 and ending after SI 2005/3374 comes into force (ie 29 December 2005).

[3] In para (1), words substituted for words "paragraph 17C(1)(*a*) of Schedule 26 to the Finance Act 2002" by the Loan Relationships and Derivative Contracts (Disregard and Bringing into Account of Profits and Losses) (Amendment) Regulations, SI 2014/3188 regs 2, 8(1), (8)(*b*) with effect from 31 December 2014.

[4] In para (1), words substituted for words "paragraph 50A credit or debit" by the Loan Relationships and Derivative Contracts (Disregard and Bringing into Account of Profits and Losses) (Amendment) Regulations, SI 2014/3188 regs 2, 8(9) with effect from 31 December 2014. Note that transitional provisions apply in relation to any company which at any time before the start of the first period of account beginning on or after 1 January 2015 uses fair value accounting in relation to a derivative contract which satisfies the conditions in reg 7(1)(*a*), 8(1)(*a*) or 9(1) (SI 2014/3188 reg 9).

9 Profits or losses arising from derivative contracts which are interest rate contracts

(1) For the purposes of [section 598(1)(*a*) of CTA 2009][3] there is prescribed all credits and debits representing the whole or part of the fair value profit or loss arising to a company in relation to its interest rate contracts in an accounting period if—

(*a*) there is a hedging relationship between the contract or a portion of the contract and any of the risks arising in respect of an asset, liability, receipt or expense ("the hedged item"); and

(*b*) fair value profits or losses arising on the hedged item or in relation to any of the risks[, in relation to which the contract was intended to act as a hedge,][2] arising in respect of the hedged item, or any portion of the hedged item, are not brought into account for the purposes of corporation tax for that period.

(2) Where paragraph (1) applies, credits and debits shall be brought into account for the purposes of [section 598(1)(*b*) of CTA 2009][4] on the assumption that an appropriate accruals basis had been used in relation to the contract for that accounting period.

[(2A) Where an interest rate contract—

(*a*) becomes a contract to which paragraph (1) applies, or

(*b*) ceases to be a contract to which paragraph (1) applies, the amount to be brought into account for the purposes of [section 598(1)(*b*) of CTA 2009][4] is such amount as is just and reasonable in the circumstances and with regard to whether as a result of the change any amounts cease to be brought into account or are brought into account more than once [and to the unexpired term of the hedged item][5].][1]

(3) Where [regulation 4 or 5A][5] apply to a contract to which this regulation applies nothing in this regulation is to require any exchange gains or losses in relation to that contract to be brought into account.

(4) In this regulation—

"an appropriate accruals basis" in relation to a derivative contract is one where—

(*a*) the contract is shown in the company's accounts at cost (which may be nil), and the cost is adjusted for any cumulative amortisation of any premium or other amount falling to be recognised in arriving at the cost of the contract;

(*b*) the aggregate of—

(i) the amount of periodical payments under the contract, or in the case of a swap contract under which only a single payment is to be made, the value of the payment and

(ii) the credits or debits representing interest arising, on the assumption that an effective interest method is used, in respect of the asset or liability representing a loan relationship which is the hedged item,

represent the credits or debits that would be given by generally accepted accounting practice in relation to an asset or liability representing a loan relationship whose terms include those of both the hedged item and the interest rate contract;

(*c*) exchange gains and losses are recognised as a result of the translation of the contract at the balance-sheet date; and

(*d*) profits and losses which arise as a result of the contract coming to an end before its stated date of maturity are amortised and brought into account over the unexpired term of the hedged item.

"an interest rate contract" means—

(i) a derivative contract whose underlying subject matter is, or includes, interest rates, or

(ii) if not falling within paragraph (*i*), a swap contract in which payments fall to be made by reference to a rate of interest or to an index determined by reference to income or retail prices.

(5), (6) . . . [5]

(7) . . . [4]

Commentary—*Simon's Taxes* **D1.851.**

Amendments—[1] Para (2A) inserted by the Loan Relationships and Derivative Contracts (Disregard and Bringing into Account of Profits and Losses) (Amendment No 2) Regulations, SI 2005/3374 regs 2, 9 with effect from 29 December 2005. This amendment has effect in relation to periods of account beginning on or after 1 January 2005 and ending after SI 2005/3374 comes into force (ie 29 December 2005).

[2] Words in para (1)(b) inserted by the Loan Relationships and Derivative Contracts (Disregard and Bringing into Account of Profits and Losses) (Amendment) Regulations, SI 2006/3236 regs 2, 4 with effect in relation to periods of account beginning on or after 1 January 2006 and ending on or after 27 December 2006.

[3] In para (1) words substituted for words "paragraph 17C(1)(*a*) of Schedule 26 to the Finance Act 2002" by the Loan Relationships and Derivative Contracts (Disregard and Bringing into Account of Profits and Losses) (Amendment) Regulations, SI 2014/3188 regs 2, 8(1), (8)(*c*) with effect from 31 December 2014.

[4] In paras (2), (2A) words substituted for words "paragraph 17C(1)(*b*) of Schedule 26 to the Finance Act 2002", and para (7) revoked, by the Loan Relationships and Derivative Contracts (Disregard and Bringing into Account of Profits and Losses) (Amendment) Regulations, SI 2014/3188 regs 2, 8(10)–(12) with effect from 31 December 2014.

Note that transitional provisions apply in relation to any company which at any time before the start of the first period of account beginning on or after 1 January 2015 uses fair value accounting in relation to a derivative contract which satisfies the conditions in reg 7(1)(*a*), 8(1)(*a*) or 9(1) (SI 2014/3188 reg 9).

[5] In para (2A) words inserted, in para (3) words substituted for words "section 606(3) of CTA 2009 or regulation 4", and paras (5), (6) revoked, by the Loan Relationships and Derivative Contracts (Disregard and Bringing into Account of Profits and Losses) (Amendment) Regulations, SI 2015/1961 regs 2, 8 with effect in relation to accounting periods beginning on or after 1 January 2016. Paras (5), (6) previously read as follows—

"(5) For the purposes of section 598(1)(*a*) of CTA 2009, there is also prescribed for any period any credits and debits which—

(a) have for that or any previous period been brought into account in the statement of recognised gains and losses or statement of changes in equity ("equity statements"); and

(b) represent fair value profits or losses which are transferred in that period from an equity statement—

(i) to the profit and loss account or income statement, or

(ii) directly to the carrying value of an asset or liability.

(6) Where credits and debits are prescribed by sub-paragraph (5) there is also prescribed, for the purposes of section 598(1)(*a*) of CTA 2009, any debits and credits corresponding to the sub-paragraph (5) credits and debits which are brought into account in the profit and loss account or income statement when—

(a) the hedged item is recognised; or

(b) a forecast transaction is no longer expected to occur.".

[9A— [Profits or losses arising from designated cash flow hedges]

(1) For the purposes of [section 598(1)(*a*) of CTA 2009][3] there is prescribed all credits and debits representing the whole or part of the fair value profit or loss arising to a company in relation to [a currency contract, a commodity contract, a debt contract or an interest rate contract (as the case may be)][2] in an accounting period if—

(*a*) *the contract or a portion of the contract ("the hedging instrument") is designated as a hedge in respect of any risks arising in respect of an asset, liability, receipt or expense ("the hedged item");*

(*b*) *fair value profits or losses arising on the hedging instrument are recognised in accordance with generally accepted accounting practice in the company's statement of recognised gains and losses or statement of changes in equity ("equity statements"); and*

[(*c*) *regulation 7, 8 or 9, as the case may be, does not apply in respect of contracts of that type.*][3]

(2) Credits and debits which—

(*a*) *are brought into account in the profit and loss account or income statement (including debits and credits previously brought into account in an equity statement and transferred to the profit and loss account or income statement), or*

(*b*) *are taken to the carrying value of an asset or liability [where the profit or loss for corporation tax purposes in relation to that asset or liability will not fall to be computed in accordance with generally accepted accounting practice*][2],

are not prescribed for the purposes of [section 598(1)(a) of CTA 2009][3]. This is subject to paragraph (3).

(3) In relation to credits or debits within paragraph (2)(*a*) [or (*b*)], there is prescribed for the purposes of [section 598(1)(*a*) of CTA 2009][3] any debits or credits corresponding to the paragraph (2)(*a*) debits or credits which are reflected in an equity statement.

[(3A) Where a derivative contract becomes a contract in relation to which debits and credits are prescribed by this regulation, or ceases to be such a contract, the amount to be brought into account for the purposes of section 598(1)(*b*) of CTA 2009 is such amount as is just and reasonable in the circumstances, and with regard to whether as a result of the change any amounts cease to be brought into account or are brought into account more than once.][3]

(4) In this regulation "an interest rate contract" has the same meaning as in regulation 9.][1], [5]

Amendments—[1] Regulation 9A inserted by the Loan Relationships and Derivative Contracts (Disregard and Bringing into Account of Profits and Losses) (Amendment No 2) Regulations, SI 2005/3374 regs 2, 10 with effect from 29 December 2005. This amendment has effect in relation to periods of account beginning on or after 1 January 2005 and ending after SI 2005/3374 comes into force (ie 29 December 2005).

[2] Words in para (1) substituted, and words in paras (2)(*b*), (3) inserted, by the Loan Relationships and Derivative Contracts (Disregard and Bringing into Account of Profits and Losses) (Amendment) Regulations, SI 2006/3236 regs 2, 5 with effect in relation to periods of account beginning on or after 1 January 2006 and ending on or after 27 December 2006.

[3] Heading to reg 9A inserted, and paras (1)(*c*), (3A) substituted, by the Loan Relationships and Derivative Contracts (Disregard and Bringing into Account of Profits and Losses) (Amendment) Regulations, SI 2014/3188 regs 2, 7 with effect in relation to periods of account beginning on or after 1 January 2015. Paras (1)(*c*), (3A) previously read as follows—

"(*c*) the company has made an election under regulation 6(3A), 6(5) or 6(5B) (as the case may be). This is subject to paragraph (2).".

"(3A) Where—

(a) amounts in respect of a currency contract, a commodity contract or a debt contract are brought into account differently as a result of an election under regulation 6(3A), or

(b) an interest rate contract ceases to be a contract to which regulation 9 applies as a result of an election under regulation 6(5B),

the amount to be brought into account for the purposes of paragraph 17C(1)(*b*) of Schedule 26 to the Finance Act 2002 is such amount as is just and reasonable in the circumstances and with regard to whether as a result of the change any amounts cease to be brought into account or are brought into account more than once, and that amount shall be brought into account on the first day of the first accounting period beginning on or after 1st January 2006.".

[4] In paras (1), (2), (3) words substituted for words "paragraph 17C(1)(*a*) of Schedule 26 to the Finance Act 2002" by the Loan Relationships and Derivative Contracts (Disregard and Bringing into Account of Profits and Losses) (Amendment) Regulations, SI 2014/3188 regs 2, 8(1), (8)(*d*) with effect from 31 December 2014.

[5] Reg 9A revoked by the Loan Relationships and Derivative Contracts (Disregard and Bringing into Account of Profits and Losses) (Amendment) Regulations, SI 2015/1961 regs 2, 9 with effect in relation to accounting periods beginning on or after 1 January 2016.

10 Bringing fair value profits or losses into account on currency and commodity contracts

(1) For the purposes of [section 598(1)(c) of CTA 2009][4]

(*a*) there is prescribed the aggregate of the credits and debits representing any [regulation 7 or 8][1] fair value profits or losses excluded in relation to a derivative contract of a company . . . [1]; and (*b*) the amount of that aggregate is brought into account for the period in which a termination event occurs.

This is subject to paragraphs (3), (5), (7) [and (9)][5].

(2) In paragraph (1) a "termination event" occurs—

(*a*) on the company ceasing to be a party to the contract; or

(*b*) if earlier, when the hedged item begins to affect the company's profit or loss.

(3) If the forecast transaction or firm commitment which is the hedged item mentioned in regulation 7 or regulation 8 is a forecast transaction of, or a firm commitment to a purchase of, anything the expenditure in relation to which—

(*a*) falls to be taken into account in computing the profits of a trade or property business carried on by the company, or

(*b*) would fall to be deducted but for any provision of the Corporation Tax Acts prohibiting the deduction of capital expenditure in respect of depreciation of an asset,

then the aggregate mentioned in paragraph (1)(a) in relation to the contract is[, subject to paragraph (3A),][1] to be brought into account in the accounting period in which the expenditure falls or would fall to be deducted.

[(3A) [Subject to paragraph (3B),][2] if paragraph (3)(*b*) applies—

(*a*) the amount to be brought into account in an accounting period is the product of—

$$\frac{DA}{E} \times FVP$$

where—

DA is the amount of depreciation recognised in the profit and loss account or income statement in relation to the hedged item in the accounting period,

E is the total expenditure on the hedged item, and

FVP is the aggregate amount of regulation 7 or 8 fair value profit;

(*b*) where the hedged item is disposed of, the balance of the aggregate amount mentioned in paragraph (1)(*a*) which has not been brought into account under sub-paragraph (*a*) of this paragraph shall be brought into account in the accounting period in which the disposal takes place.][1]

[(3B) Where the disposal mentioned in paragraph (3A)(*b*) is to a company ("the transferee") which is a member of the same group of companies, in applying paragraph (3A)(*a*) to the transferee FVP shall be treated as meaning the fair value profits and losses of the transferor.][2]

[(3C) In paragraph (3B), "group of companies" has the meaning given in [section 624(3) of CTA 2009][4].][2]

(4) In paragraph (3) "property business" has the meaning given in [section 748(4) of CTA 2009][4].

(5) Where—

(*a*) part of a contract to which this regulation applies terminates without the company ceasing to be a party to the contract, or

(*b*) part only of the hedged item begins to be recognised in determining the company's profit and loss,

paragraph (1)(b) [or paragraph (3)][1] is to apply to a proportionate amount of the aggregate.

(6) In paragraph (5) "proportionate amount" means that proportion of the relevant aggregate amount which is—

(*a*) in a case where it is part of the contract which matures, the [proportion][1] which the fair value of the part of the contract maturing bears to the fair value of the whole of the contract at that time, and

(*b*) in any other case the proportion which the fair value of the hedged item [which begins][1] to be recognised bears to the fair value of the whole of the hedged item at that time.

(7) Where immediately on ceasing to be a party to the contract ("the old contract"), the company enters into another contract ("the new contract") which meets the conditions in regulation 7 or regulation 8 in relation to the same hedged item as was the hedged item in relation to the old contract—

(*a*) paragraph (1)(*b*) shall not apply in relation to the old contract, and

(*b*) the aggregate prescribed in paragraph (1)(*a*) in relation to the old contract shall be treated for the purposes of the application of this regulation to the new contract as included in the aggregate prescribed in relation to the new contract.

(8) . . . [5]

[(9) Where regulation 6B applies—

(*a*) paragraph (1)(*b*) does not apply to the transferor, and

(*b*) the aggregate prescribed in paragraph (1)(*a*) in relation to the contract held by the transferor is treated as included in the aggregate prescribed in relation to the contract held by the transferee.

In this paragraph "the transferor" and "the transferee" have the same meaning as in section 625 of CTA 2009.][5]

(10), (11) . . . [5]

Commentary—*Simon's Taxes* **D1.850.**

Amendments—[1] This regulation amended by the Loan Relationships and Derivative Contracts (Disregard and Bringing into Account of Profits and Losses) (Amendment) Regulations, SI 2005/2012 regs 2, 10 with effect from 11 August 2005. These amendments have effect in relation to periods of account beginning on or after 1 January 2005 and ending after SI 2005/2012 comes into force (ie 11 August 2005).

[2] Words in para (3A) inserted and paras (3B), (3C) inserted by the Loan Relationships and Derivative Contracts (Disregard and Bringing into Account of Profits and Losses) (Amendment No 2) Regulations, SI 2005/3374 regs 2, 11 with effect from 29 December 2005. These amendments have effect in relation to periods of account beginning on or after 1 January 2005 and ending after SI 2005/3374 comes into force (ie 29 December 2005).

[4] The following amendments made by the Loan Relationships and Derivative Contracts (Disregard and Bringing into Account of Profits and Losses) (Amendment) Regulations, SI 2014/3188 regs 2, 8(13)–(16) with effect from 31 December 2014—

- in para (1) words substituted for words "paragraph 17C(1)(*c*) of Schedule 26 to the Finance Act 2002";
- in para (3C) words substituted for words "paragraph 28(6) of Schedule 26 to the Finance Act 2002";
- in para (4) words substituted for words "paragraph 32(2) of Schedule 29 to the Finance Act 2002 (gains and losses of a company from intangible fixed assets)".

[5] In para (1) words substituted for words "and (8)", para (9) substituted, and paras (8), (10), (11) revoked, by the Loan Relationships and Derivative Contracts (Disregard and Bringing into Account of Profits and Losses) (Amendment) Regulations, SI 2015/1961 regs 2, 10 with effect in relation to accounting periods beginning on or after 1 January 2016. Paras (8)–(11) previously read as follows—

"(8) Where as a result of the company ("the transferor company") ceasing to be a party to the contract ("the old contract")—

(*a*) section 625 of the Corporation Tax 2009 would apply but for section 628 of that Act, and

(*b*) the transferee company (within the meaning of section 625 of that Act) meets the conditions in regulation 7 or regulation 8 in relation to the contract ("the new contract") and the same hedged item as was the hedged item in relation to the old contract,

paragraph (9) applies.

(9) Where this paragraph applies—

(*a*) paragraph (1)(*b*) shall not apply in relation to the old contract; and

(*b*) the aggregate prescribed in paragraph (1)(*a*) in relation to the old contract shall be treated for the purposes of the application of this regulation to the new contract as included in the aggregate prescribed in relation to the new contract.

(10) For the purposes of section 598(1)(*a*) of CTA 2009, there is also prescribed for any period any credits and debits which—

(*a*) have for that or any previous period been brought into account in the statement of recognised gains and losses and statement of changes in equity ("equity statements"); or

(*b*) represent regulation 7 or 8 fair value profits or losses which are transferred in that period from an equity statement—

(i) to the profit and loss account or income statement, or

(ii) directly to the carrying value of an asset or liability.

(11) Where credits and debits are prescribed by sub-paragraph (10) there is also prescribed, for the purposes of section 598(1)(*a*) of CTA 2009, any debits and credits corresponding to the sub-paragraph (10) credits and debits which are brought into account in the profit and loss account or income statement when—

(*a*) the hedged item is recognised; or

(*b*) a forecast transaction is no longer expected to occur.".

10A [Bringing exchange gains into account on contracts to which regulation 7A applies

(1) For the purposes of section 598(1)(*c*) of the Corporation Tax Act 2009 there is an amount to be brought into account which is equivalent to the amount of any exchange gain specified in paragraph (2).

(2) The exchange gain specified is any exchange gain—

(*a*) arising to a company in relation to a derivative contract to which regulation 7A applies or applied, and

(*b*) which has been distributed to the shareholders of the company.

(3) The amount to be brought into account by paragraph (1) is to be brought into account for the accounting period in which the distribution is made.][1]

Amendments—[1] Reg 10A inserted by the Loan Relationships and Derivative Contracts (Disregard and Bringing into Account of Profits and Losses) (Amendment) Regulations, SI 2009/1886 regs 3, 6 with effect in relation to derivative contracts—

(a) entered into on or after 1 January 2009 and which formed part of a relevant hedging relationship up to and including 10 March 2009; or

(b) entered into on or after 10 March 2009.

11 [Profits and losses arising from loan relationships with embedded derivatives

[(1) For the purposes of [section 310(1) of CTA 2009][4] (amounts recognised in determining company's profits and loss) the amounts described in paragraph (2) are prescribed in relation to a company which is party to a creditor relationship to which—

(*a*) either—

(i) section 92 (convertible securities etc: creditor relationships), or

(ii) section 93 (relationships linked to the value of chargeable assets),

of the Finance Act 1996 applied immediately before the start of the first accounting period of the company to begin on or after 1st January 2005, and

(*b*) section 94A of the Finance Act 1996 (loan relationships with embedded derivatives) applies in the first accounting period of the company to begin on or after 1st January 2005.

(1A) Where paragraph (1) does not apply, for the purposes of [section 310(1) of CTA 2009][4] the amounts described in paragraph (3) are prescribed in relation to a company which is party to a creditor relationship to which—

(*a*) section 92, or

(*b*) section 93,

of the Finance Act 1996 applies immediately before the start of the first accounting period of the company to begin on or after 1st January 2005.][3]

(2) The prescribed amounts are all credits and debits in respect of the host contract save for—

(*a*) credits in relation to interest accruing in respect of the creditor relationship without regard to the amounts given by the effective interest method; and

(*b*) [where paragraph (1)(*a*)(i) applies,][3] credits and debits in respect of exchange gains and losses.

(3) The prescribed amounts are all credits and debits save for—

(*a*) credits in relation to interest, and

(*b*) [where paragraph (1A)(a) applies,][3] credits and debits in respect of exchange gains and losses.][1]

[(4) Where there is a change of accounting policy in drawing up a company's accounts from one period of account to the next affecting the amounts to be brought into account for accounting purposes in respect of the company's loan relationships, the amounts prescribed in paragraphs (1) to (3) that would otherwise be brought into account for the purposes of [Part 5 of the Corporation Tax 2009][4] shall not be brought into account.][2]

Amendments—[1] Regulations 11, 12 inserted by the Loan Relationships and Derivative Contracts (Disregard and Bringing into Account of Profits and Losses) (Amendment) Regulations, SI 2005/2012 regs 2, 11 with effect from 11 August 2005. These amendments have effect in relation to periods of account beginning on or after 1 January 2005 and ending after SI 2005/2012 comes into force (ie 11 August 2005).

[2] Para (4) inserted by the Loan Relationships and Derivative Contracts (Disregard and Bringing into Account of Profits and Losses) (Amendment No 2) Regulations, SI 2005/3374 regs 2, 12 with effect from 29 December 2005. This amendment has effect in relation to periods of account beginning on or after 1 January 2005 and ending after SI 2005/3374 comes into force (ie 29 December 2005).

[3] Paras (1), (1A) substituted for original para (1), words in paras (2)(b), (3)(b) inserted by the Loan Relationships and Derivative Contracts (Disregard and Bringing into Account of Profits and Losses) (Amendment) Regulations, SI 2006/3236 regs 2, 6 with effect in relation to periods of account beginning on or after 1 January 2006 and ending on or after 27 December 2006

[4] In paras (1), (1A) words substituted for words "section 85B(3) of the Finance Act 1996", and in para (4) words substituted for words "Chapter 2 of the Finance Act 1996", by the Loan Relationships and Derivative Contracts (Disregard and Bringing into Account of Profits and Losses) (Amendment) Regulations, SI 2014/3188 regs 2, 8(17)(*a*), (18) with effect from 31 December 2014.

[12—[(1) For the purposes of [section 310(1) of CTA 2009][5] the amounts described in paragraph (2) are prescribed in relation to a company which is party to a debtor relationship to which—

(*a*) either—

(i) section 92A (convertible securities etc: debtor relationships), or

(ii) section 93,

of the Finance Act 1996 applies immediately before the start of the first accounting period of the company to begin on or after 1st January 2005, and

(*b*) section 94A of the Finance Act 1996 applies in the first accounting period of the company to begin on or after 1st January 2005.

This is subject to paragraph (4).

(1A) Where paragraph (1) does not apply, for the purposes of [section 310(1) of CTA 2009][5] the amounts described in paragraph (2A) are prescribed in relation to a company which is party to a debtor relationship to which—

(*a*) section 92A, or

(*b*) section 93,

of the Finance Act 1996 applies immediately before the start of the first accounting period of the company to begin on or after 1st January 2005.

This is subject to paragraph (4).

(2) The prescribed amounts are—

(*a*) where paragraph (1)(*a*)(i) applies, [all debits and credits in respect of the host contract save for—

(i) debits in relation to interest accruing in respect of the debtor relationship,

(ii) credits and debits in respect of discounts, premiums, fees and other incidental costs to the extent that these amounts are not within section 92A(3) of the Finance Act 1996, and

(iii) debits and credits in respect of exchange gains and losses,

without regard to the amounts given by the effective interest method, and][4];

(*b*) where paragraph (1)(*a*)(ii) applies, all debits and credits in respect of the host contract save for debits in relation to interest accruing in respect of the debtor relationship without regard to the amounts given by the effective interest method.

(2A) The prescribed amounts are—

(*a*) where paragraph (1A)(*a*) applies, debits to the extent that they are within section 92A(3) of the Finance Act 1996;

(*b*) where paragraph (1A)(*b*) applies, all debits and credits in respect of the host contract save for debits in relation to interest.][3]

[(3) Where there is a change of accounting policy in drawing up a company's accounts from one period of account to the next affecting the amounts to be brought into account for accounting purposes in respect of the company's loan relationships, the amounts prescribed in paragraphs (1) and (2) that would otherwise be brought into account for the purposes of [Part 5 of the Corporation Tax 2009][5] shall not be brought into account.][2]

[(4) This regulation does not apply to a company which is a party to a debtor relationship in a case where—

(*a*) the company is carrying on a banking business or a business consisting wholly or partly in dealing in securities, and

(*b*) it entered into the debtor relationship in the ordinary course of that business.][2]][1]

Amendments—[1] Regulations 11, 12 inserted by the Loan Relationships and Derivative Contracts (Disregard and Bringing into Account of Profits and Losses) (Amendment) Regulations, SI 2005/2012 regs 2, 11 with effect from 11 August 2005. These amendments have effect in relation to periods of account beginning on or after 1 January 2005 and ending after SI 2005/2012 comes into force (ie 11 August 2005).

[2] Words in paras (1), (2) inserted, and paras (3), (4) inserted, by the Loan Relationships and Derivative Contracts (Disregard and Bringing into Account of Profits and Losses) (Amendment No 2) Regulations, SI 2005/3374 regs 2, 13 with effect from 29 December 2005. This amendment has effect in relation to periods of account beginning on or after 1 January 2005 and ending after SI 2005/3374 comes into force (ie 29 December 2005).

[3] Paras (1)–(2A) substituted for original paras (1), (2) by the Loan Relationships and Derivative Contracts (Disregard and Bringing into Account of Profits and Losses) (Amendment) Regulations, SI 2006/3236 regs 2, 7 with effect in relation to periods of account beginning on or after 1 January 2006 and ending on or after 27 December 2006.

[4] Words in para (2)(a) substituted by the Loan Relationships and Derivative Contracts (Disregard and Bringing into Account of Profits and Losses) (Amendment) Regulations, SI 2007/948 regs 2, 6 with effect from 11 April 2007. This amendment has effect in relation to periods of account ending on or after 11 April 2007.

Where a company ceased to be party to a debtor relationship to which SI 2004/3256 reg 12(1)(*a*)(i) applies before 11 April 2007, reg 6 shall not apply in respect of that loan relationship.

[5] In paras (1), (1A) words substituted for words "section 85B(3) of the Finance Act 1996", and in para (3) words substituted for words "Chapter 2 of the Finance Act 1996", by the Loan Relationships and Derivative Contracts (Disregard and Bringing into Account of Profits and Losses) (Amendment) Regulations, SI 2014/3188 regs 2, 8(17)(*b*), (18) with effect from 31 December 2014.

[12A Loan relationships as permanent as equity

(1) The amounts described in paragraph (3) are not brought into account for the purposes of Part 5 of the Corporation Tax Act 2009 in relation an asset representing a loan relationship of a company which is denominated in a currency which is not, or was not, the company's functional currency, if there is a relevant change of accounting policy.

(2) A relevant change of accounting policy is a change of accounting policy in drawing up a company's accounts from one period of account to the next where in accordance with generally accepted accounting practice—

(*a*) in the earlier period the loan relationship is treated (in accordance with SSAP 20) as permanent as equity and either—

(i) the loan relationship was brought into account at an historic rate, or

(ii) debits and credits in relation to the loan relationship were not brought into account by virtue of section 328(3) of the Corporation Tax Act 2009, and

(*b*) in the later period the loan relationship was brought into account at a spot rate of exchange.

(3) The amounts are—

(*a*) debits and credits representing the difference between the carrying value of the loan relationship recognised for accounting purposes at the end of the earlier period and the value recognised at the beginning of the later period to the extent the debits or credits are attributable to the different rates of exchange, and

(*b*) debits and credits representing exchange gains and losses arising in the later period and subsequent accounting periods in relation to the loan relationship.

(4) But an amount is not within paragraph (3)(*b*) to the extent that in any period—

(*a*) the loan relationship is a hedged item under a hedging relationship where the hedging instrument is a liability representing a loan relationship of the company or an obligation of the company under a derivative contract to pay in exchange for one currency an amount in a second currency, or

(*b*) regulation 3(5) applies in relation to the loan relationship.

(5) For the purposes of this regulation—

(*a*) where there is a change of accounting policy in drawing up a company's accounts from one period of account to the next, the "earlier period" is the first of those periods of account and the "later period" is the next period;

(*b*) "functional currency" means the currency of the primary economic environment in which a company operates;

(*c*) "historic rate" and "as permanent as equity" have the same meaning as for accounting purposes;

(*d*) "SSAP 20" means Statement of Standard Accounting Practice No 20 on Foreign Currency Translation, issued by the Accounting Standards Board on 1st April 1983.][1]

Amendments—[1] Regulation 12A inserted by the Changes in Accounting Standards (Loan Relationships and Derivative Contracts) Regulations, SI 2014/3325 reg 3 with effect from 31 December 2014. Note that if, in consequence of a relevant change in accounting policy, a company adopts a relevant accounting change for a period of account beginning on or after 1 October 2012, this amendment has effect in relation to the accounting period which coincides with that period and subsequent accounting periods (SI 2014/3325 reg 1(2)).

13 [Transitional provision: exchange losses arising from contracts to which regulation 7A applies

(1) This regulation applies to a derivative contract to which regulation 7A applies—

(*a*) which was entered into on or after 1st January 2009;

(*b*) which formed part of a relevant hedging relationship (within the meaning of regulation 7A) up to and including 10th March 2009; and

(*c*) in respect of which an exchange loss would have arisen to the company had an accounting period ended on 9th March 2009.

(2) For the purposes of section 598(1)(*c*) of the Corporation Tax Act 2009 the amount to be brought into account is the lower of—

(*a*) the exchange loss arising to the company which is incurred on the termination of the derivative contract; or

(*b*) the exchange loss which would have arisen to the company in relation to the derivative contract had an accounting period ended on 9th March 2009.

(3) Paragraph (4) applies if there is more than one derivative contract to which regulation 7A applies in relation to the same hedged item.

(4) The total amount of the exchange loss in relation to those contracts which is to be brought into account under this regulation shall not exceed the aggregate net exchange losses (if any) which—

(*a*) arose to the company on the termination of those contracts, or

(*b*) would have arisen to the company in relation to those contracts had an accounting period ended on 9 March 2009.

(5) Where paragraph (4) applies, the amount of loss to be brought into account is to be apportioned between each of the contracts on a just and reasonable basis.

(6) For the purposes of this regulation, the termination of a derivative contract shall be regarded as having occurred on the earlier of—

(*a*) the day on which the contract is terminated, or

(*b*) the last day of the first accounting period which ends on or after 10th March 2009.

(7) The amount to be brought into account for the purposes of section 598(1)(*c*) of the Corporation Tax Act 2009 is nil in a case where—

(*a*) no exchange loss arises to the company on the termination of the derivative contract;

(*b*) there is more than one derivative contract to which regulation 7A applies in relation to the same hedged item and no aggregate net exchange loss arises to the companion the termination of those contracts; or

(*c*) there is more than one derivative contract to which regulation 7A applies in relation to the same hedged item and no aggregate net exchange loss would have arisen to the company in relation to those contracts had an accounting period ended on 9th March 2009.][1]

Amendments—[1] Reg 13 inserted by the Loan Relationships and Derivative Contracts (Disregard and Bringing into Account of Profits and Losses) (Amendment) Regulations, SI 2009/1886 regs 3, 7 with effect in relation to derivative contracts—

(a) entered into on or after 1 January 2009 and which formed part of a relevant hedging relationship up to and including 10 March 2009; or

(b) entered into on or after 10 March 2009.

2004/3271

LOAN RELATIONSHIPS AND DERIVATIVE CONTRACTS (CHANGE OF ACCOUNTING PRACTICE) REGULATIONS 2004

Made by the Treasury under FA 1996 ss 85B(3), (5), 90A, Sch 9 para 19B and FA 2002 Sch 26 para 17C

Made . . . . 9 December 2004
Laid before the House of Commons . . . . 10 December 2004
Coming into force . . . . 1 January 2005

Commentary—*Simon's Taxes* **D1.7100, D1.845, D1.8102.**

1 Citation, commencement and effect

(1) These Regulations may be cited as the Loan Relationships and Derivative Contracts (Change of Accounting Practice) Regulations 2004 and shall come into force on 1st January 2005.

(2) These Regulations have effect in relation to periods of account beginning on or after 1st January 2005.

2 Interpretation

In these Regulations—

"amortised cost basis of accounting" has the meaning given by [section 313(4) of CTA 2009][4];

["CTA 2009" means the Corporation Tax Act 2009;

"CTA 2010" means the Corporation Tax Act 2010;][4]

["earlier period" and "later period" have the meanings given in [section 315(2) of CTA 2009][4];][1]

["exchange gains and losses"—

(*a*) in relation to a loan relationship shall be construed in accordance with [section 475 of CTA 2009][4]; and

(*b*) in relation to a derivative contract shall be construed in accordance with [section 705 of CTA 2009][4];][3]

"fair value accounting" has the meaning given by [section 313(5) of CTA 2009][4];

"impairment" and "impairment loss" have the meanings given by [section 476(1) of CTA 2009][4];

["qualifying transfer" means—

(*a*) a transaction to which [Chapter 1 of Part 22 of CTA 2010][4] applies,

(*b*) a transaction to which that section would apply if for "trade" there were substituted "investment business or property business", or

(*c*) a transfer of a business which consists of the effecting or carrying out of contracts of long-term insurance from one person to another person ("the transferee");

"successor" has the meaning given by [section 940B(4) of CTA 2010][4];

"transferee" shall be construed in accordance with paragraph (c) of "qualifying transfer".][2]

Amendments—[1] Definitions of "earlier period" and "later period" inserted by the Loan Relationships and Derivative Contracts (Change of Accounting Practice) (Amendment) Regulations, SI 2005/3383 regs 2, 3 with effect from 29 December 2005. The amendments have effect in relation to periods of account beginning on or after 1 January 2005.

[2] Definitions of "qualifying transfer", "successor" and "transferee" inserted by the Loan Relationships and Derivative Contracts (Change of Accounting Practice) (Amendment) (No 2) Regulations, SI 2007/3432 regs 2, 3 with effect in relation to accounting periods beginning on or after 1 January 2008: SI 2007/3432 reg 1(2).

[3] Definition of "exchange gains and losses" inserted by the Loan Relationships and Derivative Contracts (Change of Accounting Practice) (Amendment) Regulations, SI 2008/3237 regs 2, 3 with effect from 7 January 2009.

[4] The following amendments made by the Loan Relationships and Derivative Contracts (Change of Accounting Practice) (Amendment) Regulations, SI 2014/3187 regs 2, 4(1) with effect in relation to periods of account beginning on or after 1 January 2015—

- in definition of "amortised cost basis of accounting" words substituted for words "section 103(1) of the Finance Act 1996";
- definitions of "CTA 2009" and "CTA 2010" inserted;
- in definition of "earlier period" and "later period" words substituted for words "paragraph 19A of Schedule 9 to the Finance Act 1996";
- in definition of "exchange gains and losses" words substituted for words "sections 103(1A) and 103(1B) of the Finance Act 1996" and "paragraphs 54(2) and (3) of Schedule 26 to the Finance Act 2002";
- in definitions of "fair value accounting" and "impairment and impairment loss", words substituted for words "section 103(1) of the Finance Act 1996";
- in definition of "qualifying transfer" words substituted for words "section 343(1) of the Income and Corporation Taxes Act 1988 (company reconstruction without a change of ownership)"; and
- in definition of "successor" words substituted for words "section 343(1) of the Income and Corporation Taxes Act 1988".

3 [Prescribed debits and credits to be brought into account: general

[Subject to regulation 3C [and regulations 7, 8 and 12A of the Loan Relationships and Derivative Contracts (Disregard and Bringing into Account of Profits and Losses) Regulations 2004][2], the debits and credits prescribed in regulation 4 shall be brought into account in accordance with regulations 3A and 3B . . . [3].][1]

Amendments—[1] Regulation 3 substituted by the Loan Relationships and Derivative Contracts (Change of Accounting Practice) (Amendment) Regulations, SI 2006/3238 regs 2, 3 with effect from 27 December 2006.

[2] Words inserted by the Changes in Accounting Standards (Loan Relationships and Derivative Contracts) Regulations, SI 2014/3325 reg 4 with effect from 31 December 2014. Note that if, in consequence of a relevant change in accounting policy, a company adopts a relevant accounting change for a period of account beginning on or after 1 October 2012, this amendment has effect in relation to the accounting period which coincides with that period and subsequent accounting periods (SI 2014/3325 reg 1(2)).

[3] Words "in an accounting period of the company beginning on or after 1st January 2006" revoked by the Loan Relationships and Derivative Contracts (Change of Accounting Practice) (Amendment No 2) Regulations, SI 2015/1962 regs 2, 3 with effect in relation to periods of account beginning on or after 1 January 2016.

3A [Prescribed debits and credits brought into account over prescribed period

(1) Subject to regulation 3B, debits and credits prescribed in regulation 4 ("the applicable amounts") shall be brought into account in accordance with this regulation.

[(2) Subject to paragraphs (2A) and (7A), one tenth of the applicable amount must be brought into account for each year in the period of ten years beginning with the later period.

(2A) Where the applicable amounts relate to own credit risk which would be recognised in the company's accounts as an item of other comprehensive income on the application of the relevant recognition and measurement provisions of International Financial Reporting Standard 9 issued by the International Accounting Standards Board on 24th July 2014, a percentage of the applicable amounts must be brought into account for each year in the period of five years beginning with the later period as follows—

1st year	40%
2nd year	25%
3rd year	15%
4th year	10%
5th year	10%][4]

(3) If amounts representing fractions of the applicable amounts fall to be brought into account under paragraph (2) [or (2A)][4], those amounts shall be—

(*a*) apportioned between the accounting periods beginning or ending in that year, and

(*b*) brought into account in the periods to which they are allocated in accordance with that apportionment.

(4) An apportionment between accounting periods of amounts to be brought into account under paragraph (2) [or (2A)][4] for any year shall be made according to how much of the year is included in each period, and, if that year and the accounting period are the same, the apportionment shall be effected by the allocation of the whole of the amounts to that accounting period.

(5) [Subject to [paragraph (7A)][4],][3] if a company ceases to be within the charge to corporation tax before the end of the prescribed period, the whole of the applicable amounts, so far as they have not fallen to be brought into account for an earlier accounting period, shall be brought into account as a credit or debit for the accounting period ending when the company ceases to be within that charge. This paragraph does not apply if paragraph (6) applies.

(6) In a case where there is a qualifying transfer—

(*a*) these Regulations apply to the successor or transferee for the remainder of the prescribed period for the purpose of bringing into account the applicable amounts, so far as they have not fallen to be brought into account for an earlier accounting period, and

(*b*) if—

(i) there are two or more successors or transferees, or

(ii) the transfer is of part only of the business,

those applicable amounts shall be apportioned between the parties in a manner that is just and reasonable in the circumstances.

(7) Paragraph (6) does not apply where the successor or transferee is resident outside the United Kingdom unless the business to which the qualifying transfer relates is carried on by the successor or transferee through a permanent establishment in the United Kingdom.

[(7A) To the extent that the applicable amounts (or fractions of applicable amounts) represent debits or credits to which sub-paragraph (*ca*) or (*da*) of regulation 3C(2) would apply if those sub-paragraphs had been in force at the time that the debits or credits arose—

(*a*) those amounts shall not be brought into account under paragraph (2) or (5) in relation to any accounting period . . .[4];

(*b*) . . . [4]

(7B) . . . [4]][3]

(8) . . . [2]

[(9) In this regulation—

"own credit risk" has the meaning it has for accounting purposes;

"prescribed period" means the period of ten years referred to in paragraph (2) or the period of five years referred to in paragraph (2A).][4]

Modification—The Securitisation Companies (Application of Section 83(1) of the Finance Act 2005: Accounting Standards) Regulations, SI 2007/3338 (in relation to a securitisation company the prescribed period in reg 3A shall be treated as beginning with the first accounting period).

Amendments—[1] Regulations 3A–3C inserted by the Loan Relationships and Derivative Contracts (Change of Accounting Practice) (Amendment) Regulations, SI 2005/3383 regs 2, 5 with effect from 29 December 2005. The amendments have effect in relation to periods of account beginning on or after 1 January 2005.

[2] Para (8) revoked by the Loan Relationships and Derivative Contracts (Change of Accounting Practice) (Amendment) (No 2) Regulations, SI 2007/3432 regs 2, 4 with effect in relation to accounting periods beginning on or after 1 January 2008: SI 2007/3432 reg 1(2).

[3] Words in para (5), and whole of paras (7A), (7B), inserted, by the Loan Relationships and Derivative Contracts (Change of Accounting Practice) (Amendment) Regulations, SI 2008/3237 regs 2, 4 with effect in relation to periods of account beginning on or after 1 January 2008 and ending after 31 December 2008.

[4] Paras (2), (2A) substituted for previous para (2), in paras (3), (4) words inserted, in para (5) words substituted for words "paragraphs (7A) and (7B)", in para (7A) in sub-para (*a*) words "beginning on or after 1st January 2009" revoked and sub-para (*b*) revoked, para (7B) revoked, and para (9) inserted, by the Loan Relationships and Derivative Contracts (Change of Accounting Practice) (Amendment No 2) Regulations, SI 2015/1962 regs 2, 4 with effect in relation to periods of account beginning on or after 1 January 2016 where the later period begins on or after 1 January 2016. "Later period" has the meaning given in CTA 2009 s 315(2). Para (2) previously read as follows—

"(2) Subject to paragraphs (7A) and (7B), one tenth of the applicable amounts shall be brought into account for each year in the period of ten years ("the prescribed period") beginning with the later of—

(a) the first accounting period of the company beginning on or after 1st January 2006, and

(b) the later period.".

Para (7A)(*b*) previously read as follows—

"(b) the relevant fraction of those amounts shall not be brought into account under paragraph (2) or (5) in relation to any accounting period beginning on or after 1st January 2008 and ending after 31st December 2008.".

Para (7B) previously read as follows—

"(7B) In paragraph (7A)(*b*) the relevant fraction is—

$$1-(A/B)$$

where—

A is the number of days in the accounting period up to, and including, 31st December 2008, and

B is the total number of days in the accounting period.".

3B [Prescribed debits and credits in relation to dormant accounts

(1) The debits and credits prescribed in regulation 4(1)(*a*) or (*b*) which are specified in paragraph (2) ("the specified amounts") shall be brought into account in accounting periods of the company beginning on or after 1st January 2008 in accordance with this regulation, but only to the extent that they represent the reversal of amounts that have been brought into account for corporation tax in accounting periods before the later period.

(2) The specified debits and credits are those which represent an adjustment in the value for accounting purposes of a liability owed by a bank or building society to a depositor which at the end of the earlier period had no [tax-adjusted carrying value][3].

(3) One tenth of the specified amounts shall be allocated to each year in the prescribed period.

(4) If amounts representing fractions of the specified amounts fall under paragraph (3) to be allocated to a year these amounts shall be—

(*a*) apportioned between the accounting periods beginning or ending in that year, and

(*b*) brought into account in the periods to which they are so apportioned, subject to paragraph (6).

(5) An apportionment between accounting periods of amounts allocated under paragraph (3) to any year shall be made according to how much of the year is included in each period, and, if that year and the accounting period are the same, the apportionment shall be effected by the allocation of the whole of the amounts to that accounting period.

(6) Where the prescribed period began before 1st January 2008, the debits and credits specified in paragraph (2) that would have been brought into account in accounting periods beginning before that date if regulation 3A had applied to those debits and credits from the beginning of the prescribed period shall be brought into account in the first accounting period beginning on or after that date.

(7) If a company ceases to be within the charge to corporation tax before the end of the prescribed period, the whole of the specified amounts, so far as they have not fallen to be brought into account for an earlier accounting period, shall be brought into account as a credit or debit for the accounting period ending when the company ceases to be within that charge.

This paragraph does not apply if paragraph (8) applies.

(8) In a case where there is a qualifying transfer—

(*a*) these Regulations apply to the successor or transferee for the remainder of the prescribed period for the purpose of bringing into account the specified amounts, so far as they have not fallen to be brought into account for an earlier accounting period, and

(*b*) if—

(i) there are two or more successors or transferees, or

(ii) the transfer is of part only of the business,

those specified amounts shall be apportioned between the parties in a manner that is just and reasonable in the circumstances.

(9) Paragraph 8 does not apply where the successor or transferee is resident outside the United Kingdom unless the business to which the qualifying transfer relates is carried on by the successor or transferee through a permanent establishment in the United Kingdom.

(10) In this regulation—

"bank" has the meaning given by [section 1120(2) of CTA 2010][2];

"building society" has the meaning given by [section 1119][2] of that Act;

"[tax-adjusted carrying value][3]" has the meaning given by [[section 465B][3] of CTA 2009][2];

"prescribed period" has the meaning given by [regulation 3A(9)][3].][1]

Amendments—[1] Regulation 3B substituted by the Loan Relationships and Derivative Contracts (Change of Accounting Practice) (Amendment) (No 2) Regulations, SI 2007/3432 regs 2, 5 with effect in relation to accounting periods beginning on or after 1 January 2008: SI 2007/3432 reg 1(2).

[2] In para (10), the following amendments made by the Loan Relationships and Derivative Contracts (Change of Accounting Practice) (Amendment) Regulations, SI 2014/3187 regs 2, 4(2) with effect in relation to periods of account beginning on or after 1 January 2015—

– in definition of "bank" words substituted for words "section 840A of the Income and Corporation Taxes Act 1988";
– in definition of "building society" words substituted for words "section 832(1)"; and
– in definition of "carrying value" words substituted for words "paragraph 19A(4A) of Schedule 9 to the Finance Act 1996".

[3] In paras (2), (10) words substituted for words "carrying value", and in para (10) words substituted for words "section 317" and "regulation 3A(2)", by the Loan Relationships and Derivative Contracts (Change of Accounting Practice) (Amendment No 2) Regulations, SI 2015/1962 regs 2, 5 with effect in relation to periods of account beginning on or after 1 January 2016.

3C [Prescribed debits and credits not brought into account

(1) The debits and credits prescribed in regulation 4(1) which are specified in paragraph (2) shall not be brought into account in determining a company's profit or loss for any period.

(2) The specified debits and credits are—

(*a*) debits and credits in relation to a derivative contract to which a company is treated as a party by section 94A(2)(*b*) of the Finance Act 1996 where section 92A of that Act (convertible securities etc: debtor relationships) applied to the debtor relationship in relation to that contract at the end of the company's period of account immediately preceding the first period of account to begin on or after 1st January 2005;

[(*aa*) debits and credits in relation to a derivative contract to which a company is treated as party by section 94A(2)(*b*) of the Finance Act 1996 where section 93 of that Act (relationships linked to the value of chargeable assets) applied to the debtor relationship in relation to that contract at the end of the company's period of account immediately preceding the first period of account to begin on or after 1st January 2005;][2]

(*b*) debits and credits in relation to a derivative contract to which [section 616 of CTA 2009][6] applies;

(*c*) debits and credits in relation to a derivative contract which is an interest rate contract to which regulation 9 of the Disregard Regulations applies;

[(*ca*) debits and credits in relation to a derivative contract the underlying subject matter of which consists wholly or partly of a currency, to the extent that—

(i) those debits and credits represent the reversal of exchange gains and losses arising to the company in an accounting period before the later period, and

(ii) those exchange gains and losses have not been brought into account for the purposes of corporation tax by virtue of [section 606(3) of CTA 2009][6], regulations 4 to 11 of the Exchange Gains and Losses (Alternative Method of Calculation of Gain or Loss) Regulations 1994 or regulation 4 of the Disregard Regulations;][4]

(*d*) debits and credits in relation to a loan relationship specified in paragraph (3) representing the difference between the value of the loan relationship recognised for accounting purposes at the end of the earlier period and the value recognised at the beginning of the later period, where in accordance with generally accepted accounting practice—

(i) in the earlier period the loan relationship was brought into account at a contract rate, and

(ii) in the later period the loan relationship is brought into account at a spot rate of exchange,

to the extent that the debit or credit is attributable to the different rates of exchange; [2]

[(*da*) debits and credits in relation to a loan relationship which is denominated in a currency which is not, or was not, the company's functional currency, to the extent that—

(i) those debits and credits represent the reversal of exchange gains and losses arising to the company in an accounting period before the later period, and

(ii) those exchange gains and losses have not been brought into account for the purposes of corporation tax by virtue of [section 328(3) of CTA 2009][6], regulations 4 to 11 of the Exchange Gains and Losses (Alternative Method of Calculation of Gain or Loss) Regulations 1994 or regulation 3 of the Disregard Regulations;][4]

(*e*) . . . [7]

[(*f*) debits and credits in relation to a loan relationship to which a company is treated as party by section 94A(2)(*a*) of the Finance Act 1996 where section 92A(4) of that Act ([convertible securities etc: debtor relationships][3]) applied to the debtor relationship in relation to that relationship at the end of the company's period of account immediately preceding the first period of account to begin on or after 1st January 2005][2] [, . . . [8]

(*g*) credits in respect of the modification or replacement of a loan relationship specified in paragraph (3B);][5]

[(*h*) debits and credits relating to the matters mentioned in section 306A(1) of CTA 2009 in respect of a loan relationship of a company which—

(i) have in accordance with generally accepted accounting practice been recognised in the company's accounts in an accounting period beginning before 1 January 2016 as an item of other comprehensive income, and

(ii) have not subsequently been transferred to become items of profit or loss in an accounting period beginning before 1st January 2016, and

(*i*) debits and credits relating to the matters mentioned in section 594A(1) of CTA 2009 in respect of a derivative contract of a company which—

(i) have in accordance with generally accepted accounting practice been recognised in the company's accounts in an accounting period beginning before 1st January 2016 as an item of other comprehensive income, and

(ii) have not subsequently been transferred to become items of profit or loss in an accounting period beginning before 1st January 2016.][8]

(3) A loan relationship is specified if—

(*a*) it is denominated in a currency which is not the company's functional currency,

(*b*) a hedging relationship exists between the loan relationship and a derivative contract, and

(*c*) as a result of that hedging relationship, the derivative contract is within regulation 9 of the Disregard Regulations.

[(3A) Debits in respect of the reversal of a credit specified in paragraph (2)(*g*) shall not be brought into account in determining a company's profit or loss for any period.

(3B) A loan relationship is specified if—

(*a*) the company is party to the relationship as debtor,

(*b*) the debtor relationship is modified or replaced by another,

(*c*) immediately before the modification or replacement it is reasonable to assume that, without the modification or replacement and any arrangements of which the modification or replacement forms part, there would be a material risk that at some time within the next 12 months the company would be unable to pay its debts, and

(*d*) the modification or replacement is treated for accounting purposes as a substantial modification of the terms of a loan relationship of the company.

(3C) For the purposes of paragraph (3B)(*c*), a company is unable to pay its debts if—

(*a*) it is unable to pay its debts as they fall due, or

(*b*) the value of the company's assets is less than the amount of its liabilities, taking into account its contingent and prospective liabilities.][5]

[(3D) For the purposes of sub-paragraphs (*h*) and (*i*) of paragraph (2)—

(*a*) in determining what debits and credits fall within those sub-paragraphs, it is to be assumed that the accounting policy applied in drawing up the company's accounts for the last accounting period of the company beginning before 1 January 2016 ("the pre-commencement period") was also applied in previous accounting periods,

(*b*) but if the company's accounts for the pre-commencement period are in accordance with generally accepted accounting practice drawn up on an assumption as to the accounting policy in previous accounting periods which differs from that mentioned in sub-paragraph (*a*), that different assumption applies in determining what debits and credits fall within those sub-paragraphs.][8]

(4) In this regulation—

"contract rate" means the rate of exchange implied by the derivative contract in paragraph 3(*b*);

"designated", "cash flow hedge" and "income statement" have the same meaning as for accounting purposes;

"the Disregard Regulations" means the Loan Relationships and Derivative Contracts (Disregard and Bringing into Account of Profits and Losses) Regulations 2004;

"functional currency" has the meaning given in [section 17(4) of CTA 2010][6];

"hedging relationship" has the meaning given in regulation 2(5) of the Disregard Regulations.

["underlying subject matter" has the meaning given in [section 583 of CTA 2009][6].][4]][1]

Amendments—[1] Regulations 3A–3C inserted by the Loan Relationships and Derivative Contracts (Change of Accounting Practice) (Amendment) Regulations, SI 2005/3383 regs 2, 5 with effect from 29 December 2005. The amendments have effect in relation to periods of account beginning on or after 1 January 2005.

[2] In para (2), sub-paras (*aa*), (*f*) inserted, by the Loan Relationships and Derivative Contracts (Change of Accounting Practice) (Amendment) Regulations, SI 2006/3238 regs 2, 5 with effect from 27 December 2006.

[3] In para (2)(*f*) words inserted and substituted by the Loan Relationships and Derivative Contracts (Change of Accounting Practice) (Amendment) Regulations, SI 2007/950 regs 2, 3 with effect from 11 April 2007.

[4] Para (2)(*ca*), (*da*), and in para (4) definition of "underlying subject matter", inserted, by the Loan Relationships and Derivative Contracts (Change of Accounting Practice) (Amendment) Regulations, SI 2008/3237 regs 2, 5 with effect in relation to periods of account beginning on or after 1 January 2009.

[5] In para (2), sub-para (*g*) and preceding word "and" inserted, and paras (3A)–(3C) inserted, by the Loan Relationships and Derivative Contracts (Change of Accounting Practice) (Amendment) Regulations, SI 2014/3187 regs 2, 3 with effect in relation to periods of account beginning on or after 1 January 2015.

[6] The following amendments made by the Loan Relationships and Derivative Contracts (Change of Accounting Practice) (Amendment) Regulations, SI 2014/3187 regs 2, 4(3) with effect in relation to periods of account beginning on or after 1 January 2015—

- in para (2)(*b*), (*ca*)(ii),)(*da*)(ii), words substituted; and
- in para (4), in definitions of "functional currency" and "underlying subject matter", words substituted

[7] Para (2)(*e*) revoked by the Loan Relationships and Derivative Contracts (Change of Accounting Practice) (Amendment No 2) Regulations, SI 2015/1962 regs 2, 6 with effect in relation to periods of account beginning on or after 1 January 2016 where the later period begins on or after 1 January 2016. "Later period" has the meaning given in CTA 2009 s 315(2). Para (2)(*e*) previously read as follows—

"(*e*) debits and credits in relation to an interest rate, currency, commodity or debt contract to which regulation 9A of the Disregard Regulations applies;".

[8] In para (2)(*f*), word "and" revoked, para (2)(*h*), (*i*) inserted, and para (3D) inserted, by the Loan Relationships and Derivative Contracts (Change of Accounting Practice) (Amendment) Regulations, SI 2016/1234 regs 2, 3 with effect in relation to periods of account beginning on or after 1 January 2016.

4 Prescribed debits and credits

(1) Subject to [paragraphs (1A) and][3] (2), the debits and credits prescribed for the purpose of regulation 3 are any debits or credits [which represent an adjustment arising from a change in accounting policy,][6] which must be brought into account in accordance with—

[(*a*) section 308 of CTA 2009;][6]

(*b*) [section 316 of CTA 2009][4];

[(*c*) section 597 of CTA 2009;][6]

(*d*) [section 614 or 615 of CTA 2009][4].

[(1A) In relation to a liability representing a loan relationship to which a company is treated as a party by section 94A(2)(a) of the Finance Act 1996 to which, immediately before the start of the first accounting period of the company beginning on or after 1st January 2005—

(*a*) section 92A of that Act applied, but

(*b*) section 92A(4) of that Act did not apply,

in determining whether credits must be brought into account in accordance with section 85B(1)(b) of, or paragraph 19A(3) of Schedule 9 to, that Act regulation 12(3) of the Disregard Regulations shall be treated as not applying to the extent that the amount otherwise falling to be brought into account does not exceed the relevant amount specified in paragraph (1B).

(1B) The relevant amount is an amount equal to A less B, where—

A is the amount of all debits and credits in an accounting period ending on or after 27th December 2006 and before 11th April 2007 ("the relevant period") in respect of the loan relationship save for—

(*a*) debits in relation to interest accruing in respect of the debtor relationship,

(*b*) credits and debits in respect of discounts, premiums, fees and other incidental costs to the extent that these amounts are not within 92A(3) of the Finance Act 1996, and

(*c*) debits and credits in respect of exchange gains and losses,

without regard to the amounts given by the effective interest method; and

B is the amount of debits in the relevant period in respect of the loan relationship to the extent that they are within section 92A(3) of the Finance Act 1996.][3]

(2) [Subject to paragraph (2A),][5] the debits and credits falling within [paragraph (3) and (4)][1] are not prescribed.

[(2A) But paragraph (2) does not apply to debits and credits in respect of impairment losses arising on the application of the recognition and measurement provisions of International Financial Reporting Standard 9 issued by the International Accounting Standards Board on 24th July 2014.][5]
(3) The debits or credits falling within this paragraph are debits or credits in relation to an asset or liability representing a loan relationship of a company (referred to in this regulation respectively as "a relevant asset" and "a relevant liability") where the latest date on which [the asset or liability falls to be fully discharged is within the same accounting period as that in which the debits or credits falling within this paragraph arise][2].
[1]

[(4) The debits and credits falling within this paragraph are debits and credits in relation to a derivative contract to which a company is a party where—

(*a*) the company is treated as party to the contract by [section 415(3) of CTA 2009][4] and the corresponding loan relationship to which the company is treated as a party by paragraph (*b*) of that section is one to which paragraph (3) applies; or

(*b*) the Disregard Regulations do not apply to that contract and there is a hedging relationship between the derivative contract and a hedged item which is a relevant asset or relevant liability.][1]

(5) In [this regulation][3] "the Disregard Regulations" means the Loan Relationships and Derivative Contracts (Disregard and Bringing into Account of Profits and Losses) Regulations 2004 and expressions which are defined for the purposes of those Regulations have the same meanings in that paragraph (4) as they have in those Regulations.
(6), (7) . . .[1]

Modification—The Securitisation Companies (Application of Section 83(1) of the Finance Act 2005: Accounting Standards) Regulations, SI 2007/3338 (there shall be treated as prescribed by reg 4 any debit or credit that would have been brought into account in accordance with reg 3 in any previous period had FA 2005 s 83 not applied to that period).

Amendments—[1] Words in para (2) substituted; words in para (3) revoked; para (4) substituted; and paras (6), (7) revoked; by the Loan Relationships and Derivative Contracts (Change of Accounting Practice) (Amendment) Regulations, SI 2005/3383 regs 2, 6 with effect from 29 December 2005. The amendments have effect in relation to periods of account beginning on or after 1 January 2005.

[2] Words in para (3) inserted by the Loan Relationships and Derivative Contracts (Change of Accounting Practice) (Amendment) Regulations, SI 2006/3238 regs 2, 6 with effect from 27 December 2006.

[3] Words in paras (1), (5) substituted, and paras (1A), (1B) inserted, by the Loan Relationships and Derivative Contracts (Change of Accounting Practice) (Amendment) Regulations, SI 2007/950 regs 2, 4 with effect from 11 April 2007.

[4] The following amendments made by the Loan Relationships and Derivative Contracts (Change of Accounting Practice) (Amendment) Regulations, SI 2014/3187 regs 2, 4(4) with effect in relation to periods of account beginning on or after 1 January 2015—

- in para (1)(*b*) words substituted for words "paragraph 19A(3) of Schedule 9 to the Finance Act 1996 (adjustment on change of accounting policy)";
- in para (1)(*d*) words substituted for words "paragraph 50A(2) of Schedule 26 to the Finance Act 2002 (adjustment on change of accounting policy)"; and
- in para (4)(*a*) words substituted for words "section 94A(2)(b) of the Finance Act 1996".

[5] Words inserted in para (2), and para (2A) inserted, by the Loan Relationships and Derivative Contracts (Change of Accounting Practice) (Amendment) Regulations, SI 2015/1541 reg 2 with effect in relation to periods of account beginning on or after 1 January 2015.

[6] In para (1), words substituted for words "in any accounting period of a company beginning on or after 1st January 2005", and sub-paras (*a*), (*c*) substituted, by the Loan Relationships and Derivative Contracts (Change of Accounting Practice) (Amendment No 2) Regulations, SI 2015/1962 regs 2, 7 with effect in relation to periods of account beginning on or after 1 January 2016. Para (1)(*a*), (*c*) previously read as follows—

"(*a*) section 308(1)(*b*) of CTA 2009 where the debit or credit represents a prior period adjustment;".

"(*c*) section 597(1)(b) of CTA 2009 where the debit or credit represents a prior period adjustment;".

5 *Amounts recognised in determining a company's profit or loss in relation to held-to-maturity assets*

(1) Subject to paragraph (6), if the assets representing a loan relationship of a company satisfy the conditions prescribed in paragraph (5) and in accordance with generally accepted accounting practice those assets—

(*a*) *were previously dealt with for accounting purposes on an amortised cost basis of accounting and*

(*b*) *are subsequently required to be dealt with for accounting purposes on the basis of fair value accounting,*

the debits and credits to be brought into account for the purposes of [Part 5 of CTA 2009][2] *shall continue to be determined on an amortised cost basis of accounting.*

(2) Subject to paragraph (6), the amounts described in paragraphs (3) and (4) are excluded from [section 308(1) of CTA 2009][2] in the circumstances specified in those paragraphs.

(3) If the assets representing a loan relationship of a company satisfy the conditions prescribed in paragraph (5), the amount is any debit or credit representing the difference between the carrying value of the asset recognised for accounting purposes at the time the company ceased to treat the asset as held-to-maturity and the fair value of the asset immediately after that time.

(4) If the assets representing a loan relationship of a company cease to satisfy the conditions prescribed in paragraph (5), the amount is any debit or credit representing profits or losses—

(*a*) *brought into account in the statement of realised gains or losses or statement of changes in equity for the periods in which the asset was treated as available-for-sale,*

(*b*) *which are transferred from the statement of realised gains or losses or statement of changes in equity for the period in which the company ceased to satisfy the conditions in paragraph (5), and*

(*c*) *which are brought into account in the company's profit and loss account or income statement for the period in which the company ceased to satisfy the conditions in paragraph (5) and any subsequent accounting period.*

(5) The conditions prescribed in relation to an asset are that—

(*a*) *in accordance with generally accepted accounting practice, it is treated at any time as available-for-sale,*

(*b*) *in accordance with generally accepted accounting practice, it has at any previous time been treated as held-to-maturity,*

(*c*) *it becomes treated as available-for-sale as a result of the disposal by the company of one or more assets previously treated as held-to-maturity, and*

(*d*) *the amortised cost of the asset or assets disposed of (referred to in paragraph (c))* in the accounting period in which the disposal was made is [less][1] than 10% of the amortised cost of all the assets then treated by the company as held-to-maturity in that period.

(6) A company may elect that this regulation does not apply.

(7) An election under paragraph (6) applies to all of the company's assets which satisfy the conditions in paragraph (5).

(8) An election under paragraph (6)—

(*a*) *shall be made by notice in writing to the Inland Revenue,*

(*b*) *within 90 days of the end of the company's accounting period in which the disposal mentioned in paragraph (5)(c)* took place,

has effect for the succeeding accounting period and all subsequent accounting periods until the assets representing a loan relationship of the company cease to satisfy the conditions prescribed in paragraph (5).[3]

Amendments—[1] Word in para (5)(d) substituted by the Loan Relationships and Derivative Contracts (Change of Accounting Practice) (Amendment) Regulations, SI 2005/3383 regs 2, 7 with effect from 29 December 2005. The amendments have effect in relation to periods of account beginning on or after 1 January 2005.

[2] In para (1) words substituted for words "Chapter 2 of Part 4 of the Finance Act 1996", and in para (2) words substituted for words "section 85B(1) of the Finance Act 1996", by the Loan Relationships and Derivative Contracts (Change of Accounting Practice) (Amendment) Regulations, SI 2014/3187 regs 2, 4(5) with effect in relation to periods of account beginning on or after 1 January 2015.

[3] Reg 5 revoked by the Loan Relationships and Derivative Contracts (Change of Accounting Practice) (Amendment No 2) Regulations, SI 2015/1962 regs 2, 8 with effect in relation to periods of account beginning on or after 1 January 2016.

2004/3369

CHILD TRUST FUNDS ACT 2004 (COMMENCEMENT NO 2) ORDER 2004

Made by The Treasury under CTFA 2004 s 27

Made . . . . *20 December 2004*

1 Citation and interpretation

(1) This Order may be cited as the Child Trust Funds Act 2004 (Commencement No 2) Order 2004.

(2) In this Order—

"the Act" means the Child Trust Funds Act 2004;

"the earlier Order" means the Child Trust Funds Act 2004 (Commencement No 1) Order 2004).

2 Commencement of provisions of the Act

(1) Sections 1 to 24 of the Act shall come into force on 6th April 2005, subject to the following paragraphs.

(2) Paragraph (1) does not apply to provisions brought into force for all purposes by the earlier Order.

(3) Section 23(1) of the Act shall come into force for all purposes on 1st January 2005.

(4) Where a provision of the Act (other than section 23(1)) was partially brought into force by the earlier Order, that provision shall come into force for all other purposes on 6th April 2005.

2005/191

CHILD TRUST FUNDS (NON-TAX APPEALS) REGULATIONS 2005

Made . . . . *3 February 2005*
Laid before Parliament . . . . *4 February 2005*
Coming into force . . . . *25 February 2005*

Made by the Treasury under Child Trust Funds Act 2004 ss 23(1), 24(5) and 28(1) to (4)

1 Citation, commencement and duration

(1) These Regulations may be cited as the Child Trust Funds (Non-tax Appeals) Regulations 2005 and shall come into force on 25 February 2005.

(2) . . . [1]

Amendments—[1] Para (2) revoked by the Transfer of Tribunal Functions and Revenue and Customs Appeals Order, SI 2009/56 art 3, Sch 2 para 131 with effect from 1 April 2009.

2 Interpretation

In these Regulations—

"the Act" means the Child Trust Funds Act 2004;

"appeal tribunal" means an appeal tribunal constituted—

(*a*) . . . [1]

(*b*) in Northern Ireland, under Chapter 1 of Part 2 of the 1998 Order (social security appeals: Northern Ireland);

"child trust fund appeal" means an appeal under section 22 of the Act which, by virtue of section 24 of the Act, is to an appeal tribunal or lies to a Social Security Commissioner [or to the First-tier Tribunal or lies to the Upper Tribunal][1];

"Social Security Commissioner" means—

(*a*) [1] . . .

(*b*) in Northern Ireland, the Chief Social Security Commissioner or any other Social Security Commissioner appointed under the Social Security Administration (Northern Ireland) Act 1992 or a tribunal of two or more Commissioners constituted under Article 16(7) of the 1998 Order;

"the 1998 Act" means the Social Security Act 1998;

"the 1998 Order" means the Social Security (Northern Ireland) Order 1998.

Amendments—[1] In definition "appeal tribunal" para (*a*) revoked, in definition "child trust fund appeal" words inserted, and in definition "Social Security Commissioner" para (*a*) revoked, by the Tribunals, Courts and Enforcement Act 2007 (Transitional and Consequential Provisions) Order, SI 2008/2683 art 6(1), Sch 1 paras 260, 261 with effect from 3 November 2008.

3 Prescribed manner of notice of appeal

(1) The prescribed manner of giving notice of appeal[, in respect of an appeal to an appeal tribunal,][1] to the Inland Revenue under section 23(1) of the Child Trust Funds Act 2004 is as follows.

(2) The notice must—

(*a*) be given in writing,

(*b*) contain sufficient information to identify the appellant and the decision against which the appeal is being made, and

(*c*) be signed by or on behalf of the appellant.

(3) In paragraph (2)(*a*) "writing" includes writing produced by electronic communications if those electronic communications are approved by the Commissioners of Inland Revenue.

(4) In paragraph (2)(*c*) "signed", where the notice is in writing produced by electronic communications, means authenticated in any manner approved by those Commissioners.

Amendments—[1] Words in para (1) inserted by the Tribunals, Courts and Enforcement Act 2007 (Transitional and Consequential Provisions) Order, SI 2008/2683 art 6(1), Sch 1 paras 260, 262 with effect from 3 November 2008.

4 Application of section 54 of the Taxes Management Act 1970

(1) Section 54 of the Taxes Management Act 1970 (settling of appeals by agreement) shall apply to a child trust fund appeal to an appeal tribunal [or the First-tier Tribunal][2], with the following modifications.

(2) In subsection (1) for "[tribunal[1]]", in both places where that word occurs, substitute "appeal tribunal [or the First-tier Tribunal][2] ".

(3) In subsections (1) and (4) omit "assessment or", in each place where those words occur.

(4) In subsections (1) to (3) and (4)(*a*) for "inspector or other proper officer of the Crown" substitute "officer of the Board".

(5) In subsection (3)(*a*), (4)(*b*) and in the words following paragraph (*b*) in subsection (4), for "inspector or other proper officer" substitute "officer of the Board".

(6) After subsection (5) add the following subsection—

"(6) In subsection (1) "appeal tribunal" means an appeal tribunal constituted—

(*a*) . . . [2]

. . . [2] in Northern Ireland, under Chapter 1 of Part 2 of the Social Security (Northern Ireland) Order 1998 (social security appeals: Northern Ireland).".

Amendments—[1] In para (2) word substituted by the Transfer of Tribunal Functions and Revenue and Customs Appeals Order, SI 2009/56 art 3, Sch 2 para 132 with effect from 1 April 2009.

[2] In paras (1), (2) words inserted, and in para (6), in inserted sub-s (6), para (*a*) and letter "(*b*)" revoked, by the Tribunals, Courts and Enforcement Act 2007 (Transitional and Consequential Provisions) Order, SI 2008/2683 art 6(1), Sch 1 paras 260, 263 with effect from 3 November 2008.

5 Application of . . . Articles 6 to 8 of and Schedule 1 to the 1998 Order

(1) . . . [1] Articles 6 to 8 of and paragraphs 7, 11 and 12 of Schedule 1 to the 1998 Order, shall apply to a child trust fund appeal to an appeal tribunal with the following modifications.

(2) . . . [1]

(3) In paragraph 12 in Schedule 1 to the 1998 Order, for references to officers authorised by the Department substitute references to the clerk to the appeal tribunal.

Amendments—[1] In the heading, para (1), words revoked, and whole of para (2) revoked, , by the Tribunals, Courts and Enforcement Act 2007 (Transitional and Consequential Provisions) Order, SI 2008/2683 art 6(1), Sch 1 paras 260, 264 with effect from 3 November 2008.

6 Application of section 12 of the 1998 Act or Article 13 of the 1998 Order

(1) Section 12 of the 1998 Act ("section 12") or, in Northern Ireland, Article 13 of the 1998 Order ("Article 13") (appeals to an appeal tribunal [or the First-tier Tribunal][1]), shall apply to a child trust fund appeal to an appeal tribunal [or the First-tier Tribunal][1], with the following modifications.

(2) Omit subsections (1) to (6) of section 12 and paragraphs (1) to (6) of Article 13.

(3) In subsection (8) of section 12 for "an appeal under this section" substitute "a child trust fund appeal".

(4) In paragraph (8) of Article 13 for "an appeal under this Article" substitute "a child trust fund appeal".

(5) Omit subsections (8)(*a*) and (9) of section 12 and paragraphs (8)(*a*) and (9) of Article 13.

Amendments—[1] Words in para (1) inserted by the Tribunals, Courts and Enforcement Act 2007 (Transitional and Consequential Provisions) Order, SI 2008/2683 art 6(1), Sch 1 paras 260, 265 with effect from 3 November 2008.

7 Application of section 13 of the 1998 Act or Article 14 of the 1998 Order

Section 13 of the 1998 Act ("section 13") or, in Northern Ireland, Article 14 of the 1998 Order ("Article 14") (redetermination etc of appeals by tribunal), shall apply to a decision of an appeal tribunal [or the First-tier Tribunal][1] on a child trust fund appeal (other than a decision on a penalty appeal under section 21(9) of the Act as modified by section 24(2) of the Act), with the modifications that subsections (3) and (4) of section 13, and paragraphs (3) and (4) of Article 14, are omitted.

Amendments—[1] Words inserted by the Tribunals, Courts and Enforcement Act 2007 (Transitional and Consequential Provisions) Order, SI 2008/2683 art 6(1), Sch 1 paras 260, 266 with effect from 3 November 2008.

8 Application of section 14 of the 1998 Act or Article 15 of the 1998 Order

(1) Section [14(2) and (3)][1] of the 1998 Act or, in Northern Ireland, Article 15(1) to (10) of the 1998 Order (Appeal from tribunal to Commissioner [or the Upper Tribunal][1]), shall apply to a decision of an appeal tribunal [or the First-tier Tribunal][1] on a child trust fund appeal (other than a decision on a penalty appeal under section 21(9) of the Act as modified by section 24(2) of the Act), with the following modifications.

(2) In section 14—

(*a*) in subsection [(3)][1] for "under section 12 or 13 above" substitute "on a child trust fund appeal";

(*b*) in subsection (3)(*a*) for "Secretary of State" substitute "Board";

(*c*) for subsection (3)(*b*) substitute—

"(*b*) the appellant in the child trust fund appeal;"; [and][1]

[(*d*) omit subsections 3(*c*) and (*d*).][1]

(*e*) . . . [1]

(3) In Article 15—

(*a*) in paragraph (1) for "under Article 13 or 14" substitute "on a child trust fund appeal";

(*b*) in paragraph (3)(*a*) for "Department" substitute "Board";

(*c*) for paragraph (3)(*b*) substitute—

"(*b*) the appellant in the child trust fund appeal;";

(*d*) omit paragraphs (3)(*c*) and (*d*), and (4) to (6); and

(*e*) in paragraph (7) for "principal parties" substitute "Board and the appellant".

Amendments—[1] In para (1), words substituted, and words inserted, in para (2), in sub-para (*a*) reference substituted, word at end of sub-para (*c*) inserted, sub-para (*d*) substituted, and sub-para (*e*) revoked, by the Tribunals, Courts and Enforcement Act 2007 (Transitional and Consequential Provisions) Order, SI 2008/2683 art 6(1), Sch 1 paras 260, 267 with effect from 3 November 2008.

9 Application of . . . Article 15(11) to (13) of the 1998 Order

(1) . . . [1] Article 15(11) to (13) of the 1998 Order, (appeals and procedure before Commissioner), shall apply to a decision of an appeal tribunal on a child trust fund appeal, with the following modifications.

(2) So far as concerns decisions of an appeal tribunal on a penalty appeal under . . . [1] paragraph (11) of Article 15, omit the words "and applications made for leave to appeal".

Amendments—[1] In heading, paras (1), (2), words revoked, by the Tribunals, Courts and Enforcement Act 2007 (Transitional and Consequential Provisions) Order, SI 2008/2683 art 6(1), Sch 1 paras 260, 268 with effect from 3 November 2008.

10 Application of section 15 of the 1998 Act

Section 15 of the 1998 Act ([Applications for permission to appeal against a decision of the Upper Tribunal][1]) shall apply to a decision of [the Upper Tribunal][1] on a child trust fund appeal.

Amendments—[1] Words substituted for words by the Tribunals, Courts and Enforcement Act 2007 (Transitional and Consequential Provisions) Order, SI 2008/2683 art 6(1), Sch 1 paras 260, 269 with effect from 3 November 2008.

11 Application of section 16 of the 1998 Act or Article 16 of the 1998 Order

(1) Section 16 ("section 16") of and Schedule 5 to the 1998 Act or, in Northern Ireland, Article 16 ("Article 16") of and Schedule 4 to the 1998 Order (procedure), shall apply for the purposes of a child trust fund appeal with the following modifications.

[(2) Omit subsection (3) of section 16.][1]

(3) Omit paragraph (3)(*b*) of Article 16 and the word "and" immediately preceding it.

(4) Omit subsections (4) and (5) of section 16 and paragraphs (4) and (5) of Article 16.

(5) In Schedule 5 to the 1998 Act, in paragraph 1, omit "the Secretary of State," in both places where those words occur.

(6) In Schedule 4 to the 1998 Order, in paragraph 1, omit "the Department", in both places where those words occur.

Amendments—[1] Para (2) substituted by the Tribunals, Courts and Enforcement Act 2007 (Transitional and Consequential Provisions) Order, SI 2008/2683 art 6(1), Sch 1 paras 260, 270 with effect from 3 November 2008.

12 Application of section 17 of the 1998 Act or Article 17 of the 1998 Order

(1) Section 17 of the 1998 Act ("section 17") or, in Northern Ireland, Article 17 of the 1998 Order ("Article 17") (finality of decisions), shall apply to a decision of an appeal tribunal[, the First-tier Tribunal, the Upper Tribunal][1] or a Social Security Commissioner on a child trust fund appeal, with the following modifications.

(2) For subsection (1) of section 17 substitute the following subsection—

"(1) Subject to the provisions of—

(*a*) sections 12 to 16, and 28 of this Act (as modified by the Child Trust Funds (Non-tax Appeals) Regulations 2004), . . . [1]

(*b*) sections 21(9) and (10) and 22 to 24 of the Child Trust Funds Act 2004, [and][1]

[(*c*) any provisions made by or under Chapter 2 of Part 1 of the Tribunals, Courts and Enforcement Act 2007 (c 15)][1]

any decisions made in accordance with those provisions in respect of a child trust fund appeal which, in accordance with section 24 of the Child Trust Funds Act 2004, is to an appeal tribunal or lies to a Commissioner, shall be final.".

(3) For paragraph (1) of Article 17 substitute the following paragraph—

"(1) Subject to the provisions of—

(*a*) Articles 13 to 16, and 28 of this Order (as modified by the Child Trust Funds (Non-tax Appeals) Regulations 2004), and

(*b*) sections 21(9) and (10) and 22 to 24 of the Child Trust Funds Act 2004],

any decisions made in accordance with those provisions in respect of a child trust fund appeal which, in accordance with section 24 of the Child Trust Funds Act 2004, is to [the First-tier Tribunal or lies to the Upper Tribunal][1], shall be final.".

(4) Omit subsection (2)(*b*) and (*c*) of section 17 and paragraph (2)(*b*) and (*c*) of Article 17.

Amendments—[1] In para (1), words inserted, in para (2), in substituted s 17(1), word "and" at end of sub-para (1) revoked, and sub-para (c) and preceding word inserted, and words substituted, by the Tribunals, Courts and Enforcement Act 2007 (Transitional and Consequential Provisions) Order, SI 2008/2683 art 6(1), Sch 1 paras 260, 271 with effect from 3 November 2008.

13 Application of . . . Article 28 of the 1998 Order

(1) . . . [1] Article 28 of the 1998 Order ("Article 28") (correction of errors and setting aside of decisions), shall apply to a decision by an appeal tribunal or a Social Security Commissioner on a child trust fund appeal, with the following modifications.

(2) Omit . . . [1] paragraph (1A) of Article 28.

(3) . . . [1]

(4) For paragraph (3) of Article 28 substitute the following paragraph—

"(3) In this Article "relevant statutory provision" means—

(*a*) any of Articles 13 to 17 above (as modified by the Child Trust Funds (Non-tax Appeals) Regulations 2004), and

(*b*) sections 21(9) and (10) and 22 to 24 of the Child Trust Funds Act 2004.",

Amendments—[1] In heading, paras (1), (2), words revoked, and whole of para (3), revoked, by the Tribunals, Courts and Enforcement Act 2007 (Transitional and Consequential Provisions) Order, SI 2008/2683 art 6(1), Sch 1 paras 260, 272 with effect from 3 November 2008.

14 Application of section 39 of the 1998 Act or Article 39 of the 1998 Order

(1) Section 39 of the 1998 Act or, in Northern Ireland, Article 39 of the 1998 Order (interpretation etc of Chapter 2), shall apply for the purposes of a child trust fund appeal with the following modifications.

(2) In subsection (1) of section 39—

(*a*) insert at the appropriate places—

" "the Board" means the Commissioners of the Inland Revenue;

"child trust fund appeal" means an appeal under section 22 of the Child Trust Funds Act 2004 which, by virtue of section 24 of that Act, is to [the First-tier Tribunal or lies to the Upper Tribunal][2];";

[(*b*) omit the definitions of "claimant" and "relevant benefit."][1]

(3) In paragraph (1) of Article 39—

(*a*) for the definition of "Inland Revenue" substitute—

" "the Board" means the Commissioners of Inland Revenue;

"child trust fund appeal" means an appeal under section 22 of the Child Trust Funds Act 2004 which, by virtue of section 24 of that Act, is to an appeal tribunal or lies to a Social Security Commissioner;";

[(*b*) omit the definitions of "claimant" and "relevant benefit."][1]

(4) Omit subsections (2) and (3) of section 39 and paragraphs (2) and (3) of Article 39.

Amendments—[1] Paras (2)(*b*), (3)(*b*) substituted by the Transfer of Tribunal Functions and Revenue and Customs Appeals Order, SI 2009/56 art 3, Sch 2 para 134 with effect from 1 April 2009.

[2] In para (2), in inserted definition of "child trust fund appeal", words substituted by the Tribunals, Courts and Enforcement Act 2007 (Transitional and Consequential Provisions) Order, SI 2008/2683 art 6(1), Sch 1 paras 260, 273 with effect from 3 November 2008.

15 Application of sections 79, 80 and 84 of the 1998 Act or Articles 74 and 75 of the 1998 Order

(1) Sections 79, 80 and 84 of the 1998 Act or, in Northern Ireland, Articles 74 and 75 of the 1998 Order shall apply to regulations for child trust fund appeals, made under provisions of the 1998 Act or the 1998 Order applied by these Regulations, with the following modifications.

(2) In section 79—

(*a*) . . . [1]

(*b*) omit subsections (2A) and (8).

(3) In Article 74—

(*a*) in paragraph (1)—

(i) for "paragraphs (2) and (2A)" substitute "paragraph (2)";

(ii) for "Department" substitute "Treasury";

(*b*) omit paragraphs (2A) and (7).

(4) In Article 75 omit paragraphs (1) and (3).

Amendments—[1] Para (2)(*a*) revoked by the Tribunals, Courts and Enforcement Act 2007 (Transitional and Consequential Provisions) Order, SI 2008/2683 art 6(1), Sch 1 paras 260, 274 with effect from 3 November 2008.

2005/276

CAPITAL GAINS TAX (GILT-EDGED SECURITIES) ORDER 2005

Made . . . . 9 February 2005

Made by the Treasury under TCGA 1992 Sch 9 para 1

1 Citation

This Order may be cited as the Capital Gains Tax (Gilt-edged Securities) Order 2005.

2 Securities specified as gilt-edged securities

For the purposes of Schedule 9 to the Taxation of Chargeable Gains Act 1992 (gilt-edged securities) the following securities are specified—

4¾% Treasury Stock 2010;

4¾% Treasury Stock 2038.

2005/644

ENERGY ACT 2004 (NUCLEAR DECOMMISSIONING) (EXEMPT ACTIVITIES AND FURTHER CONDITIONS) REGULATIONS 2005

Made ....10 March 2005
Laid before the House of Commons ....10 March 2005
Coming into force ....1 April 2005

Made by the Treasury and the Secretary of State under Energy Act 2004 s 27(3)(b) and (5)(d)

1 Citation, commencement and interpretation

(1) These Regulations may be cited as the Energy Act 2004 (Nuclear Decommissioning) (Exempt Activities and Further Conditions) Regulations 2005 and shall come into force on 1st April 2005.

(2) In these Regulations—

a reference, without more, to a numbered section or Schedule is a reference to the corresponding provision of the Energy Act 2004;

"the NDA" means the Nuclear Decommissioning Authority (see section 1); and

"designated" means designated by means of a direction given by the Secretary of State to the NDA under section 3(3); and any other expression defined in section 37(1) bears the same meaning in these Regulations.

2 Exempt activities for the purposes of section 27 of, and Schedule 4 to, the Energy Act 2004

(1) For the purposes of section 27 and Schedule 4 (tax exemptions for NDA activities) the activities mentioned in paragraph (2) are specified.

(2) The activities are the operation of designated facilities for the treatment, storage, transportation or disposal of hazardous material, carried on for the purpose of thermal oxide reprocessing or mixed oxide manufacture where that reprocessing or manufacture is undertaken at Sellafield in Cumbria.

3 Further conditions in respect of NDA company which is a relevant site licensee

(1) The further conditions referred to in section 27(5)(*d*) (conditions in respect of NDA company which is a relevant site licensee) are those in paragraphs (2) and (3).

(2) The condition is that all the ordinary share capital of the company must have been transferred from the NDA or a wholly owned subsidiary of the NDA ("the original transfer").

(3) The condition is that where—

(*a*) a management contract is in force—

(i) which relates to the whole or part of the site, or to an installation or facility in or on that site, for which a nuclear site licence is in force; and

(ii) which is made between the NDA and the company, or between the NDA and a company which owns, directly or indirectly, at least 90 per cent of the ordinary share capital of the company; or

(*b*) the company has control of a designated installation, site or facility and directions have been given to the company under section 18(3) in respect of that installation, site or facility;

the company's memorandum and articles must be such as to secure that the restrictions imposed by paragraphs (4) and (5) will always be met.

(4) The company may not declare dividends on its shares.

(5) A transfer of the company's shares—

(*a*) may only be made to the NDA; or a wholly owned subsidiary of the NDA,

(*b*) must comprise the whole of the company's share capital, and

(*c*) must be for a consideration which is no greater than that given for the original transfer.

(6) For the purposes of paragraph (5)(*c*) where consideration is given for share capital and for something else besides, a just and reasonable apportionment shall be made between the amount given for the share capital and the amount given for the other thing.

2005/695

PENSIONS ACT 2004 (COMMENCEMENT NO 3, TRANSITIONAL PROVISIONS AND AMENDMENT) ORDER 2005

Made ....14 March 2005

Made by the Secretary of State for Work and Pensions under Pensions Act 2004 ss 300(2)(*a*) and (*b*), 315(5) and 322(1) and (5)

Citation and interpretation

1 Citation and interpretation

(1) This Order may be cited as the Pensions Act 2004 (Commencement No 3, Transitional Provisions and Amendment) Order 2005.

(2) In this Order—

"the Act" means the Pensions Act 2004;

"the 1993 Act" means the Pension Schemes Act 1993;

"the 1995 Act" means the Pensions Act 1995; and

"the Authority" means the Occupational Pensions Regulatory Authority established by section 1 of the 1995 Act.

2 Appointed days

(1) The day appointed for the coming into force of section 10 of the Act (functions exercisable by the Determinations Panel) in so far as not already brought into force, and of Schedule 2 to the Act (the reserved regulatory functions), is 6th April 2005.

(2) The day appointed for the coming into force of section 272 of the Act (debt due from the employer in the case of multi-employer schemes), in so far as not already brought into force, is 15th March 2005.

(3) The day appointed for the coming into force of section 300(1) of the Act (dissolution of the Authority) is 6th April 2005 ("the appointed day").

(4) The day appointed for the coming into force of sections 278 and 280 for the purpose only of conferring power to make regulations is 15th March 2005.

(5) The day appointed for the coming into force of paragraph 21 of Schedule 1 to the Act (Pensions Regulator – delegation) is 15th March 2005 for the purpose only of conferring power to make regulations, and 6th April 2005 for all other purposes.

(6) The day appointed for the coming into force of Schedule 13 to the Act in so far as it relates to the repeal of paragraph 1(2)(*a*) of Schedule 1 to the Welfare Reform and Pensions Act 1999, and section 320 of the Act in so far as it relates to that provision, is 1st April 2005.

(7) The day appointed for the coming into force of the provisions set out in Schedule 1 to this Order is 6th April 2005.

3 Transfer of property, rights and liabilities

(1) Subject to paragraph (2), all property, rights and liabilities to which the Authority is entitled or subject immediately before the appointed day shall, on that day, become the property, rights and liabilities of the Regulator.

(2) All property held by the Authority in relation to the carrying out of its function (as Registrar) under regulation 6(1)(*a*) of the Register of Occupational and Personal Pension Schemes Regulations 1997 (availability of information held on the register) immediately before the appointed day shall, on that day, become the property of the Secretary of State.

4 Transitional modification of section 10 of the Act

Section 10 of the Act (functions exercisable by the Determinations Panel) shall, for the purposes of paragraph (6)(*b*) and (*c*) of article 5 of this Order, be modified for so that it shall have effect as if, after subsection (4), there were inserted the following subsection—

"(4A) For the purposes of this Part, a function conferred on the Occupational Pensions Regulatory Authority ("OPRA") by or by virtue of the Pensions Act 1995 relating to—

(*a*) the review, under section 96 of that Act (review of decisions), of a determination made by OPRA before the 6th April 2005 ("the appointed day") of a question falling within OPRA's functions, or

(*b*) the reference for a decision by the court, under section 97 of that Act (references and appeals from the Authority), of any matter arising for determination by OPRA before the appointed day or of any matter arising before that day on—

(i) an application for a review of a determination; or

(ii) a review entered upon by OPRA without an application,

shall, where that function falls to be exercised by or in relation to the Regulator on or after the appointed day, also be a reserved regulatory function.".

5 Transitional provisions

(1) In this article, unless the context otherwise requires, "function of the Authority" means a function of the Authority which is transferred to the Regulator under subsection (1) of section 7 of the Act (transfer of OPRA's functions to the Regulator) on 6th April 2005 ("the appointed day").

(2) Anything done (or having effect as if done) by or in relation to the Authority before the appointed day pursuant to, or for the purposes of, any function of the Authority shall, so far as is required for continuing its effect, have effect as if done by or in relation to the Regulator pursuant to, or for the purposes of, that function.

(3) Subject to paragraph (5), anything which, immediately before the appointed day, is in the process of being done by or in relation to the Authority pursuant to, or for the purposes of, any function of the Authority shall be continued by or in relation to the Regulator pursuant to, or for the purposes of, that function.

(4) Any reference to the Authority in any document constituting or relating to anything to which paragraph (2) or (3) applies in relation to any function of the Authority shall, so far as is required for giving effect to those provisions, be construed as a reference to the Regulator.

(5) Where any function of the Authority described in paragraph (6) would, but for its dissolution, fall to be exercised on or after the appointed day, or fell to be exercised before the appointed day but has not been exercised, that function shall be exercised by the Regulator as if it were a function of the Regulator conferred on it under or by virtue of the Act.

(6) The functions of the Authority to which paragraph (5) refers are—

(*a*) the investigation of any matter falling within the Authority's functions where the matter under investigation occurred, or first occurred, before the appointed day,

(*b*) the review, under section 96 of the 1995 Act, of a determination made by the Authority before the appointed day of a question falling within the Authority's functions, and

(*c*) the reference for a decision by the court, under section 97 of the 1995 Act, of any matter arising for determination by the Authority before the appointed day or of any matter arising before that day on an application for a review of a determination or on a review entered upon by the Authority without an application.

(7) Where any function under regulation 6(1)(*a*) of the Register of Occupational and Personal Pension Schemes Regulations 1997 fell to be exercised by the Authority, as Registrar, before the appointed day but has not been exercised, or would have fallen to be exercised by the Authority on or after the appointed day, that function shall be exercised by the Secretary of State (or by a person appointed by him).

(8) Schedule 2, which makes further transitional provision, has effect.

2005/723

RETIREMENT BENEFITS SCHEMES (INCREASE IN PERMITTED MAXIMUM IN TRANSITIONAL CASES) ORDER 2005

Made . . . . *16 March 2005*
Laid before the House of Commons . . . . *16 March 2005*
Coming into force . . . . *6 April 2005*

Made by the Treasury under TA 1988 s 590(3)

1 Citation and commencement

This Order may be cited as the Retirement Benefits Schemes (Increase in Permitted Maximum in Transitional Cases) Order 2005 and shall come into force on 6th April 2005.

2 Increase in permitted maximum

In section 590(3) of the Income and Corporation Taxes Act 1988 as originally enacted for "£100,000" substitute "£105,600".

2005/724

CHARGE TO INCOME TAX BY REFERENCE TO ENJOYMENT OF PROPERTY PREVIOUSLY OWNED REGULATIONS 2005

Made . . . . *16th March 2005*
Laid before the House of Commons . . . . *16th March 2005*
Coming into force . . . . *6th April 2005*

Made by the Treasury, under FA 2004 Sch 15 paras 1, 4(5) and (6), 7(2), (4) and (5), 9(1) and (3), 14 and 20, and the Commissioners of Inland Revenue, under Finance Act 1986 s 104

1 Citation and commencement

These Regulations may be cited as the Charge to Income Tax by Reference to Enjoyment of Property Previously Owned Regulations 2005 and shall come into force on 6th April 2005.

2 Prescribed valuation date

In paragraph 4 (chargeable amount in relation to land), paragraph 7 (chargeable amount in relation to chattels) and paragraph 9 (chargeable amount in relation to intangible property) of Schedule 15 to the Finance Act 2004 the valuation date in relation to a taxable period is 6th April in the relevant year of assessment or, if later, the first day of the taxable period.

Commentary—*Simon's Taxes* **I3.731, I3.743.**

3 Prescribed rate of interest

(1) In paragraphs 7(2) and 9(1) of Schedule 15 to the Finance Act 2004 the prescribed rate is the official rate of interest at the valuation date.

(2) In this regulation, "the official rate of interest" has the meaning given in section 181 of the Income Tax (Earnings and Pensions) Act 2003.

Commentary—*Simon's Taxes* **I3.722, I3.731.**

4 Valuation and rental value

(1) The valuation of land or any interest in land for the purposes of paragraph 4 of Schedule 15 to the Finance Act 2004 and a chattel or any interest in a chattel for the purposes of paragraph 7 of Schedule 15 to the Finance Act 2004 is—

(*a*) before the first five-year anniversary, by reference to the first valuation date, and

(*b*) thereafter, by reference to the valuation date at the last five-year anniversary.

(2) The rental value of land for the purposes of paragraph 4 of Schedule 15 to the Finance Act 2004 is determined in relation to a year of assessment—

(*a*) between the end of the first taxable period and the first five-year anniversary, by reference to the annual value in relation to the first year of assessment in which paragraph 3 of Schedule 15 to the Finance Act 2004 (land) applied, and

(*b*) thereafter, by reference to the rental value for the year of assessment commencing at the last five-year anniversary.

(3) Subject to paragraph (4), in this regulation—

"five-year anniversary" means the fifth anniversary of 6th April in the year of assessment in which paragraph 3 (land) or paragraph 6 (chattels) of Schedule 15 to the Finance Act 2004 first applied to a chargeable person in relation to the relevant land or chattel or any interest in the relevant land or chattel, and subsequent anniversaries at five-year intervals;

"first valuation date" means the date on which paragraph 3 or paragraph 6 of Schedule 15 to the Finance Act 2004 first applied to a chargeable person in relation to the relevant land or chattel or any interest in the relevant land or chattel.

(4) If there is no valuation date at a five-year anniversary, the date on which paragraph 3 or paragraph 6 of Schedule 15 to the Finance Act 2004 next apply to the chargeable person in relation to the relevant land or chattel, or any interest in the relevant land or chattel, shall be treated as the date on which, and being in the year of assessment in which, paragraph 3 or paragraph 6 of that Schedule first applied to that person in relation to that land, chattel or interest.

Commentary—*Simon's Taxes* **I3.743.**

5 Exemptions from charge

(1) Paragraph 3 (land) and paragraph 6 (chattels) do not apply to a person in relation to a disposal of part of an interest in any property if—

(*a*) the disposal was by a transaction made at arm's length with a person not connected with him;

(*b*) the disposal was by a transaction such as might be expected to be made at arm's length between persons not connected with each other, and

(i) the disposal was for a consideration not in money or in the form of readily convertible assets, or

(ii) the disposal was made before 7th March 2005.

(2) In this regulation "readily convertible asset" has the meaning given in section 702 of the Income Tax (Earnings and Pensions) Act 2003.

Commentary—*Simon's Taxes* **I3.738A.**

6 Avoiding double charge

(1) This regulation provides for the avoidance, to the extent specified, of double charges to tax arising in the circumstances specified (in paragraph (2)) for the purposes of paragraph (*d*) of section 104(1) of the Finance Act 1986 (being circumstances which appear to the Board to be similar to those referred to in paragraphs (*a*) to (*c*) of that subsection).

(2) The specified circumstances are—

(*a*) a person makes a transfer by way of gift—

(i) of property representing the proceeds of the disposal of relevant property,

(ii) by virtue of which property becomes comprised in a settlement,

(*b*) the transfer is or proves to be a chargeable transfer,

(*c*) the person dies on or after 6th April 2005 and within seven years of the transfer,

(*d*) the person made an election under paragraph 21 of Schedule 15 to the Finance Act 2004 (election for application of inheritance tax provisions) in relation to the relevant property,

(*e*) the relevant property—

(i) is by virtue of section 102(3) of the Finance Act 1986 treated for the purposes of the Inheritance Tax Act 1984 as property to which the person was beneficially entitled immediately before his death, or

(ii) ceased to be property subject to a reservation and became the subject of a potentially exempt transfer by virtue of section 102(4) of the Finance Act 1986, and

(*f*) the chargeable proportion of the relevant property—

(i) is comprised in the estate of the person immediately before his death within the meaning of section 5(1) of the Inheritance Tax Act 1984 and the value attributable to it is transferred by a chargeable transfer under section 4 of that Act, or

(ii) is property transferred by the potentially chargeable transfer to which sub-paragraph (*e*)(ii) applies, value attributable to which is transferred by a chargeable transfer.

(3) Where this regulation applies, there shall be calculated, separately in accordance with sub-paragraphs (*a*) and (*b*), the total tax chargeable as a consequence of the death of the person—

(*a*) disregarding so much of the value transferred by the transfer of value to which paragraph (2)(*a*) refers as represents the proceeds of the disposal of the relevant property to which paragraph (2)(*f*) refers, and

(*b*) disregarding so much of the value transferred by the transfer of value to which paragraph (2)(*f*) refers as is represented by property to which paragraph (2)(*a*) refers.

(4) Where the amount calculated under paragraph (3)(*a*) is higher than the amount calculated under (3)(*b*)—

(*a*) only so much of that higher amount shall be payable as remains after deducting, as a credit, from the amount comprised in the higher amount which is attributable to the value of the property to which paragraph (2)(*f*) refers, a sum (not exceeding the amount so attributable) equal to so much of the tax paid—

(i) as became payable before the person's death, and

(ii) as is attributable to the value disregarded under paragraph (3)(*a*), and

(*b*) so much of the value transferred by the transfer of value to which paragraph (2)(*a*) refers as is attributable to the property to which paragraph (2)(*f*) refers shall (except in relation to chargeable transfers which were chargeable to tax, when made by the person, for the purposes of an occasion which occurred before the person's death on which tax was chargeable under section 64 or 65 of the Inheritance Tax Act 1984 (charge at ten year anniversary and charge at other times in relation to settlements without interests in possession)) be treated as reduced to a nil amount for all the purposes of the Inheritance Tax Act 1984.

(5) Where the amount calculated under paragraph (3)(*a*) is less than the amount calculated under paragraph (3)(*b*) the value of the property to which paragraph (2)(*f*) refers shall be reduced to a nil amount for all the purposes of the Inheritance Tax Act 1984.

(6) In this regulation, "relevant property" and "the chargeable proportion" have the meanings given in paragraph 21 of Schedule 15 to the Finance Act 2004.

2005/990

CHILD TRUST FUNDS (APPEALS) REGULATIONS 2005

Made . . . .*24 March 2005*

Coming into force in accordance with . . . .*regulation 1(1)*

Made by the Secretary of State for Work and Pensions under Social Security Act 1998 ss 7(6) and (7), 12(7), 14(10)(a) and (11), 16(1) and (3)(a), 28(1), 79(1) and (4) to (7) and 84, Sch 1 paras 7, 11 and 12, Sch 5 paras 1 to 6, in accordance with Tribunals and Inquiries Act 1992 s 8

1 Citation, commencement, duration and interpretation

(1) These Regulations may be cited as the Child Trust Funds (Appeals) Regulations 2005 and shall come into force on the day after they are made.

(2) . . . [2]

(3) In these Regulations, unless the context otherwise requires—

"the Act" means the Social Security Act 1998;

"the 2004 Act" means the Child Trust Funds Act 2004;

"appeal" means an appeal under section 22 of the 2004 Act to [the First-tier Tribunal][1];

"the Board" means the Commissioners of Inland Revenue;

. . . [1]

"notification period" has the meaning given in regulation 3;

"party to the proceedings" means the Board and any person who brings an appeal;

. . . [1]

(4) . . . [1]

Amendments—[1] In para (3), definitions revoked, and para (4) revoked, by the Tribunals, Courts and Enforcement Act 2007 (Transitional and Consequential Provisions) Order, SI 2008/2683, art 6(1), Sch 1, paras 290, 291(1), (2) with effect from 3 November 2008.

[2] Para (2) revoked by the Transfer of Tribunal Functions and Revenue and Customs Appeals Order, SI 2009/56 art 3, Sch 2 para 136 with effect from 1 April 2009.

2 Service of notices or documents

Where by any provision of these Regulations—

(*a*) any notice or other document is required to be given or sent to . . . [1] the Board, that notice or document shall be treated as having been so given or sent on the day that it is received by . . . [1] the Board, and

(*b*) any notice or other document is required to be given or sent to any person other than . . . [1] the Board, that notice or document shall, if sent to that person's last known address, be treated as having been given or sent on the day that it was posted.

Amendments—[1] Words in paras (*a*), (*b*) revoked by the Tribunals, Courts and Enforcement Act 2007 (Transitional and Consequential Provisions) Order, SI 2008/2683, art 6(1), Sch 1, paras 290, 292 with effect from 3 November 2008.

3 Disputes about notices of appeal

Where a dispute arises as to whether notice of an appeal was given to the Board within the period of thirty days specified in section 23(1) of the 2004 Act ("the notification period") the dispute shall be referred to, and be determined by, [the First-tier Tribunal][1].

Amendments—[1] Words substituted by the Tribunals, Courts and Enforcement Act 2007 (Transitional and Consequential Provisions) Order, SI 2008/2683, art 6(1), Sch 1, paras 290, 293 with effect from 3 November 2008.

4 Late appeals

(1) Where the conditions specified in paragraphs (2) to (8) are satisfied, an appeal may be brought within a period of one year after the expiration of the notification period.

(2), (3) . . . [1]

[(4) The Board must not treat the appeal as made in time unless the Board is satisfied that it is in the interests of justice.][1]

(5) For the purposes of paragraph (4) it is not in the interests of justice to [treat the appeal as made in time unless the Board are][1] satisfied that—

(*a*) the special circumstances specified in paragraph (6) are relevant . . . [1]; or

(*b*) some other special circumstances exist which are wholly exceptional and relevant . . . [1],

and as a result of those special circumstances, it was not practicable for the appeal to be brought within the notification period.

(6) For the purposes of paragraph (5)(*a*), the special circumstances are that—

(*a*) the [appellant][1] or a partner or dependant of the [appellant][1] has died or suffered serious illness;

(*b*) the [appellant][1] is not resident in the United Kingdom; or

(*c*) normal postal services were disrupted.

(7) In determining whether it is in the interests of justice to [treat the appeal as made in time][1], regard shall be had to the principle that the greater the amount of time that has elapsed between the expiration of the notification period and the [submission of the notice of appeal, the more compelling should be the special circumstances][1].

(8) In determining whether it is in the interests of justice to [treat the appeal as made in time][1], no account shall be taken of the following—

(*a*) that the [appellant][1] or any person acting for him was unaware of or misunderstood the law applicable to his case (including ignorance or misunderstanding of the notification period); or

(*b*) that [the Upper Tribunal][1] or a court has taken a different view of the law from that previously understood and applied.

(9), (10) . . . [1]

(11) As soon as practicable after the decision is made a copy of the decision shall be sent or given to every party to the proceedings.

Amendments—[1] Paras (2), (3), (9), (10) revoked, para (4) substituted, in para (5) words substituted and revoked, and in paras (6)–(8) words substituted, by the Tribunals, Courts and Enforcement Act 2007 (Transitional and Consequential Provisions) Order, SI 2008/2683, art 6(1), Sch 1, paras 290, 294 with effect from 3 November 2008.

5 Death of a party to an appeal

In any proceedings relating to an appeal under section 22(2), (4), (5) or (6) of the 2004 Act, on the death of a party to the proceedings (other than the Board) the personal representative of the person who has died may represent him at any hearing.

Amendments—Paras 6–25 revoked by the Tribunals, Courts and Enforcement Act 2007 (Transitional and Consequential Provisions) Order, SI 2008/2683, art 6(1), Sch 1, paras 290, 295 with effect from 3 November 2008.

2005/1114

ENERGY-SAVING ITEMS REGULATIONS 2005

Revocation—Regulations revoked by the Energy-Saving Items Regulations, SI 2007/831 reg 5, Sch, with effect in relation to expenditure incurred on or after 6 April 2007.

2005/1133

REVENUE AND CUSTOMS (INSPECTIONS) REGULATIONS 2005

Made . . . . *7 April 2005*
Laid before Parliament . . . . *8 April 2005*
Coming into force . . . . *29 April 2005*

Made by the Treasury under CRCA 2005 s 27(1) and (2)

1 Citation and commencement

These Regulations may be cited as the Revenue and Customs (Inspections) Regulations 2005 and shall come into force on 29th April 2005.

2 Interpretation

(1) In these Regulations—

"the Act" means the Commissioners for Revenue and Customs Act 2005;

"appropriate inspectors" means in relation to—

(*a*) an inspection in England and Wales, the inspectors of constabulary,

(*b*) an inspection in Scotland, the inspectors of constabulary and the Scottish inspectors acting jointly,

(*c*) an inspection in Northern Ireland, the Northern Ireland inspectors;

"Chairman" means the Commissioner for the time being designated as chairman of Her Majesty's Revenue and Customs in Letters Patent under section 1(1) of the Act;

"civil penalty" means any penalty for which the Commissioners have power under any enactment to make an assessment or a demand;

"Commissioners" means the Commissioners for Revenue and Customs;

"criminal investigation" means any investigation for the purpose of considering whether an offence has been committed or discovering by whom an offence has been committed;

"Director" means [the Director of Public Prosecutions][1];

"inspectors of constabulary" means Her Majesty's Inspectors of Constabulary;

"officer" means an officer of Revenue and Customs;

"revenue" has the meaning given by section 5(4) of the Act;

"risk" means the likelihood of an officer or the Commissioners doing or omitting to do something which affects—

(*a*) the prevention, detection or investigation of an offence by an officer or the Commissioners,

(*b*) any criminal proceedings in England and Wales conducted by the Director,

(*c*) any criminal proceedings conducted in Scotland under the direction of the Lord Advocate or a procurator fiscal, or

(*d*) any criminal proceedings conducted in Northern Ireland by the Commissioners or the Director of Public Prosecutions for Northern Ireland,

and the possible effect of such an act or omission on the prevention, detection or investigation of that offence or those proceedings.

(2) A reference to the Scottish inspectors or to the Northern Ireland inspectors has the same meaning as in section 27(6) of the Act.

Amendments—[1] In para (2), in definition of "Director", words substituted by the Public Bodies (Merger of the Director of Public Prosecutions and the Director of Revenue and Customs Prosecutions) Order, SI 2014/834 art 3(3), Sch 3 para 10 with effect from 27 March 2014.

3 Inspection Functions: England and Wales

(1) The inspectors of constabulary may carry out inspections in England and Wales for the purpose of assessing the effectiveness of the following conduct—

(*a*) any acts or omissions of an officer or the Commissioners in connection with the prevention, detection or investigation of an offence by him or them, or

(*b*) any acts or omissions of an officer or the Commissioners in connection with criminal proceedings conducted by the Director.

(2) The inspectors of constabulary may carry out inspections in England and Wales to assess the effectiveness of any matter described in regulation 6.

(3) The inspectors of constabulary may exercise the powers under this regulation on their own initiative or at the request of the Chancellor of the Exchequer or the Commissioners but the Chancellor of the Exchequer may not make a request to carry out an inspection in relation to a particular person.

(4) The chief inspector of constabulary may include in his report under section 54(4) of the Police Act 1996 (annual reports) a report on the Commissioners and officers.

4 Inspection Functions: Scotland

(1) The inspectors of constabulary and the Scottish inspectors may jointly carry out inspections in Scotland for the purpose of assessing the effectiveness of the following conduct—

(*a*) any acts or omissions of an officer or the Commissioners in connection with the prevention, detection or investigation of an offence by him or them, or

(*b*) any acts or omissions of an officer or the Commissioners in connection with criminal proceedings conducted under the direction of the Lord Advocate or a procurator fiscal.

(2) The inspectors of constabulary and the Scottish inspectors may jointly carry out inspections in Scotland to assess the effectiveness of any matter described in regulation 6.

(3) The inspectors of constabulary and the Scottish inspectors may jointly exercise the powers under this regulation on their own initiative or at the request of the Chancellor of the Exchequer or the Commissioners but the Chancellor of the Exchequer may not make a request to carry out an inspection in relation to a particular person.

5 Inspection Functions: Northern Ireland

(1) The Northern Ireland inspectors may carry out inspections in Northern Ireland for the purpose of assessing the effectiveness of the following conduct—

(*a*) any acts or omissions of an officer or the Commissioners in connection with the prevention, detection or investigation of an offence by him or them, or

(*b*) any acts or omissions of an officer or the Commissioners in connection with criminal proceedings conducted in Northern Ireland by the Commissioners or the Director of Public Prosecutions for Northern Ireland.

(2) The Northern Ireland inspectors may carry out inspections in Northern Ireland to assess the effectiveness of any of the matters described in regulation 6.

(3) The Northern Ireland inspectors may exercise the powers under this regulation on their own initiative or at the request of the Chancellor of the Exchequer or the Commissioners but the Chancellor of the Exchequer may not make a request to carry out an inspection in relation to a particular person.

6 Inspection of means of dealing with risks

The matters to which regulations 3(2), 4(2) and 5(2) apply are—

(*a*) any method devised by or for Her Majesty's Revenue and Customs for identifying and dealing with a risk;

(*b*) any measures devised by or for Her Majesty's Revenue and Customs for assuring that an officer or the Commissioners are properly applying that method, and

(*c*) the operation of any such method or measures by an officer or the Commissioners.

7 Access

(1) This regulation applies to an inspection carried out under regulation 3, 4 or 5.

(2) For the purposes of an inspection the Commissioners shall provide to the appropriate inspectors such of the following as are reasonably required by the appropriate inspectors—

(*a*) access to any premises belonging to the Commissioners;

(*b*) access to any system operated by or on behalf of the Commissioners for storing and retrieving information electronically;

(*c*) any information or documents held by the Commissioners.

(3) For the purposes of an inspection an officer shall provide to the appropriate inspectors such information or documents held by him as are reasonably required by the inspectors.

8 Inspections of guidance

The appropriate inspectors may, if the Chancellor of the Exchequer or the Commissioners request them to do so, carry out an inspection of—

(*a*) the operation of any guidance issued by the Commissioners to officers for assessing or demanding a civil penalty instead of carrying out a criminal investigation into any matter or vice versa, or

(*b*) the operation of any guidance issued by the Commissioners for using other powers to secure any revenue, for the collection and management of which the Commissioners are responsible, instead of assessing or demanding a civil penalty or carrying out a criminal investigation.

9 Reports

(1) Where—

(*a*) the inspectors of constabulary carry out an inspection under regulation 3 or 8,

(*b*) the inspectors of constabulary and the Scottish inspectors jointly carry out an inspection under regulation 4 or 8, or

(*c*) the Northern Ireland inspectors carry out an inspection under regulation 5 or 8,

they shall provide a report of the inspection to the Chancellor of the Exchequer.

(2) Subject to paragraph (3), the Chancellor of the Exchequer shall arrange for any report received by him to be published.

(3) The Chancellor of the Exchequer may exclude from publication under paragraph (2) any part of a report if, in his opinion, the publication of that part—

(*a*) would be against the interests of national security;

(*b*) might jeopardise the safety of any person;

(*c*) would contravene section 29(2) of the Act, or

(*d*) might prejudice the prevention or detection of crime or the apprehension or prosecution of offenders.

(4) The Chancellor of the Exchequer shall send a copy of the published report to the Chairman.

(5) The Commissioners shall—

(*a*) prepare comments on the published report;

(*b*) send a copy of the comments to the Chancellor of the Exchequer before such date as may be specified by him;

(*c*) publish the comments in such manner as appears to the Commissioners to be appropriate.

(6) Where the inspectors of constabulary and the Scottish inspectors provide a report of an inspection to the Chancellor of the Exchequer he shall send a copy of the published report to the Scottish Ministers.

10 Appointment of assistant inspectors and staff officers

(1) Section 56 of the Police Act 1996 (appointment of assistant inspectors and staff officers) shall have effect subject to the following modifications—

(*a*) in section 56(1) after "constabulary" insert "for the purpose of carrying out functions under the Revenue and Customs (Inspections) Regulations 2005", and

(*b*) in section 56(2) for "Members of a police force" substitute "Officers of Revenue and Customs".

(2) Section 34 of the Police (Scotland) Act 1967 (appointment of assistant inspectors and staff officers)shall have effect subject to the following modifications—

(*a*) in section 34(1) after "constabulary" insert "for the purpose of carrying out functions under the Revenue and Customs (Inspections) Regulations 2005", and

(*b*) in section 34(1A) for "Constables" substitute "Officers of Revenue and Customs".

11 Payment

(1) The Commissioners shall pay to the inspectors of constabulary, for functions carried out by those inspectors under these Regulations, such amount as may be agreed between the Commissioners and those inspectors or, in the absence of an agreement, such amount as the Treasury, after consultation with the Secretary of State, may determine.

(2) The Commissioners shall pay to the inspectors of constabulary and the Scottish inspectors, for functions carried out jointly by those inspectors under these Regulations, such amount as may be agreed between the Commissioners and those inspectors or, in the absence of an agreement, such amount as the Treasury, after consultation with the Secretary of State and Scottish Ministers, may determine.

(3) The Commissioners shall pay to the Northern Ireland inspectors for functions carried out by those inspectors under these Regulations such amount as may be agreed between the Commissioners and those inspectors or, in the absence of an agreement, such amount as the Treasury, after consultation with the Secretary of State, may determine.

2005/1449

TONNAGE TAX (FURTHER OPPORTUNITY FOR ELECTION) ORDER 2005

Made . . . . *6 June 2005*

Laid before the House of Commons . . . . *6 June 2005*

Coming into force . . . . *1 July 2005*

Made by the Treasury under FA 2000 Sch 22 para 11

1 Citation and commencement

This Order may be cited as the Tonnage Tax (Further Opportunity for Election) Order 2005 and shall come into force on 1st July 2005.

2 Further opportunity for election into tonnage tax

A tonnage tax election may be made at any time during the period beginning on 1st July 2005 and ending on 31st December 2006 ("the further period").

3—(1) In the case of a tonnage tax election made during the further period, paragraph 12 of Schedule 22 to the Finance Act 2000 (when a tonnage tax election takes effect) is adapted as follows.

(2) In sub-paragraph (2)—

(*a*) after "A tonnage tax election" insert "made during the further period"; and
(*b*) for "1st January 2000" substitute "1st January 2005".

(3) In sub-paragraph (3)—
(*a*) for "before the end of the initial period" substitute "during the further period"; and
(*b*) for "1st January 2000" substitute "1st January 2005".

(4) In sub-paragraph (4) for "before the end of the initial period" substitute "during the further period".

(5) At the end of the paragraph add—

"(7) In this paragraph "the further period" means the period provided for by article 2 of the Tonnage Tax (Further Opportunity for Election) Order 2005 (SI 2005/1449).".

2005/1907

PENSION PROTECTION FUND (TAX) (2005–06) REGULATIONS 2005

Made .... *12 July 2005*
Laid before the House of Commons .... *13 July 2005*
Coming into force .... *3 August 2005*

Made by the Treasury under FA 2005 s 102

1 Citation, commencement and effect

(1) These Regulations may be cited as the Pension Protection Fund (Tax) (2005–06) Regulations 2005 and shall come into force on 3rd August 2005.

(2) These Regulations have effect for the period beginning on 6th April 2005 and ending on 5th April 2006 only.

2 Interpretation

(1) In this regulation—
(*a*) paragraph (2) gives the meaning of the abbreviated references to Acts and instruments used in these Regulations, and
(*b*) paragraph (3) deals with other expressions used in these Regulations.

(2) In these Regulations—
"the Pensions Act" (without more) means the Pensions Act 2004;
"the 1988 Act" means the Income and Corporation Taxes Act 1988;
"the 1992 Act" means the Taxation of Chargeable Gains Act 1992;
"the 2003 Act" means the Income Tax (Earnings and Pensions) Act 2003;
"the 2005 Order" means the Pensions (Northern Ireland) Order 2005.

(3) In these Regulations—
"the Board of the Pension Protection Fund" means the body corporate established under section 107 of the Pensions Act;
"exempt approved scheme" means an exempt approved scheme within the meaning of Chapter 1 of Part 14 of the 1988 Act (see section 592(1) of that Act);
"the Fraud Compensation Fund" has the meaning given by regulation 3(1);
"fraud compensation payment"—
(*a*) in England, Wales and Scotland means a fraud compensation payment within the meaning of Part 2 of the Pensions Act (see section 182(1) of that Act), and
(*b*) in Northern Ireland means a fraud compensation payment within the meaning of Part 3 of the 2005 Order (see Article 165(1) of that Order);
"the Pension Protection Fund" has the meaning given by regulation 3(1);
"the Pensions Act Funds" has the meaning given by regulation 3(1);
"the Pensions Act levies" means the levies specified in paragraph (2) or (3) of regulation 3, as the case may require.

3 Meaning of "the Pension Protection Fund" and other expressions

(1) In these Regulations—
"the Pension Protection Fund" means the Fund required to be held, managed and applied by the Board of the Pension Protection Fund under section 110(1)(*a*) of the Pensions Act;
"the Fraud Compensation Fund" means the Fund required to be held, managed and applied by the Board of the Pension Protection Fund under section 110(1)(*b*) of the Pensions Act;
"the Pensions Act Funds" means the Pension Protection Fund and the Fraud Compensation Fund.

(2) In England, Wales and Scotland, "the Pensions Act levies" means—
(*a*) the administration levy referred to in section 117(1) of the Pensions Act;
(*b*) the initial levy referred to in section 174(1) of that Act;
(*c*) the risk-based pension protection levy referred to in section 175(1)(*a*) of that Act;

(*d*) the scheme-based pension protection levy referred to in section 175(1)(*b*) of that Act;
(*e*) the fraud compensation levy referred to in section 189(1) of that Act;
(*f*) a levy in respect of eligible schemes imposed by regulations made under section 209(7) of that Act (the Ombudsman for the Board of the Pension Protection Fund).

(3) In Northern Ireland, "the Pensions Act levies" means—
(*a*) the administration levy referred to in Article 103(1) of the 2005 Order;
(*b*) the initial levy referred to in Article 157(1) of that Order;
(*c*) the risk-based pension protection levy referred to in Article 158(1)(*a*) of that Order;
(*d*) the scheme-based pension protection levy referred to in Article 158(1)(*b*) of that Order;
(*e*) the fraud compensation levy referred to in Article 171(1) of that Order;
(*f*) a levy in respect of eligible schemes imposed by regulations made under Article 191(3) of that Order (the PPF Ombudsman).

4 Application of the Tax Acts: general
(1) The Tax Acts apply in relation to each of the Pensions Act Funds in the same way as they apply in relation to an exempt approved scheme.
(2) The general rule in paragraph (1) is subject to the further provisions contained in these Regulations.

5 Application of the 1988 Act: further provisions
Section 592(2) of the 1988 Act (exemption from income tax in respect of investments) applies in respect of income derived from investments or deposits held for each of the Pensions Act Funds—
(*a*) as if for "income tax" there were substituted "corporation tax", and
(*b*) as if after "income derived from investments or deposits" there were inserted "(including any profit, gain or loss on a loan relationship within the meaning of Chapter 2 of Part 4 of the Finance Act 1996)".

6 Section 592(3) of the 1988 Act (exemption from income tax in respect of underwriting commissions) applies in respect of underwriting commissions applied for the purposes of each of the Pensions Act Funds—
(*a*) as if for "income tax" there were substituted "corporation tax", and
(*b*) as if for "under Chapter 8 of Part 5 of ITTOIA 2005 (income not otherwise charged)" there were substituted "under Case VI of Schedule D".

7 Section 592(6A) of the 1988 Act (sums paid towards discharge of liability of an employer) applies in relation to the payment, by an employer, of any sum in respect of any of the Pensions Act levies as it applies in relation to the payment of any sum in or towards the discharge of any liability of an employer under the enactments specified in that subsection.

8—(1) If at any time section 606 of the 1988 Act (default of scheme administrator etc) applies in relation to the Pension Protection Fund, the Board of the Pension Protection Fund shall be responsible for the discharge of all duties imposed on the administrator under Chapter 1 of Part 14 of the 1988 Act (whenever arising), and liable for any tax due from the administrator in the administrator's capacity as such (whenever falling due).
(2) Section 606 of the 1988 Act does not apply in relation to the Fraud Compensation Fund.

9—(1) For the purposes of section 611AA of the 1988 Act (definition of the administrator), references to the administrator, in relation to the Pension Protection Fund, are to the person who is, or the persons who are, for the time being, appointed by the Board of the Pension Protection Fund to be responsible for the discharge of all duties imposed on the administrator under Chapter 1 of Part 14 of the 1988 Act.
(2) Section 611AA of the 1988 Act does not apply in relation to the Fraud Compensation Fund.

10 Schedule 22 to the 1988 Act (reduction of pension fund surpluses) does not apply in relation to either of the Pensions Act Funds.

11 Application of the 1992 Act: further provisions
(1) For the purposes of the 1992 Act, any gain accruing to the Board of the Pension Protection Fund from its disposal of investments shall not be a chargeable gain if, or to the extent that, at the time of the disposal, those investments were held by the Board, or on its behalf, for the purposes of one of the Pensions Act Funds.
(2) In paragraph (1) "investments" includes futures contracts and options contracts.
(3) This regulation is to be construed as one with the 1992 Act.

12 Application of the Finance Act 1996: further provisions

(1) No credit or debit shall be required or allowed to be brought into account for the purposes of Chapter 2 of Part 4 of the Finance Act 1996 (loan relationships) in respect of the Pensions Compensation Board transfer in the case of the transferor.

(2) In paragraph (1) "the Pensions Compensation Board transfer" means the transfer, by the Pensions Compensation Board to the Board of the Pension Protection Fund, of all property, rights and liabilities to which the Pensions Compensation Board was entitled immediately before the transfer.

13 Application of the 2003 Act: further provisions

Step 5 of section 54(1) of the 2003 Act (calculation of deemed employment payment under arrangements made by intermediaries) applies in relation to a payment, by the intermediary, of any sum in respect of any of the Pensions Act levies in the same way as it applies in relation to any contributions that may be deducted under that step.

14 Section 307 of the 2003 Act (exemption from employment income for death or retirement benefit provision made by employer) applies in relation to the payment of any sum in respect of any of the Pensions Act levies in the same way as it applies in respect of provision made by an employee's employer for a retirement or death benefit.

15—(1) Section 583 of the 2003 Act (unauthorised payments of pension income from approved retirement benefits schemes) applies in relation to a payment made out of funds which are held for the purposes of the Pension Protection Fund if the following two conditions are met.

(2) The first condition is that the payment is not expressly authorised under Part 2 of the Pensions Act.

(3) The second condition is that the payment is made to or for the benefit of—

(*a*) an employee, or

(*b*) an ex-spouse [or former civil partner][1] of an employee,

who has entitlements under a scheme for which the Board of the Pension Protection Fund has assumed responsibility under Chapter 3 of Part 2 of the Pensions Act.

Amendments—[1] Words in para (3)(*b*) inserted by Tax and Civil Partnership (No 2) Regulations, SI 2005/3230 reg 16, with effect from 5 December 2005 (Reg 1).

16 Fraud compensation payments and other related payments

(1) Receipt of a payment to which this regulation applies shall not be regarded as a disposal of an asset for the purposes of capital gains tax or for the purposes of corporation tax on chargeable gains.

(2) This regulation applies to—

(*a*) a fraud compensation payment under section 185 of the Pensions Act;

(*b*) an interim payment under section 186 of the Pensions Act;

(*c*) a fraud compensation payment under Article 168 of the 2005 Order;

(*d*) an interim payment under Article 169 of the 2005 Order;

(*e*) a payment made by the Board of the Pension Protection Fund under section 83 of the Pensions Act 1995;

(*f*) a payment in anticipation made by the Board of the Pension Protection Fund under section 84 of that Act;

(*g*) a payment made by the Board of the Pension Protection Fund under Article 81 of the Pensions (Northern Ireland) Order 1995;

(*h*) a payment in anticipation made by the Board of the Pension Protection Fund under Article 82 of that Order.

2005/2014

FRIENDLY SOCIETIES (MODIFICATION OF THE CORPORATION TAX ACTS) REGULATIONS 2005

Made . . . . *21 July 2005*

Laid before the House of Commons . . . . *21 July 2005*

Coming into force . . . . *12 August 2005*

Made by the Treasury under TA 1988 s 463

Revocation—These Regulations revoked by the Friendly Societies (Modifications of the Tax Acts) Regulations, SI 2012/3008 reg 16, Schedule, with effect in relation to accounting periods beginning on or after 1 January 2013.

1 Citation, commencement and effect

(1) These Regulations may be cited as the Friendly Societies (Modification of the Corporation Tax Acts) Regulations 2005 and shall come into force on 12th August 2005.

(2) These Regulations have effect for accounting periods beginning on or after 1st January 2005.

2 Interpretation

In these Regulations—

"annual return society" means a non-directive friendly society which is required to submit an annual actuarial investigation to the Financial Services Authority under rule 5.1 of the Prudential Sourcebook (Friendly Societies);

. . . [1]

"directive friendly society" and "non-directive friendly society" have the meanings in the Prudential Sourcebook (Friendly Societies);

. . . [1]

"non annual return society" means a non-directive friendly society which is not required to submit an annual actuarial investigation to the Financial Services Authority under rule 5.1 of the Prudential Sourcebook (Friendly Societies);

"partnership pension society" has the meaning in the Prudential Sourcebook (Friendly Societies);

"pension business"—

(*a*) in relation to any time before 6th April 2006, has the meaning given by section 431B of the Taxes Act, and

(*b*) in relation to any time on or after 6th April 2006, has the meaning given by section 466(2B) of the Taxes Act;

"prescribed transactions" means any of the following transactions—

(*a*) the transfer of business as between a friendly society which maintains a separate fund for long-term insurance business and a friendly society which does not do so,

(*b*) the amalgamation of a friendly society which maintains a separate fund for long-term insurance business and a friendly society which does not do so,

(*c*) the transfer of the whole or part of the business of a friendly society which does not maintain a separate fund for long-term insurance business to a company which is not a friendly society, and

(*d*) the conversion of a friendly society which does not maintain a separate fund for long-term insurance business into a company which is not a friendly society, and for the purposes of this definition a friendly society maintains a separate fund for long-term insurance business if it complies with rule 4.20 of the Prudential Sourcebook (Friendly Societies), whether that rule applies to it or voluntarily; "the Prudential Sourcebook (Insurers)" means the Interim Prudential Sourcebook for Insurers made by the Financial Services Authority under the Financial Services and Markets Act 2000; "the Prudential Sourcebook (Friendly Societies)" means the Interim Prudential Sourcebook for Friendly Societies made by the Financial Services Authority under the Financial Services and Markets Act 2000; "the Taxes Act" means the Income and Corporation Taxes Act 1988.

Amendments—[1] Definitions of "child trust fund business" and "individual savings account business" revoked, by the Friendly Societies (Modification of the Corporation Tax Acts) (Amendment) Regulations, SI 2007/2134 regs 2, 3 with effect for accounting periods beginning on or after 1 January 2007: SI 2007/2134 reg 1(2).

3 In the Corporation Tax Acts, in their application to a friendly society— "insurance business transfer scheme" means a scheme which effects—

(*a*) the transfer of the whole or part of the business of a friendly society to another friendly society;

(*b*) the amalgamation of two or more friendly societies;

(*c*) the transfer of the whole or part of the business of a friendly society to a company which is not a friendly society;

(*d*) the conversion of a friendly society into a company which is not a friendly society; or

(*e*) the transfer of the whole or part of the long-term business of an insurance company to a friendly society.

4 Modification of section 43F of the Taxes Act

Amendments—Regulation 4 revoked by the Friendly Societies (Modification of the Corporation Tax Acts) (Amendment) Regulations, SI 2007/2134 regs 2, 4 with effect in relation to transactions entered into on or after 6 June 2006: SI 2007/2134 reg 1(3).

5 Modifications of section 76 of the Taxes Act

(1) Paragraphs (2) to (6) prescribe modifications to section 76 of the Taxes Act so far as it applies to the life or endowment business carried on by friendly societies, subject to paragraph (7).

(2) In subsection (2), after "referable to" insert "taxable";

(3) In subsection (3), for "line 12, 22 or 25 of Form 40 (the revenue account)" substitute "line 12 or 25 of Form 40 (the revenue account) or column 1 of line 49 of Form 41 (long-term insurance business: analysis of premiums and expenses)";

(4) In paragraph (*a*) of Step 1 in subsection (7), after "attributable to" insert "taxable";

(5) In subsection (8)—

(*a*) after "attributable to" insert "taxable";

(*b*) in paragraph (*b*), for "the Prudential Sourcebook (Insurers)" substitute "the Prudential Sourcebook (Friendly Societies)";

[(5A) In paragraph (a) of subsection (9E) before "basic life" insert "taxable".][2]

(6) . . . [1]

(7) The modifications in paragraphs (3) and (5)(*b*) only apply to a non-directive friendly society.

Amendments—[1] Paragraph (6) revoked, by the Friendly Societies (Modification of the Corporation Tax Acts) (Amendment) Regulations, SI 2007/2134 regs 2, 5 with effect for accounting periods beginning on or after 1 January 2007: SI 2007/2134 reg 1(2).

[2] Para (5A) inserted by the Friendly Societies (Modification of the Corporation Tax Acts) (Amendment) Regulations, SI 2008/1937 regs 2, 3 with effect in relation to accounting periods beginning on or after 1 January 2008.

6 Modifications of section 431 of the Taxes Act

[(1) In this regulation—

(*a*) paragraphs (2), (2A), (5A) and (5B) prescribe modifications of section 431 of the Taxes Act so far as it applies to long-term business carried on by friendly societies, and

(*b*) paragraphs (3) to (5) and (6) prescribe modifications of that section so far as it applies to the long-term business carried on by non-directive friendly societies.][2]

(2) In subsection (2) insert the following definitions in the appropriate places—

"annual return society" means a non-directive friendly society which is required to submit an annual actuarial investigation to the Financial Services Authority under rule 5.1 of the Prudential Sourcebook (Friendly Societies);

"directive friendly society" and "non-directive friendly society" have the meanings in the Prudential Sourcebook (Friendly Societies);

"non annual return society" means a non-directive friendly society which is not required to submit an annual actuarial investigation to the Financial Services Authority under rule 5.1 of the Prudential Sourcebook (Friendly Societies);

"partnership pension society" has the meaning in the Prudential Sourcebook (Friendly Societies);

"the Prudential Sourcebook (Friendly Societies)" means the Interim Prudential Sourcebook for Friendly Societies made by the Financial Services Authority under the Financial Services and Markets Act 2000;

"tax exempt basic life assurance and general annuity business" means basic life assurance and general annuity business the profits arising from which are exempt from tax by virtue of section 460(1);

"taxable basic life assurance and general annuity business" means basic life assurance and general annuity business other than tax exempt basic life assurance and general annuity business;

"tax exempt [PHI][1] business" means—

(*a*) business specified in [section 466(1)(*b*)][2] the profits arising from which are exempt from tax by virtue of section 460(1), and

(*b*) business other than that specified in [section 466(1)(*b*) which is long term business][2] the profits arising from which are exempt from tax by virtue of section 461(1) or 461B(1);

["taxable PHI business" means—

(*a*) business specified in section 466(1)(*b*) other than tax exempt PHI business, and

(*b*) business other than that specified in section 466(1)(*b*) which is PHI business the profits arising from which are not exempt from tax by virtue of section 461(1) or 461B(1);][2]

"valuation report"—

(*c*) in the case of an annual return society, means the abstract of the actuary's report referred to in rule 5.1(2) of the Prudential Sourcebook (Friendly Societies);

(*d*) in the case of a non annual return society, means the abstract of the actuary's report referred to in section rule 5.2(2) of the Prudential Sourcebook (Friendly Societies);

[(2A) In subsection (2) in the definition of "foreign currency assets" before "gross roll-up business" in each place insert "taxable".][2]

[(2B) In the definition of "foreign business assets" before "overseas life assurance business" in both places insert "taxable".][2]

(3) In subsection (2) for the definition of "liabilities" substitute—

"liabilities"—

(*a*) in relation to an annual return society, means the liabilities of the society estimated as for the purposes of its valuation report (excluding any that have fallen due or been reinsured and any not arising under or in connection with policies or contracts effected as part of the society's insurance business); and

(*b*) in relation to a non annual return society means—

(i) in the case of a society which has sent a valuation report as at the end of a period of account to the Financial Services Authority, the liabilities of the society estimated as for the purposes of its valuation report (excluding any that have fallen due or been reinsured and any not arising under or in connection with policies or contracts effected as part of the society's insurance business), and

(ii) in the case of a society which has not sent a valuation report as at the end of a period of account to the Financial Services Authority but has caused the actuary to the society to prepare a report on the same basis as the actuary's report referred to in rule 5.2(2) of the Prudential Sourcebook (Friendly Societies), the liabilities of the society estimated as for the purposes of that report (excluding any that have fallen due or been reinsured and any not arising under or in connection with policies or contracts effected as part of the society's insurance business), and

(iii) in any other case, the liabilities of the society ascertained in accordance with subsections (7) to (9) and (13) below;".

(4) In subsection (2) for the definition of "periodical return" substitute—

"periodical return"—

(*a*) in the case of an annual return society, means the FSC1 return within the meaning in Chapter 5 of the Prudential Sourcebook (Friendly Societies); and

(*b*) in the case of a non annual return society, means the FSC2 return within the meaning in that Chapter;".

(5) In subsection (2) for the definition of "value" substitute—

"value"—

(*a*) in relation to the assets of an annual return society, means the value of the assets as taken into account for the purposes of the society's periodical return; and

(*b*) in relation to the assets of a non annual return society means—

(i) in the case of a society which has sent a valuation report as at the end of a period of account to the Financial Services Authority, the value of the assets as taken into account for the purposes of its valuation report,

(ii) in the case of a society which has not sent a valuation report as at the end of a period of account to the Financial Services Authority but has caused the actuary to the society to prepare a report on the same basis as the actuary's report referred to in rule 5.2(2) of the Prudential Sourcebook (Friendly Societies), the value of the assets as taken into account for the purposes of that report, and

(iii) in any other case, the value of the assets ascertained in accordance with subsections (10) to (13) below;".

[(5A) In subsection (2YB) before "BLAGAB income" and before "BLAGAB deductions" insert "taxable".

(5B) In subsection (2YC)(*a*) before "basic life assurance" insert "taxable".

(6) At the end of the section add the following subsections—

"(7) For the purposes of paragraph (*b*)(iii) of the definition of 'liabilities' in subsection (2) above the closing liabilities of a society for a period of account ('the relevant period of account') shall be ascertained in accordance with the formula—

$$L1 + \left((L2 - L1) \times \frac{T1}{T2} \right)$$

where—

L1 is the liabilities as at the end of the last period of account ('the preceding period of account') which precedes the relevant period of account and for which a relevant report is drawn up;

L2 is the liabilities as at the end of the first period of account ('the subsequent period of account') which follows the relevant period of account and for which a relevant report is drawn up;

T1 is the number of days from the end of the preceding period of account to the end of the relevant period of account;

T2 is the number of days from the end of the preceding period of account to the end of the subsequent period of account;

and where the formula is used to ascertain the value of the assets as at the end of a period of account, the value so ascertained shall be the value of the assets at the beginning of the next period of account.

(8) Where, for those purposes, it is necessary to ascertain the liabilities in any case where a relevant report has not been drawn up at the end of the relevant period of account, the liabilities shall be estimated on a basis compatible with that used in the previous relevant report, having regard to any changes in the nature or extent of the society's business since that report.

(9) In any case where subsection (8) above has applied, subsection (7) above shall apply as soon as the society is able to ascertain the closing liabilities in accordance with the formula set out in that subsection; and all such adjustments to the liability to tax of the society shall be made, whether by assessment or otherwise, as may be required to give effect to subsection (7) above.

(10) For the purposes of paragraph (*b*)(iii) of the definition of 'value' in subsection (2) above the value of the assets of a society as at the end of a period of account ('the relevant period of account') shall be ascertained in accordance with the formula—

$$V1 + \left((V2 - V1) \times \frac{T1}{T2} \right)$$

where—

V1 is the value of the assets at the end of the last period of account ('the preceding period of account') which precedes the relevant period of account and for which a relevant report is drawn up;

V2 is the value of the assets as at the end of the first period of account ('the subsequent period of account') which follows the relevant period of account and for which a relevant report is drawn up;

T1 is the number of days from the end of the preceding period of account to the end of the relevant period of account;

T2 is the number of days from the end of the preceding period of account to the end of the subsequent period of account;

and where the formula is used to ascertain the value of the assets as at the end of a period of account, the value so ascertained shall be the value of the assets at the beginning of the next period of account.

(11) Where, for those purposes, it is necessary to ascertain the value of the assets in any case where a relevant report has not been drawn up at the end of the relevant period of account, the value of the assets shall be estimated on a basis compatible with that used in the previous relevant report, having regard to any changes in the nature or extent of the society's business since that report.

(12) In any case where subsection (11) above has applied, subsection (10) above shall apply as soon as the society is able to ascertain the value of the assets in accordance with the formula set out in that subsection; and all such adjustments to the liability to tax of the society shall be made, whether by assessment or otherwise, as may be required to give effect to subsection (10) above.

(13) In subsections (7), (8), (10) and (11) above a "relevant report" means a valuation report or the report specified in paragraph (*b*)(ii) of the definition of "value" in subsection (2) above.".

Amendments—[1] In para (2), in the inserted definitions of "tax exempt class IV business" and "taxable class IV business", words substituted for words "class IV" in each place, by the Friendly Societies (Modification of the Corporation Tax Acts) (Amendment) Regulations, SI 2007/2134 regs 2, 6, with effect for accounting periods beginning on or after 1 January 2007: SI 2007/2134 reg 1(2).

[2] Para (1) substituted, in para (2), in the definition of "tax exempt PHI business", in paras (*a*), (*b*), words substituted definition of "taxable PHI business" substituted, paras (2A), (2B), (5A), (5B) inserted, by the Friendly Societies (Modification of the Corporation Tax Acts) (Amendment) Regulations, SI 2008/1937 regs 2, 4 with effect in relation to accounting periods beginning on or after 1 January 2008. But insertion of para (2A) shall have effect in relation to accounting periods beginning on or after 1 January 2007 (SI 2008/1937 art 1(3)).

7 Meaning of "long-term insurance fund" for a society which does not maintain separate assets

In the case of a friendly society which does not maintain a separate fund for long-term business, the following section shall be treated as inserted after section 431AA of the Taxes Act—

"431AB Friendly societies: meaning of "long-term insurance fund"

(1) "Long-term insurance fund" means the fund made up of—

(*a*) assets held primarily for the purposes of long-term business carried on by a friendly society, and

(*b*) the relevant fraction of each asset held neither primarily for the purposes of long-term business nor primarily for the purposes of some other specific business carried on by that society.

(2) For the purposes of subsection (1) "the relevant fraction" means—

$$\frac{(0.5 \times (OLB + CLB)) - (0.5 \times (OLA + CLA))}{(0.5 \times (OTB + CTB)) - (0.5 \times (OTA + CTA))}$$

where—

OLB and CLB are respectively the balances brought forward and carried forward in the fund accounts for those accounts within which the society conducts its long-term business;

OLA and CLA are respectively the opening and closing values of the assets already recognised at the beginning and end of the period of account as held for the purposes of long-term business carried on by the society;

OTB and CTB are respectively the total balances brought forward and carried forward on all the society's fund accounts; and

OTA and CTA are respectively the opening and closing values of the assets already recognised at the beginning and end of the period of account as held for the purposes of long-term business or for the purposes of other specific business carried on by the society.

(3) In calculating the values and balances for the purpose of determining the relevant fraction in subsection (2), a balance on a general management fund or a general reserve fund shall be excluded.

(4) In subsection (2), references to balances brought forward and carried forward are references to balances brought forward and carried forward as shown in the society's periodical return."

7A [Modifications of section 431H of the Taxes Act

(1) Paragraphs (2) to (4) prescribe modifications of section 431H of the Taxes Act so far as it applies to the [long-term][2] business carried on by friendly societies.

(2) For subsection (1) substitute—

"(1) This section applies in relation to a friendly society which carries on two or more of the following—

[(*a*) life assurance business,

(*b*) taxable PHI business and taxable insurance business of any other kind (other than life assurance business), and

(*c*) tax exempt PHI business and tax exempt business of any other kind.][2]

(3) In subsection (2)—

(*a*) omit the word "and" immediately following paragraph (*a*),

(*b*) after paragraph (*a*) insert—

"(*aa*) taxable PHI business,

(*ab*) tax exempt PHI business, and", and

(*c*) in paragraph (*b*) for "the" substitute "any".

(4) Omit subsections (3) and (4).][1]

Amendments—[1] Regulation 7A inserted by the Friendly Societies (Modification of the Corporation Tax Acts) (Amendment) Regulations, SI 2007/2134 regs 2, 7, with effect for accounting periods beginning on or after 1 January 2007: SI 2007/2134 reg 1(2).

[2] In para (1), words substituted, and in para (2), in the substitution, paras (*a*)–(*c*) substituted for previous paras (*a*)–(*d*), by the Friendly Societies (Modification of the Corporation Tax Acts) (Amendment) Regulations, SI 2008/1937 regs 2, 5 with effect in relation to accounting periods beginning on or after 1 January 2008.

8 Modification of section 432 of the Taxes Act

. . .

Amendments—Regulation 8 revoked by the Friendly Societies (Modification of the Corporation Tax Acts) (Amendment) Regulations, SI 2007/2134 regs 2, 8, with effect for accounting periods beginning on or after 1 January 2007: SI 2007/2134 reg 1(2).

9 Modifications of section 432A of the Taxes Act

[(1) In this regulation—

(a) paragraphs (1A), (2), (4) and (4A) prescribe modifications of section 432A of the Taxes Act so far as it applies to long-term business carried on by friendly societies, and

(*b*) paragraph (3) prescribes a further modification of that section so far as it applies to the long-term business carried on by partnership pensions societies.][2]

[(1A) In subsection (1ZC) before "PHI" insert "taxable".][2]

(2) After subsection (1A) insert the following subsections—

"(1B) Subsections (1C) to (1E) below apply where a friendly society with branches carries on more than one category of business.

(1C) In a case where—

(*a*) the society has caused the actuary to the society to prepare, as at the end of an accounting period and as at the end of the previous accounting period, reports prepared on the same basis as—

(i) the society's valuation report but which are limited to an investigation of the matters referred to in Rule 5.1(3) of the Prudential Sourcebook (Friendly Societies), or

(ii) the society's periodical return but which are limited to an investigation of the matters referred to in Rule 9.4(2) of the Prudential Sourcebook

(Insurers), in relation to the central body of the society (and not to any of its branches), and

(*b*) the society so chooses, the apportionment of the income, gains or losses of the central body shall be determined by reference to the liabilities and the value of the assets estimated for the purposes of those reports.

(1D) Subject to subsection (1C) above, the apportionment shall be of the income, gains or losses of the society, together with all its branches.

(1E) Where, by virtue of this section, income, gains or losses are referable to any of the following categories, namely—

[(*a*) gross roll-up business,][1]

(*d*) taxable basic life assurance and general annuity business, or

(*e*) taxable [PHI][1] business, that income, or those gains or losses, shall be attributable to the central body of the society and not to any of its branches unless the society shows that any business within any of those categories was written by a branch, in which case the income, gains or losses referable to any of those categories shall be attributed to any such branch in such manner as is just and reasonable.".

(3) After subsection (1E) (inserted by paragraph (2)) insert the following subsection—

"(1F) In the case of a partnership pension society, the definitions of "liabilities" and "value" in section 431(2) shall not apply, and any apportionment required by this section shall be made in such manner as is just and reasonable.".

[(4) In subsection (2) for paragraphs (*a*) to (*c*) substitute—

"(*a*) taxable basic life assurance and general annuity business,

(*b*) tax exempt basic life assurance and general annuity business,

(*c*) gross roll-up business,

(*d*) taxable PHI business, and

(*e*) tax exempt PHI business;".

[(4A) For subsection (3A) substitute—

"(3A) Amounts falling within—

(*a*) section 442A, or

(*b*) section 85(2C) of the Finance Act 1989

are directly referable to taxable basic life assurance general annuity business to the extent that the amounts are referable to that business.".][2]

(5) For subsections (6) to (6C) substitute—

"(6) For the purposes of subsection (5) above, "the relevant fraction", in relation to taxable basic life assurance and general annuity business, is—

$$\frac{A}{A+B+C+D+E}$$

where—

A is the aggregate of—

(*a*) the mean of the opening and closing liabilities of the taxable basic life assurance business (but taking that mean to be nil if it would otherwise be below nil) reduced (but not below nil) by the mean of the opening and closing net values of any assets directly referable to that category, and

(*b*) the mean of the appropriate parts (that is, the parts relating to that category) of the opening and closing amounts of the free assets amounts;

B is the aggregate of—

(*a*) the mean of the opening and closing liabilities of the tax exempt basic life assurance business (but taking that mean to be nil if it would otherwise be below nil) reduced (but not below nil) by the mean of the opening and closing net values of any assets directly referable to that category, and

(*b*) the mean of the appropriate parts (that is, the parts relating to that category) of the opening and closing amounts of the free assets amounts;

C is the aggregate of—

(*a*) the mean of the opening and closing liabilities of the gross roll-up business (but taking that mean to be nil if it would otherwise be below nil) reduced (but not below nil) by the mean of the opening and closing net values of any assets directly referable to that category, and

(*b*) the mean of the appropriate parts (that is, the parts relating to that category) of the opening and closing amounts of the free assets amounts;

D is the aggregate of—

(*a*) the mean of the opening and closing liabilities of the taxable PHI business (but taking that mean to be nil if it would otherwise be below nil) reduced (but not below nil) by the mean of the opening and closing net values of any assets directly referable to that category, and

(*b*) the mean of the appropriate parts (that is, the parts relating to that category) of the opening and closing amounts of the free assets amounts; and

E is the aggregate of—

(*a*) the mean of the opening and closing liabilities of the tax exempt PHI business (but taking that mean to be nil if it would otherwise be below nil) reduced (but not below nil) by the mean of the opening and closing net values of any assets directly referable to that category, and

(*b*) the mean of the appropriate parts (that is, the parts relating to that category) of the opening and closing amounts of the free assets amounts.

(6A) For the purposes of subsection (5) above, "the relevant fraction", in relation to tax exempt basic life assurance and general annuity business, is—

$$\frac{B}{A+B+C+D+E}$$

where A, B, C, D and E have the same meaning as in subsection (6) above.

(6B) For the purposes of subsection (5) above, "the relevant fraction", in relation to gross roll-up business, is—

$$\frac{C}{A+B+C+D+E}$$

where A, B, C, D and E have the same meaning as in subsection (6) above.

(6C) For the purposes of subsection (5) above, "the relevant fraction", in relation to taxable PHI business, is—

$$\frac{D}{A+B+C+D+E}$$

where A, B, C, D and E have the same meaning as in subsection (6) above.

(6D) For the purposes of subsection (5) above, "the relevant fraction", in relation to tax exempt PHI business, is—

$$\frac{E}{A+B+C+D+E}$$

where A, B, C, D and E have the same meaning as in subsection (6) above.

(6E) But if the denominator found in accordance with subsection (6), (6A), (6B), (6C) or (6D) above is nil, the relevant fraction for the purposes of subsection (5) above in relation to the category of business in question is such fraction as is just and reasonable."

(7) In subsection (7) for "and (6B)" substitute ", (6B), (6C) and (6D)".

(8) Omit—

(*a*) paragraph (*b*) of subsection (8) and the word "and" which precedes it;

(*b*) subsections (8ZA), (8A) and (8B).][1]

Amendments—[1] In para (1) reference substituted; in para (2), in the inserted sub-s (1E), para (*a*) substituted for previous paras (*a*)–(*c*), and words in para (*e*) substituted; and paras (4)–(8) substituted; by the Friendly Societies (Modification of the Corporation Tax Acts) (Amendment) Regulations, SI 2007/2134 regs 2, 9, with effect for accounting periods beginning on or after 1 January 2007: SI 2007/2134 reg 1(2).

[2] Para (1) substituted, and paras (1A), (4A) inserted, by the Friendly Societies (Modification of the Corporation Tax Acts) (Amendment) Regulations, SI 2008/1937 regs 2, 6 with effect in relation to accounting periods beginning on or after 1 January 2008.

9A [Modification of section 432B of the Taxes Act

. . .

Amendments—This regulation revoked by the Friendly Societies (Modification of the Corporation Tax Acts) (Amendment) Regulations, SI 2008/1937 regs 2, 7 with effect in relation to accounting periods beginning on or after 1 January 2008.

10 Modifications of section 432AA of the Taxes Act

(1) Paragraphs (2) to (4) prescribe modifications of subsection (4) of section 432AA of the Taxes Act so far as it applies to the [long-term][2] business carried on by friendly societies.

(2) In paragraph (*c*) at the beginning, insert 'taxable'.

(3) After paragraph (*c*) insert the following paragraph—

"(*ca*) tax exempt basic life assurance and general annuity business;".

(4) For paragraph (*d*) substitute the following paragraphs—

"(*d*) taxable [PHI][1] business;

(*e*) tax exempt [PHI][1] business."

Amendments—[1] In para (4), in substituted paras (*d*), (*e*), word substituted, by the Friendly Societies (Modification of the Corporation Tax Acts) (Amendment) Regulations, SI 2007/2134 regs 2, 11, with effect for accounting periods beginning on or after 1 January 2007: SI 2007/2134 reg 1(2).

[2] In para (1), words substituted by the Friendly Societies (Modification of the Corporation Tax Acts) (Amendment) Regulations, SI 2008/1937 regs 2, 8 with effect in relation to accounting periods beginning on or after 1 January 2008.

11 Modifications of section 432AB of the Taxes Act

(1) Paragraphs (2) and (3) prescribe modifications of section 432AB of the Taxes Act so far as it applies to the life or endowment business carried on by friendly societies.

(2) In subsection (3) before "basic" insert "taxable".

(3) In subsection (4) before "basic" insert "taxable".

12 Modifications of section 432E of the Taxes Act

(1) Section 432E of the Taxes Act shall apply to the life or endowment business of a friendly society with the following modifications.

(2) In subsection [(1)(*a*)][1], after the words "subsections (2) and (2A)" insert "or, as the case may be, subsection (2B)".

(3) After subsection (2A), the following subsection shall be treated as inserted—

"(2B) In a case where an amount is taken into account under subsection (2) of section 83 of the Finance Act 1989 by virtue of subsection (2F) of that section, the amount determined under subsection (2) above is increased by

$$\frac{CAS}{AS} \times RP$$

where—

CAS and AS have the same meanings as in subsection (2) above; and

RP is the amount taken into account under subsection (2) of section 83 of the Finance Act 1989 by virtue of subsection (2F) of that section."

Amendments—[1] In para (2), reference substituted by the Friendly Societies (Modification of the Corporation Tax Acts) (Amendment) Regulations, SI 2007/2134 regs 2, 12, with effect for accounting periods beginning on or after 1 January 2007: SI 2007/2134 reg 1(2).

13 Modifications of section 436 of the Taxes Act

. . .

Amendments—Regulation 13 revoked by the Friendly Societies (Modification of the Corporation Tax Acts) (Amendment) Regulations, SI 2007/2134 regs 2, 13, with effect for accounting periods beginning on or after 1 January 2007: SI 2007/2134 reg 1(2).

13A [Modifications of section 436A of the Taxes Act

(1) Paragraph (2) prescribes a modification of section 436A of the Taxes Act so far as it applies to the life or endowment business carried on by non annual return societies other than partnership pension societies.

(2) At the end of subsection (2) add—

", and

(*c*) the opening liabilities and the closing liabilities of the society shall be ascertained in accordance with paragraph (*b*) of the definition of "liabilities" in subsection (2) of section 431, and the definition of "closing liabilities" in that subsection shall not apply."

(3) Paragraph (4) prescribes a modification of section 436A of the Taxes Act so far as it applies to the life or endowment business carried on by partnership pension societies.

(4) At the end add the following subsections—

"(8) Subject to subsection (11) below, subsection (9) below applies where the amount shown in respect of Item 3 of Part I of Schedule 7 to the Friendly Societies (Accounts and Related Provisions) Regulations 1994 ("the Item 3 amount") is a positive amount; and subsection (10) below applies where the Item 3 amount is a negative amount.

(9) The amount of the increase in liabilities to policy holders (that is to say, the excess of the society's closing liabilities to policy holders over its opening liabilities to policy holders) that is taken into account for the purpose of computing the profits arising to the society from pension business shall be the Item 3 amount.

(10) The amount of the decrease in liabilities to policy holders (that is to say, the excess of the society's opening liabilities to policy holders over its closing liabilities to policy holders) that is taken into account for the purpose of computing the profits arising to the society from pension business shall be the Item 3 amount.

(11) Subject to subsection (13) below, in a case where, for any period of account, income or gains arising to a society—

(*a*) derive directly or indirectly from a transaction or transactions with a member or members of the society, and

(*b*) exceed the amount of the income or gains which would have arisen to the society if any transaction mentioned in paragraph (*a*) above had been a transaction at arm's length,

the closing liabilities of the society shall be reduced by the amount of the excess; but the opening liabilities for the next following period of account shall not be increased by the like amount.

(12) For the purposes of subsection (11) above a person associated with a member shall be treated as a member; and "associated" shall be construed in accordance with section 783(10).

(13) In any case where—

(*a*) there has been a transaction consisting of the disposal of an asset to a friendly society ("the earlier disposal"),

(*b*) section 17(1)(*a*) of the 1992 Act has applied on the earlier disposal,

(*c*) the friendly society subsequently makes a disposal of the asset ("the later disposal"), and

(*d*) subsection (11) above applies (or would, apart from this subsection, apply) to the later disposal,

any gains accruing to the society on the later disposal shall, for the purposes of subsection (11) above, be reduced by the excess (if any) of the amount treated, by virtue of the application of section 17(1)(a) of the 1992 Act, as the consideration for the earlier disposal over the actual amount of the consideration for the earlier disposal."][1]

Amendments—[1] Regulation 13A inserted by the Friendly Societies (Modification of the Corporation Tax Acts) (Amendment) Regulations, SI 2007/2134 regs 2, 14, with effect for accounting periods beginning on or after 1 January 2007: SI 2007/2134 reg 1(2).

14 Modifications of section 437 of the Taxes Act

(1) Paragraphs (2) and (3) prescribe modifications of section 437 of the Taxes Act so far as it applies to the life or endowment business carried on by friendly societies.

(2) In subsection (1C)(*a*), before "basic" insert "taxable".

(3) In subsection (1F) at the end insert—

"taxable basic life assurance and general annuity business" means basic life assurance and general annuity business the profits arising from which do not fall to be exempted from tax by virtue of section 460(1), and for the purposes of this definition it shall be assumed that the friendly society has made a claim for exemption from tax under that provision.".

15 Modifications of section 438B of the Taxes Act

. . .

Amendments—Regulation 15 revoked by the Friendly Societies (Modification of the Corporation Tax Acts) (Amendment) Regulations, SI 2007/2134 regs 2, 15, with effect for accounting periods beginning on or after 1 January 2007: SI 2007/2134 reg 1(2).

16 Modifications of section 440 of the Taxes Act

(1) The modifications of section 440 of the Taxes Act given in paragraphs (2) and (3) apply—

(*a*) where a friendly society begins or ceases to maintain a separate fund for long-term insurance business, or

(*b*) in relation to a prescribed transaction.

(2) In subsection (1), for "If" substitute "Subject to subsection (4A) below, if"

[(2A) In subsection (3) after "(*d*)" insert ", (*da*)".][1]

(3) After subsection (4) insert the following subsection—

"(4A) Subsection (1) above shall not have effect in relation to any assets which—

(*a*) cease to be within the category set out in paragraph (*e*) of subsection (4) above and come within the category set out in paragraph (*f*) of that subsection, or

(*b*) cease to be within the category set out in paragraph (*f*) of subsection (4) above and come within the category set out in paragraph (*e*) of that subsection."

(4) Paragraph (5) prescribes a modification of section 440(4) of the Taxes Act so far as it applies to the life or endowment business carried on by friendly societies.

(5) For paragraph (*d*) substitute—

"(*d*) assets linked solely to taxable basic life assurance and general annuity business;

(*da*) assets linked solely to tax exempt basic life assurance and general annuity business;".

Amendments—[1] Para (2A) inserted by the Friendly Societies (Modification of the Corporation Tax Acts) (Amendment) Regulations, SI 2007/2134 regs 2, 16, with effect for accounting periods beginning on or after 1 January 2007: SI 2007/2134 reg 1(2).

17 [Modifications of section 440A of the Taxes Act

(1) Paragraphs (2) and (3) prescribe modifications of section 440A of the Taxes Act so far as it applies to the life or endowment business carried on by friendly societies.

(2) In subsection (2)(*a*)—

(*a*) in sub-paragraph (i) before "basic life assurance" insert "taxable";

(*b*) after sub-paragraph (i) insert—

"(ia) tax exempt basic life assurance and general annuity business, or"

(3) Omit subsection (3).][1]

Amendments—[1] Regulation 17 substituted by the Friendly Societies (Modification of the Corporation Tax Acts) (Amendment) Regulations, SI 2007/2134 regs 2, 17, with effect for accounting periods beginning on or after 1 January 2007: SI 2007/2134 reg 1(2).

18 Modifications of section 441 of the Taxes Act

. . .

(2) Before paragraph (b) insert the following paragraph—

Amendments—Regulation 18 revoked by the Friendly Societies (Modification of the Corporation Tax Acts) (Amendment) Regulations, SI 2007/2134 regs 2, 18(*a*), with effect for accounting periods beginning on or after 1 January 2007: SI 2007/2134 reg 1(2).

19 Modification of section 442A(1) of the Taxes Act

(1) Paragraph (2) prescribes a modification of section 442A(1) of the Taxes Act so far as it applies to the life or endowment business carried on by friendly societies.

(2) Before "basic" insert "taxable".

20 Modification of section 460(2) of the Taxes Act

. . .

Amendments—Regulation 20 revoked by the Friendly Societies (Modification of the Corporation Tax Acts) (Amendment) Regulations, SI 2007/2134 regs 2, 18(*b*), with effect for accounting periods beginning on or after 1 January 2007: SI 2007/2134 reg 1(2).

20A [Modifications of section 502H of the Taxes Act

. . .

Amendments—This reg revoked by the Friendly Societies (Modification of the Corporation Tax Acts) (Amendment) Regulations, SI 2008/1937 regs 2, 9 with effect in relation to accounting periods beginning on or after 1 January 2008.

21 Modification of section 587B of the Taxes Act

. . .

Amendments—Regulation 21 revoked by the Friendly Societies (Modification of the Corporation Tax Acts) (Amendment) Regulations, SI 2007/2134 regs 2, 20, with effect for accounting periods beginning on or after 1 January 2007: SI 2007/2134 reg 1(2).

22 Modifications of section 755A of the Taxes Act

(1) Paragraphs (2) to (9) prescribe modifications of section 755A of the Taxes Act so far as it applies to the life or endowment business carried on by friendly societies.

(2) In subsections (3) and (10) before "BLAGAB apportioned profit", in each place where those words occur, insert "taxable".

[(3) In subsection (4) after "gross roll-up business" insert ", or tax exempt basic life assurance and general annuity business,".

(4) In subsection (4A) before "basic life assurance" insert "taxable".

(5) In subsection (6)(c) after "gross roll-up business" insert "or tax exempt basic life assurance and general annuity business".

(6) In subsection (11) before "BLAGAB" insert "taxable".][1]

(7) . . . [1]

(8) In subsection (12), in the definition of "BLAGAB apportioned profit"—

(*a*) before "BLAGAB" insert "taxable";

(*b*) before "basic life assurance" insert "taxable".

[(9) In subsection (13)(*a*) before "basic life assurance" insert "taxable".][1]

Amendments—[1] Paras (3)–(6) substituted for previous paras (3)–(7), and para (9) substituted, by the Friendly Societies (Modification of the Corporation Tax Acts) (Amendment) Regulations, SI 2007/2134 regs 2, 21, with effect for accounting periods beginning on or after 1 January 2007: SI 2007/2134 reg 1(2).

23 Modifications of section 804B of the Taxes Act

(1) Paragraphs (2) to (5) prescribe modifications of section 804B of the Taxes Act so far as it applies to the [long-term][2] business carried on by friendly societies.

(2) The modification of section 804B(4)(*a*) prescribed by paragraph (3)(*a*) shall not apply where section 804B(4) is applied by virtue of regulation 4(3) and (5) of the Double Taxation Relief (Surrender of Relievable Tax within a Group) Regulations 2001.

(3) In subsection (4)—

(*a*) in paragraph (*a*) before "basic" insert "taxable";

(*b*) for paragraph (*b*) substitute—

"(*b*) taxable [PHI][1] business,".

(4), (5) . . . [1]

Amendments—[1] In para (3)(*b*), word substituted, and paras (4), (5) revoked, by the Friendly Societies (Modification of the Corporation Tax Acts) (Amendment) Regulations, SI 2007/2134 regs 2, 22, with effect for accounting periods beginning on or after 1 January 2007: SI 2007/2134 reg 1(2).

[2] In para (1), words substituted by the Friendly Societies (Modification of the Corporation Tax Acts) (Amendment) Regulations, SI 2008/1937 regs 2, 10 with effect in relation to accounting periods beginning on or after 1 January 2008.

24 Modifications of section 804D of the Taxes Act

(1) Paragraphs (2) to (4) prescribe modifications of section 804D of the Taxes Act so far as it applies to the life or endowment business carried on by non annual return societies.

(2) In subsection (2) for the words from "by which" to the end substitute—

"by which—

(*a*) so much of the total of the amounts shown, in the society's accounts for that period, in respect of Item 1 of Part I of Schedule 7 to the Friendly Societies (Accounts and Related Provisions) Regulations 1994 as is referable to that category of business exceeds

(*b*) so much of any commissions payable and any expenses of management incurred in connection with the acquisition of the business, as shown in those accounts in respect of Item 2(*f*) and (*g*) of Part I of that Schedule, as is referable to that category of business.".

(3) In subsection (4) for the words from "claims incurred" to the end substitute "total income of that category determined under subsection (2) above.".

(4) Omit subsection (5).

25 Modification of paragraph 5 of Schedule 19AA to the Taxes Act

. . .

Amendments—Regulation 25 revoked by the Friendly Societies (Modification of the Corporation Tax Acts) (Amendment) Regulations, SI 2007/2134 regs 2, 23, with effect for accounting periods beginning on or after 1 January 2007: SI 2007/2134 reg 1(2).

26 Modifications of section 82 of the Finance Act 1989

(1) Where section 82(1)(*b*) of the Finance Act 1989 applies, as originally enacted, by virtue of paragraph 1(6) of Schedule 33 to the Finance Act 2003—

(*a*) in the case of a friendly society, subsection (1)(*b*) of that section shall be modified so that for "section 9.6 of the Prudential Sourcebook (Insurers)" there is substituted "rule 5.1 of the Prudential Sourcebook (Friendly Societies)";

(*b*) in the case of a non annual return society, at the end of that section there is treated as inserted— "(9) Where a period of account ends on a day to which a valuation report has not been prepared, or begins on a day immediately following such a day, the amount of any unappropriated surplus on valuation for the purposes of subsections (1)(*b*) and (4) shall be the amount which was taken into account at the end of the last period of account for which a valuation report was prepared."

27 Modifications of section 82B of the Finance Act 1989

(1) In the case of a non-directive friendly society, section 82B of the Finance Act 1989 shall apply with the following modifications.

(2) In paragraph (*a*) of subsection (1), for "section 9.6 of the Prudential Sourcebook (Insurers)" substitute "Rule 5.1 of the Prudential Sourcebook (Friendly Societies)".

(3) In paragraph (*b*) of subsection (1), for "Rule 9.10(*c*) of the Prudential Sourcebook (Insurers)" substitute "Paragraph 2(6) of Appendix 4 to the Prudential Sourcebook (Friendly Societies)".

(4) Where that friendly society is not required to submit an annual actuarial investigation to the Financial Services Authority under Rule 5.1 of the Prudential Sourcebook (Friendly Societies)—

(*a*) in subsection (2) for "the period of account immediately preceding the period of account in question" substitute "the period of account for which a report was submitted which most closely precedes the period of account in question ("the most closely preceding period of account")";

(*b*) in subsection (3), for "that immediately preceding period of account", wherever those words occur, substitute "the most closely preceding period of account".

28 Modification of section 83 of the Finance Act 1989

(1) Paragraph (2) prescribes a modification of section 83 of the Finance Act 1989 so far as it applies to the life or endowment business carried on by annual return societies.

(2) After subsection (2E) insert the following subsections—

"(2F) Where, in a case where the expenses charged in the management fund exceed the amount transferred from all revenue account funds, the amount determined in accordance with subsection (2G) below shall be taken into account as an increase in value of the assets of the long-term insurance fund.

(2G) Subject to subsection (2I) below, that amount is the amount found by—

(*a*) taking the aggregate amount of the society's investment income recognised in the account of the management fund;

(*b*) either adding any increase in value of the assets of the management fund, or subtracting any decrease in value of the assets of the management fund, as the case may be; and

(*c*) multiplying the amount so found by the fraction specified in subsection (2H) below.

(2H) That fraction is the fraction of which—

(*a*) the numerator is the amount transferred from the revenue account recognised for the purposes of section 83A(2), and

(*b*) the denominator is the amount transferred from all revenue account funds. (2I) Where, apart from this subsection, the amount determined in accordance with subsection (2G) above would be a negative amount, the amount determined in accordance with that subsection shall be taken to be nil.".

29 Modification of section 83A of the Finance Act 1989 – annual return societies

(1) Paragraph (2) prescribes a modification of section 83A of the Finance Act 1989 so far as it applies to the life or endowment business carried on by annual return societies.

(2) For subsection (2) substitute—

"(2) The accounts recognised for the purposes of those sections are—

(*a*) a revenue account included in, or supplied to the Financial Services Authority with, the society's valuation report which contains items relating to the society's life or endowment business in respect of the whole of the society's long-term business;

(*b*) any separate revenue account included in, or supplied to the Financial Services Authority with, the society's valuation report which contains items relating to the society's life or endowment business in respect of a with-profits fund (see subsection (6)).

(2A) In subsection (2) above 'life or endowment business' has the meaning given by section 466(1) of the Taxes Act 1988.".

30 Modifications of section 83A of the Finance Act 1989 – non-annual return societies

(1) Paragraphs (2) and (3) prescribe modifications of Section 83A of the Finance Act 1989 so far as it applies to the life or endowment business carried on by non annual return societies.

(2) For subsection (2) substitute—

"(2) The account recognised for the purposes of those sections is the income and expenditure account prepared in accordance with the requirements of the Friendly Societies (Accounts and Related Provisions) Regulations 1994.".

(3) Omit subsections [(3) to (4)][1].

Amendments—[1] In para (3) words substituted by the Friendly Societies (Modification of the Corporation Tax Acts) (Amendment) Regulations, SI 2007/2134 regs 2, 24, with effect for accounting periods beginning on or after 1 January 2007: SI 2007/2134 reg 1(2).

31 Modifications of section 85 of the Finance Act 1989

(1) Paragraph (2) prescribes a modification of section 85(1) and (2C) of the Finance Act 1989 so far as they apply to the life or endowment business carried on by friendly societies.

(2) Before "basic life assurance", wherever those words occur, insert "taxable".

32 [Modifications of section 88 of the Finance Act 1989

(1) Paragraph (2) prescribes a modification of section [88(3)(*a*)][2] and (3B) of the Finance Act 1989 so far as [it applies][2] to the life or endowment business carried on by friendly societies.

(2) Before "basic life assurance", wherever those words occur, insert "taxable".][1]

Amendments—[1] Regulation 32 substituted by the Friendly Societies (Modification of the Corporation Tax Acts) (Amendment) Regulations, SI 2007/2134 regs 2, 25, with effect for accounting periods beginning on or after 1 January 2007: SI 2007/2134 reg 1(2).

[2] In para (1), words substituted by the Friendly Societies (Modification of the Corporation Tax Acts) (Amendment) Regulations, SI 2008/1937 regs 2, 11 with effect in relation to accounting periods beginning on or after 1 January 2008.

33 Modification of paragraph 16 of Schedule 7 to the Finance Act 1991

(1) Paragraph (2) prescribes a modification of paragraph 16 of Schedule 7 to the Finance Act 1991 so far as it applies to the life or endowment business carried on by friendly societies.

(2) In sub-paragraph (7), in the definition of "general annuity contract", for "referable to general annuity business" substitute " 'referable to taxable general annuity business', and 'taxable general annuity business' means general annuity business the profits arising from which do not fall to be exempted from tax by virtue of section 460(1) of the Taxes Act 1988, and for the purposes of this definition it shall be assumed that the friendly society has made a claim for exemption from tax under that provision".

34 Modification of paragraph 17 of Schedule 7 to the Finance Act 1991

. . .

Amendments—Regulation 34 revoked by the Friendly Societies (Modification of the Corporation Tax Acts) (Amendment) Regulations, SI 2007/2134 regs 2, 26, with effect for accounting periods beginning on or after 1 January 2007: SI 2007/2134 reg 1(2).

34A [Modification of section 210A of the 1992 Act

(1) In the case of a friendly society, section 210A of the Taxation of Chargeable Gains Act 1992 shall be modified as follows.

(2) In subsection (13), in the definitions of "BLAGAB allowable losses" and "BLAGAB chargeable gains", before "basic life assurance" insert "taxable".][1]

Amendments—[1] Regulation 34A inserted by the Friendly Societies (Modification of the Corporation Tax Acts) (Amendment) Regulations, SI 2007/2134 regs 2, 27, with effect for accounting periods beginning on or after 1 January 2007: SI 2007/2134 reg 1(2).

35 Modifications of section 210B of the 1992 Act

(1) In the case of a friendly society, section 210B of the Taxation of Chargeable Gains Act 1992 shall be modified as follows.

(2) In subsection (7)(*a*), before "BLAGAB internal linked fund" insert "taxable".

(3) In subsection (8), for the definition of "BLAGAB internal linked fund" substitute—

"taxable BLAGAB internal linked fund" means an internal linked fund all the assets appropriated to which are linked solely to taxable basic life assurance and general annuity business,".

36 Modifications of section 211ZA of the 1992 Act

(1) In the case of a friendly society, section 211ZA of the Taxation of Chargeable Gains Act 1992 shall be modified as follows.

(2) In subsection (7), before "basic life assurance and general annuity business" insert "taxable".

(3) In subsection (10), before "basic life assurance and general annuity business" insert "taxable".

37 Modification of section 212 of the 1992 Act

(1) Paragraph (2) prescribes a modification of section 212 of the 1992 Act so far as it applies to the life or endowment business carried on by friendly societies.

[(2) In subsection (2) after "gross roll-up business" insert "or tax exempt basic life assurance and general annuity business".][1]

Amendments—[1] Para (2) substituted by the Friendly Societies (Modification of the Corporation Tax Acts) (Amendment) Regulations, SI 2007/2134 regs 2, 28, with effect for accounting periods beginning on or after 1 January 2007: SI 2007/2134 reg 1(2).

38 Modification of section 213 of the 1992 Act

(1) Paragraph (2) prescribes a modification of section 213(1A) of the 1992 Act so far as it applies to the life or endowment business carried on by friendly societies.

(2) In paragraph (*a*) before "basic life" insert "taxable".

39 Modification of section 214(1) of the 1992 Act

. . .

Amendments—Regulation 39 revoked by the Friendly Societies (Modification of the Corporation Tax Acts) (Amendment) Regulations, SI 2007/2134 regs 2, 29, with effect for accounting periods beginning on or after 1 January 2007: SI 2007/2134 reg 1(2).

39A [Modification of paragraph 12 of Schedule 9 to the Finance Act 1996

(1) Paragraph (2) prescribes a modification of paragraph 12 of Schedule 9 to the Finance Act 1996 so far as it applies to the life or endowment business carried on by friendly societies.

(2) In sub-paragraph (3) after "(*d*)" insert ", (*da*)".][1]

Amendments—[1] Regulation 39A inserted by the Friendly Societies (Modification of the Corporation Tax Acts) (Amendment) Regulations, SI 2007/2134 regs 2, 30, with effect for accounting periods beginning on or after 1 January 2007: SI 2007/2134 reg 1(2).

40 Modifications of Schedule 11 to the Finance Act 1996

(1) Paragraphs (2) and (3) prescribe modifications of Schedule 11 to the Finance Act 1996 so far as it applies to the [long-term][2] business carried on by friendly societies.

(2) In [paragraph][2] 4(1)(*a*)[, (2)(*a*), (7) and (10) before "basic life assurance", wherever those words occur][1], insert "taxable".

[(2A) In paragraph 3A(5) before "PHI" insert "taxable" after "(6B)" insert ", (6C), (6D)".][1]

(3) . . .[1]

Amendments—[1] In para (2) words substituted, para (2A) inserted, and para (3) revoked, by the Friendly Societies (Modification of the Corporation Tax Acts) (Amendment) Regulations, SI 2007/2134 regs 2, 31, with effect for accounting periods beginning on or after 1 January 2007: SI 2007/2134 reg 1(2).

[2] In paras (1), (2), words substituted by the Friendly Societies (Modification of the Corporation Tax Acts) (Amendment) Regulations, SI 2008/1937 regs 2, 12 with effect in relation to accounting periods beginning on or after 1 January 2008.

41 Modifications of Schedule 11 to the Finance Act 1996 as modified in relation to capital redemption business

. . .

Amendments—Regulation 41 revoked by the Friendly Societies (Modification of the Corporation Tax Acts) (Amendment) Regulations, SI 2007/2134 regs 2, 32(*a*), with effect for accounting periods beginning on or after 1 January 2007: SI 2007/2134 reg 1(2).

42 Modifications of paragraph 18 of Schedule 12 to the Finance Act 1997

. . .

Amendments—Regulation 42 revoked by the Friendly Societies (Modification of the Corporation Tax Acts) (Amendment) Regulations, SI 2007/2134 regs 2, 32(*b*), with effect for accounting periods beginning on or after 1 January 2007: SI 2007/2134 reg 1(2).

43 Modifications of paragraph 4 of Schedule 6 to the Finance Act 1999

. . .

Amendments—Regulation 43 revoked by the Friendly Societies (Modification of the Corporation Tax Acts) (Amendment) Regulations, SI 2007/2134 regs 2, 32(*c*), with effect for accounting periods beginning on or after 1 January 2007: SI 2007/2134 reg 1(2).

43A [Modification of section 255 of the Capital Allowances Act 2001

(1) Paragraph (2) prescribes a modification of section 255 of the Capital Allowances Act 2001 so far as it applies to the [long-term][2] business carried on by friendly societies.

[(2) In subsection (1)—

(*a*) for "basic life assurance and general annuity business" substitute "taxable basic life assurance and general annuity business, tax exempt basic life assurance and general annuity business", and

(*b*) for "and PHI business" substitute ", taxable PHI business and tax exempt PHI business".][2]][1]

Amendments—[1] Regulation 43A inserted by the Friendly Societies (Modification of the Corporation Tax Acts) (Amendment) Regulations, SI 2007/2134 regs 2, 33, with effect for accounting periods beginning on or after 1 January 2007: SI 2007/2134 reg 1(2).

[2] In para (1), words substituted, and para (2) substituted by the Friendly Societies (Modification of the Corporation Tax Acts) (Amendment) Regulations, SI 2008/1937 regs 2, 12 with effect in relation to accounting periods beginning on or after 1 January 2008.

44 Modifications of section 256 of the Capital Allowances Act 2001

(1) Paragraphs (2) and (3) prescribe modifications of section 256 of the Capital Allowances Act 2001 so far as it applies to the life or endowment business carried on by friendly societies.

(2) In subsection (1)(*a*) before "basic life assurance and general annuity business" insert "taxable".

(3) In subsection (2)(*a*) before "basic life assurance and general annuity business" insert "taxable".

44A [Modification of paragraph 29 of Schedule 26 to the Finance Act 2002

(1) Paragraph (2) prescribes a modification of paragraph 29 of Schedule 26 to the Finance Act 2002 so far as it applies to the life or endowment business carried on by friendly societies.

(2) In sub-paragraph (1) after "(*d*)" insert ", (*da*)".][1]

Amendments—[1] Regulation 44A inserted by the Friendly Societies (Modification of the Corporation Tax Acts) (Amendment) Regulations, SI 2007/2134 regs 2, 34, with effect for accounting periods beginning on or after 1 January 2007: SI 2007/2134 reg 1(2).

45 Modification of paragraph 36 of Schedule 29 to the Finance Act 2002

(1) Paragraph (2) prescribes a modification of paragraph 36 of Schedule 29 to the Finance Act 2002 so far as it applies to the life or endowment business carried on by friendly societies.

(2) In sub-paragraph (3) after "carries on" insert "taxable".

46 Supersession of earlier Regulations
In consequence of the provisions of these Regulations, the Regulations specified in column (1) of the Schedule shall (to the extent mentioned in column (3) of that Schedule) cease to have effect for accounting periods beginning on or after 1st January 2005.

SCHEDULE
REVOCATIONS

Regulation 46

Table

Column (1)	*Column (2)*	*Column (3)*
Regulations	*References*	*Extent of revocation*
The Friendly Societies (Modification of the Corporation Tax Acts) Regulations 1997	SI 1997/473	The whole Regulations
The Friendly Societies (Modification of the Corporation Tax Acts) (Amendment No 2) Regulations 1997	SI 1997/2877	The whole Regulations
The Individual Savings Account (Insurance Companies) Regulations 1998	SI 1998/1871	Regulation 25
The Friendly Societies (Modification of the Corporation Tax Acts) (Amendment) Regulations 1999	SI 1999/2636	The whole Regulations
The Friendly Societies (Modification of the Corporation Tax Acts) (Amendment) Regulations 2000	SI 2000/2710	The whole Regulations
The Financial Services and Markets Act 2000 (Consequential Amendments) (Taxes) Order 2001	SI 2001/3629	Articles 152 to 165
The Friendly Societies (Modification of the Corporation Tax Acts) (Amendment) Regulations 2001	SI 2001/3975	The whole Regulations
The Friendly Societies (Modification of the Corporation Tax Acts) (Amendment) Regulations 2003	SI 2003/23	The whole Regulations
The Friendly Societies (Modification of the Corporation Tax Acts) (Amendment) Regulations 2004	SI 2004/822	The whole Regulations
The Friendly Societies (Modification of the Corporation Tax Acts) (Amendment) Regulations 2005	SI 2005/2005	The whole Regulations

2005/2017

PARTNERSHIPS (RESTRICTIONS ON CONTRIBUTIONS TO A TRADE) REGULATIONS 2005

Made . . . . *20 July 2005*
Coming into force . . . . *22 July 2005*

Made by the Commissioners for Her Majesty's Revenue and Customs under TA 1988 s 118ZN(2)–(4) and FA 2004 s 122A(2)–(4)

Modification—Following the repeal of TA 1988 s 118ZN and FA 2004 s 122A, these Regulations have effect as if made under ITA 2007 ss 114, 802, by virtue of ITA 2007 s 1034, Sch 2 para 35(1).

1 Citation, commencement and effect
(1) These Regulations may be cited as the Partnerships (Restrictions on Contributions to a Trade) Regulations 2005 and shall come into force on 22nd July 2005. (2) These Regulations shall have effect from 2nd December 2004.

2 Interpretation
In these Regulations—

"any other person", in relation to an individual, includes a partnership of which the individual is a member;

"arrangement" means any scheme, arrangement or understanding of any kind (whether or not it is, or is intended to be, legally enforceable);

"bank" has the meaning given by section 840A of ICTA [section 991 of ITA 2007][1];

["capital contribution"—

(*a*) for the purposes of section 114 of ITA 2007, means the contribution to the firm for the purposes of section 104 or 110 of that Act or the contribution to the LLP for the purposes of section 107 of that Act, and

(*b*) for the purposes of section 802 of ITA 2007, has the meaning given by section 801(3) of that Act;][1]

"events" includes an omission to exercise a right;

"FA 2004" means the Finance Act 2004;

["ITA 2007" means the Income Tax Act 2007;][1]

"loan" includes—

(*a*) an advance of money, or any form of credit and "takes out a loan" shall be construed accordingly; and

(*b*) except in regulation 4(4)(*a*), any loan which, directly or indirectly, replaces the original loan (and so on, through any number of such loans); "repaying", where the context requires, includes part repayment.

Modifications—ITA 2007 Sch 2 para 35(2), (3) (modification of this regulation so as to apply for the purposes of ITA 2007).

ITA 2007 Sch 2 para 148(2), (3) (modification of this regulation so as to apply for the purposes of ITA 2007).

Amendments—[1] In definition of "bank" words substituted, definition of "capital contribution" substituted for previous definition of "contribution to the relevant trade", and definition of "ITA 2007" substituted for previous definition of "ICTA", by virtue of ITA 2007 s 1031(1), Sch 2 para 35(1), (2), (3), para 148(6) with effect for income tax purposes from 6 April 2007, and corporation tax purposes for accounting periods ending after 5 April 2007.

3 Scope of these Regulations

These Regulations apply for the purposes of—

(*a*) the relevant provisions mentioned in [section 114(1)(*a*) and (*b*) of ITA 2007][1], and

(*b*) except in regulation 5, [section 797 of ITA 2007 as mentioned in section 802(2) of that Act][1],

in computing the amount of an individual's [capital contribution][1].

Modifications—ITA 2007 Sch 2 para 35(2), (4), (5) (modification of this regulation so as to apply for the purposes of ITA 2007).

ITA 2007 Sch 2 para 148(2), (4) (modification of this regulation so as to apply for the purposes of ITA 2007).

Amendments—[1] Words substituted by virtue of the Income Tax Act 2007 s 1031(1), Sch 2 paras 35(1), (2), (4), (5), 148(6) with effect for income tax purposes from 6 April 2007, and corporation tax purposes for accounting periods ending after 5 April 2007.

4 Restrictions on computing the amount of an individual's contribution to a trade—Loans

(1) This regulation applies where—

(*a*) an individual takes out a loan in connection with his financing of the whole or part of a [capital contribution][1], and

(*b*) at least one of the following conditions is satisfied.

Condition 1

There is, at any time an agreement or arrangement, under which all or any of the financial cost of repaying the loan is, will or may be borne, or ultimately borne, by any other person.

Condition 2

All or any of the financial cost of repaying the loan is at any time borne, or ultimately borne, by any other person (except under the terms of an agreement or arrangement falling within Condition 1).

Condition 3

The liability to repay the loan is at any time assumed or released by any other person. Condition 4 The actual financial cost which the individual incurs in repaying the loan during a period mentioned in paragraph (4) is substantially less than what the financial cost to him would be on arm's length repayment terms (those costs being determined in accordance with paragraphs (3) and (4)), or is nil.

(2) Where any of Conditions 1 to 3 are satisfied, there shall be excluded when computing the amount of the individual's [capital contribution][1] at the time in question the financial cost of repaying the loan, which is, will or may be borne or ultimately borne by the other person, or the liability to repay which is assumed or released by the other person, as the case may be.

(3) In determining the financial cost on arm's length repayment terms—

(*a*) the actual amount of the loan shall be taken into account,

(*b*) it shall be assumed that the individual repays the loan personally (without recourse to any other person or fund), and

(*c*) the rate of interest, period of the loan, repayment terms and other terms of the loan shall be assumed to be such that might be expected to be applicable if the loan were made—

(i) by a bank in the ordinary course of its lending business, and

(ii) by way of a bargain made at arm's length.

(4) The comparison required by Condition 4 shall be carried out over five year periods, and computations shall be made to determine the earliest such period—

(*a*) beginning on or after 2nd December 2004 (or the date when the loan was taken out, if later) and

(*b*) for which Condition 4 is satisfied. The end of that period is referred to in paragraph (5) as "the relevant time".

(5) Where Condition 4 is satisfied, there shall be excluded when computing the amount of the individual's [capital contribution][1] at the relevant time the capital liability outstanding under the loan at the relevant time, whether due from the individual or any other person or fund.

Modifications—ITA 2007 Sch 2 para 35(2), (4) (modification of these regulations so that they apply for the purposes of ITA 2007).

ITA 2007 Sch 2 para 148(2), (5) (modification of this regulation so as to apply for the purposes of ITA 2007).

Amendments—[1] Words in paras (1)(*a*), (2), (5) substituted by virtue of ITA 2007 s 1031(1), Sch 2 paras 35(1), (2), (4), 148(6) with effect for income tax purposes from 6 April 2007, and corporation tax purposes for accounting periods ending after 5 April 2007.

5 Restrictions on computing the amount of an individual's contribution to a trade – reimbursements

(1) Where there is, at any time, an agreement or arrangement, under which all or any of the financial cost of making a [capital contribution][1] will or may be directly or indirectly reimbursed to the individual by any other person, paragraph (3) shall apply.

(2) Where, at any time, all or any of the financial cost of making a [capital contribution][1] is directly or indirectly reimbursed to the individual by any other person (except under the terms of an agreement or arrangement falling within paragraph (1)), paragraph (3) shall apply.

(3) There shall be excluded when computing the amount of the individual's [capital contribution][1] at the time in question the financial cost of making the contribution which is, will or may be directly or indirectly reimbursed by the other person, as the case may be.

Modifications—ITA 2007 Sch 2 para 35(2), (4) (modification of these regulations so that they apply for the purposes of ITA 2007).

Amendments—[1] Words substituted by virtue of the ITA 2007 s 1031(1), Sch 2 paras 35(1), (2), (4), 148(6) with effect for income tax purposes from 6 April 2007, and corporation tax purposes for accounting periods ending after 5 April 2007.

6 No amount shall be excluded from the computations more than once, and the following shall not be excluded when computing the amount of the individual's [capital contribution][1]

(*a*) any financial cost which is borne or reimbursed by another individual in the normal course of that individual's domestic, family or personal relationships;

(*b*) any loan repayments not made by the individual due to his financial inability to pay, arising as a result of events outside his control which occur after the loan was taken out; and

(*c*) any amount on which the individual is chargeable to income tax as profits of [a trade][1].

Modifications—ITA 2007 Sch 2 para 35(2), (4), (6) (modification of this regulation so as to apply for the purposes of ITA 2007).

Amendments—[1] Words substituted by virtue of ITA 2007 s 1031(1), Sch 2 paras 35(1), (2), (4), (6), 148(6) with effect for income tax purposes from 6 April 2007, and corporation tax purposes for accounting periods ending after 5 April 2007.

2005/2045

INCOME TAX (CONSTRUCTION INDUSTRY SCHEME) REGULATIONS 2005

Made . . . .*25 July 2005*
Laid before the House of Commons . . . .*25 July 2005*
Coming into force in accordance with . . . .*regulation 1*

ARRANGEMENT OF REGULATIONS

Made by the Commissioners for Her Majesty's Revenue and Customs under FA 2003 s 205, FA 2004 ss 60(7), 62(3), (6) and (7), 63(1), 65(2), 66(2) and (9), 68, 69, 70, 71, 73 and 75, Sch 11 paras 2, 3(1) and (3), 4(3) and (5), 6, 7(1) and (3), 8(2), 10, 11(1) and (4), 12(2), 15 and 16, and TMA 1970 ss 98A(1) and 113(1)

Commentary—*Simon's Taxes* **E5.540**.

PART 1
INTRODUCTION

1 Citation and commencement

These Regulations may be cited as the Income Tax (Construction Industry Scheme) Regulations 2005 and shall come into force on such day as may be appointed by the Commissioners for Her Majesty's Revenue and Customs by notice in the London, Edinburgh and Belfast Gazettes ("the appointed day").

2 Interpretation

In these Regulations—

"the Act" means the Finance Act 2004;

"approved method of electronic communications", in relation to the delivery of information or the making of a payment in accordance with a provision of these Regulations, means [the internet services provided through the Construction Industry Scheme Online for Contractors or PAYE Online for Agents or the Electronic Data Interchange services provided through the Construction Industry Scheme Online for Contractors or PAYE Online for Agents, or][4] a method of electronic communications which has been approved, by specific or general directions issued by the Commissioners for Her Majesty's Revenue and Customs, for the delivery of information of that kind or the making of a payment of that kind under that provision;

["combined amount" means an amount which includes an amount the contractor is liable to pay under these regulations and one or more of the following—

(*a*) earnings-related contributions due under the SSC Regulations;

(*b*) tax due under the PAYE Regulations;

(*c*) payments of repayments of student loans due under the Student Loan Regulations;][1]

"contract payment" has the meaning given in section 60 of the Act;

"contractor" has the meaning given in section 57 of the Act;

"construction contract" has the meaning given in section 57 of the Act;

"construction operations" has the meaning given in section 74 of the Act;

"electronic communications" has the meaning given in section 132(10) of the Finance Act 1999;

"employer reference" means the combination of letters, numbers or both used by Her Majesty's Revenue and Customs to identify an employer for the purpose of the Income Tax (Pay As You Earn) Regulations 2003;

"ICTA" means the Income and Corporation Taxes Act 1988;

"ITEPA" means the Income Tax (Earnings and Pensions) Act 2003; "notice" means notice in writing;

"PAYE Regulations" means the Income Tax (Pay As You Earn) Regulations 2003;

["SSC Regulations" means the Social Security (Contributions) Regulations 2001;][1]

["Student Loan Regulations" means the Education (Student Loans) (Repayment) Regulations 2009 or, in Northern Ireland, the Education (Student Loans) (Repayment) Regulations (Northern Ireland) 2009;][3]

"sub-contractor" has the meaning given in section 58 of the Act;

. . . [2]

"tax month" means the period beginning on the 6th day of a calendar month and ending on the 5th day of the following calendar month;

"tax year" means a year for which any Act provides for income tax to be charged;

"tax period" means—

(*a*) tax quarter if regulation 8 (quarterly tax periods) applies, or (*b*) tax month, in every other case; "tax quarter" means any of the following (inclusive) periods—

6th April to 5th July, 6th July to 5th October, 6th October to 5th January, and 6th January to 5th April;

"TMA" means the Taxes Management Act 1970;

["tribunal" means the First-tier Tribunal or, where determined by or under Tribunal Procedure Rules, the Upper Tribunal.][1]

Amendments—[1] Definitions of "combined amount", "SSC Regulations" inserted by the Income Tax (Construction Industry Scheme) (Amendment) Regulations, SI 2008/740 regs 2, 3 with effect from 6 April 2008.

[2] Entry "tax appeal Commissioners" revoked and entry for "tribunal" inserted, by the Transfer of Tribunal Functions and Revenue and Customs Appeals Order, SI 2009/56 art 3, Sch 2 paras 137, 138 with effect from 1 April 2009.

[3] Definition of "Student Loan Regulations" substituted by the Income Tax (Construction Industry Scheme) (Amendment) Regulations, SI 2012/820 regs 2, 3 with effect from 6 April 2012.

[4] In definition of "approved method of electronic communications", words inserted by the Income Tax (Construction Industry Scheme) (Amendment) Regulations, SI 2016/348 reg 2(1), (2) with effect in relation to the tax year 2016–17 and subsequent tax years.

PART 2
CONTRACTORS

3 Multiple contractors

(1) A contractor may elect, for the purposes of these Regulations, to be treated as different contractors in relation to different groups of sub-contractors.

(2) Where the contractor makes an election these Regulations apply as if—

(*a*) in respect of each group the contractor were a different contractor; and

(*b*) each group constituted all the sub-contractors to whom the contractor makes payments under contracts relating to construction operations.

(3) While an election is in force, a contractor must allocate any new sub-contractors to one of the groups.

(4) An election must be made by notice to an officer of Revenue and Customs containing—

(*a*) such information as may be necessary to identify the groups of sub-contractors, and

(*b*) a certificate that the contractor makes no payments under contracts relating to construction operations other than to sub-contractors in the groups so identified.

(5) A contractor must, subject to paragraph (6), make an election before the beginning of the tax year for which it is to have effect.

(6) A contractor who acquires the whole or part of any business of another contractor may, within 90 days of the acquisition, elect—

(*a*) to be treated as a different contractor in relation to the acquired sub-contractors, or two or more different contractors in relation to groups of the acquired sub-contractors, whether or not an election is already in force in respect of the existing sub-contractors, or

(*b*) to add some or all of the acquired sub-contractors to existing groups of sub-contractors in respect of whom an election is already in force,

and such election has effect for the tax year in which the acquisition takes place.

(7) In paragraph (6)—"business" includes any trade, concern or undertaking; "acquired sub-contractor" means a sub-contractor who contracted with the acquired business.

(8) An election continues in effect until revoked by notice given to an officer of Revenue and Customs.

(9) A notice of revocation must be given before the beginning of the tax year for which the election is to be revoked, but the revocation of an election does not prevent the making of a new election for that or a later tax year.

(10) An election which has not yet come into effect may be revoked at any time before the beginning of the tax year for which it is to have effect.

Commentary—*Simon's Taxes* **E5.542A**.

4 Monthly return

(1) A return must be made to the Commissioners for Her Majesty's Revenue and Customs in a document or format provided or approved by the Commissioners—

(*a*) not later than 14 days after the end of every tax month, by a contractor making contract payments or payments which would be contract payments but for section 60(4) of the Act (contract payments: exceptions), and

(*b*) not later than 14 days after the end of the tax month following the appointed day, by a contractor who has made a payment in the 12 months preceding the appointed day which would be a contract payment or a payment which would be a contract payment but for section 60(4) of the Act if made after the appointed day.

(2) The return under paragraph (1) must contain the following information—

(*a*) the contractor's name,

(*b*) the contractor's unique taxpayer reference (UTR) and Accounts' Office reference, (*c*) the tax month to which the return relates, and

(*d*) in respect of each sub-contractor to whom, or to whose nominee, payments under construction contracts were made by the contractor during that month,—

(i) the sub-contractor's name;

(ii) the sub-contractor's national insurance number (NINO) or company registration number (CRN), if known; and

(iii) the information specified in paragraph (3).

(3) The information specified is—

(*a*) if the sub-contractor is registered for gross payment—

(i) the sub-contractor's unique taxpayer reference (UTR), and

(ii) the total amount of payments which would be contract payments but for section 60(4) of the Act (contract payments: exceptions) made by the contractor to the sub-contractor during the tax month;

(*b*) if the sub-contractor is registered for payment under deduction—

(i) the sub-contractor's unique taxpayer reference (UTR),

(ii) the total amount of contract payments made by the contractor to the sub-contractor during the tax month,

(iii) the total amount included in those payments which the contractor is satisfied represents the direct cost to any person other than the contractor of materials used or to be used in carrying out the construction contract to which the contract payment relates, and

(iv) the total amount deducted from the payments mentioned in paragraph (3)(*b*)(ii) under section 61 of the Act (deduction on account of tax from contract payments);

(*c*) if the sub-contractor is not registered for gross payment or payment under deduction—

(i) the sub-contractor's unique taxpayer reference (UTR), if known,

(ii) the total amount of contract payments made by the contractor to the sub-contractor during the tax month,

(iii) the total amount included in those payments which the contractor is satisfied represents the direct cost to any person other than the contractor of materials used or to be used in carrying out the construction contract to which the contract payment relates,

(iv) the total amount deducted from the payments mentioned in paragraph (3)(*c*)(ii) under section 61 of the Act, and

(v) the verification reference for higher rate deduction.

[(4) The return must be transmitted to the Commissioners for Her Majesty's Revenue and Customs using an approved method of electronic communications unless paragraph (4A) applies or where a direction has been given under paragraph (4B).

(4A) This paragraph applies where a contractor is—

(*a*) an individual who is a practising member of a religious society or order whose beliefs are incompatible with the use of electronic communications,

(*b*) a partnership, if all the partners fall within sub-paragraph (*a*), or

(*c*) a company if all the directors and the company secretary fall within sub-paragraph (*a*).

(4B) Where—

(*a*) a contractor considers that it is not reasonably practicable for that contractor to transmit the monthly returns using an approved method of electronic communications, and

(*b*) it is the contractor which delivers the return (and not some other person on the contractor's behalf),

the Commissioners for Her Majesty's Revenue and Customs may, by a specific direction, authorise that contractor to transmit the return by a method other than an approved method of electronic communications.][3]

(5) The return must include a declaration by the person making the return—

(*a*) that none of the contracts to which the return relates is a contract of employment;

(*b*) indicating whether he has complied with the requirements of regulation 6 (verification etc of registration status of sub-contractor) in the case of each person to whom a payment to which the return relates is made; and

(*c*) that the return contains all the information, particulars and supporting information required by this regulation to be included in the return, and such information, particulars and supporting information are complete and accurate to the best of the contractor's knowledge and belief.

(6) If the return is not transmitted electronically, it must be signed by the contractor or a person duly authorised by the contractor to make the return.

(7) The contractor must make and keep such records as will enable him to comply with this regulation.

(8) The contractor must give the following information in writing to the sub-contractor to whom it relates not later than 14 days after the end of the tax month either in respect of the total payments made in that month or in respect of each payment made in that month—

(*a*) if the sub-contractor is registered for payment under deduction—
(i) the contractor's name,
(ii) the contractor's employer's reference,
(iii) the tax month to which the payments relate or the date of the payment,
(iv) the sub-contractor's name,
(v) the sub-contractor's unique taxpayer reference (UTR),
(vi) the total amount of contract payments made by the contractor to the sub-contractor during the tax month,
(vii) the total amount included in those payments which the contractor is satisfied represents the direct cost to any person other than the contractor of materials used or to be used in carrying out the construction contract to which the contract payment relates, and
(viii) the total amount deducted from the payments mentioned in paragraph (vi) under section 61 of the Act; and

(*b*) if the sub-contractor is not registered under Chapter 3 of the Act, the verification reference.

(9) The information required under paragraph (8) may be given by means of electronic communications if—
(*a*) the contractor has indicated to the sub-contractor that he intends to use electronic communications for the purposes of giving this information;
(*b*) the sub-contractor has consented to information being given by the contractor by means of electronic communications, and that consent has not been withdrawn;
(*c*) the information is given in an electronic format—
(i) in which the statement may be stored; and
(ii) which permits a paper copy of the information contained in the statement to be printed.

(10), (11) . . . [2]

(12) Subject to paragraph (13), section 98A of TMA (special penalties in the case of certain returns) applies to the requirements in—
(*a*) paragraph (1),
(*b*) paragraph (3)(*b*),
(*c*) paragraph (3)(*c*),
(*d*) paragraph (10).

(13) A penalty under section 98A of TMA in relation to a failure to make a return in accordance with paragraphs (1) or (10) arises for each month (or part of a month) during which the failure continues after the 19th day of the sixth month following the appointed day[, but only arises where that failure relates to a return that must be made not later than 19th October 2011][1].

Commentary—*Simon's Taxes* **E5.542B**.

Amendments—[1] In para (13), words inserted by the Finance (No 3) Act 2010, Schedule 10 and the Finance Act 2009, Schedule 55 and Sections 101 to 103 (Appointed Day, etc) (Construction Industry Scheme) Order, SI 2011/2391 art 3(3) with effect from 6 October 2011.

[2] Paras 10, 11 revoked by the Income Tax (Construction Industry Scheme) (Amendment) Regulations, SI 2015/429 reg 2(1), (2) with effect from 6 April 2015.

[3] Paras (4)–(4B) substituted for previous para (4) by the Income Tax (Construction Industry Scheme) (Amendment) Regulations, SI 2016/348 reg 2(1), (3) with effect in relation to the tax year 2016–17 and subsequent tax years.

5 Scheme representative

(1) A company ("the appointing company") which makes payments under construction contracts may appoint another company in the same group ("a scheme representative") to act on its behalf in connection with any such requirements imposed on the company by these Regulations as the appointment specifies.

(2) An appointment under paragraph (1) shall not have effect until the appointing company has notified the Commissioners for Her Majesty's Revenue and Customs.

(3) A scheme representative must make returns and payments under these Regulations in the name of the appointing company.

(4) The appointing company remains liable in relation to all the requirements imposed on it by these Regulations notwithstanding any appointment under paragraph (1).

(5) For the purposes of paragraph (1) section 413(3)(*a*) of ICTA applies to determine whether two companies are in the same group.

Commentary—*Simon's Taxes* **E5.542C**.

6 Verification etc of registration status of sub-contractor and nominee

(1) A contractor must verify with the Commissioners for Her Majesty's Revenue and Customs whether a person to whom he is proposing to make—
(*a*) a contract payment, or
(*b*) a payment which would be a contract payment but for section 60(4) of the Act (contract payments: exceptions), and, where that person has appointed a nominee, his nominee, are registered for gross payment, for payment under deduction or is not registered under Chapter 3 of the Act. This is subject to paragraph (3).

(2) For the purpose of verification the contractor must provide—

(*a*) his name, unique taxpayer reference (UTR), accounts office reference and employer's reference, and

(*b*) in relation to the person to whom he is proposing to make the payment and, where that person has appointed a nominee, his nominee—

(i) if that person or nominee is an individual, his name, unique taxpayer reference (UTR) and national insurance number;

(ii) if that person or nominee is a partner in a firm, the name of the firm and that partner, the unique taxpayer reference (UTR) of the firm, and if the partner is an individual his unique taxpayer reference (UTR) or national insurance number or if the partner is a company the unique taxpayer reference (UTR) or the company registration number;

(iii) if that person or nominee is a company, the name of the company, unique taxpayer reference (UTR) and the company registration number.

[(2A) The contractor must provide the information mentioned in paragraph (2) using an approved method of electronic communications unless paragraph (2B) applies or where a direction has been given under paragraph (2C).

(2B) This paragraph applies where a contractor is—

(*a*) an individual who is a practising member of a religious society or order whose beliefs are incompatible with the use of electronic communications,

(*b*) a partnership, if all the partners fall within sub-paragraph (*a*), or

(*c*) a company if all the directors and the company secretary fall within sub-paragraph (*a*).

(2C) Where—

(*a*) a contractor considers that it is not reasonably practicable for that contractor to provide the information using an approved method of electronic communications, and

(*b*) it is the contractor which provides the information (and not some other person on the contractor's behalf),

the Commissioners for Her Majesty's Revenue and Customs may, by a specific direction, authorise that contractor to provide the information by a method other than an approved method of electronic communications.][1]

(3) A contractor may not verify under paragraph (1) unless the contractor has a contract with the sub-contractor or has formally accepted a tender for work under a contract.

(4) A contractor need not verify if—

(*a*) the person to whom he is proposing to make the payment has been included in a return under regulation 4 in the current or previous two tax years;

(*b*) the payment is made within two years of the appointed day, if the person to whom he is proposing to make the payment has been included in a return under regulation 4 or a return under regulation 40A of the Income Tax (Sub-contractors in the Construction Industry) Regulations 1993 for the current or previous two years;

(*c*) the contractor is a company and the person to whom he is proposing to make the payment has been included in a return under regulation 4 or a return under regulation 40A of the Income Tax (Sub-contractors in the Construction Industry) Regulations 1993 for the current or previous two tax years made by another company in the same group;

(*d*) the contractor has made an election under regulation 3 and the person to whom he is proposing to make the payment has been included in a return under regulation 4 in the current or previous two years in respect of a different group of sub-contractors in relation to which the contractor is treated as a different contractor;

(*e*) the contractor acquired the contract under which the payment is to be made in a transfer of a business as a going concern where the transferor was within one of paragraphs (*a*) to (*d*) and the contractor has notified the Commissioners for Her Majesty's Revenue and Customs of the transfer.

(5) For the purposes of paragraph (4)(*c*) section 413(3)(*a*) of ICTA applies to determine whether two companies are in the same group.

(6) The Commissioners for Her Majesty's Revenue and Customs must notify a contractor that—

(*a*) a person registered for gross payment has become registered for payment under deduction or has ceased to be registered under Chapter 3 of the Act, or

(*b*) a person registered for payment under deduction has become registered for gross payment or has ceased to be registered under Chapter 3 of the Act, if a payment to that person has been included in the contractor's return under regulation 4, or a return under regulation 40A of the Income Tax (Sub-contractors in the Construction Industry) Regulations 1993, in the current or previous two tax years or that person has been verified under paragraph (1) by the contractor in that period.

(7) A contractor is entitled to assume that—

(*a*) a person verified or notified as being registered for gross payment, or

(*b*) a person verified or notified as being registered for payment under deduction, has not subsequently ceased to be so registered.

Commentary—*Simon's Taxes* **E5.542D**.

Amendments—[1] Paras (2A)–(2C) inserted by the Income Tax (Construction Industry Scheme) (Amendment) Regulations, SI 2016/348 reg 2(1), (4) with effect in relation to the tax year 2017–18 and subsequent tax years.

PART 3
PAYMENT AND RECOVERY OF AMOUNTS DEDUCTED UNDER SECTION 61

7 Payment, due date for payment of amounts deducted and receipts

(1) A contractor must pay to the Commissioners for Her Majesty's Revenue and Customs all amounts he was liable under section 61 of the Act to deduct on account of tax from contract payments made by him during that tax period—

(*a*) within 17 days after the end of the tax period, where payment is made by an approved method of electronic communications, or

(*b*) within 14 days after the end of the tax period, in any other case.

(2) The Commissioners for Her Majesty's Revenue and Customs must give a receipt to the contractor for the total amount paid under paragraph (1) if asked.

(3) But no separate receipt for the total amount paid under paragraph (1) need be given if a receipt is given for the total of—

(*a*) the amount paid under paragraph (1),

(*b*) any tax deducted under the [PAYE Regulations][1], and

(*c*) any earnings-related contributions (as defined by regulation 1(2) of the Social Security (Contributions) Regulations 2001,

paid at the same time.

Commentary—*Simon's Taxes* **E5.547A**.

Amendments—[1] Words in para (3)(*b*) substituted by the Income Tax (Construction Industry Scheme) (Amendment) Regulations, SI 2008/740 regs 2, 4 with effect from 6 April 2008.

[7A (1) Payment of an amount that is less than the amount which the contractor was liable to pay to the Commissioners for Her Majesty's Revenue and Customs under regulation 7(1), will, for the purposes of paragraph 6(2) of Schedule 56 to the Finance Act 2009 (amounts of penalty: PAYE and CIS), be treated as a payment of the full amount if the difference between the full amount and the amount paid is no more than £100 ("the tolerance"), but this is subject to paragraph (2).

(2) If a contractor makes a payment under regulation 7(1) and the total sum paid to Her Majesty's Revenue and Customs for the tax period includes not only that payment but also one or more of—

(*a*) any tax deducted under the PAYE Regulations,

(*b*) any earnings-related contributions (as defined by regulation 1(2) of the SSC Regulations, or

(*c*) any repayment due under the Student Loans Regulations 2009,

the tolerance is applied to the total sum paid to the Commissioners for Her Majesty's Revenue and Customs for the tax period to which the payments relate.][1]

Amendments—[1] Regulation 7A inserted by the Income Tax (Pay As You Earn) and the Income Tax (Construction Industry Scheme) (Amendment) Regulations, SI 2014/472 reg 21 with effect in relation to a payment made in relation to the tax year 2014–15 and subsequent tax years.

8 Quarterly tax periods

(1) This regulation applies so that the tax period is a tax quarter if a contractor—

(*a*) has reasonable grounds for believing that the average monthly amount will be less than £1,500, and

(*b*) chooses to pay tax quarterly.

(2) "The average monthly amount" is the average, for tax months falling within the current tax year, of the amounts found by the formula—

$$(P + N + L + S) - (SP + CD)$$

(3) In paragraph (2)—

P is the amount which would be payable to an officer of Revenue and Customs under regulation [67G or][1] 68 of the PAYE Regulations (periodic payments to and recoveries from the Revenue);

N is the amount which would be payable to an officer of Revenue and Customs under the SSCBA and the SSC Regulations disregarding any amount of secondary Class 1 contributions in respect of which liability has been transferred to the employed earner by an election made jointly by the employed earner and the secondary contributor for the purposes of paragraph 3B(1) of Schedule 1 to the SSCBA (transfer of liability to be borne by earner)(*a*);

L is the amount which would be payable to an officer of Revenue and Customs under regulation [54(1) or, in Northern Ireland, 49(1)][3] of the Student Loans Regulations (payment of repayments deducted to the Commissioners for Her Majesty's Revenue and Customs) disregarding the reduction referred to in paragraph (3) of [those regulations][3];

S is the amount which would be payable by the contractor to the Commissioners for Her Majesty's Revenue and Customs under regulation 7 during the tax month;
SP is the amount which would be payable by the contractor to employees by way of statutory sick pay, statutory maternity pay, [statutory paternity pay][4][, statutory shared parental pay][3] and statutory adoption pay under the SSCBA; and
CD is—

(*a*) if the contractor is a company, the amount which others would deduct from payments to it, in its position as a sub-contractor, under section 61 of the Act;

(*b*) in any other case, nil.

(4) In this regulation—
"employed earner" has the same meaning as in the SSCBA;
"SSCBA" means the Social Security Contributions and Benefit Act 1992 or, in Northern Ireland, the Social Security Contributions and Benefit (Northern Ireland) Act 1992;
. . .[1]

Commentary—*Simon's Taxes* **E5.547B**.

Amendments—[1] In para (4), definitions of "SSC Regulations" and "Student Loan Regulations" revoked by the Income Tax (Construction Industry Scheme) (Amendment) Regulations, SI 2008/740 regs 2, 5 with effect from 6 April 2008.

[2] In para (3), words in value for SP substituted by the Income Tax (Construction Industry Scheme) (Amendment No 2) Regulations, SI 2010/2495, regs 2, 3 with effect from 14 November 2010.

[3] In para (3), in definition of "P", words inserted, and in definition of "L" words substituted, by the Income Tax (Construction Industry Scheme) (Amendment) Regulations, SI 2012/820 regs 2, 4 with effect from 6 April 2012.

[4] In para (3), words substituted and inserted by the Statutory Payment Schemes (Electronic Communications) (Amendment) Regulations, SI 2015/125 reg 4(1), (2) with effect from 5 April 2015..

9 Recovery from sub-contractor of amount not deducted by contractor

(1) This regulation applies if—

(*a*) it appears to an officer of Revenue and Customs that the deductible amount exceeds the amount actually deducted, and

(*b*) condition A or B is met.

(2) In this regulation—
"the deductible amount" is the amount which a contractor was liable to deduct on account of tax from a contract payment under section 61 of the Act in a tax period;
"the amount actually deducted" is the amount actually deducted by the contractor on account of tax from a contract payment under section 61 of the Act during that tax period;
"the excess" means the amount by which the deductible amount exceeds the amount actually deducted.

(3) Condition A is that the contractor satisfies an officer of Revenue and Customs—

(*a*) that he took reasonable care to comply with section 61 of the Act and these Regulations, and

(*b*) that—

(i) the failure to deduct the excess was due to an error made in good faith, or

(ii) he held a genuine belief that section 61 of the Act did not apply to the payment.

(4) Condition B is that—

(*a*) an officer of Revenue and Customs is satisfied that the person to whom the contractor made the contract payments to which section 61 of the Act applies either—

(i) was not chargeable to income tax or corporation tax in respect of those payments, or

(ii) has made a return of his income or profits in accordance with section 8 of TMA (personal return) or paragraph 3 of Schedule 18 to the Finance Act 1998(*a*) (company tax return), in which those payments were taken into account, and paid the income tax and Class 4 contributions due or corporation tax due in respect of such income or profits; and

(*b*) the contractor requests that the Commissioners for Her Majesty's Revenue and Customs make a direction under paragraph (5).

(5) An officer of Revenue and Customs may direct that the contractor is not liable to pay the excess to the Commissioners for Her Majesty's Revenue and Customs.

(6) If condition A is not met an officer of Revenue and Customs may refuse to make a direction under paragraph (5) by giving notice to the contractor ("the refusal notice") stating—

(*a*) the grounds for the refusal, and

(*b*) the date on which the refusal notice was issued.

(7) A contractor may appeal against the refusal notice—

(*a*) by notice to an officer of Revenue and Customs,

(*b*) within 30 days of the refusal notice,

(*c*) specifying the grounds of the appeal.

(8) For the purpose of paragraph (7) the grounds of appeal are that—

(*a*) that the contractor took reasonable care to comply with section 61 of the Act and these Regulations, and

(*b*) that—

(i) the failure to deduct the excess was due to an error made in good faith, or

(ii) the contractor held a genuine belief that section 61 of the Act did not apply to the payment.

(9) If on an appeal under paragraph (7) [that is notified to the tribunal it appears][1] that the refusal notice should not have been issued [the tribunal][1] may direct that an officer of Revenue and Customs make a direction under paragraph (5) in an amount the [tribunal determines][1] is the excess for one or more tax periods falling within the relevant year.

(10) If a contractor has deducted an amount under section 61 of the Act, but has not paid it to the Commissioners for Her Majesty's Revenue and Customs as required by regulation 7 (payment, due date etc. and receipts), that amount is treated, for the purposes of determining the liability of any sub-contractor in respect of whose liability the sum was deducted, as having been paid to the Commissioners for Her Majesty's Revenue and Customs at the time required by regulation 8 (quarterly tax periods).

Commentary—*Simon's Taxes* **E5.547D**.

Amendments—[1] In para (9), words substituted by the Transfer of Tribunal Functions and Revenue and Customs Appeals Order, SI 2009/56 art 3, Sch 2 paras 137, 139 with effect from 1 April 2009.

10 Return and certificate if amount may be unpaid

(1) This regulation applies if, 17 days or more after the end of a tax period, condition [A, B or C][1] is met.

(2) Condition A is that—

(*a*) a contractor has not paid any amount under regulation 7 for that tax period, and

(*b*) an officer of Revenue and Customs is unaware of the amount (if any) which the contractor is liable to pay for that tax period.

(3) Condition B is that—

(*a*) a contractor has paid an amount under regulation 7 for that tax period, but

(*b*) an officer of Revenue and Customs is not satisfied, that it is the full amount which the contractor is liable to pay for that period.

[(3A) Condition C is that—

(*a*) the contractor has made a return under regulation 4 showing the amount which the contractor is liable to pay under regulation 7 for that tax period, but

(*b*) the contractor has not paid the full amount shown in the return.][1]

(4) [If condition A or B is met][1] an officer of Revenue and Customs may give notice to the contractor requiring the contractor within 14 days of the issue of the notice to deliver a return showing the amount which the contractor is liable to pay under regulation 7 in respect of the tax period.

(5) [If—

(*a*) the notice extends to, or

(*b*) condition C is met in, two][1] or more consecutive tax periods in a tax year,

this regulation has effect as if they were one tax period.

(6) On receiving a return made by the contractor under paragraph (4) [or if condition C is met][1], an officer of Revenue and Customs may prepare a certificate showing the amount which the contractor is liable to pay for the tax period and how much (if any) of that amount remains unpaid.

(7) Regulation 57 (certificate that sum due) deals with the use of certificates as evidence that sums are due and unpaid.

Commentary—*Simon's Taxes* **E5.547E**.

Amendments[1] Words in paras (1), (5) substituted, para (3A) inserted, and words in paras (4), (6) inserted, by the Income Tax (Construction Industry Scheme) (Amendment) Regulations, SI 2007/672 regs 2, 3 with effect from 26 March 2007.

11 Notice and certificate if amount may be unpaid

(1) This regulation applies if, 17 days or more after the end of a tax period, condition A or B is met.

(2) Condition A is that—

(*a*) a contractor has not paid any amount under regulation 7 for that tax period, and

(*b*) an officer of Revenue and Customs has reason to believe that the contractor is liable to pay an amount for that tax period.

(3) Condition B is that—

(*a*) a contractor has paid an amount under regulation 7 for that tax period, but

(*b*) an officer of Revenue and Customs is not satisfied, after seeking the contractor's explanation, that it is the full amount which the contractor is liable to pay for that period.

(4) An officer of Revenue and Customs, [whether of deductions under section 61 of the Act (deductions on account of tax from contract payments) or of combined amounts][1], may—

(*a*) specify, to the best of his judgment, the amount [due under regulation 7 or a combined amount][1] which he considers the contractor is liable to pay, and

(*b*) serve notice on the contractor requiring payment of [the specified][1] amount within 7 days of the issue of the notice ("the notice period").

(5) If condition A is met an officer of Revenue and Customs may give notice under paragraph (4) which extends to two or more consecutive tax periods in a tax year and these Regulations have effect as if they were the latest tax period specified in the notice.

(6) If, during the notice period, the contractor—

[(*a*) claims that any payment made in respect of the tax period specified in the notice is or includes the full amount the contractor is liable to pay under regulation 7, but][1]

(*b*) does not satisfy an officer of Revenue and Customs that this is the case,

the contractor may require an officer of Revenue and Customs to inspect the contractor's documents and records as if the contractor had been required to produce those documents in accordance with regulation 51 (inspection of records of contractors and sub-contractors).

(7) If there is an inspection by virtue of paragraph (6), regulation 51 applies to that inspection and the notice given by an officer of Revenue and Customs under paragraph (4) must be disregarded.

(8) If the amount specified in the notice, or any part of it, is not paid during the notice period—

(*a*) the amount unpaid is treated as[, or including,][1] an amount which the contractor was liable to pay for that tax period under regulation 7, and

(*b*) an officer of Revenue and Customs may prepare a certificate showing how much of that amount remains unpaid.

(9) But paragraph (8) does not apply if during the notice period—

(*a*) the contractor pays the full amount which the contractor is liable to pay under regulation 7 for that tax period, or

(*b*) the contractor satisfies an officer of Revenue and Customs that no amount, or no further amount, is due for that tax period.

(10) Paragraph (11) applies if the contractor pays an amount [of deductions under section 61 of the Act, whether separately or as part of a combined amount,][1] certified under this regulation which exceeds the amount the contractor would have been liable to pay in respect of that tax period apart from this regulation.

(11) The contractor is entitled to set off the excess [of deductions under section 61 of the Act][1] against any amount which the contractor is liable to pay under regulation 7 for any subsequent tax periods in the tax year.

(12) Regulation 57 deals with the use of certificates as evidence that sums are due and unpaid.

Commentary—*Simon's Taxes* **E5.547E.**

Amendments—[1] Words in para (4) inserted and substituted, para (6)(*a*) substituted, and words in paras (8)(*a*), (10), (11) inserted, by the Income Tax (Construction Industry Scheme) (Amendment) Regulations, SI 2008/740 regs 2, 6 with effect from 6 April 2008.

12 Certificate after inspection of records of contractors and sub-contractors

(1) This regulation applies if there is an inspection of a contractor's documents and records under regulation 51.

(2) An officer of Revenue and Customs may, by reference to the information obtained from the inspection, prepare a certificate showing—

(*a*) the amount which it appears that the contractor is liable to pay for the tax years or tax periods covered by the inspection; and

(*b*) any amount which remains unpaid.

(3) Regulation 57 deals with the use of certificates as evidence that sums are due and unpaid.

Commentary—*Simon's Taxes* **E5.547F.**

13 Determination of amounts payable by contractor and appeal against determination

(1) This regulation applies if—

(*a*) there is a dispute between a contractor and a sub-contractor as to—

(i) whether a payment is made under a construction contract, or

(ii) the amount, if any, deductible by the contractor under section 61 of the Act from a contract payment to a sub-contractor or his nominee, or

(*b*) an officer of Revenue and Customs has reason to believe, as a result of an inspection under regulation 51 or otherwise, that there may be an amount payable for a tax year under these Regulations by a contractor that has not been paid to them, or

(*c*) an officer of Revenue and Customs considers it necessary in the circumstances.

(2) An officer of Revenue and Customs may determine the amount which to the best of his judgment a contractor is liable to pay under these Regulations, and serve notice of his determination on the contractor.

(3) A determination under this regulation must not include amounts in respect of which a direction under regulation 9(5) has been made and directions under that regulation do not apply to amounts determined under this regulation.

(4) A determination under this regulation may—

(*a*) cover the amount payable by the contractor under section 61 of the Act for any one or more tax periods in a tax year, and

(*b*) extend to the whole of that amount, or to such part of it as is payable in respect of—

(i) a class or classes of sub-contractors specified in the notice of determination (without naming the individual sub-contractors), or

(ii) one or more named sub-contractors specified in the notice.

(5) A determination under this regulation is subject to Parts 4, 5[, 5A][2] and 6 of TMA (assessment, appeals, collection and recovery) as if—

(*a*) the determination were an assessment, and

(*b*) the amount determined were income tax charged on the contractor,

and those Parts of that Act apply accordingly with any necessary modifications, except that the amount determined is due and payable 14 days after the determination is made.

(6) If paragraph (1)(*a*) applies and an officer of Revenue and Customs does not make a determination under paragraph (2), either the contractor or the sub-contractor may on giving notice to an officer of Revenue and Customs, apply to the [tribunal][1] to determine the matter.

(7) For the purposes of paragraph 3(1)(a) of Schedule 3 to TMA (rules for assigning proceedings to General Commissioners), the relevant place for an appeal against a determination under this regulation is the place where the determination was made.[1]

(8) If paragraph (1)(*a*) applies—

(*a*) the contractor must make the deduction required by section 61 of the Act from the contract payment or the part of the contract payment, to which the dispute relates, and the amount so deducted is treated as a sum which he is liable to pay to the Commissioners for Her Majesty's Revenue and Customs under these Regulations; and

(*b*) any amount which, on a final determination of the dispute, is shown not to have been so payable is, except where regulation 56 (application by the Commissioners for Her Majesty's Revenue and Customs of sums deducted under section 61 of the Act) applies, treated as an overpayment of income tax or corporation tax by the sub-contractor.

Commentary—*Simon's Taxes* **E5.547G**.

Amendments—[1] In para (6), words substituted and para (7) revoked, by the Transfer of Tribunal Functions and Revenue and Customs Appeals Order, SI 2009/56 art 3, Sch 2 paras 137, 140 with effect from 1 April 2009.

[2] Reference inserted in para (5) by the Income Tax (Construction Industry Scheme) (Amendment) Regulations, SI 2010/717, regs 2, 3, with effect in relation to the tax year 2010–11 and subsequent tax years.

14 Interest on amounts overdue

. . .

Amendments—Regulation 14 revoked by the Finance Act 2009, Sections 101 and 102 (Interest on Late Payments and Repayments), Appointed Days and Consequential Provisions Order, SI 2014/992 art 11(*a*), with effect in relation to payments due and payable in respect of the tax year 2014–15 and subsequent tax years.

15 Interest on amount overpaid

. . .

Amendments—Regulation 15 revoked by the Finance Act 2009, Sections 101 and 102 (Interest on Late Payments and Repayments), Appointed Days and Consequential Provisions Order, SI 2014/992 art 11(*b*), with effect in relation to payments due and payable in respect of the tax year 2014–15 and subsequent tax years.

16 Recovery of amount unpaid and interest

(1) In this regulation, "the unpaid amount" means any amount or interest which a contractor is liable to pay under regulation 10(6), 11(8), 12(2)(*b*) or 13(2).

(2) Part 6 of TMA (collection and recovery) applies to the recovery of the unpaid amount [or combined amount and any interest on it][1] as if it were income tax charged on the contractor but with the modification indicated in paragraph (3).

(3) Summary proceedings for the recovery of the unpaid amount may be brought in England and Wales or Northern Ireland at any time before the end of the period which applies for the purposes of the regulation, as shown in Table 1.

1. Regulation	*2. Period*
Regulation 10(6), 11(8) and 13(2)	(*a*) 12 months after the date on which the unpaid amount [or combined amount and any interest on it][1] became payable, or
	(*b*) if a return has been required under regulation 10, 12 months after the date of the delivery of that return to the Commissioners for Her Majesty's Revenue and Customs.
Regulation 12(2)	12 months after the date of the certificate.

(4) Proceedings against a contractor may be brought for the recovery of the unpaid amount [or unpaid combined amount and any interest on it][1] without distinguishing the amounts which the employer is liable to pay in respect of each sub-contractor and without specifying the sub-contractor in question.

(5) The unpaid amount [or unpaid combined amount and any interest on it][1] is one cause of action or one matter of complaint for the purposes of proceedings under sections 65, 66 and 67 of TMA (magistrates' courts, county courts and inferior courts in Scotland).

(6) But paragraphs (4) and (5) do not prevent the bringing of separate proceedings for the recovery of each of the amounts which the contractor is liable to pay for any tax period in respect of each of the sub-contractors.

Commentary—*Simon's Taxes* **E5.547J**.

Amendments—[1] Words in paras (2)–(5) inserted by the Income Tax (Construction Industry Scheme) (Amendment) Regulations, SI 2008/740 regs 2, 7 with effect from 6 April 2008.

17 In-year repayments of provisional excess credit

(1) This regulation applies if—

(*a*) a sub-contractor is an individual or a firm,

(*b*) an application is made by that individual or a partner in the firm ("the applicant") to the Commissioners for Her Majesty's Revenue and Customs in accordance with paragraph (4),

(*c*) any income tax and Class 4 contributions due from the applicant, or the sub-contractor, on the applicant's share of the annual profits or gains arising or accruing from the trade, profession or vocation of the sub-contractor, for any earlier year, have been paid, and

(*d*) all relevant tax payment vouchers issued to the sub-contractor under regulation 7 of the Income Tax (Sub-contractors in the Construction Industry) Regulations 1993 in relation to payments made before the appointed day are produced to the Commissioners for Her Majesty's Revenue and Customs.

(2) If the Commissioners for Her Majesty's Revenue and Customs are satisfied by evidence produced by the applicant that A exceeds B, the applicant shall, subject to paragraph (5), be entitled to repayment of the excess by the Commissioners for Her Majesty's Revenue and Customs.

(3) In paragraph (2)—

A is the amount of the applicant's share of the total of sums deducted under section 61 of the Act from contract payments made to the sub-contractor and paid to the Commissioners for Her Majesty's Revenue and Customs, in so much of the year as has elapsed at the date when the application is made; and

B is the aggregate of the following amounts—

(*a*) the income tax and any Class 4 contributions payable (whether or not yet due and payable) by the applicant, on his share of the annual profits or gains arising from the trade, profession or vocation of the sub-contractor which are chargeable to tax for the whole of that year, after deducting any cumulative entitlement of the applicant at the date of the application to an allowance under section 257 or 257A of ICTA (personal allowance and married couple's allowance);

(*b*) the income tax and any Class 4 contributions payable (whether or not yet due and payable) by the applicant, on any income arising during so much of the year as has elapsed at the date of the application, from which income tax has not been deducted at source, within the meaning given by section 59B(7) of TMA (payment of income tax and capital gains tax); and

(*c*) any sum due and payable by the sub-contractor under ICTA or TMA, and, without prejudice to the generality of the foregoing, this includes any sums deducted by the sub-contractor in the capacity of a contractor, under section 61 of the Act.

(4) An application under this regulation must be made to the Commissioners for Her Majesty's Revenue and Customs containing a declaration that all of the information given in relation to paragraph (3) is correctly stated to the best of the knowledge and belief of the applicant, and where the applicant is a partner in a firm, the form shall be signed by all the partners in the firm who are individuals and, where the partner is a company, by the secretary or a director of the company.

(5) No repayment under this regulation shall be made after the end of the year to which the application relates.

Commentary—*Simon's Taxes* **E5.547K**.

PART 4

PAYMENTS EXCEPTED FROM SECTION 60

18 Small payments

(1) A payment under a construction contract is not a contract payment if—

(*a*) the conditions prescribed in paragraph (2) in relation to the person making the payment are satisfied, and

(*b*) the condition prescribed in paragraph (3) in relation to the payment is satisfied.

(2) The conditions prescribed in relation to the person making the payment are that—

(*a*) the person is one to whom any of paragraphs (*b*) to (l) of section 59(1) of the Act (contractors) applies, and

(*b*) the person has been approved by the Commissioners for Her Majesty's Revenue and Customs for the purposes of this regulation.

(3) The condition prescribed in relation to the payment is that the payment is not one made under a construction contract in respect of which the total payments so made (excluding the direct cost of materials) exceed or are likely to exceed £1000.

Commentary—*Simon's Taxes* **E5.545A**.

19 Work carried out on land owned by person to whom payment is made

(1) A payment under a construction contract is not a contract payment if—

(*a*) the conditions prescribed in paragraph (2) in relation to the person making the payment are satisfied, and

(*b*) the conditions prescribed in paragraph (3) in relation to the payment are satisfied.

(2) The conditions prescribed in relation to the person making the payment are that—

(*a*) the person is one to whom section 59(1)(*a*) of the Act [applies][1], and

(*b*) the person has been approved by the Commissioners for Her Majesty's Revenue and Customs for the purposes of this regulation.

(3) The conditions prescribed in relation to the payment are that the payment—

(*a*) is made to a body or person in respect of construction operations carried out by that body or person in relation to—

(i) property owned by that body or person, or

(ii) agricultural property of which that body or person is a tenant, and

(*b*) is not one made under a construction contract in respect of which the total payments so made (excluding the direct cost of materials) exceed or are likely to exceed £1000.

(4) For the purposes of paragraph (3)(*a*)(ii) "agricultural property" means—

(*a*) agricultural land or pasture,

(*b*) woodland or any building used in connection with the intensive rearing of livestock or fish if the woodland or building is occupied with agricultural land or pasture and the occupation is ancillary to that of the agricultural land or pasture,

(*c*) cottages, farm buildings and farm houses, together with the land occupied with them, as are of a character appropriate to the property, and

(*d*) land and buildings used for breeding and rearing horses on a stud farm and grazing of horses in connection with those activities.

Commentary—*Simon's Taxes* **E5.545A**.

Amendments—[1] Word in para (2)(*a*) inserted by the Income Tax (Construction Industry Scheme) (Amendment) Regulations, SI 2007/672 regs 2, 4 with effect from 26 March 2007.

20 Reverse premiums

(1) Subject to paragraph (2), a payment under a construction contract is not a contract payment if the payment is a reverse premium within the meaning of Schedule 6 to the Finance Act 1999(*a*) (tax treatment of receipts by way of reverse premium) (see paragraph 1 of that Schedule) [or section 99 of the Income Tax (Trading and Other Income) Act 2005 (reverse premiums)][1].

(2) Paragraph 5 of Schedule 6 to the Finance Act 1999 (exclusion of receipts taken into account for capital allowances) [and section 100(1) of the Income Tax (Trading and Other Income) Act 2005 (excluded cases) do][1] not apply for the purposes of paragraph (1).

Commentary—*Simon's Taxes* **E5.545A**.

Amendments—[1] Words in para (1) inserted, and words in para (2) substituted, by the Income Tax (Construction Industry Scheme) (Amendment) Regulations, SI 2007/672 regs 2, 5 with effect from 26 March 2007.

21 Payments as agent of a local education authority

[A payment under a construction contract is not a contract payment if the payment is made by the governing body or head teacher of a maintained school as the agent of a local authority under section 49(5)(b) of the School Standards and Framework Act 1998 (delegated budget).][1]

Commentary—*Simon's Taxes* **E5.545A**.

Amendments—[1] Reg 21 substituted by the Local Education Authorities and Children's Services Authorities (Integration of Functions) (Local and Subordinate Legislation) Order, SI 2010/1172, art 4, Sch 3 para 59 with effect from 5 May 2010: see SI 2010/1172 art 2(1).

22 Payments in respect of property used for business

(1) A payment under a construction contract is not a contract payment if the payment is made by a person to whom section 59(1)(l) of the Act applies in respect of construction operations relating to property used for the purposes of the business of—

(*a*) that person, or

(*b*) another company in the same group or of another company of which that company owns 50% or more of the shares.

(2) For the purpose of paragraph (1)—

(*a*) property is not used for the purposes of the business of a person if it is for sale or to let [(except where the sale or letting of that property is purely incidental to the business of that person)][1] or is held as an investment by that person;

(*b*) in determining whether property is used for the purposes of the business of a person incidental use of that property by any other person is disregarded;

(*c*) section 413(3)(*a*) of ICTA applies to determine whether two companies are in the same group.

Commentary—*Simon's Taxes* **E5.545A**.

Amendments—[1] Words in para (2)(*a*) inserted by the Income Tax (Construction Industry Scheme) (Amendment) Regulations, SI 2007/672 regs 2, 6 with effect from 26 March 2007.

23 Arrangements involving public bodies

(1) A payment under a construction contract is not a contract payment if—

(*a*) the person making the payment ("the public body") is within any of paragraphs (*b*) to (k) of section 59(1) of the Act, and

(*b*) the payment is made under a private finance transaction.

(2) For the purposes of this regulation, a transaction is a private finance transaction if—

(*a*) the resources are provided partly by one or more public bodies and partly by one or more private persons;

(*b*) it is designed wholly or mainly for the purpose of assisting a public body to discharge a function or is ancillary to the function of a public body; and

(*c*) the public body makes payments by instalments at annual or more frequent intervals of fees determined in accordance with factors which include—

(i) the standard attained in the performance of services by the private person or persons in relation to the discharge of the function referred to in paragraph (*b*), or

(ii) the extent, rate or intensity of use of the resources or the asset which is constructed, enhanced, replaced or installed under the transaction.

(3) For the purposes of paragraph (2), "resources" includes—

(*a*) funds (including payment for the provision of services or facilities),

(*b*) assets,

(*c*) professional skill,

(*d*) the grant of a concession or franchise, and

(*e*) any other commercial resource.

Commentary—*Simon's Taxes* **E5.545A**.

24 Charities

A payment under a construction contract is not a contract payment if the payment is made by any body of persons or trust established for charitable purposes only.

Commentary—*Simon's Taxes* **E5.545A**.

PART 5
REGISTRATION OF SUB-CONTRACTORS

25 Registration for gross payment or for payment under deduction and cancellation of registration for payment under deduction

(1) On the application for registration for gross payment or for payment under deduction under section 63 of the Act (registration for gross payment or payment under deduction), the applicant must provide such documents, records and information to establish his identity as an officer of Revenue and Customs may require, which may include—

(*a*) the applicant's birth certificate,

(*b*) the name, address, national insurance number and unique taxpayer reference of—

(i) if the applicant is an individual, the applicant,

(ii) if the applicant is a partner in a firm, any partner,

(iii) if the applicant is a company, the directors of the company or, if the company is a close company, the persons who are the beneficial owners of shares in the company,

(*c*) utility bills,

(*d*) council tax bills,

(*e*) current passport,

(*f*) driving licence,

(*g*) company registration number,

(*h*) company's memorandum and articles of association.

(2) An officer of Revenue and Customs may require that any of the documents, records or information required under paragraph (1) be produced by the applicant in person.

(3) If the Commissioners for Her Majesty's Revenue and Customs are not satisfied with the documents, records or information provided under paragraph (1), they may refuse to register the applicant for payment under deduction by notice stating the reasons for the refusal ("the refusal notice").

(4) An officer of Revenue and Customs may at any time make a determination cancelling a person's registration for payment under deduction with immediate effect by notice stating the reasons for the cancellation ("the cancellation notice") if they have reasonable grounds to suspect that the person—

(*a*) provided false or incorrect information under paragraph (1), (*b*) has fraudulently made an incorrect return or provided incorrect information (whether as a contractor or a sub-contractor) under any provision of Chapter 3 of the Act or these Regulations, or

(*c*) has knowingly failed to comply (whether as a contractor or a sub-contractor) with any such provision.

(5) A person may appeal against a notice or refusal specified in column 1 of Table 2 by giving notice to an officer of Revenue and Customs within 30 days of the event specified in column 2 stating the person's reasons for appeal stated in column 3.

Table 2

Column 1: appeal	*Column 2: timing event*	*Column 3: reasons for appeal*
Appeal against a refusal notice.	Issue of the refusal notice.	Reasons for believing the application should not have been refused.
Appeal against a cancellation notice.	Issue of the cancellation notice.	Reasons for believing the registration should not have been cancelled.
Refusal to register for payment under deduction under section 66(7) of the Act (registration following cancellation of registration for gross payment).	Cancellation of registration for gross payment	Reasons for believing the person should have been registered for payment under deduction.

(6) An appeal under paragraph (5) is to the General Commissioners or, if the person so elects in the notice, to the Special Commissioners.[1]

Commentary—*Simon's Taxes* **E5.550**.

Amendments—[1] Para (6) revoked by the Transfer of Tribunal Functions and Revenue and Customs Appeals Order, SI 2009/56 art 3, Sch 2 paras 137, 141 with effect from 1 April 2009.

26 Cancellation of registration for gross payment

For the purpose of section 66(2) of the Act (cancellation of registration for gross payment) the prescribed period is 90 days from the date of the notice given under sub-section (5) of that section.

Commentary—*Simon's Taxes* **E5.552**.

PART 6
CONDITIONS TO BE SATISFIED FOR GROSS PAYMENT

BUSINESS TEST

27 Evidence prescribed to satisfy the business test

(1) The evidence required to satisfy an officer of Revenue and Customs for the purposes of section 64 of the Act (requirements for registration for gross payment) that the applicant or company is carrying on a business in the United Kingdom which satisfies the conditions mentioned in paragraph 2(*a*) and (*b*) of Schedule 11 to the Act is prescribed in paragraph (2).

(2) The evidence is—

(*a*) the business address;

(*b*) invoices, contracts or purchase orders for construction work carried out by the applicant;

(*c*) details of payments for construction work;

(*d*) the books and accounts of the business;

(*e*) details of the business bank account, including bank statements.

Commentary—*Simon's Taxes* **E5.551**.

TURNOVER TEST

28 Minimum turnover

(1) The minimum turnover for the purposes of paragraph 3(1) of Schedule 11 to the Act is £30,000.

(2) The amount specified for the purposes of paragraph 7 of Schedule 11 to the Act is [£100,000][1].

(3) The amount specified for the purposes of paragraph 11 of Schedule 11 to the Act is [£100,000][1].

Commentary—*Simon's Taxes* **E5.551**.

Amendments—[1] In paras (2), (3), figure substituted for figure "£200,000" by the Income Tax (Construction Industry Scheme) (Amendment) Regulations, SI 2016/348 reg 2(1), (5) with effect in relation to the tax year 2016–17 and subsequent tax years.

29 Evidence prescribed to satisfy the turnover test

(1) The evidence prescribed for the purposes of paragraphs 3(1), 7(1) and 11(1) of Schedule 11 to the Act is—

(*a*) evidence of turnover of the business mentioned in paragraph 3(1), 7(1) or 11(1) of Schedule 11 to the Act, as appropriate, during the qualifying period;

(*b*) evidence of relevant payments which may include bank statements and paid cheques;

(*c*) evidence that—

(i) the aggregate amount of relevant payments received in the qualifying period equalled or exceeded the relevant turnover threshold; or

(ii) for the purposes of section 66 of the Act (cancellation of registration for gross payment – continuing compliance), the aggregate amount of relevant payments received in the qualifying period equalled or exceeded the relevant turnover threshold or the average amount of relevant payments received in the qualifying period and the previous two years equalled or exceeded the relevant turnover threshold;

(*d*) documentary evidence of operations carried out by the business during the qualifying period which demonstrate that the operations amounted to construction operations.

(2) In the case of a new business carried on by a firm or company where there is no evidence as prescribed in sub-paragraphs (*a*), (*c*) or (*d*) of paragraph 1, the evidence prescribed for the purposes of paragraphs 7(1) and 11(1) of Schedule 11 to the Act is—

(*a*) evidence of relevant payments which may include bank statements and paid cheques;

(*b*) in the case of a firm, evidence of turnover of partners during the qualifying period;

(*c*) in the case of a company, evidence of turnover of relevant persons during the qualifying period;

(*d*) evidence of construction contracts entered into by the firm or company including payment schedules where the aggregate value of these contracts exceeds [£100,000][1] and payments of at least £30,000 have been made;

(*e*) if the business mentioned in paragraph 11(1) of Schedule 11 was acquired from another person, firm or company ("the transferor"), the evidence specified in paragraph (3). This is subject to paragraph (4).

(3) The evidence specified is—

(*a*) evidence of turnover of the transferor in relation to carrying on the business during the qualifying period;

(*b*) evidence that—

(i) the aggregate amount of relevant payments received by the transferor in relation to carrying on the business in the qualifying period equalled or exceeded the relevant turnover threshold; or

(ii) for the purposes of section 66(1)(*a*) of the Act (cancellation of registration for gross payment – continuing compliance), the aggregate amount of relevant payments received by the transferor in the qualifying period in relation to carrying on the business equalled or exceeded the relevant turnover threshold or the average amount of relevant payments in relation to the business received in the qualifying period and the previous two years equalled or exceeded the relevant turnover threshold;

(*c*) invoices for operations carried out by the transferor during the qualifying period which demonstrate that the business operations amounted to construction operations;

(*d*) evidence that the transferor would have satisfied the compliance test in paragraphs 4, 8 or 12 of Schedule 11 to the Act at the date of the transfer.

(4) The evidence prescribed in paragraph (2) may only be given in relation to one application for registration for gross payment.

(5) For the purposes of this regulation and regulation 31— "relevant payment" has the meaning given in paragraph 3(2) of Schedule 11 to the Act; "relevant turnover threshold" means—

(*a*) for the purposes of paragraph 3(1) of Schedule 11 of the Act, in relation to individuals, the minimum turnover specified in regulation 28(1);

(*b*) for the purposes of paragraph 7(1) of Schedule 11 of the Act, in relation to firms, the smaller of—

(i) the sum specified in paragraph 7(2) of Schedule 11 of the Act, and

(ii) the amount specified in regulation 28(2);

(*c*) for the purposes of paragraph 11(1) of Schedule 11 of the Act, in relation to companies, the minimum turnover for the purposes of that sub-paragraph.

Commentary—*Simon's Taxes* **E5.551**.

Amendments—[1] In para (2)(*d*), figure substituted for figure "£200,000" by the Income Tax (Construction Industry Scheme) (Amendment) Regulations, SI 2016/348 reg 2(1), (6) with effect in relation to the tax year 2016–17 and subsequent tax years.

30 Number of partners or relevant persons

For the purposes of paragraphs 7(2)(*a*) and 11(2)(*a*) of Schedule 11 to the Act if the number of partners or relevant persons as the case may be has fluctuated over the qualifying period, the number of partners or relevant persons is the maximum number of partners or relevant persons at any one time in the qualifying period.

Commentary—*Simon's Taxes* **E5.551**.

31 Turnover test treated as satisfied in prescribed circumstances

A person, firm or company which does not satisfy the condition in paragraphs 3(1), 7(1) or 11(1) of Schedule 11 to the Act, as appropriate, is treated as satisfying that condition if an officer of Revenue and Customs is satisfied that—

(*a*) the business of the person, firm or company does not mainly consist of construction operations,

(*b*) in the year prior to making the application the total turnover of the business exceeded the relevant turnover threshold, and

(*c*) in the year following making the application the person, firm or company is likely to receive relevant payments in relation to construction operations which are incidental to the main business of the person, firm or company.

Commentary—*Simon's Taxes* **E5.551**.

COMPLIANCE TEST

32 Exceptions from compliance obligations

(1) The obligations and requests prescribed for the purposes of paragraphs 4(3), 8(2) and 12(2) of Schedule 11 to the Act are given in column 1 of Table 3.

(2) The circumstances prescribed in which the applicant or company is to be treated as satisfying the conditions in paragraphs 4(1), 8(1) or 12(1) of Schedule 11 to the Act as regards each of the prescribed obligations are given in column 2 of Table 3.

[Table 3

1 Prescribed obligations	*2 Prescribed circumstances*
Obligation to submit monthly contractor return within the required period.	(1) Return is submitted not later than 28 days after the due date and (2) the applicant or company has failed to comply with this obligation on not more than two occasions within the previous 12 months.
Obligation to pay— a) the amount liable to be deducted under section 61 of the Act from payments made during that tax period, or b) tax liable to be deducted under the PAYE Regulations	(1) Where the amount not paid by the due date is under £100, or (2) Where the amount not paid by the due date is at least £100— (a) the payment is made not later than 14 days after the due date and (b) the applicant or company has failed to comply with this obligation in respect of an amount of at least £100 on not more than two occasions within the previous 12 months.
Obligation to submit a self-assessment return within the required period	Return is submitted not later than 28 days after the due date.][1]

Commentary—*Simon's Taxes* **E5.551**.

Amendments—[1] Table 3 substituted by the Income Tax (Construction Industry Scheme) (Amendment) Regulations, SI 2016/348 reg 2(1), (7) with effect in relation to the tax year 2016–17 and subsequent tax years.

33 Absence abroad – evidence of living outside the United Kingdom

(1) The evidence required to satisfy the Commissioners for Her Majesty's Revenue and Customs for the purposes of paragraph 4(5)(*a*) of Schedule 11 to the Act that the applicant was not subject to any one or more of the obligations mentioned in paragraph 4(1) of that Schedule because he has been outside the United Kingdom for the whole or part of the qualifying period is prescribed in paragraphs (2) and (3).

(2) Subject to paragraph (3), if the applicant claims to have been employed or self-employed outside the United Kingdom during any part of the qualifying period, the evidence is any document from the Revenue Department or equivalent department of the country in which he claims to have been living which confirms his presence throughout that part of the qualifying period.

(3) If the applicant claims—

(*a*) not to have been employed or self-employed while outside the United Kingdom during any part of the qualifying period, or

(*b*) to have been employed or self-employed outside the United Kingdom during any part of the qualifying period but not to have been liable to tax in the country in which he claims to have been living during that part of the qualifying period,

the evidence is any document from the Social Security Department or equivalent department, or from the immigration authorities, or from any other Government department of the country in which he claims to have been living which confirms his presence throughout that part of the qualifying period.

Commentary—*Simon's Taxes* **E5.551**.

34 Absence abroad – evidence of compliance with tax obligations

(1) The evidence required to satisfy the Commissioners for Her Majesty's Revenue and Customs for the purposes of paragraph 4(5)(*b*) of Schedule 11 to the Act that the applicant has complied with any obligations imposed under the tax laws of any country in which he was living during any part of the qualifying period which are comparable to the obligations mentioned in paragraph 4(1) of that Schedule is prescribed in paragraph (2).

(2) The evidence is such notice or documents issued by the Revenue Department or equivalent department of the country in which the applicant claims to have been living as confirms that the obligations have been complied with.

Commentary—*Simon's Taxes* **E5.551**.

35 Evidence of unemployment

(1) The evidence required to satisfy the Commissioners for Her Majesty's Revenue and Customs for the purposes of paragraph 4(5)(*a*) of Schedule 11 to the Act that the applicant was not subject to any one or more of the obligations mentioned in paragraph 4(1) of that Schedule because he was unemployed is prescribed in paragraphs (2) and (3).

(2) If the applicant claims to have been living within the United Kingdom during any period, the evidence is—

(*a*) a statement from the benefit officer certifying the period during which the applicant was registered as unemployed, or

(*b*) during any period during which the applicant was not registered as unemployed, such other evidence as satisfied the Commissioners for Her Majesty's Revenue and Customs that he was unemployed during that period.

(3) If the applicant claims to have been living outside the United Kingdom during any period, the evidence is any document from the Social Security Department or equivalent department, or from the immigration authorities, or from any other Government Department of the country in which he claims to have been living, which confirms his presence there throughout that period.

(4) In paragraph (2), "benefit officer" means appropriate officer of the Department for Work and Pensions or, in Northern Ireland, the appropriate officer of the Department of Health and Social Services for Northern Ireland.

Commentary—*Simon's Taxes* **E5.551**.

36 Evidence of full-time education

(1) The evidence required to satisfy the Commissioners for Her Majesty's Revenue and Customs for the purposes of paragraph 4(5)(*a*) of Schedule 11 to the Act that the applicant was not subject to any one or more of the obligations mentioned in paragraph 4(1) of that Schedule because he was undergoing full-time education is prescribed in paragraphs (2) and (3).

(2) If the applicant claims to have been living within the United Kingdom, the evidence is a statement from the educational institution which the applicant attended, certifying the periods during which the applicant was undergoing full-time education at that institution.

(3) If the applicant claims to have been living outside the United Kingdom during any period, the evidence is a statement from the educational institution which the applicant attended, in the country in which the applicant claims to have been living, certifying the periods during which the applicant was undergoing full-time education at that institution.

Commentary—*Simon's Taxes* **E5.551**.

37 Interpretation

In this Part—

"applicant" shall be construed in accordance with section 63 of and Schedule 11 to the Act;

"qualifying period" has the meaning given in paragraph 14 of Schedule 11 to the Act.

PART 7
ELECTRONIC COMMUNICATIONS

38 Interpretation

In this Part—

"official computer system" means a computer system maintained by or on behalf of the Commissioners for Her Majesty's Revenue and Customs or an officer of Revenue and Customs;

"specified payment" means the amount due under regulation 7 (payment, due date for payment of amounts deducted and receipts) in respect of contract payments ...[1].

Commentary—*Simon's Taxes* **E5.555**.

Amendments—[1] Words repealed by the Income Tax (Construction Industry Scheme) (Amendment) Regulations, SI 2010/717, regs 2, 4 with effect in relation to the tax year 2010–11 and subsequent tax years.

39 Whether information has been delivered electronically

For the purpose of these Regulations, information is taken to have been delivered to an official computer system by an approved method of electronic communications only if it is accepted by that official computer system.

Commentary—*Simon's Taxes* **E5.555**.

40 Proof of content of electronic delivery

(1) A document certified by an officer of Revenue and Customs to be a printed-out version of any information delivered by an approved method of electronic communications is evidence, unless the contrary is proved, that the information—

(*a*) was delivered by an approved method of electronic communications on that occasion, and

(*b*) constitutes everything which was delivered on that occasion.

(2) A document which purports to be a certificate given in accordance with paragraph (1) is presumed to be such a certificate unless the contrary is proved.

Commentary—*Simon's Taxes* **E5.555**.

41 Proof of identity of person sending or receiving electronic delivery

The identity of—

(*a*) the person sending any information by an approved method of electronic communications to Her Majesty's Revenue and Customs, or

(*b*) the person receiving any information delivered by an approved method of electronic communications by Her Majesty's Revenue and Customs,

is presumed, unless the contrary is proved, to be the person recorded as such on an official computer system.

Commentary—*Simon's Taxes* **E5.555**.

42 Information sent electronically on behalf of a person

(1) Any information delivered by an approved method of electronic communications—

(*a*) to Her Majesty's Revenue and Customs, or

(*b*) to an official computer system,

on behalf of a person is taken to have been delivered by that person.

(2) But this does not apply if the person proves that the information was delivered without the person's knowledge or connivance.

Commentary—*Simon's Taxes* **E5.555**.

43 Proof of delivery of information sent electronically

(1) The use of an approved method of electronic communications is presumed, unless the contrary is proved, to have resulted in the delivery of information—

(*a*) to Her Majesty's Revenue and Customs, if the delivery of the information has been recorded on an official computer system;

(*b*) by Her Majesty's Revenue and Customs, if the despatch of the information has been recorded on an official computer system.

(2) The use of a method of electronic communications is presumed, unless the contrary is proved, not to have resulted in the delivery of information—

(*a*) to Her Majesty's Revenue and Customs, if the delivery of the information has not been recorded on an official computer system;

(*b*) by Her Majesty's Revenue and Customs, if despatch of the information has not been recorded on an official computer system.

(3) The time of receipt or despatch of any information delivered by a method of electronic communications is presumed, unless the contrary is proved, to be the time recorded on an official computer system.

Commentary—*Simon's Taxes* **E5.555**.

44 Proof of payment sent electronically

(1) The use of a method of electronic communications is presumed, unless the contrary is proved, to have resulted in the making of a payment—

(*a*) to Her Majesty's Revenue and Customs, if the making of the payment has been recorded on an official computer system;

(*b*) by Her Majesty's Revenue and Customs, if despatch of the payment has been recorded on an official computer system.

(2) The use of a method of electronic communications is presumed, unless the contrary is proved, not to have resulted in the making of a payment—

(*a*) to Her Majesty's Revenue and Customs, if the making of the payment has not been recorded on an official computer system;

(*b*) by Her Majesty's Revenue and Customs, if despatch of the payment has not been recorded on an official computer system.

(3) The time of receipt or despatch of any payment sent by a method of electronic communications is presumed, unless the contrary is proved, to be the time recorded on an official computer system.

Commentary—*Simon's Taxes* **E5.556.**

45 Mandatory electronic payment

[(1) A contractor who is a large employer within the meaning of regulation [198A (large employers)][2] of the PAYE Regulations must pay the specified payment using an approved method of electronic communications.][1]

(2) Paragraph (1) applies regardless of whether a payment of tax is due under regulation [67G or][3] 68 of the PAYE Regulations (payment and recovery of tax by employer).

(3) If the Commissioners for Her Majesty's Revenue and Customs have given directions under regulation 199(3) of the PAYE Regulations in relation to a contractor, the specified payment must be made in accordance with those directions.

[(4) A specified payment is not treated as received in full by Her Majesty's Revenue and Customs on or before the date by which that specified payment is required in accordance with regulation 7 unless it is made in a manner which secures (in a case where the specified payment is made otherwise than in cash) that, on or before that date, all transactions can be completed which need to be completed before the whole amount of the specified payment becomes available to the Commissioners for Her Majesty's Revenue and Customs.][1]

Commentary—*Simon's Taxes* **E5.556.**

Amendments—[1] Para (1) substituted, and para (4) inserted, by the Income Tax (Construction Industry Scheme) (Amendment) Regulations, SI 2010/717, regs 2, 5(*a*), (*c*) with effect in relation to the tax year 2010–11 and subsequent tax years.

[2] In para (1), words substituted by the Income Tax (Construction Industry Scheme) (Amendment) Regulations, SI 2010/717, regs 2, 5(*b*), with effect in relation to the tax year 2011–12 and subsequent tax years.

[3] In para (2), words inserted by the Income Tax (Construction Industry Scheme) (Amendment) Regulations, SI 2012/820 regs 2, 6 with effect from 6 April 2012.

46 Contractor in default if specified payment not received by applicable due date

. . .

Amendments—Regs 46, 47 repealed by the Income Tax (Construction Industry Scheme) (Amendment) Regulations, SI 2010/717, regs 2, 6 with effect in relation to the tax year 2010–11 and subsequent tax years.

47 Default notice and appeal

. . .

Amendments—Regs 46, 47 repealed by the Income Tax (Construction Industry Scheme) (Amendment) Regulations, SI 2010/717, regs 2, 6 with effect in relation to the tax year 2010–11 and subsequent tax years.

48 Default surcharge

. . .

Amendments—Regs 48 and 49 revoked by the Finance Act 2009, Schedule 56 (Appointed Day and Consequential Provisions) Order, SI 2010/466 art 4. However, these regs will continue to have effect for surcharges that arise in respect of late payments of tax where the tax was chargeable in respect of a tax period ending on or before 5 April 2010 (see SI 2010/466 art 4(3)).

49 Surcharge notice and appeal

. . .

Amendments—Regs 48 and 49 revoked by the Finance Act 2009, Schedule 56 (Appointed Day and Consequential Provisions) Order, SI 2010/466 art 4. However, these regs will continue to have effect for surcharges that arise in respect of late payments of tax where the tax was chargeable in respect of a tax period ending on or before 5 April 2010 (see SI 2010/466 art 4(3)).

PART 8

SUPPLEMENTARY PROVISIONS

50 Delegation of Commissioners for Her Majesty's Revenue and Customs' functions

(1) The following may be done by an officer of Revenue and Customs on behalf of the Commissioners for Her Majesty's Revenue and Customs—

(*a*) the registration of persons under section 63 of the Act (registration for gross payment or payment under deduction);

(*b*) the giving of directions under section 64(5) of the Act (power to make directions as to application of conditions to be satisfied by individuals applying for registration for gross payment);

(*c*) the cancellation under section 66 of the Act of a person's registration for gross payment.

(2) This regulation is without prejudice to any other power of the Commissioners for Her Majesty's Revenue and Customs to delegate their functions

51 Inspection of records of contractors and sub-contractors

(1) Whenever required to do so by a person nominated by the Commissioners for Her Majesty's Revenue and Customs, a contractor must produce to that person all contractor records, or such contractor records as may be specified by that person, for inspection at the prescribed place and at such time as that person may reasonably require.

(2) "Contractor records" means all documents and records relating to—

(*a*) the calculation and payment of sums paid by the contractor to sub-contractors (or their nominees) under contracts relating to construction operations, and (*b*) the deductions made from such sums required under section 61 of the Act, in the tax years or tax periods specified by the nominated person.

(3) Whenever required to do so by a person nominated by the Commissioners for Her Majesty's Revenue and Customs, a person who is or has within the preceding three tax years been a sub-contractor must produce to that person all sub-contractor records, or such sub-contractor records as may be specified by that person, for inspection at the prescribed place and at such time as that person may reasonably require.

(4) "Sub-contractor records" means all documents and records relating to—

(*a*) the calculation or payment of sums paid to the sub-contractor pursuant to any contract relating to construction operations under which he is or was a sub-contractor within the previous three years, and

(*b*) the direct cost of materials relating to any such contract.

(5) "The prescribed place" means such place in the United Kingdom as the contractor or sub-contractor and the nominated person may agree upon, or in the absence of agreement—

(*a*) the place in the United Kingdom at which the contractor records or sub-contractor records are normally kept, or

(*b*) if there is no such place, the contractor's or sub-contractor's principal place of business in the United Kingdom.

(6) The nominated person may—

(*a*) take copies of, or make extracts from, any document produced for inspection in accordance with paragraph (1) or (3);

(*b*) remove any document so produced if it appears to the nominated person to be necessary to do so, at a reasonable time and for a reasonable period.

(7) If any document is removed in accordance with paragraph (6)(*b*), the nominated person must provide—

(*a*) a receipt for the document, and

(*b*) a copy of the document, free of charge, to the person by whom it was produced or caused to be produced, within seven days of that person requesting a copy, if the document is reasonably required for the proper conduct of a business.

(8) If a lien is claimed on a document produced in accordance with paragraph (1) or (3), the removal of the document under paragraph (6)(*b*) is not to be regarded as breaking the lien.

(9) If records are maintained by computer, the person required to make them available for inspection must provide the nominated person with all facilities necessary for obtaining information from them.

(10) For the purposes of this regulation, a contractor and a sub-contractor must keep, for not less than three years after the end of the tax year to which they relate, all contractor records or sub-contractor records as the case may be which are not required to be sent to the Commissioners for Her Majesty's Revenue and Customs by other provisions of these Regulations.

Commentary—*Simon's Taxes* **E5.561**.

52 Inspection of records of sub-contractors – additional provisions

(1) Where a sum deducted under section 61 of the Act is treated as paid on account of the liabilities mentioned in regulation 56(2) (application by Commissioners for Her Majesty's Revenue and Customs of sums deducted under section 61), the sub-contractor, whose liabilities they are, shall—

(*a*) maintain the records specified in paragraph (2), and

(*b*) produce to a person nominated by the Commissioners for Her Majesty's Revenue and Customs for inspection those records, or such of them as may be specified by him, at such time as he may reasonably require, at the prescribed place.

(2) The records are all documents and records relating to the calculation of—

(*a*) the amounts which the sub-contractor would have been liable to pay to the Commissioners for Her Majesty's Revenue and Customs in the preceding three tax years, under the provisions mentioned in regulation 56(2), but for the withholding by a contractor of sums due to him; and

(*b*) the amounts deducted by a contractor under section 61 of the Act which the sub-contractor claims to be entitled to set off against those liabilities.

(3) "The prescribed place" means such place in the United Kingdom as the sub-contractor and the nominated person may agree upon, or in the absence of agreement—

(*a*) the place in the United Kingdom at which the documents and records mentioned in paragraph (2) are normally kept, or

(*b*) if there is no such place, the sub-contractor's principal place of business in the United Kingdom.

(4) The nominated person may—

(*a*) take copies of, or make extracts from, any document produced for inspection in accordance with paragraph (1)(*b*);

(*b*) remove any document so produced if it appears to the nominated person to be necessary to do so, at a reasonable time and for a reasonable period.

(5) If a lien is claimed on a document produced in accordance with paragraph (1)(*b*), the removal of the document under paragraph (4)(*b*) is not to be regarded as breaking the lien.
(6) If records are maintained by computer, the person required to make them available for inspection must provide the nominated person with all facilities necessary for obtaining information from them.

Commentary—*Simon's Taxes* **E5.561A**.

53 Information as to change of control of close company

(1) This regulation applies to a company which—
(*a*) is a close company,
(*b*) is a private company limited by shares, and
(*c*) is registered for gross payment or is applying to be so registered.
(2) Where there is a change in the control of the company by reason of an issue or transfer of shares in the company to a person who was not a shareholder in the company immediately before the issue or transfer, the company shall, within 30 days of the issue or of receiving information as to the transfer, give notice to the Commissioners for Her Majesty's Revenue and Customs of the name and address of the person to whom the shares were issued or transferred.
(3) In this regulation "control" has the same meaning as in section 840 of ICTA.

Commentary—*Simon's Taxes* **E5.562**.

54 Death of contractor

If a contractor dies, anything which he would have been liable to do under these Regulations must be done by his personal representatives.

Commentary—*Simon's Taxes* **E5.562**.

55 Service by post

Any notice which is authorised or required to be given, served or issued under these Regulations may be sent by post.

Commentary—*Simon's Taxes* **E5.562**.

56 Application by the Commissioners for Her Majesty's Revenue and Customs of sums deducted under section 61

(1) This regulation applies to sums deducted from contract payments made to a sub-contractor which is a company ("the qualifying sub-contractor").
(2) So much of any sum deducted under section 61 of the Act by a contractor in a tax year and paid to the Commissioners for Her Majesty's Revenue and Customs as is required shall be applied—
(*a*) first, in discharge of any liability of the qualifying sub-contractor to account for primary Class 1 contributions in respect of earnings paid to its employees in that year;
(*b*) second, in discharge of any liability of the qualifying sub-contractor for secondary Class 1 contributions in respect of earnings paid to its employees in that year;
(*c*) third, in discharge of any liability of the qualifying sub-contractor to account for tax deducted from the emoluments of its employees in accordance with Regulations made under section 684 of ITEPA (pay as you earn) in respect of that year;
(*d*) fourth, in discharge of any liability of the qualifying sub-contractor to account for deductions made by it in that year from the emoluments of its employees in accordance with regulations made under section 22(5) of the Teaching and Higher Education Act 1998, section 73B of the Education (Scotland) Act 1980, or Article 3(5) of the Education (Student Support) (Northern Ireland) Order 1998;
(*e*) fifth, in discharge of any liability of the qualifying sub-contractor to refund to the Commissioners for Her Majesty's Revenue and Customs any funding payment made by them in respect of statutory sick pay, statutory maternity pay, [statutory paternity pay][6][, statutory shared parental pay][6] or statutory adoption pay under the relevant recovery provision; and
(*f*) last, in discharge of any liability of the qualifying sub-contractor to account for sums deducted by it (in its capacity as a contractor) under section 61 of the Act from payments made to other sub-contractors.
[(2A) For any tax period where as a consequence of paragraph (2) the qualifying sub-contractor pays an amount to the Commissioners for Her Majesty's Revenue and Customs in respect of any liability referred to in that paragraph that is less than the amount the qualifying sub-contractor would have paid but for that paragraph, paragraph (2B) applies if the qualifying sub-contractor is a Real Time Information employer for the purposes of the PAYE Regulations.
(2B) The qualifying sub-contractor must deliver to the Commissioners for Her Majesty's Revenue and Customs a return under this paragraph stating the value of the sums deducted from contract payments made to the qualifying sub-contractor under section 61 of the Act in the tax year to date.
(2C) The return required by paragraph (2B) must be delivered within 14 days after the end of the tax period.
(2D) If an employer makes an error in a return under paragraph (2B), the employer must provide the correct information in the first return made under that paragraph after the discovery of the error.

(2E) But if the information given has not been corrected before 20th April following the end of the year in question, the employer must provide the correct information for the year in question in a return under this paragraph.][2]

(3) So much of any sum deducted under section 61 of the Act as is not required to discharge the sub-contractor's liabilities specified in paragraph (2) shall be repaid to the qualifying sub-contractor. This is subject to the qualifications in paragraphs (5) and (6).

(4) . . . [4]

(5) The Commissioners for Her Majesty's Revenue and Customs shall not repay any sum deducted under section 61 of the Act to the qualifying sub-contractor [unless][2]

(*a*) the tax year in which the deduction was made, has ended; and

[(*b*) the qualifying sub-contractor has paid to the Commissioners for Her Majesty's Revenue and Customs—

(i) any amounts the qualifying sub-contractor deducted from contract payments in their capacity as a contractor during that tax year, and

(ii) any amounts due under the PAYE Regulations in respect of that tax year,][3]

[but this paragraph does not apply to a qualifying sub-contractor within paragraph (5A).

(5A) A qualifying sub-contractor is within this paragraph if—

(*a*) that sub-contractor is subject to a winding-up under Part 4 of the Insolvency Act 1986, and

(*b*) that sub-contractor has—

(i) ceased trading,

(ii) permanently ceased making payments to which section 61 of the Act(a) applies in its capacity as a contractor, or

(iii) ceased trading and permanently ceased to make any payments within subparagraph (b)(ii).

(5B) Where a qualifying sub-contractor is within paragraph (5A), the Commissioners for Her Majesty's Revenue and Customs may repay any sum deducted under section 61 of the Act to that sub-contractor during the tax year in which the deduction was made.][5]

(6) If it appears to an officer of Revenue and Customs that there is an outstanding liability of the qualifying sub-contractor in respect of corporation tax due for an accounting period ending before the relevant payment is made under section 61 of the Act, the amount required to discharge that liability shall be retained by the Commissioners for Her Majesty's Revenue and Customs and applied in discharge of that liability.

(7) In paragraph (2)(*e*), "the relevant recovery provision" means—

(*a*) in respect of [. . . statutory paternity pay][1] and statutory adoption pay, regulations 4, 5, 6 and 8 of either the Statutory Paternity Pay and Statutory Adoption Pay (Administration) Regulations 2002 or the Statutory Paternity Pay and Statutory Adoption Pay (Administration) Regulations (Northern Ireland) 2002;

(aa) [16]

(*b*) in respect of statutory maternity pay, regulations 5, 6, 6A and 7A of the Statutory Maternity (Compensation of Employers) and Miscellaneous Amendment Regulations 1994 or the Statutory Maternity (Compensation of Employers) and Miscellaneous Amendment Regulations (Northern Ireland) 1994.

[(*c*) in respect of statutory shared parental pay, regulations 4, 5, 6 and 8 of either the Statutory Shared Parental Pay (Administration) Regulations 2014 or corresponding regulations made under articles 8, 9, 11 and 16(1) of the Employment (Northern Ireland) Order 2002.][6]

[(8) A return under this regulation must—

(*a*)state—

(i) the employer's HMRC office number,

(ii) the employer's PAYE reference for the purposes of the PAYE Regulations,

(iii) the employer's accounts office reference, and

(iv) the tax year to which the return relates, and

(*b*) be delivered using an approved method of electronic communications unless the qualifying sub-contractor is one to whom regulation 67D of the PAYE Regulations applies, in which case the return must be made in a document or format provided or approved by the Commissioners for Her Majesty's Revenue and Customs.][2]

Commentary—*Simon's Taxes* **E5.563**.

Amendments—[1] In paras (2)(*e*), (7)(*a*), words substituted, and para (7)(*aa*) inserted, by the Income Tax (Construction Industry Scheme) (Amendment No 2) Regulations, SI 2010/2495, regs 2, 4 with effect from 14 November 2010.

[2] Paras (2A)–(2E) inserted; in para (5), word substituted; and para (8) inserted; by the Income Tax (Construction Industry Scheme) (Amendment) Regulations, SI 2012/820 regs 2, 7 with effect from 6 April 2012.

[3] Para (5)(*b*) substituted by the Income Tax (Construction Industry Scheme) (Amendment) Regulations, SI 2013/620 regs 2, 4 with effect in relation to the tax year 2013–14 and subsequent tax years.

[4] Para 4 revoked by the Finance Act 2009, Sections 101 and 102 (Interest on Late Payments and Repayments), Appointed Days and Consequential Provisions Order, SI 2014/992 art 11(*c*), with effect in relation to payments due and payable in respect of the tax year 2014–15 and subsequent tax years.

5 Words at the end of para (5) inserted, and paras (5A), (5B) inserted by the Income Tax (Construction Industry Scheme) (Amendment) Regulations, SI 2015/429 reg 2(1), (3) with effect from 6 April 2015.

6 In para (2)(*e*), words substituted and inserted, in para (7), word in sub-para (*a*), revoked, sub-para (*aa*) revoked, and sub-para (*c*) inserted, by the Statutory Payment Schemes (Electronic Communications) (Amendment) Regulations, SI 2015/125 reg 4(1), (3), (4) with effect from 5 April 2015..

57 Certificate that sum due

(1) A certificate of an officer of Revenue and Customs that, to the best of his knowledge and belief, any amount shown in a certificate under the regulations listed in paragraph (2) has not been paid by a contractor, is sufficient evidence that the amount mentioned in the certificate is unpaid and due to the Crown.

(2) The regulations are—

regulation 10(6) (return and certificate if amount may be unpaid)

regulation 11(8) (notice and certificate if amount may be unpaid)

regulation 12(2) (certificate after inspection of records).

[(2A) An officer of Revenue and Customs may prepare a certificate showing the whole or part of a combined amount which includes deductions under section 61 of the Act without specifying the components of the combined amount.

Paragraph (1) shall apply with any necessary modifications to the certificate.][1]

(3) A certificate of an officer of Revenue and Customs that, to the best of his knowledge and belief, any amount of interest payable under . . . [1] regulation 14 (interest on amounts overdue) has not been paid by a contractor, is sufficient evidence that the amount mentioned in the certificate is unpaid and due to the Crown.

[(3A) An officer of Revenue and Customs may prepare a certificate showing the total amount of interest payable in respect of the whole or any component of the combined amount without specifying which component of the combined amount the interest relates to.

Paragraph (3) shall apply with any necessary modifications to the certificate.][1]

(4) The production of—

(*a*) the return made by the contractor under regulation 10(4), and

(*b*) the certificate of an officer of Revenue and Customs under regulation 10(6),

is sufficient evidence that the amount shown in the certificate is the amount of tax which the contractor is liable to pay to the Commissioners for Her Majesty's Revenue and Customs in respect of the tax period in question.

(5) A document which purports to be a certificate under [this regulation][1] is treated as such a certificate until the contrary is proved.

Commentary—*Simon's Taxes* **E5.564**.

Amendments—[1] Paras (2A), (3A) inserted, word in para (3) revoked, and words in para (5) substituted, by the Income Tax (Construction Industry Scheme) (Amendment) Regulations, SI 2008/740 regs 2, 8 with effect from 6 April 2008.

58 Payment by cheque

(1) For the purposes of the following provisions, if—

(*a*) any payment to the Commissioners for Her Majesty's Revenue and Customs is made by cheque, and

(*b*) the cheque is paid on its first presentation to the banker on whom it is drawn,

the payment shall be treated as made on the day which the cheque was received by the Commissioners for Her Majesty's Revenue and Customs.

(2) The provisions are—

regulation 7 payment, due date for payment of amounts deducted and receipts for payment of tax

regulation 9 recovery from sub-contractor of tax not deducted by contractor

regulation 11 notice and certificate if tax may be unpaid

. . . [1]

Commentary—*Simon's Taxes* **E5.565**.

Amendments—[1] In para 2, entry relating to regulation 14 revoked by the Finance Act 2009, Sections 101 and 102 (Interest on Late Payments and Repayments), Appointed Days and Consequential Provisions Order, SI 2014/992 art 11(*d*), with effect in relation to payments due and payable in respect of the tax year 2014–15 and subsequent tax years.

59 Appeals: supplementary provisions

[(1) Section 31A(5) and (6) of TMA applies to appeals under regulation 47 (default notice and appeal) as it applies to an appeal under section 31 of that Act.][1]

(2), (3) 1 . . .

Amendments—[1] Para (1) substituted and paras (2), (3) revoked, by the Transfer of Tribunal Functions and Revenue and Customs Appeals Order, SI 2009/56 art 3, Sch 2 paras 137, 142 with effect from 1 April 2009.

60 Transitional provisions, savings and revocation

(1) Schedule 1 (transitional provisions and savings) has effect.

(2) The Regulations listed in column 1 of Schedule 2 are revoked to the extent specified in column 3 of that Schedule.

(3) Paragraph (2) is subject to Schedule 1.

SCHEDULE 1

TRANSITIONAL PROVISIONS AND SAVINGS PART 1

Regulation 60

GENERAL PROVISIONS

Continuity of the law

1 The revocation of provisions and their making in a rewritten form in these Regulations does not affect the continuity of the law.

2 Paragraph 1 does not apply to any change in the law made by these Regulations.

3 Anything which—

(*a*) has been done, or has effect as if done, under or for the purposes of a provision of the revoked Regulations, and

(*b*) is in force or effective immediately before the commencement of these Regulations, has effect after that commencement as if done under or for the purposes of the corresponding provision of these Regulations.

4 Any reference (express or implied) in these Regulations or any document made under these Regulations to—

(*a*) a provision of these Regulations, or

(*b*) things done or falling to be done under or for the purposes of a provision of these Regulations, is to be read as including, in relation to times, circumstances or purposes in relation to which any corresponding provision of the revoked Regulations had effect, a reference to the provision of the revoked Regulations or to things done or falling to be done under or for the purposes of the provision of the revoked Regulations.

5 Any reference (express or implied) in these Regulations to—

(*a*) a provision of the Act, or

(*b*) things done or falling to be done under or for the purposes of a provision of the Act, is to be read as including, in relation to times, circumstances or purposes in relation to which any corresponding provision repealed by the Act had effect, a reference to the repealed provision or to things done or falling to be done under or for the purposes of the repealed provision.

6 Any reference (express or implied) in these Regulations to contractors, sub-contractors, construction operations or similar concepts created by the Act is to be read as including, in relation to times, circumstances or purposes in relation to which any corresponding concept which has been superseded by the Act had effect, a reference to the superseded concept.

7 Paragraphs 4, 5 and 6 apply only in so far as the context permits.

8 Paragraph 6 is without prejudice to the generality of paragraph 5.

9 These Regulations have effect in relation to sums liable, under the Income Tax (Sub-contractors in the Construction Industry) Regulations 1993, to be deducted or accounted for in respect of payments made before the appointed day as if the sum had been liable to be deducted or accounted for under these Regulations.

10 Paragraph 9 is without prejudice to the generality of paragraphs 1 to 8.

11 Paragraphs 1 to 10 have effect instead of paragraph (*b*) of section 17(2) of the Interpretation Act 1978.

General saving for old savings

12—(1) The revocation by these Regulations of a provision previously revoked subject to savings does not affect the continued operation of those savings.

(2) The revocation by these Regulations of a saving on the previous revocation of a provision does not affect the operation of the saving in so far as it is not specifically reproduced in these Regulations but remains capable of having effect.

Interpretation

13 In this Part of this Schedule, "the revoked Regulations" means the Regulations which are revoked by these Regulations.

PART 2
SPECIFIC PROVISIONS

Interest on unpaid amounts: disapplication of regulation 14 for tax years before the tax year ending 5th April 1993

1 Regulation 14 (interest on amounts overdue) does not apply in relation to unpaid amounts in respect of a tax year ending on or before 5th April 1992.

Interest on overpaid tax: disapplication of regulation 15 for tax years before the tax year ending 5th April 1993

2 Regulation 15 (interest on overpaid amount) does not apply to tax which was paid by an employer in respect of a tax year ending on or before 5th April 1993.

SCHEDULE 2
Regulation 60
REVOCATIONS

1. Regulations revoked	*2. Reference*	*3. Extent of revocation*
The Income Tax (Sub-contractors in the Construction Industry) Regulations 1993	1993/743	The whole instrument.
The Income Tax (Sub-contractors in the Construction Industry) (Amendment) Regulations 1995	1995/217	The whole instrument.
The Income Tax (Sub-contractors in the Construction Industry) (Amendment No 2) Regulations 1995	1995/448	The whole instrument.
The Income Tax (Sub-contractors in the Construction Industry) (Amendment) Regulations 1996	1996/981	The whole instrument.
The Income Tax (Sub-contractors in the Construction Industry) (Amendment) Regulations 1998	1998/2622	The whole instrument.
The Income Tax (Sub-contractors in the Construction Industry) (Amendment) Regulations 1999	1999/825	The whole instrument.
The Income Tax (Sub-contractors in the Construction Industry) (Amendment No 2) Regulations 1999	1999/2159	The whole instrument.
The Income Tax (Sub-contractors in the Construction Industry) (Amendment) Regulations 2000	2000/1151	The whole instrument.
The Income Tax (Sub-contractors in the Construction Industry) (Amendment No 2) Regulations 2000	2000/1880	The whole instrument.
The Income Tax (Sub-contractors in the Construction Industry and Employments) (Amendment) Regulations 2000	2000/2742	The whole instrument to the extent not already revoked.
The Income Tax (Sub-contractors in the Construction Industry) (Amendment) Regulations 2001	2001/1531	The whole instrument.
The Income Tax (Sub-contractors in the Construction Industry) (Amendment) Regulations 2002	2002/2225	The whole instrument.
The Income Tax (Sub-contractors in the Construction Industry and Employments) (Amendment) Regulations 2003	2003/536	The whole instrument to the extent not already revoked.
The Income Tax (Sub-contractors in the Construction Industry) (Amendment) Regulations 2004	2004/1075	The whole instrument.

2005/3311

REVENUE AND CUSTOMS (COMPLAINTS AND MISCONDUCT) REGULATIONS 2005

Revocation—These Regs revoked by the Revenue and Customs (Complaints and Misconduct) Regulations, SI 2010/1813 reg 2 with effect from 5 August 2010. However, where an allegation in respect of the conduct by an officer came to the attention of the appropriate authority before 5 August 2010, nothing in SI 2010/1813 shall apply and these Regs shall continue to have effect.

Made by the Treasury under CRCA 2005 ss 28(1) and (2), and 29(3)

Made . . . . *1 December 2005*
Laid before Parliament . . . . *2 December 2005*

Coming into force . . . .*28 December 2005*

1 Citation, commencement and extent

(1) These Regulations may be cited as the Revenue and Customs (Complaints and Misconduct) Regulations 2005 and shall come into force on 28th December 2005.

(2) These Regulations extend to England and Wales.

Revocation—These Regs revoked by the Revenue and Customs (Complaints and Misconduct) Regulations, SI 2010/1813 reg 2 with effect from 5 August 2010. However, where an allegation in respect of the conduct by an officer came to the attention of the appropriate authority before 5 August 2010, nothing in SI 2010/1813 shall apply and these Regs shall continue to have effect.

2 Interpretation

In these Regulations—

"2002 Act" means the Police Reform Act 2002;

"Commission" means the Independent Police Complaints Commission;

"Commissioners" means the Commissioners for Her Majesty's Revenue and Customs;

"Complaints Regulations" means the Police (Complaints and Misconduct) Regulations 2004;

"conduct matter" has the meaning given by section 12 of the 2002 Act;

"functions" has the meaning given by section 51(2)(*a*) of the Commissioners for Revenue and Customs Act 2005;

"Investigatory Powers Order" means the Independent Police Complaints Commission (Investigatory Powers) Order 2004;

"officers" means officers of Revenue and Customs;

"Staff Conduct Regulations" means the Independent Police Complaints Commission (Staff Conduct) Regulations 2004.

Revocation—These Regs revoked by the Revenue and Customs (Complaints and Misconduct) Regulations, SI 2010/1813 reg 2 with effect from 5 August 2010. However, where an allegation in respect of the conduct by an officer came to the attention of the appropriate authority before 5 August 2010, nothing in SI 2010/1813 shall apply and these Regs shall continue to have effect.

3 Application of provisions of Part 2 of the 2002 Act with modifications

(1) The provisions specified in paragraphs (2), (3) and (4) shall apply for the purpose of conferring functions on the Commission in relation to the Commissioners and officers.

(2) Sections 9 to 29 of the 2002 Act shall have effect with the modifications made by Schedule 1 to these Regulations.

(3) Schedule 2 to the 2002 Act shall have effect with the modifications made by Schedule 2 to these Regulations.

(4) Paragraphs 10 to 24, 27 and 29 of Schedule 3 to the 2002 Act shall have effect with the modifications made by Schedule 3 to these Regulations.

(5) Paragraphs 1 to 9, 25, 26 and 28 of Schedule 3 to the 2002 Act shall have effect with the modifications made by Schedule 3 to these Regulations.

(6) The provisions specified in—

(*a*) paragraphs (2), (3) and (4) shall have effect from the date these Regulations come into force;

(*b*) paragraph (5) shall have effect from 1st April 2006.

(7) The references in regulations 5, 8 and 9(1) to Part 2 of the 2002 Act are references to Part 2 of the 2002 Act as modified by Schedules 1, 2 and 3 to these Regulations.

Revocation—These Regs revoked by the Revenue and Customs (Complaints and Misconduct) Regulations, SI 2010/1813 reg 2 with effect from 5 August 2010. However, where an allegation in respect of the conduct by an officer came to the attention of the appropriate authority before 5 August 2010, nothing in SI 2010/1813 shall apply and these Regs shall continue to have effect.

4 Application of the Investigatory Powers Order, the Complaints Regulations and the Staff Conduct Regulations with modifications

(1) The provisions specified in paragraph (2) shall apply for the purpose of conferring functions on the Commission in relation to the Commissioners and officers.

(2) From the date these Regulations come into force—

(*a*) the Investigatory Powers Order shall have effect,

(*b*) the Complaints Regulations shall have effect with the modifications made by Part 1 of Schedule 4 to these Regulations, and

(*c*) the Staff Conduct Regulations shall have effect with the modifications made by Part 2 of Schedule 4 to these Regulations.

(3) The references in regulations 5, 8 and 9(1) to—

(*a*) the Complaints Regulations,

(*b*) the Staff Conduct Regulations,

are references to those Regulations as modified by Parts 1 and 2 of Schedule 4 to these Regulations.

Revocation—These Regs revoked by the Revenue and Customs (Complaints and Misconduct) Regulations, SI 2010/1813 reg 2 with effect from 5 August 2010. However, where an allegation in respect of the conduct by an officer came to the attention of the appropriate authority before 5 August 2010, nothing in SI 2010/1813 shall apply and these Regs shall continue to have effect.

[4A—(1) For the purpose of the application of the Complaints Regulations under regulation 4, the amendments made to those Regulations by the provisions specified in paragraph (2) shall apply.

(2) The provisions specified are—

(*a*) regulation 26 of the Serious Organised Crime and Police Act 2005 (Powers of Arrest) (Consequential Amendments) Order 2005, and

(*b*) regulation 2 of the Police (Complaints and Misconduct) (Amendment) Regulations 2006.

(3) This regulation has effect from 27th July 2006.][1]

Revocation—These Regs revoked by the Revenue and Customs (Complaints and Misconduct) Regulations, SI 2010/1813 reg 2 with effect from 5 August 2010. However, where an allegation in respect of the conduct by an officer came to the attention of the appropriate authority before 5 August 2010, nothing in SI 2010/1813 shall apply and these Regs shall continue to have effect.

Amendments—[1] This regulation inserted by the Revenue and Customs (Complaints and Misconduct) (Amendment) Regulations, SI 2006/1748 reg 3 with effect from 27 July 2006.

5 Disclosure of information

Where the Commission, or any person acting on its behalf, obtains information in the course of performing a function under these Regulations it or he may not disclose it except as permitted by Part 2 of the 2002 Act or the Complaints Regulations.

Revocation—These Regs revoked by the Revenue and Customs (Complaints and Misconduct) Regulations, SI 2010/1813 reg 2 with effect from 5 August 2010. However, where an allegation in respect of the conduct by an officer came to the attention of the appropriate authority before 5 August 2010, nothing in SI 2010/1813 shall apply and these Regs shall continue to have effect.

6 Use of information

Where the Commission, or any person acting on its behalf, obtains information in the course of performing a function under these Regulations it or he may not use it for any purpose other than the performance of a function under these Regulations.

Revocation—These Regs revoked by the Revenue and Customs (Complaints and Misconduct) Regulations, SI 2010/1813 reg 2 with effect from 5 August 2010. However, where an allegation in respect of the conduct by an officer came to the attention of the appropriate authority before 5 August 2010, nothing in SI 2010/1813 shall apply and these Regs shall continue to have effect.

7 Payments

(1) The Commissioners shall pay such amount to the Secretary of State in respect of functions performed by the Commission under these Regulations as may be agreed between the Commissioners and the Commission.

(2) In the absence of an agreement, the Commissioners shall pay such amount in respect of those functions as the Treasury, after consultation with the Secretary of State, shall determine.

Revocation—These Regs revoked by the Revenue and Customs (Complaints and Misconduct) Regulations, SI 2010/1813 reg 2 with effect from 5 August 2010. However, where an allegation in respect of the conduct by an officer came to the attention of the appropriate authority before 5 August 2010, nothing in SI 2010/1813 shall apply and these Regs shall continue to have effect.

8 Complaints about conduct occurring before 1st April 2006

Nothing in Part 2 of the 2002 Act, the Investigatory Powers Order, the Complaints Regulations or the Staff Conduct Regulations shall have effect in relation to a complaint made about the conduct of a Commissioner or an officer occurring before 1st April 2006.

Revocation—These Regs revoked by the Revenue and Customs (Complaints and Misconduct) Regulations, SI 2010/1813 reg 2 with effect from 5 August 2010. However, where an allegation in respect of the conduct by an officer came to the attention of the appropriate authority before 5 August 2010, nothing in SI 2010/1813 shall apply and these Regs shall continue to have effect.

9 Conduct matter occurring before 1st April 2006

(1) Subject to paragraph (2), nothing in Part 2 of the 2002 Act, the Investigatory Powers Order, the Complaints Regulations or the Staff Conduct Regulations shall have effect in relation to a conduct matter relating to the conduct of a Commissioner or an officer occurring before 1st April 2006.

(2) Paragraph (1) does not apply to any conduct matter which the appropriate authority may refer to the Commission under paragraph 13(2) of Schedule 3 to the 2002 Act.

Revocation—These Regs revoked by the Revenue and Customs (Complaints and Misconduct) Regulations, SI 2010/1813 reg 2 with effect from 5 August 2010. However, where an allegation in respect of the conduct by an officer came to the attention of the appropriate authority before 5 August 2010, nothing in SI 2010/1813 shall apply and these Regs shall continue to have effect.

SCHEDULE 1

MODIFICATION OF SECTIONS 9 TO 29 OF THE 2002 ACT

Regulation 3(2)

1 At the end of section 9(3) insert—

"(*g*) any person who holds or has held office or employment as a Commissioner or officer.".

Revocation—These Regs revoked by the Revenue and Customs (Complaints and Misconduct) Regulations, SI 2010/1813 reg 2 with effect from 5 August 2010. However, where an allegation in respect of the conduct by an officer came to the attention of the appropriate authority before 5 August 2010, nothing in SI 2010/1813 shall apply and these Regs shall continue to have effect.

2—(1) Section 10 shall be modified as follows.

(2) In subsection (1) after "the Commission" insert ", in relation to the Commissioners and officers,".

(3) In subsection (1)(*a*) for "police authorities and chief officers" substitute "the Commissioners".

(4) In subsection (1)(*e*) omit "and also of police practice in relation to other matters,".

(5) Omit subsection (1)(*f*).

(6) In subsection (2)(*a*) for "persons serving with the police" substitute—

"Commissioners or officers which the appropriate authority—

(i) has a duty to refer to the Commission under paragraph 4(1) of Schedule 3 or,

(ii) may refer to the Commission under paragraph 4(2) or (3) of Schedule 3;".

(7) In subsection (2)(*b*) for the words from "appears that" to the end substitute—

"appears that—

(i) there may have been conduct by such persons which constitutes or involves the commission of a criminal offence or behaviour justifying disciplinary proceedings, and

(ii) that conduct or behaviour is conduct or behaviour which the appropriate authority has a duty to refer to the Commission under paragraph 13(1) of Schedule 3 or may refer to the Commission under paragraph 13(2) or (3) of that Schedule.".

(8) In subsection (2)(*ba*) for "a person serving with the police" insert "an officer".

(9) Omit subsection (3).

(10) In subsection (4)(*a*) for "subsections (1) and (3)" insert "subsection (1)".

(11) In subsection (5)(*a*) after "functions" insert "in relation to the Commissioners and officers".

(12) Omit subsections (7)(*b*) and (*c*).

(13) In subsection (8) for the words from "control of a police force" to the end substitute "control of Her Majesty's Revenue and Customs by the Commissioners".

Revocation—These Regs revoked by the Revenue and Customs (Complaints and Misconduct) Regulations, SI 2010/1813 reg 2 with effect from 5 August 2010. However, where an allegation in respect of the conduct by an officer came to the attention of the appropriate authority before 5 August 2010, nothing in SI 2010/1813 shall apply and these Regs shall continue to have effect.

3—(1) Section 11 shall be modified as follows.

(2) In subsections (1), (2), (3), and (5) for "Secretary of State" insert "Chancellor of the Exchequer".

(3) Omit subsection (4)(*b*).

(4) In subsection (6) for the words from "under subsection (1)" to the end substitute "under subsection (1) to the Commissioners".

(5) In subsection (7) for the words from "under subsection (3)" to the end substitute "under subsection (3) to the Commissioners".

(6) Omit subsections (8) and (9).

(7) In subsection (10) for paragraphs (*a*) to (*g*) substitute—

"(*a*) the Chancellor of the Exchequer, and

(*b*) the Commissioners.".

(8) In the heading for "Reports to the Secretary of State" substitute "Reports to the Chancellor of the Exchequer".

Revocation—These Regs revoked by the Revenue and Customs (Complaints and Misconduct) Regulations, SI 2010/1813 reg 2 with effect from 5 August 2010. However, where an allegation in respect of the conduct by an officer came to the attention of the appropriate authority before 5 August 2010, nothing in SI 2010/1813 shall apply and these Regs shall continue to have effect.

4—(1) Section 12 shall be modified as follows.

(2) In subsections (1) and (2) for "a person serving with the police" substitute "a Commissioner or an officer".

(3) In subsections (2B)(*a*), [(2B)(*b*),][1] (2C)(*a*) and (2D) for "a person serving with the police" (on each occasion the words occur) substitute "an officer".

Revocation—These Regs revoked by the Revenue and Customs (Complaints and Misconduct) Regulations, SI 2010/1813 reg 2 with effect from 5 August 2010. However, where an allegation in respect of the conduct by an officer came to the attention of the appropriate authority before 5 August 2010, nothing in SI 2010/1813 shall apply and these Regs shall continue to have effect.

Amendments—[1] Reference inserted by the Revenue and Customs (Complaints and Misconduct) (Amendment) Regulations, SI 2006/1748 reg 4 with effect from 27 July 2006.

5—(1) Section 14 shall be modified as follows.

(2) In subsection (1) for the words from "control of a police force" to the end substitute "control of Her Majesty's Revenue and Customs by the Commissioners".

(3) Omit subsections (2) and (3).

Revocation—These Regs revoked by the Revenue and Customs (Complaints and Misconduct) Regulations, SI 2010/1813 reg 2 with effect from 5 August 2010. However, where an allegation in respect of the conduct by an officer came to the attention of the appropriate authority before 5 August 2010, nothing in SI 2010/1813 shall apply and these Regs shall continue to have effect.

6—(1) Section 15 shall be modified as follows.

(2) In subsection (1)—

(*a*) for the words in paragraph (*a*) substitute "the Commissioners and ";

(*b*) omit paragraph (*b*);

(*c*) for "it or he is" substitute "they are or he is" and for "that force" substitute "Her Majesty's Revenue and Customs".

(3) In subsection (3)—

(*a*) for paragraph (*a*) substitute—

"(*a*) the Commission requires the chief officer of a police force to provide a member of his force for appointment under paragraph 17A or 18A of Schedule 3,";

(*b*) omit paragraphs (*b*) and (*c*);

(*c*) omit "or Director General".

(4) In subsection (4)—

(*a*) omit paragraphs (*c*) and (*d*), and

(*b*) after paragraph (*d*) insert—

"(*e*) the Commissioners,".

(5) In subsection (5)—

(*a*) omit paragraphs (*c*) and (*d*);

(*b*) for "16, 17 or 18" substitute "17A or 18A".

(6) After subsection (5) insert—

"(5A) It shall be the duty of the [designated permanent secretary][1], the Chairman and Commissioners to ensure that a person appointed under paragraph 16,17, 17A, 18 or 18A of Schedule 3 to carry out an investigation is given all such assistance and co-operation in the carrying out of that investigation as that person may reasonably require.".

(7) Omit subsections (6) and (7).

Revocation—These Regs revoked by the Revenue and Customs (Complaints and Misconduct) Regulations, SI 2010/1813 reg 2 with effect from 5 August 2010. However, where an allegation in respect of the conduct by an officer came to the attention of the appropriate authority before 5 August 2010, nothing in SI 2010/1813 shall apply and these Regs shall continue to have effect.

Amendments—[1] In sub-para (6), in sub-s (5A) (as set out), words substituted by the Constitutional Reform and Governance Act 2010 s 19, Sch 2 para 22(1), (2) with effect from 11 November 2010 by virtue of SI 2010/2703 art 2.

7—(1) Section 16 shall be modified as follows.

(2) In subsection (1)—

(*a*) in paragraph (*a*)—

(i) for "one" substitute "a";

(ii) omit "to another";

(iii) delete "or";

(*b*) at the end of paragraph (*b*) insert "; or";

(*c*) after paragraph (*b*) insert—

"(*c*) a police force provides assistance by agreement under paragraph 17A(2) or 18A(2) of Schedule 3.".

(3) In subsection (2)—

(*a*) in paragraph (*a*) for—

(i) "one police force to another" substitute "a police force",

(ii) "the first force ("the assisting force")" substitute "that force";

(iii) in sub-paragraph (i) for "a member of the other force" substitute "a Commissioner or an officer";

(iv) in sub-paragraph (ii) for "a member of the other force" substitute "an officer";

(*b*) in paragraph (*b*)—

(i) omit "(the assisting force)";

(ii) in sub-paragraph (i) for "not a member of that force" substitute "a Commissioner or an officer";

(iii) in sub-paragraph (ii) for "not a member of that force" substitute "an officer".

(4) In subsection (3)—

(*a*) for "one police force to another" substitute "a police force";
(*b*) for "police authority maintaining that other police force" substitute "appropriate authority";
(*c*) for "the assisting force" substitute "that force";
(*d*) omit "(if any)";
(*e*) in paragraph (*b*)(i) after "generally" insert "and the Commissioners", and
(*f*) in paragraph (*b*)(ii) omit "by one police force to another".

(5) After subsection (3) there shall be inserted—

"(3A) Subsection (3) shall have effect in relation to assistance which a police force provides by agreement under paragraph 17A (2) or 18A (2) of Schedule 3 as if the reference in that subsection to required to be provided were a reference to provided by agreement under paragraph 17A(2) or 18A(2) of Schedule 3.".

(6) Omit subsections (5), (6) and (7).

Revocation—These Regs revoked by the Revenue and Customs (Complaints and Misconduct) Regulations, SI 2010/1813 reg 2 with effect from 5 August 2010. However, where an allegation in respect of the conduct by an officer came to the attention of the appropriate authority before 5 August 2010, nothing in SI 2010/1813 shall apply and these Regs shall continue to have effect.

8—(1) Section 17 shall be modified as follows.

(2) From the beginning of subsection (1) to the end of paragraph (*b*) of that subsection substitute "It shall be the duty of the Commissioners".

(3) In subsection (2)—

(*a*) for the words "every police authority and of every chief officer" substitute "the Commissioners", and
(*b*) in paragraph (*a*) for the words "that authority and or chief officer" substitute "the Commissioners".

(4) In subsection (4)—

(*a*) for the words "a police authority or chief officer" substitute "the Commissioners", and
(*b*) in paragraph (*a*) for the words "that authority and or chief officer" substitute "the Commissioners".

Revocation—These Regs revoked by the Revenue and Customs (Complaints and Misconduct) Regulations, SI 2010/1813 reg 2 with effect from 5 August 2010. However, where an allegation in respect of the conduct by an officer came to the attention of the appropriate authority before 5 August 2010, nothing in SI 2010/1813 shall apply and these Regs shall continue to have effect.

9—(1) Section 18 shall be modified as follows.

(2) In subsection (1)(*a*)—

(*a*) for paragraphs (i) and (ii) substitute "the Commissioners"; and
(*b*) for "that force" substitute "Her Majesty's Revenue and Customs".

(3) In subsection (1) for "the authority or, as the case may be, of the chief officer" substitute "the Commissioners".

(4) In subsection (2)(*a*) for "the force in question" substitute "the Commissioners".

(5) In subsection (3) for "the authority or chief officer" substitute "the Commissioners".

(6) In subsection (5)(*b*) for "police authorities and chief officers" substitute "the Commissioners".

(7) In the heading to the section for "police premises" substitute "Her Majesty's Revenue and Customs premises".

Revocation—These Regs revoked by the Revenue and Customs (Complaints and Misconduct) Regulations, SI 2010/1813 reg 2 with effect from 5 August 2010. However, where an allegation in respect of the conduct by an officer came to the attention of the appropriate authority before 5 August 2010, nothing in SI 2010/1813 shall apply and these Regs shall continue to have effect.

10—(1) Section 22 shall be modified as follows.

(2) In subsection (1) for the words from "guidance" to the end of paragraph (*c*) substitute "guidance to the Commissioners and officers".

(3) In subsection (3)—

(*a*) for paragraph (*a*) substitute—

"(*a*) the Commissioners and";

(*b*) omit paragraph (*b*).

(4) In subsection (4) for "the Secretary of State" substitute "the Chancellor of the Exchequer".

(5) Omit subsection (5)(*c*).

Revocation—These Regs revoked by the Revenue and Customs (Complaints and Misconduct) Regulations, SI 2010/1813 reg 2 with effect from 5 August 2010. However, where an allegation in respect of the conduct by an officer came to the attention of the appropriate authority before 5 August 2010, nothing in SI 2010/1813 shall apply and these Regs shall continue to have effect.

11 Omit sections 25 and 26.

Revocation—These Regs revoked by the Revenue and Customs (Complaints and Misconduct) Regulations, SI 2010/1813 reg 2 with effect from 5 August 2010. However, where an allegation in respect of the conduct by an officer came to the attention of the appropriate authority before 5 August 2010, nothing in SI 2010/1813 shall apply and these Regs shall continue to have effect.

12—(1) Section 29 shall be modified as follows.

(2) In subsection (1)—

(*a*) for the definition of "the appropriate authority" substitute the following definition—

""the appropriate authority"—

(*a*) in relation to the Chairman, the Deputy Chairman, a Commissioner or an officer or in relation to any complaint, matter or

investigation relating to the conduct of such a person, means—

(i) if that person is the Chairman or Deputy Chairman, the [designated permanent secretary][1],

(ii) if that person is a Commissioner, the Chairman, or

(iii) if that person is an officer, the Commissioners" and

(*b*) in relation to a death or serious injury matter and the relevant officer, means the Commissioners.";

(*b*) after the definition of "the appropriate authority" insert—

""the Chairman" means the chairman of the Commissioners";

(*c*) after the definition of "the Commission" insert—

""the Commissioners" means the Commissioners for Her Majesty's Revenue and Customs;";

(*d*) after the definition of "conduct matter" insert—

""the Deputy Chairman" means the Deputy Chairman of the Commissioners";

([*da*) after the definition of "the Deputy Chairman insert—

""the designated permanent secretary" means the permanent secretary in the civil service of the State designated by the Minister for the Civil Service for the purposes of this Part;";][1]

(*e*) for the definition of "disciplinary proceedings" substitute—

""disciplinary proceedings" means any proceedings or management process during which the conduct of the Chairman, Deputy Chairman, a Commissioner or an officer is considered in order to determine whether a sanction or punitive measure should be imposed against him in relation to that conduct;";

(*f*) after the definition of "local resolution" insert the following definition—

""officers" means officers of Revenue and Customs;", and

(*g*) omit the definitions of "local resolution", "relevant force", and "senior officer".

(3) In subsection (1A) for "person serving with the police (within the meaning of section 12(7))" substitute "officer" and for "such person" substitute "such officer".

(4) In subsection (1B) for "persons serving with the police" substitute "officers".

(5) Omit subsection (7).

(6) In subsection (3) for the words from "falling within" to the end of that subsection substitute "who is a Commissioner or an officer (whether at the time of the conduct or any subsequent time)".

(7) In subsection (4)—

(*a*) for paragraph (*a*) substitute—

"(*a*) a person who, at the time when the conduct was supposed to have taken place in relation to him, was a Commissioner or an officer (whether or not he was on duty in his capacity as a Commissioner or officer at that time).";

(*b*) omit paragraph (*b*)(i);

(*c*) for "person falling within subsection (3)(*a*) to (*d*)" substitute "Commissioner or officer".

Revocation—These Regs revoked by the Revenue and Customs (Complaints and Misconduct) Regulations, SI 2010/1813 reg 2 with effect from 5 August 2010. However, where an allegation in respect of the conduct by an officer came to the attention of the appropriate authority before 5 August 2010, nothing in SI 2010/1813 shall apply and these Regs shall continue to have effect.

Amendments—[1] In sub-para (2)(*a*), in definition "the appropriate authority" (as set out), in para (*a*)(i) words substituted, and sub-para (2)(*da*) inserted, by the Constitutional Reform and Governance Act 2010 s 19, Sch 2 para 22(1)–(3) with effect from 11 November 2010 by virtue of SI 2010/2703 art 2.

SCHEDULE 2

MODIFICATION OF SCHEDULE 2 TO THE 2002 ACT

Regulation 3(3)

1 After paragraph 6(2) insert—

"(2A) The Commission may make arrangements with the Commissioners under which officers of Revenue and Customs are engaged on temporary service with the Commission.".

Revocation—These Regs revoked by the Revenue and Customs (Complaints and Misconduct) Regulations, SI 2010/1813 reg 2 with effect from 5 August 2010. However, where an allegation in respect of the conduct by an officer came to the attention of the appropriate authority before 5 August 2010, nothing in SI 2010/1813 shall apply and these Regs shall continue to have effect.

2 In paragraph 17(1)(*c*) after "Secretary of State" insert ", the Treasury".

Revocation—These Regs revoked by the Revenue and Customs (Complaints and Misconduct) Regulations, SI 2010/1813 reg 2 with effect from 5 August 2010. However, where an allegation in respect of the conduct by an officer came to the attention of the appropriate authority before 5 August 2010, nothing in SI 2010/1813 shall apply and these Regs shall continue to have effect.

SCHEDULE 3

MODIFICATION OF SCHEDULE 3 TO THE 2002 ACT

Regulations 3(4) and (5)

1—(1) Paragraph 1 shall be modified as follows.

(2) For sub-paragraph (1) substitute—

"(1) Where—

(*a*) complaint is made to the [designated permanent secretary][1] about the conduct of the Chairman or Deputy Chairman, or

(*b*) the [designated permanent secretary][1] becomes aware that a complaint about the conduct of the Chairman or Deputy Chairman has been made to the Commission,

the [designated permanent secretary][1] shall take all such steps as appear to him to be appropriate for the purposes of Part 2 of this Act for obtaining and preserving evidence relating to the conduct complained of.".

(3) After sub-paragraph (1) insert—

"(1A) Where—

(*a*) a complaint is made to the Chairman about the conduct of a Commissioner, or

(*b*) the Chairman becomes aware that a complaint about the conduct of a Commissioner has been made to the Commission,

the Chairman shall take all such steps as appear to him to be appropriate for the purposes of Part 2 of this Act for obtaining and preserving evidence relating to the conduct complained of.".

(4) For sub-paragraph (2) substitute—

"(2) Where—

(*a*) a complaint is made to the Commissioners about the conduct of an officer, or

(*b*) the Commissioners become aware that a complaint about the conduct of an officer has been made to the Commission,

the Commissioners shall take all such steps as appear to them to be appropriate for the purposes of Part 2 of this Act for obtaining and preserving evidence relating to the conduct complained of.".

(5) For sub-paragraph (3) substitute—

"(3) The duty of the—

(*a*) [designated permanent secretary][1] under sub-paragraph (1);

(*b*) Chairman under sub-paragraph (1A);

(*c*) Commissioners under sub-paragraph (2),

must be performed as soon as practicable after the complaint is made or, as the case may be, he or they become aware of it.".

(6) In sub-paragraph (4) for—

(*a*) "he shall" substitute "he or they shall";

(*b*) "he is satisfied" substitute "he is or they are satisfied"; and

(*c*) "appearing to him" substitute "appearing to him or them".

(7) Omit sub-paragraph (5).

(8) In sub-paragraph (6)—

(*a*) for "a chief officer" substitute—

"the—

(*a*) [designated permanent secretary][1] ;

(*b*) Chairman;

(*c*) Commissioners,";

(*b*) the words after "a chief officer" become full out words;

(*c*) for "he may" substitute "he or they may", and

(*d*) omit "by the police authority maintaining his force or".

Revocation—These Regs revoked by the Revenue and Customs (Complaints and Misconduct) Regulations, SI 2010/1813 reg 2 with effect from 5 August 2010. However, where an allegation in respect of the conduct by an officer came to the attention of the appropriate authority before 5 August 2010, nothing in SI 2010/1813 shall apply and these Regs shall continue to have effect.

Amendments—[1] Words substituted by the Constitutional Reform and Governance Act 2010 s 19, Sch 2 para 23 with effect from with effect from 11 November 2010 by virtue of SI 2010/2703 art 2.

2—(1) Paragraph 2 shall be modified as follows.

(2) In sub-paragraph (1)(*a*) for "police authority or chief officer who is" substitute "[designated permanent secretary][1], Chairman or Commissioners who is or are".

(3) In sub-paragraph (2)—

(*a*) for "a police authority, it" substitute "[designated permanent secretary][1] or Chairman, he";

(*b*) in paragraph (*a*) for "it is itself" substitute "he is himself"; and

(*c*) in paragraph (*b*) for "it determines that it" substitute "he determines that he".

(4) In sub-paragraph (3) for—

(*a*) "a chief officer, he shall" substitute "the Commissioners, they shall";

(*b*) "he is himself" substitute "they are themselves"; and

(*c*) "he determines that he is not" substitute "they determine that they are not".

(5) In sub-paragraph (5) for "a police authority or a chief officer gives" substitute "[designated permanent secretary][1] , Chairman or Commissioners gives or give".

(6) For sub-paragraph (6) substitute—

"(6) Where—

(*a*) the [designated permanent secretary][1] or Chairman determines, in the case of any complaint made to him, that he is himself the appropriate authority,

(*b*) the Commissioners determine, in the case of any complaint made to them, that they are themselves the appropriate authority, or

(*c*) a complaint is notified to the [designated permanent secretary][1] , Chairman or Commissioners under this paragraph,

the [designated permanent secretary][1] , Chairman or Commissioners shall record the complaint.".

Revocation—These Regs revoked by the Revenue and Customs (Complaints and Misconduct) Regulations, SI 2010/1813 reg 2 with effect from 5 August 2010. However, where an allegation in respect of the conduct by an officer came to the attention of the appropriate authority before 5 August 2010, nothing in SI 2010/1813 shall apply and these Regs shall continue to have effect.

Amendments—[1] Words substituted by the Constitutional Reform and Governance Act 2010 s 19, Sch 2 para 23 with effect from 11 November 2010 by virtue of SI 2010/2703 art 2.

3—(1) Paragraph 3 shall be modified as follows.

(2) In sub-paragraph (1) for "a police authority or chief officer" substitute "the [designated permanent secretary][1], Chairman or Commissioners".

(3) In sub-paragraph (2)—

(*a*) for "police authority or chief officer" and "authority or chief officer" substitute (on each occasion) "[designated permanent secretary][1], Chairman or Commissioners"

(*b*) for "decides" substitute "decides or decide" and

(*c*) in paragraph (*c*) for "that complainant's right to appeal" substitute "whether the complainant has a right to appeal".

(4) In sub-paragraph (3)—

(*a*) for "police authority or chief officer" substitute "[designated permanent secretary][1], Chairman or Commissioners"; and

(*b*) after "paragraph" insert "if, but only if, the failure is in respect of conduct which the [designated permanent secretary][1], Chairman or Commissioners is or are required to refer to the Commission under paragraph 4(1)(*a*) or (*b*).".

(5) In sub-paragraph (4)—

(*a*) in paragraph (*b*) for "police authority or chief officer" substitute "[designated permanent secretary][1], Chairman or Commissioners"; and

(*b*) for "a police authority or chief officer" substitute "the [designated permanent secretary][1], Chairman or Commissioners".

(6) In sub-paragraph (6) for—

(*a*) "police authority or, as the case may be, the chief officer" substitute "[designated permanent secretary][1], Chairman or, as the case may be, the Commissioners"; and

(*b*) "police authority or chief officer" substitute "[designated permanent secretary][1], Chairman or Commissioners".

Revocation—These Regs revoked by the Revenue and Customs (Complaints and Misconduct) Regulations, SI 2010/1813 reg 2 with effect from 5 August 2010. However, where an allegation in respect of the conduct by an officer came to the attention of the appropriate authority before 5 August 2010, nothing in SI 2010/1813 shall apply and these Regs shall continue to have effect.

Amendments—[1] Words substituted by the Constitutional Reform and Governance Act 2010 s 19, Sch 2 para 23 with effect from 11 November 2010 by virtue of SI 2010/2703 art 2.

4—(1) Paragraph 4 shall be modified as follows.

[(1A) After sub-paragraph (1) insert—

"(1A) The obligation on the [designated permanent secretary][2] under sub-paragraph (1)(*a*) or (*b*) to refer a complaint about the conduct of a person in respect of whom he is the appropriate authority arises only if the [designated permanent secretary][1] is satisfied that the complaint contains an indication that a criminal offence may have been committed by that person.

(1B) The obligation on the Chairman or the Commissioners under sub-paragraph (1)(*a*) or (1)(*b*) to refer a complaint about the conduct of a person in respect of whom he is or they are the appropriate authority arises only if he is or they are satisfied that the complaint contains an indication that the person may have—

(*a*) committed a criminal offence; or

(*b*) behaved in a manner which would justify the bringing of disciplinary proceedings and that such behaviour (if it had taken place) would be likely to lead to the termination of that person's office or employment.".][1]

(2) In sub-paragraph (3)—

(*a*) for "a police authority" substitute "the [designated permanent secretary[2]]";

(*b*) in paragraph (*a*) for "chief officer of police of the police force maintained by that authority" substitute "Chairman"; and

(*c*) in paragraph (*b*) for "the police authority" substitute "the [designated permanent secretary[2]]".

(3) In sub-paragraph (5)(*b*) for "a police authority or chief officer" substitute "the [designated permanent secretary][2], Chairman or Commissioners".

(4) In sub-paragraph (6)—

(*a*) for "A police authority or chief officer which refers" substitute "Where the [designated permanent secretary][2], Chairman or Commissioners refers or refer";

(*b*) after "paragraph" insert "he or they"; and

(*c*) in paragraph (*b*) for "that authority or chief officer" substitute "the [designated permanent secretary][2], Chairman or Commissioners".

Revocation—These Regs revoked by the Revenue and Customs (Complaints and Misconduct) Regulations, SI 2010/1813 reg 2 with effect from 5 August 2010. However, where an allegation in respect of the conduct by an officer came to the attention of the appropriate authority before 5 August 2010, nothing in SI 2010/1813 shall apply and these Regs shall continue to have effect.

Amendments—[1] Sub-para (1A) inserted by the Revenue and Customs (Complaints and Misconduct) (Amendment) Regulations, SI 2006/1748 reg 5(1), (2) with effect from 27 July 2006.

[2] Words substituted by the Constitutional Reform and Governance Act 2010 s 19, Sch 2 para 23 with effect from 11 November 2010 by virtue of SI 2010/2703 art 2.

5—(1) Paragraph 5 shall be modified as follows.

(2) In sub-paragraph (1) for "a police authority or chief officer" substitute "the [designated permanent secretary][1], Chairman or Commissioners".

(3) In sub-paragraph (2) for "paragraph 6" substitute "sub-paragraph (2A)".

(4) After sub-paragraph (2) insert—

"(2A) In a case to which sub-paragraph (2) applies the appropriate authority shall not be required by virtue of any of the provisions of this Schedule to take any action in relation to the complaint but may handle the complaint in whatever manner it thinks fit, or take no action in relation to the complaint.".

(5) For sub-paragraph 3(*b*) substitute—

"(*b*) to the person complained against.".

Revocation—These Regs revoked by the Revenue and Customs (Complaints and Misconduct) Regulations, SI 2010/1813 reg 2 with effect from 5 August 2010. However, where an allegation in respect of the conduct by an officer came to the attention of the appropriate authority before 5 August 2010, nothing in SI 2010/1813 shall apply and these Regs shall continue to have effect.

Amendments—[1] Words substituted by the Constitutional Reform and Governance Act 2010 s 19, Sch 2 para 23 with effect from 11 November 2010 by virtue of SI 2010/2703 art 2.

6—(1) Paragraph 6 shall be modified as follows.

(2) For sub-paragraph (2) substitute—

"(2) The appropriate authority shall not be required by virtue of any provisions of this Schedule to take any action in relation to the complaint but may handle the complaint in whatever manner it thinks fit or take no action in relation to the complaint.".

(3) Omit sub-paragraphs (3) to (7).

Revocation—These Regs revoked by the Revenue and Customs (Complaints and Misconduct) Regulations, SI 2010/1813 reg 2 with effect from 5 August 2010. However, where an allegation in respect of the conduct by an officer came to the attention of the appropriate authority before 5 August 2010, nothing in SI 2010/1813 shall apply and these Regs shall continue to have effect.

7 Omit paragraphs 7, 8 and 9.

Revocation—These Regs revoked by the Revenue and Customs (Complaints and Misconduct) Regulations, SI 2010/1813 reg 2 with effect from 5 August 2010. However, where an allegation in respect of the conduct by an officer came to the attention of the appropriate authority before 5 August 2010, nothing in SI 2010/1813 shall apply and these Regs shall continue to have effect.

8—(1) Paragraph 10 shall be modified as follows.

(2) In sub-paragraph (1)—

(*a*) in paragraph (*a*) for—

(i) "a police authority or chief officer" (on both occasions where it occurs) substitute "the [designated permanent secretary][2], Chairman or Commissioners";

(ii) for "has received" substitute "has or have received"; and

(iii) for "that authority or chief officer" substitute "the [designated permanent secretary][1], Chairman or Commissioners";

(*b*) in paragraph (*b*) for "that authority or chief officer" substitute "the [designated permanent secretary][1], Chairman or Commissioners".

(3) In sub-paragraph (2)—

(*a*) for "The authority or chief officer" substitute "The [designated permanent secretary][2], Chairman or Commissioners";

(*b*) in paragraph (*a*) for "it or, as the case may be, he is" substitute "he is or, as the case may be, they are"; and

(*c*) in paragraph (*b*) for "if it or he is not" substitute "if he is or they are not".

(4) In sub-paragraph (3)—

(a) at the beginning insert "Subject to sub-paragraphs (3A) and (3B),";[1]

(*b*) for "a police authority or chief officer determines" substitute "the [designated permanent secretary][2], Chairman or Commissioners determines or determine";

(*c*) for "it or, as the case may be, he is" substitute "he is, or as the case may be, they are", and

(*d*) for "it or he" substitute "he or they".

(5) After sub-paragraph (3) insert—

"(3A) Nothing in sub-paragraph (3) shall require the Head of the Home Civil Service, as the appropriate authority, to record a conduct matter if he is satisfied that matter falls within subsection 12(1)(b) of this Act.

(3B) Nothing in sub-paragraph (3) shall require the Chairman or the Commissioners, as the appropriate authority, to record a conduct matter if he is or they are satisfied that—

(a) the matter falls within subsection 12(1)(b) of this Act; and

(b) any disciplinary proceedings which were brought would be unlikely to result in the termination of an office or employment.".[1]

Revocation—These Regs revoked by the Revenue and Customs (Complaints and Misconduct) Regulations, SI 2010/1813 reg 2 with effect from 5 August 2010. However, where an allegation in respect of the conduct by an officer came to the attention of the appropriate authority before 5 August 2010, nothing in SI 2010/1813 shall apply and these Regs shall continue to have effect.

Amendments—[1] Sub-paras (4)(*a*), (5) revoked by the Revenue and Customs (Complaints and Misconduct) (Amendment) Regulations, SI 2006/1748 reg 5(1), (3) with effect from 27 July 2006.

[2] Words substituted by the Constitutional Reform and Governance Act 2010 s 19, Sch 2 para 23 with effect from 11 November 2010 by virtue of SI 2010/2703 art 2.

9—(1) Paragraph 11 shall be modified as follows.

(2) In sub-paragraph (1)—

(a) at the beginning insert "Subject to paragraphs (2A) and (2B),";[1]

(*b*) in paragraph (*a*) for "police authority or chief officer who is" substitute "[designated permanent secretary][2], Chairman or Commissioners who is or are".

(3) After sub-paragraph (2) insert—

"(2A) Nothing in sub-paragraph (1) shall require the Head of the Home Civil Service, as the appropriate authority, to record a conduct matter if he is satisfied that the matter falls within section 12(1)(b) of this Act.

(2B) Nothing in sub-paragraph (1) shall require the Chairman or the Commissioners, as the appropriate authority, to record a conduct matter if he is or they are satisfied that—

(a) the matter falls within section 12(1)(b) of this Act; and

(b) any disciplinary proceedings which were brought would be unlikely to result in the termination of an office or employment.".[1]

Revocation—These Regs revoked by the Revenue and Customs (Complaints and Misconduct) Regulations, SI 2010/1813 reg 2 with effect from 5 August 2010. However, where an allegation in respect of the conduct by an officer came to the attention of the appropriate authority before 5 August 2010, nothing in SI 2010/1813 shall apply and these Regs shall continue to have effect.

Amendments—[1] Sub-paras (2)(*a*), (3) revoked by the Revenue and Customs (Complaints and Misconduct) (Amendment) Regulations, SI 2006/1748 reg 5(1), (3) with effect from 27 July 2006.

[2] Words substituted by the Constitutional Reform and Governance Act 2010 s 19, Sch 2 para 23 with effect from 11 November 2010 by virtue of SI 2010/2703.

10—(1) Paragraph 12 shall be modified as follows.

(2) Omit sub-paragraph (1).

(3) For sub-paragraph (2) substitute—

"(2) Where—

(*a*) the [designated permanent secretary][1] becomes aware of any recordable matter relating to the conduct of the Chairman or Deputy Chairman;

(*b*) the Chairman becomes aware of any recordable matter relating to the conduct of a Commissioner; or

(*c*) the Commissioners become aware of any recordable matter relating to the conduct of an officer,

it shall be his or their duty to take all such steps as appear to him or them to be appropriate for the purposes of Part 2 of this Act for obtaining and preserving the evidence relating to that matter.".

(4) For sub-paragraph (3) substitute—

"(3) The duty under sub-paragraph (2) of—

(*a*) the [designated permanent secretary][1];

(*b*) the Chairman;

(*c*) the Commissioners,

must be performed as soon as practicable after he becomes or they become aware of the matter in question.".

(5) In sub-paragraph (4) for—

(*a*) "he shall be under a duty, until he is" substitute "he or they shall be under a duty until he is or they are"; and

(*b*) "appearing to him" substitute "appearing to him or them".

(6) Omit sub-paragraph (5).

(7) In sub-paragraph (6)—

(*a*) for "the chief officer" substitute "the Chairman or Commissioners";

(*b*) for "he may be directed" substitute "he or they may be directed"; and

(*c*) omit "by the police authority maintaining his force or".

Revocation—These Regs revoked by the Revenue and Customs (Complaints and Misconduct) Regulations, SI 2010/1813 reg 2 with effect from 5 August 2010. However, where an allegation in respect of the conduct by an officer came to the attention of the appropriate authority before 5 August 2010, nothing in SI 2010/1813 shall apply and these Regs shall continue to have effect.

Amendments—[1] Words substituted by the Constitutional Reform and Governance Act 2010 s 19, Sch 2 para 23 with effect from 11 November 2010 by virtue of SI 2010/2703.

11—(1) Paragraph 13 shall be modified as follows.

(2) In sub-paragraph (1) for—

(*a*) "a police authority or a chief officer" substitute "the [designated permanent secretary][2], Chairman or Commissioners", and

(*b*) "the authority or chief officer is" substitute "any of those persons is or are".

[(2A) After sub-paragraph (1) insert—

"(1A) Sub-paragraph (1) is subject to sub-paragraphs (1B) and (1C).

(1B) The obligation on the [designated permanent secretary][2] under sub-paragraph (1)(a) or (1)(b) to refer a recordable conduct matter in respect of a person for whom he is the appropriate authority arises only if the [designated permanent secretary][2] is satisfied that the matter is one in respect of which there is an indication that a criminal offence may have been committed by that person.

(1C) The obligation on the Chairman or the Commissioners under sub-paragraph (1)(*a*) or (1)(*b*) to refer a recordable conduct matter in respect of a person for whom he is or they are the appropriate authority arises only if he is or they are satisfied that the matter is one in respect of which there is an indication that the person may have—

(*a*) committed a criminal offence; or

(*b*) behaved in a manner which would justify the bringing of disciplinary proceedings and that such behaviour (if it had taken place) would be likely to lead to the termination of that person's office or employment."][1]

(3) In sub-paragraph (3)—

(*a*) for "a police authority maintaining any police force" substitute "the [designated permanent secretary[2]]";

(*b*) in paragraph (*a*) for "chief officer of police of that force" substitute "Chairman"; and

(*c*) in paragraph (*b*) for "police authority" substitute "[designated permanent secretary[2]]".

(4) In sub-paragraph (5)(*b*) for "a police authority or chief officer" substitute "the [designated permanent secretary][2], Chairman or Commissioners".

(5) In sub-paragraph (6)—

(*a*) in paragraph (*a*) for "a police authority or chief officer refers" substitute "the [designated permanent secretary][2], Chairman or Commissioners refers or refer";

(*b*) in paragraph (*b*) for "that authority or chief officer does not" substitute "the [designated permanent secretary][2], Chairman or Commissioners does or do not"; and

(*c*) for "that authority or chief officer" substitute "the [designated permanent secretary][2], Chairman or Commissioners".

Revocation—These Regs revoked by the Revenue and Customs (Complaints and Misconduct) Regulations, SI 2010/1813 reg 2 with effect from 5 August 2010. However, where an allegation in respect of the conduct by an officer came to the attention of the appropriate authority before 5 August 2010, nothing in SI 2010/1813 shall apply and these Regs shall continue to have effect.

Amendments—[1] Sub-para(2A) inserted by the Revenue and Customs (Complaints and Misconduct) (Amendment) Regulations, SI 2006/1748 reg 5(1), (4) with effect from 27 July 2006.

[2] Words substituted by the Constitutional Reform and Governance Act 2010 s 19, Sch 2 para 23 with effect from 11 November 2010 by virtue of SI 2010/2703 art 2.

12—(1) Paragraph 14 shall be modified as follows.

(2) In sub-paragraph (1) for "a police authority or chief officer" substitute "the [designated permanent secretary][1], Chairman or Commissioners".

(3) In sub-paragraph (2)—

(*a*) after "recordable conduct matter" insert "referred by the [designated permanent secretary][1], Chairman or Commissioners";

(*b*) for "appropriate authority" substitute "[designated permanent secretary][1], Chairman or Commissioners";

(*c*) for "that authority" (on the first occasion those words appear) substitute "by him or them"; and

(*d*) for "that authority" (on the second occasion those words appear) substitute "he or they".

Revocation—These Regs revoked by the Revenue and Customs (Complaints and Misconduct) Regulations, SI 2010/1813 reg 2 with effect from 5 August 2010. However, where an allegation in respect of the conduct by an officer came to the attention of the appropriate authority before 5 August 2010, nothing in SI 2010/1813 shall apply and these Regs shall continue to have effect.

Amendments—[1] Words substituted by the Constitutional Reform and Governance Act 2010 s 19, Sch 2 para 23 with effect from 11 November 2010 by virtue of SI 2010/2703 art 2.

13—(1) Paragraph 14A shall be modified as follows.

(2) For sub-paragraph (1) substitute—

"(1) Where a DSI matter comes to the attention of the Commissioners, being the appropriate authority, it shall be their duty to record that matter.".

Revocation—These Regs revoked by the Revenue and Customs (Complaints and Misconduct) Regulations, SI 2010/1813 reg 2 with effect from 5 August 2010. However, where an allegation in respect of the conduct by an officer came to the attention of the appropriate authority before 5 August 2010, nothing in SI 2010/1813 shall apply and these Regs shall continue to have effect.

14—(1) Paragraph 14B shall be modified as follows.

(2) Omit sub-paragraph (1).

(3) In sub-paragraph (2)—

(*a*) for the words from "Where" to the end of paragraph (*b*) substitute "Where a DSI matter comes to the attention of the Commissioners";

(*b*) for "his duty" substitute "their duty"; and

(*c*) for "to him" substitute "to them".

(4) In sub-paragraph (3) for "chief officer's" substitute "Commissioners'" and for "he becomes" substitute "they become".

(5) In sub-paragraph (4) for "he shall" substitute "they shall", "he is" substitute "they are" and "to him" substitute "to them".

(6) Omit sub-paragraph (5).

(7) In sub-paragraph (6) for "chief officer" substitute "Commissioners", for "he" substitute "they" and omit "by the police authority maintaining his force or".

Revocation—These Regs revoked by the Revenue and Customs (Complaints and Misconduct) Regulations, SI 2010/1813 reg 2 with effect from 5 August 2010. However, where an allegation in respect of the conduct by an officer came to the attention of the appropriate authority before 5 August 2010, nothing in SI 2010/1813 shall apply and these Regs shall continue to have effect.

15—(1) Paragraph 14D shall be modified as follows.

(2) In sub-paragraph (1) for "a police authority or a chief officer" substitute "the Commissioners".

Revocation—These Regs revoked by the Revenue and Customs (Complaints and Misconduct) Regulations, SI 2010/1813 reg 2 with effect from 5 August 2010. However, where an allegation in respect of the conduct by an officer came to the attention of the appropriate authority before 5 August 2010, nothing in SI 2010/1813 shall apply and these Regs shall continue to have effect.

16—(1) Paragraph 15 shall be modified as follows.

(2) After sub-paragraph (4)(*b*) insert—

"(*bb*) an investigation by a police force under the supervision of the Commission;".

(3) In sub-paragraph (4)(*c*) substitute "the appropriate authority" for "that authority".

(4) After sub-paragraph (4)(*c*) insert—

"(*cc*) an investigation by a police force under the management of the Commission;".

(5) After sub-paragraph (4) insert—

"(4A) An investigation relating to any conduct of the Chairman, Deputy Chairman or other Commissioners under this paragraph may only be carried out in the form specified in sub-paragraph (4)(*bb*), (4)(*cc*) or (4)(*d*).".

Revocation—These Regs revoked by the Revenue and Customs (Complaints and Misconduct) Regulations, SI 2010/1813 reg 2 with effect from 5 August 2010. However, where an allegation in respect of the conduct by an officer came to the attention of the appropriate authority before 5 August 2010, nothing in SI 2010/1813 shall apply and these Regs shall continue to have effect.

17—(1) Paragraph 16 shall be modified as follows.

(2) In sub-paragraph (1) omit paragraph (*a*).

(3) Omit sub-paragraph (2).

(4) For sub-paragraph (3) substitute—

"(3) It shall be the duty of the appropriate authority to appoint an officer to investigate the complaint or matter."

(5) Omit [sub-paragraphs (4) and (5)][1].

Revocation—These Regs revoked by the Revenue and Customs (Complaints and Misconduct) Regulations, SI 2010/1813 reg 2 with effect from 5 August 2010. However, where an allegation in respect of the conduct by an officer came to the attention of the appropriate authority before 5 August 2010, nothing in SI 2010/1813 shall apply and these Regs shall continue to have effect.

Amendments—[1] Sub-para (4) substituted, and in sub-para (5), words substituted by the Revenue and Customs (Complaints and Misconduct) (Amendment) Regulations, SI 2006/1748 reg 5(1), (5), (6) with effect from 27 July 2006.

18—(1) Paragraph 17 shall be modified as follows.

(2) In sub-paragraph (2) for the words from "appoint" to the end of the sub-paragraph substitute "appoint an officer to investigate the complaint or matter.".

(3) In sub-paragraph (4)(*a*) for "sub-paragraph 2(*a*) or (*b*)" substitute "sub-paragraph (2)".

(4) Omit sub-paragraphs (6) and (6A).

Revocation—These Regs revoked by the Revenue and Customs (Complaints and Misconduct) Regulations, SI 2010/1813 reg 2 with effect from 5 August 2010. However, where an allegation in respect of the conduct by an officer came to the attention of the appropriate authority before 5 August 2010, nothing in SI 2010/1813 shall apply and these Regs shall continue to have effect.

19 After paragraph 17 insert—

"17A—

(1) This paragraph applies where the Commission determines that there should be an investigation by a police force under the supervision of the Commission.

(2) The Commission shall—

(*a*) identify the police force whose force area includes the geographical area to which the subject matter of the complaint, recordable conduct matter or DSI matter most closely relates, and

(*b*) take steps to obtain the agreement of—

(i) the chief officer of police of that force, and

(ii) the appropriate authority,

to the appointment by the Commission of that force to carry out the investigation.

(3) In the event that no agreement is reached under sub-paragraph (2) the Commission may require the chief officer of police of any police force it considers appropriate to carry out the investigation.

(4) A chief officer of police of a police force who agrees to or is required to carry out an investigation shall, if he has not already done so, appoint a person serving with the police who is a member of that force to investigate that complaint.

(5) Sub-paragraphs (3) to (5) and (7) of paragraph 17 shall apply as they apply to an investigation by the appropriate authority which the Commission has determined is one that it should supervise and the references to the appropriate authority in those sub-paragraphs shall be treated as references to the chief officer of police concerned.

(6) An appointment of a person under sub-paragraph (4) or (5) shall be notified by the chief officer of police concerned to the appropriate authority.".

Revocation—These Regs revoked by the Revenue and Customs (Complaints and Misconduct) Regulations, SI 2010/1813 reg 2 with effect from 5 August 2010. However, where an allegation in respect of the conduct by an officer came to the attention of the appropriate authority before 5 August 2010, nothing in SI 2010/1813 shall apply and these Regs shall continue to have effect.

20 After paragraph 18 insert—

"18A—

(1) This paragraph applies where the Commission determines that there should be an investigation by a police force under the management of the Commission.

(2) The Commission shall—

(*a*) identify the police force whose force area includes the geographical area to which the subject matter of the complaint, recordable conduct matter or DSI matter most closely relates, and

(*b*) take steps to obtain the agreement of—

(i) the chief officer of police of that force, and

(ii) the appropriate authority,

to the appointment by the Commission of that force to carry out the investigation.

(3) In the event that no agreement is reached under sub-paragraph (2) the Commission may require the chief officer of police of any police force it considers appropriate to carry out the investigation.

(4) A chief officer of police of a police force who agrees to or is required to carry out an investigation shall, if he has not already done so, appoint a person serving with the police who is a member of that force to investigate that complaint or matter.

(5) Sub-paragraphs (3) to (5) of paragraph 17 shall apply as they apply to an investigation by the appropriate authority which the Commission has determined is one that it should supervise and the references to the appropriate authority in those sub-paragraphs shall be treated as references to the chief officer of police concerned.

(6) An appointment of a person under sub-paragraph (4) or (5) shall be notified by the chief officer of police concerned to the appropriate authority.

(7) The person appointed to investigate the complaint or matter shall, in relation to that investigation, be under the direction and control of the Commission.".

Revocation—These Regs revoked by the Revenue and Customs (Complaints and Misconduct) Regulations, SI 2010/1813 reg 2 with effect from 5 August 2010. However, where an allegation in respect of the conduct by an officer came to the attention of the appropriate authority before 5 August 2010, nothing in SI 2010/1813 shall apply and these Regs shall continue to have effect.

21 Omit paragraphs 19(3) and (3A).

Revocation—These Regs revoked by the Revenue and Customs (Complaints and Misconduct) Regulations, SI 2010/1813 reg 2 with effect from 5 August 2010. However, where an allegation in respect of the conduct by an officer came to the attention of the appropriate authority before 5 August 2010, nothing in SI 2010/1813 shall apply and these Regs shall continue to have effect.

22—(1) Paragraph 20 shall be modified as follows.

(2) Omit sub-paragraph (1)(*a*).

(3) In paragraph 20(3) after "Director of Public Prosecutions" insert "or, as the case may be, the Director of Revenue and Customs Prosecutions".

Revocation—These Regs revoked by the Revenue and Customs (Complaints and Misconduct) Regulations, SI 2010/1813 reg 2 with effect from 5 August 2010. However, where an allegation in respect of the conduct by an officer came to the attention of the appropriate authority before 5 August 2010, nothing in SI 2010/1813 shall apply and these Regs shall continue to have effect.

23 Omit paragraphs 20A to 20I.

Revocation—These Regs revoked by the Revenue and Customs (Complaints and Misconduct) Regulations, SI 2010/1813 reg 2 with effect from 5 August 2010. However, where an allegation in respect of the conduct by an officer came to the attention of the appropriate authority before 5 August 2010, nothing in SI 2010/1813 shall apply and these Regs shall continue to have effect.

24—(1) Paragraph 21A shall be modified as follows.
(2) In sub-paragraphs (1) and (3) for "a person serving with the police" substitute "an officer".
(3) In sub-paragraph (1) after "18" insert "or 18A".
(4) In sub-paragraph (3) for "16 or 17" substitute "16, 17 or 17A".

Revocation—These Regs revoked by the Revenue and Customs (Complaints and Misconduct) Regulations, SI 2010/1813 reg 2 with effect from 5 August 2010. However, where an allegation in respect of the conduct by an officer came to the attention of the appropriate authority before 5 August 2010, nothing in SI 2010/1813 shall apply and these Regs shall continue to have effect.

25 In paragraph 22(2) for "17 or 18" substitute "17, 17A, 18 or 18A".

Revocation—These Regs revoked by the Revenue and Customs (Complaints and Misconduct) Regulations, SI 2010/1813 reg 2 with effect from 5 August 2010. However, where an allegation in respect of the conduct by an officer came to the attention of the appropriate authority before 5 August 2010, nothing in SI 2010/1813 shall apply and these Regs shall continue to have effect.

26—(1) In paragraph 23(2)(*c*) after "Director of Public Prosecutions" insert "or the Director of Revenue and Customs Prosecutions".
(2) In paragraphs 23(3), (4) and (6)(*b*) after "Director of Public Prosecutions" insert "or, as the case may be, the Director of Revenue and Customs Prosecutions".

Revocation—These Regs revoked by the Revenue and Customs (Complaints and Misconduct) Regulations, SI 2010/1813 reg 2 with effect from 5 August 2010. However, where an allegation in respect of the conduct by an officer came to the attention of the appropriate authority before 5 August 2010, nothing in SI 2010/1813 shall apply and these Regs shall continue to have effect.

27 In paragraphs 24(2)(*b*), (3), (4) and (6)(*b*) after "Director of Public Prosecutions" insert "or, as the case may be, the Director of Revenue and Customs Prosecutions".

Revocation—These Regs revoked by the Revenue and Customs (Complaints and Misconduct) Regulations, SI 2010/1813 reg 2 with effect from 5 August 2010. However, where an allegation in respect of the conduct by an officer came to the attention of the appropriate authority before 5 August 2010, nothing in SI 2010/1813 shall apply and these Regs shall continue to have effect.

28 In paragraphs 24A(4), 24B(1) and 24C(1) for "a person serving with the police" substitute (on each occasion where the words occur) "an officer".

Revocation—These Regs revoked by the Revenue and Customs (Complaints and Misconduct) Regulations, SI 2010/1813 reg 2 with effect from 5 August 2010. However, where an allegation in respect of the conduct by an officer came to the attention of the appropriate authority before 5 August 2010, nothing in SI 2010/1813 shall apply and these Regs shall continue to have effect.

29 Omit paragraph 25(2A).

Revocation—These Regs revoked by the Revenue and Customs (Complaints and Misconduct) Regulations, SI 2010/1813 reg 2 with effect from 5 August 2010. However, where an allegation in respect of the conduct by an officer came to the attention of the appropriate authority before 5 August 2010, nothing in SI 2010/1813 shall apply and these Regs shall continue to have effect.

30 In paragraph 27(3) for "any person serving with the police" substitute "any officer".

Revocation—These Regs revoked by the Revenue and Customs (Complaints and Misconduct) Regulations, SI 2010/1813 reg 2 with effect from 5 August 2010. However, where an allegation in respect of the conduct by an officer came to the attention of the appropriate authority before 5 August 2010, nothing in SI 2010/1813 shall apply and these Regs shall continue to have effect.

SCHEDULE 4

Regulation 4(2)

PART 1
MODIFICATION OF THE COMPLAINTS REGULATIONS

1 Omit regulation 4.

Revocation—These Regs revoked by the Revenue and Customs (Complaints and Misconduct) Regulations, SI 2010/1813 reg 2 with effect from 5 August 2010. However, where an allegation in respect of the conduct by an officer came to the attention of the appropriate authority before 5 August 2010, nothing in SI 2010/1813 shall apply and these Regs shall continue to have effect.

2—(1) In regulation 6(2) for the words from "consent" to the end of the paragraph substitute—
"consent—

(i) in the case of an investigation carried out by an appointed person who is an officer, of the Director of Revenue and Customs Prosecutions, or
(ii) in any other case, of the Director of Public Prosecutions,

to the imposition thereof."
(2) In regulation 6(3) for—

(*a*) "a chief officer" substitute "the [designated permanent secretary][1], Chairman or Commissioners";

(*b*) "consulting him" substitute "consulting him or them";

(*c*) "he may make" substitute "he or they may make".

Revocation—These Regs revoked by the Revenue and Customs (Complaints and Misconduct) Regulations, SI 2010/1813 reg 2 with effect from 5 August 2010. However, where an allegation in respect of the conduct by an officer came to the attention of the appropriate authority before 5 August 2010, nothing in SI 2010/1813 shall apply and these Regs shall continue to have effect.

Amendments—[1] Words substituted by the Constitutional Reform and Governance Act 2010 s 19, Sch 2 para 23 with effect from 11 November 2010 by virtue of SI 2010/2703 art 2.

3 Omit regulations 7(2)(*b*) and 7(7)(*c*).

Revocation—These Regs revoked by the Revenue and Customs (Complaints and Misconduct) Regulations, SI 2010/1813 reg 2 with effect from 5 August 2010. However, where an allegation in respect of the conduct by an officer came to the attention of the appropriate authority before 5 August 2010, nothing in SI 2010/1813 shall apply and these Regs shall continue to have effect.

4—(1) In regulation 8(1) for "a police authority or chief officer" substitute "the [designated permanent secretary][1], Chairman or Commissioners".

(2) In regulation 8(2)(*c*) for "the police force or police authority which" substitute "the [designated permanent secretary][1], Chairman or Commissioners who".

(3) In regulations 8(3)(*a*) and (7) for "police authority or chief officer" substitute "[designated permanent secretary][1], Chairman or Commissioners".

(4) In regulation 8(5) for "A police authority or chief officer" substitute "The [designated permanent secretary][1], Chairman or Commissioners".

Revocation—These Regs revoked by the Revenue and Customs (Complaints and Misconduct) Regulations, SI 2010/1813 reg 2 with effect from 5 August 2010. However, where an allegation in respect of the conduct by an officer came to the attention of the appropriate authority before 5 August 2010, nothing in SI 2010/1813 shall apply and these Regs shall continue to have effect.

Amendments—[1] Words substituted by the Constitutional Reform and Governance Act 2010 s 19, Sch 2 para 23 with effect from 11 November 2010 by virtue of SI 2010/2703 art 2.

5 Omit regulation 9.

Revocation—These Regs revoked by the Revenue and Customs (Complaints and Misconduct) Regulations, SI 2010/1813 reg 2 with effect from 5 August 2010. However, where an allegation in respect of the conduct by an officer came to the attention of the appropriate authority before 5 August 2010, nothing in SI 2010/1813 shall apply and these Regs shall continue to have effect.

6—(1) Regulation 12 shall be modified as follows.

(2) After paragraph (1)(*b*) insert—

"(*c*) preventing the disclosure of any information held by the Revenue and Customs in connection with a function of the Revenue and Customs which—

(i) is obtained from the [designated permanent secretary][1], Chairman, Commissioners or an officer, and

(ii) relates to a person whose identity is specified in the disclosure or can be deduced from it.".

(3) After paragraph (1) insert—

"(1A) Paragraph (1)(*c*) does not apply to any information about internal administrative arrangements of Her Majesty's Revenue and Customs (whether relating to Commissioners, officers or others).".

(4) After paragraph (2) insert—

"(2A) The Commission shall consult the appropriate authority in any case under paragraph (1)(*c*) before deciding whether or not it is satisfied under paragraph (2).".

(5) After paragraph (3) insert—

"(4) In this regulation "the Revenue and Customs" means—

(*a*) the Commissioners;

(*b*) an officer;

(*c*) a person acting on behalf of the Commissioners or an officer;

(*d*) a committee established by the Commissioners;

(*e*) a member of a committee established by the Commissioners;

(*f*) the Commissioners of Inland Revenue (or any committee or staff of theirs or anyone acting on their behalf);

(*g*) the Commissioners of Customs and Excise (or any committee or staff of theirs or anyone acting on their behalf), and

(*h*) a person specified in section 6(2) or 7(3) of the Commissioners for Revenue and Customs Act 2005.".

Revocation—These Regs revoked by the Revenue and Customs (Complaints and Misconduct) Regulations, SI 2010/1813 reg 2 with effect from 5 August 2010. However, where an allegation in respect of the conduct by an officer came to the attention of the appropriate authority before 5 August 2010, nothing in SI 2010/1813 shall apply and these Regs shall continue to have effect.

Amendments—[1] Words substituted for words by the Constitutional Reform and Governance Act 2010 s 19, Sch 2 para 23 with effect from 11 November 2010 by virtue of SI 2010/2703 art 2.

7—(1) In regulation 18(1) for "17 or 18" substitute "17, 17A, 18 or 18A".
(2) Omit regulations 18(1)(*d*), (2) and (3).

Revocation—These Regs revoked by the Revenue and Customs (Complaints and Misconduct) Regulations, SI 2010/1813 reg 2 with effect from 5 August 2010. However, where an allegation in respect of the conduct by an officer came to the attention of the appropriate authority before 5 August 2010, nothing in SI 2010/1813 shall apply and these Regs shall continue to have effect.

8 In regulation 21 for "person serving with the police" substitute "Commissioner or an officer".

Revocation—These Regs revoked by the Revenue and Customs (Complaints and Misconduct) Regulations, SI 2010/1813 reg 2 with effect from 5 August 2010. However, where an allegation in respect of the conduct by an officer came to the attention of the appropriate authority before 5 August 2010, nothing in SI 2010/1813 shall apply and these Regs shall continue to have effect.

9 In regulation 24—

(*a*) for "Every police authority and chief officer" substitute "The [designated permanent secretary][2], Chairman and Commissioners", and

(*b*) in paragraphs (*a*)[, (*b*) and (*ab*)][1] for "it or him" substitute "him or them".

Revocation—These Regs revoked by the Revenue and Customs (Complaints and Misconduct) Regulations, SI 2010/1813 reg 2 with effect from 5 August 2010. However, where an allegation in respect of the conduct by an officer came to the attention of the appropriate authority before 5 August 2010, nothing in SI 2010/1813 shall apply and these Regs shall continue to have effect.

Amendments—[1] In sub-para (*b*), words substituted by the Revenue and Customs (Complaints and Misconduct) (Amendment) Regulations, SI 2006/1748 reg 6(1), (2) with effect from 27 July 2006.
[2] Words substituted by the Constitutional Reform and Governance Act 2010 s 19, Sch 2 para 23 with effect from 11 November 2010 by virute of SI 2010/2703 art 3.

10—(1) In regulation 25(1) for "a police authority or chief officer" substitute "the [designated permanent secretary][1], Chairman or Commissioners".
(2) In regulation 25(3) for "(*a*) and (*b*)" substitute "(*a*), (*b*) and (*c*)".

Revocation—These Regs revoked by the Revenue and Customs (Complaints and Misconduct) Regulations, SI 2010/1813 reg 2 with effect from 5 August 2010. However, where an allegation in respect of the conduct by an officer came to the attention of the appropriate authority before 5 August 2010, nothing in SI 2010/1813 shall apply and these Regs shall continue to have effect.

Amendments—[1] Words substituted by the Constitutional Reform and Governance Act 2010 s 19, Sch 2 para 23 with effect from 11 November 2010 by virtue of SI 2010/2703 art 2.

11—(1) Regulation 26 shall be modified as follows.
(2) In paragraph (1) for—

(*a*) "chief officer" substitute "the [designated permanent secretary][2], Chairman or Commissioners";

(*b*) "on him" substitute "on him or them"; and

(*c*) "an officer" substitute "a person".

(3) In paragraph (2) for sub-paragraphs (*a*) to (*c*) substitute—

"(*a*) in the case of the [designated permanent secretary][2], to a member of the Senior Civil Service;

(*b*) in the case of the Chairman, to a member of the Senior Civil Service employed in the service of the Commissioners;

(*c*) in the case of the Commissioners, to an officer.".

(4) Omit paragraph (3).
(5) For paragraph (4) substitute—

"(4) The [designated permanent secretary][2], Chairman or Commissioners shall not, in any particular case, delegate any power or duty under paragraph (1) to a person who has acted as investigating officer in that case.".

(6) In paragraph (5) for "a chief constable" substitute "the Head of the Home Civil Service, Chairman or Commissioners".[1]

Revocation—These Regs revoked by the Revenue and Customs (Complaints and Misconduct) Regulations, SI 2010/1813 reg 2 with effect from 5 August 2010. However, where an allegation in respect of the conduct by an officer came to the attention of the appropriate authority before 5 August 2010, nothing in SI 2010/1813 shall apply and these Regs shall continue to have effect.

Amendments—[1] Sub-para (6) revoked by the Revenue and Customs (Complaints and Misconduct) (Amendment) Regulations, SI 2006/1748 reg 6(1), (3) with effect from 27 July 2006.

[2] Words substituted by the Constitutional Reform and Governance Act 2010 s 19, Sch 2 para 23 with effect from 11November 2010 by virtue of SI 2010/2703 art 2

12 Omit regulations 28, 29 and 30.

Revocation—These Regs revoked by the Revenue and Customs (Complaints and Misconduct) Regulations, SI 2010/1813 reg 2 with effect from 5 August 2010. However, where an allegation in respect of the conduct by an officer came to the attention of the appropriate authority before 5 August 2010, nothing in SI 2010/1813 shall apply and these Regs shall continue to have effect.

PART 2

MODIFICATION OF THE STAFF CONDUCT REGULATIONS

1 In regulation 2(3)(*a*)(i) for "person serving with the police" substitute "Commissioner or officer".

Revocation—These Regs revoked by the Revenue and Customs (Complaints and Misconduct) Regulations, SI 2010/1813 reg 2 with effect from 5 August 2010. However, where an allegation in respect of the conduct by an officer came to the attention of the appropriate authority before 5 August 2010, nothing in SI 2010/1813 shall apply and these Regs shall continue to have effect.

2005/3327

INCOME TAX (INDEXATION) (NO 2) ORDER 2005

Made by the Treasury under TA 1988 s 257C(3)

Made . . . . *5th December 2005*

1 Citation

This Order may be cited as the Income Tax (Indexation) (No 2) Order 2005.

2 Amounts of personal allowance, married couple's allowance and blind person's allowance for 2005–6

(1) The amounts, which, unless Parliament otherwise determines, will be treated by virtue of sections 257C(1) and 265(1A) of the Income and Corporation Taxes Act 1988 as specified for the year 2006–7 in sections 257, 257AB, 257A and 265 of that Act are set out in paragraphs (2) to (4) below.

(2) In section 257 of that Act (personal allowance)—

(*a*) in subsection (1) (personal allowance)—£5,035;

(*b*) in subsection (2) (personal allowance—age 65–74)—£7,280;

(*c*) in subsection (3) (personal allowance—age 75 and over)—£7,420;

(*d*) in subsection (5) (income limit for age-related allowances)—£20,100.

(3) In section 257A of that Act (married couple's allowance)—

(*a*) in subsection (2) (married couple's allowance—age 70 to 74 and born before 6th April 1935)—£6,065;

(*b*) in subsection (3) (married couple's allowance—age 75 and over)—£6,135;

(*c*) in subsection (5) (income limit for age-related married couple's allowance)—£20,100;

(*d*) in subsection (5A) (minimum married couple's allowance)—£2,350.

(4) In section 257AB of that Act (married couple's allowance (post 5th December 2005 marriages and civil partnerships))—

(*a*) in subsection (2)(*a*) (married couple's allowance—age 75 and over)—£6,135;

(*b*) in subsection (2)(*b*) (married couple's allowance—age 70 to 74 and born before 6th April 1935)—£6,065;

(*c*) in subsection (4) (income limit for age-related allowances)—£20,100;

(*d*) in subsection (5) (minimum married couple's allowance)—£2,350.

(5) In section 265(1) of that Act (blind person's allowance)—£1,660.

2005/3338

LLOYD'S UNDERWRITERS (TAX) REGULATIONS 2005

Made by the Commissioners for HMRC, under FA 1993 ss 182(1)(a) and (6) and 184(1), FA 1994 ss 229(1)(a) and (2) and 230(1), FA 1999 ss 132 and 133(2) and F(No 2)A 2005 s 45(11)

Made . . . . *6th December 2005*

Laid before the House of Commons . . . . *6th December 2005*

Coming into force . . . . *27th December 2005*

PART 1
GENERAL

1 Citation, commencement and effect

(1) These Regulations may be cited as the Lloyd's Underwriters (Tax) Regulations 2005 and shall come into force on 27th December 2005.

(2) These Regulations shall have effect—

(*a*) in their application to members who are individuals, for the year 2006–07 (including any actions taken before 6th April 2006, in relation to the year 2006–07) and subsequent years of assessment; and

(*b*) in their application to corporate members, for accounting periods ending after 31st December 2005 (but not in relation to profits and losses arising to corporate members which are mentioned in section 220(2) of the Finance Act 1994 and are declared in 2005).

2 Interpretation

(1) In these Regulations—

"the Commissioners" means the Commissioners for Her Majesty's Revenue and Customs;

"managing agent", in relation to a syndicate and an underwriting year, means—

(*a*) the person registered as a managing agent at Lloyd's who is currently acting as such managing agent, or

(*b*) such person who has previously acted as managing agent in relation to that syndicate and underwriting year, as the Commissioners may determine;"

"the Management Act" means the Taxes Management Act 1970;

"notice" has the meaning in section 832(1) of the Taxes Act;

"Schedule 18" means Schedule 18 to the Finance Act 1998;

"the Taxes Act" means the Income and Corporation Taxes Act 1988.

(2) In relation to members who are individuals, other expressions which are defined in Chapter 3 of Part 2 of the Finance Act 1993 have those defined meanings.

(3) In relation to corporate members, other expressions which are defined in Chapter 5 of Part 4 of the Finance Act 1994 have those defined meanings.

PART 2
DETERMINATION OF A SYNDICATE'S PROFIT OR LOSS

3 Preliminary

In this Part of these Regulations "profit or loss", in relation to a syndicate, means the aggregate amount of such of the profits or losses of all the members of the syndicate (taken together) as arise—

(*a*) directly from their membership of the syndicate, or

(*b*) from assets forming part of premium trust funds,

and "profits" and "losses" shall be construed accordingly.

4 Returns by managing agent

(1) An officer of Revenue and Customs may, by notice to a syndicate's managing agent, require him to deliver a return (a "syndicate return") of the syndicate's profit or loss for an underwriting year (the amount of that profit or loss being referred to as a "syndicate determination").

(2) A notice under paragraph (1) may be given—

(*a*) at any time after the closing year for the underwriting year in question; and

(*b*) more than once, (in particular where the syndicate continues after the end of its closing year).

(3) The return shall—

(*a*) contain such information as may reasonably be required by the notice; and

(*b*) be accompanied by such accounts, statements and reports as may reasonably be so required.

(4) The filing date for any syndicate return required by a notice under paragraph (1) is whichever is the later of—

(*a*) 1st July in the underwriting year next following that closing year; and

(*b*) the end of the period of three months beginning on the day following that on which the notice was served.

(5) If a syndicate's managing agent, having been required by a notice under paragraph (1) to deliver a return, fails to deliver the return on or before the filing date, he shall be liable to a flat-rate penalty equal to the prescribed amount multiplied by the number of days on which the failure continues.

(6) In paragraph (5) "the prescribed amount" means £60 for each fifty members of the syndicate (counting any number of members less than fifty, and any number left over, as fifty).

(7) If a syndicate's managing agent fraudulently or negligently delivers an incorrect return under paragraph (1), he shall be liable to a penalty not exceeding £3,000 multiplied by the number of members of the syndicate.

(8) In relation to a return required by a notice under paragraph (1)—

(*a*) any reference in paragraph (4) or (5) to the filing date for, or delivery of, a return is a reference to its delivery together with the accompanying documents referred to in paragraph (3)(*b*); and

(*b*) the reference in paragraph (7) to the return being incorrect includes a reference to any of those documents being incorrect.

5 Amendment of syndicate determinations and HMRC enquiries

(1) In relation to both members who are individuals and corporate members, the like provisions as are contained in paragraphs 15, 16, 24, 25, 27 to 29 and 31 to 34 of Schedule 18 shall apply with the modifications in paragraphs (2) to (6).

(2) For references to—

(*a*) the company substitute references to the syndicate's managing agent;

(*b*) the company tax return substitute references to the syndicate return;

(*c*) the company's self-assessment, tax payable or tax liability, substitute references to the syndicate determination;

(*d*) an accounting period (or periods) substitute references to the underwriting year to which the syndicate return relates (or would relate); and

(*e*) the Inland Revenue substitute references to Her Majesty's Revenue and Customs.

(3) In paragraph 15(4) for "twelve" substitute "six".

(4) In paragraph 16(3) for "nine" substitute "three".

(5) In paragraph 24(2) for "twelve" substitute "six".

(6) Omit paragraphs 32(2) and (3) and 34(1)(*a*)(ii), (2)(*a*)(ii) and (5).

(7) The giving of a notice of enquiry to a syndicate's managing agent under the like provisions as are contained in paragraph 24 of Schedule 18 shall be deemed to include the giving of notice of enquiry—

(*a*) under section 9A(1) of the Management Act to each member of the syndicate who is an individual, and who at that time has made a return under section 8 or 8A of that Act or at any subsequent time makes such a return; and

(*b*) under paragraph 24 of Schedule 18 to each member of the syndicate who at that time has made a company tax return or at any subsequent time makes such a return.

5A [Notice to provide report on technical provisions

In relation to both members who are individuals and corporate members, paragraph 2 of Schedule 11 to the Finance Act 2007 (technical provisions made by general insurers: enforcement) shall apply with the following modifications—

(*a*) in sub-paragraphs (1), (2), (4), (5) and (6) for "general insurer" in each place it occurs substitute "syndicate's managing agent"; and

(*b*) in sub-paragraph (2)—

(i) for "general insurer's" substitute "managing agent's", and

(ii) for "the company tax return" substitute "the syndicate return".][1]

Definitions—In paragraph (2) "syndicate return" means a return of a syndicate's profit or loss for an underwriting year under regulation 4 of the Lloyd's Underwriters (Tax) Regulations 2005.

Amendments—[1] Reg 5A inserted by the Lloyd's Underwriters (Tax) (Amendment) Regulations, SI 2009/2889 reg 2(1), (2) with effect in relation to a syndicate return made in respect of profits or losses declared after 31 December 2009. Note that "syndicate return" means a return of a syndicate's profit or loss for an underwriting year under reg 4 of these regulations (SI 2009/2889 reg 1(3)).

6 HMRC determinations

(1) In relation to both members who are individuals and corporate members, the like provisions as are contained in paragraphs 36 and 40 of Schedule 18 shall apply with the modifications in paragraphs (2) and (3).

(2) For references to—

(*a*) the company substitute references to the syndicate's managing agent;

(*b*) the company tax return substitute references to the syndicate return;

(*c*) the company's self-assessment or tax payable, substitute references to the syndicate determination;

(*d*) an accounting period (or periods) substitute references to the underwriting year to which the syndicate return relates (or would relate); and

(*e*) the Inland Revenue substitute references to Her Majesty's Revenue and Customs.

(3) Omit paragraphs 36(3) and (6)(*a*) and 40(1)(*b*) and (2).

7 Discovery determinations

(1) In relation to both members who are individuals and corporate members, the like provisions as are contained in paragraphs 41(2) to 44 and 46 to 49 of Schedule 18 (as they apply to discovery determinations) shall apply with the modifications in paragraphs (2) and (3).

(2) Except in paragraph 49 of Schedule 18, for references to—

(*a*) the company substitute references to the syndicate's managing agent;
(*b*) the company tax return substitute references to the syndicate return;
(*c*) the company's self-assessment or tax payable, substitute references to the syndicate determination;
(*d*) an accounting period (or periods) substitute references to the underwriting year to which the syndicate return relates (or would relate); and
(*e*) the Inland Revenue substitute references to Her Majesty's Revenue and Customs.

(3) In paragraph 41(2) of Schedule 18, omit—
(*a*) "for another accounting period" in paragraph (*a*), and
(*b*) paragraph (*b*).

8 Relief in case of mistake in syndicate return

(1) In relation to both members who are individuals and corporate members, the like provisions as are contained in paragraph 51 of Schedule 18 shall apply with the modifications in paragraph (2).

(2) For references to—
(*a*) the company substitute references to the syndicate's managing agent;
(*b*) the payment of tax, an assessment or the profits of the company for corporation tax purposes substitute references to the syndicate determination;
(*c*) the liability of the claimant or claimant company, treat them as including references to the liability of the members of the syndicate;
(*d*) an accounting period (or periods) substitute references to the underwriting year to which the syndicate return relates (or would relate); and
(*e*) the Inland Revenue substitute references to Her Majesty's Revenue and Customs.

9 Apportionments of syndicate's profit or loss

(1) Where a determination of a syndicate's profit or loss for an underwriting year is made, amended or corrected (whether under the foregoing provisions of these Regulations or on appeal), the officer may, by notice in writing to the syndicate's managing agent, require him to make to the officer, within the specified period, a return apportioning, between the members of the syndicate, the syndicate's profit or loss as stated in the determination as so made, amended or corrected.

(2) If a syndicate's managing agent, having been required by a notice under paragraph (1) to deliver a return within the specified period, fails to deliver the return within that period, he shall be liable to a penalty equal to the prescribed amount multiplied by the number of days on which the failure continues.

(3) In paragraph (2) "the prescribed amount" means £5 for each fifty members of the syndicate (counting any number of members less than fifty, and any number left over, as fifty).

(4) In this regulation "the specified period" means such period, not being less than thirty days and beginning with the day following the date of the notice under paragraph (1), as may be specified in that notice.

10 Effect of determinations on members

(1) A determination of a syndicate's profit or loss for an underwriting year (whether as originally made or as amended or corrected) and any apportionment under regulation 9 shall, for the purpose of determining the liability to tax of each member of the syndicate, be conclusive against that member that the syndicate's profit or loss for that year, or the member's share of it, as the case may be, is as there stated.

(2) Where a determination of a syndicate's profit or loss for an underwriting year is amended or corrected at any time after the issue of a notice of assessment assessing any member of the syndicate to tax—
(*a*)
(i) in relation to members who are individuals, section 31A of the Management Act (notice of appeal) and section 55 of that Act (recovery of tax not postponed), and
(ii) in relation to corporate members, paragraph 48 of Schedule 18,

shall have effect, in relation to that member, as if any reference to the date of the notice of assessment, or the date of the issue of the notice of assessment, were a reference to the date of the amendment or correction; and

(*b*) in the case of an amendment, an assessment which gives effect to the determination as amended shall not be out of time if it is made within one year of the date of the amendment.

(3) Paragraph (2)(*b*) shall not apply in the case of an HMRC amendment under regulation 6 which is made later than six years after the end of the last year during which, or during any part of which, the syndicate continues.

11 Assessment of individual members: time limits

For the purposes of sections 36 and 40 of the Management Act and paragraph 46(2) of Schedule 18 (extension of time in cases of fraudulent or negligent conduct) anything done or omitted to be done by a syndicate's managing agent shall be deemed to have been done or omitted to be done by each member of the syndicate.

12 Non-delivery of return—reasonable excuse

(1) For the purposes of these Regulations, a managing agent shall be deemed not to have failed to deliver—

(*a*) a syndicate return by the filing date referred to in regulation 4(4), or

(*b*) a return apportioning a syndicate profit or loss within the period referred to in regulation 9(4),

if he delivered it within such further time, if any, as the officer of Revenue and Customs may have allowed.

(2) Where a managing agent had a reasonable excuse for not delivering a return mentioned in paragraph (1), he shall be deemed not to have failed to deliver it—

(*a*) unless the excuse had ceased, and

(*b*) if, after the excuse ceased, he delivered it without unreasonable delay.

13 Determinations and notices of determinations

The like provisions as are contained in section 113(1B) of the Management Act shall apply to a determination or notice of a determination under regulations 6 or 7 as if the determination were an assessment and the notice of a determination were a notice of an assessment.

PART 3

14 Repayment of tax deducted etc from investment income

(1) In relation to an underwriting year, a syndicate's managing agent may, by notice in writing at any time during the period of six years beginning with the 1st March next following the end of the closing year for that year, make a claim to an officer of Revenue and Customs for the repayment of tax suffered by way of deduction on such of the syndicate's investment income as is allocated to that year in accordance with the rules or practice of Lloyd's.

(2) The syndicate's managing agent shall provide such information in support of the claim as the officer may reasonably require.

(3) Where an amount is repaid to a syndicate's managing agent under this regulation, he shall—

(*a*) apportion that amount between the members of the syndicate in proportion to their interests in that part of the syndicate's investment income which has suffered tax by way of deduction; and

(*b*) except in so far as it is required to meet a share of a loss of the syndicate, pay the amount so apportioned to each member, within 90 days of the repayment, to the members' agent of that member.

(4) The provisions of section 824 of the Taxes Act (repayment supplements: individuals and others) shall not apply to any repayment of tax made under this regulation.

(5) In this regulation "investment income", in relation to a syndicate, means the aggregate amount of the profits arising to all the members of the syndicate (taken together) from assets forming part of premium trust funds.

(6) In its application to a corporate member, this regulation shall have effect as if—

(*a*) in paragraph (3)(*b*), the reference to the members' agent of each member were a reference to each corporate member itself; and

(*b*) in paragraph (4), the reference to section 824 of the Taxes Act were a reference to section 826 of that Act (interest on tax overpaid).

PART 4

ELECTRONIC COMMUNICATIONS, CONSEQUENTIAL PROVISIONS AND REPEALS

15 Amendment to the Income and Corporation Taxes (Electronic Communications) Regulations 2003

In regulation 2(1)(*a*) of the Income and Corporation Taxes (Electronic Communications) Regulations 2003, after paragraph (ii) insert—

"(iia) the Lloyd's Underwriters (Tax) Regulations 2005,".

16 Consequential provisions and repeals

In section 184(1) of the Finance Act 1993, in the definition of "members' agent", for "Part II of Schedule 19 to this Act" substitute "the Lloyd's Underwriters (Tax) Regulations 2005".

17 In Schedule 1 to the Income Tax (Trading and Other Income) Act 2005 omit paragraph 465.

18 Regulations 3, 7 and 8 of the Lloyd's Underwriters (Tax) Regulations 1995 are hereby revoked.

2005/3422

LOAN RELATIONSHIPS AND DERIVATIVE CONTRACTS (EXCHANGE GAINS AND LOSSES USING FAIR VALUE ACCOUNTING) REGULATIONS 2005

Made by the Treasury under FA 1996 s 103(1AA) and FA 2002 Sch 26 para 54(2A)

Made . . . . 12 December 2005
Laid before the House of Commons . . . . 12 December 2005
Coming into force . . . . 2 January 2006

1 Citation, commencement and effect

These Regulations may be cited as the Loan Relationships and Derivative Contracts (Exchange Gains and Losses using Fair Value Accounting) Regulations 2005 and shall come into force on 2nd January 2006 and shall have effect in relation to periods of account beginning on or after 1st January 2005.

[2 Interpretation

In these Regulations—

"CTA 2009" means the Corporation Tax Act 2009;
"CTA 2010" means the Corporation Tax Act 2010;
"derivative contract" has the same meaning as in Part 7 of CTA 2009;
"generally accepted accounting practice" has the meaning given in section 1127 of CTA 2010;
"loan relationship" has the same meaning as in section 302 CTA 2009;
"available-for-sale", "carrying value", "designated", "fair value", "fair value hedge" and "fair value through other comprehensive income" have the same meanings as they have for accounting purposes.][1]

Amendments—[1] Reg 2 substituted by the Loan Relationships and Derivative Contracts (Exchange Gains and Losses using Fair Value Accounting) (Amendment) Regulations, SI 2015/1963 reg 2(1), (2) with effect in relation to accounting periods beginning on or after 1 January 2016. Reg 2 previously read as follows—

"**2 Interpretation**

In these Regulations—

"derivative contract" has the same meaning as in Schedule 26 to the Finance Act 2002;
"fair value accounting" has the meaning given in section 103 of the Finance Act 1996;
"generally accepted accounting practice" has the meaning given in section 50 of the Finance Act 2004;
"loan relationship" has the same meaning as in Chapter 2 of Part 4 of the Finance Act 1996; and
"designated", "fair value", "available-for-sale" and "fair value hedge" have the same meanings as they have for accounting purposes.".

3 Currency

For the purposes of these Regulations the currency with which a company computes its profits and losses as determined by [Chapter 4 of Part 2 of CTA 2010][1] shall be known as the "base currency".

Amendments—[1] Words substituted for words "sections 92 to 92E of the Finance Act 1993" by the Loan Relationships and Derivative Contracts (Exchange Gains and Losses using Fair Value Accounting) (Amendment) Regulations, SI 2015/1963 reg 2(1), (3) with effect in relation to accounting periods beginning on or after 1 January 2016.

4 Exchange gain or loss: general

In these Regulations exchange gain or loss shall not include any debits or credits referred to in regulation 4(1), (3) and (4) of the Loan Relationships and Derivative Contracts (Change of Accounting Practice) Regulations 2004.

5 Exchange gain or loss arising from loan relationship assets or liabilities

(1) Paragraphs (2) and (3) set out the rules for calculating the exchange gain or loss arising from loan relationship assets or liabilities in the following circumstances—

(*a*) the asset or liability is [measured][1] at fair value, or
(*b*) that asset or liability or part of it is a hedged item in a designated fair value hedge [and the carrying value of the hedged item is adjusted for changes in fair value attributable to the hedged risk][1].

(2) Where paragraph (1) applies and—

(*a*) an amount is recognised in the company's [accounts][1] which arises from comparing at different times the fair value of the asset or liability (or in the case of regulation 5(1)(*b*) any part of it), and
(*b*) the change in fair value is attributable to any extent to fluctuations in the spot rate of exchange between the currency in which the asset or liability is denominated and the base currency of the company,

the exchange gain or loss is calculated as set out in paragraph (3).

(3) The exchange gain or loss for any accounting period is the change in fair value between the earlier and the later time in that period that is attributable only to fluctuations in the spot rate of exchange between the currency in which the asset or liability is denominated and the base currency of the company.

Amendments—[1] In para (1), in sub-para (*a*) word substituted for words "accounted for", and in sub-para (*b*) words substituted for words "and the risk being hedged is or includes exchange risk", and in para (2)(*a*), word substituted for words "profit and loss account or income statement", by the Loan Relationships and Derivative Contracts (Exchange Gains and Losses using Fair Value Accounting) (Amendment) Regulations, SI 2015/1963 reg 2(1), (4) with effect in relation to accounting periods beginning on or after 1 January 2016.

6 If an asset is accounted for as available-for-sale [or fair value through other comprehensive income][1], the exchange gain or loss is the amount shown in the profit and loss account or income statement which fairly represents that gain or loss in accordance with generally accepted accounting practice.

Amendments—[1] Words inserted by the Loan Relationships and Derivative Contracts (Exchange Gains and Losses using Fair Value Accounting) (Amendment) Regulations, SI 2015/1963 reg 2(1), (5) with effect in relation to accounting periods beginning on or after 1 January 2016.

7 Exchange gain or loss arising from derivative contracts

(1) Paragraphs (2) and (3) set out the rules for calculating the exchange gain or loss arising from derivative contracts where such a contract is accounted for at fair value.

(2) Where—

(*a*) an amount is recognised in the company's [accounts][1] which arises from comparing at different times the fair value of the derivative contract, and

(*b*) that change in fair value is attributable to any extent to fluctuations in the spot rate of exchange between the base currency of the company and one or more currencies that form part of—

(i) the underlying subject matter of the derivative contract, or

(ii) in a case in which that currency or those currencies do not form part of the underlying subject matter of the contract, the currency or currencies in which payments under the contract fall to be made,

the exchange gain or loss is calculated as set out in paragraph (3).

(3) The exchange gain or loss for any accounting period is the change in fair value between the earlier and the later time in that period that is attributable only to fluctuations in the spot rate of exchange between the currency or currencies and the base currency.

Amendments—[1] In para (2)(*a*), word substituted for words "profit and loss account or income statement" by the Loan Relationships and Derivative Contracts (Exchange Gains and Losses using Fair Value Accounting) (Amendment) Regulations, SI 2015/1963 reg 2(1), (6) with effect in relation to accounting periods beginning on or after 1 January 2016.

8 Calculation of residual profit and loss

Regulation 9 applies where there is a fair value profit or loss in relation to a loan relationship or derivative contract which is not wholly an exchange gain or loss (as determined by regulations 5 to 7).

9—(1) Where there is a fair value profit, the residual profit is calculated by subtracting from the profit any exchange gain, and adding to it the amount of any exchange loss.

(2) Where the exchange gain exceeds the fair value profit, the difference between the two is the residual loss.

(3) Where there is a fair value loss, the residual loss is calculated by adding to the loss any exchange gain or subtracting from it any exchange loss.

(4) Where the exchange loss exceeds the fair value loss the difference between the two is the residual profit.

(5) Residual profits and losses are amounts recognised in determining a company's profit or loss for a period for the purposes of [sections 308(1) and 597(1) of CTA 2009][1].

Amendments—[1] In para (5), words substituted for words "section 85B(1) of the Finance Act 1996 and paragraph 17B(1) of Schedule 26 to the Finance Act 2002" by the Loan Relationships and Derivative Contracts (Exchange Gains and Losses using Fair Value Accounting) (Amendment) Regulations, SI 2015/1963 reg 2(1), (7) with effect in relation to accounting periods beginning on or after 1 January 2016.

2005/3448

REGISTERED PENSION SCHEMES (RELIEF AT SOURCE) REGULATIONS 2005

Made . . . . 14th December 2005

Laid before the House of Commons . . . . 15th December 2005

Coming into force . . . . *6th April 2006*

Modifications—Registered Pension Schemes (Splitting of Schemes) Regulations, SI 2006/569 reg 3 (modification of this provision in relation to sub-scheme administrators).

The Commissioners for Her Majesty's Revenue and Customs, in exercise of the powers conferred by section 192(6), (7) and (8) of the Finance Act 2004, and now exercisable by them, make the following Regulations:

1 Citation and commencement

These Regulations may be cited as the Registered Pension Schemes (Relief at Source) Regulations 2005 and shall come into force on 6th April 2006.

2 Interpretation

(1) In these Regulations "section", without more, means a section of the Finance Act 2004.

(2) In these Regulations, unless the context otherwise requires—

"the basic amount" has the meaning given by section 190(4);

"electronic signature" has the meaning given by section 7(2) of the Electronic Communications Act 2000;

"ITEPA 2003" means the Income Tax (Earnings and Pensions) Act 2003;

"ITTOIA 2005" means the Income Tax (Trading and Other Income) Act 2005;

"net contribution" means a contribution from which income tax at [the relevant rate][2] is deductible in accordance with section 192;

"person with parental responsibility" means a person—

(*a*) in England and Wales, who has such responsibility within section 3 of the Children Act 1989;

(*b*) in Scotland means a person who has parental responsibilities as defined by section 1(3) of the Children (Scotland) Act 1995; and

(*c*) in Northern Ireland, who has such responsibility within the meaning of Article 6 of the Children (Northern Ireland) Order 1995;

"pension scheme" and "registered pension scheme" have the meanings given by section 150;

"relevant individual" means the person in respect of whom contributions are payable to a pension scheme;

"scheme administrator" has the meaning given by section 270;

"tax month" means a period beginning on the 6th day of any month and ending with the 5th day of the following month;

"TMA 1970" means the Taxes Management Act 1970;

["tribunal" means the First-tier Tribunal or, where determined by or under Tribunal Procedure Rules, the Upper Tribunal.][1]

"year of assessment" means a year beginning with 6th April in any year and ending with 5th April in the following year.

Amendments—[1] In para (2), entry for "tribunal" inserted by the Transfer of Tribunal Functions and Revenue and Customs Appeals Order, SI 2009/56 art 3, Sch 2 paras 143, 144 with effect from 1 April 2009.

[2] In para (2), in definition of "net contribution", words substituted by the Scottish Rate of Income Tax (Consequential Amendments) Order, SI 2015/1810 art 6 with effect in relation to the tax year 2016–17 (the tax year appointed by the Treasury under the Scotland Act 2012 s 25(5) by virtue of SI 2015/2000) and subsequent tax years.

3 Prescribed conditions

(1) Regulations 4, 5 and 6 specify the conditions subject to which relief under section 191 (methods of giving relief for pension contributions) shall be given in accordance with section 192(1) and (2) (relief at source).

(2) The particulars specified in regulation 4(2) and the declarations required by regulations 5(2) and 6(2) must be given to the scheme administrator by the relevant individual. This paragraph is subject to the qualifications in paragraph (3) and regulation 7.

(3) In a case where—

(*a*) membership of a registered pension scheme is connected with a particular employment, and

(*b*) an individual in such employment automatically becomes a member of a registered pension scheme, subject to the right of the individual to opt out of membership of the scheme,

the employer (rather than the relevant individual) may give the scheme administrator the particulars specified in regulation 4(2), and make the declarations required by regulation 5(2) and 6.

4 Information to be given to the scheme administrator

(1) The scheme administrator must be given—

(*a*) the particulars specified in paragraph (2), and

(*b*) the declarations required by regulations 5(2) and 6(2),

before the time specified in paragraph (5).

(2) The particulars are—

(*a*) the relevant individual's full name and permanent residential address including, where the address is in the United Kingdom, the postcode.

(*b*) the relevant individual's date of birth;

(*c*) unless the relevant individual is—

(i) aged under 16, or

(ii) a citizen of a country outside the United Kingdom who is not resident in the United Kingdom,

the relevant individual's National Insurance number, or a statement that he does not have one;

(*d*) except where the scheme is an occupational pension scheme within the meaning of section 150(5), the category of status specified in paragraph (3) applicable in the relevant individual's case or, if more than one category is applicable, the category which is that individual's principal source of income.

(3) The categories of status specified for the purposes of paragraph (2)(*d*) are—

(*a*) employed, if the relevant individual is chargeable to tax under Chapter 2 of Part 2 of ITEPA 2003 for the year of assessment concerned in respect of employment income as defined in section 7 of that Act;

(*b*) pensioner, where the relevant individual is chargeable to tax under Part 9 of that Act for the year of assessment concerned in respect of a pension;

(*c*) self-employed, in the case of an individual chargeable to tax under Chapter 2 of Part 2 of ITTOIA 2005 for the year of assessment concerned in respect of annual profits or gains arising or accruing from any trade, profession or vocation carried on by the individual;

(*d*) child, where the individual is under the age of 16;

(*e*) other, in the case of a relevant individual not falling within any of sub-paragraphs (*a*) to (*d*).

(4) In the case of a relevant individual whose status falls within paragraph (3)(*e*), the particulars given must specify which of the following descriptors is applicable or, if more than one, the most applicable, namely—

(*a*) caring for one or more children aged under 16;

(*b*) caring for a person aged 16 or over;

(*c*) in full time education;

(*d*) unemployed; or

(*e*) other.

(5) The time specified in relation to the particulars in paragraph (2)(*a*) to (*d*) is when the individual first pays a net contribution.

5 Declaration that relevant individual entitled to relief

(1) Before a relevant individual pays a net contribution for the first time, the scheme administrator must be given the declaration specified in paragraph (2).

(2) The declaration is one that the total contributions to any registered pension schemes in respect of which he is entitled to relief under section 188 will not exceed the higher of—

(*a*) the basic amount, or

(*b*) the relevant individual's relevant UK earnings, within the meaning of section 189 for that tax year.

6 Declaration about accuracy of information

(1) Whenever particulars are given in accordance with regulation 4 they must be accompanied by the declaration specified in paragraph (2).

(2) The declaration is one to the effect that—

(*a*) in relation to—

(i) the particulars specified in regulation 4(2), they are, to the best of the maker's knowledge and belief, correct and complete;

(ii) the declaration specified in regulation 5(2), it is, to the best of the maker's knowledge and belief, correct;

(*b*) no later than the date specified in paragraph (3), the maker will give notice to the scheme administrator if an event occurs, as a result of which the relevant individual will no longer be entitled to relief for his contributions pursuant to section 188.

(3) The date is the later of—

(*a*) 5th April in the year of assessment in which the event referred to in sub-paragraph (2)(*b*) occurs; and

(*b*) the date which is 30 days after the occurrence of that event.

(4) If a declaration given under this regulation or regulation 5 is in writing, it shall be signed by, or on behalf of, the maker.

7 Persons under incapacity and disabled persons

(1) Where the obligations imposed by regulations 4 to 6 would fall to be discharged by a person who is—

(*a*) a child under the age of 16,

(*b*) a person incapable, by reason of mental disorder, of managing and administering his property and affairs, or (*c*) a person suffering from a physical disability, by reason of which he has difficulty executing documents in respect of the management and administration of his property and affairs,

the following provisions of this regulation apply.

(2) In a case falling within paragraph (1)(*a*) those obligations shall be discharged by the child's parent or guardian, or a person with parental responsibility for the child.

(3) In a case falling within paragraph (1)(*b*) those obligations shall be discharged—

(*a*) in England and Wales or Northern Ireland, by the person's attorney or receiver, or the person managing and administering his property and affairs;

(*b*) in Scotland, by the person's guardian within the meaning of the Adults with Incapacity (Scotland) Act 2000.

(4) In a case falling within paragraph (1)(*c*) those obligations may be discharged by a person having a power of attorney in relation to the affairs of the person referred to in that sub-paragraph.

8 Electronic communications and documents

(1) If particulars or declarations given under regulations 4 to 7—

(*a*) are not in writing, or

(*b*) are given to the scheme administrator by someone other than the relevant individual,

the following provisions of this regulation apply.

(2) In a case falling within paragraph (1) the scheme administrator shall—

(*a*) make a declaration in writing on behalf of the relevant individual under regulations 4 to 6 that the particulars given or the terms of the declarations given are those recorded in the scheme administrator's declaration, and

(*b*) send a copy of the declaration to the relevant individual.

(3) Unless the relevant individual notifies the scheme administrator, within 30 days after the date when the copy of the declaration referred to in paragraph (2) ("the original declaration") was sent to him—

(*a*) that he does not wish to become a member of the pension scheme, or

(*b*) that the original declaration was incorrect,

the original declaration shall take effect as from the date on which the copy of it was sent to the relevant individual in accordance with that paragraph.

(4) If the relevant individual notifies the scheme administrator that the original declaration should be corrected, the original declaration shall cease to have effect, and the scheme administrator shall make a new declaration and paragraphs (2) and (3) shall apply to the new declaration as they applied to the original declaration.

(5) Particulars or declarations furnished under regulation 4, 5, 6 or 7 or this regulation shall be regarded as furnished in writing for the purposes of this regulation if, although not in writing, they are furnished by means of electronic communication and contain the electronic signature of the maker.

(6) Declarations made by the scheme administrator under this regulation shall be regarded as made in writing if they are produced by electronic means.

(7) The copy of a declaration to be sent in accordance with paragraph (2)(*b*) may be sent to the relevant individual by electronic communications.

(8) In the case of a person to whom regulation 7 applies, references in this regulation to the relevant individual include any person authorised by that regulation to act on his behalf.

9 Claims: introductory

(1) Amounts recoverable by a scheme administrator under section 192(3)(*a*) shall be recovered on a claim made to Her Majesty's Revenue and Customs for the purpose of these Regulations.

(2) A claim shall be for a year of assessment (an "annual claim").

This is subject to the following qualification.

(3) A claim may also be made in accordance with regulation 10 for a tax month (an "interim claim").

10 Interim claims

(1) An interim claim may be made by a scheme administrator within 6 months after the end of the tax month for which it is made.

This is subject to the following qualifications.

(2) An interim claim may not be made for the tax month ending 5th October or for any subsequent month until the annual claim for the preceding year of assessment and any information required by a notice under regulation 15(1) in respect of that year has been made by the scheme administrator and received by an officer of Revenue and Customs.

(3) An interim claim may not be based on an estimate but may only be made to recover an amount deducted in respect of contributions paid in the tax month to which it relates.

(4) If the amount claimed is established to the satisfaction of Her Majesty's Revenue and Customs, they shall pay that amount to the claimant: if they are not so satisfied they shall pay to the claimant any lesser amount which is so established.

(5) If a scheme administrator discovers that an amount paid by Her Majesty's Revenue and Customs under paragraph (4) was excessive the scheme administrator shall bring into account in the interim claim next made after the discovery ("the subsequent claim") the amount of the excess.
If that excess exceeds the amount deducted in respect of the tax month for which the subsequent claim is made—

(*a*) the scheme administrator shall repay the amount of the excess to Her Majesty's Revenue and Customs with the claim; and

(*b*) if the scheme administrator fails so to do that amount shall immediately be recoverable by Her Majesty's Revenue and Customs in the same manner as tax charged by an assessment on the scheme administrator which has become final and conclusive.

11 Annual claims

(1) An annual claim may be made at any time within 6 years after the end of the year of assessment to which it relates.
This is subject to the following qualification.

(2) In relation to any year of assessment in which a scheme administrator has received and not repaid in full any amount on an interim claim, the administrator shall within 6 months after the end of the year of assessment make an annual claim.

(3) An annual claim—

(*a*) may not be based on an estimate but may only be made to recover an amount deducted in respect of contributions paid in respect of the year of assessment to which it relates, and

(*b*) must bring into account payments made in respect of that year.

For the purpose of this regulation "aggregate of the interim payments" means the aggregate of payments made (and not repaid) on interim claims.

(4) Where the aggregate of the interim payments shown by an annual claim exceeds the amount deducted for the year of assessment—

(*a*) the scheme administrator shall repay the amount of the excess to Her Majesty's Revenue and Customs with the claim; and

(*b*) if the administrator fails to do so, that amount shall immediately be recoverable by Her Majesty's Revenue and Customs in the same manner as tax charged by an assessment on the scheme administrator which has become final and conclusive.

(5) If a scheme administrator fails to make an annual claim under paragraph (2) within the time limited by that paragraph, an officer of Revenue and Customs may issue a notice to the scheme administrator showing the aggregate of the interim payments for the year, and stating that they are not satisfied that the amount due to the scheme administrator for the year of assessment exceeds the lower amount stated in the notice.

(6) If an annual claim is not delivered to Her Majesty's Revenue and Customs within 14 days after the issue of a notice under paragraph (5), the amount of the difference between the aggregate of the interim payments and the amount stated in the notice shall immediately be recoverable by Her Majesty's Revenue and Customs in the same manner as tax charged by an assessment on the scheme administrator which has become final and conclusive.

(7) If an annual claim has been made and the scheme administrator subsequently discovers that an error or mistake has been made in the claim the scheme administrator may make a supplementary claim within the time limited by paragraph (1).

12 Claims: supplementary provisions

(1) Section 42 of TMA 1970 (procedure for making claims) shall not apply to a claim under these Regulations.

(2) No appeal shall lie from the decision of an officer of Revenue and Customs on an interim claim.

(3) An appeal . . . [1] from the decision of an officer of Revenue and Customs on an annual claim . . . [1] shall be brought by giving written notice to the officer within 30 days of receipt of written notice of the decision.

(4) No payment made or other thing done on or in relation to an interim claim shall prejudice the decision on an annual claim.

(5) Part 5 of TMA 1970 (appeals and other proceedings) shall apply to an appeal under paragraph (3) [and, on an appeal that is notified to the tribunal, the tribunal][1] may vary the decision appealed against whether or not the variation is to the advantage of the appellant.

(6) All such assessments, payments and repayments shall be made as are necessary to give effect to the decision of an officer of Revenue and Customs on an annual claim, or to any variation of that decision on appeal.

(7) Claims under these Regulations must—

(*a*) contain such information and be in such form as the Commissioners for Her Majesty's Revenue and Customs may prescribe (and forms prescribed for annual claims may require a report to be given by the scheme administrator's auditor);

(*b*) contain declarations to the effect that—

(i) sufficient records in respect of the scheme are maintained so as to enable the requirements of these Regulations to be satisfied, and

(ii) the information contained in the claim (including the declaration referred to in paragraph (i)) is correct; and

(*c*) be signed by the scheme administrator or an individual in the service of the scheme administrator authorised by him.

Amendments—[1] In para (3), words revoked, and in para (5), words substituted, by the Transfer of Tribunal Functions and Revenue and Customs Appeals Order, SI 2009/56 art 3, Sch 2 paras 143, 145 with effect from 1 April 2009.

13 Recovery on de-registration of schemes

(1) When a scheme administrator gives information to an officer of Revenue and Customs in accordance with regulation 15(2) the amount (if any) referred to in regulation 15(2)(*b*) must be paid to Her Majesty's Revenue and Customs.

(2) If an amount payable by virtue of paragraph (1) is not paid as required, that amount shall immediately be recoverable by Her Majesty's Revenue and Customs in the same manner as tax charged by an assessment on the scheme administrator which has become final and conclusive.

14 Recovery of amounts by assessment &c

(1) Section 30 of TMA 1970 (recovery of overpayment of tax, etc) shall apply in relation to the payment by Her Majesty's Revenue and Customs of an amount—

(*a*) paid under these Regulations to which a scheme administrator was not entitled, or

(*b*) recoverable from a scheme administrator under regulations 10(5), 11(4) or (6) or 13,

as if it had been income tax repaid to the scheme administrator to which he was not entitled.

(2) An assessment made by virtue of this regulation shall be made by an officer of Revenue and Customs and, subject to the provisions of these Regulations, TMA 1970 shall apply as if the assessment were an assessment to tax for the year of assessment in respect of which the amount was paid or is recoverable.

(3) For the purposes of section 86 TMA 1970 (interest on overdue income tax and capital gains tax) the relevant date shall be the later of—

(*a*) 1st January in the year in which the amount was paid or is recoverable; or

(*b*) the date of the making of the repayment by Her Majesty's Revenue and Customs following receipt of the annual claim for that year.

(4) Section 95 of TMA 1970 (incorrect return or accounts of income tax or capital gains tax) shall apply to an amount—

(a) paid under these Regulations to a scheme administrator by reason of an incorrect claim made by him and

(b) to which the scheme administrator was not entitled,

as if that amount were tax payable by him.[1]

Amendments—[1] Para (4) revoked by the Finance Act 2008, Schedule 40 (Appointed Day, Transitional Provisions and Consequential Amendments) Order, SI 2009/571 art 9, Sch 1 paras Sch 2 paras 1, 2 with effect from 1 April 2009.

15 Information

(1) An officer of Revenue and Customs may by notice in writing require any person who is, or who at any time has been—

(*a*) a scheme administrator to whom net contributions have been paid, or

(*b*) an individual or other person who has paid such contributions,

to give the officer, within such time (not being less than 14 days) as may be provided in the notice, such information and in such form as may be prescribed in the notice.

(2) If an officer of Revenue and Customs by notice under section 157 withdraws the registration of a scheme under which net contributions have been paid, within 30 days the scheme administrator in relation to that scheme must give to that officer the following information—

(*a*) the full name, address and national insurance number of each individual who has paid net contributions after the date specified in the notice in relation to the scheme ("the relevant contributions"); and

(*b*) the amount of relief obtained under section 189 by means of the relevant contributions.

(3) If the requirements of regulations 4 to 6 or 7(2) or (3) have not been met in relation to an individual who has paid net contributions, the scheme administrator to whom such contributions have been made shall give to an officer of Revenue and Customs the information prescribed in paragraph (2) within 30 days.

16 Inspection of records

(1) Every scheme administrator to whom net contributions have been paid shall, whenever required so to do, make available for inspection by an officer of Revenue and Customs all books, documents and other records (including all particulars and declarations furnished under regulations 4 to 6 and 7(2) to 7(4)) in the scheme administrator's possession or control relating to—

(*a*) contributions paid to the scheme administrator,

(*b*) the scheme under which those contributions were paid, and

(c) the individual who paid the contributions.

(2) Where records are maintained by computer, the scheme administrator shall provide the person making the inspection with all facilities necessary to obtain information from them.

(3) All books, documents and records referred to in paragraph (1), shall be preserved by the scheme administrator so as to be available for inspection under this regulation for a period of six years following the end of the tax year to which they relate, or, where there is more than one such year, the later or latest of them.

This is subject to the following qualification.

(4) All particulars and declarations furnished under regulations 4 to 8 shall be preserved for a period of six years following the end of the tax year in which the individual to whom they relate ceased to make net contributions.

17 Transitional provision

(1) If information has been furnished to, or a declaration made to, the scheme administrator of a personal pension scheme in relation to an individual in accordance with any provision of the Personal Pension Schemes (Relief at Source) Regulations 1988 ("the 1988 Regulations"), paragraph (2) applies.

(2) If this paragraph applies, and the scheme administrator to whom information or a declaration under these Regulations would fall to be made—

(a) is the same person as the scheme administrator to whom that information was furnished (whether in the form of particulars or a certificate), or that declaration was made, under the 1988 Regulations, or

(b) is the successor, as the scheme administrator of the scheme to which the 1988 Regulations applied, of the person to whom that information was furnished or that declaration was made,

the information furnished under the 1988 Regulations, and the declaration under those Regulations, shall be treated as having been furnished or made under these Regulations.

2005/3449

REGISTERED PENSION SCHEMES (PRESCRIBED INTEREST RATES FOR AUTHORISED EMPLOYER LOANS) REGULATIONS 2005

Made . . . . 14 December 2005
Laid before the House of Commons . . . . 15 December 2005
Coming into force . . . . 6 April 2006

The Commissioners for Her Majesty's Revenue and Customs, in exercise of the powers conferred by section 179(2)(a) of the Finance Act 2004 make the following Regulations:

1 Citation and commencement

These Regulations may be cited as the Registered Pension Schemes (Prescribed Interest Rates for Authorised Employer Loans) Regulations 2005 and shall come into force on 6th April 2006.

2 Interpretation

(1) In these Regulations—

"the operative date" means the sixth working day of each month;

"the reference date" is the twelfth working day preceding the operative date in the following month;

"working day" means a day which is not a non-business day within the meaning of section 92 of the Bills of Exchange Act 1882.

(2) In these Regulations the relevant interest rate found on a reference date is the percentage rate per annum found by the following steps.

Step 1

Find the average of the base lending rates of—

(a) the Bank of Scotland;
(b) Barclays Bank plc;
(c) HSBC Bank plc;
(d) Lloyds TSB Bank plc;
(e) National Westminster Bank plc; and
(f) the Royal Bank of Scotland plc.

Step 2

If the amount found by step 1 is a multiple of 1/4%, that is the relevant interest rate.

If the amount found by step 1 is not such a multiple, round the amount up to the nearest amount which is such a multiple.

3 Prescribed rate of interest for the purposes of section 179 of the Finance Act 2004

(1) For the purposes of section 179 of the Finance Act 2004 (authorised employer loans) the prescribed rate of interest is found in accordance with paragraph (2).

(2) The prescribed rate applicable for the period beginning on one operative date and ending on the day preceding the next operative date is the percentage rate found by the formula—

$$RIR + 1$$

Here RIR is the relevant interest rate found on the reference date immediately preceding the operative date at the start of the period.

2005/3450

REGISTERED PENSION SCHEMES (MINIMUM CONTRIBUTIONS) REGULATIONS 2005

Made . . . . *14th December 2005*
Laid before the House of Commons . . . . *15th December 2005*
Coming into force . . . . *6th April 2006*

Modifications—Registered Pension Schemes (Splitting of Schemes) Regulations, SI 2006/569 reg 3 (modification of this provision in relation to sub-scheme administrators).

The Commissioners for Her Majesty's Revenue and Customs, in exercise of the powers conferred upon them by section 202(5)(*b*) of the Finance Act 2004, and now exercisable by them, make the following Regulations:

1 Citation and commencement

These Regulations may be cited as the Registered Pension Schemes (Minimum Contributions) Regulations 2005 and shall come into force on 6th April 2006.

2 Recovery of amounts representing basic rate tax

(1) Subsections (1), (1B), (4) and (5) of section 30 of the Taxes Management Act 1970 (recovery of overpayments of tax, etc) shall apply in relation to the payment by the Commissioners for Her Majesty's Revenue and Customs of an amount, by way of minimum contributions under section 202 of the Finance Act 2004, which—

(*a*) they were not required to pay, or

(*b*) they were required to pay, but which they paid to persons other than the scheme administrator of the registered pension scheme to whom they should have made the payment,

as if a sum representing income tax at the basic rate on the amount paid ("the notional repayment sum") had been income tax repaid to the person to whom, or in respect of whom, the amount was paid, and to which that person was not entitled.

(2) An assessment made by virtue of paragraph (1) shall be made by an officer of Revenue and Customs and the provisions of the Taxes Management Act 1970 shall apply to the assessment as if it were an assessment to tax for the year of assessment in respect of which the amount of the notional repayment sum was paid.

2005/3451

REGISTERED PENSION SCHEMES (PRESCRIBED SCHEMES AND OCCUPATIONS) REGULATIONS 2005

Made . . . . *14th December 2005*
Laid before the House of Commons . . . . *15th December 2005*
Coming into force . . . . *6th April 2006*

The Commissioners for Her Majesty's Revenue and Customs, in exercise of the powers conferred by paragraphs 19(3)(*c*) and 23(4)(*b*) of Schedule 36 to the Finance Act 2004, and now exercisable by them, make the following Regulations:

1 Citation, commencement and interpretation

(1) These Regulations shall be cited as the Registered Pension Schemes (Prescribed Schemes and Occupations) Regulations 2005 and shall come into force on 6th April 2006.

(2) In these Regulations "Schedule 36" means Schedule 36 to the Finance Act 2004 (pension schemes etc: transitional provisions and savings) and any other reference to a numbered Schedule is a reference to the corresponding Schedule to these Regulations.

2 Schemes prescribed for the purposes of paragraph 19(3) of Schedule 36

A pension scheme is prescribed for the purposes of paragraph 19(3) of Schedule 36 if—

(*a*) it is listed in Schedule 1; or

(*b*) it is a scheme established solely for the receipt of additional voluntary pension contributions from members of a scheme listed in Schedule 1.

3 Occupations prescribed for the purposes of paragraph 23 of Schedule 36

The occupations listed in Schedule 2 are prescribed for the purposes of paragraph 23 of Schedule 36.

SCHEDULE 1

PRESCRIBED SCHEMES

Regulation 2

The Armed Forces Pension Scheme.

The British Transport Police Force Superannuation Fund.

The Firefighters' Pension Scheme.

The Firemen's Pension Scheme (Northern Ireland).

The Gurkha Pension Scheme

The Police Pension Scheme.

The Police Service of Northern Ireland Pension Scheme.

The Police Service of Northern Ireland Full Time Reserve Pension Scheme.

SCHEDULE 2

PRESCRIBED OCCUPATIONS

Regulation 3

Athletes

Badminton Players

Boxers

Cricketers

Cyclists

Dancers

Divers (Saturation, Deep Sea and Free Swimming)

Footballers

Golfers

Ice Hockey Players

Jockeys—Flat Racing

Jockeys—National Hunt

Members of the Reserve Forces

Models

Motor Cycle Riders (Motocross or Road Racing)

Motor Racing Drivers

Rugby League Players

Rugby Union Players

Skiers (Downhill)

Snooker or Billiards Players

Speedway Riders

Squash Players

Table Tennis Players

Tennis Players (including Real Tennis)

Trapeze Artistes

Wrestlers

2005/3452

REGISTERED PENSION SCHEMES (DISCHARGE OF LIABILITIES UNDER SECTIONS 267 AND 268 OF THE FINANCE ACT 2004) REGULATIONS 2005

Made . . . . *14th December 2005*

Laid before the House of Commons . . . . *15th December 2005*

Coming into force . . . . *6th April 2006*

Modifications—Registered Pension Schemes (Splitting of Schemes) Regulations, SI 2006/569 reg 3 (modification of this provision in relation to sub-scheme administrators).

The Commissioners for Her Majesty's Revenue and Customs, in exercise of the powers conferred by sections 267(10) and 268(10) of the Finance Act 2004 make the following Regulations:

1 Citation and commencement

These Regulations may be cited as the Registered Pension Schemes (Discharge of Liabilities under Sections 267 and 268 of the Finance Act 2004) Regulations 2005 and shall come into force on 6th April 2006.

2 Interpretation

In these Regulations—

"a section 267 application" means an application under subsection (2) or (5) of section 267 of the Finance Act 2004 (which concern the scheme administrator's liability to lifetime allowance charges);

"a section 268 application" means an application under subsection (2) or (5) of section 268 of the Finance Act 2004 (which concern liability to unauthorised payments surcharges and scheme sanctions charges);

"applicant" means a person making a section 267 application or a section 268 application; and

"company" and "year of assessment" have the meanings given to them in section 832 of the Income and Corporation Taxes Act 1988.

3 Time limits for, and content of section 267 and 268 applications

(1) Any section 267 application or section 268 application must be made in writing—

(*a*) in the case of a company, not later than six years after the end of the accounting period to which it relates; or

(*b*) in the case of any other applicant, no later than five years after the 31st January next following the year of assessment to which it relates.

This is subject to the following qualification.

(2) If an assessment is made under section 36 of the Taxes Management Act 1970 (assessments for the purpose of making good any loss to the Crown from a loss of income tax, etc), the section 267 application or section 268 application (as the case may be) must be made within two years of the date on which the assessment is issued as stated in the notice of that assessment.

(3) A section 267 application or section 268 application shall set out particulars of the ground relied on under the relevant section.

4 Applications on behalf of persons who are incapacitated

. . . [1]

Amendments—[1] Reg 4 revoked by the Child Trust Funds, Registered Pension Schemes and Stamp Duty Reserve Tax (Consequential Amendments) Regulations, SI 2012/886 reg 3 with effect from 6 April 2012.

5 Supplementary applications

Where a section 267 application or section 268 application has been made and the applicant subsequently discovers that an error or mistake has been made in it, the applicant may make a supplementary application in the same manner, and within the same time, as is allowed for making the original application.

2005/3453

EMPLOYER-FINANCED RETIREMENT BENEFITS SCHEMES (PROVISION OF INFORMATION) REGULATIONS 2005

Made . . . . *14th December 2005*
Laid before the House of Commons . . . . *15th December 2005*
Coming into force . . . . *6th April 2006*

The Commissioners for Her Majesty's Revenue and Customs, in exercise of the powers conferred by section 251(1) and (2)(*e*) and (*f*) of the Finance Act 2004, and now exercisable by them, make the following Regulations:

1 Citation and commencement

These Regulations may be cited as the Employer-Financed Retirement Benefits Schemes (Provision of Information) Regulations 2005 and shall come into force on 6th April 2006.

2 Interpretation

(1) In these Regulations—

"the Act" means the Finance Act 2004; and

"ITEPA 2003" means the Income Tax (Earnings and Pensions) Act 2003.

(2) In these Regulations—

"employer-financed retirement benefits scheme" has the same meaning as in section 393A of ITEPA 2003;

"relevant benefits" has the same meaning as in section 393B of ITEPA 2003;
"responsible person" has the same meaning as in section 399A of ITEPA 2003;
"year of assessment" means a year beginning with 6th April in any year and ending with 5th April in the following year.

3 Prescribed person

The responsible person in relation to an employer-financed retirement benefits scheme is the person prescribed for the purposes of these Regulations.

4 Provision of information in relation to the coming into operation of schemes

(1) The responsible person shall supply to the Board the particulars prescribed in paragraph (3) on or before 31st January next following the end of the year of assessment during which the scheme first came into operation.

(2) For the purposes of this regulation a scheme "comes into operation" on whichever is the first date, on or after that on which these Regulations come into force, on which—

(*a*) an employer makes a contribution to that scheme; or
(*b*) relevant benefits are provided.

(3) The prescribed information for the purposes of this paragraph is—

(*a*) the name of the scheme;
(*b*) the address of the responsible person; and
(*c*) the date the scheme came into operation.

5 Provision of information in relation to relevant benefits

(1) The responsible person shall supply to the Board the particulars prescribed in paragraph (3) in respect of all relevant benefits provided during the year of assessment at the time prescribed by paragraph (4).

This is subject to the following qualification.

(2) Information is not required to be supplied under this regulation in respect of pensions which are chargeable to tax under Chapter 2 of Part 9 of ITEPA 2003.

(3) The prescribed information is—

(*a*) the name, address and national insurance number of the recipient of the relevant benefit;
(*b*) the nature of the relevant benefit provided; and
(*c*) the amount of the relevant benefit calculated in accordance with section 398(2) of ITEPA 2003.

(4) The prescribed time is not later than 7th July following the end of the year of assessment in which the relevant benefit was provided.

2005/3454

REGISTERED PENSION SCHEMES (ACCOUNTING AND ASSESSMENT) REGULATIONS 2005

Made . . . . *14 December 2005*
Laid before the House of Commons . . . . *15 December 2005*
Coming into force . . . . *6 April 2006*

Modifications—Registered Pension Schemes (Splitting of Schemes) Regulations, SI 2006/569 reg 3 (modification of this provision in relation to sub-scheme administrators).

The Commissioners for Her Majesty's Revenue and Customs, in exercise of the powers conferred upon them by sections 254(4)(*b*), (6) and (7) and 255 of the Finance Act 2004 make the following Regulations:

1 Citation and commencement

These Regulations may be cited as the Registered Pension Schemes (Accounting and Assessment) Regulations 2005 and shall come into force on 6th April 2006.

2 Interpretation

(1) In these Regulations—

"the Act" means the Finance Act 2004;
"ITEPA" means the Income Tax (Earnings and Pensions) Act 2003;
"TMA" means the Taxes Management Act 1970.

(2) In these Regulations a reference to a numbered case is a reference to the case bearing that number in Table 2.

3 The particulars required to be included in returns under section 254

[(1)] If the scheme administrator is liable to income tax in respect of a charge listed in column 1 of Table 1, the return under section 254 of the Act must include the particulars in respect of that liability specified in column 2.

Table 1

Column 1: charge	*Column 2: specified particulars*
Charge under section 207 of the Act (authorised surplus payments charge).	1 The number of employers to whom an authorised surplus payment was made. 2 The name . . . [1] and, if appropriate, company registration number of each employer to whom an authorised surplus payment was made. 3 The date the authorised surplus payment was made. 4 The amount of tax due and payable in respect of each authorised surplus payment.
Charge under section 214 of the Act (lifetime allowance charge).	1 The number of individuals liable to a lifetime allowance charge. 2 The name, date of birth, address and national insurance number of each individual liable to a lifetime allowance charge. 3 The date of the benefit crystallisation event in relation to the lifetime allowance charge. 4 The amount of tax due in respect of each chargeable amount as constitutes a lump-sum amount and each chargeable amount as constitutes a retained amount.
[Charge under section 227 of the Act (annual allowance charge).	1. The title, name and national insurance number of each individual in relation to whom the scheme administrator becomes liable to an annual allowance charge under section 237B(7)of the Act. 2. The date on which the scheme administrator becomes liable to the annual allowance charge.. 3. The amount of tax to which the scheme administrator became jointly liable in respect of each individual under section 237B(7) of the Act. [4. The tax year to which the annual allowance charge relates.][3]][2]
Charge under section 242 of the Act (deregistration charge).	The date the registration of the registered pension scheme was withdrawn.
[Charge under section 244A (overseas transfer charge).	1. The name, date of birth and national insurance number of each individual in whose case a transfer results in the scheme administrator becoming liable to the overseas transfer charge. 2. The date, and transferred value, of each transfer. 3. The reference number of the qualifying recognised overseas pension scheme to which each transfer is made. 4. The amount of tax due in respect of each transfer.][4]

[(2) Where an individual provides the scheme administrator with written confirmation that the individual does not qualify for a national insurance number, the scheme administrator must—

(*a*) provide the Commissioners with the individual's date of birth and address in order to obtain an alternative number from them, and

(*b*) provide this alternative number in place of the national insurance number (where the national insurance number is required by paragraph (1)).

(3) Paragraph (4) applies to any amended return (made in accordance with regulation 6)—

(*a*) delivered on or after 6th April 2011 in respect of a return under section 254 of the Act delivered before 6th April 2011, and

(*b*) which relates to an individual whose details were included in the return under section 254 of the Act in relation to which an amended return is being made.

(4) Where paragraph (1) requires the scheme administrator to provide the Commissioners with an individual's national insurance number and where the national insurance number is not known to the scheme administrator—

(*a*) paragraph (2) does not apply, and

(*b*) the scheme administrator may provide the date of birth in place of the national insurance number.][1]

Amendments—[1] Para (1) numbered as such, in para (1) Table amended, and paras (2)–(4) inserted, by the Registered Pension Schemes (Accounting and Assessment) (Amendment) Regulations, SI 2011/302 reg 2 with effect from 6 April 2011.

[2] In para (1), Table, entry inserted by the Registered Pension Schemes (Miscellaneous Amendments) Regulations, SI 2011/1751 reg 9 with effect from 11 August 2011.

[3] In para (1), Table, entry inserted by the Registered Pension Schemes (Reduction in Pension Rates, Accounting and Assessment) (Amendment) Regulations, SI 2013/1111 reg 2 with effect from 31 May 2013.

[4] In para (1), Table, entry inserted by FA 2017 s 10, Sch 4 para 21(1) with effect in relation to transfers made on or after 9 March 2017. Note that this amendment is to be treated as having been made by the HMRC Commissioners under the applicable powers to make regulations conferred by FA 2004 s 254 (FA 2017 Sch 4 para 21(3)).

4 The making of assessments

(1) In the cases listed in column 1 of Table 2 an officer of Revenue and Customs must issue an assessment to tax to the assessable person specified in column 2.

Table 2

Column 1	*Column 2: assessable person*
Case 1: a charge to tax arises under section 208 of the Act (unauthorised payments charge) and the person liable to the charge is a company.	The person liable to the charge under section 208(2) of the Act.
Case 2: a charge to tax arises under section 209 of the Act (unauthorised payments surcharge) and the person liable to the charge is a company.	The person liable to the charge under section 209(3) of the Act.
Case 3: a charge to tax arises under section 217(2) of the Act (lifetime allowance charge on receipt of a lump sum death benefit).	The person liable under section 217(2) of the Act.
Case 4: a charge to tax arises under section 239 of the Act (scheme sanction charge).	The scheme administrator, or the person or persons liable to the scheme sanction charge under section 239(3) of the Act.
Case 5: the correct tax due under section 254 of the Act has not been paid on or before the due date.	The scheme administrator.
[Case 6A: section 272C of the Act (former scheme administrator etc to retain liability) applies.	The person or persons specified as assuming liability under section 272C(3), (4) or (7) of the Act.
Case 7A: a charge to tax arises under regulations made under section 273ZA of the Act (income and gains from taxable property).	The person liable to the charge.][1]
Tax assessed under case 8.	31st January following the end of the tax year in which the benefit within section 393 of ITEPA is received.

(2) Subject to paragraph (3), tax assessed under this regulation is payable within 30 days after the issue of the notice of assessment.

(3) Tax assessed under cases 1 and 2 is payable on the day following the expiry of nine months from the end of the accounting period in which the unauthorised payment was made or, if later, within 30 days after the issue of the notice of assessment.

(4) An assessment under case 3 may be made at any time not later than six years after an officer of Revenue and Customs is notified of the relevant lump sum death benefit, but cannot be made later than 20 years after 31st January following the end of the tax year in which the relevant lump sum death benefit was paid.

(5) Any tax assessable under one or more cases of Table 1 may be included in one assessment if the tax so included is all due on the same date.

Amendments—[1] In para (1), in Table 2, entries inserted by the Registered Pension Schemes (Accounting and Assessment) (Amendment) Regulations, SI 2014/1928 regs 2, 3 with effect from 1 September 2014.

5 Interest on tax due under section 254 or assessed under regulation 4

(1) Tax which—

(*a*) becomes due and payable in accordance with section 254(5) of the Act, or

(*b*) is assessed under regulation 4,

carries interest at the prescribed rate from the reckonable date until payment ("the interest period").

(2) The "prescribed rate" means the rate applicable under section 178 of the Finance Act 1989 for the purposes of section 86 of TMA.

(3) In relation to each of the cases listed in column 1 of Table 3, the "reckonable date" is specified in column 2.

Column 1	*Column 2: reckonable date*
Tax due under section 254 of the Act.	The due date under section 254(5) of the Act.
Tax assessed under case 1 or 2.	The day following the expiry of nine months from the end of the accounting period in which the unauthorised payment was made.
Tax assessed under case 3.	31st January following the end of the tax year in which the relevant lump sum death benefit was paid.
Tax assessed under case 4.	31st January following the end of the tax year in which the scheme sanction charge arose.
Tax assessed under case 5.	The due date under section 254(5) of the Act.
Tax assessed under case 6[, 6A][1] or 7.	The date the tax was due before sections 272[, 272C][1] or 273 of the Act applied in relation to the pension scheme.
[Tax assessed under Case 7A.	31st January following the end of the tax year in which the charge arose.][1]
Tax assessed under case 8.	31st January following the end of the tax year in which the benefit within section 393 of ITEPA is received.

(4) Paragraph (1) applies even if the reckonable date is a non-business day as defined by section 92 of the Bills of Exchange Act 1882.

(5) Any change made to the prescribed rate during the interest period applies to the unpaid amount from the date of the change.

Amendments—[1] In para (3), in Table 3, in entry for "Tax assessed under case 6 or 7.Tax assessed under case 6 or 7", words inserted, and entry inserted by the Registered Pension Schemes (Accounting and Assessment) (Amendment) Regulations, SI 2014/1928 regs 2, 4 with effect from 1 September 2014.

6 The making of amended returns

If the scheme administrator becomes aware—

(*a*) that anything which ought to have been included in a return made under section 254 of the Act for any period has not been so included,

(*b*) that anything which ought not to have been included in a return made under section 254 of the Act for any period has been so included, or

(*c*) that any other error has occurred in a return made under section 254 of the Act for any period,

the scheme administrator must immediately make an amended return to an officer of Revenue and Customs for that period.

7 Adjustments, repayments and interest on tax overpaid

(1) If the correct tax due under section 254 of the Act has not been paid on or before the due date or if an amended return is made under regulation 6, an officer of Revenue and Customs may make such adjustments or repayments as may be required for securing that the resulting liabilities to tax (including interest on unpaid or overpaid tax) whether of the scheme administrator or of any other person are the same as they would have been if the correct tax had been paid or if a correct return had been made.

(2) Tax overpaid which is repaid to the scheme administrator or any other person carries interest at the prescribed rate from the later of the due date and the date on which the tax was paid until the date of repayment ("the interest period").

(3) The "prescribed rate" means the rate applicable under section 178 of the Finance Act 1989 for the purposes of section 824 of the Income and Corporation Taxes Act 1988.

(4) Any change made to the prescribed rate during the interest period applies to the overpaid amount from the date of the change.

8 Modifications and application of TMA

(1) Section 9(1A) of TMA (tax not to be assessed by a self-assessment) applies with the following modifications in relation to an assessment to tax under case [3, 6, 6A, 7 or 7A][1].

(2) At the end of paragraph [(*ab*)][1] delete "or".
(3) After paragraph (*b*) insert—
"(*c*) is chargeable on a person under section 217(2) of the Finance Act 2004 (liability to lifetime allowance charge by reason of the payment of a relevant lump sum death benefit),
(*d*) is chargeable on a person or persons under section 272 of the Finance Act 2004 (trustees etc liable as scheme administrator), . . . [1]
[(*da*) is chargeable on a person or persons under section 272C of the Finance Act 2004 (former scheme administrator etc to retain liability),][1]
(*e*) is chargeable on a person or persons under section 273 of the Finance Act 2004 (members liable as scheme administrator)[, or
(*f*) is chargeable on a person under regulations made under section 273ZA of the Finance Act 2004 (income and gains from taxable property).[1]]".

Amendments—[1] The following amendments made by the Registered Pension Schemes (Accounting and Assessment) (Amendment) Regulations, SI 2014/1928 regs 2, 5–7 with effect from 1 September 2014—
- in para (1), words substituted for words "3, 6 or 7";
- in para (2), reference substituted for reference "(*a*)";
- in para (3)(*d*), word "or" at the end revoked and para (3)(*da*) inserted; and
- para (3)(*f*) and preceding word inserted.

9—(1) Section 29(1)(*a*) of TMA (assessment where loss of tax discovered) applies with the following modification in relation to an assessment to tax under case 1, 2 or 3.
(2) After "any income" insert—
", unauthorised payments under section 208 of the Finance Act 2004 or surchargeable unauthorised payments under section 209 of that Act or relevant lump sum death benefit under section 217(2) of that Act".

10—(1) Section 34(1) of TMA (ordinary time limit of six years) applies with the following modifications in relation to an assessment to tax under case 8.
(2) For "income tax or" substitute "income tax,".
(3) After "capital gains tax" insert—
"or to tax chargeable under section 394(2) of the Income Tax (Earnings and Pensions) Act 2003".

11—(1) Section 36(1) of TMA (fraudulent or negligent conduct) applies with the following modifications in relation to an assessment to tax under case 8.
(2) For "income tax or" substitute "income tax,".
(3) After "capital gains tax" insert "or to tax chargeable under section 394(2) of the Income Tax (Earnings and Pensions) Act 2003".

12 In relation to any assessment under case 5—
(*a*) section 34 of TMA applies notwithstanding that the assessment may relate to a quarter or other period which is not a year of assessment, and
(*b*) for the purposes of section 36 of TMA any such assessment relates to the year of assessment in which the quarter or other period ends.

13 Modification of Schedule 18 to the Finance Act 1998
(1) Schedule 18 to the Finance Act 1998 (company tax returns, assessments and related matters) applies with the following modification in relation to an assessment to tax under case 8.
(2) In paragraph 1 after "as if it was corporation tax" insert—
"but does not include any tax which is chargeable on the person who is (or persons who are) the responsible person in relation to an employer-financed retirement benefits scheme under section 394(2) of the Income Tax (Earnings and Pensions) Act 2003".

[14 Claims for repayments of overseas transfer charge
(1) This regulation applies where the scheme administrator of a registered pension scheme becomes aware that the scheme administrator may be entitled to a repayment under section 244M of the Act in respect of overseas transfer charge on a transfer.
(2) The scheme administrator must, no later than 60 days after the date on which the scheme administrator becomes aware of that, make a claim for the repayment to the Commissioners for Her Majesty's Revenue and Customs.
(3) The claim must provide the following information—
(*a*) the member's name, date of birth and principal residential address,
(*b*) the date of the transfer and, if different, the date of the event triggering payability of the charge on the transfer,
(*c*) the date on which the scheme manager accounted for the charge on the transfer,
(*d*) why the charge on the transfer has become repayable, and

(*e*) the amount in respect of which the claim is made.

(4) In a case where the 60 days mentioned in paragraph (2) ends with a day earlier than 14 November 2017, paragraph (2) is to be treated as requiring the claim to be made no later than 14 November 2017."][1]

Amendments—[1] Reg 14 inserted by FA 2017 s 10, Sch 4 para 21(2) with effect in relation to transfers made on or after 9 March 2017. Note that this amendment is to be treated as having been made by the HMRC Commissioners under the powers to make regulations conferred by FA 2004 s 244M(7) (FA 2017 Sch 4 para 21(4)).

2005/3455

REGISTERED PENSION SCHEMES AND EMPLOYER-FINANCED RETIREMENT BENEFITS SCHEMES (INFORMATION) (PRESCRIBED DESCRIPTIONS OF PERSONS) REGULATIONS 2005

Made . . . . .14th December 2005

Laid before the House of Commons . . . . .15th December 2005

Coming into force . . . . .6th April 2006

Modifications—Registered Pension Schemes (Splitting of Schemes) Regulations, SI 2006/569 reg 3 (modification of this provision in relation to sub-scheme administrators).

The Commissioners of Inland Revenue, in exercise of the powers conferred upon them by section 252(1) of the Finance Act 2004, make the following Regulations:

1 Citation, commencement and interpretation

(1) These Regulations may be cited as the Registered Pension Schemes and Employer-Financed Retirement Benefits Schemes (Information) (Prescribed Descriptions of Persons) Regulations 2005 and shall come into force on 6th April 2006.

(2) In these Regulations any reference, without more, to a numbered section, is a reference to the section of the Finance Act 2004 which is so numbered.

2 Prescribed descriptions of persons for the purposes of section 252 of the Finance Act 2004

(1) For the purposes of section 252 (notices requiring documents or particulars about registered pension schemes and employer-financed retirement benefit schemes) the prescribed descriptions of persons are those prescribed in the following paragraphs.

For the purposes of this regulation "the relevant period" means the period which—

(*a*) begins with the time at which occurred the event in relation to which information is required by the notice under section 252, and

(*b*) ends with the end of the sixth tax year following that in which that event occurred.

(2) In relation to a pension scheme referred to in subsection (3)(*a*), (*b*) or (*c*) of section 252 the prescribed descriptions of person are—

(*a*) any person who is, or at any time during the relevant period has been, the scheme administrator,

(*b*) any person who is, or at any time during the relevant period has been, a trustee of the scheme,

(*c*) any person who is, or at any time during the relevant period has been, a sponsoring employer in relation to the scheme, and

(*d*) any person who is, or at any time within the relevant period has been, a member of the scheme,

in respect of which the notice is given.

(3) In relation to an annuity purchased with sums or assets held for the purposes of a registered pension scheme, the prescribed description of person is the insurance company or other person from whom the annuity has been purchased.

(4) In relation to an employer-financed retirement benefits scheme, the prescribed description of person—

(*a*) for the purposes of section 252(3)(*e*), is the responsible person at the time the scheme comes into operation; and

(*b*) for the purposes of section 252(3)(*f*) is the responsible person at the time that the notice under that section is issued.

(5) For the purposes of paragraph (4)—

(*a*) a scheme "comes into operation" on whichever is the first date, on or after that on which these Regulations come into force on which—

(i) an employer makes a contribution to that scheme; or

(ii) relevant benefits are provided; and

(*b*) "responsible person" has the meaning given in section 399A of the Income Tax Earnings and Pensions Act 2003.

2005/3456

REGISTERED PENSION SCHEMES (AUDITED ACCOUNTS) (SPECIFIED PERSONS) REGULATIONS 2005

Made by the Commissioners for HMRC under FA 2004 s 250(6)

Made . . . . *14th December 2005*
Laid before the House of Commons . . . . *15th December 2005*
Coming into force . . . . *6th April 2006*

1 Citation and commencement

These Regulations may be cited as the Registered Pension Schemes (Audited Accounts) (Specified Persons) Regulations 2005 and shall come into force on 6th April 2006.

2 Specified descriptions of persons in relation to the audit of registered pension scheme accounts

In relation to the audit of the accounts of a registered pension scheme, the following descriptions of person are specified namely—

[(*a*) a person specified in section 1212 of the Companies Act 2006 (individuals and firms: eligibility for appointment as a statutory auditor);][1]

(*b*) a person eligible for appointment as a scheme auditor under section 47(1) of the Pensions Act 1995 or Article 47(1) of the Pensions (Northern Ireland) Order 1995 (professional advisers).

This is subject to regulation 3.

Amendments—[1] Para (*a*) substituted by the Companies Act 2006 (Consequential Amendments) (Taxes and National Insurance) Order, SI 2008/954 arts 55, 56 with effect from 6 April 2008.

[3 Circumstances in which a person specified under regulation 2 is not to audit scheme accounts

(1) Notwithstanding regulation 2, a person shall not be a registered pension scheme's auditor if he is—

(*a*) a member of the scheme;

(*b*) employed under a contract of service by the scheme administrator;

(*c*) an employer in relation to the scheme; or

(*d*) subject to paragraph (2), ineligible, by virtue of section 1214 of the Companies Act 2006, to audit the accounts of a company which is an employer in relation to the scheme.

(2) Paragraph (1)(*d*) does not apply in relation to the accounts and auditor's statement for a relevant scheme for a scheme year—

(*a*) in which, on the first day of that scheme year, the scheme has at least 500 participating employers; or

(*b*) which immediately precedes a scheme year in which sub-paragraph (a) is satisfied.

(3) In paragraph (2)—

"relevant scheme" means a trust scheme which applies to earners in employment under different employers; and

"scheme year" means—

(*a*) a year specified for the purposes of the scheme in any document comprising the scheme or, if none, a period of 12 months commencing on 1st April or on such date as the trustees or managers select; or

(*b*) such other period (if any) exceeding 6 months but not exceeding 18 months as is selected by the trustees or managers in connection with—

(i) the commencement or termination of the scheme; or

(ii) a variation of the date on which the year or period referred to in sub-paragraph (a) is to commence.][1]

Amendments—[1] Regulation 3 substituted by the Registered Pension Schemes (Audited Accounts) (Specified Persons) (Amendment) Regulations, SI 2015/1518 reg 2 with effect from 6 April 2014. Note that the power to make the Regulations with retrospective effect is provided for in FA 2004 s 282(A1).

2005/3457

TAXES MANAGEMENT ACT 1970 (MODIFICATIONS TO SCHEDULE 3 FOR PENSION SCHEME APPEALS) ORDER 2005

Revocation—These Regulations revoked by the Transfer of Tribunal Functions and Revenue and Customs Appeals Order, SI 2009/56 art 3, Sch 2 para 187(*u*) with effect from 1 April 2009.

2005/3458

REGISTERED PENSION SCHEMES (RESTRICTION OF EMPLOYERS' RELIEF) REGULATIONS 2005

Made by the Commissioners for HMRC under FA 2004 s 196A(1)

Made . . . . *14th December 2005*
Laid before the House of Commons . . . . *15th December 2005*
Coming into force . . . . *6th April 2006*

1 Citation, commencement and interpretation

(1) These Regulations may be cited as the Registered Pension Schemes (Restriction of Employers' Relief) Regulations 2005 and shall come into force on 6th April 2006.

(2) In these Regulations—

(*a*) "arrangement" has the meaning in section 152(1);
(*b*) "period of account" has the meaning in section 832(1) of the Income and Corporation Taxes Act 1988; and
(*c*) references to a section (without more) are to that section of the Finance Act 2004.

2 Scope of these Regulations

(1) These Regulations apply in circumstances where—

(*a*) subsection (2) or (3) of section 196A applies (or both do); and
(*b*) the condition in paragraph (2) is not satisfied.

(2) The condition in this paragraph is that, in such of those subsections as apply—

(*a*) the employer-financed retirement benefits scheme referred to is a recognised overseas pension scheme within the meaning in section 150(8); and
(*b*) the individual referred to would be a relevant migrant member of that scheme by virtue of paragraph 4 of Schedule 33 to the Finance Act 2004, or regulations made under sub-paragraph (*c*) of that paragraph, modified as follows—
  (i) in paragraph 4, in the words preceding sub-paragraph (*a*), omit "in relation to any contributions,";
  (ii) in sub-paragraph (*b*) for "the time when the contributions are paid" substitute "the employer's period of account which is in question"; and
  (iii) omit sub-paragraph (*d*).

3 Restriction of employers' relief in respect of contributions

Contributions paid by an employer under a registered pension scheme, where a member is an individual referred to in section 196A(2) or (3), shall be subject to the following restrictions on relief.

4 In respect of each arrangement relating to the individual under the scheme, calculate the individual's pension input amount (modified as follows) for the employer's period of account in which the contributions are paid, in accordance with regulations 5 to 8.

5 Cash balance arrangements

(1) The individual's pension input amount for a period of account in respect of a cash balance arrangement shall be determined in accordance with sections 230 and 232, modified as follows.

(2) In both sections, for each of the references to the "pension input period" and the "pension input period of the arrangement that ends in the tax year" substitute references to the employer's period of account in question.

(3) In both section 230(4) and (5) at the end add "ignoring (if it be the case) the fact that payment of any benefits, or the amount of any recognised transfer, is subject to a contingency mentioned in section 196A(2) or (3)".

(4) In section 230(6) omit the reference to section 231.

(5) The amount of any relievable pension contributions paid by or on behalf of the individual under the arrangement during the period of account is to be subtracted from the closing value.

6 Other money purchase arrangements

(1) The individual's pension input amount for a period of account in respect of a money purchase arrangement other than a cash balance arrangement shall be determined in accordance with section 233, modified as follows.

(2) Omit section 233(1)(*a*) and the word "and" which follows it.

(3) For the reference to the "pension input period of the arrangement that ends in the tax year" substitute a reference to the employer's period of account in question.

7 Defined benefits arrangements

(1) The individual's pension input amount for a period of account in respect of a defined benefits arrangement shall be determined in accordance with sections 234 and 236, modified as follows.

(2) In both sections, for each of the references to the "pension input period" and the "pension input period of the arrangement that ends in the tax year" substitute references to the employer's period of account in question.
(3) In section 234(4) and (5), in each of the definitions of PB, LSB, PE and LSE at the end add "ignoring (if it be the case) the fact that payment of any benefits, or the amount of any recognised transfer, is subject to a contingency mentioned in section 196A(2) or (3)".
(4) In section 234(6) omit the reference to section 235.
(5) The amount of any relievable pension contributions paid by or on behalf of the individual under the arrangement during the period of account is to be subtracted from the closing value.

8 Hybrid arrangements

(1) The individual's pension input amount for a period of account in respect of a hybrid arrangement shall be determined in accordance with section 237, modified as follows.
(2) Omit the references to sections 231 and 235.
(3) Sections 230, 232 to 234 and 236 shall be modified in accordance with regulation 5, 6 or 7, as the case may be.

9 Restriction of relief

Aggregate the pension input amounts for the period of account in question in respect of each arrangement relating to the individual under the scheme.

10 An amount equal to the aggregate pension input amount in respect of that individual for the period of account in question shall not be subject to relief within the meaning in section 196A(4).

2006/129

REGISTERED PENSION SCHEMES (RELEVANT ANNUITIES) REGULATIONS 2006

Made by the Commissioners for HMRC under FA 2004 Sch 28 para 14

Made . . . .*25 January 2006*
Laid before the House of Commons . . . .*26 January 2006*
Coming into force . . . .*6 April 2006*

1 Citation, commencement and interpretation

(1) These Regulations may be cited as the Registered Pension Schemes (Relevant Annuities) Regulations 2006 and shall come into force on 6th April 2006.

(2) In these Regulations "the Act" means the Finance Act 2004.

2 Definition of "relevant annuity"

For the purposes of Part 4 of the Act (pension schemes etc) a "relevant annuity" is a level single life annuity without a guaranteed term.

3 Definition of "annual amount"

(1) For the purposes of Part 4 of the Act the "annual amount" of a relevant annuity is the rate of annual income which the tables, published for this purpose by the Government Actuary's Department, show as available if—

(*a*) a relevant annuity were purchased by the application of the sums and assets representing the [member's or dependant's][1] pension fund valued at the relevant date; and

[(*b*) the purchaser were male and the same age as the member or dependant (but in any case where that age is greater than 85, it shall be treated as 85).][2]

[(2) For the purposes of paragraph (1) the "relevant date" in relation to drawdown pension years beginning on or before the member's or dependant's 75th birthday is—

(*a*) for the first drawdown pension year falling within a reference period—

(i) the nominated date, as set out in [paragraph 10(3) or 24(3)][2] (as the case requires); or

(ii) if there has been an additional fund designation made during that year, the date on which that designation was made;][1]

(*b*) for each other [drawdown pension year][1] falling within a reference period, the date found in accordance with paragraph 10(4) or 24(4) (as the case requires);

[(3) For the purposes of paragraph (1) the "relevant date" in relation to drawdown pension years beginning after the member's or dependant's 75th birthday is—

(*a*) the nominated date, as determined in accordance with paragraph 10A(3), (4) and (5) or 24A(3) (as the case requires); or

(*b*) if there has been an additional fund designation during a drawdown pension year, the date on which that designation was made.

(4) In paragraphs (2)(*a*)(i) and (*b*) and (3)(*a*), references to numbered paragraphs are to the paragraphs of Schedule 28 to the Act.][1]

Amendments—[1] In paras (1)(*a*), (2)(*b*), words substituted, in para (2) opening words and sub-para (*a*) substituted,, para (2)(*c*), (*d*) and closing words revoked, and paras (3), (4) inserted, by the Registered Pension Schemes (Miscellaneous Amendments) Regulations, SI 2011/1751 reg 6 with effect for the tax year 2011–12 and subsequent tax years.

[2] Para (1)(*b*) substituted, and in para (2)(*a*)(i) words substituted for words "paragraph 10(3)(*a*) or 24(3)(*a*)", by the Registered Pension Schemes (Relevant Annuities) (Amendment) Regulations, SI 2012/2940 reg 2 with effect in relation to—

- relevant dates (as defined in paras (2) and (3) above) falling on or after 21 December 2012;
- reference periods beginning on or after 21 December 2012 in relation to which the relevant date falls prior to 21 December 2012; and
- drawdown pension years beginning on or after 21 December 2012 and after the member or dependant's 75th birthday, in relation to which the relevant date falls prior to 21 December 2012.

2006/130

REGISTERED PENSION SCHEMES (UPRATING PERCENTAGES FOR DEFINED BENEFITS ARRANGEMENTS AND ENHANCED PROTECTION LIMITS) REGULATIONS 2006

Made by the Commissioners for HMRC under FA 2004 s 235(3)(c), Sch 36 paras 15(5)(b), 16(5A)(b), 17(6)(b)

Made . . . .*25 January 2006*
Laid before the House of Commons . . . .*26 January 2006*
Coming into force . . . .*6 April 2006*

Commentary—*Simon's Taxes* **E7.242**.

1 Citation, commencement and interpretation

(1) These Regulations may be cited as the Registered Pension Schemes (Uprating Percentages for Defined Benefits Arrangements and Enhanced Protection Limits) Regulations 2006 and shall come into force on 6th April 2006.

(2) In these Regulations a reference to a numbered section or Schedule (without more) is a reference to the section of, or Schedule to, the Finance Act 2004 which bears that number.

(3) In the application of these Regulations to Northern Ireland, a reference to an enactment applying only in Great Britain shall be construed as including a reference to any enactment having corresponding effect in Northern Ireland.

2 Percentage referred to for the purposes of section 235(3)(c)

(1) For the purpose of section 235(3)(*c*) (defined benefits arrangements: uprating of opening value) the percentage to which these Regulations refer is the percentage found as follows.

(2) In this regulation "the relevant percentage" is any of—

(*a*) the percentage by which the individual's guaranteed minimum pension rights falls to be adjusted by virtue of one or more orders under section 148 of the Social Security Administration Act 1992;

(*b*) the percentage by which the individual's earnings factors in respect of contracted-out employment by reference to the scheme shall be taken to be increased in accordance with section 16 of the Pension Schemes Act 1993 (revaluation of earnings factors);

(*c*) the percentage by which the individual's occupational pension falls to be adjusted by virtue of the application of subsections (1) and (2) of section 84 of the Pension Schemes Act 1993 (which provide that the method of revaluation is to be the final salary method except where the trustees or managers otherwise provide); or

(*d*) the percentage by which a pension, payment of which has been deferred until after normal pension age in accordance with the rules of the pension scheme in question, falls to be increased so that the scheme's trustees or managers can be reasonably satisfied that, when the member's benefit becomes payable, the total value of the benefits provided under regulation 8 of the Occupational Pension Schemes (Preservation of Benefit) Regulations 1991(early retirement or deferred retirement) is at least equal to the amount prescribed in regulation 11 of those Regulations (value of alternatives to short service benefit).

(3) The percentage in a particular case is found as follows.

Step 1

Determine whether any of the relevant percentages applies to the defined benefit arrangement.

Step 2

If any of the relevant percentages applies to the arrangement, determine whether that percentage applies to the whole of the arrangement.

Step 3

If one relevant percentage applies to the whole of the arrangement, that is the percentage to which these Regulations refer.

Step 4

If different percentages apply to different parts of the arrangement, the percentage to which these Regulations refer is that found by the formula—

$$\left(\text{RP1}\times\frac{\text{P1}}{\text{W}}\right)+\left(\text{RP2}\times\frac{\text{P2}}{\text{W}}\right)+\left(\text{RP3}\times\frac{\text{P3}}{\text{W}}\right)+\left(\text{RP4}\times\frac{\text{P4}}{\text{W}}\right)+\left[\text{SP}\times\left(1-\frac{\text{PT}}{\text{W}}\right)\right]$$

Here—

RP is the relevant percentage;

P is the amount of that part of the individual's rights under the arrangement to which the relevant percentage applies;

W is the whole amount of the individual's rights under the arrangement; and

SP is the greater of—

(*a*) 5%, or

(*b*) the percentage (if any) by which the retail prices index for the month in which the pension input period ends is higher than it was for the month in which it began;

PT is the sum of the amounts of *P1, P2, P3* and *P4*;

(*c*) expressions with the suffix 1 refer to the percentage described in paragraph (2)(*a*);

(*d*) expressions with the suffix 2 refer to the percentage described in paragraph (2)(*b*);

(*e*) expressions with the suffix 3 refer to the percentage described in paragraph (2)(*c*);

(*f*) expressions with the suffix 4 refer to the percentage described in paragraph (2)(*d*).

This step is subject to paragraph (4).

(4) If—

(*a*) any relevant percentage is a value less than the greater of—

(i) 5%, or

(ii) the percentage (if any) by which the retail prices index for the month in which the pension input period ends is higher than it was for the month in which it began;

the value shall instead be taken to be whichever is the greater of the two values given in this sub-paragraph;

(*b*) two or more relevant percentages apply to the same part of the arrangement, the value of P1, P2, P3 or P4 (as the case may be) is found by determining which of those relevant percentages produces the greatest increase in the opening value in the pension input period in question.

3 Percentage increases in enhanced protection limits

(1) For the purposes of paragraph 15(5)(*b*) of Schedule 36 (relevant indexation percentage for the purposes of the appropriate limit in relation to a relevant event), the annual percentage rate referred to in these Regulations is found by the formula—

$$\left[\left(RP1\times\frac{P1}{W}\right)+\left(RP2\times\frac{P2}{W}\right)+\left(RP3\times\frac{P3}{W}\right)+\left(RP4\times\frac{P4}{W}\right)+\left(PP\times\left(1-\frac{PT}{W}\right)\right)\right]\div\frac{MRE}{12}$$

(2) In paragraph (1)—

terms defined in regulation 2(3) bear the same meaning as they do there;

MRE is the number of complete tax months which have elapsed since 6th April 2006 at the time when the relevant event occurs; and

PP is the greater of—

(*a*) an annual rate of 5% for the period beginning on 6th April 2006 and ending with the last day of the tax month in which the relevant event occurs, or

(*b*) the percentage (if any) by which the retail prices index for the month in which the relevant event occurs is higher than it was for April 2006;

(3) For the purposes of paragraphs 16(5A)(*b*) and 17(6)(*b*) of Schedule 36 (relevant indexation percentages for the purposes of limit on post-commencement earnings) the annual percentage rate referred to in these Regulations is that which would be found by the formula in paragraph (1) if—

(*a*) for MRE there were substituted MBE, where MBE is the number of complete tax months between the date on which the appropriate three year period ends and the date of the first relevant event; and

(*b*) in the definition of PP—

(i) in paragraph (*a*) for "6th April 2006" there were substituted "the first day of the tax month in which the appropriate period ends"; and

(ii) in paragraph (*b*) for "April 2006" there were substituted "the month in which the appropriate period ends".

(4) In this regulation "tax month" means the period beginning on the 6th day of a calendar month and ending on the 5th day of the following calendar month.

2006/131

REGISTERED PENSION SCHEMES (ENHANCED LIFETIME ALLOWANCE) REGULATIONS 2006

Made by the Commissioners for HMRC under FA 2004 ss 220(5), 221(6), 224(9), 251(1), (6), 256, Sch 36 paras 7(1)(b), 12(1), 18(6), and TMA 1970 s 113(1)

Made . . . .*25 January 2006*

Laid before the House of Commons . . . .*26 January 2006*

Coming into force . . . .*6 April 2006*

Commentary—*Simon's Taxes* **E7.216**.

PRELIMINARY

1 Citation and commencement

These Regulations may be cited as the Registered Pension Schemes (Enhanced Lifetime Allowance) Regulations 2006 and shall come into force on 6th April 2006.

2 Interpretation

(1) In these Regulations—

"the closing date" is to be read in accordance with regulation 3(4), [3A(4), 4(4), 4A(4),][1] 5(4), 6(4), 7(4) or 8(4) as the case may require;

"notification" is to be read in accordance with regulation 3(3), [3A(3), 4(3), 4A(3),][1] 5(3), 6(3), 7(3) or 8(3) as the case may require;

"the Revenue and Customs" means Her Majesty's Revenue and Customs.

["relevant lump sum death benefit" shall be construed in accordance with paragraph 16 of Schedule 32 to the Finance Act 2004;

"the specified regulations" means regulations 3, 4, 5, 6, 7 and 8 of these Regulations.][1]

["tribunal" means the First-tier Tribunal or, where determined by or under Tribunal Procedure Rules, the Upper Tribunal.][2]

(2) In these Regulations references to sections, without more, are references to sections of the Finance Act 2004, and references to provisions of Schedule 36 are references to provisions of Schedule 36 to that Act.

(3) The expressions defined or otherwise explained in the list in section 280(2) have the same definitions or explanations in these Regulations as in Part 4 of the Finance Act 2004.

Amendments—[1] In definitions "the closing date" and "notification" words substituted, and definitions "relevant lump sum death benefit" and "the specified regulations" inserted, by the Registered Pension Schemes (Enhanced Lifetime Allowance) (Amendment) Regulations, 2006/3261 regs 2, 3 with effect from 28 December 2006.

[2] In para (1), entry for "tribunal" inserted by the Transfer of Tribunal Functions and Revenue and Customs Appeals Order, SI 2009/56 art 3, Sch 2 paras 147, 148 with effect from 1 April 2009.

RELIANCE ON PROVISIONS OF THE FINANCE ACT 2004

3 Reliance on paragraph 7 of Schedule 36 (lifetime allowance enhancement: "primary protection")

(1) This regulation applies if the amount of the relevant pre-commencement pension rights of an individual (determined in accordance with paragraph 7(5) of Schedule 36) exceeds £1,500,000.

(2) The individual may give notice of intention to rely on paragraph 7 of Schedule 36 ("paragraph 7").

(3) If the individual intends to rely on paragraph 7, the individual must give a notification to the Revenue and Customs on or before the closing date.

(4) For the purposes of this regulation the closing date is 5th April 2009.

(5) Paragraph (6) applies if—

(*a*) the individual gives the notification to the Revenue and Customs, and

(*b*) the Revenue and Customs issue a certificate to the individual in response to the giving of the notification.

(6) The individual may rely on paragraph 7 during the period beginning on 6th April 2006 and ending on the day on which the Revenue and Customs—

(*a*) revoke the certificate, or

(*b*) issue an amended certificate to the individual.

(7) Paragraph (8) applies if the Revenue and Customs—

(*a*) issue a certificate to which paragraph (6) applies to the individual, and

(*b*) later issue an amended certificate ("the subsequent certificate") to the individual.

(8) The individual may rely on paragraph 7 during the period beginning on the day specified on the subsequent certificate and ending on the day on which the Revenue and Customs—

(*a*) revoke the subsequent certificate, or

(*b*) issue an amended certificate to the individual.

(9) The day so specified must not be earlier than 6th April 2006.

3A [Reliance on paragraph 11A of Schedule 36 (lifetime allowance enhancement: "primary protection": taking account of death benefit)

(1) This regulation applies if a person is paid a relevant lump sum death benefit in respect of an individual in the circumstances specified in paragraphs (*a*) and (*b*) of paragraph 11A(1) of Schedule 36.

(2) That person may give notice of intention to rely on paragraph 11A of Schedule 36 ("paragraph 11A").

(3) If that person intends to rely on paragraph 11A, that person must give a notification to the Revenue and Customs on or before the closing date.

(4) The closing date is the date specified by paragraph (5); but if paragraph (6) applies and specifies a later closing date, the closing date is the date specified in paragraph (6).

(5) The date specified by this paragraph is the date determined in accordance with the following rules.

First rule: Find the 31st January following the tax year in which the relevant lump sum death benefit is paid.

Second rule: Find the 31st January five years after that.

The date so found is the closing date.

(6) This paragraph applies if an assessment to income tax is made under section 217(2) on a person to whom a lump sum death benefit has been paid; and, if this paragraph applies, the closing date specified by this paragraph is 5th April in the tax year following the tax year in which the assessment is made.][1]

Amendments—[1] This regulation inserted by the Registered Pension Schemes (Enhanced Lifetime Allowance) (Amendment) Regulations, 2006/3261 regs 2, 4 with effect from 28 December 2006.

4 Reliance on paragraph 12 of Schedule 36 (lifetime allowances: "enhanced protection")

(1) This regulation applies in the case of an individual to whom paragraph 12(1) of Schedule 36 has applied at all times on and after 6th April 2006.

(2) The individual may give notice of intention to rely on paragraph 12 of Schedule 36 ("paragraph 12").

(3) If the individual intends to rely on paragraph 12, the individual must give a notification to the Revenue and Customs on or before the closing date.

(4) For the purposes of this regulation the closing date is 5th April 2009.

(5) Paragraph (6) applies if—

(*a*) the individual gives the notification to the Revenue and Customs, and

(*b*) the Revenue and Customs issue a certificate to the individual in response to the giving of the notification.

(6) The individual may rely on paragraph 12 during the period beginning on 6th April 2006 and ending on the day on which the Revenue and Customs—

(*a*) revoke the certificate,

(*b*) issue an amended certificate to the individual, or

(*c*) receive notice, given by the individual, that the individual no longer wishes to rely on paragraph 12.

(7) Paragraph (8) applies if the Revenue and Customs—

(*a*) issue a certificate to which paragraph (6) applies to the individual, and

(*b*) later issue an amended certificate ("the subsequent certificate") to the individual.

(8) The individual may rely on paragraph 12 during the period beginning on the day specified on the subsequent certificate and ending on the day on which the Revenue and Customs—

(*a*) revoke the subsequent certificate,

(*b*) issue an amended certificate to the individual, or

(*c*) receive notice, given by the individual, that the individual no longer wishes to rely on paragraph 12.

(9) The day so specified must not be earlier than 6th April 2006.

4A [Reliance on paragraph 15A of Schedule 36 (lifetime allowances: "enhanced protection": taking account of death benefit)

(1) This regulation applies if a person is paid a relevant lump sum death benefit in respect of an individual under an arrangement in the circumstances specified in paragraph 15A(1)(*a*) of Schedule 36.

(2) That person may give notice of intention to rely on paragraph 15A of Schedule 36 ("paragraph 15A").

(3) If that person intends to rely on paragraph 15A, that person must give a notification to the Revenue and Customs on or before the closing date.

(4) The closing date is the date specified by paragraph (5); but if paragraph (6) applies and specifies a later closing date, the closing date is the date specified in paragraph (6).

(5) The date specified by this paragraph is the date determined in accordance with the following rules.

First rule: Find the 31st January following the tax year in which the relevant lump sum death benefit is paid.

Second rule: Find the 31st January five years after that.

The date so found is the closing date.

(6) This paragraph applies if an assessment to income tax is made under section 217(2) on a person to whom a lump sum death benefit has been paid; and, if this paragraph applies, the closing date specified by this paragraph is 5th April in the tax year following the tax year in which the assessment is made.][1]

Amendments—[1] This regulation inserted by the Registered Pension Schemes (Enhanced Lifetime Allowance) (Amendment) Regulations, 2006/3261 regs 2, 5 with effect from 28 December 2006.

5 Reliance on paragraph 18 of Schedule 36 (lifetime allowance enhancement: pre-commencement pension credits)

(1) This regulation applies if a benefit crystallisation event occurs in relation to an individual in the circumstances specified in paragraph 18(1) of Schedule 36.

(2) The individual may give notice of intention to rely on paragraph 18 of Schedule 36 ("paragraph 18").

(3) If the individual intends to rely on paragraph 18, the individual must give a notification to the Revenue and Customs on or before the closing date.

(4) For the purposes of this regulation the closing date is 5th April 2009.

(5) Paragraph (6) applies if—

(*a*) the individual gives the notification to the Revenue and Customs, and (*b*) the Revenue and Customs issue a certificate to the individual in response to the giving of the notification.

(6) The individual may rely on paragraph 18 during the period beginning on 6th April 2006 and ending on the day on which the Revenue and Customs—

(*a*) revoke the certificate, or

(*b*) issue an amended certificate to the individual.

(7) Paragraph (8) applies if the Revenue and Customs—

(*a*) issue a certificate to which paragraph (6) applies to the individual, and

(*b*) later issue an amended certificate ("the subsequent certificate") to the individual.

(8) The individual may rely on paragraph 18 during the period beginning on the day specified on the subsequent certificate and ending on the day on which the Revenue and Customs—

(*a*) revoke the subsequent certificate, or

(*b*) issue an amended certificate to the individual.

(9) The day so specified must not be earlier than 6th April 2006.

6 Reliance on section 220 (lifetime allowance enhancement: registration of pension credits)

(1) This regulation applies if an individual acquires rights under a registered pension scheme in the circumstances specified in section 220(1).

(2) The individual may give notice of intention to rely on section 220.

(3) If the individual intends to rely on section 220, the individual must give a notification to the Revenue and Customs on or before the closing date.

(4) For the purposes of this regulation use the rules in this paragraph to find the closing date.

First rule: Find the 31st January following the tax year in which the pension sharing order or provision takes effect.

Second rule: Find the 31st January five years after that.

The date so found is the closing date.

(5) Paragraph (6) applies if—

(*a*) the individual gives the notification to the Revenue and Customs, and

(*b*) the Revenue and Customs issue a certificate to the individual in response to the giving of the notification.

(6) The individual may rely on section 220 during the period beginning on the day on which the pension sharing order or provision takes effect and ending on the day on which the Revenue and Customs—

(*a*) revoke the certificate, or

(*b*) issue an amended certificate to the individual.

(7) Paragraph (8) applies if the Revenue and Customs—

(*a*) issue a certificate to which paragraph (6) applies to the individual, and

(*b*) later issue an amended certificate ("the subsequent certificate") to the individual.

(8) The individual may rely on section 220 during the period beginning on the day specified on the subsequent certificate and ending on the day on which the Revenue and Customs—

(*a*) revoke the subsequent certificate, or

(*b*) issue an amended certificate to the individual.

7 Reliance on section 221 (lifetime allowance enhancement: relevant overseas individuals)

(1) This regulation applies if, at any time on or after 6th April 2006, an individual is a relevant overseas individual during any part of a period that is the active membership period in relation to an arrangement relating to the individual.

(2) The individual may give notice of intention to rely on section 221.

(3) If the individual intends to rely on section 221, the individual must give a notification to the Revenue and Customs on or before the closing date.

(4) For the purposes of this regulation use the rules in this paragraph to find the closing date.

First rule: Find the 31st January following the tax year in which the accrual period ends (see paragraph (10)).

Second rule: Find the 31st January five years after that.

The date so found is the closing date.

(5) Paragraph (6) applies if—

(*a*) the individual gives the notification to the Revenue and Customs, and

(*b*) the Revenue and Customs issue a certificate to the individual in response to the giving of the notification.

(6) The individual may rely on section 221 during the period beginning on the accrual day (see paragraph (10)) and ending on the day on which the Revenue and Customs—

(*a*) revoke the certificate, or

(*b*) issue an amended certificate to the individual.

(7) Paragraph (8) applies if the Revenue and Customs—

(*a*) issue a certificate to which paragraph (6) applies to the individual, and (*b*) later issue an amended certificate ("the subsequent certificate") to the individual.

(8) The individual may rely on section 221 during the period beginning on the day specified on the subsequent certificate and ending on the day on which the Revenue and Customs—

(*a*) revoke the subsequent certificate, or

(*b*) issue an amended certificate to the individual.

(9) The day so specified must not be earlier than the accrual day.

(10) For the purposes of this regulation—

(*a*) the accrual period ends—

(i) when the individual ceases to be a relevant overseas individual,

(ii) immediately before a benefit crystallisation event occurring in relation to the arrangement relating to the individual, or

(iii) when benefits cease to accrue to or in respect of the individual under the arrangement,

whichever is the earliest; and

(*b*) "the accrual day" is the day on which the accrual period ends.

8 Reliance on section 224 (lifetime allowance enhancement: transfer from recognised overseas pension scheme)

(1) This regulation applies if, in relation to an individual, there is a recognised overseas scheme transfer in the circumstances specified in section 224(1).

(2) The individual may give notice of intention to rely on section 224.

(3) If the individual intends to rely on section 224, the individual must give a notification to the Revenue and Customs on or before the closing date.

(4) For the purposes of this regulation use the rules in this paragraph to find the closing date.

First rule: Find the 31st January following the tax year in which the recognised overseas scheme transfer takes place.

Second rule: Find the 31st January five years after that.

The date so found is the closing date.

(5) Paragraph (6) applies if—

(*a*) the individual gives the notification to the Revenue and Customs, and

(*b*) the Revenue and Customs issue a certificate to the individual in response to the giving of the notification.

(6) The individual may rely on section 224 during the period beginning on the day on which the recognised overseas scheme transfer takes place and ending on the day on which the Revenue and Customs—

(*a*) revoke the certificate, or

(*b*) issue an amended certificate to the individual.

(7) Paragraph (8) applies if the Revenue and Customs—

(*a*) issue a certificate to which paragraph (6) applies to the individual, and

(*b*) later issue an amended certificate ("the subsequent certificate") to the individual.

(8) The individual may rely on section 224 during the period beginning on the day specified on the subsequent certificate and ending on the day on which the Revenue and Customs—

(*a*) revoke the subsequent certificate, or

(*b*) issue an amended certificate to the individual.

LOSS OF ENHANCED PROTECTION

9 Loss of enhanced protection

(1) This regulation applies if conditions A to F are met.

(2) Condition A is that an individual has one or more relevant existing arrangements (within the meaning given by paragraph 12(4) of Schedule 36).

(3) Condition B is that the lump sum condition specified in paragraph 24(2) of Schedule 36 is met in relation to the individual.

(4) Condition C is that the first notice requirement condition specified in paragraph 24(5) of Schedule 36 is not met in relation to the individual.

(5) Condition D is that the second notice requirement condition specified in paragraph 24(6) of Schedule 36 is met in relation to the individual.

(6) Condition E is that the individual has a certificate issued under regulation 4 on which the individual may rely.

(7) Condition F is that paragraph 12 of Schedule 36 has ceased to apply to the individual.

(8) Paragraph 31 of Schedule 36 applies in relation to the individual and to a registered pension scheme which is a protected pension scheme.

(9) In paragraph (8) "protected pension scheme" has the meaning given by paragraph 31 of Schedule 36.

[NOTIFICATIONS

10 Form of notification: the specified regulations

(1) This regulation applies if a notification is given under one of the specified regulations.

(2) The notification must be in a form prescribed by the Commissioners for Her Majesty's Revenue and Customs.

(3) The individual must sign and date the notification.][1]

Amendments—[1] This regulation, along with reg 10A, substituted for original reg 10 by the Registered Pension Schemes (Enhanced Lifetime Allowance) (Amendment) Regulations, 2006/3261 regs 2, 6 with effect from 28 December 2006.

10A [Form of notification: regulations 3A and 4A

(1) This regulation applies if a notification is given under regulation 3A or 4A.

(2) The notification must contain the following information—

(*a*) the name and address of the person giving the notification;

(*b*) the name of the deceased member in respect of whose death the person has received the relevant lump sum death benefit;

(*c*) the name of the registered pension scheme under which that person was entitled to receive that relevant lump sum death benefit;

(*d*) the name and address of the scheme administrator by whom the relevant lump sum death benefit was paid;

(*e*) the amount of the relevant lump sum death benefit the person received; and

(*f*) the date on which the relevant lump sum death benefit was paid.

(3) The person who gives the notification must sign and date it.][1]

Amendments—[1] This regulation, along with reg 10, substituted for original reg 10 by the Registered Pension Schemes (Enhanced Lifetime Allowance) (Amendment) Regulations, 2006/3261 regs 2, 6 with effect from 28 December 2006.

11 Preservation of documents

(1) This regulation applies if—

(*a*) an individual gives a notification to the Revenue and Customs, and

(*b*) the Revenue and Customs issue a certificate to the individual in response to the giving of the notification.

(2) The individual must preserve all documents relating to the information given in the notification for a period of six years beginning with the day on which the individual gives the notification to the Revenue and Customs.

12 Late submission of notification

(1) This regulation applies if an individual—

(*a*) gives a notification to the Revenue and Customs after the closing date,

(*b*) had a reasonable excuse for not giving the notification on or before the closing date, and

(*c*) gives the notification without unreasonable delay after the reasonable excuse ceased.

(2) If the Revenue and Customs are satisfied that paragraph (1) applies, they must consider the information provided in the notification.

(3) If there is a dispute as to whether paragraph (1) applies, the individual may require the Revenue and Customs to give notice of their decision to refuse to consider the information provided in the notification.

(4) If the Revenue and Customs gives notice of their decision to refuse to consider the information provided in the notification, the individual may appeal . . .[1].

(5) . . . [1]

(6) The notice of appeal must be given to the Revenue and Customs within 30 days after the day on which notice of their decision is given to the individual.

(7) On an [appeal that is notified to the tribunal, the tribunal][1] shall determine whether the individual gave the notification to the Revenue and Customs in the circumstances specified in paragraph (1).

(8) If the [tribunal allows][1] the appeal, [the tribunal][1] shall direct the Revenue and Customs to consider the information provided in the notification.

Amendments—[1] In para (4), words revoked, para (5) revoked, in paras (7), (8), words substituted by the Transfer of Tribunal Functions and Revenue and Customs Appeals Order, SI 2009/56 art 3, Sch 2 paras 147, 149 with effect from 1 April 2009.

[PROCEDURE ON GIVING OF NOTIFICATIONS

13 Procedure on giving of notification: the specified provisions

(1) If an individual gives a notification to the Revenue and Customs under one of the specified provisions, and there are no obvious errors or omissions in the notification (whether errors of principle, arithmetical mistakes or otherwise), the Revenue and Customs must issue a certificate to the individual.

(2) If an individual gives a notification to the Revenue and Customs under one of the specified provisions, and there are obvious errors or omissions in the notification (whether errors of principle, arithmetical mistakes or otherwise), the Revenue and Customs must return the notification to the individual.][1]

Amendments—[1] This regulation, along with reg 13A, substituted for original reg 13 by the Registered Pension Schemes (Enhanced Lifetime Allowance) (Amendment) Regulations, 2006/3261 regs 2, 7 with effect from 28 December 2006.

13A [Procedure on giving of notification: regulations 3A and 4A

(1) If a person gives a notification to the Revenue and Customs under regulation 3A or 4A, and there are no obvious errors or omissions in the notification (whether errors of principle, arithmetical mistakes or otherwise), the Revenue and Customs—

(*a*) must notify that person, in writing, that there are no obvious errors or omissions in the notification, and

(*b*) confirm that that person has given a valid notification of intention to rely on paragraph 11A or 15A (as the case may be).

(2) If a person gives a notification to the Revenue and Customs, and there are obvious errors or omissions in the notification (whether errors of principle, arithmetical mistakes or otherwise), the Revenue and Customs must return the notification to the individual.][1]

Amendments—[1] This regulation, along with reg 13, substituted for original reg 13 by the Registered Pension Schemes (Enhanced Lifetime Allowance) (Amendment) Regulations, 2006/3261 regs 2, 7 with effect from 28 December 2006.

14 Appeal against refusal to issue certificate

(1) This regulation applies if there is a dispute as to whether the Revenue and Customs are entitled to take the view that there are obvious errors or omissions in [a notification given under one of the specified regulations][1] (whether errors of principle, arithmetical mistakes or otherwise).

(2) The individual may require the Revenue and Customs to give notice of their decision to refuse to issue a certificate.

(3) If the Revenue and Customs give notice of their decision to refuse to issue a certificate, the individual may appeal . . .[2].

(4) . . .[2]

(5) The notice of appeal must be given to the Revenue and Customs within 30 days after the day on which notice of their decision is given to the individual.

(6) On an [appeal that is notified to the tribunal, the tribunal][2] shall determine whether the Revenue and Customs were entitled to take the view that there were obvious errors or omissions in the notification (whether errors of principle, arithmetical mistakes or otherwise).

(7) If the [tribunal allows][2] the appeal, [the tribunal][2] may direct the Revenue and Customs to issue a certificate to the individual with effect from a date specified by the [tribunal][2].

Amendments—[1] Words in para (1) substituted by the Registered Pension Schemes (Enhanced Lifetime Allowance) (Amendment) Regulations, 2006/3261 regs 2, 8 with effect from 28 December 2006.

[2] In para (3), words revoked, para (4) revoked, in paras (6), (7), words substituted, by the Transfer of Tribunal Functions and Revenue and Customs Appeals Order, SI 2009/56 art 3, Sch 2 paras 147, 150 with effect from 1 April 2009.

14A [Appeal against refusal to confirm validity of notification

(1) This regulation applies if there is a dispute as to whether the Revenue and Customs are entitled to take the view that there are obvious errors or omissions in a notification given under regulation 3A or 4A (whether errors of principle, arithmetical mistakes or otherwise).

(2) The person may require the Revenue and Customs to give notice of their decision to refuse to confirm the validity of the notification.

(3) If the Revenue and Customs give notice of their decision to refuse to confirm the validity of the notification, the person may appeal . . .[2].

(4) . . .[2]

(5) The notice of appeal must be given to the Revenue and Customs within 30 days after the day on which notice of their decision is given to the person.

(6) On an [appeal that is notified to the tribunal, the tribunal][2] shall determine whether the Revenue and Customs were entitled to take the view that there were obvious errors or omissions in the notification (whether errors of principle, arithmetical mistakes or otherwise).

(7) If the [tribunal allows][2] the appeal, [the tribunal][2] may direct the Revenue and Customs to confirm the validity of the notification with effect from a date specified by the [tribunal][2].][1]

Amendments—[1] This regulation inserted by the Registered Pension Schemes (Enhanced Lifetime Allowance) (Amendment) Regulations, 2006/3261 regs 2, 9 with effect from 28 December 2006.

[2] In para (3), words revoked, para (4) revoked, in paras (6), (7), words substituted, by the Transfer of Tribunal Functions and Revenue and Customs Appeals Order, SI 2009/56 art 3, Sch 2 paras 147, 151 with effect from 1 April 2009.

CERTIFICATES

15 General

(1) A certificate must be in a form prescribed by the Commissioners for Her Majesty's Revenue and Customs.

(2) A certificate must have a unique reference number.

(3) An individual to whom a certificate is issued must preserve the certificate until no further benefit crystallisation event can occur.

16 Aggregate certificates

(1) This regulation applies if—

(*a*) an individual is a relevant overseas individual during any part of a period that is the active membership period in relation to an arrangement relating to an individual, and
(*b*) condition A, B or C is met.

(2) Condition A is that—
(*a*) the individual has given a notification under regulation 7 to the Revenue and Customs in relation to a part of the active membership period, and
(*b*) the individual gives a further notification under regulation 7 to the Revenue and Customs in relation to a further part of the same active membership period.

(3) Condition B is that—
(*a*) the Revenue and Customs have issued a certificate to an individual in response to a notification under regulation 7 given by the individual in relation to a part of the active membership period, and
(*b*) the individual gives a further notification under regulation 7 to the Revenue and Customs in relation to a further part of the same active membership period.

(4) Condition C is that—
(*a*) the Revenue and Customs have issued a certificate to an individual in response to a notification under regulation 7 given by the individual in relation to a part of the active membership period, and
(*b*) the Revenue and Customs issue a further certificate to the individual in response to a further notification under regulation 7 given by the individual in relation to a further part of the same active membership period.

(5) The individual may require the Revenue and Customs to issue a single certificate (an "aggregate certificate") to the individual.

(6) An aggregate certificate supersedes the certificates mentioned in paragraphs (3)(*a*) and (4).

(7) If the Revenue and Customs issue an aggregate certificate to an individual, paragraphs (6) to (10) of regulation 7 apply as if the aggregate certificate were the certificate referred to in paragraph (5)(*b*) of that regulation.

(8) Any notification mentioned in this regulation must be given on or before the closing date; and regulation 7 applies to find the closing date for a notification mentioned in this regulation in the same way as it applies to find the closing date for a notification given under that regulation.

17 Incorrect information given in connection with notification

(1) This regulation applies if—
(*a*) after the giving of a notification, the Revenue and Customs have issued a certificate ("the first certificate") to an individual, and
(*b*) either condition A or condition B is met.

(2) Condition A is that the individual informs the Revenue and Customs that information given in the notification was incorrect or has become incorrect.

(3) Condition B is that the individual informs the Revenue and Customs that information given in connection with the notification was incorrect or has become incorrect.

(4) The Revenue and Customs may revoke the first certificate and issue an amended certificate to the individual.

(5) The amended certificate supersedes the first certificate.

(6) If an individual realises that any information given in the notification, or given in connection with the notification, was incorrect or has become incorrect, the individual must inform the Revenue and Customs without undue delay.

(7) If condition A is met, the individual must inform the Revenue and Customs in a form prescribed by the Commissioners for Her Majesty's Revenue and Customs.

18 Incorrect information given in certificate

(1) This regulation applies if—
(*a*) the Revenue and Customs have issued a certificate ("the first certificate") to an individual, and
(*b*) the individual informs the Revenue and Customs that information given in the certificate was incorrect or has become incorrect.

(2) The Revenue and Customs may—
(*a*) revoke the first certificate,
(*b*) revoke the first certificate and issue an amended certificate to the individual, or
(*c*) issue an additional certificate to the individual.

(3) The amended certificate supersedes the first certificate.

(4) This regulation is subject to regulation 16.

(5) If an individual realises that any information given in the certificate was incorrect or has become incorrect, the individual must inform the Revenue and Customs without undue delay.

19 Further supply of information given in certificate

(1) This regulation applies if, after the Revenue and Customs have issued a certificate to an individual, the individual no longer possesses information given in the certificate.

(2) The individual may require the Revenue and Customs to give the information to the individual.

COMPLIANCE

20 Review of notification after certificate issued

(1) This regulation applies if—

(*a*) an individual has given a notification to the Revenue and Customs, and

(*b*) the Revenue and Customs have issued a certificate to the individual in response to the giving of the notification.

(2) The Revenue and Customs may review any information given—

(*a*) in the notification, or

(*b*) in connection with the notification.

(3) The Revenue and Customs may begin a review under this regulation at any time within a period of twelve months beginning with the day on which the notification was given to them.

(4) The procedure to be followed on the review is set out in regulation 22.[1]

Amendments—[1] Para (4) revoked by the Registered Pension Schemes (Enhanced Lifetime Allowance) (Amendment) Regulations, SI 2010/651 reg 2 with effect from 1 April 2010. This amendment does not apply in relation to or in connection with a notice given before 1 April 2010 under reg 22 below.

21 Review of notification after receipt of further information

(1) This regulation applies if—

(*a*) an individual has given a notification to the Revenue and Customs,

(*b*) the Revenue and Customs have issued a certificate to the individual in response to the giving of the notification, and

(*c*) after the certificate has been issued, the Revenue and Customs have reason to believe that information given in the notification, given in connection with the notification, or given in the certificate, either was incorrect or has become incorrect.

(2) The Revenue and Customs may review any information given in the notification, in connection with the notification, or in the certificate.

(3) The Revenue and Customs may begin a review under this regulation at any time.

(4) . . . [1]

Amendments—[1] Para (4) revoked by the Registered Pension Schemes (Enhanced Lifetime Allowance) (Amendment) Regulations, SI 2010/651 reg 2 with effect from 1 April 2010. This amendment does not apply in relation to or in connection with a notice given before 1 April 2010 under reg 22 below.

22 Reviews of notifications: procedure to be followed

. . .

Amendments—Reg 22 revoked by the Registered Pension Schemes (Enhanced Lifetime Allowance) (Amendment) Regulations, SI 2010/651 reg 2 with effect from 1 April 2010. This amendment does not apply in relation to or in connection with a notice given before 1 April 2010 under reg 22.

23 Appeals against notices under regulation 22

. . .

Amendments—Reg 23 revoked by the Registered Pension Schemes (Enhanced Lifetime Allowance) (Amendment) Regulations, SI 2010/651 reg 2 with effect from 1 April 2010. This amendment does not apply in relation to or in connection with a notice given before 1 April 2010 under reg 22.

24 Revocation or amendment of certificate

(1) The Revenue and Customs may revoke or amend a certificate at any time if—

(*a*) after the certificate has been issued, the Revenue and Customs have reason to believe that any information given in the notification, given in connection with the notification, or given in the certificate, either was incorrect or has become incorrect, or

(*b*) after notice has been given to an individual under [paragraph 1 of Schedule 36 to the Finance Act 2008][2], the individual does not reply to the notice within the time specified in the notice.

(2) If the Revenue and Customs revoke or amend a certificate, they must give notice to the individual of the revocation or amendment.

(3) The individual may appeal . . . [1] against the revocation or amendment of the certificate.

(4) . . . [1]

(5) The notice of appeal must be given to the Revenue and Customs within 30 days after the day on which notice of the revocation or amendment is given to the individual.

(6) On an [appeal that is notified to the tribunal, the tribunal][1] shall determine whether the Revenue and Customs revoked or amended the certificate in the circumstances specified in paragraph (1).

(7) If the [tribunal allows][1] the appeal, [the tribunal][1] may direct the Revenue and Customs to issue a certificate to the individual with effect from a date specified by the [tribunal][1].

(8) If the Revenue and Customs revoke a certificate and, on appeal, the [tribunal determines][1] that the certificate should have been amended, the [tribunal][1] shall order that the certificate shall be amended in such terms as the [tribunal][1] may specify.

(9) If the Revenue and Customs amend a certificate and, on appeal, the [tribunal determines][1] that the certificate should have been amended in other terms, the [tribunal][1] Commissioners shall order that the certificate shall be amended in such terms as the [tribunal][1] Commissioners may specify.

Amendments—[1] In para (3), words revoked, para (4) revoked, in paras (6), 7), (8), words substituted, by the Transfer of Tribunal Functions and Revenue and Customs Appeals Order, SI 2009/56 art 3, Sch 2 paras 147, 152 with effect from 1 April 2009.

[2] Words in para (2)(*b*) substituted by the Registered Pension Schemes (Enhanced Lifetime Allowance) (Amendment) Regulations, SI 2010/651 reg 2 with effect from 1 April 2010. This amendment does not apply in relation to or in connection with a notice given before 1 April 2010 under reg 22 above.

SUPPLEMENTARY

25 Special classes of individuals

(1) If an individual is a person who is incapable, by reason of mental disorder, of managing and administering his property and affairs, anything under these Regulations which could have been done by the individual may be done—

(*a*) in England and Wales or Northern Ireland, by the individual's attorney or receiver, or the person managing and administering the individual's property and affairs,

(*b*) in Scotland, by the individual's guardian within the meaning of the Adults with Incapacity (Scotland) Act 2000, and

(*c*) in a country or territory outside the United Kingdom, by a person authorised by a Court having jurisdiction, in that country or territory, to regulate the property and affairs of an individual to whom this paragraph applies.

(2) If an individual is a person who is suffering from a physical disability, by reason of which that person has difficulty executing documents in respect of the management and administration of his property and affairs, anything under these Regulations which could have been done by the individual may be done—

(*a*) in the United Kingdom, by a person having a power of attorney in relation to the individual's property and affairs, and

(*b*) in a country or territory outside the United Kingdom, by a person authorised, under the laws of that country or territory, to execute documents in relation to the individual's property and affairs.

26 Personal representatives

If an individual dies, anything under these Regulations which could have been done by the individual may be done by the individual's personal representatives.

2006/132

ARMED FORCES AND RESERVE FORCES (COMPENSATION SCHEME) (EXCLUDED BENEFITS FOR TAX PURPOSES) REGULATIONS 2006

Made by the Commissioners for HMRC under ITEPA 2003 s 393B

Made . . . .*25 January 2006*

Laid before the House of Commons . . . .*26 January 2006*

Coming into force . . . .*6 April 2006*

Commentary—*Simon's Taxes* **E4.126, E7.112**.

Revocation—These regulations revoked by the Armed Forces and Reserve Forces (Compensation Scheme) Order 2011 SI 2011/517 art 94, Sch 7 with effect from 9 May 2011.

1 Citation and commencement

These Regulations may be cited as the Armed Forces and Reserve Forces (Compensation Scheme) (Excluded Benefits for Tax Purposes) Regulations 2006 and shall come into force on 6th April 2006.

Revocation—These regulations revoked by the Armed Forces and Reserve Forces (Compensation Scheme) Order 2011 SI 2011/517 art 94, Sch 7 with effect from 9 May 2011.

2 Benefits excluded from charge under Chapter 2 of Part 6 of ITEPA 2003

Any benefit provided under the Armed Forces and Reserve Forces (Compensation Scheme) Order 2005 is prescribed for the purposes of section 393B(3)(*d*) of the Income Tax Earnings and Pensions Act 2003 (prescribed benefits to be excluded benefits for the purposes of Chapter 2 of Part 6 of that Act).

Revocation—These regulations revoked by the Armed Forces and Reserve Forces (Compensation Scheme) Order 2011 SI 2011/517 art 94, Sch 7 with effect from 9 May 2011.

2006/133

REGISTERED PENSION SCHEMES (CO-OWNERSHIP OF LIVING ACCOMMODATION) REGULATIONS 2006

Made by the Commissioners for HMRC under FA 2004 s 173(8)(a)

Made . . . . *25 January 2006*
Laid before the House of Commons . . . . *26 January 2006*
Coming into force . . . . *6 April 2006*

Commentary—*Simon's Taxes* **E7.237**.

1 Citation and commencement

These Regulations may be cited as the Registered Pension Schemes (Co-ownership of Living Accommodation) Regulations 2006, and shall come into force on 6th April 2006.

2 Circumstances in which these Regulations apply

(1) These Regulations apply if, for the whole or part of a tax year, living accommodation is held—

(*a*) partly by persons for the purposes of a registered pension scheme, and

(*b*) partly by persons for other purposes.

(2) In these Regulations—

an "owner" means a person for whom the living accommodation is held;

a "pension scheme owner" means a person who is an owner by virtue of paragraph (1)(*a*);

a "scheme member" means an individual who is a member of the registered pension scheme mentioned in paragraph (1)(*a*).

3 The living accommodation benefit

(1) If these Regulations apply, a benefit is provided.

(2) In these Regulations the benefit is called "the living accommodation benefit".

(3) The amount of the living accommodation benefit is calculated in the same way as the cash equivalent of the benefit is calculated under Chapter 5.

(4) For the purposes of the calculation required by paragraph (3)—

(*a*) references in Chapter 5 to the employee are to be treated as references to an individual for whom the living accommodation is provided,

(*b*) references in Chapter 5 to the employer are to be treated as references to the registered pension scheme, and

(*c*) references in Chapter 5 to the taxable period are to be treated as references to the period (consisting of the whole or part of a tax year) for which these Regulations apply.

(5) In this regulation "Chapter 5" means Chapter 5 of Part 3 of the Income Tax (Employments and Pensions) Act 2003 (taxable benefits: living accommodation).

4 The pension scheme owner's benefit

(1) The amount of the living accommodation benefit must be apportioned among the owners according to their respective shares and interests.

(2) In these Regulations, the amount of the living accommodation benefit so apportioned to a pension scheme owner is called "the pension scheme owner's benefit".

5 The private owner's benefit

(1) The pension scheme owner's benefit must be apportioned.

(2) If the living accommodation is used to provide a benefit for persons who consist of, or include—

(*a*) one particular scheme member, or

(*b*) a member of the scheme member's family or household,

the pension scheme owner's benefit is apportioned to the scheme member.

(3) If the living accommodation is used to provide a benefit for persons who consist of, or include—

(*a*) a scheme member or a member of the scheme member's family or household, and

(*b*) another scheme member or a member of that other scheme member's family or household,

the pension scheme owner's benefit is apportioned among those scheme members.

(4) If paragraph (3)(*b*) applies in relation to more than one scheme member, the pension scheme owner's benefit is apportioned among all the scheme members in relation to whom paragraph (3)(*a*) or (3)(*b*) applies.

(5) If paragraph (3) applies, the amount of the pension scheme benefit apportioned to any particular scheme member is to be such part of that benefit as is just and reasonable.

(6) Section 721 of the Income Tax (Employments and Pensions) Act 2003 (definitions) applies for the purpose of determining the members of a scheme member's family or household.

(7) In these Regulations the amount of the pension scheme owner's benefit apportioned under this regulation to a scheme member is called "the private owner's benefit".

6 Unauthorised payments to members of registered pension schemes

(1) A pension scheme owner is to be treated as having made an unauthorised payment under section 173 of the Finance Act 2004 to a scheme member to whom regulation 5(7) applies.

(2) The amount of the unauthorised payment is equal to the amount of the private owner's benefit.

2006/134

REGISTERED PENSION SCHEMES (AUTHORISED PAYMENTS) (TRANSFERS TO THE PENSION PROTECTION FUND) REGULATIONS 2006

Made by the Commissioners for HMRC under FA 2004 s 164(f).

Made . . . . *25 January 2006*
Laid before the House of Commons . . . . *26 January 2006*
Coming into force . . . . *6 April 2006*

Commentary—*Simon's Taxes* **E7.224.**

1 Citation and commencement

These Regulations may be cited as the Registered Pension Schemes (Authorised Payments) (Transfers to the Pension Protection Fund) Regulations 2006 and shall come into force on 6th April 2006.

2 Authorised payments

For the purposes of section 164(*f*) of the Finance Act 2004 (authorised member payments), a transfer of the property, rights and liabilities of a registered pension scheme to the Board of the Pension Protection Fund is a payment of a description that is prescribed.

2006/135

REGISTERED PENSION SCHEMES (MEANING OF PENSION COMMENCEMENT LUMP SUM) REGULATIONS 2006

Made by the Commissioners for HMRC under FA 2004 Sch 29 para 1(6)

Made . . . . *25 January 2006*
Laid before the House of Commons . . . . *26 January 2006*
Coming into force . . . . *6 April 2006*

Commentary—*Simon's Taxes* **E7.224.**

Modifications—Registered Pension Schemes (Splitting of Schemes) Regulations, SI 2006/569 reg 3 (modification of this provision in relation to sub-scheme administrators).

1 Citation and commencement

These Regulations may be cited as the Registered Pension Schemes (Meaning of Pension Commencement Lump Sum) Regulations 2006, and shall come into force on 6th April 2006.

2 Application of these Regulations: general

These Regulations apply for the purposes of paragraph 1(6) of Schedule 29 to the Finance Act 2004 (regulations relating to meaning of "pension commencement lump sum").

3 Circumstances in which these Regulations apply

The circumstances in which incorrect income tax has been paid by the scheme administrator in relation to the member by way of the lifetime allowance charge are circumstances in which—

(*a*) the scheme administrator has made an overpayment by way of the lifetime allowance charge in relation to the member, and

(*b*) Her Majesty's Revenue and Customs refund the overpayment to the scheme administrator.

4 The circumstances in which a lump sum subsequently paid to the member is to be treated as a pension commencement lump sum [even though the condition in paragraph 1(1)(c) of Schedule 29 to the Finance Act 2004 is not met][2] are circumstances in which—

(*a*) Her Majesty's Revenue and Customs refund an overpayment by way of the lifetime allowance charge in relation to the member to the scheme administrator, and

(*b*) the scheme administrator pays part or all of the overpayment to the member within the period of [twelve months][1] beginning with the day on which the scheme administrator receives the overpayment from Her Majesty's Revenue and Customs.

Amendments—[1] Words substituted by the Registered Pension Schemes (Meaning of Pension Commencement Lump Sum) (Amendment) Regulations, SI 2007/3533 reg 2 with effect from 7 January 2008: SI 2007/3533 reg 1.

[2] Words substituted by the Registered Pension Schemes (Miscellaneous Amendments) Regulations, SI 2011/1751 reg 7 with effect in relation to lump sums paid on or after 6 April 2011.

2006/136

PENSION BENEFITS (INSURANCE COMPANY LIABLE AS SCHEME ADMINISTRATOR) REGULATIONS 2006

Made by the Commissioners for HMRC under FA 2004 s 273A(1), (2).

Made . . . . *25 January 2006*
Laid before the House of Commons . . . . *26 January 2006*
Coming into force . . . . *6 April 2006*

Commentary—*Simon's Taxes* **E7.241**.

Modifications—Registered Pension Schemes (Splitting of Schemes) Regulations, SI 2006/569 reg 3 (modification of this provision in relation to sub-scheme administrators).

1 Citation and commencement

These Regulations may be cited as the Pension Benefits (Insurance Company Liable as Scheme Administrator) Regulations 2005 and shall come into force on 6th April 2006.

2 Insurance company liable as scheme administrator

(1) This regulation applies where an insurance company makes a payment of—

(*a*) a pension protection lump sum death benefit,

(*b*) an annuity protection lump sum death benefit, . . .[3]

[(*c*) a drawdown pension fund lump sum death benefit][1][, or

(*d*) a flexi-access drawdown fund lump sum death benefit.][3]

(2) The insurance company is to be treated as the scheme administrator for the purposes of the operation of section 206 (special lump sum death benefits charge) in relation to the lump sum death benefit.

(3) The insurance company is responsible for the discharge of the obligations imposed on the scheme administrator under subsections (1) to (7) of section 254 (accounting for tax by scheme administrators).

[(4) The insurance company is liable to the penalties under—

(*a*) Schedule 24 to the Finance Act 2007 (penalties for errors); and

(*b*) Schedule 55 to the Finance Act 2009 (penalty for failure to make returns)

if it fails to comply with the obligations imposed by section 254(1) to (7) as applied to it by virtue of paragraphs (2) and (3).][2]

Amendments—[1] Para (1)(*c*) substituted by the Registered Pension Schemes (Miscellaneous Amendments) Regulations, SI 2011/1751 reg 2 with effect for the tax year 2011–12 and subsequent tax years.

[2] Para (4) substituted by the Pension Schemes (Miscellaneous Amendments) Order, SI 2013/1114 art 6 with effect from 1 June 2013.

[3] In para (1), word "or" at end of sub-para (*b*) repealed, and sub-para (*d*) and preceding word inserted, by the Taxation of Pensions Act 2014 s 1, Sch 1 paras 5, 30(1) with effect from 17 December 2014. This amendment is to be treated as having been made by the Commissioners for HMRC in exercise of their powers under FA 2004 s 273A (as amended by the Taxation of Pensions Act 2014 Sch 1).

2006/137

REGISTERED PENSION SCHEMES (AUTHORISED MEMBER PAYMENTS) REGULATIONS 2006

Made by the Commissioners for HMRC under FA 2004 s 164(f)

Made . . . . *25 January 2006*
Laid before the House of Commons . . . . *26 January 2006*
Coming into force . . . . *6 April 2006*

1 Citation and commencement

These Regulations may be cited as the Registered Pension Schemes (Authorised Member Payments) Regulations 2006 and shall come into force on 6th April 2006.

2 Authorised member payments: demutualisation of insurance companies and members of qualifying pension schemes

(1) Any payment made—

(*a*) by a company to—

(i) a member of a qualifying pension scheme, or

(ii) a person who is the beneficiary under a qualifying annuity contract;

(*b*) in connection with the demutualisation of an insurance company,

(*c*) as compensation to that member or person, for the loss of his rights as a member of the insurance company, and

(*d*) without reducing the total value of the sums and assets held for the purposes of the scheme, or the value or amount of the annuity, as the case may be,

is prescribed for the purposes of section 164 of the Finance Act 2004 (authorised member payments under registered pension schemes).

(2) In this regulation—

"the commencement date" means 6th April 2006;

"demutualisation" means a transfer under an insurance business transfer scheme of the whole or any part of the business carried on by a mutual insurance company to one or more companies with a share capital;

"insurance business transfer scheme" means a scheme falling within section 105 FISMA 2000;

"mutual insurance company" means an insurance company not having a share capital;

"qualifying annuity contract" means an annuity contract made with an insurance company—

(*a*)

(i) by means of which benefits provided under a pension scheme which, at the time of the purchase of the annuity, fell within one of the categories set out in paragraphs (*a*) to (*c*) and (*g*) of paragraph 1(1) of Schedule 36 to the Finance Act 2004, have been secured, and

(ii) which, immediately before the commencement date, provided for the immediate payment of benefits; or

(*b*) issued out of a trust scheme within section 620(5) of the Income and Corporation Taxes Act 1988, or

(*c*) which is a lifetime annuity within the meaning in paragraph 3 of Schedule 28 to the Finance Act 2004, or a short term annuity within the meaning in paragraph 6 of that Schedule;

"qualifying pension scheme" means a registered pension scheme which is neither an occupational pension scheme nor a public service pension scheme; and

expressions defined in section 150, 151 or 280(1) of the Finance Act 2004 have the same meanings in this regulation as they have for the purposes of Part 4 of that Act.

2006/138

PENSION SCHEMES (REDUCTION IN PENSION RATES) REGULATIONS 2006

Made by the Commissioners for HMRC under FA 2004 Sch 28 para 2(4)(e), (h)

Made	*25 January 2006*
Laid before the House of Commons	*26 January 2006*
Coming into force	*6 April 2006*

Commentary—*Simon's Taxes* **E7.224**.

1 Citation, commencement and interpretation

(1) These Regulations may be cited as the Pension Schemes (Reduction in Pension Rates) Regulations 2006 and shall come into force on 6th April 2006.

(2) In these Regulations a reference, without more, to a paragraph is a reference to a paragraph of Schedule 28 of the Finance Act 2004.

2 Forfeiture of entitlement to pension—prescribed circumstances

(1) For the purposes of paragraph 2(4)(*e*) (forfeiture of entitlement to pension) the prescribed circumstances are where forfeiture of a pension has been permitted—

(*a*) under section 92(2) or 93 of the Pensions Act 1995 ("the 1995 Act") providing that the member meets the condition set out in sub-paragraph 2(2);

(*b*) under section 92(4) or (5) of the 1995 Act;

(*c*) under Article 90(4) or (5) or 91 of the Pensions (Northern Ireland) Order 1995;

(*d*) in any of the circumstances prescribed by the Occupational Pension Schemes (Assignment, Forfeiture, Bankruptcy etc) Regulations 1997 or the Occupational Pension Schemes (Assignment, Forfeiture, Bankruptcy etc) Regulations (Northern Ireland) 1997.

(2) The condition referred to in sub-paragraph 2(1)(*a*) is that the member is not connected with—

(*a*) the sponsoring employer of the scheme in respect of which the scheme pension is payable ("the employer"); or

(*b*) a person who is connected with the employer.

(3) Section 839 of ICTA 1988 applies to determine whether persons are connected for the purposes of paragraph (2) of this regulation.

[3 Reduction of pension—prescribed circumstances

The circumstances described in regulations 4[, 4A][2] and 5 are prescribed circumstances for the purpose of paragraph 2(4)(*h*) (scheme pension – other circumstances in which reduction does not breach condition in paragraph 2(3)).][1]

Amendments—[1] Regs 3–5 substituted for previous reg 3 by the Pension Schemes (Reduction in Pension Rates) (Amendment) Regulations, SI 2009/1311 reg 2. Those Regulations come into force on 1 July 2009 and have effect from 6 April 2006.

[2] Reference inserted by the Registered Pension Schemes (Reduction in Pension Rates, Accounting and Assessment) (Amendment) Regulations, SI 2013/1111 reg 3(1), (2) with effect from 6 April 2013.

[4 Reduction of pension under certain provisions

The circumstances are that the pension is reduced under any of the following provisions—

(*a*) section 138(2) of the Pensions Act 2004 (payment of scheme benefits);

(*b*) article 122(2) of the Pensions (Northern Ireland) Order 2005 (payment of scheme benefits);

(*c*) paragraph 14(3) or 15(3) of Schedule 5 to the Gender Recognition Act 2004 (guaranteed minimum pension etc)[;

(*d*) section 237E(1) of the Finance Act 2004 (consequential benefit adjustments to be reasonable etc)][2]][1]

Amendments—[1] Regs 3–5 substituted for previous reg 3 by the Pension Schemes (Reduction in Pension Rates) (Amendment) Regulations, SI 2009/1311 reg 2. Those Regulations come into force on 1 July 2009 and have effect from 6 April 2006.

[2] Para (*d*) inserted by the Registered Pension Schemes (Reduction in Pension Rates, Accounting and Assessment) (Amendment) Regulations, SI 2013/1111 reg 3(1), (3) with effect from 6 April 2013.

[4A Reduction of pension – voluntary satisfaction of liability

The circumstances are that the pension is reduced by reason of the satisfaction by the scheme administrator on a voluntary basis of all or part of a liability of a member arising under section 227(1) of the Finance Act 2004 (annual allowance charge).][1]

Amendments—[1] Reg 4A inserted by the Registered Pension Schemes (Reduction in Pension Rates, Accounting and Assessment) (Amendment) Regulations, SI 2013/1111 reg 3(1), (4) with effect from 6 April 2013.

[5 Reduction of pension during winding-up

(1) The circumstances are that—

(*a*) an occupational pension scheme reduces the pension while the scheme is being wound up; and

(*b*) the reason for the reduction is that the sums or assets held for the purposes of the scheme are insufficient to pay the pension at the rate at which the pension was being paid at the relevant time.

(2) A reduction of pension is not within the circumstances described in this regulation if the reduction is part of avoidance arrangements.

(3) In this regulation, "avoidance arrangements" includes schemes, arrangements and understandings of any kind (whether or not legally enforceable) the main purpose, or one of the main purposes, of which is to increase the member's entitlement to a lump sum on which there is no liability to income tax.][1]

Amendments—[1] Regs 3–5 substituted for previous reg 3 by the Pension Schemes (Reduction in Pension Rates) (Amendment) Regulations, SI 2009/1311 reg 2. Those Regulations come into force on 1 July 2009 and have effect from 6 April 2006.

2006/184

TAXATION OF CHARGEABLE GAINS (GILT-EDGED SECURITIES) ORDER 2006

Made by the Treasury under TCGA 1992 Sch 9 para 1

Made . . . . *30 January 2006*

1 Citation

This Order may be cited as the Taxation of Chargeable Gains (Gilt-edged Securities) Order 2006.

2 Securities specified as gilt-edged securities

For the purposes of Schedule 9 to the Taxation of Chargeable Gains Act 1992 (gilt-edged securities) the following securities are specified—

4¼% Treasury Gilt 2011;
4¾% Treasury Stock 2020;
4¼% Treasury Stock 2036;
1¼% Index-linked Treasury Gilt 2055;
4¼% Treasury Gilt 2055.

Commentary—*Simon's Taxes* **C2.825**.

2006/206

PENSION SCHEMES (CATEGORIES OF COUNTRY AND REQUIREMENTS FOR OVERSEAS PENSION SCHEMES AND RECOGNISED OVERSEAS PENSION SCHEMES) REGULATIONS 2006

Made by the Commissioners for HMRC under FA 2004 s 150(7), (8)

Made . . . . 1 February 2006
Laid before the House of Commons . . . . 2 February 2006
Coming into force . . . . 6 April 2006

Commentary—*Simon's Taxes* **E7.222, E7.223**.

1 Citation, commencement and interpretation

(1) These Regulations may be cited as the Pension Schemes (Categories of Country and Requirements for Overseas Pension Schemes and Recognised Overseas Pension Schemes) Regulations 2006 and shall come into force on 6th April 2006.

(2) In these Regulations a reference, without more, to a numbered section or Schedule is a reference to the section of, or Schedule to, the Finance Act 2004 which is so numbered.

2 Requirements of an overseas pension scheme

(1) For the purposes of section 150(7) (meaning of overseas pension scheme) an overseas pension scheme must—

(*a*) [subject to paragraph (2A)][3]satisfy the requirements in paragraphs (2) and (3); or
(*b*) be established (outside the United Kingdom) by an international organisation for the purpose of providing benefits for, or in respect of, past service as an employee of the organisation . . .[3].

(2) This paragraph is satisfied if—

(*a*) the scheme is an occupational pension scheme and there is, in the country or territory in which it is established, a body—
  (i) which regulates occupational pension schemes; and
  (ii) which regulates the scheme in question;
(*b*) the scheme is not an occupational pension scheme and there is in the country or territory in which it is established, a body—
  (i) which regulates pension schemes other than occupational pension schemes; and
  (ii) which regulates the scheme in question; or
[(*c*) sub-paragraph (*a*) is not satisfied by reason only that no such regulatory body exists in the country or territory; or][3]
[(*d*) sub-paragraph (*b*) is not satisfied by reason only that no such regulatory body exists in the country or territory and—
  (i) the scheme is established in another member State, Norway, Iceland or Liechtenstein; or
  (ii) there is in the country or territory in which the scheme is established a body—
    (*aa*) which regulates providers of pension schemes; and
    (*bb*) which regulates the provider for the purpose of establishing the scheme in question.][3]

[(2A) An overseas public service pension scheme that falls within regulation 3(1B) is deemed to satisfy the requirements in paragraph (2).][3]

(3) This paragraph is satisfied if the scheme is recognised for tax purposes.

A scheme is "recognised for tax purposes" under the tax legislation of a country or territory in which it is established if it meets the [following conditions][2].

[Condition 1][2]

The scheme is open to persons resident in the country or territory in which it is established.

[Condition 2][2]

The scheme is established in a country or territory where there is a system of taxation of personal income under which tax relief is available in respect of pensions and—

(*a*) tax relief is not available to the member on contributions made to the scheme by the individual or, if the individual is an employee, by their employer, in respect of earnings to which benefits under the scheme relate; . . .[1]
[(*ab*) the scheme is liable to taxation on its income and gains and is of a kind specified in [Schedule 1][2] to these Regulations; or][1]
(*b*) all or most of the benefits paid by the scheme to members who are not in serious ill-health are subject to taxation.

For the purposes of this condition "tax relief" includes the grant of an exemption from tax.

[Condition 3][2]

The scheme is approved or recognised by, or registered with, the relevant tax authorities as a pension scheme in the country or territory in which it is established.

. . . [2]

(4) . . . [3]

(5) In this regulation—

"international organisation" means an organisation to which section 1 of the International Organisations Act 1968 applies by virtue of an Order in Council under subsection (1) of that section;

occupational pension scheme" has the meaning given by section 150(5); and

. . . [3]

Simon's Tax Cases—reg 2, *Equity Trust (Singapore) Ltd v R&C Comrs* [2012] EWCA Civ 192, [2012] STC 998. reg 2(3), *Equity Trust (Singapore) Ltd v R&C Comrs* [2011] EWHC 1463 (Ch), [2011] STC 1830.

Amendments—[1] In reg 2(3) primary condition 2, word in sub-para (*a*) revoked and para (*ab*) inserted, by the Pension Schemes (Categories of Country and Requirements for Overseas Pension Schemes and Recognised Overseas Pension Schemes) (Amendment) Regulations, SI 2007/1600 regs 2, 3 with effect from 1 July 2007.

[2] In para (3), words substituted, italic cross-headings substituted and Condition B revoked, by the Registered Pension Schemes and Overseas Pension Schemes (Miscellaneous Amendments) Regulations, SI 2012/884 regs 2, 3 with effect from 6 April 2012.

[3] The following amendments made by the Pension Schemes (Categories of Country and Requirements for Overseas Pension Schemes and Recognised Overseas Pension Schemes) (Amendments) Regulations, SI 2017/398 regs 2, 3 with effect from 6 April 2017—

- in para (1)(*a*), words inserted, and paras (2)(*d*), (2A) inserted;
- in para (1)(*b*), words revoked, para (4) revoked, and in para (5), definition of "UK tax-relieved scheme funds" revoked; and
- para (2)(*c*) substituted.

3 Recognised overseas pension schemes: prescribed countries or territories and prescribed [requirements]

[(1) For the purposes of section 150(8) (recognised overseas pension schemes), in addition to satisfying the requirements set out in regulation 2 above, the pension scheme must—

(*a*) except where it falls within paragraph (1A), satisfy the [the requirements in paragraphs (6) and (6A)][4]; and

(*b*) satisfy . . . [5] the following requirements—

(i) the requirement that the scheme must be established in a country or territory mentioned in paragraph (2), [and][5]

(ii) [for schemes established in Guernsey,][5] the requirement in paragraph (4)[.][5]

(iii) . . . [5]

(1A) A pension scheme falls within this paragraph if it is an overseas public service pension scheme or if it falls within regulation 2(1)(*b*).

(1B) A pension scheme is an "overseas public service pension scheme" for the purposes of paragraph (1A) [and regulation 2(2A)][5] if—

(*a*) it is established in a country or territory outside the United Kingdom and is either—

(i) so established by or under the law of that country or territory, or

(ii) approved by the government of that country or territory; and

(*b*) it is established for the purpose of providing benefits to individuals for or in respect of services rendered to that country or territory or any political subdivision or local authority thereof.][3]

(2) The countries and territories referred to in [paragraph (1)(*b*)(i)][1] are—

(*a*) the member States of the European Communities, other than the United Kingdom;

(*b*) Iceland, Liechtenstein and Norway; and

[(*c*) any country or territory in respect of which there is in force an Order in Council under section 173 of the Finance Act 2006 or section 2 of the Taxation (International and Other Provisions) Act 2010 giving effect in the United Kingdom to an agreement which contains provision about the exchange of information between the parties.] . . . [5]

(3) . . . [5]

[(4) At the time of the transfer of sums or assets which would, subject to these Regulations, constitute a recognised transfer, where the pension scheme is an exempt pension contract or an exempt pension trust within the meaning of section 157E of the Income Tax (Guernsey) Law, 1975, the scheme must not be open to non-residents of Guernsey.] . . . [5]

(4A) . . . . . . [5]

[(5) . . . . . . [5]

(6) Where tax relief in respect of benefits paid from the scheme is available to a member of the scheme who is not resident in the country or territory in which the scheme is established, the same or substantially the same tax relief must—

(*a*) also be available to members of the scheme who are resident in the country or territory; and

(*b*) apply regardless of whether the member was resident in the country or territory—

(i) when the member joined the scheme; or

(ii) for any period of time when they were a member of the scheme.

[(6A) The benefits payable to the member under the scheme, to the extent that they consist of the member's relevant transfer fund or ring-fenced transfer funds—

(*a*) are payable no earlier than they would be if pension rule 1 in section 165 applied; or

(*b*) if payable earlier, are only payable in circumstances in which they would be authorised member payments if they were made by a registered pension scheme.][5]

(7) For the purposes of paragraph (6) "tax relief"—

(*a*) is any tax relief that is available under the system of taxation of personal income in the country or territory in which the scheme is established; and

(*b*) includes the grant of an exemption from tax other than an exemption which applies by virtue of double taxation arrangements.

(8) In paragraph (7)(*b*) "double taxation arrangements" means arrangements made between the country or territory in which the scheme is established and another country or territory with a view to affording relief from double taxation.][1]

Amendments—[1] In para (2) words substituted and words inserted, and paras (5)–(8) inserted, by the Registered Pension Schemes and Overseas Pension Schemes (Miscellaneous Amendments) Regulations, SI 2012/884 regs 2, 4 with effect from 6 April 2012.

[2] In heading, word substituted for word "conditions", and paras (4), (4A) substituted for previous para (4), by the Pension Schemes (Categories of Country and Requirements for Overseas Pension Schemes and Recognised Overseas Pension Schemes) (Amendment) Regulations, SI 2012/1221 reg 2 with effect from 25 May 2012.

[3] Paras (1)–(1B) substituted for previous para (1) by the Registered Pension Schemes and Overseas Pension Schemes (Miscellaneous Amendments) Regulations, SI 2013/2259 regs 7, 8 with effect from 14 October 2013. Note that, in relation to qualifying recognised overseas pension schemes (QROPS) in existence immediately before 6 April 2012, this amendment has effect from 6 April 2012 (SI 2013/2259 reg 2).

[4] Words in para (1)(*a*) substituted, and para (6A) inserted by the Overseas Pension Schemes (Miscellaneous Amendments) Regulations, SI 2015/673 regs 2, 3 with effect from 6 April 2015.

[5] The following amendments made by the Pension Schemes (Categories of Country and Requirements for Overseas Pension Schemes and Recognised Overseas Pension Schemes) (Amendments) Regulations, SI 2017/398 regs 2, 4 with effect from 6 April 2017—

- in para (1)(*b*), words revoked, and in sub-para (1)(*b*)(i), (ii), words inserted;
- in para (1B), words inserted;
- paras (2)(*c*), (4), (6A) substituted; and
- paras (3), (4A), (5) revoked.

[[SCHEDULE 1]
SPECIFIED SCHEMES

Amendments—Schedule 1 renumbered as such by the Registered Pension Schemes and Overseas Pension Schemes (Miscellaneous Amendments) Regulations, SI 2012/884 regs 2, 5 with effect from 6 April 2012.

Regulation 2(3)

A complying superannuation plan as defined in section 995–1 (definitions) of the Income Tax Assessment Act 1997 of Australia.][1]

Amendments—[1] Schedule inserted by the Pension Schemes (Categories of Country and Requirements for Overseas Pension Schemes and Recognised Overseas Pension Schemes) (Amendment) Regulations, SI 2007/1600 regs 2, 4 with effect from 1 July 2007.

[SCHEDULE 2
SPECIFIED SCHEMES

Regulation 3(5)

A pension scheme which is a KiwiSaver scheme as defined in section 4(1) (interpretation) of the KiwiSaver Act 2006 of New Zealand.][1]

Amendments—[1] Schedule 2 inserted by the Registered Pension Schemes and Overseas Pension Schemes (Miscellaneous Amendments) Regulations, SI 2012/884 regs 2, 6 with effect from 6 April 2012.

2006/207

PENSIONS SCHEMES (APPLICATION OF UK PROVISIONS TO RELEVANT NON-UK SCHEMES) REGULATIONS 2006

Made by the Commissioners for HMRC under FA 2004 Sch 34 paras 3(2)–(6), 4(2), (4), 7, 12, 19

Made . . . . *1 February 2006*

Laid before the House of Commons . . . . *2 February 2006*

Coming into force . . . . *6 April 2006*

Commentary—*Simon's Taxes* **E7.224.**

PART 1
INTRODUCTION

1 Citation, commencement and interpretation

(1) These Regulations may be cited as the Pensions Schemes (Application of UK Provisions to Relevant Non-UK Schemes) Regulations 2006 and shall come into force on 6th April 2006.

(2) In these Regulations—

"the Act" means the Finance Act 2004 any reference (without more) to a numbered section or Schedule is a reference, as the case requires, to the section of, or Schedule to, the Act which bears that number;

"benefit crystallisation event 8" means the event which constitutes benefit crystallisation event 8 in section 216;

"recognised overseas pension scheme" has the meaning given by section 150(8); and

"relevant non-UK scheme" has the same meaning given by paragraph 1(5) of Schedule 34.

["taxable property" has the meaning in Schedule 29A to the Act;][1]

["taxable property provisions" has the meaning in paragraph 1(3) of that Schedule; and][1]

["transfer member" of a scheme has the meaning in paragraph 1(8) of Schedule 34 to the Act.][1]

Amendments—[1] Definitions inserted by the Pensions Schemes (Application of UK Provisions to Relevant Non-UK Schemes) (Amendment) Regulations, SI 2006/1960 regs 2, 3. SI 2006/1960 came into force on 11 August 2006, and these amendments have effect from 6 April 2006.

PART 2
APPLICATION AND COMPUTATION OF UK TAX CHARGES

2 Computation of a member's UK tax-relieved fund under a relevant non-UK scheme

The amount of a member's UK tax-relieved fund under a relevant non-UK scheme is the aggregate of—

(*a*) the amounts which, for each tax year before that in which the computation falls to be made, would have been arrived at in relation to arrangements under the relevant non-UK scheme relating to the individual as pension input amounts under sections 230 to 238 of the Act (annual allowance) as they apply by virtue of paragraph 8 of Schedule 34 to the Act, and

(*b*) the amount which would be so arrived at if the period beginning with 6th April of the tax year in which the computation falls to be made; and ending immediately before the making of the computation, were a tax year,

assuming that section 229(3) did not apply.

3 Computation of a member's relevant transfer fund

The amount of a member's relevant transfer fund under a relevant non-UK scheme (that scheme being referred to here as "the RNUKS") is the sum of—

(*a*) the amount crystallised by virtue of benefit crystallisation event 8 on the transfer from a UK registered scheme to the RNUKS; and

(*b*) so much of the member's UK tax-relieved fund under any other relevant non-UK scheme as has been transferred to the RNUKS but has not been subject to the unauthorised payments charge; and

(*c*) so much of the member's relevant transfer fund under any other relevant non-UK scheme as has been transferred to the RNUKS—

(i) without being subject to the unauthorised payments charge; *and*[1]

(ii) *at a time when the other relevant non-UK scheme is a recognised overseas pension scheme.*[1]

Amendments—[1] Para (3)(*c*)(ii) and preceding word "and" revoked by the Pensions Schemes (Application of UK Provisions to Relevant Non-UK Schemes) (Amendment) Regulations, SI 2006/1960 regs 2, 4. SI 2006/1960 came into force on 11 August 2006, and these amendments have effect from 6 April 2006.

3A [Computation of a member's taxable asset transfer fund

(1) The amount of a member's taxable asset transfer fund under a relevant non-UK scheme ("the RNUKS") is the sum of—

(*a*) the amount crystallised by virtue of benefit crystallisation event 8 on the transfer from a UK registered pension scheme to the RNUKS; and

(*b*) so much of the member's taxable asset transfer fund under any other relevant non-UK scheme as has been transferred to the RNUKS without being subject to the unauthorised payments charge.

(2) Accordingly, the member's taxable asset transfer fund ("TATF") shall form part of the member's relevant transfer fund ("RTF"), except in a case where the member's RTF consists solely of a UK tax-relieved fund which has been transferred to the RNUKS.][1]

Amendments—[1] This paragraph inserted by the Pensions Schemes (Application of UK Provisions to Relevant Non-UK Schemes) (Amendment) Regulations, SI 2006/1960 regs 2, 5. SI 2006/1960 came into force on 11 August 2006, and these amendments have effect from 6 April 2006.

4 Attributing payments to particular funds under a relevant non-UK scheme

(1) This regulation applies to determine to which part of a relevant non-UK scheme a payment to, or in respect of, a member is referable.

(2) It shall be assumed that—

(*a*) payments made by the scheme to or in respect of the member are made out of the member's UK tax-relieved fund in priority to any other fund under that scheme; and

(*b*) the amount of the member's UK tax-relieved fund is reduced [(but not below nil)][1] by the amount paid out of the scheme.

(3) If the member's UK tax-relieved fund is nil, or has been reduced to nil, [the following Rules apply (with an earlier Rule applying in preference to a later Rule).

Rule 1

Where an unauthorised payment is treated as made by the scheme to the transfer member by virtue of section 174A—

(*a*) the payment shall be treated as made out of the member's RTF and TATF, but

(*b*) the interest in taxable property, in respect of which the unauthorised payment is treated as made, shall represent the payment and form part of the member's RTF and TATF (an "appropriated asset"), up to an amount equal to the amount of that payment.

Rule 2

Accordingly, if a scheme transfers that appropriated asset (or an interest in a vehicle through which the scheme holds the interest in the taxable property indirectly), or part of it, to another pension scheme, that transfer shall be treated as a transfer of the whole or part, as the case may be, of the member's RTF and TATF (limited to the amount of the unauthorised payment) to that other scheme, falling (if appropriate) within regulation 3A(1)(*b*).

Rule 3

If a scheme disposes of (other than to another pension scheme) an appropriated asset (or an interest in a vehicle through which the scheme holds the interest in the taxable property indirectly), or part of it, any other property which directly or indirectly represents proceeds of either of those interests (limited to the amount of the unauthorised payment) shall form part of the member's RTF and TATF.

Rule 4

This Rule applies to payments made by the scheme to or in respect of the member, other than—

(*a*) a transfer of an interest in taxable property or an interest in a vehicle through which the scheme holds the interest in the taxable property indirectly, and

(*b*) payments treated as made by virtue of section 174A.

So far as the member's RTF and TATF are not represented by appropriated assets—

(*a*) where the member has both an RTF and a TATF, and the amount of his RTF exceeds the amount of his TATF, such payments shall, to the extent of that excess, be treated as made out of his RTF (but not his TATF) and as reducing the RTF, and subject thereto

(*b*) such payments are made out of the member's RTF and TATF in priority to any other fund under that scheme, and reduce (but not below nil) the amount of the RTF and TATF.][1]

[(4) In paragraph (3), references to payments made or treated as made by virtue of section 174A include references to payments treated as made by regulations under paragraph 37 of Schedule 29A, or paragraph 7A of Schedule 34, to the Act.][1]

Amendments—[1] Words in sub-para (2)(*b*) inserted; in para (3), words substituted; and para (4) inserted; by the Pensions Schemes (Application of UK Provisions to Relevant Non-UK Schemes) (Amendment) Regulations, SI 2006/1960 regs 2, 6–8. SI 2006/1960 came into force on 11 August 2006, and these amendments have effect from 6 April 2006.

4A [Taxable property provisions to apply to a transfer member of a relevant non-UK scheme (to payments referable to his taxable asset transfer fund)

The—

(*a*) taxable property provisions, and

(*b*) regulations made under paragraph 37 of Schedule 29A or paragraph 7A of Schedule 34,

apply to a transfer member of a relevant non-UK scheme, in relation to payments treated as made by those provisions or regulations which are referable to the member's taxable asset transfer fund under the scheme, but subject to the modifications in regulations 4B to 4D.][1]

Amendments—[1] Regulations 4A–4D inserted by the Pensions Schemes (Application of UK Provisions to Relevant Non-UK Schemes) (Amendment) Regulations, SI 2006/1960 regs 2, 9. SI 2006/1960 came into force on 11 August 2006, and these amendments have effect from 6 April 2006.

4B [Unauthorised payments charge to apply (in lieu of scheme chargeable payment)

(1) The scheme chargeable payment provisions in sections 185A to 185I shall not apply to a relevant non-UK scheme.

(2) But, during such time as an appropriated asset forms the whole or part of a transfer member's TATF—

(*a*) the scheme shall be treated as making unauthorised payments to that member equal in amount to the scheme chargeable payments (in respect of income and gains) which would have been computed in accordance with those sections, and (*b*) the transfer member shall be liable to pay the unauthorised payments charge in respect of such payments.

(3) Where the scheme's interest in taxable property is not wholly referable to the transfer member's TATF, the amount of the unauthorised payment shall be proportionately reduced.][1]

Amendments—[1] Regulations 4A–4D inserted by the Pensions Schemes (Application of UK Provisions to Relevant Non-UK Schemes) (Amendment) Regulations, SI 2006/1960 regs 2, 9. SI 2006/1960 came into force on 11 August 2006, and these amendments have effect from 6 April 2006.

4C [Modification of paragraph 15 of Schedule 29A

Paragraph 15 of Schedule 29A applies to the transfer member of a relevant non-UK scheme as if "insurance company" included any person—

(*a*) resident in a country or territory outside the European Economic Area,

(*b*) whose business consists of, or includes, the effecting or carrying out of contracts of long-term insurance (within the meaning in Part 2 of Schedule 1 to the Financial Services and Markets Act 2000 (Regulated Activities) Order 2001), and

(*c*) who is regulated in the conduct of that business by—

(i) the government of that country or territory, or

(ii) a body established under the law of that country or territory for the purpose of regulating such business.][1]

Amendments—[1] Regulations 4A–4D inserted by the Pensions Schemes (Application of UK Provisions to Relevant Non-UK Schemes) (Amendment) Regulations, SI 2006/1960 regs 2, 9. SI 2006/1960 came into force on 11 August 2006, and these amendments have effect from 6 April 2006.

4D [Modifications of paragraphs 29 and 31 of Schedule 29A

(1) This regulation applies where—

(*a*) a relevant non-UK scheme acquires an interest in taxable property;

(*b*) the interest is acquired in the circumstances mentioned in paragraph 32(3), (5) (excluding paragraphs (*a*) and (*b*)) or (6) (excluding paragraphs (*a*) and (*b*)) of Schedule 29A; and

(*c*) the whole or part of the consideration for the acquisition is rent.

(2) The amount of the consideration (or the part that is rent) shall not be the relevant rental value of the property (as provided by paragraph 34(2) of Schedule 29A).

(3) Each payment of rent (or the aggregate of such payments during a year, if there are more than one) shall be treated, for the purposes of the taxable property provisions, as if the pension scheme or other person who acquired the interest were being granted a lease for the period for which the rent is paid, in consideration of the rent (or aggregate) so paid.][1]

Amendments—[1] Regulations 4A–4D inserted by the Pensions Schemes (Application of UK Provisions to Relevant Non-UK Schemes) (Amendment) Regulations, SI 2006/1960 regs 2, 9. SI 2006/1960 came into force on 11 August 2006, and these amendments have effect from 6 April 2006.

PART 3

5 Modifications to Part 4 of the Finance Act 2004 in respect of relevant non-UK schemes

Part 4 of the Finance Act 2004 shall be modified in respect of relevant non-UK schemes, within the meaning of paragraph 1(5) of Schedule 34, in accordance with the following provisions of [this Part][1].

Amendments—[1] Words substituted for words "these Regulations" by the Taxation of Pensions Act 2014 s 1, Sch 1 para 96(1), (2) with effect in relation to lump sums paid on or after 6 April 2015. These amendments are to be treated as having been made by the Commissioners for Revenue and Customs under such of the powers conferred on them by FA 2004 Sch 34 (as amended by TPA 2014 Sch 1) as are applicable.

[6 Modification of section 165

In section 165 (pension rules)—

(*a*) in subsection (1), in pension rule 4 omit from "but a scheme pension" to the end. . . . [2]

(b) in subsection (3A), for "scheme administrator" (in both places) substitute "scheme manager".[2]*]*[1]

Amendments—[1] Reg 6 substituted by the Pensions Schemes (Application of UK Provisions to Relevant Non-UK Schemes) (Amendment) Regulations, SI 2012/1795 regs 2, 3 with effect for the tax year 2011–12 and subsequent tax years.

[2] Para (*b*) and preceding word "and" repealed by the Taxation of Pensions Act 2014 s 1, Sch 1 para 33(1), (2) with effect from 6 April 2015.

[7 Modification of section 167

In section 167 (pension death benefit rules)—

(*a*) in subsection (1), in pension death benefit rule 3 omit from "but a dependants' scheme pension" to the end. . . . [2]

(b) in subsection (2A), for "scheme administrator" (in both places) substitute "scheme manager".[2]*]*[1]

Amendments—[1] Reg 7 substituted by the Pensions Schemes (Application of UK Provisions to Relevant Non-UK Schemes) (Amendment) Regulations, SI 2012/1795 regs 2, 4 with effect for the tax year 2011–12 and subsequent tax years.

[2] Para (*b*) and preceding word "and" repealed by the Taxation of Pensions Act 2014 s 1, Sch 1 para 33(1), (2) with effect from 6 April 2015.

8 *Modification of section 227*

In section 227(3)(*b*) for "scheme administrator" substitute "scheme manager".

Amendments—[1] Reg 8 revoked by the Registered Pension Schemes (Miscellaneous Amendments) Regulations, SI 2011/1751 reg 12(1), (2) with effect for the tax year 2011–12 and subsequent tax years.

9 Modification of section 231

In section 231—

[(*a*) in subsection (3) for "the consumer prices index" substitute "the relevant index"][1]

(*b*) at the end add—

["(4) In this section "the relevant index" means—

(*a*) if there is an index of the movement of consumer prices maintained, or officially recognised, by the government of the country or territory in which the recognised overseas scheme is established, that index, or

(*b*) if there is no such index, the consumer prices index."][1]

Amendments—[1] Para (*a*) substituted, and in para (*b*) the inserted sub-s (4) substituted, by the Registered Pension Schemes (Miscellaneous Amendments) Regulations, SI 2011/1751 reg 12(1), (3) with effect in relation to pension input periods ending in the tax year 2011–12 and subsequent tax years.

10 Modification of section 235

In section 235—

(*b*) at the end of the section add—

["(4) In this section "the relevant index" means—

(*a*) if there is an index of the movement of consumer prices maintained, or officially recognised, by the government of the country or territory in which the recognised overseas scheme is established, that index, o

(*b*) if there is no such index, the consumer prices index."][1]

Amendments—[1] Para (*a*) substituted, and in para (*b*) the inserted sub-s (4) substituted, by the Registered Pension Schemes (Miscellaneous Amendments) Regulations, SI 2011/1751 reg 12(1), (2) with effect in relation to pension input periods ending in the tax year 2011–12 and subsequent tax years.

11 Modification of section 275

(1) In the heading of section 275 at the end add "and Non-EEA annuity provider".

(2) At the end of the section add—

"(3) In this Part "non-EEA annuity provider" means a person resident in a country or territory outside the European Economic Area—

(*a*) whose normal business includes the provision of annuities; and

(*b*) who is regulated in the conduct of that business—

(i) by the government of that country or territory; or

(ii) a body established under the law of that country or territory for the purpose of regulating such business.".

12 Modification of section 276

In section 276(2) for "scheme administrator" substitute "scheme manager".

13 Modification of section 279

(1) Section 279(1) shall be modified as follows.

(2) At the appropriate points in the alphabetical list insert—

"applicable pension scheme", in relation to a pension sharing order in respect of a member's spouse [, ex-spouse, civil partner or former civil partner][1], means a scheme which is—

(*a*) a recognised overseas pension scheme within the meaning of this Part; or

(*b*) a scheme which is recognised for tax purposes under the law of either the country or territory in which it is situate or that of the country or territory in which the pension sharing order is made;"; and

"ex-spouse", in relation to a member, means the other party to a marriage with the member that has been dissolved or annulled;

['former civil partner' in relation to a member means the other party to a civil partnership with the member that has been dissolved or annulled.[1]]";

(3) For the definitions of "pension credit" and "pension debit" substitute—

"pension credit" and "pension debit" mean respectively the amount by which—

(*a*) the entitlement of a member's spouse[, ex-spouse, civil partner or former civil partner][1] under an applicable pension scheme, is increased; and

(*b*) the entitlement of a member under a qualifying recognised overseas pension scheme is decreased, pursuant to a pension sharing order;".

(4) For the definition of "pension sharing order or provision" substitute—

"pension sharing order" means an order of a court, by virtue of which amounts are transferred from a recognised overseas pension scheme of a member to an applicable pension scheme of that member's spouse[, ex-spouse, civil partner or former civil partner][1], in or in connection with proceedings relating to the dissolution or annulment of the marriage [or civil partnership][1] of the parties;".

Amendments—[1] Words in sub-paras (2), (4) substituted and inserted, and words in sub-para (3) substituted, by the Tax and Civil Partnerships Regulations, SI 2007/493 reg 3 with effect from 22 February 2007.

14 Modification of Schedule 28

(1) Schedule 28 is modified as follows.

(2) In paragraph 1—

(*a*) in sub-paragraph (*a*) after "registered medical practitioner" insert "or a recognised medical practitioner";

(*b*) at the end of the paragraph add—

"In this paragraph "recognised medical practitioner" means a medical practitioner practising outside the United Kingdom who is authorised, licensed or registered to practise medicine in the country or territory, outside the United Kingdom, in which either the scheme or the member is resident.".

(3) In the following provisions for "scheme administrator" substitute "scheme manager".

The provisions are—

(*a*) paragraph 1(*a*);

(*b*) paragraph 2 (in each place where the expression occurs);

[(*ba*) paragraphs 8C and 8D (in each place where the expression occurs);][2]

[(*c*) paragraph 10 (in each place where the expression occurs);][1]

[(*ca*) paragraph 10A (in each place where the expression occurs);

(*cb*) paragraph 10B (in each place where the expression occurs);][1]

(*d*) paragraph 13(3);

(da) paragraph 14E(2);[2]][1]

(*e*) paragraph 16(1) and (2);

[(*ea*) paragraphs 22C and 22D (in each place where the expression occurs);][2]

[(*f*) paragraph 24 (in each place where the expression occurs);][1]

[(*fa*) paragraph 24A (in each place where the expression occurs);

(*fb*) paragraph 24B (in each place where the expression occurs);

(fc) paragraph 24G(2);[2]][1]

(*g*) paragraph 27(3).

(4) Omit paragraphs 3(1)(*b*), 6(1)(*c*), 17(1)(*b*) and 20(1)(*c*).

(5) In paragraph 15(2)(*b*) and (3) omit ", in the opinion of the scheme administrator".

(6) At the end of the Schedule add—

"PART 3

RELEVANT NON-UK SCHEMES—INTERPRETATION

28— Construction of references to insurance companies

(1) In this Schedule, in its application to a scheme established in a country or territory outside the European Economic Area, any reference to an insurance company includes a non-EEA annuity provider.

(2) Section 275(3) defines "non-EEA annuity provider".".

Amendments—[1] In para (3), sub-paras (*c*), (*f*) substituted, and sub-paras (*ca*), (*cb*), (*da*), (*fa*)–(*fc*) inserted, by the Pensions Schemes (Application of UK Provisions to Relevant Non-UK Schemes) (Amendment) Regulations, SI 2012/1795 regs 2, 5 with effect for the tax year 2011–12 and subsequent tax years.

[2] In para (3), paras (*ba*), (*ea*) inserted, and paras (*da*), (*fc*) repealed, by the Taxation of Pensions Act 2014 s 1, Sch 1 para 33(1), (3) with effect from 6 April 2015. The insertion of paras (*ba*), (*ea*) are to be treated as having been made by the Commissioners for HMRC under such of the powers conferred on them by FA 2004 Sch 34 (as amended by the Taxation of Pensions Act 2014 Sch 1) as are applicable.

15 Modification of Schedule 29

(1) Schedule 29 is modified as follows.

(2) In paragraph 1 after sub-paragraph (4) insert—

"[(4A) In determining whether all or part of the member's lifetime allowance is available—

(*a*) there shall be disregarded any amount treated as crystallising by virtue of a relevant BCE; but

(*b*) the amount of the allowance available shall be reduced by the amount determined in accordance with sub-paragraph (4B) or (4C), as the case may require.

(4B) Where benefit crystallisation event 8 has occurred, the member's lifetime allowance that is available shall be reduced by the aggregate of—

(*a*) the referable portion of any previous pension commencement lump sum paid to or in respect of the member by a recognised overseas pension scheme;

[(*aa*) the referable portion of any previous uncrystallised funds pension lump sum paid to or in respect of the member by a recognised overseas pension scheme;] [6] and

(*b*) the referable portion of the amount which would have crystallised by virtue of the member becoming entitled to a pension, had the scheme paying it been a registered pension scheme [and disregarding paragraph 2 of Schedule 32][4].

(4C) Where the paragraph 15 BCE has occurred, the member's lifetime allowance that is available shall be reduced by the aggregate of—

(*a*) the referable portion of any previous pension commencement lump sum to which the member became entitled under a relevant non-UK scheme since the paragraph 15 BCE occurred;

[(*aa*) the referable portion of any previous uncrystallised funds pension lump sum to which the member became entitled under a relevant non-UK scheme since the paragraph 15 BCE occurred;][6] and

(*b*) in respect of any pension to which the member has become entitled since the paragraph 15 BCE occurred, the referable portion of the amount which would have crystallised by virtue of the member's becoming entitled to the pension, had the scheme paying it been a registered pension scheme [and disregarding paragraph 2 of Schedule 32.[4]]."][1]

(3) In paragraph 2—

(*a*) in sub-paragraph (6) for the definition of AAC substitute—

"[AAC is the aggregate of—

(*a*) the amounts crystallised by each benefit crystallisation event (other than a relevant BCE) which has occurred in relation to the member before the member becomes entitled to the lump sum on each occasion on which entitlement to a pension arises[, as adjusted under sub-paragraph (7)][4]; and

(*b*) if a relevant BCE has occurred, RP.

["RP is the referable portion of the amount which would have crystallised, had the scheme paying it been a registered pension scheme and disregarding paragraphs 2 and 15A of Schedule 32, in respect of any previous pension commencement lump sum [or previous uncrystallised funds pension lump sum][6] or pension to which the member became entitled since the relevant BCE occurred, as adjusted under sub-paragraph (7) (but excluding any amount included in paragraph (*a*)).[4]]"][1]

[(*aa*) in sub-paragraph (7) for "the relevant amount" substitute "the amount which is, or would have, crystallised";][4]

(*b*) [after sub-paragraph (7)][4] insert—

"[(7ZA)] The member's becoming entitled to a pension commencement lump sum, [or to an uncrystallised funds pension lump sum,][6] or to a pension, as mentioned in [the definition of RP][1] in [sub-paragraph (6)][4] shall be treated as a benefit crystallisation event for the purposes of sub-paragraph (7).".

(*c*) after sub-paragraph (7A) insert—

"(7B) But sub-paragraph (7A)(*b*) does not apply to anything which, but for paragraph 2 or 15A of Schedule 32, would have constituted a relevant BCE."][4]

[(3A) In paragraph 3, after sub-paragraph (7) insert—

"(7ZA) Where a relevant BCE has occurred in relation to the member, subparagraph (6) has effect as if for the definition of "AC" in sub-paragraph (7) there were substituted—

""AC" is—

(*a*) in a case where the member becomes entitled to the pension before reaching the age of 75, the referable portion of the amount that, had the scheme been a registered pension scheme, would have crystallised by reason of the member becoming entitled to the pension, disregarding paragraph 3 of Schedule 32, and

(*b*) in a case where the member becomes entitled to the pension after reaching that age, the referable portion of the amount that would have been so crystallised (disregarding that paragraph) but for paragraph 2 of that Schedule, had the scheme been a registered pension scheme. ""][4]

(4) In paragraph 4—

(*a*) in sub-paragraph (1)(*a*) after "registered medical practitioner" insert "or a recognised medical practitioner";

(*b*) at the end of the paragraph add—

"[(4)] In sub-paragraph (1) "recognised medical practitioner" means a medical practitioner practising outside the United Kingdom who is authorised, licensed or registered to practise medicine in the country or territory, outside the United Kingdom, in which either the scheme or the member is resident.

[[(5)] In determining whether all or part of the member's lifetime allowance is available—

(*a*) there shall be disregarded any amount treated as crystallising by virtue of a relevant BCE; but

(*b*) the amount of the allowance available shall be reduced by the amount determined in accordance with [sub-paragraph (6) or (7)][5], as the case may require.

[(6)] Where benefit crystallisation event 8 has occurred, the member's lifetime allowance that is available shall be reduced by the aggregate of—

(*a*) the referable portion of any previous pension commencement lump sum paid to or in respect of the member by a recognised overseas pension scheme;

[(*aa*) the referable portion of any previous uncrystallised funds pension lump sum paid to or in respect of the member by a recognised overseas pension scheme;][6] and

(*b*) the referable portion of the amount which would have crystallised by virtue of the member becoming entitled to a pension, had the scheme paying it been a registered pension scheme [and disregarding paragraph 2 of Schedule 32][5].

[(7)] Where the paragraph 15 BCE has occurred, the member's lifetime allowance that is available shall be reduced by the aggregate of—

(*a*) the referable portion of any earlier pension commencement lump sum to which the member became entitled under a relevant non-UK scheme since the paragraph 15 BCE occurred;

[(*aa*) the referable portion of any earlier uncrystallised funds pension lump sum to which the member became entitled under a relevant non-UK scheme since the paragraph 15 BCE occurred;][6] and

(*b*) in respect of any pension to which the member has become entitled since the paragraph 15 BCE occurred, the referable portion of the amount which would have crystallised by virtue of the member's becoming entitled to the pension, had the scheme paying it been a registered pension scheme [and disregarding paragraph 2 of Schedule 32][5].[1]]"

[(4A) In paragraph 4A (uncrystallised funds pension lump sums) after sub-paragraph (2) insert—

"(2A) In determining for the purposes of sub-paragraph (1)(*b*) whether all or part of the member's lifetime allowance is available—

(*a*) disregard any amount treated as crystallising by virtue of a relevant BCE, and

(*b*) the amount of the allowance available is reduced by the amount determined in accordance with sub-paragraph (2B) or (2C), as the case may require.

(2B) Where benefit crystallisation event 8 has occurred, the member's lifetime allowance that is available is reduced by the aggregate of—

(*a*) the referable portion of any previous pension commencement lump sum paid to or in respect of the member by a recognised overseas pension scheme,

(*b*) the referable portion of any previous uncrystallised funds pension lump sum paid to or in respect of the member by a recognised overseas pension scheme, and

(*c*) the referable portion of the amount which would have crystallised by virtue of the member becoming entitled to a pension, had the scheme paying it been a registered pension scheme and disregarding paragraph 2 of Schedule 32.

(2C) Where the paragraph 15 BCE has occurred, the member's lifetime allowance that is available is reduced by the aggregate of—

(*a*) the referable portion of any earlier pension commencement lump sum to which the member became entitled under a relevant non-UK scheme since the paragraph 15 BCE occurred,

(*b*) the referable portion of any earlier uncrystallised funds pension lump sum to which the member became entitled under a relevant non-UK scheme since the paragraph 15 BCE occurred, and

(*c*) in respect of any pension to which the member has become entitled since the paragraph 15 BCE occurred, the referable portion of the amount which would have crystallised by virtue of the member's becoming entitled to the pension, had the scheme paying it been a registered pension scheme and disregarding paragraph 2 of Schedule 32.][6]

(5) In paragraph 5(1)(*c*) after "benefit crystallisation event" insert—

[", other than an event which constitutes a relevant BCE,"][1]

(6) At the end of paragraph 7 add—

"[(6) In determining whether all or part of the member's lifetime allowance is available—

(*a*) there shall be disregarded any amount treated as crystallising by virtue of a relevant BCE; but

(*b*) the amount of the allowance available shall be reduced by the amount determined in accordance with sub-paragraph (7) or (8), as the case may require.

(7) Where benefit crystallisation event 8 has occurred, the member's lifetime allowance that is available shall be reduced by the aggregate of—

(*a*) the referable portion of any previous pension commencement lump sum paid to or in respect of the member by a recognised overseas pension scheme;

[(*aa*) the referable portion of any previous uncrystallised funds pension lump sum paid to or in respect of the member by a recognised overseas pension scheme;][6] and

(*b*) the referable portion of the amount which would have crystallised by virtue of the member becoming entitled to a pension, had the scheme paying it been a registered pension scheme [and disregarding paragraph 2 of Schedule 32][5].

(8) Where the paragraph 15 BCE has occurred, the member's lifetime allowance that is available shall be reduced by the aggregate of—

(*a*) the referable portion of any earlier pension commencement lump sum to which the member became entitled under a relevant non-UK scheme since the paragraph 15 BCE occurred;

[(*aa*) the referable portion of any earlier uncrystallised funds pension lump sum to which the member became entitled under a relevant non-UK scheme since the paragraph 15 BCE occurred;][6] and

(*b*) in respect of any pension to which the member has become entitled since the paragraph 15 BCE occurred, the referable portion of the amount which would have crystallised by virtue of the member's becoming entitled to the pension, had the scheme paying it been a registered pension scheme [and disregarding paragraph 2 of Schedule 32][5].[1]]"

(7) At the end of paragraph 10 add—

"[(4) In determining whether all or part of the member's lifetime allowance is available—

(*a*) there shall be disregarded any amount treated as crystallising by virtue of a relevant BCE; but

(*b*) the amount of the allowance available shall be reduced by the amount determined in accordance with sub-paragraph (5) or (6), as the case may require.

(5) Where benefit crystallisation event 8 has occurred, the member's lifetime allowance that is available shall be reduced by the aggregate of—

(*a*) the referable portion of any previous pension commencement lump sum paid to or in respect of the member by a recognised overseas pension scheme;

[(*aa*) the referable portion of any previous uncrystallised funds pension lump sum paid to or in respect of the member by a recognised overseas pension scheme;][6] and

(*b*) the referable portion of the amount which would have crystallised by virtue of the member becoming entitled to a pension, had the scheme paying it been a registered pension scheme [and disregarding paragraph 2 of Schedule 32][5].

(6) Where the paragraph 15 BCE has occurred, the member's lifetime allowance that is available shall be reduced by the aggregate of—

(*a*) the referable portion of any earlier pension commencement lump sum to which the member became entitled under a relevant non-UK scheme since the paragraph 15 BCE occurred;

[(*aa*) the referable portion of any earlier uncrystallised funds pension lump sum to which the member became entitled under a relevant non-UK scheme since the paragraph 15 BCE occurred;][6] and

(*b*) in respect of any pension to which the member has become entitled since the paragraph 15 BCE occurred, the referable portion of the amount which would have crystallised by virtue of the member's becoming entitled to the pension, had the scheme paying it been a registered pension scheme [and disregarding paragraph 2 of Schedule 32][5].[1]]"

(8) In paragraph 11 after sub-paragraph (*b*) insert—

"[(*bb*) it is not paid from the relevant transfer fund of a qualifying recognised overseas pension scheme,

(*bc*) it is not paid from the UK tax-relieved fund of a relevant non-UK scheme,[2]]"

(9) In paragraph 4(1)(*a*), and paragraph 19(1)(*d*) and (2)(*e*) for "scheme administrator" substitute "scheme manager".

[(9A) In paragraph 12 (interpretation of Part 1), after sub-paragraph (1A) insert—

(1B) But sub-paragraph (1A)(b) does not apply to anything which, but for paragraph 2 of Schedule 32, would have constituted a relevant BCE."][4]

[(10) After paragraph 12 add—

"12A Interpretation of Part 1—Non-UK Schemes

(1) The referable portion of a lump sum, pension or an amount which is or would have been crystallised is—

(*a*) in a case where benefit crystallisation event 8 has occurred, the extent to which it is referable to the member's relevant transfer fund; or

(*b*) in a case where the paragraph 15 BCE has occurred, the extent to which it is referable to the member's UK tax-relieved fund.

(2) In this Part—

"the paragraph 15 BCE" means the benefit crystallisation event treated as occurring by virtue of paragraph 15 of Schedule 34;

"relevant BCE" means—

(*a*) benefit crystallisation event 8; or

(*b*) the paragraph 15 BCE;

"relevant transfer fund" shall be construed in accordance with paragraph 4(2) of Schedule 34;

"UK tax-relieved fund" shall be construed in accordance with paragraph 3(2) of Schedule 34."][3]

Definition—"Paragraph 15 BCE" means the benefit crystallisation event treated as occurring by virtue of FA 2004 Sch 34 para 15 (SI 2009/2047 reg 1(4)).

Amendments—[1] The following amendments are made by the Pensions Schemes (Application of UK Provisions to Relevant Non-UK Schemes) (Amendment) Regulations, SI 2009/2047 regs 2–8 with effect where there is a paragraph 15 BCE which is treated as occurring on a date ("the specified date") on or after 6 April 2006, and the member becomes entitled to a lump sum under a relevant non-UK scheme on or after the specified date.

– In para (2), in modified Sch 29 para 1, sub-paras (4A)–(4C) substituted for previous sub-paras (4A), (4B).
– In para (3)(*a*), in modified Sch 29 para 2(6), definitions of "AAC" and "RP" substituted for previous definition of "AAC".
– In para (3)(*b*), in modified Sch 29 para 2(6A), words substituted.
– In para (4)(*b*), in modified Sch 29 para 4, sub-paras (4)–(6) substituted for previous sub-para (4).
– In para (5), in modified Sch 29 para 5(1)(*c*), words substituted for previously inserted words.
– In para (6), in modified Sch 29 para 7, sub-paras (6)–(8) substituted for previous sub-para (6).
– In para (7), in modified Sch 29 para 10, sub-paras (4)–(6) substituted for previous sub-para (4).

[2] In para (8), in modified Sch 29 para 11, inserted sub-paras (*bb*), (*bc*) substituted for previously inserted sub-para (*bb*), by the Pensions Schemes (Application of UK Provisions to Relevant Non-UK Schemes) (Amendment) Regulations, SI 2009/2047 regs 2, 9 with effect where there is a paragraph 15 BCE, the notice given under FA 2004 Sch 34 para 15 is given on or after 23 July 2009, and the member becomes entitled to a lump sum under a relevant non-UK scheme on or after the date on which the paragraph 15 BCE is treated as occurring.

[3] Para (10) inserted by the Pensions Schemes (Application of UK Provisions to Relevant Non-UK Schemes) (Amendment) Regulations, SI 2009/2047 regs 2, 10 with effect from 13 August 2009.

[4] The following amendments made by the Pensions Schemes (Application of UK Provisions to Relevant Non-UK Schemes) (Amendment) Regulations, SI 2012/1795 regs 2, 6(2)–(4), (8) with effect in relation to any lump sum to which a person becomes entitled for the purposes of FA 2004 Part 4 on or after 6 April 2011.

– in para (2), in para (*b*) of sub-paras (4B), (4C) that are treated as inserted, words inserted;
– in para (3)(a), in definition of "AAC" that is treated as substituted, in para (*a*) words inserted, definition of "RP" substituted, and para (*aa*) inserted;
– in para (3)(b) words substituted, sub-para (7ZA) that is treated as inserted renumbered as such, and words in that sub-para substituted;,
– para (3)(c) inserted;
– para (3A) inserted; and
– para (9A) inserted.

[5] The following amendments made by the Pensions Schemes (Application of UK Provisions to Relevant Non-UK Schemes) (Amendment) Regulations, SI 2012/1795 regs 2, 6(5)–(7) with effect in relation to any lump sums paid on or after 6 April 2011.

– in para (4)(b)—
  (i) sub-paras (4)–(7) that are treated as inserted renumbered as such;
  (ii) in para (*b*) of sub-para (5) that is treated as inserted, words substituted; and
  (iii) in para (*b*) of sub-paras (6), (7) that are treated as inserted, words inserted;
– in para (6)—
  (i) in para (*b*) of sub-paras (7), (8) that are treated as inserted, words inserted;
– in para (7)—
  (i) in para (*b*) of sub-paras (5), (5) that are treated as inserted, words inserted.

[6] The following amendments made by the Taxation of Pensions Act 2014 s 1, Sch 1 para 96(1), (3)–(14) with effect in relation to lump sums paid on or after 6 April 2015. These amendments are to be treated as having been made by the Commissioners for Revenue and Customs under such of the powers conferred on them by FA 2004 Sch 34 (as amended by TPA 2014 Sch 1) as are applicable—

– in para (2), in the inserted para 1(4B), words inserted;
– in para (2), in the inserted para 1(4C), words inserted;
– in para (3)(*a*), in the inserted definition of "RP", words inserted;
– in para (3)(*b*), in the inserted para 2(7ZA), words inserted;

– in para (4)(*b*), in the inserted para 4(6), words inserted;
– in para (4)(*b*), in the inserted para 4(7), words inserted;
– para (4A) inserted;
– in para (6), in the inserted para 7(7), words inserted;
– in para (6), in the inserted para 7(8), words inserted;
– in para (7), in the inserted para 10(5), words inserted; and
– in para (7), in the inserted para 10(6), words inserted.

16 Modification of Schedule 32

In paragraph 11(6) of Schedule 32—

(*a*) for "the retail prices index" (in both places) substitute "a relevant index"; and

(*b*) at the end add—

"Here "relevant index" means—

(*a*) an index of the movement of retail prices maintained, or officially recognised, by the government of the country or territory in which the recognised overseas scheme is established; or

(*b*) if there is no such index as is mentioned in paragraph (*a*) of this definition, the retail prices index.".

17 In Schedule 34 after paragraph 19 add—

19A "Revenue and Customs discretion

(1) Sub-paragraph (2) applies to—

(*a*) the member payment provisions to a payment made (or treated by this Part as made) to or in respect of—

(i) a relieved member of a relevant non-UK scheme, or

(ii) a transfer member of such a scheme;

(*b*) the annual allowance provisions in relation to an individual who is a currently-relieved member of a currently-relieved non-UK scheme; and

(*c*) the lifetime allowance provision charge in relation to an individual who is a relieved member of a relieved non-UK pension scheme.

(2) If it appears to an officer of Revenue and Customs that, by reason of some non-compliance with the requirements set out in this Part, which in the officer's view does not materially affect the nature of a payment, the payment, or the member in respect of whom it is payable, would be treated less favourably by the strict application of the provisions mentioned in paragraph (1) than in the officer's view is appropriate, sub-paragraph (3) applies.

(3) If this sub-paragraph applies, an officer of Revenue and Customs—

(*a*) may decide, and

(*b*) if requested to do so by a member falling within any of the descriptions in paragraphs (*a*) to (*c*) of sub-paragraph (1), shall decide,

whether, notwithstanding the non-compliance referred to in sub-paragraph (2), the treatment which, but for that non-compliance, would have applied under this Part should apply to the payment or the member (as the case may be).

This is subject to the qualification in sub-paragraph (4).

(4) An officer of Revenue and Customs shall not make a decision under sub-paragraph (3) that, notwithstanding the difference referred to in sub-paragraph (2), the provisions of this Part shall apply to the payment or the member unless—

(*a*) it appears to the officer that the effect of the decision would be to reduce the total cumulative tax liability in respect of the charges mentioned in subparagraph (1) of the member whose tax liability would be affected by it, taking one year with another;

(*b*) the officer has first given at least 28 days' notice of his intention to make the decision to the member whose tax liability would by affected by it; and

(*c*) the member has—

(i) consented to the making of the decision; or

(ii) failed to respond to the notice within the period specified in paragraph (*b*).

(5) If an officer of Revenue and Customs decides under sub-paragraph (3) that—

(*a*) the conditions for the exercise of his discretion under that paragraph are not met; or

(*b*) the conditions for its exercise are met, but that it is otherwise inappropriate for him to exercise it in favour of the member,

the member may appeal against the decision.

(6) Subsections (3) to (5) of section 170 apply for the purposes of a decision by an officer of Revenue and Customs under sub-paragraph (3) as they apply to a decision under section 169(5).

(7) The Commissioners before whom an appeal under paragraph (5) is brought must consider—

(*a*) whether the conditions for the exercise of the discretion of an officer of Revenue and Customs have been met; and

(*b*) if they are satisfied that those conditions have been met, whether the discretion ought to have been exercised in favour of the member.

(8) If they decide that the conditions for the exercise of that discretion have not been met, they must dismiss the appeal.

(9) If they decide that the conditions for the exercise of that discretion have been met, they must decide whether the discretion ought to have been exercised in favour of the member.

(10) If they decide that although the conditions are met, the discretion ought not to have been exercised in favour of the member, they must dismiss the appeal.

(11) If they decide that the discretion ought to have been exercised in favour of the member they may so decide and the provisions of this Part shall apply accordingly to the member or the payment in question (as the case may be).

(12) A decision under sub-paragraph (8) or (10) is final but subject to any further appeal or any determination on, or in consequence of, a case stated.".

[PART 4

Modifications to section 636A of ITEPA 2003 in respect of relevant non-UK schemes

18—Section 636A(1B) of the Income Tax (Earnings and Pensions) Act 2003 (income tax on uncrystallised funds pension lump sums under registered pension schemes: meaning of "member's available lifetime allowance") has effect in relation to relevant non-UK schemes as if the following provisions were inserted in section 636A of that Act after subsection (1C)—

"(1D) In determining the member's available lifetime allowance for the purposes of subsection (1B)—

(*a*) disregard any amount treated as crystallising by virtue of—

(i) benefit crystallisation event 8 (see section 216 of, and Schedule 32 to, FA 2004), or

(ii) the benefit crystallisation event treated as occurring by virtue of paragraph 15 of Schedule 34 to FA 2004 ("the paragraph 15 BCE"), and

(*b*) the amount of the allowance available is reduced by the amount determined in accordance with subsection (1E) or (1F), as the case may require.

(1E) Where benefit crystallisation event 8 has occurred, the member's available lifetime allowance is reduced by the aggregate of—

(*a*) the referable portion of any previous pension commencement lump sum paid to or in respect of the member by a recognised overseas pension scheme,

(*b*) the referable portion of any previous uncrystallised funds pension lump sum paid to or in respect of the member by a recognised overseas pension scheme, and

(*c*) the referable portion of the amount which would have crystallised by virtue of the member becoming entitled to a pension, had the scheme paying it been a registered pension scheme and disregarding paragraph 2 of Schedule 32 to FA 2004;

and in this subsection "referable portion" means portion referable to the member's relevant transfer fund (within the meaning given by paragraph 4 of Schedule 34 to FA 2004).

(1F) Where the paragraph 15 BCE has occurred, the member's available lifetime allowance is reduced by the aggregate of—

(*a*) the referable portion of any earlier pension commencement lump sum to which the member became entitled under a relevant non-UK scheme since the paragraph 15 BCE occurred,

(*b*) the referable portion of any earlier uncrystallised funds pension lump sum to which the member became entitled under a relevant non-UK scheme since the paragraph 15 BCE occurred, and

(*c*) in respect of any pension to which the member has become entitled since the paragraph 15 BCE occurred, the referable portion of the amount which would have crystallised by virtue of the member's becoming entitled to the pension, had the scheme paying it been a registered pension scheme and disregarding paragraph 2 of Schedule 32 to FA 2004;

and in this subsection "referable portion" means portion referable to the member's UK tax-relieved fund (within the meaning given by paragraph 3 of Schedule 34 to FA 2004).

(1G) In subsections (1E) and (1F)—

"recognised overseas pension scheme" and "pension" have the same meaning as in Part 4 of FA 2004 (see section 280(2) of FA 2004), and

"relevant non-UK scheme" has the same meaning as in Schedule 34 to FA 2004 (see paragraph 1 of that Schedule)."][1]

Amendments—[1] Part 4 (reg 18) inserted by the Taxation of Pensions Act 2014 s 1, Sch 1 para 96(1), (15) with effect in relation to lump sums paid on or after 6 April 2015. This amendment is to be treated as having been made by the Commissioners for Revenue and Customs under such of the powers conferred on them by FA 2004 Sch 34 (as amended by TPA 2014 Sch 1) as are applicable.

2006/208

PENSION SCHEMES (INFORMATION REQUIREMENTS FOR QUALIFYING OVERSEAS PENSION SCHEMES, QUALIFYING RECOGNISED OVERSEAS PENSIONS SCHEMES AND CORRESPONDING RELIEF) REGULATIONS 2006

Made by the Commissioners for HMRC under FA 2004 s 169, Sch 33 para 5(2), Sch 36 para 51(4)

Made ....*1 February 2006*
Laid before the House of Commons ....*2 February 2006*
Coming into force ....*6 April 2006*

Commentary—*Simon's Taxes* **E7.241**.

1 Citation, commencement and interpretation

(1) These Regulations may be cited as the Pension Schemes (Information Requirements for Qualifying Overseas Pension Schemes, Qualifying Recognised Overseas Pension Schemes and Corresponding Relief) Regulations 2006 and shall come into force on 6th April 2006.

(2) In these Regulations—

"the Act" means the Finance Act 2004 and a reference to a numbered section or Schedule, without more, is a reference to the section of; or Schedule to, the Act bearing that number; . . . [1]

["HMRC" means the Commissioners for Her Majesty's Revenue and Customs;

["onward transfer" has the meaning given by section 244A;][2]

"tax identification number" means—

(*a*) if the person is resident for tax purposes in the United Kingdom, the unique taxpayer reference (UTR) allocated to that person, and

(*b*) if the person is resident for tax purposes outside the United Kingdom, the unique taxpayer reference (UTR) allocated to that person or, if they do not have one, the reference number allocated to that person by the tax authority in the country or territory in which they are resident for tax purposes; and][1]

"tax year" means a period beginning on 6th April of one year and ending on 5th April of the immediately following year.

Amendments—[1] Word "and" following definition of "the Act" revoked, and definitions of "HMRC" and "tax identification number" inserted, by the Registered Pension Schemes and Overseas Pension Schemes (Miscellaneous Amendments) Regulations, SI 2013/2259 regs 9, 10 with effect 14 October 2013.

[2] Definition of "onward transfer" inserted by FA 2017 s 10, Sch 4 para 22(1), (2) with effect in relation to transfers made on or after 9 March 2017.

2 Information—benefit crystallisation events in relation to relevant migrant members and individuals entitled to corresponding relief

(1) For the purposes of paragraph 5(2) of Schedule 33 and paragraph 51(4) of Schedule 36 (information about benefit crystallisation events in cases of relevant migrant members and individuals entitled to corresponding relief) the prescribed benefit crystallisation information is—

(*a*) the name and address of the relevant migrant member or individual (as the case may be) in respect of whom there has been a benefit crystallisation event in the tax year; and

(*b*) the date, amount and nature of the benefit crystallisation event.

(2) The information must be provided by 31st January next following the end of the tax year in which the benefit crystallisation event occurs.

3 [Information — QROPS and former QROPS]

[(1) For the purposes of section 169(4) (information to be provided by a QROPS or former QROPS), the scheme manager of a QROPS must provide to HMRC—

(*a*) the name and address of the scheme, the date of its establishment and the name of the country or territory in which it is established;

(*b*) confirmation whether or not the scheme is regulated in the country or territory in which it is established and, if so, the name and address of the regulator and the reference number, if any, allocated by that regulator;

(*c*) the name and address of the tax authority for the scheme in the country or territory in which it is established and the reference number, if any, allocated by that tax authority;

(*d*) confirmation of the basis on which the scheme satisfies the requirements imposed by regulations 2 and 3 of the Pension Schemes (Categories of Country and Requirements for Overseas Pension Schemes and Recognised Overseas Pension Schemes) Regulations 2006;

(*g*) if a scheme satisfies regulation 2(2) of those Regulations solely because it fulfils the requirement in regulation 2(2)(*c*)(ii); or if a scheme satisfies regulation 3(1)(*b*) of those Regulations solely because it fulfils the requirement in regulation 3(4), evidence demonstrating that it fulfils the requirement set out in paragraph (ii) or (4), as the case may be;

(*f*) the name, address, contact details and legal status of the scheme manager; and (g) any information or evidence required in writing, at any time, by HMRC relating to any of the matters referred to in sub-paragraphs (*a*) to (*f*).

No information is required to be provided under sub-paragraph (*c*) if the scheme was established by an organisation to which section 1 of the International Organisations Act 1968 applies by virtue of an Order in Council under subsection (1) of that section.

(1A) The information required under paragraph (1)(*a*) to (*f*) must be provided—

(*a*) five years after the date of the HMRC letter advising the QROPS of the reference number that had been allocated to it, and

(*b*) at the end of every succeeding period of five years.

This paragraph is subject to paragraph (1B).

(1B) Where this paragraph applies to a QROPS, paragraph (1A) does not apply and the information required under paragraph (1)(*a*) to (*f*) must be provided on the dates notified to the QROPS by HMRC.

(1C) Paragraph (1B) applies to a QROPS if—

(*a*) the date of the HMRC letter advising the QROPS of the reference number that had been allocated to it was before [6 April 2011][5], and

(*b*) less than fifteen years have passed since the date of that letter.

(1D) Where paragraph (1A) or (1B) applies, the required information may be provided at any time during the six months prior to the end of each five year period or the notified dates, as the case may be.][2]

[(2) When a QROPS or former QROPS makes, or is treated under the relevant provisions as making, a payment in respect of a relevant member, the scheme manager of the QROPS or former QROPS must provide to HMRC—

(*a*) the name, principal residential address, date of birth, contact details, the national insurance number or, if they do not have one, the tax identification number, if any, of the relevant member and if the relevant member has ceased to be resident for tax purposes in the United Kingdom, the date that residence ceased;

(*b*) the name, address and contact details of the QROPS or former QROPS and of the scheme manager;

(*c*) the date, amount and nature of the payment and if as a result of the payment no relevant transfer fund remains [and no ring-fenced transfer funds remain][6], a statement to that effect;

(*d*) if the payment is made to a pension scheme, the name and address of the recipient and if the recipient is a registered pension scheme(b) or a QROPS, the reference number allocated to that pension scheme by HMRC;

[(*da*) if the payment is made to a QROPS—

(i) whether the overseas transfer charge arises on the payment,

(ii) if the charge does arise, the transferred value and the amount of charge the scheme manager deducted from the payment before making it,

(iii) if the charge does not arise, why it does not, and

(iv) the total amount or value of the member's relevant transfer fund, and ring-fenced transfer funds, remaining immediately after the payment;][6]

(*e*) where the relevant member has died and the payment is made to an individual, the name, principal residential address, date of birth and the national insurance number or, if they do not have one, the tax identification number, if any, of that individual; and

(*f*) where the relevant member has died and the payment is made to a person who is not an individual, the name and address of that person.

Here "the relevant provisions" means sections 172 to 174A, paragraph 2A of Schedule 28 and paragraph 3A of Schedule 29.

This paragraph is subject to the qualifications in paragraphs (3) and (4).][3]

[(2A) Paragraphs (2B) and (2C) apply where—

(*a*) a recognised transfer is made to a QROPS, or

(*b*) an onward transfer is made by a QROPS or former QROPS.

(2B) Where an event occurring before the end of the relevant period for the transfer (see section 244A(4)) means that the transfer no longer counts as excluded from the overseas transfer charge or that entitlement to repayment under section 244M arises, the scheme manager of the QROPS or former QROPS must, within 90 days after the date the scheme manager is notified of the event, provide to HMRC notification of—

(*a*) the occurrence, nature and date of the event,

(*b*) the transferred value of the transfer,
(*c*) the amount of overseas transfer charge on the transfer,
(*d*) whether, and to what extent, the scheme manager has accounted, or intends to account, for the charge, and
(*e*) the total amount or value of the member's relevant transfer fund, and ring-fenced transfer funds, remaining immediately after the event.

This paragraph is subject to the qualification in paragraph (3A).

(2C) Where the scheme manager of the QROPS or former QROPS becomes aware that the member has at any time in the relevant period for the transfer acquired a new residential address that is neither—
(*a*) in the country or territory in which the QROPS or former QROPS is established, nor
(*b*) in an EEA state,

the scheme manager is to notify that address to HMRC within 3 months after the date on which the scheme manager becomes aware of it.][7]

(3) No obligation arises under paragraph (2) if [the following conditions are met—
(*a*) at the date of the payment more than ten years has elapsed beginning[—
(i) if the payment is in respect of one or more of the relevant member's ring-fenced transfer funds (whether or not it is also in respect of anything else), with the key date for that fund or (as the case may be) the later or latest of the key dates for those funds, and
(ii) if the payment is not to any extent in respect of the relevant member's ring-fenced transfer funds,][7]

with the date on which the relevant transfer fund in respect of the relevant member came into existence; and
(*b*) the relevant member to whom the payment is made or treated as made is a person to whom the member payment provisions do not apply (see paragraph 2 of Schedule 34).][1]

[(3A) No obligation arises under paragraph (2B) in relation to a transfer if the following conditions are met—
(*a*) at the date of the transfer more than 10 years has elapsed since the key date for the ring-fenced transfer fund arising from the transfer (see paragraph 1 of Schedule 34); and
(*b*) the relevant member to whom the transfer is made is a person to whom the member payment provisions do not apply.][7]

(4) In the case of a payment by way of a pension the obligation under paragraph (2) applies only to the first such payment.

(5) The information required by paragraph (2) must be [provided—
(*a*) within 90 days beginning with the day on which the payment is made or is treated as made; or
(*b*) by such other time as may be agreed between an officer of Revenue and Customs and the scheme manager.][1]

[(5A) Where the scheme manager is a company it must provide the names and addresses of the directors of the company to an officer of Revenue and Customs if required to do so in writing, and within such time as may be specified, by the officer.][1]

(6) For the purposes of this regulation [and regulation 3C[4]]—
"payment" has the meaning given in section 161(2); and
"relevant member" means a member of a scheme in respect of whom there is a relevant transfer fund [or any ring-fenced transfer fund][7] . . . [1]

[(7) For the purposes of this regulation[, regulation 3B and regulation 3C][4] "relevant transfer fund" has the meaning given in paragraph 4(2) of Schedule 34.][1]

Amendments—[1] In paras (3), (5) words substituted, in para (6) words revoked, and para (7) inserted, with effect in respect of information relating to payments that are made or are treated as made on or after 6 April 2012; and para (5A) inserted with effect from 6 April 2012; by the Registered Pension Schemes and Overseas Pension Schemes (Miscellaneous Amendments) Regulations, SI 2012/884 regs 7, 8.

[2] Heading substituted, and paras (1)–(1D) substituted for previous para (1), by the Registered Pension Schemes and Overseas Pension Schemes (Miscellaneous Amendments) Regulations, SI 2013/2259 regs 9, 11 with effect from 14 October 2013. Note that the obligations imposed by para (1A) have effect in relation to five-year periods ending on or after 6 April 2016 (SI 2013/2259 reg 3, as amended by the Taxation of Pensions Act 2014 s 1, Sch 1 para 97(2)). Heading and para (1) previously read as follows—

Information—qualifying recognised overseas pension schemes

(1) For the purposes of section 169(4) (meaning of qualifying recognised overseas pension scheme), a qualifying recognised overseas pension scheme must provide to an officer of Revenue and Customs—
(a) the name of the country or territory in which it is established;
(b) in the case of a scheme falling within regulation 3(4) of the Pension Schemes (Categories of Country and Requirements for Overseas Pension Schemes and Recognised Overseas Pension Schemes) Regulations 2006, evidence demonstrating that it fulfils the requirement set out in that paragraph; and
(c) any other evidence required in writing by the officer.".

[3] Para (2) substituted by the Registered Pension Schemes and Overseas Pension Schemes (Miscellaneous Amendments) Regulations, SI 2013/2259 regs 9, 12 with effect from 14 October 2013. Note that this amendment has effect in respect of information relating to payments that are made, or treated as made, on or after 14 October 2013, but in the case of a payment made by a former QROPS, does not have effect unless the former QROPS ceased to be a QROPS on or after 14 October 2013 (SI 2013/2259 reg 4).

[4] In para (6) words inserted, and in para (7) words substituted for words "and regulation 3B", by the Registered Pension Schemes and Overseas Pension Schemes (Miscellaneous Amendments) Regulations, SI 2013/2259 regs 9, 13, 14 with effect from 14 October 2013.

[5] In para (1C)(*a*), words substituted for words "1st April 2010" by the Taxation of Pensions Act 2014 s 1, Sch 1 para 97(3) with effect from 17 December 2014.

[6] In para (2)(*c*), words inserted, and para (2)(*da*) inserted, by FA 2017 s 10, Sch 4 para 22(1), (3) with effect in relation to payments made on or after 9 March 2017.

[7] Paras (2A)–(2C), (3)(*a*)(i), (ii), (3A) inserted, and in para (6), words inserted, by FA 2017 s 10, Sch 4 para 22(1), (4)–(7) with effect in relation to transfers made on or after 9 March 2017.
Note that these amendments are to be treated as having been made by the HMRC Commissioners under the powers to make regulations conferred by FA 2004 s 169(4) (FA 2017 Sch 4 para 22(15)(*b*)).

[3A Information—transfer of sums or assets to a [QROPS]

[(1) For the purposes of section 169(4), where paragraph (2) applies the scheme manager of the QROPS (or former QROPS, if the scheme has ceased to be a QROPS) must provide to HMRC such of the information specified in paragraph (3) as may be required in writing by an officer of Revenue and Customs.][2]

(2) This paragraph applies where there is a transfer to a [QROPS][2] of sums or assets which have at any time been held for the purposes of, or representing accrued rights under, a registered pension scheme from—

(*a*) a registered pension scheme; or

(*b*) another [QROPS][2].

(3) The information is—

(*a*) the date of the transfer;

(*b*) the name and address of any bank and details of any bank account which the scheme has used in relation to the transfer;

(*c*) details of the sums or assets transferred;

(*d*) where information is required from a scheme which is a transferee, the way that the sums or assets have been applied by the scheme;

(*e*) where the transfer is from a registered pension scheme, the name and address of that scheme;

(*f*) the name, principal residential address, date of birth and, if any, the national insurance number of the member who is connected with the sums or assets;

(*g*) where the member referred to in sub-paragraph (*f*) is a person to whom the member payment provisions do not apply by virtue of paragraph 2 of Schedule 34, the date that the member ceased to be resident in the United Kingdom;

(*h*) the name and address of the body that regulates the scheme and the reference number, if any, issued to the scheme by the regulator;

(*i*) the name and address of the tax authority that administers the scheme and the reference number, if any, issued to the scheme by the authority;

(*j*) evidence to show that the scheme met at the time of the transfer and continues to meet the requirements specified in regulations 2 and 3 of the Pension Schemes (Categories of Country and Requirements for Overseas Pension Schemes and Recognised Overseas Pension Schemes) Regulations 2006; and

(*k*) any other evidence relating to the transfer as may be required by the officer of Revenue and Customs.

(4) Information required in accordance with paragraph (1) must be provided—

(*a*) within 90 days beginning with the day on which the requirement is notified by the officer of Revenue and Customs; or

(*b*) by such other time as may be agreed between the officer and the scheme manager.][1]

Amendments—[1] Reg 3A inserted by the Registered Pension Schemes and Overseas Pension Schemes (Miscellaneous Amendments) Regulations, SI 2012/884 regs 7, 9 with effect from 6 April 2012.

[2] In heading, acronym substituted for words "qualifying recognised overseas pension scheme", para (1) substituted, and in para (2) words substituted for words "qualifying recognised overseas pension scheme", by the Registered Pension Schemes and Overseas Pension Schemes (Miscellaneous Amendments) Regulations, SI 2013/2259 regs 9, 15–17 with effect from 14 October 2013. Note that the substitution of para (1), so far as relating to former QROPS, has effect only in relation a scheme that ceased to be a QROPS on or after 14 October 2013 (SI 2013/2259 reg 5).

[Information provided to member of QROPS or former QROPS by scheme manager where it appears member may be first flexibly accessing pension rights

3AA (1) If a relevant event occurs in relation to a member of a QROPS or former QROPS which is to be treated as a registered pension scheme for the purposes of section 227G (when pension rights are first flexibly accessed) by virtue of paragraph 9ZA or 9ZB of Schedule 34 (non-UK schemes: application of certain charges), the scheme manager—

(*a*) must provide the member with a statement—

(i) stating the date of the relevant event; and

(ii) explaining the matters specified in paragraph (3); and

(*b*) must do so before the end of 91 days beginning with the date of the relevant event,

but this is subject to paragraphs (4) and (7).

(2) For the purposes of this regulation—

(*a*) if—

(i) the member has a member's flexi-access drawdown fund in respect of an arrangement under the scheme; and

(ii) the fund came into existence as a result of sums or assets being designated on or after 6th April 2015 as available for the payment of drawdown pension,

a relevant event occurs when a qualifying payment is made to the member from the fund;

(*b*) if section 165(3A) (pension rules) applied in the individual's case to an arrangement at any time before 6th April 2015, a relevant event occurs at the start of 6th April 2015;

(*c*) if—

(i) the member has a member's drawdown pension fund in respect of an arrangement under the scheme; and

(ii) the sums or assets that make up the fund become newly-designated funds by the operation of paragraph 8B or 8C of Schedule 28 (registered pension schemes: authorised pensions—supplementary),

a relevant event occurs when a qualifying payment is made to the member from the member's flexi-access drawdown fund in respect of the arrangement; or

(*d*) a relevant event occurs when an uncrystallised funds pension lump sum is paid to the member by the scheme.

(3) The matters mentioned in paragraph (1)(*a*)(ii) are—

(*a*) that a relevant event has occurred in relation to the member and that, as a result, the member has flexibly accessed the member's pension rights (although may first have done so previously);

(*b*) that if in any tax year the total of the pension inputs to money purchase arrangements, and certain hybrid arrangements, relating to the member exceeds £10,000—

(i) there will be an annual allowance tax charge on the excess; and

(ii) the annual allowance for pension inputs to other arrangements relating to the member will be £10,000 less than it would otherwise be;

(*c*) where paragraph (2)(*d*) applies, that the member may be liable to a charge under section 636A(1A) and (1B) (exemption for certain lump sums) of ITEPA 2003 by virtue of paragraph 1(3)(*da*) of Schedule 34 (member payment charges); and

(*d*) the duties under regulation 3AB and the circumstances in which the member will have to comply with them.

(4) The scheme manager is not required to comply with paragraph (1) if—

(*a*) the scheme manager has complied with paragraph (1) in respect of an earlier relevant event; or

(*b*) the scheme manager is, at any time before complying with paragraph (1) in relation to the relevant event, informed—

(i) by the member; or

(ii) by the scheme manager of another QROPS or former QROPS or by the scheme administrator of a registered pension scheme,

that the member flexibly accessed pension rights at a time before the relevant event occurred.

(5) In this regulation, a reference to a qualifying payment from a fund is a reference to—

(*a*) payment of income withdrawal from the fund; or

(*b*) payment of a short-term annuity purchased using sums or assets out of the fund,

but does not include payment at a time when the whole of the fund represents rights attributable to a disqualifying pension credit.

(6) In paragraph (5) "disqualifying pension credit" is to be read in accordance with paragraph 2(3) and (4) of Schedule 29 (registered pension schemes: authorised lump sums—supplementary).

(7) This regulation does not apply unless the member is—

(*a*) resident in the United Kingdom when the relevant event occurs (or would occur but for this paragraph); or

(*b*) has been resident in the United Kingdom in any of the five tax years immediately preceding the tax year in which the relevant event occurs (or would occur but for this paragraph).][1]

Amendments—[1] Regulations 3AA–3AD inserted by the Overseas Pension Schemes (Miscellaneous Amendments) Regulations, SI 2015/673 regs 4, 5 with effect from 6 April 2015.

[Passing-on by member of information under regulation 3AA if active or contributing etc

3AB (1) Paragraphs (2) and (3) apply if—

(*a*) an individual receives a statement under regulation 3AA from the scheme manager of a QROPS or former QROPS (the "flexed scheme"); and

(*b*) on the date of the relevant event concerned, or at any later time, the individual is an accruing member of—

(i) the flexed scheme;

(ii) a relevant non-UK scheme which is a QROPS or former QROPS other than the flexed scheme; or

(iii) a registered pension scheme,

and in this regulation "other relevant scheme" is a scheme mentioned in sub-paragraphs (ii) and (iii).

(2) The individual must before the end of the relevant period—

(*a*) pass on a copy of the statement; or

(*b*) otherwise give notice—

(i) of receipt of the statement; and

(ii) of the date of the relevant event concerned or (if applicable) of its having occurred more than 2 years before the start of the relevant period,

to the scheme manager or scheme administrator (as the case may be) of each other relevant scheme of which the individual is an accruing member on any day in the intervening period.

(3) Where, in the case of a particular scheme which is any other relevant scheme, the individual is not an accruing member of that other scheme on any day in the intervening period but becomes an accruing member of that scheme on a day ("the activation day") after the last day of that period, the individual must before the end of the 91 days beginning with the activation day—

(*a*) pass on a copy of the statement; or

(*b*) otherwise give notice—

(i) of receipt of the statement; and

(ii) of the date of the relevant event concerned or (if applicable) of its having occurred more than 2 years before the activation day,

to the scheme manager or scheme administrator (as the case may be) of that other relevant scheme; but this is subject to paragraph (4).

(4) Paragraph (3) does not apply in connection with the individual becoming an accruing member of any particular scheme if the individual becomes an accruing member of that scheme upon or after becoming a member of that scheme [as a result of—

(*a*) a transfer of the member's relevant transfer fund,

(*b*) a transfer of any of the member's ring-fenced transfer funds, or

(*c*) a recognised transfer,

after the date of the relevant event concerned.][2]

(5) For the purposes of this regulation, the individual is an accruing member of a pension scheme on any particular day if—

(*a*) the individual is an active member of the scheme on that day as a result of there presently being arrangements for the accrual of benefits to or in respect of the individual under a cash balance arrangement or hybrid arrangement; or

(*b*) a relevant contribution is made under the scheme on that day.

(6) For the purposes of this regulation, a relevant contribution is made under a scheme if—

(*a*) a relievable pension contribution is paid by or on behalf of the individual under a non-cash-balance money purchase arrangement relating to the individual under the scheme;

(*b*) a contribution is paid in respect of the individual by an employer of the individual under a non-cash-balance money purchase arrangement relating to the individual under the scheme; or

(*c*) a contribution—

(i) paid under the scheme by an employer of the individual; and

(ii) paid otherwise than in respect of any individual,

becomes held for the purposes of a non-cash-balance money purchase arrangement relating to the individual under the scheme, and in this paragraph "non-cash-balance money purchase arrangement" means a money purchase arrangement other than a cash balance arrangement.

(7) In this regulation—

"the relevant period" means the period of 91 days beginning with—

(*a*) the date of receipt of the statement if the individual is an accruing member of the flexed scheme or any other relevant scheme on any day in the period—

(i) beginning with the date of the relevant event concerned; and

(ii) ending with the date of receipt; or

(*b*) if not, the first day after the date of receipt when the individual is an accruing member of such a scheme; and

"the intervening period" means the period—

(*a*) beginning with the date of the relevant event concerned; and

(*b*) ending with the first day of the relevant period.][1]

Amendments—[1] Regulations 3AA–3AD inserted by the Overseas Pension Schemes (Miscellaneous Amendments) Regulations, SI 2015/673 regs 4, 5 with effect from 6 April 2015.

[2] In para (4), words substituted for words "as a result of a transfer of the member's relevant transfer fund or of a recognised transfer after the date of the relevant event concerned" by FA 2017 s 10, Sch 4 para 22(1), (8) with effect in relation to transfers made on or after 9 March 2017.

Note that this amendment is to be treated as having been made by the HMRC Commissioners under the powers to make regulations conferred by FA 2004 s 169(4) (FA 2017 Sch 4 para 22(15)(*b*)).

[Information to be given by QROPS and former QROPS: transfers of UK tax-relieved funds and . . . transfer funds after flexible access

3AC (1) Paragraph (2) applies if—

(*a*) in connection with a member of a QROPS or former QROPS which is to be treated as a registered pension scheme for the purposes of section 227G (when pension rights are first flexibly accessed) by virtue of paragraph 9ZA or 9ZB of Schedule 34 (non-UK schemes: application of certain charges) ("the transferring scheme"), there is a transfer of the whole or part of—

(i) the member's UK tax-relieved fund;

[(ia) any of the member's ring-fenced transfer funds;][2] or

(ii) the member's relevant transfer fund,

from the transferring scheme to a QROPS or to a registered pension scheme ("the recipient scheme");

(*b*) the scheme manager of the transferring scheme has reason to believe that the member first flexibly accessed pension rights before the transfer; and

(*c*) the individual—

(i) is resident in the United Kingdom when sub-paragraph (*b*) is met; or

(ii) has been resident in the United Kingdom in any of the five tax years immediately preceding the tax year in which that sub-paragraph is met.

(2) The scheme manager of the transferring scheme must provide the scheme manager or scheme administrator (as the case may be) of the recipient scheme with a statement—

(*a*) stating that the scheme manager of the transferring scheme has reason to believe that the member first flexibly accessed pension rights before the transfer; and

(*b*) specifying the date the scheme manager of the transferring scheme understands to be the date when the member first flexibly accessed pension rights.

(3) The requirement under paragraph (2) is to be complied with before—

(*a*) the end of 91 days beginning with the date of the transfer; or

(*b*) if later, the end of 91 days beginning with the date when the scheme manager of the transferring scheme first has reason for the belief mentioned in paragraph (1)(b).][1]

Amendments—[1] Regulations 3AA–3AD inserted by the Overseas Pension Schemes (Miscellaneous Amendments) Regulations, SI 2015/673 regs 4, 5 with effect from 6 April 2015.

[2] Para (1)(*a*)(ia) inserted, and in heading word "relevant" revoked, by FA 2017 s 10, Sch 4 para 22(1), (9) with effect in relation to transfers made on or after 9 March 2017.

Note that these amendments are to be treated as having been made by the HMRC Commissioners under the powers to make regulations conferred by FA 2004 s 169(4) (FA 2017 Sch 4 para 22(15)(*b*)).

[Information to be given by QROPS and former QROPS to QROPS about transfers of UK tax-relieved funds and . . . transfer funds

3AD (1) Paragraph (2) applies if in connection with a member of a QROPS or former QROPS ("the transferring scheme") there is a transfer of sums or assets ("the transfer")—

(*a*) which immediately before the transfer are comprised in—

(i) the member's UK tax-relieved fund;

[(ia) any of the member's ring-fenced transfer funds;][2] or

(ii) the member's relevant transfer fund;

(*b*) from the transferring scheme so as to be held for the purposes of, or to represent rights under, a QROPS ("the recipient scheme").

(2) The scheme manager of the transferring scheme must provide the scheme manager of the recipient scheme with a statement stating—

(*a*) the value of so many of the transferred sums or assets as are referable to the member's UK tax-relieved fund (if any);

[(*aa*) where any of the transferred sums or assets are referable to the member's UK tax-relieved fund, the value of so many of them as are referable to tax-relieved contributions, or tax-exempt provision, made under the scheme before 9 March 2017;

(*ab*) the value of so many of the transferred sums or assets as are referable to any of the member's ring-fenced transfer funds (if any);][2]

(*b*) the value of so many of the transferred sums or assets as are referable to the member's relevant transfer fund (if any); . . . [2]

(*c*) where any transferred sums or assets are—

(i) referable to the member's relevant transfer fund [or any of the member's ring-fenced transfer funds][2]; and

(ii) the transferring scheme is aware of any recognised transfer from which those sums or assets are derived,

that there was such a recognised transfer and, where . . . [2] known, the date of that transfer [and the date it was requested][2].

[(*d*) whether the overseas transfer charge arises on the transfer;

(*e*) if the charge does arise on the transfer—

(i) the transferred value of the transfer, and

(ii) the amount in respect of the charge deducted by the scheme manager from the transfer;

(*f*) if the transfer is excluded from the charge—

(i) the reason for its exclusion, and

(ii) where section 244G(2)(*a*) or (*b*) (charge paid on earlier transfer) is the reason for its exclusion, the date of the earlier transfer on which the charge was paid and the amount of charge paid on that earlier transfer; and

(*g*) the relevant period for the transfer (see section 244A(4)).][2]

(3) The requirements in paragraph (2) must be complied with before the end of 91 days beginning with the date of the transfer.

(4) In paragraph (2)(*c*)(ii) the sums or assets are "derived" from a recognised transfer regardless of whether those sums or assets are also derived from one or more relevant transfers which took place after the date of that recognised transfer.][1]

Amendments—[1] Regulations 3AA–3AD inserted by the Overseas Pension Schemes (Miscellaneous Amendments) Regulations, SI 2015/673 regs 4, 5 with effect from 6 April 2015.

[2] Paras (1)(*a*)(ia), (2)(*aa*), (*ab*), (*d*)–(*g*) inserted; word "and" at end of para (2)(*b*) revoked; words in para (2)(*c*)(i) inserted; in closing words to para (2)(*c*), words "it is" revoked and words inserted; and in heading, word "relevant" revoked; by FA 2017 s 10, Sch 4 para 22(1), (9) with effect in relation to transfers made on or after 9 March 2017.

Note that these amendments are to be treated as having been made by the HMRC Commissioners under the powers to make regulations conferred by FA 2004 s 169(4) (FA 2017 Sch 4 para 22(15)(*b*)).

[3AE Information provided by member to QROPS: onward transfers

(1) Paragraph (4) applies where a member of a QROPS or former QROPS makes a request to the scheme manager to make an onward transfer to a QROPS.

(2) But paragraph (4) does not apply if—

(*a*) the transfer will be excluded from the overseas transfer charge by section 244G, or

(*b*) the transfer will take place after the end of the relevant period (see section 244A(4)) for what would be the original transfer in relation to the requested onward transfer.

(3) In this regulation "original transfer", in relation to an onward transfer, has the meaning given by section 244A(5).

(4) The member must provide to the scheme manager—

(*a*) the member's name, date of birth and principal residential address,

(*b*) if the member is not UK resident for income tax purposes, the date when the member last ceased to be UK resident for those purposes,

(*c*) the member's national insurance number or, where applicable, confirmation that the member does not qualify for a national insurance number,

(*d*) the name and address of the QROPS to which the transfer is to be made,

(*e*) the country or territory under the law of which that QROPS is established and regulated,

(*f*) the reference number, if any, given by the Commissioners for that QROPS,

(*g*) whether the member knows for certain that the transfer would be excluded from the overseas transfer charge by one of sections 244D, 244E and 244F, and if the member does know that for certain—

(i) the section concerned (if known),

(ii) the name and address of the member's employer whose connection with the QROPS gives rise to exclusion of the transfer from the charge,

(iii) the member's job title as an employee of that employer,

(iv) the date the member's employment with that employer began, and

(v) if known, that employer's tax reference for that employment, and

(*h*) the member's acknowledgement in writing that the member—

(i) is aware that an onward transfer to a qualifying recognised overseas pension scheme may give rise to a liability to overseas transfer charge, and

(ii) is aware of the circumstances in which liability arises, in which liability is excluded from the outset and in which liability is excluded only if conditions continue to be met over a period of time.

(5) The information specified in paragraph (4) must be provided within 60 days beginning with the day the transfer request is made.

(6) The scheme manager must send the member notification of the requirements specified in this regulation within 30 days beginning with that day.][1]

Amendments—[1] Reg 3AE inserted by FA 2017 s 10, Sch 4 para 22(1), (11) with effect in relation to requests made on or after 9 March 2017.

Note that the insertion of paras (1) to (5) is to be treated as having been made by the HMRC Commissioners under the powers to make regulations conferred by FA 2004 s 169(4ZA), and the insertion of para (6) under the powers to make regulations under FA 2004 s 169(4) (FA 2017 Sch 4 para 22(15)(*a*), (*b*)).

[3AF Information provided by member to QROPS: inward and outward transfers

(1) Paragraph (2) applies where—

(*a*) a recognised transfer or onward transfer is made to a QROPS, or an onward transfer is made by a QROPS or former QROPS, and

(*b*) either—

(i) the overseas transfer charge arises in the case of the transfer, or

(ii) the transfer is required by section 244B or 244C to be initially assumed to be excluded from the overseas transfer charge by that section.

(2) Each time during the relevant period for the transfer that the member—

(*a*) becomes resident in a country or territory, or

(*b*) ceases to be resident in a country or territory,

the member must, within 60 days after the date that happens, inform the scheme manager of the QROPS or former QROPS that it has happened.

(3) In a case where the 60 days mentioned in paragraph (2) ends with a day earlier than 30 June 2017, paragraph (2) is to be treated as requiring the information to be given no later than 30 June 2017.][1]

Amendments—[1] Regs 3AF–3AL inserted by FA 2017 s 10, Sch 4 para 22(1), (11) with effect in relation to transfers made on or after 9 March 2017.

Note that the insertion reg 3AF is to be treated as having been made by the HMRC Commissioners under the powers to make regulations conferred by FA 2004 s 169(4ZA) (FA 2017 Sch 4 para 22(15)(*a*)).

[3AG Provision of information about liability for overseas transfer charge

(1) If an onward transfer is made from a QROPS or former QROPS and the overseas transfer charge arises on the transfer, the scheme manager of the QROPS or former QROPS must within 90 days after the date of the transfer provide the member with a notice stating—

(*a*) the date of the transfer,

(*b*) that overseas transfer charge arises on the transfer,

(*c*) the transferred value of the transfer,

(*d*) the amount of the charge on the transfer,

(*e*) whether, and to what extent, the scheme manager has accounted, or intends to account, for the charge, and

(*f*) where the scheme manager has accounted for the charge, the date the scheme manager did so.

(2) If an onward transfer is made from a QROPS or former QROPS and the transfer is excluded from the overseas transfer charge by or under sections 244B to 244H, the scheme manager of the QROPS or former QROPS must within 90 days after the date of the transfer provide the member with a notice stating—

(*a*) the date of the transfer,

(*b*) that the transfer is excluded from the overseas transfer charge,

(*c*) the provision by reason of which the transfer is excluded, and

(*d*) where that provision is section 244B or 244C—

(i) when the relevant period for the transfer ends, and

(ii) how the transfer may turn out not to be excluded as a result of the member changing country or territory of residence within the relevant period for the transfer.

(3) Paragraph (4) applies if—

(*a*) a recognised transfer is made to a QROPS, or

(*b*) an onward transfer is made by a QROPS or former QROPS.

(4) Where an event occurring before the end of the relevant period for the transfer (see section 244A(4)) means that the transfer no longer counts as excluded from the overseas transfer charge or that entitlement to repayment under section 244M arises, the scheme manager of the QROPS or former QROPS must, within 90 days after the date the scheme manager is notified of the event, provide the member with a notice stating—

(*a*) the amount of overseas transfer charge on the transfer,

(*b*) whether, and to what extent, the scheme manager has accounted, or intends to account, for the charge, and

(*c*) where the scheme manager has accounted for the charge, the date the scheme manager did so.][1]

Amendments—[1] Regs 3AF–3AL inserted by FA 2017 s 10, Sch 4 para 22(1), (11) with effect in relation to transfers made on or after 9 March 2017.

Note that the insertion reg 3AG is to be treated as having been made by the HMRC Commissioners under the powers to make regulations conferred by FA 2004 s 169(4) (FA 2017 Sch 4 para 22(15)(*b*)).

[3AH Accounting for overseas transfer charge on onward transfers

(1) Paragraph (2) applies where—

(*a*) overseas transfer charge arises on an onward transfer from a QROPS or former QROPS,

(*b*) the scheme manager has notified HMRC of the transfer or, where applicable, of the event triggering payability of the charge on the transfer, and

(*c*) HMRC have provided the scheme manager with an accounting reference for paying the charge on the transfer.

(2) The scheme manager must pay the charge to HMRC using the accounting reference.

(3) Payment of the charge is due at the end of the 91 days beginning with the date of issue of the accounting reference.][1]

Amendments—[1] Regs 3AF–3AL inserted by FA 2017 s 10, Sch 4 para 22(1), (11) with effect in relation to transfers made on or after 9 March 2017.

Note that the insertion of regs 3AH–3AK is to be treated as having been made by the HMRC Commissioners under the applicable powers to make regulations conferred by FA 2004 s 244L (FA 2017 Sch 4 para 22(15)(*c*)).

[3AI Assessments of unpaid overseas transfer charge on onward transfers

(1) Where the correct amount of overseas transfer charge due from a scheme manager under regulation 3AH on an onward transfer has not been paid by the time it is due, an officer of Revenue and Customs must issue an assessment to tax to the scheme manager.

(2) Tax assessed under this regulation is payable within 30 days after the issue of the notice of assessment.][1]

Amendments—[1] Regs 3AF–3AL inserted by FA 2017 s 10, Sch 4 para 22(1), (11) with effect in relation to transfers made on or after 9 March 2017.

Note that the insertion of regs 3AH–3AK is to be treated as having been made by the HMRC Commissioners under the applicable powers to make regulations conferred by FA 2004 s 244L (FA 2017 Sch 4 para 22(15)(*c*)).

[3AJ Interest on overdue overseas transfer charge

(1) Tax which—

(*a*) becomes due and payable in accordance with regulation 3AH , or

(*b*) is assessed under regulation 3AI ,

carries interest at the prescribed rate from the due date under regulation 3AH until payment ("the interest period").

(2) Paragraph (1) applies even if the due date is a non-business day as defined by section 92 of the Bills of Exchange Act 1882.

(3) The "prescribed rate" means the rate applicable under section 178 of the Finance Act 1989 for the purposes of section 86 of TMA.

(4) Any change made to the prescribed rate during the interest period applies to the unpaid amount from the date of the change.][1]

Amendments—[1] Regs 3AF–3AL inserted by FA 2017 s 10, Sch 4 para 22(1), (11) with effect in relation to transfers made on or after 9 March 2017.

Note that the insertion of regs 3AH–3AK is to be treated as having been made by the HMRC Commissioners under the applicable powers to make regulations conferred by FA 2004 s 244L (FA 2017 Sch 4 para 22(15)(*c*)).

[3AK Adjustments, repayments and interest on overpaid charge

(1) If the correct tax due under regulation 3AH has not been paid on or before the due date, an officer of Revenue and Customs may make such adjustments or repayments as may be required for securing that the resulting liabilities to tax (including interest on unpaid or overpaid tax) whether of the scheme manager or of any other person are the same as they would have been if the correct tax had been paid.

(2) Tax overpaid which is repaid to the scheme manager or any other person carries interest at the prescribed rate from the later of the due date and the date on which the tax was paid until the date of repayment ("the interest period").

(3) The "prescribed rate" means the rate applicable under section 178 of the Finance Act 1989 for the purposes of section 824 of the Income and Corporation Taxes Act 1988.

(4) Any change to the prescribed rate during the interest period applies to the overpaid amount from the date of the change.][1]

Amendments—[1] Regs 3AF–3AL inserted by FA 2017 s 10, Sch 4 para 22(1), (11) with effect in relation to transfers made on or after 9 March 2017.

Note that the insertion of regs 3AH–3AK is to be treated as having been made by the HMRC Commissioners under the applicable powers to make regulations conferred by FA 2004 s 244L (FA 2017 Sch 4 para 22(15)(*c*)).

[3AL Claims for repayments of charge on subsequent excluding events

(1) Repayment under section 244M (repayments of overseas transfer charge) to the scheme manager of a QROPS or former QROPS is conditional on making a claim to HMRC.

(2) Such a claim in respect of overseas transfer charge on a transfer—

(*a*) must be in writing,

(*b*) must be made no later than 12 months after the end of the relevant period for the transfer, and

(*c*) must provide the following information—

(i) the member's name, date of birth and principal residential address,

(ii) the date of the transfer and, if different, the date of the event triggering payability of the charge on the transfer,

(iii) the date on which the scheme manager accounted for the charge on the transfer,

(iv) why the charge on the transfer has become repayable, and

(v) the amount in respect of which the claim is made.][1]

Amendments—[1] Regs 3AF–3AL inserted by FA 2017 s 10, Sch 4 para 22(1), (11) with effect in relation to transfers made on or after 9 March 2017.

Note that the insertion of reg 3AL is to be treated as having been made by the HMRC Commissioners under the powers to make regulations conferred by FA 2004 s 244M(7) (FA 2017 Sch 4 para 22(15)(*d*)).

[3B Information—cessation of [QROPS]

For the purposes of section 169(4), [the scheme manager of][2] a pension scheme which ceases to be a [QROPS][2] must within 30 days beginning with the day on which the cessation takes place ("the cessation date") provide to [HMRC[2]]—

[(*za*) the name and address of the scheme and the date of and reason for the cessation;][2]

(*a*) the value at the cessation date of the relevant transferred sums or assets pertaining to each relevant transfer fund[, or ring-fenced transfer fund,][3] under the scheme; and

(*b*) the name, principal residential address, date of birth and . . . [2] the national insurance number [or, if they do not have one, the tax identification number, if any,][2] of each member in respect of whom there is a relevant transfer fund[, or ring-fenced transfer fund,][3] under the scheme at the cessation date.][1]

Amendments—[1] Reg 3B inserted by the Registered Pension Schemes and Overseas Pension Schemes (Miscellaneous Amendments) Regulations, SI 2012/884 regs 7, 9 with effect from 6 April 2012.

[2] In heading acronym substituted for words "qualifying recognised overseas pension scheme", in reg 3B itself words inserted, acronyms substituted for words "qualifying recognised overseas pension scheme" and "an officer of Revenue and Customs", sub-para (*za*) inserted, and in sub-para (*b*) words ", if any," revoked and words inserted, by the Registered Pension Schemes and Overseas Pension Schemes (Miscellaneous Amendments) Regulations, SI 2013/2259 regs 9, 18, 19 with effect from 14 October 2013.

[3] Words inserted in both places by FA 2017 s 10, Sch 4 para 22(1), (12) with effect in relation to transfers made on or after 9 March 2017.

Note that these amendments are to be treated as having been made by the HMRC Commissioners under the powers to make regulations conferred by FA 2004 s 169(4) (FA 2017 Sch 4 para 22(15)(*b*)).

[3C Information—changes, completion or correction

[(1) For the purposes of section 169(4), if at any time after a QROPS or former QROPS has provided HMRC with information in accordance with regulation 3, 3A or 3B it becomes apparent to the QROPS or former QROPS that—

(*a*) there is a material change affecting that information; or

(*b*) the information is incomplete or contains a material inaccuracy, the scheme manager of the QROPS or former QROPS must provide to HMRC details of the change, the complete information or correction of the inaccuracy ("the relevant obligation").

(2) Where paragraph (1) applies the details of the change, the complete information or correction of the inaccuracy must be provided—

(*a*) within 30 days beginning with the day on which the change, lack of completeness or inaccuracy becomes apparent to the QROPS or former QROPS; or

(*b*) by such other time as may be agreed between an officer of Revenue and Customs and the scheme manager.

(3) No obligation arises under paragraph (1) in respect of a former QROPS if at the time the relevant obligation arises—

(*a*) the following conditions are met—

(i) more than ten years has elapsed beginning with the date on which the relevant transfer fund in respect of the relevant member came into existence [or, where the information relates to a ring-fenced transfer fund in respect of the relevant member, more than 10 years has elapsed beginning with the date on which that ring-fenced transfer fund came into existence][3]; and

(ii) the relevant member to whom the payment is made or treated as made is a person to whom the member payment provisions do not apply (see paragraph 2 of Schedule 34); or

(*b*) there is no relevant transfer fund [and there are no ring-fenced transfer funds][3].][2]][1]

Amendments—[1] Reg 3C inserted by the Registered Pension Schemes and Overseas Pension Schemes (Miscellaneous Amendments) Regulations, SI 2012/884 regs 7, 9 with effect from 6 April 2012.

[2] Text of Reg 3C (excluding heading) substituted by the Registered Pension Schemes and Overseas Pension Schemes (Miscellaneous Amendments) Regulations, SI 2013/2259 regs 9, 20 with effect from 14 October 2013. Note that this amendment, so far as relating to former QROPS, has effect only in relation a scheme that ceased to be a QROPS on or after 14 October 2013 (SI 2013/2259 reg 5).

[3] Words in para (3)(*a*)(i), (*b*) inserted by FA 2017 s 10, Sch 4 para 22(1), (13) with effect in relation to transfers made on or after 9 March 2017.

Note that these amendments are to be treated as having been made by the HMRC Commissioners under the powers to make regulations conferred by FA 2004 s 169(4) (FA 2017 Sch 4 para 22(15)(*b*)).

4 Notice in cases of serious prejudice to proper assessment or collection of tax

(1) If an officer of Revenue and Customs has reasonable grounds for believing that the pension scheme in question—

(*a*) has failed or may fail to comply with any of the requirements imposed upon it under or by virtue of [regulation 2][1], and

(*b*) such failure is likely to have led or to lead to serious prejudice to the proper assessment or collection of tax,

paragraph (2) applies.

(2) If this paragraph applies, the officer may notify the pension scheme that he requires such information to be provided within 30 days of the issue of that notice, notwithstanding the provisions set out in [regulation 2][1].

Amendments—[1] In paras (1) (*a*), (2) words substituted by the Registered Pension Schemes and Overseas Pension Schemes (Miscellaneous Amendments) Regulations, SI 2012/884 regs 7, 10 with effect from 6 April 2012.

[5 Application and modification of the penalty provisions in Part 7 of Schedule 36 to the Finance Act 2008

(1) Where the scheme manager of a former QROPS is required to provide information under regulation 3(2), [(2B) or (2C),][3] 3A(1)[, 3AA(1)(*a*), 3AC(2), 3AD(2)][2][, 3AE(6), 3AG][3] or 3C(1), Part 7 of Schedule 36 to the Finance Act 2008 (penalties) is to apply, with the modifications specified in paragraph (2), to the scheme manager as if—

(*a*) that information had been required to be provided by an information notice given to the scheme manager under that Schedule; and

(*b*) the information notice had specified that the information had to be provided by the time required under regulation 3, 3A[, 3C, 3AA, 3AC or 3AD][2], as the case may be.

(2) The modifications of Part 7 of Schedule 36 to the Finance Act 2008 mentioned in paragraph (1) are as follows—

(*a*) in paragraph 39, sub-paragraphs (1)(*b*) and (3) are omitted;

(*b*) in paragraph 40, "or obstruction" is omitted wherever it appears;

(*c*) in paragraph 40A(4)(*b*), "take reasonable steps to" is omitted and "within 30 days beginning with the date on which the inaccuracy becomes apparent" is inserted at the end;

(*d*) paragraphs 42 and 43 are omitted;

(*e*) in paragraph 45, in sub-paragraph (1) "or the obstruction of an officer of Revenue and Customs" is omitted, in sub-paragraph (2)(*b*) "or obstruction" is omitted and in sub-paragraph (2)(*c*) "or obstruction" and ", or the obstruction stops," are omitted;

(*f*) in paragraph 46, in sub-paragraph (2) ", subject to sub-paragraph (3)" is omitted and sub-paragraph (3) is omitted;

(*g*) in paragraph 49, in sub-paragraph (1)(*a*) and (*b*) "90 days" is substituted for "30 days";

(*h*) in paragraph 49A, in sub-paragraph (1)(*a*) "an information notice" is substituted for "a notice under paragraph 5" and sub-paragraph (6) is omitted;

(*i*) paragraphs 50 and 51 are omitted.][1]

Amendments—[1] Reg 5 inserted by the Registered Pension Schemes and Overseas Pension Schemes (Miscellaneous Amendments) Regulations, SI 2013/2259 regs 9, 21 with effect from 14 October 2013.

[2] In para 1, words inserted, and in sub-para (2)(*b*), words substituted, by the Overseas Pension Schemes (Miscellaneous Amendments) Regulations, SI 2015/673 regs 4, 6 with effect from 6 April 2015.

[3] Words in para (1) inserted by FA 2017 s 10, Sch 4 para 22(1), (14) with effect in relation to transfers made on or after 9 March 2017. Note that the reference to reg 3AE(6) has effect in relation to requests made on or after 9 March 2017 (FA 2017 Sch 4 para 25(4)).

Note that this amendment is to be treated as having been made by the HMRC Commissioners under the powers to make regulations conferred by FA 2004 s 169(4) (FA 2017 Sch 4 para 22(15)(*b*)).

2006/209

REGISTERED PENSION SCHEMES (AUTHORISED PAYMENTS) REGULATIONS 2006

Made by the Commissioners for HMRC under FA 2004 s 164(f)

Made . . . . *1 February 2006*

Laid before the House of Commons . . . . *2 February 2006*

Coming into force . . . . *6 April 2006*

1 Citation and commencement

These Regulations may be cited as the Registered Pension Schemes (Authorised Payments) Regulations 2006 and shall come into force on 6th April 2006.

2 Prescribed payments

For the purposes of section 164(*f*) of the Finance Act 2004 (authorised member payments), the following payments are prescribed—

(*a*) lump sum payments arising from the commutation of equivalent pension benefits pursuant to regulation 2(1A) of—

(i) the Occupational Pension Schemes (Assignment, Forfeiture, Bankruptcy etc) Regulations 1997, or

(ii) the Occupational Pension Schemes (Assignment, Forfeiture, Bankruptcy etc) Regulations (Northern Ireland) 1997,

(*b*) payments of state scheme premiums pursuant to—

(i) section 55 of the Pension Schemes Act 1993, or

(ii) section 51 of the Pension Schemes (Northern Ireland) Act 1993,

(*c*) payments of contributions equivalent premiums pursuant to—

(i) section 55(2) of the Pension Schemes Act 1993, or

(ii) section 51(2) of the Pension Schemes (Northern Ireland) Act 1993; and

(*d*) payments for restoring members' State scheme rights pursuant to—

(i) paragraph 5(3B)(*b*) of Schedule 2 to the Pension Schemes Act 1993, or

(ii) paragraph 5(3B)(*b*) of Schedule 1 to the Pension Schemes (Northern Ireland) Act 1993.

2006/210

EMPLOYER-FINANCED RETIREMENT BENEFITS (EXCLUDED BENEFITS FOR TAX PURPOSES) REGULATIONS 2006

Made by the Commissioners for HMRC under ITEPA 2003 s 393B(3)(d)

Made . . . . *1 February 2006*

Laid before the House of Commons . . . . *2 February 2006*

Coming into force . . . . *6 April 2006*

Commentary—*Simon's Taxes* **E7.224**.

1 Citation and commencement

These Regulations may be cited as the Employer-Financed Retirement Benefits (Excluded Benefits for Tax Purposes) Regulations 2006 and come into force on 6th April 2006.

2 Excluded benefit

(1) For the purposes of section 393B(3)(*d*) of the Income Tax (Earnings and Pensions) Act 2003 (prescribed benefits to be excluded benefits for the purpose of Chapter 2 of Part 6 of that Act) a lump sum benefit which is—

(*a*) in respect of the non-accidental death of an employee during service, and

(*b*) already provided for under the rules of a scheme on 6th April 2006,

is prescribed.

(2) In paragraph (1) "scheme" means any scheme which, on 6th April 2006—

(*a*) will be an employer–financed retirement benefits scheme, or

(*b*) would be such a scheme but for the fact that it provides for a benefit which is an excluded benefit by virtue of this regulation.

(3) In paragraph (2) "employer–financed retirement benefits scheme" has the meaning given in section 393A of the Income Tax (Earnings and Pensions) Act 2003.

2006/211

REGISTERED PENSION SCHEMES (SURRENDER OF RELEVANT EXCESS) REGULATIONS 2006

Made by the Commissioners for HMRC under FA 2004 s 172A(5)(f), Sch 36 paras 3(1), 12(5)

Made . . . . *1 February 2006*
Laid before the House of Commons . . . . *2 February 2006*
Coming into force . . . . *6 April 2006*

Commentary—*Simon's Taxes* **E7.240**.

1 Citation, commencement and interpretation

(1) These Regulations may be cited as the Registered Pension Schemes (Surrender of Relevant Excess) Regulations 2006, and shall come into force on 6th April 2006.
(2) In these Regulations, references to provisions are references to provisions of the Finance Act 2004.
(3) In these Regulations, "the relevant excess" has the meaning given by paragraph 12(6) of Schedule 36.

2 Rights representing the relevant excess

The rights that are to be treated as representing the relevant excess are rights that—
(*a*) meet the qualification condition (see regulation 3), and
(*b*) are valued in accordance with the computation condition (see regulation 4).

3 The qualification condition

(1) The rights that meet the qualification condition are all the individual's uncrystallised rights with the exception of excluded rights.
(2) Rights are excluded rights if—
(*a*) they are rights surrendered or transferred in any of the circumstances specified in paragraphs (*a*), (*b*), (*c*) and (*e*) of section 172A(5) (surrenders of benefits and rights), or
(*b*) they are rights to which the individual has a prospective entitlement as a dependant of another individual.

4 The computation condition

(1) Rights are valued in accordance with the computation condition if the value of the rights surrendered—
(*a*) is determined in accordance with section 212 (valuation of uncrystallised rights) on the date of the surrender, and
(*b*) as so determined, is equal to the relevant excess.
(2) If rights are surrendered on more than one occasion, the value of the rights surrendered—
(*a*) is to be determined separately for each surrender, and
(*b*) is the aggregate of the values as so determined.

5 Surrenders and unauthorised payments

Subsections (2) and (4) of section 172A (surrenders of benefits and rights) do not apply to a surrender of rights that are to be treated as representing the relevant excess to the extent that the value of the rights surrendered, determined in accordance with regulation 4, does not exceed the relevant excess.

6 Modification of conditions of pension schemes

The rules of any pension scheme to which paragraph 1(1) of Schedule 36 (deemed registration of existing schemes) applies shall be modified so as to provide that a member may surrender rights that are to be treated as representing the relevant excess to the extent that the value of the rights surrendered, determined in accordance with regulation 4, does not exceed the relevant excess.

2006/212

PENSION SCHEMES (RELEVANT MIGRANT MEMBERS) REGULATIONS 2006

Made by the Commissioners for HMRC under FA 2004 Sch 33 para 4(c)

Made . . . . *1 February 2006*
Laid before the House of Commons . . . . *2 February 2006*
Coming into force . . . . *6 April 2006*

Commentary—*Simon's Taxes* **E7.222, E7.223**.

1 Citation and commencement

These Regulations may be cited as the Pension Schemes (Relevant Migrant Members) Regulations 2006 and shall come into force on 6th April 2006.

2 Alternative condition for relevant migrant member relief

(1) For the purposes of paragraph 4(*c*) of Schedule 33 to the Finance Act 2004 (meaning of "relevant migrant member"), the prescribed condition, in relation to the individual is set out in paragraph (2).

(2) The individual was at any time in the 10 years before the beginning of that period of residence, whether before or after the coming into force of these Regulations, entitled to tax relief in respect of contributions paid under the pension scheme under the law of the country or territory in which the individual was then resident.

2006/333

TONNAGE TAX (EXCEPTION OF FINANCIAL YEAR 2006) ORDER 2006

Made . . . . *13 February 2006*
Coming into force . . . . *1 April 2006*

The Treasury are satisfied that the percentage of the tonnage tax fleet which is Community-flagged has not decreased on average over the period prescribed in Article 2(a) of this Order.

Accordingly the Treasury, in exercise of the powers conferred upon them by paragraphs 22B(2) and 22C of Schedule 22 to the Finance Act 2000, make the following Order:

1 Citation and commencement

This Order may be cited as the Tonnage Tax (Exception of Financial Year 2006) Order 2006 and shall come into force on 1st April 2006.

2 Prescribed three year period and other definitions

For the purposes of this Order—

(*a*) the period prescribed for the purposes of paragraph 22C(1)(*a*) of Schedule 22 to the Finance Act 2000 (three year period to determine whether the percentage of the tonnage tax fleet which is Community-flagged has not decreased) is the period beginning on 2nd October 2002 and ending on 1st October 2005;

(*b*) "the tonnage tax fleet" means qualifying ships operated by single companies or qualifying companies which are members of a tonnage tax group; and

(*c*) "the percentage of the tonnage tax fleet which is Community-flagged" is—

$$\frac{CFT}{TT} \times 100$$

where—

CFT is the aggregate tonnage of qualifying ships registered in one of the Member States' registers,

TT is the aggregate tonnage of all qualifying ships, and

no qualifying ship is counted more than once in determining an aggregate.

3 Exception of financial year 2006

The financial year 2006 is designated as one in relation to which paragraph 22A of Schedule 22 to the Finance Act 2000 is not to have effect.

Commentary—*Simon's Taxes* **D7.1004**.

2006/364

REGISTERED PENSION SCHEMES (MODIFICATION OF THE RULES OF EXISTING SCHEMES) REGULATIONS 2006

Made by the Commissioners for HMRC under FA 2004 Sch 36 para 3

Made . . . . *16 February 2006*
Laid before the House of Commons . . . . *17 February 2006*
Coming into force . . . . *6 April 2006*

Modifications—Registered Pension Schemes (Splitting of Schemes) Regulations, SI 2006/569 reg 3 (modification of this provision in relation to sub-scheme administrators).

1 Citation, commencement and interpretation

(1) These Regulations may be cited as the Registered Pension Schemes (Modification of the Rules of Existing Schemes) Regulations 2006 and shall come into force on 6th April 2006.

(2) In these Regulations—

"the Act" means the Finance Act 2004 and a reference (without more) to a numbered provision is a reference to the provision of the Act bearing that number;

"the commencement day" means 6th April 2006;

"existing scheme" means a pension scheme to which paragraph 1(1) of Schedule 36 applies;

"the permitted maximum"—

(*a*) in relation to times before the commencement day, has the meaning which it has by virtue of section 590C of the Income and Corporation Taxes Act 1988; and

(*b*) in relation to times during the transitional period has the meaning which it would have had if—

(i) section 590C of the Income and Corporation Taxes Act 1988 (permitted maximum) had continued in force, and

(ii) the Treasury had made the orders required by that section, as it had effect immediately before its repeal, in respect of each tax year during that period;

"rules", in relation to an existing scheme, means the rules (whether contained in the governing instruments or otherwise) of an existing scheme;

"the transitional period", in relation to an existing scheme, means the period beginning with the commencement day and ending with the date on which, by virtue of paragraph 3(2) of Schedule 36, the modifications in these Regulations cease to have effect.

(3) In the application of these Regulations to an annuity contract falling within paragraph 1(1)(*d*) of Schedule 36, references to the trustees or managers of a scheme are to be read as references to the insurance company with whom that contract is made.

(4) For the purposes of these Regulations whether something would have prejudiced the approval of an existing scheme by the Inland Revenue or by Her Majesty's Revenue and Customs is to be determined—

(*a*) in the case of an occupational pension scheme, in accordance with the publication IR 12(2001) (known as the Occupational Pension Scheme Practice Notes) published by the former Inland Revenue Pension Scheme Office on 23rd March 2001, and

(*b*) in the case of a personal pension scheme, in accordance with the publication IR 76(2000) published by the former Inland Revenue Pension Scheme Office on 20th November 2000,

as each of those publications stood immediately before the making of these Regulations.

2 Existing schemes to which these Regulations apply

Each of the following provisions of these Regulations apply to existing schemes, unless—

(*a*) before the commencement day amendments have been adopted, to have effect on and after that day, which have a corresponding effect to the modification contained in that provision; or

(*b*) the rules of the scheme are framed in a way which means that no such amendment is necessary.

3 Schemes rules not to require the making of unauthorised payments

(1) Any provision (however framed) in the rules of an existing scheme as they stood immediately before the commencement day, which would require the trustees or managers of the scheme—

(*a*) to make a payment which, by virtue of section 160 would be an unauthorised payment, or

(*b*) to make such a payment if the consent of the sponsoring employer or any other person was given for their doing so,

shall be construed, in respect of the transitional period, as conferring a discretion upon the trustees or managers to make that payment.

This is subject to the following qualification.

(2) If, immediately before the commencement day, the consent of a sponsoring employer, or any other person, was required before the trustees or managers of a pension scheme could make any other discretionary payment under the scheme, then the discretion conferred by paragraph (1) may only be exercised with the consent of that person.

4 References to the permitted maximum

(1) If the rules of an existing scheme, as they stood immediately before the commencement day, imposed a limit on a person's entitlement to any benefit, or liability to make any contribution, by reference to the permitted maximum (whether expressly or by necessary implication), paragraph (2) applies.

(2) If this paragraph applies, the permitted maximum shall continue to apply in respect of the transitional period.

5 Limits on amounts of remuneration to be taken into account

(1) This paragraph applies in the case of the rules of an existing scheme which becomes a registered pension scheme by virtue of paragraph 1(1)(*a*), (*c*) or (*d*) of Schedule 36—

(*a*) where the existing scheme came into existence before 14th March 1989, as regards an employee who became a member of that scheme on or after 1st June 1989;

(*b*) where the existing scheme came into existence on or after 14th March 1989, as regards any employee who is a member of that scheme (whenever he became a member).

This paragraph is subject to the following qualifications.

(2) Paragraph (1) does not apply to the rules of an existing scheme in their application to an employee to whom paragraph 20 of Schedule 6 to the Finance Act 1989 did not apply, immediately before its repeal, by virtue of regulation 3(2), (3), (4), (6) or (8) or 3A(2) of the Continuation of Rights Regulations.

(3) If, and to the extent that, paragraph (1) applies, paragraphs (4) to (7) have effect—

(*a*) in respect of the transitional period and

(*b*) regardless of anything contained in the rules of the existing scheme to the contrary.

(4) In arriving at the employee's relevant annual remuneration for the purposes of calculating benefits, any excess of what would be the employee's relevant annual remuneration (apart from this paragraph) over the permitted maximum for the year of assessment in which his participation in the scheme ceases shall be disregarded.

(5) In arriving at the employee's remuneration for the year 2006–07 or any subsequent year of assessment for the purposes of any restriction on the aggregate amount of contributions payable under the scheme by the employee and the employer, there shall be disregarded any excess of what would be his remuneration for the year (apart from this paragraph) over the permitted maximum for the year.

(6) If—

(*a*) a transfer payment having been accepted by the existing scheme under its rules, the payment has been treated as entitling the employee to be regarded as having additional years of service ("inserted years"), and

(*b*) by virtue of the modification of paragraph 20 of Schedule 6 to the Finance Act 1989 contained in regulation 5 of the Continuation of Rights Regulations that paragraph did not apply to the inserted years, but did apply to the member's actual years of service,

paragraph (5) applies only to the computation of pension benefits so far as they are referable to the member's actual years of service.

(7) The amount of contributions payable under the scheme by an employee in the year 2006–07 or any subsequent year of assessment shall be limited to 15 per cent of the employee's remuneration for the year in respect of the employment.

(8) In this regulation "the Continuation of Rights Regulations" means the Retirement Benefits Schemes (Continuation of Rights of Members of Approved Schemes) Regulations 1990.

6 Payments not prejudicing HM Revenue and Customs approval

(1) If the rules of an existing scheme—

(*a*) provide for an absolute entitlement to the making of a transfer or the payment of a specified sum or rate of pension; and

(*b*) refer (in whatever terms) to the possibility of making a transfer or a payment in any greater amount which would not prejudice approval of the scheme by—

(i) the Inland Revenue, or

(ii) Her Majesty's Revenue and Customs,

the following provisions of this regulation apply.

(2) The scheme's rules shall be construed, in respect of the transitional period, as—

(*a*) authorising the trustees or managers of the scheme to make transfers or payments falling within paragraph (1)(*b*) only to the extent that the payments would have been authorised by the rules immediately before the coming into force of these Regulations; and

(*b*) to prohibit the making of transfers or payments which would not have been so authorised.

This is subject to the following qualification.

(3) If, immediately before the commencement day, the consent of a sponsoring employer, or any other person except Her Majesty's Revenue and Customs, was required before the trustees or managers of a pension scheme could make a payment of the kind referred to in paragraph (1)(*b*), then the power conferred by paragraph (2)(*a*) may only be exercised with the consent of that person.

7 Limits on payments in amounts "which would not prejudice Revenue approval"

(1) If the rules of an existing scheme provide for an absolute entitlement to—

(*a*) the making of a transfer, or

(*b*) the payment of a specified sum or rate of pension,

in an amount which would not prejudice approval of the scheme by the Inland Revenue or Her Majesty's Revenue and Customs, paragraph (2) applies.

(2) If this paragraph applies the rules of the existing scheme shall be construed, in respect of the transitional period, as prohibiting the trustees or managers of the scheme from making payments to the extent that they would not have been authorised by the rules immediately before the commencement day.

8 Recovery of tax in respect of lifetime allowance charge

(1) The rules of an existing scheme shall be modified, during the transitional period, so as to provide for the recovery, from present or future benefits or entitlement under the scheme in respect of a member, of an amount reflecting any liability of the scheme administrator in respect of the lifetime allowance charge under section 215 in respect of that member.

But this does not authorise the reduction of entitlement to a benefit which has not crystallised, except that in relation to which the lifetime allowance charge arises.

(2) The methods of recovery authorised by virtue of paragraph (1) include reduction of benefits or entitlement determined in accordance with normal actuarial practice.

This paragraph does not limit the generality of paragraph (1).

2006/365

REGISTERED PENSION SCHEMES (UNAUTHORISED PAYMENTS BY EXISTING SCHEMES) REGULATIONS 2006

Made by the Commissioners for HMRC under FA 2004 s 241(2)(e)

Made . . . . *16 February 2006*
Laid before the House of Commons . . . . *17 February 2006*
Coming into force . . . . *6 April 2006*

Modifications—Registered Pension Schemes (Splitting of Schemes) Regulations, SI 2006/569 reg 3 (modification of this provision in relation to sub-scheme administrators).

1 Citation, commencement and interpretation

These Regulations may be cited as the Registered Pension Schemes (Unauthorised Payments by Existing Schemes) Regulations 2006 and shall come into force on 6th April 2006.

2 Unauthorised member payments not to be scheme chargeable

(1) An unauthorised member payment which—

(*a*) is made in exercise of the discretion conferred by regulation 3(1) of the Registered Pension Schemes (Modification of the Rules of Existing Schemes) Regulations 2006, or

(*b*) would be so made if that regulation applied to the scheme, or

(*c*) would be so made if—

(i) those regulation applied to the scheme, and

(ii) the payment were made during the transitional period in relation to the scheme,

is a payment of a description prescribed for the purposes of section 241(2) (certain payments not to be scheme chargeable payments), but only to the extent that it is referable to subsisting rights which have accrued under defined benefits arrangements before the commencement day, or to contributions which have been paid to a scheme under money purchase arrangements before that day.

This is subject to the following qualification.

(2) In the case of an unauthorised member payment which comprises or includes a refund of additional voluntary contributions, so much of the refund payment as could have been used to provide pension benefits for the member and his dependants without prejudicing approval of the scheme, before the commencement day, by the Inland Revenue or Her Majesty's Revenue and Customs is not a payment of a description prescribed for the purposes of section 241(2).

(3) In this regulation—

"the commencement day" means 6th April 2006;

"existing scheme" means a pension scheme to which paragraph 1(1) of Schedule 36 applies;

"subsisting rights" shall be construed—

(*a*) in Great Britain, in accordance with section 67A(6) of the Pensions Act 1995; and

(*b*) in Northern Ireland, in accordance with Article 67A(6) of the Pensions (Northern Ireland) Order 1995; and

"the transitional period" means the period beginning with the commencement day and ending with the date on which, by virtue of paragraph 3(2) of Schedule 36, the modifications in Registered Pension Schemes (Modification of the Rules of Existing Schemes) Regulations 2006 cease to have effect; and

a reference (without more) to a numbered provision is a reference to the provision of the Finance Act 2004 bearing that number.

(4) For the purposes of this regulation, whether something would have prejudiced the approval of an existing scheme by the Inland Revenue or by Her Majesty's Revenue and Customs is to be determined in the case of an occupational pension scheme, in accordance with the publication IR

12(2001) (known as the Occupational Pension Scheme Practice Notes) published by the former Inland Revenue Pension Scheme Office on 23rd March 2001 as that publication stood immediately before the coming into force of these Regulations.

2006/497

TAXATION OF JUDICIAL PENSIONS (CONSEQUENTIAL PROVISIONS) ORDER 2006

Made by the Treasury under FA 2004 s 281(2), (3)

Made ....*28 February 2006*
Laid before the House of Commons ....*1 March 2006*
Coming into force ....*6 April 2006*

Commentary—*Simon's Taxes* **E4.514**.

1 Citation and commencement

This Order may be cited as the Taxation of Judicial Pensions (Consequential Provisions) Order 2006 and shall come into force on 6th April 2006.

2 Interpretation

In this Order—

"the 1993 Act" means the Judicial Pensions and Retirement Act 1993,
"the 1981 Act" means the Judicial Pensions Act 1981,
"the 1960 Act" means the Resident Magistrates' Pensions Act (Northern Ireland) 1960,
"the 1959 Act" means the County Courts Act (Northern Ireland) 1959.

3 Amendments of the 1993 Act

(1) Section 3 of the 1993 Act (the appropriate annual rate) is amended as follows.

(2) In subsection (3)—

(*a*) in paragraph (*a*)(i) (definition of "pensionable pay") omit ", within the meaning of section 590C(1) of the Income and Corporation Taxes Act 1988 (earnings cap),";

(*b*) in paragraph (*b*) (definition of "pension-capped salary") for the words from ", within the" to "assessment" substitute "does not exceed the permitted maximum for the tax year".

(3) After subsection (3) insert—

"(3A) In subsection (3)(*b*) above "the permitted maximum" means—

(*a*) in relation to the tax year 2005–06 and any earlier tax year, the permitted maximum within the meaning of section 590C(1) of the Income and Corporation Taxes Act 1988 (earnings cap) as it had effect for the tax year, and

(*b*) in relation to the tax year 2006–07 and any later tax year, the amount arrived at under subsection (3B) below.

(3B) The permitted maximum for the tax year 2006–07 and any later tax year is the permitted maximum for the previous tax year increased (if there is a relevant increase in the retail prices index for the tax year) by the appropriate percentage for the tax year.

(3C) There is a relevant increase in the retail prices index for a tax year if the retail prices index for the month of September before the tax year is higher than it was for the previous September.

(3D) And the appropriate percentage for the tax year is the same percentage as the percentage increase in the retail prices index.

(3E) But if the result of the application of subsection (3B) above in relation to a tax year would not be a multiple of £600, the permitted maximum for that tax year is what it would be apart from this subsection rounded up to the nearest amount which is such a multiple.".

(4) In subsection (6) (interpretation of section), insert at the end—

", "retail prices index", in relation to a month, means—

(*a*) the general index of retail prices (for all items) published by the Office for National Statistics for the month, or

(*b*) if that index is not published for the month, any substituted index or index figures published by that Office for the month, and

"tax year" and "the tax year 2006–07" (and corresponding expressions) have the meanings in section 279(1) of the Finance Act 2004.".

4 Voluntary contributions

(1) Section 10 of the 1993 Act (additional benefits from voluntary contributions) is amended as follows.

(2) In subsection (4) (what regulations may not do or must do) in paragraph (*b*), (which refers to a limit fixed by or under section 594 of the Income and Corporation Taxes Act 1988), omit "either or both of the following, that is to say" and sub-paragraph (ii) and the word "or" before it.

(3) In subsection (8) (interpretation)—

(*a*) omit the definition of "relevant benefits",

(*b*) in the definition of "retained benefits", omit "relevant" and for "has, or which may be expected to qualify for, tax-exemption or tax approval" substitute "is registered under Part 4 of the Finance Act 2004", and

(*c*) omit the definitions of "tax-exemption" and "tax-approval".

5 Continuity of tax treatment

Section 18 of the 1993 Act (under which the scheme constituted by Part 1 of the 1993 Act is, for tax purposes, to be regarded as amendments of the statutory schemes constituted by or under the 1981 Act) shall cease to have effect.

6 Section 19 scheme

In section 19 of the 1993 Act (benefits in respect of earnings in excess of pension-capped salary), omit subsection (4) (tax treatment).

7 Other amendments

The Schedule contains amendments of enactments other than the 1993 Act.

SCHEDULE

Article 7

1 The 1981 Act is amended as follows.

2 In section 33A (voluntary contributions)—

(*a*) in subsection (2) (what regulations may not do or must do), in paragraph (*b*), (which refers to a limit fixed by or under section 594 of the Income and Corporation Taxes Act 1988), omit "either or both of the following, that is to say" and sub-paragraph (ii) and the word "or" before it; and

(*b*) in subsection (9)—

(i) omit the definition of "relevant benefits",

(ii) in the definition of "retained benefits", omit "relevant" and for "has, or which may be expected to qualify for, tax-exemption or tax approval" substitute "is registered under Part 4 of the Finance Act 2004", and

(iii) omit the definitions of "tax-exemption" and "tax-approval".

3 The 1960 Act is amended as follows.

4 In section 9A (voluntary contributions)—

(*a*) in subsection (2) (what regulations may not do), in paragraph (*b*), (which refers to a limit fixed by or under section 594 of the Income and Corporation Taxes Act 1988), omit "either or both of the following, that is to say" and sub-paragraph (ii) and the word "or" before it; and

(*b*) in subsection (7)—

(i) omit the definition of "relevant benefits",

(ii) in the definition of "retained benefits", omit "relevant" and for "has, or which may be expected to qualify for, tax-exemption or tax approval" substitute "is registered under Part 4 of the Finance Act 2004", and

(iii) omit the definitions of "tax-exemption" and "tax-approval".

5 The 1959 Act is amended as follows.

6 In section 127A (voluntary contributions)—

(*a*) in subsection (2) (what regulations may not do), in paragraph (*b*), (which refers to a limit fixed by or under section 594 of the Income and Corporation Taxes Act 1988), omit "either or both of the following, that is to say" and sub-paragraph (ii) and the word "or" before it; and

(*b*) in subsection (7)—

(i) omit the definition of "relevant benefits",

(ii) in the definition of "retained benefits", omit "relevant" and for "has, or which may be expected to qualify for, tax-exemption or tax approval" substitute "is registered under Part 4 of the Finance Act 2004", and

(iii) omit the definitions of "tax-exemption" and "tax-approval".

2006/498

REGISTERED PENSION SCHEMES (BLOCK TRANSFERS) (PERMITTED MEMBERSHIP PERIOD) REGULATIONS 2006

Made by the Commissioners for HMRC under FA 2004 Sch 36 para 22(6)(b)

Made . . . . *28 February 2006*
Laid before the House of Commons . . . . *1 March 2006*
Coming into force . . . . *6 April 2006*

Commentary—*Simon's Taxes* **E7.240**.

1 Citation and commencement

These Regulations may be cited as the Registered Pension Schemes (Block Transfers) (Permitted Membership Period) Regulations 2006, and shall come into force on 6th April 2006.

2 Permitted membership period for block transfers

(1) For the purposes of paragraph (*b*) of paragraph 22(6) of Schedule 36 to the Finance Act 2004 the period prescribed is a period of twelve months ending with the date on which the transfer is made [("the prescribed period")][1].

[(2) But in calculating the prescribed period, any period preceding the period of twelve months ending with the date on which the transfer is made is ignored if conditions A and B are met.][1]

(3) Condition A is that immediately before 6th April 2006 the member was a member of a personal pension scheme approved under Chapter 4 of Part 14 of the Income and Corporation Taxes Act 1988 (personal pension schemes).

(4) Condition B is that the member's rights under that scheme consist solely of rights referable to either or both of the following—

(*a*) amounts paid under the provisions mentioned in section 188(3)(*c*) of the Finance Act 2004;
(*b*) payments under the provisions mentioned in paragraph 14(2) of Schedule 36 to that Act.

Amendments—[1] Words in para (1) inserted, and para (2) substituted, by the Registered Pension Schemes (Block Transfers) (Permitted Membership Period) (Amendment) Regulations, SI 2007/838 reg 2 with effect from 6 April 2007.

2006/499

REGISTERED PENSION SCHEMES (TRANSFER OF SUMS AND ASSETS) REGULATIONS 2006

Made by the Commissioners for HMRC under FA 2004 s 169(1B), (1C), (1D), (1E), Sch 28 paras 2(4)(h), (6A), 3(2B), (2C), 6(1B), (1C), 16(2A), (2B), 17(3), (4), 20(1B), (1C)

Made . . . . *28 February 2006*
Laid before the House of Commons . . . . *1 March 2006*
Coming into force . . . . *6 April 2006*

Modifications—Registered Pension Schemes (Splitting of Schemes) Regulations, SI 2006/569 reg 3 (modification of this provision in relation to sub-scheme administrators).

1 Citation and commencement

These Regulations may be cited as the Registered Pension Schemes (Transfer of Sums and Assets) Regulations 2006 and shall come into force on 6th April 2006.

2 Interpretation

In these Regulations "Part", "section" or "Schedule", without more, means a Part, section or Schedule of the Finance Act 2004.

3 Scheme pension payable by registered pension scheme—recognised transfers

(1) A transfer within section 169(1) or (1A) (recognised transfer) of sums or assets which represent rights in respect of a scheme pension to which a member of a registered pension scheme has become entitled ("the original scheme pension") is not a recognised transfer unless those sums and assets are, after the transfer, applied towards the provision of a scheme pension (a "new scheme pension").

(2) If the sums and assets are so applied, the new scheme pension is to be treated as if it were the original scheme pension for the purposes of Part 4 prescribed in table 1.

4 Scheme pension payable by insurance company

If—

(*a*) a scheme pension payable by an insurance company selected by the scheme administrator of a registered pension scheme ("the original scheme pension") ceases to be payable, and
(*b*) in consequence of the transfer of sums or assets (or both) from the insurance company to another insurance company in connection with the original scheme pension ceasing to be payable, another scheme pension becomes payable by the other insurance company ("the new scheme pension"),

the new scheme pension is to be treated as if it were the original scheme pension for the purposes of Part 4 prescribed in table 1.

Table 1
Prescribed purposes—scheme pensions

Provision	*Purpose*
[Section 165(1), pension rule 1	To determine whether the individual has reached the normal minimum pension age by reference to the day on which the original scheme pension was first paid.][1]
Section 216(1), benefit crystallisation event 2 (benefit crystallisation event on becoming entitled to a scheme pension)	To determine whether the individual has become entitled to a scheme pension by reference to the original scheme pension (to prevent a benefit crystallisation event occurring in relation to the individual becoming entitled to the new scheme pension).
Section 216(1), benefit crystallisation event 3 (benefit crystallisation event on becoming entitled to a scheme pension at an increased rate)	To determine the rate at which the scheme pension was payable on the day on which the individual became entitled to it by reference to the rate payable in relation to the original scheme pension.
Paragraph 2A(3) and (5) of Schedule 28 (unauthorised payments)	To determine—
	(i) the rate payable when the member became entitled to the pension, and
	(ii) the amount of any lump sum on which there is no liability to tax to which the member became entitled in conjunction with the pension,
	by reference to the original scheme pension.
Paragraph 1(1) and (3)(*a*) of Schedule 29 (pension commencement lump sum)	To determine whether the member has become entitled to a lump sum in connection with the member becoming entitled to the scheme pension by reference to the original scheme pension (to prevent a lump sum to which a member becomes entitled in connection with becoming entitled to the new scheme pension being a pension commencement lump sum).
Paragraph 14(3) of Schedule 29 (pension protection lump sum death benefit)	To determine—
	(i) the amount crystallised by reason of the member becoming entitled to the pension (*ac*) by reference to the member becoming entitled to the original scheme pension,
	(ii) the amount of pension paid (AP) as that paid in respect of the original scheme pension and the new scheme pension in respect of the period between the member becoming entitled to the original scheme pension and the member's death,
	(iii) the total amount of pension protection lump sum death benefit (TPLS) by reference to that paid in respect of the original scheme pension and the new scheme pension.
Paragraph 16(3) of Schedule 29 (annuity protection lump sum death benefit)	To determine—
	(i) the amount crystallised by reason of the member becoming entitled to the pension (*ac*) by reference to the member becoming entitled to the original scheme pension,

Provision	*Purpose*
	(ii) the amount of pension paid (AP) as that paid in respect of the original scheme pension and the new scheme pension in respect of the period between the member becoming entitled to the original scheme pension and the member's death, and
	(iii) the total amount of annuity protection lump sum death benefit (TPLS) by reference to that paid in respect of the original scheme pension and the new scheme pension.
[Paragraph 20(2), (3) and (5) of Schedule 36 (pre-commencement pensions)	To determine—
	(i) whether an individual has precommencement pension rights,
	(ii) whether an individual has a relevant existing pension.][2]

Amendments—[1] In Table 1 entry relating to s 165(1) inserted by the Registered Pension Schemes (Transfer of Sums and Assets) (Amendment) Regulations, SI 2011/733 regs 2, 3 with effect from 6 April 2010.

[2] In Table 1 entry relating to Sch 36 para20 (2), (3), (5) inserted by the Registered Pension Schemes (Transfer of Sums and Assets) (Amendment) Regulations, SI 2014/1449 reg 2 with effect from 1 July 2014 in respect of transfers made on or after 6th April 2014.

5 Term and reduction in the rate of scheme pension

[(1)] [1] In a case within regulation 3 or 4 a reduction of the original scheme pension is a prescribed circumstance for the purposes of paragraph 2(4) of Schedule 28 (scheme pension: satisfying conditions) if—

(*a*) the rate of the pension payable under the new scheme pension on the day on which the member becomes entitled to it is not less than the rate payable under the original scheme pension immediately before the original scheme pension ceased to be payable save to the extent that any reduction reflects the reasonable administration costs of the transfer of sums or assets; and

(*b*) where the new scheme pension is payable until the later of the member's death and the end of a term certain, that term ends on or before the date on which the term certain under the original scheme pension would have ended.

[(2) In paragraph (1)(*a*) "administration costs" includes, in particular, payments of overseas transfer charge.][1]

Amendments—[1] Para (1) numbered as such, and para (2) inserted, by FA 2017 s 10, Sch 4 para 23 with effect in relation to transfers made on or after 9 March 2017.

Note that these amendments are to be treated as made by the HMRC Commissioners under the powers to make regulations conferred by FA 2004 Sch 28 para 2(4)(*h*) (FA 2017 Sch 4 para 23(4)).

6 Lifetime annuity—unauthorised payments and prescribed purposes

(1) In a case within paragraph 3(2B)(*a*) of Schedule 28 (transfer of sums or assets on cessation of lifetime annuity) where a new lifetime annuity becomes payable, the new lifetime annuity is to be treated as if it were the original lifetime annuity for the purposes of Part 4 prescribed in table 2 to the extent that the amount of the sums and the value of the assets applied to purchase the new lifetime annuity are equal to the amount of the sums and the value of the assets transferred.

(2) In any other case within paragraph 3(2B), the relevant registered pension scheme is to be treated as making an unauthorised payment to the member of an amount equal to the aggregate of the amount of the sums and the market value of the assets transferred.

Table 2
Prescribed purposes—lifetime annuities

Provision	*Purpose*
[Section 165(1), pension rule 1	To determine whether the individual has reached the normal minimum pension age by reference to the day on which the original lifetime annuity was first paid.][2]
[Section 172A (surrender)	To determine for the purposes of section 172A(1) and (2) whether a surrender of (or agreement to surrender) rights to payments under a lifetime annuity has occurred.][1]

Provision	Purpose
Section 216(1), benefit crystallisation event 4 (benefit crystallisation event on becoming entitled to a lifetime annuity)	To determine whether the individual has become entitled to a lifetime annuity by reference to the original annuity (to prevent a benefit crystallisation event occurring in relation to the individual becoming entitled to the new lifetime annuity).
Paragraph 1(1) and (3)(*a*) of Schedule 29 (pension commencement lump sum)	To determine whether the member has become entitled to a lump sum in connection with the member becoming entitled to a lifetime annuity by reference to the original annuity (to prevent a lump sum to which a member becomes entitled in connection with becoming entitled to the new lifetime annuity being a pension commencement lump sum).
Paragraph 16(3) of Schedule 29 (annuity protection lump sum death benefit)	To determine—
	(i) the amount crystallised by reason of the member becoming entitled to the annuity (*ac*) by reference to the member becoming entitled to the original lifetime annuity,
	(ii) the amount of pension paid (AP) as that paid in respect of the original lifetime annuity and the new lifetime annuity in respect of the period between the member becoming entitled to the original lifetime annuity and the member's death,
	(iii) the total amount of annuity protection lump sum death benefit (TPLS) by reference to that paid in respect of the original lifetime annuity and the new lifetime annuity.

Amendments—[1] Entry inserted by the Registered Pension Schemes (Transfer of Sums and Assets) (Amendment) Regulations, SI 2008/1946 reg 2 with effect in relation to surrenders of and agreements to surrender rights to payments under lifetime annuities or dependants' annuities made on or after 10 October 2007.

[2] Entry relating to s 165(1) inserted by the Registered Pension Schemes (Transfer of Sums and Assets) (Amendment) Regulations, SI 2011/733 regs 2, 4 with effect from 6 April 2010.

7 [Short—term annuity—unauthorised payments

(1) In any case within paragraph 6(1B) of Schedule 28 (transfer of sums and assets on cessation of short-term annuity) except where a new short-term annuity becomes payable, the relevant registered pension scheme is to be treated as making an unauthorised payment to the member of an amount equal to the aggregate of the amount of the sums and the market value of the assets transferred.

(2) In any case within paragraph 6(1B) where a new short-term annuity becomes payable, the new short-term annuity is to be treated as if it were the original short-term annuity for the purposes prescribed in paragraph (3).

(3) The prescribed purposes are to determine, in relation to pension rule 1 in section 165(1), whether the individual has reached the normal minimum pension age by reference to the day on which the original short-term annuity was first paid.][1]

Amendments—[1] Reg 7 substituted by the Registered Pension Schemes (Transfer of Sums and Assets) (Amendment) Regulations, SI 2011/733 regs 2, 5 with effect from 6 April 2010.

8 Dependants' scheme pension payable by registered pension scheme—recognised transfers

A transfer within section 169(1) or (1A) of sums or assets which represent rights in respect of a dependants' scheme pension to which a dependant of a member of a registered pension scheme has become entitled in respect of the member ("the original dependants' scheme pension") is not a recognised transfer unless those sums and assets are, after the transfer, applied towards the provision of a dependants' scheme pension (a "new dependants' scheme pension").

9 Dependants' scheme pension payable by an insurance company—unauthorised payments

In any case within paragraph 16(2A) of Schedule 28 (transfer of sums or assets on cessation of payment of a dependants' scheme pension by an insurance company) except where a new dependants' scheme pension becomes payable, the relevant registered pension scheme is to be treated as making an unauthorised payment in respect of the member of an amount equal to the aggregate of the amount of the sums and the market value of the assets transferred.

10 [Dependants' annuity – unauthorised payments

(1) In any case within paragraph 17(3) of Schedule 28 (transfer of sums or assets on cessation of dependants' annuity) where a new dependants' annuity becomes payable, the new dependants' annuity is to be treated as if it were the original dependants' annuity for the purposes of Part 4 prescribed in table 2A to the extent that the amount of the sums and the value of the assets applied to purchase the new dependants' annuity are equal to the amount of the sums and the value of the assets transferred.

(2) In any other case within paragraph 17(3), except where a new dependants' annuity becomes payable, the relevant registered pension scheme is to be treated as making an unauthorised payment in respect of the member of an amount equal to the aggregate of the amount of the sums and the market value of the assets transferred.

Table 2A

Provision	*Purpose*
Section 172A (surrender)	To determine for the purposes of section 172A(1) and (2) whether a surrender of (or agreement to surrender) rights to payments under a dependants' annuity has occurred.][1]

Amendments—[1] Regulation 10 substituted by the Registered Pension Schemes (Transfer of Sums and Assets) (Amendment) Regulations, SI 2008/1946 reg 2(3) with effect in relation to surrenders of and agreements to surrender rights to payments under lifetime annuities or dependants' annuities made on or after 10 October 2007.

11 Dependants' short-term annuity—unauthorised payments

In any case within paragraph 20(1B) of Schedule 28 (transfer of sums or assets on cessation of dependants' short-term annuity) except where a new dependant' short-term annuity becomes payable, the relevant registered pension scheme is to be treated as making an unauthorised payment in respect of the member of an amount equal to the aggregate of the amount of the sums and the market value of the assets transferred.

12 [Member's drawdown pension fund [or flexi-access drawdown fund] and dependant's drawdown pension fund [or flexi-access drawdown fund] [and nominee's flexi-access drawdown fund and successor's flexi-access drawdown fund]—recognised transfers and prescribed purposes

(1) A transfer within section 169(1) of sums or assets which represent a [member's flexi-access drawdown fund, dependant's flexi-access drawdown fund,][2] [nominee's flexi-access drawdown fund, successor's flexi-access drawdown fund,][3] member's drawdown pension fund or dependant's drawdown pension fund under an arrangement ("the old arrangement"), is not a recognised transfer unless all of those sums and assets become held under an arrangement under which no other sums or assets are held ("the new arrangement").

(2) In a case where the sums and assets become so held, the sums and assets transferred are to be treated as remaining sums and assets held under the old arrangement for the purposes prescribed—

[(*za*) in the case of a member's flexi-access drawdown fund, in the entries in table 3 for provisions not in Schedule 28,][2]

(a) in table 3 in the case of a member's drawdown pension fund, and

(b) in table 4 in the case of a dependant's drawdown pension fund.

Table 3

Prescribed purposes—[member's flexi-access drawdown fund or][2] member's drawdown pension fund

Provision	*Purpose*
Section 165(1), pension rule 1 (normal minimum pension age)	To determine whether the individual has reached the normal minimum pension age by reference to the day on which, in the case of income withdrawal, the first payment of drawdown pension was made under the old arrangement.
Section 165(3A) (conditions for flexible drawdown arrangement)	*To determine whether the limit in section 165(1), pension rule 5 (withdrawal limit for drawdown pension year) is disapplied by reference to whether the limit was disapplied in relation to the old arrangement (so that if the flexible drawdown conditions have been met in relation to the old arrangement, these conditions are treated as having been met in relation to the new arrangement).*[2]

Section 216(1), benefit crystallisation event 1 (benefit crystallisation event on designation of sums or assets held as available for payment of drawdown pension to the individual)	To determine whether there has been a designation of sums or assets held as available for payment of drawdown pension to the individual by reference to the designation of sums or assets held under the old arrangement (to prevent a benefit crystallisation event occurring in relation to the sums or assets becoming held under a new arrangement).
Paragraph 9(1) of Schedule 28 (definition of drawdown pension year)	To determine the drawdown pension year for the purpose of paragraphs 9, 10 and 10A of Schedule 28 by reference to the day on which the member first became entitled to a drawdown pension in respect of the old arrangement, except where a determination has been made under paragraph 10B(3) in which case the drawdown pension year is to be determined by reference to that determination.
Paragraph 10(2) and (4)(a) of Schedule 28 (calculation of basis amount for drawdown pension year)	To determine, for the reference period in which the transfer is made, the annual amount of the relevant annuity which could have been purchased by the application of the sums and assets representing the member's drawdown pension fund on the nominated date, by reference to the sums and assets held under the old arrangement.
Paragraph 10A(2) of Schedule 28 (calculation of basis amount for drawdown pension year beginning after the member's 75th birthday)	To determine, for the drawdown pension year in which the transfer is made, the annual amount of the relevant annuity which could have been purchased by the application of the sums and assets representing the member's drawdown pension fund on the nominated date, by reference to the sums and assets held under the old arrangement.
Paragraph 1(1) and (3)(a) of Schedule 29 (pension commencement lump sum)	To determine whether the member has become entitled to a lump sum in connection with the member becoming entitled under an arrangement by reference to the old arrangement (to prevent a lump sum to which a member becomes entitled in connection with becoming entitled under the new arrangement being a pension commencement lump sum).

Table 4

Prescribed purposes—dependant's drawdown pension fund

Provision	*Purpose*
Section 167(2A) (conditions for flexible drawdown arrangement)	*To determine whether the limit in section 167(1), pension death benefit rule 4 (withdrawal limit for drawdown pension year) is disapplied by reference to whether the limit was disapplied in relation to the old arrangement (so that if the flexible drawdown conditions have been met in relation to the old arrangement, these conditions are treated as having been met in relation to the new arrangement).*[2]
Paragraph 23(1) of Schedule 28 (definition of drawdown pension year)	To determine the drawdown pension year for the purpose of paragraphs 23, 24 and 24A of Schedule 28 by reference to the day on which the dependant first became entitled to a dependant's drawdown pension in respect of the old arrangement, except where a determination has been made under paragraph 24B(3) in which case the drawdown pension year is to be determined by reference to that determination.
Paragraph 24(2) and (4)(a) of Schedule 28 (calculation of basis amount for drawdown pension year)	To determine, for the reference period in which the transfer is made, the annual amount of the relevant annuity which could have been purchased by the application of the sums and assets representing the dependant's drawdown pension fund on the nominated date, by reference to the sums and assets held under the old arrangement.
Paragraph 24A(2) of Schedule 28 (calculation of basis amount for drawdown pension year beginning after the dependant's 75th birthday)	To determine, for the drawdown pension year in which the transfer is made, the annual amount of the relevant annuity which could have been purchased by the application of the sums and assets representing the dependant's drawdown pension fund on the nominated date, by reference to the sums and assets held under the old arrangement.][1]

Amendments—[1] Reg 12 substituted by the Registered Pension Schemes (Transfer of Sums and Assets) (Amendment) (No 2) Regulations, SI 2011/1790 reg 2 with effect for the tax year 2011–12 and subsequent tax years.

[2] In heading to reg 12 words inserted, in para (1) words inserted, para (2)(*za*) inserted, in table 3 words inserted and entry for entry for FA 2004 s 165(3A) repealed, in table 4 entry for FA 2004 s 167(2A) repealed, by the Taxation of Pensions Act 2014 s 1, Sch 1 para 34 with effect from 6 April 2015. These amendments are to be treated as having been made by the Commissioners for Revenue and Customs under the powers to make regulations conferred by FA 2004 s 169(1D), (1E) (as amended by the Taxation of Pensions Act 2014 Sch 1)

[3] In heading to reg 12 words inserted, and in para (1) words inserted, by the Taxation of Pensions Act 2014 s 3, Sch 2 para 16 with effect from 6 April 2015. These amendments are to be treated as having been made by the Commissioners for Revenue and Customs under the powers to make regulations conferred by FA 2004 s 169(1D), (1E) (as amended by TPA 2014 Sch 2).

[13 Lifetime annuity — new annuity not a lifetime annuity for the purposes of Part 4

In a case within paragraph 3(2B)(*a*) of Schedule 28 (transfer of sums or assets on cessation of lifetime annuity) where—

(*a*) a new annuity becomes payable,

(*b*) the member becomes entitled to it on or after 6th April 2015,

(*c*) it would be a lifetime annuity but for this regulation,

(*d*) the terms of the contract for it are such that there will or could be decreases in its amount other than allowed decreases, and

(*e*) the member became entitled to the original lifetime annuity before 6th April 2015, or sums or assets (or both) derived from a transfer or a series of transfers of sums or assets (or both) from an insurance company in respect of a lifetime annuity to which the member became entitled before 6th April 2015 were applied towards the provision of the original lifetime annuity,

the new annuity is not a lifetime annuity for the purposes of Part 4.][1]

Amendments—[1] Regulations 13–18 inserted by the Registered Pension Schemes (Transfer of Sums and Assets) (Amendment) Regulations, SI 2015/633 regs 2, 3 with effect from 6 April 2015.

[14 Short-term annuity: new annuity not a short-term annuity for the purposes of Part 4

In any case within paragraph 6(1B) of Schedule 28 (transfer of sums or assets on cessation of short-term annuity) where—

(*a*) a new annuity becomes payable,

(*b*) the member becomes entitled to it on or after 6th April 2015,

(*c*) it would be a short-term annuity but for this regulation,

(*d*) the terms of the contract for it are such that there will or could be decreases in its amount other than allowed decreases, and

(*e*) the member became entitled to the original short-term annuity before 6th April 2015, or sums or assets (or both) derived from a transfer or a series of transfers of sums or assets (or both) from an insurance company in respect of a short-term annuity to which the member became entitled before 6th April 2015 were applied towards the provision of the original short-term annuity,

the new annuity is not a short-term annuity for the purposes of Part 4.][1]

Amendments—[1] Regulations 13–18 inserted by the Registered Pension Schemes (Transfer of Sums and Assets) (Amendment) Regulations, SI 2015/633 regs 2, 3 with effect from 6 April 2015.

[15 Dependants' annuity: new annuity not a dependants' annuity for the purposes of Part 4

(1) In any case within paragraph 17(3) of Schedule 28 (transfer of sums or assets on cessation of dependants' annuity) where—

(*a*) a new annuity becomes payable,

(*b*) the dependant becomes entitled to it on or after 6th April 2015,

(*c*) it would be a dependants' annuity but for this regulation,

(*d*) the terms of the contract for it are such that there will or could be decreases in its amount other than allowed decreases, and

(*e*) condition A, B, C or D is met,

the new annuity is not a dependants' annuity for the purposes of Part 4.

(2) Condition A is that the dependant became entitled to the original dependants' annuity before 6th April 2015.

(3) Condition B is that sums or assets (or both) derived from a transfer or a series of transfers of sums or assets (or both) from an insurance company, in respect of a dependants' annuity to which the dependant became entitled before 6th April 2015, were applied towards the provision of the original dependants' annuity.

(4) Condition C is that the original dependants' annuity was purchased together with a lifetime annuity payable to the member and the member became entitled to that lifetime annuity before 6th April 2015.

(5) Condition D is that sums or assets (or both) derived from a transfer or a series of transfers of sums or assets (or both) from an insurance company, in respect of a dependants' annuity that was purchased together with a lifetime annuity payable to the member and the member became entitled to that lifetime annuity before 6th April 2015, were applied towards the provision of the original dependants' annuity.
(6) For the purposes of paragraphs (4) and (5) a dependants' annuity is purchased together with a lifetime annuity if the dependants' annuity is related to the lifetime annuity.][1]

Amendments—[1] Regulations 13–18 inserted by the Registered Pension Schemes (Transfer of Sums and Assets) (Amendment) Regulations, SI 2015/633 regs 2, 3 with effect from 6 April 2015.

[16 Dependants' short-term annuity: new annuity not a dependants' short-term annuity for the purposes of Part 4

In any case within paragraph 20(1B) of Schedule 28 (transfer of sums or assets on cessation of dependants' short-term annuity) where—

(*a*) a new annuity becomes payable,
(*b*) the dependant becomes entitled to it on or after 6th April 2015,
(*c*) it would be a dependants' short-term annuity but for this regulation,
(*d*) the terms of the contract for it are such that there will or could be decreases in its amount other than allowed decreases, and
(*e*) the dependant became entitled to the original dependants' short-term annuity before 6th April 2015, or sums or assets (or both) derived from a transfer or a series of transfers of sums or assets (or both) from an insurance company in respect of a dependants' short-term annuity to which the dependant became entitled before 6th April 2015 were applied towards the provision of the original dependants' short-term annuity,

the new annuity is not a dependants' short-term annuity for the purposes of Part 4.][1]

Amendments—[1] Regulations 13–18 inserted by the Registered Pension Schemes (Transfer of Sums and Assets) (Amendment) Regulations, SI 2015/633 regs 2, 3 with effect from 6 April 2015.

[17 Nominees' short-term annuity — unauthorised payments

In any case within paragraph 27C(2) of Schedule 28 (transfer of sums or assets on cessation of nominees' short-term annuity) except where a new nominees' short-term annuity becomes payable, the relevant registered pension scheme is to be treated as making an unauthorised payment in respect of the member of an amount equal to the aggregate of the amount of the sums and the market value of the assets transferred.][1]

Amendments—[1] Regulations 13–18 inserted by the Registered Pension Schemes (Transfer of Sums and Assets) (Amendment) Regulations, SI 2015/633 regs 2, 3 with effect from 6 April 2015.

[18 Successors' short-term annuity — unauthorised payments

In any case within paragraph 27H(2) of Schedule 28 (transfer of sums or assets on cessation of successors' short-term annuity) except where a new successors' short-term annuity becomes payable, the relevant registered pension scheme is to be treated as making an unauthorised payment in respect of the member of an amount equal to the aggregate of the amount of the sums and the market value of the assets transferred.][1]

Amendments—[1] Regulations 13–18 inserted by the Registered Pension Schemes (Transfer of Sums and Assets) (Amendment) Regulations, SI 2015/633 regs 2, 3 with effect from 6 April 2015.

[19 Nominees' annuity — unauthorised payments

(1) In any case within paragraph 27AA(3) of Schedule 28 (transfer of sums or assets on cessation of a nominees' annuity) where a new nominees' annuity becomes payable, to the extent that the amount of the sums and the value of the assets applied to purchase the new nominees' annuity are equal to the amount of the sums and the value of the assets transferred, the new nominees' annuity is to be treated as if it were the original nominees' annuity to determine for the purposes of section 172A(1) and (2) (surrender of benefits or rights under a registered pension scheme) whether a surrender of (or agreement to surrender) rights to payments under a nominees' annuity has occurred.
(2) In any other case within paragraph 27AA(3) the relevant registered pension scheme is to be treated as making an unauthorised payment in respect of the member of an amount equal to the aggregate of the amount of the sums, and the market value of the assets, transferred.][1]

Amendments—[1] Regulations 19, 20 inserted by the Registered Pension Schemes (Transfer of Sums and Assets) (Amendment No 2) Regulations, SI 2015/1454 regs 2, 3 with effect for the tax year 2015–16 and subsequent years.

[20 Successors' annuity — unauthorised payments

(1) In any case within paragraph 27FA(3) of Schedule 28 (transfer of sums or assets on cessation of a successors' annuity) where a new successors' annuity becomes payable, to the extent that the amount of the sums and the value of the assets applied to purchase the new successors' annuity are equal to the amount of the sums and the value of the assets transferred, the new successors' annuity is to be treated as if it were the original successors' annuity to determine for the purposes of section 172A(1) and (2) whether a surrender of (or agreement to surrender) rights to payments under a successors' annuity has occurred.

(2) In any other case within paragraph 27FA(3) the relevant registered pension scheme is to be treated as making an unauthorised payment in respect of the member of an amount equal to the aggregate of the amount of the sums, and the market value of the assets, transferred.][1]

Amendments—[1] Regulations 19, 20 inserted by the Registered Pension Schemes (Transfer of Sums and Assets) (Amendment No 2) Regulations, SI 2015/1454 regs 2, 3 with effect for the tax year 2015–16 and subsequent years.

2006/567

REGISTERED PENSION SCHEMES (PROVISION OF INFORMATION) REGULATIONS 2006

Made by the Commissioners for HMRC under FA 2004 ss 220(5), 221(6), 224(9), 251(1)(a), (b), (4)(a), (b), (5), (6), 256, Sch 36 paras 7(1)(b), 12(1), 18(6).

Made . . . . *9 March 2006*
Laid before the House of Commons . . . . *10 March 2006*
Coming into force . . . . *6 April 2006*

Commentary—*Simon's Taxes* **E7.241.**
HMRC Manuals—Registered Pension Schemes Manual RPSM06107510 (automatic pension savings statement).
Modifications—Registered Pension Schemes (Splitting of Schemes) Regulations, SI 2006/569 reg 3 (modification of this provision in relation to sub-scheme administrators).

1 Citation, commencement and effect

These Regulations may be cited as the Registered Pension Schemes (Provision of Information) Regulations 2006, shall come into force on 6th April 2006, and have effect in relation to any reportable event which takes place on or after 6th April 2006.

2 Interpretation

(1) In these Regulations—

"the Act" means the Finance Act 2004 and a reference, without more, to a numbered section or Schedule is a reference to the section of, or Schedule to the Act bearing that number;

"associated company" has the meaning given by [section 449 of the Corporation Tax Act 2010][1];

"the Commissioners" means the Commissioners for Her Majesty's Revenue and Customs;

"director" has the meaning given by [section 67 of ITEPA 2003][1];

"event report" means the report required by regulation 3(1);

["fixed protection" means transitional protection provided for under paragraph 14 of Schedule 18 to the Finance Act 2011.][1]

["fixed protection 2014" means transitional protection provided for under Part 1 of Schedule 22 to the Finance Act 2013.][2]

["fixed protection 2016" means protection under paragraph 1(2) of Schedule 4 to FA 2016;][4]

["individual protection 2014" means transitional protection provided for under Part 1 of Schedule 6 to the Finance Act 2014;][3]

["individual protection 2016" means protection under paragraph 9(2) of Schedule 4 to FA 2016;][4]

"relevant lump sum death benefit" means a defined benefits lump sum death benefit or an uncrystallised funds lump sum death benefit;

"reportable event" means an event in relation to which information is required to be provided by virtue of these Regulations;

"reporting year" means the tax year to which an event report relates.

(2) [Section 993 ITA 2007][1] applies for the purpose of determining whether a person is connected with another for the purposes of these Regulations.

(3) Expressions defined, or otherwise explained, in section 280, have the same meaning in these Regulations as they have in Part 4 of the Act.

Amendments—[1] In para (1), in definitions of "associated company"and "director", words substituted; definition of "fixed protection" inserted; and in para 2 words substituted; by the Registered Pension Schemes (Provision of Information) (Amendment) (No 2) Regulations, SI 2011/1797 regs 2, 3 with effect from 11 August 2011.

[2] In para (1), definition of "fixed protection 2014" inserted by the Registered Pension Schemes (Provision of Information) (Amendment) Regulations, SI 2013/1742 regs 2, 3 with effect for the tax year 2014–15 and subsequent years.

[3] In para (1), definition of "individual protection 2014" inserted by the Registered Pension Schemes (Provision of Information) (Amendment) Regulations, SI 2014/1843 regs 2, 3 with effect for the tax year 2014–15 and subsequent years.

[4] In para (1), definition of "fixed protection 2016" and "individual protection 2016" inserted by FA 2016 Sch 4 paras 22, 23 with effect from 15 September 2016.

3 Provision of information by scheme administrator to the Commissioners

(1) The scheme administrator of a registered pension scheme shall provide to the Commissioners an event report in respect of all of the reportable events specified in column (1) of the Table below which have occurred in respect of the scheme during the reporting year, containing the information specified in column (2).

Table

Reportable event	*Information*
1 Unauthorised payments	
The scheme makes an unauthorised member payment or an unauthorised employer payment.	[The name of the person to whom the payment was made, and— (*a*) where the person is an individual, the national insurance number, (*b*) where the person is a company, the company registration number, or (*c*) in any other case, an alternative number obtained from [the Commissioners][4], together with the nature, amount and date of the payment.][3]
2 Payments exceeding 50% of standard lifetime allowance	
The scheme makes a lump sum death benefit payment to a person in respect of the death of a member, and that payment, either alone or when aggregated with other such payments from that scheme, amounts to more than 50% of the standard lifetime allowance applicable at the time of the member's death.	The name . . . [3] and national insurance number of the deceased member, together with the name and [national insurance number][3] of the person to whom the payment was made, and the amount and date of the payment.
3 Early provision of benefits	
The scheme provides benefits to a member of the scheme who is under the normal minimum pension age and before the benefits were provided the member was, either in the year in which they were provided or any of the preceding six years— (*a*) in relation to the sponsoring employer, or an associated company of that employer, a director or a person connected with a director; (*b*) whether alone or with others, the sponsoring employer; or (*c*) a person connected with the sponsoring employer.	The name . . . [3] and national insurance number of the member, the nature, date and amount of the benefits provided, and reasons for those benefits having been provided under normal minimum pension age.
4 Serious ill-health lump sum	
A scheme pays a member of the scheme a serious ill-health lump sum and before the payment was made the member was, either in the year in which they were provided or any of the preceding six years— (*a*) in relation to the sponsoring employer, or an associated company of that employer, a director or a person connected with a director; or (*b*) whether alone or with others, the sponsoring employer; or *c*) a person connected with the sponsoring employer.	The name . . . [3] and national insurance number of the member, and the date and amount of the payment.
5 Suspension of ill-health pension	
An ill-health pension which has been paid, pursuant to pension rule 1 in section 165(1), [ceases to be paid for any reason other than the member's death][2].	The name . . . [3] and national insurance number of the member to whom the pension had been paid, the date on which the period of non-payment began and the annual rate of the pension, to which the member was entitled, immediately before that period began.

Reportable event	*Information*
6 [Benefit crystallisation events and [non-standard lifetime allowances][15]	
A benefit crystallisation event occurs in relation to a member in respect of the scheme and— (*a*) . . . [10]	[The name and national insurance number of the member, the amount crystallised by the event, the date of the event and the reference number given by [or on behalf of][15] the Commissioners under — (*a*) the Registered Pension Schemes (Enhanced Lifetime Allowance) Regulations 2006(2) (where the member relies on an enhanced lifetime allowance or enhanced protection), . . . [9] (*b*) the Registered Pension Schemes (Lifetime Allowance Transitional Protection) Regulations 2011(3) (where the member relies on fixed protection)[, . . . [10] (*c*) the Registered Pension Schemes and Relieved Non-UK Pension Schemes (Lifetime Allowance Transitional Protection) (Notification) Regulations 2013 (where the member relies on fixed protection 2014)[, ...[15]][9] (*d*) the Registered Pension Schemes and Relieved Non-UK Pension Schemes (Lifetime Allowance Transitional Protection) (Individual Protection 2014 Notification) Regulations 2014 (where the member relies on individual protection 2014),][10] [or (*e*) Schedule 4 to the Finance Act 2016 (where the member relies on fixed protection 2016 or individual protection 2016).][15]
[(*b*) in order to reduce or eliminate liability to the lifetime allowance charge the member relies on entitlement to— (i) an enhanced lifetime allowance, (ii) enhanced protection, . . . [9] (iii) fixed protection[, . . . [105] (iv) fixed protection 2014][9] ...[15] (v) individual protection 2014.][10] [or (vi) fixed protection 2016 or individual protection 2016.][15]	
7 Pension commencement lump sum	
[The scheme makes a pension commencement lump sum payment to a member which— (*a*)exceeds 25% of the amount found by adding the amount of the payment to the entitlement amount; and (*b*) is more than 7.5%, but less than 25%, of the standard lifetime allowance for the tax year in which the sum is paid. For the purposes of this reportable event, "the entitlement amount" is— (*I*) the amount crystallised by reason of the member becoming entitled to the pension with which the lump sum payment is associated, or (*ii*) where a benefit crystallisation event did not occur by reason of the member becoming entitled to the pension with which the lump sum payment is associated, the amount that would have been so crystallised if the member had been under the age of 75 at the date the entitlement arose.][4]	The name . . . [3] and national insurance number of the member, together with— (*a*) the amount and date of payment of the lump sum; and (*b*)[the entitlement amount][4]
8 Pension commencement lump sum: primary and enhanced protection provisions of Schedule 36	

Reportable event	Information
The scheme makes a pension commencement lump sum payment to a member and the amount of the payment is an authorised payment by reason only of the application of paragraphs 24 to 30 of Schedule 36.	The name . . .[3] and national insurance number of the member, the amount and date of the payment, and the reference number given to the member by the Commissioners under the Registered Pension Schemes (Enhanced Lifetime Allowance) Regulations 2006.
[8A Stand-alone lump sum	
The scheme makes a stand-alone lump sum payment to a member where—	(*a*) The name . . . [3] and national insurance number of the member;
[(*a*) circumstance A in article 25B(2) of the Taxation of Pension Schemes (Transitional Provisions) Order 2006 ("the 2006 Order") is met,	(*b*) the amount and date of payment of the lump sum; and
(*b*) circumstance B in article 25B(3) of the 2006 Order is met; or	(*c*) the reference number, if any, given by the Commissioners under the Registered Pension Schemes (Enhanced Lifetime Allowance) Regulations 2006.][1]
(*c*) circumstance C in article 25B(4) of the 2006 Order is met and the payment is more than 7.5% of the standard lifetime allowance for the tax year in which the sum is paid.][2]	

9 Transfers to qualifying recognised overseas pension schemes

Reportable event	*Information*
The scheme makes a recognised transfer to a qualifying recognised overseas pension scheme [("QROPS")][6] which is not a registered pension scheme.	[The name and national insurance number of the member, together with—][3] [(*a*) the member's principal residential address and, where that address is not in the United Kingdom, the member's last principal residential address in the United Kingdom; [(*aa*) if the member is no longer resident in the United Kingdom, the date that the residence ceased;][7] (*b*) the member's date of birth; (*c*) the member's telephone number, if any, which the member has provided to the scheme administrator for use by the Commissioners in relation to the scheme; (*d*) the acknowledgement mentioned in regulation 11BA(2)(*b*); (*e*) the date of the recognised transfer; (*f*) in the case of a transfer of sums, the amount of the sums; (*g*) in the case of a transfer of assets, a description and valuation of each type of asset transferred including the value of any unquoted shares, quoted shares and real property; [(*ga*) whether or not overseas transfer charge arises on the transfer; (*gb*) if the transfer is excluded from the charge, the reason why it is excluded; (*gc*) if the charge arises on the transfer— (i) the transferred value, and (ii) the amount in respect of the charge deducted from the transfer;][16] (*h*) the name and address of the QROPS to which the sums or assets have been transferred; [(*ha*) the reference number, if any, given by the Commissioners for the QROPS;][16] (*I*) the country or territory under the law of which the QROPS is established and regulated; and (*j*) the name, address, business telephone number and, where available, the electronic mail address of the manager of the QROPS.][6]
[10 Investment-regulated pension scheme	
The scheme becomes, or ceases to be, an investment-regulated pension scheme.	(*a*) The date on which the scheme becomes, or ceases to be, an investment-regulated pension scheme; and *b*) whether all the investments held by the scheme comprise contracts or policies of insurance.][1]
11 Changes in scheme rules	
The scheme changes its rules to— (*a*) entitle any person to require the making of unauthorised payments; or (*b*) permit investment other than in [contracts or][1] policies of insurance.	The fact of the change and the date on which the change takes effect.
12 Changes to rules of pre-commencement scheme treated as more than one scheme	

Reportable event	*Information*
The scheme, being one which immediately before 6th April 2006 was treated in accordance with section 611 of ICTA as two or more separate schemes, changes its rules in any way.	The fact of the change and the date on which the change takes effect.
13 Change in legal structure of scheme	
The legal structure of the scheme changes from one of the following categories to another.	The date on which the change took effect, together with—
The categories are—	(*a*) the new category listed in column 1 which applies to the scheme; and
(*a*) a single trust under which all of the assets are held for the benefit of all members of the scheme [and which does not fall within category (*d*)][12];	(*b*) in the case of a change falling within category (*f*), a brief description of the nature of the new category of legal structure of the scheme.
(b) an overall trust within which there are individual trusts applying for the benefit of each member;[1]	
(c) an overall trust within which specific assets are held as, or within, sub-funds for each member;[1]	
[(*d*) a single trust under which all of the assets are held for the benefit of all members of the scheme and which provides benefits only—	
(i) in the event of the death of a member, and	
(ii) in respect of a sum assured under a policy of insurance which becomes payable on the death of that member;][12]	
(*e*) a body corporate; and	
(*f*) other.	
14 Change in number of members	
The number of scheme members falls in a different band at the end of a tax year from that in which it fell at the end of the previous tax year.	The new band applicable to the number of scheme members.
The bands are—	
[(*a*) 0 members;	
(*b*) 1 member;	
(*c*) 2 to 11 members;	
(*d*) 12 to 50 members;	
(*e*) 51 to 10,000 members; and	
(*f*) more than 10,000 members.][13]	
15 ..[4]	
16 . . . [2]	
17 ...[4]	
[18 Scheme chargeable payment	
The scheme is treated as having made a scheme chargeable payment under [...[4],][2] section 185A (income from taxable property) or [section 185F][2] (gains from taxable property).	[The fact that the scheme is to be treated as having made a scheme chargeable payment.][2]][1]
[19 Country or territory of establishment	
The scheme changes the country or territory in which it is established.	The date of the change and the country or territory in which the scheme becomes established][1]
[20 Occupational pension scheme	
The scheme becomes, or ceases to be, an occupational pension scheme.	The fact of the change and the date on which the change takes effect.][1]
[21 *Flexible drawdown arrangements*	

Reportable event	*Information*
Section 165(3A) or 167(2A) applies to an arrangement.	*The name and national insurance number of the member or dependant ("the member") who meets the flexible drawdown conditions together with the total amount of drawdown pension or dependant's drawdown pension ("drawdown pension") paid under the arrangement to the member during the reporting year and the country or territory where the sole or main address of the member was situated on the date—* *(i) the declaration under sections 165(3A)(b) or 167(2A)(b) was made in respect of the arrangement, or* *(ii) if later, the first payment of drawdown pension was made under the arrangement in the reporting year.*[11]][5]
[22 Annual Allowance	
The scheme administrator is required to provide a member with a pension savings statement under regulation 14A(1) [containing the information specified in regulation 14A(2)][14].	The tax year for which the annual allowance was exceeded and the name and national insurance number of the member together with the information specified in regulation 14A(2)(*a*).][8]
[23 Dual annual allowances	
The scheme administrator is required to provide a member with a pension savings statement under regulation 14A(1) containing the information specified in regulation 14A(10).	The tax year for which the statement is provided and the name and national insurance number of the member together with the information specified in regulation 14A(10)(*a*) and (*b*).][14]

[(2) Where an individual provides the scheme administrator of a scheme with written confirmation that the individual does not qualify for a national insurance number, the scheme administrator must—

(*a*) provide the Commissioners with the individual's date of birth and address in order to obtain an alternative number from them, and

(*b*) provide this alternative number in place of the national insurance number (where the national insurance number is required by paragraph (1)).

(2A) Paragraph (2B) applies to any amendment—

(a) delivered on or after 6th April 2011 to an event report delivered before 6th April 2011, and

(*b*) which relates to an individual whose details were included in respect of a reportable event in the event report which is being amended.

(2B) Where paragraph (1) requires the scheme administrator of the scheme to provide the Commissioners with an individual's national insurance number and where the national insurance number is not known to the scheme administrator—

(*a*) paragraph (2) does not apply, and

(*b*) the scheme administrator may provide the date of birth in place of the national insurance number.][3]

(3) For the purposes of reportable event 3 "benefits" does not include a payment—

(*a*) which is reportable as reportable event 1 or reportable event 4; or

(*b*) which falls within paragraph 10 of Schedule 29.

[(4) Subject to paragraph (4A), in the tax year 2006–07 an event report is required by virtue of reportable event 10 where—

(*a*) the scheme is an investment-regulated pension scheme, and

(*b*) the scheme was registered on or after 6th April 2006 and did not state on the application that a member of the scheme, whether alone or with others, is able to control the way in which scheme assets are used to provide pension benefits.][1]

[(4A) Paragraph (4) does not apply to a scheme treated as becoming a registered pension scheme on 6th April 2006 by virtue of paragraph 1(1) of Schedule 36 if the scheme is an investment-regulated pension scheme throughout the tax year.][1]

(5) No event report is required by virtue of reportable event 17—

(*a*) if the same event constitutes reportable event 1; or

(*b*) in respect of the payment of a life cover lump sum.

Here "life cover lump sum" has the same meaning as it has in the paragraph 21A treated as inserted into Part 2 of Schedule 29 by article 8(3) of the Taxation of Pension Schemes (Transitional Provisions) Order 2006.

(6) The event report shall—

(*a*) be in a form specified by the Commissioners, and

(*b*) be delivered (subject to the qualification in [paragraph 7 and][6] regulation 4(3)) at any time which falls—

(i) after the end of the end of the tax year to which the report relates, but

(ii) no later than the 31st January following the tax year to which the report relates.

[(7) An event report in respect of reportable event 9 must be delivered within 60 days beginning with the day of the transfer to which it relates [but, if the scheme administrator applies before the end of those 60 days for a repayment of overseas transfer charge on the transfer, the report must be delivered before the administrator applies for the repayment.][16].][6]

Note—See SI 2013/2599 reg 6(1): notwithstanding para (7) above, the period within which the event report referred to in this reg must be delivered ends on 12 December 2013 in any case where—

– the event occurred on or after 6 April 2012 and before 14 October 2013; and

– the requirement to deliver the event report arose only by virtue of the coming into force of SI 2013/2599 regs 7, 8.

Amendments—[1] In para (1), Table amended; and paras (4), (4A) substituted for para (4); by the Registered Pension Schemes (Provision of Information) (Amendment) Regulations, SI 2006/1961 regs 2, 3 with effect from 11 August 2006.

[2] In para (1), Table amended by the Registered Pension Schemes (Provision of Information) (Amendment) Regulations, SI 2008/720 regs 2, 3 with effect from 6 April 2008.

[3] In para (1), Table amended, and para (2) substituted, by the Registered Pension Schemes (Provision of Information) (Amendment) Regulations, SI 2011/301 regs 2, 3 with effect from 6 April 2011.

[4] In para (1), in Table, in entry 1 words substituted; in entry 7, column 1 substituted and in column 2 words in sub-para (*b*) substituted; in entry 9, in second column, word inserted and words substituted; entries 15 and 17 revoked; and in entry 18, in column 1 words revoked; by the Registered Pension Schemes (Provision of Information) (Amendment) (No 2) Regulations SI 2011/1797 reg 4(1), (2), (4)–(8) with effect from 11 August 2011. I

[5] In the Table, in item 6, in first column, para (*a*) substituted and entry I second column substituted and item 21 inserted by the Registered Pension Schemes (Provision of Information) (Amendment) (No 2) Regulations SI 2011/1797 reg 4(3), (9) with effect for the tax year 2012–13 and subsequent years.

[6] In the Table in entry 9, in the first column, abbreviation inserted and in the second column sub-paras substituted; in para 6(*b*), words inserted and para (7) inserted, by the Registered Pension Schemes and Overseas Pension Schemes (Miscellaneous Amendments) Regulations, SI 2012/884 regs 11, 12 with effect in relation to recognised transfers which are requested by the member on or after 6 April 2012.

[7] In the Table in entry 9, in the second column, para (*aa*) inserted by the Registered Pension Schemes (Provision of Information) (Amendment) Regulations, SI 2013/1742 regs 2, 4(1), (3) with effect in relation to recognised transfers which are requested by a member on or after 12 August 2013.

[8] In the Table, entry 22 inserted by the Registered Pension Schemes (Provision of Information) (Amendment) Regulations, SI 2013/1742 regs 2, 4(1), (4) with effect in relation to pension savings statements for pension input periods ending in tax year 2013–14 and subsequent years.

[9] In Table, in item 6, in the first column, in para (*b*)(ii), word at the end revoked, and para (*b*)(iv) and preceding word inserted, and in the second column, in para (*a*), word at the end revoked, and para (*c*) and preceding word inserted, by the Registered Pension Schemes (Provision of Information) (Amendment) Regulations, SI 2013/1742 regs 2, 4(1), (2) with effect for the tax year 2014–15 and subsequent years.

[10] In Table, in item 6, in the first column, para (*a*) revoked, in para (*b*)(iii), word at the end revoked, and para (*b*)(v) and preceding word inserted, and in the second column, in para (*b*), word at the end revoked, and para (*d*) and preceding word inserted, by the Registered Pension Schemes (Provision of Information) (Amendment) Regulations, SI 2014/1843 regs 2, 4 with effect for the tax year 2014–15 and subsequent years.

[11] In Table in para (1), entry for reportable event 21 repealed by the Taxation of Pensions Act 2014 s 1, Sch 1 para 35(1), (2) with effect in relation to reports for the tax year 2015–16 and subsequent tax years.

[12] In Table, in entry 13, first column, words inserted and para (*d*) substituted by the Registered Pension Schemes (Provision of Information) (Amendment) Regulations, SI 2015/606 regs 2, 3(1), (2) with effect in relation to changes in the legal structure of a registered pension scheme which take effect on or after 6 April 2015.

[13] In Table, in entry 14, first column, paras (*a*)–(*e*) substituted by the Registered Pension Schemes (Provision of Information) (Amendment) Regulations, SI 2015/606 regs 2, 3(1), (3) with effect in relation to changes in the number of members of a registered pension scheme on or after 6 April 2015.

[14] In Table, in entry 22, first column, words inserted, and entry 23 inserted, by the Taxation of Pensions Act 2014 s 1, Sch 1 para 90 with effect from 6 April 2015. These amendments are to be treated as having been made by the Commissioners for Revenue and Customs under such of the powers cited in the instrument containing the Regulations as are applicable (Taxation of Pensions Act 2014 Sch 1 para 91).

[15] In Table, in entry 6, first column, para (vi) inserted, in second column, words above para (*a*) inserted, para (*e*) inserted and words in heading substituted, by FA 2016 Sch 4 paras 22, 24 with effect from 15 September 2016. Heading to entry 6 previously read as follows—

"6 Benefit crystallisation events and enhanced lifetime allowance, enhanced protection, fixed protection, fixed protection 2014 or individual protection 2014".

[16] In Table, in entry 9, in second column, paras (*ga*)–(*gc*), (*ha*) inserted, and in para (7) words inserted, by FA 2017 s 10, Sch 4 para 24(1)–(3) with effect in relation to transfers made on or after 9 March 2017.

Note that these amendments are to be treated as made by the HMRC Commissioners under the applicable powers to make regulations conferred by FA 2004 s 251 (FA 2017 Sch 4 para 24(8)).

OTHER INFORMATION REQUIREMENTS

4 Provision of information in respect of a pension scheme which has been wound-up

(1) The person who, immediately before the winding-up of a registered pension scheme, was the scheme administrator shall give notice to the Commissioners of the fact that the scheme has been wound up and the date on which the winding up was concluded.

(2) No notice is required by virtue of paragraph (1) in respect of—

(*a*) an annuity contract or a trust scheme which is treated as a registered pension scheme by virtue of paragraph 1(1)(*d*), or (*f*) of Schedule 36, or article 27 of the Taxation of Pension Schemes (Transitional Provisions) Order 2006 (contracts approved under section 620 or 621 of the Income and Corporation Taxes Act 1988); . . . [1]

(*b*) a former approved superannuation fund within the meaning of paragraph 1(3) of Schedule 36[; . . . [2]

(*c*) an annuity contract which is treated as a registered pension scheme by virtue of section 153(8) other than an annuity contract to which paragraph (2A) applies[; or][2]][1]

[(*d*) an annuity policy which is treated as a registered pension scheme by virtue of article 15(5) of the Pension Schemes (Transfers, Reorganisations and Winding Up) (Transitional Provisions) Order 2006 other than an annuity policy to which paragraph (2A) applies.][2]

[(2A) This paragraph applies to an annuity contract [or annuity policy[2]]—

[(*a*) which has received a recognised transfer (within the meaning of section 169) subsequent to the one which led to—

(i) the annuity contract becoming a registered pension scheme under section 153(8), or

(ii) the annuity policy becoming a registered pension scheme under paragraph 1(1) of Schedule 36 by virtue of article 15(5) of the Pension Schemes (Transfers, Reorganisations and Winding Up) (Transitional Provisions) Order 2006;][2]

(*b*) which has received—

(i) relievable pension contributions as defined in section 188(2), or

(ii) contributions paid by an employer,

where the total of those contributions exceeds £10;

(*c*) where a declaration under section 270(2)(*b*) has been made by the scheme administrator to the Commissioners; or

(*d*) which is an investment-regulated pension scheme which directly or indirectly holds an interest in taxable property.

Here "taxable property" has the same meaning as in Part 2 of Schedule 29A and whether an interest in taxable property is held directly or indirectly shall be determined in accordance with Part 3 of that Schedule.][1]

(3) Where a pension scheme is wound up, the time prescribed in respect of any information required to be delivered under these Regulations (whether in the event report or otherwise) is any time on or before—

(*a*) the last day of the period of 3 months beginning with the day on which the winding up is completed, or

(*b*) the last day otherwise prescribed by these Regulations for the provision of that information,

whichever is the earlier.

Amendments—[1] Word in para (2)(*a*) revoked, and para (2)(*c*) and preceding word "or", and whole of para (2A), inserted by the Registered Pension Schemes (Provision of Information) (Amendment) Regulations, SI 2008/720 regs 2, 4 with effect from 6 April 2008.

[2] In para (2), word "or" at end of sub-para (*b*) revoked, sub-para (*d*) and preceding word "or" inserted, and in para (2A) words inserted and sub-para (*a*) substituted, by the Registered Pension Schemes (Provision of Information) (Amendment) Regulations, 2010/581 regs 2, 3 with effect from 6 April 2010.

5 Provision of information by employer company to the Commissioners

(1) Where a registered pension scheme makes an unauthorised employer payment to a company, the company shall provide the information specified in paragraph (2).

(2) The information required is—

(*a*) details of the scheme that made the payment;

(*b*) the nature of the payment;

(*c*) the amount of the payment; and

(*d*) the date on which the payment was made.

(3) This information shall be provided to the Commissioners no later than the 31st January following the tax year in which the payment is made.

5A [Unauthorised borrowing: Provision of information by scheme administrator to the Commissioners

(1) Where a registered pension scheme is treated as having made a scheme chargeable payment ("the payment") by virtue of sections 183 (effect of unauthorised borrowing: money purchase arrangements) or 185 (effect of unauthorised borrowing: other arrangements), the scheme administrator shall provide the information specified in paragraph (2).

(2) The information required is—

(*a*) the name and pension scheme tax reference number of the scheme that is treated as making the payment;

(*b*) the name and address of the scheme administrator;

(*c*) the tax year in which the payment is treated as having been made; and (*d*) the aggregate amount of payments treated as having been made by the scheme during that tax year.

(3) This information shall be provided to the Commissioners in an annual written report delivered at any time which falls—

(*a*) after the end of the tax year in which the payment is treated as having been made, but

(*b*) no later than the 31st January following that tax year.".

Amendments—Reg 5A inserted by the Registered Pension Schemes (Provision of Information) (Amendment) Regulations, 2010/581 regs 2, 4 with effect from 6 April 2010.

5B ***Minimum income requirement: provision of information by scheme administrator to the Commissioners for the tax year 2011–12***

Amendments—Reg 5B repealed by the Taxation of Pensions Act 2014 s 1, Sch 1 para 35(1), (3) with effect from 6 April 2015 but without prejudice to the continued operation of the revoked provisions in relation to reports for the tax year 2011–12.

6 Scheme administration

The person who has been, but has ceased to be, the scheme administrator must notify the Commissioners of the termination of his appointment, together with the date on which the termination took effect, within 30 days.

7 Percentage of standard lifetime allowance expended on the happening of a benefit crystallisation event

(1) The percentage of standard lifetime allowance expended on the happening of each relevant benefit crystallisation event for the purposes of the provisions listed in paragraph (3) is found by the application of the formula—

$$\frac{AE}{RSLA} \times \frac{100}{1}$$

Here—

AE is the amount of lifetime allowance expended on the happening of the benefit crystallisation event; and

RSLA is the relevant standard lifetime allowance at the time of that event.

(2) The amount of lifetime allowance expended on the happening of a benefit crystallisation event is the sum of *AC* and *SFTP*.

Here—

AC is the amount crystallised by the benefit crystallisation event; and

SFTP is the amount covered by a scheme-funded tax payment (within the meaning of section 215) in relation to that benefit crystallisation event.

(3) The provisions to which this paragraph applies are—

(*a*) regulation 8(2)[, (2A)[,][1] (2B)][2] and (3);

(*b*) regulation 9(2);

(*c*) regulation 14(3);

(*d*) regulation 15(2);

(*e*) regulation 16(2) and (3);

(*f*) regulation 17(2), (3) (5) and (7).

(4) The total percentage of standard lifetime allowance expended in relation to a member is the sum of the percentages found in accordance with paragraph (1) in respect of benefit crystallisation events in respect of the member.

Amendments—[1] In para (3)(*a*), words inserted by the Registered Pension Schemes (Provision of Information) (Amendment) Regulations, SI 2015/606 regs 2, 4 with effect in relation to the tax year 2015–16 and subsequent years.

[2] In para (3)(*a*), words inserted by the Registered Pension Schemes (Provision of Information) (Amendment No 2) Regulations, SI 2015/1455 regs 2, 3 with effect in relation to the tax year 2015–16 and subsequent years.

8 Death: provision of information by scheme administrator to personal representatives

(1) The scheme administrator of a registered pension scheme shall provide to the personal representatives . . .[1] of a deceased member of that scheme, the information specified in paragraphs (2)[, (2A)[,][2] (2B)][3] and (3).

(2) The information is the percentage of standard lifetime allowance expended by, and the amount and the date of payment of, a relevant lump sum death benefit by the scheme in relation to the member.

[(2A) The information is the percentage of standard lifetime allowance expended, the amount designated and the date of designation where benefit crystallisation event 5C (designation of relevant unused uncrystallised funds) occurs in relation to the member.

The information shall be provided no later than the last day of the period of 3 months beginning with the day on which the designation is made.][2]

The information shall be provided no later than the last day of the period of 3 months beginning with the day on which the final such payment is made.

[(2B) The information is the percentage of the standard lifetime allowance expended, the aggregate of the amount of such of the sums and the market value of such of the assets applied to the purchase of the annuity as are relevant unused uncrystallised funds, and the date on which the person became entitled to the annuity where benefit crystallisation event 5D (entitlement to a dependants' annuity or nominees' annuity) occurs in relation to the member.

The information shall be provided no later than the last day of the period of 3 months beginning with the day on which the person became entitled to the annuity.][3]

The information shall be provided no later than the last day of the period of 3 months beginning with the day on which the final such payment is made.

(3) The information is the total percentage of standard lifetime allowance expended, at the date of the statement, by—

(*a*) any benefit crystallisation event in respect of the deceased member's rights under the scheme to the extent that—

(i) the sums or assets subject to any such event; and

(ii) any sums or assets subsequently representing those sums or assets;

have not been transferred to another registered pension scheme, and

(*b*) where sums or assets have been transferred to the scheme from another registered pension scheme (whether directly or indirectly) in respect of the deceased member any benefit crystallisation event in connection with—

(i) those sums or assets; and

(ii) any other sums or assets held prior to the transfer which the sums and assets mentioned in sub-paragraph (i) represented,

but excluding from that percentage any amount in respect of any relevant lump sum death benefit payment in respect of the deceased member [and any amount in respect of a designation referred to in paragraph (2A)][2] [and any aggregate amount in respect of an entitlement referred to in paragraph (2B)][3].

The information shall be provided no later than the last day of the period of 2 months beginning with the day on which a request for it is received from the member's personal representatives.

Amendments—[1] In para (1), words revoked by the Registered Pension Schemes (Provision of Information) (Amendment) Regulations, SI 2008/720 regs 2, 5 with effect from 6 April 2008.

[2] Words inserted in paras (1), (3), and para (2A) inserted by the Registered Pension Schemes (Provision of Information) (Amendment) Regulations, SI 2015/606 regs 2, 5 with effect in relation to the tax year 2015–16 and subsequent years.

[3] Words inserted in paras (1), (3), and para (2B) inserted by the Registered Pension Schemes (Provision of Information) (Amendment No 2) Regulations, SI 2015/1455 regs 2, 4 with effect in relation to the tax year 2015–16 and subsequent years.

9 Death: provision of information by insurance company to personal representatives

(1) Where—

(*a*) an insurance company has paid a lifetime annuity or a scheme pension to an individual who has been a member of a registered pension scheme purchased with sums or assets held for the purposes of that scheme, and

(*b*) the member to whom that annuity or pension was payable has died,

the insurance company shall, on request by the member's personal representatives, provide them with the information specified in paragraph (2).

(2) The information is the total percentage of standard lifetime allowance expended, at the date of the statement, by—

(*a*) any benefit crystallisation event in respect of the deceased member under the registered pension scheme to the extent that—

(i) the sums and assets subject to that event, or

(ii) sums and assets subsequently representing those sums and assets,

have not been transferred to another such scheme, and

(*b*) where sums or assets have been transferred to the scheme from another registered pension scheme (whether directly or indirectly) in respect of the deceased member's rights, any benefit crystallisation event in connection with—

(i) those sums or assets; and

(ii) any other sums or assets held prior to the transfer which the sums or assets mentioned in sub-paragraph (i) represented.

(3) The information shall be provided no later than the last day of the period of 2 months beginning with the day on which the request was received.

10 Death: provision of information by personal representatives to the Commissioners

(1) Where—

(*a*) a relevant lump sum death benefit is paid in respect of a deceased member of a registered pension scheme, and (*b*) that payment, of itself or together with any other relevant lump sum death benefit [or any benefit crystallisation event 5C][1] [or 5D][2], results in a lifetime allowance charge,

[(1A) Where—

(*a*) benefit crystallisation event 5C (designation of relevant unused uncrystallised funds) occurs in respect of a deceased member of a registered pension scheme, and

(*b*) that designation, of itself, or together with any other benefit crystallisation event 5C or any [benefit crystallisation event 5D or 7][2] results in a lifetime allowance charge,

the personal representatives of the member shall provide to the Commissioners the information specified in paragraph (2A).][1]

the personal representatives of the member shall provide to the Commissioners the information specified in paragraph (2).

[(1B) Where—

(*a*) benefit crystallisation event 5D (entitlement to a dependants' annuity or nominees' annuity) occurs in respect of a deceased member of a registered pension scheme, and

(*b*) that entitlement, of itself, or together with any other benefit crystallisation event 5D or any benefit crystallisation event 5C or 7 results in a lifetime allowance charge,

the personal representatives of the member shall provide to the Commissioners the information specified in paragraph (2B).][2]

the personal representatives of the member shall provide to the Commissioners the information specified in paragraph (2).

(2) The information required is—

(*a*) the name of the pension scheme from which, and the name and address of the scheme administrator by whom, the benefits were paid;

(*b*) the name of the deceased member in respect of whom the benefits were paid;

(*c*) the amount and date of payment of the benefits; and

(*d*) the chargeable amount in respect of which a lifetime allowance charge is payable by virtue of the payments.

(2A) The information required is—

(*a*) the name of the pension scheme from which, and the name and address of the scheme administrator by whom, the benefits were paid;

(*b*) the name of the deceased member in respect of whom the benefits were paid;

(*c*) the amount and date of payment of the benefits; and

(*d*) the chargeable amount in respect of which a lifetime allowance charge is payable by virtue of the payments.

[(2B) The information required is—

(*a*) the name of the pension scheme which held the relevant unused uncrystallised funds and the name and address of the scheme administrator of that scheme;

(*b*) the name of the deceased member whose relevant unused uncrystallised funds were used to purchase the dependants' annuity or the nominees' annuity;

(*c*) the aggregate of the amount of such of the sums and the market value of such of the assets applied to the purchase of the annuity as are relevant unused uncrystallised funds;

(*d*) the date on which the dependant or the nominee (as the case may be) became entitled to the annuity; and

(*e*) the chargeable amount in respect of which a lifetime allowance charge is payable by virtue of the dependant or the nominee (as the case may be) becoming entitled to the annuity.][2]

(3) The information required shall be provided on or before the later of—

(*a*) the end of the period of 13 months beginning with the death of the member; or

(*b*) the end of the period of 30 days beginning with the date on which the personal representatives (or any of them) became aware that paragraph (1)[, (1A) or (1B),][2] applied to the deceased member.

(4) Where a requirement to provide information under this regulation arises after the period specified in paragraph (3) has expired, the information shall be provided no later than the last day of the period of 30 months beginning with the death of the member.

(5) If the personal representatives discover after the latest date for providing information under paragraph (4) any information required to be provided under paragraph (1)[, (1A) or (1B),][2], that information shall be provided no later than the last day of the period of 3 months beginning with the discovery of that information.

Amendments—[1] In paras (1)(*b*), (3)(*b*), (5), words inserted, and paras (1A), (2A) inserted by the Registered Pension Schemes (Provision of Information) (Amendment) Regulations, SI 2015/606 regs 2, 6 with effect in relation to the tax year 2015–16 and subsequent years.

[2] Words in para (1)(*b*) inserted, paras (1B), (2B) inserted, and words in paras (1A)(*b*), (3)(*b*), (5) substituted by the Registered Pension Schemes (Provision of Information) (Amendment No 2) Regulations, SI 2015/1455 regs 2, 5 with effect in relation to the tax year 2015–16 and subsequent years.

[10A Death: provision of information by scheme administrator to trustee

(1) Where—

(*a*) a registered pension scheme makes a payment of a sum on whose payment tax has been charged under section 206, and

(*b*) the payment is made to a trustee who is not a bare trustee,

the scheme administrator shall provide to the trustee the information specified in paragraph (2).

(2) The information required is—

(*a*) the amount of the lump sum death benefit on which tax has been charged under section 206,

(*b*) the amount of that tax charge,

(*c*) the name and pension scheme tax reference number of the registered pension scheme making the payment, and

(*d*) the name, date of birth and date of death of the member of the registered pension scheme in respect of whom the lump sum death benefit is paid.

(3) The scheme administrator shall provide the information specified in paragraph (2) to the trustee before—

(*a*) the end of 30 days beginning with the date of the payment to the trustee, or

(*b*) if later, the end of 8th March 2017.

(4) In paragraph (1) "bare trustee" has the meaning given by section 206(10).][1]

Amendments—[1] Regulations 10A, 10B inserted by the Registered Pension Schemes (Provision of Information) (Amendment) Regulations, SI 2017/11, regs 2, 3 with effect in relation to—

(a) payments of lump sum death benefits made by registered pension schemes to trustees on or after 6 April 2016; and

(b) payments made by trustees to beneficiaries out of sums to which sub-para (a) above applies.

[10B Death: provision of information by trustee to beneficiary

(1) Where—

(*a*) a trustee who is not a bare trustee makes a payment out of a sum on whose payment tax has been charged under section 206, and

(*b*) the payment is made out of a settlement to a beneficiary who is an individual,

the trustee shall provide to the beneficiary the information specified in paragraph (2).

(2) The information required is—

(*a*) the total of—

(i) the sum paid to the beneficiary, and

(ii) the amount of tax that has been charged in respect of that sum under section 206,

(*b*) the amount of tax that has been charged under section 206 in respect of the sum paid to the beneficiary,

(*c*) the name and pension scheme tax reference number of the registered pension scheme which paid the lump sum death benefit, and

(*d*) the name, date of birth and date of death of the member of the registered pension scheme in respect of whom the lump sum death benefit was paid.

(3) The trustee shall provide the information specified in paragraph (2) to the beneficiary before the latest of the following—

(*a*) the end of 30 days beginning with the date of the payment to the beneficiary,

(*b*) the end of 30 days beginning with the date of the receipt by the trustee of the information required to be provided by the scheme administrator under regulation 10A, and

(*c*) the end of 8th March 2017.

(4) In paragraph (1) "bare trustee" has the meaning given by section 206(10).][1]

Amendments—[1] Regulations 10A, 10B inserted by the Registered Pension Schemes (Provision of Information) (Amendment) Regulations, SI 2017/11, regs 2, 3 with effect in relation to—

(a) payments of lump sum death benefits made by registered pension schemes to trustees on or after 6 April 2016; and

(b) payments made by trustees to beneficiaries out of sums to which sub-para (a) above applies.

11 [Information provided by member to scheme administrator: enhanced lifetime allowance, enhanced protection[, fixed protection[, fixed protection 2014[,] individual protection 2014]][, fixed protection 2016 or individual protection 2016]

[(1)] [1] If the member of a registered pension scheme intends to rely on entitlement to—

(*a*) an enhanced lifetime allowance or enhanced protection by virtue of any provisions listed in section 256(1)(1), . . . [2]

(*b*) fixed protection by virtue of paragraph 14 of Schedule 18 to the Finance Act 2011, ...[4]

(*c*) fixed protection 2014 by virtue of Part 1 of Schedule 22 to the Finance Act 2013][2][, or

(*d*) fixed protection 2016 by virtue of Part 1 of Schedule 4 to the Finance Act 2016,][4]

the member must give to the scheme administrator the reference number issued by [or on behalf of][4] the Commissioners under the Registered Pension Schemes (Enhanced Lifetime Allowance) Regulations 2006 or the Registered Pension Schemes (Lifetime Allowance Transitional Protection) Regulations 2011 [or the Registered Pension Schemes and Relieved Non-UK Pension Schemes (Lifetime Allowance Transitional Protection) (Notification) Regulations 2013][2] [or Schedule 4 to the Finance Act 2016][4] in respect of that entitlement.

[(2) If the member of a registered pension scheme intends to rely on entitlement to individual protection 2014 by virtue of Part 1 of Schedule 6 to the Finance Act 2014 ("Part 1"), the member must notify the scheme administrator of—

(*a*) the reference number issued by the Commissioners under the Registered Pension Schemes and Relieved Non-UK Pension Schemes (Lifetime Allowance Transitional Protection) (Individual Protection 2014 Notification) Regulations 2014; and

(*b*) the member's relevant amount calculated in accordance with Part 1.][3]

[(3) If the member of a registered pension scheme intends to rely on individual protection 2016 by virtue of Part 2 of Schedule 4 to the Finance Act 2016, the member must notify the scheme administrator of—

(*a*) the reference number in respect of the member issued by or on behalf of the Commissioners for the purposes of paragraph 9(2) of that Schedule, and

(*b*) the member's relevant amount calculated in accordance with Part 2 of that Schedule.][4]][1]

Amendments—[1] Reg 11 substituted by the Registered Pension Schemes (Provision of Information) (Amendment) (No 2) Regulations, SI 2011/1797 regs 2, 6 with effect for the tax year 2012–13 and subsequent years.

[2] In heading words substituted, in para (1)(*a*), word revoked, para (1)(*c*) inserted, and in closing words to para (1), words inserted, by the Registered Pension Schemes (Provision of Information) (Amendment) Regulations, SI 2013/1742 regs 2, 5 with effect for the tax year 2014–15 and subsequent years.

[3] In heading, words substituted, para (1) numbered as such, and para (2) inserted, by the Registered Pension Schemes (Provision of Information) (Amendment) Regulations, SI 2014/1843 regs 2, 5 with effect for the tax year 2014–15 and subsequent years.

[4] In heading, comma substituted for word "or" and words inserted, para (1)(*d*) and preceding word inserted, in para (1), in closing words, words inserted, and para (3) inserted, by FA 2016 Sch 4 paras 22, 25 with effect from 15 September 2016.

11A [Information provided by members to scheme administrators: recycling of lump sums

Where a registered pension scheme is treated as making to a member of the scheme an unauthorised payment under paragraph 3A of Schedule 29 (recycling of lump sums), the member shall notify—

(*a*) the date on which the unauthorised payment is treated as made, and

(*b*) the amount of the payment,

to the scheme administrator within 30 days of the date on which the unauthorised payment is treated as made.][1]

Amendments—[1] Regulations 11A, 11B inserted by the Registered Pension Schemes (Provision of Information) (Amendment) Regulations, SI 2006/1961 regs 2, 4 with effect from 11 August 2006.

11B [Information provided by members to scheme administrators: pension commencement lump sums

Where—

(*a*) a registered pension scheme intends to pay a pension commencement lump sum to a member of the scheme,

(*b*) paragraph 2(5)(*a*) of Schedule 29 (available portion of the member's lump sum allowance) applies to determine the permitted maximum, and

(*c*) a benefit crystallisation event has occurred previously in relation to the member in respect of a scheme pension that crystallised under a money purchase arrangement,

the member shall provide such information as will enable the scheme administrator to calculate the available portion of the member's lump sum allowance.][1]

Amendments—[1] Regulations 11A, 11B inserted by the Registered Pension Schemes (Provision of Information) (Amendment) Regulations, SI 2006/1961 regs 2, 4 with effect from 11 August 2006.

11BA [Information provided by members to scheme administrators: recognised transfers

(1) Paragraph (2) applies where a member of a registered pension scheme makes a request to the scheme administrator to make a recognised transfer ("transfer request") in respect of a qualifying recognised overseas pension scheme.

(2) The member must provide to the scheme administrator—

(*a*) the member's—

(i) name;

(ii) date of birth;

(iii) principal residential address and, where that address is not in the United Kingdom, the member's last principal residential address in the United Kingdom;

[(iiia) if the member is no longer resident in the United Kingdom, the date that the residence ceased;][2]

(iv) national insurance number or, where applicable, confirmation in writing that the member does not qualify for a national insurance number;

(v) telephone number, if any, which the member provides for use by the scheme administrator or the Commissioners in relation to the scheme.

(vi), (vii) . . .[3]

[(*aa*) the name and address of, and (if known) the reference number given by the Commissioners for, the qualifying recognised overseas pension scheme ("the QROPS");

(*ab*) the country or territory under the law of which the QROPS is established and regulated;

(*ac*) whether the member knows for certain that the transfer would be excluded from the overseas transfer charge by one of sections 244D, 244E and 244F, and if the member does know that for certain—

(i) the section concerned (if known),

(ii) the name and address of the member's employer whose connection with the QROPS gives rise to exclusion of the transfer from the charge,

(iii) the member's job title as an employee of that employer,

(iv) the date the member's employment with that employer began, and

(v) if known, that employer's tax reference for that employment;][3]

(*b*) the member's acknowledgement in writing that the member is aware that a transfer other than a recognised transfer to a qualifying recognised overseas pension scheme of sums or assets held for the purposes of, or representing accrued rights under, an arrangement under a registered pension scheme—

(i) gives rise to a liability under section 208 (unauthorised payments charge); and

(ii) may give rise to a liability under section 209 (unauthorised payments surcharge)[; and

(*c*) the member's acknowledgement in writing that the member—

(i) is aware that a recognised transfer to a qualifying recognised overseas pension scheme may give rise to a liability to overseas transfer charge, and

(ii) is aware of the circumstances in which liability arises, in which liability is excluded from the outset and in which liability is excluded only if conditions continue to be met over a period of time.][3]

(3) The information specified in paragraph (2) must be provided within 60 days beginning with the day of the transfer request.

(4) The scheme administrator must send the member notification of the requirements specified in this regulation within 30 days beginning with the day of the transfer request.][1]

Note—See SI 2013/2599 reg 6(2): notwithstanding para (3) above, the period within which the information specified in para (2) must be provided ends on 12 December 2013 in any case where—

– the transfer request was made on or after 6 April 2012 and before 14 October 2013; and

– the requirement to provide the information arose only by virtue of the coming into force of SI 2013/2599 regs 7, 8.

See SI 2013/2599 reg 6(3): notwithstanding para (4) above, the period within which the scheme administrator must send the member notification of the requirements specified in this reg ends on 12 November 2013 in any case where—

– the transfer request was made on or after 6 April 2012 and before 14 October 2013; and

– the requirement to provide the information arose only by virtue of the coming into force of SI 2013/2599 regs 7, 8.

Amendments—[1] Reg 11BA inserted by the Registered Pension Schemes and Overseas Pension Schemes (Miscellaneous Amendments) Regulations, SI 2012/884 regs 11, 13 with effect from 6 April 2012.

[2] Para (2)(*a*)(iiia) inserted by the Registered Pension Schemes (Provision of Information) (Amendment) Regulations, SI 2013/1742 regs 2, 6 with effect in relation to recognised transfers which are requested by the member on or after 12 August 2013.

[3] In para (2): sub-para (*a*)(vi), (vii) revoked; sub-paras (*aa*)–(*ac*) inserted; and sub-para (*c*) and preceding word "and" inserted; by FA 2017 s 10, Sch 4 para 24(1), (4) with effect in relation to requests made on or after 9 March 2017. Para (2)(*a*)(vi), (vii) previously read as follows—

"(vi) the name and address of the qualifying recognised overseas pension scheme;

(vii) the country or territory under the law of which the qualifying recognised overseas pension scheme is established and regulated; and".

Note that these amendments are to be treated as made by the HMRC Commissioners under the applicable powers to make regulations conferred by FA 2004 s 251 (FA 2017 Sch 4 para 24(8)).

[11BB Information provided by members to scheme administrators: overseas transfers

(1) Paragraph (2) applies where—

(*a*) a recognised transfer is made by a registered pension scheme to a qualifying recognised overseas pension scheme, and

(*b*) either—

(i) the overseas transfer charge arises in the case of the transfer, or

(ii) the transfer is required by section 244B or 244C to be initially assumed to be excluded from the overseas transfer charge by that section.

(2) Each time during the relevant period for the transfer that the member—

(*a*) becomes resident in a country or territory, or

(*b*) ceases to be resident in a country or territory,

the member must, within 60 days after the date that happens, inform the scheme administrator of the registered pension scheme that it has happened.

(3) In a case where the 60 days mentioned in paragraph (2) ends with a day earlier than 30 June 2017, paragraph (2) is to be treated as requiring the information to be given no later than 30 June 2017.][1]

Amendments—[1] Reg 11BB inserted by FA 2017 s 10, Sch 4 para 24(1), (5) with effect in relation to transfers made on or after 9 March 2017.

Note that this amendment is to be treated as made by the HMRC Commissioners under the applicable powers to make regulations conferred by FA 2004 s 251 (FA 2017 Sch 4 para 24(8)).

11C [Information provided by individuals to scheme administrator: national insurance number

(1) Paragraph (2) applies where a scheme administrator needs an individual's national insurance number or to obtain an alternative number in respect of an individual in order to complete an event report[, other than an event report in respect of reportable event 9,][2] or a return under section 254.

(2) The individual must provide the scheme administrator with the national insurance number or the information described in paragraph (3), as appropriate, within 60 days of the date on which the scheme administrator requests the individual to provide the information.

(3) If the individual does not qualify for a national insurance number the individual must provide the scheme administrator with confirmation of this in writing, together with the individual's date of birth and address.][1]

Amendments—[1] Reg 11C inserted by the Registered Pension Schemes (Provision of Information) (Amendment) Regulations, SI 2011/301 regs 2, 4 with effect from 6 April 2011.

[2] In para (1), words inserted by the Registered Pension Schemes and Overseas Pension Schemes (miscellaneous Amendments) Regulations, SI 2012/884, regs 11, 14 with effect from 6 April 2012.

12 Information about scheme administrator's liability for a lifetime allowance charge

If the scheme administrator of a registered pension scheme has made or intends to make a payment, on account of his liability to account for tax in respect of a lifetime allowance charge on a benefit crystallisation event, the scheme administrator shall within 3 months after the benefit crystallisation event provide the member with a notice stating—

(*a*) the chargeable amount in respect of the benefit crystallisation event;
(*b*) how that chargeable amount has been calculated;
(*c*) the amount of the resulting charge to tax; and
(*d*) whether the scheme administrator has accounted for the tax or intends to do so.

[12A Provision of information about liability for overseas transfer charge

(1) If a recognised transfer is made by a registered pension scheme to a qualifying recognised overseas pension scheme and the overseas transfer charge arises on the transfer, the scheme administrator of the registered pension scheme must within 90 days after the date of the transfer provide the member with a notice stating—

(*a*) the date of the transfer,
(*b*) that overseas transfer charge arises on the transfer,
(*c*) the transferred value of the transfer,
(*d*) the amount of the charge on the transfer,
(*e*) whether, and to what extent, the scheme administrator has accounted, or intends to account, for the charge, and
(*f*) where the scheme administrator has accounted for the charge, the date the scheme administrator did so.

(2) If a recognised transfer is made by a registered pension scheme to a qualifying recognised overseas pension scheme and the transfer is excluded from the overseas transfer charge by or under sections 244B to 244H, the scheme administrator of the registered pension scheme must within 90 days after the date of the transfer provide the member with a notice stating—

(*a*) the date of the transfer,
(*b*) that the transfer is excluded from the overseas transfer charge,
(*c*) the provision by reason of which the transfer is excluded, and
(*d*) where that provision is section 244B or 244C, how the transfer may turn out not to be excluded as a result of the member changing country or territory of residence within the relevant period for the transfer.

(3) If overseas transfer charge on a transfer is repaid to the scheme administrator of a registered pension scheme, the scheme administrator must within 90 days after the date of the repayment provide the member with a notice stating—

(*a*) the date of the repayment,
(*b*) the amount of the repayment, and
(*c*) the reason for the repayment.][1]

Amendments—[1] Reg 12A inserted by FA 2017 s 10, Sch 4 para 24(1), (6) with effect in relation to transfers made on or after 9 March 2017.

Note that this amendment is to be treated as made by the HMRC Commissioners under the applicable powers to make regulations conferred by FA 2004 s 251 (FA 2017 Sch 4 para 24(8)).

13 Provision of information about unauthorised payments

(1) Where a registered pension scheme has made to a member of the scheme an unauthorised payment under section 173(1) (provision of benefits), the scheme administrator shall provide to the member before 7th July following the tax year in which the payment is made the information specified in paragraph (2).

(2) The information is—

(*a*) the nature of the benefit provided;

(*b*) the amount of the unauthorised payment which is treated as being made by the provision of the benefit; and

(*c*) the date on which the benefit was provided.

14 Information provided to members by scheme administrators about benefit crystallisation events

(1) The scheme administrator shall provide a statement containing the information in paragraph (3) to each member of the scheme [or, if the member has died, the member's personal representatives[1]]—

(*a*) who has an actual (as opposed to prospective) entitlement to be paid a pension, at least once in each tax year, or

(*b*) in respect of whom a benefit crystallisation event has occurred, within 3 months of that event.

This paragraph is subject to the following qualification.

(2) No obligation to provide a statement arises—

(*a*) under paragraph (1) if a statement is required to be provided under regulation [16, 17 or 17A][1] containing the same information as is required by paragraph (3);

(*b*) under paragraph (1)(*a*) in relation to a relevant existing pension (within the meaning of paragraph 10(2) of Schedule 36) to which an individual has an actual (as opposed to prospective) entitlement to be paid a pension on 5th April 2006;

[(*ba*) under paragraph (1)(*a*) in a tax year following the tax year in which the member reaches the age of 75;][2]

(*c*) under paragraph (1)(*b*) if a statement is required to be provided under paragraph (1)(*a*) or under regulation 8(2[, (2A) or (2B)][4].

(3) The information is the percentage of standard lifetime allowance expended by—

(*a*) benefit crystallisation events in respect of the scheme, to the extent that the sums or assets subject to any such event have not been transferred to another registered pension scheme, and

(*b*) where the first-mentioned scheme has received (whether directly or indirectly) a transfer in respect of the member, any benefit crystallisation event, prior to the transfer, in connection with—

(i) the sums or assets represented by the transfer;

(ii) sums and assets replaced by the sums or assets mentioned in paragraph (i).

Amendments—[1] Words in para (1) inserted, and words in para (2)(*a*) substituted, by the Registered Pension Schemes (Provision of Information) (Amendment) Regulations, SI 2008/720 regs 2, 6 with effect from 6 April 2008.

[2] Para 2(*ba*) inserted by the Registered Pension Schemes (Provision of Information) (Amendment) (No 2) Regulations, SI 2011/1797 regs 2, 7 with effect from 11 August 2011.

[3] In para (2)(*c*), words inserted by the Registered Pension Schemes (Provision of Information) (Amendment) Regulations, SI 2015/606 regs 2, 7 with effect in relation to the tax year 2015–16 and subsequent years.

[4] In para (2)(*c*), words substituted by the Registered Pension Schemes (Provision of Information) (Amendment No 2) Regulations, SI 2015/1455 regs 2, 6 with effect in relation to the tax year 2015–16 and subsequent years.

[14ZA Information provided to member by scheme administrator where it appears member may be first flexibly accessing pension rights

(1) If a relevant event (see paragraph (2)) occurs in relation to a member of a registered pension scheme, the scheme administrator—

(*a*) must provide the member with a statement—

(i) stating the date of the relevant event, and

(ii) explaining the matters specified in paragraph (3), and

(*b*) must do so before the end of the 31 days beginning with the date of the relevant event,

but this is subject to paragraph (4).

(2) For the purposes of this regulation—

(*a*) if—

(i) the member has a member's flexi-access drawdown fund in respect of an arrangement under the scheme, and

(ii) the fund came into being as a result of sums or assets being designated on or after 6 April 2015 as available for the payment of drawdown pension, or as a result of the operation of paragraph 8D(2) of Schedule 28,

a relevant event occurs when a qualifying payment is made to the member from the fund,

(*b*) if—

(i) the member has a member's drawdown pension fund in respect of an arrangement under the scheme, and

(ii) the sums and assets that make up the fund become newly-designated funds by the operation of paragraph 8B of Schedule 28,

a relevant event occurs when a qualifying payment is made to the member from the member's flexi-access drawdown fund in respect of the arrangement,

(*c*) a relevant event occurs when an uncrystallised funds pension lump sum is paid to the member by the scheme,

(*d*) if the member is entitled to payment of a lifetime annuity under a flexible annuity contract as defined by section 227G(8), a relevant event occurs when the first payment of the annuity is made,

(*e*) if—

(i) the member is entitled to payment of a scheme pension under a money purchase arrangement under the scheme,

(ii) the member became entitled to the scheme pension on or after 6 April 2015,

(iii) the member became entitled to the scheme pension at a time when fewer than 11 other individuals were entitled to the present payment of a scheme pension, or dependants' scheme pension, under the scheme, and

(iv) the scheme pension is not payable under an annuity contract treated under section 153(8) or (8A) as having become a registered pension scheme,

a relevant event occurs when the first payment of the scheme pension is made, and

(*f*) a relevant event occurs when a stand-alone lump sum is paid on or after 6 April 2015 to the member by the scheme in circumstances where article 25B(2) of the Taxation of Pension Schemes (Transitional Provisions) Order 2006 applies.

(3) The matters mentioned in paragraph (1)(*a*)(ii) are—

(*a*) that a relevant event has occurred in relation to the member and that, as a result, the member has flexibly accessed the member's pension rights (although may have first done so previously),

(*b*) that if in any tax year the total of the pension inputs to money purchase arrangements, and certain hybrid arrangements, relating to the member exceeds £10,000—

(i) there will be an annual allowance tax charge on the excess, and

(ii) the annual allowance for pension inputs to other arrangements relating to the member will be £10,000 less than it would otherwise be, and

(*c*) the duties under regulation 14ZB and the circumstances in which the member will have to comply with them.

(4) The scheme administrator is not required to comply with paragraph (1) in relation to the relevant event if—

(*a*) the scheme administrator has complied with paragraph (1) in respect of an earlier relevant event, or

(*b*) the scheme administrator is, at any time before complying with paragraph (1) in relation to the relevant event, informed—

(i) by the member, or

(ii) by the scheme administrator of another registered pension scheme [or the scheme manager of a qualifying recognised overseas pension scheme or former qualifying recognised overseas pension scheme][2],

that the member flexibly accessed pension rights at a time before the relevant event occurred.

(5) In this regulation, a reference to a qualifying payment from a fund is a reference to—

(*a*) payment of income withdrawal from the fund, or

(*b*) payment of a short-term annuity purchased using sums or assets out of the fund,

but does not include payment at a time when the whole of the fund represents rights attributable to a disqualifying pension credit.

(6) In paragraph (5) "disqualifying pension credit" is to be read in accordance with paragraph 2(3) and (4) of Schedule 29.][1]

Amendments—[1] Regs 14ZA–14ZE inserted by the Taxation of Pensions Act 2014 s 1, Sch 1 paras 86, 87 with effect from 6 April 2015. These amendments are to be treated as having been made by the Commissioners for Revenue and Customs under such of the powers cited in the instrument containing the Regulations as are applicable (Taxation of Pensions Act 2014 Sch 1 para 91).

[2] In para (4)(*b*)(ii), words inserted by the Registered Pension Schemes (Provision of Information) (Amendment No 2) Regulations, SI 2015/1455 regs 2, 7 with effect in relation to the tax year 2015–16 and subsequent years.

[14ZB Passing-on by member of information under regulation 14ZA if active or contributing etc

(1) Paragraphs (3) and (4) apply if—

(*a*) an individual receives a statement under regulation 14ZA from the scheme administrator of a registered pension scheme (the "flexed" registered pension scheme), and
(*b*) on the date of the relevant event concerned, or at any later time, the individual is an accruing member (see paragraph (7)) of the flexed or any other registered pension scheme.

(2) In this regulation—
"the relevant 13-week period" means the period of 91 days beginning with—
(*a*) the date of receipt if the individual is an accruing member of any registered pension scheme on any day in the period—
(i) beginning with the date of the relevant event concerned, and
(ii) ending with the date of receipt, or
(*b*) if not, the first day after the date of receipt when the individual is an accruing member of a registered pension scheme, and
"the intervening period" means the period—
(*a*) beginning with the date of the relevant event concerned, and
(*b*) ending with the first day of the relevant 13-week period.

(3) The individual must before the end of the relevant 13-week period—
(*a*) pass on a copy of the statement, or
(*b*) otherwise give notice—
(i) of receipt of the statement, and
(ii) of the date of the relevant event concerned or (if applicable) of its having occurred more than 2 years before the start of the relevant 13-week period,

to the scheme administrator of each other registered pension scheme of which the individual is an accruing member on any day in the intervening period; but this is subject to paragraph (6).

(4) Where, in the case of a particular registered pension scheme other than the flexed scheme, the individual is not an accruing member of that other scheme on any day in the intervening period but becomes an accruing member of that other scheme on a day ("the activation day") after the last day of that period, the individual must before the end of the 91 days beginning with the activation day—
(*a*) pass on a copy of the statement, or
(*b*) otherwise give notice—
(i) of receipt of the statement, and
(ii) of the date of the relevant event concerned or (if applicable) of its having occurred more than 2 years before the activation day,

to the scheme administrator of that other scheme; but this is subject to paragraphs (5) and (6).

(5) Paragraph (4) does not apply in connection with the individual becoming an accruing member of any particular scheme if the individual becomes an accruing member of that scheme upon or after becoming a member of that scheme as a result of a recognised transfer after the date of the relevant event concerned.

(6) Paragraph (3) or (4), as the case may be, does not require the information concerned to be provided to the scheme administrator of a particular scheme if the individual has complied with regulation 14ZD(3) or (4) or 14ZE(3) or (4), [or has complied with regulation 3AB(2) or (3) of the Pension Schemes (Information Requirements for Qualifying Overseas Pension Schemes, Qualifying Recognised Overseas Pension Schemes and Corresponding Relief) Regulations 2006,][2] or has previously complied with paragraph (3) or (4), in relation to the scheme administrator of that scheme.

(7) For the purposes of this regulation, the individual is an accruing member of a registered pension scheme on any particular day if—
(*a*) the individual is an active member of the scheme on that day as a result of there presently being arrangements for the accrual of benefits to or in respect of the individual under a cash balance arrangement or hybrid arrangement, or
(*b*) a relevant contribution is made under the scheme on that day.

(8) For the purposes of this regulation, a relevant contribution is made under a registered pension scheme if—
(*a*) a relievable pension contribution is paid by or on behalf of the individual under a non-cash-balance money purchase arrangement relating to the individual under the scheme,
(*b*) a contribution is paid in respect of the individual by an employer of the individual under a non-cash-balance money purchase arrangement relating to the individual under the scheme, or
(*c*) a contribution—
(i) paid under the scheme by an employer of the individual, and
(ii) paid otherwise than in respect of any individual,

becomes held for the purposes of a non-cash-balance money purchase arrangement relating to the individual under the scheme;

and in this paragraph "non-cash-balance money purchase arrangement" means a money purchase arrangement other than a cash balance arrangement.][1]

Amendments—[1] Regs 14ZA–14ZE inserted by the Taxation of Pensions Act 2014 s 1, Sch 1 paras 86, 87 with effect from 6 April 2015. These amendments are to be treated as having been made by the Commissioners for Revenue and Customs under such of the powers cited in the instrument containing the Regulations as are applicable (Taxation of Pensions Act 2014 Sch 1 para 91).

[2] In para (6), words inserted by the Registered Pension Schemes (Provision of Information) (Amendment No 2) Regulations, SI 2015/1455 regs 2, 8 with effect in relation to the tax year 2015–16 and subsequent years.

[14ZC Information [provided by] scheme administrators on recognised transfers

(1) Paragraph (2) applies if—

(*a*) in connection with a member of a registered pension scheme ("the transferring scheme"), there is a recognised transfer from the transferring scheme to another registered pension scheme [or a qualifying recognised overseas pension scheme][1] ("the recipient scheme"), and

(*b*) the scheme administrator of the transferring scheme has reason to believe that the member first flexibly accessed pension rights before the transfer.

(2) The scheme administrator of the transferring scheme must provide the scheme administrator [or the scheme manager (as the case may be)][1] of the recipient scheme with a statement—

(*a*) stating that the scheme administrator of the transferring scheme has reason to believe that the member first flexibly accessed pension rights before the transfer, and

(*b*) specifying the date the scheme administrator of the transferring scheme understands to be the date when the member first flexibly accessed pension rights.

(3) The requirement under paragraph (2) is to be complied with before—

(*a*) the end of the 31 days beginning with the date of the transfer, or

(*b*) if later, the end of the 31 days beginning with the date when the scheme administrator of the transferring scheme first has reason for the belief mentioned in paragraph (1)(*b*).

(4) References in this regulation to an individual first flexibly accessing pension rights are to be read in accordance with section 227G.][1]

Amendments—[1] Regs 14ZA–14ZE inserted by the Taxation of Pensions Act 2014 s 1, Sch 1 paras 86, 87 with effect from 6 April 2015. These amendments are to be treated as having been made by the Commissioners for Revenue and Customs under such of the powers cited in the instrument containing the Regulations as are applicable (Taxation of Pensions Act 2014 Sch 1 para 91).

[2] In heading, words substituted, and in paras (1)(*a*), (2), words inserted by the Registered Pension Schemes (Provision of Information) (Amendment) Regulations, SI 2015/606 regs 2, 8 with effect in relation to the tax year 2015–16 and subsequent years.

[14ZCA Further information provided by scheme administrators on recognised transfers to overseas schemes

(1) This regulation applies if there is a recognised transfer from a registered pension scheme to a qualifying recognised overseas pensions scheme.

(2) The scheme administrator of the registered pension scheme must provide the scheme manager of the qualifying recognised overseas pension scheme with a statement—

(*a*) stating whether or not the overseas transfer charge arose on the transfer, and

(*b*) stating—

(i) if the charge arose, the amount of the charge, and

(ii) if the transfer is excluded from the charge, the reason why it is excluded.

(3) The requirement under paragraph (2) is to be complied with before the end of the 31 days beginning with the date of the transfer.

(4) Paragraph (5) applies if overseas transfer charge on the transfer is repaid to the scheme administrator of the registered pension scheme.

(5) The scheme administrator of the registered pension scheme must provide the scheme manager of the qualifying recognised overseas pension scheme with—

(*a*) a copy of the statement under paragraph (2),

(*b*) a statement that the original statement is inaccurate and that the overseas transfer charge on the transfer has been repaid to the scheme administrator, and

(*c*) the reason why the transfer is excluded from the charge.

(6) The requirement under paragraph (5) is to be complied with before the end of the 31 days beginning with the date of the repayment.][1]

Amendments—[1] Reg 14ZCA inserted by FA 2017 s 10, Sch 4 para 24(1), (7) with effect in relation to transfers made on or after 9 March 2017.

Note that this amendment is to be treated as made by the HMRC Commissioners under the applicable powers to make regulations conferred by FA 2004 s 251 (FA 2017 Sch 4 para 24(8)).

[14ZD Individual to whom flexible drawdown arrangements applied before 6 April 2015 must tell other schemes if active or contributing etc

(1) Paragraphs (3) and (4) apply if—

(*a*) at any time before 6 April 2015, section 165(3A) applied to an arrangement relating to an individual under a registered pension scheme (the "flexed" registered pension scheme), and

(*b*) on or after 6 April 2015, the individual is an accruing member (see paragraph (9)) of the flexed or any other registered pension scheme.

(2) In this regulation "the relevant 13-week period" means the period of 91 days beginning with—

(*a*) 6 April 2015 if on that date the individual is an accruing member of any registered pension scheme, or

(*b*) if not, the first day after 6 April 2015 when the individual is an accruing member of a registered pension scheme.

(3) The individual must, before the end of the relevant 13-week period, provide the information specified in paragraph (5) to the scheme administrator of each registered pension scheme of which the individual is an accruing member on the first day of the relevant 13-week period; but this is subject to paragraphs (6) and (8).

(4) Where, in the case of a particular registered pension scheme other than the flexed scheme, the individual is not an accruing member of that other scheme on the first day of the relevant 13-week period but becomes an accruing member of that other scheme on a day ("the activation day") after the first day of that period, the individual must, before the end of the 91 days beginning with the activation day, provide the information specified in paragraph (5) to the scheme administrator of that other scheme; but this is subject to paragraphs (7) and (8).

(5) The information is that, as a result of section 227G(3), the individual is treated for the purposes of sections 227B to 227F as having first flexibly accessed pension rights at the start of 6 April 2015.

(6) Paragraph (3) does not require that information to be provided to the scheme administrator of a particular scheme if, immediately before 6 April 2015, section 165(3A) applied to an arrangement relating to the individual under that scheme.

(7) Paragraph (4) does not require that information to be provided to the scheme administrator of a particular scheme if the individual becomes an accruing member of that scheme upon or after becoming a member of that scheme as a result of a recognised transfer made to the scheme after 6 April 2015.

(8) Paragraph (3) or (4), as the case may be, does not require that information to be provided to the scheme administrator of a particular scheme if the individual has complied with regulation 14ZB(3) or (4) or 14ZE(3) or (4), [or has complied with regulation 3AB(2) or (3) of the Pension Schemes (Information Requirements for Qualifying Overseas Pension Schemes, Qualifying Recognised Overseas Pension Schemes and Corresponding Relief) Regulations 2006,][2] or has previously complied with paragraph (3) or (4), in relation to the scheme administrator of that scheme.

(9) For the purposes of this regulation, the individual is an accruing member of a registered pension scheme on any particular day if—

(*a*) the individual is an active member of the scheme on that day as a result of there presently being arrangements for the accrual of benefits to or in respect of the individual under a cash balance arrangement or hybrid arrangement, or

(*b*) a relevant contribution is made under the scheme on that day.

(10) For the purposes of this regulation, a relevant contribution is made under a registered pension scheme if—

(*a*) a relievable pension contribution is paid by or on behalf of the individual under a non-cash-balance money purchase arrangement relating to the individual under the scheme,

(*b*) a contribution is paid in respect of the individual by an employer of the individual under a non-cash-balance money purchase arrangement relating to the individual under the scheme, or

(*c*) a contribution—

(i) paid under the scheme by an employer of the individual, and

(ii) paid otherwise than in respect of any individual,

becomes held for the purposes of a non-cash-balance money purchase arrangement relating to the individual under the scheme;

and in this paragraph "non-cash-balance money purchase arrangement" means a money purchase arrangement other than a cash balance arrangement.][1]

Amendments—[1] Regs 14ZA–14ZE inserted by the Taxation of Pensions Act 2014 s 1, Sch 1 paras 86, 87 with effect from 6 April 2015. These amendments are to be treated as having been made by the Commissioners for Revenue and Customs under such of the powers cited in the instrument containing the Regulations as are applicable (Taxation of Pensions Act 2014 Sch 1 para 91).

[2] In para (8), words inserted by the Registered Pension Schemes (Provision of Information) (Amendment No 2) Regulations, SI 2015/1455 regs 2, 9 with effect in relation to the tax year 2015–16 and subsequent years.

[14ZE Member to inform other schemes if active or contributing etc and, under paragraph 8C of Schedule 28, drawdown pension fund becomes flexi-access drawdown fund [and is flexibly accessed]

(1) Paragraphs (3) and (4) apply if—

(*a*) under paragraph 8C of Schedule 28, the drawdown pension fund in respect of an arrangement relating to an individual under a registered pension scheme (the "flexed" registered pension scheme) becomes the individual's flexi-access drawdown fund in respect of the arrangement, . . . [2]

[(*b*) the individual accesses that flexi-access drawdown fund, and][2] [(*c*)] [2]on the [date ("first flexi-access date") that the individual first flexibly accesses that flexi-access drawdown fund (the "first flexiaccess")][2], or at any later time, the individual is an accruing member (see paragraph (7)) of the flexed or any other registered pension scheme.

(2) In this regulation "the relevant 13-week period" means the period of 91 days beginning with—

(*a*) the [first flexi-access date][2] if on that date the individual is an accruing member of any registered pension scheme, or

(*b*) if not, the first day after that date when the individual is an accruing member of a registered pension scheme.

(3) The individual must, before the end of the relevant 13-week period, inform the scheme administrator of each other registered pension scheme of which the individual is an accruing member on the first day of the relevant 13-week period—

(*a*) of the conversion, and

(*b*) of the [first flexi-access date][2] or (if applicable) of the [first flexi-access having occurred][2] more than 2 years before the start of the relevant 13-week period;

but this is subject to paragraph (6).

(4) Where, in the case of a particular registered pension scheme other than the flexed scheme, the individual is not an accruing member of that other scheme on the first day of the relevant 13-week period but becomes an accruing member of that other scheme on a day ("the activation day") after the first day of that period, the individual must, before the end of the 91 days beginning with the activation day, inform the scheme administrator of that other scheme—

(*a*) of the conversion, and

(*b*) of the [first flexi-access date][2] or (if applicable) of the [first flexi-access having occurred][2] more than 2 years before the activation day;

but this is subject to paragraphs (5) and (6).

(5) Paragraph (4) does not apply in connection with the individual becoming an accruing member of any particular scheme if the individual becomes an accruing member of that scheme upon or after becoming a member of that scheme as a result of a recognised transfer after the conversion date.

(6) Paragraph (3) or (4), as the case may be, does not require the information concerned to be provided to the scheme administrator of a particular scheme if the individual has complied with regulation 14ZB(3) or (4) or 14ZD(3) or (4), [or has complied with regulation 3AB(2) or (3) of the Pension Schemes (Information Requirements for Qualifying Overseas Pension Schemes, Qualifying Recognised Overseas Pension Schemes and Corresponding Relief) Regulations 2006,][3] or has previously complied with paragraph (3) or (4), in relation to the scheme administrator of that scheme.

(7) For the purposes of this regulation, the individual is an accruing member of a registered pension scheme on any particular day if—

(*a*) the individual is an active member of the scheme on that day as a result of there presently being arrangements for the accrual of benefits to or in respect of the individual under a cash balance arrangement or hybrid arrangement, or

(*b*) a relevant contribution is made under the scheme on that day.

(8) For the purposes of this regulation, a relevant contribution is made under a registered pension scheme if—

(*a*) a relievable pension contribution is paid by or on behalf of the individual under a non-cash-balance money purchase arrangement relating to the individual under the scheme,

(*b*) a contribution is paid in respect of the individual by an employer of the individual under a non-cash-balance money purchase arrangement relating to the individual under the scheme, or

(*c*) a contribution—

(i) paid under the scheme by an employer of the individual, and

(ii) paid otherwise than in respect of any individual,

becomes held for the purposes of a non-cash-balance money purchase arrangement relating to the individual under the scheme;

and in this paragraph "non-cash-balance money purchase arrangement" means a money purchase arrangement other than a cash balance arrangement.][1]

Amendments—[1] Regs 14ZA–14ZE inserted by the Taxation of Pensions Act 2014 s 1, Sch 1 paras 86, 87 with effect from 6 April 2015. These amendments are to be treated as having been made by the Commissioners for Revenue and Customs under such of the powers cited in the instrument containing the Regulations as are applicable (Taxation of Pensions Act 2014 Sch 1 para 91).

[2] In heading words inserted, in para (1)(*a*), word revoked, para (1)(*b*) inserted, para (1)(*c*) renumbered as such, and in paras (1)(*c*), (2)(*a*), (3)(*b*), (4)(*b*), word substituted by the Registered Pension Schemes (Provision of Information) (Amendment) Regulations, SI 2015/606 regs 2, 9 with effect in relation to the tax year 2015–16 and subsequent years.

[3] In para (6), words inserted by the Registered Pension Schemes (Provision of Information) (Amendment No 2) Regulations, SI 2015/1455 regs 2, 10 with effect in relation to the tax year 2015–16 and subsequent years.

14A [Annual allowance: annual provision of information by scheme administrator to member

(1) Where—

(*a*) an individual is a member ("the member") of a registered pension scheme for all or part of a pension input period ending in a tax year ("the relevant pension input period") who meets one of the conditions in paragraph (8), and

(*b*) [either—

(i)][2] the aggregate of the pension input amounts for the relevant pension input period in respect of each arrangement under the registered pension scheme relating to the member exceeds the annual allowance for that tax year, [or

(ii) both of the conditions in paragraph (9) are met,][2]

the scheme administrator must provide the member with a statement containing the information [specified in paragraph (10) if the condition in sub-paragraph (*b*)(ii) is met but otherwise containing the information][2] specified in paragraph (2) (the "pension savings statement").

[(1A) For the tax year 2015-16—

(*a*) for the purposes of this regulation the pre-alignment and post-alignment tax years are treated as a single tax year and references to "tax year", "the relevant tax year" and "the relevant pension input period" shall be construed accordingly,

(*b*) without prejudice to sub-paragraph (*a*), the condition in paragraph (1)(*b*)(i) is satisfied if the aggregate of the pension input amounts for the tax year 2015-16 exceeds £80,000, or the aggregate of the pension input amounts for the post-alignment tax year exceeds £40,000,

(*c*) without prejudice to sub-paragraph (*a*), the information required to be provided pursuant to paragraphs (2)(*a*), (2)(*c*), (10)(*a*), (10)(*b*), (10)(*c*) and (10)(*f*) must be provided separately for the pre-alignment and post-alignment tax years,

(*d*) paragraphs (2)(*b*)[, (10)(*d*) and (10)(*e*)][4] do not apply, [and][4]

(*e*) *the annual allowance for that tax year is excluded from the information required to be provided pursuant to paragraph (2)(d),* . . . [4]

(*f*) . . . [4]

(2) The information is—

(*a*) the aggregate of the pension input amounts for the relevant pension input period in respect of all the arrangements under the registered pension scheme relating to the member (see section 152),

(*b*) the annual allowance for the tax year in which the relevant pension input period ends ("the relevant tax year"),

(*c*) the aggregate of the pension input amounts in respect of all the arrangements under the registered pension scheme relating to the member for each of the pension input periods ending in the three tax years immediately preceding the relevant tax year (subject to paragraph (3)), and

(*d*) the annual allowance for each of the three preceding tax years or where one or more of the three preceding tax years is the 2008–09, 2009–10 or 2010–11 tax year, the assumed annual allowance for that tax year pursuant to paragraph 30(3)(a) of Schedule 17 to the Finance Act 2011.

(3) Where a pension input period in paragraph (2)(c) ends in the 2008–09, 2009–10 or 2010–11 tax year, the pension input amount for that pension input period must be determined on the basis that the assumptions in paragraph 30(3)(b) of Schedule 17 to the Finance Act 2011 apply to that pension input period.

(4) The scheme administrator must provide the member with the pension savings statement no later than the 6th October following the relevant tax year. This paragraph is subject to paragraphs (5) and (6).

(5) Where the relevant tax year is 2011–12, the scheme administrator must provide the member with the pension savings statement for that year no later than 6th October 2013.

(6) Where the scheme administrator has not been provided with the information concerning the member by the member's employer in respect of the relevant pension input period pursuant to regulation 15A, the scheme administrator must provide the pension savings statement—

(*a*) within 3 months following receipt of that information, or

(*b*) if later, on or before the date specified in paragraph (4) or (where the relevant tax year is 2011–12) paragraph (5).

(7) Where—

(*a*) the member meets the conditions in paragraph (1)(*a*) and (*b*), and

(*b*) paragraph 28 of Schedule 17 to the Finance Act 2011 applies (provision for a straddling pension input period),

the scheme administrator must provide the member with a pension savings statement containing the pension input amount in respect of the pre-announcement period and post-announcement period in addition to the information specified in paragraph (2).

(8) The conditions referred to in paragraph [(1)(*a*)][2] are as follows.

Condition A

The individual is an active member of the registered pension scheme referred to in paragraph (1)

Condition B

The individual is a deferred member of the registered pension scheme referred to in paragraph (1) in relation to a cash balance arrangement and the condition in section 230(5B)(*b*) (cash balance arrangements) is not met in respect of the pension input amount for the relevant pension input period.

Condition C

The individual is a deferred member of the registered pension scheme referred to in paragraph (1) in relation to a defined benefits arrangement and the condition in section 234(5B)(*b*) (defined balance arrangements) is not met in respect of the pension input amount for the relevant pension input period.

[(9) The conditions referred to in paragraph (1)(*b*)(ii) are as follows.

Condition D

The scheme administrator has reason to believe that the member has first flexibly accessed pension rights for the purposes of sections 227B to 227F.

Condition E

That the overall total of the following amounts is more than £10,000—

(*a*) for each money purchase arrangement relating to the member under the scheme, the pension input amount for the relevant pension input period in respect of the arrangement, and

(*b*) for each hybrid arrangement relating to the member under the scheme, the greater of such of input amounts A and B mentioned in section 237 as are, for the purposes of section 237, relevant input amounts for the relevant pension input period in the case of the arrangement.

(10) The information is—

(*a*) the total of—

(i) the pension input amounts for the relevant pension input period in respect of each money purchase arrangement relating to the member under the scheme, and

(ii) the pension input amounts for the relevant pension input period in respect of each hybrid arrangement under the scheme—

(*aa*) that relates to the member, and

(*bb*) for which the pension input amount for the relevant pension input period is input amount A or B mentioned in section 237,

(*b*) the total of—

(i) the pension input amounts for the relevant pension input period in respect of each defined benefits arrangement relating to the member under the scheme, and

(ii) the pension input amounts for the relevant pension input period in respect of each hybrid arrangement under the scheme—

(*aa*) that relates to the member,

(*bb*) for which the pension input amount for the relevant pension input period is input amount C mentioned in section 237, and

(*cc*) that is made before 14 October 2014 and has not become a hybrid arrangement (whether or not for the first time) on or after that day,

(*c*) for each hybrid arrangement relating to the member under the scheme—

(i) that is made on or after 14 October 2014 or has become a hybrid arrangement (whether or not for the first time) on or after that day, and

(ii) for which the pension input amount for the relevant pension input period is input amount C mentioned in section 237,

which of input amounts A, B and C mentioned in section 237 is a relevant input amount for the purposes of section 237 for the relevant pension input period in the case of the arrangement, and the amount of each of those input amounts that in the case of the arrangement is a relevant input amount for those purposes for that period,

(*d*) the unadjusted alternative annual allowance for the relevant tax year, and the fact the member's money-purchase input sub-total for the relevant tax year will be tested against a £10,000 allowance,

(*e*) the unadjusted alternative annual allowance for each of the three preceding tax years, and the fact that the member's money-purchase input sub-total for each of those preceding years will be tested against a £10,000 allowance or, if any of those preceding years is earlier than the tax year 2015-16, the annual allowance for each such earlier year, and

(*f*) for each of those three preceding years, the information given in the pension savings statement for the pension input period ending in that year under, as the case may be, sub-paragraphs (*a*) to (*c*) or paragraph (2)(*a*).

(11) If, in the case of a hybrid arrangement, input amount C mentioned in section 237—

(*a*) is a relevant input amount for the purposes of section 237 for the relevant pension input period, and

(*b*) is equal to—

(i) input amount A or B mentioned in section 237 if that is the only other relevant input amount for the purposes of section 237 for that period, or

(ii) the greater of input amounts A and B mentioned in section 237 if both are relevant input amounts for the purposes of section 237 for that period,

the pension input amount in respect of the arrangement for that period is, for the purposes of paragraph (10), treated as being input amount A or B or, as the case may be, the greater of input amounts A and B (and, in either case, not input amount C).

(12) In paragraph (10)(*d*) and (*e*) "the unadjusted alternative annual allowance", in relation to a tax year, means the amount that would be the member's alternative annual allowance under section 227B(2) for that tax year if any increases under section 228A(2) (carry forward of unused allowance from preceding 3 years) [and any reductions under section 228ZA(*c*) (tapered reduction of annual allowance: high-income individual)][4] are ignored.][2]][1]

Amendments—[1] Reg 14A inserted by the Registered Pension Schemes (Provision of Information) (Amendment) (No 2) Regulations, SI 2011/1797 regs 2, 8 with effect from 11 August 2011.

[2] In para (1) words inserted, in para (8) reference substituted for previous reference "(1)", and paras (9)–(12) inserted, by the Taxation of Pensions Act 2014 s 1, Sch 1 para 88 with effect from 6 April 2015. These amendments are to be treated as having been made by the Commissioners for Revenue and Customs under such of the powers cited in the instrument containing the Regulations as are applicable (Taxation of Pensions Act 2014 Sch 1 para 91).

[3] Para (1A) inserted by the Registered Pension Schemes (Provision of Information) (Amendment) Regulations, SI 2016/308 regs 1, 2 with effect from 6 April 2016.

[4] In para (1A)(*d*), words substituted and word inserted, para 1A(*f*) and preceding word revoked, and in para (12), words inserted, by the Registered Pension Schemes (Provision of Information) (Amendment) Regulations, SI 2017/11 regs 2, 4, 5 with effect for the tax year 2016–17 and subsequent years.

14B [Annual allowance: provision of information by scheme administrator to member on request

(1) Where a member or former member ("the member") of a registered pension scheme makes a written request to the scheme administrator of that scheme for any such information in respect of a pension input period ending in a tax year ("the relevant pension input period") as is referred to in [regulation 14A(2), (7) or (10)][2], the scheme administrator must provide the member with the information requested—

(*a*) within 3 months following receipt of the request, or

(*b*) if later, on or before 6th October following the tax year ("the relevant tax year") in which the relevant pension input period ended.

This paragraph is subject to paragraphs (2) and (3).

(2) Where the relevant tax year is 2011–12, the scheme administrator must provide the member with the information requested under paragraph (1) for that tax year no later than 6th October 2013.

(3) Where the scheme administrator has not been provided with the information concerning the member by the member's employer in respect of the relevant pension input period pursuant to regulation 15A ("the regulation 15A information"), the scheme administrator must provide the information requested under paragraph (1)—

(*a*) within 3 months following receipt of the regulation 15A information, or

(*b*) if later, on or before—

(i) 6th October following the relevant tax year, or

(ii) where the relevant tax year is 2011–12, the 6th October 2013.][1]

Amendments—[1] Reg 14B inserted by the Registered Pension Schemes (Provision of Information) (Amendment) (No 2) Regulations, SI 2011/1797 regs 2, 8 with effect from 11 August 2011.

[2] In para (1) words substituted for words "regulations 14A(2) or (7)" by the Taxation of Pensions Act 2014 s 1, Sch 1 para 89 with effect from 6 April 2015. These amendments are to be treated as having been made by the Commissioners for Revenue and Customs under such of the powers cited in the instrument containing the Regulations as are applicable (Taxation of Pensions Act 2014 Sch 1 para 91).

[14C Individual protection 2016: provision of information by scheme administrator to member on request

(1) Where—

(*a*) an individual is a member of a registered pension scheme on 5 April 2016,

(*b*) the individual makes a written request to the scheme administrator for the information mentioned in paragraph (2), and

(*c*) the request is received by the scheme administrator before 6 April 2020,

the scheme administrator must provide the individual with the information within 3 months following receipt of the request.

(2) The information is such information relating to the member's rights under the scheme as is necessary for calculating, in accordance with Part 2 of Schedule 4 to the Finance Act 2016 (individual protection 2016), the member's relevant amount for the purposes of paragraph 9(2) of that Schedule.][1]

Amendments—[1] Reg 14C inserted by FA 2016 Sch 4 paras 22, 26 with effect from 15 September 2016.

15 Information between scheme administrators

(1) This regulation applies if, and to the extent that, a member's crystallised rights under one registered pension scheme ("Scheme A"), are transferred to another such scheme ("Scheme B").

(2) The scheme administrator of Scheme A shall provide to the administrator of Scheme B, within 3 months of the transfer, a statement of the total percentage of the standard lifetime allowance expended, at the date of the statement, by—

(*a*) benefit crystallisation events in respect of Scheme A in connection with the sums and assets represented by the transfer; and

(*b*) where Scheme A has received (whether directly or indirectly) a transfer in respect of the member, any benefit crystallisation event prior to the occurrence of the transfer in connection with—

(i) the sums or assets represented by the transfer; and

(ii) sums and assets replaced by the sums and assets mentioned in paragraph (i).

[15 Information between scheme administrators: transfer of dependant's, nominee's or successor's funds

(1) This regulation applies if and to the extent to which there is a recognised transfer of sums or assets (or both) which represent—

(*a*) a dependant's flexi-access drawdown fund,

(*b*) a nominee's flexi-access drawdown fund,

(*c*) a successor's flexi-access drawdown fund, or

(*d*) a dependant's drawdown pension fund,

in respect of a registered pension scheme ("Scheme A") to another such scheme ("Scheme B").

(2) The scheme administrator of Scheme A shall provide the information specified in paragraph (3) to the scheme administrator of Scheme B within 3 months of the transfer.

(3) The information is—

(*a*) which of the descriptions in paragraphs (1)(*a*) to (*d*) applies to the drawdown fund from which the sums or assets (or both) are transferred,

(*b*) whether a successor has been nominated in respect of that drawdown fund under paragraph 27F of Schedule 28 and the name and address of any individual so nominated,

(*c*) where the sums or assets (or both) transferred represent a dependant's flexi-access drawdown fund, a nominee's flexi-access drawdown fund or a dependant's drawdown pension fund, the age at death of the deceased member,

(*d*) where the sums or assets (or both) transferred represent a successor's flexi-access drawdown fund, the age at death of the immediately preceding dependant, nominee or successor (as the case may be), and

(*e*) where the deceased member referred to in sub-paragraph (*c*), or the immediately preceding dependant, nominee or successor referred to in sub-paragraph (d) died before the age of 75—

(i) confirmation as to whether or not section 579CZA(1) or (2) of ITEPA 2003 (exemption for beneficiaries' income withdrawal in some cases)(b) apply to payments of income withdrawal from the fund from which the sums or assets (or both) are transferred, and

(ii) if section 579CZA(1) or (2) do not apply, confirmation as to which (if any) of section 579CZA(4), (5) or (6) of ITEPA 2003 apply to payments of income withdrawal from that fund.][1]

Amendments—[1] Regulation 15A inserted by the Registered Pension Schemes (Provision of Information) (Amendment) Regulations, SI 2015/606 regs 2, 10 with effect in relation to recognised transfers made on or after 6 April 2015.

15A [Annual allowance: information to be provided to scheme administrators by certain persons

(1) Where—

(*a*) an employer is a sponsoring employer of a registered pension scheme, and

(*b*) an employee of that employer or a director is an active member of that scheme in relation to an arrangement under the scheme ("the arrangement") for all or part of a pension input period ending in a tax year,

the employer must provide to the scheme administrator such information as will enable the scheme administrator to calculate the pension input amount in respect of the arrangement for the pension input period ending in that tax year.

(2) The information must be provided to the scheme administrator no later than the 6th July following the tax year in which the pension input period ends. This paragraph is subject to paragraph (3).

(3) Where the pension input period ends in the tax year 2011–12, the employer must provide the information relating to the pension input period no later than 6th July 2013.

(4) The employer must provide to the scheme administrator such information as will enable the scheme administrator to calculate the pension input amount for any of the pension input periods ending in the tax years 2008–09, 2009–10 and 2010–11, within 3 months following receipt of a written request from the scheme administrator or, (if later), on or before 6th July 2013.

(5) Where—

(*a*) regulation 14A(7) applies to a scheme administrator (obligation to provide information to a member where there is a straddling pension input period), and

(*b*) a written request is made by the scheme administrator to the employer,

the employer must provide the scheme administrator with such information as will enable the scheme administrator to comply with the obligation contained in regulation 14A(7), such information to be supplied within three months of receipt of the written request or, (if later) on or before 6th July 2013.

(6) The obligations contained in this regulation shall apply to a responsible person (see paragraph (7)) and for the purposes of applying this regulation to the responsible person, references to "employer" shall be read as referring to the responsible person.

(7) For the purposes of this regulation "responsible person" means a person who is responsible for providing the scheme administrator of a registered pension scheme with such information as will enable the scheme administrator to calculate the pension input amount in respect of a member where the member is an active member of that scheme in relation to an arrangement under the scheme for all or part of a pension input period ending in a tax year.][1]

Amendments—[1] Reg 15A inserted by the Registered Pension Schemes (Provision of Information) (Amendment) (No 2) Regulations SI 2011/1797 regs 2, 9 with effect from 11 August 2011.

16 Pensions and annuities in payment: information provided to and by insurance companies

(1) This regulation applies if a registered pension scheme has provided an insurance company with funds, otherwise than from [a drawdown pension][1] fund [or flexi-access drawdown fund][2], to secure the payment of—

(*a*) a scheme pension, or

(*b*) a lifetime annuity.

(2) The scheme administrator shall provide the insurance company, within 3 months of the date on which the recipient becomes entitled to the pension or annuity, with a statement of the total percentage of standard lifetime allowance expended, at the date of the statement by benefit crystallisation events in respect of that pension or annuity, and any pension commencement lump sum connected with that pension or annuity.

(3) The insurance company shall provide to each pensioner or annuitant, at least once in each tax year, a statement of the percentage of the standard lifetime allowance expended at the date of the statement, by benefit crystallisation events in respect of that pension or annuity and any pension commencement lump sum paid in connection with that pension or annuity.

[(4) No obligation to provide a statement arises—

(*a*) under paragraph (2) in respect of any entitlement to a pension or annuity or pension commencement lump sum which does not give rise to a benefit crystallisation event;

(*b*) under paragraph (3) in a tax year following the tax year in which the member reaches the age of 75.][1]

Amendments—[1] In para (1), words substituted, and para (4) inserted, by the Registered Pension Schemes (Provision of Information) (Amendment) (No 2) Regulations, SI 2011/1797 regs 2, 10 with effect from 11 August 2011.

[2] In para (1), words inserted by the Taxation of Pensions Act 2014 s 1, Sch 1 para 35(1), (4) with effect from 6 April 2015. This amendment is to be treated as having been made by the Commissioners for HMRC under such of the powers cited in the instrument containing the Regulations as are applicable (Taxation of Pensions Act 2014 Sch 1 para 35(7)).

17 Payments to insurance companies from [drawdown pension] funds

(1) This regulation applies if a registered pension scheme has provided an insurance company with sums or assets from [a drawdown pension][1] fund [or flexi-access drawdown fund][2], to secure the payment of—

(*a*) a scheme pension, or

(*b*) a lifetime annuity.

(2) If the sums or assets provided comprise part of the member's [drawdown pension][1] fund [or of the member's flexi-access drawdown fund][2], the scheme administrator shall provide the insurance company, within 3 months of the purchase of the pension or annuity, with a statement of the percentage of standard lifetime allowance expended by the member becoming entitled to the scheme pension or the lifetime annuity.

(3) The insurance company shall provide to each pensioner or annuitant, at least once in each tax year, a statement of the percentage of the standard lifetime allowance expended at the date of the statement, in respect of that pension or annuity.

But no statement is required if the percentage expended is nil.

(4) If the sums or assets provided comprise the whole of the member's [drawdown pension][1] fund [or of the member's flexi-access drawdown fund][2], the scheme administrator shall provide the insurance company, within 3 months of the purchase of the pension or annuity, with a statement containing the information in paragraph (5).

(5) The information is—

(*a*) the sum of the percentages of standard lifetime allowance expended by—

(i) benefit crystallisation events in respect of the scheme referred to in paragraph (4) ("A"), to the extent that the sums and assets subject to those events have not been the subject of a transfer to another registered scheme; and

(ii) where A has received (whether directly or indirectly) a transfer in respect of that member, any benefit crystallisation event prior to the transfer in connection with the sums and assets represented by the transfer and sums and assets which were replaced by the sums and assets mentioned in paragraph (i), less

(*b*) the sum of the percentages of standard lifetime allowance expended by benefit crystallisation events—

(i) which have been the subject of a statement under paragraph (2),

(ii) which have been the subject of a statement under regulation 16(2), or

(iii) which are referable to sums or assets which continue to be held by A.

(6) The insurance company shall provide to the pensioner or annuitant, once in each tax year, a statement containing the information in paragraph (7).

(7) The information is—

(*a*) the sum of the percentages of standard lifetime allowance expended by—

(i) benefit crystallisation events in respect of the scheme referred to in paragraph (4) ("A"), to the extent that the sums and assets subject to those events have not been the subject of a transfer to another registered scheme;

(ii) benefit crystallisation events in respect of a scheme pension after the pensioner first became entitled to it; and

(iii) where A has received (whether directly or indirectly) a transfer in respect of that member, any benefit crystallisation event prior to the transfer in connection with the sums and assets represented by the transfer and sums and assets which were replaced by the sums and assets mentioned in paragraph (i), less

(*b*) the sum of the percentages of standard lifetime allowance expended by benefit crystallisation events—

(i) which have been the subject of a statement under paragraph (2),

(ii) which have been the subject of a statement under regulation 16(3), or

(iii) which are referable to sums or assets which continue to be held by A.

[(8) No obligation to provide a statement arises under paragraph (3) or (6) in a tax year following the tax year in which the pensioner or annuitant reaches the age of 75.][1]

Amendments—[1] In heading, paras (1), (2), (4), words substituted; and para (8) inserted; by the Registered Pension Schemes (Provision of Information) (Amendment) (No 2) Regulations, SI 2011/1797 regs 2, 11, 12 with effect from 11 August 2011.

[2] In paras (1), (2), (4) words inserted by the Taxation of Pensions Act 2014 s 1, Sch 1 para 35(1), (5), (6) with effect from 6 April 2015. These amendments are to be treated as having been made by the Commissioners for HMRC under such of the powers cited in the instrument containing the Regulations as are applicable (Taxation of Pensions Act 2014 Sch 1 para 35(7)).

[17A Transfers between insurance companies

(1) This regulation applies if—

(*a*) a scheme pension payable by an insurance company ("Insurer A") ceases to be payable and another scheme pension becomes payable by another insurance company ("Insurer B"), in the circumstances described in regulation 4 of the Registered Pension Schemes (Transfer of Sums and Assets) Regulations 2006 (scheme pension payable by insurance company) ("the Transfer Regulations"); or

(*b*) a lifetime annuity payable by an insurance company ("Insurer A") ceases to be payable and a new lifetime annuity becomes payable by another insurance company ("Insurer B"), in the circumstances described in regulation 6 of the Transfer Regulations (lifetime annuity).

In the following provisions of this regulation "a relevant transfer" means a transfer which occurs in the circumstances described in regulation 4 or 6 of the Transfer Regulations.

(2) If in connection with a relevant transfer—

(*a*) Insurer A transfers funds to Insurer B; and

(*b*) Insurer A was required to provide a statement under regulation 16(3),

Insurer A shall provide Insurer B, within 3 months of the transfer, with a statement containing the information specified in regulation 16(3).

(3) After the relevant transfer the obligation imposed by regulation 16(3) shall be that of Insurer B.

(4) Where in connection with a relevant transfer Insurer A transfers funds to Insurer B, and Insurer A was required to provide a statement under regulation 17(3) or 17(6)—

(*a*) if the statement was provided under regulation 17(3), Insurer A must provide Insurer B, within 3 months of the transfer, with a statement containing the information specified in regulation 17(3); or

(*b*) if the statement was provided under regulation 17(6), Insurer A must provide Insurer B, within 3 months of the transfer, with a statement containing the information specified in regulation 17(7).

(5) Where paragraph (4)(*a*) applies, after the relevant transfer the obligation imposed by regulation 17(3) shall be that of Insurer B.

But no statement is required if the percentage expended is nil.

(6) Where paragraph (4)(*b*) applies, after the relevant transfer the obligation imposed by regulation 17(6) shall be that of Insurer B.][1]

Amendments—[1] Regulation 17A inserted by the Registered Pension Schemes (Provision of Information) (Amendment) Regulations, SI 2008/720 regs 2, 7 with effect from 6 April 2008.

[17B Information between insurance companies: transfer of sums or assets representing beneficiaries' annuities

(1) This regulation applies if and to the extent to which there is a transfer of sums or assets (or both) which represent—

(*a*) a lifetime annuity that is being paid pursuant to pension rule 2 in section 165 (guaranteed period for payment of scheme pension or annuity),

(*b*) a dependants' annuity,

(*c*) a nominees' annuity, or

(*d*) a successors' annuity,

as a result of which an annuity payable by an insurance company ("Insurer A") ceases to be payable and a new annuity becomes payable by another insurance company ("Insurer B") in the circumstances described in regulation 6(1), 10(1), 19(1) or 20(1) (as the case may be) of the Registered Pension Schemes (Transfer of Sums and Assets) Regulations 2006.

(2) Insurer A shall provide the information specified in paragraph (3) to Insurer B within 3 months of the transfer.

(3) The information is—

(*a*) which of the descriptions in paragraphs (1)(*a*) to (*d*) applies to the annuity in respect of which the sums or assets (or both) are transferred,

(*b*) where sums or assets (or both) are transferred in respect of a lifetime annuity that is being paid pursuant to pension rule 2 in section 165, a dependants' annuity or a nominees' annuity, the age at death of the deceased member,

(*c*) where sums or assets (or both) are transferred in respect of a successors' annuity, the age at death of the immediately preceding dependant, nominee or successor (as the case may be), and

(*d*) where the deceased member referred to in sub-paragraph (*b*), or the immediately preceding dependant, nominee or successor referred to in sub-paragraph (*c*) died before the age of 75—

(i) confirmation as to whether or not section 646B(1) to (4) of ITEPA 2003 (registered schemes: beneficiaries' annuities from unused funds) apply to payments of the annuity, and

(ii) if so, confirmation as to which of section 646B(1) to (4) apply to those payments.][1]

Amendments—[1] Regulations 17B, 17C inserted by the Registered Pension Schemes (Provision of Information) (Amendment No 2) Regulations, SI 2015/1455 regs 2, 11 with effect in respect of transfers on or after 6 April 2015.

[17C Information between insurance companies: transfer of sums or assets representing beneficiaries' short-term annuities

(1) This regulation applies if and to the extent to which there is a transfer of sums or assets (or both) which represent—

(*a*) a dependants' short-term annuity,

(*b*) a nominees' short-term annuity, or

(*c*) a successors' short-term annuity,

as a result of which a short-term annuity payable by an insurance company ("Insurer A") ceases to be payable and a new short-term annuity becomes payable by another insurance company ("Insurer B") in the circumstances described in regulation 11, 17 or 18 (as the case may be) of the Registered Pension Schemes (Transfer of Sums and Assets) Regulations 2006.

(2) Insurer A shall provide the information specified in paragraph (3) to Insurer B within 3 months of the transfer.

(3) The information is—

(*a*) which of the descriptions in paragraphs (1)(*a*) to (*c*) applies to the short-term annuity in respect of which the sums or assets (or both) are transferred,

(*b*) where sums or assets (or both) are transferred in respect of a dependants' shortterm annuity or a nominees' short-term annuity, the age at death of the deceased member,

(*c*) where sums or assets (or both) are transferred in respect of a successors' short-term annuity, the age at death of the immediately preceding dependant, nominee or successor (as the case may be), and

(*d*) where the deceased member referred to in sub-paragraph (*b*), or the immediately preceding dependant, nominee or successor referred to in sub-paragraph (*c*) died before the age of 75—

(i) confirmation as to whether or not section 646C(1) and (2) of ITEPA 2003 (registered schemes: beneficiaries' annuities from drawdown funds) apply to payments of the annuity, and

(ii) if so, confirmation as to which of section 646C(1) and (2) apply to those payments.][1]

Amendments—[1] Regulations 17B, 17C inserted by the Registered Pension Schemes (Provision of Information) (Amendment No 2) Regulations, SI 2015/1455 regs 2, 11 with effect in respect of transfers on or after 6 April 2015.

18 Record-keeping: Retention of records

(1) The persons prescribed by paragraph (2) shall preserve any documents in their possession or under their control in relation to a registered pension scheme and relating to—

(*a*) any monies received by or owing to the scheme;

(*b*) any investments or assets held by the scheme;

(*c*) any payments made by the scheme;

(*d*) any contracts to purchase a lifetime annuity in respect of a member of the scheme; and

(*e*) the administration of the scheme.

(2) In relation to a registered pension scheme the persons prescribed are—

(*a*) any person who is or has been the scheme administrator;

(*b*) any person who is or has been a trustee of the scheme;

(*c*) any person who provides or has provided administrative services to the scheme; and

(*d*) if the scheme is an occupational pension scheme, any person who is or has been a sponsoring employer or a director of an employer company.

This is subject to the following qualification.

(3) Any person who has ceased to act in relation to the scheme or ceased to provide administrative services to the scheme shall not be required to preserve documents where he has transferred all the documents to another person who has succeeded him in acting in relation to the scheme or providing administrative services to the scheme.

(4) Documents must be preserved for the tax year to which they relate and for a period of 6 years following that year.

[Modified operation of these Regulations in the case of certain pre-6 April 2015 lump sums

19 Lump sums to which paragraph 1B of Schedule 29 applies

(1) Regulations 3 to 18 have effect subject to the following provisions of this regulation.

(2) Paragraphs (3) to (8) apply if—

(*a*) a lump sum is paid by a registered pension scheme ("the paying scheme") to a member of the scheme,

(*b*) paragraph 1B of Schedule 29 applies to the lump sum, and

(*c*) the member's becoming entitled to the actual pension mentioned in paragraph 1B(2)(*h*) of Schedule 29 has the effect that—

(i) the member also becomes entitled to the lump sum, and

(ii) the member's becoming entitled to the lump sum is a benefit crystallisation event.

(3) For the purposes of—

(*a*) reportable event 6,

(*b*) regulation 3 so far as applying by virtue of that event, and

(*c*) obligations under regulation 14(1),

the benefit crystallisation event mentioned in paragraph (2)(*c*)(ii) is treated as occurring—

(i) in respect of the scheme to which the transfer mentioned in paragraph 1B(2)(*g*) of Schedule 29 was made ("the receiving scheme") and not in respect of the paying scheme, and

(ii) when the member becomes entitled to the actual pension or, if later, on 5 August 2014.

(4) For the purposes of regulations 15(2)(*a*) and 17(5)(*a*)(i) and (7)(*a*)(i), that benefit crystallisation event is treated as occurring in respect of the receiving scheme and not in respect of the paying scheme.

(5) For the purposes of—

(*a*) reportable event 7 (but not its definition of "the entitlement amount"),

(*b*) reportable event 8, and

(*c*) regulation 3 so far as applying by virtue of either of those events,

the lump sum is treated as having been paid—

(i) by the receiving scheme and not by the paying scheme, and

(ii) when the member becomes entitled to the actual pension or, if later, on 5 August 2014.

(6) For the purposes of reportable event 7 "the entitlement amount" is the total of—

(*a*) the sums held, at the time the lump sum is actually paid, for the purpose of providing the expected pension mentioned in paragraph 1B(2)(*b*) of Schedule 29, and

(*b*) the market value at that time of the assets held at that time for that purpose.

(7) The scheme administrator of the paying scheme is to provide the scheme administrator of the receiving scheme with the following information—

(*a*) the date the lump sum was paid,

(*b*) the amount of the lump sum,

(*c*) the total of—

(i) the sums held, at the time lump sum is paid, for the purpose of providing the expected pension mentioned in paragraph 1B(2)(*b*) of Schedule 29, and

(ii) the market value at that time of the assets held at that time for that purpose, and

(*d*) a statement that no further pension commencement lump sum may be paid in connection with that expected pension.

(8) The scheme administrator of the paying scheme is to comply with its obligations under paragraph (7) before—

(*a*) the end of 30 days beginning with the date of the transfer mentioned in paragraph 1B(2)(*g*) of Schedule 29, or

(*b*) if later, the end of 3 September 2014.][1]

Amendments—[1] Regulations 19, 20 and preceding crosshead inserted by FA 2014 s 43, Sch 5 para 11. This amendment is to be treated as having come into force on 19 March 2014 (FA 2014 Sch 5 para 15) and as having been made by the Commissioners for HMRC under such of the powers cited in the instrument containing the Regulations as are applicable (FA 2014 Sch 5 para 11(2)).

[20 Lump sums to which paragraph 1B of Schedule 29 fails to apply

(1) Regulations 3 to 18 have effect subject to the following provisions of this regulation.

(2) Paragraph (3) applies if—

(*a*) a lump sum is paid by a registered pension scheme ("the paying scheme") to a member of the scheme,

(*b*) paragraph 1B of Schedule 29 does not apply to the lump sum, but the conditions in paragraph 1B(2)(*a*) to (*g*) are met in the case of the lump sum, and

(*c*) as at the end of 5 October 2015 it is the case that the lump sum is to be taken as having been an unauthorised member payment.

(3) For the purposes of reportable event 1, and regulation 3 so far as applying by virtue of that event, the lump sum is treated as having been paid—

(*a*) by the receiving scheme and not by the paying scheme, and

(*b*) on 6 October 2015.][1]

Amendments—[1] Regulations 19, 20 and preceding crosshead inserted by FA 2014 s 43, Sch 5 para 11. This amendment is to be treated as having come into force on 19 March 2014 (FA 2014 Sch 5 para 15) and as having been made by the Commissioners for HMRC under such of the powers cited in the instrument containing the Regulations as are applicable (FA 2014 Sch 5 para 11(2)).

2006/568

REGISTERED PENSION SCHEMES (PRESCRIBED MANNER OF DETERMINING AMOUNT OF ANNUITIES) REGULATIONS 2006

Made by the Commissioners for HMRC under FA 2004 Sch 28 paras 3(1)(d), 6(1)(e), 17(1)(c), 20(1)(e)

Made . . . . *9 March 2006*
Laid before the House of Commons . . . . *10 March 2006*
Coming into force . . . . *6 April 2006*

Commentary—*Simon's Taxes* **E7.224**.

1 Citation, commencement and interpretation

(1) These Regulations may be cited as the Registered Pension Schemes (Prescribed Manner of Determining Amount of Annuities) Regulations 2006 and shall come into force on 6th April 2006.

(2) In these Regulations a reference to a numbered section or Schedule (without more) is a reference to the section of, or Schedule to, the Finance Act 2004 bearing that number.

2 Determining amount of member's lifetime annuity

(1) The annual amount of a member's lifetime annuity shall be determined in accordance with any of paragraphs (2) to (4).

(2) The manner of determination prescribed by this paragraph is variation from year to year—

(*a*) where the variation is in line with, or by a percentage which does not exceed, the percentage by which the amount would vary if it varied in line with, changes in—

(i) the retail prices index,

(ii) the market value of any freely marketable assets,

(iii) an index reflecting the value of freely marketable assets,

after allowing for any contractual charges;

(*b*) in accordance with an insurance company's published "Principles and Practices of Financial Management" in relation to with-profits business, as required under section 6.10 of the Financial Services Authority's Conduct of Business Sourcebook as it stood immediately before the coming into force of these Regulations; or (*c*) any combination of those factors.

(3) The manner of determination prescribed by this paragraph is variation—

(*a*) in line with, or by a percentage which does not exceed the percentage by which the amount would vary if it varied in line with, changes in any of the factors specified in paragraph (2) (or any combination of those factors); and

(*b*) by reference to an assumed annual level of growth of between 0% and 5%, selected by the member, in the relevant factor or factors.

(4) The manner of determination prescribed by this paragraph is determination in accordance with the following conditions.

Condition 1

The amount of the annuity payable is linked to any of the factors specified in sub-paragraphs [(*a*) to (*c*)][1] of paragraph (2) (or any combination of those factors).

Condition 2

A review is conducted, by the insurance company by whom the annuity is provided, at least once every [3][2] years of the value of the sums and assets which are applied towards the provision of the annuity.

Condition 3

At the time of the review, the maximum and minimum amount of income that may be drawn in each year until the next review is determined.

The maximum amount of income which the annuitant may draw is 120% of the annual rate of a level annuity which could be purchased with the sums and assets which are applied to its provision for the member, for the term for which the annuity is provided.

The minimum amount of income which the annuitant may draw is half of the annual rate of a level annuity which could be paid upon the assumptions in the preceding paragraph of this condition.

(5) For the purposes of paragraph (4), the annual rate of an annuity which could be purchased with the sums and assets applied to its provision shall be assumed to be—

(*a*) the freely marketable level annuity rate (if any) applicable in the case of the insurance company in question which could be purchased with those sums and assets; or

(*b*) if the insurance company in question does not offer level annuities, the average of three current market annuity rates for a level annuity.

(6) For the purposes of paragraph (2)—

"freely marketable assets" means assets which are sold on the open market at a price not determined by the member;

"the retail prices index" has the meaning given in section 279(1).

Amendments—[1] In para (4), in condition 1, words substituted by the Registered Pension Schemes (Miscellaneous Amendments) Regulations, SI 2011/1751 reg 10(1), (2)(*a*) with effect from 11 August 2011.

[2] In para (4), in condition 2, "3" substituted for "5" by the Registered Pension Schemes (Miscellaneous Amendments) Regulations, SI 2011/1751 reg 10(1)(2)(*b*) with effect as follows—

Where the amount of—

(a) a member's lifetime annuity; or

(b) (b) a dependant's annuity

has been determined in accordance with regulation 2 or 3 of SI 2006/568 before the coming into force of SI 2011/1751 (11 August 2011), the amendment made by reg 10(2)(*b*) has effect from the date of the next review of the value of the sums and assets which are applied towards the provision of the annuity by the insurance company by whom the annuity is provided.

3 Determining amount of dependant's annuity

(1) The amount of a dependant's annuity shall be determined in the same manner as a member's lifetime annuity.

(2) For this purpose, paragraphs (2) to (6) of regulation 2 shall apply, but subject to the following modifications—

(*a*) in paragraphs (2), (4) and (6) substitute "dependant " for "member" wherever it occurs, and

(*b*) in paragraph (3)(*b*) for "member" substitute "member or dependant".

4 Determining amount of short-term annuities

(1) The amount of a member's short-term annuity shall be determined in the same manner as a member's lifetime annuity in accordance with paragraph (2) or (3) of regulation 2.

(2) The amount of a dependant's short-term annuity shall be determined in the same manner as a member's short-term annuity, and for this purpose paragraphs (2), (3) and (6) of regulation 2 shall apply, but substituting "dependant " for "member" wherever it occurs.

2006/569

REGISTERED PENSION SCHEMES (SPLITTING OF SCHEMES) REGULATIONS 2006

Made by the Commissioners for HMRC under FA 2004 s 274A

Made . . . . *9 March 2006*
Laid before the House of Commons . . . . *10 March 2006*
Coming into force . . . . *6 April 2006*

Commentary—*Simon's Taxes* **E7.241**.

1 Citation, commencement and interpretation

(1) These Regulations may be cited as the Registered Pension Schemes (Splitting of Schemes) Regulations 2006 and shall come into force on 6th April 2006.

(2) In these Regulations—

"group of employers" means two or more employers who are formally or informally linked to each other by reasons of common management, shareholding, staff or close business interests;

"HMRC" means the Commissioners for Her Majesty's Revenue and Customs;

"split scheme" means a registered pension scheme that is being treated, in accordance with regulation 2, as having been split into two or more sub-schemes;

"sub-scheme" means a scheme which forms part of a split scheme and which is being treated as a separate pension scheme under and for the purposes set out in these regulations;

"split scheme administrator" means a scheme administrator of a split scheme;

"sub-scheme administrator" means the scheme administrator of a sub-scheme appointed in accordance with the rules of the split scheme to be responsible for the discharge of the functions conferred or imposed on the sub-scheme administrator by or under these Regulations;

"section" without more, means a section of the Finance Act 2004;

"schedule" without more, means a schedule to the Finance Act 2004.

2 Description of schemes to be split

(1) The following registered pension schemes shall be treated as split schemes for the purposes of these Regulations—

(*a*) the registered pension schemes listed in Schedule 1;

(*b*) a registered pension scheme which meets the conditions in paragraph (5);

(*c*) a successor scheme to any of the above schemes.

(2) A successor scheme is a registered pension scheme established to take over some or all of the rights and obligations of a split scheme.

(3) The scheme administrator of a successor scheme shall notify HMRC of any sub-schemes in respect of which he is assuming responsibility immediately following registration of the successor scheme.

The notification shall—

(*a*) be in a form specified by HMRC, and;

(*b*) contain any information reasonably required by HMRC

(4) Schedule 2 lists the schemes which, at the coming into force of these Regulations, are to be treated as sub-schemes of the split schemes referred to in sub-paragraph (1).

(5) The conditions referred to in sub-paragraph (1)(*b*) are as follows.

Condition A

The pension scheme falls within Paragraph 1(1)(*a*) or (*c*) of Schedule 36 to the Finance Act 2004.

Condition B

The pension scheme provides benefits to or for the benefit of the employees of two or more employers.

Condition C

The rules of the pension scheme as at 28th February 2006 provided for the establishment of separate schemes for each of the participating employers or group of employers and for the administration of such schemes to be carried out by separate scheme administrators.

(6) A successor sub-scheme is a scheme established to take over some or all of the rights and obligations of a sub-scheme.

(7) The scheme administrator of a successor sub-scheme shall notify HMRC immediately following his assumption of liability of the successor sub-scheme.

The notification shall—

(*a*) be in a form specified by HMRC, and

(*b*) contain any information reasonably required, including the name and address of the scheme administrator.

3 Responsibilities and liabilities of sub-scheme administrators

(1) The sub-scheme administrator of a sub-scheme shall assume the liabilities and responsibilities set out in Schedule 3 to these Regulations in relation to that scheme.

(2) In the provisions referred to in that Schedule any reference to the scheme administrator shall be read as a reference to the sub-scheme administrator.

(3) The split scheme administrator shall cease to have responsibility or liability in relation to the matters referred to in paragraph (1) in respect of the sub-scheme.

(4) The provisions of section 270(2) and (3) (meaning of "scheme administrator") apply to the sub-scheme administrator and the references to the scheme administrator in those subsections shall be read as references to the sub-scheme administrator).

(5) Section 272 (trustees etc liable as scheme administrator) applies to sub-scheme administrators with the following modifications—

(*a*) in subsection (1)" for "registered pension scheme"; substitute "sub-scheme";

(*b*) in subsections (1)(*a*) to (*c*), (2)(*a*) and (*b*) for "scheme administrator" (in each place) substitute "sub-scheme administrator";

(*c*) in subsections (1)(*a*) to (*c*) and (2), (3) and (5) for "pension scheme" (in each place) substitute "sub-scheme";

(*d*) in subsection (2)—

(i) in paragraph (*a*) after "by virtue of this Part" insert "as applied by regulation 3 of the Registered Pensions (Splitting of Schemes) Regulations 2006"; and

(ii) in paragraph (*b*) after "by or under this Part." insert "as applied by the Registered Pensions (Splitting of Schemes) Regulations 2006"; and

(*e*) in subsection (4) for "pension scheme" substitute "sub-scheme".

(6) Section 273 (members liable as scheme administrator) applies to members of a sub-scheme with the following modifications—

(*a*) in subsection (1) for "registered pension scheme" substitute "sub-scheme";

(*b*) in subsections (1)(*a*) and (*b*) for "pension scheme" substitute "sub-scheme";

(*c*) in subsection (1)(*a*) after " (trustees, etc)" add " (as modified by regulation 3 of the Registered Pensions (Splitting of Schemes) Regulations 2006)";

(*d*) in subsection (1)(*b*) omit the words "or section 242 (de-registration charge)";

(*e*) in subsections (2) and (4) for "pension scheme" substitute "sub-scheme";

(*f*) in subsection (5)(*a*) for "the pension scheme" substitute "the split scheme";

(*g*) in subsections (5)(*b*) and (*d*) for "the pension scheme" substitute "the sub-scheme";

(*h*) in subsection (5)(*c*) after the words "that the pension scheme was" add "part of";

(i) in subsection (10) for "the pension scheme" substitute "the sub-scheme".

(7) Section 274(2) (supplementary) applies to sub-scheme administrators with the following modifications—

(*a*) for "scheme administrator" substitute "sub-scheme administrator"; and

(*b*) for "registered pension scheme" substitute "sub-scheme".

4—(1) Section 209(5) (unauthorised payments surcharge) shall be modified as follows.

(*a*) in paragraph (*b*) delete "and";

(*b*) in paragraph (*c*) after "the scheme administrator" add "and";

(*c*) after paragraph (*c*) add—

"(*d*) the sub-scheme administrator,".

5—(1) Paragraph 11 of Schedule 31 (insertion of chapter 15A into ITEPA 2003) shall be modified as follows.

(2) After subsection (4) of the inserted section 636A insert—

"(4A) In the case of a registered pension scheme which is a split scheme for the purposes of the Registered Pensions Schemes (Splitting of Schemes) Regulations 2006, subsections (3) and (4) shall have effect as if the references to the scheme administrator were to the sub-scheme administrator (within the meaning of those Regulations).".

(3) Paragraph 1 of Schedule 35 (consequential amendments to the Taxes Management Act 1970) shall be modified as follows.

(*a*) in the substitution to section 9(1A) of the Taxes Management Act 1970, in sub-paragraph (*a*) delete "or"; and

(*b*) after sub-paragraph (*a*) add—

"(*ab*) is chargeable on the sub-scheme administrator of a sub-scheme under Part 4 of the Finance Act 2004 as modified by the Registered Pensions (Splitting of Schemes) Regulations 2006, or"

(4) Paragraph 16 of Schedule 35 (consequential amendments to section 349B(3) of ICTA) shall be modified as follows.

(5) After the substituted sub-paragraph (i) add—

"(ia) the sub-scheme administrator of a sub-scheme which forms part of a split scheme pursuant to the Registered Pensions (Splitting of Schemes) Regulations 2006;"

(6) Paragraph 33 of Schedule 35 (consequential amendments to section 824(9) of ICTA) shall be modified as follows.

(7) After the insertion of the words "scheme administrators of registered pension schemes" add—

"sub-scheme administrators of sub-schemes which form part of a split scheme pursuant to the Registered Pensions (Splitting of Schemes) Regulations 2006".

SCHEDULE 1

SCHEMES TO BE TREATED AS SPLIT SCHEMES PURSUANT TO REGULATION 2(1)(A)

Regulation 2(1)(a)

Name of Scheme	*Enabling legislation*	*Governing regulations*
Police Pension Scheme	ss 1–8 Police Pensions Act [1976][1]	The Police Pensions Regulations 1987 (SI 1987 No 257) as amended
[Police Pension Scheme (England and Wales) 2015	sections 1 to 5, 7, 8, 12, 18 and 25, paragraph 7 of Schedule 2, Schedule 3 and paragraphs 1, 2 and 5 of Schedule 7 to the Public Service Pensions Act 201	The Police Pension Regulations 2015][1]
Firefighters Pension Scheme [and Firefighters' Pension (Wales) Scheme][1]	s 26 Fire Services Act 1947 and s 34 Fire and Rescue Services Act 2004	The Firemen's Pension Scheme Order 1992 SI 1992 No 129 as amended
[Firefighters' Pension Scheme (Wales) 2015	sections 1 to 4, 7, 8, 12 and 18, paragraph 6 of Schedule 2, Schedule 3 and paragraphs 20 and 21 of Schedule 5 to the Public Service Pensions Act 2013	The Firefighters' Pension Scheme (Wales) Regulations 2015][1]
[Firefighters' Pension Scheme 2015	sections 1 to 4, 8 and 18, paragraph 6 of Schedule 2 and Schedule 3 to the Public Service Pensions Act 2013	The Firefighters' Pension Scheme (England) Regulations 2014][1]
Local Government Pension Scheme	s 7 and s 12 Superannuation Act 1972	The Local Government Pension Scheme Regulations 1997 SI 1997 No 1612 as amended
Local Government Pension Scheme (Scotland)	s 7 and s 12 Superannuation Act 1972	The Local Government Pension Scheme (Scotland) Regulations 1998 SI 1998 No 366 (S 14) as amended
Electricity Supply Pension Scheme		

Amendments—[1] Figure in column 2 substituted, words in column 1 inserted, and table entries inserted by the Registered Pension Schemes (Splitting of Schemes) (Amendment) Regulations, SI 2015/667 regs 2, 3 with effect from 6 April 2015.

SCHEDULE 2

SCHEMES TO BE TREATED AS SUB-SCHEMES PURSUANT TO REGULATION 2(4)

Regulation 2(4)

Name of sub-scheme	*Split scheme to which it relates*
[Avon & Somerset Police Authority	Police Pension Scheme
Bedfordshire Police Authority	
Cambridgeshire Police Authority	
Cheshire Police Authority	
City of London Police Authority	
Cleveland Police Authority	

Name of sub-scheme	*Split scheme to which it relates*
Cumbria Police Authority	
Derbyshire Police Authority	
Devon & Cornwall Constabulary	
Dorset Police Force Headquarters	
Durham Police Authority	
Dyfed Powys Police Authority	
Essex Police Authority	
Gloucestershire Police Authority	
Greater Manchester Police Authority	
Gwent Police Authority Office	
Hampshire Police Authority	
Hertfordshire Police Authority	
Humberside Police Authority	
Kent Police Authority	
Lancashire Police Authority	
Leicestershire Police Authority	
Lincolnshire Police Headquarters	
Merseyside Police Authority][1]	
Metropolitan Police Authority	
Norfolk Police Authority	
North Yorkshire Police Authority	
North Wales Police Authority	
Northamptonshire Police Authority	
Northumbria Police Authority	
Nottinghamshire Police Authority	
South Wales Police Authority	
South Yorkshire Police Authority	
Staffordshire Police Authority	
Suffolk Police Authority	
Surrey Police Authority	
Sussex Police	
Thames Valley Police Authority	
Warwickshire Police Authority	
West Mercia Police Authority	
West Midlands Police Authority	
West Yorkshire Police Authority	
Wiltshire Police Authority	
Central Scotland Joint Police Board	
Dumfries & Galloway Police Authority	
Fife Police Authority	
Grampian Joint Police Board	
Lothian and Borders Police Board	
Northern Joint Police Board	
Strathclyde Joint Police Fire Board	
Tayside Joint Police Board	
Avon Fire Authority	Firefighters Pension Scheme
Bedfordshire and Luton Combined Fire Authority	
Buckinghamshire and Milton Keynes Fire Authority	

Name of sub-scheme	*Split scheme to which it relates*
Cambridgeshire and Peterborough Fire Authority	
Cheshire Fire Authority	
Cleveland Fire Authority	
Cornwall Fire Authority	
County Durham and Darlington Fire and Rescue Authority	
Cumbria Fire Authority	
Derbyshire Fire Authority	
Devon Fire Authority	
Dorset Fire Authority	
East Sussex Fire Authority	
Essex Fire Authority	
Gloucestershire Fire Authority	
Greater Manchester Fire and Civil Defence Authority	
Hampshire Fire and Rescue Authority	
Hereford and Worcester Combined Fire Authority	
Hertfordshire Fire Authority	
Humberside Fire Authority	
Isle of Wight Fire Authority	
Kent and Medway Towns Fire Authority	
Lancashire Combined Fire Authority	
Leicester, Leicestershire and Rutland Combined Fire Authority	
Lincolnshire Fire Authority	
London Fire and Emergency Planning Authority	
Merseyside Fire and Civil Defence Authority	
Mid and West Wales Fire Authority	
Norfolk Fire Authority	
North Wales Fire Authority	
North Yorkshire Fire and Rescue Authority	
Northamptonshire Fire Authority	
Northumberland Fire Authority	
Nottinghamshire and City of Nottingham Fire Authority	
Oxfordshire Fire Authority	
Royal Berkshire Fire Authority	
Shropshire and Wrekin Fire Authority	
Somerset Fire Authority	
South Wales Fire Authority	
South Yorkshire Fire and Civil Defence Authority	
Stoke on Trent and Staffordshire Fire Authority	
Suffolk Fire Authority	
Surrey Fire Authority	
Tyne & Wear Fire and Civil Defence Authority	
Warwickshire Fire Authority	
West Midlands Fire and Civil Defence Authority	

Name of sub-scheme	*Split scheme to which it relates*
West Sussex Fire Authority	
West Yorkshire Fire and Civil Defence Authority	
Wiltshire and Swindon Fire Authority	
Dumfries & Galloway Fire and Rescue Authority	
Highland and Islands Fire Board	
Grampian Fire Board	
Lothian and Borders Fire Board	
Central Scotland Fire Board	
Fife Fire and Rescue Authority	
Strathclyde Fire Board	
Tayside Fire Board	
Bath & North East Somerset Council	Local Government Pension Scheme
Bedfordshire County Council	
Buckinghamshire County Council	
Cambridgeshire County Council	
Carmarthenshire County Council	
Cheshire County Council	
City and County of Cardiff Council	
City and County of Swansea	
City of London	
City of Bradford Metropolitan District Council	
Cornwall County Council	
Cumbria County Council	
Derbyshire County Council	
Devon County Council	
Dorset County Council	
Durham County Council	
East Riding of Yorkshire Council	
East Sussex County Council	
Environment Agency	
Essex County Council	
Flintshire County Council	
Gloucestershire County Council	
Gwynedd Council	
Hampshire County Council	
Hertfordshire County Council	
Isle of Wight Council	
Kent County Council	
Lancashire County Council	
Leicestershire County Council	
Lincolnshire County Council	
London Borough of Barking and Dagenham	
London Borough of Barnet	
London Borough of Bexley	
London Borough of Brent	
London Borough of Bromley	
London Borough of Camden	
London Borough of Croydon	
London Borough of Ealing	

Name of sub-scheme	*Split scheme to which it relates*
London Borough of Enfield	
London Borough of Greenwich	
London Borough of Hackney	
London Borough of Hammersmith and Fulham	
London Borough of Haringey	
London Borough of Harrow	
London Borough of Havering	
London Borough of Hillingdon	
London Borough of Hounslow	
London Borough of Islington	
London Borough of Lambeth	
London Borough of Lewisham	
London Borough of Merton	
London Borough of Newham	
London Borough of Redbridge	
London Borough of Richmond Upon Thames	
London Borough of Southwark	
London Borough of Sutton	
London Borough of Tower Hamlets	
London Borough of Waltham Forest	
London Borough of Wandsworth	
London Pensions Fund Authority	
Middlesbrough Borough Council	
Norfolk County Council	
North Yorkshire County Council	
Northamptonshire County Council	
Northumberland County Council	
Nottinghamshire County Council	
Oxfordshire County Council	
Powys County Council	
Rhondda-Cynon-Taff County Borough Council	
Royal Borough of Kensington & Chelsea	
Royal Borough of Kingston Upon Thames	
Royal Borough of Windsor and Maidenhead	
Shropshire County Council	
Somerset County Council	
South Tyneside Metropolitan Borough Council	
South Yorkshire Pensions Authority	
Staffordshire County Council	
Suffolk County Council	
Surrey County Council	
Tameside Metropolitan Borough Council	
Torfaen County Borough Council	
Warwickshire County Council	
Westminster City Council	
West Sussex County Council	
Wiltshire County Council	
Wirral District Council	
Wolverhampton City Council	
Worcestershire County Council	

Name of sub-scheme	*Split scheme to which it relates*
Aberdeen City Council	Local Government Pension Scheme (Scotland)
The City of Edinburgh Council	
The City of Glasgow Council	
Dumfries & Galloway Council	
Dundee City Council	
Falkirk Council	
Fife Council	
The Highland Council	
Orkney Islands Council	
Scottish Borders Council	
Shetland Islands Council	
Alfred McAlpine Group	Electricity Supply Pension Scheme
Areva Group	
British Energy Combined Group	
British Energy Generation Group	
Drax Power Group	
EA Technology Group	
EDF Energy Group	
Electricity Association Services Group	
E.ON UK Group	
First Hydro Group	
International Power Group	
Keadby Generation Group	
Magnox Electric Group	
Manweb Group	
National Grid Electricity Group	
Northern Electric Group	
RWE npower Group	
Southern Electric Group	
United Utilities Group	
Western Power Distribution Group	

Amendment—[1] Entries in table inserted by the Registered Pension Schemes (Splitting of Schemes) (Amendment) Regulations, SI 2007/793 reg 2 with effect from 6 April 2007.

SCHEDULE 3
RESPONSIBILITIES AND LIABILITIES OF SUB-SCHEME ADMINISTRATORS IN RESPECT OF A SUB-SCHEME

Regulation 3

PART 1
FINANCE ACT 2004

Statutory Reference	*Subject-matter*
Liabilities	
[Section 192	Deduction of relief at source][2]
Section 205	Short service refund lump sum charge
[Section 205A	Serious ill-health lump sum charge][2]
Section 206	Special lump sum death benefit s charge
Section 207	Authorised surplus payments charge
Section 215(9)	Lifetime allowance charge—amount of charge

Statutory Reference	*Subject-matter*
Section 217	Lifetime allowance charge (joint & several with the individual)
. . . [2]	. . . [2]
[Section 237B to 237E	Annual allowance charge][2]
Section 238(3) and (4)	Pension input period
Section 239	Scheme sanction charge
Information	
Section 250(1)	To make and deliver a registered pension scheme return
Section 254	Accounting for tax by scheme administrators
Interest and penalties	
Section 257	Penalty for failure to comply with a s 250 notice.
. . . [2]	. . . [2]
Section 258(2)	Penalty for failure to comply with regulations within s 251(1)(*b*)
. . . [2]	. . . [2]
. . . [1]	. . . [1]
Section 265(3)	Penalty for winding up a scheme to obtain a winding up lump sum
Section 266(2)	Penalty for transfers to "non" insured schemes (unauthorised transfer)
Section 266B	Scheme liability (inserted by Paragraph 4 Schedule 10 FA 05)
Section 267	Discharge of lifetime allowance charge in the case of good faith.
Section 268	Unauthorised payment surcharge & scheme sanction charge
Scheme administrator	
Section 271	Liability of a scheme administrator
Section 272	Trustees etc liable as scheme administrator
[Section 272A to 272C	Liability of independent trustee, scheme administrator and former scheme administrator][2]
Section 273	Members liable as scheme administrator
Section 274	Supplementary provisions
Paragraph 1 of Schedule 28	Scheme administrator to receive evidence of member's ill health.
Paragraph 15(2)(*b*) of Schedule 28	Scheme administrator to agree if a child is a dependant
Paragraph 15(3) of Schedule 28	Scheme administrator to decide whether someone is a dependant.
Paragraph 4(1) of Schedule 29	Scheme administrator to consider evidence of serious ill health
. . . [2]	. . . [2]
. . . [2]	. . . [2]
Paragraph 9(2) of Schedule 32	Changes to benefit crystallisation event 2
Paragraph 9(3) of Schedule 32	Changes to benefit crystallisation event 2 (inserted by paragraph 43(4) of Schedule 10 to the Finance Act 2005).
Paragraph 13(4) and (5) of Schedule 32	Changes to benefit crystallisation event 3 (inserted by paragraph 43(5) of Schedule 10 to the Finance Act 2005)
Paragraph 14(1A) & (1B) of Schedule 32	Changes to benefit crystallisation event 5 (inserted by paragraph 43(7) of Schedule 10 to the Finance Act 2005)

Statutory Reference	*Subject-matter*
Paragraph 5 of Schedule 34	Exemption for scheme administrator from s 205 & s 206 charges
Paragraph 17 of Schedule 34	Omits reference to scheme administrator in s 217
Paragraph 4(1), (2) and (3) of Schedule 36	Transitional provisions for deemed registered schemes
Paragraph 6 of Schedule 36	Pre-commencement liability of scheme administrator

Amendments—[1] Entry relating to s 260(6) revoked by the Pension Schemes (Miscellaneous Amendments) Order, SI 2013/1114 art 7(1), (2) with effect from 1 June 2013.

[2] Entries revoked and inserted by the Registered Pension Schemes (Splitting of Schemes) (Amendment) Regulations, SI 2015/667 regs 2, 4 with effect from 6 April 2015.

[PART 1A
OTHER LEGISLATION

. . .[2]

[*Statutory Reference*	*Subject-matter*
Schedule 24 to the Finance Act 2007	Penalty for carelessly or deliberately making an incorrect return under section 254 of the Finance Act 2004
Schedule 55 to the Finance Act 2009	Penalty for failure to make returns][2]][1]

Amendments—[1] Part 1A inserted by the Finance Act 2009, Schedules 55 and 56 (Income Tax Self Assessment and Pension Schemes) (Appointed Days and Consequential and Savings Provisions) Order, SI 2011/702 art 18 with effect from 1 April 2011. This amendment has no effect in respect of a return period ending on or before 31 December 2010 (SI 2011/702 art 21).

[2] Words "Schedule 55 to the Finance Act 2009 (penalty for failure to make returns)" revoked, and table inserted, by the Pension Schemes (Miscellaneous Amendments) Order, SI 2013/1114 art 7(1), (3) with effect from 1 June 2013.

PART 2
SECONDARY LEGISLATION

The Pension Schemes (Discharge of Liabilities under Section 267 and 268 of the Finance Act 2004) Regulations 2005

The Registered Pension Schemes (Relief at Source) Regulations 2005

The Registered Pension Schemes (Minimum Contributions) Regulations 2006

The Registered Pension Schemes (Accounting and Assessment) Regulations 2005

. . .[1]

The Registered Pension Schemes (Provision of Information) Regulations 2006

The Registered Pension Schemes (Modification of the Rules of Existing Schemes) Regulations 2006

The Pension Benefits (Insurance Company Liable as Scheme Administrator) Regulations 2006

The Registered Pension Schemes (Meaning of Pension Commencement Lump Sum) Regulations 2006

The Registered Pension Schemes and Overseas Pension Schemes (Electronic Communication of Returns and Information) Regulations 2006

. . .[1]

. . .[1]

The Registered Pension Schemes (Unauthorised Payments by Existing Schemes) Regulations 2006

[The Registered Pension Schemes etc (Information) (Prescribed Descriptions of Persons) Regulations 2010

The Registered Pension Schemes (Notice of Joint Liability for the Annual Allowance Charge) Regulations 2011

The Registered Pension Schemes (Modification of Scheme Rules) Regulations 2011][1]

Amendments—[1] Entries revoked and inserted by the Registered Pension Schemes (Splitting of Schemes) (Amendment) Regulations, SI 2015/667 regs 2, 5 with effect from 6 April 2015.

2006/570

REGISTERED PENSION SCHEMES AND OVERSEAS PENSION SCHEMES (ELECTRONIC COMMUNICATION OF RETURNS AND INFORMATION) REGULATIONS 2006

Made by the Commissioners for HMRC under FA 1999 ss 132, 133(2), FA 2002 ss 135, 136.

Made . . . . *9 March 2006*
Laid before the House of Commons . . . . *10 March 2006*
Coming into force in accordance with . . . . *regulation 1*

Commentary—*Simon's Taxes* **E7.241**.

Modifications—Registered Pension Schemes (Splitting of Schemes) Regulations, SI 2006/569 reg 3 (modification of this provision in relation to sub-scheme administrators).

PART 1
INTRODUCTION

1 Citation and commencement

These Regulations may be cited as the Registered Pension Schemes and Overseas Pension Schemes (Electronic Communication of Returns and Information) Regulations 2006 and shall come into force on such days or days as may be appointed by the Commissioners and specified in a notice in the London, Edinburgh and Belfast Gazettes.

Note—Appointed day notified as 16 October 2007 in the London, Edinburgh and Belfast Gazettes on 13 April 2007.

2 Interpretation

(1) In these Regulations—

(*a*) "the Act" means the Finance Act 2004;

(*b*) "Part 4" means Part 4 of the Act; and

(*c*) any reference to a numbered section or Schedule (without more) is a reference to the section or Schedule bearing that number in the Act.

(2) In these Regulations, except where the context otherwise requires—

"approved method of electronic communications", in relation to the delivery of information in accordance with a provision of these Regulations, means a method of electronic communications which has been approved, by specific or general directions issued by the Commissioners, for the delivery of information of that kind under that provision;

"the Commissioners" means the Commissioners for Her Majesty's Revenue and Customs;

"the ELA Regulations" means the Pension Schemes (Enhanced Lifetime Allowance) Regulations 2006;

"electronic communications" has the meaning given in section 132(10) of the Finance Act 1999;

"official computer system" means a computer system maintained by or on behalf of the Commissioners or on behalf of an officer of Revenue and Customs;

"relevant information" means information which is required or authorised by virtue of these Regulations to be delivered to Revenue and Customs by an approved method of electronic communications;

"Revenue and Customs" means Her Majesty's Revenue and Customs; and

"the tax appeal Commissioners" means, as the case requires, the General Commissioners or the Special Commissioners.[1]

Amendments—[1] Entry for "the tax appeal Commissioners" revoked by the Transfer of Tribunal Functions and Revenue and Customs Appeals Order, SI 2009/56 art 3, Sch 2 para 153(1), (2) with effect from 1 April 2009.

3 Introduction

(1) Part 2 of these Regulations makes provision about returns and information which must be delivered to Revenue and Customs by an approved method of electronic communications.

(2) Part 3 of these Regulations makes provision about returns and information which may be delivered to Revenue and Customs by an approved method of electronic communications.

PART 2
INFORMATION WHICH MUST BE DELIVERED BY ELECTRONIC COMMUNICATIONS

4 Information which must be delivered by electronic communications

(1) The information specified in Schedule 1 to these Regulations must be delivered to Revenue and Customs—

(*a*) in a form approved for that purpose; and

(*b*) by a method of electronic communications approved for that purpose.

(2) The Commissioners may make a general or specific direction requiring a scheme administrator to deliver specified information to Revenue and Customs by a particular method of electronic communications.

(3) Information specified in Schedule 1 which is delivered to Revenue and Customs in a form, or by a method, otherwise than that required by virtue of this regulation must be treated as not having been delivered.

Commentary—*Simon's Taxes* **E7.208**.
Directions—The following Directions were published by HMRC on 13 April 2007:

> The Commissioners for HMRC direct that, on and after 16 October 2007, a pension scheme administrator who is required to deliver information specified in the Registered Pension Schemes and Overseas Pension Schemes (Electronic Communication of Returns and Information) Regulations 2006 (SI 2006/570) Sch 1 (to the extent that that Schedule is brought into force by a notice in the London, Edinburgh and Belfast Gazettes dated 13 April 2007) must do so over the internet.
>
> The Commissioners further direct that—
>
> – the methods approved by them for—
>   – authenticating the identity of the person sending the relevant information,
>   – delivery of the relevant information, and
>   – authenticating the relevant information, and
> – the form approved by them in which the relevant information is to be delivered;
>
> are (save as provided below) the methods and form set out, at the time of, and for the purposes of, the delivery of the relevant information, in the terms and conditions for use of the Internet Pension Schemes Online service for scheme administrators (including XML submissions through the third party channel).
>
> But where the total submission exceeds 23.8 megabytes the information must be delivered by sending a compact disc, in the format specified by the Pension Schemes Online technical pack for software developers, to: Pension Schemes Services, Her Majesty's Revenue and Customs, Yorke House, Castle Meadow Road, Nottingham, NG2 1BG.

PART 3
INFORMATION WHICH MAY BE DELIVERED BY ELECTRONIC COMMUNICATIONS

5 Information which may be delivered by electronic communications

(1) Information specified in Schedule 2 to these Regulations may be delivered to Revenue and Customs, if—

(*a*) it is in a form approved for that purpose;
(*b*) it is sent by a method of electronic communications approved for that purpose; and
(*c*) the sender is authorised by Revenue and Customs to use electronic communications for that purpose.

(2) Information specified in Schedule 2 may be supplied by Revenue and Customs if—

(*a*) the proposed recipient has consented to the use of electronic communications for the delivery of information by Revenue and Customs; and
(*b*) that consent has not been withdrawn.

PART 4
EVIDENTIAL PROVISIONS

6 Whether relevant information has been delivered electronically

(1) For the purposes of these Regulations, relevant information is to be taken to have been delivered to an official computer system by an approved method of electronic communications only if it is accepted by that official computer system.

This is subject to the following qualification.

(2) Relevant information which is delivered to an official computer system must meet the standards of accuracy and completeness set by specific or general directions given by the Commissioners.

(3) Relevant information which fails to meet those standards must be treated as not having been delivered.

7 Proof of content of electronic delivery

(1) A document certified by Revenue and Customs to be a printed-out version of information delivered by an approved method of electronic communications is evidence, unless the contrary is proved, that the information—

(*a*) was delivered by an approved method of electronic communications on that occasion; and
(*b*) constitutes everything which was delivered on that occasion.

(2) A document which purports to be a certificate given in accordance with paragraph (1) is presumed to be such a certificate unless the contrary is proved.

8 Proof of identity of person sending or receiving electronic delivery

The identity of—

(*a*) the person sending any information delivered by an approved method of electronic communications to Revenue and Customs, or
(*b*) the person receiving any information delivered by an approved method of electronic communications by Revenue and Customs,

is presumed, unless the contrary is proved, to be the person recorded as such on an official computer system.

9 Information sent electronically on behalf of a person

(1) Any information delivered by an approved method of electronic communications—

(*a*) to Revenue and Customs, or

(*b*) to an official computer system,

on behalf of a person, is taken to have been delivered by that person.

(2) But this does not apply if the person proves that the information was delivered without the person's knowledge or connivance.

10 Proof of information sent electronically

(1) The use of an approved method of electronic communications is presumed, unless the contrary is proved, to have resulted in the delivery of information—

(*a*) to Revenue and Customs, if the delivery of the information has been recorded on an official computer system;

(*b*) by Revenue and Customs, if the despatch of the information has been recorded on an official computer system.

(2) The use of an approved method of electronic communications is presumed, unless the contrary is proved, not to have resulted in the delivery of relevant information—

(*a*) to Revenue and Customs, if the delivery of the information has not been recorded on an official computer system;

(*b*) by Revenue and Customs, if the despatch of the information has not been recorded on an official computer system.

(3) The time of receipt or despatch of any relevant information delivered by an approved method of electronic communications is presumed, unless the contrary is proved, to be the time recorded on an official computer system.

This is subject to the following qualification.

(4) The Commissioners may by a general or specific direction provide for information to be treated as delivered upon a different date (whether earlier or later) than that given by paragraph (3).

(5) Information shall not be taken to have been delivered to an official computer system by means of electronic communications unless it is accepted by the system to which it is delivered.

11 Authentication of information in document otherwise required to be signed

If—

(*a*) information specified in Schedule 2 to these Regulations is delivered to Revenue and Customs by a method of electronic communications; and

(*b*) the information is required to be signed by or on behalf of the person delivering it,

the requirement for a signature shall be treated as satisfied if the information is authenticated by or on behalf of the sender in such manner as may be approved by the Commissioners.

12 Use of unauthorised method of electronic communications

(1) This regulation applies to information—

(*a*) which is required to be delivered to Revenue and Customs under a provision of Part 2 of these Regulations; or

(*b*) which is permitted to be delivered to Revenue and Customs under a provision of Part 3 of these Regulations.

(2) The use of a method of electronic communications for the purpose of delivering such information is conclusively presumed not to have resulted in the delivery of that information, unless that method of electronic communications is for the time being approved for the delivery of information of that kind under that provision.

SCHEDULE 1

INFORMATION WHICH MUST BE SUPPLIED TO REVENUE AND CUSTOMS BY AN APPROVED METHOD OF ELECTRONIC COMMUNICATIONS

Regulation 4

A form of application for the registration of a pension scheme under section 153 (registration of pension schemes).

A return under section 250(2) (registered pension scheme return) in response to a notice under section 250(1).

A return under section 254 (accounting for tax by scheme administrators), and any amendment of that return[, which does not relate to a currently-relieved non-UK pension scheme][1].

A declaration under section 270 (scheme administrator's obligations).

[An event report in respect of a reportable event specified in entries 1 to 8A and 10 to 21 in the table in paragraph (1) of][1] regulation 3 of the Registered Pension Schemes (Provision of Information) Regulations 2006 (provision of information by scheme administrator to Revenue and Customs).

Information furnished under regulation 4 of the Registered Pension Schemes (Provision of Information) Regulations 2006 (information about a pension scheme which has been wound up).

A notice under regulation 6 of the Registered Pension Schemes (Provision of Information) Regulations 2006 (termination of scheme administrator's appointment).

Amendments—[1] Words inserted and substituted by the Registered Pension Schemes and Overseas Pension Schemes (Miscellaneous Amendments) Regulations, SI 2012/884 reg 15(1), (2) with effect from 6 April 2012.

SCHEDULE 2

INFORMATION WHICH MAY BE SUPPLIED EITHER TO OR BY REVENUE AND CUSTOMS BY AN APPROVED METHOD OF ELECTRONIC COMMUNICATIONS

Regulation 5

A notification by Revenue and Customs under section 153(6) of a decision on an application to register a pension scheme under section 153(4).

A notification by Revenue and Customs under section 157(2) (withdrawal of An amendment to a return under section 250 by the scheme administrator.registration) of withdrawal of the registration of a pension scheme under section 157(1).

A notification under section 169(2)(*a*) (recognised transfers) by a scheme manager (within the meaning of section 169(3)) that a scheme is a recognised overseas pension scheme.

An undertaking by the scheme manager under section 169(2)(*b*) that he will inform Revenue and Customs if the scheme ceases to be a recognised overseas pension scheme.

An undertaking by the scheme manager under section 169(2)(*c*) that he will comply with any prescribed information requirements.

A notification by Revenue and Customs of a decision under section 169(5), the effect of which is to exclude a recognised overseas pension scheme from being a qualifying recognised overseas pension scheme.

A notification by Revenue and Customs of a decision under section 169(7) that a recognised overseas pension scheme is to cease to be excluded from being a qualifying recognised overseas pension scheme.

A notice under section 250 requiring the scheme administrator of a registered pension scheme to deliver a return under that section.

[An amendment to a return under section 250 by the scheme administrator.][4]

[A—

(*a*) taxpayer notice under paragraph 1 of Schedule 36 to the Finance Act 2008 (information and inspection powers),

(*b*) third party notice under paragraph 2 of that Schedule,

(*c*) notice under paragraph 5 of that Schedule

that relates to a registered pension scheme; and a notice of appeal against any such notice or against the imposition of a penalty in relation to any such notice.][2]

. . . [2]

An assessment made by Revenue and Customs under section 254 or 255 (assessments on scheme administrators and others under Part 4).

A notice issued by Revenue and Customs in respect of a penalty imposed under any of sections 257 to 266 (penalties for non-compliance with requirements to provide information or furnish returns).

An application—

(*a*) under section 267 for the discharge of the scheme administrator's liability to the lifetime allowance charge;

(*b*) under section 268 for the discharge of the scheme administrator's liability to the scheme sanction charge; or

(*c*) under that section for the discharge of a person's liability to the unauthorised payments surcharge

and a notification by Revenue and Customs of their decision upon that application.

An application by a former scheme administrator under section 271(5) (release of former scheme administrator) to be released from the liability as scheme administrator, and a notification by Revenue and Customs of their decision on that application.

A notification under paragraph 10(3) of Schedule 29 (winding up lump sum: employer's undertaking).

A notification, information or an undertaking provided by a scheme manager under paragraph 5(1) of Schedule 33 given for the purpose of securing that a pension scheme is a qualifying overseas pension scheme.

A notification by Revenue and Customs of their decision under paragraph 5(3) of Schedule 33 (exclusion of overseas pension scheme from being a qualifying overseas pension scheme).

A notification by Revenue and Customs of their decision under paragraph 5(5) of Schedule 33 (overseas pension scheme ceasing to be excluded from being a qualifying overseas pension scheme).

A notification by an individual under regulation 3, 4, 5, 6, 7 or 8 of the ELA Regulations.

A requirement by an individual under regulation 12 of the ELA Regulations that Revenue and Customs give notice of their decision to refuse to consider the information in a notification by the individual; the notice given of that decision; and a notice of appeal . . . [1] against that decision.

A requirement by an individual under regulation 14 of the ELA Regulations that Revenue and Customs give notice of their refusal to issue a certificate under those Regulations; the notice given of that refusal; and a notice of appeal . . . [1] against that refusal.

A requirement by an individual under regulation 16 of the ELA Regulations that Revenue and Customs issue an aggregate certificate.

A notice given by an individual under regulation 17 of the ELA Regulations that any information given in a notification, or in connection with a notification under those Regulations, was incorrect or has become incorrect.

A notice given by an individual under regulation 18 of the ELA Regulations that information given in a certificate issued by Revenue and Customs under those Regulations was incorrect or has become incorrect.

. . . [2]

A notice by Revenue and Customs under regulation 24 of the ELA Regulations of the revocation or amendment of a certificate under those Regulations; and a notice of appeal . . . [1] against such a notice.

A certificate by Revenue and Customs under the ELA Regulations, and an amendment, under those Regulations, of such a certificate.

[An amendment to an event report in respect of a reportable event specified in entries 1 to 8A and 10 to 21 in the table in paragraph (1) of regulation 3 of the Registered Pension Schemes (Provision of Information) Regulations 2006 (provision of information by scheme administrator to the Commissioners).][4]

Information furnished by a company about an unauthorised employer payment under regulation 5 of the Registered Pension Schemes (Provision of Information) Regulations 2006.

Information furnished by personal representatives under regulation 10 of the Registered Pension Schemes (Provision of Information) Regulations 2006.

A notice of appeal against a decision by Revenue and Customs under section 153(6), 157(2), 169(5), 267, 268 or 271(6) or paragraph 5(3) of Schedule 33.

. . . [2]

A notice of appeal against an assessment under regulation 4 of the Registered Pension Schemes (Accounting and Assessment) Regulations 2005 (assessment in respect of supplementary charges under Part 4).

Information required from qualifying overseas pension schemes[, QROPS and former QROPS under regulations 2 to 3C][6] of the Pension Schemes (Information Requirements—Qualifying Overseas Pension Schemes, Qualifying Recognised Overseas Pensions Schemes and Corresponding Relief) Regulations 2006.

A notice of appeal against the imposition of a penalty under—

(*a*) section 98 of TMA 1970 by virtue of section 258 (penalties for failure to provide information required by regulations under section 251(1)(*a*) or (4) of the Finance Act 2004);

(*b*) section 257 (scheme administrator failing to make a registered pension scheme return or negligently or fraudulently making an incorrect return or delivering incorrect documents);

(c) section 259 (failure to deliver documents or particulars required by notice);[2]

(*d*) . . . [5];

(*e*) section 261 (enhanced lifetime allowance regulations: documents and information);

(*f*) section 262 (enhanced lifetime allowance regulations: failures to comply);

(*g*) section 263 (lifetime allowance enhanced protection: benefit accrual);

(*h*) section 264 (fraudulent or negligent misstatements, etc);

(*i*) section 265 (winding up wholly or mainly to facilitate payment of lump sums); or

(*j*) section 266(2) (transfer of sums representing accrued rights to a registered pension scheme which is an insured scheme otherwise than to scheme administrator of the transferee scheme or an insurance company);

[(*ja*) Schedule 24 to the Finance Act 2007 (penalties for errors) in respect of an error in a return under section 254 of the Finance Act 2004][5][; or (*k*) Schedule 55 to the Finance Act 2009 (penalty for failure to make returns)][3]

Amendments—[1] Words revoked in each place by the Transfer of Tribunal Functions and Revenue and Customs Appeals Order, SI 2009/56 art 3, Sch 2 para 153(1), (3) with effect from 1 April 2009.

[2] Entries repealed, and entry inserted, by the Registered Pension Schemes and Overseas Pension Schemes (Electronic Communication of Returns and Information) (Amendment) Regulations 2010, SI 2010/652 reg 2 with effect from 1 April 2010. Note that these amendments do not apply in relation to or in connection with a notice given before 1 April 2010 requiring the provision or production of information, particulars or documents (SI 2010/652 reg 1(2)).

[3] In final para, sub-para (*k*) and preceding word "or" inserted, by the Finance Act 2009, Schedules 55 and 56 (Income Tax Self Assessment and Pension Schemes) (Appointed Days and Consequential and Savings Provisions) Order, SI 2011/702 art 19 with effect from 1 April 2011. This amendment has no effect in respect of a return period ending on or before 31 December 2010 (SI 2011/702 art 21).

[4] Entries inserted by the Registered Pension Schemes and Overseas Pension Schemes (Miscellaneous Amendments) Regulations, SI 2012/884 reg 15(1), (3) with effect from 6 April 2012.

[5] In final para, sub-para (*d*) revoked, and sub-para (*ja*) inserted, by the Pension Schemes (Miscellaneous Amendments) Order, SI 2013/1114 art 8 with effect from 1 June 2013.

[6] Words substituted for words "and qualifying recognised overseas pension schemes under regulations 2 and 3" by the Registered Pension Schemes and Overseas Pension Schemes (Miscellaneous Amendments) Regulations, SI 2013/2259 regs 22, 23 with effect from 14 October 2013.

2006/571

REGISTERED PENSION SCHEMES (AUTHORISED MEMBER PAYMENTS) (NO 2) REGULATIONS 2006

Made by the Commissioners for HMRC under FA 2004 s 164(f)

Made . . . .*9 March 2006*
Laid before the House of Commons . . . .*10 March 2006*
Coming into force . . . .*6 April 2006*

Commentary—*Simon's Taxes* **E7.202–E7.207**.

1 Citation and commencement

These Regulations may be cited as the Registered Pension Schemes (Authorised Member Payments) (No 2) Regulations 2006 and shall come into force on 6th April 2006.

2 Payments which are authorised member payments

A payment which satisfies the conditions in article 39(1), 40(1), 41(1) or 42(1) of the Taxation of Pension Schemes (Transitional Provisions) Order 2006 is a payment which a registered pension scheme is authorised to make.

2006/572

TAXATION OF PENSION SCHEMES (TRANSITIONAL PROVISIONS) ORDER 2006

Made by the Treasury under s 283(2) of the Finance Act 2004

Made . . . .*9 March 2006*
Laid before the House of Commons . . . .*10 March 2006*
Coming into force . . . .*6 April 2006*

Commentary—*Simon's Taxes* **E7.240**.

1 Citation and commencement

(1) This Order may be cited as the Taxation of Pension Schemes (Transitional Provisions) Order 2006 and shall come into force on 6th April 2006.

(2) In this Order—

"Revenue and Customs" means Her Majesty's Revenue and Customs (see section 4 of the Commissioners for Revenue and Customs Act 2005);

"the 2004 Act" means the Finance Act 2004;

"Part 4" means Part 4 of the Finance Act 2004;

a reference to a numbered section or Schedule (without more) is a reference to the section or Schedule bearing that number in Part 4; and

expressions which are defined, or are otherwise explained, in section 280 have the same meaning in this Order as they have in Part 4.

2 Payments made from annuities

(1) In its application to any pension scheme which by virtue of paragraph 1(1) of Schedule 36 (pension schemes: transitional provisions and savings)—

(*a*) is to be treated as becoming a registered pension scheme on 6th April 2006;
(*b*) would have been so treated had it not been wound up before that date; or
(*c*) would have been so treated if the scheme administrator had not notified Revenue and Customs under paragraph 2 of Schedule 36 (opting out of deemed registration) that the pension scheme was not to become a registered pension scheme on that date,

section 161 (meaning of "payment" etc) is modified as follows.

(2) In subsection (3) after the words "of a registered pension scheme" add—

"or, if the purchase took place before 6th April 2006, a pension scheme which at the time of purchase fell within one of the categories set out in paragraph 1(1)(*a*) to (*g*) of Schedule 36.".

(3) After subsection (3) add—

"(3A) But subsection (4) does not apply to a payment made or benefit provided under or in connection with an annuity which fulfils the following conditions.

Condition 1

The annuity was purchased from an insurance company.

Condition 2

The annuity was purchased by a pension scheme which at the time of purchase fell within one of the categories set out in paragraph 1(1)(*a*) to (*g*) of Schedule 36.

Condition 3

The annuity was purchased in order to secure or provide benefits under the scheme referred to in Condition 2.

Condition 4

The terms of the annuity, or of any arrangement or agreement made in connection with that annuity do not permit a payment, the making of which would have given the Board grounds for withdrawing approval of the pension scheme under section 591B of ICTA if it had been made before 6th April 2006.

Condition 5

The terms of the annuity contract have not been altered on or after 6th April 2006 to allow a payment that would be an unauthorised payment if it had been made by a registered pension scheme."

(4) In its application to any pension scheme which falls within sub-paragraph (1)(*b*) section 161(4) is modified as follows.

(5) For the words "held for the purpose of the pension scheme" substitute "held for the purposes of a registered pension scheme".

3 Commencement provisions for unsecured pension funds

Part 4 of the 2004 Act shall be modified as set out in articles 4 and 5 in its application to any pension which—

(*a*) was paid by way of income withdrawal, income drawdown or annuity purchase deferral from a retirement benefits scheme, or a personal pension scheme approved under Part 14 of ICTA immediately before 6th April 2006; and
(*b*) on 6th April 2006 becomes an unsecured pension or a dependant's unsecured pension by virtue of a scheme which is treated as becoming a registered pension scheme on that date (see paragraph 1 of Schedule 36).

4 Modification of section 165

(1) Section 165(1) (pension rules) shall be modified as follows.

(2) In pension rule 5 after "basis amount for the unsecured pension year" add "or 100% of that amount during the first reference period as defined in paragraph 10(1A) of Schedule 28.".

(3) Section 167(1) (pension death benefit rules) shall be modified as follows.

(4) In pension death benefit rule 4 after "basis amount for the unsecured pension year" add "or 100% of that amount during the first reference period as defined in paragraph 24(1A) of Schedule 28.".

5 Modification of Schedule 28

(1) Schedule 28 (registered pension schemes: authorised pensions—supplementary) shall be modified as follows.

(2) In paragraph 10—

(*a*) in sub-paragraph (1) for "The period of five unsecured pension years" substitute "The first reference period as defined in sub-paragraph (1A) below";
(*b*) after sub-paragraph (1) insert a new sub-paragraph as follows—

"(1A) The "first reference period" is the period commencing on 6th April 2006 and terminating on the earliest of—

(*a*) the day immediately before the day fixed by the scheme administrator on which to recalculate the basis amount;

(*b*) the day immediately before the day on which the basis amount was recalculated following an annuity purchase;

(*c*) 6th April 2008.";

(*c*) in sub-paragraph (2) for "sub-paragraph (5)" substitute "sub-paragraphs (2A) and (5).";

(*d*) after sub-paragraph (2) insert the following sub-paragraph—

"(2A) For the first reference period as defined in sub-paragraph (1A), the basis amount is—

(*a*) the annual amount of the annuity calculated pursuant to section 630 of ICTA;

(*b*) the maximum annual pension calculated in accordance with the rules set out in Appendix XII Part I of the Occupational Pension Schemes Practice Notes (IR12) published by the Board on 22nd January 2001 ("the Notes");

(*c*) the annual amount of pension income which has been paid in accordance with paragraph 20.41 of the Notes in respect of a retirement benefits scheme approved for the purposes of Chapter 1 of Part 14 of ICTA, being paid as a small self-administered pension pursuant to the terms of Memorandum 119 issued on 6th May 1994 by the Board.

which could have been purchased by the application of the sums and assets which then represented the member's pension fund on the nominated date.";

(*e*) in sub-paragraph (3)(*a*) for "the reference date" substitute "the applicable reference date";

(*f*) after sub-paragraph (3) insert—

"(3A) "The applicable reference date" is the date on which the pension fund was last valued—

(*a*) in the case of a personal pension fund, pursuant to section 634A of ICTA (income withdrawal by member),

(*b*) in the case of a retirement benefits scheme (other than one falling within paragraph (*c*) below), pursuant to the rules set out in the Notes, or

(*c*) in the case of a retirement benefits scheme referred to in sub-paragraph (2A)(*c*), the date of the scheme's last triennial report as required by paragraph 20.41 of the Notes.".

(3) In paragraph 24—

(*a*) in sub-paragraph (1) for the words "The period of five unsecured pension years" substitute "The first reference period as defined in sub-paragraph (1A) below";

(*b*) after sub-paragraph (1) insert a new sub-paragraph as follows—

"(1A) The "first reference period" is the period commencing on 6th April 2006 and terminating on the earliest of—

(*a*) the day immediately before the day fixed by the scheme administrator on which to recalculate the basis amount;

(*b*) the day immediately before the day on which the basis amount was recalculated following an annuity purchase;

(*c*) 6th April 2008.";

(*c*) in sub-paragraph (2) for "sub-paragraph (5)" substitute "sub-paragraphs (2A) and (5).";

(*d*) after sub-paragraph (2) insert the following sub-paragraph—

"(2A) For the first reference period as defined in sub-paragraph (1A), the basis amount is—

(*a*) the annual amount of the annuity calculated pursuant to section 630 of ICTA,

(*b*) the maximum annual pension calculated in accordance with the rules set out in Appendix XII Part I of the Occupational Pension Schemes Practice Notes (IR12) published by the Board on 22nd January 2001 ("the Notes") or,

(*c*) the annual amount of pension income that has been paid in accordance with paragraph 20.41 of the Notes in respect of a retirement benefits scheme approved for the purposes of Chapter 1 of Part 14 of ICTA, being paid as a small self-administered pension calculated pursuant to the terms of Memorandum 119 issued by the Board on 6 May 1994

which could have been purchased by the application of the sums and assets which then represented the member's pension fund on the nominated date.";

(*e*) in sub-paragraph (3)(*a*) for "the reference date" substitute "the applicable reference date";

(*f*) after sub-paragraph (3) insert—

"(3A) "The applicable reference date" is the date on which the pension fund was last valued—

(*a*) in the case of a personal pension fund, pursuant to section 636A of ICTA (income withdrawal after the death of member),

(*b*) in the case of a retirement benefits scheme (other than one falling within paragraph (*c*) below), pursuant to the rules set out in the Notes, or (*c*) in the case of a retirement benefits scheme referred to in sub-paragraph (2A)(*c*), the date of the scheme's last triennial report as required by paragraph 20.41 of the Notes.".

5A [Reduction in rate of pension

(1) Part 4 of the 2004 Act shall be modified as set out in paragraph (2) in a case where the following conditions are satisfied—

(*a*) the pension came into payment before 3rd July 2007;

(*b*) the pension is paid to a person who was a member of the pension scheme on 5th April 2006;

(*c*) on 5th April 2006 the rules of the pension scheme included provision that there shall or may be a reduction in the rate of the pension ("the rate reduction provisions");

(*d*) the pension is paid at a rate required or permitted by the rate reduction provisions;

(*e*) the rate reduction provisions would not have prejudiced the approval of the pension scheme by the Inland Revenue or by Her Majesty's Revenue and Customs;

(*f*) the rate reduction provisions did not change in any material particular between 5th April 2006 and the date at which the pension became payable at the reduced rate.

(2) In paragraph 2(4) of Schedule 28 to the 2004 Act insert after paragraph (*d*)—

"(*da*) a reduction in respect of which an order made under section 283(2) and (3C) makes transitional provision,"

(3) For the purposes of this article, whether something would have prejudiced the approval of the pension scheme by the Inland Revenue or by Her Majesty's Revenue and Customs is to be determined—

(*a*) in the case of an occupational pension scheme approved for the purposes of Chapter 1 of Part 14 of ICTA, in accordance with the publication IR 12(2001) (known as the Occupational Pension Schemes Practice Notes) published by the former Inland Revenue Pension Schemes Office on 23rd March 2001, and

(*b*) in the case of a personal pension scheme approved under Chapter 4 of Part 14 of ICTA, in accordance with the publication IR 76(2000) published by the former Inland Revenue Pension Schemes Office on 20th November 2000,

as each of those publications stood at 5th April 2006.][1]

Amendments—[1] This paragraph inserted by the Taxation of Pension Schemes (Transitional Provisions) (Amendment) Order, SI 2008/2990 arts 2, 3 with effect in respect of payments of pension made on or after 6 April 2006. This amendment comes into force on 1 January 2009.

6 Transitional protection for continued life cover (75+)

The modifications in articles 7 and 8 apply in the case of a member of a registered pension scheme who satisfies the following conditions.

Condition A

The registered pension scheme was, immediately before 6th April 2006, a retirement benefits scheme approved for the purposes of Chapter 1 of Part 14 of ICTA (retirement benefits schemes).

Condition B

The member had a right under the pension scheme to a life cover lump sum on 5th April 2006.

Condition C

The rules of the pension scheme on 10th December 2003 included provision conferring such a right on some or all of the persons who were then members of the pension scheme, and such a right was either then conferred on the member or would have been had the member been a member of the scheme on that date.

Condition D

The rules of the scheme in relation to life cover lump sums have not been changed since 10th December 2003.

Condition E

The member was—

(*a*) in receipt of benefits from the scheme on or before 5th April 2006, or

(*b*) entitled to one or more life cover lump sums, amounting in the aggregate, to £2,500 or less.

Commentary—*Simon's Taxes* **E7.202–E7.207**.

7 Modification of section 636A ITEPA 2003

(1) ITEPA 2003 is modified as follows.

(2) In section 636A(1) (exemption for certain lump sums under registered pension schemes)—

(*a*) at the end of paragraph (*e*) omit "or";

(*b*) at the end of paragraph (*f*) add "or"; and

(*c*) after paragraph (*f*) insert—

"(*g*) a life cover lump sum.".

(3) In section 636A(7) after "unsecured pension fund lump sum death benefit" insert "life cover lump sum".

Commentary—*Simon's Taxes* **E7.202–E7.207**.

8 Modification of section 168 and Schedule 29

(1) The 2004 Act is modified as follows.

(2) In section 168(1) (lump sum death benefit rule) after paragraph (i) insert—

"(*j*) a life cover lump sum.".

(3) In Part 2 of Schedule 29 (registered pension schemes: supplementary provisions about lump sums) after paragraph 21 insert—

21 "Life cover lump sum

For the purposes of this Part a lump sum death benefit is a life cover lump sum if—

(*a*) the member had reached the age of 75 before he died;

(*b*) payment of the sum would not have prejudiced approval of the scheme for the purposes of Chapter 1 of Part 14 of ICTA if it had been made on 5th April 2006.".

Commentary—*Simon's Taxes* **E7.202–E7.207**.

9 Valuation of "primary protection" – compensation for poorly performing investments

Part 4 of 2004 Act shall be modified as set out in articles 10 and 11 in its application to any individual who has given notice of intention to rely on paragraph 7 Schedule 36 where the following conditions are met—

Condition A

The pension scheme in respect of which the individual has given notice is either—

(*a*) a money purchase arrangement that is not a cash balance arrangement; or

(*b*) a hybrid arrangement where the benefits that may be provided include money purchase benefits that are not cash balance benefits.

Condition B

An amount is paid into the pension scheme, or is determined as being so payable, between 6th April 2006 and 5th April 2009, in respect of compensation for the poor performance of an investment owned by that scheme.

Condition C

The investment in respect of which the compensation is payable was owned by the pension scheme at any time before 6th April 2006 and was offered for sale to the public on the open market.

Condition D

The amount of compensation paid, or determined as being so payable, is an amount which might reasonably have been expected to be paid between two parties in the same position as the payer and the scheme administrator acting at arm's length.

Commentary—*Simon's Taxes* **E7.202–E7.207**.

10 Modification of section 212

(1) Section 212 (valuation of uncrystallised rights for the purposes of section 210) is modified, for the purposes of calculating the value of *RR* in paragraph 7(3) of Schedule 36, as follows.

(2) In subsection (5) (valuation of money purchase arrangements other than cash balance arrangements) after paragraphs (*a*) and (*b*) add—

"together with the value, if any, of any relevant compensation on 5th April 2006.".

(3) After subsection (5) add—

"(5A) For the purposes of subsections (5) and (7) relevant compensation is the market value, calculated in accordance with section 278, of any compensation paid or payable in respect of the poor performance of an investment owned by the pension scheme on the earlier of the date of payment of the compensation or 5th April 2009.".

(4) In subsection (7) (valuation of hybrid arrangements) after paragraphs (*a*) and (*b*) add—

"together with any hybrid compensation as defined in subsection (7A) below.".

(5) After subsection (7) add—

"(7A) For the purposes of subsection (7) hybrid compensation is—

(*a*) any relevant compensation payable in respect of a money purchase arrangement which forms part of the hybrid arrangement calculated in accordance with subsection (5A); less

(*b*) the value of the hybrid arrangement calculated in accordance with subsection (7) less the value of any sums or assets representing other money purchase benefits calculated in accordance with subsection (5).

If this calculation results in a negative amount, the amount of relevant compensation to be added to the value of the member's uncrystallised rights under this subsection is nil.".

Commentary—*Simon's Taxes* **E7.202–E7.207**.

11 Modification of paragraph 8 of Schedule 36

(1) Part 2 of Schedule 36 (pre-commencement rights: lifetime allowance charge) is modified as follows.

(2) In paragraph 8(5) after the words " (valuation of uncrystallised rights for the purposes of section 210)" add—

"(as modified by article 10 of The Taxation of Pension Schemes (Transitional Provisions) Order 2006)".

Commentary—*Simon's Taxes* **E7.202–E7.207**.

12 "Primary protection" and non residents

(1) Part 4 of the 2004 Act shall have effect subject to the modifications set out in articles 13 and 14 below in its application to any individual to whom either paragraph (2) or (3) applies

(2) This paragraph applies if the following conditions are met—

Condition A

The individual has given the Inland Revenue a notice under section 221(6) of his intention to rely on that section where the active membership period in relation to the arrangement in respect of which the notice was given commenced on 6th April 2006

Condition B

The individual would have been a relevant overseas individual in the tax year 2005–06 pursuant to section 221(3) had that subsection been in force during that year.

Condition C

The individual gives or has already given notice to the Inland Revenue pursuant to paragraph 7(1)(*b*) of Schedule 36 that he intends to rely on that paragraph.

(3) This paragraph applies if the following conditions are met—

Condition A

The individual has given the Inland Revenue a notice under paragraph 7(1)(*b*) of Schedule 36 of his intention to rely on that paragraph.

Condition B

The individual gives or has already given notice to the Inland Revenue pursuant to section 221(6) that he intends to rely on that section where the active membership period in relation to the arrangement in respect of which the notice was given commenced on 6th April 2006.

Condition C

The individual would have been a relevant overseas individual in the tax year 2005–06 pursuant to section 221(3) had that subsection been in force during that year.

Commentary—*Simon's Taxes* **E7.216**.

13 Modification of section 222

(1) In subsection 222(4) (non residence: money purchase arrangements) after "OV is" for the words "the opening value of the individual's rights under the arrangement" substitute "calculated in accordance with subsection (4A).".

(2) After subsection (4) add subsection (4A)—

"(4A) For the purposes of subsection (4)—

$$OV = OVA \times \frac{SLA}{CSLA}$$

Here—

OVA is the value of the individual's rights under the arrangement on 5th April 2006 calculated in accordance with subsection (5)(*b*).

SLA is the standard lifetime allowance at the time when the part of the active membership period referred to in subsection (4) ended and

CSLA is £1,500,000 (the lifetime allowance for the tax year 2006–07).".

(3) For subsection (5)(*b*) substitute—

"(*b*) the value of the individual's rights under the arrangement on 5th April 2006 is the amount which would, on the valuation assumptions, be available for the provision of benefits to or in respect of the individual under the arrangement if the individual became entitled to the benefits on 5th April 2006.".

Commentary—*Simon's Taxes* **E7.216**.

14 Modification of section 223

(1) Section 223 (non-residence: other arrangements) is modified as follows.

(2) In subsection (4) in the definitions of PB and LSB for "at the beginning of that part of that period" substitute "on 5th April 2006 indexed in accordance with subsection (4A).".

(3) After subsection (4) insert—

"(4A) PB and LSB shall be increased by multiplying the appropriate figure by—

$$\frac{SLA}{CSLA}$$

Here—

SLA is the standard lifetime allowance at the time when the part of the active membership period referred to in subsection (4) ended and

CSLA is £1,500,000 (the lifetime allowance for the tax year 2006–07)."

Commentary—*Simon's Taxes* **E7.216**.

15 Employers or employees with pre-commencement entitlement to corresponding relief

(1) This article applies where Revenue and Customs allow contributions made between 1st April 2005 and 5th April 2006 by an employer under a pension scheme for the benefit of an employee (a "qualifying employee") to be deducted in accordance with section 76(6A) and (6C) of the Finance Act 1989—

(*a*) for the purposes of Case I or Case II of Schedule D;

(*b*) in respect of management expenses under section 75 of ICTA; or

(*c*) in respect of the expenses of an insurance company under section 76 of ICTA;

(*d*) in respect of profits of a trade, profession or vocation chargeable under section 5 of the Income Tax (Trading and Other Income) Act 2005.

(2) Where, at any time on or after 6th April 2006, the employer makes contributions under the pension scheme referred to in paragraph (1) for the benefit of the qualifying employee, Revenue and Customs may allow the contributions to be treated as if they were relevant migrant member contributions under paragraph 2 of Schedule 33 if—

(*a*) they are satisfied that the conditions in paragraph (3) are met, and

(*b*) the scheme manager complies with any prescribed benefit crystallisation information requirements imposed on the scheme manager.

(3) The conditions are that—

(*a*) the contribution consists of the expenses of paying any sum, or of providing benefits, pursuant to a pension scheme which is established outside the United Kingdom; and

(*b*) Revenue and Customs are satisfied that that scheme corresponds to such a scheme as is registered under Part 4 of the 2004 Act.

(4) For the purposes of this article and article 17, "Prescribed benefit crystallisation information requirements" means requirements imposed by regulation 2 of the Pension Schemes (Information Requirements—Qualifying Overseas Pension Schemes, Qualifying Recognised Overseas Pension Schemes and Corresponding Relief) Regulations 2006 ("the Overseas Information Requirements Regulations").

For the purposes of this article, the provisions of regulation 2 of the Overseas Information Requirements Regulations shall apply to qualifying employees.

(5) The references in paragraphs (2), (3) and (4) to a pension scheme include a pension scheme to which there has been a block transfer on or after 6th April 2006 from a pension scheme to which paragraph (2) applies.

(6) In this article "block transfer" has the same meaning as in paragraph 22(6) of Schedule 36 but treating the references there to "the member" as references to the qualifying employee.

Commentary—*Simon's Taxes* **E7.224**.

16 Modification of section 245

(1) In a case falling within article 15, section 245 (restriction of deduction for contributions by employer) is modified as follows.

(2) In subsection (5)—

(*a*) after the words " (deductions to which Schedule does not apply)" insert " (*a*)"; and

(*b*) after the words "relevant migrant member of the pension scheme in relation to the contributions," insert—

"and

(*b*) after paragraph (*g*) insert—

"(*h*) in respect of contributions which have been given relief under section 196 as applied by paragraph 2 of Schedule 33 and modified by article 15 of The Taxation of Pension Schemes (Transitional Provisions) Order 2006."."

Commentary—*Simon's Taxes* **E7.224**.

17 Application of 308A ITEPA 2003

(1) This article applies where—

(*a*) Revenue and Customs allow an employee (an "exempt employee") to be exempted from income tax under section 390 ITEPA 2003 in relation to contributions made between 6th April 2005 and 5th April 2006 by his employer under a pension scheme; and

(*b*) the conditions in paragraph (2) are met.

(2) The conditions are

Condition A

The scheme manager of the pension scheme referred to in paragraph (1)(*a*) complies with any prescribed benefit crystallisation information requirements imposed on the scheme manager.

Condition B

Revenue and Customs are satisfied that the pension scheme corresponds to such a scheme as is registered under Part 4 of this Act.

(3) For the purposes of this article, the provisions of regulation 2 of the Overseas Information Requirements Regulations shall apply to exempt employees.

(4) Section 308A of ITEPA 2003 (exemption of contributions to overseas pension scheme) shall apply in relation to any contributions made on or after 6th April 2006 for the benefit of the employee by an employer under the pension scheme as if—

(*a*) the pension scheme were a qualifying overseas pension scheme, and

(*b*) the contributions were relevant migrant member contributions.

(5) The references in paragraphs (1) and (2) to a pension scheme include a pension scheme to which there has been a block transfer on or after 6th April 2006 from a pension scheme to which paragraphs (1) and (2) apply.

(6) In this article "block transfer" has the same meaning as in paragraph 22(6) of Schedule 36 but treating the references there to "the member" as references to the exempt employee.

Commentary—*Simon's Taxes* **E7.224**.

18 "Enhanced protection" and pension commencement lump sums

If (and for so long) as paragraph 27 or 29 of Schedule 36 applies in relation to an individual, paragraph 1(1) of Schedule 29 (supplementary provision about authorised lump sums: meaning of "pension commencement lump sum") shall have effect, in relation to that individual, with the omission of paragraph (*b*) (requirement that lump sum payable only when lifetime allowance available)[, and section 239 has effect in the case of a lump sum paid to that individual as if its subsection (3)(*b*) did not include a reference to paragraph 1(1)(*b*) of Schedule 29][1].

Amendments[1] Words inserted by FA 2014 s 43, Sch 5 para 12(4). This amendment is to be treated as having come into force on 19 March 2014 (FA 2014 Sch 5 para 15) and as made by the Treasury under the powers to make orders conferred by FA 2004 s 283(2) (FA 2014 Sch 5 para 12(5)).

19 Pre-commencement pension and calculation of the "permitted maximum" pension commencement lump sum

(1) In the case of an individual who falls within paragraph 20(1) of Schedule 36 (pre-commencement pensions) paragraph (2) applies.

(2) In paragraph 2(6) of Schedule 29 after the words "AAC is the aggregate of the amounts crystallised by each benefit crystallisation event which has occurred in relation to the member" insert " (including any pre-commencement pension rights valued under paragraph 20 of Schedule 36) and the amount of any lump sum deemed to have been crystallised under paragraph 1(1A) of Schedule 29)".

20 Pre-commencement lump sum death benefits

(1) In the case of an individual who dies on or after 6th April 2006 and meets the conditions in paragraph (2) paragraph (3) applies.

(2) The conditions are—

Condition A

The individual had an actual right to one or more pre-commencement pensions immediately before his death.

Condition B

No benefit crystallisation event has occurred in relation to the individual before his death.

Condition C

After the individual's death a single benefit crystallisation event occurs in relation to that individual by reason of the payment of a lump sum death benefit in respect of that individual.

(3) Paragraph 20(2)(*b*) of Schedule 36 is to be treated as providing that the amount crystallised was the value of the individual's pre-commencement pension rights immediately before the individual's death.

21 Transfers and entitlement to lump sums exceeding 25% of uncrystallised rights

(1) Articles 22 and 23 apply if—

(*a*) a person was a member of a pension scheme—

(i) which was in existence on 5th April 2006; and

(ii) which is treated as becoming a registered pension scheme within Part 4 of the Finance Act 2004 on 6th April 2006 (see paragraph 1 of Schedule 36 to that Act); and

(*b*) on or after 6th April 2006 sums and assets held for the purposes of, or representing accrued rights, under the registered pension scheme are transferred, otherwise than by a block transfer—

(i) to another registered pension scheme; or

(ii) to a registered pension scheme from a registered pension scheme which has received a block transfer of the sums and assets referred to in sub-paragraph 1(*b*) of this article.

(2) In this article "block transfer" has the meaning given in paragraph 31(8) of Schedule 36 (entitlement to lump sums exceeding 25% of uncrystallised rights).

Commentary—*Simon's Taxes* **E7.202–E7.207**.

22 Modification of paragraph 31 of Schedule 36

(1) In a case to which this article applies, paragraph 31 of Schedule 36 is modified as follows.

(2) In sub-paragraph (1) for "sub-paragraph (2)" substitute "sub-paragraphs (2) and (2A)".

(3) After sub-paragraph (2) insert—

"(2A) Those provisions apply with the further modifications prescribed by Article 23 of the Taxation of Pension Schemes (Transitional Provisions) Order 2006 in the case of a person satisfying sub-paragraph (1) above—

(*a*) who was a member of a pension scheme which—

(i) was in existence on 5th April 2006; and

(i) is treated as becoming a registered pension scheme within Part 4 of the Finance Act 2004 on 6th April 2006 (see paragraph 1 of Schedule 36 to that Act); and

(*b*) in respect of whom sums and assets held for the purposes of, or representing accrued rights under, the registered pension scheme are transferred, otherwise than by a block transfer—

(i) to another registered pension scheme, or

(ii) to another registered pension scheme from a registered pension which has received a block transfer of the sums and assets referred to in paragraph (*b*) of this sub-paragraph.".

Commentary—*Simon's Taxes* **E7.202–E7.207**.

23 Modification of paragraph 34 of Schedule 36

(1) In a case to which this article applies, paragraph 34 of Schedule 36 is modified as follows.

(2) In sub-paragraph (2) for the words from "pension scheme and for" to the end of the paragraph (7) (as substituted) substitute—

"pension scheme and for sub-paragraphs (5) to (8) there were substituted—

"(5) If paragraph 2(2) does not apply, [1] and there has been a transfer of part or all of the sums and assets held for the purposes of, or representing accrued rights under, the registered pension scheme in relation to the individual, the permitted maximum is the greater of—

(*VULSR* × ([*ULA*][3] / [*FSLA*][2])) + *ALSA* – (*TV* / 4)

and nil.

(6) . . . [1]

(7) In this paragraph—

VULSR is the value of the individual's uncrystallised lump sum rights under the pension scheme on 5th April 2006, calculated in accordance with paragraph 32 of Schedule 36,

[ULA is the underpinned lifetime allowance,][3]

FSLA is £1,500,000 (the standard lifetime allowance for the tax year 2006–07),

ALSA is the greater of the additional lump sum amount and nil; and

TV is the value of all sums and assets held for the purposes of, or representing accrued rights under the registered pension scheme transferred from the scheme on or after 6th April 2006.".".

Commentary—*Simon's Taxes* **E7.202–E7.207**.

Amendments—[1] In substituted Sch 36 para 34(5), words revoked, and whole of para 34(6), revoked,, by the Taxation of Pension Schemes (Transitional Provisions) (Amendment) Order, SI 2008/2990 arts 2, 4 with effect in respect of lump sums paid on or after 6 April 2006. This amendment comes into force on 1 January 2009.

[2] In para (2), "FSLA" substituted for "FLSA" by the Taxation of Pension Schemes (Transitional Provisions) (Amendment) (No 2) Order, SI 2011/1782 art 2(1), (2)(*a*)(ii) with effect from 11 August 2011.

[3] In para (2), in the sub-para (5) treated as substituted, reference substituted, and in the sub-para (7) treated as substituted, definition substituted by the Taxation of Pension Schemes (Transitional Provisions) (Amendment) (No.2) Order, SI 2011/1782 art 2(1), (2)(*a*)(i), (*b*) with effect for the tax year 2012–13 and subsequent tax years.

23ZA [Pension commencement lump sums where no pension is paid before death

(1) Subject to articles 23ZD and 23ZE, in a case where an individual has received a pension commencement lump sum, or part of a pension commencement lump sum, but dies before becoming entitled to the pension in connection with the lump sum, Schedule 36 is modified as follows.

(2) For paragraph 31(3) (entitlement to lump sums exceeding 25% of uncrystallised rights—the pension condition) substitute—

"(3) The pension condition is that, the scheme administrator considers that, had the individual not died, the individual would have become entitled to all of the pensions payable to the individual under arrangements under the pension scheme (to which the individual did not have an actual entitlement on or before 5th April 2006) on the same date.".

(3) In paragraph 34(2) (entitlement to lump sums exceeding 25% of uncrystallised rights—modifications to Schedule 29)—

(*a*) in the substituted sub-paragraph (7A) for the definition of AC substitute—

"AC is the value of the individual's uncrystallised rights on the date of death under arrangements under the pension scheme in connection with which the lump sum is paid calculated in accordance with section 212 (but this is subject to sub-paragraphs (7B) and (7BA)) on the assumption that the individual became entitled to the present payment of benefits in respect of the rights on that date.";

(*b*) omit substituted sub-paragraph (7AA); and

(*c*) after the substituted sub-paragraph (7B) insert—

"(7BA) In determining AC, section 212 shall apply as if "the value assumptions" means the basis upon which the scheme administrator determined the amount of the lump sum to be paid.][1]

Amendments—[1] Articles 23ZA–23ZE inserted by the Taxation of Pension Schemes (Transitional Provisions) (Amendment) Order, SI 2011/732 arts 2, 3 with effect in relation to any time on or after 6 April 2006.

23ZB [Pension commencement lump sums and multiple pensions

(1) Article 23ZC applies where—

(*a*) there is a single pension commencement lump sum;

(*b*) the lump sum is paid in connection with at least two of the three types of pension listed in paragraph (4) from the same registered pension scheme; and

(*c*) an individual becomes entitled to all of the pensions in connection with which the pension commencement lump sum is paid within the specified period.

(2) Article 23ZD applies where—

(*a*) there is a single pension commencement lump sum;

(*b*) the scheme administrator anticipated that the lump sum would be paid in connection with at least two of the three types of pension listed in paragraph (4) from the same registered pension scheme;

(*c*) an individual received the lump sum, or part of the lump sum, but died before becoming entitled to any of the pensions; and

(*d*) the scheme administrator considers that, had the individual not died, the individual would have become entitled to all of the pensions in connection with the lump sum within the specified period.

(3) Article 23ZE applies where—

(*a*) there is a single pension commencement lump sum;

(*b*) the scheme administrator anticipated that the lump sum would be paid in connection with at least two of the three types of pension listed in paragraph (4) from the same registered pension scheme;

(*c*) an individual received the lump sum, or part of the lump sum, but died before the end of the specified period after becoming entitled to at least one but not all of the pensions; and

(*d*) the scheme administrator considers that, had the individual not died, the individual would have become entitled to all of the pensions in connection with the lump sum within the specified period.

(4) The three types of pension are—

(*a*) a scheme pension under a defined benefits arrangement;

(*b*) a scheme pension under a money purchase arrangement;

(*c*) a lifetime annuity.

(5) The "specified period" is the period of six months beginning with the earliest date on which the individual becomes entitled to any of the pensions or on which the scheme administrator considers, had the individual not died, that the individual would have become so entitled.][1]

Amendments—[1] Articles 23ZA–23ZE inserted by the Taxation of Pension Schemes (Transitional Provisions) (Amendment) Order, SI 2011/732 arts 2, 3 with effect in relation to any time on or after 6 April 2006.

23ZC [Individual becomes entitled to the pensions

(1) In a case to which this article applies, Part 4 is modified as follows.

(2) For section 166(2)(a) (lump sum rule) substitute—

"(*a*) in the case of a pension commencement lump sum, immediately before the person becomes entitled to the last of the pensions in connection with which it is paid, and".

(3) In paragraph 31(3) of Schedule 36 for "on the same date" substitute "within a period of six months beginning with the earliest date on which the individual becomes entitled to any of the pensions".][1]

Amendments—[1] Articles 23ZA–23ZE inserted by the Taxation of Pension Schemes (Transitional Provisions) (Amendment) Order, SI 2011/732 arts 2, 3 with effect in relation to any time on or after 6 April 2006.

23ZD [Individual dies before becoming entitled to any of the pensions

(1) In a case to which this article applies, Schedule 36 is modified as follows.

(2) For paragraph 31(3) substitute—

"(3) The pension condition is that, the scheme administrator considers that, had the individual not died, the individual would have become entitled to all of the pensions payable to the individual under arrangements under the pension scheme (to which the individual did not have an actual entitlement on or before 5th April 2006) within a period of six months beginning with the earliest date on which the scheme administrator considers that the individual would have become entitled to any of the pensions.".

(3) In paragraph 34(2)—

(*a*) in the substituted sub-paragraph (7A) for the definition of AC substitute—

"AC is the value of the individual's uncrystallised rights on the date of death under arrangements under the pension scheme in connection with which the lump sum is paid calculated in accordance with section 212 (but this is subject to sub-paragraphs (7B) and (7BA)) on the assumption that the individual became entitled to the present payment of benefits in respect of the rights on that date.";

(*b*) omit sub-paragraph (7AA); and

(*c*) after the substituted sub-paragraph (7B) insert—

"(7BA) In determining AC, section 212 shall apply as if "the value assumptions" means the basis upon which the scheme administrator determined the amount of the lump sum to be paid.".][1]

Amendments—[1] Articles 23ZA–23ZE inserted by the Taxation of Pension Schemes (Transitional Provisions) (Amendment) Order, SI 2011/732 arts 2, 3 with effect in relation to any time on or after 6 April 2006.

23ZE [Individual dies after becoming entitled to at least one but not all of the pensions

(1) In a case to which this article applies, Part 4 is modified as follows.

(2) For section 166(2)(a) substitute—

"(*a*) in the case of a pension commencement lump sum, immediately before the latest time when the person becomes entitled to any of the pensions in connection with which it was anticipated that it would be paid, and".

(3) For paragraph 31(3) of Schedule 36 substitute—

"(3) The pension condition is that, the scheme administrator considers that, had the individual not died, the individual would have become entitled to all of the pensions payable to the individual under arrangements under the pension scheme (to which the individual did not have an actual entitlement on or before 5th April 2006) within a period of six months beginning with the earliest date on which the individual became entitled to any of the pensions.".

(4) In paragraph 34(2) of Schedule 36—

(*a*) in the substituted sub-paragraph (7A) of paragraph 2 of Schedule 29, for the definition of AC substitute—

"AC is CB + UCB where—

CB is the amount crystallised, prior to death, on the individual becoming entitled to pensions in connection with which the lump sum is paid (see section 216) (but this is subject to sub-paragraphs (7AA) and (7B)), and

UCB is the value of the individual's uncrystallised rights on the date of death under arrangements under the pension scheme in connection with which the lump sum is paid calculated in accordance with section 212 (but this is subject to sub-paragraphs (7B) and (7BA)) on the assumption that the individual became entitled to the present payment of benefits in respect of the rights on that date.", and

(*b*) after the substituted sub-paragraph (7B) of paragraph 2 of Schedule 29, insert—

"(7BA) In determining AC, section 212 shall apply as if "the value assumptions" means the basis upon which the scheme administrator determined the amount of the lump sum to be paid.".][1]

Amendments—[1] Articles 23ZA–23ZE inserted by the Taxation of Pension Schemes (Transitional Provisions) (Amendment) Order, SI 2011/732 arts 2, 3 with effect in relation to any time on or after 6 April 2006.

23A [Modification of trivial commutation lump sum rules

Part 4 of the 2004 Act shall be modified as set out in articles 23B to 23D.][1]

Amendments—[1] Arts 23A–23D inserted by the Taxation of Pension Schemes (Transitional Provisions) (Amendment) Order, SI 2009/1172 arts 2, 3 with effect from 1 June 2009.

[23B—(1) For subsection (2)(*a*) of section 166 (lump sum rule) substitute—

"(*a*) in the case of a pension commencement lump sum, either—

(i) immediately before the person becomes entitled to the pension in connection with which it is paid (or, if the person dies before becoming entitled to the pension in connection with which it was anticipated it would be paid, immediately before death), or

(ii) if the person becomes entitled to a trivial commutation lump sum within paragraph 7A of Schedule 29, immediately before becoming so entitled,".][1]

Amendments—[1] Arts 23A–23D inserted by the Taxation of Pension Schemes (Transitional Provisions) (Amendment) Order, SI 2009/1172 arts 2, 3 with effect from 1 June 2009.

23C—(1) Schedule 29 (registered pension schemes: authorised lump sums – supplementary) is modified as follows.

(2) For paragraph (*aa*) of paragraph 1(1) (pension commencement lump sum) substitute—

"(*aa*) the member becomes entitled to it either—

(i) in connection with becoming entitled to a relevant pension (or dies after becoming entitled to it, but before becoming entitled to the relevant pension in connection with which it was anticipated that the member would become entitled to it), or

(ii) in connection with a trivial commutation lump sum within paragraph 7A,".

(3) In paragraph 7(1) (trivial commutation lump sum), after the words "trivial commutation lump sum if" insert "it is a lump sum within paragraph 7A or".

(4) After paragraph 7 insert—

"7A—(1) A lump sum is within this paragraph if—

(*a*) it does not exceed [£10,000][3];

(*b*) the member has reached [normal minimum pension age (or the ill-health condition is met)][4] . . . [2];

(*c*) it is paid when all or part of the member's lifetime allowance is available;

(*d*) except for any pension to which the member had an actual entitlement on or before 5th April 2006, it extinguishes the member's entitlement to benefits under the pension scheme;

(*e*) the PCLS conditions are satisfied.

(2) The PCLS conditions are that—

(*a*) the lump sum is paid in connection with a pension commencement lump sum ("PCLS");

(*b*) that PCLS would not have been a PCLS had the modifications in paragraph 34 of Schedule 36 not applied;

(*c*) the lump sum is paid no later than one month after the PCLS;

(*d*) since the payment of the PCLS—

(i) no contribution in respect of the member has been made into the scheme,

(ii) no recognised transfer in respect of the member has been made into or out of the scheme, and

(iii) no annuity or scheme pension has been purchased by the application of the sums or assets held by the scheme for the benefit of the member.".

(5) After paragraph 9 insert—

"9A If a lump sum is a trivial commutation lump sum by virtue of its being within paragraph 7A, the member shall be treated as not having any uncrystallised rights under an arrangement under the pension scheme immediately before it was paid.".][1]

Amendments—[1] Arts 23A–23D inserted by the Taxation of Pension Schemes (Transitional Provisions) (Amendment) Order, SI 2009/1172 arts 2, 3 with effect from 1 June 2009.

[2] In para (4), in the para 7A treated as inserted, in sub-para (1)(*b*) words revoked by the Taxation of Pension Schemes (Transitional Provisions) (Amendment) (No 2) Order, SI 2011/1782 art 2(1), (3) with effect in relation to lump sums paid on or after 6 April 2011.

[3] In para (4), in the para (7A) treated as inserted, figure in sub-para (1)(*a*) substituted by FA 2014 s 42(5) with effect for lump sums paid on or after 27 March 2014. This amendment is to be treated as having been made by the Treasury under the powers to make orders conferred by FA 2004 s 283(2) (FA 2014 s 42(9)(*b*)).

[4] In para (4), in the para (7A) treated as inserted, in sub-para (1)(*b*) words substituted for words "the age of 60" by the Taxation of Pensions Act 2014 s 1, Sch 1 para 72 with effect for determining whether a lump sum paid on or after 6 April 2015 is within the inserted para 7A, and this amendment is to be treated as having been made by the Treasury under the powers to make orders conferred by FA 2004 s 283(2).

[23D—(1) Schedule 36 (pension schemes etc: transitional provisions and savings) is modified as follows.

(2) For paragraph 31(3) (entitlement to lump sums exceeding 25% of uncrystallised rights) substitute—

"(3) The pension condition is that either—

(*a*) the individual becomes entitled to all the pensions payable to the individual under arrangements under the pension scheme (to which the individual did not have an actual entitlement on or before 5th April 2006) on the same date; or

(*b*) the individual is paid a trivial commutation lump sum within paragraph 7A of Schedule 29.".

(3) In the sub-paragraph (7A) of paragraph 2 of Schedule 29 that is substituted by paragraph 34(2) (modification of Schedule 29)—

(*a*) in the definition of "LS", for "lump sum" substitute "pension commencement lump sum"; and

(*b*) for the definition of "AC" substitute—

"AC is either—

(*a*) the amount crystallised on the individual becoming entitled to the pension in connection with which the lump sum is paid (see section 216) (but this is subject to sub-paragraphs (7AA) and (7B)), or

(*b*) the amount of the trivial commutation lump sum within paragraph 7A of Schedule 29 in connection with which the lump sum is paid, and".][1]

Amendments—[1] Arts 23A–23D inserted by the Taxation of Pension Schemes (Transitional Provisions) (Amendment) Order, SI 2009/1172 arts 2, 3 with effect from 1 June 2009.

24 Dependant's scheme pension limit

(1) Paragraph (2) applies where the member in respect of whom the dependant's scheme pension is payable was actually entitled to one or more relevant existing pensions (as defined in paragraph 10(2) of Schedule 36) on 5th April 2006.

(2) Paragraph 16A of Schedule 28 shall be modified as follows.

(3) After sub-paragraph (2) add—

"(3) This paragraph shall not apply to a scheme pension where the member was actually entitled to that pension on 5th April 2006.".

25 [Stand-alone lump sums: introductory and definition

(1) This article and articles 25A to 25D deal with stand-alone lump sums.

(2) In those articles—

this article is introductory and sets out the definition of a stand-alone lump sum;

article 25A deals with the conditions that must be met before a lump sum may be classified as a stand-alone lump sum;

article 25B deals with the circumstances in which a stand-alone lump sum may be paid;

article 25C deals with the tax consequences; and

article 25D contains further provisions.

(3) In this article and in articles 25A to 25D a "stand-alone lump sum" means a lump sum which—

(*a*) meets all the conditions A to [C][2] set out in article 25A, and

(*b*) is paid in one of the circumstances A to C set out in article 25B.][1]

Amendments—[1] Article 25 substituted, together with arts 25A–25D, for art 25 as originally enacted, by the Taxation of Pension Schemes (Transitional Provisions) (Amendment No 2) Order, SI 2006/2004, arts 2, 3, with effect from 25 July 2006.

[2] In para (3)(*a*), "C" substituted for "D" by the Taxation of Pension Schemes (Transitional Provisions) (Amendment) (No 2) Order, SI 2011/1782 art 2(1), (4) with effect in relation to lump sums paid on or after 6 April 2011.

25A [Conditions to be met by stand-alone lump sums

(1) This article sets out the conditions referred to in article 25(3)(*a*).

(2) Condition A is that, on or after 6th April 2006, the lump sum is paid to an individual under a registered pension scheme of which the individual is a member.

(3) Condition B is that the lump sum is paid in circumstances where all of the member's uncrystallised rights under the scheme come into payment on a single benefit crystallisation event.

(4) Condition C is that the lump sum is paid when the member has reached normal minimum pension age (or the ill-health condition is satisfied).

(5) Condition D is that the lump sum is paid before the member reaches the age of 75.[2]][1]

Amendments—[1] Article 25 substituted, together with arts 25A–25D, for art 25 as originally enacted, by the Taxation of Pension Schemes (Transitional Provisions) (Amendment No 2) Order, SI 2006/2004, arts 2, 3, with effect from 25 July 2006.

[2] Para (5) revoked by the Taxation of Pension Schemes (Transitional Provisions) (Amendment) (No 2) Order, SI 2011/1782 art 2(1), (5) with effect in relation to lump sums paid on or after 6 April 2011.

25B [Circumstances in which stand-alone lump sums are paid

(1) This article sets out the circumstances referred to in article 25(3)(*b*).

(2) Circumstance A is where paragraph 28 of Schedule 36 (modification of paragraph 2 of Schedule 29 in the case of a member of a pension scheme to whom enhanced protection does not apply) applies in relation to the member.

(3) Circumstance B is where—

(*a*) paragraph 29 of Schedule 36 (modification of applicable amount in the case of a member of a pension scheme to whom enhanced protection applies) applies in relation to the member, and (*b*) on 5th April 2006, and on the assumptions set out in paragraph (5), all of the member's rights under all of the member's pension schemes within paragraphs (*a*) to (*g*) of paragraph 1(1) of Schedule 36 could have been paid out to the member in the form of a lump sum.

(4) Circumstance C is where—

(*a*) on 5th April 2006 the member was a member of a pension scheme within paragraphs (*a*) to (*e*) of paragraph 1(1) of Schedule 36 and relating to an employment (the "original pension scheme"),

(*b*) on 5th April 2006, and on the assumptions set out in paragraph (5), all of the member's rights under the original pension scheme, and all of the member's rights under any other pension scheme within paragraphs (*a*) to (*e*) of paragraph 1(1) of Schedule 36 and relating to the same employment could have been paid out to the member in the form of a lump sum,

(*c*) on and after 6th April 2006, relevant benefit accrual (as defined in paragraph 13 of Schedule 36) has not occurred under the original pension scheme in relation to the member,

(*d*) on or after 6th April 2006 the member is paid a lump sum representing all of the member's rights (to which the member did not have an actual entitlement on or before 5th April 2006) under the original pension scheme,

(*e*) the circumstances set out in paragraphs (2) and (3) (circumstances A and B) do not apply.

(5) The assumptions are that—

(*a*) the member had retired on 5th April 2006;

(*b*) the valuation assumptions apply (modified, if appropriate, in accordance with paragraph 25(7) of Schedule 36); and

(*c*) the payment of the lump sum on 5th April 2006 (on the assumptions set out in paragraph 26(4) of Schedule 36) would not have given the Commissioners of Her Majesty's Revenue and Customs grounds for withdrawing the approval of the pension scheme.][1]

Amendments—[1] Article 25 substituted, together with arts 25A–25D, for art 25 as originally enacted, by the Taxation of Pension Schemes (Transitional Provisions) (Amendment No 2) Order, SI 2006/2004, arts 2, 3, with effect from 25 July 2006.

25C [Payment of stand-alone lump sums: tax consequences

(1) In subsection (1) of section 166 (lump sum rule), the list of lump sums set out in the paragraphs of that subsection shall be treated as including a stand-alone lump sum.

(2) In paragraph 15 of Schedule 32 (benefit crystallisation event 6: meaning of "relevant lump sum") the list of lump sums set out in the sub-paragraphs of that paragraph shall be treated as including a stand-alone lump sum.

(3) In subsection (1) of section 636A of ITEPA 2003 (exemption for certain lump sums under registered pension schemes), the list of lump sums set out in the paragraphs of that subsection shall be treated as including a stand-alone lump sum.

[(4) If—

(*a*) a stand-alone lump sum is paid—

(i) on or after 6 April 2015,

(ii) to a member of a pension scheme,

(iii) under a money purchase arrangement, and

(iv) in circumstances where article 25B(2) (circumstance A) applies, and

(*b*) no previous stand-alone lump sum has been paid—

(i) on or after that day,

(ii) to the member,

(iii) under a money purchase arrangement, and

(iv) in circumstances where article 25B(2) applies,

subsection (1) of section 227G of the 2004 Act (individual first flexibly accesses pension rights at earliest time given by the following subsections of that section) has effect as if there were a subsequent subsection of that section stating that the member first flexibly accesses pension rights immediately before the stand-alone lump sum is paid.][2]][1]

Amendments—[1] Article 25 substituted, together with arts 25A–25D, for art 25 as originally enacted, by the Taxation of Pension Schemes (Transitional Provisions) (Amendment No 2) Order, SI 2006/2004, arts 2, 3, with effect from 25 July 2006.
[2] Para (4) inserted by the Taxation of Pensions Act 2014 s 1, Sch 1 para 69 with effect from 17 December 2014. This amendment is to be treated as having been made by the Treasury under the powers to make orders conferred by FA 2004 s 283(2).

25D [25D Stand-alone lump sums: further provisions

(1) Paragraphs (2) and (3) apply if—

(*a*) a stand-alone lump sum is paid to a member of a pension scheme in circumstances where article 25B(2) (circumstance A) applies, or

(*b*) a stand-alone lump sum is paid to a member of a pension scheme, and a pension commencement lump sum is subsequently paid to the member (whether from the same pension scheme or from any other pension scheme) in circumstances where paragraph 28 of Schedule 36 applies to the payment of the pension commencement lump sum.

(2) The stand-alone lump sum paid must not exceed the stand-alone lump sum maximum.

The "stand-alone lump sum maximum" means the amount given by the formula "VULSR – APCLS" in sub-paragraph (3) of paragraph 28 of Schedule 36, in the modified sub-paragraph (6) of paragraph 2 of Schedule 29 (as that formula is modified in accordance with paragraph (3)).

(3) In sub-paragraph (3) of paragraph 28 of Schedule 36, in the modified sub-paragraph (6) of paragraph 2 of Schedule 29, the term "APCLS" shall be treated as referring to the aggregate of the amounts of each pension commencement lump sum and each stand-alone lump sum to which the individual has previously become entitled, as adjusted under sub-paragraph (7) (or, if the individual has not previously become entitled to a pension commencement lump sum or a stand-alone lump sum, is nil).

(4) Paragraph (5) applies if—

(*a*) an individual was a member of a pension scheme ("the original pension scheme"),

(*b*) the original pension scheme was entitled to pay a stand-alone lump sum to the member which, if it had been paid, would have been a stand-alone lump sum paid in circumstances where article 25B(4) (circumstance C) applied,

(*c*) the rights of the member under the original pension scheme are transferred to a new pension scheme (the "transferee pension scheme") as the result of a block transfer (within the meaning given by paragraph 22(6) of Schedule 36), and

(*d*) the member had no rights under the transferee pension scheme before the block transfer.

(5) The transferee pension scheme is treated as the same pension scheme as the original pension scheme (so that, accordingly, the transferee pension scheme may pay a stand-alone lump sum to the member in circumstances where article 25B(4) (circumstance C) applies).

(6) Paragraphs (7) to (9) apply if—

(*a*) an individual is a member of a pension scheme (a "stand-alone lump sum pension scheme") which is entitled to pay a stand-alone lump sum to the member in circumstances where article 25B(3) or (4) (circumstance B or C) applies;

(*b*) on or after 6th April 2006 sums and assets are transferred in relation to the member by another pension scheme under which the member has rights (a "transferor scheme") to the stand-alone lump sum pension scheme; and

(*c*) the stand-alone lump sum pension scheme subsequently makes a lump sum payment to the member.

(7) The lump sum payment made by the stand-alone lump sum pension scheme to the member is not a stand-alone lump sum unless the lump sum is also made in the circumstances set out in paragraph (8).

(8) The circumstances are that—

(*a*) neither a stand-alone lump sum nor a pension commencement lump sum has previously been paid under the pension scheme to the member, and

(*b*) the sums and assets transferred (or, if there is more than one transfer, all the sums and assets transferred), as specified in paragraph (6)(*b*), are stand-alone lump sum transfer sums.

(9) In paragraph (8)(*b*) "stand-alone lump sum transfer sums" means sums and assets transferred by the transferor scheme to the stand-alone lump sum pension scheme in the circumstances specified in paragraph (6)(b) which would have been a stand-alone lump sum on the assumptions that—

(*a*) the sums and assets had been transferred not to the stand-alone lump sum pension scheme but to the member, and

(*b*) the condition in article 25A(4) (condition C) is met.][1]

Amendments—[1] Article 25 substituted, together with arts 25A–25D, for art 25 as originally enacted, by the Taxation of Pension Schemes (Transitional Provisions) (Amendment No 2) Order, SI 2006/2004, arts 2, 3, with effect from 25 July 2006.

26 Application of paragraph 31 of Schedule 36

. . .

Amendments—Article 26 revoked by the Taxation of Pension Schemes (Transitional Provisions) (Amendment No 2) Order, SI 2006/2004, arts 2, 4, with effect from 25 July 2006.

27 Contracts approved under section 621(1)(b) of ICTA

(1) This article applies in the case of an individual who, immediately before 6th April 2006, had rights under a contract which had been approved under section 621(1)(*b*) of ICTA.

(2) Schedule 36 shall be modified as follows.

(3) In paragraph 1(1) (deemed registration of existing schemes) after paragraph (*e*) insert—

"(*ea*) a contract approved under section 621(1)(*b*) of ICTA,".

(4) In paragraph 4 after sub-paragraph (4) add

"(4A) If the pension scheme is within paragraph 1(1)(*ea*) immediately before that date, the trustee or trustees of the pension scheme, or the insurance company which is party to the contract in which the pension scheme is comprised, is or are to be treated as becoming the scheme administrator.".

(5) In paragraph 40(3) (members' contributions to pre-commencement retirement annuity contracts) after paragraph (*a*) insert—

"(*aa*) a contract approved under section 621(1)(*b*) of ICTA, where article 27(2) of the Taxation of Pension Schemes (Transitional Provisions) Order 2006 applies to the individual in question, or".

28 Pre-existing entitlement to lump sums and deferment

(1) In the case of an individual who meets the conditions set out in paragraph (2), paragraph (3) applies.

(2) The conditions are as follows.

Condition A

The individual is a member of a scheme which falls within paragraph 1(1)(*a*), (*c*), (*d*) or (*e*) of Schedule 36.

Condition B

The individual has become entitled to a tax-free lump sum under that scheme on or before 5th April 2006.

Condition C

The individual would but for an election to defer entitlement made on or after 27 July 2004, have been entitled to all or part of the pension to which the lump sum in Condition B relates on or before 5th April 2006.

Condition D

A benefit crystallisation event occurs on or after 6th April 2006 in relation to any of the rights, sums and assets of the scheme in relation to the individual.

(3) Paragraph 1 of Schedule 29 shall be modified, as follows.

(*a*) After sub-paragraph (1) add—

"(1A) Where a member of a scheme has become entitled to a tax free lump sum on or before 5th April 2006, that lump sum is to be treated as if it were a pension commencement lump sum if—

(*a*) the member who became entitled to the lump sum is a member of a scheme which falls within paragraph 1(1)(*a*), (*c*), (*d*) or (*e*) of Schedule 36,

(*b*) the member has elected to defer entitlement to all or part of the pension to which the lump sum in sub-paragraph (*a*) relates until after 5th April 2006.

The lump sum shall be treated as if the member became entitled to it on 6th April 2006 and the amount to be treated as having been crystallised at that time shall be the amount of the lump sum to which the member became entitled.

(1AA) No lifetime allowance charge shall arise in respect of the amount deemed to have been crystallised in paragraph (1A).".

(*b*) After sub-paragraph (3) add—

"(3A) But a pension—

(*a*) which becomes payable under a scheme which falls within paragraph 1(1)(*a*), (*c*), (*d*) or (*e*) of Schedule 36 in respect of which entitlement to a lump sum has already arisen prior to 6th April 2006, and

(*b*) entitlement to which has been deferred (in whole or in part) until after 5th April 2006,

is not a relevant pension.

(3B) Sub-paragraph (3A) also applies to a pension payable under any registered pension scheme which has received, (whether directly or through one or more intermediate schemes), a transfer of the sums or assets held for the purposes of the scheme referred to in that sub-paragraph to the extent that the pension is payable in respect of those sums or assets and any investment growth that has been made on them.".

Commentary—*Simon's Taxes* **E7.226–E7.236**.

29 Member's unsecured pension funds

(1) In the case of an individual who meets the conditions set out in paragraph (2), paragraphs (3) to (5) apply.

(2) The conditions are as follows.

Condition A

The individual had not reached the age of 75 on 6th April 2006.

Condition B

The individual is a member of a scheme which falls within paragraph 1(1) of Schedule 36.

Condition C

The individual was, on 5th April 2006 entitled to a pension which was not provided under a defined benefits arrangement and which—

(*a*) took the form of income drawdown under a retirement benefits scheme approved for the purposes of Chapter 1 of Part 14 of ICTA; or

(*b*) was paid from the resources of—

(i) a small self-administered scheme as defined in the Retirement Benefits Schemes (Restriction on Discretion to Approve) (Small Self-Administered Schemes) Regulations 1991, or

(ii) a small self-administered scheme that had been approved under section 590 of ICTA,

and the rules of the scheme on 5th April 2006 did not require the purchase of an annuity in respect of the individual; or

(*c*) took the form of income withdrawal under a personal pension scheme approved under Chapter 4 of Part 14 of ICTA pursuant to section 634Aof that Act.

(3) Paragraph 8 of Schedule 28 (member's unsecured pension fund) is modified as follows—

(*a*) for sub-paragraph (1A) substitute—

"(1A) For the purposes of this Part sums or assets held for the purposes of an arrangement are member-designated funds if they have at any time been applied to provide a pension which—

(*a*) took the form of income drawdown under a retirement benefits scheme approved for the purposes of Chapter 1 of Part 14 of ICTA;

(*b*) was paid from the resources of—

(i) a small self-administered scheme as defined in the Retirement Benefits Schemes (Restriction on Discretion to Approve) (Small Self-administered Schemes) Regulations 1991, or

(ii) a small self-administered scheme that had been approved under section 590 of ICTA;

and the rules of scheme on 5th April 2006 did not require the purchase of an annuity in respect of the individual; or

(*c*) took the form of income withdrawal under a personal pension scheme approved under Chapter 4 of Part 14 of ICTA pursuant to section 634Aof that Act.".

(*b*) after sub-paragraph (1A) insert—

"(1AA) The sums or assets referred to in sub-paragraph (1A) shall be treated as comprising a separate arrangement and the deemed designation of those sums or assets does not constitute benefit crystallisation event 1.

(1AB) Any sums or assets transferred from an arrangement referred to in sub-paragraph (1AA) shall be treated as comprising a separate arrangement.".

(4) For paragraph 9(1) of Schedule 28 substitute—

"**9**—(1) "Unsecured pension year" in relation to an unsecured pension referred to in paragraph 8(1A), means—

(*a*) the period beginning on 6th April 2006 and ending on the earlier of—

(i) 5th April 2007, or

(ii) the date upon which the first reference period defined in paragraph 10(1A) treated as inserted by Article 5 of the Taxation of Pension Schemes (Transitional Provisions) Order 2006 terminates; and

(*b*) each succeeding period of 12 months.".

(5) Section 216 (benefit crystallisation events and amounts crystallised) shall be modified as follows—

(*a*) in BCE2, in column 1 of the table, after the words "under any of the relevant pension schemes" add—

"except to the extent that, the scheme pension was funded by the surrender of—

(*a*) sums or assets deemed to represent an arrangement pursuant to paragraph 8(1A) (*a*) to (*c*) of Schedule 28 as modified by article 29 of the Taxation of Pension Schemes (Transitional Provisions) Order 2006; or

(*b*) sums or assets which have been transferred from an arrangement referred to in sub-paragraph (*a*) to the extent that the scheme pension is payable in respect of those sums or assets and any investment growth that has been made on them.";

(*b*) in BCE4, in column 1 of the table, after the words "under any of the relevant pension schemes" add—

"except to the extent that, the purchase of the lifetime annuity was funded by the surrender of—

(*a*) sums or assets deemed to represent an arrangement pursuant to paragraph 8(1A) (*a*) to (*c*) of Schedule 28 as modified by article 29 of the Taxation of Pension Schemes (Transitional Provisions) Order 2006; or

(*b*) sums or assets which have been transferred from an arrangement referred to in sub-paragraph (*a*) to the extent that the lifetime annuity is payable in respect of those sums or assets and any investment growth that has been made on them.";

(*c*) in BCE8, in column 1 of the table, after the words "in connection with the individual's membership of that pension scheme" add—

"unless the sums or assets transferred were—

(*a*) deemed to represent an arrangement pursuant to paragraph 8(1A) (*a*) to (*c*) of Schedule 28 as modified by article 29 of the Taxation of Pension Schemes (Transitional Provisions) Order 2006; or

(*b*) sums or assets which had been transferred from an arrangement referred to in sub-paragraph (*a*)."

For the purposes of this paragraph references to "BCE" are references to a benefit crystallisation event as set out in section 216.

29A [Member's unsecured pension funds – further provisions

(1) In the case of an individual who meets the conditions set out in paragraph (2), paragraph (3) applies.

(2) The conditions are as follows.

Condition A

The individual is a member of a scheme which falls within paragraph 1(1) of Schedule 36.

Condition B

The individual was, on 5th April 2006, entitled to a pension which was not provided under a defined benefits arrangement and which—

(*a*) took the form of income drawdown under a retirement benefits scheme approved for the purposes of Chapter 1 of Part 14 of ICTA; or

(*b*) was paid from the resources of—

(i) a small self-administered scheme as defined in the Retirement Benefits Schemes (Restriction on Discretion to Approve) (Small Self-Administered Schemes) Regulations 1991, or

(ii) a small self-administered scheme that had been approved under section 590 of ICTA,

the rules of which, on 5th April 2006, did not require the purchase of an annuity in respect of the individual; or

(*c*) took the form of income withdrawal under a personal pension scheme approved under Chapter 4 of Part 14 of ICTA pursuant to section 634A of that Act.

(3) In section 216 (benefit crystallisation events and amounts crystallised) in benefit crystallisation event 5A, in column 1 of the table, after the words "available for the payment of unsecured pension to the individual" add—

"except to the extent that, the sums and assets in the money purchase arrangement are sums or assets deemed to represent an arrangement pursuant to paragraph 8(1A) (*a*) to (*c*) of Schedule 28 as modified by article 29 of the Taxation of Pension Schemes (Transitional Provisions) Order 2006".][1]

Amendments—[1] This regulation inserted by the Taxation of Pension Schemes (Transitional Provisions) (Amendment) Order, SI 2006/1962 regs 2, 3. SI 2006/1962 came into force on 11 August 2006 and has effect in respect of—

(a) death benefit lump sum payments made, and

(b) benefit crystallisation events taking place,

on or after 6 April 2006.

30 Dependant's unsecured pension funds

(1) In the case of an individual who meets the conditions set out in paragraph (2), paragraphs (3) and (4) apply.

(2) The conditions are as follows.

Condition A

The individual had not reached the age of 75 on the 6th April 2006.

Condition B

The individual is a dependant of a member who was a member of scheme which falls within paragraph 1(1) of Schedule 36.

Condition C

On 5th April 2006 the individual was, under an arrangement which was not a defined benefits arrangement—

(*a*) entitled to a pension which took the form of income drawdown under a retirement benefits scheme approved for the purposes of Chapter 1 of Part 14 of ICTA;

(*b*) entitled to a pension that was paid from the resources of—

(i) small self-administered scheme as defined in the Retirement Benefits Schemes (Restriction on Discretion to Approve) (Small Self-administered Schemes) Regulations 1991, or

(ii) a small self-administered scheme that had been approved under section 590 of ICTA,

and the rules of the scheme on 5th April 2006 did not require the purchase of an annuity in respect of the individual;

(*c*) entitled to a pension which took the form of income withdrawal under a personal pension scheme approved under Chapter 4 of Part 14 of ICTA pursuant to section 636A of that Act; or

(*d*) prospectively entitled to an annuity payment of which has been deferred pursuant to section 636(5) of ICTA.

(3) Paragraph 22 of Schedule 28 (dependant's unsecured pension fund) is modified as follows—

(*a*) at the end of sub-paragraph (1)(*a*) omit word "and",

(*b*) omit sub-paragraph (1)(*b*),

(*c*) in sub-paragraph (2)—

(i) for paragraphs (*a*) and (*b*) substitute—

"(*a*) have at any time been applied to provide a pension which—took the form of income drawdown under a retirement benefits scheme approved for the purposes of Chapter 1 of Part 14 of ICTA;

(*b*) have at any time been applied to provide a pension which was paid from the resources of—

(i) a small self-administered scheme as defined in the Retirement Benefits Schemes (Restriction on Discretion to Approve) (Small Self-administered Schemes) Regulations 1991, or

(ii) a small self-administered scheme that had been approved under section 590 of ICTA

and the rules of scheme on 5th April 2006 did not require the purchase of an annuity in respect of the individual;

(*c*) have at any time been applied to provide a pension which took the form of income withdrawal under a personal pension scheme approved under Chapter 4 of Part 14 of ICTA pursuant to section 636Aof that Act; or

(*d*) have, immediately before the coming into force of this Part, been held for the purpose of providing an annuity, payment of which has been deferred in accordance with section 636(5) of that Act.".

(4) For 23(1) (unsecured pension year and basis amount for unsecured pension year) of Schedule 28 substitute—

"**23—**(1) "Unsecured pension year", in relation to a dependant's unsecured pension referred to in paragraph 22(2) as modified by article 30 of the Taxation of Pension Schemes (Transitional Provisions) Order 2006, means—

(*a*) the period beginning on 6th April 2006 and ending on the earlier of—

(i) 5th April 2007 or

(ii) the date that the first reference period defined in paragraph 24(1A), as modified by article 5 of the 2006 Order, terminates, and

(*b*) each succeeding period of 12 months.".

31 Individuals over the age of 75 and alternatively secured pension funds

(1) In the case of an individual who meets the conditions set out in paragraph (2), paragraph (3) applies.

(2) The conditions are as follows.

Condition A

The individual had reached the age of 75 before 6th April 2006.

Condition B

The individual is a member of a scheme which falls within paragraphs 1(1)(*a*) to (*d*) of Schedule 36.

Condition C

The individual has a prospective right to receive a pension under that scheme on 5th April 2006.

(3) Paragraph 11 of Schedule 28 (member's alternatively secured pension fund) is modified as follows—

(*a*) in sub-paragraph (1)(*a*) for "Condition A or Condition B" substitute "Condition A, Condition B or Condition C".

(*b*) after sub-paragraph (3) add—

"(3A) Condition C is that immediately before the 6th April 2006—

(*a*) the sums and assets were part of the member's pension fund which fell within sub-paragraphs 1(1)(*a*) to (*d*) of Schedule 36;

(*b*) the member had a prospective right to receive a pension under that scheme, and

(*c*) the member's pension fund was a money purchase arrangement that was not a cash balance arrangement immediately before 6th April 2006.".

(4) In the case of an individual who meets the conditions set out in paragraph (5), paragraph (6) applies.

(5) The conditions are as follows.

Condition A

The individual had reached the age of 75 before 6th April 2006.

Condition B

The individual is a member of a scheme which falls within sub-paragraph 1(1)(*a*) of Schedule 36.

Condition C

On 5th April 2006, the individual was entitled to a pension which—

(*a*) was paid from the resources of—

(i) a small self-administered scheme as defined in regulation 2 of the Retirement Benefits Schemes (Restriction on Discretion to Approve) (Small self-administered Schemes) Regulations 1991, or

(ii) a small self-administered scheme that had been approved under section 590 of ICTA,

and the rules of the scheme on 5th April 2006 did not require the purchase of an annuity in respect of the individual; and

(*b*) is not provided under a defined benefits arrangement.

(6) Paragraph 11 of Schedule 28 (member's alternatively secured pension fund) shall be modified as follows—

(*a*) after the words "held for the purposes of the arrangement as" add the words "meet condition A, B or C".

(*b*) omit sub-paragraphs (1)(*a*) and (*b*).

(*c*) after sub-paragraph (3) add—

"(3A) Condition C is that immediately before the 6th April 2006—

(*a*) the sums and assets were part of the member's pension fund which fell within sub-paragraph 1(1)(*a*) of Schedule 36; and

(*b*) the member was drawing a pension payable from the resources of—

(i) a small self-administered scheme as defined in the Retirement Benefits Schemes (Restriction on Discretion to Approve) (Small Self-administered Schemes) Regulations 1991, or

(ii) a small self-administered scheme that had been approved under section 590 of ICTA,

and the rules of scheme on 5th April 2006 did not require the purchase of an annuity in respect of the member.".

32 Dependant's alternatively secured pension funds

(1) In the case of an individual who meets the conditions set out in paragraph (2), paragraph (3) applies.

(2) The conditions are as follows.

Condition A

The individual had reached the age of 75 before 6th April 2006.

Condition B

The individual is a dependant of a member who was a member of a scheme which falls within sub-paragraph 1(1)(*a*) of Schedule 36.

Condition C

The individual was, on 5th April 2006, entitled to a pension which was not provided under a defined benefits arrangement and was payable from the resources of—

(*a*) a small self-administered scheme as defined in regulation 2 of the Retirement Benefits Schemes (Restriction on Discretion to Approve) (Small Self-administered Schemes) Regulations 1991, or

(*b*) a small self-administered scheme that had been approved under section 590 of ICTA,

and the rules of the scheme on 5th April 2006 did not require the purchase of an annuity in respect of the individual.

(3) Paragraph 25(1) of Schedule 28 (dependant's alternatively secured pension fund) shall be modified as follows—

(*a*) after the words "held for the purposes of the arrangement as" add the words "meet condition A, B or C".

(*b*) omit sub-paragraphs (1)(*a*) and (*b*).

(*c*) after sub-paragraph (3) add—

"(3A) Condition C is that immediately before the 6th April 2006—

(*a*) the sums and assets were part of the dependant's pension fund which fell within sub-paragraph 1(1)(*a*)of Schedule 36; and

(*b*) the dependant was drawing a pension payable from the resources of—

(i) a small self-administered scheme as defined in regulation 2 of the Retirement Benefits Schemes (Restriction on Discretion to Approve) (Small Self-administered Schemes) Regulations 1991, or

(ii) a small self-administered scheme that had been approved under section 590 of ICTA,

and the rules of the scheme on 5th April 2006 did not require the purchase of an annuity in respect of the dependant.".

33 Serious ill-health lump sums, pension protection lump sum death benefits and annuity protection lump sum death benefits

(1) In the case of an individual who meets the conditions set out in paragraph (2), paragraphs (3), (4) and (5) apply.

(2) The conditions are as follows.

Condition A

The individual is a member of a scheme which falls within sub-paragraphs 1(1)(*a*) to (*g*) of Schedule 36.

Condition B

The individual has an actual (rather than a prospective) right to the payment of one or more relevant existing pensions under that scheme on 6th April 2006.

(3) In paragraph 4(2) of Schedule 29 (serious ill-health lump sum) for the words "there has been no previous benefit crystallisation event" substitute—

"the member has a prospective (rather than an actual) right to the payment of one or more relevant existing pensions.".

(4) In paragraph 14(3) of Schedule 29 (pension protection lump sum death benefit)—

(*a*) for "AC is the amount crystallised by reason of the member becoming entitled to the pension (see section 216)" substitute—

"AC is the value of the individual's pre-commencement pension rights as defined in paragraph 20(3) to (5) of Schedule 36.".

(*b*) in the definition of "AP" for the words after "paid in respect of the period" substitute—
"from the period from the 6th April 2006 and the date of the member's death.".

(5) In paragraph 16(3) of Schedule 29 (annuity protection lump sum death benefit)—

(*a*) for "AC is the amount crystallised by reason of the member becoming entitled to the pension or annuity" substitute—

"AC is the value of the individual's pre-commencement pension rights as defined in paragraph 20(3) to (5) of Schedule 36.".

(*b*) in the definition of "AP" for the words after "paid in respect of the period" substitute—
"from the period from the 6th April 2006 and the date of the member's death.".

34 [Payments to children aged 23 or over

(1) Paragraph (2) applies to the payment of a pension death benefit by a pension scheme which falls within paragraph 1(1) of Schedule 36 where—

(*a*) either of Conditions A and B is satisfied and the first scheme rules condition is satisfied; or

(*b*) Condition C and the second scheme rules condition are satisfied.

(2) Paragraph 15(2) of Schedule 28 shall be modified as follows—

(*a*) at the end of paragraph (*a*) omit the word "or"; and

(*b*) after paragraph (*b*) insert—

"(*c*) has reached that age and is in full time education or undertaking vocational training, or

(*d*) on reaching that age or, if later, on ceasing full time education or vocational training is, in the opinion of the scheme administrator, suffering from physical or mental deterioration which is sufficiently serious to prevent the individual from following a normal employment or which would seriously impair his earning capacity.".

(3) The Conditions A, B and C mentioned in paragraph (1) are:

Condition A

The pension was in payment to a child ("C") of the member ("M") on 5th April 2006 or M had died on or before that date and a pension was due to come into payment to C.

Condition B

The pension was in payment to M on 5th April 2006 and C was born on or before 5th April 2007.

Condition C

An election such as is described in the second scheme rules condition had been made by M and accepted by the scheme administrator on or before 5th April 2006.

(4) The scheme rules conditions mentioned in paragraph (1) are:

First scheme rules condition

The rules of the pension scheme allowed a pension to be paid to a child ("C") of the member ("M") following M's death until C ceased full-time education or vocational training.

Second scheme rules condition

The rules of the pension scheme on 10 December 2003 allowed an irrevocable election to be made designating part of the sums or assets representing M's rights as available for the payment of a pension to C following M's death until C ceased full-time education or vocational training.

(5) For the purpose of the first scheme rules condition, a rule that the pension would not be paid to C if or after C reached a specified age (even if that is before C ceased full-time education or vocational training) does not prevent the condition being satisfied.

(6) Paragraph (2) also applies to the payment of a pension death benefit by a qualifying transferee scheme (as to which see article 34B) where either—

- (*a*) paragraph (2) had applied to payment by the original pension scheme or another transferee pension scheme; or
- (*b*) paragraph (2) would have applied—
  - (i) if there had been no block transfer on or after 6th April 2006, and
  - (ii) if payment had been by the original pension scheme.][1]

Amendments—[1] Paras 34–34B substituted by the Taxation of Pension Schemes (Transitional Provisions) (Amendment No 2) Order, SI 2009/1989 art 2 with effect in respect of payments of pension death benefit made on or after 6 April 2006.

34A [Payments to financially dependent children aged 23 or over

(1) Paragraph (2) applies to the payment of a pension death benefit by a pension scheme which falls within paragraph 1(1) of Schedule 36 where—

- (*a*) any of Conditions A to D is satisfied; and
- (*b*) the scheme rules condition is satisfied.

(2) Paragraph 15(2) of Schedule 28 shall be modified as follows—

- (*a*) at the end of paragraph (a) omit the word "or"; and
- (*b*) after paragraph (b) insert—
  - "(*c*) has reached that age and—
    - (i) is financially dependent on the member at the date of the member's death, or
    - (ii) the financial relationship with the member at the date of the member's death is one of mutual dependence.".

(3) The Conditions A to D mentioned in paragraph (1) are:

Condition A

The member's ("M's") pension was in payment on or before 1st July 2008.

Condition B

The pension death benefit was in payment on 1st July 2008.

Condition C

The entitlement to the pension death benefit arose before 1st July 2008.

Condition D

The entitlement to the pension death benefit was subject to the discretion of the trustees of the scheme and the discretion was capable of being exercised (in favour of the child having such an entitlement) so that the entitlement could have arisen before 1st July 2008.

(4) The scheme rules condition mentioned in paragraph (1) is:

Scheme rules condition

The rules of the pension scheme on 5th April 2006 allowed a pension to be paid to a child ("C") of the member ("M") following M's death if, at the date of M's death, C was financially dependent on M or C's financial relationship with M was one of mutual dependence.

(5) Paragraph (2) also applies to the payment of a pension death benefit by a qualifying transferee scheme (as to which see article 34B) where—

- (*a*) paragraph (2) had applied to payment by the original pension scheme or another transferee pension scheme; or
- (*b*) paragraph (2) would have applied—
  - (i) if there had been no block transfer on or after the relevant date, and
  - (ii) if payment had been by the original pension scheme.

(6) For the purposes of paragraph (5), the relevant date is—

- (*a*) in relation to Condition A, the later of—
  - (i) 6th April 2006, and
  - (ii) the date on which the member's pension came into payment; and
- (*b*) in relation to Condition B, C or D, the later of—
  - (i) 6th April 2006, and
  - (ii) the date of the member's death.][1]

Amendments—[1] Paras 34–34B substituted by the Taxation of Pension Schemes (Transitional Provisions) (Amendment No 2) Order, SI 2009/1989 art 2 with effect in respect of payments of pension death benefit made on or after 6 April 2006.

34B [Meaning of "qualifying transferee scheme"

(1) A pension scheme is a qualifying transferee scheme for the purposes of articles 34 and 34A if it is a pension scheme to which there has been a relevant block transfer.

(2) A block transfer is relevant if any of Conditions A to C is satisfied as a result of—

(*a*) a block transfer from a pension scheme within paragraph 1(1) of Schedule 36 ("the original pension scheme"); or

(*b*) a block transfer to a pension scheme ("a transferee pension scheme") from a pension scheme that was a transferee pension scheme in relation to the original pension scheme by virtue of the previous application of sub-paragraph (a) or the previous application (on one or more occasions) of this sub-paragraph.

(3) The Conditions A to C mentioned in paragraph (2) are:

Condition A

The member became a member of the transferee pension scheme.

Condition B

The child is a pensioner member of the transferee pension scheme.

Condition C

An irrevocable election having been made designating part of the sums or assets representing the member's rights as available for the payment of a pension to the child, the child is entitled to such payment from the transferee pension scheme.

(4) In this article, "block transfer" has the meaning given by paragraph 22(6) of Schedule 36, but with the modification that for "as is prescribed" in paragraph (b) there is substituted "as has been prescribed".][1]

Amendments—[1] Paras 34–34B substituted by the Taxation of Pension Schemes (Transitional Provisions) (Amendment No 2) Order, SI 2009/1989 art 2 with effect in respect of payments of pension death benefit made on or after 6 April 2006.

35 Enhanced protection and transfers made in connection with the winding up of a pension scheme

(1) In the case of an individual who meets the conditions in paragraph (2), paragraph 12 of Schedule 36 (transitional provisions— "enhanced protection") is modified in accordance with paragraph (3).

(2) The conditions are—

Condition A

The individual is one to whom paragraph 12 of Schedule 36 applies.

Condition B

The pension scheme of which the individual is a member makes a recognised transfer of sums or assets to an insurance company pursuant to section 169(1A) (permitted transfers).

Condition C

The transfer is made in connection with the winding up of the pension scheme from which the transfer is made.

(3) Paragraph 12(8) is modified as follows—

(*a*) after paragraph (*a*) delete the word "or"; and

(*b*) after paragraph (*b*) add—

"or;

(*c*) the transfer is a recognised transfer pursuant to section 169(1A).".

36 Transfer of crystallised rights with enhanced protection

(1) In the case of an individual who meets the conditions in paragraph (2), paragraph 15 of Schedule 36 (definition of the "relevant crystallised amount") is modified in accordance with paragraph (3).

(2) The conditions are—

Condition A

The individual is one to whom paragraph 12 of Schedule 36 applies.

Condition B

The individual is in receipt of a scheme pension.

Condition C

The pension scheme of which the individual is a member makes a recognised transfer of sums or assets in connection with the winding up of the pension scheme.

(3) Paragraph 15 is modified as follows—

(*a*) at the end of sub-paragraph (1) add—

"This paragraph is subject to sub-paragraph (1A)." and

(*b*) after that sub-paragraph insert—

"(1A) If the relevant event is a transfer of sums or assets representing crystallised rights under a scheme pension and made in connection with the winding-up of the pension scheme under which the scheme pension is paid, the relevant crystallised amount shall be nil.".

37 Modification of section 636B ITEPA 2003

(1) Section 636B of ITEPA 2003 (trivial commutation and winding-up lump sums) is modified as follows in relation to an equivalent pension benefits commutation lump sum pursuant to regulation 2(1A) of—

(*a*) the Occupational Pension Schemes (Assignment, Forfeiture, Bankruptcy etc) Regulations 1997; or

(*b*) the Occupational Pension Schemes (Assignment, Forfeiture, Bankruptcy etc) Regulations (Northern Ireland) 1997.

(2) For the heading substitute—

"Trivial commutation, winding-up lump sums etc"

(3) In subsection (1)—

(*a*) at the end of paragraph (*a*) omit "or";

(*b*) at the end of paragraph (*b*) add "or"; and

(*c*) after that paragraph insert the following paragraph—

"(*c*) an equivalent pension benefits commutation lump sum,"

(4) In subsection (4) after "In this section—"insert the following definition—

""equivalent pension benefits commutation lump sum" means a lump sum payment arising from the commutation of equivalent pension benefits pursuant to regulation 2(1A) of—

(*a*) the Occupational Pension Schemes (Assignment, Forfeiture, Bankruptcy etc) Regulations 1997; or

(*b*) the Occupational Pension Schemes (Assignment, Forfeiture, Bankruptcy etc) Regulations (Northern Ireland) 1997,".

38 Lump sum payments—general

(1) This paragraph applies to a lump sum payment—

(*a*) the entirety of which is made in accordance with the rules of the existing scheme as they stood immediately before the 6th April 2006;

(*b*) which is made on or after the 6th April 2006 but before 6th July 2006;

(*c*) to which the member became entitled before the 6th April 2006;

(*d*) which would not have given the Commissioners grounds for withdrawing approval of the scheme had it been made before the 6th April 2006; and

(*e*) which is not a lump sum paid in circumstances of the member's serious ill-health.

(2) In this article and articles 39, 40 and 41—

"the 1995 Regulations" means the Retirement Benefits Schemes (Information Powers) Regulations 1995;

"the Commissioners" means the Commissioners for Her Majesty's Revenue and Customs and, in relation to times before 18th April 2005, includes the Commissioners of Inland Revenue;

"existing scheme" means a scheme which becomes a registered pension scheme by virtue of paragraph 1(1) of Schedule 36 (pension schemes etc: transitional provisions and savings —deemed registration of existing schemes);

"lump sum paid in circumstances of the member's serious ill-health" has the meaning given in article 39(3);

"member" means a member of an existing scheme;

(3) A payment to which paragraph (1) applies shall be chargeable to income tax in accordance with section 598, 599 or 599A of ICTA (which deal respectively with charges to tax on repayment of employee's contributions, on the commutation of the entire pension in special circumstances and on payments out of surplus funds), or Chapter 13 of Part 9 of ITEPA 2003 (return of employee's additional voluntary contributions) (as the case requires)—

(*a*) to the same extent as it would have been if the provision in question had not been repealed; and

(*b*) as if the references in section 598(2), 599(3) and section 599A(2)(*b*) of ICTA to the administrator of the scheme were instead references to the scheme administrator (within the meaning of section 270) of the registered pension scheme which is treated as coming into being by virtue of paragraph 1(1) of Schedule 36.

(4) For the purposes of a lump sum payment to which paragraph (1) applies, regulations 10 and 11 of the 1995 Regulations (reporting of chargeable events) shall continue to have effect, subject to the following modifications—

(*a*) in paragraph (1) for the words preceding sub-paragraph (*a*) substitute—

"The scheme administrator of the registered pension scheme which, immediately before the coming into force of Part 4 of the Finance Act 2004, was both a retirement benefits scheme and—";

(*b*) in paragraph (3) omit sub-paragraph (*d*); and

(*c*) omit paragraph (4).

(5) In section 98(5) of the Taxes Management Act 1970 the entry in Table 1 relating to regulations under section 605(1A) of ICTA shall continue to have effect so far as it relates to regulations 10 and 11 of the 1995 Regulations as saved, with modifications, by paragraph (4).

Commentary—*Simon's Taxes* **E7.201**.

39 Lump sums—serious ill-health

(1) This article applies to a lump sum—

(*a*) paid to a member in circumstances of the member's serious ill-health; and

(*b*) which satisfies the requirements set out in sub-paragraphs (*a*) to (*d*) of article 38(1).

(2) There is no charge to tax under Part 4 on a lump sum to which paragraph (1) applies.

(3) A lump sum is paid in circumstances of the member's serious ill-health if—

(*a*) before it is paid the scheme administrator, or the administrator of the scheme which became a registered pension scheme on the 6th April 2006, received evidence from a registered medical practitioner that the member is expected to live for less than one year; and

(*b*) all of the member's uncrystallised rights under the scheme making the payment, other than those which are—

(i) required to be maintained in order to meet contracted-out rights or safeguarded rights, or

(ii) retained by the scheme in accordance with its rules as they stood immediately before the 6th April 2006 to provide benefits for the member's dependants,

are paid out as a lump sum.

(4) In paragraph (3)(*b*)(i)—

"contracted-out rights" means—

(*a*) entitlement to payment of, or accrued rights to—

(i) guaranteed minimum pensions within the meaning of section 8(2) of the Pension Schemes Act 1993; and

(ii) a pension in respect of protected rights within the meaning of section 10 of that Act;

(*b*) section 9(2B) rights within the meaning of regulation 1(2) of the Occupational Pension Schemes (Contracting-Out) Regulations 1996, or

(*c*) any of the rights in sub-paragraphs (*a*), (*b*) or (*c*) which themselves derive from any of those rights which have been the subject of a transfer payment; and

"safeguarded rights" have the same meaning as in section 68A of the Pension Schemes Act 1993.

(5) In the application of this article to Northern Ireland, a reference to a provision applying only in Great Britain shall be construed as a reference to any provision having corresponding effect in Northern Ireland.

Commentary—*Simon's Taxes* **E7.201**.

40 Lump sum death benefits—death of member

(1) This paragraph applies to a lump sum paid—

(*a*) in respect of the death, occurring before the 6th April 2006, of a member of a pension scheme;

(*b*) within two years of [the date upon which the administrator of the pension scheme could reasonably have known of the member's death][1];

(*c*) by a scheme which is treated as becoming a registered pension scheme on the 6th April 2006 by virtue of paragraph 1(1) of Schedule 36;

(*d*) in accordance with the rules of that scheme as they stood—

(i) immediately before the death; or

(ii) immediately before the 6th April 2006; and

(*e*) in circumstances which would not have [led to the Commissioners withdrawing the approval of the scheme.][1]

(2) A lump sum to which paragraph (1) applies is not a relevant lump sum death benefit as defined in paragraph 16 of Schedule 32, and the payment of such a death benefit is to be disregarded for the purposes of benefit crystallisation event 7.

(3) A lump sum to which paragraph (1) applies shall be chargeable to income tax in accordance with section 648B of ICTA as if—

(*a*) that section had not been repealed;

(*b*) references in that section to the administrator of the scheme were references to the scheme administrator of the registered pension scheme which is treated as coming into being by virtue of paragraph 1(1)(*g*) of Schedule 36;

(*c*) subsection (3) were omitted; and

(*d*) the reference in subsection (4) to the rules of the scheme were a reference to the rules of the personal pension scheme as they stood immediately before the 6th April 2006.

(4) For the purposes of a lump sum payment to which paragraph (1) applies, regulation 5 of the Personal Pension Schemes (Information Powers) Regulations 2000 ("the 2000 Regulations") shall continue to have effect, subject to the following modifications—

(*a*) references to the scheme administrator of the personal pension scheme are to be read as references to the scheme administrator of the registered pension scheme which is treated as coming into being by virtue of paragraph 1(1)(*g*) of Schedule 36; and

(*b*) in paragraph (2) of that regulation for "an approved personal pension scheme" substitute "the registered pension scheme".

(5) In section 98(5) of the Taxes Management Act 1970 the entry in Table 1 relating to regulations under section 651A(1)(*b*) to (*d*) of ICTA shall continue to have effect, so far as it relates to regulation 5 of the 2000 Regulations as saved, with modifications, by paragraph (4).

Commentary—*Simon's Taxes* **E7.201**.

Amendments—[1] In para (1)(*b*), words substituted; and in para (1)(*e*), words substituted; by the Taxation of Pension Schemes (Transitional Provisions) (Amendment) Order, SI 2006/1962 regs 2, 4. SI 2006/1962 came into force on 11 August 2006 and has effect in respect of—

(a) death benefit lump sum payments made, and

(b) benefit crystallisation events taking place,

on or after 6 April 2006.

41 Lump sum death benefits—death of a dependant

(1) This paragraph applies to a lump sum paid—

(*a*) in respect of the death, occurring before the 6th April 2006, of a dependant of a former member of a pension scheme;

(*b*) by a scheme which is treated as becoming a registered pension scheme on the 6th April 2006 by virtue of paragraph 1(1)(*g*) of Schedule 36 (personal pension schemes);

(*c*) within two years of [the date upon which the administrator of the pension scheme could reasonably have known of the dependant's death][1];

(*d*) in accordance with the rules of that scheme as they stood—

(i) immediately before the dependant's death; or

(ii) immediately before the 6th April 2006; and

(*e*) in circumstances which would not have [led to the Commissioners withdrawing the approval of the scheme.][1]

(2) Paragraphs (3) to (5) of article 40 apply for the purposes of paragraph (1) as they apply for the purposes of paragraph (1) of that article.

Commentary—*Simon's Taxes* **E7.201**.

Amendments—[1] In para (1)(*c*), words substituted; and in para (1)(*e*), words substituted; by the Taxation of Pension Schemes (Transitional Provisions) (Amendment) Order, SI 2006/1962 regs 2, 5. SI 2006/1962 came into force on 11 August 2006 and has effect in respect of—

(a) death benefit lump sum payments made, and

(b) benefit crystallisation events taking place,

on or after 6 April 2006.

42 [Protected pension age and multiple pensions

(1) In the case of a member who has a protected pension age in connection with at least two of the three types of pension listed in paragraph (2) from the same registered pension scheme, Schedule 36 is modified in accordance with paragraph (3).

(2) The three types of pension are—

(*a*) a scheme pension under a defined benefits arrangement;

(*b*) a scheme pension under a money purchase arrangement;

(*c*) a lifetime annuity.

(3) In paragraphs 22(7)(*a*) and 23(7) for "on the same date" substitute "within a period of six months beginning with the earliest date on which the individual becomes entitled to any of the benefits.][1]

Amendments—[1] Articles 42, 43 inserted by the Taxation of Pension Schemes (Transitional Provisions) (Amendment) Order, SI 2011/732 arts 2, 4 with effect in relation to any time on or after 6 April 2011.

43 [Protected pension age and multiple pensions - member dies before receiving all pensions

(1) Schedule 36 is modified in accordance with paragraphs (3) and (4) where—

(*a*) a member has a protected pension age in connection with at least two of the three types of pension listed in regulation 42(2) from the same registered pension scheme;

(*b*) the member dies before the end of the specified period after becoming entitled to at least one but not all of the benefits in respect of the pensions; and

(*c*) the scheme administrator considers that, had the individual not died, the individual would have become entitled to all of the benefits in respect of the pensions within the specified period.

(2) The "specified period" is the period of six months beginning with the earliest date on which the individual became entitled to any of the benefits in respect of the pensions.

(3) For paragraph 22(7)(*a*) substitute—

"(*a*) the scheme administrator considers that, had the individual not died, the member would have become entitled to all the benefits payable to the member under arrangements under the pension scheme (to which the member did not have an actual entitlement on or before 5th April 2006) within a period of six months beginning with the earliest date on which the individual became entitled to any of the benefits, and".

(4) For paragraph 23(7) substitute—

"(7) The retirement condition is met in relation to the member and the pension scheme if the scheme administrator considers that, had the individual not died, the member would have become entitled to all the benefits payable to the member under arrangements under the pension scheme (to which the member did not have an actual entitlement on or before 5th April 2006) within a period of six months beginning with the earliest date on which the individual became entitled to any of the benefits.][1]

Amendments—[1] Articles 42, 43 inserted by the Taxation of Pension Schemes (Transitional Provisions) (Amendment) Order, SI 2011/732 arts 2, 4 with effect in relation to any time on or after 6 April 2011.

44 [Normal minimum pension age—modification of section 165 (payment of pension rules)

(1) This article applies in the case of a member of a registered pension scheme where the primary condition in paragraph (2) and one of conditions in paragraph (3) are met.

(2) The primary condition is—

(*a*) on 5th April 2010, the member was aged between 50 and 54 (inclusive); and

(*b*) on or before that date, benefit crystallisation event 1 ("BCE1"), 2 ("BCE2") or 4 ("BCE4") had occurred in relation to that member.

(3) The conditions are—

Condition A

On or after 6th April 2010 some or all of the sums and assets held for the purposes of the arrangement in respect of which BCE1 had occurred are applied towards—

(*a*) the purchase of a short-term annuity or a lifetime annuity ("the new annuity"); or

(*b*) the provision of a scheme pension under the arrangement.

Condition B

On or after 6th April 2010 the first payment of pension by way of income withdrawal ("withdrawal pension") is made from some or all of the sums or assets held for the purposes of the arrangement in respect of which BCE1 had occurred.

Condition C

On or before 5th April 2010 some or all of the assets held for the purposes of the arrangement in respect of which BCE1 had occurred were applied towards the purchase of a short-term annuity ("the new annuity"), and the first payment of the new annuity is made on or after 6th April 2010.

Condition D

Where BCE2 or BCE4 had occurred in relation to the member on or before 5th April 2010, the first payment of scheme pension or lifetime annuity ("the new annuity") in respect of which BCE2 or BCE4 occurred, is made on or after 6th April 2010.

(4) For the purposes of determining whether pension rule 1 in section 165 (payment of pension rules) has been met in relation to a payment of the new annuity, scheme pension or withdrawal pension, the member is deemed to have reached the age of 55 immediately before the date on which the first payment of the new annuity, scheme pension or withdrawal pension is made. This paragraph is subject to paragraph (5).

(5) Where a member was chargeable to income tax at the additional rate for the tax year 2010-11, paragraph (4) shall only have effect in respect of 80% of the amount of any payment of the new annuity, scheme pension or withdrawal pension made in that tax year.

(6) For the purposes of this article "sums or assets held for the purposes of the arrangement" means sums or assets that—

(*a*) on or before 5th April 2010, have been designated under the arrangement as available for the payment of unsecured pension; or

(*b*) arise, or (directly or indirectly) derive from sums or assets which have been so designated or which so arise or derive.][1]

Amendments—[1] Articles 44, 45 inserted by the Taxation of Pension Schemes (Transitional Provisions) (Amendment) Order, SI 2011/732 arts 2, 5 with effect in relation to any time on or after 6 April 2010.

45 [Normal minimum pension age—modification of paragraph 1 of Schedule 29 (lump sum rule)

(1) This article applies in the case of a member of a registered pension scheme where the conditions in paragraph (2) are met.

(2) The conditions are that on 5th April 2010—

(*a*) the member was aged between 50 and 54 (inclusive);

(*b*) the member had become entitled to a lump sum ("the relevant lump sum") which would have been a pension commencement lump sum had it been paid on or before that date; and

(*c*) no payment of the relevant lump sum had been made.

(3) For the purposes of determining whether the condition in paragraph 1(1)(d) of Schedule 29 (pension commencement lump sum) has been met in relation to a payment of the relevant lump sum made on or after 6th April 2010, the member is deemed to have reached the age of 55 immediately before the date on which the payment of the relevant lump sum is made.][1]

Amendments—[1] Articles 44, 45 inserted by the Taxation of Pension Schemes (Transitional Provisions) (Amendment) Order, SI 2011/732 arts 2, 5 with effect in relation to any time on or after 6 April 2010.

2006/573

PENSION SCHEMES (TRANSFERS, REORGANISATIONS AND WINDING UP) (TRANSITIONAL PROVISIONS) ORDER 2006

Made by the Treasury under FA 2004 s 283(2)

Made . . . . *9 March 2006*
Laid before the House of Commons . . . . *10 March 2006*
Coming into force . . . . *6 April 2006*

Commentary—*Simon's Taxes* **E7.226–E7.236**.

GENERAL

1 Citation, commencement and interpretation

(1) This Order may be cited as the Pension Schemes (Transfers, Reorganisations and Winding Up) (Transitional Provisions) Order 2006, and shall come into force on 6th April 2006.

(2) In this Order, references to provisions of Schedule 36 are references to provisions of Schedule 36 to the Finance Act 2004.

(3) In this Order—

"normal minimum pension age" has the meaning given in section 279(1) of the Finance Act 2004, and

"the TUPE Regulations" means the Transfer of Undertakings (Protection of Employment) Regulations 1981.

2 The original pension scheme condition

(1) For the purposes of this Order the original pension scheme condition is met if conditions A and B are met.

(2) Condition A is that on 10th December 2003 a pension scheme ("the original pension scheme") was either an approved scheme for the purposes of Chapter 1 of Part 14 of the Income and Corporation Taxes Act 1988 (see section 612(1) of that Act) or was a relevant statutory scheme for the purposes of that Chapter (see section 611A of that Act).

(3) Condition B is that the original pension scheme was a scheme whose rules included provision conferring a right to retire before the normal minimum pension age on some or all of the persons who were then members of the scheme.

3 The employee condition

(1) For the purposes of this Order the employee condition is met if either condition A or condition B is met.

(2) Condition A is that, on 10th December 2003, a person ("the employee") was a person who had the right, under the original pension scheme, to retire before the normal minimum pension age.

(3) Condition B is that the employee would have been a person who, on 10th December 2003, had the right, under the original pension scheme, to retire before the normal minimum pension age had the employee been a member of the scheme on that date.

TRANSFERS DURING PERIOD BEGINNING WITH 10TH DECEMBER 2003 AND ENDING WITH 5TH APRIL 2006

4 Conditions for application of article 8

Article 8 applies if the following conditions are met—

(*a*) the original pension scheme condition (see article 2);
(*b*) the employee condition (see article 3);
(*c*) the transfer condition, either as it applies in the case of one transfer (see article 5), or as it applies in the case of two or more transfers (see article 6); and
(*d*) the new pension scheme condition (see article 7).

5 The transfer condition as it applies in the case of one transfer

(1) The transfer condition, as it applies in the case of one transfer, is met if conditions A to G are met.

(2) Condition A is that, during the period beginning with 10th December 2003 and ending with 5th April 2006, there was one transfer of an undertaking, or part of an undertaking.

(3) Condition B is that the TUPE Regulations applied to the transfer.

(4) Condition C is that by virtue of the transfer, the employee ceased to be employed by the transferor and became employed by the transferee.

(5) Condition D is that the transferor was the employer in relation to the original pension scheme.

(6) Condition E is that at the time immediately before the employee became employed by the transferee, the employee was a member of the original pension scheme.

(7) Condition F is that from the time when the employee became employed by the transferee, the employee—

(*a*) was a member of a pension scheme in relation to which the transferee was the employer, or

(*b*) was a member of one other pension scheme ("the new pension scheme") in relation to which the transferee was the employer.

(8) Condition G is that, as a result of the transfer, all the sums held for the purposes of, or representing the employee's accrued rights under, the original pension scheme have become held for the purposes of, or represented rights under, the new pension scheme.

(9) In paragraph (2) the reference to an undertaking or part of an undertaking has the same meaning as in the TUPE Regulations.

6 The transfer condition as it applies in the case of two or more transfers

(1) The transfer condition, as it applies in the case of two or more transfers, is met if conditions A to H are met.

(2) Condition A is that, during the period beginning with 10th December 2003 and ending with 5th April 2006, there were two or more transfers of an undertaking, or part of an undertaking.

(3) Condition B is that the TUPE Regulations applied to each transfer.

(4) Condition C is that by virtue of each transfer, the employee ceased to be employed by the transferor and became employed by the transferee.

(5) Condition D is that the transferor—

(*a*) in the case of the first transfer, was the employer in relation to the original pension scheme, and

(*b*) in the case of each subsequent transfer, was the employer in relation to the pension scheme of which the employee was a member immediately before the transfer.

(6) Condition E is that the employee—

(*a*) in the case of the first transfer, was a member of the original pension scheme at the time immediately before the employee became employed by the transferee, and

(*b*) in the case of each subsequent transfer, was a member of a pension scheme in relation to which the transferor was the employer at the time immediately before the employee became employed by the transferee.

(7) Condition F is that in the case of a transfer other than the final transfer, and from the time when he became employed by the transferee, the employee was a member of a pension scheme in relation to which the transferee was the employer.

(8) Condition G is that in the case of the final transfer, and from the time when he became employed by the transferee, the employee—

(*a*) was a member of a pension scheme in relation to which the transferee was the employer, or

(*b*) was a member of one other pension scheme ("the new pension scheme") in relation to which the transferee was the employer.

(9) Condition H is that, as a result of the transfers, all the sums held for the purposes of, or representing the employee's accrued rights under, the original pension scheme have become held for the purposes of, or represented rights under, the new pension scheme.

(10) In paragraph (2) the reference to an undertaking or part of an undertaking has the same meaning as in the TUPE Regulations.

7 The new pension scheme condition

(1) The new pension scheme condition is met if conditions A and B are met.

(2) Condition A is that the new pension scheme was a scheme whose rules, at the time of the transfer (where article 5 applies), or at the time of the final transfer (where article 6 applies), included provision conferring a right on some or all of the persons who were then members of that scheme to retire before the normal minimum pension age.

(3) Condition B is that, on 6th April 2006, the new pension scheme was within any of paragraphs (*a*) to (*e*) of paragraph 1(1) of Schedule 36 (deemed registration of existing schemes) (and, accordingly, is treated as having become a registered pension scheme).

8 Rights to take benefit before normal minimum pension age

(1) For the purposes of paragraph 22 of Schedule 36 (rights to take benefit before normal minimum pension age), and in relation to the employee, the new pension scheme is a protected pension scheme.

(2) The employee has the right to retire at the age specified in paragraph (3) or (4), whichever is the greater.

(3) The age specified in this paragraph is the age at which—

(*a*) immediately before the transfer, the employee had the right to retire under the original pension scheme (in a case where article 5 applies), or

(*b*) immediately before the final transfer, the employee had the right to retire under the original pension scheme (in a case where article 6 applies).

(4) The age specified in this paragraph is the age at which, on 6th April 2006, the employee has the right to retire under the new pension scheme.

REORGANISATIONS DURING PERIOD BEGINNING WITH 10TH DECEMBER 2003 AND ENDING WITH 5TH APRIL 2006

9 Conditions for application of article 12

Article 12 applies if the following conditions are met—

(*a*) the original pension scheme condition (see article 2);

(*b*) the employee condition (see article 3);

(*c*) the reorganisation condition (see article 10); and

(*d*) the new pension scheme condition (see article 11).

10 The reorganisation condition

(1) The reorganisation condition is met if conditions A to C are met.

[(2) Condition A is that, during the period beginning with 10th December 2003 and ending with 5th April 2006—

(*a*) there was a transfer in a single transaction of all the sums and assets held for the purposes of, or representing the employee's accrued rights under, the original pension scheme to another pension scheme ("the new pension scheme"),

(*b*) there was a transfer in a single transaction of all the sums and assets held for the purposes of, or representing the employee's accrued, non contracted-out rights under the original pension scheme to the new pension scheme, or

(*c*) there were transfers of sums and assets held for the purposes of, or representing the employee's accrued rights under, the original pension scheme to the new pension scheme, and those transfers were made—

(i) in two separate transactions, and

(ii) in circumstances where paragraph (2A) applies.

(2A) This paragraph applies in circumstances where—

(*a*) the employee's accrued rights under the original pension scheme included contracted-out rights;

(*b*) all the sums and assets held for the purposes of, or representing accrued, non contracted-out rights under the original pension scheme were transferred to the new pension scheme in a single transaction; and

(*c*) the sums and assets held for the purposes of, or representing contracted-out rights under the original pension scheme were transferred in a single transaction to—

(i) the new pension scheme referred to in sub-paragraph (*b*) of this paragraph, or

(ii) another pension scheme that satisfies the new pension scheme condition (see article 11).][1]

(3) Condition B is that, immediately before the transfer mentioned in paragraph (2), the employee was an active member or a deferred member of the original pension scheme.

(4) Condition C is that, immediately before and after the transfer mentioned in paragraph (2), the employee was—

(*a*) employed by a sponsoring employer of the new pension scheme, . . .[1]

(*b*) a former employee of a sponsoring employer of the new pension scheme[, or][1]

[(*c*) a former employee of a former sponsoring employer of the original pension scheme in a case where the relevant sums and assets are transferred at the same time as the relevant sums and assets held for another employee or former employee who falls within sub-paragraphs (*a*) or (*b*).][1]

(5) In this article—

"active member" has the meaning given by section 151(2) of the Finance Act 2004,

["appropriate personal pension scheme" means a scheme in respect of which an appropriate scheme certificate is in force under section 7 of the Pension Schemes Act 1993,

"contracted-out rights" means rights under or derived from an occupational pension scheme or an appropriate personal pension scheme which fell within the following categories—

(*a*) entitlement to payment of, or accrued rights to, guaranteed minimum pensions;

(*b*) protected rights; or

(*c*) section 9(2B) rights.][1]

"deferred member" has the meaning given by section 151(4) of that Act, . . .[1]

["guaranteed minimum pensions" has the meaning given by section 8 of the Pension Schemes Act 1993, "occupational pension scheme" has the meaning given by section 1(1) of the Pension Schemes Act 1993,

"protected rights" has the meaning given by section 10 of the Pension Schemes Act 1993,

"relevant sums and assets", in relation to an employee or former employee, are the sums and assets held for the purposes of, or representing the accrued rights of the employee or former employee (as the case may be) under, the original pension scheme, and

"section 9(2B) rights" has the meaning given by regulation 1(2) of the Protected Rights (Transfer Payment) Regulations 1996.][1]

"sponsoring employer" has the meaning given by section 150(6) of that Act.

Amendments—[1] Paras (2), (2A) substituted for previous para (2), in para (4)(*a*), words "or" revoked, and para (4)(*c*) and preceding word "or", and definitions in para (5), inserted, by the Pension Schemes (Transfers, Reorganisations and Winding Up) (Transitional Provisions) (Amendment) Order, SI 2010/529 arts 2, 3, with effect on and after 6 April 2006.

11 The new pension scheme condition

(1) The new pension scheme condition is met if conditions A and B are met.

(2) Condition A is that the new pension scheme was a scheme whose rules, at the time of the transfer, included provision conferring a right on some or all of the persons who were then members of that scheme to retire before the normal minimum pension age.

(3) Condition B is that, on 6th April 2006, the new pension scheme was within either of paragraphs (*a*) or (*c*) of paragraph 1(1) of Schedule 36 (deemed registration of existing schemes) (and, accordingly, is treated as having become a registered pension scheme).

12 Rights to take benefit before normal minimum pension age

The employee has the right to retire—

(*a*) at the age at which, immediately before the transfer mentioned in article 10(2), the employee had the right to retire under the original pension scheme, or

(*b*) at the age at which, on 6th April 2006, the employee has the right to retire under the new pension scheme,

whichever is the greater.

WINDING UP OF ORIGINAL PENSION SCHEME

13 Conditions for application of article 16

Article 16 applies if the following conditions are met—

(*a*) the winding up condition (see article 14); and

(*b*) the annuity purchase condition (see article 15).

14 The winding up condition

(1) The winding up condition is met if [the first or second condition is met.][1]

(*a*)–(*c*) . . . [1]

[(1A) The first condition is met if—

(*a*) a pension scheme ("the original pension scheme") is being wound up,

(*b*) the original pension scheme is within any of paragraphs (*a*) to (*d*) of paragraph 1(1) of Schedule 36 (deemed registration of existing schemes), and

(*c*) condition A, B or C is met as set out in paragraphs (2), (3) and (4).

(1B) The second condition is met if—

(*a*) a registered pension scheme which is not within any of the paragraphs 1(1)(*a*) to (*d*) of paragraph 1(1) of Schedule 36 is being wound up, and

(*b*) immediately before the commencement of the winding up, an individual member of that registered pension scheme has rights which are protected under paragraph 22 or 31 of Schedule 36 (or under both of those paragraphs).][1]

(2) Condition A is that—

(*a*) the winding up commences before 6th April 2006, and

(*b*) immediately before the commencement of the winding up, an individual member of the original pension scheme would have had rights which were protected under paragraph 22 or 31 of Schedule 36 (or under both those paragraphs) if the winding up had commenced on or after 6th April 2006.

(3) Condition B is that—

(*a*) the winding up commences before 6th April 2006,

(*b*) an individual becomes a member of the original pension scheme after the commencement of the winding up but before 6th April 2006, and

(*c*) on becoming a member of the original pension scheme, the individual would have had rights which were protected under paragraph 22 or 31 of Schedule 36 (or under both those paragraphs) if the winding up had commenced on or after 6th April 2006.

(4) Condition C is that—

(*a*) the winding up commences on or after 6th April 2006, and (*b*) immediately before the commencement of the winding up, an individual member of the original pension scheme has rights which are protected under paragraph 22 or 31 of Schedule 36 (or under both those paragraphs).

Amendments—[1] Words in para (1) inserted, paras (1)(*a*), (*b*), (*c*) revoked, and paras (1A), (1B) inserted, by the Pension Schemes (Transfers, Reorganisations and Winding Up) (Transitional Provisions) (Amendment) Order, SI 2010/529 arts 2, 4 with effect on and after 6 April 2006.

[15 The annuity purchase condition

(1) The annuity purchase condition is met if—

(*a*) condition A is met in the case of an annuity policy that has been assigned, or

(*b*) conditions A to C are met in the case of an annuity policy that has been purchased.

(2) Condition A is that all the rights of the member have been extinguished by—

(*a*) purchasing one annuity policy which satisfies the requirements prescribed under section 74(3)(*c*) of the Pensions Act 1995 ("the prescribed requirements"), or

(*b*) assigning one annuity policy which satisfies the prescribed requirements, to the member.

(3) Condition B is that the contract under which the annuity policy was purchased ("the annuity contract") does not authorise the making of any payment which would be an unauthorised payment within the meaning of Part 4 of the Finance Act 2004.

(4) Condition C is that the annuity contract does not provide for the immediate payment of benefits.

(5) If the annuity purchase condition is met, paragraph 1(1) of Schedule 36 shall be modified so as to provide in addition that—

(*a*) in the case of an annuity policy within paragraph (2)(*a*), the annuity policy is treated as having become a registered pension scheme ("the new pension scheme") on the date on which the contract was made, and

(*b*) in the case of an annuity policy within paragraph (2)(*b*), the annuity policy is treated as having become a registered pension scheme ("the new pension scheme") on the date the annuity policy was assigned.][1]

Amendments—[1] Article 15 substituted by the Pension Schemes (Transfers, Reorganisations and Winding Up) (Transitional Provisions) (Amendment) Order, SI 2010/529 arts 2, 5, with effect on and after 6 April 2006.

16 Membership of the new pension scheme

(1) For the purposes of Part 3 of Schedule 36 (pension schemes: transitional provisions and savings: pre-commencement benefit rights) the member is to be treated as having become a member of the new pension scheme as the result of a block transfer to it.

(2) In paragraph (1) "block transfer" has the meaning given by paragraph 22(6) of Schedule 36.

17 [Stand-alone lump sums

(1) Paragraph (6) applies if condition A, B or C is met.

(2) Condition A is that—

(*a*) a pension scheme is being wound up ("the original pension scheme") and the winding up commenced before 6th April 2006,

(*b*) the stand-alone lump sum condition (see paragraph (5)) would have been met immediately before the commencement of the winding up, if the pension scheme had commenced winding up on or after 6th April 2006, and

(*c*) the annuity purchase condition set out in article 15 is met.

(3) Condition B is that—

(*a*) the original pension scheme is being wound up and the winding up commenced before 6th April 2006,

(*b*) an individual became a member of the original pension scheme before 6th April 2006 but after the commencement of the winding up,

(*c*) the stand-alone lump sum condition would have been met immediately before the commencement of the winding up, if the pension scheme had commenced winding up on or after 6th April 2006, and

(*d*) the annuity purchase condition set out in article 15 is met.

(4) Condition C is that—

(*a*) the original pension scheme is being wound up and the winding up commenced on or after 6th April 2006,

(*b*) the annuity purchase condition set out in article 15 is met, and

(*c*) the stand-alone lump sum condition is met.

(5) The stand-alone lump sum condition is that a member of the original pension scheme was entitled to be paid, a stand-alone lump sum which, if it had been paid would have been a stand-alone lump sum paid in circumstances where article 25B(4) (circumstance C) of the Taxation of Pension Schemes (Transitional Provisions) Order 2006 ("the Transitional Provisions Order") applied.

(6) The new pension scheme (within the meaning of article 15(5)(*a*) or (*b*) as the case may be) is treated as the same pension scheme as the original pension scheme (so that accordingly, the new pension scheme may pay a stand-alone lump sum to the member in circumstances where Article 25B(4) (circumstance C) of the Transitional Provisions Order applies).][1]

Amendments—[1] Art 17 inserted by the Pension Schemes (Transfers, Reorganisations and Winding Up) (Transitional Provisions) (Amendment) Order, SI 2010/529 arts 2, 6, with effect on and after 6 April 2006.

2006/574

REGISTERED PENSION SCHEMES (AUTHORISED SURPLUS PAYMENTS) REGULATIONS 2006

Made by the Commissioners for HMRC under FA 2004 s 177

Made . . . .*9 March 2006*
Laid before the House of Commons . . . . *10 March 2006*
Coming into force . . . .*6 April 2006*

Commentary—*Simon's Taxes* **E7.202–E7.207**.

1 Citation, commencement and interpretation

(1) These Regulations may be cited as the Registered Pension Schemes (Authorised Surplus Payments) Regulations 2006 and shall come into force on 6th April 2006.

(2) In these Regulations—

"the 1995 Act" means the Pensions Act 1995;

"the 1988 Act" means the Income and Corporation Taxes Act 1988;

"controlling director" means a director to whom subsection (5)(*b*) of section 417 of the 1988 Act (read with sections (3), (4) and (6) of that section) applies.

(3) In the application of these Regulations to Northern Ireland, a reference to an enactment applying only in Great Britain shall be construed as a reference to the corresponding enactment in Northern Ireland.

2 Payments falling within section 37 or 76 of the Pensions Act 1995

(1) A payment is an authorised surplus payment if it satisfies either paragraph (2) or (3).

(2) A payment satisfies this paragraph if it is made in compliance with the requirements contained in section 37 (payment of surplus to employer) of the 1995 Act.

This paragraph is subject to paragraph (4).

(3) A payment satisfies this paragraph if—

(*a*) it is made in connection with the winding up of an occupational pension scheme and

(*b*) the scheme making it satisfies the requirements set out in section 76 (excess assets on winding up) of the 1995 Act.

This paragraph is subject to paragraph (4).

[(4) A payment made by an occupational pension scheme to a sponsoring employer solely in respect of the death of a member is an authorised surplus payment if—

(*a*) it satisfies the conditions in paragraphs (2) or (3), and

(*b*) the member was not connected to the sponsoring employer at the date of the member's death.][1]

(5) For the purposes of this regulation and regulation 3 a member is connected to a sponsoring employer if—

(*a*) the employer is a partnership and he is connected with—

(i) a partner in the partnership, or

(ii) a person who has been a partner in the partnership at any time during the preceding year, or

(*b*) the employer is a company and the member, or a person connected with him, is, or at any time during the preceding year has been, a controlling director of the company.

For the purposes of paragraph (5) any question whether a person is connected with another shall be determined in accordance with section 839(2) of the 1988 Act.

Amendments—[1] Para (4) substituted by the Registered Pension Schemes (Miscellaneous Amendments) Regulations, SI 2011/1751 regs 3, 4 with effect for the tax year 2011–12 and subsequent tax years.

3 Payments falling outside section 37 or 76 of the Pensions Act 1995

(1) A payment made by an occupational pension scheme to a sponsoring employer which does not satisfy paragraph (2) or (3) of regulation 2 is an authorised surplus payment if it satisfies the following conditions.

Condition A

The rules of the scheme permit such a payment to be made.

Condition B

The rules of the scheme contain a limit, calculated other than by reference to the size of the member's fund, on the maximum amount of benefits that may be paid to, or in respect of, members of the scheme.

Condition C

If the scheme is being wound up, the liabilities of the scheme have been fully discharged including any tax that may be due and there is a surplus of assets over liabilities.

Condition D

If the scheme is not being wound up, the requirements set out in section 37 of the 1995 Act would have been met if the scheme had been one to which the section applied.
This paragraph is subject to paragraph (2).
[(2) A payment made by an occupational pension scheme to a sponsoring employer solely in respect of the death of a member is an authorised surplus payment if—
(*a*) it satisfies the conditions in paragraph (1), and
(*b*) the member was not connected to the sponsoring employer at the date of the member's death.][1]

Amendments—[1] Para (2) substituted by the Registered Pension Schemes (Miscellaneous Amendments) Regulations, SI 2011/1751 regs 3, 5 with effect for the tax year 2011–12 and subsequent tax years.

2006/575

PENSION PROTECTION FUND (TAX) REGULATIONS 2006

Made by the Treasury under FA 2005 s 102

Made . . . . *9 March 2006*
Laid before the House of Commons . . . . *10 March 2006*
Coming into force . . . . *6 April 2006*

Commentary—*Simon's Taxes* **E7.224**.

1 Citation and commencement

These Regulations may be cited as the Pension Protection Fund (Tax) Regulations 2006 and shall come into force on 6th April 2006.

2 Interpretation

(1) In this regulation—
(*a*) paragraph (2) gives the meaning of the abbreviated references to Acts and instruments used in these Regulations, and
(*b*) paragraph (3) deals with other expressions used in these Regulations.
(2) In these Regulations—
"FA 2004" means the Finance Act 2004;
"ICTA" means the Income and Corporation Taxes Act 1988;
"ITEPA 2003" means the Income Tax (Earnings and Pensions) Act 2003;
["P(No. 2)A(NI) 2008" means the Pensions (No. 2) Act (Northern Ireland) 2008;
"PA 2008" means the Pensions Act 2008;][1]
"the Pensions Act" (without more) means the Pensions Act 2004;
"the Pensions Order" means the Pensions (Northern Ireland) Order 2005;
"TCGA 1992" means the Taxation of Chargeable Gains Act 1992.
(3) In these Regulations—
"the Board of the Pension Protection Fund" means the body corporate established under section 107 of the Pensions Act;
"dependant" is to be construed in accordance with paragraph 15 of Schedule 28 to FA 2004;
"dependants' scheme pension" is to be construed in accordance with paragraph 16 of Schedule 28 to FA 2004;
"the Fraud Compensation Fund" has the meaning given by regulation 3(1);
"fraud compensation payment"—
(*a*) in England, Wales and Scotland means a fraud compensation payment within the meaning of Part 2 of the Pensions Act (see section 182(1) of that Act), and
(*b*) in Northern Ireland means a fraud compensation payment within the meaning of Part 3 of the Pensions Order (see Article 165(1) of that Order);
"Part 4" means Part 4 of FA 2004 (pension schemes);
"the pension compensation provisions"—
[(*a*) in England, Wales and Scotland is to be construed in accordance with section 108 of PA 2008 (interpretation), and
(*b*) in Northern Ireland is to be construed in accordance with section 87 of P(No. 2)A(NI) 2008 (interpretation);][1]
"the Pension Protection Fund" has the meaning given by regulation 3(1);
"the Pensions Act Funds" has the meaning given by regulation 3(1);
"the Pensions Act levies" means the levies specified in paragraph (2) or (3) of regulation 3, as the case may require;
"periodic compensation"—
(*a*) in England, Wales and Scotland is to be construed in accordance with Schedule 7 to the Pensions Act (pension compensation provisions) [or, as the case may be, Schedule 5 to PA 2008 (pension compensation payable on discharge of pension compensation credit)][1], and

(*b*) in Northern Ireland is to be construed in accordance with Schedule 6 to the Pensions Order (pension compensation provisions)[or, as the case may be, Schedule 4 to P(No. 2)A(NI) 2008(a) (pension compensation payable on discharge of pension compensation credit)][1];

["PPF money purchase lump sum"—

(*a*) in England, Wales and Scotland has the meaning given by regulation 1(2) of the Pension Protection Fund (General and Miscellaneous Amendments) Regulations 2006 (citation, commencement and interpretation), and

(*b*) in Northern Ireland has the meaning given by regulation 1(2) of the Pension Protection Fund (General and Miscellaneous Amendments) Regulations (Northern Ireland) 2006 (citation, commencement and interpretation);][1]

"registered pension scheme" has the meaning given by section 832(1) of ICTA;

"Schedule 36" means Schedule 36 to FA 2004 (transitional provisions);

"scheme pension" is to be construed in accordance with paragraph 2 of Schedule 28 to FA 2004.

Amendments—[1] In para (2), definitions inserted; in para (3), in definition of "the pension compensation provisions", sub-paras (*a*), (*b*) substituted, words in definition of "periodic compensation" inserted, and definition of ""PPF money purchase lump sum" inserted; by the Pension Protection Fund (Tax) (Amendment) Regulations, SI 2013/1117 regs 2, 3 with effect from 31 May 2013.

3 Meaning of "the Pension Protection Fund" and other expressions

(1) In these Regulations—

"the Pension Protection Fund" means the Fund required to be held, managed and applied by the Board of the Pension Protection Fund under section 110(1)(*a*) of the Pensions Act;

"the Fraud Compensation Fund" means the Fund required to be held, managed and applied by the Board of the Pension Protection Fund under section 110(1)(*b*) of the Pensions Act;

"the Pensions Act Funds" means the Pension Protection Fund and the Fraud Compensation Fund.

(2) In England, Wales and Scotland "the Pensions Act levies" means—

(*a*) the administration levy referred to in section 117(1) of the Pensions Act;

(*b*) the risk-based pension protection levy referred to in section 175(1)(*a*) of that Act;

(*c*) the scheme-based pension protection levy referred to in section 175(1)(*b*) of that Act;

(*d*) the fraud compensation levy referred to in section 189(1) of that Act;

(*e*) a levy in respect of eligible schemes imposed by regulations made under section 209(7) of that Act (the Ombudsman for the Board of the Pension Protection Fund).

(3) In Northern Ireland "the Pensions Act levies" means—

(*a*) the administration levy referred to in Article 103(1) of the Pensions Order;

(*b*) the risk-based pension protection levy referred to in Article 158(1)(*a*) of that Order;

(*c*) the scheme-based pension protection levy referred to in Article 158(1)(*b*) of that Order;

(*d*) the fraud compensation levy referred to in Article 171(1) of that Order;

(*e*) a levy in respect of eligible schemes imposed by regulations made under Article 191(3) of that Order (the PPF Ombudsman).

4 Application of the Tax Acts: general

(1) The Tax Acts apply in relation to the Pension Protection Fund in the same way as they apply in relation to a registered pension scheme.

(2) The general rule in paragraph (1) is subject to the further provisions contained in these Regulations.

5 Application of Part 4 of FA 2004: further provisions

Section 151 of FA 2004 (meaning of "member") applies as if, in Part 4, "member" in relation to the Pension Protection Fund, meant—

(*a*) an individual in receipt of compensation from the Pension Protection Fund, . . . [1]

(*b*) an individual who expects to receive such compensation following the assumption of responsibility, by the Board of the Pension Protection Fund, for a scheme of which that individual was a member[, or

(*c*) an individual who receives a PPF money purchase lump sum.][1]

Amendments—[1] In para (*a*) word "or" revoked, and para (*c*) and preceding word "or" inserted, by the Pension Protection Fund (Tax) (Amendment) Regulations, SI 2013/1117 regs 2, 4 with effect from 31 May 2013.

6—(1) Section 152 of FA 2004 (meaning of "arrangement") applies as if, in Part 4, "arrangement", in relation to an individual specified in paragraph (2), meant an arrangement specified in paragraph (3).

(2) An individual is specified for the purposes of this paragraph if the individual—

(*a*) is in receipt of compensation from the Pension Protection Fund, . . . [1]

(*b*) expects to receive such compensation following the assumption of responsibility, by the Board of the Pension Protection Fund, for a scheme of which that individual was a member[, or [(*c*) receives a PPF money purchase lump sum.][1]

[(3) An arrangement is specified for the purposes of this paragraph if—

(*a*) in relation to an individual falling within paragraph (2)(*a*) or (*b*), it is an arrangement under which the individual receives (or, as the case may be, expects to receive)—

(i) compensation paid under Schedule 7 to the Pensions Act or, as the case may be, Schedule 5 to PA 2008 (pension compensation provisions), or

(ii) compensation paid under Schedule 6 to the Pensions Order or, as the case may be, Schedule 4 to P(No. 2)A(NI) 2008 (pension compensation provisions), or

(*b*) in relation to an individual falling within paragraph (2)(c), it is an arrangement under which the individual receives a PPF money purchase lump sum.][1]

Amendments—[1] In para (2)(*a*) word "or" revoked, para (2)(*c*) and preceding word "or" inserted, and para (3) substituted, by the Pension Protection Fund (Tax) (Amendment) Regulations, SI 2013/1117 regs 2, 5, 6 with effect from 31 May 2013.

7 Chapter 2 of Part 4 (registration of pension schemes) does not apply in relation to the Pension Protection Fund.

8 Section 164 of FA 2004 (authorised member payments) applies as if it also provided that the Board of the Pension Protection Fund was authorised to make the following payments to or in respect of a member—

(*a*) payments of an amount falling within section 166(2) of the Pensions Act (duty to pay scheme benefits unpaid at assessment date);

(*b*) payments of an amount falling within Article 150(2) of the Pensions Order (duty to pay scheme benefits unpaid at assessment date)[;

(*c*) a payment of a PPF money purchase lump sum.][1]

Amendments—[1] Para (*c*) inserted by the Pension Protection Fund (Tax) (Amendment) Regulations, SI 2013/1117 regs 2, 7 with effect from 31 May 2013.

9—(1) For the purposes of Part 4, payment of periodic compensation from the Pension Protection Fund to an individual is treated as payment of a scheme pension to a member of a registered pension scheme (see section 165 of FA 2004: pension rules).

(2) The payment of such compensation is treated as meeting the condition specified in paragraph 2(2)(*a*) of Schedule 28 to FA 2004 (condition relating to payer of scheme pension).

10—(1) This regulation applies if—

(*a*) either condition A or B is met, and

(*b*) condition C is met.

(2) Condition A is that the Board of the Pension Protection Fund is responsible for securing that compensation is (and has been) paid to an individual in accordance with the pension compensation provisions.

(3) Condition B is that the Board of the Pension Protection Fund is required to secure the discharge of liabilities to an individual in respect of benefits transferred to the Board under—

(*a*) Chapter 3 of Part 2 of the Pensions Act (pension protection), or

(*b*) Chapter 3 of Part 3 of the Pensions Order (pension protection).

(4) Condition C is that the Board of the Pension Protection Fund provides for the securing of—

(*a*) the payment of compensation in the circumstances specified in condition A, or

(*b*) the discharge of liabilities in the circumstances specified in condition B,

by the entry into an annuity contract or a number of such contracts.

(5) For the purposes of Part 4, payment of an annuity under an annuity contract mentioned in paragraph (4) is treated as payment of a scheme pension.

(6) If this regulation applies, so much of Pension rule 4 in section 165(1) of FA 2004 (pension rules) as provides that a scheme pension may only be paid if the member had an opportunity to select a lifetime annuity instead is treated as omitted.

11—(1) Section 166 of FA 2004 (lump sum rule) and Part 1 of Schedule 29 to that Act (authorised lump sums: lump sum rule) apply with the following modifications to the payment of lump sums by the Pension Protection Fund to an individual.

(2) Section 166(2) of FA 2004 (time at which a person becomes entitled to a lump sum) applies as if the person becomes entitled to a lump sum when a person acquires an actual (rather than a prospective) right to receive the lump sum.

(3) In Schedule 29 to FA 2004, paragraph 5(1)(*a*) is treated as omitted.

12—(1) For the purposes of Part 4, payment of periodic compensation from the Pension Protection Fund to a dependant of an individual is treated as payment of a dependants' scheme pension in respect of a member of a registered pension scheme (see section 167 of FA 2004: pension death benefit rules).

(2) The payment of such compensation is treated as meeting the condition specified in paragraph 16(2)(*a*) of Schedule 28 to FA 2004 (condition relating to payer of dependants' scheme pension).

13—(1) This regulation applies if—

(*a*) either condition A or B is met, and

(*b*) condition C is met.

(2) Condition A is that the Board of the Pension Protection Fund is responsible for securing that compensation is (and has been) paid to a dependant of an individual in accordance with the pension compensation provisions.

(3) Condition B is that the Board of the Pension Protection Fund is required to secure the discharge of liabilities to a dependant of an individual in respect of benefits transferred to the Board under—

(*a*) Chapter 3 of Part 2 of the Pensions Act (pension protection), or

(*b*) Chapter 3 of Part 3 of the Pensions Order (pension protection).

(4) Condition C is that the Board of the Pension Protection Fund provides for the securing of—

(*a*) the payment of compensation in the circumstances specified in condition A, or

(*b*) the discharge of liabilities in the circumstances specified in condition B,

by the entry into an annuity contract or a number of such contracts.

(5) For the purposes of Part 4, payment of an annuity under an annuity contract mentioned in paragraph (4) is treated as payment of a dependants' scheme pension.

(6) If this regulation applies, so much of Pension death benefit rule 3 in section 167(1) of FA 2004 (pension death benefit rules) as provides that a dependants' scheme pension may only be paid if the member or dependant had an opportunity to select a dependants' annuity instead is treated as omitted.

14—(1) Section 168 of FA 2004 (lump sum death benefit rule) and Part 2 of Schedule 29 to that Act (authorised lump sums: lump sum death benefit rule) apply to the payment of lump sums by the Pension Protection Fund to a dependant of a qualifying individual.

[(2) In paragraph (1) a "qualifying individual" means—

(*a*) an individual who was a member of a scheme for which the Board of the Pension Protection Fund has assumed responsibility, or

(*b*) an individual who was a transferee entitled to a pension compensation credit referred to in section 111(1) of PA 2008 or section 89(1) of P(No. 2)A(NI) 2008 (creation of pension compensation debits and credits).][1]

Amendments—[1] Para (2) substituted by the Pension Protection Fund (Tax) (Amendment) Regulations, SI 2013/1117 regs 2, 8 with effect from 31 May 2013.

15 Sections 175 to 181 of FA 2004 (authorised and unauthorised employer payments) do not apply in relation to the Pension Protection Fund.

16 Sections 182 to 185 of FA 2004 (borrowing) do not apply in relation to the Pension Protection Fund.

17—(1) Section 186 of FA 2004 (exemption from tax on certain types of income) applies in relation to each of the Pensions Act Funds as if in subsection (1) for the reference to income tax there were substituted a reference to corporation tax.

(2) The exemption provided by section 186(1) of FA 2004 (as modified by paragraph (1)) in relation to each of the Pensions Act Funds also applies in respect of—

(*a*) any profit, gain or loss on a loan relationship within the meaning of Chapter 2 of Part 4 of the Finance Act 1996 (loan relationships), and

(*b*) any amount received on account of the Pensions Act levies.

18—(1) Any amount recovered by an individual's employer on account of any of the Pensions Act levies is treated in the same way as relievable pension contributions paid during a tax year (see section 188 of FA 2004: relief for contributions).

(2) In paragraph (1) "tax year" has the meaning given by section 279(1) of FA 2004.

19 Relief on any amount recovered by an individual's employer on account of any of the Pensions Act levies may be given in accordance with section 193 of FA 2004 (relief under net pay arrangements).

20 Sections 197 and 198 of FA 2004 (spreading of relief) do not apply in relation to any sum paid by an employer on account of any of the Pensions Act levies.

21 Section 199 of FA 2004 (deemed contributions) applies in relation to any sum paid by an employer on account of any of the Pensions Act levies as it applies in relation to a sum paid by an employer in or towards the discharge of any liability of the employer under the enactments specified in subsection (1) of that section.

22 Section 213 of FA 2004 (surchargeable unauthorised employer payments) does not apply in relation to the Pension Protection Fund.

23—(1) For the purposes of benefit crystallisation event 2 (see the Table in section 216(1) of FA 2004) "P" is the amount of the periodic payments which will be payable to the individual in the period of 12 months beginning with the day on which the individual first becomes entitled to a periodic payment (assuming that it remains payable throughout that period at the rate at which it is payable on that day).

(2) Benefit crystallisation event 2 does not apply if—

(*a*) an individual becomes entitled to a scheme pension under a relevant pension scheme,

(*b*) the Board of the Pension Protection Fund assumes responsibility for that relevant pension scheme, and

(*c*) the individual receives periodic compensation from the Pension Protection Fund under Schedule 7 to the Pensions Act or Schedule 6 to the Pensions Order (pension compensation provisions) in respect of the scheme pension mentioned in sub-paragraph (*a*).

(3) For the purposes of benefit crystallisation event 5 "DP" is the annual rate of periodic compensation to which the individual would be entitled if, on the date on which the individual reaches 75, the individual acquired an actual (rather than a prospective) right to receive it.

(4) Subject to the provisions of this regulation, section 216 of FA 2004 (benefit crystallisation events and amounts crystallised) applies to the payment, by the Board of the Pension Protection Fund, of any amount falling within section 166(2) of the Pensions Act or Article 150(2) of the Pensions Order (duty to pay scheme benefits unpaid at assessment date) in the same way as it would apply if that payment had been made by a registered pension scheme.

(5) Schedule 32 to FA 2004 (registered pension schemes: benefit crystallisation events: supplementary) applies to give the meaning of expressions used in this regulation as it applies to give the meaning of expressions used in the Table in section 216(1) of FA 2004 (benefit crystallisation events and amounts crystallised).

[23A Section 220 of FA 2004 (pension credits from previously crystallised rights) applies as if, in relation to the Pension Protection Fund—

(*a*) in subsection (4) for "or Article 26(1) of WRP(NI)O 1999 " there were substituted ", Article 26(1) of WRP(NI)O 1999, section 111(1) of the Pensions Act 2008 or section 89(1) of the Pensions (No. 2) Act (Northern Ireland) 2008",

(*b*) in subsection (4A)(*a*) for "or Article 26(2) or (3)(*b*) of WRP(NI)O 1999" there were substituted ", Article 26(2) or (3)(*b*) of WRP(NI)O 1999, section 111(2)(*a*) or (*b*)(ii) of the Pensions Act 2008 or section 89(2)(*a*) or (*b*)(ii) of the Pensions (No. 2) Act (Northern Ireland) 2008", and

(*c*) in subsection (4A)(*b*) for "or Article 26(3)(*a*) of WRP(NI)O 1999" there were substituted ", Article 26(3)(*a*) of WRP(NI)O 1999, section 111(2)(*b*)(i) of the Pensions Act 2008 or section 89(2)(*b*)(i) of the Pensions (No. 2) Act (Northern Ireland) 2008".][1]

Amendments—[1] Reg 23A inserted by the Pension Protection Fund (Tax) (Amendment) Regulations, SI 2013/1117 regs 2, 9 with effect from 31 May 2013.

24 Section 242 of FA 2004 (de-registration charge) does not apply in relation to the Pension Protection Fund.

25 Chapter 6 of Part 4 (schemes that are not registered pension schemes) does not apply in relation to the Pension Protection Fund.

26—(1) References in Part 4 to the scheme administrator, in relation to a pension scheme (see section 270 of FA 2004: meaning of "scheme administrator"), are to be treated as references to the scheme administrator of the Pension Protection Fund.

(2) For the purposes of paragraph (1) the "scheme administrator of the Pension Protection Fund" means the person appointed by the Board of the Pension Protection Fund to be responsible for the discharge of the functions conferred or imposed on the scheme administrator of the Pension Protection Fund by and under Part 4.

27—(1) If section 272 of FA 2004 (trustees etc liable as scheme administrator) applies in relation to the Pension Protection Fund, the Board of the Pension Protection Fund assumes liability by reason of that section applying in relation to that Fund.

(2) For the purposes of section 272(4) of FA 2004 (specification of persons assuming liability) the Board of the Pension Protection Fund are treated as persons who assume liability by virtue of being specified under Head 2.

28 Section 273 of FA 2004 (members liable as scheme administrator) does not apply in relation to the Pension Protection Fund.

[28A Section 279(1) of FA 2004 (other definitions) applies as if, in relation to the Pension Protection Fund—

(*a*) "pension credit" included any pension compensation credit mentioned in section 111(1)(*b*) of PA 2008 or section 89(1)(*b*) of P(No. 2)A(NI) 2008 (creation of pension compensation debits and credits),

(*b*) "pension debit" included any pension compensation debit mentioned in section 111(1)(*a*) of PA 2008 or section 89(1)(*a*) of P(No. 2)A(NI) 2008 (creation of pension compensation debits and credits), and

(*c*) "pension sharing order or provision" included any pension compensation sharing order or provision mentioned in section 109 of PA 2008 or section 88 of P(No. 2)A(NI) 2008 (activation of pension compensation sharing).][1]

Amendments—[1] Reg 28A inserted by the Pension Protection Fund (Tax) (Amendment) Regulations, SI 2013/1117 regs 2, 10 with effect from 31 May 2013.

29—(1) A lifetime allowance enhancement factor may operate in accordance with paragraph 7 of Schedule 36 (primary protection) in relation to all benefit crystallisation events occurring in relation to an individual in the circumstances specified in paragraph (2).

(2) The circumstances are where some or all of the individual's relevant pre-commencement rights are rights under a pension arrangement relating to that individual under a pension scheme for which the Board of the Pension Protection Fund assumes responsibility in accordance with—

(*a*) Chapter 3 of Part 2 of the Pensions Act (pension protection), or

(*b*) Chapter 3 of Part 3 of the Pensions Order (pension protection).

(3) This regulation is to be construed as one with paragraph 7 of Schedule 36.

30—(1) This regulation applies if there is a transfer to the Board of the Pension Protection Fund of all sums and assets held for the purposes of, or representing accrued rights under, an arrangement relating to an individual under a registered pension scheme.

(2) For the purposes of paragraph 12 of Schedule 36 (enhanced protection) the transfer is treated as a permitted transfer by virtue of sub-paragraph (8)(*b*) of that paragraph

(3) This regulation is to be construed as one with paragraph 12 of Schedule 36.

31—(1) For the purposes of Part 3 of Schedule 36 (pre-commencement benefit rights), the transfer of the property, rights and liabilities of a scheme to the Board of the Pension Protection Fund in accordance with a relevant transfer notice is treated as a block transfer within the meaning given by paragraph 22(6) of Schedule 36.

(2) But for the purposes of determining the compensation payable where the Board of the Pension Protection Fund assumes responsibility for a scheme in accordance with Chapter 3 of Part 2 of the Pensions Act or Chapter 3 of Part 3 of the Pensions Order (pension protection), paragraph (1) does not affect the application of—

(*a*) Schedule 7 to the Pensions Act (pension compensation provisions) or regulations made under that Schedule, or

(*b*) Schedule 6 to the Pensions Order (pension compensation provisions) or regulations made under that Schedule.

(3) In paragraph (1) a "relevant transfer notice" means—

(*a*) a transfer notice given under section 160 of the Pensions Act (transfer notice), or

(*b*) a transfer notice given under Article 144 of the Pensions Order (transfer notice).

32 Paragraphs 35 and 36 of Schedule 36 (winding-up lump sums paid by former approved superannuation funds and right to payment of lump sum death benefit) do not apply in relation to the Pension Protection Fund.

33 Application of the Inheritance Tax Act 1984: further provisions

Section 58 of the Inheritance Tax Act 1984 (relevant property) applies in relation to property which is held for the purposes of the Pension Protection Fund as it applies in relation to property which is held for the purposes of a registered pension scheme.

34 Section 151 of the Inheritance Tax Act 1984 (treatment of pension rights) applies in relation to an interest in or under the Pension Protection Fund as it applies in relation to an interest in or under a registered pension scheme.

35 Application of ICTA: further provisions

(1) Section 413(3) of ICTA (group relief: interpretation) applies as if it provided that two companies shall be deemed to be members of a group of companies if—

(*a*) one company is the 75 per cent subsidiary of the other and neither company is the Board of the Pension Protection Fund, or

(*b*) both companies are 75 per cent subsidiaries of the Board of the Pension Protection Fund.

(2) This regulation is to be construed as one with Chapter 4 of Part 10 of ICTA (group relief).

36—(1) If the Board of the Pension Protection Fund acquires more than half the ordinary share capital of a company (so that, accordingly, the condition in paragraph (*a*) of section 769(1) of ICTA is met), there is no change in the ownership of the company for the purposes of sections 767A to 768E of ICTA (change in ownership of company).

(2) This regulation is to be construed as one with sections 767A to 768E of ICTA.

37 Application of TCGA 1992: further provisions

(1) For the purposes of section 170 of TCGA 1992 (groups of companies), none of the following may be a member of a group—

(*a*) the Board of the Pension Protection Fund;

(*b*) the Pension Protection Fund;

(*c*) the Fraud Compensation Fund.

(2) This regulation is to be construed as one with TCGA 1992.

38—(1) For the purposes of TCGA 1992, any gain accruing to the Board of the Pension Protection Fund from its disposal of investments shall not be a chargeable gain if, or to the extent that, at the time of the disposal, those investments were held by the Board, or on its behalf, for the purposes of one of the Pensions Act Funds.

(2) In paragraph (1) "investments" includes futures contracts and options contracts.

(3) This regulation is to be construed as one with TCGA 1992.

39 Application of ITEPA 2003: further provisions

Step 5 of section 54(1) of ITEPA 2003 (calculation of deemed employment payment under arrangements made by intermediaries) applies in relation to a payment, by the intermediary, of any sum in respect of any of the Pensions Act levies in the same way as it applies in relation to any contributions that may be deducted under that step.

40 Section 307 of ITEPA 2003 (exemption from employment income for death or retirement benefit provision made by employer) applies in relation to the payment of any sum in respect of any of the Pensions Act levies in the same way as it applies in respect of provision made by an employee's employer for a retirement or death benefit.

41 Section 579A of ITEPA 2003 (pensions) applies in relation to periodic compensation from the Pension Protection Fund as it applies to any pension under a registered pension scheme.

[42 Unless it is a lump sum falling within any of paragraphs (*a*) to (*c*) of regulation 42A, a lump sum paid under any of the following provisions is treated as if it were a lump sum paid under a registered pension scheme to which section 636A of ITEPA 2003 (exemption for certain lump sums under registered pension schemes) applies—

(*a*) Schedule 7 to the Pensions Act or Schedule 6 to the Pensions Order (pension compensation provisions), or

(*b*) Schedule 5 to PA 2008 or Schedule 4 to P(No. 2)A(NI) 2008 (pension compensation provisions).][1]

Amendments—[1] Regs 42, 42A substituted for previous reg 42 by the Pension Protection Fund (Tax) (Amendment) Regulations, SI 2013/1117 regs 2, 11 with effect from 31 May 2013.

[42A Each of the following is to be treated as if it were a lump sum, paid to a member under a registered pension scheme, in relation to which section 636B of ITEPA 2003 (trivial commutation and winding-up lump sums) applies—

(*a*) a PPF money purchase lump sum,

(*b*) a lump sum under paragraph 24 of Schedule 7 to the Pensions Act or paragraph 24 of Schedule 6 to the Pensions Order (commutation of periodic compensation), where the portion of periodic compensation commuted exceeds 25%, and

(*c*) a lump sum under paragraph 9 of Schedule 5 to PA 2008 or paragraph 9 of Schedule 4 to P(No. 2)A(NI) 2008 (commutation of periodic compensation), where the portion of periodic compensation commuted exceeds 25%.][1]

Amendments—[1] Regs 42, 42A substituted for previous reg 42 by the Pension Protection Fund (Tax) (Amendment) Regulations, SI 2013/1117 regs 2, 11 with effect from 31 May 2013.

43 Application of the Finance Act 2003: further provisions

(1) Paragraph 8 of Schedule 4 to the Finance Act 2003 (debt as consideration) does not apply in relation to the Pension Protection Fund if—

(*a*) the Board of the Pension Protection Fund acquires a chargeable interest as part of its assumption of responsibility for a scheme in accordance with Chapter 3 of Part 2 of the Pensions Act or Chapter 3 of Part 3 of the Pensions Order (pension protection), and

(*b*) the chargeable interest is held by the Board of the Pension Protection Fund as an investment.

(2) Paragraph 1 of Schedule 7 to the Finance Act 2003 (group relief) applies in relation to a group of companies of which the Board of the Pension Protection Fund is a member as if, in the case of each reference to 75%, there were substituted a reference to 50%.

(3) For the purposes of paragraph 3(1) of Schedule 7 to the Finance Act 2003 (withdrawal of group relief) there is no withdrawal of group relief if the vendor is the Board of the Pension Protection Fund.

(4) This regulation is to be construed as one with Part 4 of the Finance Act 2003 (stamp duty land tax).

44 Fraud compensation payments and other related payments

(1) Receipt of a payment to which this regulation applies shall not be regarded as a disposal of an asset for the purposes of capital gains tax or for the purposes of corporation tax on chargeable gains.

(2) This regulation applies to—

(*a*) a fraud compensation payment under section 185 of the Pensions Act;

(*b*) an interim payment under section 186 of the Pensions Act;

(*c*) a fraud compensation payment under Article 168 of the Pensions Order;

(*d*) an interim payment under Article 169 of the Pensions Order;

(*e*) a payment made by the Board of the Pension Protection Fund under section 83 of the Pensions Act 1995;

(*f*) a payment in anticipation made by the Board of the Pension Protection Fund under section 84 of that Act;

(*g*) a payment made by the Board of the Pension Protection Fund under Article 81 of the Pensions (Northern Ireland) Order 1995;

(*h*) a payment in anticipation made by the Board of the Pension Protection Fund under Article 82 of that Order.

2006/614

REGISTERED PENSION SCHEMES (AUTHORISED PAYMENTS—ARREARS OF PENSION) REGULATIONS 2006

Made by the Commissioners for HMRC under FA 2004 s 164(f)

Made . . . . *9 March 2006*

Laid before the House of Commons . . . . *10 March 2006*

Coming into force . . . . *6 April 2006*

Commentary—*Simon's Taxes* **E7.224.**

1 Citation and commencement

These Regulations may be cited as the Registered Pension Schemes (Authorised Payments—Arrears of Pension) Regulations 2006 and shall come into force on 6th April 2006.

2 Payment of arrears of pension to be an authorised payment

(1) Where a registered pension scheme pays to a member of the scheme an amount representing accrued arrears of pension, paragraph (2) applies.

(2) Paragraph (3) applies to so much of the payment mentioned in paragraph (1) as—

(*a*) does not exceed the amount accrued during the period—

(i) ending with the date on which he became entitled to the pension ("the actual start date"); and

(ii) beginning with the earliest date from which the member could, at the actual start date, have required the scheme administrator, in accordance with the rules of the scheme, to make a payment of arrears of pension; and

(*b*) constitutes taxable pension income within section 579B of ITEPA 2003.

(3) The amount to which this paragraph applies is a payment of a prescribed description for the purposes of section 164(*f*).

(4) In this regulation—

"entitled" has the meaning given in section 165(3); and

a reference to a numbered section, without more, is a reference to the section of the Finance Act 2004 bearing that number.

2006/643

FILMS (DEFINITION OF "BRITISH FILM") ORDER 2006

Made by the Secretary of State under the Films Act 1985 Sch 1 para 10(2)

Made . . . . *31 March 2006*

Coming into force . . . . *1 April 2006*

1 Citation, commencement and interpretation

(1) This Order may be cited as the Films (Definition of "British Film") Order 2006 and shall come into force on the day after the day on which it is made.

(2) "The Schedule" means Schedule 1 to the Films Act 1985, and a reference to a numbered paragraph is a reference to the paragraph bearing that number in the Schedule.

2 Transitional provisions

(1) An application for certification under paragraph 2 which is made in relation to a film for which the first day of principal photography is on or after 1st April 2006 shall be determined by the Secretary of State in accordance with the Schedule as modified by this Order.

(2) An application for certification under paragraph 2 which is made in relation to a film for which the first day of principal photography is before 1st April 2006 shall be determined by the Secretary of State in accordance with the Schedule as in force immediately before the commencement of this Order if production is completed before 1st January 2007; otherwise it shall be determined in accordance with the Schedule as modified by this Order.

(3) For this purpose the production of a film is completed when the film is first in a form in which it can reasonably be regarded as ready for copies of it to be made and distributed for presentation to the general public.

3 Modification of the Schedule

In paragraph 1(1) (preliminary) omit the definitions of "Commonwealth country" and "film production activity".

4 For paragraph 4 (British films for purposes of the Schedule) substitute—

"**4** (1) A film is a British film for the purposes of this Schedule if the requirements specified in sub-paragraphs (2) and (3) are met.

(2) The first requirement is that throughout the period during which the film is being made the maker of the film is—

(*a*) a person ordinarily resident in a member State, or

(*b*) a company which is registered in a member State and of which the central management and control of business is exercised in a member State.

(3) The second requirement is that the film passes the relevant cultural test (see paragraph 4A, 4B or 4C).

(4) For the purposes of this paragraph and paragraphs 4A to 4D a state shall be treated as if it were a member State if—

(*a*) it is a party to an agreement under Article 310 of the Treaty establishing the European Community, and

(*b*) the agreement requires a maker of a film who is ordinarily resident or registered in that state to be treated for the purposes of this Schedule in the same way as a maker of a film who is ordinarily resident or registered in a member State.

(5) Her Majesty may by Order in Council provide for films to be treated as British films for the purposes of this Schedule if they are made in accordance with the terms of any agreement between Her Majesty's Government in the United Kingdom and any other government, international organisation or authority.

(6) This paragraph has effect subject to paragraph 5 (excluded films).

4A (1) The cultural test for a film other than a documentary (see paragraph 4B) or an animation (see paragraph 4C) is as follows.

(2) A film passes the cultural test if it is awarded at least 16 points in total.

(3) Up to 4 points shall be awarded in respect of the content of the film as follows—

(*a*) 1 point if at least 50% of the film is set in the United Kingdom;

(*b*) 1 point if at least one of the three principal characters depicted in the film (or, if there are three or fewer characters depicted in the film, any of them) is a British character;

(*c*) 1 point if the film depicts a British story;

(*d*) 1 point if at least 50% of the original dialogue is recorded in the English language or in a recognised regional or minority language.

(4) Up to 15 points shall be awarded in respect of work carried out in the making of the film as follows—

(*a*) up to 6 points depending on the percentage of principal photography that is carried out in the United Kingdom as follows—

(i) 6 points for 75%,

(ii) 5 points for 62.5%,

(iii) 4 points for 50%,

(iv) 3 points for 37.5%,

(v) 2 points for 25%,

(vi) 1 point for 10%;

(*b*) up to 4 points depending on the percentage of the work on visual effects that is carried out in the United Kingdom as follows—

(i) 4 points for 75%,

(ii) 3 points for 50%,

(iii) 2 points for 25%,

(iv) 1 point for 10%;

(*c*) 1 point if at least 75% of the work on special effects is carried out in the United Kingdom;

(*d*) up to 2 points depending on the percentage of the work on performing and recording the original music score created for the film that is carried out in the United Kingdom as follows—

(i) 2 points for 75%,

(ii) 1 point for 50%;

(*e*) 1 point if at least 75% of the work on audio post production is carried out in the United Kingdom;

(*f*) 1 point if at least 75% of the work on image processing is carried out in the United Kingdom.

(5) Up to 13 points shall be awarded in respect of the personnel involved in the making of the film as follows—

(*a*) 2 points if the director (or, if there is more than one, the lead director) is a qualifying person;

(*b*) up to 2 points depending on the number of the scriptwriters who are qualifying persons as follows—

(i) if there is only one scriptwriter, 2 points if he is a qualifying person,

(ii) if there are only two scriptwriters, 2 points if both of them are qualifying persons, 1 point if one of them is,

(iii) if there are only three scriptwriters, 2 points if two or more of them are qualifying persons, 1 point if one of them is,

(iv) if there are more than three scriptwriters, 2 points if two or more of the three lead scriptwriters are qualifying persons, 1 point if one of the three lead scriptwriters is a qualifying person;

(*c*) 1 point if at least one of the producers (or, if there are more than three, of the three lead producers) is a qualifying person;

(*d*) 1 point if the composer (or, if there is more than one, the lead composer) is a qualifying person;

(*e*) up to 2 points depending on the number of the actors who are qualifying persons as follows—

(i) if there are more than three actors, 2 points if two or more of the three lead actors are qualifying persons, 1 point if one of the three lead actors is a qualifying person,

(ii) if there are only three actors, 2 points if two or more of them are qualifying persons, 1 point if one of them is,

(iii) if there are only two actors, 2 points if both of them are qualifying persons, 1 point if one of them is,

(iv) if there is only one actor, 2 points if he is a qualifying person;

(*f*) 1 point if at least 50% of the cast are qualifying persons;

(*g*) up to 3 points depending on the number of the heads of department who are qualifying persons as follows—

(i) 3 points for five or more,

(ii) 2 points for three or four,

(iii) 1 point for one or two;

(*h*) 1 point if at least 50% of the production crew are qualifying persons.

4B (1) The cultural test for a documentary is as follows.

(2) A film passes the cultural test if it is awarded at least 16 points in total.

(3) Up to 4 points shall be awarded in respect of the content of the film as follows—

(*a*) 1 point if at least 50% of the film is set in the United Kingdom;

(*b*) 1 point if at least one of the three principal characters depicted in the film (or, if there are three or fewer characters depicted in the film, any of them) is a British character;

(*c*) 1 point if the film depicts a British story;

(*d*) 1 point if at least 50% of the original dialogue is recorded in the English language or in a recognised regional or minority language.

(4) Up to 15 points shall be awarded in respect of work carried out in the making of the film as follows—

(*a*) up to 6 points depending on the percentage of the work on shooting and visual effects that is carried out in the United Kingdom as follows—

(i) 6 points for 75%,

(ii) 5 points for 62.5%,

(iii) 4 points for 50%,

(iv) 3 points for 37.5%,

(v) 2 points for 25%,

(vi) 1 point for 10%;

(*b*) up to 4 points depending on the percentage of the work on research and development that is carried out in the United Kingdom as follows—

(i) 4 points for 75%,

(ii) 3 points for 50%,

(iii) 2 points for 25%,

(iv) 1 point for 10%;

(*c*) 1 point if at least 75% of the work on special effects is carried out in the United Kingdom;

(*d*) up to 2 points depending on the percentage of the work on performing and recording the original music score created for the film that is carried out in the United Kingdom as follows—

(i) 2 points for 75%,

(ii) 1 point for 50%;

(*e*) 1 point if at least 75% of the work on audio post production is carried out in the United Kingdom;

(*f*) 1 point if at least 75% of the work on image processing is carried out in the United Kingdom.

(5) Up to 13 points shall be awarded in respect of the personnel involved in the making of the film as follows—

(*a*) 2 points if the director (or, if there is more than one, the lead director) is a qualifying person;

(*b*) up to 2 points depending on the number of the scriptwriters who are qualifying persons as follows—

(i) if there is only one scriptwriter, 2 points if he is a qualifying person,

(ii) if there are only two scriptwriters, 2 points if both of them are qualifying persons, 1 point if one of them is,

(iii) if there are only three scriptwriters, 2 points if two or more of them are qualifying persons, 1 point if one of them is,

(iv) if there are more than three scriptwriters, 2 points if two or more of the three lead scriptwriters are qualifying persons, 1 point if one of the three lead scriptwriters is a qualifying person;

(*c*) 1 point if at least one of the producers (or, if there are more than three, of the three lead producers) is a qualifying person;

(*d*) 1 point if the composer (or, if there is more than one, the lead composer) is a qualifying person;

(*e*) up to 2 points depending on the number of the participants who are qualifying persons as follows—

(i) if there are more than three participants, 2 points if two or more of the three lead participants are qualifying persons, 1 point if one of the three lead participants is a qualifying person,

(ii) if there are only three participants, 2 points if two or more of them are qualifying persons, 1 point if one of them is,

(iii) if there are only two participants, 2 points if both of them are qualifying persons, 1 point if one of them is,

(iv) if there is only one participant, 2 points if he is a qualifying person;

(*f*) 1 point if at least 50% of all of the participants are qualifying persons;

(*g*) up to 3 points depending on the number of the heads of department who are qualifying persons as follows—

(i) 3 points for four,

(ii) 2 points for three,

(iii) 1 point for one or two;

(*h*) 1 point if at least 50% of the production crew are qualifying persons.

4C (1) The cultural test for an animation is as follows.

(2) A film passes the cultural test if it is awarded at least 16 points in total.

(3) Up to 4 points shall be awarded in respect of the content of the film as follows—

(*a*) 1 point if at least 50% of the film is set in the United Kingdom;

(*b*) 1 point if at least one of the three principal characters depicted in the film (or, if there are three or fewer characters depicted in the film, any of them) is a British character;

(*c*) 1 point if the film depicts a British story;

(*d*) 1 point if at least 50% of the original dialogue is recorded in the English language or in a recognised regional or minority language.

(4) Up to 15 points shall be awarded in respect of work carried out in the making of the film as follows—

(*a*) up to 6 points depending on the percentage of the work on shooting, visual design, layout and storyboarding that is carried out in the United Kingdom as follows—

(i) 6 points for 75%,

(ii) 5 points for 62.5%,

(iii) 4 points for 50%,

(iv) 3 points for 37.5%,

(v) 2 points for 25%,

(vi) 1 point for 10%;

(*b*) up to 4 points depending on the percentage of the work on visual effects that is carried out in the United Kingdom as follows—

(i) 4 points for 75%,

(ii) 3 points for 50%,

(iii) 2 points for 25%,

(iv) 1 point for 10%;

(*c*) 1 point if at least 75% of the work on special effects is carried out in the United Kingdom;

(*d*) up to 2 points depending on the percentage of the work on performing and recording the original music score created for the film that is carried out in the United Kingdom as follows—

(i) 2 points for 75%,

(ii) 1 point for 50%;

(*e*) 1 point if at least 75% of the work on voice recording and audio post production is carried out in the United Kingdom;

(*f*) 1 point if at least 75% of the work on image processing is carried out in the United Kingdom.

(5) Up to 13 points shall be awarded in respect of the personnel involved in the making of the film as follows—

(*a*) 2 points if the director (or, if there is more than one, the lead director) is a qualifying person;

(*b*) up to 2 points depending on the number of the scriptwriters who are qualifying persons as follows—

(i) if there is only one scriptwriter, 2 points if he is a qualifying person,

(ii) if there are only two scriptwriters, 2 points if both of them are qualifying persons, 1 point if one of them is,

(iii) if there are only three scriptwriters, 2 points if two or more of them are qualifying persons, 1 point if one of them is,

(iv) if there are more than three scriptwriters, 2 points if two or more of the three lead scriptwriters are qualifying persons, 1 point if one of the three lead scriptwriters is a qualifying person;

(*c*) 1 point if at least one of the producers (or, if there are more than three, of the three lead producers) is a qualifying person;

(*d*) 1 point if the composer (or, if there is more than one, the lead composer) is a qualifying person;

(*e*) up to 2 points depending on the number of the actors who are qualifying persons as follows—

(i) if there are more than three actors, 2 points if two or more of the three lead actors are qualifying persons, 1 point if one of the three lead actors is a qualifying person,

(ii) if there are only three actors, 2 points if two or more of them are qualifying persons, 1 point if one of them is,

(iii) if there are only two actors, 2 points if both of them are qualifying persons, 1 point if one of them is,

(iv) if there is only one actor, 2 points if he is a qualifying person;

(*f*) 1 point if at least 50% of the cast are qualifying persons;

(*g*) up to 3 points depending on the number of the heads of department who are qualifying persons as follows—

(i) 3 points for five or more,

(ii) 2 points for three or four,

(iii) 1 point for one or two;

(*h*) 1 point if at least 50% of the production crew are qualifying persons.

4D (1) In paragraphs 4A to 4C—

"cast" means all the actors and performers but not the extras who appear in a film;

"heads of department" has the meaning given by sub-paragraph (2);

"participant" means a presenter, narrator, subject or other person who participates and appears in a documentary;

"production crew" means all the persons directly involved in the production of a film who do not appear in the film;

"qualifying person" means a citizen of, or a person ordinarily resident in, a member State;

"recognised regional or minority language" means Welsh, Scottish-Gaelic, Irish, Scots, Ulster Scots or Cornish;

"special effects" means artificial techniques or processes, which are not visual effects, used to create an illusion in a film;

"visual effects" means digital alterations to a film's images.

(2) "Heads of department" means—

(*a*) in paragraph 4A, the lead cinematographer, the lead production designer, the lead costume designer, the lead editor, the lead sound designer, the lead visual effects supervisor and the lead hair and makeup supervisor;

(*b*) in paragraph 4B, the lead cameraman, the lead sound recordist, the lead editor and the lead researcher;

(*c*) in paragraph 4C, the lead layout supervisor, the lead production designer, the lead character designer, the lead editor, the lead sound designer, the lead visual effects supervisor and the lead modelling supervisor.

(3) For the purposes of paragraphs 4A to 4C—

(*a*) a film is set in the United Kingdom if it is set in a country which is now part of the United Kingdom; and

(*b*) a film depicts a British story if the subject matter of the film or the underlying material on which the film is based is British.

(4) The amount of work that is carried out in the United Kingdom or elsewhere shall be determined—

(*a*) for the purposes of paragraph 4A(4)(*a*) (principal photography), by reference to the number of days spent on the work;

(*b*) for the purposes of paragraphs 4A(4)(*b*) to (*f*), 4B(4)(*a*) to (*f*) and 4C(4)(*a*) to (*f*) (other matters), by reference to the amount of expenditure on the work.

(5) No points shall be awarded under any provision of paragraph 4A(4), 4B(4) or 4C(4) (points awarded in respect of the making of the film) in respect of work the expenditure on which is, in the opinion of the Secretary of State, insignificant in relation to the expenditure on all the work carried out in the making of the film.".

5 Omit paragraphs 6 (ascertainment of labour costs and playing time), 7 (determination of requisite amount of labour costs) and 8 (power of Secretary of State to direct alteration of labour costs).

2006/843

LOAN RELATIONSHIPS AND DERIVATIVE CONTRACTS (DISREGARD AND BRINGING INTO ACCOUNT OF PROFITS AND LOSSES) REGULATIONS 2006

Made by the Treasury under FA 1996 s 84A(3A), FA 2002 Sch 26 paras 16(3A), 17C(1)

Made . . . . *21 March 2006*
Laid before the House of Commons . . . . *21 March 2006*
Coming into force . . . . *22 March 2006*

Revocation—These Regulations revoked by FA 2009 s 43, Sch 21 para 10 with effect in relation to exchange gains and losses arising in accounting periods beginning on or after 22 April 2009 (subject to the provisions in FA 2009 Sch 21 para 11(2)–(5) in relation to exchange gains and losses arising in straddling accounting periods).

2006/912

ENERGY-SAVING ITEMS REGULATIONS 2006

Made by the Treasury under ITTOIA 2005 s 312(5)(c)

Made . . . . *23 March 2006*
Laid before the House of Commons . . . . *24 March 2006*
Coming into force . . . . *6 April 2006*

Revocation—Regulations revoked by the Energy-Saving Items Regulations, SI 2007/831 reg 5, Sch, with effect in relation to expenditure incurred on or after 6 April 2007.

2006/964

AUTHORISED INVESTMENT FUNDS (TAX) REGULATIONS 2006

Made by the Treasury under F(No 2)A 2005 ss 17(3), 18, FA 1995 s 152

Made . . . . *29 March 2006*
Coming into force . . . . *1 April 2006*

Commentary—*Simon's Taxes* **D8.140**.

PART 1
PRELIMINARY PROVISIONS AND INTERPRETATION
PRELIMINARY PROVISIONS

1 Citation, commencement and effect

(1) These Regulations may be cited as the Authorised Investment Funds (Tax) Regulations 2006, and shall come into force on 1st April 2006.

(2) These Regulations have effect—

(*a*) for the purposes of income tax—

(i) for the tax year 2006–07 and subsequent tax years, and

(ii) for distributions made on or after 6th April 2006;

(*b*) for the purposes of corporation tax—

(i) on income, for accounting periods beginning on or after 1st April 2006,

(ii) on chargeable gains, in relation to disposals made on or after 1st April 2006, and

(iii) for distributions made on or after 1st April 2006; and

(*c*) for the purposes of capital gains tax, in relation to disposals made on or after 6th April 2006.

(3) . . . [1]

Commentary—*Simon's Taxes* **D8.150.**

Amendment—[1] Para (3) revoked by the Authorised Investment Funds (Tax) (Amendment No 2) Regulations, SI 2007/794 regs 2, 8 with effect from 6 April 2007.

2 Structure of these Regulations

The structure of these Regulations is as follows—

this Part contains preliminary provisions and provides for interpretation;

[Part 1A deals with the genuine diversity of ownership condition;][3]

Part 2 deals with the tax treatment of authorised investment funds;

[Part 2A deals with qualified investor schemes][2]

[Part 2B deals with diversely owned AIFs;][3]

Part 3 deals with distributions made by authorised investment funds;

Part 4 deals with the treatment of participants in authorised investment funds;
[Part 4A deals with Property AIFs;][1]
[Part 4B deals with Tax Elected Funds;][3]
Part 5 deals with compliance;
Part 6 contains further provisions relating to authorised investment funds;
[Part 6A contains provisions relating to Funds Investing in Non-Reporting Offshore Funds (FINROFs);][4]
Part 7 contains consequential amendments and modifications of enactments; and
Part 8 contains final provisions.

Commentary—*Simon's Taxes* **D8.150.**

Amendments—[1] Entry inserted by the Authorised Investment Funds (Tax) (Amendment) Regulations, SI 2008/705 regs 2, 3 with effect from 6 April 2008.

[2] Entry inserted by the Authorised Investment Funds (Tax) (Amendment No 3) Regulations, SI 2008/3159 regs 3, 4 with effect from 1 January 2009. In relation to a qualified investor scheme authorised by the Financial Services Authority before 1 January 2009, this amendment has effect subject to SI 2008/3159 reg 31.

[3] Entries for Parts 1A, 2B and 4B inserted by the Authorised Investment Funds (Tax) (Amendment) Regulations, SI 2009/2036 regs 2, 3 with effect from 1 September 2009.

[4] Entry for Part 6A inserted by the Authorised Investment Funds (Tax) (Amendment) Regulations, SI 2010/294, regs 2 and 3, with effect from 6 March 2010 (see reg 1(2)).

INTERPRETATION

3 Definition of "authorised investment funds"

In these Regulations "authorised investment funds" means—

(*a*) open-ended investment companies, and
(*b*) authorised unit trust schemes.

Commentary—*Simon's Taxes* **D8.151.**

4 Definition of "open-ended investment company"

In these Regulations "open-ended investment company" means a company incorporated in the United Kingdom to which section 236 of FISMA 2000 applies.

Commentary—*Simon's Taxes* **D8.151.**

5 Interpretation of expressions relating to authorised unit trust schemes

(1) In these Regulations "unit trust scheme" has the meaning given by section 237 of FISMA 2000.
(2) For the purposes of these Regulations a unit trust scheme is authorised in relation to an accounting period if an order under section 243 of FISMA 2000 is in force in relation to that scheme during the whole or part of that accounting period.
(3) In these Regulations "unit holder" means a person entitled to a share of the investments subject to the trusts of a unit trust scheme.

Commentary—*Simon's Taxes* **D8.151.**

6 Further definitions generally relevant for authorised investment funds

(1) In these Regulations the "legal owner" means—

(*a*) in relation to an open-ended investment company, the open-ended investment company, and
(*b*) in relation to an authorised unit trust, the trustees of the trust.

(2) In these Regulations the "scheme property" means—

(*a*) in relation to an open-ended investment company, the property subject to the collective investment scheme constituted by the company, and
(*b*) in relation to an authorised unit trust, the property subject to the collective investment scheme constituted by the trust.

(3) In these Regulations the "manager" means—

(*a*) in relation to an open-ended investment company, the authorised corporate director, and
(*b*) in relation to an authorised unit trust, the person who is the manager of the trust for the purposes of Chapter 3 of Part 17 of FISMA 2000 (authorised unit trust schemes).

(4) In these Regulations, unless a contrary intention appears, "units" means the rights or interests (however described) of the participants in the authorised investment fund.
(5) In these Regulations "accumulation unit" means—

(*a*) in relation to an open-ended investment company, a share in the company in respect of which income is credited periodically to the capital part of the scheme property of the company, and
(*b*) in relation to an authorised unit trust, a unit in the trust in respect of which income is credited periodically to the capital part of the scheme property of the trust.

(6) In these Regulations a "participant", in relation to an authorised investment fund, means a beneficial owner of units in the fund, except where the units are held on trust (other than a bare trust) or are comprised in the estate of a deceased person, and in such a case the participant, in relation to the fund, means the trustees of the trust, or, as the case may be, the deceased's personal representatives.
[(7) In these Regulations "instrument constituting the fund" means—

(*a*) in relation to an open-ended investment company, the instrument of incorporation, and (*b*) in relation to an authorised unit trust scheme, the trust deed.

(8) In these Regulations "genuine diversity of ownership condition" has the meaning given by regulation 9A.][1]

Commentary—*Simon's Taxes* **D8.151.**

Amendments—[1] Paras (7), (8) inserted by the Authorised Investment Funds (Tax) (Amendment) Regulations, SI 2009/2036 regs 2, 4 with effect from 1 September 2009.

7 Umbrella companies and umbrella schemes: interpretation

(1) In these Regulations "umbrella company" has the meaning given by section 468A(4) of ICTA, and a reference to a part of an umbrella company is to be construed in accordance with that provision.

(2) For the purposes of these Regulations each of the parts of an umbrella company is regarded as an open-ended investment company and the umbrella company as a whole shall not be so regarded.

(3) In relation to a part of an umbrella company, any reference—

(*a*) to investments or to scheme property of an open-ended investment company has effect as a reference to such of the investments or to such of the scheme property as under the arrangements form part of the separate pool to which that part of the umbrella company relates, and

(*b*) a person for the time being having rights in that part is regarded as the owner of shares in the open-ended investment company which that part is regarded as being by virtue of paragraph (2), and not as the owner of shares in the umbrella company itself.

(4) In relation to a part of an umbrella company, any references in these Regulations to the instrument of incorporation or the prospectus in issue for the time being . . . [1] of an open-ended investment company have effect, for the purposes of these Regulations, as references to such parts of the instrument of incorporation or of that prospectus . . . [1] as apply to that part of the umbrella company.

(5) In these Regulations "umbrella scheme" has the meaning given by section 468(8) of ICTA, and a reference to a part of an umbrella scheme is to be construed in accordance with that provision.

(6) For the purposes of these Regulations each of the parts of an umbrella scheme is regarded as an authorised unit trust and the umbrella scheme as a whole is not regarded as an authorised unit trust or as any other form of collective investment scheme.

(7) In relation to a part of an umbrella scheme, any reference—

(*a*) to investments or to scheme property subject to the trusts of an authorised unit trust has effect as a reference to such of the investments or to such of the scheme property as under the arrangements form part of the separate pool to which that part of the umbrella scheme relates, and

(*b*) to a unit holder, has effect as a reference to a person for the time being having rights in that separate pool.

(8) In relation to a part of an umbrella scheme, any references in these Regulations to the prospectus in issue for the time being . . . [1] of an authorised unit trust have effect, for the purposes of these Regulations, as references to such parts of that prospectus . . . [1] as apply to that part of the umbrella scheme.

Commentary—*Simon's Taxes* **D8.151.**

[1] Words in paras (4), (8) revoked by the Authorised Investment Funds (Tax) (Amendment) Regulations, SI 2010/294, regs 2, 21, with effect from 6 March 2010 (see reg 1(2)).

8 General interpretation

In these Regulations—

"authorised corporate director", in relation to an open-ended investment company, means a corporate director of the company acting in the capacity as the director having responsibility for the management of its scheme property, being an authorised person within the meaning given by section 31(2) of FISMA 2000, or if there is no such director, the person for the time being having responsibility for the management of the scheme property of the company and acting in that capacity;

"collective investment scheme" has the meaning given by section 235 of FISMA 2000;

the "Commissioners" means the Commissioners for Revenue and Customs;

["connected person" has the meaning given in—

(*a*) sections 993 and 994 of ITA 2007 (connected persons) in the case of a person chargeable to income tax, and

(*b*) section 839 of ICTA (connected persons) in the case of a person chargeable to corporation tax;][2]

"creditor relationship" has the meaning given by section 103(1) of FA 1996;

"derivative contract" means—

(*a*) a contract which is a derivative contract within the meaning of Schedule 26 to FA 2002, or (*b*) a contract which is, in the accounting period in question, treated as if it were a derivative contract by virtue of paragraph 36 of that Schedule (contracts relating to holdings in unit trust schemes, open-ended investment companies and offshore funds);

"investments" do not include cash awaiting investment;

"net asset value" means the value of the assets of the authorised investment fund, after the deduction of specified liabilities;

["non-reporting fund" has the same meaning as in regulation 4(2) of the Offshore Funds Regulations;

"offshore fund" means a fund within the meaning of section 355 of the Taxation (International and Other Provisions) Act 2010;

"Offshore Funds Regulations" means the Offshore Funds (Tax) Regulations 2009;][4]

"owner of shares", in relation to an open-ended investment company, means a beneficial owner of shares in the company, except where the shares are held on trust (other than a bare trust) or are comprised in the estate of a deceased person, and in such a case the owner of shares, in relation to the company, means the trustees of the trust, or, as the case may be, the deceased's personal representatives;

["prospectus" includes a proposed prospectus, supplements to a prospectus and supplements to a proposed prospectus;][3]

["reportable income" has the same meaning as in Chapter 5 of Part 3 of the Offshore Funds Regulations;][4]

"reporting date" means the final day of each annual and each half-yearly accounting period of the authorised investment fund;

["reporting fund" means an offshore fund to which Part 3 of the Offshore Funds Regulations applies;][4]

"residence declaration" is to be construed in accordance with regulation 31;

["Statement of Recommended Practice" means, in relation to any accounting period for which it is required or permitted to be used, the Statement of Recommended Practice relating to authorised investment funds issued by the Investment Management Association in November 2008;][3]

"tax year"—

(*a*) in relation to income tax, means a year of assessment within the meaning of ICTA (see section 832(1) of that Act), and

(*b*) in relation to capital gains tax, means a year of assessment within the meaning of TCGA 1992 (see section 288(1) of that Act).

["tribunal" means the First-tier Tribunal or, where determined by or under Tribunal Procedure Rules, the Upper Tribunal.][1], [4]

Commentary—*Simon's Taxes* **D8.151.**

Amendments—[1] Entry for "tribunal" inserted by the Transfer of Tribunal Functions and Revenue and Customs Appeals Order, SI 2009/56 art 3, Sch 2 paras 154, 155 with effect from 1 April 2009.

[2] Entry for "connected person" inserted by the Authorised Investment Funds (Tax) (Amendment) Regulations, SI 2009/2036 regs 2, 5 with effect from 1 September 2009.

[3] Definitions for "prospectus" and "statement of recommended practice" inserted by the Authorised Investment Funds (Tax) (Amendment) Regulations, SI 2010/294, regs 2 and 4, with effect from 6 March 2010 (see reg 1(2)).

[4] Definitions of "non-reporting fund", "offshore fund", Offshore Funds Regulations", "reportable income" and "reporting fund" inserted by the Authorised Investment Funds (Tax) (Amendment) Regulations, SI 2011/244 regs 2, 3 with effect as follows—

(a) for the purposes of corporation tax—
- on income, for accounting periods ending on or after 6 March 2011, and
- on chargeable gains, in relation to disposals made on or after 6 March 2011, and

(b) for the purposes of capital gains tax, in relation to disposals made on or after 6 March 2011.

These amendments are subject to the following transitional provision (SI 2011/244 reg 8)—

- This provision applies to an authorised investment fund ("the fund") which, on 5 March 2011, met the following requirement: that the fund did not meet the investment condition in reg 85D of these Regulations by virtue of holding an interest in an offshore fund that is treated as creditor relationship rights under CTA 2009 s 490 (a "relevant interest").
- A relevant interest shall continue to be treated as not being an interest in a non-reporting fund for the purposes of reg 85E of these Regulations for the period beginning on 6 March 2011 and ending on 5 July 2011.

9 Abbreviations and general index

(1) The Schedule to these Regulations (which contains abbreviations and defined expressions that apply for the purposes of these Regulations) has effect.

(2) Part 1 of the Schedule gives the meaning of the abbreviated references to Acts used in these Regulations.

(3) Part 2 of the Schedule lists the places where expressions used in these Regulations are defined or otherwise explained—

(*a*) in these Regulations for the purposes of these Regulations, or

(*b*) in these Regulations for the purposes of a Part or Chapter of these Regulations.

[PART 1A
THE GENUINE DIVERSITY OF OWNERSHIP CONDITION

9A The genuine diversity of ownership condition

(1) For the purposes of these Regulations, the genuine diversity of ownership condition is as follows.

(2) The genuine diversity of ownership condition is that an authorised investment fund must—

(*a*) meet conditions A to C throughout the accounting period; or

(*b*) comply with paragraph (8).

(3) Condition A is that the fund documents—

(*a*) contain a statement that units in the fund will be widely available,

(*b*) specify the intended categories of investor, and

(*c*) specify that the manager of the fund must market and make available the units in the fund in accordance with paragraph 9A(6)(*a*).

(4) Condition B is that neither—

(*a*) the specification of the intended categories of investor, nor

(*b*) any other terms or conditions governing participation in the fund, whether or not specified in the fund documents,

have a limiting or deterring effect.

(5) In paragraph (4) a limiting or deterring effect means an effect which—

(*a*) limits investors to a limited number of specific persons or specific groups of connected persons, or

(*b*) deters a reasonable investor within the intended categories of investor from investing in the fund.

(6) Condition C is that—

(*a*) units in the fund must be marketed and made available—

(i) sufficiently widely to reach the intended categories of investors, and

(ii) in a manner appropriate to attract those categories of investors; and

(*b*) a person who is in an intended category of investor can, upon request to the manager of the fund, obtain information about that fund and acquire units in it.

Condition C is subject to paragraph (7).

(7) Condition C shall be treated as being met even if at the relevant time the fund has no capacity to receive additional investments, unless—

(*a*) the capacity of the fund to receive investments in it is fixed by the fund documents (or otherwise), and

(*b*) a pre-determined number of specific persons or specific groups of connected persons make investments in the fund which collectively exhausts all, or substantially all, of that capacity.

(8) An authorised investment fund . . . [3] also meets the genuine diversity of ownership condition if—

(*a*) an investor in the fund is a unit trust scheme[, an offshore fund or another authorised investment fund][3] (a "feeder fund");

(*b*) conditions A to C are met in relation to the authorised investment fund after taking into account—

(i) the fund documents relating to the feeder fund, and

(ii) the intended investors in the feeder fund; and

(*c*) the authorised investment fund and the feeder fund have the same manager (or proposed manager).

(9) In this Part "fund documents" means—

(*a*) the instrument constituting the fund, and

(*b*) the fund's prospectus in issue for the time being . . . [2].][1]

Amendments—[1] Part 1A inserted by the Authorised Investment Funds (Tax) (Amendment) Regulations, SI 2009/2036 regs 2, 6 with effect from 1 September 2009.

[2] In para (9)(b), words "(including any supplements to the prospectus)" revoked by the Authorised Investment Funds (Tax) (Amendment) Regulations, SI 2010/294, regs 2, 23, with effect from 6 March 2010 (see reg 1(2)).

[3] In para (8), words "which is a Property AIF" revoked, and words in sub-para (*a*) inserted, by the Authorised Investment Funds (Tax) (Amendment No 2) Regulations, SI 2011/2192 regs 2, 3 with effect as follows—

– for the purposes of corporation tax:

(a) on income, for accounting periods starting on or after 1 October 2011, and

(b) on chargeable gains, in relation to disposals made on or after 1 October 2011, and

– for the purposes of capital gains tax, in relation to disposals made on or after 1 October 2011.

[4] Definitions of "non-reporting fund", "offshore fund", Offshore Funds Regulations", "reportable income" and "reporting fund" inserted by the Authorised Investment Funds (Tax) (Amendment) Regulations, SI 2011/244 regs 2, 3 with effect as follows—

(a) for the purposes of corporation tax—

– on income, for accounting periods ending on or after 6 March 2011, and

– on chargeable gains, in relation to disposals made on or after 6 March 2011, and

(b) for the purposes of capital gains tax, in relation to disposals made on or after 6 March 2011.

These amendments are subject to the following transitional provision (SI 2011/244 reg 8)—

- This provision applies to an authorised investment fund ("the fund") which, on 5 March 2011, met the following requirement: that the fund did not meet the investment condition in reg 85D of these Regulations by virtue of holding an interest in an offshore fund that is treated as creditor relationship rights under CTA 2009 s 490 (a "relevant interest").
- A relevant interest shall continue to be treated as not being an interest in a non-reporting fund for the purposes of reg 85E of these Regulations for the period beginning on 6 March 2011 and ending on 5 July 2011.

9B [Clearance in relation to the genuine diversity of ownership condition

(1) An application for clearance that an authorised investment fund meets the genuine diversity of ownership condition (see regulation 9A) may be made in writing to the Commissioners by the manager (or proposed manager) of an authorised investment fund.

(2) An application for clearance must be accompanied by the fund documents in the form in which it is proposed that those documents will apply at the beginning of the first accounting period of the fund for which clearance is sought.

(3) If regulation 9A(2)(b) and (8) applies, an application for clearance by the authorised investment fund must be accompanied by—

(*a*) the documents specified in paragraph (2), and

(*b*) the fund documents of the feeder fund in the form in which it is proposed that those documents will apply at the beginning of the first accounting period of the fund for which clearance is sought.

(4) The Commissioners may require the manager (or proposed manager) to provide further particulars if they believe that full particulars of the fund have not been provided.

(5) The Commissioners must notify the applicant within 28 days of the receipt of the particulars (or, if paragraph (4) applies, of all further particulars required) that they—

(*a*) give clearance that the fund meets the genuine diversity of ownership condition,

(*b*) give that clearance subject to conditions, or

(*c*) refuse to give that clearance.

(6) An authorised investment fund (and investors in that fund) may not rely on a clearance given under this regulation if—

(*a*) at the beginning of the first accounting period of the fund to which the clearance relates (and at the beginning of each subsequent accounting period), a relevant statement in the fund documents in issue for the time being is not in accordance with a relevant statement in the documents considered by the Commissioners before giving clearance,

(*b*) the fund acts or is operated in contravention of a relevant statement in the fund documents,

(*c*) the fund documents are materially amended, or

(*d*) the fund is operated otherwise than in accordance with condition C of the genuine diversity of ownership condition (see regulation 9A(6)).

(7) If regulation 9A(2)(*b*) and (8) applies an authorised investment fund (and investors in that fund) may not rely on a clearance given under this regulation if any of sub-paragraphs (*a*) to (*d*) of paragraph (6) apply in relation to either the authorised investment fund or the feeder fund.

(8) Paragraph (6)(*c*) does not apply if the manager of the fund has obtained a clearance given under this regulation which applies to the amendment.

(9) For the purposes of paragraph (6)(*c*), a material amendment is one that may reasonably be construed as causing, or likely to cause, the fund to fail to meet the genuine diversity of ownership condition in relation to any accounting period.][1]

Amendments—[1] Part 1A inserted by the Authorised Investment Funds (Tax) (Amendment) Regulations, SI 2009/2036 regs 2, 6 with effect from 1 September 2009.

PART 2

THE TAX TREATMENT OF AUTHORISED INVESTMENT FUNDS

LOAN RELATIONSHIPS AND DERIVATIVE CONTRACTS: EXCLUSION OF CAPITAL PROFITS, GAINS OR LOSSES

10 General rule for loan relationships: exclusion of capital profits, gains or losses

(1) This regulation applies if any profits, gains or losses arising to an authorised investment fund from a creditor relationship in an accounting period are capital profits, gains or losses.

(2) For the purposes of Chapter 2 of Part 4 of FA 1996 (loan relationships) those profits, gains or losses must not be brought into account as credits or debits.

(3) Regulation 12 explains what is meant by "capital profits, gains or losses" in the case of an authorised investment fund that prepares accounts in accordance with UK generally accepted accounting practice.

[(4) This regulation is subject to regulation 14B (tax treatment of qualified investor schemes.][1]

Commentary—*Simon's Taxes* **D8.152.**

Amendments—[1] Para (4) inserted by the Authorised Investment Funds (Tax) (Amendment No 3) Regulations, SI 2008/3159 regs 3, 5 with effect from 1 January 2009. In relation to a qualified investor scheme authorised by the Financial Services Authority before 1 January 2009, this amendment has effect subject to SI 2008/3159 reg 31.

11 General rule for derivative contracts: exclusion of capital profits, gains or losses

(1) This regulation applies if any profits, gains or losses arising to an authorised investment fund from a derivative contract in an accounting period are capital profits, gains or losses.

(2) For the purposes of Schedule 26 to FA 2002 (derivative contracts) those profits, gains or losses must not be brought into account as credits or debits.

(3) Regulation 12 explains what is meant by "capital profits, gains or losses" in the case of an authorised investment fund that prepares accounts in accordance with UK generally accepted accounting practice.

[(4) This regulation is subject to regulation 14B (tax treatment of qualified investor schemes).][1]

Commentary—*Simon's Taxes* **D8.152.**

Amendments—[1] Para (4) inserted by the Authorised Investment Funds (Tax) (Amendment No 3) Regulations, SI 2008/3159 regs 3, 6 with effect from 1 January 2009. In relation to a qualified investor scheme authorised by the Financial Services Authority before 1 January 2009, this amendment has effect subject to SI 2008/3159 reg 31.

12 Accounts prepared in accordance with UK generally accepted accounting practice

(1) In the case of an authorised investment fund that prepares accounts in accordance with UK generally accepted accounting practice, capital profits, gains or losses arising from a creditor relationship in an accounting period, or capital profits, gains or losses arising from a derivative contract in an accounting period, are such profits, gains or losses as fall to be dealt with under [the heading "net capital gains/losses"][2] in the statement of total return for the accounting period.

(2) For the purposes of paragraph (1), the statement of total return for an accounting period is the statement of total return which, in accordance with the Statement of Recommended Practice used for the accounting period, must be included in the accounts contained in the annual report of the authorised investment fund which deals with the accounting period.

(3) . . . [3]

Commentary—*Simon's Taxes* **D8.152.**

Amendments—[1] Words in para (3)(*a*) substituted by the Authorised Investment Funds (Tax) (Amendment) Regulations, SI 2008/705 regs 2, 4 with effect from 6 April 2008.

[2] In para (1), words substituted for previous sub-paras (*a*), (*b*) by the Authorised Investment Funds (Tax) (Amendment No 3) Regulations, SI 2008/3159 regs 3, 7 with effect from 1 January 2009. In relation to a qualified investor scheme authorised by the Financial Services Authority before 1 January 2009, this amendment has effect subject to SI 2008/3159 reg 31.

[3] Para (3) revoked by the Authorised Investment Funds (Tax) (Amendment) Regulations, SI 2010/294, regs 2, 5, with effect from 6 March 2010 (see reg 1(2)).

[1] INTEREST DISTRIBUTIONS AND DEFICITS1 INTEREST DISTRIBUTIONS AND DEFICITS

Amendments—[1] In heading, words "Loan relationships: treatment of" revoked by the Authorised Investment Funds (Tax) (Amendment) Regulations, SI 2015/485 reg 2(1), (2) with effect for accounting periods beginning on or after 26 March 2015, subject to transitional provisions for accounting periods straddling that date: SI 2015/485 reg 1(3).

[12A Deduction of expenses

Where an authorised investment fund makes an interest distribution for a distribution period, the amount that can be deducted under Step 2 in section 4(2) of CTA 2010 (amounts that can be relieved against the company's total profits of the period) cannot exceed an amount that would reduce the total profits chargeable to corporation tax for the accounting period in which the last day of the distribution period falls to below the total amount chargeable to corporation tax in accordance with Part 4 of CTA 2009 for that accounting period.][1]

Amendments—[1] Regulation 12A inserted by the Authorised Investment Funds (Tax) (Amendment) Regulations, SI 2015/485 reg 2(1), (3) with effect for accounting periods beginning on or after 26 March 2015, subject to transitional provisions for accounting periods straddling that date: SI 2015/485 reg 1(3).

13 Treatment of interest distributions for purposes of loan relationships

(1) Chapter 2 of Part 4 of FA 1996 (loan relationships) has effect in relation to an authorised investment fund and to an interest distribution paid by that fund as it would have effect if the interest distribution were interest payable on a loan to the authorised investment fund and were, accordingly, interest under a loan relationship to which the authorised investment fund were a party.

[(1A) But paragraph (1) only applies to the extent that the interest distribution is derived from income [other than income chargeable to corporation tax in accordance with Part 4 of CTA 2009 and][5] in respect of which the legal owner is charged to corporation tax.][3]

(2) For the purposes of these Regulations, an interest distribution is treated as paid if it is credited to the capital part of the scheme property of an authorised investment fund on behalf of a participant in respect of the participant's accumulation units.

(3) This regulation is subject to regulation 14 [and regulation 14B (tax treatment of qualified investor schemes)][1].

[(4) In this regulation an "interest distribution" includes a TEF distribution (non-dividend) (see regulation 69Z61(3))[2]

Commentary—*Simon's Taxes* **D8.153.**

Amendments—[1] Words in para (3) inserted by the Authorised Investment Funds (Tax) (Amendment No 3) Regulations, SI 2008/3159 regs 3, 8 with effect from 1 January 2009. In relation to a qualified investor scheme authorised by the Financial Services Authority before 1 January 2009, this amendment has effect subject to SI 2008/3159 reg 31.

[2] Para (4) inserted by the Authorised Investment Funds (Tax) (Amendment) Regulations, SI 2009/2036 regs 2, 7 with effect from 1 September 2009.

[4] Para (1A) substituted by the Authorised Investment Funds (Tax) (Amendment) Regulations, SI 2012/519 regs 2, 3 with effect in relation to any distribution made on or after 1.30pm on 27 February 2012 (SI 2012/519 reg 1).

[5] In para (1A), words inserted by the Authorised Investment Funds (Tax) (Amendment) Regulations, SI 2015/485 reg 2(1), (4) with effect for accounting periods beginning on or after 26 March 2015, subject to transitional provisions for accounting periods straddling that date: SI 2015/485 reg 1(3).

14 Treatment of deficits on loan relationships

Section 83(2)(*c*) of FA 1996 (carrying back of non-trading deficit on loan relationships) shall not have effect in relation to the loan relationships of an authorised investment fund (so that, accordingly, if for any accounting period there is a deficit on the loan relationships of the authorised investment fund, the deficit may not be carried back to be set off against profits for earlier accounting periods). [This is subject to regulation 14B (tax treatment of qualified investor schemes)][1]

Commentary—*Simon's Taxes* **D8.153.**

Amendments—[1] Words inserted by the Authorised Investment Funds (Tax) (Amendment No 3) Regulations, SI 2008/3159 regs 3, 9 with effect from 1 January 2009. In relation to a qualified investor scheme authorised by the Financial Services Authority before 1 January 2009, this amendment has effect subject to SI 2008/3159 reg 31.

[Authorised investment funds having interests in offshore non-reporting funds

14ZA Interests in offshore non-reporting funds: general

(1) Regulation 14ZB applies if—

(*a*) an authorised investment fund disposes of an asset which is an interest in a non-reporting fund ("the asset"); and

(*b*) the conditions in paragraph (2) are satisfied for the period beginning with the date on which the authorised investment fund acquired the asset and ending on the date of the disposal.

(2) The conditions are that—

(*a*) the authorised investment fund has access to the accounts of the non-reporting fund,

(*b*) the authorised investment fund had sufficient information about the non-reporting fund referred to in paragraph (1)(*a*) to enable it to prepare computations of reportable income for the non-reporting fund for every accounting period which, if the non-reporting fund were a reporting fund, would be a reporting period ending within the period mentioned in paragraph (1)(*b*),

(*c*) the authorised investment fund has prepared such computations, and

(*d*) any excess of the authorised investment fund's share of the reportable income of the non-reporting fund over the authorised investment fund's share of the distributions made by the non-reporting fund is included in the amount available for income allocation by the authorised investment fund for each reporting period of the authorised investment fund which falls within the period mentioned in paragraph (1)(*b*).

(3) An authorised investment fund has an interest in a non-reporting fund if and to the extent that it has an interest in such a fund for the purposes of the Offshore Funds Regulations.

(4) For the purposes of the computations mentioned in paragraph (2)(*b*), regulation 80 of the Offshore Funds Regulations applies if (and only if) the non-reporting fund is a UCITS fund.

(5) In this regulation, "UCITS fund" has the same meaning as in regulation 12 of the Offshore Funds Regulations and "reporting period" has the same meaning as in regulation 91 of those Regulations.][1]

Commentary—*Simon's Taxes* **D8.153.**

Amendments—[1] Regs 14ZA, 14ZB, 14ZC inserted by the Authorised Investment Funds (Tax) (Amendment) Regulations, SI 2011/244 regs 2, 4with effect as follows—

(a) for the purposes of corporation tax—
- on income, for accounting periods ending on or after 6 March 2011, and
- on chargeable gains, in relation to disposals made on or after 6 March 2011, and

(b) for the purposes of capital gains tax, in relation to disposals made on or after 6 March 2011.

These amendments are subject to the following transitional provision (SI 2011/244 reg 8)—

- This provision applies to an authorised investment fund ("the fund") which, on 5 March 2011, met the following requirement: that the fund did not meet the investment condition in reg 85D of these Regulations by virtue of holding an interest in an offshore fund that is treated as creditor relationship rights under CTA 2009 s 490 (a "relevant interest").
- A relevant interest shall continue to be treated as not being an interest in a non-reporting fund for the purposes of reg 85E of these Regulations for the period beginning on 6 March 2011 and ending on 5 July 2011.

[14ZB Treatment of disposal of interest in non-reporting fund

No tax shall be charged on the authorised investment fund under regulation 17 of the Offshore Funds Regulations on the disposal by the authorised investment fund of an asset which is an interest in a non-reporting fund at the time of the disposal.][1]

Commentary—*Simon's Taxes* **D8.153.**

Amendments—[1] Regs 14ZA, 14ZB, 14ZC inserted by the Authorised Investment Funds (Tax) (Amendment) Regulations, SI 2011/244 regs 2, 4with effect as follows—

(a) for the purposes of corporation tax—
- on income, for accounting periods ending on or after 6 March 2011, and
- on chargeable gains, in relation to disposals made on or after 6 March 2011, and

(b) for the purposes of capital gains tax, in relation to disposals made on or after 6 March 2011.

These amendments are subject to the following transitional provision (SI 2011/244 reg 8)—
- This provision applies to an authorised investment fund ("the fund") which, on 5 March 2011, met the following requirement: that the fund did not meet the investment condition in reg 85D of these Regulations by virtue of holding an interest in an offshore fund that is treated as creditor relationship rights under CTA 2009 s 490 (a "relevant interest").
- A relevant interest shall continue to be treated as not being an interest in a non-reporting fund for the purposes of reg 85E of these Regulations for the period beginning on 6 March 2011 and ending on 5 July 2011.

[14ZC Treatment of interest in non-reporting fund: cases where the conditions in regulation 14ZA(2) would not be satisfied

(1) This regulation applies in relation to an asset of an authorised investment fund ("the asset") which—

(*a*) is an interest in a non-reporting fund, but

(*b*) in relation to which the conditions in regulation 14ZA(2) would not (apart from this regulation) be satisfied for the whole of the period specified in regulation 14ZA(1)(*b*) in relation to the asset.

(2) Paragraph (4) applies if the authorised investment fund, in relation to the asset, reasonably expects to satisfy the conditions in regulation 14ZA(2) for the period beginning with a date to be determined in accordance with paragraph (3) ("the deemed start date") and ending on the date of the disposal of the asset.

(3) The deemed start date is a date to be determined by the authorised investment fund but which must not be earlier than 6th March 2011.

(4) The authorised investment fund is treated for all purposes (including for the purposes of determining the beginning of the period mentioned in regulation 14ZA(1)(*b*)) as if it had, on the deemed start date, disposed of the asset (and not satisfied the conditions in regulation 14ZA(2)) and immediately reacquired the asset for a consideration equal to its market value on the deemed start date.

(5) The authorised investment fund must notify the Commissioners of the deemed start date by making an appropriate entry in its tax return for the accounting period in which the deemed start date falls.][1]

Commentary—*Simon's Taxes* **D8.153.**

Amendments—[1] Regs 14ZA, 14ZB, 14ZC inserted by the Authorised Investment Funds (Tax) (Amendment) Regulations, SI 2011/244 regs 2, 4with effect as follows—

(a) for the purposes of corporation tax—
- on income, for accounting periods ending on or after 6 March 2011, and
- on chargeable gains, in relation to disposals made on or after 6 March 2011, and

(b) for the purposes of capital gains tax, in relation to disposals made on or after 6 March 2011.

These amendments are subject to the following transitional provision (SI 2011/244 reg 8)—
- This provision applies to an authorised investment fund ("the fund") which, on 5 March 2011, met the following requirement: that the fund did not meet the investment condition in reg 85D of these Regulations by virtue of holding an interest in an offshore fund that is treated as creditor relationship rights under CTA 2009 s 490 (a "relevant interest").
- A relevant interest shall continue to be treated as not being an interest in a non-reporting fund for the purposes of reg 85E of these Regulations for the period beginning on 6 March 2011 and ending on 5 July 2011.

[Treatments applying to authorised investment funds with specific investment purposes

14ZD Index tracking funds

(1) This regulation applies if—

(*a*) an authorised investment fund has an interest in a non-reporting fund, and

(*b*) the conditions in paragraph (2) are met throughout the relevant period.

(2) The conditions are that—

(*a*) in accordance with either the authorised investment fund's prospectus or the instrument constituting the authorised investment fund, the aim of the authorised investment fund's investment policy is to replicate the performance of a qualifying index,

(*b*) the main purpose of the investment in the non-reporting fund is to represent the composition of the qualifying index, and

(*c*) the capital and income returns of the authorised investment fund replicate as closely as practicable the returns of the investments comprised in the qualifying index.

(3) For the purposes of paragraph (2) an index is a "qualifying index" if—

(*a*) it is based solely on the value of securities listed on a recognised stock exchange or admitted to trading on a regulated market,

(*b*) either a competent authority for the United Kingdom or an authority responsible for regulating offshore funds recognises the index on the basis that—

(i) its composition is sufficiently diverse,

(ii) it represents an adequate benchmark for the market to which it refers, and

(iii) it is published in such a way that it is widely available, and

(*c*) it is calculated and published by a body which is managed independently from the management of the authorised investment fund.

(4) Regulation 17 of the Offshore Funds Regulations does not apply in respect of a disposal of the interest in the non-reporting fund by the authorised investment fund.

(5) In this regulation "the relevant period" means the period—

(*a*) starting on the day the authorised investment fund acquires the interest in the non-reporting fund (or any part of it), and

(*b*) ending on the day of the disposal of the interest.

(6) In this regulation—

(*a*) a "competent authority in the United Kingdom" means the authority which is a competent authority for the United Kingdom for the purposes of Directive 2009/65/EC of the European Parliament and of the Council on the coordination of laws, regulations and administrative provisions relating to undertakings for collective investment in transferable securities (UCITS), and

(*b*) "regulated market" has the same meaning as in Directive 2004/39/EC of the European Parliament and of the Council on markets in financial instruments (see article 4.1(14)).][1]

Amendments—[1] Reg 14ZD inserted by the Authorised Investment Funds (Tax) (Amendment No 2) Regulations, SI 2011/2192 regs 2, 4 with effect as follows—

– for the purposes of corporation tax:

(a) on income, for accounting periods starting on or after 1 October 2011, and

(b) on chargeable gains, in relation to disposals made on or after 1 October 2011, and

– for the purposes of capital gains tax, in relation to disposals made on or after 1 October 2011.

14A [Authorised investment funds with limited investment powers—stamp duty reserve tax

. . .

Amendments—Regulation 14A revoked by the Stamp Duty Reserve Tax (Finance Act 1999, Schedule 19) (Consequential Amendments) Regulations, SI 2014/1932 reg 4 with effect in relation to any surrender made or effected on or after 30 March 2014.

[PART 2A
QUALIFIED INVESTOR SCHEMES

14B Tax treatment of qualified investor schemes

(1) The provisions in paragraph (2) shall not apply to a qualified investor scheme in relation to an accounting period of the scheme unless the genuine diversity of ownership condition (see regulation [9A][2]) is met in relation to that accounting period.

(2) The provisions referred to in paragraph (1) are—

(*a*) the provisions of Part 2 of these Regulations,

[(*aa*) the provisions of Part 4 of these Regulations,][2]

(*b*) the provisions of Part 4A of these Regulations,

(*c*) where the qualified investor scheme is an authorised unit trust scheme, section 468(1A) of ICTA,

(*d*) where the qualified investor scheme is an open-ended investment company, section 468A(1) of ICTA,

(*e*) in subsection (1) of section 99 of TCGA 1992 (as modified by these Regulations) the words "except that nothing in this section" to the end of that sub-section, and

(*f*) section 100 of TCGA 1992.

(3) Where the genuine diversity of ownership condition is not met in relation to an accounting period of the scheme—

(*a*) section 13A of ICTA applies to the qualified investor scheme, whether or not that section would apply apart from this sub-paragraph; and

[(*b*) the total amount available for income allocation to participants must only be allocated in accordance with paragraph (1)(*b*) of regulation 17 (allocation of income).][3]

(4) In these Regulations a "qualified investor scheme" means a fund, authorised by the Financial Services Authority, in which a statement that the fund is a qualified investor scheme is included in the instrument constituting the scheme.

(5) . . . [2]][1]

Amendments—[1] Part 2A (paras 14B–14D) inserted by the Authorised Investment Funds (Tax) (Amendment No 3) Regulations, SI 2008/3159 regs 3, 11 with effect from 1 January 2009. In relation to a qualified investor scheme authorised by the Financial Services Authority before 1 January 2009, this amendment has effect subject to SI 2008/3159 reg 31.

[2] In para (1), figure substituted, para (2)(*aa*) inserted, and para (5) revoked, by the Authorised Investment Funds (Tax) (Amendment) Regulations, SI 2009/2036 regs 2, 8 with effect from 1 September 2009.

[3] Para (3)(*b*) substituted by the Authorised Investment Funds (Tax) (Amendment) Regulations, SI 2010/294, regs 2, 6, with effect from 6 March 2010, but see regs 24–26 for transitional provisions relating to distribution dates for earlier accounting periods, and entry into the FINROF regime.

14C The genuine diversity of ownership condition

Amendments—Paras 14C, 14D revoked by the Authorised Investment Funds (Tax) (Amendment) Regulations, SI 2009/2036 regs 2, 9 with effect from 1 September 2009.

14D Clearance in relation to the genuine diversity of ownership condition

Amendments—Paras 14C, 14D revoked by the Authorised Investment Funds (Tax) (Amendment) Regulations, SI 2009/2036 regs 2, 9 with effect from 1 September 2009.

[PART 2B

DIVERSELY OWNED AIFS

14E Tax treatment of diversely owned AIFs

(1) This regulation applies to an authorised investment fund in respect of an accounting period if—

(*a*) the fund carries out an investment transaction in that period, and

(*b*) the fund meets the genuine diversity of ownership condition in relation to that period.

(2) In these Regulations an authorised investment fund to which this regulation applies is referred to as a "diversely owned AIF".

(3) If the profits or losses, as the case may be, arising from an investment transaction are capital profits, gains or losses, that investment transaction shall be treated as a non-trading transaction of the diversely owned AIF for the purposes of corporation tax.

(4) Chapter 2 of Part 3 of CTA 2009 (income taxed as trade profits) does not apply to capital profits and losses arising from such an investment transaction.

(5) For the purposes of these Regulations "investment transaction" means a transaction specified in [regulation 2 of the Investment Transactions (Tax) Regulations 2014][2].

(6) For the purposes of paragraphs (3) and (4) capital profits, gains or losses arising from an investment transaction in an accounting period are such profits, gains or losses as fall to be dealt with under the heading "net capital gains/losses" in the statement of total return for an accounting period.

(7) For the purposes of paragraph (6), the "statement of total return for an accounting period" has the same meaning as in regulation 12(2).][1]

Amendments—[1] Part 2B (regs 14E–14N) inserted by the Authorised Investment Funds (Tax) (Amendment) Regulations, SI 2009/2036 regs 2, 10 with effect from 1 September 2009.

[2] In sub-para (5), words substituted for words "regulation 14F" by the Investment Transactions (Tax) Regulations, SI 2014/685 reg 7(1), (2) with effect from 8 April 2014.

14F Meaning of "investment transaction"

Amendments—Regulations 14F–14N revoked by the Investment Transactions (Tax) Regulations, SI 2014/685 reg 7(1), (3) with effect from 8 April 2014.

14G Meaning of relevant contracts: general

Amendments—[1] Part 2B (regs 14E–14N) inserted by the Authorised Investment Funds (Tax) (Amendment) Regulations, SI 2009/2036 regs 2, 10 with effect from 1 September 2009.

[2] Regulations 14F–14N revoked by the Investment Transactions (Tax) Regulations, SI 2014/685 reg 7(1), (3) with effect from 8 April 2014.

14H Meaning of relevant contract: options

Amendments—Regulations 14F–14N revoked by the Investment Transactions (Tax) Regulations, SI 2014/685 reg 7(1), (3) with effect from 8 April 2014.

14I Meaning of relevant contract: futures

Amendments—Regulations 14F–14N revoked by the Investment Transactions (Tax) Regulations, SI 2014/685 reg 7(1), (3) with effect from 8 April 2014.

14J Meaning of relevant contract: options and futures—general provisions

Amendments—Regulations 14F–14N revoked by the Investment Transactions (Tax) Regulations, SI 2014/685 reg 7(1), (3) with effect from 8 April 2014.

14K Meaning of relevant contract: contract for differences

Amendments—Regulations 14F–14N revoked by the Investment Transactions (Tax) Regulations, SI 2014/685 reg 7(1), (3) with effect from 8 April 2014.

14L Loan relationships or related transactions

Amendments—Regulations 14F–14N revoked by the Investment Transactions (Tax) Regulations, SI 2014/685 reg 7(1), (3) with effect from 8 April 2014.

14M Units in a collective investment scheme

Amendments—Regulations 14F–14N revoked by the Investment Transactions (Tax) Regulations, SI 2014/685 reg 7(1), (3) with effect from 8 April 2014.

14N Carbon emission trading products

Amendments—Regulations 14F–14N revoked by the Investment Transactions (Tax) Regulations, SI 2014/685 reg 7(1), (3) with effect from 8 April 2014.

PART 3
DISTRIBUTIONS MADE BY AUTHORISED INVESTMENT FUNDS

PRELIMINARY

15 Interpretation

[(1) In these Regulations—

(*a*) "income allocation" means the distribution of an amount to participants; and

(*b*) "distribution" includes the crediting of an amount to the capital part of the scheme property on behalf of a participant in respect of the participant's accumulation units.][1]

(2) In these Regulations "distribution period", in relation to an authorised investment fund, means a period by reference to which the total amount available for [income allocation to participants][1] is ascertained.

(3) . . . [1]

(4) In these Regulations the "distribution date" for a distribution period of an authorised investment fund means—

(*a*) the date specified by or in accordance with the terms of the trust or the instrument of incorporation of the company for any distribution for that distribution period, or

(*b*) if no date is specified, the last day of that distribution period.

Commentary—*Simon's Taxes* **D8.154.**

Amendment—[1] Para (1) substituted, words in para (2) substituted, and para (3) revoked, by the Authorised Investment Funds (Tax) (Amendment) Regulations, SI 2010/294, regs 2, 7, with effect from 6 March 2010, but see regs 24–26 for transitional provisions relating to distribution dates for earlier accounting periods, and entry into the FINROF regime.

16 Funds excluded from the ambit of this Part

This Part does not apply to an authorised investment fund if the fund—

(*a*) is a registered pension scheme within the meaning of Part 4 of the Finance Act 2004, or

(*b*) is treated, under paragraph 1(1) of Schedule 36 to that Act, as having become such a scheme.

Commentary—*Simon's Taxes* **D8.154.**

. . . .

Amendments—Part heading, "Distribution accounts: general" revoked.

17 [Allocation of income]

[(1) The total amount available for income allocation must be allocated in one of the following ways—

(*a*) for distribution as yearly interest (see regulations 18 to 21); or

(*b*) for distribution as dividends (see regulation 22).][2]

[(1A) Paragraph (1) does not apply in relation to an authorised investment fund to which Part 4A or 4B applies.][1]

(2) . . . [4]

Commentary—*Simon's Taxes* **D8.155.**

Amendments—[1] Para (1A) inserted by the Authorised Investment Funds (Tax) (Amendment) Regulations, SI 2009/2036 regs 2, 11 with effect from 1 September 2009.

[2] Regulation heading substituted, and paras (1) and (2) substituted by the Authorised Investment Funds (Tax) (Amendment) Regulations, SI 2010/294, regs 2, 8, with effect from 6 March 2010, but see regs 24–26 for transitional provisions relating to distribution dates for earlier accounting periods, and entry into the FINROF regime.

[3] In para (2), words inserted by the Unauthorised Unit Trusts (Tax) Regulations, SI 2013/2819 reg 42 with effect from 6 April 2014.

[4] Para (2) revoked by the Authorised Investment Funds (Tax) (Amendment) Regulations, SI 2015/485 reg 2(1), (5) with effect for accounting periods beginning on or after 26 March 2015, subject to transitional provisions for accounting periods straddling that date: SI 2015/485 reg 1(3). Para (2) previously read as follows—

"(2) Amounts chargeable to corporation tax in accordance with Part 4 of CTA 2009 or regulation 15 of the Unauthorised Unit Trusts (Tax) Regulations 2013 must not be included in any amount of income allocated for distribution as yearly interest."

INTEREST DISTRIBUTIONS

18 Interest distributions: general

(1) Paragraph (2) applies where the total amount [available for income allocation is allocated][1] for distribution as yearly interest.

(2) The Tax Acts shall have effect as if the total amount were payments of yearly interest made on the distribution date by the authorised investment fund to the participants in proportion to their rights.

(3) In these Regulations an "interest distribution" means a payment of yearly interest treated as made by virtue of paragraph (2) (including a payment of interest treated as made to a participant who is not chargeable to income tax).

(4) This regulation is subject to—

(*a*) regulation 19 (the qualifying investments test), and

(*b*) regulation 23 (treatment of de minimis amounts).

Commentary—*Simon's Taxes* **D8.156.**

[1] Words in para (1) substituted by the Authorised Investment Funds (Tax) (Amendment) Regulations, SI 2010/294, regs 2, 9, with effect from 6 March 2010, but see regs 24–26 for transitional provisions relating to distribution dates for earlier accounting periods, and entry into the FINROF regime.

19 The qualifying investments test

(1) No amount may be shown as available for distribution as yearly interest unless the authorised investment fund in question satisfies the qualifying investments test throughout the distribution period.

(2) An authorised investment fund satisfies the qualifying investments test throughout a distribution period (the "relevant period") if, at all times in that period, the market value of the qualifying investments exceeds 60% of the market value of all the investments of the fund.

(3) Regulations 20 and 21 deal with the meaning of the expression "qualifying investments".

Commentary—*Simon's Taxes* **D8.156.**

20 Meaning of "qualifying investments"

In these Regulations "qualifying investments", in relation to an authorised investment fund, means the investments of that fund which fall within any of the following categories (read, as appropriate, with any applicable provision in regulation 21)—

Category 1

Money placed at interest.

Category 2

Securities.

Category 3

Shares in a building society.

Category 4

Qualifying units in another authorised investment fund.

[Category 4A

Qualifying units in an offshore fund.][1]

Category 5

Derivative contracts whose underlying subject matter consists wholly of any one or more of the matters referred to in categories 1 to [4A][2] and currency.

Category 6

Contracts for differences whose underlying subject matter consists wholly of any one or more of interest rates, creditworthiness and currency.

Category 7

Derivative contracts not within categories 5 or 6 where there is a hedging relationship between the derivative contract and an asset within categories 1 to [4A][2].

Category 8

Alternative finance arrangements.

Commentary—*Simon's Taxes* **D8.156.**

[1] Entry for Category 4A inserted by the Authorised Investment Funds (Tax) (Amendment) Regulations, SI 2010/294, regs 2, 10, with effect for accounting periods beginning on or after 6 March 2010 (see reg 1(2)).

[2] In Category 5 and Category 7, reference substituted by the Authorised Investment Funds (Tax) (Amendment No 2) Regulations, SI 2011/2192 regs 2, 5 with effect as follows—

- for the purposes of corporation tax:
  - (a) on income, for accounting periods starting on or after 1 October 2011, and
  - (b) on chargeable gains, in relation to disposals made on or after 1 October 2011, and
- for the purposes of capital gains tax, in relation to disposals made on or after 1 October 2011.

21 Meaning of "qualifying investments": further provisions

(1) This regulation applies for the purposes of regulation 20.

(2) For the purposes of category 2 "securities" do not include shares in a company.

(3) For the purposes of category 4 units in another authorised investment fund are qualifying units at any time in the relevant period if, and only if, the other authorised investment fund would itself (on the relevant assumption) satisfy the qualifying investments test throughout that period.

(4) For the purposes of paragraph (3) the relevant assumption is that the only investments of the other authorised investment fund which are to be regarded as qualifying investments are those falling within categories 1 to 3 and 5 to 8.

(5) In paragraph (4) references to investments of an authorised investment fund—

(*a*) in the case of an open-ended investment company are references to investments comprised in the scheme property of that company, but do not include references to cash awaiting investment, and

(*b*) in the case of an authorised unit trust are references to investments subject to the trusts of that authorised unit trust, but do not include references to cash awaiting investment.

[(5A) For the purpose of category 4A, units in an offshore fund are qualifying units at any time in the relevant period if, and only if, the offshore fund would itself (on the relevant assumption) satisfy the qualifying investments test throughout that period.
(5B) For the purposes of paragraph (5A), the relevant assumption is that the only investments of the offshore fund which are to be regarded as qualifying investments are those falling within categories 1 to 3 and 5 to 8.
(5C) In paragraph (5B), references to investments of an offshore fund—

(*a*) in the case of an offshore fund which is a company, are references to investments which are the investments of the company, but do not include cash awaiting investment, and

(*b*) in the case of any other offshore fund, are references to investments subject to the trust or other arrangements constituting the investments of the other offshore fund, but do not include cash awaiting investment.][1]

(6) For the purposes of categories 5 and 6 "underlying subject matter" has the same meaning as in paragraph 11 of Schedule 26 to FA 2002.
(7) For the purposes of categories 5 and 6 underlying subject matter may consist of currency only if and to the extent that there is a hedging relationship between the contract and a qualifying investment falling within categories 1 to 4.
(8) In paragraph (7) "hedging relationship" has the meaning given by paragraph 12(14) of Schedule 26 to FA 2002.
(9) For the purposes of category 6 a "contract for differences" has the same meaning as in paragraph 12 of Schedule 26 to FA 2002.
(10) For the purposes of category 7 a fund has a hedging relationship between a derivative contract on the one hand ("the hedging instrument") and an asset on the other ("the hedged item") if and to the extent that—

(*a*) the hedging instrument and the hedged item are designated by the fund as a hedge, or

(*b*) in any other case the hedging instrument is intended to act as a hedge of the exposure to changes in fair value of a hedged item which is a recognised asset or an identified portion of such an asset that is attributable to a particular risk and could affect the total net return of the fund.

(11) For the purposes of category 8 "alternative finance arrangements" has the meaning given by section 46(1) of the Finance Act 2005.

Commentary—*Simon's Taxes* **D8.156.**

1 Paras (5A)–(5C) inserted by the Authorised Investment Funds (Tax) (Amendment) Regulations, SI 2010/294, regs 2, 11, with effect for accounting periods beginning on or after 6 March 2010 (see reg 1(2)).

DIVIDEND DISTRIBUTIONS

22 Dividend distributions: general

(1) Paragraph (2) applies where the total amount [available for income allocation is allocated][1] for distribution as dividends.
(2) The Tax Acts shall have effect as if the total amount were dividends on shares paid on the distribution date by the authorised investment fund to the participants in proportion to their rights [(but see regulation 96A (modification of CTA 2009))][2].
(3) In these Regulations a "dividend distribution" means a dividend treated as paid by virtue of paragraph (2) (including a dividend treated as paid to a participant who is not chargeable to corporation tax).
(4) This regulation is subject to regulation 23 (treatment of de minimis amounts).

Commentary—*Simon's Taxes* **D8.157.**

Amendments—1 Words in para (1) substituted by the Authorised Investment Funds (Tax) (Amendment) Regulations, SI 2010/294, regs 2, 12, with effect from 6 March 2010, but see regs 24–26 for transitional provisions relating to distribution dates for earlier accounting periods, and entry into the FINROF regime.

2 Words in para (2) inserted by the Authorised Investment Funds (Tax) (Amendment) Regulations, SI 2012/519 regs 2, 4 with effect in relation to any distribution made at or after 1.30pm on 27 February 2012 (SI 2012/519 reg 1).

DE MINIMIS AMOUNTS

23 Provisions applying if amounts available for distribution are de minimis

(1) An authorised investment fund is not treated as making a distribution for a distribution period if conditions A to D are met.
(2) Condition A is that, in accordance with rules made by the Financial Services Authority, the authorised investment fund has an agreed de minimis limit.
(3) Condition B is that the authorised investment fund—

[(*a*) has calculated that the total income available for income allocations is a de minimis amount, and

(*b*) chooses to waive the allocation of that de minimis amount.][1]

(4) Condition C is that the de minimis amount is carried forward to the next distribution period as an amount available for distribution to participants.

(5) Condition D is that none of the units of the authorised investment fund in issue on the distribution date are in bearer form.

(6) If this regulation applies, the authorised investment fund is not required to comply with the requirements of section 234A of ICTA (information relating to distributions) in respect of the de minimis amount for the distribution period in question.

(7) In this regulation—

the "de minimis limit", in relation to an authorised investment fund, means an amount in respect of which a distribution of income of the fund is not required if the total amount [available for income allocation][1] to participants does not exceed that amount, and

"de minimis amount" means an amount falling within the de minimis limit.

Commentary—*Simon's Taxes* **D8.157.**

[1] Paras (3)(*a*), (*b*) substituted, and words in para (7) substituted, by the Authorised Investment Funds (Tax) (Amendment) Regulations, SI 2010/294, regs 2, 13, with effect from 6 March 2010, but see regs 24–26 for transitional provisions relating to distribution dates for earlier accounting periods, and entry into the FINROF regime.

PART 4

THE TREATMENT OF PARTICIPANTS IN AUTHORISED INVESTMENT FUNDS

CHAPTER 1

PRELIMINARY PROVISIONS

24 Structure of this Part

The structure of this Part of these Regulations is as follows—

this Chapter contains preliminary provisions;

Chapter 2 contains provisions relating to the tax treatment of participants chargeable to income tax;

Chapter 3 contains provisions relating to the tax treatment of participants chargeable to corporation tax;

. . . [1]

Amendments—[1] Words revoked by the Authorised Investment Funds (Tax) (Amendment No 3) Regulations, SI 2008/3159 regs 3, 12 with effect from 1 January 2009. In relation to a qualified investor scheme authorised by the Financial Services Authority before 1 January 2009, this amendment has effect subject to SI 2008/3159 reg 31.

25 Funds excluded from the ambit of this Part

This Part does not apply to an authorised investment fund if the fund—

(*a*) is a registered pension scheme within the meaning of Part 4 of the Finance Act 2004, or

(*b*) is treated, under paragraph 1(1) of Schedule 36 to that Act, as having become such a scheme.

CHAPTER 2

PARTICIPANTS CHARGEABLE TO INCOME TAX

DEDUCTION OF TAX FROM INTEREST DISTRIBUTIONS: GENERAL

26 Deduction of tax where interest distributions made

(1) This regulation applies if an interest distribution is made for a distribution period to a participant chargeable to income tax.

(2) Any obligation to deduct a sum under [section 874 of ITA 2007][2] is subject to the provisions of this regulation.

(3) In this Part the "deduction obligation" means the obligation specified in paragraph (2).

(4) The deduction obligation does not apply to the interest distribution if—

(*a*) the participant is a company;

(*b*) the participant consists of the trustees of a unit trust scheme;

(*c*) the reputable intermediary condition is met with respect to a participant on the distribution date (see regulation 27); . . . [3]

(*d*) the residence condition is met with respect to a participant on the distribution date (see regulation 30); . . .

(*e*) . . . [1] [, or

(*f*) the offshore marketing condition is met with respect to the class of units in relation to which the distribution is made (see regulation 33A).][3]

(5) But if the participant is a company which is the trustee of the trust to which (or under which) the interest distribution is made (or received), the deduction obligation is not excluded by virtue of paragraph (4)(*a*).

(6) In its application to an interest distribution to a participant in respect of accumulation units, the deduction obligation is an obligation to deduct a sum out of the amount being credited to scheme capital on the participant's behalf.

Commentary—*Simon's Taxes* **D8.158.**

Amendments—[1] Para (4)(*e*) and preceding word "or" revoked, by the Authorised Investment Funds (Tax) (Amendment No 2) Regulations, SI 2007/794 regs 2, 3, 8 with effect from 6 April 2007.

[2] In para (2), words substituted for words "section 349(2) of ICTA" by the Authorised Investment Funds (Tax) (Amendment) (No 2) Regulations 2013/2994 regs 2, 3(*a*) with effect from 19 December 2013.

[3] In para (4), word "or" at end of sub-para (*c*) revoked, and sub-para (*f*) and preceding word "or" inserted, by the Authorised Investment Funds (Tax) (Amendment) (No 2) Regulations 2013/2994 regs 2, 3(*b*) with effect in relation units acquired on or after 19 December 2013.

27 The reputable intermediary condition

(1) The reputable intermediary condition is met with respect to a participant on the distribution date if conditions A to C are met.

(2) Condition A is that the interest distribution is paid on behalf of the participant to a company.

(3) Condition B is that the legal owner has reasonable grounds for believing that the participant is not . . . [1] resident in the United Kingdom.

(4) Condition C is that the company mentioned in paragraph (2)—

(*a*) is subject to the EC Money Laundering Directive,

(*b*) is subject to equivalent non-EC provisions, or

(*c*) is a company which—

(i) is resident in a regulating country or territory, and

(ii) is an associated company of a company which is subject to paragraph (*a*) or (*b*).

Commentary—*Simon's Taxes* **D8.158.**

Amendments—[1] In para (3), word "ordinarily" revoked by the Authorised Investment Funds (Tax) (Amendment) (No 2) Regulations 2013/2994 regs 2, 7 with effect for the purposes of a person's liability to income tax for the tax year 2014–15 and any subsequent tax year.

28 The reputable intermediary condition: further provisions

(1) This regulation applies for the purposes of Condition C in regulation 27.

(2) A company is subject to the EC Money Laundering Directive if it is a credit institution or financial institution as defined by Article 1 of Directive 91/308/EEC, as amended by Directive 2001/97/EC

(3) A company is subject to equivalent non-EC provisions if it is required by the law of any country or territory which is not a member State to comply with requirements similar to those which, under Article 3 of that Directive (as so amended), member States must ensure are complied with by credit institutions and financial institutions.

(4) A country or territory is a regulating country or territory if it either is a member State or imposes requirements similar to those which, under Article 3 of that Directive (as so amended), member States must ensure are complied with by credit institutions and financial institutions.

(5) A company is to be treated as another's associated company if it would be so treated for the purposes of Part 11 of ICTA (close companies) (see section 416 of that Act).

Commentary—*Simon's Taxes* **D8.158.**

29 Consequences of reasonable but incorrect belief

(1) This regulation applies if conditions A to D are met.

(2) Condition A is that an interest distribution is made to a participant.

(3) Condition B is that the legal owner, in reliance on the reputable intermediary condition being met with respect to the participant, does not comply with the deduction obligation in relation to the interest distribution.

(4) Condition C is that the deduction obligation would apply but for the reputable intermediary condition being met.

(5) Condition D is that (contrary to the belief of the legal owner) the participant is in fact . . . [1] resident in the United Kingdom.

(6) Section 350 of ICTA (charge to tax where payments made under section 349) and Schedule 16 to that Act (collection of income tax on company payments which are not distributions) have effect as if the deduction obligation applied.

Commentary—*Simon's Taxes* **D8.158.**

Amendments—[1] In para (5), word "ordinarily" revoked by the Authorised Investment Funds (Tax) (Amendment) (No 2) Regulations 2013/2994 regs 2, 8 with effect for the purposes of a person's liability to income tax for the tax year 2014–15 and any subsequent tax year.

30 The residence condition

(1) The residence condition is met with respect to a participant on the distribution date if any of conditions A to E is met.

(2) Condition A is that, in relation to an interest distribution which is not made to or received under a trust, there is a valid declaration, made by the participant, that the participant is not . . . [1] resident in the United Kingdom.

(3) Condition B is—

(*a*) that the participant holds the units as the personal representative of a deceased person, and (*b*) that the deceased, before his death, made a declaration, valid at the time of his death, that he was not . . . [1] resident in the United Kingdom.

(4) Condition C is—

(*a*) that the participant holds the units as the personal representative of a deceased person, and

(*b*) that the personal representative has made a declaration that the deceased, immediately before his death, was not . . . [1] resident in the United Kingdom.

(5) Condition D is that, in the case of an interest distribution made to or received under a trust where the whole of the income is, or falls to be treated as, or under any provision of the Tax Acts is deemed to be, the income of a person other than the trustees of that trust, there is a valid declaration, made by the person in question that [the person is][1] not resident in the United Kingdom.

(6) Condition E is that, in circumstances in which condition D does not apply and with respect to a participant in the case of an interest distribution made to or received under a trust, there is a valid declaration, made by the trustees of that trust that—

(*a*) the trustees are not resident in the United Kingdom, and

(*b*) each beneficiary of the trust is . . . [1] not resident in the United Kingdom.

Commentary—*Simon's Taxes* **D8.158.**

Amendments—[1] In paras (2), (3)(*b*), (4)(*b*) word "ordinarily" revoked, in para (5) words substituted for words "he is either not ordinarily resident or, in the case of a company", and in para (6)(*b*), words "either not ordinarily resident or, in the case of a beneficiary which is a company," revoked, by the Authorised Investment Funds (Tax) (Amendment) (No 2) Regulations 2013/2994 regs 2, 9 with effect in relation to the making of declarations on or after 6 April 2014. Any declarations made before that date continue to have effect in respect of interest distributions made on or after that date as if those amendments had not been made.

31 Residence declarations

(1) A declaration made for the purposes of regulation 30 must—

(*a*) be in such form as may be required or authorised by the Commissioners;

(*b*) be made in writing to the legal owner of the authorised investment fund in question; and

(*c*) contain any details or undertakings required by paragraphs (2) to (4) below.

(2) A declaration made for the purposes of condition A or B in regulation 30 must contain—

(*a*) the name and principal residential address of the person making it; and

(*b*) an undertaking that he will notify the legal owner if he becomes . . . [1] resident in the United Kingdom.

(3) A declaration made for the purposes of condition C in regulation 30 must contain the name of the deceased and his principal residential address immediately before his death.

(4) A declaration made for the purposes of condition D or E in regulation 30 must contain—

(*a*) the names and principal residential addresses of the trustees of the trust or, in the case of a trustee which is a company, the name of the company and the address of its registered or principal office;

(*b*) the names and principal residential addresses of the beneficiaries of the trust or, in the case of a beneficiary which is a company, the name of the company and the address of its registered or principal office; and

(*c*) an undertaking that the trustees of the trust will notify the legal owner of the authorised investment fund in question if—

(i) they become resident in the United Kingdom,

(ii) any beneficiary of the trust named in the declaration becomes . . . [1] resident in the United Kingdom, or

(iii) any person who becomes a beneficiary of the trust after the making of the declaration either is at the time of becoming a beneficiary, or subsequently becomes, . . . [1] resident in the United Kingdom.

Commentary—*Simon's Taxes* **D8.158.**

Amendments—[1] In para (2)(*b*), word "ordinarily" revoked, and in para (4)(*c*)(ii), (iii), words "ordinarily resident or, in the case of a company," revoked, by the Authorised Investment Funds (Tax) (Amendment) (No 2) Regulations 2013/2994 regs 2, 10 with effect in relation to the making of declarations on or after 6 April 2014. Any declarations made before that date continue to have effect in respect of interest distributions made on or after that date as if those amendments had not been made.

32 References to beneficiaries in regulations 30 and 31

In regulations 30 and 31 references to a beneficiary are references to any person who is known to the trustees of the trust to be either—

(*a*) a person who is or will or may become, entitled to any income of the trust, whether in the form of income or not, or

(*b*) a person to whom any such income may be paid, or for whose benefit any such income may be applied, whether in the form of income or not, in the exercise of a discretion by them.

Commentary—*Simon's Taxes* **D8.158.**

33 Interest distributions: the position of the legal owner

(1) For the purposes of determining whether an interest distribution should be made with or without any deduction, the legal owner is entitled to treat a declaration made for the purposes of regulation 30 as valid.

(2) But the legal owner may not treat a declaration as valid if condition A or B is met.
(3) Condition A is that the legal owner receives a notification in compliance with an undertaking under regulation 31 that a person in question has become resident . . . [1] in the United Kingdom.
(4) Condition B is that the legal owner comes into possession of information by some other means which indicates that such a person is or may be resident . . . [1] in the United Kingdom.

Commentary—*Simon's Taxes* **D8.158.**

Amendments—[1] In paras (3), (4) words "or ordinarily resident" revoked by the Authorised Investment Funds (Tax) (Amendment) (No 2) Regulations 2013/2994 regs 2, 11 with effect in relation to the making of declarations on or after 6 April 2014. Any declarations made before that date continue to have effect in respect of interest distributions made on or after that date as if those amendments had not been made.

[33A The offshore marketing condition

The offshore marketing condition is met with respect to a class of units if—

(*a*) marketing of units of that class is not directed to investors resident in the United Kingdom, and

(*b*) before units of that class are acquired, information in relation to those units is available to investors to the effect that—

(i) no sum representing income tax will be deducted from any interest distribution in relation to those units, and

(ii) an investor must notify HM Revenue and Customs of any distribution in relation to such units if the investor is chargeable to income tax for the tax year in which the distribution date falls.][1]

Amendments—[1] Reg 33A inserted by the Authorised Investment Funds (Tax) (Amendment) (No 2) Regulations 2013/2994 regs 2, 4 with effect in relation units acquired on or after 19 December 2013.

34–46(*Regulations 34–46 revoked by the Authorised Investment Funds (Tax) (Amendment No 2) Regulations, SI 2007/794 regs 2, 8 with effect from 6 April 2007.*)

[Annual payments to non-residents

46A Annual Payments—duty to deduct income tax

(1) An annual payment made to a participant which meets the conditions in paragraphs (2) to (6) is not a qualifying annual payment for the purposes of Chapter 6 of Part 15 of ITA 2007 (deduction from annual payments and royalties).
(2) The payment must be charged to income tax under Chapter 7 of Part 5 of ITTOIA 2005 (annual payments not otherwise charged).
(3) The payment must be made in respect of the participant's interest in an authorised investment fund other than a Property AIF.
(4) The payment and the amount of the payment must be directly or indirectly referable to, and must not be more than, any management fees paid to the manager of the authorised investment fund in respect of the participant's interest in the fund.
(5) Any management fees must not exceed an amount representing a reasonable commercial amount in all the circumstances.
(6) At the time the payment is made, the person making the payment must have reasonable grounds for believing [that—

(*a*) the participant is not resident in the United Kingdom, or

(*b*) the payment is made in respect a class of units in relation to which of the offshore marketing condition in regulation 33A is met.][2]][1]

Amendments—[1] Regs 46A, 46B inserted by the Authorised Investment Funds (Tax) (Amendment) Regulations, SI 2013/1772 reg 2 with effect in relation to annual payments made on or after 7 August 2013.
[2] In para (6), words substituted by the Authorised Investment Funds (Tax) (Amendment) (No 2) Regulations 2013/2994 regs 2, 5 with effect in relation units acquired on or after 19 December 2013.

[46B Consequences of reasonable but incorrect belief

(1) This regulation applies if—

(a) an annual payment is made to a participant without a sum representing income tax on the payment being deducted from it,

(b) at the time the payment is made, the condition in [regulation 46A(6)(*a*)][2] is met,

(c) the payment would be a qualifying annual payment but for that condition being met, and

(d) at the time the payment is made, the participant is resident in the United Kingdom.

(2) Section 900 (deduction from commercial payments made by individuals) and section 901 (deduction from annual payments made by other persons) of ITA 2007 apply as if the payment were a qualifying annual payment.][1]

Amendments—[1] Regs 46A, 46B inserted by the Authorised Investment Funds (Tax) (Amendment) Regulations, SI 2013/1772 reg 2 with effect in relation to annual payments made on or after 7 August 2013.
[2] In para (1)(*b*), words substituted for words "regulation 46A(6)" by the Authorised Investment Funds (Tax) (Amendment) (No 2) Regulations 2013/2994 regs 2, 6 with effect in relation units acquired on or after 19 December 2013.

CHAPTER 3
PARTICIPANTS CHARGEABLE TO CORPORATION TAX

INTEREST DISTRIBUTIONS

47 The obligation to deduct tax

(1) This regulation applies if an interest distribution is made for a distribution period to a participant chargeable to corporation tax.

(2) The deduction obligation does not apply to the interest distribution.

(3) But if the participant is a company which is the trustee of the trust to which (or under which) the interest distribution is made (or received), the deduction obligation is not excluded by virtue of paragraph (2).

(4) In its application to an interest distribution to a participant in respect of accumulation units, the deduction obligation is an obligation to deduct a sum out of the amount being invested on the participant's behalf.

Commentary—*Simon's Taxes* **D8.159.**

DIVIDEND DISTRIBUTIONS

48 General

(1) Paragraph (2) applies if—

(*a*) a dividend distribution for a distribution period is made to a participant by the legal owner of an authorised investment fund, and

(*b*) on the distribution date for that distribution period the participant is within the charge to corporation tax.

(2) [Subject to paragraphs (2A)[,(2B) and (2BA)][5],][1] for the purpose of computing the corporation tax chargeable upon the participant, the unfranked part of the dividend distribution is treated—

(*a*) as an annual payment and not as a dividend distribution or an interest distribution; and

(*b*) as having been received by the participant after deduction of [tax at a rate equal to the basic rate of income tax][4] for the [tax year][1] in which the distribution date falls, from a corresponding gross amount.

[(2A) But paragraph (2) does not apply to a dividend distribution to which [Chapter 2 of Part 3 of CTA 2009][3] applies [unless the dividend distribution is made to—

(*a*) an insurance company in respect of any non-BLAGAB long-term business carried on by it, or

(*b*) an insurance special purpose vehicle that is not an insurance company in respect of any long-term business carried on by it that does not consist wholly of PHI business.

Expressions used in paragraph (a) or (b) have the same meaning as they have in Part 2 of FA 2012.][6]

(2B) If, on the distribution date, the participant is the manager of the authorised investment fund, paragraph (2) shall not apply to the extent that the rights in respect of which the dividend distribution is made are held by him in the ordinary course of the manager's business as manager of the fund.][1]

[(2BA) Paragraph (2)(*b*) does not apply to so much of any dividend distribution as on a just and reasonable apportionment is attributable to an unallowable arrangement.

(2BB) For the purposes of paragraph (2BA), an unallowable arrangement is an arrangement the main purpose or one of the main purposes of which is to secure that an amount of tax, or an increased amount of tax, is treated as deducted under paragraph (2)(b).

(2BC) In paragraph (2BB), "arrangement" includes any arrangement, agreement, scheme, transaction, series of transactions or understanding (whether or not legally enforceable).][5]

[(2C) Regulation 48A makes provision in relation to the unfranked part of the dividend distribution treated as an annual payment under paragraph (2)(*a*) and regulation 48B makes provision in relation to the tax treated as deducted under paragraph (2)(*b*).][4]

(3) Regulation 49 explains how to calculate the unfranked part of the dividend distribution.

[(4) This regulation does not apply in respect of a holding in a qualified investor scheme if the scheme has not met the genuine diversity of ownership condition in regulation [9A][2] in relation to an accounting period.][1]

Commentary—*Simon's Taxes* **D8.159.**

Amendments—[1] In para (2) words inserted, in para (2)(*b*) words substituted, and paras (2A), (2B), (4) inserted, by the Authorised Investment Funds (Tax) (Amendment No 3) Regulations, SI 2008/3159 regs 3, 13 with effect from 1 January 2009. In relation to a qualified investor scheme authorised by the Financial Services Authority before 1 January 2009, this amendment has effect subject to SI 2008/3159 reg 31.

[2] In para (4), figure substituted by the Authorised Investment Funds (Tax) (Amendment) Regulations, SI 2009/2036 regs 2, 12 with effect from 1 September 2009.

[3] Words in (2A) substituted for by the Authorised Investment Funds (Tax) (Amendment) Regulations, SI 2010/294, regs 2, 14, with effect from 6 March 2010 (see reg 1(2)).

[4] In para (2)(*b*), words substituted for words, and para (2C) inserted, by the Authorised Investment Funds (Tax) (Amendment No 2) Regulations, SI 2010/1642 regs 2, 4 with effect in relation to distributions made at or after 13.45 on 22 June 2010 (SI 2010/1642 reg 1).

5 In para (2), references substituted for, and paras (2BA), (2BB), (2BC) inserted, by the Authorised Investment Funds (Tax) (Amendment) Regulations, SI 2012/519 regs 2, 5 with effect in relation to any distribution made at or after 1.30pm on 27 February 2012 (SI 2012/519 reg 1).

6 Words in para (2A) inserted by the Authorised Investment Funds (Tax) (Amendment No 3) Regulations, SI 2012/3043 reg 2(1), (2) with effect in relation to dividend distributions made on or after 1 January 2013.

48A [Income treated as an annual payment treated as foreign income

If there is a foreign element of the tax treated as deducted under regulation 48(2)(*b*) (see regulation 48B), a corresponding proportionate part of the distribution which is treated as an annual payment under regulation 48(2)(*a*) is treated as if it were income that—

(*a*) arises in a territory of the kind mentioned in regulation 48B(3)(*a*), and

(*b*) is income by reference to which the tax treated under that provision as payable was computed.][1]

Amendments—[1] Regs 48A, 48B inserted, by the Authorised Investment Funds (Tax) (Amendment No 2) Regulations, SI 2010/1642 regs 2, 5 with effect in relation to distributions made at or after 13.45 on 22 June 2010 (SI 2010/1642 reg 1).

48B [Tax treated as deducted from a dividend distribution

(1) The tax treated as deducted under regulation 48(2)(*b*) ("the deemed deduction") is treated as income tax.

(2) But paragraph (1) does not apply to any foreign element of the deemed deduction.

(3) Instead, for the purposes of the Tax Acts the foreign element of the deemed deduction is treated as if it were tax—

(*a*) payable under the law of a territory outside the United Kingdom with which there are not in force any arrangements under section 2(1) of TIOPA 2010 (double taxation relief by agreement),

(*b*) calculated by reference to income arising or any chargeable gain accruing, in the territory, and

(*c*) corresponding to United Kingdom corporation tax.

(4) The amount of the foreign element of the deemed deduction is the amount, if any, by which the participant's portion of the legal owner's liability to corporation tax in respect of the gross income is reduced by any relief which is given, or falls to be given by way of a credit under section 18 of TIOPA 2010 (entitlement to credit for foreign tax reduces UK tax by amount of the credit).

(5) For the purposes of paragraph (4) the participant's portion shall be determined by reference to the proportions in which participants have rights in the authorised investment fund in the distribution period in question.][1]

Amendments—[1] Regs 48A, 48B inserted, by the Authorised Investment Funds (Tax) (Amendment No 2) Regulations, SI 2010/1642 regs 2, 5 with effect in relation to distributions made at or after 13.45 on 22 June 2010 (SI 2010/1642 reg 1).

49 Calculation of unfranked part of dividend distribution

(1) This is how to calculate the unfranked part of the dividend distribution—

$$U = \frac{(A \times C)}{D}$$

(2) In paragraph (1)—

U = the unfranked part of the dividend distribution to the participant;

A = the amount of the dividend distribution;

[C = such amount of the gross income as derives from income in respect of which the legal owner is charged to corporation tax, as reduced by—

(*a*) any amount carried forward from an earlier accounting period and allowed as a deduction in computing the legal owner's liability to corporation tax for the accounting period in which the last day of the distribution period falls, and

(*b*) an amount equal to the legal owner's net liability to corporation tax in respect of the gross income.][2]

D = the amount of the gross income, as reduced by an amount equal to the legal owner's net liability to corporation tax in respect of the gross income.

[(2A) ...[2]

(3) Any reference in this regulation to the legal owner's net liability to corporation tax in respect of the gross income is a reference to the amount of the liability of the legal owner to corporation tax in respect of that gross income less the amount (if any) of any reduction of that liability which is given or falls to be given in accordance with any arrangements having effect by virtue of section 788 of ICTA (relief by agreement with other territories) or by way of a credit under section 790(1) of that Act (unilateral relief).

Commentary—*Simon's Taxes* **D8.159.**

Amendments—[1] Fomer para (2A) inserted by the Authorised Investment Funds (Tax) (Amendment No 3) Regulations, SI 2008/3159 regs 3, 14 with effect from 1 January 2009. In relation to a qualified investor scheme authorised by the Financial Services Authority before 1 January 2009, this amendment has effect subject to SI 2008/3159 reg 31.

[2] In para (2), definition of "C" substituted, and para (2A) revoked, by the Authorised Investment Funds (Tax) (Amendment) Regulations, SI 2012/519 regs 2, 6 with effect in relation to any distribution made in respect of a distribution period ending at or after 1.30 pm on 27 February 2012 (SI 2012/519 reg 1).

[50 References to gross income

For the purposes of this Chapter, references to gross income are references to the net revenue before taxation determined in accordance with the Statement of Recommended Practice.][1]

Commentary—*Simon's Taxes* **D8.159.**

[1] Reg 50 substituted by the Authorised Investment Funds (Tax) (Amendment) Regulations, SI 2010/294, regs 2, 15, with effect from 6 March 2010, but see regs 24–26 for transitional provisions relating to distribution dates for earlier accounting periods, and entry into the FINROF regime.

51 [Participants chargeable to corporation tax: holdings in qualified investor schemes where scheme does not meet the genuine diversity of ownership condition

(1) This regulation applies if—

(*a*) a participant has a holding in a qualified investor scheme, and

(*b*) the scheme has not met the genuine diversity of ownership condition in regulation [9A][2] in relation to an accounting period.

(2) Section 212 of TCGA 1992 (annual deemed disposal of holdings of unit trusts etc) does not apply to the participant in relation to that accounting period.

(3) Paragraph 4 of Schedule 10 to FA 1996 (company holdings in unit trusts and offshore funds) shall not apply to the participant in relation to that accounting period.][1]

Commentary—*Simon's Taxes* **D8.159.**

Amendments—[1] Regulation 51 substituted by the Authorised Investment Funds (Tax) (Amendment No 3) Regulations, SI 2008/3159 regs 3, 15 with effect from 1 January 2009. In relation to a qualified investor scheme authorised by the Financial Services Authority before 1 January 2009, this amendment has effect subject to SI 2008/3159 reg 31.

[2] In para (1)(*b*), figure substituted by the Authorised Investment Funds (Tax) (Amendment) Regulations, SI 2009/2036 regs 2, 13 with effect from 1 September 2009.

52 Repayments of tax

(1) This regulation applies if, in relation to a dividend distribution, any tax is treated as having been deducted by virtue of regulation 48(2)(*b*).

(2) The amount to which the participant is entitled by way of repayment of that tax must not exceed the amount of the participant's portion of the legal owner's net liability to corporation tax in respect of the gross income.

(3) In calculating the amount to which the participant is entitled by way of repayment of that tax, tax treated as having been deducted by virtue of regulation 48(2)(*b*) is set off in priority to any other tax under section 7(2) of ICTA and under paragraph 5 of Schedule 16 to that Act.

(4) For the purposes of paragraph (2) the participant's portion shall be determined by reference to the proportions in which participants have rights in the authorised investment fund in the distribution period in question.[1]

Commentary—*Simon's Taxes* **D8.159.**

Amendments—[1] Reg 52 revoked by the Authorised Investment Funds (Tax) (Amendment No 2) Regulations, SI 2010/1642 regs 2, 6 with effect in relation to distributions made at or after 13.45 on 22 June 2010 (SI 2010/1642 reg 1).

52A Companies carrying on general insurance business: treatment of certain amounts of tax as foreign tax

Amendments—Reg 52A revoked by the Authorised Investment Funds (Tax) (Amendment No 2) Regulations, SI 2010/1642 regs 2, 7 with effect in relation to distributions made at or after 13.45 on 22 June 2010 (SI 2010/1642 reg 1).

52B [Diversely owned AIFs and financial traders: treatment of shares and units

(1) This regulation and regulation 52C apply if a financial trader has held, or holds, shares or units in a diversely owned AIF.

(2) In computing the trading profits or losses of the financial trader for the relevant period, the following amounts must be brought into account—

(*a*) all distributions received by or credited to the financial trader in respect of such shares or units for the relevant period; and

(*b*) any amount required to be brought into account under regulation 52C.

(3) In this regulation and in regulation 52D(2) references to distributions are subject to section 130 of CTA 2009 (insurers receiving distributions etc).

(4) In this regulation and in regulations 52C and 52D—

"relevant period" means—

(*a*) in the case of a financial trader within the charge to corporation tax, an accounting period, and

(*b*) in the case of a financial trader within the charge to income tax, a period of account;

"financial trader" has the meaning given by regulation 52E.][1]

Amendments—[1] Paras 52B–52E inserted by the Authorised Investment Funds (Tax) (Amendment) Regulations, SI 2009/2036 regs 2, 14 with effect from 1 September 2009.

52C [Financial traders: amounts to be brought into account in respect of shares or units held in diversely owned AIFs

(1) The only amounts that are to be brought into account in computing the trading profits or losses in respect of the shares or units in the diversely owned AIF for the relevant period are—

(*a*) amounts that are brought into account in accordance with Cases 1 to 4, and

(*b*) amounts within regulation 52B(2)(*a*).

This is subject to section 130 of CTA 2009 (insurers receiving distributions etc) and regulation 52D.

(2) Case 1 applies if the financial trader held the shares or units in a diversely owned AIF at the beginning of the relevant period and holds those shares or units throughout that period.

Where Case 1 applies, the amount to be brought into account is the difference between the market value of the shares or units at the end of the immediately preceding relevant period and the market value of those shares or units at the end of the relevant period.

(3) Case 2 applies if a financial trader acquired shares or units in a diversely owned AIF during the relevant period and retains those shares or units throughout the relevant period.

Where Case 2 applies, the amount to be brought into account is the difference between the market value of the shares or units at the end of the relevant period and the acquisition cost of those shares or units.

(4) Case 3 applies if the financial trader held shares or units in a diversely owned AIF at the beginning of the relevant period and disposes of those shares or units during that period.

Where Case 3 applies the amount to be brought into account is the difference between the market value of the shares or units at the end of the immediately preceding relevant period and the disposal value of the shares or units.

(5) Case 4 applies if the financial trader acquires shares or units in a diversely owned AIF during the relevant period and disposes of those shares or units during that period.

Where Case 4 applies the amount to be brought into account is the difference between the acquisition cost of the shares or units and the disposal value of those shares or units.

(6) In this regulation—

"acquisition cost" means the value of the consideration given for the acquisition of the shares or units;

"disposal value" means the value of the consideration received for the disposal of the shares or units;

"market value" means—

(*a*) in the case of shares or units in a diversely owned AIF where both the buying and selling prices of units are published regularly by the manager of the fund, an amount equal to the buying price (that is the lower price) so published on any particular date or, if none were published on that date, on the latest date before;

(*b*) in the case of shares or units in a diversely owned AIF where a single price is published regularly by the manager of the fund, the price so published on any particular date, or if none were published on that date, on the latest date before.][1]

Amendments—[1] Paras 52B–52E inserted by the Authorised Investment Funds (Tax) (Amendment) Regulations, SI 2009/2036 regs 2, 14 with effect from 1 September 2009.

52D [Shares and units not within regulation 52C

(1) Regulation 52C does not apply in respect of any shares or units in a diversely owned AIF in relation to which—

(*a*) conditions A and B are both satisfied, or

(*b*) condition C is satisfied.

(2) Condition A is that the shares or units in the diversely owned AIF form part of the financial trader's stock in trade and all the profits and losses, including distributions, arising in relation to the shares or units in the diversely owned AIF are included in the computation of the financial trader's trading profits for the relevant period.

(3) Condition B is that the shares or units in the diversely owned AIF are accounted for under generally accepted accounting practice on the basis of fair value accounting.

(4) Condition C is that the shares or units in the diversely owned AIF are a relevant holding in respect of which the provisions of section 490 of CTA 2009 apply in relation to the financial trader.

(5) In paragraph (4) "relevant holding" means—

(*a*) any rights under a unit trust scheme;

(*b*) [an interest][2] in an offshore fund; or

(*c*) any shares in an open-ended investment company.][1]

Amendments—[1] Paras 52B–52E inserted by the Authorised Investment Funds (Tax) (Amendment) Regulations, SI 2009/2036 regs 2, 14 with effect from 1 September 2009.

[2] In para (5)(*b*), word substituted for words "a material interest" by the Offshore Funds (Tax) (Amendment No. 2) Regulations, SI 2013/1411 reg 14(*a*) with effect from 28 June 2013.

52E [Meaning of financial trader

(1) In regulations 52B, 52C and 52D "financial trader" means a person who is carrying on a business which is—

(*a*) a banking business,

(*b*) an insurance business, or

(*c*) a business consisting wholly or in part of dealing in trading assets such that any profit on such assets would form part of the trading profits of that business.

This paragraph is subject to paragraphs (2) and (3).

(2) "An insurance business" in paragraph (1)(*b*) does not include life assurance business carried on by an insurance company and in the event that such a company carries on both life assurance business and any other insurance business that company will not be a financial trader in respect of the life assurance business.

(3) If—

(*a*) a financial trader, "A", directly or indirectly transfers trading assets to a diversely owned AIF under or as part of an arrangement which has an unallowable purpose, and

(*b*) a connected person, "B"—

(i) holds shares or units in that diversely owned AIF at the time of the transfer; or

(ii) directly or indirectly acquires shares or units in that diversely owned AIF at a later time,

B is treated as being a financial trader in relation to those shares or units.

(4) In paragraphs (1) and (3) "trading assets" means—

(*a*) stocks or shares;

(*b*) a relevant contract within regulation 14G;

(*c*) a loan relationship within regulation 14L;

(*d*) units in a collective investment scheme within regulation 14M;

(*e*) securities within regulation 14F;

(*f*) foreign currency; or

(*g*) a carbon emission trading product within regulation 14N,

a profit on the sale of which would form part of the trading profits of the financial trader.

(5) An arrangement includes any scheme, understanding or transaction of any kind, whether or not legally enforceable and whether involving a single transaction or two or more transactions.

(6) An arrangement has an unallowable purpose if the main purpose or one of the main purposes for either A or B being party to the arrangement is to obtain a tax advantage or an income tax advantage for any person.

(7) In paragraph (6)—

"tax advantage" has the meaning given by section of 840ZA of ICTA; and

"income tax advantage" has the meaning given by section 683 of ITA 2007.][1]

Amendments—[1] Paras 52B–52E inserted by the Authorised Investment Funds (Tax) (Amendment) Regulations, SI 2009/2036 regs 2, 14 with effect from 1 September 2009.

CHAPTER 4

CHARGE TO TAX ON SUBSTANTIAL QIS HOLDINGS IN QUALIFIED INVESTOR SCHEMES

Amendments—Part 4, Chapter 4 (regs 53–69) revoked by the Authorised Investment Funds (Tax) (Amendment No 3) Regulations, SI 2008/3159 regs 3, 17 with effect from 1 January 2009. In relation to a qualified investor scheme authorised by the Financial Services Authority before 1 January 2009, this amendment has effect subject to SI 2008/3159 reg 31.

[PART 4A PROPERTY AIFS][1]

Amendments—[1] Part 4 (regs 69A–69Z41) inserted by the Authorised Investment Funds (Tax) (Amendment) Regulations, SI 2008/705 regs 2, 5 with effect from 6 April 2008.

[CHAPTER 1

PRELIMINARY PROVISIONS

69A Property AIFs

(1) This Part enables an open-ended investment company which meets the conditions in regulations 69D to 69O—

(*a*) to benefit from the exemption from corporation tax in accordance with regulation 69Y(1), and

(*b*) to have liabilities to tax imposed on the company and on participants in accordance with Chapters 3, 4 and 5 of this Part.

(2) In these Regulations an open-ended investment company to which this Part applies may be referred to as a "Property AIF".][1]

Amendments—[1] Part 4 (regs 69A–69Z41) inserted by the Authorised Investment Funds (Tax) (Amendment) Regulations, SI 2008/705 regs 2, 5 with effect from 6 April 2008.

[69B Structure of this Part

The structure of this Part of these Regulations is as follows—

This Chapter contains preliminary provisions;

Chapter 2 deals with entry into and membership of the Property AIF regime;

Chapter 3 deals with the tax treatment of Property AIFs;

Chapter 4 deals with distributions made by Property AIFs;

Chapter 5 deals with the treatment of participants in Property AIFs;

Chapter 6 deals with compliance in relation to the Property AIF regime; and

Chapter 7 contains provisions relating to an open-ended investment company's leaving the Property AIF regime.][1]

Amendments—[1] Part 4 (regs 69A–69Z41) inserted by the Authorised Investment Funds (Tax) (Amendment) Regulations, SI 2008/705 regs 2, 5 with effect from 6 April 2008.

[69C Key concepts

(1) In this Part "entry" means the time when this Part begins to apply to an open-ended investment company.

(2) In this Part "cessation" means the time when this Part ceases to apply to an open-ended investment company.

(3) In this Part, in relation to an open-ended investment company—

(*a*) "F (pre-entry)" means the open-ended investment company before this Part begins to apply to it,

(*b*) "F (tax-exempt)" means the open-ended investment company in so far as it carries on property investment business (within the meaning of regulation 69F) while this Part applies to it,

(*c*) "F (residual)" means the open-ended investment company in so far as it carries on business other than property investment business while this Part applies to it, and

(*d*) "F (post-cessation)" means the open-ended investment company after this Part has ceased to apply to it.

[(4) In this Part, a "dedicated feeder fund" in relation to a property AIF means a fund which—

(*a*) is a unit trust scheme;

(*b*) is dedicated to investment in the property AIF for which it is a feeder fund (in accordance with its prospectus); and

(*c*) holds at least 85% of its assets in the form of shares in that property AIF.][2]][1]

Amendments—[1] Part 4 (regs 69A–69Z41) inserted by the Authorised Investment Funds (Tax) (Amendment) Regulations, SI 2008/705 regs 2, 5 with effect from 6 April 2008.

[2] Para (4) inserted by the Authorised Investment Funds (Tax) (Amendment No 2) Regulations, SI 2012/1783 regs 2, 3 with effect for the purposes of capital gains tax, in relation to disposals made on or after 1 August 2012, and for the purposes of corporation tax on chargeable gains, in relation to disposals made on or after 1 August 2012.

[CHAPTER 2

ENTRY INTO AND MEMBERSHIP OF THE PROPERTY AIF REGIME

CONDITIONS OF MEMBERSHIP OF THE PROPERTY AIF REGIME

69D Conditions for this Part to apply to company

In order for this Part to apply to an open-ended investment company in respect of an accounting period, the following conditions must be met—

(*a*) the property investment business condition (see regulation 69E);

(*b*) the genuine diversity of ownership condition (see regulation [9A][2]);

(*c*) the corporate ownership condition (see regulation 693K);

(*d*) the loan creditor condition (see regulation 694M);

(*e*) the balance of business conditions (see regulation 69N); and

(*f*) the notification condition (see regulation 69O).][1]

Amendments—[1] Part 4 (regs 69A–69Z41) inserted by the Authorised Investment Funds (Tax) (Amendment) Regulations, SI 2008/705 regs 2, 5 with effect from 6 April 2008.

[2] In para (*b*), figure substituted by the Authorised Investment Funds (Tax) (Amendment) Regulations, SI 2009/2036 regs 2, 15 with effect from 1 September 2009.

[69DA Conditions for this Part to apply to a company where the company is also a qualified investor scheme

. . .

Amendments—Reg revoked by the Authorised Investment Funds (Tax) (Amendment) Regulations, SI 2009/2036 regs 2, 16 with effect from 1 September 2009.

[THE PROPERTY INVESTMENT BUSINESS CONDITION

69E The property investment business condition

(1) The property investment business condition is that the open-ended investment company must meet conditions A and B throughout the accounting period.

(2) Condition A is that the company's instrument of incorporation and its prospectus . . . [2] include a statement that the company's investment objectives are—

(*a*) to carry on property investment business, and

(*b*) to manage cash raised from investors for investment in the property investment business.

(3) Condition B is that the company must carry on property investment business.

(4) In this Part "prospectus" includes any supplements to a prospectus.][1]

Amendments—[1] Part 4 (regs 69A–69Z41) inserted by the Authorised Investment Funds (Tax) (Amendment) Regulations, SI 2008/705 regs 2, 5 with effect from 6 April 2008.

[2] In para (2), words revoked, and para (4), revoked, by the Authorised Investment Funds (Tax) (Amendment) Regulations, SI 2010/294, regs 2, 23, with effect from 6 March 2010 (see reg 1(2)).

[69F Meaning of "property investment business"

(1) In this Part "property investment business" means business consisting of any one or more of—

(*a*) property rental business (see regulation 69H);

(*b*) owning shares in UK-REITs; and

(*c*) owning shares or units in an entity [within section 528(4A)(j) of CTA 2010 (overseas equivalent to UK REIT)][3].

(2) In these Regulations "UK-REIT" [has the meaning given in section 518(4) of CTA 2010][3].

(3)–(6) . . . [3]

(7) . . . [2]

(8) This regulation is subject to the further provisions in regulation 69G.][1]

Amendments—[1] Part 4 (regs 69A–69Z41) inserted by the Authorised Investment Funds (Tax) (Amendment) Regulations, SI 2008/705 regs 2, 5 with effect from 6 April 2008.

[2] Para (7) revoked by the Authorised Investment Funds (Tax) (Amendment No 2) Regulations, SI 2011/2192 regs 2, 6 with effect as follows—

– for the purposes of corporation tax:

(a) on income, for accounting periods starting on or after 1 October 2011, and

(b) on chargeable gains, in relation to disposals made on or after 1 October 2011, and

– for the purposes of capital gains tax, in relation to disposals made on or after 1 October 2011.

[3] In para (1)(*c*), words substituted for words "in circumstances in which conditions A to C are met", in para (2), words substituted for words "means a company or group to which Part 4 of FA 2006 applies", and paras (3)–(6) revoked, by the Real Estate Investment Trust (Amendments to the Corporation Tax Act 2010 and Consequential Amendments) Regulations, SI 2014/518 reg 3(1), (2) with effect for accounting periods beginning on or after 1 April 2014.

[69G Property investment business: further provisions

(1) If an open-ended investment company to which this Part applies receives a distribution from a UK-REIT—

(*a*) the distribution is income of F (tax-exempt) to the extent that the distribution represents business of C (tax-exempt) carried on by the UK-REIT, and

(*b*) the distribution is income of F (residual) to the extent that the distribution represents business other than business of C (tax-exempt) carried on by the UK-REIT.

(2) In paragraph (1) "C (tax-exempt)" shall be construed in accordance with Part 4 of the Finance Act 2006.

(3) If an open-ended investment company to which this Part applies receives a distribution from an entity within regulation 69F(1)(*c*), the distribution is income of F (tax-exempt) except to the extent that the distribution is identified, at the time at which it is made, as arising from any activity of the entity that is not property rental business.

(4) For the purposes of this Part an asset is involved in property investment business if—

(*a*) it is an estate, interest or right in or over land by the exploitation of which property rental business is conducted;

(*b*) it consists of shares owned by the open-ended investment company in a UK-REIT; or

(*c*) it consists of shares [or units][2] owned by the open-ended investment company in an entity within regulation 69F(1)(*c*).][1]

Amendments—[1] Part 4 (regs 69A–69Z41) inserted by the Authorised Investment Funds (Tax) (Amendment) Regulations, SI 2008/705 regs 2, 5 with effect from 6 April 2008.

[2] Words in para (4)(*c*) inserted by the Authorised Investment Funds (Tax) (Amendment No 3) Regulations, SI 2008/3159 regs 3, 19 with effect from 1 January 2009. In relation to a qualified investor scheme authorised by the Financial Services Authority before 1 January 2009, this amendment has effect subject to SI 2008/3159 reg 31.

[69H Meaning of "property rental business"

(1) In this Part "property rental business" means—

(*a*) property rental business within the meaning given by section 104 of FA 2006, and

(*b*) the relevant business of an intermediate holding vehicle (see regulation 69I).

(2) For the purposes of paragraph (1)(*b*) the relevant business of an intermediate holding vehicle is its property rental business within the meaning given by section 104 of FA 2006, but disregarding subsection (1)(*a*) of that section.

(3) For the purposes of this Part an asset is involved in property rental business if—

(*a*) it is an estate, interest or right in or over land by the exploitation of which property rental business is conducted, or

(*b*) it consists of shares owned by the open-ended investment company in an intermediate holding vehicle.][1]

Amendments—[1] Part 4 (regs 69A–69Z41) inserted by the Authorised Investment Funds (Tax) (Amendment) Regulations, SI 2008/705 regs 2, 5 with effect from 6 April 2008.

[69I Meaning of "intermediate holding vehicle"

(1) For the purposes of regulation 69H, an entity is an "intermediate holding vehicle" in an accounting period if it meets conditions A to F throughout the accounting period.

(2) Condition A is that the vehicle is a company, trust or partnership.

(3) Condition B is that the vehicle is not a collective investment scheme.

(4) Condition C is that the vehicle is wholly owned by the open-ended investment company (the "parent") or another intermediate holding vehicle or series of intermediate holding vehicles wholly owned by the parent, unless and to the extent that local legislation or regulations relating to the intermediate holding vehicle holding the property specified in paragraph (5) requires a proportion of local ownership.

(5) Condition D is that the function of the intermediate holding vehicle is solely to enable the holding, by the parent, of estates, interests or rights in or over land outside the United Kingdom by the exploitation of which property rental business is conducted.

(6) Condition E is that the intermediate holding vehicle has its accounts consolidated with those of the parent.

(7) Condition F is that all property rental income of the intermediate holding vehicle (or the full proportion of that income representing the interest of the parent in the intermediate holding vehicle) must be reflected in the distribution accounts of the parent at the same time as that income is reflected in the accounts of the intermediate holding vehicle.][1]

Amendments—[1] Part 4 (regs 69A–69Z41) inserted by the Authorised Investment Funds (Tax) (Amendment) Regulations, SI 2008/705 regs 2, 5 with effect from 6 April 2008.

[THE GENUINE DIVERSITY OF OWNERSHIP CONDITION

69J The genuine diversity of ownership condition

. . .

Amendments—Reg 69J revoked by the Authorised Investment Funds (Tax) (Amendment) Regulations, SI 2009/2036 regs 2, 17 with effect from 1 September 2009.

[THE CORPORATE OWNERSHIP CONDITION

69K The corporate ownership condition

(1) The corporate ownership condition is that the open-ended investment company must meet conditions A to C and (if applicable) condition D at the time that this Part begins to apply to the company and throughout the accounting period.

This is subject to regulation 69L(1).

(2) Condition A is that no body corporate is beneficially entitled (directly or indirectly) to 10% or more of the net asset value of the fund.

(3) Condition A is treated as met if—

(*a*) the company has taken reasonable steps to prevent a body corporate from acquiring a holding of 10% or more of the net asset value of the fund,

(*b*) a body corporate has nevertheless acquired such a holding,

(*c*) immediately upon becoming aware of the situation, the company has taken steps to ensure that the holding is reduced below 10% of the net asset value of the fund, and

(*d*) the company has continued, with all reasonable speed, to take steps to ensure that the holding is so reduced.

(4) Condition B is that the company's instrument of incorporation and its prospectus include provisions under which any body corporate which becomes a [participant][2] in the company—

(*a*) must undertake not to acquire 10% or more of the share capital of the company, and

(*b*) must undertake, on becoming aware that it has acquired 10% or more of the share capital of the company, to reduce its holding of that share capital below 10%.

(5) Condition C is that the company's instrument of incorporation and its prospectus include provisions under which a body corporate acquiring shares in the company must give a certificate in accordance with paragraph (6) or (7).

(6) The certificate is a certificate that the body corporate acquiring shares holds the shares as beneficial owner.

(7) The certificate is a certificate that the body corporate acquiring shares holds some or all of those shares otherwise than as a beneficial owner, but that the body corporate—

(*a*) holds less than 10% of the share capital of the company on behalf of itself or any one other corporate beneficial owner, and

(*b*) has obtained the undertakings in the terms specified in sub-paragraphs (*a*) and (*b*) of paragraph (4) from every other body corporate on whose behalf it owns shares in the company otherwise than as a beneficial owner.

(8) Condition D is that, in a case in which the body corporate acquiring shares in the company gives a certificate in accordance with paragraph (7), the body corporate acquiring the shares has undertaken to disclose the following information to the manager of the company if the manager so requires—

(*a*) the names of any body corporate on whose behalf the body corporate owns shares in the company otherwise than as a beneficial owner, and

(*b*) the extent of the holding of that body corporate in the company.][1]

Amendments—[1] Part 4 (regs 69A–69Z41) inserted by the Authorised Investment Funds (Tax) (Amendment) Regulations, SI 2008/705 regs 2, 5 with effect from 6 April 2008.

[2] In para (4), word substituted by the Authorised Investment Funds (Tax) (Amendment No 3) Regulations, SI 2008/3159 regs 3, 21 with effect from 1 January 2009. In relation to a qualified investor scheme authorised by the Financial Services Authority before 1 January 2009, this amendment has effect subject to SI 2008/3159 reg 31.

[69L The corporate ownership condition: further provisions

(1) The open-ended investment company meets conditions B and C of the corporate ownership condition if it provides in its instrument of incorporation and its prospectus that a body corporate is prohibited from acquiring shares in the open-ended investment company.

(2) The open-ended investment company meets conditions B and C of the corporate ownership condition if—

(*a*) it provides in its instrument of incorporation and its prospectus that a body corporate is prohibited from acquiring shares [as a participant][2] in the open-ended investment company,

(*b*) a body corporate ("BC") acquires shares in the open-ended investment company,

(*c*) BC does not hold those shares as beneficial owner, and

(*d*) BC gives a certificate in accordance with paragraph (3).

(3) The certificate is a certificate—

(*a*) that BC does not hold any of the shares in the open-ended investment company as beneficial owner, and

(*b*) that none of the beneficial owners of BC's shares in the open-ended investment company is a body corporate.

(4) Paragraph (5) applies if the trustees of a unit trust scheme—

(*a*) hold shares in the open-ended investment company, and

(*b*) are chargeable, in the United Kingdom, either to income tax or to corporation tax in their capacity as trustees of that unit trust scheme.

(5) For the purposes of regulation 69K [the unit trust scheme is treated][2] as the beneficial owners of the shares; and a person holding units in the unit trust shall not be treated as beneficially entitled (directly or indirectly) to 10% or more of the net asset value of the open-ended investment company's fund by virtue of holding the units.

(6) In this Part "body corporate" means—

(*a*) a body corporate incorporated under the laws of any part of the United Kingdom or any other territory, or

(*b*) an entity which is treated as a body corporate for tax purposes—

(i) in accordance with the law of a territory outside the United Kingdom with which relevant arrangements have been entered into, or

(ii) in accordance with an international agreement containing relevant arrangements.

(7) In paragraph (6) "relevant arrangements" means arrangements which—

(*a*) have been entered into with a view to affording relief from double taxation, and

(*b*) have effect by virtue of an Order in Council under section 788 of ICTA.][1]

Amendments—[1] Part 4 (regs 69A–69Z41) inserted by the Authorised Investment Funds (Tax) (Amendment) Regulations, SI 2008/705 regs 2, 5 with effect from 6 April 2008.

[2] In para (2)(*a*) words inserted, and in para (5) words substituted, by the Authorised Investment Funds (Tax) (Amendment No 3) Regulations, SI 2008/3159 regs 3, 22 with effect from 1 January 2009. In relation to a qualified investor scheme authorised by the Financial Services Authority before 1 January 2009, this amendment has effect subject to SI 2008/3159 reg 31.

THE LOAN CREDITOR CONDITION

69M The loan creditor condition

(1) The loan creditor condition is that the open-ended investment company must meet conditions A to C throughout the accounting period in the case of any loan relationship to which the company is party as debtor.

(2) Condition A is that, in the case of a debtor relationship of the company, the person standing in the position of a creditor as respects the debt in question is not entitled to an amount by way of interest which depends to any extent on—

(*a*) the results of all or part of the open-ended investment company's business, or

(*b*) the value of any of the company's assets.

(3) For the purposes of condition A, a loan shall not be treated as dependent on the results of the company's business by reason only that the terms of the loan provide—

(*a*) for the interest to be reduced in the event of results improving, or

(*b*) for the interest to be increased in the event of results deteriorating.

(4) Condition B is that, in the case of a debtor relationship of the company, the person standing in the position of a creditor as respects the debt in question is not entitled to an amount by way of interest which exceeds a reasonable commercial return on the consideration lent.

(5) Condition C is that, in the case of a debtor relationship of the company, the person standing in the position of a creditor as respects the debt in question is entitled on repayment to an amount which—

(*a*) does not exceed the consideration lent, or

(*b*) is reasonably comparable with the amount generally repayable (in respect of an equal amount of consideration) under the terms of issue of securities listed on a recognised stock exchange.

(6) In this regulation "loan relationship" and "debtor relationship" shall be construed in accordance with Chapter 2 of Part 4 of FA 1996 (loan relationships).][1]

Amendments—[1] Part 4 (regs 69A–69Z41) inserted by the Authorised Investment Funds (Tax) (Amendment) Regulations, SI 2008/705 regs 2, 5 with effect from 6 April 2008.

[THE BALANCE OF BUSINESS CONDITIONS

69N The balance of business conditions

(1) The balance of business conditions are that conditions A and B must be met.

(2) Condition A is that the net income of F (tax-exempt) for an accounting period (determined in accordance with regulation 69Z1) is—

(*a*) at least 40% of the open-ended investment company's net income (as defined in regulation 69Z) where this Part applies to a newly qualified company in its first accounting period, or

(*b*) at least 60% of the open-ended investment company's net income (as defined in regulation 69Z) where this Part applies to a company in an accounting period in any other circumstances.

(3) Condition B is that the value of the assets involved in property investment business is—

(*a*) at least 40% of the total value of the assets held by the open-ended investment company at the end of the accounting period where this Part applies to a newly qualified company in its first accounting period, or

(*b*) at least 60% of the total value of the assets held by the open-ended investment company at the end of the accounting period where this Part applies to a company in an accounting period in any other circumstances.

(4) For the purposes of condition B—

(*a*) assets must be valued in accordance with generally accepted accounting practice,

(*b*) where generally accepted accounting practice offers a choice of valuation between cost basis and fair value, fair value must be used, and

(*c*) no account shall be taken of liabilities secured against or otherwise relating to assets (whether generally or specifically).

(5) In this Part a "newly qualified company" means a company—

(*a*) to which this Part applies immediately upon its authorisation, and

(*b*) which has not been an authorised investment fund before that authorisation.][1]

Amendments—[1] Part 4 (regs 69A–69Z41) inserted by the Authorised Investment Funds (Tax) (Amendment) Regulations, SI 2008/705 regs 2, 5 with effect from 6 April 2008.

[THE NOTIFICATION CONDITION

69O The notification condition

(1) The notification condition is that conditions A and B must be met.

(2) Condition A is—

(*a*) that the manager of an existing open-ended investment company has given notice for this Part to apply to the company, or

(*b*) if it is proposed to incorporate an open-ended investment company, that the person expected to become the manager of the open-ended investment company on its incorporation (the "applicant") has given notice for this Part to apply to the company.

(3) Condition B is that the notice given under paragraph (2) has taken effect.

(4) If notice is given under paragraph (2)(*a*), the company must obtain any necessary shareholder and regulatory approvals to its instrument of incorporation and prospectus before giving the notice.

(5) If notice is given under paragraph (2)(*b*), the terms of the proposed company's instrument of incorporation must be such that the proposed company, on its incorporation, will be required to meet—

(*a*) the property investment business condition (see regulation 69E), and (*b*) the genuine diversity of ownership condition (see regulation [9A][2]).

(6) In this Part—

the "applicant" means the person referred to in paragraph (2)(*b*),

an "existing company notice" means a notice given under paragraph (2)(*a*), and

a "future company notice" means a notice given under paragraph (2)(*b*).][1]

Amendments—[1] Part 4 (regs 69A–69Z41) inserted by the Authorised Investment Funds (Tax) (Amendment) Regulations, SI 2008/705 regs 2, 5 with effect from 6 April 2008.

[2] In para (5)(*b*), figure substituted by the Authorised Investment Funds (Tax) (Amendment) Regulations, SI 2009/2036 regs 2, 18 with effect from 1 September 2009.

[69P Form and timing of notice under regulation 69O

(1) A notice under regulation 69O must be given in writing to the Commissioners.

(2) An existing company notice must be given at least 28 days before the beginning of the specified period.

This is subject to the following paragraphs of this regulation.

(3) A future company notice must be given at least 42 days before the date of the expected incorporation and authorisation.

This is subject to the following paragraphs of this regulation.

(4) A notice under regulation 69O may be withdrawn or amended at any time before it takes effect—

(*a*) by the manager (in the case of an existing company notice), or

(*b*) by the applicant (in the case of a future company notice).

(5) If a notice under regulation 69O is amended before it is due to take effect, regulation 69O shall apply to the amended notice.

(6) But if HM Revenue and Customs give notice that they are satisfied that the amended notice is valid, the amended notice shall take effect as if given on the date of the original notice.

(7) An existing company notice may be given at any time before the beginning of the specified period if—

(*a*) HM Revenue and Customs have given clearance under regulation [9B][2], and

(*b*) the manager of the open-ended investment company certifies that there have been no changes in substance between—

(i) the form in which the company's instrument of incorporation and its prospectus were considered by HM Revenue and Customs before giving the clearance, and

(ii) the form in which it is proposed that those documents will apply at the beginning of the specified period.

(8) A future company notice may be given at any time before the proposed company is authorised and incorporated if—

(*a*) HM Revenue and Customs have given clearance under regulation [9B][2], and

(*b*) the applicant certifies that there have been no changes in substance between—

(i) the form in which the proposed company's instrument of incorporation and its prospectus were considered by HM Revenue and Customs before giving the clearance, and

(ii) the form in which it is proposed that those documents will apply at the time when the proposed company is authorised.][1]

Amendments—[1] Part 4 (regs 69A–69Z41) inserted by the Authorised Investment Funds (Tax) (Amendment) Regulations, SI 2008/705 regs 2, 5 with effect from 6 April 2008.

[2] In paras (7)(*a*), (8)(*a*) figure substituted by the Authorised Investment Funds (Tax) (Amendment) Regulations, SI 2009/2036 regs 2, 19 with effect from 1 September 2009.

[69Q Contents of notice under regulation 69O

(1) This regulation applies if notice is given under regulation 69O.

(2) An existing company notice must specify the accounting period from the beginning of which this Part is to apply to the company (the "specified accounting period").

(3) An existing company notice must be accompanied by—

(*a*) a statement by the manager of the open-ended investment company that the conditions specified in [regulation 9A and][2] regulations 69E to 69N are reasonably expected to be met in respect of the company throughout the specified accounting period;

(*b*) the following documents relating to the company—

(i) its instrument of incorporation, and

(ii) its prospectus;

(*c*) a copy of the application to the Financial Services Authority for agreement to changes in the company's instrument of incorporation and its prospectus; and

(*d*) copies of any documents accompanying the application mentioned in sub-paragraph (*c*) to the extent that those documents do not fall within sub-paragraphs (*a*) and (*b*).

(4) A future company notice must specify that this Part will apply to the proposed company from the date of its incorporation and authorisation.

(5) A future company notice must be accompanied by—

(*a*) a statement by the applicant that the conditions specified in [regulation 9A and][2] regulations 69E to 69N are reasonably expected to be met in respect of the proposed company throughout its first accounting period;

(*b*) the following documents relating to the proposed company—

(i) its proposed instrument of incorporation, and

(ii) its . . . [3] prospectus . . . [3];

(*c*) a copy of the application to the Financial Services Authority for approval of the proposed company as an open-ended investment company; and

(*d*) copies of any documents accompanying the application mentioned in sub-paragraph (*c*) to the extent that those documents do not fall within sub-paragraphs (*a*) and (*b*).][1]

Amendments—[1] Part 4 (regs 69A–69Z41) inserted by the Authorised Investment Funds (Tax) (Amendment) Regulations, SI 2008/705 regs 2, 5 with effect from 6 April 2008.

[2] In paras (3)(*a*), (5)(*a*) words inserted by the Authorised Investment Funds (Tax) (Amendment) Regulations, SI 2009/2036 regs 2, 20 with effect from 1 September 2009.

[3] In para (5)(b)(ii), words revoked by the Authorised Investment Funds (Tax) (Amendment) Regulations, SI 2010/294, regs 2, 23, with effect from 6 March 2010 (see reg 1(2)).

[PROCEDURAL MATTERS RELATING TO THE GIVING OF NOTICE FOR THIS PART TO APPLY

69R Notice: further provisions: quashing notices

(1) This regulation applies if any of conditions A to C are met.

(2) Condition A is that an existing company notice is given, but the notice is not accompanied by the documents specified in regulation 69Q(3)(*b*).

(3) Condition B is that a future company notice is given, but the notice is not accompanied by the documents specified in regulation 69Q(5)(*b*).

(4) Condition C is that a person gives a notice under regulation 69O in circumstances where the documents supplied do not demonstrate that the open-ended investment company (or the proposed open-ended investment company) will meet all the conditions of membership of the Property AIF regime.

(5) HM Revenue and Customs may give a notice (a "quashing notice") quashing the notice given under regulation 69O—

(*a*) to the manager of the open-ended investment company if an existing company notice has been given, or

(*b*) to the applicant if a future company notice has been given.][1]

Amendments—[1] Part 4 (regs 69A–69Z41) inserted by the Authorised Investment Funds (Tax) (Amendment) Regulations, SI 2008/705 regs 2, 5 with effect from 6 April 2008.

[69S Procedure relating to quashing notices

(1) HM Revenue and Customs must not give a quashing notice until—

(*a*) they have given a notice (a "preliminary notice") to the person giving the notice under regulation 69O specifying the reasons why the preliminary notice is given, and

(*b*) they have given the person giving the notice under regulation 69O a period of 28 days to rectify the matters specified in the preliminary notice.

Paragraph (1)(*b*) is subject to paragraphs (7) to (9).

(2) HM Revenue and Customs must give a preliminary notice within a period of 28 days beginning with the day on which they receive the notice given under regulation 69O.

(3) HM Revenue and Customs must—

(*a*) give a quashing notice, or

(*b*) give notice to the manager of the open-ended investment company or to the applicant (as the case may be) that they are satisfied that the matters specified in the preliminary notice have been rectified,

within a period of 28 days beginning on the day specified in paragraph (4).

(4) The day specified is whichever is the earlier to occur of—

(*a*) the day immediately following the expiry of the period specified in the preliminary notice, and

(*b*) the day on which HM Revenue and Customs receive notice from the manager of the open-ended investment company or from the applicant (as the case may be) that the manager or applicant thinks—

(i) that the matters specified in the preliminary notice have been rectified, or

(ii) that the original notice given under regulation 69O is valid.

(5) If HM Revenue and Customs give a preliminary notice, the open-ended investment company (or, as the case may be, the proposed open-ended investment company) in respect of which the notice is given may not enter the Property AIF regime until HM Revenue and Customs have notified the manager of the company (or, as the case may be, the applicant) that they are satisfied that the matters specified in the preliminary notice have been rectified.

(6) If HM Revenue and Customs give a quashing notice, and the person to whom the notice is given appeals, the open-ended investment company (or, as the case may be, the proposed open-ended investment company) in respect of which the notice is given may not enter the Property AIF regime until the appeal is determined.
(7) The period of 28 days mentioned in paragraph (1)(*b*) is replaced by the period referred to in paragraph (9) if, within that 28 day period, the conditions specified in paragraph (8) are met.
(8) The conditions are that—

(*a*) HM Revenue and Customs and the applicant are in agreement as to the changes needed to the notice or to the documents accompanying the notice (or to both),

(*b*) the applicant has given notice to HM Revenue and Customs stating that the changes referred to in sub-paragraph (*a*) will take a specified period (which is longer than 28 days) to effect, and

(*c*) HM Revenue and Customs have given notice to the applicant accepting the statement made in the notice given under sub-paragraph (*b*).

(9) The period is the specified period mentioned in paragraph (8)(*b*).][1]

Amendments—[1] Part 4 (regs 69A–69Z41) inserted by the Authorised Investment Funds (Tax) (Amendment) Regulations, SI 2008/705 regs 2, 5 with effect from 6 April 2008.

[69T Appeal against quashing notice

(1) A person to whom a quashing notice is given may appeal . . . [2].
(2) The notice of appeal must be given to HM Revenue and Customs within a period of 28 days beginning with the day on which the quashing notice is given.
(3) On an appeal [that is notified to the tribunal, the tribunal][2] shall determine whether it was just and reasonable for HM Revenue and Customs to give the quashing notice.
(4) If the [tribunal allows][2] the appeal—

(*a*) [the tribunal may][2] direct that this Part shall apply to the open-ended investment company (or, as the case may be to the proposed open-ended investment company), and

(*b*) [the tribunal may][2] specify the date from which this Part shall so apply.

(5) The date mentioned in paragraph (4)(*b*)—

(*a*) must not be earlier than the beginning of the specified accounting period if an existing company notice has been given, and

(*b*) must not be earlier than the date of incorporation and authorisation if a future company notice has been given.][1]

Amendments—[1] Part 4 (regs 69A–69Z41) inserted by the Authorised Investment Funds (Tax) (Amendment) Regulations, SI 2008/705 regs 2, 5 with effect from 6 April 2008.

[2] In para (1), words revoked, in paras (3), (4), words substituted, by the Transfer of Tribunal Functions and Revenue and Customs Appeals Order, SI 2009/56 art 3, Sch 2 paras 154, 156 with effect from 1 April 2009.

[CLEARANCE APPLICATIONS

69U Clearance in relation to the genuine diversity of ownership condition

. . .

Amendments—Reg 69U revoked by the Authorised Investment Funds (Tax) (Amendment) Regulations, SI 2009/2036 regs 2, 21 with effect from 1 September 2009.

[CONSEQUENCES OF ENTRY

69V Effects of entry

(1) Property rental business of F (pre-entry) shall be treated for the purposes of corporation tax as ceasing at entry.
(2) Assets which immediately before entry are involved in property rental business of F (pre-entry) shall be treated for the purposes of corporation tax as being sold by F (pre-entry) immediately before entry and reacquired by F (tax-exempt) immediately after entry.
(3) For the purposes of corporation tax, on entry one accounting period of the open-ended investment company shall end and another shall begin.
(4) On entry a new distribution period of the open-ended investment company shall begin.
(5) The sale and reacquisition deemed under paragraph (2) shall not have effect for the purposes of tax in respect of chargeable gains.
(6) For the purposes of CAA 2001, the sale and reacquisition deemed under paragraph (2)—

(*a*) shall not give rise to allowances or charges, and

(*b*) shall not make it possible to make an election under section 198 or 199 of that Act (apportionment).

(7) For the purposes of CAA 2001, anything done by or to F (pre-entry) before entry in relation to an asset which is deemed under paragraph (2) to be sold and reacquired shall be treated after entry as having been done by or to F (tax-exempt).][1]

Amendments—[1] Part 4 (regs 69A–69Z41) inserted by the Authorised Investment Funds (Tax) (Amendment) Regulations, SI 2008/705 regs 2, 5 with effect from 6 April 2008.

[69W— Duration

Once this Part has begun to apply to an open-ended investment company it shall continue to apply unless and until it ceases to apply in accordance with Chapter 7 of this Part.][1]

Amendments—[1] Part 4 (regs 69A–69Z41) inserted by the Authorised Investment Funds (Tax) (Amendment) Regulations, SI 2008/705 regs 2, 5 with effect from 6 April 2008.

[CHAPTER 3

THE TAX TREATMENT OF PROPERTY AIFS

CATEGORIES OF BUSINESS

69X [Ring-fencing of tax-exempt business

(1) For the purposes of corporation tax, the business of F (tax-exempt) shall be treated as a separate business (distinct from—

(*a*) any business carried on by F (pre-entry),

(*b*) any business carried on by F (residual), and

(*c*) any business carried on by F (post-cessation)).

(2) For the purposes of corporation tax, F (tax-exempt) shall be treated as a separate company (distinct from—

(*a*) F (pre-entry),

(*b*) F (residual), and

(*c*) F (post-cessation)).

(3) In particular—

(*a*) a loss incurred by F (tax-exempt) may not be set off against the net income of F (residual),

(*b*) a loss incurred in respect of F (residual) may not be set off against the net income of F (tax exempt),

(*c*) a loss incurred in respect of F (pre-entry) may not be set off against the net income of F (tax-exempt) (but this regulation does not prevent a loss of that kind from being set off against profits of F (residual)),

(*d*) a loss incurred by F (tax-exempt) may not be set off against profits arising to F (post-cessation) (in respect of business of any kind), and

(*e*) receipts accruing after entry but relating to business of F (pre-entry) shall not be treated as receipts of F (tax-exempt).

(4) In paragraph (3) a reference to a loss includes a reference to a deficit, expense, charge or allowance.

(5) Section 392B of ICTA (ring-fencing of losses from overseas property business) shall not apply to business of F (tax-exempt).

(6) Paragraphs 5B and 5C of Schedule 28AA to ICTA (transfer pricing: exemption for small and medium enterprises) shall not apply to an open-ended investment company to which this Part applies (whether to F (tax-exempt) or to F (residual)).][1]

Amendments—[1] Part 4 (regs 69A–69Z41) inserted by the Authorised Investment Funds (Tax) (Amendment) Regulations, SI 2008/705 regs 2, 5 with effect from 6 April 2008.

[CHARGEABILITY TO TAX

69Y Chargeability to corporation tax

(1) The net income of F (tax-exempt) (see regulation 69Z1) shall not be charged to corporation tax.

(2) The net income of F (residual) (see regulation 69Z3) shall be charged to corporation tax at the rate applicable for open-ended investment companies (see section 468A(1) of ICTA).][1]

Amendments—[1] Part 4 (regs 69A–69Z41) inserted by the Authorised Investment Funds (Tax) (Amendment) Regulations, SI 2008/705 regs 2, 5 with effect from 6 April 2008.

[69Z Meaning of "net income"

(1) In this Part the "net income" of an open-ended investment company for an accounting period means, in the case of an open-ended investment company that prepares accounts in accordance with UK generally accepted accounting practice, the amount falling to be dealt with under the heading "[net revenue/(expense) before taxation]"[2] in the company's statement of total return for the accounting period.

(2) In paragraph (1) "the company's statement of total return for the accounting period" is to be construed in accordance with regulation 12.][1]

Amendments—[1] Part 4 (regs 69A–69Z41) inserted by the Authorised Investment Funds (Tax) (Amendment) Regulations, SI 2008/705 regs 2, 5 with effect from 6 April 2008.

[2] In para (1) words substituted by the Authorised Investment Funds (Tax) (Amendment No 3) Regulations, SI 2008/3159 regs 3, 23 with effect from 1 January 2009. In relation to a qualified investor scheme authorised by the Financial Services Authority before 1 January 2009, this amendment has effect subject to SI 2008/3159 reg 31.

[69Z1 Calculation of net income of F (tax-exempt)

(1) This regulation applies to determine the net income of F (tax-exempt) for the purposes of this Part.

(2) Section 21A of ICTA (calculation of profits of Schedule A business) shall apply to income arising from the business of F (tax-exempt).

(3) Paragraph 2(3) of section 15(1) of ICTA (Schedule A: disregard of credits and debits from loan relationships and derivative contracts) shall not apply in respect of—

(*a*) a loan relationship if or in so far as it relates to tax-exempt business,

(*b*) a hedging derivative contract if or in so far as it relates to tax-exempt business, or

(*c*) embedded derivatives if or in so far as the host contract is entered into for the purposes of tax-exempt business.

(4) For the purposes of paragraph (3)—

(*a*) a derivative contract is hedging in relation to a company if or in so far as it is acquired as a hedge of risk in relation to an asset by the exploitation of which tax-exempt business is conducted,

(*b*) a derivative contract is hedging in relation to a company if or in so far as it is acquired as a hedge of risk in relation to a liability incurred in connection with tax-exempt business,

(*c*) a designation of a contract as wholly or partly hedging for the purposes of a company's accounts shall be conclusive, and

(*d*) "embedded derivatives" and "host contract" shall be construed—

(i) in accordance with section 94A of FA 1996 in relation to loan contracts with embedded derivatives,

(ii) in accordance with paragraph 2A of Schedule 26 to FA 2002 in relation to non-financial contracts with embedded derivatives,

(iii) in accordance with paragraph 2B of Schedule 26 to FA 2002 in relation to hybrid derivatives.

(5) In paragraph (4)(*a*) the reference to an asset includes a reference to—

(*a*) the value of an asset, and

(*b*) profits attributable to it.

(6) Net income shall be computed without regard to items giving rise to credits or debits which would be within Schedule 26 to FA 2002 (derivative contracts) but for paragraph 4(2)(*b*) of that Schedule (exclusion of share-based and unit-trust-based contracts).

(7) Income and expenditure relating partly to tax-exempt business and partly to non-tax-exempt business shall be apportioned reasonably.

(8) Section 3(1) of CAA 2001 (claims for capital allowances) shall not apply; and any allowance which the company could claim under that section shall be made automatically and reflected in the calculation of net income.][1]

Amendments—[1] Part 4 (regs 69A–69Z41) inserted by the Authorised Investment Funds (Tax) (Amendment) Regulations, SI 2008/705 regs 2, 5 with effect from 6 April 2008.

[69Z2 Components of income arising to F (residual)

(1) For the purposes of this Part the income arising to F (residual) consists of—

(*a*) distributions qualifying for exemption under section 208 of ICTA, and

(*b*) income arising from the business of F (residual).

(2) Section 21A of ICTA (calculation of profits of Schedule A business) shall apply to income arising from the business of F (residual) if and to the extent that income arising from the business of F (residual) is chargeable to corporation tax under Schedule A.][1]

Amendments—[1] Part 4 (regs 69A–69Z41) inserted by the Authorised Investment Funds (Tax) (Amendment) Regulations, SI 2008/705 regs 2, 5 with effect from 6 April 2008.

[69Z3 Calculation of net income of F (residual)

Use this regulation to determine the net income of F (residual) for the purposes of this Part.

First rule

Determine the amount of the income arising to F (residual).

Second rule

Deduct any amounts whose deduction is required or allowed under the Corporation Tax Acts (including any distributions qualifying for exemption under section 208 of ICTA).

In this Part the amount so found is called the "pre-distribution amount".

Third rule

Deduct the amount attributed to PAIF distributions (interest) under regulation 69Z14(*b*).

The result is the net income of F (residual).][1]

Amendments—[1] Part 4 (regs 69A–69Z41) inserted by the Authorised Investment Funds (Tax) (Amendment) Regulations, SI 2008/705 regs 2, 5 with effect from 6 April 2008.

[BREACHES OF CONDITIONS

69Z4 Breach of the genuine diversity of ownership condition

(1) This regulation applies if an open-ended investment company to which this Part applies is in breach of the genuine diversity of ownership condition.

(2) Within 28 days of becoming aware of the breach, the company must provide the following information to the Commissioners—

(*a*) the date on which the condition first ceased to be met;

(*b*) the date on which the company became aware of the breach;

(*c*) details of the condition that was breached;

(*d*) the nature of the breach;

(*e*) the steps the company proposes to take to rectify the breach; and

(*f*) the date by which the company proposes to rectify the breach.

(3) The date referred to in paragraph (2)(*f*) must be the earliest date by which the objective of complying with the genuine diversity of ownership condition may reasonably be achieved.

(4) The Commissioners may give a termination notice to the company if—

(*a*) the steps that the company proposes to take will not rectify the breach, or

(*b*) the date by which the company proposes to rectify the breach is not the earliest date by which the objective of remedying the genuine diversity ownership condition may reasonably be achieved.

(5) If there are three different breaches of the genuine diversity of ownership condition in three different accounting periods in a period of ten years beginning with the first day of the accounting period in which the company becomes aware of the first of those breaches, the Commissioners may give a termination notice to the company.][1]

Amendments—[1] Part 4 (regs 69A–69Z41) inserted by the Authorised Investment Funds (Tax) (Amendment) Regulations, SI 2008/705 regs 2, 5 with effect from 6 April 2008.

[69Z5 Breach of the corporate ownership condition

(1) This regulation applies if an open-ended investment company to which this Part applies is in breach of the corporate ownership condition.

(2) If there is a breach which is caused by the action of a shareholder in the company and the company has not taken reasonable steps to prevent the breach (so that, accordingly, there is a charge to corporation tax under regulation 69Z12) (a "specified breach"), this Part shall continue to apply to the company despite the breach (but see paragraph (3) and regulation 69Z8).

(3) If there are three specified breaches in a period of ten years beginning with the first day of the accounting period in which the first specified breach occurs, the Commissioners may give a termination notice to the company.][1]

Amendments—[1] Part 4 (regs 69A–69Z41) inserted by the Authorised Investment Funds (Tax) (Amendment) Regulations, SI 2008/705 regs 2, 5 with effect from 6 April 2008.

[69Z6 Breach of the loan creditor condition

(1) This regulation applies if an open-ended investment company to which this Part applies is in breach of the loan creditor condition.

(2) If the company is inadvertently in breach of the loan creditor condition but rectifies the breach within a period of 28 days beginning with the day on which the company first becomes aware of the breach, this Part shall continue to apply to the company despite the breach (but see paragraphs (5) and (6) and regulation 69Z8).

(3) If the company is inadvertently in breach of the loan creditor condition but does not rectify the breach within a period of 28 days beginning with the day on which the company first becomes aware of the breach, the Commissioners may give a termination notice to the company.

(4) If the company is intentionally or negligently in breach of the loan creditor condition, the Commissioners may give a termination notice to the company.

(5) If the company is in breach of the same condition specified in paragraphs (2) to (5) of regulation 69M in two different accounting periods in a period of ten years beginning with the first day of the accounting period in which the company becomes aware of the first of those breaches, the Commissioners may give a termination notice to the company.

(6) If the company is in breach of the conditions specified in paragraphs (2) to (5) of regulation 69M in three different accounting periods in a period of ten years beginning with the first day of the accounting period in which the company becomes aware of the first of those breaches, the Commissioners may give a termination notice to the company.][1]

Amendments—[1] Part 4 (regs 69A–69Z41) inserted by the Authorised Investment Funds (Tax) (Amendment) Regulations, SI 2008/705 regs 2, 5 with effect from 6 April 2008.

[69Z7 Breach of balance of business conditions

(1) Paragraph (2) applies if a newly qualified company—

(*a*) is in breach of condition A set out in regulation 69N(2)(*a*) in its first accounting period, or

(*b*) is in breach of condition B set out in regulation 69N(3)(*a*) at the end of its first accounting period.

(2) This Part shall cease to apply to the company at the end of its first accounting period and regulation 69Z41 shall apply.

(3) Paragraphs (4) to (7) apply if an open-ended-investment company to which this Part applies—

(*a*) is in breach of condition A set out in regulation 69N(2)(*b*) in an accounting period, or

(*b*) is in breach of condition B set out in regulation 69N(3)(*b*) at the end of an accounting period.

(4) If the conditions specified in paragraph (6) are met, this Part shall continue to apply to the company despite the breach (but see paragraph (7) and regulation 69Z8).

(5) If the conditions specified in paragraph (6) are not met, the Commissioners may give a termination notice to the company.

(6) The conditions are that—

(*a*) property investment business is at least 50% of the company's net income in the accounting period,

(*b*) the value of the assets involved in property investment business is at least 50% of the total value of assets held by the company at the end of the accounting period.

(7) If this regulation applies to a company in three different accounting periods in a period of ten years beginning with the first day of the accounting period in which the company becomes aware of the first of those breaches, the Commissioners may give a termination notice to the company.][1]

Amendments—[1] Part 4 (regs 69A–69Z41) inserted by the Authorised Investment Funds (Tax) (Amendment) Regulations, SI 2008/705 regs 2, 5 with effect from 6 April 2008.

[69Z8 Multiple breaches of separate conditions

(1) This regulation applies in relation to an open-ended investment company to which this Part applies if—

(*a*) there has been a breach of at least two of the conditions in [regulation 9A or][2] regulations 69E to 69N,

(*b*) at least one of the conditions breached is contained in a different regulation from that containing another of those breached, and

(*c*) there have been five breaches in a period of ten years beginning with the first day of the accounting period in which the first breach occurs.

(2) The Commissioners may give a termination notice to the company.][1]

Amendments—[1] Part 4 (regs 69A–69Z41) inserted by the Authorised Investment Funds (Tax) (Amendment) Regulations, SI 2008/705 regs 2, 5 with effect from 6 April 2008.

[2] In para (1)(*a*), words inserted by the Authorised Investment Funds (Tax) (Amendment) Regulations, SI 2009/2036 regs 2, 22 with effect from 1 September 2009.

[FURTHER PROVISIONS

69Z9 Profit/financing costs in the case of a Property AIF that is a qualified investor scheme

(1) This regulation applies if conditions A and B are met.

(2) Condition A is that an open-ended investment company to which this Part applies is a qualified investor scheme.

(3) Condition B is that the result of the following calculation is less than 1.25 in respect of an accounting period—

Income/Financing Costs

(4) In paragraph (3)—

"Income" means the amount of the net income of F (tax-exempt) arising in the accounting period (before the offset of capital allowances, of losses from a previous accounting period, and of amounts taken into account under regulation 69Z1(3)), and

"Financing Costs" means the amount of the financing costs incurred in that period in respect of the business of F (tax-exempt).

(5) An amount shall be charged to corporation tax.

(6) That amount is determined as follows—

Step One

Determine the financing costs which, given the actual income, would produce the result of 1.25 in the calculation specified in paragraph (3) (the "theoretical financing costs").

Step Two

Determine the amount by which the actual financing costs exceed the theoretical financing costs ("the excess financing cost").

Step Three

Divide the main rate at which corporation tax is charged for the accounting period by the rate at which corporation tax is charged on an open-ended investment company for the accounting period (see section 468A(1) of ICTA) to determine the multiplier.

Step Four

Multiply the excess financing cost by the multiplier.

The result is the amount charged to tax.

(7) For the purposes of paragraphs (3) and (4) "financing costs" are the costs of debt finance; and in calculating the costs of debt finance in respect of an accounting period the matters to be taken into account include—

(*a*) costs giving rise to debits in respect of debtor relationships of the company under Chapter 2 of Part 4 of FA 1996 (loan relationships), other than debits in respect of exchange losses from such relationships (within the meaning of section 103(1A) and (1B) of that Act),

(*b*) any exchange gain or loss from a debtor relationship within the meaning of that Chapter in relation to debt finance,

(*c*) any credit or debit falling to be brought into account under Schedule 26 to FA 2002 (derivative contracts) in relation to debt finance,

(*d*) the financing cost implicit in a payment under a finance lease, and

(*e*) any other costs arising from what would be considered, in accordance with generally accepted accounting practice, to be a financing transaction.

(8) No loss, deficit, expense or allowance may be set off against the amount charged to tax by paragraph (5).][1]

Amendments—[1] Part 4 (regs 69A–69Z41) inserted by the Authorised Investment Funds (Tax) (Amendment) Regulations, SI 2008/705 regs 2, 5 with effect from 6 April 2008.

[69Z10 Cancellation of tax advantage

(1) This regulation applies if a company to which this Part applies has tried to obtain a tax advantage for itself or another person.

(2) The Commissioners may give a notice to the company specifying the tax advantage.

(3) If the Commissioners give a notice to the company under paragraph (2) a tax advantage obtained by the company shall be counteracted, in accordance with the notice, by an adjustment by way of—

(*a*) an assessment;

(*b*) the cancellation of a right of repayment;

(*c*) a requirement to return a repayment already made; or

(*d*) the computation or recomputation of profits or gains, or liability to tax, on a basis specified by the Commissioners in the notice.

(4) The Commissioners may (in addition to the adjustment under paragraph (3)) assess the company to such additional amount of income tax under Case VI of Schedule D as they think is equivalent to the value of the tax advantage.

(5) For the purposes of this regulation "tax advantage" has the meaning given by section 709 of ICTA.

(6) But a company does not obtain a tax advantage by reason only of this Part applying to it, unless it does anything (whether before or during the application of this Part) which is wholly or principally designed to create or inflate or apply a loss, deduction or expense (whether or not suffered or incurred by the company).][1]

Amendments—[1] Part 4 (regs 69A–69Z41) inserted by the Authorised Investment Funds (Tax) (Amendment) Regulations, SI 2008/705 regs 2, 5 with effect from 6 April 2008.

[69Z11 Appeal against notice under regulation 69Z10

(1) If a notice is given to a company under regulation 69Z10, the company may appeal . . .[2].

(2) The notice of appeal must be given to HM Revenue and Customs within a period of 28 days beginning with the day on which the notice under regulation 69Z10 is given.

(3) On an appeal [that is notified to the tribunal, the tribunal][2] may—

(*a*) affirm, vary or cancel the notice, and

(*b*) affirm, vary or quash an assessment made under regulation 69Z10(4).][1]

Amendments—[1] Part 4 (regs 69A–69Z41) inserted by the Authorised Investment Funds (Tax) (Amendment) Regulations, SI 2008/705 regs 2, 5 with effect from 6 April 2008.

[2] In para (1), words revoked, and in para (3), words substituted, by the Transfer of Tribunal Functions and Revenue and Customs Appeals Order, SI 2009/56 art 3, Sch 2 paras 154, 157 with effect from 1 April 2009.

[69Z12 Distribution to holder of excessive rights: charge to tax

(1) This regulation applies if an open-ended investment company to which this Part applies—

(*a*) makes a distribution to, or in respect of, a holder of excessive rights (see regulation 69Z13), and

(*b*) the company has not taken reasonable steps to prevent the possibility of such a distribution being made.

(2) The company is treated as having received an amount of income calculated in accordance with paragraph (3).

(3) The amount of the income is determined by the formula—

I x P

(4) In paragraph (3)—

I is the net income of F (tax-exempt) distributable in accordance with regulation 69Z14(*a*);

P is the percentage of the rights to the net asset value of the company held by, or on behalf of, the holder of excessive rights.

(5) The amount determined in accordance with paragraph (3) shall be charged to corporation tax as if it were income of F (residual) chargeable under Case VI of Schedule D arising in the accounting period in which the distribution mentioned in paragraph (1) was made by the company.
(6) No loss, deficit, expense or allowance may be set off against the amount charged to tax by paragraph (5).][1]

Amendments—[1] Part 4 (regs 69A–69Z41) inserted by the Authorised Investment Funds (Tax) (Amendment) Regulations, SI 2008/705 regs 2, 5 with effect from 6 April 2008.

[69Z13 Meaning of "holder of excessive rights"

(1) In this Part a "holder of excessive rights" means a body corporate which—
(*a*) is a participant in an open-ended investment company to which this Part applies, and
(*b*) is beneficially entitled to shares representing rights to 10% or more of the net asset value of the company.
(2) Paragraphs (4) and (5) of regulation 69L apply for the purposes of paragraph (1) as they apply for the purposes of regulation 69K.
(3) In this Part an "excessive holding" means the holding of a holder of excessive rights.][1]

Amendments—[1] Part 4 (regs 69A–69Z41) inserted by the Authorised Investment Funds (Tax) (Amendment) Regulations, SI 2008/705 regs 2, 5 with effect from 6 April 2008.

[CHAPTER 4
DISTRIBUTIONS MADE BY PROPERTY AIFS

69Z14 [Allocation of income]

[The total amount available for income allocation in an open-ended investment company to which this Part applies shall be attributed][2]
(*a*) first, to property income distributions up to the amount of the net income of F (tax-exempt) (determined in accordance with regulation 69Z1),
(*b*) secondly, to PAIF distributions (interest) up to the pre-distribution amount (determined in accordance with regulation 69Z3), and
(*c*) finally, to PAIF distributions (dividends).][1]

Amendments—[1] Part 4 (regs 69A–69Z41) inserted by the Authorised Investment Funds (Tax) (Amendment) Regulations, SI 2008/705 regs 2, 5 with effect from 6 April 2008.
[2] Regulation heading substituted, and words in first para substituted, by the Authorised Investment Funds (Tax) (Amendment) Regulations, SI 2010/294, regs 2, 16, with effect from 6 March 2010, but see regs 24–26 for transitional provisions relating to distribution dates for earlier accounting periods, and entry into the FINROF regime (see reg 1(2)).

[69Z15 Property income distributions

(1) This regulation applies if—
(*a*) an open-ended investment company to which this Part applies makes a distribution, and
(*b*) the amount distributed includes sums attributed to property income distributions.
(2) The Tax Acts shall have effect as if the sums were payments made on the distribution date by the company to the participants in proportion to their rights.
(3) Regulation 69Z18 (property income distributions: liability to tax of participants) explains how a property income distribution received by a participant is treated.
(4) In these Regulations a "property income distribution" means a sum attributed to property income distributions which is distributed (including a payment made to a participant who is not chargeable to income tax or corporation tax).][1]

Amendments—[1] Part 4 (regs 69A–69Z41) inserted by the Authorised Investment Funds (Tax) (Amendment) Regulations, SI 2008/705 regs 2, 5 with effect from 6 April 2008.

[69Z16 PAIF distributions (interest)

(1) This regulation applies if—
(*a*) an open-ended investment company to which this Part applies makes a distribution, and
(*b*) the amount distributed includes sums attributed to PAIF distributions (interest).
(2) The Tax Acts shall have effect as if the sums were payments of yearly interest made on the distribution date by the company to the participants in proportion to their rights.
(3) In this Part a "PAIF distribution (interest)" means a sum attributed to PAIF distributions (interest) which is distributed (including a payment made to a participant who is not chargeable to income tax).][1]

Amendments—[1] Part 4 (regs 69A–69Z41) inserted by the Authorised Investment Funds (Tax) (Amendment) Regulations, SI 2008/705 regs 2, 5 with effect from 6 April 2008.

[69Z17 PAIF distributions (dividends)

(1) This regulation applies if—
(*a*) an open-ended investment company to which this Part applies makes a distribution, and
(*b*) the amount distributed includes sums attributed to PAIF distributions (dividends).
(2) The Tax Acts shall have effect as if the sums were dividends on shares paid on the distribution date by the company to the participants in proportion to their rights.

(3) In this Part a "PAIF distribution (dividends)" means a sum attributed to PAIF distributions (dividends) which is distributed (including a dividend treated as paid to a participant who is not chargeable to corporation tax).][1]

Amendments—[1] Part 4 (regs 69A–69Z41) inserted by the Authorised Investment Funds (Tax) (Amendment) Regulations, SI 2008/705 regs 2, 5 with effect from 6 April 2008.

[CHAPTER 5

THE TREATMENT OF PARTICIPANTS IN PROPERTY AIFS

TREATMENT OF DISTRIBUTIONS: LIABILITY TO TAX OF PARTICIPANTS

69Z18 Property income distributions: liability to tax of participants

(1) A property income distribution received by a participant in an open-ended investment company to which this Part applies shall be treated—

- (*a*) in the case of a participant within the charge to corporation tax, as profits of a Schedule A business, and
- (*b*) in the case of a participant within the charge to income tax, as the profits of a UK property business (within the meaning of section 264 of ITTOIA 2005).

(2) A distribution received by a participant who is not resident in the United Kingdom—

- (*a*) if the participant is a company within the charge to corporation tax, shall be chargeable to tax as profits of a Schedule A business,
- (*b*) if the participant is a person other than a company within the charge to corporation tax, shall be chargeable to tax as profits of a UK property business (within the meaning of section 264 of ITTOIA 2005), and
- (*c*) in either case shall not be chargeable to tax by virtue of sections 971 and 972 of ITA 2007 (non-resident landlords).

(3) Paragraph (1) shall not apply in relation to a participant if and in so far as the participant—

- (*a*) is a dealer in respect of distributions (within the meaning of section 95 of ICTA),
- (*b*) is a dealer in securities who is charged to tax under Part 2 of ITTOIA 2005 (trading income) in respect of distributions made by companies,
- (*c*) is an individual member of Lloyd's (within the meaning given by section 184(1) of FA 1993) and the distribution is made in respect of assets forming part of—
  - (i) a premium trust fund of his (within the meaning given by section 174 of FA 1993), or
  - (ii) an ancillary trust fund of his (within the meaning given by section 176 of FA 1993), or
- (*d*) is a corporate member of Lloyd's (within the meaning given by section 230(1) of FA 1994) and the distribution is made in respect of assets forming part of—
  - (i) a premium trust fund of his (within the meaning given by section 222 of FA 1994), or
  - (ii) an ancillary trust fund of his (within the meaning given by section 223 of FA 1994).

(4) Section 114(1)(*a*) of ICTA (partnerships with companies as members) does not disapply paragraph (1).

(5) Sections 231 of ICTA and 397 of ITTOIA 2005 (tax credits in respect of qualifying distributions) shall not apply to property income distributions.

(6) Property income distributions received by one participant acting in one capacity shall be treated, for the purposes of paragraph (1), as the profits of a single business which is separate from—

- (*a*) any other Schedule A business carried on by the participant,
- (*b*) any other UK property business (within the meaning of section 264 of ITTOIA 2005) carried on by the participant,
- (*c*) any overseas property business (within the meaning of section 70A(4) of ICTA) carried on by the participant, and
- (*d*) any overseas property business (within the meaning of section 265 of ITTOIA 2005) carried on by the participant.

(7) In the case of a participant which is a partnership, paragraph (6) applies to receipts by a partner of a share of any distribution as it applies to receipts by a participant.][1]

Amendments—[1] Part 4 (regs 69A–69Z41) inserted by the Authorised Investment Funds (Tax) (Amendment) Regulations, SI 2008/705 regs 2, 5 with effect from 6 April 2008.

[69Z19 PAIF distributions (interest): liability to tax of participants

[(1) A PAIF distribution (interest) received by a participant in an open-ended investment company to which this Part applies shall be treated—

- (*a*) in the case of a participant within the charge to corporation tax, as if it were interest arising from a loan relationship; and
- (*b*) in the case of a participant within the charge to income tax, as if it were a payment of yearly interest falling within Chapter 2 of Part 4 of ITTOIA 2005.][2]

(2) Sections 231 of ICTA and 397 of ITTOIA 2005 (tax credits in respect of qualifying distributions) shall not apply to PAIF distributions (interest).][1]

Amendments—[1] Part 4 (regs 69A–69Z41) inserted by the Authorised Investment Funds (Tax) (Amendment) Regulations, SI 2008/705 regs 2, 5 with effect from 6 April 2008.

[2] Para (1) substituted by the Authorised Investment Funds (Tax) (Amendment No 3) Regulations, SI 2008/3159 regs 3, 24 with effect from 1 January 2009. In relation to a qualified investor scheme authorised by the Financial Services Authority before 1 January 2009, this amendment has effect subject to SI 2008/3159 reg 31.

[69Z20 Property distributions (dividends): liability to tax of participants

(1) A PAIF distribution (dividends) received by a participant in an open-ended investment company to which this Part applies shall be treated as if it were a dividend on shares.

(2) If a PAIF distribution (dividends) is made for a distribution period to a participant chargeable to corporation tax, regulations 48 to 52A shall not apply to the distribution.][1]

Amendments—[1] Part 4 (regs 69A–69Z41) inserted by the Authorised Investment Funds (Tax) (Amendment) Regulations, SI 2008/705 regs 2, 5 with effect from 6 April 2008.

[69Z21 Distributions made after cessation

(1) This regulation applies if an open-ended investment company—

(*a*) is a company to which this Part applies in respect of an accounting period,

(*b*) makes a distribution in respect of that accounting period, and

(*c*) the distribution is made after cessation.

(2) Regulations 69Z18 to 69Z20 apply in relation to the distribution.][1]

Amendments—[1] Part 4 (regs 69A–69Z41) inserted by the Authorised Investment Funds (Tax) (Amendment) Regulations, SI 2008/705 regs 2, 5 with effect from 6 April 2008.

[DEDUCTION OF TAX FROM DISTRIBUTIONS

69Z22 Deduction of tax from property income distributions

(1) On making a property income distribution, an open-ended investment company to which this Part applies must deduct a sum representing income tax at the basic rate in force for the tax year in which the distribution date falls.

(2) A property income distribution shall be treated as having been received by the participant after deduction of income tax at the basic rate for the year of assessment in which the distribution date falls, from a corresponding gross amount.

(3) The sum is accordingly taken into account under sections 59B and 59D of TMA 1970 (see also paragraph 8 of Schedule 18 to the Finance Act 1998) in determining the income tax or corporation tax payable by, or repayable to, the participant.

(4) This regulation is subject to regulation 69Z24 (distribution payments to be made without deduction of tax).][1]

Amendments—[1] Part 4 (regs 69A–69Z41) inserted by the Authorised Investment Funds (Tax) (Amendment) Regulations, SI 2008/705 regs 2, 5 with effect from 6 April 2008.

[69Z23 Deduction of tax from PAIF distributions (interest)

(1) On making a PAIF distribution (interest), an open-ended investment company to which this Part applies must deduct a sum representing income tax at the [basic rate][2] in force for the tax year in which the PAIF distribution (interest) is made.

(2) Accordingly, the sum is one to which section 874 of ITA 2007 applies.

(3) . . .[2]

(4) This regulation is subject to regulation 69Z24 (distribution payments to be made without deduction of tax).][1]

Amendments—[1] Part 4 (regs 69A–69Z41) inserted by the Authorised Investment Funds (Tax) (Amendment) Regulations, SI 2008/705 regs 2, 5 with effect from 6 April 2008.

[2] In para (1) words substituted, and para (3) revoked, by the Authorised Investment Funds (Tax) (Amendment No 3) Regulations, SI 2008/3159 regs 3, 25 with effect from 1 January 2009. In relation to a qualified investor scheme authorised by the Financial Services Authority before 1 January 2009, this amendment has effect subject to SI 2008/3159 reg 31.

[69Z24 Distribution payments to be made without deduction of tax

(1) [Subject to paragraphs (3A) and (3B),][2] on making a distribution, an open-ended investment company to which this Part applies must not deduct any sum representing income tax if the company reasonably believes that conditions A and B are met.

(2) Condition A is that if the distribution were made by a UK-REIT out of the profits of C (tax-exempt), the distribution would be required to be made without any deduction representing income tax.

(3) Condition B is that if the distribution were a distribution of yearly interest, the distribution would be required to be made without any deduction representing income tax.

[(3A) But neither condition A nor condition B is met, in relation to a unit trust scheme, where—

(*a*) the distribution is made to the trustee of the scheme;

(*b*) the trustee is chargeable to corporation tax or income tax on the distribution in the United Kingdom; and

(*c*) the trustee has made a request in writing to the Property AIF that the Property AIF should deduct tax from the distribution.

(3B) The Property AIF must not specify that the trustee of any unit trust scheme seeking to acquire shares in the Property AIF must have tax deducted from any distribution.][2]

(4) If at the time it makes a distribution the company reasonably believes that conditions A and B are met, but in fact those conditions are not both met, these Regulations shall apply to the distribution as if it were never one which could be made without deduction of tax.

(5) In paragraph (2) "profits of C (tax-exempt)" shall be construed in accordance with Part 4 of FA 2006.][1]

Amendments—[1] Part 4 (regs 69A–69Z41) inserted by the Authorised Investment Funds (Tax) (Amendment) Regulations, SI 2008/705 regs 2, 5 with effect from 6 April 2008.

[2] Words in para (1), and paras (3A), (3B) inserted, by the Authorised Investment Funds (Tax) (Amendment No 3) Regulations, SI 2008/3159 regs 3, 26 with effect from 1 January 2009. In relation to a qualified investor scheme authorised by the Financial Services Authority before 1 January 2009, this amendment has effect subject to SI 2008/3159 reg 31.

[69Z24A Manufactured dividends representing property income distributions

(1) This regulation applies to the extent that a manufactured dividend which is paid by a dividend manufacturer is representative of property income distributions to which regulation 69Z15 applies.

(2) The amount of the manufactured dividend falling within paragraph (1) is referred to in this regulation as "the manufactured PID amount".

(3) The recipient of the manufactured PID amount is treated as having received a distribution to which regulation 69Z18 applies.

(4) In relation to the dividend manufacturer—

(*a*) if the dividend manufacturer is a company and the manufactured dividend is paid in the course of a trade carried on in the United Kingdom, the manufactured PID amount shall be treated as an expense of the trade;

(*b*) if the manufactured dividend is paid in connection with investment business, the manufactured PID amount shall be treated for the purposes of section 75 of ICTA as expenses of management; and

(*c*) in the case of a company carrying on life assurance business, so much of the manufactured PID amount as would be referable by virtue of section 432A of ICTA to basic life assurance and general annuity business if it were received by the company shall be treated for the purposes of section 76 of ICTA as if it were an expense payable falling to be brought into account at step 3 of section 76(7).

(5) Regulations 69Z22, 69Z24 and 69Z29 to 69Z35 apply to the dividend manufacturer as if—

(*a*) the dividend manufacturer were an open-ended investment company to which this Part applies; and

(*b*) the manufactured PID amount were a distribution to which those regulations apply.][1]

Amendments—[1] Regs 69Z24A–69Z24D inserted by the Authorised Investment Funds (Tax) (Amendment No 3) Regulations, SI 2008/3159 regs 3, 27 with effect in relation to manufactured dividends paid on or after 1 January 2009. In relation to a qualified investor scheme authorised by the Financial Services Authority before 1 January 2009, these amendments have effect subject to SI 2008/3159 reg 31.

[69Z24B Manufactured dividends representing PAIF distributions (interest)

(1) This regulation applies to the extent that a manufactured dividend which is paid by a dividend manufacturer is representative of a PAIF distribution (interest) to which regulation 69Z16 applies.

(2) The amount of the manufactured dividend to which this regulation applies is referred to in this regulation as the "manufactured PAIF interest amount".

(3) If the recipient of the manufactured dividend is a company within the charge to corporation tax it is treated as having received, in relation to the manufactured PAIF interest amount, an amount to which section 97 of FA 1996 applies.

(4) If the recipient of the manufactured dividend is within the charge to income tax it is treated as having received, in relation to the manufactured PAIF interest amount, an amount to which regulation 69Z19 applies.

(5) If the dividend manufacturer is a company within the charge to corporation tax, section 97 of FA 1996 is treated as applying to the manufactured PAIF interest amount.

(6) Regulations 69Z23, 69Z24 and 69Z29 to 69Z35 apply to the dividend manufacturer in relation to the manufactured PAIF interest amount as if the dividend manufacturer were an open-ended investment company to which this Part applies.][1]

Amendments—[1] Regs 69Z24A–69Z24D inserted by the Authorised Investment Funds (Tax) (Amendment No 3) Regulations, SI 2008/3159 regs 3, 27 with effect in relation to manufactured dividends paid on or after 1 January 2009. In relation to a qualified investor scheme authorised by the Financial Services Authority before 1 January 2009, these amendments have effect subject to SI 2008/3159 reg 31.

[69Z24C Manufactured dividends—PAIF distributions (dividends)

(1) This regulation applies to the extent that a manufactured dividend which is paid by a dividend manufacturer is representative of a PAIF distribution (dividends) to which regulation 69Z17 applies.

(2) The recipient of the manufactured dividend is treated as having received, to that extent, an amount to which regulation 69Z20 applies.

(3) If the dividend manufacturer is a company, paragraph 2(2)(b) of Schedule 23A to ICTA has effect in relation to the amount of the manufactured dividend to which paragraph (1) applies.][1]

Amendments—[1] Regs 69Z24A–69Z24D inserted by the Authorised Investment Funds (Tax) (Amendment No 3) Regulations, SI 2008/3159 regs 3, 27 with effect in relation to manufactured dividends paid on or after 1 January 2009. In relation to a qualified investor scheme authorised by the Financial Services Authority before 1 January 2009, these amendments have effect subject to SI 2008/3159 reg 31.

[69Z24D Interpretation

In regulations 69Z24A to 69Z24C, "manufactured dividend" and "dividend manufacturer" have the meanings given by Schedule 23A to ICTA.][1]

Amendments—[1] Regs 69Z24A–69Z24D inserted by the Authorised Investment Funds (Tax) (Amendment No 3) Regulations, SI 2008/3159 regs 3, 27 with effect in relation to manufactured dividends paid on or after 1 January 2009. In relation to a qualified investor scheme authorised by the Financial Services Authority before 1 January 2009, these amendments have effect subject to SI 2008/3159 reg 31.

[Conversions and exchanges

69Z24E Conversion to property AIF

(1) This regulation applies if—

(*a*) a fund ("the pre-conversion fund") which is not a property AIF becomes, or intends to become, a property AIF,

(*b*) the unit-holders in the pre-conversion fund dispose of the units which they hold in that fund ("the original units") and, as part of an arrangement, acquire units of the same, or substantially the same, value as the original units in the fund which is, or is intended to become, the dedicated feeder fund for the property AIF, and

(*c*) the further requirement of regulation 69Z24G is met.

(2) Sections 127 to 131 of TCGA apply in relation to the disposal and subsequent acquisition of units specified in this regulation.

(3) A fund converting to a property AIF in accordance with this regulation shall be treated as meeting condition A in regulation 69K (the corporate ownership condition) where the conditions in paragraph (4) are met, notwithstanding that the holding of a body corporate in the property AIF may exceed the percentage mentioned in regulation 69K(3)(*a*) during the relevant period.

(4) The conditions in this paragraph are that—

(*a*) during the relevant period, no distributions are declared or made,

(*b*) any distribution which was declared before the beginning of the relevant period is paid before the beginning of that period, and

(*c*) the units held by the body corporate in the property AIF are exchanged for units in the dedicated feeder fund as soon as reasonably practicable.

(5) In this regulation, "the relevant period" is the period beginning with the time at which the fund becomes a property AIF and ending with the time at which the units in the dedicated feeder fund for the property AIF are issued to a participant which is a body corporate.][1]

Amendments—[1] Regs 69Z24E–69Z24H inserted by the Authorised Investment Funds (Tax) (Amendment No 2) Regulations, SI 2012/1783 regs 2, 4 with effect for the purposes of capital gains tax, in relation to disposals made on or after 1 August 2012, and for the purposes of corporation tax on chargeable gains, in relation to disposals made on or after 1 August 2012.

[69Z24F Exchange of units

(1) This regulation applies if—

(*a*) there is—

(i) an exchange of units in a dedicated feeder fund for shares in the property AIF for which that fund is the dedicated feeder fund, or

(ii) an exchange of shares in a property AIF for units in the dedicated feeder fund for that property AIF, and

(*b*) the further requirement of regulation 69Z24G is met.

(2) The units to be exchanged in accordance with either paragraph (1)(*a*) or (*b*) must represent the same, or substantially the same, share of the net asset value of the property AIF as the units which are held immediately after the exchange.

(3) Sections 127 to 131 of TCGA 1992 apply in relation to a disposal or acquisition of units or shares specified in paragraph (1).][1]

Amendments—[1] Regs 69Z24E–69Z24H inserted by the Authorised Investment Funds (Tax) (Amendment No 2) Regulations, SI 2012/1783 regs 2, 4 with effect for the purposes of capital gains tax, in relation to disposals made on or after 1 August 2012, and for the purposes of corporation tax on chargeable gains, in relation to disposals made on or after 1 August 2012.

[69Z24G Further requirement

The further requirement is that if a transaction involves the acquisition of units in a dedicated feeder fund, that it is undertaken with the agreement of the manager of the property AIF.][1]

Amendments—[1] Regs 69Z24E–69Z24H inserted by the Authorised Investment Funds (Tax) (Amendment No 2) Regulations, SI 2012/1783 regs 2, 4 with effect for the purposes of capital gains tax, in relation to disposals made on or after 1 August 2012, and for the purposes of corporation tax on chargeable gains, in relation to disposals made on or after 1 August 2012.

[69Z24H Application of section 137 of TCGA

Section 137 of TCGA (restriction on application of tax treatment) applies to any transaction specified in regulations 69Z24E or 69Z24F in the circumstances mentioned in that section.][1]

Amendments—[1] Regs 69Z24E–69Z24H inserted by the Authorised Investment Funds (Tax) (Amendment No 2) Regulations, SI 2012/1783 regs 2, 4 with effect for the purposes of capital gains tax, in relation to disposals made on or after 1 August 2012, and for the purposes of corporation tax on chargeable gains, in relation to disposals made on or after 1 August 2012.

[CHAPTER 6

COMPLIANCE IN RELATION TO THE PROPERTY AIF REGIME

COMPANY TAX RETURN

69Z25 Documents to be included with company tax return

(1) An open-ended investment company to which this Part applies must include documents A and B in its company tax return.

(2) Document A is a calculation of the net income of F(tax-exempt) and F(residual) in accordance with regulations 69Z1 to 69Z3.

(3) Document B is a reconciliation between—

(*a*) the net income of the company (see regulation 69Z), and

(*b*) [the total amount available for income allocation][2] as attributed in accordance with regulation 69Z14.

(4) In paragraph (1) "company tax return" means the return required to be delivered pursuant to a notice under paragraph 3 of Schedule 18 to the Finance Act 1998, as read with paragraph 4 of that Schedule.

(5) Section 98 of TMA 1970 applies to any failure to furnish any information, give any certificate or produce any document or record in accordance with any provision of this Chapter as it applies to any such failure in the case of any provision specified in the second column of the Table below that section.][1]

Amendments—[1] Part 4 (regs 69A–69Z41) inserted by the Authorised Investment Funds (Tax) (Amendment) Regulations, SI 2008/705 regs 2, 5 with effect from 6 April 2008.

[2] Words in para (3)(*b*) substituted for by the Authorised Investment Funds (Tax) (Amendment) Regulations, SI 2010/294, regs 2, 17, with effect from 6 March 2010, but see regs 24–26 for transitional provisions relating to distribution dates for earlier accounting periods, and entry into the FINROF regime (see reg 1(2)).

[BREACHES OF CONDITIONS IN CHAPTER 2

69Z26 Information to be provided by company to which this Part applies

(1) This regulation applies if an open-ended investment company to which this Part applies—

(*a*) does not meet a condition set out in Chapter 2 of this Part (entry into and membership of the Property AIF regime), and

(*b*) becomes aware that it does not meet the condition.

(2) As soon as reasonably practicable, the company must provide the following information to the Commissioners—

(*a*) the date on which the condition first ceased to be met and the date (if any) on which the condition was satisfied again;

(*b*) details of the condition that was breached;

(*c*) the nature of the breach; and

(*d*) what (if anything) the company has done to prevent the breach recurring.

(3) This regulation does not apply if the breach of condition is one to which regulation 69Z27 applies.][1]

Amendments—[1] Part 4 (regs 69A–69Z41) inserted by the Authorised Investment Funds (Tax) (Amendment) Regulations, SI 2008/705 regs 2, 5 with effect from 6 April 2008.

[HOLDERS OF EXCESSIVE RIGHTS

69Z27 Information relating to holders of excessive rights

(1) This regulation applies if an open-ended investment company to which this Part applies becomes aware that it has made a distribution to, or in respect of, a holder of excessive rights.

(2) As soon as reasonably practicable, the company must provide the following information to the Commissioners—

(*a*) the name of every person to whom, or in respect of whom, the distribution specified in paragraph (1) was made;

(*b*) the address of every such person;

(*c*) the amount or value of the distribution;

(*d*) particulars of those persons' interests in the company, including details of the percentage of rights to the net asset value of the company represented by the shares held by those persons;

(*e*) the steps the company took to prevent the acquisition of any excessive holding; and (*f*) the steps the company has taken, or is taking, to ensure that there is no longer any excessive holding in the company.][1]

Amendments—[1] Part 4 (regs 69A–69Z41) inserted by the Authorised Investment Funds (Tax) (Amendment) Regulations, SI 2008/705 regs 2, 5 with effect from 6 April 2008.

[INFORMATION ABOUT POSSIBLE BREACHES OF CONDITIONS OF MEMBERSHIP OF PROPERTY AIF REGIME

69Z28 Information to be provided to officers of Revenue and Customs

(1) This regulation applies if an officer of Revenue and Customs thinks that an open-ended investment company to which this Part applies—

(*a*) does not meet, or may not meet, a condition specified in Chapter 2 of this Part, or

(*b*) has not rectified a breach of such a condition.

(2) The officer may serve a notice on the manager of the company.

(3) The notice may require the manager to provide any of the information specified in regulation 69Z26(2) or, as the case may be, regulation 69Z27(2).

(4) The manager must comply with the notice within a period of 28 days beginning with the day on which the notice is served.][1]

Amendments—[1] Part 4 (regs 69A–69Z41) inserted by the Authorised Investment Funds (Tax) (Amendment) Regulations, SI 2008/705 regs 2, 5 with effect from 6 April 2008.

[ACCOUNTING FOR TAX DEDUCTED FROM PROPERTY INCOME DISTRIBUTIONS

69Z29 Payments in an accounting period

(1) This regulation applies if—

(*a*) an open-ended investment company to which this Part applies makes a distribution in an accounting period of the company, and

(*b*) the distribution includes sums attributed to property income distributions or to PAIF distributions (interest) (or to both) (referred to in this Chapter as a "relevant distribution").

(2) The company must deliver a return to an officer of Revenue and Customs for each return period—

(*a*) which falls within the accounting period, and

(*b*) in which the company makes a relevant distribution.

(3) The return periods are—

(*a*) the quarters ending on 31st March, 30th June, 30th September and 31st December (the "quarter days"); and

(*b*) any shorter period which—

(i) starts on the first day of an accounting period and ends with the first or only quarter day in that accounting period;

(ii) begins immediately after the last or only quarter day in that accounting period and ends on the last day of that accounting period; or

(iii) is an accounting period which starts and ends within a quarter.

(4) The company must deliver the return during a period of 14 days beginning with the day immediately following the end of the return period.

(5) The return must show the amount of—

(*a*) any relevant distributions made by the company in the return period, and

(*b*) the tax (if any) payable by the company in respect of those payments.

(6) The company must deliver, with the return for the return period which ends on the last day of an accounting period, a reconciliation statement showing, in relation to any distribution made during the accounting period, the amounts (if any) which are attributable to each of paragraphs (*a*) to (*c*) of regulation 69Z14 (attribution of distributions).][1]

Amendments—[1] Part 4 (regs 69A–69Z41) inserted by the Authorised Investment Funds (Tax) (Amendment) Regulations, SI 2008/705 regs 2, 5 with effect from 6 April 2008.

[69Z30 Collection and payment of tax

(1) Tax in respect of a relevant distribution is due at the time by which the return on which the distribution must be included is required to be delivered.

(2) The tax due is equal to the sum which the company is required to deduct from the relevant distribution under—

(*a*) regulation 69Z22(1) (deduction of tax from property income distributions), and

(*b*) regulation 69Z23(1) (deduction of tax from PAIF distributions (interest)).

(3) The tax is due from the company making the relevant distribution.

(4) The tax is payable without an officer of Revenue and Customs making any assessment.][1]

Amendments—[1] Part 4 (regs 69A–69Z41) inserted by the Authorised Investment Funds (Tax) (Amendment) Regulations, SI 2008/705 regs 2, 5 with effect from 6 April 2008.

[69Z31 Assessments where relevant distribution included in return

(1) This regulation applies if any tax in respect of a relevant distribution which is included in a return under this Chapter has not been paid at or before the time mentioned in regulation 69Z30.

(2) An officer of Revenue and Customs may make an assessment on the person who made the relevant distribution.

(3) Tax may be assessed under this regulation whether or not it has been paid when the assessment is made.][1]

Amendments—[1] Part 4 (regs 69A–69Z41) inserted by the Authorised Investment Funds (Tax) (Amendment) Regulations, SI 2008/705 regs 2, 5 with effect from 6 April 2008.

[69Z32 Assessments in other cases

(1) This regulation applies if an officer of Revenue and Customs thinks—

(*a*) that there is a relevant distribution which should have been included in a return under this Chapter and which has not been so included, or

(*b*) that a return under this Chapter is otherwise incorrect.

(2) An officer of Revenue and Customs may make an assessment on the person who made the relevant distribution to the best of the officer's judgement.][1]

Amendments—[1] Part 4 (regs 69A–69Z41) inserted by the Authorised Investment Funds (Tax) (Amendment) Regulations, SI 2008/705 regs 2, 5 with effect from 6 April 2008.

[69Z33 Application of Income Tax Acts provisions about time limits for assessments

(1) The provisions of the Income Tax Acts about the time within which an assessment may be made apply to assessments under this Chapter, so far as those provisions refer or relate to—

(*a*) the tax year for which an assessment is made, or

(*b*) the year to which an assessment relates.

(2) Paragraph (1) applies despite the fact that an assessment under this Chapter may relate to a return period which is not a tax year.

(3) The provisions of section 36 of TMA 1970 (fraudulent or negligent conduct) about the circumstances in which an assessment may be made out of time apply accordingly on the basis that any such assessment relates to the tax year in which the return period ends.

(4) Section 87 of TMA 1970 (interest on overdue income tax deducted at source) applies for the purposes of a payment due under regulation 69Z30 or an assessment made under regulation 69Z31 or 69Z32.][1]

Amendments—[1] Part 4 (regs 69A–69Z41) inserted by the Authorised Investment Funds (Tax) (Amendment) Regulations, SI 2008/705 regs 2, 5 with effect from 6 April 2008.

[69Z34 Certificates of deduction of tax

(1) A company making a relevant distribution which is subject to deduction of tax by virtue of regulation 69Z22(1) must furnish the recipient with a statement that complies with condition A or B. This is subject to paragraph (5).

(2) The duty imposed by paragraph (1) is enforceable at the suit or instance of the recipient.

(3) Condition A is that the statement is in writing showing—

(*a*) the gross amount of the payment,

(*b*) the amount of tax deducted, and

(*c*) the actual amount paid.

(4) Condition B is that the statement is in writing—

(*a*) showing—

(i) the gross amount of the distribution made to the participant,

(ii) the number and class of units held by the participant in respect of which the distribution is made,

(iii) the net amount of the distribution per unit,

(iv) whether any tax has been deducted from the distribution, and

(v) the date the distribution was made;

(*b*) providing details to allow the participant to access an electronic means of calculating the amounts that would be shown in a statement provided in accordance with condition A; and

(*c*) providing the participant with an alternative method of obtaining the details of those amounts without recourse to electronic means.

(5) If an appropriate statement for the purposes of section 234A of ICTA is provided by the company in accordance with regulation 70(4) and (5)—

(*a*) condition A does not apply, and

(*b*) the statement required by condition B must be included in the appropriate statement.

(6) Where paragraph (5) applies, "distribution" in regulation 70(4) and (5) shall be taken to include the property income distribution and the statement must show the percentage of the gross distribution attributable to the property income distribution.][1]

Amendments—[1] Regulation substituted by the Authorised Investment Funds (Tax) (Amendment) Regulations, SI 2009/2036 regs 2, 23 with effect from 1 September 2009.

[69Z35 Company's duty to deliver amended return

(1) This regulation applies if an open-ended investment company to which this Part applies makes a distribution, and then becomes aware that—

(*a*) anything which should have been included in a return delivered by the company under these Regulations has not been so included,

(*b*) anything which should not have been included in a return delivered by the company under these Regulations has been so included, or

(*c*) any other error has occurred in a return delivered by the company under these Regulations.

(2) The company must deliver an amended return correcting the error to an officer of Revenue and Customs without delay.

(3) If the company delivers an amended return such assessments, adjustments, setoffs or payments or repayments of tax as are necessary for achieving the objective mentioned in paragraph (4) must be made.

(4) The objective is that the resulting liabilities to income and corporation tax (including interest on unpaid or overpaid tax) of the company or any other person are the same as they would have been if a correct return had been delivered.][1]

Amendments—[1] Part 4 (regs 69A–69Z41) inserted by the Authorised Investment Funds (Tax) (Amendment) Regulations, SI 2008/705 regs 2, 5 with effect from 6 April 2008.

[CHAPTER 7

LEAVING THE PROPERTY AIF REGIME

69Z36 Termination by notice: company

(1) This regulation applies if an open-ended investment company to which this Part applies gives a notice under this regulation specifying a date at the end of which this Part is to cease to apply to the company.

(2) This Part shall cease to apply to the company at the end of that date.

(3) A notice under paragraph (1) must be given in writing to the Commissioners.

(4) The date specified under paragraph (1) must be after the date on which the Commissioners receive the notice.][1]

Amendments—[1] Part 4 (regs 69A–69Z41) inserted by the Authorised Investment Funds (Tax) (Amendment) Regulations, SI 2008/705 regs 2, 5 with effect from 6 April 2008.

[69Z37 Termination by notice: Commissioners

(1) This regulation applies if the Commissioners give a notice in writing under this paragraph to an open-ended investment company to which this Part applies (a "termination notice").

(2) This Part shall cease to apply to the company.

(3) The Commissioners may give a termination notice only if—

(*a*) a provision contained in this Part provides that the Commissioners may give a termination notice,

(*b*) there is an intentional or negligent breach of a condition in Chapter 2, or

(*c*) there is an attempt to gain a tax advantage to which regulation 69Z10 applies.

(4) A termination notice must state the reason for it.

(5) If a termination notice is given to an open-ended investment company, this Part shall be taken to have ceased to apply to the open-ended investment company at the end of the accounting period before the accounting period during which the event occurs (or the last event occurs) which caused the Commissioners to give the notice.][1]

Amendments—[1] Part 4 (regs 69A–69Z41) inserted by the Authorised Investment Funds (Tax) (Amendment) Regulations, SI 2008/705 regs 2, 5 with effect from 6 April 2008.

[69Z38 Appeal against termination notice

(1) An open-ended investment company to which a termination notice is given may appeal . . .[2].

(2) The notice of appeal must be given to HM Revenue and Customs within a period of 28 days beginning with the day on which the termination notice is given.

(3) On an appeal [that is notified to the tribunal, the tribunal][2] shall determine whether it was just and reasonable for HM Revenue and Customs to give the termination notice.

(4) If [the tribunal decides][2] that it was, [the tribunal must][2] confirm the notice.

(5) If [the tribunal decides][2] that it was not, [the tribunal must][2] set aside the notice.][1]

Amendments—[1] Part 4 (regs 69A–69Z41) inserted by the Authorised Investment Funds (Tax) (Amendment) Regulations, SI 2008/705 regs 2, 5 with effect from 6 April 2008.

[2] In para (1), words revoked, in paras (3), (4), (5), words substituted, by the Transfer of Tribunal Functions and Revenue and Customs Appeals Order, SI 2009/56 art 3, Sch 2 paras 154, 158 with effect from 1 April 2009.

[69Z39 Company ceasing to be authorised etc

(1) This regulation applies if an open-ended investment company to which this Part applies—

(*a*) ceases to be authorised by the Financial Services Authority,

(*b*) ceases to be an open-ended investment company, or

(*c*) ceases to carry on property investment business.

(2) This Part shall cease to apply to the company at the end of the date on which the company ceases to be authorised by the Financial Services Authority, to be an open-ended investment company, or to carry on property investment business (as the case may be).][1]

Amendments—[1] Part 4 (regs 69A–69Z41) inserted by the Authorised Investment Funds (Tax) (Amendment) Regulations, SI 2008/705 regs 2, 5 with effect from 6 April 2008.

[69Z40 Mergers

(1) This regulation applies if an open-ended investment company to which this Part applies—

(*a*) is party to a merger or takeover, and

(*b*) as a result, ceases to meet one or more of the conditions for this Part to apply.

(2) On the occurrence of the merger or takeover—

(*a*) an accounting period of the company shall end at the end of the date of the merger or takeover, and

(*b*) this Part shall cease to apply to the company at the end of that date.][1]

Amendments—[1] Part 4 (regs 69A–69Z41) inserted by the Authorised Investment Funds (Tax) (Amendment) Regulations, SI 2008/705 regs 2, 5 with effect from 6 April 2008.

[69Z41 Effects of cessation

(1) The business of F (tax-exempt) shall be treated for the purposes of corporation tax as ceasing immediately before cessation.

(2) Assets which immediately before cessation are involved in the business of F (tax-exempt) shall be treated for the purposes of corporation tax as being sold by F (tax-exempt) immediately before cessation and reacquired immediately after cessation by F (post-cessation).

(3) For the purposes of corporation tax, on cessation one accounting period of F (residual) shall end and an accounting period of F (post-cessation) shall begin.

(4) The sale and reacquisition deemed under paragraph (2) shall not have effect for the purposes of tax in respect of chargeable gains.

(5) For the purposes of CAA 2001, the sale and re-acquisition deemed under paragraph (2)—

(*a*) shall not give rise to allowances or charges, and

(*b*) shall not make it possible to make an election under section 198 or 199 of that Act (apportionment).

(6) For the purposes of CAA 2001, anything done by or to F (tax-exempt) before cessation in relation to an asset which is deemed under paragraph (2) to be sold and re-acquired shall be treated after cessation as having been done by or to F (post-cessation).][1]

Amendments—[1] Part 4 (regs 69A–69Z41) inserted by the Authorised Investment Funds (Tax) (Amendment) Regulations, SI 2008/705 regs 2, 5 with effect from 6 April 2008.

[PART 4B
TAX ELECTED FUNDS

CHAPTER 1
PRELIMINARY PROVISIONS

69Z42 Tax Elected Funds

(1) This Part makes provision in relation to an authorised investment fund which meets the conditions in regulations 69Z45 to 69Z48.

(2) In these Regulations an authorised investment fund to which this Part applies may be referred to as a "Tax Elected Fund".][1]

Amendments—[1] Part 4B (regs 69Z42– 69Z73) inserted by the Authorised Investment Funds (Tax) (Amendment) Regulations, SI 2009/2036 regs 2, 24 with effect from 1 September 2009.

[69Z43 Structure of this Part

The structure of this Part is as follows—

this Chapter contains preliminary provisions;

Chapter 2 deals with entry into and membership of the Tax Elected Funds regime;

Chapter 3 deals with the tax treatment of Tax Elected Funds;

Chapter 4 deals with distributions made by Tax Elected Funds;

Chapter 5 deals with the treatment of participants in Tax Elected Funds;

Chapter 6 deals with compliance in relation to the Tax Elected Funds regime; and

Chapter 7 contains provisions relating to an authorised investment fund's leaving the Tax Elected Funds regime.][1]

Amendments—[1] Part 4B (regs 69Z42– 69Z73) inserted by the Authorised Investment Funds (Tax) (Amendment) Regulations, SI 2009/2036 regs 2, 24 with effect from 1 September 2009.

[69Z44 Interpretation

In this Part—

"entry" means the time when this Part begins to apply to an authorised investment fund;

"cessation" means the time when this Part ceases to apply to an authorised investment fund;
"overseas property business" has the meaning given in section 206 of CTA 2009;
"UK property business" has the meaning given in section 205 of CTA 2009.][1]

Amendments—[1] Part 4B (regs 69Z42– 69Z73) inserted by the Authorised Investment Funds (Tax) (Amendment) Regulations, SI 2009/2036 regs 2, 24 with effect from 1 September 2009.

[CHAPTER 2

ENTRY INTO AND MEMBERSHIP OF THE TAX ELECTED FUNDS REGIME

CONDITIONS OF MEMBERSHIP OF THE TAX ELECTED FUNDS REGIME

69Z45 Conditions for this Part to apply to fund

In order for this Part to apply to an authorised investment fund in respect of an accounting period—

(*a*) the following conditions (the "TEF conditions") must be met—

(i) the property condition (see regulation 69Z46);

(ii) the genuine diversity of ownership condition (see regulation 9A);

(iii) the loan creditor condition (see regulation 694Z47); and

(iv) the scheme documentation condition (see regulation 69Z48); and

(*b*) an application for this Part to apply must be accepted by HM Revenue and Customs (see regulations 69Z49 to 69Z53).[1]

Amendments—[1] Part 4B (regs 69Z42– 69Z73) inserted by the Authorised Investment Funds (Tax) (Amendment) Regulations, SI 2009/2036 regs 2, 24 with effect from 1 September 2009.

THE TEF CONDITIONS

69Z46 The property condition

The property condition is that the authorised investment fund does not have a UK property business or an overseas property business.[1]

Amendments—[1] Part 4B (regs 69Z42– 69Z73) inserted by the Authorised Investment Funds (Tax) (Amendment) Regulations, SI 2009/2036 regs 2, 24 with effect from 1 September 2009.

[69Z47 The loan creditor condition

(1) The loan creditor condition is that the authorised investment fund must meet conditions A to C throughout the accounting period in the case of any loan relationship to which the fund is party as a debtor.

(2) Condition A is that, in the case of a debtor relationship of the fund, the person standing in the position of a creditor as respects the debt in question is not entitled to an amount by way of interest which depends to any extent on—

(*a*) the results of all or part of the authorised investment fund's business, or

(*b*) the value of any of the fund's assets.

(3) For the purposes of condition A, a loan shall not be treated as dependent on the results of the fund's business by reason only that the terms of the loan provide—

(*a*) for the interest to be reduced in the event of results improving, or

(*b*) for the interest to be increased in the event of results deteriorating.

(4) Condition B is that, in the case of a debtor relationship of the fund, the person standing in the position of a creditor as respects the debt in question is not entitled to an amount by way of interest which exceeds a reasonable commercial return on the consideration lent.

(5) Condition C is that, in the case of a debtor relationship of the fund, the person standing in the position of a creditor as respects the debt in question is entitled on repayment to an amount which—

(*a*) does not exceed the consideration lent, or

(*b*) is reasonably comparable with the amount generally repayable (in respect of an equal amount of consideration) under the terms of issue of securities listed on a recognised stock exchange.

(6) In this regulation "loan relationship" and "debtor relationship" shall be construed in accordance with Part 5 of CTA 2009 (loan relationships).][1]

Amendments—[1] Part 4B (regs 69Z42– 69Z73) inserted by the Authorised Investment Funds (Tax) (Amendment) Regulations, SI 2009/2036 regs 2, 24 with effect from 1 September 2009.

[69Z48 The scheme documentation condition

The scheme documentation condition is that the instrument constituting the authorised investment fund and its prospectus must include provisions which require the fund to meet the property condition and the loan creditor condition on entry and throughout the accounting period.[1]

Amendments—[1] Part 4B (regs 69Z42– 69Z73) inserted by the Authorised Investment Funds (Tax) (Amendment) Regulations, SI 2009/2036 regs 2, 24 with effect from 1 September 2009.

[APPLICATION FOR THIS PART TO APPLY

69Z49 Application process

(1) An application for this Part to apply to an authorised investment fund may be made by—

(*a*) the manager of an existing authorised investment fund, or

(*b*) if it is proposed to establish an authorised investment fund, the person expected to become the manager of the fund once established (the "applicant").

(2) Before making an application in relation to an existing authorised investment fund, the fund must obtain any necessary shareholder or unit holder approval and must have applied for any necessary regulatory approval in respect of the instrument constituting the fund and the prospectus.

(3) The manager or applicant must notify HM Revenue and Customs when any necessary regulatory authorisation has been given.

(4) Where in relation to an existing authorised investment fund this Part has previously applied to the fund—

(*a*) no application may be made if a termination notice was issued in relation to the fund, or

(*b*) if an election was made under regulation 69Z70 that this Part should cease to apply, no application can be made in relation to any accounting period which begins within six years of the cessation.

(5) In this Part—

"applicant" means the person referred to in paragraph (1)(*b*);

"application" means an application under this regulation;

"existing fund application" means an application made under paragraph (1)(*a*); and

"future fund application" means an application made under paragraph (1)(*b*).][1]

Amendments—[1] Part 4B (regs 69Z42– 69Z73) inserted by the Authorised Investment Funds (Tax) (Amendment) Regulations, SI 2009/2036 regs 2, 24 with effect from 1 September 2009.

[69Z50 Form and timing of application under regulation 69Z49

(1) An application must be made in writing to the Commissioners.

(2) An existing fund application must be received by HM Revenue and Customs at least 28 days before the beginning of the specified accounting period (see regulation 69Z51(2)).
This is subject to paragraph (8).

(3) A future fund application must be received by HM Revenue and Customs at least 42 days before the date the fund is expected to be established and authorisation given.
This is subject to paragraph (9).

(4) Within a period of 28 days (or 14 days in the case of an application within paragraph (8) or (9)) beginning on the day on which the application is received, HM Revenue and Customs must—

(*a*) notify the manager or applicant that the application is accepted, or

(*b*) issue a refusal notice.

(5) An application may be withdrawn or amended at any time before it is accepted—

(*a*) by the manager (in the case of an existing fund application), or

(*b*) by the applicant (in the case of a future fund application).

(6) If an application is amended before it is accepted, regulation 69Z49 shall apply to the amended application.

(7) But if HM Revenue and Customs give notice that they are satisfied that the amended application is valid, the amended application shall take effect as if made on the date of the original application.

(8) An existing fund application may be received by HM Revenue and Customs at least 14 days before the beginning of the specified accounting period if—

(*a*) HM Revenue and Customs have given clearance under regulation 9B, and

(*b*) the manager of the authorised investment fund certifies that there have been no changes in substance between—

(i) the form in which the instrument constituting the fund and its prospectus were considered by HM Revenue and Customs before giving the clearance, and

(ii) the form in which it is proposed that those documents will apply at the beginning of the specified accounting period.

(9) A future fund application may be received by HM Revenue and Customs at least 14 days before the proposed fund is authorised and established if—

(*a*) HM Revenue and Customs have given clearance under regulation 9B, and

(*b*) the applicant certifies that there have been no changes in substance between—

(i) the form in which the instrument constituting the fund and its prospectus were considered by HM Revenue and Customs before giving the clearance, and

(ii) the form in which it is proposed that those documents will apply at the time when the proposed fund is authorised.][1]

Amendments—[1] Part 4B (regs 69Z42– 69Z73) inserted by the Authorised Investment Funds (Tax) (Amendment) Regulations, SI 2009/2036 regs 2, 24 with effect from 1 September 2009.

[69Z51 Contents of application under regulation 69Z49

(1) An application must include the following information.

(2) An existing fund application must specify the accounting period from the beginning of which the application seeks to apply this Part to the fund (the "specified accounting period").

(3) An existing fund application must be accompanied by—

(*a*) a statement by the manager of the authorised investment fund that the TEF conditions are reasonably expected to be met in respect of the fund throughout the specified accounting period;

(*b*) the following documents relating to the fund—

(i) the instrument constituting the fund, and

(ii) its prospectus;

(*c*) a statement by the manager as to whether or not this Part has previously applied to the fund and where this Part has previously applied that statement must include—

(i) the dates of entry and cessation, and

(ii) a statement by the manager that a termination notice has never been issued in respect of the fund;

(*d*) a statement by the manager that either—

(i) shareholder or unit holder consent to the application is not required, or

(ii) shareholder or unit holder consent has been given, in which case the statement must specify the date of the shareholder or unit holder resolution giving consent;

(*e*) a copy of the application to the Financial Services Authority for approval for any changes in the instrument constituting the fund and its prospectus; and

(*f*) copies of any documents accompanying the application mentioned in sub-paragraph (*e*) to the extent that those documents do not fall within sub-paragraphs (*a*) to (*d*).

(4) A future fund application must specify the date it is expected the fund will be established and authorisation given and seek to apply this Part to the proposed fund from that date.

(5) A future fund application must be accompanied by—

(*a*) a statement by the applicant that the TEF conditions are reasonably expected to be met in respect of the proposed fund throughout its first accounting period;

(*b*) the following documents relating to the proposed fund—

(i) the proposed instrument constituting the fund, and

(ii) its . . .[2] prospectus . . .[2];

(*c*) a copy of the application to the Financial Services Authority for authorisation of the proposed fund as an authorised investment fund; and

(*d*) copies of any documents accompanying the application mentioned in sub-paragraph (*c*) to the extent that those documents do not fall within sub-paragraphs (*a*) and (*b*).][1]

Amendments—[1] Part 4B (regs 69Z42– 69Z73) inserted by the Authorised Investment Funds (Tax) (Amendment) Regulations, SI 2009/2036 regs 2, 24 with effect from 1 September 2009.

[2] In para (5)(b)(ii), words revoked by the Authorised Investment Funds (Tax) (Amendment) Regulations, SI 2010/294, regs 2, 23, with effect from 6 March 2010 (see reg 1(2)).

[PROCEDURAL MATTERS RELATING TO THE MAKING OF APPLICATIONS FOR THIS PART TO APPLY

69Z52 Refusing an application: refusal notice

(1) If any of conditions A to C are met HM Revenue and Customs must refuse the application and give a notice (a "refusal notice")—

(*a*) to the manager of the authorised investment fund if an existing fund application has been made, or

(*b*) to the applicant if a future fund application has been made.

(2) Condition A is that—

(*a*) the documents supplied do not demonstrate that the authorised investment fund (or the proposed authorised investment fund) will meet all the TEF conditions, or

(*b*) the statement given in accordance with regulation 69Z51(3)(*a*) or (5)(*a*) does not demonstrate that the fund (or proposed fund) can reasonably be expected to meet all the TEF conditions throughout the specified accounting period or the first accounting period.

(3) Condition B is that the application is not accompanied by the documents and statements specified in regulation 69Z51(3) in the case of an existing fund application or regulation 69Z51(5) in the case of a future fund application.

(4) Condition C is that any necessary shareholder, unit holder or regulatory authorisation or approval has not been given.

(5) A refusal notice must specify the reason for refusing the application.][1]

Amendments—[1] Part 4B (regs 69Z42– 69Z73) inserted by the Authorised Investment Funds (Tax) (Amendment) Regulations, SI 2009/2036 regs 2, 24 with effect from 1 September 2009.

[69Z53 Appeal against refusal notice

(1) A person to whom a refusal notice is given may appeal.

(2) The notice of appeal must be given to HM Revenue and Customs within a period of 28 days beginning with the day on which the refusal notice is given.

(3) On an appeal that is notified to the tribunal, the tribunal shall determine whether it was just and reasonable for HM Revenue and Customs to give the refusal notice.

(4) If the tribunal allow the appeal—

(*a*) they may direct that this Part shall apply to the authorised investment fund (or, as the case may be, to the proposed authorised investment fund), and

(*b*) they may specify the date from which this Part shall so apply.

(5) The date mentioned in paragraph (4)(*b*)—

(*a*) must not be earlier than the beginning of the specified accounting period if an existing fund application has been made, and

(*b*) must not be earlier than the date of authorisation by the Financial Services Authority if a future fund application has been made.][1]

Amendments—[1] Part 4B (regs 69Z42– 69Z73) inserted by the Authorised Investment Funds (Tax) (Amendment) Regulations, SI 2009/2036 regs 2, 24 with effect from 1 September 2009.

[CONSEQUENCES OF ENTRY

69Z54 Effects of entry

On entry a new distribution period of the authorised investment fund shall begin.][1]

Amendments—[1] Part 4B (regs 69Z42– 69Z73) inserted by the Authorised Investment Funds (Tax) (Amendment) Regulations, SI 2009/2036 regs 2, 24 with effect from 1 September 2009.

[69Z55 Duration

Once this Part has begun to apply to an authorised investment fund it shall continue to apply unless and until it ceases to apply in accordance with Chapter 7 of this Part.][1]

Amendments—[1] Part 4B (regs 69Z42– 69Z73) inserted by the Authorised Investment Funds (Tax) (Amendment) Regulations, SI 2009/2036 regs 2, 24 with effect from 1 September 2009.

[CHAPTER 3

THE TAX TREATMENT OF TAX ELECTED FUNDS

69Z56 Components of income

(1) For the purposes of corporation tax, the income arising to a Tax Elected Fund consists of—

(*a*) dividend income;

(*b*) property investment income, being—

(i) distributions of profits of C (tax-exempt) in relation to shares held in a UK-REIT, and

(ii) property income distributions in relation to shares held in a Property AIF;

(*c*) property business income (arising on a breach of the property condition), being—

(i) profits of a UK property business that are not within sub-paragraph (*b*), and

(ii) income from an overseas property business; and

(*d*) other income.

(2) In this regulation, "C (tax-exempt)" shall be construed in accordance with Part 4 of FA 2006.][1]

Amendments—[1] Part 4B (regs 69Z42– 69Z73) inserted by the Authorised Investment Funds (Tax) (Amendment) Regulations, SI 2009/2036 regs 2, 24 with effect from 1 September 2009.

[69Z57 Treatment of property investment income

(1) Section 7(2) of ICTA (treatment of certain payments and repayments of income tax: set off of tax) shall not apply to payments of property investment income.

(2) Property investment income arising to a Tax Elected Fund shall be treated for the purposes of the Tax Acts as a distribution that is exempt for the purposes of Part 9A of CTA 2009 (company distributions) but shall not be treated as franked investment income.][1]

Amendments—[1] Part 4B (regs 69Z42– 69Z73) inserted by the Authorised Investment Funds (Tax) (Amendment) Regulations, SI 2009/2036 regs 2, 24 with effect from 1 September 2009.

[69Z58 Treatment of distributions

Section 931R of CTA 2009 (election that distribution should not be exempt) shall not apply in relation to distributions received by a Tax Elected Fund.][1]

Amendments—[1] Part 4B (regs 69Z42– 69Z73) inserted by the Authorised Investment Funds (Tax) (Amendment) Regulations, SI 2009/2036 regs 2, 24 with effect from 1 September 2009.

[CHAPTER 4

DISTRIBUTIONS MADE BY TAX ELECTED FUNDS

69Z59 [Allocation of income]

[(1) The total amount available for income allocation in a Tax Elected Fund shall be attributed as follows.][2]

(2) There shall be attributed to TEF distributions (dividends)—

(*a*) dividend income,

(*b*) property investment income, and

(*c*) property business income.

(3) Other income shall be attributed to TEF distributions (non-dividend).][1]

Amendments—[1] Part 4B (regs 69Z42–69Z73) inserted by the Authorised Investment Funds (Tax) (Amendment) Regulations, SI 2009/2036 regs 2, 24 with effect from 1 September 2009.

[2] Heading substituted, and para (1) substituted, by the Authorised Investment Funds (Tax) (Amendment) Regulations, SI 2010/294, regs 2, 18, with effect from 6 March 2010, but see regs 24–26 for transitional provisions relating to distribution dates for earlier accounting periods, and entry into the FINROF regime (see reg 1(2)).

[69Z60 TEF distributions (dividends)

(1) This regulation applies if—

(*a*) a Tax Elected Fund makes a distribution, and

(*b*) the amount distributed includes sums attributed to TEF distributions (dividends).

(2) The Tax Acts shall have effect as if the sums were dividends on shares paid on the distribution date by the fund to the participants in proportion to their rights.

(3) In this Part a "TEF distribution (dividend)" means a sum attributed to TEF distributions (dividends) which is distributed (including a dividend treated as paid to a participant who is not chargeable to corporation tax).

(4) This regulation is subject to regulation 23 (treatment of de minimis amounts).][1]

Amendments—[1] Part 4B (regs 69Z42–69Z73) inserted by the Authorised Investment Funds (Tax) (Amendment) Regulations, SI 2009/2036 regs 2, 24 with effect from 1 September 2009.

[69Z61 TEF distributions (non-dividend)

(1) This regulation applies if—

(*a*) a Tax Elected Fund makes a distribution, and

(*b*) the amount distributed includes sums attributed to TEF distributions (non-dividend).

(2) The Tax Acts shall have effect as if the sums were payments of yearly interest made on the distribution date by the fund to the participants in proportion to their rights.

(3) In these Regulations a "TEF distribution (non-dividend)" means a sum attributed to TEF distributions (non-dividend) which is distributed (including a payment made to a participant who is not chargeable to income tax).

(4) This regulation is subject to regulation 23 (treatment of de minimis amounts).][1]

Amendments—[1] Part 4B (regs 69Z42–69Z73) inserted by the Authorised Investment Funds (Tax) (Amendment) Regulations, SI 2009/2036 regs 2, 24 with effect from 1 September 2009.

[CHAPTER 5

THE TREATMENT OF PARTICIPANTS IN TAX ELECTED FUNDS

TEF DISTRIBUTION (DIVIDEND)

69Z62 Participants chargeable to corporation tax

(1) If a TEF distribution (dividend) is made for a distribution period to a participant within the charge to corporation tax, regulations 48 to 52A (dividend distributions) shall apply with the modifications specified in paragraph (2).

(2) The specified modifications are—

(*a*) for "dividend distribution" in each place it occurs there shall be substituted "TEF distribution (dividend)";

[(*b*) in regulation 50 (references to gross income) for "the net revenue before taxation shall be determined in accordance with the Statement of Recommended Practice" there shall be substituted "the amount attributed to TEF distributions (dividends) in accordance with regulation 69Z59 (allocation of income);][2]

(*c*) for "an authorised investment fund" in each place it occurs there shall be substituted "a Tax Elected Fund"; and

(*d*) for "the authorised investment fund" in each place it occurs there shall be substituted "the Tax Elected Fund".][1]

Amendments—[1] Part 4B (regs 69Z42–69Z73) inserted by the Authorised Investment Funds (Tax) (Amendment) Regulations, SI 2009/2036 regs 2, 24 with effect from 1 September 2009.

[2] Para (2)(*b*) substituted by the Authorised Investment Funds (Tax) (Amendment) Regulations, SI 2010/294, regs 2, 19, with effect from 6 March 2010, but see regs 24–26 for transitional provisions relating to distribution dates for earlier accounting periods, and entry into the FINROF regime (see reg 1(2)).

[TEF DISTRIBUTIONS (NON-DIVIDEND)

69Z63 Obligation to deduct tax from TEF distributions (non-dividend)

(1) If a TEF distribution (non-dividend) is made for a distribution period to a participant within the charge to income tax, regulations 26 to 33 (deduction of tax from interest distributions: general) shall apply with the modification specified in paragraph (3).

(2) If a TEF distribution (non-dividend) is made for a distribution period to a participant within the charge to corporation tax, regulation 47 (the obligation to deduct tax) shall apply with the modification specified in paragraph (3).

(3) The modification specified is that for "interest distribution" in each place it occurs there shall be substituted "TEF distribution (non-dividend)".][1]

Amendments—[1] Part 4B (regs 69Z42– 69Z73) inserted by the Authorised Investment Funds (Tax) (Amendment) Regulations, SI 2009/2036 regs 2, 24 with effect from 1 September 2009.

[69Z64 Modification of section 490 of CTA 2009

Section 490 of CTA 2009 (holdings in OEICs, unit trusts and offshore funds treated as creditor relationship rights) shall apply to a participant in a TEF as if in subsections (4) and (5) for "interest distribution" there were substituted "TEF distribution (non-dividend)".][1]

Amendments—[1] Part 4B (regs 69Z42– 69Z73) inserted by the Authorised Investment Funds (Tax) (Amendment) Regulations, SI 2009/2036 regs 2, 24 with effect from 1 September 2009.

[CHAPTER 6

COMPLIANCE IN RELATION TO THE TAX ELECTED FUNDS REGIME

BREACHES OF TEF CONDITIONS

69Z65 Breach of conditions: general

(1) This regulation applies if a Tax Elected Fund—

(*a*) does not meet one of the TEF conditions, and

(*b*) becomes aware that it does not meet the condition.

(2) Within 28 days of becoming aware of the breach, the fund must provide the following information to the Commissioners—

(*a*) the date on which the condition first ceased to be met;

(*b*) the date on which the fund became aware of the breach;

(*c*) details of the condition that was breached;

(*d*) the nature of the breach;

(*e*) the steps the fund proposes to take to rectify the breach;

(*f*) the date by which the fund proposes to rectify the breach; and

(*g*) where there has been a previous breach of the TEF conditions, details of the condition that was breached on that occasion, the date of that breach and the date that breach was rectified.

(3) The date referred to in paragraph (2)(*f*) must be the earliest date by which the objective of complying with the relevant condition may reasonably be achieved.

(4) The Commissioners must give a termination notice to the fund if—

(*a*) the steps that the fund proposes to take will not rectify the breach;

(*b*) the date by which the fund proposes to rectify the breach is not the earliest date by which the objective of remedying the relevant condition may reasonably be achieved;

(*c*) the fund is intentionally or negligently in breach of a condition; or

(*d*) there are three breaches of the same TEF condition in a period of ten years beginning with the first day of the accounting period in which the fund becomes aware of the first of those breaches.][1]

Amendments—[1] Part 4B (regs 69Z42– 69Z73) inserted by the Authorised Investment Funds (Tax) (Amendment) Regulations, SI 2009/2036 regs 2, 24 with effect from 1 September 2009.

[69Z66 Breach of the property condition, genuine diversity of ownership condition or scheme documentation condition

(1) This regulation applies if a Tax Elected Fund is in breach of the property condition, genuine diversity of ownership condition or scheme documentation condition.

(2) If the fund is inadvertently in breach but rectifies the breach within a reasonable time of the fund becoming aware of the breach, this Part shall continue to apply to the fund despite the breach (but see regulations 69Z65(4)(*d*) and 69Z68).

(3) If the fund is inadvertently in breach but does not rectify the breach within a reasonable time of the fund first becoming aware of the breach, the Commissioners must give a termination notice to the fund.][1]

Amendments—[1] Part 4B (regs 69Z42– 69Z73) inserted by the Authorised Investment Funds (Tax) (Amendment) Regulations, SI 2009/2036 regs 2, 24 with effect from 1 September 2009.

[69Z67 Breach of the loan creditor condition

(1) This regulation applies if a Tax Elected Fund is in breach of the loan creditor condition.

(2) If the fund is inadvertently in breach but rectifies the breach within a period of 28 days beginning with the day on which the fund first becomes aware of the breach, this Part shall continue to apply to the fund despite the breach (but see paragraph (4) and regulations 69Z65(4)(*d*) and 69Z68).

(3) If the fund is inadvertently in breach but does not rectify the breach within a period of 28 days beginning with the day on which the fund first becomes aware of the breach, the Commissioners must give a termination notice to the fund.

(4) If the fund is in breach of the same condition specified in paragraphs (2) to (5) of regulation 69Z47 in two different accounting periods in a period of ten years beginning with the first day of the accounting period in which the fund becomes aware of the first of those breaches, the Commissioners must give a termination notice to the fund.][1]

Amendments—[1] Part 4B (regs 69Z42– 69Z73) inserted by the Authorised Investment Funds (Tax) (Amendment) Regulations, SI 2009/2036 regs 2, 24 with effect from 1 September 2009.

[69Z68 Multiple breaches of separate conditions

The Commissioners must give a termination notice to a Tax Elected Fund if—

(*a*) there has been a breach of at least two of the TEF conditions, and

(*b*) there have been four breaches in a period of ten years beginning with the first day of the accounting period in which the first breach occurs.][1]

Amendments—[1] Part 4B (regs 69Z42– 69Z73) inserted by the Authorised Investment Funds (Tax) (Amendment) Regulations, SI 2009/2036 regs 2, 24 with effect from 1 September 2009.

[INFORMATION ABOUT POSSIBLE BREACHES OF THE TEF CONDITIONS

69Z69 Information to be provided to officers of Revenue and Customs

(1) This regulation applies if an officer of Revenue and Customs thinks that a Tax Elected Fund—

(*a*) does not meet, or may not meet, one of the TEF conditions, or

(*b*) has not rectified a breach of such a condition.

(2) The officer may serve a notice (an "information notice") on the manager of the fund requiring the manager to provide any of the information specified in regulation 69Z65(2) within a specified period.

(4) If the manager does not comply with the information notice within the specified period the Commissioners must give a termination notice.

(5) In this regulation the specified period is a period of 28 days beginning with the day on which the notice is served or, on an application by the manager, such longer period as the officer of Revenue and Customs thinks is reasonable.][1]

Amendments—[1] Part 4B (regs 69Z42– 69Z73) inserted by the Authorised Investment Funds (Tax) (Amendment) Regulations, SI 2009/2036 regs 2, 24 with effect from 1 September 2009.

[CHAPTER 7

LEAVING THE TAX ELECTED FUNDS REGIME

69Z70 Termination by election: authorised investment fund

(1) This regulation applies if a Tax Elected Fund gives a notice under this regulation electing that this Part is to cease to apply to the fund at the end of a specified accounting period.

(2) This Part shall cease to apply to the fund at the end of that accounting period.

(3) A notice under paragraph (1) must—

(*a*) be given in writing to the Commissioners,

(*b*) be given before the end of the accounting period specified in paragraph (1), and

(*c*) give the reasons for the fund leaving the TEF regime.][1]

Amendments—[1] Part 4B (regs 69Z42– 69Z73) inserted by the Authorised Investment Funds (Tax) (Amendment) Regulations, SI 2009/2036 regs 2, 24 with effect from 1 September 2009.

69Z71 [Termination by notice: Commissioners

(1) This regulation applies if the Commissioners give a notice in writing under this paragraph to a Tax Elected Fund (a "termination notice").

(2) This Part shall cease to apply to the fund.

(3) The Commissioners may give a termination notice only if a provision contained in this Part provides that the Commissioners must give a termination notice.

(4) A termination notice must state the reason for it.

(5) If a termination notice is given to an authorised investment fund, this Part shall be taken to have ceased to apply to the fund at the end of the accounting period immediately preceding the accounting period in which the notice was given.

(6) But regulations 13 (treatment of interest distributions for the purpose of loan relationships), 69Z61 (TEF distributions (non-dividend)) and 69Z63 (obligation to deduct tax from TEF distributions (non-dividend)) shall apply in relation to any TEF distribution (non-dividend) made before the notice was given.][1]

Amendments—[1] Part 4B (regs 69Z42– 69Z73) inserted by the Authorised Investment Funds (Tax) (Amendment) Regulations, SI 2009/2036 regs 2, 24 with effect from 1 September 2009.

69Z72 [Appeal against termination notice

(1) An authorised investment fund to which a termination notice is given may appeal.

(2) The notice of appeal must be given to HM Revenue and Customs within a period of 28 days beginning with the day on which the termination notice is given.

(3) On an appeal that is notified to the tribunal, the tribunal shall determine whether it was just and reasonable for HM Revenue and Customs to give the termination notice.

(4) If they decide that it was, they must confirm the notice.
(5) If they decide that it was not, they must set aside the notice.][1]

Amendments—[1] Part 4B (regs 69Z42– 69Z73) inserted by the Authorised Investment Funds (Tax) (Amendment) Regulations, SI 2009/2036 regs 2, 24 with effect from 1 September 2009.

69Z73 [Mergers

(1) This regulation applies if a Tax Elected Fund—
 (*a*) is party to a merger or takeover, and
 (*b*) as a result, ceases to meet one or more of the TEF conditions.
(2) On the occurrence of the merger or takeover—
 (*a*) an accounting period of the fund shall end at the end of the date of the merger or takeover, and
 (*b*) this Part shall cease to apply to the fund at the end of that date.][1]

Amendments—[1] Part 4B (regs 69Z42– 69Z73) inserted by the Authorised Investment Funds (Tax) (Amendment) Regulations, SI 2009/2036 regs 2, 24 with effect from 1 September 2009.

PART 5
COMPLIANCE

INFORMATION RELATING TO DISTRIBUTIONS

70 Application of section 234A of ICTA

(1) Section 234A of ICTA (information relating to distributions) applies in relation to an authorised investment fund with any necessary modifications.
(2) In the appropriate statement sent under that section to a participant within the charge to corporation tax, the legal owner of the authorised investment fund must include a statement showing the legal owner's net liability to corporation tax in respect of the gross income.
(3) In paragraph (2)—
 "gross income" has the same meaning as in regulation 50, and
 "net liability to corporation tax" is to be construed in accordance with regulation 49(3).
[(4) In the case of a Property AIF and a Tax Elected Fund, an appropriate statement for the purposes of section 234A of ICTA includes a written statement—
 (*a*) showing the details specified in paragraph (5),
 (*b*) providing details to allow the participant to access an electronic means of calculating the amounts that would be shown in a written statement that would, apart from this paragraph, be provided in accordance with subsection (6) (in the case of a PAIF distribution (interest) or a TEF distribution (non-dividend)) or subsection (7) (in the case of a PAIF distribution (dividends) or a TEF distribution (dividend)) of section 234A, and
 (*c*) providing the participant with an alternative method of obtaining the details of those amounts without recourse to electronic means.
(5) The specified details are—
 (*a*) the gross amount of the distribution made to the participant,
 (*b*) the number and class of units held by the participant in respect of which the distribution is made,
 (*c*) the net amount of the distribution per unit,
 (*d*) whether any tax has been deducted from the distribution,
 (*e*) the date the distribution was made, and
 (*f*) the percentage of the gross distribution attributable—
  (i) in the case of a Property AIF, to PAIF distribution (interest) and to PAIF distribution (dividends), or
  (ii) in the case of a Tax Elected Fund, to TEF distribution (dividend) and to TEF distribution (non-dividend).][1]

Commentary—*Simon's Taxes* **D8.161.**

Amendments—[1] Paras (4), (5) inserted by the Authorised Investment Funds (Tax) (Amendment) Regulations, SI 2009/2036 regs 2, 25 with effect from 1 September 2009.

INTEREST DISTRIBUTIONS [AND TEF DISTRIBUTIONS (NON-DIVIDEND)]

Amendments—Words in heading inserted by the Authorised Investment Funds (Tax) (Amendment) Regulations, SI 2009/2036 regs 2, 26, 27 with effect from 1 September 2009.

71 Notification of interest distributions [and TEF distributions (non-dividend)] made without deduction of tax

(1) If, during a tax year, an authorised investment fund has made interest distributions [and TEF distributions (non-dividend)][1] without deduction of tax, the legal owner must give notice of that fact to the Commissioners within 14 days of the end of that tax year.
(2) Notice given under paragraph (1)—
 (*a*) must be in writing, and

(*b*) has effect for the tax year in which it is given and for subsequent tax years until the notice is withdrawn.

(3) An authorised investment fund that fails to comply with paragraph (1) is liable to a penalty not exceeding £3,000 determined in accordance with section 100 of TMA 1970.

(4) Sections 100A, 100B, 102, 103(4) and 118(2) of TMA 1970 apply to a penalty determined in accordance with paragraph (3).

Commentary—*Simon's Taxes* **D8.161.**

Amendments—[1] Words in cross-heading and in para (1) inserted by the Authorised Investment Funds (Tax) (Amendment) Regulations, SI 2009/2036 regs 2, 26, 27 with effect from 1 September 2009.

72 Information about interest distributions [and TEF distributions (non-dividend)] made without deduction of tax

(1) The Commissioners may by notice require a person specified in paragraph (2) to provide them with such information as they may reasonably require for the purpose of determining whether interest distributions [and TEF distributions (non-dividend)][1] were properly made by that person without deduction of tax.

(2) The persons specified are—

(*a*) an open-ended investment company;

(*b*) the authorised corporate director of an open-ended investment company;

(*c*) a trustee of an authorised unit trust.

(3) The information to be provided may include copies of any relevant books, documents or other records.

(4) The information must be provided within such time (not being less than 14 days) as may be specified in the notice.

Commentary—*Simon's Taxes* **D8.161.**

Amendments—[1] Words in cross-heading and in para (1) inserted, by the Authorised Investment Funds (Tax) (Amendment) Regulations, SI 2009/2036 regs 2, 26, 28 with effect from 1 September 2009.

73 Inspection of records

(1) A person specified in regulation 72(2) must, whenever required to do so, make available for inspection by an officer of the Commissioners authorised for that purpose, at such time as that officer may reasonably require, all such copies of books, documents or other records in their possession or under their control as may be required by the Commissioners under regulation 72.

(2) Every qualifying certificate supplied to a legal owner under Chapter 2 of Part 4 (participants chargeable to income tax) must be preserved by the legal owner in such manner as may be approved by the Commissioners for two years after it has ceased to be otherwise required under the provisions of these Regulations.

Commentary—*Simon's Taxes* **D8.161.**

74 Use of information

(1) Information obtained by the Commissioners under regulation 72 or 73—

(*a*) must not be used for the purpose of ascertaining the tax liability (if any) of any person other than the persons specified in paragraph (2), and

(*b*) must otherwise be used only for the purposes of these Regulations.

(2) The persons specified in this paragraph are—

(*a*) the open-ended investment company in question;

(*b*) the trustees of the authorised unit trust in question;

(*c*) a participant who is beneficially entitled to an interest distribution [or a TEF distribution (non-dividend)][1] made without deduction of tax to whom the information obtained relates;

(*d*) where the whole of an interest distribution [or a TEF distribution (non-dividend)][1] made to or received under a trust without deduction of tax is, or falls to be treated as, or under any provision of the Tax Acts is deemed to be, the income of a person other than the trustees of that trust, that person in so far as the information obtained relates to him; and

(*e*) where an interest distribution [or a TEF distribution (non-dividend)][1] is made to or received under a trust without deduction of tax and sub-paragraph (*d*) does not apply, the trustees of that trust and any beneficiary of the trust to whom the information obtained relates.

(3) In paragraph (2)(*e*) "any beneficiary of the trust" means—

(*a*) any person who is, or will or may become, entitled to any income of the trust, whether in the form of income or not, and

(*b*) any person to whom any such income may be paid, or for whose benefit any such income may be applied, whether in the form of income or not, in the exercise of a discretion by the trustees of the trust.

(4) Paragraph (1) does not prevent any disclosure of information authorised under section 182(5) of the Finance Act 1989.

Commentary—*Simon's Taxes* **D8.161.**

Amendments—[1] In paras (2)(*c*), (*d*), (*e*), words inserted, by the Authorised Investment Funds (Tax) (Amendment) Regulations, SI 2009/2036 regs 2, 29 with effect from 1 September 2009.

RESIDENCE DECLARATIONS

75 Inspection of residence declarations

(1) The legal owner of an authorised investment fund must, on being required to do so by a notice given by an officer of the Commissioners, make available for inspection by such an officer—

(*a*) any residence declarations made to the authorised investment fund under Chapter 2 of Part 4 (participants chargeable to income tax), or

(*b*) any specified declaration or description of declarations.

(2) If a notice has been given to the legal owner under paragraph (1), the declarations shall be made available within such time as may be specified in the notice and the person carrying out the inspection may take copies of or extracts from them.

Commentary—*Simon's Taxes* **D8.161.**

PART 6

FURTHER PROVISIONS RELATING TO AUTHORISED INVESTMENT FUNDS

CHAPTER 1

GENERAL

76 Ownership of shares of different denominations in open-ended investment companies

(1) This regulation applies if conditions A and B are met.

(2) Condition A is that in respect of a given class of shares specified in the instrument of incorporation of an open-ended investment company, shares issued of that class consist of both smaller denomination shares and larger denomination shares.

(3) Condition B is that a participant owns both smaller denomination shares and larger denomination shares of that class.

(4) For the purposes of the provisions relating to ownership of shares in a company contained in the Tax Acts and TCGA 1992, the shares owned by the participant are treated as securities of the same class.

(5) Each larger denomination share is to be treated for those purposes as if it were comprised of the relevant number of smaller denomination shares.

(6) The market value of each smaller denomination share is to be taken for those purposes to be the relevant proportion of the market value of each larger denomination share.

(7) In this regulation—

"smaller denomination shares" means shares to which are attached rights specified in the company's instrument of incorporation that are expressed in the smaller of two denominations;

"larger denomination shares" means shares to which are attached rights so specified that are expressed in the larger of two denominations;

"relevant number" means the number calculated by reference to the relevant proportion; and

"relevant proportion" means the proportion, determined by the company's instrument of incorporation, which the rights attaching to each smaller denomination share bear to the rights attaching to each larger denomination share.

Commentary—*Simon's Taxes* **D8.162.**

77 Non-discrimination in respect of different classes of shares

[(1) This regulation applies if there is an amount available for income allocation.][1]

(2) There must not be any discrimination between participants in respect of different classes of shares.

(3) There is no such discrimination if condition A and either condition B or C is met.

(4) Condition A is that the differences are wholly attributable to differences between the amounts or treatment for accounting purposes of the charges or expenses which—

(*a*) are permitted by the instrument of incorporation of the open-ended investment company concerned or the prospectus in issue for the time being of that company . . . [2] or by the trust deed under which the authorised unit trust is constituted, and

(*b*) are payable out of the scheme property of that authorised investment fund in respect of the shares of those classes.

(5) Condition B is that the authorised investment fund is able to show that the differences between the amounts or treatment for accounting purposes of the charges or expenses referred to in condition A apply for bona fide commercial reasons.

(6) Condition C is that the differences are not such as to enable the participants in any one of those classes to obtain a tax advantage which they would not obtain if there were no differences between the amounts or treatment for accounting purposes of those charges or expenses.

(7) In paragraph (6) "tax advantage" has the same meaning as in Chapter 1 of Part 17 of ICTA (cancellation of tax advantages from transactions in securities).

Commentary—*Simon's Taxes* **D8.162.**

[1] Para (1) substituted by the Authorised Investment Funds (Tax) (Amendment) Regulations, SI 2010/294, regs 2, 20, with effect from 6 March 2010, but see regs 24–26 for transitional provisions relating to distribution dates for earlier accounting periods, and entry into the FINROF regime (see reg 1(2)).

[2] In para (4)(a), words revoked by the Authorised Investment Funds (Tax) (Amendment) Regulations, SI 2010/294, regs 2, 23, with effect from 6 March 2010 (see reg 1(2)).

CHAPTER 2

AMALGAMATION OF AN AUTHORISED UNIT TRUST WITH, AND CONVERSION OF AN AUTHORISED UNIT TRUST TO, AN OPEN-ENDED INVESTMENT COMPANY

78 Circumstances in which this Chapter applies

(1) This Chapter applies if, in connection with a scheme of reorganisation, conditions A to E are met.

(2) Condition A is that the whole of the scheme property of an authorised unit trust that is available for transfer is transferred on a given date under an arrangement to an open-ended investment company.

(3) Condition B is that the consideration under the arrangement consists of or includes the issue, on the transfer date, of shares in the acquiring company to the holders of units in the target trust in exchange for those units.

(4) Condition C is that the consideration shares are issued to the holders of units in proportion to their holdings of the exchanged units.

(5) Condition D is that the consideration under the arrangement does not include anything else in addition to the issue of the consideration shares, other than (where applicable) the assumption or discharge by the acquiring company of liabilities of the trustees of the target trust.

(6) Condition E is that under the arrangement all the units in the target trust are extinguished.

(7) In this Chapter—

the "target trust" means the authorised unit trust mentioned in paragraph (2);

the "transfer date" means the given date mentioned in paragraph (2);

the "acquiring company" means the open-ended investment company mentioned in paragraph (2); and

"the whole of the scheme property of an authorised unit trust that is available for transfer" means the whole of the property subject to the trusts of the target trust, other than any property which is retained for the purpose of discharging liabilities of the trustees of the target trust;

the "consideration shares" means the shares in the acquiring company mentioned in paragraph (4); and

the "exchanged units" means the units in the target trust mentioned in paragraph (4).

Commentary—*Simon's Taxes* **D8.163.**

79 Ending of accounting period of the target trust

(1) An accounting period of the target trust (the "pre-transfer accounting period") ends immediately before the transfer date; and, for the purposes of the Corporation Tax Acts, the whole of the scheme property of the target trust that is available for transfer is treated as having been transferred immediately after the end of that accounting period.

(2) This regulation applies despite anything in section 12(1) to (7) of ICTA (periods of assessment for corporation tax).

Commentary—*Simon's Taxes* **D8.163.**

80 Carrying forward of excess management expenses

(1) This regulation applies if condition A or B is met.

(2) Condition A is that, in respect of the pre-transfer accounting period of the target trust, the trustees are entitled, under section 75(9) of ICTA (carry forward of management expenses and sums treated as management expenses), to carry forward an excess amount to the next accounting period of the trust.

(3) Condition B is that—

(*a*) the pre-transfer accounting period is the final accounting period of the target trust, and

(*b*) the trustees are entitled, under section 75(9) of ICTA, to carry forward an excess amount to what would have been the next accounting period of the trust were the trust to have an accounting period beginning on the transfer date.

(4) With effect from the transfer date, the entitlement is translated into a right in the acquiring company to treat the amount as if it had been carried forward under section 75(9) of ICTA to the first of its accounting periods to end on or after the transfer date.

Commentary—*Simon's Taxes* **D8.163.**

81 Distributions by authorised unit trust after the end of its pre-transfer accounting period

(1) This regulation applies if, in respect of any post-transfer distribution date of the target trust, there is an amount which falls to be treated, in accordance with regulation [22][1] (dividend distributions: general), as dividends on shares paid on that distribution date by the target trust to its participants in proportion to their rights.

(2) The amount shall instead be treated as dividends on shares paid on that date by the acquiring company to those persons in proportion to their rights.

(3) In this regulation "post-transfer distribution date" of a target trust means a distribution date of that trust which—

(*a*) occurs on or after the transfer date, and

(*b*) is the distribution date for a distribution period of the trust ending before the transfer date.

Commentary—*Simon's Taxes* **D8.163.**

Amendments—[1] Reference in para (1) substituted by the Authorised Investment Funds (Tax) (Amendment No 2) Regulations, SI 2007/794 regs 2, 4 with effect from 6 April 2007.

82 Continuing validity of residence declarations

(1) This regulation applies if—

(*a*) before the transfer date, a unit holder has made a residence declaration to the trustees of the target trust, and

(*b*) immediately before the transfer date, the trustees of the target trust treated the residence declaration as valid.

(2) The acquiring company may treat the residence declaration as valid.

Commentary—*Simon's Taxes* **D8.163.**

83 Powers of the acquiring company

(1) On and after the transfer date, the acquiring company has the powers set out in paragraphs (2) and (3).

(2) The acquiring company may continue anything which—

(*a*) immediately before the transfer date was in the process of being done by the trustees of the target trust for the purposes of tax in relation to accounting periods of the target trust ending before that date, and

(*b*) is not continued by those trustees on or after the transfer date.

(3) The acquiring company may do anything which—

(*a*) immediately before the transfer date was not in the process of being done by the trustees of the target trust for the purposes of tax in relation to accounting periods of the target trust ending before that date and is not done by them for those purposes, and

(*b*) might reasonably have been expected to be done by those trustees for those purposes had the scheme of reorganisation not taken place.

Commentary—*Simon's Taxes* **D8.163.**

84 Assessments made on discovery

The provisions of this Chapter do not affect any enactment in the Tax Acts which provides for assessments to be made where an officer of the Commissioners discovers that a set-off, matching, repayment of tax, or payment of tax credit or provision for relief in any other form ought not to have been made, given or otherwise allowed, or is or has become excessive.

Commentary—*Simon's Taxes* **D8.163.**

85 Prevention of double relief

For the purposes of the Tax Acts, nothing in this Chapter has the effect of enabling—

(*a*) any set-off or matching of an amount to be made,

(*b*) any repayment of an amount of tax or payment of an amount of tax credit to be made, or

(*c*) any other relief to be given,

more than once in respect of the same amount or relief.

Commentary—*Simon's Taxes* **D8.163.**

[PART 6A

FUNDS INVESTING IN NON-REPORTING OFFSHORE FUNDS

CHAPTER 1

PRELIMINARY PROVISIONS

85A FINROFs

(1) This Part applies to—

(*a*) an authorised investment fund which meets the investment condition in regulation 85D (the investment condition);

(*b*) an authorised investment fund in respect of which an election has been made in accordance with regulation 85F (elective FINROFs);

(*c*) a participant in a fund mentioned in paragraph (*a*) or (*b*); and

(*d*) a participant in a fund which has left the FINROF regime, where the participant has not made a valid election under regulation 85Z11 (participant's power to elect for deemed disposal).

(2) A fund to which this Part applies shall be known as a Fund Investing in Non-Reporting Offshore Funds ("FINROF").][1]

Amendments—[1] Part 6A (regs 85A–85Z11) inserted by the Authorised Investment Funds (Tax) (Amendment) Regulations, SI 2010/294, regs 2, 21, with effect from 6 March 2010, subject to transitional provisions in regs 25, 26 (see reg 1(2)).

[85B Structure of this Part

The structure of this Part is as follows—

This Chapter contains preliminary provisions;

Chapter 2 deals with entry into the Funds Investing in Non-Reporting Offshore Funds regime ("FINROF regime");

Chapter 3 deals with the tax treatment of FINROFs and of participants in FINROFs;

Chapter 4 deals with exceptions, etc from the charge to tax;

Chapter 5 deals with disposal of units in FINROFs;

Chapter 6 deals with income gains and computation of income gains;

Chapter 7 deals with deduction of income gains in computing chargeable gains;

Chapter 8 deals with leaving the FINROF regime.][1]

Amendments—[1] Part 6A (regs 85A–85Z11) inserted by the Authorised Investment Funds (Tax) (Amendment) Regulations, SI 2010/294, regs 2, 21, with effect from 6 March 2010, subject to transitional provisions in regs 25, 26 (see reg 1(2)).

[85C Interpretation

In this Part—

"gross asset value" means the value of the investments comprising the scheme property of the authorised investment fund before the deduction of specified liabilities, but does not include cash awaiting investment;

. . . [2]][1]

Amendments—[1] Part 6A (regs 85A–85Z11) inserted by the Authorised Investment Funds (Tax) (Amendment) Regulations, SI 2010/294, regs 2, 21, with effect from 6 March 2010, subject to transitional provisions in regs 25, 26 (see reg 1(2)).

[2] Entries relating to "non reporting fund", "offshore fund", "Offshore Funds Regulations" and "reporting fund" revoked by the Authorised Investment Funds (Tax) (Amendment) Regulations, SI 2011/244 regs 2, 9(1) with effect as follows—

(a) for the purposes of corporation tax—

– on income, for accounting periods ending on or after 6 March 2011, and

– on chargeable gains, in relation to disposals made on or after 6 March 2011, and

(b) for the purposes of capital gains tax, in relation to disposals made on or after 6 March 2011.

These amendments are subject to the following transitional provision (SI 2011/244 reg 8)—

– This provision applies to an authorised investment fund ("the fund") which, on 5 March 2011, met the following requirement: that the fund did not meet the investment condition in reg 85D of these Regulations by virtue of holding an interest in an offshore fund that is treated as creditor relationship rights under CTA 2009 s 490 (a "relevant interest").

– A relevant interest shall continue to be treated as not being an interest in a non-reporting fund for the purposes of reg 85E of these Regulations for the period beginning on 6 March 2011 and ending on 5 July 2011.

[85D The investment condition

(1) The investment condition is met in relation to an authorised investment fund if the total amount invested in non-reporting funds or FINROFs is more than [50%][2] of the gross asset value of the authorised investment fund.

(2) This regulation is subject to regulation 85E.][1]

Amendments—[1] Part 6A (regs 85A–85Z11) inserted by the Authorised Investment Funds (Tax) (Amendment) Regulations, SI 2010/294, regs 2, 21, with effect from 6 March 2010, subject to transitional provisions in regs 25, 26 (see reg 1(2)).

[2] In para (1), figure substituted by the Authorised Investment Funds (Tax) (Amendment) Regulations, SI 2011/244 regs 2, 5 with effect from 6 March 2011.

[85E Interests in funds treated as not being interests in non-reporting funds

(1) For the purposes of regulation 85D(1) the interests specified in paragraph (2) shall not be regarded as interests in non-reporting funds.

[(2) The interests specified are—

(*a*) any interest in an offshore fund in respect of which, by virtue of regulation 29 or 30 of the Offshore Funds Regulations, no liability to tax would arise under regulation 17 of those Regulations on a disposal of that interest; and

(*b*) any interest of an authorised investment fund in a non-reporting fund which meets the conditions in regulation 14ZA(2).][2]][1]

Amendments—[1] Part 6A (regs 85A–85Z11) inserted by the Authorised Investment Funds (Tax) (Amendment) Regulations, SI 2010/294, regs 2, 21, with effect from 6 March 2010, subject to transitional provisions in regs 25, 26 (see reg 1(2)).

[2] Para (2) substituted by the Authorised Investment Funds (Tax) (Amendment) Regulations, SI 2011/244 regs 2, 6 with effect as follows—

(a) for the purposes of corporation tax—

– on income, for accounting periods ending on or after 6 March 2011, and

– on chargeable gains, in relation to disposals made on or after 6 March 2011, and

(b) for the purposes of capital gains tax, in relation to disposals made on or after 6 March 2011.

These amendments are subject to the following transitional provision (SI 2011/244 reg 8)—

– This provision applies to an authorised investment fund ("the fund") which, on 5 March 2011, met the following requirement: that the fund did not meet the investment condition in reg 85D of these Regulations by virtue of holding an interest in an offshore fund that is treated as creditor relationship rights under CTA 2009 s 490 (a "relevant interest").

– A relevant interest shall continue to be treated as not being an interest in a non-reporting fund for the purposes of reg 85E of these Regulations for the period beginning on 6 March 2011 and ending on 5 July 2011.

[85F Elective FINROFs

(1) An authorised investment fund which does not meet the investment condition may elect to be treated as a FINROF (an "elective FINROF").

This is subject to paragraph (4).

(2) An election under paragraph (1) must—

(*a*) be made in writing to HM Revenue and Customs by the manager; and

(*b*) specify the date from which the fund is to be so treated.

(3) But the manager must not specify a date which is more than 3 months before the date of the election mentioned in paragraph (2).

(4) Before making an election, the fund must have obtained any necessary regulatory approval in respect of the instrument constituting the fund and the prospectus.[1]

Amendments—[1] Part 6A (regs 85A–85Z11) inserted by the Authorised Investment Funds (Tax) (Amendment) Regulations, SI 2010/294, regs 2, 21, with effect from 6 March 2010, subject to transitional provisions in regs 25, 26 (see reg 1(2)).

[CHAPTER 2

ENTRY INTO FUNDS INVESTING IN NON-REPORTING OFFSHORE FUND ("FINROF") REGIME

85G Entry into FINROF regime: the basic rule

This Part applies to an authorised investment fund from—

(*a*) the date on which the fund first met the condition in regulation 85D (the investment condition); or

(*b*) the date specified in the notice given under regulation 85F (elective FINROFs),

whichever is the earlier.][1]

Amendments—[1] Part 6A (regs 85A–85Z11) inserted by the Authorised Investment Funds (Tax) (Amendment) Regulations, SI 2010/294, regs 2, 21, with effect from 6 March 2010, subject to transitional provisions in regs 25, 26 (see reg 1(2)).

[85H The requirement to notify where regulation 85D is satisfied

(1) The legal owner of an authorised investment fund which is a FINROF by virtue of regulation 85D must notify HM Revenue and Customs of the date on which the fund first met the investment condition within a period of 3 months beginning with the date on which the fund first met that condition.

(2) For the purposes of paragraph (1), no account shall be taken of the period before the date of any previous valid election under regulation 85Z9 (leaving the FINROF regime).

(3) An authorised investment fund that fails to comply with this regulation is liable to a penalty not exceeding £3,000 determined in accordance with section 100 of TMA 1970.

(4) Sections 100A, 100B, 102, 103(4) and 118(2) of TMA 1970 apply to a penalty determined in accordance with paragraph (3).

(5) This regulation is subject to regulation 85J (inadvertent fulfilment of investment condition).][1]

Amendments—[1] Part 6A (regs 85A–85Z11) inserted by the Authorised Investment Funds (Tax) (Amendment) Regulations, SI 2010/294, regs 2, 21, with effect from 6 March 2010, subject to transitional provisions in regs 25, 26 (see reg 1(2)).

[85I The requirement to notify participants when a fund enters the FINROF regime

(1) The legal owner must notify the participants in a fund that the fund has entered the FINROF regime and inform them that any gains made on the disposal of units in the fund shall be treated as an income gain rather than a capital gain, in accordance with Chapter 3 of this Part.

(2) The notification under paragraph (1) must be given within a period of 3 months beginning with the date on which this Part first applied to the fund.

(3) For the purposes of paragraph (2), no account shall be taken of the period before the date of any previous valid election under regulation 85Z9 (leaving the FINROF regime).

(4) An authorised investment fund that fails to comply with this regulation is liable to a penalty not exceeding £3,000 determined in accordance with section 100 of TMA 1970.

(5) Sections 100A, 100B, 102, 103(4) and 118(2) of TMA 1970 apply to a penalty determined in accordance with paragraph (4).

(6) This regulation is subject to regulation 85J.][1]

Amendments—[1] Part 6A (regs 85A–85Z11) inserted by the Authorised Investment Funds (Tax) (Amendment) Regulations, SI 2010/294, regs 2, 21, with effect from 6 March 2010, subject to transitional provisions in regs 25, 26 (see reg 1(2)).

[85J Inadvertent fulfilment of investment condition

(1) If this regulation applies a fund shall be treated as if it had never met the investment condition and consequently none of the provisions of this Part (including the penalty provisions in regulations 85H and 85I) apply to the fund.

(2) This regulation applies where—

(*a*) an authorised investment fund meets the investment condition but as soon as possible after becoming aware that the condition is met, the legal owner gives notice in writing to HM Revenue and Customs of the steps that the fund has taken, or proposes to take, to ensure that the fund no longer meets that condition,

(*b*) the fund ceases the meet the investment condition before the end of a 4 month period beginning with the date that the fund first met the condition and the legal owner gives notice in writing to HM Revenue and Customs that the fund no longer meets the condition, and

(*c*) HM Revenue and Customs issue a notice in writing that this regulation applies.

(3) HM Revenue and Customs must, within a period of 28 days beginning with the date on which they receive notice from the legal owner that the fund no longer meets the investment condition, issue a notice in writing to the legal owner that—

(*a*) this regulation applies, or

(*b*) this regulation does not apply as HM Revenue and Customs are not satisfied that the conditions in sub-paragraphs (*a*) and (*b*) of paragraph (2) are met for the reasons specified in the notice.][1]

Amendments—[1] Part 6A (regs 85A–85Z11) inserted by the Authorised Investment Funds (Tax) (Amendment) Regulations, SI 2010/294, regs 2, 21, with effect from 6 March 2010, subject to transitional provisions in regs 25, 26 (see reg 1(2)).

[85K Appeal against refusal to provide written notice

(1) A legal owner to whom a notice is issued under paragraph (3)(*b*) of regulation 85J (a "refusal notice") may appeal.

(2) The notice of appeal must be given to HM Revenue and Customs within a period of 28 days beginning with the day on which HM Revenue and Customs issued the refusal notice.

(3) On an appeal that is notified to the tribunal, the tribunal shall determine whether it was just and reasonable for HM Revenue and Customs to issue the refusal notice.

(4) If the tribunal determine that it was just and reasonable for HM Revenue and Customs to issue the refusal notice, this Part applies to the fund from the date on which it first met the investment condition and the legal owner must notify the participants in the fund in accordance with regulation 85I.

(5) If the tribunal determine that it was not just and reasonable for HM Revenue and Customs to issue the refusal notice, paragraph (1) of regulation 85J shall apply.][1]

Amendments—[1] Part 6A (regs 85A–85Z11) inserted by the Authorised Investment Funds (Tax) (Amendment) Regulations, SI 2010/294, regs 2, 21, with effect from 6 March 2010, subject to transitional provisions in regs 25, 26 (see reg 1(2)).

[85L Disposal of an interest in an authorised investment fund prior to its becoming a FINROF

(1) This regulation applies if an authorised investment fund either meets the investment condition or becomes an elective FINROF in accordance with regulation 85F.

(2) A participant in the fund may make an election to be treated for the purposes of TCGA 1992—

(*a*) as disposing of all the units that they hold in the authorised investment fund on the deemed disposal date, and

(*b*) as immediately upon that disposal, acquiring units in the FINROF.

(3) The disposal referred to in paragraph (2)(*a*) is treated as made for a consideration equal to the market value of the participant's holding of units in the fund on the deemed disposal date.

(4) The acquisition referred to in paragraph (2)(*b*) is treated as made for a consideration equal to the consideration for the disposal referred to in paragraph (2)(*a*).

(5) If the participant is chargeable to income tax, the election mentioned in paragraph (2) must be made by being included in a return made for the tax year which includes the deemed disposal date.

(6) If the participant is chargeable to corporation tax, the election mentioned in paragraph (2) must be made by being included in the participant's company tax return for the accounting period which includes the deemed disposal date.

(7) In this regulation—

(*a*) "company tax return" has the same meaning as in Schedule 18 to the Finance Act 1998, and

(*b*) "deemed disposal date" means the date on which this Part begins to apply to the authorised investment fund.][1]

Amendments—[1] Part 6A (regs 85A–85Z11) inserted by the Authorised Investment Funds (Tax) (Amendment) Regulations, SI 2010/294, regs 2, 21, with effect from 6 March 2010, subject to transitional provisions in regs 25, 26 (see reg 1(2)).

[CHAPTER 3

TAX TREATMENT OF FINROFS AND OF PARTICIPANTS IN FINROFS

85M The charge to tax: general provisions

(1) There is a charge to tax if—

(*a*) a person disposes of an asset,

(*b*) either condition A or condition B is met, and

(*c*) as a result of the disposal, an income gain (see regulation 85Z) arises to the person making the disposal.

(2) Condition A is that the asset consists of units in a FINROF at the time of the disposal.

(3) Condition B is that—

(*a*) the asset consists of units in an authorised investment fund that had been a FINROF for some of the material period; and

(*b*) no valid election under regulation 85Z11 (participant's power to elect for deemed disposal) was made in relation to the asset.

(4) In paragraph (3) "the material period" means a period beginning with the date of acquisition of the asset and ending with the date of the disposal.][1]

Amendments—[1] Part 6A (regs 85A–85Z11) inserted by the Authorised Investment Funds (Tax) (Amendment) Regulations, SI 2010/294, regs 2, 21, with effect from 6 March 2010, subject to transitional provisions in regs 25, 26 (see reg 1(2)).

[85N The charge to tax: further provisions

(1) The income gain arising is treated for all purposes of the Tax Acts as income which arises at the time of the disposal to the person making the disposal (or treated as making the disposal).

(2) The tax is charged on the person making the disposal (or treated as making the disposal).

(3) In the case of a person chargeable to income tax, tax is charged under Chapter 8 of Part 5 of ITTOIA 2005 (miscellaneous income: income not otherwise charged) for the year of assessment in which the disposal is made, but sections 688(1) (income charged) and 689 (person liable) of ITTOIA 2005 do not apply.

(4) In the case of a person chargeable to corporation tax, tax is charged under Chapter 8 of Part 10 of CTA 2009 (miscellaneous income: income not otherwise charged) for the accounting period in which the disposal is made.][1]

Amendments—[1] Part 6A (regs 85A–85Z11) inserted by the Authorised Investment Funds (Tax) (Amendment) Regulations, SI 2010/294, regs 2, 21, with effect from 6 March 2010, subject to transitional provisions in regs 25, 26 (see reg 1(2)).

[85O Application of certain provisions of TCGA 1992

The following enactments have effect in relation to income tax or corporation tax in respect of income gains as they have effect in relation to capital gains tax or corporation tax in respect of chargeable gains—

(*a*) section 2(1) of TCGA 1992 (persons chargeable to capital gains tax);

(*b*) section 10 of TCGA 1992 (non-resident with a United Kingdom branch or agency);

(*c*) section 10B of TCGA 1992 (non-resident company with United Kingdom permanent establishment).][1]

Amendments—[1] Part 6A (regs 85A–85Z11) inserted by the Authorised Investment Funds (Tax) (Amendment) Regulations, SI 2010/294, regs 2, 21, with effect from 6 March 2010, subject to transitional provisions in regs 25, 26 (see reg 1(2)).

[85P Application of section 10A of TCGA 1992

(1) Section 10A of TCGA 1992 (temporary non-residence) applies for the purposes of this Part with the following modifications.

(2) The section applies as if, in subsection (2)—

(*a*) the reference to section 86A were omitted;

(*b*) for the reference to capital gains tax there were substituted a reference to income tax;

(*c*) in paragraph (*a*), for the reference to chargeable gains and losses there were substituted a reference to income gains;

(*d*) paragraphs (*b*) and (*c*) were omitted; and

(*e*) for the references to gains or losses there were substituted a reference to income gains.

(3) The section applies as if, in subsection (3)—

(*a*) for the reference to gains and losses there were substituted a reference to income gains; and

(*b*) for the reference to any gain or loss there were substituted a reference to any income gains.

(4) The section applies as if, in subsection (4) were omitted.

(5) The section applies as if, in subsection (5)—

(*a*) for the reference to gains and losses there were substituted a reference to income gains;

(*b*) for the reference to any chargeable gain or allowable loss there were substituted a reference to an any income gain; and

(*c*) for the reference to section 10 or 16(3) there were substituted a reference to regulation 85O(*b*) (application of certain provisions of TCGA).

(6) The section applies as if, in subsection (6) were omitted.

(7) The section applies as if, in subsection (7), for the reference to capital gains tax there were substituted a reference to income tax.

(8) The section applies as if, in subsection (9C)—

(*a*) for the reference to capital gains tax there were substituted a reference to income tax; and

(*b*) for the reference to chargeable gains there were substituted a reference to income gains.][1]

Amendments—[1] Part 6A (regs 85A–85Z11) inserted by the Authorised Investment Funds (Tax) (Amendment) Regulations, SI 2010/294, regs 2, 21, with effect from 6 March 2010, subject to transitional provisions in regs 25, 26 (see reg 1(2)).

[CHAPTER 4

EXCEPTIONS, ETC FROM THE CHARGE TO TAX

85Q Exceptions from the charge to tax

(1) No liability to tax arises under regulation 85M (the charge to tax: general provisions) if condition A or B is met.

(2) Condition A is that the participant is required to treat units in the FINROF as a loan relationship to which the provisions of Chapter 3 of Part 6 of CTA 2009 apply.

(3) Condition B is that the participant is required to treat units in the FINROF as a derivative contract to which the provisions of Part 7 of CTA 2009 apply.][1]

Amendments—[1] Part 6A (regs 85A–85Z11) inserted by the Authorised Investment Funds (Tax) (Amendment) Regulations, SI 2010/294, regs 2, 21, with effect from 6 March 2010, subject to transitional provisions in regs 25, 26 (see reg 1(2)).

[85R Trading stock etc

(1) No liability to tax arises under regulation 85M if condition A or B is met.

(2) Condition A is that the units in the fund are held as trading stock.

(3) Condition B is that the disposal of the units is taken into account in computing the profits of a trade.][1]

Amendments—[1] Part 6A (regs 85A–85Z11) inserted by the Authorised Investment Funds (Tax) (Amendment) Regulations, SI 2010/294, regs 2, 21, with effect from 6 March 2010, subject to transitional provisions in regs 25, 26 (see reg 1(2)).

[85S Long-term insurance funds of insurance companies

(1) No liability to tax arises under regulation 85M in respect of disposals of units of an insurance company's long-term insurance fund.

(2) In paragraph (1) "insurance company" and "long-term insurance fund" have the same meaning as is section 431(2) of ICTA.][1]

Amendments—[1] Part 6A (regs 85A–85Z11) inserted by the Authorised Investment Funds (Tax) (Amendment) Regulations, SI 2010/294, regs 2, 21, with effect from 6 March 2010, subject to transitional provisions in regs 25, 26 (see reg 1(2)).

[85T Charitable companies and charitable trusts

(1) A charitable company shall be exempt from corporation tax in respect of an income gain if the gain is applicable and is applied for charitable purposes.

(2) A charitable trust shall be exempt from income tax in respect of an income gain if the gain is applicable and is applied for charitable purposes.

(3) Paragraphs (4) and (5) apply if—

(*a*) property held on charitable trusts ceases to be subject to charitable trusts, and

(*b*) that property represents directly or indirectly an income gain.

(4) The trustees are treated as if they had disposed of and immediately reacquired that property for a consideration equal to its market value.

(5) An income gain accruing on the disposal arising under paragraph (4) is treated as an income gain not accruing to a charity.

(6) In this regulation "charity" and "charitable company" have the same meaning as in section 506 of ICTA.][1]

Amendments—[1] Part 6A (regs 85A–85Z11) inserted by the Authorised Investment Funds (Tax) (Amendment) Regulations, SI 2010/294, regs 2, 21, with effect from 6 March 2010, subject to transitional provisions in regs 25, 26 (see reg 1(2)).

[CHAPTER 5

DISPOSAL OF UNITS IN FINROFS

85U Application of this Chapter

This Chapter applies if a participant disposes of an asset and at the time of the disposal—

(*a*) the asset consists of units in a FINROF, or

(*b*) the asset consists of units in an authorised investment fund that is not a FINROF and the requirements specified in paragraph (3) of regulation 85M are met.][1]

Amendments—[1] Part 6A (regs 85A–85Z11) inserted by the Authorised Investment Funds (Tax) (Amendment) Regulations, SI 2010/294, regs 2, 21, with effect from 6 March 2010, subject to transitional provisions in regs 25, 26 (see reg 1(2)).

[85V Disposal of an asset: the basic rule

(1) There is a disposal of an asset for the purposes of this Part if there would be a disposal of an asset for the purposes of TCGA 1992.

(2) Paragraph (1) is subject to the following regulations in this Chapter.][1]

Amendments—[1] Part 6A (regs 85A–85Z11) inserted by the Authorised Investment Funds (Tax) (Amendment) Regulations, SI 2010/294, regs 2, 21, with effect from 6 March 2010, subject to transitional provisions in regs 25, 26 (see reg 1(2)).

[85W Provisions applicable on death

(1) Notwithstanding anything in paragraph (*b*) of subsection (1) of section 62 of TCGA 1992 (general provisions applicable on death: no deemed disposal by the deceased), where a person dies and the assets of which the deceased was competent to dispose at the time of death include units in a FINROF, then, for the purposes of these Regulations—

(*a*) immediately before the acquisition referred to in paragraph (*a*) of that subsection, those units shall be deemed to be disposed of by the deceased for such a consideration as is mentioned in that subsection; but

(*b*) nothing in this regulation affects the determination, in accordance with regulation 85U, of the question whether that deemed disposal is one to which this Chapter applies.

(2) Subject to paragraph (1), section 62 of TCGA 1992 applies for the purposes of these Regulations as it applies for the purposes of that Act, and the reference in that paragraph to the assets of which a deceased person was competent to dispose are to be construed in accordance with subsection (10) of that section.][1]

Amendments—[1] Part 6A (regs 85A–85Z11) inserted by the Authorised Investment Funds (Tax) (Amendment) Regulations, SI 2010/294, regs 2, 21, with effect from 6 March 2010, subject to transitional provisions in regs 25, 26 (see reg 1(2)).

[85X Application of section 135 of TCGA 1992

(1) Section 135 of TCGA 1992 (exchange of securities for those in another company treated as not involving a disposal) does not apply for the purposes of this Part to the extent that—

(*a*) the interest in the entity that is company A for the purposes of that section that is exchanged is units in a FINROF, and

(*b*) the interest in the entity that is company B for those purposes that is exchanged is not units in such a fund.

(2) In a case where section 135 of TCGA 1992 would apply apart from paragraph (1), the exchange in question shall for the purposes of this Part constitute a disposal of units in the FINROF for a consideration equal to their market value at the time of the exchange.][1]

Amendments—[1] Part 6A (regs 85A–85Z11) inserted by the Authorised Investment Funds (Tax) (Amendment) Regulations, SI 2010/294, regs 2, 21, with effect from 6 March 2010, subject to transitional provisions in regs 25, 26 (see reg 1(2)).

[85Y Application of section 136 of TCGA 1992

(1) Section 136 of TCGA 1992 (scheme of reconstruction involving issue of securities treated as exchange not involving disposal) does not apply for the purposes of this Part to the extent that—

(*a*) the interest in the entity that is company A for the purposes of that section that is exchanged is units in a FINROF, and

(*b*) the interest in the entity that is company B for those purposes that is exchanged is not units in such a fund.

(2) In a case where section 136 of TCGA 1992 would apply apart from paragraph (1), the deemed exchange in question shall for the purposes of this Part constitute a disposal of units in the FINROF for a consideration equal to their market value at the time of the deemed exchange.][1]

Amendments—[1] Part 6A (regs 85A–85Z11) inserted by the Authorised Investment Funds (Tax) (Amendment) Regulations, SI 2010/294, regs 2, 21, with effect from 6 March 2010, subject to transitional provisions in regs 25, 26 (see reg 1(2)).

[CHAPTER 6

INCOME GAINS AND COMPUTATION OF INCOME GAINS

85Z General provisions

(1) An income gain arises to a person on the disposal of an asset if a basic gain arises on the disposal.

(2) The disposal gives rise to an income gain of an amount equal to the basic gain on the disposal.

(3) The following provisions of this Chapter explain how the basic gain is computed.][1]

Amendments—[1] Part 6A (regs 85A–85Z11) inserted by the Authorised Investment Funds (Tax) (Amendment) Regulations, SI 2010/294, regs 2, 21, with effect from 6 March 2010, subject to transitional provisions in regs 25, 26 (see reg 1(2)).

[85Z1 The basic gain and its computation

(1) In the case of a participant chargeable to income tax, the basic gain is a gain of the amount which would be the gain on that disposal for the purposes of TCGA 1992 if the gain were computed without regard to any charge to income tax arising under this Part.

(2) In the case of a participant chargeable to corporation tax, the basic gain is a gain of the amount which would be the gain on that disposal for the purposes of TCGA 1992 if the gain were computed—

(*a*) without regard to any charge to corporation tax arising under this Part, and

(*b*) without regard to any indexation allowance on the disposal under TCGA 1992.

(3) The computation of the basic gain is subject to—

(*a*) regulation 85W (provisions applicable on death);
(*b*) regulation 85X (application of section 135 of TCGA 1992);
(*c*) regulation 85Y (application of section 136 of TCGA 1992);
(*d*) regulation 85Z2 (earlier disposal to which the no gain/no loss basis applies);
(*e*) regulation 85Z3 (modifications of TCGA 1992); and
(*f*) regulation 85Z4 (losses).][1]

Amendments—[1] Part 6A (regs 85A–85Z11) inserted by the Authorised Investment Funds (Tax) (Amendment) Regulations, SI 2010/294, regs 2, 21, with effect from 6 March 2010, subject to transitional provisions in regs 25, 26 (see reg 1(2)).

[85Z2 Earlier disposal to which the no gain/no loss basis applies

(1) This regulation applies if—
(*a*) a participant is chargeable to corporation tax, and
(*b*) the amount of any chargeable gain or allowable loss which would arise on the disposal would fall to be computed in a way which, in whole or in part, would take account of the indexation allowance on an earlier disposal to which section 56(2) of TCGA 1992 (disposals on a no gain/no loss basis) applies.
(2) The basic gain on the disposal is computed as if—
(*a*) no indexation allowance had been available on any such earlier disposal, and
(*b*) subject to that, neither a gain nor a loss had arisen to the person making such an earlier disposal.][1]

Amendments—[1] Part 6A (regs 85A–85Z11) inserted by the Authorised Investment Funds (Tax) (Amendment) Regulations, SI 2010/294, regs 2, 21, with effect from 6 March 2010, subject to transitional provisions in regs 25, 26 (see reg 1(2)).

[85Z3 Modifications of TCGA 1992

(1) If the disposal forms part of a transfer to which section 162 of TCGA 1992 (roll-over relief on transfer of business) applies, the basic gain arising on the disposal is computed without regard to any deduction which falls to be made under that section in computing a chargeable gain.
(2) If the disposal is made otherwise than under a bargain at arm's length and a claim for relief is made in respect of that disposal under section 165 or 260 of TCGA 1992 (relief for gifts), the claim does not affect the computation of the basic gain arising on the disposal.][1]

Amendments—[1] Part 6A (regs 85A–85Z11) inserted by the Authorised Investment Funds (Tax) (Amendment) Regulations, SI 2010/294, regs 2, 21, with effect from 6 March 2010, subject to transitional provisions in regs 25, 26 (see reg 1(2)).

[85Z4 Losses

(1) If the effect of any computation under regulations 85Z1 to 85Z3 would be to produce a loss, the basic gain on the disposal is nil.
(2) Paragraph (1) applies notwithstanding section 16 of TCGA 1992 (losses determined in like manner as gains).
(3) Accordingly, for the purposes of these Regulations, no loss is to be treated as arising on the disposal.][1]

Amendments—[1] Part 6A (regs 85A–85Z11) inserted by the Authorised Investment Funds (Tax) (Amendment) Regulations, SI 2010/294, regs 2, 21, with effect from 6 March 2010, subject to transitional provisions in regs 25, 26 (see reg 1(2)).

[CHAPTER 7

DEDUCTION OF INCOME GAINS IN COMPUTING CHARGEABLE GAINS

85Z5 Scope of this Chapter

(1) This Chapter applies if—
(*a*) a disposal gives rise to an income gain, and
(*b*) that disposal also constitutes the disposal of the units concerned for the purposes of TCGA 1992.
(2) In this Chapter, the disposal specified in paragraph (1)(*b*) is called the "TCGA disposal".][1]

Amendments—[1] Part 6A (regs 85A–85Z11) inserted by the Authorised Investment Funds (Tax) (Amendment) Regulations, SI 2010/294, regs 2, 21, with effect from 6 March 2010, subject to transitional provisions in regs 25, 26 (see reg 1(2)).

[85Z6 Treatment of the TCGA disposal: general rules

(1) This regulation applies for the purposes of the computation of the chargeable gain arising on the TCGA disposal.
(2) The provisions of this regulation have effect in relation to the TCGA disposal in substitution for section 37(1) of TCGA 1992 (deduction of consideration chargeable to tax on income).
(3) In the computation of the gain arising on the TCGA disposal, a sum equal to the income gain shall be deducted from the sum which would otherwise constitute the amount or value of the consideration for the disposal.
(4) Paragraph (3) is subject to the following provisions of this Chapter.
(5) Paragraph (6) applies if the TCGA disposal is of such a nature that, by virtue of section 42 of TCGA (part disposal), an apportionment falls to be made of certain expenditure.
(6) No deduction is to be made by virtue of paragraph (3) in determining the amount or value of the consideration for the purpose of the fraction in section 42(2) of TCGA 1992.][1]

Amendments—[1] Part 6A (regs 85A–85Z11) inserted by the Authorised Investment Funds (Tax) (Amendment) Regulations, SI 2010/294, regs 2, 21, with effect from 6 March 2010, subject to transitional provisions in regs 25, 26 (see reg 1(2)).

[85Z7 Modification of section 162 TCGA 1992

(1) This regulation applies if the TCGA disposal forms part of a transfer to which section 162 of TCGA applies (roll-over relief on transfer of business in exchange wholly or partly for shares).

(2) For the purposes of subsection (4) of section 162 of TCGA 1992 (determination of the amount of the deduction from the gain on the old assets) "B" in the fraction in that subsection (the value of the whole of the consideration received by the transferor in exchange for the business) is to be taken to be what it would be if the value of the consideration other than shares so received by the transferor were reduced by an amount equal to the income gain.][1]

Amendments—[1] Part 6A (regs 85A–85Z11) inserted by the Authorised Investment Funds (Tax) (Amendment) Regulations, SI 2010/294, regs 2, 21, with effect from 6 March 2010, subject to transitional provisions in regs 25, 26 (see reg 1(2)).

[85Z8 Application of section 128 of TCGA 1992

(1) This regulation applies if there is a disposal to which this Part applies by virtue of—

(*a*) regulation 85X (application of section 135 of TCGA 1992), and

(*b*) regulation 85Y (application of section 136 of TCGA 1992).

(2) TCGA 1992 has effect as if an amount equal to the income gain to which that disposal gives rise were given (by the person making the exchange) as consideration for the new holding (within the meaning of section 128 of that Act (consideration given or received for new holding on a reorganisation)).][1]

Amendments—[1] Part 6A (regs 85A–85Z11) inserted by the Authorised Investment Funds (Tax) (Amendment) Regulations, SI 2010/294, regs 2, 21, with effect from 6 March 2010, subject to transitional provisions in regs 25, 26 (see reg 1(2)).

[CHAPTER 8

LEAVING THE FINROF REGIME

85Z9 Leaving the FINROF regime

(1) The provisions of this Part apply to a FINROF until the date specified in an election under this regulation made by the manager.

(2) An election under this regulation must be made to HM Revenue and Customs in writing and must comply with the following provisions of this regulation.

(3) An election may only be made in respect of a FINROF if—

(*a*) the FINROF does not meet the investment condition—

(i) at the date specified in the election, and

(ii) at the date on which the election is made,

(*b*) the FINROF has been subject to this Part for at least one complete accounting period, and

(*c*) the fund has obtained any necessary regulatory approval of the instrument constituting the fund and the prospectus.

(4) An election under this regulation must specify the date from which this Part ceases to apply to the FINROF.

(5) But the date specified in paragraph (4) must not be earlier than the date which is 3 months before the date on which the election is made.][1]

Amendments—[1] Part 6A (regs 85A–85Z11) inserted by the Authorised Investment Funds (Tax) (Amendment) Regulations, SI 2010/294, regs 2, 21, with effect from 6 March 2010, subject to transitional provisions in regs 25, 26 (see reg 1(2)).

[85Z10 Requirement to notify participants when a fund leaves the FINROF regime

(1) If an election is made under regulation 85Z9, the legal owner must notify the participants in a fund that this Part no longer applies to the fund but continues to apply to a participant unless an election is made in accordance with regulation 85Z11.

(2) The notification under paragraph (1) must be made within a period of 3 months beginning with the date mentioned in regulation 85Z9(5).

(3) An authorised investment fund which fails to comply with this regulation is liable to a penalty not exceeding £3,000 determined in accordance with section 100 of TMA 1970.

(4) Sections 100A, 100B, 102, 103(4) and 118(2) of TMA 1970 apply to a penalty determined in accordance with paragraph (3).][1]

Amendments—[1] Part 6A (regs 85A–85Z11) inserted by the Authorised Investment Funds (Tax) (Amendment) Regulations, SI 2010/294, regs 2, 21, with effect from 6 March 2010, subject to transitional provisions in regs 25, 26 (see reg 1(2)).

[85Z11 Participant's power to elect for deemed disposal

(1) Notwithstanding an election made under regulation 85Z9, this Part continues to apply to a participant in a FINROF unless the participant makes an election in accordance with paragraph (2).

(2) A participant in the fund may make an election to be treated—

(*a*) as disposing of the units owned by the participant in the FINROF at their market value on the deemed disposal date, and

(*b*) as acquiring units in the authorised investment fund on the deemed disposal date.

(3) The income gain arising on the deemed disposal referred to in paragraph (2)(*a*) shall be determined in accordance with Chapter 6 of this Part.

(4) The acquisition referred to in paragraph (2)(*b*) is treated as made for a consideration equal to the consideration for the disposal referred to in paragraph (2)(*a*).

(5) An election may not be made under paragraph (2) unless the income gain arising on the disposal referred to in paragraph (2)(*a*) (determined in accordance with Chapter 6 of this Part) is greater than zero.

(6) If the participant is chargeable to income tax, the election mentioned in paragraph (2) must be made by being included in a return made for the tax year which includes the deemed disposal date.

(7) If the participant is chargeable to corporation tax, the election mentioned in paragraph (2) must be made by being included in the participant's company tax return for the accounting period which includes the deemed disposal date.

(8) In this regulation—

"company tax return" has the same meaning as in Schedule 18 to the Finance Act 1998; and

the "deemed disposal date" means the date on which, in accordance with regulation 85Z9, the fund ceases to be a FINROF.][1]

Amendments—[1] Part 6A (regs 85A–85Z11) inserted by the Authorised Investment Funds (Tax) (Amendment) Regulations, SI 2010/294, regs 2, 21, with effect from 6 March 2010, subject to transitional provisions in regs 25, 26 (see reg 1(2)).

PART 7
CONSEQUENTIAL AMENDMENTS AND MODIFICATIONS OF ENACTMENTS

CHAPTER 1

AMENDMENTS OF REFERENCES TO REPEALED ENACTMENTS

86 Introduction

Regulations 87 to 92—

(*a*) amend references in enactments to provisions repealed by section 17(1) of the Finance (No 2) Act 2005, and

(*b*) make incidental, consequential and supplemental provision.

87 Amendments of TMA 1970

(1) TMA 1970 is amended as follows.

(2) In section 98 (penalties in relation to special returns)—

(*a*) in subsection (4E) for "Chapter 3 of Part 12 of the principal Act" substitute "regulations made under section 17(3) of the Finance (No 2) Act 2005 (as at 1st April 2006, see the Authorised Investment Funds (Tax) Regulations 2006 (SI 2006/964))".

(*b*) in the first column of the Table—

(i) omit the entry relating to section 468P(6) of ICTA,

(ii) omit the entry relating to regulations under section 468PB(3) of ICTA, and

(iii) at the end insert—

"regulations under section 17(3) of the Finance (No 2) Act 2005".

88 Amendment of ICTA

(1) ICTA is amended as follows.

(2) In section 468(1) (authorised unit trusts) for "section 468L" substitute "regulations made under section 17(3) of the Finance (No 2) Act 2005 (as at 1st April 2006, see regulation 18(3) of the Authorised Investment Funds (Tax) Regulations 2006 (SI 2006/964))".

89 Amendment of TCGA 1992

(1) TCGA 1992 is amended as follows.

(2) In section 99B(3) (calculation of the disposal cost of accumulation units) for "section 468H of ICTA" substitute "regulations made under section 17(3) of the Finance (No 2) Act 2005 (as at 1st April 2006, see regulation 15 of the Authorised Investment Funds (Tax) Regulations 2006 (SI 2006/964))".

90 Amendment of FA 1996

(1) FA 1996 is amended as follows.

(2) In paragraph 4(4) of Schedule 10 (loan relationships: company holdings in unit trusts and offshore funds) for "section 468L(3) of the Taxes Act 1988" substitute "regulations made under section 17(3) of the Finance (No 2) Act 2005 (as at 1st April 2006, see regulation 18(3) of the Authorised Investment Funds (Tax) Regulations 2006 (SI 2006/964))".

91 Amendments of ITTOIA 2005

(1) ITTOIA 2005 is amended as follows.

(2) In section 373(2) (open-ended investment company interest distributions) for "subsections (6) and (7)" substitute "subsection (7)".

(3) In section 376(2) (authorised unit trust interest distributions) for "subsections (6) and (7)" substitute "subsection (7)".

92 Amendment of the Finance Act 2005

(1) The Finance Act 2005 is amended as follows.

(2) In Schedule 2 (alternative finance arrangements: further provisions), omit paragraph 4.

CHAPTER 2

MODIFICATIONS OF THE TAX ACTS

93 Introduction

In their application in relation to—

(*a*) authorised investment funds,

(*b*) shareholders or unit holders in authorised investment funds, and

(*c*) transactions involving authorised investment funds,

the Tax Acts have effect with the modifications specified in regulations 94 to [96A][1].

Amendments—[1] Reference substituted by the Authorised Investment Funds (Tax) (Amendment) Regulations, SI 2012/519 regs 2, 7 with effect in relation to any distribution made at or after 1.30pm on 27 February 2012 (SI 2012/519 reg 1).

[93A [Modifications of TMA 1970

(1) TMA 1970 is modified as follows.

(2) In section 98(4E) (special returns etc)—

(*a*) in paragraph (*a*) for "trustees of an authorised unit trust" substitute "legal owner of an authorised investment fund";

(*b*) in paragraph (*b*)—

(i) for "trustees" substitute "legal owner", and

(ii) for "do not comply" substitute "does not comply"; and

(*c*) in paragraph (*d*) for "trustees" substitute "legal owner".][1]

Amendment—[1] Regulation inserted by the Authorised Investment Funds (Tax) (Amendment No 2) Regulations, SI 2007794 regs 2, 5 with effect from 6 April 2007.

94 Modifications of ICTA

(1) ICTA is modified as follows.

(2) In section 402 (surrender of relief between members of groups and consortia) after subsection (3) the following subsection is treated as inserted—

"(3AA) For the purposes of this Chapter—

(*a*) an open-ended investment company cannot be either the surrendering company or the claimant company, and

(*b*) an authorised unit trust shall not be regarded as a company.".

(3) In section 413 (interpretation of Chapter 4), in subsection (2), the following definitions are treated as inserted at the appropriate places—

" "authorised unit trust" has the meaning given by section 468(6);

"open-ended investment company" has the meaning given by section 468A(2);".

(4) In section 413 after subsection (3) the following subsection is treated as inserted—

"(3A) For the purposes of paragraph (*a*) of subsection (3) above an open-ended investment company cannot be the third company mentioned in that paragraph.".

[(4A) After paragraph (*b*) of section 432A(1ZA) of ICTA (apportionment of income and gains), there is treated as inserted—

"(*ba*) income from property income distributions to which regulation 69Z15 of the Authorised Investment Funds (Tax) Regulations 2006 apply (property income distributions by an open-ended investment company."][2]

(5) In section 832 (interpretation of the Tax Acts) after subsection (2) [the following subsection is treated as inserted][1]

"(2A) The definition of "ordinary share capital" does not include the issued share capital of an open-ended investment company.".

(6) In section 834 (interpretation of the Corporation Tax Acts), in subsection (3), the words "except in so far as regulations made under section 17(3) of the Finance (No 2) Act 2005 make other provision for dividends treated as paid by virtue of those Regulations" are treated as substituted for the words from "except in so far as" to the end.

(7) In Schedule 20 (charities: qualifying investments and loans) after paragraph 6 the following paragraph is treated as inserted—

"6A Shares in an open-ended investment company.".

Amendment—[1] Words in para (5) substituted by the Authorised Investment Funds (Tax) (Amendment No 2) Regulations, SI 2007/794 regs 2, 6 with effect from 6 April 2007.

[2] Para (4A) inserted by the Authorised Investment Funds (Tax) (Amendment No 3) Regulations, SI 2008/3159 regs 3, 28 with effect in relation to property income distributions paid on or after 1 January 2009. In relation to a qualified investor scheme authorised by the Financial Services Authority before 1 January 2009, this amendment has effect subject to SI 2008/3159 reg 31.

95 [Modifications of FA 1996

. . .

Amendments—Regulation 95 revoked by CTA 2009 s 1326, Sch 3 Pt 1. CTA 2009 applies for accounting periods ending on or after 1 April 2009 (for corporation tax purposes) and for tax years 2009-10 onwards (for income and capital gains tax purposes).

Note that new paras (1A), (1B) were purported to be inserted by the Authorised Investment Funds (Tax) (Amendment) Regulations, SI 2009/2036 regs 2, 30 with effect from 1 September 2009, but that reg 30 was revoked by the Authorised Investment Funds (Tax) (Amendment No 2) Regulations, SI 2009/2199, reg 2 with effect from 31 August 2009 (ie before SI 2009/2036 came into effect).

96 Modifications of ITTOIA 2005

(1) ITTOIA 2005 is modified as follows.

[(1A) In the application of the provisions specified in paragraph (1B) in relation to a Property AIF and a Tax Elected Fund—

(*a*) for "the total" substitute "an", and

(*b*) the amount available for distribution as PAIF distribution (interest) or TEF distribution (non-dividend), as the case may be, shall be treated as the amount available for distribution as yearly interest.

(1B) The specified provisions are—

(*a*) section 373(1) (open-ended investment company interest distributions), and

(*b*) section 376(1) (authorised unit trust interest distributions).][1]

(2) The words ", except in so far as regulations made under section 17(3) of the Finance (No 2) Act 2005 make other provision for dividends treated as paid by virtue of those regulations" are treated as inserted at the end of each of the provisions specified in paragraph (3).

(3) The provisions specified are—

(*a*) section 374(1) (date when open-ended investment company interest distributions made),

(*b*) section [377(1)][1] (date when authorised unit trust interest distributions made),

(*c*) section 387(1) (date when open-ended investment company dividend distributions made), and

(*d*) section 390(1) (date when authorised unit trust dividend distributions made).

(4) In sections 375(1) (interpretation of sections 373 and 374) and 388(1) (interpretation of sections 386 and 387) the definition of "the OEIC Regulations" is treated as omitted.

(5) In those provisions, the following definitions are treated as substituted for the definitions of "open-ended investment company", "owner of shares" and "umbrella company"—

" "open-ended investment company" means a company incorporated in the United Kingdom to which section 236 of FISMA 2000 applies,

"owner of shares", in relation to an open-ended investment company, has the meaning given in regulations made under section 17(3) of the Finance (No 2) Act 2005, and

"umbrella company" has the meaning given by section 468A of ICTA.".

(6) In sections 375(3) and 388(3) the words "regulations under section 17(3) of the Finance (No 2) Act 2005 (as at 1st April 2006, see regulation 6(2) of the Authorised Investment Funds (Tax) Regulations 2006 (SI 2006/964))" are treated as substituted for the words from "Chapter 3 of Part 12 of ICTA" to the end.

Amendments—[1] Paras (1A), (1B) inserted, and in para (3)(*b*) figure substituted, by the Authorised Investment Funds (Tax) (Amendment) Regulations, SI 2009/2036 regs 2, 31 with effect from 1 September 2009.

96A [Modification of CTA 2009

(1) CTA 2009 is modified as follows.

(2) In section 490 (holdings in OEICs, unit trusts and offshore funds treated as creditor relationship rights)—

(*a*) for subsection (2) the following subsection is treated as substituted—

"(2) The Corporation Tax Acts have effect for the accounting period in accordance with subsections (3) and (3A) as if—

(*a*) the relevant holding were rights under a creditor relationship of the company, and

(*b*) any distribution in respect of the relevant holding were not a distribution (and accordingly is within Part 5)."

(*b*) after subsection (3) the following subsections are treated as inserted—

"(3A) To the extent that any distribution to which subsection (2)(*b*) applies relates to an unfranked part of a dividend distribution—

(*a*) regulation 48(2)(b) of the Authorised Investment Funds (Tax) Regulations 2006 applies to determine the amount of the distribution and any tax treated as deducted from that distribution, and

(b) regulations 48A and 48B of those Regulations apply to determine the amount of any foreign income and the foreign element of the tax treated as deducted.

(3B) For the purposes of subsection (3A)—

(a) "dividend distribution" has the meaning given by regulation 22(3) of the Authorised Investment Funds (Tax) Regulations 2006, and

(b) regulation 49 of those Regulations explains how to calculate the unfranked part of the dividend distribution."; and

(c) subsections (4) and (5) are treated as omitted.][1]

Amendments—[1] Reg 96A and preceding heading inserted by the Authorised Investment Funds (Tax) (Amendment) Regulations, SI 2012/519 regs 2, 8 with effect in relation to any distribution made at or after 1.30 pm on 27 February 2012 (SI 2012/519 reg 1).

CHAPTER 3

MODIFICATIONS OF TCGA 1992

PRELIMINARY

97 Introduction

In its application in relation to—

(a) authorised investment funds,

(b) shareholders or unit holders in authorised investment funds, and

(c) transactions involving authorised investment funds

TCGA 1992 has effect with the modifications specified in regulations 98 to 110.

GENERAL

98 Application of TCGA 1992: general

(1) TCGA 1992 has effect in relation to—

(a) open-ended investment companies,

(b) holdings in, and the assets of, such companies, and

(c) transactions involving such companies,

in like manner as the manner in which it has effect in relation to authorised unit trusts, to rights under, and the assets subject to, such trusts and to transactions for purposes connected with such trusts.

(2) References in TCGA 1992 to companies, to holdings in, and the assets of, companies and to transactions involving companies accordingly have effect (or do not have effect as the case may be) in relation to open-ended investment companies, to holdings in, and the assets of, such companies, and to transactions involving such companies, in like manner as the manner in which they have effect (or do not have effect) in relation to authorised unit trusts, to rights under, and the assets subject to, such trusts, and to transactions for purposes connected with such trusts.

(3) This regulation has effect subject to the other modifications contained in this Chapter.

GENERAL MODIFICATIONS OF TCGA 1992

99 General modifications: introduction

The modifications specified in regulations 100 to 104 have effect subject to the modifications specified in regulations 105 to 110.

100 General modification: authorised unit trust

(1) The modifications specified in this regulation are that references, however expressed, in TCGA 1992 to—

(a) an authorised unit trust (other than references in a definition of an authorised unit trust, an unauthorised unit trust or a unit trust scheme),

(b) a unit trust scheme as denoting or including (whether expressly or by implication) an authorised unit trust (other than references in a definition of an authorised unit trust, an unauthorised unit trust or a unit trust scheme),

(c) the trustees of an authorised unit trust within sub-paragraph (a) or of a unit trust scheme within sub-paragraph (b),

have effect as if they included references to an open-ended investment company.

(2) Paragraph (1) does not apply—

(a) to references in any of the provisions specified in paragraph (3), or

(b) to references to provisions which include reference, whether made expressly or by implication, to an open-ended investment company.

(3) The provisions specified are—

(a) section 99(1) (application of Act to unit trust scheme),

(b) . . .[1]

(c) section 100(2) (exemption for units in unit trust scheme), and

(d) section 272(5) (valuation of rights of unit holders).

Amendments—[1] Sub-para (3)(*b*) revoked by the Collective Investment Schemes (Tax Transparent Funds, Exchanges, Mergers and Schemes of Reconstruction) Regulations, SI 2013/1400 reg 14(*a*) with effect in relation to disposals on or after 8 June 2013.

101 General modification: manager of authorised unit trust

(1) The modifications specified in this regulation are that references, however expressed, in TCGA 1992 to the manager of an authorised unit trust or of a unit trust scheme within regulation 100(1)(*b*) have effect as if they included references to the authorised corporate director of the open-ended investment company concerned.

(2) Paragraph (1) does not apply—

(*a*) to section 272(5) (valuation of rights of unit holders), or

(*b*) to references in provisions which include reference, whether made expressly or by implication, to the authorised corporate director of an open-ended investment company.

102 General modification: unit in authorised unit trust

(1) The modifications specified in this regulation are that references, however expressed, in TCGA 1992 to—

(*a*) a unit or an interest in, or rights under, an authorised unit trust,

(*b*) a unit or an interest in, or rights under, a unit trust scheme within regulation 100(1)(*b*), or

(*c*) an entitlement to a share of, or in, the investments subject to the trusts of an authorised unit trust or a unit trust scheme within regulation 100(1)(*b*),

have effect as if they included references to a share in the open-ended investment company concerned.

(2) Paragraph (1) does not apply—

(*a*) to section 99(1) (application of Act to unit trust scheme),

(*b*) . . . [1]

(*c*) to section 272(5) (valuation of rights of unit holders), or

(*d*) to references in provisions which include reference, whether made expressly or by implication, to shares in, or an owner of shares in, an open-ended investment company.

Amendments—[1] Sub-para (2)(*b*) revoked by the Collective Investment Schemes (Tax Transparent Funds, Exchanges, Mergers and Schemes of Reconstruction) Regulations, SI 2013/1400 reg 14(*b*) with effect in relation to disposals on or after 8 June 2013.

103 General modification: accumulation units in authorised unit trusts

(1) The modifications specified in this regulation are that references, however expressed, in TCGA 1992 to accumulation units in an authorised unit trust or in a unit trust scheme within regulation 100(1)(*b*) have effect as if they included references to accumulation shares in an open-ended investment company.

(2) In paragraph (1) "accumulation shares in an open-ended investment company" means shares in the company in respect of which income is credited periodically to the capital part of the scheme property of the company.

104 General modification: holder of unit in authorised unit trust

(1) The modifications specified in this regulation are that references, however expressed, in TCGA 1992 to the holder of a unit within regulation 102(1) (other than references in a definition of a unit holder) have effect as if they included references to the owner of a share in the open-ended investment company concerned.

(2) Paragraph (1) does not apply—

(*a*) to section 99(1) (application of Act to unit trust scheme),

(*b*) . . . [1]

(*c*) to section 272(5) (valuation of rights of unit holders), or

(*d*) to references in provisions which include reference, whether made expressly or by implication, to shares in, or an owner of shares in, an open-ended investment company.

Amendments—[1] Sub-para (2)(*b*) revoked by the Collective Investment Schemes (Tax Transparent Funds, Exchanges, Mergers and Schemes of Reconstruction) Regulations, SI 2013/1400 reg 14(*c*) with effect in relation to disposals on or after 8 June 2013.

SPECIFIC MODIFICATIONS OF TCGA 1992

105 Modification of section 99 of TCGA 1992

In section 99 of TCGA 1992 (application of Act to unit trust schemes), in subsection (2), the words "sections 99A and 99AA" are treated as substituted for "section 99A".

106 Insertion of section 99AA of TCGA 1992

Amendments—Regulation 106 revoked by the Collective Investment Schemes (Tax Transparent Funds, Exchanges, Mergers and Schemes of Reconstruction) Regulations, SI 2013/1400 reg 14(*d*) with effect in relation to disposals on or after 8 June 2013.

107 Modification of section 170 of TCGA 1992

In section 170 of TCGA 1992 (groups of companies: interpretation), after subsection (4), the following subsection is treated as inserted—

"(4A) An open-ended investment company cannot be the principal company of a group.".

108— Modifications of section 272 of TCGA 1992

(1) Section 272 of TCGA 1992 (valuation: general) is modified as follows.

(2) . . . [1]

(3) After subsection (5) the following subsection is treated as inserted—

"(5AA) In this Act "market value" in relation to shares of a given class in an open-ended investment company the prices of which are published regularly by the authorised corporate director of that company (whether or not those shares are also quoted in The Stock Exchange Daily Official List) shall mean an amount equal to the price so published on the relevant date, or if no price was published on that date, on the latest date before that date.".

Amendments—[1] Para (2) revoked by the Market Value of Shares, Securities and Strips Regulations, SI 2015/616 reg 4 with effect from 6 April 2015.

109— Modifications of section 288 of TCGA 1992

(1) Section 288 of TCGA 1992 (interpretation) is modified as follows.

(2) In subsection (1)—

(*a*) . . . [1]

(*b*) the following definitions are treated as inserted at the appropriate places in alphabetical order—

" "authorised corporate director" has the meaning given in regulations made under section 17(3) of the Finance (No 2) Act 2005 (as at 1st April 2006, see regulation 8 of the Authorised Investment Funds (Tax) Regulations 2006 (SI 2006/964));"

" "open-ended investment company" has the meaning given in regulations made under section 17(3) of the Finance (No 2) Act 2005 (as at 1st April 2006, see regulation 4 of the Authorised Investment Funds (Tax) Regulations 2006 (SI 2006/964));"

" "owner of shares" has the meaning given in regulations made under section 17(3) of the Finance (No 2) Act 2005 (as at 1st April 2006, see regulation 8 of the Authorised Investment Funds (Tax) Regulations 2006 (SI 2006/964));".

Amendments—[1] Sub-para (2)(*a*) revoked by the Collective Investment Schemes (Tax Transparent Funds, Exchanges, Mergers and Schemes of Reconstruction) Regulations, SI 2013/1400 reg 14(*e*) with effect in relation to disposals on or after 8 June 2013.

110 Modification of Schedule A1 to TCGA 1992

In Schedule A1 to TCGA 1992 (application of taper relief), in paragraph 16(2) (special rules for postponed gains), at the end of paragraph (*f*) the word ", or" is treated as added and the following paragraph is then also treated as added—

"(*g*) regulations 67(4) and 68(4) of the Authorised Investment Funds (Tax) Regulations 2006."

PART 8
FINAL PROVISIONS

111 Instruments revoked

The following statutory instruments are revoked—

The Open-ended Investment Companies (Tax) Regulations 1997;
The Open-ended Investment Companies (Tax) (Amendment) Regulations 1997;
The Open-ended Investment Companies (Tax) (Amendment) Regulations 2002;
The Open-ended Investment Companies (Tax) (Amendment) Regulations 2003.

SCHEDULE
ABBREVIATIONS AND DEFINED EXPRESSIONS

PART 1
ABBREVIATIONS OF ACTS

TMA 1970	The Taxes Management Act 1970 (c 9).
ICTA	The Income and Corporation Taxes Act 1988 (c 1)
TCGA 1992	The Taxation of Chargeable Gains Act 1992 (c 12)
[FA 1993	The Finance Act 1993 (c 34)][1]
[FA 1994	The Finance Act 1994 (c 9)][1]

FA 1996	The Finance Act 1996 (c 8)
FISMA 2000	The Financial Services and Markets Act 2000 (c 8)
FA 2002	The Finance Act 2002 (c 23).
ITEPA 2003	The Income Tax (Earnings and Pensions) Act 2003 (c 1)
ITTOIA 2005	The Income Tax (Trading and Other Income) Act 2005 (c 5)
[FA 2006	The Finance Act 2006 (c 25)][1]
[ITA 2007	The Income Tax Act 2007 (c 3)][1]
[CTA 2009	The Corporation Tax Act 2009 (c 4)][2]
[CTA 2010	The Corporation Tax Act 2010 (c. 4)][5]
[TIOPA 2010	The Taxation (International and Other Provisions) Act 2010 (c 8)][3]
[FA 2012	The Finance Act 2012 (c. 14)][4]

Amendments—[1] Entries inserted by the Authorised Investment Funds (Tax) (Amendment) Regulations, SI 2008/705 regs 2, 6 with effect from 6 April 2008.

[2] Entry inserted by the Authorised Investment Funds (Tax) (Amendment) Regulations, SI 2009/2036 regs 2, 32 with effect from 1 September 2009.

[3] Entry for TIOPA 2010 inserted by the Authorised Investment Funds (Tax) (Amendment No 2) Regulations, SI 2010/1642 regs 2, 8 with effect in relation to distributions made at or after 13.45 on 22 June 2010 (SI 2010/1642 reg 1).

[4] Entry for FA 2012 inserted by the Authorised Investment Funds (Tax) (Amendment No 3) Regulations, SI 2012/3043 reg 2(1), (3) with effect in relation to dividend distributions made on or after 1 January 2013.

[5] Definition of CTA 2010 inserted by the Real Estate Investment Trust (Amendments to the Corporation Tax Act 2010 and Consequential Amendments) Regulations, SI 2014/518 reg 3(1), (3) with effect for accounting periods beginning on or after 1 April 2014.

PART 2
INDEX OF EXPRESSIONS DEFINED OR OTHERWISE EXPLAINED IN THESE REGULATIONS

Accumulation unit	Regulation 6(5)
Acquiring company (in Chapter 2 of Part 6)	Regulation 78(7)
Alternative finance arrangements (in Part 3)	Regulation 21(11)
[Applicant (in Part 4A)	Regulation 69O(6)][2]
[Applicant (in Part 4B)	Regulation 69Z49(5)][4]
[Application (in Part 4B)	Regulation 69Z49(5)][4]
Authorised (in relation to unit trust schemes)	Regulation 5(2)
Authorised corporate director	Regulation 8
Authorised investment funds	Regulation 3
[Balance of business conditions (in Part 4A)	Regulation 69N][2]
[Body corporate (in Part 4A)	Regulation 69L(6)][2]
Capital profits, gains or losses (in Part 2)	Regulation 12
[Cessation (in Part 4A)	Regulation 69C(2)][2]
[Cessation (in Part 4B)	Regulation 69Z44][4]
Chargeable measuring date (in Chapter 4 of Part 4)	*Regulation 56(2)*[3]
Collective investment scheme	Regulation 8
Commissioners	Regulation 8
Consideration shares (in Chapter 2 of Part 6)	Regulation 78(7)
Contract for differences (in Part 3)	Regulation 21(9)
[Corporate ownership condition (in Part 4A)	Regulation 69K][2]
Creditor relationship	Regulation 8
[Dedicated feeder fund	Regulation 69C(4)][7]
Deduction obligation (in Part 4)	Regulation 26(3)
Derivative contract	Regulation 8
Difference in value (in Chapter 4 of Part 4)	*Regulation 55(2)*[3]
Disposal (in Chapter 4 of Part 4)	*Regulation 59*[3]
Distribution	*Regulation 15(1)*[5]

[Distribution	[Regulation 15(1)(*b*)][5]
Distribution accounts	*Regulation 15(3)*[5]
Distribution date	Regulation 15(4)
[Distribution income (in Part 4B)	Regulation 69Z56(1)(*a*)][4]
Distribution period	Regulation 15(2)
[Diversely owned AIF	Regulation 14E(2)][4]
Dividend distribution	Regulation 22(3)
Earlier measuring date (in Chapter 4 of Part 4)	*Regulation 55(2)*[3]
[Elective FINROF (in Part 6A)	Regulation 85F][5]
[Entry (in Part 4A)	Regulation 69C(1)][2]
[Entry (in Part 4B)	Regulation 69Z44][4]
[Excessive holding (in Part 4A)	Regulation 69Z13(3)][2]
Exchanged units (in Chapter 2 of Part 6)	Regulation 78(7)
[Existing company notice (in Part 4A)	Regulation 69O(6)][2]
[Existing fund application (in Part 4B)	Regulation 69Z49(5)][4]
[FINROF (in Part 6A)	Regulation 85A][5]
First measuring date (in Chapter 4 of Part 4)	*Regulation 64*[3]
[Fund documents	Regulation 9A(10)][4]
[Future company notice (in Part 4A)	Regulation 69O(6)][2]
[Future fund application (in Part 4B)	Regulation 69Z49(5)][4]
[F (post-cessation) (in Part 4A)	Regulation 69C(3)(*d*)][2]
[F (pre-entry) (in Part 4A)	Regulation 69C(3)(*a*)][2]
[F (residual) (in Part 4A)	Regulation 69C(3)(*c*)][2]
[F (tax-exempt) (in Part 4A)	Regulation 69C(3)(*b*)][2]
[Genuine diversity of ownership condition . . .[4]	Regulation [9A][4]][2]
[Gross asset value (in Part 6A)	Regulation 85C][5]
[Holder of excessive rights (in Part 4A)	Regulation 69Z13][2]
[Income allocation	Regulation 15(1)(*a*)][5]
[Information notice (in Part 4B)	Regulation 69Z67(2)][4]
[Instrument constituting the fund	Regulation 6(7)][4]
[Instrument constituting the scheme	Regulation [6(7)][4]][3]
Interest distribution	Regulation 18(3)
Investments	Regulation 8
[Investment condition (in Part 6A)	Regulation 85D][5]
. . .[8]	. . .[8]
Later measuring date (in Chapter 4 of Part 4)	*Regulation 55(2)*[3]
Legal owner	Regulation 6(1)
[Loan creditor condition (in Part 4A)	Regulation 69M][2]
[Loan creditor condition (in Part 4B)	Regulation 69Z47][4]
Manager	Regulation 6(3)
Market value (in Chapter 4 of Part 4)	*Regulation 55(4) and (5)*[3]
Measuring date (in Chapter 4 of Part 4)	*Regulation 55*[3]
Net asset value	Regulation 8
[Net income (in Part 4A)	Regulation 69Z][2]
[Net income of F (residual) (in Part 4A)	Regulation 69Z2][2]
[Net income of F (tax-exempt) (in Part 4A)	Regulation 69Z1][2]
[Newly qualified company (in Part 4A)	Regulation 69N(5)][2]
[Non-reporting fund	Regulation 8][6]
. . .	. . .[6]
[Offshore fund	Regulation 8[6]
[Offshore Funds Regulations	Regulation 8][6]

. . .	. . . [6]
. . .	. . . [6]
Open-ended investment company	Regulation 4
Owner of shares	Regulation 8
[PAIF distribution (dividends) (in Part 4A)	Regulation 69Z17(3)][2]
[PAIF distribution (interest) (in Part 4A)	Regulation 69Z16(3)][2]
Participant	Regulation 6(6)
[Pre-distribution amount (in Part 4A)	Regulation 69Z3][2]
Pre-transfer accounting period (in Chapter 2 of Part 6)	Regulation 79(1)
[Property AIF	Regulation 69A(2)][2]
[Property business income (in Part 4B)	Regulation 69Z56(1)(*c*)][4]
[Property condition (in Part 4B)	Regulation 69Z46][4]
[Property income distribution	Regulation 69Z15(4)][2]
[Property investment business (in Part 4A)	Regulation 69F(1)][2]
[Property investment income (in Part 4B)	Regulation 69Z56(1)(b)][4]
[Property rental business (in Part 4A)	Regulation 69H(1)][2]
[Prospectus (in Part 4A)	*Regulation 69E(4)][5]*
[Prospectus	Regulation 8][5]
Qualifying certificate	Regulation 35
Qualified investor scheme	Regulation [14B(4)][3]
Qualifying investments	Regulation 20
Qualifying units (in another authorised investment fund) (in Part 3)	Regulation 21(3)
[Refusal notice (in Part 4B)	Regulation 69Z52(1)][4]
[Relevant distribution (in Chapter 6 of Part 4A)	Regulation 69Z29(1)(*b*)][2]
Relevant period (in Part 3)	Regulation 19(2)
[Reportable income	Regulation 8][6]
Reporting date	Regulation 8
[Reporting fund	Regulation 8][6]
. . .	. . . [6]
[Reputable intermediary condition (in Part 4)	Regulation 27][1]
[Residence condition (in Part 4)	Regulation 30][1]
Residence declaration	Regulation 8
Scheme property	Regulation 6(2)
Securities (in Part 3)	Regulation 21(2)
[Specified accounting period (in Part 4A)	Regulation 69Q(2)][2]
[Specified accounting period (in Part 4B)	Regulation 69Z51(2)][4]
[Statement of Recommended Practice	Regulation 8][5]
Substantial QIS holding (in Chapter 4 of Part 4)	*Regulation 54*[3]
Target trust (in Chapter 2 of Part 6)	Regulation 78(7)
[Tax Elected Fund	Regulation 69Z42(2)][4]
Tax year	Regulation 8
[TEF conditions (in Part 4B)	Regulation 69Z45(a)][4]
[TEF distribution (dividend) (in Part 4B)	Regulation 69Z60(3)][4]
[TEF distribution (non-dividend)	Regulation 69Z61(3)][4]
[Termination notice (in Part 4A)	Regulation 69Z37(1)][2]
[Termination notice (in Part 4B)	Regulation 69Z70(1)][4]
Transfer date (in Chapter 2 of Part 6)	Regulation 78(7)
[UK-REIT	Regulation 69F(2)][2]
Umbrella company	Regulation 7(1)
Umbrella scheme	Regulation 7(4)

Underlying subject matter (in Part 3)	Regulation 21(6)
Unit holder	Regulation 5(3)
Unit trust scheme	Regulation 5(1)
Units	Regulation 6(4)
The whole of the scheme property of an authorised unit trust that is available for transfer (in Chapter 2 of Part 6)	Regulation 78(7)

Amendments—[1] Entries inserted by the Authorised Investment Funds (Tax) (Amendment No 2) Regulations, SI 2007/794 regs 2, 7 with effect from 6 April 2007.

[2] Entries inserted by the Authorised Investment Funds (Tax) (Amendment) Regulations, SI 2008/705 regs 2, 7 with effect from 6 April 2008.

[3] Entries revoked, in definition of "Qualified investor scheme" reference substituted for reference "53(3)", and definition of "instrument constituting the scheme" inserted, by the Authorised Investment Funds (Tax) (Amendment No 3) Regulations, SI 2008/3159 regs 3, 29 with effect from 1 January 2009. In relation to a qualified investor scheme authorised by the Financial Services Authority before 1 January 2009, these amendments have effect subject to SI 2008/3159 reg 31.

[4] Entries inserted and amended by the Authorised Investment Funds (Tax) (Amendment) Regulations, SI 2009/2036 regs 2, 32 with effect from 1 September 2009.

[5] Entries for "Prospectus (in Part 4A)", "distribution" and "distribution accounts" revoked, and entries inserted, by the Authorised Investment Funds (Tax) (Amendment) Regulations, SI 2010/294, regs 2, 22, with effect from 6 March 2010 (see reg 1(2)).

[6] Entries relating to "non reporting fund (in Part 6A)", "offshore fund (in Part 6A), "Offshore Funds Regulations 2009 (in Part 6A)" and "reporting fund (in Part 6A)" revoked, and entries inserted, by the Authorised Investment Funds (Tax) (Amendment) Regulations, SI 2011/244 regs 2, 7 with effect as follows—

(a) for the purposes of corporation tax—
- on income, for accounting periods ending on or after 6 March 2011, and
- on chargeable gains, in relation to disposals made on or after 6 March 2011, and

(b) for the purposes of capital gains tax, in relation to disposals made on or after 6 March 2011.

These amendments are subject to the following transitional provision (SI 2011/244 reg 8)—
- This provision applies to an authorised investment fund ("the fund") which, on 5 March 2011, met the following requirement: that the fund did not meet the investment condition in reg 85D of these Regulations by virtue of holding an interest in an offshore fund that is treated as creditor relationship rights under CTA 2009 s 490 (a "relevant interest").
- A relevant interest shall continue to be treated as not being an interest in a non-reporting fund for the purposes of reg 85E of these Regulations for the period beginning on 6 March 2011 and ending on 5 July 2011.

[7] Entry relating to "Dedicated feeder fund" inserted by the Authorised Investment Funds (Tax) (Amendment No 2) Regulations, SI 2012/1783 regs 2, 5 with effect for the purposes of capital gains tax, in relation to disposals made on or after 1 August 2012, and for the purposes of corporation tax on chargeable gains, in relation to disposals made on or after 1 August 2012.

[8] Definition of "investment transaction" revoked by the Investment Transactions (Tax) Regulations, SI 2014/685 reg 7(1), (4) with effect from 8 April 2014.

2006/1182

INVESTMENT TRUSTS AND VENTURE CAPITAL TRUSTS (DEFINITION OF CAPITAL PROFITS, GAINS OR LOSSES) ORDER 2006

Made by the Treasury under FA 1996 Sch 10 paras 1A(2)(b), 1B(2)(b), 9(1), FA 2002 Sch 26 paras 38(2)(b), 38A(2)(b)

Made . . . . *26 April 2006*
Laid before the House of Commons . . . . *27 April 2006*
Coming into force . . . . *18 May 2006*

Amendment—This Order revoked by CTA 2009 s 1326, Sch 3 Pt 1. CTA 2009 applies for accounting periods ending on or after 1 April 2009 (for corporation tax purposes) and for tax years 2009–10 onwards (for income and capital gains tax purposes).

2006/1465

REGISTERED PENSION SCHEMES (AUTHORISED REDUCTIONS) REGULATIONS 2006

Made by the Commissioners for HMRC under FA 2004 Sch 28 para 2(4)(h), (4A), (8)

Made . . . . *6 June 2006*
Laid before the House of Commons . . . . *6 June 2006*
Coming into force . . . . *27 June 2006*

1 Citation, commencement and effect

These Regulations may be cited as the Registered Pension Schemes (Authorised Reductions) Regulations 2006, shall come into force on 27th June 2006 and shall have effect in relation to all times on and after 6th April 2006.

2 Effect of cessation of pension in connection with admission to Chelsea Hospital

The reduction of a scheme pension upon the admission of the pensioner to Royal Hospital at Chelsea in accordance with section 24 of the Chelsea and Kilmainham Hospitals Act 1826 (pension forfeited upon becoming an in-pensioner at Chelsea) does not prevent that pension from satisfying the condition in sub-paragraph (3) of paragraph 2 of Schedule 28 to the Finance Act 2004 (pension payable in any relevant 12 month period to be not less than that for the previous such period).

2006/1543

TAX AVOIDANCE SCHEMES (PRESCRIBED DESCRIPTIONS OF ARRANGEMENTS) REGULATIONS 2006

Made by the Treasury under FA 2004 s 306(1)(a), (b)

Made . . . .*15 June 2006*
Laid before the House of Commons . . . .*15 June 2006*
Coming into force . . . .*1 August 2006*

Modification—The National Insurance Contributions (Application of Part 7 of the Finance Act 2004) Regulations, SI 2012/1868 (these Regulations apply to notifiable contribution arrangements and notifiable contribution proposals with modifications as noted below, and any reference in these Regulations to FA 2004 ss 306–313C and s 314A shall be construed as a reference to the corresponding provision of SI 2012/1868).

Simon's Tax Cases—*R (on the appn of Graham and ors) v R&C Comrs* [2016] EWHC 1197 (Admin), [2017] STC 1.

PART 1
PRELIMINARY

1 Citation, commencement and effect

(1) These Regulations may be cited as the Tax Avoidance Schemes (Prescribed Descriptions of Arrangements) Regulations 2006, and shall come into force on 1st August 2006.

(2) These Regulations do not have effect—

(*a*) for the purposes of section 308(1) of FA 2004 (duties of promoter relating to any notifiable proposal), if the relevant date falls before 1st August 2006;

(*b*) for the purposes of section 308(3) of FA 2004 (duties of promoter relating to any notifiable arrangements), if the date on which the promoter first becomes aware of any transaction forming part of notifiable arrangements falls before 1st August 2006;

(*c*) for the purposes of section 309(1) of FA 2004 (duty of person dealing with promoter outside United Kingdom), and of section 310 of that Act (duty of parties to notifiable arrangements not involving promoter) if the date on which any transaction forming part of notifiable arrangements is entered into falls before 1st August 2006.

(3) In paragraph (2)(*a*) "the relevant date" has the meaning given by section 308(2) of FA 2004.

Modification—NIC (Application of Part 7 of the Finance Act 2004) Regulations, SI 2012/1868 reg 25(2) (modification of this regulation to omit paras (2), (3) in relation to NIC avoidance schemes and proposals).

2 Interpretation: general

(1) This paragraph gives the meaning of the abbreviated references to Acts used in these Regulations—

"CAA 2001" means the Capital Allowances Act 2001;
["CTA 2009" means the Corporation Tax Act 2009;
"CTA 2010" means the Corporation Tax Act 2010;][2]
"FA 2004" means the Finance Act 2004;
"ICTA 1988" means the Income and Corporation Taxes Act 1988;
["ITA 2007" means the Income Tax Act 2007;][2]
"ITEPA 2003" means the Income Tax (Earnings and Pensions) Act 2003;
"ITTOIA 2005" means the Income Tax (Trading and Other Income) Act 2005;
"TCGA 1992" means the Taxation of Chargeable Gains Act 1992.

(2) In these Regulations—

"business" has the meaning given by regulation 3;
["HMRC" means Her Majesty's Revenue and Customs;][1]
["generally accepted accounting practice" has the meaning given by section 1127 of CTA 2010;][2]
"the Information Regulations" means the Tax Avoidance Schemes (Information) Regulations 2004;

["the material date" means whichever of the following is applicable—

(a) for a proposal notifiable under section 308(1) of FA 2004, the relevant date (as defined in section 308(2) of FA 2004);

(b) for arrangements notifiable under section 308(3) of FA 2004, the date the promoter first becomes aware of any transaction forming part of the notifiable arrangements; or

(c) for arrangements notifiable under section 309 or 310 of FA 2004, the date the person enters into any transaction forming part of the notifiable arrangements.][1]

. . .[1]

"plant or machinery lease" has the meaning given by [section 70K CAA 2001][1];

"the Promoters Regulations" means the Tax Avoidance Schemes (Promoters and Prescribed Circumstances) Regulations 2004;

"small or medium-sized enterprise" has the meaning given by regulation 4;.

(3) For the purposes of these Regulations section 839 of ICTA 1988 applies to determine whether persons are connected.

Amendments—[1] In para (2), definitions of "HMRC" and "the material date" inserted, definitions of " 'lease', 'lessor' and 'lessee' " revoked, and in definition of "plant or machinery lease" words substituted by the Tax Avoidance Schemes (Prescribed Descriptions of Arrangements) (Amendment) Regulations, SI 2010/2834 regs 2, 3 with effect from 1 January 2011.

[2] In para (1), definitions of "CTA 2009", "CTA 2010" and "ITA 2007" inserted, and in para (2), definition of "generally accepted accounting practice" inserted by the Tax Avoidance Schemes (Prescribed Descriptions of Arrangements) (Amendment) Regulations, SI 2016/99 regs 2, 3 with effect from 23 February 2016. These amendments do not have effect—

- for the purposes of FA 2004 s 308(1) (duties of promoter relating to any notifiable proposal), if the relevant date, as defined in FA 2004 s 308(2), falls before 23 February 2016;
- for the purposes of FA 2004 s 308(3) (duties of promoter relating to any notifiable arrangements), if the date on which the promoter first becomes aware of any transaction forming part of notifiable arrangements falls before 23 February 2016; and
- for the purposes of FA 2004 ss 309(1) (duty of person dealing with promoter outside United Kingdom), 310 (duty of parties to notifiable arrangements not involving promoter), if the date on which any transaction forming part of notifiable arrangements is entered into falls before 23 February 2016.

3 Meaning of "business"

In these Regulations "business" means—

(*a*) a company;

(*b*) a partnership; or

(*c*) any person whose profits are charged to income tax, otherwise than by virtue of his being a partner—

(i) as trading income under Part 2 of ITTOIA 2005 (trading income), or

(ii) as property income under section 268 of ITTOIA 2005 (charge to tax on profits of a property business).

4 Meaning of "small or medium-sized enterprise"

(1) For the purposes of these Regulations a "small or medium-sized enterprise" means a micro, small or medium-sized enterprise as defined in the Recommendation.

(2) In this regulation—

"the Recommendation" means the Commission Recommendation of 6th May 2003, and

"the Annex" means the Annex to the Recommendation.

(3) Paragraph (1) is subject to the following provisions.

(4) If a company ("C") is a micro, small or medium-sized enterprise, disregarding any partner enterprise or linked enterprise, and, taken alone, it would satisfy the employee limit and at least one of the financial limits, but—

(*a*) the number of employees, annual turnover or annual balance sheet total (as the case may be) of a partner enterprise or linked enterprise to which it is related has been taken into account in determining whether the employee limits or the financial limits have been exceeded, and

(*b*) a partner enterprise or linked enterprise to which C is related would, disregarding the number of employees, and the annual turnover and annual balance sheet totals of C, exceed the employee limit, or either of the financial limits,

Article 4(2) of the Annex is to be disregarded in determining whether C is a small or medium-sized enterprise for an accounting period in which it exceeds the employee or financial limits.

In this paragraph references to the employee limit and the financial limits are to the limits respectively on the number of employees, and the annual turnover and balance sheet totals, contained in Article 2(1) of the Annex.

PART 2
GENERAL

5 Prescribed descriptions of arrangements

(1) The following arrangements are prescribed for the purposes of Part 7 of the FA 2004 (disclosure of tax avoidance schemes)—

(*a*) in relation to income tax, corporation tax and capital gains tax, any arrangements which fall within any description specified in a provision of these Regulations listed in paragraph (2);

(*b*) in relation to inheritance tax, any arrangements which fall within any description specified in a provision of these Regulations listed in paragraph (2)(*a*) or (*c*).][4]

(2) The provisions are—

(*a*) regulation 6 (description 1: confidentiality in cases involving a promoter);

(*b*) regulation 7 (description 2: confidentiality in cases not involving a promoter);

(*c*) regulation 8 (description 3: premium fee);

(*d*) . . .[2]

(*e*) regulation 10 (description 5: standardised tax products);

(*f*) regulation 12 (description 6: loss schemes); . . .[1]

(*g*) regulation 13 (description 7: leasing arrangements); [. . .[4]

(*h*) regulation 18 (description 8: employment income provided through third parties)[and][3]

(*i*) regulation 19 (description 9: financial products).][4]

(3) For the purpose only of determining whether arrangements are prescribed by regulations 6, 7, 8 and 13 of these Regulations, regulation 6 of the Promoters Regulations (persons not to be treated as promoters: legal professional privilege) shall be disregarded.

Modification—NIC (Application of Part 7 of the Finance Act 2004) Regulations, SI 2012/1868 reg 25(3) (modification of this reg in relation to NIC avoidance schemes or proposals).

Amendments—[1] In para (2), word "and" in sub-para (*f*) revoked, and in sub-para (*g*) word substituted for previous full stop, by the Tax Avoidance Schemes (Prescribed Descriptions of Arrangements) (Amendment) Regulations, SI 2009/2033 reg 2 with effect from 1 September 2009. Note that SI 2009/2033 is revoked by the Tax Avoidance Schemes (Prescribed Descriptions of Arrangements) (Amendment) Regulations, SI 2013/2595 regs 2, 11 with effect from 4 November 2013.

[2] Para (2)(*d*) revoked by the Tax Avoidance Schemes (Prescribed Descriptions of Arrangements) (Amendment) Regulations, SI 2010/2834 regs 2, 4 with effect from 1 January 2011.

[3] Para (2)(h) substituted by the Tax Avoidance Schemes (Prescribed Descriptions of Arrangements) (Amendment) Regulations, SI 2013/2595 regs 2, 9 with effect from 4 November 2013.

[4] Para (1) substituted, in para (2)(*g*), word "and" revoked, and para (2)(*i*) and preceding word inserted by the Tax Avoidance Schemes (Prescribed Descriptions of Arrangements) (Amendment) Regulations, SI 2016/99 regs 2, 4 with effect from 23 February 2016. These amendments do not have effect—

– for the purposes of FA 2004 s 308(1) (duties of promoter relating to any notifiable proposal), if the relevant date, as defined in FA 2004 s 308(2), falls before 23 February 2016;
– for the purposes of FA 2004 s 308(3) (duties of promoter relating to any notifiable arrangements), if the date on which the promoter first becomes aware of any transaction forming part of notifiable arrangements falls before 23 February 2016; and
– for the purposes of FA 2004 ss 309(1) (duty of person dealing with promoter outside United Kingdom), 310 (duty of parties to notifiable arrangements not involving promoter), if the date on which any transaction forming part of notifiable arrangements is entered into falls before 23 February 2016.

PART 3
PRESCRIBED ARRANGEMENTS

Modification—NIC (Application of Part 7 of the Finance Act 2004) Regulations, SI 2012/1868 reg 25(4) (modification of this Part in relation to NIC avoidance schemes and proposals).

[6 Description 1: Confidentiality where promoter involved

(1) Arrangements are prescribed if—

(*a*) any element of the arrangements (including the way in which the arrangements are structured) gives rise to the tax advantage expected to be obtained under the arrangements; and

(*b*) it might reasonably be expected that a promoter would wish the way in which that element of those arrangements secures, or might secure, a tax advantage to be kept confidential from any other promoter at any time following the material date.

(2) Arrangements are prescribed [if it might reasonably be expected that a promoter would][2], but for the requirements of these Regulations, wish to keep [the way in which any element of those arrangements (including the way in which the arrangements are structured)][2] that secures, or might secure, the tax advantage confidential from HMRC at any time following the material date, and a reason for doing so is to facilitate repeated or continued use of the same element, or substantially the same element, in the future.

[(2A) Cases where arrangements will be prescribed under paragraph (2) include, but are not limited to, where—

(a) a promoter does not provide to the user of the arrangements ("the user"), or prevents or discourages the user from retaining, any promotional materials, data or written professional advice relating to those arrangements; and

(b) it might reasonably be expected that the reason for doing so is to keep the arrangements confidential from HMRC in order to facilitate repeated or continued use of any element of those arrangements.][2]

(3) In a case where—

(*a*) by virtue of regulation 6 of the Promoters Regulations (persons not to be treated as promoters: legal professional privilege), no person is to be treated as the promoter in relation to the arrangements; or

(*b*) by virtue of section 309(1) of FA 2004 (duty of person dealing with promoter outside United Kingdom), a user of the arrangements has a duty to provide prescribed information,

for paragraph (2) substitute—

[(2) Arrangements are prescribed if it might reasonably be expected that the user of the arrangements would, but for the requirements of these regulations, wish to keep the way in which any element of those arrangements (including the way in which the arrangements are structured) that secures the tax advantage confidential from HMRC at any time following the material date.][2]][1]

Amendments—[1] Reg 6 substituted by the Tax Avoidance Schemes (Prescribed Descriptions of Arrangements) (Amendment) Regulations, SI 2010/2834 regs 2, 5 with effect from 1 January 2011.

[2] In para (2), words substituted, para (2A) inserted, and words in para (3) substituted, by the Tax Avoidance Schemes (Prescribed Descriptions of Arrangements) (Amendment) Regulations, SI 2013/2595 regs 2–5 with effect from 4 November 2013.

7 Description 2: Confidentiality where no promoter involved

[(1)] [2]Arrangements are prescribed if—

(*a*) no person is a promoter in relation to them;

(*b*) the intended user of the arrangements is a business which is not a small or medium-sized enterprise;

(*c*) any element of the arrangements (including the way in which the arrangements are structured) gives rise to the tax advantage expected to be obtained under the arrangements;

[(*d*) [it might reasonably be expected that a user would][2], but for the requirements of these Regulations, wish to keep the way in which that element secures the advantage confidential from HMRC at any time following the material date; and][1]

[(*e*) a reason for the user's wishing to keep the element confidential from HMRC is—

(i) to facilitate repeated or continued use of the same element, or substantially the same element, in the future; or

(ii) to reduce the risk of HMRC using that information to open an enquiry into any return or account which a person is required by or under any enactment to deliver to HMRC; or

(iii) to reduce the risk of HMRC using that information to withhold payment of all or part of an amount claimed separately from a return under—

(*aa*) section 261B of the Taxation of Chargeable Gains Act 1992 (treating trade loss etc as CGT loss); or

(*bb*) Part 4 of the [ITA 2007][3] (loss relief).][1]

[(2) Arrangements are also prescribed if—

(a) paragraphs (1)(a) to (c) are met; and

(b) if there had been a promoter in relation to the arrangements, it might reasonably have been expected that they would, but for the requirements of these Regulations, wish to have kept the way in which any element of the arrangements (including the way in which the arrangements were structured) that secured the tax advantage confidential from HMRC at any time following the material date, and a reason for doing so would be to facilitate repeated or continued use of the same element, or substantially the same element, in the future.][2]

Amendments—[1] Paras (1)(*d*), (*e*) substituted by the Tax Avoidance Schemes (Prescribed Descriptions of Arrangements) (Amendment) Regulations, SI 2010/2834 regs 2, 6 with effect from 1 January 2011.

[2] Para (1) numbered as such, in para (1)(*d*), words substituted, and para (2) inserted, by the Tax Avoidance Schemes (Prescribed Descriptions of Arrangements) (Amendment) Regulations, SI 2013/2595 regs 2, 6–8 with effect from 4 November 2013.

[3] In para (1)(*e*)(iii)(*bb*), words substituted for words "Income Tax Act 2007" by the Tax Avoidance Schemes (Prescribed Descriptions of Arrangements) (Amendment) Regulations, SI 2016/99 regs 2, 5 with effect from 23 February 2016. This amendment does not have effect—

– for the purposes of FA 2004 s 308(1) (duties of promoter relating to any notifiable proposal), if the relevant date, as defined in FA 2004 s 308(2), falls before 23 February 2016;
– for the purposes of FA 2004 s 308(3) (duties of promoter relating to any notifiable arrangements), if the date on which the promoter first becomes aware of any transaction forming part of notifiable arrangements falls before 23 February 2016; and
– for the purposes of FA 2004 ss 309(1) (duty of person dealing with promoter outside United Kingdom), 310 (duty of parties to notifiable arrangements not involving promoter), if the date on which any transaction forming part of notifiable arrangements is entered into falls before 23 February 2016.

8 Description 3: Premium Fee

(1) Arrangements are prescribed if they are such that it might reasonably be expected that a promoter or a person connected with a promoter of arrangements that are the same as, or substantially similar to, the arrangements in question, would, but for the requirements [of][1] these Regulations, be able to obtain a premium fee from a person experienced in receiving services of the type being provided. But arrangements are not prescribed by this regulation if—

(*a*) no person is a promoter in relation to them; and

(*b*) the tax advantage which may be obtained under the arrangements is intended to be obtained by an individual or a business which is a small or medium-sized enterprise.

(2) For the purposes of paragraph (1), and in relation to any arrangements, a "premium fee" is a fee chargeable by virtue of any element of the arrangements (including the way in which they are structured) from which the tax advantage expected to be obtained arises, and which is—

(*a*) to a significant extent attributable to that tax advantage, or

(*b*) to any extent contingent upon the obtaining of that tax advantage [as a matter of law][1].

Amendments—[1] in para (1), words substituted for words, and in para (2)(*b*) words inserted, by the Tax Avoidance Schemes (Prescribed Descriptions of Arrangements) (Amendment) Regulations, SI 2010/2834 regs 2, 7 with effect from 1 January 2011.

9 . . .

. . .

Amendments—Reg 9 and preceding heading revoked by the Tax Avoidance Schemes (Prescribed Descriptions of Arrangements) (Amendment) Regulations, SI 2010/2834 regs 2, 8 with effect from 1 January 2011.

[10 Description 5: standardised tax products

(1) Subject to regulation 11, arrangements are prescribed if a promoter makes the arrangements available for implementation by more than one person and the conditions in paragraph (2) are met.

(2) The conditions are that an informed observer (having studied the arrangements and having regard to all relevant circumstances) could reasonably be expected to conclude that—

(*a*) the arrangements have standardised, or substantially standardised, documentation—

(i) the purpose of which is to enable a person to implement the arrangements;

(ii) the form of which is determined by the promoter; and

(iii) the substance of which does not need to be tailored, to any material extent, to enable a person to implement the arrangements;

(*b*) a person implementing the arrangements must enter into a specific transaction or series of specific transactions;

(*c*) the transaction or series of transactions is standardised, or substantially standardised, in form; and

(*d*) either the main purpose of the arrangements is to enable a person to obtain a tax advantage or the arrangements would be unlikely to be entered into but for the expectation of obtaining a tax advantage.][1]

Modification—NIC (Application of Part 7 of the Finance Act 2004) Regulations, SI 2012/1868 reg 25(5) (modification of this regulation in relation to NIC avoidance schemes and proposals).

Amendments—[1] Regulation 10 substituted by the Tax Avoidance Schemes (Prescribed Descriptions of Arrangements) (Amendment) Regulations, SI 2016/99 regs 2, 6 with effect from 23 February 2016. This amendment does not have effect—

- for the purposes of FA 2004 s 308(1) (duties of promoter relating to any notifiable proposal), if the relevant date, as defined in FA 2004 s 308(2), falls before 23 February 2016;
- for the purposes of FA 2004 s 308(3) (duties of promoter relating to any notifiable arrangements), if the date on which the promoter first becomes aware of any transaction forming part of notifiable arrangements falls before 23 February 2016; and
- for the purposes of FA 2004 ss 309(1) (duty of person dealing with promoter outside United Kingdom), 310 (duty of parties to notifiable arrangements not involving promoter), if the date on which any transaction forming part of notifiable arrangements is entered into falls before 23 February 2016.

11 Arrangements excepted from Description 5

(1) The arrangements specified in this regulation are—

(*a*) those described in paragraph (2); and

(*b*) those which are of the same, or substantially the same, description as arrangements which were first made available for implementation before 1st August 2006.[2]

(2) [The following arrangements are excepted from being prescribed under regulation 10][2]—

(*a*) arrangements which consist solely of one or more plant or machinery leases . . . [1];

(*b*) an enterprise investment scheme ([Part 5 of ITA 2007 and Schedule 5B][2] to TCGA 1992);

(*c*) arrangements using a venture capital trust (see [Part 6 of ITA 2007][2] and Schedule 5C to TCGA 1992);

(*d*) arrangements qualifying under the corporate venturing scheme (see Schedule 15 to the Finance Act 2000);

(*e*) arrangements qualifying for community investment tax relief (see Schedules 16 and 17 to the Finance Act 2002);

(*f*) an account which satisfies the conditions in the Individual Savings Account Regulations 1998;

(*g*) an approved share incentive plan (see Chapter 6 of Part 7 of, and Schedule 2 to, ITEPA 2003);

(*h*) an approved share option scheme (see Chapter 7 of Part 7 of, and Schedule 3 to, ITEPA 2003);

(i) an approved CSOP scheme (see Chapter 8 of Part 7 of, and Schedule 4 to, ITEPA 2003);

(*j*) the grant of one or more qualifying options which meet the requirements of Schedule 5 to ITEPA 2003 (enterprise management incentives)—

(i) together only with such other steps as are reasonably necessary in all the circumstances for the purposes of facilitating it, or

(ii) which fall to be notified to the Board in accordance with Part 7 of that Schedule;

(*k*) a registered pension scheme (see section 150(2) of FA 2004);

(*l*) an overseas pension scheme in respect of which tax relief is granted in the United Kingdom under section 615 of ICTA 1988 (exemption from tax for superannuation payments in respect of persons not resident in the United Kingdom or in respect of trades carried on wholly or partly outside the United Kingdom);

(*m*) a pension scheme which is a relevant non-UK pension scheme within the meaning given by paragraph 1(5) of Schedule 34 to FA 2004;

(*n*) a scheme to which section 731 of ITTOIA 2005 applies (periodical payments of personal injury damages).

[(*o*) arrangements which would be prescribed by regulation 19 but for regulation 21.][2]

Amendments—[1] In para (2)(*a*), words revoked, by the Tax Avoidance Schemes (Prescribed Descriptions of Arrangements) (Amendment) Regulations, SI 2010/2834 regs 2, 9 with effect from 1 January 2011.

[2] The following amendments made by the Tax Avoidance Schemes (Prescribed Descriptions of Arrangements) (Amendment) Regulations, SI 2016/99 regs 2, 7 with effect from 23 February 2016—

– para (1) revoked;
– in para (2), words substituted for words "The arrangements referred to in paragraph (1)(*a*) are";
– in para (2)(*b*), words substituted for words "Chapter 3 of Part 7 of ICTA 1988 and Schedules 5B and 5BA", and in para (2)(*c*), words substituted for words "Part 5 of ITA 2007 and Schedule 5B"; and
– para (2)(*o*) inserted.

These amendment do not have effect—

– for the purposes of FA 2004 s 308(1) (duties of promoter relating to any notifiable proposal), if the relevant date, as defined in FA 2004 s 308(2), falls before 23 February 2016;
– for the purposes of FA 2004 s 308(3) (duties of promoter relating to any notifiable arrangements), if the date on which the promoter first becomes aware of any transaction forming part of notifiable arrangements falls before 23 February 2016; and
– for the purposes of FA 2004 ss 309(1) (duty of person dealing with promoter outside United Kingdom), 310 (duty of parties to notifiable arrangements not involving promoter), if the date on which any transaction forming part of notifiable arrangements is entered into falls before 23 February 2016.

12 Description 6: Loss schemes

Arrangements are prescribed if—

(*a*) the promoter expects more than one individual to implement the same, or substantially the same, arrangements; and

(*b*) the arrangements are such that an informed observer (having studied them) could reasonably conclude—

(i) that the main benefit of those arrangements which could be expected to accrue to some or all of the individuals participating in them is the provision of losses, and

(ii) that those individuals would be expected to use those losses to reduce their liability to income tax or capital gains tax.

Modification—NIC (Application of Part 7 of the Finance Act 2004) Regulations, SI 2012/1868 reg 25(6) (revocation of regs 12–17A in relation to NIC avoidance schemes and proposals).

Amendments—[1] In para (2)(*a*), words revoked, by the Tax Avoidance Schemes (Prescribed Descriptions of Arrangements) (Amendment) Regulations, SI 2010/2834 regs 2, 8 with effect from 1 January 2011.

[2] The following amendments made by the Tax Avoidance Schemes (Prescribed Descriptions of Arrangements) (Amendment) Regulations, SI 2016/99 regs 2, 7 with effect from 23 February 2016—

– para (1) revoked;
– in para (2), words substituted for words "The arrangements referred to in paragraph (1)(*a*) are";
– in para (2)(*b*), words substituted for words "Chapter 3 of Part 7 of ICTA 1988 and Schedules 5B and 5BA", and in para (2)(*c*), words substituted for words "Part 5 of ITA 2007 and Schedule 5B"; and
– para (2)(*o*) inserted.

These amendment do not have effect—

– for the purposes of FA 2004 s 308(1) (duties of promoter relating to any notifiable proposal), if the relevant date, as defined in FA 2004 s 308(2), falls before 23 February 2016;
– for the purposes of FA 2004 s 308(3) (duties of promoter relating to any notifiable arrangements), if the date on which the promoter first becomes aware of any transaction forming part of notifiable arrangements falls before 23 February 2016; and
– for the purposes of FA 2004 ss 309(1) (duty of person dealing with promoter outside United Kingdom), 310 (duty of parties to notifiable arrangements not involving promoter), if the date on which any transaction forming part of notifiable arrangements is entered into falls before 23 February 2016.

13 Description 7: Leasing arrangements

(1) Arrangements are prescribed if—

(*a*) the arrangements include a plant or machinery lease . . . [1];

(*b*) one of the additional conditions is met (see regulation 15);

(*c*) the relevant value condition is met (see regulation 16); and (*d*) the lease is not a short-term lease (see regulation 17).

(2) But arrangements are not prescribed by this regulation if—

(*a*) no person is a promoter in relation to them; and

(*b*) the tax advantage which may be obtained under the arrangements is intended to be obtained by an individual or a business which is a small or medium-sized enterprise.

Modification—NIC (Application of Part 7 of the Finance Act 2004) Regulations, SI 2012/1868 reg 25(6) (revocation of regs 12–17A in relation to NIC avoidance schemes and proposals).

Amendments—[1] In para (1)(*a*), words revoked, by the Tax Avoidance Schemes (Prescribed Descriptions of Arrangements) (Amendment) Regulations, SI 2010/2834 regs 2, 10 with effect from 1 January 2011.

14 Meaning of "plant or machinery lease"

Amendments—Reg 14 revoked, by the Tax Avoidance Schemes (Prescribed Descriptions of Arrangements) (Amendment) Regulations, SI 2010/2834 regs 2, 11 with effect from 1 January 2011.

15 The additional conditions

(1) The first additional condition is that the arrangements are designed in such a way that one or more of the plant or machinery leases, comprised in the arrangements, are or would be entered into by—

(*a*) one party who has or would have a right or entitlement to claim capital allowances under Part 2 of CAA 2001 (plant and machinery allowances) in respect of the expenditure incurred on the plant or machinery, and

(*b*) another party who is not, or would not be, within the charge to corporation tax.

(2) A lease satisfies this condition if sub-paragraphs (*a*) and (*b*) of paragraph (1) are met, regardless of whether there are or would be (in addition to the parties mentioned in those sub-paragraphs) other parties to the lease who satisfy neither of those conditions.

(3) A party who acts merely as a guarantor under the lease is to be disregarded for the purposes of paragraph (1)(*b*).

(4) The second additional condition is that the arrangements include provision designed to—

(*a*) remove from the lessor the whole, or the greater part, of any risk, which would otherwise fall directly or indirectly upon the lessor, of sustaining a loss if payments due under the lease are not made in accordance with its terms, and

(*b*) do so by the provision of money or a money debt.

For the purposes of this paragraph "money" and "money debt" have the same meanings as they have in section 702(6) of ITEPA 2003.

(5) The third additional condition is that the arrangements are designed to consist of, or include—

(*a*) a sale and finance leaseback arrangement (within the meaning of section 221 of CAA 2001), or

(*b*) a lease and finance leaseback (within the meaning of section [228A(2)][1] of CAA 2001).

The third additional condition is subject to the following paragraphs of this regulation.

(6) In a case falling within paragraph (5)(*a*) the third additional condition does not apply if the arrangements are designed in such a way that—

(*a*) the assets leased or to be leased under the sale and finance leaseback are or will be unused and not second-hand at the time when the assets are acquired or created; and

(*b*) the interval between the acquisition or creation of the asset and the sale of the asset under the sale and finance leaseback arrangement is not more than four months.

(7) The third additional condition does not apply if plant or machinery which is, or which the promoter expects to become, a fixture, is leased with relevant land, unless the plant or machinery is used for storage or production.

Here "used for storage or production" means used for the purposes of—

(*a*) storing, moving or displaying goods to be sold in the course of a trade;

(*b*) manufacturing goods or materials;

(*c*) subjecting goods or materials to a process;

(*d*) storing goods or materials—

(i) which are to be used in the manufacture of other goods or materials;

(ii) which are to be subjected to a process in the course of a trade;

(iii) which having been subjected in the course of a trade to process, manufactured or produced, have not yet been delivered to a purchaser; or

(iv) upon their arrival in the United Kingdom from a place outside it.

(8) But paragraph (7) does not apply (so that, accordingly, the third additional condition is met) if the arrangements are designed in such a way that—

(*a*) the qualifying expenditure incurred on the fixture referred to in paragraph (7) amounts or will amount to more than 50% of the aggregate value of the assets subject to the lease, and

(*b*) the rent payable under the lease is directly or indirectly dependent on the availability of capital allowances under Part 2 of CAA 2001 in respect of expenditure on any plant or machinery comprised in the lease.

(9) In determining the value of the assets comprised in the lease the following rules apply.

Rule 1
The value of the land subject to the lease is the market value of the lessor's interest.
Rule 2
The value of the plant or machinery subject to the lease is to be determined in the same manner as for the purposes of regulation 16(1).
(10) In this regulation—
"fixture" has the meaning given by section 173(1) of CAA 2001;
"relevant land" has the meaning given by section 173(2) of CAA 2001.

Modification—NIC (Application of Part 7 of the Finance Act 2004) Regulations, SI 2012/1868 reg 25(6) (revocation of regs 12–17A in relation to NIC avoidance schemes and proposals).

Amendments—[1] In para (5)(*b*), words substituted by the Tax Avoidance Schemes (Prescribed Descriptions of Arrangements) (Amendment) Regulations, SI 2010/2834 regs 2, 12 with effect from 1 January 2011.

16 The relevant value condition

(1) The relevant value condition is met if—
(*a*) the lower of the cost to the lessor, or the market value, of any one asset forming part of the plant and machinery leased or to be leased under the arrangements is at least £10,000,000; or
(*b*) the aggregate of the lower of the costs to the lessor, or the market values, of all of the assets forming part of the plant and machinery leased or to be leased under the arrangements is at least £25,000,000.
(2) For the purposes of paragraph (1) the market value of plant or machinery leased or to be leased under the arrangements is to be determined on the assumption of a disposal—
(*a*) by an absolute owner;
(*b*) free from all encumbrances; and
(*c*) in the open market.
(3) "Absolute owner" in the application of paragraph (2)(*a*) to Scotland, means the owner.

Modification—NIC (Application of Part 7 of the Finance Act 2004) Regulations, SI 2012/1868 reg 25(6) (revocation of regs 12–17A in relation to NIC avoidance schemes and proposals).

17 Short-term leases

(1) For the purposes of regulation 13(1)(*d*) a lease whose term is 2 years or less is a short-term lease. But a lease is not a short-term lease if any of the following Conditions apply.
In those Conditions "L" is the lessee.
(2) Condition A is that the lease contains an option exercisable by L to extend the term so that the total term exceeds 2 years.
(3) Condition B is that at the time of the inception of the lease, other arrangements have been entered into which contemplate the extension of the lease to L which, if carried out, would extend the term of the lease so that it exceeds 2 years.
(4) Condition C is that—
(*a*) a person leases an asset to L under a lease that would, apart from this paragraph, be a short-term lease,
(*b*) the inception of that lease is on or after the date on which these Regulations come into force,
(*c*) at or about the time of the inception of that lease, arrangements are entered into for the asset to be leased to one or more other persons under one or more other leases, and
(*d*) in the aggregate, the term of the lease to L and the terms of the leases to such of those other persons as are connected with L exceed 2 years.
[(5) In this regulation "inception" has the meaning given by section 70YI CAA 2001.][1]

Modification—NIC (Application of Part 7 of the Finance Act 2004) Regulations, SI 2012/1868 reg 25(6) (revocation of regs 12–17A in relation to NIC avoidance schemes and proposals).

Amendments—[1] Para (5) inserted by the Tax Avoidance Schemes (Prescribed Descriptions of Arrangements) (Amendment) Regulations, SI 2010/2834 regs 2, 13 with effect from 1 January 2011.

[18 Description 8: Employment income provided through third parties

(1) Arrangements are prescribed if—
(a) Conditions 1 and 2 are met and Condition 3 is not met; or
(b) Conditions 1, 2 and 3 are met and at least one of Conditions 4 and 5 is met.
(2) Condition 1 is met if the arrangements involve at least one of the following—
(a) a relevant third person taking a relevant step under section 554B;
(b) any person taking a relevant step under section 554C or 554D; or
(c) B taking a step under section 554Z18 or 554Z19.
(3) Condition 2 is met if the main benefit, or one of the main benefits, of the arrangements is that an amount that would otherwise count as employment income under section 554Z2(1) is reduced or eliminated.
(4) Condition 3 is met if, by reason of at least one of sections 554E to 554X or regulations made under section 554Y, Chapter 2 of Part 7A does not apply.
(5) Condition 4 is met if the arrangements involve one or more contrived or abnormal steps without which the main benefit in paragraph (3) would not be obtained.

(6) Condition 5 is met if the arrangements involve—

(a) a relevant step being treated as taking place; and

(b) Chapter 2 of Part 7A applying as a consequence of sub-paragraph (a).

(7) In this regulation—

(a) references to sections or Parts are to those in ITEPA unless otherwise stated;

(b) "B" has the meaning given for Part 7A by sections 554A(1)(a) and 554Z17(7) read together;

(c) "contrived or abnormal" has the same meaning as in section 207 of the Finance Act 2013; and

(d) "relevant third person" has the same meaning as in section 554A(7).][1]

Amendments—[1] Reg 18 substituted for previous reg 17A by the Tax Avoidance Schemes (Prescribed Descriptions of Arrangements) (Amendment) Regulations, SI 2013/2595 regs 2, 10(2) with effect from 4 November 2013.

[19 Description 9: Financial products

(1) Subject to regulation 21, arrangements are prescribed if—

(*a*) condition 1 is met, and

(*b*) it would be reasonable to expect an informed observer (having studied the arrangements and having regard to all relevant circumstances) to conclude that—

(i) condition 2 is met, and

(ii) either condition 3 or condition 4 is met.

(2) Condition 1 is that the arrangements include at least one financial product specified in regulation 20(1) (a "specified financial product").

(3) Condition 2 is that the main benefit, or one of the main benefits, of including a specified financial product in the arrangements is to give rise to a tax advantage.

(4) Condition 3 is that a specified financial product included in the arrangements contains at least one term which is unlikely to have been entered into by the persons concerned were it not for the tax advantage.

(5) Condition 4 is that the arrangements involve one or more contrived or abnormal steps without which the tax advantage could not be obtained.

(6) For the purposes of this regulation condition 3 is treated as not having been met if—

(*a*) the specified financial product includes a term requiring that it is held for a minimum period of time before it is redeemed and—

(i) section 135 or 136 of TCGA 1992 applies to the specified financial product, and

(ii) condition 3 is met only by virtue of that term; or

(*b*) the specified financial product includes a term whereby the issuing company can secure that the date for redemption falls before the end of the permitted period and—

(i) but for that term, the specified financial product would be an equity note, and

(ii) condition 3 is met only by virtue of that term.

(7) In paragraph (6)(*b*) "equity note" and "the permitted period" have the meanings given by section 1016 of CTA 2010.

(8) For the purposes of condition 4 a step is not to be treated as being contrived or abnormal if—

(*a*) that step involves only the transfer of an asset to which the condition in paragraph 15A(2)(*b*) of Schedule 7AC to TCGA 1992 applies; or

(*b*) that step involves only the issue of shares and—

(i) that step is taken to eliminate or substantially reduce the economic risk of holding a loan relationship or a derivative contract, or part of such a loan relationship or a derivative contract, which is attributable to fluctuations in exchange rates, and

(ii) the shares are treated for accounting purposes as a liability of the company in accordance with generally accepted accounting practice.

(9) For the purposes of this regulation, neither condition 3 nor condition 4 is treated as having been met if—

(*a*) the specified financial product includes a term providing for conversion into, or redemption in, a currency other than sterling, and

(*b*) both condition 3 and condition 4 are met only by virtue of that term.][1]

Amendments—[1] Regulations 19–21 inserted by the Tax Avoidance Schemes (Prescribed Descriptions of Arrangements) (Amendment) Regulations, SI 2016/99 regs 2, 9 with effect from 23 February 2016. This amendment does not have effect—

– for the purposes of FA 2004 s 308(1) (duties of promoter relating to any notifiable proposal), if the relevant date, as defined in FA 2004 s 308(2), falls before 23 February 2016;

– for the purposes of FA 2004 s 308(3) (duties of promoter relating to any notifiable arrangements), if the date on which the promoter first becomes aware of any transaction forming part of notifiable arrangements falls before 23 February 2016; and

– for the purposes of FA 2004 ss 309(1) (duty of person dealing with promoter outside United Kingdom), 310 (duty of parties to notifiable arrangements not involving promoter), if the date on which any transaction forming part of notifiable arrangements is entered into falls before 23 February 2016.

[20 (1) The financial products specified in this paragraph are—

(*a*) a loan,

(*b*) a share,
(*c*) a derivative contract within the meaning given by section 576 of CTA 2009,
(*d*) a repo in respect of securities within the meaning given by section 263A(A1) of TCGA 1992,
(*e*) a creditor repo, creditor quasi-repo, debtor repo or a debtor quasi-repo (within the meanings given by sections 543, 544, 548 and 549 of CTA 2009 respectively),
(*f*) a stock lending arrangement within the meaning given by section 263B(1) of TCGA 1992,
(*g*) an alternative finance arrangement within Chapter 6 of Part 6 of CTA 2009 or Part 10A of ITA 2007,
(*h*) a contract which, whether alone or in combination with one or more other contracts—
(i) is in accordance with generally accepted accounting practice required to be treated as a loan, deposit or other financial asset or obligation, or
(ii) would be required to be so treated by the person entering into the arrangements were that person a company to which the Companies Act 2006 applies.

(2) Paragraph (1) does not specify a financial product held within an account which satisfies the conditions in regulation 4 of the Individual Savings Account Regulations 1998.][1]

Amendments—[1] Regulations 19–21 inserted by the Tax Avoidance Schemes (Prescribed Descriptions of Arrangements) (Amendment) Regulations, SI 2016/99 regs 2, 9 with effect from 23 February 2016. This amendment does not have effect—
- for the purposes of FA 2004 s 308(1) (duties of promoter relating to any notifiable proposal), if the relevant date, as defined in FA 2004 s 308(2), falls before 23 February 2016;
- for the purposes of FA 2004 s 308(3) (duties of promoter relating to any notifiable arrangements), if the date on which the promoter first becomes aware of any transaction forming part of notifiable arrangements falls before 23 February 2016; and
- for the purposes of FA 2004 ss 309(1) (duty of person dealing with promoter outside United Kingdom), 310 (duty of parties to notifiable arrangements not involving promoter), if the date on which any transaction forming part of notifiable arrangements is entered into falls before 23 February 2016.

[21 Arrangements excepted from Description 9

Arrangements are excepted from being prescribed under regulation 19 if—
(*a*) a promoter is a participating entity, or is part of a participating group, within the meaning of section 286 of the Finance Act 2014; and
(*b*) HMRC has confirmed, or could reasonably be expected to confirm, to the promoter that the arrangements are acceptable transactions under the Code of Practice on Taxation for Banks (as published by the Commissioners for Her Majesty's Revenue and Customs on 31st May 2013).][1]

Amendments—[1] Regulations 19–21 inserted by the Tax Avoidance Schemes (Prescribed Descriptions of Arrangements) (Amendment) Regulations, SI 2016/99 regs 2, 9 with effect from 23 February 2016. This amendment does not have effect—
- for the purposes of FA 2004 s 308(1) (duties of promoter relating to any notifiable proposal), if the relevant date, as defined in FA 2004 s 308(2), falls before 23 February 2016;
- for the purposes of FA 2004 s 308(3) (duties of promoter relating to any notifiable arrangements), if the date on which the promoter first becomes aware of any transaction forming part of notifiable arrangements falls before 23 February 2016; and
- for the purposes of FA 2004 ss 309(1) (duty of person dealing with promoter outside United Kingdom), 310 (duty of parties to notifiable arrangements not involving promoter), if the date on which any transaction forming part of notifiable arrangements is entered into falls before 23 February 2016.

PART 4
FURTHER PROVISIONS

18 Revocations

The Tax Avoidance Schemes (Prescribed Descriptions of Arrangements) Regulations 2004 and the Tax Avoidance Schemes (Prescribed Descriptions of Arrangements) (Amendment) Regulations 2004 are revoked.[1]

Amendments—[1] Part 4 revoked by the Tax Avoidance Schemes (Prescribed Descriptions of Arrangements) (Amendment) Regulations, SI 2013/2595 regs 2, 10(1) with effect from 4 November 2013.

2006/1639

PARTNERSHIPS (RESTRICTIONS ON CONTRIBUTIONS TO A TRADE) REGULATIONS 2006

Made by the Commissioners for Her Majesty's Revenue and Customs under FA 2004 ss 122A(2) to (4) and approved by a resolution of the House of Commons under FA 2004 s 122A(5)

Made . . . .*21 June 2006*
Coming into force . . . .*22 June 2006*

Note—Following the commencement of ITA 2007 ss 114, 802, these regulations have effect as if made under those sections: see ITA 2007 Sch 2 para 148(1).

1 Citation, commencement and effect

(1) These Regulations may be cited as the Partnerships (Restrictions on Contributions to a Trade) Regulations 2006 and shall come into force on the day after the day on which they are made.

(2) These Regulations shall have effect from 20th December 2005.

2 Interpretation

In these Regulations—

["ITA 2007" means the Income Tax Act 2007;][1]

"ITTOIA" means the Income Tax (Trading and Other Income) Act 2005;

["relevant individual" means—

(*a*) a limited partner (within the meaning given by section 106 of ITA 2007),

(*b*) a member of a limited liability partnership, or

(*c*) a non-active partner (within the meaning given by section 112 of ITA 2007),

where the partnership carries on a trade in which the individual makes a film-related loss (as defined in section 800(2) of ITA 2007) for which the individual makes a claim as mentioned in section 802(1) of that Act;][1]

"profit-sharing arrangements" has the meaning in section 850(6) of ITTOIA.

Amendments—[1] Definitions of "ITA 2007" and "relevant individual" substituted by ITA 2007 s 1031(1), Sch 2 para 148(1), (2), (3) with effect for income tax purposes from 6 April 2007 and corporation tax purposes for accounting periods ending after 5 April 2007.

3 Scope of these Regulations

These Regulations apply where (and if there are successive events, in each case where)—

(*a*) a relevant individual disposes of his right to profits arising from a firm's trade (within the meaning in [section 799 of ITA 2007][1]),

(*b*) the result of the disposal is that his share of the profits (or any part of the profits) arising from the trade is reduced or extinguished, or his share of the losses (or any part of the losses) arising from the trade is increased,

(*c*) another person ("the new partner") becomes a partner in the firm, and

(*d*) the new partner contributes or agrees to contribute an amount as capital to the partnership.

Amendments—[1] Words in para (*a*) substituted by ITA 2007 s 1031(1), Sch 2 para 148(1), (2), (4) with effect for income tax purposes from 6 April 2007 and corporation tax purposes for accounting periods ending after 5 April 2007.

4 Exclusion when computing the amount of the relevant individual's contribution to the trade

Where these Regulations apply—

(*a*) apportion the amount referred to in regulation 3(*d*) between the partners in the firm immediately before the new partner becomes a partner, according to their profit-sharing arrangements at that time,

(*b*) the amount apportioned to the relevant individual under paragraph (*a*) shall be excluded when computing the amount of that individual's [capital contribution][1] (but not so as to produce a contribution less than nil), at the time of whichever of the events referred to in regulation 3 is the latest to occur, for the purposes of [section 797(2)(*b*) of ITA 2007][1], and

(*c*) accordingly, recalculate that individual's [capital contribution][1], as at the time of that event, for the purposes of determining—

(i) whether that event is an exit event within the meaning of [section 797(2)(*b*) of ITA 2007][1], and

[(ii) the amount of income treated as received in accordance with section 797(5) of that Act][1].

Amendments—[1] Words in paras (*b*), (*c*), and para (*c*)(ii), substituted by ITA 2007 s 1031(1), Sch 2 para 148(1), (2), (5) with effect for income tax purposes from 6 April 2007 and corporation tax purposes for accounting periods ending after 5 April 2007.

2006/1957

REGISTERED PENSION SCHEMES (EXTENSION OF MIGRANT MEMBER RELIEF) REGULATIONS 2006

Made by the Commissioners for HMRC under FA 2004 Sch 33 para 4(2), (3)

Made . . . . *20 July 2006*
Laid before the House of Commons . . . . *21 July 2006*
Coming into force . . . . *11 August 2006*

1 Citation, commencement, effect and interpretation

(1) These Regulations may be cited as the Registered Pension Schemes (Extension of Migrant Member Relief) Regulations 2006, shall come into force on 11th August 2006 and shall have effect in relation to all times on or after 6th April 2006.

(2) In these Regulations—

"the Act" means the Finance Act 2004;
"block transfer" has the same meaning as it has in paragraph 22(6) of Schedule 36;
"the receiving scheme" means the scheme referred to in the relevant provisions;
"the relevant provisions" means paragraphs (*a*), (*b*) and (*c*) of paragraph 4(1) of Schedule 33 (meaning of relevant migrant member); and
"Schedule" means a Schedule to the Act.

2 References in relevant provisions treated as including references to other schemes
(1) Paragraphs (2) to (4) prescribe circumstances in which references in the relevant provisions to the pension scheme are to be read as including other schemes.
(2) The circumstance prescribed by this paragraph is that there has been a block transfer to the receiving scheme on or after 6th April 2006.
In the circumstance prescribed by this paragraph, references in the relevant provisions to the pension scheme are to either the receiving scheme or to the scheme from which the block transfer takes place.
(3) The circumstance prescribed by this paragraph is that there has been a series of transfers, all of which were block transfers from one overseas pension scheme to another and the last of which was a transfer to the receiving scheme occurring on or after 6th April 2006.
In the circumstance prescribed by this paragraph, references in the relevant provisions to the pension scheme are to either the receiving scheme or to any of the overseas pension schemes from which a block transfer, which forms part of the series, has taken place.
(4) The circumstance prescribed by this paragraph is that—
(*a*) under the rules of a pension scheme ("the original scheme") on and after a specified date it is no longer possible for further accruals to occur;
(*b*) a further pension scheme ("the new scheme") has been established to provide benefits in respect of rights accruing to members of the original scheme after the specified date;
(*c*) more than one member of the original scheme has become a member of the new scheme in relation to all rights accruing after the specified date;
(*d*) rights do not accrue to any member of the new scheme after the specified date under the original scheme.
In the circumstance prescribed by this paragraph references in the relevant provisions to the pension scheme are to either the new scheme or the original scheme.

2006/1958

PENSIONS SCHEMES (TAXABLE PROPERTY PROVISIONS) REGULATIONS 2006

Made by the Treasury under FA 2004 s 273ZA, Sch 29A paras 33(4), 34(4), 36, 37

Made . . . .*20 July 2006*
Laid before the House of Commons . . . .*21 July 2006*
Coming into force . . . .*11 August 2006*

1 Citation, commencement and effect
(1) These Regulations may be cited as the Pensions Schemes (Taxable Property Provisions) Regulations 2006 and shall come into force on 11th August 2006.
(2) These Regulations shall have effect from 6th April 2006.

2 Interpretation
In these Regulations—
"taxable property" has the meaning in Schedule 29A;
"taxable property provisions" has the meaning in paragraph 1(3) of that Schedule; and
any reference (without more) to a numbered section or Schedule is a reference to that section of, or Schedule to, the Finance Act 2004.

3 Provisions supplementing Schedule 29A
Paragraphs 33 and 34 of Schedule 29A shall apply to land outside the United Kingdom as if—
(*a*) "chargeable interest" (in section 48(1) of the Finance Act 2003) applied to such land, and
(*b*) in relation to such land, the meaning of "lease" in paragraphs 1 and 19 of Schedule 17A to the Finance Act 2003, included any interest corresponding to a lease,
and "rent" and "tenant" shall be construed accordingly.

4 Paragraph 32 of Schedule 29A (and the remainder of the taxable property provisions excepting paragraph 34 of that Schedule) shall apply to—
(*a*) a licence to use or occupy residential property (for a consideration which is wholly or partly rent), and

(*b*) the right to use, or participate in arrangements relating to the use of, taxable property or a description of taxable property to which the property in question belongs (for a consideration which is wholly or partly rent),

as if each payment of rent represented the grant, to the pension scheme or other person who acquired the interest in taxable property, of a lease of the taxable property for the period for which the rent is paid, and in consideration of the rent so paid.

5 Paragraph 33 of Schedule 29A shall apply to—

(*a*) tangible moveable property,

(*b*) a licence to use or occupy residential property (for a consideration wholly or partly other than rent), and

(*c*) the right to use, or participate in arrangements relating to the use of, taxable property or a description of taxable property to which the property in question belongs (for a consideration wholly or partly other than rent),

as they apply to a chargeable interest in property.

6 Paragraph 34 of Schedule 29A shall apply to tangible moveable property.

7 Application of paragraphs 3 and 4 of Schedule 17A to the Finance Act 2003

(1) The following provisions—

(*a*) paragraph 3(1) and (2) of Schedule 17A to the Finance Act 2003 (leases that continue after a fixed term), and

(*b*) paragraph 4(1), (2) and (5) of that Schedule (treatment of leases for indefinite term),

apply for the purposes of paragraph 34(2) of Schedule 29A, for determining the amount of rent payable, with the following modifications.

(2) Each extension of the original fixed term by paragraph 3(2) or 4(1) of Schedule 17A shall be treated as the grant of a new lease for the period of the extension.

(3) Accordingly, an investment-regulated pension scheme is to be treated as making an unauthorised payment within section 174A(1) to a member of the scheme, on the occasion of each such extension.

8 Application of paragraph 8 of Schedule 17A to the Finance Act 2003

(1) Paragraph 8(1) and (2) of Schedule 17A to the Finance Act 2003 (adjustment where rent ceases to be uncertain) shall apply for the purposes of paragraph 34(2) of Schedule 29A, for determining the amount of rent payable, with the following modifications.

(2) If the result of the recalculation as at the date referred to in paragraph 8(1)(*a*) or (*b*) of Schedule 17A is that the rent paid or payable in respect of the first five years of the term is greater than the rent originally calculated, an investment-regulated pension scheme is to be treated as making an unauthorised payment within section 174A(1) to a member of the scheme, based on the difference between the two calculations.

9 Variation of a lease to give rise to an additional unauthorised payment

(1) An investment-regulated pension scheme is to be treated as making an unauthorised payment within section 174A(1) to a member of the pension scheme, if—

(*a*) a lease of taxable property is varied (whether or not in pursuance of a provision in the lease) so as to increase the amount of the rent; and

(*b*) the increase falls to be regarded as abnormal (within the meaning of paragraph 15 of Schedule 17A to the Finance Act 2003).

(2) The variation shall be treated for the purposes of the taxable property provisions as if it were the grant of a lease in consideration of the additional rent made payable by the variation.

10 Scheme chargeable payment on income and gains from non-UK. taxable property

(1) This regulation applies to a registered pension scheme which—

(*a*) is for the time being established in a country or territory outside the United Kingdom, and

(*b*) falls within the circumstances mentioned in section 273ZA(1)(*a*) and (*c*).

(2) Liability to pay the scheme sanction charge so far as relating to a scheme chargeable payment treated as made by the pension scheme—

(*a*) under section 185A (income from taxable property) by virtue of the pension scheme holding an interest in the property, or

(*b*) under section 185F (gains from taxable property) by virtue of a gain treated as accruing to the pension scheme in respect of an interest in the property,

("the property enjoyment scheme sanction charge") shall be determined under this regulation and not under section 239 (see section 239(6)).

(3) Any member of the pension scheme resident . . . [1] in the United Kingdom, for the purposes of whose arrangement the interest in taxable property referred to in section 273ZA(1)(*a*) is held, is liable to pay the property enjoyment scheme sanction charge, subject to [paragraphs (4) and (5)][2].

(4) Where the interest in taxable property is held by the pension scheme for the purposes of more than one arrangement, the property enjoyment scheme sanction charge shall be apportioned between the members whose arrangements they are, on a just and reasonable basis.

[(5) Where a member is temporarily non-resident at a time when a scheme chargeable payment would, but for this regulation, be treated as made by virtue of section 185F, that member shall be liable to the property enjoyment scheme sanction charge so far as relating to that scheme chargeable payment, as if that scheme chargeable payment were treated as made in the period of return.][2]

(6) . . .[2]

(7) Where paragraph (5) applies, nothing in any enactment imposing any limit on the time within which an assessment to tax may be made shall prevent an assessment to the property enjoyment scheme sanction charge from being made on the member at any time before the end of two years after the 31st January next following the tax year in which the [period of return][2] falls.

[(8) In this regulation—

(*a*) "period of return" has the meaning given in paragraph 115 of Schedule 45 to the Finance Act 2013 (statutory residence test: anti-avoidance),

(*b*) "temporarily non-resident" has the meaning given in paragraph 110 of that Schedule.][2]

Amendments—[1] In para (3), words "or ordinarily resident" revoked by the Income Tax (Removal of Ordinary Residence) Regulations, SI 2013/605 reg 5 with effect in relation to a scheme chargeable payment treated as made in the tax year 2013–14 or any subsequent tax years.

[2] In paras (3), (7), words substituted, para (5) substituted, para (6) revoked, and para (8) inserted by the Temporary Non-Residence (Miscellaneous Amendments) Regulations, SI 2013/1810 reg 3(1), (2) with effect in relation to a scheme chargeable payment treated as made in the tax year 2013–14 and any subsequent tax year.

2006/1959

INVESTMENT-REGULATED PENSION SCHEMES (EXCEPTION OF TANGIBLE MOVEABLE PROPERTY) ORDER 2006

Made by the Treasury under FA 2004 Sch 29A para 11

Made . . . . *20 July 2006*
Laid before the House of Commons . . . . *21 July 2006*
Coming into force . . . . *11 August 2006*

1 Citation, commencement, effect and interpretation

(1) This Order may be cited as the Investment-regulated Pension Schemes (Exception of Tangible Moveable Property) Order 2006 and shall come into force on 11th August 2006.

(2) This Order has effect from 6th April 2006.

(3) In these Regulations—

"market value" is to be determined in accordance with section 272 of the Taxation of Chargeable Gains Act 1992; and

"connected persons" (and cognate expressions) have the meaning in section 839 of the Income and Corporation Taxes Act 1988.

2 Exclusions from tangible moveable property

The following property shall not be regarded as taxable property for the purposes of the taxable property provisions (within the meaning in paragraph 1(3) of Schedule 29A to the Finance Act 2004)—

(*a*) gold bullion (that is, gold of a purity not less than 995 thousandths, which is in the form of a bar, or of a wafer, of a weight accepted by the bullion markets);

(*b*) any item of tangible moveable property (whose market value does not exceed £6,000)—

(i) held by a vehicle (within the meaning in paragraph 20(2) of Schedule 29A to the Finance Act 2004) solely for the purposes of the administration or management of the vehicle;

(ii) in which the relevant investment-regulated pension scheme does not hold an interest directly; and

(iii) where a member of the pension scheme or a person connected with such a member does not occupy or use, or have any right to occupy or use, the property.

2006/1960

PENSIONS SCHEMES (APPLICATION OF UK PROVISIONS TO RELEVANT NON-UK SCHEMES) (AMENDMENT) REGULATIONS 2006

Made by the Commissioners for HMRC under FA 2004 Sch 34 paras 4(2), (4), 7, 7A

Made . . . . *20 July 2006*
Laid before the House of Commons . . . . *21 July 2006*
Coming into force . . . . *11 August 2006*

1 Citation, commencement and effect

(1) These Regulations may be cited as the Pensions Schemes (Application of UK Provisions to Relevant Non-UK Schemes) (Amendment) Regulations 2006 and shall come into force on 11th August 2006.

(2) These Regulations shall have effect from 6th April 2006.

2 Amendment of the Pensions Schemes (Application of UK Provisions to Relevant Non-UK Schemes) Regulations 2006

The Pensions Schemes (Application of UK Provisions to Relevant Non-UK Schemes) Regulations 2006 are amended as follows.

3 In regulation 1(2) insert at the end—

""taxable property" has the meaning in Schedule 29A to the Act;

"taxable property provisions" has the meaning in paragraph 1(3) of that Schedule; and

"transfer member" of a scheme has the meaning in paragraph 1(8) of Schedule 34 to the Act."

4 In regulation 3(*c*) omit paragraph (ii) and the word "and" which precedes it.

5 After regulation 3 insert—

3A "Computation of a member's taxable asset transfer fund

(1) The amount of a member's taxable asset transfer fund under a relevant non-UK scheme ("the RNUKS") is the sum of—

(*a*) the amount crystallised by virtue of benefit crystallisation event 8 on the transfer from a UK registered pension scheme to the RNUKS; and

(*b*) so much of the member's taxable asset transfer fund under any other relevant non-UK scheme as has been transferred to the RNUKS without being subject to the unauthorised payments charge.

(2) Accordingly, the member's taxable asset transfer fund ("TATF") shall form part of the member's relevant transfer fund ("RTF"), except in a case where the member's RTF consists solely of a UK tax-relieved fund which has been transferred to the RNUKS."

6 In regulation 4(2)(*b*) after "reduced" insert "(but not below nil)".

7 In regulation 4(3) for "it shall be assumed" to the end substitute—

"the following Rules apply (with an earlier Rule applying in preference to a later Rule).

Rule 1

Where an unauthorised payment is treated as made by the scheme to the transfer member by virtue of section 174A—

(*a*) the payment shall be treated as made out of the member's RTF and TATF, but

(*b*) the interest in taxable property, in respect of which the unauthorised payment is treated as made, shall represent the payment and form part of the member's RTF and TATF (an "appropriated asset"), up to an amount equal to the amount of that payment.

Rule 2

Accordingly, if a scheme transfers that appropriated asset (or an interest in a vehicle through which the scheme holds the interest in the taxable property indirectly), or part of it, to another pension scheme, that transfer shall be treated as a transfer of the whole or part, as the case may be, of the member's RTF and TATF (limited to the amount of the unauthorised payment) to that other scheme, falling (if appropriate) within regulation 3A(1)(*b*).

Rule 3

If a scheme disposes of (other than to another pension scheme) an appropriated asset (or an interest in a vehicle through which the scheme holds the interest in the taxable property indirectly), or part of it, any other property which directly or indirectly represents proceeds of either of those interests (limited to the amount of the unauthorised payment) shall form part of the member's RTF and TATF.

Rule 4

This Rule applies to payments made by the scheme to or in respect of the member, other than—

(*a*) a transfer of an interest in taxable property or an interest in a vehicle through which the scheme holds the interest in the taxable property indirectly, and

(*b*) payments treated as made by virtue of section 174A.

So far as the member's RTF and TATF are not represented by appropriated assets—

(*a*) where the member has both an RTF and a TATF, and the amount of his RTF exceeds the amount of his TATF, such payments shall, to the extent of that excess, be treated as made out of his RTF (but not his TATF) and as reducing the RTF, and subject thereto

(*b*) such payments are made out of the member's RTF and TATF in priority to any other fund under that scheme, and reduce (but not below nil) the amount of the RTF and TATF.

8 After regulation 4(3) add—

"(4) In paragraph (3), references to payments made or treated as made by virtue of section 174A include references to payments treated as made by regulations under paragraph 37 of Schedule 29A, or paragraph 7A of Schedule 34, to the Act."

9 After regulation 4 insert—

4A "Taxable property provisions to apply to a transfer member of a relevant non-UK scheme (to payments referable to his taxable asset transfer fund)

The—

(*a*) taxable property provisions, and

(*b*) regulations made under paragraph 37 of Schedule 29A or paragraph 7A of Schedule 34,

apply to a transfer member of a relevant non-UK scheme, in relation to payments treated as made by those provisions or regulations which are referable to the member's taxable asset transfer fund under the scheme, but subject to the modifications in regulations 4B to 4D.

4B Unauthorised payments charge to apply (in lieu of scheme chargeable payment)

(1) The scheme chargeable payment provisions in sections 185A to 185I shall not apply to a relevant non-UK scheme.

(2) But, during such time as an appropriated asset forms the whole or part of a transfer member's TATF—

(*a*) the scheme shall be treated as making unauthorised payments to that member equal in amount to the scheme chargeable payments (in respect of income and gains) which would have been computed in accordance with those sections, and

(*b*) the transfer member shall be liable to pay the unauthorised payments charge in respect of such payments.

(3) Where the scheme's interest in taxable property is not wholly referable to the transfer member's TATF, the amount of the unauthorised payment shall be proportionately reduced.

4C Modification of paragraph 15 of Schedule 29A

Paragraph 15 of Schedule 29A applies to the transfer member of a relevant non-UK scheme as if "insurance company" included any person—

(*a*) resident in a country or territory outside the European Economic Area,

(*b*) whose business consists of, or includes, the effecting or carrying out of contracts of long-term insurance (within the meaning in Part 2 of Schedule 1 to the Financial Services and Markets Act 2000 (Regulated Activities) Order 2001), and

(*c*) who is regulated in the conduct of that business by—

(i) the government of that country or territory, or

(ii) a body established under the law of that country or territory for the purpose of regulating such business.

4D Modifications of paragraphs 29 and 31 of Schedule 29A

(1) This regulation applies where—

(*a*) a relevant non-UK scheme acquires an interest in taxable property;

(*b*) the interest is acquired in the circumstances mentioned in paragraph 32(3), (5) (excluding paragraphs (*a*) and (*b*)) or (6) (excluding paragraphs (*a*) and (*b*)) of Schedule 29A; and

(*c*) the whole or part of the consideration for the acquisition is rent.

(2) The amount of the consideration (or the part that is rent) shall not be the relevant rental value of the property (as provided by paragraph 34(2) of Schedule 29A).

(3) Each payment of rent (or the aggregate of such payments during a year, if there are more than one) shall be treated, for the purposes of the taxable property provisions, as if the pension scheme or other person who acquired the interest were being granted a lease for the period for which the rent is paid, in consideration of the rent (or aggregate) so paid."

2006/1962

TAXATION OF PENSION SCHEMES (TRANSITIONAL PROVISIONS) (AMENDMENT) ORDER 2006

Made by the Treasury under FA 2004 s 283(2), (3A), (3B), (3C)

Made . . . . *20 July 2006*

Laid before the House of Commons . . . . *21 July 2006*

Coming into force . . . . *11 August 2006*

1 Citation, commencement and effect

This Order may be cited as the Taxation of Pension Schemes (Transitional Provisions) (Amendment) Order 2006, shall come into force on 11th August 2006 and have effect in respect of—

(*a*) death benefit lump sum payments made, and

(*b*) benefit crystallisation events taking place,

on or after 6th April 2006.

2 Amendment of the Taxation of Pension Schemes (Transitional Provisions) Order 2006

(1) The Taxation of Pension Schemes (Transitional Provisions) Order 2006 is amended as follows.

3 (*inserts* Taxation of Pension Schemes (Transitional Provisions) Order, SI 2006/572 art 29A)

4 (*amends* Taxation of Pension Schemes (Transitional Provisions) Order, SI 2006/572 art 40(1))

5 (*amends* Taxation of Pension Schemes (Transitional Provisions) Order, SI 2006/572 art 41(1))

2006/1963

TAXATION OF PENSION SCHEMES (CONSEQUENTIAL AMENDMENTS) (NO 2) ORDER 2006

Made by the Treasury under FA 2004 s 281(2), (4)

Made . . . . *20 July 2006*
Laid before the House of Commons . . . . *21 July 2006*
Coming into force . . . . *11 August 2006*

1 Citation, commencement and effect

(1) This Order may be cited as the Taxation of Pension Schemes (Consequential Amendments) (No 2) Order 2006 and shall come into force on 11th August 2006.

(2) Article 2 of this Order has effect in relation to any time on or after 6th April 2006.

2 Consequential amendment of section 408 of the Income Tax (Earnings and Pensions) Act 2003

(1) Section 408(1) of the Income Tax (Earnings and Pensions) Act 2003 is amended as follows.

(2) After "registered pension scheme" insert "or an employer-financed retirement benefit scheme".

3 Consequential amendment to section 128 of the Finance Act 1995

(1) Section 128 (limit of income chargeable on non-residents: income tax) of the Finance Act 1995 is amended as follows.

(2) In subsection (3)(cc) after the words "section 577" omit "or 605" and omit "and retirement annuity contracts".

(3) After subsection (3)(*cc*) insert—

"(*cca*) it is chargeable to tax under chapter 5A, Part 9 of ITEPA 2003 because it is a pension under a registered pension scheme where that scheme—

(i) falls within paragraph 1(1)(*f*) of Schedule 36 of the Finance Act 2004, and

(ii) was, immediately before 6th April 2006, a retirement annuity contract to which section 605 of ITEPA 2003 applied;".

4 Consequential amendment to section 336 of the Income and Corporation Taxes Act 1988

(1) Section 336 (temporary residents in the United Kingdom) of the Income and Corporation Taxes Act 1988 is amended as follows.

(2) In subsection (1A)(*b*)(ia) omit the words "an annuity contract that is" and after the words "registered pension scheme" insert "that fell within paragraph 1(1)(*f*) of Schedule 36 to the Finance Act 2004".

2006/2864

REAL ESTATE INVESTMENT TRUSTS (BREACH OF CONDITIONS) REGULATIONS 2006

Made by the Treasury under FA 2006 ss 114–116, 122, 129(2)(a), (b), 134(1), 144.

Made . . . . *1 November 2006*
Laid before the House of Commons . . . . *1 November 2006*
Coming into force . . . . *1 January 2007*

Commentary—*Simon's Taxes* **D7.1117**.

1 Citation, commencement and interpretation

(1) These Regulations may be cited as the Real Estate Investment Trust (Breach of Conditions) Regulations 2006 and shall come into force on 1st January 2007.

[(1A) In these Regulations—

(*a*) a reference to Part 4 is a reference to Part 4 of the Finance Act 2006,

(*b*) a reference to a section (without more) is a reference to that section of the Finance Act 2006, and

(*c*) a reference to a paragraph of Schedule 17 is a reference to that paragraph of Schedule 17 to the Finance Act 2006.][1]

(2) In these Regulations—

"the Commissioners" means the Commissioners for Her Majesty's Revenue and Customs;

"the holder of excessive rights" means a person falling within section 114(1)(*a*), (*b*) or (*c*) being—

(*a*) a company as defined in section 832(1) of the Income and Corporation Taxes Act 1988; or

(*b*) an entity which is treated as a body corporate for tax purposes—

(i) in accordance with the law of a territory outside the United Kingdom with which arrangements have been entered into to provide relief from double taxation; or

(ii) in accordance with an international agreement containing such arrangements

where those arrangements have effect by virtue of an Order in Council under section 788 of the Income and Corporation Taxes Act 1988;

["JV Regulations" means the Real Estate Investment Trusts (Joint Ventures) Regulations 2006;][1]

["JVG Regulations" means the Real Estate Investment Trusts (Joint Venture Groups) Regulations 2007;][1]

"*MCT*" means—

(*a*) in relation to a company to which Part 4 applies, the rate of tax applicable to the company under section 119(2) (rate of corporation tax: profits of C (residual)); and

(*b*) in relation to a group to which Part 4 applies, the rate of tax applicable to the members of the group under section 119(2) as modified by virtue of paragraph 17 of Schedule 17; . . . [1]

["specified accounting period" means the accounting period referred to in regulation 7(1)(*a*);][1]

["UK property rental business" means the property rental business of a UK resident company or the property rental business in the United Kingdom of a company which is not a UK resident company; and][1]

["UK resident company" means a company which is resident in the United Kingdom, and is not resident in another place in accordance with the law of that place relating to taxation.][1]

(3) The following provisions of these Regulations, other than regulations 10 and 12, apply to groups to which Part 4 applies as they apply to companies to which that Part applies, and for that purpose references in the following regulations to the company are to the principal company save that the references in regulations 6, [7, 7A, 7B,][1] 8 and 9 are to be read as references to the group.

HMRC Manuals—Guidance on Real Estate Investment Trusts Manual, GREIT02115 ("maximum shareholding": definition of company and meaning of beneficially entitled).

GREIT02115 ("maximum shareholding": meaning of direct and indirect control of voting rights).

Amendments—[1] Para (1A) inserted; in para (2), in definition of "MCT", word "and" in para (*b*) and words following para (*b*), repealed, and definitions of "JV Regulations", "JVG Regulations", "specified accounting period", "UK property rental business" and "UK resident company" inserted; and references in para (3) inserted; by the Real Estate Investment Trusts (Breach of Conditions) (Amendment) Regulations, SI 2007/3540 regs 2, 3 with effect in relation to accounting periods beginning on or after 1 January 2007: SI 2007/3540 reg 1(2).

Breach of conditions in section 106

2–10 . . .

Revocation—Regulations 2–10 revoked by CTA 2010 s 1181, Sch 3 Pt 1 with effect for corporation tax purposes for accounting periods ending on or after 1 April 2010, and for income tax and capital gains tax purposes for the tax year 2010–11 and subsequent tax years.

Rewrite destinations—These Regulations were rewritten in CTA 2010 as follows—

reg 2 (breach of conditions for company – take-overs and demergers) — s 562.
reg 3 (breach of condition for company – actions of others) — s 562.
reg 4 (breach of condition for company – other) — s 562.
reg 5 (breach of requirements as to properties) — ss 563, 575.
reg 6 (breach of distribution condition) — ss 564, 565.
reg 7 (breach of condition 2 in s 108(3)) — ss 566, 574, 576.
reg 7A (tax charge for specified accounting period) — ss 566, 567.
reg 7B (breach of balance of business conditions) — ss 568, 576.
reg 8 (multiple breaches of separate conditions) — s 577.
reg 9 (breach of condition – information requirements) — s 561.
reg 10 (distribution to a person with more than the maximum shareholding: charge to tax) — ss 551, 552.

Breach of section 114: maximum shareholding

11 Distribution to holder of excessive rights: information

(1) This regulation applies if a company to which Part 4 applies makes a distribution to, or in respect of, a holder of excessive rights.

(2) When the company makes its return under regulation 4 of the Real Estate Investment Trusts (Assessment and Recovery of Tax) Regulations 2006 for the quarter in which the date of any distribution falls, the company must provide the Commissioners with the following information—

(*a*) the name and address of every person to, or in respect of, whom the distribution was made;

(*b*) the amount or value of the distribution;

(*c*) particulars of those persons' interests in the company including details of the percentages they form of the total issued share capital, ordinary share capital or any other share capital of the company;

(*d*) particulars of the transaction giving rise to the distribution; and

(*e*) what (if anything) the company has done to avoid the possibility of such a distribution being made.

HMRC Manuals—Guidance on Real Estate Investment Trusts Manual, GREIT07010 (breaches of conditions: information requirements).

Breach of section 115(2)—profit: financing costs ratio

12–14 . . .

Revocation—Regulations 12–14 revoked by CTA 2010 s 1181, Sch 3 Pt 1 with effect for corporation tax purposes for accounting periods ending on or after 1 April 2010, and for income tax and capital gains tax purposes for the tax year 2010–11 and subsequent tax years.

Rewrite destinations—These Regulations were rewritten in CTA 2010 as follows—

reg 12 (charge to tax where profit: financing-cost ratio less than 1.25 – REITs which are not Group REITs) — s 543.

reg 13 (charge to tax where profit: financing-cost ratio – Group REITs) — s 543.

reg 14 (termination by notice – specified number of s 117 notices) – s 573.

2006/2865

REAL ESTATE INVESTMENT TRUSTS (FINANCIAL STATEMENTS OF GROUP REAL ESTATE INVESTMENT TRUSTS) REGULATIONS 2006

Made by the Commissioners for HMRC under FA 2006 s 144, Sch 17 para 31(7)

Made . . . .*1 November 2006*

Laid before the House of Commons . . . .*1 November 2006*

Coming into force . . . .*1 January 2007*

Commentary—*Simon's Taxes* **D7.1155**.

Preliminary

1 Citation, commencement and effect

(1) These Regulations may be cited as the Real Estate Investment Trusts (Financial Statements of Group Real Estate Investment Trusts) Regulations 2006, and shall come into force on 1st January 2007.

(2) These Regulations have effect in relation to accounting periods beginning on and after 1st January 2007.

2 Interpretation

(1) In these Regulations—

(*a*) a reference to Part 4 is a reference to Part 4 of the Finance Act 2006,

(*b*) a reference to a section (without more) is a reference to that section of the Finance Act 2006,

(*c*) a reference to Schedule 17 is a reference to Schedule 17 to the Finance Act 2006, and

(*d*) a reference to paragraph 31 (however expressed) is a reference to paragraph 31 of Schedule 17.

(2) In these Regulations—

"financing costs" has the meaning given by section 115(4);

"G (property rental business)" has the meaning given by paragraph 2(*b*) of Schedule 17;

"G (residual)" has the meaning given by paragraph 2(*c*) of Schedule 17;

"the Joint Ventures Regulations" means the Real Estate Investment Trusts (Joint Ventures) Regulations 2006;

"open-ended investment company" has the meaning given by section 17(4)(*e*) of the Finance (No 2) Act 2005;

"the principal company" is to be construed in accordance with section 134(2);

"significant influence" is to be construed in accordance with regulation 3(1);

"UK business" is to be construed in accordance with paragraph 3(3) of Schedule 17.

(3) In these Regulations—

"for accounting purposes" means for the purposes of accounts drawn up in accordance with generally accepted accounting practice;

"fair value accounting" means a basis of accounting under which assets or liabilities are shown in the company's balance sheet at their fair value;

"generally accepted accounting practice" has the meaning given by section 50 of the Finance Act 2004;

"joint venture" and "venturer" have the same meaning as for accounting purposes.

3 Significant influence and profits available for distribution to equity holders

(1) For the purposes of these Regulations a member of a group has significant influence over another entity if—

(*a*) the member holds a percentage of the beneficial interest in the other entity, and

(*b*) the members of the group hold more than 20% of the beneficial interest in that other entity.

(2) For the purposes of these Regulations percentages of beneficial interest in an entity must be determined by reference to entitlement to profits available for distribution to equity holders.

(3) Profits available for distribution to equity holders do not include any profits or assets available to equity holders otherwise than as equity holders.

(4) For the purpose of determining profits available for distribution to equity holders in relation to an entity other than a company these Regulations have effect as if—

(*a*) the entity were a company resident in the United Kingdom, and

(*b*) the rights of persons in the entity were shares in the company.

General

4 Scope of these Regulations

(1) These Regulations apply in respect of a group to which Part 4 applies in relation to an accounting period of the principal company.

(2) In accordance with Schedule 17 the principal company must prepare—

(*a*) a financial statement for G (property rental business) for the accounting period (see paragraph 31(2)(*a*)),

(*b*) a financial statement for G (residual) for the accounting period (see paragraph 31(2)(*c*)), and

(*c*) a financial statement for G (property rental business) in respect of its UK business (see paragraph 31(2)(*b*)).

(3) In these Regulations—

(*a*) regulations 5 to 11 make further provision relating to the content of—

(i) a financial statement for G (property rental business) for an accounting period, and

(ii) a financial statement for G (residual) for an accounting period;

(*b*) regulation 12 makes further provision relating to the content of a financial statement for G (property rental business) in respect of its UK business; and

(*c*) regulation 13 contains further provisions.

Financial statements for G (property rental business) and G (residual)

5 General

(1) In accordance with paragraph 31(3), a financial statement for G (property rental business) for an accounting period and a financial statement for G (residual) for an accounting period must specify—

(*a*) income (in the manner specified in paragraph 31(3)(*a*)),

(*b*) expenses (in the manner specified in paragraph 31(3)(*b*)),

(*c*) profits before tax (in the manner specified in paragraph 31(3)(*c*)), and

(*d*) assets valued (in the manner specified in paragraph 31(3)(*d*)).

(2) The financial statement for G (property rental business) for an accounting period and the financial statement for G (residual) for an accounting period must exclude the following items—

(*a*) transactions between one member of the group and another member of the group;

(*b*) income and expenses payable between one member of the group and another member of the group;

(*c*) the value of holdings of one member of the group in another member of the group; and

(*d*) any balances held by one member of the group that relate to another member of the group.

(3) In accordance with paragraph 31(5), where a non-member of the group holds a percentage of the beneficial interest in a member (other than the principal company), the financial statement for G (property rental business) for an accounting period and the financial statement for G (residual) for an accounting period must exclude that percentage of income, expenses, gains, losses, assets and liabilities of the member.

(4) A reconciliation must be provided between—

(*a*) the financial statement for G (property rental business) for an accounting period and the financial statement for G (residual) for that accounting period, and (*b*) the audited financial statements of the group for that accounting period (whether in the form of consolidated statements or of statements of individual members of the group).

(5) The expenses must show the following amounts separately—

(*a*) financing costs, and

(*b*) all other expenses.

(6) Financing costs—

(*a*) in the case of the financial statement for G (property rental business) for an accounting period, must include Financing Costs (external) (see regulation 6), and

(*b*) in the case of the financial statement for G (residual) for an accounting period, must include financing costs payable by a member of the group in respect of financing used in the business of G (residual).

HMRC Manuals—Guidance on Real Estate Investment Trusts Manual, GREIT12115–12145 (group conditions and rules: financial statements for G).

6 Financing costs (external)

(1) In the case of the financial statement for G (property rental business) for an accounting period, the amount of Financing Costs (external) is determined as follows—

Step 1

Determine the amount of the financing costs incurred in respect of the property rental business of G (property rental business) owed by group entities to non-group entities (the "outside financing costs").

Step 2

Determine the percentages of the outside financing costs incurred in respect of—

(*a*) the UK business of G (property rental business), and

(*b*) other matters.

The amount of Financing Costs (external) is the percentage of the outside financing costs incurred in respect of the UK business of G (property rental business).

(2) If the outside financing costs are owed by a group entity (other than the principal company) and a non-group entity holds a percentage of the beneficial interest in that group entity, the outside financing costs must exclude that percentage of those costs.

(3) For the purposes of paragraph (2), percentages of beneficial interest must be determined by reference to beneficial entitlement to profits available for distribution to equity holders.

(4) In this regulation—

"group entity" means—

(*a*) a member of the group, or

(*b*) an entity which, under these Regulations, is treated as a member of the group for accounting purposes and for the purposes of the financial statements specified in regulation 4(2) (see regulations 9 to 11); and

"non-group entity" means an entity which is not a group entity.

HMRC Manuals—Guidance on Real Estate Investment Trusts Manual, GREIT12155 (group conditions and rules: financial statements – financing costs (external)).

[7 Treatment of certain exceptional items

(1) This regulation applies to the items specified in sub-paragraphs (ii) and (iii) of section 108(2)(*b*) (the "specified items").

(2) The financial statement for G (property rental business) for an accounting period and the financial statement for G (residual) for an accounting period must show the specified items.

(3) For the purposes of paragraph 7 of Schedule 17 (which modifies section 108 (conditions for balance of business)), the specified items are excluded from—

(*a*) the amount of the income, expenses and profits accruing from any business, and

(*b*) the amount of the assets involved in any business.][1]

Amendments—[1] Regulation 7 substituted by the Real Estate Investment Trusts (Financial Statements of Group Real Estate Investment Trusts) (Amendment) Regulations, SI 2007/3536 regs 2, 3 with effect for accounting periods beginning on or after 1 January 2008, and ending on or after 7 January 2008: SI 2007/3536 reg 1(2).

8 Beneficial interests in entities other than group companies

(1) This regulation applies if—

(*a*) a member of a group holds a percentage of the beneficial interest in another entity, and

(*b*) that other entity is not a member of the group.

(2) The member of the group must account for income received from that other entity—

(*a*) on the basis that the beneficial interest is held as an investment, and

(*b*) in accordance with generally accepted accounting practice.

(3) The financial statement for G (residual) must—

(*a*) show the beneficial interest in that other entity as an asset of the member of the group, and

(*b*) account for that beneficial interest in accordance with fair value accounting.

(4) The general rules in paragraphs (2) and (3) are subject to further provisions relating to—

(*a*) a joint venture (see regulation 9),

(*b*) an open-ended investment company (see regulation 10), and
(*c*) certain other non-corporate entities (see regulation 11).

[9 Joint ventures

(1) This regulation applies if—

(*a*) a member of a group (the "venturing group") is a venturer in a joint venture, and
(*b*) notice has been given—

(i) in accordance with the Joint Ventures Regulations for those Regulations to apply to the joint venture, or
(ii) in accordance with the Real Estate Investment Trusts (Joint Venture Groups) Regulations 2007 for those Regulations to apply to the joint venture.

(2) If the joint venture takes the form of a company, the joint venture must be treated, for accounting purposes, as a member of the venturing group for the purposes of the financial statements specified in regulation 4(2).

(3) If the joint venture takes the form of another group ("the joint venture group"), the principal company of the venturing group must reflect the relevant information in its financial statements.

(4) In paragraph (3) the "relevant information" means the information specified in sub-paragraphs (3) and (4) of paragraph 31 as set out in the financial statements of the principal company of the joint venture group.][1]

Amendments—[1] Regulation 9 substituted by the Real Estate Investment Trusts (Financial Statements of Group Real Estate Investment Trusts) (Amendment) Regulations, SI 2007/3536 regs 2, 4 with effect for accounting periods beginning on or after 1 January 2008, and ending on or after 7 January 2008: SI 2007/3536 reg 1(2).

10 Open-ended investment companies

(1) This regulation applies if a member of a group has significant influence over an open-ended investment company.

(2) For the purposes of the financial statements specified in regulation 4(2), the open-ended investment company must be treated, for accounting purposes, as a member of the group.

11 Other non-corporate entities

(1) This regulation applies if a member of a group has significant influence over a non-corporate entity.

(2) For the purposes of the financial statements specified in regulation 4(2), that other entity must be treated, for accounting purposes, as a member of the group.

Financial statements for G (property rental business) in respect of its UK business

12 Contents of the financial statement

(1) In accordance with paragraph 31(4), a financial statement for G (property rental business) in respect of its UK business must specify profits calculated in accordance with section 120 in relation to each member of the group.

(2) In accordance with paragraph 31(5), where a non-member of the group holds a percentage of the beneficial interest in a member (other than the principal company), the financial statement for G (property rental business) in respect of its UK business must exclude that percentage of income, expenses, gains, losses, assets and liabilities of the member.

(3) The financial statement must also show the following amounts separately—

(*a*) capital allowances, and
(*b*) financing costs.

Further provisions

13 Time by which financial statements must be supplied

(1) The financial statements specified in regulation 4(2) must be supplied with the company tax return for the relevant accounting period.

(2) Accordingly, the filing date for those financial statements must be determined in accordance with paragraph 14 of Schedule 18 to the Finance Act 1998.

2006/2866

REAL ESTATE INVESTMENT TRUSTS (JOINT VENTURES) REGULATIONS 2006

Made by the Treasury under FA 2006 s 138

Made . . . . *1 November 2006*
Laid before the House of Commons . . . . *1 November 2006*
Coming into force . . . . *1 January 2007*

Revocation—These Regulations revoked by CTA 2010 s 1181, Sch 3 Pt 1 with effect for corporation tax purposes for accounting periods ending on or after 1 April 2010, and for income tax and capital gains tax purposes for the tax year 2010–11 and subsequent tax years.

Rewrite destinations—These Regulations were rewritten in CTA 2010 as follows—

reg 1 (citation, commencement and interpretation) — ss 584, 598.
reg 2 (notice) — ss 585, 586.
reg 3 (conditions) — ss 584, 586, 591, 598.
reg 4 (duration) — s 590.
reg 5 (financial statements) — s 588.
reg 6 (requirements for venturing companies) —s 588.
reg 7 (tax charges and exemptions) — ss 588, 594.
reg 8 (non-resident joint-venture companies and single-company UK REITs) — s 588.
reg 9 (notice) — ss 585, 586.
reg 10 (conditions) — ss 584, 586, 591, 598.
reg 11 (duration) — s 590.
reg 12 (financial statements) s 588.
reg 13 (tax charges and exemptions) — ss 588, 594.
reg 14 (joint ventures – entry charges) — ss 595, 597.
reg 15 (non-resident joint-venture companies and group REITs) — s 588.

2006/2867

REAL ESTATE INVESTMENT TRUSTS (ASSESSMENT AND RECOVERY OF TAX) REGULATIONS 2006

Made by the Treasury under FA 2006 s 122, Sch 17 paras 4 and 19

Made . . . . *1 November 2006*
Laid before the House of Commons . . . . *1 November 2006*
Coming into force . . . . *1 January 2007*

Commentary—*Simon's Taxes* **D7.1127, D7.1128.**

HMRC Manuals—Guidance on Real Estate Investment Trusts Manual, GREIT08060 (administration by UK-REIT).
GREIT08065–08070 and 08080 (administration: quarterly returns and reconciliations, with examples).
GREIT08075 and 08085–08095 (administration: attributions and reconciliations, with examples).
GREIT08115–08120 (administration: quarterly returns).
GREIT08125 (administration: gross payment).

PART 1
INTRODUCTORY

1 Citation, commencement and interpretation

(1) These Regulations may be cited as the Real Estate Investment Trusts (Assessment and Recovery of Tax) Regulations 2006 and shall come into force on 1st January 2007.

(2) In these Regulations—

(*a*) "ICTA" means the Income and Corporation Taxes Act 1988
(*b*) "FA 2006" means the Finance Act 2006;
(*c*) "TMA" means the Taxes Management Act 1970
(*d*) "TCGA" means the Taxation of Chargeable Gains Act 1992;
(*e*) a reference to a numbered section or Schedule (without more) is a reference to a section of, or Schedule to, FA 2006 bearing that number;

(3) In these Regulations—

"C (residual)" has the meaning given by section 105(3)(*c*);
"C (post-cessation)" has the meaning given by section 105(3)(*d*);
"C (tax-exempt)" has the meaning given by section 105(3)(*b*);
"G (post-cessation)" has the meaning given by paragraph 2(*d*) of Schedule 17;
"G (property rental business)" has the meaning given by paragraph 3(2)(*b*) of that Schedule;
"profits" means income and gains; and
"UK profits" shall be construed in accordance with paragraph 3(2) of Schedule 17.

2 Introduction

(1) These Regulations provide for the deduction of sums representing tax—

(*a*) where a company to which Part 4 of FA 2006 applies makes a distribution of profits of C (tax-exempt) or,
(*b*) in a case where Part 4 of FA 2006 applies to a group by virtue of section 134(1), where the principal company makes a distribution out of the UK profits of G (property rental business).

(2) Part 2 of these Regulations applies in the case of a company to which Part 4 of FA 2006 applies but which is not part of a group to which that Part applies.

(3) Part 3 of these Regulations modifies Part 2 of these Regulations in the case of—

(*a*) C (post-cessation) where the company to which Part 4 of FA 2006 applied was not part of a group to which that Part applied;

(*b*) a group to which Part 4 of FA 2006 applies; and

(*c*) each UK resident company which is a member of G (post-cessation).

PART 2
COMPANIES TO WHICH PART 4 OF FA 2006 APPLIES, BUT WHICH ARE NOT PART OF A GROUP

3 Deduction of tax

(1) This regulation applies if a company to which Part 4 of FA 2006 applies, and which is not part of a group to which that Part applies, makes a distribution of profits of C (tax-exempt) ("a relevant distribution").

(2) The company must, on making a relevant distribution, deduct from it a sum representing tax at the basic rate in force for the year in which it is made, unless (or to the extent that) regulation 7 authorises the distribution to be made without deduction of tax.

4 Payments in an accounting period

(1) This regulation applies if the company makes a relevant distribution in an accounting period of the company.

(2) The company must deliver a return to an officer of Revenue and Customs for each return period in which the company makes a relevant distribution and which falls within the accounting period.

(3) The return periods are—

(*a*) the quarters ending upon 31st March, 30th June, 30th September and 31st December ("the quarter days"); and

(*b*) any shorter period which—

(i) starts on the first day of an accounting period and ends with the first or only quarter day in that accounting period;

(ii) begins immediately after the last or only quarter day in that accounting period and ends on the last day of that accounting period; or

(iii) is an accounting period which starts and ends within a quarter.

(4) The company must deliver the return within 14 days after the end of the return period.

(5) The return must show the amount of—

(*a*) any relevant distributions made by the company in the return period, and

(*b*) the tax (if any) payable by the company in respect of those payments.

(6) The company must deliver, with the return for the return period which ends on the last day of an accounting period, a reconciliation statement showing, in relation to any distribution made during the accounting period, the amounts (if any) which are attributable to each of paragraphs (*a*) to (*e*) of section 123.

5 Collection and payment of tax

(1) Tax in respect of a relevant distribution is due, from the company making it, at the time by which the return on which the distribution must be included is required to be delivered.

(2) The tax due is equal to the sum which the company is required to deduct from the relevant distribution under regulation 3(2).

(3) The tax is payable without an officer of Revenue and Customs making any assessment.

6 Certificates of deduction of tax

(1) A company making a relevant distribution which is subject to deduction of tax by virtue of section 122 must furnish the recipient with a statement in writing showing—

(*a*) the gross amount of the payment,

(*b*) the amount of tax deducted, and

(*c*) the actual amount paid.

(2) The duty imposed by paragraph (1) is enforceable at the suit or instance of the recipient.

7 Gross payment of distributions

(1) A payment of a relevant distribution must be made without deduction of income tax if the company reasonably believes that—

(*a*) the person beneficially entitled to the payment is a person or body to which one of paragraphs (2) and (3) applies;

(*b*) the recipient is a person or body to which paragraph (4) applies, and the payment satisfies the condition in paragraph (5);

(*c*) the recipient is a partnership to which paragraph (6) applies; or

(*d*) the distribution arises in respect of shares held as investments of the Overseas Service Pension Fund established pursuant to section 7(1) of the Overseas Aid Act 1966.

This paragraph is subject to the qualifications in paragraphs (7) and (8).

(2) This paragraph applies to—
(*a*) a company resident in the United Kingdom for corporation tax purposes; and
(*b*) a company that—
(i) is not resident in the United Kingdom;
(ii) carries on a trade in the United Kingdom through a permanent establishment; and
(iii) is required to bring the relevant distribution into account in computing the chargeable profits (within the meaning of section 11(2) of ICTA).

[(2A) But paragraph (2) does not apply to a Tax Elected Fund.

(2B) In paragraph (2A) "Tax Elected Fund" has the meaning given by regulation 69Z42(2) of the Authorised Investment Funds (Tax) Regulations 2006.][1]

(3) This paragraph applies to—
(*a*) a local authority;
(*b*) a health service body within the meaning of section 519A(2) of ICTA;
(*c*) a public office or department of the Crown to which section 829(1) of that Act applies;
(*d*) a charity within the meaning of section 506(1) of that Act;
(*e*) a body for the time being mentioned in section 507(1) of that Act (bodies which are allowed the same exemption from tax as charities the whole income of which is applied to charitable purposes);
(*f*) an Association of a description specified in section 508 of that Act (scientific research organisations); and
(*g*) the European Investment Fund.

(4) This paragraph applies to a payment which is made to—
(*a*) the trustees of a scheme entitled to exemption under section 613(4) of that Act (Parliamentary pension funds);
(*b*) the scheme administrator of a registered pension scheme;
(*c*) the sub-scheme administrator of a sub-scheme which forms part of a split scheme pursuant to the Registered Pension Schemes (Splitting of Schemes) Regulations 2006;
(*d*) the account provider for a child trust fund within the meaning of section 1(2) of the Child Trust Funds Act 2004 or the nominee of the account provider;
(*e*) the account manager of an account within the meaning of regulation 4(1) of the Individual Savings Account Regulations 1998 or the nominee of the account manager;
(*f*) the plan manager of a plan within the meaning of regulation 4(1) of the Personal Equity Plan Regulations 1989 or the nominee of the plan manager;

and satisfies the condition in paragraph (5).

(5) The condition is that the payment is to be applied for the purposes of the fund, scheme, account or plan mentioned in paragraph (4) in respect of which the recipient has duties.

(6) This paragraph applies to a partnership each member of which is a person or body mentioned in paragraph (2), (3), or (4), provided that, in the case of a person or body mentioned in paragraph (4) its share of the partnership profits are to be applied for the purposes of the fund, scheme, account or plan in respect of which that person or body has duties.

(7) If the owner of securities in a company that is a Real Estate Investment Trust has sold or transferred the right to receive a relevant distribution (whether before or after the sale or transfer), without selling or transferring those securities, the company must deduct tax at the basic rate.

(8) If the company reasonably believes, at the time that it makes a payment without deduction of tax, that paragraph (2), (3), (4) or (6) applies, but in fact none of those paragraphs applies, these Regulations shall apply to the payment as if it were never one which could be made without deduction of tax.

(9) Upon discovering that the payment mentioned in paragraph (8) is one from which tax should have been deducted, the company making it must deliver an amended return in accordance with regulation 11.

HMRC Manuals—Guidance on Real Estate Investment Trusts Manual, GREIT09180 (dividend strips).

Amendments—[1] Paras (2A), (2B) inserted by the Authorised Investment Funds (Tax) (Amendment) Regulations, SI 2009/2036 regs 2, 33 with effect from 1 September 2009.

8 Assessments where relevant distribution included in return

(1) This regulation applies if any tax in respect of a relevant distribution which is included in a return under these Regulations has not been paid at or before the time mentioned in regulation 5.

(2) An officer of Revenue and Customs may make an assessment on the person who made the relevant distribution.

(3) Tax may be assessed under this regulation whether or not it has been paid when the assessment is made.

9 Assessments in other cases

(1) This regulation applies if an officer of Revenue and Customs thinks—
(*a*) that there is a relevant distribution which should have been included in a return under these Regulations and which has not been so included, or

(*b*) that a return under these Regulations is otherwise incorrect.

(2) An officer of Revenue and Customs may make an assessment on the person who made the relevant distribution to the best of the officer's judgement.

10 Application of Income Tax Acts provisions about time limits for assessments

(1) The provisions of the Income Tax Acts about the time within which an assessment may be made apply to assessments under these Regulations, so far as those provisions refer or relate to—

(*a*) the tax year for which an assessment is made, or

(*b*) the year to which an assessment relates.

(2) Paragraph (1) applies despite the fact that an assessment under these Regulations may relate to a return period which is not a tax year.

(3) The provisions of section 36 of TMA (fraudulent or negligent conduct) about the circumstances in which an assessment may be made out of time apply accordingly on the basis that any such assessment relates to the tax year in which the return period ends.

(4) Section 87 of TMA (late payments of tax on assessments made or payments due under Schedule 16 to ICTA) applies for the purposes of a payment due under regulation 4 or an assessment made under regulation 8 or 9.

11 Company's duty to deliver amended return

(1) This regulation applies if a company which has made a relevant distribution becomes aware that—

(*a*) anything which should have been included in a return delivered by the company under these Regulations has not been so included,

(*b*) anything which should not have been included in a return delivered by the company under these Regulations has been so included, or

(*c*) any other error has occurred in a return delivered by the company under these Regulations.

(2) The company must deliver an amended return correcting the error to an officer of Revenue and Customs without delay.

(3) If the company delivers an amended return such assessments, adjustments, setoffs or payments or repayments of tax as are necessary for achieving the objective mentioned in paragraph (4) must be made.

(4) The objective is that the resulting liabilities to income and corporation tax (including interest on unpaid or overpaid tax) of the company or any other person are the same as they would have been if a correct return had been delivered.

PART 3

COMPANY TO WHICH PART 4 OF FA 2006 FORMERLY APPLIED, AND GROUPS

12—(1) Part 2 of these Regulations applies—

(*a*) to a group to which Part 4 of FA 2006 applies;

(*b*) to a company to which Part 4 of FA 2006 formerly applied, but which was not part of a group to which that Part applied, and

(*c*) to a group to which Part 4 of FA 2006 formerly applied

with the following modifications.

(2) In a case falling within paragraph (1)(*a*) the modifications are that—

(*a*) references to the company shall be read as references to the principal company;

(*b*) references to a relevant distribution shall be read as references to a distribution out of amounts shown in the financial statements of G (property rental business) as—

(i) the profits of the UK-resident members of the group; and

(ii) gains accruing to UK-resident members of the group.

(3) In a case falling within paragraph (1)(*b*) references to company shall be read as references to a company to which Part 4 formerly applied.

(4) In a case falling within paragraph (1)(*c*)—

(*a*) references to company shall be read as references to the principal company of G (post-cessation); and

(*b*) references to relevant distribution are to be read as references to a distribution out of amounts shown in the financial statements of G (property rental business) as—

(i) the profits of the UK-resident members of the group; and

(ii) gains accruing to UK-resident members of the group.

(5) . . . [1]

Amendments—[1] Para (5) revoked by the Real Estate Investment Trusts (Assessment and Recovery of Tax) (Amendment) Regulations, SI 2006/3222 reg 2 with effect from 26 December 2006. This amendment removes reg 12(5) that was originally included as a result of a minor drafting error.

2006/3170

TAXATION OF CHARGEABLE GAINS (GILT-EDGED SECURITIES) (NO 2) ORDER 2006

Made by the Treasury, under TCGA 1992 Sch 9 para 1

Made . . . . *28 November 2006*

Commentary—*Simon's Taxes* **C2.825**.

1 Citation

This Order may be cited as the Taxation of Chargeable Gains (Gilt-edged Securities) (No 2) Order 2006.

2 Securities specified as gilt-edged securities

For the purposes of Schedule 9 to the Taxation of Chargeable Gains Act 1992 (gilt-edged securities) the following securities are specified—

4% Treasury Gilt 2016;
1¼% Index-Linked Treasury Gilt 2017;
1¼% Index-Linked Treasury Gilt 2027;
4¼% Treasury Gilt 2027;
4¼% Treasury Gilt 2046.

2006/3262

LLOYD'S UNDERWRITERS (DOUBLE TAXATION RELIEF) (CORPORATE MEMBERS) REGULATIONS 2006

Made by the Commissioners for Her Majesty's Revenue and Customs under FA 1994 s 229

Made . . . . *6th December 2006*
Laid before the House of Commons . . . . *7th December 2006*
Coming into force . . . . *31st December 2006*

Preliminary

1 Citation, commencement and effect

(1) These Regulations may be cited as the Lloyd's Underwriters (Double Taxation Relief) (Corporate Members) Regulations 2006 and shall come into force on 31st December 2006.
(2) These Regulations shall have effect in relation to accounting periods ending on or after the date on which these Regulations come into force.

2 Interpretation

(1) This paragraph gives the meaning of abbreviated references to legislation used in these Regulations—

"ICTA" means the Income and Corporation Taxes Act 1988;
"Chapter 2 of Part 18" means Chapter 2 of Part 18 of ICTA (rules governing relief by way of credit).

(2) In these Regulations—

"foreign amount of tax" has the meaning given by regulation 5(4);
"foreign tax" means tax chargeable under the law of a territory outside the United Kingdom.

General Scope of these Regulations

3 General provisions

(1) These Regulations make provision for giving credit for foreign tax payable in respect of profits or losses arising from a corporate member's underwriting business in an accounting period.
(2) Relief from corporation tax shall be given under Chapters 1 and 2 of Part 18 of ICTA in respect of the foreign tax payable by allowing the amount of the pool of adjusted sums of foreign tax for an accounting period as a credit against the corporation tax payable on the profits arising from the corporate member's underwriting business.
(3) In these Regulations—

(*a*) regulations 5 to 10 apply to determine how the amount of the pool of adjusted sums of foreign tax for an accounting period is ascertained, and
(*b*) regulation 11 explains how the amount of the pool of adjusted sums of foreign tax for an accounting period is allowed as a credit against the corporation tax payable on the profits arising from the corporate member's underwriting business.

4 Application of sections in Chapter 2 of Part 18

The following sections of Chapter 2 of Part 18 apply for the purposes of these Regulations—

section 792 (interpretation of credit code);

sections 793 to 795A (general rules);

sections 797 to 798C (the measure of the foreign income);

sections 805 and 806 (elections and claims).

The Pool of Adjusted Sums of Foreign Tax

5 Allocation of foreign tax to accounting periods

(1) The amount of the pool of adjusted sums of foreign tax for an accounting period is calculated by reference to the foreign tax payable for the corresponding foreign period of accounting.

(2) Adjusted sums of foreign tax must be calculated separately for each relevant territory outside the United Kingdom.

(3) For the purposes of these Regulations an accounting period corresponds to a foreign period of accounting if the foreign period of accounting ends in the period of twelve months immediately preceding the beginning of the accounting period.

Regulation 6 contains further provisions that apply if an accounting period or a foreign period of accounting is not a period of twelve months.

(4) In these Regulations an amount of foreign tax payable for a corresponding foreign period of accounting is called a foreign amount of tax.

6 Further provisions relating to accounting periods and to foreign periods of accounting

(1) If a foreign period of accounting is more than twelve months—

(*a*) the period must be split into successive periods of twelve months and a final period not exceeding twelve months, and

(*b*) the profit of the corporate member's underwriting business and the amount of foreign tax must be apportioned rateably.

(2) If a foreign period of accounting is less than twelve months and more than one such period ends in the period of twelve months immediately preceding the beginning of the accounting period, the accounting period corresponds to all those foreign periods of accounting.

(3) If a foreign period of accounting ends at a time which is within the immediately preceding twelve months period of more than one accounting period, the accounting period to which the foreign period of accounting corresponds is the first accounting period to begin after the foreign period of accounting ends.

(4) In paragraph (3) "the immediately preceding twelve months period" means the period of twelve months immediately preceding an accounting period.

7 Adjustments of foreign amounts of tax

(1) If necessary, foreign amounts of tax must be adjusted in accordance with the provisions of this regulation to determine the adjusted sums of foreign tax.

(2) The effective rate of foreign tax must be determined in accordance with the equation—

$$\mathrm{ERFT} = \frac{\mathrm{F}}{\mathrm{P}} \times 100$$

(3) In this regulation—

ERFT = the effective rate of foreign tax;

F = the foreign tax payable for the corresponding foreign period of accounting;

P = the profit of the corporate member's underwriting business arising in the relevant territory outside the United Kingdom for the foreign period of accounting in respect of which the foreign tax is payable.

(4) If the effective rate of foreign tax for a corresponding foreign period of accounting is less than, or equal to, the average rate of corporation tax fixed for companies generally for the accounting period corresponding to the foreign period of accounting, the amount of the adjusted sum of foreign tax is the foreign amount of tax.

(5) If the effective rate of foreign tax for a corresponding foreign period of accounting is greater than the average rate of corporation tax fixed for companies generally for the accounting period corresponding to the foreign period of accounting, the amount of the adjusted sum of foreign tax is determined in accordance with the equation—

$$\mathrm{ASFT} = \frac{\mathrm{CTR}}{\mathrm{ERFT}} \times \mathrm{FT}$$

(6) In paragraph (5)—

ASFT = the amount of the adjusted sum of foreign tax;

CTR = the average rate of corporation tax fixed for companies generally for the accounting period corresponding to the foreign period of accounting;
FT = the foreign amount of tax.

8 Calculation of amount of pool of adjusted sums of foreign tax

(1) The amount of the pool of adjusted sums of foreign tax for an accounting period is determined in accordance with the equation—

$$PASFT = AASFT + ATA + BFA$$

(2) In paragraph (1)—

PASFT = the amount of the pool of adjusted sums of foreign tax;
AASFT = the aggregate amount of adjusted sums of foreign tax;
ATA = an additional transitional amount (see regulation 9(2));
BFA = the amount brought forward from the previous accounting period (see regulation 11(2)).

(3) If regulation 10 applies, the amount of an adjusted sum of foreign tax must be determined in accordance with that regulation.

9 Transitional provision

(1) This regulation applies if, for the first accounting period for which these Regulations apply—

(*a*) a corporate member has an amount of tax chargeable under the law of a territory outside the United Kingdom for which relief has not been given, and
(*b*) that amount of tax relates to foreign periods of accounting earlier than the period to which the first accounting period corresponds.

(2) If the corporate member so chooses, that amount of tax may be added to the pool of adjusted sums of foreign tax for that first accounting period.

(3) If paragraph (2) applies, the amount of tax must be adjusted in accordance with the provisions of regulation 7 if necessary.

(4) In any other case, relief must be given for that amount of tax before relief is given under these Regulations.

10 Refunds of foreign tax

(1) This regulation applies if—

(*a*) relief for foreign tax paid is given by way of credit against United Kingdom tax on profits arising from a corporate member's underwriting business, and
(*b*) an amount of that foreign tax ("the repaid amount") is subsequently repaid to the member.

(2) For the purposes of regulations 5 to 8 the repaid amount must be dealt with in accordance with paragraphs (3) and (4).

(3) For the purposes of regulation 7—

(*a*) the repaid amount is to be treated as if it were a foreign amount of tax repayable for the corresponding foreign period of accounting, and
(*b*) the following are to be adjusted by deducting the repaid amount—
(i) the foreign tax payable for the corresponding foreign period of accounting (see paragraphs (2) and (3) of regulation 7), and
(ii) the foreign amount of tax (see paragraphs (5) and (6) of regulation 7).

(4) For the purposes of regulation 8 the repaid amount (adjusted, if necessary, under paragraph (3)) must be deducted from the amount AASFT.

(5) Paragraph (6) applies if—

(*a*) any credit for foreign tax has been allowed to a corporate member under any arrangements, and
(*b*) the amount of that credit is subsequently rendered excessive by reason of an adjustment of the amount of any tax payable under the laws of a territory outside the United Kingdom.

(6) The corporate member shall give notice in writing to an Officer of Revenue and Customs that an adjustment has been made that has rendered the amount of the credit excessive.

(7) A notice under paragraph (6) must be given within one year from the time of the making of the adjustment.

(8) A corporate member which fails to comply with the requirements imposed by paragraphs (6) and (7) in relation to any adjustment shall be liable to a penalty of an amount not exceeding the amount by which the credit allowed has been rendered excessive by reason of the adjustment.

(9) If the condition in paragraph (10) is met, any assessments may be made as are necessary to ensure that the total amount of the corporate member's income or chargeable gains is assessed, and the proper credit, if any, is given in respect of that income or those gains.

(10) The condition is that it appears that the assessment to corporation tax made on the corporate member in respect of the income or chargeable gains—

(*a*) is not made in respect of the full amount of that income or those gains, or
(*b*) is incorrect having regard to the repaid amount.

(11) Where the income is, or the chargeable gains are, entrusted to any person in the United Kingdom for payment, any such assessment may be made on the recipient of the income or gains; and, in the case of an assessment to corporation tax in respect of the income, may be assessed under Case VI of Schedule D.

Double Taxation Relief Given

11 How relief is given

(1) Relief from corporation tax for an accounting period in respect of foreign tax shall be given by allowing the amount of the pool of adjusted sums of foreign tax for that accounting period as a credit against corporation tax payable on the profits arising from a corporate member's underwriting business—

(*a*) in that accounting period, or

(*b*) in such one or more preceding accounting periods, beginning not more than three years before the accounting period mentioned in sub-paragraph (*a*),

or partly in the one way and partly in the other as the corporate member may choose.

(2) Any amount in the pool of adjusted sums of foreign tax for an accounting period that is not allowed as a credit against corporation tax in accordance with paragraph (1) shall be carried forward and added to the pool of adjusted sums of foreign tax for the next accounting period (see regulation 8(1)).

2006/3271

OVERSEAS LIFE INSURANCE COMPANIES REGULATIONS 2006

Made by the Treasury under FA 2003 s 156

Made ....*7th December 2006*

Laid before the House of Commons ....*8th December 2006*

Coming into force ....*31st December 2006*

Commentary—*Simon's Taxes* **D4.116; D4.117**.

1 Citation, commencement and effect

These Regulations may be cited as the Overseas Life Insurance Companies Regulations 2006, shall come into force on 31st December 2006 and shall have effect in relation to periods of account (whenever beginning) which end on or after that day.

2 Interpretation

In these Regulations—

"overseas life insurance company" has the meaning given in section 156(5) of the Finance Act 2003;

"period of account" has the meaning given in section 832(1) of the Income and Corporation Taxes Act 1988.

3 Modifications of the Income and Corporation Taxes Act

In relation to an overseas life insurance company, the Income and Corporation Taxes Act 1988 shall have effect as if it were subject to the following modifications.

4

Amendments—Regulation 4 revoked by the Overseas Life insurance Companies (Amendment) Regulations, SI 2007/2146 regs 2, 3 with effect for periods of account beginning on or after 1 January 2007 which end on or after 14 August 2007: SI 2007/2146 reg 1(2).

5—(1) Modify section 76 (expenses of insurance companies) as follows.

(2) For subsection (3) substitute—

"(3) For the purposes of this section "expenses payable" means—

(*a*) where the company is a UK-authorised firm, expenses brought into account in the periodical return of the company for a period of account in line 12, 22 or 25 of Form 40 (the revenue account) in relation to the long-term business carried on by the company at a permanent establishment in the United Kingdom;

[(*b*) where the company is an EEA firm or a Treaty firm—

(i) so much of the expenses included in item II.8 or 9(a) of the [long-term business technical account][2] included in IAD accounts as are attributable to a permanent establishment in the United Kingdom through which the company carries on life assurance business; or

(ii) so much of the expenses included in the income statement included in IAS accounts as are equivalent to expenses that would be included in item II.8 or 9(a) of the [long-term business technical account][2] included in any IAD accounts and are so attributable;][1]

but does not include any of the amounts falling within subsections (4), (5) or (6).".

(3) In subsection (7), in Step 2—

(*a*) in paragraph [(*c*)][3] (*b*) omit "or", and

(*b*) at the end insert—

", or

[(*e*)] [3] equal to the amount—

$$S1 \times \left(\frac{FOTRA}{TBLAGAB}\right)$$

where—

S1 is the amount given by Step 1,

FOTRA is the amount of any profits and gains arising from a FOTRA security, or from any loan relationship represented by it (after applying the provisions of section 154(2) to (7) of the Finance Act 1996), excluded by virtue of the tax exemption condition of that security,

TBLAGAB means the income from the investments of an overseas life insurance company referable in accordance with section 432A to the basic life assurance and general annuity business of the permanent establishment in the United Kingdom through which the company carries on life assurance business, and

"FOTRA security" and "tax exemption condition" have the same meaning as in section 154(8) of the Finance Act 1996.".

(4) . . . [1]

Amendments—[1] In para (2), modified TA 1988 s 76(3)(*b*) substituted, and para (4) revoked, by the Overseas Life insurance Companies (Amendment) Regulations, SI 2007/2146 regs 2, 4 with effect for periods of account beginning on or after 1 January 2007 which end on or after 14 August 2007: SI 2007/2146 reg 1(2).

[2] Words in para (2), in the substituted sub-s (3)(*b*)(i), (ii), substituted, and para (5) inserted, by the Overseas Life Insurance Companies (Amendment No 2) Regulations, SI 2007/3449 regs 2, 3 with effect in relation to periods of account which begin on or after 1 January 2008: SI 2007/3449 reg 1(2).

[3] In sub-para (3)(*a*), letter "(*c*)" substituted for previous letter "(*b*)", and in sub-para (3)(*b*), inserted para (*e*) labelled as such (formerly labelled as para "(*d*)"), by the Overseas Life Insurance Companies (Amendment) Regulations, SI 2008/1924 reg 3 with effect in relation to periods of account beginning on or after 1 January 2008 which end on or after 12 August 2008: SI 2008/1924 reg 1(2).

6—(1) Modify section 431(2) (interpretative provisions relating to insurance companies) as follows.

[(1ZA) Modify subsection (2) in accordance with paragraphs (1A) to (5).][3]

[(1A) In the definition of "foreign business assets" omit—

(*a*) "either",

(*b*) "or" at the end of paragraph (*a*), and

(*c*) paragraph (*b*).][3]

(2) In the definition of "insurance company"—

(*a*) in paragraph (*a*), after "contracts of insurance" insert "(a "UK-authorised firm")", and

(*b*) in paragraph (*b*)—

[(i) for "paragraph 5(*d*) of Schedule 3 to that Act" substitute "sub-paragraph (*d*) or (*da*) of paragraph 5 of Schedule 3 to that Act (an "EEA firm")";][2]

(ii) after "Schedule 4 to that Act" insert "(a "Treaty firm")", and

(iii) in sub-paragraph (ii) for "branch or agency" substitute "permanent establishment".

[(2A) In the case of an EEA firm or a Treaty firm, for the definition of "liabilities" substitute—

""liabilities", where the company concerned is an EEA firm or a Treaty firm—

(*a*) does not include liabilities that have been reinsured, but

(*b*) subject to that, means liabilities (including those which arise from deposit back arrangements) as determined in accordance with actuarial principles for the purposes of any return equivalent to a periodical return and required to be made by the company under the law of the territory in which the company is resident;"][3]

(3) In the definition of "overseas life insurance company" for "branch or agency" substitute "permanent establishment".

(4) Substitute the following definitions in the appropriate places—

. . . [3]

""value", in relation to assets and where the company concerned is an overseas life insurance company, means—

(*a*) their value as taken into account for the purposes of the company's periodical return, or

(*b*) where their value is not taken into account for the purposes of such a periodical return, their value as taken into account for the purposes of any return equivalent to a periodical return and required to be made by the company under the law of the territory in which the company is resident;";

""insurance business transfer scheme" means a scheme falling within section 105 of the Financial Services and Markets Act 2000 and includes a reference to—

(*a*) an excluded scheme falling within Case 2, 3[, 4 or 5][3] of subsection (3) of that section; and

(*b*) a qualifying overseas transfer;".

(5) Insert the following definitions in the appropriate places—

""free assets amount", in relation to an overseas life insurance company, means the excess of the value of the relevant assets over the [relevant liabilities][3], and for the purposes of this definition—

(*a*) relevant assets are such assets of the company's long-term insurance fund as fall to be attributed, for the purposes of section 11AA(2), to the permanent establishment in the United Kingdom through which the company carries on long-term business; [and][3]

(*b*) relevant liabilities are—

(i) such liabilities of the long-term business as fall to be attributed, for the purposes of section 11AA(2), to the permanent establishment; and

(ii) any money debts (within the meaning of Chapter 2 of Part 4 of the Finance Act 1996) of the company which are not within sub-paragraph (i) above but which are owed in respect of that business and fall to be attributed, for the purposes of section 11AA(2), to the permanent establishment; . . . [3]

(c) . . . [3]

""IAD accounts" means the accounts drawn up in accordance with the Council Directive of 19th December 1991 on the annual accounts and consolidated accounts of insurance undertakings (No91/674/EEC);";

[""IAS accounts" means accounts prepared in accordance with international accounting standards;";][1]

""long-term insurance fund", in the case of an overseas life insurance company where the company is an EEA firm or a Treaty firm, [means—

(*a*) the technical account for [life-assurance][2] business of the company included in the IAD accounts; or

[(*aa*) where the technical account included in the IAD accounts for non-life-insurance business of the company is used for all business, such part of that account as relates to the long-term business of the company; or][2]

(*b*) such part of the income statement . . . [2] as relates to the life assurance business of the company included in the IAS accounts;

and references to assets of the long-term insurance fund shall be read as references to assets from which any income or gain is or would be included in [either that technical account or that part of the technical account or that part of the income statement][2], and][1];";

""periodical return" means, in relation to an overseas life insurance company, where the company is an EEA firm or a Treaty firm, the IAD accounts [or the IAS accounts][1];";

""qualifying overseas transfer" means so much of any transfer of the whole or any part of the business of an overseas life insurance company carried on through a permanent establishment in the United Kingdom as takes place in accordance with any authorisation granted outside the United Kingdom for the purposes of Article 14 of the Council Directive of 5th November 2002 concerning life assurance (No2002/83/EC);".

[(6) In subsection (2YC), at the end insert—

"so far as that income and those gains fall to be attributed, for the purposes of section 11AA(2), to the permanent establishment in the United Kingdom through which the company carries on life assurance business.".

(7) In subsection (2YD), at the end insert—

"so far as those amounts and that deduction fall to be attributed, for the purposes of section 11AA(2), to the permanent establishment in the United Kingdom through which the company carries on life assurance business."][3]

Amendments—[1] In para (5), definition of "IAS accounts" inserted; and in the definition of "long-term insurance fund" words substituted; by the Overseas Life insurance Companies (Amendment) Regulations, SI 2007/2146 regs 2, 5 with effect for periods of account beginning on or after 1 January 2007 which end on or after 14 August 2007: SI 2007/2146 reg 1(2).

[2] Para (2)(*b*)(i) substituted; in para (5), in definition of "long-term insurance fund, words in para (*a*) substituted for words "life assurance", para (*aa*) inserted, and in para (*b*) words "as relates to" revoked and words substituted for words "that technical account or income statement"; by the Overseas Life Insurance Companies (Amendment No 2) Regulations, SI 2007/3449 regs 2, 4 with effect in relation to periods of account which begin on or after 1 January 2008: SI 2007/3449 reg 1(2).

[3] In para (1), reference revoked; paras (1ZA), (2A) inserted; para (1A) substituted; in para (4), the substituted definition of "liabilities" revoked, and in the substituted definition of "insurance business transfer scheme", words substituted for words; in para (5), in the inserted definition of "free assets amount", words substituted, word inserted at end of para (*a*), and para (*c*) and preceding word "and" revoked; and sub-ss (6), (7) inserted; by the Overseas Life Insurance Companies (Amendment) Regulations, SI 2008/1924 reg 4 with effect in relation to periods of account beginning on or after 1 January 2008 which end on or after 12 August 2008: SI 2008/1924 reg 1(2).

7 In section 431D (meaning of "overseas life assurance business"), in subsection (1), after "means life assurance business" insert "carried on through a permanent establishment in the United Kingdom by an overseas life insurance company".

[7A—(1) Modify section 431G (company carrying on life assurance business) as follows.

(2) In subsection (1) after "life assurance business" insert "through a permanent establishment in the United Kingdom".

(3) In subsections (2) and (3)(*a*) and (*b*), after "life assurance business" insert "carried on through a permanent establishment in the United Kingdom".][1]

Amendments—[1] This regulation inserted by the Overseas Life insurance Companies (Amendment) Regulations, SI 2007/2146 regs 2, 6 with effect for periods of account beginning on or after 1 January 2007 which end on or after 14 August 2007: SI 2007/2146 reg 1(2).

[7B In section 431H (company carrying on life assurance business and other insurance business), in subsection (1), after "any other kind" insert "through a permanent establishment in the United Kingdom".][1]

Amendments—[1] This regulation inserted by the Overseas Life insurance Companies (Amendment) Regulations, SI 2007/2146 regs 2, 6 with effect for periods of account beginning on or after 1 January 2007 which end on or after 14 August 2007: SI 2007/2146 reg 1(2).

8—(1) Modify section 432A (apportionment of income and gains) as follows.

(2) . . . [2]

(3) After subsection (9A) insert—

"(9AA) In this section—

"assets" means those assets that fall to be attributed, for the purposes of section 11AA(2), to the permanent establishment in the United Kingdom through which the company carries on life assurance business;

"liabilities" means those liabilities that fall to be attributed, for the purposes of section 11AA(2), to the permanent establishment in the United Kingdom through which the company carries on life assurance business.".

Amendments—[1] Paragraph (2) substituted by the Overseas Life insurance Companies (Amendment) Regulations, SI 2007/2146 regs 2, 7 with effect for periods of account beginning on or after 1 January 2007 which end on or after 14 August 2007: SI 2007/2146 reg 1(2).

[2] Para (2) revoked by the Overseas Life Insurance Companies (Amendment) Regulations, SI 2008/1924 reg 5 with effect from 12 August 2008.

9—(1) Modify section 432B (apportionment of receipts brought into account) as follows.

(2) In subsection (3) after "business" insert [(in the first place][1]) "of the permanent establishment in the United Kingdom through which the company carries on life assurance business".

(3) . . . [2]

Amendments—[1] In para (2) words substituted for words, and in para (3) new sub-para (*a*) substituted for sub-paras (*a*), (*b*), by the Overseas Life insurance Companies (Amendment) Regulations, SI 2007/2146 regs 2, 8 with effect for periods of account beginning on or after 1 January 2007 which end on or after 14 August 2007: SI 2007/2146 reg 1(2).

[2] Para (3) revoked by the Overseas Life Insurance Companies (Amendment) Regulations, SI 2008/1924 reg 6 with effect from 12 August 2008.

10 After section 434A (computation of losses and limitation on relief) insert—

"434AA Treatment of annuities

An overseas life insurance company shall not be entitled to treat as paid out of profits or gains brought into charge to income tax any part of the annuities paid by the company which is referable to its life assurance business.".

11—(1) Modify section 440 (transfers of assets etc) as follows.

(2) In subsection (2), in paragraph (*b*), for "is within another of those categories" substitute "is not within the corresponding category".

(3) In subsection (4)—

(*a*) in paragraphs (*a*) [and (*d*) to (*f*)][1] before "assets" insert "UK", and

(*b*) at the end insert—

"(*h*) assets of the company which are not UK assets.".

(4) After subsection (4) insert—

"(4AA) Section 13 of the Capital Allowances Act [2001][2] (use for qualifying activity of plant or machinery provided for other purposes) shall apply in relation to any case in which an asset or part of an asset held by an overseas life insurance company—

(*a*) ceases to be within the category set out in paragraph (*h*) of subsection (4) above; and

(*b*) at the same time comes within another of the categories set out in that subsection.

[(4AB) Where goodwill is acquired by an EEA firm or a Treaty firm ("the transferee") as a result of an insurance business transfer scheme which has effect to transfer long-term business from any person who is not such a firm to the transferee—

(*a*) if the goodwill (or part of it) was within the category set out in paragraph (*e*) of subsection (4) above immediately before the acquisition, the goodwill (or part) shall for the purposes of subsections (2) and (3) above be treated as being within that category immediately afterwards, and

(*b*) if the goodwill (or part of it) was within the category set out in paragraph (*f*) of subsection (4) above immediately before the acquisition, the goodwill (or part) shall for the purposes of subsections (2) and (3) above be treated as being within that category immediately afterwards.[2]]".

(5) At the end insert—

"(7) For the purposes of this section UK assets are assets which fall to be attributed, for the purposes of section 11AA(2), to the permanent establishment in the United Kingdom through which the company carries on life assurance business.

(8) Where the transferor company mentioned in subsection (2) is an overseas life insurance company, this section shall have effect, as regards the time immediately before the acquisition.

(9) Where the acquiring company mentioned in subsection (2) is an overseas life insurance company, this section shall have effect as regards the time immediately after the acquisition.".

Amendments—[1] In para (3)(*a*), words substituted for words by the Overseas Life insurance Companies (Amendment) Regulations, SI 2007/2146 regs 2, 9 with effect for periods of account beginning on or after 1 January 2007 which end on or after 14 August 2007: SI 2007/2146 reg 1(2).

[2] In para (4), in inserted sub-s (4AA) word inserted, and sub-s (4AB) inserted, by the Overseas Life Insurance Companies (Amendment No 2) Regulations, SI 2007/3449 regs 2, 5 with effect in relation to periods of account which begin on or after 1 January 2008: SI 2007/3449 reg 1(2).

12—(1) Modify section 440A (securities) as follows.

(2) In subsection (2)—

(*a*) in paragraph (*a*) before "securities" in the first place where it occurs insert "UK",

(*b*) in paragraphs [(*d*) and][1] (*e*) before "securities" insert "UK",

(*c*) in paragraph (*d*) omit "and", and

(*d*) at the end insert

", and

(*g*) the non-UK securities shall be treated for those purposes as a separate holding which is not of any of the descriptions mentioned in the preceding paragraphs.".

(3) After subsection (6) insert—

"(6A) For the purposes of this section—

(*a*) UK securities are such securities as are assets which fall to be attributed, for the purposes of section 11AA(2), to the permanent establishment in the United Kingdom through which the company carries on life assurance business; and

(*b*) non-UK securities are securities which are not UK securities.".

Amendments—[1] In para (2)(*b*), words substituted by the Overseas Life insurance Companies (Amendment) Regulations, SI 2007/2146 regs 2, 10 with effect for periods of account beginning on or after 1 January 2007 which end on or after 14 August 2007: SI 2007/2146 reg 1(2).

13 In section 440B (modifications where tax charged under Case I of Schedule D)—

(*a*) for subsection (3) substitute—

"(3) [Subsection (1) of section 440 has][1] effect as if the only categories specified in subsection (4) of that section were—

(*a*) UK assets of the long-term insurance fund,

(*b*) other UK assets, and

(*c*) assets of the company which are not UK assets,

and UK assets has the meaning given by section 440(7).", and

(*b*) for subsection (4) substitute—

"(4) Section 440A applies as if for paragraphs (*a*)[, (*d*) and (*e*)][1] of subsection (2) there were substituted—

"[(*a*) so many of the UK securities as are included in the company's long-term insurance fund shall be treated for the purposes of corporation tax as a separate holding which is an asset of that fund,][1]

(*b*) any remaining UK securities shall be treated for those purposes as a separate holding which is not of the description mentioned in the preceding paragraph, and

(*c*) the non-UK securities shall be treated for those purposes as a separate holding which is not of any of the descriptions mentioned in the preceding paragraphs."."

Amendments—[1] In para (*a*), in substituted sub-s (3), words substituted for words; in para (*b*), in substituted sub-s (4), words substituted and sub-s (4)(*a*) substituted; by the Overseas Life insurance Companies (Amendment) Regulations, SI 2007/2146 regs 2, 11 with effect for periods of account beginning on or after 1 January 2007 which end on or after 14 August 2007: SI 2007/2146 reg 1(2).

14 In section 442A (taxation of investment return where risk reinsured) after subsection (6) insert—

"(7) In the case of an overseas life insurance company, the investment return treated as accruing under this section in any accounting period in relation to a policy or contract shall be treated as chargeable profits within section 11(2) of the Taxes Act 1988 where the policy or contract is one which in that accounting period gives rise, or but for the reinsurance arrangement would give rise, to such profits.".

[14ZA In section 444AA (transfers of business: deemed periodical returns)(*b*), in subsection (5), in a case where the transferor is an EEA firm or a Treaty firm, for paragraphs (*a*) and (*b*) substitute—

"(*a*) in respect of the amount of the relevant long-term business provisions immediately before the transfer, and

(*b*) in respect of the value, immediately before the transfer, of the assets transferred.][1]

Amendments—[1] This regulation inserted by the Overseas Life Insurance Companies (Amendment) Regulations, SI 2008/1924 reg 7 with effect in relation to periods of account beginning on or after 1 January 2008 which end on or after 12 August 2008. But, this amendment has effect only in relation to transfers of business taking place on or after 1 July 2008 (SI 2008/1924 reg 1(2), (3)).

[14ZB In section 444ABA (relevant non-transferred assets)(c), in subsection (1), in a case where the transferor is an EEA firm or a Treaty firm, for the definition of BTO substitute—

"BTO is the lesser of VA and APL, where—

(*a*) VA is the value of the assets transferred by the insurance business transfer scheme shown (or treated as shown) in the periodical return of the transferor for the period of account of the transferor including the transfer date, and

(*b*) APL is the amount of the profit or loss for the financial year shown in the balance sheet in the periodical return for the last period of account of the transferor ending before the transfer date, together with—

(i) in the case of IAD accounts, the amount of profit or loss shown as being brought forward in that balance sheet, and

(ii) in the case of IAS accounts, the amount of retained earnings shown as being brought forward in that balance sheet.][1]

Amendments—[1] This regulation inserted by the Overseas Life Insurance Companies (Amendment) Regulations, SI 2008/1924 reg 7 with effect in relation to periods of account beginning on or after 1 January 2008 which end on or after 12 August 2008. But, this amendment has effect only in relation to transfers of business taking place on or after 1 July 2008 (SI 2008/1924 reg 1(2), (3)).

14ZC—(1) In a case where the transferor is an EEA or a Treaty firm, modify section 444ABB (retained assets)(d) as follows.

(2) In subsection (1)—

(*a*) for "RL13" (in both places) substitute "RL"; and

(*b*) in the definition of RL13, for "AL13" substitute "APL".

(3) In subsection (1A) for paragraphs (a) to (c) substitute—

"(*a*) APL is the amount of the profit or loss for the financial year shown in the balance sheet in the periodical return for the last period of account of the transferor ending before the transfer date, together with—

(i) in the case of IAD accounts, the amount of profit or loss shown as brought forward in that balance sheet, and

(ii) in the case of IAS accounts, the amount of retained earnings shown as brought forward in that balance sheet;

(*b*) VE is the amount (if any) by which VA exceeds VTL where—

(i) VA is the value of the assets transferred by the insurance business transfer scheme shown (or treated as shown) in the periodical return of the transferor for the period of account of the transferor including the transfer date, and

(ii) VTL is the value of the liabilities transferred by the insurance business transfer scheme (but excluding those which arise from deposit back arrangements); and

(*c*) relevant retained liabilities are any liabilities of the company's long-term business which are owed by the company immediately after the transfer date and are shown (or treated as shown) as entries—

(i) at items C3 (net of reinsurance) and G in IAD accounts, or

(ii) at equivalent items in the balance sheet in IAS accounts.".][1]

Amendments—[1] This regulation inserted by the Overseas Life Insurance Companies (Amendment) Regulations, SI 2008/1924 reg 7 with effect in relation to periods of account beginning on or after 1 January 2008 which end on or after 12 August 2008. But, this amendment has effect only in relation to transfers of business taking place on or after 1 July 2008 (SI 2008/1924 reg 1(2), (3)).

[14A—(1) In a case where the transferor is an EEA firm or a Treaty firm, modify section 444ABD (transferor's period of account including transfer) as follows.

(2) In subsection (1), for paragraphs (*a*) and (*b*) substitute—

"(*a*) the value of the liabilities transferred by the insurance business transfer scheme (but excluding those which arise from deposit back arrangements), exceeds

(*b*) the value, immediately before the transfer, of the assets transferred by the insurance business transfer scheme,".

(3) In subsection (1E) for "amount" (in the first place) substitute "value".][1]

Amendments—[1] This regulation substituted by the Overseas Life Insurance Companies (Amendment) Regulations, SI 2008/1924 reg 8 with effect in relation to periods of account beginning on or after 1 January 2008 which end on or after 12 August 2008.

15—(1) In a case where the transferor is an EEA firm or a Treaty firm, modify section 444AC (transfer schemes: reduction of income of transferee) as follows.

(2) In subsection (4) for the words from "lesser of" to the end substitute—

"the amount of the profit or loss for the financial year shown in the balance sheet in the periodical return for the last period of account of the transferor ending before the transfer date, together with—

(*a*) in the case of IAD accounts, the amount of profit or loss shown as being brought forward in that balance sheet, and

(*b*) in the case of IAS accounts, the amount of retained earnings shown as being brought forward in that balance sheet.".

(3) Omit subsection (5).][1]

Amendments—[1] This regulation substituted by the Overseas Life Insurance Companies (Amendment) Regulations, SI 2008/1924 reg 9 with effect in relation to periods of account beginning on or after 1 January 2008 which end on or after 12 August 2008. But, this amendment has effect only in relation to transfers of business taking place on or after 1 July 2008 (SI 2008/1924 reg 1(2), (3)).

15A . . .

Amendments—This regulation revoked by the Overseas Life Insurance Companies (Amendment) Regulations, SI 2008/1924 reg 10 with effect in relation to periods of account beginning on or after 1 January 2008 which end on or after 12 August 2008. But, this amendment has effect only in relation to transfers of business taking place on or after 1 July 2008 (SI 2008/1924 reg 1(2), (3)).

[15B In a case where the transferor or the transferee is an EEA firm or a Treaty firm (or both are), omit section 444AE (transfers of business: FAFTS).][1]

Amendments—[1] This regulation inserted by the Overseas Life Insurance Companies (Amendment) Regulations, SI 2008/1924 reg 11 with effect in relation to periods of account beginning on or after 1 January 2008 which end on or after 12 August 2008.

[15C In section 444AEA (transfer schemes: anti-avoidance rule), in subsection (6), in the definition of "surplus-increasing transfer of assets", in a case where the transferor is an EEA firm or a Treaty firm, for "increases the amount of total surplus shown in line 39 of Form 58" substitute "gives rise to an amount that increases the profits or reduces the losses shown".][1]

Amendments—[1] This regulation inserted by the Overseas Life Insurance Companies (Amendment) Regulations, SI 2008/1924 reg 12 with effect in relation to periods of account beginning on or after 1 January 2008 which end on or after 12 August 2008. But, this amendment has effect only in relation to transfers of business taking place on or after 1 July 2008 (SI 2008/1924 reg 1(2), (3)).

16 In section 444AL (interpretation of sections 444AF to 444AK), in subsection (3), in a case where the transferor is an EEA firm or a Treaty firm—

(*a*) for "insurance company" substitute "overseas life insurance company where the company is an EEA firm or a Treaty firm", and (*b*) for "surplus on valuation as shown in the periodical return" substitute "balance on the technical account – long-term business, so far as it relates to life assurance business carried on in the United Kingdom through a permanent establishment".

17 In section 460(10A) (exemption from tax in respect of life or endowment business) after "scheme" insert "or a qualifying overseas transfer".

18—

Amendments—This regulation revoked by the Overseas Life insurance Companies (Amendment) Regulations, SI 2007/2146 regs 2, 13 with effect for periods of account beginning on or after 1 January 2007 which end on or after 14 August 2007: SI 2007/2146 reg 1(2).

19 Modifications of the Finance Act 1989

In relation to an overseas life insurance company, the Finance Act 1989 shall have effect as if it were subject to the following modifications.

20 In section 82 (calculation of profits: bonuses etc), in subsection (2) at the end insert "to the extent that such amounts fall to be attributed, for the purposes of section 11AA(2) of the Taxes Act 1988, to the permanent establishment in the United Kingdom through which the company carries on life assurance business".

21 In section 82A (calculation of profits: policy holders' tax), in subsection (1) at the end insert "and that such tax falls to be attributed, for the purposes of section 11AA(2) of the Taxes Act 1988, to the permanent establishment in the United Kingdom through which the company carries on life assurance business".

22—(1) Modify section 83 (receipts to be taken into account) as follows.

(2) In subsection (2)(*a*) and (*d*) after "income" insert—

"so far as such income falls to be attributed, for the purposes of section 11AA(2) of the Taxes Act 1988, to the permanent establishment in the United Kingdom through which the company carries on life assurance business".

[(2A) In subsection (2A), in the case of an EEA firm or a Treaty firm, omit paragraph (*ac*).][2]

(3), (4) . . . [1]

(5) In subsection (8) after the definition of "add" insert—

""assets" means those assets that fall to be attributed, for the purposes of section 11AA(2), to the permanent establishment in the United Kingdom through which the company carries on life assurance business;".

Amendments—[1] Paragraphs (3), (4) revoked by the Overseas Life insurance Companies (Amendment) Regulations, SI 2007/2146 regs 2, 14 with effect in relation to such periods of account only where the transfer of business or demutualisation concerned took place before 21 March 2007: SI 2007/2146 reg 1(3).

[2] Paragraph (2A) inserted by the Overseas Life Insurance Companies (Amendment) Regulations, SI 2008/1924 reg 13 with effect in relation to periods of account beginning on or after 1 January 2008 which end on or after 12 August 2008.

[22A In section 83XA (structural assets), in subsection (3), in the case of an EEA firm or a Treaty firm, for paragraph (*a*) substitute—

"(*a*) assets listed under 1 and 2 in C(II) in Article 6 of the Council Directive of 19th December 1991 on the annual accounts and consolidated accounts of insurance undertakings (No 91/674/EEC), and".][1]

Amendments—[1] This regulation inserted by the Overseas Life insurance Companies (Amendment) Regulations, SI 2007/2146 regs 2, 15 with effect for periods of account beginning on or after 1 January 2007 which end on or after 14 August 2007: SI 2007/2146 reg 1(2).

[22B In the case of an EEA firm or a Treaty firm, omit sections 83YC to 83YF (financing-arrangement-funded transfers).][1]

Amendments—[1] This regulation inserted by the Overseas Life insurance Companies (Amendment) Regulations, SI 2008/1924 reg 14 with effect in relation to periods of account beginning on or after 1 January 2008 which end on or after 12 August 2008.

23—

Amendments—This regulation revoked by the Overseas Life insurance Companies (Amendment) Regulations, SI 2008/1924 reg 15 with effect in relation to periods of account beginning on or after 1 January 2008 which end on or after 12 August 2008.

24—(1) Modify section 83A (meaning of "brought into account"), as follows.

(2) After subsection (2) insert—

"(2A) In the case of an EEA firm or a Treaty firm, subject to the following provisions of this section, the accounts recognised for the purposes of those sections [are—

(*a*) such technical accounts (or such parts of those accounts) included in the IAD accounts, or

(*b*) such parts of the income statements included in the IAS accounts, as relate to the whole of the company's long-term business or such of that business as is carried on through the permanent establishment in the United Kingdom through which the company carries on life assurance business.[1]]".

(3) At the end insert—

"(7) In the case of a UK-authorised firm references in this section to the company's long-term business shall be treated as references to the whole of that business or to the whole of that business other than business in respect of which preparation of a revenue account for the purposes of Chapter 9 of the Prudential Sourcebook (Insurers) is not required.".

Amendments—[1] In para (2), in inserted sub-s (2A), words substituted by the Overseas Life Insurance Companies (Amendment No 2) Regulations, SI 2007/3449 regs 2, 7 with effect in relation to periods of account which begin on or after 1 January 2008: SI 2007/3449 reg 1(2).

[24A In section 85A(6) (excess adjusted Case I profits)—

(*a*) in paragraph (*a*), at the end insert "to the extent such income falls to be attributed, for the purposes of section 11AA(2) of that Act, to the permanent establishment in the United Kingdom through which the company carries on life assurance business",

(*b*) in paragraph (*b*), at the end insert "to the extent such gains fall to be attributed, for the purposes of section 11AA(2) of that Act, to the permanent establishment in the United Kingdom through which the company carries on life assurance business".][1]

Amendments—[1] This regulation inserted by the Overseas Life insurance Companies (Amendment) Regulations, SI 2007/2146 regs 2, 17 with effect for periods of account beginning on or after 1 January 2007 which end on or after 14 August 2007: SI 2007/2146 reg 1(2).

25

Amendments—This regulation revoked by the Overseas Life Insurance Companies (Amendment) Regulations, SI 2008/1924 reg 16 with effect in relation to periods of account beginning on or after 1 January 2008 which end on or after 12 August 2008.

26—

Amendments—This regulation revoked by the Overseas Life Insurance Companies (Amendment) Regulations, SI 2008/1924 reg 17 with effect in relation to periods of account beginning on or after 1 January 2008 which end on or after 12 August 2008.

27 Modification of the Taxation of Chargeable Gains Act 1992

In relation to an overseas life insurance company, the Taxation of Chargeable Gains Act 1992 shall have effect as if it were subject to the following modifications.

28 In section 10B (non-resident company with United Kingdom permanent establishment), in subsection (1)(*b*) omit "situated in the United Kingdom and".

29 In section 185 (deemed disposal of assets on company ceasing to be resident in UK), in subsection (4)—

(*a*) in paragraph (*a*) omit "are situated in the United Kingdom and", and

(*b*) in paragraph (*b*) omit "are so situated and".

30 In section 212 (annual deemed disposal of holdings of unit trusts etc) after subsection (5) insert—

"(5A) In its application to an overseas life insurance company, this section shall have effect as if the references in subsections (1) and (2) to assets were to such of the assets concerned as fall to be attributed, for the purposes of section 11AA(2) of the Taxes Act, to the permanent establishment in the United Kingdom through which the company carries on life assurance business.".

31 In section 213 (spreading of gains and losses under section 212), in subsection (4) after "long-term business" insert "in the United Kingdom through a permanent establishment".

32 In Schedule 7A (restriction on set-off of pre-entry losses), after paragraph 1(4) insert—

"(4A) Where—

(*a*) an asset is held by an overseas life insurance company, and

(*b*) section 440 of the Taxes Act applies at any time in relation to the asset,

the asset shall not be treated for the purposes of sub-paragraph (3A)(*b*) above as having become a chargeable asset at that time.".

33 Modification of the Finance (No 2) Act 1992

. . .

Amendments—This regulation revoked by the Overseas Life insurance Companies (Amendment) Regulations, SI 2007/2146 regs 2, 19 with effect for periods of account beginning on or after 1 January 2007 which end on or after 14 August 2007: SI 2007/2146 reg 1(2).

34 Modification of the Finance Act 1995

(1) In relation to an overseas life insurance company, the Finance Act 1995 shall have effect as if it were subject to the following modifications.

(2) In Schedule 8, in paragraph 55(1)—

(*a*) for "33, 37, 38 and 45(1) and (3)" substitute "33 and 37", and

(*b*) omit the words from "paragraph 46" to the end.

35 Modification of the Finance Act 1996

(1) In relation to an overseas life insurance company, the Finance Act 1996 shall have effect as if it were subject to the following modifications.

(2) In Schedule 9, in paragraph 12 (continuity of treatment: groups etc), in subsection (1)(*d*) omit [the words from "within the meaning" to "overseas life insurance company)"][1].

Amendments—[1] Words in para (2) substituted for words " "by paragraph 6(9) of Schedule 19AC to that Act"", by the Overseas Life insurance Companies (Amendment) Regulations, SI 2007/2146 regs 2, 20 with effect for periods of account beginning on or after 1 January 2007 which end on or after 14 August 2007: SI 2007/2146 reg 1(2).

36 Modification of the Capital Allowances Act 2001

(1) In relation to an overseas life insurance company, the Capital Allowances Act 2001 shall have effect as if it were subject to the following modifications.

[(2) In section 255 (apportionment of allowance and charges), after subsection (1B) insert—

"(2) In its application to an overseas life insurance company, subsection (1A) has effect as if the references to liabilities were only to such liabilities as are attributable to the permanent establishment in the United Kingdom through which the company carries on the business concerned.".][1]

Amendments—[1] Para (2) substituted by the Overseas Life insurance Companies (Amendment) Regulations, SI 2007/2146 regs 2, 21 with effect for periods of account beginning on or after 1 January 2007 which end on or after 14 August 2007: SI 2007/2146 reg 1(2).

37 Modification of the Finance Act 2002

In relation to an overseas life insurance company, the Finance Act 2002 shall have effect as if it were subject to the following modifications.

38, 39

Amendments—Regulations 38, 39 revoked by the Overseas Life insurance Companies (Amendment) Regulations, SI 2007/2146 regs 2, 22 with effect for periods of account beginning on or after 1 January 2007 which end on or after 14 August 2007: SI 2007/2146 reg 1(2).

40 In Schedule 26—

(*a*) in the case of an EEA firm or a Treaty firm, in paragraph 4 (contracts excluded by virtue of their underlying subject matter), in sub-paragraph (2A)—

(i) after paragraph (*a*) insert—

"(*aa*) the company is an EEA firm or a Treaty firm within the meaning of Chapter 1 Part 12 of ICTA;", and

(ii) in paragraph (*b*) for the words "is an approved derivative for the purposes of Rule [3.2.5 of the Insurance][1] Prudential Sourcebook" substitute "is a derivative instrument falling within article 23.3 of the EC Consolidated Life Directive (EC/2002/83)".

(*b*) in paragraph 28 (transactions within groups), in sub-paragraph (2)(*d*) omit [the words from "within the meaning" to the end][1].

Amendments—[1] In para (*a*)(ii), (*b*) words substituted by the Overseas Life insurance Companies (Amendment) Regulations, SI 2007/2146 regs 2, 23 with effect for periods of account beginning on or after 1 January 2007 which end on or after 14 August 2007: SI 2007/2146 reg 1(2).

41 In Schedule 29, in paragraph 89 (transfer of life assurance business), in sub-paragraph (1)(*b*) omit [the words from "within the meaning" to "overseas life insurance company)"][1]

Amendments—[1] In para (2), words substituted by the Overseas Life insurance Companies (Amendment) Regulations, SI 2007/2146 regs 2, 24 with effect for periods of account beginning on or after 1 January 2007 which end on or after 14 August 2007: SI 2007/2146 reg 1(2).

42 Modification of the Insurance Companies (Overseas Life Assurance Business) (Compliance) Regulations 1995

(1) In relation to an overseas life insurance company, the Insurance Companies (Overseas Life Assurance Business) (Compliance) Regulations 1995 shall have effect as if they were subject to the following modifications.

(2) In paragraph 2(1), in the definition of "relevant business", for "branch or agency" substitute "permanent establishment".

43 Repeals and revocations

(1) The enactments specified in Part 1 of the Schedule are repealed to the extent specified.

(2) The instruments specified in Part 2 of the Schedule are revoked to the extent specified.

SCHEDULE
REPEALS AND REVOCATION

Regulation 41

PART 1

Enactment	*Extent of Repeal*
Income and Corporation Taxes Act 1988 (c 1)	Section 444B. Schedule 19AC.
Finance Act 1989 (c 26)	Section 89A. Schedule 8A.
Taxation of Chargeable Gains Act 1992 (c 12)	Section 214B. Schedule 7B.
Finance Act 1993 (c 34)	Section 97. Section 98. Section 101. Section 102. Schedule 9. Schedule 10. Schedule 11.
Finance Act 1995 (c 4)	In Schedule 8, in paragraph 55(1) the words from "paragraph 46" to the end. In Schedule 8, paragraphs 35, 38, 39, 40, 42, 44, 45, 46, 48 and 49. In Schedule 9, paragraphs 2 and 6.
Finance Act 1996 (c 8)	Section 164(3). In Schedule 28, paragraph 5. In Schedule 31, paragraph 8(4) and (5).
Finance Act 1997 (c 16)	Section 67(5).
Finance (No 2) Act 1997 (c 58)	In Schedule 3, paragraph 13.
Finance Act 2000 (c 17)	Section 75(4). In section 75(6), the words "In this section—" and paragraph (*a*). In Schedule 29, paragraph 39.
Capital Allowances Act 2001 (c 2)	In Schedule 2, paragraph 64(2).

PART 2

Instrument	*Extent of Revocation*
The Manufactured Dividends (Tax) Regulations 1997 (SI 1997/993)	Regulation 2(3)(*a*).
The Insurance Companies (Capital Redemption Business) (Modification of the Corporation Tax Acts) Regulations 1999 (SI 1999/498)	Regulation 8.
The Individual Savings Account (Insurance Companies) (Amendment) Regulations 2000 (SI 2000/2075)	Regulation 1A.
The Overseas Life Assurance Fund (Amendment) Order 2000 (SI 2000/2188)	Regulation 5.
The Financial Services and Markets Act 2000 (Consequential Amendments) (Taxes) Order 2001 (SI 2001/3629)	Article 49. Article 52(1)(l) and (2)(o). Article 59. Article 60(1)(*d*) and (2)(*b*).

	Article 72. Article 73(1)(*b*) and (2)(*b*).
The Overseas Life Insurance Companies Regulations 2004 (SI 2004/2200)	The whole instrument.
The Finance Act 2004, Sections 38 to 40 and 45 and Schedule 6 (Consequential Amendment of Enactments) Order 2004 (SI 2004/2310)	Paragraph 36 of the Schedule.
The Overseas Life Insurance Companies (Amendment) Regulations 2005 (SI 2005/3375)	The whole instrument.

Commentary—*Simon's Taxes* **D4.116, D4.117**.

2006/3281

FILMS (CERTIFICATION) REGULATIONS 2006

Made by the Secretary of State under Films Act 1985, Sch 1, para 10(1)

Made . . . . *7th December 2006*
Laid before Parliament . . . . *11th December 2006*
Coming into force in accordance with . . . . *regulation 1*

Commentary—*Simon's Taxes* **D7.1219**.

1 Citation and commencement

(1) These Regulations may be cited as the Films (Certification) Regulations 2006.

(2) This Order shall come into force only if the Films (Definition of "British Film") (No 2) Order 2006 comes into force, and shall do so on the day that Order comes into force.

(3) If the Films (Definition of "British Film") (No 2) Order 2006 does not come into force before 31st March 2007, this Order is revoked with effect from that date.

Note—Films (Definition of "British Film") (No 2) Order 2006, SI 2006/3430, came into force on 1 January 2007.

2 Interpretation

In these Regulations—

"the Act" means the Films Act 1985;

"co-production film" means a film which by virtue of any Order in Council made under paragraph 4(5) of Schedule 1 to the Act is to be treated as if it is a British film for the purposes of Schedule 1 to the Act;

"core expenditure" has the same meaning as in section 34(1) of the Finance Act 2006;

"film production company" has the same meaning as in section 32 of the Finance Act 2006.

"group of companies" means a company and all other companies which are its subsidiaries within the meaning of section 736 of the Companies Act 1985.

"other expenditure" means all the expenditure on the work carried out in the making of the film which is not core expenditure;

"producer" means the person by whom the arrangements necessary for the making of the film are undertaken;

"theatrical release" means exhibition to the paying public at the commercial cinema;

"UK expenditure" has the same meaning as in section 35(1) of the Finance Act 2006.

3 Applications

An application under paragraph 2(1) of Schedule 1 to the Act for the certification of a film as a British film, other than a co-production film, shall be made in writing to the Secretary of State.

4 Particulars

The application shall set out the particulars of the film described in the Schedule.

5 Evidence

(1) The application shall be accompanied by a statutory declaration made by the applicant as to the truth of the particulars given in the application.

(2) A statutory declaration shall be deemed to be properly made by the applicant if it has been made on behalf of the company by the Secretary or one of the directors of the company or a by any person duly authorised by the company to make the declaration on its behalf.

6—[(1) Where an application for final certification seeks to rely on any point that may be awarded under paragraph 4A(5), 4B(5), 4C(5), 4A(6), 4B(6) or 4C(6) of Schedule 1 to the Act, the application shall be accompanied by a report prepared by a person referred to in paragraph (2) verifying the particulars in paragraphs 18 to 20 of the Schedule.][1]

(2) The person referred to in this paragraph is a person who is eligible for appointment as a company auditor under section 25 of the Companies Act 1989 and is not and was not at any time while the film was being made—

(*a*) in partnership with the applicant or any officer or servant of the applicant;

(*b*) in the employment of the applicant or any officer or servant of the applicant; or

(*c*) an officer or servant of the applicant or, if the applicant is a member of a group of companies, of any other company in that group.

Amendments—[1] Para (1) substituted by the Films (Certification) (Amendment) Regulations, SI 2007/3478 reg 2 with effect from 1 January 2008: SI 2007/3478 reg 1(1).

7 Transitional provision

(1) Subject to paragraphs (2) and (3), the following Regulations are revoked—

(*a*) the Films (Certification) Regulations 1985 (No 994);

(*b*) the Films (Certification) (Amendment) Regulations 1999 (No 2224)

(*c*) the Films (Certification) (Amendment) (No 2) Regulations 1999 (No 2334).

(*d*) the Films (Certification) (Amendment) Regulations 2006 (No 642).

(2) If an application falls to be determined by the Secretary of State in accordance with Schedule 1 to the Act as in force immediately before 1st April 2006 the Films (Certification) Regulations 1985 shall continue to have effect to the application as if the Films (Certification) (Amendment) Regulations 2006 [and these Regulations][1] had not been made.

(3) If an application falls to be determined by the Secretary of State in accordance with Schedule 1 to the Act as in force immediately before the commencement of these Regulations the Films (Certification) Regulations 1985 shall continue to have effect to the application as if these Regulations had not been made.

Amendments—[1] Words in para (2) inserted by the Films (Certification) (Amendment) Regulations, SI 2007/3478 reg 3 with effect from 1 January 2008: SI 2007/3478 reg 1(1).

SCHEDULE
PARTICULARS

Regulation 4

1 Title of the film or, in the case of a series of films or a part thereof, the title of the series or part.

2 Total playing time in minutes and seconds of the film, including credits and titles.

3 Whether the application is for interim or final certification.

4 Whether the film is intended for theatrical release.

5 Name of the applicant.

6 Address of the applicant's principal place of business.

7 Address of the applicant's registered office.

8 Registered number of the applicant.

9 Date of registration of the applicant.

10 Date of the first day of principal photography.

11 Date on which the film was completed for the purposes of Schedule 1 to the Act.

12 If the applicant seeks treatment of a series of films as a single film in reliance upon paragraph 1(2) of Schedule 1 to the Act—

(*a*) the number of parts in the series;

(*b*) the combined playing time in minutes and seconds of those parts, including credits and titles, and

(*c*) the reasons why the series constitutes a self-contained work or is series of documentaries with a common theme.

13 Type of film: documentary, animation or standard.

14 If the film is a documentary, the reasons why the film should be considered to be a documentary.

15 If the film is an animation, the reasons why the film should be considered to be an animation.

16 The reasons why any point should be awarded under paragraphs 4A(3), 4B(3) or 4C(3) of Schedule 1 to the Act.

17 The reasons why any point should be awarded under paragraphs 4A(4), 4B(4) or 4C(4) of Schedule 1 to the Act.

18 If the applicant seeks to rely on paragraph 4A(5)(*a*)(i) of Schedule 1 to the Act, the total number of days of principal photography and the number of days of principal photography carried out in the United Kingdom.

19 If the applicant seeks to rely on the rest of paragraph 4A(5), 4B(5) and 4C(5), the total expenditure of the work in relation to which the applicant is applying for points to be awarded and the expenditure of such work carried out in the United Kingdom.

20 The nationality [or][1] ordinary residence of all the persons mentioned in paragraphs 4A(6), 4B(6) or 4C(6) of Schedule 1 to the Act in relation to whom the applicant is applying for a point to be awarded.

Amendments—[1] Word substituted by the Films (Certification) (Amendment) Regulations, SI 2007/3478 reg 4 with effect from 1 January 2008: SI 2007/3478 reg 1(1).

21 Total core expenditure.

22 Total UK expenditure.

23 Total non-UK expenditure by each country the expenditure is carried out in.

24 Other expenditure on the work carried out in the making of the film which is not core expenditure.

25 Shooting script in the English language.

26 A complete synopsis or treatment of the screenplay in the English language.

27 Shooting schedule.

28 Production budget.

29 Copy of the chain of tile.

30 If any part of the film is derived from any previous film ("the previous film")—

(*a*) for each part of the film so derived and in respect of which—

(i) the two films do not have the same film production company or producer, and

(ii) the previous film has not been certified under Schedule 1 to the Act,

the playing time in minutes and seconds of that part;

(*b*) the combined playing time in minutes and seconds of all the parts referred to in sub-paragraph (*a*); and

(*c*) if the applicant seeks to rely on paragraph 5(2) of Schedule 1 to the Act the reasons why the subject matter of the film makes it appropriate for paragraph 5(1) of Schedule 1 to the Act not to be applied.

2006/3296

TAXATION OF SECURITISATION COMPANIES REGULATIONS 2006

Made . . . . 11th December 2006

Coming into force in accordance with . . . . regulation 1

Commentary—*Simon's Taxes* **D7.13.**

The Treasury make the following Regulations in exercise of the powers conferred upon them by section 84 of the Finance Act 2005.

A draft of this instrument was laid before and approved by a resolution of the House of Commons in accordance with section 84(7) of the Finance Act 2005.

PRELIMINARY

1 Citation, commencement and effect

(1) These Regulations may be cited as the Taxation of Securitisation Companies Regulations 2006 and shall come into force on the day after the day on which they are made.

(2) These Regulations have effect for periods of account beginning on or after 1st January 2007.

2 Interpretation

(1) In these Regulations—

"asset-holding company" has the meaning given by regulation 6;

"capital market arrangement" and "capital market investment" have the same meaning as in section 72B(1) of the Insolvency Act 1986 (see paragraphs 1, 2 and 3 of Schedule 2A to that Act);

"commercial paper funded company" has the meaning given by regulation 9;

"financial asset" has the meaning it has for generally accepted accounting practice (subject to paragraph (2)) but—

(*a*) [subject to paragraph (*b*)(ii)][1] includes derivative contracts as defined for the purposes of Schedule 26 to the Finance Act 2002 (see paragraph 2(1) of that Schedule) whether otherwise constituting an asset or a liability, and

[(*b*) does not include—

(i) shares (other than shares in a securitisation company which is party to the capital market arrangement);

(ii) derivative contracts as defined for the purposes of Schedule 26 to the Finance Act 2002 where the underlying subject matter is or includes shares (other than shares in a securitisation company which is party to the capital market arrangement) or land;

(iii) loan relationships with embedded derivatives within section 94A(1) of the Finance Act 1996 (loan relationships with embedded derivatives) where the underlying subject matter of the embedded derivative is or includes shares or land;

(iv) relevant assets within paragraph 7(1) of Schedule 6 to the Finance (No. 2) Act 2005 (loan relationships with embedded derivatives) where the underlying subject matter of any embedded derivative is or includes shares or land.][1]

"ICTA" means the Income and Corporation Taxes Act 1988;

"independent persons" means persons who are not connected with a company (and see paragraph (3));

["insurance special purpose vehicle" has the same meaning as in section 431(2) of ICTA;][2]

"intermediate borrowing company" has the meaning given by regulation 7;

"note-issuing company" has the meaning given by regulation 5;

"related transaction" is to be construed in accordance with paragraphs (4) and (5);

"retained profit" is to be construed in accordance with regulation 10;

"securitisation company" has the meaning given by regulation 4;

"specified regulations" means regulations 14 (corporation tax charge) and 16 to 20 (application, modification and non-application of provisions of the Corporation Tax Acts);

"warehouse company" has the meaning given by regulation 8.

(2) For the purposes of these Regulations whether an asset acquired, held or managed by a company is a financial asset shall be determined at the time that asset is first acquired, held or managed by that company.

(3) Section 839 of ICTA (connected persons) applies for the purposes of the definition of "independent persons", except that in applying the definition of "control" in that section a person is not to be treated as a participator in a company by reason only that he is a loan creditor of the company.

(4) For the purpose of these Regulations one or more transactions are to be regarded as related transactions, in the case of any arrangements, if it would be reasonable to assume, from either or both of—

(*a*) the likely effect of the transactions, and

(*b*) the circumstances in which the transactions are entered into or effected,

that none of the transactions would have been entered into or effected independently of the arrangements.

(5) Transactions are not prevented from being related transactions, in the case of any arrangements, just because the transactions—

(*a*) are not between the same parties, or

(*b*) are not between the parties to the capital market arrangements.

Amendments—[1] Words in para (1)(*a*), in definition of "financial asset", inserted, and para (1)(*b*) substituted, by the Taxation of Securitisation Companies (Amendment) Regulations, SI 2007/3339 reg 2(1), (2) with effect from the beginning of periods of account beginning on or after 1 January 2007 and current on 3 December 2007: SI 2007/3339 reg 1(2).

These amendments do not apply to a company to which the Taxation of Securitisation Companies Regulations, SI 2006/3296 apply in relation to a capital market arrangement in existence on 3 December 2007: SI 2007/3339 reg 1(3).

[2] In para (1), definition of "insurance special purpose vehicle" inserted by the Taxation of Securitisation Companies (Amendment No 2) Regulations, SI 2007/3401 reg 2(1), (2) with effect from the beginning of periods of account beginning on or after 1 January 2007 and current on 4 December 2007: SI 2007/3401 reg 1(2).

3 Scope of these Regulations

(1) These Regulations make provision as to the application of the Corporation Tax Acts in relation to a securitisation company.

(2) The Regulations deal with the following matters—

(*a*) they define "securitisation company" and related expressions (see regulations 4 to 10);

(*b*) they specify securitisation companies to which specified regulations do not apply (see regulations 11 to 12);

(*c*) they specify companies to which these Regulations do not apply (see [regulations 13 and 13A][1]);

(*d*) they make provision as to profit of a securitisation company to be brought into account for an accounting period for corporation tax purposes (see regulation 14);

(*e*) they make supplementary provision (see regulations 15 to 21).

Amendments—[1] In para (2)(*c*), words substituted by the Taxation of Securitisation Companies (Amendment) Regulations, SI 2007/3339 reg 2(1), (3) with effect from the beginning of periods of account beginning on or after 1 January 2007 and current on 3 December 2007: SI 2007/3339 reg 1(2).

MEANING OF "SECURITISATION COMPANY" AND RELATED EXPRESSIONS

4 Meaning of "securitisation company"

(1) For the purposes of these Regulations a "securitisation company" means a company that meets conditions A and B.

(2) Condition A is that the company is—

(*a*) a note-issuing company (see regulation 5),

(*b*) an asset-holding company (see regulation 6),

(*c*) an intermediate borrowing company (see regulation 7),

(*d*) a warehouse company (see regulation 8), or

(*e*) a commercial paper funded company (see regulation 9).

(3) Condition B is that the company has a retained profit (see regulation 10).

5 Meaning of "note-issuing company"

(1) For the purposes of these Regulations a "note-issuing company" means a company that meets conditions A to D.

(2) Condition A is that the company is within section 84(2)(*a*) of the Finance Act 2005.

(3) Condition B is that the securities that represent the capital market investment referred to in section 84(2)(*a*)(ii) of that Act are issued wholly or mainly to independent persons.

(4) Condition C is that the total value of the capital market investments made under the capital market arrangement referred to in section 84(2)(*a*)(iii) of that Act is at least £10 million.

(5) Condition D is that the company's only business apart from the activity mentioned in section 84(2)(*a*)(i) of that Act (being party as debtor to a capital market investment), and apart from any incidental activities, [consists in—

(*a*) one][1] or both of the following activities—

[(i)] [1] acquiring, holding and managing financial assets forming the whole or part of the security for the capital market arrangement; or

[(ii)] [1] acting as guarantor in respect of loan relationships, derivative contracts, finance leases or other liabilities of other companies where the whole, or substantially the whole, of the company's rights in respect of the guarantee (including any right of subrogation) form the whole or part of the security for the capital market arrangement[; or

(*b*) being party to a creditor relationship with an insurance special purpose vehicle.][1]

Amendments—[1] In para (5), words substituted, previous sub-paras (*a*), (*b*) renumbered as paras (i), (ii) of new sub-para (*a*), and sub-para (*b*) and preceding word "or" inserted, by the Taxation of Securitisation Companies (Amendment No 2) Regulations, SI 2007/3401 reg 2(1), (3) with effect from the beginning of periods of account beginning on or after 1 January 2007 and current on 4 December 2007: SI 2007/3401 reg 1(2).

6 Meaning of "asset-holding company"

(1) For the purposes of these Regulations an "asset-holding company" means a company that meets conditions A and B.

(2) Condition A is that the company's business, apart from any incidental activities, consists in acquiring, holding and managing financial assets forming the whole or part of the security for a capital market arrangement entered into by a note-issuing company.

(3) Condition B is that the company's [initial][1] liabilities representing debtor relationships are owed wholly or mainly to a note-issuing company or intermediate borrowing company.

Amendments—[1] In para (3), word inserted by the Taxation of Securitisation Companies (Amendment) Regulations, SI 2007/3339 reg 2(1), (4) with effect from the beginning of periods of account beginning on or after 1 January 2007 and current on 3 December 2007: SI 2007/3339 reg 1(2).

7 Meaning of "intermediate borrowing company"

(1) For the purposes of these Regulations an "intermediate borrowing company" means a company that meets conditions A and B.

(2) Condition A is that the company's only business, apart from any incidental activities, is to enter into and be a party to creditor relationships with—

(*a*) an asset-holding company,

[(*aa*) a partnership that would be an asset-holding company if it were a company,][1]

(*b*) a company that would be an asset-holding company if the assets forming the security for the capital market arrangement were financial assets,

(*c*) a partnership that would be an asset-holding company if it were a company and the assets forming the security for the capital market arrangement were financial assets, . . . [2]

(*d*) another intermediate borrowing company[, or

(*e*) an insurance special purpose vehicle.][2]

(3) Condition B is that the company's [initial][1] liabilities representing debtor relationships are owed wholly or mainly to a note-issuing company or another intermediate borrowing company.

Amendments—[1] Para (2)(*aa*), and word in para (3), inserted, by the Taxation of Securitisation Companies (Amendment) Regulations, SI 2007/3339 reg 2(1), (5) with effect from the beginning of periods of account beginning on or after 1 January 2007 and current on 3 December 2007: SI 2007/3339 reg 1(2).

[2] In para (2)(*c*), word "or" revoked, and para (2)(*e*) and preceding word "or" inserted, by the Taxation of Securitisation Companies (Amendment No 2) Regulations, SI 2007/3401 reg 2(1), (4) with effect from the beginning of periods of account beginning on or after 1 January 2007 and current on 4 December 2007: SI 2007/3401 reg 1(2).

8 Meaning of "warehouse company"

[(1)] [1] For the purposes of these Regulations a "warehouse company" means a company whose business, apart from any incidental activities, consists in acquiring and holding financial assets for the purpose—

(*a*) of transferring them to a company (whether or not yet in existence) that at the time of the transfer is, or as a result of the transfer will become, an asset-holding or note-issuing company, or

(*b*) of itself becoming an asset-holding or note-issuing company.

[(2) For the purposes of these Regulations the business of a warehouse company described in paragraph (1) shall be referred to as a "warehouse arrangement".][1]

Amendments—[1] Para (1) renumbered as such, and para (2) inserted, by the Taxation of Securitisation Companies (Amendment) Regulations, SI 2007/3339 reg 2(1), (6) with effect from the beginning of periods of account beginning on or after 1 January 2007 and current on 3 December 2007: SI 2007/3339 reg 1(2).

9 Meaning of "commercial paper funded company"

For the purposes of these Regulations a "commercial paper funded company" means—

(*a*) a company that was an asset-holding company but whose obligations under debtor relationships to a note-issuing company or intermediate borrowing company—

(i) have been transferred to, or

(ii) have been replaced by obligations under debtor relationships to,

one or more companies carrying on a business of banking, or

(*b*) a company that was an intermediate borrowing company but whose obligations under debtor relationships to a note-issuing company—

(i) have been transferred to, or

(ii) have been replaced by obligations under debtor relationships to,

one or more companies carrying on a business of banking.

10 Meaning of "retained profit"

(1) For the purposes of these Regulations the "retained profit" of a securitisation company for an accounting period is the amount required by the capital market arrangement[, or][1] related transaction [or a warehouse arrangement][1] to be retained, made available to be retained, or designated as profits of the securitisation company (however described).

(2) If retained profit relates to two or more accounting periods, it shall be apportioned on a just and reasonable basis between them.

(3) If in an accounting period the securitisation company has insufficient funds available to meet the retained profit required by the capital market arrangement or a related transaction—

(*a*) the amount of the retained profit for the purposes of these Regulations is the amount actually retained as profit for that accounting period, and

(*b*) in a later accounting period the amount of the retained profit may be increased by up to the amount of the shortfall in the earlier period.

Amendments—[1] In para (1), word substituted, and words inserted, by the Taxation of Securitisation Companies (Amendment) Regulations, SI 2007/3339 reg 2(1), (7) with effect from the beginning of periods of account beginning on or after 1 January 2007 and current on 3 December 2007: SI 2007/3339 reg 1(2).

COMPANIES TO WHICH SPECIFIED REGULATIONS DO NOT APPLY

11 Securitisation companies that do not meet the payments condition

(1) The specified regulations do not apply to a securitisation company that—

(*a*) does not meet the payments condition, or

(*b*) at any time has not met the payments condition.

(2) The payments condition is that in any accounting period R is equal to or less than the sum of P + RA + RP.

(3) In paragraph (2)—

R is, subject to paragraph (6), the aggregate of—

(*a*) amounts received by the securitisation company in the accounting period, and

(*b*) amounts which have been—

(i) retained as RA in that accounting period, or

(ii) taken into account as RA for the purposes of this regulation in a previous accounting period, where those amounts are no longer reasonably required to be retained as RA;

P is the aggregate amount of—

(*a*) payments made by the securitisation company in the accounting period and the following 18 months except payments which have already been taken into account for the purposes of this regulation for a previous accounting period, and

(*b*) payments made by the securitisation company in the previous accounting period but not taken into account for the purposes of this regulation;

RA is the aggregate of amounts retained by the securitisation company in the accounting period, which have not already been taken into account for the purposes of this regulation in a previous accounting period, which are reasonably required to—

(*a*) provide for losses or expenses arising from the company's business, or

(*b*) maintain or enhance the company's creditworthiness; and

RP is the amount of the retained profit of the securitisation company in the accounting period.

(4) If a securitisation company receives amounts or makes payments of amounts in a currency other than its functional currency, that amount shall be translated into the functional currency by reference to the appropriate exchange rate for the last day of the accounting period.

(5) For the purposes of this regulation the aggregate amount of payments made includes any payment which was not made but which would have been made but for—

(*a*) a legal prohibition, or

(*b*) a reasonable excuse for failing to make that payment,

but if any such payment is subsequently made it shall be disregarded.

(6) In the case of a company which has elected in accordance with regulation 13(2) that these Regulations shall apply—

(*a*) in the first accounting period to which these Regulations apply, R includes an amount that would be given by the formula—

$$R - P - RA - RP$$

in relation to the previous accounting period ("the relevant accounting period");

(*b*) sub-paragraph (*b*)(ii) of the definition of R in paragraph (3) shall apply as if there were included in those amounts the aggregate of amounts retained by the company in previous accounting periods, in which these Regulations did not apply, which were reasonably required to—

(i) provide for losses or expenses arising from the company's business, or

(ii) maintain or enhance the company's creditworthiness.

(7) For the purposes of the formula in paragraph (6)(*a*)—

R is the aggregate of amounts received by the company in the relevant accounting period;

P is the aggregate amount of payments made by the company in the relevant accounting period;

RA is the aggregate of amounts retained by the company for the relevant accounting period which were reasonably required to—

(*a*) provide for losses or expenses arising from the company's business, or

(*b*) maintain or enhance the company's creditworthiness; and

RP is the amount that would be the retained profit of the company in the relevant accounting period if these Regulations applied.

(8) In this regulation—

"appropriate exchange rate" has the meaning given in section 92D(2)(*b*) of the Finance Act 1993;

"functional currency" has the meaning given in section 92E(3) of the Finance Act 1993;

"payment" includes part of a payment.

12 Securitisation companies that have an unallowable purpose

(1) The specified regulations do not apply to a securitisation company that—

(*a*) has an unallowable purpose, or

(*b*) at any time has had an unallowable purpose.

(2) For the purpose of these Regulations a securitisation company has an unallowable purpose if the purpose for which the securitisation company is a party to—

(*a*) the capital market arrangement,

(*b*) any related transaction, or

(*c*) any transaction in pursuance of the capital market arrangement,

includes a purpose which is not amongst the business or other commercial purposes of the securitisation company.

(3) If one of the purposes for which a securitisation company is at any time a party to—

(*a*) any capital market arrangement,

(*b*) any related transaction in the case of any capital market arrangement, or

(*c*) any transaction in pursuance of any capital market arrangement, is a tax avoidance purpose, that purpose shall be taken to be a business or other commercial purpose of the securitisation company only where it is not the main purpose, or one of the main purposes, for which the company is party to the arrangements or transaction at that time.

(4) In this regulation—

"tax avoidance purpose" means any purpose that consists in securing a tax advantage for any other person;

"tax advantage" has the same meaning as in [section 840ZA][1] of ICTA (tax avoidance).

Amendments—[1] In para (4), in definition of "tax advantage", words substituted by the Taxation of Securitisation Companies (Amendment) Regulations, SI 2007/3339 reg 2(1), (7) with effect from the beginning of periods of account beginning on or after 1 January 2007 and current on 3 December 2007: SI 2007/3339 reg 1(2).

COMPANIES TO WHICH THESE REGULATIONS DO NOT APPLY

13 Securitisation companies on 1st January 2007

(1) These Regulations do not apply to a company which before the start of the first accounting period of the company beginning on or after 1st January 2007—

(*a*) is a securitisation company within section 83 of the Finance Act 2005 (application of accounting standards to securitisation companies), or

(*b*) is a company in relation to which the following conditions are met—

(i) it is party as debtor to a capital market investment,

(ii) securities representing that capital market investment are issued, and

(iii) the capital market investment is part of a capital market arrangement.

This is subject to paragraph (2).

(2) The company may elect by notice in writing to Her Majesty's Revenue and Customs, within 18 months of the end of that period, that these Regulations shall apply.

(3) An election under paragraph (2) is irrevocable.

13A [Securitisation companies to which section 83 of the Finance Act 2005 does not apply

These Regulations do not apply to a company in a case where—

(*a*) section 83(1) of the Finance Act 2005 does not apply by virtue of an election under regulation 2 of the Securitisation Companies (Application of Section 83(1) of the Finance Act 2005: Accounting Standards) Regulations 2007, and

(*b*) the company continues to be party to the arrangement or transaction referred to in paragraph (1)(*b*) of regulation 2 of those Regulations.][1]

Amendments—[1] Regulation inserted by the Taxation of Securitisation Companies (Amendment) Regulations, SI 2007/3339 reg 2(1), (9) with effect from the beginning of periods of account beginning on or after 1 January 2007 and current on 3 December 2007: SI 2007/3339 reg 1(2).

APPLICATION OF THE CORPORATION TAX ACTS

14 Corporation tax charge

(1) The profit of a securitisation company to be brought into account for an accounting period for corporation tax purposes is the aggregate of—

(*a*) the greater of—

(i) nil; and

(ii) the amount given by the formula—

RP – DS + D, and

(*b*) the amount specified in paragraph (3).

(2) In paragraph (1)—

RP is the amount of the retained profit of the securitisation company for the accounting period;

DS is the amount of any distribution received in that accounting period from another securitisation company which is party to the capital market arrangement where the distribution is made from that company's retained profit;

D is the greater of—

(*a*) the amount equal to the aggregate of any dividends paid by the securitisation company in that and any previous accounting period, less—

(i) RP for the accounting period,

(ii) the aggregate of profits calculated under this regulation for previous accounting periods,

(iii) the aggregate of DS calculated under this regulation for previous accounting periods, and

(iv) the amount of any dividends paid out of profits arising in any previous accounting period in which these Regulations did not apply; and

(*b*) nil.

(3) The specified amount is any credit that would be brought into account by the securitisation company in the accounting period in consequence of paragraph 12A of Schedule 9 to the Finance Act 1996 (transferee leaving group after replacing transferor as party to loan relationship) or paragraph 30A of Schedule 26 to the Finance Act 2002 (transferee leaving group after replacing transferor as party to derivative contract).

(4) The amount of profit calculated under this regulation shall be brought into account for corporation tax purposes instead of any other amount that would fall to be brought into account.

SUPPLEMENTARY PROVISION

15 Application, modification and non-application of provisions of the Corporation Tax Acts

(1) In relation to a securitisation company, ICTA has effect as if it were subject to the following modification.

(2) In section 12 (basis of, and periods for, assessment), in subsection (3) after paragraph (*e*) insert—

"(*f*) the company becoming or ceasing to be a securitisation company to which regulation 14 of the Taxation of Securitisation Companies Regulations 2006 applies.".

16 Paragraphs (*b*) to (*f*) in section 209(2) (meaning of distribution) of ICTA shall not apply in relation to any interest paid or other distribution made by a securitisation company.

17 For the purposes of Chapter 4 of Part 10 (group relief) of ICTA, a securitisation company shall not be treated as the member of any group or consortium.

18—(1) Section 171 (transfers within a group: general provisions) of the Taxation of Chargeable Gains Act 1992 shall not apply if "company B" in subsection (1) of that section is a securitisation company.

(2) Section 179A (reallocation within group of gain or loss accruing under section 179) of that Act shall not apply if "company C" in that section is a securitisation company.

19—(1) Paragraph 2 of Schedule 9 to the Finance Act 1996 (loan relationships: special computational provisions: late interest) shall not apply if the person standing in the position of a creditor as respects a loan relationship within that paragraph is a securitisation company.

(2) Paragraph 12 of that Schedule (continuity of treatment: groups etc) shall not apply if the "transferee company" or "transferor company" in subparagraph (1) of that paragraph is a securitisation company.

[(3) Paragraph 17 of that Schedule (deeply discounted securities where companies have a connection) shall not apply if the person standing in the position of a creditor as respects a security within that paragraph is a securitisation company.

(4) Paragraph 18 of that Schedule (deeply discounted securities of close companies) shall not apply if the person standing in the position of a creditor as respects a security within that paragraph is a securitisation company.][1]

Amendments—[1] Paras (3), (4) inserted by the Taxation of Securitisation Companies (Amendment) Regulations, SI 2007/3339 reg 2(1), (10) with effect from the beginning of periods of account beginning on or after 1 January 2007 and current on 3 December 2007: SI 2007/3339 reg 1(2).

20 Paragraph 28 of Schedule 26 to the Finance Act 2002 (derivative contracts: transactions within groups) shall not apply if the "transferee company" or "transferor company" in subparagraph (1) of that paragraph is a securitisation company.

21 Section 83 of the Finance Act 2005 (application of accounting standards to securitisation companies) shall not apply to a securitisation company.

2006/3389

GROUP RELIEF FOR OVERSEAS LOSSES (MODIFICATION OF THE CORPORATION TAX ACTS FOR NON-RESIDENT INSURANCE COMPANIES) (NO 2) REGULATIONS 2006

Made by the Treasury, under TA 1988 Sch 18A para 16(2) to (5)

Made . . . . *18th December 2006*

Laid before the House of Commons . . . . *18th December 2006*

Coming into force . . . . *8th January 2007*

Revocation—These Regulations revoked by the Group Relief for Overseas Losses (Modification of the Corporation Tax Acts for Non-resident Insurance Companies) Regulations, SI 2008/2646, reg 5(*a*) with effect for accounting periods beginning on or after 28 October 2008.

2006/3399

FINANCE ACT 2006, SECTION 53(1) (FILMS AND SOUND RECORDINGS) (APPOINTED DAY) ORDER 2006

Made by the Treasury under FA 2006 s 53(1)

Made . . . .*18th December 2006*

1 This Order may be cited as the Finance Act 2006, Section 53(1) (Films and Sound Recordings) (Appointed Day) Order 2006.

2 The day appointed for the purposes of section 53(1) of the Finance Act 2006 is 1st January 2007.

2007/46

FINANCE ACT 2004, SECTION 61(2), (RELEVANT PERCENTAGE) ORDER 2007

Made by the Treasury under FA 2004 s 61(2)

Made . . . . 11 *January 2007*
Laid before the House of Commons . . . . 11 *January 2007*
Coming into force . . . . 1 *February 2007*

1 This Order may be cited as the Finance Act 2004, Section 61(2), (Relevant Percentage) Order 2007 and shall come into force on 1st February 2007.

2 For the purposes of section 61(1) of the Finance Act 2004 (deductions on account of tax from contract payments) the relevant percentage is—

(*a*) 20% if the person for whose labour (or for whose employees' or officers' labour) the payment in question is made is registered for payment under deduction, or

(*b*) 30% if that person is not so registered.

2007/303

CAPITAL ALLOWANCES (LEASES OF BACKGROUND PLANT OR MACHINERY FOR A BUILDING) ORDER 2007

Made by the Treasury under CAA 2001 s 70T

Made . . . . 6 *February 2007*
Laid before the House of Commons . . . . 7 *February 2007*
Coming into force . . . . 28 *February 2007*

HMRC Manuals—Business Leasing Manual, BLM21320–21325 (defining long funding leases: meaning of "background plant or machinery").
BLM21330 (examples of background plant or machinery).
BLM21335 (plant or machinery treated as background plant or machinery).
BLM21340 (plant or machinery that is not to be treated as background plant or machinery).
BLM21345 (order of priority within the regulations).

1 Citation, commencement and effect

(1) This Order may be cited as the Capital Allowances (Leases of Background Plant or Machinery for a Building) Order 2007 and comes into force on 28th February 2007.

(2) This Order has effect in relation to times on and after 1st April 2006.

2 Examples of background plant or machinery

(1) The descriptions of plant or machinery in paragraph (2) are prescribed examples of the kinds of plant or machinery that may be regarded as falling within the definition of background plant or machinery for a building in determining whether any particular plant or machinery does or does not fall within that definition.

(2) The descriptions of plant or machinery are—

(*a*) heating and air conditioning installations,
(*b*) ceilings which are part of an air conditioning system,
(*c*) hot water installations,
(*d*) electrical installations that provide power to a building, such as high and low voltage switchgear, all sub-mains distribution systems and standby generators,
(*e*) mechanisms, including automatic control systems, for opening and closing doors, windows and vents,
(*f*) escalators and passenger lifts,
(*g*) window cleaning installations,
(*h*) fittings such as fitted cupboards, blinds, curtains and associated mechanical equipment,
(*i*) demountable partitions,
(*j*) protective installations such as lightning protection, sprinkler and other equipment for containing or fighting fires, fire alarm systems and fire escapes, and
(*k*) building management systems.

(3) This article is subject to article 4.

3 Plant or machinery deemed to be background plant or machinery

(1) The following descriptions of plant or machinery are deemed to be background plant or machinery.

(2) The descriptions of plant or machinery are—

(*a*) lighting installations including all fixed light fittings and emergency lighting systems,

(*b*) telephone, audio-visual and data installations incidental to the occupation of the building,

(*c*) computer networking facilities incidental to the occupation of the building,

(*d*) sanitary appliances and other bathroom fittings including hand driers, counters, partitions, mirrors, shower and locker facilities,

(*e*) kitchen and catering facilities for producing and storing food and drink for the occupants of the building,

(*f*) fixed seating,

(*g*) signs,

(*h*) public address systems, and

(*i*) intruder alarm systems and other security equipment including surveillance equipment.

4 Plant or machinery deemed not to be background plant or machinery

(1) The following descriptions of plant or machinery are deemed not to be background plant or machinery.

(2) The descriptions of plant or machinery are plant or machinery used for any of the purposes in paragraph (3).

(3) The purposes are—

(*a*) storing, moving or displaying goods to be sold in the course of a trade, whether wholesale or retail,

(*b*) manufacturing goods or materials,

(*c*) subjecting goods or materials to a process,

(*d*) storing goods or materials—

(i) which are to be used in the manufacture of other goods or materials,

(ii) which are to be subjected, in the course of a trade, to a process,

(iii) which, having been manufactured or produced or subjected in the course of a trade to a process, have not yet been delivered to any purchaser, or

(iv) on their arrival in the United Kingdom from a place outside the United Kingdom.

(4) This article is subject to article 3.

2007/304

LONG FUNDING LEASES (ELECTIONS) REGULATIONS 2007

Made by the Treasury under FA 2006, Sch 8, paragraph 16

Made . . . . .6 *February 2007*
Laid before the House of Commons . . . . .7 *February 2007*
Coming into force . . . . .28 *February 2007*

1 Citation, commencement, interpretation and effect

(1) These Regulations may be cited as the Long Funding Leases (Elections) Regulations 2007, shall come into force on 28th February 2007 and shall have effect in respect of leases finalised on or after 1st April 2006.

(2) In these Regulations—

"CAA" means the Capital Allowances Act 2001; and

"TMA" means the Taxes Management Act 1970.

(3) In these Regulations—

"eligible lease" has the meaning given by regulation 3;

"lessor" has the meaning given in section 70YI of CAA;

"qualifying incidental lease" has the meaning given by regulation 4; and

other terms defined or otherwise explained in Chapter 6A of CAA have the same meaning in these Regulations as they have there.

2 Election

(1) A lessor may make an election ("a long funding lease election") in respect of all his eligible leases and qualifying incidental leases.

In these Regulations "electing lessor" means a lessor who makes such an election.

(2) A long-funding lease election—

(*a*) must be made within the permitted time;

(*b*) must be made in the return for the relevant chargeable period or for the year of assessment to which the election relates, either by inclusion in the return as originally made or by an amendment to that return;

(*c*) must specify the date from which it is to take effect ("the effective date"); and (*d*) may be withdrawn by amending that return within the permitted time (but is otherwise irrevocable).

Sub-paragraph (*c*) is subject to the qualification in paragraph (4).

(3) The permitted time is—

(*a*) for income tax purposes, the period beginning with the end of the year of assessment to which the election relates, and ending 12 months after the 31st January next following that year of assessment;

(*b*) for corporation tax purposes, the period beginning with the time when the relevant chargeable period ends and ending with the second anniversary of that time.

(4) The effective date may not be earlier than the later of—

(*a*) 1st April 2006; and

(*b*) the beginning of the relevant chargeable period or the year of assessment to which the election relates (as the case requires).

(5) If a long funding lease election has been made, the electing lessor shall be treated as if all the electing lessor's eligible and qualifying incidental leases finalised on or after the effective date (including those finalised in subsequent chargeable periods or years of assessment) had been long funding leases for the purposes of Part 2 of CAA since they were finalised.

(6) For the purposes of this regulation—

"chargeable period" has the meaning given by section 6 of CAA;

"relevant chargeable period" means the chargeable period in which the effective date falls; and

"the year of assessment to which the election relates" means the tax year in which ends the basis period in which falls the effective date.

HMRC Manuals—Business Leasing Manual, BLM24010 (defining long funding leases: who can make an election?).

BLM24015 (plant or machinery lessor, with example).

BLM24020 (effect of election on lessee).

BLM24025 (effective date of election).

BLM24030 (consequences of making an election).

BLM24035 (how to make an election).

BLM24040 (time limit for making an election).

BLM24045 (withdrawing an election, with example).

3 Eligible leases

An eligible lease is one which meets the following conditions.

Condition A

The lease is a plant or machinery lease.

Condition B

The lease is not, apart from the provisions of these Regulations, a long funding lease.

Condition C

The lease was finalised, as defined in paragraph 23 of Schedule 8 of the Finance Act 2006, on or after 1 April 2006.

Condition D

The term of the lease is 12 months or more.

Condition E

The plant or machinery made available under the lease—

(*a*) was unused and not second-hand at the commencement of the term of the lease;

(*b*) if leased previously, was last leased under a long funding lease (under the provisions of Part 2 of CAA or pursuant to these Regulations) before the commencement of the term of the lease;

(*c*) was the subject of a valid election under section 227 of CAA before the electing lessor made a return for the period in which the commencement of the term of the lease occurred; or

(*d*) replaces (whether by one or more substitutions) plant or machinery of the same type and quantity previously made available by the electing lessor to the lessee under a lease which is an eligible lease by virtue of one of the preceding paragraphs of this condition.

Condition F

The lease is not a lease for the provision of a car as defined in section 81 of CAA.

Condition G

The lease does not provide for the leasing of any asset whose market value is more than £10 million at its commencement.

Condition H

The lease is not one to which section 70R or section 70U of CAA applies.

Condition I

If the original lessor's interest under the lease has been assigned—

(*a*) the assignment, or where there is more than one assignment, both or all of them, must have occurred within 4 months of the commencement of the term of the lease; and (*b*) the original lessor, and any person later owning the leased assets and through whom the lessor making the long funding lease election derives title to them, must not claim, or have claimed, capital allowances at any time in respect of those assets.

HMRC Manuals—Business Leasing Manual, BLM24055 (defining long funding leases: date lease finalised).
BLM24060 (term of lease).
BLM24065 (plant or machinery must be new, etc).
BLM24070 (election under CAA 2001 s 227).
BLM24075 (replacement plant or machinery).
BLM24080 (asset value not to exceed £10m).
BLM24085 (background plant or machinery, etc).
BLM24090 (assignments).

4 Qualifying incidental leases

A qualifying incidental lease is a lease of plant or machinery which—

(*a*) is wholly incidental to an eligible lease; and

(*b*) disregarding Condition D in regulation 3, would have been an eligible lease.

HMRC Manuals—Business Leasing Manual, BLM24095 (defining long funding leases: qualifying incidental leases).

2007/494

REGISTERED PENSION SCHEMES (STANDARD LIFETIME AND ANNUAL ALLOWANCES) ORDER 2007

Made by the Treasury under FA 2004 ss 218(3) and 228(2)

Made . . . . *21 February 2007*
Laid before House of Commons . . . . *22 February 2007*
Coming into force . . . . *6 April 2007*

Commentary—*Simon's Taxes* **E7.211–E7.216**.

1 Citation and commencement

This Order may be cited as the Registered Pension Schemes (Standard Lifetime and Annual Allowances) Order 2007 and shall come into force on 6th April 2007.

2 Standard lifetime allowance

The standard lifetime allowance—

(*a*) for the tax year 2007–08 is £1,600,000;
(*b*) for the tax year 2008–09 is £1,650,000;
(*c*) for the tax year 2009–10 is £1,750,000;
(*d*) for the tax year 2010–11 is £1,800,000.

3 Annual allowance

The annual allowance for the tax year—

(*a*) for the tax year 2007–08 is £225,000;
(*b*) for the tax year 2008–09 is £235,000;
(*c*) for the tax year 2009–10 is £245,000;
(*d*) for the tax year 2010–11 is £255,000.

2007/678

CORPORATION TAX (SURRENDER OF TERMINAL LOSSES ON FILMS AND CLAIMS FOR RELIEF) REGULATIONS 2007

Made by the Treasury under FA 2006 s 45(5)

Made . . . . *5 March 2007*
Laid before the House of Commons . . . . *6 March 2007*
Coming into force . . . . *27 March 2007*

Commentary—*Simon's Taxes* **D7.1211**.

1 Citation and commencement

These Regulations may be cited as the Corporation Tax (Surrender of Terminal Losses on Films and Claims for Relief) Regulations 2007 and shall come into force on 27th March 2007.

2 Interpretation

In these Regulations—

"FA" followed by a year means the Finance Act of that year;

"TMA" means the Taxes Management Act 1970; and

"Part 8" means Part 8 of Schedule 18 to FA 1998 (claims for group relief).

3 Provision corresponding to Part 8 of Schedule 18 to FA 1998

The provision made by regulations 4 to 15 corresponds to the provision made by Part 8.

The Table below shows the correspondence between those regulations and the paragraphs of Part 8.

Table

Regulation	*Paragraph of Part 8 to which the regulation corresponds*
4	66 (introduction)
5	67 (claims to be included in company tax return)
6	68 (content of claims)
7	69 (claims for more or less than the amount available for surrender)
8	70 (consent to surrender)
9	71 (notice of consent)
10	72 (notice of consent requiring amendment of return)
11	73 (withdrawal or amendment of claim)
12	74 (time limit for claims)
13	75 (reduction in amount available for surrender)
14	75A (assessment on other claimant companies)
15	76 (assessment to recover excessive group relief)

4 Introduction of provisions on claims for relief in respect of terminal losses

Regulations 5 to 15 apply to claims for relief made by virtue of section 45(3) of FA 2006 (terminal losses of company A may be surrendered to company B and treated as a loss of company B).

5 Claim to be included in company B's return

(1) A claim to treat the terminal loss surrendered by company A as if it were a loss brought forward by company B must be included in company B's tax return for the accounting period for which the claim is made.

(2) It may be included in the return originally made or by amendment.

6 Content of claims

(1) A claim to treat the terminal loss surrendered by company A as if it were a loss brought forward by company B must specify—

(*a*) the amount of relief claimed, and

(*b*) the name of company A.

(2) The amount specified must be an amount which is quantified at the time the claim is made.

(3) A claim to treat the terminal loss surrendered by company A as if it were a loss brought forward by company B must also state whether or not there is a company mentioned in paragraph (4) that was not resident in the United Kingdom in either or both of the following periods—

(*a*) the accounting period of company A to which the surrender relates,

(*b*) the corresponding accounting period of company B.

(4) Those companies are company A, company B and any other company by reference to which company A or company B are members of the same group.

7 Claims for more or less than the terminal loss available for surrender

(1) A claim to treat the terminal loss surrendered by company A as if it were a loss brought forward by company B may be made for less than the amount available for surrender at the time the claim is made.

(2) A claim is ineffective if the amount claimed exceeds the terminal loss available for surrender at the time the claim is made.

(3) For these purposes the terminal loss available for surrender is calculated as follows, subject to paragraphs (4) and (5).

First step

Determine the total amount available for surrender under section 45 of FA 2006—

(*a*) on the basis of the information in company A's company tax return, and

(*b*) disregarding any amendments whose effect is deferred under paragraph 31(3) of Schedule 18 to FA 1998.

Second step

Then deduct the total of all amounts for which notices of consent have been given by company A and not withdrawn.

(4) Where one or more claims are withdrawn on the same day as one or more claims are made, the withdrawals are given effect first.

(5) Where more than one claim is made on the same day, and the claims together take the amount claimed over the limit of what is available for surrender, an officer of Revenue and Customs may determine which of the claims is to be ineffective.

8 Consent to surrender

(1) A claim for terminal loss surrendered by company A as if it were a loss brought forward by company B requires the consent of company A.

(2) The necessary consent must be given—

(*a*) by notice in writing,

(*b*) to the officer of Revenue and Customs to whom company A makes its company tax returns,

(*c*) at or before the time the claim is made.

Otherwise the claim is ineffective.

(3) A claim to treat the terminal loss surrendered by company A as if it were a loss brought forward by company B is ineffective unless it is accompanied by a copy of the notice of consent to surrender given by company A.

9 Notice of consent

(1) Notice of consent by company A must contain all of the following details—

(*a*) the name of company A;

(*b*) the name of company B;

(*c*) the amount of the terminal loss being surrendered;

(*d*) the accounting period of company A to which the surrender relates;

(*e*) the tax district references of company A and company B.

Otherwise the notice is ineffective.

(2) A notice of consent may not be amended, but it may be withdrawn and replaced by another notice of consent.

(3) A notice of consent may be withdrawn by notice to the officer of Revenue and Customs to whom the notice of consent was given.

(4) Except where the consent is withdrawn under regulation 13 (withdrawal in consequence of reduction of the amount available for surrender), the notice of withdrawal must be accompanied by a notice signifying the consent of company B to the withdrawal.

Otherwise the notice is ineffective.

(5) Company B must, so far as it may do so, amend its company tax return for the accounting period for which the claim was made so as to reflect the withdrawal of consent.

10 Notice of consent requiring amendment of return

(1) Where notice of consent by company A is given after that company has made a company tax return for the period to which the surrender relates, company A must at the same time amend its return so as to reflect the notice of consent.

(2) Where a notice of consent given by company A relates to a loss in respect of which relief has been given to company A, company A must at the same time amend its tax return for the period or, if more than one, each of the periods in which relief for that loss has been given in accordance with section 45(2) of FA 2006 so as to reflect the new notice of consent.

(3) The time limits otherwise applicable to amendment of a company tax return do not prevent an amendment being made under paragraph (1) or (2).

(4) But if company A fails to comply with paragraph (1) or (2), the notice of consent is ineffective.

11 Withdrawal or amendment of claim

(1) A claim to treat the terminal loss surrendered by company A as if it were a loss brought forward by company B may be withdrawn by company B only by amending its company tax return.

(2) A claim to treat the terminal loss surrendered by company A as if it were a loss brought forward by company B may not be amended by company B, but must be withdrawn and replaced by another claim.

12 Time limit for claims

(1) A claim to treat the terminal loss surrendered by company A as if it were a loss brought forward by company B may be withdrawn by company B at any time up to whichever is the last of the following dates—

(*a*) the first anniversary of the filing date for the company tax return of company B for the accounting period for which the claim is made;

(*b*) if notice of enquiry is given into that return, 30 days after the enquiry is completed;

(*c*) if after such an enquiry an officer of Revenue and Customs amends the return under paragraph 34(2) of Schedule 18 to FA 1998, 30 days after the date on which the amendment is issued;

(*d*) if an appeal is brought against such an amendment, 30 days after the date on which the appeal is finally determined.

(2) A claim to treat the terminal loss surrendered by company A as if it were a loss brought forward by company B may be made or withdrawn at a later time if an officer of Revenue and Customs allows it.

(3) The time limits otherwise applicable to amendment of a company tax return do not apply to an amendment to the extent that it makes or withdraws a claim to treat the terminal loss surrendered by company A as if it were a loss brought forward by company B within the time allowed by this regulation.

(4) The references in paragraph (1) to an enquiry into a company tax return do not include an enquiry restricted to a previous amendment making or withdrawing a claim to treat the terminal loss surrendered by company A as if it were a loss brought forward by company B.

An enquiry is so restricted if—

(*a*) the scope of the enquiry is limited as mentioned in paragraph 25(2) of Schedule 18 to FA 1998 (limiting scope of enquiry into a company tax return);

(*b*) the amendment giving rise to the enquiry consisted of the making or withdrawal of a claim to treat the terminal loss surrendered by company A as if it were a loss brought forward by company B.

13 Reduction in amount available for surrender

(1) This regulation applies if, after company A has given one or more notices of consent to a claim by company B to treat the terminal loss surrendered by company A as if it were a loss brought forward by company B, the total available to be so treated is reduced to less than the amount stated in the notice, or the total amount of the amounts stated in the notices, as being available to be so treated.

(2) Company A must within 30 days withdraw the notice of consent, or as many of the notices as is necessary to bring the total amount surrendered within the new total amount available to be treated as a loss carried forward by company B, and may give one or more new notices of consent.

(3) Company A must give notice in writing of the withdrawal of consent, and send a copy of any new notice of consent—

(*a*) to each of the companies affected; and

(*b*) to an officer of Revenue and Customs.

(4) If company A fails to act in accordance with paragraph (2) an officer of Revenue and Customs may by notice to company A give such directions as he thinks fit as to which notice or notices are to be ineffective or are to have effect in a lesser amount.

The power shall not be exercised to any greater extent than is necessary to secure that the total amount stated in the notice or notices is consistent with the total amount available to be treated as a loss carried forward by company B by virtue of section 45 of FA 2006.

(5) An officer of Revenue and Customs must at the same time send a copy of the notice to company B.

(6) Company B upon receipt of—

(*a*) a notice of the withdrawal of consent, or a copy of a new notice of consent under paragraph (3), or

(*b*) a copy of a notice containing directions by an officer of Revenue and Customs under paragraph (4),

must, so far as it may do so, amend its company tax return for the accounting period for which the claim is made so that it is consistent with the new position with regard to consent to surrender.

(7) Company A may appeal against any directions given by an officer of Revenue and Customs under paragraph (4).

(8) Notice of appeal must be given—

(*a*) in writing,

(*b*) within 30 days after the notice containing the directions was issued,

(*c*) to the officer of Revenue and Customs by whom the notice was given.

14 Assessment on other claimant companies

(1) This regulation applies where, after company A has given notice of consent to surrender, company B has become liable to tax in consequence of receiving—

(*a*) notice of the withdrawal of consent, or a copy of a new notice of consent under regulation 13(3); or

(*b*) a copy of a notice containing directions by an officer of Revenue and Customs under regulation 13(4).

(2) If any of the tax is unpaid six months after company B's time limit for claims, an officer of Revenue and Customs may make an assessment to tax in the name of company B on any other company which has obtained relief as a result of the surrender.

(3) The assessment must not be made more than two years after that time limit.

(4) The amount of the assessment must not exceed—

(*a*) the amount of the unpaid tax, or

(*b*) if less, the amount of tax which the other company saves by virtue of the surrender.

(5) A company assessed to an amount of tax under paragraph (2) is entitled to recover from company B—

(*a*) a sum equal to that amount, and

(*b*) any interest on that amount which it has paid under section 87A of TMA (interest on unpaid corporation tax).

(6) For the purposes of this regulation company B's time limit for claims is the last of the dates mentioned in regulation 12(1) on which company B could make or withdraw a claim to treat the terminal loss surrendered by company A as if it were a loss brought forward by company B.

15 Assessment to recover excess relief

(1) If an officer of Revenue and Customs discovers that any relief given in respect of a claim by company B to treat the terminal loss surrendered by company A as if it were a loss brought forward by company B is or has become excessive, he may make an assessment to tax which in his opinion ought to be charged.

(2) This power—

(*a*) is in addition to the power to make a discovery assessment under paragraph 41(1) of Schedule 18 to FA 1998; and

(*b*) does not prevent the making of such adjustments by way of discharge or repayment of tax or otherwise as may be required where company B has obtained too much relief, or company A has forgone relief in respect of a corresponding amount.

(3) If an assessment under this regulation is made because company B fails, or is unable, to amend its company tax return under regulation 13(6), the assessment is not out of time if it is made within one year from—

(*a*) the date on which company A gives notice of the withdrawal of consent, or (if later) sends a new notice of consent, to company B under regulation 13(3), or

(*b*) the date on which an officer of Revenue and Customs sends the company B a copy of a notice containing his directions under regulation 13(4).

2007/766

TRANSFER OF THE NORTHERN IRELAND WATER SERVICE (TAX) REGULATIONS 2007

Made by the Treasury under F(No 2)A 2005 s 67

Made . . . . *8 March 2007*

Laid before the House of Commons . . . . *9 March 2007*

Coming into force . . . . *1 April 2007*

1 Citation and commencement

These Regulations may be cited as the Transfer of the Northern Ireland Water Service (Tax) Regulations 2007 and come into force on 1st April 2007.

2 Interpretation

In these Regulations—

"CAA" means the Capital Allowances Act 2001;

"TCGA" means the Taxation of Chargeable Gains Act 1992;

"relevant transfer" has the meaning given in section 67(1) of the Finance (No 2) Act 2005;

"successor company" has the meaning given in Article 269 of the Water and Sewerage Services (Northern Ireland) Order 2006;

"transferor" means the Department for Regional Development;

"wholly owned subsidiary" has the meaning given in Article 4 of the Companies (Northern Ireland) Order 1986.

3 Capital allowances: transfer of plant or machinery

(1) This regulation applies where—

(*a*) there is a relevant transfer of plant or machinery; and

(*b*) the plant or machinery would have been treated for the purposes of CAA (had the transferor incurred expenditure qualifying for allowances under Part 2 of that Act on the provision of the plant or machinery) as disposed of by the transferor to the successor company on the transfer taking effect.

(2) Where this regulation applies, the Secretary of State may determine the amount which is to be taken for the purposes of Part 2 of CAA to be the amount of capital expenditure incurred by the successor company on the provision of plant or machinery.

(3) A determination referred to in paragraph (2) may only be made with the consent of the Treasury.

(4) Expressions used in this regulation and in Part 2 of CAA have the same meanings in this regulation as in that Part.

4 Capital allowances: determination of capital value of industrial buildings etc

(1) This regulation applies where there is a relevant transfer of a relevant interest in an industrial building or structure.

(2) Where this regulation applies the Secretary of State may determine—

(*a*) the amount to be taken as the amount of the residue of qualifying expenditure immediately after the transfer; and

(*b*) the period to be taken as the period from the date of the transfer to the end of the period of 25 years beginning with the day on which the building or structure was first used.

(3) A determination referred to in paragraph (2) may only be made with the consent of the Treasury.

(4) Expressions used in this regulation and in Part 3 of CAA have the same meanings in this regulation as in that Part.

5 Amendment of company tax return following determination by Secretary of State

(1) Where the Secretary of State makes a determination in accordance with regulations 3(2) or 4(2) the successor company—

(*a*) may amend its company tax return where necessary in accordance with paragraph 15(4) of Schedule 18 to the Finance Act 1998; or

(*b*) shall amend its company tax return not more than twelve months after the end of the accounting period in which the determination occurred where the date of the determination makes it impossible to comply with the time limits set out in paragraph 15(4) of Schedule 18 to that Act.

(2) Where a company does not make an amended return in accordance with sub-paragraph (*b*), an officer of Revenue and Customs may make an assessment or determination—

(*a*) in accordance with paragraph 46 of Schedule 18 to the Finance Act 1998; or

(*b*) not later than two years after the end of the accounting period in which the determination occurred,

whichever is the later.

6 Chargeable gains: transfer values

Where there is a relevant transfer, to the extent that section 171 of TCGA would otherwise apply to the transfer, that section shall not apply.

7 Chargeable gains: degrouping charges

(1) This regulation applies if the successor company acquires an asset from the transferor by way of a relevant transfer at a time when both are members of the same group of companies.

(2) Where paragraph (1) applies the successor company shall not be treated as having acquired the asset from the transferor for the purposes of section 179 of TCGA (company ceasing to be member of group).

(3) Expressions used in this regulation and in section 179 of TCGA have the same meanings in this regulation as in that section.

8 Ownership of successor company: issue of securities

Any security (other than a share) issued by the successor company or its wholly owned subsidiary pursuant to Article 271 of the Water and Sewerage Services (Northern Ireland) Order 2006 shall be treated for the purposes of the Corporation Tax Acts as if it had been issued for new consideration, such new consideration being equal to the principal sum payable under the security.

9 Modification of transfer schemes

(1) Where a transfer scheme is treated as modified under, or by an order made under paragraph 3 of Schedule 11 to the Water and Sewerage Services (Northern Ireland) Order 2006 the successor company—

(*a*) may amend its company tax return in accordance with paragraph 15(4) of Schedule 18 to the Finance Act 1998; or

(*b*) shall amend its company tax return not more than twelve months after the end of the accounting period in which the modification occurred where the date of the modification makes it impossible to comply with the time limits set out in paragraph 15(4) of Schedule 18 to that Act.

(2) Where a company does not make an amended return in accordance with sub-paragraph (*b*), an officer of Revenue and Customs may make an assessment or determination—

(*a*) in accordance with paragraph 46 of Schedule 18 to the Finance Act 1998; or

(*b*) not later than two years after the end of the accounting period in which the modification occurred,

whichever is the later.

2007/792

EMPLOYEE SHARE SCHEMES (ELECTRONIC COMMUNICATION OF RETURNS AND INFORMATION) REGULATIONS 2007

Revocation—These Regulations revoked by FA 2014 s 51, Sch 8 para 88. This amendment is treated as having come into force on 6 April 2014.

2007/826

REGISTERED PENSION SCHEMES (BRIDGING PENSIONS) REGULATIONS 2007

Made by the Treasury under FA 2004 Sch 28 paras 2(5) and 2(8)

Made . . . . *13 March 2007*
Laid before the House of Commons . . . . *14 March 2007*
Coming into force . . . . *6 April 2007*

Commentary—*Simon's Taxes* **E2.250**.

1 Citation, commencement and effect

(1) These Regulations may be cited as the Registered Pension Schemes (Bridging Pensions) Regulations 2007 and shall come into force on 6th April 2007.

(2) These Regulations have effect in relation to payments of scheme pensions made on or after 6th April 2006.

2 Prescribed percentage of the basic pension rate

(1) The prescribed percentage of the rate of the basic pension under paragraph 2(5)(*c*) of Schedule 28 to the Finance Act 2004 is that found by the formula—

$$125 + \left(125\frac{A}{B}\right)$$

Here—

A is the total number of years of a member's employment to which the pension scheme relates which is not or has not been contracted-out employment, and

B is the total number of years of a member's employment to which the pension scheme relates.

(2) In paragraph (1) "the basic pension" and "contracted-out employment" have the meanings given by paragraph 2(5A) of Schedule 28 to the Finance Act 2004.

2007/831

ENERGY-SAVING ITEMS REGULATIONS 2007

Made by the Treasury under ITTOIA 2005 ss 312 and 314

Made . . . . *13 March 2007*
Laid before the House of Commons . . . . *14 March 2007*
Coming into force . . . . *6 April 2007*

Revocation—These Regulations revoked by the Energy-Saving Items (Income Tax) Regulations, SI 2007/3278 reg 8 with effect in respect of expenditure incurred on or after 6 April 2007.

2007/850

TONNAGE TAX (EXCEPTION OF FINANCIAL YEAR 2007) ORDER 2007

Made . . . . *14 March 2007*
Coming into force . . . . *1 April 2007*

The Treasury are satisfied that the percentage of the tonnage tax fleet which is Community-flagged has not decreased on average over the period prescribed in Article 2(*a*) of this Order.

The Treasury, in exercise of the powers conferred upon them by paragraphs 22B(2) and 22C(1) of Schedule 22 to the Finance Act 2000, make the following Order:

Commentary—*Simon's Taxes* **D7.1004**.

1 Citation and commencement

This Order may be cited as the Tonnage Tax (Exception of Financial Year 2007) Order 2007 and shall come into force on 1st April 2007.

2 Prescribed three year period and other definitions

For the purposes of this Order—

(*a*) the period prescribed for the purposes of paragraph 22C(1)(*a*) of Schedule 22 to the Finance Act 2000 (three year period to determine whether the percentage of the tonnage tax fleet which is Community-flagged has not decreased) is the period beginning on 2nd October 2003 and ending on 1st October 2006;

(*b*) "the tonnage tax fleet" means qualifying ships operated by single companies or qualifying companies which are members of a tonnage tax group; and

(*c*) "the percentage of the tonnage tax fleet which is Community-flagged" is—

$$\frac{CFT}{TT} \times 100$$

where—

CFT is the aggregate tonnage of qualifying ships registered in one of the Member States' registers,

TT is the aggregate tonnage of all qualifying ships, and

no qualifying ship is counted more than once in determining an aggregate.

3 Exception of financial year 2007

The financial year 2007 is designated as one in relation to which paragraph 22A of Schedule 22 to the Finance Act 2000 is not to have effect.

2007/945

BUSINESS PREMISES RENOVATION ALLOWANCES REGULATIONS 2007

Made by the Treasury under CAA 2001 ss 360C(2)(a), (3) and 360D(4)

Made . . . . *21 March 2007*

Laid before the House of Commons . . . . *21 March 2007*

Coming into force . . . . *11 April 2007*

Commentary—*Simon's Taxes* **B3.1101**.

1 Citation and commencement

These Regulations may be cited as the Business Premises Renovation Allowances Regulations 2007 and shall come into force on 11th April 2007.

2 Interpretation

In these Regulations "the Act" means the Capital Allowances Act 2001.

["General Block Exemption Regulation" means Commission Regulation (EU) No 651/2014 of 17 June 2014 declaring certain categories of aid compatible with the internal market in application of Articles 107 and 108 of the Treaty on the Functioning of the European Union.][1]

Amendments—[1] Definition inserted by the Business Premises Renovation Allowances (Amendment) Regulations, SI 2014/1687 regs 2, 3 with effect in relation to expenditure incurred on or after 22 July 2014.

[2A Expiry Date for incurring qualifying expenditure

For the purposes of Part 3A of the Act, "the expiry date" is prescribed as—

(*a*) 1 April 2017, for corporation tax purposes; and

(*b*) 6 April 2017, for income tax purposes.][1]

Amendments—[1] Reg 2A inserted by the Business Premises Renovation Allowances (Amendment) Regulations, SI 2012/868 regs 2, 3 with effect from 11 April 2012.

3 Designation of areas as disadvantaged areas

The following areas are designated as disadvantaged areas for the purposes of section 360C of the Act (meaning of "qualifying building")—

(*a*) areas specified as development areas by the [Assisted Areas Order 2014][1];

(*b*) Northern Ireland.

Amendments—[1] Words in para (*a*) substituted for words "Assisted Areas Order 2007" by the Business Premises Renovation Allowances (Amendment) Regulations, SI 2014/1687 regs 2, 4 with effect in relation to expenditure incurred on or after 22 July 2014.

4 Meaning of "qualifying business premises"

(1) For the purposes of Part 3A of the Act (business premises renovation allowances) premises are not qualifying business premises where—

(*a*) the person entitled to the relevant interest in the premises is carrying on a relevant trade; or

(*b*) the premises are used, or used in part, for the purposes of such a trade.

(2) In this regulation—

"relevant interest" has the meaning given by Chapter 4 of Part 3A of the Act (the relevant interest in the qualifying building);

["relevant trade" means a trade—

[(*a*) in the fishery and aquaculture sector;

(*b*) in the coal sector, steel sector, shipbuilding sector or synthetic fibres sector;

(*c*) in the transport sector or in related infrastructure;

(*d*) relating to the development of broadband networks;

(*e*) relating to energy generation, distribution and infrastructure;

(*f*) in the primary agricultural production sector; or

(*g*) carried on by any undertaking which—

(i) is subject to an outstanding recovery order made by virtue of Article 108(2) of the Treaty on the Functioning of the European Union; or

(ii) it is reasonable to assume would be regarded as an undertaking in difficulty for the purposes of the General Block Exemption Regulation.][2], [1]

(3) This regulation applies in relation to part of a trade as it applies in relation to a trade.

[(4) In this regulation "undertaking" has the same meaning as it has for the purposes of section 45DB (exclusions from allowances under section 45DA) of the Act.][1]

[(5) In this regulation "broadband network", "coal sector", "energy generation, distribution and infrastructure", "fishery and aquaculture sector", "primary agricultural production sector", "shipbuilding sector", "steel sector", "synthetic fibres sector" and "transport sector" have the same meaning as they have for the purposes of the General Block Exemption Regulation.][2]

Amendments—[1] In para (2), definition of "relevant trade" substituted, and para (4) inserted, by the Business Premises Renovation Allowances (Amendment) Regulations, SI 2012/868 regs 2, 4 with effect in relation to expenditure incurred on or after 11 April 2012.

[2] In para (2), definition of "relevant trade" substituted, and para (5) inserted, by the Business Premises Renovation Allowances (Amendment) Regulations, SI 2014/1687 regs 2, 5 with effect in relation to expenditure incurred on or after 22 July 2014.

[5 Meaning of "qualifying expenditure"

(1) For the purposes of Part 3A of the Act, expenditure is not qualifying expenditure if the expenditure is incurred on or in connection with a qualifying building and the building is not in a disadvantaged area on the date the expenditure is incurred.

(2) For the purposes of Part 3A of the Act, expenditure is not qualifying expenditure if, and to the extent that,—

(*a*) the amount of the expenditure ("current expenditure"); or

(*b*) the current expenditure and the aggregate amount of the single project investment expenditure in respect of which allowances under Part 3A of the Act have previously been made,

exceeds 20 million euros.

(3) In this regulation "single project investment expenditure" means expenditure—

(*a*) incurred by any person within a period of three years prior to the date on which the current expenditure is incurred; and,

[(*b*) which, together with the current expenditure, would be treated as incurred as part of a single investment project for the purposes of paragraph 13 of Article 14 of the General Block Exemption Regulation.][2]

(4) In this regulation "disadvantaged area" has the same meaning as that which applies for the purposes of section 360C of the Act.

(5) For the purposes of this regulation, expenditure incurred in a currency other than the euro is to be converted into its equivalent in euros using the spot rate of exchange for the day on which the expenditure is incurred.][1]

Amendments—[1] Reg 5 inserted by the Business Premises Renovation Allowances (Amendment) Regulations, SI 2012/868 regs 2, 5 with effect in relation to expenditure incurred on or after 11 April 2012.

[2] Para (3)(*b*) substituted by the Business Premises Renovation Allowances (Amendment) Regulations, SI 2014/1687 regs 2, 6 with effect in relation to expenditure incurred on or after 22 July 2014.

2007/963

FINANCE ACT 1995, SECTION 127(12), (DESIGNATED TRANSACTIONS) REGULATIONS 2007

Made by the Treasury under FA 1995 s 127(12)(c)

Made . . . . *22 March 2007*

Laid before the House of Commons . . . . *22 March 2007*

Coming into force . . . . *12 April 2007*

Commentary—*Simon's Taxes* **B1.211**.

1 Citation and commencement

These Regulations may be cited as the Finance Act 1995, Section 127(12), (Designated Transactions) Regulations 2007 and shall come into force on 12th April 2007.

2 Transaction designated as an investment transaction

(1) A transaction is designated as an investment transaction for the purposes of section 127 of the Finance Act 1995 (persons not treated as United Kingdom representatives) if conditions A to C are met.

(2) Condition A is that the transaction is a transaction—

(*a*) in Community tradeable emissions allowances, or

(*b*) in transferable units issued pursuant to the Kyoto Protocol.

(3) Condition B is that the transaction does not give rise to a chargeable gain falling within section 10 of the Taxation of Chargeable Gains Act 1992 (non-resident with United Kingdom branch or agency).

(4) Condition C is that the transaction does not otherwise fall within section 127(12).

(5) For the purposes of this regulation—

"Community tradeable emissions allowances" are transferable allowances which relate to the making of emissions of greenhouse gases, and are allocated as part of a system made for the purpose of implementing any Community obligation of the United Kingdom relating to such emissions;

"Kyoto Protocol" means the Kyoto Protocol to the United Nations Framework Convention on Climate Change signed at Kyoto on 11th December 1997;

"section 127(12)" means section 127(12) of the Finance Act 1995 (meaning of "investment transaction" for the purposes of determining whether a person is capable of being the UK representative of a non-resident taxpayer); and

"units" include assigned amount units, certified emission reductions, emission reduction units and removal units.

2007/964

FINANCE ACT 2003, PARAGRAPH 3(3) OF SCHEDULE 26, (DESIGNATED TRANSACTIONS) REGULATIONS 2007

Made by the Treasury under FA 2003 Sch 26 para 3(3)

Made . . . .*22 March 2007*

Laid before the House of Commons . . . .*22 March 2007*

Coming into force . . . .*12 April 2007*

Commentary—*Simon's Taxes* **D4.123**.

1 Citation and commencement

These Regulations may be cited as the Finance Act 2003, Paragraph 3(3) of Schedule 26, (Designated Transactions) Regulations 2007 and shall come into force on 12th April 2007.

2 Transaction designated as an investment transaction

(1) A transaction is designated as an investment transaction for the purposes of Schedule 26 to the Finance Act 2003 (non-resident companies: transactions through investment manager and others) if conditions A to C are met.

(2) Condition A is that the transaction is a transaction—

(*a*) in Community tradeable emissions allowances, or

(*b*) in transferable units issued pursuant to the Kyoto Protocol.

(3) Condition B is that the transaction does not give rise to a chargeable gain falling within section 10B of the Taxation of Chargeable Gains Act 1992 (non-resident company with United Kingdom permanent establishment) (and accordingly taken into account for the purposes of section 11(2A) of the Income and Corporation Taxes Act 1988 (profits attributable to a permanent establishment)).

(4) Condition C is that the transaction does not otherwise fall within paragraph 3(3).

(5) For the purposes of this regulation—

"Community tradeable emissions allowances" are transferable allowances which relate to the making of emissions of greenhouse gases, and are allocated as part of a system made for the purpose of implementing any Community obligation of the United Kingdom relating to such emissions;

"Kyoto Protocol" means the Kyoto Protocol to the United Nations Framework Convention on Climate Change signed at Kyoto on 11th December 1997;

"paragraph 3(3)" means paragraph 3(3) of Schedule 26 to the Finance Act 2003 (meaning of "investment transaction" for the purposes of determining whether a person is an agent of independent status in respect of investment transactions);

"units" include assigned amount units, certified emission reductions, emission reduction units and removal units.

2007/1050

CORPORATION TAX (TAXATION OF FILMS) (TRANSITIONAL PROVISIONS) REGULATIONS 2007

Made . . . .*28 March 2007*

Coming into force in accordance with . . . .*regulation 1*

The Treasury in exercise of the powers conferred upon them by section 52 of the Finance Act 2006 make the following Regulations.

A draft of this instrument was laid before and approved by a resolution of the House of Commons in accordance with section 52(4) of the Finance Act 2006.

Commentary—*Simon's Taxes* **D7.1215**.

Cross-reference—See CTA 2009 Sch 2 para 131 (these regs have effect as if made under CTA 2009 Sch 2 para 130 and are modified accordingly).

Preliminary

1 Citation, commencement and effect

(1) These Regulations may be cited as the Corporation Tax (Taxation of Films) (Transitional Provisions) Regulations 2007 and shall come into force on the day after the day on which they are made.

(2) The provisions of Chapter 3 of Part 3 of the Finance Act 2006 (films and sound recordings) applied by these Regulations shall have effect as if they had been in force at all material times.

Modification—This regulation modified as follows by CTA 2009 Sch 2 para 131(1)–(3). In para (2), words "and Part 15 and section 812 of the Corporation Tax Act 2009 (film production)" substituted for words "(films and sound recordings)".

2 Interpretation

In these Regulations a reference to a "Chapter", "Part", "section" or "Schedule" without more is a reference to a Chapter, Part, section or Schedule of the Finance Act 2006, unless the context otherwise requires.

Modification—This regulation modified so as to be revoked for the purpose of CTA 2009 Sch 2 para 130, by CTA 2009 Sch 2 para 131(1), (2), (4).

3 Application of enactments

The provisions of Chapter 3 of Part 3, the enactments amended by that Chapter and the Corporation Tax Acts apply with the modifications provided in regulations 4 to 12 in relation to films that commenced principal photography before 1st January 2007 but are not completed before that date.

Modification—This regulation modified as follows by CTA 2009 Sch 2 para 131(1), (2), (5). Words "Part 15 and section 812 of the Corporation Tax Act 2009, Chapter 3 of Part 3 of the Finance Act 2006" substituted for words "Chapter 3 of Part 3".

Modifications to the Finance Act 2006

4 Modification of section 32 (meaning of "film production company")

In section 32 (meaning of "film production company"), in subsection (3), in relation to a film that commenced principal photography before 1st April 2006, omit "pre-production," in both places.

Modification—This regulation modified as follows by CTA 2009 Sch 2 para 131(1), (2), (6). Words "section 1182 of the Corporation Tax Act 2009" substituted for words "section 32" (and corresponding change in the heading for reg 4).

5 Modification of section 40 (conditions of relief: British film)

In section 40 (conditions of relief: British film) at the end insert "for the purposes of film tax relief".

Modification—This regulation modified as follows by CTA 2009 Sch 2 para 131(1), (2), (7). Words "section 1197 of the Corporation Tax Act 2009" substituted for words "section 40" (and corresponding change in the heading for reg 5).

6 Modification of section 46 (films: withdrawal of existing reliefs (corporation tax))

(1) Modify section 46 (films: withdrawal of existing reliefs (corporation tax)) as follows.

(2) In the provisions listed below for the words "commences principal photography on or after 1st January 2007" substitute "is certified by the Secretary of State under Schedule 1 to the Films Act 1985 as a British film for the purposes of film tax relief and is intended for theatrical release at the time the film commences principal photography".

The provisions are—

subsection (1)(*a*);
subsection (1)(*b*)(i);
subsection (3)(*a*); and
subsection (3)(*b*)(i).

(3) In subsections (1)(*b*)(ii) and (3)(*b*)(ii) for "1st October 2007" substitute "31st March 2008".

Modification—This regulation modified as follows by CTA 2009 Sch 2 para 131(1), (2), (8). In para (1), after "section 46", words "of the Finance Act 2006" inserted (and corresponding change in the heading for reg 6).

7 Modification of section 47 (films: withdrawal of existing reliefs (income tax))

(1) Modify section 47 (films: withdrawal of existing reliefs (income tax))as follows.

(2) In the provisions listed below for the words "commences principal photography on or after 1st January 2007" substitute "is certified by the Secretary of State under Schedule 1 to the Films Act 1985 as a British film for the purposes of film tax relief and is intended for theatrical release at the time the film commences principal photography".

The provisions are—

subsection (1)(*a*);
subsection (1)(*b*)(i);
subsection (3)(*a*); and
subsection (3)(*b*)(i).

(3) In subsections (1)(*b*)(ii) and (3)(*b*)(ii) for "1st October 2007" substitute "31st March 2008".

Modification—This regulation modified as follows by CTA 2009 Sch 2 para 131(1), (2), (9). In para (1), after "section 47", words "of the Finance Act 2006" inserted, (and corresponding change in the heading for reg 7).

8 Modification of section 51 (supplementary provisions)

(1) In the substitution made by section 51(1) (supplementary provisions) for paragraph 80 (exclusion of films and sound recordings) of Schedule 29 to the Finance Act 2002 (corporation tax: gains and losses from intangible fixed assets) modify substituted paragraph 80A(2) as follows.

(2) In paragraphs (*a*) and (*b*) for the words "that commenced principal photography before 1st January 2007" substitute "to which Schedule 4 of the Finance Act 2006 does not apply".

(3) In paragraph (*b*) for "1st October 2007" substitute "31st March 2008".

Modification—This regulation modified as follows by CTA 2009 Sch 2 para 131(1), (2), (10). Reg 8 substituted as follows—

> **"8 Modification of section 812 of the Corporation Tax Act 2009 (intangible fixed assets: films)**
>
> In section 812(1) of the Corporation Tax Act 2009—
>
> (*a*) in paragraph (*a*) for "that began principal photography before 1st January 2007" substitute "to which Chapter 2 of Part 15 of the Corporation Tax Act 2009 does not apply", and
>
> (*b*) in paragraph (*b*) for "1st October 2007" substitute "31st March 2008".".

9 Modification of Schedule 4 (taxation of activities of film production company)

In Schedule 4 (taxation of activities of film production company), in paragraph 1 (films to which this Schedule applies) for the words "commence principal photography on or after 1st January 2007" substitute "are certified by the Secretary of State under Schedule 1 to the Films Act 1985 as British films for the purposes of film tax relief and are intended for theatrical release at the time principal photography commences".

Modification—This regulation modified as follows by CTA 2009 Sch 2 para 131(1), (2), (11). Reg 9 substituted as follows—

> **"9 Modification of section 1188 of the Corporation Tax Act 2009 (taxation of activities of film production company)**
>
> In section 1188(1) of the Corporation Tax Act 2009 (taxation of activities of film production company) after "a film" insert "if the film—
>
> (*a*) is certified by the Secretary of State under Schedule 1 to the Films Act 1985 as a British film for the purposes of film tax relief, and
>
> (*b*) is intended for theatrical release at the time principal photography commences".

10 Modifications of Schedule 5 (film tax relief: further provisions)

(1) Modify Schedule 5 (film tax relief: further provisions) as follows.

(2) In paragraph 1(1) omit the words from ", and" to the end.

(3) After paragraph 15 insert—

> **"15A** After section 6 of that Act insert—
>
> "6A Where the Secretary of State refuses an application for interim or final certification of a film as a British film for the purposes of film tax relief, Schedule 1A to this Act has effect with respect to the certification by the Secretary of State of a master negative, tape or disc of a film as a qualifying film, tape or disc for the purposes of section 40D of the Finance (No 2) Act 1992 (election for sections 40A and 40B not to apply) or Chapter 9 of Part 2 of the Income Tax (Trading and Other Income) Act 2005 (election relating to tax treatment of films expenditure).".".

(4) In paragraph 17, in the substituted paragraph 1 of Schedule 1 to the Films Act 1985 after "Schedule" insert "and Schedule 1A" in each place.

(5) In paragraph 19, in the substituted paragraph 3 of Schedule 1 to the Films Act 1985, in subparagraph (4) after "otherwise" insert "and except in relation to sections 46 and 47 (films: withdrawal of existing reliefs) of, and paragraph 1 of Schedule 4 (taxation of activities of film production company) to, the Finance Act 2006".

(6) After paragraph 20 insert—

"20A For paragraphs 4A to 4C of that Schedule substitute—

"4A—(1) The cultural test for a film other than a documentary (see paragraph 4B) or an animation (see paragraph 4C) is as follows.

(2) Subject to sub-paragraph (7), a film passes the cultural test if it is awarded at least 16 points in total.

(3) Up to 16 points shall be awarded in respect of the content of the film as follows—

(*a*) up to 4 points depending on the percentage of the film that is set in the United Kingdom as follows—

(i) 4 points for at least 75%;

(ii) 3 points for at least 66%;

(iii) 2 points for at least 50%;

(iv) 1 point for at least 25%;

(*b*) up to 4 points depending on the number of the characters depicted in the film that are British as follows—

(i) if there are more than three characters depicted in the film, 4 points if two or three of the three lead characters are British or, if only one of the three lead characters is British, 2 points if he is the first or second lead, 1 point if he is the third lead;

(ii) if there are only three characters depicted in the film, 4 points if two or three of them are British or, if only one of them is British, 2 points if he is the first or second lead, 1 point if he is the third lead;

(iii) if there are only two characters depicted in the film, 4 points if both of them are British, 2 points if one of them is;

(iv) if there is only one character depicted in the film, 4 points if he is British;

(*c*) 4 points if the film depicts a British story;

(*d*) up to 4 points depending on the percentage of the original dialogue that is recorded in the English language or in a recognised regional or minority language as follows—

(i) 4 points for at least 75%;

(ii) 3 points for at least 66%;

(iii) 2 points for at least 50%;

(iv) 1 point for at least 25%.

(4) Up to 4 points may be awarded in respect of the contribution of the film to the promotion, development and enhancement of British culture.

(5) Up to 3 points shall be awarded in respect of work carried out in the making of the film as follows—

(*a*) 2 points if at least 50% of the work carried out on any of the following is carried out in the United Kingdom—

(i) principal photography;

(ii) visual effects;

(iii) special effects;

(*b*) 1 point if at least 50% of the work carried out on any of the following is carried out in the United Kingdom—

(i) performing and recording the music score created for the film;

(ii) audio post production;

(iii) picture post production.

(6) Up to 8 points shall be awarded in respect of the personnel involved in the making of the film as follows—

(*a*) 1 point if the director (or, if there is more than one, the lead director) is a qualifying person;

(*b*) 1 point if at least one of the scriptwriters (or, if there are more than three, of the three lead scriptwriters) is a qualifying person;

(*c*) 1 point if at least one of the producers (or, if there are more than three, of the three lead producers) is a qualifying person;

(*d*) 1 point if the composer (or, if there is more than one, the lead composer) is a qualifying person;
(*e*) 1 point if at least one of the actors (or, if there are more than three, of the three lead actors) is a qualifying person;
(*f*) 1 point if at least 50% of the cast are qualifying persons;
(*g*) 1 point if at least one of the heads of department is a qualifying person;
(*h*) 1 point if at least 50% of the production crew are qualifying persons.

(7) A film that is awarded all the points available under sub-paragraphs (3)(*d*) (language), (5) (where work carried out) and (6) (personnel) does not pass the cultural test unless—
(*a*) it is awarded at least 2 points under sub-paragraph (3)(*a*) (setting),
(*b*) it is awarded at least 2 points under sub-paragraph (3)(*b*) (characters), or
(*c*) it is awarded 4 points under sub-paragraph (3)(*c*) (story).

4B—(1) The cultural test for a documentary is as follows.

(2) Subject to sub-paragraph (7), a film passes the cultural test if it is awarded at least 16 points in total.

(3) Up to 16 points shall be awarded in respect of the content of the film as follows—
(*a*) up to 4 points depending on the percentage of the film that is set in the United Kingdom as follows—
(i) 4 points for at least 75%;
(ii) 3 points for at least 66%;
(iii) 2 points for at least 50%;
(iv) 1 point for at least 25%;
(*b*) up to 4 points depending on the number of the characters depicted in the film that are British as follows—
(i) if there are more than three characters depicted in the film, 4 points if two or three of the three lead characters are British or, if only one of the three lead characters is British, 2 points if he is the first or second lead, 1 point if he is the third lead;
(ii) if there are only three characters depicted in the film, 4 points if two or three of them are British or, if only one of them is British, 2 points if he is the first or second lead, 1 point if he is the third lead;
(iii) if there are only two characters depicted in the film, 4 points if both of them are British, 2 points if one of them is;
(iv) if there is only one character depicted in the film, 4 points if he is British;
(*c*) 4 points if the film depicts a British story;
(*d*) up to 4 points depending on the percentage of the original dialogue that is recorded in the English language or in a recognised regional or minority language as follows—
(i) 4 points for at least 75%;
(ii) 3 points for at least 66%;
(iii) 2 points for at least 50%;
(iv) 1 point for at least 25%.

(4) Up to 4 points may be awarded in respect of the contribution of the film to the promotion, development and enhancement of British culture.

(5) Up to 3 points shall be awarded in respect of work carried out in the making of the film as follows—
(*a*) 2 points if at least 50% of the work carried out on any of the following is carried out in the United Kingdom—
(i) shooting;
(ii) visual effects;
(iii) research and development;
(iv) special effects;
(*b*) 1 point if at least 50% of the work carried out on any of the following is carried out in the United Kingdom—
(i) performing and recording the music score created for the film;
(ii) audio post production;
(iii) picture post production.

(6) Up to 8 points shall be awarded in respect of the personnel involved in the making of the film as follows—

(*a*) 1 point if the director (or, if there is more than one, the lead director) is a qualifying person;
(*b*) 1 point if at least one of the scriptwriters (or, if there are more than three, of the three lead scriptwriters) is a qualifying person;
(*c*) 1 point if at least one of the producers (or, if there are more than three, of the three lead producers) is a qualifying person;
(*d*) 1 point if the composer (or, if there is more than one, the lead composer) is a qualifying person;
(*e*) 1 point if at least one of the participants (or, if there are more than three, of the three lead participants) is a qualifying person;
(*f*) 1 point if at least 50% of the participants are qualifying persons;
(*g*) 1 point if at least one of the heads of department is a qualifying person;
(*h*) 1 point if at least 50% of the production crew are qualifying persons.

(7) A film that is awarded all the points available under sub-paragraphs (3)(*d*) (language), (5) (where work carried out) and (6) (personnel) does not pass the cultural test unless—
(*a*) it is awarded at least 2 points under sub-paragraph (3)(*a*) (setting),
(*b*) it is awarded at least 2 points under sub-paragraph (3)(*b*) (characters), or
(*c*) it is awarded 4 points under sub-paragraph (3)(*c*) (story).

4C—(1) The cultural test for an animation is as follows.
(2) Subject to sub-paragraph (7), a film passes the cultural test if it is awarded at least 16 points in total.
(3) Up to 16 points shall be awarded in respect of the content of the film as follows—
(*a*) up to 4 points depending on the percentage of the film that is set in the United Kingdom as follows—
(i) 4 points for at least 75%;
(ii) 3 points for at least 66%;
(iii) 2 points for at least 50%;
(iv) 1 point for at least 25%;
(*b*) up to 4 points depending on the number of the characters depicted in the film that are British as follows—
(i) if there are more than three characters depicted in the film, 4 points if two or three of the three lead characters are British or, if only one of the three lead characters is British, 2 points if he is the first or second lead, 1 point if he is the third lead;
(ii) if there are only three characters depicted in the film, 4 points of two or three of them are British or, if only one of them is British, 2 points if he is the first or second lead, 1 point if he is the third lead;
(iii) if there are only two characters depicted in the film, 4 points both of them are British, 2 points if one of them is;
(iv) if there is only one character depicted in the film, 4 points if he is British;
(*c*) 4 points if the film depicts a British story;
(*d*) up to 4 points depending on the percentage of the original dialogue that is recorded in the English language or in a recognised regional or minority language as follows—
(i) 4 points for at least 75%;
(ii) 3 points for at least 66%;
(iii) 2 points for at least 50%;
(iv) 1 point for at least 25%.

(4) Up to 4 points may be awarded in respect of the contribution of the film to the promotion, development and enhancement of British culture.
(5) Up to 3 points shall be awarded in respect of work carried out in the making of the film as follows—
(*a*) 2 points if at least 50% of the work carried out on any of the following is carried out in the United Kingdom—
(i) shooting;
(ii) visual design;
(iii) layout and storyboarding;
(iv) visual effects;
(v) special effects;

(*b*) 1 point if at least 50% of the work carried out on any of the following is carried out in the United Kingdom—
(i) performing and recording the music score created for the film;
(ii) voice recording;
(iii) audio post production;
(iv) picture post production.

(6) Up to 8 points shall be awarded in respect of the personnel involved in the making of the film as follows—

(*a*) 1 point if the director (or, if there is more than one, the lead director) is a qualifying person;
(*b*) 1 point if at least one of the scriptwriters (or, if there are more than three, of the three lead scriptwriters) is a qualifying person;
(*c*) 1 point if at least one of the producers (or, if there are more than three, of the three lead producers) is a qualifying person;
(*d*) 1 point if the composer (or, if there is more than one, the lead composer) is a qualifying person;
(*e*) 1 point if at least one of the actors (or, if there are more than three, of the three lead actors) is a qualifying person;
(*f*) 1 point if at least 50% of the cast are qualifying persons;
(*g*) 1 point if at least one of the heads of department is a qualifying person;
(*h*) 1 point if at least 50% of the production crew are qualifying persons.

(7) A film that is awarded all the points available under sub-paragraphs (3)(*d*) (language), (5) (where work carried out) and (6) (personnel) does not pass the cultural test unless—

(*a*) it is awarded at least 2 points under sub-paragraph (3)(*a*) (setting),
(*b*) it is awarded at least 2 points under sub-paragraph (3)(*b*) (characters), or
(*c*) it is awarded 4 points under sub-paragraph (3)(*c*) (story).".

20B In paragraph 4D of that Schedule—

(*a*) in sub-paragraph (4)(*a*) for "paragraph 4A(4)(*a*)" substitute "paragraph 4A(5)(*a*)(i)";
(*b*) for sub-paragraph (4)(*b*) substitute—
"(*b*) for the purposes of the rest of paragraph 4A(5) and paragraphs 4B(5) and 4C(5) (other matters), by reference to the amount of expenditure on the work.";
(*c*) in sub-paragraph (5) for "paragraph 4A(4), 4B(4) or 4C(4) (points awarded in respect of the making of the film)" substitute "paragraph 4A(5), 4B(5) or 4C(5) (where work carried out)".".

(7) After paragraph 25 insert—

"PART 2A

CERTIFICATION OF MASTER NEGATIVE, TAPE OR DISC OF A FILM AS A QUALIFYING FILM, TAPE OR DISC FOR THE PURPOSES OF SECTION 40D OF THE FINANCE (NO 2) ACT 1992 OR CHAPTER 9 OF PART 2 OF ITTOIA 2005

25A After Schedule 1 to the Films Act 1985 insert—

"SCHEDULE 1A

CERTIFICATION OF MASTER NEGATIVE, TAPE OR DISC OF A FILM AS A QUALIFYING FILM, TAPE OR DISC FOR THE PURPOSES OF SECTION 40D OF THE FINANCE (NO 2) ACT 1992 OR CHAPTER 9 OF PART 2 OF THE INCOME TAX (TRADING AND OTHER INCOME) ACT 2005

Section 6A

Preliminary

1— (1) In this Schedule—

"maker", in relation to a film, means the person by whom the arrangements necessary for the making of the film are undertaken;

"master disc", in relation to a film, means the original master film disc or the original master audio disc of the film;

"master negative", in relation to a film, means the original master negative of the film and its soundtrack (if any);

"master tape", in relation to a film, means the original master film tape or the original master audio tape of the film;

(2) Any reference in this Schedule to a master negative, tape or disc certified under paragraph 3(1) or to a certificate issued under that provision includes a reference to a master negative, tape or disc certified in pursuance of section 72(7)(*b*) of the Finance Act 1982 as originally enacted or to a certificate issued in pursuance of that provision.

Applications for certification of master negatives, tapes and discs

2— (1) An application for the certification by the Secretary of State of a master negative, master tape or master disc of a film as a qualifying film, qualifying tape or qualifying disc for the purposes of section 40D of the Finance (No 2) Act 1992, or Chapter 9 of Part 2 of the Income Tax (Trading and Other Income) Act 2005, may be made by any person who has incurred expenditure on the production or acquisition of that negative, tape, or disc.

(2) In sub-paragraph (1) the reference to the acquisition of a master negative, tape or disc includes a reference to the acquisition of any description of rights in it.

(3) On an application under this paragraph for the certification of a master negative, tape or disc the applicant shall—

(*a*) produce to the Secretary of State such books and other documents relating to it; and

(*b*) furnish to the Secretary of State such other information with respect to it,

as the Secretary of State may require for the purpose of determining the application.

(4) Any information furnished for the purposes of sub-paragraph (3) shall, if the Secretary of State so directs, be accompanied by a statutory declaration as to the truth of the information made by the person furnishing it.

Certification by Secretary of State of master negatives, tapes and discs

3— (1) If the Secretary of State is satisfied that a master negative, tape or disc with respect to which an application is made under paragraph 2 is a master negative, tape or disc of a film which, in his opinion, is a British film for the purposes of this Schedule, he shall certify that negative, tape or disc as a qualifying film, qualifying tape or qualifying disc for the purposes of section 40D of the Finance (No 2) Act 1992 or, as the case may be, Chapter 9 of Part 2 of the Income Tax (Trading and Other Income) Act 2005.

(2) If the Secretary of State is for any reason not satisfied as mentioned in sub-paragraph (1) he shall refuse the application.

(3) If it appears to the Secretary of State that any negative, tape or disc certified by him under sub-paragraph (1) ought for any reason not to have been so certified he shall revoke its certification.

(4) Where an application is made under paragraph 2 in relation to a negative, tape or disc of a film which has already been certified by the Secretary of State under sub-paragraph (1) on a prior application, the Secretary of State may issue the applicant with a duplicate or copy of the certificate issued on that prior application.

British films for purposes of the Schedule

4— (1) A film is a British film for the purposes of this Schedule if it passes the relevant cultural test (see paragraph 4A, 4B or 4C).

(2) For the purposes of this paragraph and paragraphs 4A to 4D a state shall be treated as if it were a member State if—

(*a*) it is a party to an agreement under Article 310 of the Treaty establishing the European Community, and

(*b*) the agreement requires a maker of a film who is ordinarily resident or registered in that state to be treated for the purposes of this Schedule in the same way as a maker of a film who is ordinarily resident or registered in a member State.

(3) This paragraph has effect subject to paragraph 5 (excluded films).

4A—(1) The cultural test for a film other than a documentary (see paragraph 4B) or an animation (see paragraph 4C) is as follows.

(2) A film passes the cultural test if it is awarded at least 16 points in total.

(3) Up to 4 points shall be awarded in respect of the content of the film as follows—

- (*a*) 1 point if at least 50% of the film is set in the United Kingdom;
- (*b*) 1 point if at least one of the three principal characters depicted in the film (or, if there are three or fewer characters depicted in the film, any of them) is a British character;
- (*c*) 1 point if the film depicts a British story;
- (*d*) 1 point if at least 50% of the original dialogue is recorded in the English language or in a recognised regional or minority language.

(4) Up to 15 points shall be awarded in respect of work carried out in the making of the film as follows—

- (*a*) up to 6 points depending on the percentage of principal photography that is carried out in the United Kingdom as follows—
  - (i) 6 points for 75%,
  - (ii) 5 points for 62.5%,
  - (iii) 4 points for 50%,
  - (iv) 3 points for 37.5%,
  - (v) 2 points for 25%,
  - (vi) 1 point for 10%;
- (*b*) up to 4 points depending on the percentage of the work on visual effects that is carried out in the United Kingdom as follows—
  - (i) 4 points for 75%,
  - (ii) 3 points for 50%,
  - (iii) 2 points for 25%,
  - (iv) 1 point for 10%;
- (*c*) 1 point if at least 75% of the work on special effects is carried out in the United Kingdom;
- (*d*) up to 2 points depending on the percentage of the work on performing and recording the original music score created for the film that is carried out in the United Kingdom as follows—
  - (i) 2 points for 75%,
  - (ii) 1 point for 50%;
- (*e*) 1 point if at least 75% of the work on audio post production is carried out in the United Kingdom;
- (*f*) 1 point if at least 75% of the work on image processing is carried out in the United Kingdom.

(5) Up to 13 points shall be awarded in respect of the personnel involved in the making of the film as follows—

- (*a*) 2 points if the director (or, if there is more than one, the lead director) is a qualifying person;
- (*b*) up to 2 points depending on the number of the scriptwriters who are qualifying persons as follows—
  - (i) if there is only one scriptwriter, 2 points if he is a qualifying person,
  - (ii) if there are only two scriptwriters, 2 points if both of them are qualifying persons, 1 point if one of them is,
  - (iii) if there are only three scriptwriters, 2 points if two or more of them are qualifying persons, 1 point if one of them is,
  - (iv) if there are more than three scriptwriters, 2 points if two or more of the three lead scriptwriters are qualifying persons, 1 point if one of the three lead scriptwriters is a qualifying person;
- (*c*) 1 point if at least one of the producers (or, if there are more than three, of the three lead producers) is a qualifying person;
- (*d*) 1 point if the composer (or, if there is more than one, the lead composer) is a qualifying person;
- (*e*) up to 2 points depending on the number of the actors who are qualifying persons as follows—

(i) if there are more than three actors, 2 points if two or more of the three lead actors are qualifying persons, 1 point if one of the three lead actors is a qualifying person,

(ii) if there are only three actors, 2 points if two or more of them are qualifying persons, 1 point if one of them is,

(iii) if there are only two actors, 2 points if both of them are qualifying persons, 1 point if one of them is,

(iv) if there is only one actor, 2 points if he is a qualifying person;

(*f*) 1 point if at least 50% of the cast are qualifying persons;

(*g*) up to 3 points depending on the number of the heads of department who are qualifying persons as follows—

(i) 3 points for five or more,

(ii) 2 points for three or four,

(iii) 1 point for one or two;

(*h*) 1 point if at least 50% of the production crew are qualifying persons.

4B—(1) The cultural test for a documentary is as follows.

(2) A film passes the cultural test if it is awarded at least 16 points in total.

(3) Up to 4 points shall be awarded in respect of the content of the film as follows—

(*a*) 1 point if at least 50% of the film is set in the United Kingdom;

(*b*) 1 point if at least one of the three principal characters depicted in the film (or, if there are three or fewer characters depicted in the film, any of them) is a British character;

(*c*) 1 point if the film depicts a British story;

(*d*) 1 point if at least 50% of the original dialogue is recorded in the English language or in a recognised regional or minority language.

(4) Up to 15 points shall be awarded in respect of work carried out in the making of the film as follows—

(*a*) up to 6 points depending on the percentage of the work on shooting and visual effects that is carried out in the United Kingdom as follows—

(i) 6 points for 75%,

(ii) 5 points for 62.5%,

(iii) 4 points for 50%,

(iv) 3 points for 37.5%,

(v) 2 points for 25%,

(vi) 1 point for 10%;

(*b*) up to 4 points depending on the percentage of the work on research and development that is carried out in the United Kingdom as follows—

(i) 4 points for 75%,

(ii) 3 points for 50%,

(iii) 2 points for 25%,

(iv) 1 point for 10%;

(*c*) 1 point if at least 75% of the work on special effects is carried out in the United Kingdom;

(*d*) up to 2 points depending on the percentage of the work on performing and recording the original music score created for the film that is carried out in the United Kingdom as follows—

(i) 2 points for 75%,

(ii) 1 point for 50%;

(*e*) 1 point if at least 75% of the work on audio post production is carried out in the United Kingdom;

(*f*) 1 point if at least 75% of the work on image processing is carried out in the United Kingdom.

(5) Up to 13 points shall be awarded in respect of the personnel involved in the making of the film as follows—

(*a*) 2 points if the director (or, if there is more than one, the lead director) is a qualifying person;

(*b*) up to 2 points depending on the number of the scriptwriters who are qualifying persons as follows—

(i) if there is only one scriptwriter, 2 points if he is a qualifying person,

(ii) if there are only two scriptwriters, 2 points if both of them are qualifying persons, 1 point if one of them is,

(iii) if there are only three scriptwriters, 2 points if two or more of them are qualifying persons, 1 point if one of them is,

(iv) if there are more than three scriptwriters, 2 points if two or more of the three lead scriptwriters are qualifying persons, 1 point if one of the three lead scriptwriters is a qualifying person;

(*c*) 1 point if at least one of the producers (or, if there are more than three, of the three lead producers) is a qualifying person;

(*d*) 1 point if the composer (or, if there is more than one, the lead composer) is a qualifying person;

(*e*) up to 2 points depending on the number of the participants who are qualifying persons as follows—

(i) if there are more than three participants, 2 points if two or more of the three lead participants are qualifying persons, 1 point if one of the three lead participants is a qualifying person,

(ii) if there are only three participants, 2 points if two or more of them are qualifying persons, 1 point if one of them is,

(iii) if there are only two participants, 2 points if both of them are qualifying persons, 1 point if one of them is,

(iv) if there is only one participant, 2 points if he is a qualifying person;

(*f*) 1 point if at least 50% of all of the participants are qualifying persons;

(*g*) up to 3 points depending on the number of the heads of department who are qualifying persons as follows—

(i) 3 points for four,

(ii) 2 points for three,

(iii) 1 point for one or two;

(*h*) 1 point if at least 50% of the production crew are qualifying persons.

4C—(1) The cultural test for an animation is as follows.

(2) A film passes the cultural test if it is awarded at least 16 points in total.

(3) Up to 4 points shall be awarded in respect of the content of the film as follows—

(*a*) 1 point if at least 50% of the film is set in the United Kingdom;

(*b*) 1 point if at least one of the three principal characters depicted in the film (or, if there are three or fewer characters depicted in the film, any of them) is a British character;

(*c*) 1 point if the film depicts a British story;

(*d*) 1 point if at least 50% of the original dialogue is recorded in the English language or in a recognised regional or minority language.

(4) Up to 15 points shall be awarded in respect of work carried out in the making of the film as follows—

(*a*) up to 6 points depending on the percentage of the work on shooting, visual design, layout and storyboarding that is carried out in the United Kingdom as follows—

(i) 6 points for 75%,

(ii) 5 points for 62.5%,

(iii) 4 points for 50%,

(iv) 3 points for 37.5%,

(v) 2 points for 25%,

(vi) 1 point for 10%;

(*b*) up to 4 points depending on the percentage of the work on visual effects that is carried out in the United Kingdom as follows—

(i) 4 points for 75%,

(ii) 3 points for 50%,

(iii) 2 points for 25%,

(iv) 1 point for 10%;

(*c*) 1 point if at least 75% of the work on special effects is carried out in the United Kingdom;

(*d*) up to 2 points depending on the percentage of the work on performing and recording the original music score created for the film that is carried out in the United Kingdom as follows—

(i) 2 points for 75%,

(ii) 1 point for 50%;

(*e*) 1 point if at least 75% of the work on voice recording and audio post production is carried out in the United Kingdom;

(*f*) 1 point if at least 75% of the work on image processing is carried out in the United Kingdom.

(5) Up to 13 points shall be awarded in respect of the personnel involved in the making of the film as follows—

(*a*) 2 points if the director (or, if there is more than one, the lead director) is a qualifying person;

(*b*) up to 2 points depending on the number of the scriptwriters who are qualifying persons as follows—

(i) if there is only one scriptwriter, 2 points if he is a qualifying person,

(ii) if there are only two scriptwriters, 2 points if both of them are qualifying persons, 1 point if one of them is,

(iii) if there are only three scriptwriters, 2 points if two or more of them are qualifying persons, 1 point if one of them is,

(iv) if there are more than three scriptwriters, 2 points if two or more of the three lead scriptwriters are qualifying persons, 1 point if one of the three lead scriptwriters is a qualifying person;

(*c*) 1 point if at least one of the producers (or, if there are more than three, of the three lead producers) is a qualifying person;

(*d*) 1 point if the composer (or, if there is more than one, the lead composer) is a qualifying person;

(*e*) up to 2 points depending on the number of the actors who are qualifying persons as follows—

(i) if there are more than three actors, 2 points if two or more of the three lead actors are qualifying persons, 1 point if one of the three lead actors is a qualifying person,

(ii) if there are only three actors, 2 points if two or more of them are qualifying persons, 1 point if one of them is,

(iii) if there are only two actors, 2 points if both of them are qualifying persons, 1 point if one of them is,

(iv) if there is only one actor, 2 points if he is a qualifying person;

(*f*) 1 point if at least 50% of the cast are qualifying persons;

(*g*) up to 3 points depending on the number of the heads of department who are qualifying persons as follows—

(i) 3 points for five or more,

(ii) 2 points for three or four,

(iii) 1 point for one or two;

(*h*) 1 point if at least 50% of the production crew are qualifying persons.

4D—(1) In paragraphs 4A to 4C—

"cast" means all the actors and performers but not the extras who appear in a film;

"heads of department" has the meaning given by sub-paragraph (2);

"participant" means a presenter, narrator, subject or other person who participates and appears in a documentary;

"production crew" means all the persons directly involved in the production of a film who do not appear in the film;

"qualifying person" means a citizen of, or a person ordinarily resident in, a member State;

"recognised regional or minority language" means Welsh, Scottish-Gaelic, Irish, Scots, Ulster Scots or Cornish;

"special effects" means artificial techniques or processes, which are not visual effects, used to create an illusion in a film;

"visual effects" means digital alterations to a film's images.

(2) "Heads of department" means—

(*a*) in paragraph 4A, the lead cinematographer, the lead production designer, the lead costume designer, the lead editor, the lead sound designer, the lead visual effects supervisor and the lead hair and makeup supervisor;

(*b*) in paragraph 4B, the lead cameraman, the lead sound recordist, the lead editor and the lead researcher;

(*c*) in paragraph 4C, the lead layout supervisor, the lead production designer, the lead character designer, the lead editor, the lead sound designer, the lead visual effects supervisor and the lead modelling supervisor.

(3) For the purposes of paragraphs 4A to 4C—

(*a*) a film is set in the United Kingdom if it is set in a country which is now part of the United Kingdom; and

(*b*) a film depicts a British story if the subject matter of the film or the underlying material on which the film is based is British.

(4) The amount of work that is carried out in the United Kingdom or elsewhere shall be determined—

(*a*) for the purposes of paragraph 4A(4)(*a*) (principal photography), by reference to the number of days spent on the work;

(*b*) for the purposes of paragraphs 4A(4)(*b*) to (*f*), 4B(4)(*a*) to (*f*) and 4C(4)(*a*) to (*f*) (other matters), by reference to the amount of expenditure on the work..

(5) No points shall be awarded under any provision of paragraph 4A(4), 4B(4) or 4C(4) (points awarded in respect of the making of the film) in respect of work the expenditure on which is, in the opinion of the Secretary of State, insignificant in relation to the expenditure on all the work carried out in the making of the film.

Excluded films

5— (1) Subject to sub-paragraph (2), a film is not a British film for the purposes of this Schedule by virtue of paragraph 4(1) if parts of the film are derived from—

(*a*) any film of which the master negative, tape or disc is certified under paragraph 3(1), or

(*b*) any film not made by the same maker as the first-mentioned film, and the playing time of those parts exceeds 10 per cent of the total playing time of the film.

(2) The Secretary of State may direct that sub-paragraph (1) shall not apply in relation to a film if in his opinion—

(*a*) it is a documentary; and

(*b*) its subject matter makes it appropriate for sub-paragraph (1) not to be applied.

Determination of disputes

6— (1) Any person who is aggrieved by any decision of the Secretary of State to refuse an application under paragraph 2 or to revoke any certification under paragraph 3(1) may, subject to rules of court, apply to the High Court, and the decision of that Court shall be final.

(2) In relation to any person whose principal place of business is in Scotland, sub-paragraph (1) shall have effect as if for any reference to the High Court there were substituted a reference to the Court of Session.

Application for certification

7— (1) The Films (Certification) Regulations 1985 shall apply to an application for certification under paragraph 2 as if a reference to Schedule 1 in those Regulations were a reference to this Schedule.

(2) For the purposes of subparagraph (1) the application under paragraph 2 shall be treated as an application to be determined by the Secretary of State in accordance with Schedule 1 as in force immediately before the commencement of the Films (Certification) Regulations 2006".".

Modification—This regulation modified as follows by CTA 2009 Sch 2 para 131(1), (2), (12)–(14). In para (1), after "Schedule 5" words "to the Finance Act 2006" inserted (and corresponding change in the heading for regulation 10), para (2) revoked, and in para (5), words "of the Finance Act 2006 (films: withdrawal of existing reliefs) and section 1188(1) of the Corporation Tax Act 2009 (taxation of activities of film production company)" substituted for words after "sections 46 and 47".

Modification of other enactments

11 Modification of the Finance (No 2) Act 1992

(1) Modify the Finance (No 2) Act 1992 as follows.

(2) In section 40D (election for sections 40A and 40B not to apply), in subsection (2)(*b*)—

(*a*) for "Schedule 1" substitute "Schedule 1A"; and

(*b*) at the end insert "or certified by the Secretary of State under paragraph 3 of Schedule 1 to that Act as a British film for the purposes of film tax relief".

(3) In section 43 (interpretation of sections 41 and 42), in subsection (1), in the definitions of "qualifying disc", "qualifying film" and "qualifying tape"—

(*a*) for "Schedule 1" substitute "Schedule 1A"; and

(*b*) at the end insert "or certified by the Secretary of State under paragraph 3 of Schedule 1 to that Act as a British film for the purposes of film tax relief".

12 Modification of ITTOIA 2005

In section 132 (meaning of "original master version" and "certified master version") of ITTOIA 2005, in subsection (3)—

(*a*) for "Schedule 1" substitute "Schedule 1A"; and

(*b*) at the end insert "or certified by the Secretary of State under paragraph 3 of Schedule 1 to that Act as a British film for the purposes of film tax relief".

Consequential provision

13 Returns, amendments to returns and assessments

(1) Where the provisions of Chapter 3 of Part 3, of the enactments amended by that Chapter and the Corporation Tax Acts apply in accordance with these Regulations, returns must be made or amended, and assessments may be made in relation to past accounting periods or tax years (whether before or after the commencement of that Chapter) in accordance with those provisions as modified by these Regulations.

(2) Any return, amendment or assessment necessary to give effect to paragraph (1) may be made notwithstanding any limitation on the time within which a return, amendment or assessment may normally be made.

Modification—This regulation modified as follows by CTA 2009 Sch 2 para 131(1), (2), (15). In para (1), words "Part 15 or section 812 of the Corporation Tax Act 2009, of Chapter 3 of Part 3 of the Finance Act 2006" substituted for words "Chapter 3 of Part 3", and words "whenever beginning" substituted for words "whether before or after the commencement of that Chapter".

2007/2126

INTERNATIONAL MUTUAL ADMINISTRATIVE ASSISTANCE IN TAX MATTERS ORDER 2007

Made . . . . *25 July 2007*

A draft of this Order was laid before the House of Commons in accordance with section 173(7) of the Finance Act 2006 and approved by a resolution of that House.

Accordingly, Her Majesty, in exercise of the powers conferred upon Her by section 173(1) to (3) of the Finance Act 2006, by and with the advice of Her Privy Council, orders as follows—

Commentary—*Simon's Taxes* **A2.104, E6.455**.

1 Citation

This Order may be cited as the International Mutual Administrative Assistance in Tax Matters Order 2007.

2 Mutual administrative assistance arrangements to have effect

It is declared that—

(*a*) arrangements relating to international tax enforcement that fall within the joint Council of Europe/Organisation for Economic Co-operation and Development Convention on Mutual Administrative Assistance in Tax Matters, signed on behalf of the United Kingdom on 24 May 2007, have been made in relation to the other signatory territories, and

(*b*) it is expedient that those arrangements have effect.

2007/2145

INSURANCE COMPANIES (TAX EXEMPT BUSINESS) REGULATIONS 2007

Made by the Treasury under TA 1988 ss 460(15) and (16), 461(12) and (13) and 461B(8) and (9)

Made . . . . *23 July 2007*
Laid before the House of Commons . . . . *24 July 2007*
Coming into force . . . . *14 August 2007*

Revocation—These Regulations revoked by the Friendly Societies (Modifications of the Tax Acts) Regulations, SI 2012/3008 reg 16, Schedule, with effect in relation to accounting periods beginning on or after 1 January 2013.

1 Citation, commencement and effect

(1) These Regulations may be cited as the Insurance Companies (Tax Exempt Business) Regulations 2007 and shall come into force on 14th August 2007.

(2) Subject to paragraph (3), these Regulations have effect for periods of account ending on or after the date on which these Regulations come into force.

(3) Where any part of a company's business is exempt from corporation tax by virtue of section 460(11), 461(4) or 461B(5) of the Taxes Act 1988, these Regulations have effect for periods of account beginning on or after 1st January 2007 (whenever ending).

2 Interpretation

In these Regulations—

"the Taxes Act 1988" means the Income and Corporation Taxes Act 1988;

"tax exempt business" means business which is exempt from corporation tax by virtue of any of the following provisions of the Taxes Act 1988—

(*a*) section 460(11) or (12);

(*b*) section 461(4) or (4A); and

(*c*) section 461B(5) or (6A).

3 Modifications of the Taxes Act 1988

Where any part of the business of a company is tax exempt business, the Taxes Act 1988 has effect subject to the following modifications.

4 Modification of section 431

(1) Section 431 (interpretative provisions relating to insurance companies) is modified as follows.

(2) In subsection (2), insert at the appropriate places—

""tax exempt life assurance business" has the meaning given by section 431FA;", and

""tax exempt other business" has the meaning given by section 431FB;".

5 Insertion of sections 431FA and 431FB

After section 431F (meaning of "basic life assurance and general annuity business") insert—

"431FA Meaning of "tax exempt life assurance business"

(1) In this Chapter "tax exempt life assurance business" means business which is exempt from corporation tax by virtue of section 460(11) or (12).

(2) For the purposes of this Chapter, tax exempt life assurance business shall be treated as not being life assurance business.

431FB Meaning of "tax exempt other business"

(1) In this Chapter "tax exempt other business" means business which is exempt from corporation tax by virtue of section 461(4) or (4A) or 461B(5) or (6A).

(2) For the purposes of this Chapter, tax exempt other business shall be treated as being neither PHI business nor general insurance business."

6 Modifications of section 431H

(1) Section 431H (company carrying on life assurance business and other insurance business) is modified as follows.

(2) For subsection (1) substitute—

"(1) This section applies in relation to an insurance company which carries on two or more of the following—

(*a*) life assurance business,

(*b*) tax exempt life assurance business,

(*c*) tax exempt other business, and

(*d*) insurance business of any other kind."

(3) In subsection (2)—

(*a*) omit the word "and" immediately following paragraph (*a*),

(*b*) after paragraph (*a*) insert—

"(*aa*) tax exempt life assurance business,

(*ab*) tax exempt other business, and", and

(*c*) in paragraph (*b*), for "the" substitute "any".

7 Modifications of section 432A

(1) Section 432A (apportionment of income and gains) is modified as follows.

(2) In subsection (2)—

(*a*) omit the word "and" immediately following paragraph (*b*), and

(*b*) for paragraph (*c*) substitute—

"(*c*) PHI business,

(*d*) tax exempt life assurance business, and

(*e*) tax exempt other business."

(3) In subsection (6)—

(*a*) in the fraction, for the denominator "*A* + *B* + *C*" substitute "*A* + *B* + *C* + *D* + *E*",

(*b*) omit the word "and" immediately following the definition of *B*, and

(*c*) after the definition of *C* insert—

"*D* is the aggregate of—

(*a*) the mean of the opening and closing liabilities of the tax exempt life assurance business (but taking that mean to be nil if it would otherwise be below nil), and

(*b*) the mean of the appropriate parts (that is, the parts relating to that category) of the opening and closing amounts of the free assets amounts,

reduced (but not below nil) by the mean of the opening and closing net values of any assets directly referable to that category; and

E is the aggregate of—

(*a*) the mean of the opening and closing liabilities of the tax exempt other business (but taking that mean to be nil if it would otherwise be below nil), and

(*b*) the mean of the appropriate parts (that is, the parts relating to that category) of the opening and closing amounts of the free assets amounts,

reduced (but not below nil) by the mean of the opening and closing net values of any assets directly referable to that category."

(4) In subsection (6A)—

(*a*) in the fraction, for the denominator "*A* + *B* + *C*" substitute "*A* + *B* + *C* + *D* + *E*", and

(*b*) for "and *C*" substitute ", *C*, *D* and *E*".

(5) In subsection (6B)—

(*a*) in the fraction, for the denominator "*A* + *B* + *C*" substitute "*A* + *B* + *C* + *D* + *E*", and

(*b*) for "and *C*" substitute ", *C*, *D* and *E*".

(6) After subsection (6B) insert—

"(6BA) For the purposes of subsection (5) above "the relevant fraction", in relation to tax exempt life assurance business, is—

$$\frac{D}{A+B+C+D+E}$$

where A, B, C, D and E have the same meaning as in subsection (6) above.

(6BB) For the purposes of subsection (5) above "the relevant fraction", in relation to tax exempt other business, is—

$$\frac{E}{A+B+C+D+E}$$

where A, B, C, D and E have the same meaning as in subsection (6) above."

(7) In subsection (6C), for "or (6B)" substitute ", (6B), (6BA) or (6BB)".

(8) In subsection (7), for "and (6B)" substitute ", (6B), (6BA) and (6BB)".

(9) In subsection (8ZA), for "and *C*" substitute ", *C*, *D* and *E*".

8 Modifications of section 432AA

(1) Section 432AA (Schedule A business or overseas property business) is modified as follows.

(2) In subsection (4)—

(*a*) omit the word "and" immediately following paragraph (*b*), and

(*b*) after paragraph (*c*) insert—

"(*d*) tax exempt life assurance business; and

(*e*) tax exempt other business."

9 Modifications of section 432C

(1) Section 432C (section 432B apportionment: non-participating funds) is modified as follows.

(2) In subsection (5), in the definition of *B*, after "PHI business" (in both places) insert ", tax exempt life assurance business or tax exempt other business".

(3) In subsection (9), in the definition of *D*—

(*a*) for "or PHI business" substitute ", PHI business, tax exempt life assurance business or tax exempt other business", and

(*b*) for "either" substitute "any".

10 Modifications of section 440

(1) Section 440 (transfers of assets etc) is modified as follows.

(2) In subsection (4)—

(*a*) after paragraph (*a*) insert—

"(*b*) assets which are linked solely to tax exempt life assurance business;", and

(*b*) in paragraph (*e*), for "either" substitute "any".

11 Modification of section 440A

(1) Section 440A (securities) is modified as follows.

(2) In subsection (2)(*a*)—

(*a*) omit the word "or" immediately following sub-paragraph (i), and

(*b*) after sub-paragraph (ii) insert—

"(iii) tax exempt life assurance business, or

(iv) tax exempt other business,".

12 Modifications of section 755A

(1) Section 755A (treatment of chargeable profits and creditable tax apportioned to company carrying on life assurance business) is modified as follows.

(2) In subsection (4), for the words from "as is referable" to the end substitute—

"as is referable to—

(*a*) gross roll-up business,

(*b*) tax exempt life assurance business, or

(*c*) tax exempt other business,

carried on by the UK company."

(3) In subsection (6)(*c*), for "gross roll-up business" substitute "a category of business specified in paragraphs (*a*) to (*c*) of subsection (4) above".

(4) In subsection (13)—

(*a*) omit the word "or" immediately following paragraph (*a*), and

(*b*) after paragraph (*ba*) insert—

"(*bb*) tax exempt life assurance business, or

(*bc*) tax exempt other business,".

13 Modification of section 212 of the Taxation of Chargeable Gains Act 1992

(1) Where any part of the business of a company is tax exempt life assurance business, section 212 of the Taxation of Chargeable Gains Act 1992 (annual deemed disposal of holdings of unit trusts) is modified as follows.

(2) In subsection (2), after "gross roll-up business" insert "or tax exempt life assurance business".

14 Modification of paragraph 3A of Schedule 11 to the Finance Act 1996

(1) Where any part of the business of a company is tax exempt business, paragraph 3A of Schedule 11 to the Finance Act 1996 (loan relationships: special provisions for insurers) is modified as follows.

(2) In sub-paragraph (5), after "(6B)" insert ", (6BA), (6BB)".

15 Modification of section 255 of the Capital Allowances Act 2001

(1) Where any part of the business of a company is tax exempt business, section 255 of the Capital Allowances Act 2001 (apportionment of allowances and charges) is modified as follows.

(2) In subsection (1), for "and PHI business" substitute ", PHI business, tax exempt life assurance business and tax exempt other business".

2007/2157

MONEY LAUNDERING REGULATIONS 2007

Made . . . . *24 July 2007*

Laid before Parliament . . . . *25 July 2007*

Coming into force . . . . *15 December 2007*

Revocation—These Regulations revoked by the Money Laundering, Terrorist Financing and Transfer of Funds (Information on the Payer) Regulations, SI 2017/692 reg 110 with effect from 26 June 2017, subject to savings in reg 110(2)–(4).

Note that these Regulations shall continue to have effect where the conduct constituting a contravention of these Regulations, or an offence under these Regulations, began before 26 June 2017 (SI 2017/692 reg 110(2)).

Commentary—*Simon's Taxes* **A7.115.**

Press releases etc—HMRC Notice 27 June 2017—Money laundering supervision: fees (see *Simon's Weekly Tax Intelligence 2017, Issue 27*).

HMRC Issue Briefing—Tackling tax avoidance. 6 September 2012 (see *Simon's Weekly Tax Intelligence 2012, Issue 36*).

The Treasury are a government department designated for the purposes of section 2(2) of the European Communities Act 1972 in relation to measures relating to preventing the use of the financial system for the purpose of money laundering;

The Treasury, in exercise of the powers conferred on them by section 2(2) of the European Communities Act 1972 and by sections 168(4)(*b*), 402(1)(*b*), 417(1) and 428(3) of the Financial Services and Markets Act 2000, make the following Regulations:

PART 1
GENERAL

1 Citation, commencement etc

(1) These Regulations may be cited as the Money Laundering Regulations 2007 and come into force on 15th December 2007.

(2) These Regulations are prescribed for the purposes of sections 168(4)(*b*) (appointment of persons to carry out investigations in particular cases) and 402(1)(*b*) (power of the Authority to institute proceedings for certain other offences) of the 2000 Act.

(3) The Money Laundering Regulations 2003 are revoked.

Revocation—These Regulations revoked by the Money Laundering, Terrorist Financing and Transfer of Funds (Information on the Payer) Regulations, SI 2017/692 reg 110 with effect from 26 June 2017, subject to savings in reg 110(2)–(4).

2 Interpretation

(1) In these Regulations—

"the 2000 Act" means the Financial Services and Markets Act 2000;

"Annex I financial institution" has the meaning given by regulation 22(1);

["auction platform" has the meaning given by regulation 3(13A);][6]

"auditor", except in regulation 17(2)(*c*) and (*d*), has the meaning given by regulation 3(4) and (5);

"authorised person" means a person who is authorised for the purposes of the 2000 Act;

"the Authority" means the Financial Services Authority;

"the banking consolidation directive" means Directive 2006/48/EC of the European Parliament and of the Council of 14th June 2006 relating to the taking up and pursuit of the business of credit institutions;

"beneficial owner" has the meaning given by regulation 6;

["bill payment service provider" means an undertaking which provides a payment service enabling the payment of utility and other household bills;][1]

"business relationship" means a business, professional or commercial relationship between a relevant person and a customer, which is expected by the relevant person, at the time when contact is established, to have an element of duration;

"cash" means notes, coins or travellers' cheques in any currency;

"casino" has the meaning given by regulation 3(13);

"the Commissioners" means the Commissioners for Her Majesty's Revenue and Customs;

"consumer credit financial institution" has the meaning given by regulation 22(1);

"credit institution" has the meaning given by regulation 3(2);

"customer due diligence measures" has the meaning given by regulation 5;

"DETI" means the Department of Enterprise, Trade and Investment in Northern Ireland;

["the electronic money directive" means Directive 2009/110/EC of the European Parliament and of the Council of 16th September 2009 on the taking up, pursuit and prudential supervision of the business of electronic money institutions;

"electronic money institution" has the meaning given by regulation 2(1) of the Electronic Money Regulations 2011;][4]

["the emission allowance auctioning regulation" means Commission Regulation (EU) No. 1031/2010 of 12 November 2010 on the timing, administration and other aspects of auctioning of greenhouse gas emission allowances pursuant to Directive 2003/87/EC of the European Parliament and of the Council establishing a scheme for greenhouse gas emission allowances trading within the Community;][6]

"estate agent" has the meaning given by regulation 3(11);

"external accountant" has the meaning given by regulation 3(7);

"financial institution" has the meaning given by regulation 3(3);

"firm" means any entity, whether or not a legal person, that is not an individual and includes a body corporate and a partnership or other unincorporated association;

"high value dealer" has the meaning given by regulation 3(12);

"the implementing measures directive" means Commission Directive 2006/70/EC of 1st August 2006 laying down implementing measures for the money laundering directive;

"independent legal professional" has the meaning given by regulation 3(9);

"insolvency practitioner", except in regulation 17(2)(*c*) and (*d*), has the meaning given by regulation 3(6);

. . . [7]

"local weights and measures authority" has the meaning given by section 69 of the Weights and Measures Act 1985 (local weights and measures authorities);

"the markets in financial instruments directive" means Directive 2004/39/EC of the European Parliament and of the Council of 12th April 2004 on markets in financial instruments;

"money laundering" means an act which falls within section 340(11) of the Proceeds of Crime Act 2002;

"the money laundering directive" means Directive 2005/60/EC of the European Parliament and of the Council of 26th October 2005 on the prevention of the use of the financial system for the purpose of money laundering and terrorist financing;

"money service business" means an undertaking which by way of business operates a currency exchange office, transmits money (or any representations of monetary value) by any means or cashes cheques which are made payable to customers;

"nominated officer" means a person who is nominated to receive disclosures under Part 7 of the Proceeds of Crime Act 2002 (money laundering) or Part 3 of the Terrorism Act 2000 (terrorist property);

"non-EEA state" means a state that is not an EEA state;

"notice" means a notice in writing;

"occasional transaction" means a transaction (carried out other than as part of a business relationship) amounting to 15,000 euro or more, whether the transaction is carried out in a single operation or several operations which appear to be linked;

"the OFT" means the Office of Fair Trading;

"ongoing monitoring" has the meaning given by regulation 8(2);

["payment services" has the meaning given by regulation 2(1) of the Payment Services Regulations 2009;][1]

"regulated market"—

(*a*) within the EEA, has the meaning given by point 14 of Article 4(1) of the markets in financial instruments directive; and

(*b*) outside the EEA, means a regulated financial market which subjects companies whose securities are admitted to trading to disclosure obligations which are contained in international standards and are equivalent to the specified disclosure obligations;

"relevant person" means a person to whom, in accordance with regulations 3 and 4, these Regulations apply;

["the Solvency 2 Directive" means Directive 2009/138/EC of the European Parliament and of the Council of 25 November 2009 on the taking-up and pursuit of the business of Insurance and Reinsurance (Solvency II);][7]

"the specified disclosure obligations" means disclosure requirements consistent with—

(*a*) Article 6(1) to (4) of Directive 2003/6/EC of the European Parliament and of the Council of 28th January 2003 on insider dealing and market manipulation;

(*b*) Articles 3, 5, 7, 8, 10, 14 and 16 of Directive 2003/71/EC of the European Parliament and of the Council of 4th November 2003 on the prospectuses to be published when securities are offered to the public or admitted to trading;

(*c*) Articles 4 to 6, 14, 16 to 19 and 30 of Directive 2004/109/EC of the European Parliament and of the Council of 15th December 2004 relating to the harmonisation of transparency requirements in relation to information about issuers whose securities are admitted to trading on a regulated market; or

(*d*) Community legislation made under the provisions mentioned in sub-paragraphs (*a*) to (*c*);

"supervisory authority" in relation to any relevant person means the supervisory authority specified for such a person by regulation 23;

"tax adviser" (except in regulation 11(3)) has the meaning given by regulation 3(8);

["telecommunication, digital and IT payment service provider" means an undertaking which provides payment services falling within paragraph 1(*g*) of Schedule 1 to the Payment Services Regulations 2009;][1]

"terrorist financing" means an offence under—

(*a*) section 15 (fund-raising), 16 (use and possession), 17 (funding arrangements), 18 (money laundering) or 63 (terrorist finance: jurisdiction) of the Terrorism Act 2000;

(*b*) paragraph 7(2) or (3) of Schedule 3 to the Anti-Terrorism, Crime and Security Act 2001 (freezing orders);

(*c*) . . .[3]

[(*d*) regulation 10 of the ISIL (Da'esh) and Al-Qaida (Asset-Freezing) Regulations 2011 (SI 2011/2742 as renamed by SI 2016/937); or][8]

[(*e*) section 11, 12, 13, 14, 15 or 18 of the Terrorist Asset-Freezing etc. Act 2010 (offences relating to the freezing of funds etc. of designated persons)][3];][2]

"trust or company service provider" has the meaning given by regulation 3(10).

(2) In these Regulations, references to amounts in euro include references to equivalent amounts in another currency.

(3) Unless otherwise defined, expressions used in these Regulations and the money laundering directive have the same meaning as in the money laundering directive and expressions used in these Regulations and in the implementing measures directive have the same meaning as in the implementing measures directive.

Revocation—These Regulations revoked by the Money Laundering, Terrorist Financing and Transfer of Funds (Information on the Payer) Regulations, SI 2017/692 reg 110 with effect from 26 June 2017, subject to savings in reg 110(2)–(4).

Amendments—[1] In para (1), definitions inserted by the Payment Services Regulations SI 2009/209 reg 126, Sch 6 para 6(*a*) with effect from 1 November 2009.

[2] In definition of "terrorist financing" sub-para (*e*) and immediately preceding word "or" inserted by the Terrorism (United Nations Measures) Order (Consequential Amendments) Regulations SI 2009/1912 reg 2(*b*) with effect from 10 August 2009.

[3] In definition of "terrorist financing" sub-para (*c*) repealed and sub-para (*e*) substituted by the Terrorist Asset-Freezing etc Act 2010 s 45(1), Sch 1 para 6 with effect from 16 December 2010.

[4] In para (1), definitions substituted for previous definition by the Electronic Money Laundering Regulations, SI 2011/99 regs 1, 79, Sch 4 para 19(*a*) with effect from 30 April 2011.

[6] Definitions of "auction platform" and "the emission allowance auctioning regulation" inserted by the Recognised Auction Platforms Regulations, SI 2011/2699 reg 11(1), (2) with effect from 12 December 2011.

[7] In para (1), definition of "the life assurance consolidation directive" revoked, and definition of "the Solvency 2 Directive" inserted, by the Solvency 2 Regulations, SI 2015/575 reg 60, Sch 2 para 25(1), (2)(*a*), (*b*) with effect from 1 January 2016.

[8] In para (1), in definition of "terrorist financing", para (*d*) substituted by the Al-Qaida (Asset-Freezing) (Amendment) Regulations, SI 2016/937 reg 8, Schedule para 2 with effect from 22 September 2016.

3 Application of the Regulations

(1) Subject to regulation 4, these Regulations apply to the following persons acting in the course of business carried on by them in the United Kingdom ("relevant persons")—

(*a*) credit institutions;

(*b*) financial institutions;

(*c*) auditors, insolvency practitioners, external accountants and tax advisers;

(*d*) independent legal professionals;

(*e*) trust or company service providers;

(*f*) estate agents;

(*g*) high value dealers;

(*h*) casinos.

[(1A) Regulations 2, 20, 21, 23, 24, 35 to 42, and 44 to 48 apply to an auction platform acting in the course of business carried on by it in the United Kingdom, and such an auction platform is a relevant person for the purposes of those provisions.][2]

(2) "Credit institution" means—

(*a*) a credit institution as defined in [Article 4(1)][1] of the banking consolidation directive; or

(*b*) a branch (within the meaning of Article 4(3) of that directive) located in an EEA state of an institution falling within sub-paragraph (*a*) (or an equivalent institution whose head office is located in a non-EEA state) wherever its head office is located,

when it accepts deposits or other repayable funds from the public or grants credits for its own account (within the meaning of the banking consolidation directive)[, or when it bids directly in auctions in accordance with the emission allowance auctioning regulation on behalf of its clients][3].

(3) "Financial institution" means—

(*a*) an undertaking, including a money service business, when it carries out one or more of the activities listed in points 2 to 12[, 14 and 15][1] of Annex 1 to the banking consolidation directive (the relevant text of which is set out in Schedule 1 to these Regulations), other than—

(i) a credit institution;

[(ii) an undertaking whose only listed activity is as a creditor under an agreement which—

(*aa*) falls within section 12(*a*) of the Consumer Credit Act 1974 (debtor-creditor-supplier agreements), (bb) provides fixed sum credit (within the meaning given in section 10 of the Consumer Credit Act 1974 (running-account credit and fixed-sum credit)) in relation to the provision of services, and

(cc) provides financial accommodation by way of deferred payment or payment by instalments over a period not exceeding 12 months;][4]

[(iii)] an undertaking whose only listed activity is trading for own account in one or more of the products listed in point 7 of Annex 1 to the banking consolidation directive where the undertaking does not have a customer,

and, for this purpose, "customer" means a third party which is not a member of the same group as the undertaking;

(b) an insurance company duly authorised in accordance with [the Solvency 2 Directive][5], when it carries out [any activities or operations referred to in Article 2(3) of that Directive][5];

[(c) a person, other than a person falling within Article 2 of the markets in financial instruments directive, whose regular occupation or business is the provision to other persons of an investment activity on a professional basis, when providing or performing investment services or activities (within the meaning of that directive) or when bidding directly in auctions in accordance with the emission allowance auctioning regulation on behalf of clients;][3]

(ca) a person falling within Article 2(1)(i) of the markets in financial instruments directive, when bidding directly in auctions in accordance with the emission allowance auctioning regulation on behalf of clients of the person's main business.][3]

(d) a collective investment undertaking, when marketing or otherwise offering its units or shares;

(e) an insurance intermediary as defined in Article 2(5) of Directive 2002/92/EC of the European Parliament and of the Council of 9th December 2002 on insurance mediation, with the exception of a tied insurance intermediary as mentioned in Article 2(7) of that Directive, when it acts in respect of contracts of long-term insurance within the meaning given by article 3(1) of, and Part II of Schedule 1 to, the Financial Services and Markets Act 2000 (Regulated Activities) Order 2001;

(f) a branch located in an EEA state of a person referred to in sub-paragraphs (a) to (e) (or an equivalent person whose head office is located in a non-EEA state), wherever its head office is located, when carrying out any activity mentioned in sub-paragraphs (a) to (e);

(g) the National Savings Bank;

(h) the Director of Savings, when money is raised under the auspices of the Director under the National Loans Act 1968.

(4) "Auditor" means any firm or individual who is a statutory auditor within the meaning of Part 42 of the Companies Act 2006 (statutory auditors), when carrying out statutory audit work within the meaning of section 1210 of that Act.

(5) Before the entry into force of Part 42 of the Companies Act 2006 the reference in paragraph (4) to—

(a) a person who is a statutory auditor shall be treated as a reference to a person who is eligible for appointment as a company auditor under section 25 of the Companies Act 1989 (eligibility for appointment) or article 28 of the Companies (Northern Ireland) Order 1990; and

(b) the carrying out of statutory audit work shall be treated as a reference to the provision of audit services.

(6) "Insolvency practitioner" means any person who acts as an insolvency practitioner within the meaning of section 388 of the Insolvency Act 1986 (meaning of "act as insolvency practitioner") or article 3 of the Insolvency (Northern Ireland) Order 1989.

(7) "External accountant" means a firm or sole practitioner who by way of business provides accountancy services to other persons, when providing such services.

(8) "Tax adviser" means a firm or sole practitioner who by way of business provides advice about the tax affairs of other persons, when providing such services.

(9) "Independent legal professional" means a firm or sole practitioner who by way of business provides legal or notarial services to other persons, when participating in financial or real property transactions concerning—

(a) the buying and selling of real property or business entities;

(b) the managing of client money, securities or other assets;

(c) the opening or management of bank, savings or securities accounts;

(d) the organisation of contributions necessary for the creation, operation or management of companies; or

(e) the creation, operation or management of trusts, companies or similar structures,

and, for this purpose, a person participates in a transaction by assisting in the planning or execution of the transaction or otherwise acting for or on behalf of a client in the transaction.

(10) "Trust or company service provider" means a firm or sole practitioner who by way of business provides any of the following services to other persons—

(*a*) forming companies or other legal persons;

(*b*) acting, or arranging for another person to act—

(i) as a director or secretary of a company;

(ii) as a partner of a partnership; or

(iii) in a similar position in relation to other legal persons;

(*c*) providing a registered office, business address, correspondence or administrative address or other related services for a company, partnership or any other legal person or arrangement;

(*d*) acting, or arranging for another person to act, as—

(i) a trustee of an express trust or similar legal arrangement; or

(ii) a nominee shareholder for a person other than a company whose securities are listed on a regulated market,

when providing such services.

(11) "Estate agent" means—

(*a*) a firm; or

(*b*) sole practitioner,

who, or whose employees, carry out estate agency work . . . [4], when in the course of carrying out such work.

[(11A) For the purposes of paragraph (11) "estate agency work" is to be read in accordance with section 1 of the Estate Agents Act 1979 (estate agency work), but for those purposes references in that section to disposing of or acquiring an interest in land are (despite anything in section 2 of that Act) to be taken to include references to disposing of or acquiring an estate or interest in land outside the United Kingdom where that estate or interest is capable of being owned or held as a separate interest.][4]

(12) "High value dealer" means a firm or sole trader who by way of business trades in goods (including an auctioneer dealing in goods), when he receives, in respect of any transaction, a payment or payments in cash of at least 15,000 euros in total, whether the transaction is executed in a single operation or in several operations which appear to be linked.

(13) "Casino" means the holder of a casino operating licence and, for this purpose, a "casino operating licence" has the meaning given by section 65(2) of the Gambling Act 2005 (nature of licence).

[(13A) "Auction platform" means a platform which auctions two-day spot or five-day futures, within the meanings given by Article 3(4) and (5) of the emission allowance auctioning regulation, when it carries out activities covered by that regulation.][2]

(14) In the application of this regulation to Scotland, for "real property" in paragraph (9) substitute "heritable property".

Revocation—These Regulations revoked by the Money Laundering, Terrorist Financing and Transfer of Funds (Information on the Payer) Regulations, SI 2017/692 reg 110 with effect from 26 June 2017, subject to savings in reg 110(2)–(4).

Amendments—[1] In paras (2)(*a*), (3)(*a*), words substituted by the Electronic Money Laundering Regulations, SI 2011/99 regs 1, 79, Sch 4 para 19(*b*) with effect from 30 April 2011.

[2] Paras (1A), (13A) inserted by the Recognised Auction Platforms Regulations, SI 2011/2699 reg 11(1), (3) with effect from 12 December 2011.

[3] In para (2) words inserted, para (3)(*c*) substituted, and para (3)(*ca*) inserted, by the Financial Services and Markets Act 2000 (Regulated Activities) (Amendment) Order, SI 2012/1906 art 7 with effect from 20 July 2012.

[4] In para (3)(*a*), para (iii) renumbered as such and para (ii) inserted, in para (11) words revoked, and para (11A) inserted, by the Money Laundering (Amendment) Regulations, SI 2012/2298 regs 2, 3 with effect from 1 October 2012.

[5] In para (3)(*b*), words substituted for words "the life assurance consolidation directive" and words "activities covered by that directive", by the Solvency 2 Regulations, SI 2015/575 reg 60, Sch 2 para 25(1), (2)(*a*), (*c*) with effect from 1 January 2016.

4 Exclusions

(1) These Regulations do not apply to the following persons when carrying out any of the following activities—

(*a*) a society registered under the Industrial and Provident Societies Act 1965, when it—

(i) issues withdrawable share capital within the limit set by section 6 of that Act (maximum shareholding in society); or

(ii) accepts deposits from the public within the limit set by section 7(3) of that Act (carrying on of banking by societies);

(*b*) a society registered under the Industrial and Provident Societies Act (Northern Ireland) 1969, when it—

(i) issues withdrawable share capital within the limit set by section 6 of that Act (maximum shareholding in society); or

(ii) accepts deposits from the public within the limit set by section 7(3) of that Act (carrying on of banking by societies);

(*c*) a person who is (or falls within a class of persons) specified in any of paragraphs 2 to 23, 25 to 38 or 40 to 49 of the Schedule to the Financial Services and Markets Act 2000 (Exemption) Order 2001, when carrying out any activity in respect of which he is exempt;

[(*ca*) a local authority within the meaning given in article 3 of the Financial Services and Markets Act 2000 (Regulated Activities) Order 2001, when carrying on an activity which would be a regulated activity for the purposes of the Financial Services and Markets Act 2000 but for article 72G of that Order;][2]

(*d*) a person who was an exempted person for the purposes of section 45 of the Financial Services Act 1986 (miscellaneous exemptions) immediately before its repeal, when exercising the functions specified in that section;

(*e*) a person whose main activity is that of a high value dealer, when he engages in financial activity on an occasional or very limited basis as set out in paragraph 1 of Schedule 2 to these Regulations; or

[(*f*) a person, when he prepares a home report.][1]

(2) These Regulations do not apply to a person who falls within regulation 3 solely as a result of his engaging in financial activity on an occasional or very limited basis as set out in paragraph 1 of Schedule 2 to these Regulations.

(3) Parts 2 to 5 of these Regulations do not apply to—

(*a*) the Auditor General for Scotland;

(*b*) the Auditor General for Wales;

(*c*) the Bank of England;

(*d*) the Comptroller and Auditor General;

(*e*) the Comptroller and Auditor General for Northern Ireland;

(*f*) the Official Solicitor to the Supreme Court, when acting as trustee in his official capacity;

(*g*) the Treasury Solicitor.

[(4) In paragraph (1)(*f*), "home report" means the documents prescribed for the purposes of section 98, 99(1) or 101(2) of the Housing (Scotland) Act 2006.][1]

Revocation—These Regulations revoked by the Money Laundering, Terrorist Financing and Transfer of Funds (Information on the Payer) Regulations, SI 2017/692 reg 110 with effect from 26 June 2017, subject to savings in reg 110(2)–(4).

Amendments—[1] Paras (1)(*f*), (4) substituted by the Money Laundering (Amendment) Regulations, SI 2012/2298 regs 2, 4 with effect from 1 October 2012.

[2] Para 1(*ca*) inserted by the Financial Services and Markets Act 2000 (Consumer Credit) (Miscellaneous Provisions) (No 2) Order, SI 2014/506 art 4 with effect from 1 April 2014.

PART 2
CUSTOMER DUE DILIGENCE

5 Meaning of customer due diligence measures

"Customer due diligence measures" means—

(*a*) identifying the customer and verifying the customer's identity on the basis of documents, data or information obtained from a reliable and independent source;

(*b*) identifying, where there is a beneficial owner who is not the customer, the beneficial owner and taking adequate measures, on a risk-sensitive basis, to verify his identity so that the relevant person is satisfied that he knows who the beneficial owner is, including, in the case of a legal person, trust or similar legal arrangement, measures to understand the ownership and control structure of the person, trust or arrangement; and

(*c*) obtaining information on the purpose and intended nature of the business relationship.

Revocation—These Regulations revoked by the Money Laundering, Terrorist Financing and Transfer of Funds (Information on the Payer) Regulations, SI 2017/692 reg 110 with effect from 26 June 2017, subject to savings in reg 110(2)–(4).

6 Meaning of beneficial owner

(1) In the case of a body corporate, "beneficial owner" means any individual who—

(*a*) as respects any body other than a company whose securities are listed on a regulated market, ultimately owns or controls (whether through direct or indirect ownership or control, including through bearer share holdings) more than 25% of the shares or voting rights in the body; or

(*b*) as respects any body corporate, otherwise exercises control over the management of the body.

(2) In the case of a partnership (other than a limited liability partnership), "beneficial owner" means any individual who—

(*a*) ultimately is entitled to or controls (whether the entitlement or control is direct or indirect) more than a 25% share of the capital or profits of the partnership or more than 25% of the voting rights in the partnership; or

(*b*) otherwise exercises control over the management of the partnership.

(3) In the case of a trust, "beneficial owner" means—

(*a*) any individual who is entitled to a specified interest in at least 25% of the capital of the trust property;

(*b*) as respects any trust other than one which is set up or operates entirely for the benefit of individuals falling within sub-paragraph (*a*), the class of persons in whose main interest the trust is set up or operates;

(*c*) any individual who has control over the trust.

(4) In paragraph (3)—

"specified interest" means a vested interest which is—

(*a*) in possession or in remainder or reversion (or, in Scotland, in fee); and

(*b*) defeasible or indefeasible;

"control" means a power (whether exercisable alone, jointly with another person or with the consent of another person) under the trust instrument or by law to—

(*a*) dispose of, advance, lend, invest, pay or apply trust property;

(*b*) vary the trust;

(*c*) add or remove a person as a beneficiary or to or from a class of beneficiaries;

(*d*) appoint or remove trustees;

(*e*) direct, withhold consent to or veto the exercise of a power such as is mentioned in sub-paragraph (*a*), (*b*), (*c*) or (*d*).

(5) For the purposes of paragraph (3)—

(*a*) where an individual is the beneficial owner of a body corporate which is entitled to a specified interest in the capital of the trust property or which has control over the trust, the individual is to be regarded as entitled to the interest or having control over the trust; and

(*b*) an individual does not have control solely as a result of—

(i) his consent being required in accordance with section 32(1)(*c*) of the Trustee Act 1925 (power of advancement);

(ii) any discretion delegated to him under section 34 of the Pensions Act 1995 (power of investment and delegation);

(iii) the power to give a direction conferred on him by section 19(2) of the Trusts of Land and Appointment of Trustees Act 1996 (appointment and retirement of trustee at instance of beneficiaries); or

(iv) the power exercisable collectively at common law to vary or extinguish a trust where the beneficiaries under the trust are of full age and capacity and (taken together) absolutely entitled to the property subject to the trust (or, in Scotland, have a full and unqualified right to the fee).

(6) In the case of a legal entity or legal arrangement which does not fall within paragraph (1), (2) or (3), "beneficial owner" means—

(*a*) where the individuals who benefit from the entity or arrangement have been determined, any individual who benefits from at least 25% of the property of the entity or arrangement;

(*b*) where the individuals who benefit from the entity or arrangement have yet to be determined, the class of persons in whose main interest the entity or arrangement is set up or operates;

(*c*) any individual who exercises control over at least 25% of the property of the entity or arrangement.

(7) For the purposes of paragraph (6), where an individual is the beneficial owner of a body corporate which benefits from or exercises control over the property of the entity or arrangement, the individual is to be regarded as benefiting from or exercising control over the property of the entity or arrangement.

(8) In the case of an estate of a deceased person in the course of administration, "beneficial owner" means—

(*a*) in England and Wales and Northern Ireland, the executor, original or by representation, or administrator for the time being of a deceased person;

(*b*) in Scotland, the executor for the purposes of the Executors (Scotland) Act 1900.

(9) In any other case, "beneficial owner" means the individual who ultimately owns or controls the customer or on whose behalf a transaction is being conducted.

(10) In this regulation—

"arrangement", "entity" and "trust" means an arrangement, entity or trust which administers and distributes funds;

"limited liability partnership" has the meaning given by the Limited Liability Partnerships Act 2000.

Revocation—These Regulations revoked by the Money Laundering, Terrorist Financing and Transfer of Funds (Information on the Payer) Regulations, SI 2017/692 reg 110 with effect from 26 June 2017, subject to savings in reg 110(2)–(4).

7 Application of customer due diligence measures

(1) Subject to regulations 9, 10, 12, 13, 14, 16(4) and 17, a relevant person must apply customer due diligence measures when he—

(*a*) establishes a business relationship;

(*b*) carries out an occasional transaction;

(*c*) suspects money laundering or terrorist financing;

(*d*) doubts the veracity or adequacy of documents, data or information previously obtained for the purposes of identification or verification.

(2) Subject to regulation 16(4), a relevant person must also apply customer due diligence measures at other appropriate times to existing customers on a risk-sensitive basis.

(3) A relevant person must—

(*a*) determine the extent of customer due diligence measures on a risk-sensitive basis depending on the type of customer, business relationship, product or transaction; and

(*b*) be able to demonstrate to his supervisory authority that the extent of the measures is appropriate in view of the risks of money laundering and terrorist financing.

(4) Where—

(*a*) a relevant person is required to apply customer due diligence measures in the case of a trust, legal entity (other than a body corporate) or a legal arrangement (other than a trust); and

(*b*) the class of persons in whose main interest the trust, entity or arrangement is set up or operates is identified as a beneficial owner,

the relevant person is not required to identify all the members of the class.

(5) Paragraph (3)(*b*) does not apply to the National Savings Bank or the Director of Savings.

Revocation—These Regulations revoked by the Money Laundering, Terrorist Financing and Transfer of Funds (Information on the Payer) Regulations, SI 2017/692 reg 110 with effect from 26 June 2017, subject to savings in reg 110(2)–(4).

8 Ongoing monitoring

(1) A relevant person must conduct ongoing monitoring of a business relationship.

(2) "Ongoing monitoring" of a business relationship means—

(*a*) scrutiny of transactions undertaken throughout the course of the relationship (including, where necessary, the source of funds) to ensure that the transactions are consistent with the relevant person's knowledge of the customer, his business and risk profile; and

(*b*) keeping the documents, data or information obtained for the purpose of applying customer due diligence measures up-to-date.

(3) Regulation 7(3) applies to the duty to conduct ongoing monitoring under paragraph (1) as it applies to customer due diligence measures.

Revocation—These Regulations revoked by the Money Laundering, Terrorist Financing and Transfer of Funds (Information on the Payer) Regulations, SI 2017/692 reg 110 with effect from 26 June 2017, subject to savings in reg 110(2)–(4).

9 Timing of verification

(1) This regulation applies in respect of the duty under regulation 7(1)(*a*) and (*b*) to apply the customer due diligence measures referred to in regulation 5(*a*) and (*b*).

(2) Subject to paragraphs (3) to (5) and regulation 10, a relevant person must verify the identity of the customer (and any beneficial owner) before the establishment of a business relationship or the carrying out of an occasional transaction.

(3) Such verification may be completed during the establishment of a business relationship if—

(*a*) this is necessary not to interrupt the normal conduct of business; and

(*b*) there is little risk of money laundering or terrorist financing occurring,

provided that the verification is completed as soon as practicable after contact is first established.

(4) The verification of the identity of the beneficiary under a life insurance policy may take place after the business relationship has been established provided that it takes place at or before the time of payout or at or before the time the beneficiary exercises a right vested under the policy.

(5) The verification of the identity of a bank account holder may take place after the bank account has been opened provided that there are adequate safeguards in place to ensure that—

(*a*) the account is not closed; and

(*b*) transactions are not carried out by or on behalf of the account holder (including any payment from the account to the account holder),

before verification has been completed.

Revocation—These Regulations revoked by the Money Laundering, Terrorist Financing and Transfer of Funds (Information on the Payer) Regulations, SI 2017/692 reg 110 with effect from 26 June 2017, subject to savings in reg 110(2)–(4).

10 Casinos

(1) A casino must establish and verify the identity of—

(*a*) all customers to whom the casino makes facilities for gaming available—

(i) before entry to any premises where such facilities are provided; or

(ii) where the facilities are for remote gaming, before access is given to such facilities; or

(*b*) if the specified conditions are met, all customers who, in the course of any period of 24 hours—

(i) purchase from, or exchange with, the casino chips with a total value of 2,000 euro or more;

(ii) pay the casino 2,000 [euro][1] or more for the use of gaming machines; or

(iii) pay to, or stake with, the casino 2,000 euro or more in connection with facilities for remote gaming.

(2) The specified conditions are—

(*a*) the casino verifies the identity of each customer before or immediately after such purchase, exchange, payment or stake takes place, and

(*b*) the Gambling Commission is satisfied that the casino has appropriate procedures in place to monitor and record—

(i) the total value of chips purchased from or exchanged with the casino;

(ii) the total money paid for the use of gaming machines; or

(iii) the total money paid or staked in connection with facilities for remote gaming,

by each customer.

(3) In this regulation—

"gaming", "gaming machine", "remote operating licence" and "stake" have the meanings given by, respectively, sections 6(1) (gaming & game of chance), 235 (gaming machine), 67 (remote gambling) and 353(1) (interpretation) of the Gambling Act 2005;

"premises" means premises subject to—

(*a*) a casino premises licence within the meaning of section 150(1)(*a*) of the Gambling Act 2005 (nature of licence); or

(*b*) a converted casino premises licence within the meaning of paragraph 65 of Part 7 of Schedule 4 to the Gambling Act 2005 (Commencement No 6 and Transitional Provisions) Order 2006;

"remote gaming" means gaming provided pursuant to a remote operating licence.

Revocation—These Regulations revoked by the Money Laundering, Terrorist Financing and Transfer of Funds (Information on the Payer) Regulations, SI 2017/692 reg 110 with effect from 26 June 2017, subject to savings in reg 110(2)–(4).

Amendments—[1] Word in para (1)(*b*)(ii) inserted by the Money Laundering (Amendment) Regulations, SI 2007/3299 reg 2(*a*), with effect from 15 December 2007: SI 2007/3299 reg 1.

11 Requirement to cease transactions etc

(1) Where, in relation to any customer, a relevant person is unable to apply customer due diligence measures in accordance with the provisions of this Part, he—

(*a*) must not carry out a transaction with or for the customer through a bank account;

(*b*) must not establish a business relationship or carry out an occasional transaction with the customer;

(*c*) must terminate any existing business relationship with the customer;

(*d*) must consider whether he is required to make a disclosure by Part 7 of the Proceeds of Crime Act 2002 or Part 3 of the Terrorism Act 2000.

(2) Paragraph (1) does not apply where a lawyer or other professional adviser is in the course of ascertaining the legal position for his client or performing his task of defending or representing that client in, or concerning, legal proceedings, including advice on the institution or avoidance of proceedings.

(3) In paragraph (2), "other professional adviser" means an auditor, accountant or tax adviser who is a member of a professional body which is established for any such persons and which makes provision for—

(*a*) testing the competence of those seeking admission to membership of such a body as a condition for such admission; and

(*b*) imposing and maintaining professional and ethical standards for its members, as well as imposing sanctions for non-compliance with those standards.

Revocation—These Regulations revoked by the Money Laundering, Terrorist Financing and Transfer of Funds (Information on the Payer) Regulations, SI 2017/692 reg 110 with effect from 26 June 2017, subject to savings in reg 110(2)–(4).

12 Exception for trustees of debt issues

(1) A relevant person—

(*a*) who is appointed by the issuer of instruments or securities specified in paragraph (2) as trustee of an issue of such instruments or securities; or

(*b*) whose customer is a trustee of an issue of such instruments or securities,

is not required to apply the customer due diligence measure referred to in regulation 5(b) in respect of the holders of such instruments or securities.

(2) The specified instruments and securities are—

(*a*) instruments which fall within article 77 [or 77A][1] of the Financial Services and Markets Act 2000 (Regulated Activities) Order 2001; and

(*b*) securities which fall within article 78 of that Order.

Revocation—These Regulations revoked by the Money Laundering, Terrorist Financing and Transfer of Funds (Information on the Payer) Regulations, SI 2017/692 reg 110 with effect from 26 June 2017, subject to savings in reg 110(2)–(4).

Amendments—[1] In para (2)(*a*), words inserted by the Financial Services and Markets Act 2000 (Regulated Activities) (Amendment) Order, SI 2010/86 art 10 with effect from 24 February 2010.

13 Simplified due diligence

(1) A relevant person is not required to apply customer due diligence measures in the circumstances mentioned in regulation 7(1)(*a*), (*b*) or (*d*) where he has reasonable grounds for believing that the customer, transaction or product related to such transaction, falls within any of the following paragraphs.

(2) The customer is—

(*a*) a credit or financial institution which is subject to the requirements of the money laundering directive; or

(*b*) a credit or financial institution (or equivalent institution) which—

(i) is situated in a non-EEA state which imposes requirements equivalent to those laid down in the money laundering directive; and

(ii) is supervised for compliance with those requirements.

(3) The customer is a company whose securities are listed on a regulated market subject to specified disclosure obligations.

(4) The customer is an independent legal professional and the product is an account into which monies are pooled, provided that—

(*a*) where the pooled account is held in a non-EEA state—

(i) that state imposes requirements to combat money laundering and terrorist financing which are consistent with international standards; and

(ii) the independent legal professional is supervised in that state for compliance with those requirements; and

(*b*) information on the identity of the persons on whose behalf monies are held in the pooled account is available, on request, to the institution which acts as a depository institution for the account.

(5) The customer is a public authority in the United Kingdom.

(6) The customer is a public authority which fulfils all the conditions set out in paragraph 2 of Schedule 2 to these Regulations.

(7) The product is—

(*a*) a life insurance contract where the annual premium is no more than 1,000 euro or where a single premium of no more than 2,500 euro is paid;

(*b*) an insurance contract for the purposes of a pension scheme where the contract contains no surrender clause and cannot be used as collateral;

(*c*) a pension, superannuation or similar scheme which provides retirement benefits to employees, where contributions are made by an employer or by way of deduction from an employee's wages and the scheme rules do not permit the assignment of a member's interest under the scheme (other than an assignment permitted by section 44 of the Welfare Reform and Pensions Act 1999 (disapplication of restrictions on alienation) or section 91(5)(*a*) of the Pensions Act 1995 (inalienability of occupational pension)); or

(*d*) electronic money, within the meaning of Article [2(2)][1] of the electronic money directive, where—

(i) if the device cannot be recharged, the maximum amount stored in the device is no more than [250 euro or, in the case of electronic money used to carry out payment transactions within the United Kingdom, 500 euro][1]; or

(ii) if the device can be recharged, a limit of 2,500 euro is imposed on the total amount transacted in a calendar year, except when an amount of 1,000 euro or more is redeemed in the same calendar year [by the electronic money holder (within the meaning of Article 11 of the electronic money directive)][1]..

(8) The product and any transaction related to such product fulfils all the conditions set out in paragraph 3 of Schedule 2 to these Regulations.

(9) The product is a child trust fund within the meaning given by section 1(2) of the Child Trust Funds Act 2004.

[(10) The product is a junior ISA within the meaning given by regulation 2B of the Individual Savings Account Regulations 1998.][2]

Revocation—These Regulations revoked by the Money Laundering, Terrorist Financing and Transfer of Funds (Information on the Payer) Regulations, SI 2017/692 reg 110 with effect from 26 June 2017, subject to savings in reg 110(2)–(4).

Amendments—[1] In para (7)(*d*), in opening words and in sub-para(*d*)(ii) words substituted by the Electronic Money Laundering Regulations, SI 2011/99 regs 1, 79, Sch 4 para 19(*c*) with effect from 30 April 2011.

[2] Para 10 inserted by the Money Laundering (Amendment) Regulations, SI 2011/1781 reg 2 with effect from 1 November 2011.

14 Enhanced customer due diligence and ongoing monitoring

(1) A relevant person must apply on a risk-sensitive basis enhanced customer due diligence measures and enhanced ongoing monitoring—

(*a*) in accordance with paragraphs (2) to (4);

(*b*) in any other situation which by its nature can present a higher risk of money laundering or terrorist financing.

(2) Where the customer has not been physically present for identification purposes, a relevant person must take specific and adequate measures to compensate for the higher risk, for example, by applying one or more of the following measures—

(*a*) ensuring that the customer's identity is established by additional documents, data or information;

(*b*) supplementary measures to verify or certify the documents supplied, or requiring confirmatory certification by a credit or financial institution which is subject to the money laundering directive;

(*c*) ensuring that the first payment is carried out through an account opened in the customer's name with a credit institution.

(3) A credit institution ("the correspondent") which has or proposes to have a correspondent banking relationship with a respondent institution ("the respondent") from a non-EEA state must—

(*a*) gather sufficient information about the respondent to understand fully the nature of its business;

(*b*) determine from publicly-available information the reputation of the respondent and the quality of its supervision;

(*c*) assess the respondent's anti-money laundering and anti-terrorist financing controls;

(*d*) obtain approval from senior management before establishing a new correspondent banking relationship;

(*e*) document the respective responsibilities of the respondent and correspondent; and

(*f*) be satisfied that, in respect of those of the respondent's customers who have direct access to accounts of the correspondent, the respondent—

(i) has verified the identity of, and conducts ongoing monitoring in respect of, such customers; and

(ii) is able to provide to the correspondent, upon request, the documents, data or information obtained when applying customer due diligence measures and ongoing monitoring.

(4) A relevant person who proposes to have a business relationship or carry out an occasional transaction with a politically exposed person must—

(*a*) have approval from senior management for establishing the business relationship with that person;

(*b*) take adequate measures to establish the source of wealth and source of funds which are involved in the proposed business relationship or occasional transaction; and

(*c*) where the business relationship is entered into, conduct enhanced ongoing monitoring of the relationship.

(5) In paragraph (4), "a politically exposed person" means a person who is—

(*a*) an individual who is or has, at any time in the preceding year, been entrusted with a prominent public function by—

(i) a state other than the United Kingdom;

(ii) a Community institution; or

(iii) an international body,

including a person who falls in any of the categories listed in paragraph 4(1)(a) of Schedule 2;

(*b*) an immediate family member of a person referred to in sub-paragraph (*a*), including a person who falls in any of the categories listed in paragraph 4(1)(*c*) of Schedule 2; or

(*c*) a known close associate of a person referred to in sub-paragraph (*a*), including a person who falls in either of the categories listed in paragraph 4(1)(*d*) of Schedule 2.

(6) For the purpose of deciding whether a person is a known close associate of a person referred to in paragraph (5)(*a*), a relevant person need only have regard to information which is in his possession or is publicly known.

Revocation—These Regulations revoked by the Money Laundering, Terrorist Financing and Transfer of Funds (Information on the Payer) Regulations, SI 2017/692 reg 110 with effect from 26 June 2017, subject to savings in reg 110(2)–(4).

15 Branches and subsidiaries

(1) A credit or financial institution must require its branches and subsidiary undertakings which are located in a non-EEA state to apply, to the extent permitted by the law of that state, measures at least equivalent to those set out in these Regulations with regard to customer due diligence measures, ongoing monitoring and record-keeping.

(2) Where the law of a non-EEA state does not permit the application of such equivalent measures by the branch or subsidiary undertaking located in that state, the credit or financial institution must—

(*a*) inform its supervisory authority accordingly; and

(*b*) take additional measures to handle effectively the risk of money laundering and terrorist financing.

(3) In this regulation "subsidiary undertaking"—

(*a*) except in relation to an incorporated friendly society, has the meaning given by section 1162 of the Companies Act 2006 (parent and subsidiary undertakings) and, in relation to a body corporate in or formed under the law of an EEA state other than the United Kingdom, includes an undertaking which is a subsidiary undertaking within the meaning of any rule of law in force in that state for purposes connected with implementation of the European Council Seventh Company Law Directive 83/349/EEC of 13th June 1983 on consolidated accounts;

(*b*) in relation to an incorporated friendly society, means a body corporate of which the society has control within the meaning of section 13(9)(*a*) or (*aa*) of the Friendly Societies Act 1992 (control of subsidiaries and other bodies corporate).

(4) Before the entry into force of section 1162 of the Companies Act 2006 the reference to that section in paragraph (3)(*a*) shall be treated as a reference to section 258 of the Companies Act 1985 (parent and subsidiary undertakings).

Revocation—These Regulations revoked by the Money Laundering, Terrorist Financing and Transfer of Funds (Information on the Payer) Regulations, SI 2017/692 reg 110 with effect from 26 June 2017, subject to savings in reg 110(2)–(4).

16 Shell banks, anonymous accounts etc

(1) A credit institution must not enter into, or continue, a correspondent banking relationship with a shell bank.

(2) A credit institution must take appropriate measures to ensure that it does not enter into, or continue, a corresponding banking relationship with a bank which is known to permit its accounts to be used by a shell bank.

(3) A credit or financial institution carrying on business in the United Kingdom must not set up an anonymous account or an anonymous passbook for any new or existing customer.

(4) As soon as reasonably practicable on or after 15th December 2007 all credit and financial institutions carrying on business in the United Kingdom must apply customer due diligence measures to, and conduct ongoing monitoring of, all anonymous accounts and passbooks in existence on that date and in any event before such accounts or passbooks are used.

(5) A "shell bank" means a credit institution, or an institution engaged in equivalent activities, incorporated in a jurisdiction in which it has no physical presence involving meaningful decision-making and management, and which is not part of a financial conglomerate or third-country financial conglomerate.

(6) In this regulation, "financial conglomerate" and "third-country financial conglomerate" have the meanings given by regulations 1(2) and 7(1) respectively of the Financial Conglomerates and Other Financial Groups Regulations 2004.

Revocation—These Regulations revoked by the Money Laundering, Terrorist Financing and Transfer of Funds (Information on the Payer) Regulations, SI 2017/692 reg 110 with effect from 26 June 2017, subject to savings in reg 110(2)–(4).

17 Reliance

(1) A relevant person may rely on a person who falls within paragraph (2) (or who the relevant person has reasonable grounds to believe falls within paragraph (2)) to apply any customer due diligence measures provided that—

(*a*) the other person consents to being relied on; and

(*b*) notwithstanding the relevant person's reliance on the other person, the relevant person remains liable for any failure to apply such measures.

(2) The persons are—

(*a*) a credit or financial institution which is an authorised person;

[(*aa*) a consumer credit financial institution;][3]

(*b*) a relevant person who is—

(i) an auditor, insolvency practitioner, external accountant, tax adviser or independent legal professional; and

(ii) supervised for the purposes of these Regulations by one of the bodies listed in . . . [3] Schedule 3;

(*c*) a person who carries on business in another EEA state who is—

(i) a credit or financial institution, auditor, insolvency practitioner, external accountant, tax adviser or independent legal professional;

(ii) subject to mandatory professional registration recognised by law; and

(iii) supervised for compliance with the requirements laid down in the money laundering directive in accordance with section 2 of Chapter V of that directive; or

(*d*) a person who carries on business in a non-EEA state who is—

(i) a credit or financial institution (or equivalent institution), auditor, insolvency practitioner, external accountant, tax adviser or independent legal professional;

(ii) subject to mandatory professional registration recognised by law;

(iii) subject to requirements equivalent to those laid down in the money laundering directive; and

(iv) supervised for compliance with those requirements in a manner equivalent to section 2 of Chapter V of the money laundering directive.

(3) In paragraph (2)(*c*)(i) and (*d*)(i), "auditor" and "insolvency practitioner" includes a person situated in another EEA state or a non-EEA state who provides services equivalent to the services provided by an auditor or insolvency practitioner.

(4) Nothing in this regulation prevents a relevant person applying customer due diligence measures by means of an outsourcing service provider or agent provided that the relevant person remains liable for any failure to apply such measures.

[(5) In this regulation, "financial institution" excludes—

(*a*) any money service business;

(*b*) any authorised payment institution, EEA authorised payment institution or small payment institution (within the meaning of the Payment Services Regulations 2009) which provides payment services mainly falling within paragraph 1(*f*) of Schedule 1 to those Regulations][; and[1]

(*c*) any electronic money institution or EEA authorised electronic money institution (within the meaning of the Electronic Money Regulations 2011) which provides payment services mainly falling within paragraph 1(f) of Schedule 1 to the Payment Services Regulations 2009;][2]

Revocation—These Regulations revoked by the Money Laundering, Terrorist Financing and Transfer of Funds (Information on the Payer) Regulations, SI 2017/692 reg 110 with effect from 26 June 2017, subject to savings in reg 110(2)–(4).

Amendments—[1] Para (5) substituted by the Payment Services Regulations SI 2009/209 reg 126, Sch 6 para 6(*b*) with effect from 1 November 2009.

[2] Para (5)(*c*) and preceding word "and" inserted by the Electronic Money Laundering Regulations, SI 2011/99 regs 1, 79, Sch 4 para 19(*d*) with effect from 30 April 2011.

[3] In para (2), sub-para *(aa)* inserted and in sub-para (*b*)(ii) words revoked, by the Money Laundering (Amendment) Regulations, SI 2012/2298 regs 2, 5 with effect from 1 October 2012.

18 Directions where Financial Action Task Force applies counter-measures

Amendments—Reg 18 revoked by the Money Laundering (Amendment) Regulations, SI 2012/2298 regs 2, 6 with effect from 1 October 2012.

PART 3
RECORD-KEEPING, PROCEDURES AND TRAINING

19 Record-keeping

(1) Subject to paragraph (4), a relevant person must keep the records specified in paragraph (2) for at least the period specified in paragraph (3).

(2) The records are—

(*a*) a copy of, or the references to, the evidence of the customer's identity obtained pursuant to regulation 7, 8, 10, 14 or 16(4);

(*b*) the supporting records (consisting of the original documents or copies) in respect of a business relationship or occasional transaction which is the subject of customer due diligence measures or ongoing monitoring.

(3) The period is five years beginning on—

(*a*) in the case of the records specified in paragraph (2)(*a*), the date on which—

(i) the occasional transaction is completed; or

(ii) the business relationship ends; or

(*b*) in the case of the records specified in paragraph (2)(*b*)—

(i) where the records relate to a particular transaction, the date on which the transaction is completed;

(ii) for all other records, the date on which the business relationship ends.

(4) A relevant person who is relied on by another person must keep the records specified in paragraph (2)(*a*) for five years beginning on the date on which he is relied on for the purposes of regulation 7, 10, 14 or 16(4) in relation to any business relationship or occasional transaction.

(5) A person referred to in regulation 17(2)(*a*) or (*b*) who is relied on by a relevant person must, if requested by the person relying on him within the period referred to in paragraph (4)—

(*a*) as soon as reasonably practicable make available to the person who is relying on him any information about the customer (and any beneficial owner) which he obtained when applying customer due diligence measures; and

(*b*) as soon as reasonably practicable forward to the person who is relying on him copies of any identification and verification data and other relevant documents on the identity of the customer (and any beneficial owner) which he obtained when applying those measures.

(6) A relevant person who relies on a person referred to in regulation 17(2)(*c*) or (*d*) (a "third party") to apply customer due diligence measures must take steps to ensure that the third party will, if requested by the relevant person within the period referred to in paragraph (4)—

(*a*) as soon as reasonably practicable make available to him any information about the customer (and any beneficial owner) which the third party obtained when applying customer due diligence measures; and (*b*) as soon as reasonably practicable forward to him copies of any identification and verification data and other relevant documents on the identity of the customer (and any beneficial owner) which the third party obtained when applying those measures.

(7) Paragraphs (5) and (6) do not apply where a relevant person applies customer due diligence measures by means of an outsourcing service provider or agent.

(8) For the purposes of this regulation, a person relies on another person where he does so in accordance with regulation 17(1).

Revocation—These Regulations revoked by the Money Laundering, Terrorist Financing and Transfer of Funds (Information on the Payer) Regulations, SI 2017/692 reg 110 with effect from 26 June 2017, subject to savings in reg 110(2)–(4).

20 Policies and procedures

(1) A relevant person must establish and maintain appropriate and risk-sensitive policies and procedures relating to—

(*a*) customer due diligence measures and ongoing monitoring;

(*b*) reporting;

(*c*) record-keeping;

(*d*) internal control;

(*e*) risk assessment and management;

(*f*) the monitoring and management of compliance with, and the internal communication of, such policies and procedures,

in order to prevent activities related to money laundering and terrorist financing.

(2) The policies and procedures referred to in paragraph (1) include policies and procedures—

(*a*) which provide for the identification and scrutiny of—

(i) complex or unusually large transactions;

(ii) unusual patterns of transactions which have no apparent economic or visible lawful purpose; and

(iii) any other activity which the relevant person regards as particularly likely by its nature to be related to money laundering or terrorist financing;

(*b*) which specify the taking of additional measures, where appropriate, to prevent the use for money laundering or terrorist financing of products and transactions which might favour anonymity;

(*c*) to determine whether a customer is a politically exposed person;

(*d*) under which—

(i) an individual in the relevant person's organisation is a nominated officer under Part 7 of the Proceeds of Crime Act 2002 and Part 3 of the Terrorism Act 2000;

(ii) anyone in the organisation to whom information or other matter comes in the course of the business as a result of which he knows or suspects or has reasonable grounds for knowing or suspecting that a person is engaged in money laundering or terrorist financing is required to comply with Part 7 of the Proceeds of Crime Act 2002 or, as the case may be, Part 3 of the Terrorism Act 2000; and

(iii) where a disclosure is made to the nominated officer, he must consider it in the light of any relevant information which is available to the relevant person and determine whether it gives rise to knowledge or suspicion or reasonable grounds for knowledge or suspicion that a person is engaged in money laundering or terrorist financing.

(3) Paragraph (2)(*d*) does not apply where the relevant person is an individual who neither employs nor acts in association with any other person.

(4) A credit or financial institution [and an auction platform][2] must establish and maintain systems which enable it to respond fully and rapidly to enquiries from financial investigators accredited under section 3 of the Proceeds of Crime Act 2002 (accreditation and training), persons acting on behalf of the Scottish Ministers in their capacity as an enforcement authority under that Act, officers of Revenue and Customs or constables as to—

(*a*) whether it maintains, or has maintained during the previous five years, a business relationship with any person; and

(*b*) the nature of that relationship.

(5) A credit or financial institution [and an auction platform][2] must communicate where relevant the policies and procedures which it establishes and maintains in accordance with this regulation to its branches and subsidiary undertakings which are located outside the United Kingdom.

[(5A) A relevant person who is an issuer of electronic money must appoint an individual to monitor and manage compliance with, and the internal communication of, the policies and procedures relating to the matters referred to in paragraph (1)(a) to (e), and in particular to—

(*a*) identify any situations of higher risk of money laundering or terrorist financing;

(*b*) maintain a record of its policies and procedures, risk assessment and risk management including the application of such policies and procedures;

(*c*) apply measures to ensure that such policies and procedures are taken into account in all relevant functions including in the development of new products, dealing with new customers and in changes to business activities; and

(*d*) provide information to senior management about the operation and effectiveness of such policies and procedures at least annually.][1]

(6) In this regulation—

"politically exposed person" has the same meaning as in regulation 14(4);

"subsidiary undertaking" has the same meaning as in regulation 15.

Revocation—These Regulations revoked by the Money Laundering, Terrorist Financing and Transfer of Funds (Information on the Payer) Regulations, SI 2017/692 reg 110 with effect from 26 June 2017, subject to savings in reg 110(2)–(4).

Amendments—[1] Para (5A) inserted by the Electronic Money Laundering Regulations, SI 2011/99 regs 1, 79, Sch 4 para 19(*e*) with effect from 30 April 2011.

[2] in paras (4), (5), words inserted by the Recognised Auction Platforms Regulations, SI 2011/2699 reg 11(1), (4) with effect from 12 December 2011.

21 Training

A relevant person must take appropriate measures so that all relevant employees of his are—

(*a*) made aware of the law relating to money laundering and terrorist financing; and

(*b*) regularly given training in how to recognise and deal with transactions and other activities which may be related to money laundering or terrorist financing.

Revocation—These Regulations revoked by the Money Laundering, Terrorist Financing and Transfer of Funds (Information on the Payer) Regulations, SI 2017/692 reg 110 with effect from 26 June 2017, subject to savings in reg 110(2)–(4).

PART 4
SUPERVISION AND REGISTRATION

Interpretation

22 Interpretation

(1) In this Part—

"Annex I financial institution" means any undertaking which falls within regulation 3(3)(*a*) other than—

(*a*) a consumer credit financial institution;

(*b*) a money service business; . . . [1]

(*c*) an authorised person;

[(*d*) a bill payment service provider; or

(*e*) a telecommunication, digital and IT payment service provider;][1]

"consumer credit financial institution" means any undertaking which falls within regulation 3(3)(*a*) and which requires, under section 21 of the Consumer Credit Act 1974 (businesses needing a licence), a licence to carry on a consumer credit business, other than—

(*a*) a person covered by a group licence issued by the OFT under section 22 of that Act (standard and group licences);

(*b*) a money service business; . . . [1]

(*c*) an authorised person;

[(*d*) a bill payment service provider; or

(*e*) a telecommunication, digital and IT payment service provider][1].

["recognised investment exchange" has the same meaning as in section 285 of the 2000 Act (exemption for recognised investment exchanges and clearing houses).][2]

(2) In paragraph (1), "consumer credit business" has the meaning given by section 189(1) of the Consumer Credit Act 1974 (definitions) and, on the entry into force of section 23(*a*) of the Consumer Credit Act 2006 (definitions of "consumer credit business" and "consumer hire business"), has the meaning given by section 189(1) of the Consumer Credit Act 1974 as amended by section 23(*a*) of the Consumer Credit Act 2006.

Revocation—These Regulations revoked by the Money Laundering, Terrorist Financing and Transfer of Funds (Information on the Payer) Regulations, SI 2017/692 reg 110 with effect from 26 June 2017, subject to savings in reg 110(2)–(4).

Amendments—[1] In para (1), in definition of "Annex I financial institution", in para (*b*) word "or" revoked, and paras (*d*), (*e*) inserted, and in definition of "consumer credit financial institution", in para (*b*) word "or" revoked, and paras (*d*), (*e*) inserted, by the Payment Services Regulations SI 2009/209 reg 126, Sch 6 para 6(*c*) with effect from 1 November 2009.

[2] In para (1), definition of "recognised investment exchange" inserted by the Money Laundering (Amendment) Regulations, SI 2012/2298 regs 2, 7 with effect from 1 October 2012.

Supervision

23 Supervisory authorities

(1) Subject to paragraph (2), the following bodies are supervisory authorities—

(*a*) the Authority is the supervisory authority for—

(i) credit and financial institutions which are authorised persons;

(ii) trust or company service providers which are authorised persons;

(iii) Annex I financial institutions;

[(iv) electronic money institutions;][2]
[(v) auction platforms;][3]
[(vi) credit unions in Northern Ireland;][4]
[(vii) recognised investment exchanges;][5]

(*b*) the OFT is the supervisory authority for—
(i) consumer credit financial institutions;
(ii) . . . [6]

(*c*) each of the professional bodies listed in Schedule 3 is the supervisory authority for relevant persons who are regulated by it;

(*d*) the Commissioners are the supervisory authority for—
(i) high value dealers;
(ii) money service businesses which are not supervised by the Authority;
(iii) trust or company service providers which are not supervised by the Authority or one of the bodies listed in Schedule 3;
(iv) auditors, external accountants and tax advisers who are not supervised by one of the bodies listed in Schedule 3;
[(v) bill payment service providers which are not supervised by the Authority;
(vi) telecommunication, digital and IT payment service providers which are not supervised by the Authority][1]. [(vii) estate agents][6].

(*e*) the Gambling Commission is the supervisory authority for casinos;

(*f*) DETI is the supervisory authority for—
(i) . . . [4]
(ii) insolvency practitioners authorised by it under article 351 of the Insolvency (Northern Ireland) Order 1989;

(*g*) *the Secretary of State is the supervisory authority for insolvency practitioners authorised by him under section 393 of the Insolvency Act 1986 (grant, refusal and withdrawal of authorisation).*[7]

(2) Where under paragraph (1) there is more than one supervisory authority for a relevant person, the supervisory authorities may agree that one of them will act as the supervisory authority for that person.

(3) Where an agreement has been made under paragraph (2), the authority which has agreed to act as the supervisory authority must notify the relevant person or publish the agreement in such manner as it considers appropriate.

(4) Where no agreement has been made under paragraph (2), the supervisory authorities for a relevant person must cooperate in the performance of their functions under these Regulations.

Revocation—These Regulations revoked by the Money Laundering, Terrorist Financing and Transfer of Funds (Information on the Payer) Regulations, SI 2017/692 reg 110 with effect from 26 June 2017, subject to savings in reg 110(2)–(4).

Cross-reference—See the Money Laundering (Amendment) (No 2) Regulations, SI 2011/2833 reg 3 (requirement for the Treasury to review the operation and effect of SI 2011/2833 and to publish a report).

Amendments—[1] Para (1)(*d*)(v), (vi) inserted by the Payment Services Regulations SI 2009/209 reg 126, Sch 6 para 6(*d*) with effect from 1 November 2009.

[2] Para (1)(*a*)(iv) inserted by the Electronic Money Laundering Regulations, SI 2011/99 regs 1, 79, Sch 4 para 19(*f*) with effect from 30 April 2011.

[3] Para (1)(*a*)(v) inserted by the Recognised Auction Platforms Regulations, SI 2011/2699 reg 11(1), (5) with effect from 12 December 2011.

[4] In para (1), sub-para (*a*)(vi) inserted and sub-para (*f*)(i) revoked, by the Money Laundering (Amendment No 2) Regulations, SI 2011/2833 reg 2(*a*) with effect from 31 March 2012.

[5] Para (1)(*a*)(vii) inserted by the Money Laundering (Amendment) Regulations, SI 2012/2298 regs 2, 8 with effect from 1 October 2012.

[6] Para (1)(*b*)(ii) revoked, and para (1)(*d*)(vii) inserted by the Public Bodies (Abolition of the National Consumer Council and Transfer of the Office of Fair Trading's Functions in relation to Estate Agents etc) Order, SI 2014/631 art (5)(3), Sch 3 para (2)(1), (2) with effect from 31 March 2014.

[7] Para (1)(*g*) revoked by the Deregulation Act 2015 (Insolvency) (Consequential Amendments and Transitional and Savings Provisions) Order, SI 2015/1641 art 4, Sch 1 para 6 with effect from 1 October 2015, subject to transitional provisions and savings: see SI 2015/1641 arts 8, 9.

24 Duties of supervisory authorities

(1) A supervisory authority must effectively monitor the relevant persons for whom it is the supervisory authority and take necessary measures for the purpose of securing compliance by such persons with the requirements of these Regulations.

[(1A) The Authority, when carrying out its supervisory functions in relation to an auction platform—

(*a*) must effectively monitor the auction platform's compliance with—
(i) the customer due diligence requirements of Articles 19 and 20(6) of the emission allowance auctioning regulation;
(ii) the monitoring and record keeping requirements of Article 54 of the emission allowance auctioning regulation; and

(iii) the notification requirements of Article 55(2) and (3) of the emission allowance auctioning regulation; and

(*b*) may monitor the auction platform's compliance with regulations 20 and 21 of these Regulations.][1]

(2) A supervisory authority which, in the course of carrying out any of its functions under these Regulations, knows or suspects that a person is or has engaged in money laundering or terrorist financing must promptly inform the Serious Organised Crime Agency.

(3) A disclosure made under paragraph (2) is not to be taken to breach any restriction, however imposed, on the disclosure of information.

(4) The functions of the Authority under these Regulations shall be treated for the purposes of Parts 1, 2 and 4 of Schedule 1 to the 2000 Act (the Financial Services Authority) as functions conferred on the Authority under that Act.

Revocation—These Regulations revoked by the Money Laundering, Terrorist Financing and Transfer of Funds (Information on the Payer) Regulations, SI 2017/692 reg 110 with effect from 26 June 2017, subject to savings in reg 110(2)–(4).

Amendments—[1] Para (1A) inserted by the Recognised Auction Platforms Regulations, SI 2011/2699 reg 11(1), (6) with effect from 12 December 2011.

[24A Disclosure by supervisory authorities

(1) A supervisory authority may disclose to another supervisory authority information it holds relevant to its functions under these Regulations, provided the disclosure is made for purposes connected with the effective exercise of the functions of either supervisory authority under these Regulations.

(2) Information disclosed to a supervisory authority under paragraph (1) may not be further disclosed by that authority, except—

(*a*) in accordance with paragraph (1);

(*b*) with a view to the institution of, or otherwise for the purposes of, any criminal or other enforcement proceedings; or

(*c*) as otherwise required by law.][1]

Revocation—These Regulations revoked by the Money Laundering, Terrorist Financing and Transfer of Funds (Information on the Payer) Regulations, SI 2017/692 reg 110 with effect from 26 June 2017, subject to savings in reg 110(2)–(4).

Amendments—[1] Reg 24A inserted by the Money Laundering (Amendment) Regulations, SI 2012/2298 regs 2, 9 with effect from 1 October 2012.

Registration of high value dealers, money service businesses and trust or company service providers

25 Duty to maintain registers

(1) The Commissioners must maintain registers of—

(*a*) high value dealers;

(*b*) money service businesses for which they are the supervisory authority; . . . [1]

(*c*) trust or company service providers for which they are the supervisory authority

[(*d*) bill payment service providers for which they are the supervisory authority; and

(*e*) telecommunication, digital and IT payment service providers for which they are the supervisory authority][1].

(2) The Commissioners may keep the registers in any form they think fit.

(3) The Commissioners may publish or make available for public inspection all or part of a register maintained under this regulation.

Revocation—These Regulations revoked by the Money Laundering, Terrorist Financing and Transfer of Funds (Information on the Payer) Regulations, SI 2017/692 reg 110 with effect from 26 June 2017, subject to savings in reg 110(2)–(4).

Amendments—[1] In para (1), in para (*b*), word "and" revoked, and paras (*d*), (*e*) inserted, by the Payment Services Regulations SI 2009/209 reg 126, Sch 6 para 6(*e*) with effect from 1 November 2009.

26 Requirement to be registered

(1) A person in respect of whom the Commissioners are required to maintain a register under regulation 25 must not act as a—

(*a*) high value dealer;

(*b*) money service business; . . . [1]

(*c*) trust or company service provider,

[(*d*) bill payment service provider; or

(*e*) telecommunication, digital and IT payment service provider,][1]

unless he is included in the register.

(2) Paragraph (1) and regulation 29 are subject to the transitional provisions set out in regulation 50.

Revocation—These Regulations revoked by the Money Laundering, Terrorist Financing and Transfer of Funds (Information on the Payer) Regulations, SI 2017/692 reg 110 with effect from 26 June 2017, subject to savings in reg 110(2)–(4).

Amendments—[1] In para (1), in para (*b*), word "or" revoked, and paras (*d*), (*e*) inserted, by the Payment Services Regulations SI 2009/209 reg 126, Sch 6 para 6(*f*) with effect from 1 November 2009.

27 Applications for registration in a register maintained under regulation 25

(1) An applicant for registration in a register maintained under regulation 25 must make an application in such manner and provide such information as the Commissioners may specify.

(2), (3) . . . [1]

(4) If at any time after the applicant has provided the Commissioners with any information under paragraph (1) or (3)—

(*a*) there is a material change affecting any matter contained in that information; or

(*b*) it becomes apparent to that person that the information contains a significant inaccuracy,

he must provide the Commissioners with details of the change or, as the case may be, a correction of the inaccuracy within 30 days beginning with the date of the occurrence of the change (or the discovery of the inaccuracy) or within such later time as may be agreed with the Commissioners.

(5) The obligation in paragraph (4) applies also to material changes or significant inaccuracies affecting any matter contained in any supplementary information provided pursuant to that paragraph.

(6) Any information to be provided to the Commissioners under this regulation must be in such form or verified in such manner as they may specify.

Revocation—These Regulations revoked by the Money Laundering, Terrorist Financing and Transfer of Funds (Information on the Payer) Regulations, SI 2017/692 reg 110 with effect from 26 June 2017, subject to savings in reg 110(2)–(4).

28 Fit and proper test

(1) The Commissioners must refuse to register an applicant as a money service business or trust or company service provider if they are satisfied that—

(*a*) the applicant;

(*b*) a person who effectively directs, or will effectively direct, the business or service provider;

(*c*) a beneficial owner of the business or service provider; or

(*d*) the nominated officer of the business or service provider,

is not a fit and proper person [with regard to the risk of money laundering or terrorist financing][1].

(2), (3) . . . [1]

Revocation—These Regulations revoked by the Money Laundering, Terrorist Financing and Transfer of Funds (Information on the Payer) Regulations, SI 2017/692 reg 110 with effect from 26 June 2017, subject to savings in reg 110(2)–(4).

Amendments—[1] Words in para (1) inserted and paras (2), (3) revoked, by the Money Laundering (Amendment) Regulations, SI 2012/2298 regs 2, 10 with effect from 1 October 2012.

29 Determination of applications under regulation 27

(1) Subject to regulation 28, the Commissioners may refuse to register an applicant for registration in a register maintained under regulation 25 only if—

(*a*) any requirement of, or imposed under, regulation 27 has not been complied with;

(*b*) it appears to the Commissioners that any information provided pursuant to regulation 27 is false or misleading in a material particular; or

(*c*) the applicant has failed to pay a charge imposed by them under regulation 35(1).

(2) The Commissioners must within 45 days beginning either with the date on which they receive the application or, where applicable, with the date on which they receive any further information required under regulation 27(3), give the applicant notice of—

(*a*) their decision to register the applicant; or

(*b*) the following matters—

(i) their decision not to register the applicant;

(ii) the reasons for their decision;

[(iii) the right to a review under regulation 43A; and][1]

(iv) the right to appeal under regulation [43][1].

(3) The Commissioners must, as soon as practicable after deciding to register a person, include him in the relevant register.

Revocation—These Regulations revoked by the Money Laundering, Terrorist Financing and Transfer of Funds (Information on the Payer) Regulations, SI 2017/692 reg 110 with effect from 26 June 2017, subject to savings in reg 110(2)–(4).

Amendments—[1] Para (2)(*b*)(iii) substituted, and in para (2)(*b*)(iv), reference substituted, by the Transfer of Tribunal Functions and Revenue and Customs Appeals Order, SI 2009/56 art 3, Sch 2 paras 168, 169 with effect from 1 April 2009.

30 Cancellation of registration in a register maintained under regulation 25

(1) The Commissioners must cancel the registration of a money service business or trust or company service provider in a register maintained under regulation 25(1) if, at any time after registration, they are satisfied that he or any person mentioned in regulation 28(1)(*b*), (*c*) or (*d*) is not a fit and proper person within the meaning of regulation [28][3].

[(2) The Commissioners may cancel a person's registration in a register maintained by them under regulation 25 if, at any time after registration—

(*a*) it appears to them that that any condition in regulation 29(1) is met; or

(*b*) the person has failed to comply with any requirement of a notice given under regulation 37.][3]

[(2A) The Commissioners may cancel the registration of a money service business in a register maintained under regulation 25(1)(*b*) where the money service business—

(*a*) is providing a payment service in the United Kingdom, or is purporting to do so;

(*b*) is not included in the register of payment service providers maintained by the Authority under regulation 4(1) of the Payment Service Regulations 2009; and (*c*) is not a person mentioned in paragraphs (c) to (h) of the definition of a payment service provider in regulation 2(1) of the Payment Services Regulations 2009, or a person to whom regulation 3 or 121 of those Regulations applies.][2]

(3) Where the Commissioners decide to cancel a person's registration they must give him notice of—

(*a*) their decision and, subject to paragraph (4), the date from which the cancellation takes effect;

(*b*) the reasons for their decision;

[(*c*) the right to a review under regulation 43A; and][1]

(*d*) the right to appeal under regulation [43][1].

(4) If the Commissioners—

(*a*) consider that the interests of the public require the cancellation of a person's registration to have immediate effect; and

(*b*) include a statement to that effect and the reasons for it in the notice given under paragraph (3),

the cancellation takes effect when the notice is given to the person.

Revocation—These Regulations revoked by the Money Laundering, Terrorist Financing and Transfer of Funds (Information on the Payer) Regulations, SI 2017/692 reg 110 with effect from 26 June 2017, subject to savings in reg 110(2)–(4).

Amendments—[1] Para (3)(*c*) substituted, and in para (3)(*d*), reference substituted by the Transfer of Tribunal Functions and Revenue and Customs Appeals Order, SI 2009/56 art 3, Sch 2 paras 168, 170 with effect from 1 April 2009.

[2] Para (2A) inserted by the Payment Services Regulations, SI 2012/1791 reg 2 with effect from 1 October 2012.

[3] In para (1), reference substituted , and para (2) substituted, by the Money Laundering (Amendment) Regulations, SI 2012/2298 regs 2, 11 with effect from 1 October 2012.

Requirement to inform the authority

31 Requirement on authorised person to inform the Authority

(1) An authorised person whose supervisory authority is the Authority must, before acting as a money service business or a trust or company service provider or within 28 days of so doing, inform the Authority that he intends, or has begun, to act as such.

(2) Paragraph (1) does not apply to an authorised person who—

(*a*) immediately before 15th December 2007 was acting as a money service business or a trust or company service provider and continues to act as such after that date; and

(*b*) before 15th January 2008 informs the Authority that he is or was acting as such.

(3) Where an authorised person whose supervisory authority is the Authority ceases to act as a money service business or a trust or company service provider, he must immediately inform the Authority.

(4) Any requirement imposed by this regulation is to be treated as if it were a requirement imposed by or under the 2000 Act.

(5) Any information to be provided to the Authority under this regulation must be in such form or verified in such manner as it may specify.

Revocation—These Regulations revoked by the Money Laundering, Terrorist Financing and Transfer of Funds (Information on the Payer) Regulations, SI 2017/692 reg 110 with effect from 26 June 2017, subject to savings in reg 110(2)–(4).

Registration of Annex I financial institutions, estate agents etc

32 Power to maintain registers

(1) The supervisory authorities mentioned in paragraph (2), (3) or (4) may, in order to fulfil their duties under regulation 24, maintain a register under this regulation.

(2) The Authority may maintain a register of Annex I financial institutions.

(3) The OFT may maintain registers of—

(*a*) consumer credit financial institutions; and

(*b*) . . .[1]

(4) The Commissioners may maintain registers of—

(*a*) auditors;

(*b*) external accountants; and

(*c*) tax advisers,

who are not supervised by the Secretary of State, DETI or any of the professional bodies listed in Schedule 3.

[(4A The Commissioners may maintain a register of estate agents.][1]

(5) Where a supervisory authority decides to maintain a register under this regulation, it must take reasonable steps to bring its decision to the attention of those relevant persons in respect of whom the register is to be established.

(6) A supervisory authority may keep a register under this regulation in any form it thinks fit.

(7) A supervisory authority may publish or make available to public inspection all or part of a register maintained by it under this regulation.

Revocation—These Regulations revoked by the Money Laundering, Terrorist Financing and Transfer of Funds (Information on the Payer) Regulations, SI 2017/692 reg 110 with effect from 26 June 2017, subject to savings in reg 110(2)–(4).

Amendments—[1] Para (3)(*b*) revoked, and para (4A) inserted by the Public Bodies (Abolition of the National Consumer Council and Transfer of the Office of Fair Trading's Functions in relation to Estate Agents etc) Order, SI 2014/631 art (5)(3), Sch 3 para (2)(1), (3) with effect from 31 March 2014.

33 Requirement to be registered

Where a supervisory authority decides to maintain a register under regulation 32 in respect of any description of relevant persons and establishes a register for that purpose, a relevant person of that description may not carry on the business or profession in question for a period of more than six months beginning on the date on which the supervisory authority establishes the register unless he is included in the register.

Revocation—These Regulations revoked by the Money Laundering, Terrorist Financing and Transfer of Funds (Information on the Payer) Regulations, SI 2017/692 reg 110 with effect from 26 June 2017, subject to savings in reg 110(2)–(4).

34 Applications for and cancellation of registration in a register maintained under regulation 32

(1) Regulations 27, 29 (with the omission of the words "Subject to regulation 28" in regulation 29(1)) and 30(2), (3) and (4) apply to registration in a register maintained by the Commissioners under regulation 32 as they apply to registration in a register maintained under regulation 25.

(2) Regulation 27 applies to registration in a register maintained by the Authority or the OFT under regulation 32 as it applies to registration in a register maintained under regulation 25 and, for this purpose, references to the Commissioners are to be treated as references to the Authority or the OFT, as the case may be.

(3) The Authority and the OFT may refuse to register an applicant for registration in a register maintained under regulation 32 only if—

(*a*) any requirement of, or imposed under, regulation 27 has not been complied with;

(*b*) it appears to the Authority or the OFT, as the case may be, that any information provided pursuant to regulation 27 is false or misleading in a material particular; or

(*c*) the applicant has failed to pay a charge imposed by the Authority or the OFT, as the case may be, under regulation 35(1).

(4) The Authority or the OFT, as the case may be, must, within 45 days beginning either with the date on which it receives an application or, where applicable, with the date on which it receives any further information required under regulation 27(3), give the applicant notice of—

(*a*) its decision to register the applicant; or

(*b*) the following matters—

(i) that it is minded not to register the applicant;

(ii) the reasons for being minded not to register him; and

(iii) the right to make representations to it within a specified period (which may not be less than 28 days).

(5) The Authority or the OFT, as the case may be, must then decide, within a reasonable period, whether to register the applicant and it must give the applicant notice of—

(*a*) its decision to register the applicant; or

(*b*) the following matters—

(i) its decision not to register the applicant;

(ii) the reasons for its decision; and

(iii) the right to appeal under regulation 44(1)(*b*).

(6) The Authority or the OFT, as the case may be, must, as soon as reasonably practicable after deciding to register a person, include him in the relevant register.

[(7) The Authority or the OFT may cancel a person's registration in a register maintained by them under regulation 32 if, at any time after registration—

(*a*) it appears to them that any condition in paragraph (3) is met; or

(*b*) the person has failed to comply with any requirement of a notice given under regulation 37.][1]

(8) Where the Authority or the OFT proposes to cancel a person's registration, it must give him notice of—

(*a*) its proposal to cancel his registration;

(*b*) the reasons for the proposed cancellation; and

(*c*) the right to make representations to it within a specified period (which may not be less than 28 days).

(9) The Authority or the OFT, as the case may be, must then decide, within a reasonable period, whether to cancel the person's registration and it must give him notice of—

(*a*) its decision not to cancel his registration; or

(*b*) the following matters—

(i) its decision to cancel his registration and, subject to paragraph (10), the date from which cancellation takes effect;

(ii) the reasons for its decision; and

(iii) the right to appeal under regulation 44(1)(*b*).

(10) If the Authority or the OFT, as the case may be—

(*a*) considers that the interests of the public require the cancellation of a person's registration to have immediate effect; and

(*b*) includes a statement to that effect and the reasons for it in the notice given under paragraph (9)(*b*),

the cancellation takes effect when the notice is given to the person.

(11) In paragraphs (3) and (4), references to regulation 27 are to be treated as references to that paragraph as applied by paragraph (2) of this regulation.

Revocation—These Regulations revoked by the Money Laundering, Terrorist Financing and Transfer of Funds (Information on the Payer) Regulations, SI 2017/692 reg 110 with effect from 26 June 2017, subject to savings in reg 110(2)–(4).

Amendments—[1] Para (7) substituted by the Money Laundering (Amendment) Regulations, SI 2012/2298 regs 2, 12 with effect from 1 October 2012.

Financial provisions

35 Costs of supervision

(1) The Authority, the OFT and the Commissioners may impose charges—

(*a*) on applicants for registration;

(*b*) on relevant persons supervised by them.

(2) Charges levied under paragraph (1) must not exceed such amount as the Authority, the OFT or the Commissioners (as the case may be) consider will enable them to meet any expenses reasonably incurred by them in carrying out their functions under these Regulations or for any incidental purpose.

(3) Without prejudice to the generality of paragraph (2), a charge may be levied in respect of each of the premises at which a person carries on (or proposes to carry on) business.

[(4) The Authority must pay to the Treasury any amounts received by the Financial Services Authority during the financial year beginning with 1st April 2012 year by way of penalties imposed under regulation 42 after deducting any amounts the Financial Services Authority has, prior to 1st April 2013, applied towards expenses incurred by it in carrying out its functions under these Regulations or for any incidental purpose.

(4A) The Authority must in respect of the financial year beginning with 1st April 2013 and each subsequent financial year pay to the Treasury any amounts received by it during the year by way of penalties imposed under regulation 42.

(4B) The Treasury may give directions to the Authority as to how the Authority is to comply with its duties under paragraphs (4) and (4A).

(4C) The directions may in particular—

(*a*) specify the time when any payment is required to be made to the Treasury, and

(*b*) require the Authority to provide the Treasury at specified times with information relating to penalties that the Authority has imposed under regulation 42.

(4D) The Treasury must pay into the Consolidated Fund any sums received by them under this regulation.][1]

(5) In paragraph (2), "expenses" in relation to the OFT includes expenses incurred by a local weights and measures authority or DETI pursuant to arrangements made for the purposes of these Regulations with the OFT—

(*a*) by or on behalf of the authority; or

(*b*) by DETI.

Revocation—These Regulations revoked by the Money Laundering, Terrorist Financing and Transfer of Funds (Information on the Payer) Regulations, SI 2017/692 reg 110 with effect from 26 June 2017, subject to savings in reg 110(2)–(4).

Amendments—[1] Paras (4)–(4D) substituted for previous para (4) by the Payment to Treasury of Penalties Regulations, SI 2013/429 reg 2 with effect from 1 April 2013.

PART 5
ENFORCEMENT

Powers of designated authorities

36 Interpretation

In this Part—

"designated authority" means—

(*a*) the Authority;

(*b*) the Commissioners; [and][1]

(*c*) the OFT; . . . [1]

(*d*) . . . [1]

"officer", except in regulations 40(3), 41 and 47 means—

(*a*) an officer of the Authority, including a member of the Authority's staff or an agent of the Authority;

(*b*) an officer of Revenue and Customs;

(*c*) an officer of the OFT; [or][1]

(*d*) a relevant officer; . . . [1]

(*e*) . . . [1]

"recorded information" includes information recorded in any form and any document of any nature;

"relevant officer" means—

(*a*) in Great Britain, an officer of a local weights and measures authority;

(*b*) in Northern Ireland, an officer of DETI acting pursuant to arrangements made with the OFT for the purposes of these Regulations.

Revocation—These Regulations revoked by the Money Laundering, Terrorist Financing and Transfer of Funds (Information on the Payer) Regulations, SI 2017/692 reg 110 with effect from 26 June 2017, subject to savings in reg 110(2)–(4).

Cross-reference—See the Money Laundering (Amendment) (No 2) Regulations, SI 2011/2833 reg 3 (requirement for the Treasury to review the operation and effect of SI 2011/2833 and to publish a report).

Amendments—[1] In definition of "designated authority", in para (*b*) word "and" inserted and para (*d*) and preceding word "and" revoked, and in definition of "officer", in para (*c*) word "or" inserted and para (*e*) and preceding word "or" revoked, by the Money Laundering (Amendment) (No 2) Regulations, SI 2011/2833 reg 2(*c*) with effect from 31 March 2012.

37 Power to require information from, and attendance of, relevant and connected persons

(1) An officer may, by notice to a relevant person or to a person connected with a relevant person, require the relevant person or the connected person, as the case may be—

(*a*) to provide such information as may be specified in the notice;

(*b*) to produce such recorded information as may be so specified; or

(*c*) to attend before an officer at a time and place specified in the notice and answer questions.

[(2) For the purposes of paragraph (1)—

(*a*) "relevant person" includes a person whom a designated authority believes, or has reasonable grounds to suspect, is or has at any time been a relevant person; and

(*b*) a person is connected with a relevant person if the person is, or has at any time been, in relation to the relevant person, a person listed in Schedule 4 to these Regulations.][2]

(3) An officer may exercise powers under this regulation only if the information sought to be obtained as a result is reasonably required in connection with the exercise by the designated authority for whom he acts of its functions under these Regulations.

(4) Where an officer requires information to be provided or produced pursuant to paragraph (1)(*a*) or (*b*)—

(*a*) the notice must set out the reasons why the officer requires the information to be provided or produced; and

(*b*) such information must be provided or produced—

(i) before the end of such reasonable period as may be specified in the notice; and

(ii) at such place as may be so specified.

(5) In relation to information recorded otherwise than in legible form, the power to require production of it includes a power to require the production of a copy of it in legible form or in a form from which it can readily be produced in visible and legible form.

(6) The production of a document does not affect any lien which a person has on the document.

(7) A person may not be required under this regulation to provide or produce information or to answer questions which he would be entitled to refuse to provide, produce or answer on grounds of legal professional privilege in proceedings in the High Court, except that a lawyer may be required to provide the name and address of his client.

(8) Subject to paragraphs (9) and (10), a statement made by a person in compliance with a requirement imposed on him under paragraph (1)(*c*) is admissible in evidence in any proceedings, so long as it also complies with any requirements governing the admissibility of evidence in the circumstances in question.

(9) In criminal proceedings in which a person is charged with an offence to which this paragraph applies—

(*a*) no evidence relating to the statement may be adduced; and

(*b*) no question relating to it may be asked,

by or on behalf of the prosecution unless evidence relating to it is adduced, or a question relating to it is asked, in the proceedings by or on behalf of that person.

(10) Paragraph (9) applies to any offence other than one under—

(*a*) section 5 of the Perjury Act 1911 (false statements without oath);

(*b*) section 44(2) of the Criminal Law (Consolidation) (Scotland) Act 1995 (false statements and declarations); or

(*c*) Article 10 of the Perjury (Northern Ireland) Order 1979 (false unsworn statements).

(11) In the application of this regulation to Scotland, the reference in paragraph (7) to—

(*a*) proceedings in the High Court is to be read as a reference to legal proceedings generally; and

(*b*) an entitlement on grounds of legal professional privilege is to be read as a reference to an entitlement on the grounds of confidentiality of communications[—

(i) between a professional legal adviser and his client; or

(ii) made in connection with or in contemplation of legal proceedings and for the purposes of those proceedings][1].

Revocation—These Regulations revoked by the Money Laundering, Terrorist Financing and Transfer of Funds (Information on the Payer) Regulations, SI 2017/692 reg 110 with effect from 26 June 2017, subject to savings in reg 110(2)–(4).

Amendments—[1] Para (11)(*b*)(i), (ii) inserted by the Money Laundering (Amendment) Regulations, SI 2007/3299 reg 2(*b*), with effect from 15 December 2007: SI 2007/3299 reg 1.

[2] Para (2) substituted by the Money Laundering (Amendment) Regulations, SI 2012/2298 regs 2, 13 with effect from 1 October 2012.

38 Entry, inspection without a warrant etc

(1) Where an officer has reasonable cause to believe that any premises are being used by a relevant person in connection with his business or professional activities, he may on producing evidence of his authority at any reasonable time—

(*a*) enter the premises;
(*b*) inspect the premises;
(*c*) observe the carrying on of business or professional activities by the relevant person;
(*d*) inspect any recorded information found on the premises;
(*e*) require any person on the premises to provide an explanation of any recorded information or to state where it may be found;
(*f*) in the case of a money service business or a high value dealer, inspect any cash found on the premises.

(2) An officer may take copies of, or make extracts from, any recorded information found under paragraph (1).

(3) Paragraphs (1)(*d*) and (*e*) and (2) do not apply to recorded information which the relevant person would be entitled to refuse to disclose on grounds of legal professional privilege in proceedings in the High Court, except that a lawyer may be required to provide the name and address of his client and, for this purpose, regulation 37(11) applies to this paragraph as it applies to regulation 37(7).

(4) An officer may exercise powers under this regulation only if the information sought to be obtained as a result is reasonably required in connection with the exercise by the designated authority for whom he acts of its functions under these Regulations.

(5) In this regulation, "premises" means any premises other than premises used only as a dwelling.

Revocation—These Regulations revoked by the Money Laundering, Terrorist Financing and Transfer of Funds (Information on the Payer) Regulations, SI 2017/692 reg 110 with effect from 26 June 2017, subject to savings in reg 110(2)–(4).

39 Entry to premises under warrant

(1) A justice may issue a warrant under this paragraph if satisfied on information on oath given by an officer that there are reasonable grounds for believing that the first, second or third set of conditions is satisfied.

(2) The first set of conditions is—

(*a*) that there is on the premises specified in the warrant recorded information in relation to which a requirement could be imposed under regulation 37(1)(*b*); and
(*b*) that if such a requirement were to be imposed—
(i) it would not be complied with; or
(ii) the recorded information to which it relates would be removed, tampered with or destroyed.

(3) The second set of conditions is—

(*a*) that a person on whom a requirement has been imposed under regulation 37(1)(*b*) has failed (wholly or in part) to comply with it; and
(*b*) that there is on the premises specified in the warrant recorded information which has been required to be produced.

(4) The third set of conditions is—

(*a*) that an officer has been obstructed in the exercise of a power under regulation 38; and
(*b*) that there is on the premises specified in the warrant recorded information or cash which could be inspected under regulation 38(1)(*d*) or (*f*).

(5) A justice may issue a warrant under this paragraph if satisfied on information on oath given by an officer that there are reasonable grounds for suspecting that—

(*a*) an offence under these Regulations has been, is being or is about to be committed by a relevant person; and
(*b*) there is on the premises specified in the warrant recorded information relevant to whether that offence has been, or is being or is about to be committed.

(6) A warrant issued under this regulation shall authorise an officer—

(*a*) to enter the premises specified in the warrant;
(*b*) to search the premises and take possession of any recorded information or anything appearing to be recorded information specified in the warrant or to take, in relation to any such recorded information, any other steps which may appear to be necessary for preserving it or preventing interference with it;
(*c*) to take copies of, or extracts from, any recorded information specified in the warrant;

SIs

(*d*) to require any person on the premises to provide an explanation of any recorded information appearing to be of the kind specified in the warrant or to state where it may be found;

(*e*) to use such force as may reasonably be necessary.

(7) Where a warrant is issued by a justice under paragraph (1) or (5) on the basis of information [on oath][1] given by an officer of the Authority, for "an officer" in paragraph (6) substitute "a constable".

(8) In paragraphs (1), (5) and (7), "justice" means—

(*a*) in relation to England and Wales, a justice of the peace;

(*b*) in relation to Scotland, a justice within the meaning of section 307 of the Criminal Procedure (Scotland) Act 1995 (interpretation);

(*c*) in relation to Northern Ireland, a lay magistrate.

(9) In the application of this regulation to Scotland, the references in paragraphs [(1), (5) and (7)][1] to information on oath are to be read as references to evidence on oath.

Revocation—These Regulations revoked by the Money Laundering, Terrorist Financing and Transfer of Funds (Information on the Payer) Regulations, SI 2017/692 reg 110 with effect from 26 June 2017, subject to savings in reg 110(2)–(4).

Amendments—[1] Words in para (7) inserted, and words in para (9) substituted, by the Money Laundering (Amendment) Regulations, SI 2007/3299 reg 2(*c*), with effect from 15 December 2007: SI 2007/3299 reg 1.

40 Failure to comply with information requirement

(1) If, on an application made by—

(*a*) a designated authority; or

(*b*) a local weights and measures authority or DETI pursuant to arrangements made with the OFT—

(i) by or on behalf of the authority; or

(ii) by DETI,

it appears to the court that a person (the "information defaulter") has failed to do something that he was required to do under regulation 37(1), the court may make an order under this regulation.

(2) An order under this regulation may require the information defaulter—

(*a*) to do the thing that he failed to do within such period as may be specified in the order;

(*b*) otherwise to take such steps to remedy the consequences of the failure as may be so specified.

(3) If the information defaulter is a body corporate, a partnership or an unincorporated body of persons which is not a partnership, the order may require any officer of the body corporate, partnership or body, who is (wholly or partly) responsible for the failure to meet such costs of the application as are specified in the order.

(4) In this regulation, "court" means—

(*a*) in England and Wales and Northern Ireland, the High Court or the county court;

(*b*) in Scotland, the Court of Session or the sheriff [court][1].

Revocation—These Regulations revoked by the Money Laundering, Terrorist Financing and Transfer of Funds (Information on the Payer) Regulations, SI 2017/692 reg 110 with effect from 26 June 2017, subject to savings in reg 110(2)–(4).

Amendments—[1] Word in para (4)(*b*) inserted by the Money Laundering (Amendment) Regulations, SI 2007/3299 reg 2(*d*), with effect from 15 December 2007: SI 2007/3299 reg 1.

41 Powers of relevant officers

(1) A relevant officer may only exercise powers under regulations 37 to 39 pursuant to arrangements made with the OFT—

(*a*) by or on behalf of the local weights and measures authority of which he is an officer ("his authority"); or

(*b*) by DETI.

(2) Anything done or omitted to be done by, or in relation to, a relevant officer in the exercise or purported exercise of a power in this Part shall be treated for all purposes as having been done or omitted to be done by, or in relation to, an officer of the OFT.

(3) Paragraph (2) does not apply for the purposes of any criminal proceedings brought against the relevant officer, his authority, DETI or the OFT, in respect of anything done or omitted to be done by the officer.

(4) A relevant officer shall not disclose to any person other than the OFT and his authority or, as the case may be, DETI information obtained by him in the exercise of such powers unless—

(*a*) he has the approval of the OFT to do so; or

(*b*) he is under a duty to make the disclosure.

Revocation—These Regulations revoked by the Money Laundering, Terrorist Financing and Transfer of Funds (Information on the Payer) Regulations, SI 2017/692 reg 110 with effect from 26 June 2017, subject to savings in reg 110(2)–(4).

Civil penalties, review and appeals

42 Power to impose civil penalties

(1) A designated authority may impose a penalty of such amount as it considers appropriate on a . . . [4] person [(except an auction platform)][3] who fails to comply with any requirement in regulation 7(1), (2) or (3), 8(1) or (3), 9(2), 10(1), 11(1), 14(1), 15(1) or (2), 16(1), (2), (3) or (4), 19(1), (4), (5) or (6), 20(1), (4) or (5), 21, 26, 27(4) or 33 . . . [4].

[(1A) A designated authority may impose a penalty of such amount as it considers appropriate on an auction platform which fails to comply with—

(*a*) the customer due diligence requirements of Article 19 or 20(6) of the emission allowance auctioning regulation;

(*b*) the monitoring and record keeping requirements of Article 54 of the emission allowance auctioning regulation; or

(*c*) regulation 20(1), (4) or (5) or 21 of these Regulations;

[4]][3]

[(1B) A designated authority may impose a penalty of such amount as it considers appropriate on a person who fails to comply with any requirement of a notice given under regulation 37(1).

(1C) In paragraphs (1), (1A) and (1B), "appropriate" means effective, proportionate and dissuasive.][4]

(2) The designated authority must not impose a penalty on a person under paragraph (1)[, (1A) or (1B)][4] where there are reasonable grounds for it to be satisfied that the person took all reasonable steps and exercised all due diligence to ensure that the requirement would be complied with.

(3) In deciding whether a person has failed to comply with a requirement of these Regulations, the designated authority must consider whether he followed any relevant guidance which was at the time—

(*a*) issued by a supervisory authority or any other appropriate body;

(*b*) approved by the Treasury; and

(*c*) published in a manner approved by the Treasury as suitable in their opinion to bring the guidance to the attention of persons likely to be affected by it.

(4) In paragraph (3), an "appropriate body" means any body which regulates or is representative of any trade, profession, business or employment carried on by the [person][1].

(5) Where the Commissioners decide to impose a penalty under this regulation, they must give the person notice of—

(*a*) their decision to impose the penalty and its amount;

(*b*) the reasons for imposing the penalty;

(*c*) the right to a review under regulation [43A][2]; and

(*d*) the right to appeal under regulation [43][2].

(6) Where the Authority, the OFT or DETI proposes to impose a penalty under this regulation, it must give the person notice of—

(*a*) its proposal to impose the penalty and the proposed amount;

(*b*) the reasons for imposing the penalty; and

(*c*) the right to make representations to it within a specified period (which may not be less than 28 days).

(7) The Authority, the OFT or DETI, as the case may be, must then decide, within a reasonable period, whether to impose a penalty under this regulation and it must give the person notice of—

(*a*) its decision not to impose a penalty; or

(*b*) the following matters—

(i) its decision to impose a penalty and the amount;

(ii) the reasons for its decision; and

(iii) the right to appeal under regulation 44(1)(*b*).

(8) A penalty imposed under this regulation is payable to the designated authority which imposes it.

Revocation—These Regulations revoked by the Money Laundering, Terrorist Financing and Transfer of Funds (Information on the Payer) Regulations, SI 2017/692 reg 110 with effect from 26 June 2017, subject to savings in reg 110(2)–(4).

Amendments—[1] Words in para (4) substituted, by the Money Laundering (Amendment) Regulations, SI 2007/3299 reg 2(*e*), with effect from 15 December 2007: SI 2007/3299 reg 1.

[2] In para (5)(*c*), (*d*), words substituted respectively, by the Transfer of Tribunal Functions and Revenue and Customs Appeals Order, SI 2009/56 art 3, Sch 2 paras 168, 171 with effect from 1 April 2009.

[3] Words in para (1) and whole of para (1A) inserted, by the Recognised Auction Platforms Regulations, SI 2011/2699 reg 11(1), (7) with effect from 12 December 2011.

[4] In paras (1), (1A), words revoked, paras (1B), (1C) inserted, and in para (2), words substituted, by the Money Laundering (Amendment) Regulations, SI 2012/2298 regs 2, 14 with effect from 1 October 2012.

43 [Appeals against decisions of the Commissioners][1]

(1) This regulation applies to decisions of the Commissioners made under—

[(*za*) regulation 28, to the effect that a person is not a fit and proper person;][2]

(*a*) regulation 29, to refuse to register an applicant;

(*b*) regulation 30, to cancel the registration of a registered person; and

(*c*) regulation 42, to impose a penalty.

(2) Any person who is the subject of a decision to which this regulation applies may [appeal to the tribunal in accordance with regulation 43F][1].

[(3) The provisions of Part 5 of the Value Added Tax Act 1994 (appeals), subject to the modifications set out in paragraph 1 of Schedule 5 to these Regulations, apply in respect of appeals to a tribunal made under this regulation as they apply in respect of appeals made to the tribunal under section 83 (appeals) of that Act.

(4) A tribunal hearing an appeal under paragraph (2) has the power to—

(*a*) quash or vary any decision of the supervisory authority, including the power to reduce any penalty to such amount (including nil) as it thinks proper, and

(*b*) substitute its own decision for any decision quashed on appeal.

(5) The modifications in Schedule 5 have effect for the purposes of appeals made under this regulation.

(6) For the purposes of appeals under this regulation, the meaning of "tribunal" is as defined in section 82 of the Value Added Tax Act 1994.][1]

Revocation—These Regulations revoked by the Money Laundering, Terrorist Financing and Transfer of Funds (Information on the Payer) Regulations, SI 2017/692 reg 110 with effect from 26 June 2017, subject to savings in reg 110(2)–(4).

Amendments—[1] Heading substituted, in para (2), words substituted, and paras (3)–(6) substituted for previous paras (3)–(5), by the Transfer of Tribunal Functions and Revenue and Customs Appeals Order, SI 2009/56 art 3, Sch 2 paras 168, 172 with effect from 1 April 2009, subject to transitional and savings provisions in Sch 3 para 2.

[2] Para (1)(*za*) inserted by the Money Laundering (Amendment) Regulations, SI 2012/2298 regs 2, 15 with effect from 1 October 2012.

[43A Offer of review

(1) The Commissioners must offer a person (P) a review of a decision that has been notified to P if an appeal lies under regulation 43 in respect of the decision.

(2) The offer of the review must be made by notice given to P at the same time as the decision is notified to P.

(3) This regulation does not apply to the notification of the conclusions of a review.][1]

Revocation—These Regulations revoked by the Money Laundering, Terrorist Financing and Transfer of Funds (Information on the Payer) Regulations, SI 2017/692 reg 110 with effect from 26 June 2017, subject to savings in reg 110(2)–(4).

Amendments—[1] Regulations 43A–43F inserted by the Transfer of Tribunal Functions and Revenue and Customs Appeals Order, SI 2009/56 art 3, Sch 2 paras 168, 173 with effect from 1 April 2009.

[43B Review by the Commissioners

(1) The Commissioners must review a decision if—

(*a*) they have offered a review of the decision under regulation 43A, and

(*b*) P notifies the Commissioners accepting the offer within 30 days from the date of the document containing the notification of the offer.

(2) But P may not notify acceptance of the offer if P has already appealed to the tribunal under regulation 43F.

(3) The Commissioners shall not review a decision if P has appealed to the tribunal under regulation 43F in respect of the decision.][1]

Revocation—These Regulations revoked by the Money Laundering, Terrorist Financing and Transfer of Funds (Information on the Payer) Regulations, SI 2017/692 reg 110 with effect from 26 June 2017, subject to savings in reg 110(2)–(4).

Amendments—[1] Regulations 43A–43F inserted by the Transfer of Tribunal Functions and Revenue and Customs Appeals Order, SI 2009/56 art 3, Sch 2 paras 168, 173 with effect from 1 April 2009.

[43C Extensions of time

(1) If under regulation 43A, the Commissioners have offered P a review of a decision, the Commissioners may within the relevant period notify P that the relevant period is extended.

(2) If notice is given the relevant period is extended to the end of 30 days from—

(*a*) the date of the notice, or

(*b*) any other date set out in the notice or a further notice.

(3) In this regulation "relevant period" means—

(*a*) the period of 30 days referred to in regulation 43B(1)(*b*), or

(*b*) if notice has been given under paragraph (1) that period as extended (or as most recently extended) in accordance with paragraph (2).][1]

Revocation—These Regulations revoked by the Money Laundering, Terrorist Financing and Transfer of Funds (Information on the Payer) Regulations, SI 2017/692 reg 110 with effect from 26 June 2017, subject to savings in reg 110(2)–(4).

Amendments—[1] Regulations 43A–43F inserted by the Transfer of Tribunal Functions and Revenue and Customs Appeals Order, SI 2009/56 art 3, Sch 2 paras 168, 173 with effect from 1 April 2009.

[43D Review out of time

(1) This regulation applies if—

(*a*) the Commissioners have offered a review of a decision under regulation 43A, and

(*b*) P does not accept the offer within the time allowed under regulation 43B(1)(*b*) or 43C(2).

(2) The Commissioners must review the decision under regulation 43B if—

(*a*) after the time allowed, P notifies the Commissioners in writing requesting a review out of time,

(*b*) the Commissioners are satisfied that P had a reasonable excuse for not accepting the offer or requiring review within the time allowed, and

(*c*) the Commissioners are satisfied that P made the request without unreasonable delay after the excuse had ceased to apply.

(3) The Commissioners shall not review a decision if P has appealed to the tribunal under regulation 43F in respect of the decision.][1]

Revocation—These Regulations revoked by the Money Laundering, Terrorist Financing and Transfer of Funds (Information on the Payer) Regulations, SI 2017/692 reg 110 with effect from 26 June 2017, subject to savings in reg 110(2)–(4).
Amendments—[1] Regulations 43A–43F inserted by the Transfer of Tribunal Functions and Revenue and Customs Appeals Order, SI 2009/56 art 3, Sch 2 paras 168, 173 with effect from 1 April 2009.

[43E Nature of review etc

(1) This regulation applies if the Commissioners are required to undertake a review under regulation 43B or 43D.

(2) The nature and extent of the review are to be such as appear appropriate to the Commissioners in the circumstances.

(3) For the purpose of paragraph (2), the Commissioners must, in particular, have regard to steps taken before the beginning of the review—

(*a*) by the Commissioners in reaching the decision, and

(*b*) by any person in seeking to resolve disagreement about the decision.

(4) The review must take account of any representations made by P at a stage which gives the Commissioners a reasonable opportunity to consider them.

(5) The review may conclude that the decision is to be—

(*a*) upheld,

(*b*) varied, or

(*c*) cancelled.

(6) The Commissioners must give P notice of the conclusions of the review and their reasoning within—

(*a*) a period of 45 days beginning with the relevant date, or

(*b*) such other period as the Commissioners and P may agree.

(7) In paragraph (6) "relevant date" means—

(*a*) the date the Commissioners received P's notification accepting the offer of a review (in a case falling within regulation 43A), or

(*b*) the date on which the Commissioners decided to undertake the review (in a case falling within regulation 43D).

(8) Where the Commissioners are required to undertake a review but do not give notice of the conclusions within the time period specified in paragraph (6), the review is to be treated as having concluded that the decision is upheld.

(9) If paragraph (8) applies, the Commissioners must notify P of the conclusion which the review is treated as having reached.][1]

Revocation—These Regulations revoked by the Money Laundering, Terrorist Financing and Transfer of Funds (Information on the Payer) Regulations, SI 2017/692 reg 110 with effect from 26 June 2017, subject to savings in reg 110(2)–(4).
Amendments—[1] Regulations 43A–43F inserted by the Transfer of Tribunal Functions and Revenue and Customs Appeals Order, SI 2009/56 art 3, Sch 2 paras 168, 173 with effect from 1 April 2009.

[43F Bringing of appeals against decisions of the Commissioners

(1) An appeal under regulation 43 is to be made to the tribunal before—

(*a*) the end of the period of 30 days beginning with the date of the document notifying the decision to which the appeal relates, or

(*b*) if later, the end of the relevant period (within the meaning of regulation 43C).

(2) But that is subject to paragraphs (3) to (5).

(3) In a case where the Commissioners are required to undertake a review under regulation 43B—

(*a*) an appeal may not be made until the conclusion date, and

(*b*) any appeal is to be made within the period of 30 days beginning with the conclusion date.

[(4) In a case where the Commissioners are requested to undertake a review in accordance with section 43D—

(*a*) an appeal may not be made—

(i) unless the Commissioners have notified P as to whether or not a review will be undertaken, and

(ii) if the Commissioners have notified P that a review will be undertaken, until the conclusion date;

(*b*) any appeal where paragraph (*a*)(ii) applies is to be made within the period of 30 days beginning with the conclusion date;

(*c*) if the Commissioners have notified P that a review will not be undertaken, an appeal may be made only if the tribunal gives permission to do so.][2]

(5) In a case where regulation 43E(8) applies, an appeal may be made at any time from the end of the period specified in regulation 43E(6) to the date 30 days after the conclusion date.

(6) An appeal may be made after the end of the period specified in paragraph (1), (3)(*b*), (4)(*b*) or (5) if the tribunal gives permission to do so.

(7) In this regulation "conclusion date" means the date of the document notifying the conclusions of the review.][1]

Revocation—These Regulations revoked by the Money Laundering, Terrorist Financing and Transfer of Funds (Information on the Payer) Regulations, SI 2017/692 reg 110 with effect from 26 June 2017, subject to savings in reg 110(2)–(4).

Amendments—[1] Regulations 43A–43F inserted by the Transfer of Tribunal Functions and Revenue and Customs Appeals Order, SI 2009/56 art 3, Sch 2 paras 168, 173 with effect from 1 April 2009.

[2] Para (4) substituted by the Revenue and Customs (Amendment of Appeal Provisions for Out of Time Reviews) Order, SI 2014/1264 art 11 with effect in relation to requests for a review out of time notified to HMRC on or after 14 May 2014.

44 Appeals

(1) A person may appeal from a decision by—

(*a*) . . . [1]

(*b*) the Authority, the OFT or DETI under regulation 34 or 42.

(2) An appeal from a decision by—

(*a*) . . . [1]

(*b*) the Authority is to the [Upper Tribunal][2];

(*c*) the OFT is to the [First-tier Tribunal][3]; and

(*d*) DETI is to the High Court.

(3) . . . [1]

(4) The provisions of Part 9 of the 2000 Act (hearings and appeals), subject to the modifications set out in paragraph 2 of Schedule 5, apply in respect of appeals to the [Upper Tribunal][2] made under this regulation as they apply in respect of references made to that Tribunal under that Act.

(5) . . . [3]

(6) . . . [1]

(7) Notwithstanding paragraph (2)(*c*), until the coming into force of section 55 of the Consumer Credit Act 2006 (the Consumer Credit Appeals Tribunal), an appeal from a decision by the OFT is to the Financial Services and Markets Tribunal and, for these purposes, the coming into force of that section shall not affect—

(*a*) the hearing and determination by the Financial Service and Markets Tribunal of an appeal commenced before the coming into force of that section ("the original appeal"); or

(*b*) any appeal against the decision of the Financial Services and Markets Tribunal with respect to the original appeal.

(8) The modifications in Schedule 5 have effect for the purposes of appeals made under this regulation.

Revocation—These Regulations revoked by the Money Laundering, Terrorist Financing and Transfer of Funds (Information on the Payer) Regulations, SI 2017/692 reg 110 with effect from 26 June 2017, subject to savings in reg 110(2)–(4).

Amendments—[1] Paras (1)(*a*), (2)(*a*), (3), (6) revoked by the Transfer of Tribunal Functions and Revenue and Customs Appeals Order, SI 2009/56 art 3, Sch 2 paras 168, 174 with effect from 1 April 2009, subject to transitional and savings provisions in Sch 3 para 2.

[2] Words in paras (2)(*b*), (4) substituted by the Transfer of Tribunal Functions Order, SI 2010/22 art 5(2), Sch 3 paras 140, 141 with effect from 6 April 2010 (SI 2010/22 art 1(2), (*f*)).

[3] In para (2)(*c*), words substituted, and para (5) revoked, by the Transfer of Functions of the Consumer Credit Appeals Tribunal Order, SI 2009/1835 art 4(2), Sch 2 para 1 with effect from 1 September 2009.

Criminal offences

45 Offences

(1) A person [(except an auction platform)][1] who fails to comply with any requirement in regulation 7(1), (2) or (3), 8(1) or (3), 9(2), 10(1), 11(1)(*a*), (*b*) or (*c*), 14(1), 15(1) or (2), 16(1), (2), (3) or (4), 19(1), (4), (5) or (6), 20(1), (4) or (5), 21, 26, 27(4) or 33 . . . [2] is guilty of an offence and liable—

(*a*) on summary conviction, to a fine not exceeding the statutory maximum;

(*b*) on conviction on indictment, to imprisonment for a term not exceeding two years, to a fine or to both.

[(1A) An auction platform which fails to comply with the customer due diligence requirements of Article 19 or 20(6) of the emission allowance auctioning regulation, the monitoring and record keeping requirements of Article 54 of that regulation, or regulation 20(1), (4) or (5) or 21 of these Regulations, is guilty of an offence and liable—

(*a*) on summary conviction, to a fine not exceeding the statutory maximum;

(*b*) on conviction on indictment, to imprisonment for a term not exceeding two years, to a fine or to both.][1]

(2) In deciding whether a person has committed an offence under paragraph (1) [or (1A)][1], the court must consider whether he followed any relevant guidance which was at the time—

(*a*) issued by a supervisory authority or any other appropriate body;

(*b*) approved by the Treasury; and

(*c*) published in a manner approved by the Treasury as suitable in their opinion to bring the guidance to the attention of persons likely to be affected by it.

(3) In paragraph (2), an "appropriate body" means any body which regulates or is representative of any trade, profession, business or employment carried on by the alleged offender.

(4) A person is not guilty of an offence under this regulation if he took all reasonable steps and exercised all due diligence to avoid committing the offence.

(5) Where a person is convicted of an offence under this regulation, he shall not also be liable to a penalty under regulation 42.

Revocation—These Regulations revoked by the Money Laundering, Terrorist Financing and Transfer of Funds (Information on the Payer) Regulations, SI 2017/692 reg 110 with effect from 26 June 2017, subject to savings in reg 110(2)–(4).

Cross references—FA 2014 Sch 34 para 6(4)(*j*) (application of this reg in relation to the issue of conduct notices to promoters of tax avoidance schemes).

Amendments—[1] Words in paras (1), (2), and whole of para (1A) inserted, by the Recognised Auction Platforms Regulations, SI 2011/2699 reg 11(1), (8) with effect from 12 December 2011.

[2] In para (1), words revoked by the Money Laundering (Amendment) Regulations, SI 2012/2298 regs 2, 16 with effect from 1 October 2012.

46 Prosecution of offences

(1) Proceedings for an offence under regulation 45 may be instituted by—

(*a*) . . . [2] order of the Commissioners;

(*b*) the OFT;

(*c*) a local weights and measures authority;

(*d*) DETI;

(*e*) the Director of Public Prosecutions; or

(*f*) the Director of Public Prosecutions for Northern Ireland.

(2) Proceedings for an offence under regulation 45 may be instituted only against a relevant person or, where such a person is a body corporate, a partnership or an unincorporated association, against any person who is liable to be proceeded against under regulation 47.

(3) Where proceedings under paragraph (1) are instituted by order of the Commissioners, the proceedings must be brought in the name of an officer of Revenue and Customs.

(4) Where a local weights and measures authority in England or Wales proposes to institute proceedings for an offence under regulation 45 it must give the OFT notice of the intended proceedings, together with a summary of the facts on which the charges are to be founded.

(5) A local weights and measures authority must also notify the OFT of the outcome of the proceedings after they are finally determined.

(6) A local weights and measures authority must, whenever the OFT requires, report in such form and with such particulars as the OFT requires on the exercise of its functions under these Regulations.

(7) Where the Commissioners investigate, or propose to investigate, any matter with a view to determining—

(*a*) whether there are grounds for believing that an offence under regulation 45 has been committed by any person; or

(*b*) whether such a person should be prosecuted for such an offence,

that matter is to be treated as an assigned matter within the meaning of section 1(1) of the Customs and Excise Management Act 1979.

(8) Paragraphs (1) and (3) to (6) do not extend to Scotland.

[(9) In its application to the Commissioners acting in Scotland, paragraph (7)(*b*) shall be read as referring to the Commissioners determining whether to refer the matter to the Crown Office and Procurator Fiscal Service with a view to the Procurator Fiscal determining whether a person should be prosecuted for such an offence.][1]

Revocation—These Regulations revoked by the Money Laundering, Terrorist Financing and Transfer of Funds (Information on the Payer) Regulations, SI 2017/692 reg 110 with effect from 26 June 2017, subject to savings in reg 110(2)–(4).

Amendments—[1] Para (9) inserted by the Money Laundering (Amendment) Regulations, SI 2007/3299 reg 2(*f*), with effect from 15 December 2007: SI 2007/3299 reg 1.

[2] In para (1)(*a*), words revoked by the Public Bodies (Merger of the Director of Public Prosecutions and the Director of Revenue and Customs Prosecutions) Order, SI 2014/834 art 3(3), Sch 3 para 21 with effect from 27 March 2014.

47 Offences by bodies corporate etc

(1) If an offence under regulation 45 committed by a body corporate is shown—

(*a*) to have been committed with the consent or the connivance of an officer of the body corporate; or

(*b*) to be attributable to any neglect on his part,

the officer as well as the body corporate is guilty of an offence and liable to be proceeded against and punished accordingly.

(2) If an offence under regulation 45 committed by a partnership is shown—

(*a*) to have been committed with the consent or the connivance of a partner; or

(*b*) to be attributable to any neglect on his part,

the partner as well as the partnership is guilty of an offence and liable to be proceeded against and punished accordingly.

(3) If an offence under regulation 45 committed by an unincorporated association (other than a partnership) is shown—

(*a*) to have been committed with the consent or the connivance of an officer of the association; or

(*b*) to be attributable to any neglect on his part,

that officer as well as the association is guilty of an offence and liable to be proceeded against and punished accordingly.

(4) If the affairs of a body corporate are managed by its members, paragraph (1) applies in relation to the acts and defaults of a member in connection with his functions of management as if he were a director of the body.

(5) Proceedings for an offence alleged to have been committed by a partnership or an unincorporated association must be brought in the name of the partnership or association (and not in that of its members).

(6) A fine imposed on the partnership or association on its conviction of an offence is to be paid out of the funds of the partnership or association.

(7) Rules of court relating to the service of documents are to have effect as if the partnership or association were a body corporate.

(8) In proceedings for an offence brought against the partnership or association—

(*a*) section 33 of the Criminal Justice Act 1925 (procedure on charge of offence against corporation) and Schedule 3 to the Magistrates' Courts Act 1980 (corporations) apply as they do in relation to a body corporate;

(*b*) section 70 (proceedings against bodies corporate) of the Criminal Procedure (Scotland) Act 1995 applies as it does in relation to a body corporate;

(*c*) section 18 of the Criminal Justice (Northern Ireland) Act 1945 (procedure on charge) and Schedule 4 to the Magistrates' Courts (Northern Ireland) Order 1981 (corporations) apply as they do in relation to a body corporate.

(9) In this regulation—

"officer"—

(*a*) in relation to a body corporate, means a director, manager, secretary, chief executive, member of the committee of management, or a person purporting to act in such a capacity; and

(*b*) in relation to an unincorporated association, means any officer of the association or any member of its governing body, or a person purporting to act in such capacity; and

"partner" includes a person purporting to act as a partner.

PART 6
MISCELLANEOUS

48 Recovery of charges and penalties through the court

Any charge or penalty imposed on a person by a supervisory authority under regulation 35(1) or 42(1) is a debt due from that person to the authority, and is recoverable accordingly.

Revocation—These Regulations revoked by the Money Laundering, Terrorist Financing and Transfer of Funds (Information on the Payer) Regulations, SI 2017/692 reg 110 with effect from 26 June 2017, subject to savings in reg 110(2)–(4).

49 Obligations on public authorities

(1) The following bodies and persons must, if they know or suspect or have reasonable grounds for knowing or suspecting that a person is or has engaged in money laundering or terrorist financing, as soon as reasonably practicable inform the Serious Organised Crime Agency—

(*a*) the Auditor General for Scotland;

(*b*) the Auditor General for Wales;

(*c*) the Authority;

(*d*) the Bank of England;

(*e*) the Comptroller and Auditor General;

(*f*) the Comptroller and Auditor General for Northern Ireland;

(*g*) the Gambling Commission;

(*h*) the OFT;

(*i*) the Official Solicitor to the Supreme Court;

(*j*) the Pensions Regulator;

(*k*) the Public Trustee;

(*l*) the Secretary of State, in the exercise of his functions under enactments relating to companies and insolvency;

(*m*) the Treasury, in the exercise of their functions under the 2000 Act;

(*n*) the Treasury Solicitor;

(*o*) a designated professional body for the purposes of Part 20 of the 2000 Act (provision of financial services by members of the professions);

(*p*) a person or inspector appointed under section 65 (investigations on behalf of Authority) or 66 (inspections and special meetings) of the Friendly Societies Act 1992;

(*q*) an inspector appointed under section 49 of the Industrial and Provident Societies Act 1965 (appointment of inspectors) or section 18 of the Credit Unions Act 1979 (power to appoint inspector);

(*r*) an inspector appointed under section 431 (investigation of a company on its own application), 432 (other company investigations), 442 (power to investigate company ownership) or [446D (appointment of replacement inspectors)][1] of the Companies Act 1985 . . .[1];

(*s*) a person or inspector appointed under section 55 (investigations on behalf of Authority) or 56 (inspections and special meetings) of the Building Societies Act 1986;

(*t*) a person appointed under section 167 (appointment of persons to carry out investigations), 168(3) or (5) (appointment of persons to carry out investigations in particular cases), 169(1)(*b*) (investigations to support overseas regulator) or 284 (power to investigate affairs of a scheme) of the 2000 Act, or under regulations made under section 262(2)(k) (open-ended investment companies) of that Act, to conduct an investigation; and

(*u*) a person authorised to require the production of documents under section 447 of the Companies Act 1985 (Secretary of State's power to require production of documents), Article 440 of the Companies (Northern Ireland) Order 1986 or section 84 of the Companies Act 1989 (exercise of powers by officer).

(2) A disclosure made under paragraph (1) is not to be taken to breach any restriction on the disclosure of information however imposed.

Revocation—These Regulations revoked by the Money Laundering, Terrorist Financing and Transfer of Funds (Information on the Payer) Regulations, SI 2017/692 reg 110 with effect from 26 June 2017, subject to savings in reg 110(2)–(4).

Amendments—[1] In para (1)(*r*) words substituted and words revoked by the Companies Act 2006 (Consequential Amendments and Transitional Provisions) Order SI 2011/1265 art 30 with effect from 12 May 2011; see art (1)(2).

[49A Disclosure by the Commissioners

(1) The Commissioners may disclose to the Authority information held in connection with their functions under these Regulations if the disclosure is made for the purpose of enabling or assisting the Authority to discharge any of its functions under the Payment Services Regulations 2009 [or the Electronic Money Regulations 2011][2].

(2) Information disclosed to the Authority under subsection (1) may not be disclosed by the Authority or any person who receives the information directly or indirectly from the Authority except—

(*a*) to, or in accordance with authority given by, the Commissioners;

(*b*) with a view to the institution of, or otherwise for the purposes of, any criminal proceedings;

(c) with a view to the institution of any other proceedings by the Authority, for the purposes of any such proceedings instituted by the Authority, or for the purposes of any reference to the Tribunal under the Payment Services Regulations 2009; or

(*d*) in the form of a summary or collection of information so framed as not to enable information relating to any particular person to be ascertained from it.

(3) Any person who discloses information in contravention of subsection (2) is guilty of an offence and liable—

(*a*) on summary conviction, to imprisonment for a term not exceeding three months, to a fine not exceeding the statutory maximum, or to both;

(*b*) on conviction on indictment, to imprisonment for a term not exceeding two years to a fine, or to both.

(4) It is a defence for a person charged with an offence under this regulation of disclosing information to prove that they reasonably believed

(*a*) that the disclosure was lawful; or

(*b*) that the information had already and lawfully been made available to the public.][1]

Revocation—These Regulations revoked by the Money Laundering, Terrorist Financing and Transfer of Funds (Information on the Payer) Regulations, SI 2017/692 reg 110 with effect from 26 June 2017, subject to savings in reg 110(2)–(4).

Amendments—[1] Reg inserted, by the Payment Services Regulations SI 2009/209 reg 126, Sch 6 para 6(*g*) with effect from 1 November 2009.

[2] In para (1) words inserted by the Electronic Money Laundering Regulations, SI 2011/99 regs 1, 79, Sch 4 para 19(*g*) with effect from 9 February 2011.

50 Transitional provisions: requirement to be registered

(1) Regulation 26 does not apply to an existing money service business, an existing trust or company service provider [, an existing high value dealer, an existing bill payment service provider or an existing telecommunication, digital and IT payment service provider][1] until—

(*a*) where it has applied in accordance with regulation 27 before the specified date for registration in a register maintained under regulation 25(1) (a "new register")—

(i) the date it is included in a new register following the determination of its application by the Commissioners; or

(ii) where the Commissioners give it notice under regulation 29(2)(*b*) of their decision not to register it, the date on which the Commissioners state that the decision takes effect or, where a statement is included in accordance with paragraph (3)(*b*), the time at which the Commissioners give it such notice;

(*b*) in any other case, the specified date.

(2) The specified date is—

(*a*) in the case of an existing money service business, 1st February 2008;

(*b*) in the case of an existing trust or company service provider, 1st April 2008;

(*c*) in the case of an existing high value dealer, the first anniversary which falls on or after 1st January 2008 of the date of its registration in a register maintained under regulation 10 of the Money Laundering Regulations 2003;

[(*d*) in the case of an existing bill payment service provider or an existing telecommunication, digital and IT payment service provider, 1st March 2010][1].

(3) In the case of an application for registration in a new register made before the specified date by an existing money service business, an existing trust or company service provider[, an existing high value dealer, an existing bill payment service provider or an existing telecommunication, digital and IT payment service provider][1], the Commissioners must include in a notice given to it under regulation 29(2)(*b*)—

(*a*) the date on which their decision is to take effect; or

(*b*) if the Commissioners consider that the interests of the public require their decision to have immediate effect, a statement to that effect and the reasons for it.

(4) In the case of an application for registration in a new register made before the specified date by an existing money services business or an existing trust or company service provider, the Commissioners must give it a notice under regulation 29(2) by—

(*a*) in the case of an existing money service business, 1st June 2008;

(*b*) in the case of an existing trust or company service provider, 1st July 2008; or

(*c*) where applicable, 45 days beginning with the date on which they receive any further information required under regulation 27(3).

(5) In this regulation—

["existing bill payment service provider" and "existing telecommunication, digital and IT payment service provider" mean a bill payment service provider or a telecommunication, digital and IT payment service provider carrying on business in the United Kingdom immediately before 1st November 2009;][1]

"existing money service business" and an "existing high value dealer" mean a money service business or a high value dealer which, immediately before 15th December 2007, was included in a register maintained under regulation 10 of the Money Laundering Regulations 2003;

"existing trust or company service provider" means a trust or company service provider carrying on business in the United Kingdom immediately before 15th December 2007.

Revocation—These Regulations revoked by the Money Laundering, Terrorist Financing and Transfer of Funds (Information on the Payer) Regulations, SI 2017/692 reg 110 with effect from 26 June 2017, subject to savings in reg 110(2)–(4).

Amendments—[1] In paras (1), (3), words substituted, para (2)(*d*) inserted, and in para (5), definition "existing bill payment service provider" and "existing telecommunication, digital and IT payment service provider" inserted, by the Payment Services Regulations SI 2009/209 reg 126, Sch 6 para 6(*h*) with effect from 1 November 2009.

51 Minor and consequential amendments

Schedule 6, which contains minor and consequential amendments to primary and secondary legislation, has effect.

Revocation—These Regulations revoked by the Money Laundering, Terrorist Financing and Transfer of Funds (Information on the Payer) Regulations, SI 2017/692 reg 110 with effect from 26 June 2017, subject to savings in reg 110(2)–(4).

SCHEDULE 1

ACTIVITIES LISTED IN POINTS 2 TO 12[, 14 AND 15][1] OF ANNEX I TO THE BANKING CONSOLIDATION DIRECTIVE

Revocation—These Regulations revoked by the Money Laundering, Terrorist Financing and Transfer of Funds (Information on the Payer) Regulations, SI 2017/692 reg 110 with effect from 26 June 2017, subject to savings in reg 110(2)–(4).

Amendments—[1] Words substituted by the Electronic Money Laundering Regulations, SI 2011/99 regs 1, 79, Sch 4 para 19(*h*)(i) with effect from 30 April 2011.

Regulation 3(3)(a)

2 Lending including, inter alia: consumer credit, mortgage credit, factoring, with or without recourse, financing of commercial transactions (including forfeiting).

3 Financial leasing.

[**4** Payment services as defined in Article 4(3) of Directive 2007/64/EC of the European Parliament and of the Council of 13 November 2007 on payment services in the internal market.

5 Issuing and administering other means of payment (including travellers' cheques and bankers' drafts) insofar as this activity is not covered by point 4.][1]

6 Guarantees and commitments.

7 Trading for own account or for account of customers in:

(*a*) money market instruments (cheques, bills, certificates of deposit, etc);

(*b*) foreign exchange;

(*c*) financial futures and options;
(*d*) exchange and interest-rate instruments; or
(*e*) transferable securities.

8 Participation in securities issues and the provision of services related to such issues.

9 Advice to undertakings on capital structure, industrial strategy and related questions and advice as well as services relating to mergers and the purchase of undertakings.

10 Money broking.

11 Portfolio management and advice.

12 Safekeeping and administration of securities.

14 Safe custody services.

[**15** Issuing electronic money.][2]

Revocation—These Regulations revoked by the Money Laundering, Terrorist Financing and Transfer of Funds (Information on the Payer) Regulations, SI 2017/692 reg 110 with effect from 26 June 2017, subject to savings in reg 110(2)–(4).

Amendments—[1] Points 4, 5 substituted by the Payment Services Regulations SI 2009/209 reg 126, Sch 6 para 6(*i*) with effect from 1 November 2009.

[2] Point 15 inserted by the Electronic Money Laundering Regulations, SI 2011/99 regs 1, 79, Sch 4 para 19(*h*)(ii) with effect from 30 April 2011.

SCHEDULE 2
FINANCIAL ACTIVITY, SIMPLIFIED DUE DILIGENCE AND POLITICALLY EXPOSED PERSONS

Regulations 4(1)(*e*) and (2), 13(6) and (8) and 14(5)

Revocation—These Regulations revoked by the Money Laundering, Terrorist Financing and Transfer of Funds (Information on the Payer) Regulations, SI 2017/692 reg 110 with effect from 26 June 2017, subject to savings in reg 110(2)–(4).

Financial activity on an occasional or very limited basis

1 For the purposes of regulation 4(1)(*e*) and (2), a person is to be considered as engaging in financial activity on an occasional or very limited basis if all the following conditions are fulfilled—
(*a*) the person's total annual turnover in respect of the financial activity does not exceed £64,000;
(*b*) the financial activity is limited in relation to any customer to no more than one transaction exceeding 1,000 euro, whether the transaction is carried out in a single operation, or a series of operations which appear to be linked;
(*c*) the financial activity does not exceed 5% of the person's total annual turnover;
(*d*) the financial activity is ancillary and directly related to the person's main activity;
(*e*) the financial activity is not the transmission or remittance of money (or any representation of monetary value) by any means;
(*f*) the person's main activity is not that of a person falling within regulation 3(1)(*a*) to (*f*) or (*h*);
(*g*) the financial activity is provided only to customers of the person's main activity and is not offered to the public.

Simplified due diligence

2 For the purposes of regulation 13(6), the conditions are—
(*a*) the authority has been entrusted with public functions pursuant to the [Treaty on European Union, the Treaty on the Functioning of the European Union or EU secondary legislation][1];
(*b*) the authority's identity is publicly available, transparent and certain;
(*c*) the activities of the authority and its accounting practices are transparent;
(*d*) either the authority is accountable to a Community institution or to the authorities of an EEA state, or otherwise appropriate check and balance procedures exist ensuring control of the authority's activity.

Amendments—[1] In para (*a*) words substituted by the Treaty of Lisbon (Changes in Terminology or Numbering) Order, SI 2012/1809 art 3 Schedule Pt 2 with effect from 1 August 2012. Note that this amendment does not affect the application of para 2 to things done before 1st December 2009 (the date on which the Treaty of Lisbon came into force): SI 2012/1809 art 2.

3 For the purposes of regulation 13(8), the conditions are—
(*a*) the product has a written contractual base;

(*b*) any related transaction is carried out through an account of the customer with a credit institution which is subject to the money laundering directive or with a credit institution situated in a non-EEA state which imposes requirements equivalent to those laid down in that directive;

(*c*) the product or related transaction is not anonymous and its nature is such that it allows for the timely application of customer due diligence measures where there is a suspicion of money laundering or terrorist financing;

(*d*) the product is within the following maximum threshold—

(i) in the case of insurance policies or savings products of a similar nature, the annual premium is no more than 1,000 euro or there is a single premium of no more than 2,500 euro;

(ii) in the case of products which are related to the financing of physical assets where the legal and beneficial title of the assets is not transferred to the customer until the termination of the contractual relationship (whether the transaction is carried out in a single operation or in several operations which appear to be linked), the annual payments do not exceed 15,000 euro;

(iii) in all other cases, the maximum threshold is 15,000 euro;

(*e*) the benefits of the product or related transaction cannot be realised for the benefit of third parties, except in the case of death, disablement, survival to a predetermined advanced age, or similar events;

(*f*) in the case of products or related transactions allowing for the investment of funds in financial assets or claims, including insurance or other kinds of contingent claims—

(i) the benefits of the product or related transaction are only realisable in the long term;

(ii) the product or related transaction cannot be used as collateral; and

(iii) during the contractual relationship, no accelerated payments are made, surrender clauses used or early termination takes place.

Politically exposed persons

4—(1) For the purposes of regulation 14(5)—

(*a*) individuals who are or have been entrusted with prominent public functions include the following—

(i) heads of state, heads of government, ministers and deputy or assistant ministers;

(ii) members of parliaments;

(iii) members of supreme courts, of constitutional courts or of other high-level judicial bodies whose decisions are not generally subject to further appeal, other than in exceptional circumstances;

(iv) members of courts of auditors or of the boards of central banks;

(v) ambassadors, chargés d'affaires and high-ranking officers in the armed forces; and

(vi) members of the administrative, management or supervisory bodies of state-owned enterprises;

(*b*) the categories set out in paragraphs (i) to (vi) of sub-paragraph (*a*) do not include middle-ranking or more junior officials;

(*c*) immediate family members include the following—

(i) a spouse;

(ii) a partner;

(iii) children and their spouses or partners; and

(iv) parents;

(*d*) persons known to be close associates include the following—

(i) any individual who is known to have joint beneficial ownership of a legal entity or legal arrangement, or any other close business relations, with a person referred to in regulation 14(5)(*a*); and

(ii) any individual who has sole beneficial ownership of a legal entity or legal arrangement which is known to have been set up for the benefit of a person referred to in regulation 14(5)(*a*).

(2) In paragraph (1)(*c*), "partner" means a person who is considered by his national law as equivalent to a spouse.

[SCHEDULE 3
PROFESSIONAL BODIES

Regulations 17(2)(b), 23(1)(c) and 32(4)

Revocation—These Regulations revoked by the Money Laundering, Terrorist Financing and Transfer of Funds (Information on the Payer) Regulations, SI 2017/692 reg 110 with effect from 26 June 2017, subject to savings in reg 110(2)–(4).

1 Association of Accounting Technicians

2 Association of Chartered Certified Accountants

3 Association of International Accountants

4 Association of Taxation Technicians

[**4A** Chartered Institute of Legal Executives][2]

5 Chartered Institute of Management Accountants

6 . . . [2]

7 Chartered Institute of Taxation

8 Council for Licensed Conveyancers

9 Faculty of Advocates

10 Faculty Office of the Archbishop of Canterbury

11 General Council of the Bar

12 General Council of the Bar of Northern Ireland

13 Insolvency Practitioners Association

14 Institute of Certified Bookkeepers

15 Institute of Chartered Accountants in England and Wales

16 Institute of Chartered Accountants in Ireland

17 Institute of Chartered Accountants of Scotland

18 Institute of Financial Accountants

19 International Association of Book-keepers

20 Law Society

21 Law Society of Northern Ireland

22 Law Society of Scotland][1]

Amendments—[1] Schedule 3 substituted by the Money Laundering (Amendment) Regulations, SI 2012/2298 regs 2, 17, schedule, with effect from 1 October 2012.

[2] Para 4A inserted, and para 6 revoked, by the Money Laundering (Amendment) Regulations, SI 2015/11 regs 2, 3 with effect from 6 February 2015.

SCHEDULE 4
CONNECTED PERSONS

Regulation 37(2)

Revocation—These Regulations revoked by the Money Laundering, Terrorist Financing and Transfer of Funds (Information on the Payer) Regulations, SI 2017/692 reg 110 with effect from 26 June 2017, subject to savings in reg 110(2)–(4).

Corporate bodies

1 If the relevant person is a body corporate ("BC"), a person who is or has been—
(*a*) an officer or manager of BC or of a parent undertaking of BC;
(*b*) an employee of BC;
(*c*) an agent of BC or of a parent undertaking of BC

Partnerships

2 If the relevant person is a partnership, a person who is or has been a member, manager, employee or agent of the partnership.

Unincorporated associations

3 If the relevant person is an unincorporated association of persons which is not a partnership, a person who is or has been an officer, manager, employee or agent of the association.

Individuals

4 If the relevant person is an individual, a person who is or has been an employee or agent of that individual.

SCHEDULE 5
MODIFICATIONS IN RELATION TO APPEALS

Regulation 44(8)

Revocation—These Regulations revoked by the Money Laundering, Terrorist Financing and Transfer of Funds (Information on the Payer) Regulations, SI 2017/692 reg 110 with effect from 26 June 2017, subject to savings in reg 110(2)–(4).

PART 1
PRIMARY LEGISLATION

The Value Added Tax Act 1994 (c 23)

[**1** Part 5 of the Value Added Tax Act 1994 (appeals) is modified by omitting sections 83A to 84, 85A and 85B.][1]

Amendments—[1] This para substituted by the Transfer of Tribunal Functions and Revenue and Customs Appeals Order, SI 2009/56 art 3, Sch 2 paras 168, 175 with effect from 1 April 2009.

The Financial Services and Markets Act 2000 (c 8)

2 Part 9 of the 2000 Act (hearings and appeals) is modified as follows—

(*a*) in the application of [sections 133 to 133B][1] to any appeal commenced before the coming into force of section 55 of the Consumer Credit Act 2006, for all the references to "the Authority", substitute "the Authority or the OFT (as the case may be)";

(*b*) . . . [1]

[(*c*) in section 133A omit subsections (1), (2), (3) and (5);][1] and

(*d*) in [section 133A(4)][1] for "decision notice" in both places where it occurs substitute "notice under regulation 34(5) or (9) or 42(7) of the Money Laundering Regulations 2007".

Amendments—[1] Words in sub-paras(*a*), (*d*) substituted, sub-para (b) revoked, and sub-para (c) substituted, by the Transfer of Tribunal Functions Order, SI 2010/22 art 5(2), Sch 3 paras 140, 142 with effect from 6 April 2010 (SI 2010/22 art 1(2), (*f*)).

PART 2
SECONDARY LEGISLATION[1]

Amendments—[1] Part 2 revoked by the Transfer of Tribunal Functions Order, SI 2010/22 art 5(2), Sch 3 paras 140, 142(*b*) with effect from 6 April 2010 (SI 2010/22 art 1(2), (*f*)).

SCHEDULE 6
MINOR AND CONSEQUENTIAL AMENDMENTS

Regulation 51

Revocation—These Regulations revoked by the Money Laundering, Terrorist Financing and Transfer of Funds (Information on the Payer) Regulations, SI 2017/692 reg 110 with effect from 26 June 2017, subject to savings in reg 110(2)–(4).

PART 1
PRIMARY LEGISLATION

The Value Added Tax Act 1994 (c 23)

1 In section 83 of the Value Added Tax Act 1994 (appeals), omit paragraph (zz).

The Northern Ireland Act 1998 (c 47)

2 In paragraph 25 of Schedule 3 to the Northern Ireland Act 1998 (reserved matters), for "2003" substitute "2007".

The Criminal Justice and Police Act 2001 (c 16)

3 In Part 1 of Schedule 1 to the Criminal Justice and Police Act 2001 (powers of seizure to which section 50 of the 2001 Act applies), after paragraph 73I insert—

"The Money Laundering Regulations 2007

73J
The power of seizure conferred by regulation 39(6) of the Money Laundering Regulations 2007 (entry to premises under warrant).".

PART 2
SECONDARY LEGISLATION

The Independent Qualified Conveyancers (Scotland) Regulations 1997

4 Regulation 28 of the Independent Qualified Conveyancers (Scotland) Regulations 1997 is revoked.

The Executry Practitioners (Scotland) Regulations 1997

5 Regulation 26 of the Executry Practitioners (Scotland) Regulations 1997 is revoked.

The Cross-Border Credit Transfers Regulations 1999

6 In regulation 12(2) of the Cross-Border Credit Transfers Regulations 1999, for "2003" substitute "2007".

The Terrorism Act 2000 (Crown Servants and Regulators) Regulations 2001

7 In regulation 2 of the Terrorism Act 2000 (Crown Servants and Regulators) Regulations 2001, in the definition of "relevant business", for "has the meaning given by regulation 2(2) of the Money Laundering Regulations 2003" substitute "means an activity carried on in the course of business by any of the persons listed in regulation 3(1)(*a*) to (*h*) of the Money Laundering Regulations 2007".

The Representation of the People (England and Wales) Regulations 2001

8 In regulation 114(3)(*b*) of the Representation of the People (England and Wales) Regulations 2001, for "2003" substitute "2007".

The Representation of the People (Scotland) Regulations 2001

9 In regulation 113(3)(*b*) of the Representation of the People (Scotland) Regulations 2001, for "2003" substitute "2007".

The Financial Services and Markets Act 2000 (Regulated Activities) Order 2001

10 In article 72E(9) of the Financial Services and Markets Act 2000 (Regulated Activities) Order 2001, for "2003" substitute "2007".

The Proceeds of Crime Act 2002 (Failure to Disclose Money Laundering: Specified Training) Order 2003

11 In article 2 of the Proceeds of Crime Act 2002 (Failure to Disclose Money Laundering: Specified Training) Order 2003, for "regulation 3(1)(*c*)(ii) of the Money Laundering Regulations 2003" substitute "regulation 21 of the Money Laundering Regulations 2007".

The Public Contracts (Scotland) Regulations 2006

12 In regulation 23(1)(*f*) of the Public Contracts (Scotland) Regulations 2006, for "2003" substitute "2007".

The Utilities Contracts (Scotland) Regulations 2006

13 In regulation 26(1)(*f*) of the Utilities Contracts (Scotland) Regulations 2006, for "2003" substitute "2007".

The Public Contracts Regulations 2006

14 (*amended* the Public Contracts Regulations 2006 reg 23(1)(*e*); *repealed by* the Public Procurement (Amendments, Repeals and Revocations) Regulations, SI 2016/275 reg 4, Sch 3 Pt 2).

The Utilities Contracts Regulations 2006

15 (*amended* the Utilities Contracts Regulations 2006 reg 26(1)(*e*); *repealed by* the Public Procurement (Amendments, Repeals and Revocations) Regulations, SI 2016/275 reg 4, Sch 3 Pt 2).

2007/2483

FINANCE ACT 2007 (SCHEDULES 13 AND 14) ORDER 2007

Made by the Treasury under FA 2007 s 47(4) and (5)

Made . . . . *30 August 2007*

Commentary—*Simon's Taxes* **D9.1001**.

1 Citation

This Order may be cited as the Finance Act 2007 (Schedules 13 and 14) Order 2007.

2 Schedule 13 to the Finance Act 2007

Schedule 13 to the Finance Act 2007 (sale and repurchase of securities) shall have effect in relation to an arrangement that comes into force on or after 1st October 2007.

3 Schedule 14 to the Finance Act 2007

The amendments made by Schedule 14 to the Finance Act 2007 (sale and repurchase of securities: minor and consequential amendments), with the exception of the amendments made by paragraphs 10 and 18 of that Schedule, shall have effect in relation to an arrangement that comes into force on or after 1st October 2007.

4—(1) The amendments made by paragraph 10 of Schedule 14 to the Finance Act 2007 shall have effect as follows.

(2) In a case where there is a debtor repo within the meaning of paragraph 2 of Schedule 13 to the Finance Act 2007, the amendments shall have effect in relation to an arrangement that comes into force on or after 1st October 2007.

(3) In a case where there is a stock lending arrangement within the meaning of section 263B(1) of the Taxation of Chargeable Gains Act 1992, the amendments shall have effect in relation to an arrangement under which the lender transfers securities to the borrower otherwise than by way of sale on or after 1st October 2007.

5—(1) The amendments made by paragraph 18 of Schedule 14 to the Finance Act 2007 shall have effect as follows.

(2) In a case where there is an arrangement to which Schedule 13 to the Finance Act 2007 applies, the amendments shall have effect in relation to an arrangement that comes into force on or after 1st October 2007.

(3) In a case where there is a stock lending arrangement within the meaning of section 263B(1) of the Taxation of Chargeable Gains Act 1992, the amendments shall have effect in relation to an arrangement under which the lender transfers securities to the borrower otherwise than by way of sale on or after 1st October 2007.

(4) In any other case, the amendments shall have effect in relation to disposals on or after 1st October 2007.

6 Interpretation

Paragraph 14(6) of Schedule 13 to the Finance Act 2007 applies for the purpose of determining the times at which an arrangement is in force.

2007/2485

SALE AND REPURCHASE OF SECURITIES (MODIFICATION OF SCHEDULE 13 TO THE FINANCE ACT 2007) REGULATIONS 2007

Made by the Treasury under FA 2007 Sch 13 para 15

Made . . . . *30 August 2007*
Laid before the House of Commons . . . . *31 August 2007*
Coming into force . . . . *1 October 2007*

Commentary—*Simon's Taxes* **D9.1001**.

1 Citation, commencement and interpretation

(1) These Regulations may be cited as the Sale and Repurchase of Securities (Modification of Schedule 13 to the Finance Act 2007) Regulations 2007, shall come into force on 1st October 2007, and shall have effect in relation to arrangements that come into force on or after that day.

(2) Paragraph 14(6) of Schedule 13 to the Finance Act 2007 applies for the purpose of determining the time at which an arrangement is in force.

(3) In these Regulations—

"non-standard repo case" shall be construed in accordance with paragraph 15(2) of Schedule 13;

"redemption arrangements" shall be construed in accordance with paragraph 15(6) of Schedule 13;

"Schedule 13" means Schedule 13 to the Finance Act 2007.

2 Non-standard repo cases: substitution of securities

(1) In a non-standard repo case where—

(*a*) condition B is met in relation to the repo (see paragraph 15(4) of Schedule 13), and

(*b*) securities ("the substituted securities") are substituted for other securities,

Schedule 13 applies with the modifications specified in paragraph (2).

(2) Paragraphs 2 (meaning of debtor repo), 6 (ignoring sale and subsequent purchase for purposes of chargeable gains: debtor repos), 7 (meaning of creditor repo) and 11 (ignoring purchase and subsequent sale for purposes of chargeable gains: creditor repos) of Schedule 13 apply as if any references in any of those paragraphs to "securities or similar securities" (however expressed) included a reference to the substituted securities.

3 Redemption arrangements: modifications of Schedule 13

(1) In a case involving redemption arrangements—

(*a*) paragraphs 2 (meaning of debtor repo) and 3 (meaning of debtor quasi-repo) of Schedule 13 apply with the modifications specified in paragraphs (2) and (3), and

(*b*) paragraphs 7 (meaning of creditor repo) and 8 (meaning of creditor quasi-repo) of Schedule 13 apply with the modifications specified in paragraphs (4) and (5).

(2) Any reference in paragraphs 2 and 3 to an arrangement that makes provision conferring a right or imposing an obligation on the borrower to buy securities at any subsequent time shall be treated as if it included a reference to an arrangement under which the borrower has the right or obligation to receive an amount equivalent to the proceeds of redemption of the securities.

(3) Any reference in paragraphs 2 and 3 to the buying of securities extinguishing the financial liability in respect of the advance recorded in the accounts of the borrower in accordance with generally accepted accounting practice shall be treated as if it included a reference to a payment of an amount equivalent to the proceeds of redemption of the securities extinguishing the financial liability in respect of the advance recorded in the accounts of the borrower in accordance with generally accepted accounting practice.

(4) Any reference in paragraphs 7 and 8 to an arrangement that makes provision conferring a right or imposing an obligation on the lender to sell securities at any subsequent time shall be treated as if it included a reference to an arrangement under which the lender has the right or obligation to pay the proceeds of redemption of the securities to any person.

(5) Any reference in paragraphs 7 and 8 to the subsequent sale of securities extinguishing the financial asset in respect of the advance recorded in the accounts of the lender in accordance with generally accepted accounting practice shall be treated as if it included a reference to the payment of an amount equivalent to the proceeds of redemption of the securities extinguishing the financial asset in respect of the advance recorded in the accounts of the lender in accordance with generally accepted accounting practice.

4 Redemption arrangements: consequences for tax in respect of chargeable gains

(1) In a case where paragraph 2 of Schedule 13 applies with the modifications specified in regulation 3, sub-paragraphs (3) to (5) of paragraph 6 of Schedule 13 apply as if those sub-paragraphs provided that, in such a case, the borrower shall be treated for the purposes of tax in respect of chargeable gains as having disposed of the securities transferred by him to the lender under the arrangement—

(*a*) on the occasion of the redemption of the securities, and

(*b*) for an amount equivalent to the proceeds of redemption.

(2) In a case where paragraph 7 of Schedule 13 applies with the modifications specified in regulation 3, sub-paragraphs (3) to (5) of paragraph 11 of Schedule 13 apply as if those sub-paragraphs provided that, in such a case, the lender shall be treated for the purposes of tax in respect of chargeable gains as having acquired the securities transferred to him under the arrangement—

(*a*) on the occasion of the redemption of the securities, and

(*b*) for an amount equivalent to the proceeds of redemption.

2007/2486

SALE AND REPURCHASE OF SECURITIES (MODIFICATION OF ENACTMENTS) REGULATIONS 2007

Made by the Treasury under ITA 2007 ss 612, 613 and 614 and TCGA 1992 ss 263F, 263G and 263H

Made . . . .*30 August 2007*
Laid before the House of Commons . . . .*31 August 2007*
Coming into force . . . .*1 October 2007*

Commentary—*Simon's Taxes* **D9.1001**.

1 Citation, commencement and interpretation

(1) These Regulations may be cited as the Sale and Repurchase of Securities (Modification of Enactments) Regulations 2007 and shall come into force on 1st October 2007.

(2) These Regulations shall have effect in relation to arrangements where the transfer of securities referred to in section 607(1)(*b*) of ITA 2007 takes place on or after 1st October 2007.

(3) In these Regulations—

"ITA 2007" means the Income Tax Act 2007;

"non-standard repo case" shall be construed in accordance with section 612(2) of ITA 2007;

"redemption arrangements" shall be construed in accordance with section 613(2) of ITA 2007;

"TCGA 1992" means the Taxation of Chargeable Gains Act 1992.

2 Non-standard repo cases: substitution of securities

(1) This regulation applies in a non-standard repo case where—

(*a*) condition B is met in relation to the repo (see section 612(4) of ITA 2007), and

(*b*) securities ("the substituted securities") are substituted for other securities.

(2) Sections 601 to 610 of ITA 2007 (repos) and section 263A of TCGA 1992 (agreements for sale and repurchase of securities) apply as if any references in any of those sections to "securities or similar securities" (however expressed) included a reference to the substituted securities.

3 Redemption arrangements: modifications of enactments relating to income tax

(1) In a case involving redemption arrangements, sections 601 to 610 of ITA 2007 apply with the modifications specified in paragraph (2).

(2) Sections 601 to 610 apply as if any references in any of those sections to the repurchase of the securities (however expressed) included a reference to an arrangement under which the borrower has the right or obligation to receive an amount equivalent to the proceeds of redemption of the securities.

4 Redemption arrangements: modifications of enactments relating to capital gains tax

(1) In a case involving redemption arrangements, section 263A of TCGA 1992 applies with the following modifications.

(2) Subsection (1A) applies as if it provided that the interim holder shall be treated for the purposes of capital gains tax as acquiring the securities—

(*a*) on the occasion of the redemption of the securities, and

(*b*) for an amount equivalent to the proceeds of redemption.

(3) Subsection (1B) applies as if it provided that the original owner shall be treated for the purposes of capital gains tax as disposing of the securities—

(*a*) on the occasion of the redemption of the securities, and

(*b*) for an amount equivalent to the proceeds of redemption.

2007/2488

MANUFACTURED INTEREST (TAX) REGULATIONS 2007

Made by the Treasury under ITA 2007 s 585

Made . . . . *30 August 2007*
Laid before the House of Commons . . . . *31 August 2007*
Coming into force . . . . *1 October 2007*

Commentary—*Simon's Taxes* **D9.713**.

Amendments—These Regulations revoked by the Manufactured Interest (Tax) (Amendment) Regulations, SI 2009/2810 reg 2 with effect in relation to payments of manufactured interest made or treated as made on or after 1.15 pm on 21 October 2009.

2007/2532

FINANCE ACT 2007, SCHEDULE 25 (COMMENCEMENT AND TRANSITIONAL PROVISIONS) ORDER 2007

Made by the Treasury under FA 2007 Sch 25 para 23

Made . . . . *30 August 2007*

Commentary—*Simon's Taxes* **C5.117H.**

1 Citation and interpretation

(1) This Order may be cited as the Finance Act 2007, Schedule 25 (Commencement and Transitional Provisions) Order 2007.

(2) In this Order—

"the 2006 Order" means the Gambling Act 2005 (Commencement No 6 and Transitional Provisions) Order 2006; and

"BGDA 1981" means the Betting and Gaming Duties Act 1981.

2 Provisions coming into force on 1st September 2007

The provisions of Schedule 25 to the Finance Act 2007, other than the provisions specified in paragraph 23(1) of that Schedule (which came into force on the day that Act was passed), come into force on 1st September 2007.

3 Transitional provisions

In section 505(1)(*f*)(ii) of the Income and Corporation Taxes Act 1988 (charitable companies: exemption for profits from lotteries) and section 530(2) of the Income Tax Act 2007 (charitable trusts: exemption for profits from lotteries) the references to "lottery operating licence" include an operating licence which is treated as being held by a society by virtue of paragraph 68 of Schedule 4 to the 2006 Order.

4 In section 12(4) of BGDA 1981 (definitions for purposes of Part 1 of that Act) the reference to "general betting operating licence" includes an operating licence granted by virtue of paragraph 40(4) of Schedule 4 to the 2006 Order.

5—(1) In section 20C(2) of BGDA 1981 (definitions for purposes of Part 2 of that Act) the references to "bingo premises licence" include a bingo club licence which is to have effect, by virtue of paragraph 62 of Schedule 4 to the 2006 Order, to authorise the licensed premises to be used for providing facilities for gambling as if it were a bingo premises licence.

(2) In paragraph (1) "bingo club licence" has the same meaning as in paragraph 1(1) of Schedule 4 to the 2006 Order.

6—(1) Paragraph 5(1) of Schedule 3 to BGDA (exemptions from bingo duty: small scale amusements provided commercially) is subject to the following transitional provisions.

(2) In paragraph (*a*) the reference to "family entertainment centre" includes premises in respect of which—

(*a*) an application for a family entertainment centre gaming machine permit under Schedule 10 to the Gambling Act 2005 is treated by virtue of paragraph 98 of Schedule 4 to the 2006 Order as having been granted, or

(*b*) a permit under section 34 of the Gaming Act 1968 is to have effect, by virtue of paragraph 62 of Schedule 4 to the 2006 Order, to authorise the premises to be used for the purposes of providing facilities for gambling as if it were a family entertainment centre premises licence.

(3) In paragraph (*b*) the reference to "an adult gaming centre premises licence" includes a permit under section 34 of the Gaming Act 1968 which is to have effect, by virtue of paragraph 62 of Schedule 4 to the 2006 Order, to authorise the premises to which the permit relates to be used for the purposes of providing facilities for gambling as if it were an adult gaming centre premises licence.

2007/2709

TRIBUNALS, COURTS AND ENFORCEMENT ACT 2007 (COMMENCEMENT NO 1) ORDER 2007

Made by the Lord Chancellor under TCEA 2007 s 148(5)

Made . . . . *13 September 2007*

1 Citation and interpretation

(1) This Order may be cited as the Tribunals, Courts and Enforcement Act 2007 (Commencement No 1) Order 2007.

(2) In this Order, "the Act" means the Tribunals, Courts and Enforcement Act 2007.

2 Provisions coming into force on 19th September 2007

The following provisions of the Act come into force on 19th September 2007—

(*a*) sections 1, 2, 7(1) and (9), 9(3), 10(3), 11(5)(*f*) and (6) to (8), 13(6), (8)(*f*), (9), (10), (14) and (15), 18(10) and (11), 20(3), (6) and (7), 21(6), 22, 27(5) and (6), 30 to 42, 45(3), 49, 54, 58, 59, 61 and 144(1), (5) and (7);

(*b*) section 46 to the extent that it relates to Schedule 5;

(*c*) section 48(1) to the extent that it relates to the following paragraphs of Schedule 8—

(i) paragraphs 31(1) to (3), 62, 63 and 65(1) and (2); and

(ii) paragraph 65(3) to the extent that it relates to the Senior President of Tribunals;

(*d*) section 48(2) to the extent that it relates to paragraphs 1, 2 and 12(2) of Schedule 9;

(*e*) sections 50(1) to (5) and (7), 51 and 52 for the purposes of paragraph 3 of Schedule 1;

(*f*) section 144(11) to the extent that it relates to Part 1 and section 51;
(*g*) in Schedule 1, paragraphs 1 to 11;
(*h*) in Schedule 4, paragraph 15;
(*i*) Schedule 5;
(*j*) Schedule 6; and
(*k*) in Schedule 7, paragraphs 25(2) to (7) and 26 to 28.

3 Provisions coming into force on 1st November 2007

The following provisions of the Act come into force on 1st November 2007—

(*a*) sections 44, 45(1) and (2) and 146;
(*b*) section 48(1) to the extent that it relates to the following paragraphs of Schedule 8—
(i) paragraphs 2, 3, 8 to 12, 14, 15, 17, 19 to 23, 30(*a*) to (*c*), 32, 33(1) and (2), 49 to 52 and 56 to 61;
(ii) paragraphs 4, 5, 7 and 53 to the extent that they relate to the Administrative Justice and Tribunals Council and to the Scottish Committee of the Administrative Justice and Tribunals Council; and
(iii) paragraph 18 to the extent that it relates to the Administrative Justice and Tribunals Council;
(*c*) in Schedule 7—
(i) paragraphs 1 to 6, 10(1)(*a*) and (*b*), (2)(*a*) and (*b*), (3)(*a*) and (*b*) and (4), 12, 13, 14(1), (2), (3)(*a*) and (4), 15 to 18, 20, 21(1), (2), (4) and (5), 22(1)(*a*) and (*b*) and (2), 23 and 25(1);
(ii) paragraphs 11 and 22(3) to the extent that they relate to the Administrative Justice and Tribunals Council and to the Scottish Committee of the Administrative Justice and Tribunals Council; and
(iii) paragraph 21(6) to the extent that it relates to reports made by the Administrative Justice and Tribunals Council; and
(*d*) in Part 1 of Schedule 23, the entries relating to—
(i) the House of Commons Disqualification Act 1975;
(ii) the Northern Ireland Assembly Disqualification Act 1975;
(iii) the Race Relations Act 1976;
(iv) the Estate Agents Act 1979;
(v) sections 1, 2, 3, 4 and 13(5)(*c*) of the Tribunals and Inquiries Act 1992;
(vi) the Scotland Act 1998 (Cross-Border Public Authorities) (Adaptation of Functions etc) Order 1999 to the extent that Schedule 9 applies to sections 2 and 4 of the Tribunals and Inquiries Act 1992;
(vii) the Freedom of Information Act 2000; and
(viii) the Scottish Public Services Ombudsman Act 2002 (Consequential Provisions and Modifications) Order 2004.

4 Provisions coming into force on 1st December 2007

Section 48(1) of the Act comes into force on 1st December 2007 to the extent that it relates to paragraphs 35 to 39 of Schedule 8.

5 Provisions coming into force on 1st April 2008

The following provisions of the Act come into force on 1st April 2008—

(*a*) sections 139 and 140; and
(*b*) Schedule 22.

6 Provisions coming into force on 1st June 2008

The following provisions of the Act come into force on 1st June 2008—

(*a*) all paragraphs of Schedule 7, except paragraph 24, to the extent that they are not already in force; and
(*b*) section 48(1) to the extent that it relates to the following paragraphs of Schedule 8—
(i) paragraphs 4 and 5 to the extent that they relate to the Welsh Committee of the Administrative Justice and Tribunals Council;
(ii) paragraphs 7, 18 and 53, to the extent that they are not already in force; and
(iii) paragraph 30(*d*).

2007/3000

INCOME TAX (BENEFITS RECEIVED BY FORMER OWNER OF PROPERTY) (ELECTION FOR INHERITANCE TAX TREATMENT) REGULATIONS 2007

Made by the Treasury, under FA 2004 Sch 15 para 23(2)

Made . . . . *19 October 2007*
Laid before House of Commons . . . . *22 October 2007*
Coming into force . . . . *14 November 2007*

1 Citation and commencement

These Regulations may be cited as the Income Tax (Benefits Received by Former Owner of Property) (Election for Inheritance Tax Treatment) Regulations 2007 and shall come into force on 14th November 2007.

2 Manner in which election to be made

An election under paragraph 21 or 22 of Schedule 15 to the Finance Act 2004 (power to elect for inheritance tax treatment of pre-owned assets) is to be made in writing on the form designated IHT 500 in the Schedule to these Regulations.

SCHEDULE

FORM IHT 500

Regulation 2

HM Revenue & Customs

Election for Inheritance Tax to apply to asset previously owned

Fill in this form if you are chargeable to Income Tax on the benefit you receive from property you previously owned but want to elect for the property to be treated as part of your estate for Inheritance Tax purposes.

You should read the notes IHT501 as you fill in this form. Please provide information for all sections, inserting 'not applicable' where appropriate.

About the person making the election

Title

Surname

First name(s)

Date of birth *DD MM YYYY*

HMRCIncome Tax office

HMRCIncome Tax office reference

Unique Taxpayer Reference (UTR)

National Insurance number

Address

Postcode

About the property subject to the election

The property is:

an interest in land a chattel intangible property

Description of the property

Name(s) of the legal owners of the property

Details of disposal(s) or contribution(s)

What is the nature and extent of your interest in the property?

Is the property conditionally exempt from Inheritance Tax or Capital Gains Tax on an earlier event?

Yes ☐ No ☐

If 'Yes', please provide details

Name(s) of anyone else who receives a benefit from the property

The election

I elect that the property specified above is to form part of my estate for Inheritance Tax purposes under the provisions of paragraphs 21 to 23, Schedule 15 to the Finance Act 2004.

Signature of person making the election

Date DD MM YYYY

Capacity

The election applies from the year of Assessment [illegible]

April

When you have completed this form send it to:

Pre-owned Assets Section
HMRC Inheritance Tax
PO Box 38
Castle Meadow Road
Nottingham
NG2 1BB

Document Exchange: **DX 701201 Nottingham 4.**

Probate and Inheritance Tax helpline:
0845 30 20 900.

For further guidance go to:
www.hmrc.gov.uk/poa/index.htm

Page 2

2007/3104

TAX AVOIDANCE SCHEMES (PENALTY) REGULATIONS 2007

Made by the Treasury under TMA 1970 s 98C(2A) to (2C)(a)

Made . . . .*30 October 2007*

Coming into force in accordance with . . . .*regulation 1*

Note—National Insurance Contributions (Application of Part 7 of the Finance Act 2004) Regulations, SI 2012/1868 reg 28 (these Regulations apply to notifiable contribution arrangements and notifiable contribution proposals as they apply to income tax. Any reference in these Regulations to FA 2004 ss 306–313C and s 314A shall be construed as a reference to the corresponding provision of SI 2012/1868. Any reference in these Regulations to TMA 1970 s 98C shall be construed as a reference to SI 2012/1868 reg 22.

1 Citation and commencement

These Regulations may be cited as the Tax Avoidance Schemes (Penalty) Regulations 2007 and shall come into force 21 days after they are made.

2 Interpretation

In these Regulations—

"FA 2004" means the Finance Act 2004; and

"TMA 1970" means the Taxes Management Act 1970.

[3 For the purposes of section 98C(2A) of TMA 1970, the prescribed sum is £5,000.][1]

Amendments—[1] Reg 3 substituted by the Tax Avoidance Schemes (Penalty) (Amendment) Regulations, SI 2010/2743 regs 2, 3 with effect from 1 January 2011.

[4 For the purposes of section 98C(2B) of TMA 1970, the prescribed sum is £5,000.][1]

Amendments—[1] Reg 4 substituted by the Tax Avoidance Schemes (Penalty) (Amendment) Regulations, SI 2010/2743 regs 2, 4 with effect from 1 January 2011.

2007/3175

POLICE AND CRIMINAL EVIDENCE ACT 1984 (APPLICATION TO REVENUE AND CUSTOMS) ORDER 2007

Made by the Treasury under PACE 1984 s 114 (2) and (3)

Made .... *8 November 2007*
Laid before Parliament .... *9 November 2007*
Coming into force .... *1 December 2007*

Commentary—*Simon's Taxes* **A6.11**.

Amendments—Revoked by the Police and Criminal Evidence Act 1984 (Application to Revenue and Customs) Order, SI 2015/1783 art 20(*a*) with effect from 4 November 2015.

1 Citation and commencement

This Order may be cited as the Police and Criminal Evidence Act 1984 (Application to Revenue and Customs) Order 2007 and shall come into force on 1st December 2007.

2 Interpretation

(1) In this Order—

"the Act" means the Police and Criminal Evidence Act 1984;

"the Commissioners" means the Commissioners for Her Majesty's Revenue and Customs;

"the customs and excise Acts" has the meaning given to it by section 1 of the Customs and Excise Management Act 1979;

"former Inland Revenue matter" means a matter specified in section 54(4) (*b*) or (*f*) of, or in paragraphs 3, 7, 10, [14, 15][1], 19 or 24 to 29 of Schedule 1 to, the Commissioners for Revenue and Customs Act 2005;

"office of Revenue and Customs" means premises wholly or partly occupied by Her Majesty's Revenue and Customs;

"relevant indictable offence" means an indictable offence which relates to a matter in relation to which Her Majesty's Revenue and Customs have functions apart from a former Inland Revenue matter;

"relevant investigation" means a criminal investigation conducted by officers of Revenue and Customs which relates to a matter in relation to which Her Majesty's Revenue and Customs have functions apart from a former Inland Revenue matter.

(2) A person is in Revenue and Customs detention for the purpose of this Order if—

(*a*) he has been taken to an office of Revenue and Customs after being arrested for an offence; or

(*b*) he is arrested at an office of Revenue and Customs after attending voluntarily at the office or accompanying an officer of Revenue and Customs to it,

and is detained there or detained elsewhere in the charge of an officer of Revenue and Customs, and nothing shall prevent a detained person from being transferred between Revenue and Customs detention and police detention.

Amendments—[1] In para (1), in definition of of "former Inland Revenue matter", reference substituted by the Police and Criminal Evidence Act 1984 (Application to Revenue and Customs) (Amendment) Order, SI 2010/360 art 2(1), (2) with effect from 19 March 2010.

3 Application

(1) The provisions of the Act contained in Schedule 1 to this Order which relate to investigations of offences conducted by police officers or to persons detained by the police shall apply to relevant investigations conducted by officers of Revenue and Customs and to persons detained by such officers.

This is subject to the modifications in paragraphs (2) and (3) and articles 4 to 19 and Schedule 2.

(2) The Act shall have effect as if the words and phrases in Column 1 of Part 1 of Schedule 2 to this Order were replaced by the substitute words and phrases in Column 2 of that Part.

SIs

(3) Where in the Act any act or thing is to be done by a constable of a specified rank, that act or thing shall be done by an officer of Revenue and Customs of at least the grade specified in Column 2 of Part 2 of Schedule 2 to this Order, and the Act shall be construed accordingly.

4 Exceptions

Nothing in the application of the Act to Revenue and Customs confers on an officer of Revenue and Customs any power—

(*a*) to charge a person with any offence;

(*b*) to release a person on bail; or

(*c*) to detain a person for an offence after he has been charged with that offence.

5 Seizure and retention of things found upon search

(1) Where in the Act a constable is given power to seize and retain any thing found upon a lawful search of person or premises, an officer of Revenue and Customs shall have the same power notwithstanding that the thing found is not evidence of an offence which relates to a matter in relation to which Her Majesty's Revenue and Customs have functions.

(2) Nothing in the application of the Act to Revenue and Customs prevents any thing lawfully seized by a person under any enactment from being accepted and retained by an officer of Revenue and Customs.

(3) Section 21 of the Act (access and copying) shall not apply to any thing seized as liable to forfeiture under the customs and excise Acts.

6 Excluded and special procedure material

In its application by virtue of article 3 above the Act shall have effect as if the following section were inserted after section 14—

"14A Exception for Revenue and Customs

Material in the possession of a person who acquired or created it in the course of any trade, business, profession or other occupation or for the purpose of any paid or unpaid office and which relates to a matter in relation to which Her Majesty's Revenue and Customs have functions, is neither excluded material nor special procedure material for the purposes of any enactment such as is mentioned in section 9(2) above.".

7 Restriction on other powers to apply for production of documents

In its application by virtue of article 3 above the Act shall have effect as if the following section were inserted after section 14A—

"14B Revenue and Customs: restriction on other powers to apply for production of documents

(1) An officer of Revenue and Customs may make an application for the delivery of, or access to, documents under a provision specified in subsection (3) only if the condition in subsection (2) is satisfied.

(2) The condition is that the officer thinks that an application under Schedule 1 would not succeed because the material required does not consist of or include special procedure material.

(3) The provisions are—

(*a*) section 20BA and Schedule 1AA of the Taxes Management Act 1970 (serious tax fraud);

(*b*) paragraph 11 of Schedule 11 to the Value Added Tax Act 1994 (VAT);

(*c*) paragraph 4A of Schedule 7 to the Finance Act 1994 (insurance premium tax);

(*d*) paragraph 7 of Schedule 5 to the Finance Act 1996 (landfill tax);

(*e*) paragraph 131 of Schedule 6 to the Finance Act 2000 (climate change levy);

(*f*) paragraph 8 of Schedule 7 to the Finance Act 2001 (aggregates levy);

(*g*) Part 6 of Schedule 13 to the Finance Act 2003 (stamp duty land tax).".

8 Modification of section 18 of the Act (Entry and search after arrest)

(1) Section 18 of the Act (entry and search after arrest)is modified as follows.

(2) For subsection 18 (1) substitute—

"(1) Subject to the following provisions of this section, an officer of Revenue and Customs may enter and search any premises occupied or controlled by a person who is under arrest for any relevant indictable offence if he has reasonable grounds for suspecting that there is on the premises evidence, other than items subject to legal privilege, that relates—

(*a*) to that offence; or

(*b*) to some other indictable offence which is connected with or similar to that offence.".

9 Modification of section 35 of the Act (Designated police stations)

(1) Section 35 of the Act (designated police stations)is modified as follows.

(2) For subsection 35(1) substitute—

"(1) The Director of Detection shall designate offices of Revenue and Customs which, subject to sections 30(3) and (5), are to be the offices to be used for the purposes of detaining arrested persons."

(3) For subsection 35(2) substitute—

"(2) The Director of Detection's duty under subsection (1) above is to designate offices of Revenue and Customs appearing to him to provide enough accommodation for that purpose.".

(4) For subsection 35(3) substitute—

"(3) Without prejudice to section 12 of the Interpretation Act 1978 (continuity of duties) the Director of Detection—

(*a*) may designate an office which was not previously designated; and

(*b*) may direct that a designation of an office previously made shall cease to operate.".

10 Modification of section 36 of the Act (Custody officers at police stations)

(1) Section 36 of the Act (custody officers at police stations) is modified as follows.

(2) For subsection (2) substitute—

"(2) A custody officer for an office of Revenue and Customs designated under section 35(1) above shall be appointed—

(*a*) by the Director of Detection; or

(*b*) by such other officer of Revenue and Customs as the Director of Detection may direct.".

11 Modification of section 41 of the Act (Limits on period of detention without charge)

(1) Section 41 of the Act (limits on period of detention without charge) is modified as follows.

(2) For subsection (2)(*b*) substitute—

"(*b*) in the case of a person arrested outside England and Wales, shall be—

(i) the time at which that person arrives at the office of Revenue and Customs in England and Wales in which the offence for which he was arrested is being investigated; or

(ii) the time 24 hours after the time of that person's entry into England and Wales.".

12 Modification of section 50 of the Act (Records of detention)

(1) Section 50 of the Act (records of detention) is modified as follows.

(2) For subsection (1) substitute—

"(1) The Commissioners shall keep written records showing on an annual basis—

(*a*) the number of persons kept in Revenue and Customs detention for more than 24 hours and subsequently released without charge;

(*b*) the number of applications for warrants of further detention and the results of the applications; and

(*c*) in relation to each warrant of further detention—

(i) the period of further detention authorised by it;

(ii) the period which the person named in it spent in Revenue and Customs detention on its authority; and

(iii) whether he was charged or released without charge."

(3) For subsection (2) substitute—

"(2) Every annual report made by the Commissioners shall contain information about the matters mentioned in subsection (1) above in respect of the period to which the report relates.".

13 Modification of section 55 of the Act (Intimate searches)

(1) Section 55 of the Act (intimate searches) shall have effect as if it related only to things such as are mentioned in subsection (1)(*a*) of that section.

(2) The annual report of the Commissioners shall contain information about searches under section 55 which have been carried out during the period to which the report relates.

14 Modification of section 64 of the Act (Destruction of fingerprints and samples)

Amendments—[1] Art 14 revoked by the Police and Criminal Evidence Act 1984 (Application to Revenue and Customs) (Amendment) Order, SI 2014/788 arts 2, 3 with effect from 11 April 2014.

15 Modification of section 77 of the Act (Definition of independent person)
Section 77(3) of the Act (definition of independent person) shall be modified to the extent that the definition of "independent person" shall, in addition to the persons mentioned therein, also include an officer of Revenue and Customs or any other person acting under the authority of the Commissioners.

16 Use of reasonable force
Where any provision of the Act as applied to Revenue and Customs—
(*a*) confers a power on an officer of Revenue and Customs, and
(*b*) does not provide that the power may only be exercised with the consent of some person other than that officer,
the officer may use reasonable force, if necessary, in the exercise of the power.

17 Arrest without warrant
Section 24(2) of the Act (arrest without warrant) does not limit—
(*a*) section 138(1) of the Customs and Excise Management Act 1979;
(*b*) section 20 and paragraph 4 of Schedule 3 to the Criminal Justice (International Co-operation) Act 1990;
(*c*) any other enactment, including any enactment contained in subordinate legislation, for the time being in force which confers upon officers of Revenue and Customs the power to arrest or detain persons.

18 Search of persons
Where an officer of Revenue and Customs searches premises in reliance on a warrant under section 8 of, or paragraph 12 of Schedule 1 to, the Act (power of justice of the peace to authorise entry and search of premises), he may search any person found on the premises—
(*a*) where he has reasonable cause to believe that person to be in possession of material which is likely to be of substantial value (whether by itself or together with other material) to the investigation of the offence;
(*b*) but no person should be searched except by a person of the same sex.

19 Authorisation
Powers and functions in the provisions of the Act contained in Schedule 1 to this Order may be exercised only by officers of Revenue and Customs acting with the authority (which may be general or specific) of the Commissioners.

20 Revocation
The following instruments are revoked—
(*a*) the Police and Criminal Evidence Act 1984 (Application to Customs and Excise) Order 1981;
(*b*) the Police and Criminal Evidence Act 1984 (Application to Customs and Excise) Order 1987;
(*c*) the Police and Criminal Evidence Act 1984 (Application to Customs and Excise) (Amendment) Order 1995; and
(*d*) the Police and Criminal Evidence Act 1984 (Application to Customs and Excise) (Amendment) Order 1996.

SCHEDULE 1

PROVISIONS OF THE ACT APPLIED TO REVENUE AND CUSTOMS

Article 3(1)

Section 8 (power of justice of the peace to authorise entry and search of premises)
Section 9 (special provisions as to access) and Schedule 1 (special procedure)
Section 15 (search warrants-safeguards)
Section 16 (execution of warrants)
[Section 17(1)(*a*)(i), (1)(*b*), (1)(*cb*), (1)(*d*), (2), (4)][1] (entry for purpose of arrest etc)
Section 18 (entry and search after arrest) (subject to the modification in article 8)
Section 19 (general power of seizure etc)
Section 20 (extension of powers of seizure to computerised information)
Section 21 (access and copying) (subject to the modification in article 5)
[Section 22(1) to (4) and (7)][1] (retention)
[Section 24(2), (4), (5)][1] (arrest without warrant: constables) (subject to the modification in article 17)
Section 28 (information to be given on arrest)
Section 29 (voluntary attendance at police station etc)
Section 30(1) to (4) (*a*) and (5) to (11) (arrest elsewhere than at police station)

Section 31 (arrest for further offence)
Section 32(1) to (9) (search upon arrest) (subject to the modifications in article 5)
Section 34(1) to (5) (limitations on police detention)
Section 35(1), (2), (3) and (4) (designated police stations) (subject to the modification in article 9)
Section 36(1), (2), (3), (4), (5), (6), (7), (8), (9) and (10) (custody officers at police stations) (subject to the modification in article 10)
Section 37 (duties of custody officer before charge)
Section 39 (responsibilities in relation to persons detained)
Section 40 (review of police detention)
Section 41(1), (2), (4) and (6) to (9) (limits on period of detention without charge) (subject to the modification in article 11)
Section 42(1), (2) and (4) to (11) (authorisation of continued detention)
Section 43(1) to (12) and (14) to (19) (warrants of further detention)
Section 44 (extension of warrants of further detention)
Section 50 (records of detention) (subject to the modification in article 12)
Section 51(*d*) (savings)
Section 54 (searches of detained persons)
Section 55 (intimate searches) (subject to the modifications in articles 5 and 13)
Section 56(1) to (9) (right to have someone informed when arrested)
Section 57 (additional rights of children and young persons)
Section 58(1) to (11) (access to legal advice)
Section 62 (intimate samples)
Section 63 (other samples)
[Section 63D (destruction of fingerprints and DNA profiles)
Section 63E (retention of section 63D material pending investigation or proceedings)
Section 63G (retention of section 63D material by virtue of section 63F(5): consent of Commissioner)
Section 63H (retention of section 63D material: persons arrested for or charged with a minor offence)
Section 63I (retention of material: persons convicted of a recordable offence)
Section 63J (retention of material: persons convicted of an offence outside England and Wales)
Section 63K (retention of section 63D material: exception for persons under 18 convicted of first minor offence)
Section 63L (retention of section 63D material: persons given a penalty notice)
Section 63M (retention of section 63D material for purposes of national security)
Section 63N (retention of section 63D material given voluntarily)
Section 63O (retention of section 63D material with consent)
Section 63P (section 63D material obtained for one purpose and used for another)
Section 63Q (destruction of copies of section 63D material)
Section 63R (destruction of samples)
Section 63S (destruction of impressions of footwear)
Section 63T (use of retained material)
Section 63U (exclusions for certain regimes)][2]
Section 66 (codes of practice)
Section 67 (codes of practice-supplementary)
Section 77 (confessions by mentally handicapped persons) (subject to the modification in article 15)
Section 107 (police officers performing duties of higher rank)

Amendments—[1] Entries substituted by the Police and Criminal Evidence Act 1984 (Application to Revenue and Customs) (Amendment) Order, SI 2010/360 art 2(1), (3) with effect from 19 March 2010.

[2] Entries substituted by the Police and Criminal Evidence Act 1984 (Application to Revenue and Customs) (Amendment) Order, SI 2014/788 arts 2, 4 with effect from 11 April 2014.

SCHEDULE 2

Article 3(2)

PART 1

SUBSTITUTION OF EQUIVALENT WORDS AND PHRASES IN THE ACT

Where in the Act a word or phrase specified in Column 1 is used, in the application of the Act to Revenue and Customs, there shall be substituted the equivalent word or phrase in column 2—

Column 1	*Column 2*
WORDS AND PHRASES USED IN THE ACT	SUBSTITUTED WORDS AND PHRASES
chief officer of police	director
constable	officer of Revenue and Customs
designated police station	designated office of Revenue and Customs
officer of a force maintained by a police authority	officer of Revenue and Customs
Police detention (except in section 118 and in section 39(1)(*a*) the second time the words occur)	Revenue and Customs detention
Police officer	Officer of Revenue and Customs
Police station	Office of Revenue and Customs
Rank	Grade
Station	Office of Revenue and Customs
The police	Her Majesty's Revenue and Customs

PART 2

EQUIVALENT TITLES OF OFFICERS

Where in the Act an act or thing is to be done by a constable of the rank specified in Column 1, that same act or thing shall, in the application of the Act to Revenue and Customs, be done by an officer of Revenue and Customs of at least an equivalent grade specified in Column 2—

Column 1	*Column 2*
RANK OF CONSTABLE	GRADE OF OFFICER
Sergeant	Officer
Inspector	Higher officer
Chief Inspector	Higher officer
Superintendent	Senior officer

2007/3186

CORPORATION TAX (IMPLEMENTATION OF THE MERGERS DIRECTIVE) REGULATIONS 2007

Made by the Treasury under Finance Act 2007 s 110.

Made . . . .*8 November 2007*
Laid before the House of Commons . . . .*8 November 2007*
Coming into force . . . .*29 November 2007*

The Treasury are satisfied in accordance with section 110(3) of the Finance Act 2007 that the following Regulations are necessary for the purpose of complying with the United Kingdom's obligations under the Mergers Directive.

1 Citation, commencement and effect

(1) These Regulations may be cited as the Corporation Tax (Implementation of the Mergers Directive) Regulations 2007.

(2) These Regulations shall come into force on 29th November 2007 and shall have effect as set out in regulation 3.

2 Interpretation

In these Regulations—

"TCGA 1992" means the Taxation of Chargeable Gains Act 1992;
"ICTA" means the Income and Corporation Taxes Act 1988;
"CAA 2001" means the Capital Allowances Act 2001;
"FA 1988" means the Finance Act 1988;
"FA 1996" means the Finance Act 1996; and
"FA 2002" means the Finance Act 2002.

3 Amendments of primary legislation

(1) Schedule 1, which contains amendments to TCGA 1992, ICTA, FA 1996, FA 2002, CAA 2001 relating to cross-border transfers of business, has effect in relation to transfers which take place on or after 1st January 2007.

(2) Schedule 2, which contains amendments to TCGA 1992, ICTA, FA 1988, FA 1996, FA 2002 and CAA 2001 relating to cross-border mergers, has effect but subject as follows—

(*a*) paragraphs 1 to 14 have effect—

(i) in relation to mergers relating to the formation of an SE or SCE which take place on or after 18th August 2006, and

(ii) in relation to all other mergers which take place on or after 1st January 2007;

(*b*) paragraph 15 has effect in relation to transfers of a registered office which take effect on or after 18th August 2006.

(3) Schedule 3, which contains amendments to TCGA 1992, FA 1996 and FA 2002 relating to mergers and treatment of transparent entities, has effect—

(*a*) in relation to mergers relating to the formation of an SE or SCE which take place on or after 18th August 2006, and

(*b*) in relation to all other mergers which take place on or after 1st January 2007.

Regulations—The Corporation Tax (Implementation of the Mergers Directive), SI 2008/1579 reg 4(1) (reg 3(1) is deemed always to have had effect as if it also provided for Sch 1 to have effect, so far as relating to cross-border mergers—

(a) in relation to mergers relating to the formation of an SE or SCE which take place on or after 18 August 2006, and

(b) in relation to all other mergers which take place on or after 1 January 2007.).

The Corporation Tax (Implementation of the Mergers Directive), SI 2008/1579 reg 4(2) (reg 3(3) is deemed always to have had effect as if it also provided for Sch 3 to have effect, so far as relating to cross-border transfers of business, in relation to transfers which take place on or after 1 January 2007.).

SCHEDULE 1

CROSS-BORDER TRANSFERS OF BUSINESS

Regulation 3(1)

Regulations—The Corporation Tax (Implementation of the Mergers Directive), SI 2008/1579 reg 4(1) (reg 3(1) is deemed always to have had effect as if it also provided for Sch 1 to have effect, so far as relating to cross-border mergers—

(a) in relation to mergers relating to the formation of an SE or SCE which take place on or after 18 August 2006, and

(b) in relation to all other mergers which take place on or after 1 January 2007.).

PART 1

AMENDMENTS OF TGCA 1992

1 TCGA 1992 is amended as follows.

Division of UK business

2—(1) Section 140A (transfer of a UK trade) is amended as follows.

(2) (*amends* TCGA 1992 s 140A(1))

(3) (*inserts* TCGA 1992 s 140A(1A)–(1D))

(4) (*amends* TCGA 1992 s 140A(2)–(4))

(5) (*amends* TCGA 1992 s 140A(4))

(6) (*repeals* TCGA 1992 s 140A(5)–(7))

(7) (*amends* heading to TCGA 1992 s 140A)

3 (*amends* TCGA 1992 s 140B)

Division of non-UK business

4—(1) Section 140C (transfer of non-UK trade) is amended as follows.

(2) (*amends* TCGA 1992 s 140C(1))

(3) (*inserts* TCGA 1992 s 140C(1A)–(1C))

(4) (*amends* TCGA 1992 s 140C(3), (8))

(5) (*repeals* TCGA 1992 s 140C(6), (7)–(9))

(6) (*amends* heading to TCGA 1992 s 140C)

5 (*amends* TCGA 1992 s 140D)

Treatment of securities issued on transfer of assets

6 (*inserts* TCGA 1992 s 140DA)

Held over gains

7 (*inserts* TCGA 1992 s 140(6AA))

8 (*inserts* TCGA 1992 s 154(2D))

9 (*inserts* TCGA 1992 s 179(1AA))

Loan relationships

10

Revocation—Para 10 revoked by the Corporation Tax (Implementation of the Mergers Directive), SI 2008/1579 reg 5 with effect from 8 July 2008.

Note—The repeal of TCGA 1992 s 116(8A), (8B) by para 10 is deemed never to have had effect. Accordingly, para 10 is revoked and is treated as if it were never included in these regulations (SI 2008/1579 reg 5).

PART 2
AMENDMENTS OF ICTA

Regulations—The Corporation Tax (Implementation of the Mergers Directive), SI 2008/1579 reg 4(1) (reg 3(1) is deemed always to have had effect as if it also provided for Sch 1 to have effect, so far as relating to cross-border mergers—

(a) in relation to mergers relating to the formation of an SE or SCE which take place on or after 18 August 2006, and
(b) in relation to all other mergers which take place on or after 1 January 2007.).

11 ICTA is amended as follows.

Exempt distributions

12 (*inserts* TA 1988 s 209(1A))

13 (*inserts* TA 1988 s 213A)

14 (*amends* TA 1988 s 218(1))

PART 3
AMENDMENTS OF FA 1996

Regulations—The Corporation Tax (Implementation of the Mergers Directive), SI 2008/1579 reg 4(1) (reg 3(1) is deemed always to have had effect as if it also provided for Sch 1 to have effect, so far as relating to cross-border mergers—

(a) in relation to mergers relating to the formation of an SE or SCE which take place on or after 18 August 2006, and
(b) in relation to all other mergers which take place on or after 1 January 2007.).

15 Schedule 9 to FA 1996 (loan relationships: special computational provisions) is amended as follows.

Loan relationships

16 (*inserts* FA 1996 Sch 9 paras 12D–12G)

17 In paragraph 12A (transferee leaving group)—
(*a*) (*inserts* FA 1996 Sch 9 para 12(5A))
(*b*) (*amends* FA 1996 Sch 9 para 12(8))

PART 4
AMENDMENTS OF FA 2002

Regulations—The Corporation Tax (Implementation of the Mergers Directive), SI 2008/1579 reg 4(1) (reg 3(1) is deemed always to have had effect as if it also provided for Sch 1 to have effect, so far as relating to cross-border mergers—

(a) in relation to mergers relating to the formation of an SE or SCE which take place on or after 18 August 2006, and
(b) in relation to all other mergers which take place on or after 1 January 2007.).

18 FA 2002 is amended as follows.

Derivative contracts

19 (*inserts* FA 1996 Sch 26 paras 30D–30F)

20—(1) Paragraph 30A of Schedule 26 (transferee leaving group) is amended as follows.
(2) (*inserts* FA 1996 Sch 26 para 30A(5A))
(3) (*amends* FA 1996 Sch 26 para 30A(8))

Intangible fixed assets

21—(1) Paragraph 85 of Schedule 29 (transfer of UK trade between companies resident in different EU member states) is amended as follows.

(2) (*substitutes* FA 1996 Sch 29 para 85(1))
(3)–(5) (*amend* FA 1996 Sch 29 para 85(4), (5) and section heading)

22—(1) Paragraph 87 of Schedule 29 (transfer of non-UK trade) is amended as follows,
(2) (*substitutes* FA 1996 Sch 29 para 87(1))
(3), (4) (*amend* FA 1996 Sch 29 para 87(7)and setion heading)

23 (*inserts* FA 1996 Sch 29 para 58(6))

24 (*amends* FA 1996 Sch 29 para 127(1)(*b*)(ii), (iii))

PART 5
AMENDMENT OF CAA 2001

Regulations—The Corporation Tax (Implementation of the Mergers Directive), SI 2008/1579 reg 4(1) (reg 3(1) is deemed always to have had effect as if it also provided for Sch 1 to have effect, so far as relating to cross-border mergers—

(a) in relation to mergers relating to the formation of an SE or SCE which take place on or after 18 August 2006, and
(b) in relation to all other mergers which take place on or after 1 January 2007.).

Capital allowances

25—(1) Section 561 of CAA 2001 (transfer of UK trade to a company in another member state) is amended as follows.
(2) (*substitutes* CAA 2001 s 561(1))
(3), (4) (*amend* CAA 2001 s 561(2)(*b*) and section heading)

SCHEDULE 2

EUROPEAN CROSS-BORDER MERGERS

Regulation 3(2)

PART 1
AMENDMENTS OF TCGA 1992

1 TCGA 1992 is amended as follows.

2 (*substitutes* TCGA 1992 ss140E–140G)

3 (*amends* TCGA 1992 s 24(1))

4 (*inserts* TCGA 1992 s 122(1A))

Held over gains

5 (*substitutes* TCGA 1992 s 140(6B))

6 (*substitutes* TCGA 1992 s 154(2A), (2B))

7 (*substitutes* TCGA 1992 s 179(1B), (1C))

PART 2
AMENDMENTS OF FA 1996

Loan relationships

8 (*substitutes* FA 1996 Sch 9 para 12B)

PART 3
AMENDMENTS OF FA 2002

9 FA 2002 is amended as follows.

Derivative contracts

10 (*substitutes* FA 2002 Sch 26 para 30B)

Intangible assets

11, 12(*substitute* FA 2002 Sch 29 paras 85A, 87A)

13 (*amends* FA 2002 Sch 29 para 88(1), (5))

PART 4

AMENDMENTS OF CAA 2001, FA 1988 AND ICTA

CAPITAL ALLOWANCES

14 (*substitutes* CAA 2001 s 561A)

RESIDENCE OF SCE

15—(1) Section 66A of FA 1988 (residence of SE) is amended as follows.
(2) (*substitutes* FA 1988 s 66A(1))
(3), (4) (*amend* FA 1988 s 66A(2), (3) and section heading)

Tax treatment of SCE

16 (*amends* FA 1988 s 486(12))

SCHEDULE 3

MERGERS, &C: TREATMENT OF TRANSPARENT ENTITIES

Regulation 3(3)

Regulations—The Corporation Tax (Implementation of the Mergers Directive), SI 2008/1579 reg 4(2) (reg 3(3) is deemed always to have had effect as if it also provided for Sch 3 to have effect, so far as relating to cross-border transfers of business, in relation to transfers which take place on or after 1 January 2007.).

PART 1

AMENDMENT OF TCGA 1992

Chargeable gains

1 (*inserts* TCGA 1992 ss 140H–140L)

PART 2

AMENDMENT OF FA 1996

Regulations—The Corporation Tax (Implementation of the Mergers Directive), SI 2008/1579 reg 4(2) (reg 3(3) is deemed always to have had effect as if it also provided for Sch 3 to have effect, so far as relating to cross-border transfers of business, in relation to transfers which take place on or after 1 January 2007.).

Loan relationships

2 (*inserts* FA 1996 Sch 9 paras 12H, 12J)

PART 3

AMENDMENTS OF FA 2002

Regulations—The Corporation Tax (Implementation of the Mergers Directive), SI 2008/1579 reg 4(2) (reg 3(3) is deemed always to have had effect as if it also provided for Sch 3 to have effect, so far as relating to cross-border transfers of business, in relation to transfers which take place on or after 1 January 2007.).

Derivative contracts

3 FA 2002 is amended as follows.

4 (*inserts* FA 2002 Sch 26 paras 30G–30I)

Intangible assets

5 (*inserts* FA 2002 Sch 29 paras 85B–85D)

2007/3278

ENERGY-SAVING ITEMS (INCOME TAX) REGULATIONS 2007

Made by the Treasury under ITTOIA 2005 ss 312 and 314

Made . . . . *15 November 2007*
Laid before the House of Commons . . . . *16 November 2007*
Coming into force . . . . *6 December 2007*

Commentary—*Simon's Taxes* **B6.207**.

1 Citation, commencement and interpretation

(1) These Regulations may be cited as the Energy-Saving Items (Income Tax) Regulations 2007, shall come into force on 6th December 2007, and shall have effect in respect of expenditure incurred on or after 6th April 2007.

(2) In these Regulations—

"ITTOIA 2005" means the Income Tax (Trading and Other Income) Act 2005;

"deduction" means a deduction allowed under section 312 of ITTOIA 2005 (deduction for expenditure on energy-saving items);

"maximum amount" shall be construed in accordance with regulation 3(1);

"relevant expenditure" means—

(*a*) expenditure incurred in acquiring and installing an energy-saving item in a dwelling-house, or

(*b*) in so far as it is for the benefit of a dwelling-house, expenditure incurred in acquiring and installing an energy-saving item in a building containing that dwelling-house.

2 Items of an energy-saving nature

The following descriptions of items of an energy-saving nature are specified for the purposes of section 312(5)(*c*) of ITTOIA 2005—

(*a*) hot water system insulation;

(*b*) draught proofing;

(*c*) solid wall insulation; and

(*d*) floor insulation.

3 Restrictions on relevant expenditure to be taken into account: general

(1) The maximum amount of the relevant expenditure which may be taken into account in calculating the deduction is £1,500 per dwelling-house.

(2) Paragraph (1) applies irrespective of the number of persons incurring relevant expenditure or entitled to a deduction in respect of a dwelling-house.

(3) If the person entitled to the deduction has received a contribution from any other person towards the relevant expenditure incurred, that contribution shall be excluded in calculating the relevant expenditure incurred by the person entitled to the deduction.

(4) Further rules (to be applied in the order stated) are set out in—

(*a*) regulation 4 (first further rule: apportionment of relevant expenditure benefiting more than one property);

(*b*) regulation 5 (second further rule: restriction of relevant expenditure to the maximum amount);

(*c*) regulation 6 (third further rule: apportionment of relevant expenditure if a dwelling-house or building is owned jointly or in common or is subject to differing estates or interests).

4 First further rule: apportionment of relevant expenditure benefiting more than one property

(1) This regulation applies to relevant expenditure which is incurred in acquiring and installing an energy-saving item—

(*a*) in more than one dwelling-house,

(*b*) in a building containing more than one dwelling-house, or

(*c*) in a building containing one or more dwelling-houses and one or more properties which are not dwelling-houses.

(2) The relevant expenditure must be apportioned on a just and reasonable basis to all the properties which benefit from it.

(3) The amount of the relevant expenditure for which a deduction is allowable in respect of a dwelling-house shall not exceed the amount which is apportioned to that dwelling-house.

5 Second further rule: restriction of relevant expenditure to the maximum amount

(1) This regulation applies if the relevant expenditure benefiting a particular dwelling-house (including any relevant expenditure apportioned to the dwelling-house under regulation 4) exceeds the maximum amount.

(2) The relevant expenditure must be restricted to the maximum amount.

6 Third further rule: apportionment of relevant expenditure if a dwelling-house or building is owned jointly or in common or is subject to differing estates or interests

(1) This regulation applies if relevant expenditure is incurred benefiting a dwelling-house and the dwelling-house or the building containing it—

(*a*) is owned jointly or in common by the person entitled to the deduction and by other persons, or

(*b*) is subject to differing estates or interests.

(2) The relevant expenditure (restricted if necessary to the maximum amount) must be apportioned on a just and reasonable basis.

(3) The amount of the deduction to which the person entitled to it is entitled shall not exceed the amount apportioned to that person in accordance with paragraph (2).

7 Further provisions

(1) This regulation applies if any question arises under regulations 3(3) or 4 to 6 as to the amount of the deduction to which a person may be entitled.

(2) The amount shall be treated as if it were an amount specified in a paragraph of subsection (1) of section 42 of ICTA 1988 (appeals against determinations under sections 34 to 36 or Chapter 4 of Part 3 of the Income Tax (Trading and Other Income) Act 2005), and the procedure set out in that section shall apply accordingly.

8 Revocation of the Energy-Saving Items Regulations 2007 (SI 2007/831)

The Energy-Saving Items Regulations 2007 (SI 2007/831) are revoked.

2007/3338

SECURITISATION COMPANIES (APPLICATION OF SECTION 83(1) OF THE FINANCE ACT 2005: ACCOUNTING STANDARDS) REGULATIONS 2007

Made by the Treasury under FA 2005 s 83(7A) and (7B)

Made . . . . *3 December 2007*

Laid before the House of Commons . . . . *4 December 2007*

Coming into force . . . . *27 December 2007*

Commentary—*Simon's Taxes* **B2.107**.

1 Citation and commencement

These Regulations may be cited as the Securitisation Companies (Application of Section 83(1) of the Finance Act 2005: Accounting Standards) Regulations 2007 and shall come into force on 27th December 2007.

2 Application of section 83(1) of the Finance Act 2005: accounting standards

(1) This regulation applies where—

(*a*) subsection (1) of section 83 of the Finance Act 2005 (application of accounting standards to securitisation companies) applies to a company in relation to a period of account ending before 1st January 2008, and

(*b*) the company—

(i) became party to a capital market arrangement referred to in subsection (3)(*c*) of that section or a related transaction before 1st January 2008 and continues to be party to that arrangement or transaction, or

(ii) is a warehouse company where any of the financial assets referred to in subsection (6) of that section were acquired before 1st January 2008.

(2) Subsection (1) of section 83 of the Finance Act 2005 shall apply in relation to periods of account ending on or after 1st January 2008 but before [1st January 2037][1].

This is subject to paragraph (3).

(3) Paragraph (2) shall not apply to a company that elects that the paragraph shall not apply to it.

(4) An election under paragraph (3)—

(*a*) must be made in writing to Her Majesty's Revenue and Customs,

(*b*) must be made before the end of the first accounting period ending on or after 1st January 2008, and

(*c*) is irrevocable.

Amendments—[1] In para 2, words substituted for words "1st January 2017" by the Securitisation Companies (Application of Section 83(1) of the Finance Act 2005: Accounting Standards) (Amendment) Regulations, SI 2016/1182 reg 2 with effect from 28 December 2016.

3 Modification of provisions of, and made under, the Corporation Tax Acts

(1) This regulation applies in relation to the first period of account of a securitisation company in the case of which section 83(1) of the Finance Act 2005 does not apply by virtue of that section itself or regulation 2 ("the first period") where—

(*a*) the company continues to be party to a capital market arrangement or a related transaction, or

(*b*) the company would continue to be a warehouse company if that section continued to apply.

(2) Where this regulation applies—

(*a*) there shall be treated as arising any adjustment that would have been made in accordance with section 64 of the Finance Act 2002 (adjustment on change of basis) in any previous period of account had section 83 of the Finance Act 2005 not applied to that period;

(*b*) in relation to the Loan Relationships and Derivative Contracts (Change of Accounting Practice) Regulations 2004—

(i) the prescribed period in regulation 3A shall be treated as beginning with the first period, and

(ii) there shall be treated as prescribed by regulation 4 any debit or credit that would have been brought into account in accordance with regulation 3 in any previous period had section 83 of the Finance Act 2005 not applied to that period.

This is subject to paragraph (3).

(3) Any amount brought into account on the application of this regulation must be just and reasonable in the circumstances and with regard to whether as a result any amounts cease to be brought into account or are brought into account more than once.

4 Interpretation

For the purposes of these Regulations—

(*a*) "party" to a capital market arrangement or a related transaction includes a party to an agreement which—

(i) forms part of the arrangement,

(ii) provides for the raising of finance as part of the arrangement, or

(iii) is necessary for the purposes of implementing the arrangement;

(*b*) one or more transactions are to be regarded as related transactions, in the case of any capital market arrangement, if it would be reasonable to assume, from either or both of—

(i) the likely effect of the transactions, and

(ii) the circumstances in which the transactions are entered into or effected,

that none of the transactions would have been entered into or effected independently of the arrangement;

(*c*) transactions are not prevented from being related transactions, in the case of any capital market arrangement, just because the transactions—

(i) are not between the same parties, or

(ii) are not between the parties to the capital market arrangement.

2007/3402

TAXATION OF INSURANCE SECURITISATION COMPANIES REGULATIONS 2007

Made by the Treasury under FA 2005 s 84

Made . . . . .4 *December 2007*
Laid before the House of Commons . . . . .5 *December 2007*
Coming into force . . . . .28 *December 2007*

Commentary—*Simon's Taxes* **B2.107**.

Preliminary

1 Citation, commencement and effect

(1) These Regulations may be cited as the Taxation of Insurance Securitisation Companies Regulations 2007 and shall come into force on 28th December 2007 immediately after the coming into force of the Taxation of Securitisation Companies (Amendment No 2) Regulations 2007.

(2) These Regulations have effect from the beginning of periods of account beginning on or after 1st January 2007 and current on 4th December 2007.

2 Interpretation

(1) In these Regulations—

"capital market arrangement" and "capital market investment" have the same meaning as in section 72B(1) of the Insolvency Act 1986 (see paragraphs 1, 2 and 3 of Schedule 2A to that Act);

"ICTA" means the Income and Corporation Taxes Act 1988;

"independent persons" means persons who are not connected with a company (and see paragraph (3));

"insurance special purpose vehicle" and "Insurance Prudential Sourcebook" have the same meanings as in section 431(2) of ICTA.

(2) Section 839 of ICTA (connected persons) applies for the purposes of the definition of "independent persons", except that in applying the definition of "control" in that section a person is not to be treated as a participator in a company by reason only that he is a loan creditor of the company.

3 Scope of these Regulations

(1) These Regulations make provision as to the application of the Corporation Tax Acts in relation to an insurance securitisation company.

(2) The Regulations deal with the following matters—

(*a*) they define "insurance securitisation company" (see regulation 4);

(*b*) they provide that the Regulations do not apply if an insurance securitisation company has an unallowable purpose (see regulation 5);

(*c*) they make provision for the application of accounting standards to an insurance securitisation company (see regulation 6);

(*d*) they make supplementary provision in relation to the application, modification and non-application of provisions of the Corporation Tax Acts (see regulations 7 to 11).

Insurance Securitisation Companies

4 Meaning of insurance securitisation company

(1) For the purposes of these Regulations an "insurance securitisation company" means a company that is an insurance special purpose vehicle and—

(*a*) meets conditions A to C, or

(*b*) whose liabilities representing debtor relationships are owed wholly or mainly to a note-issuing company or intermediate borrowing company within the Taxation of Securitisation Companies Regulations 2006.

(2) Condition A is that the company is within section 84(2)(*a*) of the Finance Act 2005.

(3) Condition B is that the securities that represent the capital market investment referred to in section 84(2)(*a*)(ii) of that Act are issued wholly or mainly to independent persons.

(4) Condition C is that the total value of the capital market investments made under the capital market arrangement referred to in section 84(2)(*a*)(iii) of that Act is at least £10 million.

5 Insurance securitisation companies that have an unallowable purpose

(1) These Regulations do not apply or will cease to apply to an insurance securitisation company that—

(*a*) has an unallowable purpose, or

(*b*) at any time has had an unallowable purpose.

(2) Where these Regulations cease to apply by virtue of this regulation the accounting period of the company shall end.

(3) For the purpose of these Regulations an insurance securitisation company has an unallowable purpose if the purpose for which the company is a party to—

(*a*) the capital market arrangement,

(*b*) any related transaction, or

(*c*) any transaction in pursuance of the capital market arrangement,

includes a purpose which is not amongst the business or other commercial purposes of the company.

(4) If one of the purposes for which an insurance securitisation company is at any time a party to—

(*a*) any capital market arrangement,

(*b*) any related transaction in the case of any capital market arrangement, or

(*c*) any transaction in pursuance of any capital market arrangement,

is a tax avoidance purpose, that purpose shall be taken to be a business or other commercial purpose of the company only where it is not the main purpose, or one of the main purposes, for which the company is party to the arrangements or transaction at that time.

(5) For the purpose of this regulation—

(*a*) one or more transactions are to be regarded as related transactions, in the case of any arrangements, if it would be reasonable to assume, from either or both of—

(i) the likely effect of the transactions, and

(ii) the circumstances in which the transactions are entered into or effected,

that none of the transactions would have been entered into or effected independently of the arrangements; and

(*b*) transactions are not prevented from being related transactions, in the case of any arrangements, just because the transactions—

(i) are not between the same parties, or

(ii) are not between the parties to the capital market arrangements.

(6) In this regulation—

"tax avoidance purpose" means any purpose that consists in securing a tax advantage for any other person;

"tax advantage" has the same meaning as in section 840ZA of ICTA (tax avoidance).

6 Application of accounting standards to insurance securitisation companies

For the purposes of the Corporation Tax Acts as they apply to an insurance securitisation company, generally accepted accounting practice shall be taken to be UK generally accepted accounting practice as it applied for a period of account ending on 31 December 2006 but excluding the application of Financial Reporting Standard 26 issued in December 2004 by the Accounting Standards Board.

Supplementary Provisions

7 Application, modification and non-application of provisions of the Corporation Tax Acts

In relation to an insurance securitisation company the provisions of the Corporation Tax Acts have effect in accordance with regulations 8 to 11.

8 ICTA

(1) ICTA has effect as follows.

(2) In section 209(2) (meaning of distribution) paragraphs (*b*) to (*f*) shall not apply in relation to any interest paid or other distribution made by an insurance securitisation company.

(3) For the purposes of Chapter 4 of Part 10 (group relief) an insurance securitisation company shall not be treated as the member of any group or consortium.

9 The Taxation of Chargeable Gains Act 1992

(1) Taxation of Chargeable Gains Act 1992 has effect as follows.

(2) Section 171 (transfers within a group: general provisions) shall not apply if "company B" in subsection (1) of that section is an insurance securitisation company.

(3) Section 179A (reallocation within group of gain or loss accruing under section 179) shall not apply if "company C" in that section is an insurance securitisation company.

10 The Finance Act 1996

(1) The Finance Act 1996 has effect as follows.

(2) In Schedule 9 (loan relationships: special computational provisions)—

(*a*) paragraph 2 (late interest) shall not apply if the person standing in the position of a creditor as respects a loan relationship within that paragraph is an insurance securitisation company;

(*b*) paragraph 12 (continuity of treatment: groups etc) shall not apply if the "transferee company" or "transferor company" in subparagraph (1) of that paragraph is an insurance securitisation company;

(*c*) paragraph 17 (deeply discounted securities where companies have a connection) shall not apply if the "issuing company" or the company standing in the position of a creditor in subparagraph (1) of that paragraph is an insurance securitisation company;

(*d*) paragraph 18 (deeply discounted securities of companies) shall not apply if the "issuing company" or the company standing in the position of a creditor in subparagraph (1) of that paragraph is an insurance securitisation company.

11 The Finance Act 2002

(1) The Finance Act 2002 has effect as follows.

(2) Paragraph 28 of Schedule 26 (derivative contracts: transactions within groups) shall not apply if the "transferee company" or "transferor company" in subparagraph (1) of that paragraph is an insurance securitisation company.

2007/3425

REAL ESTATE INVESTMENT TRUSTS (JOINT VENTURE GROUPS) REGULATIONS 2007

Made by the Treasury under FA 2006 ss 138 and 144

Made . . . . *4 December 2007*
Laid before the House of Commons . . . . *5 December 2007*
Coming into force . . . . *31 December 2007*

Revocation—These Regulations revoked by CTA 2010 s 1181, Sch 3 Pt 1 with effect for corporation tax purposes for accounting periods ending on or after 1 April 2010, and for income tax and capital gains tax purposes for the tax year 2010–11 and subsequent tax years.

Rewrite destinations—These Regulations were rewritten in CTA 2010 as follows—

reg 3 (interpretation: general) — s 584.
reg 4 (interpretation: specific terms) — ss 587, 589, 592, 598.
reg 5 (notice) — ss 585, 587.
reg 6 (conditions for giving notice) — ss 584, 587.
reg 7 (duration and effect of notice) — ss 589, 590, 591.
reg 8 (joint-venture group: conditions for balance of business) — s 591.
reg 9 (joint-venture group: financial statements) — s 592.
reg 10 (venturing company: conditions for tax-exempt business and balance of business) — s 589.
reg 11 (venturing company: financial statements) — ss 589, 593.
reg 12 (venturing company: profit: financing-cost ratio) — s 589.
reg 13 (tax charges and exemptions: single-company REITs) — ss 589, 594, 598.
reg 14 (changes in company shareholdings: entry charges) — ss 596, 597.
reg 15 (non-resident members of joint-venture group: single-company REITs) — s 589.

reg 16 (early exit) — s 589.
reg 17 (notice) — ss 585, 587.
reg 18 (conditions for giving notice) — ss 584, 587.
reg 19 (duration and effect of notice) — ss 589, 590, 591.
reg 20 (joint-venture group: conditions for balance of business) — s 591.
reg 21 (joint-venture group: financial statements) — s 592.
reg 22 (venturing group: financial statements) — ss 589, 593.
reg 23 (tax charges and exemptions: group REITs) — ss 589, 594, 598.
reg 24 (changes in company shareholdings: entry charges) — s 596.
reg 25 (non-resident members of joint-venture group: group REITs) — s 589.
reg 26 (early exit) — s 589.

2007/3426

SCIENTIFIC RESEARCH ORGANISATIONS REGULATIONS 2007

Made by the Treasury under TA 1988 s 508(1A) and (1B)

Made . . . . *5 December 2007*
Laid before the House of Commons . . . . *5 December 2007*
Coming into force . . . . *1 January 2008*

Commentary—*Simon's Taxes* **C5.135.**

PART 1
INTRODUCTION

1 Citation, commencement and effect

(1) These Regulations may be cited as the Scientific Research Organisations Regulations 2007 and shall come into force on 1st January 2008.

(2) These Regulations have effect in relation to accounting periods that begin on or after that date.

2 Interpretation

(1) In these Regulations a reference to a section without more is a reference to that section of the Income and Corporation Taxes Act 1988.

(2) In these Regulations—

"constitutional document" means the memorandum of association, articles of association or other similar instrument regulating the functions of the Association;

"intellectual property" has the meaning it has in paragraph 2(2) of Schedule 29 to the Finance Act 2002;

"relevant income" means the amount determined in accordance with regulation 7 (relevant income of an accounting period); and

"100% subsidiary company" means a company—

(*a*) the entire ordinary share capital of which is beneficially owned directly or indirectly by the Association, or

(*b*) which is one limited by guarantee and of which the Association is the only member.

(3) Section 838 (subsidiaries) shall apply for the purpose of determining whether a company is a 100% subsidiary company of an Association but construing references in section 838(1)(*b*) to 75 per cent as to 100%.

PART 2
ASSOCIATIONS, OBJECT AND PROFITS

3 Associations for the purposes of section 508

The following shall be deemed to be an Association for the purposes of section 508(1)(*a*)—

(*a*) a body formed by the combining of two or more persons for a purpose common to those persons, or

(*b*) a body corporate comprised of two or more members.

4 Association's object

(1) In relation to an accounting period, an Association shall be deemed to have as its object the undertaking of research and development which may lead to or facilitate an extension of any class or classes of trade if—

(*a*) the Association's constitutional document states that the object of the Association is the undertaking of research and development which may lead to or facilitate an extension of any class or classes of trade;

(*b*) the stated object is the only object of the Association;

(*c*) the Association satisfies the income spending condition in regulation 5;

(*d*) regulation 6 (breach of income spending condition) does not apply;

(*e*) regulation 15 (breach of arrangements for disseminating the results of research and development) does not apply; and

(*f*) regulation 17 (breach of intellectual property requirements) does not apply.

This paragraph is subject to paragraph (2).

(2) Where an Association's constitutional document does not satisfy sub-paragraph (*b*) of paragraph (1) that sub-paragraph shall be deemed to be satisfied if—

(*a*) in relation to the accounting period immediately preceding the first accounting period in relation to which these Regulations have effect, an Association is approved by the Secretary of State for the purposes of section 508, and

(*b*) the object or objects stated in the constitutional document in relation to the accounting period for which the approval was given has not or have not in any way been altered or replaced.

5 Income spending condition

(1) The income spending condition in relation to an accounting period is that the Association must apply, or intend to apply, at least 75% of the amount of its relevant income of the accounting period to activities that are treated as research and development which may lead to or facilitate an extension of any class or classes of trade.

This is subject to paragraphs (2) and (3).

(2) Paragraph (3) applies in a case where an Association—

(*a*) intends to apply an amount of its relevant income of an accounting period to activities that are treated as research and development, and

(*b*) intends to so apply the amount after the accounting period in which the relevant income arose.

(3) Where this paragraph applies—

(*a*) the activities, to which the amount referred to in paragraph (2) is to be applied, must be planned or programmed to be undertaken by or on behalf of the Association; and

(*b*) the plan or programme of activities must have been prepared on or before the last day of the accounting period.

6 Breach of income spending condition

(1) This regulation applies where an Association fails to apply the amount (or any part of it) referred to in regulation 5(2) to the planned or programmed activities referred to in regulation 5(3) before the fifth anniversary of the last day of the accounting period in which the relevant income arose.

(2) Where this regulation applies the Association shall be deemed not to have complied with the condition in section 508(1)(*a*) in relation to any accounting period which falls in whole or in part in the calendar year that ends on the sixth anniversary of the last day of the accounting period in which the relevant income arose.

7 Relevant income of an accounting period

For the purposes of regulation 5, the amount of an Association's relevant income of an accounting period is the amount of its gross income of the accounting period less any amount paid by the Association in the accounting period in respect of pension deficit funding.

8 Gross income of an accounting period

(1) For the purposes of regulation 7, the gross income of an accounting period shall be determined in accordance with generally accepted accounting practice but subject to paragraphs (2) to (4).

(2) The amount of the gross income of an accounting period is the amount of—

(*a*) the revenue of the period, and

(*b*) subject to paragraph (4), any chargeable gains arising to the Association in the period.

(3) For the purposes of paragraph (2) the revenue of the period includes in particular—

(*a*) gross investment income;

(*b*) interest;

(*c*) dividends;

(*d*) royalties;

(*e*) grants of funding for the undertaking of research and development;

(*f*) grants from public funds;

(*g*) any payment of a sum of money received by the Association which, if the Association were a charity, would be a qualifying donation received by it within the meaning of—

(i) section 339 (charges on income: donations to charity), or

(ii) section 25 of the Finance Act 1990 (donations to charity by individuals), and

(*h*) any other amounts received by the Association which, if the Association were a charity, would be treated for the purposes of the Tax Acts in relation to the Association as a donation to it.

(4) Where in an accounting period an Association sells or otherwise disposes of real property to a 100% subsidiary company of the Association any chargeable gain arising to the Association on the sale or disposal of the real property shall not be included in the determination of the gross income of the accounting period.

(5) In paragraph (1) "generally accepted accounting practice" has the meaning it has in section 50(1) of the Finance Act 2004.

9 Pension deficit funding

(1) For the purposes of regulation 7, an amount is paid in respect of pension deficit funding if—

(*a*) it is paid directly or indirectly to the trustees or managers of an occupational pension scheme to which Part 3 of the Pensions Act 2004 applies;

(*b*) the amount paid—

(i) is recommended by an actuary, or

(ii) made in compliance with a direction, notice or order of the Pensions Regulator made under the Pensions Act 2004;

(*c*) the amount paid discharges, in whole or part, an obligation of the Association to make good any deficiency in the assets of the scheme required to meet the scheme's liabilities;

(*d*) the obligation discharged by the amount paid is in respect of only those of the scheme's liabilities which arise before the first day of the first accounting period in relation to which these Regulations have effect; and

(*e*) the obligation discharged by the amount paid is in respect of only those of the scheme's liabilities to beneficiaries who undertook scientific research the purpose of which was to facilitate an extension of any class or classes of trade.

(2) In paragraph (1) "scientific research" means any activities in the fields of natural or applied science for the extension of knowledge.

10 Relevant income of an earlier accounting period applied in a later accounting period

For the purposes of regulation 5, in determining the percentage of the amount of the relevant income of an accounting period ("the relevant period") applied, or intended to be applied, to activities treated as research and development, any amount which—

(*a*) arose in an earlier accounting period, and

(*b*) is applied, or intended to be applied, in the relevant period,

shall not be taken into account.

11 Non-distribution of profits

(1) In relation to an accounting period, an Association shall be deemed not to have complied with the condition in section 508(1)(*b*) if in the accounting period the Association directly or indirectly distributes, or intends to so distribute, in any manner or form any of its profits of that accounting period or any other accounting period to any of its members, subscribers or shareholders.

This is subject to paragraph (2).

(2) Payments made by an Association to a member, subscriber or shareholder—

(*a*) of reasonable remuneration for goods, labour, power supplied or services rendered,

(*b*) of reasonable interest for money lent, or

(*c*) of reasonable rent for any premises,

shall be treated as not being a distribution of profits for the purposes of paragraph (1) if such payments are not prohibited by the Association's constitutional document.

PART 3

RESEARCH AND DEVELOPMENT CAPABLE OF EXTENDING TRADE

12 Undertaking of research and development leading to or facilitating an extension of a class of trade

In relation to an accounting period, the undertaking of research and development is deemed to be capable of leading to or facilitating an extension of a class of trade if—

(*a*) the research and development is undertaken in accordance with regulation 13;

(*b*) the results of any research and development are or will be disseminated in accordance with regulation 14; and

(*c*) the intellectual property requirements in regulation 16 are satisfied.

13 Manner of undertaking research and development

Research and development is undertaken in accordance with this regulation if—

(*a*) the Association directly undertakes by using its own facilities activities that are treated as research and development;

(*b*) a person under the terms of a contract with the Association undertakes on behalf of the Association activities that are treated as research and development; or (*c*) a 100% subsidiary company of the Association undertakes on behalf of the Association activities that are treated as research and development.

14 Arrangements for disseminating the results of research and development

(1) For the purposes of regulation 12, the Association must disseminate the results of any research and development in accordance with the arrangements referred to in paragraph (2).

(2) The arrangements for the dissemination of the results of any research and development must be made, on or before the last day of the accounting period, and must ensure that the results of any research and development undertaken in the accounting period are to be—

(*a*) made available upon request and without charge, subject to paragraph (3);

(*b*) made available, subject to paragraph (4)—

(i) to all the members and shareholders of, and all the subscribers to, the Association who undertake the class of trade that may be facilitated or extended by the research and development; or

(ii) to all the members and shareholders of, and all the subscribers to, the Association; or

(iii) generally to the public; and

(*c*) made available not later than one year after the completion of the research and development.

(3) Paragraph (2)(*a*) does not prevent an Association from recovering from a recipient of the results of any research and development the reasonable costs of publishing or distributing the results to the recipient.

(4) Where any member or shareholder of, or subscriber to, the Association is connected with the Association paragraph (2)(*b*) does not apply and instead the arrangements must ensure that the results of any research and development undertaken in the accounting period are made available—

(*a*) generally to the public, or

(*b*) to any person who undertakes the class of trade that may be facilitated or extended by the research and development whether or not the person is or is not a member or shareholder of, or subscriber to, the Association.

Section 839 (connected persons) shall apply for the purpose of determining whether a member, shareholder or subscriber is connected with the Association.

15 Breach of arrangements for disseminating the results of research and development

(1) This regulation applies where—

(*a*) the arrangements referred to in paragraph (2) of regulation 14 are altered or replaced after the end of an accounting period in respect of which a claim under section 508 is made with the effect that the requirements of that paragraph cease to met in relation to research and development undertaken in that accounting period; or

(*b*) any results of any research and development undertaken in an accounting period in respect of which a claim under section 508 is made are disseminated other than in accordance with the arrangements referred to in that paragraph.

(2) Where this regulation applies the Association shall be deemed not to have satisfied the condition in section 508(1)(*a*) in relation to the accounting period in which the alteration or replacement occurs or in which the dissemination occurs.

16 Intellectual property requirements

For the purposes of regulation 12, the intellectual property requirements are that any intellectual property from any research and development undertaken by or on behalf of an Association in an accounting period—

(*a*) must be solely and beneficially owned by the Association for a period of not less than one year from the date on which the accounting period ends;

(*b*) in a case where the intellectual property is sold, transferred, assigned, licensed or otherwise made available by an Association to any person—

(i) in the accounting period, or

(ii) in the period that ends one year from the date on which the accounting period ends,

the intellectual property must also be made available by the Association to all the members and shareholders of, and all the subscribers to, the Association; or

(*c*) in a case where the funding of the research and development is—

(i) shared by the Association and another person or body ("shared funding"), and

(ii) as a consequence of the shared funding the Association is unable to secure sole beneficial ownership of any intellectual property from the research and development,

the Association must secure in the accounting period a right to use or exploit any intellectual property from the research and development for a period of not less than one year from the date on which the accounting period ends.

17 Breach of intellectual property requirements

(1) This regulation applies where in respect of any intellectual property from research and development undertaken by or on behalf of an Association in an accounting period in respect of which a claim under section 508 is made the circumstances are such that none of the requirements in regulation 16(*a*), (*b*) or (*c*) is satisfied in relation to the intellectual property.

(2) Where this regulation applies at any time in an accounting period, the Association shall be deemed not to have satisfied the condition in section 508(1)(*a*) in relation to that accounting period (whether or not the intellectual property involved arose in or existed in that accounting period or in an earlier accounting period).

2007/3507

RECOVERY OF FOREIGN TAXES REGULATIONS 2007

Made by the Treasury under FA 2006 s 175(1)

Made . . . .*12 December 2007*

Laid before the House of Commons . . . .*13 December 2007*

Coming into force . . . .*3 January 2008*

Commentary—*Simon's Taxes* **D4.324**.

1 Citation and commencement

These Regulations may be cited as the Recovery of Foreign Taxes Regulations 2007 and shall come into force on 3rd January 2008.

2 Interpretation

In these Regulations—

"applicant authority" means an authority in a foreign territory which makes a request for recovery in accordance with [arrangements having effect by virtue of section 173 of the Finance Act 2006][1];

"the Commissioners" means the Commissioners for Her Majesty's Revenue and Customs, or an officer of Her Majesty's Revenue and Customs;

"a contested claim" is one which is subject to action challenging either the foreign claim or the instrument permitting enforcement brought by an interested party before the competent body of the foreign territory in which the applicant authority is situated in accordance with the laws in force there;

"enforcement action" means action to enforce a foreign claim by way of legal proceedings, distress, diligence or other process which might be taken to enforce a United Kingdom claim for income tax of the same amount;

"a final decision" is one against which no appeal lies or against which an appeal lies within a period that has expired without an appeal having been brought by either party to the proceedings;

["a foreign claim" means a debt relating to any relevant foreign tax;][1]

"instrument permitting enforcement" means—

(*a*) any instrument issued by an applicant authority in a foreign territory in relation to a sum claimed by that authority within the jurisdiction of that territory; or

(*b*) a decision on that claim given in favour of that authority by a court or tribunal or other competent body in that territory which permits recovery of that claim in that territory or part thereof;

"request for recovery" means a request for recovery of a [foreign claim][1] by an applicant authority;

"the Taxes Acts" has the meaning given in section 118(1) of the Taxes Management Act 1970;

"transmission by electronic means" includes transmission by means of an electronic communications system (and cognate expressions shall be construed accordingly).

Amendments—[1] Words in definitions "applicant authority" and "request for recovery" substituted, and definition inserted, by the Recovery of Foreign Taxes (Amendment) Regulations, SI 2010/794, regs 2, 3 with effect from 6 April 2010.

3 Relevant foreign tax claim

(1) For the purposes of these Regulations a [foreign claim][1] shall be treated as if it were a claim for income tax under the Taxes Acts subject to what follows.

(2) The Commissioners may take such enforcement action [in relation to a foreign claim][1] as they would for a claim for income tax under the Taxes Acts in the same amount.

Amendments—[1] Words in para (1) substituted and words in para (2) inserted, by the Recovery of Foreign Taxes (Amendment) Regulations, SI 2010/794, regs 2, 4 with effect from 6 April 2010.

[4 Requests for recovery

(1) A request for recovery shall be in writing.

(2) A request for recovery shall give the sterling equivalent of the amount of the foreign claim, using the latest selling rate for sterling recorded on the most representative exchange market or markets of the territory in which the applicant authority is situated on the date when the request for recovery is made.][1]

Amendments—[1] Reg 4 substituted by the Recovery of Foreign Taxes (Amendment) Regulations, SI 2010/794, regs 2, 5 with effect from 6 April 2010.

5 Procedure on receipt of request

When the Commissioners receive a request for recovery they—

(*a*) shall acknowledge receipt of the request in writing to the applicant authority, and

(*b*) may request additional information or documentation from the applicant authority if the agreed information and documentation has not been supplied in accordance with regulation 4(1)(*b*).

6 Requests for recovery—further provisions

For the purposes of these Regulations—

(*a*) a request for recovery made by an applicant authority shall be taken to be duly made in accordance with arrangements relating to international tax enforcement unless the contrary is proved, and

(*b*) except as set out in regulations 9, 10 and 11, no question may be raised as to a person's liability on the foreign claim.

7 Communication of information

Information sent to the Commissioners as part of a request for recovery may only be communicated by them to—

(*a*) the person mentioned in the request for assistance;

(*b*) those persons and authorities responsible for the recovery of the claims, and solely for that purpose, or

(*c*) the judicial authorities dealing with matters concerning the recovery of claims.

8 Adjustment of a foreign claim

(1) This regulation applies where the amount of a foreign claim is amended for any reason.

(2) Where the amendment leads to a reduction in the amount of the foreign claim the following rules apply.

Rule 1

The Commissioners shall continue the action which they have undertaken with a view to recovery but that action shall be limited to the amount still outstanding.

Rule 2

If at the time the Commissioners are informed of the reduction in the amount of the foreign claim, an amount exceeding the amount still outstanding has already been recovered by them, but this amount has not yet been transferred to the applicant authority, the Commissioners shall repay the excess to the person who appears to them to be entitled to it.

(3) Where the amendment leads to an increase in the amount of the foreign claim the following rules apply.

Rule 1

The additional request shall as far as possible be dealt with by the Commissioners at the same time as the original request.

Rule 2

Where, in view of the state of progress of the existing recovery procedure, consolidation of the additional request with the original request is not possible, the Commissioners shall treat that request as a new claim but shall be required to comply with it only if it concerns an amount not less than the minimum amount referred to in regulation 4(3).

9 Cancellation or payment of a claim

In any case where the Commissioners take enforcement action in relation to a foreign claim, and upon receipt of notice in writing by the applicant authority that—

(*a*) the taxpayer has made payment in satisfaction of that claim; or

(*b*) the claim has been terminated or cancelled for some other reason;

they shall cease any enforcement action in relation to that claim.

10 Disputed claims

(1) No enforcement action under these Regulations shall be taken against a person if he shows that proceedings relevant to his liability on the foreign claim are pending, or are about to be instituted, before a court, tribunal or other competent body in the foreign territory in question.

(2) For this purpose proceedings relevant to a person's liability on a foreign claim are pending until a final decision is made.

11 Claims determined in taxpayer's favour

(1) No enforcement action under these Regulations shall be taken against a person if a final decision on the foreign claim has been given in his favour by a court, tribunal or other competent body in the foreign territory in question.

(2) If a person shows that such a decision has been given in respect of part of the claim, no enforcement action under these Regulations shall be taken in relation to that part.

12 Limitation

(1) The period of limitation or prescription in relation to any issue arising on the recovery of any foreign claim shall be that applicable under the laws in force in the foreign territory in which the applicant authority is situated.

(2) For the purposes of paragraph (1) any step taken by the Commissioners in recovery of a foreign claim in pursuance of a request for assistance shall be deemed to have been taken in the foreign territory in which the applicant authority is situated where that step, if it had been taken by that applicant authority, would have had the effect of suspending or interrupting the period of limitation or prescription in accordance with the laws in force in that territory.

[13 Interest

(1) A foreign claim carries interest in respect of the relevant foreign tax and any penalty claimed if arrangements having effect by virtue of section 173 of the Finance Act 2006 so provide.

(2) Where the arrangements provide that the rate of interest is that which applies under the law of the territory in which the applicant authority is situated, the claim carries interest at that rate for the period determined in accordance with those laws.

(3) Where paragraph (2) applies, the applicant authority must provide details to the Commissioners—

(*a*) of the daily rate of interest to be applied, and

(*b*) of the period for which interest runs.

(4) Where the arrangements provide that the rate of interest is that which applies in respect of any tax or duty imposed under the domestic law of the United Kingdom, the claim carries interest at the rate applicable to income tax under section 178 of the Finance Act 1989 from the date of recognition until payment.

(5) In paragraph (4), "the date of recognition" means the earlier of—

(*a*) the day following the expiry of three months from the date of receipt by the Commissioners of the request for recovery of the foreign claim, and

(*b*) the date the receipt of the request for recovery is acknowledged in writing by the Commissioners to the applicant authority.

(6) Paragraph (4) applies even if the date of recognition is a non-business day within the meaning of section 92 of the Bills of Exchange Act 1882.

(7) Interest is payable under this regulation without any deduction of income tax.

(8) For the purposes of this regulation, where—

(*a*) any payment is made by cheque to Her Majesty's Revenue and Customs, and

(*b*) the cheque is paid on its first presentation to the banker on whom it is drawn;

the payment shall be treated as made on the day on which the cheque is received by the Commissioners.

(9) Interest charged under this regulation shall be recoverable as if it were interest charged under a provision of the Taxes Management Act 1970.][1]

Amendments—[1] Reg 13 substituted by the Recovery of Foreign Taxes (Amendment) Regulations, SI 2010/794, regs 2, 6 with effect from 6 April 2010.

14 Evidence

(1) An instrument permitting enforcement of a foreign claim recognised by the Commissioners as an instrument authorising enforcement of the claim in the United Kingdom, together with a certificate of an officer of Revenue and Customs that payment of the claim has not been made to him, or to the best of his knowledge and belief, to any other officer, or to any person acting on his behalf, or on behalf of another officer, or to the applicant authority, is sufficient evidence that the sum mentioned in the instrument is unpaid and is due to the applicant authority.

(2) A certificate of an officer of Revenue and Customs that interest is payable under either regulation 13(2) or 13(3) and that payment of the interest has not been made to him, or, to the best of his knowledge and belief, to any other officer, or to any person acting on his behalf or on behalf of another officer, or to the applicant authority, is sufficient evidence that the interest is unpaid and due to the applicant authority.

(3) For the purposes of this regulation, any document purporting to be such a certificate as is mentioned in paragraphs (1) and (2) is deemed to be such a certificate unless the contrary is proved.

15 Enforcement in Scotland

(1) For the purposes of enforcement in Scotland, an original, official or certified copy of a final decision on a foreign claim by a court, tribunal or other competent body in the foreign territory in which the applicant authority is situated shall be of the same force and effect as an extract of a decree of the Court of Session for the payment of money bearing a warrant for execution.

(2) For the purposes of paragraph (1), a final decision on a foreign claim is a final decision on a foreign claim which permits recovery of that claim in the foreign territory in which the applicant authority is situated or in part thereof.

2007/3532

REGISTERED PENSION SCHEMES (AUTHORISED MEMBER PAYMENTS) REGULATIONS 2007

Made by the Commissioners for Her Majesty's Revenue and Customs under FA 2004 s 164(f)

Made . . . . *14 December 2007*
Laid before the House of Commons . . . . *17 December 2007*
Coming into force . . . . *7 January 2008*

1 Citation and commencement

These Regulations may be cited as the Registered Pension Schemes (Authorised Member Payments) Regulations 2007 and shall come into force on 7th January 2008.

2 Prescribed authorised member payment relating to inherited estate on reattribution

(1) For the purposes of section 164(*f*) of the Finance Act 2004 (authorised member payments) a payment made by a registered pension scheme to or in respect of a person who is or has been a member of the pension scheme is of a description that is prescribed if the payment meets conditions A, B and C

(2) Condition A is that the payment is made as part of a scheme which—

(*a*) makes a reattribution of the inherited estate of a person who carries on with-profits business, and

(*b*) is made or sanctioned by a court of competent jurisdiction.

(3) Condition B is that the payment is made to or in respect of the registered pension scheme's with-profits policyholders in exchange for giving up rights and interests over the inherited estate.

(4) Condition C is that the payment does not reduce the total value of the sums and assets held for the purposes of the registered pension scheme.

(5) In this regulation—

"inherited estate" has the same meaning as in the Conduct of Business sourcebook issued by the Financial Services Authority;

a "reattribution" means a redefinition of rights and interests of the with-profits policyholders mentioned in paragraph (3) over the inherited estate; and

"with-profits business" has the same meaning as in the Conduct of Business sourcebook issued by the Financial Services Authority.

2007/3537

EMPLOYER-FINANCED RETIREMENT BENEFITS (EXCLUDED BENEFITS FOR TAX PURPOSES) REGULATIONS 2007

Made by the Commissioners for Her Majesty's Revenue and Customs under ITEPA 2003 s 393B(3)(*d*) and (4A)

Made . . . . *14 December 2007*
Laid before the House of Commons . . . . *17 December 2007*
Coming into force . . . . *8 January 2008*

Commentary—*Simon's Taxes* **E4.841**.

1 Citation and commencement

(1) These Regulations may be cited as the Employer-Financed Retirement Benefits (Excluded Benefits for Tax Purposes) Regulations 2007 and come into force on 8th January 2008.

(2) [Subject to paragraph (3), these][1] Regulations have effect for the tax year 2006–07 and subsequent tax years.

[(3) These Regulations have effect—

(*a*) so far as they relate to tuition fees, as described in paragraph 18 of the Schedule, for the tax year 2009-2010 and subsequent tax years; and (*b*) so far as they relate to resettlement commutation, resettlement grants, gratuity earnings and the provision of independent inquest advice, as described in paragraphs 19, 20 and 21 of the Schedule, for the tax year 2010-2011 and subsequent tax years.][1]

Amendments—[1] In para (2), words substituted, and para (3) inserted, by the Employer-Financed Retirement Benefits (Excluded Benefits for Tax Purposes) (Amendment) Regulations, SI 2011/2281 regs 2–4 with effect from 7 October 2011.

2 Interpretation

(1) In these Regulations—

["armed forces" means the regular forces and the reserve forces as defined in section 374 of the Armed Forces Act 2006 and former members of both;][1]

"employee" includes a former employee;

"employer" includes—

(*a*) a former employer; and

(*b*) a person who has assumed the responsibility for providing a benefit in place of the person who employed the employee;

"ill-health" means physical or mental impairment;

"ITEPA 2003" means the Income Tax (Earnings and Pensions) Act 2003;

["medical discharge" means the discharge from service of a member of the armed forces because the member is medically unfit to continue in service due to injury or illness caused or worsened by service in the armed forces;][1]

"relevant benefit" means a benefit to which Chapter 2 of Part 6 of ITEPA 2003 applies.

(2) References to a member of a person's family shall be construed in accordance with section 721(4) of ITEPA 2003, but this is subject to regulation 3(4).

Amendments—[1] In para (1), definitions of "armed forces" and "medical discharge" inserted by the Employer-Financed Retirement Benefits (Excluded Benefits for Tax Purposes) (Amendment) Regulations, SI 2011/2281 regs 2, 5 with effect from 7 October 2011.

3 Excluded benefits

(1) A relevant benefit—

(*a*) that is provided (or to be provided) in any of the circumstances mentioned in paragraphs (*a*) to (*c*) of section 393B(1) of ITEPA 2003;

(*b*) that is described in the Schedule; and

(*c*) that is provided to a qualifying person,

is an excluded benefit for the purposes of section 393B(3)(d) of ITEPA 2003.

(2) The following are qualifying persons for the purposes of paragraph (1)—

[(*a*) in the case of the benefits described in the following paragraphs of the Schedule, the employee: paragraph 2 (accommodation provided for performance of duties—employees), paragraph 16 (equipment for disabled employees) and paragraph 17 (health-screening and medical check-ups),][1]

(*b*) in the case of the benefit described in paragraph 3 of the Schedule (accommodation provided for performance of duties—members of employees' families), a member of the employee's family,

(*c*) in the case of any other benefit described in Part 1 of the Schedule—

(i) the employee, and

(ii) after any of the events specified in paragraph (3), a member of the employee's family,

[(*ca*) in the case of the benefits described in paragraph 18 (tuition fees for armed forces personnel) of Part 3 of the Schedule (other benefits)—

(i) a member of the armed forces, and

(ii) after the death or medical discharge of a member of the armed forces, a member of his or her family,

(*cb*) in the case of the benefits described in paragraph 19 (armed forces resettlement commutation and resettlement grants schemes) of the Schedule, a member of the armed forces, and

(*cc*) in the case of the benefits described in paragraph 20 (the armed forces gratuity earnings scheme) of the Schedule—

(i) a member of the armed forces, and

(ii) after the death of a member of the armed forces, a member of his or her family or the personal representatives of the member of the armed forces, and

(*cd*) in the case of the benefits described in paragraph 21 (independent inquest advice service) of the Schedule—

(i) a member of the family of the armed forces member, or

(ii) a brother or sister of the member of the armed forces.][2]

[(*ce*) in the case of the benefits described in paragraph 22 (trivial benefits) of the Schedule—][3]

(i) the employee, and

(ii) a member of the employee's family or household.][3]

(*d*) in the case of any other benefit described in Part 3 of the Schedule—

(i) the employee, and

(ii) after the employee's death, a member of the employee's family.

(3) The events mentioned in paragraph (2)(*c*)(ii) are—

(*a*) the employee's death;

(*b*) the employee's taking up residence elsewhere (than in the living accommodation concerned) as a result of ill-health;

(*c*) the employee's taking up residence elsewhere (than in the living accommodation concerned) following—

(i) a separation,

(ii) the annulment or divorce of a marriage, or

(iii) the nullity or dissolution of a civil partnership.

(4) Where the event mentioned in paragraph (3)(*c*)(ii) or (iii) has occurred, the ex-spouse or ex-civil partner shall be treated as a member of the employee's family.

Amendments—[1] Para (2)(*a*) substituted by the Employer-Financed Retirement Benefits (Excluded Benefits for Tax Purposes) (Amendment) Regulations, SI 2009/2886 regs 2, 3 with effect for the tax year 2006–07 and subsequent tax years.

[2] Para (2)(*ca*)–(*cd*), inserted by the Employer-Financed Retirement Benefits (Excluded Benefits for Tax Purposes) (Amendment) Regulations, SI 2011/2281 regs 2, 6 with effect from 7 October 2011.

[3] Para (2)(*ce*) inserted by the Employer-Financed Retirement Benefits (Excluded Benefits for Tax Purposes) (Amendment) Regulations, SI 2016 regs 2, 3 with effect for the tax year 2016–17 and subsequent tax years.

SCHEDULE

Regulation 3

PART 1
LIVING ACCOMMODATION AND RELATED BENEFITS

Accommodation provided by local authority

1 Living accommodation if—

(*a*) it is provided by a local authority, and

(*b*) Chapter 5 of Part 3 of ITEPA 2003 (taxable benefits: living accommodation) would not have applied to the provision of that accommodation by virtue of section 98 of that Act (accommodation provided by local authority) if the employee had remained in that employment.

Accommodation provided for performance of duties-employees

2—(1) Living accommodation if—

(*a*) the employee had been in continuous occupation of the same or similar living accommodation during the five years immediately preceding the employee's retirement,

(*b*) throughout that period of five years—

(i) Chapter 5 of Part 3 of ITEPA 2003 did not apply to the provision of that accommodation by virtue of section 99 of that Act (accommodation provided for performance of duties), and

(ii) for any tax year before 2003–04, the accommodation attracted similar treatment for tax purposes by virtue of an enactment that was restated by section 99,

(*c*) the employee continued to occupy the same or similar accommodation after retirement.

(2) In determining whether the occupation of living accommodation is continuous, the following breaks in occupation shall be disregarded—

(*a*) any one break not exceeding six months,

(*b*) breaks not exceeding one month each,

(*c*) breaks (of any duration) resulting from the employee's ill health.

(3) Living accommodation is not within this paragraph if it is improved property.

Accommodation provided for performance of duties – members of employees' families

3—(1) Living accommodation provided to a member of the employee's family after the employee's death if—

(*a*) the employee died before retirement and Condition A is satisfied; or

(*b*) the employee died after retirement and Condition B is satisfied.

(2) Condition A is that—

(*a*) the employee had been in occupation of the same or similar living accommodation at any time during the five years immediately preceding the employee's death,

(*b*) at any time during that period of five years—

(i) Chapter 5 of Part 3 of ITEPA 2003 did not apply to the provision of that accommodation by virtue of section 99 of that Act, or

(ii) for a tax year before 2003–04, the accommodation attracted similar treatment for tax purposes by virtue of an enactment that was restated by section 99,

(3) Condition B is that the living accommodation was living accommodation described in paragraph 2 immediately before the employee's death.

(4) In determining whether the occupation of living accommodation is continuous, the breaks in occupation mentioned in paragraph 2(2) shall be disregarded.

(5) Living accommodation is not within this paragraph if it is improved property.

Accommodation provided for ministers of religion

4—(1) Living accommodation if—

(*a*) the employee had been employed as a minister of a religious denomination—

(i) for the period of five years immediately preceding the employee's retirement,

(ii) immediately preceding the employee's death, or

(iii) if the employee retired immediately after a period of ill-health, immediately preceding the beginning of that period, and

(*b*) at any time while the employee had been a minister, either—

(i) Chapter 5 of Part 3 of ITEPA 2003 did not apply to the provision of that or some other living accommodation provided to the employee by the employer by virtue of section 99 of that Act, or

(ii) for a tax year before 2003–04, such accommodation attracted similar treatment for tax purposes by virtue of an enactment that was restated by section 99.

(2) The condition in sub-paragraph (1)(*a*)(iii) is not satisfied unless and until the employer has received evidence from a registered medical practitioner that the employee is incapable of carrying on the occupation.

Accommodation provided as result of security threat

5 Living accommodation if—

(*a*) at any time before the employee's retirement or death—

(i) Chapter 5 of Part 3 of ITEPA 2003 did not apply to the provision of that or similar accommodation provided to the employee by the employer by virtue of section 100 of that Act (accommodation provided as result of security threat), and

(ii) for any tax year before 2003–04, such accommodation attracted similar treatment for tax purposes by virtue of an enactment that was restated by section 100,

(*b*) except that the employment has been terminated, the conditions set out in paragraphs (*a*) to (*c*) of section 100 continue to be satisfied.

Removal expenses

6—(1) A benefit provided by the employer in connection with a change of residence if—

(*a*) it is a benefit of a description within section 280 of ITEPA 2003;

(*b*) there would have been no liability to income tax by virtue of section 271 of ITEPA 2003 if—

(i) the benefit had been provided in the course of the employment,

(ii) the change of residence had met the conditions in section 273 of ITEPA 2003,

(iii) the last day of the tax year after that in which the change of residence occurred had constituted the limitation day;

(*c*) the former residence is living accommodation described in this Part.

(2) If the cash equivalent of the benefit determined in accordance with the rules in section 203 of ITEPA 2003 exceeds £8,000—

(*a*) the excess is not within the description in this paragraph; and

(*b*) in determining whether there would have been no liability to income tax by virtue of section 271 of ITEPA 2003 for the purposes of sub-paragraph (1)(*b*), the excess shall be disregarded.

Repairs and alterations to living accommodation

7 Works—

(*a*) in respect of which there would have been no liability to income tax by virtue of section 313 of ITEPA 2003 if they had been carried out in relation to living accommodation provided by reason of the employee's employment;

(*b*) that are carried out in relation to living accommodation described in this Part; and

(*c*) that do not have the effect of the living accommodation becoming improved property.

Council tax etc paid for living accommodation

8 Payments or reimbursements if—

(*a*) they are of a description within section 314(2) of ITEPA 2003;

(*b*) section 314 would have applied to them if the living accommodation had been of a description within subsection (1) of that section;

(*c*) they are in respect of living accommodation described in this Part.

PART 2
INTERPRETATION OF PART 1

Similar accommodation

9—(1) All living accommodation is similar to other living accommodation unless, at the time the employee or member of the employee's family starts to occupy the new accommodation, its market value exceeds that of the accommodation occupied immediately prior to it by more than 20%.

(2) Where the living accommodation is not capable of being sold separately (whether because it forms part of larger premises in multiple occupation or otherwise), its market value shall be taken to be such amount as would be obtained if the factors that prevented its separate sale were disregarded.

Improved property

10—(1) Living accommodation is improved property if works have been carried out to it which—

(*a*) materially improve it; and

(*b*) are not carried out wholly for the purposes of complying with a statutory requirement or a requirement imposed by a government department, a statutory body or a person holding a statutory office.

(2) For the purposes of sub-paragraph (1), a property is materially improved by works if—

(*a*) its market value on the date the works are substantially completed ("MVW") exceeds what would have been its market value on that date if the works had not been carried out ("MV"); and

(*b*) the amount by which MVW exceeds MV is greater than 20% of MV.

(3) Where the living accommodation is not capable of being sold separately (whether because it forms part of larger premises in multiple occupation or otherwise), both MVW and MV shall be taken to be such amount as would be obtained if the factors that prevented its separate sale were disregarded.

(4) For the purposes of sub-paragraph (1)(*b*)—

"statutory body" means a body set up by or under an enactment (including an enactment comprised in, or an instrument made under, an Act of the Scottish Parliament);

"statutory office" means a body set up by or under such an enactment; and

"statutory requirement" means a requirement imposed by provision made by or under such an enactment.

PART 3
OTHER BENEFITS

Non-cash benefits received before 6th April 1998

11 The provision of a non-cash benefit if—

(*a*) it was received in connection with the termination of the employee's employment,

(*b*) that termination took place before 6th April 1998.

Welfare counselling

12 The provision of welfare counselling which would have been exempted by virtue of the Income Tax (Benefits in Kind) (Exemption for Welfare Counselling) Regulations 2000 if it had been provided in the course of the employee's employment.

Recreational benefits

13 The provision of recreational benefits if no liability to income tax would have arisen by virtue of section 261 of ITEPA 2003 if it had been provided in the course of the employee's employment.

Annual parties and similar functions

14 The provision of an annual party or similar annual function if no liability to income tax would have arisen by virtue of section 264 of ITEPA 2003 if it had been provided in the course of the employee's employment.

Writing of wills etc

15 The provision of a service for the writing of a will or similar testamentary document if the cash equivalent of the benefit determined in accordance with the rules in section 203 of ITEPA 2003 does not exceed £150.

Equipment for disabled employees

16—(1) The provision of a benefit which—

(*a*) was first provided in the course of the employee's employment; and

(*b*) satisfied Conditions 1 to 5 of regulation 3 of the Income Tax (Benefits in Kind) (Exception for Employment Costs resulting from Disability) Regulations 2002 ("the 2002 Regulations") at that time.

(2) The replacement, whenever provided, for a hearing aid or other equipment, services or facilities mentioned in Condition 3 of the 2002 Regulations where the aid, equipment, services or facilities are no longer usable or appropriate to the needs of the employee.

[Health-screening and medical check-ups

17—(1) The provision of a health-screening assessment or medical check-up if—

(*a*) no liability to income tax would have arisen by virtue of section 320B of ITEPA 2003 if it had been provided in the course of the employee's employment; and

(*b*) at least one health-screening assessment or medical check-up (as defined in that section) had been provided to the employee in the course of the employee's employment.

(2) A health-screening assessment or medical check-up that was provided during the tax year 2006–07, 2007–08 or 2008–09 shall be taken to satisfy the condition in sub-paragraph (1)(*a*) if it would have satisfied that condition if section 320B of ITEPA 2003 had had effect for the tax year concerned.][1]

Amendments—[1] Para 17 inserted by the Employer-Financed Retirement Benefits (Excluded Benefits for Tax Purposes) (Amendment) Regulations, SI 2009/2886 regs 2, 4 with effect for the tax year 2006–07 and subsequent tax years.

[Tuition fees for armed forces personnel

18—(1) The payment of tuition fees for higher level learning and qualification level learning.

(2) For the purposes of this paragraph—

"higher level learning" means full or part time study towards the achievement of a higher level learning qualification;

"higher level learning qualification" means a qualification at Level 3 or above on the Qualifications and Credit Framework or such other equivalent qualification in respect of which qualifying persons may claim tuition fees;

"qualification level learning" means a first qualification at Level 3 or above on the Qualifications and Credit Framework, a first vocational qualification which is the equivalent of the preceding qualification, a first undergraduate degree (including a foundation degree), a first Higher National Certificate, a first Higher National Diploma or such other equivalent qualifications in respect of which qualifying persons may claim tuition fees;

"the Qualifications and Credit Framework" is a national framework which accommodates qualifications and operates across England, Wales and Northern Ireland;

"tuition fees" means the fees charged by the provider of a course of study leading to a higher level learning qualification or to qualification level learning and such fees may include registration, examination and accreditation fees.][1]

Amendments—[1] Para 18 inserted by the Employer-Financed Retirement Benefits (Excluded Benefits for Tax Purposes) (amendment) Regulations, SI 2011/2281 regs 2, 7 with effect from 7 October 2011.

[Armed Forces Resettlement Commutation and Resettlement Grants Schemes

19 The provision of a lump sum in connection with resettlement commutation or resettlement grants of the description given in the Armed Forces (Redundancy, Resettlement and Gratuity Earnings Schemes) (No 2) Order 2010.][1]

Amendments—

Para 19 inserted by the Employer-Financed Retirement Benefits (Excluded Benefits for Tax Purposes) (amendment) Regulations, SI 2011/2281 regs 2, 7 with effect from 7 October 2011.

[Armed Forces Gratuity Earnings Scheme

20 The provision of gratuity earnings of the description given in the Armed Forces (Redundancy, Resettlement and Gratuity Earnings Schemes) (No 2) Order 2010.][1]

Amendments—[1] Para 20 inserted by the Employer-Financed Retirement Benefits (Excluded Benefits for Tax Purposes) (amendment) Regulations, SI 2011/2281 regs 2, 7 with effect from 7 October 2011.

[Independent Inquest Advice Service

21 The provision of independent inquest advice in connection with the death in service of a member of the armed forces.][1]

Amendments—[1] Para 21 inserted by the Employer-Financed Retirement Benefits (Excluded Benefits for Tax Purposes) (Amendment) Regulations, SI 2011/2281 regs 2, 7 with effect from 7 October 2011.

[Trivial benefits

22 (1) The provision of a benefit which would have been exempted by virtue of sections 323A and 323B of ITEPA 2003 (exemption from income tax for trivial benefits provided by employers) if it had been provided in the course of the employee's employment.

(2) For the purposes of sub-paragraph (1)—

(*a*) section 323A(2) of ITEPA 2003 (close company restriction) applies where—

(i) the former employer is a close company when the benefit is provided, and

(ii) the former employee is—

(*aa*) a person who was a director or other office-holder at any time when the former employer was a close company, or

(*bb*) a member of the family or household of such a person, and

(*b*) a benefit provided to a member of the family or household of the former employee is included in the calculation of the amount allocated under section 323B(4) of ITEPA 2003 (amount allocated in respect of a benefit).][1]

Amendments—[1] Para 22 inserted by the Employer-Financed Retirement Benefits (Excluded Benefits for Tax Purposes) (Amendment) Regulations, SI 2016/1036 regs 2, 4 with effect for the tax year 2016–17 and subsequent tax years.

2008/403

SERIOUS CRIME ACT 2007 (DISCLOSURE OF INFORMATION BY REVENUE AND CUSTOMS) ORDER 2008

Made by the Treasury under SCA 2007 ss 85(7) and 89(1)

Made . . . . *19 February 2008*
Laid before Parliament . . . . *19 February 2008*
Coming into force . . . . *11 March 2008*

Commentary—*Simon's Taxes* **A3.413**.

1 Citation and commencement

This Order may be cited as the Serious Crime Act 2007 (Disclosure of Information by Revenue and Customs) Order 2008 and shall come into force on 11th March 2008.

2 Interpretation

In this Order "the CAB" means the Criminal Assets Bureau in Ireland established under section 3(1) of the Criminal Assets Bureau Act 1996.

3 Disclosure of information by Revenue and Customs

The following persons are specified in relation to the CAB for the purposes of section 85(7) of the Serious Crime Act 2007 (disclosure of information by Revenue and Customs)—

(*a*) the Chief Bureau Officer;

(*b*) the bureau legal officer; and

(*c*) any person appointed as a bureau officer under section 8 of the Criminal Assets Bureau Act 1996.

2008/562

INCOME TAX (PURCHASED LIFE ANNUITIES) REGULATIONS 2008

Made by the Commissioners for Her Majesty's Revenue and Customs under TA 1988 s 658(3) and ITTOIA 2005 s 724

Made . . . .*5 March 2008*
Laid before the House of Commons . . . .*5 March 2008*
Coming into force . . . .*6 April 2008*

PART 1
INTRODUCTION

1 Citation, commencement and application

(1) These Regulations may be cited as The Income Tax (Purchased Life Annuities) Regulations 2008 and come into force on 6th April 2008.

(2) These Regulations apply to an annuity under which the first payment to the annuitant is made on or after 6th April 2008, subject to the transitional provision in regulation 27.

2 Interpretation

In these Regulations—

"the 1956 Regulations" means the Income Tax (Purchased Life Annuities) Regulations 1956;

"the 2005 Act" means the Income Tax (Trading and Other Income) Act 2005;

"annuitant" means the person beneficially entitled for the time being to the payments on account of an annuity;

"annuity" means a purchased life annuity within the meaning of section 423 of the 2005 Act;

"the Commissioners" means the Commissioners for Her Majesty's Revenue and Customs;

"insurer" means a United Kingdom insurer or a non-United Kingdom insurer, as the case may be;

"non-United Kingdom insurer" means any person carrying on life annuity business and who—

(*a*) is resident outside the United Kingdom; and

(*b*) does not carry on such business through a permanent establishment in the United Kingdom;

"relevant EEA State" means an EEA State, other than the United Kingdom;

"relevant person" means—

(*a*) a United Kingdom insurer; or

(*b*) a tax representative appointed in accordance with Part 3; or

(*c*) a person appointed in accordance with arrangements made under regulation 18;

"relevant records" means the records referred to in regulation 21(1);

"tax representative" means the person appointed in accordance with Part 3 to act as such for a non-United Kingdom insurer;

"the partial tax exemption" means the exemption provided by Chapter 7 of Part 6 of the 2005 Act; and

"United Kingdom insurer" means—

(*a*) any person resident in the United Kingdom carrying on life annuity business; or

(*b*) any person not so resident who carries on life annuity business through a permanent establishment in the United Kingdom.

PART 2
PROCEDURE WHERE ANNUITY IS PURCHASED

3 Application of this Part

This Part applies where—

(*a*) an annuitant purchases an annuity from a United Kingdom insurer;

(*b*) a tax representative is appointed in accordance with Part 3; or

(*c*) a person is appointed in accordance with arrangements made under regulation 18.

4 Initial steps

(1) The relevant person must provide the annuitant with the form on which the annuitant is to make the declaration in accordance with regulation 5, within such time as is reasonable to enable the annuitant to comply with this Part before the first annuity payment becomes due and payable.

(2) The form mentioned in paragraph (1) must include such of the following information as is known (at the appropriate place in each case) before it is provided to the annuitant—

(*a*) the name of the insurer;

(*b*) the insurer's life office reference number;

(*c*) a reference number for the quotation that relates to the annuity in question or the policy number for that annuity, if the latter is available;

(*d*) the name or names of the person or persons on whose life or lives the annuity depends;

(*e*) the gross amount of each payment to be made under the annuity;

(*f*) the frequency of the payment referred to in sub-paragraph (*e*); and

(*g*) the date on which the first payment under the annuity is to be made.

(3) Where the relevant person is either—

(*a*) a tax representative appointed in accordance with Part 3; or
(*b*) a person appointed in accordance with arrangements made under regulation 18;

that person must comply with the requirements of paragraphs (1) and (2) within 30 days of the date of the first payment being made under the annuity.

5 Annuitant to provide information and make declaration

(1) The annuitant must, upon receipt of the form referred to in regulation 4—

(*a*) provide, at the appropriate part of the form in each case, the information specified in paragraph (2); and
(*b*) make a declaration—
  (i) as to whether the annuity is a purchased life annuity which is eligible for the partial tax exemption; and
  (ii) confirming the accuracy of the other information provided on the form.

(2) The information specified is—

(*a*) the full name and home address (including the postal code) of each annuitant;
(*b*) the national insurance number for each annuitant; and
(*c*) the name, address and reference of the office of Her Majesty's Revenue and Customs to which each annuitant sends their tax return, or to which the last claim for an exemption under the 1956 Regulations was submitted.

(3) Where there is more than one annuitant, any of them may make the declaration referred to in paragraph (1)(*b*), provided that the declaration properly reflects all the material facts about the annuity.

6 Form to be returned on completion

(1) The annuitant must—

(*a*) complete the form and make the declaration in accordance with regulation 5; and
(*b*) return the form to the person who provided it, together with any other information and documents that are required to accompany it.

(2) Until the annuitant complies with paragraph (1), the annuity must be treated as one for which no part of the payments are eligible for the partial tax exemption.

7 What must be done on receipt of the completed form

(1) This regulation applies where the annuitant has complied with regulations 5 and 6(1).

(2) The relevant person must calculate the exempt capital element of the annuity in accordance with the mortality [table][1] which, at the time when the annuity payments become due and payable, [is prescribed][1] in paragraph (3).

[(3) The mortality table prescribed for the purposes of sections 720(4) and 721(4) of the 2005 Act is the table which specifies mortality rates according to "lives" and which is comprised in Table A11 set out in Appendix A on pages 181 to 183 of the booklet entitled "Continuous Mortality Investigation Reports Number 17", published by the Institute of Actuaries and the Faculty of Actuaries in 1999.][1]

(4) For the purposes of this regulation the relevant person must assume that the information provided by the annuitant on the form referred to in regulation 6 is correct unless there are reasonable grounds to believe otherwise.

(5) When calculating the exempt capital element, the relevant person must—

(*a*) if the annuity is one to which section 720 of the 2005 Act applies, calculate the exempt proportion; or
(*b*) if the annuity is one to which section 721 of the 2005 Act applies, calculate the amount of the exempt sum.

(6) If the annuitant has made a declaration under regulation 5(1)(*b*) that would lead the relevant person to reasonably conclude that the annuity is ineligible for the partial tax exemption, the insurer must make a statement, on the appropriate part of the form, that the annuity has no exempt capital element.

(7) The relevant person must state, on the appropriate parts of the form—

(*a*) if paragraph (5)(*a*) applies, the exempt proportion, or
(*b*) if paragraph (5)(*b*) applies, the exempt sum and

notify the annuitant of the amount so calculated.

(8) The relevant person must complete the appropriate parts of the form in accordance with this regulation, and must—

(*a*) sign and date the form; and
(*b*) state the business address and position in the organisation of the individual who completes the form.

(9) The relevant person must send the form fully completed with the information required by regulation 4(2) (including the reference number for the annuity) to the annuitant.

(10) The relevant person must comply with paragraphs (1) to (9) within 30 days beginning with—

(*a*) the date of receipt of the form referred to in regulation 5 (or, if the declaration and the other information required by the form are received on different dates, the date of receipt of the latter); or (*b*) the date of the first payment under the annuity.

(11) The relevant person must send a true photostat copy of the form referred to in paragraph (9) to such office of Her Majesty's Revenue and Customs as the Commissioners may from time to time specify, within 3 months of the date of first payment under the annuity.

Amendments—[1] In para (2), words substituted, and para (3) substituted, by the Income Tax (Purchased Life Annuities) (Amendment) Regulations, SI 2012/2902 reg 2 with effect in relation to any annuity the contract for which is made on or after 21 December 2012. Note that In the case of any annuity the contract for which is made before 21 December 2012 and under which the first annuity payment becomes due and payable on or after that date, the relevant person is entitled to comply with this regulation as if the amendments made by SI 2012/2902 had effect in relation to the annuity.

8 What the relevant person must do if no completed form is received

(1) If the annuitant does not send a completed form to the relevant person in accordance with regulation 6 the latter must send, to such office of Her Majesty's Revenue and Customs as the Commissioners may from time to time specify, such details of the annuity policy specified in regulation 4 as are known to the relevant person.

(2) The relevant person must comply with this regulation within 3 months of the end of the month in which the first payment under the annuity is due and payable.

PART 3
ADDITIONAL REQUIREMENTS WHERE ANNUITY IS PURCHASED FROM A NON-UNITED KINGDOM INSURER

9 Application of this Part

This Part applies where an annuitant has purchased an annuity from a non-United Kingdom insurer.

10 Nomination of a tax representative

(1) Subject to regulations 17 and 18, a non-United Kingdom insurer who sells or intends to sell annuities to annuitants in the United Kingdom, must nominate a United Kingdom resident tax representative.

(2) A person shall not be a tax representative unless—

(*a*) if an individual, that person is resident in the United Kingdom and has a fixed place of residence there; or

(*b*) if not an individual, that person has a business establishment in the United Kingdom; and

(*c*) there has been a nomination approved by the Commissioners in accordance with regulation 11.

11 Procedure for nomination

(1) A nomination to the Commissioners of a tax representative by a non-United Kingdom insurer must be made in writing and must contain the following information—

(*a*) the full name or title under which the non-United Kingdom insurer is registered in the country in which his principal place of business is situated and the address in that country of the principal place of business;

(*b*) the business address of any permanent establishment which the non-United Kingdom insurer has in the United Kingdom;

(*c*) the name of the person nominated as a tax representative, and—

(i) if an individual, the address of that person's fixed place of residence in the United Kingdom; or

(ii) if not an individual, the address of that person's business establishment in the United Kingdom; and

(*d*) the office of Her Majesty's Revenue and Customs to which, and the tax reference under which, the person nominated submits tax returns.

(2) A nomination under this regulation must be accompanied by a declaration that the person nominated is willing and able to secure that the relevant duties are discharged by or on behalf of the non-United Kingdom insurer, signed—

(*a*) if the person nominated is an individual, by that individual; or

(*b*) if the person nominated is not an individual—

(i) by a proper officer as defined by section 108(3) of the Taxes Management Act 1970 in the case of a company; and

(ii) by any partner who is an individual in the case of a partnership.

(3) The insurer must make a nomination under this regulation within 3 months of the first instance on which payments under an annuity commence.

12 Decision as to nomination

(1) Within the period of 30 days beginning with the date of receipt of a nomination under regulation 11, the Commissioners must give notice to the non-United Kingdom insurer and the person nominated that they—

(*a*) approve the person nominated by the non-United Kingdom insurer as the insurer's tax representative;

(*b*) refuse to approve the person nominated by the non-United Kingdom insurer as the insurer's tax representative on one or more of the grounds specified in paragraph (4); or

(*c*) require the non-United Kingdom insurer or the person nominated, or both, to supply within the period of 30 days beginning with the date on which the notice in paragraph (1) was received, such further information as they may reasonably require in order to satisfy the Commissioners that the person nominated is a fit and proper person to be a tax representative.

(2) A notice under paragraph (1)(*c*) must specify the further information that the Commissioners require.

(3) Where the non-United Kingdom insurer or the person nominated, supplied, or both of them supply, information pursuant to a notice under paragraph (1)(*c*), the Commissioners must within the period of 30 days beginning with the date on which the information is received—

(*a*) give notice to the non-United Kingdom insurer and the person nominated—

(i) that they approve the person nominated; or

(ii) that they refuse to approve the person nominated, stating on which of the grounds specified in paragraph (4) they rely, or

(*b*) give further notice under paragraph (1)(*c*).

(4) The grounds on which the Commissioners may refuse to approve the person nominated by the non-United Kingdom insurer are that—

(*a*) the requirements of regulation 11 have not been complied with; or

(*b*) the Commissioners have reasonable grounds to believe that the nominated person is unwilling or unable to assume any of the obligations that are prescribed in these Regulations.

(5) Where the Commissioners refuse to approve the person nominated they must give the insurer notice in writing to that effect, stating the reason for the refusal.

(6) Where the Commissioners refuse to approve the person nominated on the ground set out in paragraph (4)(*a*), the insurer must—

(*a*) submit a further nomination for that person; or

(*b*) nominate another person as tax representative,

within 30 days beginning with the date of receipt of the notice under paragraph (5).

(7) Where the Commissioners refuse to approve the person nominated on the ground set out in paragraph (4)(*b*), the insurer must nominate another person in accordance with regulation 11 within 3 months beginning with the date of receipt of the notice under paragraph (5).

(8) A nomination made under paragraph (6) or (7) must contain the information required by regulation 11 and the Commissioners must give their decision on that nomination in accordance with this regulation.

13 Notification of changes

The insurer must notify the Commissioners of any changes to the information that was provided in the nomination made under regulation 11 as soon as practicable.

14 Termination of appointment of a tax representative—other than death or bankruptcy, etc

(1) The appointment of a tax representative may be terminated at any time, either by the insurer or the tax representative, or by the Commissioners' withdrawing their approval of the tax representative's nomination.

(2) Where the Commissioners withdraw their approval of the nomination, they must state on which of the grounds specified in paragraph (3) they rely and send notice in writing of the withdrawal to the insurer and the tax representative.

(3) The grounds on which the Commissioners may withdraw approval of the appointment are where they have reason to believe that the tax representative—

(*a*) has failed to fulfil any obligations under these Regulations;

(*b*) no longer satisfies the requirements of regulation 10(2); or

(*c*) for some other reason is not fit to act as such.

(4) The tax representative or the non-United Kingdom insurer may terminate the appointment on any ground whatsoever.

(5) Where the appointment is terminated under paragraph (4) the person terminating the appointment must send notice in writing of the termination to the other party to the appointment and to the Commissioners.

(6) Where the appointment is terminated under this regulation the insurer must, within 3 months starting with the date on which notice of the termination under paragraph (5) was given—

(*a*) nominate another person as tax representative;

(*b*) make an application under regulation 17 to be released from the requirement to nominate a tax representative; or

(*c*) make other arrangements with the Commissioners in accordance with regulation 18.

(7) Where a nomination is made under paragraph (6)(*a*), that nomination must contain the information required by regulation 11 and the Commissioners must give their decision on the nomination in accordance with regulation 12.

15 Termination of appointment of a tax representative—death or bankruptcy, etc

(1) Where the person nominated as a tax representative—

(*a*) is an individual who—

(i) becomes bankrupt or in Scotland, whose estate is sequestered;

(ii) makes any arrangement or composition with their creditors generally; or

(iii) dies, or

(*b*) is a company or partnership which is dissolved or wound up,

the appointment ceases and the non-United Kingdom insurer must comply with paragraphs (2) and (3).

(2) The insurer must—

(*a*) nominate another person as tax representative;

(*b*) make an application under regulation 17 to be released from the requirement to nominate a tax representative; or

(*c*) make other arrangements with the Commissioners in accordance with regulation 18,

within the period of 3 months beginning with the date of the event in question.

(3) Where a nomination is made under paragraph (2)(*a*), that nomination must contain the information required by regulation 11 and the Commissioners must give their decision on the nomination in accordance with regulation 12.

16 Tax representative to remain in post until successor appointed

Where a tax representative's appointment is terminated in accordance with regulation 14, the representative must continue to act as tax representative until a successor's nomination is approved by the Commissioners.

17 Release of non-United Kingdom insurer from requirement to nominate a tax representative

(1) Where the non-United Kingdom insurer makes a declaration that the insurer will conduct life annuity business in accordance with the law applicable in the United Kingdom (including these Regulations), the Commissioners may agree to release the insurer from the requirement to have a tax representative.

(2) Paragraph (1) is subject to paragraph (3) and regulation 4(3).

(3) Where the insurer—

(*a*) is resident in a relevant EEA State; and

(*b*) the disclosure by that person to the Commissioners of information with respect to holders of annuities is a criminal offence under the law of that State,

the insurer is not bound by the requirements of regulation 7(11).

(4) The Commissioners may at any time give notice to the non-United Kingdom insurer of their decision to withdraw their agreement to release the insurer from the requirement that there be a tax representative, other than where the circumstances described in paragraph (3) exist.

(5) An application by a non-United Kingdom insurer to be released from the requirement to have a tax representative must be made in writing to the Commissioners within the period specified in regulation 11(3).

(6) The Commissioners must, within the period of 30 days beginning with the date on which an application under paragraph (5) was received, give notice to the insurer that they—

(*a*) agree to release the insurer from the requirement to have a tax representative;

(*b*) refuse to agree to release the insurer from that requirement; or

(*c*) require the insurer to supply, within the period of 30 days beginning with the date of the notice, such information as they may reasonably require to enable them to determine whether there are sufficient grounds to release the insurer from that requirement.

(7) A notice under paragraph (6)(*c*) must specify the information that the Commissioners require.

(8) Where the insurer supplies information required by a notice under paragraph (6)(*c*) the Commissioners must, within the period of 30 days beginning with the date on which that information was received—

(*a*) give notice to the insurer that they agree to release the insurer from the requirement that there be a tax representative;

(*b*) give notice to the insurer that they refuse to do so; or

(*c*) give a further notice under paragraph (6)(*c*).

(9) Where—

(*a*) the Commissioners give notice that they refuse to release the insurer from the requirement that there be a tax representative;

(*b*) it ceases to be a criminal offence under the law of the relevant EEA State in which the non-United Kingdom insurer is resident for that person to disclose to the Commissioners information with respect to the holders of annuities; or

(*c*) the Commissioners give notice to the non-United Kingdom insurer of their decision to withdraw their agreement to release the insurer from the requirement that there be a tax representative, paragraph (10) applies.

(10) If this paragraph applies, the non-United Kingdom insurer must either nominate a person as a tax representative, or make other arrangements with the Commissioners in accordance with regulation 18, within the period of 3 months beginning with either—

(i) the date of the notice; or

(ii) the date on which disclosure to the Commissioners ceased to be a criminal offence,

as the case may be.

(11) Where the non-United Kingdom insurer nominates a person as a tax representative in accordance with paragraph (10), that nomination must contain the information required by regulation 11 and the Commissioners must give their decision on that nomination in accordance with regulation 12.

18 Other arrangements

(1) A non-United Kingdom insurer may make other arrangements with the Commissioners for the purpose of securing the discharge by the insurer or on the insurer's behalf of the obligations under United Kingdom law.

(2) A non-United Kingdom insurer must, within the period specified in regulation 11(3), give notice in writing to the Commissioners applying to—

(*a*) make arrangements for the purpose specified in paragraph (1); and

(*b*) be released from the duty to either nominate a tax representative or the requirement to nominate a tax representative.

(3) The notice referred to in paragraph (2) must—

(*a*) set out the other arrangements that the non-United Kingdom insurer wishes to make with the Commissioners; and

(*b*) give reasons why the requirement either to nominate a tax representative or have to apply to be released from the requirement to nominate a tax representative, should not apply.

(4) The Commissioners must, within the period of 30 days beginning with the date on which an application under paragraph (2) was received, give notice to the insurer that they—

(*a*) agree to the proposed arrangements, with such modification as they may specify;

(*b*) refuse to agree to those arrangements; or

(*c*) require the insurer to supply, within the period of 30 days beginning with the date of the notice, such information as they may reasonably require to enable them to determine whether they should agree to those arrangements.

(5) A notice under paragraph (4)(*a*) must specify the modifications to the arrangements that the Commissioners require.

(6) A notice under paragraph (4)(*c*) must specify the further information that the Commissioners require.

(7) Where the non-United Kingdom insurer indicates the ability to comply with the modifications required by the Commissioners, or supplies information pursuant to a notice under paragraph (4)(*c*) as the case may be, the Commissioners must, within the period of 30 days beginning with the date on which the indication or the information is received—

(*a*) give notice to the insurer—

(i) that they approve the arrangement set out in the application;

(ii) that they refuse to approve the arrangement, stating the reason for the refusal; or

(*b*) give further notice under paragraph (4)(*c*).

(8) If the Commissioners have reason to believe that any arrangements which have been made under this regulation do not secure the discharge by the non-United Kingdom insurer or on the insurer's behalf of the obligations under United Kingdom law, they must give notice to the insurer that those arrangements are no longer in force with effect from the date of the notice.

(9) Where notice is given by the Commissioners in accordance with paragraph (8)—

(*a*) subject to compliance with any modifications specified under paragraph (5), the non-United Kingdom insurer must nominate a person as a tax representative within the period of 3 months from the date of the notice;

(*b*) that nomination must contain the information specified in regulation 11; and

(*c*) the Commissioners must give their decision on that nomination in accordance with regulation 12.

19 Appointment by the Commissioners of a non-United Kingdom insurer's tax representative

(1) Where the non-United Kingdom insurer has failed—

(*a*) to nominate a person as tax representative in accordance with regulations 10 and 11;

(*b*) following the refusal of the Commissioners to approve a person so nominated, to nominate another person as tax representative in accordance with regulation 12(6)(*b*) or (7);

(*c*) following the withdrawal by the Commissioners of their approval of a person nominated, to nominate another person as tax representative in accordance with regulation 14(6);

[(*d*) following—

(i) the termination of the appointment of the insurer's tax representative under regulation 14(4); or

(ii) the occurrence of one of the events described in regulation 15(1),

to nominate another person as a tax representative in accordance with either regulation 14(6) or 15(2), as the case may be;][1]

(*e*) following the giving of a notice by the Board in accordance with regulation 18(8), to nominate a person as tax representative in accordance with regulation 18(9);

(*f*) following—

(i) the refusal of the Commissioners to agree to release the insurer from the requirement that there be a tax representative;

(ii) the disclosure to the Commissioners of information with respect to relevant annuities ceasing to be a criminal offence under the law of the relevant EEA State in which the insurer is resident; or

(iii) the giving of a notice by the Commissioners of their intention to withdraw from their agreement to release the insurer from the requirement that there be a tax representative,

to nominate a person as tax representative in accordance with regulation 17(10);

(*g*) following the termination of the appointment of a person under this paragraph, to nominate another person in accordance with paragraph (2) of this regulation;

the Commissioners may appoint a person who satisfies the requirements of paragraphs (2) and (3) to be the non-United Kingdom insurer's tax representative.

(2) A person appointed by the Commissioners to be the tax representative of a non-United Kingdom insurer must be a person who has a significant business or economic connection with the non-United Kingdom insurer and may in particular be—

(*a*) a company which is connected within the meaning of section 839 of the Income and Corporation Taxes Act 1988; or

(*b*) the permanent establishment in the United Kingdom of any such company.

(3) Before being appointed under this regulation, the person must make a declaration to the Commissioners in similar terms to the declaration specified in regulation 11(2).

(4) The Commissioners must give notice in writing of their decision to the person appointed under this regulation and to the non-United Kingdom insurer and, subject to regulation 20(6), the date of the appointment is the date of the notice.

(5) The Commissioners may at any time terminate the appointment of the person appointed by them as the tax representative under this regulation by giving notice in writing to the person appointed and to the non-United Kingdom insurer.

(6) If the Commissioners terminate an appointment under paragraph (5), the non-United Kingdom insurer must nominate another person as tax representative within the period of 3 months beginning with the date on which that notice is given.

(7) The non-United Kingdom insurer may at any time nominate a person as tax representative in place of the person appointed by the Commissioners and, if the Commissioners approve the nomination of that person, at the same time as the Commissioners give notice of their decision approving it they must give notice in writing to the person appointed by them that the latter's appointment ceased on the date of the appointment of the substitute.

(8) If the non-United Kingdom insurer nominates another person in accordance with paragraph (7), that nomination must contain the information required by regulation 11 and the Commissioners must give their decision on that nomination in accordance with regulation 12.

Amendments—[1] Para (1)(*d*) substituted by the Income Tax (Purchased Life Annuities) (Amendment) Regulations, SI 2008/1481 reg 2 with effect from 1 July 2008.

20 Appeals against decisions of the Commissioners

(1) A non-United Kingdom insurer to whom notice has been given of a decision of the Commissioners—

(*a*) refusing to approve a person nominated as tax representative;

(*b*) withdrawing their approval of a person nominated as tax representative;

(*c*) appointing a person as tax representative;

(*d*) that arrangements made under regulation 18 are no longer in force;

(*e*) refusing to agree to release the insurer from the requirement that there be a tax representative; or

(*f*) to withdraw from their agreement to release the insurer from the requirement to have a tax representative,

may appeal against the decision contained in that notice by giving notice in writing to the Commissioners within the period of 30 days after the date of the notice of the decision in question.

(2) A person who has been appointed to be the tax representative of a non-United Kingdom insurer under regulation 12(1) may appeal against the decision contained in that notice by giving notice to the Commissioners within the period of 30 days after the date of the notice of the decision sought to be appealed.

(3) An appeal under paragraph (1) or (2) is to the Special Commissioners.[1]

(4) The provisions in Part 5 of the Taxes Management Act 1970 (appeals and other proceedings) . . . [1] apply to an appeal under this regulation and [on an appeal that is notified to the tribunal, the tribunal must][1] confirm the decision contained in the notice unless . . . [1] satisfied that it ought to be quashed.

(5) Where a non-United Kingdom insurer appeals against a decision of the Commissioners referred to in paragraph (1)(*a*), (*b*), (*d*), (*e*) or (*f*), and the decision is confirmed on appeal, the period of 3 months within which another person must be nominated as tax representative does not begin to run until such time as there is no possibility of a further appeal against that decision.

(6) Where a non-United Kingdom insurer appeals against a decision of the Commissioners appointing a person as tax representative, or the person appointed by the Commissioners to be the tax representative of a non-United Kingdom insurer appeals against the decision to appoint, the date of the appointment of that person is the first date on which there is no possibility of a further appeal against that decision.

(7) Where a non-United Kingdom insurer appeals against a decision of the Commissioners referred to in paragraph (1)(*a*) and the decision of the Commissioners is quashed on appeal, the date of the appointment of the person nominated as the tax representative of the non-United Kingdom insurer is the first date on which there is no possibility of a further appeal against the decision quashing the decision of the Commissioners.

Amendments—[1] Para (3) revoked, in para (4), words revoked and words substituted, by the Transfer of Tribunal Functions and Revenue and Customs Appeals Order, SI 2009/56 art 3, Sch 2 paras 182, 183 with effect from 1 April 2009.

PART 4
RECORD-KEEPING AND PROVISION OF INFORMATION

21 Obligation to keep proper records

A relevant person shall, in respect of each annuity, keep relevant records to enable the Commissioners to ascertain the terms of the annuity and to whether there has been or is likely to be any contravention of the requirements of Chapter 7 of Part 6 of the 2005 Act or these Regulations.

22 Information to be provided to the Commissioners

(1) The Commissioners may by notice require any person to whom premiums under an annuity are or have at any time been payable, within such period as may be specified in the notice, to furnish them with such information as they may reasonably require to enable them to ascertain or verify any of the matters mentioned in regulation 21.

(2) The period specified in a notice given under paragraph (1) shall be not less than 30 days beginning with the date on which the notice is given.

23 Inspection of records

(1) The Commissioners may by notice require any person to whom premiums under an annuity are or have at any time been payable, to make available for inspection by an officer duly authorised for that purpose, at such a time as that officer may reasonably require, any documents (in any format) that—

(*a*) are in that person's possession or control; and

(*b*) are relevant records.

(2) The period specified in a notice given under paragraph (1) shall be not less than 30 days beginning with the date on which the notice was given.

24 Period for which records to be kept

An insurer must, in respect of each annuity, keep the relevant records for a period of three years beginning with the date on which the contract for the annuity was terminated.

25 Transfer of records

(1) This regulation applies in any case where the obligations under any annuity of the person that issued, entered into or effected it ("the original relevant person") are at any time the obligations of another person ("the transferee") to whom there has been a transfer of the whole or part of a business previously carried on by the original relevant person.

(2) The original relevant person must, in respect of that annuity, deliver to the transferee the records that it was required to keep under regulation 21, within the period of three months beginning with the date of the transfer.

PART 5
MISCELLANEOUS

26 Penalties

(1) The Table in section 98 of the Taxes Management Act 1970 is modified in accordance with this regulation.

(2) In column 1, there shall be treated as having been added at the end—

"Regulations 21 and 22 of the Income Tax (Purchased Life Annuities) Regulations 2007."

(3) In column 2, there shall be treated as having been added—

"Regulations 7, 23 and 25 of the Income Tax (Purchased Life Annuities) Regulations 2007."

27 Transitional provision

In the case of an annuity—

(*a*) the contract for which was made during the period beginning with 6th April 2007 and ending with (and including) 5th April 2008;

(*b*) under which the payments by the insurer to the annuitant are made in arrears; and

(*c*) under which the first payment to the annuitant is made on or after 6th April 2008,

the mortality tables applicable shall be the ones which were in force when the annuity was made and not those prescribed by regulation 7(3).

28 Revocations

The following instruments are revoked—

(*a*) the Income Tax (Purchased Life Annuities) Regulations 1956;

(*b*) the Income Tax (Purchased Life Annuities) (Amendment) Regulations 1960;

(*c*) the Income Tax (Purchased Life Annuities) (Amendment) Regulations 1990; and

(*d*) the Income Tax (Purchased Life Annuities) (Amendment) Regulations 1991.

2008/568

FINANCE ACT 2007, SCHEDULE 24 (COMMENCEMENT AND TRANSITIONAL PROVISIONS) ORDER 2008

Made by the Treasury under FA 2007 s 97

Made . . . . *3 March 2008*

1 Citation and interpretation

(1) This Order may be cited as the Finance Act 2007, Schedule 24 (Commencement and Transitional Provisions) Order 2008.

(2) In this Order "Schedule 24" means Schedule 24 to the Finance Act 2007 and a reference to a paragraph (without more) is a reference to that paragraph of Schedule 24.

(3) In this Order—

"HMRC" means Her Majesty's Revenue and Customs;

"relevant documents" means documents given to HMRC of a kind listed in the Table in paragraph 1;

"relevant tax" means any tax mentioned in the Table in paragraph 1; and

"tax period" has the meaning given in paragraph 28(g).

2 Appointed days

The days appointed for the coming into force of Schedule 24 are—

(*a*) 1st April 2008 in relation to relevant documents relating to tax periods commencing on or after that date;

(*b*) 1st April 2008 in relation to assessments falling within paragraph 2 for tax periods commencing on or after that date;

(*c*) 1st July 2008 in relation to relevant documents relating to claims under the Thirteenth Council Directive (arrangements for the refund of value added tax to persons not established in Community territory) for years commencing on or after that date;

(*d*) 1st January 2009 in relation to relevant documents relating to claims under the Eighth Council Directive (arrangements for the refund of value added tax to taxable persons not established in the territory of the country) for years commencing on or after that date;

(*e*) 1st April 2009 in relation to documents relating to all other claims for repayments of relevant tax made on or after 1st April 2009 which are not related to a tax period; and

(*f*) in any other case, 1st April 2009 in relation to documents given where a person's liability to pay relevant tax arises on or after that date.

3 Transitional provision

Notwithstanding article 2, no person shall be liable to a penalty under Schedule 24 in respect of any tax period for which a return is required to be made before 1st April 2009.

4 Saving

Notwithstanding paragraph 29(*d*) (consequential amendments), sections 60 and 61 of the Value Added Tax Act 1994 (VAT evasion) shall continue to have effect with respect to conduct involving dishonesty which does not relate to an inaccuracy in a document or a failure to notify HMRC of an under-assessment by HMRC.

Commentary—*Simon's Taxes* **A6.604**.

2008/1464

TAXATION OF BENEFITS UNDER GOVERNMENT PILOT SCHEMES (UP-FRONT CHILDCARE FUND) ORDER 2008

Made by the Treasury under FA 1996 s 151(1)(a) and (7)(a)

Made . . . . *9 June 2008*
Laid before the House of Commons . . . . *9 June 2008*
Coming into force . . . . *1 July 2008*

1 Citation and commencement

This Order may be cited as the Taxation of Benefits under Government Pilot Schemes (Up-Front Childcare Fund) Order 2008 and shall come into force on 1st July 2008.

2 Income tax exemption under Part 2 of the Income Tax (Earnings and Pensions) Act 2003

The Income Tax Acts shall have effect in relation to any amount of benefit payable by virtue of the Government pilot scheme known as the Up-Front Childcare Fund as if it was exempt from income tax as employment income under Part 2 of the Income Tax (Earnings and Pensions) Act 2003.

2008/1520

ENERGY-SAVING ITEMS (CORPORATION TAX) REGULATIONS 2008

Made by the Treasury under TA 1988 ss 31ZA and 31ZC

Made . . . . *11 June 2008*
Laid before the House of Commons . . . . *12 June 2008*
Coming into force . . . . *7 July 2008*

Commentary—*Simon's Taxes* **B9.303**.

1 Citation, commencement and interpretation

(1) These Regulations may be cited as the Energy-Saving Items (Corporation Tax) Regulations 2008, shall come into force on 7th July 2008, and shall have effect in respect of expenditure incurred on or after 8th July 2008.

(2) In these Regulations—

"ICTA 1988" means the Income and Corporation Taxes Act 1988;

"deduction" means a deduction allowed under section 31ZA of ICTA 1988 (deduction for expenditure on energy-saving items);

"maximum amount" shall be construed in accordance with regulation 3(1);

"relevant expenditure" means—

(*a*) expenditure incurred in acquiring and installing an energy-saving item in a dwelling-house, or

(*b*) in so far as it is for the benefit of a dwelling-house, expenditure incurred in acquiring and installing an energy-saving item in a building containing that dwelling-house.

2 Items of an energy-saving nature

The following descriptions of items of an energy-saving nature are specified for the purposes of section 31ZA(5) of ICTA 1988—

(*a*) hot water system insulation;
(*b*) draught proofing;
(*c*) cavity wall insulation;
(*d*) solid wall insulation;
(*e*) floor insulation; and
(*f*) loft insulation.

3 Restrictions on relevant expenditure to be taken into account: general

(1) The maximum amount of the relevant expenditure which may be taken into account in calculating the deduction is £1,500 per dwelling-house.

(2) Paragraph (1) applies irrespective of the number of persons incurring relevant expenditure or entitled to a deduction in respect of a dwelling-house.

(3) If the company entitled to the deduction has received a contribution from any other person towards the relevant expenditure incurred, that contribution shall be excluded in calculating the relevant expenditure incurred by the company entitled to the deduction.

(4) Further rules (to be applied in the order stated) are set out in—

(*a*) regulation 4 (first further rule: apportionment of relevant expenditure benefiting more than one property);

(*b*) regulation 5 (second further rule: restriction of relevant expenditure to the maximum amount);

(*c*) regulation 6 (third further rule: apportionment of relevant expenditure if a dwelling-house or building is owned jointly or in common or is subject to differing estates or interests).

4 First further rule: apportionment of relevant expenditure benefiting more than one property

(1) This regulation applies to relevant expenditure which is incurred in acquiring and installing an energy-saving item—

(*a*) in more than one dwelling-house,

(*b*) in a building containing more than one dwelling-house, or

(*c*) in a building containing one or more dwelling-houses and one or more properties which are not dwelling-houses.

(2) The relevant expenditure must be apportioned on a just and reasonable basis to all the properties which benefit from it.

(3) The amount of the relevant expenditure for which a deduction is allowable in respect of a dwelling-house shall not exceed the amount which is apportioned to that dwelling-house.

5 Second further rule: restriction of relevant expenditure to the maximum amount

(1) This regulation applies if the relevant expenditure benefiting a particular dwelling-house (including any relevant expenditure apportioned to the dwelling-house under regulation 4) exceeds the maximum amount.

(2) The relevant expenditure must be restricted to the maximum amount.

6 Third further rule: apportionment of relevant expenditure if a dwelling-house or building is owned jointly or in common or is subject to differing estates or interests

(1) This regulation applies if relevant expenditure is incurred benefiting a dwelling-house and the dwelling-house or the building containing it—

(*a*) is owned jointly or in common by the company entitled to the deduction and by other persons, or

(*b*) is subject to differing estates or interests.

(2) The relevant expenditure (restricted if necessary to the maximum amount) must be apportioned on a just and reasonable basis.

(3) The amount of the deduction to which the company entitled to it is entitled shall not exceed the amount apportioned to that company in accordance with paragraph (2).

7 Further provisions

(1) This regulation applies if any question arises under regulations 3(3) or 4 to 6 as to the amount of the deduction to which a company may be entitled.

(2) The amount shall be treated as if it were an amount specified in a paragraph of subsection (1) of section 42 of ICTA 1988 (appeals against determinations under sections 34 to 36 or Chapter 4 of Part 3 of the Income Tax (Trading and Other Income) Act 2005), and the procedure set out in that section shall apply accordingly.

2008/1579

CORPORATION TAX (IMPLEMENTATION OF THE MERGERS DIRECTIVE) REGULATIONS 2008

Made . . . . *16 June 2008*
Laid before the House of Commons . . . . *17 June 2008*
Coming into force . . . . *8 July 2008*

The Treasury make the following Regulations in exercise of the powers conferred by section 110 of the Finance Act 2007.

The Treasury are satisfied in accordance with section 110(3) of the Finance Act 2007 that the following Regulations are necessary for the purposes of complying with the United Kingdom's obligations under the Mergers Directive.

1 Citation, commencement and effect

(1) These Regulations may be cited as the Corporation Tax (Implementation of the Mergers Directive) Regulations 2008.

(2) These Regulations shall come into force on 8th July 2008.

(3) For the effect of certain provisions of these Regulations, see regulations 3 and 6.

2 Interpretation

In these Regulations—

"TCGA 1992" means the Taxation of Chargeable Gains Act 1992,

"FA 1996" means the Finance Act 1996, and

"FA 2002" means the Finance Act 2002.

3 Amendments to primary legislation

(1) Schedules 1 to 3 to these Regulations make amendments to TCGA 1992, FA 1996 and FA 2002 relating to cross-border mergers and cross-border transfers of business.

(2) Those Schedules have effect—

(*a*) so far as relating to mergers—

(i) in relation to mergers relating to the formation of an SE or SCE which take place on or after 18th August 2006, and

(ii) in relation to all other mergers which take place on or after 1st January 2007, and

(*b*) so far as relating to transfers, in relation to transfers which take place on or after 1st January 2007.

4 Commencement of 2007 Regulations

(1) Regulation 3(1) of the Corporation Tax (Implementation of the Mergers Directive) Regulations 2007 is deemed always to have had effect as if it also provided for Schedule 1 to those Regulations to have effect, so far as relating to cross-border mergers—

(*a*) in relation to mergers relating to the formation of an SE or SCE which take place on or after 18th August 2006, and

(*b*) in relation to all other mergers which take place on or after 1st January 2007.

(2) Regulation 3(3) of those Regulations is deemed always to have had effect as if it also provided for Schedule 3 to those Regulations to have effect, so far as relating to cross-border transfers of business, in relation to transfers which take place on or after 1st January 2007.

5 Revocation

(1) The repeal of section 116(8A) and (8B) of TCGA 1992 by paragraph 10 of Schedule 1 to the Corporation Tax (Implementation of the Mergers Directive) Regulations 2007 is deemed never to have had effect.

(2) Accordingly, that paragraph—

(*a*) is revoked, and

(*b*) is treated as if it were never included in those Regulations.

6 Transitional: references to Companies Act 2006

(1) Until section 658 of the Companies Act 2006 (rule against limited company acquiring own shares) comes into force, references to that section in the provisions specified in Schedule 4 (transitional: references to Companies Act 2006) have effect as if they were references to section 143 of the Companies Act 1985 (general rule against companies acquiring own shares).

(2) This regulation, so far as it has effect in relation to any provision specified in that Schedule, has the same effect as that provision has by virtue of regulation 3 of the Corporation Tax (Implementation of the Mergers Directive) Regulations 2007 (as read with regulation 4 of these Regulations).

SCHEDULE 1

AMENDMENTS TO TCGA 1992

Regulation 3

(*amends* TCGA 1992 ss 116(8A), 140F(2), 140J(1)(*a*), 140L(1), *inserts* 140GA)

SCHEDULE 2

AMENDMENTS TO FA 1996

Regulation 3

(*amends* FA 1996 Sch 9)

SCHEDULE 3

AMENDMENTS TO FA 2002

Regulation 3

(*amends* FA 2002 Schs 26, 29)

SCHEDULE 4

TRANSITIONAL: REFERENCES TO COMPANIES ACT 2006

Regulation 6

1 The provisions mentioned in regulation 6 are as follows.

2 In TCGA 1992—

(*a*) section 140A(1C) (transfer of a UK trade),

(*b*) section 140C(1C)(transfer of a non-UK trade),

(*c*) section 140E(2)(*d*) (merger leaving assets within UK tax charge), and

(*d*) section 140F(2)(*e*) (merger: assets outside UK tax charge).

3 In FA 1996—

(*a*) paragraph 12B(2)(*d*) of Schedule 9 (European cross-border merger),

(*b*) paragraph 12C(2)(*e*) of Schedule 9 (double taxation relief on European cross-border merger),

(*c*) paragraph 12D(4) of Schedule 9 (cross-border transfer of business within European Community), and

(*d*) paragraph 12E(4) of Schedule 9 (double taxation relief on cross-border transfer of business within European Community).

4 In FA 2002—

(*a*) paragraph 30B(2)(*d*) of Schedule 26 (European cross-border merger),

(*b*) paragraph 30C(2)(*e*) of Schedule 26 (double taxation relief on European cross-border merger),

(*c*) paragraph 30D(4) of Schedule 26 (cross-border transfer of business within European Community),

(*d*) paragraph 30E(4) of Schedule 26 (double taxation relief on cross-border transfer of business within European Community),

(*e*) paragraph 85(1C) of Schedule 29 (transfer of UK business between companies resident in different EU member States),

(*f*) paragraph 85A(2)(*d*) of Schedule 29 (European cross-border merger: transfer of UK business),

(*g*) paragraph 87(1D) of Schedule 29 (transfer of non-UK business), and

(*h*) paragraph 87A(2)(*g*) of Schedule 29 (European cross-border merger: transfer of non-UK business).

2008/1588

TAXATION OF CHARGEABLE GAINS (GILT-EDGED SECURITIES) ORDER 2008

Made by the Treasury under TCGA 1992 Sch 9 para 1

Made . . . . 19 June 2008

Commentary—*Simon's Taxes* **19.321**.

1 Citation

This Order may be cited as the Taxation of Chargeable Gains (Gilt-edged Securities) Order 2008.

2 Securities specified as gilt-edged securities

For the purposes of Schedule 9 to the Taxation of Chargeable Gains Act 1992 (Gilt-edged Securities) the following securities are specified—

1 1/8% Index-Linked Treasury Gilt 2037
5 1/4% Treasury Gilt 2012
5% Treasury Gilt 2018
4 1/2% Treasury Gilt 2042
1 7/8% Index-Linked Treasury Gilt 2022
4 3/4% Treasury Gilt 2030
0 3/4% Index-Linked Treasury Gilt 2047
4 1/2% Treasury Gilt 2013

2008/1926

FINANCING-ARRANGEMENT-FUNDED TRANSFERS TO SHAREHOLDERS REGULATIONS 2008

Made by the Treasury under FA 1989 s 83YE(1) and (4)

Made . . . .*22 July 2008*
Laid before the House of Commons . . . .*22 July 2008*
Coming into force . . . .*12 August 2008*

Preliminary

1 Citation, commencement and effect

(1) These Regulations may be cited as the Financing-Arrangement-Funded Transfers to Shareholders Regulations 2008 and shall come into force on 12th August 2008.

(2) These Regulations have effect in relation to periods of account beginning on or after 1st January 2008.

2 Interpretation

In these Regulations—

a "relevant financing arrangement" means a relevant financing arrangement in relation to a non-profit fund within section 83YC(4) of the Finance Act 1989;

a "section 83YC(3) amount" means an amount within section 83YC(3) of the Finance Act 1989;

a "section 83YC(3) period of account" means a period of account for which there is a section 83YC(3) amount;

a "section 83YD arrangement" means a relevant financing arrangement in respect of which there is a section 83YD(2) amount;

a "section 83YD(2) amount" means an amount within section 83YD(2) of the Finance Act 1989;

a "section 83YD(2) period of account" means a period of account for which there is a section 83YD(2) amount.

The treatment of section 83YC(3) amounts

3 Amounts wholly attributable to life assurance business or to gross roll-up business

(1) This regulation applies if, at the end of a section 83YC(3) period of account, each relevant financing arrangement of an insurance company has as a condition of the arrangement that—

(*a*) in the case of a loan, any repayment may only be made if the company has an amount of surplus from carrying on life assurance business or gross roll-up business and the repayment is made from that surplus, or

(*b*) in the case of a financial reinsurance arrangement, any recapture of liabilities may only be made if the company has an amount of surplus from carrying on life assurance business or gross roll-up business.

(2) The section 83YC(3) amount is wholly referable to life assurance business or to gross roll-up business (as the case may be).

4 Other cases where relevant financing arrangements meet the loan condition only: life assurance business and PHI business

(1) This regulation applies if, in a section 83YC(3) period of account—

(*a*) an insurance company carries on both life assurance business and PHI business, and

(*b*) each relevant financing arrangement of the company in force in that period of account meets the loan condition (and not the reinsurance condition).

(2) The part of the section 83YC(3) amount referable to life assurance business is—

$$\frac{LABL}{LABL + PHIL}$$

where—

"*LABL*" is the mean of the opening and closing liabilities of the company's life assurance business relating to the non-profit fund for the section 83YC(3) period of account, and

"*PHIL*" is the mean of the opening and closing liabilities of the company's PHI business relating to the non-profit fund for that period of account.

5 Other cases where relevant financing arrangements meet the loan condition only: gross roll-up business and basic life assurance and general annuity business

(1) This regulation applies if, in a section 83YC(3) period of account—

(*a*) an insurance company carries on both gross roll-up business and basic life assurance and general annuity business, and (*b*) each relevant financing arrangement of the company in force in that period of account meets the loan condition (and not the reinsurance condition).

(2) The part of the section 83YC(3) amount referable to gross roll-up business is—

$$\frac{GRBL}{LABL + PHIL}$$

where—

"*GRBL*" is the mean of the opening and closing liabilities of the company's gross roll-up business relating to the non-profit fund for the section 83YC(3) period of account, and

"*LABL*" and "*PHIL*" each have the same meaning as in regulation 4(2).

6 Other cases where relevant financing arrangements meet the reinsurance condition only: life assurance business and PHI business

(1) This regulation applies if, in a section 83YC(3) period of account—

(*a*) an insurance company carries on both life assurance business and PHI business, and

(*b*) each relevant financing arrangement of the company in force in that period of account meets the reinsurance condition (and not the loan condition).

(2) The part of the section 83YC(3) amount referable to life assurance business is—

$$\frac{LABL + LFRAL}{LABL + PHIL + TFRAL}$$

where—

"*LFRAL*" is the mean of the opening and closing life assurance liabilities reinsured under relevant financing arrangements relating to the non-profit fund for that period of account,

"*TFRAL*" is the mean of the total opening and closing liabilities reinsured under relevant financing arrangements relating to the non-profit fund for that period of account, and

"*LABL*" and "*PHIL*" each have the same meaning as in regulation 4(2).

7 Other cases where relevant financing arrangements meet the reinsurance condition only: gross roll-up business and basic life assurance and general annuity business

(1) This regulation applies if, in a section 83YC(3) period of account—

(*a*) an insurance company carries on both gross roll-up business and basic life assurance and general annuity business, and

(*b*) each relevant financing arrangement of the company in force in that period of account meets the reinsurance condition (and not the loan condition).

(2) The part of the section 83YC(3) amount referable to gross roll-up business is—

$$\frac{GRBL + GFRAL}{LABL + PHIL + TFRAL}$$

where—

"*GFRAL*" is the mean of the opening and closing gross roll-up business liabilities reinsured under relevant financing arrangements relating to the non-profit fund for that period of account,

"*GRBL*" has the same meaning as in regulation 5(2),

"*LABL*" and "*PHIL*" each have the same meaning as in regulation 4(2), and

"*TFRAL*" has the same meaning as in regulation 6(2).

8 Relevant financing arrangements of more than one type

(1) This regulation applies if, in a section 83YC(3) period of account—

(*a*) an insurance company carries on—

(i) both life assurance business and PHI business, or

(ii) both gross roll-up business and basic life assurance and general annuity business; and

(*b*) the relevant financing arrangements of the company in force in that period of account include—

(i) at least one arrangement that meets the loan condition (and not the reinsurance condition), and

(ii) at least one arrangement that meets the reinsurance condition (and not the loan condition).

(2) The part of the section 83YC(3) amount referable to life assurance business is determined in accordance with regulation 6(2).

(3) The part of the section 83YC(3) amount referable to gross roll-up business is determined in accordance with regulation 7(2).

The treatment of section 83YD(2) amounts

9 Amounts wholly attributable to life assurance business or to gross roll-up business

(1) This regulation applies if, at the beginning of a section 83YD(2) period of account, each relevant financing arrangement of an insurance company has as a condition of the arrangement that—

(*a*) in the case of a loan, any repayment may only be made if the company has an amount of surplus from carrying on life assurance business or gross roll-up business and the repayment is made from that surplus, or

(*b*) in the case of a financial reinsurance arrangement, any recapture of liabilities may only be made if the company has an amount of surplus from carrying on life assurance business or gross roll-up business.

(2) The section 83YD(2) amount is wholly referable to life assurance business or to gross roll-up business (as the case may be).

10 Other cases where relevant financing arrangements meet the loan condition only: life assurance business and PHI business

(1) This regulation applies if, in a section 83YD(2) period of account—

(*a*) an insurance company carries on both life assurance business and PHI business,

(*b*) each relevant financing arrangement of the company in force in that period of account meets the loan condition (and not the reinsurance condition), and

(*c*) there has been only one section 83YC(3) amount in that period of account and all preceding periods of account.

(2) The part of the section 83YD(2) amount referable to life assurance business is a fraction of that amount, determined in accordance with regulation 4(2), for the period of account in which the section 83YC(3) amount arose in respect of the section 83YD arrangement.

11 Other cases where relevant financing arrangements meet the loan condition only: gross roll-up business and basic life assurance and general annuity business

(1) This regulation applies if, in a section 83YD(2) period of account—

(*a*) an insurance company carries on both gross roll-up business and basic life assurance and general annuity business,

(*b*) each relevant financing arrangement of the company in force in that period of account meets the loan condition (and not the reinsurance condition), and

(*c*) there has been only one section 83YC(3) amount in that period of account and all preceding periods of account.

(2) The part of the section 83YD(2) amount referable to gross roll-up business is a fraction of that amount, determined in accordance with regulation 5(2), for the period of account in which the section 83YC(3) amount arose in respect of the section 83YD arrangement.

12 Other cases where relevant financing arrangements meet the reinsurance condition: life assurance business and PHI business

(1) This regulation applies if, in a section 83YD(2) period of account—

(*a*) an insurance company carries on both life assurance business and PHI business,

(*b*) each relevant financing arrangement of the company in force in that period of account—

(i) meets the reinsurance condition (and not the loan condition), or

(ii) meets both the reinsurance condition and the loan condition, and

(*c*) there has been only one section 83YC(3) amount in that period of account and all preceding periods of account.

(2) The part of the section 83YD(2) amount referable to life assurance business is a fraction of that amount, determined in accordance with regulation 6(2), for the period of account in which the section 83YC(3) amount arose in respect of the section 83YD arrangement.

13 Other cases where relevant financing arrangements meet the reinsurance condition: gross roll-up business and basic life assurance and general annuity business

(1) This regulation applies if, in a section 83YD(2) period of account—

(*a*) an insurance company carries on both gross roll-up business and basic life assurance and general annuity business,

(*b*) each relevant financing arrangement of the company in force in that period of account—

(i) meets the reinsurance condition (and not the loan condition), or

(ii) meets both the reinsurance condition and the loan condition, and

(*c*) there has been only one section 83YC(3) amount in that period of account and all preceding periods of account.

(2) The part of the section 83YD(2) amount referable to gross roll-up business is a fraction of that amount, determined in accordance with regulation 7(2), for the period of account in which the section 83YC(3) amount arose in respect of the section 83YD arrangement.

14 Cases involving more than one section 83YC(3) amount

(1) This regulation applies if—

(*a*) there has been more than one section 83YC(3) amount for a period of account (or for more than one period of account),

(*b*) that period of account is (or those periods of account are) earlier than the section 83YD(2) period of account, and

(*c*) regulation 9 does not apply.

(2) The insurance company may claim that the section 83YD(2) amount is such a fraction of the amount determined under section 83YD(4) of the Finance Act 1989 as is just and reasonable in the circumstances.

2008/1936

FINANCE ACT 2008 SECTION 135 (DISASTER OR EMERGENCY) ORDER 2008

Made by the Treasury under FA 2008 s 135

Made . . . . *22 July 2008*
Laid before the House of Commons . . . . *22 July 2008*
Coming into force . . . . *13 August 2008*

The Treasury, in accordance with section 135(9) of the Finance Act 2008, consider the disaster referred to in the following Order to be of national significance.

1 Citation, commencement and interpretation

This order may be cited as the Finance Act 2008 Section 135 (Disaster or Emergency) Order 2008 and comes into force on 13th August 2008.

2 Specification of disaster

For the purposes of section 135 of the Finance Act 2008 (interest on unpaid tax in case of disaster etc of national significance), floods, caused by weather conditions, which occurred in the United Kingdom in June and July 2007 are a disaster.

3 Specified date

For the purposes of section 135(4)(*a*) of the Finance Act 2008 (relief period), the date specified is 1st June 2007.

2008/1942

FRIENDLY SOCIETIES (TRANSFERS OF OTHER BUSINESS) (MODIFICATION OF THE CORPORATION TAX ACTS) REGULATIONS 2008

Made by the Treasury under TA 1988 s 461D(4) and (5)

Made . . . . *22 July 2008*
Laid before House of Commons . . . . *22 July 2008*
Coming into force . . . . *12 August 2008*

Revocation—These Regulations revoked by the Friendly Societies (Modifications of the Tax Acts) Regulations, SI 2012/3008 reg 16, Schedule, with effect in relation to accounting periods beginning on or after 1 January 2013.

2008/2353

SERIOUS CRIME ACT 2007 (SPECIFIED ANTI-FRAUD ORGANISATIONS) ORDER 2008

Made by the Secretary of State under SCA 2007 s 68(8)

Made . . . . *2 September 2008*
Laid before Parliament . . . . *5 September 2008*
Coming into force . . . . *1 October 2008*

1 Citation and commencement

This Order may be cited as the Serious Crime Act 2007 (Specified Anti-fraud Organisations) Order 2008 and shall come into force on 1st October 2008.

2 Specified anti-fraud organisations

The following anti-fraud organisations are specified pursuant to section 68 of the Serious Crime Act 2007—

(*a*) CIFAS;
(*b*) Experian Limited;
(*c*) Insurance Fraud Investigators Group;
(*d*) N Hunter Limited;
(*e*) The Insurance Fraud Bureau;
(*f*) The Telecommunications United Kingdom Fraud Forum Limited.

2008/2603

TAXATION OF BENEFITS UNDER GOVERNMENT PILOT SCHEMES (BETTER OFF IN WORK CREDIT) ORDER 2008

Made by the Treasury under FA 1996 s 151(1)(a) and (7)(a)

Made . . . . *6 October 2008*
Laid before the House of Commons . . . . *6 October 2008*
Coming into force . . . . *27 October 2008*

Commentary—*Simon's Taxes* **E4.401, E4.701**.

1 Citation and commencement
This Order may be cited as the Taxation of Benefits under Government Pilot Schemes (Better off in Work Credit) Order 2008 and shall come into force on 27th October 2008.

2 Interpretation
In this Order, "Better off in Work Credit" means benefit payable by virtue of the Government pilot scheme known by that name.

3 Exemption from income tax
The Income Tax Acts shall have effect in relation to any amount of Better off in Work Credit as if it was wholly exempt from income tax and accordingly to be disregarded in computing the amount of any receipts brought into account for income tax purposes.

2008/2646

GROUP RELIEF FOR OVERSEAS LOSSES (MODIFICATION OF THE CORPORATION TAX ACTS FOR NON-RESIDENT INSURANCE COMPANIES) REGULATIONS 2008

Made by the Treasury under TA 1988 Sch 18A paras 16(2) to (4)

Made . . . . *7 October 2008*
Laid before the House of Commons . . . . *7 October 2008*
Coming into force . . . . *28 October 2008*

Commentary—*Simon's Taxes* **D7.5114**.

1 Citation, commencement and effect
(1) These Regulations may be cited as the Group Relief for Overseas Losses (Modification of the Corporation Tax Acts for Non-resident Insurance Companies) Regulations 2008 and shall come into force on 28th October 2008.
(2) These Regulations shall have effect for accounting periods beginning on or after 28th October 2008.

2 Modification of the Corporation Tax Acts
(1) For the purposes of Part 2 of Schedule 18A to the Income and Corporation Taxes Act 1988, the Corporation Tax Acts, and provisions made under them, shall have effect with the modifications—
(*a*) in regulation 3, in relation to EEA life insurance companies, and
(*b*) in regulation 4, in relation to EEA general insurers.
(2) For the purposes of these Regulations—
"EEA general insurer" means an EEA company whose business consists of, or includes, the effecting or carrying out of contracts falling within Part 1 of Schedule 1 to the Financial Services and Markets Act 2000 (Regulated Activities) Order 2001; and
"EEA life insurance company" means an EEA company whose business consists of, or includes, the effecting or carrying out of contracts falling within Part 2 of Schedule 1 to the Financial Services and Markets Act 2000 (Regulated Activities) Order 2001.
(3) In paragraph (2)—

"EEA company" means a non-resident company—

(*a*) which is resident in an EEA territory; or

(*b*) which is not so resident but which carries on a trade in an EEA territory through a permanent establishment.

(4) In paragraph (3)—

"EAA territory" has the meaning given in section 413(2) of the Income and Corporation Taxes Act 1988, and

"non-resident" means a company which is not resident in the United Kingdom.

3 Modification of section 431(2) of the Income and Corporation Taxes Act 1988

(1) It shall be assumed that the definition of "insurance special purpose vehicle" in section 431(2) of the Income and Corporation Taxes Act 1988 includes an EEA life insurance company but does not include an insurance special purpose vehicle treated as a BLAGAB group reinsurer.

(2) In paragraph (1) "BLAGAB group reinsurer" has the meaning given in paragraph 1 of Schedule 19ABA to the Income and Corporation Taxes Act 1988.

4 Modification of the Insurance Companies (Reserves) (Tax) Regulations 1996

It shall be assumed that regulation 8 of the Insurance Companies (Reserves) (Tax) Regulations 1996 applies to an EEA general insurer.

5 Revocations

The following instruments are hereby revoked—

(*a*) the Group Relief for Overseas Losses (Modification of the Corporation Tax Acts for Non-resident Insurance Companies) (No 2) Regulations 2006; and

(*b*) the Group Relief (Modification of the Corporation Tax Acts for Non-resident Insurance Companies) (No 2) (Amendment) Regulations 2007.

2008/2682

INCOME TAX (DEPOSIT-TAKERS AND BUILDING SOCIETIES) (INTEREST PAYMENTS) REGULATIONS 2008

Made by the Commissioners for HMRC under ITA 2007 ss 852, 871.

Made .... *9 October 2008*

Laid before the House of Commons .... *10 October 2008*

Coming into force .... *31 October 2008*

Commentary—*Simon's Taxes* **D7.813, D7.720**.

PART 1

INTRODUCTION

1 Citation, commencement and effect

(1) These Regulations may be cited as the Income Tax (Deposit-takers and Building Societies) (Interest Payments) Regulations 2008 and shall come into force on 31st October 2008.

(2) These Regulations shall have effect in relation to payments of interest made on or after 31st October 2008.

2 Interpretation

In these Regulations—

"certificate" means a certificate of non-liability to tax [on savings income][2] given in accordance with regulation 5;

"the Commissioners" means the Commissioners for Her Majesty's Revenue and Customs;

"electronic communication" includes any communication conveyed by means of an electronic communications network;

"electronic signature" has the meaning given by section 7(2) of the Electronic Communications Act 2000;

"ITA 2007" means the Income Tax Act 2007;

"ITTOIA 2005" means the Income Tax (Trading and Other Income) Act 2005;

"notice" means notice in writing;

"officer" means an officer of Revenue and Customs;

["relevant dormant account" has the meaning given in section 39(2) of the Finance Act 2008;][1]

"relevant financial institution" means a deposit-taker or building society as the case requires;

["repayment claim" means a repayment claim mentioned in section 5(6) of the Dormant Bank and Building Society Accounts Act 2008, and other terms used in regulations 4A and 4B and in that Act have the same meaning in those regulations as in that Act;][1]

"section 851" means section 851 of ITA 2007 (duty to deduct sums representing income tax);

"tax year" means a year beginning with 6th April in any year and ending with 5th April in the following year.

Amendments—[1] Definitions of "relevant dormant account" and "repayment claim" inserted by the Dormant Bank and Building Society Account (Tax) Regulations, SI 2011/22 regs 5, 6 with effect in relation to interest paid or credited on or after 1 February 2011.

[2] In definition of "certificate", words inserted by the Income Tax (Deposit-takers and Building Societies) (Interest Payments) (Amendment) Regulations, SI 2015/653 regs 2, 3 with effect from 6 April 2015.

3 Scope of these Regulations

(1) These Regulations make the following provisions.

(2) Part 2 makes provision in respect of payments of interest by relevant financial institutions relating to relevant investments (regulations 4 to 13).

(3) Part 3 makes provision in respect of payments of interest by relevant financial institutions relating to investments which are not relevant investments (regulation 14).

(4) Part 4 makes provision in relation to information requirements (regulations 15 to 18).

(5) Part 5 makes general provisions relating to continuity of certificates and declarations, consequential amendments, savings and revocations (regulations 19 to 20).

PART 2
PAYMENTS OF INTEREST IN RELATION TO RELEVANT INVESTMENTS

4 Gross payments

(1) Section 851 does not apply in relation to—

(*a*) a payment of interest, or

(*b*) part of a payment of interest within regulation 13(2)(*a*) (joint accounts),

where, in respect of the person beneficially entitled to the payment or the part of the payment, a certificate has been supplied (see regulation 5) and has not ceased to be valid (see regulation 11). This is subject to regulation 13(3).

(2) But paragraph (1) does not apply if—

(*a*) the provisions of section 629 of ITTOIA 2005 (income paid to relevant children of settlor) apply to the payment; or

(*b*) a notice of deduction under regulation 12 has been issued in relation to the payment and it has not been cancelled.

(3) Where a certificate has been supplied and it has not ceased to be valid, a relevant financial institution which operates a system which refunds an amount corresponding to tax deducted from payments of interest made previously in the tax year shall—

(*a*) refund any such amount in relation to the investment to which the certificate relates, and

(*b*) recover an amount corresponding to the amount refunded on a written application to the Commissioners.

This is subject to paragraph (4).

(4) Paragraph (3) shall not apply where a relevant financial institution has given a statement under section 975 of ITA 2007 (statements about deduction of income tax), if—

(*a*) the statement relates to the tax year in which the certificate was given; and

(*b*) the statement was given prior to the receipt of the certificate.

[4A Dormant accounts—postponement of obligation to deduct sum representing income tax

(1) Section 851 does not apply to a payment of interest in respect of a relevant dormant account before the time (if any) at which the balance of the account is paid out to the holder of the relevant dormant account following a repayment claim (such payment being referred to in this regulation as the repayment claim being "settled"), subject to paragraph (4).

(2) In paragraph (3) and regulation 4B, the period between—

(*a*) the time when a dormant account first becomes a relevant dormant account, and

(*b*) the time at which a repayment claim to the balance of the account is settled,

is referred to, in relation to the account, as the "relevant dormant period."

(3) Where a repayment claim to the balance of a dormant account is settled, all interest paid or credited to the account, or included in the balance of the account, during and at the end of the relevant dormant period, shall be treated for the purposes of section 851—

(*a*) as paid at the time the repayment claim is settled; and

(*b*) as if the account were at that time an investment, and a relevant investment for the purposes of Chapter 2 of Part 15 of ITA 2007 (deduction by deposit-takers and building societies).

(4) Section 851 does not apply to a payment of interest in respect of a relevant dormant account which, at the time it first became a relevant dormant account, was a plan provided for by regulations made under Chapter 3 of Part 6 of ITTOIA 2005 (individual investment plans).][1]

Amendments—[1] Regs 4A, 4B inserted by the Dormant Bank and Building Society Account (Tax) Regulations, SI 2011/22 regs 5, 7 with effect in relation to interest paid or credited on or after 1 February 2011.

[4B The duty to deduct a sum representing income tax under section 874 of ITA 2007 (duty to deduct from certain payments of yearly interest) does not apply to a payment of interest in respect of a relevant dormant account, made by or through a reclaim fund, deposit-taker or building society, during or at the end of the relevant dormant period for the account.][1]

Amendments—[1] Regs 4A, 4B inserted by the Dormant Bank and Building Society Account (Tax) Regulations, SI 2011/22 regs 5, 7 with effect in relation to interest paid or credited on or after 1 February 2011.

5 Certificate of non-liability to tax [on savings income][1]

A certificate of non-liability to tax [on savings income][1] must—

(*a*) certify that the person beneficially entitled to a payment of interest or, where regulation 13 (joint accounts) applies, to part of a payment of interest, is unlikely to be liable to pay any amount by way of income tax [on savings income][1] for the tax year in which that payment is made,

(*b*) be supplied by a prescribed person (regulation 6),

(*c*) be supplied to the relevant financial institution within the prescribed time limit (regulation 7),

(*d*) be in the prescribed form (regulation 8), and

(*e*) contain the prescribed contents (regulation 9).

Amendments—[1] In heading and text, words inserted by the Income Tax (Deposit-takers and Building Societies) (Interest Payments) (Amendment) Regulations, SI 2015/653 regs 2, 4(*a*), (*b*) with effect from 6 April 2015.

6 Prescribed persons

(1) A prescribed person is—

(*a*) a person—

(i) in whose name an investment is held,

(ii) who is beneficially entitled to a payment of interest on that investment, and

(iii) who was aged 16 or over at the beginning of the tax year in which the payment is made;

(*b*) the parent or guardian of a person who is beneficially entitled to a payment of interest where that person is under the age of 16 at the beginning of the tax year in which the payment is made;

(*c*) a person—

(i) who is beneficially entitled to a payment of interest, and

(ii) who is under the age of 16 at the beginning of the tax year in which the payment is made but who will become 16 during that tax year;

(*d*) the donee of a power of attorney authorising the donee to administer the financial affairs of a person beneficially entitled to a payment of interest;

[(*e*) if the person beneficially entitled to a payment of interest is resident in England and Wales and lacks capacity to make a decision for himself for the purposes of section 2 of the Mental Capacity Act 2005 – a parent, guardian, spouse, civil partner, son or daughter of the person;

(*ea*) if the person beneficially entitled to a payment of interest is resident in Scotland or Northern Ireland and is suffering from mental disorder – a parent, guardian, spouse, civil partner, son or daughter of the person;][2]

[(*f*) if the person beneficially entitled to a payment of interest is resident in England and Wales—

(i) a person appointed pursuant to an order under section 16(2)(a) of the Mental Capacity Act 2005; or

(ii) a person appointed a deputy under section 16(2)(b) of that Act;

(*fa*) if the person beneficially entitled to a payment of interest is resident in Scotland and is incapable by reason of mental disorder of managing and administering their property and affairs – a receiver or other person appointed by any court to act in relation to their property and affairs;

(*fb*) if the person beneficially entitled to a payment of interest is resident in Northern Ireland and is incapable by reason of mental disorder of managing and administering their property and affairs – a receiver or other person appointed by any court to act in relation to their property and affairs; or][2]

(*g*) a person appointed by the Secretary of State under—

(i) paragraph (1) of regulation 33 of the Social Security (Claims and Payments) Regulations 1987 (persons unable to act), whose appointment has not been revoked or terminated, or who has not resigned, under paragraph (2) of that regulation; or

(ii) paragraph (2) of regulation 28 of the Child Benefit and Guardian's Allowance (Administration) Regulations 2003 (appointment of persons to act on behalf of those unable to act), whose appointment has not been revoked, or who has not resigned, under paragraph (3) of that regulation, or whose appointment has not been terminated under paragraph (4) of that regulation[or

(iii) paragraph (1) of regulation 57 of the Universal Credit, Personal Independence Payment, Jobseeker's Allowance and Employment and Support Allowance (Claims and Payments) Regulations 2013 (persons unable to act), whose appointment has not been revoked or ended, or who has not resigned, under paragraph (8) of that regulation.][1]

(2) In this regulation—

"daughter or son" means a daughter or son aged 16 or over and includes a stepdaughter or stepson and an adopted or illegitimate daughter or son; and

"mental disorder" has the meaning given by—

(*a*) . . . [2]

(*b*) section 328 of the Mental Health (Care and Treatment) (Scotland) Act 2003 (meaning of "mental disorder") in Scotland, and

(*c*) Article 3 of the Mental Health (Northern Ireland) Order 1986 (definition of "mental disorder" and related expressions) in Northern Ireland.

Amendments—[1] Para (1)(*g*)(iii) and preceding word inserted by the Universal Credit, Personal Independence Payment, Jobseeker's Allowance and Employment and Support Allowance (Claims and Payments) Regulations, SI 2013/380 reg 4, Sch 3, para 5 with effect, for the purpose of personal independence payment, from 8 April 2013, and for the purposes of universal credit, jobseeker's allowance and employment and support allowance, from 29 April 2013.

[2] Para (1)(*e*), (*ea*) substituted for previous para (1)(*e*), para (1)(*f*)–(*fb*) substituted for previous para (1)(*f*), and in para (2), in definition of "mental disorder", sub-para (*a*) revoked by the Income Tax (Deposit-takers and Building Societies) (Interest Payments) (Amendment) Regulations, SI 2015/653 regs 2, 5 with effect from 6 April 2015.

7 Supply within prescribed time limit

(1) A certificate is treated as supplied to the relevant financial institution on the date it is given to the relevant financial institution or recorded by the relevant financial institution in accordance with paragraph (1)(*b*) of regulation 8 and nothing in paragraphs (2) or (3) of that regulation affects that date.

(2) The prescribed time limit is—

(*a*) where regulation 6(1)(*c*) applies, before the end of the tax year in which the person beneficially entitled to the payment attains the age of 16; and

(*b*) in any other case, before the end of the tax year in which the payment is made.

8 Prescribed form of a certificate

(1) A certificate must be—

(*a*) in writing, signed by a prescribed person, or

(*b*) if not in writing, recorded in writing by the relevant financial institution on behalf of a prescribed person.

(2) If the relevant financial institution operates a record system under which the original certificate is not retained, the relevant financial institution must make a record of the certificate.

(3) Where paragraph (1)(*b*) or (2) applies—

(*a*) a copy of the record of the certificate must be sent by the relevant financial institution to the prescribed person within 30 days of that record being made;

(*b*) the prescribed person must notify the relevant financial institution of any corrections required within 30 days from the date the copy is sent; and

(*c*) the relevant financial institution must incorporate any such corrections in a revised record which must be sent to the prescribed person as soon as possible.

(4) A certificate shall be regarded as being in writing if it was supplied—

(*a*) by telephonic facsimile transmission; or

(*b*) by electronic communication containing an electronic signature of the prescribed person.

(5) A certificate or a record of a certificate must be retained by a relevant financial institution in such manner as may be approved by the Commissioners for two years after the relevant financial institution has ceased to pay interest without deduction of a sum representing income tax in relation to a relevant investment.

9 Prescribed contents of a certificate

(1) A certificate must contain—

(*a*) the information prescribed in paragraphs (2) and (4); and

(*b*) the undertaking prescribed in paragraph (5).

(2) In relation to the person beneficially entitled to the payment of interest, the prescribed information is that person's—

(*a*) name,

(*b*) permanent residential address (including post code),

(*c*) date of birth, and

(*d*) national insurance number if the circumstances in paragraph (3) apply, except where, in a particular case, an officer has indicated that this information is not required.

(3) The circumstances referred to in paragraph (2)(*d*) are that the person beneficially entitled to the payment of interest—

(*a*) was aged 16 or over at the beginning of the tax year in which the payment was made, and

(*b*) was liable to pay Class 1 or Class 2 contributions within the meaning of section 1(2) of the Social Security Contributions and Benefits Act 1992, at any time within the period of three years ending with the date on which the certificate is signed.

(4) In relation to the investment to which the certificate relates, the prescribed information is—

(*a*) the name of the relevant financial institution,
(*b*) the account number, and
(*c*) the branch, sort code or roll number as appropriate, of the relevant financial institution where the account is held, if the account cannot otherwise be identified.

(5) The prescribed person must undertake to notify the relevant financial institution that if—
(*a*) that person, being the person beneficially entitled to the payment of interest, or
(*b*) the person so entitled,

becomes liable to pay any amount by way of income tax [on savings income][1] for the tax year in which the payment is made, that person will notify the relevant financial institution in accordance with regulation 10.

Amendments—[1] In para (5), words inserted by the Income Tax (Deposit-takers and Building Societies) (Interest Payments) (Amendment) Regulations, SI 2015/653 regs 2, 4(*c*) with effect from 6 April 2015.

10 Notification of liability to income tax [on savings income][1] in accordance with regulation 9(5)

A notification given in accordance with the undertaking in regulation 9(5) must contain details of the investment to which the certificate relates, including the account number and where necessary for identifying the account, the branch, sort code or roll number as appropriate, of the relevant financial institution.

Amendments—[1] In heading, words inserted by the Income Tax (Deposit-takers and Building Societies) (Interest Payments) (Amendment) Regulations, SI 2015/653 regs 2, 4(*a*) with effect from 6 April 2015.

11 Certificate ceasing to be valid

(1) A certificate ceases to be valid in any of the circumstances specified in paragraph (2).

(2) The circumstances specified in this paragraph are—
(*a*) the receipt by the relevant financial institution of a notification under regulation 10 that the person beneficially entitled to a payment of interest arising on an account specified in the notification has become liable to pay an amount by way of income tax [on savings income][1] for the tax year in which the payment is made;
(*b*) in the case of a certificate supplied by a prescribed person within regulation 6(1)(*b*), the ending of the tax year in which the person beneficially entitled to the payment of interest reaches the age of 16;
(*c*) the failure by a person who has given a certificate under regulation 6(1)(*c*) to become the holder of the investment to which the certificate relates before the first payment of interest after the end of the tax year in which the age of 16 is reached;
(*d*) the issue of a notice of deduction under regulation 12;
(*e*) the notification of the relevant financial institution that the person beneficially entitled to the payment of interest in respect of whom the certificate was given has died.

Amendments—[1] In para (2)(*a*), words inserted by the Income Tax (Deposit-takers and Building Societies) (Interest Payments) (Amendment) Regulations, SI 2015/653 regs 2, 4(*d*) with effect from 6 April 2015.

12 Notice of deduction

(1) If an officer thinks that a person beneficially entitled to a payment of interest is or has become liable to pay an amount by way of income tax [on savings income][1] the officer must notify the prescribed person accordingly.

(2) If the prescribed person does not satisfy the officer within 30 days of the notification under paragraph (1) that the person beneficially entitled to the payment is not, or has not become, liable to pay an amount by way of income tax [on savings income][1], the officer shall issue a notice of deduction to the relevant financial institution.

(3) A notice of deduction must—
(*a*) give the name of the person beneficially entitled to the payment of interest;
(*b*) give the account number of the account in respect of which the payment of interest is made;
(*c*) give the branch, sort code or roll number as appropriate, of the relevant financial institution where the account is held, if the account cannot otherwise be identified; and
(*d*) require a sum representing income tax to be deducted under section 851.

(4) Following the issue of a notice of deduction under this regulation no further certificate shall be accepted from or in respect of the person beneficially entitled to the payment of interest relating to the account specified in the notice.

This is subject to paragraph (7).

(5) A sum representing income tax shall be deducted under section 851 as soon as it is reasonably practicable to do so and in any event not later than 30 days following the date of issue of the notice.

(6) Where an officer is satisfied that the person referred to in the notice was not liable at the date of the notice and has not since become liable, or is no longer liable, to tax [on savings income][1], the notice of deduction must be cancelled and notice of the cancellation must be given to that person and to the relevant financial institution.

(7) Where notice of the cancellation is given by an officer under paragraph (6) a further certificate may be supplied by or in respect of the person beneficially entitled to the payment of interest.

Amendments—[1] In paras (1), (2), (6), words inserted by the Income Tax (Deposit-takers and Building Societies) (Interest Payments) (Amendment) Regulations, SI 2015/653 regs 2, 4(*e*) with effect from 6 April 2015.

13 Joint accounts

(1) Where—

(*a*) more than one person is beneficially entitled to a payment of interest on a relevant investment, and

(*b*) a certificate is given by or in respect of—

(i) one or more (but not all) of the persons beneficially entitled to the payment of interest, or

(ii) each person beneficially entitled to the payment of interest but one or more of the certificates has ceased to be valid at any time due to the occurrence of one of the circumstances specified in sub-paragraphs (*a*), (*b*), (*c*), or (*d*) of regulation 11(2) (circumstances in which a certificate ceases to be valid),

for the purposes of these Regulations and section 851, it shall be assumed that those persons are beneficially entitled to the payment of interest in equal shares.

(2) Where paragraph (1) applies, payment of—

(*a*) so much of the interest as corresponds to the share of any person by, or in respect of whom, a certificate was supplied and has not ceased to be valid shall be made without deduction of tax under regulation 4, and

(*b*) the remainder of the interest—

(i) must be made under deduction of tax in accordance with section 851, and

(ii) the amount so deducted must be treated as income tax paid by the person or persons to whom the payment is treated as being made for all purposes of the Income Tax Acts.

This is subject to paragraph (4).

(3) Where paragraph (2)(*b*) applies, in the case of a certificate which ceases to be valid the deduction of tax pursuant to section 851 must be made—

(*a*) as soon as the certificate has ceased to be valid, or

(*b*) where regulation 12 (notice of deduction) applies, in accordance with paragraph (5) of that regulation.

(4) Where paragraph (1) applies—

(*a*) a relevant financial institution may by notice inform an officer that the whole of the payment of interest referred to in the notice shall be made under deduction of tax in accordance with section 851; and

(*b*) an amount representing income tax shall accordingly be deducted by the relevant financial institution from the payment to which the notice relates and which is made after the date of the notice.

(5) A relevant financial institution may by notice to an officer ("the cancellation notice")—

(*a*) cancel a notice given under paragraph (4), and

(*b*) where a notice is so cancelled, paragraph (2) shall apply to any payment of interest to which the notice formerly related and which is made after the date of the cancellation notice.

PART 3
DECLARATIONS OF NON-UK RESIDENCE (INVESTMENTS WHICH ARE NOT RELEVANT INVESTMENTS)

14 Prescribed form of a declaration

(1) A declaration made under any of sections 858 to 861 of ITA 2007 must be—

(*a*) in writing signed by an appropriate person, or

(*b*) if not in writing, recorded in writing by the relevant financial institution, on behalf of an appropriate person.

(2) If the relevant financial institution operates a record system under which the original declaration is not retained, the relevant financial institution must make a record of the declaration.

(3) Where paragraph (1)(*b*) or (2) applies—

(*a*) a copy of the record of the declaration must be sent by the relevant financial institution to the appropriate person within 30 days of that record being made;

(*b*) the appropriate person must notify the relevant financial institution of any corrections required within 30 days from the date the copy is sent; and

(*c*) the relevant financial institution must incorporate any such corrections in a revised record which must be sent to the appropriate person as soon as possible.

(4) The declaration has effect at the later of the date on which—

(*a*) it was given to the relevant financial institution,

(*b*) a copy of the record in paragraph (3)(*a*) was sent, or

(*c*) a revised copy of the record in paragraph (3)(*c*) was sent.

(5) A declaration shall be regarded as being in writing if it was made—

(*a*) by telephonic facsimile transmission, or

(*b*) by electronic communication containing an electronic signature of the appropriate person.

(6) A declaration or record of a declaration must be retained by a relevant financial institution in such manner as may be approved by the Commissioners for two years after the investment has been repaid or has become a relevant investment.

PART 4
INFORMATION REQUIREMENTS

15 Information to be provided to an officer—(relevant investments)

(1) This regulation applies to payments of interest made by relevant financial institutions in respect of relevant investments.

(2) An officer may by notice require a relevant financial institution to provide such information (including copies of any relevant books, documents and other records) as that officer may reasonably require for the purposes of these Regulations and, in particular, in relation to the matters covered in paragraph (3).

(3) The matters are—

(*a*) verifying payments of interest made without deduction of tax in accordance with these Regulations;

(*b*) determining whether a certificate has been supplied in accordance with Part 2;

(*c*) verifying amounts of interest paid by the relevant financial institution to which this regulation applies; and

(*d*) verifying amounts representing income tax deducted by the relevant financial institution from such payments in accordance with section 851.

(4) The information required must be provided within such time (not being less than 14 days) as stated in the notice.

16 Information to be provided to an officer—(investments which are not relevant investments)

(1) This regulation applies to payments of interest made without deduction of tax by relevant financial institutions in respect of investments which are not relevant investments.

(2) Where this regulation applies, an officer may by notice require a relevant financial institution to provide such information (including copies of any relevant books, documents and other records) as that officer may reasonably require for the purposes of determining whether payments of interest by that relevant financial institution were properly made without deduction of tax.

(3) The information required must be provided within such time (not being less than 14 days) as may be provided by the notice.

17 Inspection of records

(1) An officer may require a relevant financial institution to produce all books, documents and other records, or such of these as may be specified, either in the possession of or under the control of the relevant financial institution, for inspection at such time and place as that officer may reasonably require under this Part.

(2) Where records are maintained by computer the person required to make them available for inspection shall provide the officer making the inspection with all the facilities necessary for obtaining information from these.

18 Use of information

(1) Subject to paragraph (2), information obtained by an officer under this Part—

(*a*) must not be used for the purpose of ascertaining the tax liability (if any) of any person other than—

(i) a person beneficially entitled to a payment of interest specified in regulation 15(1) or 16(1) to whom the information obtained relates, and

(ii) the relevant financial institution; and

(*b*) must otherwise be used only for the purposes of these Regulations.

(2) Paragraph (1) shall not be construed as preventing any disclosure of information within section 182(5) of the Finance Act 1989.

PART 5
GENERAL PROVISIONS

19 Continuity of certificates and declarations of non-UK residence following transfer of business

Where a relevant financial institution ("the original institution") transfers the whole or part of its business to another relevant financial institution ("the successor institution")—

(*a*) a certificate under regulation 5, or

(*b*) a declaration made under any of sections 858 to 861 of ITA 2007 (declaration of non-UK residence), supplied to the original institution in relation to an investment shall be treated as supplied to the successor institution.

20 Consequential amendments, savings and revocation

(1) Schedule 1 (consequential amendments) and Schedule 2 (transitional provisions and savings) have effect.

(2) The Regulations listed in column 1 of Schedule 3 are revoked.

(3) Paragraph (2) is subject to Schedule 2.

SCHEDULE 1

CONSEQUENTIAL AMENDMENTS

Regulation 20

1 Regulation 16 of the Reporting of Savings Income Information Regulations 2003 (audit and related issues) is amended as follows.

2 In paragraph (5)—

(*a*) for sub-paragraph (i) substitute—

"(i) regulations 8(5) and 14(6) of the Income Tax (Deposit-takers and Building Societies) (Interest Payments) Regulations 2008"; and

(*b*) omit sub-paragraphs (ii) and (iii).

3 In paragraph (6)(*b*)—

(*a*) in paragraph (ii) for "Chapter 4 of Part 12 of the Income and Corporation Taxes Act 1988" substitute "Chapter 2 of Part 15 of the Income Tax Act 2007";

(*b*) for paragraph (iii) substitute—

"(iii) the Income Tax (Deposit-takers and Building Societies) (Interest Payments) Regulations 2008, and"; and

(*c*) omit sub-paragraph (iv).

SCHEDULE 2

TRANSITIONAL PROVISIONS AND SAVINGS

Regulation 20

PART 1

GENERAL PROVISIONS

Continuity of the Law

1 The revocation of provisions and their making in a rewritten form by these Regulations does not affect the continuity of the law.

2 Paragraph 1 does not apply to any change in the law made by these Regulations.

3 Anything which—

(*a*) has been done, or has effect as if done, under or for the purposes of a provision of the revoked Regulations, and

(*b*) is in force or effective immediately before the commencement of these Regulations,

has effect after that commencement as if done under or for the purposes of the corresponding provision of these Regulations.

4 Any reference (express or implied) in these Regulations or any document made under these Regulations to—

(*a*) a provision of these Regulations, or

(*b*) things done or falling to be done under or for the purposes of a provision of these Regulations,

is to be read as including, in relation to times, circumstances or purposes in relation to which any corresponding provision of the revoked Regulations had effect, a reference to the provision of the revoked Regulations or to things done or falling to be done under or for the purposes of the provision of the revoked Regulations.

5 Any reference (express or implied) in these Regulations to—

(*a*) a provision of ITA 2007, or

(*b*) things done or falling to be done under or for the purposes of a provision of ITA 2007,

is to be read as including, in relation to times, circumstances or purposes in relation to which any corresponding provision repealed by that Act had effect, a reference to the repealed provision or to things done or falling to be done under or for the purposes of the repealed provision.

6 Paragraphs 4 and 5 apply only so far as the context permits.

7 Paragraphs 1 to 5 have effect instead of paragraph (*b*) of section 17(2) of the Interpretation Act 1978.

General Saving for Old Savings

8—(1) The revocation by these Regulations of a provision previously revoked subject to savings does not affect the continued operation of those savings.
(2) The revocation by these Regulations of a saving on the previous revocation of a provision does not affect the operation of the saving in so far as it is not specifically reproduced in these Regulations but remains capable of having effect.

PART 2
SPECIFIC PROVISIONS

9—(1) Declarations made under regulation 11 of the Income Tax (Building Societies) (Dividends and Interest) Regulations 1990 or treated as having effect as if made under that provision shall have effect as if made under section 858(3), 859(3), 860(3) or 861(3) of ITA 2007.
(2) Declarations within paragraph (1) shall be preserved by a building society for two years after the investment has been repaid or become a relevant investment.

SCHEDULE 3
REVOCATIONS

Regulation 20

Column (1)	*Column (2)*
Regulations revoked	*References*
The Income Tax (Building Societies) (Dividends and Interest) Regulations 1990	SI 1990/2231
The Income Tax (Building Societies) (Dividends and Interest) (Amendment) Regulations 1992	SI 1992/11
The Income Tax (Building Societies) (Dividends and Interest) (Amendment No 2) Regulations 1992	SI 1992/2915
The Income Tax (Building Societies) (Dividends and Interest) (Amendment) Regulations 1994	SI 1994/296
The Income Tax (Building Societies) (Dividends and Interest) (Amendment) Regulations 1995	SI 1995/1184
The Income Tax (Building Societies) (Dividends and Interest) (Amendment) Regulations 1996	SI 1996/223
The Income Tax (Building Societies) (Dividends and Interest) (Amendment) Regulations 2001	SI 2001/404
The Income Tax (Building Societies) (Dividends and Interest) (Amendment) Regulations 2005	SI 2005/3474
The Income Tax (Deposit-takers) (Interest Payments) Regulations 1990	SI 1990/2232
The Income Tax (Deposit-takers) (Interest Payments) (Amendment) Regulations 1992	SI 1992/13
The Income Tax (Deposit-takers) (Interest Payments) (Amendment) Regulations 1994	SI 1994/295
The Income Tax (Deposit-takers) (Interest Payments) (Amendment) Regulations 2001	SI 2001/406
The Income Tax (Building Societies) (Audit Powers) Regulations 1992	SI 1992/10

Column (1)	Column (2)
The Income Tax (Deposit-takers) (Audit Powers) Regulations 1992	SI 1992/12
The Income Tax (Deposit-takers) (Non-residents) Regulations 1992	SI 1992/14

2008/2684

FIRST-TIER TRIBUNAL AND UPPER TRIBUNAL (CHAMBERS) ORDER 2008

Made . . . . *13 October 2008*
Laid before Parliament . . . . *15 October 2008*
Coming into force . . . . *3 November 2008*

Revocation—This Order revoked by the First-tier Tribunal and Upper Tribunal (Chambers) Order, SI 2010/2655 art 1(2), Schedule with effect from 29 November 2010.

2008/2692

QUALIFICATIONS FOR APPOINTMENT OF MEMBERS TO THE FIRST-TIER TRIBUNAL AND UPPER TRIBUNAL ORDER 2008

Made . . . . *15th October 2008*
Laid before Parliament . . . . *15th October 2008*
Coming into force . . . . *3rd November 2008*

The Lord Chancellor, with the concurrence of the Senior President of Tribunals, makes the following Order in exercise of the powers conferred by paragraph 2(2) of Schedule 2 and paragraph 2(2) of Schedule 3 to the Tribunals, Courts and Enforcement Act 2007.

1 [(1)] This Order may be cited as the Qualifications for Appointment of Members to the First-tier Tribunal and Upper Tribunal Order 2008 and shall come into force on 3rd November 2008.
[(2) In this Order "registered medical practitioner" means a fully registered person within the meaning of the Medical Act 1983 whether or not they hold a licence to practise under that Act.]

2 (1) A person is eligible for appointment as a member of the First-tier Tribunal or the Upper Tribunal who is not a judge of those tribunals if paragraph (2), (3) or (4) applies.
(2) This paragraph applies to a person who is—
(*a*) a registered medical practitioner;
(*b*) a registered nurse;
(*c*) a registered dentist;
[(*ca*) a registered optometrist;]
(*d*) a clinical psychologist;
(*e*) an educational psychologist;
(*f*) a pharmacologist;
(*g*) a veterinary surgeon or a veterinary practitioner registered under the Veterinary Surgeons Act 1966;
(*h*) a Member or Fellow of the Royal Institution of Chartered Surveyors; or
(*i*) an accountant who is a member of—
(i) the Institute of Chartered Accountants in England and Wales;
(ii) the Institute of Chartered Accountants in Scotland;
(iii) the Institute of Chartered Accountants in Ireland;
(iv) the Institute of Certified Public Accountants in Ireland;
(v) the Association of Chartered Certified Accountants;
(vi) the Chartered Institute of Management Accountants; or
(vii) the Chartered Institute of Public Finance and Accountancy.
(3) This paragraph applies to a person. . . who is experienced in dealing with the physical or mental needs of disabled persons because they—
(*a*) work with disabled persons in a professional or voluntary capacity; or
(*b*) are themselves disabled.
[(3A) A person is not eligible for appointment under paragraph (3) if they are a registered medical practitioner.]
(4) This paragraph applies to a person who has substantial experience—

(*a*) of service in Her Majesty's naval, military, or air forces;
(*b*) of educational, child care, health, or social care matters;
(*c*) of dealing with victims of violent crime;
(*d*) in transport operations and its law and practice;
(*e*) in the regulatory field;
(*f*) in consumer affairs;
(*g*) in an industry, trade or business sector and the matters that are likely to arise as issues in the course of disputes with regulators of such industries, trades or businesses;
(*h*) in tax matters and related tax procedures;
(*i*) in a business, trade[, charity] or not-for-profit organisation;
[(*j*) in immigration services or the law and procedure relating to immigration;
(*k*) of data protection;
(*l*) of freedom of information (including environmental information) rights;
(*m*) of service as a Member or Senior Officer of a local authority in England].
[(*n*) in environmental matters;][1]
[(*o*) in the drainage of land;
(*p*) in farming and the ownership or management of agricultural property;
(*q*) in relation to housing or housing conditions;
(*r*) in matters relating to landlord and tenant relationships;
(*s*) in valuation.][2]

Amendments—[1] In para (4), sub-para (*n*) inserted by the Qualifications for Appointment of Members to the First-tier Tribunal and Upper Tribunal (Amendment) Order, SI 2012/897 arts 2, 3 with effect from 16 April 2012.
[2] In para (4), sub-paras (*o*)–(*s*) inserted by the Qualifications for Appointment of Members to the First-tier Tribunal and Upper Tribunal (Amendment) Order, SI 2013/1185 arts 2, 3 with effect from 1 July 2013.

2008/2698

TRIBUNAL PROCEDURE (UPPER TRIBUNAL) RULES 2008

Made by the Tribunal Procedure Committee, after consulting in accordance with TCEA 2007 Sch 5 para 28(1), under TCEA 2007 ss 10(3), 16(9), 22, 29(3), (4), Sch 5.

The Lord Chancellor has allowed the Rules in accordance with TCEA 2007 Sch 5 para 28(3).

Made . . . . *9 October 2008*
Laid before Parliament . . . . *15 October 2008*
Coming into force . . . . *3 November 2008*

PART 1
INTRODUCTION

1 Citation, commencement, application and interpretation

(1) These Rules may be cited as the Tribunal Procedure (Upper Tribunal) Rules 2008 and come into force on 3rd November 2008.
(2) These Rules apply to proceedings before the Upper Tribunal [except proceedings in the Lands Chamber][2].
(3) In these Rules—

"the 2007 Act" means the Tribunals, Courts and Enforcement Act 2007;

["appellant" means—

(a) a person who makes an appeal, or applies for permission to appeal, to the Upper Tribunal;
(b) in proceedings transferred or referred to the Upper Tribunal from the First-tier Tribunal, a person who started the proceedings in the First-tier Tribunal; or
(c) a person substituted as an appellant under rule 9(1) (substitution and addition of parties);][1]

["applicant" means—

(*a*) a person who applies for permission to bring, or does bring, judicial review proceedings before the Upper Tribunal and, in judicial review proceedings transferred to the Upper Tribunal from a court, includes a person who was a claimant or petitioner in the proceedings immediately before they were transferred; or
(*b*) a person who refers a financial services case [or a wholesale energy case][11] to the Upper Tribunal;][5]

["appropriate national authority" means, in relation to an appeal, the Secretary of State, the Scottish Ministers[, the Department of the Environment in Northern Ireland][8] or the Welsh Ministers, as the case may be;

["asylum case" means proceedings before the Upper Tribunal on appeal against a decision in proceedings under section 82, 83 or 83A of the Nationality, Immigration and Asylum Act 2002 in which a person claims that removal from, or a requirement to leave, the United Kingdom would breach the United Kingdom's obligations under the Convention relating to the Status of Refugees done at Geneva on 28 July 1951 and the Protocol to the Convention;][4]

["authorised person" means—

(*a*) an examiner appointed by the Secretary of State under section 66A of the Road Traffic Act 1988;

(*b*) an examiner appointed by the Department of the Environment in Northern Ireland under Article 74 of the Road Traffic (Northern Ireland) Order 1995; or

(*c*) any person authorised in writing by the Department of the Environment in Northern Ireland for the purposes of the Goods Vehicles (Licensing of Operators) Act (Northern Ireland) 2010;

and includes a person acting under the direction of such an examiner or other authorised person, who has detained the vehicle to which an appeal relates;][8]

["disability discrimination in schools case" means proceedings concerning discrimination in the education of a child or young person or related matters;][12]

. . .[1]

"dispose of proceedings" includes, unless indicated otherwise, disposing of a part of the proceedings;

"document" means anything in which information is recorded in any form, and an obligation under these Rules or any practice direction or direction to provide or allow access to a document or a copy of a document for any purpose means, unless the Upper Tribunal directs otherwise, an obligation to provide or allow access to such document or copy in a legible form or in a form which can be readily made into a legible form;

["fast-track case" means an asylum case or an immigration case where the person who appealed to the First-tier Tribunal—

(*a*) was detained under the Immigration Acts at a place specified in [rule 2(3) of the Schedule to the Tribunal Procedure (First-tier Tribunal) (Immigration and Asylum Chamber) Rules 2014][13] when the notice of decision that was the subject of the appeal to the First-tier Tribunal was served on the appellant;

(*b*) remains so detained; and

(*c*) the First-tier Tribunal or the Upper Tribunal has not directed that the case cease to be treated as a fast-track case;][4]

["financial sanctions case" means an appeal to the Upper Tribunal under section 147(6) of the Policing and Crime Act 2017;][15]

["financial services case" means a reference to the Upper Tribunal in respect of—

[(*a*) a decision of the Financial Conduct Authority;

(*aa*) a decision of the Prudential Regulation Authority;][9]

(*b*) a decision of the Bank of England;

(*c*) a decision of the Pensions Regulator; . . .[11]

(*d*) a decision of a person relating to the assessment of any compensation or consideration under the Banking (Special Provisions) Act 2008 or the Banking Act 2009;] [or[5]

(*e*) any determination, calculation or dispute which may be referred to the Upper Tribunal under the Financial Services and Markets Act 2000 (Contribution to Costs of Special Resolution Regime) Regulations 2010(2) (and in these Rules a decision in respect of which a reference has been made to the Upper Tribunal in a financial services case includes any such determination, calculation or, except for the purposes of rule 5(5), dispute relating to the making of payments under the Regulations).][6]

. . .[10]

"hearing" means an oral hearing and includes a hearing conducted in whole or in part by video link, telephone or other means of instantaneous two-way electronic communication;

["immigration case" means proceedings before the Upper Tribunal on appeal against a decision in proceedings under section 40A of the British Nationality Act 1981, section 82 of the Nationality, Immigration and Asylum Act 2002, or regulation 26 of the Immigration (European Economic Area) Regulations 2006 that are not an asylum case;][4]

["immigration judicial review proceedings" means judicial review proceedings which are designated as an immigration matter—

(*a*) in a direction made in accordance with Part 1 of Schedule 2 to the Constitutional Reform Act 2005 specifying a class of case for the purposes of section 18(6) of the 2007 Act; or

(*b*) in an order of the High Court in England and Wales made under section 31A(3) of the Senior Courts Act 1981, transferring to the Upper Tribunal an application of a kind described in section 31A(1) of that Act;][10]

"interested party" means—

(*a*) a person who is directly affected by the outcome sought in judicial review proceedings, and has been named as an interested party under rule 28 or 29 (judicial review), or has been substituted or added as an interested party under rule 9 [(addition, substitution and removal of parties)][5] . . . [5];

(*b*) in judicial review proceedings transferred to the Upper Tribunal under section 25A(2) or (3) of the Judicature (Northern Ireland) Act 1978 or section 31A(2) or (3) of the Supreme Court Act 1981, a person who was an interested party in the proceedings immediately before they were transferred to the Upper Tribunal; [and

(*c*) in a financial services case [or a wholesale energy case][11], any person other than the applicant who could have referred the case to the Upper Tribunal and who has been added or substituted as an interested party under rule 9 (addition, substitution and removal of parties);][5]

[(*d*) in a financial sanctions case, any person other than the appellant upon whom the Treasury has imposed a monetary penalty under Part 8 of the Policing and Crime Act 2017 in connection with the same matters as led to the decision that is the subject of the appeal and who has been added or substituted as an interested party under rule 9 (addition, substitution and removal of parties);][15]

"judicial review proceedings" means proceedings within the jurisdiction of the Upper Tribunal pursuant to section 15 or 21 of the 2007 Act, whether such proceedings are started in the Upper Tribunal or transferred to the Upper Tribunal;

. . . [1]

"mental health case" means proceedings before the Upper Tribunal on appeal against a decision in proceedings under the Mental Health Act 1983 or paragraph 5(2) of the Schedule to the Repatriation of Prisoners Act 1984;

["national security certificate appeal" means an appeal under section 28 of the Data Protection Act 1998 or section 60 of the Freedom of Information Act 2000 (including that section as applied and modified by regulation 18 of the Environmental Information Regulations 2004);][3]

"party" means a person who is an appellant, an applicant, a respondent or an interested party in proceedings before the Upper Tribunal, a person who has referred a question [or matter][5] to the Upper Tribunal or, if the proceedings have been concluded, a person who was an appellant, an applicant, a respondent or an interested party when the [Upper][10] Tribunal finally disposed of all issues in the proceedings;

"permission" includes leave in cases arising under the law of Northern Ireland;

"practice direction" means a direction given under section 23 of the 2007 Act;

["QCS Board" means a Board constituted under Part 2 of the Transport Act 2000;

"quality contracts scheme" has the meaning provided for in section 124(3) (quality contracts scheme) of the Transport Act 2000;

"quality contracts scheme case" means proceedings in the Upper Tribunal under Part 2 of the Transport Act 2000;][14]

["relevant minister" means the Minister or designated person responsible for the signing of the certificate to which a national security certificate appeal relates;][3]

["reference", in a financial services case, includes an appeal;][5]

"respondent" means—

(*a*) in an appeal, or application for permission to appeal, against a decision of another tribunal, any person other than the appellant who—

(i) was a party before that other tribunal;

(ii) . . . [1]

(iii) otherwise has a right of appeal against the decision of the other tribunal and has given notice to the Upper Tribunal that they wish to be a party to the appeal;

(*b*) in an appeal [other than a road transport case][8], the person who made the decision;

(*c*) in judicial review proceedings—

(i) in proceedings started in the Upper Tribunal, the person named by the applicant as the respondent;

(ii) in proceedings transferred to the Upper Tribunal under section 25A(2) or (3) of the Judicature (Northern Ireland) Act 1978 or section 31A(2) or (3) of the Supreme Court Act 1981, a person who was a defendant in the proceedings immediately before they were transferred;

(iii) in proceedings transferred to the Upper Tribunal under section 20(1) of the 2007 Act, a person to whom intimation of the petition was made before the proceedings were transferred, or to whom the Upper Tribunal has required intimation to be made;

[(*ca*) in proceedings transferred or referred to the Upper Tribunal from the First-tier Tribunal, a person who was a respondent in the proceedings in the First-tier Tribunal;][1]

(*d*) in a reference under the Forfeiture Act 1982, the person whose eligibility for a benefit or advantage is in issue; . . . [5]

[(*da*) in a financial services case—

(i) where the case is a multiple regulator case, both the primary and secondary regulator as defined in Schedule 3 to these rules (but subject to the operation of paragraph 4A(3) of that Schedule);

(ii) where the case is a single regulator case, the maker of the decision in respect of which a reference has been made; or][9]

[(*db*) in a wholesale energy case, in relation to Great Britain, the Gas and Electricity Markets Authority or, in relation to Northern Ireland, the Northern Ireland Authority for Utility Regulation; or][11]

(*e*) a person substituted or added as a respondent under rule 9 (substitution and addition of parties);

["road transport case" means an appeal against a decision of a traffic commissioner or the Department of the Environment in Northern Ireland;][8]

["special educational needs case" means proceedings concerning the education of a child or young person who has or may have special educational needs, including proceedings relating to—

(*a*) an EHC needs assessment within the meaning of section 36(2) of the Children and Families Act 2014(b); . . . [14]

[(*aa*) a detained person's EHC needs assessment within the meaning of section 70(5) of the Children and Families Act 2014(; or][14]

(*b*) an EHC plan within the meaning of section 37(2) of that Act,

of such a child or young person;][12]

["tribunal" does not include a traffic commissioner;][2]

["wholesale energy case" means a reference to the Upper Tribunal in respect of a decision of—

(*a*) in relation to Great Britain, the Gas and Electricity Markets Authority under the Electricity and Gas (Market Integrity and Transparency) (Enforcement etc.) Regulations 2013; or

(*b*) in relation to Northern Ireland, the Northern Ireland Authority for Utility Regulation under the Electricity and Gas (Market Integrity and Transparency) (Enforcement etc.) Regulations (Northern Ireland) 2013;][11]

. . . [1]

"working day" means any day except a Saturday or Sunday, Christmas Day, Good Friday or a bank holiday under section 1 of the Banking and Financial Dealings Act 1971.

["young person" means, in relation to a special educational needs case or a disability discrimination in schools case, a person over compulsory school age but under 25;][12]

Amendments—[1] In para (3), definition of "appellant" substituted, definitions of "disability discrimination in schools case", "legal representative" and "special educational needs case" revoked, in definition of "respondent", sub-para (*a*)(ii) revoked and sub-para (*ca*) inserted, by the Tribunal Procedure (Amendment) Rules, SI 2009/274 rules 3, 5 with effect from 1 April 2009.

[2] In paras (2), (3) words inserted by the Tribunal Procedure (Amendment No 2) Rules, SI 2009/1975 rules 7, 8 with effect from 1 September 2009.

[3] Definitions inserted by the Tribunal Procedure (Amendment) Rules, SI 2010/43, rules 5, 6, with effect from 18 January 2010.

[4] Definitions inserted by the Tribunal Procedure (Amendment No 2) Rules, SI 2010/44, rules 2, 3, with effect from 15 February 2010.

[5] Definition of "applicant" substituted, definitions of "financial services case" and "reference" inserted, in definition of "interested party" words in sub-para (*a*) substituted and word "and" revoked, and sub-para (*c*) and preceding word "and" inserted, in definition of "party" words inserted, in definition of "respondent" in sub-para (*d*) word "or" revoked, by the Tribunal Procedure (Upper Tribunal) (Amendment) Rules, SI 2010/747 rules 2, 4 with effect from 6 April 2010.

[6] In definition of "financial services case" sub-para (*e*) and preceding word "or" inserted by the Tribunal Procedure (Amendment) Rules SI 2011/651 rule 8(1), (2) with effect from 1 April 2011.

[8] In definition of "appropriate national authority", words inserted, definition of "authorised person" substituted, in definition of "respondent", words substituted, and definition of "road transport case" inserted, by the Tribunal Procedure (Amendment No 2) Rules, SI 2012/1363 rules 4, 5 with effect from 1 July 2012.

[9] In definition of "financial services case" paras (*a*), (*aa*) substituted for previous para (*a*), and in definition of "respondent" para (*da*) substituted, by the Tribunal Procedure (Amendment No 2) Rules, SI 2013/606 rule 2(1), (2) with effect from 1 April 2013.

[10] In para (3), definition of "fresh claim proceedings" revoked, definition of "immigration judicial review proceedings" inserted, and in the definition of "party" word inserted, by the Tribunal Procedure (Amendment No 4) Rules, SI 2013/2067 rules 2, 4 with effect from 1 November 2013.

[11] In definition of "applicant", words in para (*b*) inserted, in definition of "financial services case", word in para (*c*) revoked, in definition of "interested party", words in para (*c*) inserted, in definition of "respondent", para (*db*) inserted, and definition of "wholesale energy case" inserted by the Tribunal Procedure (Amendment) Rules, SI 2014/514 rules 2, 4 with effect from 6 April 2014.

[12] Definitions of "disability discrimination in schools case", "special educational needs case" and "young person" inserted by the Tribunal Procedure (Amendment No 3) Rules, SI 2014/2128 rules 2, 4(*a*), (*c*), (*d*) with effect from 1 September 2014.

13 In definition of "fast-track case" words substituted by the Tribunal Procedure (Amendment No 3) Rules, SI 2014/2128 rules 2, 4(*b*) with effect from 20 October 2014.

14 Definitions of ""QCS Board", "quality contracts scheme", and "quality contracts scheme case" inserted, and in definition of "special educational needs case", in sub-para (*a*), word "or" revoked and sub-para (*aa*) inserted, by the Tribunal Procedure (Amendment) Rules, SI 2015/1510 rules 2, 3 with effect from 21 August 2015.

15 Definition of ""financial sanctions case" inserted, and in definition of "interested party", para (*d*) inserted, by the Tribunal Procedure (Amendment) Rules, SI 2017/723 rules 5, 7 with effect from 27 July 2017.

2 Overriding objective and parties' obligation to co-operate with the Upper Tribunal

(1) The overriding objective of these Rules is to enable the Upper Tribunal to deal with cases fairly and justly.

(2) Dealing with a case fairly and justly includes—

(*a*) dealing with the case in ways which are proportionate to the importance of the case, the complexity of the issues, the anticipated costs and the resources of the parties;

(*b*) avoiding unnecessary formality and seeking flexibility in the proceedings;

(*c*) ensuring, so far as practicable, that the parties are able to participate fully in the proceedings;

(*d*) using any special expertise of the Upper Tribunal effectively; and

(*e*) avoiding delay, so far as compatible with proper consideration of the issues.

(3) The Upper Tribunal must seek to give effect to the overriding objective when it—

(*a*) exercises any power under these Rules; or

(*b*) interprets any rule or practice direction.

(4) Parties must—

(*a*) help the Upper Tribunal to further the overriding objective; and

(*b*) co-operate with the Upper Tribunal generally.

3 Alternative dispute resolution and arbitration

(1) The Upper Tribunal should seek, where appropriate—

(*a*) to bring to the attention of the parties the availability of any appropriate alternative procedure for the resolution of the dispute; and

(*b*) if the parties wish and provided that it is compatible with the overriding objective, to facilitate the use of the procedure.

(2) Part 1 of the Arbitration Act 1996 does not apply to proceedings before the Upper Tribunal.

PART 2
GENERAL POWERS AND PROVISIONS

4 Delegation to staff

(1) Staff appointed under section 40(1) of the 2007 Act (tribunal staff and services) may, with the approval of the Senior President of Tribunals, carry out functions of a judicial nature permitted or required to be done by the Upper Tribunal.

(2) The approval referred to at paragraph (1) may apply generally to the carrying out of specified functions by members of staff of a specified description in specified circumstances.

(3) Within 14 days after the date on which the Upper Tribunal sends notice of a decision made by a member of staff under paragraph (1) to a party, that party may apply in writing to the Upper Tribunal for that decision to be considered afresh by a judge.

5 Case management powers

(1) Subject to the provisions of the 2007 Act and any other enactment, the Upper Tribunal may regulate its own procedure.

(2) The Upper Tribunal may give a direction in relation to the conduct or disposal of proceedings at any time, including a direction amending, suspending or setting aside an earlier direction.

(3) In particular, and without restricting the general powers in paragraphs (1) and (2), the Upper Tribunal may—

(*a*) extend or shorten the time for complying with any rule, practice direction or direction;

(*b*) consolidate or hear together two or more sets of proceedings or parts of proceedings raising common issues, or treat a case as a lead case;

(*c*) permit or require a party to amend a document;

(*d*) permit or require a party or another person to provide documents, information, evidence or submissions to the Upper Tribunal or a party;

(*e*) deal with an issue in the proceedings as a preliminary issue;

(*f*) hold a hearing to consider any matter, including a case management issue;

(*g*) decide the form of any hearing;

(*h*) adjourn or postpone a hearing;

(*i*) require a party to produce a bundle for a hearing;

(*j*) stay (or, in Scotland, sist) proceedings;

(*k*) transfer proceedings to another court or tribunal if that other court or tribunal has jurisdiction in relation to the proceedings and—

(i) because of a change of circumstances since the proceedings were started, the Upper Tribunal no longer has jurisdiction in relation to the proceedings; or

(ii) the Upper Tribunal considers that the other court or tribunal is a more appropriate forum for the determination of the case;

(*l*) suspend the effect of its own decision pending an appeal or review of that decision;

(*m*) in an appeal, or an application for permission to appeal, against the decision of another tribunal, suspend the effect of that decision pending the determination of the application for permission to appeal, and any appeal;

[(*n*) require any person, body or other tribunal whose decision is the subject of proceedings before the Upper Tribunal to provide reasons for the decision, or other information or documents in relation to the decision or any proceedings before that person, body or tribunal.][1]

[(4) The Upper Tribunal may direct that a fast-track case cease to be treated as a fast-track case if—

(*a*) all the parties consent; [or][6]

(*b*) the Upper Tribunal is satisfied that . . . [6] the appeal or application could not be justly determined if it were treated as a fast-track case. . . . [6]

(*c*) . . . [6]][2]

[(5) In a financial services case, the Upper Tribunal may direct that the effect of the decision in respect of which the reference has been made is to be suspended pending the determination of the reference, if it is satisfied that to do so would not prejudice—

(*a*) the interests of any persons (whether consumers, investors or otherwise) intended to be protected by that notice; . . . [4]

(*b*) the smooth operation or integrity of any market intended to be protected by that notice[; or][4]

[(*c*) the stability of the financial system of the United Kingdom.][4]

(6) Paragraph (5) does not apply in the case of a reference in respect of a decision of the Pensions Regulator.][3]

[(5A) In a financial sanctions case, the Upper Tribunal may direct that the payment of a monetary penalty that is the subject of an appeal be suspended pending the determination of the appeal or its withdrawal.][7]

[(7) In a wholesale energy case, the Upper Tribunal may direct that the effect of the decision in respect of which the reference has been made is to be suspended pending the determination of the reference.][5]

Amendments—[1] Para (3)(*n*) substituted by the Tribunal Procedure (Amendment No 2) Rules, SI 2009/1975 rules 7, 9 with effect from 1 September 2009.

[2] Para (4) inserted by the Tribunal Procedure (Amendment No 2) Rules, SI 2010/44 rules 2, 4, with effect from 15 February 2010.

[3] Paras (5), (6) inserted by the Tribunal Procedure (Upper Tribunal) (Amendment) Rules, SI 2010/747 rules 2, 5 with effect from 6 April 2010.

[4] In para (5), word "or" at end of sub-para (*a*) revoked, and sub-para (*c*) and preceding word "or" inserted, by the Tribunal Procedure (Amendment No 2) Rules, SI 2013/606 rule 2(1), (3) with effect from 1 April 2013.

[5] Para (7) inserted by the Tribunal Procedure (Amendment) Rules, SI 2014/514 rules 2, 5 with effect from 6 April 2014.

[6] In para (4), in sub-para (*a*) word inserted, in sub-para (*b*) words revoked, and sub-para (*c*) revoked, by the Tribunal Procedure (Amendment No 3) Rules, SI 2014/2128 rules 2, 5 with effect from 20 October 2014.

[7] Para (5A) inserted by the Tribunal Procedure (Amendment) Rules, SI 2017/723 rules 5, 8 with effect from 27 July 2017.

6 Procedure for applying for and giving directions

(1) The Upper Tribunal may give a direction on the application of one or more of the parties or on its own initiative.

(2) An application for a direction may be made—

(*a*) by sending or delivering a written application to the Upper Tribunal; or

(*b*) orally during the course of a hearing.

(3) An application for a direction must include the reason for making that application.

(4) Unless the Upper Tribunal considers that there is good reason not to do so, the Upper Tribunal must send written notice of any direction to every party and to any other person affected by the direction.

(5) If a party or any other person sent notice of the direction under paragraph (4) wishes to challenge a direction which the Upper Tribunal has given, they may do so by applying for another direction which amends, suspends or sets aside the first direction.

7 Failure to comply with rules etc

(1) An irregularity resulting from a failure to comply with any requirement in these Rules, a practice direction or a direction, does not of itself render void the proceedings or any step taken in the proceedings.

(2) If a party has failed to comply with a requirement in these Rules, a practice direction or a direction, the Upper Tribunal may take such action as it considers just, which may include—

(*a*) waiving the requirement;

(*b*) requiring the failure to be remedied;

(*c*) exercising its power under rule 8 (striking out a party's case); or (*d*) except in [a mental health case, an asylum case or an immigration case][1], restricting a party's participation in the proceedings.

(3) Paragraph (4) applies where the First-tier Tribunal has referred to the Upper Tribunal a failure by a person to comply with a requirement imposed by the First-tier Tribunal—

(*a*) to attend at any place for the purpose of giving evidence;

(*b*) otherwise to make themselves available to give evidence;

(*c*) to swear an oath in connection with the giving of evidence;

(*d*) to give evidence as a witness;

(*e*) to produce a document; or

(*f*) to facilitate the inspection of a document or any other thing (including any premises).

(4) The Upper Tribunal may exercise its power under section 25 of the 2007 Act (supplementary powers of the Upper Tribunal) in relation to such non-compliance as if the requirement had been imposed by the Upper Tribunal.

Amendments—[1] In para (2)(*d*), words substituted by the Tribunal Procedure (Amendment No 2) Rules, SI 2010/44 rules 2, 5, with effect from 15 February 2010.

8 Striking out a party's case

[(1A) Except for paragraph (2), this rule does not apply to an asylum case or an immigration case.][2]

[(1) The proceedings, or the appropriate part of them, will automatically be struck out—

(*a*) if the appellant or applicant has failed to comply with a direction that stated that failure by the appellant or applicant to comply with the direction would lead to the striking out of the proceedings or part of them; or

[(*b*) in immigration judicial review proceedings, when a fee has not been paid, as required, in respect of an application under rule 30(4) or upon the grant of permission.][4]][3]

(2) The Upper Tribunal must strike out the whole or a part of the proceedings if the Upper Tribunal—

(*a*) does not have jurisdiction in relation to the proceedings or that part of them; and

(*b*) does not exercise its power under rule 5(3)(k)(i) (transfer to another court or tribunal) in relation to the proceedings or that part of them.

(3) The Upper Tribunal may strike out the whole or a part of the proceedings if—

(*a*) the appellant or applicant has failed to comply with a direction which stated that failure by the appellant or applicant to comply with the direction could lead to the striking out of the proceedings or part of them;

(*b*) the appellant or applicant has failed to co-operate with the Upper Tribunal to such an extent that the Upper Tribunal cannot deal with the proceedings fairly and justly; or

(*c*) in proceedings which are not an appeal from the decision of another tribunal or judicial review proceedings, the Upper Tribunal considers there is no reasonable prospect of the appellant's or the applicant's case, or part of it, succeeding.

(4) The Upper Tribunal may not strike out the whole or a part of the proceedings under paragraph (2) or (3)(*b*) or (*c*) without first giving the appellant or applicant an opportunity to make representations in relation to the proposed striking out.

(5) If the proceedings have been struck out under paragraph (1) or (3)(*a*), the appellant or applicant may apply for the proceedings, or part of them, to be reinstated.

(6) An application under paragraph (5) must be made in writing and received by the Upper Tribunal within 1 month after the date on which the Upper Tribunal sent notification of the striking out to the appellant or applicant.

(7) This rule applies to a respondent [or an interested party][1] as it applies to an appellant or applicant except that—

(*a*) a reference to the striking out of the proceedings is to be read as a reference to the barring of the respondent [or interested party][1] from taking further part in the proceedings; and

(*b*) a reference to an application for the reinstatement of proceedings which have been struck out is to be read as a reference to an application for the lifting of the bar on the respondent [or interested party][1] . . .[1] taking further part in the proceedings.

(8) If a respondent [or an interested party][1] has been barred from taking further part in proceedings under this rule and that bar has not been lifted, the Upper Tribunal need not consider any response or other submission made by that respondent [or interested party, and may summarily determine any or all issues against that respondent or interested party][1].

Amendments—[1] In para (7), words inserted and word revoked, and in sub-s (8), words inserted, by the Tribunal Procedure (Amendment) Rules, SI 2009/274 rules 3, 6 with effect from 1 April 2009.

[2] Para (1A) inserted by the Tribunal Procedure (Amendment No 2) Rules, SI 2010/44 rules 2, 6, with effect from 15 February 2010.

[3] Para (1) substituted by the Tribunal Procedure (Upper Tribunal) (Amendment) Rules, SI 2011/2343 rules 2, 5 with effect from 17 October 2011.

[4] Para (1)(*b*) substituted by the Tribunal Procedure (Amendment No 4) Rules, SI 2013/2067 rules 2, 5 with effect from 1 November 2013.

[Addition, substitution and removal of parties

9—(1) The Upper Tribunal may give a direction adding, substituting or removing a party as an appellant, a respondent or an interested party.
(2) If the Upper Tribunal gives a direction under paragraph (1) it may give such consequential directions as it considers appropriate.
(3) A person who is not a party may apply to the Upper Tribunal to be added or substituted as a party.
(4) If a person who is entitled to be a party to proceedings by virtue of another enactment applies to be added as a party, and any conditions applicable to that entitlement have been satisfied, the Upper Tribunal must give a direction adding that person as a respondent or, if appropriate, as an appellant.][1]
[(5) In an asylum case, the United Kingdom Representative of the United Nations High Commissioner for Refugees ("the United Kingdom Representative") may give notice to the Upper Tribunal that the United Kingdom Representative wishes to participate in the proceedings.
(6) If the United Kingdom Representative gives notice under paragraph (5)—
(i) the United Kingdom Representative is entitled to participate in any hearing; and
(ii) all documents which are required to be sent or delivered to parties must be sent or delivered to the United Kingdom Representative.][2]

Amendments—[1] Rule 9 substituted by the Tribunal Procedure (Amendment No 2) Rules, SI 2009/1975 rules 7, 10 with effect from 1 September 2009.
[2] Paras (5), (6) inserted by the Tribunal Procedure (Amendment No 2) Rules, SI 2010/44 rules 2, 7, with effect from 15 February 2010.

[10 Orders for costs
(1) The Upper Tribunal may not make an order in respect of costs (or, in Scotland, expenses) in proceedings [transferred or referred by, or on appeal from,][2] another tribunal except—
[(*aa*) in a national security certificate appeal, to the extent permitted by paragraph (1A);][3]
(*a*) in proceedings [transferred by, or on appeal from,][2] the Tax Chamber of the First-tier Tribunal; or
(*b*) to the extent and in the circumstances that the other tribunal had the power to make an order in respect of costs (or, in Scotland, expenses).
[(1A) In a national security certificate appeal—
(*a*) the Upper Tribunal may make an order in respect of costs or expenses in the circumstances described at paragraph (3)(*c*) and (*d*);
(*b*) if the appeal is against a certificate, the Upper Tribunal may make an order in respect of costs or expenses against the relevant Minister and in favour of the appellant if the Upper Tribunal allows the appeal and quashes the certificate to any extent or the Minister withdraws the certificate;
(*c*) if the appeal is against the application of a certificate, the Upper Tribunal may make an order in respect of costs or expenses—
(i) against the appellant and in favour of any other party if the Upper Tribunal dismisses the appeal to any extent; or
(ii) in favour of the appellant and against any other party if the Upper Tribunal allows the appeal to any extent.][3]
(2) The Upper Tribunal may not make an order in respect of costs or expenses under section 4 of the Forfeiture Act 1982.
(3) In other proceedings, the Upper Tribunal may not make an order in respect of costs or expenses except—
(*a*) in judicial review proceedings;
(*b*) . . .[2]
(*c*) under section 29(4) of the 2007 Act (wasted costs) [and costs incurred in applying for such costs][5]; . . .[4]
(*d*) if the Upper Tribunal considers that a party or its representative has acted unreasonably in bringing, defending or conducting the proceedings [. . .[8]
(*e*) if, in a financial services case [or a wholesale energy case][7], the Upper Tribunal considers that the decision in respect of which the reference was made was unreasonable[; or.][4]
(*f*) if, in a financial sanctions case, the Upper Tribunal considers that the decision to impose or uphold a monetary penalty in respect of which the appeal was made was unreasonable;][8]
(4) The Upper Tribunal may make an order for costs (or, in Scotland, expenses) on an application or on its own initiative.
(5) A person making an application for an order for costs or expenses must—
(*a*) send or deliver a written application to the Upper Tribunal and to the person against whom it is proposed that the order be made; and
(*b*) send or deliver with the application a schedule of the costs or expenses claimed sufficient to allow summary assessment of such costs or expenses by the Upper Tribunal.
(6) An application for an order for costs or expenses may be made at any time during the proceedings but may not be made later than 1 month after the date on which the Upper Tribunal sends—

(*a*) a decision notice recording the decision which finally disposes of all issues in the proceedings; or

[(*b*) notice under rule 17(5) that a withdrawal which ends the proceedings has taken effect.][5]

(7) The Upper Tribunal may not make an order for costs or expenses against a person (the "paying person") without first—

(*a*) giving that person an opportunity to make representations; and

(*b*) if the paying person is an individual and the order is to be made under paragraph (3)(*a*), (*b*) or (*d*), considering that person's financial means.

(8) The amount of costs or expenses to be paid under an order under this rule may be ascertained by—

(*a*) summary assessment by the Upper Tribunal;

(*b*) agreement of a specified sum by the paying person and the person entitled to receive the costs or expenses ("the receiving person"); or

(*c*) assessment of the whole or a specified part of the costs or expenses[, including the costs or expenses of the assessment,][5] incurred by the receiving person, if not agreed.

(9) Following an order for assessment under paragraph (8)(*c*), the paying person or the receiving person may apply—

(*a*) in England and Wales, to the High Court or the Costs Office of the Supreme Court (as specified in the order) for a detailed assessment of the costs on the standard basis or, if specified in the order, on the indemnity basis; and the Civil Procedure Rules 1998 shall apply, with necessary modifications, to that application and assessment as if the proceedings in the tribunal had been proceedings in a court to which the Civil Procedure Rules 1998 apply;

(*b*) in Scotland, to the Auditor of the Court of Session for the taxation of the expenses according to the fees payable in that court; or

(*c*) in Northern Ireland, to the Taxing Office of the High Court of Northern Ireland for taxation on the standard basis or, if specified in the order, on the indemnity basis.

[(10) Upon making an order for the assessment of costs, the [Upper][6] Tribunal may order an amount to be paid on account before the costs or expenses are assessed.][5]][1]

Simon's Tax Cases—10, *Capital Air Services Ltd v R&C Comrs* [2011] STC 617; *Leeds City Council v R&C Comrs* [2014] UKUT 350 (TCC), [2015] STC 168; *Drummond v R&C Comrs* [2016] UKUT 221 (TCC), [2016] STC 1870.

Amendments—[1] Rule 10 substituted by the Tribunal Procedure (Amendment) Rules, SI 2009/274 rules 3, 7 with effect from 1 April 2009.

[2] In para (1), (1)(*a*), words substituted, and para (3)(*b*) revoked, by the Tribunal Procedure (Amendment No 2) Rules, SI 2009/1975 rules 7, 11 with effect from 1 September 2009.

[3] Paras (1)(*aa*), (1A) inserted by the Tribunal Procedure (Amendment) Rules, SI 2010/43, rules 5, 7, with effect from 18 January 2010.

[4] In para (3)(*c*), word revoked, and para (3)(*e*) and preceding word inserted, by the Tribunal Procedure (Upper Tribunal) (Amendment) Rules, SI 2010/747 rules 2, 6 with effect from 6 April 2010.

[5] In paras (3), (8)(*c*) words inserted, para (6)(*b*) substituted, and para (10) inserted, by the Tribunal Procedure (Amendment) Rules, SI 2013/477 rules 49–53 with effect from 1 April 2013.

[6] Word in para (10) inserted by the Tribunal Procedure (Amendment No 4) Rules, SI 2013/2067 rules 2, 6 with effect from 1 November 2013.

[7] In para (3)(*e*), words inserted by the Tribunal Procedure (Amendment) Rules, SI 2014/514 rules 2, 6 with effect from 6 April 2014.

[8] In para (3)(*d*), word "or" at the end revoked, and para (*f*) and preceding word inserted, by the Tribunal Procedure (Amendment) Rules, SI 2017/723 rules 5, 9 with effect from 27 July 2017.

11 Representatives

(1) [Subject to paragraph (5A),][5] a party may appoint a representative (whether a legal representative or not) to represent that party in the proceedings [save that a party in an asylum or immigration case may not be represented by any person prohibited from representing by section 84 of the Immigration and Asylum Act 1999][4].

(2) If a party appoints a representative, that party (or the representative if the representative is a legal representative) must send or deliver to the Upper Tribunal . . . [1] written notice of the representative's name and address.

[(2A) If the Upper Tribunal receives notice that a party has appointed a representative under paragraph (2), it must send a copy of that notice to each other party.][1]

(3) Anything permitted or required to be done by a party under these Rules, a practice direction or a direction may be done by the representative of that party, except signing a witness statement.

(4) A person who receives due notice of the appointment of a representative—

(*a*) must provide to the representative any document which is required to be provided to the represented party, and need not provide that document to the represented party; and

(*b*) may assume that the representative is and remains authorised as such until they receive written notification that this is not so from the representative or the represented party.

(5) [Subject to paragraph (5B),][5] at a hearing a party may be accompanied by another person whose name and address has not been notified under paragraph (2) but who, subject to paragraph (8) and with the permission of the Upper Tribunal, may act as a representative or otherwise assist in presenting the party's case at the hearing.

[(5A) In [immigration judicial review][6] proceedings, a party may appoint as a representative only a person authorised under the Legal Services Act 2007 to undertake the conduct of litigation in the High Court.

(5B) At a hearing of [immigration judicial review][6] proceedings, rights of audience before the Upper Tribunal are restricted to persons authorised to exercise those rights in the High Court under the Legal Services Act 2007.][5]

(6) Paragraphs (2) to (4) do not apply to a person who accompanies a party under paragraph (5).

(7) In a mental health case if the patient has not appointed a representative the Upper Tribunal may appoint a legal representative for the patient where—

(*a*) the patient has stated that they do not wish to conduct their own case or that they wish to be represented; or

(*b*) the patient lacks the capacity to appoint a representative but the Upper Tribunal believes that it is in the patient's best interests for the patient to be represented.

(8) In a mental health case a party may not appoint as a representative, or be represented or assisted at a hearing by—

(*a*) a person liable to be detained or subject to guardianship or after-care under supervision, or who is a community patient, under the Mental Health Act 1983; or

(*b*) a person receiving treatment for mental disorder at the same hospital [or][2] home as the patient.

[(9) In this rule "legal representative" means [a person who, for the purposes of the Legal Services Act 2007, is an authorised person in relation to an activity which constitutes the exercise of a right of audience or the conduct of litigation within the meaning of that Act][3], [a qualified person as defined in section 84(2) of the Immigration and Asylum Act 1999,][4] an advocate or solicitor in Scotland or a barrister or solicitor in Northern Ireland.][1]

[(10) In an asylum case or an immigration case, an appellant's representative before the First-tier Tribunal will be treated as that party's representative before the Upper Tribunal, unless the Upper Tribunal receives notice—

(*a*) of a new representative under paragraph (2) of this rule; or

(*b*) from the appellant stating that they are no longer represented.][4]

Amendments—[1] In para (2), words revoked, and paras (2A), (9) inserted, by the Tribunal Procedure (Amendment) Rules, SI 2009/274 rules 3, 8 with effect from 1 April 2009.

[2] In para (8)(*b*) word inserted by the Tribunal Procedure (Amendment No 2) Rules, SI 2009/1975 rules 7, 12 with effect from 1 September 2009.

[3] In para (9), words substituted by the Tribunal Procedure (Amendment) Rules, SI 2010/43, rules 5, 8, with effect from 18 January 2010.

[4] Words in paras (1), (9), and whole of para (10), inserted, by the Tribunal Procedure (Amendment No 2) Rules, SI 2010/44 rules 2, 8, with effect from 15 February 2010.

[5] In paras (1), (5), words inserted, and paras (5A), (5B) inserted, by the Tribunal Procedure (Upper Tribunal) (Amendment) Rules, SI 2011/2343 rules 2, 6 with effect from 17 October 2011.

[6] In paras (5A), (5B) words substituted by the Tribunal Procedure (Amendment No 4) Rules, SI 2013/2067 rules 2, 7 with effect from 1 November 2013.

12 Calculating time

(1) An act required by these Rules, a practice direction or a direction to be done on or by a particular day must be done by 5pm on that day.

(2) If the time specified by these Rules, a practice direction or a direction for doing any act ends on a day other than a working day, the act is done in time if it is done on the next working day.

(3) In a special educational needs case or a disability discrimination in schools case, the following days must not be counted when calculating the time by which an act must be done—

(*a*) 25th December to 1st January inclusive; and

(*b*) any day in August.

[(3A) In an asylum case or an immigration case, when calculating the time by which an act must be done, in addition to the days specified in the definition of "working days" in rule 1 (interpretation), the following days must also not be counted as working days—

(*a*) 27th to 31st December inclusive. . . . [2]

(*b*) . . . [2]][1]

(4) Paragraph (3) [or (3A)][1] does not apply where the Upper Tribunal directs that an act must be done by or on a specified date.

(5) . . . [2]

Amendments—[1] Para (3A) and words in para (4) inserted by the Tribunal Procedure (Amendment No 2) Rules, SI 2010/44 rules 2, 9, with effect from 15 February 2010.

[2] Para (5) revoked by the Tribunal Procedure (Amendment No 3) Rules, SI 2014/2128 rules 2, 6(b) with effect from 1 September 2014.

[3] Para (3A)(*b*) and preceding word "and" revoked, by the Tribunal Procedure (Amendment No 3) Rules, SI 2014/2128 rules 2, 6 with effect from 20 October 2014.

13 Sending and delivery of documents

(1) Any document to be provided to the Upper Tribunal under these Rules, a practice direction or a direction must be—

(*a*) sent by pre-paid post or [by document exchange, or delivered by hand,][1] to the address specified for the proceedings;

(*b*) sent by fax to the number specified for the proceedings; or

(*c*) sent or delivered by such other method as the Upper Tribunal may permit or direct.

(2) Subject to paragraph (3), if a party provides a fax number, email address or other details for the electronic transmission of documents to them, that party must accept delivery of documents by that method.

(3) If a party informs the Upper Tribunal and all other parties that a particular form of communication, other than pre-paid post or delivery by hand, should not be used to provide documents to that party, that form of communication must not be so used.

(4) If the Upper Tribunal or a party sends a document to a party or the Upper Tribunal by email or any other electronic means of communication, the recipient may request that the sender provide a hard copy of the document to the recipient. The recipient must make such a request as soon as reasonably practicable after receiving the document electronically.

(5) The Upper Tribunal and each party may assume that the address provided by a party or its representative is and remains the address to which documents should be sent or delivered until receiving written notification to the contrary.

[(6) Subject to paragraph (7), if a document submitted to the Upper Tribunal is not written in English, it must be accompanied by an English translation.

(7) In proceedings that are in Wales or have a connection with Wales, a document or translation may be submitted to the [Upper][3] Tribunal in Welsh.][2]

Amendments—[1] Words in para (1)(*a*) substituted by the Tribunal Procedure (Amendment) Rules, SI 2009/274 rules 3, 10 with effect from 1 April 2009.

[2] Paras (6), (7) inserted by the Tribunal Procedure (Amendment No 2) Rules, SI 2010/44 rules 2, 10, with effect from 15 February 2010.

[3] Word in para (7) inserted by the Tribunal Procedure (Amendment No 4) Rules, SI 2013/2067 rules 2, 8 with effect from 1 November 2013.

14 Use of documents and information

(1) The Upper Tribunal may make an order prohibiting the disclosure or publication of—

(*a*) specified documents or information relating to the proceedings; or

(*b*) any matter likely to lead members of the public to identify any person whom the Upper Tribunal considers should not be identified.

(2) The Upper Tribunal may give a direction prohibiting the disclosure of a document or information to a person if—

(*a*) the Upper Tribunal is satisfied that such disclosure would be likely to cause that person or some other person serious harm; and

(*b*) the Upper Tribunal is satisfied, having regard to the interests of justice, that it is proportionate to give such a direction.

(3) If a party ("the first party") considers that the Upper Tribunal should give a direction under paragraph (2) prohibiting the disclosure of a document or information to another party ("the second party"), the first party must—

(*a*) exclude the relevant document or information from any documents that will be provided to the second party; and

(*b*) provide to the Upper Tribunal the excluded document or information, and the reason for its exclusion, so that the Upper Tribunal may decide whether the document or information should be disclosed to the second party or should be the subject of a direction under paragraph (2).

(4) The Upper Tribunal must conduct proceedings as appropriate in order to give effect to a direction given under paragraph (2).[1]

(5) If the Upper Tribunal gives a direction under paragraph (2) which prevents disclosure to a party who has appointed a representative, the Upper Tribunal may give a direction that the documents or information be disclosed to that representative if the Upper Tribunal is satisfied that—

(*a*) disclosure to the representative would be in the interests of the party; and

(*b*) the representative will act in accordance with paragraph (6).

(6) Documents or information disclosed to a representative in accordance with a direction under paragraph (5) must not be disclosed either directly or indirectly to any other person without the Upper Tribunal's consent.

(7) Unless the Upper Tribunal gives a direction to the contrary, information about mental health cases and the names of any persons concerned in such cases must not be made public.

[(8) The Upper Tribunal may, on its own initiative or on the application of a party, give a direction that certain documents or information must or may be disclosed to the Upper Tribunal on the basis that the Upper Tribunal will not disclose such documents or information to other persons, or specified other persons.

(9) A party making an application for a direction under paragraph (8) may withhold the relevant documents or information from other parties until the Upper Tribunal has granted or refused the application.
(10) In a case involving matters relating to national security, the Upper Tribunal must ensure that information is not disclosed contrary to the interests of national security.
(11) The Upper Tribunal must conduct proceedings and record its decision and reasons appropriately so as not to undermine the effect of an order made under paragraph (1), a direction given under paragraph (2) or (8) or the duty imposed by paragraph (10).][1]

Amendments—[1] Para (4) revoked, and paras (8)–(11) inserted, by the Tribunal Procedure (Amendment No 2) Rules, SI 2009/1975 rules 7, 13 with effect from 1 September 2009.

15 Evidence and submissions

(1) Without restriction on the general powers in rule 5(1) and (2) (case management powers), the Upper Tribunal may give directions as to—
- (*a*) issues on which it requires evidence or submissions;
- (*b*) the nature of the evidence or submissions it requires;
- (*c*) whether the parties are permitted or required to provide expert evidence, and if so whether the parties must jointly appoint a single expert to provide such evidence;
- (*d*) any limit on the number of witnesses whose evidence a party may put forward, whether in relation to a particular issue or generally;
- (*e*) the manner in which any evidence or submissions are to be provided, which may include a direction for them to be given—
  - (i) orally at a hearing; or
  - (ii) by written submissions or witness statement; and
- (*f*) the time at which any evidence or submissions are to be provided.

(2) The Upper Tribunal may—
- (*a*) admit evidence whether or not—
  - (i) the evidence would be admissible in a civil trial in the United Kingdom; or
  - (ii) the evidence was available to a previous decision maker; or
- (*b*) exclude evidence that would otherwise be admissible where—
  - (i) the evidence was not provided within the time allowed by a direction or a practice direction;
  - (ii) the evidence was otherwise provided in a manner that did not comply with a direction or a practice direction; or
  - (iii) it would otherwise be unfair to admit the evidence.

[(2A) In an asylum case or an immigration case—
- (*a*) if a party wishes the Upper Tribunal to consider evidence that was not before the First-tier Tribunal, that party must send or deliver a notice to the Upper Tribunal and any other party—
  - (i) indicating the nature of the evidence; and
  - (ii) explaining why it was not submitted to the First-tier Tribunal; and
- (*b*) when considering whether to admit evidence that was not before the First-tier Tribunal, the Upper Tribunal must have regard to whether there has been unreasonable delay in producing that evidence.][1]

(3) The Upper Tribunal may consent to a witness giving, or require any witness to give, evidence on oath, and may administer an oath for that purpose.

Amendments—[1] Para (2A) inserted by the Tribunal Procedure (Amendment No 2) Rules, SI 2010/44 rules 2, 11, with effect from 15 February 2010.

16 Summoning or citation of witnesses and orders to answer questions or produce documents

(1) On the application of a party or on its own initiative, the Upper Tribunal may—
- (*a*) by summons (or, in Scotland, citation) require any person to attend as a witness at a hearing at the time and place specified in the summons or citation; or
- (*b*) order any person to answer any questions or produce any documents in that person's possession or control which relate to any issue in the proceedings.

(2) A summons or citation under paragraph (1)(*a*) must—
- (*a*) give the person required to attend 14 days' notice of the hearing or such shorter period as the Upper Tribunal may direct; and
- (*b*) where the person is not a party, make provision for the person's necessary expenses of attendance to be paid, and state who is to pay them.

(3) No person may be compelled to give any evidence or produce any document that the person could not be compelled to give or produce on a trial of an action in a court of law in the part of the United Kingdom where the proceedings are due to be determined.
[(4) A person who receives a summons, citation or order may apply to the Upper Tribunal for it to be varied or set aside if they did not have an opportunity to object to it before it was made or issued.
(5) A person making an application under paragraph (4) must do so as soon as reasonably practicable after receiving notice of the summons, citation or order.

(6) A summons, citation or order under this rule must—

(*a*) state that the person on whom the requirement is imposed may apply to the Upper Tribunal to vary or set aside the summons, citation or order, if they did not have an opportunity to object to it before it was made or issued; and

(*b*) state the consequences of failure to comply with the summons, citation or order.][1]

Amendments—[1] Paras (4)–(6) substituted for previous para (4) by the Tribunal Procedure (Amendment) Rules, SI 2009/274 rules 3, 11 with effect from 1 April 2009.

17 Withdrawal

(1) Subject to paragraph (2), a party may give notice of the withdrawal of its case, or any part of it—

(*a*) . . . [2] by sending or delivering to the Upper Tribunal a written notice of withdrawal; or

(*b*) orally at a hearing.

(2) Notice of withdrawal will not take effect unless the Upper Tribunal consents to the withdrawal except in relation to an application for permission to appeal.

(3) A party which has withdrawn its case may apply to the Upper Tribunal for the case to be reinstated.

(4) An application under paragraph (3) must be made in writing and be received by the Upper Tribunal within 1 month after—

(*a*) the date on which the Upper Tribunal received the notice under paragraph (1)(*a*); or

(*b*) the date of the hearing at which the case was withdrawn orally under paragraph (1)(*b*).

(5) The Upper Tribunal must notify each party in writing [that a withdrawal has taken effect][2] under this rule.

[(6) Paragraph (3) does not apply to a financial services case other than a reference against a penalty.][1]

Amendments—[1] Para (6) inserted, by the Tribunal Procedure (Upper Tribunal) (Amendment) Rules, SI 2010/747 rules 2, 7 with effect from 6 April 2010.

[2] In para (1)(*a*), words revoked, and in para (5), words substituted, by the Tribunal Procedure (Amendment) Rules, SI 2013/477 rules 49, 54 with effect from 1 April 2013.

[17A Appeal treated as abandoned or finally determined in an asylum case or an immigration case

(1) A party to an asylum case or an immigration case before the Upper Tribunal must notify the [Upper][2] Tribunal if they are aware that—

(*a*) the appellant has left the United Kingdom;

(*b*) the appellant has been granted leave to enter or remain in the United Kingdom;

(*c*) a deportation order has been made against the appellant; or

(*d*) a document listed in paragraph 4(2) of Schedule 2 to the Immigration (European Economic Area) Regulations 2006 has been issued to the appellant.

(2) Where an appeal is treated as abandoned pursuant to section 104(4) or (4A) of the Nationality, Immigration and Asylum Act 2002 or paragraph 4(2) of Schedule 2 to the Immigration (European Economic Area) Regulations 2006, or as finally determined pursuant to section 104(5) of the Nationality, Immigration and Asylum Act 2002, the Upper Tribunal must send the parties a notice informing them that the appeal is being treated as abandoned or finally determined.

(3) Where an appeal would otherwise fall to be treated as abandoned pursuant to section 104(4A) of the Nationality, Immigration and Asylum Act 2002, but the appellant wishes to pursue their appeal, the appellant must send or deliver a notice, which must comply with any relevant practice directions, to the Upper Tribunal and the respondent so that it is received within thirty days of the date on which the notice of the grant of leave to enter or remain in the United Kingdom was sent to the appellant.

(4) Where a notice of grant of leave to enter or remain is sent electronically or delivered personally, the time limit in paragraph (3) is twenty eight days.

(5) Notwithstanding rule 5(3)(*a*) (case management powers) and rule 7(2) (failure to comply with rules etc), the Upper Tribunal must not extend the time limits in paragraph (3) and (4).][1]

Amendments—[1] Rule 17A inserted by the Tribunal Procedure (Amendment No 2) Rules, SI 2010/44 rules 2, 12, with effect from 15 February 2010.

[2] Word in para (1) inserted by the Tribunal Procedure (Amendment No 4) Rules, SI 2013/2067 rules 2, 9 with effect from 1 November 2013.

18 Notice of funding of legal services

If a party is granted funding of legal services at any time, that party must as soon as practicable—

(*a*)

(i) if [civil legal services (within the meaning of section 8 of the Legal Aid, Sentencing and Punishment of Offenders Act 2012) are provided under arrangements made for the purposes of Part 1 of that Act or by][1] the Northern Ireland Legal Services Commission, send a copy of the [certificate or][1] funding notice to the Upper Tribunal; or

(ii) if funding is granted by the Scottish Legal Aid Board, send a copy of the legal aid certificate to the Upper Tribunal; and

(*b*) notify every other party in writing that funding has been granted.

Amendments—[1] In para (*a*)(i), words substituted andinserted by the Tribunal Procedure (Amendment) Rules, SI 2013/477 rules 49, 55 with effect from 1 April 2013.

[19 Confidentiality in social security and child support cases

(1) Paragraph (4) applies to an appeal against a decision of the First-tier Tribunal—

(*a*) in proceedings under the Child Support Act 1991 in the circumstances described in paragraph (2), other than an appeal against a reduced benefit decision (as defined in section 46(10)(*b*) of the Child Support Act 1991, as that section had effect prior to the commencement of section 15(*b*) of the Child Maintenance and Other Payments Act 2008); or

(*b*) in proceedings where the parties to the appeal include former joint claimants who are no longer living together in the circumstances described in paragraph (3).

(2) The circumstances referred to in paragraph (1)(*a*) are that—

(*a*) in the proceedings in the First-tier Tribunal in respect of which the appeal has been brought, there was an obligation to keep a person's address confidential; or

(*b*) an absent parent, non-resident parent or person with care would like their address or the address of the child to be kept confidential and has given notice to that effect to the Upper Tribunal—

(i) in an application for permission to appeal or notice of appeal;

(ii) within 1 month after an enquiry by the Upper Tribunal; or

(iii) when notifying any subsequent change of address after proceedings have been started.

(3) The circumstances referred to in paragraph (1)(*b*) are that—

(*a*) in the proceedings in the First-tier Tribunal in respect of which the appeal has been brought, there was an obligation to keep a person's address confidential; or

(*b*) one of the former joint claimants would like their address to be kept confidential and has given notice to that effect to the Upper Tribunal—

(i) in an application for permission to appeal or notice of appeal;

(ii) within 1 month after an enquiry by the Upper Tribunal; or

(iii) when notifying any subsequent change of address after proceedings have been started.

(4) Where this paragraph applies, the Secretary of State or other decision maker and the Upper Tribunal must take appropriate steps to secure the confidentiality of the address and of any information which could reasonably be expected to enable a person to identify the address, to the extent that the address or that information is not already known to each other party.

(5) In this rule—

"absent parent", "non-resident parent" and "person with care" have the meanings set out in section 3 of the Child Support Act 1991;

"joint claimants" means the persons who made a joint claim for a jobseeker's allowance under the Jobseekers Act 1995, a tax credit under the Tax Credits Act 2002 or in relation to whom an award of universal credit is made under Part 1 of the Welfare Reform Act 2012.][1]

Amendments—[1] Rule 19 substituted by the Tribunal Procedure (Amendment No 3) Rules, SI 2014/2128 rules 2, 7 with effect from 20 October 2014.

20 Power to pay expenses and allowances

(1) In proceedings brought under section 4 of the Safeguarding Vulnerable Groups Act 2006 . . . [1], the Secretary of State may pay such allowances for the purpose of or in connection with the attendance of persons at hearings as the Secretary of State may, with the consent of the Treasury, determine.

(2) Paragraph (3) applies to proceedings on appeal from a decision of—

(*a*) the First-tier Tribunal in proceedings under the Child Support Act 1991, section 12 of the Social Security Act 1998 or paragraph 6 of Schedule 7 to the Child Support, Pensions and Social Security Act 2000;

(*b*) the First-tier Tribunal in a war pensions and armed forces case (as defined in the Tribunal Procedure (First-tier Tribunal) (War Pensions and Armed Forces Compensation Chamber) Rules 2008); or

(*c*) a Pensions Appeal Tribunal for Scotland or Northern Ireland.

(3) The Lord Chancellor (or, in Scotland, the Secretary of State) may pay to any person who attends any hearing such travelling and other allowances, including compensation for loss of remunerative time, as the Lord Chancellor (or, in Scotland, the Secretary of State) may determine.

Amendments—[1] Words in para (1) revoked by the Tribunal Procedure (Amendment) Rules, SI 2009/274 rules 3, 12 with effect from 1 April 2009.

[Procedure for applying for a stay of a decision pending an appeal

20A—(1) This rule applies where another enactment provides in any terms for the Upper Tribunal to stay or suspend, or to lift a stay or suspension of, a decision which is or may be the subject of an appeal to the Upper Tribunal ("the substantive decision") pending such appeal.

(2) A person who wishes the Upper Tribunal to decide whether the substantive decision should be stayed or suspended must make a written application to the Upper Tribunal which must include—

(*a*) the name and address of the person making the application;

(*b*) the name and address of any representative of that person;
(*c*) the address to which documents for that person should be sent or delivered;
(*d*) the name and address of any person who will be a respondent to the appeal;
(*e*) details of the substantive decision and any decision as to when that decision is to take effect, and copies of any written record of, or reasons for, those decisions; and
(*f*) the grounds on which the person making the application relies.

(3) In the case of an application under paragraph (2) [in a road transport case][2]
(*a*) the person making the application must notify the [decision maker][2] when making the application;
(*b*) within 7 days of receiving notification of the application the [decision maker][2] must send or deliver written reasons for refusing or withdrawing the stay—
(i) to the Upper Tribunal; and
(ii) to the person making the application, if the [decision maker][2] has not already done so.

(4) If the Upper Tribunal grants a stay or suspension following an application under this rule—
(*a*) the Upper Tribunal may give directions as to the conduct of the appeal of the substantive decision; and
(*b*) the Upper Tribunal may, where appropriate, grant the stay or suspension subject to conditions.

(5) Unless the Upper Tribunal considers that there is good reason not to do so, the Upper Tribunal must send written notice of any decision made under this rule to each party.][1]

Amendments—[1] Rule inserted by the Tribunal Procedure (Amendment No 2) Rules, SI 2009/1975 rules 7, 14 with effect from 1 September 2009.
[2] In para (3), words substituted by the Tribunal Procedure (Amendment No 2) Rules, SI 2012/1363 rules 4, 6 with effect from 1 July 2012.

PART 3
[PROCEDURE FOR CASES IN][1] THE UPPER TRIBUNAL

Amendments—[1] Words substituted by the Tribunal Procedure (Amendment) Rules, SI 2009/274 rules 3, 13 with effect from 1 April 2009.

21 Application to the Upper Tribunal for permission to appeal

(1) This rule applies to an application for permission to appeal to the Upper Tribunal against any decision.[1]

(2) A person may apply to the Upper Tribunal for permission to appeal to the Upper Tribunal against a decision of another tribunal only if—
(*a*) they have made an application for permission to appeal to the tribunal which made the decision challenged; and
(*b*) that application has been refused or has not been admitted [or has been granted only on limited grounds][3].

(3) An application for permission to appeal must be made in writing and received by the Upper Tribunal no later than—
(*a*) in the case of an application under section 4 of the Safeguarding Vulnerable Groups Act 2006, 3 months after the date on which written notice of the decision being challenged was sent to the appellant; . . . [2]
[(*aa*) . . . [4], in an asylum case or an immigration case where the appellant is in the United Kingdom at the time that the application is made—
(i) [14][4] days after the date on which notice of the First-tier Tribunal's refusal of permission was sent to the appellant; or
(ii) if the case is a fast-track case, four working days after the date on which notice of the First-tier Tribunal's refusal of permission was sent to the appellant;][2]
(*ab*) . . . [4]
(*b*) otherwise, a month after the date on which the tribunal that made the decision under challenge sent notice of its refusal of permission to appeal, or refusal to admit the application for permission to appeal, to the appellant.

(3A) . . . [4]

(4) The application must state—
(*a*) the name and address of the appellant;
(*b*) the name and address of the representative (if any) of the appellant;
(*c*) an address where documents for the appellant may be sent or delivered;
(*d*) details (including the full reference) of the decision challenged;
(*e*) the grounds on which the appellant relies; and
(*f*) whether the appellant wants the application to be dealt with at a hearing.

(5) The appellant must provide with the application a copy of—
(*a*) any written record of the decision being challenged;
(*b*) any separate written statement of reasons for that decision; and

(*c*) if the application is for permission to appeal against a decision of another tribunal, the notice of refusal of permission to appeal, or notice of refusal to admit the application for permission to appeal, from that other tribunal.

(6) If the appellant provides the application to the Upper Tribunal later than the time required by paragraph (3) or by an extension of time allowed under rule 5(3)(*a*) (power to extend time)—

(*a*) the application must include a request for an extension of time and the reason why the application was not provided in time; and

(*b*) unless the Upper Tribunal extends time for the application under rule 5(3)(*a*) (power to extend time) the Upper Tribunal must not admit the application.

(7) If the appellant makes an application to the Upper Tribunal for permission to appeal against the decision of another tribunal, and that other tribunal refused to admit the appellant's application for permission to appeal because the application for permission or for a written statement of reasons was not made in time—

(*a*) the application to the Upper Tribunal for permission to appeal must include the reason why the application to the other tribunal for permission to appeal or for a written statement of reasons, as the case may be, was not made in time; and

(*b*) the Upper Tribunal must only admit the application if the Upper Tribunal considers that it is in the interests of justice for it to do so.

[(8) In this rule, a reference to notice of a refusal of permission to appeal is to be taken to include a reference to notice of a grant of permission to appeal on limited grounds.][3]

Note—In rule 21(2)(*a*), the reference to the tribunal which made the decision challenged is to be read as a reference to the First-tier Tribunal (SI 2009/196 art 9).

Amendments—[1] Para (1) revoked by the Tribunal Procedure (Amendment No 2) Rules, SI 2009/1975 rules 7, 15 with effect from 1 September 2009.

[2] Word "and" in para (3)(*a*) revoked, and para (3)(*aa*) inserted, by the Tribunal Procedure (Amendment No 2) Rules, SI 2010/44 rules 2, 13, with effect from 15 February 2010.

[3] Words in para (2)(*b*) inserted, and para (8) inserted by the Tribunal Procedure (Amendment) Rules, SI 2014/514 rules 2, 7 with effect from 6 April 2014.

[4] In para (3)(*aa*), words revoked, in para (3)(*aa*)(i), words substituted, and paras (3)(*ab*), (3A) revoked, by the Tribunal Procedure (Amendment No 3) Rules, SI 2014/2128 rules 2, 8 with effect from 20 October 2014.

22 Decision in relation to permission to appeal

(1) [Except where rule 22A (special procedure for providing notice of a refusal of permission to appeal in an asylum case) applies][4] if the Upper Tribunal refuses permission to appeal [or refuses to admit a late application for permission][3], it must send written notice of the refusal and of the reasons for the refusal to the appellant.

(2) If the Upper Tribunal gives permission to appeal—

(*a*) the Upper Tribunal must send written notice of the permission, and of the reasons for any limitations or conditions on such permission, to each party;

(*b*) subject to any direction by the Upper Tribunal, the application for permission to appeal stands as the notice of appeal and the Upper Tribunal must send to each respondent a copy of the application for permission to appeal and any documents provided with it by the appellant; and

(*c*) the Upper Tribunal may, with the consent of the appellant and each respondent, determine the appeal without obtaining any further response.

[(3) Paragraph (4) applies where the Upper Tribunal, without a hearing, determines an application for permission to appeal—

(*a*) against a decision of—

(i) the Tax Chamber of the First-tier Tribunal;

(ii) the Health, Education and Social Care Chamber of the First-tier Tribunal;

[(iia) the General Regulatory Chamber of the First-tier Tribunal;][2]

[(iib) the Property Chamber of the First-tier Tribunal;][3]

(iii) the Mental Health Review Tribunal for Wales; or

(iv) the Special Educational Needs Tribunal for Wales; or

(*b*) under section 4 of the Safeguarding Vulnerable Groups Act 2006.][1]

(4) In the circumstances set out at paragraph (3) the appellant may apply for the decision to be reconsidered at a hearing if the Upper Tribunal—

(*a*) refuses permission to appeal [or refuses to admit a late application for permission][3]; or

(*b*) gives permission to appeal on limited grounds or subject to conditions.

(5) An application under paragraph (4) must be made in writing and received by the Upper Tribunal within 14 days after the date on which the Upper Tribunal sent written notice of its decision regarding the application to the appellant.

Amendments—[1] Para (3) substituted by the Tribunal Procedure (Amendment) Rules, SI 2009/274 rules 3, 14 with effect from 1 April 2009.

[2] Para (3)(*a*)(iia) inserted by the Tribunal Procedure (Amendment No 2) Rules, SI 2009/1975 rules 7, 16 with effect from 1 September 2009.

[3] In paras (1), (4)(*a*), words inserted, and para (3)(*a*)(iib) inserted, by the Tribunal Procedure (Amendment) Rules, SI 2014/514 rules 2, 8 with effect from 6 April 2014.

[4] In para (1) words substituted by the Tribunal Procedure (Amendment No 3) Rules, SI 2014/2128 rules 2, 9 with effect from 20 October 2014.

[22A Special procedure for providing notice of a refusal of permission to appeal in an asylum case

(1) This rule applies to a decision in an asylum case to refuse permission to appeal or to refuse to admit a late application for permission to appeal, where—

(*a*) the appellant is not the Secretary of State;

(*b*) at the time the application is made the appellant is in the United Kingdom; and

(*c*) the decision is not made in a fast-track case.

(2) The Upper Tribunal must provide written notice of the refusal and of the reasons for the refusal ("the notice") to the Secretary of State as soon as reasonably practicable.

(3) The Secretary of State must—

(*a*) send the notice to the appellant not later than 30 days after the Upper Tribunal provided it to the Secretary of State; and

(*b*) as soon as practicable after doing so, inform the Upper Tribunal of the date on which, and the means by which, it was sent.

(4) If the Secretary of State does not give the Upper Tribunal the information required by paragraph (3)(*b*) within 31 days after the notice was provided to the Secretary of State, the Upper Tribunal must send the notice to the appellant as soon as reasonably practicable.][1]

Amendments—[1] Rule 22A inserted by the Tribunal Procedure (Amendment No 3) Rules, SI 2014/2128 rules 2, 10 with effect from 20 October 2014.

23 Notice of appeal

[(1) This rule applies—

(*a*) to proceedings on appeal to the Upper Tribunal for which permission to appeal is not required, except proceedings to which rule 26A[, 26B or 26C][6] applies;

(*b*) if another tribunal has given permission for a party to appeal to the Upper Tribunal; or

(*c*) subject to any other direction by the Upper Tribunal, if the Upper Tribunal has given permission to appeal and has given a direction that the application for permission to appeal does not stand as the notice of appeal.

[(1A) In an asylum case or an immigration case in which the First-tier Tribunal has given permission to appeal, subject to any direction of the First-tier Tribunal or the Upper Tribunal, the application for permission to appeal sent or delivered to the First-tier Tribunal stands as the notice of appeal and accordingly paragraphs (2) to (6) of this rule do not apply.][2]

(2) The appellant must provide a notice of appeal to the Upper Tribunal so that it is received within 1 month after—

(*a*) the date that the tribunal that gave permission to appeal sent notice of such permission to the appellant; or

[(*b*) if permission to appeal is not required, the date on which notice of decision to which the appeal relates—

(i) was sent to the appellant; or

(ii) in a quality contracts scheme case, if the notice was not sent to the appellant, the date on which the notice was published in a newspaper in accordance with the requirement of section 125 (notice and consultation requirements) of the Transport Act 2000.][5][1]

(3) The notice of appeal must include the information listed in rule 21(4)(*a*) to (*e*) (content of the application for permission to appeal) and, where the Upper Tribunal has given permission to appeal, the Upper Tribunal's case reference.

(4) If another tribunal has granted permission to appeal, the appellant must provide with the notice of appeal a copy of—

(*a*) any written record of the decision being challenged;

(*b*) any separate written statement of reasons for that decision; and

(*c*) the notice of permission to appeal.

(5) If the appellant provides the notice of appeal to the Upper Tribunal later than the time required by paragraph (2) or by an extension of time allowed under rule 5(3)(*a*) (power to extend time)—

(*a*) the notice of appeal must include a request for an extension of time and the reason why the notice was not provided in time; and

(*b*) unless the Upper Tribunal extends time for the notice of appeal under rule 5(3)(*a*) (power to extend time) the Upper Tribunal must not admit the notice of appeal.

[(6) When the Upper Tribunal receives the notice of appeal it must send a copy of the notice and any accompanying documents—

(*a*) to each respondent; or

(*b*) in a road transport case, to—

(i) the decision maker;

(ii) the appropriate national authority; and

(iii) in a case relating to the detention of a vehicle, the authorised person.][4]][1]

[(7) Paragraph (6)(*a*) does not apply in a quality contracts scheme case, in respect of which Schedule A1 makes alternative and further provision.][5]

Amendments—[1] Paras (1), (2), (6) substituted by the Tribunal Procedure (Amendment No 2) Rules, SI 2009/1975 rules 7, 17 with effect from 1 September 2009.

[2] Para (1A) inserted by the Tribunal Procedure (Amendment No 2) Rules, SI 2010/44 rules 2, 14, with effect from 15 February 2010.

[4] Para (6)(*b*) substituted by the Tribunal Procedure (Amendment No 2) Rules, SI 2012/1363 rules 4, 7 with effect from 1 July 2012.

[5] Para (2)(*b*) substituted and para (7) inserted by the Tribunal Procedure (Amendment) Rules, SI 2015/1510 arts 2, 4 with effect from 21 August 2015.

[6] In para (1)(*a*), words substituted for words "or 26B" by the Tribunal Procedure (Amendment) Rules, SI 2017/723 rules 5, 10 with effect from 27 July 2017.

24 Response to the notice of appeal

[(1) This rule and rule 25 do not apply to—

(*a*) a road transport case, in respect of which Schedule 1 makes alternative provision; or

(*b*) a financial sanctions case in respect of which Schedule 4 makes alternative provision.][8]

(1A) Subject to any direction given by the Upper Tribunal, a respondent may provide a response to a notice of appeal.][2]

(2) Any response provided under paragraph [(1A)][3] must be in writing and must be sent or delivered to the Upper Tribunal so that it is received—

[(*a*) if an application for permission to appeal stands as the notice of appeal, no later than one month after the date on which the respondent was sent notice that permission to appeal had been granted;][4]

[(*aa*) in a fast-track case, [two days][6] before the hearing of the appeal; or][4]

[(*ab*) in a quality contracts scheme case, no later than 1 month after the date on which a copy of the notice of appeal is sent to the respondent;][7]

(*b*) in any other case, no later than 1 month after the date on which the Upper Tribunal sent a copy of the notice of appeal to the respondent.

(3) The response must state—

(*a*) the name and address of the respondent;

(*b*) the name and address of the representative (if any) of the respondent;

(*c*) an address where documents for the respondent may be sent or delivered;

(*d*) whether the respondent opposes the appeal;

(*e*) the grounds on which the respondent relies, including [(in the case of an appeal against the decision of another tribunal)][2] any grounds on which the respondent was unsuccessful in the proceedings which are the subject of the appeal, but intends to rely in the appeal; and

(*f*) whether the respondent wants the case to be dealt with at a hearing.

(4) If the respondent provides the response to the Upper Tribunal later than the time required by paragraph (2) or by an extension of time allowed under rule 5(3)(*a*) (power to extend time), the response must include a request for an extension of time and the reason why the [response][1] was not provided in time.

(5) When the Upper Tribunal receives the response it must send a copy of the response and any accompanying documents to the appellant and each other party.

[(6) Paragraph (5) does not apply in a quality contracts scheme case, in respect of which Schedule A1 makes alternative and further provision.][7]

Note—Publisher's note: SI 2015/1510 art 5(1) inserts para (1)(*ab*). It is the publisher's belief that the intention was to insert para (2)(*ab*), and the amendment has been made on that basis.

Amendments—[1] Word in para (4) substituted by the Tribunal Procedure (Amendment) Rules, SI 2009/274 rules 3, 15 with effect from 1 April 2009.

[2] Paras (1), (1A) substituted for previous para (1), in para (2)(*a*), words substituted, and in para (3)(*e*), words inserted, by the Tribunal Procedure (Amendment No 2) Rules, SI 2009/1975 rules 7, 18 with effect from 1 September 2009.

[3] In para (2), reference substituted by the Tribunal Procedure (Amendment) Rules, SI 2010/43, rules 5, 9, with effect from 18 January 2010.

[4] Para (2)(*a*) substituted, and para (2)(*aa*) inserted, by the Tribunal Procedure (Amendment No 2) Rules, SI 2010/44 rules 2, 15, with effect from 15 February 2010.

[5] In para (1), words substituted by the Tribunal Procedure (Amendment No 2) Rules, SI 2012/1363 rules 4, 8 with effect from 1 July 2012.

[6] In para (2)(*aa*), words substituted by the Tribunal Procedure (Amendment No 3) Rules, SI 2014/2128 rules 2, 11 with effect from 20 October 2014.

[7] Paras (2)(*ab*), (6) inserted by the Tribunal Procedure (Amendment) Rules, SI 2015/1510 arts 2, 5 with effect from 21 August 2015.

[8] Para (1) substituted by the Tribunal Procedure (Amendment) Rules, SI 2017/723 rules 5, 11 with effect from 27 July 2017. Para (1) previously read as follows—

"(1) This rule and rule 25 do not apply to a road transport case, in respect of which Schedule 1 makes alternative provision.".

25 Appellant's reply

(1) Subject to any direction given by the Upper Tribunal, the appellant may provide a reply to any response provided under rule 24 (response to the notice of appeal).

(2) [Subject to paragraph (2A), any][1] reply provided under paragraph (1) must be in writing and must be sent or delivered to the Upper Tribunal so that it is received within one month after the date on which the Upper Tribunal sent a copy of the response to the appellant.

[(2A) In an asylum case or an immigration case, the time limit in paragraph (2) is—

(*a*) one month after the date on which the Upper Tribunal sent a copy of the response to the appellant, or five days before the hearing of the appeal, whichever is the earlier; and

(*b*) in a fast-track case, the day of the hearing.][1]

[(2B) In a quality contracts scheme case, the time limit in paragraph (2) is 1 month from the date on which the respondent sent a copy of the response to the appellant.][2]

(3) When the Upper Tribunal receives the reply it must send a copy of the reply and any accompanying documents to each respondent.

[(4) Paragraph (3) does not apply in a quality contracts scheme case, in respect of which Schedule A1 makes alternative and further provision.][2]

Amendments—[1] In para (2), words substituted, and para (2A) inserted, by the Tribunal Procedure (Amendment No 2) Rules, SI 2010/44 rules 2, 16, with effect from 15 February 2010.

[2] Paras (2B), (4) inserted by the Tribunal Procedure (Amendment) Rules, SI 2015/1510 arts 2, 6 with effect from 21 August 2015.

26 References under the Forfeiture Act 1982

(1) If a question arises which is required to be determined by the Upper Tribunal under section 4 of the Forfeiture Act 1982, the person to whom the application for the relevant benefit or advantage has been made must refer the question to the Upper Tribunal.

(2) The reference must be in writing and must include—

(*a*) a statement of the question for determination;

(*b*) a statement of the relevant facts;

(*c*) the grounds upon which the reference is made; and

(*d*) an address for sending documents to the person making the reference and each respondent.

(3) When the Upper Tribunal receives the reference it must send a copy of the reference and any accompanying documents to each respondent.

(4) Rules 24 (response to the notice of appeal) and 25 (appellant's reply) apply to a reference made under this rule as if it were a notice of appeal.

[26A Cases transferred or referred to the Upper Tribunal, applications made directly to the Upper Tribunal and proceedings without notice to a respondent]

[(1) Paragraphs (2) and (3) apply to—

(*a*) a case transferred or referred to the Upper Tribunal from the First-tier Tribunal; or

(*b*) a case, other than an appeal or a case to which rule 26 (references under the Forfeiture Act 1982) applies, which is started by an application made directly to the Upper Tribunal.][2]

(2) In a case to which this paragraph applies—

(*a*) the Upper Tribunal must give directions as to the procedure to be followed in the consideration and disposal of the proceedings; ...[4]

[(*aa*) in a reference under Schedule 1D of the Charities Act 1993, the Upper Tribunal may give directions providing for an application to join the proceedings as a party and the time within which it may be made; and][4]

(*b*) the preceding rules in this Part will only apply to the proceedings to the extent provided for by such directions.

(3) If a case or matter to which this paragraph applies is to be determined without notice to or the involvement of a respondent—

(*a*) any provision in these Rules requiring a document to be provided by or to a respondent; and

(*b*) any other provision in these Rules permitting a respondent to participate in the proceedings

does not apply to that case or matter.][1]

[(4) Schedule 2 makes further provision for national security certificate appeals transferred to the Upper Tribunal.][3]

Amendments—[1] Rule 26A inserted by the Tribunal Procedure (Amendment) Rules, SI 2009/274 rules 3, 16 with effect from 1 April 2009.

[2] Para (1) substituted by the Tribunal Procedure (Amendment No 2) Rules, SI 2009/1975 rules 7, 19 with effect from 1 September 2009.

[3] Para (4) inserted by the Tribunal Procedure (Amendment) Rules, SI 2010/43, rules 5, 10 with effect from 18 January 2010.

[4] In para (2), in sub-para (*a*), word revoked, and sub-para (*aa*) inserted, by the Tribunal Procedure (Amendment) Rules, SI 2012/500, rule 5 with effect from 6 April 2012.

[26B Financial services cases [and wholesale energy cases][2]

Schedule 3 makes provision for financial services cases [and wholesale energy cases][2].][1]

Amendments—[1] Rule 26B inserted by the Tribunal Procedure (Upper Tribunal) (Amendment) Rules, SI 2010/747 rules 2, 9 with effect from 6 April 2010.

[2] Words in heading and text inserted by the Tribunal Procedure (Amendment) Rules, SI 2014/514 rules 2, 9, 10 with effect from 6 April 2014.

[26C Financial sanctions cases

Schedule 4 makes provision for financial sanctions cases.][1]

Amendments—[1] Rule 26C inserted by the Tribunal Procedure (Upper Tribunal) (Amendment) Rules, SI 2017/723 rules 5, 12 with effect from 27 July 2017.

PART 4
JUDICIAL REVIEW PROCEEDINGS IN THE UPPER TRIBUNAL

27 Application of this Part to judicial review proceedings transferred to the Upper Tribunal

(1) When a court transfers judicial review proceedings to the Upper Tribunal, the Upper Tribunal—

(*a*) must notify each party in writing that the proceedings have been transferred to the Upper Tribunal; and

(*b*) must give directions as to the future conduct of the proceedings.

(2) The directions given under paragraph (1)(*b*) may modify or disapply for the purposes of the proceedings any of the provisions of the following rules in this Part.

(3) In proceedings transferred from the Court of Session under section 20(1) of the 2007 Act, the directions given under paragraph (1)(*b*) must—

(*a*) if the Court of Session did not make a first order specifying the required intimation, service and advertisement of the petition, state the Upper Tribunal's requirements in relation to those matters;

(*b*) state whether the Upper Tribunal will consider summary dismissal of the proceedings; and

(*c*) where necessary, modify or disapply provisions relating to permission in the following rules in this Part.

28 Applications for permission to bring judicial review proceedings

(1) A person seeking permission to bring judicial review proceedings before the Upper Tribunal under section 16 of the 2007 Act must make a written application to the Upper Tribunal for such permission.

(2) Subject to paragraph (3), an application under paragraph (1) must be made promptly and, unless any other enactment specifies a shorter time limit, must be sent or delivered to the Upper Tribunal so that it is received no later than 3 months after the date of the decision[, action or omission][1] to which the application relates.

(3) An application for permission to bring judicial review proceedings challenging a decision of the First-tier Tribunal may be made later than the time required by paragraph (2) if it is made within 1 month after the date on which the First-tier Tribunal sent—

(*a*) written reasons for the decision; or

(*b*) notification that an application for the decision to be set aside has been unsuccessful, provided that that application was made in time.

(4) The application must state—

(*a*) the name and address of the applicant, the respondent and any other person whom the applicant considers to be an interested party;

(*b*) the name and address of the applicant's representative (if any);

(*c*) an address where documents for the applicant may be sent or delivered;

(*d*) details of the decision challenged (including the date, the full reference and the identity of the decision maker);

(*e*) that the application is for permission to bring judicial review proceedings;

(*f*) the outcome that the applicant is seeking; and

(*g*) the facts and grounds on which the applicant relies.

(5) If the application relates to proceedings in a court or tribunal, the application must name as an interested party each party to those proceedings who is not the applicant or a respondent.

(6) The applicant must send with the application—

(*a*) a copy of any written record of the decision in the applicant's possession or control; and

(*b*) copies of any other documents in the applicant's possession or control on which the applicant intends to rely.

(7) If the applicant provides the application to the Upper Tribunal later than the time required by paragraph (2) or (3) or by an extension of time allowed under rule 5(3)(*a*) (power to extend time)—

(*a*) the application must include a request for an extension of time and the reason why the application was not provided in time; and

(*b*) unless the Upper Tribunal extends time for the application under rule 5(3)(*a*) (power to extend time) the Upper Tribunal must not admit the application.

(8) [Except where rule 28A(2)(*a*) (special provisions for [immigration judicial review][3] proceedings) applies,][2] when the Upper Tribunal receives the application it must send a copy of the application and any accompanying documents to each person named in the application as a respondent or interested party.

Amendments—[1] In para (2), words inserted by the Tribunal Procedure (Amendment) Rules, SI 2009/274 rules 3, 17 with effect from 1 April 2009.

[2] In para (8), words inserted by the Tribunal Procedure (Upper Tribunal) (Amendment) Rules, SI 2011/2343 rules 2, 7 with effect from 17 October 2011.

[3] In para (8), words substituted by the Tribunal Procedure (Amendment No 4) Rules, SI 2013/2067 rules 2, 10 with effect from 1 November 2013.

[28A Special provisions for [immigration judicial review] proceedings

(1) The Upper Tribunal must not accept an application for permission to bring [immigration judicial review][2] proceedings unless it is either accompanied by any required fee or the Upper Tribunal accepts an undertaking that the fee will be paid.

(2) Within 9 days of making an application referred to in paragraph (1), an applicant must provide—

(*a*) a copy of the application and any accompanying documents to each person named in the application as a respondent or an interested party; and

(*b*) the Upper Tribunal with a written statement of when and how this was done.][1]

Amendments—[1] Rule 28A inserted by the Tribunal Procedure (Upper Tribunal) (Amendment) Rules, SI 2011/2343 rules 2, 8 with effect from 17 October 2011.

[2] In heading and in para (1), words substituted by the Tribunal Procedure (Amendment No 4) Rules, SI 2013/2067 rules 2, 11 with effect from 1 November 2013.

29 Acknowledgment of service

(1) A person who is sent [or provided with][3] a copy of an application for permission under rule 28(8) (application for permission to bring judicial review proceedings) [or rule 28A(2)(a) (special provisions for [immigration judicial review][4] proceedings)][3] and wishes to take part in the proceedings must [provide][3] to the Upper Tribunal an acknowledgment of service so that it is received no later than 21 days after the date on which the Upper Tribunal sent[, or in [immigration judicial review][4] proceedings the applicant provided,][3] a copy of the application to that person.

(2) An acknowledgment of service under paragraph (1) must be in writing and state—

(*a*) whether the person intends to [support or][1] oppose the application for permission;

(*b*) their grounds for any [support or][1] opposition under sub-paragraph (*a*), or any other submission or information which it considers may assist the Upper Tribunal; and

(*c*) the name and address of any other person not named in the application as a respondent or interested party whom the person providing the acknowledgment considers to be an interested party.

(2A) In [immigration judicial review][4] proceedings, a person who provides an acknowledgement of service under paragraph (1) must also provide a copy to—

(a) the applicant; and

(b) any other person named in the application under rule 28(4)(a) or acknowledgement of service under paragraph (2)(c)

no later than the time specified in paragraph (1).][3]

(3) A person who is [provided with][3] a copy of an application for permission under rule 28(8) [or 28A(2)(*a*)][3] but does not provide an acknowledgment of service [to the Upper Tribunal][3] may not take part in the application for permission [unless allowed to do so by the Upper Tribunal][2], but may take part in the subsequent proceedings if the application is successful.

Amendments—[1] In para (2), words inserted by the Tribunal Procedure (Amendment) Rules, SI 2009/274 rules 3, 17 with effect from 1 April 2009.

[2] In para (3) words inserted by the Tribunal Procedure (Amendment) Rules SI 2011/651 rule 8(1), (3) with effect from 1 April 2011.

[3] In para (1) words inserted and word substituted; para (2A) inserted; and in para (3), words substituted and words inserted; by the Tribunal Procedure (Upper Tribunal) (Amendment) Rules, SI 2011/2343 rules 2, 9 with effect from 17 October 2011.

[4] In para (1) in both places, and in para (2A), words substituted , by the Tribunal Procedure (Amendment No 4) Rules, SI 2013/2067 rules 2, 12 with effect from 1 November 2013.

30 Decision on permission or summary dismissal, and reconsideration of permission or summary dismissal at a hearing

(1) The Upper Tribunal must send to the applicant, each respondent and any other person who provided an acknowledgment of service to the Upper Tribunal, and may send to any other person who may have an interest in the proceedings, written notice of—

(*a*) its decision in relation to the application for permission; and

[(*b*) the reasons for any—

(i) refusal of the application or refusal to admit the late application, or

(ii) limitations or conditions on permission.][3]

(2) In proceedings transferred from the Court of Session under section 20(1) of the 2007 Act, where the Upper Tribunal has considered whether summarily to dismiss of the proceedings, the Upper Tribunal must send to the applicant and each respondent, and may send to any other person who may have an interest in the proceedings, written notice of—

(*a*) its decision in relation to the summary dismissal of proceedings; and (*b*) the reasons for any decision summarily to dismiss part or all of the proceedings, or any limitations or conditions on the continuation of such proceedings.

(3) Paragraph (4) applies where the Upper Tribunal, without a hearing—

(*a*) determines an application for permission to bring judicial review proceedings by—

(i) refusing permission or refusing to admit the late application, or

(ii) giving permission on limited grounds or subject to conditions.][3]

(*b*) in proceedings transferred from the Court of Session, summarily dismisses part or all of the proceedings, or imposes any limitations or conditions on the continuation of such proceedings.

(4) [Subject to paragraph (4A), in][2] the circumstances specified in paragraph (3) the applicant may apply for the decision to be reconsidered at a hearing.

[(4A) Where the Upper Tribunal refuses permission to bring immigration judicial review proceedings [or refuses to admit a late application for permission to bring such proceedings][3] and considers the application to be totally without merit, it shall record that fact in its decision notice and, in those circumstances, the applicant may not request the decision to be reconsidered at a hearing.][2]

(5) An application under paragraph (4) must be made in writing and must be sent or delivered to the Upper Tribunal so that it is received within 14 days[, or in [immigration judicial review][2] proceedings 9 days,][1] after the date on which the Upper Tribunal sent written notice of its decision regarding the application to the applicant.

Amendments—[1] In para (5), words inserted by the Tribunal Procedure (Upper Tribunal) (Amendment) Rules, SI 2011/2343 rules 2, 10 with effect from 17 October 2011.

[2] In para (4) words substituted for word "In", para (4A) inserted, and in para (5) words substituted, by the Tribunal Procedure (Amendment No 4) Rules, SI 2013/2067 rules 2, 13 with effect from 1 November 2013. Note that the amendments relating to paras (4) and (4A) do not apply to fresh claim proceedings where an application for permission to bring judicial review proceedings was issued in the Upper Tribunal before 1 November 2013, or an application for permission to apply for judicial review was transferred to the Upper Tribunal by the High Court under the Senior Courts Act 1981 s 31A before 1 November 2013. "Fresh claim proceedings" has the meaning in rule 1(3) of these Rules as it was in force immediately before 1 November 2013 (SI 2013/2067 rule 29).

[3] Paras (1)(*b*), (3)(*a*) substituted, and in para (4A), words inserted by the Tribunal Procedure (Amendment) Rules, SI 2014/514 rules 2, 11 with effect from 6 April 2014.

31 Responses

(1) Any person to whom the Upper Tribunal has sent notice of the grant of permission under rule 30(1) (notification of decision on permission), and who wishes to contest the application or support it on additional grounds, must provide detailed grounds for contesting or supporting the application to the Upper Tribunal.

(2) Any detailed grounds must be provided in writing and must be sent or delivered to the Upper Tribunal so that they are received not more than 35 days after the Upper Tribunal sent notice of the grant of permission under rule 30(1).

32 Applicant seeking to rely on additional grounds

The applicant may not rely on any grounds, other than those grounds on which the applicant obtained permission for the judicial review proceedings, without the consent of the Upper Tribunal.

33 Right to make representations

Each party and, with the permission of the Upper Tribunal, any other person, may—

(*a*) submit evidence, except at the hearing of an application for permission;

(*b*) make representations at any hearing which they are entitled to attend; and

(*c*) make written representations in relation to a decision to be made without a hearing.

[33A Amendments and additional grounds resulting in transfer of proceedings to the High Court in England and Wales

(1) This rule applies only to judicial review proceedings arising under the law of England and Wales.

(2) In relation to such proceedings—

(*a*) the powers of the Upper Tribunal to permit or require amendments under rule 5(3)(*c*) extend to amendments which would, once in place, give rise to an obligation or power to transfer the proceedings to the High Court in England and Wales under section 18(3) of the 2007 Act or paragraph (3);

(*b*) except with the permission of the Upper Tribunal, additional grounds may not be advanced, whether by an applicant or otherwise, if they would give rise to an obligation or power to transfer the proceedings to the High Court in England and Wales under section 18(3) of the 2007 Act or paragraph (3).

(3) Where the High Court in England and Wales has transferred judicial review proceedings to the Upper Tribunal under any power or duty and subsequently the proceedings are amended or any party advances additional grounds—

(*a*) if the proceedings in their present form could not have been transferred to the Upper Tribunal under the relevant power or duty had they been in that form at the time of the transfer, the Upper Tribunal must transfer the proceedings back to the High Court in England and Wales;

(*b*) subject to sub-paragraph (*a*), where the proceedings were transferred to the Upper Tribunal under section 31A(3) of the Senior Courts Act 1981(power to transfer judicial review proceedings to the Upper Tribunal), the Upper Tribunal may transfer proceedings back to the High Court in England and Wales if it appears just and convenient to do so.][1]

Amendments—[1] Rule 33A inserted by the Tribunal Procedure (Upper Tribunal) (Amendment) Rules, SI 2011/2343 rules 2, 11 with effect from 17 October 2011.

PART 5
HEARINGS

34 Decision with or without a hearing

(1) Subject to [paragraphs (2) and (3)][1], the Upper Tribunal may make any decision without a hearing.

(2) The Upper Tribunal must have regard to any view expressed by a party when deciding whether to hold a hearing to consider any matter, and the form of any such hearing.

[(3) In immigration judicial review proceedings, the Upper Tribunal must hold a hearing before making a decision which disposes of proceedings.

(4) Paragraph (3) does not affect the power of the Upper Tribunal to—

(*a*) strike out a party's case, pursuant to rule 8(1)(*b*) or 8(2);

(*b*) consent to withdrawal, pursuant to rule 17;

(*c*) determine an application for permission to bring judicial review proceedings, pursuant to rule 30; or

(*d*) make a consent order disposing of proceedings, pursuant to rule 39,

without a hearing.][1]

Amendments—[1] In para (1) words substituted, and paras (3), (4) inserted, by the Tribunal Procedure (Amendment No 4) Rules, SI 2013/2067 rules 2, 14 with effect from 1 November 2013.

35 Entitlement to attend a hearing

[(1)] [1]Subject to rule 37(4) (exclusion of a person from a hearing), each party is entitled to attend a hearing.

[(2) In a national security certificate appeal the relevant Minister is entitled to attend any hearing.][1]

Amendments—[1] Para (1) numbered as such, and para (2) inserted, by the Tribunal Procedure (Amendment) Rules, SI 2010/43, rules 5, 11, with effect from 18 January 2010.

36 Notice of hearings

(1) The Upper Tribunal must give each party entitled to attend a hearing reasonable notice of the time and place of the hearing (including any adjourned or postponed hearing) and any change to the time and place of the hearing.

(2) The period of notice under paragraph (1) must be at least 14 days except that—

(*a*) in applications for permission to bring judicial review proceedings, the period of notice must be at least 2 working days; . . .[1]

[(*aa*) in a fast-track case the period of notice must be at least one working day; and][1]

(*b*) [in any case other than a fast-track case][1] the Upper Tribunal may give shorter notice—

(i) with the parties' consent; or

(ii) in urgent or exceptional cases.

Amendments—[1] Word "and" at end of para (2)(*a*) revoked, and para (2)(*aa*) and words in para (2)(*b*) inserted, by the Tribunal Procedure (Amendment No 2) Rules, SI 2010/44 rules 2, 17, with effect from 15 February 2010.

[36A Special time limits for hearing an appeal in a fast-track case

(1) Subject to rule 36(2)(*aa*) (notice of hearings) and paragraph (2) of this rule, where permission to appeal to the Upper Tribunal has been given in a fast-track case, the Upper Tribunal must start the hearing of the appeal not later than—

(*a*) [five][2] working days after the date on which the First-tier Tribunal or the Upper Tribunal sent notice of its grant of permission to appeal to the appellant; or

(*b*) where the notice of its grant of permission to appeal is sent electronically or delivered personally, two working days after the date on which the First-tier Tribunal or the Upper Tribunal sent notice of its grant of permission to appeal to the appellant.

(2) If the Upper Tribunal is unable to arrange for the hearing to start within the time specified in paragraph (1), it must set a date for the hearing as soon as is reasonably practicable.][1]

Amendments—[1] Rule 36A inserted by the Tribunal Procedure (Amendment No 2) Rules, SI 2010/44 rules 2, 18, with effect from 15 February 2010.

[2] In para (1)(*a*), word substituted by the Tribunal Procedure (Amendment No 3) Rules, SI 2014/2128 rules 2, 13 with effect from 20 October 2014.

37 Public and private hearings

(1) Subject to the following paragraphs, all hearings must be held in public.

(2) The Upper Tribunal may give a direction that a hearing, or part of it, is to be held in private.

[(2A) In a national security certificate appeal, the Upper Tribunal must have regard to its duty under rule 14(10) (no disclosure of information contrary to the interests of national security) when considering whether to give a direction that a hearing, or part of it, is to be held in private.][3]

(3) Where a hearing, or part of it, is to be held in private, the Upper Tribunal may determine who is entitled to attend the hearing or part of it.

(4) The Upper Tribunal may give a direction excluding from any hearing, or part of it—

(*a*) any person whose conduct the Upper Tribunal considers is disrupting or is likely to disrupt the hearing;

(*b*) any person whose presence the Upper Tribunal considers is likely to prevent another person from giving evidence or making submissions freely;

(*c*) any person who the Upper Tribunal considers should be excluded in order to give effect to [the requirement at rule 14(11) (prevention of disclosure or publication of documents and information)][2]; . . . [1]

(*d*) any person where the purpose of the hearing would be defeated by the attendance of that person[; or

(*e*) a person under [18, other than a young person who is a party in a special educational needs case or a disability discrimination in schools case][4]][1].

(5) The Upper Tribunal may give a direction excluding a witness from a hearing until that witness gives evidence.

Amendments—[1] In para (4), word "or" in sub-para (*c*) revoked, and sub-para (*e*) and preceding word "or" inserted, by the Tribunal Procedure (Amendment) Rules, SI 2009/274 rules 3, 19 with effect from 1 April 2009.

[2] In para (4)(*c*), words substituted by the Tribunal Procedure (Amendment No 2) Rules, SI 2009/1975 rules 7, 20 with effect from 1 September 2009.

[3] Para (2A) inserted by the Tribunal Procedure (Amendment) Rules, SI 2010/43, rules 5, 12, with effect from 18 January 2010.

[4] In para (4)(*e*), words substituted by the Tribunal Procedure (Amendment No 3) Rules, SI 2014/2128 rules 2, 13 with effect from 1 September 2014.

38 Hearings in a party's absence

If a party fails to attend a hearing, the Upper Tribunal may proceed with the hearing if the Upper Tribunal—

(*a*) is satisfied that the party has been notified of the hearing or that reasonable steps have been taken to notify the party of the hearing; and

(*b*) considers that it is in the interests of justice to proceed with the hearing.

PART 6
DECISIONS

39 Consent orders

(1) The Upper Tribunal may, at the request of the parties but only if it considers it appropriate, make a consent order disposing of the proceedings and making such other appropriate provision as the parties have agreed.

(2) Notwithstanding any other provision of these Rules, the [Upper][2] Tribunal need not hold a hearing before making an order under paragraph (1) . . . [1].

Amendments—[1] In para (2), words revoked by the Tribunal Procedure (Amendment) Rules, SI 2009/274 rules 3, 20 with effect from 1 April 2009.

[2] Word in para (2) inserted by the Tribunal Procedure (Amendment No 4) Rules, SI 2013/2067 rules 2, 15 with effect from 1 November 2013.

40 Decisions

(1) The Upper Tribunal may give a decision orally at a hearing.

[(1A) Subject to paragraph (1B), in immigration judicial review proceedings, a decision which disposes of proceedings shall be given at a hearing.

(1B) Paragraph (1A) does not affect the power of the Upper Tribunal to—

(*a*) strike out a party's case, pursuant to rule 8(1)(*b*) or 8(2);

(*b*) consent to withdrawal, pursuant to rule 17;

(*c*) determine an application for permission to bring judicial review proceedings, pursuant to rule 30; or

(*d*) make a consent order disposing of proceedings, pursuant to rule 39,

without a hearing.][6]

(2) . . . [1] [Except where [rule 22 (decision in relation to permission to appeal) or rule 22A (special procedure for providing notice of a refusal of permission to appeal in an asylum case)][7] applies,][4] The Upper Tribunal must provide to each party as soon as reasonably practicable after making [a decision (other than a decision under Part 7) which finally disposes of all issues in the proceedings or of a preliminary issue dealt with following a direction under rule 5(3)(*e*)[5]]—

(*a*) a decision notice stating the [Upper][5] Tribunal's decision; and

(*b*) notification of any rights of review or appeal against the decision and the time and manner in which such rights of review or appeal may be exercised.

(3) [Subject to rule [14(11) (prevention of disclosure or publication of documents and information)][2],][1] the Upper Tribunal must provide written reasons for its decision with a decision notice provided under paragraph (2)(*a*) unless—

(*a*) the decision was made with the consent of the parties; or

(*b*) the parties have consented to the Upper Tribunal not giving written reasons.

(4) The [Upper][2] Tribunal may provide written reasons for any decision to which paragraph (2) does not apply.

[(5) In a national security certificate appeal, when the Upper Tribunal provides a notice or reasons to the parties under this rule, it must also provide the notice or reasons to the relevant Minister and the Information Commissioner, if they are not parties.][3]

Amendments—[1] In para (2), words revoked, and in para (3), words inserted, by the Tribunal Procedure (Amendment) Rules, SI 2009/274 rules 3, 21 with effect from 1 April 2009.

[2] In para (3), words substituted, and in para (4), word inserted, by the Tribunal Procedure (Amendment No 2) Rules, SI 2009/1975 rules 7, 21 with effect from 1 September 2009.

[3] Para (5) inserted by the Tribunal Procedure (Amendment) Rules, SI 2010/43, rules 5, 13, with effect from 18 January 2010.

[4] Words in para (2) inserted by the Tribunal Procedure (Amendment No 2) Rules, SI 2010/44 rules 2, 19, with effect from 15 February 2010.

[5] In para (2), words substitute, and in sub-para (*a*) word inserted, by the Tribunal Procedure (Amendment) Rules, SI 2013/477 rules 49, 56 with effect from 1 April 2013.

[6] Paras (1A), (1B) inserted by the Tribunal Procedure (Amendment No 4) Rules, SI 2013/2067 rules 2, 16 with effect from 1 November 2013.

[7] In para (2), words substituted by the Tribunal Procedure (Amendment No 3) Rules, SI 2014/2128 rules 2, 14 with effect from 20 October 2014.

40A Special procedure for providing notice of a decision relating to an asylum case

Amendments—Rule 40A revoked by the Tribunal Procedure (Amendment No 3) Rules, SI 2014/2128 rules 2, 15 with effect from 20 October 2014.

PART 7

CORRECTING, SETTING ASIDE, REVIEWING AND APPEALING DECISIONS OF THE UPPER TRIBUNAL

41 Interpretation

In this Part—

"appeal"[, except in rule 44(2) (application for permission to appeal),][1] means the exercise of a right of appeal under section 13 of the 2007 Act; and

"review" means the review of a decision by the Upper Tribunal under section 10 of the 2007 Act.

Amendments—[1] Words in definition of "appeal" inserted by the Tribunal Procedure (Amendment) Rules, SI 2009/274 rules 3, 22 with effect from 1 April 2009.

42 Clerical mistakes and accidental slips or omissions

The Upper Tribunal may at any time correct any clerical mistake or other accidental slip or omission in a decision or record of a decision by—

(*a*) sending notification of the amended decision, or a copy of the amended record, to all parties; and

(*b*) making any necessary amendment to any information published in relation to the decision or record.

43 Setting aside a decision which disposes of proceedings

(1) The Upper Tribunal may set aside a decision which disposes of proceedings, or part of such a decision, and re-make the decision or the relevant part of it, if—

(*a*) the Upper Tribunal considers that it is in the interests of justice to do so; and

(*b*) one or more of the conditions in paragraph (2) are satisfied.

(2) The conditions are—

(*a*) a document relating to the proceedings was not sent to, or was not received at an appropriate time by, a party or a party's representative;

(*b*) a document relating to the proceedings was not sent to the Upper Tribunal at an appropriate time;

(*c*) a party, or a party's representative, was not present at a hearing related to the proceedings; or

(*d*) there has been some other procedural irregularity in the proceedings.

(3) [Except where paragraph (4) applies,][1] a party applying for a decision, or part of a decision, to be set aside under paragraph (1) must make a written application to the Upper Tribunal so that it is received no later than 1 month after the date on which the [Upper][2] Tribunal sent notice of the decision to the party.

[(4) In an asylum case or an immigration case, the written application referred to in paragraph (3) must be sent or delivered so that it is received by the Upper Tribunal—

(*a*) where the person who appealed to the First-tier Tribunal is in the United Kingdom at the time that the application is made, no later than twelve days after the date on which the Upper Tribunal or, as the case may be in an asylum case, the Secretary of State for the Home Department, sent notice of the decision to the party making the application; or

(*b*) where the person who appealed to the First-tier Tribunal is outside the United Kingdom at the time that the application is made, no later than thirty eight days after the date on which the Upper Tribunal sent notice of the decision to the party making the application.

(5) Where a notice of decision is sent electronically or delivered personally, the time limits in paragraph (4) are ten working days.][1]

Amendments—[1] Words at start of para (3), and whole of paras (4), (5), inserted, by the Tribunal Procedure (Amendment No 2) Rules, SI 2010/44 rules 2, 21, with effect from 15 February 2010.

[2] Word in para (3) inserted by the Tribunal Procedure (Amendment No 4) Rules, SI 2013/2067 rules 2, 17 with effect from 1 November 2013.

44 Application for permission to appeal

(1) [Subject to [paragraphs (4A) and (4B)][6],][5] a person seeking permission to appeal must make a written application to the Upper Tribunal for permission to appeal.

(2) Paragraph (3) applies to an application under paragraph (1) in respect of a decision—

(*a*) on an appeal against a decision in a social security and child support case (as defined in the Tribunal Procedure (First-tier Tribunal) (Social Entitlement Chamber) Rules 2008);

(*b*) on an appeal against a decision in proceedings in the War Pensions and Armed Forces Compensation Chamber of the First-tier Tribunal; . . . [1]

[(*ba*) on an appeal against a decision of a Pensions Appeal Tribunal for Scotland or Northern Ireland; or][1]

(*c*) in proceedings under the Forfeiture Act 1982.

(3) Where this paragraph applies, the application must be sent or delivered to the Upper Tribunal so that it is received within 3 months after the date on which the Upper Tribunal sent to the person making the application—

(*a*) written notice of the decision;

(*b*) notification of amended reasons for, or correction of, the decision following a review; or

(*c*) notification that an application for the decision to be set aside has been unsuccessful.

[(3A) An application under paragraph (1) in respect of a decision in an asylum case or an immigration case must be sent or delivered to the Upper Tribunal so that it is received within the appropriate period after the Upper Tribunal or, as the case may be in an asylum case, the Secretary of State for the Home Department, sent any of the documents in paragraph (3) to the party making the application.

(3B) The appropriate period referred to in paragraph (3A) is as follows—

(*a*) where the person who appealed to the First-tier Tribunal is in the United Kingdom at the time that the application is made—

(i) [twelve working days][4]; or

(ii) if the party making the application is in detention under the Immigration Acts, seven working days; and

(*b*) where the person who appealed to the First-tier Tribunal is outside the United Kingdom at the time that the application is made, thirty eight days.

(3C) Where a notice of decision is sent electronically or delivered personally, the time limits in paragraph (3B) are—

(*a*) in sub-paragraph (*a*)(i), ten working days;

(*b*) in sub-paragraph (*a*)(ii), five working days; and

(*c*) in sub-paragraph (*b*), ten working days.][2]

[(3D) An application under paragraph (1) in respect of a decision in a financial services case must be sent or delivered to the Upper Tribunal so that it is received within 14 days after the date on which the Upper Tribunal sent to the person making the application—

(*a*) written notice of the decision;

(*b*) notification of amended reasons for, or correction of, the decision following a review; or

(*c*) notification that an application for the decision to be set aside has been unsuccessful.][3]

(4) Where paragraph (3)[, (3A)[, (3D) or (4C);][6]][3] does not apply, an application under paragraph (1) must be sent or delivered to the Upper Tribunal so that it is received within 1 month after the latest of the dates on which the Upper Tribunal sent to the person making the application—

(*a*) written reasons for the decision;

(*b*) notification of amended reasons for, or correction of, the decision following a review; or

(*c*) notification that an application for the decision to be set aside has been unsuccessful.

[(4A) Where a decision that disposes of immigration judicial review proceedings is given at a hearing, a party may apply at that hearing for permission to appeal, and the Upper Tribunal must consider at the hearing whether to give or refuse permission to appeal.

(4B) Where a decision that disposes of immigration judicial review proceedings is given at a hearing and no application for permission to appeal is made at that hearing—

(*a*) the Upper Tribunal must nonetheless consider at the hearing whether to give or refuse permission to appeal; and

(*b*) if permission to appeal is given to a party, it shall be deemed for the purposes of section 13(4) of the 2007 Act to be given on application by that party.

(4C) Where a decision that disposes of immigration judicial review proceedings is given pursuant to rule 30 and the Upper Tribunal records under rule 30(4A) that the application is totally without merit, an application under paragraph (1) must be sent or delivered to the Upper Tribunal so that it is received within 7 days after the later of the dates on which the Upper Tribunal sent to the applicant—

(*a*) written reasons for the decision; or

(*b*) notification of amended reasons for, or correction of, the decision following a review.][6]

(5) The date in paragraph (3)(*c*) or (4)(*c*) applies only if the application for the decision to be set aside was made within the time stipulated in rule 43 (setting aside a decision which disposes of proceedings) or any extension of that time granted by the Upper Tribunal.

(6) If the person seeking permission to appeal provides the application to the Upper Tribunal later than the time required by paragraph (3)[, (3A)][2][, (3D)][3] or (4), or by any extension of time under rule 5(3)(a) (power to extend time)—

(*a*) the application must include a request for an extension of time and the reason why the application notice was not provided in time; and

(*b*) unless the Upper Tribunal extends time for the application under rule 5(3)(*a*) (power to extend time) the Upper Tribunal must refuse the application.

(7) An application under paragraph (1) [or (4A)(*a*)][5] must—

(*a*) identify the decision of the [Upper][6] Tribunal to which it relates;

(*b*) identify the alleged error or errors of law in the decision; and

(*c*) state the result the party making the application is seeking.

Amendments—[1] In para (2), in sub-para (*b*), word "or" revoked, and sub-para (*ba*) inserted, by the Tribunal Procedure (Amendment) Rules, SI 2009/274 rules 3, 23 with effect from 1 April 2009.

[2] Paras (3A)–(3C), and references in para (6), inserted, by the Tribunal Procedure (Amendment No 2) Rules, SI 2010/44 rules 2, 22, with effect from 15 February 2010.

[3] Para (3D) inserted, reference in para (4) substituted and reference in para (6) inserted, by the Tribunal Procedure (Upper Tribunal) (Amendment) Rules, SI 2010/747 rules 2, 10 with effect from 6 April 2010.

[4] In para (3B)(*a*)(i), words substituted by the Tribunal Procedure (Amendment) Rules, SI 2011/651 rule 8(1), (4) with effect from 1 April 2011.

[5] Words in paras (1), (7) inserted, by the Tribunal Procedure (Upper Tribunal) (Amendment) Rules, SI 2012/2890 rules 2, 3 with effect from 11 December 2012.

[6] In paras (1), (4) words substituted, paras (4A)–(4C) substituted for previous para (4A), and in para (7)(*a*), word inserted, by the Tribunal Procedure (Amendment No 4) Rules, SI 2013/2067 rules 2, 18 with effect from 1 November 2013.

45 Upper Tribunal's consideration of application for permission to appeal

(1) On receiving an application for permission to appeal the Upper Tribunal may review the decision in accordance with rule 46 (review of a decision), but may only do so if—

(*a*) when making the decision the Upper Tribunal overlooked a legislative provision or binding authority which could have had a material effect on the decision; or

(*b*) since the Upper Tribunal's decision, a court has made a decision which is binding on the Upper Tribunal and which, had it been made before the Upper Tribunal's decision, could have had a material effect on the decision.

(2) If the Upper Tribunal decides not to review the decision, or reviews the decision and decides to take no action in relation to the decision or part of it, the Upper Tribunal must consider whether to give permission to appeal in relation to the decision or that part of it.

(3) The Upper Tribunal must [provide][1] a record of its decision to the parties as soon as practicable.

(4) If the Upper Tribunal refuses permission to appeal it must [provide][1] with the record of its decision—

(*a*) a statement of its reasons for such refusal; and

(*b*) notification of the right to make an application to the relevant appellate court for permission to appeal and the time within which, and the method by which, such application must be made.

(5) The Upper Tribunal may give permission to appeal on limited grounds, but must comply with paragraph (4) in relation to any grounds on which it has refused permission.

Amendments—[1] In paras (3), (4) word substituted by the Tribunal Procedure (Amendment No 4) Rules, SI 2013/2067 rules 2, 19 with effect from 1 November 2013.

46 Review of a decision

[(1) The Upper Tribunal may only undertake a review of a decision pursuant to rule 45(1) (review on an application for permission to appeal).][1]

(2) The Upper Tribunal must notify the parties in writing of the outcome of any review and of any rights of review or appeal in relation to the outcome.

(3) If the Upper Tribunal decides to take any action in relation to a decision following a review without first giving every party an opportunity to make representations, the notice under paragraph (2) must state that any party that did not have an opportunity to make representations may apply for such action to be set aside and for the decision to be reviewed again.

Amendments—[1] Para (1) substituted by the Tribunal Procedure (Upper Tribunal) (Amendment) Rules, SI 2011/2343 rules 2, 12 with effect from 17 October 2011.

47 [Setting aside] a decision in proceedings under the Forfeiture Act 1982

(1) A person who referred a question to the Upper Tribunal under rule 26 (references under the Forfeiture Act 1982) must refer the Upper Tribunal's previous decision in relation to the question to the Upper Tribunal if they—

(*a*) consider that the decision should be [set aside and re-made under this rule][1]; or

(*b*) have received a written application for the decision to be [set aside and re-made under this rule][1] from the person to whom the decision related.

(2) The Upper Tribunal may [set aside the decision, either in whole or in part, and re-make it][1] if—

(*a*) ...[1]

(*b*) the decision was made in ignorance of, or was based on a mistake as to, some material fact; or

(*c*) there has been a relevant change in circumstances since the decision was made.

[(3) Rule 26(2) to (4), Parts 5 and 6 and this Part apply to a reference under this rule as they apply to a reference under rule 26(1).][1]

Amendments—[1] In heading, paras (1) (*a*), (*b*), (2), words substituted; para 2(*a*) revoked; and para (3) substituted for previous paras (3)–(5); by the Tribunal Procedure (Upper Tribunal) (Amendment) Rules, SI 2011/2343 rules 2, 13 with effect from 17 October 2011.

[48 Power to treat an application as a different type of application

The [Upper][2] Tribunal may treat an application for a decision to be corrected, set aside or reviewed, or for permission to appeal against a decision, as an application for any other one of those things.][1]

Amendments—[1] Rule 48 inserted by the Tribunal Procedure (Amendment No 3) Rules, SI 2010/2653 rule 8 with effect from 29 November 2010.

[2] Word inserted by the Tribunal Procedure (Amendment No 4) Rules, SI 2013/2067 rules 2, 20 with effect from 1 November 2013.

[SCHEDULE A1

PROCEDURE IN QUALITY CONTRACTS SCHEME CASES]

Rule 23

Amendments—[1] Schedule A1 inserted by the Tribunal Procedure (Amendment) Rules, SI 2015/1510 arts 2, 7 with effect from 21 August 2015.

[1 This Schedule applies to quality contracts scheme cases.][1]

Amendments—[1] Schedule A1 inserted by the Tribunal Procedure (Amendment) Rules, SI 2015/1510 arts 2, 7 with effect from 21 August 2015.

[Notice of appeal

2 The appellant must send or deliver to the Upper Tribunal the notice of appeal together with the following materials —

(*a*) a copy of the notice of the decision being challenged;

(*b*) a copy of any separate written statement of reasons;

(*c*) copies of the most significant documents (or relevant extracts) on which the appellant relies in support of the grounds stated in its notice of appeal, including—

(i) the quality contracts scheme (or relevant extracts); and

(ii) any report of the QCS Board (or relevant extracts); and

(*d*) a list of the materials referred to in sub-paragraphs (*a*) to (*c*) and where such materials may be accessed (e.g. link to internet webpage).][1]

Amendments—[1] Schedule A1 inserted by the Tribunal Procedure (Amendment) Rules, SI 2015/1510 arts 2, 7 with effect from 21 August 2015.

[3 The appellant must, at the same time as sending its notice of appeal to the Upper Tribunal in accordance with paragraph 2, send a copy of the notice of appeal and of the additional materials to the respondent.][1]

Amendments—[1] Schedule A1 inserted by the Tribunal Procedure (Amendment) Rules, SI 2015/1510 arts 2, 7 with effect from 21 August 2015.

[4 The Upper Tribunal must send a copy of the notice of appeal and a copy of the list referred to in paragraph 2(*d*) to the appropriate national authority.][1]

Amendments—[1] Schedule A1 inserted by the Tribunal Procedure (Amendment) Rules, SI 2015/1510 arts 2, 7 with effect from 21 August 2015.

[**5** The Upper Tribunal may, upon receipt of the notice of appeal, direct the respondent to—

(*a*) give notice in at least one newspaper circulating in the area to which the scheme relates that a notice of appeal has been received;

(*b*) give written notice to the persons consulted under section 125(3) (notice and consultation requirements) of the Transport Act 2000 and (if the case may be) those not consulted under section 125(3) but who in the opinion of the QCS Board, under section 126D(1)(*b*) (consideration of proposed schemes by boards) of that Act, ought to have been so consulted, that a notice of appeal has been received;

(*c*) make arrangements for a place or website where copies of the notice of appeal and any response or reply and in each case their accompanying documents may be inspected;

(*d*) ensure that each notice provided for in sub-paragraphs (*a*) and (*b*) states—

(i) where copies of the notice of appeal and other documents relating to the proceedings may be inspected; and

(ii) where information about the procedure for applying to be added as a party may be found.][1]

Amendments—[1] Schedule A1 inserted by the Tribunal Procedure (Amendment) Rules, SI 2015/1510 arts 2, 7 with effect from 21 August 2015.

[Response to the notice of appeal

6 A respondent must send or deliver to the Upper Tribunal its response to the notice of appeal together with the following materials —

(*a*) a copy of the most significant documents (or relevant extracts) on which the respondent relies in support of the response;

(*b*) a list of those documents.][1]

Amendments—[1] Schedule A1 inserted by the Tribunal Procedure (Amendment) Rules, SI 2015/1510 arts 2, 7 with effect from 21 August 2015.

[**7** The respondent must, at the same time as providing its response to the Upper Tribunal in accordance with paragraph 6, provide copies of that response and of those materials to—

(*a*) the appellant; and

(*b*) the appropriate national authority.][1]

Amendments—[1] Schedule A1 inserted by the Tribunal Procedure (Amendment) Rules, SI 2015/1510 arts 2, 7 with effect from 21 August 2015.

[**8** Any directions given by the Upper Tribunal to the respondent under paragraph 5 are also to be regarded as directions to the respondent to make available for inspection copies of its response and accompanying materials.][1]

Amendments—[1] Schedule A1 inserted by the Tribunal Procedure (Amendment) Rules, SI 2015/1510 arts 2, 7 with effect from 21 August 2015.

[Appellant's reply

9 The appellant must send or deliver to the Upper Tribunal its reply (if any) to a response under paragraph 6 together with the following materials—

(*a*) a copy of any additional documents (or relevant extracts) relied on in support of the reply;

(*b*) a list of those documents.][1]

Amendments—[1] Schedule A1 inserted by the Tribunal Procedure (Amendment) Rules, SI 2015/1510 arts 2, 7 with effect from 21 August 2015.

[**10** The appellant must, at the same time as providing its reply to the Upper Tribunal in accordance with paragraph 9, provide a copy of that reply and of those materials to the respondent.][1]

Amendments—[1] Schedule A1 inserted by the Tribunal Procedure (Amendment) Rules, SI 2015/1510 arts 2, 7 with effect from 21 August 2015.

[**11** The Upper Tribunal must send a copy of the appellant's reply and a copy of the list of documents referred to in paragraph 9(*b*) to the appropriate national authority.][1]

Amendments—[1] Schedule A1 inserted by the Tribunal Procedure (Amendment) Rules, SI 2015/1510 arts 2, 7 with effect from 21 August 2015.

[**12** Any directions given by the Upper Tribunal to the respondent under paragraph 5 are also to be regarded as directions to the respondent to make available for inspection copies of the appellant's reply and accompanying materials.][1]

Amendments—[1] Schedule A1 inserted by the Tribunal Procedure (Amendment) Rules, SI 2015/1510 arts 2, 7 with effect from 21 August 2015.

[Adding further parties

13 Any person who wishes to be added as a party to the proceedings, and has given notice to the respondent that they received the notice of the appeal in consequence of a direction made under paragraph 5, must apply to the Upper Tribunal in accordance with rule 9 within 1 month of the date on which they received notice of the appeal.][1]

Amendments—[1] Schedule A1 inserted by the Tribunal Procedure (Amendment) Rules, SI 2015/1510 arts 2, 7 with effect from 21 August 2015.

[14 Any application to be added as a party must state—

(*a*) the name and address of the person making the application;

(*b*) the name and address of the representative (if any) of that person;

(*c*) an address where documents for that person may be sent or delivered;

(*d*) whether or not copies of the notice of appeal, any response and any reply has been inspected, along with their accompanying documents;

(*e*) whether the person making the application supports or opposes the appeal; and

(*f*) the grounds relied upon for adding the person as a party.][1]

Amendments—[1] Schedule A1 inserted by the Tribunal Procedure (Amendment) Rules, SI 2015/1510 arts 2, 7 with effect from 21 August 2015.

[15 The person making the application must provide the following materials with the application—

(*a*) a copy of the most significant documents (or relevant extracts) on which the person relies in support of the application, if not already listed by a party; and

(*b*) a list of the documents referred to in sub-paragraph (*a*).][1]

Amendments—[1] Schedule A1 inserted by the Tribunal Procedure (Amendment) Rules, SI 2015/1510 arts 2, 7 with effect from 21 August 2015.

[16 The Upper Tribunal must notify the parties of any application to be joined as a party and send a copy of the list of documents with the notification.][1]

Amendments—[1] Schedule A1 inserted by the Tribunal Procedure (Amendment) Rules, SI 2015/1510 arts 2, 7 with effect from 21 August 2015.

[17 The Upper Tribunal may give further directions relating to any application to be added as a party and generally as to the conduct of the case.][1]

Amendments—[1] Schedule A1 inserted by the Tribunal Procedure (Amendment) Rules, SI 2015/1510 arts 2, 7 with effect from 21 August 2015.

[SCHEDULE 1

Rule 24(1)

Procedure after the notice of appeal in [road transport cases]

1 This Schedule applies to [road transport cases][1].

Amendments—[1] In Schedule heading and para 1, words substituted by the Tribunal Procedure (Amendment No 2) Rules, SI 2012/1363 rules 4, 9 with effect from 1 July 2012.

2 The only parties to the appeal are the appellant and any person added as a party under rule 9 [(addition, substitution and removal of parties)][1].

Amendments—[1] Words substituted by the Tribunal Procedure (Upper Tribunal) (Amendment) Rules, SI 2010/747 rules 2, 11 with effect from 6 April 2010.

3 On receipt of a copy of a notice of appeal under rule 23(6)(*b*), the [decision maker][1] must send to the Upper Tribunal a copy (and, on request, further copies) of—

(*a*) a written record of the decision appealed against and reasons for the decision;

(*b*) all documents produced to the [decision maker][1] in connection with the decision;

(*c*) if a public inquiry was held, the transcript of the inquiry or, if no such transcript was produced, the [decision maker's][1] note of the inquiry; and

[(*d*) in an appeal under—

(i) section 50 of the Public Passenger Vehicles Act 1981(a) or section 37 of the Goods Vehicles (Licensing of Operators) Act 1995(b), or

(ii) section 35 of the Goods Vehicles (Licensing of Operators) Act (Northern Ireland) 2010,

a list of the names and addresses of objectors and representors.][1]

Amendments—[1] Words substituted, and para (*d*) substituted, by the Tribunal Procedure (Amendment No 2) Rules, SI 2012/1363 rules 4, 9 with effect from 1 July 2012.

4 On receipt of a list under paragraph 3(*d*) the Upper Tribunal must send a copy of the notice of appeal—

(*a*) where the appellant had applied for, or for the variation of, an operator's licence, to each person who made an objection to the application;

(*b*) where the appellant had made an objection to an application for, or (in the case of a goods vehicle operator's licence) for the variation of, an operator's licence, to the person who made the application and to every other person who made an objection to the application; . . .[1]

(*c*) in an appeal under section 37(5) of the Goods Vehicles (Licensing of Operators) Act 1995, [to][2] each person who made representations under section 12(4) or 19(2) of that Act against the application for, or for the variation of, the operator's licence in question.

[(*d*) in an appeal under section 35(5) of the Goods Vehicles (Licensing of Operators) Act (Northern Ireland) 2010, to each person who made representations under section 11(4) or 18(2) of that Act.][1]

Amendments—[1] In para (*b*) word "and" revoked, and para (*d*) inserted, by the Tribunal Procedure (Amendment No 2) Rules, SI 2012/1363 rules 4, 9 with effect from 1 July 2012.

[2] Word in para (*c*) inserted by the Tribunal Procedure (Amendment) Rules, SI 2013/477 rules 49, 57(*a*) with effect from 1 April 2013. Note that this amendment is repeated in SI 2014/2128 rule 16.

5 The appropriate national authority and any person to whom the Upper Tribunal has sent a copy of the notice of appeal under paragraph 4 may apply for a direction under rule 9(2) adding them as a respondent.

6 An application under paragraph 5 must be sent or delivered to the Upper Tribunal so that it is received within 14 days of the date that the Upper Tribunal sent a copy of the notice of appeal to the person making the application.

7 If a person . . .[1] makes an application in accordance with paragraphs 5 and 6, the Upper Tribunal must give a direction under rule 9(2) adding that person as a respondent.

Amendments—[1] Words revoked by the Tribunal Procedure (Amendment) Rules, SI 2013/477 rules 49, 57(*b*) with effect from 1 April 2013.

8

Amendments—Para 8 revoked by the Tribunal Procedure (Amendment) Rules, SI 2013/477 rules 49, 57(*c*) with effect from 1 April 2013.

9 The Upper Tribunal must notify each other party of any application under paragraph 3 and the Upper Tribunal's decision in respect of each such application.

10 Any party may make a request to the Upper Tribunal for copies of specified documents provided by the [decision maker][1] under paragraph 3.

Amendments—[1] Words substituted for words "traffic commissioner", by the Tribunal Procedure (Amendment No 2) Rules, SI 2012/1363 rules 4, 9 with effect from 1 July 2012.

11 On receiving a request under paragraph 9 the Upper Tribunal—

(*a*) must provide the requested copies unless it considers the request unreasonable; and

(*b*) if it considers the request unreasonable, give details of why it considers the request unreasonable.][1]

Amendments—[1] Schedule inserted by the Tribunal Procedure (Amendment No 2) Rules, SI 2009/1975 rules 7, 22 with effect from 1 September 2009.

[SCHEDULE 2

ADDITIONAL PROCEDURE IN NATIONAL SECURITY CERTIFICATE CASES

Rule 26A(4)

1 This Schedule applies only to national security certificate appeals.

2 Following the transfer of the appeal from the First-tier Tribunal, the Upper Tribunal must provide a copy of the notice of appeal to the respondent, the relevant Minister and the Information Commissioner.

3 The relevant Minister must send or deliver to the Upper Tribunal a copy of the certificate to which the appeal relates, and a response to the notice of appeal, not later than 42 days after the date on which the relevant Minister received a copy of the notice of appeal.

4 In an appeal under section 28(4) of the Data Protection Act 1998 or section 60(1) of the Freedom of Information Act 2000 (including that subsection as applied and modified by regulation 18 of the Environmental Information Regulations 2004), the relevant Minister's response must state whether the relevant Minister intends to oppose the appeal and, if so set out—

(*a*) a summary of the circumstances relating to the issue of the certificate;

(*b*) the reason for the issue of the certificate;

SIs

(*c*) the grounds on which the relevant Minister relies in opposing the appeal; and
(*d*) a statement of the evidence on which the relevant Minister relies in support of those grounds.

5 In an appeal under section 28(6) of the Data Protection Act 1998 or section 60(4) of the Freedom of Information Act 2000 (including that subsection as applied and modified by regulation 18 of the Environmental Information Regulations 2004), the relevant Minister's response must state whether the relevant Minister intends to make representations in relation to the appeal and, if so set out—

(*a*) the extent to which the relevant Minister intends to support or oppose the appeal;
(*b*) the grounds on which the relevant Minister relies in supporting or opposing the appeal; and
(*c*) a statement of the evidence on which the relevant Minister relies in support of those grounds.

6 The Upper Tribunal must—

(*a*) subject to paragraph 11, provide the relevant Minister's response and any other response to the appellant, the Information Commissioner and any respondent; and
(*b*) send a copy of any other response to the relevant Minister.

7 On grounds of the need to ensure that information is not disclosed contrary to the interests of national security, the relevant Minster may—

(*a*) object to the disclosure of the relevant Minister's response to the appellant, the Information Commissioner or any respondent, by sending a notice to the Upper Tribunal with the response; or
(*b*) object to the disclosure of any other response to the Information Commissioner or any respondent, by sending a notice to the Upper Tribunal within 42 days of the date on which the relevant Minister received a copy of the response.

8 A notice under paragraph 7 must—

(*a*) state the reason for the objection; and
(*b*) in the case of a notice under paragraph 7(*a*) and to the extent that it is possible to do so, be accompanied by a version of the relevant Minister's response in a form that can be shown to the appellant, the Commissioner or, as the case may be, a respondent.

9 Before the Upper Tribunal gives a direction, issues a summons or citation, or produces or publishes a written record of, or reasons for, a decision—

(*a*) the Upper Tribunal must notify the relevant Minister of the proposed action; and
(*b*) if the relevant Minister considers that the proposal would cause information that is or would be exempt by virtue of a provision in Part 2 of the Freedom of Information Act 2000 to be disclosed, the relevant Minister may object to the proposal by sending a notice to the Upper Tribunal [so that the Upper Tribunal receives the notice within 14 days of the date that the Minister received notice of the proposal][1].

Amendments—[1] Words substituted by the Tribunal Procedure (Upper Tribunal) (Amendment) Rules, SI 2010/747 rules 2, 12 with effect from 6 April 2010.

10 When deciding whether to uphold an objection made by the relevant Minister—

(*a*) any hearing must take place in the absence of the parties;
(*b*) if the Upper Tribunal is minded to overrule the relevant Minister's objection, or to require the relevant Minister to provide a version of the relevant Minister's response in a form other than one provided under paragraph 8(*b*) above, the Upper Tribunal must invite the relevant Minister to make representations; and
(*c*) if the Upper Tribunal overrules an objection in relation to the disclosure of a response, the [Upper][1] Tribunal must not disclose, or require the relevant Minister to disclose, any material the subject of the objection unless the relevant Minister relies upon that material in opposing the appeal.

Amendments—[1] Word in para (*c*) inserted by the Tribunal Procedure (Amendment No 4) Rules, SI 2013/2067 rules 2, 21(*a*) with effect from 1 November 2013.

11 Where the relevant Minister may object to the disclosure of a response or proposed action by the Upper Tribunal, the Upper Tribunal may not proceed with that disclosure or that proposed action unless—

(*a*) the time for the relevant Minister to object has expired; and
(*b*) the relevant Minister has not objected, or the [Upper][2] Tribunal has overruled the relevant Minister's objection and, in the case of the disclosure of a response, may proceed with the disclosure under paragraph 10(*c*).][1]

Amendments—[1] Schedule 2 inserted by the Tribunal Procedure (Amendment) Rules, SI 2010/43, rules 5, 14, with effect from 18 January 2010.

[2] Word in para (*b*) inserted by the Tribunal Procedure (Amendment No 4) Rules, SI 2013/2067 rules 2, 21(*b*) with effect from 1 November 2013.

[SCHEDULE 3

PROCEDURE IN FINANCIAL SERVICES CASES [AND WHOLESALE ENERGY CASES]

Rule 26B

Amendments—Words in heading inserted by the Tribunal Procedure (Amendment) Rules, SI 2014/514 rules 2, 12 with effect from 6 April 2014.

Interpretation

1 In this Schedule—

["further material" means—

(*a*) in a single regulator case, documents which—

(i) were considered by the respondent in reaching or maintaining the decision to give the notice in respect of which the reference has been made; or

(ii) were obtained by the respondent in connection with the matter to which that notice relates (whether they were obtained before or after giving the notice) but which were not considered by it in reaching or maintaining that decision;

but does not include documents on which the respondent relies in support of the referred action;

(*b*) in a multiple regulator case—

(i) in relation to a respondent who is the primary regulator, documents which—

(*aa*) were considered by that regulator in reaching or maintaining its decision to give the notice in respect of which the reference has been made; or

(*bb*) were obtained by that regulator in connection with the matter to which that notice relates (whether they were obtained before or after the notice was given) but which were not considered by that regulator in reaching or maintaining its decision;

(ii) in relation to a respondent who is the secondary regulator, documents which—

(*aa*) were considered by that regulator in reaching or maintaining its decision to take the secondary regulator action in relation to the notice in respect of which the reference has been made; or

(*bb*) were obtained by that regulator in connection with the matter to which that notice relates (whether they were obtained before or after the notice was given) but which were not considered by that regulator in reaching or maintaining its decision;

but does not include documents on which either the primary regulator or the secondary regulator relies;][2]

["multiple regulator case" means a case where—

(*a*) any of the Financial Conduct Authority, the Prudential Regulation Authority or the Bank of England has given the notice in respect of which the reference has been made; and

(*b*) such notice stated that another of those regulators had decided to take one of the following actions—

(i) to refuse a consent where such consent is required under the 2000 Act;

(ii) to give a conditional consent under the 2000 Act; or

(iii) to direct another regulator to take an action or not to take an action under the 2000 Act;][2]

["primary regulator" means, in a multiple regulator case, the regulator giving the notice;][2]

"reference notice" means the written notice required in making a reference in a financial services case [or a wholesale energy case][3];

["referred action" means—

(*a*) in a single regulator case, the act (or proposed act) on the part of the respondent that gave rise to the reference; and

(*b*) in a multiple regulator case, the act (or proposed act) on the part of the primary regulator that gave rise to the reference;][2]

["secondary regulator action" means an action taken by a secondary regulator, as stated in the notice given by the primary regulator;][2]

["secondary regulator" means, in a multiple regulator case, a regulator specified in the notice other than the primary regulator;][2]

["single regulator case" means a case that is not a multiple regulator case;][2]

"the 2000 Act" means the Financial Services and Markets Act 2000[;][1]

"the 2013 Regulations" means the Electricity and Gas (Market Integrity and Transparency) (Enforcement etc.) Regulations 2013;

"the 2013 (NI) Regulations" means the Electricity and Gas (Market Integrity and Transparency) (Enforcement etc.) Regulations (Northern Ireland) 2013.][13]

Amendments—[1] Schedule 3 inserted by the Tribunal Procedure (Upper Tribunal) (Amendment) Rules, SI 2010/747 rules 2, 13 with effect from 6 April 2010.

[2] Definitions inserted, and definitions of "further material" and "referred action" substituted, by the Tribunal Procedure (Amendment No 2) Rules, SI 2013/606 rule 2(1), (4) with effect from 1 April 2013.

[3] Words inserted in definition of "reference notice", and definitions of "the 2013 Regulations" and "the 2013 (NI) Regulations" inserted by the Tribunal Procedure (Amendment) Rules, SI 2014/514 rules 2, 13(*a*), (*b*) with effect from 6 April 2014.

Reference notice

[**2** (1) A reference notice must be signed by or on behalf of the applicant and sent or delivered by the applicant to the Upper Tribunal.

(2) A reference notice must be received by the Upper Tribunal no later than 28 days after notice was given of the decision in respect of which the reference is made.

(3) The reference notice must state—

(*a*) the name and address of the applicant;

(*b*) the name and address of the applicant's representative (if any);

(*c*) if no representative is named under sub-paragraph (*b*), an address where documents for the applicant may be sent or delivered; and

(*d*) the issues that the applicant wishes the Upper Tribunal to consider.

(4) The applicant must send or deliver to the Upper Tribunal with the reference notice a copy of the notice of the decision in respect of which the reference has been made.

[(5) At the same time the applicant must send a copy of the reference notice—

(*a*) in a single regulator case, to the respondent; and

(*b*) in a multiple regulator case, to each of the primary and secondary regulators.][2]][1]

Amendments—[1] Schedule 3 inserted by the Tribunal Procedure (Upper Tribunal) (Amendment) Rules, SI 2010/747 rules 2, 13 with effect from 6 April 2010.

[2] Sub-para (5) substituted by the Tribunal Procedure (Amendment No 2) Rules, SI 2013/606 rule 2(1), (5) with effect from 1 April 2013.

Register of references and decisions

[**3** (1) The Upper Tribunal must keep a register of references and decisions in financial services cases [and wholesale energy cases][3].

(2) The register must be open to inspection by any person without charge and at all reasonable hours.

[(3) The Upper Tribunal may direct that the register is not to include particulars of a reference if it is satisfied that it is necessary to do so having regard [in particular to—

(*a*) any unfairness to the applicant or, except as regards a reference in respect of a decision of the Prudential Regulation Authority, any prejudice to the interests of consumers that might otherwise result;

(*b*) as regards a reference in respect of a decision of the Financial Conduct Authority, any detriment to the stability of the UK financial system;

(*c*) as regards a reference in respect of a decision of the Prudential Regulation Authority, any prejudice to the safety and soundness of persons authorised by it, or where section 2C of the 2000 Act applies, any prejudice to securing the appropriate degree of protection for policy holders; or

(*d*) as regards a reference under the 2013 Regulations or the 2013 (NI) Regulations any detriment to the stability of the wholesale energy market as defined in those Regulations.][3]

(4) Upon receiving a reference notice, the Upper Tribunal must—

(*a*) subject to any direction given under sub-paragraph (3), enter particulars of the reference in the register; and

(*b*) notify the parties either that it has done so or that it will not include particulars in the register, as the case may be.

[(5) In a multiple regulator case, notification under sub-paragraph (4)(*b*) must be given to each of the primary and secondary regulators.][2]][1]

Amendments—[1] Schedule 3 inserted by the Tribunal Procedure (Upper Tribunal) (Amendment) Rules, SI 2010/747 rules 2, 13 with effect from 6 April 2010.

[2] Sub-para (5) inserted by the Tribunal Procedure (Amendment No 2) Rules, SI 2013/606 rule 2(1), (6) with effect from 1 April 2013.

[3] Words in sub-para (1) inserted, and in sub-para (3), words substituted by the Tribunal Procedure (Amendment) Rules, SI 2014/514 rules 2, 13(*c*) with effect from 6 April 2014.

[Respondent's statement of case in a single regulator case]

[4 (1) The respondent [in a single regulator case][2] must send or deliver a written statement ("a statement of case") in support of the referred action so that it is received by the Upper Tribunal no later than 28 days after the day on which the respondent received from the Upper Tribunal the notification required by paragraph 3(4)(*b*).

(2) The statement of case must—

(*a*) identify the statutory provisions providing for the referred action;

(*b*) state the reasons for the referred action; and

(*c*) set out all the matters and facts upon which the respondent relies to support the referred action.

(3) The respondent must provide with the statement of case a list of—

(*a*) any documents on which the respondent relies in support of the referred action; and

(*b*) any further material which in the opinion of the respondent might undermine the decision to take that action.

(4) At the same time as it sends or delivers the statement of case, the respondent must send to the applicant a copy of the statement of case and of the list referred to in sub-paragraph (3).][1]

Amendments—[1] Schedule 3 inserted by the Tribunal Procedure (Upper Tribunal) (Amendment) Rules, SI 2010/747 rules 2, 13 with effect from 6 April 2010.

[2] Heading substituted and words in sub-para (1) inserted, by the Tribunal Procedure (Amendment No 2) Rules, SI 2013/606 rule 2(1), (7) with effect from 1 April 2013.

Respondents' statements of case in a multiple regulator case

[4A (1) This paragraph applies in a multiple regulator case.

(2) The primary regulator must send or deliver either—

(*a*) a written statement (a "statement of case") in support of the referred action; or

(*b*) a written notification that it does not itself advance a case in support of the referred action,

so that it is received by the Upper Tribunal no later than 28 days after the day on which the primary regulator received from the Upper Tribunal the notification required by paragraph 3(4)(*b*).

(3) A primary regulator providing a written notification under sub-paragraph (2)(*b*) must send or deliver a copy to the secondary regulator and the applicant and upon so doing—

(*a*) the primary regulator shall not be required to take further steps in the proceedings unless the Upper Tribunal gives a direction to the contrary under rule 6; and

(*b*) the respondent shall be the secondary regulator unless the Upper Tribunal orders otherwise.

(4) The secondary regulator must send or deliver a written statement ("a statement of case") in support of its decision to take the secondary regulator action so that it is received by the Upper Tribunal no later than 28 days after the day on which the secondary regulator received from the Upper Tribunal the notification required by paragraph 3(4)(*b*).

(5) A statement of case must—

(*a*) identify the statutory provisions providing for the referred action;

(*b*) state the reasons in support for the referred action; and

(*c*) set out all the matters and facts upon which the regulator relies to support the referred action.

(6) A regulator must provide with the statement of case a list of—

(*a*) all documents on which it relies in support of the referred action;

(*b*) any further material which, in the opinion of the regulator, might undermine its decision to—

(i) in the case of a primary regulator; take the referred action; and

(ii) in the case of a secondary regulator; take the secondary regulator action.

(7) The primary regulator and the secondary regulator must send to the applicant and the other regulator a copy of any statement of case required by sub-paragraphs (2) and (4) above and of the list referred to in sub-paragraph (6).][1]

Amendments—[1] Para 4A inserted by the Tribunal Procedure (Amendment No 2) Rules, SI 2013/606 rule 2(1), (8) with effect from 1 April 2013.

Applicant's reply

[5—(1) The applicant must send or deliver a written reply so that it is received by the Upper Tribunal no later than 28 days after—

[(*a*) in a single regulator case, on the date on which the applicant received a copy of the statement of case;

(*aa*) in a multiple regulator case, on the first date on which the applicant was in receipt of all the statements and, where relevant, notifications required under paragraphs 4A(2) and 4A(4); or][2]

(*b*) if [a respondent][2] amends its statement of case, the date on which the applicant received a copy of the amended statement of case.

(2) The reply must—

(*a*) state the grounds on which the applicant relies in the reference;
(*b*) identify all matters contained in [the respondent's statement of case (or, where applicable, respondents' statements of case)][2] which are disputed by the applicant; . . . [2]
(*c*) state the applicant's reasons for disputing them.

(3) The applicant must send with the reply a list of all the documents on which the applicant relies in support of his case.

(4) At the same time the applicant must send to [all other parties][2] a copy of the reply and of the list referred to in sub-paragraph (3).

[(5) Where the primary regulator has provided a written notification under paragraph 4A(2)(*b*), if the applicant wishes the Tribunal to direct that further steps in the proceedings be taken by the primary regulator, an application must be made at the time of sending the reply.][2]

Amendments—[1] Schedule 3 inserted by the Tribunal Procedure (Upper Tribunal) (Amendment) Rules, SI 2010/747 rules 2, 13 with effect from 6 April 2010.

[2] In sub-para (1), paras (*a*), (*aa*) substituted for previous para (*a*), and words in para (*b*) substituted; in sub-para (2)(*b*) words substituted and word "and" revoked; in sub-para (4) words substituted; and sub-para (5) inserted; by the Tribunal Procedure (Amendment No 2) Rules, SI 2013/606 rule 2(1), (9) with effect from 1 April 2013.

Secondary disclosure by [a respondent]

[6—(1) After the applicant's reply has been sent or delivered, if there is any further material which might reasonably be expected to assist the applicant's case as disclosed by the applicant's reply and which is not listed in the list [(or lists)][2] provided in accordance with paragraph 4(3) [(or paragraph 4A(6) where applicable)][2], the respondent [(or the respondents)][2] must send or deliver to the Upper Tribunal a list [(or lists)][2] of such further material.

(2) Any list required to be sent or delivered by sub-paragraph (1) must be sent or delivered so that it is received no later than 14 days after the day on which the respondent [in question][2] received the applicant's reply.

(3) At the same time as it sends or delivers any list required by sub-paragraph (1) [a respondent must send a copy to the applicant (and where applicable the other parties)][2].][1]

Amendments—[1] Schedule 3 inserted by the Tribunal Procedure (Upper Tribunal) (Amendment) Rules, SI 2010/747 rules 2, 13 with effect from 6 April 2010.

[2] Words in heading substituted, words in sub-paras (1), (2) inserted, and words in sub-para (3) substituted, by the Tribunal Procedure (Amendment No 2) Rules, SI 2013/606 rule 2(1), (10) with effect from 1 April 2013.

Exceptions to disclosure

[7—(1) A list provided in accordance with paragraph 4(3)[, 4A(6)][2] or 6(1) need not include any document that relates to a case involving a person other than the applicant which was taken into account by the respondent [providing the list][2] in the applicant's case only for the purposes of comparison with other cases.

(2) A list provided in accordance with paragraph 4(3)[, 4A(6)][2], 5(3) or 6(1) need not include any document that is material the disclosure of which for the purposes of or in connection with any legal proceedings is prohibited by section 17 of the Regulation of Investigatory Powers Act 2000.

(3) A list provided in accordance with paragraph 4(3)[, 4A(6)][2], 5(3) or 6(1) need not include any document in respect of which an application has been or is being made under sub-paragraph (4).

(4) A party may apply to the Upper Tribunal (without giving notice to any other party) for a direction authorising the party making the application not to include in the list required by paragraph 4(3)[, 4A(6)][2], 5(3) or 6(1) a document on the ground that disclosure of the document—
(*a*) would not be in the public interest; or
(*b*) would not be fair, having regard to—
(i) the likely significance of the document to the applicant in relation to the matter referred to the Upper Tribunal; and
(ii) the potential prejudice to the commercial interests of a person other than the applicant which would be caused by disclosure of the document.

(5) For the purpose of deciding an application by a party under sub-paragraph (4), the Upper Tribunal may—
(*a*) require the document to be produced to the Upper Tribunal together with a statement of the reasons why its inclusion in the list would—
(i) in the case of an application under sub-paragraph (4)(*a*), not be in the public interest; or
(ii) in the case of an application under sub-paragraph (4)(*b*), not be fair; and
(*b*) invite any other party to make representations.

(6) If the Upper Tribunal refuses an application under sub-paragraph (4), it must direct the party—
(*a*) to revise its list so as to include the document; and
(*b*) to send or deliver a copy of the revised list to the Upper Tribunal and to any other party.

[(7) A party ("P") who has sent or delivered a list under paragraph 4(3), 4A(6), 5(3) or 6(1) must, upon the request of another party, provide that other party with a copy of any document which P has which is specified in the list, or make it available for inspection or copying, and if P does not have it, tell the other party where to the best of P's knowledge and belief it may be found.][2]
(8) Sub-paragraph (7) does not apply to any document that is a protected item.
(9) In this paragraph "protected item" has the meaning provided by section 413 of the 2000 Act, section 311(2) of the Pensions Act 2004 or article 283(2) of the Pensions (Northern Ireland) Order 2005 [or regulation 52(2) of the 2013 Regulations or regulation 51(2) of the 2013 (NI) Regulations][3].][1]

Amendments—[1] Schedule 3 inserted by the Tribunal Procedure (Upper Tribunal) (Amendment) Rules, SI 2010/747 rules 2, 13 with effect from 6 April 2010.
[2] Words in sub-paras (1)–(4) inserted, and sub-para (7) substituted, by the Tribunal Procedure (Amendment No 2) Rules, SI 2013/606 rule 2(1), (11) with effect from 1 April 2013.
[3] Words in sub-para (9) inserted by the Tribunal Procedure (Amendment) Rules, SI 2014/514 rules 2, 13(*d*) with effect from 6 April 2014.

Subsequent notices in relation to the referred action

[8—Where, after a reference notice has been sent or delivered, [a respondent][2] gives the applicant any further, amended or supplementary notice in relation to the referred action, [that respondent][2] must without delay send or deliver a copy of that notice to the Upper Tribunal.][1]

Amendments—[1] Schedule 3 inserted by the Tribunal Procedure (Upper Tribunal) (Amendment) Rules, SI 2010/747 rules 2, 13 with effect from 6 April 2010.
[2] Words substituted by the Tribunal Procedure (Amendment No 2) Rules, SI 2013/606 rule 2(1), (12) with effect from 1 April 2013.

References by third parties

[9—(1) In the case of any reference made by an applicant under section 393 of the 2000 Act[, regulation 40 of the 2013 Regulations or regulation 40 of the 2013 (NI) Regulations][3] (third party rights) these rules apply subject to the modifications set out in this paragraph.
(2) In this paragraph—

(*a*) if the reference was made under section 393(9) of the 2000 Act[, regulation 40(9) of the 2013 Regulations or regulation 40(9) of the 2013 (NI) Regulations][3] (reference to the Upper Tribunal by a third party to whom a decision notice was copied), the notice of the decision in respect of which the reference has been made is the decision notice which was copied to the applicant by the respondent [that gave the notice][2]; and

(*b*) if the reference was made under section 393(11) of the 2000 Act[, regulation 40(11) of the 2013 Regulations or regulation 40(11) of the 2013 (NI) Regulations][3] (reference to the Upper Tribunal by a third party who alleges that they were not given a copy of a decision notice), the notice of the decision in respect of which the reference has been made is the decision notice which the applicant alleges was not copied to them.

(3) If the reference was made under section 393(11) of the 2000 Act[, regulation 40(11) of the 2013 Regulations or regulation 40(11) of the 2013 (NI) Regulations][3], paragraph 2(4) does not apply.
[(4) The duties of a respondent to—

(*a*) set out information under paragraphs 4(2), 4A(2), 4A(4) or 4A(5); or

(*b*) list material under paragraphs 4(3), 4A(6) or 6(1);

apply only to information or material which relate to the matters referred to the Upper Tribunal in accordance with section 393(9) or (as the case may be) section 393(11) of the 2000 Act[, regulation 40(9) or, as the case may be, regulation 40(11) of the 2013 Regulations, or regulation 40(9) or, as the case may be, regulation 40(11) of the 2013 (NI) Regulations][3].][2]][1]

Amendments—[1] Schedule 3 inserted by the Tribunal Procedure (Upper Tribunal) (Amendment) Rules, SI 2010/747 rules 2, 13 with effect from 6 April 2010.
[2] Words in sub-para (2)(*a*) inserted, and sub-para (4) substituted, by the Tribunal Procedure (Amendment No 2) Rules, SI 2013/606 rule 2(1), (13) with effect from 1 April 2013.
[3] Words inserted by the Tribunal Procedure (Amendment) Rules, SI 2014/514 rules 2, 13(*e*) with effect from 6 April 2014.

[SCHEDULE 4

PROCEDURE IN FINANCIAL SANCTIONS CASES

Rule 26C

Amendments—Schedule 4 inserted by the Tribunal Procedure (Upper Tribunal) (Amendment) Rules, SI 2017/723 rules 5, 13 with effect from 27 July 2017.

[Interpretation

1 In this Schedule—

"2017 Act" means the Policing and Crime Act 2017.

"financial sanctions legislation" has the meaning provided by section 143(4) of the 2017 Act.

"further material" means documents which—

(*a*) were considered by the Treasury in reaching a decision under section 147(3) of the 2017 Act to impose the monetary penalty that is the subject of the appeal; or

(*b*) were considered by the Minister in reaching a decision under section 147(4) of the 2017 Act to uphold the monetary penalty that is the subject of the appeal; or

(*c*) were obtained by either the Treasury or the Minister in connection with a decision described above (whether they were obtained before or after making the decision) but which were not considered by them in reaching that decision, but does not include documents on which the respondent relies in support of the decision made.][1]

Amendments—[1] Schedule 4 inserted by the Tribunal Procedure (Upper Tribunal) (Amendment) Rules, SI 2017/723 rules 5, 13 with effect from 27 July 2017.

[Notice of appeal

2 (1) A notice of appeal must be made in writing and received by the Upper Tribunal no later than 28 days after notice was given of the decision under challenge.

(2) The notice of appeal must state—

(*a*) the name and address of the appellant;

(*b*) the name and address of the appellant's representative (if any);

(*c*) if no representative is named under sub-paragraph (*b*), an address where documents for the appellant may be sent or delivered;

(*d*) details (including the full reference) of the decision challenged; and

(*e*) the grounds on which the appellant relies.

(3) The appellant must provide with the notice of appeal a copy of—

(*a*) any written record of the Treasury's decision under section 147(3) of the 2017 Act;

(*b*) any written record of the Minister's decision under section 147(4) of the 2017 Act;

(*c*) any separate written statement of reasons for either of those decisions.

(4) If the appellant provides the notice of appeal to the Upper Tribunal later than the time required by sub-paragraph (1) or by an extension of time allowed under rule 5(3)(*a*) (power to extend time)—

(*a*) the notice of appeal must include a request for an extension of time and the reason why the notice of appeal was not provided in time; and

(*b*) unless the Upper Tribunal extends time for the application under rule 5(3)(*a*) (power to extend time) the Upper Tribunal must not admit the notice of appeal.

(5) At the same time as it sends the notice to the Upper Tribunal, the appellant must send a copy of the notice and any accompanying documents to the respondent.][1]

Amendments—[1] Schedule 4 inserted by the Tribunal Procedure (Upper Tribunal) (Amendment) Rules, SI 2017/723 rules 5, 13 with effect from 27 July 2017.

[Respondent's statement of case

3 (1) On receipt of a copy of a notice of appeal, the respondent must send or deliver a written statement ("a statement of case") in support of the decision taken so that it is received by the Upper Tribunal no later than 28 days after the day on which the respondent received from the Upper Tribunal the copy of the notice of appeal.

(2) The statement of case must—

(*a*) identify the provisions of the financial sanctions legislation by reference to which the decision was made;

(*b*) state the reasons for the decision; and

(*c*) set out all the matters and facts upon which the respondent relies to support the decision.

(3) The respondent must provide with the statement of case a list of—

(*a*) any documents (or relevant extracts) on which the respondent relies in support of the decision; and

(*b*) any further material (or relevant extracts) which in the opinion of the respondent might undermine the decision taken.

(4) At the same time as it sends or delivers the statement of case to the Upper Tribunal, the respondent must send to the appellant a copy of the statement of case and of the list referred to in sub-paragraph (3).][1]

Amendments—[1] Schedule 4 inserted by the Tribunal Procedure (Upper Tribunal) (Amendment) Rules, SI 2017/723 rules 5, 13 with effect from 27 July 2017.

[Appellant's reply

4 (1) The appellant must send or deliver a written reply so that it is received by the Upper Tribunal no later than 28 days after the date on which the appellant received a copy of the statement of case.

(2) The reply must—

(*a*) identify all matters contained in the respondent's statement of case which are disputed by the appellant; and

(*b*) state the appellant's reasons for disputing them.

(3) The appellant must send with the reply a list of all the documents (or relevant extracts) on which the appellant relies in support of the appellant's case.

(4) At the same time as it sends or delivers the written reply required by sub-paragraph (1) to the Upper Tribunal, the appellant must send to the respondent a copy of the reply and of the list referred to in sub-paragraph (3).][1]

Amendments—[1] Schedule 4 inserted by the Tribunal Procedure (Upper Tribunal) (Amendment) Rules, SI 2017/723 rules 5, 13 with effect from 27 July 2017.

[Secondary disclosure by the respondent

5—(1) After the appellant's reply has been sent or delivered, if there is any further material (or relevant extracts) which might reasonably be expected to assist the appellant's case as disclosed by the appellant's reply and which is not listed in the list provided in accordance with paragraph 4(3), the respondent must send or deliver to the Upper Tribunal a list of such further material (or relevant extracts).

(2) Any list required to be sent or delivered by sub-paragraph (1) must be sent or delivered so that it is received no later than 14 days after the day on which the respondent received the appellant's reply.

(3) At the same time as it sends or delivers any list required by sub-paragraph (1) to the Upper Tribunal, the respondent must send a copy to the appellant.][1]

Amendments—[1] Schedule 4 inserted by the Tribunal Procedure (Upper Tribunal) (Amendment) Rules, SI 2017/723 rules 5, 13 with effect from 27 July 2017.

[Exceptions to disclosure

6—(1) A list provided in accordance with paragraph 3(3), 4(3) or 5(1) need not include any document:

(*a*) that is material the disclosure of which for the purposes of or in connection with any legal proceedings is prohibited by section 17 of the Regulation of Investigatory Powers Act 2000; or

(*b*) in respect of which an application has been or is being made under sub-paragraph (2).

(2) A party may apply to the Upper Tribunal (without giving notice to any other party) for a direction authorising the party making the application not to include in the list required by paragraph 3(3), 4(3) or 5(1) a document on the ground that disclosure of the document—

(*a*) would not be in the public interest; or

(*b*) should not otherwise be given.

(3) For the purpose of deciding an application by a party under sub-paragraph (2), the Upper Tribunal may—

(*a*) require the document to be produced to the Upper Tribunal together with a statement of the reasons why—

(i) in the case of an application under sub-paragraph (2)(*a*), its disclosure would not be in the public interest; or

(ii) in the case of an application under sub-paragraph (2)(*b*), its disclosure should not be given; and

(*b*) invite the other party to make representations.

(4) If the Upper Tribunal refuses an application under sub-paragraph (2), it must direct the party—

(*a*) to revise its list so as to include the document; and

(*b*) to send or deliver a copy of the revised list to the Upper Tribunal and to the other party.

(7) A party ("P") who has sent or delivered a list under paragraph 3(3), 4(3) or 5(1) must, upon the request of the other party, provide that party with a copy of any document which P has which is specified in the list, or make it available for inspection or copying, and if P does not have it, tell the other party where to the best of P's knowledge and belief it may be found.

(8) Sub-paragraph (7) does not apply to any document in respect of which a claim to legal professional privilege, or (in Scotland) to confidentiality of communications as between client and professional legal adviser, could be maintained in legal proceedings.][1]

Note—Publisher's note: the text of this para as published includes sub-paras (7), (8). It is the Publisher's view that the intention was that these sub-paras should be numbered (5), (6) respectively, and that accordingly, the reference in sub-para (8) as published should be to sub-para (5).

Amendments—[1] Schedule 4 inserted by the Tribunal Procedure (Upper Tribunal) (Amendment) Rules, SI 2017/723 rules 5, 13 with effect from 27 July 2017.

2008/2834

APPEALS FROM THE UPPER TRIBUNAL TO THE COURT OF APPEAL ORDER 2008

Made . . . .*29 October 2008*
Coming into force in accordance with . . . .*article 1*

The Lord Chancellor makes the following Order in exercise of the power conferred by section 13(6) of the Tribunals, Courts and Enforcement Act 2007.

A draft of this Order was laid before Parliament and approved by a resolution of each House of Parliament in accordance with section 49(5) of that Act.

1 This Order may be cited as the Appeals from the Upper Tribunal to the Court of Appeal Order 2008 and shall come into force on 3rd November 2008.

2 Permission to appeal to the Court of Appeal in England and Wales or leave to appeal to the Court of Appeal in Northern Ireland shall not be granted unless the Upper Tribunal or, where the Upper Tribunal refuses permission, the relevant appellate court, considers that—

(*a*) the proposed appeal would raise some important point of principle or practice; or
(*b*) there is some other compelling reason for the relevant appellate court to hear the appeal.

2008/2835

FIRST-TIER TRIBUNAL AND UPPER TRIBUNAL (COMPOSITION OF TRIBUNAL) ORDER 2008

Made . . . .*29 October 2008*
Coming into force . . . .*3 November 2008*

The Lord Chancellor makes the following Order in exercise of the powers conferred by section 145(1) of, and paragraph 15 of Schedule 4 to, the Tribunals, Courts and Enforcement Act 2007.

In accordance with paragraph 15(8) of that Act the Lord Chancellor has consulted the Senior President of Tribunals.

In accordance with section 49(5) of that Act a draft of this instrument was laid before Parliament and approved by a resolution of each House of Parliament.

1 Citation and commencement

This Order may be cited as the First-tier Tribunal and Upper Tribunal (Composition of Tribunal) Order 2008 and comes into force on 3rd November 2008.

2 Number of members of the First-tier Tribunal

(1) The number of members of the tribunal who are to decide any matter that falls to be decided by the First-tier Tribunal must be determined by the Senior President of Tribunals in accordance with paragraph (2).

(2) The Senior President of Tribunals must have regard to—

(*a*) where the matter which falls to be decided by the tribunal fell to a tribunal in a list in Schedule 6 to the Tribunals, Courts and Enforcement Act 2007 before its functions were transferred by order under section 30(1) of that Act, any provision made by or under any enactment for determining the number of members of that tribunal; and
(*b*) the need for members of tribunals to have particular expertise, skills or knowledge.

3 Number of members of the Upper Tribunal

(1) The number of members of the tribunal who are to decide any matter that falls to be decided by the Upper Tribunal is one unless determined otherwise under paragraph (2).

(2) The tribunal may consist of two or three members if the Senior President of Tribunals so determines.

4 Tribunal consisting of single member

(1) Where a matter is to be decided by a single member of a tribunal, it must be decided by a judge of the tribunal unless paragraph (2) applies.

(2) The matter may be decided by one of the other members of the tribunal if the Senior President of Tribunals so determines.

5 Tribunal consisting of two or more members

The following articles apply where a matter is to be decided by two or more members of a tribunal.

6 The number of members who are to be judges of the tribunal and the number of members who are to be other members of the tribunal must be determined by the Senior President of Tribunals.

7 The Senior President of Tribunals must select one of the members (the "presiding member") to chair the tribunal.

8 If the decision of the tribunal is not unanimous, the decision of the majority is the decision of the tribunal; and the presiding member has a casting vote if the votes are equally divided.

2009/56

TRANSFER OF TRIBUNAL FUNCTIONS AND REVENUE AND CUSTOMS APPEALS ORDER 2009

Made . . . . *18th January 2009*

Coming into force . . . . *1st April 2009*

The Lord Chancellor and the Treasury make the following Order in exercise of the powers conferred by sections 30(1) and (4), 31(1), (2) and (9) and 38 of, and paragraph 30 of Schedule 5 to, the Tribunals, Courts and Enforcement Act 2007 and section 124(1) to (7) of the Finance Act 2008.

A draft of this Order was laid before Parliament and approved by resolution of each House of Parliament in accordance with section 49(5) of the Tribunals, Courts and Enforcement Act 2007 and section 124(9) of the Finance Act 2008.

1 Citation and commencement

(1) This Order may be cited as the Transfer of Tribunal Functions and Revenue and Customs Appeals Order 2009.

(2) This Order comes into force on 1st April 2009.

2 The existing tribunals

In this Order "existing tribunals" means—

(*a*) the Commissioners for the general purposes of the income tax established under section 2 of the Taxes Management Act 1970;

(*b*) the Commissioners for the special purposes of the Income Tax Acts established under section 4 of the Taxes Management Act 1970;

(*c*) the VAT and duties tribunals established under Schedule 12 to the Value Added Tax Act 1994;

(*d*) the tribunal established under section 706 of the Income and Corporation Taxes Act 1988; and

(*e*) the tribunal established under section 704 of the Income Tax Act 2007.

3 Transfer of functions, consequential and other amendments

(1) Schedule 1 contains amendments to primary legislation which—

(*a*) transfer functions of existing tribunals, and

(*b*) make consequential and other provision (including provision about reviews of decisions by Her Majesty's Revenue and Customs).

(2) Schedule 2 contains amendments to secondary legislation which—

(*a*) transfer functions of existing tribunals, and

(*b*) make consequential and other provision (including provision about reviews of decisions by Her Majesty's Revenue and Customs).

4 Abolition of existing tribunals

The existing tribunals (apart from the Commissioners for the general purposes of the income tax) are abolished.

5 Transfer of members of existing tribunals

A person who, immediately before this Order comes into force, holds an office listed in column 1 of any of the following tables is to hold the office or offices listed in the corresponding entry in column 2 of that table—

The Special Commissioners	
1 Office held	2 Office or offices to be held
Commissioner for the special purposes of the Income Tax Acts appointed under section 4 of the Taxes Management Act 1970	Transferred-in judge of the Upper Tribunal
Deputy Commissioner for the special purposes of the Income Tax Acts appointed under section 4A of the Taxes Management Act 1970	Transferred-in judge of the First-tier Tribunal and deputy judge of the Upper Tribunal

VAT and duties tribunals	
1 Office held	*2 Office or offices to be held*

President of VAT and duties tribunals appointed under paragraph 2 of Schedule 12 to the Value Added Tax Act 1994	Transferred-in judge of the Upper Tribunal
Person appointed to a panel of chairmen of a VAT and duties tribunal under paragraph 7 of Schedule 12 to the Value Added Tax Act 1994	Transferred-in judge of the First-tier Tribunal and deputy judge of the Upper Tribunal
Person appointed to a panel of other members of a VAT and duties tribunal under paragraph 7 of Schedule 12 to the Value Added Tax Act 1994	Transferred-in other member of the First-tier Tribunal

Tribunal established under section 706 ICTA 1988	
1 Office held	*2 Office or offices to be held*
Chairman of the tribunal appointed under section 706(1)(*a*) of the Income and Corporation Taxes Act 1988	Transferred-in judge of the Upper Tribunal
Other member of the tribunal appointed under section 706(1)(*b*) of the Income and Corporation Taxes Act 1988	Transferred-in other member of the First-tier Tribunal

Tribunal established under section 704 ITA 2007	
1 Office held	*2 Office or offices to be held*
Chairman of the tribunal appointed under section 704(1)(*a*) of the Income Taxes Act 2007	Transferred-in judge of the Upper Tribunal
Other member of the tribunal appointed under section 704(1)(*b*) of the Income Taxes Act 2007	Transferred-in other member of the First-tier Tribunal

6 Transitionals and savings

Schedule 3 contains—

(*a*) transitional provision, and

(*b*) saving provision.

SCHEDULE 1

CONSEQUENTIAL AMENDMENTS AND SUPPLEMENTAL PROVISIONS—PRIMARY LEGISLATION

Article 3

Note—The amendments made by this Schedule are already in force and are therefore not reproduced.

SCHEDULE 2

CONSEQUENTIAL AMENDMENTS AND SUPPLEMENTAL PROVISIONS—SECONDARY LEGISLATION

Article 3

Note—The amendments made by this Schedule are already in force and are therefore not reproduced.

SCHEDULE 3

TRANSITIONAL AND SAVING PROVISIONS

Article 6

General

1—(1) In this Schedule—

"commencement date" means the date on which this Order comes into force;

"enactment" includes subordinate legislation (within the meaning of the Interpretation Act 1978);

"HMRC" means Her Majesty's Revenue and Customs;

"tribunal" means the First-tier Tribunal or, where determined by or under Tribunal Procedure Rules, the Upper Tribunal.

(2) For the purposes of this Schedule there are "current proceedings" if, before the commencement date—

(*a*) any party has served notice on an existing tribunal for the purpose of beginning proceedings before the existing tribunal, and

(*b*) the existing tribunal has not concluded proceedings arising by virtue of that notice.

Former VAT and duties tribunals matters (except VAT)

2—(1) This paragraph applies in relation to the following decisions—

(*a*) any relevant decision which HMRC notify before the commencement date, unless—

(i) the period to require a review of the decision has expired before that date, or

(ii) a review of the decision has been required before that date;

(*b*) any relevant review decision which HMRC notify before the commencement date unless—

(i) the period to serve notice of appeal against the decision on an existing tribunal has expired before that date, or

(ii) notice of appeal against the decision has been served on an existing tribunal before that date.

(2) On and after the commencement date, the following enactments continue to apply (subject to sub-paragraphs (3) and (4)) as they applied immediately before that date—

(*a*) the review and appeal provisions,

(*b*) rule 4(2) of the Value Added Tax Tribunals Rules 1986, and

(*c*) any other enactments that apply in relation to relevant decisions or relevant review decisions.

(3) Those enactments apply subject to Tribunal Procedure Rules.

(4) Any reference to an existing tribunal is to be substituted with a reference to the tribunal.

(5) Any time period which has started to run before the commencement date and has not expired will continue to apply.

(6) In this paragraph—

"relevant decision" means a decision to which a review and appeal provision applies (apart from a relevant review decision);

"relevant review decision" means a decision—

(*a*) that is made on a review of a relevant decision, and

(*b*) to which a review and appeal provision applies,

and includes a relevant decision that is treated as having been confirmed under a review and appeal provision.

"review and appeal provisions" means—

(*a*) sections 14 to 16 of the Finance Act 1994,

(*b*) sections 59 and 60 of the Finance Act 1994,

(*c*) sections 54 to 56 of the Finance Act 1996,

(*d*) paragraphs 121 to 123 of Schedule 6 to the Finance Act 2000,

(*e*) sections 40 to 42 of the Finance Act 2001,

(*f*) sections 33 to 37 of the Finance Act 2003,

(*g*) regulations 9 to 13 of the Export (Penalty) Regulations 2003,

(*h*) regulations 4 to 7 of the Control of Cash (Penalties) Regulations 2007,

(*i*) [regulations 94 to 100 of the Money Laundering, Terrorist Financing and Transfer of Funds (Information on the Payer) Regulations 2017][1], . . .

(*j*) . . . [1]

Amendments—[1] In para (6), in definition of "review and appeal provisions", in para (*i*) words substituted for words "regulations 43 and 44 of the Money Laundering Regulations 2007", and para (*j*) revoked, by the Money Laundering, Terrorist Financing and Transfer of Funds (Information on the Payer) Regulations, SI 2017/692 reg 109, Sch 7 para 23 with effect from 26 June 2017. Para (*j*) previously read as follows—

"(*j*) regulations 12 and 13 of the Transfer of Funds (Information on the Payer) Regulations 2007.".

3—(1) This paragraph applies in relation to a relevant decision if, before the commencement date—

(*a*) HMRC have notified the relevant decision, and

(*b*) a review of the decision has begun under a review and appeal provision (whether or not a relevant review decision has been notified).

(2) On and after the commencement date the following enactments continue to apply (subject to sub-paragraphs (3) and (4)), as they applied immediately before that date—

(*a*) the review and appeal provisions,

(*b*) rule 4(2) of the VAT Tribunals Rules 1986, and

(*c*) any other enactments that apply in relation to relevant decisions or relevant review decisions.

(3) Those enactments apply subject to Tribunal Procedure Rules.

(4) Any reference to an existing tribunal is to be substituted with a reference to the tribunal.

(5) Any time period which has started to run before the commencement date and has not expired will continue to apply.

(6) On and after the commencement date, no notification offering or requiring a review may be given under any review and appeal provision or any other enactments that are applicable to the decision as they apply after that date.

(7) In this paragraph "review and appeal provision", "relevant decision" and "relevant review decision" have the same meaning as in paragraph 2.

Former VAT and duties tribunals matters: VAT

4—(1) This paragraph applies if, before the commencement date—

(*a*) HMRC have notified a decision relating to a matter to which section 83 of the Value Added Tax Act 1994 applies, and

(*b*) no party has served notice on a VAT and duties tribunal for the purpose of beginning proceedings before such a tribunal in relation to that decision.

(2) On and after the commencement date, the following enactments continue to apply (subject to sub-paragraphs (3) and (4)) as they applied immediately before that date—

(*a*) the Value Added Tax Act 1994,

(*b*) rule 4(2) of the VAT Tribunals Rules 1986, and

(*c*) any other enactments that are applicable to the decision.

(3) Those enactments apply subject to Tribunal Procedure Rules.

(4) Any reference to an existing tribunal is to be substituted with a reference to the tribunal.

(5) Any time period which has started to run before the commencement date and has not expired will continue to apply.

Matters formerly heard by existing tribunals (except VAT and duties tribunals)

5—(1) This paragraph applies if, before the commencement date—

(*a*) a notice of appeal has been given to HMRC; but

(*b*) no party has served notice on an existing tribunal for the purpose of beginning proceedings before the existing tribunal in relation to that appeal.

(2) Where the date on which a review is required or offered falls on or before 31 March 2010, the period for HMRC to give notice of their conclusions for the purposes of the relevant provision is to be 90 days (but without prejudice to any power to agree to a different period).

(3) In this paragraph—

"review" means a review under—

(*a*) section 49B or 49C of the Taxes Management Act 1970, or

(*b*) any other enactment which, as amended by this Order, contains provisions corresponding to section 49B or 49C for review to be required or offered;

"relevant provision" means—

(*a*) in the case of a review under section 49B or 49C of the Taxes Management Act 1970, section 49E(6) of that Act, or

(*b*) in the case of a review under any other enactment amended by this Order, the provision that corresponds to section 49E(6) of the Taxes Management Act 1970 in relation to that review.

Current proceedings

6 Any current proceedings are to continue on and after the commencement date as proceedings before the tribunal.

7—(1) This paragraph applies to current proceedings that are continued before the tribunal by virtue of paragraph 6.

(2) Where a hearing before an existing tribunal (except for the Commissioners for the general purposes of the income tax) began before the commencement date but was not completed by that date, the tribunal must be comprised for the continuation of that hearing of the person or persons who began it.

(3) The tribunal may give any direction to ensure that proceedings are dealt with fairly and justly and, in particular, may—

(*a*) apply any provision in procedural rules which applied to the proceedings before the commencement date; or

(*b*) disapply any provision of Tribunal Procedure Rules.

(4) In sub-paragraph (3) "procedural rules" means any provision (whether called rules or not) regulating practice or procedure before an existing tribunal.
(5) Any direction or order made or given in proceedings which is in force immediately before the commencement date remains in force on and after that date as if it were a direction or order of the tribunal relating to proceedings before that tribunal.
(6) A time period which has started to run before the commencement date and which has not expired will continue to apply.
(7) An order for costs may only be made if, and to the extent that, an order could have been made before the commencement date (on the assumption, in the case of costs actually incurred after that date, that they had been incurred before that date).

Cases to be remitted by courts

8 Any case to be remitted by a court on or after the commencement date in relation to an existing tribunal shall be remitted to the tribunal.

Decisions of VAT and duties tribunals and courts: interest and payment

9—(1) This paragraph applies in relation to any decision of a VAT and duties tribunal made before the commencement date.
(2) On and after that date, the following provisions continue to apply as they applied immediately before that date—

(*a*) section 84(8) of the Value Added Tax Act 1994 (VAT),
(*b*) section 60(6) to (8) of the Finance Act 1994 (insurance premium tax),
(*c*) paragraphs 8 and 10 of Schedule 6 to the Finance Act 1994 (air passenger duty),
(*d*) section 56(3) to (5) of the Finance Act 1996 (landfill tax),
(*e*) paragraph 123(4) to (6) of Schedule 6 to the Finance Act 2000 (climate change levy),
(*f*) section 42(4) to (6) of the Finance Act 2001 (aggregates levy),
(*g*) paragraph 14(4) of Schedule 3 to the Finance Act 2001 (excise and customs).

10—(1) This paragraph applies if an appeal from a decision of a VAT and duties tribunal, or from a court, is made before the commencement date.
(2) Section 85B of the Value Added Tax Act 1994 does not apply in relation to that decision.

Decisions of existing tribunals: rights of appeal, reviews and irregularities

11—(1) This paragraph applies to a decision of an existing tribunal if, immediately before the commencement date—

(*a*) an appeal lies to a court from that decision,
(*b*) an application may be or has been made to an existing tribunal seeking a review of that decision, or
(*c*) the existing tribunal wishes to correct an irregularity.

(2) Except as provided for in sub-paragraph (3), on and after the commencement date such rights of appeal shall lie from the decision as would lie from a decision of the First-tier Tribunal made on or after that date.
(3) Subject to the modifications specified in sub-paragraphs (4) and (5) the following enactments continue to apply for the purposes of a case to be stated, a review, or for correcting an irregularity in respect of any decision of the Commissioners for the general purposes of the income tax made before the commencement date, as if the amendments in this Order had not been made—

(*a*) sections 56 and 58 of the Taxes Management Act 1970,
(*b*) regulations 17 and 20 to 24 of the General Commissioners (Jurisdiction and Procedure) Regulations 1994, and
(*c*) the General Commissioners of Income Tax (Costs) Regulations 2001.

(4) Section 56(6) of the Taxes Management Act 1970 is modified so that for "the Commissioners" there is substituted "the tribunal".
(5) Section 58 of the Taxes Management Act 1970 is modified as follows—

(*a*) omit subsection (2B); and
(*b*) in subsection (2C) omit "or on an appeal under section 56A of this Act".

(6) In article 4 of the Tribunals, Courts and Enforcement Act 2007 (Commencement No 6 and Transitional Provisions) Order 2008—

(*a*) for "section 56 of the 1970 Act (statement of case for opinion of the High Court)" substitute "sections 56(3) and (11) and 58 of the 1970 Act (statement of case for opinion of the High Court) and regulations 17 and 20 to 24 of the General Commissioners (Jurisdiction and Procedure) Regulations 1994 (review of tribunal's final determination, stated case procedures and correction of irregularities)"; and (*b*) after "commenced" insert ", and the amendments to the 1970 Act and the revocation of the General Commissioners (Jurisdiction and Procedure) Regulations 1994, the General Commissioners (Jurisdiction and Procedure) (Amendment) Regulations 1999, the General Commissioners (Jurisdiction and Procedure) (Amendment) Regulations 2005 and the General Commissioners and Special Commissioners (Jurisdiction and Procedure) (Amendment) Regulations 2007 (as they relate to the General Commissioners) in the Transfer of Tribunal Functions and Revenue and Customs Appeals Order 2009 had not been made".

Existing tribunals—staff

12 Staff appointed to the existing tribunals (except to the Commissioners for the general purposes of the income tax) before the commencement date are, on and after that date, to be treated, for the purpose of any enactment, as if they had been appointed by the Lord Chancellor under section 40(1) of the Tribunals, Courts and Enforcement Act 2007 (tribunal staff and services).

Transitional: general

13—(1) In so far as appropriate in consequence of this Order, a reference in an enactment, instrument or other document to an existing tribunal, or a member or official of an existing tribunal (however expressed) is to be taken to be a reference to the tribunal.
(2) Sub-paragraph (1) does not apply to any reference that is amended by Schedule 1 or 2.

2009/196

FIRST-TIER TRIBUNAL AND UPPER TRIBUNAL (CHAMBERS) (AMENDMENT) ORDER 2009

Made.......................................*9 February 2009*
Laid before Parliament.......................*13 February 2009*
Coming into force..............................*1 April 2009*

The Lord Chancellor, with the concurrence of the Senior President of Tribunals, makes the following Order in exercise of the power conferred by sections 7(1) and (9) and 145 of the Tribunals, Courts and Enforcement Act 2007.

Note—This Order revoked, except for the purposes of article 9, by the First-tier Tribunal and Upper Tribunal (Chambers) Order, SI 2010/2655 art 1(2), Schedule with effect from 29 November 2010.

9 Transitional provision

(1) This article applies to an appeal which lies to the to the Upper Tribunal by virtue of paragraph 11(2) of Schedule 3 to the Transfer of Tribunal Functions and Revenue and Customs Appeals Order 2009 (transitional provisions) against a decision of—
(*a*) the Commissioners for the general purposes of the income tax established under section 2 of the Taxes Management Act 1970;
(*b*) the Commissioners for the special purposes of the Income Tax Acts established under section 4 of the Taxes Management Act 1970;
(*c*) the VAT and duties tribunals established under Schedule 12 to the Value Added Tax Act 1994;
(*d*) the tribunal established under section 706 of the Income and Corporation Taxes Act 1988; or
(*e*) the tribunal established under section 704 of the Income Tax Act 2007.
(2) In rule 21(2)(*a*) of the Tribunal Procedure (Upper Tribunal) Rules 2008 (application to the Upper Tribunal for permission to appeal) the reference to the tribunal which made the decision challenged is to be read as a reference to the First-tier Tribunal.

2009/273

TRIBUNAL PROCEDURE (FIRST-TIER TRIBUNAL) (TAX CHAMBER) RULES 2009

Made.......................................*5 February 2009*
Laid before Parliament.......................*13 February 2009*
Coming into force..............................*1 April 2009*

After consulting in accordance with paragraph 28(1) of Schedule 5 to the Tribunals, Courts and Enforcement Act 2007, the Tribunal Procedure Committee has made the following Rules in exercise of the power conferred by sections 9(3), 22 and 29(3) of, and Schedule 5 to, that Act.

The Lord Chancellor has allowed the Rules in accordance with paragraph 28(3) of Schedule 5 to the Tribunals, Courts and Enforcement Act 2007.

PART 1
INTRODUCTION

1 Citation, commencement, application and interpretation

(1) These Rules may be cited as the Tribunal Procedure (First-tier Tribunal) (Tax Chamber) Rules 2009 and come into force on 1st April 2009.

[(2) These Rules apply to proceedings before the Tax Chamber of the First-tier Tribunal.][1]

(3) In these Rules—

"the 2007 Act" means the Tribunals, Courts and Enforcement Act 2007;

"appellant" means—

(*a*) the person who starts proceedings (whether by bringing or notifying an appeal, by making an originating application, by a reference, or otherwise);

(*b*) in proceedings started jointly by more than one person, such persons acting jointly or each such person, as the context requires;

(*c*) a person substituted as an appellant under rule 9 (substitution and addition of parties);

"Basic case" means a case allocated to the Basic category under rule 23 (allocation of cases to categories);

["CAA case" means an application under section 563 of the Capital Allowances Act 2001;][3]

"Complex case" means a case allocated to the Complex category under rule 23 (allocation of cases to categories);

["Compliance Officer" means the Compliance Officer for IPSA;][1]

"Default Paper case" means a case allocated to the Default Paper category under rule 23 (allocation of cases to categories);

"document" means anything in which information is recorded in any form, and an obligation under these Rules to provide or allow access to a document or a copy of a document for any purpose means, unless the Tribunal directs otherwise, an obligation to provide or allow access to such document or copy in a legible form or in a form which can be readily made into a legible form;

["financial restrictions civil penalty case" means an appeal under paragraph 26(3) or 28(1) of Schedule 7 to the Counter-Terrorism Act 2008;][3]

"hearing" means an oral hearing and includes a hearing conducted in whole or in part by video link, telephone or other means of instantaneous two-way electronic communication;

["HMRC" means Her Majesty's Revenue and Customs but also includes—

(*a*) the Serious Organised Crime Agency when carrying out functions under section 317 of the Proceeds of Crime Act 2002; and

(*b*) the Director of Border Revenue when carrying out functions under section 7 of the Borders, Citizenship and Immigration Act 2009;][1]

["IPSA" means the Independent Parliamentary Standards Authority;

"MP expenses case" means an appeal under the Parliamentary Standards Act 2009;][1]

"party" means a person who is (or was at the time that the Tribunal disposed of the proceedings) an appellant or respondent in proceedings before the Tribunal;

"practice direction" means a direction given under section 23 of the 2007 Act;

["respondent" means—

(*a*) in a case other than an MP expenses case—

(i) HMRC, where HMRC is not an appellant;

(ii) in proceedings brought by HMRC alone, a person against whom the proceedings are brought or to whom the proceedings relate;

(*b*) in a MP expenses case, the Compliance Officer; and

(*c*) in any case, a person substituted or added as a respondent under rule 9 (substitution and addition of parties);][1]

"Standard case" means a case allocated to the Standard category under rule 23 (allocation of cases to categories);

. . .[2]

"Tribunal" means the First-tier Tribunal.

Amendments—[1] Para (2) substituted, in para (3) definitions of "Compliance Officer", "IPSA", and "MP expense case" inserted, and definitions of "HMRC" and "respondent" substituted, by the Tribunal Procedure (Amendment No 3) Rules, SI 2010/2653 rule 6(1)–(3) with effect from 29 November 2010.

[2] In para (3) definition of "Tax Chamber" repealed by the Tribunal Procedure (Amendment) Rules, SI 2011/651 rule 5(1), (2) with effect from 1 April 2011.

[3] Definitions of "CAA case" and "financial restrictions civil penalty case" inserted by the Tribunal Procedure (Amendment) Rules, SI 2013/477 rules 33, 34 with effect from 1 April 2013.

2 Overriding objective and parties' obligation to co-operate with the Tribunal

(1) The overriding objective of these Rules is to enable the Tribunal to deal with cases fairly and justly.

(2) Dealing with a case fairly and justly includes—

(*a*) dealing with the case in ways which are proportionate to the importance of the case, the complexity of the issues, the anticipated costs and the resources of the parties;
(*b*) avoiding unnecessary formality and seeking flexibility in the proceedings;
(*c*) ensuring, so far as practicable, that the parties are able to participate fully in the proceedings;
(*d*) using any special expertise of the Tribunal effectively; and
(*e*) avoiding delay, so far as compatible with proper consideration of the issues.

(3) The Tribunal must seek to give effect to the overriding objective when it—
(*a*) exercises any power under these Rules; or
(*b*) interprets any rule or practice direction.

(4) Parties must—
(*a*) help the Tribunal to further the overriding objective; and
(*b*) co-operate with the Tribunal generally.

Simon's Tax Cases—*R&C Comrs v Ingenious Games LLP and others* [2014] UKUT 62 (TCC), [2014] STC 1416.

3 Alternative dispute resolution and arbitration

(1) The Tribunal should seek, where appropriate—
(*a*) to bring to the attention of the parties the availability of any appropriate alternative procedure for the resolution of the dispute; and
(*b*) if the parties wish and provided that it is compatible with the overriding objective, to facilitate the use of the procedure.

(2) Part 1 of the Arbitration Act 1996 does not apply to proceedings before the Tribunal.

PART 2
GENERAL POWERS AND PROVISIONS

4 Delegation to staff

(1) Staff appointed under section 40(1) of the 2007 Act (tribunal staff and services) may, with the approval of the Senior President of Tribunals, carry out functions of a judicial nature permitted or required to be done by the Tribunal.

(2) The approval referred to at paragraph (1) may apply generally to the carrying out of specified functions by members of staff of a specified description in specified circumstances.

(3) Within 14 days after the date that the Tribunal sends notice of a decision made by a member of staff pursuant to an approval under paragraph (1) to a party, that party may make a written application to the Tribunal requiring that decision to be considered afresh by a judge.

5 Case management powers

(1) Subject to the provisions of the 2007 Act and any other enactment, the Tribunal may regulate its own procedure.

(2) The Tribunal may give a direction in relation to the conduct or disposal of proceedings at any time, including a direction amending, suspending or setting aside an earlier direction.

(3) In particular, and without restricting the general powers in paragraphs (1) and (2), the Tribunal may by direction—
(*a*) extend or shorten the time for complying with any rule, practice direction or direction, unless such extension or shortening would conflict with a provision of another enactment setting down a time limit;
(*b*) consolidate or hear together two or more sets of proceedings or parts of proceedings raising common issues, or treat a case as a lead case (whether in accordance with rule 18 (lead cases) or otherwise);
(*c*) permit or require a party to amend a document;
(*d*) permit or require a party or another person to provide documents, information or submissions to the Tribunal or a party;
(*e*) deal with an issue in the proceedings as a preliminary issue;
(*f*) hold a hearing to consider any matter, including a case management hearing;
(*g*) decide the form of any hearing;
(*h*) adjourn or postpone a hearing;
(*i*) require a party to produce a bundle for a hearing;
(*j*) stay (or, in Scotland, sist) proceedings;
(*k*) transfer proceedings to another tribunal if that other tribunal has jurisdiction in relation to the proceedings and, because of a change of circumstances since the proceedings were started—
(i) the Tribunal no longer has jurisdiction in relation to the proceedings; or
(ii) the Tribunal considers that the other tribunal is a more appropriate forum for the determination of the case;
(*l*) suspend the effect of its own decision pending the determination by the Tribunal or the Upper Tribunal, as the case may be, of an application for permission to appeal, a review or an appeal.

Simon's Tax Cases—*R&C Comrs v Ingenious Games LLP and others* [2014] UKUT 62 (TCC), [2014] STC 1416.

6 Procedure for applying for and giving directions

(1) The Tribunal may give a direction on the application of one or more of the parties or on its own initiative.

(2) An application for a direction may be made—

(*a*) by sending or delivering a written application to the Tribunal; or

(*b*) orally during the course of a hearing.

(3) An application for a direction must include the reasons for making that application.

(4) Unless the Tribunal considers that there is good reason not to do so, the Tribunal must send written notice of any direction to every party and to any other person affected by the direction.

(5) If a party or other person sent notice of the direction under paragraph (4) wishes to challenge a direction which the Tribunal has given, they may do so by applying for another direction which amends, suspends or sets aside the first direction.

7 Failure to comply with rules etc

(1) An irregularity resulting from a failure to comply with any requirement in these Rules, a practice direction or a direction does not of itself render void the proceedings or any step taken in the proceedings.

(2) If a party has failed to comply with a requirement in these Rules, a practice direction or a direction, the Tribunal may take such action as it considers just, which may include—

(*a*) waiving the requirement;

(*b*) requiring the failure to be remedied;

(*c*) exercising its power under rule 8 (striking out a party's case);

(*d*) restricting a party's participation in proceedings; or

(*e*) exercising its power under paragraph (3).

(3) The Tribunal may refer to the Upper Tribunal, and ask the Upper Tribunal to exercise its power under section 25 of the 2007 Act (Upper Tribunal to have powers of High Court or Court of Session) in relation to, any failure by a person to comply with a requirement imposed by the Tribunal—

(*a*) to attend at any place for the purpose of giving evidence;

(*b*) otherwise to make themselves available to give evidence;

(*c*) to swear an oath in connection with the giving of evidence;

(*d*) to give evidence as a witness;

(*e*) to produce a document; or

(*f*) to facilitate the inspection of a document or any other thing (including any premises).

8 Striking out a party's case

(1) The proceedings, or the appropriate part of them, will automatically be struck out if the appellant has failed to comply with a direction that stated that failure by a party to comply with the direction would lead to the striking out of the proceedings or that part of them.

(2) The Tribunal must strike out the whole or a part of the proceedings if the Tribunal—

(*a*) does not have jurisdiction in relation to the proceedings or that part of them; and

(*b*) does not exercise its power under rule 5(3)(k)(i) (transfer to another court or tribunal) in relation to the proceedings or that part of them.

(3) The Tribunal may strike out the whole or a part of the proceedings if—

(*a*) the appellant has failed to comply with a direction which stated that failure by the appellant to comply with the direction could lead to the striking out of the proceedings or part of them;

(*b*) the appellant has failed to co-operate with the Tribunal to such an extent that the Tribunal cannot deal with the proceedings fairly and justly; or

(*c*) the Tribunal considers there is no reasonable prospect of the appellant's case, or part of it, succeeding.

(4) The Tribunal may not strike out the whole or a part of the proceedings under paragraphs (2) or (3)(*b*) or (*c*) without first giving the appellant an opportunity to make representations in relation to the proposed striking out.

(5) If the proceedings, or part of them, have been struck out under paragraphs (1) or (3)(*a*), the appellant may apply for the proceedings, or part of them, to be reinstated.

(6) An application under paragraph (5) must be made in writing and received by the Tribunal within 28 days after the date that the Tribunal sent notification of the striking out to the appellant.

(7) This rule applies to a respondent as it applies to an appellant except that—

(*a*) a reference to the striking out of the proceedings must be read as a reference to the barring of the respondent from taking further part in the proceedings; and

(*b*) a reference to an application for the reinstatement of proceedings which have been struck out must be read as a reference to an application for the lifting of the bar on the respondent taking further part in the proceedings.

(8) If a respondent has been barred from taking further part in proceedings under this rule and that bar has not been lifted, the Tribunal need not consider any response or other submissions made by that respondent, and may summarily determine any or all issues against that respondent.

Simon's Tax Cases—*R&C Comrs v Fairford Group plc and another* [2014] UKUT 329 (TCC), [2015] STC 156; *R&C Comrs v BPP Holdings Ltd and others* [2014] UKUT 496 (TCC), [2015] STC 415; *R&C Comrs v BPP Holdings Ltd and others* [2016] EWCA Civ 121, [2016] STC 841.

9 Substitution and addition of parties

(1) The Tribunal may give a direction substituting a party if—

(*a*) the wrong person has been named as a party; or

(*b*) the substitution has become necessary because of a change in circumstances since the start of proceedings.

(2) The Tribunal may give a direction adding a person to the proceedings as a respondent.

(3) A person who is not a party to proceedings may make an application to be added as a party under this rule.

(4) If the Tribunal refuses an application under paragraph (3) it must consider whether to permit the person who made the application to provide submissions or evidence to the Tribunal.

(5) If the Tribunal gives a direction under paragraph (1) or (2) it may give such consequential directions as it considers appropriate.

10 Orders for costs

(1) The Tribunal may only make an order in respect of costs (or, in Scotland, expenses)—

(*a*) under section 29(4) of the 2007 Act (wasted costs) [and costs incurred in applying for such costs][2];

(*b*) if the Tribunal considers that a party or their representative has acted unreasonably in bringing, defending or conducting the proceedings; . . . [1]

(*c*) if—

(i) the proceedings have been allocated as a Complex case under rule 23 (allocation of cases to categories); and

(ii) the taxpayer (or, where more than one party is a taxpayer, one of them) has not sent or delivered a written request to the Tribunal, within 28 days of receiving notice that the case had been allocated as a Complex case, that the proceedings be excluded from potential liability for costs or expenses under this sub-paragraph; [or

(*d*) in a MP expenses case, if—

(i) the case has been allocated as a Complex case under rule 23 (allocation of cases to categories); and

(ii) the appellant has not sent or delivered a written request to the Tribunal, within 28 days of receiving notice that the case had been allocated as a Complex case, that the proceedings be excluded from potential liability for costs or expenses under this sub-paragraph.][1]

(2) The Tribunal may make an order under paragraph (1) on an application or of its own initiative.

(3) A person making an application for an order under paragraph (1) must—

(*a*) send or deliver a written application to the Tribunal and to the person against whom it is proposed that the order be made; and

(*b*) send or deliver with the application a schedule of the costs or expenses claimed in sufficient detail to allow the Tribunal to undertake a summary assessment of such costs or expenses if it decides to do so.

(4) An application for an order under paragraph (1) may be made at any time during the proceedings but may not be made later than 28 days after the date on which the Tribunal sends—

(*a*) a decision notice recording the decision which finally disposes of all issues in the proceedings; or

(*b*) notice [under rule 17(2) of its receipt of a withdrawal][2] which ends the proceedings.

(5) The Tribunal may not make an order under paragraph (1) against a person (the "paying person") without first—

(*a*) giving that person an opportunity to make representations; and

(*b*) if the paying person is an individual, considering that person's financial means.

(6) The amount of costs (or, in Scotland, expenses) to be paid under an order under paragraph (1) may be ascertained by—

(*a*) summary assessment by the Tribunal;

(*b*) agreement of a specified sum by the paying person and the person entitled to receive the costs or expenses (the "receiving person"); or

(*c*) assessment of the whole or a specified part of the costs or expenses[, including the costs or expenses of the assessment,][2] incurred by the receiving person, if not agreed.

(7) Following an order for assessment under paragraph (6)(*c*) the paying person or the receiving person may apply—

(*a*) in England and Wales, to a county court, the High Court or the Costs Office of the Supreme Court (as specified in the order) for a detailed assessment of the costs on the standard basis or, if specified in the order, on the indemnity basis; and the Civil Procedure Rules 1998 shall apply, with necessary modifications, to that application and assessment as if the proceedings in the tribunal had been proceedings in a court to which the Civil Procedure Rules 1998 apply;

(*b*) in Scotland, to the Auditor of the Sheriff Court or the Court of Session (as specified in the order) for the taxation of the expenses according to the fees payable in that court; or

(*c*) in Northern Ireland, to the Taxing Office of the High Court of Northern Ireland for taxation on the standard basis or, if specified in the order, on the indemnity basis.

[(7A) Upon making an order for the assessment of costs, the Tribunal may order an amount to be paid on account before the costs or expenses are assessed.][2]

(8) In this rule "taxpayer" means a party who is liable to pay, or has paid, the tax, duty, levy or penalty to which the proceedings relate or part of such tax, duty, levy or penalty, or whose liability to do so is in issue in the proceedings;

Simon's Tax Cases—*Market & Opinion Research International Ltd v R&C Comrs* [2015] UKUT 12 (TCC), [2015] STC 1205.

Amendments—[1] In para (1), word "or" in sub-para (*b*) revoked and sub-para (*d*) and preceding word "or" inserted, by the Tribunal Procedure (Amendment No 3) Rules, SI 2010/2653 rule 6(1), (4) with effect from 29 November 2010.

[2] In paras (1)(*a*), (6)(*c*) words inserted, in para (4) words substituted for words "of a withdrawal under rule 17 (withdrawal)", and para (7A) inserted, by the Tribunal Procedure (Amendment) Rules, SI 2013/477 rules 33, 35–38 with effect from 1 April 2013.

11 Representatives

(1) A party may appoint a representative (whether a legal representative or not) to represent that party in the proceedings.

(2) If a party appoints a representative, that party (or the representative if the representative is a legal representative) must send or deliver to the Tribunal and to each other party to the proceedings written notice of the representative's name and address.

(3) Anything permitted or required to be done by a party under these Rules, a practice direction or a direction may be done by the representative of that party, except signing a witness statement.

(4) A person who receives due notice of the appointment of a representative—

(*a*) must provide to the representative any document which is required to be provided to the represented party, and need not provide that document to the represented party; and

(*b*) may assume that the representative is and remains authorised as such until they receive written notification that this is not so from the representative or the represented party.

(5) At a hearing a party may be accompanied by another person who, with the permission of the Tribunal, may act as a representative or otherwise assist in presenting the party's case at the hearing.

(6) Paragraphs (2) to (4) do not apply to a person (other than an appointed representative) who accompanies a party in accordance with paragraph (5).

(7) In this rule "legal representative" means [a person who, for the purposes of the Legal Services Act 2007, is an authorised person in relation to an activity which constitutes the exercise of a right of audience or the conduct of litigation within the meaning of that Act][1], an advocate or solicitor in Scotland, or a barrister or solicitor in Northern Ireland.

Amendments—[1] In para (7), words substituted by the Tribunal Procedure (Amendment) Rules, SI 2010/43, rule 16, with effect from 18 January 2010.

12 Calculating time

(1) An act required by these Rules, a practice direction or a direction to be done on or by a particular day must be done before 5pm on that day.

(2) If the time specified by these Rules, a practice direction or a direction for doing any act ends on a day other than a working day, the act is done in time if it is done on the next working day.

(3) In this rule "working day" means any day except a Saturday or Sunday, Christmas Day, Good Friday or a bank holiday under section 1 of the Banking and Financial Dealings Act 1971.

13 Sending and delivery of documents

(1) Any document to be provided to the Tribunal under these Rules, a practice direction or a direction must be—

(*a*) sent by pre-paid post or document exchange, or delivered by hand, to the address specified for the proceedings; or

(*b*) sent or delivered by such other method as the Tribunal may permit or direct.

(2) Subject to paragraph (3), if a party or representative provides a fax number, email address or other details for the electronic transmission of documents to them, that party or representative must accept delivery of documents by that method.

(3) If a party informs the Tribunal and all other parties that a particular form of communication (other than pre-paid post or delivery by hand) should not be used to provide documents to that party, that form of communication must not be so used.

(4) If the Tribunal or a party sends a document to a party or the Tribunal by email or any other electronic means of communication, the recipient may request that the sender provide a hard copy of the document to the recipient. The recipient must make such a request as soon as reasonably practicable after receiving the document electronically.
(5) The Tribunal and each party may assume that the address provided by a party or its representative is and remains the address to which documents should be sent or delivered until receiving written notification to the contrary.

14 Use of documents and information

The Tribunal may make an order prohibiting the disclosure or publication of—
(*a*) specified documents or information relating to the proceedings; or
(*b*) any matter likely to lead members of the public to identify any person whom the Tribunal considers should not be identified.

15 Evidence and submissions

(1) Without restriction on the general powers in rule 5(1) and (2) (case management powers), the Tribunal may give directions as to—
(*a*) issues on which it requires evidence or submissions;
(*b*) the nature of the evidence or submissions it requires;
(*c*) whether the parties are permitted or required to provide expert evidence, and if so whether the parties must jointly appoint a single expert to provide such evidence;
(*d*) any limit on the number of witnesses whose evidence a party may put forward, whether in relation to a particular issue or generally;
(*e*) the manner in which any evidence or submissions are to be provided, which may include a direction for them to be given—
(i) orally at a hearing; or
(ii) by written submissions or witness statement; and
(*f*) the time at which any evidence or submissions are to be provided.
(2) The Tribunal may—
(*a*) admit evidence whether or not the evidence would be admissible in a civil trial in the United Kingdom; or
(*b*) exclude evidence that would otherwise be admissible where—
(i) the evidence was not provided within the time allowed by a direction or a practice direction;
(ii) the evidence was otherwise provided in a manner that did not comply with a direction or a practice direction; or
(iii) it would otherwise be unfair to admit the evidence.
(3) The Tribunal may consent to a witness giving, or require any witness to give, evidence on oath, and may administer an oath for that purpose.

16 Summoning or citation of witnesses and orders to answer questions or produce documents

(1) On the application of a party or on its own initiative, the Tribunal may—
(*a*) by summons (or, in Scotland, citation) require any person to attend as a witness at a hearing at the time and place specified in the summons or citation;
(*b*) order any person to answer any questions or produce any documents in that person's possession or control which relate to any issue in the proceedings.
(2) A summons or citation under paragraph (1)(*a*) must—
(*a*) give the person required to attend at least 14 days' notice of the hearing, or such shorter period as the Tribunal may direct; and
(*b*) where the person is not a party, make provision for the person's necessary expenses of attendance to be paid, and state who is to pay them.
(3) No person may be compelled to give any evidence or produce any document that the person could not be compelled to give or produce on a trial of an action in a court of law in the part of the United Kingdom where the proceedings are due to be determined.
(4) A person who receives a summons, citation or order may apply to the Tribunal for it to be varied or set aside if they did not have an opportunity to object to it before it was made or issued.
(5) A person making an application under paragraph (4) must do so as soon as reasonably practicable after receiving notice of the summons, citation or order.
(6) A summons, citation or order under this rule must—
(*a*) state that the person on whom the requirement is imposed may apply to the Tribunal to vary or set aside the summons, citation or order, if they did not have an opportunity to object to it before it was made or issued; and
(*b*) state the consequences of failure to comply with the summons, citation or order.

Simon's Tax Cases—*Clavis Liberty Fund LP1 v R&C Comrs and others* [2015] UKUT 72 (TCC), [2015] STC 1645.

17 Withdrawal

(1) Subject to any provision in an enactment relating to withdrawal or settlement of particular proceedings, a party may give notice to the Tribunal of the withdrawal of the case made by it in the Tribunal proceedings, or any part of that case—

(*a*) . . . [1] by sending or delivering to the Tribunal a written notice of withdrawal; or

(*b*) orally at a hearing.

(2) The Tribunal must notify each . . . [1] party in writing of [its receipt of][1] a withdrawal under this rule.

(3) A party who has withdrawn their case may apply to the Tribunal for the case to be reinstated.

(4) An application under paragraph (3) must be made in writing and be received by the Tribunal within 28 days after—

(*a*) the date that the Tribunal received the notice under paragraph (1)(*a*); or

(*b*) the date of the hearing at which the case was withdrawn orally under paragraph (1)(*b*).

Amendments—[1] In para (1)(*a*), words "at any time before a hearing to consider the disposal of the proceedings (or, if the Tribunal disposes of the proceedings without a hearing, before that disposal)," repealed, in para (2), word "other" repealed and words inserted, by the Tribunal Procedure (Amendment) Rules, SI 2013/477 rules 33, 39 with effect from 1 April 2013.

18 Lead cases

(1) This rule applies if—

(*a*) two or more cases have been started before the Tribunal;

(*b*) in each such case the Tribunal has not made a decision disposing of the proceedings; and

(*c*) the cases give rise to common or related issues of fact or law.

(2) The Tribunal may give a direction—

(*a*) specifying one or more cases falling under paragraph (1) as a lead case or lead cases; and

(*b*) staying (or, in Scotland, sisting) the other cases falling under paragraph (1) ("the related cases").

(3) When the Tribunal makes a decision in respect of the common or related issues—

(*a*) the Tribunal must send a copy of that decision to each party in each of the related cases; and

(*b*) subject to paragraph (4), that decision shall be binding on each of those parties.

(4) Within 28 days after the date that the Tribunal sent a copy of the decision to a party under paragraph (3)(*a*), that party may apply in writing for a direction that the decision does not apply to, and is not binding on the parties to, that case.

(5) The Tribunal must give directions in respect of cases which are stayed or sisted under paragraph (2)(*b*), providing for the disposal of or further steps in those cases.

(6) If the lead case or cases are withdrawn or disposed of before the Tribunal makes a decision in respect of the common or related issues, the Tribunal must give directions as to—

(*a*) whether another case or other cases are to be heard as a lead case or lead cases; and

(*b*) whether any direction affecting the related cases should be set aside or amended.

PART 3
PROCEDURE BEFORE THE TRIBUNAL

CHAPTER 1

STARTING PROCEEDINGS AND ALLOCATION OF CASES TO CATEGORIES

19 Proceedings without notice to a respondent

If a case or matter is to be determined without notice to or the involvement of a respondent—

(*a*) any provision in these Rules requiring a document to be provided by or to a respondent; and

(*b*) any other provision in these Rules permitting a respondent to participate in the proceedings

does not apply to that case or matter.

20 Starting appeal proceedings

[(1) A person making or notifying an appeal to the Tribunal under any enactment must start proceedings by sending or delivering a notice of appeal to the Tribunal.][1]

(2) The notice of appeal must include—

(*a*) the name and address of the appellant;

(*b*) the name and address of the appellant's representative (if any);

(*c*) an address where documents for the appellant may be sent or delivered;

(*d*) details of the decision appealed against;

(*e*) the result the appellant is seeking; and

(*f*) the grounds for making the appeal.

(3) The appellant must provide with the notice of appeal a copy of any written record of any decision appealed against, and any statement of reasons for that decision, that the appellant has or can reasonably obtain.

[(4) If the notice of appeal is provided after the end of any period specified in an enactment referred to in paragraph (1) but the enactment provides that an appeal may be made or notified after that period with the permission of the Tribunal—

(*a*) the notice of appeal must include a request for such permission and the reason why the notice of appeal was not provided in time; and

(*b*) unless the Tribunal gives such permission, the Tribunal must not admit the appeal.][1]

(5) When the Tribunal receives the notice of appeal it must give notice of the proceedings to the respondent.

Amendments—[1] Paras (1), (4) substituted by the Tribunal Procedure (Amendment No 3) Rules, SI 2010/2653 rule 6(1), (5) with effect from 29 November 2010.

21 Starting proceedings by originating application or reference

(1) Where an enactment provides for a person or persons to make an originating application or reference to the Tribunal, the appellant must start proceedings by providing an application notice or notice of reference to the Tribunal within any time limit imposed by that enactment.

(2) The application notice or notice of reference must state—

(*a*) the name and address of the appellant;

(*b*) the name and address of the appellant's representative (if any);

(*c*) an address where documents for the appellant may be sent or delivered;

(*d*) the name and address of each respondent (if any);

(*e*) the facts relevant to the originating application or reference;

(*f*) the result the appellant is seeking (if any); and

(*g*) the grounds for making the originating application or reference.

(3) If the appellant provides the application notice or notice of reference to the Tribunal later than the time required by paragraph (1) or by any extension of time under rule 5(3)(*a*) (power to extend time)—

(*a*) the application notice or notice of reference must include a request for an extension of time and the reason why the application notice or notice of reference was not provided in time; and

(*b*) unless the Tribunal extends time for the application notice or notice of reference under rule 5(3)(*a*) (power to extend time) the Tribunal must not admit the application notice or notice of reference.

[(3A) The power of the Tribunal under these Rules to extend time for starting proceedings shall not apply in a CAA case.][1]

(4) When the Tribunal receives an application notice or a notice of reference it must send a copy of the notice and any accompanying document to any respondent.

Amendments—[1] Para (3A) inserted by the Tribunal Procedure (Amendment) Rules, SI 2013/477 rules 33, 40 with effect from 1 April 2013.

22 Hardship applications

(1) This rule applies where an enactment provides, in any terms, that an appeal may not proceed if the liability to pay the amount in dispute is outstanding unless HMRC or the Tribunal consent to the appeal proceeding.

(2) When starting proceedings, the appellant must include or provide the following in or with the notice of appeal—

(*a*) a statement as to whether the appellant has paid the amount in dispute;

(*b*) if the appellant has not paid the amount in dispute, a statement as to the status or outcome of any application to HMRC for consent to the appeal proceeding; and

(*c*) if HMRC have refused such an application, an application to the Tribunal for consent to the appeal proceeding.

(3) An application under paragraph (2)(*c*) must include the reasons for the application and a list of any documents the appellant intends to produce or rely upon in support of that application.

(4) If the appellant requires the consent of HMRC or the Tribunal before the appeal may proceed, the Tribunal must stay the proceedings until any applications to HMRC or the Tribunal in that respect have been determined.

23 Allocation of cases to categories

[(1) When the Tribunal receives a notice of appeal, application notice or notice of reference, the Tribunal must give a direction—

(*a*) in an MP expenses case[, a financial restrictions civil penalty case or a CAA case][2], allocating the case to one of the categories set out in paragraph (2)(*c*) or (*d*); and

(*b*) in any other case, allocating the case to one of the categories set out in paragraph (2).][1]

(2) The categories referred to in paragraph (1) are—

(*a*) Default Paper cases, which will usually be disposed of without a hearing;

(*b*) Basic cases, which will usually be disposed of after a hearing, with minimal exchange of documents before the hearing;

(*c*) Standard cases, which will usually be subject to more detailed case management and be disposed of after a hearing; and (*d*) Complex cases, in respect of which see paragraphs (4) and (5) below.

(3) The Tribunal may give a further direction re-allocating a case to a different category at any time, either on the application of a party or on its own initiative.

(4) The Tribunal may allocate a case as a Complex case under paragraph (1) or (3) only if the Tribunal considers that the case—

(*a*) will require lengthy or complex evidence or a lengthy hearing;

(*b*) involves a complex or important principle or issue; or

(*c*) involves a large financial sum.

(5) If a case is allocated as a Complex case—

(*a*) rule 10(1)(*c*) (costs in Complex cases) applies to the case; and

(*b*) rule 28 (transfer of Complex cases to the Upper Tribunal) applies to the case.

Simon's Tax Cases—*Capital Air Services Ltd v R&C Comrs* [2010] STC 2726.

Amendments—[1] Para (1) substituted by the Tribunal Procedure (Amendment No 3) Rules, SI 2010/2653 rule 6(1), (6) with effect from 29 November 2010.

[2] Words in para (1)(*a*) inserted by the Tribunal Procedure (Amendment) Rules, SI 2013/477 rules 33, 41 with effect from 1 April 2013.

CHAPTER 2

PROCEDURE AFTER ALLOCATION OF CASES TO CATEGORIES

24 Basic cases

(1) This rule applies to Basic cases.

(2) Rule 25 (respondent's statement of case) does not apply and, subject to paragraph (3) and any direction given by the Tribunal, the case will proceed directly to a hearing.

(3) If the respondent intends to raise grounds for contesting the proceedings at the hearing which have not previously been communicated to the appellant, the respondent must notify the appellant of such grounds.

(4) If the respondent is required to notify the appellant of any grounds under paragraph (3), the respondent must do so—

(*a*) as soon as reasonably practicable after becoming aware that such is the case; and

(*b*) in sufficient detail to enable the appellant to respond to such grounds at the hearing.

25 Respondent's statement of case

[(1) A respondent must send or deliver a statement of case to the Tribunal, the appellant and any other respondent so that it is received—

(*a*) in a Default Paper case, within 42 days after the Tribunal sent the notice of appeal or a copy of the application notice or notice of reference;

(*b*) in an MP expenses case, within 28 days after the Tribunal sent the notice of appeal; or

(*c*) in a Standard or Complex case other than an MP expenses case, within 60 days after the Tribunal sent the notice of appeal or a copy of the application notice or notice of reference.][1]

(2) A statement of case must—

(*a*) in an appeal, state the legislative provision under which the decision under appeal was made; and

(*b*) set out the respondent's position in relation to the case.

(3) A statement of case may also contain a request that the case be dealt with at a hearing or without a hearing.

(4) If a respondent provides a statement of case to the Tribunal later than the time required by paragraph (1) or by any extension allowed under rule 5(3)(*a*) (power to extend time), the statement of case must include a request for an extension of time and the reason why the statement of case was not provided in time.

Amendments—[1] Para (1) substituted by the Tribunal Procedure (Amendment No 3) Rules, SI 2010/2653 rule 6(1), (7) with effect from 29 November 2010.

26 Further steps in a Default Paper case

(1) This rule applies to Default Paper cases.

(2) The appellant may send or deliver a written reply to the Tribunal so that it is received within 30 days after the date on which the respondent sent to the appellant the statement of case to which the reply relates.

(3) The appellant's reply may—

(*a*) set out the appellant's response to the respondent's statement of case;

(*b*) provide any further information (including, where appropriate, copies of the documents containing such information) which has not yet been provided to the Tribunal and is relevant to the case; and

(*c*) contain a request that the case be dealt with at a hearing.

(4) The appellant must send or deliver a copy of any reply provided under paragraph (2) to each respondent at the same time as it is provided to the Tribunal.

(5) If the appellant provides a reply to the Tribunal later than the time required by paragraph (2) or by any extension allowed under rule 5(3)(*a*) (power to extend time), the reply must include a request for an extension of time and the reason why the reply was not provided in time.
(6) Following receipt of the appellant's reply, or the expiry of the time for the receipt of the appellant's reply then, unless it directs otherwise and subject in any event to paragraph (7), the Tribunal must proceed to determine the case without a hearing.
(7) If any party has made a written request to the Tribunal for a hearing, the Tribunal must hold a hearing before determining the case.

27 Further steps in a Standard or Complex case

(1) This rule applies to Standard and Complex cases.
(2) Subject to any direction to the contrary, within 42 days after the date the respondent sent the statement of case (or, where there is more than one respondent, the date of the final statement of case) each party must send or deliver to the Tribunal and to each other party a list of documents—

(*a*) of which the party providing the list has possession, the right to possession, or the right to take copies; and
(*b*) which the party providing the list intends to rely upon or produce in the proceedings.

(3) A party which has provided a list of documents under paragraph (2) must allow each other party to inspect or take copies of the documents on the list (except any documents which are privileged).

28 Transfer of Complex cases to the Upper Tribunal

(1) If a case has been allocated as a Complex case the Tribunal may, with the consent of the parties, refer a case [or a preliminary issue][1] to the President of the Tax Chamber [of the First-tier Tribunal][2] with a request that the case [or issue][1] be considered for transfer to the Upper Tribunal.
[(2) If a case or issue has been referred by the Tribunal under paragraph (1), the President of the Tax Chamber may, with the concurrence of the President of the Tax and Chancery Chamber of the Upper Tribunal, direct that the case or issue be transferred to and determined by the Upper Tribunal.][1]

Amendments—[1] In para (1) words inserted, and para (2) substituted, by the Tribunal Procedure (Amendment No 3) Rules, SI 2010/2653 rule 6(1), (8) with effect from 29 November 2010.
[2] In para (1) words inserted by the Tribunal Procedure (Amendment) Rules, SI 2011/651 rule 5(1), (3) with effect from 1 April 2011.

CHAPTER 3

HEARINGS

29 Determination with or without a hearing

(1) Subject to rule 26(6) (determination of a Default Paper case without a hearing) and the following paragraphs in this rule, the Tribunal must hold a hearing before making a decision which disposes of proceedings, or a part of proceedings, unless—

(*a*) each party has consented to the matter being decided without a hearing; and
(*b*) the Tribunal considers that it is able to decide the matter without a hearing.

(2) This rule does not apply to decisions under Part 4 (correcting, setting aside, reviewing and appealing Tribunal decisions).
(3) The Tribunal may dispose of proceedings, or a part of proceedings, without a hearing under rule 8 (striking out a party's case).

30 Entitlement to attend a hearing

Subject to rules 19 (proceedings without notice to a respondent) and 32(4) (exclusion from a hearing), each party to proceedings is entitled to attend a hearing.

31 Notice of hearings

(1) The Tribunal must give each party entitled to attend a hearing reasonable notice of the time and place of any hearing (including any adjourned or postponed hearing) and any changes to the time and place of any hearing.
(2) In relation to a hearing to consider the disposal of proceedings, the period of notice under paragraph (1) must be at least 14 days except that the Tribunal may give less than 14 days' notice—

(*a*) with the parties' consent; or
(*b*) in urgent or exceptional circumstances.

32 Public and private hearings

(1) Subject to the following paragraphs, all hearings must be held in public.
(2) The Tribunal may give a direction that a hearing, or part of it, is to be held in private if the Tribunal considers that restricting access to the hearing is justified—

(*a*) in the interests of public order or national security;
(*b*) in order to protect a person's right to respect for their private and family life;
(*c*) in order to maintain the confidentiality of sensitive information;
(*d*) in order to avoid serious harm to the public interest; or
(*e*) because not to do so would prejudice the interests of justice.

(3) Where a hearing, or part of it, is to be held in private, the Tribunal may determine who is permitted to attend the hearing or part of it.

(4) The Tribunal may give a direction excluding from any hearing, or part of it—

(*a*) any person whose conduct the Tribunal considers is disrupting or is likely to disrupt the hearing;

(*b*) any person whose presence the Tribunal considers is likely to prevent another person from giving evidence or making submissions freely;

(*c*) any person where the purpose of the hearing would be defeated by the attendance of that person; or

(*d*) a person under the age of eighteen years.

(5) The Tribunal may give a direction excluding a witness from a hearing until that witness gives evidence.

(6) If the Tribunal publishes a report of a decision resulting from a hearing which was held wholly or partly in private, the Tribunal must, so far as practicable, ensure that the report does not disclose information which was referred to only in a part of the hearing that was held in private (including such information which enables the identification of any person whose affairs were dealt with in the part of the hearing that was held in private) if to do so would undermine the purpose of holding the hearing in private.

33 Hearings in a party's absence

If a party fails to attend a hearing the Tribunal may proceed with the hearing if the Tribunal—

(*a*) is satisfied that the party has been notified of the hearing or that reasonable steps have been taken to notify the party of the hearing; and

(*b*) considers that it is in the interests of justice to proceed with the hearing.

CHAPTER 4

DECISIONS

34 Consent orders

(1) The Tribunal may, at the request of the parties but only if it considers it appropriate, make a consent order disposing of the proceedings and making such other appropriate provision as the parties have agreed.

(2) Notwithstanding any other provision of these Rules, the Tribunal need not hold a hearing before making an order under paragraph (1), or provide reasons for the order.

35 Notice of decisions and reasons

(1) The Tribunal may give a decision orally at a hearing.

(2) The Tribunal must provide to each party within 28 days after making [a decision (other than a decision under Part 4) which finally disposes of all issues in proceedings or of a preliminary issue dealt with following a direction under rule 5(3)(*e*)][1], or as soon as practicable thereafter, a decision notice which—

(*a*) states the Tribunal's decision; and

(*b*) notifies the party of any right of appeal against the decision and the time within which, and the manner in which, the right of appeal may be exercised.

(3) Unless each party agrees that it is unnecessary, the decision notice must—

(*a*) include a summary of the findings of fact and reasons for the decision; or

(*b*) be accompanied by full written findings of fact and reasons for the decision.

(4) If the Tribunal provides no findings and reasons, or summary findings and reasons only, in or with the decision notice, a party to the proceedings may apply for full written findings and reasons, and must do so before making an application for permission to appeal under rule 39 (application for permission to appeal).

(5) An application under paragraph (4) must be made in writing and be sent or delivered to the Tribunal so that it is received within 28 days after the date that the Tribunal sent or otherwise provided the decision notice under paragraph (2) to the party making the application.

(6) The Tribunal must send a full written statement of findings and reasons to each party within 28 days after receiving an application for full written reasons made in accordance with paragraphs (4) and (5), or as soon as practicable thereafter.

Amendments—[1] In para (2),words substituted for words "a decision which finally disposes of all issues in proceedings (except a decision under Part 4)" by the Tribunal Procedure (Amendment) Rules, SI 2013/477 rules 33, 42 with effect from 1 April 2013.

PART 4
CORRECTING, SETTING ASIDE, REVIEWING AND APPEALING TRIBUNAL DECISIONS

36 Interpretation

In this Part—

"appeal" means the exercise of a right of appeal against a decision of the Tribunal; and
"review" means the review of a decision by the Tribunal under section 9 of the 2007 Act.

37 Clerical mistakes and accidental slips or omissions

The Tribunal may at any time correct any clerical mistake or other accidental slip or omission in a decision, direction or any document produced by it, by—

(*a*) sending notification of the amended decision or direction, or a copy of the amended document, to all parties; and

(*b*) making any necessary amendment to any information published in relation to the decision, direction or document.

38 Setting aside a decision which disposes of proceedings

(1) The Tribunal may set aside a decision which disposes of proceedings, or part of such a decision, and re-make the decision, or the relevant part of it, if—

(*a*) the Tribunal considers that it is in the interests of justice to do so; and

(*b*) one or more of the conditions in paragraph (2) is satisfied.

(2) The conditions are—

(*a*) a document relating to the proceedings was not sent to, or was not received at an appropriate time by, a party or a party's representative;

(*b*) a document relating to the proceedings was not sent to the Tribunal at an appropriate time;

(*c*) there has been some other procedural irregularity in the proceedings; or

(*d*) a party, or a party's representative, was not present at a hearing related to the proceedings.

(3) A party applying for a decision, or part of a decision, to be set aside under paragraph (1) must make a written application to the Tribunal so that it is received no later than 28 days after the date on which the Tribunal sent notice of the decision to the party.

(4) If the Tribunal sets aside a decision or part of a decision under this rule, the Tribunal must notify the parties in writing as soon as practicable.

39 Application for permission to appeal

(1) A person seeking permission to appeal must make a written application to the Tribunal for permission to appeal.

(2) An application under paragraph (1) must be sent or delivered to the Tribunal so that it is received no later than 56 days after the latest of the dates that the Tribunal sends to the person making the application—

[(*za*) the relevant decision notice;][1]

[(*a*) where—

(i) the decision disposes of all issues in the proceedings; or

(iii) subject to paragraph (2A), the decision disposes of a preliminary issue dealt with following a direction under rule 5(3)(e),

full written reasons for the decision;][1]

(*b*) notification of amended reasons for, or correction of, the decision following a review; or

(*c*) notification that an application for the decision to be set aside has been unsuccessful.

[(2A) The Tribunal may direct that the 56 days within which a party may send or deliver an application for permission to appeal against a decision that disposes of a preliminary issue shall run from the date of the decision that disposes of all issues in the proceedings.][1]

(3) The date in paragraph (2)(*c*) applies only if the application for the decision to be set aside was made within the time stipulated in rule 38 (setting aside a decision which disposes of proceedings), or any extension of that time granted by the Tribunal.

(4) If the person seeking permission to appeal sends or delivers the application to the Tribunal later than the time required by paragraph (2) or by any extension of time under rule 5(3)(*a*) (power to extend time)—

(*a*) the application must include a request for an extension of time and the reason why the application notice was not provided in time; and

(*b*) unless the Tribunal extends time for the application under rule 5(3)(*a*) (power to extend time) the Tribunal must not admit the application.

(5) An application under paragraph (1) must—

(*a*) identify the decision of the Tribunal to which it relates;

(*b*) identify the alleged error or errors in the decision; and

(*c*) state the result the party making the application is seeking.

Amendments—[1] Para (2)(*za*) inserted, para (2)(*a*) substituted, and para (2A) inserted, by the Tribunal Procedure (Amendment) Rules, SI 2013/477 rules 33, 43 with effect from 1 April 2013.

40 Tribunal's consideration of application for permission to appeal

(1) On receiving an application for permission to appeal the Tribunal must first consider, taking into account the overriding objective in rule 2, whether to review the decision in accordance with rule 41 (review of a decision).

(2) If the Tribunal decides not to review the decision, or reviews the decision and decides to take no action in relation to the decision, or a part of it, the Tribunal must consider whether to give permission to appeal in relation to the decision or that part of it.

(3) The Tribunal must send a record of its decision to the parties as soon as practicable.

(4) If the Tribunal refuses permission to appeal it must send with the record of its decision—

(*a*) a statement of its reasons for such refusal; and

(*b*) notification of the right to make an application to the Upper Tribunal for permission to appeal and the time within which, and the method by which, such application must be made.

(5) The Tribunal may give permission to appeal against part only of the decision or on limited grounds, but must comply with paragraph (4) in relation to any part of the decision or grounds on which it has refused permission.

41 Review of a decision

(1) The Tribunal may only undertake a review of a decision—

(*a*) pursuant to rule 40(1) (review on an application for permission to appeal); and

(*b*) if it is satisfied that there was an error of law in the decision.

(2) The Tribunal must notify the parties in writing of the outcome of any review, unless the Tribunal decides to take no action following the review.

(3) The Tribunal may not take any action in relation to a decision following a review without first giving every party an opportunity to make representations in relation to the proposed action.

42 Power to treat an application as a different type of application

The Tribunal may treat an application for a decision to be corrected, set aside or reviewed, or for permission to appeal against a decision, as an application for any other one of those things.

2009/275

APPEALS (EXCLUDED DECISIONS) ORDER 2009

Made by the Lord Chancellor under the Tribunals, Courts and Enforcement Act 2007 ss 11(5)(f) and 13(8)(f).

Made . . . . *5 February 2009*
Laid before Parliament . . . . *13 February 2009*
Coming into force . . . . *1 April 2009*

1 Citation and commencement

This Order may be cited as the Appeals (Excluded Decisions) Order 2009 and comes into force on 1st April 2009.

2 [Excluded decisions

For the purposes of section 11(1) of the Tribunals, Courts and Enforcement Act 2007, the following decisions of the First-tier Tribunal are excluded decisions—

(*a*) a decision under section 103 of the Immigration and Asylum Act 1999 (appeals); and

(*b*) a decision under paragraphs 22, 23, 24, 29, 30, 31, 32 and 33 of Schedule 2 to the Immigration Act 1971.][1]

Amendments—[1] Art 2 substituted by the Tribunals, Courts and Enforcement Act 2007 (Miscellaneous Provisions) Order, SI 2010/41 arts 2, 3 with effect from 15 February 2010.

3 For the purposes of sections 11(1) and 13(1) of the Tribunals, Courts and Enforcement Act 2007, the following decisions of the First-tier Tribunal or the Upper Tribunal are excluded decisions—

(*a*) any decision under section 20(7), (8B) or (8G)(*b*) (power to call for documents of taxpayer and others), 20B(1B) or (6) (restrictions on powers under sections 20 and 20A) or 20BB(2)(*a*) (falsification etc of documents) of the Taxes Management Act 1970;

(*b*) any decision under section 35A(2) (variation of undertakings), 79A(2) (variation of undertakings) or 219(1A) (power to require information) of the Inheritance Tax Act 1984;

(*c*) any decision under section 152(5) (notification of taxable amount of certain benefits) or 215(7) (advance clearance by Board of distributions and payments) of the Income and Corporation Taxes Act 1988;

(*d*) any decision under section 138(4) of the Taxation of Chargeable Gains Act 1992 (procedure for clearance in advance);

(*e*) any decision under section 187(5) or (6) (returns and information) of, or paragraph 3(2) or 6(2) of Schedule 21 (restrictions on powers under section 187) to, the Finance Act 1993;

(*f*) any decision under paragraph 91(5) of Schedule 15 to the Finance Act 2000 (corporate venturing scheme: advance clearance);

(*g*) any decision under paragraph 88(5) of Schedule 29 to the Finance Act 2002 (gains and losses from intangible fixed assets: transfer of business or trade);

(*h*) any decision under paragraph 2, 4, 7, 9, 10, 11 or 24 of Schedule 13 to the Finance Act 2003 (stamp duty land tax: information powers);

(*i*) any decision under section 306A (doubt as to notifiability), 308A (supplemental information), 313B (reasons for non-disclosure: supporting information) or 314A (order to disclose) of the Finance Act 2004;

(*j*) any decision under section 697(4) of the Income Tax Act 2007 (opposed notifications: determinations by tribunal);

(*k*) any decision under regulation 10(3) of the Venture Capital Trust (Winding up and Mergers) (Tax) Regulations 2004 (procedure for Board's approval);

(*l*) any decision under regulation 5A (doubt as to notifiability), 7A (supplemental information), 12B (reasons for non-disclosure: supporting information) or 12C (order to disclose) of the National Insurance Contributions (Application of Part 7 of the Finance Act 2004) Regulations 2007;

(*m*) any procedural, ancillary or preliminary decision made in relation to an appeal against a decision under section 40A of the British Nationality Act 1981, section 82 . . . [2] of the Nationality, Immigration and Asylum Act 2002, or regulation 26 of the Immigration (European Economic Area) Regulations 2006.][1]

Amendments—[1] Art 3 substituted by the Tribunals, Courts and Enforcement Act 2007 (Miscellaneous Provisions) Order, SI 2010/41 arts 2, 3 with effect from 15 February 2010.

[2] In para (*m*), words revoked by the Immigration (Appeals) (Consequential Amendments and Saving Provision) Order, SI 2015/383 art 3 with effect fom 6 April 2015.

4 Revocations

The Appeals (Excluded Decisions) Order 2008 and the Appeals (Excluded Decisions) (Amendment) Order 2008 are revoked.

2009/403

FINANCE ACT 2008, SCHEDULE 39 (APPOINTED DAY, TRANSITIONAL PROVISION AND SAVINGS) ORDER 2009

Made by the Treasury under FA 2008 s 118(2) and (3)

Made . . . . *26 February 2009*

Commentary—*Simon's Taxes* **A6.708**.

1 Citation and interpretation

(1) This Order may be cited as the Finance Act 2008, Schedule 39 (Appointed Day, Transitional Provision and Savings) Order 2009.

(2) In this Order a reference to a paragraph (without more) is a reference to that paragraph of Schedule 39 to the Finance Act 2008.

(3) In this Order—

"the Taxes Acts" has the meaning given in section 118(1) of the Taxes Management Act 1970;

"TMA 1970" means the Taxes Management Act 1970;

"VATA 1994" means the Value Added Tax Act 1994.

2 Appointed days

(1) The day appointed for the coming into force of paragraphs 32 to 36 is 1st April 2009.

(2) Subject to article 10(2), the day appointed for the coming into force of paragraphs 1 to 31 and 37 to 66 is 1st April 2010.

3 Transitional provisions and savings

Paragraph 33 is disregarded where, for the purposes of section 33A of VATA 1994 (refunds of VAT to museums and galleries), the day on which the supply was made or the acquisition or importation took place was on or before 31st March 2006.

4 Paragraph 34 is disregarded—

(*a*) where, for the purposes of section 77 of VATA 1994 (assessments: time limits and supplementary assessments), the end of the prescribed accounting period or the importation, acquisition or event giving rise to the penalty, as appropriate, occurred on or before 31st March 2006, and (*b*) where, after a person's death, a sum is assessed as due by reason of some conduct (however described) of the deceased, including a sum due by way of penalty, interest or surcharge, and the date of the death is on or before 31st March 2006.

5 Paragraph 35 is disregarded where, for the purposes of a claim under section 78 of VATA 1994 (interest in certain cases of official error), the end of the applicable period to which the claim relates was on or before 31st March 2006.

6 Paragraph 36 is disregarded where, for the purposes of section 80 of VATA 1994 (credit for, or repayment of, overstated or overpaid VAT), the relevant date is on or before 31st March 2006.

7 Section 36(1A)(*b*) and (*c*) of TMA 1970 (fraudulent and negligent conduct) shall not apply where the year of assessment is 2008-09 or earlier, except where the assessment on the person ("P") is for the purposes of making good to the Crown a loss of tax attributable to P's negligent conduct or the negligent conduct of a person acting on P's behalf.

8 Paragraph 46(2A)(*b*) and (*c*) of Schedule 18 to the Finance Act 1998 (general time limits for assessments) shall not apply where the end of the accounting period to which the assessment relates is on or before 31st March 2010, except in a case involving negligence on the part of—

(*a*) the company, or
(*b*) a person acting on behalf of the company, or
(*c*) a person who was a partner of the company at the relevant time.

9 Section 77(4A)(*c*) and (*d*) of VATA 1994 (value added tax: assessments: time limits and supplementary assessments) shall not apply where the end of the prescribed accounting period or the importation, acquisition or event giving rise to the penalty, as appropriate, occurred on or before 31 March 2010, except where VAT has been lost in circumstances giving rise to a penalty under section 67 of VATA 1994 (failure to notify and unauthorised issue of invoices).

10—(1) This article applies where an event specified in paragraph 4 below relates to a year of assessment in respect of which a person ("P") has not been given notice under—

(*a*) section 8 of TMA 1970 (personal return),
(*b*) section 8A of TMA 1970 (trustee's return), or
(*c*) section 12AA of TMA 1970 (partnership return),

within one year of the end of the year of assessment.

(2) Where this article applies, the day appointed for the coming into force of paragraphs 1 to 31 and 37 to 65 is 1st April 2012.

(3) But this article does not apply if, as regards P and a year of assessment, any income which ought to have been assessed to income tax or chargeable gains which ought to have been assessed to capital gains tax, have not been assessed, or an assessment to tax has become insufficient, or any relief which has been given has become excessive.

(4) The events referred to in paragraph (1) above are—

(*a*) an assessment on P to income tax or capital gains tax,
(*b*) a claim by or on behalf of P, provided for by any provision of the Taxes Acts, and
(*c*) a notice given by P under section 711 of the Income Tax (Earnings and Pensions Act) 2003 (right to make a return).

(5) Nothing in this article has any application where P is a company.

2009/404

FINANCE ACT 2008, SCHEDULE 36 (APPOINTED DAY AND SAVINGS) ORDER 2009

Made by the Treasury under FA 2008 s 113(2) and (3)

Made . . . .*26 February 2009*

1 Citation and interpretation

(1) This Order may be cited as the Finance Act 2008, Schedule 36 (Appointed Day and Savings) Order 2009.

(2) In this Order a reference to a paragraph (without more) is a reference to that paragraph of Schedule 36 to the Finance Act 2008.

2 Appointed day

The day appointed for the coming into force of Schedule 36 to the Finance Act 2008 is 1st April 2009.

3 Savings
Where a notice is given under section 19A of the Taxes Management Act 1970 ("TMA 1970") (power to call for documents for purposes of enquiries) on or before 31st March 2009, for the purposes of that notice—

(*a*) the provisions contained in that section and in section 97AA of TMA 1970 (penalties for failure to produce documents under section 19A) shall continue to have effect on and after 1st April 2009;

(*b*) the amendments made by paragraphs 71 and 75 (consequential amendments) shall be disregarded.

4 Where a notice is given under section 20 of TMA 1970 (power to call for documents of taxpayer and others) on or before 31st March 2009, for the purposes of that notice—

(*a*) the provisions contained in that section and in section 20BB of TMA 1970 (offence of falsification etc of documents) shall continue to have effect on and after 1st April 2009;

(*b*) the amendments made by paragraphs 68, 70 and 76 (consequential amendments) shall be disregarded.

5 Where a notice is given under paragraph 6 of Schedule 1A to TMA 1970 (power to call for documents for the purposes of enquiries) on or before 31st March 2009, for the purposes of that notice—

(*a*) the provisions contained in paragraphs 6 and 6A (power to appeal against notice to produce documents) of that Schedule shall continue to have effect on and after 1st April 2009;

(*b*) the amendments made by paragraphs 72 and 75 (consequential amendments) shall be disregarded.

6 Where a notice is given under section 767C of the Income and Corporation Taxes Act (change in company ownership: information) on or before 31st March 2009, for the purposes of that notice—

(*a*) the provisions contained in that section shall continue to have effect on and after 1st April 2009;

(*b*) the amendments made by paragraph 73(*a*), 80, 81 and 82 (consequential amendments) shall be disregarded.

7 Where a notice is given under paragraph 27 of Schedule 18 to the Finance Act 1998 (company tax returns) on or before 31st March 2009, the provisions contained in paragraphs 27, 28 and 29 of that Schedule (notice to produce documents etc for purposes of enquiry into company tax return, power to appeal against such notices and penalty for failure to produce such documents etc) shall continue to have effect on and after 1st April 2009 for the purposes of that notice.

8 Where a notice is given for the purposes of regulation 5 (amendment of syndicate determinations and HMRC enquiries) of the Lloyd's Underwriters (Tax) Regulations 2005 on or before 31st March 2009, the provisions of paragraphs 27 to 29 of Schedule 18 to the Finance Act 1998 shall continue to have effect on and after 1st April 2009, with appropriate modification, for the purposes of that regulation.

9 In relation to a notice given on or before 31st March 2009, for the purposes of the application of section 20 of TMA 1970 (with sections 20B and 20BB of that Act) to—

(*a*) section 110ZA of the Social Security Administration Act 1992 (Class 1, 1A, 1B or 2 contributions: powers to call for documents etc),

(*b*) section 104ZA of the Social Security Administration (Northern Ireland) Act 1992 (Class 1, 1A, 1B or 2 contributions: powers to call for documents etc), and

(*c*) section 25 of the Tax Credits Act 2002 (payments of working tax credit by employers),

the amendments made respectively by paragraphs 84, 85 and 90 shall be disregarded.

10 In relation to a notice given on or before 31st March 2009, for the purposes of the application of—

(*a*) subsections (1) to (8) and 8(*c*) to 9 of section 20 of TMA 1970 (powers to call for information relevant to liability to income tax, corporation tax or capital gains tax), and

(*b*) sections 20B, 20BB and 20D of that Act so far as relating to those subsections,

to section 174 of the Finance Act 2006 (international tax enforcement arrangements: information powers), the amendments made by paragraph 91 shall be disregarded.

11 Where a notice is given on or before 31st March 2009, the amendments made by paragraph 78 (amendment to section 12(3) (secrecy) of the National Savings Bank Act 1971) shall be disregarded so far as they affect the notice.

12 In consequence of the preceding provisions of this Order, the amendments made by paragraph 92 shall be disregarded so far as they affect any notice referred to in those provisions, given on or before 31st March 2009.

2009/511

FINANCE ACT 2008, SCHEDULE 41 (APPOINTED DAY AND TRANSITIONAL PROVISIONS) ORDER 2009

Made . . . . *5 March 2009*

The Treasury make the following Order in exercise of the powers conferred by sections 122 and 123 of the Finance Act 2008:

1 Citation and interpretation

(1) This Order may be cited as the Finance Act 2008, Schedule 41 (Appointed Day and Transitional Provisions) Order 2009.

(2) In this Order a reference to a paragraph (without more) is a reference to that paragraph of Schedule 41 to the Finance Act 2008.

(3) In this Order—

"relevant excise provision" has the meaning given in paragraph 3(1);

"relevant obligation" means an obligation specified in the Table in paragraph 1;

"unauthorised issue of an invoice" has the meaning given in paragraph 2(2).

2 Appointed day

The day appointed for the coming into force of Schedule 41 to the Finance Act 2008 is 1st April 2010.

3 That Schedule has effect—

(*a*) in relation to any relevant obligation arising on or after that date;

(*b*) in relation to any unauthorised issue of an invoice taking place on or after that date;

(*c*) in relation to any act which enables HMRC to assess an amount as duty under a relevant excise provision and which is done on or after that date; and

(*d*) in relation to any act giving rise to a penalty under paragraph 4 (handling goods subject to unpaid excise duty) which is done on or after that date.

4 Transitional provisions

Paragraph 25 (consequential repeals), paragraph 29 of Schedule 24 to the Finance Act 2007 and paragraph 21 of Schedule 40 to the Finance Act 2008 repeal the following provisions only in so far as those provisions relate to conduct involving dishonesty which gives rise to a penalty under Schedule 41 to the Finance Act 2008—

(*a*) in the Value Added Tax Act 1994—

(i) sections 60 and 61 (VAT evasion), and

(ii) section 67(1)(*b*) (failure to notify);

(*b*) in the Finance Act 1994—

(i) section 8 (penalty for evasion of excise duty), and

(ii) paragraphs 12 and 13 of Schedule 7 (insurance premium tax: civil penalties);

(*c*) paragraphs 18 and 19 of Schedule 5 to the Finance Act 1996 (landfill tax: civil penalties: evasion and misdeclaration or neglect);

(*d*) paragraphs 98 and 99 of Schedule 6 to the Finance Act 2000 (climate change levy: civil penalties: evasion, liability of directors and misdeclaration or neglect);

(*e*) in Schedule 6 to the Finance Act 2001—

(i) paragraphs 7 and 8 (aggregates levy: civil penalties: evasion, liability of directors and misdeclaration or neglect); and

(ii) paragraph 9A(5)(*b*) (penalty under paragraph 7 above); and

(*f*) section 133(2) to (4) of the Finance Act 2002 (aggregates levy: amendments to provisions about civil penalties).

2009/571

FINANCE ACT 2008, SCHEDULE 40 (APPOINTED DAY, TRANSITIONAL PROVISIONS AND CONSEQUENTIAL AMENDMENTS) ORDER 2009

Made by the Treasury under FA 2008 s 122

Made . . . . *9 March 2009*
Laid before the House of Commons . . . . *10 March 2009*
Coming into force . . . . *1 April 2009*

1 Citation and interpretation

(1) This Order may be cited as the Finance Act 2008, Schedule 40 (Appointed Day, Transitional Provisions and Consequential Amendments) Order 2009 and comes into force on 1st April 2009.

(2) In this Order a reference to a paragraph (without more) is a reference to that paragraph of Schedule 40 to the Finance Act 2008.

(3) In this Order—

"filing date", in relation to a relevant document, means—

(i) where the document is required to be given to HMRC, the date by which it is required to be given, and

(ii) where the document is not required to be given to HMRC, the date on which it is given;

"HMRC" means Her Majesty's Revenue and Customs;

"relevant documents" means documents given to HMRC of a kind inserted in the Table in paragraph 1 of Schedule 24 by paragraph 2(4) or (5);

"relevant tax" means any tax inserted in the Table in paragraph 1 of Schedule 24 by paragraph 2(4) or (5);

"Schedule 24" means Schedule 24 to the Finance Act 2007; and

"tax period" has the meaning given in paragraph 28(*g*) of Schedule 24.

2 Appointed day

The day appointed for the coming into force of Schedule 40 to the Finance Act 2008 is 1st April 2009.

3 In their application in relation to penalties payable under paragraph 1 of Schedule 24 (error in taxpayer's document), the entries inserted by paragraph 2(4) and (5) shall have effect in relation to—

(*a*) relevant documents—

(i) which relate to tax periods commencing on or after 1st April 2009, and

(ii) for which the filing date is on or after 1st April 2010;

(*b*) relevant documents relating to all claims for repayments of relevant tax made on or after 1st April 2010 which are not related to a tax period;

(*c*) relevant documents produced under regulations under section 256 of the Inheritance Tax Act 1984 ("IHTA 1984") (regulations about accounts, etc), where the date of death is on or after 1st April 2009; and

(*d*) in any other case, relevant documents given where a person's liability to pay relevant tax arises on or after 1st April 2010.

4 In their application in relation to penalties payable under paragraph 1A of Schedule 24 (error in taxpayer's document attributable to another person), the entries inserted by paragraph 2(4) and (5) shall have effect in relation to—

(*a*) relevant documents—

(i) which relate to tax periods commencing on or after 1st April 2009, and

(ii) for which the filing date is on or after 1st April 2010;

(*b*) relevant documents relating to all claims for repayments of relevant tax made on or after 1st April 2010 which are not related to a tax period;

(*c*) relevant documents produced under regulations under section 256 of IHTA 1984 (regulations about accounts, etc) where the date of death is on or after 1st April 2009; and

(*d*) in any other case, relevant documents given where a person's liability to pay relevant tax arises on or after 1st April 2010.

5 In their application in relation to assessments falling within paragraph 2 of Schedule 24 (under-assessment by HMRC), the entries inserted by paragraph 2(4) and (5) shall have effect in relation to tax periods commencing on or after 1st April 2009, where the filing date for the relevant document is on or after 1st April 2010.

6 Transitional provisions

(1) Paragraph 21 (consequential repeals) repeals the provisions listed in paragraph (2) only in so far as those provisions relate to conduct involving dishonesty which relates to—

(*a*) an inaccuracy in a document, or

(*b*) a failure to notify HMRC of an under-assessment by HMRC.

(2) The provisions referred to in paragraph (1) are—

(*a*) in the Finance Act 1994—

(i) section 8 (penalty for evasion of excise duty), and

(ii) paragraphs 12 and 13 of Schedule 7 (insurance premium tax: civil penalties),

(*b*) paragraphs 18 and 19 of Schedule 5 to the Finance Act 1996 (landfill tax: civil penalties: evasion and misdeclaration or neglect),

(*c*) paragraphs 98 and 99 of Schedule 6 to the Finance Act 2000 (climate change levy: civil penalties: evasion, liability of directors and misdeclaration or neglect),

(*d*) in Schedule 6 to the Finance Act 2001—

(i) paragraphs 7 and 8 (aggregates levy: civil penalties: evasion, liability of directors and misdeclaration or neglect), and

(ii) paragraph 9A(5)(*b*) (penalty under paragraph 7 above),

(*e*) section 133(2) to (4) of the Finance Act 2002 (aggregates levy: amendments to provisions about civil penalties).

7 Notwithstanding paragraph 29(*d*) of Schedule 24 (consequential amendments), sections 60 and 61 of the Value Added Tax Act 1994 (VAT evasion) shall continue to have effect with respect to conduct involving dishonesty which does not relate to an inaccuracy in a document or a failure to notify HMRC of an under-assessment by HMRC.

8 Consequential amendments to enactments

Schedule 1 contains amendments of enactments in consequence of the provisions omitted by paragraph 21 and by paragraph 29 of Schedule 24.

9 Schedule 2 contains consequential amendments to secondary legislation.

SCHEDULE 1
CONSEQUENTIAL AMENDMENTS—PRIMARY LEGISLATION

Article 8

TAXES MANAGEMENT ACT 1970

1–4 (*amend* TMA 1970 ss 59C(4), 100B(1), 107A)

BETTING AND GAMING DUTIES ACT 1981

5 The Betting and Gaming Duties Act 1981 is amended as follows.

6 In paragraph 15(1)(*a*)(ii) of Schedule 1 after "section 8 of the Finance Act 1994 (penalty for evasion)" insert "or a penalty for a deliberate inaccuracy under paragraph 1 of Schedule 24 to the Finance Act 2007 (penalties for errors)".

FINANCE ACT 1982

7, 8 (*amend* FA 1982 Sch 18 para 10)

INCOME AND CORPORATION TAXES ACT 1988

9, 10 (*amend* TA 1988 s 827)

FINANCE ACT 1994

11 (*amends* FA 1994 Sch 7 (IPT))

VALUE ADDED TAX ACT 1994

12–17 (*amend* VATA 1994)

FINANCE ACT 1996

18, 19 (*amend* FA 1996 Sch 5 (landfill tax))

FINANCE ACT 2000

20 (*amends* FA 2000 Sch 6 (climate change levy))

FINANCE ACT 2001

21–25 (*amend* FA 2001 ss 25(5), 45(3), Sch 4, Sch 7)

FINANCE ACT 2004

26 (*amends* FA 2004 s 313)

INCOME TAX (TRADING AND OTHER INCOME) ACT 2005

27–29 (*amend* ITTOIA 2005 ss 54(2), 869(4))

SCHEDULE 2

CONSEQUENTIAL AMENDMENTS—SECONDARY LEGISLATION

Article 9

(*amends* the Registered Pension Schemes (Relief at Source) Regulations 2005 and the Duty Stamps Regulations 2006)

2009/1171

REGISTERED PENSION SCHEMES (AUTHORISED PAYMENTS) REGULATIONS 2009

Made by the Commissioners for HMRC under FA 2004 s 164(1)(f) and (2)

Made . . . .*6 May 2009*
Laid before the House of Commons . . . .*8 May 2009*
Coming into force in accordance with . . . .*regulation 1*

PART 1

INTRODUCTION

1 Citation, commencement and effect

(1) These Regulations may be cited as the Registered Pension Schemes (Authorised Payments) Regulations 2009 and shall come into force on 1st June 2009.

(2) These Regulations shall have effect—

(*a*) for payments of a description within Part 2, in relation to payments made on or after 1st December 2009; . . .[1]

(*b*) for payments of a description within Part 3 or Part 4, in relation to payments made on or after 6th April 2006[; . . .[2]

(*c*) for payments of a description within Part 5, in relation to payments made on or after 8th August 2012[; and][1]

(*d*) for payments of a description within Part 6, in relation to payments made on or after 6th April 2017."][2]

Amendments—[1] In para (2), word at end of sub-para (*a*) revoked, and sub-para (*c*) and preceding word inserted, by the Registered Pension Schemes (Authorised Payments) (Amendment) (No 2) Regulations, SI 2012/1881 regs 2, 3 with effect from 8 August 2012.

[2] In para (2), word "and" at end of sub-para (*b*) revoked, and sub-para (*d*) and preceding word "and" inserted, by the Registered Pension Schemes (Authorised Payments) (Amendment) Regulations, SI 2017/397 regs 2, 3 with effect from 6 April 2017.

2 Interpretation

(1) Any reference in these Regulations to a numbered section or a paragraph of a Schedule, without more, is a reference to the section or paragraph of the Finance Act 2004 bearing that number.

(2) Any reference in these Regulations to a person's being entitled to a payment—

(*a*) if it is a payment of pension (or intended to be such a payment), shall be construed in accordance with section 165(3) (pension rules), and related expressions shall be construed accordingly;

(*b*) if it is a payment of a lump sum (or intended to be such a payment), shall be construed in accordance with section 166(2) (lump sum rule), and related expressions shall be construed accordingly.

(3) For the purpose of these Regulations, whether a person is connected with another person is determined in accordance with section 993 of the ITA 2007 (meaning of "connected" persons).

(4) For the purpose of these Regulations,

(*a*) a pension scheme is related to another pension scheme if each of them is—

(i) a registered pension scheme that is an occupational pension scheme or a public service pension scheme, and

(ii) a pension scheme relating to the same employment; but

(*b*) if the context is whether a person is or is not a controlling director of a sponsoring employer of a pension scheme, only registered pension schemes that are occupational pension schemes are related to other such pension schemes.

(5) In these Regulations—

"controlling director" has the meaning given by section 273(9) (members liable as scheme administrator);

"excluded transfer" means—

(*a*) a recognised transfer; or

(*b*) any other transfer to the pension scheme of any sums or assets held for the purposes of, or representing accrued rights under, another pension scheme.

3 Prescribed payments and taxation

A payment by a registered pension scheme to or in respect of a member that is described in Part 2 of these Regulations—

(*a*) is a payment of a prescribed description for the purposes of section 164(1)(*f*) (authorised member payments);

(*b*) if paid to the member, shall be treated as a trivial commutation lump sum paid to the member for the purposes of Part 9 of ITEPA 2003 (pension income); and

(*c*) if not paid to the member, shall be treated as a trivial commutation lump sum death benefit paid to the recipient for the purposes of Part 9 of ITEPA 2003.

[3A—(1) This regulation applies to a lump sum if—

(*a*) the sum ("the earlier sum") is paid under a registered pension scheme to a member of the scheme,

(*b*) the earlier sum is paid to the member in connection with a pension under a registered pension scheme to which it is expected that the member will become entitled ("the expected pension"),

(*c*) the earlier sum is paid before the member becomes entitled to the expected pension,

(*d*) either—

(i) the earlier sum is paid on or after 19 September 2013 but before 27 March 2014, or

(ii) the earlier sum is paid before 19 September 2013, a contract for a lifetime annuity is entered into to provide the expected pension, and on or after 19 March 2014 the contract is cancelled,

(*e*) all of the sums and assets for the time being representing the sums and assets that when the earlier sum was paid were held for the purpose of providing the expected pension are, before the member becomes entitled to the expected pension, used in paying a further lump sum to the member ("the further sum"),

(*f*) the further sum is paid on or after 6 July 2014 but before 6 April 2015, and

(*g*) either—

(i) the payment of the further sum is a payment described in regulation 11, 11A or 12, or

(ii) the further sum is a trivial commutation lump sum within paragraph 7A of Schedule 29 and the earlier sum is the pension commencement lump sum in connection with which the further sum is paid.

(2) If this regulation applies to the earlier sum, and the payment of the further sum is a payment described in regulation 11, 11A or 12—

(*a*) the payment of the earlier sum is a payment of a prescribed description for the purposes of section 164(1)(*f*), and

(*b*) section 636A of ITEPA 2003 (exemption from income tax for certain lump sums) applies in relation to the earlier sum as if the earlier sum were a pension commencement lump sum.

(3) When deciding for the purposes of this regulation whether the further sum is a trivial commutation lump sum within paragraph 7A of Schedule 29, sub-paragraph (2)(*c*) of that paragraph is to be omitted.

(4) If this regulation applies to the earlier sum, and only the sums and assets mentioned in paragraph (1)(*e*) are used in paying the further sum, section 636B of ITEPA 2003 applies in relation to the further sum with the omission of its subsection (3).

(5) If this regulation applies to the earlier sum, and the sums and assets mentioned in paragraph (1)(*e*) are used together with other sums and assets in paying the further sum—

(*a*) section 636B of ITEPA 2003 applies in relation to the further sum as if instead of the further sum there were two separate trivial commutation lump sums as follows—

(i) one ("the first part of the further sum") consisting of so much of the further sum as is attributable to the sums and assets mentioned in paragraph (1)(*e*), and

(ii) another consisting of the remainder of the further sum,

(*b*) the first part of the further sum is to be treated for the purposes of section 636B of ITEPA 2003 as having been paid immediately before the remainder of the further sum,

(*c*) section 636B of ITEPA 2003 applies in relation to the first part of the further sum with the omission of its subsection (3), and

(*d*) for the purposes of applying section 636B(3) of ITEPA 2003 in relation to the remainder of the further sum, the rights to which the first part of the further sum relates are to be treated as rights that are not uncrystallised rights immediately before the remainder of the further sum is paid.

(6) For the purposes of paragraph (1), if the circumstances are as described in paragraph (1)(*d*)(ii), the member is treated as not having become entitled to the expected pension as a result of the cancelled contract having been entered into.][1]

Amendments—[1] Reg 3A inserted by FA 2014 s 43, Sch 5 para 6(1). This amendment is to be treated as having come into force on 19 March 2014 (FA 2014 Sch 5 para 15) and having been made by the Commissioners for HMRC under the powers to make regulations conferred by FA 2004 s 164(1)(*f*), (2) (FA 2014 Sch 5 para 6(2).

4 A payment by a registered pension scheme that is described in Part 3 of these Regulations, to the extent specified in the regulation concerned—

(*a*) is a payment of a prescribed description for the purposes of section 164(1)(*f*) of the Finance Act 2004;

(*b*) shall be treated as pension paid to the recipient under a registered pension scheme for the purposes of Part 9 of ITEPA 2003; and

(*c*) shall be treated for those purposes as pension accruing in the tax year in which it is paid.

5 A payment by a registered pension scheme that is described in Part 4 of these Regulations—

(*a*) is a payment of a prescribed description for the purposes of section 164(1)(*f*) of the Finance Act 2004; and

(*b*) shall be treated as a pension commencement lump sum paid under a registered pension scheme for the purposes of Part 9 of ITEPA 2003.

[5A A payment by a registered pension scheme that is described in Part 5 of these Regulations—

(*a*) is a payment of a prescribed description for the purposes of section 164(1)(f) of the Finance Act 2004; and

(*b*) shall be treated as a short service refund lump sum for the purposes of Part 9 of ITEPA 2003.][1]

Amendments—[1] Reg 5A inserted by the Registered Pension Schemes (Authorised Payments) (Amendment) (No 2) Regulations, SI 2012/1881 regs 2, 4 with effect from 8 August 2012.

[5B A payment by a registered pension scheme that is described in Part 6 of these Regulations is a payment of a prescribed description for the purposes of section 164(1)(*f*) of the Finance Act 2004.][1]

Amendments—[1] Regulation 5B inserted by the Registered Pension Schemes (Authorised Payments) (Amendment) Regulations, SI 2017/397 regs 2, 4 with effect from 6 April 2017.

PART 2
COMMUTATION PAYMENTS

6 Payment after relevant accretion

(1) A payment made after there has been a relevant accretion in respect of the member if—

(*a*) the payment extinguishes the member's entitlement to benefits under the pension scheme;

(*b*) it does not exceed [£10,000][1];

(*c*) it does not exceed the value of the accretion; and

(*d*) it is made no later than the relevant date.

(2) Regulation 7 defines "relevant accretion".

(3) In a case where the accretion is a relevant accretion by virtue of having occurred after the event described in regulation 7(2)(*b*), the scheme pension or annuity concerned shall be ignored in determining whether the member's entitlement to benefits under the scheme has been extinguished.

(4) For the purposes of paragraph (1)(*d*) the relevant date is—

Amendments—[1] In para (1)(*b*), figure substituted by FA 2014 s 42(6)(*a*) with effect for payments made on or after 27 March 2014. This amendment is to be treated as having been made by the Commissioners for HMRC under the powers to make regulations conferred by FA 2004 s 164(1)(*f*), (2) (FA 2014 s 42(11)).

(*a*) if the accretion has occurred before 1st December 2009, 1st June 2010, otherwise

(*b*) six months after the date the accretion occurs.

7 Meaning of "relevant accretion"

(1) The following are relevant accretions for the purposes of regulation 6 if they occur after either of the events mentioned in paragraph (2)—

(*a*) a payment ("the payment in") is received by the scheme in respect of the member, other than a contribution into the pension scheme or an excluded transfer into the pension scheme;

(*b*) there is an allocation to the arrangement in the amount by which the value of the sums and assets held for the purposes of the arrangement exceeds the value the scheme administrator had believed they had; and

(*c*) the scheme administrator becomes aware that the member is entitled to a benefit under the pension scheme, provided—

(i) the scheme administrator had not been aware of the entitlement before the event in paragraph (2), and

(ii) the scheme administrator could not reasonably have been expected to be aware of it before that event.

(2) The events are—

(*a*) there is a recognised transfer to another registered pension scheme or to a qualifying recognised overseas pension scheme in respect of the member; and

(*b*) a scheme pension or annuity is purchased for the member by the pension scheme from an insurance company.

(3) In order for the purchase of a scheme pension or annuity on or after 6th April 2006 to be an event within paragraph (2)(*b*), all or a part of the member's lifetime allowance must be available at the time of the purchase.

[(3A) For the purposes of determining whether all or part of the member's lifetime allowance is available under paragraph (3)—

(*a*) the fact that benefit crystallisation event 5 or benefit crystallisation event 5B has occurred in relation to the member is to be disregarded, and

(*b*) anything which, but for paragraph 2 or 15A of Schedule 32(c), would have been such a benefit crystallisation event is to be treated as if it were such an event.][1]

(4) The value of a relevant accretion is—

(*a*) in the case of a payment in within paragraph (1)(*a*), the amount of the payment; or

(*b*) in the case of an allocation within paragraph (1)(*b*), the amount by which the value of the sums and assets exceeds the value they had been believed to have;

(*c*) in the case described in paragraph (1)(*c*), the value of the benefit to which the member is entitled.

(5) . . .[2]

Amendments—[1] Para (3A) inserted by the Registered Pension Schemes (Miscellaneous Amendments) Regulations, SI 2011/1751 reg 8(1), (2) with effect for the tax year 2011–12 and subsequent tax years.

[2] Para (5) revoked by the Registered Pension Schemes (Authorised Payments) (Amendment) Regulations, SI 2013/1818 reg 2(1), (3) with effect from 6 April 2015.

8 Payments under the Financial Services Compensation Scheme

(1) A payment made by way of compensation under the Financial Services Compensation Scheme if—

(*a*) the payment does not exceed [£10,000][1]; and

(*b*) it extinguishes the member's entitlement to benefits under the pension scheme.

(2) The reference in paragraph (1) to the Financial Services Compensation Scheme is to the scheme established by Part 15 of the Financial Services and Markets Act 2000.

Amendments—[1] In para (1)(*a*), figure substituted by FA 2014 s 42(6)(*a*) with effect for payments made on or after 27 March 2014. This amendment is to be treated as having been made by the Commissioners for HMRC under the powers to make regulations conferred by FA 2004 s 164(1)(*f*), (2) (FA 2014 s 42(11)).

9 Payments to or in respect of members who were untraceable

. . .

Amendments—Reg 9 revoked by the Registered Pension Schemes (Miscellaneous Amendments) Regulations, SI 2011/1751 reg 8(1), (3) with effect for the tax year 2011–12 and subsequent tax years.

[10 Payments to members receiving annuities

A payment by a registered pension scheme to a member which would be a payment that is described in regulation 11, 11A(1)(*a*) to (*c*) or 12 but for the continuance after the payment of an annuity if the member has not previously received a payment, by that scheme, under this regulation.][1]

Amendments—[1] Reg 10 substituted by the Taxation of Pensions Act 2014 s 1, Sch 1 para 73(1), (2) with effect for payments made on or after 6 April 2015. This amendment is to be treated as having been made by the Commissioners for HMRC under the powers to make regulations conferred by FA 2004 s 164(1)(*f*), (2).

11 De minimis rule for pension schemes

(1) A payment by a public service pension scheme or an occupational pension scheme if—

(*a*) the member has reached [normal minimum pension age or the ill-health condition is met (see paragraph 1 of Schedule 28)][3] . . .[1];

(*b*) the member—

(i) is not a controlling director of a sponsoring employer of this or of any related scheme, and

(ii) is not a person connected to such a person;

(*c*) the payment does not exceed [£10,000][2];

(*d*) the commutation value of the benefits to which the member is entitled under this and any related scheme does not exceed [£10,000][2] in total;

(*e*) the payment extinguishes the member's entitlement to benefits under this scheme; and

(*f*) no recognised transfer was made out of this or any related scheme in respect of the member during the 3 years preceding the date of the payment.

(2) For the purposes of paragraph (1)(*d*), the commutation value is equal to the amount of the lump sum that, if paid, would extinguish the member's entitlement to benefits under the scheme concerned.

Amendments—[1] In para (1)(*a*), words revoked by the Registered Pension Schemes (Miscellaneous Amendments) Regulations, SI 2011/1751 reg 8(1), (5) with effect for the tax year 2011–12 and subsequent tax years

[2] In para (1)(*c*), (*d*), figure substituted by FA 2014 s 42(6)(*a*), (*c*) with effect for payments made on or after 27 March 2014. These amendments are to be treated as having been made by the Commissioners for HMRC under the powers to make regulations conferred by FA 2004 s 164(1)(*f*), (2) (FA 2014 s 42(11)).

[3] In para (1)(*a*), words substituted for words "the age of 60" by the Taxation of Pensions Act 2014 s 1, Sch 1 para 73(1), (3) with effect for payments made on or after 6 April 2015. This amendment is to be treated as having been made by the Commissioners for HMRC under the powers to make regulations conferred by FA 2004 s 164(1)(*f*), (2).

[11A—(1) A payment to a member by a pension scheme which is not a public service pension scheme or an occupational pension scheme in respect of an arrangement under that scheme if—

(*a*) the member has reached [normal minimum pension age or the ill-health condition is met (see paragraph 1 of Schedule 28)][3];

(*b*) the payment does not exceed [£10,000][2];

(*c*) the payment extinguishes the member's entitlement to benefits under the arrangement; and

(*d*) the condition in paragraph (2) is satisfied.

(2) The condition is that the member has not previously received more than [two payments][2] under this regulation.][1]

Amendments—[1] Reg 11A inserted by the Registered Pension Schemes (Authorised Payments) (Amendment) Regulations, SI 2012/522 reg 2 with effect in relation to payments made on or after 6 April 2012.

[2] In para (1)(*b*), figure substituted, and in para (2), words substituted, by FA 2014 s 42(6)(*a*), (*d*) with effect for payments made on or after 27 March 2014. These amendments are to be treated as having been made by the Commissioners for HMRC under the powers to make regulations conferred by FA 2004 s 164(1)(*f*), (2) (FA 2014 s 42(11)).

[3] In para (1)(*a*), words substituted for words "the age of 60" by the Taxation of Pensions Act 2014 s 1, Sch 1 para 73(1), (3) with effect for payments made on or after 6 April 2015. This amendment is to be treated as having been made by the Commissioners for HMRC under the powers to make regulations conferred by FA 2004 s 164(1)(*f*), (2).

12 Payments by larger pension schemes

(1) A payment by a public service pension scheme or an occupational pension scheme if—

(*a*) there are at least 50 members;

(*b*) any of conditions A, B or C is satisfied;

(*c*) the member has reached [normal minimum pension age or the ill-health condition is met (see paragraph 1 of Schedule 28)][3] . . . [1];

(*d*) the member—

(i) is not a controlling director of a sponsoring employer of this or any related scheme, and

(ii) is not a person connected to such a person;

(*e*) the payment does not exceed [£10,000][2];

(*f*) the payment extinguishes the member's entitlement to benefits under this scheme;

(*g*) ignoring any transfer within paragraph (5), no excluded transfer was made into this scheme in relation to the member during the 5 years preceding the date of the payment; and

(*h*) no recognised transfer was made out of this scheme in respect of the member during the 3 years preceding the date of the payment.

(2) Condition A is that the scheme was in existence on 1st July 2008.

(3) Condition B is that—

(*a*) the payment is in respect of a defined benefits arrangement; and

(*b*) the aggregate amount of the sums and assets held for the purposes of defined benefits arrangements is more than half of the aggregate amount of all the sums and assets held for the purposes of this scheme.

(4) Condition C is that in respect of at least 20 members the aggregate amount of the sums and assets held for the purpose of the arrangement exceed [£10,000][2].

(5) A transfer is within this paragraph if it is a transfer of sums and assets described in paragraph 12(8)(*b*), (*c*) or (*d*) of Schedule 36 (enhanced protection—permitted transfers).

(6) In paragraphs (3) and (4), the "aggregate amount" is an amount equal to the aggregate of the amount of the sums and the market value of the assets concerned.

Amendments—[1] In para (1)(*c*), words revoked by the Registered Pension Schemes (Miscellaneous Amendments) Regulations, SI 2011/1751 reg 8(1), (5) effect for the tax year 2011–12 and subsequent tax years

[2] In paras (1)(*e*), (4), figure substituted by FA 2014 s 42(6)(*a*), (*e*) with effect for payments made on or after 27 March 2014. These amendments are to be treated as having been made by the Commissioners for HMRC under the powers to make regulations conferred by FA 2004 s 164(1)(*f*), (2) (FA 2014 s 42(11)).

[3] In para (1)(*c*), words substituted for words "the age of 60" by the Taxation of Pensions Act 2014 s 1, Sch 1 para 73(1), (3) with effect for payments made on or after 6 April 2015. This amendment is to be treated as having been made by the Commissioners for HMRC under the powers to make regulations conferred by FA 2004 s 164(1)(*f*), (2).

PART 3
PENSION ERRORS

13 Pensions paid in error

(1) A payment made in error which is intended to represent a payment permitted by the pension rules or the pension death benefit rules to or in respect of a member, if the scheme administrator or insurance company making the payment (in either case, "the payer") believed that—

(*a*) the recipient was entitled to the payment, and

(b) the recipient was entitled to it in that amount.

(2) A payment is not within paragraph (1) if the error is that the recipient is no longer alive (as to which see regulation 15).

(3) Regulation 4 applies to—

(a) the whole of the payment; or

(b) if the recipient was entitled to an authorised payment apart from under this regulation, the amount by which the payment exceeds the amount of the authorised payment.

14 Pensions paid after discovery of error

(1) A payment made after the discovery of an error if either—

(a) it is made after there is a payment within regulation 13 to the same person and (apart from the discovery of the error) is of a similar nature to that payment; or

(b) if the error had not been discovered until after the payment, it would have been a payment within regulation 13.

(2) A payment is not within paragraph (1) unless it falls within paragraph (3), (4) or (5).

(3) A payment is within this paragraph if it is made even though the payer took reasonable steps to prevent its being made or its being made in that amount.

(4) A payment is within this paragraph if it is made while the scheme administrator is considering whether the rules of the scheme should be amended so that such payments or payments in such amounts will be permitted by the pension rules or the pension death benefit rules (as the case may be), provided the scheme administrator has not taken an unreasonable amount of time to decide.

(5) A payment is within this paragraph if it is made while the scheme administrator is in the process of amending the rules of the scheme so that such payments or payments in such amounts will be permitted by the pension rules or the pension death benefit rules (as the case may be), provided the scheme administrator has not taken an unreasonable amount of time to amend the rules.

(6) Regulation 4 applies to—

(a) the whole of the payment; or

(b) if the recipient was entitled to an authorised payment apart from under this regulation, the amount by which the payment exceeds the amount of the authorised payment.

15 Pensions continuing to be paid after death

(1) A payment which is intended to represent the payment of a pension permitted by the pension rules or the pension death benefit rules to or in respect of a member if—

(a) the member or dependant concerned ("the person") has died;

(b) the payment is made no later than six months after the date of the person's death;

(c) the payment would not have been an unauthorised payment if it had been made on the day before the person died; and

(d) either of the conditions in paragraph (2) is satisfied.

(2) The conditions mentioned in paragraph (1)(d) are—

(a) the scheme administrator or insurance company making the payment (in either case, "the payer") did not know, and could not reasonably have been expected to know, that the person had died before the payment was made;

(b) where the payer knew of the person's death before the payment was made, the payer took reasonable steps to prevent the payment's being made or its being made in that amount.

(3) Regulation 4 applies to the whole of the payment.

16 Payments of arrears of pension after death

(1) A payment of pension under the pension scheme to or in respect of a member who has died if—

(a) the payment is in respect of a defined benefits arrangement;

(b) . . . [1]

(c) the member—

(i) was not a controlling director of a sponsoring employer of this or any related scheme, and

(ii) was not a person connected to such a person; and

(d) either—

(i) the conditions in paragraph (2) are satisfied, or

(ii) where the member died on or after 6th April 2006, the conditions in paragraph (3) are satisfied.

(2) The conditions where the member died before 6th April 2006 are that—

(a) the payment represents accrued arrears of pension;

(b) the payment was allowed or required by the rules of this scheme as they stood immediately before the member died; and

(c) the existence of the rule or rules concerned would not have prejudiced approval of the scheme by the Inland Revenue or Her Majesty's Revenue and Customs.

(3) The conditions where the member died on or after 6th April 2006 are that—

(*a*) the payment represents accrued arrears of scheme pension the member's entitlement to which the scheme administrator had not established until after the member's death;
(*b*) the payment would not have been an unauthorised payment if the payment had been made immediately before the member's death and the member had been entitled to it; and
(*c*) the scheme administrator could not reasonably have been expected to make the payment before the member's death.

(4) Regulation 4 applies to so much of the payment as does not exceed the amount accrued during the period—
(*a*) beginning with the earliest date from which the member could have required the scheme administrator to make the payment if the member had been entitled to it; and
(*b*) ending with the member's death.

(5) If the member died on or after 6th April 2006, the making of the payment shall be treated as a benefit crystallisation event for the purposes of the lifetime allowance charge, namely benefit crystallisation event 9.

(6) The amount crystallised for the purposes of benefit crystallisation event 9 is the amount of the payment to which regulation 4 applies.

(7) For the purpose of paragraph (2)(*c*), whether something would have prejudiced the approval of a scheme by the Inland Revenue or by Her Majesty's Revenue and Customs is to be determined in accordance with the publication IR 12(2001) (known as the Occupational Pension Schemes Practice Notes) published by the former Inland Revenue Pension Schemes Office on 23rd March 2001, as that publication stood—
(*a*) if the member died before 23rd March 2001, on that date,
(*b*) otherwise, on the date of the member's death.

Amendments—[1] Para (1)(*b*) revoked by the Registered Pension Schemes (Miscellaneous Amendments) Regulations, SI 2011/1751 reg 8(1), (6) with effect in relation to any payment of pension made in respect of a member who died on or after 6 April 2011.

PART 4
LUMP SUM ERRORS

17 Commencement lump sums based on pension errors

(1) A payment of a lump sum the whole of which is intended to represent a pension commencement lump sum, but which exceeds the permitted maximum, if—
(*a*) the lump sum exceeds the permitted maximum only because it has been calculated by reference to the amount of a relevant pension; and
(*b*) either—
(i) the payment of the pension is a payment within regulation 13 or 14 (1)(*b*), or
(ii) paragraph (3) applies.

(2) The discovery that the lump sum exceeds the permitted maximum before the payment is made does not prevent the payment's being within paragraph (1) if the payer took reasonable steps to prevent its being made or its being made in that amount.

(3) This paragraph applies where—
(*a*) the lump sum is paid before the pension by reference to which its amount was calculated;
(*b*) the pension is not in the event paid, or paid in the amount originally intended, because an error is discovered; and
(*c*) if the error had not been discovered and the pension had been paid as intended, its payment would have been a payment within regulation 13.

(4) The member's becoming entitled to the pension commencement lump sum that forms part of the payment within paragraph (1) shall be treated as a benefit crystallisation event for the purposes of the lifetime allowance charge, namely benefit crystallisation event 9 (and this does not prevent the member's becoming so entitled from also having effect for the purposes of benefit crystallisation event 6).

(5) The amount crystallised for the purposes of benefit crystallisation event 9 is the amount by which the lump sum exceeds the permitted maximum.

18 Commencement lump sums paid in error—money purchase arrangements

(1) A payment of a lump sum the whole of which is intended to represent a pension commencement lump sum, but which exceeds the permitted maximum, if—
(*a*) the lump sum exceeds the permitted maximum only because it has been calculated by reference to the annuity purchase price or the scheme pension purchase price;
(*b*) an error in that calculation means that the amount concerned is greater than it would have been; and
(*c*) paragraph (3) applies.

(2) The discovery that the lump sum exceeds the permitted maximum before the payment is made does not prevent the payment's being within paragraph (1) if the payer took reasonable steps to prevent its being made or its being made in that amount.

(3) This paragraph applies where—

(*a*) the lump sum is paid before the lifetime annuity or scheme pension is purchased; and

(*b*) the lifetime annuity or scheme pension is not in the event purchased, or purchased for the amount originally intended, because the error is discovered.

(4) The member's becoming entitled to the pension commencement lump sum that forms part of the payment within paragraph (1) shall be treated as a benefit crystallisation event for the purposes of the lifetime allowance charge, namely benefit crystallisation event 9 (and this does not prevent the member's becoming so entitled from also having effect for the purposes of benefit crystallisation event 6).

(5) The amount crystallised for the purposes of benefit crystallisation event 9 is the amount by which the lump sum exceeds the permitted maximum.

19 Commencement lump sums paid after death

(1) A payment of a lump sum under the pension scheme to or in respect of a member who has died if—

(*a*) the payment is in respect of a defined benefits arrangement;

(*b*) the scheme administrator had not established the member's entitlement to the payment until after the member's death;

(*c*) the scheme administrator could not reasonably have been expected to make the payment before the member died;

(*d*) the payment would have been a pension commencement lump sum if it had been made immediately before the member's death and the member had been entitled to it;

(*e*) it is made no later than the end of the period of one year beginning with the earlier of—

(i) the day on which the scheme administrator first knew of the member's death, and

(ii) the day on which the scheme administrator could first reasonably be expected to have known of it; and

(*f*) the member was neither—

(i) a controlling director of a sponsoring employer of this or any related scheme, nor

(ii) a person connected to such a person.

(2) The making of the payment shall be treated as a benefit crystallisation event for the purposes of the lifetime allowance charge, namely benefit crystallisation event 9.

(3) The amount crystallised for the purposes of benefit crystallisation event 9 is the amount of the payment.

[PART 5
MISCELLANEOUS LUMP SUMS

20 Part refund payments relating to short service

(1) A payment of a lump sum by an occupational pension scheme if—

(a) the member's pensionable service was terminated before normal pension age but the member is not entitled to short service benefit by virtue of section 71 of the Pension Schemes Act 1993 (basic principle as to short service benefit);

(b) there has been no previous benefit crystallisation event in relation to the member and the pension scheme;

(c) it is paid when the member has not reached the age of 75;

(d) it does not exceed an amount equal to the aggregate of the member's contributions under the pension scheme;

(e) the payment extinguishes the member's entitlement to benefits under the scheme except to the extent that the entitlement is prohibited from being extinguished by rules of the pension scheme described in paragraph (2)(a); and

(f) at the time that the lump sum is paid the condition in paragraph (2) is satisfied.

(2) The condition in this paragraph is satisfied if—

(a) rules of the pension scheme ("the prohibition rules") have the effect of prohibiting a member's entitlement to benefits under the scheme from being extinguished by the payment of a lump sum;

(b) at the time that the prohibition rules took effect a provision ("the relevant provision") made by or under any enactment—

(i) was in force; and

(ii) had the effect of prohibiting a member's entitlement to benefits under the scheme from being extinguished by the payment of a lump sum; and

(c) the relevant provision has been repealed or revoked or has otherwise ceased to apply.

(3) A payment mentioned in paragraph (1) shall be subject to the charge specified in section 205 of the Finance Act 2004 (short service refund lump sum charge) and shall accordingly be treated as a short service refund lump sum for the purposes of the application of that section.

(4) In this regulation "pensionable service", "normal pension age" and "short service benefit" have the same meaning as in the Pension Schemes Act 1993 (see section 181(1) of that Act).][1]

[(5) In paragraph (1)(d) the reference to the member's contributions includes—

(a) any amount paid under section 7 of the Social Security Act 1986 (incentive payments to schemes becoming contracted-out between 1986 and 1993),

(b) any amount paid by the Commissioners for Her Majesty's Revenue and Customs under section 42A(3) of the Pension Schemes Act 1993 or section 38A(3) of the Pension Schemes (Northern Ireland) Act 1993 (rebates), and

(c) any amount recovered by the member's employer under regulations falling within paragraph (6) in respect of minimum payments made to the scheme in relation to any period before 6th April 2012.

(6) Those regulations are regulations which were made under—

(a) section 8(3) of the Pension Schemes Act 1993 (recovery of minimum payments), or

(b) section 4(3) of the Pension Schemes (Northern Ireland) Act 1993 (corresponding provisions for Northern Ireland).][2]

Amendments—[1] Part 5 (reg 20) inserted by the Registered Pension Schemes (Authorised Payments) (Amendment) (No 2) Regulations, SI 2012/1881 regs 2, 5 with effect from 8 August 2012.

[2] Paras 5, 6 inserted by the Registered Pension Schemes (Authorised Payments) (Amendment) Regulations, SI 2013/1818 reg 2(1), (2) with effect from 6 April 2013.

[PART 6

PENSION ADVICE ALLOWANCE PAYMENT

(21)

(1) A payment made by an arrangement in respect of which the conditions in paragraph (2) are satisfied.

(2) The conditions are that—

(*a*) the payment is made for—

(i) retirement financial advice provided to the person, or

(ii) the implementation of such advice;

(*b*) the payment is requested in writing by the person;

(*c*) the written request contains a declaration by the person that the conditions in sub-paragraphs (*d*), (*e*) and (*f*) are satisfied;

(*d*) no more than two pension advice allowance payments have been requested and made in respect of the person;

(*e*) no pension advice allowance payment has been requested and made in respect of the person in the tax year in which the request is made;

(*f*) the advice is regulated financial advice, provided by a financial advisor regulated and authorised by the Financial Conduct Authority to provide such advice;

(*g*) the payment is made by the registered pension scheme directly to the financial advisor; and

(*h*) the payment does not exceed £500.

(3) In this regulation—

(*a*) "arrangement" means

(i) a "money purchase arrangement" within the meaning given by section 152(2); or

(ii) a "hybrid arrangement" within the meaning given by section 152(8);

(*b*) "retirement financial advice" means advice in respect of the person's financial position, including their pension arrangements and the use of their pension funds;

(*c*) "regulated financial advice" has the meaning given in Article 53 of the Financial Services and Markets Act 2000 (Regulated Activities) Order 2001.][1]

Amendments—[1] Part 6 (reg 21) inserted by the Registered Pension Schemes (Authorised Payments) (Amendment) Regulations, SI 2017/397 regs 2, 5 with effect from 6 April 2017.

2009/May

INVESTMENT MANAGER (SPECIFIED TRANSACTIONS) REGULATIONS 2009

Made by the Commissioners for Her Majesty's Revenue and Customs under FA 1995 s 127(12) and (13), FA 2003 Sch 26 para 3(3) and (4) and ITA 2007 s 827(2) and (3).

These Regulations specify the types of transaction which constitute an "investment transaction" for the purposes of the Investment Manager Exemption and came into force on 12 May 2009.

The Investment Manager (Specified Transactions) Regulations 2009 came into force on 12 May 2009. The Regulations have effect for income tax purposes for the tax year 2009–10 and subsequent tax years, and for corporation tax purposes in relation to accounting periods ending on or after 12 May 2009. The Regulations specify the types of transaction which constitute an "investment transaction" for the purposes of the Investment Manager Exemption.

Revocations—These Regulations revoked by the Investment Manager (Investment Transactions) Regulations, 2014/April reg 3 with effect from 8 April 2014.

1 Citation, commencement and effect

(1) These Regulations may be cited as the Investment Manager (Specified Transactions) Regulations 2009 and come into force on 12 May 2009.

(2) These Regulations have effect—

(*a*) for income tax purposes for the tax year 2009–10 and subsequent tax years; and

(*b*) for corporation tax purposes in relation to accounting periods ending on or after 12 May 2009.

Revocations—These Regulations revoked by the Investment Manager (Investment Transactions) Regulations, 2014/April reg 3 with effect from 8 April 2014.

2 Interpretation

In these Regulations—

"loan relationship" has the meaning given by regulation 7; and

"non–resident person" means a person who is not resident in the United Kingdom.

Revocations—These Regulations revoked by the Investment Manager (Investment Transactions) Regulations, 2014/April reg 3 with effect from 8 April 2014.

3 Specified transactions

Any transaction falling within any of regulations 4 to 6 and 8 to 11 is of a description specified for the purposes of—

(*a*) section 127 of the Finance Act 1995 (persons not treated as UK representatives);

(*b*) paragraph 3 of Schedule 26 to the Finance Act 2003 (investment managers); and

(*c*) section 827 of the Income Tax Act 2007 (meaning of "investment manager" and "investment transaction").

Revocations—These Regulations revoked by the Investment Manager (Investment Transactions) Regulations, 2014/April reg 3 with effect from 8 April 2014.

4 Transactions in stocks or shares

Any transaction in stocks or shares falls within this regulation.

Revocations—These Regulations revoked by the Investment Manager (Investment Transactions) Regulations, 2014/April reg 3 with effect from 8 April 2014.

5 Transactions in relevant contracts

(1) Any transaction in a relevant contract falls within this regulation.

(2) For the purposes of this regulation a "relevant contract" is—

(*a*) an option;

(*b*) a future; or

(*c*) a contract for differences.

(3) For the purposes of paragraph (2) an "option" includes an instrument which entitles the holder to subscribe for shares in a company or assets representing a loan relationship of a company; and for these purposes it is immaterial whether the shares or assets to which the instrument relates exist or are identifiable.

(4) For the purposes of paragraph (3) the reference to a loan relationship of a company is to be construed in accordance with regulation 7 but with references in that regulation to "the non– resident person" treated as references to the company.

(5) For the purposes of paragraph (2) a "future" is a contract for the sale of property under which delivery is to be made—

(*a*) at a future date agreed when the contract is made, and

(*b*) at a price so agreed.

(6) For the purposes of paragraph (5)(*b*) a price is taken to be agreed when the contract is made—

(*a*) notwithstanding that the price is left to be determined by reference to the price at which a contract is to be entered into on a market or exchange or could be entered into at a time and place specified in the contract; or

(*b*) in a case where the contract is expressed to be by reference to a standard lot and quality notwithstanding that provision is made for a variation in the price to take account of any variation in quantity or quality on delivery.

(7) For the purposes of paragraph (2) and (5) references to an option or a future do not include references to a contract whose terms provide—

(*a*) that, after setting off their obligations to each other under the contract, a cash payment is to be made by one party to the other in respect of the excess, if any, and do not provide for the delivery of any property;

(*b*) that each party is liable to make to the other party a cash payment in respect of all that party's obligations to the other under the contract and do not provide for the delivery of any property; or

(*c*) for the delivery of any property other than property a transaction in which would fall within any of regulations 4 to 6 and 8 to 11 of these Regulations where the property is delivered.

Nothing in this paragraph has effect to exclude from references to an option or a future, an option or a future whose underlying subject matter is currency.

(8) In paragraph (7) "underlying subject matter" means—
(*a*) in relation to an option, the property which would fall to be delivered if the option were exercised, and
(*b*) in relation to a future, the property which, if the future were to run to delivery, would fall to be delivered at the date and price agreed when the contract is made.

(9) For the purposes of paragraph (2) "a contract for differences" is a contract the purpose or pretended purpose of which is to make a profit or avoid a loss by reference to fluctuations in—
(*a*) the value or price of property described in the contract, or
(*b*) an index or other factor designated in the contract.

(10) For the purposes of paragraph (9)(*b*) an index or other factor may be determined by reference to any matter and, for these purposes, a numerical value may be attributed to any variation in a matter.

(11) For the purposes of paragraph (2) none of the following is a contract for differences—
(*a*) an option;
(*b*) an future;
(c a contract of insurance;
(*d*) a contract effected in the course of capital redemption business;
(*e*) a contract of indemnity;
(*f*) a guarantee;
(*g*) a warranty;
(*h*) a loan relationship.

(12) For the purposes of paragraph (11)—
(*a*) "capital redemption business" means any business of a company carrying on insurance business in so far as it consists of the effecting on the basis of actuarial calculations, and the carrying out, of contracts under which, in return for one or more fixed payments, a sum or series of sums of a specified amount become payable at a future time or over a period; and
(*b*) "loan relationship" is to be construed in accordance with regulation 8 but with references to "the non–resident person" in that regulation treated as including references to a UK resident company.

(13) For the purposes of this regulation where an option, a future or a contract for differences relates to land, such option, future or contract for differences will not be a relevant contract except in cases where the option, the future or the contract for differences uses an index referred to in paragraph (9)(*b*) and the index is—
(*a*) publicly accessible;
(*b*) comprised of a significant number of properties; and
(*c*) not maintained by—
(i) the non–resident person;
(ii) the investment manager of the non–resident person; or
(iii) a person or persons connected with the non–resident person or the investment manager of the non–resident person.

(14) In paragraph (13) "investment manager" means a person providing investment or asset management services in the United Kingdom to a non–resident person.

(15) For the purposes of this regulation—
(*a*) sections 993 and 994 of the Income Tax Act 2007(connected persons and the meaning of control) apply in the case of a person chargeable to income tax; and
(*b*) section 839 of the Income and Corporation Taxes Act 1988 (connected persons and the meaning of control) apply in the case of a person chargeable to corporation tax.

Revocations—These Regulations revoked by the Investment Manager (Investment Transactions) Regulations, 2014/April reg 3 with effect from 8 April 2014.

6 Transactions involving loan relationships or related transactions

Any transaction which results in a non–resident person becoming a party to a loan relationship or a related transaction in respect of a loan relationship falls within this regulation.

Revocations—These Regulations revoked by the Investment Manager (Investment Transactions) Regulations, 2014/April reg 3 with effect from 8 April 2014.

7 Loan relationships: supplemental provisions

(1) For the purposes of regulation 7 a non–resident person has a "loan relationship" where that person stands (whether by reference to a security or otherwise) in the position of a creditor or debtor as respects any money debt and either—
(*a*) that debt is one arising from a transaction for the lending of money; or
(*b*) that debt is not one which arose from a transaction for the lending of money but is one—
(i) on which interest is payable to or by the non–resident person;
(ii) in relation to which exchange gains or losses arise to the non–resident person; or
(iii) as respects which the conditions in paragraph (2) are satisfied.

(2) The conditions referred to in paragraph (1)(*b*)(iii) are that—
(*a*) the non–resident person stands in the position of creditor in relation to the money debt; and

(*b*) the money debt is one from which a discount (whether of an income or capital nature) arises to the non–resident.

(3) In this regulation "exchange gains or losses" means—

(*a*) profits or gains, or

(*b*) losses,

which arise as a result of comparing at different times the expression in one currency of the whole or some part of the valuation put by the non–resident person in another currency on an asset or liability of the non–resident person.

(4) For the purposes of this regulation a "money debt" is a debt which is, or has at any time been, one that falls, or that may at the choice of the debtor or of the creditor fall, to be settled—

(*a*) by the payment of money,

(*b*) by the transfer of a right to settlement under a debt which is itself a money debt, or

(*c*) by the issue or transfer of shares in any company, disregarding any other alternative exercisable by either party.

(5) Subject to paragraph (6), where an instrument is issued by any person for the purpose of representing security for, or the rights of a creditor in respect of, any money debt, then (whatever the circumstances of the issue of the instrument) that debt shall be taken for the purposes of these Regulations to be a debt arising from a transaction for the lending of money.

(6) For the purposes of these Regulations a debt shall not be taken to arise from a transaction for the lending of money to the extent that it is a debt arising from rights conferred by shares in a company.

(7) For the purposes of this regulation so far as relating to exchange gains and losses, any currency held by the company shall be treated as a money debt.

(8) For the purposes of this regulation "money" includes money expressed in a currency other than sterling.

(9) For the purposes of regulation 6 a "related transaction" in relation to a loan relationship means any disposal or acquisition (in whole or in part) of rights or liabilities under that relationship.

Revocations—These Regulations revoked by the Investment Manager (Investment Transactions) Regulations, 2014/April reg 3 with effect from 8 April 2014.

8 Transactions in units in collective investment schemes

(1) Any transaction in units in a collective investment scheme falls within this regulation.

(2) In this regulation—

(*a*) "collective investment scheme" means any arrangements with respect to property of any description, including money, the purpose or effect of which is to enable persons taking part in the arrangements (whether by becoming owners of the property or any part of it or otherwise) to participate in or receive profits or income arising from the acquisition, holding, management or disposal of the property or sums paid out of such profits or income; and

(*b*) "units" means the rights or interests (however described) of the persons who are to participate in a collective investment scheme.

(3) The arrangements must be such that the persons who are to participate ("participants") do not have day–to–day control over the management of the property, whether or not they have the right to be consulted or to give directions.

(4) The arrangements must also have either of the following characteristics—

(*a*) the contributions of the participants and the profits or income out of which payments are to be made to them are pooled; or

(*b*) the property is managed as a whole by or on behalf of the operator of the collective investment scheme.

(5) If arrangements provide for such pooling as is mentioned in paragraph (4)(*a*) in relation to separate parts of the property, the arrangements are not to be regarded as constituting a single collective investment scheme unless the participants are entitled to exchange rights in one part for rights in another.

Revocations—These Regulations revoked by the Investment Manager (Investment Transactions) Regulations, 2014/April reg 3 with effect from 8 April 2014.

9 Transactions in securities

(1) Any transaction in securities falls within this regulation.

(2) For the purposes of this regulation a "transaction in securities" is any transaction in securities of any description not falling within regulations 4 to 6 and 8.

Revocations—These Regulations revoked by the Investment Manager (Investment Transactions) Regulations, 2014/April reg 3 with effect from 8 April 2014.

10 Transactions in buying or selling foreign currency

Any transaction consisting in the buying or selling of any foreign currency falls within this regulation.

Revocations—These Regulations revoked by the Investment Manager (Investment Transactions) Regulations, 2014/April reg 3 with effect from 8 April 2014.

11 Transactions in carbon emission trading products

(1) Any transaction in a carbon emission trading product falls within this regulation.

(2) For the purposes of this regulation a "transaction in a carbon emission trading product" is any transaction which meets conditions A to C.

(3) Condition A is that the transaction is a transaction—

(*a*) in Community tradable emissions allowances, or

(*b*) in transferable units issued pursuant to the Kyoto Protocol.

(4) Condition B is that the transaction is not one which gives rise to either—

(*a*) a chargeable gain falling within section 10 of the Taxation of Chargeable Gains Act 1992 (non–resident with United Kingdom branch or agency), or

(*b*) a chargeable gain falling within section 10B of that Act (non–resident company with United Kingdom permanent establishment) (and accordingly taken into account for the purposes of section 11(2A) of the Income and Corporation Taxes Act 1988 (profits attributable to a permanent establishment)).

(5) Condition C is that the transaction does not otherwise fall within any other regulation of these Regulations.

(6) In this regulation—

"Community tradable emissions allowances" means transferable allowances which relate to the making of emissions of greenhouse gases, and are allocated as part of a system made for the purpose of implementing any community obligation of the United Kingdom relating to such emissions;

"the Kyoto Protocol" means the Kyoto Protocol to the United Nations Framework Convention on Climate Change signed at Kyoto on 11th December 1997; and

"units" includes assigned amount units, certified emission reductions, emission reduction units and removal units.

Revocations—These Regulations revoked by the Investment Manager (Investment Transactions) Regulations, 2014/April reg 3 with effect from 8 April 2014.

2009/1343

RESEARCH AND DEVELOPMENT (QUALIFYING BODIES) (TAX) ORDER 2009

Made by the Treasury under CTA 2009 s 1142(1)(e)

Made . . . . *1 June 2009*
Laid before the House of Commons . . . . *2 June 2009*
Coming into force . . . . *23 June 2009*

Revocation—These Regulations revoked by the Research and Development (Qualifying Bodies) (Tax) Order, SI 2012/286 art 3 with effect from 28 February 2012.

2009/1916

INFORMATION NOTICE: RESOLUTION OF DISPUTES AS TO PRIVILEGED COMMUNICATIONS REGULATIONS 2009

Made by the Commissioners for HMRC under FA 2008 Sch 36 para 23(3) and (4)

Made . . . . *16 July 2009*
Laid before the House of Commons . . . . *17 July 2009*
Coming into force . . . . *7 August 2009*

1 Citation and commencement

These Regulations may be cited as the Information Notice: Resolution of Disputes as to Privileged Communications Regulations 2009 and come into force on 7th August 2009.

2 Interpretation

In these Regulations—

"document" means information, a document or part of a document;

a "document in dispute" is a document over which there is a dispute between HMRC and a person who has been given an information notice as to whether the document is privileged;

"officer" means an officer of Revenue and Customs;

a "person acting on behalf of" a taxpayer or a third party means any person who is acting on behalf of a taxpayer or third party in relation to an information notice;

"Schedule 36" means Schedule 36 to the Finance Act 2008;

"taxpayer" means a person who is given a notice under paragraph 1 of Schedule 36;

"third party" means a person who is given a notice under paragraph 2 or paragraph 5 of Schedule 36;

"working day" means any day except a Saturday, Sunday, Christmas Day, Good Friday or a bank holiday under section 1 of the Banking and Financial Dealings Act 1971.

3 Application of these Regulations

These Regulations apply where there is a dispute between HMRC and a person to whom an information notice has been given either—

(*a*) during the course of correspondence, or

(*b*) during the course of an inspection of premises under Schedule 36,

as to whether a document is privileged.

4 Requirement to provide information and produce documents not in dispute

Nothing in these Regulations shall affect—

(*a*) the requirement under an information notice to provide information or produce a document, which is not in dispute; or

(*b*) the power under Schedule 36 to inspect premises.

5 Procedure where information notice given in correspondence is in dispute

(1) The following procedure applies where there is a dispute falling within regulation 3(*a*).

(2) On receipt of the information notice, the taxpayer, third party or person acting on their behalf shall—

(*a*) by the date given in the notice for providing information or producing documents, specify in a list each document, required under the information notice, which is in dispute, with a description of the nature and contents of that document;

(*b*) serve that list on HMRC.

(3) But no description of a document or type of document is required where such description would itself give rise to a dispute over privilege.

(4) Within twenty working days of receiving the list referred to in sub-paragraph (2), HMRC must notify the person who served the list of any documents on the list that it requires to be produced and which it considers are not privileged.

(5) On receipt of notification under paragraph (4), the taxpayer, third party or person acting on their behalf must make an application to the First-tier Tribunal to consider and resolve the dispute and must include copies of the documents which remain in dispute with that application.

(6) The taxpayer, third party or person acting on their behalf shall provide HMRC with proof of service under paragraph (2)(*b*).

(7) Service for the purposes of paragraph (2)(*b*) must take place within a reasonable time to be agreed between the taxpayer, third party or person acting on their behalf and HMRC but in any event no later than twenty working days after the date given in the notice for providing information or producing documents.

(8) An application under paragraph (5) must be made within a reasonable time to be agreed between the taxpayer, third party or person acting on their behalf and HMRC but in any event no later than twenty working days of the date of the notification required under paragraph (4).

6 Procedure where information notice given during inspection of premises is in dispute

(1) The following procedure applies where there is a dispute falling within regulation 3(*b*).

(2) On receipt of the information notice, the taxpayer, third party or person acting on their behalf shall indicate to the officer carrying out the inspection each document, required under the information notice, which is in dispute.

(3) The taxpayer, third party or person acting on their behalf must place the document or documents in dispute, or a copy of such document or documents, in an appropriate container which prevents the contents being visible.

(4) The container shall be—

(*a*) sealed, labelled and signed by that person;

(*b*) countersigned by the officer; and

(*c*) given into the custody of the officer.

(5) The officer shall deliver the container to the First-tier Tribunal with the seal intact within forty-two working days of having taken custody of it together with an application to that Tribunal to consider and resolve the dispute.

7 Compliance with information notice

Where a taxpayer or third party who has received an information notice, or a person acting on their behalf, complies with the procedure set out in regulation 5 or, as the case may be, regulation 6, those persons shall be treated as having complied with the information notice in relation to the documents in dispute until the First-tier Tribunal decides the status of the document or until an agreement has been reached under regulation 10.

8 Finding of the First-tier Tribunal

When an application is made under regulation 5(5) or 6(5), the First-tier Tribunal shall—

(*a*) resolve the dispute by confirming whether and to what extent the document, is or is not privileged;

(*b*) direct which part or parts of a document (if any) shall be disclosed.

9 The First-tier Tribunal must ensure that any document in dispute, or any copy of such document, is not inappropriately disclosed to any person pending the Tribunal's consideration of the status of the document.

10 Resolution of disputes by agreement

A dispute falling within regulation 3 may be resolved at any time by HMRC and the person to whom an information notice has been given reaching an agreement, whether in writing or otherwise.

2009/1926

GENERAL INSURERS' TECHNICAL PROVISIONS (APPROPRIATE AMOUNT) (TAX) REGULATIONS 2009

Made by the Commissioners for HMRC under FA 2007 Sch 11 paras 1(4), 3(7) and 3(15).

Made .... *17 July 2009*

Laid before the House of Commons .... *20 July 2009*

Coming into force .... *1 September 2009*

PART 1

INTRODUCTORY PROVISIONS

1 Citation, commencement and effect

(1) These Regulations may be cited as the General Insurers' Technical Provisions (Appropriate Amount) (Tax) Regulations 2009 and come into force on 1st September 2009.

(2) In relation to a general insurer, other than a member of a Lloyd's syndicate, these Regulations shall have effect in relation to periods of account ending on or after 31st December 2009.

(3) In relation to a member of a Lloyd's syndicate, these Regulations shall have effect in relation to a syndicate return made in respect of profits or losses declared after 31st December 2009.

2 Interpretation

(1) In these Regulations a reference to Schedule 11 is a reference to Schedule 11 to the Finance Act 2007.

(2) In these Regulations—

"Schedule 3 to the Accounts and Reports Regulations" means Schedule 3 to the Large and Medium-sized Companies and Groups (Accounts and Reports) Regulations 2008; and

"syndicate return" means a return of a syndicate's profit or loss for an underwriting year made under regulation 4 of the Lloyd's Underwriters (Tax) Regulations 2005.

PART 2

GENERAL INSURERS (OTHER THAN MEMBERS OF LLOYD'S SYNDICATES)

3 Appropriate amount of technical provisions: general insurers (other than a member of a Lloyd's syndicate)

This Part applies to a general insurer other than a member of a Lloyd's syndicate.

4 For a period of account, the appropriate amount of the technical provisions for the purposes of paragraph 1 of Schedule 11 is the aggregate of—

(*a*) the amount of the provision for unearned premiums determined in accordance with paragraph 50 of Schedule 3 to the Accounts and Reports Regulations;

(*b*) the amount of the provision for unexpired risks determined in accordance with paragraph 51 of that Schedule; and

(*c*) the estimated amount of the liabilities in respect of claims outstanding arising from the general insurer's general business determined in accordance with regulations 5 to 8.

5 Estimated amount of claims outstanding: confirmation by general insurer

(1) For the purposes of regulation 4, the amount of the liabilities in respect of claims outstanding arising from the general insurer's general business is the amount of those liabilities stated in the general insurer's accounts for the period if conditions A to C are satisfied.

(2) Condition A is—

(*a*) that the general insurer gives confirmation in writing that the amount of the liabilities stated in the accounts is not an excessive estimate of the amount of the liabilities, and

(*b*) the confirmation is founded on or supported by an opinion in writing given to the general insurer by an actuary or other suitably skilled person (which may include a director or employee of the general insurer) stating that the amount is not an excessive estimate of the amount of the liabilities.

Regulation 6 contains provisions supplementing condition A.

(3) Condition B is that the opinion referred to in condition A must reflect the circumstances prevailing at the time at which the technical provisions are adopted by the general insurer.

(4) Condition C is that the amount of the liabilities stated in the accounts is determined in accordance with regulation 8 (provisions supplementing regulations 5 and 7).

6 Provisions supplementing condition A

(1) In the case of a controlled foreign company which is a general insurer within the meaning of paragraph 3(1)(*b*) of Schedule 11—

(*a*) references to "general insurer" in regulation 5(2)(*a*) and in this regulation (other than in sub-paragraph (*b*) of this paragraph) are to be construed as references to the company referred to in paragraph 3(2)(*b*) of Schedule 11, and

(*b*) the reference to "general insurer" in regulation 5(2)(*b*) is to be construed as a reference to the controlled foreign company.

(2) For the purposes of condition A in regulation 5, an estimate of the amount of the liabilities is an excessive estimate unless the estimate includes no more than a reasonable margin to take into account the nature or type of risks to which the liabilities relate and the uncertainty associated with those risks.

(3) If the opinion referred to in condition A is given to the general insurer by a director, or by an employee who is not a director of the general insurer, the confirmation must include a statement identifying the status of the person who gave the opinion to the general insurer.

(4) Subject to paragraph (5), the confirmation referred to in condition A must accompany the general insurer's company tax return which relates to the period of account (and if more than one company tax return relates to the period of account the confirmation need only be given with the return which relates to the earliest period in the period of account).

(5) If, at the time the company tax return is made, the general insurer has a reasonable excuse for not providing the confirmation with the company tax return, the confirmation may be provided to an officer of Revenue and Customs separately from the return but must be provided as soon as reasonably possible after the return is made.

(6) In this regulation "company tax return" means a return under paragraph 3 of Schedule 18 to the Finance Act 1998.

7 Estimated amount of claims outstanding where conditions in regulation 5 are not satisfied

(1) This regulation applies in a case where any of conditions A to C in regulation 5 is not satisfied.

(2) For the purposes of regulation 4, the amount of the liabilities in respect of claims outstanding arising from the general insurer's general business is the general insurer's undiscounted best estimate of the future cash flows in respect of claims outstanding.

(3) For the purposes of paragraph (2)—

(*a*) the reference to "best estimate" shall be construed as a reference to the mean of the distribution of the potential outcomes of the claims to which the estimate relates, and

(*b*) the best estimate of the future cash flows must be the best estimate available at the time at which the technical provisions are adopted by the general insurer.

8 Provisions supplementing regulations 5 and 7

(1) This regulation supplements regulations 5 and 7.

(2) Any calculation, computation or estimate required to determine the amount of the liabilities in respect of claims outstanding must be made in accordance the standards specified in paragraph (3) in force at the time at which the technical provisions are adopted by the general insurer.

(3) The specified standards are—

(*a*) all generic technical actuarial standards and relevant specific technical actuarial standards published by the Board for Actuarial Standards in relation to the performance of actuarial functions, or

(*b*) where the general insurer is not resident in the United Kingdom, such other standards or provisions of the law of the territory in which the general insurer is domiciled as may reasonably be regarded as equivalent in effect to the standards referred to in sub-paragraph (*a*).

In this paragraph, "the Board for Actuarial Standards" means the operating body of that name of the Financial Reporting Council.

(4) Any calculation, computation or estimate required to determine the amount of the liabilities in respect of claims outstanding must take into account—

(*a*) the nature or type of risks to which the liabilities in respect of claims outstanding relate, and
(*b*) the volatility and uncertainty associated with those risks.

(5) Without prejudice to the generality of paragraph (4), the reference in that paragraph to taking into account includes, in particular, taking into account liabilities—

(*a*) on the basis of general insurance business reporting categories described in Annex 11.3 to Chapter 11 of Volume 1 of IPRU(INS), or
(*b*) on the basis of grouping of risks in accordance with the descriptions of accounting classes for general insurance business set out in Appendix 9.16 to Volume 2 of IPRU(INS).

(6) In paragraph (5), "IPRU(INS)" means the Interim Prudential Sourcebook for Insurers made by the Financial Services Authority under the Financial Services and Markets Act 2000.

(7) Any estimate of the amount of the liabilities in respect of claims outstanding shall be determined—

(*a*) net of reinsurance ceded, and
(*b*) in accordance with paragraph 53 of Schedule 3 to the Accounts and Reports Regulations.

(8) A reference to claims outstanding includes—

(*a*) the expense of handling a future claim (whether allocated or unallocated), and
(*b*) a future claim which has been incurred as a liability of the general insurer but which is—
 (i) not reported to the general insurer at the time at which the technical provisions are adopted, or
 (ii) reported, but not fully reported, to the general insurer at that time.

(9) A reference in this Part to the time at which technical provisions are adopted is a reference—

(*a*) to the time at which the directors of the general insurer approve the general insurers' annual accounts for the purposes of section 414 of the Companies Act 2006;
(*b*) in the case of a general insurer to which that section does not apply, to such similar time as may apply under equivalent provisions of the law of the territory in which the general insurer is domiciled; or
(*c*) in the case of general business carried on by a permanent establishment in the United Kingdom of a general insurer which is not resident in the United Kingdom and for which accounts of the permanent establishment are prepared for the period of account, the time at which the general insurer approves those accounts.

PART 3
MEMBERS OF LLOYD'S SYNDICATES

9 Appropriate amount of technical provisions: members of closed Lloyd's syndicates

(1) This regulation applies to a general insurer which is a member of a closed Lloyd's syndicate. In this regulation, a closed Lloyd's syndicate is a Lloyd's syndicate that is not an open Lloyd's syndicate.

(2) For a period of account, the appropriate amount of the technical provisions for the purposes of paragraph 1 of Schedule 11 is the member's allowable reinsurance to close amount in respect of the syndicate.

(3) For the purposes of paragraph (2), the allowable reinsurance to close amount for the period of account is the lesser of—

(*a*) the reinsurance to close amount for the period of account which is treated as a technical provision in accordance with regulation 11 (reinsurance to close amounts); and
(*b*) subject to paragraphs (4), the aggregate of the member's share of—
 (i) the amount of the provision for unearned premiums determined in accordance with paragraph 50 of Schedule 3 to the Accounts and Reports Regulations;
 (ii) the amount of the provision for unexpired risks determined in accordance with paragraph 51 of that Schedule; and
 (iii) the amount of the liabilities in respect of claims outstanding arising from the general business of the syndicate.

(4) For the purposes of paragraph (3)(*b*), amounts are to be determined on the assumption that—

(*a*) the syndicate is an open Lloyd's syndicate, and
(*b*) no reinsurance to close amounts have been paid in respect of the syndicate by any member of the syndicate.

10 Appropriate amount of technical provisions: members of open Lloyd's syndicates

(1) This regulation applies to any general insurer which is a member of an open Lloyd's syndicate.

(2) For a period of account, the appropriate amount of the technical provisions for the purposes of paragraph 1 of Schedule 11 is the aggregate of the member's share of—

(*a*) the amount of the provision for unearned premiums determined in accordance with paragraph 50 of Schedule 3 to the Accounts and Reports Regulations;

(*b*) the amount of the provision for unexpired risks determined in accordance with paragraph 51 of that Schedule 3; and

(*c*) the amount of the liabilities in respect of claims outstanding arising from the general business of the syndicate.

11 Reinsurance to close amounts

(1) The reinsurance to close amount to be treated as a technical provision in the case of a member of a Lloyd's syndicate for a period of account is whichever is the lesser of—

(*a*) the total of the reinsurance to close amounts which the member pays or gives, or is treated as paying or giving, in respect of the underwriting year for which profits or losses are declared; and

(*b*) the total of the reinsurance to close amounts which the member receives, or is treated as receiving, in respect of the underwriting year for which profits or losses are declared.

This paragraph is subject to paragraph (2).

(2) If a company—

(*a*) pays or gives, or is treated as paying or giving, a reinsurance to close amount to a member in respect of an underwriting year for which profits or losses are declared, and

(*b*) the company is connected to the member,

the amount which the member receives, or is treated as receiving, shall also be treated as a reinsurance to close amount paid by the member in respect of that underwriting year.

(3) For the purposes of paragraph (2), section 839(5) to (8) of the Income and Corporation Taxes Act 1988 (connected persons) applies for the purpose of determining whether a company is connected to a member.

12 Provisions supplementing regulations 9 and 10: determination of member's share of provisions

(1) For the purposes of regulations 9(3)(*b*) and 10(2), a member's share of the amounts referred to in those regulations shall be determined by reference to the member's proportionate entitlement to participate in the underwriting business of the syndicate.

(2) For the purposes of regulations 9(3)(*b*)(iii) and 10(2)(*c*), in determining the amount referred to in those provisions, regulations 5 to 8 shall apply with the following modifications—

(*a*) a reference to "the general insurer's general business" shall be treated as a reference to the general business of the syndicate;

(*b*) the reference in regulation 5(1) to "the general insurer's accounts" shall be treated as a reference to the syndicate's accounts;

(*c*) references in regulations 5(3), 7(3) and 8(8) to "the general insurer" shall be treated as a reference to the syndicate;

(*d*) regulation 6(1) shall be treated as omitted;

(*e*) the reference in regulation 6(4) and (5) to the "general insurer's company tax return" shall be treated as a reference to the syndicate return which relates to the period of account;

(*f*) the reference in regulation 6(5) to "general insurer" shall be treated as a reference to the syndicate's managing agent;

(*g*) regulation 6(6) shall be treated as omitted;

(*h*) the reference in regulation 7(2) to "the general insurer's undiscounted best estimate" shall be treated as a reference to the best estimate of the syndicate's managing agent;

(*i*) regulation 8(3)(*b*) shall be treated as omitted; and

(*j*) for regulation 8(9) there shall be treated as substituted—

"(9) A reference in this Part to the time at which technical provisions are adopted is a reference to the time at which the syndicate's managing agent approves the syndicate's profit or loss accounts for the period of account by signing them.".

2009/2031

SPECIAL ANNUAL ALLOWANCE CHARGE (APPLICATION TO MEMBERS OF CURRENTLY-RELIEVED NON-UK PENSION SCHEMES) ORDER 2009

Made by the Treasury under FA 2009 Sch 35 para 20(1) and (2)

Made . . . .*21 July 2009*
Laid before the House of Commons . . . .*22 July 2009*
Coming into force . . . .*12 August 2009*

1 Citation, commencement and interpretation

(1) This Order may be cited as the Special Annual Allowance Charge (Application to Members of Currently-Relieved Non-UK Pension Schemes) Order 2009 and shall come into force on 12th August 2009.

2 This Order shall have effect for the tax year 2009–10 and subsequent tax years.

(1) In this Order a reference to Schedule 35 is a reference to Schedule 35 to the Finance Act 2009.

3 Application of the special annual allowance charge

(1) The provisions in Schedule 35 shall apply to individuals who are members of currently-relieved non-UK pension schemes as if those schemes were registered pension schemes.

(2) Paragraph (1) shall have effect subject to the modifications of Schedule 35 specified in this Order.

4 Modifications of Schedule 35

For the words "scheme administrator", in each place where they occur, substitute the words "scheme manager".

5—(1) In paragraph 3 of Schedule 35 the calculation of the total adjusted pension input amount for members of currently-relieved non-UK pension schemes shall be arrived at with the following modifications.

(2) Section 230(1) and 234(1) of FA 2004 (cash balance and defined benefits arrangements) shall apply as if the increase in the value of the individual's rights under an arrangement under the pension scheme relating to the individual during the tax year were the greater of—

(*a*) the appropriate fraction of what it otherwise would be (see paragraph (3)); and

(*b*) the amount of any contributions paid under the arrangement during the tax year by or on behalf of the individual (otherwise than by an employer) in respect of which relief is given by virtue of—

(i) Schedule 33 to FA 2004 (overseas pensions schemes: migrant member relief),

(ii) paragraph 51 of Schedule 36 to FA 2004 (individuals with pre-commencement entitlement to corresponding relief), or

(iii) double tax arrangements,

and section 237 of FA 2004 (hybrid arrangements) shall apply accordingly.

(3) The appropriate fraction referred to in paragraph (2)(*a*) is—

$$\frac{TE}{EI}$$

where—

EI is the total amount of employment income of the individual from any relevant employment or employments for the tax year, excluding any such income which is exempt income (within the meaning of section 8 of ITEPA 2003), and

TE is so much of EI as constitutes taxable earnings from any such employment (within the meaning of section 10(2) of ITEPA 2003).

(4) For the purposes of paragraph (3) an employment is a relevant employment if it is an employment with an employer who is a sponsoring employer in relation to the currently-relieved non-UK pension scheme.

(5) Section 233(1) of FA 2004 (other money purchase arrangements) shall apply as if—

(*a*) the reference in section 233(1)(*a*) of FA 2004 to relievable pension contributions paid by or on behalf of the individual under an arrangement under the pension scheme relating to the individual were to those in respect of which relief from tax is given by virtue of—

(i) Schedule 33 to FA 2004 (overseas pensions schemes: migrant member relief),

(ii) paragraph 51 of Schedule 36 to FA 2004 (individuals with pre-commencement entitlement to corresponding relief), or

(iii) double tax arrangements; and

(*b*) the reference in section 233(1)(*b*) of FA 2004 to contributions paid in respect of the individual under such an arrangement by an employer of the individual were to the appropriate fraction of the contributions so paid (as to which see paragraph (6)),

and section 237 of FA 2004 shall apply accordingly.

(6) The appropriate fraction referred to in paragraph (5)(*b*) is—

$$\frac{TE}{EI}$$

where—

EI is the total amount of employment income of the individual from any employment or employments with the employer for the tax year, excluding any such income which is exempt income (within the meaning of section 8 of ITEPA 2003), and

TE is so much of EI as constitutes taxable earnings from any such employment (within the meaning of section 10(2) of ITEPA 2003).

6—(1) Paragraph 6 of Schedule 35 shall be modified as follows.

(2) In sub-paragraph (2)—

(*a*) after the words "under sub-paragraph (3)" insert "as modified by article 5 of the Special Annual Allowance Charge (Application to Members of Currently-Relieved Non-UK Pension Schemes) Order 2009 ("the 2009 Order")"; and

(*b*) after the words "in accordance with paragraph 3(2)" insert "as modified by article 4 of the 2009 Order".

(3) Sub-paragraph (3) shall apply as if the amount arrived at were the appropriate fraction of what it otherwise would be (see paragraph (4)).

(4) The appropriate fraction referred to in paragraph (3) is—

$$\frac{TE}{EI}$$

where—

EI is the total amount of employment income of the individual from any relevant employment or employments for the tax year, excluding any such income which is exempt income (within the meaning of section 8 of ITEPA 2003), and

TE is so much of EI as constitutes taxable earnings from any such employment (within the meaning of section 10(2) of ITEPA 2003).

(5) For the purposes of paragraph (4) an employment is a relevant employment if it is an employment with an employer who is a sponsoring employer in relation to the currently-relieved non-UK pension scheme.

(6) In sub-paragraph (6) after the words "(but as if references to the pension input period were to the tax year and whether or not the arrangement is a defined benefits arrangement)." insert "This sub-paragraph is subject to sub-paragraph (7)".

(7) After sub-paragraph (6) insert—

"(7) The references to "amount" in subsections (2), (3) and (5) of section 236 shall be read as references to an amount referable to a member's UK tax-relieved fund only.".

7—(1) Paragraph 13 of Schedule 35 shall be modified as follows.

(2) In sub-paragraphs (2)(*a*) and (6) the references to "employer" and "employment" shall be read as including "former employer" and "former employment" where the individual was—

(*a*) an employee of that former employer;

(*b*) resident outside the UK, and either—

(i) a member of an occupational pension scheme or a group personal pension scheme relating to that former employment or,

(ii) a member of a public service pension scheme.

(3) In sub-paragraph (2)(*b*) the reference to "persons mentioned in sub-paragraph (1)(*d*)" shall be read as including persons who are employees of the former employer referred to in paragraph (2).

8—(1) Paragraph 15 of Schedule 35 shall be modified as follows.

(2) For sub-paragraph (4) substitute—

"(4) "Relevant relievable pension contributions" are contributions which—

(*a*) are relievable pension contributions in relation to the individual, and are paid to the pension scheme under the arrangement in the tax year;

(*b*) are contributions in respect of which the individual is given relief from tax under double tax arrangements and which are paid under the arrangement in the tax year; or

(*c*) are contributions paid under the arrangement by the individual for which a deduction is given under Chapter 2 of Part 5 of ITEPA 2003 for the tax year in accordance with paragraph 51 of Schedule 36 to FA 2004,

but this is subject as follows.".

9—For sub-paragraph (3) of paragraph 16 of Schedule 35 substitute—

"(3) In relation to a money purchase arrangement that is not a cash balance arrangement, a pre-22 April 2009 pension input amount is so much of the amount arrived at under paragraph 3(2) as is attributable to contributions—

(*a*) which are paid in the period beginning with 6 April 2009 and ending with [22][1] April 2009, other than any contributions paid pursuant to an agreement for the payment of contributions on a quarterly or more frequent basis; and—

(*b*) in respect of which relief is given by virtue of—

(i) Schedule 33 to FA 2004 (overseas pensions schemes: migrant member relief),

(ii) paragraph 51 of Schedule 36 to FA 2004 (individuals with pre-commencement entitlement to corresponding relief), or

(iii) double tax arrangements.".

Amendments—[1] Figure substituted by the Special Annual Allowance Charge (Protected Pension Input Amounts) Order, SI 2010/429 art 11 with effect for the tax year 2009–10 and subsequent tax years.

10—(1) Paragraph 17 of Schedule 35 shall be modified as follows.

(2) In sub-paragraph (4) the definition of "infrequent money purchase contributions amount" shall be read as including any relevant contributions under overseas pension schemes paid in a tax year in which the individual was not resident in the UK.

(3) For sub-paragraph (6) substitute—

"(6) "Relevant contributions" for a tax year in which an individual is resident in the UK means contributions made to money purchase arrangements (other than cash balance arrangements) which—

(*a*) are relievable pension contributions in relation to the individual, and are paid to the pension scheme under the arrangement in the tax year;

(*b*) are contributions in respect of which the individual is given relief from tax under double tax arrangements and which are paid under the arrangement in the tax year;

(*c*) are contributions paid under the arrangement by the individual for which a deduction is given under Chapter 2 of Part 5 of ITEPA 2003 for the tax year in accordance with paragraph 51 of Schedule 36 to FA 2004; or

(*d*) are contributions paid by an employer of the individual in respect of the individual.".

(4) After sub-paragraph (6) insert—

"(7) "Relevant contributions" for a tax year in which an individual was not resident in the UK means contributions made to money purchase arrangements (other than cash balance arrangements) under an overseas pension scheme which—

(*a*) are paid by or behalf of an individual; or

(*b*) are paid by an employer of the individual in respect of the individual.".

11 For paragraph 18 of Schedule 35 substitute—

"**18**—(1) Part 4 of FA 2004 applies in relation to a contributions refund lump sum as if it were a short service refund lump sum in excess of the limit specified in section 205(4) of that Act (so that it is not an unauthorised payment and is liable to tax at the rate chargeable on a short service refund lump sum).

This sub-paragraph is subject to sub-paragraph (2).

(2) Section 205 of FA 2004 shall apply with respect to a contributions refund lump sum paid to or in respect of an individual who is a member of a currently-relieved non-UK pension scheme so as to make the person to whom the sum is paid (rather than the scheme administrator) liable to any charge imposed by section 205 FA 2004.".

2009/2033

TAX AVOIDANCE SCHEMES (PRESCRIBED DESCRIPTIONS OF ARRANGEMENTS) (AMENDMENT) REGULATIONS 2009

Made by the Treasury under FA 2004 ss 306(1)(a) and (b) and section 317(2) of the Finance Act 2004

Made . . . . *21 July 2009*

Laid before the House of Commons . . . . *23 July 2009*

Coming into force . . . . *1 September 2009*

1 Citation and commencement

These Regulations may be cited as the Tax Avoidance Schemes (Prescribed Descriptions of Arrangements) (Amendment) Regulations 2009 and shall come into force on 1st September 2009.

2 Amendment to the Tax Avoidance Schemes (Prescribed Descriptions of Arrangements) Regulations 2006

(*amends* the Tax Avoidance Schemes (Prescribed Descriptions of Arrangements) Regulations, SI 2006/1543)

3 Time for providing information: transitional provisions

(1) Where paragraph (2) applies, the prescribed period or time (as the case may be) to be found in accordance with regulation 4 of the Tax Avoidance Schemes (Information) Regulations 2004 (time for providing information under section 308, 308A, 309 or 310) shall end on 31st October 2009 instead of the day on which it would end by virtue of that regulation.

(2) This paragraph applies in respect of proposals or arrangements (as the case may be) that are notifiable by virtue of regulation 17A of the Tax Avoidance Schemes (Prescribed Descriptions of Arrangements) Regulations 2009.

(*a*) for the purposes of section 308(1) of the Finance Act 2004 if the relevant date in relation to a proposal falls within the period beginning with 23rd April 2009 and ending with 31st August 2009;

(*b*) for the purposes of section 308(3) of the Finance Act 2004 if the date on which the promoter first becomes aware of any transaction forming part of the arrangements falls within the period beginning with 23rd April 2009 and ending with 31st August 2009;

(*c*) for the purposes of sections 309 and 310 of the Finance Act 2004 if the date on which any transaction forming part of the arrangements is entered into falls within the period beginning with 23rd April 2009 and ending with 31st August 2009.

(3) In paragraph (2)(*a*) "the relevant date" has the meaning given by section 308(2) of the Finance Act 2004.

2009/2034

INVESTMENT TRUSTS (DIVIDENDS) (OPTIONAL TREATMENT AS INTEREST DISTRIBUTIONS) REGULATIONS 2009

Made by the Treasury under FA 2009 s 45

Made . . . . *21 July 2009*
Laid before the House of Commons . . . . *23 July 2009*
Coming into force . . . . *1 September 2009*

PART 1
PRELIMINARY PROVISIONS

1 Citation, commencement and effect

(1) These Regulations may be cited as the Investment Trusts (Dividends) (Optional Treatment as Interest Distributions) Regulations 2009 and shall come into force on 1st September 2009.

(2) These Regulations have effect in relation to amounts distributed on or after 1st September 2009.

2 Structure of these Regulations

The structure of these Regulations is as follows—

this Part contains preliminary provisions;
Part 2 deals with the optional treatment of dividends as interest distributions;
Part 3 deals with the duty to deduct tax from interest distributions; and
Part 4 deals with information and record keeping relating to distributions.

3 Interpretation

(1) In these Regulations—

the "Commissioners" means the Commissioners for Her Majesty's Revenue and Customs;
"ICTA" means the Income and Corporation Taxes Act 1988;
"interest distribution" has the meaning given in regulation 5(2);
"period of account" has the meaning given in section 832(1) of ICTA; and
"qualifying interest income" means the amount determined in accordance with regulation 8.

(2) In these Regulations "recipient", in relation to an interest distribution of an investment trust or prospective investment trust, means the beneficial owner of the interest distribution, except where the distribution is held on trust (other than under a bare trust) or forms part of the estate of a deceased person; and, in such a case, the recipient means the trustees of the trust on which the interest distribution is held or, as the case may be, the deceased person's personal representatives.

PART 2
OPTIONAL TREATMENT OF DIVIDENDS AS INTEREST DISTRIBUTIONS

4 Circumstances in which dividends may be treated as interest distributions

(1) Subject to paragraph (2), regulation 5 applies if—

(*a*) a company is an investment trust or a prospective investment trust as respects an accounting period;

(*b*) an amount is distributed by the company as a dividend in respect of a period of account which includes that accounting period; and (*c*) the amount distributed in relation to the period of account is distributed on or before the first anniversary of the day on which that period of account ends.

(2) In a case where an amount is distributed by the company as a dividend in respect of a period of account which includes two or more accounting periods of the company, the company must be an investment trust or prospective investment trust as respects all of those accounting periods.

5 Treatment of dividends as interest distributions

(1) If this regulation applies, the company may designate as an interest distribution all or part of the amount distributed as a dividend or dividends in respect of the period of account which includes the accounting period.

(2) A dividend, or part of a dividend, in respect of which a designation under this regulation has been made is referred to in these Regulations as an "interest distribution".

(3) A designation under paragraph (1) becomes irrevocable at the time the interest distribution is made.

(4) The aggregate of the amounts distributed as interest distributions in relation to an accounting period may not exceed the amount of the company's qualifying interest income for the accounting period.

Regulation 8 explains how a company's qualifying interest income for an accounting period is calculated.

(5) For the purposes of paragraph (4), where an interest distribution is made in respect of a period of account which includes more than one accounting period the amount distributed as the interest distributions in relation to each accounting period is—

(A × I) / T

where—

"A" is the amount of qualifying interest income for the accounting period;

"I" is the total of the amounts distributed as interest distributions in respect of the period of account; and

"T" is the total amount of the qualifying interest income in respect of all the accounting periods in the period of account.

6 Notification of designation of dividends as interest distributions

If a company makes a designation under regulation 5, the application by the company for approval as an investment trust under section 842 of ICTA (investment trusts) as respects the accounting period to which the designation relates must include details of the total amount distributed, or to be distributed, as interest distributions in respect of the accounting period.

Amendments—Reg 6 revoked by the Investment Trust (Dividends) (Optional Treatment as Interest Distributions) (Amendment) Regulations, SI 2011/2951 regs 2, 3 with effect in relation to amounts distributed in respect of accounting periods beginning on or after 1 January 2012.

7 Interest distributions not to be treated as distributions for purposes of the Tax Acts

An amount distributed as an interest distribution by an investment trust or prospective investment trust shall be treated for the purposes of the Tax Acts as if the amount distributed is not a distribution.

8 Qualifying interest income

(1) The company's amount of qualifying interest income for an accounting period is the amount by which the aggregate of the company's relevant credits exceeds the aggregate of the company's relevant debits given for that period.

(2) Subject to paragraph (3) and regulation 9, the company's relevant credits and relevant debits are—

(*a*) credits and debits given for the accounting period for the purposes of Part 5 of the Corporation Tax Act 2009 (loan relationships); and

(*b*) credits and debits given for the accounting period for the purposes of Part 7 of that Act (derivative contracts) in relation to—

(i) derivative contracts the underlying subject matter of which consists wholly of assets representing loan relationships or currency or both, and

(ii) contracts for differences the underlying subject matter of which consists wholly of any one or more of interest rates, creditworthiness and currency.

(3) The company's relevant debits for an accounting period do not include debits arising under regulation 10 in respect of interest distributions made in respect of the accounting period.

(4) If, in relation to an accounting period, the aggregate of the company's relevant debits exceeds the aggregate of the company's relevant credits the amount of the qualifying interest income for that period shall be treated as nil.

(5) In this regulation expressions used in Parts 5 and 7 of the Corporation Tax Act 2009 have the same meaning as they have in those Parts.

9 Qualifying interest income: further provisions

(1) In the circumstances specified in paragraph (2), the underlying subject matter of a derivative contract is treated for the purposes of regulation 8 as consisting wholly of assets representing loan relationships or currency or both (as the case may be).

(2) The circumstances specified are where the underlying subject matter consists only of—

(*a*) assets representing loan relationships or currency or both, and

(*b*) other underlying subject matter which is—

(i) subordinate in relation to those assets, or

(ii) of small value in comparison with the value of the underlying subject matter.

(3) In the circumstances specified in paragraph (4), the underlying subject matter of a contract for differences is treated for the purposes of regulation 8 as consisting wholly of one or more of interest rates, creditworthiness and currency (the "principal subject matter").

(4) The circumstances specified are where the underlying subject matter consists only of—

(*a*) the principal subject matter, and

(*b*) other underlying subject matter which is—

(i) subordinate in relation to the principal subject matter, or

(ii) of small value in comparison with the value of the underlying subject matter.

(5) For the purposes of paragraphs (2) and (4), whether part of the underlying subject matter of a contract of a company is subordinate or of small value is to be determined by reference to the time when the company enters into or acquires the contract.

10 Interest distributions: effect for investment trust or prospective investment trust

(1) This regulation applies in respect of an accounting period if a company—

(*a*) is an investment trust or prospective investment trust in respect of the accounting period, and

(*b*) makes an interest distribution in relation to the accounting period.

(2) Subject to paragraph (3), the Corporation Tax Acts have effect in relation to the company as if the interest distribution made by the company in relation to the accounting period were interest under a debtor relationship of the company (and, accordingly is an amount recognised in determining the company's profit or loss for the period).

(3) Paragraph (2) does not apply to the extent that the aggregate of the amount distributed as interest distributions in relation to the accounting period exceeds the amount of the company's qualifying interest income for that period.

(4) In paragraph (2) "debtor relationship" has the same meaning as in section 302(6) of the Corporation Tax Act 2009 (loan relationships).

11 Interest distributions: effect for recipients

(1) In relation to a recipient of an interest distribution within the charge to corporation tax, the Corporation Tax Acts have effect as if the interest distribution were interest under a creditor relationship of that person.

(2) In paragraph (1) "creditor relationship" has the same meaning as in section 302(5) of the Corporation Tax Act 2009 (loan relationships).

(3) In relation to a recipient of an interest distribution within the charge to income tax, the Income Tax Acts have effect as if the interest distribution were a payment of yearly interest on the date the interest distribution is made.

(4) If a recipient of an amount distributed by a company—

(*a*) is informed (whether directly by the company or by a person who receives the amount on behalf of the recipient) that the amount is distributed to the recipient as an interest distribution, and

(*b*) is so informed at, or as soon as reasonably possible after, the time the amount is distributed,

the recipient shall treat that amount as an interest distribution (whether or not the amount distributed is an interest distribution for the purposes of the Corporation Tax Acts in relation to the company).

12 Failure to obtain approval as an investment trust

[No amount may be distributed as an interest distribution by a company in relation to an accounting period for which the company is not approved, or is treated as not having been approved, in accordance with regulations made under section 1159 of the Corporation Tax Act 2010.][1]

Amendments—[1] Reg 12 substituted by the Investment Trusts (Dividends) (Optional Treatment as Interest Distributions) (Amendment) Regulations, SI 2011/2951 regs 2, 4 with effect in relation to amounts distributed in respect of accounting periods beginning on or after 1 January 2012.

PART 3

DUTY TO DEDUCT TAX FROM INTEREST DISTRIBUTIONS

Duty to deduct tax interest distributions

13 Duty to deduct tax from interest distributions: general

(1) Any obligation to deduct a sum under section 874(2) of the Income Tax Act 2007 is subject to the provisions of this regulation.

(2) In this Part the "deduction obligation" means the obligation specified in paragraph (1).

(3) The deduction obligation does not apply to the interest distribution if—

(*a*) the recipient is a company (whether or not the company is resident in the United Kingdom for tax purposes);

(*b*) the recipient consists of the trustees of a unit trust scheme;

(*c*) the reputable intermediary condition in regulation 14 is met with respect to the recipient on the date the interest distribution is made; or

(*d*) the residence condition in regulation 17 is met with respect to the recipient on the date the interest distribution is made.

(4) But if the recipient is a company acting in the capacity of a trustee of a trust, the deduction obligation is not excluded by virtue of paragraph (3)(*a*).

(5) In this regulation, "unit trust scheme" has the meaning given by section 237 of the Financial Services and Markets Act 2000.

The reputable intermediary condition

14 The reputable intermediary condition

(1) The reputable intermediary condition is met with respect to a recipient on the date the interest distribution is made if conditions A to C are met.

(2) Condition A is that the interest distribution is made on behalf of the recipient to a company.

(3) Condition B is that the investment trust or prospective investment trust making the interest distribution has reasonable grounds for believing that the recipient is not . . . [1] resident in the United Kingdom.

(4) Condition C is that the company mentioned in paragraph (2)—

(*a*) is subject to the EC Money Laundering Directive,

(*b*) is subject to equivalent non-EC provisions, or

(*c*) is a company which—

(i) is resident in a regulated country or territory, and

(ii) is an associated company of a company which is subject to sub-paragraph (*a*) or (*b*).

Amendments—[1] In para (3), word revoked by the Income Tax (Removal of Ordinary Residence) Regulations, SI 2013/605 reg 6(1), (2) with effect in relation to interest distributions made on or after 6 April 2014.

15 The reputable intermediary condition: further provisions

(1) This regulation applies for the purposes of Condition C in regulation 14.

(2) A company is subject to the EC Money Laundering Directive if it is a credit institution or financial institution as defined by Article 1 of Directive 91/308/EEC, as amended by Directive 2001/97/EC.

(3) A company is subject to equivalent non-EC provisions if it is required by the law of any country or territory which is not a member State to comply with requirements similar to those which, under Article 3 of Directive 91/308/EEC (as so amended), member States must ensure are complied with by credit institutions and financial institutions.

(4) A country or territory is a regulated country or territory if it either is a member State or imposes requirements similar to those, which, under Article 3 of that Directive (as so amended), member States must ensure are complied with by credit institutions and financial institutions.

(5) A company is to be treated as another's associated company if it would be so treated for the purposes of Part 11 of ICTA (see section 416 of that Act).

16 The reputable intermediary condition: consequences of reasonable but incorrect belief

(1) This regulation applies if conditions A to D are met.

(2) Condition A is that an interest distribution is made by an investment trust or prospective investment trust.

(3) Condition B is that the investment trust or prospective investment trust, in reliance on the reputable intermediary condition being met with respect to the recipient of the interest distribution, does not comply with the deduction obligation in relation to the interest distribution.

(4) Condition C is that the deduction obligation would apply but for the reputable intermediary condition being met.

(5) Condition D is that (contrary to the belief of the investment trust or prospective investment trust) the recipient is in fact . . . [1] resident in the United Kingdom.

(6) The following provisions of the Income Tax Act 2007 have effect as if the deduction obligation applied—

(*a*) section 874 (duty to deduct from certain payments of yearly interest), and

(*b*) Chapter 15 of Part 15 (collection: deposit-takers, building societies and certain companies).

Amendments—[1] In para (5), word revoked by the Income Tax (Removal of Ordinary Residence) Regulations, SI 2013/605 reg 6(1), (3) with effect in relation to interest distributions made on or after 6 April 2014.

The residence condition

17 The residence condition

(1) The residence condition is met with respect to a recipient on the date the interest distribution is made if any of conditions A to E is met.

(2) Condition A is that, in relation to an interest distribution which is not made to or received under a trust, there is a valid declaration, made by the recipient, that the recipient is not . . . [1] resident in the United Kingdom.

(3) Condition B is—

(*a*) that the recipient receives the interest distribution as the personal representative of a deceased person, and

(*b*) that the deceased person had made a declaration, which was valid at the time of the deceased person's death, that the deceased person was not . . . [1] resident in the United Kingdom.

(4) Condition C is—

(*a*) that the recipient receives the interest distribution as a personal representative of a deceased person, and

(*b*) that the personal representative has made a declaration that the deceased, immediately before the time at which the deceased died, was not . . . [1] resident in the United Kingdom.

(5) Condition D is that, in the case of an interest distribution made to or received under a trust where the whole of the income is, or falls to be treated as, or under any provision of the Tax Acts is deemed to be, the income of a person other than the trustees of that trust, there is a valid declaration, made by the person in question that the person is . . . [1] not resident in the United Kingdom.

(6) Condition E is that, in circumstances in which condition D does not apply and with respect to a recipient in the case of an interest distribution made to or received under a trust, there is a valid declaration, made by the trustees of that trust, that—

(*a*) the trustees are not resident in the United Kingdom, and

(*b*) each beneficiary of the trust is . . . [1] not resident in the United Kingdom.

Amendments—[1] In paras (2), (3)(*b*), (4)(*b*), word revoked, and in paras (5), (6)(*b*), words revoked by the Income Tax (Removal of Ordinary Residence) Regulations, SI 2013/605 reg 6(1), (4) with effect in relation to the making of declarations on or after 6 April 2014. Any declarations made before that date continue to have effect in respect of interest distributions made on or after that date as if those amendments had not been made (SI 2013/605 reg 2(*d*)).

18 The residence condition: declarations

(1) A declaration for the purposes of regulation 17 must—

(*a*) be in such form as may be required or authorised by the Commissioners;

(*b*) be made in writing to the investment trust or prospective investment trust making the interest distribution in question; and

(*c*) contain any details or undertakings required by paragraphs (2) to (4).

(2) A declaration made for the purposes of condition A or B in regulation 17 must contain—

(*a*) the name and principal residential address of the person making it; and

(*b*) an undertaking that the investment trust or prospective investment trust will be notified by that person if the person becomes . . . [1] resident in the United Kingdom.

(3) A declaration made for the purposes of condition C in regulation 17 must contain the name of the deceased and the principal residential address of the deceased immediately before the time at which the deceased died.

(4) A declaration made for the purposes of condition D or E in regulation 17 must contain—

(*a*) the names and principal residential addresses of the trustees of the trust or, in the case of a trustee which is a company, the name of the company and the address of its registered or principal office;

(*b*) the names and principal residential addresses of the beneficiaries of the trust or, in the case of a beneficiary which is a company, the name of the company and the address of its registered or principal office; and

(*c*) an undertaking that the trustees of the trust will notify the investment trust or prospective investment trust if—

(i) they become resident in the United Kingdom,

(ii) any beneficiary of the trust named in the declaration becomes . . . [1] resident in the United Kingdom, or

(iii) any person who becomes a beneficiary of the trust after making the declaration either is at the time of becoming a beneficiary, or subsequently becomes, . . . [1] resident in the United Kingdom.

Amendments—[1] In para (2)(*b*), word revoked, and in para (4)(*c*)(ii), (iii), words revoked by the Income Tax (Removal of Ordinary Residence) Regulations, SI 2013/605 reg 6(1), (5) with effect in relation to the making of declarations on or after 6 April 2014. Any declarations made before that date continue to have effect in respect of interest distributions made on or after that date as if those amendments had not been made (SI 2013/605 reg 2(*d*)).

19 References to beneficiaries in regulations 17 and 18

In regulations 17 and 18 references to a beneficiary are references to any person who is known to the trustees of the trust to be either—

(*a*) a person who is, or will, or may become, entitled to any income of the trust, whether in the form of income or not, or

(*b*) a person to whom any such income may be paid, or for whose benefit any such income may be applied, whether in the form of income or not, in the exercise of a discretion by the trustees.

20 Interest distributions: declarations and position of investment trust or prospective investment trust

(1) For the purposes of determining whether an interest distribution should be made with or without any deduction required by the deduction obligation, an investment trust or prospective investment trust is entitled to treat a declaration made for the purposes of regulation 17 as valid.

(2) But the investment trust or prospective investment trust may not treat the declaration as valid if condition A or B is met.

(3) Condition A is that the investment trust or prospective investment trust receives a notification in compliance with an undertaking under regulation 18 that a person to whom the undertaking relates has become resident . . . [1] in the United Kingdom.

(4) Condition B is that the investment trust or prospective investment trust comes into possession of information by some other means which indicates that such a person is or may be resident . . . [1] in the United Kingdom.

Amendments—[1] In paras (3), (4) words revoked by the Income Tax (Removal of Ordinary Residence) Regulations, SI 2013/605 reg 6(1), (6) with effect in relation to the making of declarations on or after 6 April 2014. Any declarations made before that date continue to have effect in respect of interest distributions made on or after that date as if those amendments had not been made (SI 2013/605 reg 2(*d*)).

PART 4
INFORMATION AND RECORD KEEPING RELATING TO DISTRIBUTIONS

21 Information relating to distributions

(1) If an amount is distributed as an interest distribution, section 234A of ICTA (information relating to distributions: further provisions) shall apply to the company making the interest distribution as if the amount distributed were a payment of interest.

(2) In the case of an investment trust or prospective investment trust, an appropriate statement for the purposes of section 234A of ICTA includes a written statement—

(*a*) showing—

(i) the gross amount of the distribution made to the recipient,

(ii) the number and class of shares held by the recipient in respect of which the distribution is made,

(iii) the net amount of the distribution per share,

(iv) whether any tax has been deducted from the distribution,

(v) the date the distribution was made,

(vi) the percentage of the gross distribution attributable to the amount treated as an interest distribution and the percentage attributable to dividend;

(*b*) providing details to allow the recipient to access an electronic means of calculating the amounts that would be shown in a written statement that would apart, from this paragraph, be provided in accordance with subsection (6) or (7) of section 234A; and

(*c*) providing the recipient with an alternative method of obtaining the details of those amounts without recourse to electronic means.

22 Notification of interest distributions made without deduction of tax

(1) If, during a tax year, a company has made interest distributions without deduction of tax, the company must give notice of that fact to the Commissioners within 14 days of the end of that tax year.

(2) Notice given under paragraph (1)—

(*a*) must be given in writing, and

(*b*) has effect for the tax year in which the distribution was made and for subsequent tax years until the notice is withdrawn.

(3) A company that fails to comply with paragraph (1) is liable to a penalty not exceeding £3,000 determined in accordance with section 100 of the Taxes Management Act 1970.

(4) Sections 100A, 100B, 102, 103(4) and 118(2) of the Taxes Management Act 1970 apply to a penalty determined in accordance with paragraph (3).

23 Duty to keep and preserve records

(1) A company must—

(a) keep such books, records and other documents as may be needed to enable the company to demonstrate that the information supplied in any written statement for the purposes of section 234A of ICTA is correct and complete,
(b) keep copies of all declarations made under Part 3 of these Regulations received by the company,
(c) keep such books, records and other documents as may be needed in relation to amounts distributed as interest distributions (whether or not the interest distributions were made without deduction of tax) for the purposes of demonstrating when and to whom those amounts were distributed, and
(d) preserve those books, records, other documents and declarations in accordance with this regulation.

In this regulation the books, records, other documents and declarations a company is required to keep and preserve are referred to as the "relevant records".

(2) The relevant records must be preserved until the end of the day that is the sixth anniversary of the end of the tax year in which the distribution is made to which the relevant records relate.

(3) Subject to paragraph (4), the duty under paragraphs (1) and (2) to preserve relevant records may be discharged—
(a) by preserving them in any form and by any means, or
(b) by preserving the information contained in them in any form and by any means.

(4) Paragraph (3) does not apply in the case of any kind of record or document to which paragraph 22(3) of Schedule 18 to the Finance Act 1998 (preservation of information etc) applies.

2009/2037

CORPORATION TAX (LAND REMEDIATION RELIEF) ORDER 2009

Made by the Treasury under CTA 2009 ss 1145(2), 1145(3), 1146(3A), (3B), 1146A(3), (4), 1147(3), (3A), (3B) and 1149(3), (3A), (3B) and FA 2009 Sch 7 para 27

Made . . . . *21 July 2009*
Laid before the House of Commons . . . . *23 July 2009*
Coming into force . . . . *13 August 2009*

1 Citation, commencement and effect

(1) This Order may be cited as the Corporation Tax (Land Remediation Relief) Order 2009.

(2) This Order shall come into force on 13th August 2009 and shall have effect in relation to expenditure incurred on or after 1st April 2009.

2 Interpretation

In this Order—

"the Act" means the Corporation Tax Act 2009;
"arsenic" means the element whose chemical symbol is As and whose atomic number is 33;
"arsenical compounds" mean any compound one of whose constituent elements is arsenic;
"Japanese Knotweed" is the plant matter also known as Fallopia japonica, Reynoutria japonica or Polygonum cuspidatum;
"radon" means the element whose chemical symbol is Rn and whose atomic number is 86.

3 Land in a contaminated state

(1) Section 1145(2) of the Act (land "in a contaminated state") shall not apply where the following are present in, on or under the land—
(a) arsenic,
(b) arsenical compounds,
(c) Japanese Knotweed, or
(d) radon.

(2) This article is limited so that it has effect only in relation to—
(a) that part of the land where the items listed in paragraph (1) are present, and
(b) expenditure incurred for the purpose of remedying or mitigating the effects of relevant harm caused by the presence of one or more of the listed items.

4 Relevant contaminated land remediation: specified activity

(1) For the purposes of Condition C in section 1146 of the Act ("relevant contaminated land remediation"), a specified activity is the removal of relevant material from the land in question to a licensed landfill site.

(2) For the purposes of this article—
(a) "relevant material" means material which contains or may contain Japanese Knotweed;
(b) "licensed landfill site" means a site in respect of which a permit has been granted under the following—

[(i) the Environmental Permitting (England and Wales) Regulations 2016,][1]
(ii) the Pollution Prevention and Control (Scotland) Regulations 2000,
(iii) the Pollution Prevention and Control (Northern Ireland) Regulations 2003, or
(iv) Council Directive 1999/31/EC of 26th April 1999 on the landfill of waste.

Amendments—[1] Para (2)(*b*)(i) substituted by the Environmental Permitting (England and Wales) Regulations, SI 2016/1154 reg 75, Sch 29 Pt 2 para 32 with effect from 1 January 2017. This amendment extends to England and Wales only and applies in relation to areas specified in SI 2016/1154 reg 1(2)–(5).

5 Relevant contaminated land remediation: specified enactments

For the purposes of Condition C in section 1146 of the Act the following are specified enactments—

Statute	*Section*	*Explanatory note*
Building Act 1984	section 77	dangerous buildings
	section 79	ruinous and dilapidated buildings and neglected sites
Environmental Protection Act 1990	section 78E	duty of enforcing authority to require remediation of contaminated land
	section 79	statutory nuisances and inspections therefore
	section 80	summary proceedings for statutory nuisances
	section 81	supplementary provisions
	section 82	summary proceedings by persons aggrieved by statutory nuisances
Town and Country Planning Act 1990	section 215	power to require proper maintenance of land
Planning (Listed Buildings and Conservation Areas) Act 1990	section 48	repair notices preliminary to acquisition under section 47
Town and Country Planning (Scotland) Act 1997	section 179	notice requiring proper maintenance of land
Planning (Listed Buildings and Conservation Areas) (Scotland) Act 1997	section 43	repair notices preliminary to acquisition under section 42
Building (Scotland) Act 2003	section 28	defective buildings
Pollution Control and Local Government (Northern Ireland) Order 1978	article 65	defective buildings
	article 66	ruinous and dilapidated buildings
Planning (Northern Ireland) Order 1991	article 39	orders requiring discontinuance of use or alteration or removal of buildings or works
	article 109	compulsory acquisition of listed buildings

6 Relevant derelict land remediation: specified purposes

(1) For the purposes of Condition B in section 1146A of the Act ("relevant derelict land remediation"), the specified purposes are the removal of—

(*a*) post-tensioned concrete heavyweight construction,
(*b*) building foundations and machinery bases,
(*c*) reinforced concrete pilecaps,
(*d*) reinforced concrete basements, or
(*e*) redundant services which are located below the ground.

(2) For the purposes of this article, "services" means any pipes, wiring, cables, tunnels or other similar equipment or infrastructure used in relation to the following—

(*a*) gas supply,
(*b*) water supply, drainage or sewerage,
(*c*) electricity supply, or
(*d*) telecommunications.

7 Exception from condition that land be in a contaminated state at time of acquisition

Where land is in a contaminated state by virtue of the presence in, on or under it of Japanese Knotweed the following conditions need not be met—

(*a*) Condition B as specified by section 1147(3)(*a*) (deduction for capital expenditure), and
(*b*) Condition B as specified by section 1149(3)(*a*) (additional deduction for qualifying land remediation expenditure).

2009/2039

LLOYD'S UNDERWRITERS (EQUALISATION RESERVES) (TAX) REGULATIONS 2009

Made by the Treasury under FA 2009 s 47

Made . . . . *21 July 2009*
Laid before the House of Commons . . . . *23 July 2009*
Coming into force . . . . *1 September 2009*

Revocation—These Regulations revoked by the Lloyd's Underwriters (Transitional Equalisation Reserves) (Tax) Regulations, SI 2015/1983 reg 5(*b*) with effect from 1 January 2016.

1 *Citation, commencement and effect*

(1) These Regulations may be cited as the Lloyd's Underwriters (Equalisation Reserves) (Tax) Regulations 2009 and shall come into force on 1st September 2009.
(2) These Regulations have effect in relation to accounting periods ending on or after 31st December 2008.

Revocation—These Regulations revoked by the Lloyd's Underwriters (Transitional Equalisation Reserves) (Tax) Regulations, SI 2015/1983 reg 5(*b*) with effect from 1 January 2016.

2 *Interpretation*

In these Regulations—
(*a*) *"underwriting business" means, in relation to a corporate member or a partnership member, its underwriting business as a member of Lloyd's; and*
(*b*) *references to section 444BA are references to section 444BA of the Income and Corporation Taxes Act 1988 (equalisation reserves for general business).*

Revocation—These Regulations revoked by the Lloyd's Underwriters (Transitional Equalisation Reserves) (Tax) Regulations, SI 2015/1983 reg 5(*b*) with effect from 1 January 2016.

3 *Reserves maintained by Lloyd's members which are equivalent to equalisation reserves*

(1) This regulation applies in a case where an equivalent Lloyd's reserve is maintained by a corporate member or a partnership member.
(2) For the purposes of this regulation a corporate member or a partnership member maintains an equivalent Lloyd's reserve if, and only if, the reserve is maintained by the member as if the equalisation reserves rules referred to in subsection (11) of section 444BA apply to the member notwithstanding that those rules do not otherwise apply to the member.
(3) Where this regulation applies, section 444BA shall apply with the modifications specified in regulation 4.

Revocation—These Regulations revoked by the Lloyd's Underwriters (Transitional Equalisation Reserves) (Tax) Regulations, SI 2015/1983 reg 5(*b*) with effect from 1 January 2016.

4 *Modifications of section 444BA Income and Corporation Taxes Act 1988 and equalisation reserves rules*

(1) The modifications to section 444BA referred to in regulation 3 are as follows—
(*a*) *in subsection (1), the words "and to sections 444BB to 444BD" shall be treated as omitted;*
(*b*) *subject to paragraph (2), the equalisation reserves rules shall be treated as applying to the corporate member or partnership member (as the case may be);*
(*c*) *references to "an insurance company" and "the insurance company" shall be treated as references to the corporate member or the partnership member (as the case may be);*
(*d*) *references to "business" shall be treated as references to the underwriting business of the corporate member or the partnership member (as the case may be);*
(*e*) *references to an "equalisation reserve" shall be treated as references to an "equivalent Lloyd's reserve"; and*
(*f*) *subsection (10) shall be treated as omitted.*

(2) For the purposes of the equalisation reserves rules treated as applied by paragraph (1), any calculation of the average of the amount of the annualised net written premiums shall be made without reference to any period prior to 1st January 2005.
(3) In paragraph (3), the reference to "annualised net written premiums" has the meaning given by the equalisation reserves rules.

Revocation—These Regulations revoked by the Lloyd's Underwriters (Transitional Equalisation Reserves) (Tax) Regulations, SI 2015/1983 reg 5(*b*) with effect from 1 January 2016.

5 Further modification for purposes of computing profits or losses arising in the first accounting period to which these Regulations apply

(1) This regulation applies for the purposes of computing the profits or losses of a corporate member or a partnership member arising in the first accounting period of the member in relation to which these Regulations have effect.

(2) In computing the profits or losses arising in the accounting period in accordance with section 444BA (as applied by and with the modifications made by these Regulations) any amount—

- (*a*) *which is transferred into the equivalent Lloyd's reserve before or after the date these Regulations come into force,*
- (*b*) *which is an amount to which subsection (2)(a)* of section 444BA applies by virtue of these Regulations, and
- (*c*) *which is transferred into the reserve in respect of underwriting business written on or after 1st January 2005 and before 1st January 2006,*

shall be deductible for the purposes of computing the profits or losses for that accounting period.

Revocation—These Regulations revoked by the Lloyd's Underwriters (Transitional Equalisation Reserves) (Tax) Regulations, SI 2015/1983 reg 5(*b*) with effect from 1 January 2016.

2009/2192

INTERNATIONAL MOVEMENT OF CAPITAL (REQUIRED INFORMATION) REGULATIONS 2009

Made by the HMRC Commissioners under FA 2009 s 37 and Sch 17 paras 4(2), 6(4), 8(4), 9(1)(*e*) and 14(2)

Made	*10 August 2009*
Laid before the House of Commons	*11 August 2009*
Coming into force	*1 September 2009*

1 Citation, commencement and effect

(1) These Regulations may be cited as the International Movement of Capital (Required Information) Regulations 2009 and shall come into force on 1st September 2009.

(2) These Regulations shall have effect in relation to events taking place and transactions carried out on or after 1st July 2009.

2 Interpretation

(1) In these Regulations—

"group company" means any company which is resident in the United Kingdom and which would be deemed to be a member of the group of companies which includes the reporting body for the purposes of Chapter IV of Part X of the Income and Corporation Taxes Act 1988 if in section 413(3) of that Act the words "51 per cent" were substituted for the words "75 per cent";

"ICTA" means the Income and Corporation Taxes Act 1988;

"redeemable", in relation to shares, means that the shares satisfy one or both of the following conditions—

- (*a*) that, by virtue of the terms of their issue or the exercise of a right by any person or the existence of any arrangements, they are liable to be redeemed, cancelled or repaid, in whole or in part;
- (*b*) that, by virtue of any material arrangements, the holder has a right to require another person to acquire the shares or is obliged in any circumstances to dispose of them or another person has a right or is in any circumstances obliged to acquire them;

and arrangements are material arrangements if the company which issued the shares or a company connected with that company is a party to the arrangements;

"Schedule 17" means Schedule 17 (international movement of capital) to the Finance Act 2009.

(2) For the purposes of these Regulations, whether a person is connected with another shall be determined as it would in accordance with the provisions of subsections (2) to (8) of section 839 (connected persons) of ICTA if the words "paragraph 12 of Schedule 17 to the Finance Act 2009" were substituted for the words "section 416" in the definition of "control" in subsection (8).

(3) In these Regulations, references to a reporting body include a body corporate which would be a reporting body if it had not entered into an arrangement under paragraph 6 of Schedule 17.

3 Information

(1) Paragraphs (2) and (3) specify the information (in this regulation referred to as "the required information") to be contained in the report which is required to be made to an officer of Revenue and Customs under paragraph 4(1) of Schedule 17.

(2) The required information as it relates to a foreign subsidiary connected with the event or transaction is—

(*a*) its name, and
(*b*) the territory from the laws of which it derives its status as a body corporate.

(3) The required information as it relates to an event or transaction is a full description of the event or transaction (and, in the case of a transaction, a full description of all the steps taken in the course of the transaction) and includes in particular—
(*a*) the date on which the event took place or the transaction was carried out,
(*b*) for a transaction, the name of each party to it,
(*c*) the reason for the event or transaction, and
(*d*) an estimate of the effect of the event or transaction on the liability to tax in the United Kingdom of the reporting body and of any group company.

4 Value of the event or transaction

(1) The value of an event or transaction is to be determined for the purposes of paragraph 8 of Schedule 17 in accordance with this regulation.

(2) The value of an issue or transfer of shares or debentures is the market value of the shares or debentures.

(3) The value of an event or transaction which results in a foreign subsidiary becoming, or ceasing to be, a controlling partner in a partnership is the market value of the share of the subsidiary in the assets of the partnership immediately after it becomes a controlling partner or, as the case may be, immediately before it ceases to be a controlling partner.

(4) For the purposes of paragraphs (2) and (3), the value of an event or transaction that is one of a series is the aggregate of the value of all the events and transactions in the series.

5 Excluded transactions

(1) A transaction is excluded for the purposes of Schedule 17 if—
(*a*) it is a transaction within paragraph 8(2)(*a*) to (*c*) of Schedule 17 that is entered into pursuant to cash pooling arrangements in respect of which the conditions specified in paragraph (2) have been met; or
(*b*) it is described in one of the paragraphs in the Schedule (excluded transactions) to these Regulations and meets such conditions (if any) as are specified there.

(2) The conditions mentioned in paragraph (1)(*a*) are that before the transaction takes place—
(*a*) the parties to the cash pooling arrangements notify an officer of Revenue and Customs in writing of the terms of the arrangements;
(*b*) an officer of Revenue and Customs gives notice in writing to the parties that transactions entered into pursuant to the cash pooling arrangements after the date of the notice will be excluded transactions for the purposes of Schedule 17.

(3) The Schedule (excluded transactions) to these Regulations has effect.

6 Nomination arrangements

(1) This regulation contains provision about an arrangement under paragraph 6 of Schedule 17.

(2) The parties to an arrangement must give notice to an officer of Revenue and Customs within 28 days of entering into it.

(3) The notice must be in writing and signed by all the parties to the arrangement.

(4) The notice must state—
(*a*) the name of each party,
(*b*) the tax reference of each party, and
(*c*) which party is the nominated reporting body.

(5) The parties to an arrangement are treated as having withdrawn from it if they fail to give notice in accordance with paragraphs (2) to (4).

(6) A party to an arrangement is treated as having withdrawn from it if that party ceases to be controlled by the foreign parent.

(7) A party which withdraws from or is treated as having withdrawn from an arrangement must give notice in writing of that fact to an officer of Revenue and Customs and to any other party to the arrangement within 28 days of the date of withdrawal or, as the case may be, the date on which it ceases to be controlled by the foreign parent.

SCHEDULE

EXCLUDED TRANSACTIONS

Regulation 5(1)(*b*) and (3)

1 The following transactions are excluded transactions mentioned in regulation 5(1)(*b*).

2 (1) The first transaction is the issue of shares by the foreign subsidiary to the reporting body or to a group company.

(2) The conditions are that the issue—
(*a*) is of shares that are not redeemable; and
(*b*) is either—

(i) at market value and for consideration paid in cash to the foreign subsidiary, or

(ii) in or towards payment for any business undertaking or property acquired by the foreign subsidiary at market value.

3 (1) The second transaction is the issue of shares by the foreign subsidiary to a person not connected with the reporting body.

(2) The conditions are—

(*a*) that the issue—

(i) is at market value and for consideration paid to the foreign subsidiary, and

(ii) is not to a nominee or trustee for a person who is connected with the reporting body;

(*b*) that no arrangements exist as a consequence of which the reporting body or a person connected with the reporting body, or a nominee or trustee for that person or the reporting body, is or may become entitled to the shares so issued or to any of them or to any interest in them or in any of them.

4 (1) The third transaction is the issue of shares by the foreign subsidiary to all persons who are its shareholders at the time of the issue.

(2) The conditions are that the issue—

(*a*) is in respect of and in proportion to the shares held by the shareholders in the foreign subsidiary at the time of the issue; and

(*b*) either—

(i) is of shares that are not redeemable, or

(ii) where no shares are issued to a company which is resident in the United Kingdom or to a nominee or trustee for such a company, is at market value for consideration paid in cash to the foreign subsidiary.

5 (1) The fourth transaction is the issue of debentures by the foreign subsidiary to the reporting body or to a group company.

(2) The condition is that the circumstances specified in sub-paragraph (3) are not associated with or present in connection with the issue of the debentures.

(3) The circumstances are that a loan, whether or not of the same amount as that secured by the debentures, is made by a company which is not resident in the United Kingdom to a company which is resident in the United Kingdom.

6 (1) The fifth transaction is the issue of debentures by the foreign subsidiary to persons not connected with the reporting body.

(2) The conditions are—

(*a*) that the issue—

(i) is at market value and for consideration paid to the foreign subsidiary, and

(ii) is not to a nominee or trustee for a person who is connected with the reporting body;

(*b*) that no arrangements exist as a consequence of which the reporting body or a person connected with the reporting body, or a nominee or trustee for that person or the reporting body, is or may become entitled to the debentures so issued or to any of them or to any interest in them or in any of them.

7 (1) The sixth transaction is the transfer by the reporting body or a company (whether or not it is resident in the United Kingdom) of shares or debentures of the foreign subsidiary to a person not connected with the reporting body.

(2) The conditions are—

(*a*) that the transfer—

(i) is at market value for consideration paid to the transferor company, and

(ii) is not to a nominee or trustee for a person who is connected with the reporting body;

(*b*) that no arrangements exist as a consequence of which—

(i) the reporting body, or

(ii) a nominee or trustee for the reporting body, or

(iii) a person connected with the reporting body, or

(iv) a nominee or trustee for a person connected with the reporting body,

is or may become entitled to the shares or debentures transferred or to any of them or to any interest in them or in any of them.

8 The seventh transaction is a transfer by the reporting body of shares or debentures of the foreign subsidiary to a group company.

9 (1) The eighth transaction is a transfer within sub-paragraph (2) to the reporting body or a group company.

(2) A transfer is within this sub-paragraph if it—

(*a*) is not by the reporting body,
(*b*) is of shares or debentures of a foreign subsidiary in which the reporting body has an interest, and
(*c*) is permitted or caused by the reporting body.

10 The ninth transaction consists in the reporting body or a group company giving security over the shares of a foreign subsidiary in connection with borrowing money from a lender who is unconnected to the reporting body or the group company.

2009/2971

MUTUAL SOCIETIES (TRANSFERS OF BUSINESS) (TAX) REGULATIONS 2009

Made by the Treasury under FA 2009 s 124

Made . . . .*9 November 2009*
Laid before the House of Commons . . . .*10 November 2009*
Coming into force . . . .*1 December 2009*

PART 1

PRELIMINARY PROVISIONS AND INTERPRETATION

1 Citation, commencement and effect

(1) These Regulations may be cited as the Mutual Societies (Transfers of Business) (Tax) Regulations 2009 and shall come into force on 1st December 2009.

(2) Regulations 2 to 11, 15 to 25, and 31 to 34 shall have effect—

(*a*) in relation to any relevant transfer which takes place on or after 22 April 2009; and
(*b*) in relation to any land transaction which forms part of a relevant transfer to which these Regulations apply where the effective date of that land transaction is on or after 22 April 2009.

(3) Regulations 12 to 14, 26 to 30, and 35 shall have effect in relation to any relevant transfer which takes place on or after 1st December 2009.

2 Interpretation

(1) In these Regulations—

"CTA" means the Corporation Tax Act 2009;
"FA, followed by a year" means the Finance Act of that year;
"ICTA" means the Income and Corporation Taxes Act 1988;
"TCGA" means the Taxation of Chargeable Gains Act 1992;
"75% subsidiary" has the meaning given by section 838 of ICTA;
"business" includes engagements;
"chargeable intangible asset" has the meaning given by section 741 of CTA (meaning of "chargeable intangible asset");
"commercial company" means a company formed and registered under the Companies Act 2006 (or treated as formed and registered under that Act) which is a public company limited by shares;
"creditor relationship" has the meaning given by section 302(5) of CTA ("loan relationship", "creditor relationship", "debtor relationship");
"debtor relationship" has the meaning given by section 302(6) of CTA ("loan relationship", "creditor relationship", "debtor relationship");
"effective date" has the meaning given by section 119 of FA 2003 (meaning of "effective date" of a transaction);
"fair value accounting" has the meaning given by section 313 of CTA (basis of accounting);
"land transaction" has the meaning given by section 43(1) of FA 2003 (land transactions);
"loan relationship" includes matters treated as a loan relationship by Part 6 of CTA (relationships treated as loan relationships);
["registered society" means a registered society within the meaning given by section 1(1) of the Co-operative and Community Benefit Societies Act 2014, other than a society registered as a credit union;][1]
"relevant transfer" has the meaning given by regulation 3;
"subsidiary of a mutual society" means a company within the meaning of the Companies Act 2006—

(*a*) in which a building society, [a registered society][1] or a friendly society, as the case may be, holds a majority of the voting rights or of which that society is a member and alone controls, pursuant to an agreement with other shareholders or members, a majority of the voting rights; and (*b*) in relation to which that society has the right to appoint or remove a majority of the company's board of directors;

"tax-neutral" has the meaning given by section 776 of CTA (meaning of tax neutral transfer).

(2) In regulations 5 to 7 and 16 to 18 "asset" has the meaning given by section 21 of TCGA (assets and disposals).

(3) In regulations 6, 7, 9, 17, 18 and 25 references to a company being a member of a group of companies are to be read in accordance with section 170 of TCGA (interpretation of sections 171 to 181).

(4) In regulations 13 and 29 "group" has the meaning given by Chapter 8 of Part 8 of CTA (intangible fixed assets).

(5) In these Regulations references to a person being connected with another are to be read in accordance with section 839 of ICTA (connected persons).

Amendments—[1] Definition of "registered society" inserted, and words substituted for words "an industrial and provident society", by the Co-operative and Community Benefit Societies and Credit Unions Act 2010 (Consequential Amendments) Regulations, SI 2014/1815 reg 2, Sch para 26(1)–(3) with effect from 1 August 2014.

3 Meaning of relevant transfer

(1) A "relevant transfer" by a building society is—

(*a*) an amalgamation of two or more building societies ("the transferor") by the establishment of a successor building society ("the transferee") in accordance with section 93 of the Building Societies Act 1986 (amalgamations);

(*b*) a transfer by a building society ("the transferor") of the whole of its business to another building society ("the transferee") in accordance with section 94 of the Building Societies Act 1986 (transfers of engagements);

(*c*) a transfer by a building society ("the transferor") of part of its business to another building society ("the transferee") in accordance with section 94 (transfers of engagements) of the Building Societies Act 1986;

(*d*) a transfer by a building society ("the transferor") of the whole of its business to a commercial company ("the transferee") in accordance with section 97 of the Building Societies Act 1986 (transfers of business to commercial company); or

(*e*) a transfer by a building society ("the transferor") of the whole of its business to a subsidiary of a mutual society ("the transferee") in accordance with section 97 of the Building Societies Act 1986 (transfers of business to commercial company).

(2) A "relevant transfer" by [a registered society][2] is—

(*a*) an amalgamation of two or more [registered societies][2] ("the transferor") into one [registered society][2] ("the transferee") in accordance with section 50 of the Industrial and Provident Societies Act 1965 (amalgamation of societies);

(*b*) a transfer by [a registered society][2] ("the transferor") of the whole of its business to another [registered society][2] ("the transferee") in accordance with section 51 of the Industrial and Provident Societies Act 1965 (transfer of engagements between societies);

(*c*) a transfer by [a registered society][2] ("the transferor") of part of its business to one or more [registered societies][2] ("the transferee") in accordance with section 51 of the Industrial and Provident Societies Act 1965 (transfer of engagements between societies);

(*d*) a conversion of [a registered society][2] ("the transferor") into a company ("the transferee") in accordance with section 52 of the Industrial and Provident Societies Act 1965 (conversion into, amalgamation with, or transfer of engagements to company);

(*e*) an amalgamation of [a registered society][2] ("the transferor") with a company ("the transferee") in accordance with section 52 of the Industrial and Provident Societies Act 1965 (conversion into, amalgamation with, or transfer of engagements to company); or

(*f*) a transfer by [a registered society][2] ("the transferor") of the whole of its business to a company ("the transferee") in accordance with section 52 of the Industrial and Provident Societies Act 1965 (conversion into, amalgamation with, or transfer of engagements to company).

(3) A "relevant transfer" by a friendly society is—

(*a*) an amalgamation of two or more friendly societies ("the transferor") by the establishment of a successor society ("the transferee") in accordance with section 85 of the Friendly Societies Act 1992 (amalgamation of friendly societies);

(*b*) a transfer by a friendly society ("the transferor") of the whole of its business to a person ("the transferee") referred to in section 86 of the Friendly Societies Act 1992 (transfer of engagements by or to friendly society);

(*c*) a transfer by a friendly society ("the transferor") of part of its business to a person ("the transferee") referred to in section 86 of the Friendly Societies Act 1992 (transfer of engagements by or to friendly society);

(*d*) a transfer by a friendly society ("the transferor") of the whole of its business to a person ("the transferee") specified by the [appropriate authority][1] in accordance with section 90 of the Friendly Societies Act 1992 (power of authority to effect transfer of engagements); or (*e*) a conversion of a friendly society ("the transferor") into a company ("the transferee") in accordance with section 91 of the Friendly Societies Act 1992 (conversion of friendly society into company).

Amendments—[1] In para (2)(*d*), words substituted by the Financial Services Act 2012 (Mutual Societies) Order, SI 2013/496, art 2(*c*), Sch 11, para 17 with effect from 1 APril 2013..

[2] Words substituted for words "an industrial and provident society", "industrial and provident society", and "industrial and provident societies", by the Co-operative and Community Benefit Societies and Credit Unions Act 2010 (Consequential Amendments) Regulations, SI 2014/1815 reg 2, Sch para 26(1), (3)–(5) with effect from 1 August 2014.

PART 2
BUILDING SOCIETIES

4 Relevant transfer by a building society

(1) This regulation applies if there is a relevant transfer by a building society.

(2) The Corporation Tax Acts shall have effect in relation to the relevant transfer subject to paragraphs (3) to (18).

(3) For the purposes of the allowances and charges provided for by the Capital Allowances Act 2001 a trade which is transferred or amalgamated as a result of the relevant transfer shall not be treated as permanently discontinued nor shall a new trade be treated as set up and commenced, and—

(*a*) there shall be made to or on the transferee in accordance with that Act all such allowances and charges as would, if the transferor had continued to carry on the trade, have fallen to be made to or on the transferor; and

(*b*) the amount of any such allowance or charge shall be computed as if—

(i) the transferee had been carrying on the trade since the transferor began to do so, and

(ii) everything done to or by the transferor had been done to or by the transferee (but so that no sale or transfer which, on the transfer of the trade, is made to the transferee by the transferor of any assets in use for the purpose of the trade shall be treated as giving rise to any such allowance or charge).

(4) The transferee shall be entitled to such relief under section 393(1) of ICTA (losses other than terminal losses), as for a loss sustained by the transferee in carrying on the trade, for any amount for which the transferor would have been entitled to relief if it had continued to carry on the trade. This paragraph is subject to paragraph (5) and to any claim made by the transferor under section 393A(1) of ICTA (losses: set off against profits of the same, or an earlier, accounting period).

(5) If the amount of relevant liabilities exceeds the value of relevant assets, the transferee shall be entitled to relief by virtue of paragraph (4) only if, and only to the extent that, the amount of that excess is less than the amount mentioned in that paragraph.

(6) For the purposes of paragraph (5)—

(*a*) the value of assets (other than money) shall be taken to be the price which they might reasonably be expected to have fetched on a sale in the open market immediately before the predecessor ceased to carry on the trade; and

(*b*) the amount of liabilities shall be taken to be their amount at that time.

(7) Subsection (2A) of section 393A of ICTA (losses: set off against profits of the same, or an earlier, accounting period) shall not apply to any loss which (but for this paragraph) would fall within subsection (2B) of that section by virtue of the transferor ceasing to carry on the trade, and subsection (7) of that section shall not apply for the computation of any such loss.

(8) If, on the transferor ceasing to carry on the trade, the transferee begins to carry on the activities of the trade as part of its trade, then that part of the trade carried on by the transferee shall be treated for the purposes of this regulation as a separate trade, if the effect of so treating it is that paragraph (2) has effect on that event in relation to that separate trade.

(9) If, on the transferor ceasing to carry on part of a trade, the transferee begins to carry on the activities of that part as its trade or part of its trade, the transferor shall for the purposes of this regulation be treated as having carried on that part of its trade as a separate trade if the effect of so treating it is that paragraph (2) has effect on that event in relation to that separate trade.

(10) If, under paragraphs (8) or (9), any activities of the transferor fall, on that transferor ceasing or beginning to carry them on, to be treated as a separate trade, such apportionments of receipts, expenses, assets or liabilities shall be made as may be just and reasonable.

(11) If, by virtue of paragraph (10), any item falls to be apportioned and, at the time of the apportionment, it appears that it is material as respects the liability to tax (for whatever period) of two or more building societies or a commercial company or a subsidiary of a mutual society, any question which arises as to the manner in which the item shall be apportioned shall be determined, for the purposes of the tax of those building societies, commercial company or subsidiary of a mutual in like manner as an appeal, and all those companies shall be entitled to be a party to those proceedings.

(12) If the amount of relevant liabilities does not exceed the value of relevant assets—

(*a*) paragraph (10) shall have effect as if for the words following "separate trade," to the end of the paragraph there were substituted "any necessary apportionment shall be made of receipts or expenses."; and (*b*) paragraph (11) shall have effect as if for "item" there were substituted "sum".

(13) In this regulation—

"relevant assets" means—

(*a*) assets vested in the transferor immediately before it ceased to carry on the trade, which were not transferred to the transferee; and

(*b*) consideration given to the transferor by the transferee in respect of the relevant transfer or change of the entity carrying on the business as a consequence of the relevant transfer;

and for the purposes of sub-paragraph (*b*) the assumption by the transferee of any liabilities of the transferor shall not be treated as the giving of consideration to the transferor by the transferee;

"relevant liabilities" means liabilities outstanding and vested in the transferor immediately before it ceased to carry on the trade which were not transferred to the transferee; but a liability representing the transferor's share capital, share premium account, reserves or relevant loan stock is not a relevant liability.

(14) Where the transferor transferred a liability to the transferee but the creditor concerned agreed to accept settlement of part of the liability as settlement of the whole, the liability shall be treated for the purposes of paragraph (13) as not having been transferred to the transferee except as to that part.

(15) For the purposes of paragraph (13), a liability representing the transferor's share capital, share premium account, reserves or relevant loan stock shall be treated as not doing so, if, in the period of one year ending with the day on which the transferor ceased to carry on the trade, the liability arose on a conversion of a liability not representing its share capital, share premium account, reserves or relevant loan stock.

(16) Where a liability of the transferor representing its relevant loan stock is not a relevant liability for the purposes of paragraph (5) but is secured on an asset of the transferor not yet transferred to the transferee, the value of the asset shall, for the purposes of paragraph (5), be reduced by an amount equal to the amount of the liability.

(17) In this regulation "relevant loan stock" means any loan stock or similar security (whether secured or unsecured) except any in the case of which paragraph (18) applies.

(18) This paragraph applies where, at the time the liability giving rise to the loan stock or other security was incurred, the person who was the creditor was carrying on a trade of lending money.

5 Transfer of an asset—taxation of chargeable gains

If—

(*a*) there is a relevant transfer within regulation 3(1)(*e*); and

(*b*) there is a disposal of an asset by the transferor to the transferee,

the transferor and the transferee shall be treated for the purposes of corporation tax in respect of chargeable gains as if the asset were acquired from the transferor for a consideration of such amount as would secure that on the disposal neither a gain nor a loss would accrue to the transferor.

6 Transfer of an asset—taxation of chargeable gains—company ceasing to be member of group

If—

(*a*) there is a relevant transfer within regulation 3(1)(*a*), (*b*) or (*e*);

(*b*) the transferor and the transferee are not members of the same group at the time of the relevant transfer; and

(*c*) as a result of the relevant transfer, a company ceases to be a member of the same group as the transferor,

section 179 of TCGA (company ceasing to be a member of group: post-appointed day cases) shall not apply in respect of any asset acquired by the company referred to in paragraph (*c*) from the transferor or from any other member of the same group as the transferor.

7 Transfer of an asset—company ceasing to be a member of a group—further provisions

(1) This regulation applies if there is a relevant transfer within regulation 3(1)(*a*), (*b*) or (*e*).

(2) If this regulation applies and the transferor and the transferee—

(*a*) as a result of the relevant transfer become members of the same group; but

(*b*) subsequently cease to be members of the same group,

paragraph (3) applies.

(3) If paragraph (2) is satisfied, section 179 of TCGA (company ceasing to be a member of group: post-appointed day cases) shall not have effect as respects—

(*a*) any asset acquired by the transferee as a consequence of the relevant transfer from the transferor or any other member of the same group; or

(*b*) any asset acquired as a consequence of the relevant transfer from the transferor, or any other member of the same group, by any company which is a member of the same group as the transferor at the time of the relevant transfer.

(4) If this regulation applies and, as a result of the relevant transfer, a company which was a member of the same group as the transferor at the time of the relevant transfer—

(*a*) ceases to be a member of that group;

(*b*) becomes a member of the same group as the transferee; and

(*c*) subsequently ceases to be a member of that group,

section 179 of TCGA shall have effect when the company ceases to be a member of the same group as the transferee as respects any relevant asset acquired by that company otherwise than from the transferee as if that asset had been acquired from the transferee.

This paragraph is subject to paragraph (6).

(5) In paragraph (4) "relevant asset" means any asset acquired by the company referred to in that paragraph from—

(*a*) the transferor; or

(*b*) any other company which is a member of the same group as the transferor at the time of the relevant transfer,

when the company referred to in that paragraph and the transferor, or the company referred to in that paragraph, the transferor and the other company, were members of the same group.

(6) Paragraph (4) shall not apply if the company referred to in that paragraph which acquired that asset and the company from which that asset was acquired (one being a 75 per cent subsidiary of the other) cease simultaneously to be members of the same group as the transferee but continue to be members of the same group as one another.

8 Transfer of loan relationship or derivative contract

(1) This regulation applies if—

(*a*) there is a relevant transfer by a building society;

(*b*) the transferor has consistently applied appropriate accounting treatment in accordance with generally accepted accounting practice up to and including the date of the relevant transfer in respect of all loan relationships and derivative contracts shown in its balance sheet; and

(*c*) as a result of the relevant transfer the transferee directly or indirectly replaces the transferor as a party to—

(i) the loan relationships; or

(ii) the derivative contracts.

(2) The transferee shall bring into account, in accordance with paragraphs (3) to (15), amounts in respect of the transfer adjustment.

(3) The "transfer adjustment" is the difference, if any, that arises on a comparison of the closing accounting balance sheet figure, adjusted for tax as appropriate, in respect of the loan relationships or the derivative contracts in the transferor's accounts and the opening accounting balance sheet figure, adjusted for tax as appropriate, in respect of the loan relationships or derivative contracts in the transferee's accounts.

(4) If the transferor carries out simultaneous relevant transfers of its business, within regulation 3(1)(*c*) of part of its business the "transfer adjustment" in respect of each transferee is to be computed by reference to the difference between the opening accounting balance sheet figure, adjusted for tax as appropriate, for the transferred loan relationships and derivative contracts in each transferee's accounts and the closing accounting balance sheet figure, adjusted for tax as appropriate, for those same loan relationships and derivative contracts in the transferor's accounts.

(5) For the purposes of paragraphs (3) and (4), where, in the Tax Acts, an accounting balance sheet figure is adjusted for tax, it is that adjusted figure that is to be used when calculating the transfer adjustment.

(6) The credits and debits to be brought into account as profits or deficits or losses for the purposes of Part 3, 5, 6 or 7 of CTA in respect of the transferee's transfer adjustment shall be determined in accordance with this regulation.

(7) The transferee shall bring one-sixth of the transfer adjustment ("the applicable amount") into account for each year of a six year period ("the prescribed period") beginning with the day on which the relevant transfer takes place. This is subject to paragraphs (8), (10) and (16).

(8) If there are two or more accounting periods falling in a year, the applicable amount for the year shall be apportioned between the accounting periods.

(9) An apportionment between accounting periods of an applicable amount in accordance with paragraph (8) shall be made according to the proportion of the year which is included in each accounting period.

(10) If the transferee ceases to be within the charge to corporation tax before the end of the prescribed period, the whole of the applicable amounts, so far as they have not been brought into account in an earlier accounting period, shall be brought into account as a credit or debit for the period ending when the transferee ceases to be within that charge. This paragraph is subject to paragraph (11).

(11) If before the end of the prescribed period—

(*a*) the transferee transfers the business by way of a relevant transfer within regulation 3(1)(*a*) or (*b*) to a successor building society ("A"); and,

(*b*) as a result of the transfer, the transferee ceases to be within the charge to corporation tax, that relevant transfer will not cause the whole of the applicable amounts, so far as they have not been brought into account in an earlier period, to be brought into account for the period in which that relevant transfer takes place.

(12) Where there is a relevant transfer to which paragraph (11) applies, paragraph (7) will apply to the applicable amounts which have not been brought into account by the transferee as if references to "the transferee" were references to "A".

(13) If this regulation applies and the transferor has been bringing debits and credits into account in accordance with regulation 3A of the Loan Relationships and Derivative Contracts (Change of Accounting Practice) Regulations 2004, the relevant transfer shall be treated for the purposes of regulation 3A(6) of those Regulations as though it were a qualifying transfer.

(14) In paragraph (1)(*c*) the reference to "the transferee directly or indirectly replaces the transferor as a party" has the same meaning given by—

(*a*) regulation 10 in the case of a loan relationship; and

(*b*) regulation 11 in the case of a derivative contract.

(15) Paragraph (7) does not apply if the transferee has made an election under paragraph (16).

(16) If the amount of the transfer adjustment does not exceed £1.5 million, the transferee may elect to bring into account the full amount of the transfer adjustment in the accounting period in which the relevant transfer takes place.

(17) An election under paragraph (16)—

(*a*) must be made—

(i) by notice in writing to an officer of Revenue and Customs; and

(ii) no later than 12 months after the end of the accounting period in which the relevant transfer took place;

(*b*) must specify the amount of the transfer adjustment; and

(*c*) is irrevocable.

(18) In this regulation—

"generally accepted accounting practice" has the meaning given by section 50(1) of FA 2004 (generally accepted accounting practice);

"officer of Revenue and Customs" has the meaning given by section 2 of the Commissioners for Revenue and Customs Act 2005 (officers of revenue and customs).

9 Transfer of loan relationship or derivative contract—further provisions

(1) This regulation applies if—

(*a*) there is a relevant transfer within regulation 3(1)(*a*), (*b*), (*d*) or (*e*); and

(*b*) before the date of the relevant transfer there had been a transfer to a company of—

(i) a loan relationship to which section 336 of CTA (transfers of loans on group transactions) applied; or

(ii) a derivative contract to which section 625 of CTA (group member replacing another as party to a derivative contract) applied;

but this is subject to paragraph (6).

(2) Paragraph (3) applies if, as a result of the relevant transfer, the company referred to in paragraph (1)(*b*) ceases to be a member of the same group as the transferor—

(*a*) before the end of the relevant six year period referred to in—

(i) section 344(4) of CTA (transferee leaving group after replacing transferor as party to loan relationship); or

(ii) section 630(4) of CTA (introduction to sections 631 and 632); and

(*b*) whilst still a party to the relevant loan relationship or derivative contract.

(3) If paragraph (2) is satisfied—

(*a*) the company referred to in paragraph (1)(*b*) shall be treated as not having ceased to be a member of the same group as the transferor;

(*b*) in the case of a loan relationship, section 345 of CTA (transferee leaving group otherwise than because of an exempt distribution) shall not apply to the loan relationship as a result of the relevant transfer; and

(*c*) in the case of a derivative contract, section 631 of CTA (transferee leaving group otherwise than because of exempt distribution) shall not apply to the derivative contract as a result of the relevant transfer.

(4) Paragraph (5) applies if the company referred to in paragraph (1)(*b*) ceases to be a member of the same group as the transferee—

(*a*) before the end of the relevant six year period referred to in—

(i) section 344(4) of CTA (transferee leaving group after replacing transferor as party to loan relationship); or

(ii) section 630(4) of CTA (introduction to sections 631 and 632); and

(*b*) whilst still a party to the relevant loan relationship or derivative contract.

(5) If paragraph (4) is satisfied—

(*a*) in the case of a loan relationship, section 345 of CTA (transferee leaving group otherwise than because of an exempt distribution) shall apply to the loan relationship as a result of the relevant transfer; and

(*b*) in the case of a derivative contract, section 631 of CTA (transferee leaving group otherwise than because of exempt distribution) shall apply to the derivative contract as a result of the relevant transfer.

(6) This regulation does not apply where a transferor of a loan relationship is regarded as using fair value accounting in respect of that loan relationship.

(7) A transferor shall be regarded for the purposes of this regulation as using fair value accounting in respect of a loan relationship only if the credits and debits to be brought into account for the purposes of these Regulations as respects that loan relationship are determined on that basis.

(8) It does not matter for the purposes of paragraph (7) if the transferor does not otherwise use fair value accounting in respect of the loan relationship.

10 Meaning of transferee replacing building society as party to a loan relationship

(1) References in regulation 8 to a transferee replacing a transferor as a party to a loan relationship include references to a transferee becoming party to a loan relationship which—

(*a*) confers rights within paragraph (2);

(*b*) imposes obligations within paragraph (2); or

(*c*) both confers such rights and imposes such obligations.

(2) Rights or obligations are within this paragraph if they are equivalent to those of the transferor under a loan relationship to which that transferor has ceased to be a party as a result of the relevant transfer.

(3) For the purposes of paragraph (2), a transferor's rights under a creditor relationship are equivalent to rights under another creditor relationship if each set of rights gives the holder of an asset representing the relationship in question—

(*a*) the same rights against the same persons as to capital, interest and dividends; and

(*b*) the same remedies to enforce those rights.

(4) For the purposes of paragraph (3), any difference in—

(*a*) the total nominal amounts of the assets representing each loan relationship;

(*b*) the form in which they are held; or

(*c*) the way in which they can be transferred,

is ignored.

(5) For the purposes of paragraph (2), a transferee's obligations under a debtor relationship are equivalent to obligations under another debtor loan relationship if under each set of obligations the holder of the liability representing the loan relationship in question has—

(*a*) the same obligations to the same persons as to capital, interest and dividends; and

(*b*) the same remedies to enforce those obligations.

(6) For the purposes of paragraph (5), any difference in—

(*a*) the total nominal amounts of the assets representing the creditor loan relationship corresponding to each relationship;

(*b*) the form in which they are held; or

(*c*) the way in which they can be transferred,

is ignored.

11 Meaning of transferee replacing building society as a party to a derivative contract

(1) References in regulation 8 to a transferee replacing a transferor as a party to a derivative contract include references to the transferee becoming party to a derivative contract which—

(*a*) confers rights within paragraph (2);

(*b*) imposes obligations within paragraph (2); or

(*c*) both confers such rights and imposes such obligations.

(2) Rights or obligations are within this paragraph if they are equivalent to those of the transferor under a derivative contract to which that transferor has ceased to be a party as a result of the relevant transfer.

12 Transfer of intangible fixed assets

(1) This regulation applies if—

(*a*) there is a relevant transfer within regulation 3(1)(*e*) which includes intangible fixed assets;

(*b*) those assets are chargeable intangible assets in relation to the transferor immediately before the relevant transfer; and

(*c*) those assets are chargeable intangible assets in relation to the transferee immediately after the relevant transfer.

(2) The transfer of those assets is tax-neutral for the purposes of—

(*a*) these Regulations; and

(*b*) Part 8 of CTA (intangible fixed assets).

(3) For the application of sections 780 (deemed realisation and reacquisition at market value) and 785 (principal company becoming member of another group) of CTA where this regulation applies, see regulation 13.

(4) This regulation and regulations 13 and 14 apply to goodwill as they apply to intangible fixed assets.

13 Transfer of intangible fixed assets—further provisions

(1) This regulation applies if—

(*a*) there is a relevant transfer within regulation 3(1)(*a*), (*b*) or (*e*) which includes intangible fixed assets;

(*b*) those assets are—

(i) chargeable intangible assets in relation to the transferor immediately before the relevant transfer; and

(ii) chargeable intangible assets in relation to the transferee immediately after the relevant transfer; and

(*c*) the transfer of those assets is tax-neutral for the purposes of these Regulations or Part 8 of CTA (intangible fixed assets).

(2) If because of the relevant transfer a company ceases to be a member of the same group as the transferor, that event does not cause—

(*a*) section 780 of CTA (deemed realisation and reacquisition at market value); or

(*b*) section 785 of that Act (principal company becoming member of another group),

to apply as respects any assets acquired by the company from the transferor or any other member of the same group as the transferor.

(3) If the transferor and transferee are members of the same group at the time of the relevant transfer but later cease to be, that later event does not cause section 780 or 785 of CTA to apply in relation to any asset to which this regulation applies.

(4) Paragraph (3) applies to—

(*a*) any asset acquired by the transferee on or before the relevant transfer from the transferor, or from any other member of the same group; or

(*b*) any asset acquired from the transferor or from any other member of the same group by a company (other than the transferee) that is a member of that group at the time of the relevant transfer.

(5) Paragraph (6) applies if a company which is a member of the same group as the transferor at the time of the relevant transfer—

(*a*) ceases to be a member of that group and becomes a member of the same group as the transferee, and

(*b*) later ceases to be a member of that group.

(6) Section 780 of CTA (deemed realisation and reacquisition at market value) applies on that later event as if any asset to which this paragraph applies that has not been acquired from the transferee had been so acquired.

(7) Paragraph (6) applies to—

(*a*) any asset acquired by the company referred to in paragraph (5) from the transferor when that company and the transferor were members of the same group, or

(*b*) any asset acquired by the company referred to in paragraph (5) from another company which is a member of the same group at the time of the relevant transfer when the company referred to in paragraph (5), the transferor and the other company were members of the same group.

(8) Paragraph (6) does not apply if—

(*a*) the company which acquired the asset is a 75% subsidiary of the company from which it was acquired or vice versa;

(*b*) those companies cease simultaneously to be members of the same group as the transferee; and

(*c*) those companies continue to be members of the same group as one another.

14 Intangible fixed assets transferred as if at no gain or no loss

(1) This regulation applies if—

(*a*) there is a relevant transfer by a building society; and

(*b*) the transferor is treated—

(i) for the purposes of these Regulations; or

(ii) by virtue of the provisions referred to in paragraph (2),

as disposing of any assets for a consideration of such amount as would secure that neither a gain nor a loss would accrue to the transferor on that disposal.

(2) The provisions referred to in this paragraph are—

(*a*) section 215 of TCGA (disposal of assets on amalgamation of building societies); and

(*b*) section 216 of that Act (assets transferred from society to company).

(3) The assets, in the hands of the transferee, shall be treated as not satisfying the general rule set out in section 882(1) of CTA (application of Part 8 to assets created or acquired on or after 1 April 2002).

PART 3
INDUSTRIAL AND PROVIDENT SOCIETIES

15 Interpretation

In this Part—

"carrying value" has the meaning given by section 317 of CTA (carrying value);

"discount" has the meaning given by section 480(5) of CTA (relevant non-lending relationships involving discounts);

"notional carrying value" in relation to an asset or liability has the same meaning as it has for section 340(6) of CTA (group transfers and transfers of insurance business: transfer at notional carrying value).

16 Transfer of an asset—taxation of chargeable gains

If—

(*a*) there is a relevant transfer within regulation 3(2)(*d*), (*e*) or (*f*); and

(*b*) there is a disposal of an asset by the transferor to the transferee,

the transferor and the transferee shall be treated for the purposes of corporation tax in respect of chargeable gains as if the asset were acquired from the transferor for a consideration of such amount as would secure that on the disposal neither a gain nor a loss would accrue to the transferor.

17 Transfer of an asset—taxation of chargeable gains—company ceasing to be a member of group

If—

(*a*) there is a relevant transfer within regulation 3(2)(*a*), (*b*), (*d*), (*e*) or (*f*);

(*b*) the transferor and the transferee are not members of the same group at the time of the relevant transfer; and

(*c*) as a result of the relevant transfer, a company ceases to be a member of the same group as the transferor,

section 179 of TCGA (company ceasing to be a member of group: post-appointed day cases) shall not apply in respect of any asset acquired by the company referred to in paragraph (*c*) . . . [1] from the transferor or from any other member of the same group as the transferor.

Commentary—*Simon's Taxes* **D7.630.**

Amendments—[1] Words revoked by the Mutual Societies (Transfers of Business) (Tax) (Amendment) Regulations, SI 2011/37 reg 3 with effect in relation to any relevant transfer (within the meaning of these regs) which takes place on or after 2 February 2011..

18 Transfer of an asset—company ceasing to be a member of a group—further provisions

(1) This regulation applies if there is a relevant transfer within regulation 3(2)(*a*), (*b*), (*d*), (*e*) or (*f*).

(2) If there is a relevant transfer to which this regulation applies, and the transferor and the transferee—

(*a*) are members of the same group at the time of the relevant transfer; but

(*b*) subsequently cease to be members of the same group,

paragraph (3) applies.

(3) If paragraph (2) is satisfied, section 179 of TCGA (company ceasing to be a member of group: post-appointed day cases) shall not have effect as respects—

(*a*) any asset acquired by the transferee as a consequence of the relevant transfer from the transferor or any other member of the same group; or

(*b*) any asset acquired as a consequence of the transfer from the transferor, or any other member of the same group, by any company which is a member of the same group as the transferor at the time of the relevant transfer.

(4) If this regulation applies and, as a result of the relevant transfer, a company which was a member of the same group as the transferor at the time of the relevant transfer—

(*a*) ceases to be a member of that group;

(*b*) becomes a member of the same group as the transferee; and

(*c*) subsequently ceases to be a member of that group,

section 179 of TCGA shall have effect when the company ceases to be a member of the same group as the transferee as respects any relevant asset acquired by that company otherwise than from the transferee as if that asset had been acquired from the transferee.

This paragraph is subject to paragraph (6).

(5) In paragraph (4) "relevant asset" means any asset acquired by the company referred to in that paragraph from—

(*a*) the transferor; or

(*b*) any other company which is a member of the same group as the transferor at the time of the relevant transfer,

when the company referred to in that paragraph and the transferor, or the company referred to in that paragraph, the transferor and the other company, were members of the same group.

(6) Paragraph (4) shall not apply if the company referred to in that paragraph which acquired that asset and the company from which that asset was acquired (one being a 75 per cent subsidiary of the other) cease simultaneously to be members of the same group as the transferee but continue to be members of the same group as one another.

19 Transfer of loan relationship

(1) Subject to paragraph (7), this regulation applies if—

(*a*) there is a relevant transfer by [a registered society][1]; and

(*b*) as a result of that transfer, the transferee directly or indirectly replaces the transferor as a party to a loan relationship (as to which see regulation 20).

(2) The credits and debits to be brought into account for the purposes of Parts 3, 5 and 6 of CTA as a result of the relevant transfer shall be determined in accordance with paragraphs (3) to (10).

(3) Subject to paragraph (5), for the accounting period in which the relevant transfer takes place, the transferor shall be treated as having entered into the relevant transfer for consideration of an amount equal to the notional carrying value of the asset or liability representing the loan relationship at the time of the relevant transfer.

(4) For any accounting period in which the transferee is a party to the loan relationship, the transferee shall be treated as if it had acquired the asset or liability representing the loan relationship for consideration of an amount equal to the notional carrying value of the asset or liability in the accounts of the transferor at the time of the relevant transfer.

(5) If a discount arises in respect of the relevant transfer, the consideration referred to in paragraph (3) shall be treated as increased by the amount of that discount.

(6) Schedule 28AA to ICTA (provision not at arm's length) does not apply in relation to the amounts in respect of which credits or debits are to be brought into account under this regulation.

(7) This regulation does not apply where the transferor is regarded as using fair value accounting in respect of the loan relationship (as to which see regulation 21).

(8) The transferor shall be regarded for the purposes of this Part as using fair value accounting in respect of a loan relationship only if the credits and debits to be brought into account for the purposes of these Regulations as respects the relationship are determined on that basis.

(9) It does not matter for the purposes of paragraph (8) if the transferor does not otherwise use fair value accounting in respect of the loan relationship.

(10) For the purposes of this regulation, subsection (5) of section 480 of CTA (relevant non-lending relationships involving discounts) applies as it applies for the purposes of that section.

(11) This regulation is subject to—

(*a*) section 332 of CTA (repo, stock lending and other transactions); and

(*b*) regulation 26.

Amendments—[1] Words substituted for words "an industrial and provident society", by the Co-operative and Community Benefit Societies and Credit Unions Act 2010 (Consequential Amendments) Regulations, SI 2014/1815 reg 2, Sch para 26(1), (3) with effect from 1 August 2014.

20 Meaning of transferee replacing transferor as a party to a loan relationship

(1) References in regulation 19 to a transferee replacing a transferor as a party to a loan relationship include references to a transferee becoming party to a relationship which—

(*a*) confers rights within paragraph (2);

(*b*) imposes obligations within paragraph (2); or

(*c*) both confers such rights and imposes such obligations.

(2) Rights or obligations are within this paragraph if they are equivalent to those of the transferor under a loan relationship to which that transferor ceased to be a party as a result of the relevant transfer.

(3) For the purposes of paragraph (2), a transferor's rights under a creditor relationship are equivalent to rights under another creditor relationship if each set of rights gives the holder of an asset representing the relationship in question—

(*a*) the same rights against the same persons as to capital, interest and dividends; and

(*b*) the same remedies to enforce those rights.

(4) For the purposes of paragraph (3), any difference in—

(*a*) the total nominal amounts of the assets representing each relationship;

(*b*) the form in which they are held; or

(*c*) the way in which they can be transferred,

is ignored.

(5) For the purposes of paragraph (2), a transferee's obligations under a debtor relationship are equivalent to obligations under another debtor relationship if under each set of obligations the holder of the liability representing the relationship in question has—

(*a*) the same obligations to the same persons as to capital, interest and dividends; and (*b*) the same remedies to enforce those obligations.

(6) For the purposes of paragraph (5), any difference in—

(*a*) the total nominal amounts of the assets representing the creditor relationship corresponding to each relationship;

(*b*) the form in which they are held; or

(*c*) the way in which they can be transferred,

is ignored.

21 Transfer of loan relationship where fair value accounting is used

(1) This regulation applies if regulation 19 would apply but for the fact that the transferor is regarded as using fair value accounting in respect of the loan relationship.

(2) The credits and debits to be brought into account for the purposes of Parts 3, 5 and 6 of CTA as a result of the relevant transfer shall be determined in accordance with paragraphs (3) to (5).

(3) The amount which is to be brought into account by the transferor in respect of the relevant transfer ("the transferor's amount") is—

(*a*) if the amount relates to an asset, either—

(i) the fair value of the asset as at the date when the transferee becomes party to the loan relationship; or

(ii) the fair value of the rights under or interest in the loan relationship as at that date; and

(*b*) if the amount relates to a liability, the fair value of the liability as at that date.

(4) Subject to paragraph (5), for any accounting period in which the transferee is a party to the loan relationship, for the purpose of determining the credits and debits to be brought into account in respect of the relationship for the purposes of these Regulations, the transferee shall be treated as if it had acquired the asset or liability representing the relationship for consideration of an amount equal to the transferor's amount.

(5) If a discount arises in respect of the transfer, the transferor's amount shall be treated as increased by the amount of the discount.

(6) This regulation is subject to—

(*a*) section 332 of CTA (repo, stock lending and other transactions); and

(*b*) regulation 26.

22 Replacement of [registered society] as party to a derivative contract

(1) Subject to paragraph (7), this regulation applies if—

(*a*) there is a relevant transfer by [a registered society][1]; and

(*b*) as a result of that transfer the transferee directly or indirectly replaces the transferor as a party to a derivative contract (as to which see regulation 23).

(2) The credits and debits to be brought into account for the purposes of Part 3 or 7 of CTA as a result of the relevant transfer shall be determined in accordance with paragraphs (3) to (6).

(3) Subject to paragraph (5), for the accounting period in which the relevant transfer takes place, the transferor shall be treated as having entered into the derivative contract for consideration of an amount equal to the notional carrying value of that contract (as to which see paragraph (8)).

(4) For any accounting period in which the transferee is a party to the derivative contract, the transferee shall be treated as if it had acquired that derivative contract for consideration of an amount equal to the notional carrying value of that contract in the accounts of the transferor (as to which see paragraph (8)).

(5) If a discount arises in respect of the relevant transfer, the consideration referred to in paragraph (3) shall be treated for the purposes of that paragraph as increased by the amount of the discount.

(6) Schedule 28AA to ICTA (provision not at arm's length) does not apply in relation to the amounts in respect of which credits or debits are to be brought into account under this regulation.

(7) This regulation does not apply where the transferor is regarded as using fair value accounting in respect of the derivative contract (as to which see regulation 24).

(8) For the purposes of this regulation the notional carrying value of a derivative contract is the amount which would have been its carrying value in the accounts of the transferor if a period of account had ended immediately before the date on which the transferor had ceased to be a party to that derivative contract.

(9) For the purposes of this regulation, subsection (5) of section 480 of CTA (relevant non-lending relationships involving discounts) applies as it applies for the purposes of that section.

(10) This regulation is subject to regulation 27.

Amendments—[1] In para (1)(*a*) words substituted for words "an industrial and provident society", and in heading words substituted for words "industrial and provident society", by the Co-operative and Community Benefit Societies and Credit Unions Act 2010 (Consequential Amendments) Regulations, SI 2014/1815 reg 2, Sch para 26(1), (3), (4) with effect from 1 August 2014.

23 Meaning of transferee replacing transferor as party to a derivative contract

(1) References in regulation 22 to a transferee replacing a transferor as a party to a derivative contract include references to the transferee becoming party to a derivative contract which—

(*a*) confers rights within paragraph (2),

(*b*) imposes liabilities within paragraph (2), or

(*c*) both confers such rights and imposes such liabilities.

(2) Rights or liabilities are within this paragraph if they are equivalent to those of the transferor under a derivative contract to which the transferor has ceased to be a party as a result of the relevant transfer.

24 Transfer of derivative contract where fair value accounting is used

(1) This regulation applies in a case where regulation 22 would apply but for the fact that the transferor is regarded as using fair value accounting as respects the derivative contract.

(2) Subject to paragraph (4), the amount which is to be brought into account by the transferor in respect of a relevant transfer is the fair value of the derivative contract as at the date of that transfer.

(3) For any accounting period in which the transferee is a party to the derivative contract, for the purpose of determining the credits and debits to be brought into account in respect of the contract for the purposes of these Regulations, the transferee shall be treated as if it had acquired the contract for consideration of an amount equal to the fair value of the contract as at the date of the transfer.

(4) If a discount arises in respect of the relevant transfer, the amount to be brought into account under paragraph (2) shall be treated as increased by the amount of the discount.

(5) For the purposes of this regulation, subsection (5) of section 480 of CTA (relevant non-lending relationships involving discounts) applies as it applies for the purposes of that section.

(6) This regulation is subject to regulation 27.

25 Transfer of loan relationship or derivative contract—further provisions

(1) This regulation applies if—

(*a*) there is a relevant transfer within regulation 3(2)(*a*), (*b*), (*d*), (*e*) or (*f*); and

(*b*) before the date of the relevant transfer there had been a transfer to a company of—

(i) a loan relationship to which section 336 of CTA (transfers of loans on group transactions) applied; or

(ii) a derivative contract to which section 625 of CTA (group member replacing another as party to derivative contract) applied,

but this is subject to paragraph (6).

(2) Paragraph (3) applies if as a result of the relevant transfer the company referred to in paragraph (1)(*b*) ceases to be a member of the same group as the transferor—

(*a*) before the end of the relevant six year period referred to in—

(i) section 344(4) of CTA (transferee leaving group after replacing transferor as party to loan relationship); or

(ii) section 630(4) of CTA (introduction to sections 631 and 632); and

(*b*) whilst still a party to the relevant loan relationship or derivative contract.

(3) If paragraph (2) is satisfied—

(*a*) the company referred to in paragraph (1)(*b*) shall be treated as not having ceased to be a member of the same group as the transferor;

(*b*) in the case of a loan relationship, section 345 of CTA (transferee leaving group otherwise than because of exempt distribution) shall not apply to the loan relationship as a result of the relevant transfer; and

(*c*) in the case of a derivative contract, section 631 of CTA (transferee leaving group otherwise than because of exempt distribution) shall not apply to the derivative contract as a result of the relevant transfer.

(4) Paragraph (5) applies if the company referred to in paragraph (1)(*b*) ceases to be a member of the same group as the transferee—

(*a*) before the end of the relevant six year period referred to in—

(i) section 344(4) of CTA (transferee leaving group after replacing transferor as party to loan relationship); or

(ii) section 630(4) of CTA (introduction to sections 631 and 632); and

(*b*) whilst still a party to the relevant loan relationship or derivative contract.

(5) If paragraph (4) is satisfied—

(*a*) in the case of a loan relationship, section 345 of CTA (transferee leaving group otherwise than because of exempt distribution) shall apply to the loan relationship as a result of the relevant transfer; and

(*b*) in the case of a derivative contract, section 631 of CTA (transferee leaving group otherwise than because of exempt distribution) shall apply to the derivative contract as a result of the relevant transfer.

(6) This regulation does not apply where the transferor of a loan relationship is regarded as using fair value accounting in respect of that loan relationship.

(7) The transferor shall be regarded for the purposes of this Part as using fair value accounting in respect of a loan relationship only if the credits and debits to be brought into account for the purposes of these Regulations as respects that loan relationship are determined on that basis.
(8) It does not matter for the purposes of paragraph (7) if the transferor does not otherwise use fair value accounting in respect of the loan relationship.
(9) This regulation is subject to—

- (*a*) regulation 26 if there has been a transfer of a loan relationship to which section 336 of CTA (transfers of loans on group transactions) applied; or
- (*b*) regulation 27 if there has been a transfer of a derivative contract to which section 625 of CTA (group member replacing another as party to a derivative contract) applied.

26 Transferor of loan relationship is party to avoidance

(1) Regulations 19, 21 and 25 do not apply if conditions A and B are met.
(2) Condition A is that the transferor is a party to arrangements under which there is likely to be a transfer of rights or liabilities under the loan relationship by the transferee to another person in circumstances in which—

- (*a*) sections 336 and 340 of CTA; or
- (*b*) regulation 19, 21 or 25,

would not apply.
(3) Condition B is that the purpose, or one of the main purposes, of the arrangements is to obtain a tax advantage for the transferor or a person connected with the transferor.
(4) In this regulation "transfer" includes any arrangement which equates in substance to a transfer.

27 Transferor of derivative contract is party to avoidance

(1) Regulations 22, 24 and 25 do not apply if conditions A and B are met.
(2) Condition A is that the transferor is a party to arrangements under which there is likely to be a transfer of rights or liabilities under the derivative contract by the transferee to another person in circumstances in which—

- (*a*) section 625 of CTA; or
- (*b*) regulation 22, 24 or 25,

would not apply.
(3) Condition B is that the purpose, or one of the main purposes, of the arrangements is to obtain a tax advantage for the transferor or a person connected with the transferor.
(4) In this regulation "transfer" includes any arrangement which equates in substance to a transfer.

28 Transfer of intangible fixed assets

(1) This regulation applies if—

- (*a*) there is a relevant transfer within regulation 3(2)(*a*), (*b*), (*d*), (*e*) or (*f*) which includes intangible fixed assets;
- (*b*) those assets are chargeable intangible assets in relation to the transferor immediately before the relevant transfer; and
- (*c*) those assets are chargeable intangible assets in relation to the transferee immediately after the relevant transfer.

(2) The transfer of those assets is tax-neutral for the purposes of—

- (*a*) these Regulations; and
- (*b*) Part 8 of CTA (intangible fixed assets).

(3) For the application of sections 780 (deemed realisation and reacquisition at market value) and 785 (principal company becoming member of another group) of CTA where this regulation applies, see regulation 29.
(4) This regulation and regulations 29 and 30 apply to goodwill as they apply to intangible fixed assets.

29 Transfer of intangible fixed assets—further provisions

(1) This regulation applies if—

- (*a*) there is a relevant transfer within regulation 3(2)(*a*), (*b*), (*d*), (*e*) or (*f*) which includes intangible fixed assets;
- (*b*) those assets are—
  - (i) chargeable intangible assets in relation to the transferor immediately before the relevant transfer; and
  - (ii) chargeable intangible assets in relation to the transferee immediately after the relevant transfer; and
- (*c*) the transfer is tax-neutral for the purposes of these Regulations or Part 8 of CTA (intangible fixed assets).

(2) If because of the relevant transfer a company ceases to be a member of the same group as the transferor, that event does not cause—

- (*a*) section 780 of CTA (deemed realisation and reacquisition at market value); or
- (*b*) section 785 of that Act (principal company becoming member of another group),

to apply as respects any assets acquired by the company from the transferor or any other member of the same group as the transferor.

(3) If the transferor and transferee are members of the same group at the time of the relevant transfer but later cease to be, that later event does not cause section 780 or 785 of CTA to apply in relation to any asset to which this regulation applies.

(4) Paragraph (3) applies to—

(*a*) any asset acquired by the transferee on or before the relevant transfer from the transferor, or from any other member of the same group; or

(*b*) any asset acquired from the transferor or from any other member of the same group by a company (other than the transferee) that is a member of that group at the time of the relevant transfer.

(5) Paragraph (6) applies if a company which is a member of the same group as the transferor at the time of the relevant transfer—

(*a*) ceases to be a member of that group and becomes a member of the same group as the transferee, and

(*b*) later ceases to be a member of that group.

(6) Section 780 of CTA (deemed realisation and reacquisition at market value) applies on that later event as if any asset to which this paragraph applies that has not been acquired from the transferee had been so acquired.

(7) Paragraph (6) applies to—

(*a*) any asset acquired by the company referred to in paragraph (5) from the transferor when that company and the transferor were members of the same group; or

(*b*) any asset acquired by the company referred to in paragraph (5) from another company which is a member of the same group at the time of the relevant transfer when the company referred to in paragraph (5), the transferor and the other company were members of the same group.

(8) Paragraph (6) does not apply if—

(*a*) the company which acquired the asset is a 75% subsidiary of the company from which it was acquired or vice versa;

(*b*) those companies cease simultaneously to be members of the same group as the transferee; and

(*c*) those companies continue to be members of the same group as one another.

30 Intangible fixed assets transferred as if at no gain or no loss

(1) This regulation applies if—

(*a*) there is a relevant transfer by [a registered society][1]; and

(*b*) the transferor is treated—

(i) for the purposes of these Regulations; or

(ii) by virtue of section 486 of ICTA (industrial and provident societies and co-operative associations),

as disposing of any assets for a consideration of such amount as would secure that neither a gain nor a loss would accrue to the transferor on that disposal.

(2) The assets, in the hands of the transferee, shall be treated as not satisfying the general rule set out in section 882(1) of CTA (application of Part 8 to assets created or acquired on or after 1 April 2002).

Amendments—[1] In para (1)(*a*) words substituted for words "an industrial and provident society", by the Co-operative and Community Benefit Societies and Credit Unions Act 2010 (Consequential Amendments) Regulations, SI 2014/1815 reg 2, Sch para 26(1), (3) with effect from 1 August 2014.

31 Exemption from stamp duty land tax

A land transaction made in connection with a relevant transfer within regulation 3(2)(*b*), (*c*), (*d*), (*e*) or (*f*) shall be exempt from charge under Part 4 of FA 2003.

32 Exemption from stamp duty

Any instrument, document or agreement required to give effect to a relevant transfer by [a registered society][2] shall not be chargeable to stamp duty under the Stamp Act 1891.

Amendments—[1] Words substituted for words "an industrial and provident society", by the Co-operative and Community Benefit Societies and Credit Unions Act 2010 (Consequential Amendments) Regulations, SI 2014/1815 reg 2, Sch para 26(1), (3) with effect from 1 August 2014.

PART 4
FURTHER PROVISIONS RELATING TO RELEVANT TRANSFERS

33 Stamp duty land tax—group relief

(1) Paragraph 3 of Schedule 7 to FA 2003 (withdrawal of group relief) does not apply if—

(*a*) there is a relevant transfer;

(*b*) before the date of that relevant transfer there had been a land transaction to which Part 1 of Schedule 7 to FA 2003 applied; and

(*c*) as a result of that relevant transfer, the purchaser in relation to the land transaction referred to in sub-paragraph (*b*) ceases to be a member of the same group as the transferor—
  (i) before the end of the period of three years beginning with the effective date of that land transaction; or
  (ii) in pursuance of, or in connection with, arrangements made before the end of that three year period.

(2) In this regulation, references to a company being a member of a group of companies are to be read in accordance with paragraph 1 of Schedule 7 to FA 2003.

34 Transitional provision

(1) This regulation applies if a relevant transfer takes place on or after 22 April 2009 but before the date on which these Regulations come into force.

(2) Subject to paragraph (4) nothing in these Regulations shall have effect so as to—
  (*a*) impose a charge to tax (or increase a charge to tax) on a party to the relevant transfer;
  (*b*) reduce a relief from tax, including a tax credit, available to a party to the relevant transfer; or
  (*c*) reduce losses available to a party to the relevant transfer;

where that charge or reduction arises only as a result of the application of these Regulations.

(3) If paragraph (2) applies—
  (*a*) any charge to tax (or increase in a charge to tax) on a party to the relevant transfer;
  (*b*) any reduction in relief from tax available to a party to the relevant transfer; or
  (*c*) any reduction in losses available to a party to the relevant transfer;

shall be disregarded.

(4) Paragraphs (2) and (3) do not apply in relation to—
  (*a*) any charge to tax (or increase in a charge to tax);
  (*b*) any reduction in relief from tax; or
  (*c*) any reduction in losses;

which may arise as a result of anything done or occurring on or after the date on which these Regulations come into force.

35 Arrangements the purpose of which is to secure a tax advantage

(1) This regulation applies if a relevant transfer forms part of an unallowable arrangement.

(2) If paragraph (1) is satisfied the following Cases shall apply.

Case 1

Case 1 is where as a result of the arrangement any party to the relevant transfer obtains a relief from tax (including a tax credit) or an increased relief from tax.

Where Case 1 applies, the relief from tax, or increased relief from tax, shall not be allowed.

Case 2

Case 2 is where as a result of the arrangement any party to the relevant transfer obtains a repayment of tax or an increased repayment of tax.

Where Case 2 applies, the repayment of tax, or the increased repayment, shall not be allowed.

Case 3

Case 3 is where as a result of the arrangement any party to the relevant transfer avoids, reduces or delays a charge or assessment to tax.

Where Case 3 applies, a charge or an assessment to tax may be made upon that party.

Case 4

Case 4 is where as a result of the arrangement any party to the relevant transfer avoids a possible assessment to tax.

Where Case 4 applies, an assessment to tax may be made upon that party.

(3) For the purposes of this regulation an arrangement is an unallowable arrangement where the purpose, or one of the main purposes, of a person in being a party to the relevant transfer is to obtain a tax advantage as a result of that transfer for that person or any other person.

2009/2997

SAVING GATEWAY ACCOUNTS REGULATIONS 2009

Made . . . . *11 November 2009*

Coming into force in accordance with . . . . *regulation 1*

A draft of this instrument has been laid before Parliament in accordance with section 28(4) and (7) of the Saving Gateway Accounts Act 2009 and approved by a resolution of each House of Parliament. Accordingly, the Treasury make the following Regulations in exercise of the powers conferred by sections 2(2) and (3), 3(1)(*b*), (5) and (6), 4 to 7, 8(1) and (4), 9 to 12, 16, 17, 24(4) and 28(1) and (2) of the Saving Gateway Accounts Act 2009:

PART 1
INTRODUCTORY AND ELIGIBILITY

1 Citation and commencement

These Regulations may be cited as the Saving Gateway Accounts Regulations 2009 and shall come into force on the appointed day.

2 Interpretation

(1) In these Regulations—

(*a*) the following expressions have the meanings given in the Saving Gateway Accounts Act 2009 ("the Act")—

"approved account provider" (see section 4(1));

"the Commissioners" (see section 1(2));

a "death payment" (see section 4(2)(*b*));

"eligible person" (see section 3(1) as supplemented by regulations 3 and 4);

the "first month of the account's operation" (see section 4(5)), and references to the sixth or any other month of the account's operation, and cognate expressions, have corresponding meanings;

"maturity payment" (see section 4(2)(*a*));

"maturity period" (see section 4(2)(*a*));

"month" (see section 4(5)), except in the expression "the first month of the account's operation;

(*b*) "notice of eligibility" (see section 2);

(*c*) the "qualifying balance" of a Saving Gateway account (see section 8(2));

(*d*) "the relevant date" (see section 1(3));

(*e*) "relevant person" (see section 17(2));

(*f*) "Saving Gateway account" (see section 1(1));

(*g*) "tax appeal" (see section 24(3));

(*h*) except where the context otherwise requires—

"accepting deposits", in regulation 14, has the meaning in section 22 of FISMA 2000, taken with Schedule 2 of that Act and any order made under section 22;

"account", except in regulations 8, 10(2)(*k*), 20(1) and (2) and 21, means a Saving Gateway account;

"appointed day" means the day appointed under section 31 of the Act for the purposes of section 8 of the Act;

"credit union" means a society registered as a credit union under the Industrial and Provident Societies Act 1965, or the Credit Unions (Northern Ireland) Order 1985;

"EEA State" means a State, other than the United Kingdom, which is a Contracting Party to the EEA agreement;

"electronic communications" includes any communications by an electronic communications network (within the meaning in the Communications Act 2003);

"electronic signature" has the meaning given by section 7(2) of the Electronic Communications Act 2000;

"FISMA 2000" means the Financial Services and Markets Act 2000;

"full name" includes shortened details sufficient to identify the individual;

"ITA 2007" means the Income Tax Act 2007;

"ITTOIA 2005" means the Income Tax (Trading and Other Income) Act 2005;

"insolvency event" means the procedures listed in the definition of "insolvency event" in regulation 19(15) of the Payment Services Regulations 2009

"the Management Act" means the Taxes Management Act 1970;

"notice" means notice in writing; and "notify" shall be construed accordingly;

"reference number", except in regulation 5(1), means an eligible person's reference number as stated on his or her notice of eligibility;

"tax year" means a period beginning with 6th April in one year and ending with 5th April in the next, and "the tax year 2009–10" means the tax year beginning with 6th April 2009;

"UK institution" means an institution which is incorporated in, or formed under the law of any part of, the United Kingdom.

(2) The table below indexes other definitions in these Regulations:

Term defined	*Regulation*

(*a*) "account holder"	10(1)(*a*)
(*b*) "agreed terms"	10(1)(*h*)
(*c*) "the disqualifying circumstances"	16
(*d*) "the eligibility window"	3(3)
(*e*) "qualifying circumstances"	14(1)

3 Eligible persons—entitlement to working tax credit or child tax credit

(1) A person is an eligible person by reason of entitlement (alone or with another person) to working tax credit or child tax credit, within the meaning in section 3(5) of the Act, only if he or she satisfies the following conditions.

(2) Those conditions are—

Condition 1

There is a decision under sections 18 to 21 of the 2002 Act, other than on the basis of estimated income (a "final award"), that the person was entitled (alone or with another person) to working tax credit or child tax credit (not being at a nil rate) for the tax year 2009–10, or a subsequent tax year.

Condition 2

(*a*) The relevant income for that tax year ("the relevant tax year") did not exceed £16,040, or

(*b*) the person's entitlement to working tax credit or child tax credit for the relevant tax year arose by virtue of section 7(2) of the 2002 Act (automatic entitlement where the claimant or one of the claimants is entitled to a prescribed social security benefit).

Where a higher amount is determined for the purposes of section 7(1)(*a*) of the 2002 Act in relation to child tax credit (income threshold for child tax credit) in relation to the relevant tax year, that higher amount shall be substituted for the figure of £16,040 in paragraph (*a*).

Condition 3

The final award for the relevant tax year (and calculation of the relevant income on which it is based) has not been overturned.

Condition 4

If—

(*c*) the Commissioners have given the person a final notice under section 17 of the 2002 Act, relating to the relevant tax year, and

(*d*) the notice contained a requirement to make a declaration or statement under section 17(2)(*a*), (4)(*a*) or (6)(*a*) of the 2002 Act (annual declaration form),

the person has made the declarations or statements required by the time at which eligibility is being determined.

Condition 5

The eligibility window for that final award has not ended.

(3) In this regulation—

the "eligibility window", in relation to a final award, means the period—

(*a*) beginning when that final award was made, and

(*b*) ending 12 months after the date of that final award;

"estimated income" means estimated current year income, declared or stated as mentioned in section 17(8)(*a*) or (*b*) of the 2002 Act, unless the estimate has been treated as confirmed in the amount estimated, in accordance with section 17(8) of the 2002 Act;

"relevant income", in relation to a person or persons and a tax year, means the relevant income determined in accordance with section 7 of the 2002 Act, and with regulations made under that section, in relation to a claim by the person or persons for working tax credit or child tax credit for the tax year;

"the 2002 Act" means the Tax Credits Act 2002.

4 Eligible persons—connection with the UK

(1) The connection with the United Kingdom mentioned in section 3(1)(*b*) of the Act is that the person is ordinarily resident in the United Kingdom.

(2) A Crown servant posted overseas or his or her partner shall be treated as ordinarily resident in the United Kingdom.

(3) A person shall be treated as ordinarily resident in the United Kingdom if he or she is exercising in the United Kingdom his or her rights as a worker pursuant to Council Regulation (EEC) No 1612/68.

(4) A person who is in the United Kingdom as a result of his or her deportation, expulsion or other removal by compulsion of law from another country to the United Kingdom shall be treated as being ordinarily resident in the United Kingdom.

(5) In paragraph (2)—

"Crown servant posted overseas" has the meaning in regulation 5(2) of the Tax Credits (Residence) Regulations 2003;
the "partner" of a Crown servant posted overseas means a person falling within the description in regulation 6(1) (read with regulation 2(1)) of those Regulations.

5 Notices of eligibility

(1) The notice of eligibility to be issued under section 2(1) of the Act shall contain (in addition to the expiry date) the following particulars—

(*a*) the full name of the eligible person; and

(*b*) his or her Saving Gateway reference number.

(2) The notice shall be issued by being sent to the eligible person by post, except in a case where there is a person acting under regulation 13(8), in which case it may be sent to that person.

(3) A further notice of eligibility may be issued to an eligible person at the discretion of the Commissioners, where the expiry date of a previous notice has passed, and the person has not opened a Saving Gateway account.

6 Opening of account by a person who has received a notice of eligibility

(1) For the purposes of these Regulations, an account is opened with an approved account provider on the date when all the following conditions are satisfied (but no later than the expiry date specified in the notice of eligibility):

Condition 1

(2) The applicant produces his or her notice of eligibility to the approved account provider or, where the approved account provider's business systems provide for the opening of accounts without production of the relevant notice of eligibility, the applicant makes a true declaration to the approved account provider of the following information:

(*a*) the expiry date of the notice, and

(*b*) the applicant's reference number (as stated on the notice).

Condition 2

The applicant enters into agreed terms with the approved account provider (see regulation 10(1)(*h*)) which include the application and declaration required by regulation 13.

Condition 3

Where that application is not in writing the applicant has agreed, or is treated as having agreed, the contents of the copy of the declaration required by regulation 13(2).

(3) Where—

(*a*) an account is opened in accordance with paragraph (1), and

(*b*) there is a right to cancel (or automatic cancellation of) the agreed terms, and the period during which it may be exercised or occur has not expired,

the account shall not be treated as open for the purposes of regulation 22 (monthly return and financial claim) and regulation 5(3) until the period during which that right may be exercised or cancellation occur has expired without the right being exercised or cancellation occurring.

7 Maturity period (and payment of maturity payments or death payments)

(1) Subject to paragraph (3), the maturity period for an account is the period—

(*a*) beginning simultaneously with the first month of the account's operation (see section 4(5) of the Act), and

(*b*) ending with the last day of the twenty fourth month of the account's operation.

(2) The approved account provider must credit the account with the amount of the maturity payment, or otherwise pay the maturity payment to the account holder, within 21 days from the end of the maturity period for the account.

(3) If the account holder of an account dies before the end of the account's maturity period calculated under paragraph (1), paragraph (2) shall not apply and the account provider shall pay to the account holder's personal representatives an amount (a "death payment") equal to the amount of the maturity payment to which the account holder would have become entitled if the maturity period for the account had ended immediately before the death.

(4) A death payment shall be made within 21 days of the end of the month in which the account provider receives sufficient evidence of the death of the account holder and of the status of the personal representatives.

8 Account ceasing to be a Saving Gateway account (and rollover certificates)

(1) An account ceases to be a Saving Gateway account—

(*a*) on the death of the account holder;

(*b*) for the purposes of section 8(4) of the Act, when the account provider has credited the account with the amount of the maturity payment, or otherwise paid the maturity payment to the account holder; or

(*c*) for all other purposes, at the end of the maturity period for the account.

(2) Where an account ceases to be a Saving Gateway account under paragraph (1)(*c*) for the purposes there mentioned ("on maturity"), if the account holder so requires by notice to the account provider, given within 6 months of that date, the account provider shall give to the account holder a certificate containing the information mentioned in paragraph (3) and the declaration mentioned in paragraph (4).

(3) The information mentioned in this paragraph is—

(*a*) the account holder's full name;

(*b*) his or her permanent address including postcode;

(*c*) the name of the account provider with which the account was held on maturity;

(*d*) the number allocated to it by that account provider;

(*e*) the date on which it matured; and

(*f*) the credit balance of the account (if any) on maturity, and the amount of the maturity payment made or to be made.

(4) The declaration mentioned in this paragraph is a declaration by the account provider that the account was a Saving Gateway account throughout its maturity period and that the information given in the certificate is correct.

9 Government contribution rate

In the calculation of A x B to determine the maturity payment in relation to a Saving Gateway account in section 8(1) of the Act, the multiplier B is 50 pence.

PART 2

OTHER REQUIREMENTS TO BE SATISFIED IN RELATION TO ACCOUNTS

10 General requirements for accounts

(1) A Saving Gateway account must satisfy the requirements that—

(*a*) it is the account of a single person ("the account holder") who is "the applicant" in regulations 6(1) and 13;

(*b*) the account holder is or has been an eligible person;

(*c*) no person may open more than one Saving Gateway account in their lifetime;

(*d*) it is a cash deposit account (including a share account held with a building society within the meaning of the Building Societies Act 1986, and a deposit by way of subscription for shares in a credit union);

(*e*) the account is denominated in sterling;

(*f*) the account is covered by the Financial Services Compensation Scheme, or another deposit-guarantee scheme introduced and officially recognised in a Member State or EEA State, in accordance with Article 3(1) of Council Directive 94/19/EEC;

(*g*) the account must be in the beneficial ownership of the account holder, and not be held on behalf of any other person; and

(*h*) the account must at all times be managed in accordance with the Act and these Regulations by an approved account provider and under terms agreed and recorded in an agreement (the "agreed terms") made between the account provider and the account holder.

(2) Apart from other requirements of the Act and these Regulations, the agreed terms shall include (or comply with, as the case may be) the conditions that—

(*a*) if the account is held by the account holder until the end of the account's maturity period, the account provider shall pay the account holder a maturity payment (see section 8 of the Act);

(*b*) if the account holder dies, while still holding the account, before the end of the account's maturity period, the account provider shall pay a death payment in accordance with regulation 7(3) and (4);

(*c*) there is no restriction on the maximum or minimum amount or on timing (subject to the account provider's normal business hours) of withdrawals of the credit balance of the account;

(*d*) there is no requirement that a minimum credit balance must be maintained in the account (with the result that an account with a nil balance is not automatically closed);

(*e*) the account provider shall permit payment of sums into the account by cheque, direct debit, standing order, direct credit (other than standing order) or cash (unless, in the case of cash, the provider offers both internet and non-internet accounts, and the non-internet accounts accept cash);

(*f*) no deductions or withdrawals from the account (by way of charges or otherwise) shall be made by the account provider;

(*g*) the account provider shall have no right of charge, lien, set-off, mortgage or other security against the money in the account;

(*h*) the account provider shall satisfy himself that any person to whom he delegates any of his functions or responsibilities under the agreed terms is competent to carry out those functions or responsibilities;

(i) where there is a right to transfer the account under regulation 19(1), the whole of the account shall be transferred free of expense to the other approved account provider subject to and in accordance with regulation 19;

(j) where the account is transferred to the account provider by a transfer under regulation 19, that no charges or expenses are due in respect of that transfer;

(k) the account provider shall notify the account holder if by reason of any failure to satisfy the provisions of these Regulations an account is or will become no longer exempt from tax by virtue of regulation 3 of the Saving Gateway Accounts (No 2) Regulations 2009.

(3) In applying paragraph (1)(*c*), any account opened and cancelled as mentioned in regulation 6(2) shall be ignored.

11 Limit on sums paid into the account

(1) The total of the sums paid into an account in a month (excluding any interest or other sums paid by the approved account provider under the agreed terms) shall not exceed £25.

(2) In calculating the limit in paragraph (1) for the purpose of any payment into the account, previous withdrawals from the account shall be ignored.

12 Statements for an account

(1) Except where a passbook is provided in accordance with paragraph (5), the account provider must issue a statement for the account—

(*a*) at least six monthly, and

(*b*) where an account is transferred to another account provider under regulation 19, as at the transfer date.

(2) The statement date in the case of a six monthly statement must be the end of the sixth, twelfth, eighteenth or twenty fourth month of the account's operation, as the case may be.

(3) The statement shall be sent to the account holder within 30 days of the statement date.

(4) Statements shall include the following information—

(*a*) the full name of the account holder;

(*b*) his or her address, including postcode;

(*c*) the statement date;

(*d*) the balance of the account at the previous statement date (if any), and otherwise at the opening of the account;

(*e*) all payments into and withdrawals from the account during the statement period ending on the statement date;

(*f*) a provisional calculation of the maturity payment (based on the qualifying balance achieved between the opening of the account and the statement date); and

(*g*) the closing balance of the account at the statement date.

(5) An account provider may comply with its obligations under this regulation (other than under paragraph (4)(*f*), if paragraph (6) applies) by issuing the account holder with a passbook for the account which, on presentation at a branch of the account provider, is up-dated to include the same information as a statement, omitting references in paragraph (4) to a statement date or statement period.

(6) The information in paragraph (4)(*f*) may, at the option of the account provider, be provided in a notice to the account holder which is separate from the statement or passbook.

13 Conditions for application to open an account

(1) An application by a person who has received a notice of eligibility ("the applicant") to open an account with an approved account provider must be made to the approved account provider, and satisfy the conditions in paragraphs (2) to (4).

(2) An application must incorporate a true declaration by the applicant that he or she—

(*a*) has not previously opened a Saving Gateway account (excepting any account opened and closed as mentioned in regulation 6(2)); and

(*b*) is ordinarily resident in the United Kingdom, or is so treated as ordinarily resident under regulation 4(2) to (5);

and where the application is not in writing, must authorise the approved account provider to record the terms of the declaration in a written declaration made on behalf of the applicant.

(3) An application must contain—

(*a*) the applicant's full name and date of birth,

(*b*) his or her address, including postcode,

(*c*) the reference number, as stated on his or her notice of eligibility; and

(*d*) an authorisation to the approved account provider to make on the account holder's behalf any claims to relief from tax in respect of the account.

(4) Where the application is not in writing, the approved account provider shall make the written declaration mentioned in paragraph (2), and notify the applicant of its contents, and such declaration shall take effect from the date on which the applicant agrees the contents (subject to any corrections), and if he or she neither agrees or disagrees with the contents within 14 days, he or she shall be treated as having agreed them.

(5) An account provider shall decline to accept an application if he has reason to believe that—

(*a*) the notice of eligibility has expired, or is not or might not be genuine,

(*b*) the applicant's declaration (see Condition 1 in regulation 6(1) if applicable, and paragraph (2) of this regulation) or application is or might be untrue, or contains matters which are or might be untrue, or

(*c*) opening an account would be a breach of, or failure to comply with, any requirement in or a direction made under the Money Laundering Regulations 2007.

(6) An application made under this regulation shall be regarded as in writing if it is made—

(*a*) by telephonic facsimile transmission containing the signature of the individual, or

(*b*) by electronic communication containing an electronic signature of the individual.

(7) Declarations made by the account provider under paragraph (4) shall be regarded as made in writing if they are produced by electronic means, and the copy of the declaration to be sent to the applicant in accordance with paragraph (4) may be sent by telephonic facsimile transmission or by electronic communication.

(8) Where a person is or may be entitled to a benefit or tax credit specified in section 3(2) of the Act but is unable for the time being to act, the following persons may act for that person—

(*a*) a deputy or receiver appointed by the Court of Protection with power to make a claim for a benefit or tax credit on behalf of that person;

(*b*) in Scotland, a tutor, curator or guardian acting or appointed in terms of law who is administering the estate of that person;

(*c*) in Northern Ireland, a controller appointed by the High Court, with power to make a claim for a benefit or tax credit on behalf of that person;

(*d*) where there is no person mentioned in sub-paragraphs (*a*) to (*c*), a person appointed on behalf of the person under—

(i) regulation 33(1) of the Social Security (Claims and Payments) Regulations 1987,

(ii) regulation 33(1) of the Social Security (Claims and Payments) Regulations (Northern Ireland) 1987, or

(iii) regulation 18(3) of the Tax Credits (Claims and Notifications) Regulations 2002.

14 Account provider—qualifications and Commissioners' approval

(1) This regulation specifies the circumstances ("qualifying circumstances") in which a person may be approved by the Commissioners as an account provider.

(2) The qualifying circumstances are the following—

(*a*) the person must make an application to the Commissioners for approval in a form specified by the Commissioners;

(*b*) the person must undertake with the Commissioners (subject to regulation 13(5))—

(i) to accept properly completed applications from any person who has received a notice of eligibility and, where there is a right to transfer the account under regulation 19(1)(*a*), to accept transfers of an account in accordance with that regulation; or

(ii) in the case of a credit union, to accept properly completed applications from any person who has received a notice of eligibility and, where there is a right to transfer the account under regulation 19(1)(*a*), to accept transfers of an account in accordance with that regulation, if the applicant or account holder is a member, or fulfils or is treated as fulfilling a qualification for admission to membership, of the credit union;

(*c*) the person must demonstrate to the satisfaction of the Commissioners that the person can correctly operate the procedures in regulation 22, and receive electronic communications for the purposes of these Regulations from H.M. Revenue and Customs;

(*d*) an approved account provider must be—

(i) a UK institution which has permission under Part 4 of FISMA 2000 to carry on the regulated activity of accepting deposits;

(ii) an EEA firm mentioned in paragraph 5(*b*) of Schedule 3 to FISMA 2000 (credit institution) which has permission under paragraph 15 of that Schedule to carry on the activity of accepting deposits, as a result of qualifying for authorisation under paragraph 12(1) or (2) of that Schedule (exercise of passport rights by EEA firms); or

(iii) a credit institution (within the same meaning) incorporated outside the EEA which has permission under Part 4 of FISMA 2000 to carry on the regulated activity of accepting deposits through a branch in the United Kingdom;

(*e*) an approved account provider must not be prevented from acting as such by any limitation or requirement imposed under section 42 or 43 of FISMA 2000, or by any prohibition or prohibition order in or made under that Act;

(*f*) an account provider which is a credit institution within sub-paragraph (*d*)(ii) or (iii), and which does not intend to carry out all its functions as an account provider in the United Kingdom, must fulfil one of the requirements mentioned in regulation 15.

(3) The terms of the Commissioners' approval may include conditions designed to ensure that the provisions of these Regulations are satisfied.

15 Approved account provider—appointment of tax representative

(1) This regulation specifies the requirements mentioned in regulation 14(2)(*f*).

(2) The first requirement is that—

(*a*) a person who falls within section 698(2) of ITTOIA 2005 is for the time being appointed by the account provider to be responsible for securing the discharge of the duties mentioned in paragraph (5) which fall to be discharged by the account provider, and

(*b*) his or her identity and the fact of the appointment have been notified to the Commissioners by the account provider.

(3) The second requirement is that there are for the time being other arrangements with the Commissioners for a person other than the account provider to secure the discharge of such duties.

(4) The third requirement is that there are for the time being other arrangements with the Commissioners designed to secure the discharge of such duties.

(5) The duties mentioned in this paragraph are those that fall to be discharged by an account provider under the Act and these Regulations.

(6) The appointment of a person in pursuance of the first requirement shall be treated as terminated in circumstances where—

(*a*) the Commissioners have reason to believe that the person concerned—

(i) has failed to secure the discharge of any of the duties mentioned in paragraph (5), or

(ii) does not have adequate resources to discharge those duties, and

(*b*) the Commissioners have notified the account provider and that person that they propose to treat his or her appointment as having terminated from the date specified in the notice.

(7) Where, in accordance with the first requirement, a person is at any time responsible for securing the discharge of duties, the person concerned—

(*a*) shall be entitled to act on the account provider's behalf for any of the purposes of the provisions relating to the duties;

(*b*) shall secure (where appropriate by acting on the account provider's behalf) the account provider's compliance with and discharge of the duties; and

(*c*) shall be personally liable in respect of any failure of the account provider to comply with or discharge any such duty as if the duties imposed on the account provider were imposed jointly and severally on the account provider and the person concerned.

16 Account provider—withdrawal by Commissioners of approval

(1) This regulation specifies the circumstances ("the disqualifying circumstances") in which the Commissioners may by notice withdraw their approval of a person as an account provider.

(2) The disqualifying circumstances are that the Commissioners have reason to believe—

(*a*) that any provision of the Act or these Regulations, or any term of an undertaking given in accordance with regulation 14(2)(*b*) or condition under regulation 14(3), is not or at any time has not been satisfied, either in respect of an account managed by the account provider or otherwise; or

(*b*) that a person to whom they have given approval to act as an account provider is not qualified so to act.

(3) The notice to which paragraph (1) refers shall specify—

(*a*) the date from which the Commissioners' approval is withdrawn; and

(*b*) the disqualifying circumstances.

(4) On receiving the notice referred to in paragraph (1), subject to any appeal under section 23(1)(*b*) of the Act, the account provider shall notify the account holder of the right to transfer the account under regulation 19(1)(*a*), and the notice shall inform the account holder of the rights under regulation 18(3).

17 Approved account provider ceasing to act

(1) A person shall give notice to the Commissioners and to the account holder of an account which it manages of its intention to cease to act as the approved account provider not less than 30 days before it so ceases so that its obligations to the Commissioners under the account can be conveniently discharged at or about the time it ceases so to act.

(2) The notice to the account holder shall inform him or her of the right to transfer the account under regulation 19(1)(*a*), and of the rights under regulation 18(3).

18 Account provider ceasing to qualify

(1) A person shall cease to qualify as an approved account provider and shall notify the Commissioners within 30 days of the relevant event in sub-paragraphs (*a*) to (*d*), of that relevant event, where—

(*a*) the person no longer fulfils the conditions of regulation 14;

(*b*) there is an insolvency event in relation to the account provider;

(*c*) an application has been made for a bank insolvency order or a bank administration order; or (*d*) in the case of a credit institution within regulation 14(2)(*d*)(ii) or (iii), action corresponding to that described in sub-paragraph (*b*) or (*c*) has been taken by or in relation to the institution under the law of an EEA State or other State.

(2) On giving the notice referred to in paragraph (1), the person shall also notify the account holder of the right to transfer the account under regulation 19(1)(*a*), and the notice shall inform the account holder of the rights under paragraph (3).

(3) Where an account holder—

(*a*) receives a notice under paragraph (2), or regulation 16(4) or 17, and

(*b*) gives instructions to the account provider in accordance with regulation 19(1)(*a*), with the consequence that the account is transferred pursuant to regulation 19 to another approved account provider ("the transferee") within 30 days of the sending of the notice,

the period between the account provider ceasing to be approved, or act or qualify as an approved account provider, and the transfer to the transferee, shall be ignored in determining whether the account has at all times been managed by an approved account provider.

19 Transfer of accounts to other account providers

(1) Where—

(*a*) in a case falling within regulation 16, 17 or 18, the account holder, within 14 days of the sending to him or her of the notice under regulation 16(4), 17(2) or 18(2), instructs the account provider to transfer the account to another named approved account provider,

(*b*) in a case where both account providers have agreed to the transfer of the account, the account holder instructs the account provider to transfer the account to another named approved account provider, or

(*c*) arrangements are made by an account provider (subject to complying with regulation 16, 17 or 18, as the case may be) to transfer all its accounts to another approved account provider,

the transfer shall have effect and be treated as a transfer of the account.

(2) Any transfer relating to an account shall be made directly between one account provider ("the transferor") and another approved account provider ("the transferee"), and the account shall not be affected for the purposes of these Regulations by reason of the transfer.

(3) The account holder shall make a fresh application under regulation 13 (with any necessary modifications to reflect the fact that it is made on a transfer) to the transferee.

(4) The transferor shall on the date of the transfer give the transferee a notice containing the information mentioned in paragraph (5) and the declaration mentioned in paragraph (6).

(5) The information mentioned in this paragraph is—

(*a*) the date of the transfer,

(*b*) the account holder's full name and reference number,

(*c*) the date of the opening of the account, and the expected end of the maturity period under regulation 7(1)(*b*),

(*d*) the qualifying balance of the account achieved up to the date of the transfer, and

(*e*) the total of the sums paid into the account (calculated in accordance with regulation 11(1) and (2)) in the month in which the transfer is made.

(6) The declaration mentioned in this paragraph is a declaration by the transferor that—

(*a*) it has fulfilled all its obligations to the account holder, the Commissioners or otherwise, which are imposed by these Regulations;

(*b*) it has transferred to the transferee or its nominee all the funds in the account;

(*c*) it will forward any further payment received in respect of the account to the transferee, on receipt of the payment; and

(*d*) the information contained in the notice is correct.

20 Recoupment of maturity payments and death payments etc

(1) Where—

(*a*) the account holder was not an eligible person at the relevant date;

(*b*) there is a breach of section 6(2)(*a*) or (*b*) of the Act in relation to an account;

(*c*) there is a breach of Condition 1 in regulation 6(1) in relation to an account; or

(*d*) there is a breach of regulation 10(1)(*c*) or 13(2) in relation to an account;

the account is void and the persons mentioned in paragraph (3) shall account to the Commissioners for any maturity payment or death payment wrongly made in respect of the account.

(2) Where—

(*a*) a person was entitled to a benefit under the terms of section 3(1)(*a*) of the Act, or was an eligible person by reason of entitlement to working tax credit or child tax credit under the terms of regulation 3, but such entitlement has been overturned, or it has subsequently been determined that payment of the relevant benefit or tax credit should not have been made, or should have been made at a different rate; or (*b*) an amount is paid by the Commissioners to an account provider in pursuance of the Act, due to a mis-statement in a monthly return or financial claim, or a mistake by an officer of Revenue and Customs;

the persons mentioned in paragraph (3) shall account to the Commissioners for any maturity payment, death payment or overpayment wrongly made in respect of the account.

(3) The persons mentioned in paragraphs (1) and (2) are—

(*a*) the account provider (to the extent that it has assets relating to the account, or directly or indirectly representing any of the payments, in its possession or control);

(*b*) the account holder, or former account holder (to the extent that the payments have been made or credited to the account holder);

(*c*) any person in whom the maturity payments, death payments or overpayments, or any property directly or indirectly representing any of them, is vested (whether beneficially or otherwise);

and they shall be jointly and severally liable.

(4) Sections 49 (late notice of appeal) and 54 (settling of appeals by agreement) of the Management Act apply in relation to appeals under section 23 of the Act, other than tax appeals.

(5) Where a person accountable under this regulation is notified by the Commissioners that an amount is due from him or her under it, that amount shall be treated for the purposes of Part 6 of the Management Act (collection and recovery) as if it were tax charged in an assessment and due and payable.

(6) The time limits in sections 34 to 36 of the Management Act shall apply to amounts payable under this regulation as they apply to assessments.

21 "Repair" of invalid accounts

(1) Except in the case of a breach of regulation 10(1)(*b*) or (*c*) or 13(2), or the case mentioned in regulation 20(2)(*a*), (where no repair of an account is possible), it is an overriding requirement to be satisfied in relation to an account that the account provider and account holder, as the case may be, take any steps necessary to remedy any breach of these Regulations.

(2) Where a breach is remedied as mentioned in paragraph (1), the account shall, to the extent of that breach, be treated as having been a valid account at all times, except for the purposes of sections 19 to 21 of the Act (penalties).

PART 3
REQUIREMENTS RELATING TO ADMINISTRATION OF ACCOUNTS

22 Monthly return and financial claim

(1) In this regulation—

"initial return period", in relation to an account provider, means the period—

(*a*) beginning on the date on which the approval of the provider takes effect, or the appointed day (whichever is the later), and

(*b*) ending simultaneously with the end of the then current month.

(2) The following provisions of this regulation apply to an account provider in relation to—

(*a*) that provider's initial return period, and

(*b*) each succeeding month,

during which, or any part of which, it acted as an account provider.

(3) Within 14 days of the end of—

(*a*) a provider's initial return period, and

(*b*) any succeeding period mentioned in paragraph (2),

the account provider shall deliver by means of electronic communications to the Commissioners, a return for that period, in a form specified by the Commissioners.

(4) The return shall include a declaration of the information in paragraph (5), and a claim as mentioned in paragraph (6).

(5) The information (to be given in relation to the return period) is—

(*a*) for each account opened by the account provider in accordance with regulation 6, or transferred to the account provider in accordance with regulation 19—

(i) the account holder's full name and date of birth,

(ii) the account holder's reference number, and

(iii) the date of opening or transfer of the account;

(*b*) for each account whose twelfth month of operation ends simultaneously with the end of the return period—

(i) the account holder's full name and date of birth,

(ii) the account holder's reference number,

(iii) a provisional calculation of the maturity payment, based on the qualifying balance achieved between the account's opening and the end of the return period, and

(iv) the balance of the account at the end of the return period (disregarding any interest or sums mentioned in section 8(3)(*a*) or (*b*) of the Act);

(*c*) for each account closed before the end of the account's maturity period other than due to the death of the account holder, the account holder's full name, date of birth and reference number, and the date of closure of the account;

(*d*) for each account so closed due to the death of the account holder—

(i) the account holder's full name and date of birth,

(ii) the account holder's reference number,

(iii) the date of death, and

(iv) the amount of the death payment made or due to be made;

(*e*) for each account whose maturity period ended at the end of the return period—

(i) the account holder's full name and date of birth,

(ii) the account holder's reference number,

(iii) the amount of the maturity payment credited or due to be credited to the account, and

(iv) the balance of the account at the end of the maturity period (disregarding any interest or sums mentioned in section 8(3)(*a*) or (*b*) of the Act);

or a statement, in each relevant case, that there were no items falling within the relevant category.

(6) The claim (where there is an item falling with paragraph (5)(*d*) or (*e*)) is a claim for payment of an amount equal to the aggregate of those maturity payments and death payments, as the case may be.

(7) Paragraph (5)(*a*) shall apply notwithstanding any transfer of the account to another provider under regulation 19, before the end of the return period in question.

(8) The Commissioners (subject to checking and if necessary correcting the amount of the claim) shall pay the account provider—

(*a*) where the return is made by the due date in paragraph (3), within 7 days of the due date, and

(*b*) where the return is made later than the due date, within 7 days of receipt of the return.

(9) Where the Commissioners require further information to verify a claim, the 7 days shall be calculated from the date on which the information is received.

23 Records to be kept by account provider

(1) An account provider shall during the period mentioned in paragraph (2) keep sufficient records to enable it to show that the requirements of the Act and of these Regulations have been satisfied.

(2) In particular, an account provider shall produce (when required to do so by an officer of Revenue and Customs)—

(*a*) any application made under regulation 13 (where an account has been opened);

(*b*) copies of account statements for an account, or notices given under regulation 12(6);

(*c*) working papers supporting the calculation of each amount returned under regulation 22(5)(*d*)(iv) or (*e*)(iii); and

(*d*) evidence of the date on which a maturity payment or death payment was made;

or electronic copies, within the period of 3 years from when the record was made, issued or given, or the account ceased to be a Saving Gateway account (whichever is later), notwithstanding any transfer of the account pursuant to regulation 19.

24 Information to be provided to the Commissioners

The Commissioners may by notice require any relevant person to furnish them, within such time (not being less than 14 days) as may be provided in the notice, such information about any account (including copies of or extracts from any books or other records) as they may reasonably require for the purposes of the Act or these Regulations.

25 Inspection of records by officer of Revenue and Customs

The Commissioners may by notice require any relevant person, within such time (not being less than 14 days) as may be provided in the notice, to make available for inspection at a place within the United Kingdom by an officer of Revenue and Customs authorised for that purpose all documents (including books and other records) in his possession or under his control relating to Saving Gateway accounts.

2009/2998

SAVING GATEWAY ACCOUNTS (NO 2) REGULATIONS 2009

Made by the Treasury under Saving Gateway Accounts Act 2009 s 14, 24(4) and 28(1), (2)

Made . . . . *11 November 2009*

Coming into force in accordance with . . . . *regulation 1*

1 Citation and commencement

These Regulations may be cited as the Saving Gateway Accounts (No 2) Regulations 2009 and shall come into force on the appointed day.

2 Interpretation

In these Regulations—

"account", except in regulations 5(1)(*d*) and (*e*) and 6, means a Saving Gateway account;

"the Act" means the Saving Gateway Accounts Act 2009;

"the appointed day" means the day appointed under section 31 of the Act, for the purposes of section 8 of the Act;

"building society bonus" excludes any bonus, distribution of funds or the conferring of rights in relation to shares—

(i) in connection with an amalgamation, transfer of engagements or transfer of business of a building society, and

(ii) mentioned in section 96 or 100 of the Building Societies Act 1986,

and "payment under a building society bonus scheme" shall be construed accordingly;

"interest" in regulation 3, where paid by a building society or credit union, includes a dividend paid by, and in respect of a share account held with, the society or credit union (and "dividend" includes any distribution, whether or not described as a dividend);

"the principal Regulations" means the Saving Gateway Accounts Regulations 2009;

other expressions defined in the principal Regulations have the same meanings as they have in those definitions.

3 Exemption from tax of account income, maturity payments and death payments

Subject to compliance with the principal Regulations (and in particular with regulation 11 of those Regulations)—

(*a*) no tax shall be chargeable on the account provider or his nominee, or on the account holder, in respect of—

(i) interest paid or credited in respect of an account;

(ii) profit share return from arrangements falling within section 49 of the Finance Act 2005, paid or credited by a financial institution (within the meanings in Chapter 5 of Part 2 of that Act), in respect of an account;

(iii) a payment under a building society bonus scheme, so far as the bonus is calculated by reference to an account (and if paid directly by the society into the account, the payment shall not count towards the payment limits in regulation 11 of the principal Regulations);

(*b*) any gain or loss accruing on and attributable to a maturity payment or death payment shall not be a chargeable gain or allowable loss for capital gains tax purposes; and

(*c*) income arising from an account shall not be regarded as income for any income tax purposes (including section 629 of ITTOIA 2005).

4 Tax liabilities and reliefs—account provider to act on behalf of account holder

An account provider may under these Regulations make tax claims, conduct appeals and agree on behalf of the account holder liabilities for and reliefs from tax in respect of an account.

5 Tax liabilities and reliefs—supplementary provisions

(1) Where—

(*a*) any relief or exemption from tax given in respect of income or gains under an account is found not to be due or to be excessive;

(*b*) the account holder was not an eligible person at the relevant date;

(*c*) a person was—

(i) entitled to a benefit under the terms of section 3(1)(*a*) of the Act, or

(ii) an eligible person by reason of entitlement to working tax credit or child tax credit under the terms of regulation 3 of the principal Regulations,

but such entitlement has been overturned, or it has subsequently been determined that payment of the relevant benefit or tax credit should not have been made, or should have been made at a different rate;

(*d*) an account does not comply with the requirements imposed by section 4(2)(*a*) and (*b*) of the Act, or by regulations 10 to 21 of the principal Regulations; or

(*e*) there is a breach of section 6(2)(*a*) or (*b*) of the Act in relation to an account;

the persons mentioned in paragraph (2) shall account to the Commissioners for any tax from which relief has been incorrectly given under regulation 3 in respect of an account.

(2) The persons mentioned in paragraph (1) are—

(*a*) the account provider (to the extent that it has assets relating to the account, or directly or indirectly representing the tax, in its possession or control);

(*b*) the account holder, or former account holder;

(*c*) any person in whom the money in the account, or any property directly or indirectly representing it, is vested (whether beneficially or otherwise);

and they shall be jointly and severally liable.

(3) The relevant provisions of Part 5 of the Management Act (within the meaning in section 48(3) of that Act) other than section 50 of that Act shall apply to tax appeals, with the necessary modifications mentioned in section 48(2)(*b*)(ii) of that Act.

6 Assessments for withdrawing relief and recovering tax

(1) Where—

(*a*) any relief or exemption from tax given in respect of income or gains under an account is found not to be due or to be excessive, or

(*b*) the full amount of tax in respect of the income or gains under an account has not otherwise been fully accounted for and paid to the Commissioners on behalf of the account holder,

an assessment to tax may be made by the Commissioners in the amount or further amount which in their opinion ought to be charged.

(2) An assessment to which paragraph (1) refers may be made on the account provider or on the account holder.

(3) If the assessment is made to recover tax in respect of income under an account it shall be made under section 369 of ITTOIA 2005.

2009/3001

OFFSHORE FUNDS (TAX) REGULATIONS 2009

Made by the Treasury under FA 2008 ss 41(1), 42

Made . . . . *12 November 2009*
Coming into force . . . . *1 December 2009*

PART 1
INTRODUCTION

Commentary—*Simon's Taxes* **B5.701**.

Preliminary provisions

1 Citation, commencement and effect

(1) These Regulations may be cited as the Offshore Funds (Tax) Regulations 2009 and shall come into force on 1st December 2009.

(2) These Regulations have effect—

(*a*) for the purposes of income tax—

(i) for the tax year 2009-10 and subsequent tax years, and

(ii) for distributions made on or after 1st December 2009;

(*b*) for the purposes of corporation tax—

(i) on income, for accounting periods ending on or after 1st December 2009 and for distributions made on or after that date, and

(ii) on chargeable gains, in relation to disposals made on or after 1st December 2009; and

(*c*) for the purposes of capital gains tax, in relation to disposals made on or after 1st December 2009.

(3) Paragraph (2) is subject to Schedule 1 to these Regulations (transitional provisions and savings).

Commentary—*Simon's Taxes* **B5.701, B5.702**.

2 Structure of these Regulations

The structure of these Regulations is as follows—

this Part contains introductory provisions;

Part 2 deals with the treatment of participants in non-reporting funds;

Part 3 deals with reporting funds and the treatment of participants in reporting funds;

[Part 3A deals with annual payments to non-resident participants;][1]

Part 4 makes consequential amendments to primary legislation.

Commentary—*Simon's Taxes* **B5.701, B5.702**.

Amendments—[1] Entry for "Part 3A" inserted by the Offshore Funds (Tax) (Amendment No 3) Regulations, SI 2013/1770 reg 2(2) with effect for the purposes of income tax for the tax year 2013–14 and subsequent tax years.

General provisions

3 Definition of "offshore fund"

(1) In these Regulations "offshore fund" has the meaning given by section 40A(2) of FA 2008 (read with the provisions of the relevant group of sections).

(2) Paragraph (1) does not apply to the use of the words "offshore fund" in the expression "material interest in an offshore fund".

Commentary—*Simon's Taxes* **B5.701, B5.702.**

4 Classification of offshore funds

(1) Offshore funds consist of—

(*a*) non-reporting funds (see Part 2 of these Regulations), and

(*b*) reporting funds (see Part 3 of these Regulations).

(2) [In a period of account][1] an offshore fund is a non-reporting fund unless it is a fund to which Part 3 of these Regulations applies . . . [1].

Commentary—*Simon's Taxes* **B5.705.**

Amendments—[1] In para (2), words inserted and words revoked, by the Offshore Funds (Tax) (Amendment) Regulations, SI 2011/1211 regs 2, 28 with effect as follows—

– for the purposes of income tax for distributions made, or treated as made, on or after 27 May 2011;

– for the purposes of corporation tax: on chargeable gains, in relation to disposals made on or after 27 May 2011; and for distributions made, or treated as made, on or after that date;

– for the purposes of capital gains tax, in relation to disposals made on or after 27 May 2011.

Treatment of umbrella arrangements and of funds comprising more than one class of interest

5 Treatment of umbrella arrangements

In these Regulations, in relation to an offshore fund constituted by a part of umbrella arrangements (within the meaning of section 40C of FA 2008)—

(*a*) a reference to the assets of an offshore fund is to such of the assets of the umbrella arrangements as under the arrangements form part of the separate pool to which that part of the umbrella arrangements relates;

(*b*) a reference to the income of an offshore fund is to the income arising from those assets; and

(*c*) a reference to a participant in an offshore fund is to a person for the time being owning an interest in that separate pool.

6 Treatment of funds comprising more than one class of interest

In these Regulations, in relation to an offshore fund constituted by a class of interest in the main arrangements (within the meaning of section 40D of FA 2008)—

(*a*) a reference to the assets of an offshore fund is to the assets of the main arrangements;

(*b*) a reference to the income of an offshore fund is to such of the income of the main fund as is attributable to interests of that class under the arrangements constituting the main arrangements; and

(*c*) a reference to a participant in an offshore fund is to a person for the time being owning an interest of that class.

Interpretation

7 Meaning of "participant"

In these Regulations references to a participant in a fund are to be read in accordance with section 40A(5) of FA 2008.

8 Meaning of "interest" (of a participant in an offshore fund)

(1) For the purposes of these Regulations the interest of a participant in an offshore fund is the investment held by a participant taking part in arrangements (or arrangements constituting a fund) to which the relevant group of sections applies.

(2) Paragraph (1) does not apply to the use of the word "interest" in the expression "material interest in an offshore fund".

9 Meaning of "guaranteed return fund"

(1) For the purposes of these Regulations an offshore fund is a guaranteed return fund if conditions A to C are met.

(2) Condition A is that the return on the shares or other interests in the fund is defined by reference to an index.

(3) Condition B is that the assets of the fund which are held to produce the return on the shares or other interests concerned cannot give rise to a return which, if it arose directly to an individual resident in the United Kingdom, would be chargeable to income tax.

(4) Condition C is that it is reasonable to assume that the main purpose, or one of the main purposes, of the arrangements constituting the offshore fund is or was the production for participants of a return that equates, in substance, to the return on an investment of money at interest.

10 Meaning of "market value"

(1) For the purposes of these Regulations the market value of any asset is to be determined in like manner as it would be determined for the purposes of TCGA 1992.

(2) But, in the case of an interest in an offshore fund for which there are separate published buying and selling prices, section 272(5) of that Act (meaning of "market value" in relation to rights of unit holders in a unit trust scheme) shall apply with any necessary modifications for determining the market value of the interest for the purposes of these Regulations.

11 Meaning of "transparent fund"

For the purposes of these Regulations a fund is a "transparent fund" if, in the case of holders of interests in the fund who are individuals resident in the United Kingdom, any sums which form part of the income of the fund are of such a nature that those holders—

(*a*) are chargeable to tax under a provision specified in section 830(2) of ITTOIA 2005 in respect of such of those sums as are referable to their interests, or

(*b*) if any of that income is derived from assets within the United Kingdom, would be so chargeable had the assets been outside the United Kingdom.

12 General interpretation

In these Regulations—

"HMRC" means Her Majesty's Revenue and Customs;

"period of account", in relation to an offshore fund, means any period for which accounts of the offshore fund are drawn up;

"proposed prospectus" includes—

(*a*) any document supplementing or amending the proposed prospectus, and

(*b*) any document fulfilling the same function as a proposed prospectus;

"prospectus" includes—

(*a*) any document supplementing or amending the prospectus, and

(*b*) any document fulfilling the same function as a prospectus;

["regulated market" has the same meaning as in Directive 2004/39/EC of the European Parliament and the Council on markets in financial instruments (see article 4.1(14));][1]

the "relevant group of sections" means sections 40A to 42A of FA 2008;

"tax year"—

(*a*) in relation to income tax, has the meaning given by section 4(2) of ITA 2007, and

(*b*) in relation to capital gains tax, has the meaning given by section 288(1ZA) of TCGA 1992;

"tribunal" means the First-tier Tribunal or, where determined by or under Tribunal Procedure Rules, the Upper Tribunal;

"UCITS fund" means a fund which is an undertaking for collective investments in transferable securities that is authorised by a European Union Member State in accordance with Article 4 of Council Directive 85/611/EEC.

Amendments—[1] Definition of "regulated market" inserted by the Offshore Funds (Tax) (Amendment) Regulations, SI 2011/1211 regs 2, 29 with effect as follows—

- for the purposes of income tax for distributions made, or treated as made, on or after 27 May 2011;
- for the purposes of corporation tax: on chargeable gains, in relation to disposals made on or after 27 May 2011; and for distributions made, or treated as made, on or after that date;
- for the purposes of capital gains tax, in relation to disposals made on or after 27 May 2011.

Transitional provisions etc

13 Transitional provisions and savings, repeals, abbreviations and general index

(1) Schedule 1 to these Regulations (which contains transitional provisions and savings) has effect.

(2) Schedule 2 to these Regulations (which contains repeals) has effect.

(3) The repeals contained in Schedule 2 have effect subject to the saving contained in paragraph 3(4) of Schedule 1.

(4) Schedule 3 to these Regulations (which contains abbreviations and defined expressions that apply for the purposes of these Regulations) has effect.

(5) Part 1 of Schedule 3 gives the meaning of the abbreviated references to Acts used in these Regulations.

(6) Part 2 of Schedule 3 lists the places where expressions used in these Regulations are defined or otherwise explained—

(*a*) in these Regulations for the purposes of these Regulations, or

(*b*) in these Regulations for the purposes of a Part or Chapter of these Regulations.

PART 2
THE TREATMENT OF PARTICIPANTS IN NON-REPORTING FUNDS

CHAPTER 1
PRELIMINARY PROVISIONS

14 Structure of this Part

The structure of this Part is as follows—

(*a*) this Chapter contains preliminary provisions;

(*b*) Chapter 2 deals with charges to tax on participants in non-reporting funds;

(*c*) Chapter 3 deals with exceptions from the charge to tax;

(*d*) Chapter 4 deals with disposals of interests in non-reporting funds;
(*e*) Chapter 5 deals with offshore income gains and the computation of offshore income gains;
(*f*) Chapter 6 deals with the deduction of offshore income gains in computing chargeable gains;
(*g*) Chapter 7 deals with the conversion of a non-reporting fund into a reporting fund.

15 Meaning of "material disposal"

In these Regulations a "material disposal" means a disposal to which this Part applies.

CHAPTER 2

CHARGES TO TAX ON PARTICIPANTS IN NON-REPORTING FUNDS

Charge to tax on certain amounts treated as distributions

16 Treatment of certain amounts as distributions

(1) This regulation applies if a non-reporting fund which is a transparent fund has an interest in a reporting fund.
(2) In the case of any excess specified in regulation [94(1) or (2)][1] which is treated, under that regulation, as made to the non-reporting fund, the Tax Acts have effect as if the excess were additional income of the participants in the non-reporting fund in proportion to their rights.
(3) The additional income is treated as arising on the same date as the excess is treated as made to the non-reporting fund.
(4) If a participant in the non-reporting fund is chargeable to income tax, the additional income is charged as relevant foreign income within the meaning given by section 830 of ITTOIA 2005.
(5) If a participant in the non-reporting fund is chargeable to corporation tax, the additional income is charged under Chapter 8 of Part 10 of CTA 2009 (miscellaneous income: income not otherwise charged).

Commentary—*Simon's Taxes* **B5.705**.

Amendments—[1] In para (2), words substituted, by the Offshore Funds (Tax) (Amendment) Regulations, SI 2011/1211 regs 2, 30 with effect as follows—

– for the purposes of income tax for distributions made, or treated as made, on or after 27 May 2011;
– for the purposes of corporation tax: on chargeable gains, in relation to disposals made on or after 27 May 2011; and for distributions made, or treated as made, on or after that date;
– for the purposes of capital gains tax, in relation to disposals made on or after 27 May 2011.

Charge to tax on disposal of asset

17 The charge to tax

(1) There is a charge to tax if—
(*a*) a person disposes of an asset,
(*b*) either condition A or condition B is met, and
(*c*) as a result of the disposal, an offshore income gain arises to the person making the disposal.
(2) Condition A is that the asset is an interest in a non-reporting fund at the time of the disposal.
(3) Condition B is that—
(*a*) the asset is an interest in a reporting fund at the time of the disposal,
(*b*) the reporting fund was previously a non-reporting fund (becoming a reporting fund as the result of an application under regulation 52),
(*c*) the interest was an interest in a non-reporting fund during some or all of the material period,
(*d*) an election under regulation 48 was not prevented by paragraph (5) of that regulation, and
(*e*) no election has been made under regulation 48(2).
[(3A) Where the asset is an interest in a reporting fund acquired in consequence of an arrangement to which section 135 (exchange of securities for those in another company treated as not involving a disposal) or section 136 (scheme of reconstruction involving issue of securities treated as exchange not involving a disposal) of TCGA 1992 applied, the reporting fund referred to in sub-paragraph (*b*) of condition B is the fund that was company A for the purposes of either of those sections and the interest referred to in sub-paragraph (*c*) of condition B is the interest in that fund.][1]
(4) For the purposes of paragraph (3)(*c*) the "material period" means a period beginning with the day on which consideration was given for the acquisition of the asset or on 1st January 1984 (whichever is the later) and ending with the day on which the fund became a reporting fund.
[(4A) For the purposes of paragraph (4), where the asset was acquired on the vesting of variable remuneration represented by profit allocated under section 863I of ITTOIA 2005 (allocation of profit to the AIFM firm), the date on which the variable remuneration was awarded is treated as the date on which consideration was given for the acquisition of the asset.
(4B) Terms used in paragraph (4A) which are also used in section 863I of ITTOIA 2005 have the same meaning as in that section.][2]
(5) Chapter 5 of this Part deals with offshore income gains and the computation of offshore income gains.

Commentary—*Simon's Taxes* **B5.705**.

Amendments—[1] Para (3A) inserted by the Offshore Funds (Tax) (Amendment) Regulations, SI 2013/661 reg 2 with effect in relation to disposals made on or after 3pm on 20 March 2013.

[2] Paras (4A), (4B) inserted by the Offshore Funds (Tax) (Amendment) Regulations, SI 2014/931 reg 2(1), (2) with effect in relation to disposals made on or after 12 August 2014..

18 The charge to tax: further provisions

(1) The offshore income gain arising is treated for all the purposes of the Tax Acts as income which arises at the time of the disposal to the person making the disposal (or treated as making the disposal).

(2) The tax is charged on the person making the disposal (or treated as making the disposal).

(3) In the case of a person chargeable to income tax, tax is charged under Chapter 8 of Part 5 of ITTOIA 2005 (miscellaneous income: income not otherwise charged) for the year of assessment in which the disposal is made, but sections 688(1) and 689 of ITTOIA 2005 (income charged and person liable) do not apply.

(4) In the case of a person chargeable to corporation tax, tax is charged under Chapter 8 of Part 10 of CTA 2009 (miscellaneous income: income not otherwise charged) for the accounting period in which the disposal is made.

(5) Paragraph (1) is subject to—

(*a*) regulation 19 (income treated as arising under regulation 17: remittance basis);

(*b*) regulation 20(1) (offshore income gain arising to non-resident trustees not treated as income of settlor);

(*c*) regulation 20(5) (application to gains of non-resident settlements);

(*d*) regulation 24(6) (application of section 13 of TCGA 1992).

[(6) Nothing in regulation 17 of these Regulations applies to—

(*a*) an authorised investment fund to which regulation 14ZB[, 14ZD(1)][1] or Part 6A of the Authorised Investment Fund (Tax) Regulations 2006 applies, . . . [3]

(*b*) an investment trust company to which regulation 43 or 45 of the Investment Trust (Approved Company) (Tax) Regulations 2011 apply[, or[3].][2]

"(*c*) the trustees of an exempt unauthorised unit trust to which regulations 22 or 23 of the Unauthorised Unit Trusts (Tax) Regulations 2013 applies.][3]

Commentary—*Simon's Taxes* **B5.705**.

Amendments—[1] In para (6), words inserted by the Authorised Investment Funds (Tax) (Amendment No 2) Regulations, SI 2011/2192 reg 7 with effect as follows—

– for the purposes of corporation tax:
  (a) on income, for accounting periods starting on or after 1 October 2011, and
  (b) on chargeable gains, in relation to disposals made on or after 1 October 2011, and
– for the purposes of capital gains tax, in relation to disposals made on or after 1 October 2011.

[2] Para (6) substituted by the Investment Trust (Approved Company) (Tax) Regulations, SI 2011/2999 reg 46 with effect in relation to disposals made on or after 1 January 2012.

[3] In para (6)(*a*), word "or" revoked, and sub-para (6)(*c*) and preceding word inserted, by the Unauthorised Unit Trusts (Tax) Regulations, SI 2013/2819 reg 43 with effect from 6 April 2014. Note that an unauthorised unit trust is not a non-exempt unauthorised unit trust, and these amendments do not apply in relation to the trust, if at all times in the period beginning with 24 May 2012 and ending with 5 April 2014 it had at least one unit holder which was, and at least one unit holder which was not, an eligible investor (ie a mixed unauthorised unit trust); this ceases to apply in relation to the trust if subsequently it no longer has any unit holders which are eligible investors (SI 2013/2819 reg 32).

19 Income treated as arising under regulation 17: remittance basis

(1) This regulation applies to income treated as arising under regulation 17 to an individual in a tax year if—

(*a*) section 809B, 809D or 809E of ITA 2007 (remittance basis) applies to the individual for that year, and

(*b*) the individual is not domiciled in the United Kingdom in that year.

(2) The income is treated as relevant foreign income of the individual.

(3) For the purposes of Chapter A1 of Part 14 of ITA 2007 (remittance basis)—

(*a*) any consideration obtained on the disposal of the asset is treated as deriving from the income, and

(*b*) unless the consideration so obtained is of an amount equal to or exceeding the market value of the asset, the asset is treated as deriving from the income.

(4) In paragraph (3)—

(*a*) "the asset" means the asset the disposal of which causes the income to be treated as arising, and

(*b*) "the disposal" means the disposal mentioned in sub-paragraph (*a*) of that paragraph.

(5) This regulation does not apply for the purposes of regulation 20.

Commentary—*Simon's Taxes* **B5.705**.

Offshore funds and gains of non-resident settlements

20 Application to gains of non-resident settlements

(1) If an offshore income gain arises to a settlement in a tax year and the trustees of the settlement are [not][1] resident in the United Kingdom in the tax year, the gain is not regarded as income for the purposes of Chapter 5 of Part 5 of ITTOIA 2005 (settlements: amounts treated as income of settlor).

(2) If—

(*a*) offshore income gains arise to the trustees of a settlement in a tax year, and

(*b*) section 87 of TCGA 1992 (gains of non-resident settlements) applies to the settlement for that year,

the OIG amount for the settlement for that year is the amount of the offshore income gains.

(3) Sections 12, 87 to 90A and 96 to 98 of, and Schedule 4C to, TCGA 1992 apply in relation to OIG amounts as if—

(*a*) references to section 2(2) amounts (except those in paragraph 7B(2)(*b*) and (4) of Schedule 4C) were to OIG amounts,

(*b*) references to chargeable gains (except the one in paragraph 1(5) of Schedule 4C) were to offshore income gains,

(*c*) references to anything accruing were to it arising (and similar references, except the one in paragraph 1(5) of Schedule 4C, were read accordingly),

(*d*) sections 87(4), 88(2) to (5) and 97(6) and paragraphs 1(3A), 3 to 7 and 12 of Schedule 4C were omitted, and

(*e*) regulation 21 did not apply.

(4) Section 87A of TCGA 1992 applies for a tax year by virtue of paragraph (3) before it applies for that year otherwise than by virtue of that paragraph.

(5) If this regulation applies, the person to whom the offshore income gain arises is treated as the person making the disposal.

Commentary—*Simon's Taxes* **B5.705**.

Amendments—[1] In para (1), word substituted for words "neither resident nor ordinarily" by the Income Tax (Removal of Ordinary Residence) Regulations, SI 2013/605 reg 7(1), (2) with effect for the purposes of a person's liability to income tax for the tax year 2013–14 or any subsequent tax years.

Offshore funds and the transfer of assets abroad

21 Application of transfer of assets abroad provisions

(1) Chapter 2 of Part 13 of ITA 2007 (transfer of assets abroad) applies in relation to an offshore income gain arising to a person resident or domiciled outside the United Kingdom as if the offshore income gain were income becoming payable to the person.

(2) Income treated as arising under that Chapter by virtue of paragraph (1) is regarded as "foreign" for the purposes of section 726, 730 or 735 of that Act.

(3) Paragraph (1) does not apply in relation to an offshore income gain if (and to the extent that) it is treated, by virtue of regulation 24, as arising to a person resident . . . [1] in the United Kingdom.

(4) The following provisions apply if regulation 20 applies in relation to an offshore income gain (the "relevant offshore income gain").

(5) If—

(*a*) by virtue of regulation 20 an offshore income gain is treated as arising in a tax year to a person resident . . . [1] in the United Kingdom, and

(*b*) it is so treated by reason of the relevant offshore income gain (or part of it),

for that and subsequent tax years paragraph (1) does not apply in relation to the relevant offshore income gain (or that part).

(6) If, by virtue of paragraph (1) as it applies in relation to the relevant offshore income gain, income is treated under Chapter 2 of Part 13 of ITA 2007 as arising in a tax year, the OIG amount in question must be reduced (with effect from the following tax year) by the amount of the income.

Commentary—*Simon's Taxes* **B5.705**.

Amendments—[1] In paras (3), (5)(*a*), words "or ordinarily resident" revoked by the Income Tax (Removal of Ordinary Residence) Regulations, SI 2013/605 reg 7(1), (3) with effect for the purposes of a person's liability to income tax for the tax year 2013–14 or any subsequent tax years.

Application of TCGA 1992

22 Application of certain provisions of TCGA 1992

(1) The following enactments have effect in relation to income tax or corporation tax in respect of offshore income gains as they have effect in relation to capital gains tax or corporation tax in respect of chargeable gains—

(*a*) section 2(1) of TCGA 1992 (persons chargeable to capital gains tax);

(*b*) section 10 of TCGA 1992 (non-resident with a United Kingdom branch or agency);

(*c*) section 10B of TCGA 1992 (non-resident company with United Kingdom permanent establishment).

(2) Paragraph (1) is subject to paragraphs (3) and (4).

(3) In the application of section 10 of TCGA 1992 in accordance with paragraph (1), paragraphs (*a*) and (*b*) of subsection (1) (assets on the disposal of which chargeable gains are taxable) have effect with the omission of the words "situated in the United Kingdom and".

(4) In the application of section 10B of TCGA 1992 in accordance with paragraph (1), paragraphs (*a*) and (*b*) of subsection (1) (assets on the disposal of which chargeable profits arise for the purposes of corporation tax) have effect with the omission of the words "situated in the United Kingdom and".

Commentary—*Simon's Taxes* **B5.705**.

[23 Temporary non-residents

(1) This regulation applies where an individual ("the taxpayer") is temporarily non-resident.

(2) The taxpayer is chargeable to income tax as if offshore income gains within paragraph (3) were offshore income gains arising to the taxpayer in the period of return.

(3) The offshore income gains within this paragraph are those that—

(*a*) arise to the taxpayer in the temporary period of non-residence, and

(*b*) would be treated under section 13 of TCGA 1992 (attribution of gains to members of non-resident companies) as it applies to offshore income gains by virtue of regulation 24 as having arisen to the taxpayer in that period if the residence assumption were made.

(4) The residence assumption is—

(*a*) that the taxpayer had been resident in the United Kingdom for the tax year in which the offshore income gain arose to the company, or

(*b*) if that tax year was a split year as respects the taxpayer, that offshore income gain had arisen to the company in the UK part of it.

(5) But a gain is not within paragraph (3) if, ignoring this regulation, the taxpayer is chargeable to income tax in respect of it (and could not cease to be so chargeable by making a claim under section 6 of the Taxation (International and Other Provisions) Act 2010).

(6) Paragraph (2) is subject to regulation 23A.

(7) If section 809B, 809D or 809E of ITA 2007 (remittance basis) applies to the taxpayer for the year of return, any offshore income gains to which regulation 19(2) applies falling within paragraph (3) of this regulation by virtue of sub-paragraph (a) of that paragraph that were remitted to the United Kingdom at any time in the temporary period of non-residence are to be treated as remitted to the United Kingdom in the period of return.

(8) In this regulation—

(*a*) "remitted to the United Kingdom" has the same meaning as in Chapter A1 of Part 14 of ITA 2007,

(*b*) "split year" has the meaning given in paragraph 43 of Schedule 45 to the Finance Act 2013,

(*c*) "temporarily non-resident" has the meaning given in paragraph 110 of that Schedule,

(*d*) "the UK part" of a split year has the meaning given in paragraph 56 of that Schedule.

(9) In this regulation and regulation 23A—

(*a*) "period of return" has the meaning given in paragraph 115 of Schedule 45 to the Finance Act 2013,

(*b*) "temporary period of non-residence" has the meaning given in paragraph 113 of that Schedule, and

(*c*) "the year of return" has the meaning given in section 10A(11) of TCGA 1992.][1]

Commentary—*Simon's Taxes* **B5.705**.

Amendments—[1] Regulations 23, 23A substituted for previous reg 23 by the Temporary Non-Residence (Miscellaneous Amendments) Regulations, SI 2013/1810 reg 4 with effect for the purposes of income tax for the tax year 2013–14 and subsequent tax years.

[23A Regulation 23: supplementary

(1) Regulation 23(2) does not apply to an offshore income gain accruing on the disposal by the taxpayer of an asset if—

(*a*) the asset was acquired by the taxpayer in the temporary period of non-residence,

(*b*) it was so acquired otherwise than by means of a relevant disposal that by virtue of section 58, 73 or 258(4) TCGA 1992 is treated as having been a disposal on which neither a gain nor a loss accrued, and

(*c*) the asset is not an interest created by or arising under a settlement.

(2) Nothing in any double taxation relief arrangements is to be read as preventing the taxpayer from being chargeable to income tax in respect of any offshore income gains treated under regulation 23 as accruing to the taxpayer in the period of return (or as preventing a charge to that tax from arising as a result).

(3) Nothing in any enactment imposing any limit on the time within which an assessment to income tax may be made prevents any assessment for the year of departure from being made in the taxpayer's case at any time before the end of the second anniversary of the 31 January next following the year of return.

(4) In this regulation—

(*a*) "relevant disposal" has the meaning given in section 10AA(2) of TCGA 1992, and (*b*) "the year of departure" has the meaning given in paragraph 114 of Schedule 45 to the Finance Act 2013.][1]

Amendments—[1] Regulations 23, 23A substituted for previous reg 23 by the Temporary Non-Residence (Miscellaneous Amendments) Regulations, SI 2013/1810 reg 4 with effect for the purposes of income tax for the tax year 2013–14 and subsequent tax years.

24 Application of section 13 of TCGA 1992

(1) Section 13 of TCGA 1992 (chargeable gains accruing to certain non-resident companies) applies for the purposes of this Part with the following modifications.

(2) The section applies as if—

(*a*) for any reference to a chargeable gain there were substituted a reference to an offshore income gain; and

(*b*) for any reference to anything accruing there were substituted a reference to it arising (with similar references being read accordingly).

(3) The section applies as if, in subsection (5), paragraphs (*b*) and (*c*) were omitted.

(4) The section applies as if, in subsection (7), for the reference to capital gains tax there were substituted a reference to income tax or corporation tax.

(5) The section applies as if subsection (8) were omitted.

(6) If this regulation applies, the person to whom the offshore income gain arises is treated as the person making the disposal.

(7) To the extent that an offshore income gain is treated, by virtue of this regulation, as having accrued to any person resident . . . [1] in the United Kingdom, that gain shall not be deemed to be the income of any individual for the purposes of Chapter 2 of Part 13 of ITA 2007 (transfer of assets abroad).

Commentary—*Simon's Taxes* **B5.705**.

Amendments—[1] In para (7), words "or ordinarily resident" revoked by the Income Tax (Removal of Ordinary Residence) Regulations, SI 2013/605 reg 7(1), (4) with effect for the purposes of a person's liability to income tax for the tax year 2013–14 or any subsequent tax years.

CHAPTER 3

EXCEPTIONS ETC FROM THE CHARGE TO TAX

25 Exceptions from the charge

(1) No liability to tax arises under regulation 17 if any of conditions A to E is met.

(2) Condition A is that the participant is required to treat the interest in the fund as a loan relationship under Chapter 3 of Part 6 of CTA 2009.

(3) Condition B is that the participant is required to treat the interest in the fund as a derivative contract to which the provisions of Part 7 of CTA 2009 apply.

(4) Condition C is that the asset is an intangible fixed asset to which the provisions of Part 8 of CTA 2009 apply.

(5) Condition D is that the asset consists of excluded indexed securities as defined in section 433 of ITTOIA 2005.

(6) Condition E is that the asset is a right arising under a policy of insurance.

Commentary—*Simon's Taxes* **B5.706**.

26 Trading stock etc

(1) No liability to tax arises under regulation 17 if condition A or B is met.

(2) Condition A is that the interest in the fund is held as trading stock.

(3) Condition B is that the disposal of the interest is taken into account in computing the profits of a trade.

Commentary—*Simon's Taxes* **B5.706**.

27 Long-term insurance funds of insurance companies

(1) No liability to tax arises under regulation 17 in respect of disposals of assets of an insurance company's long-term insurance fund.

(2) In paragraph (1) "insurance company" and "long-term insurance fund" have the same meaning as in section 431(2) of ICTA.

Commentary—*Simon's Taxes* **B5.706**.

28 Loans other than participating loans

(1) No liability to tax arises under regulation 17 if the asset is a loan which is not a participating loan.

(2) For the purposes of paragraph (1) a "participating loan" means a loan where the amount payable on redemption exceeds the issue price by an amount which is determined in whole or in part by reference to the income of the non-reporting fund.

Commentary—*Simon's Taxes* **B5.706**.

29 Interests in transparent funds

(1) No liability to tax arises under regulation 17 if—

(*a*) the disposal is the disposal of an interest in an offshore fund falling within paragraph (*b*) or (*c*) of section 40A(2) of FA 2008, and

(*b*) the fund is a transparent fund.

This is subject to paragraphs (2) and (3).

(2) But there is a charge to tax under regulation 17 if—

(*a*) there is a disposal of an interest in a transparent fund, and

(*b*) during a period beginning with the date the interest (or any part of it) was acquired and ending with the date of the disposal, the offshore fund has at any time held interests in other non-reporting funds which amounted in total to more than 5% by value of the offshore fund's assets.

(3) And there is a charge to tax under regulation 17 if—

(*a*) there is a disposal of an interest in a transparent fund,

(*b*) the fund is a non-reporting fund, and

(*c*) the fund fails to make sufficient information available to participants in the fund to enable those participants to meet their tax obligations in the United Kingdom with respect to their shares of the income of the fund.

(4) If, on the disposal by an offshore fund of an interest in another non-reporting fund, no liability would arise under regulation 17 by virtue of this regulation, that interest is not taken into account for the purposes of paragraph (2)(*b*).

Commentary—*Simon's Taxes* **B5.706**.

30 Rights in certain existing holdings

(1) No liability to tax arises under regulation 17 in respect of any rights in an offshore fund to which this regulation applies if the rights are acquired by a person—

(*a*) before 1st December 2009, or

(*b*) in accordance with paragraph (2).

(2) Rights are acquired in accordance with this paragraph if—

(*a*) the rights are acquired by the participant in accordance with a legally enforceable agreement in writing that was entered into by the participant before 30th April 2009,

(*b*) in the case of an agreement which was conditional, the conditions are met before that date, and

(*c*) the agreement is not varied on or after that date.

(3) Rights of a person in a fund are rights in an offshore fund to which this regulation applies if, on the date on which the person acquired the rights, those rights did not constitute a material interest in an offshore fund within the meaning of that expression given by section 759 of ICTA.

Commentary—*Simon's Taxes* **B5.706**.

31 Charitable companies and charitable trusts

(1) A charitable company shall be exempt from corporation tax in respect of an offshore income gain if the gain is applicable and applied for charitable purposes.

(2) See section 535 of ITA 2007 for an exemption for income tax purposes for offshore income gains accruing to a charitable trust.

(3) Paragraphs (4) and (5) apply if—

(*a*) property held on charitable trusts ceases to be subject to charitable trusts, and

(*b*) that property represents directly or indirectly an offshore income gain.

(4) The trustees are treated as if they had disposed of and immediately reacquired that property for a consideration equal to its market value.

(5) An offshore income gain accruing on the disposal arising under paragraph (4) is treated as an offshore income gain not accruing to a charity.

(6) In this regulation "charity" and "charitable company" have the same meaning as in section 506 of ICTA.

Commentary—*Simon's Taxes* **B5.706**.

[31A Unlisted trading company exception

(1) No liability to tax arises under regulation 17 if conditions A to D are met.

(2) Condition A is that the disposal is a disposal of an interest in an offshore fund.

(3) Condition B is that the sole or main purpose of the fund is to invest in qualifying companies.

(4) Condition C is that throughout the period starting with the date on which the interest was acquired and ending 12 months before the date of the disposal the fund met the investment condition. This is subject to paragraph (6).

(5) Condition D is that participants in the fund have access to, and are able to obtain copies of, sufficient information to demonstrate that the fund intends to dispose of any holdings of shares or securities within regulation 31B(1)(*b*) or (*d*).

(6) Condition C is treated as met in relation to the period—

(*a*) starting at the beginning of the first period of account of the fund, and (*b*) ending on the earlier of—

(i) the expiry of 3 months, and

(ii) the date the fund meets the investment condition,

if the only asset of the fund during that period is cash.

(7) For the purposes of this regulation and regulation 31B—

"cash" means cash deposited in a bank account or similar account, but not cash acquired wholly or partly for the purpose of realising a gain on its disposal;

"qualifying company" means a trading company or the holding company of a trading group or a trading subgroup, where—

(*a*) the shares of the company are not listed on a recognised stock exchange or admitted to trading on a regulated market, and

(*b*) the activities of the trading company or, in the case of a holding company, the activities of the members of the group or subgroup taken together, do not include to a substantial extent the carrying out of investment transactions undertaken in the course of a trade.

(8) In paragraph (7) in the definition of "qualifying company", "holding company", "trading company", "trading group" and "trading subgroup" have the same meanings as in Schedule 7AC to TCGA 1992 (see paragraphs 20 to 24 and 26 and 27 of that Schedule).][1]

Commentary—*Simon's Taxes* **B5.706**.

Amendments—[1] Regs31A–31C inserted by the Offshore Funds (Tax) (Amendment) Regulations, SI 2011/1211 regs 2, 19 with effect as follows—

- for the purposes of income tax for distributions made, or treated as made, on or after 27 May 2011;
- for the purposes of corporation tax: on chargeable gains, in relation to disposals made on or after 27 May 2011; and for distributions made, or treated as made, on or after that date;
- for the purposes of capital gains tax, in relation to disposals made on or after 27 May 2011.

[31B Unlisted trading company exception: the investment condition

(1) The investment condition is that at least 90% of the value of the assets of the fund consists of—

(*a*) direct or indirect holdings in qualifying companies,

(*b*) holdings of shares or securities listed on a recognised stock exchange or admitted to trading on a regulated market which the fund intends to dispose of as soon as reasonably practicable, taking into account market conditions and commercial and contractual constraints, and which—

(i) were acquired by the fund in exchange for shares or securities in a qualifying company, or

(ii) were shares in a qualifying company at the time of their acquisition by the fund,

(*c*) holdings of shares or securities listed on a recognised stock exchange or admitted to trading on a regulated market, which are holdings in a company that would be a qualifying company if it were not so listed or admitted, where it is reasonable to believe that the shares or securities will cease to be so listed or admitted within 12 months,

(*d*) shares or securities which have ceased to be within sub-paragraph (*c*) because it is no longer reasonable to believe that they will cease to be listed or admitted, which the fund intends to dispose of as soon as reasonably practicable taking into account market conditions and commercial and contractual constraints.

(2) For the purposes of the investment condition—

(*a*) any holding of cash shall be disregarded, and

(*b*) a holding in a qualifying company is held indirectly if it is held by a corporate body which is a 51% subsidiary of the fund.

(3) For the purposes of paragraph (2) section 1154 of CTA 2010 applies to determine whether a corporate body is a 51% subsidiary of a fund.][1]

Commentary—*Simon's Taxes* **B5.706**.

Amendments—[1] Regs31A–31C inserted by the Offshore Funds (Tax) (Amendment) Regulations, SI 2011/1211 regs 2, 19 with effect as follows—

- for the purposes of income tax for distributions made, or treated as made, on or after 27 May 2011;
- for the purposes of corporation tax: on chargeable gains, in relation to disposals made on or after 27 May 2011; and for distributions made, or treated as made, on or after that date;
- for the purposes of capital gains tax, in relation to disposals made on or after 27 May 2011.

[31C Unlisted trading company exception: further provision

No liability to tax arises under regulation 17 if—

(*a*) the disposal is of an interest in an offshore fund whose business consists solely of holding an interest in another offshore fund ("X"), and

(*b*) conditions B to D of regulation 31A apply in relation to X.][1]

Commentary—*Simon's Taxes* **B5.706**.

Amendments—[1] Regs31A–31C inserted by the Offshore Funds (Tax) (Amendment) Regulations, SI 2011/1211 regs 2, 19 with effect as follows—

- for the purposes of income tax for distributions made, or treated as made, on or after 27 May 2011;

- for the purposes of corporation tax: on chargeable gains, in relation to disposals made on or after 27 May 2011; and for distributions made, or treated as made, on or after that date;
- for the purposes of capital gains tax, in relation to disposals made on or after 27 May 2011.

CHAPTER 4

DISPOSALS OF INTERESTS IN NON-REPORTING FUNDS

Basic provisions

32 Application of this Chapter

This Chapter applies if a participant disposes of an asset and at the time of the disposal—

(*a*) the asset is an interest in a non-reporting fund, or

(*b*) the asset is an interest in a reporting fund and the requirements specified in paragraph (3) of regulation 17 (read, as appropriate, with paragraphs (4) and (5) of that regulation) are met.

33 Disposal of an asset: the basic rule

(1) There is a disposal of an asset for the purposes of these Regulations if there would be a disposal of an asset for the purposes of TCGA 1992.

(2) Paragraph (1) is subject to the following provisions of this Chapter.

Further provisions

34 Provisions applicable on death

(1) Notwithstanding anything in paragraph (*b*) of subsection (1) of section 62 of TCGA 1992 (general provisions applicable on death: no deemed disposal by the deceased), where a person dies and the assets of which the deceased was competent to dispose at the time of death include an interest in a non-reporting fund, then, for the purposes of these Regulations—

(*a*) immediately before the acquisition referred to in paragraph (*a*) of that subsection, that interest shall be deemed to be disposed of by the deceased for such a consideration as is mentioned in that subsection; but

(*b*) nothing in this regulation affects the determination, in accordance with regulation 32, of the question whether that deemed disposal is one to which this Chapter applies.

(2) Subject to paragraph (1), section 62 of TCGA 1992 applies for the purposes of these Regulations as it applies for the purposes of that Act, and the reference in that paragraph to the assets of which a deceased person was competent to dispose are to be construed in accordance with subsection (10) of that section.

Commentary—*Simon's Taxes* **B5.707**.

35 Application of section 135 of TCGA 1992

(1) Section 135 of TCGA 1992 (exchange of securities for those in another company treated as not involving a disposal) does not apply for the purposes of this Part to the extent that—

(*a*) *the interest in the entity that is company A for the purposes of that section that is exchanged is an interest in a non-reporting fund, and*

(*b*) *the interest in the entity that is company B for those purposes that is exchanged is not an interest in such a fund.*

(2) In a case where section 135 of TCGA 1992 would apply apart from paragraph (1), the exchange in question shall for the purposes of this Part constitute a disposal of interests in the non-reporting fund for a consideration equal to their market value at the time of the exchange.[1]

Commentary—*Simon's Taxes* **B5.707**.

Amendments—[1] Reg 36A substituted for previous regs 35, 36 by the Collective Investment Schemes (Tax Transparent Funds, Exchanges, Mergers and Schemes of Reconstruction) Regulations, SI 2013/1400 reg 15(*a*) with effect from 8 June 2013.

36 Application of section 136 of TCGA 1992

(1) Section 136 of TCGA 1992 (scheme of reconstruction involving issue of securities treated as exchange not involving disposal) does not apply for the purposes of this Part to the extent that—

(*a*) *the interest in the entity that is company A for the purposes of that section that is exchanged is an interest in a non-reporting fund, and*

(*b*) *the interest in the entity that is company B for those purposes that is exchanged is not an interest in such a fund.*

(2) In a case where section 136 of TCGA 1992 would apply apart from paragraph (1), the deemed exchange in question shall for the purposes of this Part constitute a disposal of interests in the non-reporting fund for a consideration equal to their market value at the time of the deemed exchange.[1]

Commentary—*Simon's Taxes* **B5.707**.

Amendments—[1] Reg 36A substituted for previous regs 35, 36 by the Collective Investment Schemes (Tax Transparent Funds, Exchanges, Mergers and Schemes of Reconstruction) Regulations, SI 2013/1400 reg 15(*a*) with effect from 8 June 2013.

[36A (1) The following sections of TCGA 1992 do not apply to the extent that an interest in a non-reporting fund is exchanged or treated as exchanged for an asset which is not an interest in a non-reporting fund.

(2) The sections are—

(a) section 103G (exchange of units for those in another collective investment scheme),

(b) section 103H (scheme of reconstruction involving issue of units),

(c) section 135 (exchange of securities for those in another company), and

(d) section 136 (scheme of reconstruction involving issue of securities).

(3) In a case where one of those sections would apply apart from paragraph (1), the exchange or deemed exchange shall for the purposes of this Part constitute a disposal of interests in the non-reporting fund for a consideration equal to their market value at the time of the exchange or deemed exchange.][1]

Amendments—[1] Reg 36A substituted for previous regs 35, 36 by the Collective Investment Schemes (Tax Transparent Funds, Exchanges, Mergers and Schemes of Reconstruction) Regulations, SI 2013/1400 reg 15(*a*) with effect from 8 June 2013.

37 Exchange of interests of different classes

(1) If conditions A to D are met, section 127 of TCGA 1992 (equation of original shares and new holding) does not prevent an exchange from constituting a disposal for the purposes of these Regulations.

(2) Condition A is that an offshore fund is constituted by a class of interest ("class A") in main arrangements.

(3) Condition B is that a participant exchanges an interest of class A for an interest in another offshore fund constituted by a different class of interest ("class B") in those main arrangements.

(4) Condition C is that the interest of class A is at the time of the exchange an interest in a non-reporting fund.

(5) Condition D is that the interest of class B is at the time of the exchange an interest which is not an interest in a non-reporting fund.

(6) Any disposal to which this regulation applies is to be treated as a disposal for a consideration equal to the market value of the rights at the time of the exchange.

Commentary—*Simon's Taxes* **B5.707**.

CHAPTER 5

OFFSHORE INCOME GAINS AND THE COMPUTATION OF OFFSHORE INCOME GAINS

38 General provisions

(1) An offshore income gain arises to a person on the disposal of an asset if a basic gain arises on the disposal.

(2) The disposal gives rise to an offshore income gain of an amount equal to the basic gain on the disposal.

(3) The following provisions of this Chapter explain how the basic gain is computed.

39 The basic gain and its computation

(1) In the case of a participant chargeable to income tax, the basic gain is a gain of the amount which would be the gain on that disposal for the purposes of TCGA 1992 if the gain were computed without regard to any charge to income tax arising under this Part.

(2) In the case of a participant chargeable to corporation tax, the basic gain is a gain of the amount which would be the gain on that disposal for the purposes of TCGA 1992 if the gain were computed—

(*a*) without regard to any charge to corporation tax arising under this Part, and

(*b*) without regard to any indexation allowance on the disposal under TCGA 1992.

(3) The computation of the basic gain is subject to—

(*a*) regulation 34 (provisions applicable on death);

[(*aa*) regulation 36A (exchanges and schemes of reconstruction);][1]

(*d*) regulation 37 (exchange of interests of different classes;

(*e*) regulation 40 (earlier disposal to which the no gain/no loss basis applies);

(*f*) regulation 41 (modifications of TCGA 1992);

(*g*) regulation 42 (losses);

(*h*) regulation 43 (special rules for certain existing holdings).

Commentary—*Simon's Taxes* **B5.708**.

Amendments—[1] Para (3)(*aa*) substituted for previous para (3)(*b*), (*c*) by the Collective Investment Schemes (Tax Transparent Funds, Exchanges, Mergers and Schemes of Reconstruction) Regulations, SI 2013/1400 reg 15(*b*) with effect from 8 June 2013.

40 Earlier disposal to which the no gain/no loss basis applies

(1) This regulation applies if—

(*a*) a participant is chargeable to corporation tax, and

(*b*) the amount of any chargeable gain or allowable loss which would arise on the disposal would fall to be computed in a way which, in whole or in part, would take account of the indexation allowance on an earlier disposal to which section 56(2) of TCGA 1992 (disposals on a no gain/no loss basis) applies.

(2) The basic gain on the disposal is computed as if—

(*a*) no indexation allowance had been available on any such earlier disposal, and

(*b*) subject to that, neither a gain nor a loss had arisen to the person making such an earlier disposal.

Commentary—*Simon's Taxes* **B5.708**.

41 Modifications of TCGA 1992

(1) If the disposal forms part of a transfer to which section 162 of TCGA 1992 (roll-over relief on transfer of business) applies, the basic gain arising on the disposal is computed without regard to any deduction which falls to be made under that section in computing a chargeable gain.

(2) If the disposal is made otherwise than under a bargain at arm's length and a claim for relief is made in respect of that disposal under section 165 or 260 of TCGA 1992 (relief for gifts), the claim does not affect the computation of the basic gain arising on the disposal.

Commentary—*Simon's Taxes* **B5.708**.

42 Losses

(1) If the effect of any computation under regulations 39 to 41 would be to produce a loss, the basic gain on the disposal is nil.

(2) Paragraph (1) applies notwithstanding section 16 of TCGA 1992 (losses determined in like manner as gains).

(3) Accordingly, for the purposes of these Regulations, no loss is to be treated as arising on the disposal.

Commentary—*Simon's Taxes* **B5.708**.

43 Special rules for certain existing holdings

(1) This regulation applies if—

(*a*) a person acquired rights (the "protected rights") in an offshore fund—

(i) before 1st December 2009, or

(ii) in accordance with paragraph (2),

(*b*) immediately before 1st December 2009 those rights did not constitute a material interest in an offshore fund within the meaning of that expression given by section 759 of ICTA, and

(*c*) on or after 1st December 2009 the person acquires additional rights in the offshore fund (the "non-protected rights").

(2) Rights are acquired in accordance with this paragraph if—

(*a*) the rights are acquired by the participant in accordance with a legally enforceable agreement in writing that was entered into by the participant before 30th April 2009,

(*b*) in the case of an agreement which was conditional, the conditions are met before that date, and

(*c*) the agreement is not varied on or after that date.

(3) For the purposes of tax in respect of chargeable gains—

(*a*) section 104 of TCGA 1992 (share pooling: general interpretative provisions) applies as if the protected rights were assets of a different class from the non-protected rights, and

(*b*) all the protected rights must be treated as disposed of before any of the non-protected rights may be so treated.

Commentary—*Simon's Taxes* **B5.708**.

CHAPTER 6

DEDUCTION OF OFFSHORE INCOME GAINS IN COMPUTING CHARGEABLE GAINS

44 Ambit of this Chapter

(1) This Chapter applies if—

(*a*) a material disposal gives rise to an offshore income gain, and

(*b*) that disposal also constitutes the disposal of the interest concerned for the purposes of TCGA 1992.

(2) In this Chapter the disposal specified in paragraph (1)(*b*) is called the "TCGA disposal".

Commentary—*Simon's Taxes* **B5.703**.

45 Treatment of the TCGA disposal: general rules

(1) This regulation applies for the purposes of the computation of the chargeable gain arising on the TCGA disposal.

(2) The provisions of this regulation have effect in relation to the TCGA disposal in substitution for section 37(1) of TCGA 1992 (deduction of consideration chargeable to tax on income).

(3) In the computation of the gain arising on the TCGA disposal, a sum equal to the offshore income gain shall be deducted from the sum which would otherwise constitute the amount or value of the consideration for the disposal.

(4) Paragraph (3) is subject to the following provisions of this Chapter.

(5) Paragraph (6) applies if the TCGA disposal is of such a nature that, by virtue of section 42 of TCGA 1992 (part disposals), an apportionment falls to be made of certain expenditure.
(6) No deduction is to be made by virtue of paragraph (3) in determining the amount or value of the consideration for the purposes of the fraction in section 42(2) of TCGA 1992.

Commentary—*Simon's Taxes* **B5.709**.

46 Modification of section 162 of TCGA 1992

(1) This regulation applies if the TCGA disposal forms part of a transfer to which section 162 of TCGA 1992 applies (roll-over relief on transfer of business in exchange wholly or partly for shares).
(2) For the purposes of subsection (4) of section 162 of TCGA 1992 (determination of the amount of the deduction from the gain on the old assets) "B" in the fraction in that subsection (the value of the whole of the consideration received by the transferor in exchange for the business) is to be taken to be what it would be if the value of the consideration other than shares so received by the transferor were reduced by an amount equal to the offshore income gain.

Commentary—*Simon's Taxes* **B5.709**.

47 Application of section 128 of TCGA 1992

(1) This regulation applies if there is a disposal to which this Part applies by virtue of—
[(*aa*) regulation 36A (exchanges and schemes of reconstruction), or][1]
(*c*) regulation 37 (exchange of interests of different classes).
(2) TCGA 1992 has effect as if an amount equal to the offshore income gain to which that disposal gives rise were given (by the person making the exchange) as consideration for the new holding (within the meaning of section 128 of that Act (consideration given or received for new holding on a reorganisation)).

Commentary—*Simon's Taxes* **B5.709**.

Amendments—[1] Para (1)(*aa*) substituted for previous para (3)(*a*), (*b*) by the Collective Investment Schemes (Tax Transparent Funds, Exchanges, Mergers and Schemes of Reconstruction) Regulations, SI 2013/1400 reg 15(*c*) with effect from 8 June 2013.

CHAPTER 7

THE CONVERSION OF A NON-REPORTING FUND INTO A REPORTING FUND

48 Consequences of conversion for participants

(1) This regulation applies if an offshore fund ceases to be a non-reporting fund and becomes a reporting fund.
(2) A participant in the fund may make an election to be treated—
(*a*) as disposing of the interest owned by the participant in the non-reporting fund at its market value on the disposal date, and
(*b*) as acquiring a holding in the reporting fund at the beginning of the reporting fund's first period of account.
This is subject to [paragraphs (5) and (5A)][1].
(3) Chapter 5 of this Part applies to determine the offshore income gain arising on the deemed disposal referred to in paragraph (2)(*a*).
(4) The deemed acquisition referred to in paragraph (2)(*b*) is treated as made for the same amount as the deemed disposal referred to in paragraph (2)(*a*).
(5) An election may not be made under paragraph (2) unless the offshore income gain arising on the deemed disposal referred to in paragraph (2)(*a*) (determined in accordance with paragraph (3)) is greater than zero.
[(5A If the interest owned by the participant represents variable remuneration represented by profit allocated under section 863I of ITTOIA 2005 (allocation of profit to the AIFM firm), an election may not be made under paragraph (2) if the fund ceases to be a non-reporting fund and becomes a reporting fund before the remuneration has vested in the participant.][1]
(6) If the participant is chargeable to income tax, the election mentioned in paragraph (2) must be made by being included in a return made for the tax year which includes the disposal date.
(7) If the participant is chargeable to corporation tax, the election mentioned in paragraph (2) must be made by being included in the participant's company tax return for the accounting period which includes the disposal date.
(8) In this regulation—
"company tax return" has the same meaning as in Schedule 18 to the Finance Act 1998;
the "disposal date" means the final day of the last period of account before the fund becomes a reporting fund.

Commentary—*Simon's Taxes* **B5.710**.

Amendments—[1] In para (2), words substituted for words "paragraph (5)", and para (5A) inserted by the Offshore Funds (Tax) (Amendment) Regulations, SI 2014/931 reg 2(1), (2) with effect in relation to disposals made on or after 12 August 2014..

PART 3
REPORTING FUNDS AND THE TREATMENT OF PARTICIPANTS IN REPORTING FUNDS

CHAPTER 1

PRELIMINARY PROVISIONS

49 Structure [and application] of this Part

(1) The structure of this Part is as follows—

(*a*) this Chapter contains preliminary provisions;
(*b*) Chapter 2 deals with entry into the reporting fund regime;
(*c*) Chapter 3 deals with the general duties of reporting funds;
(*d*) Chapter 4 deals with the preparation of accounts;
(*e*) Chapter 5 deals with the computation of reportable income;
(*f*) Chapter 6 deals with transactions by certain reporting funds which are not treated as trading;
[(*fa*) Chapter 6A deals with transparent reporting funds;][1]
(*g*) Chapter 7 deals with reports to participants;
(*h*) Chapter 8 deals with the tax treatment of participants in reporting funds;
(i) Chapter 9 deals with the provision of information to HMRC;
(j) Chapter 10 deals with breaches of reporting fund requirements;
(k) Chapter 11 deals with leaving the reporting fund regime;
(l) Chapter 12 deals with constant NAV funds.

(2) This Part contains provisions applying to—

(*a*) funds that are not constant NAV funds (see Chapters 2 to 11), . . . [1]
[(*aa*) transparent reporting funds (see Chapter 6A), and][1]
(*b*) constant NAV funds (see Chapter 12).

[(3) Chapters 4 to 6 do not apply to transparent reporting funds.][1]

Commentary—*Simon's Taxes* **B5.716–B5.718**.

Amendments—[1] Words in heading, paras (1)(*fa*), (2)(*aa*), (3) inserted, and in para (2)(*a*) word "and" revoked, by the Offshore Funds (Tax) (Amendment) Regulations, SI 2011/1211 regs 2, 22 with effect as follows—

– for the purposes of income tax for distributions made, or treated as made, on or after 27 May 2011;
– for the purposes of corporation tax: on chargeable gains, in relation to disposals made on or after 27 May 2011; and for distributions made, or treated as made, on or after that date;
– for the purposes of capital gains tax, in relation to disposals made on or after 27 May 2011.

50 Meaning of "reporting fund"

In these Regulations a "reporting fund" means an offshore fund to which this Part applies for a period of account.

[50A Meaning of "equalisation arrangements", "full equalisation arrangements" and "equalisation amount"

For the purposes of this Part—

(*a*) a reporting fund operates equalisation arrangements if it has given a statement under regulation 53(1)(h) that it intends to operate such arrangements;
(*b*) a reporting fund operates full equalisation arrangements if in relation to any interest acquired by way of initial purchase in the reporting period—
  (i) the equalisation amount included in the consideration for the purchase is specified by the fund in a statement in writing to the participant making the acquisition, or
  (ii) the equalisation amount per unit of interest in the fund is included in the report made available in accordance with regulation 90;
(*c*) "equalisation amount" has the meaning given in regulation 72(2).][1]

Commentary—*Simon's Taxes* **B5.710, B5.715**.

Amendments—[1] Reg 50A inserted by the Offshore Funds (Tax) (Amendment) Regulations, SI 2011/1211 regs 2, 5 with effect as follows, and subject to transitional provision in reg 16(1)—

– for the purposes of income tax for distributions made, or treated as made, on or after 27 May 2011;
– for the purposes of corporation tax: on chargeable gains, in relation to disposals made on or after 27 May 2011; and for distributions made, or treated as made, on or after that date;
– for the purposes of capital gains tax, in relation to disposals made on or after 27 May 2011.

CHAPTER 2

ENTRY INTO THE REPORTING FUND REGIME

Applications for this Part to apply

51 Who may make an application

(1) The manager of an eligible offshore fund may make an application for this Part to apply to the fund.

(2) If it is proposed to establish an offshore fund which, on its establishment, is to be an eligible offshore fund, the person expected to become the manager of the fund on its establishment (the "applicant") may make an application for this Part to apply to the fund on its establishment.

(3) In this Part—

the "applicant" means the person referred to in paragraph (2);

an "application" means an existing fund application or a future fund application;

an "eligible offshore fund" means an offshore fund which is not a guaranteed return fund;

an "existing fund application" means an application made under paragraph (1);

a "future fund application" means an application made under paragraph (2);

the "manager", in relation to an offshore fund, includes the manager or other person who has or is expected to have day to day control of the property of the fund.

Commentary—*Simon's Taxes* **B5.715**.

52 Conversion of non-reporting fund into reporting fund

(1) The manager of a non-reporting fund may make an application for this Part to apply to a fund if the fund is an eligible offshore fund, and—

(*a*) has never been a reporting fund, or

(*b*) has been a reporting fund, but ceased to be such a fund because it gave notice under regulation 116.

(2) The provisions of this Part that apply to an existing fund application also apply to an application made under paragraph (1).

Commentary—*Simon's Taxes* **B5.715**.

53 Contents of an application

(1) An application must include the following—

(*a*) a statement of the first period of account for which it is proposed that this Part should apply to the fund;

(*b*) an undertaking that no period of account will exceed 18 months;

(*c*) a statement whether or not the fund intends to prepare its accounts in accordance with international accounting standards, and, if it does not, a statement of which generally accepted accounting practice it intends to use;

(*d*) in a case in which the fund does not intend to prepare its accounts in accordance with international accounting standards, a statement specifying the entries in the fund's accounts that are considered to equate to "total comprehensive income for the period" as that expression is used in international accounting standards;

(*e*) in a case in which the fund does not intend to prepare its accounts in accordance with international accounting standards, a statement specifying how the fund intends—

(i) to comply with regulation 66(1)(*b*), or

(ii) to calculate the adjustment required by regulation 66(2);

(*f*) an undertaking to meet the requirements relating to reports to participants in the fund (see Chapter 7);

(*g*) an undertaking to meet the requirements relating to the provision of information to HMRC (see Chapter 9).

[(*h*) a statement whether or not the fund intends to operate equalisation arrangements;

(*i*) in a case in which the fund does intend to operate equalisation arrangements, a statement whether or not the fund intends to operate full equalisation arrangements;

(*j*) in a case in which the fund does not intend to operate equalisation arrangements, a statement specifying whether or not the fund intends to make income adjustments in a reporting period;

(*k*) in a case in which the fund intends to make income adjustments in a reporting period, a statement specifying—

(i) whether the fund intends to make those adjustments on the basis of [reportable income)][2] (see [regulation 72A][2]) or on the basis of accounting income (see [regulation 72B][2]), and

(ii) the length of the computation period (see [regulation 72C[[2]);

(*l*) in a case in which the fund intends to make income adjustments in a reporting period on the basis of accounting income—

(i) a statement by the fund manager specifying how the accounting income is to be determined,

(ii) a statement by the fund manager that, on the basis of this determination, it is reasonable to expect that the difference between the amount of [reportable income][2] per unit calculated using this method and the amount of reported income per unit calculated on the basis of reported income will be 10% or less of the latter of those amounts, and

(iii) an undertaking by the manager to meet the requirements relating to alternative income adjustments and notice to HMRC (see [regulation 72B(6)][2]).][1]

(2) An existing fund application must be accompanied by the prospectus.

(3) A future fund application must be accompanied by the proposed prospectus.

(4) The application must be in English.

(5) If the prospectus or the proposed prospectus (as the case may be) is not in English, it must be accompanied by an English translation.

(6) In the case of an offshore fund constituted in the manner described in regulation 5 or 6, the requirements of this regulation may be met by providing material which is—

(*a*) applicable to an entity which includes the fund, and

(*b*) relevant for the application for this Part to apply to the fund.

Commentary—*Simon's Taxes* **B5.715**.

Amendments—[1] In para (1), sub-paras (*h*)–(*l*) inserted by the Offshore Funds (Tax) (Amendment) Regulations, SI 2011/1211 regs 2, 6 with effect as follows, and subject to transitional provision in reg 16(1)—

- for the purposes of income tax for distributions made, or treated as made, on or after 27 May 2011;
- for the purposes of corporation tax: on chargeable gains, in relation to disposals made on or after 27 May 2011; and for distributions made, or treated as made, on or after that date;
- for the purposes of capital gains tax, in relation to disposals made on or after 27 May 2011.

Note the transitional provisions in SI 2011/1211 regs 14–16. The manager of a transitional fund must give the statements required by para (1)(*h*)–(*l*) by a notice in writing to HMRC within one year of 27 May 2011 (SI 2011/1211 reg 15(1)).

[2] The following amendments made by the Offshore Funds (Tax) (Amendment No. 2) Regulations, SI 2013/1411 regs 2, 3 with effect from 28 June 2013, subject to transitional provision in reg 1(3), (5)—

- in para (1)(*k*)(i), words substituted for words "reported income", "regulation 92A" and "regulation 92B";
- in para (1)(*k*)(ii), words substituted for words "regulation 92C";
- in para (1)(*l*)(i), words substituted for words "reported income"; and
- in para (1)(*l*)(iii), words substituted for words "regulation 92B(5)".

54 Form, timing and withdrawal of application

(1) An application must be made in writing to HMRC.

[(2) The application must be received by HMRC before the later of—

(*a*) the end of the first period of account for which it is proposed that this Part should apply to the fund, and

(*b*) the expiry of a period of 3 months beginning with the first day on which interests in the fund are made available to investors resident in the United Kingdom.

(3) The application may be withdrawn—

(*a*) at any time during a period beginning with the day the application is made and ending on the expiry of a period of 28 days beginning on the day on which HMRC give notice under regulation 55(1) or (5), or

(*b*) at any later time, but before the end of the first reporting period, if HMRC are satisfied that the fund is not in breach of the requirements imposed by Part 3.][1]

(4) The application must be withdrawn—

(*a*) by the manager (in the case of an existing fund application), or

(*b*) by the applicant (in the case of a future fund application).

Commentary—*Simon's Taxes* **B5.710, B7.515**.

Amendments—[1] Paras (2), (3) substituted by the Offshore Funds (Tax) (Amendment) Regulations, SI 2011/1211 regs 2, 31 with effect as follows—

- for the purposes of income tax for distributions made, or treated as made, on or after 27 May 2011;
- for the purposes of corporation tax: on chargeable gains, in relation to disposals made on or after 27 May 2011; and for distributions made, or treated as made, on or after that date;
- for the purposes of capital gains tax, in relation to disposals made on or after 27 May 2011.

Procedure on applications

55 Response by HMRC to application

(1) Within 28 days beginning with the day on which HMRC receive the application, HMRC must give notice to the person who made the application—

(*a*) accepting the application,

(*b*) rejecting the application, or

(*c*) asking for further information in order to consider the application.

(2) HMRC must not accept an application if any item mentioned in regulation 53 is not supplied.

(3) HMRC must not accept an application if they consider that there will be a significant difference, in computing reportable income (see Chapter 5 [or 6A][1]), between—

(*a*) the result given by the use of international accounting standards, and

(*b*) the result given by the use of the accounting practice specified in the application and by the use of the entries in the fund's accounts, specified in the application, that are considered to equate to "total comprehensive income for the period" as that expression is used in international accounting standards (see regulation 63).

[(3A) Where the fund intends to make income adjustments on the basis of accounting income (see regulation 53(1)(l)), HMRC must not accept an application if they do not consider that it is reasonable to expect that the difference between the amount of reported income per unit calculated using this method and the amount of [reportable income][2] per unit calculated on the basis of reported income will be 10% or less of the latter of those amounts.][1]

(4) Paragraph (5) applies if—

(*a*) HMRC have given notice under paragraph (1)(*c*), and

(*b*) the person who made the application provides further information within a period of 28 days beginning with the day on which HMRC ask for further information, or within such longer period as is agreed by HMRC.

(5) Within 28 days beginning with the day on which HMRC receive the further information, HMRC must give notice to the person who made the application—

(*a*) accepting the application, or

(*b*) rejecting the application.

Commentary—*Simon's Taxes* **B5.710, B7.515.**

Amendments—[1] In para (3), words inserted, and para (3A) inserted, by the Offshore Funds (Tax) (Amendment) Regulations, SI 2011/1211 regs 2, 7 with effect as follows, and subject to transitional provision in reg 16(1)—

– for the purposes of income tax for distributions made, or treated as made, on or after 27 May 2011;

– for the purposes of corporation tax: on chargeable gains, in relation to disposals made on or after 27 May 2011; and for distributions made, or treated as made, on or after that date;

– for the purposes of capital gains tax, in relation to disposals made on or after 27 May 2011.

[2] In para (3A), words substituted for words "reported income" by the Offshore Funds (Tax) (Amendment No. 2) Regulations, SI 2013/1411 regs 2, 4 with effect from 28 June 2013, subject to transitional provision in reg 1(3), (5).

56 Appeal against rejection of application

(1) If HMRC reject an application, the person who made the application may appeal.

(2) The notice of appeal must be given to HMRC within a period of 42 days beginning with the day on which the notice rejecting the application is given.

(3) On an appeal, the tribunal may uphold or quash the rejection of the application.

(4) If the tribunal quashes the rejection of the application, this Part applies as if HMRC had accepted the application in the form in which it was considered by the tribunal.

Commentary—*Simon's Taxes* **B5.710, B7.515.**

[CHAPTER 2A

AMENDMENT TO APPLICATION FOR THIS PART TO APPLY

Amendment to Application for this Part to Apply

56A Amending a statement relating to equalisation

(1) The manager of a reporting fund may apply to amend any statement under regulation 53(1)(*h*) to (*l*) in relation to a reporting period and subsequent reporting periods by application in writing to HMRC before the end of the first reporting period in relation to which the amendment is to have effect.

(2) Paragraphs (4) to (8) do not apply in relation to an application to amend a statement under regulation 53(1)(*h*) and (*i*) or under regulation 53(1)(*i*) if the amendment sought is that the fund intends to operate full equalisation arrangements.

(3) An application to which paragraph (2) applies must be accepted by HMRC within 28 days beginning with the day on which HMRC receive the application.

(4) An application under paragraph (1) must specify—

(*a*) the reason for the application,

(*b*) the amendment sought to the statement, and

(*c*) the first reporting period in which the amendment is to apply.

(5) Within 28 days beginning with the day on which HMRC receive the application, HMRC must give notice to the manager—

(*a*) accepting the application,

(*b*) rejecting the application, or

(*c*) asking for further information in order to consider the application.

(6) HMRC must not accept an application if—

(*a*) they consider the application is made for reasons other than commercial or administrative reasons, or

(*b*) an application was accepted under this regulation in relation to either of the previous two reporting periods.

(7) Paragraph (8) applies if—

(*a*) HMRC have given notice under paragraph (5)(*c*), and

(*b*) the manager provides further information within a period of 28 days beginning with the day on which HMRC ask for further information or within such longer period as is agreed by HMRC.

(8) Within 28 days beginning with the day on which HMRC receive the further information, HMRC must give notice to the manager—

(*a*) accepting the application, or

(*b*) rejecting the application.][1]

Commentary—*Simon's Taxes* **B5.710, B7.515.**

Amendments—[1] Chapter 2A (regs 56A, 56B) inserted by the Offshore Funds (Tax) (Amendment) Regulations, SI 2011/1211 regs 2, 8 with effect as follows, and subject to transitional provision in reg 16(1)—

– for the purposes of income tax for distributions made, or treated as made, on or after 27 May 2011;

– for the purposes of corporation tax: on chargeable gains, in relation to disposals made on or after 27 May 2011; and for distributions made, or treated as made, on or after that date;
– for the purposes of capital gains tax, in relation to disposals made on or after 27 May 2011.

[56B Appeal against refusal of application to amend a statement

(1) If HMRC reject an application the manager may appeal.

(2) The notice of appeal must be given to HMRC within a period of 42 days beginning with the day on which the notice rejecting the application is given.

(3) On an appeal, the tribunal may uphold or quash the rejection of the application.

(4) If the tribunal quashes the rejection of the application, this Part applies as if HMRC had accepted the application.][1]

Commentary—*Simon's Taxes* **B5.710. B7.515.**

Amendments—[1] Chapter 2A (regs 56A, 56B) inserted by the Offshore Funds (Tax) (Amendment) Regulations, SI 2011/1211 regs 2, 8 with effect as follows, and subject to transitional provision in reg 16(1)—
– for the purposes of income tax for distributions made, or treated as made, on or after 27 May 2011;
– for the purposes of corporation tax: on chargeable gains, in relation to disposals made on or after 27 May 2011; and for distributions made, or treated as made, on or after that date;
– for the purposes of capital gains tax, in relation to disposals made on or after 27 May 2011.

CHAPTER 3

THE GENERAL DUTIES OF REPORTING FUNDS

57 Effects of entry into the reporting fund regime

(1) If HMRC accept an application, the offshore fund becomes a reporting fund on whichever is the later of—

(*a*) the first day of the first period of account mentioned in regulation 53(1)(*a*), or

(*b*) the day on which the fund is established.

[This paragraph and paragraphs (2) and (3) are subject to paragraph (4).][1]

(2) This Part applies to the fund and to its participants on and after the date specified in paragraph (1).

(3) Once this Part has begun to apply to a fund, it shall continue to apply unless and until it ceases to apply in accordance with Chapter 11 of this Part.

[(4) Where an application has been withdrawn under regulation 54(3)(b), the fund and its participants shall be treated as if the fund had never been a reporting fund.][1]

Commentary—*Simon's Taxes* **B5.710, B7.515.**

Amendments—[1] Words in para (1), and whole of para (4), inserted, by the Offshore Funds (Tax) (Amendment) Regulations, SI 2011/1211 regs 2, 32 with effect as follows—
– for the purposes of income tax for distributions made, or treated as made, on or after 27 May 2011;
– for the purposes of corporation tax: on chargeable gains, in relation to disposals made on or after 27 May 2011; and for distributions made, or treated as made, on or after that date;
– for the purposes of capital gains tax, in relation to disposals made on or after 27 May 2011.

58 General duties of reporting funds

A reporting fund must—

(*a*) prepare accounts in accordance with the requirements of Chapter 4 [(except in the case of transparent reporting funds)][1];

(*b*) provide a computation of its reportable income in accordance with the requirements of Chapter 5 [or 6A, as the case may be][1];

(*c*) provide reports to participants in accordance with the requirements of Chapter 7; and

(*d*) provide information to HMRC in accordance with the requirements of Chapter 9.

Commentary—*Simon's Taxes* **B5.715.**

Amendments—[1] Words inserted by the Offshore Funds (Tax) (Amendment) Regulations, SI 2011/1211 regs 2, 23 with effect as follows—
– for the purposes of income tax for distributions made, or treated as made, on or after 27 May 2011;
– for the purposes of corporation tax: on chargeable gains, in relation to disposals made on or after 27 May 2011; and for distributions made, or treated as made, on or after that date;
– for the purposes of capital gains tax, in relation to disposals made on or after 27 May 2011.

CHAPTER 4

THE PREPARATION OF ACCOUNTS

59 Accounts to be prepared in accordance with acceptable accounting policy

A reporting fund must prepare accounts—

(*a*) in accordance with international accounting standards, or

(*b*) in accordance with the generally accepted accounting practice specified in the application.

Commentary—*Simon's Taxes* **B5.716.**

60 Change in accounting policy

(1) This regulation applies if—

(*a*) there is a change of accounting policy in drawing up a reporting fund's accounts from one period of account (in this Chapter called the "earlier period") to the next (in this Chapter called the "later period"), and

(*b*) the approach in each of those periods accords with the law and practice applicable in relation to that period.

(2) If there is a difference between—

(*a*) the accounting value of an asset or liability of the offshore fund at the end of the earlier period, and

(*b*) the accounting value of that asset or liability at the beginning of the later period,

a corresponding debit or credit (as the case may be) must be brought into account for the purposes of these Regulations in the later period.

(3) In paragraph (2) "accounting value" means the carrying value of the asset or liability recognised for accounting purposes.

Commentary—*Simon's Taxes* **B5.716**.

61 Change in accounting practice to a generally accepted accounting practice

(1) This regulation applies if—

(*a*) there is a change of accounting practice in drawing up a reporting fund's accounts from the earlier period to the later period, and

(*b*) the fund prepares accounts for the later period in accordance with a generally accepted accounting practice.

(2) If the accounts for the later period are not prepared in accordance with international accounting standards, the offshore fund must give notice to HMRC—

(*a*) applying for approval of the generally accepted accounting practice, and

(*b*) providing the statement mentioned in regulation 53(1)(*d*).

(3) If the accounts for the later period are prepared in accordance with international accounting standards, the offshore fund must give notice to HMRC.

(4) Within 28 days beginning with the day on which HMRC receive an application under paragraph (2), HMRC must give notice to the offshore fund—

(*a*) accepting the application, or

(*b*) rejecting the application.

(5) If HMRC reject an application, the offshore fund may appeal.

(6) The notice of appeal must be given to HMRC within a period of 42 days beginning with the day on which the notice rejecting the application is given.

(7) On an appeal, the tribunal may uphold or quash the rejection of the application.

Commentary—*Simon's Taxes* **B5.716**.

CHAPTER 5

THE COMPUTATION OF REPORTABLE INCOME

General

62 Duty to provide computation

(1) This Chapter explains how reportable income is computed.

(2) A reporting fund must provide a computation of its reportable income for a period of account.

Commentary—*Simon's Taxes* **B5.717**.

63 Computation of reportable income: general

(1) The starting point for computing the reportable income of a reporting fund for a period of account is—

(*a*) in a case in which the fund prepares its accounts in accordance with international accounting standards, the "total comprehensive income for the period" as that expression is used in international accounting standards, or

(*b*) in any other case, the entries in the fund's accounts that are considered to equate to "total comprehensive income for the period" as that expression is used in international accounting standards.

(2) The starting point specified in paragraph (1) must be adjusted having regard to—

(*a*) capital items [and miscellaneous items][2] (see regulations 64 and 65),

(*b*) special classes of income (see regulations 66 to 71), and

[(*c*) any arrangements to adjust income based on the number of units in issue (see regulations 72 to 72B).][1]

(3) In the case of any one item, an adjustment under paragraph (2) may be made only once (even if more than one of the regulations mentioned in that paragraph apply to that item).

(4) The reportable income of the reporting fund for the period of account is the amount computed in accordance with the provisions of this Chapter and of Chapter 6.

(5) But if the computation gives rise to a negative amount, the reportable income is nil.

Commentary—*Simon's Taxes* **B5.717**.

Amendments—[1] Para (2)(*c*) substituted by the Offshore Funds (Tax) (Amendment No 2) Regulations, SI 2013/1411 regs 2, 5 with effect from 28 June 2013, subject to transitional provision in reg 1(3), (5). Para (2)(*c*) previously read as follows—

"(*c*) equalisation arrangements (see regulation 72).".

[2] In para (2)(*a*), words inserted by the Offshore Funds (Tax) (Amendment) Regulations, SI 2017/240 reg 2(1), (2)(*a*) with effect for each reporting period beginning on or after 1 April 2017.

Adjustments for capital items [and miscellaneous items][1]

64 Treatment of capital items following IMA SORP

(1) The capital items for which an adjustment is required are such profits, gains or losses as would fall to be dealt with under the heading "net capital gains/losses" in the statement of total return for the period of account if the accounts for that period were to be prepared in accordance with the IMA SORP.

(2) The amount specified in regulation 63(1) must be adjusted by—

(*a*) deducting gains that fall within the heading specified in paragraph (1), . . .[1]

(*b*) adding losses that fall within that heading[, and

(*c*) sums payable or allocated to the manager of a fund calculated by reference to an increase in the net asset value of the fund or a formula designed to reward the manager's performance.][1]

(3) A profit or loss from a trade may not be treated as a capital item for the purposes of this regulation.

This paragraph is subject to regulation 80.

(4) For the purposes of paragraph (1) the IMA SORP applies to determine the "net capital gains/losses" of an offshore fund for a period of account in the same way that it applies to determine the "net capital gains/losses" of an authorised investment fund for an accounting period.

(5) In this regulation—

"authorised investment fund" has the meaning given in the Authorised Investment Funds (Tax) Regulations 2006;

"the IMA SORP" means, in relation to any period of account for which it is required or permitted to be used, the Statement of Recognised Practice relating to authorised investment funds issued by the Investment Management Association in November 2008, as from time to time modified, amended or revised.

Commentary—*Simon's Taxes* **B5.717**.

Amendments—[1] In heading, words inserted, in para (2)(*a*) word revoked, and para (2)(*c*) and preceding word inserted, by the Offshore Funds (Tax) (Amendment) Regulations, SI 2017/240 reg 2(1), (2)(*b*), (3) with effect for each reporting period beginning on or after 1 April 2017.

65 Treatment of other capital items [and miscellaneous items][1]

(1) The amount specified in regulation 63(1) must also be adjusted by adding the amounts specified in paragraph (2).

(2) Those amounts are—

(*a*) expenses directly related to acquisition or disposal of investments (other than those taken into account in arriving at the amounts specified in sub-paragraph (*a*) or (*b*) of regulation 64(2)), and

(*b*) costs relating to the setting up, merger or dissolution of the fund.

Commentary—*Simon's Taxes* **B5.717**.

Amendments—[1] In heading, words inserted by the Offshore Funds (Tax) (Amendment) Regulations, SI 2017/240 reg 2(1), (2)(*c*) with effect for each reporting period beginning on or after 1 April 2017.

Adjustments for special classes of income

66 Effective interest income or comparable amounts

(1) This regulation applies if the accounting practice used does not include—

(*a*) the effective interest method for computing interest income (as described in international accounting standard 39 and equivalent United Kingdom financial reporting standards), or

(*b*) another method of accounting for interest in such a way that the difference between the purchase price of an asset and the expected redemption price of the asset is taken into account as part of the interest income over the expected life of the asset.

(2) The amount specified in regulation 63(1) must be adjusted by the addition of the net income computed by taking into account the expected redemption price of any interest bearing assets over the expected life of the asset.

(3) The sum mentioned in paragraph (2) may be computed by any reasonable method which—

(*a*) takes into account the full expected gain or loss on the asset, and

(*b*) gives a reasonably comparable result to the effective interest method.

Commentary—*Simon's Taxes* **B5.717**.

67 Income from wholly-owned subsidiaries

(1) This regulation applies if a reporting fund has a wholly-owned subsidiary.

(2) For the purposes of this regulation, a company is a wholly-owned subsidiary of an offshore fund if and so long as the whole of the issued share capital of the company is—

(*a*) in the case of an offshore fund falling within paragraph (*a*) of the definition of "offshore fund" in section 40A(2) of FA 2008, directly [or indirectly][1] owned by the fund;

(*b*) in the case of an offshore fund falling within paragraph (*b*) of the definition of "offshore fund" in that enactment, directly [or indirectly][1] owned by the trustees of the fund for the benefit of the fund;

(*c*) in the case of an offshore fund falling within paragraph (*c*) of the definition of "offshore fund" in that enactment, owned in a manner which, as near as may be, corresponds either to paragraph (*a*) or paragraph (*b*) above.

(3) But in the case of a company which has only one class of issued share capital, the reference in paragraph (2) to the whole of the issued share capital shall be construed as a reference to at least 95% of that share capital.

(4) That percentage of the receipts, expenditure, assets and liabilities of the subsidiary which is equal to the percentage of the issued share capital of the company concerned which is owned as mentioned in paragraph (2) shall be regarded as the receipts, expenditure, assets and liabilities of the fund.

(5) There shall be left out of account—

(*a*) the interest of the fund in the subsidiary, and

(*b*) any distributions or other payments made by the subsidiary to the fund or by the fund to the subsidiary.

(6) The adjustments required under regulations 64 and 65 must be made to the amount determined under paragraph (4).

Commentary—*Simon's Taxes* **B5.717**.

Amendments—[1] In para (2)(*a*) words substituted, and in para (2)(*b*) words inserted, by the Offshore Funds (Tax) (Amendment) Regulations, SI 2011/1211 regs 2, 33 with effect as follows—

- for the purposes of income tax for distributions made, or treated as made, on or after 27 May 2011;
- for the purposes of corporation tax: on chargeable gains, in relation to disposals made on or after 27 May 2011; and for distributions made, or treated as made, on or after that date;
- for the purposes of capital gains tax, in relation to disposals made on or after 27 May 2011.

68 Income from other reporting funds

(1) This regulation applies if a reporting fund ("RF1") has an interest in another reporting fund ("RF2").

(2) The excess (if any) of the income reported by RF2 in respect of RF1's interest in RF2 over the amount distributed by RF2 to RF1 must be added by RF1 to the amount specified in regulation 63(1) after making the adjustments specified in regulations 64 and 65.

(3) The adjustment specified in paragraph (2) must be made in the computation of the reportable income of RF1 for the period of account [in which the fund distribution date of RF2 falls or, if earlier, in which the date on which the reported income from RF2 in respect of that reporting period is recognised in the accounts of RF1][1].

(4) . . . [1]

(5) If [RF2 does not make a report available in accordance with regulation 90(5)][1], RF1 must—

(*a*) include its best estimate of reported income from RF2 as an adjustment to the computation of its reportable income for the period of account in which the latest possible fund distribution date for RF2 falls (to the extent that any such amount has not already been recognised in the computation of RF1's reportable income for that or any earlier period of account), and

(*b*) make any necessary corrections to its best estimate in its computation of reportable income for the first later period of account in which it has sufficient information to make those corrections.

Commentary—*Simon's Taxes* **B5.717**.

Amendments—[1] In para (3), words substituted, para (4) revoked, and in para (5) words substituted, by the Offshore Funds (Tax) (Amendment) Regulations, SI 2011/1211 regs 2, 34 with effect as follows—

- for the purposes of income tax for distributions made, or treated as made, on or after 27 May 2011;
- for the purposes of corporation tax: on chargeable gains, in relation to disposals made on or after 27 May 2011; and for distributions made, or treated as made, on or after that date;
- for the purposes of capital gains tax, in relation to disposals made on or after 27 May 2011.

[68A Index tracking funds

(1) This regulation applies if—

(*a*) a reporting fund has an interest in a non-reporting fund, and

(*b*) the conditions in paragraph (2) are met for a period of account.

(2) The conditions are that—

(*a*) in accordance with the reporting fund's rule or the instrument constituting the reporting fund, the aim of the fund's investment policy is to replicate the performance of a qualifying index,

(*b*) the main purpose of the investment in the non-reporting fund is to represent the composition of the qualifying index, and

(*c*) the capital and income returns of the reporting fund replicate as closely as practicable the returns of the investments comprised in the qualifying index.

(3) For the purposes of paragraph (2) an index is a "qualifying index" if—

(*a*) it is based solely on the value of securities listed on a recognised stock exchange or admitted to trading on a regulated market,

(*b*) an authority responsible for regulating offshore funds recognises the index on the basis that—

(i) its composition is sufficiently diverse,

(ii) it represents an adequate benchmark for the market to which it refers, and

(iii) it is published in such a way that it is widely available, and

(*c*) it is calculated and published by a body which is managed independently from the management of the reporting fund.

(4) Regulations 69 to 71 do not apply in respect of the interest in the non-reporting fund.][1]

Commentary—*Simon's Taxes* **B5.717**.

Amendments—[1] Reg 68A inserted by the Offshore Funds (Tax) (Amendment) Regulations, SI 2011/1211 regs 2, 35 with effect as follows—

– for the purposes of income tax for distributions made, or treated as made, on or after 27 May 2011;

– for the purposes of corporation tax: on chargeable gains, in relation to disposals made on or after 27 May 2011; and for distributions made, or treated as made, on or after that date;

– for the purposes of capital gains tax, in relation to disposals made on or after 27 May 2011.

69 Income from non-reporting funds: first case

(1) This regulation applies if—

(*a*) a reporting fund has an interest in a non-reporting fund, and

(*b*) the conditions in paragraph (2) are met for a period of account.

(2) The conditions are that—

(*a*) . . . [1]

(*b*) the reporting fund has access to the accounts of the non-reporting fund;

(*c*) the reporting fund has sufficient information about the non-reporting fund to enable it to prepare a computation of reportable income for the non-reporting fund; and

(*d*) the reporting fund can reasonably expect to be able to rely on continued access to that information for the period in which it will hold the investment in the non-reporting fund.

(3) Regulation [68(1) to (3)][1] applies as if the reporting fund were RF1 and the non-reporting fund were RF2.

(4) For the purposes of the computation mentioned in paragraph (2)(*c*), regulation 80 applies if (and only if) the non-reporting fund is a UCITS fund.

[(5) For the purposes of applying regulation 68, "fund distribution date" means the date six months after the end of the period of account in which the income arose.

(6) If the period of account referred to in paragraph (5) is more than 12 months, there shall be two periods of account and two fund distribution dates for the purposes of applying regulation 68.

The first fund distribution date is the date six months after the end of the first 12 months in the period of account.

The second fund distribution date is the date six months after the end of the period of account in which the income arose.][1]

Commentary—*Simon's Taxes* **B5.717**.

Amendments—[1] Para (2)(*a*) revoked, in para (3) words substituted, and paras (5), (6) inserted, by the Offshore Funds (Tax) (Amendment) Regulations, SI 2011/1211 regs 2, 36 with effect as follows—

– for the purposes of income tax for distributions made, or treated as made, on or after 27 May 2011;

– for the purposes of corporation tax: on chargeable gains, in relation to disposals made on or after 27 May 2011; and for distributions made, or treated as made, on or after that date;

– for the purposes of capital gains tax, in relation to disposals made on or after 27 May 2011.

70 Income from non-reporting funds: second case

(1) This regulation applies if a reporting fund has an interest in a non-reporting fund, but the conditions in regulation 69(2) are not met for a period of account.

(2) No adjustments may be made under regulations 64 and 65 in respect of the interest in the non-reporting fund.

(3) But if the condition specified in paragraph (4) is met, losses made by a reporting fund in earlier periods of account on an investment in a non-reporting fund may be set against gains made on the investment in the non-reporting fund to reduce the reportable income of the reporting fund, but only to the extent that the losses—

(*a*) have not previously had the effect of reducing income for the period of account in which they were incurred, or

(*b*) have not been used previously to reduce gains arising to the non-reporting fund.

(4) The condition specified is that the losses in earlier periods of account were all made during periods in which this Part applied continuously to the reporting fund.

Commentary—*Simon's Taxes* **B5.717**.

71 Income from non-reporting funds if first case ceases to apply

(1) This regulation applies if—

(*a*) a reporting fund has an interest in a non-reporting fund, and (*b*) the conditions in regulation 69(2) have been met for an earlier period of account but are no longer met for a later period of account.

(2) Regulation 70 applies for the later period of account and for all subsequent periods of account.

Commentary—*Simon's Taxes* **B5.717**.

Adjustments for equalisation arrangements

[72 Treatment of reporting funds operating equalisation arrangements

(1) This regulation applies if a reporting fund operates equalisation arrangements.

(2) If a person acquires an interest in the fund by way of initial purchase, the reportable income must be increased by an amount equal to that part of the acquisition price which is attributable to the undistributed income which has accrued to the fund in the period of account up to the time of the acquisition and which is taken into account in determining the acquisition price ("the equalisation amount").

(3) If a participant disposes of an interest in the fund by way of redemption, the reportable income must be reduced by an amount equal to that part of the redemption price which is attributable to the undistributed income which has accrued to the fund in the period of account up to the time of the redemption and which is taken into account in determining the redemption price.

(4) For the purposes of these Regulations a person acquires an interest in an offshore fund by way of initial purchase if the acquisition is by way of subscription for or allotment of new shares, units or other interests issued or created by the fund or by way of direct purchase from the managers of the fund acting in their capacity as managers of the fund.

(5) For the purposes of this regulation a person disposes of an interest in a fund by way of redemption if the disposal is by way of cancellation of the units, shares or other interest or by way of direct sale to the managers of the fund acting in their capacity as managers of thefund.][1]

Commentary—*Simon's Taxes* **B5.717**.

Amendments—[1] Reg 72 substituted by the Offshore Funds (Tax) (Amendment) Regulations, SI 2011/1211 regs 2, 9 with effect as follows, and subject to transitional provision in reg 16(1)—

- for the purposes of income tax for distributions made, or treated as made, on or after 27 May 2011;
- for the purposes of corporation tax: on chargeable gains, in relation to disposals made on or after 27 May 2011; and for distributions made, or treated as made, on or after that date;
- for the purposes of capital gains tax, in relation to disposals made on or after 27 May 2011.

[Adjustments where funds do not operate equalisation arrangements

72A Reporting Funds not operating equalisation: income adjustments based on reportable income for computation periods

(1) This regulation applies if a reporting fund does not operate equalisation arrangements and—

(a) the fund has given a statement under regulation 53(1)(k) that it intends to make income adjustments in a reporting period on the basis of reportable income, or

(b) regulation 72B(7) applies.

(2) The reportable income of the fund for a reporting period is the sum of the reportable income per unit for all the computation periods in the reporting period multiplied by the number of units in the fund in issue at the end of the reporting period.

(3) But if the sum results in a negative amount, the reportable income for that period is nil.

(4) Where a period of account consists of two reporting periods, the reportable income for the period of account is the sum of the reportable income for both those reporting periods.

(5) The reportable income per unit for a computation period is calculated by dividing the reportable income of the fund for the computation period by the average number of units in the fund in issue during the computation period.

(6) For the purposes of paragraph (5), the reportable income of the fund for a computation period means the reportable income of the fund for that period computed in accordance with this Chapter (ignoring regulation 63(5) and this regulation) and Chapter 6 of this Part.

(7) In the computation referred to in paragraph (6), this Chapter and Chapter 6 of this Part apply as if references to a period of account of the fund were references to a computation period.][1]

Amendments—[1] Regulations 72A–72C and preceding cross-head inserted by the Offshore Funds (Tax) (Amendment No. 2) Regulations, SI 2013/1411 regs 2, 6 with effect from 28 June 2013, subject to transitional provision in reg 1(3), (5).

[72B Reporting Funds not operating equalisation: income adjustments based on accounting income for computation periods

(1) This regulation applies if a reporting fund does not operate equalisation arrangements and the fund has given a statement under regulation 53(1)(k) that it intends to make income adjustments in a reporting period on the basis of accounting income.

(2) The reportable income of the fund for a reporting period is calculated as follows—

(AIU×RI / AI) x U

where—

AIU is the sum of the accounting income per unit for all the computation periods in the reporting period,

RI is the reportable income of the fund for the reporting period computed in accordance with this Chapter (ignoring this regulation), Chapter 6 of this Part and regulation 93,
AI is the sum of accounting income for all the computation periods in the reporting period, and
U is the number of units in the fund in issue at the end of the reporting period.

This is subject to paragraphs (6) and (7).

(3) Where a period of account consists of two reporting periods, the reportable income for the period of account is the sum of the reportable income for both those reporting periods.

(4) But if the sum results in a negative amount, the reportable income for that period is nil.

(5) The accounting income per unit for a computation period is calculated by dividing accounting income for the computation period by the average number of units in the fund in issue during the computation period.

(6) Where RI is zero the reportable income per unit of the fund for a reporting period is zero.

(7) Where the difference in the amount of reportable income per unit for any reporting period in a period of account calculated using this method and the amount of reportable income per unit for that reporting period calculated on the basis of reportable income is or is likely to be more than 10% of the latter of those amounts—

(a) the fund must make income adjustments in that and future periods of account on the basis of reportable income, and

(b) the manager must give notice to HMRC of the change in the method of income adjustment with the information provided to HMRC in relation to that period under regulation 106 (reporting requirements).

(8) In this Part "accounting income" means an amount proportionally related to the reportable income of the fund determined from the interim or management accounts of the fund, but this amount must not be less than zero.][1]

Amendments—[1] Regulations 72A–72C and preceding cross-head inserted by the Offshore Funds (Tax) (Amendment No. 2) Regulations, SI 2013/1411 regs 2, 6 with effect from 28 June 2013, subject to transitional provision in reg 1(3), (5).

[72C Supplementary provisions: average number of units and computation period

(1) For the purposes of regulations 72A(5) and 72B(5), the average number of units in the fund in issue during the computation period is the sum of the units in the fund in issue during the period after each unit has been multiplied by the fraction of the period for which it is held.

(2) In this Part a "computation period" means a period determined by a fund in accordance with the following rules.

Rule 1

A new computation period must start—

(a) at the beginning of a reporting period, and

(b) immediately after the end of a previous computation period.

Rule 2

A computation period must end—

(a) at the end of a reporting period, and

(b) at the end of a period in relation to which income is allocated to participants for distribution or accumulation.

Rule 3

If a reporting period consists of more than one computation period those periods must be of approximately equal length.][1]

Amendments—[1] Regulations 72A–72C and preceding cross-head inserted by the Offshore Funds (Tax) (Amendment No. 2) Regulations, SI 2013/1411 regs 2, 6 with effect from 28 June 2013, subject to transitional provision in reg 1(3), (5).

CHAPTER 6

TRANSACTIONS BY CERTAIN REPORTING FUNDS WHICH ARE NOT TREATED AS TRADING

Conditions to be met by reporting funds for this Chapter to apply

73 Introductory

(1) A reporting fund meets the conditions for this Chapter to apply in respect of a period of account if it meets—

(*a*) the equivalence condition (see regulation 74), and

(*b*) the genuine diversity of ownership condition (see regulations 75 and 76).

(2) In this Part a "diversely owned fund" means a reporting fund in respect of which the conditions mentioned in paragraph (1) are met for a period of account.

74 The equivalence condition

(1) The equivalence condition is met if the fund meets condition A[, B or C][1] throughout the period of account.

(2) Condition A is that the fund is recognised by the Financial Services Authority within the meaning of section 264 . . . [2] or 272 of FISMA 2000.

(3) Condition B is that the fund is a UCITS fund.

[(4) Condition C is that the fund—

(*a*) is constituted in another EEA state and authorised by the competent authority in that state to market to retail or professional investors, and

(*b*) is required either by the competent authority in that state or by other binding arrangements to limit its borrowing and its exposure under derivative contracts and forward transactions to 100% of its net asset value.

(5) In paragraph (4), the competent authority in an EEA state is the authority designated in accordance with Article 97 of Council Directive 2009/65/EC in relation to that fund.][1]

Commentary—*Simon's Taxes* **B5.718**.

Amendments—[1] In para (1), words substituted, and paras (4), (5) inserted, by the Offshore Funds (Tax) (Amendment) Regulations, SI 2011/1211 regs 2, 37 with effect as follows—

– for the purposes of income tax for distributions made, or treated as made, on or after 27 May 2011;

– for the purposes of corporation tax: on chargeable gains, in relation to disposals made on or after 27 May 2011; and for distributions made, or treated as made, on or after that date;

– for the purposes of capital gains tax, in relation to disposals made on or after 27 May 2011.

[2] In para (2), words ", 270" revoked by the Alternative Investment Fund Managers Regulations, SI 2013/1773 reg 81, Sch 2 para 20 with effect from 22 July 2013.

75 The genuine diversity of ownership condition

(1) The genuine diversity of ownership condition is met if the fund meets[,or, in relation to a fund constituted by a class of interests in the main arrangements, the main arrangements meet,][1] conditions A to C throughout the period of account.

(2) Condition A is that the fund produces documents, available to investors and to HMRC, which contain—

(*a*) a statement specifying the intended categories of investor,

(*b*) an undertaking that interests in the fund will be widely available, and

(*c*) an undertaking that interests in the fund will be marketed and made available in accordance with the requirements of paragraph (4)(*a*).

(3) Condition B is—

(*a*) that the specification of the intended categories of investor do not have a limiting or deterrent effect, and

(*b*) that any other terms or conditions governing participation in the fund do not have a limiting or deterrent effect.

(4) Condition C is—

(*a*) that interests in the fund must be marketed and made available—

(i) sufficiently widely to reach the intended categories of investors, and

(ii) in a manner appropriate to attract those categories of investors, and

(*b*) that a person who falls within one of the intended categories of investors can, upon request to the manager of this fund, obtain information about the fund and acquire units in it.

[(5) A fund also meets the genuine diversity of ownership condition if—

(*a*) an investor in the fund is an offshore fund, an open-ended investment company or an authorised unit trust scheme ("the feeder fund"),

(b) conditions A to C are met in relation to the fund after taking into account—

(i) the fund documents relating to the feeder fund, and

(ii) the intended investors in the feeder fund, and

(*c*) the fund and the feeder fund have the same manager (or proposed manager).][1]

Commentary—*Simon's Taxes* **B5.718**.

Amendments—[1] In para (1), words inserted, and para (5) inserted, by the Offshore Funds (Tax) (Amendment) Regulations, SI 2011/1211 regs 2, 38 with effect as follows—

– for the purposes of income tax for distributions made, or treated as made, on or after 27 May 2011;

– for the purposes of corporation tax: on chargeable gains, in relation to disposals made on or after 27 May 2011; and for distributions made, or treated as made, on or after that date;

– for the purposes of capital gains tax, in relation to disposals made on or after 27 May 2011.

76 The genuine diversity of ownership condition: further provisions

(1) For the purposes of regulation 75(3) a limiting or deterring effect means an effect which—

(*a*) limits investors to a limited number of specific persons or specific groups of connected persons, or

(*b*) deters a reasonable investor falling within one of the intended categories of investor from investing in the fund.

(2) Condition C (see regulation 75(4) shall be treated as being met even if at the relevant time the fund has no capacity to receive additional investments, unless—

(*a*) the capacity of the fund to receive investments in it is fixed by the fund documents (or otherwise), and (*b*) a pre-determined number of specific persons or specific groups of connected persons make investments in the fund which collectively exhausts all, or substantially all, of that capacity.

(3) For the purposes of this regulation—

(*a*) sections 993 and 994 of ITA 2007 (connected persons) apply in the case of a person chargeable to income tax, and

(*b*) section 839 of ICTA (connected persons) applies in the case of a person chargeable to corporation tax.

Commentary—*Simon's Taxes* **B5.718**.

Clearances in relation to the equivalence and genuine diversity of ownership conditions

77 Who may apply for clearance

(1) The following may apply for clearance that the fund meets the equivalence condition and the genuine diversity of ownership condition—

(*a*) the manager of an eligible offshore fund;

(*b*) the manager of a non-reporting fund who makes an application under regulation 52.

(2) If it is proposed to establish an offshore fund which, on its establishment, is to be an eligible offshore fund, the applicant may apply for clearance that the fund will meet the equivalence condition and the genuine diversity of ownership condition on its establishment.

Commentary—*Simon's Taxes* **B5.718**.

78 Procedure for obtaining clearance

(1) The relevant person specified in regulation 77 (the "relevant person") must apply in writing to HMRC for clearance that the fund meets the equivalence condition and the genuine diversity of ownership condition.

(2) A document submitted in accordance with paragraph (1) must be accompanied by the documents specified in regulation 75(2).

(3) HMRC may require the relevant person to provide further particulars if HMRC believe that full particulars of the fund have not been provided.

(4) HMRC must notify the relevant person within 28 days beginning with the day on which HMRC receive the documents mentioned in paragraphs (1) and (2) (or, as the case may be, the further particulars mentioned in paragraph (3))—

(*a*) giving clearance that the fund meets the equivalence condition and the genuine diversity of ownership condition,

(*b*) giving that clearance subject to conditions, or

(*c*) refusing to give that clearance.

Commentary—*Simon's Taxes* **B5.718**.

79 Circumstances in which clearance may not be relied upon

(1) An offshore fund (and investors in that fund) may not rely on a clearance given under regulation 78 if any of conditions A to D is met.

(2) Condition A is that at the beginning of the first period of account of the fund to which the clearance relates (and at the beginning of each subsequent period of account), a relevant statement in the instrument constituting the fund or in its prospectus in issue for the time being is not in accordance with a relevant statement in the documents considered by HMRC before giving clearance.

(3) Condition B is that the fund is operated otherwise than in accordance with condition C of the genuine diversity of ownership condition (see regulations 75 and 76).

(4) Condition C is that the fund acts or is operated in contravention of a relevant statement in the instrument constituting the fund or in its prospectus.

(5) Condition D is that the documents specified in regulation 75(2) are materially amended.

(6) Condition D does not apply if the relevant person specified in regulation 77 has obtained a clearance given under regulation 78 which applies to the documents in their amended form.

(7) For the purposes of condition D, a material amendment is one that may reasonably be construed as causing, or likely to cause, the fund to fail to meet the equivalence condition or the genuine diversity of ownership condition in relation to any period of account.

Commentary—*Simon's Taxes* **B5.718**.

Investment transactions carried out by diversely owned funds

80 Treatment of investment transactions carried out by diversely owned funds

(1) This regulation applies if a diversely owned fund carries out an investment transaction in an accounting period.

(2) The investment transaction is treated as a non-trading transaction.

[(3) For the purposes of these Regulations an "investment transaction" is an investment transaction specified by regulation 2 of the Investment Transactions (Tax) Regulations 2014.][1]

Amendments—[1] Para 3 inserted by the Investment Transactions (Tax) Regulations, SI 2014/685 reg 8(1), (2) with effect from 8 April 2014.

81 Meaning of "investment transaction"

Amendments—Regulations 81–89 revoked by the Investment Transactions (Tax) Regulations, SI 2014/685 reg 8(1), (3) with effect from 8 April 2014.

82 Meaning of "relevant contract": general

Amendments—Regulations 81–89 revoked by the Investment Transactions (Tax) Regulations, SI 2014/685 reg 8(1), (3) with effect from 8 April 2014.

83 Meaning of "relevant contract": options

Amendments—Regulations 81–89 revoked by the Investment Transactions (Tax) Regulations, SI 2014/685 reg 8(1), (3) with effect from 8 April 2014.

84 Meaning of "relevant contract": futures

Amendments—Regulations 81–89 revoked by the Investment Transactions (Tax) Regulations, SI 2014/685 reg 8(1), (3) with effect from 8 April 2014.

85 Options and futures: further provisions

Amendments—Regulations 81–89 revoked by the Investment Transactions (Tax) Regulations, SI 2014/685 reg 8(1), (3) with effect from 8 April 2014.

86 Meaning of "relevant contract": contracts for differences

Amendments—Regulations 81–89 revoked by the Investment Transactions (Tax) Regulations, SI 2014/685 reg 8(1), (3) with effect from 8 April 2014.

87 Interpretation of regulation 81(*c*)

Amendments—Regulations 81–89 revoked by the Investment Transactions (Tax) Regulations, SI 2014/685 reg 8(1), (3) with effect from 8 April 2014.

88 Meaning of "units in a collective investment scheme"

Amendments—Regulations 81–89 revoked by the Investment Transactions (Tax) Regulations, SI 2014/685 reg 8(1), (3) with effect from 8 April 2014.

89 Meaning of "transaction in a carbon emission trading product"

Amendments—Regulations 81–89 revoked by the Investment Transactions (Tax) Regulations, SI 2014/685 reg 8(1), (3) with effect from 8 April 2014.

[CHAPTER 6A

TRANSPARENT REPORTING FUNDS

TRANSPARENT Reporting Funds

89A Transparent reporting funds

(1) This Chapter explains how reportable income is computed in the case of a transparent reporting fund.

(2) For the purposes of these Regulations a "transparent reporting fund" is a reporting fund which is a transparent fund.][1]

Commentary—*Simon's Taxes* **B5.718A**.

Amendments—[1] Chapter 6A (regs 89A–89E) inserted by the Offshore Funds (Tax) (Amendment) Regulations, SI 2011/1211 regs 2, 24 with effect as follows—

– for the purposes of income tax for distributions made, or treated as made, on or after 27 May 2011;
– for the purposes of corporation tax: on chargeable gains, in relation to disposals made on or after 27 May 2011; and for distributions made, or treated as made, on or after that date;
– for the purposes of capital gains tax, in relation to disposals made on or after 27 May 2011.

[89B Reportable income: general

(1) A transparent reporting fund must provide a computation of its reportable income for a period of account.

(3) The reportable income of a transparent reporting fund for a period of account is comprised of—

(*a*) each of the separate sums of income for the period which fall within paragraph (*a*) or (*b*) of regulation 11 (meaning of transparent funds), and

(*b*) the adjustments made to those sums in accordance with regulations 89C to 89E.

(4) For the purposes of this Part the adjustments referred to in paragraph (3)(*b*) are excesses of reported income of the fund over the sums which form part of the income of the fund within paragraph (3)(*a*).][1]

Commentary—*Simon's Taxes* **B5.718A**.

Amendments—[1] Chapter 6A (regs 89A–89E) inserted by the Offshore Funds (Tax) (Amendment) Regulations, SI 2011/1211 regs 2, 24 with effect as follows—

– for the purposes of income tax for distributions made, or treated as made, on or after 27 May 2011;
– for the purposes of corporation tax: on chargeable gains, in relation to disposals made on or after 27 May 2011; and for distributions made, or treated as made, on or after that date;
– for the purposes of capital gains tax, in relation to disposals made on or after 27 May 2011.

[89C Adjustment in relation to income from other reporting funds

(1) This regulation applies if a transparent reporting fund ("TRF") has an interest in another reporting fund ("RF").

(2) The reportable income of TRF in relation to that interest shall include the excess (if any) of the income reported by RF in respect of TRF's interest in RF over the amount distributed by RF in relation to that interest.

(3) The excess is treated as reportable income of TRF for the period of account in which the fund distribution date of RF falls.

(4) If RF does not make a report available in accordance with regulation 90(5), TRF must—

(*a*) include its best estimate of reported income from RF as an adjustment to the computation of its reportable income in relation to that interest for the period of account in which the latest possible fund distribution date for RF falls (to the extent that any such amount has not already been recognised in the computation of TRF's reportable income for that or any earlier period of account), and

(*b*) make any necessary corrections to its best estimate in its computation of reportable income for the first later period of account in which it has sufficient information to make those corrections.][1]

Commentary—*Simon's Taxes* **B5.718A.**

Amendments—[1] Chapter 6A (regs 89A–89E) inserted by the Offshore Funds (Tax) (Amendment) Regulations, SI 2011/1211 regs 2, 24 with effect as follows—

– for the purposes of income tax for distributions made, or treated as made, on or after 27 May 2011;
– for the purposes of corporation tax: on chargeable gains, in relation to disposals made on or after 27 May 2011; and for distributions made, or treated as made, on or after that date;
– for the purposes of capital gains tax, in relation to disposals made on or after 27 May 2011.

[89D Adjustment in relation to income from non-reporting funds: first case

(1) This regulation applies if—

(*a*) a transparent reporting fund has an interest in a non-reporting fund, and

(*b*) the conditions in paragraph (2) are met for a period of account.

(2) The conditions are that—

(a) the transparent reporting fund has access to the accounts of the non-reporting fund;

(*b*) the transparent reporting fund has sufficient information about the non-reporting fund to enable it to prepare a computation of reportable income for the non-reporting fund; and

(*c*) the transparent reporting fund can reasonably expect to rely on continued access to that information for the period in which it will hold the investment in the non-reporting fund.

(3) Regulation 89C applies as if the transparent reporting fund were TRF and the non-reporting fund were RF.

(4) For the purposes of the computation mentioned in paragraph (2)(*b*), regulation 80 applies if (and only if) the non-reporting fund is a UCITS fund.][1]

Commentary—*Simon's Taxes* **B5.718A.**

Amendments—[1] Chapter 6A (regs 89A–89E) inserted by the Offshore Funds (Tax) (Amendment) Regulations, SI 2011/1211 regs 2, 24 with effect as follows—

– for the purposes of income tax for distributions made, or treated as made, on or after 27 May 2011;
– for the purposes of corporation tax: on chargeable gains, in relation to disposals made on or after 27 May 2011; and for distributions made, or treated as made, on or after that date;
– for the purposes of capital gains tax, in relation to disposals made on or after 27 May 2011.

[89E Adjustment in relation to income from non-reporting funds: second case

(1) This regulation applies if a transparent reporting fund has an interest in a non-reporting fund, but the conditions in regulation 89D(2) are not met for a period of account.

(2) The reportable income of the transparent reporting fund for a period of account in relation to that interest shall include an amount equal to the increase in the fair value of the interest in the non-reporting fund in that period.

(3) But if the condition specified in paragraph (4) is met, decreases in the fair value of that interest in earlier periods of account may be set against the increase referred to in paragraph (2) to reduce the amount of the increase, but—

(*a*) not to below zero, and

(*b*) only to the extent that the decreases in fair value have not previously had the effect of reducing the amount of a fair value increase.

(4) The condition specified is that the decrease in fair value in earlier periods of account all occurred during periods in which this Part applied continuously to the transparent reporting fund.

(5) In this regulation "fair value" in relation to an interest in a non-reporting fund means the amount which, at the time the value is to be determined, is the amount for which the interest could be exchanged between knowledgeable and willing parties dealing at arm's length.][1]

Commentary—*Simon's Taxes* **B5.718A.**

Amendments—[1] Chapter 6A (regs 89A–89E) inserted by the Offshore Funds (Tax) (Amendment) Regulations, SI 2011/1211 regs 2, 24 with effect as follows—

– for the purposes of income tax for distributions made, or treated as made, on or after 27 May 2011;

– for the purposes of corporation tax: on chargeable gains, in relation to disposals made on or after 27 May 2011; and for distributions made, or treated as made, on or after that date;
– for the purposes of capital gains tax, in relation to disposals made on or after 27 May 2011.

CHAPTER 7

REPORTS TO PARTICIPANTS

90 Report to participants for a reporting period

(1) A reporting fund must make a report available to each [relevant][1] participant for each reporting period.

(2) For the purposes of these Regulations a report is made available if the fund—

(*a*) sends the report to a [relevant][1] participant by post,

(*b*) sends the report to a [relevant][1] participant by means of an electronic communications service,

(*c*) makes the report available on a website accessible to relevant participants and to HMRC, or

(*d*) publishes the report in a newspaper which is published in English in the United Kingdom and readily available in all parts of the United Kingdom.

(3) In [this regulation][1] "relevant participants" means participants who—

(*a*) are resident in the United Kingdom, or

(*b*) are reporting funds,

during any part of the reporting period.

(4) If the fund does not provide the report to a [relevant][1] participant by sending it to the participant by post, the fund must, if so required by the participant, make the report available to the participant in some further manner (whether or not that further manner is also specified in regulation 90(2)) as the fund and the participant may agree.

(5) The reporting fund must make the report available within a period of six months beginning with the day immediately following the final day of the reporting period.

(6) The report must be in English.

Commentary—*Simon's Taxes* **B5.719**.

Amendments—[1] In paras (1), (2)(*a*), (*b*), (4) word inserted, and in para (3) words substituted, by the Offshore Funds (Tax) (Amendment) Regulations, SI 2011/1211 regs 2, 39 with effect as follows—

– for the purposes of income tax for distributions made, or treated as made, on or after 27 May 2011;
– for the purposes of corporation tax: on chargeable gains, in relation to disposals made on or after 27 May 2011; and for distributions made, or treated as made, on or after that date;
– for the purposes of capital gains tax, in relation to disposals made on or after 27 May 2011.

91 Meaning of "reporting period"

In these Regulations a "reporting period" of a reporting fund means a period determined in accordance with the following rules—

First rule

If the reporting fund's period of account is twelve months or less, the reporting period is the same as the period of account.

Second rule

If the reporting fund's period of account is more than twelve months, there are two reporting periods. The first reporting period is a period consisting of the first twelve months of the period of account. The second reporting period is a period consisting of the remainder of the period of account.

Commentary—*Simon's Taxes* **B5.719**.

92 Contents of report to participants[: non-transparent funds]

(1) [In the case of reporting funds which are not transparent funds,][2] the report to participants for a reporting period must include the following information—

(*a*) the amount actually distributed to participants per unit of interest in the fund in respect of the reporting period;

[(*b*) the amount per unit of any excess treated as additional distributions made to participants in the fund in respect of the reporting period;][3]

(*c*) the dates on which distributions were made;

(*d*) the fund distribution date (see regulation 94(4));

(*e*) a statement whether or not the fund remains a reporting fund at the date the fund makes the report available.

[(*f*) if the fund operates full equalisation arrangements and has not given a statement under regulation 50A(b)(i), the equalisation amount per unit of interest in the fund in relation to any interest acquired by way of initial purchase in the reporting period.][1]

(2) In these Regulations the "reported income" of a reporting fund for a reporting period means the reportable income of the fund for the reporting period, computed by or on behalf of the fund, and provided, in the report for the reporting period, to the participants in the fund.

(3) For the purposes of paragraph (1)—

[[(*a*) the amount in paragraph (*b*) is the amount of any excess specified in regulation 94(1) divided by the number of units in the fund in issue at the end of the reporting period.][3]

(iv) in the case of a reporting fund which does not operate equalisation arrangements and which makes income adjustments in a reporting period on the basis of accounting income, the amount determined in accordance with regulation 92B(2),

(*b*) the amount actually distributed to participants per unit of interest in the fund in respect of the reporting period must be computed at the time the distribution is made,

(*ba*) subject to paragraphs (3A) and (3B), the fund may chose to calculate the equalisation amount per unit of interest in the fund either on the basis of—

(i) the sum of all the equalisation amounts in relation to all acquisitions by way of initial purchase in the reporting period divided by the total number of units acquired by way of initial purchase in the period, or

(ii) the equalisation amount in relation to the acquisition by the participant to whom the report is made available divided by the number of units acquired on that acquisition, and][1]

(*c*) the amount per unit of interest in the fund must be expressed to at least four decimal places of a pound (or other currency unit) of value per unit.

[(3A) A fund cannot change the basis for calculating the equalisation amount per unit of interest in the fund more than once in three successive reporting periods.

(3B) In any reporting period all reports to participants must use the same basis for calculating the equalisation amount per unit of interest in the fund.][1]

(4) If the amount of the reported income per unit of interest in the fund for the reporting period is equal to, or less than, the amount actually distributed to participants per unit of interest in the fund in respect of the reporting period, the amount to be stated for the purposes of paragraph (1)(*b*) is nil.

(5) This regulation is subject to regulation 93.

Commentary—*Simon's Taxes* **B5.719**.

Amendments—[1] Para (1)(*f*) inserted, in para (3) sub-paras (*a*)–(*ba*) substituted for previous sub-paras (*a*), (*b*), and paras (3A), (3B) inserted, by the Offshore Funds (Tax) (Amendment) Regulations, SI 2011/1211 regs 2, 10 with effect as follows, and subject to transitional provision in reg 16(1)—

– for the purposes of income tax for distributions made, or treated as made, on or after 27 May 2011;
– for the purposes of corporation tax: on chargeable gains, in relation to disposals made on or after 27 May 2011; and for distributions made, or treated as made, on or after that date;
– for the purposes of capital gains tax, in relation to disposals made on or after 27 May 2011.

[2] In heading and para (1), word inserted, by the Offshore Funds (Tax) (Amendment) Regulations, SI 2011/1211 regs 2, 25 with effect as follows—

– for the purposes of income tax for distributions made, or treated as made, on or after 27 May 2011;
– for the purposes of corporation tax: on chargeable gains, in relation to disposals made on or after 27 May 2011; and for distributions made, or treated as made, on or after that date;
– for the purposes of capital gains tax, in relation to disposals made on or after 27 May 2011.

[3] Paras (1)(*b*), (3)(*a*) substituted by the Offshore Funds (Tax) (Amendment No 2) Regulations, SI 2013/1411 regs 2, 7 with effect from 28 June 2013, subject to transitional provision in reg 1(3), (5). Paras (1)(*b*), (3)(*a*) previously read as follows—

"(*b*) the excess of the amount of the reported income per unit of interest in the fund for the reporting period over the amount actually distributed to participants per unit of interest in the fund in respect of the reporting period;".

"(*a*) the reported income per unit of a reporting fund for a reporting period is—

(i) in the case of a reporting fund which operates equalisation arrangements, computed by dividing the reported income of the fund for the reporting period by the number of units in the fund in issue at the end of the reporting period,

(ii) in the case of a reporting fund which does not operates equalisation arrangements and does not make income adjustments, computed by dividing the reported income of the fund for the reporting period by the number of units in the fund in issue at the end of the reporting period,

(iii) in the case of a reporting fund which does not operate equalisation arrangements and which makes income adjustments in a reporting period on the basis of reported income, the amount determined in accordance with regulation 92A(2),

(iv) in the case of a reporting fund which does not operate equalisation arrangements and which makes income adjustments in a reporting period on the basis of accounting income, the amount determined in accordance with regulation 92B(2),".

[92A Funds which do not operate equalisation arrangements: income adjustments on the basis of reported income

(1) This regulation applies if a reporting fund does not operate equalisation arrangements and—

(*a*) *the fund has given a statement under regulation 53(1)(k)* that it intends to make income adjustments in a reporting period on the basis of reported income, or

(*b*) *regulation 92B(5) applies.*

(2) The reported income per unit of the fund for a reporting period is the sum of the reported income per unit for all the computation periods in the reporting period.

(3) The reported income per unit for a computation period is calculated by dividing the reported income of the fund for the computation period by the average number of units in the fund in issue during the computation period.
(4) For the purposes of paragraph (3) the reported income of the fund for a computation period means the reportable income of the fund for that period computed in accordance with Chapters 5 and 6 of this Part.
(5) In the computation referred to in paragraph (4) Chapters 5 and 6 of this Part apply as if references to a period of account of the fund were references to a computation period.
(6) For the purposes of paragraph (3) and regulation 92B(3) the average number of units in issue during a computation period is the sum of the units in the fund in issue during the period after each unit has been multiplied by the fraction of the period for which it is held.][1], [2]

Commentary—*Simon's Taxes* **B5.719**.

Amendments—[1] Regs 92A–92C inserted, by the Offshore Funds (Tax) (Amendment) Regulations, SI 2011/1211 regs 2, 11 with effect as follows, and subject to transitional provision in reg 16(1)—

- for the purposes of income tax for distributions made, or treated as made, on or after 27 May 2011;
- for the purposes of corporation tax: on chargeable gains, in relation to disposals made on or after 27 May 2011; and for distributions made, or treated as made, on or after that date;
- for the purposes of capital gains tax, in relation to disposals made on or after 27 May 2011.

[2] Regs 92A–92C revoked by the Offshore Funds (Tax) (Amendment No. 2) Regulations, SI 2013/1411 regs 2, 8 with effect from 28 June 2013, subject to transitional provision in reg 1(3), (5).

[92B Funds which do not operate equalisation arrangements: income adjustments on the basis of accounting income

(1) This regulation applies if a reporting fund does not operate equalisation arrangements and the fund has given a statement under regulation 53(1)(k) that it intends to make income adjustments in a reporting period on the basis of accounting income.
(2) The reported income per unit of the fund for a reporting period is calculated as follows—

AIU × RI / AI

where—

AIU is the sum of the accounting income per unit for all the computation periods in the reporting period,

RI is the reported income of the fund for the reporting period, and

AI is the sum of accounting income for all the computation periods in the reporting period.

This is subject to paragraphs (4) and (5).
(3) The accounting income per unit for a computation period is calculated by dividing accounting income for the computation period by the average number of units in the fund in issue during the computation period.
(4) Where RI is zero the reported income per unit of the fund for a reporting period is zero.
(5) Where the difference in the amount of reported income per unit calculated using this method and the amount of reported income per unit calculated on the basis of reported income is or is likely to be more than 10% of the latter of those amounts—

(*a*) *the fund must make income adjustments in that and future reporting periods on the basis of reported income, and*
(*b*) *the manager must give notice to HMRC of the change in the method of income adjustment with the information provided to HMRC in relation to that period under regulation 106 (reporting requirements).*

(6) In this Part "accounting income" means an amount proportionally related to the reportable income of the fund determined from the interim or management accounts of the fund, but this amount must not be less than zero.][1], [2]

Commentary—*Simon's Taxes* **B5.719**.

Amendments—[1] Regs 92A–92C inserted, by the Offshore Funds (Tax) (Amendment) Regulations, SI 2011/1211 regs 2, 11 with effect as follows, and subject to transitional provision in reg 16(1)—

- for the purposes of income tax for distributions made, or treated as made, on or after 27 May 2011;
- for the purposes of corporation tax: on chargeable gains, in relation to disposals made on or after 27 May 2011; and for distributions made, or treated as made, on or after that date;
- for the purposes of capital gains tax, in relation to disposals made on or after 27 May 2011.

[2] Regs 92A–92C revoked by the Offshore Funds (Tax) (Amendment No. 2) Regulations, SI 2013/1411 regs 2, 8 with effect from 28 June 2013, subject to transitional provision in reg 1(3), (5).

[92C Funds which do not operate equalisation arrangements: computation period

In this Part a "computation period" means a period determined by a fund in accordance with the following rules.

Rule 1

A new computation period must start—

(*a*) *at the beginning of a reporting period, and*
(*b*) *immediately after the end of a previous computation period.*

Rule 2

A computation period must end—

(*a*) *at the end of a reporting period, and*

(*b*) *on any date on which income is allocated to participants for distribution or accumulation.*

Rule 3

Subject to rules 1 and 2, if a reporting period consists of more than one computation period those periods must be of approximately equal length.][1], [2]

Commentary—*Simon's Taxes* **B5.719**.

Amendments—[1] Regs 92A–92C inserted, by the Offshore Funds (Tax) (Amendment) Regulations, SI 2011/1211 regs 2, 11 with effect as follows, and subject to transitional provision in reg 16(1)—

– for the purposes of income tax for distributions made, or treated as made, on or after 27 May 2011;
– for the purposes of corporation tax: on chargeable gains, in relation to disposals made on or after 27 May 2011; and for distributions made, or treated as made, on or after that date;
– for the purposes of capital gains tax, in relation to disposals made on or after 27 May 2011.

[2] Regs 92A–92C revoked by the Offshore Funds (Tax) (Amendment No. 2) Regulations, SI 2013/1411 regs 2, 8 with effect from 28 June 2013, subject to transitional provision in reg 1(3), (5).

[92D Contents of reports to participants: transparent reporting funds

In the case of transparent reporting funds, the report to participants for a reporting period must—

(*a*) contain sufficient information to enable those participants to meet their tax obligations in the United Kingdom with respect to their interests in the fund, and

(*b*) include a statement whether or not the fund remains a reporting fund at the date the fund makes the report available.][1]

Commentary—*Simon's Taxes* **B5.719**.

Amendments—[1] Reg 92D inserted by the Offshore Funds (Tax) (Amendment) Regulations, SI 2011/1211 regs 2, 26 with effect as follows—

– for the purposes of income tax for distributions made, or treated as made, on or after 27 May 2011;
– for the purposes of corporation tax: on chargeable gains, in relation to disposals made on or after 27 May 2011; and for distributions made, or treated as made, on or after that date;
– for the purposes of capital gains tax, in relation to disposals made on or after 27 May 2011.

93 Lengthy periods of account where full information not available

(1) This regulation applies if a reporting fund—

(*a*) has a period of account which is longer than twelve months, and

(*b*) has difficulty in computing its reportable income for the reporting period constituting the first twelve months of that period of account (the "relevant reporting period").

(2) For the purpose of preparing its report to participants for the relevant reporting period, the fund may elect—

(*a*) to compute its reportable income based on such information as is reasonably available, or

(*b*) to make a just and reasonable apportionment of the income of the period of account.

(3) The computation of reportable income for the reporting period following the relevant reporting period must include all amounts not accounted for in the relevant reporting period.

Commentary—*Simon's Taxes* **B5.719**.

CHAPTER 8

THE TAX TREATMENT OF PARTICIPANTS IN REPORTING FUNDS

Tax treatment of the reported income of the fund in the hands of participants

94 Reported income: general provisions

(1) In the case of a reporting fund which is not a transparent fund, the Tax Acts have effect as if the excess (if any) of the reported income of the fund in respect of a reporting period over the distributions made by the fund in respect of the reporting period were additional distributions made to the participants in the fund in proportion to their rights.

(2) In the case of a reporting fund which is a transparent fund, the Tax Acts have effect as if the excess (if any) of the reported income of the fund in respect of a reporting period over the income of the fund for the reporting period were additional income of the participants in the fund in proportion to their rights.

[(2A) But to the extent that the participant's rights in the fund are rights to which regulation 30 (rights in certain existing holdings) applies, the excess specified in [paragraphs (1) and (2)][2] shall be reduced proportionately.][1]

(3) The excess specified in paragraphs (1) and (2) is treated as made, on the fund distribution date, [or on such earlier date as the reported income in respect of that reporting period is recognised in the participant's accounts,][2] to participants holding an interest in the fund at the end of the reporting period.

[(3A) If—

(*a*) a participant disposes of an interest in a reporting fund in a reporting period ("the earlier period"), and

(*b*) section 106A of TCGA 1992 (identification of securities: capital gains tax) applies to identify the whole or any part of that interest with an interest acquired in the next reporting period, then, for the purposes of paragraph (3), the disposal of the interest so identified shall be ignored and the participant shall be treated as holding that interest at the end of the earlier period.][2]

(4) In these Regulations the "fund distribution date" for a reporting period of a reporting fund [means the date six months following the last day of the reporting period.][2]

Commentary—*Simon's Taxes* **B5.720**.

Amendments—[1] Para (2A) inserted by the Offshore Funds (Tax) (Amendment) Regulations, SI 2009/3139 regs 2, 4 with effect as follows—

- for income tax purposes for the tax year 2009–10 and subsequent tax years and for distributions made on or after 1 December 2009;
- for corporation tax purposes, on income for accounting periods ending on or after 1 December 2009 and for distributions made on or after that date, and on chargeable gains in relation to disposals made on or after 1 December 2009; and
- for capital gains tax purposes, in relation to disposals made on or after 1 December 2009.

[2] In para (2A), words substituted, in para (3), words inserted, para (3A) inserted, and in para (4), words substituted, by the Offshore Funds (Tax) (Amendment) Regulations, SI 2011/1211 regs 2, 39 with effect as follows—

- for the purposes of income tax for distributions made, or treated as made, on or after 27 May 2011;
- for the purposes of corporation tax: on chargeable gains, in relation to disposals made on or after 27 May 2011; and for distributions made, or treated as made, on or after that date;
- for the purposes of capital gains tax, in relation to disposals made on or after 27 May 2011.

[94A Equalisation amounts not treated as distributions

(1) This regulation applies if—

(*a*) a participant has acquired by way of initial purchase an interest in a reporting fund, and

(*b*) the reporting fund operates full equalisation arrangements.

[(2) Where this regulation applies, distributions are reduced in accordance with either option 1 or option 2.

Option 1

Under this option—

(*a*) the amount of any actual distributions to the participant in respect of the reporting period is reduced by the equalisation amount, and

(*b*) the amount of any excess treated as additional distributions made to the participant is reduced by the amount, if any, by which the equalisation amount exceeds the amount of any actual distributions to the participant in respect of the reporting period.

Option 2

Under this option—

(*a*) the amount of any excess treated as additional distributions made to the participant is reduced by the equalisation amount, and

(*b*) the amount of any actual distributions to the participant in respect of the reporting period is reduced by the amount, if any, by which the equalisation amount exceeds the excess.][2]

(3) But the amount of any excess treated as additional distributions or any actual distributions shall not be reduced to below nil.

(4) For the purposes of paragraph (2) the excess is the amount treated as additional distributions made to the participant in accordance with regulation 94(1) and (2).][1]

Commentary—*Simon's Taxes* **B5.720**.

Amendments—[1] Reg 94A inserted by the Offshore Funds (Tax) (Amendment) Regulations, SI 2009/3139 regs 2, 12 with effect as follows—

- for income tax purposes for the tax year 2009–10 and subsequent tax years and for distributions made on or after 1 December 2009;
- for corporation tax purposes, on income for accounting periods ending on or after 1 December 2009 and for distributions made on or after that date, and on chargeable gains in relation to disposals made on or after 1 December 2009; and
- for capital gains tax purposes, in relation to disposals made on or after 1 December 2009.

[2] Para (2) substituted by the Offshore Funds (Tax) (Amendment No. 2) Regulations, SI 2013/1411 regs 2, 9 with effect from 28 June 2013. This amendment does not apply in relation to interests in offshore funds acquired in a reporting period which began before 28 June 2013. "Reporting period" has the same meaning as in reg 91 (SI 2013/1411 reg 1(4), (5)).

95 Participants chargeable to income tax: corporate funds

(1) This regulation applies if—

(*a*) a reporting fund makes a distribution to a participant chargeable to income tax in respect of a reporting period, and

(*b*) the fund falls within section 40A(2)(*a*) of FA 2008.

(2) This regulation also applies if some or all of the excess specified in regulation 94(1) is treated as made by such a fund to such a participant.

(3) If section 378A of ITTOIA 2005 (offshore fund distributions) applies to any amount falling within paragraph (1) or (2), the amount is charged to income tax in accordance with that section.

(4) If paragraph (3) does not apply to any amount falling within paragraph (1) or (2), but the participant is entitled to a tax credit on receiving a distribution falling within paragraph (1), section 397A of ITTOIA 2005 (savings and investment income: dividends from non-UK resident companies) also applies to the excess falling within paragraph (2).

Commentary—*Simon's Taxes* **B5.720**.

96 Participants chargeable to income tax: other non-transparent funds

(1) This regulation applies if—

(*a*) a reporting fund makes a distribution to a participant chargeable to income tax in respect of a reporting period,

(*b*) the fund falls within paragraph (*b*) or (*c*) of section 40A(2) of FA 2008, and

(*c*) the fund is not a transparent fund.

(2) This regulation also applies if some or all of the excess specified in regulation 94(1) is treated as made by such a fund to such a participant.

(3) Any amount to which paragraph (1) or (2) applies is charged to income tax—

(*a*) under section 378A of ITTOIA 2005 (offshore fund distributions), or

(*b*) (if that section does not apply) under Chapter 8 of Part 5 of ITTOIA 2005 (miscellaneous income: income not otherwise charged) for the year of assessment in which the distribution is made, but sections 688(1) and 689 of ITTOIA 2005 (income charged and person liable) do not apply.

Commentary—*Simon's Taxes* **B5.720**.

97 Participants chargeable to income tax: transparent funds

(1) This regulation applies if—

(*a*) a reporting fund is a transparent fund, and

(*b*) some or all of the excess specified in regulation 94(2) is treated as income of a participant by virtue of that provision.

(2) Any amount to which paragraph (1) applies is charged to income tax under Chapter 8 of Part 5 of ITTOIA 2005 as relevant foreign income within the meaning given by section 830 of ITTOIA 2005 for the year of assessment in which the distribution is made, but sections 688(1) and 689 of ITTOIA 2005 do not apply.

Commentary—*Simon's Taxes* **B5.720**.

98 Participants chargeable to corporation tax

(1) This regulation applies if some or all of the excess specified in regulation 94 is treated as made to a participant chargeable to corporation tax.

(2) The amount is exempt if it would be exempt if it were an actual distribution made by the fund.

Commentary—*Simon's Taxes* **B5.720**.

Disposals and deemed disposals of interests

99 Disposals of interests

(1) If a participant has an interest in a reporting fund and disposes of the interest, the participant disposes of an asset for the purposes of tax in respect of chargeable gains.

(2) For the purposes of the disposal referred to in paragraph (1), an amount equal to the accumulated undistributed income is treated as expenditure—

(*a*) given for the acquisition of the asset, and

(*b*) falling within section 38(1)(*a*) of TCGA 1992 (acquisition and disposal costs).

[(2A) But where regulation 94A has applied, the expenditure given for the acquisition of the asset shall be treated as reduced by an amount equal to the amount of any reduction [in the actual distribution under regulation 94A(2)][2].][1]

(3) In paragraph (2) the "accumulated undistributed income" means the aggregate of amounts specified in regulation 94 on which the participant has been charged to tax under any of regulations 95 to 98.

(4) The expenditure mentioned in paragraph (2) is treated as incurred, in the case of each amount referred to in paragraph (3), on the fund distribution date for the reporting period in respect of which the amount is treated as distributed.

(5) But if the participant receives an amount in respect of the interest in the reporting fund which is chargeable to income tax, and that amount is received (or treated as received) after the date of the disposal referred to in paragraph (1), the amount is treated as received immediately before that disposal for the purposes of tax in respect of chargeable gains.

(6) This regulation is subject to regulation 17.

Commentary—*Simon's Taxes* **B5.721**.

Amendments—[1] Para (2A) inserted by the Offshore Funds (Tax) (Amendment) Regulations, SI 2009/3139 regs 2, 13 with effect as follows—

- for income tax purposes for the tax year 2009–10 and subsequent tax years and for distributions made on or after 1 December 2009;
- for corporation tax purposes, on income for accounting periods ending on or after 1 December 2009 and for distributions made on or after that date, and on chargeable gains in relation to disposals made on or after 1 December 2009; and
- for capital gains tax purposes, in relation to disposals made on or after 1 December 2009.

2 In para (2A), words substituted for words "under regulation 94A(2)(*b*)" by the Offshore Funds (Tax) (Amendment No. 2) Regulations, SI 2013/1411 regs 2, 10 with effect from 28 June 2013. This amendment does not apply in relation to interests in offshore funds acquired in a reporting period which began before 28th June 2013. "Reporting period" has the same meaning as in reg 91 (SI 2013/1411 reg 1(4), (5)).

100 Deemed disposals of interests

(1) This regulation applies if an offshore fund ceases to be a reporting fund and becomes a non-reporting fund.

(2) A participant in the fund may make an election to be treated for the purposes of TCGA 1992—

(*a*) as disposing of an interest in the reporting fund at the end of that fund's final period of account, and

(*b*) as acquiring an interest in the non-reporting fund at the beginning of that fund's first period of account.

This is subject to paragraph (3).

(3) The election mentioned in paragraph (2) may only be made if a report has been made available to the participant under regulation 90 for the reporting fund's final period of account.

(4) The disposal referred to in paragraph (2)(*a*) is treated as made for a consideration equal to the net asset value of the participant's interest in the fund at the end of the period of account for which the final reported income is reported to the participant.

(5) The acquisition referred to in paragraph (2)(*b*) is treated as made for the same amount as the disposal referred to in paragraph (2)(*a*).

(6) If the participant is chargeable to income tax, the election mentioned in paragraph (2) must be made by being included in a return made for the tax year which includes the disposal date.

(7) If the participant is chargeable to corporation tax, the election mentioned in paragraph (2) must be made by being included in the participant's company tax return for the accounting period which includes the disposal date.

(8) In this regulation—

"company tax return" has the same meaning as in Schedule 18 to the Finance Act 1998;

"disposal date" means the final day of the reporting fund's final period of account.

Commentary—*Simon's Taxes* **B5.721**.

Charitable companies and charitable trusts

101 Special provisions applying to charitable companies and charitable trusts

(1) This regulation applies if—

(*a*) a charitable company is a participant in a reporting fund, or

(*b*) the trustees of a charitable trust are participants in a reporting fund.

(2) No liability to tax arises in respect of any amount which, under regulation 94(1), is treated as distributed to a charitable company or the trustees of a charitable trust.

(3) Paragraph (2) of regulation 99 (read with paragraphs (3) and (4) of that regulation) does not apply to the disposal of an interest in a reporting fund by a charitable company or the trustees of a charitable trust.

(4) In this regulation "charity" and "charitable company" have the same meaning as in section 506 of ICTA.

Commentary—*Simon's Taxes* **B5.721**.

Anti-avoidance provisions

102 Treatment of financial traders if conditions specified in regulation 73 are met

(1) This group of regulations applies if a financial trader holds, or has held, an interest in a diversely owned fund.

(2) In this Chapter—

"this group of regulations" means this regulation and regulations 103 to 105;

"financial trader" has the meaning given by regulation 105.

(3) In computing the trading profits or losses of the financial trader for the relevant period, the following amounts must be brought into account—

(*a*) all distributions received by or credited to the financial trader in respect of the interest for the relevant period, and

(*b*) any amount required to be brought into account under regulation 103.

(4) In this group of regulations "relevant period" means—

(*a*) in the case of a financial trader within the charge to income tax, a period of account, and

(*b*) in the case of a financial trader within the charge to corporation tax, an accounting period.

(5) In this group of regulations references to distributions are subject to section 130 of CTA 2009 (insurers receiving distributions etc).

Commentary—*Simon's Taxes* **B5.722**.

103 Amounts brought into account in computing trading profits or losses of financial traders

(1) The only amounts that may be brought into account in computing the trading profits or losses of the financial trader in respect of the interest in the reporting fund for the relevant period are—

(*a*) amounts within regulation 102(3)(*a*), and

(*b*) amounts brought into account in accordance with Cases A to D.

(2) Paragraph (1) is subject to section 130 of CTA 2009 and to regulation 104.

(3) Case A applies if the financial trader holds the interest at the beginning of the relevant period and continues to hold the interest throughout the relevant period.

If Case A applies, the amount to be brought into account is the difference between the market value of the interest at the end of the relevant period and the market value of the interest at the end of the period immediately preceding the relevant period.

(4) Case B applies if the financial trader acquires the interest during the relevant period and continues to hold the interest throughout the remainder of the relevant period.

If Case B applies, the amount to be brought into account is the difference between the market value of the interest at the end of the relevant period and the acquisition cost of the interest.

(5) Case C applies if the financial trader holds the interest at the beginning of the relevant period and disposes of the interest during the period.

If Case C applies the amount to be brought into account is the difference between the disposal value of the interest and the market value of the interest at the end of the period immediately preceding the relevant period.

(6) Case D applies if the financial trader acquires and disposes of the interest during the relevant period.

If Case D applies the amount to be brought into account is the difference between the disposal value of the interest and its acquisition cost.

Commentary—*Simon's Taxes* **B5.722**.

104 Interests not within regulation 103

(1) Regulation 103 does not apply in respect of an interest in a reporting fund if—

(*a*) conditions A and B are met, or

(*b*) condition C is met.

(2) Condition A is that the interest forms part of the financial trader's stock in trade and all the profits and losses, including distributions, arising in respect of the interest are included in the computation of the financial trader's trading profits for the relevant period.

(3) Condition B is that the interest is accounted for under generally accepted accounting practice on the basis of fair value accounting.

(4) Condition C is that the interest is a relevant holding in respect of which the provisions of section 490 of CTA 2009 (holdings in OEICs, unit trusts and offshore funds treated as creditor relationship rights) apply in relation to the financial trader.

(5) In paragraph (4) a "relevant holding" means—

(*a*) any rights under a unit trust scheme,

(*b*) a material interest in an offshore fund, or

(*c*) any shares in an open-ended investment company.

Commentary—*Simon's Taxes* **B5.722**.

105 Meaning of "financial trader"

(1) In this Chapter "financial trader" means a person who is carrying on a business which is—

(*a*) a banking business,

(*b*) an insurance business, or

(*c*) a business consisting wholly or in part of dealing in trading assets such that any profit on such assets would form part of the trading profits of that business.

This is subject to paragraphs (2) and (3).

(2) For the purposes of paragraph (1)(*b*) an insurance business does not include life assurance business carried on by an insurance company and if such a company carries on both life assurance business and any other insurance business the company must not be treated as a financial trader in respect of the life assurance business.

(3) If—

(*a*) a financial trader ("A") directly or indirectly transfers trading assets to a diversely owned fund under, or as part of, an arrangement which has an unallowable purpose, and

(*b*) a connected person ("B")—

(i) holds an interest in the diversely owned fund at the time of the transfer, or

(ii) directly or indirectly acquires an interest in the diversely owned fund at a later time,

B is treated as being a financial trader in relation to that interest.

(4) In this regulation "trading assets" means—

(*a*) stocks or shares;

(*b*) a relevant contract (construed in accordance with regulations 82 to 86);

(*c*) a loan relationship (construed in accordance with regulation 87);

(*d*) units in a collective investment scheme (construed in accordance with regulation 88);

(*e*) securities of any description not falling within any of sub-paragraphs (*a*) to (*d*);

(*f*) foreign currency; or

(*g*) a carbon emission trading product (construed in accordance with regulation 89);

a profit on the sale of which would form part of the trading profits of the financial trader.

(5) An arrangement includes any scheme, understanding or transaction of any kind, whether or not legally enforceable and whether involving a single transaction or two or more transactions.

(6) An arrangement has an unallowable purpose if the main purpose or one of the main purposes for either A or B being party to the arrangement is to obtain a tax advantage or an income tax advantage for any person.

(7) In paragraph (6)—

"tax advantage" has the meaning given by section of 840ZA of ICTA;

"income tax advantage" has the meaning given by section 683 of ITA 2007.

Commentary—*Simon's Taxes* **B5.722.**

CHAPTER 9

THE PROVISION OF INFORMATION TO HMRC

106 Reporting requirements

(1) A reporting fund must provide the following information to HMRC in relation to each period of account—

(*a*) [subject to paragraph (3),][1] its audited accounts . . . [1];

(*b*) its computation of its reportable income for the period of account based on its audited accounts (see Chapter 5 [or 6A, as the case may be][1]);

(*c*) a copy of the report made available to participants for each reporting period falling within the period of account (including, for each reporting period, the information specified in regulation 92(1) [or 92D, as the case may be][1]);

(*d*) the reported income of the fund for each reporting period falling within the period of account;

(*e*) the amount actually distributed to participants in respect of each reporting period falling within the period of account;

(*f*) the number of units in the fund in issue at the end of each reporting period falling within the period of account;

(*g*) the amount of the reported income per unit of interest in the fund in respect of each reporting period falling within the period of account;

(*h*) a declaration confirming that the fund has complied with the obligations specified in regulations 53 and 58.

(2) The information specified in paragraph (1) must be provided within six months of the end of the period of account.

[(3) A reporting fund may provide unaudited accounts for a period of account if HMRC are satisfied, in relation to that period, that—

(*a*) it would be impossible [to provide audited accounts or unreasonable to expect them to be provided, and][2]

(*b*) there is no reason to believe that the unaudited accounts cannot be relied upon for the purposes of calculating reportable income.][1]

Commentary—*Simon's Taxes* **B5.723.**

Amendments—[1] In para (1), in sub-para (*a*) words inserted and words revoked, and in sub-paras (*b*), (*c*) words inserted, and para (3) inserted, by the Offshore Funds (Tax) (Amendment) Regulations, SI 2011/1211 regs 2, 27, 41 with effect as follows—

– for the purposes of income tax for distributions made, or treated as made, on or after 27 May 2011;

– for the purposes of corporation tax: on chargeable gains, in relation to disposals made on or after 27 May 2011; and for distributions made, or treated as made, on or after that date;

– for the purposes of capital gains tax, in relation to disposals made on or after 27 May 2011.

[2] In para (3)(*a*), words substituted for words "or unreasonable to provide audited accounts, and" by the Offshore Funds (Tax) (Amendment No. 2) Regulations, SI 2013/1411 regs 2, 11 with effect from 28 June 2013.

107 Information obligations of reporting funds

(1) HMRC may give notice requiring a reporting fund or its managers, within such time, not being less than 42 days, as is specified in the notice, to provide any information, particulars or documents, in the possession or power of the reporting fund or its managers, as HMRC may reasonably require for the purposes of determining whether the fund has met, or continues to meet, its obligations under Chapter 3 of this Part.

(2) Before a notice is given to a reporting fund by HMRC under paragraph (1), the fund must have been given a reasonable opportunity to deliver the information, particulars or documents, or to make them available (the "initial request"); and HMRC must not give notice under paragraph (1) until the initial request has been given to the fund.

(3) HMRC must give the initial request to the reporting fund or its manager within a period of one year beginning with the day that the fund provides the information specified in regulation 106(1).

(4) HMRC may extend the time specified in paragraph (1) if they consider it reasonable to do so.

(5) A person to whom a notice under paragraph (1) is given may appeal.

(6) The notice of appeal must be given to HMRC within a period of 42 days beginning with the day on which the notice under paragraph (1) is given.

(7) On an appeal, the tribunal may uphold, vary or quash the notice.

Commentary—*Simon's Taxes* **B5.723**.

CHAPTER 10

BREACHES OF REPORTING FUND REQUIREMENTS

108 Types of breaches

(1) This Chapter applies if a reporting fund is in breach of a requirement imposed in this Part.

(2) A breach of a requirement imposed in this Part is—

(*a*) a minor breach, or

(*b*) a serious breach.

(3) For the purposes of these Regulations, a breach of a requirement imposed in this Part is a "serious breach" if it is—

(*a*) a breach specified as a serious breach in a provision of this Chapter, or

(*b*) a breach which is not a minor breach.

(4) For the purposes of these Regulations, a breach of a requirement imposed in this Part is a "minor breach" if it is a breach (other than a breach specified as a serious breach in a provision of this Chapter)—

(*a*) for which there is a reasonable excuse, or

(*b*) which is inadvertent and remedied as soon as reasonably possible.

This paragraph is subject to the following provisions of this regulation.

(5) For the purposes of this Part a minor breach is not regarded as a breach if the reporting fund corrects the breach without any HMRC intervention.

(6) For the purposes of these Regulations there is an "HMRC intervention" in relation to a reporting fund if HMRC request the fund to provide them with information relating to a requirement imposed in this Part.

This is subject to paragraph (7).

(7) There is no HMRC intervention in relation to a reporting fund if—

(*a*) the fund takes the initiative to correct a minor breach, and

(*b*) HMRC request the fund to provide them with information so that they may deal with the initiative taken.

(8) Regulation 109 deals with the consequences of minor breaches.

(9) Regulation 114 deals with the consequences of serious breaches.

Commentary—*Simon's Taxes* **B5.724**.

109 Consequences of minor breaches

(1) If a reporting fund is in breach of a requirement imposed in this Part and the breach is a minor breach, the fund continues to be treated as a reporting fund.

(2) Paragraph (1) is subject to the following provisions of this Chapter.

(3) If paragraph (1) applies on four separate occasions in a period of ten years beginning with the first day of the period of account in which the first breach occurs, the fourth breach is a serious breach.

(4) If a single event results in more than one minor breach within a single period of account, there is only one minor breach in that period of account for the purposes of this Chapter.

Commentary—*Simon's Taxes* **B5.724**.

110 Differences between reported income and reportable income

(1) This regulation applies if there is a difference between—

(*a*) the reportable income of a reporting fund for a period of account, and

(*b*) the reported income of the fund for all reporting periods comprised in the period of account.

(2) The following amounts must be determined for each reporting period comprised in the period of account—

(*a*) the amount of the reported income for the reporting period, and

(*b*) the amount of the reportable income for the period of account that is referable to that reporting period.

(3) If the difference between the two amounts specified in paragraph (2) is 10% or less of the reportable income, there is no breach of a requirement imposed in this Part.

(4) If the difference between the two amounts specified in paragraph (2) is more than 10% but not more than 15% of the reportable income—

(*a*) an amount equal to the difference must be added to the reported income—

(i) for the reporting period in which the error is established, or

(ii) for the following reporting period; or

(*b*) the reporting fund must make a supplementary report for the period of account in which the difference occurs before the end of a period of three months beginning immediately after the period of account in which the error is established.

(5) If the difference between the two amounts specified in paragraph (2) is more than 15% of the reportable income, the reporting fund must make a supplementary report to participants for the period of account in which the difference occurs before the end of a period of three months beginning immediately after the period of account in which the error is established.

(6) The supplementary report mentioned in paragraphs (4) and (5) must be made to those persons who were participants in the fund at the end of the period of account in which the difference occurs.

(7) If paragraph (4) or (5) applies and the action specified in the applicable paragraph is taken as soon as reasonably possible, there is a minor breach.

(8) If paragraph (4) or (5) applies but the action specified in the applicable paragraph is not taken as soon as reasonably possible, there is a serious breach.

(9) For the purposes of paragraph (4) an error is established for a reporting period if, during that reporting period—

(*a*) HMRC conclude—

(i) that an error has been made in respect of an earlier reporting period, and

(ii) that, as a result of the error, the difference between the reported income for the reporting period and the reportable income for the period of account in which the reporting period is comprised is more than 10% but not more than 15%; and

(*b*) HMRC give notice to the reporting fund of the matters specified in sub-paragraph (*a*).

(10) For the purposes of paragraph (5) an error is established for a period of account if, during that period of account—

(*a*) HMRC conclude—

(i) that an error has been made in respect of an earlier period of account, and

(ii) that, as a result of the error, the difference between the reported income and the reportable income for the period of account is more than 15%; and

(*b*) HMRC give notice to the reporting fund of the matters specified in sub-paragraph (*a*).

Commentary—*Simon's Taxes* **B5.724.**

111 Provision of report that is incorrect or incomplete

(1) This regulation applies if—

(*a*) a reporting fund provides a report specified in paragraph (2) that is incorrect or incomplete, and

(*b*) regulation 110 does not apply.

(2) The reports specified are—

(*a*) the report to participants in accordance with the requirements of Chapter 7 of this Part, and

(*b*) the report to HMRC in accordance with the requirements of Chapter 9 of this Part.

(3) If the reporting fund provides a correct report as soon as reasonably possible, there is a minor breach.

(4) If the reporting fund does not provide a correct report as soon as reasonably possible, there is a serious breach.

Commentary—*Simon's Taxes* **B5.724.**

112 Cases where information is not provided

(1) This regulation applies if, on the relevant date, a reporting fund has not provided—

(*a*) the information specified in regulation 106(1) to HMRC in relation to a period of account (the "requisite period of account"), and

(*b*) a report to each participant for each reporting period comprised in the requisite period of account.

(2) In paragraph (1) the "relevant date" means the day immediately following the expiry of the period of six months beginning immediately after the end of the requisite period of account.

(3) If the reporting fund provides the information mentioned in paragraph (1)(*a*) and the reports mentioned in paragraph (1)(*b*) within a period of four months beginning with the relevant date, the breach is not regarded as a breach for the purposes of this Part.

(4) If the reporting fund does not provide the information mentioned in paragraph (1)(*a*) and the reports mentioned in paragraph (1)(*b*) within a period of four months beginning with the relevant date but does provide that information and those reports within a period of twelve months beginning with the relevant date, there is a minor breach.

(5) If the reporting fund does not provide the information mentioned in paragraph (1)(*a*) and the reports mentioned in paragraph (1)(*b*) within a period of twelve months beginning with the relevant date, there is a serious breach.

Commentary—*Simon's Taxes* **B5.724.**

113 Serious breaches

(1) There is a serious breach if condition A, B, C or D is met.

(2) Condition A is that a period of account of a reporting fund exceeds 18 months.

(3) Condition B is that a reporting fund has used an accounting practice which—

(*a*) is not in accordance with international accounting standards, and

(*b*) has not been approved by HMRC (see regulations 53, 55 and 61).

(4) Condition C is that—

(*a*) a reporting fund fails, or its managers fail, to provide the information, particulars or documents within the time specified in a notice given under regulation 107(1), and

(*b*) there is no appeal against the notice within the time specified in regulation 107(6).

(5) Condition D is that—

(*a*) on an appeal against a notice given under regulation 107(1), the tribunal varies the notice,

(*b*) a reporting fund fails, or its managers fail, to provide the information, particulars or documents within the time specified in the notice (as so varied), and

(*c*) there is no appeal against the decision of the tribunal.

Commentary—*Simon's Taxes* **B5.724**.

114 Consequences of serious breaches

(1) This regulation applies if conditions A and B are met.

(2) Condition A is that—

(*a*) a reporting fund is in breach of a requirement imposed in this Part, and

(*b*) the breach is a serious breach.

(3) Condition B is that HMRC give notice to the fund—

(*a*) stating that the fund is in breach of a requirement imposed in this Part and that the breach is a serious breach, and

(*b*) specifying the serious breach.

(4) The fund is treated as a non-reporting fund for the reporting period in which HMRC give the notice and for all subsequent periods.

This is subject to paragraphs (5) and (6).

(5) If regulation 113(4) applies, the fund is treated as a non-reporting fund for the reporting period in which the notice is given and for all subsequent periods.

(6) If regulation 113(5) applies, the fund is treated as a non-reporting fund for the reporting period in which the notice as varied is given and for all subsequent periods.

Commentary—*Simon's Taxes* **B5.724**.

115 Appeal against exclusion from the reporting fund regime

(1) If HMRC give notice to a fund under regulation 114(3) (an "exclusion notice"), the fund may appeal.

(2) The notice of appeal must be given to HMRC within a period of 42 days beginning with the day on which the exclusion notice is given.

(3) On an appeal, the tribunal may uphold or quash the exclusion notice.

Commentary—*Simon's Taxes* **B5.724**.

CHAPTER 11

LEAVING THE REPORTING FUND REGIME

116 Termination by notice given by reporting fund

(1) If a reporting fund gives a notice under this regulation specifying a day (the "specified day") at the end of which this Part is to cease to apply to the fund, this Part shall cease to apply to the fund at the end of that day.

(2) The specified day must be the last day of a period of account of the reporting fund.

(3) A notice under paragraph (1) must be given in writing to HMRC before the specified day.

(4) If the fund gives a notice under paragraph (1), the fund must also make the notice available to each participant before the specified day.

(5) Paragraphs (2) to (4) of regulation 90 apply to determine whether the notice is made available to a participant in the same way as they apply to determine whether a report for a reporting period is made available to a participant.

(6) This regulation is subject to regulation 117.

Commentary—*Simon's Taxes* **B5.725**.

117 Reporting fund not complying with requirements

(1) This regulation applies if—

(*a*) a reporting fund gives a notice under regulation 116, and

(*b*) the fund has not complied with all requirements imposed in this Part for all periods during which it was a reporting fund.

(2) For the purposes of these Regulations the fund is treated as a fund to which regulation 114 has applied and not as a fund to which regulation 116 has applied.

Commentary—*Simon's Taxes* **B5.725**.

CHAPTER 12

CONSTANT NAV FUNDS

Interpretation

118 Meaning of "constant NAV fund"

(1) In these Regulations a "constant NAV fund" means an offshore fund that meets conditions A and B.

(2) Condition A is that the net asset value of the fund (expressed in the currency in which units are issued) will not fluctuate by more than an insignificant amount throughout the fund's existence.

(3) Condition B is that condition A is met as a result of—

(*a*) the nature of the fund's assets, and

(*b*) the frequency with which the fund distributes its income.

Commentary—*Simon's Taxes* **B5.726**.

Modified application of this Part

119 General

In the case of a constant NAV fund, Chapters 2 to 11 of this Part apply with the following modifications.

Commentary—*Simon's Taxes* **B5.726**.

120 Modified application of Chapter 2

(1) Chapter 2 applies with the following modifications.

(2) In regulation 53 for paragraph (1) substitute—

"(1) An application must include the following—

(*a*) a statement of the first period of account for which it is proposed that the fund should be treated as a constant NAV fund for the purposes of these Regulations,

(*b*) a statement that the fund is, or will be, a constant NAV fund at the beginning of that first period of account, and

(*c*) an undertaking to notify HMRC if the offshore fund ceases to be a constant NAV fund.".

(3) Regulations 55 and 56 do not apply.

121 Modified application of Chapter 3

(1) Chapter 3 applies with the following modifications.

(2) For regulation 57 substitute—

"57A Effects of entry into the reporting fund regime

(1) Unless HMRC reject an application because an item specified in regulation 53(1) has not been supplied, the offshore fund becomes a constant NAV fund on whichever is the later of—

(*a*) the first day of the first period of account mentioned in regulation 53(1)(*a*), or

(*b*) the day on which the fund is established.

(2) This Part applies to the constant NAV fund and to its participants on and after the date specified in paragraph (1).

(3) Once this Part has begun to apply to a constant NAV fund, it shall continue to apply unless and until the fund notifies HMRC that it has ceased to be a constant NAV fund.

(4) See regulation 108A for the consequences where the net asset value of the fund has risen by more than an insignificant amount and the fund has not notified HMRC that it has ceased to be a constant NAV fund.".

(3) Regulation 58 does not apply.

122 Disapplication of Chapters 4 to 9

Chapters 4 to 9 do not apply.

123 Modified application of Chapter 10

For regulations 108 to 115 substitute—

"108A Consequences of rise in net asset value of fund

(1) This regulation applies if—

(*a*) this Part applies to a constant NAV fund,

(*b*) the net asset value of the fund (expressed in the currency in which units are issued) has risen by more than an insignificant amount, and

(*c*) the fund has not notified HMRC that it has ceased to be a constant NAV fund.

(2) But this regulation does not apply if the net asset value of a constant NAV fund (expressed in the currency in which units are issued) has fallen by more than an insignificant amount.

(3) A participant who disposes of an interest in the fund and who makes a chargeable gain on the disposal is treated as making an offshore income gain.".

124 Disapplication of Chapter 11

Chapter 11 does not apply.

[PART 3A

ANNUAL PAYMENTS TO NON-RESIDENTS]

Amendments—Part 3A (regs 124A, 124B) inserted by the Offshore Funds (Tax) (Amendment No 3) Regulations, SI 2013/1770 reg 2(3) with effect for the purposes of income tax for the tax year 2013–14 and subsequent tax years.

[124A Annual Payments – duty to deduct income tax

(1) An annual payment made to a participant which meets the conditions in paragraphs (2) to (6) is not a qualifying annual payment for the purposes of Chapter 6 of Part 15 of ITA 2007 (deduction from annual payments and royalties).

(2) The payment must be charged to income tax under Chapter 7 of Part 5 of ITTOIA 2005 (annual payments not otherwise charged).

(3) The payment must be made in respect of the participant's interest in an offshore fund.

(4) The payment and the amount of the payment must be directly or indirectly referable to, and must not be more than, any management fees paid to the manager of the offshore fund in respect of the participant's interest in the fund.

(5) Any management fee must not exceed an amount representing a reasonable commercial amount in all the circumstances.

(6) At the time the payment is made, the person making the payment must have reasonable grounds for believing that the participant is not resident in the United Kingdom.][1]

Amendments—[1] Part 3A (regs 124A, 124B) inserted by the Offshore Funds (Tax) (Amendment No 3) Regulations, SI 2013/1770 reg 2(3) with effect for the purposes of income tax for the tax year 2013–14 and subsequent tax years.

[124B Consequences of reasonable but incorrect belief

(1) This regulation applies if—

(*a*) an annual payment is made to a participant without a sum representing income tax on the payment being deducted from it,

(*b*) at the time the payment is made, the condition in regulation 124A(6) is met,

(*c*) the payment would be a qualifying annual payment but for that condition being met, and

(*d*) at the time the payment is made, the participant is resident in the United Kingdom.][1]

(2) Section 900 (deduction from commercial payments made by individuals) and section 901 (deduction from annual payments made by other persons) of ITA 2007 apply as if the payment were a qualifying annual payment.

Amendments—[1] Part 3A (regs 124A, 124B) inserted by the Offshore Funds (Tax) (Amendment No 3) Regulations, SI 2013/1770 reg 2(3) with effect for the purposes of income tax for the tax year 2013–14 and subsequent tax years.

PART 4

CONSEQUENTIAL AMENDMENTS

125 Amendment of the Inheritance Tax Act 1984

In section 174(1)(*a*) of the Inheritance Tax Act 1984 (income tax and unpaid inheritance tax) for "Chapter V of Part XVII of the Taxes Act 1988, arising on a disposal which is deemed to occur on the death by virtue of section 757(3) of that Act" substitute "regulations made under section 41(1) of the Finance Act 2008, arising on a disposal which is deemed, under such regulations (see regulation 34 of the Offshore Funds (Tax) Regulations 2009 (SI 2009/3001)), to occur on the death".

126 Amendment of ICTA

(1)–(6) (*amend* TA 1988 ss 396(2), 505(3), 587B(9), 834A, 842(3A))

127 Amendment of TCGA 1992

(1)–(4) (*amend* TCGA 1992 ss 108(1), 212, Sch 7AD para 7)

128 Amendment of ITTOIA 2005

(1)–(4) (*amend* ITTOIA 2005 ss 378A(7), 632, 830(4))

129 Amendment of ITA 2007

(1)–(6) (*amend* ITA 2007 ss 152(8), 482, 535, 734(5), 1016(2))

130 Amendment of FA 2008

(1)–(4) (*amend* FA 2008 Sch 7 paras 100–102)

131 Amendment of CTA 2009

(1)–(3) (*amend* CTA 2009 ss 489, 490)

SCHEDULE 1

TRANSITIONAL PROVISIONS AND SAVINGS

Regulation 1(3) and 13(1)

Commentary—*Simon's Taxes* **B5.727**.

1 In this Schedule—

"distributing fund" means a fund which, immediately before 1st December 2009, was a distributing fund for the purposes of Chapter 5 of Part 17 of ICTA [or a fund treated as a distributing fund in accordance with paragraph 3(3A)][1];

"existing fund" means a fund to which, immediately before 1st December 2009, section 756A of ICTA applied;

"non-qualifying fund" means a fund which, immediately before 1st December 2009, was a non-qualifying fund for the purposes of Chapter 5 of Part 17 of ICTA;

the "overlap period" means the period of account of an existing fund which has begun, but not ended, on the day these Regulations come into force;

the "succeeding period" means the period of account of the fund immediately following the overlap period.

Commentary—*Simon's Taxes* **B5.727**.

Amendments—[1] Words in definition of "distributing fund" insertedby the Offshore Funds (Tax) (Amendment) Regulations, SI 2009/3139 regs 2, 5(1), (2) with effect as follows—

– for income tax purposes for the tax year 2009–10 and subsequent tax years and for distributions made on or after 1 December 2009;
– for corporation tax purposes, on income for accounting periods ending on or after 1 December 2009 and for distributions made on or after that date, and on chargeable gains in relation to disposals made on or after 1 December 2009; and
– for capital gains tax purposes, in relation to disposals made on or after 1 December 2009.

2 (1) This paragraph applies in the case of an existing fund which, on 1st December 2009, becomes a non-reporting fund.

(2) A participant begins to have an interest in the non-reporting fund at the beginning of the accounting period of the non-reporting fund current on 1st December 2009.

(3) An offshore income gain arising to a person on the disposal of an asset must be computed in accordance with Part 2, but is to have regard to the entirety of the period of the person's ownership of the asset.

Commentary—*Simon's Taxes* **B5.727**.

3 (1) This paragraph applies in the case of an existing fund [and umbrella arrangements but is subject to paragraph (3B)][1].

[(2) The fund or any person within paragraph 18(1) of Schedule 27 to ICTA may apply in writing to HMRC for the fund to be treated as a distributing fund in respect of the overlap period or any earlier period of account.

(3) If the fund or any person within paragraph 18(1) of Schedule 27 to ICTA has made a successful application under sub-paragraph (2), the fund or that person may apply in writing to HMRC for the fund to be continued to be treated as a distributing fund in respect of the succeeding period.

(3ZA) But no application may be made under paragraph (3) if HMRC have accepted an application for Part 3 to apply to the fund.][2]

[(3A) Where an existing fund is part of umbrella arrangements (within the meaning of section 40C of FA 2008) or is part of arrangements comprising more than one class of interest (within the meaning of section 40D of FA 2008), separate arrangements under the umbrella arrangements, and each class of interest under the main arrangements, established on or after 1st December 2009, may apply in writing to HMRC to be treated as a distributing fund in respect of a period of account if—

(*a*) that period has the same accounting reference date as the overlap period or succeeding period of the existing fund, and

(*b*) the existing fund is treated as a distributing fund in respect of the contemporaneous overlap period or succeeding period.

(3B) This paragraph does not apply in respect of any period of account which ends after 31st May [2012][2].][1]

(4) The repeal by these Regulations of the enactments specified in Schedule 2 does not affect the continued operation of those provisions for the purposes of this paragraph.

Commentary—*Simon's Taxes* **B5.727**.

Amendments—[1] In sub-para (1), words inserted, and sub-paras (3A), (3B) inserted, by the Offshore Funds (Tax) (Amendment) Regulations, SI 2009/3139 regs 2, 5(1), (3) with effect as follows—

– for income tax purposes for the tax year 2009–10 and subsequent tax years and for distributions made on or after 1 December 2009;
– for corporation tax purposes, on income for accounting periods ending on or after 1 December 2009 and for distributions made on or after that date, and on chargeable gains in relation to disposals made on or after 1 December 2009; and
– for capital gains tax purposes, in relation to disposals made on or after 1 December 2009.

[2] Sub-paras (2), (3), (3A) substituted for previous sub-paras (2), (3), and in sub-para (3A) year substituted, by the Offshore Funds (Tax) (Amendment) Regulations, SI 2011/1211 regs 2, 42 with effect as follows—

– for the purposes of income tax for distributions made, or treated as made, on or after 27 May 2011;

– for the purposes of corporation tax: on chargeable gains, in relation to disposals made on or after 27 May 2011; and for distributions made, or treated as made, on or after that date;
– for the purposes of capital gains tax, in relation to disposals made on or after 27 May 2011.

[3A In the case of a reporting fund which has an interest in a distributing fund, income from the distributing fund is treated as income from a reporting fund but no adjustment shall be made to that income under regulation 68 (income from other reporting funds).][1]

Commentary—*Simon's Taxes* **B5.727**.

Amendments—[1] Paras 3A–3C inserted by the Offshore Funds (Tax) (Amendment) Regulations, SI 2009/3139 regs 2, 5(1), (4) with effect as follows—

– for income tax purposes for the tax year 2009–10 and subsequent tax years and for distributions made on or after 1 December 2009;
– for corporation tax purposes, on income for accounting periods ending on or after 1 December 2009 and for distributions made on or after that date, and on chargeable gains in relation to disposals made on or after 1 December 2009; and
– for capital gains tax purposes, in relation to disposals made on or after 1 December 2009.

[3B (1) This paragraph applies in the case of a distributing fund which has an interest in a reporting fund.

(2) The reporting fund is treated as a qualifying fund for the purposes of Part 2 of Schedule 27 of ICTA (modifications of conditions for certification in certain cases).

(3) The amount of the adjustment required by paragraph 8(1) of Schedule 27 in respect of the excess income of the qualifying fund for any account period is the amount of the excess of the income reported by the reporting fund in respect of the distributing fund's interest in the reporting fund over the amount distributed by the reporting fund to the distributing fund.][1]

Commentary—*Simon's Taxes* **B5.727**.

Amendments—[1] Paras 3A–3C inserted by the Offshore Funds (Tax) (Amendment) Regulations, SI 2009/3139 regs 2, 5(1), (4) with effect as follows—

– for income tax purposes for the tax year 2009–10 and subsequent tax years and for distributions made on or after 1 December 2009;
– for corporation tax purposes, on income for accounting periods ending on or after 1 December 2009 and for distributions made on or after that date, and on chargeable gains in relation to disposals made on or after 1 December 2009; and
– for capital gains tax purposes, in relation to disposals made on or after 1 December 2009.

[3C In the case of an exchange of an interest in a distributing fund for an interest in a reporting fund, regulation 37 (exchange of interests of different classes) shall not apply.][1]

Commentary—*Simon's Taxes* **B5.727**.

Amendments—[1] Paras 3A–3C inserted by the Offshore Funds (Tax) (Amendment) Regulations, SI 2009/3139 regs 2, 5(1), (4) with effect as follows—

– for income tax purposes for the tax year 2009–10 and subsequent tax years and for distributions made on or after 1 December 2009;
– for corporation tax purposes, on income for accounting periods ending on or after 1 December 2009 and for distributions made on or after that date, and on chargeable gains in relation to disposals made on or after 1 December 2009; and
– for capital gains tax purposes, in relation to disposals made on or after 1 December 2009.

4 (1) This paragraph applies in the case of an existing fund which does not become a reporting fund immediately following its last account period as a distributing fund.

(2) A participant in the fund may make an election to be treated for the purposes of TCGA 1992—

(*a*) as disposing of an interest in the distributing fund at the end of that fund's last account period, and

(*b*) as acquiring an interest in the non-reporting fund immediately following the disposal treated as made by paragraph (*a*).

(3) The disposal referred to in paragraph (*a*) of sub-paragraph (2) is treated as made for a consideration equal to the net asset value of the participant's interest in the fund at the end of the final accounting period.

(4) The acquisition referred to in paragraph (*b*) of sub-paragraph (2) is treated as made for the same amount as the disposal referred to in paragraph (*a*) of that sub-paragraph.

(5) If the participant is chargeable to income tax, the election mentioned in sub-paragraph (2) must be made by being included in a return made for the tax year which includes the disposal date.

(6) If the participant is chargeable to corporation tax, the election mentioned in sub-paragraph (2) must be made by being included in the participant's company tax return for the accounting period which includes the disposal date.

(7) In this paragraph—

"company tax return" has the same meaning as in Schedule 18 to the Finance Act 1998;

"disposal date" means the final day of the distributing fund's final accounting period.

Commentary—*Simon's Taxes* **B5.727**.

5 (1) This paragraph applies in the case of an existing fund which—

(*a*) immediately before 1st December 2009 was a non-qualifying fund, and

(*b*) on 1st December 2009 becomes a reporting fund.

(2) Regulation 48 applies as if, for references to the non-reporting fund, there were substituted references to the existing fund.

(3) Chapter 5 of Part 17 of ICTA applies to determine the offshore income gain arising by virtue of the application of regulation 48.

Commentary—*Simon's Taxes* **B5.727**.

6 (1) This paragraph applies in the case of an existing fund which—

(*a*) makes a successful application under paragraph 3 to continue to be treated as a distributing fund after 1st December 2009, and

(*b*) becomes a reporting fund immediately following the end of the overlap period or the succeeding period.

(2) For the purposes of regulations 17 and 99 the fund is treated as a reporting fund for the entirety of a continuous period—

(*a*) beginning with the day the fund becomes a distributing fund, and

(*b*) ending on the last day of the overlap period or the succeeding period (as the case may be).

(3) If for any part of the period specified in sub-paragraph (2) the fund is not a distributing fund, the period is not continuous for the purposes of that sub-paragraph.

Commentary—*Simon's Taxes* **B5.727**.

7 (1) This paragraph applies in the case of an arrangement ("Fund X") which, immediately before 1st December 2009, did not fall to be classified as an offshore fund, but which, on 1st December 2009, falls to be classified as an offshore fund.

(2) Fund X may make an application, in accordance with Part 3, in relation to the period of account that is current on 1st December 2009.

(3) The application must be received by HMRC on or before 31st May 2010.

Commentary—*Simon's Taxes* **B5.727**.

SCHEDULE 2

REPEALS

Regulation 13(2)

Short title and chapter	*Extent of repeal*
Income and Corporation Taxes Act 1988 (c 1)	Chapter 5 of Part 17.
	In section 834A, in Part 1 of the Table, the entry relating to section 761(1)(*b*)(i).
	Schedules 27 and 28.
Finance Act 1988 (c 39)	In Schedule 13, paragraph 12.
Finance Act 1990 (c 29)	In Schedule 14, paragraphs 10 and 11.
Taxation of Chargeable Gains Act 1992 (c 12)	In section 108(1)(*c*), the words ", or have at any time been,".
	In section 212, subsections (5) to (7).
	In Schedule 10, paragraph 14(43) to (49) and (63).
Finance Act 1995 (c 4)	Section 134.
Finance Act 1996 (c 8)	In Schedule 28, in paragraph 6, the words "and in paragraph 5(5) of Schedule 27 to that Act".
Finance Act 2002 (c 23)	In Schedule 9, paragraph 4(5) and (6).
Finance Act 2004 (c 12)	In Schedule 26, paragraphs 1(1), 2(1), 4 to 9 and 13 to 16.
Income Tax (Trading and Other Income) Act 2005 (c 5)	In Schedule 1, paragraphs 308, 309 and 350.
Finance (No 2) Act 2005 (c 22)	Section 23.
Finance Act 2006 (c 25)	In Schedule 12, paragraph 47.
Income Tax Act 2007 (c 3)	In section 1016(2), in Part 3 of the Table, the entry relating to section 761(1)(*b*)(i) of ICTA.
	In Schedule 1, paragraphs 179 to 181.
Finance Act 2008 (c 9)	In Schedule 7, paragraphs 92 to 96.
	In Schedule 17, paragraph 30.

SIs

SCHEDULE 3
ABBREVIATIONS AND DEFINED EXPRESSIONS

Regulation 13(4)

PART 1
ABBREVIATIONS OF ACTS

TMA 1970	The Taxes Management Act 1970 (c 9)
ICTA	The Income and Corporation Taxes Act 1988 (c 1)
TCGA 1992	The Taxation of Chargeable Gains Act 1992 (c 12)
FA 1996	The Finance Act 1996 (c 8)
FISMA 2000	The Financial Services and Markets Act 2000 (c 8)
ITTOIA 2005	The Income Tax (Trading and Other Income) Act 2005 (c 5)
ITA 2007	The Income Tax Act 2007 (c 3)
FA 2008	The Finance Act 2008 (c 9)
CTA 2009	The Corporation Tax Act 2009 (c 4)
[CTA 2010	The Corporation Tax Act 2010 (c 4)][1]

Amendments—[1] Entry for CTA 2010 inserted by the Offshore Funds (Tax) (Amendment) Regulations, SI 2011/1211 regs 2, 43 with effect as follows—

- for the purposes of income tax for distributions made, or treated as made, on or after 27 May 2011;
- for the purposes of corporation tax: on chargeable gains, in relation to disposals made on or after 27 May 2011; and for distributions made, or treated as made, on or after that date;
- for the purposes of capital gains tax, in relation to disposals made on or after 27 May 2011.

PART 2
INDEX OF EXPRESSIONS DEFINED OR OTHERWISE EXPLAINED IN THESE REGULATIONS

[Accounting income (in Part 3)	Regulation 72B(8)][2]
[Acquisition by way of initial purchase (in Part 4)	Regulation 72(4)][1]
Applicant (in Part 3)	Regulation 51(3)
Application (in Part 3)	Regulation 51(3)
Basic gain	Chapter 5 of Part 2
[Computation period (in Part 4)	Regulation 92C][1]
Constant NAV fund	Regulation 118
Diversely owned fund	Regulation 73(2)
Eligible offshore fund (in Part 3)	Regulation 51(3)
[Equalisation amount per unit of interest (in Part 4)	Regulation 92(3)(ba)][1]
[Equalisation amount (in Part 4)	Regulation 72(2)][1]
Equivalence condition	Regulation 74
Existing fund application (in Part 3)	Regulation 51(3)
Financial trader (in Chapter 8 of Part 3)	Regulation 105
Fund distribution date	Regulation 94(4)
[Fund operating equalisation arrangements (in Part 4)	Regulation 50A(a)][1]
[Fund operating full equalisation arrangements (in Part 4)	Regulation 50A(b)][1]
Future fund application (in Part 3)	Regulation 51(3)

Genuine diversity of ownership condition	Regulations 75 and 76
Guaranteed return fund	Regulation 9
HMRC	Regulation 12
HMRC intervention	Regulation 108(6)
Interest (of a participant in an offshore fund)	Regulation 8
. . . [3]	. . . [3]
Main arrangements	Regulation 6
Manager (in Part 3)	Regulation 51(3)
Market value	Regulation 10
Material disposal	Regulation 15
Minor breach	Regulation 108(4)
Non-reporting fund	Regulation 4(2)
Offshore fund	Regulation 3
Offshore income gain	Chapter 5 of Part 2
OIG amount	Regulation 20(2)
Participant (in a fund)	Regulation 7
Period of account	Regulation 12
Proposed prospectus	Regulation 12
Prospectus	Regulation 12
[Regulated market	Regulation 12][1]
Relevant group of sections	Regulation 12
Reportable income	Chapter 5 of Part 3
Reported income	Regulation 92(2)
Reporting fund	Regulation 50
Reporting period	Regulation 91
Serious breach	Regulation 108(3)
Tax year	Regulation 12
TCGA disposal (in Chapter 6 of Part 2)	Regulation 44(2)
This group of regulations (in Chapter 8 of Part 3)	Regulation 102(2)
Transparent fund	Regulation 11
[Transparent reporting fund	Regulation 89A(2)][1]
Tribunal	Regulation 12
UCITS fund	Regulation 12
Umbrella arrangements	Regulation 5

Amendments—[1] In definition of "investment transaction", words revoked, and definitions for ""Accounting income", Acquisition by way of initial purchase", "Computation period", "Equalisation amount per unit of interest", "Equalisation amount", "Fund operating equalisation arrangements", "Fund operating full equalisation arrangements", "Regulated market", and "Transparent reporting fund" inserted, by the Offshore Funds (Tax) (Amendment) Regulations, SI 2011/1211 regs 2, 44 with effect as follows—

– for the purposes of income tax for distributions made, or treated as made, on or after 27 May 2011;
– for the purposes of corporation tax: on chargeable gains, in relation to disposals made on or after 27 May 2011; and for distributions made, or treated as made, on or after that date;
– for the purposes of capital gains tax, in relation to disposals made on or after 27 May 2011.

[2] Definition of "accounting income" substituted by the Offshore Funds (Tax) (Amendment No. 2) Regulations, SI 2013/1411 regs 2, 12 with effect from 28 June 2013, subject to transition provision in reg1(3), (5)). Definition previously read—

"Accounting income (in Part 4)	Regulation 92B(6)".

[3] Definition of "investment transaction" revoked by the Investment Transactions (Tax) Regulations, SI 2014/685 reg 8(1), (4) with effect from 8 April 2014.

2009/3024

FINANCE ACT 2008, SECTION 128 AND PART 2 OF SCHEDULE 43 (APPOINTED DAY, TRANSITIONAL PROVISION AND SAVINGS) ORDER 2009

Made . . . . *9 November 2009*

The Commissioners for Her Majesty's Revenue and Customs, in exercise of the powers conferred by section 129(4) and (5) of the Finance Act 2008 make the following Order:

1 Citation and interpretation

(1) This Order may be cited as The Finance Act 2008, Section 128 and Part 2 of Schedule 43 (Appointed Day, Transitional Provision and Savings) Order 2009.

2 In this Order "FA 2008" means the Finance Act 2008.

3 Appointed day

The day appointed for the coming into force of Section 128 of, and Part 2 of Schedule 43 to, FA 2008 is 23rd November 2009.

4 Transitional Provision and Savings

(1) If, before the commencement date, a warrant has been granted under—

(*a*) section 63 of the Taxes Management Act 1970 (recovery of tax in Scotland);

(*b*) section 121B of the Social Security Administration Act 1992 (recovery of contributions etc in Scotland);

(*c*) section 52 of the Finance Act 1997 (recovery of relevant tax in Scotland); or

(*d*) paragraph 3 of Schedule 12 to the Finance Act 2003 (recovery of stamp duty land tax by diligence in Scotland).

that warrant shall continue to have effect according to the provisions under which it was granted.

5 (1) The amendments made by paragraph 13(1) and (2) of Schedule 43 to FA 2008 to the Debtors (Scotland) Act 1987 shall not have effect in relation to—

(*a*) actions commenced under section 1 (time to pay directions); or

(*b*) applications made under section 5 (time to pay orders);

before the commencement date.

(2) The amendment made by paragraph 13(3) of Schedule 43 to FA 2008 to the definition of "summary warrant" in section 106 (interpretation) of the Debtors (Scotland) Act 1987 shall not apply to summary warrants granted before the commencement date.

2009/3055

REGISTERED PENSION SCHEMES (MODIFICATION OF THE RULES OF EXISTING SCHEMES) REGULATIONS 2009

Made by the Treasury under FA 2004 s 282(A1), Sch 36 para 3

Made . . . . *19 November 2009*

Laid before the House of Commons . . . . *19 November 2009*

Coming into force . . . . *11 December 2009*

Commentary—*Simon's Taxes* **E7.211–E7.215**.

1 Citation, commencement and effect

(1) These Regulations may be cited as the Registered Pension Schemes (Modification of the Rules of Existing Schemes) Regulations 2009 and shall come into force on 11th December 2009.

(2) Regulation 2 shall have effect in relation to any time on or after 6th April 2006.

2 Scheme rule amendments not to require the approval of H M Revenue and Customs

(1) Any provision (however framed) in the rules of an existing scheme, as they stood immediately before 6th April 2006, to make an amendment to a rule of a scheme which would require the agreement, consent, approval of, or confirmation of continued approval of the scheme by—

(*a*) the Inland Revenue, the Board of Inland Revenue, the Commissioners of Inland Revenue, or any officer of any of them (whether referred to as such or by reference to another title), or

(*b*) Her Majesty's Revenue and Customs, the Commissioners for Her Majesty's Revenue and Customs or an officer of Revenue and Customs,

shall be disregarded during the transitional period, to the extent that the provision requires such agreement, consent, approval or confirmation of continued approval of the scheme.

(2) In this regulation—

"existing scheme" means a pension scheme to which paragraph 1(1) of Schedule 36 to the Finance Act 2004 applies,

"rules", in relation to an existing scheme, means the rules (whether contained in the governing instruments or otherwise) of an existing scheme,
"the transitional period", in relation to an existing scheme, means the period beginning with the 6th April 2006 and ending with the date on which, by virtue of paragraph 3(2) of Schedule 36 to the Finance Act 2004, the modifications in these Regulations cease to have effect.

2009/3173

CORPORATION TAX (FINANCING COSTS AND INCOME) REGULATIONS 2009

Made by the Treasury under FA 2009 Sch 15 paras 17(3), 24, 25(4) and (5), 26, 29(3), 36 and 38

Made . . . . *2 December 2009*
Laid before the House of Commons . . . . *3 December 2009*
Coming into force in accordance with . . . . *regulation 1*

Revocation—

These Regulations revoked by F(No 2)A 2017 s 20, Sch 5 para 11(3)(*a*) with effect in relation to periods of account of the worldwide group that begin on or after 1 April 2017. In relation to periods of account that straddle 1 April 2017 see Sch 5 para 26(2)–(10). **Please note** that Part 2A of the Yellow Book was sent to print before the Act had received Royal Assent. This amendment is therefore based on the 8 September 2017 Finance Bill. Please check F(No 2)A 2017 for confirmation of this amendment.

PART 1
PRELIMINARY PROVISIONS AND INTERPRETATION

1 Citation, commencement and effect

(1) These Regulations may be cited as the Corporation Tax (Financing Costs and Income) Regulations 2009 and, subject to paragraph (2), shall come into force on 1st January 2010.
(2) Circumstance 4 in regulations 13(2) and 28(2) come into force on 1st April 2010.
(3) These Regulations have effect in relation to periods of account beginning on or after 1st January 2010.

REVOCATION—

These Regulations revoked by F(No 2)A 2017 s 20, Sch 5 para 11(3)(*a*) with effect in relation to periods of account of the worldwide group that begin on or after 1 April 2017. In relation to periods of account that straddle 1 April 2017 see Sch 5 para 26(2)–(10). **Please note** that Part 2A of the Yellow Book was sent to print before the Act had received Royal Assent. This amendment is therefore based on the 8 September 2017 Finance Bill. Please check F(No 2)A 2017 for confirmation of this amendment.

2 Introduction and structure of Regulations

(1) These Regulations make provision about the treatment for the purposes of corporation tax of certain financing costs and certain financing income of companies that are members of a group.
(2) The structure of these Regulations is as follows—
Part 1 makes provision in relation to general and preliminary matters;
Part 2 makes provision in relation to the disallowance of deductions;
Part 3 makes provision in relation to the exemption of financing income.

REVOCATION—

These Regulations revoked by F(No 2)A 2017 s 20, Sch 5 para 11(3)(*a*) with effect in relation to periods of account of the worldwide group that begin on or after 1 April 2017. In relation to periods of account that straddle 1 April 2017 see Sch 5 para 26(2)–(10). **Please note** that Part 2A of the Yellow Book was sent to print before the Act had received Royal Assent. This amendment is therefore based on the 8 September 2017 Finance Bill. Please check F(No 2)A 2017 for confirmation of this amendment.

3 Interpretation

(1) For the purposes of these Regulations—
(*a*) *"Schedule 15" means Schedule 15 of the Finance Act 2009 (tax treatment of financing costs and income);*
(*b*) *a company is an "immediate parent" of another company if it directly owns more than 50% of the ordinary share capital of that other company;*
(*c*) *a company is an "ultimate UK parent" in relation to a group if it—*
(i) *is a member of the group,*
(ii) *is a corporate entity,*
(iii) *is not a subsidiary (whether direct or indirect) of a corporate entity resident in the United Kingdom,*
(iv) *is not a collective investment scheme, and*

(v) *is a company to which Part 3 and Part 4 of Schedule 15 apply.*

(2) In this regulation, "collective investment scheme" has the meaning given by paragraph 80(2) of Schedule 15.

REVOCATION—

These Regulations revoked by F(No 2)A 2017 s 20, Sch 5 para 11(3)(*a*) with effect in relation to periods of account of the worldwide group that begin on or after 1 April 2017. In relation to periods of account that straddle 1 April 2017 see Sch 5 para 26(2)–(10). **Please note** that Part 2A of the Yellow Book was sent to print before the Act had received Royal Assent. This amendment is therefore based on the 8 September 2017 Finance Bill. Please check F(No 2)A 2017 for confirmation of this amendment.

PART 2
DISALLOWANCE OF DEDUCTIONS

CHAPTER 1

APPOINTMENT OF AUTHORISED COMPANY

4 Appointment of authorised company

(1) An appointment under paragraph 17 of Schedule 15 must be made in accordance with this regulation.

(2) The company seeking to be appointed ("the applicant company") must make an application in writing to an officer of Revenue and Customs at least 3 months before the time specified in paragraph 19(2) of Schedule 15 (submission of statement of allocated disallowances).

(3) The application must be sent to the tax office that deals with the corporation tax affairs of the applicant company.

(4) The application must specify—

(*a*) *the name and the tax office reference of the applicant company,*

(*b*) *the names and the tax office references of the other companies to which Part 3 of Schedule 15 applies,*

(*c*) *the first period of account of the worldwide group in relation to which the appointment is to apply, and*

(*d*) *except in relation to the ultimate parent, the name of the immediate parent of the applicant company and each of the other companies to which Part 3 of Schedule 15 applies.*

(5) The application must contain a statement by the applicant company and by each of the other companies to which Part 3 of Schedule 15 applies—

(*a*) *that the appointment is made under paragraph 17 of Schedule 15,*

(*b*) *that the applicant company will act on behalf of all the companies to which Part 3 of Schedule 15 applies for all relevant periods of account for which the appointment has effect,*

(*c*) *that no application will be made by a company to amend its company tax return in relation to a financing expense amount specified under paragraph 21(4)(b)* of Schedule 15 other than through a revised statement submitted by the applicant company in accordance with paragraph 20 of Schedule 15, and

(*d*) *agreeing to be bound by any statement of allocated disallowances or revised statement delivered by the applicant company.*

(6) The application must be accompanied by a specimen copy of a statement of allocated disallowances that the applicant company proposes to submit in relation to the relevant period of account.

REVOCATION—

These Regulations revoked by F(No 2)A 2017 s 20, Sch 5 para 11(3)(*a*) with effect in relation to periods of account of the worldwide group that begin on or after 1 April 2017. In relation to periods of account that straddle 1 April 2017 see Sch 5 para 26(2)–(10). **Please note** that Part 2A of the Yellow Book was sent to print before the Act had received Royal Assent. This amendment is therefore based on the 8 September 2017 Finance Bill. Please check F(No 2)A 2017 for confirmation of this amendment.

5 Supplemental provisions: timing and effect

(1) An appointment under paragraph 17 of Schedule 15 has effect on the date ("the three month date") that is three months after the application is delivered to the tax office in accordance with regulation 4(3).

This is subject to paragraphs (2) to (4).

(2) An officer of Revenue and Customs may accept the application before the three month date.

(3) Where paragraph (2) applies, the officer of Revenue and Customs may amend the list of companies to which Part 3 of Schedule 15 applies specified under regulation 4(4)(*b*) to exclude any company that is not a company to which Part 3 of Schedule 15 applies for the relevant period of account.

(4) An appointment under paragraph 17 of Schedule 15 is of no effect if before the three month date an officer of Revenue and Customs refuses the application on the grounds that—

(*a*) *the specimen statement of allocated disallowances provided in accordance with regulation 4(6) is not adequate for the purposes of Part 3 of Schedule 15, or*

(*b*) *a company to which Part 3 of Schedule 15 applies has been omitted from the list of companies specified under regulation 4(4)(b).*

REVOCATION—

These Regulations revoked by F(No 2)A 2017 s 20, Sch 5 para 11(3)(*a*) with effect in relation to periods of account of the worldwide group that begin on or after 1 April 2017. In relation to periods of account that straddle 1 April 2017 see Sch 5 para 26(2)–(10). **Please note** that Part 2A of the Yellow Book was sent to print before the Act had received Royal Assent. This amendment is therefore based on the 8 September 2017 Finance Bill. Please check F(No 2)A 2017 for confirmation of this amendment.

6 Duration of appointment

Once an appointment under paragraph 17 of Schedule 15 has effect, it continues to have effect until it ceases to have effect in accordance with regulations 7, 8 or 9.

REVOCATION—

These Regulations revoked by F(No 2)A 2017 s 20, Sch 5 para 11(3)(*a*) with effect in relation to periods of account of the worldwide group that begin on or after 1 April 2017. In relation to periods of account that straddle 1 April 2017 see Sch 5 para 26(2)–(10). **Please note** that Part 2A of the Yellow Book was sent to print before the Act had received Royal Assent. This amendment is therefore based on the 8 September 2017 Finance Bill. Please check F(No 2)A 2017 for confirmation of this amendment.

7 Revocation of appointment by notice

(1) An appointment under paragraph 17 of Schedule 15 ceases to have effect if revoked by the company appointed under that paragraph by notice in writing to an officer of Revenue and Customs at the tax office that deals with the corporation tax affairs of that company.

(2) The appointment ceases to have effect in relation to the relevant period of account in which the notice is given or such subsequent relevant period of account as may be specified in the notice.

REVOCATION—

These Regulations revoked by F(No 2)A 2017 s 20, Sch 5 para 11(3)(*a*) with effect in relation to periods of account of the worldwide group that begin on or after 1 April 2017. In relation to periods of account that straddle 1 April 2017 see Sch 5 para 26(2)–(10). **Please note** that Part 2A of the Yellow Book was sent to print before the Act had received Royal Assent. This amendment is therefore based on the 8 September 2017 Finance Bill. Please check F(No 2)A 2017 for confirmation of this amendment.

8 Revocation of appointment on authorised company ceasing to be a relevant group company

(1) An appointment under paragraph 17 of Schedule 15 ceases to have effect if the company appointed under that paragraph ceases to be a company to which Part 3 of Schedule 15 applies.

(2) The appointment ceases to have effect in relation to the relevant period of account in which the company ceased to be a company to which Part 3 of Schedule 15 applies and subsequent periods of account.

REVOCATION—

These Regulations revoked by F(No 2)A 2017 s 20, Sch 5 para 11(3)(*a*) with effect in relation to periods of account of the worldwide group that begin on or after 1 April 2017. In relation to periods of account that straddle 1 April 2017 see Sch 5 para 26(2)–(10). **Please note** that Part 2A of the Yellow Book was sent to print before the Act had received Royal Assent. This amendment is therefore based on the 8 September 2017 Finance Bill. Please check F(No 2)A 2017 for confirmation of this amendment.

9 Revocation of appointment on a company becoming or ceasing to be a company to which Part 3 of Schedule 15 applies

(1) An appointment under paragraph 17 of Schedule 15 ceases to have effect if a company becomes or ceases to be a company to which Part 3 of Schedule 15 applies.

(2) The appointment ceases to have effect in relation to the relevant period of account in which the company becomes or ceases to be a company to which Part 3 of Schedule 15 applies and subsequent periods of account.

(3) But paragraph (1) does not apply if within three months of a company becoming or ceasing to be a company to which Part 3 of Schedule 15 applies, the reporting body notifies an officer of Revenue and Customs at the tax office that deals with its corporation tax affairs of the change.

(4) A notification under paragraph (3) must—

(*a*) *be in writing, and*

(*b*) *specify the name and the tax office reference of the company that has become or ceased to be a company to which Part 3 of Schedule 15 applies.*

(5) Where a new company has become a company to which Part 3 of Schedule 15 applies the notification must be accompanied by a statement by that company—

(*a*) *that the company appointed under paragraph 17 of Schedule 15 will act on its behalf for all relevant periods of account for which the appointment has effect;*

(*b*) *that no application will be made to amend a financing expense amount specified under paragraph 21(4)(b)* of Schedule 15 other than through a revised statement submitted by the reporting body in accordance with paragraph 20 of Schedule 15;

(*c*) *agreeing to be bound by a statement of allocated disallowances or a revised statement delivered by the reporting body.*

REVOCATION—

These Regulations revoked by F(No 2)A 2017 s 20, Sch 5 para 11(3)(*a*) with effect in relation to periods of account of the worldwide group that begin on or after 1 April 2017. In relation to periods of account that straddle 1 April 2017 see Sch 5 para 26(2)–(10). **Please note** that Part 2A of the Yellow Book was sent to print before the Act had received Royal Assent. This amendment is therefore based on the 8 September 2017 Finance Bill. Please check F(No 2)A 2017 for confirmation of this amendment.

CHAPTER 2

STATEMENT OF ALLOCATED DISALLOWANCES

10 Submission of statement of allocated disallowances

(1) A statement of allocated disallowances must be submitted to the tax office dealing with the corporation tax affairs of—

(*a*) *in a case in which an appointment under paragraph 17 of Schedule 15 has effect in relation to the relevant period of account, the company appointed under that paragraph, or*

(*b*) *in a case in which such an appointment does not have effect in relation to the relevant period of account—*

(i) *the ultimate parent where that entity is resident in the United Kingdom, or*

(ii) *in any other case, the UK ultimate parent.*

(2) In a case within paragraph (1)(*b*)(ii), if there is more than one UK ultimate parent the statement of allocated disallowances must be submitted to the tax office dealing with the corporation tax affairs of each.

REVOCATION—

These Regulations revoked by F(No 2)A 2017 s 20, Sch 5 para 11(3)(*a*) with effect in relation to periods of account of the worldwide group that begin on or after 1 April 2017. In relation to periods of account that straddle 1 April 2017 see Sch 5 para 26(2)–(10). **Please note** that Part 2A of the Yellow Book was sent to print before the Act had received Royal Assent. This amendment is therefore based on the 8 September 2017 Finance Bill. Please check F(No 2)A 2017 for confirmation of this amendment.

11 Information to be given in connection with a statement of allocated disallowances

A statement of allocated disallowances must be accompanied by the following information—

(*a*) *the full name and the unique taxpayer number in relation to each company listed in the statement in accordance with paragraph 21(4)(a)* of Schedule 15,

(*b*) *where a company has delivered a tax return for a relevant accounting period and as a result of submitting a statement or revised statement—*

(i) *there is a change in the amount of profits on which corporation tax is chargeable for the period, or*

(ii) *any other information contained in the return is incorrect,*

details of the change mentioned in paragraph (i) or the information mentioned in paragraph (ii).

REVOCATION—

These Regulations revoked by F(No 2)A 2017 s 20, Sch 5 para 11(3)(*a*) with effect in relation to periods of account of the worldwide group that begin on or after 1 April 2017. In relation to periods of account that straddle 1 April 2017 see Sch 5 para 26(2)–(10). **Please note** that Part 2A of the Yellow Book was sent to print before the Act had received Royal Assent. This amendment is therefore based on the 8 September 2017 Finance Bill. Please check F(No 2)A 2017 for confirmation of this amendment.

12 Statement of allocated disallowances treated as received within specified time

(1) A statement of allocated disallowances which is not received by HMRC by the time specified ("the specified time") in paragraph 19(2) of Schedule 15, shall be treated as if it were so received in one of the circumstances specified in paragraph (2).

(2) The specified circumstances are—

(*a*) *the statement was submitted without unreasonable delay and this regulation has not applied in relation to any previous statement of allocated disallowances, or*

(*b*) *the statement was submitted as soon as possible but was not received by the specified time for exceptional reasons beyond the control of the reporting body.*

REVOCATION—

These Regulations revoked by F(No 2)A 2017 s 20, Sch 5 para 11(3)(*a*) with effect in relation to periods of account of the worldwide group that begin on or after 1 April 2017. In relation to periods of account that straddle 1 April 2017 see Sch 5 para 26(2)–(10). **Please note** that Part 2A of the Yellow Book was sent to print before the Act had received Royal Assent. This amendment is therefore based on the 8 September 2017 Finance Bill. Please check F(No 2)A 2017 for confirmation of this amendment.

13 Revised statement of allocated disallowances treated as received within specified time

(1) A revised statement of allocated disallowances which is not received by HMRC by the time specified ("the specified time") in paragraph 20(2) of Schedule 15, shall be treated as if it were so received if conditions A and B are met.

(2) Condition A is that the statement is received in one of the following circumstances.

Circumstance 1

A notice of enquiry is given before the specified time in relation to the company tax return of a company to which Part 3 of Schedule 15 applies, the enquiry is not completed until after the specified time and the revised statement is received by HMRC by the last of the following dates—

(*a*) *30 days after the enquiry is completed;*

(*b*) *if the return is amended by notice under paragraph 34(2) of Schedule 18 to the Finance Act 1998, 30 days after the notice is given;*

(*c*) *if an appeal is brought against such an amendment, 30 days after the date on which the appeal is finally determined.*

Circumstance 2

A determination under paragraph 36 of Schedule 18 to the Finance Act 1998 is made in relation to a company to which Part 3 of Schedule 15 applies which is superseded by a self-assessment in accordance with paragraph 40 of that Schedule and the revised statement is received by HMRC within 30 days of delivery of the company tax return.

Circumstance 3

A discovery assessment or discovery determination is made under paragraph 41 of Schedule 18 to the Finance Act 1998 in relation to a company to which Part 3 of Schedule 15 applies and the revised statement is received by HMRC by the last of the following dates—

(*d*) *30 days after the discovery assessment or discovery determination is made;*

(*e*) *if an appeal is brought against the discovery assessment or discovery determination, 30 days after the date on which the appeal is finally determined.*

Circumstance 4

An amendment is made under paragraph 34(2A) of Schedule 18 to the Finance Act 1998 in relation to a company to which Part 3 of Schedule 15 applies and the revised statement is received by HMRC by the last of the following dates—

(*f*) *30 days after the notice of the amendment is given;*

(*g*) *if an appeal is brought against such an amendment, 30 days after the date on which the appeal is finally determined.*

(3) Condition B is that the amount of the difference between—

(*a*) *the financing expense amounts specified in accordance with paragraph 21(4)(b)* of Schedule 15 in the statement of allocated disallowances, and

(*b*) *the amounts so specified in the revised statement,*

does not exceed the change made to the amount of profit on which corporation tax is chargeable as a result of the enquiry, determination, assessment or amendment referred to in paragraph (2).

REVOCATION—

These Regulations revoked by F(No 2)A 2017 s 20, Sch 5 para 11(3)(*a*) with effect in relation to periods of account of the worldwide group that begin on or after 1 April 2017. In relation to periods of account that straddle 1 April 2017 see Sch 5 para 26(2)–(10). **Please note** that Part 2A of the Yellow Book was sent to print before the Act had received Royal Assent. This amendment is therefore based on the 8 September 2017 Finance Bill. Please check F(No 2)A 2017 for confirmation of this amendment.

14 Statement of allocated disallowances treated as complying with paragraph 21 of Schedule 15

A statement of allocated disallowances which does not comply with paragraph 21 of Schedule 15 because of an obvious error or omission in the statement (whether an error of principle, an arithmetical mistake or otherwise) shall be treated as if it did so comply if the error or omission is corrected by the reporting body as soon as it becomes apparent.

REVOCATION—

These Regulations revoked by F(No 2)A 2017 s 20, Sch 5 para 11(3)(*a*) with effect in relation to periods of account of the worldwide group that begin on or after 1 April 2017. In relation to periods of account that straddle 1 April 2017 see Sch 5 para 26(2)–(10). **Please note** that Part 2A of the Yellow Book was sent to print before the Act had received Royal Assent. This amendment is therefore based on the 8 September 2017 Finance Bill. Please check F(No 2)A 2017 for confirmation of this amendment.

CHAPTER 3

FAILURE OF REPORTING BODY TO SUBMIT A STATEMENT OF ALLOCATED DISALLOWANCES

15 Reduction of financing expense amounts

(1) The financing expense amounts of a company that must be reduced under paragraph 25(2) of Schedule 15 must be reduced in the following order until the amount of the reduction is equal to the amount determined under paragraph 25(3) of that Schedule.

First, reduce any amounts that meet condition A in paragraph 54(2) of Schedule 15 and would be brought into account in respect of a loan relationship under Part 5 of the Corporation Tax Act 2009 (other loan relationships).

Second, reduce any other amounts that meet condition A in paragraph 54(2) of Schedule 15.

Third, reduce any amounts that meet condition B in paragraph 54(4) of Schedule 15.

Fourth, reduce any amounts that meet condition C in paragraph 54(5) of Schedule 15.

(2) But a company required to make reductions under paragraph 25 of Schedule 15 may elect to make such reductions differently.

(3) An election under paragraph (2)—

(*a*) *must be made in the company's tax return,*

(*b*) *must specify the particular reductions made, and*

(*c*) *may be withdrawn, with or without making a new election, at any time that the company may amend its company tax return under paragraph 15(4) of Schedule 18 to the Finance Act 1998.*

(4) A company required to make reductions under paragraph 25 of Schedule 15 must notify its ultimate UK parent of the particular reductions made.

(5) A notice under paragraph (4) must be made no later than the date on which the company delivers its company tax return and must be accompanied by—

(*a*) *any election made under paragraph (2), and*

(*b*) *details of any error made by the company in calculating its net financing deduction for the relevant period together with the correct amount.*

REVOCATION—

These Regulations revoked by F(No 2)A 2017 s 20, Sch 5 para 11(3)(*a*) with effect in relation to periods of account of the worldwide group that begin on or after 1 April 2017. In relation to periods of account that straddle 1 April 2017 see Sch 5 para 26(2)–(10). **Please note** that Part 2A of the Yellow Book was sent to print before the Act had received Royal Assent. This amendment is therefore based on the 8 September 2017 Finance Bill. Please check F(No 2)A 2017 for confirmation of this amendment.

16 Information to be provided in relation to a company required to make default reductions

(1) An ultimate UK parent must send a company required to make default reductions details of the amounts of—

(*a*) *the tested expense amount, and*

(*b*) *the total disallowed amount,*

for the worldwide group for the relevant period of account.

(2) The information in paragraph (1) must be supplied to the company required to make default reductions before the filing date for the company's tax return (see paragraph 14 of Schedule 18 to the Finance Act 1998).

REVOCATION—

These Regulations revoked by F(No 2)A 2017 s 20, Sch 5 para 11(3)(*a*) with effect in relation to periods of account of the worldwide group that begin on or after 1 April 2017. In relation to periods of account that straddle 1 April 2017 see Sch 5 para 26(2)–(10). **Please note** that Part 2A of the Yellow Book was sent to print before the Act had received Royal Assent. This amendment is therefore based on the 8 September 2017 Finance Bill. Please check F(No 2)A 2017 for confirmation of this amendment.

17 Non-compliance

(1) If an ultimate UK parent does not provide the information specified by regulation 16 within the requisite time period, HMRC must determine to the best of their information and belief the amounts of the tested expense amount and the total disallowed amount for the worldwide group for the relevant period of account.

(2) A notice of determination under this regulation must be sent to the company required to make the default reduction and to the ultimate UK parent stating the date on which the determination is issued.

(3) No determination under this regulation may be made more than 3 years after the day on which the power becomes exercisable.

(4) If after a determination has been made under this regulation, the ultimate UK parent provides the information specified by regulation 16, that information shall supersede the determination.

(5) But paragraph (4) does not apply if the information is supplied more than 3 years after the determination is made.

REVOCATION—

These Regulations revoked by F(No 2)A 2017 s 20, Sch 5 para 11(3)(*a*) with effect in relation to periods of account of the worldwide group that begin on or after 1 April 2017. In relation to periods of account that straddle 1 April 2017 see Sch 5 para 26(2)–(10). **Please note** that Part 2A of the Yellow Book was sent to print before the Act had received Royal Assent. This amendment is therefore based on the 8 September 2017 Finance Bill. Please check F(No 2)A 2017 for confirmation of this amendment.

18 Amendment of tax return by company

(1) A company required to make default reductions may amend its company tax return so as to reflect a reduction under paragraph 25 of Schedule 15 within 3 years of the end of the relevant period of account.

(2) But where one of the following circumstances applies the company may amend its tax return at any time before the specified date.

Circumstance 1

Where there is an enquiry into the company tax return of the company, the specified date is the last of the following dates—

(*a*) *30 days after the enquiry is completed;*

(*b*) *if after the enquiry HMRC amend the return under paragraph 34(2) of Schedule 18 to the Finance Act 1998, 30 days after notice of the amendment is issued;*

(*c*) *if an appeal is brought against such an amendment, 30 days after the date on which the appeal is finally determined.*

Circumstance 2

Where a determination under paragraph 36 of Schedule 18 to the Finance Act 1998 is made in relation to the company which is superseded by a self-assessment in accordance with paragraph 40 of that Schedule, the specified date is 30 days after delivery of the company tax return.

Circumstance 3

Where a discovery assessment or discovery determination is made under paragraph 41 of Schedule 18 to the Finance Act 1998 in relation to the company, the specified date is the last of the following dates—

(*d*) *30 days after the discovery assessment or discovery determination is made,*

(*e*) *if an appeal is brought against such the discovery assessment or discovery determination, 30 days after the date on which the appeal is finally determined.*

Circumstance 4

Where a determination under regulation 17 is made in relation to the company which is superseded by the provision of information under paragraph (4) of that regulation, the specified date is 30 days after the provision of that information.

REVOCATION—

These Regulations revoked by F(No 2)A 2017 s 20, Sch 5 para 11(3)(*a*) with effect in relation to periods of account of the worldwide group that begin on or after 1 April 2017. In relation to periods of account that straddle 1 April 2017 see Sch 5 para 26(2)–(10). **Please note** that Part 2A of the Yellow Book was sent to print before the Act had received Royal Assent. This amendment is therefore based on the 8 September 2017 Finance Bill. Please check F(No 2)A 2017 for confirmation of this amendment.

PART 3
EXEMPTION OF FINANCING INCOME

CHAPTER 1
APPOINTMENT OF AUTHORISED COMPANY

19 Appointment of authorised company

(1) An appointment under paragraph 29 of Schedule 15 must be made in accordance with this regulation.

(2) The company seeking to be appointed ("the applicant company") must make an application in writing to an officer of Revenue and Customs at least 3 months before the time specified in paragraph 31(2) of Schedule 15 (submission of statement of allocated exemptions).

(3) The application must be sent to the tax office that deals with the corporation tax affairs of the applicant company.

(4) The application must specify—

(*a*) *the name and the tax office reference of the applicant company,*

(*b*) *the names and the tax office references of the other companies to which Part 4 of Schedule 15 applies,*

(*c*) *the first period of account of the worldwide group in relation to which the appointment is to apply, and*

(*d*) *except in relation to the ultimate parent, the name of the immediate parent of the applicant company and each of the other companies to which Part 3 of Schedule 15 applies.*

(5) The application must contain a statement by the applicant company and by each of the other companies to which Part 4 of Schedule 15 applies—

(*a*) *that the appointment is made under paragraph 17 of Schedule 15,*

(*b*) *that the applicant company will act on behalf of all the companies to which Part 4 of Schedule 15 applies for all relevant periods of account for which the appointment has effect,*

(*c*) *that no application will be made by a company to amend its company tax return in relation to a financing income amount specified under paragraph 33(4)(b)* of Schedule 15 other than through a revised statement submitted by the applicant company in accordance with paragraph 32 of Schedule 15, and

(*d*) *agreeing to be bound by any statement of allocated exemptions or revised statement delivered by the applicant company.*

(6) The application must be accompanied by a specimen copy of a statement of allocated exemptions that the applicant company proposes to submit in relation to the relevant period of account.

REVOCATION—

These Regulations revoked by F(No 2)A 2017 s 20, Sch 5 para 11(3)(*a*) with effect in relation to periods of account of the worldwide group that begin on or after 1 April 2017. In relation to periods of account that straddle 1 April 2017 see Sch 5 para 26(2)–(10). **Please note** that Part 2A of the Yellow Book was sent to print before the Act had received Royal Assent. This amendment is therefore based on the 8 September 2017 Finance Bill. Please check F(No 2)A 2017 for confirmation of this amendment.

20 Supplemental provisions: timing and effect

(1) An appointment under paragraph 29 of Schedule 15 has effect on the date ("the three month date") that is three months after the application is delivered to the tax office in accordance with regulation 19(3).

This is subject to paragraphs (2) to (4).

(2) An officer of Revenue and Customs may accept the application before the three month date.

(3) Where paragraph (2) applies, the officer of Revenue and Customs may amend the list of companies to which Part 4 of Schedule 15 applies specified under regulation 19(4)(*b*) to exclude any company that is not a company to which Part 4 of Schedule 15 applies for the relevant period of account.

(4) An appointment under paragraph 29 of Schedule 15 is of no effect if before the three month date an officer of Revenue and Customs refuses the application on the grounds that—

(*a*) *the specimen statement of allocated exemptions provided in accordance with regulation 19(6) is not adequate for the purposes of Part 4 of Schedule 15, or*

(*b*) *a company to which Part 4 of Schedule 15 applies has been omitted from the list of companies specified under regulation 19(4)(b).*

REVOCATION—

These Regulations revoked by F(No 2)A 2017 s 20, Sch 5 para 11(3)(*a*) with effect in relation to periods of account of the worldwide group that begin on or after 1 April 2017. In relation to periods of account that straddle 1 April 2017 see Sch 5 para 26(2)–(10). **Please note** that Part 2A of the Yellow Book was sent to print before the Act had received Royal Assent. This amendment is therefore based on the 8 September 2017 Finance Bill. Please check F(No 2)A 2017 for confirmation of this amendment.

21 Duration of appointment

Once an appointment under paragraph 29 of Schedule 15 has effect, it continues to have effect until it ceases to have effect in accordance with regulations 22, 23 or 24.

REVOCATION—

These Regulations revoked by F(No 2)A 2017 s 20, Sch 5 para 11(3)(*a*) with effect in relation to periods of account of the worldwide group that begin on or after 1 April 2017. In relation to periods of account that straddle 1 April 2017 see Sch 5 para 26(2)–(10). **Please note** that Part 2A of the Yellow Book was sent to print before the Act had received Royal Assent. This amendment is therefore based on the 8 September 2017 Finance Bill. Please check F(No 2)A 2017 for confirmation of this amendment.

22 Revocation of appointment by notice

(1) An appointment under paragraph 29 of Schedule 15 ceases to have effect if revoked by the company appointed under that paragraph by notice in writing to an officer of Revenue and Customs at the tax office that deals with the corporation tax affairs of that company.

(2) The appointment ceases to have effect in relation to the relevant period of account in which the notice is given or such subsequent relevant period of account as may be specified in the notice.

REVOCATION—

These Regulations revoked by F(No 2)A 2017 s 20, Sch 5 para 11(3)(*a*) with effect in relation to periods of account of the worldwide group that begin on or after 1 April 2017. In relation to periods of account that straddle 1 April 2017 see Sch 5 para 26(2)–(10). **Please note** that Part 2A of the Yellow Book was sent to print before the Act had received Royal Assent. This amendment is therefore based on the 8 September 2017 Finance Bill. Please check F(No 2)A 2017 for confirmation of this amendment.

23 Revocation of appointment on authorised company ceasing to be a UK group company

(1) An appointment under paragraph 29 of Schedule 15 ceases to have effect if the company appointed under that paragraph ceases to be a company to which Part 4 of Schedule 15 applies.

(2) The appointment ceases to have effect in relation to the relevant period of account in which the company ceased to be a company to which Part 4 of Schedule 15 applies and subsequent periods of account.

REVOCATION—

These Regulations revoked by F(No 2)A 2017 s 20, Sch 5 para 11(3)(*a*) with effect in relation to periods of account of the worldwide group that begin on or after 1 April 2017. In relation to periods of account that straddle 1 April 2017 see Sch 5 para 26(2)–(10). **Please note** that Part 2A of the Yellow Book was sent to print before the Act had received Royal Assent. This amendment is therefore based on the 8 September 2017 Finance Bill. Please check F(No 2)A 2017 for confirmation of this amendment.

24 Revocation of appointment on a company becoming or ceasing to be a company to which Part 4 of Schedule 15 applies

(1) An appointment under paragraph 29 of Schedule 15 ceases to have effect if a company becomes or ceases to be a company to which Part 4 of Schedule 15 applies.

(2) The appointment ceases to have effect in relation to the relevant period of account in which the company becomes or ceases to be a company to which Part 4 of Schedule 15 applies and subsequent periods of account.

(3) But paragraph (1) does not apply if within three months of a company becoming or ceasing to be a company to which Part 4 of Schedule 15 applies, the reporting body notifies an officer of Revenue and Customs at the tax office that deals with its corporation tax affairs of the change.

(4) A notification under paragraph (3) must—

(*a*) *be in writing, and*

(*b*) *specify the name and the tax office reference of the company that has become or ceased to be a company to which Part 4 of Schedule 15 applies.*

(5) Where a new company has become a company to which Part 4 of Schedule 15 applies the notification must be accompanied by a statement by that company—

(*a*) *that the company appointed under paragraph 29 of Schedule 15 will act on its behalf for all relevant periods of account for which the appointment has effect;*

(*b*) *that no application will be made to amend a financing income amount specified under paragraph 33(4)(b)* of Schedule 15 other than through a revised statement submitted by the reporting body in accordance with paragraph 20 of Schedule 15;

(*c*) *agreeing to be bound by a statement of allocated exemptions or a revised statement delivered by the reporting body.*

REVOCATION—

These Regulations revoked by F(No 2)A 2017 s 20, Sch 5 para 11(3)(*a*) with effect in relation to periods of account of the worldwide group that begin on or after 1 April 2017. In relation to periods of account that straddle 1 April 2017 see Sch 5 para 26(2)–(10). **Please note** that Part 2A of the Yellow Book was sent to print before the Act had received Royal Assent. This amendment is therefore based on the 8 September 2017 Finance Bill. Please check F(No 2)A 2017 for confirmation of this amendment.

CHAPTER 2

STATEMENT OF ALLOCATED EXEMPTIONS

25 Submission of statement of allocated exemptions

(1) A statement of allocated exemptions must be submitted to the tax office dealing with the corporation tax affairs of—

(*a*) *in a case in which an appointment under paragraph 29 of Schedule 15 has effect in relation to the relevant period of account, the company appointed under that paragraph, or*

(*b*) *in a case in which such an appointment does not have effect in relation to the relevant period of account—*

(i) *the ultimate parent where that entity is resident in the United Kingdom, or*

(ii) *in any other case, the UK ultimate parent.*

(2) In a case within paragraph (1)(*b*)(ii), if there is more than one UK ultimate parent the statement of allocated exemptions must be submitted to the tax office dealing with the corporation tax affairs of each.

REVOCATION—

These Regulations revoked by F(No 2)A 2017 s 20, Sch 5 para 11(3)(*a*) with effect in relation to periods of account of the worldwide group that begin on or after 1 April 2017. In relation to periods of account that straddle 1 April 2017 see Sch 5 para 26(2)–(10). **Please note** that Part 2A of the Yellow Book was sent to print before the Act had received Royal Assent. This amendment is therefore based on the 8 September 2017 Finance Bill. Please check F(No 2)A 2017 for confirmation of this amendment.

26 Information to be given in connection with a statement of allocated exemptions

A statement of allocated exemptions must be accompanied by the following information—

(*a*) *the full name and the unique taxpayer number in relation to each company listed in the statement in accordance with paragraph 33(4)(a)* of Schedule 15;

(*b*) *where a company has delivered a tax return for a relevant accounting period and as a result of submitting a statement or revised statement—*

(i) *there is a change in the amount of profits on which corporation tax is chargeable for the period, or*

(ii) *any other information contained in the return is incorrect,*

details of the change mentioned in paragraph (i) or the information mentioned in paragraph (ii).

REVOCATION—

These Regulations revoked by F(No 2)A 2017 s 20, Sch 5 para 11(3)(*a*) with effect in relation to periods of account of the worldwide group that begin on or after 1 April 2017. In relation to periods of account that straddle 1 April 2017 see Sch 5 para 26(2)–(10). **Please note** that Part 2A of the Yellow Book was sent to print before the Act had received Royal Assent. This amendment is therefore based on the 8 September 2017 Finance Bill. Please check F(No 2)A 2017 for confirmation of this amendment.

27 Statement of allocated exemptions treated as received within specified time

(1) A statement of allocated exemptions which is not received by HMRC by the time specified ("the specified time") in paragraph 31(2) of Schedule 15, shall be treated as if it were so received in one of the circumstances specified in paragraph (2).

(2) The specified circumstances are—

(*a*) *the statement was submitted without unreasonable delay and this regulation has not applied in relation to any previous statement of allocated exemptions, or*

(*b*) *the statement was submitted as soon as possible but was not received by the specified time for exceptional reasons beyond the control of the reporting body.*

REVOCATION—

These Regulations revoked by F(No 2)A 2017 s 20, Sch 5 para 11(3)(*a*) with effect in relation to periods of account of the worldwide group that begin on or after 1 April 2017. In relation to periods of account that straddle 1 April 2017 see Sch 5 para 26(2)–(10). **Please note** that Part 2A of the Yellow Book was sent to print before the Act had received Royal Assent. This amendment is therefore based on the 8 September 2017 Finance Bill. Please check F(No 2)A 2017 for confirmation of this amendment.

28 Revised statement of allocated exemptions treated as received within specified time

(1) A revised statement of allocated exemptions which is not received by HMRC by the time specified ("the specified time") in paragraph 32(2) of Schedule 15, shall be treated as if it were so received if conditions A and B are met.

(2) Condition A is that the statement is received in one of the following circumstances.

Circumstance 1

A notice of enquiry is given before the specified time in relation to the company tax return of a company to which Part 4 of Schedule 15 applies, the enquiry is not completed until after the specified time and the revised statement is received by HMRC by the last of the following dates—

(*a*) *30 days after the enquiry is completed;*

(*b*) *if the return is amended by notice under paragraph 34(2) of Schedule 18 to the Finance Act 1998, 30 days after the notice is given;*

(*c*) *if an appeal is brought against such an amendment, 30 days after the date on which the appeal is finally determined.*

Circumstance 2

A determination under paragraph 36 of Schedule 18 to the Finance Act 1998 is made in relation to a company to which Part 4 of Schedule 15 applies which is superseded by an a self-assessment in accordance with paragraph 40 of that Schedule and the revised statement is received by HMRC within 30 days of delivery of the company tax return.

Circumstance 3

A discovery assessment or discovery determination is made under paragraph 41 of Schedule 18 to the Finance Act 1998 in relation to a company to which Part 4 of Schedule 15 applies and the revised statement is received by HMRC by the last of the following dates—

(*d*) *30 days after the discovery assessment or discovery determination is made;*

(*e*) *if an appeal is brought against the discovery assessment or discovery determination, 30 days after the date on which the appeal is finally determined.*

Circumstance 4

An amendment is made under paragraph 34(2A) of Schedule 18 to the Finance Act 1998 in relation to a company to which Part 3 of Schedule 15 applies and the revised statement is received by HMRC by the last of the following dates—

(*f*) *30 days after the notice of the amendment is given;*

(*g*) *if an appeal is brought against such an amendment, 30 days after the date on which the appeal is finally determined.*

(3) Condition B is that the amount of the difference between—

(*a*) *the financing income amounts specified in accordance with paragraph 33(4)(b)* of Schedule 15 in the statement of allocated exemptions, and

(*b*) *the amounts so specified in the revised statement,*

does not exceed the change made to the amount of profit on which corporation tax is chargeable as a result of the enquiry, assessment or determination referred to in paragraph (2).

REVOCATION—

These Regulations revoked by F(No 2)A 2017 s 20, Sch 5 para 11(3)(*a*) with effect in relation to periods of account of the worldwide group that begin on or after 1 April 2017. In relation to periods of account that straddle 1 April 2017 see Sch 5 para 26(2)–(10). **Please note** that Part 2A of the Yellow Book was sent to print before the Act had received Royal Assent. This amendment is therefore based on the 8 September 2017 Finance Bill. Please check F(No 2)A 2017 for confirmation of this amendment.

29 Statement of allocated exemptions treated as complying with paragraph 26 of Schedule 15

A statement of allocated exemptions which does not comply with paragraph 33 of Schedule 15 because of an obvious error or omission in the statement (whether an error of principle, an arithmetical mistake or otherwise) shall be treated as if it did so comply if the error or omission is corrected by the reporting body as soon as it becomes apparent.

REVOCATION—

These Regulations revoked by F(No 2)A 2017 s 20, Sch 5 para 11(3)(*a*) with effect in relation to periods of account of the worldwide group that begin on or after 1 April 2017. In relation to periods of account that straddle 1 April 2017 see Sch 5 para 26(2)–(10). **Please note** that Part 2A of the Yellow Book was sent to print before the Act had received Royal Assent. This amendment is therefore based on the 8 September 2017 Finance Bill. Please check F(No 2)A 2017 for confirmation of this amendment.

CHAPTER 3

FAILURE OF REPORTING BODY TO SUBMIT A STATEMENT OF ALLOCATED EXEMPTIONS

30 Information to be provided in relation to a company required to make default reductions

(1) An ultimate UK parent must send a company required to make default reductions details of the amounts of—

(*a*) *the total of the unrestricted reductions,*

(*b*) *the total disallowed amount, and*

(*c*) *the tested income amount,*

for the worldwide group for the relevant period of account.

(2) The information in paragraph (1) must be supplied to the company required to make default reductions before the filing date for the company's tax return (see paragraph 14 of Schedule 18 to the Finance Act 1998).

REVOCATION—

These Regulations revoked by F(No 2)A 2017 s 20, Sch 5 para 11(3)(*a*) with effect in relation to periods of account of the worldwide group that begin on or after 1 April 2017. In relation to periods of account that straddle 1 April 2017 see Sch 5 para 26(2)–(10). **Please note** that Part 2A of the Yellow Book was sent to print before the Act had received Royal Assent. This amendment is therefore based on the 8 September 2017 Finance Bill. Please check F(No 2)A 2017 for confirmation of this amendment.

31 Non-compliance

(1) If an ultimate UK parent does not provide the information specified by regulation 30 within the requisite time period, HMRC must determine to the best of their information and belief the amounts of the total of the unrestricted reductions, the total disallowed amount and the tested income amount for the worldwide group for the relevant period of account.

(2) A notice of determination under this regulation must be sent to the company required to make the default reduction and to the ultimate UK parent stating the date on which the determination is issued.

(3) No determination under this regulation may be made more than 3 years after the day on which the power becomes exercisable.

(4) If after a determination has been made under this regulation, the ultimate UK parent provides the information specified by regulation 30, that information shall supersede the determination.

(5) But paragraph (4) does not apply if the information is supplied more than 3 years after the determination is made.

REVOCATION—

These Regulations revoked by F(No 2)A 2017 s 20, Sch 5 para 11(3)(*a*) with effect in relation to periods of account of the worldwide group that begin on or after 1 April 2017. In relation to periods of account that straddle 1 April 2017 see Sch 5 para 26(2)–(10). **Please note** that Part 2A of the Yellow Book was sent to print before the Act had received Royal Assent. This amendment is therefore based on the 8 September 2017 Finance Bill. Please check F(No 2)A 2017 for confirmation of this amendment.

32 Amendment of tax return by company

(1) A company required to make default reductions may amend its company tax return so as to reflect a reduction under paragraph 25 of Schedule 15 within 3 years of the end of the relevant period of account.

(2) But where one of the following circumstances applies the company may amend its tax return at any time before the specified date.

Circumstance 1

Where there is an enquiry into the company tax return of the company, the specified date is the last of the following dates—

(*a*) *30 days after the enquiry is completed;*

(*b*) *if after the enquiry HMRC amend the return under paragraph 34(2) of Schedule 18 to the Finance Act 1998, 30 days after notice of the amendment is issued;*

(*c*) *if an appeal is brought against such an amendment, 30 days after the date on which the appeal is finally determined.*

Circumstance 2

Where a determination under paragraph 36 of Schedule 18 to the Finance Act 1998 is made in relation to the company which is superseded by a self-assessment in accordance with paragraph 40 of that Schedule, the specified date is 30 days of delivery of the company tax return.

Circumstance 3

Where a discovery assessment or discovery determination is made under paragraph 41 of Schedule 18 to the Finance Act 1998 in relation to the company, the specified date is the last of the following dates—

(*d*) *30 days after the discovery assessment or discovery determination is made,*

(*e*) *if an appeal is brought against such the discovery assessment or discovery determination, 30 days after the date on which the appeal is finally determined.*

Circumstance 4

Where a determination under regulation 31 is made in relation to the company which is superseded by the provision of information under paragraph (4) of that regulation, the specified date is 30 days after the provision of that information.

REVOCATION—

These Regulations revoked by F(No 2)A 2017 s 20, Sch 5 para 11(3)(*a*) with effect in relation to periods of account of the worldwide group that begin on or after 1 April 2017. In relation to periods of account that straddle 1 April 2017 see Sch 5 para 26(2)–(10). **Please note** that Part 2A of the Yellow Book was sent to print before the Act had received Royal Assent. This amendment is therefore based on the 8 September 2017 Finance Bill. Please check F(No 2)A 2017 for confirmation of this amendment.

2009/3217

CORPORATION TAX (TAX TREATMENT OF FINANCING COSTS AND INCOME) (ACCEPTABLE FINANCIAL STATEMENTS) REGULATIONS 2009

Made by the Treasury under FA 2009 Sch 15 para 88(3)(*b*)

Made . . . . *3 December 2009*
Laid before the House of Commons . . . . *7 December 2009*
Coming into force . . . . *1 January 2010*

Commentary—*Simon's Taxes* **DIVISION 1.3, D5.401.**

Revocation—

These Regulations revoked by F(No 2)A 2017 s 20, Sch 5 para 11(3)(*b*) with effect in relation to periods of account of the worldwide group that begin on or after 1 April 2017. In relation to periods of account that straddle 1 April 2017 see Sch 5 para 26(2)–(10). **Please note** that Part 2A of the Yellow Book was sent to print before the Act had received Royal Assent. This amendment is therefore based on the 8 September 2017 Finance Bill. Please check F(No 2)A 2017 for confirmation of this amendment.

1 Citation, commencement and effect

(1) These Regulations may be cited as the Corporation Tax (Tax Treatment of Financing Costs and Income) (Acceptable Financial Statements) Regulations 2009.

(2) These Regulations shall come into force on 1st January 2010.

(3) Subject to paragraph (4), these Regulations shall have effect in relation to periods of account beginning on or after 1st January 2010.

(4) Paragraph (5) of regulation 2 shall have effect only in relation to periods of account beginning on or after 1st April 2011.

REVOCATION—

These Regulations revoked by F(No 2)A 2017 s 20, Sch 5 para 11(3)(*b*) with effect in relation to periods of account of the worldwide group that begin on or after 1 April 2017. In relation to periods of account that straddle 1 April 2017 see Sch 5 para 26(2)–(10). **Please note** that Part 2A of the Yellow Book was sent to print before the Act had received Royal Assent. This amendment is therefore based on the 8 September 2017 Finance Bill. Please check F(No 2)A 2017 for confirmation of this amendment.

2 Acceptable financial statements

(1) Financial statements are acceptable for the purposes of paragraph 88 of Schedule 15 to the Finance Act 2009 (non-compliant financial statements of worldwide group) if they meet one of conditions A to D.

(2) Condition A is that the financial statements are drawn up in accordance with international accounting standards adopted with modifications by the European Commission in accordance with Regulation (EC) No 1606/2002 of the European Parliament and of the Council of 19th July 2002 on the application of international accounting standards.

(3) Condition B is that the financial statements are drawn up in accordance with UK generally accepted accounting practice.

(4) Condition C is that the financial statements are drawn up in accordance with generally accepted accounting principles or practice of one of the following territories—

(*a*) *Canada,*
(*b*) *China,*
(*c*) *Japan,*
(*d*) *South Korea,*
(*e*) *the United States of America.*

(5) Condition D is that the financial statements are drawn up in accordance with generally accepted accounting principles or practice of India.

REVOCATION—

These Regulations revoked by F(No 2)A 2017 s 20, Sch 5 para 11(3)(*b*) with effect in relation to periods of account of the worldwide group that begin on or after 1 April 2017. In relation to periods of account that straddle 1 April 2017 see Sch 5 para 26(2)–(10). **Please note** that Part 2A of the Yellow Book was sent to print before the Act had received Royal Assent. This amendment is therefore based on the 8 September 2017 Finance Bill. Please check F(No 2)A 2017 for confirmation of this amendment.

2009/3227

NORTHERN ROCK PLC (TAX CONSEQUENCES) REGULATIONS 2009

Made by the Treasury under Banking (Special Provisions) Act 2008 s 10

Made . . . . *8 December 2009*
Laid before the House of Commons . . . . *8 December 2009*
Coming into force . . . . *1 January 2010*

1 Citation and commencement

These Regulations may be cited as the Northern Rock plc (Tax Consequences) Regulations 2009 and shall come into force on 1st January 2010.

2 Interpretation

In these Regulations—

"ACo" means Northern Rock plc, company registered number 03273685, or, except in relation to regulation 7, any wholly owned subsidiary of that company;

"BCo" means Gosforth Subsidiary No1 plc, company registered number 06952311, or any wholly owned subsidiary of that company;

"CTA 2009" means the Corporation Tax Act 2009;

"relevant time" means any time when both ACo and BCo are wholly owned by the Treasury;

"relevant transfer" means—

(*a*) a transfer or novation of any securities, or of any property, rights or liabilities, between ACo and BCo, or

(*b*) the grant of a lease, sublease, licence or sub-licence by ACo to BCo or by BCo to ACo,

in relation to, in connection with, or by or under, the Northern Rock plc Transfer Order 2009 at a relevant time.

3 Chargeable gains: no gain or loss disposal

(1) For the purposes of the Taxation of Chargeable Gains Act 1992, a disposal constituted by a relevant transfer is to be treated in relation to ACo and BCo as being for a consideration such that neither a gain nor a loss accrues to the transferor.

(2) For the purposes of any tax provision, paragraph (1) is to be treated as one of the no gain/no loss provisions in section 288(3A) of the Taxation of Chargeable Gains Act 1992 (meaning of "the no gain/no loss provisions").

4 Corporation tax: trading assets and trading liabilities

(1) For the purposes of Part 3 of CTA 2009 (trading income) ("Part 3"), a relevant transfer of a trading asset or a trading liability is to be treated in relation to ACo and BCo as being for a consideration such that neither a profit nor a loss accrues to the transferor.

(2) For the purposes of this regulation—

"trading asset" means an asset the proceeds of disposal of which would, but for this regulation, be brought into account as a receipt under Part 3 otherwise than in accordance with section 297 (trading credits and debits to be brought into account under Part 3), section 573 (trading credits and debits to be brought into account under Part 3) or section 747 (assets held for purposes of trade) of CTA 2009;

"trading liability" means a liability the payment for the assumption of which would, but for this regulation, be brought into account as an expense under Part 3 otherwise than in accordance with section 297 or section 573 of CTA 2009.

(3) Schedule 28AA to the Income and Corporation Taxes Act 1988 (provisions not at arm's length) does not apply in relation to a relevant transfer to which paragraph (1) applies.

5 Corporation tax: loan relationships

(1) For the purposes of Chapter 4 of Part 5 of CTA 2009 (continuity of treatment on transfers within groups or on reorganisations), in relation to a relevant transfer, ACo and BCo are to be treated as if, for the purposes of the transfer, they were members of the same group.

(2) But a relevant transfer within paragraph (1) is not to be treated as a case within section 336 of CTA 2009 (transfers of loans on group transactions) for the purposes of section 344 of the Act (introduction).

6 Corporation tax: intangible assets

(1) For the purposes of Part 8 of CTA 2009 (intangible fixed assets), a relevant transfer of a chargeable intangible asset is to be treated as tax-neutral.

(2) Schedule 28AA to the Income and Corporation Taxes Act 1988 (provisions not at arm's length) does not apply in relation to a relevant transfer to which paragraph (1) applies.

(3) For the purposes of section 882 of CTA 2009 (application of Part 8 to assets created or acquired on or after 1st April 2002), assets acquired by ACo or BCo on a relevant transfer are to be treated as if they were acquired from a person who at the time of the acquisition is a related party.

(4) Expressions used in this regulation and Part 8 of CTA 2009 have the same meaning in this regulation as they have in that Part.

7 Income tax: interest paid by banks

(1) For the purposes of section 878 of the Income Tax Act 2007 (interest paid by banks), ACo is to be treated as a bank in relation to payments of interest made by ACo after 31st December 2009 on any securities or liabilities to which this regulation applies.

(2) This regulation applies to—

(*a*) securities issued by ACo on or before 31st December 2009, and

(*b*) liabilities incurred under an agreement entered into by ACo on or before that date,

which are not transferred by a relevant transfer and in relation to which section 878 of the Income Tax Act 2007 applied to payments of interest made on or before 31st December 2009, or would have applied if a payment of interest had been made on or before that date.

8 Stamp duty

No stamp duty is chargeable on an instrument effecting or implementing a relevant transfer.

9 Stamp duty reserve tax

(1) No stamp duty reserve tax is chargeable on an agreement to transfer chargeable securities made in relation to, in connection with, or by or under, the Northern Rock plc Transfer Order 2009.

(2) In paragraph (1) "chargeable securities" has the meaning given in section 99 of the Finance Act 1986 (interpretation).

2009/3313

CORPORATION TAX (EXCLUSION FROM SHORT-TERM LOAN RELATIONSHIPS) REGULATIONS 2009

Made by the Treasury under FA 2009 Sch 15 para 62(4)

Made . . . . *15 December 2009*

Coming into force . . . . *1 January 2010*

Revocation—

These Regulations revoked by F(No 2)A 2017 s 20, Sch 5 para 11(3)(*c*) with effect in relation to periods of account of the worldwide group that begin on or after 1 April 2017. In relation to periods of account that straddle 1 April 2017 see Sch 5 para 26(2)–(10). **Please note** that Part 2A of the Yellow Book was sent to print before the Act had received Royal Assent. This amendment is therefore based on the 8 September 2017 Finance Bill. Please check F(No 2)A 2017 for confirmation of this amendment.

1 Citation, commencement and interpretation

(1) These Regulations may be cited as the Corporation Tax (Exclusion from Short-Term Loan Relationships) Regulations 2009.

(2) These Regulations shall come into force on 1st January 2010.

(3) In these Regulations "FA 2009" means the Finance Act 2009.

REVOCATION—

These Regulations revoked by F(No 2)A 2017 s 20, Sch 5 para 11(3)(*c*) with effect in relation to periods of account of the worldwide group that begin on or after 1 April 2017. In relation to periods of account that straddle 1 April 2017 see Sch 5 para 26(2)–(10). **Please note** that Part 2A of the Yellow Book was sent to print before the Act had received Royal Assent. This amendment is therefore based on the 8 September 2017 Finance Bill. Please check F(No 2)A 2017 for confirmation of this amendment.

2 Exclusion from short-term loan relationship

For the purposes of paragraph 60 of Schedule 15 to FA 2009 (intra-group short-term finance: financing expense), a finance arrangement is not to be taken as a short-term loan relationship for the relevant period or any parts of the relevant period where—

(*a*) *any part or all of the finance arrangement is made for a long-term funding purpose; or*

(*b*) *the finance arrangement is a long-term aggregated loan relationship.*

REVOCATION—

These Regulations revoked by F(No 2)A 2017 s 20, Sch 5 para 11(3)(*c*) with effect in relation to periods of account of the worldwide group that begin on or after 1 April 2017. In relation to periods of account that straddle 1 April 2017 see Sch 5 para 26(2)–(10). **Please note** that Part 2A of the Yellow Book was sent to print before the Act had received Royal Assent. This amendment is therefore based on the 8 September 2017 Finance Bill. Please check F(No 2)A 2017 for confirmation of this amendment.

3 Meaning of long-term funding purpose

(1) A finance arrangement is made for a long-term funding purpose where at the date the finance arrangement is made—

(*a*) *to the extent that the finance arrangement provides for the creation of money debt, it is reasonable to expect that all the money debt created under it will not be settled within 12 months of the money debt first being created under it, and*

(*b*) *to the extent that the finance arrangement is otherwise a loan relationship, it is reasonable to expect that it will not terminate within 12 months of its coming into force; or*

(*c*) *the conditions in regulation 4 are met.*

(2) For the purposes of this regulation circumstances where it is reasonable to expect that the finance arrangement will not be settled or terminated within 12 months include circumstances where—

(*a*) *the finance arrangement may be settled or terminated by use of borrowing; or*

(*b*) *the finance arrangement may be settled or terminated temporarily by funds available for a limited period of time.*

REVOCATION—

These Regulations revoked by F(No 2)A 2017 s 20, Sch 5 para 11(3)(*c*) with effect in relation to periods of account of the worldwide group that begin on or after 1 April 2017. In relation to periods of account that straddle 1 April 2017 see Sch 5 para 26(2)–(10). **Please note** that Part 2A of the Yellow Book was sent to print before the Act had received Royal Assent. This amendment is therefore based on the 8 September 2017 Finance Bill. Please check F(No 2)A 2017 for confirmation of this amendment.

4 Anti-avoidance

(1) A sequence of finance arrangements is considered to be a single finance arrangement made for a long-term funding purpose if the following conditions are met.

(2) The first condition is that the sequence of finance arrangements when taken together will not be settled or terminated within 12 months.

(3) The second condition is that the sequence of finance arrangements is part of a scheme or arrangement the main purpose, or one of the main purposes, of which is to characterise a loan relationship as a short-term loan relationship for the purposes of paragraph 60 of Schedule 15 to FA 2009.

REVOCATION—

These Regulations revoked by F(No 2)A 2017 s 20, Sch 5 para 11(3)(*c*) with effect in relation to periods of account of the worldwide group that begin on or after 1 April 2017. In relation to periods of account that straddle 1 April 2017 see Sch 5 para 26(2)–(10). **Please note** that Part 2A of the Yellow Book was sent to print before the Act had received Royal Assent. This amendment is therefore based on the 8 September 2017 Finance Bill. Please check F(No 2)A 2017 for confirmation of this amendment.

5 Long-term aggregated loan relationship

(1) A number of finance arrangements are long-term aggregated loan relationships if the following conditions are met.

(2) The first condition is that the finance arrangements exist between the same two companies.

(3) The second condition is that there are no repayment terms relating specifically to each separate finance arrangement.

(4) The third condition is that accounts show the finance arrangements as a single net balance between the companies at all times.

(5) The fourth condition is that the finance arrangements when taken together do not meet the conditions mentioned in paragraph 62(1) of Schedule 15 to FA 2009.

REVOCATION—

These Regulations revoked by F(No 2)A 2017 s 20, Sch 5 para 11(3)(*c*) with effect in relation to periods of account of the worldwide group that begin on or after 1 April 2017. In relation to periods of account that straddle 1 April 2017 see Sch 5 para 26(2)–(10). **Please note** that Part 2A of the Yellow Book was sent to print before the Act had received Royal Assent. This amendment is therefore based on the 8 September 2017 Finance Bill. Please check F(No 2)A 2017 for confirmation of this amendment.

2009/3314

DISTRIBUTIONS (EXCLUDED COMPANIES) REGULATIONS 2009

Made by the Treasury under CTA 2009 s 931C(2)(*b*), (6)

Made . . . . *15 December 2009*
Coming into force . . . . *15 December 2009*

1 Citation, commencement and effect

(1) These Regulations may be cited as the Distributions (Excluded Companies) Regulations 2009 and shall come into force on the day on which they are made.

(2) These Regulations shall have effect for accounting periods which are current on the day on which these Regulations are made and for accounting periods which begin after that day.

2 Excluded companies

(1) A territory which satisfies section 931C(1)(*a*) and (*b*) is nevertheless not a qualifying territory for the purpose of section 931B in respect of the payer of the distribution if the payer is an excluded company.

(2) For the purposes of this regulation, an excluded company is one which is excluded from one or more of the benefits of any double taxation relief arrangements for the time being in force in relation to that territory.

2009/3315

REAL ESTATE INVESTMENT TRUSTS (PRESCRIBED ARRANGEMENTS) REGULATIONS 2009

Made by the Treasury under FA 2006 s 136A and FA 2009 Sch 34 para 8(2)

Made . . . . *15 December 2009*
Coming into force . . . . *15 December 2009*

1 Citation, commencement and effect

(1) These Regulations may be cited as the Real Estate Investment Trusts (Prescribed Arrangements) Regulations 2009 and shall come into force forthwith.

(2) These Regulations shall have effect in relation to prescribed arrangements made on or after 7th May 2009 and during an accounting period which ends on or after 15th December 2009.

2 Interpretation

(1) In these Regulations—

(*a*) a reference to Part 4 is a reference to Part 4 of the Finance Act 2006 (real estate investment trusts), and

(*b*) a reference to a section (without more) is a reference to that section of the Finance Act 2006.

(2) For the purposes of these Regulations, "person" includes, but is not limited to—

(*a*) a legal person,

(*b*) a natural person,

(*c*) a partnership,

(*d*) a limited partnership,

(*e*) a limited liability partnership,

(*f*) a trust, and

(*g*) any other body of persons.

(3) For the purposes of these Regulations—

"arrangements" include any agreement, understanding, scheme, share reorganisation, transaction or series of transactions (whether or not legally enforceable), and

"prescribed arrangements" are arrangements (whether or not part of other arrangements) which have the purpose, or one of the main purposes, of allowing a REIT company to meet one or more of the conditions set out in sections 107 (conditions for tax exempt business) and 108 (conditions for balance of business) where, but for the arrangements, those conditions would not be satisfied.

3 Situations in which these Regulations apply

(1) These Regulations apply if conditions A and B are satisfied.

(2) Condition A is that an amount ("the specified amount")—

(*a*) falls to be taken into account as part of a REIT company's tax exempt or residual business, or

(*b*) ceases to be taken into account as part of such business.

(3) For the purposes of condition A, the specified amount may be taken into account (or may cease to be taken into account) as a liability, an expense, an asset or income.

(4) Condition B is that the specified amount arises directly or indirectly from, or in consequence of, or otherwise in connection with, prescribed arrangements.

4 Excluded arrangements

(1) For the purposes of these Regulations, arrangements are not prescribed arrangements if at least one of the following conditions is satisfied.

(2) Condition 1 is that the arrangements have been effected solely for genuine commercial purposes.

(3) Condition 2 is that the arrangements are made between persons dealing at arm's length.

5 Persons to be treated as member of REIT group in certain situations

(1) Where a REIT company enters into prescribed arrangements with a person ("the person in question"), subject to paragraph (3), the entities listed in paragraph (2) shall be treated as members of the same REIT group for the purposes of the application of Part 4, from the beginning of the accounting period in which the arrangements are made.

(2) The entities are—

(*a*) the REIT company,

(*b*) the person in question, and

(*c*) any person in which either the person in question, or the REIT company, have a direct or indirect interest.

(3) But a person within paragraph (2)(*c*) shall not be treated as a member of the REIT group where it can be shown that the person falls outside the scope of the prescribed arrangements.

6 Effect of regulations for corporation tax purposes

(1) This regulation applies if—

(*a*) a company enters into prescribed arrangements which take effect during the accounting period specified in a notice given under section 109 (notice), and

(*b*) that Part ceases to apply to it by reason of section 129 (termination notice: Commissioners).

(2) Any corporation tax paid by the company pursuant to section 112 (entry charge) shall be fully taken into account for the purposes of assessing its liability to corporation tax.

2009/3333

TAX CREDITS (EXCLUDED COMPANIES) REGULATIONS 2009

Made by the Treasury under ITTOIA 2005 ss 397BA(3)(*b*) and (7)

Made . . . . *15 December 2009*
Coming into force . . . . *22 April 2009*

1 Citation, commencement and effect

These Regulations may be cited as the Tax Credits (Excluded Companies) Regulations 2009 and shall have effect from 22nd April 2009 for the tax year 2009–2010 and subsequent tax years.

2 Excluded companies

(1) A territory which satisfies section 397BA(2)(*a*) and (*b*) of the Income Tax (Trading and Other Income) Act 2005 is nevertheless not a qualifying territory for the purposes of section 397AA of that Act in relation to the company which makes the relevant distribution if that company is an excluded company.

(2) For the purposes of this regulation, an excluded company is one which is excluded from one or more of the benefits of any double taxation relief arrangements for the time being in force in relation to that territory.

2010/4

EMPLOYERS' DUTIES (IMPLEMENTATION) REGULATIONS 2010

Made . . . . *5 January 2010*
Laid before Parliament . . . . *12 January 2010*
Coming into force . . . . *1 September 2012*

The Secretary of State makes the following Regulations in exercise of the powers conferred by sections 12, 29(2) and (4), 30(8), 99 and 144(2) and (4) of the Pensions Act 2008:

1 Citation, commencement and interpretation

(1) These Regulations may be cited as the Employers' Duties (Implementation) Regulations 2010 and shall come into force on [1st June 2012, immediately after the time when the amendments to these Regulations made by the Automatic Enrolment (Miscellaneous Amendments) Regulations 2012 come into force][1].

(2) In these Regulations—

"the Act" means the Pensions Act 2008;

["deferral date" means the date specified in a notice given by an employer under regulation 4B(1) or (2);][3]

"employer"[", except in regulations 4B and 4C,][3] has the meaning given by—

(*a*) section 88(7) of the Act; and

(*b*) regulation 2(2);

"the employers' duties" means sections 2 to 9 of the Act;

"HMRC" means Her Majesty's Revenue and Customs;

"PAYE income" has the same meaning as in section 683 of the Income Tax (Earnings and Pensions) Act 2003;

"PAYE reference number" means a number issued by HMRC to a corresponding PAYE scheme, enabling an employer to pay over amounts deducted to HMRC;

"PAYE scheme" means the HMRC record [applicable][1] to an employer who—

(*a*) employs; or

(*b*) intends to employ,

a worker or workers to whom PAYE income is payable;

"scheme administrator" has the same meaning as in section 270 of the Finance Act 2004; and

["staging date" means the date prescribed in accordance with regulation 2(1) on which the employers' duties apply to employers.][1]

Amendments—[1] In paras (1), (2), words substituted by the Automatic Enrolment (Miscellaneous Amendments) Regulations, SI 2012/255 regs 2, 3. The amendment of para (3) takes effect at the beginning of 1 June 2012, and the amendment of para (1) takes effect immediately thereafter.

[2] In para (2), definition of "staging date" substituted by the Employers' Duties (Implementation) (Amendment) Regulations, SI 2012/1813 reg 2(1), (2) with effect from 1 October 2012.

[3] In para (2), definition of "deferral date" inserted, and in definition of "employer", words inserted, by the Employers' Duties (Implementation) (Amendment) Regulations, SI 2017/347 regs 2, 3(1) with effect from 1 April 2017.

2 Application of the employers' duties to employers

[(1) Except where an employer satisfies the conditions for early automatic enrolment in regulation 3, the employers' duties do not apply to employers described in the first column of the table in regulation 4 until—

(*a*) the corresponding staging date prescribed in the final column of that table; or

(*b*) in a case to which paragraph (1A) applies—

(i) the corresponding staging date prescribed in the final column of that table in regulation 4; or

(ii) where the employer so chooses, the corresponding staging date prescribed in the final column of the table as modified by regulation 4A.][2]

[(1A) This paragraph applies in a case where, on 1st April 2012, the employer—

(*a*) had less than 50 workers; and

(*b*) had, or was part of, one or more PAYE schemes in which there were 50 or more persons.][2]

(2) For the purposes of these Regulations [(except for regulations 4B and 4C)][3], an employer is a person within the meaning of section 88(7) of the Act who—

(*a*) has[, or is part of,][1] a PAYE scheme of any size, determined by the Regulator in accordance with paragraphs (3) and (4); or

(*b*) meets any other description contained in the first column of the table in regulation 4 (including having no PAYE scheme).

(3) The size of an employer's PAYE scheme means the number of persons within that scheme.

(4) The number of persons within a PAYE scheme is based on the latest information available to the Regulator, as at 1st April 2012.

(5) Where—

(*a*) the employers' duties first apply to an employer in accordance with the table in regulation 4; and

(*b*) for any reason, an employer has another PAYE scheme (or schemes),

the employers' duties apply to that employer in respect of the scheme (or schemes) mentioned in subparagraph (*b*) from the staging date applicable in relation to subparagraph (*a*) (and this is so even where the staging date mentioned in the table for any such scheme (or schemes) is later than the staging date referred to in subparagraph (*a*)).

(6) Any employer who first pays PAYE income in respect of a worker between—

(*a*) 1st April 2012; and

(*b*) up to (but not including) [1st October 2017][2],

is to be treated as a new employer in accordance with the relevant entry in the first column of the table in regulation 4.

(7) Where paragraph (6) applies, the employers' duties do not apply to such an employer until PAYE income is first payable in respect of any worker and then only in accordance with the table in regulation 4.

[(8) Where—

(*a*) an employer first pays PAYE income in respect of any worker on or after 1st October 2017; and

(*b*) the employers' duties do not already apply to that employer,

the employers' duties apply to that employer from the day on which the employer's first worker begins to be employed by the employer.][3]

[(9) This paragraph applies in the case of an employer who does not have a PAYE scheme in respect of any worker after 1st April 2017.

(10) Where paragraph (9) applies and the employers' duties do not already apply to that employer, the employers' duties apply to that employer from the date on which [the employer's first worker begins to be employed by the employer][2].][2]

Amendments—[1] In para (2)(*a*), words inserted by the Automatic Enrolment (Miscellaneous Amendments) Regulations, SI 2012/255 regs 2, 4 with effect from the beginning of 1 June 2012.

[2] Para (1) substituted, paras (1A), (9), (10) inserted, and in paras (6)(*b*), (8)(*a*), words inserted, by the Employers' Duties (Implementation) (Amendment) Regulations, SI 2012/1813 reg 2(1), (3) with effect from 1 October 2012.

[3] In para (2), words inserted, para (8) substituted, and in para (1), words substituted, by the Employers' Duties (Implementation) (Amendment) Regulations, SI 2017/347 regs 2, 3(2) with effect from 1 April 2017.

3 Early automatic enrolment

(1) [Where the conditions in paragraphs (3) and (4) are both satisfied, the employers' duties apply to an employer from the early automatic enrolment date referred to in paragraph (5).][1]

[(1A) This regulation does not apply where the employer has chosen a staging date in accordance with regulation 2(1)(*b*)(ii).][1]

(2) Where the condition in paragraph (3) is satisfied but the condition in paragraph (4) is not satisfied, the employers' duties apply to an employer from the staging date corresponding to that employer's description . . . [1]

(3) The first condition is that an employer must fall within any description in the first column of the table in regulation 4.

(4) The second condition is that an employer has chosen an early automatic enrolment date [referred to in paragraph (5)][1] for the employers' duties to apply, which is earlier than the date mentioned in the final column of that table corresponding to that employer, and has—

(*a*) . . . [1]

(*b*) [where, on the date the employer notifies the Regulator in accordance with subparagraph (c), the duty in section 3(2) of the Act (automatic enrolment) applies in relation to at least one of that employer's jobholders,][3] secured the agreement of the [trustees or managers][1] (or scheme administrator or provider) of [a pension scheme][2] that that scheme [is][3] to be used by the employer to comply with those duties from that early automatic enrolment date; and

[(*c*) notified the Regulator accordingly in writing, at any time—

[(i) where paragraph (5)(*a*) or (*d*) applies, on or before the early automatic enrolment date;][3]

(ii) where paragraph (5)(*b*) applies, before 1st November 2012; or

(iii) where paragraph (5)(*c*) applies, no later than the first day of the period of one month before the date specified in that sub-paragraph.][1]

[(5) The early automatic enrolment date is—

(*a*) any date in the final column of the table in regulation 4 which is earlier than the staging date corresponding to that employers' description;

(*b*) 1st December 2012; . . . [3]

(*c*) in the case of an employer of 50,000 or more persons by PAYE scheme size or any other description, one of the following dates to be chosen by the employer—

(i) 1st July 2012;

(ii) 1st August 2012; or

(iii) 1st September 2012[; or][1]

(*d*) in the case of an employer who has no jobholder to whom the duty in section 3(2) of the Act applies on the date the employer notifies the Regulator in accordance with paragraph (4)(*c*)(i), any date which is earlier than the staging date corresponding to that employer's description.][3]

Amendments—[1] Paras (1), (4)(*c*) substituted, in para (2), words revoked, in para (4), words substituted, para (4)(*a*) revoked, and para (5) inserted, by the Automatic Enrolment (Miscellaneous Amendments) Regulations, SI 2012/255 regs 2, 5 with effect from the beginning of 1 June 2012.

[2] Para (1A) inserted, and in para (4)(*b*), words substituted, by the Employers' Duties (Implementation) (Amendment) Regulations, SI 2012/1813 reg 2(1), (4) with effect from 1 October 2012.

[3] In para (4)(*b*), words inserted and substituted, in para (4)(*c*)(i), words substituted, in para (5)(*b*), word revoked, and para (5)(*d*) and preceding word inserted by the Occupational and Personal Pension Schemes (Automatic Enrolment) (Miscellaneous Amendments) Regulations, SI 2016/311 reg 2(1), (2) with effect from 6 April 2016.

4 Staging of the employers' duties

(1) The table in this regulation sets out the application of the employers' duties.

(2) . . . [2]

(3) . . . [2]

Employer (by PAYE scheme size or other description)	. . . [2]	*Staging date*
120,000 or more	. . . [2]	1st October 2012
50,000–119,999	. . . [2]	1st November 2012
30,000–49,999	. . . [2]	1st January 2013
20,000–29,999	. . . [2]	1st February 2013
10,000–19,999	. . . [2]	1st March 2013
6,000–9,999	. . . [2]	1st April 2013
4,100–5,999	. . . [2]	1st May 2013
4,000–4,099	. . . [2]	1st June 2013
3,000–3,999	. . . [2]	1st July 2013
2,000–2,999	. . . [2]	1st August 2013
1,250–1,999	. . . [2]	1st September 2013
800–1,249	. . . [2]	1st October 2013
500–799	. . . [2]	1st November 2013
350–499	. . . [2]	1st January 2014
250–349	. . . [2]	1st February 2014
[160-249	. . . [2]	1st April 2014
90-159	. . . [2]	1st May 2014
62-89	. . . [2]	1st July 2014
61	. . . [2]	1st August 2014
60	. . . [2]	1st October 2014
59	. . . [2]	1st November 2014
58	. . . [2]	1st January 2015
54-57	. . . [2]	1st March 2015
50-53	. . . [2]	1st April 2015
Less than 30 with the last 2 characters in their PAYE reference numbers 92, A1-A9, B1-B9, AA-AZ, BA-BW, M1-M9, MA-MZ, Z1-Z9, ZA-ZZ, 0A-0Z, 1A-1Z or 2A-2Z	. . . [2]	1st June 2015
Less than 30 with the last 2 characters in their PAYE reference numbers BX	. . . [2]	1st July 2015
40-49	. . . [2]	1st August 2015
Less than 30 with the last 2 characters in their PAYE reference numbers BY	. . . [2]	1st September 2015
30-39	. . . [2]	1st October 2015

Less than 30 with the last 2 characters in their PAYE reference numbers BZ	. . . [2]	1st November 2015
Less than 30 with the last 2 characters in their PAYE reference numbers 02-04, C1-C9, D1-D9, CA-CZ, or DA-DZ	. . . [2]	1st January 2016
Less than 30 with the last 2 characters in their PAYE reference numbers 00, 05-07, E1-E9 or EA-EZ	. . . [2]	1st February 2016
Less than 30 with the last 2 characters in their PAYE reference numbers 01, 08-11, F1-F9, G1-G9, FA-FZ or GA-GZ	. . . [2]	1st March 2016
Less than 30 with the last 2 characters in their PAYE reference numbers 12-16, 3A-3Z, H1-H9 or HA-HZ	. . . [2]	1st April 2016
Less than 30 with the last 2 characters in their PAYE reference numbers I1-I9 or IA-IZ	. . . [2]	1st May 2016
Less than 30 with the last 2 characters in their PAYE reference numbers 17-22, 4A-4Z, J1-J9 or JA-JZ	. . . [2]	1st June 2016
Less than 30 with the last 2 characters in their PAYE reference numbers 23-29, 5A-5Z, K1-K9 or KA-KZ	. . . [2]	1st July 2016
Less than 30 with the last 2 characters in their PAYE reference numbers 30-37, 6A-6Z, L1-L9 or LA-LZ	. . . [2]	1st August 2016
Less than 30 with the last 2 characters in their PAYE reference numbers N1-N9 or NA-NZ	. . . [2]	1st September 2016
Less than 30 with the last 2 characters in their PAYE reference numbers 38-46, 7A-7Z, O1-O9 or OA-OZ	. . . [2]	1st October 2016
Less than 30 with the last 2 characters in their PAYE reference numbers 47-57, 8A-8Z, Q1-Q9, R1-R9, S1-S9, T1-T9, QA-QZ, RA-RZ, SA-SZ or TA-TZ	. . . [2]	1st November 2016
Less than 30 with the last 2 characters in their PAYE reference numbers 58-69, 9A-9Z, U1-U9, V1-V9, W1-W9, UA-UZ, VA-VZ or WA-WZ	. . . [2]	1st January 2017
Less than 30 with the last 2 characters in their PAYE reference numbers 70-83, X1-X9, Y1-Y9, XA-XZ, or YA-YZ	. . . [2]	1st February 2017
Less than 30 with the last 2 characters in their PAYE reference numbers P1-P9 or PA-PZ	. . . [2]	1st March 2017
Less than 30 with the last 2 characters in their PAYE reference numbers 84-91 or 93-99	. . . [2]	1st April 2017
Less than 30 persons in the PAYE scheme not meeting any other description contained in the first column of this table	. . . [2]	1st April 2017

Employer who does not have a PAYE scheme	. . . [2]	1st April 2017
New employer (PAYE income first payable between 1st April 2012 and 31st March 2013)	. . . [2]	1st May 2017
New employer (PAYE income first payable between 1st April 2013 and 31st March 2014)	. . . [2]	1st July 2017
New employer (PAYE income first payable between 1st April 2014 and 31st March 2015)	. . . [2]	1st August 2017
New employer (PAYE income first payable between 1st April 2015 and 31st December 2015)	. . . [2]	1st October 2017
New employer (PAYE income first payable between 1st January 2016 and 30th September 2016)	. . . [2]	1st November 2017
New employer (PAYE income first payable between 1st October 2016 and 30th June 2017)	. . . [2]	1st January 2018
New employer (PAYE income first payable between 1st July 2017 and 30th September 2017)	. . . [2]	1st February 2018][1]

Amendments—[1] In para (3), Table entries substituted, by the Employers' Duties (Implementation) (Amendment) Regulations, SI 2012/1813 reg 2(1), (5) with effect from 1 October 2012.

[2] Paras (2), (3) revoked, and column 2 of Table revoked, by the Occupational and Personal Pension Schemes (Automatic Enrolment) (Miscellaneous Amendments) Regulations, SI 2016/311 reg 2(1), (3) with effect from 6 April 2016.

[4A (1) For the purposes of regulation 2(1)(*b*)(ii), the date in the final column of the table in regulation 4 is modified in accordance with paragraph (2).

(2) Where the staging date in the final column of the table in regulation 4 is in the period—

(*a*) beginning with 1st October 2012 and ending on 1st November 2012, the modified date is 1st August 2015;

(*b*) beginning with 1st January 2013 and ending on 1st February 2013, the modified date is 1st October 2015;

(*c*) beginning with 1st March 2013 and ending on 1st April 2013, the modified date is 1st January 2016;

(*d*) beginning with 1st May 2013 and ending on 1st June 2013, the modified date is 1st February 2016;

(*e*) beginning with 1st July 2013 and ending on 1st August 2013, the modified date is 1st March 2016;

(*f*) beginning with 1st September 2013 and ending on 1st October 2013, the modified date is 1st April 2016;

(*g*) beginning with 1st November 2013 and ending on 1st January 2014, the modified date is 1st May 2016;

(*h*) beginning with 1st February 2014 and ending on 1st April 2014, the modified date is 1st July 2016;

(*i*) beginning with 1st May 2014 and ending on 1st July 2014, the modified date is 1st September 2016;

(*j*) beginning with 1st August 2014 and ending on 1st October 2014, the modified date is 1st November 2016;

(*k*) beginning with 1st November 2014 and ending on 1st January 2015, the modified date is 1st February 2017; or

(*l*) beginning with 1st March 2015 and ending on 1st April 2015, the modified date is 1st April 2017.][1]

Amendments—[1] Regulation 4A inserted by the Employers' Duties (Implementation) (Amendment) Regulations, SI 2012/1813, reg 2(1), (6) with effect from 1 October 2012.

[4B Deferral of automatic enrolment for post-staging employers

(1) Where—

(*a*) an employer ("E") gives to a worker, on the day on which the worker begins to be employed by E, notice that E intends to defer automatic enrolment for the worker until the deferral date; and

(*b*) the requirements in regulation 4C in relation to the notice are met, the worker's automatic enrolment date is the deferral date if on that date section 3 of the Act (automatic enrolment) applies to the worker as a jobholder of E.

(2) Where—

(*a*) a worker employed by E becomes a jobholder to whom section 3 of the Act applies;

(*b*) E gives the worker notice that E intends to defer automatic enrolment until the deferral date; and

(*c*) the requirements in regulation 4C in relation to the notice are met,

the worker's automatic enrolment date is the deferral date if on that date section 3 of the Act applies to the worker as a jobholder of E.

(3) If section 3 of the Act does not apply to a worker falling within paragraph (1)(*a*) and (*b*) or (2)(*a*) to (*c*) on the deferral date, arrangements prescribed under section 3(2) of the Act do not apply in relation to any employment of the worker by E in the period beginning with the starting day and ending with the deferral date.

(4) A notice under paragraph (1) or (2) may be given on the starting day or within the period of six weeks beginning with the day after the starting day.

(5) The deferral date may be any date in the period of three months [after][2] the starting day.

(6) If E gives a worker a notice under paragraph (1), E may not give the worker a notice under paragraph (2) in relation to any occasion on or before the deferral date on which the worker becomes a jobholder to whom section 3 applies.

(7) In this regulation—

(*a*) references to "E" (or to an "employer") are to a person falling within the meaning of "employer" in section 88(7) of the Act—

(i) [who first pays PAYE income in respect of any worker on or after 1st October 2017; or][2]

(ii) who does not have a PAYE scheme, where E's first worker begins to be employed by E after 1st April 2017,

where the employers' duties did not apply before that date;

(*b*) "starting day" means—

(i) in the case of a notice under paragraph (1), the day on which the worker begins to be employed by E; or

(ii) in the case of a notice under paragraph (2), the day on which the worker becomes a jobholder to whom section 3 of the Act applies.][1]

Amendments—[1] Regulations 4B, 4C inserted by the Employers' Duties (Implementation) (Amendment) Regulations, SI 2017/347, regs 2, 4 with effect from 1 April 2017.

[2] In para (5), word substituted for words "beginning with", and para (7)(*a*)(i) substituted by the Employers' Duties (Miscellaneous Amendments) Regulations, SI 2017/868 reg 2 with effect from 1 October 2017. Para (7)(*a*)(i) previously read as follows—

"(i) who pays PAYE income, where E's first worker begins to be employed by E on or after 1st October 2017; or".

[4C Deferral of automatic enrolment: notice requirements

(1) A notice (referred to in this regulation as "the notice") under regulation 4B(1) or (2) must be in writing.

(2) In the case of workers who are jobholders and who are not active members of a qualifying scheme, the notice must include the information described in paragraph (4) or (6) and the information described in paragraphs (7) to (9).

(3) In the case of workers who are not jobholders and who are not active members of a qualifying scheme, the notice must include the information described in paragraph (5) or (6) and the information described in paragraphs (7) to (9).

(4) A statement that the jobholder may, by giving written notice to the employer, require the employer to make arrangements for the jobholder to become an active member of an automatic enrolment scheme and that the jobholder is entitled to employer's contributions.

(5) A statement that the worker may, where he or she is working, or ordinarily works, in Great Britain and is aged at least 16 and under 75 and is not a member of a pension scheme that satisfies the requirements of section 9 of the Act, by giving written notice to the employer, require the employer to make arrangements for the worker to become an active member of such a pension scheme.

(6) A statement—

(*a*) that sets out the amount of the lower qualifying earnings limit ("the lower qualifying earnings limit") specified in section 13(1)(a) of the Act; and

(*b*) that by giving written notice to the employer, the worker who is aged at least 16 and under 75 and—

(i) who earns more than the lower qualifying earnings limit and is not an active member of a qualifying scheme, may require the employer to arrange for that worker to become an active member of an automatic enrolment scheme and is entitled to employer's contributions; or

(ii) who earns no more than the lower qualifying earnings limit and is not a member of a pension scheme that satisfies the requirements of section 9 of the Act, may require the employer to arrange for that worker to become an active member of such a pension scheme but is not entitled to employer's contributions.

(7) A statement that the employer has deferred automatic enrolment until the deferral date and which specifies that date.

(8) A statement—

(*a*) that sets out the amount of earnings ("the specified amount") that are payable as specified in section 3(1)(*c*) of the Act; and

(*b*) that the employer will automatically enrol the worker into an automatic enrolment scheme on the deferral date if, on that date—

(i) the worker is aged 22 or more but under state pension age;

(ii) the worker is working, or is ordinarily working, in Great Britain;

(iii) earnings of more than the specified amount are payable to the worker; and

(iv) the worker is not already an active member of a qualifying scheme.

(9) A statement that a written notice from the worker must be signed by the worker or, if it is given by means of an electronic communication, must include a statement that the worker personally submitted the notice.

(10) In this regulation, "employer" has the meaning given in regulation 4B(7).][1]

Amendments—[1] Regulations 4B, 4C inserted by the Employers' Duties (Implementation) (Amendment) Regulations, SI 2017/347, regs 2, 4 with effect from 1 April 2017.

5 Transitional periods for money purchase and personal pension schemes

For the purposes of section 29 of the Act (transitional periods for money purchase and personal pension schemes)—

(*a*) the first transitional period . . . [1], beginning with the coming into force of section 20 (quality requirement: UK money purchase schemes)[, ends on, but includes, 5th April 2018][1]; and

(*b*) the second transitional period is one year, [beginning with 6th April 2018 and ending on, but including, 5th April 2019][1].

Amendments—[1] In para (*a*), words revoked and words inserted, and in para (*b*), words substituted, by the Employers' Duties (Implementation) (Amendment) Regulations, SI 2016/719, reg 2(1), (2) with effect from 1 October 2016.

6 Transitional period for defined benefits and hybrid schemes

For the purposes of section 30 of the Act (transitional period for defined benefits and hybrid schemes), the transitional period for defined benefits and hybrid schemes . . . [1], beginning with the day on which section 3 (automatic enrolment) comes into force[, ends on, but includes, 30th September 2017][1].

Amendments—[1] Words revoked and words inserted by the Employers' Duties (Implementation) (Amendment) Regulations, SI 2016/719, reg 2(1), (3) with effect from 1 October 2016.

2010/5

EMPLOYERS' DUTIES (REGISTRATION AND COMPLIANCE) REGULATIONS 2010

Made . . . . *5 January 2010*
Laid before Parliament . . . . *12 January 2010*
Coming into force . . . . *1 October 2012*

The Secretary of State makes the following Regulations in exercise of the powers conferred by sections 11, 38(2), (3) and (4), 40(4), 41(5), 43(3), 52(3), 54(3), 60, 99 and 144(2) and (4) of the Pensions Act 2008:

PART 1
GENERAL

1 Citation, commencement and interpretation

(1) These Regulations may be cited as the Employers' Duties (Registration and Compliance) Regulations 2010 and shall come into force on [1st July 2012, immediately after the time when the amendments to these Regulations made by the Automatic Enrolment (Miscellaneous Amendments) Regulations 2012 come into force][1].

(2) In these Regulations—

"the Act" means the Pensions Act 2008;

"automatic re-enrolment date" has the same meaning as in section 5(8) of the Act;

"contributions made by an employer" means contributions payable by the employer—

(*a*) on the employer's own account (but in respect of the worker), or (*b*) on behalf of the worker out of deductions from the worker's earnings;

"the employers' duties" means sections 2 to 9 of the Act;

"employer duty provisions" has the same meaning as in section 34(3) of the Act;

"employer pension scheme reference" means—

[(*a*) in relation to an occupational pension scheme (except a scheme established under section 67 of the Act)—

(i) reference given by the Regulator (R) to the trustees or managers of the scheme (T) following the provision of registrable information to R by T; and

(ii) any reference provided to the employer by T evidencing the relationship between the employer and the scheme;][1]

(*b*) in relation to a scheme established under section 67 of the Act, a reference given by that scheme prior to registration to an employer using the same scheme to comply with the employer duty provisions; or

(*c*) in relation to a personal pension scheme, a reference given by that scheme prior to registration to an employer using the same scheme to comply with the employer duty provisions;

"HMRC" means Her Majesty's Revenue and Customs;

"joining notice" means a notice given under section 9(2) of the Act (workers without qualifying earnings);

"late payment report" means a notice given by a trustee or manager of a trust or occupational or personal pension scheme to the Regulator under—

(*a*) section 49(9)(*b*) of the Pensions Act 1995;

(*b*) section 88(1) of that Act; or

(*c*) section 111A(7A) of the Pension Schemes Act 1993;

"opt in notice" means a notice given under section 7(3) of the Act (jobholder's right to opt in);

"opt out notice" means a notice given under section 8 of the Act (jobholder's right to opt out);

"PAYE income" has the same meaning as in section 683 of the Income Tax (Earnings and Pensions) Act 2003;

"PAYE scheme" means the HMRC record [applicable][1] to an employer who—

(*a*) employs; or

(*b*) intends to employ,

a worker or workers to whom PAYE income is payable;

"registrable information" has the same meaning as in section 60 of the Pensions Act 2004;

"registration" means the process by which employers are required to provide the Regulator with information about action they have taken or intend to take for the purposes of—

(*a*) any provision of sections 2 to 9 of the Act; and

(*b*) any regulations made under those sections,

as set out in regulations 2 to 4 of these Regulations;

"retail price index" means—

(*a*) the general index of retail prices (for all items) published by the Office for National Statistics; or

(*b*) where that index is not published for a month, any substituted index or figures published by that Office;

"staging date" has the same meaning as in regulation 1 of the Employers' Duties (Implementation) Regulations 2010; and

["the staging period" means the period which—

(a) begins when the employers' duties first apply to an employer of any description, under the Employers' Duties (Implementation) Regulations 2010; and

(b) ends when the employers' duties apply to all employers described in those Regulations.][2]

Amendments—[1] In para (1), words substituted, in para (2), in definition of "employer pension scheme reference", sub-para (*a*) substituted, and in definition of "PAYE scheme", word substituted, by the Automatic Enrolment (Miscellaneous Amendments) Regulations, SI 2012/255 regs 8, 9. The amendment of para (2) takes effect at the beginning of 1 July 2012, and the amendment of para (1) takes effect immediately thereafter.

[2] In para (2), definition of "staging period" revoked by the Employers' Duties (Miscellaneous Amendments) Regulations, SI 2017/868 regs 3, 4 with effect from 1 October 2017.

PART 2
REGISTRATION

2 Registration: General

(1) An employer must provide information to the Regulator in the following cases—

[(*a*) [on or][2] after the staging date for that employer;

(b) where the staging period has ended, within a period starting from the day on which PAYE income is payable in respect of any worker; [and][2]*]*[3]

[(*c*) on or after an automatic re-enrolment date for that employer.][2]

(2) Where an employer must provide the Regulator with information under [regulation 3 or 4 but the final day of the period in regulation 3(1)][1] or 4(1) which applies to that employer is not a working day, an employer may provide the Regulator with information on or before the next working day (and for the purposes of this paragraph "working day" means a day which is not a Saturday, Sunday, bank holiday or other public holiday).

[(*d*) in a case where regulation 2(8) (application of the employers' duties to employers) of the Employers' Duties (Implementation) Regulations 2010 applies, from the day on which the employer's first worker begins to be employed by the employer;

(*e*) in a case where—

(i) regulation 2(9) and (10) of the Employers' Duties (Implementation) Regulations 2010 applies; and

(ii) the employer's first worker began to be employed by the employer in the period beginning with 2nd April 2017 and ending with 30th September 2017,

from the day on which PAYE income is payable in respect of any worker; and

(*f*) in a case where—

(i) regulation 2(9) and (10) of the Employers' Duties (Implementation) Regulations 2010 applies; and

(ii) the employer's first worker begins to be employed by the employer on or after 1st October 2017,

from the day on which the employer's first worker begins to be employed by the employer.][3]

(3) In this regulation—

(*a*) "bank holiday" means a day specified in paragraphs 1 and 2 of Schedule 1 to the Banking and Financial Dealings Act 1971; and

(*b*) "information" means the information specified in regulations 3 and 4 required to be provided to the Regulator about action employers have taken or intend to take for the purposes of—

(i) sections 2 to 9 of the Act, or

(ii) any regulations made under those sections.

[(4) In this Part, "automatic re-enrolment date" means an automatic re-enrolment date occurring by virtue of section 6(1)(*b*) of the Act (timing of automatic re-enrolment).][2]

Amendments—[1] In para (2), words substituted by the Automatic Enrolment (Miscellaneous Amendments) Regulations, SI 2012/255 regs 8, 10 with effect from the beginning of 1 July 2012.

[2] In para (1)(*a*), words inserted, in para (1)(*b*), word substituted, para (1)(*c*) substituted, and para (4) inserted, by the Occupational and Personal Pension Schemes (Automatic Enrolment) (Miscellaneous Amendments) Regulations, SI 2016/311 reg 3(1)–(3) with effect from 6 April 2016.

[3] Para (1)(*b*) revoked, and para (1)(*d*)–(*f*) inserted, by the Employers' Duties (Miscellaneous Amendments) Regulations, SI 2017/868 regs 3, 5 with effect from 1 October 2017.

3 Registration: After staging date and new PAYE schemes

(1) Where—

(*a*) paragraph (1)(*a*) of regulation 2 applies, an employer must provide the information specified in paragraphs (2) and (3) of this regulation within the period of [5 months][2] [beginning with][3] the staging date; . . .[3]

(*b*) [paragraph (1)(*d*) or (1)(*f*)][3] of regulation 2 applies, an employer must provide the information specified in paragraphs (2) and (3) of this regulation within the period of [5 months][2] [beginning with the day on which the employer's first worker begins to be employed by the employer][3],

in relation to each of its PAYE schemes[, or

(*c*) paragraph (1)(*e*) of regulation 2 applies, an employer must provide the information specified in paragraphs (2) and (3) of this regulation within the period of 5 months beginning with the day on which PAYE income is payable in respect of any worker.][1]

(2) The specified information is—

(*a*) the employer's—

(i) [name,][1] address and postcode, and

(ii) registered companies house number, where one exists;

(*b*)

(i) the name, telephone number, ordinary working address, and

[(ii) registered companies house number where one exists or, where such a number does not exist—

(*aa*) the employer's industrial and provident society number;

(*bb*) but if the number mentioned in sub-paragraph (*aa*) does not exist, the employer's registered charity number;

(*cc*) but if the number mentioned in sub-paragraph (*bb*) does not exist, the employer's VAT registration number, if one exists;][1]

of any person providing that specified information on behalf of the employer;

(*c*) the capacity in which the person providing the information in sub-paragraph (*a*) works for (or has a relationship to) that employer;

(*d*) where the employer must arrange active membership of an automatic enrolment scheme under section 3(2) of the Act—

[(i) subject to paragraph (iii) the number of jobholders automatically enrolled with effect from—

(*aa*) the employer's staging date;

(*bb*) where sub-paragraph (*aa*) does not apply and the employer has not used a deferral date the date the employer's duties first apply to the employer;][1]

(ii) if the employer uses more than one pension scheme under those arrangements, the number of jobholders who became active members of each pension scheme[, and

(iii) on the deferral date—

(*aa*) the deferral date or the last such date where the employer uses more than one; and

(*bb*) the number of jobholders automatically enrolled with effect from that date;][1]

[(*e*) where an employer is subject to transitional arrangements under section 30 of the Act (transitional period for defined benefits and hybrid schemes) the number of jobholders to whom that section applies;][1]

[(*f*) the number of workers in an employer's PAYE scheme who, immediately before whichever is applicable of—

(i) the staging date; or

(ii) the day on which the employers' duties first apply to the employer,

were active members of a qualifying scheme or, if the employer uses more than one qualifying scheme to comply with the employers' duties, each of those schemes;][1]

(*g*) the number of workers in an employer's PAYE scheme in respect of whom sub-paragraphs (*d*), (*e*) or (*f*) of this paragraph do not apply.

(3) Where an employer must arrange for a jobholder to become an active member of an automatic enrolment scheme under section 3(2) of the Act, that employer must also provide the following information to the Regulator about any pension scheme used to comply with those duties—

(*a*) where that scheme—

(i) is an occupational pension scheme, its name and, unless registrable information has already been provided to the Regulator by the trustees or managers of that scheme, its address, or

(ii) is a personal pension scheme, the name and address of the provider of that scheme; and

(*b*) the employer pension scheme reference.

(4) All information provided to the Regulator by (or on behalf of) an employer under this regulation must be accompanied by a declaration that the information is, to the best of the employer's knowledge and belief, correct and complete.

Amendments—[1] The following amendments made by the Automatic Enrolment (Miscellaneous Amendments) Regulations, SI 2012/255 regs 8, 11 with effect from the beginning of 1 July 2012—

– in para (2)(*a*)(i), words inserted, and para (2)(*d*)(iii) and preceding word inserted; and

– para (2)(*a*)(ii), (*d*)(i), (*e*), (*f*) substituted.

[2] in para (1), words substituted in each place by the Automatic Enrolment (Miscellaneous Amendments) Regulations, SI 2013/2556 reg 4(1), (2) with effect from 1 April 2014.

[3] In para (1)(*a*), words substituted for words "starting from", and word "or" revoked; in para (1)(*b*), words substituted for words "paragraph (1)(*b*)" and words "starting from the day on which PAYE income is payable in respect of any worker"; and para (1)(*c*) and preceding word inserted, by the Employers' Duties (Miscellaneous Amendments) Regulations, SI 2017/868 regs 3, 6 with effect from 1 October 2017.

4 Registration: Re-registration

[(1) Where paragraph (1)(*c*) of regulation 2 applies, an employer must provide the information specified in paragraph (3) of this regulation in relation to each of its PAYE schemes—

(*a*) where it is the employer's first automatic re-enrolment date, within the period of 5 months beginning with the third anniversary of the employer's staging date; and

(*b*) in any other case, within the period of 5 months beginning with the third anniversary of the employer's previous automatic re-enrolment date,

and the time at which an employer provides that information is referred to in this regulation as the "point of re-registration".][2]

(2) . . . [2]

(3) The specified information is—

(*a*) that specified in paragraph (2)(*a*) to (*c*) of regulation 3;

(*b*) that specified in paragraph (3)(*a*) and (*b*) of that regulation;

(*c*) where the employer must arrange active membership of an automatic enrolment scheme for any worker who is a jobholder under section 5(2) of the Act—

(i) the number of jobholders automatically [re-enrolled][1], as at the point of re-registration, . . .[1]

(ii) if the employer uses more than one pension scheme under those arrangements, the number of jobholders automatically [re-enrolled][1] into each pension scheme, as at the point of re-registration . . .[2]

[(*ca*) the automatic re-enrolment date;][2]

(*d*) where an employer is subject to [section 30][1] of the Act, the number of jobholders to whom those sections apply;

[(*e*) the number of workers in the employer's PAYE scheme who, immediately before the point of re-registration, were active members of a qualifying scheme or, if the employer uses more than one qualifying scheme to comply with the employers' duties, the number of workers in each of those schemes;][2]

(*f*) the number of workers in an employer's PAYE scheme in respect of whom sub-paragraphs (*c*), (*d*) or (*e*) of this paragraph do not apply.

(4) All information provided to the Regulator by (or on behalf of) an employer under this regulation must be accompanied by a declaration that the information is, to the best of the employer's knowledge and belief, correct and complete.

Amendments—[1] In para (3)(*c*)(i), (ii), (*d*), words substituted, and in para (3)(*c*)(i), word revoked, by the Automatic Enrolment (Miscellaneous Amendments) Regulations, SI 2012/255 regs 8, 12 with effect from the beginning of 1 July 2012—

[2] Paras (1), (3)(*e*) substituted, paras (2), (3)(*c*)(iii) and preceding word revoked, and para 3)(*ca*) inserted, by the Occupational and Personal Pension Schemes (Automatic Enrolment) (Miscellaneous Amendments) Regulations, SI 2016/311 reg 3(1), (4)–(6) with effect from 6 April 2016.

PART 3
COMPLIANCE

Records and Information

5 Requirement to keep records

(1) The persons in paragraph (2) must—

(*a*) keep the records listed within the regulation applicable to them;

(*b*) preserve the records for a period in accordance with regulation 8; and

(*c*) provide those records, on request, to the Regulator.

(2) The persons are, subject to paragraphs (5) and (6), any person who is—

(*a*) an employer;

(*b*) a trustee or manager of an occupational pension scheme; or

(*c*) a provider of a personal pension scheme.

(3) Regulation 6 applies in respect of a person falling within paragraph (2)(*a*).

(4) Regulation 7 applies in respect of a person falling within paragraph (2)(*b*) or (*c*).

(5) Where a person does not fall within paragraph (2), that person may keep, preserve or provide the records listed in regulations 6 and 7 on behalf of a person falling within paragraph (2) but only where a person falling within paragraph (2) authorises the other person to do so.

(6) A person who has ceased to act as a person falling within paragraph (2) shall not be required to keep records, where that person has transferred all the records to another person who has succeeded them in that capacity.

(7) All records must be kept in such form and manner so that they are—

(*a*) capable of being arranged according to the corresponding employer pension scheme reference; and

(*b*) legible or can be provided to the Regulator in a legible form.

6 Records: Employers

(1) A person falling within paragraph (2)(*a*) of regulation 5 must keep the following records in relation to an occupational or personal pension scheme used by them to comply with the employers' duties—

(*a*) where that scheme—

(i) is an occupational pension scheme, its name and address,

(ii) is a personal pension scheme, the name and address of the provider of that scheme, or

(iii) does not have its main administration in the United Kingdom, the address of that scheme and the name of any authority which exercises functions corresponding to the functions of the Regulator in the country or territory outside the United Kingdom where that scheme is situated;

(*b*) the employer pension scheme reference;

(*c*) where section 21 of the Act (quality requirement: UK defined benefits schemes) applies, a copy of the certificate issued in respect of a jobholder under section 7(1) of the Pension Schemes Act 1993;

(*d*) where section 22 of the Act (test scheme standard) applies, any evidence which shows that a scheme satisfies the test scheme standard within the meaning of that section, given in accordance with any regulations made under subsection (4) of that section;

(*e*) the name, national insurance number (where one exists) and date of birth of—

(i) every jobholder of an employer who became an active member of an automatic enrolment scheme pursuant to arrangements made under section 3 of the Act,

(ii) every jobholder of an employer who was not an active member of a qualifying scheme but who by notice required the employer to arrange for the jobholder to become an active member of an automatic enrolment scheme pursuant to arrangements made under section 7 of the Act, and

(iii) every worker who by notice required an employer to arrange for the worker to become an active member of a pension scheme pursuant to arrangements made under section 9 of the Act;

(*f*) every jobholder's automatic enrolment date, and the date with effect from which every worker became an active member of a pension scheme that satisfies the requirements of section 9 of the Act, pursuant to arrangements made under that section;

(*g*) an opt in notice in respect of every jobholder who gave notice under section 7(3) of the Act;

(*h*) a joining notice in respect of every worker who gave notice under section 9(2) of the Act; and

(i) an opt out notice in respect of every jobholder that gives notice under section 8 of the Act.

(2) A person falling within paragraph (2)(*a*) of regulation 5 must also keep the following records in respect of every jobholder or worker falling within paragraph (1)(*e*) where contributions fall to be deducted by an employer under section 33 of the Act and regulations made under that section—

(*a*) their gross earnings in any relevant pay reference period;

(*b*) evidence of the contributions that the jobholder's employer must pay in respect of the jobholder, in order to satisfy the quality requirement for the pension scheme used by the employer to comply with the employers' duties;

(*c*) the contributions payable by an employer during each relevant pay reference period and, if different, the contributions made; and

(*d*) the date on which the contributions made by an employer were paid to the pension scheme used by the employer to comply with the employers' duties.

[(2A) Where an employer (E) gives to a person (P) employed by E a notice under section 4 of the Act (postponement or disapplication of automatic enrolment) that meets the requirements prescribed in Part 6 of the Occupational and Personal Pension Schemes (Automatic Enrolment) Regulations 2010 E must keep a record of—

(*a*) P's full name;

(*b*) P's national insurance number (where available); and

(*c*) the date E gave the notice to P.][1]

(3) In this regulation—

(*a*) "earnings" has the meaning given by section 13(3) of the Act; and

(*b*) "relevant pay reference period" means—

(i) a period of one week, or

(ii) in the case of a person who is paid their regular wage or salary by reference to a period longer than a week, that period.

Amendments—[1] Para (2A) inserted by the Automatic Enrolment (Miscellaneous Amendments) Regulations, SI 2012/255 regs 8, 13 with effect from the beginning of 1 July 2012.

7 Records: Trustees, managers and providers

(1) A person falling within paragraph (2)(*b*) or (*c*) of regulation 5 must keep the following records—

(*a*) the employer pension scheme reference;

(*b*)

(i) the date on which every jobholder became an active member of a pension scheme, by virtue of arrangements made under section 3 [or 7][1] of the Act, and

(ii) the date with effect from which every worker became an active member of a pension scheme that satisfies the requirements of section 9 of the Act, by virtue of arrangements made under that section;

(*c*) where—

(i) a jobholder gives an opt out notice to an employer, and

(ii) any regulations under section 8(5)(*e*) of the Act require that employer to inform a pension scheme that such a notice has been received by it,

the name of the jobholder mentioned in the opt out notice and the date on which that scheme was informed by virtue of that requirement; and

(*d*) where a jobholder had been an active member of a qualifying scheme, the date on which the jobholder ceased active membership of that scheme.

(2) A person falling within paragraph (2)(*b*) or (*c*) of regulation 5 must also keep the following records in relation to all persons who are members of a qualifying scheme—

(*a*) their full name, date of birth, gender and national insurance number (as received by the trustee or manager of an occupational pension scheme or provider of a personal pension scheme);

(i) their postal residential address, and

(ii) where that address is in the United Kingdom, the postcode,

last known by or notified to that scheme or employer; and

(*c*) whether—

(i) a member is an active member of a scheme, or

(ii) a member is no longer an active member of a scheme.

Amendments—[1] In para (1)(*b*)(i), words inserted by the Automatic Enrolment (Miscellaneous Amendments) Regulations, SI 2012/255 regs 8, 14 with effect from the beginning of 1 July 2012.

8 Period of preservation of records

(1) Except where paragraph (2) applies, a record listed in regulations 6 and 7 must be preserved for a period of 6 years, starting on the day on which the record must first be kept.

(2) Paragraph (1) does not apply to any record which is kept under paragraph (1)(i) of regulation 6 or under paragraph (1)(*c*) of regulation 7, in which case the record must be preserved for 4 years, starting on the day on which the record must first be kept.

Payment Failures

9 Unpaid relevant contributions

For the purposes of section 38(2) of the Act, the prescribed period after the appropriate date is 3 months.

10 Contributions: Requirement to pay interest

(1) For the purposes of section 38(2)(*e*) of the Act, the rate at which interest must be paid on an amount required by a notice to be paid ("the rate") is determined by the Regulator in accordance with paragraph (2).

(2) The rate comprises a fixed component and a flexible component where—

(*a*) the fixed component is 4.2%; and

(*b*) the flexible component is—

(i) the percentage change in the retail price index applicable for the month during which the Regulator issues a notice, or

(ii) where the retail price index applicable for the month during which the Regulator issues a notice is not published, the percentage change in that index for the preceding month.

(3) For the purposes of section 38(2)(*e*) of the Act, the period in respect of which interest must be paid on an amount required by a notice—

(*a*) begins with the appropriate date; and

(*b*) ends when an employer complies with a notice by—

(i) taking, or refraining from taking, the steps specified in a compliance notice, or

(ii) paying into a pension scheme an amount in respect of relevant contributions that had not been paid, as specified in an unpaid contributions notice.

(4) In this regulation, "interest" means simple interest calculated from day to day.

11 Contributions: Estimating contributions

(1) The Regulator may estimate the amount of contributions that an employer has failed to pay on behalf or in respect of a worker by applying the formula—

$(E / 12) \times 8\% \times N \times M$

where—

E is the maximum qualifying earnings in a pay reference period of 12 months, as defined by section 13(1)(*b*) of the Act;

N is either—

(*a*) the number of jobholders in respect of whom the Regulator is of the opinion that the employer has—

(i) contravened one or more of the employer duty provisions, or

(ii) not paid relevant contributions on or before the due date (within the meaning of section 37(3) of the Act); or

(*b*) where in the Regulator's opinion the number in (*a*) is not known, the number of persons in the employer's PAYE scheme,

at the time that the Regulator makes the estimate; and

M is the number of months from—

(*a*) the contravention of one or more of the employer duty provisions; or

(*b*) the failure to pay contributions on behalf or in respect of the worker,

until the Regulator makes the estimate.

(2) Other than information provided by the employer, when estimating the amount of contributions under this regulation, the Regulator may use the sources of information set out in paragraph (3).
(3) The sources of information are—

(*a*) a late payment report;
(*b*) anything reported or sent to the Regulator by any person, including—
(i) a trustee or manager of an occupational pension scheme,
(ii) a provider of a personal pension scheme, and
(iii) a member of either an occupational or personal pension scheme; or
(*c*) any information disclosed to the Regulator under section 88 of the Pensions Act 2004 (tax information).

Penalties

12 Fixed penalty notices
Where the Regulator issues a fixed penalty notice to a person under subsection (1) or (2) of section 40 of the Act, the penalty is £400.

13 Escalating penalty notices
(1) Where an escalating penalty notice is issued to a person—

(*a*) in respect of a failure to comply with a third party compliance notice under section 36 of the Act; or
(*b*)
(i) in respect of a failure to comply with a notice specified in paragraph (2)(*a*) or (*b*), and
(ii) that failure was by a person other than an employer,

the prescribed daily rate is £200.
(2) Paragraph (3) applies where an escalating penalty notice is issued to an employer in respect of a failure to comply with—

(*a*) a compliance notice under section 35 of the Act;
(*b*) a notice under section 72 of the Pensions Act 2004 (provision of information); or
(*c*) an unpaid contributions notice under section 37 of the Act.

(3) Except where paragraph (1) applies, the prescribed daily rate is to be determined in accordance with Table 1 and the following paragraphs.

Table 1

Number of persons	*Prescribed daily rate (£)*
1–4	50
5–49	500
50–249	2500
250–499	5000
500 or more	10000

(4) In the first column of Table 1, the expression "Number of persons" is to be construed in accordance with paragraphs (5)[, (5A)][1] and (6).
(5) Where—

[(*a*) paragraph (2)(*a*) or (*b*) applies, it is the relevant number except that—
(i) in the circumstances set out in paragraph (5A) the number of persons is the number of persons in the employer's PAYE scheme or schemes that are employed by the employer; or
(ii) where the circumstances set out in paragraph (5A) do not apply and, in the Regulator's opinion the relevant number is not known, paragraph (7) applies;][1]
(*b*) paragraph (2)(*c*) applies, it is—
(i) the number of workers in respect of whom the Regulator is of the opinion that the employer has not paid relevant contributions on or before the due date (within the meaning of section 37(3) of the Act); or
[(ii) where in the Regulator's opinion the number in paragraph (i) is not known, the relevant number except that—
(*aa*) where paragraph (5A) applies the number of persons is the number of persons in the employer's PAYE scheme or schemes that are employed by the employer; or
(*bb*) where paragraph (5A) does not apply and, in the Regulator's opinion, the relevant number is not known, paragraph (7) applies.][1]

but where in the Regulator's opinion the number in (ii) is not known, paragraph (7) applies.

[(5A) This paragraph applies where—

(*a*) the Regulator is of the opinion that an employer's PAYE scheme (or where the Regulator is of the opinion that the employer has more than one PAYE scheme, the schemes) includes persons who are not employed by the employer; and

(*b*) the number of persons in the employer's PAYE scheme (or where the Regulator is of the opinion that the employer has more than one PAYE scheme, the schemes) who are employed by the employer is known to the Regulator.][1]

(6) In this regulation, the Regulator must use the latest information reasonably available to it up to and including the day on which the Regulator issues an escalating penalty notice[, including][1]—

(*a*) where paragraph (2)(*a*) and (*b*) apply, [information][1] disclosed to it under section 88 of the Pensions Act 2004; and

(*b*) where paragraph (2)(*c*) applies[, information][1]—

(i) contained in a late payment report,

(ii) contained in a report given to the Regulator under section 70 of the Pensions Act 2004, or

(iii) disclosed to it under section 88 of the Pensions Act 2004.

(7) Where this paragraph applies, the prescribed daily rate must be treated as being £50.

[(8) In this regulation, "relevant number" means the number of persons within an employer's PAYE scheme or, where the Regulator is of the opinion that the employer has more than one PAYE scheme, the total number of persons within those schemes.][1]

Amendments—[1] In paras (4), (6), words inserted, para (5)(*a*) substituted and words in para (5)(*b*) substituted, and paras (5A), (8) inserted, by the Automatic Enrolment (Miscellaneous Amendments) Regulations, SI 2012/255 regs 8, 15 with effect from the beginning of 1 July 2012.

14 Penalty notices: Prohibited recruitment conduct

(1) This regulation applies where the Regulator issues a penalty notice to an employer if the Regulator is of the opinion that the employer—

(*a*) has contravened section 50 of the Act; or

(*b*) has failed to comply with a compliance notice under section 51 of the Act.

(2) The penalty is to be determined in accordance with Table 2 and the following paragraphs.

Table 2

Number of persons	*Penalty* (£)
1–4	1000
5–49	1500
50–249	2500
250 or more	5000

(3) In the first column of Table 2, the expression "Number of persons" is to be construed in accordance with paragraphs (4)[, (4A)][1] and (5).

[(4) It is the relevant number except that—

(*a*) where paragraph (4A) applies the number of persons is the number of persons in the employer's PAYE scheme or schemes that are employed by the employer;

(*b*) where paragraph (4A) does not apply and, in the Regulator's opinion the relevant number is not known, paragraph (6) applies.

(4A) This paragraph applies where—

(*a*) the Regulator is of the opinion that an employer's PAYE scheme includes (or where the Regulator is of the opinion that the employer has more than one PAYE scheme, the schemes include) persons who are not employed by the employer; and

(*b*) the number of persons in the employer's PAYE scheme (or where the Regulator is of the opinion that the employer has more than one PAYE scheme, the schemes) who are employed by the employer is known to the Regulator.][1]

(5) In this regulation, the Regulator must use the latest information—

(*a*) reasonably available to it up to and including the day on which it issues a penalty notice; and

(*b*) [including information][1] disclosed to it under section 88 of the Pensions Act 2004.

(6) Where this paragraph applies, the penalty must be treated as being £1000.

[(7) In this regulation, "relevant number" means the number of persons within an employer's PAYE scheme or, where the Regulator is of the opinion that the employer has more than one PAYE scheme, the total number of persons within those schemes.][1]

Amendments—[1] In paras (3), (5)(*b*), words inserted, paras (4), (4A) substituted for para (4), and para (7) inserted, by the Automatic Enrolment (Miscellaneous Amendments) Regulations, SI 2012/255 regs 8, 16 with effect from the beginning of 1 July 2012.

Review and Issue of Notices

15 Review and issue of notices

(1) The period within which an application to review a notice may be made under section 43(1)(*a*) of the Act (written application of a person) is 28 days, starting from the day a notice is issued to a person.

(2) The period within which a notice may be reviewed under section 43(1)(*b*) of the Act (review by the Regulator) is 18 months, starting from the day a notice is issued to a person.

(3) The presumptions in paragraph (4) apply where notices to which section 43 applies are issued (including compliance notices issued under section 51 of the Act and penalty notices issued under section 52 of the Act).

(4) For the purposes of this regulation, it is presumed that—

(*a*) where a notice is given a date by the Regulator, it was posted or otherwise sent on that day;

(*b*) if a notice is posted or otherwise sent to a person's last known or notified address, it was issued on the day on which that notice was posted or otherwise sent; and

(*c*) a notice was received by the person to whom it was addressed.

Inducements

16 Inducements

For the purposes of subsection (3) of section 54 of the Act, the Regulator may not issue a compliance notice in respect of a contravention of that section unless the contravention occurred within—

(*a*) 6 months before the time when a complaint was made to the Regulator about the contravention; or

(*b*) 4 years before the time when the Regulator informed the employer of an investigation of the contravention, if no complaint was made before that time.

2010/22

TRANSFER OF TRIBUNAL FUNCTIONS ORDER 2010

Made . . . .*6 January 2010*

Coming into force in accordance with . . . .*article 1*

The Lord Chancellor makes the following Order in exercise of the powers conferred by sections 30(1) and (4), 31(1), (2) and (9) and 38 of, and paragraph 30 of Schedule 5 to, the Tribunals, Courts and Enforcement Act 2007.

The Welsh Ministers have consented to the making of this Order in so far as their consent is required by section 30(8) of that Act.

A draft of this Order was laid before Parliament and approved by a resolution of each House of Parliament in accordance with section 49(5) of that Act.

1 Citation, commencement and extent

(1) This Order may be cited as the Transfer of Tribunal Functions Order 2010 and, subject to paragraph (2), comes into force on 18th January 2010.

(2) The following provisions of this Order come into force on 6th April 2010—

(*a*) paragraph (5);

(*b*) article 2(2), (3)(*b*) and (4);

(*c*) article 3 in respect of the Financial Services and Markets Tribunal;

(*d*) Schedule 1 in respect of the Financial Services and Markets Tribunal and the Pensions Regulator Tribunal;

(*e*) in Schedule 2, paragraphs 3(*c*)(i), 4(*c*), 5 to 9, 12 to 14, 15(*c*), 17(*b*), 18(*b*), 20 to 23, 43 to 49, 74 to 89, 92(*h*) to (k) and 141 to 151;

(*f*) in Schedule 3, paragraphs 16 to 38, 90 to 94, 140 to 142, 143(*d*), 144 to 146, 148 to 158, 176 to 189 and 191 to 200; and

(*g*) Part 2 of Schedule 4.

(3) Subject as follows, this Order extends to England and Wales, Scotland and Northern Ireland.

(4) Except as provided by paragraph (5), an amendment, repeal or revocation of any enactment by any provision of Schedule 2, 3 or 4 extends to the part or parts of the United Kingdom to which the enactment extends.

(5) The amendments, repeals and revocations made by the following provisions do not extend to Northern Ireland—

(*a*) in Schedule 2, paragraphs 5(*b*), 9(*b*), 77 to 79, 83 to 85, 88, 142(*b*) and 143(*b*);

(*b*) in Schedule 3, paragraphs 90 to 94;

(*c*) in Part 2 of Schedule 4, the entries relating to—

(i) the Tribunals, Courts and Enforcement Act 2007 in so far as it relates to paragraph 40 of Schedule 10;
(ii) the Pensions Act 2008;
(iii) the Pensions Regulator Tribunal Rules 2005; and
(iv) the Lord Chancellor (Transfer of Functions and Supplementary Provisions) (No 2) Order 2006.

2 Transfer of functions of certain tribunals

(1) The functions of the following tribunals are transferred to the First-tier Tribunal—
(*a*) tribunals drawn from the Adjudication Panel for England;
(*b*) the Claims Management Services Tribunal;
(*c*) the Gambling Appeals Tribunal;
(*d*) the Immigration Services Tribunal; and
(*e*) the Family Health Services Appeal Authority.

(2) The functions of the Financial Services and Markets Tribunal are transferred to the Upper Tribunal.

(3) The functions of the following tribunals are transferred to the First-tier Tribunal and the Upper Tribunal with the question as to which one of them is to exercise the functions in a particular case being determined by, or under, Tribunal Procedure Rules—
(*a*) the Information Tribunal; and
(*b*) subject to paragraph (4), the Pensions Regulator Tribunal.

(4) The functions of the Pensions Regulator Tribunal exercisable in relation to Northern Ireland are not transferred.

3 Abolition of tribunals

The tribunals mentioned in article 2(1), (2) and (3)(*a*) are abolished.

4 Persons becoming judges and other members of the First-tier Tribunal and the Upper Tribunal

A person who, immediately before this Order comes into force, holds an office listed in a part of Schedule 1, is to hold the office or offices set out in the corresponding entry in the table below.

Part of Schedule 1	*Office or offices*
Part 1	Transferred-in judge of the Upper Tribunal
Part 2	Transferred-in other member of the Upper Tribunal
Part 3	Deputy judge of the Upper Tribunal and transferred in judge of the First-tier Tribunal
Part 4	Transferred-in judge of the First-tier Tribunal
Part 5	Transferred-in other member of the First-tier Tribunal

5 Consequential, transitional and saving provisions

(1) Schedule 2 contains amendments to primary legislation as a consequence of the transfers effected by this Order.

(2) Schedule 3 contains amendments to secondary legislation as a consequence of the transfers effected by this Order.

(3) Schedule 4 contains repeals and revocations as a consequence of the amendments in Schedules 2 and 3.

(4) Schedule 5 contains transitional and saving provisions.

SCHEDULE 5

TRANSITIONAL AND SAVING PROVISIONS

Article 5(4)

Interpretation of Schedule 5

1 In this Schedule—

"old tribunal" means a tribunal, the functions of which are transferred by article 2, but does not include the Pensions Regulator Tribunal in respect of its functions exercisable in Northern Ireland;

"new tribunal" means—

(*a*) the Upper Tribunal, in respect of—

(i) the functions of the Financial Services and Markets Tribunal and the Pensions Regulator Tribunal;

(ii) the functions of the Information Tribunal of deciding appeals under section 28 of the Data Protection Act 1998 or section 60 of the Freedom of Information Act 2000 (including that section as applied and modified by regulation 18 of the Environmental Information Regulations 2004) (appeals in relation to national security certificates);

(*b*) the First-tier Tribunal, in respect of—

(i) the tribunal functions mentioned in article 2(1);

(ii) the functions of the Information Tribunal other than those mentioned in paragraph (*a*)(ii);

"transfer date" means the date on which the functions of an old tribunal are transferred to a new tribunal by article 2.

Transitional and saving provisions

2 Any proceedings before an old tribunal which are pending immediately before the transfer date shall continue on and after the transfer date as proceedings before the new tribunal.

3 (1) The following sub-paragraphs apply where proceedings are continued in a new tribunal by virtue of paragraph 2.

(2) Where a hearing began before the transfer date but was not completed by that date, the new tribunal must be comprised for the continuation of that hearing of the person or persons who began it.

(3) The new tribunal may give any direction to ensure that proceedings are dealt with fairly and, in particular, may—

(*a*) apply any provision in procedural rules which applied to the proceedings before the transfer date; or

(*b*) disapply provisions of Tribunal Procedure Rules.

(4) In sub-paragraph (3) "procedural rules" means provision (whether called rules or not) regulating practice or procedure before a tribunal.

(5) Any direction or order given or made in proceedings which is in force immediately before the transfer date remains in force on and after that date as if it were a direction or order of the new tribunal.

(6) A time period which has started to run before the transfer date and which has not expired shall continue to apply.

(7) An order for costs may only be made if, and to the extent that, an order for costs could have been made by the old tribunal before the transfer date.

4 Paragraph 5 applies where—

(*a*) an appeal lies to a court from any decision made by an old tribunal before the transfer date;

(*b*) that right of appeal has not been exercised; and

(*c*) the time to exercise that right of appeal has not expired prior to the transfer date.

5 In the circumstances set out at paragraph 4, such of the following provisions as is appropriate shall apply as if the decision were a decision made on or after the transfer date by the new tribunal—

(*a*) section 11 of the Tribunals, Courts and Enforcement Act 2007 (right to appeal to Upper Tribunal);

(*b*) section 13 of the Tribunals, Courts and Enforcement Act 2007 (right to appeal to Court of Appeal);

(*c*) section 78(9A) to (9D) or section 78B(4) to (7) of the Local Government Act 2000 (as inserted or amended by Schedule 2 to this Order).

6 Any case to be remitted by a court on or after the transfer date and which, if it had been remitted before the transfer date, would have been remitted to an old tribunal, shall be remitted to the new tribunal.

7 Staff appointed to an old tribunal before the transfer date are to be treated on and after that date, for the purpose of any enactment, as if they had been appointed by the Lord Chancellor under section 40(1) of the Tribunals, Courts and Enforcement Act 2007 (tribunal staff and services).

8 A decision made by an old tribunal before the transfer date is to be treated on or after the transfer date as a decision of the new tribunal.

2010/294

AUTHORISED INVESTMENT FUNDS (TAX) (AMENDMENT) REGULATIONS 2010

Made ....*10 February 2010*

Laid before the House of Commons ....*11 February 2010*

Coming into force ....*6 March 2010*

The Treasury make the following Regulations in exercise of the powers conferred by sections 17(3) and 18 of the Finance (No 2) Act 2005 and sections 41(1) and 42 of the Finance Act 2008.

Preliminary

1 Citation, commencement and effect

(1) These Regulations may be cited as the Authorised Investment Funds (Tax) (Amendment) Regulations 2010 and come into force on 6th March 2010.

(2) These Regulations have effect from 6th March 2010.

This is subject to paragraph (3) and regulations 24 to 26.

(3) Regulations 10 (amendment of regulation 20 of the principal Regulations) and 11 (amendment of regulation 21 of the principal Regulations) have effect for accounting periods beginning on or after 6 March 2010.

2–23

Transitional provisions

24 Transitional provisions relating to distribution dates for earlier accounting periods

(1) Regulations 6 to 9, 12, 13 and 15 to 20 of these Regulations do not apply in relation to a distribution if conditions A to C are met.

(2) Condition A is that the distribution date in relation to a distribution relates to an accounting period ending on or before 5th March 2010.

(3) Condition B is that the distribution date in relation to a distribution falls on or after 6th March 2010 but on or before 5th July 2010.

(4) Condition C is that that authorised investment fund has elected, in accordance with the transitional provisions in the Collective Investment Schemes Sourcebook (Accounting Amendments) Instrument 2010 made by the Financial Services Authority on 28th January 2010, to comply with the rules in the Authority's Collective Investment Schemes Sourcebook as they were in force on 5th March 2010.

(5) For the purposes of this regulation—

(*a*) "distribution" has the meaning given in regulation 15(1)(*b*) of the principal Regulations (interpretation); and

(*b*) "distribution date" has the meaning given in regulation 15(4) of the principal Regulations.

25 Transitional provisions relating to entry into the FINROF regime: the first case

(1) This regulation applies to an authorised investment fund which, on 6th March 2010, is investing more than 20% of its gross asset value in non-reporting funds.

(2) Part 6A of the principal Regulations (inserted by these Regulations) applies to such an authorised investment fund from 6th July 2010.

(3) But if the authorised investment fund satisfies the requirements of paragraph (1) on 6th July 2010 that date shall, for the purposes of regulation 85G(*a*) (entry into FINROF regime: the basic rule) of the principal Regulations (inserted by these Regulations), be treated as the date from which the authorised investment fund first met the investment condition in regulation 85D of the principal Regulations (inserted by these Regulations)

(4) In this regulation "gross asset value" and "non-reporting fund" have the meanings given in regulation 85C of the principal Regulations (inserted by these Regulations).

26 Transitional provisions relating to entry into the FINROF regime: the second case

(1) This regulation applies to an authorised investment fund which holds investments in an offshore fund that is reasonably expected by the manager of the authorised investment fund to gain distributing fund status under the transitional rules in paragraph 3 of Schedule 1 to the Offshore Fund (Tax) Regulations 2009.

(2) Investments in the offshore fund mentioned in paragraph (1) shall be treated as investments in a reporting fund for the purposes of Part 6A of the principal Regulations (inserted by these Regulations).

(3) In this regulation "offshore fund" and "reporting fund" have the meanings given in regulation 85C of the principal Regulations (inserted by these Regulations).

2010/416

TAXATION OF CHARGEABLE GAINS (GILT-EDGED SECURITIES) ORDER 2010

Made by the Treasury under TCGA 1992 Sch 9 para 1

Made . . . . *23 February 2010*

1 Citation

This Order may be cited as the Taxation of Chargeable Gains (Gilt-edged Securities) Order 2010.

2 Securities specified as gilt-edged securities

For the purposes of Schedule 9 to the Taxation of Chargeable Gains Act 1992 (Gilt-edged Securities) the following securities are specified—

4¼% Treasury Gilt 2049
4½% Treasury Gilt 2019
1¼% Index-Linked Treasury Gilt 2032
3¼% Treasury Gilt 2011
4% Treasury Gilt 2022
4¼% Treasury Gilt 2039
2¼% Treasury Gilt 2014
4½% Treasury Gilt 2034
3¾% Treasury Gilt 2019
0⅝% Index-Linked Treasury Gilt 2042
0½% Index-Linked Treasury Gilt 2060
4% Treasury Gilt 2060
2¾% Treasury Gilt 2015
0½% Index-Linked Treasury Gilt 2050
0⅝% Index-Linked Treasury Gilt 2040.

2010/466

FINANCE ACT 2009, SCHEDULE 56 (APPOINTED DAY AND CONSEQUENTIAL PROVISIONS) ORDER 2010

Made by the Treasury under FA 2009 s 107

Made . . . . *25 February 2010*
Laid before the House of Commons . . . . *26 February 2010*
Coming into force . . . . *6 April 2010*

1 Citation, commencement and interpretation

This Order may be cited as the Finance Act 2009, Schedule 56 (Appointed Day and Consequential Provisions) Order 2010 and shall come into force on 6th April 2010.

2 In this Order—

"Schedule 56" means Schedule 56 to the Finance Act 2009;

"tax quarter" means any of the following (inclusive) periods—

6th April to 5th July, 6th July to 5th October, 6th October to 5th January and 6th January to 5th April;

"tax month" means the period beginning on the 6th day of a calendar month and ending on the 5th day of the following calendar month;

"tax period" means a tax quarter or tax month;

"section 254 period" means each period of three months ending with 31st March, 30th June, 30th September or 31st December as provided for in section 254(2) of the Finance Act 2004.

3 Appointed day

(1) In relation to those amounts of tax which are specified in paragraph (2), and are—

(*a*) chargeable in respect of a tax period starting on or after 6th April 2010, or

(*b*) chargeable in respect of a section 254 period ending on or after 30th September 2010

the day appointed for the coming into force of Schedule 56 is 6th April 2010.

(2) The amounts of tax referred to in paragraph (1) are the following amounts specified in column 3 of the Table in paragraph 1 of Schedule 56—

(*a*) items 2, 3 and 4, and

(*b*) items 17, 23 and 24 but only insofar as the tax falls within any of items 2,3 or 4.

4 Consequential provisions and savings

(1) Regulations 203 (default surcharge) and 204 (surcharge notice and appeal) of the Income Tax (Pay As You Earn) Regulations 2003 are omitted subject to the savings set out in paragraph (3).

(2) Regulations 48 (default surcharge) and 49 (surcharge notice and appeal) of the Income Tax (Construction Industry Scheme) Regulations 2005 are omitted subject to the savings set out in paragraph (3).

(3) The regulations referred to in paragraphs (1) and (2) shall continue to have effect in relation to surcharges arising in respect of late payments of tax where the tax was chargeable in respect of a tax period ending on or before 5th April 2010.

(4) Paragraph 110 of Schedule 2 (consequential amendments and supplemental provisions—secondary legislation) to the Transfer of Tribunal Functions and Revenue and Customs Appeals Order 2009 is omitted.

2010/650

REGISTERED PENSION SCHEMES ETC (INFORMATION) (PRESCRIBED DESCRIPTIONS OF PERSONS) REGULATIONS 2010

Made by the HMRC Commissioners under FA 2008 Sch 36 para 34B(8)

Made . . . . *8 March 2010*

Laid before the House of Commons . . . . *10 March 2010*

Coming into force . . . . *1 April 2010*

1 Citation, commencement and interpretation

(1) These Regulations may be cited as the Registered Pension Schemes etc (Information) (Prescribed Descriptions of Persons) Regulations 2010 and shall come into force on 1st April 2010.

(2) In these Regulations, "the description" means the prescribed description of person for the purposes of sub-paragraph (8) of paragraph 34B of Schedule 36 to the Finance Act 2008 (information and inspection powers: registered pension schemes etc).

2 Prescribed descriptions of persons: registered pension schemes

(1) In relation to a registered pension scheme, the descriptions are—

(*a*) any person who is, or at any time during the relevant period has been, the scheme administrator;

(*b*) any person who is, or at any time during the relevant period has been, a trustee of the scheme;

(*c*) any person who is, or at any time during the relevant period has been, a sponsoring employer in relation to the scheme; and

(*d*) any person who receives a notice under paragraph 5 of Schedule 36 to the Finance Act 2008 which requires information or the production of a document for the purposes of identifying the scheme administrator.

(2) The relevant period is the period which—

(*a*) begins with the time the event in relation to which information is required by the third party notice or notice under paragraph 5 of Schedule 36 to the Finance Act 2008 occurred; and

(*b*) ends with the end of the sixth tax year following the one in which that event occurred.

(3) "Sponsoring employer" has the meaning given by subsection (6) of section 150 of the Finance Act 2004.

[2A Prescribed descriptions of persons: QROPS and former QROPS

(1) In relation to a QROPS or former QROPS the description is any person who is, or at any time during the relevant period has been, the scheme manager.

(2) For the purposes of paragraph (1) the relevant period has the meaning given in regulation 2(2), subject to the substitution of "tenth" for "sixth" in regulation 2(2)(*b*).][1]

Amendments—[1] Reg 2A inserted by the Registered Pension Schemes and Overseas Pension Schemes (Miscellaneous Amendments) Regulations, SI 2013/2259 regs 24, 25 with effect from 14 October 2013.

3 Prescribed description of persons: annuities purchased with pension scheme assets

(1) In relation to an annuity purchased with sums or assets held for the purposes of a registered pension scheme[, a pre-2006 pension scheme, a QROPS or a former QROPS][1], the description is the insurance company or other person from whom the annuity has been purchased.

(2) "Insurance company" has the meaning given by section 275 of the Finance Act 2004.

Amendments—[1] In para (1), words substituted for words "or a pre-2006 pension scheme" by the Registered Pension Schemes and Overseas Pension Schemes (Miscellaneous Amendments) Regulations, SI 2013/2259 regs 24, 25 with effect from 14 October 2013.

4 Prescribed descriptions of persons: employer-financed retirement benefit schemes

(1) In relation to the coming into operation of an employer-financed retirement benefits scheme, the description is the responsible person at the time the scheme comes into operation.

(2) In relation to the provision of relevant benefits under an employer-financed retirement benefits scheme, the description is the responsible person at the time the third party notice or notice under paragraph 5 of Schedule 36 to the Finance Act 2008 is issued.

(3) In relation to either the coming into operation of or the provision of relevant benefits under an employer-financed retirement benefits scheme, the description is also any person who receives a notice under paragraph 5 of Schedule 36 to the Finance Act 2008 which requires information or the production of a document for the purposes of identifying the responsible person.

(4) A scheme comes into operation on the earlier of—

(*a*) the first date on or after the coming into force of these Regulations on which an employer makes a contribution to the scheme; and

(*b*) the first date on or after the coming into force of these Regulations on which relevant benefits are provided.

(5) "Relevant benefits" has the meaning given by section 393B of the Income Tax (Earnings and Pensions) Act 2003.

2010/673

MFET LIMITED (APPLICATION OF SECTIONS 731, 733 AND 734 OF THE INCOME TAX (TRADING AND OTHER INCOME) ACT 2005) ORDER 2010

Made . . . . *9th March 2010*
Laid before House of Commons . . . . *10th March 2010*
Coming into force . . . . *1st April 2010*

The Treasury make the following Order in exercise of the power conferred by section 732(2) of the Income Tax (Trading and Other Income) Act 2005.

1 Citation, commencement and interpretation

(1) This Order may be cited as the MFET Limited (Application of Sections 731, 733 and 734 of the Income Tax (Trading and Other Income) Act 2005) Order 2010 and shall come into force on 1st April 2010.

(2) In this Order "MFET Limited" and "Eligible Person" have the meanings given in respectively section 731(7) and (8) of the Income Tax (Trading and Other Income) Act 2005 (treated as inserted by article 2(2)(b)).

2 Application of sections 731, 733 and 734 of the Income Tax (Trading and Other Income) Act 2005

(1) Sections 731, 733 and 734 of the Income Tax (Trading and Other Income) Act 2005 (periodical payments of personal injury damages etc) shall have effect with the following modifications in relation to payments made pursuant to a scheme or arrangement administered by MFET Limited to an Eligible Person.

(2) In section 731 (periodical payments of personal injury damages)—

(*a*) in subsection (2), the "or" at the end of paragraph (d) is treated as omitted and after paragraph (e) there is treated as inserted—

", or

(*f*) a scheme or arrangement administered by MFET Limited, so far as it relates to payments to an Eligible Person.";

(*b*) after subsection (6) there is treated as inserted—

"(7) In this section "MFET Limited" means the company limited by guarantee of that name (company number 7121661).

(8) In this section and sections 733 and 734 "Eligible Person" has the meaning given in the Articles of Association of MFET Limited which were adopted by special resolution passed on 5th March 2010.".

(3) In section 733(a) (persons entitled to exemptions for personal injury payments etc)—

(*a*) after "the person" there is treated as inserted "("A") who is an Eligible Person or who is";

(*b*) "("A")" is treated as omitted.

(4) In section 734(1)(a) (payments from trusts for injured persons) after "who is" there is treated as inserted "an Eligible Person or who is".

2010/809

EXCHANGE GAINS AND LOSSES (BRINGING INTO ACCOUNT GAINS OR LOSSES) (AMENDMENT) REGULATIONS 2010

Made . . . . *15 March 2010*
Laid before the House of Commons . . . . *16 March 2010*

Coming into force . . . .*6 April 2010*

The Treasury make the following Regulations in exercise of the powers conferred by section 151E of the Taxation of Chargeable Gains Act 1992, paragraph 26(5) of Schedule 23 to the Finance Act 2002 and sections 328(5) to (7) and 606(5) to (7) of the Corporation Tax Act 2009.

1 Citation, commencement and effect

(1) These Regulations may be cited as the Exchange Gains and Losses (Bringing into Account Gains or Losses) (Amendment) Regulations 2010 and shall come into force on 6th April 2010.

(2) Subject to regulations 13 and 14(4), these Regulations shall have effect in relation to a disposal of an asset made on or after 6th April 2010.

(3) In these Regulations, "the principal Regulations" means the Exchange Gains and Losses (Bringing into Account Gains or Losses) Regulations 2002.

2 Amendments to the Exchange Gains and Losses (Bringing into Account Gains or Losses) Regulations 2002

The principal Regulations are amended in accordance with regulations 3 to 12.

3–12

Note—The amendments made by regs 3–12 are already in force and are therefore not reproduced here.

13 Further provisions—cases within regulation 3(3)(*a*) or (*b*) of the principal Regulations

These Regulations shall not have effect in relation to a disposal of an asset where the circumstances prescribed by regulation 3(3)(*a*) or (*b*) of the principal Regulations are satisfied.

14 Further provisions—no gain/no loss disposals

(1) This regulation applies in relation to an asset as regards which regulation 8(2)(*a*) of the principal Regulations has had effect in respect of a no gain/no loss disposal before 6th April 2010 but the net gain or net loss accruing at the time of that disposal has not been brought into account as a chargeable gain or allowable loss in accordance with regulation 8(2)(*b*), 10(3) or 12(3).
This is subject to paragraph (4).

(2) On the first disposal of the asset which is not a no gain/no loss disposal, the net gain or net loss referred to in paragraph (1) shall be brought into account in accordance with regulation 4 of the principal Regulations (as substituted by regulation 4 of these Regulations).

(3) In paragraph (2) "a no gain/no loss disposal" has the meaning given in regulation 2(1) of the principal Regulations (as substituted by regulation 3(2) of these Regulations).

(4) In a case to which this regulation applies, the company making the disposal of the asset may elect that these Regulations shall not apply.

(5) An election under paragraph (4) must—

(*a*) be made in writing to HMRC within 12 months of the date of the disposal referred to in paragraph (2),

(*b*) identify the asset which is the subject of the disposal,

(*c*) include a computation of the net gain or net loss, and

(6) An election under paragraph 4 above is irrevocable.

2010/922

REGISTERED PENSION SCHEMES (STANDARD LIFETIME AND ANNUAL ALLOWANCES) ORDER 2010

Made by the Treasury under FA 2004 ss 218(2), 228(2)

Made . . . .*24 March 2010*

Laid before the House of Commons . . . .*24 March 2010*

Coming into force . . . .*15 April 2010*

Commentary—*Simon's Taxes* **E7.216**.

1 Citation and commencement

This Order may be cited as the Registered Pension Schemes (Standard Lifetime and Annual Allowances) Order 2010 and shall come into force on 15th April 2010.

2 Standard lifetime allowance

The standard lifetime allowance for the tax years 2011–12, 2012–13, 2013–14, 2014–15 and 2015–16 is £1,800,000.[1]

Amendments—[1] Art 2 revoked by FA 2011 s 67, Sch 18 para 12 with effect for the tax year 2012–13 and subsequent tax years, subject to transitional provisions in FA 2011 Sch 18 paras 13, 14. See also FA 2004 s 218 (individual's lifetime allowance and standard lifetime allowance).

3 Annual allowance

The annual allowance for the tax years 2011–12, 2012–13, 2013–14, 2014–15 and 2015–16 is £255,000.[1]

Cross-reference—FA 2004 s 227 (annual allowance charge).
FA 2004 s 228 (annual allowance).
Amendments—[1] Art 3 revoked by FA 2011 s 66, Sch 17 para 26(2) with effect for the tax year 2011–12 and subsequent tax years, subject to transitional provisions in FA 2011 Sch 17 paras 27–34.

2010/1187

FINANCIAL ASSISTANCE SCHEME (TAX) REGULATIONS 2010

Made by the Treasury under FA 2009 s 73

Made . . . . *6 April 2010*
Laid before the House of Commons . . . . *7 April 2010*
Coming into force . . . . *1 May 2010*

PART 1
PRELIMINARY

1 Citation, commencement and interpretation

(1) These Regulations may be cited as the Financial Assistance Scheme (Tax) Regulations 2010 and shall come into force on 1st May 2010.
(2) In these Regulations, unless otherwise stated, any reference to a numbered regulation is a reference to that regulation of the FAS Regulations.
(3) In these Regulations—
"assistance" means—
interim assistance,
non-lump sum assistance,
a lump sum payment under regulation 17D (lump sum payments), and
a payment under regulation 18A (death benefit guarantees) in cases where that payment is in the form of a lump sum;
"the FA 2004" means the Finance Act 2004;
"the FAS" means the financial assistance scheme;
"the FAS Regulations" means the Financial Assistance Scheme Regulations 2005;
"the FAS scheme manager" means the person appointed by the Secretary of State by regulations under section 286 of the Pensions Act 2004 to manage the FAS;
"interim assistance" means—
an interim ill health payment from the FAS, and
an initial payment from the FAS;
"non-lump sum assistance" means—
an annual payment from the FAS under regulation 17 (annual payments),
an ill health payment from the FAS, and
an annual payment from the FAS under regulation 17C (annual payments for certain applications in cases of severe ill health);
"qualifying member" has the meaning given by regulation 15(1); and
"qualifying pension scheme" has the meaning given in regulation 9.

PART 2
TAX RELIEFS, ETC

2 Transfer of registered pension scheme assets, etc, to the Secretary of State

A transfer of the property, rights and liabilities of a registered pension scheme to the Secretary of State is to be treated as if it were a payment authorised by section 164(1) of the FA 2004 (authorised member payments).

3 Payments to the Secretary of State

(1) This regulation applies where as a result of the transfer of the property, rights and liabilities of a registered pension scheme to the Secretary of State an employer is required to pay a sum to the Secretary of State.
(2) Where section 199 of the FA 2004 (deemed contributions) would have applied if the payment had been made to the trustees or managers of the scheme, that section applies in relation to the payment in the same way as it applies in relation to a sum paid to the trustees or managers of a registered pension scheme.
(3) Where the payment does not fall within paragraph (2), section 200 of the FA 2004 (no other relief for employers in connection with contributions) applies in relation to it in the same way that section applies in relation to a sum other than a contribution paid in connection with the cost of providing benefits under a registered pension scheme.

4 Lump sum payments by the Financial Assistance Scheme

Subsections (1) and (2) of section 636A of the Income Tax (Earnings and Pensions) Act 2003 (exemption for certain lump sums under registered pension schemes) apply to a lump sum payment under regulation 17D and a payment made under regulation 18A in the form of a lump sum as they apply to the lump sums listed in subsection (1).

PART 3
LIFETIME ALLOWANCE

5 Application of relevant lifetime allowance provisions

(1) The relevant lifetime allowance provisions apply in relation to assistance from the FAS as they apply in relation to benefits that are provided under a registered pension scheme.

(2) For the purposes of the relevant lifetime allowance provisions, unless the context requires otherwise—

(*a*) a qualifying member is to be treated as if that qualifying member were a member of a registered pension scheme; and

(*b*) the FAS is to be treated as if it were a registered pension scheme and the FAS scheme manager is to be treated as its scheme administrator.

(3) Subject to regulations 6 to 11 of these Regulations, the relevant lifetime allowance provisions are—

(*a*) sections 214 to 226 and 263 of the FA 2004 (lifetime allowance charge and penalty in relation to relevant benefit accrual);

(*b*) Part 2 of Schedule 36 to the FA 2004 (lifetime allowance charge transitional provisions);

(*c*) orders made under section 218(3) of the FA 2004 (individual's lifetime allowance and standard lifetime allowance); and

(*d*) enhanced lifetime allowance regulations.

(4) "Enhanced lifetime allowance regulations" has the meaning given by section 256(2) of the FA 2004 (enhanced lifetime allowance regulations).

6 Amount of charge

For the purposes of section 215 of the FA 2004 (amount of charge) a payment under regulation 18A in the form of a lump sum is to be treated as if it was a lump sum death benefit.

7 Benefit crystallisation events and amounts crystallised

(1) In relation to assistance from the FAS, this table sets out—

(*a*) the events which are benefit crystallisation events in relation to the individual; and

(*b*) the amount which is crystallised by each of those events

in place of section 216 of the FA 2004 (lifetime allowance charge—benefit crystallisation events and amounts crystallised).

Benefit crystallisation events	*Amount crystallised*
1 Subject to paragraph (3), the individual becoming entitled for the first time to interim assistance in respect of membership of a qualifying pension scheme.	(20 *c* P) − *RPSBCE*
2 Subject to paragraphs (3) and (4), the individual becoming entitled for the first time to one of the forms of non-lump sum assistance in respect of membership of a qualifying pension scheme in a case where the individual has not previously become entitled to one of the forms of interim assistance in respect of that scheme.	(20 *c* P) − *RPSBCE*
3 The individual becoming entitled for the first time to an annual payment under regulation 17 in respect of membership of a qualifying pension scheme having previously become entitled to an initial payment in respect of that scheme.	Where paragraph (5) applies— (20 *c P*17) − *BCE*1 Where paragraph (5) does not apply, nil.

Benefit crystallisation events	*Amount crystallised*
4 The individual becoming entitled for the first time to an ill health payment from the FAS in respect of membership of a qualifying pension scheme having previously become entitled to an interim ill health payment in respect of that scheme.	Where paragraph (6) applies— (20 *c P*17*A*) – *BCE*1 Where paragraph (6) does not apply, nil.
5 The individual becoming entitled to a lump sum payment under regulation 17D in respect of membership of a qualifying pension scheme in a case where the individual has not previously become entitled to interim assistance in respect of that scheme.	The amount of the lump sum paid to the individual.
6 A person becoming entitled to a lump sum in respect of the individual under regulation 18A in respect of the individual's membership of a qualifying pension scheme.	The amount of the lump sum.

(2) For the purposes of these Regulations, an individual becomes entitled to—

(*a*) assistance from the FAS when that individual first acquires an actual (rather than a prospective) right to receive that assistance and the amount of that assistance has been determined by the FAS scheme manager; and

(*b*) a lump sum under regulation 17D immediately before the individual becomes entitled to the non-lump sum assistance to which the lump sum relates.

(3) The individual becoming entitled to interim assistance, an annual payment under regulation 17 or an ill health payment from the FAS in respect of membership of a qualifying pension scheme does not result in a benefit crystallisation event where that entitlement is solely as a result of the transfer to the Secretary of State of property, rights and liabilities which represent the rights to which the individual had, prior to the transfer, become entitled in respect of a scheme pension under that scheme.

(4) The individual becoming entitled to an annual payment under regulation 17 or an ill health payment from the FAS does not result in a benefit crystallisation event where the individual had previously become entitled to—

(*a*) an initial payment or an interim ill health payment, as the case may be, from the FAS prior to the coming into force of these Regulations; or

(*b*) a payment under regulation 17H (payments to qualifying members receiving a pension from the qualifying pension scheme before entitlement to an annual payment or ill health payment).

(5) This paragraph applies where the value of (20 *c* P17) is more than the value of BCE1.

(6) This paragraph applies where the value of (20 *c* P17A) is more than the value of BCE1.

(7) In this regulation—

"BCE 1" is the amount crystallised at the first benefit crystallisation event in the table in paragraph (1) following the individual becoming entitled to the relevant interim assistance;

"P" is the value of the assistance which will be payable to the individual in the period of 12 months beginning with the day on which the individual becomes entitled to assistance (assuming assistance remains payable throughout that period at the rate at which it is payable on that day);

"P17" is the value of the assistance which would have been payable to the individual in the period of 12 months beginning with the day on which the individual became entitled to an initial payment if—

the individual had become entitled to assistance in the form of an annual payment under regulation 17 on that day,

that assistance had remained payable throughout that period at the rate at which it would have been payable on that day, and

the individual had chosen not to commute any of that assistance for a lump sum;

"P17A" is the value of the assistance which would have been payable to the individual in the period of 12 months beginning with the day on which the individual became entitled to an interim ill health payment if—

the individual had become entitled to assistance in the form of an ill health payment on that day,

that assistance had remained payable throughout that period at the rate at which it would have been payable on that day, and

the individual had chosen not to commute any of that assistance for a lump sum; and

"RPSBCE" is the amount, if any, crystallised by the second or fifth benefit crystallisation event, as the case may be, under section 216 of the FA 2004 in respect of rights under the registered pension scheme of which the individual was a member prior to the transfer of the property, rights and liabilities which represent those rights to the Secretary of State.

8 Persons liable to charge

Section 217 of the FA 2004 (persons liable to charge) applies as if—

(*a*) in subsection (1), the words after "individual" were omitted; and

(*b*) in subsections (2), (3) and (4), the references to a "relevant lump sum death benefit" were references to a payment under regulation 18A in the form of a lump sum.

9 Availability of individual's lifetime allowance

(1) Section 219(6) of the FA 2004 (availability of individual's lifetime allowance) applies as if after the words in brackets there appeared "and regulation 7(2)(*b*) of the Financial Assistance Scheme (Tax) Regulations 2010".

(2) A payment under regulation 18A in the form of a lump sum is to be treated as the payment of a lump sum death benefit for the purposes of section 219(7) of the FA 2004.

10 Transitional provisions: Part 2 of Schedule 36 to the FA 2004

For the purposes of paragraph 12(2)(*b*) of Schedule 36 to the FA 2004 (enhanced protection), a transfer of the property, rights and liabilities of a registered pension scheme to the Secretary of State is to be treated as a permitted transfer.

11 Information and penalties

(1) Subject to regulation 12(2) of these Regulations, the Registered Pension Schemes (Provision of Information) Regulations 2006 do not apply in relation to the FAS.

(2) Sections 261 and 262 of the FA 2004 (enhanced lifetime allowance regulations: documents and information—penalties) apply to the reporting obligation in regulation 13 of these Regulations as if it was imposed by enhanced lifetime allowance regulations.

(3) Section 98 of the Taxes Management Act 1970 (special returns, etc: penalties) applies to the reporting obligations in regulations 14 to 18 of these Regulations as if they were listed in the second column of the Table in that section.

12 Percentage of standard lifetime allowance expended on the happening of a benefit crystallisation event

(1) The percentage of standard lifetime allowance expended on the happening of each benefit crystallisation event for the purposes of these Regulations is found by applying the formula—

$(AC / RSLA)$ c 100

where—

"AC" is the amount crystallised by the benefit crystallisation event; and

"RSLA" is the relevant standard lifetime allowance at the time of that event.

(2) The total percentage of standard lifetime allowance expended in relation to a qualifying member is the sum of—

(*a*) the percentages found in accordance with this regulation in respect of that member; and

(*b*) the percentages found in accordance with regulation 7 of the Registered Pension Schemes (Provision of Information) Regulations 2006 (percentage of standard lifetime allowance expended on the happening of a registered pension scheme benefit crystallisation event) in respect of that member.

13 Information provided by qualifying members to the FAS scheme manager about enhanced lifetime allowance

If a qualifying member intends to rely on entitlement to an enhanced lifetime allowance, or to enhanced protection, the qualifying member must notify the FAS scheme manager of the reference number issued by the Commissioners for Her Majesty's Revenue and Customs under the Registered Pension Schemes (Enhanced Lifetime Allowance) Regulations 2006 in respect of that entitlement.

14 Information provided by the FAS scheme manager to qualifying members about liability for a lifetime allowance charge

If assistance other than a payment under regulation 18A in the form of a lump sum results in a lifetime allowance charge, within three months of the benefit crystallisation event the FAS scheme manager must provide the qualifying member with a notice stating—

(*a*) the chargeable amount in respect of the benefit crystallisation event;
(*b*) how that chargeable amount has been calculated; and
(*c*) the amount of the resulting charge to tax.

15 Information provided by the FAS scheme manager to qualifying members about benefit crystallisation events

(1) The FAS scheme manager must provide a statement containing the information in paragraph (2) to each qualifying member—
(*a*) who has become entitled to receive assistance, at least once in each tax year; or
(*b*) in respect of whom a benefit crystallisation event has occurred, within three months of that event,

or, if the member has died, the FAS scheme manager must provide the statement to the member's personal representatives.

(2) The information is the percentage of standard lifetime allowance expended in relation to the member by—
(*a*) benefit crystallisation events in respect of the FAS; and
(*b*) benefit crystallisation events under section 216 of the FA 2004 prior to the transfer to the Secretary of State mentioned in regulation 2 of these Regulations except for a benefit crystallisation event which relates to a liability or pension obligation which is not discharged under section 161 of the Pensions Act 2004 as modified by paragraph 3D of Schedule 1 to the FAS Regulations 2005.

(3) No obligation to provide a statement under paragraph (1)(*b*) arises if a statement is required to be provided under sub-paragraph (*a*) of that paragraph or under regulation 16(1)(*a*) of these Regulations.

(4) For the purposes of paragraph (1)(*a*), a qualifying member becomes entitled to receive assistance in the circumstances set out in regulation 7(2) of these Regulations.

16 Information provided by the FAS scheme manager to personal representatives

(1) The FAS scheme manager must notify to the personal representatives of a deceased qualifying member—
(*a*) the percentage of standard lifetime allowance expended by, and the amount and the date of payment of, a payment in the form of a lump sum under regulation 18A in relation to the member; and
(*b*) the total percentage of standard lifetime allowance expended in relation to the member, at the date of the notification, by—
(i) benefit crystallisation events in respect of the FAS; and
(ii) benefit crystallisation events under section 216 of the FA 2004 prior to the transfer to the Secretary of State mentioned in regulation 2 of these Regulations except for a benefit crystallisation event which relates to a liability or pension obligation which is not discharged under section 161 of the Pensions Act 2004 as modified by paragraph 3D of Schedule 1 to the FAS Regulations 2005,

but excluding from that percentage any amount covered by paragraph (*a*).

(2) The information required by paragraph (1)(*a*) must be provided no later than the last day of the period of three months beginning with the day on which the assistance payment is made.

(3) The information required by paragraph (1)(*b*) must be provided no later than the last day of the period of two months beginning with the day on which a request for it is received from the member's personal representatives.

17 Information provided by the FAS scheme manager to Her Majesty's Revenue and Customs

(1) If assistance results in a lifetime allowance charge or would have done but for the qualifying member's entitlement to an enhanced lifetime allowance, or to enhanced protection, within three months of the benefit crystallisation event the FAS scheme manager must provide a report to Her Majesty's Revenue and Customs setting out—
(*a*) the name, date of birth, address and national insurance number of the member;
(*b*) the date of the relevant benefit crystallisation event;
(*c*) the amount crystallised by the event;
(*d*) if the member has benefited from an enhanced lifetime allowance or enhanced protection, the reference number issued under the Registered Pension Schemes (Enhanced Lifetime Allowance) Regulations 2006 in respect of that entitlement; and
(*e*) in cases where the member is liable to a lifetime allowance charge, the amount of tax due in respect of each chargeable amount as constitutes a lump sum amount and each chargeable amount as constitutes a retained amount.

(2) For the purposes of paragraph (1)(*e*), a chargeable amount that constitutes a retained amount includes cases where it is assumed under regulation 7 of these Regulations that the member has not chosen to commute any portion of non-lump sum assistance for a lump sum.

18 Information provided by personal representatives to Her Majesty's Revenue and Customs

(1) Where—

(*a*) a payment in the form of a lump sum is made in respect of a deceased qualifying member under regulation 18A; and

(*b*) that payment, of itself or together with any other such payment or any relevant lump sum death benefit paid by a registered pension scheme in respect of the individual, results in a lifetime allowance charge,

the personal representatives of the member shall provide to Her Majesty's Revenue and Customs the information specified in paragraph (2).

(2) The information is—

(*a*) a statement that a payment in the form of a lump sum has been paid by the FAS under regulation 18A;

(*b*) the name of any registered pension scheme from which, and the name and address of the scheme administrator by whom, the benefits were paid;

(*c*) the name of the deceased member in respect of whom the benefits were paid;

(*d*) the amount and date of the payment by the FAS;

(*e*) the amount and date of the payment of any benefits by a registered pension scheme; and

(*f*) the chargeable amount in respect of which a lifetime allowance charge is payable by virtue of the payments.

(3) The information required shall be provided on or before the later of—

(*a*) the end of the period of 13 months beginning with the death of the member; or

(*b*) the end of the period of 30 days beginning with the date on which the personal representatives (or any of them) became aware that paragraph (1) applied to the deceased member.

(4) Where a requirement to provide information under this regulation arises after the period specified in paragraph (3) has expired, the information shall be provided no later than the last day of the period of 30 months beginning with the death of the member.

(5) If the personal representatives discover after the latest date for providing information under paragraph (4) any information required to be provided under paragraph (1), that information shall be provided no later than the last day of the period of 3 months beginning with the discovery of that information.

(6) Where personal representatives are required to provide information under this regulation by virtue of a payment or payments in the form of a lump sum being made under regulation 18A in respect of the deceased member along with the payment of one or more relevant lump sum death benefits under Part 4 of the FA 2004 in respect of the deceased member, regulation 10 of the Registered Pension Schemes (Provision of Information) Regulations 2006 does not apply in relation to the payment or payments under Part 4 of the FA 2004.

PART 4

MISCELLANEOUS

19 Transitional provisions: lump sums

For the purposes of—

(*a*) paragraph 2 of Schedule 29 to the FA 2004 as modified by paragraph 28(3) of Schedule 36 to that Act; and

(*b*) regulation 25D of the Taxation of Pension Schemes (Transitional Provisions) Order 2006,

the reference to a pension commencement lump sum in the definition of "APCLS" in paragraph 2(6) of Schedule 29 shall be taken to include a lump sum under regulation 17D.

2010/1640

SAVING GATEWAY ACCOUNTS ACT 2009 (REVOCATION OF COMMENCEMENT) ORDER 2010

Made . . . .*22 June 2010*

The Treasury make the following Order in exercise of the powers conferred by sections 28(1) and 31 of the Saving Gateway Accounts Act 2009:

1 Citation

This Order may be cited as the Saving Gateway Accounts Act 2009 (Revocation of Commencement) Order 2010.

2 Revocation

The Saving Gateway Accounts Act 2009 (Commencement No 2) Order 2010 is revoked.

2010/1813

REVENUE AND CUSTOMS (COMPLAINTS AND MISCONDUCT) REGULATIONS 2010

Made . . . . *14 July 2010*
Laid before Parliament . . . . *15 July 2010*
Coming into force . . . . *5 August 2010*

The Treasury make the following Regulations in exercise of the powers conferred by sections 28(1), (2) and (6) and 29(3) of the Commissioners for Revenue and Customs Act 2005.

Commentary—*Simon's Taxes* **A5.403**.

PART 1
GENERAL

1 Citation and commencement

These Regulations may be cited as the Revenue and Customs (Complaints and Misconduct) Regulations 2010 and shall come into force on 5th August 2010.

2 Revocation and transitional provision

(1) Subject to paragraph (2), the Revenue and Customs (Complaints and Misconduct) Regulations 2005 and the Revenue and Customs (Complaints and Misconduct) (Amendment) Regulations 2006 are revoked.

(2) Where an allegation in respect of the conduct by an officer came to the attention of the appropriate authority before the 5th August 2010, nothing in these Regulations shall apply and the Revenue and Customs (Complaints and Misconduct) Regulations 2005 shall continue to have effect.

3 Interpretation

(1) In these Regulations—

"2002 Act" means the Police Reform Act 2002;

"appropriate authority"—

(*a*) in relation to the Commissioners or an officer or in relation to any complaint, matter or investigation relating to the conduct of such a person, means—

(i) if that person is the Chairman, the Chief Executive or the Permanent Secretary for Tax, the Head of the Home Civil Service,

(ii) if that person is a Commissioner, the Chief Executive unless that Commissioner is the Chairman, the Permanent Secretary for Tax or the Chief Executive, or

(iii) if that person is an officer, the Commissioners (other than the Chairman, the Chief Executive and the Permanent Secretary for Tax), and

(*b*) in relation to a death or serious injury matter and the relevant officer, means the Commissioners (other than the Chairman, the Chief Executive and the Permanent Secretary for Tax);

"the Chairman" means the Chairman of the Board of HMRC;

"the Chief Executive" means the Chief Executive of HMRC;

"chief officer" means the chief officer of police of any police force;

"the Commissioners" unless a contrary intention appears, means the Commissioners for Her Majesty's Revenue and Customs and for the purposes of these Regulations includes the Chairman (and unless a contrary intention appears, "Commissioner" is to be construed accordingly);

"complainant" shall be construed in accordance with paragraph (4);

"complaint" has the meaning given by regulation 9 (complaints, matters and persons to which these Regulations apply);

"conduct" includes acts, omissions and statements (whether actual, alleged or inferred);

"conduct matter" has the meaning given by regulation 9;

"death or serious injury matter" and "DSI matter" have the meaning given by regulation 9;

"disciplinary proceedings" means any proceedings or management process during which the conduct of the Commissioners or an officer is considered in order to determine whether a sanction or punitive measure should be imposed against that person in relation to that conduct;

"document" means anything in which information of any description is recorded;

"function" in relation to the Commissioners or officers has the meaning given by section 51(2) of the Commissioners for Revenue and Customs Act 2005;

"HMRC" means Her Majesty's Revenue and Customs;

"information" includes estimates and projections, and statistical analyses;

"IPCC" means the Independent Police Complaints Commission and has the meaning given by section 9(1) of the 2002 Act;

"officer" means, unless the context otherwise requires, an officer of Revenue and Customs;

"the Permanent Secretary for Tax" means HMRC's Permanent Secretary for Tax;
"the person complained against", in relation to a complaint, means the person whose conduct is the subject-matter of the complaint;
"the person investigating", in relation to a complaint, recordable conduct matter or DSI matter, means the person appointed or designated to investigate that complaint or matter;
"recordable conduct matter" means—

(*a*) a conduct matter that is required to be recorded by the appropriate authority under regulation 23 (conduct matters arising in civil proceedings) or 24 (recording etc of conduct matters in other cases), or has been so recorded; or

(*b*) except in paragraph (3) of regulation 19 (initial handling and recording of complaints), any matter brought to the attention of the appropriate authority under that paragraph;

"relevant offence" means—

(*a*) an offence for which the sentence is fixed by law,

(*b*) an offence for which a person of 18 years or over (not previously convicted) may be sentenced to imprisonment for a term of seven years or more (or might be so sentenced but for the restrictions imposed by section 33 of the Magistrates' Courts Act 1980);

"serious injury" means a fracture, a deep cut, a deep laceration or an injury causing damage to an internal organ or the impairment of any bodily function.

(2) In these Regulations "the relevant officer", in relation to a DSI matter, means the officer—

(*a*) who arrested the person who has died or suffered serious injury,

(*b*) in whose custody that person was at the time of the death or serious injury, or

(*c*) with whom that person had the contact in question;

and where there is more than one such officer it means, subject to paragraph (3), the one who so dealt with that person last before the death or serious injury occurred.

(3) Where it cannot be determined which of two or more officers dealt with a person last before a death or serious injury occurred, the "relevant officer" is the most senior of them.

(4) References in these Regulations to the complainant, in relation to anything which is or purports to be a complaint, are references—

(*a*) except in the case of anything which is or purports to be a complaint falling within regulation 9(1)(*d*) (complaints, matters and persons to which these Regulations apply), to the person by whom the complaint or purported complaint was made; and

(*b*) in that case, to the person on whose behalf the complaint or purported complaint was made;

but where any person is acting on another's behalf for the purposes of any complaint or purported complaint, anything that is to be or may be done under these Regulations by or in relation to the complainant may be done, instead, by or in relation to the person acting on the complainant's behalf.

(5) Subject to paragraph (6), references in these Regulations, in relation to any conduct or anything purporting to be a complaint about any conduct, to a member of the public include references to any person who is a Commissioner or an officer (whether at the time of the conduct or any subsequent time).

(6) In these Regulations references, in relation to any conduct or to anything purporting to be a complaint about any conduct, to a member of the public do not include references to—

(*a*) a person who, at the time when the conduct was supposed to have taken place in relation to that person, was a Commissioner or an officer (whether or not that person was on duty in that person's capacity as a Commissioner or officer at that time), or

(*b*) a person who at the time when that person is supposed to have been adversely affected by it, or to have witnessed it, was on duty in that person's capacity as a Commissioner or officer.

(7) For the purposes of these Regulations, a person is adversely affected if that person suffers any form of loss or damage, distress or inconvenience, if that person is put in danger or if that person is otherwise unduly put at risk of being adversely affected.

(8) References in these Regulations to the investigation of any complaint or matter by the appropriate authority on its own behalf, under the supervision of the IPCC, under the management of the IPCC or by the IPCC itself shall be construed as references to its investigation in accordance with—

(*a*) regulation 44 (investigations by the appropriate authority on its own behalf),

(*b*) regulation 45 (investigations supervised by the IPCC),

(*c*) regulation 46 (investigations by a police force under the management or under the supervision of the IPCC),

(*d*) regulation 47 (investigations managed by the IPCC), or

(*e*) regulation 48 (investigations by the IPCC itself).

4 Application: general

These Regulations shall apply for the purpose of conferring functions on the IPCC in relation to the Commissioners and officers, in the exercise of their functions in or in relation to England and Wales.

5 Application of the 2002 Act

(1) Sections 9 (the Independent Police Complaints Commission), 19 (use of investigatory powers by or on behalf of the IPCC), 22 (power of the IPCC to issue guidance), 23 (regulations), 24 (consultation on regulations) and 27 (conduct of the IPCC's staff) of the 2002 Act shall apply to the Commissioners and officers with the following modifications.

(2) In section 22 of the 2002 Act—

(*a*) for subsection (1) substitute—

"(1) The Commission may issue guidance to Her Majesty's Revenue and Customs and any person it sees fit concerning the exercise or performance by the persons to whom the guidance is issued, of any powers or duties specified in subsection (2).";

(*b*) in subsection (2) for "persons serving with the police" substitute "persons serving with Her Majesty's Revenue and Customs";

(*c*) for subsection (3) substitute—

"(3) Before issuing any guidance under this section, the Commission shall consult Her Majesty's Revenue and Customs and any person it sees fit.";

(*d*) in subsection (4) for "the Secretary of State" substitute "the Chancellor of the Exchequer";

(*e*) omit subsection (5)(*c*).

(3) In section 23 of the 2002 Act—

(*a*) in subsection (2)(k), for "a person serving with the police" substitute "a person serving with Her Majesty's Revenue and Customs";

(*b*) in subsection (2)(p), for "chief officers" substitute "the Commissioners for Her Majesty's Revenue and Customs".

(4) In section 24 of the 2002 Act—

(*a*) at the end of paragraph (*a*) insert "and Her Majesty's Revenue and Customs";

(*b*) omit paragraphs (*b*) and (*c*).

6 Temporary service and copies of accounts

(1) The IPCC may make arrangements with the Commissioners under which officers are engaged on temporary service with the IPCC.

(2) Copies of the statement referred to in paragraph 17(1)(*c*) of Schedule 2 to the 2002 Act (accounts) shall also be sent to the Treasury.

7 General functions of the IPCC in relation to the Commissioners and officers

(1) The functions of the IPCC in relation to the Commissioners and officers shall be—

(*a*) to secure the maintenance by the IPCC itself, and by the Commissioners, of suitable arrangements with respect to the matters mentioned in paragraph (2);

(*b*) to keep under review all arrangements maintained with respect to those matters;

(*c*) to secure that arrangements maintained with respect to those matters comply with the requirements of the following provisions of this Part, are efficient and effective and contain and manifest an appropriate degree of independence;

(*d*) to secure that public confidence is established and maintained in the existence of suitable arrangements with respect to those matters and with the operation of the arrangements that are in fact maintained with respect to those matters;

(*e*) to make such recommendations, and to give such advice, for the modification of the arrangements maintained with respect to those matters, as appear, from the carrying out by the IPCC of its other functions, to be necessary or desirable.

(2) Those matters are—

(*a*) the handling of complaints made about the conduct of the Commissioners or officers which the appropriate authority—

(i) has a duty to refer to the IPCC under regulation 28(1) (reference of complaints to the IPCC), or

(ii) may refer to the IPCC under regulation 28(4) or (5);

(*b*) the recording of matters from which it appears that—

(i) there may have been conduct by such persons which constitutes or involves the commission of a criminal offence or behaviour justifying disciplinary proceedings, and

(ii) that conduct or behaviour is conduct or behaviour which the appropriate authority has a duty to refer to the IPCC under regulation 30(1) (reference of conduct matters to the IPCC) or may refer to the IPCC under regulation 30(5) or (6) of these Regulations;

(*c*) the recording of matters from which it appears that a person has died or suffered serious injury during, or following, contact with an officer;

(*d*) the manner in which any such complaints or any such matters as are mentioned in sub-paragraph (*b*) or (*c*) are investigated or otherwise handled and dealt with.

(3) It shall be the duty of the IPCC—

(*a*) to exercise the powers and perform the duties conferred on it by the following provisions of these Regulations in the manner that it considers best calculated for the purpose of securing the proper carrying out of its functions under paragraph (1), and

(*b*) to secure that arrangements exist which are conducive to, and facilitate, the reporting of misconduct by persons in relation to whose conduct the IPCC has functions.

(4) It shall also be the duty of the IPCC—

(*a*) to enter into arrangements with the chief inspector of constabulary for the purpose of securing co-operation, in the carrying out of their respective functions in relation to the Commissioners and officers, between the IPCC and the inspectors of constabulary, and

(*b*) to provide those inspectors with all such assistance and co-operation as may be required by those arrangements, or as otherwise appears to the IPCC to be appropriate, for facilitating the carrying out by those inspectors of their functions.

(5) Subject to the other provisions of these Regulations, the IPCC may do anything which appears to it to be calculated to facilitate, or is incidental or conducive to, the carrying out of its functions.

(6) The IPCC may, in connection with the making of any recommendation or the giving of any advice to any person for the purpose of carrying out its function under paragraph (1)(*e*), impose any such charge on that person for anything done by the IPCC for the purposes of, or in connection with, the carrying out of that function as it thinks fit.

(7) Nothing in these Regulations shall confer any function on the IPCC in relation to so much of any complaint or conduct matter as relates to the direction and control of HMRC by the Commissioners.

8 Reports to the Chancellor of the Exchequer

(1) As soon as practicable after the end of each of its financial years, the IPCC shall also make a report to the Chancellor of the Exchequer ("the Chancellor") on the carrying out of its functions during that year.

(2) The IPCC shall also make such reports to the Chancellor about matters relating generally to the carrying out of its functions as the Chancellor may, from time to time, require.

(3) The IPCC may, from time to time, make such other reports to the Chancellor as it considers appropriate for drawing the Chancellor's attention to matters which—

(*a*) have come to the IPCC's notice, and

(*b*) are matters that it considers should be drawn to the Chancellor's attention by reason of their gravity or of other exceptional circumstances.

(4) The IPCC shall prepare such reports containing advice and recommendations as it thinks appropriate for the purpose of carrying out its function under regulation 7(1)(*e*) (general functions of the IPCC in relation to Commissioners and officers).

(5) Where the Chancellor receives any report under this regulation, the Chancellor shall—

(*a*) in the case of every annual report under paragraph (1), and

(*b*) in the case of any other report, if and to the extent that the Chancellor considers it appropriate to do so,

lay a copy of the report before Parliament and cause the report to be published.

(6) The IPCC shall send a copy of every annual report under paragraph (1) to the Commissioners.

(7) The IPCC shall send a copy of every report under paragraph (3) to the Commissioners.

(8) The IPCC shall send a copy of every report under paragraph (4) to—

(*a*) the Chancellor of the Exchequer, and

(*b*) the Commissioners.

(9) The IPCC shall send a copy of every report made or prepared by it under paragraphs (3) or (4) to such of the persons (in addition to those specified in the preceding paragraphs) who—

(*a*) are referred to in the report, or

(*b*) appear to the IPCC otherwise to have a particular interest in its contents,

as the IPCC thinks fit.

9 Complaints, matters and persons to which these Regulations apply

(1) In these Regulations references to a complaint are references (subject to the following provisions of this regulation) to any complaint about the conduct of a Commissioner or an officer which is made (whether in writing or otherwise) by—

(*a*) a member of the public who claims to be the person in relation to whom the conduct took place;

(*b*) a member of the public not falling within sub-paragraph (*a*) who claims to have been adversely affected by the conduct;

(*c*) a member of the public who claims to have witnessed the conduct;

(*d*) a person acting on behalf of a person falling within any of sub-paragraphs (*a*) to (*c*).

(2) In these Regulations "conduct matter" means (subject to the following provisions of this regulation, and regulation 19(3)) any matter which is not and has not been the subject of a complaint but in the case of which there is an indication (whether from the circumstances or otherwise) that a Commissioner or an officer may have—

(*a*) committed a criminal offence, or

(*b*) behaved in a manner which would justify the bringing of disciplinary proceedings.

(3) In these Regulations "death or serious injury matter" ("DSI matter") means any circumstance (other than those which are or have been the subject of a complaint or which amount to a conduct matter)—

(*a*) in or in consequence of which a person has died or has sustained serious injury, and

(*b*) in relation to which the requirements of either paragraph (4) or (5) are satisfied.

(4) The requirements of this paragraph are that at the time of the death or serious injury the person—

(*a*) had been arrested by an officer and had not been released from that arrest, or

(*b*) was otherwise detained in the custody of an officer.

(5) The requirements of this paragraph are that—

(*a*) at or before the time of the death or serious injury the person had contact (of whatever kind, and whether direct or indirect) with an officer who was acting in the execution of duties, and

(*b*) there is an indication that the contact may have caused (whether directly or indirectly) or contributed to the death or serious injury.

(6) In paragraph (3) the reference to a person includes an officer, but in relation to such a person "contact" in paragraph (5) does not include contact that the officer has whilst acting in the execution of duties.

(7) The complaints that are complaints for the purposes of these Regulations by virtue of paragraph (1)(*b*) do not, except in a case falling within paragraph (8), include any made by or on behalf of a person who claims to have been adversely affected as a consequence only of having seen or heard the conduct, or any of the alleged effects of the conduct.

(8) A case falls within this paragraph if—

(*a*) it was only because the person in question was physically present, or sufficiently nearby, when the conduct took place or the effects occurred that the person was able to see or hear the conduct or its effects, or

(*b*) the adverse effect is attributable to, or was aggravated by, the fact that the person in relation to whom the conduct took place was already known to the person claiming to have suffered the adverse effect.

(9) For the purposes of this regulation a person shall be taken to have witnessed conduct if, and only if—

(*a*) that person acquired knowledge of that conduct in a manner which would make that person a competent witness capable of giving admissible evidence of that conduct in criminal proceedings, or

(*b*) that person possesses or controls anything which would in any such proceedings constitute admissible evidence of that conduct.

(10) For the purposes of these Regulations a person falling within paragraph (1)(*a*) to (*c*) shall not be taken to have authorised another person to act on that person's behalf unless—

(*a*) that other person is for the time being designated for the purposes of these Regulations by the IPCC as a person through whom complaints may be made, or is of a description of persons so designated, or

(*b*) the other person has been given, and is able to produce, the written consent to such action, of the person on whose behalf that action is taken.

10 Handling of complaints, conduct matters and DSI matters etc

These Regulations shall have effect subject to regulation 11 (direction and control matters).

11 Direction and control matters

Nothing in these Regulations shall have effect with respect to so much of any complaint as relates to the direction and control of HMRC by the Commissioners.

PART 2
COMPLAINTS AND MISCONDUCT

12 Co-operation, assistance and information

(1) It shall be the duty of the Commissioners to ensure that they are kept informed, in relation to HMRC, about all matters falling within paragraph (2).

(2) Those matters are—

(*a*) matters with respect to which any provision of these Regulations has effect;

(*b*) anything which is done under or for the purposes of any such provision; and

(*c*) any obligations to act or refrain from acting that have arisen by or under these Regulations, but have not yet been complied with or have been contravened.

(3) Where the IPCC requires the chief officer of a police force to provide a member of that person's force for appointment under regulation 46 or 47, it shall be the duty of the chief officer to whom the requirement is addressed to comply with it.

(4) It shall be the duty of the Commissioners to provide the IPCC and every member of the IPCC's staff with all such assistance as the IPCC or that member of staff may reasonably require for the purposes of, or in connection with, the carrying out of any investigation by the IPCC under these Regulations.

(5) It shall be the duty of the Commissioners to ensure that a person appointed under regulation 42 to carry out an investigation is given all such assistance and co-operation in the carrying out of that investigation as that person may reasonably require.

(6) It shall be the duty of the Head of the Home Civil Service and the Commissioners to ensure that a person appointed under regulation 44, 45, 46 or 47 to carry out an investigation is given all such assistance and co-operation in the carrying out of that investigation as that person may reasonably require.

13 Disclosure of information

Where the IPCC, or any person acting on its behalf, obtains information in the course of performing a function under these Regulations, that information may not be disclosed except as permitted under these Regulations or as otherwise prescribed by law.

14 Use of information

Where the IPCC or any person acting on its behalf, obtains information in the course of performing a function under these Regulations, that information may not be used for any purpose other than in the performance of a function under these Regulations or as otherwise prescribed by law.

15 Payments

(1) The Commissioners shall pay such amount to the Secretary of State in respect of functions performed by the IPCC under these Regulations as may be agreed between the Commissioners and the IPCC.

(2) In the absence of an agreement, the Commissioners shall pay such amount in respect of those functions as the Treasury, after consultation with the Secretary of State, shall determine.

16 Payment for assistance with investigations

(1) This regulation applies where—

(*a*) a police force is required to provide assistance in connection with an investigation under Part 6 of these Regulations (investigations);

(*b*) a police force is required to provide assistance in such a connection to the IPCC; or

(*c*) a police force provides assistance by agreement under regulation 46(2).

(2) For the purposes of this regulation—

(*a*) assistance is required to be provided by a police force in connection with an investigation under Part 6 of these Regulations if the chief officer of that force complies with a requirement under regulation 12(3) (co-operation, assistance and information) that is made in connection with—

(i) an investigation relating to the conduct of a person who, at the time of the conduct, was a Commissioner or an officer, or

(ii) an investigation of a DSI matter in relation to which the relevant officer was, at the time of the death or serious injury, an officer; and

(*b*) assistance is required to be provided in such a connection by a police force to the IPCC if the chief officer of that force complies with a requirement under regulation 12(6) that is made in connection with—

(i) an investigation relating to the conduct of a person who, at the time of the conduct, was a Commissioner or an officer, or

(ii) an investigation of a DSI matter in relation to which the relevant officer was, at the time of the death or serious injury, an officer.

(3) Where the assistance is required to be provided by a police force, the appropriate authority shall pay to the [local policing body][1] maintaining that force such contribution towards the costs of the assistance—

(*a*) as may be agreed between them; or

(*b*) in the absence of an agreement, as may be determined in accordance with any arrangements which—

(i) have been agreed to by [local policing bodies][1] generally and the Commissioners, and

(ii) are for the time being in force with respect to the making of contributions towards the costs of assistance provided, in connection with investigations under Part 6 of these Regulations; or

(*c*) in the absence of any such arrangements, as may be determined by the Secretary of State.

(4) Paragraph (3) shall have effect in relation to assistance which a police force provides by agreement under regulation 46(2) as if the reference in that paragraph to required to be provided were a reference to provided by agreement under regulation 46(2).

(5) Where the assistance is required to be provided by a police force to the IPCC, the IPCC shall pay to the [local policing body][1] maintaining the assisting force such contribution (if any) towards the costs of the assistance—

(*a*) as may be agreed between the IPCC and that authority; or

(*b*) in the absence of an agreement, as may be determined in accordance with any arrangements which—

(i) have been agreed to by [local policing bodies][1] generally and by the IPCC, and

(ii) are for the time being in force with respect to the making of contributions towards the costs of assistance provided, in connection with investigations under this Part, to the IPCC; or

(*c*) in the absence of any such arrangements, as may be determined by the Secretary of State.

Amendments—[1] In paras (3) and (5), words substituted, and in paras 3(*b*)(*I*) and 5(*b*)(*I*), words substituted, by the Revenue and Customs (Complaints and Misconduct) (Amendment) Regulations, SI 2011/3061 reg 2 with effect from 16 January 2012.

PART 3
HANDLING OF COMPLAINTS AND CONDUCT MATTERS ETC

17 Duties to preserve evidence relating to complaints

(1) This regulation applies where condition A or B is met.

(2) Condition A is that—

(*a*) a complaint is made to an appropriate authority about the conduct of an individual, and

(*b*) that authority is the appropriate authority in relation to that individual.

(3) Condition B is that—

(*a*) an appropriate authority becomes aware that a complaint has been made to the IPCC, and

(*b*) that authority is the appropriate authority in relation to that individual.

(4) The appropriate authority shall take all such steps as appear to that authority to be appropriate for the purposes of these Regulations for obtaining and preserving evidence relating to the conduct complained of.

(5) The duty of the appropriate authority under paragraph (4) must be performed as soon as practicable after the complaint is made or after it becomes aware of the complaint.

(6) After that, the appropriate authority shall be under a duty, until it is satisfied that it is no longer necessary to do so, to continue to take the steps from time to time appearing to that authority to be appropriate for the purposes of these Regulations for obtaining and preserving evidence relating to the conduct complained of.

(7) It shall be the duty of the appropriate authority to take all such specific steps for obtaining or preserving evidence relating to any conduct that is the subject-matter of a complaint as it may be directed by the IPCC to take for the purposes of this regulation.

18 Delegation of powers and duties

(1) Subject to paragraph (3), the appropriate authority may delegate all or any of the powers or duties conferred or imposed on it by or under these Regulations to a person mentioned in paragraph (2).

(2) Those powers or duties may be delegated—

(*a*) in the case of the Head of the Home Civil Service, to a member of the Senior Civil Service;

(*b*) in the case of the Chief Executive, to a member of the Senior Civil Service employed in the service of the Commissioners;

(*c*) in the case of a Commissioner (other than the Chief Executive), to an officer.

(3) The appropriate authority shall not, in any particular case, delegate any power or duty under paragraph (1) to a person who has acted as investigating officer in that case.

19 Initial handling and recording of complaints

(1) Where a complaint is made to the IPCC—

(*a*) it shall ascertain whether the complainant is content for the appropriate authority to be notified of the complaint, and

(*b*) it shall give notification of the complaint to the appropriate authority if, and only if, the complainant is so content.

(2) Where a complaint is made to an appropriate authority, the authority shall—

(*a*) determine whether or not it is the appropriate authority in relation to the complaint, and

(*b*) if it determines that it is not, give notification of the complaint to the appropriate authority for the individual complained against.

(3) Where the IPCC—

(*a*) is prevented by paragraph (1)(*b*) from notifying any complaint to the appropriate authority, and

(*b*) considers that it is in the public interest for the subject-matter of the complaint to be brought to the attention of the appropriate authority and recorded under regulation 24,

the IPCC may bring that matter to the appropriate authority's attention under that regulation as if it were a recordable conduct matter, and (if it does so) the following provisions of these Regulations shall have effect accordingly as if it were such a matter.

(4) Where the IPCC or the appropriate authority gives notification of a complaint under paragraph (1) or (2) or the IPCC brings any matter to the appropriate authority's attention under paragraph (3), the person who gave the notification or, as the case may be, the IPCC shall notify the complainant—

(*a*) that the notification has been given and of what it contained, or

(*b*) that the matter has been brought to the appropriate authority's attention to be dealt with otherwise than as a complaint.

(5) Where—

(*a*) an appropriate authority, in the case of any complaint made to it, decides that it is the appropriate authority, or

(*b*) a complaint is notified to the appropriate authority under this regulation,

the appropriate authority shall record the complaint.

(6) Nothing in this regulation shall require the notification or recording by any person of any complaint about any conduct if—

(*a*) that person is satisfied that the subject-matter of the complaint has been, or is already being, dealt with by means of criminal or disciplinary proceedings against the person whose conduct it was, or

(*b*) the complaint has been withdrawn.

20 Keeping of records

The appropriate authority shall keep records, in such form as the IPCC shall determine, of—

(*a*) every complaint and purported complaint that is made to it;

(*b*) every conduct matter recorded by it under regulation 23(3) (conduct matters arising in civil proceedings);

(*c*) every DSI matter recorded by it under regulation 32 (duty to record DSI matters);

(*d*) every exercise of a power or performance of a duty under these Regulations.

21 Failures to notify or record a complaint

(1) This regulation applies where anything which is or purports to be a complaint in relation to which regulation 19 (initial handling and recording of complaints) has effect is received by the Head of the Home Civil Service, the Chief Executive or the Commissioners (other than the Chairman, the Chief Executive and the Permanent Secretary) (whether in consequence of having been made directly or of a notification under that regulation).

(2) Where the Head of the Home Civil Service, the Chief Executive or the Commissioners (other than the Chairman, the Chief Executive and the Permanent Secretary) decides or decide not to take action under regulation 19 for notifying or recording the whole or any part of what has been received, the Head of the Home Civil Service, the Chief Executive or the Commissioners (other than the Chairman, the Chief Executive and the Permanent Secretary) shall notify the complainant of the following matters—

(*a*) the decision to take no action, and, if that decision relates to only part of what was received, the part in question;

(*b*) the grounds on which the decision was made; and

(*c*) whether the complainant has a right to appeal against that decision under this regulation.

(3) The complainant shall have a right of appeal to the IPCC against any failure by the Head of the Home Civil Service, the Chief Executive or the Commissioners (other than the Chairman, the Chief Executive and the Permanent Secretary) to make a determination under regulation 19 or to notify or record anything under that regulation if, but only if, the failure is in respect of conduct which the Head of the Home Civil Service, the Chief Executive or the Commissioners (other than the Chairman, the Chief Executive and the Permanent Secretary) is required to refer to the IPCC under regulation 28(1)(*a*) or (*b*) (reference of complaints to the IPCC).

(4) On an appeal under this regulation, the IPCC shall—

(*a*) determine whether any action under regulation 19 should have been taken in the case in question, and

(*b*) if the IPCC finds in the complainant's favour, give to the Head of the Home Civil Service, the Chief Executive or the Commissioners (other than the Chairman, the Chief Executive and the Permanent Secretary) such directions as the IPCC considers appropriate, as to the action to be taken for making a determination, or for notifying or recording what was received,

and it shall be the duty of the Head of the Home Civil Service, the Chief Executive or the Commissioners (other than the Chairman, the Chief Executive and the Permanent Secretary) to comply with any directions given under sub-paragraph (*b*).

(5) Directions under paragraph (4)(*b*) may require action taken in pursuance of the directions to be treated as taken in accordance with any such provision of regulation 19 as may be specified in the direction.

(6) The IPCC—

(*a*) shall give notification both to the Head of the Home Civil Service, the Chief Executive or the Commissioners (other than the Chairman, the Chief Executive and the Permanent Secretary), as the case may be, and to the complainant, of any determination made by it under this regulation, and

(*b*) shall give notification to the complainant of any direction given by it to the Head of the Home Civil Service, the Chief Executive or the Commissioners (other than the Chairman, the Chief Executive and the Permanent Secretary) under this regulation.

22 Handling of complaints by the appropriate authority

(1) This regulation applies where a complaint has been recorded by the appropriate authority unless the complaint—

(*a*) is one which has been, or must be, referred to the IPCC under regulation 28 (reference of complaints to the IPCC), and

(*b*) is not for the time being either referred back to the authority under regulation 29 (duties of the IPCC on references under regulation 28) or the subject of a determination under regulation 38 (power of the IPCC to determine the form of an investigation).

(2) The appropriate authority shall not be required by virtue of any provisions of these Regulations to take any action in relation to the complaint but may handle the complaint in whatever manner it thinks fit, or take no action in relation to the complaint.

23 Conduct matters arising in civil proceedings

(1) This regulation applies where—

(*a*) the appropriate authority has received notification (whether or not under this regulation) that civil proceedings relating to any matter have been brought by a member of the public against it, or it otherwise appears to the appropriate authority that such proceedings are likely to be so brought, and

(*b*) it appears to the appropriate authority (whether at the time of the notification or at any time subsequently) that those proceedings involve or would involve a conduct matter.

(2) The appropriate authority—

(*a*) shall consider whether it is the appropriate authority in relation to the conduct matter in question, and

(*b*) if it is not, shall notify the person who is the appropriate authority about the proceedings, or the proposal to bring them, and about the circumstances that make it appear as mentioned in paragraph (1)(*b*).

(3) Where the appropriate authority determines for the purposes of this regulation that it is the appropriate authority in relation to any conduct matter, it shall record that matter.

(4) Where the appropriate authority records any matter under this regulation it—

(*a*) shall first determine whether the matter is one which it is required to refer to the IPCC under regulation 30 (reference of conduct matters to the IPCC) or is one which it would be appropriate so to refer, and

(*b*) if it is not required so to refer the matter and does not do so, may deal with the matter in such other manner (if any) as it may determine.

(5) Nothing in paragraph (3) shall require the appropriate authority to record any conduct matter if it is satisfied that the matter has been, or is already being, dealt with by means of criminal or disciplinary proceedings against the person to whose conduct the matter relates.

(6) For the purposes of this regulation civil proceedings involve a conduct matter if—

(*a*) they relate to such a matter, or

(*b*) they are proceedings that relate to a matter in relation to which a conduct matter, or evidence of a conduct matter, is or may be relevant.

24 Recording etc of conduct matters in other cases

(1) Where—

(*a*) a conduct matter comes (otherwise than as mentioned in regulation 23 (conduct matters arising in civil proceedings)) to the attention of the appropriate authority in relation to that matter, and

(*b*) it appears to the appropriate authority that the conduct involved in that matter falls within paragraph (2),

it shall be the duty of the appropriate authority to record that matter.

(2) Conduct falls within this paragraph if (assuming it to have taken place)—

(*a*) it appears to have resulted in the death of any person or in serious injury to any person;

(*b*) a member of the public has been adversely affected by it; or

(*c*) it is of a description specified in paragraph (3).

(3) The following descriptions of conduct are specified for the purposes of paragraph (2)—

(*a*) a serious assault, as defined in guidance issued by the IPCC;

(*b*) a serious sexual offence, as defined in guidance issued by the IPCC;

(*c*) serious corruption, as defined in guidance issued by the IPCC;
(*d*) a criminal offence or behaviour liable to result in disciplinary proceedings which was aggravated by discriminatory behaviour on the grounds of a person's race, sex, religion, or other status identified in guidance by the IPCC;
(*e*) a relevant offence;
(*f*) conduct whose gravity or other exceptional circumstances make it appropriate to record the matter in which the conduct is involved; or
(*g*) conduct which is alleged to have taken place in the same incident as one in which conduct within sub-paragraphs (*a*) to (*e*) is alleged.

(4) Where the appropriate authority records any matter under this regulation it—
(*a*) shall first determine whether the matter is one which it is required to refer to the IPCC under regulation 30 (reference of conduct matters to the IPCC) or is one which it would be appropriate to so refer, and
(*b*) if it is not required so to refer the matter and does not do so, may deal with the matter in such other manner (if any) as it may determine.

(5) Nothing in paragraph (1) shall require the appropriate authority to record any conduct matter if it is satisfied that the matter has been, or is already being, dealt with by means of criminal or disciplinary proceedings against the person to whose conduct the matter relates.

(6) If it appears to the IPCC—
(*a*) that any matter that has come to its attention is a recordable conduct matter, but
(*b*) that that matter has not been recorded by the appropriate authority,

the IPCC may direct the appropriate authority to record that matter; and it shall be the duty of that authority to comply with the direction.

25 Duties to preserve evidence relating to conduct matters

(1) Where the appropriate authority becomes aware of any recordable matter relating to the conduct of an individual, it shall be the duty of that authority to take all such steps as appear to it to be appropriate for the purposes of these Regulations for obtaining and preserving the evidence relating to that matter.

(2) The duty of the appropriate authority under paragraph (1) must be performed as soon as practicable after it becomes aware of the matter in question.

(3) After that, the appropriate authority shall be under a duty until it is satisfied that it is no longer necessary to do so, to continue to take the steps from time to time appearing to it to be appropriate for the purposes of these Regulations for obtaining and preserving evidence relating to the matter.

(4) It shall be the duty of the appropriate authority to take all such specific steps for obtaining or preserving evidence relating to any recordable conduct matter, as it may be directed by the IPCC to take for the purposes of these Regulations.

26 Complaints against a person who has subsequently ceased to serve with HMRC

Where a complaint or conduct matter relates to the conduct of a person who has ceased to be a Commissioner or an officer since the time of the conduct, these Regulations shall apply in relation to such person as if they did not include any requirement for an appropriate authority to determine whether disciplinary proceedings should be brought against a person whose conduct is reported to the appropriate authority.

PART 4
REFERRAL OF MATTERS TO THE IPCC

27 Recording and reference of conduct and DSI matters

(1) Any conduct matter which is required to be referred to the IPCC shall be referred in such manner as the IPCC specifies and—
(*a*) if the matter falls within paragraph (1)(*a*) or (*b*) of regulation 30, not later than the end of the day following the day on which it first becomes clear to the appropriate authority that the conduct matter is one to which that paragraph applies, and
(*b*) if the matter falls within paragraph (1)(*c*) of that regulation, not later than the end of the day following the day on which the IPCC notifies the appropriate authority that the conduct matter is to be referred.

(2) Any DSI matter which is required to be referred to the IPCC shall be referred in such manner as the IPCC specifies and—
(*a*) in a case where the IPCC directs that the matter be referred to it, within time limits defined in guidance issued by the IPCC, but no later than the end of the day following the day on which the IPCC so directs;
(*b*) in any other case, within time limits defined in guidance issued by the IPCC, but no later than the end of the day following the day on which the matter first comes to the attention of the appropriate authority.

28 Reference of complaints to the IPCC

(1) It shall be the duty of the appropriate authority to refer a complaint to the IPCC where the complaint is—

(*a*) one alleging that the conduct complained of has resulted in death or serious injury;

(*b*) any complaint not falling within paragraph (*a*) but alleging conduct which constitutes—

(i) a serious assault, as defined in guidance issued by the IPCC;

(ii) a serious sexual offence, as defined in guidance issued by the IPCC;

(iii) serious corruption, as defined in guidance issued by the IPCC;

(iv) a criminal offence or behaviour which is liable to lead to a disciplinary sanction and which in either case was aggravated by discriminatory behaviour on the grounds of a person's race, sex, religion, or other status identified in guidance by the IPCC;

(v) a relevant offence;

(*c*) a complaint which arises from the same incident as one in which any conduct falling within paragraph (*a*) or (*b*) is alleged; or

(*d*) one in respect of which the IPCC notifies the appropriate authority that it requires the complaint in question to be referred to the IPCC for its consideration.

(2) The obligation on the Head of the Home Civil Service under paragraph (1)(*a*) or (*b*) to refer a complaint about the conduct of a person in respect of whom the Head of the Home Civil Service is the appropriate authority arises only if the Head of the Home Civil Service is satisfied that the complaint contains an indication that a criminal offence may have been committed by that person.

(3) The obligation on the Chief Executive or the Commissioners (other than the Chairman, the Chief Executive and the Permanent Secretary for Tax) under paragraph (1)(*a*) or (*b*) to refer a complaint about the conduct of a person in respect of whom the Chief Executive is or the Commissioners are the appropriate authority arises only if the Chief Executive is or the Commissioners are satisfied that the complaint contains an indication that the person may have—

(*a*) committed a criminal offence, or

(*b*) behaved in a manner which would justify the bringing of disciplinary proceedings and that such behaviour (if it had taken place) would be likely to lead to the termination of that person's office or employment.

(4) In a case where there is no obligation under paragraph (1) to make a reference, the appropriate authority may refer a complaint to the IPCC if that authority considers that it would be appropriate to do so by reason of—

(*a*) the gravity of the subject-matter of the complaint; or

(*b*) any exceptional circumstances.

(5) In a case in which a reference under paragraph (1) or (4) is neither made nor required to be made, the Head of the Home Civil Service may refer a complaint to the IPCC if—

(*a*) it is one in relation to which the Chief Executive is the appropriate authority; and

(*b*) the Head of the Home Civil Service considers that it would be appropriate to do so by reason of—

(i) the gravity of the subject-matter of the complaint, or

(ii) any exceptional circumstances.

(6) Where a complaint is required to be referred to the IPCC under paragraph (1)(*a*), (*b*) or (*c*), notification of the complaint shall be given to the IPCC—

(*a*) not later than the end of the day following the day on which it first becomes clear to the appropriate authority that the complaint is one to which that sub-paragraph applies, and

(*b*) in such manner as the IPCC specifies.

(7) Where a complaint is required to be referred to the IPCC under paragraph (1)(*d*), notification of the complaint shall be given to the IPCC—

(*a*) not later than the end of the day following the day on which the IPCC notifies the appropriate authority that the complaint is to be referred, and

(*b*) in such manner as the IPCC specifies.

(8) Subject to paragraph (10), the power—

(*a*) of the IPCC by virtue of paragraph (1)(*d*) to require a complaint to be referred to it, and

(*b*) of the appropriate authority to refer a complaint to the IPCC under paragraph (2) or (3),

shall each be exercisable at any time irrespective of whether the complaint is already being investigated by any person or has already been considered by the IPCC.

(9) Where the appropriate authority refers a complaint to the IPCC under this regulation it shall give a notification of the making of the reference—

(*a*) to the complainant, and

(*b*) except in a case where it appears to the appropriate authority that to do so might prejudice a possible future investigation of the complaint, to the person complained against.

(10) A complaint that has already been referred to the IPCC under this regulation on a previous occasion—

(*a*) shall not be required to be referred again under this regulation unless the IPCC so directs, and (*b*) shall not be referred in exercise of any power conferred by this regulation unless the IPCC consents.

29 Duties of the IPCC on references under regulation 28

(1) It shall be the duty of the IPCC, in the case of every complaint referred to it by the appropriate authority, to determine whether or not it is necessary for the complaint to be investigated.
(2) Where the IPCC determines under this regulation that it is not necessary for a complaint to be investigated, it may, if it thinks fit, refer the complaint back to the appropriate authority in accordance with paragraph (3).
(3) In a case to which paragraph (2) applies, the appropriate authority shall not be required by virtue of any provisions of these Regulations to take any action in relation to the complaint but may handle the complaint in whatever manner it thinks fit, or take no action in relation to the complaint.
(4) Where the IPCC refers a complaint back under paragraph (2), it shall give a notification of the making of the reference back—

(*a*) to the complainant, and
(*b*) to the person complained against.

30 Reference of conduct matters to the IPCC

(1) It shall be the duty of the appropriate authority to refer a recordable conduct matter to the IPCC (whether or not the case falls within regulation 23), if—

(*a*) that matter relates to any incident or circumstances in or in consequence of which any person has died or suffered serious injury;
(*b*) that matter is of a description specified in paragraph (2); or
(*c*) the IPCC notifies the appropriate authority that it requires that matter to be referred to the IPCC for its consideration.

(2) Any matter which relates to conduct falling within the following descriptions is specified for the purposes of paragraph (1)(*b*)—

(*a*) a serious assault, as defined in guidance issued by the IPCC;
(*b*) a serious sexual offence, as defined in guidance issued by the IPCC;
(*c*) serious corruption, as defined in guidance issued by the IPCC;
(*d*) a criminal offence or behaviour which is liable to lead to a disciplinary sanction and which in either case was aggravated by discriminatory behaviour on the grounds of a person's race, sex, religion, or other status identified in guidance issued by the IPCC;
(*e*) a relevant offence; or
(*f*) conduct which is alleged to have taken place in the same incident as one in which conduct within sub-paragraphs (*a*) to (*e*) is alleged.

(3) The obligation on the Head of the Home Civil Service under paragraph (1)(*a*) or (*b*) to refer a recordable conduct matter in respect of a person for whom the Head of the Home Civil Service is the appropriate authority arises only if the Head of the Home Civil Service is satisfied that the matter is one in respect of which there is an indication that a criminal offence may have been committed by that person.
(4) The obligation on the appropriate authority under paragraph (1)(*a*) or (*b*) to refer a recordable conduct matter in respect of a person for whom it is the appropriate authority arises only if it is satisfied that the matter is one in respect of which there is an indication that the person may have—

(*a*) committed a criminal offence, or
(*b*) behaved in a manner which would justify the bringing of disciplinary proceedings and that such behaviour (if it had taken place) would be likely to lead to the termination of that person's office or employment.

(5) In any case where there is no obligation under paragraph (1) to make a reference, the appropriate authority may refer a recordable conduct matter to the IPCC if that authority considers that it would be appropriate to do so by reason of—

(*a*) the gravity of the matter, or
(*b*) any exceptional circumstances.

(6) In a case in which a reference under paragraph (1) or (5) is neither made nor required to be made, the Head of the Home Civil Service may refer any recordable conduct matter to the IPCC if—

(*a*) it is one in relation to which the Chief Executive is the appropriate authority, and
(*b*) the Head of the Home Civil Service considers that it would be appropriate to do so by reason of—
  (i) the gravity of the matter, or
  (ii) any exceptional circumstances.

(7) Where there is an obligation under this regulation to refer any matter to the IPCC, it must be so referred within such period as may be provided for by regulation 27.
(8) Subject to paragraph (10), the power—

(*a*) of the IPCC by virtue of paragraph (1)(*c*) to require a matter to be referred to it, and
(*b*) of the appropriate authority to refer any matter to the IPCC under paragraph (5) or (6),

shall each be exercisable at any time irrespective of whether the matter is already being investigated by any person or has already been considered by the IPCC.

(9) Where—

(*a*) the appropriate authority refers a matter to the IPCC under this regulation, and

(*b*) it does not consider that to do so might prejudice a possible future investigation of that matter,

it shall give a notification of the making of the reference to the person to whose conduct that matter relates.

(10) A matter that has already been referred to the IPCC under this regulation on a previous occasion—

(*a*) shall not be required to be referred again under this regulation unless the IPCC so directs, and

(*b*) shall not be referred in exercise of any power conferred by this regulation unless the IPCC consents.

31 Duties of the IPCC on references under regulation 30

(1) It shall be the duty of the IPCC, in the case of every recordable conduct matter referred to it by the appropriate authority under regulation 30, to determine whether or not it is necessary for the matter to be investigated.

(2) Where the IPCC determines under this regulation that it is not necessary for a recordable conduct matter referred by the appropriate authority to be investigated, it may if it thinks fit refer the matter back to the appropriate authority to be dealt with by it in such manner (if any) as the appropriate authority may determine.

(3) Where—

(*a*) the IPCC refers a matter back to the appropriate authority under this regulation, and

(*b*) the IPCC does not consider that to do so might prejudice a possible future investigation of that matter,

the IPCC shall give a notification of the making of the reference to the person to whose conduct that matter relates.

PART 5
HANDLING DEATH AND SERIOUS INJURY (DSI)

32 Duty to record DSI matters

(1) Where a DSI matter comes to the attention of the appropriate authority, it shall be the duty of the appropriate authority to record that matter.

(2) If it appears to the IPCC—

(*a*) that any matter that has come to its attention is a DSI matter, but

(*b*) that that matter has not been recorded by the appropriate authority,

the IPCC may direct the appropriate authority to record that matter; and it shall be the duty of that authority to comply with the direction.

33 Duty to preserve evidence relating to DSI matters

(1) Where a DSI matter comes to the attention of the appropriate authority it shall be the duty of that authority to take all such steps as appear to it to be appropriate for the purposes of these Regulations for obtaining and preserving evidence relating to that matter.

(2) The duty of the appropriate authority under paragraph (1) must be performed as soon as practicable after it becomes aware of the matter in question.

(3) After that, the appropriate authority shall be under a duty to continue to take the steps from time to time appearing to it to be appropriate for the purposes of these Regulations for obtaining and preserving evidence relating to the matter, until it is satisfied that it is no longer necessary to do so.

(4) It shall be the duty of the appropriate authority to take all such specific steps for obtaining or preserving evidence relating to any DSI matter as it may be directed to take for the purposes of this regulation by the IPCC.

34 Reference of DSI matters to the IPCC

(1) It shall be the duty of the appropriate authority to refer a DSI matter to the IPCC.

(2) The appropriate authority must do so within the period specified in regulation 27(2) (recording and reference of conduct matters).

(3) A matter that has already been referred to the IPCC under this regulation on a previous occasion shall not be required to be referred again under this regulation unless the IPCC so directs.

35 Duties of IPCC on references under regulation 34

(1) It shall be the duty of the IPCC, in the case of every DSI matter referred to it by the appropriate authority, to determine whether or not it is necessary for the matter to be investigated.

(2) Where the IPCC determines under this regulation that it is not necessary for a DSI matter to be investigated, it may if it thinks fit refer the matter back to the appropriate authority to be dealt with by it in such manner (if any) as the appropriate authority may determine.

36 Procedure where conduct matter is revealed during investigation of DSI matter

(1) If during the course of an investigation of a DSI matter it appears to a person designated under regulation 47 or 48 or appointed to undertake an investigation under the management of the IPCC under regulation 46, that there is an indication that the person whose conduct is in question may have—

(*a*) committed a criminal offence, or

(*b*) behaved in a manner which would justify the bringing of disciplinary proceedings,

the person so appointed shall make a submission to that effect to the IPCC.

(2) If, after considering a submission under paragraph (1), the IPCC determines that there is such an indication, it shall—

(*a*) notify the appropriate authority in relation to the DSI matter and (if different) the appropriate authority in relation to the person whose conduct is in question of its determination, and

(*b*) send to it (or each of them) a copy of the submission under paragraph (1).

(3) If during the course of an investigation of a DSI matter it appears to a person appointed under regulation 44 or 45 or appointed to undertake an investigation under the supervision of the IPCC under regulation 46, that there is an indication that the person whose conduct is in question may have—

(*a*) committed a criminal offence, or

(*b*) behaved in a manner which would justify the bringing of disciplinary proceedings,

the person so appointed shall make a submission to that effect to the appropriate authority in relation to the DSI matter.

(4) If, after considering a submission under paragraph (3), the appropriate authority determines that there is such an indication, it shall—

(*a*) if it is not the appropriate authority in relation to the person whose conduct is in question, notify that other authority of its determination and send to that authority a copy of the submission under paragraph (3), and

(*b*) notify the IPCC of its determination and send to it a copy of the submission under paragraph (3).

(5) Where the appropriate authority in relation to the person whose conduct is in question—

(*a*) is notified of a determination by the IPCC under paragraph (2),

(*b*) (in a case where it is also the appropriate authority in relation to the DSI matter) makes a determination under paragraph (4), or

(*c*) (in a case where it is not the appropriate authority in relation to the DSI matter) is notified by that other authority of a determination by it under paragraph (4),

it shall record the matter under regulation 24 (recording etc of conduct matters in other cases) as a conduct matter (and the other provisions of these Regulations shall apply in relation to that matter accordingly).

(6) Where a DSI matter is recorded under regulation 24 as a conduct matter by virtue of paragraph (5)—

(*a*) the person investigating the DSI matter shall (subject to any determination made by the IPCC under regulation 38(6)) continue the investigation as if appointed or designated to investigate the conduct matter, and

(*b*) the other provisions of these Regulations shall apply in relation to that matter accordingly.

PART 6
INVESTIGATIONS

37 Inspections of HMRC premises on behalf of the IPCC

(1) Where—

(*a*) the IPCC requires the Commissioners to allow a person nominated for the purpose by the IPCC to have access to any premises occupied for the purposes of HMRC and to documents and other things on those premises, and

(*b*) the requirement is imposed for any of the purposes mentioned in paragraph (2),

it shall be the duty of the Commissioners to secure that the required access is allowed to the nominated person.

(2) Those purposes are—

(*a*) the purposes of any examination by the IPCC of the efficiency and effectiveness of the arrangements made by the Commissioners for handling complaints or dealing with recordable conduct matters or DSI matters;

(*b*) the purposes of any investigation by the IPCC under this Part or of any investigation carried out under its supervision or management.

(3) A requirement imposed under this regulation for the purposes mentioned in paragraph (2)(*a*) must be notified to the Commissioners at least 48 hours before the time at which access is required.

(4) Where—

(*a*) a requirement imposed under this regulation for the purposes mentioned in paragraph (2)(*a*) requires access to any premises, document or thing to be allowed to any person, but

(*b*) there are reasonable grounds for not allowing that person to have the required access at the time at which that person seeks to have it,

the obligation to secure that the required access is allowed shall have effect as an obligation to secure that the access is allowed to that person at the earliest practicable time after there cease to be any such grounds as that person may specify.

(5) The provisions of this regulation are in addition to, and without prejudice to—

(*a*) the rights of entry, search and seizure that are or may be conferred on—

(i) a person designated for the purposes of regulation 48 (investigations by the IPCC itself), or

(ii) any person who otherwise acts on behalf of the IPCC,

in that person's capacity as a constable or as a person with the powers and privileges of a constable; or

(*b*) the obligations of the Commissioners under regulations 12 (co-operation, assistance and information) and 53 (provision of information to the IPCC).

38 Power of the IPCC to determine the form of an investigation

(1) This regulation applies where—

(*a*) a complaint or recordable conduct matter or DSI matter is referred to the IPCC; and

(*b*) the IPCC determines that it is necessary for the complaint or matter to be investigated.

(2) It shall be the duty of the IPCC to determine the form which the investigation shall take.

(3) In making a determination under paragraph (2) the IPCC shall have regard to the seriousness of the case and the public interest.

(4) The only forms which the investigation may take in accordance with a determination made under this regulation are—

(*a*) an investigation by the appropriate authority on its own behalf;

(*b*) an investigation by the appropriate authority under the supervision of the IPCC;

(*c*) an investigation by a police force under the supervision of the IPCC;

(*d*) an investigation by the appropriate authority under the management of the IPCC;

(*e*) an investigation by a police force under the management of the IPCC;

(*f*) an investigation by the IPCC.

(5) An investigation under this regulation relating to any conduct of the Commissioners may only be carried out in the form specified in paragraph (4)(*c*), (4)(*e*) or (4)(*f*).

(6) The IPCC may at any time make a further determination under this regulation to replace an earlier one.

(7) Where a determination under this regulation replaces an earlier determination under this regulation, or relates to a complaint or matter in relation to which the appropriate authority has already begun an investigation on its own behalf, the IPCC may give—

(*a*) the appropriate authority, and

(*b*) any person previously appointed to carry out the investigation,

such directions as it considers appropriate for the purpose of giving effect to the new determination.

(8) It shall be the duty of a person to whom a direction is given under paragraph (7) to comply with it.

(9) The IPCC shall notify the appropriate authority of any determination that it makes under this regulation in relation to a particular complaint or recordable conduct matter or DSI matter.

39 Appointment of persons to carry out investigations

No person shall be appointed to carry out an investigation under regulation 44, 45, 46 or 47—

(*a*) unless that person has an appropriate level of knowledge, skills and experience to plan and manage the investigation;

(*b*) if that person's involvement could reasonably give rise to a concern as to whether that person could act impartially under these Regulations; or

(*c*) if that person works, directly or indirectly, under the management of the person whose conduct is being investigated.

40 Power of the IPCC to impose requirements in relation to an investigation which it is supervising

(1) For the purposes of regulation 45(6) the requirements which may be imposed by the IPCC on a person appointed to investigate a complaint, recordable conduct matter or DSI matter are, subject to paragraphs (2) and (3), any reasonable requirements as to the conduct of the investigation as appear to the IPCC to be necessary.

(2) Where at any stage of an investigation of a complaint, recordable conduct matter or DSI matter the possibility of criminal proceedings arises, the IPCC shall not, under paragraph (1), impose any requirement relating to the obtaining or preservation of evidence of a criminal offence without first obtaining the [consent of the Director of Public Prosecutions to the imposition of any such requirement.][1]

(3) The IPCC shall not, under paragraph (1), impose any requirement relating to the resources to be made available by the appropriate authority, for the purposes of an investigation, without first consulting it and having regard to any representations it may make.

Amendments—[1] In para (2), words substituted by the Public Bodies (Merger of the Director of Public Prosecutions and the Director of Revenue and Customs Prosecutions) Order, SI 2014/834 art 3(3), Sch 3 paras 30, 31 with effect from 27 March 2014.

41 Combining and splitting investigations

(1) An appropriate authority which is carrying out an investigation on its own behalf may—

(*a*) combine that investigation with another such investigation, or

(*b*) split that investigation into two or more such separate investigations,

if it considers that it is more efficient and effective, or is otherwise in the public interest, to do so.

(2) Subject to paragraph (3), where the IPCC is supervising, managing or carrying out an investigation, it may—

(*a*) combine that investigation with another investigation, or

(*b*) split that investigation into two or more separate investigations,

if it considers that it is more efficient and effective, or is otherwise in the public interest, to do so.

(3) The IPCC shall not take any action under paragraph (2) in relation to a supervised or managed investigation except after consultation with the appropriate authority.

(4) Nothing in this regulation shall prevent the IPCC from determining—

(*a*) that where an investigation is split into two or more separate investigations, those investigations may take different forms, or

(*b*) that two or more separate investigations which take different forms (including an investigation being carried out by the appropriate authority on its own behalf) may be combined into a single investigation.

42 Power of the IPCC to discontinue an investigation

(1) If, following a determination under regulation 29 (duties of the IPCC on reference under regulation 28), 31 (duties of the IPCC on reference under regulation 30) or 35 (duties of the IPCC on reference under regulation 34), it appears at any time to the IPCC (whether on an application by the appropriate authority or otherwise) that a complaint or matter that is being investigated—

(*a*) by the appropriate authority on its own behalf, or

(*b*) under the supervision or management of the IPCC,

is of a description of complaint or matter specified in paragraph (5), the IPCC may by order require the discontinuance of the investigation.

(2) Where the IPCC makes an order under this regulation or discontinues an investigation being carried out in accordance with regulation 48 (investigations by the IPCC itself), it shall give notification of the discontinuance—

(*a*) to the appropriate authority;

(*b*) to every person entitled to be kept properly informed in relation to the subject matter of the investigation under regulation 55 (duty to provide information for other persons); and

(*c*) in a case where the investigation that is discontinued is an investigation of a complaint, to the complainant.

(3) Where an investigation of a complaint or recordable conduct matter or DSI matter is discontinued in accordance with this regulation—

(*a*) the IPCC may give the appropriate authority directions to do any such things as it is authorised to direct under paragraphs (11) and (12);

(*b*) the IPCC may itself take any such steps of a description specified in regulations so made as it considers appropriate for purposes connected with the discontinuance of the investigation; and

(*c*) subject to the preceding paragraphs, neither the appropriate authority nor the IPCC shall take any further action in accordance with the provisions of these Regulations in relation to that complaint or matter.

(4) The appropriate authority shall comply with any directions given to it under paragraph (3).

(5) The descriptions of complaint or matter are—

(*a*) one in which the complainant refuses to co-operate to the extent that the IPCC considers that it is not reasonably practicable to continue the investigation;

(*b*) one which the IPCC considers is vexatious, oppressive or otherwise an abuse of the procedures for dealing with complaints, conduct matters or DSI matters;

(*c*) one which is repetitious, as defined in paragraph (6); and (*d*) one which the IPCC otherwise considers is such as to make it not reasonably practicable to proceed with the investigation.

(6) A complaint is repetitious only if—

(*a*) it is substantially the same as a previous complaint (whether made by or on behalf of the same or a different complainant), or it concerns substantially the same conduct as a previous conduct matter;

(*b*) it contains no fresh allegations which significantly affect the account of the conduct complained of;

(*c*) no fresh evidence, being evidence which was not reasonably available at the time the previous complaint was made, is tendered in support of it; and

(*d*) as respects the previous complaint or conduct matter, either—

(i) the requirements of regulation 67(9) or 68(11) (determination by the appropriate authority of what action to take) were complied with;

(ii) the IPCC gave the appropriate authority a direction under paragraph (11)(*b*) (requirement to dispense with the requirements of these Regulations); or

(iii) the complainant gave such notification of the withdrawal of the complaint as is mentioned in regulation 43(1)(*a*) (complainant withdraws the complaint).

(7) The cases in which the IPCC is authorised to discontinue an investigation that is being carried out in accordance with regulation 48 are any cases where the complaint, conduct matter or DSI matter under investigation falls within paragraph (5) of this regulation.

(8) Any application by an appropriate authority to the IPCC for an order that it discontinue an investigation shall be in writing and shall be accompanied by—

(*a*) a copy of the complaint, and

(*b*) a memorandum from the appropriate authority containing a summary of the investigation undertaken so far and explaining the reasons for the application to discontinue the investigation.

(9) The appropriate authority shall—

(*a*) send the complainant a copy of any such application on the same day as the day on which the application is sent to the IPCC, and

(*b*) supply any further information requested by the IPCC for the purpose of considering that application.

(10) The IPCC shall not require the discontinuance of an investigation in a case where there has been no application to do so by the appropriate authority unless it has consulted with that authority.

(11) A direction given to an appropriate authority by the IPCC under paragraph (3) may—

(*a*) require the appropriate authority to produce an investigation report on the discontinued investigation under regulation 66 and to take any subsequent steps under these Regulations;

(*b*) where the investigation concerned a complaint, require the appropriate authority to dispense with the requirements of these Regulations as respects that complaint;

(*c*) direct the appropriate authority to handle the matter in whatever manner (if any) that authority thinks fit.

(12) For the purposes of this regulation the steps that may be taken by the IPCC where an investigation is discontinued are—

(*a*) to produce an investigation report on the discontinued investigation and take any subsequent steps required under these Regulations;

(*b*) where the investigation concerned a complaint, to dispense with the requirements of these Regulations as respects that complaint;

(*c*) to handle the matter in whatever manner it thinks fit.

43 Withdrawn and discontinued complaints

(1) If an appropriate authority receives from a complainant notification in writing signed by the complainant or by a solicitor or other authorised agent on the complainant's behalf to the effect either—

(*a*) that the complainant withdraws the complaint, or

(*b*) that the complainant does not wish any further steps to be taken in consequence of the complaint,

the appropriate authority shall forthwith record the withdrawal or the fact that the complainant does not wish any further steps to be taken, as the case may be, and subject to the following provisions of this regulation, the provisions of these Regulations shall cease to apply in respect of that complaint.

(2) Where a complainant gives such notification as is mentioned in paragraph (1) to the IPCC but, so far as is apparent to the IPCC, has not sent that notification to the appropriate authority, then—

(*a*) the IPCC shall send a copy of the notification to the appropriate authority;

(*b*) that appropriate authority shall record the withdrawal or the fact that the complainant does not wish any further steps to be taken, as the case may be; and

(*c*) subject to the following provisions of this regulation, the provisions of these Regulations shall cease to apply in respect of that complaint.

(3) Where a complainant gives such notification as is mentioned in paragraph (1) to an appropriate authority, or where the appropriate authority receives a copy of a notification under paragraph (2), and it relates to a complaint—

- (*a*) which was referred to the IPCC under regulation 28(1) (reference of complaints to the IPCC) and which has not been referred back to the appropriate authority under regulation 29(2);
- (*b*) which the appropriate authority knows is currently the subject of an appeal to the IPCC under regulation 21 (failures to notify or record a complaint), or 74 (appeals to the IPCC with respect to an investigation; or
- (*c*) which was notified to the appropriate authority by the IPCC under regulation 19(1) (initial handling and recording of complaints),

the appropriate authority shall notify the IPCC that it has recorded the withdrawal of the complaint or the fact that the complainant does not wish any further steps to be taken, as the case may be.

(4) In a case falling within paragraph (3)(*a*), the IPCC shall determine whether it is in the public interest for the complaint to be treated as a recordable conduct matter, and shall notify the appropriate authority of its decision.

(5) In a case falling within sub-paragraphs (*b*) or (*c*) of paragraph (3), the appropriate authority shall also—

- (*a*) determine whether it is in the public interest for the complaint to be treated as a recordable conduct matter, and
- (*b*) notify the IPCC of its determination and the reasons for the determination.

(6) Where a determination is made that a complaint is to be treated as a recordable conduct matter, the provisions of these Regulations shall apply to that matter.

(7) Where a complainant gives such notification as is mentioned in paragraph (1) to an appropriate authority, or where an appropriate authority receives a copy of a notification under paragraph (2), and that notification relates to a complaint which does not fall within any of sub-paragraphs (*a*) to (*c*) of paragraph (3)—

- (*a*) the appropriate authority shall determine whether it is in the public interest for the complaint to be treated as a recordable conduct matter;
- (*b*) if the complaint is to be treated as a recordable conduct matter, the provisions of these Regulations shall apply to that matter;
- (*c*) if the complaint is not to be treated as a recordable conduct matter, the provisions of these Regulations shall cease to apply in respect of that complaint.

(8) In a case where—

- (*a*) a complaint has been subjected to an investigation by the appropriate authority on its own behalf;
- (*b*) the complaint is currently subject to an appeal to the IPCC under regulation 74; and
- (*c*) the appropriate authority has notified the IPCC under paragraph (5)(*b*) that it has determined that the complaint is not to be treated as a recordable conduct matter,

the IPCC shall consider whether it is in the public interest for that determination to be reversed, and if so it shall instruct the appropriate authority to reverse the decision.

(9) Where a complainant indicates the wish to withdraw the complaint or the wish that no further steps are to be taken in consequence of the complaint, but the complainant fails to provide a notification to that effect in writing signed by or on behalf of the complainant—

- (*a*) in the case of an indication received by the appropriate authority, the authority shall take the steps set out in paragraph (10);
- (*b*) in the case of an indication received by the IPCC, the IPCC shall refer the matter to the appropriate authority which shall take the steps set out in paragraph (10).

(10) Those steps are—

- (*a*) the appropriate authority shall write to the complainant to ascertain whether the complainant wishes to withdraw the complaint or does not wish any further steps to be taken in consequence of the complaint;
- (*b*) if the complainant indicates the wish to withdraw the complaint or does not wish any further steps to be taken in consequence of the complaint, or if the complainant fails to reply within 21 days from the date of the communication under sub-paragraph (*a*), the appropriate authority shall treat the indication as though it had been received in writing signed by the complainant;
- (*c*) if the complainant indicates the wish not to withdraw the complaint, or the wish that further steps be taken in consequence of the complaint, the appropriate authority shall start or resume the investigation as the case may be.

(11) The appropriate authority shall notify the person complained against if—

- (*a*) it records the withdrawal of a complaint or the fact that the complainant does not wish any further steps to be taken;
- (*b*) it determines that a complaint shall be treated as a recordable conduct matter;
- (*c*) the IPCC determines that a complaint shall be treated as a recordable conduct matter;

(*d*) the IPCC instructs it to reverse a decision not to treat a complaint as a recordable conduct matter; or

(*e*) the provisions of these Regulations cease to apply in respect of a complaint.

(12) But nothing in paragraph (11) shall require the appropriate authority to make a notification if it has previously decided under regulation 61(3) (copies of complaints etc) not to notify the person complained against of the complaint because it is of the opinion that that—

(*a*) might prejudice any criminal investigation or pending proceedings, or

(*b*) would be contrary to the public interest.

44 Investigations by the appropriate authority on its own behalf

(1) This regulation applies where the appropriate authority is required by virtue of any determination made by the IPCC under regulation 38 (power of the IPCC to determine the form of an investigation) to make arrangements for a complaint or recordable conduct matter or DSI matter to be investigated by the appropriate authority on its own behalf.

(2) It shall be the duty of the appropriate authority to appoint an officer to investigate the complaint or matter.

(3) The person to be appointed under this regulation to investigate any DSI matter in relation to which the relevant officer is the Chairman, the Chief Executive or the Permanent Secretary for Tax is the Head of the Home Civil Service.

45 Investigations supervised by the IPCC

(1) This regulation applies where the IPCC has determined that it should supervise the investigation by the appropriate authority of any complaint or recordable conduct matter or DSI matter.

(2) On being given notice of that determination, the appropriate authority shall, if it has not already done so, appoint an officer to investigate the complaint or matter.

(3) The IPCC may require that no appointment is made under paragraph (2) unless it has given notice to the appropriate authority that it approves the person whom that authority proposes to appoint.

(4) Where a person has already been appointed to investigate the complaint or matter, or is selected under this regulation for appointment, and the IPCC is not satisfied with that person, the IPCC may require the appropriate authority, as soon as reasonably practicable after being required to do so—

(*a*) to select another person falling within paragraph (2) to investigate the complaint or matter, and

(*b*) to notify the IPCC of the person selected.

(5) Where a selection made in pursuance of a requirement under paragraph (4) has been notified to the IPCC, the appropriate authority shall appoint that person to investigate the complaint or matter if, but only if, the IPCC notifies the authority that it approves the appointment of that person.

(6) The person appointed to investigate the complaint or matter shall comply with all the requirements of regulation 40.

46 Investigation by a police force under the management or under the supervision of the IPCC

(1) This regulation applies where the IPCC determines that there should be an investigation by a police force under the management or supervision of the IPCC.

(2) The IPCC shall—

(*a*) identify the police force whose force area includes the geographical area to which the subject matter of the complaint, recordable conduct matter or DSI matter most closely relates, and

(*b*) take steps to obtain the agreement of—

(i) the chief officer of police of that force, and

(ii) the appropriate authority,

to the appointment by the IPCC of that force to carry out the investigation.

(3) In the event that no agreement is reached under paragraph (2) the IPCC may require the chief officer of police of any police force it considers appropriate to carry out the investigation.

(4) A chief officer of police of a police force who agrees to or is required to carry out an investigation shall, if that person has not already done so, appoint a person serving with the police who is a member of that force to investigate that complaint or matter.

(5) Paragraphs (3) to (6) of regulation 45 (investigations supervised by the IPCC) shall apply as they apply to an investigation by the appropriate authority which the IPCC has determined is one that it should supervise; and the references to the appropriate authority in those paragraphs shall be treated as references to the chief officer of police concerned.

(6) An appointment of a person under paragraph (4) or (5) shall be notified by the chief of police concerned to the appropriate authority.

(7) The person appointed to investigate the complaint or matter shall, in relation to an investigation under the management of the IPCC, be under the direction and control of the IPCC.

(8) The person appointed to investigate the complaint or matter shall comply with all such requirements in relation to the carrying out of that investigation as may be imposed by these Regulations.

47 Investigations managed by the IPCC

(1) This regulation applies where the IPCC has determined that it should manage the investigation by the appropriate authority of any complaint or recordable conduct matter or DSI matter.

(2) Paragraphs (2) to (5) of regulation 45 shall apply as they apply in the case of an investigation which the IPCC has determined is one that it should supervise.

(3) The person appointed to investigate the complaint or matter shall, in relation to that investigation, be under the direction and control of the IPCC.

48 Investigations by the IPCC itself

(1) This regulation applies where the IPCC has determined that it should itself carry out the investigation of a complaint or recordable conduct matter or DSI matter.

(2) The IPCC shall designate both—

(*a*) a member of the IPCC's staff to take charge of the investigation on behalf of the IPCC, and

(*b*) all such other members of the IPCC's staff as are required by the IPCC to assist that member.

(3) A member of the IPCC's staff who—

(*a*) is designated under paragraph (2) in relation to any investigation, but

(*b*) does not already, by virtue of section 97(8) of the Police Act 1996, have all the powers and privileges of a constable throughout England and Wales and the adjacent United Kingdom waters,

shall, for the purposes of the carrying out of the investigation and all purposes connected with it, have all those powers and privileges throughout England and Wales and those waters.

(4) A member of the IPCC's staff who is not a constable shall not, as a result of paragraph (3), be treated as being in police service for the purposes of—

(*a*) section 280 of the Trade Union and Labour Relations (Consolidation) Act 1992 (person in police service excluded from definitions of "worker" and "employee"); or

(*b*) section 200 of the Employment Rights Act 1996 (certain provisions of that Act not to apply to persons in police service).

(5) References in this regulation to the powers and privileges of a constable—

(*a*) are references to any power or privilege conferred by or under any enactment (including one passed after the making of these Regulations) on a constable; and

(*b*) shall have effect as if every such power were exercisable, and every such privilege existed, throughout England and Wales and the adjacent United Kingdom waters (whether or not that is the case apart from this paragraph).

(6) In this regulation "United Kingdom waters" means the sea and other waters within the seaward limits of the United Kingdom's territorial sea.

49 Relinquishing the IPCC's supervision or management of an investigation

(1) This regulation applies where the IPCC—

(*a*) relinquishes the management of an investigation in favour of a supervised investigation or an investigation by the appropriate authority on its own behalf, or

(*b*) relinquishes the supervision of an investigation in favour of an investigation by the appropriate authority on its own behalf.

(2) The IPCC—

(*a*) shall notify the appropriate authority, the complainant, any interested person within the meaning of regulation 55 (duty to provide information for other persons) and the person complained against of its decision, and the reasons for that decision; and

(*b*) shall send to the appropriate authority any documentation and evidence gathered during its investigations as will assist the appropriate authority to carry out its functions under these Regulations.

(3) But nothing in paragraph (2)(*a*) shall require the IPCC to make a notification to the person complained against if it is of the opinion that that might prejudice any criminal investigation or pending proceedings or would be contrary to the public interest.

50 Circumstances in which an investigation or other procedure may be suspended

(1) Subject to the provisions of this regulation, proceedings under these Regulations shall proceed without delay.

(2) In a case investigated by the IPCC or under the management of the IPCC, the IPCC may suspend any investigation or other procedure under these Regulations which would, if it were to continue, prejudice any criminal proceedings. Before referring a case to misconduct proceedings, the IPCC shall decide whether misconduct proceedings may prejudice any criminal proceedings.

(3) For any period during which the IPCC considers misconduct proceedings would prejudice any criminal proceedings, no such misconduct proceedings shall take place.

(4) Where a witness who is or may be a witness in any criminal proceedings is to be or may be asked to provide evidence in misconduct proceedings, the IPCC shall consult the relevant prosecutor (and when doing so must inform the prosecutor of the names and addresses of all such witnesses) before making a decision under paragraph (2).

(5) For the purposes of this regulation, "relevant prosecutor" means the Director of Public Prosecutions or any other person who has or is likely to have responsibility for criminal proceedings.

(6) In a case under the supervision of the IPCC or undertaken by the appropriate authority on its own behalf, the appropriate authority may, subject to paragraph (7), suspend any investigation or other procedure under these Regulations which would, if it were to continue, prejudice any criminal investigation or proceedings.

(7) The IPCC may direct that any investigation or other procedure under these Regulations which is liable to be suspended under paragraph (6) shall continue if it is of the view that it is in the public interest to make such a direction.

(8) The IPCC shall consult the appropriate authority before making such a direction.

51 Resumption of investigation after criminal proceedings

(1) Where the whole or part of the investigation of a complaint has been suspended until the conclusion of criminal proceedings, and after the conclusion of those proceedings the complainant has failed to express the wish for the investigation to start or to be resumed, the IPCC or, as the case may be, the appropriate authority, shall take the steps set out in paragraph (2).

(2) The IPCC or the appropriate authority shall take all reasonable steps to contact the complainant to ascertain whether the complainant wants the investigation to start or to be resumed as the case may be.

(3) If the complainant expresses the wish for the investigation to start or be resumed, the IPCC or the appropriate authority shall start or resume the investigation as the case may be.

(4) If the complainant indicates that the complainant does not want the investigation to start or to be resumed, or if the complainant fails to reply within 21 days of the date of the letter to the complainant by the IPCC or the appropriate authority, the IPCC or the appropriate authority, as the case may be, shall determine whether it is in the public interest for the complaint to be treated as a recordable conduct matter.

(5) If the IPCC or the appropriate authority determines that it is not in the public interest for the complaint to be treated as a recordable conduct matter, the provisions of these Regulations shall cease to apply to the complaint.

(6) If the IPCC or the appropriate authority determines that it is in the public interest for the complaint to be treated as a recordable conduct matter, it shall be treated as such under these Regulations.

(7) The IPCC or the appropriate authority shall notify the person complained against if paragraph (5) or (6) applies.

(8) But nothing in paragraph (7) shall require the IPCC or the appropriate authority to make a notification if it is of the opinion that that might prejudice any criminal investigation or pending proceedings or would be contrary to the public interest.

52 Restrictions on proceedings pending the conclusion of an investigation

(1) No criminal or disciplinary proceedings shall be brought in relation to any matter which falls to be determined under these Regulations until a report on that investigation has been submitted to the IPCC or to the appropriate authority under regulation 66 (final reports on investigations: complaints, conduct matters and certain DSI matters) or 69 (final reports on investigations: other DSI matters).

(2) Nothing in this regulation shall prevent the bringing of criminal or disciplinary proceedings in respect of any conduct at any time after the discontinuance of the investigation in accordance with the provisions of these Regulations which relate to that conduct.

(3) The restrictions imposed by this regulation in relation to the bringing of criminal proceedings shall not apply to the bringing of criminal proceedings by the Director of Public Prosecutions . . . [1] in any case in which it appears to that person that there are exceptional circumstances which make it undesirable to delay the bringing of such proceedings.

Amendments—[1] In para (3), words revoked by the Public Bodies (Merger of the Director of Public Prosecutions and the Director of Revenue and Customs Prosecutions) Order, SI 2014/834 art 3(3), Sch 3 paras 30, 32 with effect from 27 March 2014.

PART 7
PROVISION OF INFORMATION

53 Provision of information to the IPCC

(1) It shall be the duty of the Commissioners at such times, in such circumstances and in accordance with such other requirements as may be set out in these Regulations, to provide the IPCC with all such information and documents as may be specified or described in these Regulations.

(2) It shall also be the duty of the Commissioners—

(*a*) to provide the IPCC with all such other information and documents specified or described in a notification given by the IPCC to the Commissioners, and (*b*) to produce or deliver up to the IPCC all such evidence and other things so specified or described,

as appear to the IPCC to be required by it for the purposes of the carrying out of any of its functions.

(3) Anything falling to be provided, produced or delivered up by any person in pursuance of a requirement imposed under paragraph (2) must be provided, produced or delivered up in such form, in such manner and within such period as may be specified in—

(*a*) the notification imposing the requirement; or

(*b*) in any subsequent notification given by the IPCC to that person for the purposes of this paragraph.

(4) Nothing in this regulation shall require the Commissioners—

(*a*) to provide the IPCC with any information or document, or to produce or deliver up any other thing, before the earliest time at which it is practicable for the Commissioners to do so; or

(*b*) to provide, produce or deliver up anything at all in a case in which it never becomes practicable for the Commissioners to do so.

(5) A requirement imposed under this regulation may authorise or require information or documents to which it relates to be provided to the IPCC electronically.

54 Duty to keep the complainant informed

(1) Subject to regulation 60, in any case in which there is an investigation of a complaint in accordance with the provisions of these Regulations—

(*a*) by the IPCC, or

(*b*) under its management,

it shall be the duty of the IPCC to provide the complainant with all such information as will keep the complainant properly informed of all the matters specified in paragraph (4) while the investigation is being carried out and subsequently.

(2) Subject to regulation 60, in any case in which there is an investigation of a complaint in accordance with the provisions of these Regulations—

(*a*) by the appropriate authority on its own behalf, or

(*b*) under the supervision of the IPCC,

it shall be the duty of the appropriate authority to provide the complainant with all such information as will keep the complainant properly informed, while the investigation is being carried out and subsequently, of all the matters specified in paragraph (4).

(3) Where paragraph (2) applies, it shall be the duty of the IPCC to give the appropriate authority all such directions as it considers appropriate for securing that that authority complies with its duty under that paragraph; and it shall be the duty of the appropriate authority to comply with any direction so given.

(4) The matters of which the complainant must be kept properly informed are—

(*a*) the progress of the investigation;

(*b*) any provisional findings of the person carrying out the investigation;

(*c*) whether any report has been submitted under regulation 69 (final reports on investigations: other DSI matters);

(*d*) the action (if any) that is taken in respect of the matters dealt with in any such report; and

(*e*) the outcome of any such action.

(5) It shall be the duty of a person appointed to carry out an investigation under these Regulations to provide the IPCC or, as the case may be, the appropriate authority, with all such information as the IPCC or that authority may reasonably require for the purpose of performing its duty under this regulation.

55 Duty to provide information for other persons

(1) A person has an interest in being kept properly informed about the handling of a complaint or recordable conduct matter or DSI matter which is the subject of an investigation in accordance with the provisions of these Regulations if—

(*a*) it appears to the IPCC or to an appropriate authority that that person is a person falling within paragraph (2) or (3); and

(*b*) that person has indicated consent to the provision of information in accordance with this regulation and that consent has not been withdrawn.

(2) A person falls within this paragraph if, in the case of a complaint or recordable conduct matter, that person—

(*a*) is a relative of a person whose death is the alleged result from the conduct complained of or to which the recordable conduct matter relates;

(*b*) is a relative of a person whose serious injury is the alleged result from that conduct and that person is incapable of making a complaint;

(*c*) has suffered serious injury as the alleged result of that conduct.

(3) A person falls within this paragraph if, in the case of a DSI matter, that person—

(*a*) is a relative of the person who has died;

(*b*) is a relative of the person who has suffered serious injury and that person is incapable of making a complaint;

(*c*) is the person who has suffered serious injury.

(4) A person who does not fall within paragraph (2) or (3) has an interest in being kept properly informed about the handling of a complaint, recordable conduct matter or DSI matter if—

(*a*) the IPCC or an appropriate authority considers that that person has an interest in the handling of the complaint, conduct matter or DSI matter which is sufficient to make it appropriate for information to be provided to that person in accordance with this regulation; and

(*b*) that person has indicated consent to the provision of information in accordance with this regulation.

(5) In relation to a complaint, this section confers no rights on the complainant.

(6) A person who has an interest in being kept properly informed about the handling of a complaint, conduct matter or DSI matter is referred to in this regulation as an "interested person".

(7) In any case in which there is an investigation of the complaint, recordable conduct matter or DSI matter in accordance with the provisions of these Regulations—

(*a*) by the IPCC, or

(*b*) under its management,

it shall be the duty of the IPCC to provide the interested person with all such information as will keep the interested person properly informed of all the matters specified in paragraph (10) while the investigation is being carried out and subsequently.

(8) In any case in which there is an investigation of the complaint, recordable conduct matter or DSI matter in accordance with the provisions of these Regulations—

(*a*) by the appropriate authority on its own behalf, or

(*b*) under the supervision of the IPCC,

it shall be the duty of the appropriate authority to provide the interested person with all such information as will keep the interested person properly informed of all the matters specified in paragraph (10) while the investigation is being carried out and subsequently.

(9) Where paragraph (8) applies, it shall be the duty of the IPCC to give the appropriate authority all such directions as it considers appropriate for securing that that authority complies with its duty under that paragraph; and it shall be the duty of the appropriate authority to comply with any direction given to it under this paragraph.

(10) The matters of which the interested person must be kept properly informed are—

(*a*) the progress of the investigation;

(*b*) any provisional findings of the person carrying out the investigation;

(*c*) whether the IPCC or the appropriate authority has made a determination under regulation 36 (procedure where conduct matter is revealed during investigation of a DSI matter);

(*d*) whether any report has been submitted under regulation 66 or 69;

(*e*) the action (if any) that is taken in respect of the matters dealt with in any such report; and

(*f*) the outcome of any such action.

(11) The duties imposed by this regulation on the IPCC and the appropriate authority in relation to any complaint, recordable conduct matter or DSI matter shall be performed in such manner, and shall have effect subject to such exceptions, as may be provided for by regulation 60.

(12) Paragraph (5) of regulation 54 (duty to keep the complainant informed) applies for the purposes of this regulation as it applies for the purposes of that regulation.

(13) In this regulation "relative" means any spouse, partner, parent or adult child.

56 Written notices

(1) If during the course of an investigation of a complaint or matter which falls to be determined under these Regulations it appears to the person investigating that there is an indication that the person whose conduct is in question may have—

(*a*) committed a criminal offence, or

(*b*) behaved in a manner which would justify the bringing of disciplinary proceedings,

the person investigating the complaint or matter must give a notification to the person whose conduct is in question that complies with paragraph (2) .

(2) The notification must—

(*a*) provide sufficient details of the complaint or matter in question so that the person whose conduct is in question may make representations to the person investigating the complaint or matter;

(*b*) give the information about the effect of regulation 57 (duty to consider submissions from the person whose conduct is in question);

(*c*) set out the time limits for providing the person investigating the complaint or matter with relevant statements and relevant documents for the purposes of regulation 57(2);

(*d*) give such information that may be set out in guidance.

(3) Paragraphs (1) and (2) do not apply for so long as the person investigating the complaint or the matter considers that giving the notification might prejudice—

(*a*) the investigation, or
(*b*) any other investigation (including, in particular, a criminal investigation).

(4) In this regulation and regulations 57 and 58, the person whose conduct is in question—
(*a*) in relation to an investigation of a complaint, means the person in respect of whom it appears to the person investigating that there is the indication mentioned in paragraph (1);
(*b*) in relation to an investigation of a recordable conduct matter, means the person to whose conduct the investigation relates.

(5) In this regulation—
(*a*) "relevant document" means—
(i) a document relating to any complaint or matter under investigation, and
(ii) includes such a document containing suggestions as to lines of inquiry to be pursued or witness to be interviewed;
(*b*) "relevant statement" means an oral or written statement relating to any complaint or matter under investigation.

57 Duty to consider submissions from the person whose conduct is in question

(1) This regulation applies where a notification under regulation 56 (written notices) has been issued to the person whose conduct is in question.

(2) If before the expiry of the appropriate time limit notified in pursuance of regulation 56(2)—
(*a*) the person whose conduct is in question provides the person investigating the complaint or matter with a relevant statement or a relevant document, or
(*b*) any person provides the person investigating the complaint or matter with a relevant document,

the person investigating must consider the statement or document.

58 Duty to provide certain information to the appropriate authority

(1) This regulation applies during the course of an investigation under these Regulations.

(2) The person investigating the complaint or matter must supply the appropriate authority with such information in that person's possession as the appropriate authority may reasonably request for the purpose mentioned in paragraph (3).

(3) That purpose is determining whether the person whose conduct is in question should be, or should remain, suspended from duty.

59 Manner in which duties to provide information to the complainant are to be performed

(1) For the purposes of regulations 54(4) (duty to keep the complainant informed) and 55(10) (duty to provide information for other persons), the manner in which the IPCC or, as the case may be, an appropriate authority, shall perform the duties imposed by those regulations is as follows.

(2) The IPCC, in a case falling within regulation 54(1) or 55(7) (investigation of a complaint, conduct matter or DSI matter by or under the management of the IPCC), shall inform the complainant or, as the case may be, the interested person—
(*a*) of the progress of the investigation promptly, and in any event—
(i) if there has been no previous notification, within four weeks of the start of the investigation; and
(ii) in any other case, within four weeks of the previous notification; and
(*b*) of any provisional findings of the person carrying out the investigation as frequently as the IPCC determines to be appropriate in order for the complainant to be kept properly informed.

(3) An appropriate authority, in a case falling within regulation 54(2) (duty to keep the complainant informed or 55(8) (duty to provide information for other persons), shall inform the complainant or the interested person (as the case may be)—
(*a*) of the progress of the investigation promptly and in any event—
(i) if there has been no previous notification, within four weeks of the start of the investigation; and
(ii) in any other case, within four weeks of the previous notification; and
(*b*) of any provisional findings of the person carrying out the investigation as frequently as the appropriate authority determines to be appropriate in order for the complainant to be kept properly informed.

(4) When an investigation has been completed, each complainant and interested person shall be notified—
(*a*) of the date on which the final report under regulation 66 (final reports on investigations: complaints, conduct matters and certain DSI matters) is likely to be submitted; and
(*b*) of the date on which the notification under regulation 67(11) (action by the IPCC in response to an investigation report under regulation 66) or 68(12) (action by the appropriate authority in response to an investigation report under regulation 66) is likely to be given.

(5) In performing the duties imposed by regulations 54(1) and (2), 55(7) and (8), 67(11) and 68(12), the IPCC or, as the case may be, the appropriate authority, shall determine whether it is appropriate to offer, or to accede to a request for, a meeting with a complainant or, as the case may be, an interested person.

(6) As soon as practicable after any such meeting, the IPCC or, as the case may be, the appropriate authority, shall send to the complainant or interested person a written record of the meeting and an account of how any concerns of that person will be addressed.

(7) As soon as practicable after any misconduct hearing or other action that is taken in respect of the matters dealt with in any report submitted under regulation 66, the IPCC or, as the case may be, the appropriate authority, shall notify any complainant and interested person of the outcome of that hearing or action, including the fact and outcome of any appeal against the findings of or sanctions imposed by such a hearing.

(8) If the IPCC or, as the case may be, the appropriate authority, considers that an investigation has made minimal or no progress since the previous notification, then the next notification may be made by any means that in the opinion of the IPCC or, as the case may be, the appropriate authority, is suitable.

60 Exceptions to the duty to keep the complainant informed and to provide information for other persons

(1) Subject to paragraph (2), the duties mentioned in regulation 54(1) and (2) (duty to keep the complainant informed), regulation 55(7) and (8) (duty to provide information for other persons) and in regulations 67(11) and 68(12) shall not apply in circumstances where in the opinion of the IPCC, or, as the case may be, of the appropriate authority, the non-disclosure of information is necessary for the purpose of—

(*a*) preventing the premature or inappropriate disclosure of information that is relevant to, or may be used in, any actual or prospective criminal proceedings;

(*b*) preventing the disclosure of information in any circumstances in which its non-disclosure—

(i) is in the interests of national security;

(ii) is for the purposes of the prevention or detection of crime, or the apprehension or prosecution of offenders;

(iii) is required on proportionality grounds; or

(iv) is otherwise necessary in the public interest; or

(*c*) preventing the disclosure of any information held by HMRC in connection with its functions which—

(i) is obtained from the Head of the Home Civil Service, the Chief Executive, the Commissioners or an officer, and

(ii) relates to a person whose identity is specified in the disclosure or can be deduced from it.

(2) Paragraph (1)(*c*) does not apply to any information relating to internal administrative arrangements of HMRC (whether relating to the Commissioners, officers or others).

(3) The IPCC or, as the case may be, the appropriate authority, shall not conclude that the non-disclosure of information is necessary under paragraph (1) unless it is satisfied that—

(*a*) there is a real risk of the disclosure of that information causing an adverse effect; and

(*b*) that adverse effect would be significant.

(4) The IPCC shall consult the appropriate authority in any case under paragraph (1)(*c*) before deciding whether or not it is satisfied under paragraph (3).

(5) Without prejudice to the generality of paragraph (1), the IPCC, or, as the case may be, the appropriate authority, shall consider whether the non-disclosure of information is justified under that paragraph in circumstances where—

(*a*) that information is relevant to, or may be used in, any actual or prospective disciplinary proceedings;

(*b*) the disclosure of that information may lead to the contamination of the evidence of witnesses during such proceedings;

(*c*) the disclosure of that information may prejudice the welfare or safety of any third party;

(*d*) that information constitutes criminal intelligence.

61 Copies of complaints etc

(1) Where a complaint is recorded under regulation 19(6) (initial handling and recording of complaints), the appropriate authority shall—

(*a*) supply to the complainant a copy of the record made of that complaint; and

(*b*) subject to paragraphs (2) to (4), supply to the person complained against a copy of the complaint.

(2) A copy of a complaint supplied under this regulation may be in a form which keeps anonymous the identity of the complainant or of any other person.

(3) The appropriate authority may decide not to supply such a copy of a complaint if it is of the opinion that to do so—

(*a*) might prejudice any criminal investigation or pending proceedings, or
(*b*) would otherwise be contrary to the public interest.

(4) Where the appropriate authority decides not to supply such a copy, it shall keep that decision under regular review.

62 Notification of actions and decisions

(1) So far as not covered by regulation 67(11) and (12) and regulation 74(11) and (12) (appeals to the IPCC with respect to an investigation), where the IPCC takes any action or decisions in consequence of it having received a memorandum under regulation 67(9) or regulation 74(3), it shall notify such action or decisions, together with an explanation of its reasons for having taken them, to—

(*a*) the appropriate authority;
(*b*) the complainant and any other interested person within the meaning of regulation 55(2) and (3); and
(*c*) subject to paragraph (2), the person complained against.

(2) The IPCC may decide not to give such a notification and explanation to the person complained against if it is of the opinion that that notification might prejudice any criminal investigation, pending proceedings, or review of the complaint.

63 Information for complainant about disciplinary recommendations

(1) Where—

(*a*) the IPCC makes recommendations under regulation 71 (duties with respect to disciplinary proceedings) in the case of an investigation of a complaint, and
(*b*) the appropriate authority notifies the IPCC that the recommendations have been accepted,

the IPCC shall notify the complainant and every person entitled to be kept properly informed in relation to the complaint under regulation 55 of that fact and of the steps that have been, or are to be taken, by the appropriate authority to give effect to it.

(2) Where in the case of an investigation of a complaint the appropriate authority—

(*a*) notifies the IPCC that it does not (either in whole or in part) accept recommendations made by the IPCC under regulation 71, or
(*b*) fails to take steps to give full effect to any such recommendations,

it shall be the duty of the IPCC to determine what further steps (if any) to take under that regulation.

(3) It shall be the duty of the IPCC to notify the complainant and every person entitled to be kept properly informed in relation to the complaint under regulation 55—

(*a*) of any determination under paragraph (2) not to take further steps under regulation 71; and
(*b*) where it determines under that paragraph to take further steps under that regulation, of the outcome of the taking of those steps.

64 Register to be kept by the IPCC

(1) The IPCC shall establish and maintain a register of all information supplied to it by the appropriate authority under these Regulations.

(2) Subject to paragraph (3), the IPCC may publish or otherwise disclose to any person any information held on the register provided that the publication or disclosure is necessary for or conducive to the purpose of—

(*a*) learning lessons from the handling of, or demonstrating the thoroughness and effectiveness of, investigations by the IPCC or of managed or supervised investigations;
(*b*) raising public awareness of the complaints system; or
(*c*) improving the complaints system.

(3) Information may not be published or disclosed in circumstances where in the opinion of the IPCC the non-disclosure of information is necessary for the purposes mentioned in regulation 60(1)(*a*) and (*b*) (exceptions to the duty to keep the complainant informed and to provide information for other persons).

65 Manner and time limits of notifications

(1) Any notification to be given under these Regulations shall—

(*a*) unless otherwise specified in these Regulations or determined in guidance issued by the IPCC, be given in writing; and
(*b*) unless otherwise specified in these Regulations, be made within such period as the IPCC may determine in guidance.

(2) No time limit mentioned in these Regulations or determined by the IPCC shall apply in any case where exceptional circumstances prevent that time limit being complied with.

PART 8

REPORTS AND RECOMMENDATIONS

66 Final reports on investigations: complaints, conduct matters and certain DSI matters

(1) This regulation applies on the completion of an investigation of—

(*a*) a complaint, or

(*b*) a conduct matter.

(2) A person appointed under regulation 44 (investigation by the appropriate authority on its own behalf) shall submit a report on that person's investigation to the appropriate authority.

(3) A person appointed under regulation 45 (investigations supervised by the IPCC), 46 (investigations by a police force under the management or under the supervision of the IPCC), or 47 (investigations managed by the IPCC) shall—

(*a*) submit a report on that person's investigation to the IPCC; and

(*b*) send a copy of that report to the appropriate authority.

(4) In relation to a matter that was formerly a DSI matter but has been recorded as a conduct matter in pursuance of regulation 36(5) (procedure where conduct matter is revealed during investigation of a DSI matter), the references in paragraphs (2) and (3) of this regulation to the appropriate authority are references to—

(*a*) the appropriate authority in relation to the DSI matter; and

(*b*) (where different) the appropriate authority in relation to the person whose conduct is in question.

(5) A person designated under regulation 48 (investigations by the IPCC itself) as the person in charge of an investigation by the IPCC itself shall submit a report on the investigation to the IPCC.

(6) A person submitting a report under this regulation shall not be prevented by any obligation of secrecy imposed by any rule of law or otherwise from including all such matters in the report as that person thinks fit.

(7) A person who has submitted a report on an investigation under this regulation on an investigation within regulation 57(1) (duty to consider submissions from the person whose conduct is in question) must supply the appropriate authority with such copies of further documents or other items in that person's possession as the authority may request.

(8) The appropriate authority may only make a request under paragraph (7) in respect of a copy of a document or other item if the authority—

(*a*) considers that the document or item is of relevance to the investigation, and

(*b*) requires a copy of the document or the item for either or both of the purposes mentioned in paragraph (9).

(9) Those purposes are—

(*a*) complying with any obligation which the authority has under the disciplinary proceedings in relation to any person whose conduct is the subject-matter of the investigation;

(*b*) ensuring that any such officer (a person whose conduct is in question) receives a fair hearing at any disciplinary proceedings in respect of any such conduct of that officer.

67 Action by the IPCC in response to an investigation report under regulation 66

(1) This regulation applies where—

(*a*) a report on an investigation carried out under the management of the IPCC is submitted to it under paragraph (3) of regulation 66 (final report on investigations: complaints, conduct matters and certain DSI matters); or

(*b*) a report on an investigation carried out by a person designated by the IPCC is submitted to it under paragraph (5) of that regulation.

(2) On receipt of the report, the IPCC—

(*a*) if it appears that the appropriate authority has not already been sent a copy of the report, shall send a copy of the report to that authority;

(*b*) shall determine whether the conditions set out in paragraphs (3) and (4) are satisfied in respect of the report;

(*c*) if it determines that those conditions are so satisfied, shall notify the Director of Public Prosecutions . . . [1] of the determination and send the Director a copy of the report; and

(*d*) shall notify the appropriate authority and the persons mentioned in paragraph (7) of its determination under sub-paragraph (*b*) and of any action taken by it under sub-paragraph (*c*).

(3) The first condition is that the report indicates that a criminal offence may have been committed by a person to whose conduct the investigation related.

(4) The second condition is that the circumstances are such that, in the opinion of the IPCC, it is appropriate for the matters dealt with in the report to be considered by the Director of Public Prosecutions . . . [1].

(5) The Director of Public Prosecutions . . . [1] shall notify the IPCC of any decision of the Director to take, or not to take, action in respect of the matters dealt with in any report a copy of which has been sent to the Director under paragraph (2)(*c*).

(6) It shall be the duty of the IPCC to notify the persons mentioned in paragraph (7) if criminal proceedings are brought against any person by the Director of Public Prosecutions . . . [1] in respect of any matters dealt with in a report copied to the Director under paragraph (2)(*c*).

(7) Those persons are—

(a) in the case of a complaint, the complainant and every person entitled to be kept properly informed in relation to the complaint under regulation 55 (duty to provide information for other persons); and

(b) in the case of a recordable conduct matter, every person entitled to be kept properly informed in relation to that matter under that regulation.

(8) On receipt of the report, the IPCC shall also notify the appropriate authority that it must—

(a) determine—

(i) whether any officer (person whose conduct is in question) has a case to answer in respect of their conduct or has no case to answer, and

(ii) what action (if any) the authority is required to, or will in its discretion, take in respect of the matters dealt with in the report; and

(b) determine what other action (if any) the authority will in its discretion take in respect of those matters.

(9) On receipt of a notification under paragraph (8) the appropriate authority shall make those determinations and submit a memorandum to the IPCC which—

(a) sets out the determinations the authority has made; and

(b) if the appropriate authority has decided in relation to any person whose conduct is the subject-matter of the report that disciplinary proceedings should not be brought against that person, sets out its reasons for so deciding.

(10) On receipt of a memorandum under paragraph (9), the IPCC shall—

(a) consider the memorandum and whether the appropriate authority has made the determinations under paragraph (8)(a) that the IPCC considers appropriate in respect of the matters dealt with in the report;

(b) determine, in the light of its consideration of those matters, whether or not to make recommendations under regulation 71 (duties with respect to disciplinary proceedings); and

(c) make such recommendations (if any) under that regulation as it thinks fit.

(11) On the making of a determination under paragraph (10)(b) the IPCC shall give a notification—

(a) in the case of a complaint, to the complainant and to every person entitled to be kept properly informed in relation to the complaint under regulation 55; and

(b) in the case of a recordable conduct matter, to every person entitled to be kept properly informed in relation to that matter under that regulation.

(12) The notification required by paragraph (11) is one setting out—

(a) the findings of the report;

(b) the IPCC's determination under paragraph (10)(b); and

(c) the action which the appropriate authority is to be recommended to take as a consequence of the determination.

(13) Regulation 60 shall have effect in relation to the duties imposed on the IPCC by paragraph (11) of this regulation.

(14) Except so far as may be otherwise provided by these Regulations, the IPCC shall be entitled (notwithstanding any obligation of secrecy imposed by any rule of law or otherwise) to discharge the duty to give a person mentioned in paragraph (11) notification of the findings of the report by sending that person a copy of the report.

(15) In relation to a DSI matter in respect of which a determination has been made under regulation 36(2) or (4) (procedure where conduct matter is revealed during the investigation of a DSI matter), the references in this regulation to the appropriate authority are references to the appropriate authority in relation to the person whose conduct is in question.

Amendments—[1] In paras (2)(c), (4)–(6), words revoked by the Public Bodies (Merger of the Director of Public Prosecutions and the Director of Revenue and Customs Prosecutions) Order, SI 2014/834 art 3(3), Sch 3 paras 30, 33 with effect from 27 March 2014.

68 Action by the appropriate authority in response to an investigation report under regulation 66

(1) This regulation applies where—

(a) a report of an investigation is submitted to the appropriate authority in accordance with regulation 66(2); or

(b) a copy of a report on an investigation carried out under the supervision of the IPCC is sent to the appropriate authority in accordance with regulation 66(3).

(2) On receipt of the report or (as the case may be) of the copy, the appropriate authority—

(a) shall determine whether the conditions set out in paragraphs (3) and (4) are satisfied in respect of the report;

(b) if it determines that those conditions are so satisfied, shall notify the Director of Public Prosecutions . . . [1] of the determination and send the Director a copy of the report; and

(c) shall notify the persons mentioned in paragraph (7) of its determination under sub-paragraph (a) and of any action taken by it under sub-paragraph (b).

(3) The first condition is that the report indicates that a criminal offence may have been committed by a person to whose conduct the investigation related.

(4) The second condition is that the circumstances are such that, in the opinion of the appropriate authority, it is appropriate for the matters dealt with in the report to be considered by the Director of Public Prosecutions . . . [1].

(5) The Director of Public Prosecutions . . . [1] shall notify the appropriate authority of any decision of the Director to take, or not to take, action in respect of the matters dealt with in any report a copy of which has been sent to the Director under paragraph (2).

(6) It shall be the duty of the appropriate authority to notify the persons mentioned in paragraph (7) if criminal proceedings are brought against any person by the Director of Public Prosecutions . . . [1] in respect of any matters dealt with in a report copied to the Director under paragraph (2)(*b*).

(7) Those persons are—

(*a*) in the case of a complaint, the complainant and every person entitled to be kept properly informed in relation to the complaint under regulation 55 (duty to provide information for other persons); and

(*b*) in the case of a recordable conduct matter, every person entitled to be kept properly informed in relation to that matter under that regulation.

(8) In the case of a report falling within paragraph (1)(*b*) which relates to a recordable conduct matter, the appropriate authority shall also notify the IPCC of its determination under paragraph (2)(*a*).

(9) On receipt of such a notification that the appropriate authority has determined that the conditions in paragraphs (3) and (4) are not satisfied in respect of the report, the IPCC—

(*a*) shall make its own determination as to whether those conditions are so satisfied; and

(*b*) if it determines that they are so satisfied, shall direct the appropriate authority to notify the Director of Public Prosecutions . . . [1] of the IPCC's determination and send the Director a copy of the report.

(10) It shall be the duty of the appropriate authority to comply with any direction given to it under paragraph (9)(*b*).

(11) On receipt of the report or (as the case may be) copy, the appropriate authority shall also—

(*a*) determine—

(i) whether any person to whose conduct the investigation related has a case to answer in respect of their conduct or has no case to answer, and

(ii) what action (if any) the authority is required to, or will in its discretion, take in respect of the matters dealt with in the report; and

(*b*) determine what other action (if any) the authority will in its discretion take in respect of those matters.

(12) On the making of the determinations under paragraph (11) the appropriate authority shall give a notification—

(*a*) in the case of a complaint, to the complainant and to every person entitled to be kept properly informed in relation to the complaint under regulation 55; and

(*b*) in the case of a recordable conduct matter, to every person entitled to be kept properly informed in relation to that matter under that regulation.

(13) The notification required by paragraph (12) is one setting out—

(*a*) the findings of the report;

(*b*) the determinations the authority has made under paragraph (11); and

(*c*) the complainant's right of appeal under regulation 74 (appeals to the IPCC with respect to an investigation).

(14) Regulation 60 shall have effect in relation to the duties imposed on the appropriate authority by paragraph (12) of this regulation.

(15) Except so far as may be otherwise provided by these Regulations, the appropriate authority shall be entitled (notwithstanding any obligation of secrecy imposed by any rule of law or otherwise) to discharge the duty to give a person mentioned in paragraph (12) notification of the findings of the report by sending that person a copy of the report.

(16) In relation to a DSI matter in respect of which a determination has been made under regulation 36(2) or (4), the references in this regulation to the appropriate authority are references to the appropriate authority in relation to the person whose conduct is in question.

Amendments—[1] In paras (2)(*b*), (4)–(6), (9)(*b*), words revoked by the Public Bodies (Merger of the Director of Public Prosecutions and the Director of Revenue and Customs Prosecutions) Order, SI 2014/834 art 3(3), Sch 3 paras 30, 34 with effect from 27 March 2014.

69 Final reports on investigations: other DSI matters

(1) This regulation applies on the completion of an investigation of a DSI matter in respect of which neither the IPCC nor the appropriate authority has made a determination under regulation 36(2) or (4) (procedure where conduct matter is revealed during investigation of DSI matter).

(2) The person investigating shall—

(*a*) submit a report on the investigation to the IPCC; and

(*b*) send a copy of that report to the appropriate authority.

(3) A person submitting a report under this regulation shall not be prevented by any obligation of secrecy imposed by any rule of law or otherwise from including all such matters in that report as that person thinks fit.

70 Action by the IPCC in response to an investigation report under regulation 69

(1) On receipt of the report referred to in regulation 69, the IPCC shall determine whether the report indicates that an officer may have—

(*a*) committed a criminal offence; or

(*b*) behaved in a manner which would justify the bringing of disciplinary proceedings.

(2) If the IPCC determines under paragraph (1) that there is no indication in the report that an officer may have—

(*a*) committed a criminal offence; or

(*b*) behaved in a manner which would justify the bringing of disciplinary proceedings,

it shall make such recommendations or give such advice (if any) under regulation 7 as it considers necessary or desirable.

(3) Paragraph (2) does not affect any power of the IPCC to make recommendations or give advice under regulation 7 in other cases (whether arising under these Regulations or otherwise).

(4) If the IPCC determines under paragraph (1) that the report indicates that an officer may have—

(*a*) committed a criminal offence; or

(*b*) behaved in a manner which would justify the bringing of disciplinary proceedings,

it shall notify the appropriate authority in relation to the person whose conduct is in question of its determination, and, if it appears that the appropriate authority has not already been sent a copy of the report, send a copy of the report to that authority.

(5) Where the appropriate authority in relation to the person whose conduct is in question is notified of a determination by the IPCC under paragraph (4), it shall record the matter under regulation 24 (recording etc of conduct matters in other cases) as a conduct matter (and the other provisions of these Regulations shall apply in relation to that matter accordingly).

(6) Where a DSI matter is recorded under regulation 24 as a conduct matter by virtue of paragraph (5)—

(*a*) the person investigating the DSI matter shall (subject to any determination made by the IPCC under regulation 38(6) (power of the IPCC to determine the form of an investigation—further determination)) investigate the conduct matter as if appointed or designated to do so, and

(*b*) the other provisions of these Regulations shall apply in relation to that matter accordingly.

71 Duties with respect to disciplinary proceedings

(1) This regulation applies where, in the case of any investigation, the appropriate authority—

(*a*) has given, or is required to give, a notification under regulation 68(12) (action by the appropriate authority in response to an investigation report under regulation 66) of the action it is proposing to take in relation to the matters dealt with in any report of the investigation; or

(*b*) has submitted, or is required to submit, a memorandum to the IPCC under regulation 67 (action by the IPCC in response to an investigation report under regulation 66) or 74 (appeals to the IPCC with respect to an investigation) setting out the action that it is proposing to take in relation to those matters.

(2) Subject to regulation 52 (restrictions on proceedings pending the conclusion of an investigation) and to any recommendations or directions under this regulation, it shall be the duty of the appropriate authority—

(*a*) to take the action which has been or is required to be notified or, as the case may be, which is or is required to be set out in the memorandum; and

(*b*) in a case where that action consists of or includes the bringing of disciplinary proceedings, to secure that those proceedings, once brought, are proceeded with to a proper conclusion.

(3) Where this regulation applies by virtue of paragraph (1)(*b*), the IPCC may make a recommendation to the appropriate authority in respect of any person whose conduct is in question—

(*a*) that the person has a case to answer in respect of their conduct or has no case to answer in relation to their conduct to which the investigation related;

(*b*) that disciplinary proceedings of the form specified in the recommendation are brought against that person in respect of the conduct to which the investigation related; or

(*c*) that any disciplinary proceedings brought against that person are modified so as to deal with such aspects of that conduct as may be so specified;

and it shall be the duty of the appropriate authority to notify the IPCC whether it accepts the recommendation and (if it does) to set out in the notification the steps that it is proposing to take to give effect to it.

(4) If, after the IPCC has made a recommendation under this regulation, the appropriate authority does not take steps to secure that full effect is given to the recommendation—

(*a*) the IPCC may direct the appropriate authority to take steps for that purpose; and (*b*) it shall be the duty of the appropriate authority to comply with the direction.

(5) A direction under paragraph (4) may, to such extent as the IPCC thinks fit, set out the steps to be taken by the appropriate authority in order to give effect to the recommendation.

(6) Where the IPCC gives the appropriate authority a direction under this regulation, it shall supply the appropriate authority with a statement of its reasons for doing so.

(7) Where disciplinary proceedings have been brought in accordance with a recommendation or direction under this regulation, it shall be the duty of the authority to ensure that they are proceeded with to a proper conclusion.

(8) The IPCC may at any time withdraw a direction given under this regulation; and paragraph (7) shall not impose any obligation in relation to any time after the withdrawal of the direction.

(9) The appropriate authority shall keep the IPCC informed—

(*a*) in a case in which this regulation applies by virtue of paragraph (1)(*b*), of whatever action it takes in pursuance of its duty under paragraph (2); and

(*b*) in every case of a recommendation or direction under this regulation, of whatever action it takes in response to that recommendation or direction.

72 Complaints against a person whose identity is unascertained

(1) Where a complaint or conduct matter relates to the conduct of a person whose identity is unascertained at the time at which the complaint is made or the conduct matter is recorded, or whose identity is not ascertained during or subsequent to, the investigation of the complaint or recordable conduct matter, these Regulations shall apply in relation to such a person as if it did not include—

(*a*) any requirement for the person complained against to be given a notification or an opportunity to make representations;

(*b*) any requirement for the IPCC or the appropriate authority to determine whether a criminal offence may have been committed by the person whose conduct has been the subject-matter of an investigation, or to take any action in relation to such a determination;

(*c*) any requirement for an appropriate authority to determine whether disciplinary proceedings should be brought against a person whose conduct is the subject-matter of a report.

(2) Where the identity of such a person is subsequently ascertained, the IPCC and the appropriate authority shall take such action in accordance with these Regulations as they see fit, regardless of any previous action taken.

PART 9

APPEALS

73 Appeals to the IPCC: failures to notify or record a complaint

(1) An appeal under regulation 21 (failures to notify or record a complaint) against any failure referred to in regulation 21(3) shall be made within 28 days of the date on which notification of that failure is made or sent to the complainant under regulation 21(2).

(2) Any such appeal shall be made in writing and shall state—

(*a*) details of the complaint;

(*b*) the date on which the complaint was made;

(*c*) the name of the Head of the Home Civil Service, the Chief Executive or the Commissioner (other than the Chairman, the Chief Executive and the Permanent Secretary) who gave notification of the failure;

(*d*) the grounds for the appeal; and

(*e*) the date on which the complainant was notified of the determination or of the failure to record the complaint.

(3) Where the IPCC receives such an appeal it shall—

(*a*) notify the Head of the Home Civil Service, the Chief Executive or the Commissioners (other than the Chairman, the Chief Executive and the Permanent Secretary) concerned of the appeal, and

(*b*) request any information from any person which it considers necessary to dispose of the appeal.

(4) Where the IPCC receives an appeal which fails to comply with one or more of the requirements mentioned in paragraph (2), it may decide to proceed as if those requirements had been complied with.

(5) The Head of the Home Civil Service, the Chief Executive or the Commissioners (other than the Chairman, the Chief Executive and the Permanent Secretary) shall supply to the IPCC any information requested under paragraph (3)(*b*).

(6) The IPCC shall determine the outcome of the appeal as soon as practicable.

(7) The IPCC shall notify the complainant and the Head of the Home Civil Service, the Chief Executive or the Commissioners (other than the Chairman, the Chief Executive and the Permanent Secretary) concerned of the reasons for its determination.

(8) The IPCC may extend the time period mentioned in paragraph (1) in any case where it is satisfied that by reason of the special circumstances of the case it is just to do so.

74 Appeals to the IPCC with respect to an investigation

(1) This regulation applies where a complaint has been subjected to—

(*a*) an investigation by the appropriate authority on its own behalf; or

(*b*) an investigation under the supervision of the IPCC.

(2) The complainant shall have the following rights of appeal to the IPCC—

(*a*) a right of appeal on the grounds that the complainant has not been provided with adequate information—

(i) about the findings of the investigation; or

(ii) about any determination of the appropriate authority relating to the taking (or not taking) of action in respect of any matters dealt with in the report on the investigation;

(*b*) a right of appeal against the findings of the investigation;

(*c*) a right of appeal against any determination by the appropriate authority that a person to whose conduct the investigation related has a case to answer in respect of that person's conduct or has no case to answer;

(*d*) a right of appeal against any determination by the appropriate authority relating to the taking (or not taking) of action in respect of any matters dealt with in the report; and

(*e*) a right of appeal against any determination by the appropriate authority under regulation 68(2)(*a*) (action by the appropriate authority in response to an investigation report under regulation 66), as a result of which it is not required to send the Director of Public Prosecutions . . . [1] a copy of the report.

(3) On the bringing of an appeal under this regulation, the IPCC may require the appropriate authority to submit a memorandum to the IPCC which—

(*a*) sets out whether the appropriate authority has determined that a person to whose conduct the investigation related has a case to answer in respect of that person's conduct or has no case to answer;

(*b*) if the appropriate authority is proposing to take any action, sets out what action it is proposing to take;

(*c*) if the appropriate authority has decided in relation to a person to whose conduct the investigation related, that disciplinary proceedings should not be brought against that person, sets out its reasons for so deciding; and

(*d*) if the appropriate authority made a determination under regulation 68(2)(*a*) as a result of which it is not required to send the Director of Public Prosecutions . . . [1], a copy of the report relating to the investigation, sets out the reasons for that determination;

and it shall be the duty of the appropriate authority to comply with any requirement under this paragraph.

(4) Where the IPCC so requires on the bringing of any appeal under this regulation in the case of an investigation by the appropriate authority on its own behalf, the appropriate authority shall provide the IPCC with a copy of the report of the investigation.

(5) On an appeal under this regulation, the IPCC shall determine such of the following as it considers appropriate in the circumstances—

(*a*) whether the complainant has been provided with adequate information about the matters mentioned in paragraph (2)(*a*);

(*b*) whether the findings of the investigation need to be reconsidered; and

(*c*) whether the appropriate authority—

(i) has made such a determination as is mentioned in paragraph (3)(*a*) that the IPCC considers to be appropriate in respect of matters dealt with in the report, and

(ii) has determined that it is required to or will, in its discretion, take the action (if any) that the IPCC considers to be so appropriate; and

(*d*) whether the conditions set out in regulation 68(3) and (4) are satisfied in respect of the report on the investigation.

(6) Where, on an appeal under this regulation, the IPCC determines that the complainant has not been provided with adequate information about any matter, the IPCC shall give the appropriate authority all such directions as the IPCC considers appropriate for securing that the complainant is properly informed.

(7) Nothing in paragraph (6) shall authorise the IPCC to require the disclosure of any information the disclosure of which to the appellant has been or is capable of being withheld by virtue of regulation 60.

(8) Where, on an appeal under this regulation, the IPCC determines that the findings of the investigation need to be reconsidered, it shall either—

(*a*) review those findings without an immediate further investigation; or

(*b*) direct that the complaint be re-investigated.

(9) Where, on an appeal under this regulation, the IPCC determines that the appropriate authority has not made a determination as to whether there is a case for a person to whose conduct the investigation related to answer that the IPCC considers appropriate or has not determined that it is required to or will, in its discretion, take the action in respect of the matters dealt with in the report that the IPCC considers appropriate, the IPCC shall—

(*a*) determine, in the light of that determination, whether or not to make recommendations under regulation 71 (duties with respect to disciplinary proceedings); and

(*b*) make such recommendations (if any) under that regulation as it thinks fit.

(10) Where, on an appeal under this regulation, the IPCC determines that the conditions set out in regulation 68(3) and (4) are satisfied in respect of the report, it shall direct the appropriate authority—

(*a*) to notify the Director of Public Prosecutions . . . [1], of the IPCC's determination; and

(*b*) to send the Director a copy of the report.

(11) The IPCC shall give notification of any determination under this regulation—

(*a*) to the appropriate authority;

(*b*) to the complainant;

(*c*) to every person entitled to be kept properly informed in relation to the complaint under regulation 55 (duty to provide information for other persons); and

(*d*) except in a case where it appears to the IPCC that to do so might prejudice any proposed review or re-investigation of the complaint, to the person complained against.

(12) The IPCC shall also give notification of any directions given to the appropriate authority under this regulation—

(*a*) to the complainant;

(*b*) to every person entitled to be kept properly informed in relation to the complaint under regulation 55; and

(*c*) except in a case where it appears to the IPCC that to do so might prejudice any proposed review or re-investigation of the complaint, to the person complained against.

(13) It shall be the duty of the appropriate authority to comply with any directions given to it under this regulation.

(14) Any appeal made by a complainant under this regulation shall be made within 28 days of the date on which the appropriate authority sends a notification to the complainant of its determination under regulation 68(12) as to what action (if any) it will take in respect of the matters dealt with in the investigation report.

(15) Any such appeal shall be in writing and shall state—

(*a*) details of the complaint;

(*b*) the date on which the complaint was made;

(*c*) the grounds for the appeal; and

(*d*) the date on which the complainant received notification under regulation 68(12).

(16) Where the IPCC receives such an appeal, it shall request any information from any person which it considers necessary to dispose of the appeal.

(17) Where the IPCC receives an appeal which fails to comply with one or more of the requirements mentioned in paragraph (15), it may decide to proceed as if those requirements had been complied with.

(18) The appropriate authority shall supply to the IPCC any further information requested of it under paragraph (16).

(19) The IPCC shall determine the outcome of the appeal as soon as practicable.

(20) The IPCC shall notify the complainant and the appropriate authority of the reasons for its determination.

(21) The IPCC may extend the time period mentioned in paragraph (14) in any case where it is satisfied that by reason of the special circumstances of the case it is just to do so.

Amendments—[1] In paras (2)(*e*), (3)(*d*), (10)(*a*), words revoked by the Public Bodies (Merger of the Director of Public Prosecutions and the Director of Revenue and Customs Prosecutions) Order, SI 2014/834 art 3(3), Sch 3 paras 30, 35 with effect from 27 March 2014.

75 Reviews and re-investigations following an appeal

(1) On a review under regulation 74(8)(*a*) (appeals to the IPCC with respect to an investigation) of the findings of an investigation, the powers of the IPCC shall be, according to its determination on that review, to do one or more of the following—

(*a*) to uphold the findings in whole or in part;

(*b*) to give the appropriate authority such directions as the IPCC thinks fit—

(i) as to the carrying out by the appropriate authority of its own review of the findings,

(ii) as to the information to be provided to the complainant, and

(iii) generally as to the handling of the matter in future;

(*c*) to direct that the complaint be re-investigated.

(2) Where the IPCC directs under regulation 74 or paragraph (1) that a complaint be re-investigated, it shall make a determination of the form that the re-investigation should take.

(3) Paragraphs (3) to (8) of regulation 38 (power of the IPCC to determine the form of an investigation) shall apply in relation to a determination under paragraph (2) as they apply in the case of a determination under that regulation.

(4) The provisions of these Regulations shall apply in relation to any re-investigation in pursuance of a direction under regulation 74(9) or paragraph (1) as they apply in relation to any investigation in pursuance of a determination under regulation 38.

(5) The IPCC shall give notification of any determination made by it under this regulation—

(*a*) to the appropriate authority;

(*b*) to the complainant;

(*c*) to every person entitled to be kept properly informed in relation to the complaint under regulation 55 (duty to provide information for other persons); and

(*d*) except in a case where it appears to the IPCC that to do so might prejudice any proposed re-investigation of the complaint, to the person complained against.

(6) The IPCC shall also give notification of any directions given to the appropriate authority under this regulation—

(*a*) to the complainant;

(*b*) to every person entitled to be kept properly informed in relation to the complaint under regulation 55; and

(*c*) except in a case where it appears to the IPCC that to do so might prejudice any proposed review or re-investigation of the complaint, to the person complained against.

2010/1878

FINANCE ACT 2009, SECTIONS 101 TO 103 (APPOINTED DAY AND SUPPLEMENTAL PROVISION) ORDER 2010

Made . . . . *21 July 2010*

The Treasury make the following Order in exercise of the powers conferred by section 104(3) to (5) of the Finance Act 2009.

Commentary—*Simon's Taxes* **A4.620, A4.629**.

1 Citation

This Order may be cited as the Finance Act 2009, Sections 101 to 103 (Appointed Day and Supplemental Provision) Order 2010.

2 Appointed day

The day appointed as the day on which sections 101 to 103 of the Finance Act 2009 come into force for the purposes of bank payroll tax (including any penalties assessed in relation to that tax) is 31st August 2010.

3 Supplemental provision

Interest charged under section 101 of the Finance Act 2009 (late payment interest on sums due to HMRC) on an amount enforceable as if it were bank payroll tax may be enforced as if it were an amount of bank payroll tax.

2010/1879

TAXES AND DUTIES (INTEREST RATE) REGULATIONS 2010

Made . . . . *21 July 2010*
Laid . . . . *22 July 2010*
Coming into force . . . . *31 August 2010*

The Treasury make the following Order in exercise of the powers conferred by section 103 of the Finance Act 2009.

Revocation—

These regulations revoked by the Taxes and Duties, etc (Interest Rate) Regulations, SI 2011/2446 reg 7 with effect from 31 October 2011.

2010/1904

TAXES (DEFINITION OF CHARITY) (RELEVANT TERRITORIES) REGULATIONS 2010

Made . . . . *23rd July 2010*
Laid before the House of Commons . . . . *26th July 2010*

Coming into force . . . . *20th August 2010*

The Commissioners for Her Majesty's Revenue and Customs make the following Regulations in exercise of the powers conferred by paragraph 2 of Schedule 6 to the Finance Act 2010:

1 These Regulations may be cited as the Taxes (Definition of Charity) (Relevant Territories) Regulations 2010 and come into force on 20th August 2010.

2 The territories specified in the Schedule to these Regulations are relevant territories for the purposes of the meaning of a relevant territory in paragraph 2(3) of Schedule 6 to the Finance Act 2010 (the jurisdiction condition of the definition of "charity" in paragraph 1 of Schedule 6 to the Finance Act 2010).

SCHEDULE

Regulation 2

[The Republic of Iceland

The Kingdom of Norway][1]

[The Principality of Liechtenstein][2]

Amendments—[1] Entries inserted by the Taxes (Definition of Charity) (Relevant Territories) (Amendment) Regulations, SI 2010/1904 reg 2, Schedule with effect from 20 August 2010.

[2] Entry inserted by the Taxes (Definition of Charity) (Relevant Territories) (Amendment) Regulations, SI 2014/1807 reg 2 with effect from 31 July 2014.

2010/2655

FIRST-TIER TRIBUNAL AND UPPER TRIBUNAL (CHAMBERS) ORDER 2010

Made . . . . *28 October 2010*
Laid before Parliament . . . . *2 November 2010*
Coming into force . . . . *29 November 2010*

The Lord Chancellor, with the concurrence of the Senior President of Tribunals, makes the following Order in exercise of the power conferred by section 7(1) and (9) of the Tribunals, Courts and Enforcement Act 2007.

1 Citation, commencement and revocations

(1) This Order may be cited as the First-tier Tribunal and Upper Tribunal (Chambers) Order 2010 and comes into force on 29th November 2010.

(2) The Orders listed in the first column of the Schedule to this Order are revoked to the extent specified in the second column.

2 First-tier Tribunal Chambers

The First-tier Tribunal shall be organised into the following chambers—

(*a*) the General Regulatory Chamber;
(*b*) the Health, Education and Social Care Chamber;
(*c*) the Immigration and Asylum Chamber;
[(*cc*) the Property Chamber;][1]
(*d*) the Social Entitlement Chamber;
(*e*) the Tax Chamber;
(*f*) the War Pensions and Armed Forces Compensation Chamber.

Amendments—[1] Para (*cc*) inserted by First-tier Tribunal and Upper Tribunal (Chambers) (Amendment) Order, SI 2013/1187 arts 2, 3 with effect from 1 July 2013.

3 Functions of the General Regulatory Chamber

To the General Regulatory Chamber are allocated all functions related to—

(*a*) proceedings in respect of the decisions and actions of regulatory bodies which are not allocated to the Health, Education and Social Care Chamber by article 4 or to the Tax Chamber by article 7;
(*b*) matters referred to the First-tier Tribunal under Schedule 1D to the Charities Act 1993 (references to Tribunal);
(*c*) the determination of remuneration for carrying mail-bags in a ship or aircraft.

4 Functions of the Health, Education and Social Care Chamber

To the Health, Education and Social Care Chamber are allocated all functions related to—

(*a*) an appeal against a decision related to children with special educational needs;
(*b*) a claim of disability discrimination in the education of a child;
(*c*) an application or an appeal against a decision or determination related to work with children or vulnerable adults;

(*d*) an appeal against a decision related to registration in respect of the provision of health or social care;
(*e*) an application in respect of, or an appeal against a decision related to, the provision of health care or health services;
(*f*) an appeal against a decision related to registration in respect of social workers and social care workers;
(*g*) an appeal against a decision related to the provision of childcare;
(*h*) an appeal against a decision related to an independent school or other independent educational institution;
(*i*) applications and references by and in respect of patients under the provisions of the Mental Health Act 1983 or paragraph 5(2) of the Schedule to the Repatriation of Prisoners Act 1984.

5 Functions of the Immigration and Asylum Chamber of the First-tier Tribunal

To the Immigration and Asylum Chamber of the First-tier Tribunal are allocated all functions related to immigration and asylum matters, with the exception of matters allocated to—
(*a*) the Social Entitlement Chamber by article 6(*a*);
(*b*) the General Regulatory Chamber by article 3(*a*).

[5A Functions of the Property Chamber

To the Property Chamber are allocated all functions conferred on the First-tier Tribunal relating to—
(*a*) a reference by the Chief Land Registrar and any other application, matter or appeal under the Land Registration Act 2002;
(*b*) proceedings under any of the enactments referred to in section 6A(2) of the Agriculture (Miscellaneous Provisions) Act 1954 or the Hill Farming Act 1946;
(*c*) housing etc, under the Housing Act 2004;
(*d*) leasehold property;
(*e*) residential property;
(*f*) rents;
(*g*) the right to buy;
[(*h*) proceedings relating to mobile homes and caravan sites.][2]]
[(*I*) proceedings for approval by the First-tier Tribunal of the exercise of a power of entry, made under paragraph 6B of Schedule 9 to the Local Government Finance Act 1988 or under section 25A of the Local Government Finance Act 1992.][3]][1]

Amendments—[1] Article 5A inserted by First-tier Tribunal and Upper Tribunal (Chambers) (Amendment) Order, SI 2013/1187 arts 2, 4 with effect from 1 July 2013.
[2] Para (*h*) substituted by the First-tier Tribunal and Upper Tribunal (Chambers) (Amendment) Order, SI 2014/1901 art 2(1), (2) with effect from 8 August 2014.
[3] Para (*I*) inserted by the First-tier Tribunal and Upper Tribunal (Chambers) (Amendment) Order, SI 2015/1563 art 2(1), (2) with effect from 1 October 2015..

6 Functions of the Social Entitlement Chamber

To the Social Entitlement Chamber are allocated all functions related to appeals—
(*a*) in cases regarding support for asylum seekers, failed asylum seekers, persons designated under section 130 of the Criminal Justice and Immigration Act 2008, or the dependants of any such persons;
(*b*) in criminal injuries compensation cases;
(*c*) regarding entitlement to, payments of, or recovery or recoupment of payments of, social security benefits, child support, vaccine damage payments, health in pregnancy grant and tax credits, with the exception of—
(i) appeals under section 11 of the Social Security Contributions (Transfer of Functions, etc) Act 1999 (appeals against decisions of Her Majesty's Revenue and Customs);
(ii) appeals in respect of employer penalties or employer information penalties (as defined in section 63(11) and (12) of the Tax Credits Act 2002);
(iii) appeals under regulation 28(3) of the Child Trust Funds Regulations 2004;
(*d*) regarding saving gateway accounts with the exception of appeals against requirements to account for an amount under regulations made under section 14 of the Saving Gateway Accounts Act 2009;
(*e*) regarding child trust funds with the exception of appeals against requirements to account for an amount under regulations made under section 22(4) of the Child Trust Funds Act 2004 in relation to section 13 of that Act;
[(*ea*) appealable decisions within the meaning of section 56(3) of the Childcare Payments Act 2014;][1]
(*f*) regarding payments in consequence of diffuse mesothelioma;
(*g*) regarding a certificate or waiver decision in relation to NHS charges;
(*h*) regarding entitlement to be credited with earnings or contributions;

(*i*) against a decision as to whether an accident was an industrial accident.

Amendments—[1] Para (*ea*) inserted by the First-tier Tribunal and Upper Tribunal (Chambers) (Amendment) Order, SI 2015/1563 art 2(1), (3) with effect from 1 October 2015..

7 Functions of the Tax Chamber

To the Tax Chamber are allocated all functions, except those functions allocated to the Social Entitlement Chamber by article 6 or to the Tax and Chancery Chamber of the Upper Tribunal by article 13, related to an appeal, application, reference or other proceeding in respect of—

(*a*) a function of the Commissioners for Her Majesty's Revenue and Customs or an officer of Revenue and Customs;

(*b*) the exercise by the Serious Organised Crime Agency of general Revenue functions or Revenue inheritance tax functions (as defined in section 323 of the Proceeds of Crime Act 2002);

(*c*) the exercise by the Director of Border Revenue of functions under section 7 of the Borders, Citizenship and Revenue Act 2009;

(*d*) a function of the Compliance Officer for the Independent Parliamentary Standards Authority.

8 Functions of the War Pensions and Armed Forces Compensation Chamber

To the War Pensions and Armed Forces Compensation Chamber are allocated all functions related to appeals under the War Pensions (Administrative Provisions) Act 1919 and the Pensions Appeal Tribunals Act 1943.

9 Upper Tribunal Chambers

The Upper Tribunal shall be organised into the following chambers—

(*a*) the Administrative Appeals Chamber;

(*b*) the Immigration and Asylum Chamber of the Upper Tribunal;

(*c*) the Lands Chamber;

(*d*) the Tax and Chancery Chamber.

10 Functions of the Administrative Appeals Chamber

To the Administrative Appeals Chamber are allocated all functions related to—

(*a*) an appeal—

(i) against a decision made by the First-tier Tribunal, except an appeal allocated to the Tax and Chancery Chamber by article 13(*a*) or the Immigration and Asylum Chamber of the Upper Tribunal by article 11(*a*);

(ii) under section 5 of the Pensions Appeal Tribunals Act 1943 (appeals against assessment of extent of disablement) against a decision of the Pensions Appeal Tribunal in Northern Ireland established under paragraph 1(3) of the Schedule to the Pensions Appeal Tribunals Act 1943 (constitution, jurisdiction and procedure of Pensions Appeal Tribunals);

(iii) against a decision of the Pensions Appeal Tribunal in Scotland established under paragraph 1(2) of the Schedule to the Pensions Appeal Tribunals Act 1943;

(iv) against a decision of the Mental Health Review Tribunal for Wales established under section 65 of the Mental Health Act 1983 (Mental Health Review Tribunals);

(v) against a decision of the Special Educational Needs Tribunal for Wales;

(vi) under section 4 of the Safeguarding Vulnerable Groups Act 2006 (appeals);

(vii) transferred to the Upper Tribunal from the First-tier Tribunal under Tribunal Procedure Rules, except an appeal allocated to the Tax and Chancery Chamber by article 13(1)(*e*);

[(viii) against a decision in a road transport case;][1]

(*b*) an application, except an application allocated to another chamber by article 11(*c*)[, (*d*) or (*e*)][3], 12(*c*) or 13(*g*), for the Upper Tribunal—

(i) to grant the relief mentioned in section 15(1) of the Tribunals, Courts and Enforcement Act 2007 (Upper Tribunal's "judicial review" jurisdiction);

(ii) to exercise the powers of review under section 21(2) of that Act (Upper Tribunal's "judicial review" jurisdiction: Scotland);

(*c*) a matter referred to the Upper Tribunal by the First-tier Tribunal—

(i) under section 9(5)(*b*) of the Tribunals, Courts and Enforcement Act 2007 (review of decision of First-tier Tribunal), or

(ii) under Tribunal Procedure Rules relating to non-compliance with a requirement of the First-tier Tribunal,

except where the reference is allocated to another chamber by article 11(*b*) or 13(*f*);

(*d*) a determination or decision under section 4 of the Forfeiture Act 1982;

(*e*) proceedings, or a preliminary issue, transferred under Tribunal Procedure Rules to the Upper Tribunal from the First-tier Tribunal, except those allocated to [the Lands Chamber by article 12(*cc*) or to][2] the Tax and Chancery Chamber by article 13(1)(*e*).

Amendments—[1] Para (*a*)(viii) substituted by the First-tier Tribunal and Upper Tribunal (Chambers) (Amendment) Order, SI 2012/1673 arts 2, 3 with effect from 20 July 2012.

[2] Words in para (*e*) inserted by the First-tier Tribunal and Upper Tribunal (Chambers) (Amendment) Order, SI 2013/1187 arts 2, 5 with effect from 1 July 2013.

[3] Words in para (*b*) substituted for words "or (*d*)" by the First-tier Tribunal and Upper Tribunal (Chambers) (Amendment No 2) Order, SI 2013/2068 arts 2, 3 with effect from 1 November 2013.

11 Functions of the Immigration and Asylum Chamber of the Upper Tribunal

To the Immigration and Asylum Chamber of the Upper Tribunal are allocated all functions related to—

(*a*) an appeal against a decision of the First-tier Tribunal made in the Immigration and Asylum Chamber of the First-tier Tribunal;

(*b*) a matter referred to the Upper Tribunal under section 9(5)(*b*) of the Tribunals, Courts and Enforcement Act 2007 or under Tribunal Procedure Rules by the Immigration and Asylum Chamber of the First-tier Tribunal;

[(*c*) an application for the Upper Tribunal to grant relief mentioned in section 15(1) of the Tribunals, Courts and Enforcement Act 2007 (Upper Tribunal's "judicial review" jurisdiction), or to exercise the power of review under section 21(2) of that Act (Upper Tribunal's "judicial review" jurisdiction: Scotland), which is made by a person who claims to be a minor from outside the United Kingdom challenging a defendant's assessment of that person's age;

(*d*) an application for the Upper Tribunal to exercise the powers of review under section 21(2) of the Tribunals, Court and Enforcement Act (Upper Tribunal's "judicial review" jurisdiction: Scotland), which relates to a decision of the First-tier Tribunal mentioned in paragraph (a);

(*e*) an application for the Upper Tribunal to grant relief mentioned in section 15(1) of the Tribunals, Courts and Enforcement Act 2007 (Upper Tribunal's "judicial review" jurisdiction), which is designated as an immigration matter—

(i) in a direction made in accordance with Part 1 of Schedule 2 to the Constitutional Reform Act 2005 specifying a class of case for the purposes of section 18(6) of the Tribunals, Courts and Enforcement Act 2007; or

(ii) in an order of the High Court in England and Wales made under section 31A(3) of the Senior Courts Act 1981, transferring to the Upper Tribunal an application of a kind described in section 31A(1) of that Act.][1]

Amendments—[1] Paras (*c*)–(*e*) substituted for previous paras (*c*), (*d*), by the First-tier Tribunal and Upper Tribunal (Chambers) (Amendment No 2) Order, SI 2013/2068 arts 2, 4 with effect from 1 November 2013.

12 Functions of the Lands Chamber

To the Lands Chamber are allocated—

(*a*) all functions related to—

(i) compensation and other remedies for measures taken which affect the ownership, value, enjoyment or use of land or water, or of rights over or property in land or water;

[(ii) appeals from decisions of—

(*aa*) the First-tier Tribunal made in the Property Chamber other than appeals allocated to the Tax and Chancery Chamber by article 13(*h*);

(*ab*) leasehold valuation tribunals in Wales, residential property tribunals in Wales, rent assessment committees in Wales, the Agricultural Land Tribunal in Wales or the Valuation Tribunal for Wales;

(*ac*) the Valuation Tribunal for England;][1]

(iii) the determination of questions of the value of land or an interest in land arising in tax proceedings;

(iv) proceedings in respect of restrictive covenants, blight notices or the obstruction of light;

(*b*) the Upper Tribunal's function as arbitrator under section 1(5) of the Lands Tribunal Act 1949;

(*c*) an application for the Upper Tribunal to grant the relief mentioned in section 15(1) of the Tribunals, Courts and Enforcement Act 2007 (Upper Tribunal's "judicial review" jurisdiction) which relates to a decision of a tribunal mentioned in sub-paragraph (*a*)(ii);

[(*cc*) any case which may be transferred under Tribunal Procedure Rules to the Upper Tribunal from the Property Chamber of the First-tier Tribunal in relation to functions listed in article 5A(*c*) to (*h*);][1]

(*d*) any other functions transferred to the Upper Tribunal by the Transfer of Tribunal Functions (Lands Tribunal and Miscellaneous Amendments) Order 2009.

Amendments—[1] Para (*a*)(ii) substituted, and para (*cc*) inserted, by the First-tier Tribunal and Upper Tribunal (Chambers) (Amendment) Order, SI 2013/1187 arts 2, 6 with effect from 1 July 2013.

13 Functions of the Tax and Chancery Chamber

(1) To the Tax and Chancery Chamber are allocated all functions related to—

(*a*) an appeal against a decision of the First-tier Tribunal made—

(i) in the Tax Chamber;

(ii) in the General Regulatory Chamber in a charities case;

(*b*) a reference or appeal in respect of—

(i) a decision of the [Financial Conduct Authority or the Prudential Regulation Authority][2];

(ii) a decision of the Bank of England;

(iii) a decision of a person related to the assessment of any compensation or consideration under the Banking (Special Provisions) Act 2008;

(iv) a determination or dispute within the meaning of regulation 14(5) or 15 of the Financial Services and Management Act 2000 (Contribution to Costs of Special Resolution Regime) Regulations 2010;

[(*ba*) an appeal in respect of a decision of a Minister under section 147(4)(*a*) or (*b*) of the Policing and Crime Act 2017;][3]

(*c*) a reference in respect of a decision of the Pensions Regulator;

(*d*) an application under paragraph 50(1)(*d*) of Schedule 36 to the Finance Act 2008;

(*e*) proceedings, or a preliminary issue, transferred to the Upper Tribunal under Tribunal Procedure Rules—

(i) from the Tax Chamber of the First-tier Tribunal;

(ii) from the General Regulatory Chamber of the First-tier Tribunal in a charities case;

(*f*) a matter referred to the Upper Tribunal under section 9(5)(*b*) of the Tribunals, Courts and Enforcement Act 2007 or under Tribunal Procedure Rules relating to non-compliance with a requirement of the First-tier Tribunal—

(i) by the Tax Chamber of the First-tier Tribunal;

(ii) by the General Regulatory Chamber of the First-tier Tribunal in a charities case;

(*g*) an application for the Upper Tribunal to grant the relief mentioned in section 15(1) of the Tribunals, Courts and Enforcement Act 2007 (Upper Tribunal's "judicial review" jurisdiction), or to exercise the powers of review under section 21(2) of that Act (Upper Tribunal's "judicial review" jurisdiction: Scotland), which relates to—

(i) a decision of the First-tier Tribunal mentioned in paragraph (1)(*a*)(i) or (ii);

(ii) a function of the Commissioners for Her Majesty's Revenue and Customs or an officer of Revenue and Customs, with the exception of any function in respect of which an appeal would be allocated to the Social Entitlement Chamber by article 6;

(iii) the exercise by the Serious Organised Crime Agency of general Revenue functions or Revenue inheritance tax functions (as defined in section 323 of the Proceeds of Crime Act 2002), with the exception of any function in relation to which an appeal would be allocated to the Social Entitlement Chamber by article 6;

(iv) a function of the Charity Commission, or one of the bodies mentioned in sub-paragraph (*b*) or (*c*);

[(*h*) an appeal against a decision of the First-tier Tribunal made in the Property Chamber in a case mentioned in article 5A(*a*).][1]

(2) In this article "a charities case" means an appeal or application in respect of a decision, order or direction of the Charity Commission, or a reference under Schedule 1D to the Charities Act 1993.

Amendments—[1] Para (1)(*h*) inserted by the First-tier Tribunal and Upper Tribunal (Chambers) (Amendment) Order, SI 2013/1187 arts 2, 7 with effect from 1 July 2013.

[2] In para)1)(*b*)(i), words substituted for words "Financial Services Authority" by the First-tier Tribunal and Upper Tribunal (Chambers) (Amendment) Order, SI 2014/1901 art 2(1), (3) with effect from 8 August 2014.

[3] Para (1)(*ba*) inserted by the First-tier Tribunal and Upper Tribunal (Chambers) (Amendment) Order, SI 2017/722 arts 2, 3 with effect from 27 July 2017.

14 Resolution of doubt or dispute as to chamber

If there is any doubt or dispute as to the chamber in which a particular matter is to be dealt with, the Senior President of Tribunals may allocate that matter to the chamber which appears to the Senior President of Tribunals to be most appropriate.

15 Re-allocation of a case to another chamber

At any point in the proceedings, the Chamber President of the chamber to which a case or any issue in that case has been allocated by or under this Order may, with the consent of the corresponding Chamber President, allocate that case or that issue to another chamber within the same tribunal, by giving a direction to that effect.

SCHEDULE

REVOCATIONS

article 1(2)

Orders revoked	*Extent to which revoked*
The First-tier Tribunal and Upper Tribunal (Chambers) Order 2008, SI 2008/2684.	The whole Order.
The First-tier Tribunal and Upper Tribunal (Chambers) (Amendment) Order 2009, SI 2009/196.	The whole Order, except for the purposes of article 9 (transitional provision).
The First-tier Tribunal and Upper Tribunal (Chambers) (Amendment No 2) Order 2009, SI 2009/1021.	The whole Order.
The First-tier Tribunal and Upper Tribunal (Chambers) (Amendment No 3) Order 2009, SI 2009/1590.	The whole Order.
The First-tier Tribunal and Upper Tribunal (Chambers) (Amendment) Order 2010 SI 2010/40.	The whole Order.

2010/2880

SINGLE USE CARRIER BAGS CHARGE (WALES) REGULATIONS 2010

Made . . . . *30 November 2010*

Coming into force . . . . *1 October 2011*

The Welsh Ministers make these Regulations in exercise of the powers conferred by sections 77(2) and 90(3)(a) and (b) of, and paragraphs 1, 2, 3(1)(a) and (2)(a), 4 to 8, 9(1) and (2), 10, 12, 16 to 19 and 21 of Schedule 6 to, the Climate Change Act 2008.

The Welsh Ministers are satisfied in accordance with paragraph 23 of Schedule 6 to that Act that every county council and county borough council in Wales will act in accordance with the principles referred to in that paragraph when exercising a power conferred by these Regulations to impose a civil sanction.

A draft of these Regulations has been laid before, and approved by resolution of, the National Assembly for Wales pursuant to section 77(4)(a) and (b) of, and paragraph 27(3) of Schedule 6 to, the Climate Change Act 2008.

PART 1

INTRODUCTION

1 Title, commencement and application

(1) The title of these Regulations is the Single Use Carrier Bags Charge (Wales) Regulations 2010.

(2) These Regulations apply in relation to Wales and come into force on 1 October 2011.

2 Interpretation

(1) In these Regulations—

["the charge" ("*y tâl*") means the minimum consideration that must be paid by a customer by virtue of regulation 6(2);][1]

["consideration" ("*cydnabyddiaeth*") includes any chargeable VAT;][1]

"enforcement costs recovery notice" ("*hysbysiad adennill costau gorfodi*") has the meaning given in regulation 16(1);

"functions" ("*swyddogaethau*") includes powers and duties;

"late payment penalty" ("*cosb am dalu'n hwyr*") means any increase in an amount payable—

(a) as a fixed monetary penalty, by virtue of paragraph 10 of Schedule 2;

(b) as a variable monetary penalty, by virtue of paragraph 9 of Schedule 3;

(c) as a non-compliance penalty, by virtue of paragraph 8 of Schedule 4;

"non-compliance penalty notice" ("*hysbysiad o gosb am beidio â chydymffurfio*") has the meaning given in paragraph 5(4) of Schedule 4;

"record" ("*cofnod*") means the information specified in regulation 8(3);

"reporting year" ("*blwyddyn adrodd*") means—

(a) the period starting on the date on which these Regulations come into force and ending on 6 April 2012;

(b) thereafter, the period commencing 7 April in one year and ending on 6 April the following year; the first such period to commence 7 April 2012;

"specified sum" ("*swm penodedig*") has the meaning given in paragraph 4(2) of Schedule 2.

(2) References to—

(a) a notice of intent in relation to a fixed monetary penalty, are references to a notice of intent served under paragraph 3(1) of Schedule 2;

(b) a final notice in relation to a fixed monetary penalty, are references to a final notice served under paragraph 6(5) of Schedule 2;

(c) to a notice of intent in relation to a discretionary requirement, are references to a notice of intent served under paragraph 3(1) of Schedule 3;

(d) to a final notice in relation to a discretionary requirement, are references to a final notice served under paragraph 5(6) of Schedule 3;

(e) to a notice of intent in relation to a non-compliance penalty, are references to a notice of intent served under paragraph 3(1) of Schedule 4.

["VAT" ("*TAW*") has the meaning given in section 96 of the Value Added Tax Act 1994.][1]

(3) References to single use carrier bags attracting the charge are references to those single use carrier bags to which regulation 6 applies.

Amendments—[1] In para 1, definition of "the charge" substituted and definitions of "consideration" and "VAT" inserted by the Single Use Carrier Bags Charge (Wales) (Amendment) Regulations SI 2011/2184 reg 3 with effect from 1 October 2011.

3 Meaning of "single use carrier bag"

(1) In these Regulations "single use carrier bag" ("*bag siopa untro*") means a bag fitting the description in paragraph (2) or (3)—

(2) A bag fits the description in this paragraph if—

(a) it is made wholly or mainly of paper, plant-based material or natural starch; and

(b) it is not specifically manufactured for multiple reuse.

(3) A bag fits the description in this paragraph if it is a plastic bag—

(a) which does not meet all of the specifications in paragraph (4); or

(b) which meets all of the specifications in paragraph (4) but is not intended for multiple reuse (*see* paragraph (5)).

(4) The specifications are—

(a) both of the bag's dimensions are greater than 404 millimetres ("mm");

(b) at least one of the bag's dimensions is greater than 439 mm;

(c) the bag is manufactured from material which is greater than 49 microns in thickness.

(5) A plastic bag is intended for multiple reuse if—

(a) it is purchased by the customer; and

(b) when worn out, it is returnable to the seller from whom it was purchased to be replaced free of charge.

(6) In this regulation—

"dimensions" ("*dimensiynau*") means width or height;

"plastic bag" ("*bag plastig*") means a bag which is made wholly or mainly of plastic.

4 Meaning of "seller"

(1) In these Regulations "seller" ("*gwerthwr*") means a person who in the course of trade or business—

(a) sells goods from a place in Wales;

(b) sells goods which are delivered to persons in Wales.

But this is subject to paragraph (2).

(2) Where a person (A) sells goods in A's capacity as an officer or employee of another person (B), then for the purposes of these Regulations B is the seller in those circumstances, and not A.

5 Administrator

(1) A local authority is to administer the provision made by these Regulations and accordingly, is the administrator for its area.

(2) In paragraph (1) the reference to a local authority is a reference to a county or county borough council.

PART 2
THE CHARGE

[6 Requirement to charge

(1) A seller must charge for every single use carrier bag supplied new—

(a) at the place in Wales where the goods are sold, for the purpose of enabling the goods to be taken away;

(b) for the purpose of enabling the goods to be delivered to persons in Wales.

This is subject to regulation 7.

(2) The amount that a seller must charge is such amount as ensures that the consideration paid by a customer for each single use carrier bag is not less than 5 pence.][1]

Amendments—[1] Reg 6 substituted by the Single Use Carrier Bags Charge (Wales) (Amendment) (Regulations) SI 2011/2184 reg 4 with effect from 1 October 2011.

7 Exemption from the requirement to charge

Regulation 6 does not apply in relation to the supply of single use carrier bags of the kinds described in Schedule 1 and that Schedule has effect accordingly.

PART 3
RECORDS AND PUBLICATION

7A Application of this Part

(1) This Part applies to a seller in relation to any reporting year in which the seller meets the condition in paragraph (2).

(2) The condition is that on the first day of the reporting year the seller employs ten or more full time equivalent members of staff .][1]

Amendments—[1] Reg 7A inserted by the Single Use Carrier Bags Charge (Wales) (Amendment) Regulations 2011 (SI 2011/2184) reg 5 with effect from 1 October 2011.

[8 Record-keeping

(1) A seller must keep a record of the information specified in paragraph (3) for every reporting year.

(2) Records must be retained by a seller for a period of three years beginning on 31 May in the reporting year following that to which a record relates.

(3) The information is—

- (a) the number of single use carrier bags supplied which attract the charge;
- (b) the amount received by way of consideration for single use carrier bags which attract the charge;
- (c) the amount received by way of the charge;
- (d) the net proceeds of the charge;
- (e) a breakdown of how the amount which represents the difference between the amount received by way of the charge and the net proceeds of the charge has been arrived at, including—
  - (i) the apportionment between any chargeable VAT and reasonable costs;
  - (ii) the apportionment between different heads of reasonable costs;
- (f) the uses to which the net proceeds of the charge have been put.

(4) The following are the amounts specified for the purposes of the definition of "net proceeds of the charge" in paragraph 7(4) of Schedule 6 to the Climate Change Act 2008—

- (a) any amount in excess of the charge received by way of consideration for single use carrier bags which attract the charge;
- (b) any amount of chargeable VAT received by way of the charge;
- (c) the amount of any reasonable costs.

(5) In this regulation "reasonable costs" ("*costau rhesymol*") means—

- (a) costs reasonably incurred by a seller to enable the seller to comply with these Regulations;
- (b) costs reasonably incurred by a seller to enable the seller to communicate information about the charge to customers.

This is subject to paragraph (6).

(6) In relation to the first reporting year, "reasonable costs" includes costs reasonably incurred by a seller before the date on which these Regulations come into force—

- (a) to enable the seller to comply with these Regulations;
- (b) to enable the seller to communicate information about the charge to customers.][1]

Amendments—[1] Reg 8 substituted by the Single Use Carrier Bags Charge (Wales) (Amendment) Regulations SI 2011/2184 reg 6 with effect from 1 October 2011.

9 Availability of records

(1) This regulation applies where a person mentioned in paragraph (4) requests a seller in writing to supply a record for a reporting year.

(2) If the request is received during the retention period for the record in question, the seller must provide a copy of that record to the person who requested it within 28 days of receiving the written request.

(3) The retention period is the three year period for which any particular record must be retained under regulation 8(2).

(4) The persons are—

- (a) the Welsh Ministers;
- (b) a member of the public.

10 Publication of records

(1) A seller must publish the record for a reporting year if the conditions in paragraph (2) are met by the seller in relation to the reporting year in question.

(2) The conditions are—

(a) that the seller is a taxable person for the purposes of the Value Added Tax Act 1994;

(b) that the seller supplies 1000 or more single use carrier bags which attract the charge.

(3) A seller must publish the record on or before 31 May in the reporting year following that to which the record relates.

(4) The record must remain published until 31 May in the following reporting year.

(5) Publication must be by way of—

(a) the seller's internet site; or

(b) the display of a notice containing the record in all of the seller's premises in Wales to which customers have access.

(6) If a seller publishes the record by way of its internet site—

(a) the record must be displayed prominently on the seller's home page; or

(b) if the record is to be displayed elsewhere on the seller's internet site, a link to the record must be displayed prominently on the seller's home page.

(7) If a seller publishes the record in the way described in paragraph (5)(b), the notice must be displayed in a prominent position so that it is clearly visible to, and readable by, customers.

PART 4
BREACHES

11 Breaches

(1) A seller breaches these Regulations if, as a result of having failed to take all reasonable steps necessary to enable it to do so, a seller fails to comply with a requirement mentioned in paragraph (2).

(2) The requirements are—

(a) the requirement to charge in accordance with regulation 6;

(b) the requirement to keep records in accordance with regulation 8;

(c) the requirement to retain records in accordance with regulation 8;

(d) the requirement to supply records in accordance with regulation 9;

(e) the requirement to publish records in accordance with regulation 10.

(3) A seller breaches these Regulations if, without reasonable cause, a seller—

(a) gives false or misleading information to an administrator;

(b) otherwise obstructs or fails to assist an administrator in the conduct of its functions under these Regulations.

PART 5
CIVIL SANCTIONS

12 Civil sanctions

The following Schedules have effect—

(a) Schedule 2, which makes provision for fixed monetary penalties;

(b) Schedule 3, which makes provision for discretionary requirements.

13 Combination of penalties

[(1) An administrator may not serve a notice of intent in relation to a fixed monetary penalty on a seller in any of the following circumstances—

(a) where a discretionary requirement has been imposed on that seller in relation to the same breach;

(b) where the seller has discharged liability to a fixed monetary penalty in respect of the same breach by payment of a specified sum;

(c) where a fixed monetary penalty has previously been imposed in respect of the same act or omission.][1]

(2) An administrator may not serve a notice of intent in relation to a discretionary requirement on a seller in any of the following circumstances—

(a) where a fixed monetary penalty has been imposed on that seller in relation to the same breach;

(b) where the seller has discharged liability to a fixed monetary penalty in respect of the same breach by payment of a specified sum;

(c) where a discretionary requirement has previously been imposed in respect of the same act or omission.

Amendments—[1] Para 1 substituted by the Single Use Carrier Bags (Wales) (Amendment) Regulations SI 2011/2186 reg 7 with effect from 1 October 2011.

PART 6
ENFORCEMENT AND NON-COMPLIANCE

14 Enforcement powers

(1) An administrator has the powers of enforcement in this regulation.
(2) The powers are—
  (a) to make test purchases of goods for the purposes of ascertaining whether these Regulations are being complied with;
  (b) to inspect any goods and to enter any premises at any reasonable time (other than domestic premises) for the purposes of ascertaining whether these Regulations are being complied with;
  (c) if an administrator reasonably believes that there has been a failure to comply with a requirement of these Regulations—
    (i) to question a seller or officers or employees of a seller;
    (ii) to require the production of documents or the provision of information.
(3) In this regulation "domestic premises" ("*mangre ddomestig*") means premises used wholly or mainly as a private dwelling.
(4) An administrator seeking to exercise a power under paragraph (2)(b) or (c) must produce evidence of identity and authority if requested by a person who is, or appears to be—
  (a) the seller, or an officer or employee of the seller;
  (b) an owner or occupier of any premises in which the administrator seeks to exercise the power concerned.
(5) Nothing in paragraph (2) compels the production of any document of which—
  (a) in England and Wales or Northern Ireland, that person would on grounds of legal professional privilege be entitled to withhold production on an order for discovery in an action in the County Court or High Court; or
  (b) in Scotland, that person would on grounds of confidentiality of communications be entitled to withhold production on an order for the production of documents in an action in the Court of Session.

15 Non-monetary discretionary requirements: enforcement

Schedule 4 makes provision for the imposition of monetary penalties in cases where a seller fails to comply with a non-monetary discretionary requirement and that Schedule has effect accordingly.

16 Enforcement costs recovery

(1) An administrator may serve a notice ("an enforcement costs recovery notice") on a seller on whom a discretionary requirement is imposed requiring that seller to pay the costs incurred by the administrator in relation to the imposition of the discretionary requirement up to the time of its imposition ("enforcement costs").
(2) Enforcement costs include, in particular—
  (a) investigation costs;
  (b) administration costs;
  (c) costs of obtaining expert advice (including legal advice).
(3) An enforcement costs recovery notice must specify the amount required to be paid and must include information as to—
  (a) how payment may be made;
  (b) the date by which payment must be made;
  (c) the right of appeal; and
  (d) the consequences of failure to make payment by the date it is due.
(4) The date referred to in paragraph (3)(b) must be at least 28 days later than the date on which the enforcement costs recovery notice is served on the seller.
(5) Enforcement costs must be paid by the seller by the date specified in the enforcement costs recovery notice.
(6) But paragraph (5) is subject to the remaining provisions of this regulation and to regulation 21(4) (suspension of requirements and notices pending appeal).
(7) If a decision of an administrator under this regulation is the subject of an appeal, then to the extent that that decision is upheld, the seller must pay the enforcement costs within 28 days of the day on which the appeal is determined.
(8) An administrator must provide a detailed breakdown of the costs specified in an enforcement costs recovery notice if requested to do so by the seller on whom the notice is served.
(9) A seller is not liable to pay any costs shown by that seller to have been unnecessarily incurred.
(10) A seller may appeal—
  (a) against a decision of an administrator to impose a requirement to pay costs;
  (b) against a decision of an administrator as to the amount of those costs.

17 Recovery of payments

An administrator may recover any fixed monetary penalty, variable monetary penalty, non-compliance penalty, enforcement costs or late payment penalty—

(a) as a civil debt;

(b) on the order of a court, as if payable under a court order.

18 Publicity for imposition of civil sanctions

(1) An administrator may give a publicity notice to a seller on whom a civil sanction has been imposed.

(2) The following is the information specified for the purposes of paragraph 19(2)(b) of Schedule 6 to the Climate Change Act 2008—

(a) the type of civil sanction concerned;

(b) the grounds on which the sanction was imposed;

(c) if the sanction was a fixed or variable monetary penalty, the amount of that penalty;

(d) if the sanction was a non-monetary discretionary requirement, the nature of the requirement in question.

(3) A publicity notice must—

(a) specify the manner of publication required;

(b) specify the time for compliance with the notice;

(c) require the seller to provide evidence of compliance with the notice within a time specified in the notice.

(4) If a seller fails to comply with a publicity notice within the time specified under paragraph (3)(b), the administrator may—

(a) publicise the information required to be publicised by the notice; and

(b) recover the costs of doing so from the seller in question.

(5) Where an administrator publicises information under paragraph (4)(a) it must do so in a way it considers most likely to bring the information to the attention of members of the public in its area.

PART 7

ADMINISTRATION

19 Scope of administrators' powers

The functions conferred on an administrator by these Regulations are exercisable by an administrator in, and in relation to, its area.

20 Withdrawing or amending a notice

(1) An administrator may at any time in writing—

(a) withdraw a notice of intent or a final notice in relation to a fixed monetary penalty;

(b) withdraw a notice of intent or final notice in relation to a variable monetary penalty or reduce the amount specified in the notice;

(c) withdraw a notice of intent or a final notice in relation to a non-monetary discretionary requirement or amend the steps specified in the notice so as to reduce the amount of work necessary to comply with the notice;

(d) withdraw a notice of intent in relation to a non-compliance penalty or reduce the amount specified in the notice;

(e) withdraw a non-compliance penalty notice or reduce the amount specified in the notice;

(f) withdraw an enforcement costs recovery notice or reduce the amount specified in the notice.

(2) An administrator must consult the seller in question before withdrawing or amending a notice under paragraph (1).

(3) But paragraph (2) does not apply in any case where it is impracticable to consult the seller concerned.

21 Appeals

(1) An appeal under these Regulations is to the First-tier Tribunal ("the Tribunal").

(2) In any appeal where the commission of a breach is an issue requiring determination, the administrator must prove that breach on the balance of probabilities.

(3) In any other case the Tribunal must determine the standard of proof.

(4) A requirement or notice which is the subject of an appeal is suspended pending the determination of the appeal.

(5) The Tribunal may, in relation to the imposition of a requirement or service of a notice—

(a) withdraw the requirement or notice;

(b) confirm the requirement or notice;

(c) take such steps as the administrator could take in relation to the act or omission giving rise to the requirement or notice;

(d) remit the decision whether to confirm the requirement or notice, or any matter relating to that decision, to the administrator.

22 Guidance as to use of civil sanctions

(1) An administrator must publish guidance about its use of civil sanctions under these Regulations.

(2) The guidance must contain the relevant information (see paragraphs (5) and (6)).

(3) An administrator must revise the guidance where appropriate.

(4) An administrator must have regard to the guidance or revised guidance in exercising its functions.

(5) In the case of guidance relating to a fixed monetary penalty, the relevant information referred to in paragraph (2) is information as to—

(a) the circumstances in which the penalty is likely to be imposed;
(b) the circumstances in which the penalty may not be imposed;
(c) the amount of the penalty;
(d) how liability for the penalty may be discharged and the effect of discharge;
(e) rights to make representations and objections; and
(f) rights of appeal.

(6) In the case of guidance relating to a discretionary requirement, the relevant information referred to in paragraph (2) is information as to—

(a) the circumstances in which the requirement is likely to be imposed;
(b) the circumstances in which the requirement may not be imposed;
(c) in the case of a variable monetary penalty, the matters likely to be taken into account by the administrator in determining the amount of the penalty (including, where relevant, any discounts for voluntary reporting of non-compliance);
(d) rights to make representations and objections; and
(e) rights of appeal.

23 Additional guidance

(1) An administrator must publish guidance about how it will exercise the powers conferred by regulation 15 and Schedule 4 (non-compliance penalties) and regulation 16 (enforcement costs recovery).

(2) The guidance must include, in particular, information as to—

(a) the circumstances in which the powers are likely to be exercised;
(b) matters to be taken into account in determining the amounts involved;
(c) rights of appeal.

(3) An administrator must revise the guidance where appropriate.

(4) An administrator must have regard to the guidance or revised guidance in exercising its functions.

24 Consultation on guidance

Before publishing any guidance or revised guidance under these Regulations an administrator must consult—

(a) the Welsh Ministers;
(b) the Local Better Regulation Office;
(c) the Confederation of British Industry;
(d) the Federation of Small Businesses;
(e) the British Retail Consortium.

25 Publication of enforcement action

(1) An administrator must from time to time publish reports specifying—

(a) the cases in which a civil sanction for a breach of these Regulations has been imposed;
(b) where the civil sanction is a fixed monetary penalty, the cases in which liability to the penalty has been discharged in accordance with paragraph 4 of Schedule 2 (discharge of liability following notice of intent).

(2) In paragraph (1)(a) the reference to cases in which the civil sanction has been imposed does not include cases where the sanction has been imposed but overturned on appeal.

(3) An administrator must not publish a report in any case where the Welsh Ministers notify the administrator in writing that it would be inappropriate to do so.

Jane Davidson

Minister for Environment, Sustainability and Housing, one of the Welsh Ministers

30 November 2010

SCHEDULE 1

Regulation 7

Exemptions

1 (1) The kinds of single use carrier bags to which regulation 6 does not apply are—

[(za) bags used solely to contain one or more items of the following kinds—

(i) unpackaged food for human or animal consumption;
(ii) unpackaged loose seeds, bulbs, corms or rhizomes;
(iii) any unpackaged axe, knife, knife blade or razor blade;
(iv) unpackaged goods contaminated by soil;
(v) items from the categories specified in sub-paragraph (2);][1]

(a) ...[1]
(b) ...[1]
(c) ...[1]
(d) ...[1]
(e) bags used solely to contain packaged—
(i) uncooked fish or fish products;
(ii) uncooked meat or meat products;
(iii) uncooked poultry or poultry products,

and in respect of which the maximum dimensions are 205 millimetres ("mm") (width) x 125 mm (gusset width) x 458 mm (height inclusive of handles);

(f) ...[1]
(g) bags used to contain purchases made on board ships, trains, aircraft, coaches or buses;
(h) bags used to contain purchases made in an area designated by the Secretary of State as a security restricted area under section 11A of the Aviation Security Act 1982;
[(i) mail order dispatch and courier bags;][1]
(j) bags which—
(i) are made wholly from paper;
(ii) have maximum dimensions of 175 mm (width) x 260 mm (height);
(iii) do not have a gusset; and
(iv) do not have a handle;
(k) bags which—
(i) are made wholly or mainly from plastic;
(ii) have maximum dimensions of 125 mm (width) x 125 mm (height);
(iii) do not have a gusset; and
(iv) do not have a handle;
(l) bags which—
(i) are made wholly from paper;
(ii) have maximum dimensions of 80 mm (width) x 50 mm (gusset width) x 155 mm (height); and
(iii) do not have a handle;
(m) gusseted liners used to line or cover boxes, crates or other containers of a similar nature;
(n) bags used solely to contain live aquatic creatures in water;
(o) ...[1]

(2) The specified categories are—

(a) medicinal products or listed appliances sold in accordance with a prescription issued by a registered medical practitioner, a dentist, a supplementary prescriber, a nurse independent prescriber, an independent nurse prescriber, an optometrist independent prescriber, a pharmacist independent prescriber or an EEA health professional;
(b) where sold or supplied otherwise than in accordance with paragraph (a), pharmacy medicine.

(3) In this paragraph—

"dentist" ("*deintydd*") means a person registered in the dentists register kept under section 14 of the Dentists Act 1984;

"EEA health professional" ("*proffesiynolyn iechyd yr AEE*") has the meaning given in regulation 1(2) of the Medicines for Human Use (Prescribing by EEA Practitioners) Regulations 2008;

"independent nurse prescriber" ("*nyrs sy'n rhagnodi'n annibynnol*") has the meaning given in regulation 2(1) of the National Health Service (Pharmaceutical Services) Regulations 1992;

"listed appliances" ("*cyfarpar rhestredig*") means listed appliances within the meaning of any of the following—

(a) section 80 of the National Health Service (Wales) Act 2006;
(b) article 63 of the Health and Personal Social Services (Northern Ireland) Order 1972;
(c) section 27 of the National Health Service (Scotland) Act 1978;
(d) section 126 of the National Health Service Act 2006;

"medicinal product" ("*cynnyrch meddyginiaethol*") has the meaning given in section 130 of the Medicines Act 1968;

"pharmacy medicine" ("*meddyginiaeth fferyllol*") means a medicinal product which is not a prescription only medicine and which—

(a) in accordance with section 52 of the Medicines Act 1968, can only be sold or supplied under the conditions specified in sub-section (1)(a) to (c) of that section; or

(b) but for the fact that it is sold or supplied in accordance with section 55 of that Act, could only lawfully be sold or supplied under those conditions;

"prescription only medicine" ("*meddyginiaeth drwy bresgripsiwn yn unig*") means a medicinal product—

(a) of a description or falling within a class specified in an order made under section 58 of the Medicines Act 1968;

(b) to which section 58 of that Act applies by virtue of an order made under section 104 of that Act;

"supplementary prescriber" ("*rhagnodydd atodol*"), "nurse independent prescriber" ("*nyrs-ragnodydd annibynnol*"), "optometrist independent prescriber" ("*optometrydd-ragnodydd annibynnol*") and "pharmacist independent prescriber" ("*fferyllydd-ragnodydd annibynnol*") each have the meanings respectively ascribed to them in article 1(2) of the Prescription Only Medicines (Human Use) Order 1997;

"unpackaged" ("*heb ei becynnu*") means wholly or partly unwrapped.

Amendments—[1] In para 1(1), para (*za*) inserted; paras (*a*)–(*d*), (*f*) and (*o*) omitted and para (*l*) substituted by the Single Use Carrier Bags Charge (Wales) (Amendment) Regulations SI 2011/2184 reg 8 with effect from 1 October 2011.

SCHEDULE 2
FIXED MONETARY PENALTIES

Regulation 12

PART 1
IMPOSITION OF FIXED MONETARY PENALTIES AND PROCEDURE

Power to impose fixed monetary penalty

1 (1) An administrator may by notice impose a fixed monetary penalty on a seller who breaches these Regulations in the circumstances specified in regulation 11(1).

(2) An administrator may exercise the power conferred by sub-paragraph (1) in relation to a case if it is satisfied on the balance of probabilities that the breach has occurred.

Fixed monetary penalties

2 The amount of penalty which can be imposed by an administrator as a fixed monetary penalty in any case is the amount specified in the second column of the table in Part 2 by reference to the kind of breach concerned.

Notice of Intent

3 (1) Where an administrator proposes to impose a fixed monetary penalty on a seller, the administrator must serve a notice of intent on that seller.

(2) A notice of intent must—

(a) state the amount of the penalty;

(b) offer the seller the opportunity to discharge its liability to the penalty by paying the specified sum within 28 days beginning with the day on which the notice is received;

(c) include information as to—

(i) the grounds for the proposal to impose the fixed monetary penalty;

(ii) the effect of payment of the specified sum;

(iii) the right to make representations and objections conferred by paragraph 5;

(iv) the circumstances in which the administrator may not impose the fixed monetary penalty;

(v) the 28 day period within which liability to the fixed monetary penalty may be discharged by virtue of paragraph 4;

(vi) the 28 day period within which representations and objections may be made;

(vii) how payment may be made.

Discharge of liability following notice of intent

4 (1) A seller's liability to a fixed monetary penalty is discharged if the seller pays the specified sum within 28 days beginning with the day on which the notice of intent to which it relates was received.

(2) The specified sum is the amount specified in the third column of the table in Part 2 by reference to the kind of breach concerned.

Making representations and objections

5 (1) This paragraph applies if a seller does not discharge its liability to a fixed monetary penalty by payment of the specified sum.
(2) Within 28 days of the day on which the notice of intent was received by the seller, the seller may make written representations and objections to the administrator in relation to the proposed imposition of the fixed monetary penalty.

Decision whether to impose a fixed monetary penalty

6 (1) At the end of the 28 day period for making representations and objections under paragraph 5, the administrator must decide whether to impose the fixed monetary penalty.
(2) In making a decision under this paragraph an administrator must take into consideration any representations or objections made by the seller in accordance with that paragraph.
(3) An administrator may not decide to impose a fixed monetary penalty in any of the following circumstances—

- (a) if liability to a fixed monetary penalty in respect of the same breach has been discharged by payment of the specified sum;
- (b) if a fixed monetary penalty has previously been imposed in respect of the same breach;
- (c) if a discretionary requirement has been imposed in respect of the same act or omission;

(4) Without restricting the power under sub-paragraph (1), an administrator may decide not to impose a fixed penalty if the administrator considers that in all the circumstances of the case it would be inexpedient to do so.
(5) Where the administrator decides to impose the fixed monetary penalty it must do so by serving the final notice on the seller.
(6) The final notice must comply with paragraph 7.

Contents of final notice

7 The final notice must include information as to—

- (a) the grounds for imposing the fixed monetary penalty;
- (b) the administrator's response to any representation and objections made by the seller;
- (c) the amount of the penalty;
- (d) how payment may be made;
- (e) the period of 56 days within which payment must be made;
- (f) the effect of paragraph 9 (early payment discount);
- (g) the effect of paragraph 10 (late payment penalty);
- (h) rights of appeal; and
- (i) the consequences of non-payment.

Payment

8 (1) A fixed monetary penalty must be paid by a seller within 56 days beginning with the day on which the final notice imposing it was received.

But this is subject to regulation 21(4) (suspension of requirements and notices pending appeal).
(2) If a decision to impose a fixed monetary penalty is the subject of an appeal then if that decision is upheld, the penalty must be paid by the seller within 28 days beginning with the day on which the appeal is determined.

Early payment discount

9 A seller may discharge its liability to a fixed monetary penalty by paying 50% of the amount of the penalty within 28 days beginning with the day on which the final notice imposing it was received.

Late payment penalty

10 If a fixed monetary penalty is not paid within the period allowed in accordance with paragraph 8 the amount of the penalty is increased by 50%.

Grounds of appeal

11 (1) A seller may appeal against an administrator's decision to impose a fixed monetary penalty.
(2) The grounds of appeal are—

- (a) that the decision was based on an error of fact;
- (b) that the decision was wrong in law;
- (c) that the decision was unreasonable for any other reason;
- (d) any other reason.

PART 2

FIXED MONETARY PENALTY AMOUNTS AND SPECIFIED SUMS

Breach	*Amount of penalty which can be imposed as a fixed monetary penalty*	*Specified sums*
Failure to comply with the requirement to charge in accordance with regulation 6 (regulation 11(1) and (2))	£200	£100
Failure to keep records in accordance with regulation 8 (regulation 11(1) and (2))	£100	£50
Failure to retain records in accordance with regulation 8 (regulation 11(1) and (2))	£100	£50
Failure to supply records in accordance with regulation 9 (regulation 11(1) and (2))	£100	£50
Failure to publish records in accordance with regulation 10 (regulation 11(1) and (2))	£100	£50

SCHEDULE 3

DISCRETIONARY REQUIREMENTS

Regulation 12

PART 1

IMPOSITION OF DISCRETIONARY REQUIREMENTS AND PROCEDURE

Power to impose discretionary requirements

1 (1) An administrator may by notice impose one or more discretionary requirements on a seller who breaches these Regulations.

(2) An administrator may exercise the power conferred by sub-paragraph (1) in relation to a case if it is satisfied on the balance of probabilities that the breach has occurred.

Variable monetary penalties: maximum amounts

2 The maximum penalty which may be imposed by an administrator as a variable monetary penalty in respect of any particular kind of breach is the amount specified in the second column of the table in Part 2 by reference to the kind of breach concerned.

Notice of intent

3 (1) Where an administrator proposes to impose one or more discretionary requirements on a seller, the administrator must serve a notice of intent on that seller.

(2) The notice of intent must—

(a) if the administrator proposes to impose a non-monetary discretionary requirement—

(i) specify the steps that the administrator proposes the seller be required to take;

(ii) specify the time period within which the administrator proposes that those steps are to be completed;

(b) if the administrator proposes to impose a variable monetary penalty, specify the amount of penalty proposed;

(c) include information as to—

(i) the grounds for the proposal to impose the one or more discretionary requirements;

(ii) the right to make representations and objections conferred by paragraph 4;

(iii) the circumstances in which the administrator may not impose the one or more discretionary requirements;

(iv) the 28 day period within which representations and objections may be made;

(v) in the case of a variable monetary penalty, how payment may be made.

Making representations and objections

4 Within 28 days beginning with the day on which the notice of intent is received by the seller, the seller may make written representations and objections to the administrator in relation to the proposed imposition of the one or more discretionary requirements.

Decision whether to impose discretionary requirements

5 (1) After the end of the 28 day period for making representations and objections under paragraph 4, the administrator must decide whether to—

(a) impose the one or more discretionary requirements with or without modifications; or

(b) impose any other discretionary requirement that the administrator has the power to impose under this Schedule.

(2) In making a decision under this paragraph an administrator must take into consideration any representations or objections made by the seller in accordance with paragraph 4.

(3) An administrator may not decide to impose a discretionary requirement in any of the following circumstances—

(a) if a discretionary requirement has previously been imposed in relation to the same act or omission;

(b) if liability to a fixed monetary penalty in respect of the same breach has been discharged by payment of a specified sum;

(c) if a fixed monetary penalty has been imposed in respect of the same breach.

(4) An administrator may not decide under this paragraph to impose a fixed monetary penalty in place of a discretionary requirement.

(5) Without restricting the power under sub-paragraph (1), an administrator may decide not to impose a discretionary requirement if the administrator considers that in all the circumstances of the case it would be inexpedient to do so.

(6) Where an administrator decides to impose a discretionary requirement it must do so by serving the final notice on the seller.

(7) The final notice must comply with paragraph 6.

Contents of a final notice

6 The final notice must include information as to—

(a) the grounds for imposing the one or more discretionary requirements;

(b) the administrator's response to any representation and objections made by the seller, including the effect (if any) on the amount of any variable monetary penalty imposed;

(c) where the discretionary requirement is a non-monetary discretionary requirement—

(i) the steps the seller is required to take;

(ii) the period within which those steps must be completed;

(d) where the discretionary requirement is a variable monetary penalty—

(i) the amount of the penalty;

(ii) how payment may be made;

(iii) the period within which payment must be made;

(iv) the effect of paragraph 8 (early payment discount)

(v) the effect of paragraph 9 (late payment penalty);

(e) rights of appeal; and

(f) the consequences of failing to comply with the notice.

Payment

7 (1) A variable monetary penalty must be paid by a seller within 56 days beginning with the day on which the final notice imposing it was received.

But this is subject to regulation 21(4) (suspension of requirements and notices pending appeal).

(2) If the decision to impose a variable monetary penalty is the subject of an appeal then to the extent that that decision is upheld, the penalty must be paid by the seller within 28 days beginning with the day on which the appeal is determined.

Early payment discount

8 A seller may discharge its liability to a variable monetary penalty by paying 50% of the amount of the penalty within 28 days beginning with the day on which the final notice imposing it is received.

Late payment penalty

9 If a variable monetary penalty is not paid within the period allowed in accordance with paragraph 7 the amount payable is increased by 50%.

Grounds of appeal

10 (1) A seller may appeal against an administrator's decision to impose a discretionary requirement.

(2) The grounds of appeal are—

(a) that the decision was based on an error of fact;

(b) that the decision was wrong in law;

(c) in case of a variable monetary penalty, that the amount of the penalty is unreasonable;
(d) in the case of a non-monetary discretionary requirement, that the nature of the requirement is unreasonable;
(e) that the decision was unreasonable for any other reason;
(f) any other reason.

PART 2
VARIABLE MONETARY PENALTIES: MAXIMUM AMOUNTS

Breach	*Maximum amount which may be imposed as a variable monetary penalty*
Failure to comply with the requirement to charge in accordance with regulation 6 (regulation 11(1) and (2))	£5,000
Failure to keep records in accordance with regulation 8 (regulation 11(1) and (2))	£5,000
Failure to retain records in accordance with regulation 8 (regulation 11(1) and (2))	£5,000
Failure to supply records in accordance with regulation 9 (regulation 11(1) and (2))	£5,000
Failure to publish records in accordance with regulation 10 (regulation 11(1) and (2))	£5,000
Without reasonable cause, giving false or misleading information to an administrator (regulation 11(3))	£20,000
Without reasonable cause, otherwise obstructing or failing to assist an administrator in the conduct of its functions under these Regulations (regulation 11(3))	£20,000

SCHEDULE 4
NON-MONETARY DISCRETIONARY REQUIREMENTS: ENFORCEMENT
Regulation 15

1 (1) In this Schedule—

"specified steps" ("*camau penodedig*") means the steps specified in a final notice under paragraph 6(c)(i) of Schedule 3;

"specified period" ("*cyfnod penodedig*") means the period specified in a final notice under paragraph 6(c)(ii) of Schedule 3.

(2) A reference in this Schedule to a complete failure is a reference to a seller having taken none of the specified steps within the specified period.

(3) A reference in this Schedule to a partial failure is a reference to a seller having taken at least one, but not all, of the specified steps within the specified period.

Power to impose non-compliance penalties

2 (1) If a seller fails to comply with a non-monetary discretionary requirement an administrator may by notice impose a non-compliance penalty on the seller.

(2) A non-compliance penalty may be imposed in respect of a complete or partial failure to comply with a non-monetary discretionary requirement.

(3) A non-compliance penalty may be imposed irrespective of whether a variable monetary penalty was imposed in addition to the non-discretionary requirement to which the non-compliance penalty relates.

(4) The amount of a non-compliance penalty is to be determined by the administrator.

(5) But the maximum penalty which may be imposed by an administrator as a non-compliance penalty is the amount specified in sub-paragraph (6) by reference to the kind of failure concerned.

(6) The maximum penalties are—

(a) £5,000 in relation to a partial failure;
(b) £5,000 in relation to a complete failure.

Notice of intent

3 (1) Where an administrator proposes to impose a non-compliance penalty on a seller, the administrator must serve on that seller a notice of what is proposed (a "notice of intent").
(2) A notice of intent must include information as to—

(a) the kind of failure in relation to which the administrator proposes to impose the non-compliance penalty;
(b) the specified steps which remain to be taken by the seller concerned;
(c) the amount of the penalty proposed;
(d) how payment may be made;
(e) the date by which payment would be due;
(f) the consequences of failure to make payment by the date it is due;
(g) the right to make representations and objections conferred by paragraph 4;
(h) the 28 day period within which representations and objections may be made;
(i) the circumstances (if any) in which the administrator may be inclined to reduce the amount of the penalty proposed.

Making representations and objections

4 Within 28 days beginning with the date on which the notice of intent is received by the seller, the seller may make written representations and objections to the administrator in relation to the proposed imposition of a non-compliance penalty.

Decision whether to impose a non-compliance penalty

5 (1) After the end of the 28 day period for making representations and objections under paragraph 4, the administrator must decide whether to impose the non-compliance penalty with or without modifications.
(2) Without restricting the power under sub-paragraph (1), an administrator may decide not to impose a non-compliance penalty if the administrator considers that in all the circumstances of the case it would be inexpedient to do so.
(3) In making a decision under this paragraph an administrator must take into consideration any representations or objections made by the seller in accordance with paragraph 4.
(4) Where an administrator decides to impose a non-compliance penalty it must do so by serving a notice ("a non-compliance penalty notice") on the seller.
(5) A non-compliance penalty notice must comply with paragraph 6.

Contents of a non-compliance penalty notice

6 (1) A non-compliance penalty notice must include information as to—

(a) the grounds for imposing the non-compliance penalty;
(b) the administrator's response to any representations and objections made by the seller, including the effect (if any) on the amount of the penalty imposed;
(c) the amount of the penalty;
(d) how payment may be made;
(e) the date by which payment must be made;
(f) the right of appeal; and
(g) the consequences of failure to make payment by the date it is due.

(2) A non-compliance penalty must be paid by a seller within 56 days beginning with the date on which the notice imposing it was received.
(3) But this is subject to sub-paragraph (4) and regulation 21(4) (suspension of requirements and notices pending determination of an appeal).
(4) If the requirements of the non-monetary discretionary requirement are complied with before the 56 days expire, the non-compliance penalty is not payable.
(5) A seller on whom a non-compliance penalty notice is served may appeal against it.
(6) The grounds of appeal are—

(a) that the decision to serve the notice was based on an error of fact;
(b) that the decision was wrong in law;
(c) that the amount of the penalty was unreasonable;
(d) that the decision was unfair or unreasonable for any other reason;
(e) any other reason.

Payment of non-compliance penalties following appeal

7 If a non-compliance penalty notice is the subject of an appeal, then to the extent that the notice is upheld, the penalty must be paid by the seller within 28 days beginning with the day on which the appeal is determined.

Non-compliance penalties: late payment penalty

8 If a non-compliance penalty is not paid within the period allowed by paragraph 6(2) or (as the case may be) by paragraph 7, the amount payable is increased by 50%.

2010/2913

LONDON OLYMPIC GAMES AND PARALYMPIC GAMES TAX REGULATIONS 2010

Made . . . . 7 December 2010

Laid before the House of Commons . . . . 8 December 2010

Coming into force . . . . 1 January 2011

The Treasury, in exercise of the powers conferred by section 68 of the Finance Act 2006 and sections 966(6) and 970(5) of the Income Tax Act 2007, make the following Regulations.

1 Citation and commencement

These Regulations may be cited as the London Olympic Games and Paralympic Games Tax Regulations 2010 and come into force on 1 January 2011.

2 Interpretation

(1) In these Regulations—

"accreditation card" means an Olympic Identity and Accreditation Card, or a Paralympic Identity and Accreditation Card, issued and validated by LOCOG;

"CAS" means the Court of Arbitration for Sport;

"CTA 2009" means the Corporation Tax Act 2009;

"CTA 2010" means the Corporation Tax Act 2010;

"IF" means an organisation recognised by the IOC as an International Federation;

"IOC" means the International Olympic Committee;

"IPC" means the International Paralympic Committee;

"IPSF" means an organisation recognised by the IPC as an International Paralympic Sport Federation;

"ITA 2007" means the Income Tax Act 2007;

"ITEPA 2003" means the Income Tax (Earnings and Pensions) Act 2003;

"ITTOIA 2005" means the Income Tax (Trading and Other Income) Act 2005;

"LOCOG" means the London Organising Committee of the Olympic Games and Paralympic Games Limited registered at Companies House under Company No 05267819;

"London 2012" means the Olympic Games and Paralympic Games;

"NOC" means a National Olympic Committee recognised by the IOC;

"NPC" means a National Paralympic Committee recognised by the IPC;

"Olympic Games" means the Games of the XXX Olympiad that are to take place in 2012;

"Paralympic Games" means the Games of the XIV Paralympics that are to take place in 2012;

"WADA" means the World Anti-Doping Agency.

(2) In these Regulations "income" means—

(*a*) employment income as defined by section 7(2) of ITEPA 2003 (meaning of employment income), including income that would be employment income but for the provisions of regulation 3;

(*b*) profits of a trade, profession or vocation that are chargeable under section 5 (charge to tax on trade profits), section 229 (adjustment income: income charged) and section 242 (charge to tax on post-cessation receipts) of ITTOIA 2005;

(*c*) annual payments that are chargeable under section 683 of ITTOIA 2005 (annual payments not otherwise charged); and

(*d*) income that is chargeable under section 687 of ITTOIA 2005 (income not otherwise charged); including profits, annual payments and income that would be so chargeable but for the provisions of regulation 3.

(3) In regulations 4(1)(b), 6(1)(b) and 7(1)(b)—

(*a*) a payment or transfer is made to the individual carrying out the London 2012 activity where it is made to that individual or where it is treated for income tax purposes as made to that individual in the course of a trade, profession or vocation pursuant to section 13(5) of ITTOIA 2005 (visiting performers: treatment of payment or transfer);

(*b*) a payment or transfer is connected with a London 2012 activity where the London 2012 activity is a relevant activity for the purposes of section 13 of ITTOIA 2005 (visiting performers) and the payment or transfer has a connection of the prescribed kind with that activity pursuant to that section.

3 Exemption from income tax etc

(1) Income to which regulation 4, 6, 7 or 8 applies—

(*a*) shall not be taxable earnings or taxable specific income as defined by section 10 of ITEPA 2003 (meaning of "taxable earnings" and "taxable specific income");

(*b*) shall be exempt from income tax that would otherwise be chargeable on that income under—

(i) section 5 (charge to tax on trade profits), section 229 (adjustment income: income charged) and section 242 (charge to tax on post cessation receipts) of ITTOIA 2005;
(ii) section 683 of ITTOIA 2005 (annual payments); or
(iii) section 687 of ITTOIA 2005 (income not otherwise charged).

(2) A payment or transfer to which regulation 4, 6 or 7 applies is exempt from income tax that would otherwise be chargeable on that payment or transfer by virtue of section 13 of ITTOIA 2005 (visiting performers).

(3) Sections 900 and 901 (duty to deduct from annual payments) and section 966 (duty to deduct and account for sums representing income tax) of ITA 2007 do not apply to income, a payment or transfer to which regulation 4, 6, 7 or 8 applies.

(4) This regulation is subject to regulations 9 and 11.

4 Accredited individual

(1) This regulation applies to—
(*a*) income received by an individual to whom regulation 5 applies where that income is received wholly and exclusively in return for that individual carrying out a London 2012 activity in the UK during the relevant period;
(*b*) a payment or transfer—
(i) connected with a London 2012 activity carried out in the UK during the relevant period by an individual to whom regulation 5(2)(a) or (b) applies; and
(ii) made to the individual carrying out that London 2012 activity.

(2) In this regulation and regulation 5 "London 2012 activity" means—
(*a*) in relation to a competitor—
(i) performing in a sporting event at London 2012; or
(ii) activity primarily to support or promote London 2012, the Olympic or Paralympic Movement;
(*b*) in relation to any other individual to whom regulation 5 applies the activity necessary to perform the London 2012 function listed in regulation 5—
(i) for which that individual receives an accreditation card; or
(ii) for which that individual would have received an accreditation card if it were his or her only London 2012 function.

(3) In this regulation "relevant period" means 30th March 2012 to 8th November 2012.

5 Accredited individual: London 2012 functions

(1) This regulation applies to an individual who—
(*a*) is neither resident nor ordinarily resident in the UK in the tax year during which the London 2012 activity is carried out;
(*b*) has an accreditation card; and
(*c*) has one or more of the London 2012 functions specified in paragraph (2).

(2) The London 2012 functions are—
(*a*) competitor;
(*b*) media worker;
(*c*) representative of an Official Body;
(*d*) service technician;
(*e*) team official;
(*f*) technical official.

(3) In this regulation—

"competitor" means an individual who has been entered by a NOC or NPC to perform in a sporting event which forms part of London 2012;

"media worker" means a media manager, a media producer, a media technician, a media support worker, a radio or television worker or a written, photographic or electronic journalist;

"Official Body" means a Sovereign, a Head of State, a Government, a NOC, a NPC, a city that has been selected by the IOC or IPC to host a future Olympics and Paralympics or Youth Olympics, a city that has been selected by the IOC or IPC to be a candidate to host a future Olympics and Paralympics or Youth Olympics, a city that the IOC or IPC recognises as an applicant to host a future Olympics and Paralympics or Youth Olympics, the IOC, the IPC, an IF, an IPSF, CAS or WADA;

"representative of an Official Body" means an individual who represents, is part of the support staff of, or is a closing ceremony production worker of, an Official Body, or provides observer, drug testing, analysis or arbitration services to CAS or WADA;

"service technician" means an individual who repairs, operates or maintains the equipment on which competitors rely for their performance or safety;

"team official" means an individual who is part of the reserve athlete, support athlete, coaching, technical, carer or medical staff of a NOC or NPC;

"technical official" means an individual who has been selected by LOCOG, an IF or IPSF to officiate at London 2012 and includes technical delegates, classifiers, judges and referees.

6 Ceremony performer

(1) Where an individual is neither resident nor ordinarily resident in the UK in the tax year during which he or she carries out a London 2012 activity, this regulation applies to—

(*a*) income received by that individual wholly and exclusively in return for that activity;

(*b*) a payment or transfer connected with that activity and made to the individual carrying out that activity.

(2) In this regulation "London 2012 activity" means a performance at, or at the rehearsal of, an opening or closing ceremony of London 2012.

7 RHB worker and OBS worker

(1) Where a RHB worker or an OBS worker carries out a London 2012 activity in the UK during the relevant period this regulation applies to—

(*a*) income received by that worker wholly and exclusively in return for carrying out that activity;

(*b*) a payment or transfer connected with that activity and made to the individual carrying out that activity.

(2) A RHB worker is an individual who is neither resident nor ordinarily resident in the UK in the tax year during which the London 2012 activity is carried out and is—

(*a*) employed by a RHB;

(*b*) directly contracted to work for a RHB; or

(*c*) employed by a person that is directly contracted to work for a RHB.

(3) An OBS worker is an individual who is neither resident nor ordinarily resident in the UK in the tax year during which the London 2012 activity is carried out and is—

(*a*) employed by the OBS;

(*b*) directly contracted to work for the OBS; or

(*c*) employed by a person that is directly contracted to work for the OBS.

(4) In this regulation—

"London 2012 activity" means activity which is necessary for the broadcast of London 2012;

"OBS" means the organisation responsible for producing international television and radio signals and providing broadcasters with the facilities and services necessary for broadcasting London 2012 (the Olympic Broadcasting Services);

"relevant period" means 6th April 2011 to 5th April 2013;

"RHB" means an organisation to whom the IOC or LOCOG has granted the exclusive television, Internet or radio rights to broadcast the Olympic Games or the Paralympic Games in a particular territory (a Rights-Holding Broadcast Organisation).

8 London 2012 Partner worker

(1) This regulation applies to income received by a London 2012 Partner worker, wholly and exclusively in return for carrying out a London 2012 activity in the UK during the relevant period.

(2) A London 2012 Partner worker is an individual who is neither resident nor ordinarily resident in the UK in the tax year during which the London 2012 activity is carried out and—

(*a*) is employed by a London 2012 Partner; or

(*b*) holds an accreditation card, or is providing timing, scoring or on-venue result services, and is—

(i) directly contracted to work for a London 2012 Partner; or

(ii) employed by a person that is directly contracted to work for a London 2012 Partner.

(3) A London 2012 Partner is a Commercial Delivery Partner or a connected person to that Commercial Delivery Partner.

(4) A Commercial Delivery Partner is a person that—

(*a*) holds a London 2012 association right;

(*b*) has been granted a paragraph 4 authorisation; and

(*c*) provides services to LOCOG, for the purposes of delivering London 2012, wholly or partly in return for which it receives its paragraph 4 authorisation.

(5) In this regulation—

"connected person" has the meaning given by section 1122 and 1123 of CTA 2010 ("connected" persons);

"London 2012 association right" means a London Olympics association right as defined by paragraph 1 of Schedule 4 to the London Olympic Games and Paralympic Games Act 2006;

"London 2012 activity" means a service provided to LOCOG, for the purposes of delivering London 2012, wholly or partly in return for which a Commercial Delivery Partner receives its paragraph 4 authorisation;

"paragraph 4 authorisation" means authorisation by LOCOG under paragraph 4 of Schedule 4 to the London Olympic Games and Paralympic Games Act 2006 to market and advertise themselves or their products for commercial purposes by reference to their association with London 2012;

"relevant period" means 30th March 2012 to 8th November 2012.

9 Exclusion of certain income, payments or transfers

(1) Regulation 3 does not apply to income, a payment or transfer in the circumstances set out in paragraph (2) or (3).

(2) Where the income, payment or transfer arises in relation to a competitor performing in a sporting event of the Olympic Games, as a result of—

(*a*) a contract entered into on or after the 25th July 2012; or

(*b*) any amendment, on or after the 25th July 2012, of a contract entered into before the 25th July 2012.

(3) Where the income, payment or transfer arises in relation to a competitor performing in a sporting event of the Paralympic Games, as a result of—

(*a*) a contract entered into on or after the 29th August 2012; or

(*b*) any amendment, on or after the 29th August 2012, of a contract entered into before the 29th August 2012.

(4) In this regulation "competitor" has the same meaning as in regulation 5.

10 Permanent establishment

(1) Activity carried out for which income is received or a payment or transfer is made to which regulation 4, 7 or 8 (as modified by paragraph (3)) applies will not create a permanent establishment of the employer of the individual carrying out the activity for the purposes of section 5(2) of CTA 2009 (territorial scope of charge).

(2) Income received by the employer of the individual for carrying out activity to which paragraph (1) applies is exempt from income tax that would otherwise be chargeable on that income by virtue of section 6(2) of ITTOIA 2005 (territorial scope of charge to tax).

(3) For the purposes of this regulation—

(*a*) in regulation 7—

(i) a RHB worker or an OBS worker includes an individual who is resident or ordinarily resident in the UK in the tax year during which the activity is carried out;

(ii) the relevant period is 30th March 2012 to 8th November 2012.

(*b*) in regulation 8—

(i) a London 2012 Partner worker who is providing timing, scoring or on-venue result services includes an individual who is resident or ordinarily resident in the UK in the tax year during which the activity is carried out;

(ii) the relevant period for the activity of providing timing, scoring or on-venue result services is 1st January 2011 to 31st December 2012.

(4) This regulation is subject to regulation 11.

11 Tax avoidance

(1) Regulation 3 does not apply if conditions A and B are met.

(*a*) Condition A is that arrangements have been made which, but for this regulation would result in a person obtaining an exemption under regulation 3 in respect of income, a payment or transfer.

(*b*) Condition B is that those arrangements have, or form part of arrangements which have, as their main purpose, or one of their main purposes, the obtaining of that exemption.

(2) Regulation 10(1) does not apply if conditions C and D are met.

(*a*) Condition C is that arrangements have been made which, but for this regulation would result in a person obtaining the benefit of regulation 10(1) in respect of an activity.

(*b*) Condition D is that those arrangements have, or form part of arrangements which have, as their main purpose, or one of their main purposes, the obtaining of that benefit.

(3) Regulation 10(2) does not apply if conditions E and F are met.

(*a*) Condition E is that arrangements have been made which, but for this regulation would result in a person obtaining an exemption under regulation 10(2) in respect of income, a payment or transfer.

(*b*) Condition F is that those arrangements have, or form part of arrangements which have, as their main purpose, or one of their main purposes, the obtaining of that exemption.

2010/2929

TAX TREATMENT OF FINANCING COSTS AND INCOME (AVAILABLE AMOUNT) REGULATIONS 2010

Made . . . . *8 December 2010*
Laid before the House of Commons . . . . *9 December 2010*
Coming into force . . . . *1 January 2011*

Revocation—

These Regulations revoked by F(No 2)A 2017 s 20, Sch 5 para 11(3)(*d*) with effect in relation to periods of account of the worldwide group that begin on or after 1 April 2017. In relation to periods of account that straddle 1 April 2017 see Sch 5 para 26(2)–(10). **Please note** that Part 2A of the Yellow Book was sent to print before the Act had received Royal Assent. This amendment is therefore based on the 8 September 2017 Finance Bill. Please check F(No 2)A 2017 for confirmation of this amendment.

The Commissioners for Her Majesty's Revenue and Customs make the following regulations in exercise of the powers conferred by section 332(1)(g) of the Taxation (International and Other Provisions) Act 2010.

1 Citation and commencement

(1) These Regulations may be cited as the Tax Treatment of Financing Costs and Income (Available Amount) Regulations 2010 and come into force on 1st January 2011.

(2) These Regulations have effect in relation to periods of account of the worldwide group beginning on or after 1st January 2011.

REVOCATION—

These Regulations revoked by F(No 2)A 2017 s 20, Sch 5 para 11(3)(*d*) with effect in relation to periods of account of the worldwide group that begin on or after 1 April 2017. In relation to periods of account that straddle 1 April 2017 see Sch 5 para 26(2)–(10). **Please note** that Part 2A of the Yellow Book was sent to print before the Act had received Royal Assent. This amendment is therefore based on the 8 September 2017 Finance Bill. Please check F(No 2)A 2017 for confirmation of this amendment.

2 Interpretation

For the purposes of these Regulations—

"CTA 2009" means the Corporation Tax Act 2009;

"alternative finance arrangements" has the meaning given in section 501(2) of CTA 2009 (introduction to chapter: definitions etc);

"alternative finance return" has the meaning given in sections 511 to 513 of CTA 2009 (purchase and resale arrangements, diminishing shared ownership arrangements and other arrangements);

"loan relationship" has the meaning given in section 302 of CTA 2009 (definitions of loan relationship, creditor relationship and debtor relationship);

"manufactured interest" has the meaning given in section 539(5) of CTA 2009 (introduction to chapter: definitions etc);

"relevant non-lending relationship" has the meaning given in sections 479 (relevant non-lending relationships not involving discounts) and 480 (relevant non-lending relationships involving discounts) of CTA 2009.

REVOCATION—

These Regulations revoked by F(No 2)A 2017 s 20, Sch 5 para 11(3)(*d*) with effect in relation to periods of account of the worldwide group that begin on or after 1 April 2017. In relation to periods of account that straddle 1 April 2017 see Sch 5 para 26(2)–(10). **Please note** that Part 2A of the Yellow Book was sent to print before the Act had received Royal Assent. This amendment is therefore based on the 8 September 2017 Finance Bill. Please check F(No 2)A 2017 for confirmation of this amendment.

3 Specified matters

The following matters are specified for the purposes of section 332(1) of the Taxation (International and Other Provisions) Act 2010 to the extent that they are not included in the available amount by virtue of any of paragraphs (a) to (f) of that subsection—

(a) *interest payable in respect of a relevant non-lending relationship;*

(b) *alternative finance return under alternative finance arrangements;*

(c) *manufactured interest;*

(d) *a finance charge treated in accordance with section 551(4) of CTA 2009 (relief for borrower for finance charges in respect of the advance) as interest payable under a debt;*

(e) *a finance charge treated in accordance with any of the following provisions of the Corporation Tax Act 2010 as interest payable under a transaction or a loan relationship—*

(i) *section 761(3) (deemed loan relationship if borrower is a company),*

(ii) *section 762(3) (deemed loan relationship if borrower is a partnership with a corporate member),*
(iii) *section 766(3) (deemed loan relationship), or*
(iv) *section 769(3) (deemed loan relationship).*

REVOCATION—

These Regulations revoked by F(No 2)A 2017 s 20, Sch 5 para 11(3)(*d*) with effect in relation to periods of account of the worldwide group that begin on or after 1 April 2017. In relation to periods of account that straddle 1 April 2017 see Sch 5 para 26(2)–(10). **Please note** that Part 2A of the Yellow Book was sent to print before the Act had received Royal Assent. This amendment is therefore based on the 8 September 2017 Finance Bill. Please check F(No 2)A 2017 for confirmation of this amendment.

2010/3025

TAX TREATMENT OF FINANCING COSTS AND INCOME (CORRECTION OF MISMATCHES) REGULATIONS 2010

Made . . . . *21 December 2010*
Laid before the House of Commons . . . . *21 December 2010*
Coming into force . . . . *13 January 2011*

Revocation—

These Regulations revoked by F(No 2)A 2017 s 20, Sch 5 para 11(3)(*e*) with effect in relation to periods of account of the worldwide group that begin on or after 1 April 2017. In relation to periods of account that straddle 1 April 2017 see Sch 5 para 26(2)–(10). **Please note** that Part 2A of the Yellow Book was sent to print before the Act had received Royal Assent. This amendment is therefore based on the 8 September 2017 Finance Bill. Please check F(No 2)A 2017 for confirmation of this amendment.

The Commissioners for Her Majesty's Revenue and Customs make the following regulations in exercise of the powers conferred by sections 336A(1), (4) and (5) and 353B of the Taxation (International and Other Provisions) Act 2010.

PART 1
PRELIMINARY MATTERS AND INTERPRETATION

1 Citation and commencement

(1) These Regulations may be cited as the Tax Treatment of Financing Costs and Income (Correction of Mismatches) Regulations 2010 and come into force on 13th January 2011.
(2) These Regulations have effect in relation to periods of account beginning on or after 1st January 2010.
(3) But paragraph (2) is subject to regulations 17 (election that specified regulations are not to apply to the worldwide group) and 18 (election that these Regulations are not to apply to periods of account beginning before they are made).

REVOCATION—

These Regulations revoked by F(No 2)A 2017 s 20, Sch 5 para 11(3)(*e*) with effect in relation to periods of account of the worldwide group that begin on or after 1 April 2017. In relation to periods of account that straddle 1 April 2017 see Sch 5 para 26(2)–(10). **Please note** that Part 2A of the Yellow Book was sent to print before the Act had received Royal Assent. This amendment is therefore based on the 8 September 2017 Finance Bill. Please check F(No 2)A 2017 for confirmation of this amendment.

2 Interpretation

(1) In these Regulations—
"CTA 2009" means the Corporation Tax Act 2009;
"TIOPA 2010" means the Taxation (International and Other Provisions) Act 2010;
"Part 7" means Part 7 of TIOPA 2010 (tax treatment of financing costs and income);
"accounting period" is to be read in accordance with Chapter 2 of Part 2 of CTA 2009 (accounting periods);
"debtor relationship" has the meaning given in section 302 of CTA 2009 ("loan relationship" and other definitions);
"deeply discounted security" has the meaning given in Chapter 8 of Part 4 of the Income Tax (Trading and Other Income) Act 2005 (profits from deeply discounted securities);
"fair value accounting" means a basis of accounting under which assets or liabilities are shown in the company's balance sheet at their fair value;
"fair value adjustment" means—
(*a*) *an adjustment which brings into account a profit or loss in relation to an asset or liability representing a loan relationship where for the accounting period in question fair value accounting is used, or*

(b) *where fair value accounting is used in relation to only part of an asset or a liability, an adjustment which brings into account a profit or loss in relation to that part,*

and in either case includes an adjustment to bring into account a profit or loss recognised as a result of applying hedge accounting to a fair value hedge;

"fair value hedge" has the meaning for the time being given by international accounting standards;

"financing expense amount" in relation to a company means a financing expense amount of the company other than a financing expense amount that is treated by any provision within Chapter 7 of Part 7 ("financing expense amount" and "financing income amount") as not being a financing expense amount;

"hedge accounting" has the meaning for the time being given by international accounting standards;

"loan relationship" has the meaning given in section 302 of CTA 2009;

"period of account" means a period of account of the worldwide group;

"relevant financial relationship" has the meaning given in paragraph (2).

(2) In these Regulations, "relevant financial relationship", in relation to a company, means—

(a) *a loan relationship of the company where the company stands in the position of a debtor as respects the debt in question;*

(b) *a relationship treated as a loan relationship by virtue of any provision of Part 6 of CTA 2009 (relationships treated as loan relationships, etc), where the company stands in the position of a debtor as respects the debt in question;*

(c) *an arrangement treated by section 761(2) of the Corporation Tax Act 2010 (deemed loan relationship if borrower is a company) or section 762(2) of that Act (deemed loan relationship if borrower is partnership with corporate member) as if it were a loan relationship of the company or partnership, as the case may be, where the company stands in the position of a debtor as respects the debt in question, but excluding a money debt owed by or to a firm in relation to which the company is required to bring credits and debits into account in accordance with section 380(3) of CTA 2009 (partnerships involving companies).*

(3) In regulations 14 and 16, the expressions "amortised cost" and "effective interest rate method" have the meaning for the time being given by international accounting standards;

(4) In these Regulations, in any case in which either of sections 347 and 348 of TIOPA 2010 (non-compliant and non-existent financial statements of the worldwide group) applies, references to "financial statements" are to those financial statements of the group by reference to which Part 7 is applied.

REVOCATION—

These Regulations revoked by F(No 2)A 2017 s 20, Sch 5 para 11(3)(*e*) with effect in relation to periods of account of the worldwide group that begin on or after 1 April 2017. In relation to periods of account that straddle 1 April 2017 see Sch 5 para 26(2)–(10). **Please note** that Part 2A of the Yellow Book was sent to print before the Act had received Royal Assent. This amendment is therefore based on the 8 September 2017 Finance Bill. Please check F(No 2)A 2017 for confirmation of this amendment.

PART 2

CORRECTION OF MISMATCHES BETWEEN TAX TREATMENT AND ACCOUNTING TREATMENT

3 Fair value adjustments

(1) This regulation applies if the conditions given in regulation 4 are satisfied for a period of account.

(2) In any case in which Amount A exceeds Amount B in relation to the same relevant financial relationship, there shall be excluded from the available amount the lower of—

(a) *the amount of the fair value adjustment made in relation to the relevant financial relationship, and*

(b) *the amount of the excess.*

(3) In any case in which Amount B exceeds Amount A in relation to the same relevant financial relationship, there shall be included in the available amount the lower of—

(a) *the amount of the fair value adjustment made in relation to the relevant financial relationship, and*

(b) *the amount of the excess.*

(4) In this regulation—

(a) *Amount A in relation to a relevant financial relationship of a relevant group company in an accounting period is the amount in respect of the relevant financial relationship which is disclosed in the financial statements of the worldwide group for a period of account and included in the available amount for that period of account, and*

(b) *Amount B in relation to a relevant financial relationship of a relevant group company in an accounting period is the amount which would be brought into account for the purposes of*

Part 5 of CTA 2009 (loan relationships) in respect of the relevant financial relationship if that amount were calculated by deducting the total financing income amounts relating to the relevant financial relationship from the total financing expense amounts relating to the relevant financial relationship.

(5) In any case in which the accounting period of the relevant group company does not coincide with the period of account, it is assumed for the purposes of paragraph (4)(*b*) that the accounting period of the relevant group company is—

(*a*) *the same as the period of account, if the relevant group company is a member of the worldwide group throughout that period of account;*

(*b*) *in any other case, that part of the period of account during which the relevant group company is a member of the worldwide group.*

(6) In any case in which, but for this paragraph, Amount B would be a negative amount, Amount B is taken to be zero.

REVOCATION—

These Regulations revoked by F(No 2)A 2017 s 20, Sch 5 para 11(3)(*e*) with effect in relation to periods of account of the worldwide group that begin on or after 1 April 2017. In relation to periods of account that straddle 1 April 2017 see Sch 5 para 26(2)–(10). **Please note** that Part 2A of the Yellow Book was sent to print before the Act had received Royal Assent. This amendment is therefore based on the 8 September 2017 Finance Bill. Please check F(No 2)A 2017 for confirmation of this amendment.

4 Conditions for the application of regulation 3

(1) The first condition is that a relevant group company is a party to a relevant financial relationship in a relevant accounting period.

(2) The second condition is that a debit in respect of the relevant financial relationship is a financing expense amount of the company.

(3) The third condition is that an amount in respect of the relevant financial relationship is included in the available amount otherwise than by virtue of regulation 3.

(4) The fourth condition is that a fair value adjustment is made in relation to the relevant financial relationship by the relevant group company in the relevant accounting period.

REVOCATION—

These Regulations revoked by F(No 2)A 2017 s 20, Sch 5 para 11(3)(*e*) with effect in relation to periods of account of the worldwide group that begin on or after 1 April 2017. In relation to periods of account that straddle 1 April 2017 see Sch 5 para 26(2)–(10). **Please note** that Part 2A of the Yellow Book was sent to print before the Act had received Royal Assent. This amendment is therefore based on the 8 September 2017 Finance Bill. Please check F(No 2)A 2017 for confirmation of this amendment.

5 Late interest treated as not accruing until paid

(1) This regulation applies in relation to a debit in respect of interest payable under a debtor relationship of a relevant group company if the conditions given in regulation 6 are satisfied.

(2) In the period of account in which the interest to which the debit relates is paid, the amount of the debit shall be included in the available amount to the extent that it is not included in the available amount for that period by virtue of any other enactment.

REVOCATION—

These Regulations revoked by F(No 2)A 2017 s 20, Sch 5 para 11(3)(*e*) with effect in relation to periods of account of the worldwide group that begin on or after 1 April 2017. In relation to periods of account that straddle 1 April 2017 see Sch 5 para 26(2)–(10). **Please note** that Part 2A of the Yellow Book was sent to print before the Act had received Royal Assent. This amendment is therefore based on the 8 September 2017 Finance Bill. Please check F(No 2)A 2017 for confirmation of this amendment.

6 Conditions for the application of regulation 5

(1) The first condition is that the debit is to be brought into account in a relevant accounting period for the purposes of Part 5 of CTA 2009 by virtue of section 373 of that Act (late interest treated as not accruing until paid in some cases).

(2) The second condition is that the debit is a financing expense amount of the company in the period of account in which the interest to which the debit relates is paid.

(3) The third condition is that the debit would be brought into account for the purposes of Part 5 of CTA 2009 in an accounting period beginning on or after 1st January 2010 if section 373 of CTA 2009 did not apply.

REVOCATION—

These Regulations revoked by F(No 2)A 2017 s 20, Sch 5 para 11(3)(*e*) with effect in relation to periods of account of the worldwide group that begin on or after 1 April 2017. In relation to periods of account that straddle 1 April 2017 see Sch 5 para 26(2)–(10). **Please note** that Part 2A of the Yellow Book was sent to print before the Act had received Royal Assent. This amendment is therefore based on the 8 September 2017 Finance Bill. Please check F(No 2)A 2017 for confirmation of this amendment.

7 Adjustment for period of account in which late interest would be a financing expense amount but for section 373 of CTA 2009

(1) This regulation applies in relation to a debit in respect of interest which has accrued under a debtor relationship of a relevant group company if the conditions given in regulation 8 are satisfied.

(2) In the period of account in which the debit would be a financing expense amount of a company but for section 373 of CTA 2009, any amount in respect of the debit that would be included in the available amount but for this paragraph shall be excluded from the available amount.

REVOCATION—

These Regulations revoked by F(No 2)A 2017 s 20, Sch 5 para 11(3)(*e*) with effect in relation to periods of account of the worldwide group that begin on or after 1 April 2017. In relation to periods of account that straddle 1 April 2017 see Sch 5 para 26(2)–(10). **Please note** that Part 2A of the Yellow Book was sent to print before the Act had received Royal Assent. This amendment is therefore based on the 8 September 2017 Finance Bill. Please check F(No 2)A 2017 for confirmation of this amendment.

8 Conditions for the application of regulation 7

(1) The first condition is that but for section 373 of CTA 2009 the debit would be a financing expense amount of the company in a period of account.

(2) The second condition is that the debit would be brought into account for the purposes of Part 5 of CTA 2009 in an accounting period beginning on or after 1st January 2010 if section 373 of CTA 2009 did not apply.

REVOCATION—

These Regulations revoked by F(No 2)A 2017 s 20, Sch 5 para 11(3)(*e*) with effect in relation to periods of account of the worldwide group that begin on or after 1 April 2017. In relation to periods of account that straddle 1 April 2017 see Sch 5 para 26(2)–(10). **Please note** that Part 2A of the Yellow Book was sent to print before the Act had received Royal Assent. This amendment is therefore based on the 8 September 2017 Finance Bill. Please check F(No 2)A 2017 for confirmation of this amendment.

9 Postponed debits in relation to deeply discounted securities

(1) This regulation applies in relation to a debit in respect of a debtor relationship of a relevant group company if the conditions given in regulation 10 are satisfied.

(2) In the period of account in which the deeply discounted security to which the debit relates is redeemed, the amount of the debit shall be included in the available amount to the extent that it is not included in the available amount for that period by virtue of any other enactment.

REVOCATION—

These Regulations revoked by F(No 2)A 2017 s 20, Sch 5 para 11(3)(*e*) with effect in relation to periods of account of the worldwide group that begin on or after 1 April 2017. In relation to periods of account that straddle 1 April 2017 see Sch 5 para 26(2)–(10). **Please note** that Part 2A of the Yellow Book was sent to print before the Act had received Royal Assent. This amendment is therefore based on the 8 September 2017 Finance Bill. Please check F(No 2)A 2017 for confirmation of this amendment.

10 Conditions for the application of regulation 9

(1) The first condition is that either of sections 407 and 409 of CTA 2009 (postponement until redemption of debits for deeply discounted securities of connected companies and of close companies) requires the debit to be brought into account for the purposes of Part 5 of CTA 2009 in a relevant accounting period.

(2) The second condition is that the debit is a financing expense amount of the company in the period of account in which the deeply discounted security is redeemed.

(3) The third condition is that a debit in respect of the deeply discounted security would be brought into account for the purposes of Part 5 of CTA 2009 in an accounting period beginning on or after 1st January 2010 if neither of sections 407 and 409 of CTA 2009 applied.

REVOCATION—

These Regulations revoked by F(No 2)A 2017 s 20, Sch 5 para 11(3)(*e*) with effect in relation to periods of account of the worldwide group that begin on or after 1 April 2017. In relation to periods of account that straddle 1 April 2017 see Sch 5 para 26(2)–(10). **Please note** that Part 2A of the Yellow Book was sent to print before the Act had received Royal Assent. This amendment is therefore based on the 8 September 2017 Finance Bill. Please check F(No 2)A 2017 for confirmation of this amendment.

11 Adjustment where debits in respect of deeply discounted securities would be brought into account but for either of sections 407 and 409 of CTA 2009

(1) This regulation applies in relation to a debit in respect of a debtor relationship of a relevant group company if the conditions given in regulation 12 are satisfied.

(2) In the period of account in which the debit would be a financing expense amount of a company but for either of sections 407 and 409 of CTA 2009, any amount in respect of the debit that would be included in the available amount but for this paragraph shall be excluded from the available amount.

REVOCATION—

These Regulations revoked by F(No 2)A 2017 s 20, Sch 5 para 11(3)(*e*) with effect in relation to periods of account of the worldwide group that begin on or after 1 April 2017. In relation to periods of account that straddle 1 April 2017 see Sch 5 para 26(2)–(10). **Please note** that Part 2A of the Yellow Book was sent to print before the Act had received Royal Assent. This amendment is therefore based on the 8 September 2017 Finance Bill. Please check F(No 2)A 2017 for confirmation of this amendment.

12 Conditions for the application of regulation 11

(1) The first condition is that but for either of sections 407 and 409 of CTA 2009 the debit would be a financing expense amount of the company for a period of account.

(2) The second condition is that the debit would be brought into account for the purposes of Part 5 of CTA 2009 in an accounting period beginning on or after 1st January 2010 if neither of sections 407 and 409 of CTA 2009 applied.

REVOCATION—

These Regulations revoked by F(No 2)A 2017 s 20, Sch 5 para 11(3)(*e*) with effect in relation to periods of account of the worldwide group that begin on or after 1 April 2017. In relation to periods of account that straddle 1 April 2017 see Sch 5 para 26(2)–(10). **Please note** that Part 2A of the Yellow Book was sent to print before the Act had received Royal Assent. This amendment is therefore based on the 8 September 2017 Finance Bill. Please check F(No 2)A 2017 for confirmation of this amendment.

13 Loan relationships with embedded derivatives

(1) This regulation applies in relation to a debit if the conditions given in regulation 14 are satisfied.

(2) In the period of account in which the debit is brought into account by the relevant group company, the amount referred to in paragraph (3) shall be included in the available amount to the extent that it is not included in the available amount for that period of account by virtue of any other enactment.

(3) The amount is such part of the debit as is directly attributable to the requirement referred to in regulation 14(4).

REVOCATION—

These Regulations revoked by F(No 2)A 2017 s 20, Sch 5 para 11(3)(*e*) with effect in relation to periods of account of the worldwide group that begin on or after 1 April 2017. In relation to periods of account that straddle 1 April 2017 see Sch 5 para 26(2)–(10). **Please note** that Part 2A of the Yellow Book was sent to print before the Act had received Royal Assent. This amendment is therefore based on the 8 September 2017 Finance Bill. Please check F(No 2)A 2017 for confirmation of this amendment.

14 Conditions for the application of regulation 13

(1) The first condition is that a debit is brought into account under Part 5 of CTA 2009 in respect of a loan relationship to which section 415 of CTA 2009 (loan relationships with embedded derivatives) applies.

(2) The second condition is that the debit is a financing expense amount of the company.

(3) The third condition is that an amount in respect of the loan relationship is included in the available amount otherwise than by virtue of regulation 13.

(4) The fourth condition is that the debit is required by international accounting standards to be measured at amortised cost using the effective interest rate method.

REVOCATION—

These Regulations revoked by F(No 2)A 2017 s 20, Sch 5 para 11(3)(*e*) with effect in relation to periods of account of the worldwide group that begin on or after 1 April 2017. In relation to periods of account that straddle 1 April 2017 see Sch 5 para 26(2)–(10). **Please note** that Part 2A of the Yellow Book was sent to print before the Act had received Royal Assent. This amendment is therefore based on the 8 September 2017 Finance Bill. Please check F(No 2)A 2017 for confirmation of this amendment.

15 Debt restructuring

(1) This regulation applies in relation to a debit if the conditions given in regulation 16 are satisfied.

(2) In the period of account in which the debit is brought into account by the relevant group company, the amount referred to in paragraph (3) shall be included in the available amount to the extent that it is not included in the available amount for that period of account by virtue of any other enactment.

(3) The amount is such part of the debit as is directly attributable to the requirement referred to in regulation 16(5).

REVOCATION—

These Regulations revoked by F(No 2)A 2017 s 20, Sch 5 para 11(3)(*e*) with effect in relation to periods of account of the worldwide group that begin on or after 1 April 2017. In relation to periods of account that straddle 1 April 2017 see Sch 5 para 26(2)–(10). **Please note** that Part 2A of the Yellow Book was sent to print before the Act had received Royal Assent. This amendment is therefore based on the 8 September 2017 Finance Bill. Please check F(No 2)A 2017 for confirmation of this amendment.

16 Conditions for the application of regulation 15

(1) The first condition is that a relevant group company is a party to a relevant financial relationship in a relevant accounting period.

(2) The second condition is that a debit in respect of the relevant financial relationship is a financing expense amount of the relevant group company.

(3) The third condition is that an amount in respect of the relevant financial relationship is included in the available amount otherwise than by virtue of regulation 15.

(4) The fourth condition is that under international accounting standards the relevant financial relationship has been recognised using fair value accounting in the accounts of the relevant group company, in the relevant accounting period or in a previous accounting period, as a new financial liability upon the occurrence of one of the following events—

(*a*) *an exchange of the relevant financial relationship for an existing financial liability in substantially different terms, or*

(*b*) *a substantial modification of the terms of an existing financial liability or part of it,*

where in either case the event is accounted for, in relation to the existing financial liability, as an extinguishment of that liability.

(5) The fifth condition is that after the initial recognition of the relevant financial relationship using fair value accounting, the debit is required by international accounting standards to be measured at amortised cost using the effective interest rate method.

REVOCATION—
These Regulations revoked by F(No 2)A 2017 s 20, Sch 5 para 11(3)(*e*) with effect in relation to periods of account of the worldwide group that begin on or after 1 April 2017. In relation to periods of account that straddle 1 April 2017 see Sch 5 para 26(2)–(10). **Please note** that Part 2A of the Yellow Book was sent to print before the Act had received Royal Assent. This amendment is therefore based on the 8 September 2017 Finance Bill. Please check F(No 2)A 2017 for confirmation of this amendment.

[16A Employer asset-backed pension contribution mismatches

(1) This regulation applies in relation to a finance charge if the conditions in regulation 16B are satisfied.

(2) In the period of account in which the finance charge is brought into account by the relevant group company, an amount equal to that finance charge shall be included in the available amount to the extent that it is not included in the available amount for that period of account by virtue of any other enactment.][1], [2]

Amendments—[1] Regulations 16A, 16B inserted by the Tax Treatment of Financing Costs and Income (Correction of Mismatches: Partnerships and Pensions) Regulations, SI 2012/3111 reg 3 with effect in relation to periods of account of the worldwide group beginning on or after 1 January 2012, subject to transitional provisions in SI 2012/3111 reg 4 (SI 2012/3111 is revoked by F(No 2)A 2017 s 20, Sch 5 para 11(3)(*g*) with effect in relation to periods of account of the worldwide group that begin on or after 1 April 2017).

[2] These Regulations revoked by F(No 2)A 2017 s 20, Sch 5 para 11(3)(*e*) with effect in relation to periods of account of the worldwide group that begin on or after 1 April 2017. In relation to periods of account that straddle 1 April 2017 see Sch 5 para 26(2)–(10). **Please note** that Part 2A of the Yellow Book was sent to print before the Act had received Royal Assent. This amendment is therefore based on the 8 September 2017 Finance Bill. Please check F(No 2)A 2017 for confirmation of this amendment.

[16B Conditions for the application of regulation 16A

(1) The first condition is that the finance charge is treated as interest payable under a transaction or a loan relationship under any of the following provisions of the Corporation Tax Act 2010—

(*a*) *section 761(3) (deemed loan relationship if borrower is a company),*

(*b*) *section 762(3) (deemed loan relationship if borrower is a partnership with corporate member),*

(*c*) *section 766(3) (deemed loan relationship), or*

(*d*) *section 769(3) (deemed loan relationship).*

(2) The second condition is that the finance charge is a financing expense of the company.

(3) The third condition is that the finance charge must arise in relation to—

(*a*) *an acceptable structured finance arrangement in connection with a contribution paid by an employer under a registered pension scheme in respect of which the employer is entitled to relief under Chapter 4 of Part 4 of the Finance Act 2004 (registered pension schemes: tax reliefs and exemptions), or*

(*b*) *a finance arrangement which would be an acceptable structured finance arrangement in connection with a contribution paid by an employer under a registered pension scheme if the contribution was paid on or after 22 February 2012 and in respect of which the employer is entitled to relief under Chapter 4 of Part 4 of the Finance Act 2004.*

(4) In paragraph (3), "acceptable structured finance arrangement" has the meaning given in section 196C (employer asset-backed contributions: "acceptable structured finance arrangement" (1)), section 196E (employer asset-backed contributions: "acceptable structured finance arrangement" (2)) or section 196G (employer asset-backed contributions: "acceptable structured finance arrangement" (3)) of the Finance Act 2004, as the case may be.][1], [2]

Amendments—[1] Regulations 16A, 16B inserted by the Tax Treatment of Financing Costs and Income (Correction of Mismatches: Partnerships and Pensions) Regulations, SI 2012/3111 reg 3 with effect in relation to periods of account of the worldwide group beginning on or after 1 January 2012, subject to transitional provisions in SI 2012/3111 reg 4 (SI 2012/3111 is revoked by F(No 2)A 2017 s 20, Sch 5 para 11(3)(*g*) with effect in relation to periods of account of the worldwide group that begin on or after 1 April 2017).

[2] These Regulations revoked by F(No 2)A 2017 s 20, Sch 5 para 11(3)(*e*) with effect in relation to periods of account of the worldwide group that begin on or after 1 April 2017. In relation to periods of account that straddle 1 April 2017 see Sch 5 para 26(2)–(10). **Please note** that Part 2A of the Yellow Book was sent to print before the Act had received Royal Assent. This amendment is therefore based on the 8 September 2017 Finance Bill. Please check F(No 2)A 2017 for confirmation of this amendment.

PART 3
ELECTIONS

17 Election that specified regulations are not to apply to the worldwide group

(1) A worldwide group may elect that one or more of the following regulations and pairs of regulations will not apply to it—

(*a*) *3;*
(*b*) *5 and 7;*
(*c*) *9 and 11;*
(*d*) *13;*
(*e*) *15.*

(2) The election must specify to which regulations or pairs of regulations it relates.
(3) The election must comply with the requirements imposed by regulation 19.
(4) The election is irrevocable.

REVOCATION—

These Regulations revoked by F(No 2)A 2017 s 20, Sch 5 para 11(3)(*e*) with effect in relation to periods of account of the worldwide group that begin on or after 1 April 2017. In relation to periods of account that straddle 1 April 2017 see Sch 5 para 26(2)–(10). **Please note** that Part 2A of the Yellow Book was sent to print before the Act had received Royal Assent. This amendment is therefore based on the 8 September 2017 Finance Bill. Please check F(No 2)A 2017 for confirmation of this amendment.

18 Election that these Regulations are not to apply to periods of account beginning before they are made

(1) A worldwide group may elect that these Regulations are not to apply in relation to periods of account beginning before the date on which these Regulations are made.
(2) The election must comply with the requirements imposed by regulation 19.
(3) The election is irrevocable.

REVOCATION—

These Regulations revoked by F(No 2)A 2017 s 20, Sch 5 para 11(3)(*e*) with effect in relation to periods of account of the worldwide group that begin on or after 1 April 2017. In relation to periods of account that straddle 1 April 2017 see Sch 5 para 26(2)–(10). **Please note** that Part 2A of the Yellow Book was sent to print before the Act had received Royal Assent. This amendment is therefore based on the 8 September 2017 Finance Bill. Please check F(No 2)A 2017 for confirmation of this amendment.

19 Election requirements

(1) The election must be made by the later of—

(*a*) *31st March 2011;*
(*b*) *12 months from the end of the first period of account that begins on or after 1st January 2010.*

(2) The election must be made by the reporting body.
(3) The election must be signed by the appropriate person in relation to the reporting body.
(4) In this regulation the "appropriate person", in relation to a company, means—

(*a*) *the proper officer of the company, or*
(*b*) *such other person as may have the express, implied or apparent authority of the company to act on its behalf for the purposes of these Regulations.*

(5) Subsections (3) and (4) of section 108 of the Taxes Management Act 1970 (responsibility of company officers: meaning of "proper officer") apply for the purposes of this regulation as they apply for the purposes of that section.
(6) An election which does not comply with the conditions set out in this regulation is of no effect.
(7) In this regulation, "the reporting body" has the meaning given by section 277 of TIOPA 2010 (meaning of "the reporting body").

REVOCATION—

These Regulations revoked by F(No 2)A 2017 s 20, Sch 5 para 11(3)(*e*) with effect in relation to periods of account of the worldwide group that begin on or after 1 April 2017. In relation to periods of account that straddle 1 April 2017 see Sch 5 para 26(2)–(10). **Please note** that Part 2A of the Yellow Book was sent to print before the Act had received Royal Assent. This amendment is therefore based on the 8 September 2017 Finance Bill. Please check F(No 2)A 2017 for confirmation of this amendment.

2011/22

DORMANT BANK AND BUILDING SOCIETY ACCOUNTS (TAX) REGULATIONS 2011

Made .... *10 January 2011*
Laid before the House of Commons .... *11 January 2011*
Coming into force .... *1 February 2011*

These Regulations are made by the Treasury and the Commissioners for Her Majesty's Revenue and Customs. The powers exercised by the Treasury are those conferred by sections 694 to 696, 699 and 701 of the Income Tax (Trading and Other Income) Act 2005 and the powers exercised by the Commissioners for Her Majesty's Revenue and Customs are those conferred by section 17(5) and (6) of the Taxes Management Act 1970, sections 852 and 871 of the Income Tax Act 2007 and section 39(1) of the Finance Act 2008.

1 Citation, commencement and effect

(1) These Regulations may be cited as the Dormant Bank and Building Society Accounts (Tax) Regulations 2011 and shall come into force on 1st February 2011.

(2) Regulations 2 to 4 have effect in relation to notices under section 17(1) of the Taxes Management Act 1970 served on or after 1st February 2011.

(3) Regulations 5 to 7 have effect in relation to interest paid or credited on or after 1st February 2011.

(4) Regulation 8 has effect in relation to interest arising on or after 1st February 2011.

3–7 Not reproduced (note: regs 3, 4 revoked by SI 2012/756).

8 (1) For the purposes of Chapter 2 of Part 4 of The Income Tax (Trading and Other Income) Act 2005 (Savings and investment income: interest), interest arising in respect of a relevant dormant account shall be treated as arising at the time (if any) at which the balance of the account is paid out following a repayment claim.

(2) In paragraph (1), "relevant dormant account" has the meaning given in section 39(2) of the Finance Act 2008 and other terms used in that paragraph and in section 39 of that Act have the same meaning in that paragraph as in that section.

2011/711

TAXES, ETC (FEES FOR PAYMENT BY INTERNET) REGULATIONS 2011

Made .... *9th March 2011*
Laid before the House of Commons .... *10th March 2011*
Coming into force .... *1st April 2011*

Revocation—These Regulations revoked by the Taxes, etc. (Fees for Payment by Telephone) Regulations, SI 2016/333 with effect from 1 April 2016.

2011/712

QUALIFYING CARE RELIEF (SPECIFIED SOCIAL CARE SCHEMES) ORDER 2011

Made .... *10th March 2011*
Laid before the House of Commons .... *11th March 2011*
Coming into force .... *4th April 2011*

The Treasury make the following Order in exercise of powers conferred by section 806A(4) and (5) of the Income Tax (Trading and other Income) Act 2005.

1 Citation, commencement and effect

(1) This Order may be cited as the Qualifying Care Relief (Specified Social Care Schemes) Order 2011.

(2) This Order shall come into force on 4th April 2011.

(3) This Order shall have effect for the tax year 2010–2011 and subsequent tax years.

2 Interpretation

In this Order—

"L" is a local authority or a health service body within section 986 (meaning of "health service body") of the Corporation Tax Act 2010.

"looked after child" means a child—

(*a*) in England and Wales, to whom section 22C (ways in which looked after children are to be accommodated and maintained) of the Children Act 1989 applies,
(*b*) [in Scotland, to whom section 17(6) of the Children (Scotland) Act 1995 applies, and][1]
(*c*) in Northern Ireland, to whom Article 27(2) (accommodation and maintenance for children) of the Children (Northern Ireland) Order 1995 applies.

["school age" has the meaning given in section 31 of the Education (Scotland) Act 1980,][1]
"section 806A" means section 806A (meaning of providing shared lives care) of the Income Tax (Trading and Other Income) Act 2005,
"X" is a person who, by reason of age, illness, disability or other vulnerability, is in need of care, and
"Y" is the individual in section 806A(1).

Amendments—[1] Para (*b*) substituted, and definition of "school age" inserted, by the Qualifying Care Relief (Specified Social Care Schemes) (Amendment) Order, SI 2012/794 art 2(1)–(3) with effect for the tax year 2011–12 and subsequent tax years.

3 Specified social care schemes: overview

[For the purposes of paragraph (*c*) of subsection (2) of section 806A, a specified social care scheme means a scheme, service or arrangement that provides—
(*a*) adult placement care (article 4),
(*b*) kinship care (article 5), or
(*c*) staying put care (article 6), or
(*d*) for a parent and his or her child to live with Y (article 7).][1]

Amendments—[1] Art 3 substituted by the Qualifying Care Relief (Specified Social Care Schemes) (Amendment) Order, SI 2012/794 art 2(1), (4) with effect for the tax year 2011–12 and subsequent tax years.

4 Specified social care schemes for adult placement care

(1) A specified social care scheme in relation to adult placement care must meet Conditions A to C.
(2) Condition A is that X is placed with Y.
(3) Condition B is that Y is—
(*a*) in England, an adult placement carer within the meaning of the Health and Social Care Act 2008 (Regulated Activities) Regulations 2010,
(*b*) in Wales, an adult placement carer within the meaning of the Adult Placement Schemes (Wales) Regulations 2004,
(*c*) in Scotland, a person with whom X has been accommodated by an adult placement service within the meaning of section 47(1)(j) of the Public Services Reform (Scotland) Act 2010 , or
(*d*) in Northern Ireland, an adult placement carer within the meaning of the Adult Placement Agencies Regulations (Northern Ireland) 2007.
(4) Condition C is that Y receives payment from L for providing adult placement care to X.
(5) Until the coming into force of section 47(1)(j) of the Public Services Reform (Scotland) Act 2010, the reference to that provision in sub-paragraph (*c*) of paragraph 3 is to section 2(16) of the Regulation of Care (Scotland) Act 2001.

5 Specified social care schemes for kinship care

(1) A specified social care scheme in relation to kinship care must meet Conditions A to F.
(2) Condition A is that X has not yet attained 18 years of age.
(3) Condition B is that X is a looked after child.
(4) Condition C is that Y receives payment from L for providing kinship care to X.
(5) Condition D is that Y is—
(*a*) related to X either by blood, marriage or civil partnership, but is not a parent or step-parent of X, or
(*b*) known to X and with whom X has a pre-existing relationship.
(6) Condition E is that Y is regarded by L as a suitable person to care for X.
(7) Condition F is that, in relation to X, Y is not a person in respect of whom a court has made—
(*a*) a residence order, . . . [1]
(*aa*) (in relation to orders made in England and Wales) a child arrangements order that names Y as a person with whom X is to live, or][1]
(*b*) a special guardianship order.

Amendments—[1] Word "or" in para (7)(*a*) revoked , and para (7)(*aa*) inserted by the Child Arrangements Order (Consequential Amendments to Subordinate Legislation) Order, SI 2014/712 art 21 with effect from 22 April 2014.

6 Specified social care schemes for staying put care

(1) A specified social care scheme in relation to staying put care must meet Conditions A to D.
(2) Condition A is that X—
(*a*) has reached the age of 18 but is under 21, or
(*b*) is—
(i) in further education,
(ii) in higher education, or
(iii) pursuing vocational training.

(3) In Scotland, Condition A is also met where X—

(*a*) is over school age but under 19 years, and

(*b*) was, at the time when he ceased to be of school age or at any subsequent time, a looked after child.

(4) Condition B is that, if X is aged 18 years or over, immediately before reaching 18 years X was a looked after child.

(5) In Scotland, where Condition A is met as described in paragraph (3), Condition B need not be met.

(6) Condition C is that Y receives payment from L for providing staying put care to X.

(7) Condition D is that X has a pathway plan.][1]

Amendments—[1] Art 6 substituted by the Qualifying Care Relief (Specified Social Care Schemes) (Amendment) Order, SI 2012/794 art 2(1), (5) with effect for the tax year 2011–12 and subsequent tax years.

[7 Specified social care schemes providing for a parent and his or her child to live with Y

(1) A specified social care scheme providing for a parent and his or her child to live with Y must meet Conditions A to C in this regulation.

(2) Condition A is that L has arranged for the parent and child to live with Y.

(3) Condition B is that Y provides care for the parent and child.

(4) Condition C is that Y receives payment from L for providing the accommodation and care for the parent and child.][1]

Amendments—[1] Art 7 inserted by the Qualifying Care Relief (Specified Social Care Schemes) (Amendment) Order, SI 2012/794 art 2(1), (6) with effect for the tax year 2011–12 and subsequent tax years.

2011/976

PENALTIES, OFFSHORE INCOME ETC (DESIGNATION OF TERRITORIES) ORDER 2011

Made . . . . 28 March 2011

Coming into force . . . . 6 April 2011

The Treasury make the following Order in exercise of the powers conferred by paragraph 21A(1) to (4) of Schedule 24 to the Finance Act 2007.

In accordance with paragraph 21A(7) of Schedule 24 to that Act, a draft of this instrument was laid before the House of Commons and approved by a resolution of that House.

1 Citation and commencement

This Order may be cited as the Penalties, Offshore Income etc (Designation of Territories) Order 2011 and comes into force on 6th April 2011.

2 Designation of territories

The territories specified in the left hand column of the Table in the Schedule to this Order are designated as category 1 territories for the purposes of Schedule 24 to the Finance Act 2007 (penalties for errors).

3 The territories specified in the right hand column of the Table in the Schedule to this Order are designated as category 3 territories for the purposes of Schedule 24 to the Finance Act 2007.

SCHEDULE

Articles 2 and 3

Designated Territories

Category 1 territories	*Category 3 territories*
Anguilla	Albania
Aruba	Algeria
Australia	Andorra
Belgium	. . .[1]
Bulgaria	. . .[1]
Canada	. . .[1]
Cayman Islands	. . .[1]
Cyprus	. . .[1]
Czech Republic	Bonaire, Sint Eustatius and Saba
Denmark (not including Faroe Islands and Greenland)	Brazil

Estonia
Finland
France
Germany
Greece
Guernsey
Hungary
Ireland
Isle of Man
Italy
Japan
Korea, South
Latvia
[Liechtenstein][1]
Lithuania
Malta
Montserrat
Netherlands (not including Bonaire, Sint Eustatius and Saba)
New Zealand (not including Tokelau)
Norway
Poland
Portugal
Romania
Slovakia
Slovenia
Spain
Sweden
[Switzerland][1]
United States of America (not including overseas territories and possessions)

Cameroon
Cape Verde
Colombia
Congo, Republic of the
Cook Islands
Costa Rica
Curaçao
Cuba
Democratic People's Republic of Korea
. . . [1]
Dominican Republic
Ecuador
El Salvador
Gabon
. . . [1]
Guatemala
Honduras
Iran
Iraq
Jamaica
Kyrgyzstan
Lebanon
Macau
Marshall Islands
. . . [1]
Micronesia, Federated States of
Monaco
Nauru
Nicaragua
Niue
Palau
Panama
Paraguay
Peru
. . . [1]
. . . [1]
. . . [1]
. . . [1]
Seychelles
Sint Maarten
Suriname
Syria
Tokelau
Tonga
Trinidad and Tobago
United Arab Emirates
Uruguay

Amendments—[1] In Table, entries in left-hand column inserted and entries in right-hand column revoked by the Penalties, Offshore Income etc. (Designation of Territories) (Amendment) Order, SI 2013/1618 with effect from 24 July 2013.

2011/1079

INTERNATIONAL MUTUAL ADMINISTRATIVE ASSISTANCE IN TAX MATTERS ORDER 2011

Made . . . . *7 April 2011*

At the Court at Windsor Castle, the 7th day of April 2011.

Present,

The Queen's Most Excellent Majesty in Council

A draft of this Order was laid before the House of Commons in accordance with section 173(7) of the Finance Act 2006 and approved by a resolution of that House.

Accordingly, Her Majesty, in exercise of the power conferred upon Her by sections 173(1) to (3) of the Finance Act 2006, by and with the advice of Her Privy Council, orders as follows—

1 Citation

This Order may be cited as the International Mutual Administrative Assistance in Tax Matters Order 2011.

2 Mutual administrative assistance arrangements to have effect

It is declared that—

(*a*) the arrangements relating to international tax enforcement set out in the joint Council of Europe/Organisation for Economic Co-operation and Development Convention on Mutual Administrative Assistance in Tax Matters, as varied by the arrangements specified in the Protocol set out in the Schedule to this Order, have been made with the other signatories, and

(*b*) it is expedient that the arrangements should have effect.

SCHEDULE

Article 2

PROTOCOL AMENDING THE CONVENTION ON MUTUAL ADMINISTRATIVE ASSISTANCE IN TAX MATTERS

Preamble

The member States of the Council of Europe and the member countries of the Organisation for Economic Co-operation and Development (OECD), signatories of this Protocol,

Considering that the Convention on Mutual Administrative Assistance in Tax Matters, done at Strasbourg on 25 January 1988 (hereinafter "the Convention"), was concluded before agreement was reached on the internationally agreed standard to exchange information in tax matters;

Considering that a new cooperative environment has emerged since the Convention was concluded;

Considering that it is desirable that a multilateral instrument is made available to allow the widest number of States to obtain the benefit of the new co-operative environment and at the same time to implement the highest international standards of co-operation in the tax field;

Have agreed as follows:

ARTICLE I

1 The seventh recital of the Preamble to the Convention shall be deleted and replaced by the following:

"Convinced therefore that States should carry out measures or supply information, having regard to the necessity of protecting the confidentiality of information, and taking account of international instruments for the protection of privacy and flows of personal data;"

2 The following shall be added after the seventh recital of the Preamble to the Convention:

"Considering that a new co-operative environment has emerged and that it is desirable that a multilateral instrument is made available to allow the widest number of States to obtain the benefits of the new co-operative environment and at the same time implement the highest international standards of co-operation in the tax field;"

ARTICLE II

Article 4 of the Convention shall be deleted and replaced by the following:

"Article 4—General provision

1

The Parties shall exchange any information, in particular as provided in this section, that is foreseeably relevant for the administration or enforcement of their domestic laws concerning the taxes covered by this Convention.

2

Deleted.

3

Any Party may, by a declaration addressed to one of the Depositaries, indicate that, according to its internal legislation, its authorities may inform its resident or national before transmitting information concerning him, in conformity with Articles 5 and 7."

ARTICLE III

1 The term "and" in paragraph 1.b of Article 18 of the Convention shall be replaced by the term ", or".

2 The reference to "Article 19" in paragraph 1.f of Article 18 of the Convention shall be replaced by a reference to "Article 21.2.g".

ARTICLE IV

Article 19 of the Convention shall be deleted.

ARTICLE V

Article 21 of the Convention shall be deleted and replaced by the following:

"Article 21—Protection of persons and limits to the obligation to provide assistance

1

Nothing in this Convention shall affect the rights and safeguards secured to persons by the laws or administrative practice of the requested State.

2

Except in the case of Article 14, the provisions of this Convention shall not be construed so as to impose on the requested State the obligation:

(*a*) to carry out measures at variance with its own laws or administrative practice or the laws or administrative practice of the applicant State;

(*b*) to carry out measures which would be contrary to public policy (ordre public);

(*c*) to supply information which is not obtainable under its own laws or its administrative practice or under the laws of the applicant State or its administrative practice;

(*d*) to supply information which would disclose any trade, business, industrial, commercial or professional secret, or trade process, or information, the disclosure of which would be contrary to public policy (ordre public);

(*e*) to provide administrative assistance if and insofar as it considers the taxation in the applicant State to be contrary to generally accepted taxation principles or to the provisions of a convention for the avoidance of double taxation, or of any other convention which the requested State has concluded with the applicant State;

(*f*) to provide administrative assistance for the purpose of administering or enforcing a provision of the tax law of the applicant State, or any requirement connected therewith, which discriminates against a national of the requested State as compared with a national of the applicant State in the same circumstances;

(*g*) to provide administrative assistance if the applicant State has not pursued all reasonable measures available under its laws or administrative practice, except where recourse to such measures would give rise to disproportionate difficulty;

(*h*) to provide assistance in recovery in those cases where the administrative burden for that State is clearly disproportionate to the benefit to be derived by the applicant State.

3

If information is requested by the applicant State in accordance with this Convention, the requested State shall use its information gathering measures to obtain the requested information, even though the requested State may not need such information for its own tax purposes. The obligation contained in the preceding sentence is subject to the limitations contained in this Convention, but in no case shall such limitations, including in particular those of paragraphs 1 and 2, be construed to permit a requested State to decline to supply information solely because it has no domestic interest in such information.

4

In no case shall the provisions of this Convention, including in particular those of paragraphs 1 and 2, be construed to permit a requested State to decline to supply information solely because the information is held by a bank, other financial institution, nominee or person acting in an agency or a fiduciary capacity or because it relates to ownership interests in a person."

ARTICLE VI

Paragraphs 1 and 2 of Article 22 shall be deleted and replaced with the following:

"1

Any information obtained by a Party under this Convention shall be treated as secret and protected in the same manner as information obtained under the domestic law of that Party and, to the extent needed to ensure the necessary level of protection of personal data, in accordance with the safeguards which may be specified by the supplying Party as required under its domestic law.

2

Such information shall in any case be disclosed only to persons or authorities (including courts and administrative or supervisory bodies) concerned with the assessment, collection or recovery of, the enforcement or prosecution in respect of, or the determination of appeals in relation to, taxes of that Party, or the oversight of the above. Only the persons or authorities mentioned above may use the information and then only for such purposes. They may, notwithstanding the provisions of paragraph 1, disclose it in public court proceedings or in judicial decisions relating to such taxes."

ARTICLE VII

Paragraph 2 of Article 27 of the Convention shall be deleted and replaced by the following:

"2

Notwithstanding paragraph 1, those Parties which are member States of the European Union can apply, in their mutual relations, the possibilities of assistance provided for by the Convention in so far as they allow a wider co-operation than the possibilities offered by the applicable European Union rules."

ARTICLE VIII

1 The following paragraphs shall be added at the end of Article 28 of the Convention:

"4

Any member State of the Council of Europe or any member country of OECD which becomes a Party to the Convention after the entry into force of the Protocol amending this Convention, opened for signature on 27th May 2010 (the "2010 Protocol"), shall be a Party to the Convention as amended by that Protocol, unless they express a different intention in a written communication to one of the Depositaries.

5

After the entry into force of the 2010 Protocol, any State which is not a member of the Council of Europe or of the OECD may request to be invited to sign and ratify this Convention as amended by the 2010 Protocol. Any request to this effect shall be addressed to one of the Depositaries, who shall transmit it to the Parties. The Depositary shall also inform the Committee of Ministers of the Council of Europe and the OECD Council. The decision to invite States which so request to become Party to this Convention shall be taken by consensus by the Parties to the Convention through the co-ordinating body. In respect of any State ratifying the Convention as amended by the 2010 Protocol in accordance with this paragraph, this Convention shall enter into force on the first day of the month following the expiration of a period of three months after the date of deposit of the instrument of ratification with one of the Depositaries.

6

The provisions of this Convention, as amended by the 2010 Protocol, shall have effect for administrative assistance related to taxable periods beginning on or after 1 January of the year following the one in which the Convention, as amended by the 2010 Protocol, entered into force in respect of a Party, or where there is no taxable period, for administrative assistance related to charges to tax arising on or after 1 January of the year following the one in which the Convention, as amended by the 2010 Protocol, entered into force in respect of a Party. Any two or more Parties may mutually agree that the Convention, as amended by the 2010 Protocol, shall have effect for administrative assistance related to earlier taxable periods or charges to tax.

7

Notwithstanding paragraph 6, for tax matters involving intentional conduct which is liable to prosecution under the criminal laws of the applicant Party, the provisions of this Convention, as amended by the 2010 Protocol, shall have effect from the date of entry into force in respect of a Party in relation to earlier taxable periods or charges to tax."

2 The following subparagraph shall be added after subparagraph e of paragraph 1 of Article 30 of the Convention:

"(f) to apply paragraph 7 of Article 28 exclusively for administrative assistance related to taxable periods beginning on or after 1 January of the third year preceding the one in which the Convention, as amended by the 2010 Protocol, entered into force in respect of a Party, or where there is no taxable period, for administrative assistance related to charges to tax arising on or after 1 January of the third year preceding the one in which the Convention, as amended by the 2010 Protocol, entered into force in respect of a Party."

3 The words "and any Party to this Convention" shall be added after the words "member countries of the OECD" in paragraph 1 of Article 32 of the Convention.

ARTICLE IX

1 This Protocol shall be open for signature by the Signatories to the Convention. It is subject to ratification, acceptance or approval. A signatory may not ratify, accept or approve this Protocol unless it has previously or simultaneously ratified, accepted or approved the Convention. Instruments of ratification, acceptance or approval shall be deposited with one of the Depositaries.

2 This Protocol shall enter into force on the first day of the month following the expiration of a period of three months after the date on which five Parties to the Convention have expressed their consent to be bound by the Protocol in accordance with the provisions of paragraph 1.

3 In respect of any Party to the Convention which subsequently expresses its consent to be bound by it, the Protocol shall enter into force on the first day of the month following the expiration of a period of three months after the date of the deposit of the instrument of ratification, acceptance or approval.

ARTICLE X

1 The Depositary with whom an act, notification or communication has been accomplished, shall notify the member States of the Council of Europe, the member countries of OECD and any Party to the Convention as amended by this Protocol of:

(*a*) any signature;
(*b*) the deposit of any instrument of ratification, acceptance or approval;
(*c*) any date of entry into force of this Protocol in accordance with the provisions of Article IX;
(*d*) any other act, notification or communication relating to this Protocol.

2 The Depositary receiving a communication or making a notification in pursuance of the provisions of paragraph 1 shall inform the other Depositary thereof.

3 The Depositaries shall transmit to the member States of the Council of Europe and the member countries of the OECD a certified copy of this Protocol.

4 When this Protocol enters into force in accordance with Article IX, one of the Depositaries shall establish the text of the Convention as amended by this Protocol and shall send a certified copy to all the Parties to the Convention as amended by this Protocol.

In witness whereof the undersigned, being duly authorised thereto, have signed the Protocol.

Done at Paris, this 27th day of May 2010, in English and French, both texts being equally authentic, in two copies, one of which shall be deposited in the archives of the Council of Europe and the other in the archives of the OECD.

2011/1157

SKIPTON FUND LIMITED (APPLICATION OF SECTIONS 731, 733 AND 734 OF THE INCOME TAX (TRADING AND OTHER INCOME) ACT 2005) ORDER 2011

Made . . . . *26 April 2011*
Laid before the House of Commons . . . . *27 April 2011*
Coming into force . . . . *18 May 2011*

The Treasury make the following Order in exercise of the powers conferred by section 732(2) of the Income Tax (Trading and Other Income) Act 2005:

1 Citation, commencement and interpretation

(1) This Order may be cited as the Skipton Fund Limited (Application of Sections 731, 733 and 734 of the Income Tax (Trading and Other Income) Act 2005) Order 2011 and shall come into force on 18th May 2011.

(2) In this Order "Skipton Fund Limited" and "Qualifying Person" have the meanings given in respectively section 731(7) and (8) of the Income Tax (Trading and Other Income) Act 2005 (treated as inserted by article 2(2)(*b*)).

2 Application of sections 731, 733 and 734 of the Income Tax (Trading and Other Income) Act 2005

(1) Sections 731, 733 and 734 of the Income Tax (Trading and Other Income) Act 2005 shall have effect with the following modifications in relation to payments made pursuant to a scheme or arrangement administered by Skipton Fund Limited to a Qualifying Person.

(2) In section 731 (periodical payments of personal injury damages etc)—

(*a*) in subsection (2)—

(i) the "or" at the end of the paragraph (d) is treated as omitted;

(ii) after paragraph (*e*) there is treated as inserted—

", or

(*f*) a scheme or arrangement administered by Skipton Fund Limited, so far as it relates to a Qualifying Person.";

(*b*) after subsection (6) there is treated as inserted—

"(7) In this section "Skipton Fund Limited" means the company limited by guarantee of that name (company number 5084964).

(8) In this section and sections 733 and 734 "Qualifying person" has the meaning given in the agreement entered into between the Secretary of State for Health and Skipton Fund Limited dated 24th March 2011[, as amended on 30th April 2012][1].

(3) In section 733(a) (persons entitled to exemption for personal injury payments etc)—

(*a*) after "the person" there is treated as inserted "("A") who is a Qualifying Person or who is";

(*b*) "("A") is treated as omitted.

(4) In section 734(1)(*a*) (payments from trusts for injured persons) after "who is" there is to be treated as inserted "a Qualifying Person or who is".

Amendments—[1] In para (2)(*b*), words inserted by the Skipton Fund Limited (Application of Sections 731, 733 and 734 of the Income Tax (Trading and Other Income) Act 2005) (Amendment) Order, SI 2012/1188 art 2 with effect from 23 May 2012.

2011/1211

OFFSHORE FUNDS (TAX) (AMENDMENT) REGULATIONS 2011

Made . . . . *4 May 2011*
Laid before the House of Commons . . . . *5 May 2011*
Coming into force . . . . *27 May 2011*

The Treasury make the following Regulations in exercise of the powers conferred by section 354 of the Taxation (International and Other Provisions) Act 2010.

PART 1
INTRODUCTION

1 Citation, commencement and effect

(1) These Regulations may be cited as the Offshore Funds (Tax) (Amendment) Regulations 2011 and shall come into force on 27th May 2011.

(2) These Regulations have effect—

(*a*) for the purposes of income tax for distributions made, or treated as made, on or after 27th May 2011;

(*b*) for the purposes of corporation tax—
(i) on chargeable gains, in relation to disposals made on or after that date, and
(ii) for distributions made, or treated as made, on or after that date;
(*c*) for the purposes of capital gains tax, in relation to disposals made on or after that date.
This is subject to regulation 16(1).

2 Amendment of the Offshore Funds (Tax) Regulations 2009

The Offshore Funds (Tax) Regulations 2009 ("the principal Regulations") are amended as follows.

3 Structure of these Regulations and interpretation

(1) The structure of these Regulations is as follows—
this Part contains introductory provisions;
Part 2 deals with equalisation arrangements;
Part 3 deals with an exception from the charge to tax in relation to funds investing in certain types of unlisted trading company;
Part 4 deals with transparent funds;
Part 5 makes other amendments to the principal Regulations;
Part 6 makes amendments to primary legislation.
(2) In these Regulations—
"equalisation arrangements" has the meaning given by regulation 50A of the principal Regulations (inserted by regulation 5 of these Regulations);
"transparent fund" has the same meaning as in regulation 11 of the principal Regulations.

PART 2
EQUALISATION ARRANGEMENTS

CHAPTER 1
Introduction and amendments to principal Regulations

4 Introduction

This Part makes the following provisions in relation to equalisation arrangements—
(*a*) this Chapter makes amendments to the principal Regulations,
(*b*) Chapter 2 makes transitional provisions.

CHAPTER 2

Transitional provisions

14 Transitional provisions: introduction

(1) This Chapter applies to offshore funds which are reporting funds at the date these Regulations come into force.
(2) In this Chapter a reference to regulation 53(1) or any sub-paragraph of that regulation is a reference to regulation 53(1) (contents of an application) of the principal Regulations as amended by regulation 6 of these Regulations.
(3) In this Chapter—
"HMRC" means Her Majesty's Revenue and Customs;
"transitional fund" means a fund to which this Chapter applies.

15 Transitional provisions: general provisions

(1) The manager of a transitional fund must give the statements required by sub-paragraphs (*h*) to (*l*) of regulation 53(1) by a notice in writing to HMRC within one year of the date these Regulations come into force.
(2) A transitional fund will be treated as having operated equalisation arrangements, full equalisation arrangements or as not operating equalisation arrangements in accordance with those statements from the time that the fund first became a reporting fund for the purposes of any report made to participants after the date these Regulations come into force.
This is subject to regulation 16.

16 Transitional provisions: special cases

(1) The amendments made by this Part shall not apply in relation to a reporting period which ended before the date these Regulations come into force if the manager of a transitional fund so elects by notice in writing given with the notice under regulation 15(1).
(2) If no notice is given under regulation 15(1) or if paragraph (3) applies, a transitional fund shall be treated as having given a statement under regulation 53(1)(*k*)(i) and be treated from the time that the fund first became a reporting fund as not operating equalisation arrangements and as intending to make adjustments on the basis of reported income.
(3) This paragraph applies if—

(*a*) a transitional fund has given a statement that it does not intend to operate equalisation arrangements and intends to make income adjustments on the basis of accounting income (see regulation 53(1)(*l*)), and

(*b*) HMRC do not consider that it is reasonable to expect that the difference between the amount of reported income per unit calculated using this method and the amount of reported income per unit calculated on the basis of reported income will be 10% or less of the latter of those amounts.

(4) Where paragraph (3) applies HMRC must give notice to the manager of the transitional fund within 28 days of receiving the notice under regulation 15(1).

(5) The notice under paragraph (4) must state that paragraph (2) of this regulation applies to the fund.

17 Appeal against a refusal to accept a statement

(1) If HMRC give notice under regulation 16(4), the manager of the transitional fund may appeal.

(2) The notice of appeal must be given to HMRC within a period of 42 days beginning with the day on which the notice under regulation 16(4) is given.

(3) On an appeal, the tribunal may uphold or quash the notice.

(4) If the tribunal quashes the notice, this Chapter applies as if regulation 16(3) had never applied.

2011/1295

TAXATION OF CHARGEABLE GAINS (GILT-EDGED SECURITIES) ORDER 2011

Made . . . . .19 May 2011

The Treasury make the following Order in exercise of the powers conferred by paragraph 1 of Schedule 9 to the Taxation of Chargeable Gains Act 1992.

1 Citation

This Order may be cited as the Taxation of Chargeable Gains (Gilt-edged Securities) Order 2011.

2 Securities specified as gilt-edged securities

For the purposes of Schedule 9 to the Taxation of Chargeable Gains Act 1992 (Gilt-edged Securities) the following securities are specified—

3¾ % Treasury Gilt 2020
4¼ % Treasury Gilt 2040
2% Treasury Gilt 2016
3¾ % Treasury Gilt 2021.

2011/1502

TAXATION OF EQUITABLE LIFE (PAYMENTS) ORDER 2011

Made . . . . .15 June 2011
Coming into force in accordance with article 1(1)

The Treasury make the following Order in exercise of the powers conferred by section 1(3) and (4) of the Equitable Life (Payments) Act 2010

In accordance with section 1(5) of that Act, a draft of this Order was laid before Parliament and approved by a resolution of each House of Parliament.

1 Citation, commencement, effect and interpretation

(1) This Order may be cited as the Taxation of Equitable Life (Payments) Order 2011 and shall come into force on the day after the day on which it is made.

(2) This Order has effect in relation to authorised payments made after the day on which this Order is made.

(3) In this Order "authorised payment" means a payment to which section 1 of the Equitable Life (Payments) Act 2010 applies.

2 Capital gains tax

An authorised payment shall be disregarded for the purposes of capital gains tax.

3 Corporation tax

An authorised payment shall be disregarded for the purposes of the Corporation Tax Acts.

4 Income tax

An authorised payment shall be disregarded for the purposes of the Income Tax Acts.

5 Inheritance tax

(1) For the purposes of the Inheritance Tax Act 1984—

(*a*) in determining the value of a person's estate immediately before that person's death, no account shall be taken of any value attributable to a right to, or interest in, an authorised payment made after that person's death; and

(*b*) in determining the value of relevant property immediately before a ten-year anniversary for the purposes of the charge under section 64 of the Inheritance Tax Act 1984, no account shall be taken of any value attributable to a right to, or interest in, an authorised payment made on or after that ten-year anniversary.

(2) In this article—

"estate" has the meaning given by section 272 of the Inheritance Tax Act 1984;
"relevant property" has the meaning given by section 58 of that Act; and
"ten-year anniversary" has the meaning given by section 61 of that Act.

6 Tax Credits

In calculating investment income in accordance with regulation 10 of the Tax Credits (Definition and Calculation of Income) Regulations 2002, an authorised payment shall be disregarded.

2011/1752

REGISTERED PENSION SCHEMES (LIFETIME ALLOWANCE TRANSITIONAL PROTECTION) REGULATIONS 2011

Made . . . . *20 July 2011*
Laid before the House of Commons . . . . *21 July 2011*
Coming into force . . . . *11 August 2011*

The Commissioners for Her Majesty's Revenue and Customs make these Regulations in exercise of the powers conferred on them by paragraph 14(2) and (15) of Schedule 18 to the Finance Act 2011 and section 251(1) of the Finance Act 2004 and now exercisable by them.

Note—These Regulations are to continue to have effect and, so far as they were made under FA 2011 Sch 18 para 14(2), (15), are to be treated as if they were made under FA 2011 Sch 18 paras 16, 17(1) (see FA 2013 s 46(5)).

1 Citation, commencement and interpretation

These Regulations may be cited as the Registered Pension Schemes (Lifetime Allowance Transitional Protection) Regulations 2011 and shall come into force on 11th August 2011.

2 In these Regulations—

"paragraph 14" means paragraph 14 of Schedule 18 to the Finance Act 2011;
"paragraph 14(4) event" means an event described in sub-paragraph (4) of paragraph 14;
"paragraph 14 notice" means a notice of an intention to rely on paragraph 14; and
"tribunal" means the First-tier Tribunal or, where determined in accordance with the Tribunal Procedure (First-tier Tribunal) (Tax Chamber) Rules 2009, the Upper Tribunal.

3 Reliance on paragraph 14

(1) Subject to paragraph (2), an individual may rely on paragraph 14 if—

(*a*) the individual has given a paragraph 14 notice to Her Majesty's Revenue and Customs, and

(*b*) Her Majesty's Revenue and Customs have accepted that notice by issuing a certificate to the individual.

(2) An individual may not rely on paragraph 14 if—

(*a*) Her Majesty's Revenue and Customs have refused to accept a paragraph 14 notice in accordance with regulation 6,

(*b*) Her Majesty's Revenue and Customs have revoked the certificate in accordance with regulation 11, or

(*c*) a paragraph 14(4) event has occurred.

4 The paragraph 14 notice

(1) A paragraph 14 notice must include the following information—

(*a*) the title, full name, address (including post code, if applicable) and date of birth of the individual submitting the paragraph 14 notice,

(*b*) the national insurance number of the individual or, where the individual does not qualify for a national insurance number, the reasons for this,

(*c*) a declaration that paragraph 7 of Schedule 36 to the Finance Act 2004 (primary protection) does not make provision for a lifetime allowance enhancement factor in the case of the individual, and

(*d*) a declaration that paragraph 12 of that Schedule (enhanced protection) will not apply in relation to the individual on and after 6th April 2012.

(2) A paragraph 14 notice must be—

(*a*) in a form prescribed by Her Majesty's Revenue and Customs, and

[(*b*) received by Her Majesty's Revenue and Customs on or before the following dates—

(i) if it relates to an individual described in sub-paragraph (1) of paragraph 14, 5 April 2012; or

(ii) if it relates to an individual described in sub-paragraph (1A) of paragraph 14, 5 April 2014.][1]

(3) The individual must sign and date the paragraph 14 notice.

Amendments—[1] Para (2)(b) substituted by the Registered Pension Schemes and Relieved Non-UK Pension Schemes (Lifetime Allowance Transitional Protection) (Amendment) Regulations, SI 2013/1740 reg 3(1), (2) with effect from 12 August 2013.

5 Issue of certificate by Her Majesty's Revenue and Customs

(1) If Her Majesty's Revenue and Customs accept the paragraph 14 notice, they must issue a certificate to the individual.

(2) The certificate must have a unique reference number.

6 Refusal by Her Majesty's Revenue and Customs to accept notice

(1) Her Majesty's Revenue and Customs may refuse to accept the paragraph 14 notice if it does not satisfy the requirements in regulation 4.

(2) If Her Majesty's Revenue and Customs refuse to accept the paragraph 14 notice the individual may require that Her Majesty's Revenue and Customs provide reasons for the refusal.

7 Appeal against refusal to accept notice

(1) The individual may appeal against a refusal by Her Majesty's Revenue and Customs to accept the paragraph 14 notice.

(2) The notice of appeal must be given to Her Majesty's Revenue and Customs before the end of the period of 30 days beginning with the day on which the refusal to accept the paragraph 14 notice was given.

(3) Where an appeal under this regulation is notified to the tribunal, the tribunal must determine whether Her Majesty's Revenue and Customs were entitled to take the view that the notice did not satisfy the requirements in regulation 4.

(4) If the tribunal allows the appeal, the tribunal may direct Her Majesty's Revenue and Customs to accept the paragraph 14 notice and issue a certificate to the individual.

8 Incorrect information given in, or in connection with, the paragraph 14 notice

If the individual realises that any information given in the paragraph 14 notice or given to Her Majesty's Revenue and Customs in connection with that notice was incorrect or has become incorrect, the individual must provide Her Majesty's Revenue and Customs with the correct information without undue delay.

9 Requirement to inform Her Majesty's Revenue and Customs of a paragraph 14(4) event

Where Her Majesty's Revenue and Customs have issued a certificate the individual must—

(*a*) inform Her Majesty's Revenue and Customs when a paragraph 14(4) event occurs, and

(*b*) provide that information before the end of the period of 90 days beginning with the day on which the event occurred.

10 Replacement of a certificate by Her Majesty's Revenue and Customs

(1) Her Majesty's Revenue and Customs may issue a certificate, replacing the previous certificate, if they have reason to believe that information given in, or in connection with, the paragraph 14 notice was incorrect or has become incorrect.

(2) A certificate issued in accordance with regulation 10(1) must have a unique reference number.

11 Revocation of a certificate by Her Majesty's Revenue and Customs

Her Majesty's Revenue and Customs may revoke a certificate if they—

(*a*) have reason to believe that a paragraph 14(4) event has occurred,

(*b*) have reason to believe that any of the conditions in sub-paragraph (1) of paragraph 14 have not been met, or

(*c*) have given notice to the individual under paragraph 1 of Schedule 36 to the Finance Act 2008 in connection with paragraph 14 and the individual does not reply to that notice within the time specified in the notice.

12 Appeal against revocation or replacement of a certificate

(1) The individual may require Her Majesty's Revenue and Customs to provide reasons for revoking or replacing the certificate.

(2) Paragraphs (1) and (2) of regulation 7 apply to a decision to revoke or replace the certificate as they apply to the refusal to accept the paragraph 14 notice.

(3) Where an appeal under this regulation is notified to the tribunal, the tribunal must determine whether Her Majesty's Revenue and Customs replaced or revoked the certificate in accordance with regulations 10(1) or 11.

(4) If the tribunal allows the appeal, the tribunal may direct Her Majesty's Revenue and Customs to issue a certificate to the individual.

13 Preservation of documents

(1) Where Her Majesty's Revenue and Customs have issued a certificate the individual must preserve the certificate until no further benefit crystallisation event can occur . . . [1] in relation to the individual.

(2) The requirement to preserve the certificate ceases where the certificate has been revoked.

Amendments—[1] In para (1), words "in relation to any sums or assets held for the purposes of a registered pension scheme" revoked by the Registered Pension Schemes and Relieved Non-UK Pension Schemes (Lifetime Allowance Transitional Protection) (Amendment) Regulations, SI 2013/1740 reg 3(1), (3) with effect from 12 August 2013.

2011/1783

REGISTERED PENSION SCHEMES (RELEVANT INCOME) REGULATIONS 2011

Made . . . .*20 July 2011*
Laid before the House of Commons . . . .*21 July 2011*
Coming into force . . . .*11 August 2011*

The Treasury make the following Regulations in exercise of the powers conferred by paragraphs 14B(2)(b) and 24D(2)(b) of Schedule 28 to, and section 282(A1) of, the Finance Act 2004 as the latter section has effect under paragraph 108 of Schedule 16 to the Finance Act 2011.

1 Citation, commencement and effect

(1) These Regulations may be cited as the Registered Pension Schemes (Relevant Income) Regulations 2011 and come into force on 11th August 2011.

(2) These Regulations have effect for the tax year beginning on 6th April 2011 and subsequent tax years.

2 Payments not to be regarded as relevant income

The payments described in regulations 3 and 4 are not to be regarded as relevant income for the purpose of ascertaining whether a member or dependant satisfies the minimum income requirement in paragraphs 14A(1) or 24C(1) of Schedule 28 to the Finance Act 2004.

3 (1) Payments of a scheme pension payable by the scheme administrator and made in respect of a defined benefits arrangement where the pension scheme under which that arrangement is made has fewer than 20 pensioner members unless the payments fall within paragraph (4) or (5).

(2) Payments of a scheme pension made in respect of a money purchase arrangement and payable by the scheme administrator where fewer than 20 pensioner members of the pension scheme under which that arrangement is made are entitled to payment of such a scheme pension unless the payments fall within paragraph (4) or (6).

(3) Payments under an overseas pension scheme which, if the scheme were a registered pension scheme would fall within paragraph (1) or (2).

(4) Paragraphs (1) and (2) do not apply in the case of payments of a scheme pension payable under an annuity contract where that annuity contract is made with an insurance company or a non-EEA annuity provider and was purchased by the application of sums and assets held for the purposesof—

- (*a*) a registered pension scheme
- (*b*) an overseas pension scheme, or
- (*c*) if the purchase took place before 6th April 2006 a pension scheme which at the time of purchase fell within one of the categories set out in paragraph 1(1)(a) to (g) of Schedule 36.

(5) Paragraph (1) does not apply in the case of payments of a scheme pension or dependants' scheme pension payable in respect of a defined benefits arrangement where—

- (*a*) the pension scheme under which that arrangement was made ("the relevant pension scheme") had 20 or more members in relation to whom a defined benefits arrangement was in existence on or before 5th April 2011, and
- (*b*) the defined benefits arrangement under the relevant pension scheme was in existence in relation to the member on or before 5th April 2011.

(6) Paragraph (2) does not apply in the case of payments of a scheme pension payable under an annuity contract where that annuity contract is treated as having become a registered pension scheme under section 153(8A) of the Finance Act 2004.

(7) For the purposes of this regulation a "non-EEA annuity provider" means a person resident in a country or territory outside the European Economic Area—

- (*a*) whose normal business includes the provision of annuities; and
- (*b*) who is regulated in the conduct of that business by—

(i) the government of that country or territory, or

(ii) a body established under the law of that country or territory for the purpose of regulating such business.

4 (1) Excess payments of a lifetime annuity or dependants' annuity unless the payments fall within paragraph (4).

(2) Excess payments are payments that exceed the amount of the minimum annuity guaranteed to be paid each year under the annuity contract for the annuity over its full term.

(3) For the purposes of this regulation "full term" means the minimum period over which a lifetime annuity or a dependants' annuity must be payable in accordance with the applicable provision of paragraphs 3(1), 17(1)(*d*) or (*e*) of Schedule 28 to the Finance Act 2004.

(4) Paragraph (1) does not apply to payments of a lifetime or dependants' annuity where the annual amount of the annuity—

(*a*) cannot decrease, or

(*b*) is determined in accordance with the manner prescribed in regulation 2(2)(*a*)(i) (variation in line with the RPI) of the Registered Pension Schemes (Prescribed Manner of Determining Amount of Annuities) Regulations 2006.

2011/1784

CORPORATION TAX ACT 2010 (FACTORS DETERMINING SUBSTANTIAL COMMERCIAL INTERDEPENDENCE) ORDER 2011

Made . . . .*20 July 2011*

Laid before the House of Commons . . . .*21 July 2011*

Coming into force . . . .*11 August 2011*

The Treasury makes the following Order in exercise of the powers conferred by section 27(3) of the Corporation Tax Act 2010 and section 55(5) of the Finance Act 2011.

1 Citation, commencement and effect

(1) This Order may be cited as the Corporation Tax Act 2010 (Factors Determining Substantial Commercial Interdependence) Order 2011.

(2) This Order shall come into force on 11th August 2011.

(3) This Order shall have effect for accounting periods ending on or after 1st April 2011.

2 Factors taken into account in determining substantial commercial interdependence

In determining for the purposes of section 27 of the Corporation Tax Act 2010 (attribution to persons of rights and powers of their associates) whether a relationship between two companies amounts to "substantial commercial interdependence", the following factors are to be taken into account—

(*a*) the degree to which the companies are financially interdependent,

(*b*) the degree to which the companies are economically interdependent, and

(*c*) the degree to which the companies are organisationally interdependent.

3 "Financially interdependent"

Two companies are "financially interdependent" for the purposes of article 2 if (in particular)—

(*a*) one gives financial support (directly or indirectly) to the other, or

(*b*) each has a financial interest in the affairs of the same business.

4 "Economically interdependent"

Two companies are "economically interdependent" for the purposes of article 2 if (in particular)—

(*a*) the companies seek to realise the same economic objective,

(*b*) the activities of one benefit the other, or

(*c*) the companies have common customers.

5 "Organisationally interdependent"

Two companies are "organisationally interdependent" for the purposes of article 2 if (in particular) the businesses of the companies have or use—

(*a*) common management,

(*b*) common employees,

(*c*) common premises, or

(*d*) common equipment.

2011/1791

REGISTERED PENSION SCHEMES (MODIFICATION OF SCHEME RULES) REGULATIONS 2011

Made . . . . *20 July 2011*
Laid before the House of Commons . . . . *21 July 2011*
Coming into force . . . . *11 August 2011*

The Commissioners for Her Majesty's Revenue and Customs make the following Regulations in exercise of the power conferred by section 237F of the Finance Act 2004.

1 Citation and commencement

These Regulations may be cited as the Registered Pension Schemes (Modification of Scheme Rules) Regulations 2011 and come into force on 11th August 2011.

2 Modification of scheme rules

(1) This regulation applies where a scheme administrator of a registered pension scheme ("the scheme") satisfies all or part of a member's liability to the annual allowance charge, either on a voluntary basis or pursuant to a liability under section 237B of the Finance Act 2004.
(2) The rules of the scheme shall be modified so as to allow for a consequential adjustment to be made to the entitlement of the member to benefits under the scheme on a basis that is just and reasonable having regard to normal actuarial practice. This paragraph is subject to paragraph (3).
(3) Any modification to the scheme's rules made by virtue of paragraph (2) is subject to section 159 of the Pension Schemes Act 1993 or section 155 of the Pension Schemes (Northern Ireland) Act 1993 (inalienability of guaranteed minimum pension etc).

2011/1792

REGISTERED PENSION SCHEMES (PRESCRIBED REQUIREMENTS OF FLEXIBLE DRAWDOWN DECLARATION) REGULATIONS 2011

Made . . . . *20 July 2011*
Laid before the House of Commons . . . . *21 July 2011*
Coming into force . . . . *11 August 2011*

The Commissioners for Her Majesty's Revenue and Customs make the following Regulations in exercise of the powers conferred by sections 251(1)(*a*), (4)(*b*), (5) and 282(A1) of, and paragraphs 14E(1) and 24G(1) of Schedule 28 to, the Finance Act 2004 and now exercisable by them.

Revocation—These Regulations repealed by the Taxation of Pensions Act 2014 s 1, Sch 1 para 32(3) with effect from 6 April 2015.

2011/1793

REGISTERED PENSION SCHEMES (NOTICE OF JOINT LIABILITY FOR THE ANNUAL ALLOWANCE CHARGE) REGULATIONS 2011

Made . . . . *20 July 2011*
Laid before the House of Commons . . . . *21 July 2011*
Coming into force . . . . *11 August 2011*

The Commissioners for Her Majesty's Revenue and Customs make these Regulations in exercise of the powers conferred by sections 237B(5)(*b*) and (*c*) and 251(4)(*a*) of the Finance Act 2004 and now exercisable by them.

1 Citation, commencement and interpretation

(1) These Regulations may be cited as the Registered Pension Schemes (Notice of Joint Liability for the Annual Allowance Charge) Regulations 2011 and shall come into force on 11th August 2011.
(2) In these Regulations—

"the further notice" means a notice given by an individual to a scheme administrator in accordance with regulation 4;
"the notice" means a notice given by an individual to a scheme administrator in accordance with section 237B(3) of the Finance Act 2004; and
"relevant tax year" means the tax year to which the notice relates.

2 Particulars to be included in the notice

(1) An individual must include the following particulars in the notice—

(a) the individual's title, full name and address (including post code, if applicable),

(b) the individual's national insurance number, subject to paragraph (4),

(c) the amount of the annual allowance charge for which the individual and the scheme administrator will be jointly and severally liable, and

(d) the tax year in which the annual allowance charge arises.

(2) Where the amount specified in the notice is £2,000 or less, the individual must confirm in the notice that the amount of the individual's liability to the annual allowance charge for the relevant tax year exceeds £2,000.

(3) Where the notice is given to the scheme administrator in the relevant tax year and it is anticipated that in the relevant tax year—

(a) the individual will become entitled to all of the benefits under the pension scheme to which the notice relates ("the relevant scheme"), or

(b) benefit crystallisation events 5, 5A or 5B will occur in relation to the individual under the relevant scheme,

the individual must state in the notice the date on which it is anticipated that the event specified in sub-paragraph (a) or (b) will occur.

(4) Where the individual does not qualify for a national insurance number the individual must set out in the notice the reasons for this in place of the national insurance number.

(5) The notice must be in writing, signed and dated by the individual.

(6) Where the notice is in an electronic format, the requirement in paragraph (5) that the notice must be signed will be satisfied if the notice includes a statement that the individual has personally submitted the notice.

3 Declaration to be included in the notice

(1) The individual must declare in the notice that the individual understands that—

(a) the notice cannot be revoked, and

(b) future benefits to be paid to the individual from the pension scheme will be adjusted to take account of the payment of the annual allowance charge made by the scheme administrator.

(2) The individual must declare that the amount specified in the notice has been calculated at the correct relevant rate as described in section 237B(4) of the Finance Act 2004.

4 Amendment to the notice

(1) Where the individual's liability to the annual allowance charge in relation to the relevant tax year changes after the submission of the notice to the scheme administrator, the individual may amend the notice by sending a further notice to the scheme administrator.

(2) The further notice must comply with regulations 2 and 3.

(3) The further notice must be given to the scheme administrator no later than 31st July following the end of the period of 4 years beginning with the last day of the relevant tax year.

5 Acknowledgement of receipt of the notice and further notice

A scheme administrator must send an acknowledgement to the individual upon receipt of the notice or further notice.

2011/1797

REGISTERED PENSION SCHEMES (PROVISION OF INFORMATION) (AMENDMENT) (NO 2) REGULATIONS 2011

Made . . . . *20 July 2011*

Laid before the House of Commons . . . . *21 July 2011*

Coming into force . . . . *11 August 2011*

The Commissioners for Her Majesty's Revenue and Customs make the following Regulations in exercise of the powers conferred by sections 251(1)(a), (2), (4) and (5) of the Finance Act 2004, and now exercisable by them.

1 Citation, commencement and effect

(1) These Regulations may be cited as the Registered Pension Schemes (Provision of Information) (Amendment) (No 2) Regulations 2011 and come into force on 11th August 2011.

(2) The amendments in regulation 4(3) and (9), and regulation 6 have effect for the tax year 2012–13 and subsequent years.

2 Amendment of the Registered Pension Schemes (Provision of Information) Regulations 2006

The Registered Pension Schemes (Provision of Information) Regulations 2006 are amended as follows.

3 (1) Regulation 2 (interpretation) is amended as follows.

(2) In paragraph (1)—

(*a*) in the definition of "associated company", for "section 416 of ICTA", substitute "section 449 of the Corporation Tax Act 2010",

(*b*) in the definition of "director", for "section 417 of ICTA", substitute "section 67 of ITEPA 2003", and

(*c*) after the definition of "event report" insert—

""fixed protection" means transitional protection provided for under paragraph 14 of Schedule 18 to the Finance Act 2011.".

(3) In paragraph (2), for "section 839 of ICTA", substitute "section 993 ITA 2007".

4 (1) The table appended to Regulation 3(1) (provision of information by scheme administrators to the Commissioners) is amended as follows.

(2) In the second column of entry 1 (unauthorised payments), in sub paragraph (*c*), for "HMRC" substitute "the Commissioners".

(3) In entry 6 (benefit crystallisation events and enhanced lifetime allowance or enhanced protection)—

(a) for the heading substitute—

"Benefit crystallisation events and enhanced lifetime allowance, enhanced protection or fixed protection",

(*b*) in the first column, for paragraph (b) substitute—

"(*b*) in order to reduce or eliminate liability to the lifetime allowance charge the member relies on entitlement to—

(i) an enhanced lifetime allowance,

(ii) enhanced protection, or

(iii) fixed protection.", and

(*c*) for the entry in the second column, substitute—

"The name and national insurance number of the member, the amount crystallised by the event, the date of the event and the reference number given by the Commissioners under—

(*a*) the Registered Pension Schemes (Enhanced Lifetime Allowance) Regulations 2006 (where the member relies on an enhanced lifetime allowance or enhanced protection), or

(*b*) the Registered Pension Schemes (Lifetime Allowance Transitional Protection) Regulations 2011 (where the member relies on fixed protection).".

(4) In entry 7 (pension commencement lump sum), for the text in column 1 substitute—

"The scheme makes a pension commencement lump sum payment to a member which—

(*a*) exceeds 25% of the amount found by adding the amount of the payment to the entitlement amount; and

(*b*) is more than 7.5%, but less than 25%, of the standard lifetime allowance for the tax year in which the sum is paid.

For the purposes of this reportable event, "the entitlement amount" is—

(i) the amount crystallised by reason of the member becoming entitled to the pension with which the lump sum payment is associated, or

(ii) where a benefit crystallisation event did not occur by reason of the member becoming entitled to the pension with which the lump sum payment is associated, the amount that would have been so crystallised if the member had been under the age of 75 at the date the entitlement arose.";

(5) In the second column of entry 7, for the words in paragraph (b), substitute "the entitlement amount".

(6) In the second column of entry 9 (transfers to qualifying recognised overseas pension schemes), in paragraph (a), after "country" insert "or territory" and for "located" substitute "situated".

(7) Omit entries 15 (alternatively secured pension) and 17 (lump sum payment after the death of a member aged 75 or over).

(8) In entry 18 (scheme chargeable payment), in column 1 omit "section 181A (alternatively secured pensions: minimum level of payment);" and

(9) After entry 20 (occupational pension scheme) insert—

"21 Flexible drawdown arrangements	

Section 165(3A) or 167(2A) applies to an arrangement.	The name and national insurance number of the member or dependant ("the member") who meets the flexible drawdown conditions together with the total amount of drawdown pension or dependant's drawdown pension ("drawdown pension") paid under the arrangement to the member during the reporting year and the country or territory where the sole or main address of the member was situated on the date— (i) the declaration under sections 165(3A)(*b*) or 167(2A)(*b*) was made in respect of the arrangement, or (ii) if later, the first payment of drawdown pension was made under the arrangement in the reporting year."[1]

Amendments—[1] Para (9) repealed by the Taxation of Pensions Act 2014 s 1, Sch 1 para 35(1), (8) with effect in relation to reports for the tax year 2015–16 and subsequent tax years.

5

AMENDMENTS—

Reg 5 repealed by the Taxation of Pensions Act 2014 s 1, Sch 1 para 35(1), (9) with effect from 6 April 2015 but without prejudice to the continued operation of the revoked provisions in relation to reports for the tax year 2011–12.

6 For regulation 11 (information provided by member to scheme administrator: enhanced lifetime allowance) substitute—

"11 Information provided by member to scheme administrator: enhanced lifetime allowance, enhanced protection or fixed protection

If the member of a registered pension scheme intends to rely on entitlement to—

(*a*) an enhanced lifetime allowance or enhanced protection by virtue of any provisions listed in section 256(1), or

(*b*) fixed protection by virtue of paragraph 14 of Schedule 18 to the Finance Act 2011

the member must give to the scheme administrator the reference number issued by the Commissioners under the Registered Pension Schemes (Enhanced Lifetime Allowance) Regulations 2006 or the Registered Pension Schemes (Lifetime Allowance Transitional Protection) Regulations 2011 in respect of that entitlement.".

7 In regulation 14 (information provided to members by scheme administrators about benefit crystallisation events), after paragraph (2)(*b*) insert—

"(*ba*) under paragraph (1)(*a*) in a tax year following the tax year in which the member reaches the age of 75;".

8 After regulation 14 insert—

"14A Annual allowance: annual provision of information by scheme administrator to member

(1) Where—

(*a*) an individual is a member ("the member") of a registered pension scheme for all or part of a pension input period ending in a tax year ("the relevant pension input period") who meets one of the conditions in paragraph (8), and

(*b*) the aggregate of the pension input amounts for the relevant pension input period in respect of each arrangement under the registered pension scheme relating to the member exceeds the annual allowance for that tax year,

the scheme administrator must provide the member with a statement containing the information specified in paragraph (2) (the "pension savings statement").

(2) The information is—

(*a*) the aggregate of the pension input amounts for the relevant pension input period in respect of all the arrangements under the registered pension scheme relating to the member (see section 152),

(*b*) the annual allowance for the tax year in which the relevant pension input period ends ("the relevant tax year"), (*c*) the aggregate of the pension input amounts in respect of all the arrangements under the registered pension scheme relating to the member for each of the pension input periods ending in the three tax years immediately preceding the relevant tax year (subject to paragraph (3)), and

(*d*) the annual allowance for each of the three preceding tax years or where one or more of the three preceding tax years is the 2008–09, 2009–10 or 2010–11 tax year, the assumed annual allowance for that tax year pursuant to paragraph 30(3)(*a*) of Schedule 17 to the Finance Act 2011.

(3) Where a pension input period in paragraph (2)(*c*) ends in the 2008–09, 2009–10 or 2010–11 tax year, the pension input amount for that pension input period must be determined on the basis that the assumptions in paragraph 30(3)(*b*) of Schedule 17 to the Finance Act 2011 apply to that pension input period.

(4) The scheme administrator must provide the member with the pension savings statement no later than the 6th October following the relevant tax year. This paragraph is subject to paragraphs (5) and (6).

(5) Where the relevant tax year is 2011–12, the scheme administrator must provide the member with the pension savings statement for that year no later than 6th October 2013.

(6) Where the scheme administrator has not been provided with the information concerning the member by the member's employer in respect of the relevant pension input period pursuant to regulation 15A, the scheme administrator must provide the pension savings statement—

(*a*) within 3 months following receipt of that information, or

(*b*) if later, on or before the date specified in paragraph (4) or (where the relevant tax year is 2011–12) paragraph (5).

(7) Where—

(*a*) the member meets the conditions in paragraph (1)(*a*) and (*b*), and

(*b*) paragraph 28 of Schedule 17 to the Finance Act 2011 applies (provision for a straddling pension input period),

the scheme administrator must provide the member with a pension savings statement containing the pension input amount in respect of the pre-announcement period and post-announcement period in addition to the information specified in paragraph (2).

(8) The conditions referred to in paragraph (1) are as follows.

Condition A

The individual is an active member of the registered pension scheme referred to in paragraph (1)

Condition B

The individual is a deferred member of the registered pension scheme referred to in paragraph (1) in relation to a cash balance arrangement and the condition in section 230(5B)(*b*) (cash balance arrangements) is not met in respect of the pension input amount for the relevant pension input period.

Condition C

The individual is a deferred member of the registered pension scheme referred to in paragraph (1) in relation to a defined benefits arrangement and the condition in section 234(5B)(*b*) (defined balance arrangements) is not met in respect of the pension input amount for the relevant pension input period.

14B Annual allowance: provision of information by scheme administrator to member on request

(1) Where a member or former member ("the member") of a registered pension scheme makes a written request to the scheme administrator of that scheme for any such information in respect of a pension input period ending in a tax year ("the relevant pension input period") as is referred to in regulations 14A(2) or (7), the scheme administrator must provide the member with the information requested—

(*a*) within 3 months following receipt of the request, or

(*b*) if later, on or before 6th October following the tax year ("the relevant tax year") in which the relevant pension input period ended.

This paragraph is subject to paragraphs (2) and (3).

(2) Where the relevant tax year is 2011–12, the scheme administrator must provide the member with the information requested under paragraph (1) for that tax year no later than 6th October 2013.

(3) Where the scheme administrator has not been provided with the information concerning the member by the member's employer in respect of the relevant pension input period pursuant to regulation 15A ("the regulation 15A information"), the scheme administrator must provide the information requested under paragraph (1)—

(*a*) within 3 months following receipt of the regulation 15A information, or

(*b*) if later, on or before—

(i) 6th October following the relevant tax year, or

(ii) where the relevant tax year is 2011–12, the 6th October 2013.".

9 After regulation 15 (information between scheme administrators) insert—

"15A Annual allowance: information to be provided to scheme administrators by certain persons

(1) Where—

(*a*) an employer is a sponsoring employer of a registered pension scheme, and

(*b*) an employee of that employer or a director is an active member of that scheme in relation to an arrangement under the scheme ("the arrangement") for all or part of a pension input period ending in a tax year,

the employer must provide to the scheme administrator such information as will enable the scheme administrator to calculate the pension input amount in respect of the arrangement for the pension input period ending in that tax year.

(2) The information must be provided to the scheme administrator no later than the 6th July following the tax year in which the pension input period ends. This paragraph is subject to paragraph (3).

(3) Where the pension input period ends in the tax year 2011–12, the employer must provide the information relating to the pension input period no later than 6th July 2013.

(4) The employer must provide to the scheme administrator such information as will enable the scheme administrator to calculate the pension input amount for any of the pension input periods ending in the tax years 2008–09, 2009–10 and 2010–11, within 3 months following receipt of a written request from the scheme administrator or, (if later), on or before 6th July 2013.

(5) Where—

(*a*) regulation 14A(7) applies to a scheme administrator (obligation to provide information to a member where there is a straddling pension input period), and

(*b*) a written request is made by the scheme administrator to the employer,

the employer must provide the scheme administrator with such information as will enable the scheme administrator to comply with the obligation contained in regulation 14A(7), such information to be supplied within three months of receipt of the written request or, (if later) on or before 6th July 2013.

(6) The obligations contained in this regulation shall apply to a responsible person (see paragraph (7)) and for the purposes of applying this regulation to the responsible person, references to "employer" shall be read as referring to the responsible person.

(7) For the purposes of this regulation "responsible person" means a person who is responsible for providing the scheme administrator of a registered pension scheme with such information as will enable the scheme administrator to calculate the pension input amount in respect of a member where the member is an active member of that scheme in relation to an arrangement under the scheme for all or part of a pension input period ending in a tax year."

10 In regulation 16 (pensions and annuities in payment: information provided to and by insurance companies)—

(*a*) in paragraph (1) for "an unsecured pension" substitute "a drawdown pension"; and

(*b*) after paragraph (3) insert—

"(4) No obligation to provide a statement arises—

(a) under paragraph (2) in respect of any entitlement to a pension or annuity or pension commencement lump sum which does not give rise to a benefit crystallisation event;

(b) under paragraph (3) in a tax year following the tax year in which the member reaches the age of 75.".

11 In the heading above regulation 17 (payments to insurance companies from unsecured pension funds), for "unsecured pension" substitute "drawdown pension".

12 In regulation 17—

(*a*) in paragraph (1) for "an unsecured pension" substitute "a drawdown pension",

(*b*) in paragraphs (2) and (4) for "unsecured pension" substitute "drawdown pension".

(*c*) after paragraph (7) insert—

"(8) No obligation to provide a statement arises under paragraph (3) or (6) in a tax year following the tax year in which the pensioner or annuitant reaches the age of 75.".

2011/1798

EMPLOYER SUPPORTED CHILDCARE (RELEVANT EARNINGS AND EXCLUDED AMOUNTS) REGULATIONS 2011

Made . . . .*20th July 2011*
Laid before the House of Commons . . . .*21st July 2011*
Coming into force . . . .*11th August 2011*

The Treasury make the following Regulations in exercise of the powers conferred by section 270B(3)(b) and (4) of the Income Tax (Earnings and Pensions) Act 2003 and paragraph 9 of Schedule 8 to the Finance Act 2011.

1 Citation, commencement and effect

These Regulations may be cited as the Employer Supported Childcare (Relevant Earnings and Excluded Amounts) Regulations 2011 and come into force on 11th August 2011 with effect from 6th April 2011.

2 Interpretation

In these Regulations—

"ITEPA" means the Income Tax (Earnings and Pensions) Act 2003;

"PAYE Regulations" means the Income Tax (Pay As You Earn) Regulations 2003.

3 Relevant earnings

For the purposes of section 270B(1)(a) of ITEPA "relevant earnings" (in addition to salary, wages or fees as in section 270B(3)(a)) means—

(a) guaranteed contractual bonuses;
(b) contractual commission;
(c) guaranteed overtime payments;
(d) location or cost of living allowances;
(e) shift allowances;
(f) skills allowances;
(g) retention and recruitment allowances; and
(h) market rate supplements.

4 Excluded amounts

(1) For the purposes of section 270B(1)(b) of ITEPA "excluded amounts" means—

(a) contributions under a pension scheme if the employee has authorised the employer to make the deductions from relevant payments (as defined by regulation 4 of the PAYE Regulations) for which relief at source is given under section 192(1) of the Finance Act 2004;
(b) contributions under a pension scheme allowed under section 193(2) of the Finance Act 2004 (relief under net pay arrangements) to be deducted by the employer from the employee's employment income for the tax year in accordance with the PAYE Regulations;
(c) donations for which a deduction is made under section 713 of ITEPA (payroll giving) in calculating the employee's net taxable earnings from employment by the employer for the tax year in accordance with the PAYE Regulations;
(d) expenses within Chapter 3 of Part 3 of ITEPA (expenses payments) which the employer is authorised to exclude from the employee's taxable earnings for the tax year in accordance with the PAYE Regulations;
(e) payments in respect of removal expenses to which section 271 of ITEPA applies (as defined in section 272 of ITEPA) and which are taxable earnings of the employee from employment by the employer for the tax year;
(f) amounts equivalent to the amount of the personal allowance under section 35(1) of the Income Tax Act 2007, and in addition if applicable, the amount of the blind person's allowance under section 38 of the Income Tax Act 2007.

(2) Paragraph (1)(f) does not apply if after taking into account any relevant earnings and excluded amounts in paragraph (1)(a) to (e) the relevant earnings amount is £150,000 or more.

2011/2391

FINANCE (NO 3) ACT 2010, SCHEDULE 10 AND THE FINANCE ACT 2009, SCHEDULE 55 AND SECTIONS 101 TO 103 (APPOINTED DAY, ETC) (CONSTRUCTION INDUSTRY SCHEME) ORDER 2011

Made . . . .*29th September 2011*

The Treasury make this Order exercising the powers in sections 26(2) to 26(4) of the Finance (No 3) Act 2010, and sections 104(3) to 104(5) and 106(2) to 106(5) of the Finance Act 2009.

1 This Order may be cited as the Finance (No 3) Act 2010, Schedule 10 and the Finance Act 2009, Schedule 55 and Sections 101 to 103 (Appointed Day, etc) (Construction Industry Scheme) Order 2011.

2 6th October 2011 is appointed as the day the following provisions come into force:

(a) paragraphs 5, 6 and 10 of Schedule 10 to the Finance (No 3) Act 2010 (and, but only as relevant to those provisions, paragraph 1 of that Schedule);

(b) these paragraphs of Schedule 55 to the Finance Act 2009 ("Schedule 55"): 1 (but only in relation to item 6 in the Table in paragraph 1(5) of that Schedule ("item 6")), 7 to 13, and—but only as relevant to those provisions—14 to 24, 26, and 27(1) to 27(4);

(c) sections 101 to 103 of the Finance Act 2009, but only in relation to a penalty under paragraphs 7 to 13 of Schedule 55.

3 (1) Articles 2(a) and 2(b) only have effect in relation to a return within item 6, and for which the filing date for the purposes of Schedule 55 is after 19th October 2011.

(2) The provisions in article 2(b) come into force subject to those in article 2(a).

(3) On 6th October 2011, this paragraph amends regulation 4(13) of the Income Tax (Construction Industry Scheme) Regulations 2005 by inserting the following after "appointed day": ", but only arises where that failure relates to a return that must be made not later than 19th October 2011".

2011/2446

TAXES AND DUTIES, ETC (INTEREST RATE) REGULATIONS 2011

Made . . . . *10th October 2011*

Laid before the House of Commons . . . . *10th October 2011*

Coming into force . . . . *31st October 2011*

The Treasury make the following Regulations in exercise of the powers conferred by section 103 of the Finance Act 2009.

1 Citation and commencement

These Regulations may be cited as the Taxes and Duties, etc (Interest Rate) Regulations 2011 and come into force on 31st October 2011.

2 Interpretation

In these Regulations—

"Bank of England rate" means the official bank rate as announced at the relevant meeting;

"operative date" means the 13th working day following the relevant meeting;

"relevant meeting" means the most recent meeting of the Bank of England Monetary Policy Committee;

"working day" means any day other than a non-business day within the meaning of section 92 of the Bills of Exchange Act 1882.

3 Late payment interest rate

(1) Except where regulation 5 applies, the late payment interest rate for the purposes of section 101 of the Finance Act 2009 (late payment interest on sums due to HMRC), is the percentage per annum found by applying the following formula—

Bank of England rate + 2.5.

(2) The interest rate found under paragraph (1) applies on and after the operative date.

4 Repayment interest rate

(1) Except where regulation 5 applies, the repayment interest rate for the purposes of section 102 of the Finance Act 2009 (repayment interest on sums to be paid by HMRC), is the higher of—

(a) 0.5% per annum; and

(b) the percentage per annum found by applying the following formula—

Bank of England rate—1.

(2) The interest rate found under paragraph (1) applies on and after the operative date.

5 Initial rates of interest

(1) This regulation applies immediately on the coming into force of these Regulations until the first operative date after the coming into force of these Regulations.

(2) The late payment interest rate and repayment interest rate shall be the respective percentages per annum found by applying regulation 3(1) and regulation 4(1) as if the references in those regulations to the Bank of England rate were references to the official bank rate announced at the meeting of the Bank of England Monetary Policy Committee on, or most recently before, the 13th working day before the coming into force of these Regulations.

6 Effect of change in rates of interest

Where the late payment interest rate or repayment interest rate changes in accordance with these Regulations with effect from an operative date, the change has effect in respect of interest running from before that date as well as interest running from or after that date.

7 Earlier instrument revoked

The Taxes and Duties (Interest Rate) Regulations 2010 are revoked.

2011/2696

EMPLOYMENT INCOME PROVIDED THROUGH THIRD PARTIES (EXCLUDED RELEVANT STEPS) REGULATIONS 2011

Made . . . . *9th November 2011*

Laid before the House of Commons . . . . *10th November 2011*

Coming into force . . . . *6th December 2011*

The Commissioners for Her Majesty's Revenue and Customs, in exercise of the powers conferred by section 554Y of the Income Tax (Earnings and Pensions) Act 2003, make the following Regulations:

1 Citation, commencement and application

(1) These Regulations may be cited as the Employment Income Provided Through Third Parties (Excluded Relevant Steps) Regulations 2011 and come into force on 6th December 2011.

(2) The Regulations have effect in relation to relevant steps taken on and after 9th December 2010.

2 Interpretation

In these Regulations—

"Part 7A" means Part 7A of the Income Tax (Earnings and Pensions) Act 2003 (employment income provided through third parties); and

"relevant non-UK scheme" means a scheme within paragraph 1(5) of Schedule 34 to FA 2004.

3 Disapplication of Chapter 2 of Part 7A: relevant steps arising or deriving from UK tax-relieved funds and relevant transfer funds

(1) Chapter 2 of Part 7A (treatment of relevant steps for income tax purposes) does not apply by reason of a relevant step if the subject of the relevant step is a sum of money or asset which represents or which has (wholly or partly) arisen or derived (directly or indirectly) from a sum of money or assets which represents or has represented—

(a) a UK tax-relieved fund under a relevant non-UK scheme, or

(b) a relevant transfer fund under a relevant non-UK scheme.

(2) Paragraph (3) applies if the sum of money or asset which is the subject of the relevant step only partly—

(a) represents, or

(b) arises or derives from a sum of money or assets which represents or has represented,

a fund mentioned in paragraph (1).

(3) The relevant step is to be treated for the purposes of this Part as being two separate relevant steps—

(a) one in relation to the sum of money or asset so far as it represents or arises or derives from a sum of money or assets which represents or has represented a fund mentioned in paragraph (1), and

(b) one in relation to the sum of money or asset so far as it does not represent or arise or derive from a sum of money or assets which represents or has represented a fund mentioned in paragraph (1),

and paragraph (1) applies only in relation to the separate relevant step mentioned in sub-paragraph (a).

(4) In order to give effect to paragraph (3), the sum of money or asset which is the subject of the relevant step is to be apportioned between the two separate relevant steps on a just and reasonable basis.

(5) In paragraph (1)—

"relevant transfer fund" has the meaning given in paragraph 4(2) of Schedule 34 to FA 2004;

"UK tax-relieved fund" has the meaning given in paragraph 3(2) of Schedule 34 to FA 2004.

4 Disapplication of Chapter 2 of Part 7A: relevant steps arising or deriving from a payment from a registered pension scheme that has been subject to the unauthorised payments charge

(1) Chapter 2 of Part 7A does not apply by reason of a relevant step if the subject of the relevant step is a sum of money or asset which has (wholly or partly) arisen or derived (directly or indirectly) from a payment—

(a) made by a registered pension scheme,

(b) that was subject to the unauthorised payments charge.

(2) Paragraph (3) applies if the sum of money or asset which is the subject of the relevant step only partly arises or derives from a payment mentioned in paragraph (1).

(3) The relevant step is to be treated for the purposes of Part 7A as being two separate relevant steps—

(a) one in relation to the sum of money or asset so far as it arises or derives from a payment mentioned in paragraph (1), and

(b) one in relation to the sum of money or asset so far as it does not arise or derive from a payment mentioned in paragraph (1),

and paragraph (1) applies only in relation to the separate relevant step mentioned in sub-paragraph (a).

(4) In order to give effect to paragraph (3), the sum of money or asset which is the subject of the relevant step is to be apportioned between the two separate relevant steps on a just and reasonable basis.

(5) In this regulation, "the unauthorised payments charge" means the charge under section 208 of FA 2004.

5 Modification of section 554S in Part 7A

For the purposes of applying these Regulations, section 554S(2) in Part 7A applies as if after the reference to section 554W (and before the reference to section 554X) there were a reference to these Regulations.

2011/2833

MONEY LAUNDERING (AMENDMENT NO 2) REGULATIONS 2011

Made . . . . *23rd November 2011*

Laid before Parliament . . . . *24th November 2011*

Coming into force . . . . *31st March 2012*

The Treasury are a government department designated for the purposes of section 2(2) of the European Communities Act 1972 in relation to the prevention of money laundering and terrorist financing;

The Treasury, in exercise of the powers conferred on them by section 2(2) of the European Communities Act 1972, make the following Regulations:

1 Citation and commencement

These Regulations may be cited as the Money Laundering (Amendment No2) Regulations 2011 and come into force on 31st March 2012.

2 Change of supervisory authority for Northern Ireland credit unions

(*amends* the Money Laundering Regulations, SI 2007/2157 regs 23, 36)

3 Review

(1) The Treasury must from time to time—

(a) carry out a review of regulation 2,

(b) set out the conclusions of the review in a report, and

(c) publish the report.

(2) The report must in particular—

(a) set out the objectives intended to be achieved by the amendments made by regulation 2,

(b) assess the extent to which those objectives are achieved, and

(c) assess whether those objectives remain appropriate and, if so, the extent to which they could be achieved with a system that imposes less regulation.

(3) The first report under this regulation must be published before the end of the period of five years beginning with 31st March 2012 in conjunction with the Treasury's report setting out the conclusions of its review under article 3 of the Financial Services and Markets Act 2000 (Exemption) (Amendment No 2) Order 2011.

(4) Reports under this regulation are afterwards to be published at intervals not exceeding five years.

2011/2931

MARD REGULATIONS 2011

Made . . . . *8th December 2011*
Laid before the House of Commons . . . . *9th December 2011*
Coming into force . . . . *1st January 2012*

The Treasury make regulations 1 to 7 and 9 to 18 of these Regulations exercising their powers in paragraph 10 of Schedule 25 to the Finance Act 2011.

The Commissioners for Her Majesty's Revenue and Customs make regulations 1(1) and 8 of these Regulations exercising the powers in paragraph 9 of that Schedule.

1 Citation, commencement and interpretation

(1) These Regulations may be cited as the MARD Regulations 2011 and come into force on 1 January 2012.

(2) The Articles mentioned in these Regulations are those of MARD.

(3) Regulations 2(1), 4(1), 5(1), 6, 7(2), 7(4) and 13(2) each applies to any Article it mentions only where the relevant UK authority is the requested authority in that Article.

(4) Regulations 9, 10(1), 11, 12 and 13(3) each applies to any Article it mentions only where an applicant authority of the United Kingdom is the applicant authority in that Article.

Claims, etc to the United Kingdom (ie relevant UK authority is the requested authority in MARD)

2 Exchange of information

(1) The relevant UK authority must comply with the provision made by Article 5 in relation to the requested authority.

(2) This is subject to Articles 5(2) and 5(3).

3 A United Kingdom public authority that is to make a refund in Article 6 may follow that Article.

4 (1) The relevant UK authority must make and carry out the agreement and arrangements for which Article 7(1) makes provision in relation to the requested authority, to the extent that this will promote the mutual assistance provided for in MARD.

(2) This is subject to Articles 7(3) and 21(2).

5 Enforcement of foreign claims in the UK

(1) The relevant UK authority must comply with the provision made by Articles 8, 9(1), 13(2), 13(3), 13(5), 14(1), 16, 18(4) and 19(3) in relation to the requested authority.

(2) For Article 8: this is subject to Article 8(2).

(3) For Article 16: paragraph (1) and regulation 7 apply in a way that gives effect to Article 17.

6 (1) The relevant UK authority may follow Article 13(4), first sentence.

(2) Where it does so, that authority must follow Article 13(4), second sentence.

7 (1) Articles 12, 14(1), 14(2), 15(2) second and third sub-paragraphs, and 18 apply to a foreign claim.

(2) The relevant UK authority must follow Article 15(2), first sub-paragraph, second sentence.

(3) The provision in paragraph (1) for Articles 12 and 14 also apply where the foreign claim is based on a revised instrument in Article 15(2), third sub-paragraph.

(4) The relevant UK authority may follow Articles 18(1) and 18(2).

(5) The relevant UK authority may follow Article 18(3) where the United Kingdom is the Member State in that Article.

8 In the application of the Finance Act 2009, Schedule 49 to any kind of foreign claim for which the relevant UK authority is the Commissioners, the sum payable in paragraph 1(1) of that Schedule includes a foreign claim.

Claims, etc from the United Kingdom (ie a UK authority is the applicant authority in MARD)

9 Request for notification of certain documents relating to claims

Any applicant authority of the United Kingdom must ensure compliance or comply with the provision made by Articles 8(1) and 8(2) in relation to the applicant authority.

10 Requests for recovery, and conditions governing them

(1) Any applicant authority of the United Kingdom must comply with the provision made by Articles 10(2) and 11 in relation to the applicant authority.

(2) A request in either Article by an applicant authority of the United Kingdom must comply with Article 12(1) (except for the obligations that Article places on the requested Member State). The request may be accompanied by the other documents as mentioned in Article 12(2).

11 Disputes

Any applicant authority of the United Kingdom must comply with the provision made by Articles 14(3) and 14(4), third sub-paragraph, third sentence in relation to the applicant authority.

12 Amendment or withdrawal of UK request for recovery assistance

Any applicant authority of the United Kingdom must comply with the provision made by Article 15 in relation to the applicant authority.

Claims within MARD: general

13 Questions on limitation

(1) Article 19 applies to a foreign claim and to a claim for which the applicant Member State is the United Kingdom, as appropriate.

(2) The relevant UK authority must comply with the provision made by Article 19(3) in relation to the requested authority.

(3) Any applicant authority of the United Kingdom must comply with the provision made by Article 19(3) in relation to the applicant authority.

14 Costs

(1) The relevant UK authority and an applicant authority of the United Kingdom may follow respectively Article 20(2), second sub-paragraph in relation to the requested and applicant authorities, as appropriate to the circumstances.

(2) United Kingdom public authorities must seek to ensure compliance with Article 20(2), first sub-paragraph and with Article 20(3).

15 Standard forms and means of communication

(1) Article 21(1) applies where the United Kingdom is the requested Member State or the applicant Member State in that Article, as appropriate.

(2) This is subject to Article 21(3).

16 Use of languages

(1) The documents mentioned in Article 22(1) sent from the United Kingdom must comply with that Article.

(2) Where those documents are sent to the United Kingdom, the second sentence of that Article applies provided that the United Kingdom public authority concerned has agreed with the sending Member State as mentioned in that sentence.

(3) This paragraph applies in relation to documents covered by Article 22(3) where the relevant UK authority is the requested authority or an applicant authority of the United Kingdom is the applicant authority in that Article.

The former authority may impose, and the latter authority must obey, the requirement in that Article. Either authority may enter the bilateral agreement in that Article.

(4) English is the only official language in cases where the United Kingdom is the requested Member State in Articles 22(1) and 22(3), or is the applicant Member State in Article 22(2).

17 Disclosure of information and documents

(1) Articles 23(1) and 23(6) apply where the United Kingdom is the Member State receiving the information within those Articles.

(2) Any United Kingdom public authority in question must seek to ensure that the United Kingdom complies with Articles 23(3) and 23(5) where the United Kingdom is the Member State providing the information, or is the Member State from which it originates, within those Articles.

(3) The relevant UK authority may follow Article 23(4), first sentence where it is the requested authority in that Article.

(4) An applicant authority of the United Kingdom may follow Article 23(4), first sentence where it is the applicant authority in that Article.

(5) Paragraphs (3) and (4) are subject to the second and third sentences of Article 23(4), and to Article 23(5), being satisfied.

Statutory instruments revoked

18 Statutory instruments revoked

The Regulations in the table in the Schedule are revoked.

SCHEDULE

TABLE OF STATUTORY INSTRUMENTS REVOKED

Regulation 18

(1)	(2)
Regulations revoked	References
The Recovery of Duties and Taxes Etc Due in Other Member States (Corresponding UK Claims, Procedure and Supplementary) Regulations 2004	SI 2004/674

The Recovery of Agricultural Levies Due in Other Member States Regulations 2004	SI 2004/800
The Recovery of Duties and Taxes Etc Due in Other Member States (Corresponding UK Claims, Procedure and Supplementary) (Amendment) Regulations 2005	SI 2005/1709
The Recovery of Duties and Taxes Etc Due in Other Member States (Corresponding UK Claims, Procedure and Supplementary) (Amendment) Regulations 2007	SI 2007/3508
The Schedule 39 to the Finance Act 2002 and Recovery of Taxes etc Due in Other Member States (Amendment) Regulations 2010	SI 2010/792

2011/2999

INVESTMENT TRUST (APPROVED COMPANY) (TAX) REGULATIONS 2011

Made . . . . 14th December 2011
Coming into force . . . . 1st January 2012

The Treasury make the following regulations in exercise of the powers conferred by sections 622A, 1158(6) and 1159 of the Corporation Tax Act 2010 and section 354 of the Taxation (International and Other Provisions) Act 2010.

In accordance with sections 622A(3), 1158(8) and 1159(4) of the Corporation Tax Act 2010 and section 372(3)(b) of the Taxation (International and Other Provisions) Act 2010, a draft of these Regulations was laid before the House of Commons and approved by a resolution of that House.

PART 1
INTRODUCTORY AND GENERAL PROVISIONS

1 Citation, commencement and effect

(1) These Regulations may be cited as the Investment Trust (Approved Company) (Tax) Regulations 2011 and come into force on 1 January 2012.

(2) Subject to paragraph (3), these Regulations have effect in relation to accounting periods beginning on or after 1 January 2012.

(3) Regulations 43, 45 and 46 have effect in relation to disposals made on or after 1 January 2012.

2 Structure of these Regulations

The structure of these Regulations is as follows—

This Part contains introductory and general provisions;

Part 2 contains the following provisions about investment trusts—

Chapter 1 deals with applications for approval as an investment trust,

Chapter 2 deals with cases where the eligibility conditions are treated as being met,

Chapter 3 deals with the requirements to be met by investment trusts whilst approved,

Chapter 4 deals with breaches of the requirements to be met by investment trusts and subsequent withdrawal of approval,

Chapter 5 deals with an approved company treating itself as not being an investment trust;

Part 3 contains provisions about transactions by investment trusts which are treated as entered into otherwise than in the course of a trade; and

Part 4 contains provisions about investment trusts having interests in offshore non-reporting funds and index tracking funds, and makes consequential provision.

3 Interpretation

(1) In these Regulations—

"company tax return" has the same meaning as in paragraph 3(1) of Schedule 18 to the Finance Act 1998,

"CTA 2009" means the Corporation Tax Act 2009,

"CTA 2010" means the Corporation Tax Act 2010,

"the Offshore Funds Regulations" means the Offshore Funds (Tax) Regulations 2009,

"tribunal" means the First-tier Tribunal or, where determined by or under Tribunal Procedure Rules, the Upper Tribunal.

(2) For the purposes of these Regulations the market value of any asset is to be determined in a like manner as it would be determined for the purposes of the Taxation of Chargeable Gains Act 1992.

PART 2
INVESTMENT TRUSTS

CHAPTER 1
APPLICATION PROCEDURE

4 Interpretation

In this Part—

"the eligibility conditions" mean conditions A to C in section 1158 of CTA 2010,

"the income distribution requirement" has the meaning given in regulation 21(9).

5 Application for approval as an investment trust

(1) A company may apply to the Commissioners for approval as an investment trust in accordance with this Chapter.

(2) A company which makes such an application is referred to in this Chapter as "the applicant".

6 Contents of application

(1) An application under regulation 5 must include the particulars specified in this regulation.

(2) The application must—

(a) specify the date of the first day of an accounting period in respect of which the applicant seeks approval as an investment trust ("the specified date"),

(b) contain a statement that the applicant meets, or is expected to meet, in respect of the accounting period referred to in sub-paragraph (a)—

(i) the eligibility conditions, and

(ii) the requirements of Chapter 3 of this Part,

(c) contain an undertaking given in relation to the accounting period referred to in sub-paragraph (a) and each subsequent accounting period in respect of which it is or expects to be an investment trust, that the applicant will meet—

(i) the eligibility conditions, and

(ii) the requirements of Chapter 3 of this Part,

(d) include a copy of the applicant's current published investment policy, and

(e) provide evidence to show that the shares making up the applicant's ordinary share capital (or, if there are such shares of more than one class, those of each class) are admitted to trading on a regulated market.

This regulation is subject to regulations 7, 8, 9 and 13.

7 Contents of application: accounting period not commenced at time of application

(1) This regulation applies if at the time the application is made the applicant has not commenced an accounting period.

(2) If this regulation applies the applicant must—

(a) specify a provisional date for the purposes of regulation 6(2)(a), and

(b) where a provisional date is specified, as soon as reasonably practicable, confirm in writing to the Commissioners the date of the first day of the accounting period in respect of which the applicant seeks approval as an investment trust.

8 Contents of application: shares not admitted to trading at time of application

(1) This regulation applies if at the time the application is made the shares making up the applicant's ordinary share capital (or, if there are such shares of more than one class, those of each class) are not admitted to trading on a regulated market.

(2) If this regulation applies, the application—

(a) for the purposes of regulation 6(2)(d), may include a copy of the applicant's prospectus instead of the current published investment policy, and

(b) must explain how the applicant will be in a position to comply with condition B in section 1158(3) of CTA 2010 by the specified date.

(3) The applicant must provide evidence to the Commissioners that the shares making up the applicant's ordinary share capital (or, if there are such shares of more than one class, those of each class) are admitted to trading on a regulated market—

(a) before the end of a period of 60 days beginning with the date on which the shares were so admitted, or

(b) by such other date as the Commissioners may agree.

9 Form, timing and withdrawal of application

(1) An application must be made in writing to the Commissioners.

(2) The application must be made to the Commissioners before the end of the period of 90 days beginning with the last day of the first accounting period for which approval is sought.

(3) The applicant may withdraw the application at any time during the period beginning with the day on which the application is made and ending 28 days after the day on which the Commissioners give notice under regulation 10 accepting the application.

10 Response by Commissioners to application

(1) Within 28 days beginning with the date on which the application is made, the Commissioners must give notice in writing to the applicant—

(a) accepting the application,

(b) rejecting the application, or

(c) asking for further information in order to consider the application.

(2) The Commissioners must not accept an application if any particular or information mentioned in regulation 6, 7 or 8 is not supplied.

(3) Paragraph (4) applies if—

(a) the Commissioners have given a notice under paragraph (1)(c), and

(b) the applicant provides the further information within the period of 28 days beginning with the day on which the Commissioners ask for the further information, or within such longer period as may be agreed by the Commissioners.

(4) Within 28 days beginning with the day on which they receive the further information, the Commissioners must give notice to the applicant—

(a) accepting the application, or

(b) rejecting the application.

(5) If the Commissioners reject the application, the notice given to the applicant under paragraph (1)(b) or (4)(b) must contain a statement of the reason for which the application was rejected.

11 Appeal against rejection of the application

(1) If the Commissioners reject an application, the applicant may appeal.

(2) The notice of appeal must be given to the Commissioners within a period of 42 days beginning with the day on which the notice rejecting the application is given.

(3) On an appeal, the tribunal may uphold or quash the rejection of the application.

(4) If the tribunal quashes the rejection of the application, these Regulations apply as if the Commissioners had accepted the application in the form in which it was considered by the tribunal.

12 Effect of acceptance of application

If the Commissioners accept (or are treated as accepting) an application, the applicant is approved as an investment trust—

(a) for the accounting period commencing on the specified date (or commencing on such later date as may be confirmed in accordance with regulation 7(2)(b)), and

(b) for each subsequent accounting period,

but this is subject to regulations 13 and 25 to 31.

13 Acceptance of application conditional on receipt of specified information

(1) An acceptance by the Commissioners of an application is conditional on the provision of any information or particulars required by regulations 7(2)(b) and 8(3).

(2) If the applicant does not provide any such information or particulars, the application shall be treated as if it had not been made and the company treated as if it had not been an investment trust for any of the period to which the application mentioned in paragraph (1) related.

CHAPTER 2

CASES WHERE ELIGIBILITY CONDITIONS TREATED AS BEING MET

14 Delay in admission of company's ordinary share capital to trading on a regulated market

(1) Paragraph (3) applies if at the date on which the application under regulation 5 is made the applicant—

(a) has commenced procedures to obtain admission of the shares making up its ordinary share capital (or, if there are such shares of more than one class, those of each class) to trading on a regulated market but has not obtained admission, or

(b) has given a commitment in its prospectus to commence such procedures but has not started those procedures.

(2) Paragraph (3) also applies if a company which has been approved as an investment trust issues shares of a class ("the new shares") which is different from any of those which make up its ordinary share capital.

(3) Condition B in section 1158(3) of CTA 2010 is to be treated as met for the period of 60 days beginning with—

(a) in the case of paragraph (1), the date of the application, or

(b) in the case of paragraph (2), the date on which the new shares were issued.

15 Winding up of company approved as investment trust

(1) Paragraph (2) applies if—

(a) a company is being wound up,

(b) the company was approved as an investment trust in respect of the accounting period which ended immediately before the winding up started (see section 12 of CTA 2009),

(c) the company satisfied the eligibility conditions in respect of the accounting period referred to in sub-paragraph (b), and

(d) subject to paragraph (4), the company makes no new investments during the realisation period.

(2) Conditions A and B in section 1158 of CTA 2010 are to be treated as met in respect of the realisation period.

This paragraph is subject to regulation 16.

(3) In paragraphs (1) and (2) the "realisation period" is the period beginning with the date on which the winding up started and ending with the date on which the winding up is completed.

(4) For the purposes of paragraph (1)(d)—

(a) the placing on deposit of the proceeds of the disposal of assets of the company, or

(b) the purchase of gilts with the proceeds of the disposal of assets of the company,

shall not be treated as the making of a new investment by the company.

(5) In this regulation and regulation 16, references to "a company being wound up" and "winding up" are to be construed in accordance with section 12 of CTA 2009.

16 Winding up of company approved as investment trust—further conditions

(1) Paragraph (2) of regulation 15 shall only apply if paragraphs (2) to (4) of this regulation are met.

(2) The Commissioners must be notified in writing that the company is being wound up.

(3) The notice under paragraph (2) must be given within one year beginning with the date on which the winding up started.

(4) The Commissioners must be satisfied that the realisation period referred to in regulation 15 has not been unreasonably prolonged.

CHAPTER 3

INVESTMENT TRUST: REQUIREMENTS TO BE MET WHILST APPROVED

17 Investment trust to comply with requirements of this Chapter

A company must comply with the provisions of this Chapter in relation to each accounting period in respect of which it is approved as an investment trust.

18 Investment trust must not be a close company

(1) An investment trust must not be a close company at any time in an accounting period.

(2) See section 439 of CTA 2010 for the definition of "close company".

19 The income distribution requirement

[(1) The maximum amount an investment trust is permitted to retain in respect of an accounting period is the highest of the following amounts—

(*a*) 15% of its income for the accounting period,

(*b*) where paragraph (1A) applies, the accumulated revenue losses brought forward from previous accounting periods, and

(*c*) any amount of income that the investment trust is required to retain in respect of the accounting period by virtue of a restriction imposed by law.][1]

[(1A) This paragraph applies if in the accounting period the amount of income the investment trust is permitted to retain under this regulation and regulation 21 (taken together and ignoring this paragraph and paragraph (1)(*b*)) does not exceed the amount of any accumulated revenue losses brought forward from previous accounting periods.][1]

(2) The investment trust must distribute as a dividend the amount required to comply with paragraph (1) before the filing date for the investment trust's company tax return for the accounting period.

(3) Where the investment trust company's tax return has been amended as a result of a notice served under paragraph 15 or 34 of Schedule 18 to the Finance Act 1998, any further distribution that is required by virtue of the amendment must be made before the end of the period of 180 days beginning with the date of the amendment.

(4) In this regulation and regulation 23, "filing date" has the meaning given in paragraph 14 of Schedule 18 to the Finance Act 1998.

(5) This regulation is subject to regulations 21 and 22.

Amendments—[1] Para 1 substituted and para (1A) inserted by the Investment Trust (Approved Company) (Tax) (Amendment) Regulations, SI 2013/1406 reg 2(1), (2) with effect in relation to accounting periods beginning on or after 28 June 2013.

20 Calculation of income

(1) Paragraphs (2) and (3) apply for the purposes of [regulation 19(1)(*a*)][1] in determining the income of the investment trust for an accounting period.

(2) The amounts to be brought into account under Part 5 of CTA 2009 in respect of the investment trust's loan relationships are to be determined without reference to any debtor relationships of the investment trust.

(3) Income treated as arising under regulation 18(1) (the charge to tax: further provisions) of the Offshore Funds Regulations is to be ignored.

Amendments—[1] In para (1), words substituted for words "regulation 19(1)" by the Investment Trust (Approved Company) (Tax) (Amendment) Regulations, SI 2013/1406 reg 2(1), (3) with effect in relation to accounting periods beginning on or after 28 June 2013.

21 The income distribution requirement: reduction in amount of income permitted to be retained

(1) This regulation applies where conditions A to C are met.

(2) Condition A is that the investment trust is a participant in an offshore reporting fund within the meaning of regulation 50 (meaning of "reporting fund") of the Offshore Funds Regulations.

(3) Condition B is that there is an amount which falls to be reported to the investment trust in accordance with regulation 92(1)(b) (contents of a report to participants: non-transparent funds) of the Offshore Funds Regulations.

(4) Condition C is that the amount referred to in condition B is accounted for by the investment trust through the capital column of the income statement in accordance with the AIC Statement of Recommended Practice, or would have been so accounted for if that Statement had been applied correctly.

(5) Where this regulation applies the amount which the investment trust may retain in accordance with regulation 19(1) is reduced by an amount equal to 85% of the amount referred to in condition B.

(6) If the application of paragraph (5) has the effect that the sum which an investment trust is permitted to retain ("the retainable amount") is calculated to be less than zero, the investment trust must distribute as a dividend a further sum which is equal to the difference between the retainable amount and zero.

(7) The further distribution mentioned in paragraph (6) must be made in relation to the accounting period in which the fund distribution date for the offshore reporting fund in question falls.

(8) In this regulation—

- (a) "fund distribution date" has the meaning given in regulation 94 (reported income: general provisions) of the Offshore Funds Regulations, and
- (b) "AIC Statement of Recommended Practice" means the Statement of Recommended Practice relating to Investment Trust Companies, issued by the Association of Investment Trust Companies in January 2009.

(9) The distribution required under this regulation together with the distribution required under regulation 19 comprise "the income distribution requirement".

(10) This regulation is subject to regulation 22.

22 The income distribution requirement: exceptions

(1) Regulations 19 and 21 do not apply in relation to an accounting period if the amount that the investment trust would be required to distribute in accordance with those regulations, taken together, would be less than £30,000.

(2) . . . [1]

(3) If the accounting period mentioned in [paragraph (1)][1] is shorter than 12 months, the amount of £30,000 mentioned in [that paragraph][1] is proportionately reduced.

Amendments—[1] Para (2) revoked, and in para (3), words substituted for words "paragraphs (1) and (2)" and "paragraphs (1) and (2)(b)(ii)" by the Investment Trust (Approved Company) (Tax) (Amendment) Regulations, SI 2013/1406 reg 2(1), (4) with effect in relation to accounting periods beginning on or after 28 June 2013.

23 Requirement to notify Commissioners of revised investment policy

(1) An investment trust must notify the Commissioners if it revises its published investment policy.

(2) The investment trust must provide the Commissioners with a copy of any revised investment policy before the filing date for its company tax return for the accounting period in which the investment policy was revised.

24 Requirement to notify Commissioners of breach

(1) An investment trust must give notice in accordance with paragraph (2) if it has breached—

- (a) any of the eligibility conditions (see regulation 4), or
- (b) any other requirement of these Regulations (apart from this regulation).

(2) The notice must—

(a) be given in writing to the Commissioners as soon as reasonably practicable after the investment trust becomes aware of any breach referred to in paragraph (1), and
(b) specify the steps, if any, that have been taken, or are to be taken, to correct the breach.

CHAPTER 4

BREACH OF THE REGULATIONS AND WITHDRAWAL OF APPROVAL

25 Types of breach

(1) This Chapter applies if an investment trust is in breach of a requirement imposed by these Regulations.

(2) A breach is—
(a) a minor breach, or
(b) a serious breach.

(3) For the purposes of these Regulations, a breach is a "serious breach" if it is—
(a) a breach specified as a serious breach in this Chapter, or
(b) a breach which is not a minor breach.

(4) For the purposes of these Regulations, a breach is a "minor breach" if it is a breach (other than a breach specified as a serious breach in this Chapter)—
(a) for which there is a reasonable excuse, and
(b) which is inadvertent and corrected as soon as reasonably practicable.

(5) For the purposes of this Chapter a minor breach is not regarded as a breach if the investment trust—
(a) notifies the Commissioners of the breach in accordance with regulation 24, and
(b) corrects the breach as soon as reasonably practicable without any intervention by the Commissioners.

(6) For the purposes of this regulation there is an "intervention by the Commissioners" in relation to an investment trust if the Commissioners ask it to provide them with information relating to a requirement imposed by Chapter 3.
This paragraph is subject to paragraph (7).

(7) There is no intervention by the Commissioners in relation to an investment trust if—
(a) the investment trust notifies the Commissioners of the breach in accordance with regulation 24,
(b) the investment trust complies with regulation 25(5), and
(c) the Commissioners request the investment trust to provide them with information so that they may determine whether the breach has been corrected.

26 Serious breach

For the purposes of this Chapter a breach of regulation 18 (investment trust must not be a close company) is a serious breach.

27 Multiple breaches

(1) Subject to the following provisions of this Chapter, if an investment trust is in breach of a requirement imposed by these Regulations, and the breach is a minor breach, it continues to be treated as approved as an investment trust.

(2) If paragraph (1) applies—
(a) on three separate occasions in a period of ten years beginning with the first day of the accounting period in which the first breach occurs, and
(b) in relation to the same requirement,
the third breach is a serious breach.

(3) If paragraph (1) applies—
(a) on four separate occasions in a period of ten years beginning with the first day of the accounting period in which the first breach occurs, and
(b) in relation to more than one of the requirements,
the fourth breach is a serious breach.

(4) If a single event results in more than one minor breach within a single accounting period there is only one minor breach in that period in relation to that event for the purposes of this Chapter.

28 Breach of the income distribution requirement

(1) Subject to paragraph (4), there is a breach of the income distribution requirement if—
(a) there is a difference between—
(i) the amount that the investment trust is required to distribute in relation to an accounting period in accordance with regulations 19 and 21, and
(ii) the amount which the investment trust distributed in relation to that accounting period, and
(b) the amount referred to in paragraph (ii) is less than the amount referred to in paragraph (i).

(2) If the difference between the two amounts specified in paragraph (1) is greater than 1% but less than or equal to 5% of the income of the investment trust for the accounting period then, subject to paragraph (5), the breach is a minor breach.

(3) If the difference between the two amounts specified in paragraph (1) is greater than 5% of the income of the investment trust for the accounting period, the breach is a serious breach.

(4) If the difference between the two amounts specified in paragraph (1) is less than or equal to 1% of the income of the investment trust for the accounting period then, subject to paragraph (5), the investment trust is to be treated as not having breached the income distribution requirement.

(5) Paragraph (4) only applies if the failure to comply with the income distribution requirement was inadvertent.

(6) For the purpose of this regulation, the income of the investment trust includes income that falls to be reported to it in accordance with regulation 92(1)(b) (contents of report to participants: non-transparent funds) of the Offshore Funds Regulations.

29 Consequences of serious breaches

(1) This regulation applies if conditions A and B are met.

(2) Condition A is that—

(a) the investment trust is in breach of a requirement imposed by these Regulations, and

(b) the breach is a serious breach.

(3) Condition B is that the Commissioners give notice in writing to the investment trust—

(a) stating that the investment trust is in breach of a requirement imposed by these Regulations and that the breach is a serious breach, and

(b) specifying the serious breach.

(4) The investment trust is to be treated as a company which has not been approved as an investment trust for the accounting period in which the serious breach occurred (or, if there is more than one serious breach, the first of them) and, subject to paragraph (5), for all subsequent accounting periods.

(5) A company to which this regulation applies may make an application under regulation 5 in respect of any accounting period subsequent to the accounting period in which the serious breach occurred.

30 Breach of the eligibility conditions

(1) This regulation applies if an investment trust is in breach of any of the eligibility conditions.

(2) The investment trust is to be treated as a company which has not been approved as an investment trust for the accounting period in which the breach of the eligibility condition occurred (or, if there is more than one breach, the first of them) and, subject to paragraph (3), for all subsequent accounting periods.

(3) A company to which this regulation applies may make an application under regulation 5 in respect of any accounting period subsequent to the accounting period in which the breach of an eligibility condition occurred.

CHAPTER 5

APPROVED COMPANY TREATING ITSELF AS NOT BEING AN INVESTMENT TRUST

31 Company tax return submitted on basis that company is not an investment trust

(1) This regulation applies if—

(a) a company (apart from this regulation) is approved as an investment trust in respect of an accounting period,

(b) the company makes a company tax return for that period, and

(c) the self-assessment of the amount of tax which is payable by it included in the return is made on the basis that the company is not an investment trust with respect to that period.

(2) If this regulation applies the company is treated as not having been approved as an investment trust for the accounting period referred to in paragraph (1) with effect from the first day of that period and, subject to paragraph (3), for all subsequent accounting periods.

(3) A company to which this regulation applies may make an application under regulation 5 in respect of any accounting period subsequent to the accounting period to which the company tax return relates.

PART 3

TRANSACTIONS TO BE TREATED AS ENTERED INTO OTHERWISE THAN IN THE COURSE OF A TRADE

32 Treatment of transactions carried out by investment trusts

(1) This regulation applies if an investment trust carries out an investment transaction in an accounting period.

(2) The investment transaction is treated as a transaction entered into otherwise than in the course of a trade for the purposes of the Corporation Tax Acts.

[(3) For the purposes of this Part an "investment transaction" is an investment transaction specified by regulation 2 of the Investment Transactions (Tax) Regulations 2014.][1]

Amendments—[1] Para 3 inserted by the Investment Transactions (Tax) Regulations, SI 2014/685 reg 9(1), (2) with effect from 8 April 2014.

33 Meaning of "investment transaction"

Amendments—Regulations 33–41 revoked by the Investment Transactions (Tax) Regulations, SI 2014/685 reg 9(1), (3) with effect from 8 April 2014.

34 Meaning of "relevant contract"

Amendments—Regulations 33–41 revoked by the Investment Transactions (Tax) Regulations, SI 2014/685 reg 9(1), (3) with effect from 8 April 2014.

[1] Regulations 33–41 revoked by the Investment Transactions (Tax) Regulations, SI 2014/685 reg 9(1), (3) with effect from 8 April 2014.

35

Amendments—Regulations 33–41 revoked by the Investment Transactions (Tax) Regulations, SI 2014/685 reg 9(1), (3) with effect from 8 April 2014.

36 Meaning of "relevant contract": futures

Amendments—Regulations 33–41 revoked by the Investment Transactions (Tax) Regulations, SI 2014/685 reg 9(1), (3) with effect from 8 April 2014.

37 Options and futures: further provisions

Amendments—Regulations 33–41 revoked by the Investment Transactions (Tax) Regulations, SI 2014/685 reg 9(1), (3) with effect from 8 April 2014.

38 Meaning of "relevant contract": contracts for difference

Amendments—Regulations 33–41 revoked by the Investment Transactions (Tax) Regulations, SI 2014/685 reg 9(1), (3) with effect from 8 April 2014.

39 Interpretation of regulation 33(c)

Amendments—Regulations 33–41 revoked by the Investment Transactions (Tax) Regulations, SI 2014/685 reg 9(1), (3) with effect from 8 April 2014.

40 Meaning of "units in a collective investment scheme"

Amendments—Regulations 33–41 revoked by the Investment Transactions (Tax) Regulations, SI 2014/685 reg 9(1), (3) with effect from 8 April 2014.

41 Meaning of "transaction in a carbon emission trading product"

Amendments—Regulations 33–41 revoked by the Investment Transactions (Tax) Regulations, SI 2014/685 reg 9(1), (3) with effect from 8 April 2014.

PART 4
INVESTMENT TRUST HAVING AN INTEREST IN OFFSHORE NON-REPORTING FUNDS AND INDEX TRACKING FUNDS

42 Interests in offshore non-reporting funds: general

(1) Regulation 43 applies if—

(a) an investment trust disposes of an asset which is an interest in a non-reporting fund ("the asset"), and

(b) the conditions in paragraph (2) are satisfied for the period starting with the date on which the investment trust acquired the asset and ending with the day of the disposal.

(2) The conditions are that—

(a) the investment trust has access to the accounts of the non-reporting fund,

(b) the investment trust had sufficient information about the non-reporting fund referred to in paragraph (1)(a) to enable it to prepare computations of reportable income for the non-reporting fund for every accounting period which, if the non-reporting fund were a reporting fund, would be a reporting period ending within the period mentioned in paragraph (1)(b),

(c) the investment trust has prepared such computations, and

(d) any excess of the investment trust's share of the reportable income of the non-reporting fund over the investment trust's share of the distributions made by the non-reporting fund is included in the amount available for distribution by the investment trust for each accounting period of the investment trust which falls within the period mentioned in paragraph (1)(b).

(3) An investment trust has an interest in a non-reporting fund if and to the extent that it has an interest in such a fund for the purposes of the Offshore Funds Regulations.

(4) For the purposes of the computations mentioned in paragraph (2)(b), regulation 80 (treatment of investment transactions carried out by diversely owned funds) of the Offshore Funds Regulations applies if (and only if) the non-reporting fund is a UCITS fund.

(5) In this regulation, "UCITS fund" has the same meaning as in regulation 12 (general interpretation) of the Offshore Funds Regulations and "reporting period" has the same meaning as in regulation 91 (meaning of "reporting period") of those Regulations.

43 Treatment of disposal of interest in non-reporting fund

No tax shall be charged on the investment trust under regulation 17 (the charge to tax) of the Offshore Funds Regulations on the disposal by the investment trust of an asset which is an interest in a non-reporting fund at the time of the disposal.

44 Treatment of interest in non-reporting fund: cases where conditions in regulation 42(2) would not be satisfied

(1) This regulation applies in relation to an asset of an investment trust ("the asset")—

(a) which is an interest in a non-reporting fund, but

(b) in relation to which the conditions in regulation 42(2) would not (apart from this regulation) be satisfied for the whole of the period specified in regulation 42(1)(b) in relation to the asset.

(2) Paragraph (4) applies if the investment trust, in relation to the asset, reasonably expects to satisfy the conditions in regulation 42(2) for the period beginning with a date to be determined in accordance with paragraph (3) ("the deemed start date") and ending with the date of the disposal of the asset.

(3) The deemed start date is a date to be determined by the investment trust which must not be earlier than 1st January 2012.

(4) The investment trust is treated for all purposes (including for the purposes of determining the beginning of the period mentioned in regulation 42(1)(b)) as if it had, on the deemed start date, disposed of the asset (and not satisfied the conditions in regulation 42(2)) and immediately reacquired the asset for a consideration equal to its market value on the deemed start date.

(5) The investment trust must notify the Commissioners of the deemed start date by making an appropriate entry in its company tax return for the accounting period in which the deemed start date falls.

45 Index tracking funds

(1) This regulation applies if—

(a) an investment trust has an interest in a non-reporting fund,

(b) the conditions in paragraph (2) are met throughout the relevant period.

(2) The conditions are that—

(a) in accordance with the instrument constituting the investment trust, the aim of the investment trust's policy is to replicate the performance of a qualifying index,

(b) the main purpose of the investment in the non-reporting fund is to represent the composition of the qualifying index, and

(c) the capital and income returns of the investment trust replicate as closely as practicable the returns of the investment comprised in the qualifying index.

(3) For the purposes of paragraph (2) an index is a "qualifying index" if—

(a) it is based solely on the value of securities listed on a recognised stock exchange or admitted to trading on a regulated market,

(b) either a competent authority for the United Kingdom or an authority responsible for regulating offshore funds recognises the index on the basis that—

(i) its composition is sufficiently diverse,

(ii) it represents an adequate benchmark for the market to which it refers, and

(iii) it is published in such a way that it is widely available, and

(c) it is calculated and published by a body which is managed independently from the management of the investment trust.

(4) Regulation 17 of the Offshore Funds Regulations does not apply in respect of a disposal by the investment trust of the interest in the non-reporting fund.

(5) In this regulation the "relevant period" means the period—

(a) starting with the day on which the investment trust acquires the interest in the non-reporting fund (or any part of it), and

(b) ending with the day of the disposal of the interest.

(6) In this regulation—

(a) a "competent authority for the United Kingdom" means the authority which is a competent authority for the United Kingdom for the purposes of Directive 2009/65/EC of the European Parliament and of the Council on the coordination of laws, regulations and administrative provisions relating to undertakings for collective investment in transferable securities (UCITS), and

(b) "regulated market" has the same meaning as in Directive 2004/39/EC of the European Parliament and of the Council on markets in financial instruments (see article 4.1(14)).

46 Consequential amendment

For paragraph (6) of regulation 18 (the charge to tax: further provisions) of the Offshore Funds Regulations, substitute—

"(6) Nothing in regulation 17 of these Regulations applies to—

(a) an authorised investment fund to which regulation 14ZB, 14ZD(1) or Part 6A of the Authorised Investment Fund (Tax) Regulations 2006 applies, or

(b) an investment trust company to which regulation 43 or 45 of the Investment Trust (Approved Company) (Tax) Regulations 2011 apply.".

2012/286

RESEARCH AND DEVELOPMENT (QUALIFYING BODIES) (TAX) ORDER 2012

Made . . . . .6th February 2012

Laid before the House of Commons . . . . .7th February 2012

Coming into force . . . . .28th February 2012

The Treasury make the following Order in exercise of the powers conferred by sections 1142(1)(e), (3) and (4) of the Corporation Tax Act 2009.

1 Citation, commencement and effect

(1) This Order may be cited as the Research and Development (Qualifying Bodies) (Tax) Order 2012 and shall come into force on 28th February 2012.

(2) In relation to a body specified in column (1) of the Schedule to this Order, this Order has effect in relation to expenditure incurred on or after the date set out in column (3) opposite the entry in column (1) for that body.

2 Bodies prescribed for the purposes of Part 13 of the Corporation Tax Act 2009

Each of the bodies specified in column (1) of the Schedule to this Order is a body prescribed for the purposes of Part 13 of the Corporation Tax Act 2009 (additional relief for expenditure on research and development).

3 The Research and Development (Qualifying Bodies) (Tax) Order 2009 is revoked.

SCHEDULE

PRESCRIBED BODIES

(1) *Name of prescribed body*	*(2)* *Address*	*(3)* *Date*
Aristotle University of Thessaloniki	Thessaloniki, Greece	1 April 2002
Azienda Ospendaliera Universitaria Pisana	Messina, Italy	12 October 2010
British University in Egypt	El Sherouk City, Misr, Egypt	1 April 2002
Colorado School of Mines	Golden, Colorado, USA	1 April 2002
Colorado State University	Fort Collins, Colorado, USA	1 April 2002
Cornell University	Ithaca, New York, USA	1 April 2002
Delft University of Technology	Delft, Netherlands	1 April 2002
Ecole Polytechnique Federal de Lausanne	Lausanne, Switzerland	1 April 2002
Faculty Hospital Motol Prague	Prague, Czech Republic	12 October 2010
Fakultni Nemocnice Brno	Brno, Czech Republic	12 October 2010
Fakultni Nemocnice Ostrava	Ostrava, Czech Republic	12 October 2010
Freie University Berlin	Berlin, Germany	1 April 2002
Hospitais Da Universidade De Coimbra	Coimbra, Portugal	1 April 2002
Indian Institute of Technology Bombay	Maharashtra, India	1 April 2002
Indian Institute of Technology Kanpur	Kanpur, India	1 April 2002
Indiana University	Bloomington, Indiana, USA	22 March 2010
Institute of Computer Science	Crete, Greece	1 April 2002
Interuniversitair Micro-Elektronica Centrum	Leuven, Belgium	1 April 2002
Iowa State University	Ames, Iowa, USA	1 April 2002

Kansas State University	Manhattan, Kansas, USA	1 April 2002
Karlsruhe Institute of Technology	Karlsruhe, Germany	26 July 2011
Karolinska University Hospital	Stockohlm, Sweden	22 March 2010
Kazakh-British Technical University	Almaty, Kazakhstan	1 April 2002
King Abdulaziz University	Jeddah, Saudi Arabia	7 November 2011
Klinikum der Universität München	Munich, Germany	12 October 2010
Lawrence Berkeley National Laboratory	Berkeley, California, USA	1 April 2002
Martin-Luther University	Halle-Wittenburg, Germany	1 April 2002
Louisiana State University	Louisiana, USA	1 April 2002
Massachusetts Institute of Technology	Massachusetts, USA	1 April 2002
Massey University	Auckland, New Zealand	1 April 2002
McMaster University	Hamilton, Ontario, Canada	22 March 2010
Medical University of Lodz	Lodz, Poland	12 October 2010
Medizinische Universität Wien	Vienna, Austria	12 October 2010
Michigan State University	Michigan, USA	01 April 2002
Nanyang Technological University	Singapore	26 July 2011
National Medical University Vinnitsa	Vinnitsa, Ukraine	12 October 2010
National Technical University of Athens	Athens, Greece	22 February 2011
Norwegian University of Science & Technology	Trondheim, Norway	26 May 2010
Ohio State University	Columbus, Ohio, USA	1 April 2002
Otto-von-Guericke-Universität Magdeburg	Magdeburg, Germany	1 April 2002
OTRI- Universidad de Cordoba	Cordoba, Spain	22 March 2010
Politecnico Di Milano	Milan, Italy	1 April 2002
Pusan National University	Pusan, South Korea	26 July 2011
Ruhr Universität	Bochum, Germany	1 April 2002
RWTH Aachen University	Aachen, Germany	1 April 2002
St. James's Hospital	Dublin, Ireland	1 April 2002
Southern Illinois University	Illinois, USA	1 April 2002
Stanford University	Stanford, California, USA	1 April 2002
Swedish University of Agriculture Sciences	Uppsala, Sweden	1 April 2002
Swiss Federal Institute of Technology (ETH) Zurich	Zurich, Switzerland	1 April 2002
Technische Universität Clausthal	Clausthal-Zellerfeld, Germany	1 April 2002
Technische Universität Dresden	Dresden, Germany	1 April 2002
Technische Universität Munchen	Munich, Germany	1 April 2002
Texas A&M University	Texas, USA	1 April 2002
The Pennsylvania State University	Pennsylvania, USA	1 April 2002
The University of Antwerp	Antwerp, Belgium	22 March 2010
The University of Oklahoma	Norman, Oklahoma, USA	22 February 2011

The University of the West Indies	Kingston, Jamaica	1 April 2002
Tufts University	Massachusetts, USA	1 April 2002
UMC St Radbound	Nijmegen, Netherlands	12 October 2010
UMC Utrecht	Utrecht, Netherlands	1 April 2002
Umhat Alexandrovska Sofia	Sofia, Bulgaria	12 October 2010
Universidad de Las Palmas de Gran Canaria	Gran Canaria, Spain	1 April 2002
Universidad De Valladolid	Valladolid, Spain	1 April 2002
Universidade Do Minho	Braga, Portugal	22 February 2011
Universitair Ziekenhuis Gent	Gent, Belgium	1 April 2002
Universitat Politècnica de Catalonia of Jordi Girona	Barcelona, Spain	1 April 2002
Universite de Lausanne (UNIL)	Lausanne, Switzerland	1 April 2002
University Hospitals of Cleveland	Cleveland, USA	1 April 2002
University of Alberta	Edmonton, Alberta, Canada,	1 April 2002
University of Applied Sciences Braunschweig/ Wolfenbüttel	Wolfenbuttel, Germany	1 April 2002
University of Bergen	Bergen, Norway	1 April 2002
University of Berlin	Berlin, Germany	1 April 2002
University of British Columbia	British Columbia, Canada	1 April 2002
University of California at Davis	Davis, California, USA	1 April 2002
University of California, Berkeley	California, USA	1 April 2002
University of Dusseldorf	Dusseldorf, Germany	1 April 2002
University of Florida	Gainesville, Florida, USA	1 April 2002
University of Guelph	Ontario, Canada	1 April 2002
University of Hacettepe	Ankara, Turkey	1 April 2002
University of Hanover	Hanover, Germany	15 February 2011
University of Heidelberg	Heidelberg, Germany	22 March 2010
University of Houston	Houston, Texas, USA	1 April 2002
University of Limerick	Limerick, Ireland	17 May 2011
University of Manitoba	Winnipeg, Canada	1 April 2002
University of Massachusetts Medical School	Massachusetts, USA	1 April 2002
University of Memphis	Memphis, Tennessee, USA	22 March 2010
University of Michigan	Ann Arbor, Michigan, USA	1 April 2002
University of Minnesota	Minneapolis, USA	1 April 2002
University of Missouri-Columbia	Columbia, USA	1 April 2002
University of Munich	Munich, Germany	1 April 2002
University of Munster	Munster, Germany	1 April 2002
University of New England	Armidale, Australia	1 April 2002
University of New South Wales	Sydney, Australia	1 April 2002
University of Oslo	Oslo, Norway	22 March 2010
University of Pennsylvania	Pennsylvania, USA	1 April 2002
University of Pisa	Pisa, Italy	5 April 2011
University of Potsdam	Potsdam, Germany	1 April 2002
University of Queensland	Brisbane, Australia	1 April 2002
University of Santiago de Compostela	Santiago de Compostella, Spain	1 April 2002

University of Seville	Seville, Spain	1 April 2002
University of Sydney	New South Wales, Australia	1 April 2002
University of Stuttgart	Stuttgart, Germany	22 February 2011
University of Technology, Sydney	Broadway, Australia	1 April 2002
University of Tennessee	Knoxville, Tennessee, USA	1 April 2002
University of Texas	Austin, Texas	1 April 2002
University of Trento	Trento, Italy	5 April 2011
University of Tulsa	Tulsa, Oklahoma, USA	1 April 2002
University of Turku	Turku, Finland	15 February 2011
University of Utah	Salt Lake City, Utah, USA	1 April 2002
University of Utah School of Medicine	Salt Lake City, Utah, USA	1 April 2002
University of Utrecht	Utrecht, Netherlands	1 April 2002
University of Veterinary Medicine, Hannover	Hannover, Germany	1 April 2002
University of Wisconsin	Madison, Wisconsin, USA	1 April 2002
Uppasala University	Uppsala, Sweden	22 March 2010
Virginia Polytechnic Institute and State University	Blacksburg, Virginia, USA	1 April 2002
Washington University	St Louis, Missouri, USA	22 March 2010
Waterford Institute of Technology	Waterford, Ireland	17 May 2011
Westfaelische Wilhelms- Universität	Munster, Germany	1 April 2002
Wichita State University	Wichita, Kansas, USA	17 May 2011
Yale University School of Medicine	New Haven, Connecticut, USA	22 March 2010

2012/458

BANK LEVY (DOUBLE TAXATION RELIEF) REGULATIONS 2012

Made . . . . *21st February 2012*

Laid before the House of Commons . . . . *22nd February 2012*

Coming into force . . . . *14th March 2012*

The Treasury is satisfied that the reciprocity condition is met and accordingly make the following Regulations in exercise of the powers conferred by paragraph 67 of Schedule 19 to the Finance Act 2011.

Introduction

1 Citation, commencement and effect

(1) These Regulations may be cited as the Bank Levy (Double Taxation Relief) Regulations 2012 and come into force on 14th March 2012.

(2) These Regulations have effect in relation to periods of account ending on or after 1st January 2011.

2 Application of these Regulations

These Regulations apply where—

(a) the bank levy is charged in relation to—

(i) the relevant group which is a foreign banking group or a relevant non-banking group, or

(ii) the relevant entity which is a relevant foreign bank,

(b) an equivalent foreign levy is imposed on that relevant group or relevant entity by the law of a foreign territory, and

(c) the equivalent foreign levy is specified in regulation 3.

3 Specified equivalent foreign levy

The equivalent foreign levy in respect of which these Regulations are made is Art 235 ter ZE du code génèral des impôts imposed by the law of France.

Double taxation relief by way of credit

4 Double taxation relief

(1) Where these Regulations apply, an amount of the equivalent foreign levy paid is allowed as a credit against the bank levy for a chargeable period (see regulation 5).

(2) Subject to the provisions of these Regulations, the amount of the bank levy for the chargeable period is reduced by the amount of the credit.

(3) But the amount of the bank levy shall not be reduced to below nil.

(4) The credit under paragraph (2) requires a claim.

5 Calculation of the credit

Take steps 1 to 4 to determine how much of the equivalent foreign levy is available as a credit against the bank levy.

Step 1

Determine the amount ("A") of assets of the relevant group or the relevant entity as at the end of the chargeable period by reference to which the equivalent foreign levy is calculated.

Step 2

Determine the amount ("B") of UK assets as at the end of the chargeable period by reference to which the equivalent foreign levy is calculated.

Step 3

Determine the amount of the equivalent foreign levy paid ("C") in relation to the chargeable period.

If a proportion (Z%) of the period in relation to which the equivalent foreign levy is calculated falls in any other chargeable period, Z% of the equivalent foreign levy shall be attributable to that other period.

Step 4

The amount of the equivalent foreign levy available as a credit against the bank levy is $(B / A) \times C$.

6 Determining assets and UK assets

(1) This regulation applies to determine the assets and the UK assets of the relevant group or relevant entity.

(2) In the case of the relevant group, the amount of the assets and the UK assets are determined by reference to—

- (a) the amounts recognised in the group's consolidated financial statements for the chargeable period as prepared under international accounting standards or UK GAAP, or
- (b) if no such financial statements are prepared, the amounts which would have been so recognised had consolidated financial statements for the group been prepared for the chargeable period under international accounting standards.

(3) In the case of the relevant entity, assets and UK assets are determined by reference to—

- (a) the amounts recognised in the entity's financial statements for the chargeable period as prepared under international accounting standards or UK GAAP, or
- (b) if no such financial statements are prepared, the amounts which would have been so recognised had such financial statements been prepared for the chargeable period under international accounting standards or under UK GAAP if that is what the entity prepares its financial statements under.

(4) For the purposes of these Regulations, "UK assets" means—

- (a) in relation to the relevant group—
  - (i) the assets of any relevant UK sub-group which is a member of the relevant group,
  - (ii) the assets of any UK resident entity which is a member of the relevant group but is not a member of a relevant UK sub-group,
  - (iii) the assets of a non-UK resident entity which is a member of the relevant group and is a member of a UK sub-group but is not a member of a relevant UK sub-group, and
  - (iv) the assets of any permanent establishment through which any member of the relevant group carries on a trade in the UK; and
- (b) in relation to the relevant entity, the assets of any permanent establishment through which the entity carries on a trade in the UK.

(5) Paragraph 26 (including sub-paragraph (4)) of Schedule 19 to the Finance Act 2011 applies for the purposes of determining the assets of a permanent establishment.

7 Exchange rates

Where the equivalent foreign levy is imposed in a currency other than sterling, for the purposes of regulation 5 the amount of equivalent foreign currency is to be translated into its sterling equivalent by reference to the spot rate of exchange for the last day of the chargeable period in relation to which the credit is claimed.

Claim for double taxation relief

8 General time limit for making a claim

(1) A claim for credit under regulation 4(1) must be made not more than—

(a) four years after the end of the accounting period in relation to which the bank levy is treated as an amount of corporation tax chargeable on the responsible member (see paragraph 50 of Schedule 19 to the Finance Act 2011) or the relevant entity (see paragraph 51 of that Schedule), or

(b) if later, one year after the end of the accounting period in which the equivalent foreign levy is paid.

(2) If the chargeable period in relation to which the bank levy is charged falls in more than one accounting period, the accounting period referred to in paragraph (1)(a) shall be the latest of those periods.

9 Relevant groups: responsible member to make claim

Where the bank levy is charged as provided for by paragraph 4 of Schedule 19 to the Finance Act 2011 (bank levy to be charged in relation to certain groups of entities) any claim for credit under regulation 4(1) must be made by the responsible member.

Limits on credit

10 Restriction of credit

(1) Where the bank levy is charged in relation to the relevant group, if the parent entity is not resident in the foreign territory ("territory A") the law of which imposes the equivalent foreign levy, the credit under regulation 4(1) is only available to reduce the amount of the bank levy charged in relation to relevant chargeable equity and liabilities of the relevant group.

(2) In paragraph (1), "relevant chargeable equity and liabilities" means chargeable equity and liabilities that would be recognised in relevant accounts for the chargeable period had such accounts been prepared for the member or members of the group ("the relevant member or members") resident in territory A.

(3) In paragraph (2), "relevant accounts" mean a consolidated financial statement or financial statement—

(a) prepared under international accounting standards or under UK GAAP if that is what the relevant member or members prepare financial statements under, and

(b) in which the UK assets subject to the equivalent foreign levy in respect of which the credit is given would be recognised.

11 Reduction in credit: payment by reference to equivalent foreign levy

(1) Paragraph (2) applies if—

(a) credit for an equivalent foreign levy is to be allowed to an entity under these Regulations, and

(b) a payment is made by a tax authority to that entity, or to any other person, by reference to the equivalent foreign levy.

(2) The amount of the credit must be recalculated by repeating steps 3 and 4 in regulation 5, reducing the amount of the equivalent foreign levy by reference to the payment referred to in paragraph (1)(b).

12 Priority of credits

(1) Where credits are allowed in relation to equivalent foreign levies imposed by the law of two or more foreign territories under these Regulations or under these Regulations and any Regulations made under paragraph 66 (arrangements affording double taxation relief) or paragraph 67 (power to provide for double taxation relief) of Schedule 19 to the Finance Act 2011, the credits apply to reduce the bank levy in the order specified in paragraph (2), subject to paragraphs (3) and (4).

(2) The order is—

First, any credit allowed in relation to the equivalent foreign levy imposed by the law of the foreign territory in which the parent entity is resident.

Second, any credit allowed in relation to the equivalent foreign levy imposed by the law of the foreign territory in which a direct subsidiary ("the first subsidiary") is resident or a permanent establishment of the parent entity is located.

Third, any credit allowed in relation to an equivalent foreign levy imposed by the law of the foreign territory in which a direct subsidiary ("the second subsidiary") is resident or a permanent establishment of the first subsidiary is located.

Fourth, any credit allowed in relation to an equivalent foreign levy imposed by the law of the foreign territory in which a direct subsidiary of the second subsidiary is resident or a permanent establishment of the second subsidiary is located, and so on in relation to any fourth and further subsidiaries.

(3) If an entity has direct subsidiaries ("the elected subsidiaries") in more than one foreign territory which imposes an equivalent foreign levy, the responsible member shall elect as to the order ("the elected order") in which the credits allowed in relation to the equivalent foreign levies shall be applied.

(4) If any of the elected subsidiaries themselves have direct subsidiaries in more than one foreign territory which imposes an equivalent foreign levy, paragraphs (2) and (3) shall apply to those direct subsidiaries in the elected order and paragraph (2) shall apply as if each elected subsidiary were a parent entity.

(5) For the purposes of this regulation, where an equivalent foreign levy is not imposed by the law of the foreign territory in which an entity ("E") is resident, any direct subsidiary of E shall be treated as the direct subsidiary of the entity which is the parent entity of E.

Action after adjustment of amount payable by way of bank levy or equivalent foreign levy

13 Consequences of adjustment of the bank levy or equivalent foreign levy

(1) Paragraph (2) applies to a claim or assessment if—

(a) the amount of credit given under regulation 4(1) is reduced under regulation 11, or becomes excessive or insufficient by reason of any adjustment of the amount of any bank levy or equivalent foreign levy,

(b) the reduction or adjustment gives rise to the claim or assessment, and

(c) the claim or assessment is made not later than 6 years from the date on which all material determinations have been made, whether in the UK or elsewhere.

(2) Nothing in the Tax Acts limiting the time for the making of assessments, or limiting the time for the making of claims for relief, applies to the assessment or claim.

(3) In paragraph (1)(c) "material determination" means an assessment, reduction, adjustment or other determination that is material in determining whether any, and (if so) what, credit is to be given.

14 Duty to give notice that adjustment has rendered credit excessive

(1) This regulation applies if—

(a) any credit has been allowed under regulation 4(1), and

(b) later, the amount of that credit is reduced under regulation 11, or becomes excessive as a result of an adjustment of the amount of the equivalent foreign levy.

(2) The relevant entity or, in the case of the relevant group, the responsible member must give notice that a reduction has been made or that the amount of the credit has become excessive as a result of the making of an adjustment.

(3) Notice under paragraph (2) is to be given—

(a) to an officer of Revenue and Customs, and

(b) within one year from when the reduction or adjustment is made.

2012/459

BANK LEVY (DOUBLE TAXATION ARRANGEMENTS) (FEDERAL REPUBLIC OF GERMANY) REGULATIONS 2012

Made . . . . *21st February 2012*
Laid before the House of Commons . . . . *22nd February 2012*
Coming into force . . . . *14th March 2012*

The Treasury make the following Regulations in exercise of the powers conferred by paragraph 66(8) and (9) of Schedule 19 to the Finance Act 2011.

Introduction

1 Citation, commencement and effect

(1) These Regulations may be cited as the Bank Levy (Double Taxation Arrangements) (Federal Republic of Germany) Regulations 2012 and come into force on 14th March 2012.

(2) These Regulations have effect in relation to periods of account ending on or after 1st January 2011.

(3) But regulation 10 has effect in relation to periods of account beginning on or after 14th March 2012.

2 Interpretation

In these Regulations—

"double taxation arrangements" means the Convention and the Protocol;

"Convention" means the Convention between the Federal Republic of Germany and the United Kingdom of Great Britain and Northern Ireland for the avoidance of double charging of bank levies signed on 7th December 2011 in London;

"German bank levy" means the equivalent foreign levy imposed by the Federal Republic of Germany;

"Protocol" means the Protocol attached to the Convention;

"UK permanent establishment" means a permanent establishment through which a trade is carried on in the United Kingdom by a relevant foreign bank which is a relevant entity or a member of a relevant group.

3 Application of these Regulations

These Regulations apply in relation to the provision of relief from the bank levy provided by the Convention where the bank levy and the German bank levy are charged in relation to a UK permanent establishment.

Double taxation relief by way of credit

4 Double taxation relief

(1) Where these Regulations apply, the amount of the German bank levy paid which is attributable to the UK permanent establishment in relation to a chargeable period is allowed as a credit against the bank levy for that chargeable period.

(2) Subject to the provisions of these Regulations, the amount of the bank levy for the chargeable period is reduced by the amount of the credit.

(3) But the amount of the bank levy shall not be reduced to below nil.

(4) The amount of the German bank levy attributable to the UK permanent establishment is the amount determined in accordance with paragraph 1 of the Protocol in relation to the chargeable period.

(5) If a proportion (Z%) of the period in relation to which the German bank levy is calculated falls in any other chargeable period, Z% of the German bank levy shall be attributable to that other period.

5 Exchange rates

For the purposes of regulation 4, the amount of German bank levy is to be translated into its sterling equivalent by reference to the spot rate of exchange for the last day of the chargeable period in relation to which the credit is claimed.

Claim for double taxation relief

6 General time limit for making a claim

(1) A claim for credit under regulation 4(1) must be made not more than—

(a) four years after the end of the accounting period in relation to which the bank levy is treated as an amount of corporation tax chargeable on the responsible member (see paragraph 50 of Schedule 19 to the Finance Act 2011) or the relevant entity (see paragraph 51 of that Schedule), or

(b) if later, one year after the end of the accounting period in which the German bank levy is paid.

(2) If the chargeable period in relation to which the bank levy is charged falls in more than one accounting period, the accounting period referred to in paragraph (1)(a) shall be the latest of those periods.

7 Relevant groups: responsible member to make claim

Where the bank levy is charged as provided for by paragraph 4 of Schedule 19 to the Finance Act 2011 (bank levy to be charged in relation to certain groups of entities) any claim for credit under regulation 4(1) must be made by the responsible member.

Limits on credit

8 Restriction of credit

(1) The credit under regulation 4(1) is only available to reduce the amount of the bank levy so far as it is attributable to chargeable equity and liabilities of the UK permanent establishment.

(2) Bank levy is to be attributed for the purposes of paragraph (1) on a just and reasonable basis.

9 Reduction in credit: payment by reference to German bank levy

(1) Paragraph (2) applies if—

(a) credit for the German bank levy is to be allowed to an entity under these Regulations, and

(b) a payment is made by a tax authority to that entity, or to any other person, by reference to the German bank levy.

(2) The amount of the credit must be recalculated under regulation 4 reducing the amount of the German bank levy by reference to the payment referred to in paragraph (1)(b).

10 Priority of credits

(1) Where credits are allowed in relation to equivalent foreign levies (including the German bank levy) under these Regulations and under any Regulations made under paragraph 66 (arrangements affording double taxation relief) or paragraph 67 (power to provide for double taxation relief) of Schedule 19 to the Finance Act 2011, the credits apply to reduce the bank levy in the order specified in paragraph (2), subject to paragraphs (3) and (4).

(2) The order is—

First, any credit allowed in relation to the equivalent foreign levy imposed by the law of the foreign territory in which the parent entity is resident.

Second, any credit allowed in relation to the equivalent foreign levy imposed by the law of the foreign territory in which a direct subsidiary ("the first subsidiary") is resident or a permanent establishment of the parent entity is located.

Third, any credit allowed in relation to an equivalent foreign levy imposed by the law of the foreign territory in which a direct subsidiary ("the second subsidiary") is resident or a permanent establishment of the first subsidiary is located.

Fourth, any credit allowed in relation to an equivalent foreign levy imposed by the law of the foreign territory in which a direct subsidiary of the second subsidiary is resident or a permanent establishment of the second subsidiary is located, and so on in relation to any fourth and further subsidiaries.

(3) If an entity has direct subsidiaries ("the elected subsidiaries") in more than one foreign territory which imposes an equivalent foreign levy, the responsible member shall elect as to the order ("the elected order") in which the credits allowed in relation to the equivalent foreign levies shall be applied.

(4) If any of the elected subsidiaries themselves have direct subsidiaries in more than one foreign territory which imposes an equivalent foreign levy, paragraphs (2) and (3) shall apply to those direct subsidiaries in the elected order and paragraph (1) shall apply as if each elected subsidiary were a parent entity.

(5) For the purposes of this regulation, where an equivalent foreign levy is not imposed by the law of the foreign territory in which an entity ("E") is resident, any direct subsidiary of E shall be treated as the direct subsidiary of the entity which is the parent entity of E.

Action after adjustment of amount payable by way of bank levy or German bank levy

11 Consequences of adjustment of the bank levy or German bank levy

(1) Paragraph (2) applies to a claim or assessment if—

(a) the amount of credit given under regulation 4 is reduced under regulation 9, or becomes excessive or insufficient by reason of any adjustment of the amount of any bank levy or German bank levy,

(b) the reduction or adjustment gives rise to the claim or assessment, and

(c) the claim or assessment is made not later than 6 years from the time when all material determinations have been made, whether in the UK or elsewhere.

(2) Nothing in the Tax Acts limiting the time for the making of assessments, or limiting the time for the making of claims for relief, applies to the assessment or claim.

(3) In paragraph (1)(c) "material determination" means an assessment, reduction, adjustment or other determination that is material in determining whether any, and (if so) what, credit is to be given.

12 Duty to give notice that adjustment has rendered credit excessive

(1) This regulation applies if—

(a) any credit has been allowed under regulation 4, and

(b) later, the amount of that credit is reduced under regulation 9, or becomes excessive as a result of an adjustment of the amount of the German bank levy.

(2) The relevant entity or, in the case of a relevant group, the responsible member must give notice that a reduction has been made or that the amount of the credit has become excessive as a result of the making of an adjustment.

(3) Notice under paragraph (2) is to be given—

(a) to an officer of Revenue and Customs, and

(b) within one year from when the reduction or adjustment is made.

Cases about being taxed otherwise than in accordance with the Convention

13 Giving effect to solutions to cases and mutual agreements resolving cases

(1) Paragraphs (2) and (4) apply if under, and for the purposes of, the double taxation arrangements—

(a) an entity presents, to the Commissioners for Her Majesty's Revenue and Customs or to a competent authority in the Federal Republic of Germany, a case concerning the entity's being taxed (whether in the United Kingdom or the Federal Republic of Germany) otherwise than in accordance with the double taxation arrangements, and

(b) the Commissioners arrive at a solution to the case or make a mutual agreement with a competent authority in the Federal Republic of Germany for the resolution of the case.

(2) The Commissioners are to give effect to the solution or mutual agreement despite anything in any enactment, and any such adjustment as is appropriate in consequence may be made.

(3) An adjustment under paragraph (2) may be made by way of discharge or repayment of tax, the allowance of credit against tax payable in the United Kingdom, the making of an assessment or otherwise.

(4) A claim for relief under any provision of the Tax Acts or the enactments relating to capital gains tax may be made in pursuance of the solution or mutual agreement at any time before the end of the period of 12 months following the notification of the solution or mutual agreement to the entity affected, even if that involves making the claim after a deadline imposed by another enactment.

(5) In this regulation "competent authority in the Federal Republic of Germany" means the Federal Ministry of Finance or the agency to which it has delegated its powers.

14 Effect of, and deadline for, presenting a case

(1) This regulation applies to the presentation of a case concerning an entity's being taxed (whether in the United Kingdom or the Federal Republic of Germany) otherwise than in accordance with the double taxation arrangements.

(2) The presentation of any such case under and in accordance with the double taxation arrangements—

(a) does not constitute a claim for relief under the Tax Acts or the enactments relating to capital gains tax, and

(b) is accordingly not subject to section 42 of the Taxes Management Act 1970 or any other enactment relating to the making of such claims.

(3) Any such claim must be presented before the end of the later of—

(a) the period of 3 years following the first notification of the action resulting in the entity being charged otherwise than in accordance with the double taxation arrangements, and

(b) the period of 6 years following the end of the chargeable period to which the case relates.

2012/689

TAXES, ETC (FEES FOR PAYMENT BY TELEPHONE) REGULATIONS 2012

Made . . . . *5th March 2012*
Laid before the House of Commons . . . . *6th March 2012*
Coming into force . . . . *2nd April 2012*

Revocation—These Regulations revoked by the Taxes, etc. (Fees for Payment by Telephone) Regulations, SI 2016/333 with effect from 1 April 2016.

2012/701

LONDON LEGACY DEVELOPMENT CORPORATION (TAX CONSEQUENCES) REGULATIONS 2012

Made . . . . *6th March 2012*
Laid before the House of Commons . . . . *7th March 2012*
Coming into force . . . . *31st March 2012*

The Treasury, in exercise of the powers conferred by Part 3 of Schedule 24 to the Localism Act 2011, make the following Regulations.

1 Citation and commencement

These Regulations may be cited as the London Legacy Development Corporation (Tax Consequences) Regulations 2012 and come into force on 31st March 2012.

2 Interpretation

In these Regulations—

"CTA 2009" means the Corporation Tax Act 2009;

"CTA 2010" means the Corporation Tax Act 2010;

"LLDC" means the London Legacy Development Corporation;

"LTGDC" means the London Thames Gateway Development Corporation;

"LTGDC relevant transfer" means a transfer of LTGDC's trading stock from LTGDC to LLDC in relation to, in connection with, or by or under, the London Legacy Development Corporation and the London Thames Gateway Development Corporation (No 1) Transfer Scheme 2012;

"OPLC" means the Olympic Park Legacy Company Limited, company registered number 06900359;

"OPLC relevant transfer" means a transfer of property, rights and liabilities from OPLC to LLDC, in relation to, in connection with, or by or under, the London Legacy Development Corporation and the Olympic Park Legacy Company Transfer Scheme 2012;
"trading stock" has the same meaning as in section 163 of CTA 2009.

3 Transfers from OPLC to LLDC

(1) This regulation applies to an OPLC relevant transfer.
(2) For the purposes of any enactment about income tax or corporation tax—
(a) OPLC and LLDC are to be treated as the same person, and
(b) a relevant transfer is to be disregarded for those purposes.
(3) A relevant transfer is not to be regarded for the purposes of Part 8 of CTA 2009 (intangible fixed assets) as involving any realisation of an asset by OPLC or acquisition of an asset by LLDC.
(4) A relevant transfer is not to be regarded for the purposes of Part 14 of CTA 2010 (change in company ownership) as resulting in a change of ownership of a company.
(5) A relevant transfer does not give rise to any liability to stamp duty land tax.

4 Transfers from LTGDC to LLDC

(1) This regulation applies to a LTGDC relevant transfer.
(2) Paragraphs (3) and (4) have effect in computing for any corporation tax purpose both—
(a) the profits of LTGDC's trade in relation to which the stock transferred is trading stock immediately before the relevant transfer takes effect, and
(b) the consideration given by LLDC, or the expenditure incurred by it, for the acquisition of the stock.
(3) The stock must be taken to have been—
(a) disposed of by LTGDC in the course of its trade, and
(b) disposed of and acquired when the relevant transfer takes effect.
(4) The stock must be valued as if the disposal and acquisition were for a consideration which in relation to LTGDC would have resulted in neither a profit nor a loss being brought into account in respect of the disposal in the accounting period of LTGDC which ends with, or is current at, the time when the relevant transfer takes effect.

2012/735

FINANCE ACT 2010, SCHEDULE 6, PART 1 (FURTHER CONSEQUENTIAL AND INCIDENTAL PROVISION ETC) ORDER 2012

Made . . . . 8th March 2012
Laid before the House of Commons . . . . 9th March 2012
Coming into force . . . . 1st April 2012

The Commissioners for Her Majesty's Revenue and Customs make the following Order in exercise of the powers conferred by paragraph 29(1) and (2) of Schedule 6 to the Finance Act 2010.
The provision made by this Order appears appropriate in consequence of, or otherwise in connection with, Part 1 of that Schedule.

1 Citation, commencement and effect

This Order may be cited as the Finance Act 2010, Schedule 6, Part 1 (Further Consequential and Incidental Provision etc) Order 2012 and comes into force on 1st April 2012.

2 (1) Article 5 has effect in relation to—
(a) a supply of goods or services (including anything treated as such a supply) made on or after 1st April 2012,
(b) an acquisition of goods from another member State on or after 1st April 2012, and
(c) an importation of goods from a place outside the member States on or after 1st April 2012.
(2) In paragraph 1—
"acquisition of goods from another member State" shall be construed in accordance with section 11 of VATA 1994;
"another member State" has the meaning given by section 96(1) of VATA 1994;
"importation of goods from a place outside the member States" shall be construed in accordance with section 15 of VATA 1994;
"supply" shall be construed in accordance with section 5 of VATA 1994.

3 Article 6 has effect—
(a) for corporation tax purposes, for accounting periods beginning on or after 1st April 2012, and
(b) for capital gains tax purposes, for the tax year 2012-13 and subsequent tax years.

4 Article 7 has effect—

(a) for corporation tax purposes, for accounting periods beginning on or after 1st April 2012, and

(b) for income tax purposes, for the tax year 2012-13 and subsequent tax years.

5 Definition of "charity" for the purposes of value added tax

(1) The definition of "charity" in section 1(1) of the Charities Act 2011 ceases to apply for the purposes of enactments relating to value added tax to which it would otherwise apply.

(2) Accordingly, by virtue of paragraph 33(2) of Schedule 6 to the Finance Act 2010, the definition of "charity" in Part 1 of that Schedule applies for the purposes of those enactments.

6 Definition of "charity" for the purposes of capital gains tax

(1) The definition of "charity" in section 1(1) of the Charities Act 2011 ceases to apply for the purposes of the enactments relating to capital gains tax to which it would otherwise apply.

(2) Accordingly, by virtue of paragraph 33(2) of Schedule 6 to the Finance Act 2010, the definition of "charity" in Part 1 of that Schedule applies for the purposes of those enactments.

7 Amendment of CTA 2009

In Schedule 4 to CTA 2009 (index of defined expressions), in the entry for "charity", for "section 1119 of CTA 2010" substitute "paragraph 1 of Schedule 6 to FA 2010".

2012/736

FINANCE ACT 2010, SCHEDULE 6, PART 2 (COMMENCEMENT) ORDER 2012

Made . . . . *8th March 2012*

The Treasury make the following Order in exercise of the powers conferred by paragraph 34(1)(b), (2) and (3) of Schedule 6 to the Finance Act 2010:

1 Citation and interpretation

(1) This Order may be cited as the Finance Act 2010, Schedule 6, Part 2 (Commencement) Order 2012.

(2) In this Order "Schedule 6" means Schedule 6 to the Finance Act 2010.

2 Provisions coming into force

The repeals and other amendments made by Part 2 of Schedule 6 described in articles 3 to 22 of this Order come into force as follows.

3 Paragraph 8 of Schedule 6 (amendment of FA 1982)

The amendment of section 129(1) of FA 1982 (stamp duty: exemption from duty on grants, transfers to charities etc) made by paragraph 8 of Schedule 6 comes into force in relation to any conveyance, transfer or lease made or agreed to be made on or after 1st April 2012.

4 Paragraph 9 of Schedule 6 (amendment of FA 1983)

The amendment of section 46(3) of FA 1983 (Historic Buildings and Monuments Commission for England) made by paragraph 9 of Schedule 6 comes into force on 1st April 2012.

5 Paragraph 10 of Schedule 6 (amendment of IHTA 1984)

(1) The repeal of the definitions of "charity" and "charitable" in section 272 of IHTA 1984 (general interpretation) made by paragraph 10 of Schedule 6 comes into force in relation to a transfer of value made on or after 1st April 2012.

(2) In this article "transfer of value" has the meaning given by section 3 of IHTA 1984.

6 Paragraph 11 of Schedule 6 (amendment of FA 1986)

The amendment of section 90(7) of FA 1986 (stamp duty reserve tax: exceptions from principal charge) made by paragraph 11 of Schedule 6 comes into force in relation to any agreement to transfer securities made on or after 1st April 2012.

7 Paragraph 12 of Schedule 6 (amendment of FA 1989)

The repeal of sub-paragraph (10) of paragraph 4 of Schedule 5 to FA 1989 (employee share ownership trusts) made by paragraph 12 of Schedule 6 comes into force in relation to trusts established on or after 6th April 2012.

8 Paragraph 13 of Schedule 6 (amendment of TCGA 1992)

(1) The amendment of section 222(8B)(b)(iii) of TCGA 1992 (relief on disposal of private residence) made by paragraph 13(1) and (2) of Schedule 6 comes into force in relation to living accommodation provided for a director on or after 6th April 2012 if that accommodation was not already provided for the director immediately before that date.

(2) In this article "director" has the meaning given by section 222(8D) of TCGA 1992.

9 (1) The repeals mentioned in paragraph (2) come into force—

(a) for corporation tax purposes, for accounting periods beginning on or after 1st April 2012, and
(b) for capital gains tax purposes, for the tax year 2012–13 and subsequent tax years.

(2) The repeals referred to in paragraph (1) are—

(a) the repeal of section 256(6) and (8) of TCGA 1992 (charities) made by paragraph 13(1) and (3) of Schedule 6,
(b) the repeal of section 256C(6) of TCGA 1992 (attributing gains to the non-exempt amount: charitable companies) made by paragraph 13(1) and (4) of Schedule 6, and
(c) the repeal of section 256D(7) of TCGA 1992 (how gains are attributed to the non-exempt amount: charitable companies) made by paragraph 13(1) and (5) of Schedule 6.

10 Paragraph 15 of Schedule 6 (amendment of FA 1999)

The amendments of paragraph 6(3) of Schedule 19 to FA 1999 (exclusion of charge to stamp duty reserve tax in certain cases of change of ownership) made by paragraph 15(1) and (2) of Schedule 6 come into force in relation to surrenders (within the meaning given by paragraph 2(1) of Schedule 19 to FA 1999) occurring on or after 1st April 2012.

11 The amendment of paragraph 15(c) of Schedule 19 to FA 1999 made by paragraph 15(1) and (3) of Schedule 6 comes into force on 1st April 2012.

12 Paragraph 16 of Schedule 6 (amendment of CAA 2001)

The amendments of section 63(2)(a) and (aa) of CAA 2001 (cases in which disposal value is nil) made by paragraph 16 of Schedule 6 come into force—

(a) for corporation tax purposes, for accounting periods beginning on or after 1st April 2012, and
(b) for income tax purposes, for the tax year 2012–13 and subsequent tax years.

13 Paragraph 17 of Schedule 6 (amendment of ITEPA 2003)

The amendments of ITEPA 2003 made by paragraph 17 of Schedule 6 come into force for the tax year 2012–13 and subsequent tax years.

14 Paragraphs 18, 19 and 20 of Schedule 6 (amendment of FA 2003)

(1) The—

(a) repeal of sub-paragraph (4) of paragraph 1 of Schedule 8 to FA 2003 (SDLT: charities relief), and
(b) amendment of sub-paragraph (2) of paragraph 4 of Schedule 8 to FA 2003 (SDLT: charitable trusts)

made by paragraphs 18,19 and 20 of Schedule 6 come into force in relation to a land transaction of which the effective date is on or after 1st April 2012.

(2) In this article "land transaction" has the meaning given by section 43 of FA 2003 and "effective date" has the meaning given by section 119 of that Act.

15 Paragraph 21 of Schedule 6 (amendment of ITTOIA 2005)

(1) Subject to the following provisions of this article, the amendments of ITTOIA 2005 made by paragraph 21 of Schedule 6 come into force for the tax year 2012–13 and subsequent tax years.

(2) The amendments mentioned in paragraph (3) come into force in relation to insurances and contracts made on or after 6th April 2012.

(3) The amendments referred to in paragraph (2) are—

(a) the amendment of section 545(1) of ITTOIA 2005 (definitions for Chapter 9 of Part 4) made by paragraph 21(1) and (3) of Schedule 6, and
(b) the amendment of Part 2 of Schedule 4 to ITTOIA 2005 (index of defined expressions) made by paragraph 21(1) and (5)(a) of Schedule 6, so far as the amendment applies in relation to Chapter 9 of Part 4 of ITTOIA 2005.

16 Paragraph 22 of Schedule 6 (amendment of F(No 2)A 2005)

The amendment of section 18(3)(b)(i) of F(No 2)A 2005 (authorised investment funds: specific powers) made by paragraph 22 of Schedule 6 comes into force on 1st April 2012.

17 Paragraph 23 of Schedule 6 (amendment of ITA 2007)

The amendments of ITA 2007 made by paragraph 23(1) to (5) and (7) of Schedule 6 come into force for the tax year 2012–13 and subsequent tax years.

18 The repeal of the definition of "charity" in section 989 of ITA 2007 made by paragraph 23(1) and (6) of Schedule 6, so far as it applies for purposes other than those of Chapter 2 of Part 8 of that Act, comes into force for the tax year 2012–13 and subsequent tax years.

19 Paragraph 24 of Schedule 6 (amendment of FA 2008)

The repeal of the definition of "charity" in paragraph 60(2) of Schedule 36 to FA 2008 (references to carrying on a business) made by paragraph 24 of Schedule 6 comes into force on 1st April 2012.

20 Paragraph 26 of Schedule 6 (amendment of FA 2009)

The repeal of the definition of "charity" in paragraph 8 of Schedule 49 to FA 2009 (general interpretation) made by paragraph 26 of Schedule 6 comes into force on 1st April 2012.

21 Paragraph 27 of Schedule 6 (amendment of CTA 2010)

The amendments of CTA 2010 made by paragraph 27 of Schedule 6 come into force—

(a) for corporation tax purposes, for accounting periods beginning on or after 1st April 2012, and

(b) for income tax purposes, for the tax year 2012–13 and subsequent tax years.

22 Paragraph 28 of Schedule 6 (amendment of TIOPA 2010)

The amendment of section 326(3) of TIOPA 2010 (charities) made by paragraph 28 of Schedule 6 comes into force for accounting periods beginning on or after 1st April 2012.

2012/764

POSTAL SERVICES ACT 2011 (TAXATION) REGULATIONS 2012

Made . . . . 8th March 2012

Laid before the House of Commons . . . . 9th March 2012

Coming into force in accordance with regulation 1(1)

The Treasury make the following Regulations in exercise of the power conferred by sections 23 and 89(2) of the Postal Services Act 2011.

PART 1
PRELIMINARY

1 Citation, commencement and effect

(1) These Regulations may be cited as the Postal Services Act 2011 (Taxation) Regulations 2012 and come into force immediately after the coming into force of both—

(a) the first order made under section 17(2) (transfer of qualifying accrued rights to new public scheme) of the Act by virtue of an order made under section 25(4) and (5) of the Act ("the specified day order"); and

(b) the first order made under section 21(1) (transfer of assets of the RMPP) of the Act by virtue of the specified day order.

(2) Regulation 3 has effect in relation to the accounting period which begins on or before and ends on or after the date on which the first order made under section 17(2) of the Act comes into force by virtue of the specified day order, and subsequent accounting periods.

(3) Regulations 4 and 5 have effect in relation to accounting periods beginning on or after the date on which the first order made under section 17(2) of the Act comes into force by virtue of the specified day order.

2 Interpretation

(1) In these Regulations—

"accounting period" is to be read in accordance with Chapter 2 of Part 2 of the Corporation Tax Act 2009 (accounting periods);

"Accrued Rights" means the rights transferred from the RMPP to the new public scheme pursuant to an order made under section 17(2) of the Act;

"the Accrued Rights Transfer" means the transfer of Accrued Rights from the RMPP to the new public scheme;

"the Act" means the Postal Services Act 2011;

"the Assets Transfer" means the transfer of assets of the RMPP pursuant to an order made under section 21(1) of the Act;

"excluded contributions" means contributions paid to the RMPP in advance of 31st March 2012 in respect of amounts falling due after that date under the existing Schedule of Contributions of the RMPP;

"the final accounting period" means the accounting period which ended immediately before the first qualifying accounting period;

"the first qualifying accounting period" means the first accounting period which begins on or after the date on which the first order made under section 17(2) of the Act comes into force by virtue of an order made under section 25(4) and (5) of the Act;

"the new public scheme" means the new public scheme established pursuant to an order made under section 17(1) of the Act;

"Part 4" means Part 4 (pension schemes etc) of the Finance Act 2004;

"POL" means the Post Office Limited (registered number 02154540);

"RMGL" means the Royal Mail Group Limited (registered number 04138203);

"the Transfer" means the Accrued Rights Transfer and the Assets Transfer;

"the Transitional Provisions Order" means the Taxation of Pension Schemes (Transitional Provisions) Order 2006;

a reference to a numbered section or Schedule (without more) is a reference to the section or Schedule bearing that number in the Finance Act 2004; and

expressions which are defined, or are otherwise explained, in section 280 (abbreviations and general index) have the same meaning in these Regulations as they have in Part 4.

(2) For the purposes of paragraph (1) "Schedule of Contributions" has the same meaning as in section 227(2) of the Pension Act 2004.

PART 2

CORPORATION TAX

3 De-recognition of the obligations and assets of the RMPP

(1) Paragraph (2) applies where—

(a) RMGL or POL recognises a debit or credit in its accounts, in accordance with generally accepted accounting practice; and

(b) the debit or credit is recognised in that company's accounts as a consequence of—

(i) the Accrued Rights Transfer;

(ii) the division of the RMPP in accordance with an order made under section 18 of the Act (division of the RMPP into different sections);

(iii) an amendment of the RMPP in accordance with an order made under section 19 of the Act (amendments of the RMPP) in connection with an order under section 17 or section 18 of the Act; or

(iv) the Assets Transfer.

(2) In computing the profits, gains or losses of that company for the purposes of corporation tax, no amount is to be brought into account in respect of the debit or credit.

(3) In this regulation—

(a) "accounts" has the meaning given by section 17(1) of the Corporation Tax Act 2010 (interpretation); and

(b) "generally accepted accounting practice" has the same meaning as in section 1127 of the Corporation Tax Act 2010 (generally accepted accounting practice and related expressions).

4 Extinguishment of relevant losses of RMGL

(1) With effect from the first day of the first qualifying accounting period, the relevant losses of RMGL are to be treated for the purposes of corporation tax as extinguished.

(2) The amount of the relevant losses that are to be treated as extinguished in accordance with paragraph (1) is the sum of the relevant loss incurred in each accounting period prior to the final accounting period.

(3) In this regulation a loss is a relevant loss for an accounting period ("the relevant accounting period") if—

(a) the loss was incurred in the trade carried on by RMGL in the relevant accounting period; and

(b) the loss is included in the losses carried forward to the first qualifying accounting period as an unrelieved loss in accordance with section 45 of the Corporation Tax Act 2010 (carry forward of trade loss against subsequent trade profits),

but this paragraph is subject to paragraph (4).

(4) A loss is not a relevant loss for the purposes of paragraph (3) to the extent that it is attributable to deductions in the computation of the loss for an accounting period for contributions that are excluded contributions.

(5) For the purposes of this regulation—

(a) losses incurred by RMGL are the losses computed in accordance with section 47 of the Corporation Tax Act 2009 (losses calculated on the same basis as profits); and

(b) a loss is an unrelieved loss for an accounting period if no relief has been given in respect of the loss under section 37 (relief for trade losses against total profits) or Part 5 of the Corporation Tax Act 2010 (group relief).

5 Extinguishment of trading losses of POL

(1) With effect from the first day of the first qualifying accounting period, the relevant losses of POL are to be treated for the purposes of corporation tax as extinguished.

(2) In this regulation "relevant losses" means the aggregate of the losses incurred in each accounting period prior to the final accounting period calculated in accordance with paragraph (3). This paragraph is subject to paragraph (4).

(3) The amount of the loss for each accounting period ("the relevant accounting period") is found by—

(a) calculating—

(i) the amount of the loss incurred in the trade carried on by POL in the relevant accounting period which is carried forward to the first qualifying accounting period as an unrelieved loss in accordance with section 45 of the Corporation Tax Act 2010 ("L"); and

(ii) the amount of deductions in the computation of the loss for that relevant accounting period for, or in connection with, contributions in respect of qualifying members of the RMPP ("P"); and

(b) comparing the figures given by L and P for each accounting period and where—

(i) L is greater than P, the relevant loss for that period is the amount equal to P;

(ii) L is less than P, the relevant loss for that period is the amount equal to L; and

(iii) L and P are the same, the relevant loss for that period is the amount equal to P.

(4) A loss is not a relevant loss for the purposes of this regulation to the extent that it is attributable to deductions in the computation of the loss for an accounting period for payments in relation to contributions that are excluded contributions.

(5) For the purposes of this regulation—

(a) losses incurred by POL are the losses computed in accordance with section 47 of the Corporation Tax Act 2009; and

(b) a loss is an unrelieved loss for an accounting period if no relief has been given in respect of the loss under section 37 or Part 5 of the Corporation Tax Act 2010.

6 Exemption from corporation tax

(1) BCL is exempt from corporation tax for any accounting period [in which it is wholly owned by the Crown within the meaning of sections 14 and 15(1) of the Act].[1].

[(1A) Where BCL ceases to be wholly owned by the Crown otherwise than at the end of an accounting period—

(a) the accounting period during which it ceases to be wholly owned by the Crown is treated for the purposes of corporation tax as ending when it so ceases; and

(b) its profits and losses are to be computed accordingly for those purposes.][1]

(2) For the purposes of this regulation "BCL" means the private company limited by shares incorporated on 8th February 2012 with the registered number 07941521 and with the name BIS (Postal Services Act 2011) Company Limited.

Amendments—[1] Words in para (1) substituted and para (1A) inserted by the Postal Services Act 2011 (Taxation) (Amendment) Regulations, SI 2016/881 reg 2 with effect for accounting periods commencing on or after 1 April 2015.

PART 3

INCOME TAX

CHAPTER 1

TRANSFER OF ACCRUED RIGHTS FROM THE RMPP TO THE NEW PUBLIC SCHEME

7 New public scheme to be treated as a registered pension scheme

The new public scheme is to be treated as a registered pension scheme for the purposes of Part 4.

8 Transfer to be treated as a recognised transfer

(1) For the purposes of Part 4, the Transfer is to be treated as a recognised transfer of sums or assets held for the purposes of, or representing accrued rights under, the RMPP in connection with a member of that scheme within the meaning of section 169(1).

(2) Paragraph (3) applies where the Accrued Rights Transfer has resulted in the transfer to the new public scheme of Accrued Rights in respect of a scheme pension to which a member of the RMPP has become entitled ("the original scheme pension").

(3) The sums and assets which represented rights in respect of the original scheme pension are to be treated, after the Accrued Rights Transfer, as being applied towards the provision of a scheme pension for the purposes of regulations 3 and 5 of the Registered Pension Schemes (Transfer of Sums and Assets) Regulations 2006 (the "Transfer of Sums and Assets Regulations").

(4) Paragraph (5) applies where the Accrued Rights Transfer has resulted in the transfer to the new public scheme of Accrued Rights in respect of a dependants' scheme pension to which a dependant of a member of the RMPP has become entitled in respect of the member ("the original dependants' scheme pension").

(5) The sums and assets which represented rights in respect of the original dependants' scheme pension are to be treated, after the Accrued Rights Transfer, as being applied towards the provision of a dependants' scheme pension for the purposes of regulation 8 of the Transfer of Sums and Assets Regulations.

CHAPTER 2

CONTINUED APPLICATION OF "A DAY" TRANSITIONAL PROVISIONS AFTER THE ACCRUED RIGHTS TRANSFER

9 "Enhanced protection" to continue after the Accrued Rights Transfer

Where the Accrued Rights Transfer has taken place—

(a) the Transfer is to be treated as a permitted transfer within the meaning of paragraph 12(7) of Schedule 36 for the purposes of paragraphs 12, 13 and 15 ("enhanced protection") of that Schedule; and

(b) that permitted transfer is to be treated as falling within paragraph 12(8)(c).

10 Rights to take benefit before normal minimum pension age to continue after the Accrued Rights Transfer

(1) Paragraphs (2) and (3) apply where—

(a) the RMPP was a protected pension scheme under paragraph 22(2) of Schedule 36 in relation to a member; and

(b) the Accrued Rights Transfer has taken place.

(2) The Transfer is to be treated as a block transfer within the meaning of paragraph 22(6) of Schedule 36 for the purposes of paragraphs 21 and 22 (rights to take benefit before normal minimum pension age) of that Schedule.

(3) In relation to the retirement condition in paragraph 22(7) of Schedule 36—

(a) the requirement in paragraph (a) is to be treated as met if the member becomes entitled to all the benefits payable to the member under arrangements under both the RMPP and the new public scheme (to which the member did not have an actual entitlement on or before 5th April 2006) on the same date; and

(b) in respect of the requirement in paragraph (b), direct or indirect references to a sponsoring employer in Condition 1, 2 or 3 in sub-paragraphs (7A), (7B), (7C) or (7E) (as the case may be), are to be read as references to a sponsoring employer of the RMPP.

11 Entitlement to lump sums exceeding 25% of uncrystallised rights to continue after the Accrued Rights Transfer

(1) Paragraph (2) applies where—

(a) the RMPP was a protected pension scheme under paragraph 31(4) of Schedule 36 in relation to a member; and

(b) the Accrued Rights Transfer has taken place.

(2) The Transfer is to be treated as a block transfer within the meaning of paragraph 22(6) of Schedule 36 for the purposes of paragraphs 31 to 34 (entitlement to lump sums exceeding 25% of uncrystallised rights) of that Schedule.

12 Transitional protection for stand-alone lump sums to continue after the Accrued Rights Transfer

(1) Paragraph (2) applies where—

(a) the RMPP was entitled to pay a stand-alone lump sum under article 25(3) (stand-alone lump sums: definition) of the Transitional Provisions Order to an individual which, if it had been paid, would have been a stand-alone lump sum paid in circumstances where article 25B(4) (circumstance C) applied; and

(b) the Accrued Rights Transfer has taken place.

(2) The Transfer is to be treated as a block transfer within the meaning of paragraph 22(6) of Schedule 36 for the purposes of article 25D(4)(c) of the Transitional Provisions Order.

13 Transitional protection for continued life cover (75+) to continue after the Accrued Rights Transfer

(1) Paragraph (2) applies where—

(a) the conditions A to C and E in article 6 of the Transitional Provisions Order were satisfied in relation to a member of the RMPP; and

(b) the Accrued Rights Transfer has taken place.

(2) Conditions A to C and E in article 6 of the Transitional Provisions Order are to be treated as satisfied in respect of the new public scheme and the RMPP.

(3) Condition D in article 6 of the Transitional Provisions Order is to be treated as satisfied in respect of the new public scheme where the rules of that scheme in relation to life cover lump sums are the same as the equivalent rules of the RMPP relating to those sums on 10thDecember 2003.

14 Transitional protection in relation to dependants' scheme pension limit to continue after the Accrued Rights Transfer

(1) Paragraph (2) applies where—

(a) a member of the RMPP in respect of whom a dependants' scheme pension is payable was actually entitled to one or more relevant existing pensions, as defined in paragraph 10(2) of Schedule 36, under that scheme on 5th April 2006; and

(b) the Accrued Rights Transfer has taken place.

(2) The transitional protection afforded by article 24 (disapplication of dependants' scheme pension limit) of the Transitional Provisions Order applies to a dependants' scheme pension payable under the new public scheme in respect of that member.

15 Transitional provision in relation to serious ill-health lump sums and pension protection lump sum death benefits to continue after the Accrued Rights Transfer

(1) Paragraphs (3) and (5) apply where—

(a) the Accrued Rights Transfer has taken place; and

(b) the requirements in paragraph (2) are met.

(2) The requirements are that, in relation to article 33(2) (serious ill-health lump sums, pension protection lump sum death benefits and annuity protection lump sum death benefits) of the Transitional Provisions Order—

(a) condition A was met in respect of an individual in relation to the RMPP immediately before the Accrued Rights Transfer; and

(b) condition B had been met in respect of that individual in relation to the RMPP.

(3) Article 33(3) (modification of paragraph 4(2) of Schedule 29 (serious ill-health lump sum)) of the Transitional Provisions Order is to be treated as applying to the new public scheme subject to the modification in paragraph (4).

(4) A pension paid by the new public scheme is to be treated as a relevant existing pension, as defined by paragraph 10(2) of Schedule 36, if it would have been a relevant existing pension had it been paid by the RMPP.

(5) Article 33(4) (modification of paragraph 14(3) of Schedule 29 (pension protection lump sum death benefit)) of the Transitional Provisions Order is to be treated as applying to the new public scheme as if it provided as follows—

"(4) In paragraph 14(3) of Schedule 29 (pension protection lump sum death benefit)—

(a) for the definition of "AC" substitute—

"AC is the value of the individual's pre-commencement pension rights under the RMPP as defined in paragraph 20(3) and (5) of Schedule 36",

(b) for the definition of "AP" substitute—

"AP is the aggregate of the amounts of pension paid—

(a) under the RMPP in respect of the period before the Accrued Rights Transfer, and

(b) under the new public scheme in respect of the period on and after the day on which the Accrued Rights Transfer takes place,

between 6th April 2006 and the member's death.", and

(c) for the definition of TPLS substitute—

"TPLS is the total amount of pension protection lump sum death benefit previously paid in respect of the pension paid under—

(a) the RMPP in respect of the period before the Accrued Rights Transfer, and

(b) the new public scheme in respect of the period on and after the day on which the Accrued Rights Transfer takes place.".

16 Transitional protection in relation to payments to children aged 23 or over to continue after the Accrued Rights Transfer

(1) Paragraph (2) applies where the Accrued Rights Transfer has resulted in the transfer from the RMPP to the new public scheme of Accrued Rights in respect of which article 34 (payments to children aged 23 or over) of the Transitional Provisions Order applied.

(2) The Transfer is to be treated as a block transfer within the meaning of article 34B(4) for the purposes of article 34(6).

17 (1) Paragraph (2) applies where the Accrued Rights Transfer has resulted in the transfer from the RMPP to the new public scheme of Accrued Rights in respect of which article 34A (payments to financially dependent children aged 23 or over) of the Transitional Provisions Order applied.

(2) The Transfer is to be treated as a block transfer within the meaning of article 34B(4) for the purposes of article 34A(5).

18 (1) Paragraph (2) applies where—

(a) Condition D in article 34A(3) of the Transitional Provisions Order was met in relation to a pension death benefit payable in respect of a member of the RMPP so that article 34A was capable of applying to the payment of a pension death benefit; and

(b) the Accrued Rights Transfer has taken place.

(2) The Transfer is to be treated as a block transfer within the meaning of article 34B(4) for the purpose of article 34A(5).

19 Transitional protection in relation to lump sum death benefits to continue after the Accrued Rights Transfer

(1) Paragraph (2) applies where—

(a) the Accrued Rights Transfer has resulted in the transfer from the RMPP to the new public scheme of Accrued Rights in respect of a member; and

(b) after the Accrued Rights Transfer a lump sum is paid under the new public scheme in respect of the death of that member which—

(i) meets the condition in sub-paragraph (b) of article 40(1) (lump sum death benefits—death of member) in respect of the administrator of the RMPP for the period before the Accrued Rights Transfer and in respect of the administrator of the new public scheme for the period on and after the day on which the Accrued Rights Transfer takes place; and

(ii) had the Transfer not taken place, would have met the conditions in sub-paragraphs (a) and (c) to (e) of article 40(1) of the Transitional Provisions Order.

(2) Article 40(2) is to be treated as applying to the payment of the lump sum under the new public scheme.

CHAPTER 3

MISCELLANEOUS PROVISIONS

20 Liability of scheme administrator of the new public scheme in respect of an individual's annual allowance charge for the tax year in which the Accrued Rights Transfer takes place

(1) Paragraph (2) applies where—

(a) the Accrued Rights Transfer has taken place; and

(b) the requirements in section 237B(1) (liability of scheme administrator) are met in respect of an individual in relation to the RMPP for the tax year in which the Accrued Rights Transfer took place.

(2) The Transfer is to be treated as a transfer of all the sums or assets held for the purposes of, or representing accrued rights under, the RMPP so as to become held for the purposes of, or to represent rights under, the new public scheme within the meaning of section 237B(9).

21 Transitional protection under paragraph 14 of Schedule 18 to the Finance Act 2011 ("fixed protection") to continue after the Accrued Rights Transfer

(1) Paragraphs (2) and (3) apply where—

(a) the Accrued Rights Transfer has resulted in the transfer from the RMPP to the new public scheme of Accrued Rights in respect of an individual—

(i) who was an active member of the RMPP immediately before the Accrued Rights Transfer; and

(ii) to whom paragraph 14 (lifetime allowance charge: transitional provision) of Schedule 18 to the Finance Act 2011 applies.

(2) In paragraph 14(13)—

(a) paragraph (a) is disapplied; and

(b) for paragraph (b) substitute—

"(b) the percentage by which the retail prices index for the month of September in the previous tax year is higher than it was for the same month in the period of 12 months (or nil per cent if it is not higher)."

(3) The "retail prices index" means—

(a) the general index of retail prices (for all items) published by the Statistics Board; or

(b) if that index is not published for the relevant month, any substituted index or index figures published by the Statistics Board.

22 Calculation of pension input amount where there is an adjustment to benefit entitlement after the Accrued Rights Transfer

(1) Paragraph (2) applies where—

(a) the Accrued Rights Transfer has resulted in the transfer from the RMPP to the new public scheme of Accrued Rights; and

(b) as a result of the Transfer there is an adjustment to reduce the entitlement of an individual to benefits under the new public scheme and a corresponding adjustment to increase the entitlement of that individual to benefits under the RMPP.

(2) The adjustment and corresponding adjustment referred to in subsection (1)(b) are to be disregarded when arriving at the pension input amount for the RMPP and the new public scheme under sections 234 to 236A (pension input amount: defined benefits arrangements).

23 Provision in relation to double taxation relief arrangements

(1) Paragraph (2) applies where—

(a) immediately prior to the Accrued Rights Transfer a member of the RMPP had pensionable service in respect of the period prior to 1st October 1969;

(b) at any time after the Accrued Rights Transfer the recipient of a pension in respect of that member is resident outside the United Kingdom in a country which has entered into a double taxation relief arrangement with the United Kingdom; and

(c) as a result of the Transfer, there has been a change to the tax treatment of the pension payable in respect of that member in the new scheme under that double taxation relief arrangement.

(2) The tax charged under Chapter 5A (pensions under registered pension schemes) of Part 9 of the Income Tax (Earnings and Pensions) Act 2003 in respect of the member's pension under the new public scheme must not exceed the tax which would have been charged in respect of that pension under that section had the pension been paid by the RMPP.

(3) For the purposes of this regulation, a "double taxation relief arrangement" means an arrangement that has effect under section 2(1) of the Taxation (International and Other Provisions) Act 2010.

24 Further protection in relation to changes to tax treatment of Accrued Rights as a result of the Transfer

(1) Paragraph 2 applies where—

(a) the Accrued Rights Transfer has resulted in the transfer from the RMPP to the new public scheme of Accrued Rights in respect of a member;

(b) as a result of the Transfer, there has been a change to the tax treatment of one or both of the following—

(i) those Accrued Rights under the new public scheme;

(ii) the member's rights under the RMPP; and

(c) no other provision in these Regulations applies to that change.

(2) The tax charged under the provisions in paragraph (3) in respect of the member's Accrued Rights under the new public scheme and the member's rights under the RMPP must not exceed the tax which would have been charged under those provisions in respect of those rights had the Transfer not taken place.

(3) The provisions are—

(a) section 208 (unauthorised payments charge);

(b) section 209 (unauthorised payments surcharge) in relation to surchargeable unauthorised member payments within the meaning of section 210;

(c) section 214 (lifetime allowance charge);

(d) section 227 (annual allowance charge); and

(e) Chapter 5A of Part 9 of the Income Tax (Earnings and Pensions) Act 2003.

PART 4

STAMP DUTY, STAMP DUTY LAND TAX AND STAMP DUTY RESERVE TAX

25 Stamp Duty

Stamp duty is not chargeable on an instrument making or executing the Assets Transfer.

26 Stamp Duty Land Tax

A land transaction entered into on, or in consequence of, or in connection with, the Assets Transfer is exempt from the charge to stamp duty land tax.

27 A land transaction entered into on, or in consequence of, or in connection with, the Assets Transfer is not a notifiable transaction within the meaning of section 77 of the Finance Act 2003.

28 Stamp Duty Reserve Tax

Stamp duty reserve tax is not chargeable on an agreement to transfer chargeable securities made in relation to, in connection with, or by or under, the Assets Transfer.

2012/822

INCOME TAX (PAY AS YOU EARN) (AMENDMENT) REGULATIONS 2012

Made . . . . *14th March 2012*
Laid before the House of Commons . . . . *15th March 2012*
Coming into force . . . . *6th April 2012*

The Commissioners for Her Majesty's Revenue and Customs make the following Regulations in exercise of the powers conferred by sections 59A(10), 59B(8), 98A and 113(1) of the Taxes Management Act 1970, section 133 of the Finance Act 1999, section 136 of the Finance Act 2002 and sections 684, 706, 707 and 710 of the Income Tax (Earnings and Pensions) Act 2003 and now exercisable by them:

PART 1
GENERAL

Note—Transitional provisions only are reproduced. Amendments made by these Regulations are already in force and have therefore not been reproduced.

1 Citation, commencement and interpretation

(1) These Regulations may be cited as the Income Tax (Pay As You Earn) (Amendment) Regulations 2012 and come into force on 6th April 2012.

(2) In these Regulations, "the 2003 Regulations" means the Income Tax (Pay As You Earn) Regulations 2003.

PART 2
REAL TIME INFORMATION

CHAPTER 1

AMENDMENTS TO THE 2003 REGULATIONS

(*amends* SI 2003/2682)

CHAPTER 2

TRANSITIONAL PROVISIONS

53 Information about employees

Subject to regulation 55, on becoming a Real Time Information employer, an employer must provide to HMRC the following information—

(a) the information specified in paragraphs 2 to 4 of Schedule A1 to the 2003 Regulations, as inserted by these Regulations,

(b) the income tax year in which the employer became a Real Time Information employer,

(c) the following information about each of the employer's employees during the tax year in which the employer became a Real Time Information employer—

(i) the employee's name,

(ii) the employee's date of birth,

(iii) the employee's current gender,

(iv) if known, the employee's national insurance number,

(v) the employee's address,

(vi) the number used by the employer to identify the employee, if any,

(vii) the date on which the employee's employment commenced, if that date is in the tax year in which the employer became a Real Time Information employer,

(viii) if applicable, the date on which the employee's employment ceased,

(ix) if applicable, an indication that an occupational pension is being paid to the employee and that the employer is the pension payer,

(x) if applicable, an indication that the employee is a seconded expatriate,

(xi) if applicable, an indication that relevant payments are made in respect of the employee to a person other than the employee,

[(xia) if applicable, an indication that payments are made to a person listed in paragraph 14A of Schedule A1 to the 2003 Regulations,][1]

(xii) if applicable, an indication that relevant payments are made to the employee on an irregular basis,

(xiii) the tax code operated on relevant payments made to the employee, and

(xiv) if applicable, an indication that the tax code operated on relevant payments made to the employee is operated on the non-cumulative basis.

Amendments—[1] Para (*c*)(xia) inserted by the Income Tax (Pay As You Earn) (Amendment) Regulations, SI 2013/521 regs 38, 39 with effect from 6 April 2013 in relation to the tax year 2013–14 and subsequent tax years.

54 Information about payments to employees

(1) Within one month of making the first return under regulation 67B or 67D of the 2003 Regulations . . . [1] a Real Time Information employer must provide to HMRC the information specified in paragraph (2) in respect of—

(a) each employee who has been employed in the tax year the return was made in but whose employment had ceased before the date on which the return was made, and

(b) each employee to whom relevant payments are made on an irregular basis and—

(i) in respect of whom information was not included on that return, and

(ii) to whom the employer does not expect to make a relevant payment within one month of making the return.

(2) The information specified in this paragraph is the information specified in paragraphs 2 to 4, 8 to 13, [14A,][1] 15 to 17 and 45 of Schedule A1 to the 2003 Regulations . . . [1].

Modification—Regulation 54 applies as if para (2) included a requirement to provide the information specified in the Social Security (Contributions) Regulations, SI 2001/1004 Sch 4A paras 6, 7, 10 and, if applicable, paras 5, 8, 9 (SI 2012/821 reg 15).

Amendments—[1] In para (1) words ", as inserted by these Regulations," revoked, and in para (2) words inserted and words ", as inserted by these Regulations" revoked, by the Income Tax (Pay As You Earn) (Amendment) Regulations, SI 2013/521 regs 38, 40 with effect from 6 April 2013 in relation to the tax year 2013–14 and subsequent tax years.

55 Provision of information under regulations 53 and 54

(1) If an employer is one to whom paragraph (3) applies, the information required by regulation 53 must be provided before the employer makes any returns under regulation 67B or 67D of the 2003 Regulations, as inserted by these Regulations.

(2) Any other employer may provide the information required by regulation 53 as part of the first return the employer makes under regulation 67B or 67D of the 2003 Regulations, as inserted by these Regulations.

(3) This paragraph applies to an employer who, on the day the employer becomes a Real Time Information employer, employs 250 or more employees.

(4) The information required by regulations 53 and 54 must be provided using an approved method of electronic communications unless the employer is one to whom regulation 67D of the 2003 Regulations, as inserted by these Regulations, applies in which case the information must be provided in the form specified by HMRC.

56 Postponement of first return under regulation 67B or 67D of the 2003 Regulations

(1) This regulation applies if a return due under regulation 67B or 67D of the 2003 Regulations, as inserted by these Regulations, is the first return made under either of those provisions by an employer.

(2) HMRC may notify the employer that the return must not be sent until such a date as HMRC notifies.

(3) If a second or subsequent return falls to be made by the employer under either of those provisions before the date notified by HMRC, it is also to be made on that date.

Modification—A notification under regulation 56 applies to returns under the Social Security (Contributions) Regulations, SI 2001/1004 Sch 4 paras 21A and 21D, as if they were returns under the Income Tax (Pay as You Earn) Regulations, SI 2003/2682 regs 67B (real time returns of information about relevant payments) and 67D (exceptions to regulation 67B) (SI 2012/821 reg 16).

57 Regulations 53 to 56: interpretation

Terms used in regulations 53 to 56 have the same meaning as they have in the 2003 Regulations, as amended by these Regulations.

2012/847

DATA-GATHERING POWERS (RELEVANT DATA) REGULATIONS 2012

Made . . . . *14 March 2012*

Coming into force . . . . *1 April 2012*

A draft of these Regulations was laid before, and approved by a resolution of, the House of Commons under paragraph 44(2) of Schedule 23 to the Finance Act 2011.

Accordingly the Treasury make the following Regulations in exercise of the power conferred by paragraph 1(3) of Schedule 23 to the Finance Act 2011.

1 Citation, commencement and interpretation

These Regulations may be cited as the Data-gathering Powers (Relevant Data) Regulations 2012 and come into force on 1st April 2012.

[2 In these Regulations—

"company registration number" has the same meaning as "registered number" in section 1066 of the Companies Act 2006;

"identifying information" means information which identifies a person or an account and includes—

(*a*) any unique or generic identifier or reference number allocated by, or used by, the data-holder for the purposes of identifying a person or account, or classifying the trade of a person or account;

(*b*) name, address (including email, website, and any other electronic address), and telephone number associated with a person or account;

(*c*) company registration number or national insurance number, unique taxpayer reference, VAT number, any other unique government-issued identifier associated with a person or account;

(*d*) in relation to a person, whether that person is an individual, partnership, limited company, or has any other legal status;

"Schedule 23" means Schedule 23 to the Finance Act 2011;

"VAT number" has the same meaning as "registration number" in paragraph (1) of regulation 2 of the Value Added Tax Regulations 1995.][1]

Amendments—[1] Regulation 2 substituted by the Data-gathering Powers (Relevant Data) (Amendment) Regulations, SI 2016/979 regs 2, 3 with effect from 1 November 2016.

3 Salaries, fees, commission etc

(1) The relevant data for a data-holder of the type described in paragraph 9(1)(*a*) of Schedule 23 are information relating to all payments made by the employer that relate to the employment (referred to in this regulation as "employment related payments").

(2) The relevant data for a data-holder of the type described in paragraph 9(1)(*b*) are information relating to payments by any other person who has made employment related payments to the employer's employees or to the employees of another person.

(3) Information relating to apportioned expenses incurred partly in respect of employment related payments and partly in, or in connection with, other matters are relevant data for the purposes of paragraph 9(1)(*a*) and 9(1)(*b*).

(4) The relevant data for a data-holder of the type described in paragraph 9(1)(*c*) are information and documents relating to the donations made under Part 12 of the Income Tax (Earnings and Pensions) Act 2003 (payroll giving).

(5) For the purposes of paragraph 9(1)(*d*) and, where relevant, paragraph 9(4)—

(a) the relevant data are information relating to relevant payments made in connection with a business, or a part of a business;

(b) particulars of the following payments are not relevant data—

(i) payments from which income tax is deductible; and

(ii) payments made to any one person where the total of those payments, particulars of which would otherwise fall to be provided, does not exceed £500.

4 The relevant data for a data-holder of the type described in paragraph 11 of Schedule 23 are the data described in paragraph 11(2)(*b*).

5 Interest etc

(1) The relevant data for a data-holder of the type described in paragraph 12 of Schedule 23 are information and documents relating to accounts or sums on which relevant interest is payable, including but not limited to the data in regulations 8, 9 and 10.

(2) "Relevant interest" means interest paid or credited—

(*a*) on money received or retained in the United Kingdom; and

(*b*) either without deduction of income tax or after deduction of income tax.

6 Information relating to the following payments is not relevant data for the purposes of a data-holder of the type described in paragraph 12—

(*a*) a payment in respect of a certificate of deposit within the meaning given by section 1019 of the Income Tax Act 2007;

(*b*) a payment in respect of an investment or a deposit held by a branch of a person to whom a data-holder notice is issued, where the branch is situated in a territory other than the United Kingdom;

(*c*) . . . [1]

(*d*) a payment in respect of an investment under a plan provided for by regulations made under Chapter 3 of Part 6 of the Income Tax (Trading and Other Income) Act 2005;

(*e*) a payment to or a receipt for a person other than an individual (in whatever capacity the individual is acting), except where the case falls within regulation 9(*c*) or 10(*d*) [or where the relevant data-holder is carrying on a trade or business and, in the ordinary course of the operations thereof, receives or retains money in such circumstances that interest becomes payable thereon][1];

(*f*) any other payment not falling within any of paragraphs (*a*) to (*e*) which is specified in the data-holder notice as being a payment in respect of which information is not required.

Amendments—[1] Para (*c*) revoked, and words in para (*e*) inserted, by the Data-gathering Powers (Relevant Data) (Amendment) Regulations, SI 2013/1811 regs 2, 3 with effect from 1 September 2013.

7 (1) Information is not relevant data for the purposes of a data-holder of the type described in paragraph 12 if it is in respect of a relevant dormant account before the balance of the account is paid out to the account-holder following a repayment claim (such payment being referred to in this regulation as the repayment claim being "settled").

(2) Where a repayment claim to the balance of a dormant account is settled, all interest paid, credited or included in the balance of the account, during and at the end of the relevant dormant period, is relevant data for the purposes of paragraph 12 and shall be treated—

(*a*) as paid at the time the repayment claim is settled; and

(*b*) as if the bank or building society in question had retained the balance of the account, in the ordinary course of the operations of its trade or business.

(3) If the data-holder notice specifies the year of assessment in which the relevant dormant period for any account ends, the notice shall (unless it states otherwise) be deemed to require as relevant data the inclusion of information for all relevant dormant accounts, in respect of which repayment claims were settled in that year.

(4) Information in respect of a relevant dormant account which, at the time it first became a relevant dormant account, was a plan provided for by regulations made under Chapter 3 of Part 6 of the Income Tax (Trading and Other Income) Act 2005 (individual investment plans) is not relevant data for the purpose of paragraph 12.

(5) In this regulation—

"relevant dormant account" has the meaning in section 39(2) of the Finance Act 2008;

"relevant dormant period" means the period between the time when a dormant account becomes a relevant dormant account and the time at which a repayment claim is settled; and

"repayment claim" means a repayment claim mentioned in section 5(6) of the Dormant Bank and Building Society Accounts Act 2008 ("the Dormant Accounts Act").

Other terms used have the same meaning as in the Dormant Accounts Act.

8 If a payment is made in circumstances in which a certificate has been supplied under regulation 4 of the Income Tax (Deposit-takers and Building Societies) (Interest Payments) Regulations 2008 . . .[1] the relevant data are—

(*a*) the name and address of the person or persons by or on behalf of whom a certificate has been given in connection with the payment ("the beneficiary") if other than the person or persons to whom the payment was made;

(*b*) the date of birth of the beneficiary;

(*c*) the national insurance number or tax identification number of the beneficiary (or confirmation that a national insurance number or tax identification number is not held) for any account in respect of which the payment was made opened on or after 6th April 2013, and for any account opened earlier if such number is provided to the deposit-taker or building society;

(*d*) notification of the fact that the account in respect of which the payment was made is or was one in connection with which a certificate or certificates had been given which had not ceased to be valid at the 5th April in the year in which the payment was made or at the date of closure of the account, if earlier in that year;

(*e*) the reference number of the account referred to in paragraph (*d*) and, where necessary for identifying the account, the branch of the payer where the account is held;

(*f*) where the payment was made to two or more account-holders each of whom was beneficially entitled to the payment, notification of that fact and, if known, the number of such persons;

(*g*) the national insurance numbers or tax identification numbers of persons referred to in paragraph (*f*) other than the beneficiary referred to in paragraphs (*b*) and (*c*) (or confirmation that a national insurance number or tax identification number is not held) for any account opened on or after 6th April 2013, and for any account opened earlier if such number is provided to the deposit-taker or building society;

(*h*) where a certificate was given by or on behalf of one, or more, but not all, of the persons referred to in paragraph (*f*) and had not ceased to be valid at the 5th April in the year in which the payment was made or at the date of closure of the account, if earlier in that year, notification of those facts;

(*i*) where the payment was the first payment made in respect of an account, notification of that fact;

(*j*) where the payment was in a currency other than sterling and the amount of the payment is recorded in that currency in the data provided under a data-holder notice notification of the fact that the amount is so recorded and the specification of the currency concerned.

Amendments—[1] Words revoked by the Data-gathering Powers (Relevant Data) (Amendment) Regulations, SI 2015/672 reg 2 with effect from 1 April 2015.

9 In cases to which regulation 8 does not apply, the relevant data relating to payments in respect of deposits are—

(*a*) the reference number of the account in respect of which a payment was made and, where necessary for identifying the account, the branch of the payer where the account is held;

(*b*) where a payment was made to two or more account holders, notification of that fact and, if known, the number of such persons;

(*c*) where the payment was made without deduction of tax by virtue of a declaration made after 5th April 2001 under section 858, 859, 860 or 861 of the Income Tax Act 2007—

(i) the name and principal residential address of the individual beneficially entitled to the payment or, if more than one, of each individual entitled to the payment; or

(ii) where the person beneficially entitled to the payment is a Scottish partnership, all the partners in which are individuals, the name and principal residential address of each of the partners;

(*d*) in a case falling within paragraph (c) notification of the fact that the account in respect of which the payment was made was one in respect of which a declaration had been made as mentioned in that paragraph;

(*e*) the national insurance number or tax identification number (or confirmation that a national insurance number or tax identification number is not held) of the person or, where paragraph (b) applies, each person to whom a payment was made for any account opened on or after 6th April 2013, and for any account opened earlier if such number is provided to the deposit-taker or building society;

(*f*) where a payment made in the course of the year was the first payment in respect of an account, notification of that fact;

(*g*) where a payment was in a currency other than sterling and the amount of the payment is recorded in that currency in the data provided under a data-holder notice notification of the fact that the amount is so recorded and the specification of the currency concerned.

10 In cases to which regulation 8 does not apply, the relevant data relating to payments and receipts of interest other than payments in respect of deposits are—

(*a*) identification of the security or investment in respect of which the payment was made or received;

(*b*) where a payment or receipt was in a currency other than sterling and the amount of the payment is recorded in that currency in the data provided under a data-holder notice notification of the fact that the amount is so recorded and the specification of the currency concerned;

(*c*) where a payment was made to, or the receipt was for, two or more persons, notification of that fact and, if known, the number of such persons;

(*d*) where a payment was made without deduction of tax by virtue of a declaration made under regulation 31 of the Authorised Investment Funds (Tax) Regulations 2006, the name and principal residential address of the person beneficially entitled to the payment, or if more than one, of each person beneficially entitled to the payment;

(*e*) in a case falling within paragraph (*d*), notification of the fact that the account in respect of which the payment was made was one in respect of which the declaration had been made.

11 Income, assets etc belonging to others

The relevant data for a data-holder of the type described in paragraph 13 of Schedule 23 are—

(*a*) information relating to the money or value received; and

(*b*) the name and address of the beneficial owner of the money or value.

[11A Merchant acquirers etc

(1) The relevant data for a data-holder of the type described in paragraph 13A of Schedule 23 are—

(*a*) in relation to a retailer, information relating to payment card transactions recorded against a merchant account, including the currency these payment card transactions were made in;

[(*b*) identifying information relating to a retailer to whom the data-holder has a contractual obligation to make payments, including any identifying information about the retailer's merchant account; and

(*c*) identifying information relating to an account or system into which payments are made by the data-holder to the retailer.][2]

(2) In this regulation—

"merchant account" means an account held by a retailer with the relevant data-holder, by reference to which the amount due to be paid by the relevant data-holder to the retailer in settlement of payment card transactions is calculated; and

. . . [2]

["payment card transaction" and "retailer" have the meanings given by paragraph 13A of Schedule 23.][2]][1]

Amendments—[1] Regulation 11A inserted by the Data-gathering Powers (Relevant Data) (Amendment) Regulations, SI 2013/1811 regs 2, 5 with effect from 1 September 2013.

[2] Para (1)(*b*), (*c*) substituted for para (1)(*b*)–(*f*), in para (2), definition of "VAT number" revoked, and words at the end inserted by the Data-gathering Powers (Relevant Data) (Amendment) Regulations, SI 2016/979 regs 2, 4 with effect from 1 November 2016.

[11B Electronic stored-value payment service providers

(1) The relevant data for a data-holder of the type described in paragraph 13B(*c*) of Schedule 23 are—

(*a*) in relation to a payment recipient, information relating to transactions, including the currency the transactions were made in;

(*b*) identifying information relating to a payment recipient; and (*c*) identifying information relating to an account or system into which payments are credited to, or on behalf of, a payment recipient by the data-holder.

(2) In this regulation—

"electronic stored-value payment services" has the meaning given by paragraph 13B of Schedule 23;

"payment recipient" means the recipient of a payment from a transaction for which the data-holder provided electronic stored-value payment services.][1]

Amendments—[1] Regulations 11B, 11C inserted by the Data-gathering Powers (Relevant Data) (Amendment) Regulations, SI 2016/979 regs 2, 5 with effect from 1 November 2016.

[11C Business intermediaries

(1) The relevant data for a data-holder of the type described in paragraph 13C(*d*) of Schedule 23 are—

(*a*) in relation to suppliers—

(i) information relating to transactions that the data-holder enabled or facilitated; and

(ii) information that the Commissioners consider is likely to assist them to quantify or otherwise determine the quantity or value of transactions of suppliers, whether or not the data-holder processed the payment for those transactions;

(*b*) identifying information relating to suppliers for whom the data-holder enables or facilitates transactions; and

(*c*) identifying information relating to an account or system into which payments are credited to, or on behalf of, suppliers by the data-holder.

(2) In this regulation "suppliers" has the meaning given by paragraph 13C of Schedule 23.][1]

Amendments—[1] Regulations 11B, 11C inserted by the Data-gathering Powers (Relevant Data) (Amendment) Regulations, SI 2016/979 regs 2, 5 with effect from 1 November 2016.

12 Payments derived from securities

The relevant data for a data-holder of the type described in paragraph 14 of Schedule 23 are—

(*a*) whether the relevant data-holder is the beneficial owner (or sole beneficial owner) of the securities or payment in question;

(*b*) if not—

(i) details of the beneficial owner (or other beneficial owners); and

(ii) if those details are not known or if different, details of the person for whom the securities are held or to whom the payment is or may be paid on; and

(*c*) if there is more than one beneficial owner or more than one person of the kind mentioned in paragraph (*b*)(ii), their respective interests in the securities or payment.

13 The relevant data for a data-holder of the type described in paragraph 15 of Schedule 23 are details of the amounts paid that were received from or paid on behalf of another person including the name and address of each such person.

14 Grants and subsidies out of public funds

The relevant data for a data-holder of the type described in paragraph 16 of Schedule 23 are—

(*a*) the name and address of the person to whom the payment has been made or on whose behalf the payment has been received;

(*b*) the amount of the payment so made or received; and

(*c*) the address of any property in respect of which the payment has been made.

15 Licences, approvals etc

The relevant data for a data-holder of the type described in paragraph 17 of Schedule 23 are—

(*a*) the name and address of anyone who is or has been the holder of a licence or approval or to whom an entry in the register relates or related;

(*b*) particulars of the licence, approval or entry;

(*c*) information relating to any application for such a licence or approval or for entry on that register.

16 Rent and other payments arising from land

(1) The relevant data for a data-holder of the type described in paragraph 18 of Schedule 23 are—

(*a*) information relating to the terms applying to the lease, occupation or use of land;

(*b*) information relating to any consideration given for the grant or assignment of the tenancy;

(*c*) information relating to any person on whose behalf the land is managed or the payments received, including particulars of payments arising from the land.

(2) In this regulation—

(*a*) "lease" includes an agreement for a lease, and any tenancy, but does not include a mortgage or heritable security;

(*b*) "lessee" includes a successor in title of a lease; and
(*c*) in relation to Scotland, "assignment" means an assignation.

17 Dealing etc in securities

(1) The relevant data for a data-holder of the type described in paragraph 19 of Schedule 23 are—
(*a*) information and documents relating to securities transactions in respect of which that person is a relevant data-holder; and
(*b*) in relation to a person who carries on a business of effecting public issues or placings or otherwise effects public issues or placings, information relating to the issue, allotment or placing of the public issues or placings.

(2) In this regulation—
(*a*) "placing" means a placing of shares or securities in a company; and
(*b*) "public issue" means a public issue of shares or securities in a company.

18 Dealing in other property

The relevant data for a data-holder of the type described in paragraph 20 of Schedule 23 are—
(*a*) particulars of any transactions effected through a clearing house;
(*b*) particulars of any transaction which meets the following conditions—
(i) the transaction is effected by or through that person;
(ii) in the transaction, an asset which is tangible moveable property is disposed of; and
(iii) the amount or value of the consideration for the disposal exceeds, in the hands of the recipient, £6,000.

19 Lloyd's

The relevant data for a data-holder of the type described in paragraph 21 of Schedule 23 are information and documents relating to, and to the activities of, the syndicate of underwriting members of Lloyd's.

20 Investment plans etc

The relevant data for a data-holder of the type described in paragraph 22 of Schedule 23 are—
(*a*) information and documents relating to the plan, including investments which are or have been held under the plan;
(*b*) information and documents relating to the child trust fund including investments which are or have been held under the fund.

21 Petroleum activities

The relevant data for a data-holder of the type described in paragraph 23 of Schedule 23 are—
(*a*) particulars of transactions in connection with any activities authorised by a petroleum licence as a result of which any person is or might be liable to tax by virtue of section 276 of the Taxation of Chargeable Gains Act 1992, section 1313 of the Corporation Tax Act 2009 or section 874 of the Income Tax (Trading and Other Income) Act 2005;
(*b*) particulars of earnings or money treated as earnings, which constitute employment income (see section 7(2)(*a*) or (*b*) of the Income Tax (Earnings and Pensions) Act 2003) or other payments paid or payable in respect of duties or services performed in an area in which those activities may be carried on under the petroleum licence;
(*c*) particulars of the persons to whom such earnings, money or other payments were paid and are payable;
(*d*) information and documents relating to the oil field.

22 Insurance activities

The relevant data for a data-holder of the type described in paragraph 24 of Schedule 23 are—
(*a*) information and documents relating to contracts of insurance entered into in the course of an insurance business;
(*b*) if paragraph 24(*b*) or (*c*) applies, information and documents relating to the contracts of insurance.

23 Environmental activities

The relevant data for a data-holder of the type described in paragraph 25 of Schedule 23 are—
(*a*) information and documents relating to aggregates levy matters in which the person is or has been involved;
(*b*) information and documents relating to climate change levy matters in which the person is or has been involved;
(*c*) information and documents relating to any landfill disposal.

24 Settlements

The relevant data for a data-holder of the type described in paragraph 26 of Schedule 23 are information and documents relating to the settlement in question and to income or gains arising to the settlement.

25 Charities

The relevant data for a data-holder of the type described in paragraph 27 of Schedule 23 are information relating to donations to the charity that are eligible for tax relief under any of the following provisions—

(*a*) section 257 of the Taxation of Chargeable Gains Act 1992 (gifts to charities etc);

(*b*) section 63(2)(*a*) or (*aa*) of the Capital Allowances Act 2001(cases in which disposal value is nil);

(*c*) Part 12 of the Income Tax (Earnings and Pensions) Act 2003 (payroll giving);

(*d*) section 108 of the Income Tax (Trading and Other Income) Act 2005 (gifts of trading stock to charities etc);

(*e*) Chapter 2 or 3 of Part 8 of the Income Tax Act 2007 (gift aid, gifts of shares, securities and real property to charities etc);

(*f*) section 105 of the Corporation Tax Act 2009 (gifts of trading stock to charities etc); and

(*g*) Part 6 of the Corporation Tax Act 2010 (charitable donations relief).

2012/1258

FINANCE ACT 2004, SECTION 180(5) (MODIFICATION) REGULATIONS 2012

Made . . . . *10th May 2012*
Laid before the House of Commons . . . . *11th May 2012*
Coming into force . . . . *1st June 2012*

The Treasury, in exercise of the power conferred by section 70 of the Finance Act 2011, make the following Regulations:

1 Citation, commencement and effect

(1) These Regulations may be cited as the Finance Act 2004, Section 180(5) (Modification) Regulations 2012 and come into force on 1st June 2012.

(2) Regulation 2 has effect in relation to any payments made on or after 6th April 2012.

2 Disregard of section 180(5)(*b*) of the Finance Act 2004

In its application to a pension scheme established under section 67 of the Pensions Act 2008 (duty on Secretary of State to establish a pension scheme), section 180 of the Finance Act 2004 (scheme administration employer payments) has effect as if subsection (5)(*b*) were omitted.

2012/1709

BRITISH WATERWAYS BOARD (TAX CONSEQUENCES) ORDER 2012

Made . . . . *at 12 noon on 2nd July 2012*
Laid before the House of Commons . . . . *at 3 pm on 2nd July 2012*
Coming into force . . . . *at 3.30 pm on 2nd July 2012*

The Treasury make the following Order in exercise of the powers conferred by section 25 of the Public Bodies Act 2011.

1 Citation and commencement

This Order may be cited as the British Waterways Board (Tax Consequences) Order 2012 and comes into force at 3.30 pm on 2nd July 2012.

2 Interpretation

In this Order—

"TCGA 1992" means the Taxation of Chargeable Gains Act 1992;

"CAA 2001" means the Capital Allowances Act 2001;

"CTA 2009" means the Corporation Tax Act 2009;

"BWB" means the British Waterways Board;

"CRT" means the Canal & River Trust, company registration number 07807276;

"CRT CIC" means the Canal & River Trading CIC, company registration number 08069602;

"relevant transfer" means—

(a) a transfer of property, rights and liabilities from BWB to CRT, or

(b) a transfer of property, rights and liabilities from BWB to CRT CIC,

by, or under, the British Waterways Board Transfer Scheme 2012.

3 Capital allowances: transfer of a trade

(1) This article applies where BWB is carrying on a trade and, as a result of a relevant transfer—

(a) BWB ceases to carry on that trade, and

(b) CRT or CRT CIC begins to carry on that trade.

(2) For the purposes of the allowances and charges provided for by CAA 2001, the trade is not to be treated as permanently discontinued, nor a new trade as set up; but paragraphs (3) and (4) are to apply.

(3) There are to be made to or on CRT, or CRT CIC, in accordance with CAA 2001, all such allowances and charges as would, if BWB had continued to carry on the trade, have fallen to be made to or on BWB.

(4) The amounts of those allowances and charges are to be computed as if—

(a) CRT or CRT CIC had been carrying on the trade since BWB began to do so, and

(b) everything done to or by BWB had been done to or by CRT or CRT CIC,

but so that a relevant transfer, so far it relates to assets in use for the purposes of the trade, is not treated as giving rise to an allowance or charge.

4 Capital allowances: transfer involving part of a trade

(1) Where BWB is carrying on a trade and, as a result of a relevant transfer—

(a) BWB ceases to carry on that trade, and

(b) CRT or CRT CIC begins to carry on activities of that trade as part of a trade carried on by it,

then that part of the trade carried on by CRT, or CRT CIC, is treated for the purposes of article 3 as a separate trade.

(2) Where BWB is carrying on a trade and, as a result of a relevant transfer—

(a) BWB ceases to carry on a part of that trade, and

(b) CRT or CRT CIC begins to carry on activities of that part of that trade,

then BWB is treated for the purposes of article 3 and paragraph (1) as having carried on that part of its trade as a separate trade.

(3) Where activities fall to be treated under this article as a separate trade, such apportionments of receipts, expenses, assets and liabilities are to be made for the purposes of CAA 2001 as may be just and reasonable.

5 Chargeable gains: no gain or loss on disposal

(1) For the purposes of TCGA 1992, a disposal constituted by a relevant transfer is to be treated in relation to BWB and CRT, or CRT CIC, as made for a consideration such that no gain or loss accrues to BWB.

(2) For the purposes of any tax provision, paragraph (1) is to be treated as one of the no gain/no loss provisions in section 288(3A) of TCGA 1992 (meaning of "the no gain/no loss provisions").

6 Corporation tax: computation of profits and losses in respect of transfer of trade

(1) This article applies where BWB is carrying on a trade or part of a trade and, as a result of a relevant transfer—

(a) BWB ceases to carry on that trade or part of a trade, and

(b) CRT or CRT CIC begins to carry on that trade or part.

(2) For the purposes of computing, in relation to the time when a relevant transfer takes effect and at subsequent times, the relevant trading profits or losses of BWB and CRT, or CRT CIC,—

(a) the trade or part is to be treated as having been a separate trade at the time of its commencement and as having been carried on by CRT or CRT CIC at all times since its commencement as a separate trade, and

(b) the trade carried on by CRT or CRT CIC after the time when a relevant transfer takes effect is to be treated as the same trade as that which CRT or CRT CIC is treated, by virtue of sub-paragraph (a), as having carried on as a separate trade before that time.

(3) Where a trade or part of a trade falls to be treated under this article as a separate trade, such apportionments of receipts, expenses, assets, and liabilities are to be made for the purposes of computing relevant trading profits or losses as may be just and reasonable.

(4) In this article "relevant trading profits or losses" means profits or losses under Part 3 of CTA 2009 in respect of the trade or part of a trade in question.

7 Corporation tax: loan relationships

(1) For the purposes of Part 5 of CTA 2009 (loan relationships), in relation to a relevant transfer, BWB and CRT, or CRT CIC, are to be treated as if, for the purposes of the transfer, they were members of the same group.

(2) In paragraph (1) the reference to being members of the same group is to be read in accordance with section 335(6) of that Act.

8 Stamp duty

Stamp duty is not chargeable on an instrument making or executing a relevant transfer.

9 Stamp duty land tax

(1) A land transaction entered into on, or in consequence of, or in connection with, a relevant transfer is exempt from the charge to stamp duty land tax.

(2) Where in the case of a transaction ("the relevant transaction") that is exempt by virtue of paragraph (1) ("the exemption")—

(a) a disqualifying event occurs—

(i) before the end of the period of three years beginning with the effective date of the relevant transaction, or

(ii) in pursuance of, or in connection with, arrangements made before the end of that period,

and

(b) at the time of the disqualifying event CRT, or CRT CIC, holds a chargeable interest—

(i) that was acquired by CRT, or CRT CIC, under the relevant transaction, or

(ii) that is derived from such an interest so acquired,

the exemption in relation to the relevant transaction is withdrawn in whole, or in an appropriate proportion in the case of CRT where applicable, and tax is chargeable in accordance with paragraph (3).

(3) The amount chargeable is the amount—

(a) that would have been chargeable on CRT or CRT CIC in respect of the relevant transaction but for the exemption, or

(b) in the case of CRT where applicable, an appropriate proportion of the tax that would have been so chargeable.

(4) For the purposes of paragraph (2) a "disqualifying event" means—

(a) for a relevant transaction involving either CRT or CRT CIC—

(i) CRT ceasing to be established for charitable purposes only, or

(ii) the subject matter of the relevant transaction, or any interest or right derived from it, being used or held by CRT otherwise than for qualifying charitable purposes;

(b) for a relevant transaction involving CRT CIC, it ceasing to be a wholly-owned subsidiary of CRT.

(5) For the purposes of sub-paragraph (a) of paragraph (2) "effective date" has the same meaning as in section 119 of the Finance Act 2003.

(6) For the purposes of this article—

(a) "appropriate proportion" means an appropriate proportion having regard to—

(i) what was acquired by CRT under the relevant transaction and what is held by CRT at the time of the disqualifying event, and

(ii) the extent to which what is held by CRT at that time becomes used or held for purposes other than qualifying charitable purposes;

(b) "qualifying charitable purposes" has the same meaning as in paragraph 1(2) of Schedule 8 to the Finance Act 2003 and references to "purchaser" are to be read as references to CRT.

2012/1836

TAX AVOIDANCE SCHEMES (INFORMATION) REGULATIONS 2012

Made . . . . *12th July 2012*

Laid before the House of Commons . . . . *13th July 2012*

Coming into force . . . . *1st September 2012*

The Commissioners for Her Majesty's Revenue and Customs in exercise of the powers conferred by section 98C(2A),(2B) and (2C)(b) of the Taxes Management Act 1970, section 132 of the Finance Act 1999, section 135 of the Finance Act 2002 and sections 306A(6), 307(5), 308(1) and (3), 308A(5) and (6)(a), 309(1), 310, 312(2) and (5), 312A(2) and (5), 313(1) and (3), 313ZA(3) and (4), 313A(4)(a), 313B(2)(a), 313C(1) and (3)(a), 317(2) and 318(1) of the Finance Act 2004, make the following Regulations:

Note—NIC (Application of Part 7 of the Finance Act 2004) Regulations, SI 2012/1868 reg 26(1) (any reference in these Regulations to FA 2004 ss 306–313C and s 314A shall be construed as a reference to the corresponding provision of the NIC (Application of Part 7 of the Finance Act 2004) Regulations, SI 2012/1868, and any reference in these Regulations to TMA 1970 s 98C shall be construed as a reference to SI 2012/1868 reg 22.)

Press releases—HMRC Issue Briefing—Tackling tax avoidance. 6 September 2012 (see Simon's Weekly Tax Intelligence 2012, Issue 36).

1 Citation and commencement

These Regulations may be cited as the Tax Avoidance Schemes (Information) Regulations 2012 and shall come into force on 1st September 2012.

2 Interpretation

(1) In these Regulations a reference to a numbered section (without more) is a reference to the section of the Finance Act 2004 which is so numbered.

(2) In these Regulations—

"employment" has the same meaning as it has for the purposes of the employment income Parts of the Income Tax (Earnings and Pensions) Act 2003 (see section 4 of that Act) and includes offices to which the provisions of those Parts that are expressed to apply to employments apply equally (see section 5 of that Act); and "employee" and "employer" have corresponding meanings;

"the filing date" is—

(a) whichever date in regulation 12(4)(a) to (c) applies to the relevant return or in the case of inheritance tax the last day of the period mentioned in regulation 9(5)(b); or

(b) in the case of regulation 10(7) the date by which the relevant return is required to be delivered;

["the prescribed taxes" means capital gains tax, corporation tax, income tax, inheritance tax, stamp duty land tax and annual tax on enveloped dwellings.][1]

(3) In reckoning any period under regulation 5 (apart from paragraph (8)), or regulations [8A, 13A,][2] 14, 15 and 16, any day which is a non-business day within the meaning of section 92 of the Bills of Exchange Act 1882 (computation of time) shall be disregarded.

(4) In regulations 10(2) and (3), 11(4) and 12(2) expressions which are used in Part 4 of the Finance Act 2003 have the same meaning as in that Part.

Modifications—See the National Insurance Contributions (Application of Part 7 of the Finance Act 2004) Regulations, SI 2012/1868 reg 26(1), (2) for the modification of this regulation is its applications to notifiable contribution arrangements and notifiable contribution proposals.

Amendments—[1] In para (2), definition of "the prescribed taxes" substituted by the Tax Avoidance Schemes (Information) (Amendment, etc) Regulations, SI 2013/2592 regs 3, 4 with effect from 4 November 2013. That definition previously read '"the prescribed taxes" means capital gains tax, corporation tax, income tax, inheritance tax and stamp duty land tax.'.

[2] Words in para (3) inserted by the Tax Avoidance Schemes (Information) (Amendment, etc) Regulations, SI 2013/2592 regs 3, 15 with effect from 4 November 2013.

3 Revocations

(1) The Regulations described in the Schedule to these Regulations are revoked.

(2) Anything begun under or for the purpose of any Regulations revoked by these Regulations shall be continued under or, as the case may be, for the purpose of the corresponding provision of these Regulations.

(3) Where any document refers to a provision of a regulation revoked by these Regulations, such reference shall, unless the context otherwise requires, be construed as a reference to the corresponding provision of these Regulations.

4 Prescribed information in respect of notifiable proposals and arrangements

(1) The information which must be provided to HMRC by a promoter under section 308(1) or (3) (duties of promoter) in respect of a notifiable proposal or notifiable arrangements is sufficient information as might reasonably be expected to enable an officer of HMRC to comprehend the manner in which the proposal or arrangements are intended to operate, including—

(a) the promoter's name and address;

(b) details of the provision of the Arrangements Regulations, [the ATED Arrangements Regulations,][1] the IHT Arrangements Regulations or the SDLT Arrangements Regulations by virtue of which the arrangements or the proposed arrangements are notifiable;

(c) a summary of the arrangements or proposed arrangements and the name (if any) by which they are known;

(d) information explaining each element of the arrangements or proposed arrangements (including the way in which they are structured) from which the tax advantage expected to be obtained under those arrangements arises; and

(e) the statutory provisions, relating to any of the prescribed taxes, on which that tax advantage is based.

(2) The information which must be provided to HMRC by a client under section 309 (duty of person dealing with promoter outside the United Kingdom) in respect of notifiable arrangements is sufficient information as might reasonably be expected to enable an officer of HMRC to comprehend the manner in which the arrangements are intended to operate, including—

(a) the client's name and address;

(b) the name and address of the promoter;

(c) details of the provision of the Arrangements Regulations, [the ATED Arrangements Regulations,][1] the IHT Arrangements Regulations or the SDLT Arrangements Regulations by virtue of which the arrangements are notifiable;

(d) a summary of the arrangements, and the name (if any) by which they are known;

(e) information explaining each element of the arrangements (including the way in which they are structured) from which the tax advantage expected to be obtained under the arrangements arises; and
(f) the statutory provisions, relating to any of the prescribed taxes, on which that tax advantage is based.

(3) The information which must be provided to HMRC by a person obliged to do so by section 310 (duty of parties to notifiable arrangements not involving promoter) is sufficient information as might reasonably be expected to enable an officer of HMRC to comprehend the manner in which the arrangements of which that transaction forms part are intended to operate, including—
(a) the name and address of the person entering into the transaction;
(b) details of the provision of the Arrangements Regulations, [the ATED Arrangements Regulations,][1] the IHT Arrangements Regulations or the SDLT Arrangements Regulations by virtue of which the arrangements are notifiable;
(c) a summary of the arrangements and the name (if any) by which they are known;
(d) information explaining each element of the arrangements (including the way in which they are structured) from which the tax advantage expected to be obtained under the arrangements arises; and
(e) the statutory provisions, relating to any of the prescribed taxes, on which that tax advantage is based.

(4) If, but for this paragraph—
(a) a person would be obliged to provide information in relation to two or more notifiable arrangements,
(b) those arrangements are substantially the same (whether they relate to the same parties or different parties), and
(c) the person has already provided information under paragraph (2) or (3) in relation to any of the other arrangements,

the person need not provide further information under paragraph (2) or (3).

(5) In this regulation—

"the Arrangements Regulations" means the Tax Avoidance Schemes (Prescribed Descriptions of Arrangements) Regulations 2006;

["the ATED Arrangements Regulations" means the Annual Tax on Enveloped Dwellings Avoidance Schemes (Prescribed Descriptions of Arrangements) Regulations 2013;][1]

"the IHT Arrangements Regulations" means the Inheritance Tax Avoidance Schemes (Prescribed Descriptions of Arrangements) Regulations 2011;

"the SDLT Arrangements Regulations" means the Stamp Duty Land Tax Avoidance Schemes (Prescribed Descriptions of Arrangements) Regulations 2005.

Modifications—See the National Insurance Contributions (Application of Part 7 of the Finance Act 2004) Regulations, SI 2012/1868 reg 26(1), (3) for the modification of this regulation is its applications to notifiable contribution arrangements and notifiable contribution proposals.

Amendments—[1] In paras (1)(*b*), (2)(*c*), (3)(*b*), words inserted, and in para (5) definition of "the ATED Arrangements Regulations" inserted, by the Tax Avoidance Schemes (Information) (Amendment, etc) Regulations, SI 2013/2592 regs 3, 5–8 with effect from 4 November 2013.

5 Time for providing information under section 308, 308A, 309 or 310

(1) The period or time (as the case may be) within which—
(a) the prescribed information under section 308, 309 or 310, and
(b) the information or documents which will support or explain the prescribed information under section 308A (supplemental information),

must be provided to HMRC is found in accordance with the following paragraphs of this regulation.

(2) Where a proposal or arrangements (not being otherwise notifiable) is or are treated as notifiable by virtue of an order under section 306A(1) (doubt as to notifiability) the prescribed period is the period of 10 days beginning on the day after that on which the order is made.

(3) In the case of a requirement to provide specified information about, or documents relating to, the notifiable proposal or arrangements which arises by virtue of an order under section 308A(2), the prescribed period is the period of 10 days beginning on the day after that on which the order is made.

(4) In any other case of a notification under section 308(1), the prescribed period is the period of 5 days beginning on the day after the relevant date.

(5) In any other case of a notification under section 308(3), the prescribed period is the period of 5 days beginning on the day after that on which the promoter first becomes aware of any transaction forming part of arrangements to which that subsection applies.

(6) In the case of a notification under section 309(1), the prescribed period is the period of 5 days beginning on the day after that on which the client enters into the first transaction forming part of notifiable arrangements to which that subsection applies.

(7) In the case of a notification under section 310 which arises by virtue of the application of regulation 6 of the Tax Avoidance Schemes (Promoters and Prescribed Circumstances) Regulations 2004 (persons not to be treated as promoters: legal professional privilege), the prescribed time is any time during the period of 5 days beginning on the day after that on which the person enters into the first transaction forming part of the notifiable arrangements.

(8) In any other case of a notification under section 310 the prescribed time is any time during the period of 30 days beginning on the day after that on which the person enters into the first transaction forming part of the notifiable arrangements.

Modifications—NIC (Application of Part 7 of the Finance Act 2004) Regulations, SI 2012/1868 reg 26(4) (this reg modified in relation to NIC avoidance schemes and proposals).

The Tax Avoidance Schemes (Information) (Amendment, etc) Regulations, SI 2013/2592 reg 2. In respect of proposals or arrangements that are notifiable by virtue of the Annual Tax on Enveloped Dwellings Avoidance Schemes (Prescribed Descriptions of Arrangements) Regulations, SI 2013/2571 reg 4, where—

- for the purposes of FA 2004 s 308(1) the relevant date in relation to a proposal falls within the period beginning with 31 January 2013 and ending on 3 November 2013, or
- for the purposes of FA 2004 s 308(3) the date on which the promoter first becomes aware of any transaction forming part of the arrangements falls within the period beginning with 31 January 2013 and ending on 3 November 2013,

the period, or time, to be found in accordance with this regulation shall end on 17 January 2014 instead of the day on which it would otherwise end by virtue of this regulation.

6 Prescribed information under sections 312 and 312A

For the purposes of sections 312(2) and (5) (duty of promoter to notify client of number) and 312A(2) [and (2A) (duty of client to provide information to parties)][1] the prescribed information is—

(a) the name and address of the promoter;

(b) the name, or a brief description of the notifiable arrangements or proposal;

(c) the reference number (or if more than one, any one reference number) allocated by HMRC under section 311 (arrangements to be given reference number) to the notifiable arrangements or proposed notifiable arrangements;

(d) the date that the reference number was—

(i) sent by the promoter to the client; or (as the case may be)

(ii) sent to any other person by the client under section 312A(2) [or (2A)][1].

Amendments—[1] Words substituted for words"(duty of client to notify parties of number)", and in para (*d*)(ii), words inserted by the Tax Avoidance Schemes (Information) (Amendment) Regulations, SI 2015/948 regs 2, 3 with effect from 16 April 2015.

7 Time for providing information under section 312A

In the case of a notification under section 312A(2) [or (2A)][1] the prescribed period is the period of 30 days beginning on—

(a) the day on which the client first becomes aware of any transaction forming part of notifiable arrangements or proposed notifiable arrangements; or, if later,

(b) the day on which the prescribed information is notified to the client by the promoter under section 312.

Modification—NIC (Application of Part 7 of the Finance Act 2004) Regulations, SI 2012/1868 reg 26(5) (this reg modified in relation to NIC avoidance schemes and proposals).

Amendments—[1] Words inserted by the Tax Avoidance Schemes (Information) (Amendment) Regulations, SI 2015/948 regs 2, 4 with effect from 16 April 2015.

8 Exemption from duty under section 312A

The duty of a client to notify other persons under section 312A(2) does not apply to an employer of an employee where the employee by reason of employment receives or expects to receive a tax advantage in respect of income tax or capital gains tax as a result of notifiable arrangements or proposed notifiable arrangements.[1]

Modification—NIC (Application of Part 7 of the Finance Act 2004) Regulations, SI 2012/1868 reg 26(6) (this reg modified in relation to NIC avoidance schemes and proposals).

Amendments—[1] Regulation 8 revoked by the Tax Avoidance Schemes (Information) (Amendment) Regulations, SI 2015/948 regs 2, 5 with effect from 16 April 2015.

[8A Prescribed information under section 312B: information and timing

(1) For the purposes of section 312B (duty of client to provide information to promoter)—

(a) the prescribed period is 10 days from the later of the date that the client receives the reference number allocated by HMRC under section 311 to the notifiable arrangements, and the date the client first enters into a transaction which forms part of the notifiable arrangements; and

(b) the prescribed information is—

(i) any identification number allocated to the client by HMRC ("unique taxpayer number") and the client's national insurance number; or

(ii) confirmation that the client does not have a unique taxpayer number or a national insurance number or has neither number.][1]

Amendments—[1] Reg 8A inserted by the Tax Avoidance Schemes (Information) (Amendment, etc) Regulations, SI 2013/2592 regs 3, 16 with effect from 4 November 2013.

[8B Exemption from duty under section 313

Where an employee receives prescribed information from an employer under section 312A(2) or (2A) in circumstances where the employer has a duty to notify HMRC under section 313ZC in respect of that employee, then no duty arises under section 313(1) in respect of that employee.][1]

Amendments—[1] Regulation 8B inserted by the Tax Avoidance Schemes (Information) (Amendment) Regulations, SI 2015/948 regs 2, 6 with effect from 16 April 2015.

9 Prescribed cases under section 313(3)(a)

(1) The prescribed cases for the purposes of section 313(3)(a) (cases in which the information is to be included in returns) are as follows.

(2) Subject to regulation [10(7)][2] and (8), in the case of a person who—

(a) expects an advantage to arise in respect of that person's liability to pay, entitlement to a repayment of, or to a deferment of the liability to pay, income tax or capital gains tax as a result of notifiable arrangements; and

(b) is required to make a return to HMRC by a notice under section 8 or 8A of the Taxes Management Act 1970 (income tax and capital gains tax: personal return and trustee's return), in respect of income tax or capital gains tax,

the prescribed information shall be included in the return (under the section which applies) which relates to the year of assessment in which the person first enters into a transaction forming part of the notifiable arrangements and in the return for each subsequent year of assessment until the advantage ceases to apply to that person.

(3) Subject to regulation [10(7)][2] and (8) in the case of a company which—

(a) expects a tax advantage to arise in respect of its liability to pay, entitlement to a repayment of, or to a deferment of its liability to pay, corporation tax as a result of notifiable arrangements; and

(b) is required to make a return to HMRC by a notice under paragraph 3 of Schedule 18 to the Finance Act 1998 (company tax return), in respect of corporation tax,

the prescribed information shall be included in the return under that paragraph covering the period in which the company first enters into a transaction forming part of the notifiable arrangements and in the return covering each subsequent period until the tax advantage ceases to apply to the company.

(4) Subject to regulation [10(7)][2] and (8) in the case of a partnership—

(a) which expects an advantage to arise in respect of a partner's liability to pay, entitlement to a repayment of, or to a deferment of the liability to pay income tax, capital gains tax or corporation tax in respect of partnership profits or gains as a result of notifiable arrangements; and

(b) in respect of which a return is required to be made to HMRC by virtue of a notice under section 12AA of the Taxes Management Act 1970 (partnership return) in respect of income tax, capital gains tax or corporation tax,

in addition to any duty under paragraph (2) or (3) the prescribed information shall be included in the return under that section covering the period in which the partnership first enters into a transaction forming part of the notifiable arrangements and in the returns covering each subsequent period until the tax advantage ceases to apply to the partner in question.

(5) Subject to regulation 10(7) and (8) in the case of a person who—

(a) expects an advantage to arise in respect of that person's liability to pay, entitlement to a repayment of, or to a deferment of the liability to pay inheritance tax as a result of notifiable arrangements; and

(b) is required to make a return to HMRC under section 216 of the Inheritance Tax Act 1984 (accounts and information) in respect of a transaction forming part of the notifiable arrangements within a period of 12 months from the end of the month in which the first transaction forming part of the arrangements is entered into,

the prescribed information shall be included in the return under that section.

[(6) Subject to regulation 10(7) and (8) in the case of a person who—

(a) expects an advantage to arise in respect of that person's liability to pay, entitlement to a repayment of, or deferment of the liability to pay, annual tax on enveloped dwellings as a result of notifiable arrangements; and

(b) is required to make a return to HMRC under section 159 of the Finance Act 2013 in respect of annual tax on enveloped dwellings;

the prescribed information shall be included in the return under that section.][1]

Modifications—See the National Insurance Contributions (Application of Part 7 of the Finance Act 2004) Regulations, SI 2012/1868 reg 26(1), (7) for the modification of this regulation is its applications to notifiable contribution arrangements and notifiable contribution proposals.

Amendments—[1] Para (6) inserted by the Tax Avoidance Schemes (Information) (Amendment, etc) Regulations, SI 2013/2592 regs 3, 9 with effect from 4 November 2013.

[2] In paras (2), (3), (4), reference substituted for reference "10(4), (7)" by the Tax Avoidance Schemes (Information) (Amendment) Regulations, SI 2015/948 regs 2, 7 with effect from 16 April 2015.

10 Prescribed cases under section 313(3)(b)

(1) The prescribed cases for the purposes of section 313(3)(b) (cases in which the information is to be provided separately) are as follows.

(2) In a case where a purchaser expects an advantage to arise in respect of that person's liability to pay, entitlement to a repayment of, or to a deferment of the liability to pay stamp duty land tax as a result of notifiable arrangements the prescribed information shall be provided separately to HMRC in such form and manner as they may specify.

(3) If paragraph (2) applies in relation to a land transaction entered into as purchaser by or on behalf of a partnership notification of the prescribed information by or in relation to the responsible partners may instead be done by or in relation to a representative partner or partners.

(4) . . . [2]

(5) In the case of a person who would be obliged to comply with a duty under regulation 9(2) to (4), but is not required, in respect of a year of assessment, accounting period or tax year—

(a) in the case of notifiable arrangements to which regulation 9(2) applies, to make a return under either of the provisions referred to in regulation 9(2)(b);

(b) in the case of notifiable arrangements to which regulation 9(3) applies, to make a return under the provision referred to in regulation 9(3)(b); or

(c) in the case of notifiable arrangements to which regulation 9(4) applies, to make a return under the provision referred to in regulation 9(4)(b);

the prescribed information shall be provided separately to HMRC in such form and manner as they may specify.

(6) In the case of a person who—

(a) expects an advantage to arise in respect of that person's liability to pay, entitlement to a repayment of, or to a deferment of the liability to pay inheritance tax as a result of notifiable arrangements; and

(b) is not required to make a return to HMRC under section 216 of the Inheritance Tax Act 1984 in respect of a transaction forming part of the notifiable arrangements within a period of 12 months from the end of the month in which the first transaction forming part of the arrangements is entered into,

the prescribed information shall be provided separately to HMRC in such form and manner as they may specify.

[(6A) In the case of a person who—

(a) expects an advantage to arise in respect of that person's liability to pay, entitlement to a repayment of, or deferment of the liability to pay, annual tax on enveloped dwellings as a result of notifiable arrangements; and

(b) is not required to make a return to HMRC under section 159 of the Finance Act 2013 in respect of a transaction forming part of the notifiable arrangements within a period of 30 days beginning with the later of—

(i) the effective date of the first transaction which forms part of the arrangements; or

(ii) the date of the receipt of the reference number allocated under the provisions of section 311;

the prescribed information shall be provided separately to HMRC.][1]

(7) In a case of a person who would, but for this paragraph, be obliged to comply with a duty under regulation 9 and—

(a) the relevant return is not delivered by the filing date; or

(b) the relevant return is delivered by the filing date but does not include the prescribed information;

the prescribed information shall be provided separately to HMRC in such form and manner as they may specify.

(8) In a case where—

(a) a person is required to provide information relating to more than one reference number;

(b) the information is included in a return under regulation 9; and

(c) the number of reference numbers in relation to which information is required exceeds the number of spaces allocated to the information on the return form;

the information relating to so many of the reference numbers as exceeds the number of allocated spaces shall be provided separately to HMRC in such form and manner as they may specify.

(9) In addition to the duty under any other paragraph above, or regulation 9, in a case where the arrangements give rise to a claim submitted separately from the return under—

(a) section 261B of the Taxation of Chargeable Gains Act 1992 (treating trade loss etc as CGT loss); or

(b) Part 4 of the Income Tax Act 2007 (loss relief);

the prescribed information shall be provided separately to HMRC in such form and manner as they may specify.

Modifications—See the National Insurance Contributions (Application of Part 7 of the Finance Act 2004) Regulations, SI 2012/1868 reg 26(1), (8) for the modification of this regulation is its applications to notifiable contribution arrangements and notifiable contribution proposals.

Amendments—[1] Para (6A) inserted by the Tax Avoidance Schemes (Information) (Amendment, etc) Regulations, SI 2013/2592 regs 3, 10 with effect from 4 November 2013.

[2] Para (4) revoked by the Tax Avoidance Schemes (Information) (Amendment) Regulations, SI 2015/948 regs 2, 8 with effect from 16 April 2015.

11 Prescribed information under section 313(1)

(1) For the purposes of section 313(1) (duty of parties to notifiable arrangements to notify Board of number, etc) the prescribed information is that specified in whichever of paragraph (2), (3) or (4) is applicable.

(2) In cases prescribed in regulation 9 the prescribed information is—

(a) the reference number (or if more than one, any one reference number) allocated by HMRC under section 311 to the notifiable arrangements or proposed notifiable arrangements; and

(b) the year of assessment, tax year or accounting period (as the case may be) in which, or the date on which, the person providing the information expects a tax advantage to be obtained.

(3) In the cases prescribed in regulation 10 (apart from paragraph (2) [and any case relating to annual tax on enveloped dwellings][1]) the prescribed information is—

(a) the name and address of the person providing it;

(b) any National Insurance number, tax reference number, PAYE reference number or other personal identifier allocated by HMRC to the person to whom the information relates;

(c) the reference number (or if more than one, any one reference number) allocated by HMRC under section 311 to the notifiable arrangements or proposed notifiable arrangements;

(d) the year of assessment, tax year or accounting period (as the case may be) in which, or the date on which, the person providing the information . . . [2] expects to obtain a tax advantage by virtue of the notifiable arrangements;

(e) the name of the person providing the declaration as to the accuracy and completeness of the notification; and

(f) the capacity in which the person mentioned in sub-paragraph (e) is acting.

(4) In the case prescribed at regulation 10(2) the prescribed information is—

(a) the name and address of the purchaser;

(b) the reference number (or if more than one, any one reference number) allocated by HMRC under section 311 to the notifiable arrangements or proposed notifiable arrangements;

(c) the address of the property forming the subject of the arrangements ("the property");

(d) the title number of the property (if any is allocated);

(e) the unique transaction reference number(if a land transaction return has been submitted to HMRC at the time the prescribed information is provided);

(f) the market value of the property, taking into account all chargeable interests in the property held by the same person or connected persons;

(g) the effective date of the first land transaction which forms part of the arrangements;

(h) the name of the person providing the declaration as to the accuracy and completeness of the notification; and

(i) the capacity in which that person is acting.

[(5) In the cases prescribed in regulation 10(6A), (7) and (8), where they relate to annual tax on enveloped dwellings, the prescribed information is—

(a) the name and address of the person providing the information;

(b) any tax reference number or other personal identifier allocated by HMRC or a foreign tax authority to the person to whom the information relates;

(c) where a foreign tax authority has allocated a personal identifier, the name of the country on behalf of which that foreign tax authority acts;

(d) the reference number (or if more than one, any one reference number) allocated by HMRC under section 311 to the notifiable arrangements or proposed notifiable arrangements;

(e) the address of the property forming the subject of the arrangements ("the property");

(f) the title number of the property (if any is allocated);

(g) the first chargeable period (within the meaning of section 94(8) of the Finance Act 2013) in which the person providing the information expects to obtain a tax advantage by virtue of the notifable arrangements;

(h) the name of the person providing the declaration as to the accuracy and completeness of the notification, where different from information provided under sub-paragraph (a); and

(i) the capacity in which the person mentioned in sub-paragraph (h) is acting.][1]

Modifications—See the National Insurance Contributions (Application of Part 7 of the Finance Act 2004) Regulations, SI 2012/1868 reg 26(1), (9) for the modification of this regulation is its applications to notifiable contribution arrangements and notifiable contribution proposals.

Amendments—[1] Words in para (3), and whole of para (5), inserted, by the Tax Avoidance Schemes (Information) (Amendment, etc) Regulations, SI 2013/2592 regs 3, 11, 12 with effect from 4 November 2013.

[2] In para (3)(*d*), words "or, in the case of regulation 10(4), an employee of that person," revoked by the Tax Avoidance Schemes (Information) (Amendment) Regulations, SI 2015/948 regs 2, 9 with effect from 16 April 2015.

12 Time for providing information under section 313(3)(b)

(1) The prescribed times for providing information in the cases prescribed in regulation 10 are as follows.

(2) In the case of regulation 10(2) any time during the period of 30 days beginning with the later of—

(a) the effective date of the first land transaction which forms part of the arrangements; or

(b) the date of the receipt of the reference number allocated under the provisions of section 311.

(3) . . . [2]

(4) In the case of regulation 10(5)—

(a) for regulation 10(5)(a), any time during the period ending on 31st January next following the end of the year of assessment in question;

(b) for regulation 10(5)(b), any time during the period ending on the date defined as the filing date for the purposes of paragraph 14 of Schedule 18 to the Finance Act 1998 in respect of the period of account in question;

(c) for regulation 10(5)(c), any time during the period ending on the earliest date by which the person in question could be required to file a return under section 12AA of the Taxes Management Act 1970, determined in accordance with whichever of subsections (4) and (5) of that section is applicable.

(5) In the case of regulation 10(6) any time during the period of 12 months from the end of the month in which the first transaction forming part of the arrangements is entered into.

[(5A) In the cases of regulation 10(6A), (7) and (8), where it relates to annual tax on enveloped dwellings, any time during the period of 30 days beginning with the later of—

(a) the effective date of the first transaction which forms part of the arrangements; or

(b) the date of the receipt of the reference number allocated under the provisions of section 311.][1]

(6) In the case of regulation 10(7) and (8)[, except where they relate to annual tax on enveloped dwellings,][1] any time during the period ending on the filing date for the relevant return.

(7) In the case of regulation 10(9) the time that the claim is made.

Modifications—See the National Insurance Contributions (Application of Part 7 of the Finance Act 2004) Regulations, SI 2012/1868 reg 26(1), (9) for the modification of this regulation is its applications to notifiable contribution arrangements and notifiable contribution proposals.

Amendments—[1] Para (5A), and words in para (6), inserted, by the Tax Avoidance Schemes (Information) (Amendment, etc) Regulations, SI 2013/2592 regs 3, 13 with effect from 4 November 2013.

[2] Para (3) revoked by the Tax Avoidance Schemes (Information) (Amendment) Regulations, SI 2015/948 regs 2, 10 with effect from 16 April 2015.

13 Prescribed information under section 313ZA: information and timing

(1) For the purposes of section 313ZA(3) (duty of promoter to provide client lists)-

[(a) the prescribed period is—

(i) 30 days; or

(ii) where the circumstances in sub-paragraph (d)(iii) apply, 60 days in respect of the information prescribed under sub-paragraph (b)(iii) only.][1]

(b) the prescribed information is—

(i) any reference number allocated by HMRC under section 311 to the arrangements (or to a proposal for them) to which the information provided relates;

(ii) the name and address of each client in relation to whom the relevant date (within the meaning of section 312(3)) occurs in the relevant period in relation to which the information is being provided;

[(iii) any identification number allocated by HMRC ("unique taxpayer number") and national insurance number for each client in relation to whom the relevant date (within the meaning of section 312(3)) occurs in the relevant period in relation to which the information is being provided;

(iv) the promoter's name and address; and

(v) the end date of the relevant period in relation to which the information is being provided.][1]

(c) in sub-paragraph (b)(ii) the address of the client is the address to which the promoter has sent or would have sent the prescribed information under section 312.

[(d) at the end of the prescribed period under sub-paragraph (a)(i), where the promoter is unable to provide any unique taxpayer number or national insurance number, the prescribed information under sub-paragraph (b) must include confirmation that one of the following applies—

(i) the client has complied with section 312B and does not have a unique taxpayer number or national insurance number or has neither number;

(ii) the client has not complied with section 312B;

(iii) on the sixteenth day after the end of the relevant period, the prescribed period under regulation 8A(1)(a) had not yet expired;

(e) at the end of the prescribed period under sub-paragraph (a)(ii), where the promoter is unable to provide any unique taxpayer number or national insurance number, the prescribed information under sub-paragraph (b) must include confirmation that either sub-paragraph (d)(i) or sub-paragraph (d)(ii) applies.][1]

(2) For the purposes of section 313ZA(4) the relevant period is each calendar quarter.

Modifications—See the National Insurance Contributions (Application of Part 7 of the Finance Act 2004) Regulations, SI 2012/1868 reg 26(1), (10) for the modification of this regulation is its applications to notifiable contribution arrangements and notifiable contribution proposals.

Amendments—[1] Para (1)(a) substituted, paras (1)(b)(iii)–(v) substituted for previous paras (1)(b)(iii), (iv), and paras (1)(d), (e) inserted, by the Tax Avoidance Schemes (Information) (Amendment, etc) Regulations, SI 2013/2592 regs 3, 17–19 with effect from 4 November 2013.

[13A Prescribed information under section 313ZB: information and timing

(1) For the purposes of section 313ZB (further information from promoters)—

(a) the prescribed period is 10 days from the date that the promoter receives the written notice under section 313ZB; and

(b) the prescribed information is—

(i) the name and address of any person described in section 313ZB(2) (but only those who will, or are likely to, either sell the arrangements to another person, or achieve a tax advantage by implementing the arrangements);

(ii) any identification number allocated by HMRC to any person mentioned at sub-paragraph (b)(i); and

(iii) sufficient information as might reasonably be expected to enable an officer of HMRC to comprehend the manner in which any person mentioned at sub-paragraph (b)(i) is involved in the arrangements.

(2) Paragraph (1)(b) only extends to information held by the promoter at the time of receipt of a written notice under section 313ZB(2).][1]

Amendments—[1] Reg 13A inserted by the Tax Avoidance Schemes (Information) (Amendment, etc) Regulations, SI 2013/2592 regs 3, 20 with effect from 4 November 2013.

[13B Prescribed information under section 313ZC: information and timing

(1) For the purposes of section 313ZC (duty of employer to notify HMRC of details of employees etc) the prescribed time for providing prescribed information is 14 days after the end of the final tax period in respect of the tax year in which any person first enters into a transaction forming part of the notifiable arrangements and on the same date in each subsequent year until an advantage ceases to apply to the employee and the employer.

In this paragraph, "tax period" has the meaning given in regulation 2(1) (interpretation) of the Income Tax (Pay As You Earn) Regulations 2003.

(2) For the purposes of section 313ZC the prescribed information is—

(a) the name, address and reference number of the employer;

(b) the name and any National Insurance Number of the employee;

(c) the reference number (or, if more than one, any one reference number) allocated by HMRC under section 311 (arrangements to be given reference number) to the notifiable arrangements or proposed notifiable arrangements;

(d) where the employee obtains or might reasonably be expected to obtain a tax advantage by virtue of the notifiable arrangements, the tax year in which the employee obtains or expects to obtain the tax advantage;

(e) where a tax advantage is obtained or might reasonably be expected to be obtained only by a person other than the employee by virtue of the notifiable arrangements, confirmation that the employee's tax advantage is expected to be nil; and

(f) the name and address of the promoter, and any name given to the notifiable arrangement when it was notified.][1]

Amendments—[1] Regulation 13B inserted by the Tax Avoidance Schemes (Information) (Amendment) Regulations, SI 2015/948 regs 2, 11 with effect from 16 April 2015.

14 Time for providing information under section 313A and 313B

(1) In the case of a requirement under or by virtue of section 313A(1) (pre-disclosure enquiry), the prescribed period is the period of 10 days beginning on the day after that on which the notice is issued.

(2) In the case of a requirement under or by virtue of section 313B(1) (reasons for non-disclosure: supporting information), the prescribed period is the period of 14 days beginning on the day after that on which the order is made.

15 Prescribed information under section 313C: information and timing

(1) For the purposes of section 313C(1) (information provided to introducers) the prescribed information is—

(a) P's name and address; . . . [1]

(b) the name and address of each person who has provided P with any information relating to the proposal[; and

(c) the name and address of each person with whom P has made a marketing contact.][1]

(2) For the purposes of section 313C(3)(a) the prescribed period is 10 days.

Modification—NIC (Application of Part 7 of the Finance Act 2004) Regulations, SI 2012/1868 reg 26(11) (this reg modified in relation to NIC avoidance schemes and proposals).

Amendments—[1] Word "and" at the end of para (1)(*a*) revoked, and para (1)(*c*) and preceding word inserted by the Tax Avoidance Schemes (Information) (Amendment) Regulations, SI 2015/948 regs 2, 12 with effect from 16 April 2015.

16 Higher rate of penalty following a failure to comply with an order under section 306A or 314A

(1) For the purposes of section 98C(2A) of the Taxes Management Act 1970 (higher rate of penalty after the making of an order under section 306A) the prescribed period is the period of 10 days beginning on the date on which the order is made.

(2) For the purposes of section 98C(2B) of the Taxes Management Act 1970 (higher rate of penalty after the making of an order under section 314A) the prescribed period is the period of 10 days beginning on the date on which the order is made.

17 Electronic delivery of information

(1) Information required to be delivered to HMRC or to any other person by virtue of these Regulations may be delivered in such form and by such means of electronic communications as are for the time being authorised for that purpose.

(2) The use of a particular means of electronic communications is authorised for the purposes of paragraph (1) only if—

(a) it is authorised by directions given by HMRC under section 132(5) of the Finance Act 1999 (voluntary filing by electronic means of returns and other documents); and

(b) the user complies with any conditions imposed by HMRC under that section.

(3) Nothing in this regulation prevents the delivery of information by electronic communications if the information is contained in a return which is—

(a) authorised to be delivered electronically by virtue of regulations under section 132 of the Finance Act 1999; or

(b) required to be so delivered by virtue of regulations under section 135 of the Finance Act 2002 (mandatory e-filing).

Modification—NIC (Application of Part 7 of the Finance Act 2004) Regulations, SI 2012/1868 reg 26(12) (this reg modified in relation to NIC avoidance schemes and proposals).

18 Amendment of the Tax Avoidance Schemes (Promoters and Prescribed Circumstances) Regulations 2004

In regulation 6 of the Tax Avoidance Schemes (Promoters and Prescribed Circumstances) Regulations 2004(1) for "paragraph (1) or (2) (as the case may be) of regulation 3 of the Tax Avoidance Schemes (Information) Regulations 2004" substitute "regulation 4(1) of the Tax Avoidance Schemes (Information) Regulations 2012".

Modification—NIC (Application of Part 7 of the Finance Act 2004) Regulations, SI 2012/1868 reg 26(13) (this reg revoked in relation to NIC avoidance schemes and proposals).

SCHEDULE

REVOCATIONS

Regulation 3

Statutory Instrument Number	Title of Regulations	Extent of revocation
SI 2004/1864	The Tax Avoidance Schemes (Information) Regulations 2004	The whole regulations
SI 2004/2613	The Tax Avoidance Schemes (Promoters, Prescribed Circumstances and Information) (Amendment) Regulations 2004	Regulation 3
SI 2005/1869	The Tax Avoidance Schemes (Information) (Amendment) Regulations 2005	The whole regulations

SI 2006/1544	The Tax Avoidance Schemes (Information) (Amendment) Regulations 2006	The whole regulations
SI 2007/2153	The Tax Avoidance Schemes (Information) (Amendment) Regulations 2007	The whole regulations
SI 2007/3103	The Tax Avoidance Schemes (Information) (Amendment) (No 2) Regulations 2007	The whole regulations
SI 2008/1947	The Tax Avoidance Schemes (Information) (Amendment) Regulations 2008	The whole regulations
SI 2009/611	The Tax Avoidance Schemes (Information) (Amendment) Regulations 2009	The whole regulations
SI 2010/410	The Tax Avoidance Schemes (Information) (Amendment) Regulations 2010	The whole regulations
SI 2010/2928	The Tax Avoidance Schemes (Information) (Amendment) Regulations (No 2) 2010	The whole regulations
SI 2011/171	The Tax Avoidance Schemes (Information) (Amendment) Regulations 2011	The whole regulations

2012/1843

TAXATION OF CHARGEABLE GAINS (GILT-EDGED SECURITIES) ORDER 2012

Made . . . . 12th July 2012

The Treasury makes the following Order in exercise of the powers conferred by paragraph 1 of Schedule 9 to the Taxation of Chargeable Gains Act 1992.

1 Citation

This Order may be cited as the Taxation of Chargeable Gains (Gilt-edged Securities) Order 2012.

2 Securities specified as gilt-edged securities

For the purpose of the Taxation of Chargeable Gains Act 1992 the following securities are specified as "gilt-edged securities"—

0 $^{3}/_{4}$ % Index-linked Treasury Gilt 2034
1 $^{3}/_{4}$ % Treasury Gilt 2017
3 $^{3}/_{4}$ % Treasury Gilt 2052
0 $^{3}/_{8}$ % Index-Linked Treasury Gilt 2062
0 $^{1}/_{8}$ % Index-Linked Treasury Gilt 2029.

2012/1868

NATIONAL INSURANCE CONTRIBUTIONS (APPLICATION OF PART 7 OF THE FINANCE ACT 2004) REGULATIONS 2012

Made . . . . 16th July 2012
Laid before Parliament . . . . 17th July 2012
Coming into force . . . . 1st September 2012

The Treasury make the following Regulations in exercise of the powers conferred upon them by sections 132A(1) and 189(4) and (5) of the Social Security Administration Act 1992.

PART 1
INTRODUCTION

1 Citation and commencement

These Regulations may be cited as the National Insurance Contributions (Application of Part 7 of the Finance Act 2004) Regulations 2012 and shall come into force on 1st September 2012.

2 Interpretation

In these Regulations—

"the Descriptions Regulations" means the Tax Avoidance Schemes (Prescribed Descriptions of Arrangements) Regulations 2006 as modified by these Regulations.

"the Information Regulations" means the Tax Avoidance (Information) Regulations 2012 as modified by these Regulations.

"introducer", in relation to a notifiable contribution proposal, has the meaning given by regulation 7(2);

"HMRC" means the Commissioners for Her Majesty's Revenue and Customs;

"notifiable arrangements" and "notifiable proposal" have the meaning given to them in section 306 of the Finance Act 2004;

"Part 7" means Part 7 of the Finance Act 2004 (disclosure of tax avoidance schemes) and a reference to a numbered section (without more) is a reference to a section of Part 7;

"prescribed" means prescribed by the Information Regulations, unless the context otherwise requires;

"promoter", in relation to notifiable contribution arrangements or a notifiable contribution proposal, has the meaning given by regulation 7;

"reference number" means the reference number allocated under regulation 12 or section 311 as the case may be;

"tribunal" means the First-tier Tribunal or, where determined by or under Tribunal Procedure Rules, the Upper Tribunal.

["working day" means a day which is not a Saturday or a Sunday, Christmas Day, Good Friday or a bank holiday under the Banking and Financial Dealings Act 1971(d) in any part of the United Kingdom.][1]

Amendments—[1] Definition of "working day" inserted by the National Insurance Contributions (Application of Part 7 of the Finance Act 2004) (Amendment) Regulations, SI 2015/531 regs 2, 3 with effect from 12 April 2015.

3 Structure of the Regulations

(1) Regulations 5 to 21 make provision corresponding to Part 7 (other than section 314 (legal professional privilege)) in so far as that Part applies to income tax.

(2) Regulations 22 to 24 make provision corresponding to section 98C and section 118(2) of the Taxes Management Act 1970 (penalties for failure to comply with Part 7 of the Finance Act 2004) and other provisions of the Taxes Management Act 1970 in so far as they relate to a penalty under section 98C.

(3) Regulations 25 to 28 modify regulations made under Part 7 in so far as they apply to income tax.

4 Revocations

(1) The regulations described in Regulation 29 are revoked.

(2) Anything begun under or for the purpose of any regulations revoked by these Regulations shall be continued under or, as the case may be, for the purpose of the corresponding provision of these Regulations.

(3) Where any document refers to a provision of a regulation revoked by these Regulations, such reference shall, unless the context otherwise requires, be construed as a reference to the corresponding provision of these Regulations.

PART 2
PROVISIONS CORRESPONDING TO PART 7 OF THE FINANCE ACT 2004

5 Application of Part 2

(1) This Part applies to—

(a) notifiable contribution arrangements; and

(b) notifiable contribution proposals

which fall within any description prescribed by the Descriptions Regulations.

(2) The Table below shows which of the following regulations corresponds to which provision of Part 7.

Section within Part 7	*Corresponding provision of these Regulations*
Section 306 (meaning of "notifiable arrangements" and "notifiable proposal")	Regulation 5
Section 306A (doubt as to notifiability)	Regulation 6
Section 307 (meaning of promoter)	Regulation 7
Section 308 (duties of promoter)	Regulation 8
Section 308A (supplemental information)	Regulation 9
Section 309 (duty of person dealing with promoter outside the United Kingdom)	Regulation 10

Section 310 (duty of parties to notifiable arrangements not involving promoter)	Regulation 11
[Section 310A (duty to provide further information requested by HMRC)	Regulation 11A
Section 310B (failure to provide information under section 310A: application to the Tribunal)	Regulation 11B][1]
Section 311 (arrangements to be given reference number)	Regulation 12
Section 312 (duty of promoter to notify client of number)	Regulation 13
Section 312A (duty of client to notify parties of number)	Regulation 14
Section 313 (duty of parties to notifiable arrangements to notify Board of number etc)	Regulation 15
Section 313ZA (duty of promoter to provide details of clients)	Regulation 16
Section 313A (pre-disclosure enquiry)	Regulation 17
Section 313B (reasons for non-disclosure: supporting information)	Regulation 18
Section 313C (information provided to introducers)	Regulation 19
Section 314A (order to disclose)	Regulation 20
Section 316 (information to be provided in form and manner specified by Board)	Regulation 21

Amendments—[1] In para (2), Table entries relating to "Section 310A" and "Section 310B" inserted by the National Insurance Contributions (Application of Part 7 of the Finance Act 2004) (Amendment) Regulations, SI 2015/531 regs 2, 4 with effect from 12 April 2015.

6 Doubt as to notifiabilty

(1) HMRC may apply to the tribunal for an order that—

(a) a proposal is to be treated as a notifiable contribution proposal; or

(b) arrangements are to be treated as notifiable contribution arrangements.

(2) An application must specify—

(a) the proposal or arrangements in respect of which the order is sought; and

(b) the promoter.

(3) On an application the tribunal may make the order only if satisfied that HMRC—

(a) have taken all reasonable steps to establish whether the proposal is a notifiable contribution proposal or the arrangements are notifiable contribution arrangements; and

(b) have reasonable grounds for suspecting that the proposal may be a notifiable contribution proposal or the arrangements may be notifiable contribution arrangements.

(4) Reasonable steps under paragraph (3)(a) may (but need not) include taking action under regulation 17 or 18.

(5) Grounds for suspicion under paragraph (3)(b) may include—

(a) the fact that the relevant arrangements fall within a description prescribed by the Descriptions Regulations;

(b) an attempt by the promoter to avoid or delay providing information or documents about the proposal or arrangements under or by virtue of regulation 17 or 18;

(c) the promoter's failure to comply with a requirement under or by virtue of regulation 17 or 18 or section 313A or 313B in relation to another proposal or other arrangements.

(6) Where an order is made under this regulation in respect of a proposal or arrangements, the period for the purposes of paragraphs (1) and (3) of regulation 8 is that prescribed.

(7) An order under this regulation in relation to a proposal or arrangements is without prejudice to the possible application of regulation 8, other than by virtue of this regulation, to the proposal or arrangements.

7 Meaning of promoter

(1) For the purposes of this Part a person is a promoter—

(a) in relation to a notifiable contribution proposal if, in the course of a relevant business, the person ("P")—

(i) is to any extent responsible for the design of the proposed arrangements;

(ii) makes a firm approach to another person ("C") in relation to the proposal with a view to P making the proposal available for implementation by C or any other person; or

(iii) makes the notifiable contribution proposal available for implementation by other persons; and

(b) in relation to notifiable contribution arrangements, if the person ("P") is by virtue of sub-paragraph (a)(ii) or (iii) a promoter in relation to a notifiable contribution proposal which is implemented by those arrangements or if, in the course of a relevant business, P is to any extent responsible for—

(i) the design of the arrangements, or

(ii) the organisation or management of the arrangements.

(2) For the purposes of this Part a person is an introducer in relation to a notifiable contribution proposal if the person makes a marketing contact with another person in relation to the proposal.

(3) In this regulation "relevant business" means any trade, profession or business which—

(a) involves the provision to other persons of services relating to national insurance contributions, or

(b) is carried on by a bank, as defined by section 1120 of the Corporation Tax Act 2010, or by a securities house, as defined by section 1009(3) of that Act.

(4) For the purposes of this regulation anything done by a company is to be taken to be done in the course of a relevant business if it is done for the purposes of a relevant business falling within paragraph (3)(b) carried on by another company which is a member of the same group.

(5) Section 170 of the Taxation of Chargeable Gains Act 1992 has effect for determining for the purposes of paragraph (4) whether two companies are members of the same group, but as if in that section—

(a) for each of the references to a 75% subsidiary there were substituted a reference to a 51% subsidiary, and

(b) subsection (3)(b) and subsections (6) to (8) were omitted.

(6) For the purposes of this Part a person makes a firm approach to another person in relation to a notifiable contribution proposal if the person makes a marketing contact with the other person in relation to the proposal at a time when the proposed arrangements have been substantially designed.

(7) For the purposes of this Part a person makes a marketing contact with another person in relation to a notifiable contribution proposal if—

(a) the person communicates information about the proposal to the other person;

(b) the communication is made with a view to that other person, or any other person, entering into transactions forming part of the proposed arrangements; and

(c) the information communicated includes an explanation of the advantage in relation to any contribution that might be expected to be obtained from the proposed arrangements.

(8) For the purposes of paragraph (6) proposed contribution arrangements have been substantially designed at any time if by that time the nature of the transactions to form part of them has been sufficiently developed for it to be reasonable to believe that a person who wished to obtain the advantage mentioned in paragraph (7)(c) might enter into—

(a) transactions of the nature developed; or

(b) transactions not substantially different from transactions of that nature.

(9) A person is not to be treated as a promoter or introducer for the purposes of this Part by reason of anything done in circumstances prescribed by the Tax Avoidance Schemes (Promoters and Prescribed Circumstances) Regulations 2004 as modified by these Regulations.

(10) In the application of this Part to a proposal which is not a notifiable contribution proposal or arrangements which are not notifiable contribution arrangements, a reference to a promoter or introducer is a reference to a person who would be a promoter or introducer under paragraphs (1) to (9) if the proposal were a notifiable contribution proposal or arrangements were notifiable contribution arrangements.

8 Duties of promoter

(1) A person who is a promoter in relation to a notifiable contribution proposal must, within the prescribed period after the relevant date, provide HMRC with the prescribed information relating to the notifiable contribution proposal.

(2) In paragraph (1) "the relevant date" means the earliest of the following—

(a) the date on which the promoter first makes a firm approach to another person in relation to a notifiable contribution proposal;

(b) the date on which the promoter makes the notifiable contribution proposal available for implementation by any other person; or

(c) the date on which the promoter first becomes aware of any transaction forming part of notifiable contribution arrangements implementing the notifiable contribution proposal.

(3) A person who is a promoter in relation to notifiable contribution arrangements must, within the prescribed period after the date on which the person first becomes aware of any transaction forming part of the notifiable contribution arrangements, provide HMRC with the prescribed information relating to those arrangements, unless those arrangements implement a proposal in respect of which notice has been given under paragraph (1).

(4) Paragraph (5) applies where a person complies with paragraph (1) in relation to a notifiable contribution proposal for arrangements and another person is—

(a) also a promoter in relation to the notifiable contribution proposal or is a promoter in relation to a notifiable contribution proposal for arrangements which are substantially the same as the proposed arrangements (whether they relate to the same or different parties); or

(b) a promoter in relation to notifiable contribution arrangements implementing the notifiable contribution proposal or notifiable contribution arrangements which are substantially the same as notifiable contribution arrangements implementing the notifiable contribution proposal (whether they relate to the same or different parties).

(5) Any duty of the other person under paragraph (1) or (3) in relation to the notifiable contribution proposal or notifiable contribution arrangements is discharged if—

(a) the person who complied with paragraph (1) has notified the identity and address of the other person to HMRC or the other person holds the reference number allocated to the proposed notifiable contribution arrangements under regulation 12; and

(b) the other person holds the information provided to HMRC in compliance with paragraph (1).

(6) Paragraph (7) applies where a person complies with section 308(1) in relation to a notifiable proposal and another person is—

(a) a promoter in relation to a notifiable contribution proposal for arrangements which are substantially the same as the notifiable proposal (whether they relate to the same or different parties); or

(b) a promoter in relation to notifiable contribution arrangements which are substantially the same as notifiable arrangements implementing the notifiable proposal (whether they relate to the same or different parties).

(7) Any duty of the other person under paragraph (1) or (3) in relation to the notifiable contribution proposal or notifiable contribution arrangements is discharged if—

(a) the person who complied with section 308(1) in relation to the notifiable proposal has notified the identity and address of the other person to HMRC or the other person holds the reference number allocated to the proposed notifiable arrangements under section 311; and

(b) the other person holds the information provided to HMRC in compliance with section 308(1).

(8) Paragraph (9) applies where a person complies with paragraph (3) in relation to notifiable contribution arrangements and another person is—

(a) a promoter in relation to a notifiable contribution proposal for arrangements which are substantially the same as the notifiable contribution arrangements (whether they relate to the same or different parties); or

(b) also a promoter in relation to the notifiable contribution arrangements or notifiable contribution arrangements which are substantially the same (whether they relate to the same or different parties).

(9) Any duty of the other person under paragraph (1) or (3) in relation to the notifiable contribution proposal or notifiable contribution arrangements is discharged if—

(a) the person who complied with paragraph (3) has notified the identity and address of the other person to HMRC or the other person holds the reference number allocated to the notifiable contribution arrangements under regulation 12; and

(b) the other person holds the information provided to HMRC in compliance with paragraph (3).

(10) Paragraph (11) applies where a person complies with section 308(3) in relation to notifiable arrangements and another person is a promoter in relation to a notifiable contribution proposal for arrangements or notifiable contribution arrangements which are substantially the same as the notifiable arrangements (whether they relate to the same or different parties).

(11) Any duty of the other person under paragraph (1) or (3) in relation to the notifiable contribution proposal or notifiable contribution arrangements is discharged if—

(a) the person who complied with section 308(3) in relation to the notifiable contribution arrangements has notified the identity and address of the other person to HMRC or the other person holds the reference number allocated to the notifiable contribution arrangements under section 311;and

(b) the other person holds the information provided to HMRC in compliance with section 308(3).

(12) Where a person is a promoter in relation to two or more notifiable contribution proposals or sets of notifiable contribution arrangements which are substantially the same (whether they relate to the same parties or different parties), that person need not provide information under paragraph (1) or (3) if that person has already provided information under either of those paragraphs in relation to any of the other contribution proposals or contribution arrangements.

9 Supplemental information

(1) This regulation applies where—

(a) a promoter ("P") has provided information in purported compliance with paragraph (1) or (3) of regulation 8; but

(b) HMRC believe that P has not provided all the prescribed information.

(2) HMRC may apply to the tribunal for an order requiring P to provide specified information about, or documents relating to, the notifiable contribution proposal or notifiable contribution arrangements.
(3) The tribunal may make an order under paragraph (2) in respect of information or documents only if satisfied that HMRC have reasonable grounds for suspecting that the information or documents—
  (a) form part of the prescribed information; or
  (b) will support or explain the prescribed information.
(4) A requirement by virtue of paragraph (2) shall be treated as part of P's duty under paragraph (1) or (3) of regulation 8.
(5) In so far as P's duty under paragraph (1) or (3) of regulation 8 arises out of a requirement by virtue of paragraph (2) above, the period for the purposes of those paragraphs of regulation 8 and the date after which it begins are those prescribed.
(6) In so far as P's duty under paragraph (1) or (3) of regulation 8 arises out of a requirement by virtue of paragraph (2) above, the prescribed period may be extended by HMRC by direction.

10 Duty of person dealing with promoter outside United Kingdom

(1) Any person ("the client") who enters into any transaction forming part of any notifiable contribution arrangements in relation to which—
  (a) a promoter is resident outside the United Kingdom, and
  (b) no promoter is resident in the United Kingdom,
must provide HMRC with the prescribed information relating to the notifiable contribution arrangements within the prescribed period.
(2) Compliance with regulation 8(1) by any promoter in relation to the notifiable contribution arrangements discharges the duty of the client under paragraph (1).

11 Duty of parties to notifiable contribution arrangements not involving promoter

Any person who enters into any transaction forming part of notifiable contribution arrangements as respects which neither that person nor any other person in the United Kingdom is liable to comply with regulation 8 or regulation 10 must at the prescribed time provide HMRC with the prescribed information relating to the notifiable contribution arrangements.

[11A Duty to provide further information requested by HMRC

(1) This regulation applies where—
  (a) a person has provided the prescribed information about notifiable contribution proposals or notifiable contribution arrangements in compliance with regulation 8, 10 or 11, or
  (b) a person has provided information in purported compliance with regulation 10 or 11 but HMRC believe that the person has not provided all the prescribed information.
(2) HMRC may require the person to provide—
  (a) further specified information about the notifiable contribution proposals or notifiable contribution arrangements (in addition to the prescribed information under regulation 8, 10 or 11);
  (b) documents relating to the notifiable contribution proposals or notifiable contribution arrangements.
(3) Where HMRC impose a requirement on a person under this regulation, the person must comply with the requirement within—
  (a) the period of 10 working days beginning with the day on which HMRC imposed the requirement, or
  (b) such longer period as HMRC may direct.][1]

Amendments—[1] Regulations 11A, 11B inserted by the National Insurance Contributions (Application of Part 7 of the Finance Act 2004) (Amendment) Regulations, SI 2015/531 regs 2, 5 with effect from 12 April 2015.

[11B Failure to provide information under regulation 11A: application to the Tribunal

(1) This regulation applies where HMRC—
  (a) have required a person to provide information or documents under regulation 11A, but
  (b) believe that the person has failed to provide the information or documents required.
(2) HMRC may apply to the tribunal for an order requiring the person to provide the information or documents required.
(3) The tribunal may make an order under paragraph (2) only if satisfied that HMRC have reasonable grounds for suspecting that the information or documents will assist HMRC in considering the notifiable contribution proposals or notifiable contribution arrangements.
(4) Where the tribunal makes an order under paragraph (2), the person must comply with it within—
  (a) the period of 10 working days beginning with the day on which the tribunal made the order, or
  (b) such longer period as HMRC may direct.][1]

Amendments—[1] Regulations 11A, 11B inserted by the National Insurance Contributions (Application of Part 7 of the Finance Act 2004) (Amendment) Regulations, SI 2015/531 regs 2, 5 with effect from 12 April 2015.

12 Arrangements to be given reference number

(1) Where a person complies or purports to comply with regulation 8(1) or (3), regulation 10(1) or regulation 11 in relation to any notifiable contribution proposal or notifiable contribution arrangements, HMRC—

(a) may within 30 days allocate a reference number in relation to the notifiable contribution arrangements, or in the case of a notifiable contribution proposal, to the proposed notifiable contribution arrangements; and

(b) if they do so, must notify that number to the person and (where the person is one who has complied or purported to comply with paragraph (1) or (3) of regulation 8) to any other person—

(i) who is a promoter in relation to the notifiable contribution proposal (or arrangements implementing the notifiable contribution proposal) or the notifiable contribution arrangements (or proposal implemented by the notifiable contribution arrangements), and

(ii) whose identity and address has been notified to HMRC by the person,

except that where the arrangements or proposal concern both national insurance contributions and tax, HMRC shall allocate a single reference number in respect of both matters.

(2) The allocation of a reference number to any notifiable contribution arrangements (or proposed notifiable contribution arrangements) is not to be regarded as constituting any indication by HMRC that the arrangements could as a matter of law result in the obtaining by any person of an advantage in relation to a contribution.

13 Duty of promoter to notify client of number

(1) This regulation applies where a person who is a promoter in relation to notifiable contribution arrangements is providing (or has provided) services to any person ("the client") in connection with the notifiable contribution arrangements.

(2) The promoter must, within 30 days after the relevant date, provide the client with the prescribed information relating to any reference number (or, if more than one, any one reference number) that has been notified to the promoter (whether by HMRC or any other person) in relation to—

(a) the notifiable contribution arrangements; or

(b) any arrangements, including notifiable arrangements, which are substantially the same as the notifiable contribution arrangements (whether involving the same or different parties).

(3) In paragraph (2) "the relevant date" means the later of—

(a) the date on which the promoter becomes aware of any transaction which forms part of the notifiable contribution arrangements; and

(b) the date on which the reference number is notified to the promoter.

(4) But where the conditions in paragraph (5) are met the duty imposed on the promoter under paragraph (2) to provide the client with information in relation to notifiable contribution arrangements is discharged.

(5) Those conditions are that—

(a) the promoter is also a promoter in relation to a notifiable contribution proposal and provides services to the client in connection with them both;

(b) the notifiable contribution proposal and the notifiable contribution arrangements are substantially the same; and

(c) the promoter has provided to the client, in a form and manner specified by HMRC, prescribed information relating to the reference number that has been notified to the promoter in relation to the proposed notifiable contribution arrangements.

(6) HMRC may give notice that, in relation to notifiable contribution arrangements specified in the notice, promoters are not under the duty under paragraph (2) after the date specified in the notice.

14 Duty of client to notify parties of number

(1) This regulation applies where a person (the "client") to whom a person who is a promoter in relation to notifiable contribution arrangements or a notifiable contribution proposal is providing (or has provided) services in connection with the notifiable contribution arrangements or notifiable contribution proposal receives prescribed information relating to the reference number allocated to—

(a) the notifiable contribution arrangements,

(b) the notifiable contribution proposal, or

(c) proposed notifiable arrangements, or notifiable arrangements, which are substantially the same as the notifiable contribution proposal or notifiable contribution arrangements.

(2) The client must, within the prescribed period, provide the prescribed information relating to the reference number to any other person—

(a) who the client might reasonably be expected to know is or is likely to be a party to the arrangements or proposed arrangements, and

(b) who might reasonably be expected to gain an advantage by reason of the arrangements or proposed arrangements.

(3) HMRC may give notice that, in relation to notifiable contribution arrangements or a notifiable contribution proposal specified in the notice, persons are not under the duty under paragraph (2) after the date specified in the notice.

(4) The duty under paragraph (2) does not apply in the prescribed circumstances.

15 Duty of parties to notifiable contribution arrangements to notify HMRC of number etc

(1) Any person who is a party to any notifiable contribution arrangements must, at the prescribed time or times, provide HMRC with the prescribed information relating to—

(a) any reference number notified to him, whether the reference number was allocated under regulation 12 or section 311, and

(b) the time when he obtains or expects to obtain by virtue of the arrangements an advantage in relation to any contribution.

(2) HMRC may give notice that, in relation to notifiable contribution arrangements specified in the notice, persons are not under the duty under paragraph (1) after the date specified in the notice.

16 Duty to provide details of clients

(1) This regulation applies where a person who is a promoter in relation to notifiable contribution arrangements is providing (or has provided) services to any person ("the client") in connection with the notifiable contribution arrangements and either—

(a) the promoter is subject to the reference number information requirement; or

(b) the promoter has failed to comply with regulation 8(1) or (3) in relation to the notifiable contributions arrangements (or the notifiable contribution proposal for them) but would be subject to the reference number information requirement if a reference number had been allocated to the notifiable contribution arrangements.

(2) For the purposes of this regulation "the reference number information requirement" is the requirement under regulation 13(2) to provide to the client prescribed information relating to the reference number allocated to the notifiable contribution arrangements.

(3) The promoter must, within the prescribed period after the end of the relevant period, provide HMRC with the prescribed information in relation to the client.

(4) In paragraph (3) "the relevant period" means the prescribed period during which the promoter is or would be subject to the reference number information requirement.

(5) The promoter need not comply with paragraph (3) in relation to any notifiable contribution arrangements at any time after HMRC have given notice under regulation 13(6) in relation to the arrangements.

17 Pre-disclosure enquiry

(1) Where HMRC suspect that a person ("P") is the promoter or introducer of a proposal or arrangements which may be a notifiable contribution proposal or notifiable contribution arrangements, HMRC may by written notice require P to state—

(a) whether in P's opinion the proposal or arrangements are notifiable by P, and

(b) if not, the reasons for P's opinion.

(2) A notice must specify the proposal or arrangements to which it relates.

(3) For the purpose of paragraph (1)(b)—

(a) it is not sufficient to refer to the fact that a lawyer or other professional has given an opinion,

(b) the reasons must show, by reference to this Part and the Descriptions Regulations why P thinks the proposal or arrangements are not notifiable by P, and

(c) in particular, if P asserts that the arrangements do not fall within any description prescribed by the Descriptions Regulations the reasons must provide sufficient information to enable HMRC to confirm the assertion.

(4) P must comply with a requirement under or by virtue of paragraph (1) within—

(a) the prescribed period, or

(b) such longer period as HMRC may direct.

18 Reasons for non-disclosure: supporting information

(1) Where HMRC receive from a person ("P") a statement of reasons why a proposal or arrangements are not notifiable by P, HMRC may apply to the tribunal for an order requiring P to provide specified information or documents in support of the reasons.

(2) P must comply with a requirement under or by virtue of paragraph (1) within—

(a) the prescribed period, or

(b) such longer period as HMRC may direct.

(3) The power under paragraph (1)—

(a) may be exercised more than once, and

(b) applies whether or not the statement of reasons was received under regulation 17(1)(b).

19 Information provided to introducers

(1) Where HMRC suspect—

(a) that a person ("P") is an introducer in relation to a proposal; and

(b) that the proposal may be a notifiable contribution proposal,

HMRC may by written notice require P to provide HMRC with the prescribed information in relation to each person who has provided P with any information relating to the proposal.

(2) A notice must specify the proposal to which it relates.

(3) P must comply with a requirement under paragraph (1) within—

(a) the prescribed period; or

(b) such longer period as HMRC may direct.

20 Order to disclose

(1) HMRC may apply to the tribunal for an order that—

(a) a proposal is a notifiable contribution proposal, or

(b) arrangements are notifiable contribution arrangements.

(2) An application must specify—

(a) the proposal or arrangements in respect of which the order is sought, and

(b) the promoter.

(3) On an application the tribunal may make the order only if satisfied that section 132A(3) of the Social Security Administration Act 1992 applies to the relevant arrangements and that they are within a description prescribed by the Descriptions Regulations.

21 Information to be provided in form and manner specified by HMRC

(1) HMRC may specify the form and manner in which information required to be provided by any of the information provisions must be provided if the provision is to be complied with.

(2) The "information provisions" are regulations 8(1) and (3), 10(1), 11, [11A,][1] 13(2), 14(2), 15(1) and 16(3) and the Information Regulations.

Amendments—[1] In para (2), reference inserted by the National Insurance Contributions (Application of Part 7 of the Finance Act 2004) (Amendment) Regulations, SI 2015/531 regs 2, 6 with effect from 12 April 2015.

PART 3

PROVISIONS CORRESPONDING TO SECTION 98C AND SECTION 118(2) OF THE TAXES MANAGEMENT ACT 1970 AND MODIFICATIONS OF RELATED PROVISIONS

22 Notification under Part 2

(1) A person who fails to comply with any of the provisions of Part 2 mentioned in paragraph (2) below shall be liable—

(a) to a penalty not exceeding—

(i) in the case of a provision mentioned in sub-paragraph (a), (b)[, (c) or (ca)][1] of that paragraph, £600 for each day during the initial period (but see also paragraphs (5), (7) and (8) below); and

(ii) in any other case, £5,000; and

(b) if the failure continues after a penalty is imposed under sub-paragraph (a) above, to a further penalty or penalties not exceeding £600 for each day on which the failure continues after the day on which the penalty under sub-paragraph (a) was imposed (but excluding any day for which a penalty under this paragraph has already been imposed).

This is subject to paragraph (14).

(2) Those provisions are—

(a) regulation 8(1) and (3) (duty of promoter in relation to notifiable contribution proposals and notifiable contribution arrangements),

(b) regulation 10(1) (duty of person dealing with promoter outside United Kingdom),

(c) regulation 11 (duty of parties to notifiable contribution arrangements not involving promoter),

[(ca) regulation 11A (duty to provide further information requested by HMRC),][1]

(d) regulation 13(2) (duty of promoter to notify client of reference number),

(e) regulation 14(2) (duty of client to notify parties of reference number),

(f) regulation 16 (duty of promoter to provide details of clients),

(g) regulations 17 and 18 (duty of promoter to respond to inquiry), and

(h) regulation 19 (duty of introducer to give details of persons who have provided information).

(3) In this regulation "the initial period" means the period—

(a) beginning with the relevant day; and

(b) ending with the earlier of the day on which the penalty under paragraph (1)(a)(i) is determined and the last day before the failure ceases;

and for this purpose "the relevant day" is the day specified in relation to the failure in the following table.

TABLE

Failure	*Relevant day*

A failure to comply with paragraph (1) or (3) of regulation 8 in so far as the paragraph applies by virtue of an order under regulation 6	The first day of the prescribed period
A failure to comply with paragraph (1) or (3) of regulation 8 in so far as the paragraph applies by virtue of an order under regulation 9(2)	The first day after the end of the prescribed period (as it may have been extended by a direction under regulation 9(6))
Any other failure to comply with paragraph (1) of regulation 8	The first day after the end of the prescribed period
Any other failure to comply with paragraph (3) of regulation 8	The first day after the end of the prescribed period
A failure to comply with paragraph (1) of regulation 10	The first day after the end of the prescribed period
A failure to comply with regulation 11	The first day after the latest time by which regulation 11 must be complied with in the case concerned
[A failure to comply with regulation 11A	The first day after the end of the period within which the person must comply with regulation 11A][1]

(4) The amount of a penalty under paragraph (1)(a)(i) is to be arrived at after taking account of all relevant considerations, including the desirability of its being set at a level which appears appropriate for deterring the person, or other persons, from similar failures to comply on future occasions having regard (in particular)—

(a) in the case of a penalty for a [promoter's][1] failure to comply with regulation 8(1) or (3) [or regulation 11A][1], to the amount of any fees received, or likely to have been received, by the [promoter][1] in connection with the notifiable contribution proposal (or arrangements implementing the notifiable contribution proposal), or with the notifiable contribution arrangements;

(b) in the case of a penalty for the [relevant][1] person's failure to comply with regulation 10(1)[,11 or 11A][1], to the amount of any advantage gained, or sought to be gained, by the [relevant][1] person in relation to any contribution.

[(4A) In paragraph 4—

(a) "promoter" has the same meaning as in regulation 7, and

(b) "relevant person" means a person who enters into any transaction forming part of notifiable contribution arrangements within the meaning of regulation 5.][1]

(5) If the maximum penalty under paragraph (1)(a)(i) above appears inappropriately low after taking account of those considerations, the penalty is to be of such amount not exceeding £1 million as appears appropriate having regard to those considerations.

(6) Where it appears to an officer of Revenue and Customs that a penalty under paragraph (1)(a)(i) above has been determined on the basis that the initial period begins with a day later than that which the officer considers to be the relevant day, an officer of Revenue and Customs may commence proceedings for a re-determination of the penalty.

(7) Where a failure to comply with a provision mentioned in paragraph (2) concerns a proposal or arrangements in respect of which an order has been made under regulation 6 (doubt as to notifiability), the amounts specified in paragraph (1)(a)(i) and (b) shall be increased to the sum prescribed by the Tax Avoidance Schemes (Penalty) Regulations 2007 (as modified by these Regulations).

(8) Where a failure to comply with a provision mentioned in paragraph (2) concerns a proposal or arrangements in respect of which an order has been made under regulation 20 (order to disclose), the amounts specified in paragraph (1)(a)(i) and (b) shall be increased to the sum prescribed by the Tax Avoidance Schemes (Penalty) Regulations 2007 (as modified by these Regulations) in relation to the days falling after the prescribed period.

(9) The making of an order under regulation 6 or 20 does not of itself mean that, for the purposes of regulation 23, a person either did or did not have a reasonable excuse for non-compliance before the order was made.

(10) Where an order is made under regulation 6 or 20 then for the purposes of regulation 23—

(a) the person identified in the order as the promoter of the proposal or arrangements cannot, in respect of any time after the end of the period mentioned in paragraph (8), rely on doubt as to notifiability as an excuse for failure to comply with regulation 8, and

(b) any delay in compliance with that regulation after the end of that period is unreasonable unless attributable to something other than doubt as to notifiability.

[(10A) Where a person fails to comply with—

(a) regulation 10 and the promoter for the purposes of that regulation is a monitored promoter for the purposes of Part 5 of the Finance Act 2014, or

(b) regulation 11 and the notifiable contribution arrangements for the purposes of that regulation are arrangements of such a monitored promoter,

then for the purposes of regulation 23 (interpretation) legal advice which the person took into account is to be disregarded in determining whether the person had a reasonable excuse, if the advice was given or procured by that monitored promoter.][1]

[(10B) In determining for the purpose of regulation 23 whether or not a person who is a monitored promoter within the meaning of Part 5 of the Finance Act 2014 had a reasonable excuse for a failure to do anything required to be done under a provision mentioned in paragraph (2), reliance on legal advice is to be taken automatically not to constitute a reasonable excuse if either—

(a) the advice was not based on a full and accurate description of the facts, or

(b) the conclusions in the advice that the person relied on were unreasonable.][1]

(11) A person who fails to comply with regulation 15(1) (duty of parties to notifiable contribution arrangements to notify HMRC of number, etc) or regulation 10 of the Information Regulations shall be liable to a penalty of the relevant sum.

This is subject to paragraph (14).

(12) In paragraph (11) "the relevant sum" means—

(a) in relation to a person not falling within sub-paragraph (b) or (c) below, £100 in respect of each scheme to which the failure relates,

(b) in relation to a person who has previously failed to comply with regulation 15(1) or regulation 10 of the Information Regulations on one (and only one) occasion during the period of 36 months ending with the date on which the current failure to comply with that provision began, £500 in respect of each scheme to which the current failure relates (whether or not the same as the scheme to which the previous failure relates), or

(c) in relation to a person who has previously failed to comply with regulation 15(1) or regulation 10 of the Information Regulations on two or more occasions during the period of 36 months ending with the date on which the current failure to comply with that provision began, £1,000 in respect of each scheme to which the current failure relates (whether or not the same as the schemes to which any of the previous failures relates).

(13) In paragraph (12) above "scheme" means any notifiable contribution arrangements which fall within any description prescribed by the Descriptions Regulations.

(14) Where the notifiable contribution arrangements or proposed notifiable contribution arrangements are, or are substantially the same as, a notifiable arrangements or proposed notifiable arrangements under Part 7 in relation to which a penalty has been imposed under section 98C of the Taxes Management Act 1970 in respect of a failure to comply with the provisions of Part 7, this regulation shall not apply to impose a penalty in respect of the failure to comply with the corresponding provision of these Regulations.

Amendments—[1] The following amendments made by the National Insurance Contributions (Application of Part 7 of the Finance Act 2004) (Amendment) Regulations, SI 2015/531 regs 2, 6 with effect from 12 April 2015—

– in para (1)(a)(i), words substituted for words "or (c);
– paras (2)(ca), (4A), (10A), (10B) and table entry in para (3) inserted;
– in para (4)(a), words inserted word words substituted for wod "persons" and "person"; and
– in para (4)(b), words inserted and words substituted for words "or 11".

23 Interpretation

For the purposes of this Part—

(a) a person shall be deemed not to have failed to do anything required to be done within a limited time if it was done within such further time, if any, as HMRC may have allowed; and

(b) where a person had a reasonable excuse for not doing anything required to be done—

(i) that person shall be deemed not to have failed to do it unless the excuse ceased; and

(ii) after the excuse ceased, that person shall be deemed not to have failed to do it if it was done without unreasonable delay after the excuse had ceased.

24 Modification of Part 10 of the Taxes Management Act 1970

(1) Part 10 of the Taxes Management Act 1970 so far as it relates to a penalty under section 98C of that Act shall apply in relation to a penalty under regulation 22 with the following modifications.

(2) In section 100 (determination of penalties by officer of Board) for subsection (2)(f) (penalties to which subsection (1) of the section does not apply) substitute—

"(f) regulation 22(1)(a) of the National Insurance Contributions (Application of Part 7 of the Finance Act 2004) Regulations 2012.".

PART 4
MODIFICATION OF REGULATIONS UNDER PART 7

25 Modification of the Descriptions Regulations

(1) The Descriptions Regulations apply to notifiable contribution arrangements and notifiable contribution proposals with the following modifications and any reference in those Regulations to sections 306 to 313C and section 314A shall be construed as a reference to the corresponding provision of these Regulations (see regulation 5(2)).

(2) In regulation 1 (citation, commencement and effect) omit paragraphs (2) and (3).

(3) In regulation 5 (prescribed descriptions of arrangements)—

(a) in paragraph (1) for "income tax, corporation tax and capital gains tax" substitute "national insurance contributions", and

(b) in paragraph (2) omit sub-paragraphs (f) to (h).

(4) In Part 3—

(a) for "tax advantage" wherever it occurs substitute "advantage within the meaning given by section 132A(7) of the Social Security Administration Act 1992"; and

(b) for "a tax advantage" wherever it occurs substitute "an advantage within the meaning given by section 132A(7) of the Social Security Administration Act 1992".

(5) In regulation 10 (Description 5: standardised tax products), in the heading and paragraphs (1) and (3) for "tax product" substitute "national insurance contributions product".

(6) Omit regulations 12 to 17A.

26 The Information Regulations

(1) The Information Regulations apply to notifiable contribution arrangements and notifiable contribution proposals with the following modifications and—

(a) any reference in those Regulations to sections 306 to 313C and section 314A shall be construed as a reference to the corresponding provision of these Regulations (see regulation 5(2)); and

(b) any reference in those Regulations to section 98C of the Taxes Management Act 1970 shall be construed as a reference to regulation 22 of these Regulations.

(2) In regulation 2 (interpretation)—

(a) insert the following definition immediately before the definition of "employment"—

""contributions" means national insurance contributions;";

(b) after the definition of "filing date" insert—

""notifiable contribution arrangements" has the meaning given by section 132A(3) of the Social Security Administration Act 1992;

"notifiable contribution proposal" has the meaning given by section 132A(3) of the Social Security Administration Act 1992;";

(c) omit the definition of "the prescribed taxes".

(3) In regulation 4 (prescribed information in respect of notifiable proposals and arrangements)—

(a) wherever the words appear—

(i) for "any of the prescribed taxes" substitute "the contributions";

(ii) for "notifiable arrangements" substitute "notifiable contribution arrangements";

(iii) for "notifiable proposal" substitute "notifiable contribution proposal"; and

(iv) for "tax advantage" substitute "advantage";

(b) in paragraphs (1)(b), (2)(c) and (3)(b) omit ", the IHT Arrangements Regulations or the SDLT Arrangements Regulations"; and

(c) in paragraph (5) omit the definitions of "the IHT Arrangements Regulations" and "the SDLT Arrangements Regulations".

(4) In regulation 5 (time for providing information under section 308, 308A, 309 or 310)—

(a) in paragraph (2) for "proposal or arrangements" substitute "contribution proposal or contribution arrangements";

(b) in paragraph (3) for "notifiable proposal or arrangements" substitute "notifiable contribution proposal or notifiable contribution arrangements"; and

(c) in paragraphs (6), (7) and (8) for "notifiable arrangements" substitute "notifiable contribution arrangements".

(5) In regulation 7 (time for providing information under section 312A) for "notifiable arrangements" substitute "notifiable contribution arrangements".

(6) In regulation 8 (exemption from duty under section 312A)—

(a) for "a tax advantage in respect of income tax or capital gains tax" substitute "an advantage"; and

(b) for "notifiable arrangements" substitute "notifiable contribution arrangements".

(7) Omit regulation 9.

(8) For regulation 10 (prescribed cases under section 313(3)(b)) substitute—

"10 Prescribed information under regulation 15 of the National Insurance Contributions (Application of Part 7 of the Finance Act 2004) Regulations 2012: timing and manner of delivery

(1) For the purposes of regulation 15 of the National Insurance Contributions (Application of Part 7 of the Finance Act 2004) Regulations 2012 (duty of parties to notifiable contribution arrangements to notify HMRC of number, etc) the prescribed information is—

(a) the reference number allocated by HMRC under regulation 12 to the notifiable contribution arrangements or notifiable contribution proposal;

(b) the earnings period in which the person making the notification expects an advantage to be obtained; and

(c) the employer's name, address and Unique Taxpayer Reference (UTR).

(2) The prescribed information shall be provided by the employer to HMRC in such form and manner as they may specify.

(3) Unless paragraph (4) applies, the prescribed time at which a person who is a party to notifiable contribution arrangements must provide HMRC with information under regulation 15 is whichever of (a) or (b) below applies in respect of the tax year in which the employer first enters into a transaction forming part of the notifiable contribution arrangements and whichever applies in respect of each subsequent year until an advantage ceases to apply to any person—

(a) in the case of a non-Real Time Information employer any time before the date on which the return under paragraph 22(1) of Schedule 4 to the Social Security (Contributions) Regulations 2001 (return by employer at end of year) is or would be due; or

(b) in the case of a Real Time Information employer, 14 days after the end of the final tax period of the tax year.

In this paragraph, "non-Real Time Information employer" and "Real Time Information employer" have the meanings given in paragraph 1 of Schedule 4 to the Social Security Contributions Regulations 2001 (interpretation; provisions derived from the Income Tax Acts and the Income Tax (Pay As You Earn) Regulations 2003).

(4) Where the advantage which is expected to arise from the notifiable contribution arrangements relates to Class 1A contributions only, and the transactions which comprise the notifiable contribution arrangements do not give rise to an advantage in relation to tax, the prescribed time is any time before the date on which the return under regulation 80(1) of the Social Security (Contributions) Regulations 2001 (return by employer) is or would be due—

(a) for the year in which the employer first enters into a transaction forming part of the notifiable contribution arrangements; and

(b) for each subsequent year until the advantage ceases to apply to any person.

In this paragraph the term "an advantage in relation to tax" shall be construed in accordance with section 318(1).".

(9) Omit regulations 11 and 12.

(10) In regulation 13(1)(b)(i) (prescribed information under section 313ZA: information and timing) before "arrangements" insert "contribution".

(11) In regulation 15(1)(b) (prescribed information under section 313C: information and timing) before "proposal" insert "contribution".

(12) In regulation 17 (electronic delivery of information)—

(a) in paragraph (2)—

(i) for sub-paragraph (a) substitute—

"(a) it is authorised by virtue of Part 7A of the Social Security (Contributions) Regulations 2001 (electronic communications); and";

(ii) in paragraph (b) for "section" substitute "Part".

(b) in paragraph (3)(a) for "regulations under section 132 of the Finance Act 1999" substitute "Part 7A of the Social Security (Contributions) Regulations 2001 (electronic communications)".

(13) Omit regulation 18.

27 The Tax Avoidance Schemes (Promoters and Prescribed Circumstances) Regulations 2004

(1) The Tax Avoidance Schemes (Promoters and Prescribed Circumstances) Regulations 2004 apply to notifiable contribution arrangements and notifiable contribution proposals as they apply to income tax with the following modifications and any reference in those Regulations to sections 306 to 313C and section 314A shall be construed as a reference to the corresponding provision of these Regulations (see regulation 5(2)).

(2) In regulation 1 (citation, commencement and interpretation) for paragraph (2) substitute—

"(2) In these Regulations—

"notifiable contribution arrangements" and "notifiable contribution proposal" have the meanings given by section 132A(3) of the Social Security Administration Act 1992.".

(3) In regulation 4 (persons not to be treated as promoters under section 307(1)(a)(i) or (b)(i))—

(a) for "tax advice" wherever it occurs substitute "advice about national insurance contributions"; and

(b) for "tax advantage" wherever it occurs substitute "advantage".

(4) In regulation 6 (legal professional privilege) for "section 314" substitute "section 132A(6) of the Social Security Administration Act 1992".

28 The Tax Avoidance Schemes (Penalty) Regulations 2007

The Tax Avoidance Schemes (Penalty) Regulations 2007 apply to notifiable contribution arrangements and notifiable contribution proposals as they apply to income tax and—

(a) any reference in those Regulations to sections 306 to 313C and section 314A shall be construed as a reference to the corresponding provision of these Regulations (see regulation 5(2)); and

(b) any reference in those Regulations to section 98C of the Taxes Management Act 1970 shall be construed as a reference to regulation 22 of these Regulations.

PART 5

29 Revocations

The following instruments are revoked.

(a) the National Insurance Contributions (Application of Part 7 of the Finance Act 2004) Regulations 2007;

(b) the National Insurance Contributions (Application of Part 7 of the Finance Act 2004) (Amendment) Regulations 2008;

(c) the National Insurance Contributions (Application of Part 7 of the Finance Act 2004) (Amendment) Regulations 2009;

(d) the National Insurance Contributions (Application of Part 7 of the Finance Act 2004) (Amendment) (No 2) Regulations 2009; and

(e) the National Insurance Contributions (Application of Part 7 of the Finance Act 2004) (Amendment) Regulations 2010.

2012/1898

BUSINESS INVESTMENT RELIEF REGULATIONS 2012

Made . . . . *18th July 2012*

Laid before the House of Commons . . . . *19th July 2012*

Coming into force . . . . *10th August 2012*

The Commissioners for Her Majesty's Revenue and Customs make the following Regulations in exercise of the powers conferred by section 809VJ(4) and (5) of the Income Tax Act 2007:

1 Citation, commencement and effect

(1) These Regulations may be cited as the Business Investment Relief Regulations 2012 and shall come into force on 10th August 2012.

(2) These Regulations have effect in relation to qualifying investments made on or after 6 April 2012.

2 Circumstances in which grace period may be extended

The grace period allowed for an appropriate mitigation step by section 809VJ of the Income Tax Act 2007 may be extended by an officer of Revenue and Customs if regulation 3 or 4 applies.

3 Lock-up agreements

(1) This regulation applies if conditions 1 and 2 are met.

(2) Condition 1 is that—

(a) the target company has ceased to be a private limited company by virtue of having some or all of its shares listed on a recognised stock exchange; or

(b)

(i) the target company has become a subsidiary of another company ("the new company"); and

(ii) the new company is a body corporate some or all of whose shares are listed on a recognised stock exchange (or are to be so listed).

(3) Condition 2 is that P is unable to comply with an appropriate mitigation step without breaching the terms of a lock-up agreement.

(4) For the purposes of this regulation "lock-up agreement" means a contract—

(a) entered into by P with one or more relevant parties which is directly related to the listing of shares in the target company or, as the case may be, the new company, on a recognised stock exchange; and

(b) that imposes restrictions on the time or manner in which P may—

(i) dispose of some or all of P's holding in the target company; or

(ii) dispose of some or all of any shares in the new company received by P in return for P's holding in the target company.

(5) For the purposes of this regulation "relevant party" means—

(a) the target company;

(b) the new company;

(c) professional advisors retained by the target company or the new company in relation to the listing of the shares of the target company (or, as the case may be, the shares of the new company) on a recognised stock exchange.

4 Statutory and legal bars

This regulation applies if—

(a) P is prevented from taking an appropriate mitigation step by a prohibition imposed by or under any enactment; or

(b) the taking of an appropriate mitigation step by P would breach the terms of an order imposed by any court.

2012/2933

BANK LEVY: INTERNATIONAL TAX ENFORCEMENT ARRANGEMENTS (FEDERAL REPUBLIC OF GERMANY) ORDER 2012

Made . . . . *22nd November 2012*
Laid before the House of Commons . . . . *23rd November 2012*
Coming into force . . . . *15th December 2012*

The Treasury make the following Order in exercise of the powers conferred by paragraph 67A(1) of Schedule 19 to the Finance Act 2011.

1 Citation, commencement and effect

This Order may be cited as the Bank Levy: International Tax Enforcement Arrangements (Federal Republic of Germany) Order 2012 and comes into force on 15th December 2012.

2 International tax enforcement arrangements to have effect

It is declared that—

(a) the international tax enforcement arrangements specified in Article 9 of the Convention set out in Part 1 of the Schedule to the Double Taxation Relief (Bank Levy) (Federal Republic of Germany) Order 2012 and paragraph 2 of the Protocol set out in Part 2 of that Schedule have been made in relation to the Federal Republic of Germany;

(b) the international tax enforcement arrangements have been made in association with double taxation arrangements specified in that Order; and

(c) it is expedient that those international tax enforcement arrangements should have effect.

2012/3008

FRIENDLY SOCIETIES (MODIFICATIONS OF THE TAX ACTS) REGULATIONS 2012

Made . . . . *3rd December 2012*
Laid before the House of Commons . . . . *4th December 2012*
Coming into force . . . . *31st December 2012*

The Treasury make the following Regulations in exercise of the powers conferred by sections 151(3), (4) and (6), 158(5) and (7), 166(6) and (8) and 167(4) and (6) of the Finance Act 2012.

1 Citation, commencement, effect and interpretation

(1) These Regulations may be cited as the Friendly Societies (Modifications of the Tax Acts) Regulations 2012 and shall come into force on 31st December 2012.

(2) These Regulations have effect in relation to accounting periods beginning on or after 1st January 2013.

(3) In these Regulations "FA 2012" means "the Finance Act 2012".

2 Friendly societies subject to the same basic rules as mutual insurers

The Corporation Tax Acts, in so far as they apply to—

(a) the life assurance business and other long-term business carried on by friendly societies,

(b) any part of the business of an insurance company which is exempt from corporation tax as a result of section 158 or section 166 (transfers from friendly societies to insurance companies etc) of FA 2012, or

(c) any part of the business of a friendly society which is exempt from corporation tax as a result of section 167 of FA 2012 (transfers between friendly societies),

have effect with the modifications specified in regulations 3 to 15.

3 In Schedule 7 to the Finance Act 1991, paragraph 16 (transitional relief for old general annuity contracts) applies as if in sub-paragraph (7)—

(a) in the definition of "general annuity contract" after "referable to" there were inserted "taxable", and

(b) at the appropriate place there were inserted—

""taxable general annuity business" means general annuity business the profits arising from which do not fall to be exempted from tax by virtue of section 153 (exemption for certain BLAGAB or eligible PHI business) or section 158 (transfers from friendly societies to insurance companies etc) of the Finance Act 2012, and for the purposes of this definition it shall be assumed that the friendly society has made a claim for exemption from tax under section 153 of that Act.".

4 Section 255 of CAA 2001 (apportionment of allowances and charges) applies as if for subsection (1) there were substituted—

"(1) This section applies if the long-term business of the company consists of two or more of—

(a) basic life assurance and general annuity business,

(b) non-BLAGAB long-term business, or

(c) tax exempt business.

(1A) In subsection (1)(c) "tax exempt business" has the same meaning as in section 57A of FA 2012 (section 57: meaning of "tax exempt business").".

5 Section 57 of FA 2012 (meaning of basic life assurance and general annuity business) applies as if in subsection (2)—

(a) the "or" at the end of paragraph (f) were omitted, and

(b) at the end of paragraph (g) there were inserted—

", or

(h) tax exempt business".

6 After section 57 of FA 2012 (meaning of basic life assurance and general annuity business) there is treated as inserted—

"57A Section 57: meaning of "tax exempt business"

In this Part "tax exempt business" means business in respect of which an insurance company or a friendly society is exempt from corporation tax on its profits by virtue of—

(a) section 153 (exemption for certain BLAGAB or eligible PHI business),

(b) section 158 (transfers from friendly societies to insurance companies etc),

(c) section 164 (societies registered before 1 June 1973, etc),

(d) section 165 (incorporated friendly societies),

(e) section 166 (transfers from friendly societies etc),

(f) section 167 (transfers between friendly societies).".

7 Section 63 of FA 2012 (meaning of "long-term business" and "PHI business") applies as if after subsection (2) there were inserted—

"(3) But "PHI business" does not include tax exempt business.".

8 Section 66 of FA 2012 (separate businesses for BLAGAB and other long-term business) applies as if—

(a) for subsections (1) to (3) there were substituted—

"(1) If an insurance company carries on two or more of—

(a) basic life assurance and general annuity business,

(b) tax exempt business, or

(c) other long-term business

the general rule is that each business within paragraphs (a), (b) and (c) carried on by that company is to be treated for corporation tax purposes as a separate business carried on by that company.

(2) The business within subsection (1)(a) is to consist of the basic life assurance and general annuity business.

(3) The business within subsection (1)(b) is to consist of the tax exempt business.

(3A) The business within subsection (1)(c) is to consist of the other long-term business.", and

(b) in subsection (5)(a) for "(3)" there were substituted "(3A)".

9 Section 67 (exemption where BLAGAB small part of long-term business) applies as if—

(a) for subsection (3) there were substituted—

"(3) There are instead to be two businesses that are to be regarded for corporation tax purposes as consisting of—

(a) that basic life assurance and general annuity business and the other long-term business, and

(b) tax exempt business.", and

(b) in subsection (4) for "that single trade" there were substituted "the trade in subsection (3)(a)".

10 Section 97 of FA 2012 (application of Chapter) applies as if for subsection (1) there were substituted—

"(1) This Chapter applies in the case of an insurance company that carries on basic life assurance and general annuity business and one or both of—

(a) tax exempt business, or

(b) other long-term business.".

11 Section 98 of FA 2012 (commercial allocation) applies as if after subsection (2) there were inserted—

"(2A) But in determining those items, the credits or other income, the debits or other losses and the expenses in relation to tax exempt business are not to be taken into account.".

12 Section 114 of FA 2012 (application of Chapter) applies as if—

(a) in subsection (1)—

(i) for ", has", there were substituted "carries on two or more of",

(ii) the "and" at the end of paragraph (a) were omitted, and

(iii) after paragraph (a) there were inserted—

"(aa) a tax exempt business, and",

(b) in subsection (2)—

(i) in paragraph (a) "two" were omitted, and

(ii) in paragraph (b) "(a) and (b)" were omitted, and

(c) in subsection (5)—

(i) the "and" at the end of paragraph (a) were omitted, and

(ii) after paragraph (a) there were inserted—

"(aa) calculating the profits of the tax exempt business, and".

13 In section 115 of FA 2012 (commercial allocation of accounting profit or loss and tax adjustments) subsections (1) and (2) apply as if "two" were omitted.

14 Section 172 of FA 2012 (minor definitions) applies as if in subsection (2) after "that Part", there were inserted—

"except where the context otherwise requires".

15 Section 174 of FA 2012 (index of defined terms) applies as if in the table in the second column ("where explained") in relation to the expression "basic life and general annuity business (abbreviated to "BLAGAB")" after "section 57" there were inserted "(a) to (g)".

16 Revocation

The Regulations specified in the Schedule are revoked.

SCHEDULE

Regulation 16

Regulations	*References*

The Friendly Societies (Modification of the Corporation Tax Acts) Regulations 2005	SI 2005/2014
The Friendly Societies (Modification of the Corporation Tax Acts) (Amendment) Regulations 2007	SI 2007/2134
The Insurance Companies (Tax Exempt Business) Regulations 2007	SI 2007/2145
The Friendly Societies (Modification of the Corporation Tax Acts) (Amendment) Regulations 2008	SI 2008/1937
The Friendly Societies (Transfers of Other Business) (Modification of the Corporation Tax Acts) Regulations 2008	SI 2008/1942

2012/3009

INSURANCE COMPANIES (TRANSITIONAL PROVISIONS) REGULATIONS 2012

Made . . . . *3rd December 2012*
Laid before the House of Commons . . . . *4th December 2012*
Coming into force . . . . *31st December 2012*

The Treasury make the following Regulations in exercise of the powers conferred by paragraphs 6(3), 7(2)(e), 8(2) and 37 of Schedule 17 (Part 2: Transitional Provision) to the Finance Act 2012.

1 Citation, commencement and interpretation

(1) These Regulations may be cited as the Insurance Companies (Transitional Provisions) Regulations 2012 and come into force on 31st December 2012

(2) In these Regulations—

"category" means a category in the Table;

"Schedule 17" means Schedule 17 to the Finance Act 2012;

"specified businesses" means the businesses described in paragraph 8(1)(a) to (c) of Schedule 17;

"the Table" means the Table set out in regulation 4.

2 Overview

In these Regulations—

(a) regulations 3 to 6 make provision in relation to determining the amount of the particular items that when taken together result in the total transitional difference;

(b) regulation 7 specifies particular items that are excluded items;

(c) subject to regulation 15, regulations 8 to 14 make provision to apportion particular items that are relevant computational items between the specified businesses;

(d) regulation 15 makes provision in relation to items apportioned to basic life assurance and general annuity business where section 67 of the Finance Act 2012 (exception where BLAGAB small part of long-term business) applies;

(e) regulation 16 amends paragraph 20 of Schedule 17.

3 Comparison of items in the 2012 periodical return and the 2012 balance sheet

(1) To determine the particular items that when taken together result in the total transitional difference, the insurance company must compare—

(a) the amounts included in the 2012 periodical return for the entry for each category specified in column 1 of the Table, with

(b) the amounts included in the 2012 balance sheet for the entry for that category specified in column 2 of the Table.

(2) The difference between those amounts is the particular item in relation to each category. This is subject to regulation 5(6).

(3) The comparison must be made separately in relation to with-profits funds and non-profit funds and separately in relation to each with-profits fund.

(4) Where no entry is specified as a comparator in relation to any category, the amount is treated as nil.

(5) In determining the total amount for an entry, assets are given a positive figure and liabilities are given a negative figure.

(6) For the purposes of paragraph (5), amounts in line 51 of Form 14 are treated as liabilities.
(7) If the amount for the entry for a particular category in column 2 exceeds the amount shown in column 1 the particular item is a positive figure.
(8) If the amount for the entry for a particular category in column 1 exceeds the amount shown in column 2, the particular item is a negative figure.

4 Comparison Table

The Table for the purposes of the comparison referred to in regulation 3 is as follows—

Category	*Column 1* *Amounts shown in the 2012 periodical return*	*Column 2* *Amounts shown in the 2012 balance sheet attributable to long-term business*
1	None	Deferred acquisition costs (however described in the balance sheet) and other tax deductible amounts, which represent costs relieved for tax in an accounting period ending on or before 31 December 2012 but which are debited in accounts for an accounting period beginning after that date
2	None	Amount included as an asset in respect of the value of future profits arising from a business (or part of a business) transferred to the company (but excluding an asset so far as it is regarded for accounting purposes as internally-generated)
3	None	Loan liability where receipt of the loan was brought into account in line 15 of Form 40 of any periodical return which is, or which represents, an outstanding contingent loan
4	None	Liability under a financial reinsurance arrangement which represents an outstanding reinsurance amount
5	None	Amount in respect of intangible assets to which Part 8 of CTA 2009 (intangible fixed assets) would apply but for section 902 of that Act
6	Amount in respect of the admissible value of structural assets held in a non-profit fund, reduced by any increase and increased by any decrease reflected in that value to the extent that subsection (1) of section 83XA of the Finance Act 1989 (structural assets) has not applied to that increase or decrease	Amount in respect of structural assets
7	None	Deferred income reserves and other amounts which represent income taxed in an accounting period ending on or before 31 December 2012 but which are credited in accounts for an accounting period beginning after that date

8	Amounts included in line 21 of Form 14 to the extent they relate to deferred policyholder tax	The closing deferred policyholder tax balance for the period of account where it is a net liability (subject to regulation 5(2) and (3))
9	Amounts— (a) that are not taxable or not deductible under Part 3 of CTA 2009 (Trading Income) as that Part applies to insurance companies, or (b) that are unrecognised capital amounts included in line 51 of Form 14, (subject to regulation 5(2), (4) and (5))	Amounts— (c) that are not taxable or not deductible under Part 3 of CTA 2009 as that Part applies to insurance companies, or (d) that relate to a non-profit fund included in the fund for future appropriations or the unallocated divisible surplus, (subject to regulation 5(2) and (5))
10	Amounts in relation to which the taxability or deductibility (or the timing of taxability or deductibility) in computing the company's life assurance trade profits is determined in accordance with a specific provision of the Corporation Tax Acts applying to such an amount where the same provision applies before and after the commencement of Part 2 of the Finance Act 2012	Equivalent amounts in relation to which the taxability or deductibility (or the timing of taxability or deductibility) in computing the company's life assurance trade profits is determined in accordance with a specific provision of the Corporation Tax Acts applying to such an amount where the same provision applies before and after the commencement of Part 2 of the Finance Act 2012
11	Amount in respect of linked assets (or part asset)	Amount in respect of linked assets (or part asset)
12	Mathematical reserves net of reinsured liabilities (subject to regulation 5(2))	Technical provisions net of reinsured liabilities (subject to regulation 5(2))
13	Amount included in line 51 of Form 14 relating to with-profits funds	Fund for future appropriations or the unallocated divisible surplus except in so far as it includes amounts arising in a non-profit fund
14	Amount included in line 51 of Form 14 relating to non-profit funds except in so far as this includes— (a) amounts brought into account by section 83YA of the Finance Act 1989 (changes in value of assets brought into account: non-profit companies), or (b) unrecognised capital amounts, reduced by the amount of any increase, and increased by the amount of any decrease, reflected in the admissible value of structural assets held in a non-profit fund to the extent that subsection (1) of section 83XA of the Finance Act 1989 (structural assets) has not applied to that increase or decrease (see also regulation 5(1))	None

15	None (subject to regulation 5(2) and (4))	The closing deferred policyholder tax balance for the period of account where it is a net asset (subject to regulation 5(2) and (3))
16	Amounts reflected in the cumulative taxed surplus which are not taken into account in determining any particular item in relation to categories 1 to 15 and which are referable to particular policies	Amounts reflected in the amount attributed to shareholders as at 31 December 2012 which are not taken into account in determining any particular item in relation to categories 1 to 15 and which are referable to particular policies
17	Amounts reflected in the cumulative taxed surplus which are not taken into account in determining any particular item in relation to any other category	Amounts reflected in the amount attributed to shareholders as at 31 December 2012 which are not taken into account in determining any particular item in relation to any other category

5 Adjustments to Table amounts

(1) The amount in column 1 of category 14 cannot be reduced except as expressly provided in category 14.

(2) Where the calculation of the mathematical reserves or the technical provisions referred to in category 12 includes amounts in respect of deferred tax, paragraphs (3) to (5) apply.

(3) Amounts in column 2 of category 12 which relate to deferred policyholder tax are excluded from category 12 and are included in the determination of the particular item in category 8 or category 15 as the case may be.

(4) If the aggregate of amounts in column 1 of category 12 which relate to deferred policyholder tax is a positive figure, that aggregate amount is excluded from category 12 and is included—

(a) in column 1 of category 15 to the extent that it does not exceed the amount in column 2 of category 15 (as adjusted under paragraph (3)), and

(b) in column 1 of category 9 in so far as it exceeds the amount in column 2 of category 15.

(5) Amounts in respect of deferred tax not within paragraphs (3) or (4) are excluded from the amount in category 12 and are included as an amount in category 9.

(6) If the total of all the particular items in relation to category 15 determined by the comparisons made under regulation 3 (adjusted under paragraphs (2) to (4) of this regulation) exceeds the deferred policyholder tax—

(a) the particular items in relation to category 15 are reduced by the amount of the excess (but not below nil), and

(b) the particular items in relation to category 8 are increased by the same amount.

Where this paragraph applies and there is more than one particular item in relation to category 15, the extent to which each item is adjusted under subparagraphs (a) and (b) is determined on a just and reasonable basis.

(7) For the purposes of paragraph (6), "deferred policyholder tax" means—

(a) the amount included in the accounts of the company for the accounting period ending on 31 December 2012 in respect of deferred tax so far as it is wholly attributable to policyholder tax, and

(b) amounts in column 2 to which paragraph (3) applies.

6 Table definitions

In the Table and regulation 5—

"admissible value" has the meaning given in section 83XA(9) of the Finance Act 1989;

"the closing deferred policyholder tax balance for the period of account" shall be interpreted in accordance with section 108 of the Finance Act 2012;

"deferred income reserves" means the fee, commission or other income received in respect of contracts with policyholders which for accounting purposes is deferred and recognised as income over more than one period of account;

"deferred policyholder tax" means the amount included in the 2012 periodical return or in the accounts of the company for the accounting period ending on 31 December 2012 in respect of deferred tax so far as it is wholly attributable to policyholder tax (except in regulation 5(6) in which case see regulation 5(7));

"life assurance trade profits" means profits arising from life assurance business calculated in accordance with the provisions applicable for the purposes of the taxation of such profits under section 35 of CTA (charge on trade profits);

"linked assets" means assets of an insurance company which are identified in its records as assets by reference to the value of which benefits provided for under a policy or contract are to be determined and in cases where only part of an asset is so identified, references to a linked asset are references to that part;

"mathematical reserves" are those reserves which are determined in accordance with section 1.2 of the Insurance Prudential Sourcebook;

"outstanding contingent loan" has the meaning given in paragraph 7(3) of Schedule 17;

"outstanding re-insurance amount" has the meaning given in paragraph 7(4) of Schedule 17;

"structural assets" has the meaning given in section 83XA(3) of the Finance Act 1989;

"unrecognised capital amounts" shall be interpreted in accordance with section 83YB(3) and (4) of the Finance Act 1989;

"wholly attributable to policyholder tax" shall be interpreted in accordance with section 108(2) of the Finance Act 2012.

7 Excluded items

(1) A particular item is an excluded item for the purposes of paragraph 7 of Schedule 17 if it relates to an item in any of categories 1 to 10.

(2) Paragraph 7(6) of Schedule 17 applies to such items.

8 Apportionment in relation to a with-profit fund (1): category 13

(1) This regulation applies to a relevant computational item which relates to category 13 to the extent that—

(a) the amount of the entries for that category are attributable to the component amounts in categories 1, 2, 5, 7 and 8, and

(b) those component amounts in categories 1, 2, 5, 7 and 8 are referable to particular policies.

(2) The relevant computational item (or part of the item) must be apportioned between the specified businesses by reference to the policies referable to each specified business to which the entries in column 1 and column 2 in the Table relate.

9 Apportionment in relation to a with-profit fund (2): category 15

(1) This regulation applies to a relevant computational item which relates to a with-profit fund and is an item within category 15.

(2) The relevant computational item must be apportioned to the business described in paragraph 8(1)(a) of Schedule 17 (basic life assurance and general annuity business).

10 Apportionment in relation to a with-profit fund (3)

(1) This regulation applies to a relevant computational item which relates to a with-profit fund where neither regulation 8 or 9 applies.

(2) Each relevant computational item must be apportioned between the specified businesses in the same proportion as the bonuses declared for that with-profit fund are referable to each of the specified businesses in respect of the accounting period ending on 31 December 2012.

(3) But if the bonuses declared in respect of the accounting period ending on 31 December 2012—

(a) are nil,

(b) are of a negligible amount by reference to the liabilities to the policyholders of the fund at that date, or

(c) would otherwise give a result which is not representative of the respective contribution of the specified businesses to the fund,

the company must apportion each relevant computational item between the specified businesses in a way which fairly reflects the proportion of the fund that each of the specified businesses represents as at 31 December 2012.

(4) Where a company is one to which paragraph 3 or paragraph 4 of Schedule 17 applies, paragraphs (2) and (3) of this regulation apply as if the references to the accounting period ending on 31 December 2012 were references to the last accounting period which ended before 31 December 2012.

11 Apportionment in relation to a non-profit fund: categories 11, 12, 15 and 16

(1) This regulation applies to a relevant computational item which relates to a non-profit fund and is an item within—

(a) category 11,

(b) category 12,

(c) category 15, or

(d) category 16.

(2) Each relevant computational item must be apportioned between the specified businesses by reference to the policies referable to each specified business to which the entries in column 1 and column 2 in the Table relate.

12 Apportionment in relation to unrelieved FAFTS charge

(1) This regulation applies to an amount treated as a relevant computational item under paragraph 16 of Schedule 17.

(2) The relevant computational item must be apportioned between the businesses described in paragraphs 8(1)(a) and (b) of Schedule 17 in the same proportion as if it was an amount to which the Financing-Arrangement-Funded Transfers to Shareholders Regulations 2008 applied and the relevant computational item was a section 83YC(3) amount within the meaning of those Regulations.

13 Apportionment in relation to a non-profit fund: category 14

(1) This regulation applies to a relevant computational item which relates to category 14.

(2) Each relevant computational item must be apportioned between the specified businesses as follows—

(a) a fraction equal to the applicable relevant fraction must be apportioned to the business described in paragraph 8(1)(b) of Schedule 17 (gross roll up business);

(b) a fraction equal to—

1 - *AAF*

must be apportioned to the business described in paragraph 8(1)(c) of Schedule 17 (PHI business), where AAF is the applicable appropriate fraction; and

(c) the remainder must be apportioned to the business described in paragraph 8(1)(a) of Schedule 17 (basic life assurance and general annuity business).

(3) The applicable relevant fraction is, on the assumptions in paragraph (5), the total of—

(a) the relevant fractions in relation to appropriate periods of account beginning on or after 9 December 2009, and

(b) the relevant fraction in relation to the last period of account beginning before 9 December 2009 where section 47(4) of the Finance Act 2010 (apportionment of asset value increases) would apply,

weighted in accordance with the amount of the relevant computational item to which each of those fractions applies as a proportion of the total of those amounts.

(4) The applicable appropriate fraction is, on the assumptions in paragraph (5), the total of—

(a) the appropriate fractions in relation to appropriate periods of account beginning on or after 9 December 2009, and

(b) the appropriate fraction in relation to the last period of account beginning before 9 December 2009 where section 47(4) of the Finance Act 2010 (apportionment of asset value increases) would apply,

weighted in accordance with the amount of the relevant computational item to which each of those fractions applies as a proportion of the total of those amounts.

(5) The assumptions are that—

(a) section 432CA of ICTA (apportionment of asset value increase where line 51 amount decreases) applies in relation to the period of account ending on 31 December 2012,

(b) the period of account ending on 31 December 2012 is an "appropriate period of account" for the purposes of that section, and

(c) "the affected amount" for the purposes of that section is equal to the relevant computational item to which this regulation applies.

(6) In this regulation—

"appropriate period of account" has the same meaning as in section 432CA(5) of ICTA (apportionment of asset value increase where line 51 amount decreases);

"the appropriate fraction" has the meaning given in section 432C(5) of ICTA (section 432B apportionment non-participating funds);

"the relevant fraction" has the meaning given in section 432C(9) of ICTA (section 432B apportionment non-participating funds).

14 Apportionment in relation to a non-profit fund: other categories

(1) This regulation applies to a relevant computational item to which regulations 8 to 13 do not apply.

(2) Each relevant computational item must be apportioned between the specified businesses as follows—

(a) a fraction equal to the relevant fraction calculated for the accounting period ending on 31 December 2012 in accordance with section 432C(9) of ICTA, is to be apportioned to the business described in paragraph 8(1)(b) of Schedule 17 (gross roll up business);

(b) a fraction equal to—

1 - *AF*

is to be apportioned to the business described in paragraph 8(1)(c) of Schedule 17 (PHI business), where AF is the appropriate fraction calculated for the accounting period ending on 31 December 2012 in accordance with 432C(5) of ICTA; and

(c) the remainder is to be apportioned to the business described in paragraph 8(1)(a) of Schedule 17 (basic life assurance and general annuity business).

15 Apportionment to BLAGAB where section 67 of Finance Act 2012 applies

(1) If section 67 of the Finance Act 2012 (exception where BLAGAB small part of long-term business) ("section 67") applies to an insurance company for the accounting period beginning on 1 January 2013, any amount that would apart from this regulation be apportioned to basic life assurance and general annuity business under these Regulations must instead be apportioned to gross roll-up business.

(2) If section 67 applies to an insurance company in a subsequent accounting period when the full amount of the receipts or expenses within paragraph 9 of Schedule 17 of the business has not been treated as arising to the company, the receipts or expenses are to continue to be dealt with in accordance with the provisions of Schedule 17 but are treated as arising for that accounting period and the remainder of the 10 year period in question as receipts or expenses within paragraph 10 of Schedule 17.

(3) But paragraph (2) does not apply if paragraph 14 of Schedule 17 applies.

16 Amendment to paragraph 20 of Schedule 17

In paragraph 20 of Schedule 17 (overseas life insurance companies)—

(a) in sub-paragraph (a), after "standards" insert "or the Council Directive of 19th December 1991 on the annual accounts and consolidated accounts of insurance undertakings (No 91/674/EEC)", and

(b) in sub-paragraph (b), after "statements" insert "or the technical accounts (or part of the technical accounts)".

2012/3024

CONTROLLED FOREIGN COMPANIES (EXCLUDED TERRITORIES) REGULATIONS 2012

Made . . . . 3rd December 2012

Laid before the House of Commons . . . . 5th December 2012

Coming into force . . . . 1st January 2013

The Commissioners for Her Majesty's Revenue and Customs make these Regulations in exercise of the powers conferred by section 371KB(2) and (3) of the Taxation (International and Other Provisions) Act 2010.

1 Citation, commencement and effect

(1) These Regulations may be cited as the Controlled Foreign Companies (Excluded Territories) Regulations 2012 and come into force on 1st January 2013.

(2) These Regulations have effect for accounting periods of CFCs beginning on or after 1st January 2013.

2 Interpretation

In these Regulations—

"TIOPA 2010" means the Taxation (International and Other Provisions) Act 2010;

"the Schedule" means the Schedule to these Regulations.

3 Excluded territories

A territory listed in Part 1 of the Schedule is an excluded territory for the purposes of Chapter 11 of Part 9A of TIOPA 2010 (the excluded territories exemption).

4 Modified excluded territories exemption to apply in specified cases

(1) For the purposes of Chapter 11 of Part 9A of TIOPA 2010, the requirements of section 371KB(1)(b) and (c) of that Act do not have to be met in order for the excluded territories exemption to apply for a CFC's accounting period if—

(a) for the purposes of that Chapter, the CFC is for the accounting period resident in—

(i) Australia,

(ii) Canada,

(iii) France,

(iv) Germany,

(v) Japan, or

(vi) the United States of America;

(b) requirement A is met (if applicable); and

(c) requirement B is met.

(2) Requirement A is applicable only if the CFC is resident as mentioned in paragraph (1)(a) by virtue of section 371TA(1)(b) of TIOPA 2010.

(3) Requirement A is that the CFC would still be resident as mentioned in paragraph (1)(a) were the following subsections to be substituted for section 371KC(3) of TIOPA 2010—

"(3) But section 371TA(1)(b) is to be applied only if the CFC or persons with interests in the CFC are subject to taxation under the law of the territory in question on all of the CFC's income arising during the accounting period.

(3A) For the purposes of subsection (3), the CFC's income does not include any dividend or other distribution received, other than one for which the company paying the dividend or other distribution is entitled to a deduction against its profits for tax purposes under the law of the territory in which it is resident.".

(4) Requirement B is that at no time during the accounting period is the CFC's business carried on, to any extent, through a permanent establishment which the CFC has in a territory outside the territory in which it is resident for the accounting period for the purposes of Chapter 11 of Part 9A of TIOPA 2010.

5 Further requirement to be met for excluded territories exemption to apply

For the purposes of Chapter 11 of Part 9A of TIOPA 2010, Part 2 of the Schedule specifies a further requirement which must be met in order for the excluded territories exemption to apply for a CFC's accounting period.

SCHEDULE

Regulations 3 and 5

PART 1
EXCLUDED TERRITORIES

Afghanistan
Algeria
Angola
Argentina
Armenia
Aruba
Australia
Austria
Azerbaijan
Bangladesh
Barbados
Belarus
Belgium
Belize
Benin
Bolivia
Botswana
Brazil
Brunei
Burundi
Cameroon
Canada
China
Colombia
Croatia
Cuba
Czech Republic
Fiji
Finland
France
Gabon
Gambia
Germany
Ghana
Greece
Guyana
Honduras
Iceland
India
Indonesia
Iran
Israel
Italy
Ivory Coast
Jamaica
Japan
Kenya
Lesotho
Libya
Luxembourg
Malawi
Malaysia
Malta
Mexico
Panama
Papua New Guinea
Peru
Philippines
Poland
Portugal
Puerto Rico
Republic of Korea
Russia
Saudi Arabia
Senegal
Sierra Leone
Slovakia
Slovenia
Solomon Islands
South Africa
Spain
Sri Lanka
Swaziland
Sweden
Tanzania
Thailand
Trinidad and Tobago
Tunisia
Turkey
Uganda
Ukraine

Democratic Republic of the Congo
Denmark
Dominican Republic
Ecuador
Egypt
El Salvador
Falkland Islands
Faroe Islands
Monaco
Morocco
Namibia
Netherlands
New Zealand
Nigeria
Norway
Pakistan
United States of America
Uruguay
Venezuela
Vietnam
Zambia
Zimbabwe

PART 2

SPECIFIED FURTHER REQUIREMENT

If at any time during the accounting period the CFC carries on insurance business in relation to which the CFC is regulated in any territory, none of that business is carried on in Luxembourg at that time.

2012/3041

CONTROLLED FOREIGN COMPANIES (EXCLUDED BANKING BUSINESS PROFITS) REGULATIONS 2012

Made . . . . *5th December 2012*
Laid before the House of Commons . . . . *7th December 2012*
Coming into force . . . . *1st January 2013*

The Commissioners for Her Majesty's Revenue and Customs make the following Regulations in exercise of the powers conferred by section 371FD of the Taxation (International and Other Provisions) Act 2010.

1 Citation, commencement and effect

(1) These Regulations may be cited as the Controlled Foreign Companies (Excluded Banking Business Profits) Regulations 2012.

(2) These Regulations come into force on 1st January 2013 and have effect for accounting periods of CFCs beginning on or after 1st January 2013.

2 Interpretation

(1) In these Regulations—

"BIPRU 11" means the rules of that name set out in the [PRA Handbook][1];

"GENPRU 2 Annex 2" means the rules of that name set out in the [PRA Handbook][1];

"group consolidated accounts" means group accounts prepared in accordance with the requirements of Chapter 4 of Part 15 of the Companies Act 2006;

"group regulatory return" means consolidated financial information disclosed by a bank in accordance with BIPRU 11;

["the PRA Handbook" means the Handbook made by the Prudential Regulation Authority under the Financial Services and Markets 2000 Act (as that Handbook has effect from time to time);][2]

"regulatory return period" means the period to which a group regulatory return relates;

"total risk weighted assets" means the amount shown as such in the group regulatory return for a regulatory return period;

"total tier one capital" means the amount shown as such (or as "total tier 1 capital") in the group regulatory return for a regulatory return period;

"UK banking group" means a group for which consolidated financial information is required to be compiled under BIPRU 11.

(2) In these Regulations, the following expressions have the meaning given by the [PRA Handbook[1]]—

(a) "bank",
(b) "exposure",
(c) "group",
(d) "risk weighted exposure amount".

(3) In these Regulations, "net total tier one capital" so far as it is used in relation to a CFC means the CFC's total tier one capital after deductions, as calculated in accordance with the capital resources table shown in GENPRU 2 Annex 2.

Amendments—[1] In para (1), in definitions of "BIPRU 11" and "GENPRU 2 Annex 2", words substituted, and definition of "the PRA Handbook" substituted for definition of "the FSA Handbook", and in para (2), words substituted by the Financial Services Act 2012 (Consequential Amendments and Transitional Provisions) Order, SI 2014/3041 art 3, Sch 2 para 243 with effect from 1 April 2013.

3 Disapplication of Step 3 in section 371FA(1)

(1) Paragraph (2) applies to an accounting period of a CFC if the CFC meets the conditions specified in regulation 4, as supplemented by regulation 5.

(2) Step 3 in section 371FA(1) is not to apply in relation to the CFC's trading finance profits in that accounting period so far as they arise from banking business carried on by the CFC in relation to which the CFC is regulated in the territory in which it is resident.

4 Regulatory capital requirements test

(1) The first condition is that throughout the accounting period ("the relevant accounting period") the CFC is a member of a UK banking group ("the CFC's UK banking group").

(2) The second condition is that the CFC's tier one capital ratio at the end of the relevant accounting period does not exceed the capital ratio limit.

(3) The third condition is that it is reasonable to suppose that the average tier one capital ratio of the CFC during the relevant accounting period did not exceed the capital ratio limit.

5 Supplementary provisions

For the purposes of regulation 4—

(1) The capital ratio limit is 125% of the group tier one capital ratio of the CFC's UK banking group for its last regulatory return period ending before the beginning of the relevant accounting period.

(2) The group tier one capital ratio of a UK banking group for a regulatory return period is to be calculated using the following formula—

100% x AB

where—

(a) A is the total tier one capital of the group for the regulatory return period or, if different, the amount calculated in the same way but using amounts (calculated in accordance with BIPRU 11) shown in the group consolidated accounts (if any) for the same period, and

(b) B is the total risk weighted assets of the group for the regulatory return period or, if different, the amount calculated in the same way but using amounts (calculated in accordance with BIPRU 11) shown in the group consolidated accounts (if any) for the same period.

(3) A CFC's tier one capital ratio at a time is to be calculated using the following formula—

100% x CD

where—

(a) C is the net total tier one capital of the CFC at that time, and

(b) D is the aggregate of the risk weighted exposure amounts of the CFC for all its exposures at that time.

(4) In the formula in paragraph (3), C and D are to be determined on the assumptions that BIPRU 11 applies to the CFC and that the CFC is required by those rules to make a disclosure of financial information other than as part of a group regulatory return.

2012/3044

INSURANCE COMPANIES AND CFCS (AVOIDANCE OF DOUBLE CHARGE) REGULATIONS 2012

Made .... *6th December 2012*
Laid before the House of Commons .... *7th December 2012*
Coming into force .... *31st December 2012*

The Treasury make the following Regulations in exercise of the powers conferred by section 213A of the Taxation of Chargeable Gains Act 1992.

1 Citation, commencement and effect

(1) These Regulations may be cited as the Insurance Companies and CFCs (Avoidance of Double Charge) Regulations 2012 and come into force on 31st December 2012.

(2) These Regulations have effect in relation to accounting periods beginning on or after 1st January 2013.

2 Introduction

(1) These Regulations apply in any case where—

(a) an insurance company to which the I-E rules apply is deemed to make a disposal under section 212 of the Taxation of Chargeable Gains Act 1992 (annual deemed disposal of holdings of unit trusts etc) of an interest in an offshore fund,

(b) the offshore fund is a CFC, and

(c) there is (or, but for these Regulations, would be) a CFC charge on the company referable to its relevant interest in the CFC for the accounting period in which the disposal is deemed to have been made.

(2) These Regulations modify the operation of—

(a) the CFC rules (see regulations 3 to 5), and

(b) section 212 of the Taxation of Chargeable Gains Act 1992 (see regulation 6).

(3) In these Regulations—

"principal CFC" means the CFC referred to in paragraph (1);

"associated CFC" means an offshore fund which is a CFC in which the insurance company has an indirect interest by virtue of having an interest in the principal CFC.

3 CFC control test

The CFC rules apply to the insurance company by reference to its interest in the principal CFC or any associated CFC only if the insurance company controls the principal CFC by virtue of section 371RE of TIOPA 2010 (control determined by reference to accounting standards).

4 CFCs which are equity funds

(1) The CFC rules do not apply to the insurance company by reference to its interest in the principal CFC or any associated CFC if—

(a) at least 95% of the total assets of the CFC consists of shares, and

(b) no more than 5% of the sum of the CFC's assumed taxable total profits and exempt distribution income consists of interest or returns which are economically equivalent to interest.

(2) But this regulation does not apply if the insurance company enters into any arrangements the main purpose or one of the main purposes of which is—

(a) to secure a tax advantage for itself or any other company in relation to the operation of the CFC rules, or

(b) to avoid bringing an amount into account under Part 5 or 6 of CTA 2009 (loan relationships and relationships treated as loan relationships etc).

(3) In this regulation—

"arrangement" includes any agreement, scheme, transaction or understanding (whether or not legally enforceable);

"assumed taxable total profits" has the same meaning as in Part 9A of TIOPA 2010 (see section 371VA);

"economically equivalent to interest" has the same meaning as in section 486B(2) of CTA 2009;

"exempt distribution income" has the same meaning as in section 371CC(9) of TIOPA 2010;

"share" has the same meaning as in section 476(1) of CTA 2009;

"tax advantage" has the meaning given by section 1139 of CTA 2010.

5 Modification relating to I-E calculation

Section 371BH of TIOPA 2010 (companies carrying on BLAGAB) applies as if in subsection (6) after "step 1" there were inserted "or 2".

6 Modification of section 212 of the Taxation of Chargeable Gains Act 1992

(1) For the purposes of section 212 of the Taxation of Chargeable Gains Act 1992 the market value at the time of the deemed disposal under that section is adjusted as follows.

(2) The market value is treated as reduced by the total chargeable profits of the principal CFC and any associated CFC in any qualifying accounting period in so far as those profits are apportioned to the insurance company under the CFC rules and give rise to a CFC charge.

(3) But if the insurance company has received a distribution from the principal CFC or any associated CFC in any accounting period in which the disposal is deemed to have been made, the market value at the time of the deemed disposal is adjusted on a just and reasonable basis having regard to all the circumstances.

(4) For the purposes of paragraph (2), a "qualifying accounting period" is an accounting period of the principal CFC and any associated CFC which ends in an accounting period of the company in which a disposal of the company's interest in the principal CFC is deemed to have been made under section 212.

(5) In this regulation, "accounting period" and "chargeable profits", in relation to a CFC, have the same meanings as in Part 9A of TIOPA 2010 (see section 371VA of that Act).

2012/3070

VISITING FORCES AND INTERNATIONAL MILITARY HEADQUARTERS (EU SOFA) (TAX DESIGNATION) ORDER 2012

Made . . . . *12th December 2012*

Coming into force in accordance with Article 1(2)

At the Court at Buckingham Palace, the 12th day of December 2012

Present,

The Queen's Most Excellent Majesty in Council

Her Majesty, in exercise of the powers conferred upon Her by section 303 of the Income Tax (Earnings and Pensions) Act 2003, section 833 of the Income Tax Act 2007, section 155 of the Inheritance Tax Act 1984, by and with the advice of Her Privy Council, makes the following Order—

1 Citation and commencement

(1) This Order may be cited as the Visiting Forces and International Military Headquarters (EU SOFA) (Tax Designation) Order 2012.

(2) This Order shall come into force immediately after the coming into force of the EU SOFA in respect of the United Kingdom.

2 Interpretation

In this Order—

"the EU SOFA" means the Agreement between the member states of the European Union concerning the status of military and civilian staff seconded to the institutions of the European Union, of the headquarters and forces which may be made available to the European Union in the context of the preparation and execution of the tasks referred to in Article 17(2) of the Treaty on European Union, including exercises, and of the military and civilian staff of the member states put at the disposal of the European Union to act in this context;

"the Treaty on European Union" means the Treaty on European Union signed at Maastricht on 7 February 1992 (as amended by the Treaty of Lisbon).

3 Designation

For the purpose of giving effect to Article 16 of the EU SOFA, each of the countries specified in the First Schedule to this Order, and the international military headquarters specified in the Second Schedule to this Order, are hereby designated for the purposes of—

(a) section 303 of the Income Tax (Earnings and Pensions) Act 2003;
(b) section 833 of the Income Tax Act 2007; and
(c) section 155 of the Inheritance Tax Act 1984.

SCHEDULE 1
DESIGNATED COUNTRIES

Article 3

Austria, Belgium, Bulgaria, Cyprus, Czech Republic, Denmark, Estonia, Finland, France, Germany, Greece, Hungary, Ireland, Italy, Latvia, Lithuania, Luxembourg, Malta, Netherlands, Poland, Portugal, Romania, Slovakia, Slovenia, Spain, Sweden.

SCHEDULE 2
DESIGNATED INTERNATIONAL MILITARY HEADQUARTERS

Article 3

The European Union Operational Headquarters at Northwood.

2012/3071

VISITING FORCES AND INTERNATIONAL MILITARY HEADQUARTERS (NATO AND PFP) (TAX DESIGNATION) ORDER 2012

Made . . . . 12th December 2012

Coming into force in accordance with Article 1(2)

At the Court at Buckingham Palace, the 12th day of December 2012

Present,

The Queen's Most Excellent Majesty in Council

Her Majesty, in exercise of the powers conferred upon Her by section 74A of the Finance Act 1960, section 155 of the Inheritance Tax Act 1984, section 303 of the Income Tax (Earnings and Pensions) Act 2003 and section 833 of the Income Tax Act 2007, by and with the advice of Her Privy Council, makes the following Order—

1 Citation and commencement

(1) This Order may be cited as the Visiting Forces and International Military Headquarters (NATO and PfP) (Tax Designation) Order 2012.

(2) This Order shall come into force on the day after the date on which it is made.

2 Revocations

The Orders in Schedule 1 are revoked.

3 Interpretation

In this Order—

"NATO" means the North Atlantic Treaty Organisation based on the North Atlantic Treaty dated 4th April 1949;

"the NATO SOFA" means the Agreement regarding the Status of Forces of Parties to the North Atlantic Treaty dated 19th June 1951;

"the Paris Protocol" means the Protocol on the Status of International Military Headquarters set up pursuant to the North Atlantic Treaty dated 28th August 1952;

"PfP" means the Partnership for Peace programme of practical bilateral cooperation between individual Partner countries and NATO;

"the PfP SOFA" means the Agreement among the State Parties to the North Atlantic Treaty and the Other States Participating in the Partnership for Peace regarding the Status of their Forces dated 19th June 1995.

4 NATO designation

For the purpose of giving effect to Article X of the NATO SOFA and Article VII of the Paris Protocol each of the countries specified in the Second Schedule to this Order, and each of the headquarters specified in the Fourth Schedule to this Order, is hereby designated for the purposes of section 74A of the Finance Act 1960, section 155 of the Inheritance Tax Act 1984, section 303 of the Income Tax (Earnings and Pensions) Act 2003 and section 833 of the Income Tax Act 2007.

5 PfP designation

For the purpose of giving effect to Article I of the PfP SOFA each of the countries specified in the Third Schedule to this Order is hereby designated for the purposes of section 74A of the Finance Act 1960, section 155 of the Inheritance Tax Act 1984, section 303 of the Income Tax (Earnings and Pensions) Act 2003 and section 833 of the Income Tax Act 2007.

SCHEDULE 1

Article 2

Designation Orders revoked

Orders revoked	*References*
The Visiting Forces and Allied Headquarters (Income Tax and Death Duties) (Designation) Order 1961	SI 1961/580
The Visiting Forces and Allied Headquarters (Stamp Duties) (Designation) Order 1961	SI 1960/581
The Visiting Forces and Allied Headquarters (Income Tax and Capital Gains Tax) (Designation) Order 1998	SI 1998/1513
The Visiting Forces (Income Tax and Capital Gains Tax) (Designation) Order 1998	SI 1998/1514
The Visiting Forces and Allied Headquarters (Inheritance Tax) (Designation) Order 1998	SI 1998/1515
The Visiting Forces (Inheritance Tax) (Designation) Order 1998	SI 1998/1516
The Visiting Forces and Allied Headquarters (Stamp Duties) (Designation) Order 1998	SI 1998/1517
The Visiting Forces (Stamp Duties) (Designation) Order 1998	SI 1998/1518

SCHEDULE 2

DESIGNATED NATO COUNTRIES

Article 4

Albania, Belgium, Bulgaria, Canada, Croatia, Czech Republic, Denmark, Estonia, France, Germany, Greece, Hungary, Iceland, Italy, Latvia, Lithuania, Luxembourg, Netherlands, Norway, Poland, Portugal, Romania, Slovakia, Slovenia, Spain, Turkey, United States of America.

SCHEDULE 3

DESIGNATED PFP COUNTRIES

Article 5

Armenia, Austria, Azerbaijan, Belarus, Bosnia and Herzegovina, Finland, Georgia, Ireland, Kazakhstan, Kyrgyz Republic, Malta, Moldova, Montenegro, Russia, Serbia, Sweden, Switzerland, Tajikistan, the former Yugoslav Republic of Macedonia, Turkmenistan, Ukraine, Uzbekistan.

SCHEDULE 4

DESIGNATED HEADQUARTERS

Article 4

Headquarters of the Supreme Allied Commander Transformation (HQ SACT)
Supreme Headquarters Allied Powers Europe (SHAPE)
Maritime Component Command Headquarters Northwood (CC-MAR HQ Northwood)
Commander Submarines Allied Naval Forces North (COMSUBNORTH)
NATO Airborne Early Warning and Control Force (NAEW&CF)
NATO Joint Electronic Warfare Core Staff (NATO JEWCS)
Headquarters United Kingdom—Netherlands Amphibious Force (UKNLAF)
Headquarters United Kingdom—Netherlands Landing Force (UKNLLF)
The European Air Group (EAG)
The Intelligence Fusion Centre (IFC)
Headquarters Allied Rapid Reaction Corps (HQ ARRC)

2013/13

TAXATION OF CHARGEABLE GAINS (GILT-EDGED SECURITIES) ORDER 2013

Made . . . .*10th January 2013*

The Treasury make the following Order in exercise of the powers conferred by paragraph 1 of Schedule 9 to the Taxation of Chargeable Gains Act 1992:

1 Citation

This Order may be cited as the Taxation of Chargeable Gains (Gilt-edged Securities) Order 2013.

2 Securities specified as gilt-edged securities

For the purpose of the Taxation of Chargeable Gains Act 1992 the following securities are specified as "gilt-edged securities"—

$3^1/_4$% Treasury Gilt 2044
$0^1/_8$% Index-linked Treasury Gilt 2024
$0^1/_4$% Index-linked Treasury Gilt 2052
$0^1/_8$% Index-linked Treasury Gilt 2044
$1^3/_4$% Treasury Gilt 2022
1% Treasury Gilt 2017.

2013/420

PROFITS FROM PATENTS (EEA RIGHTS) ORDER 2013

Made . . . .*26th February 2013*
Laid before the House of Commons . . . .*27th February 2013*
Coming into force . . . .*1 April 2013*

The Treasury make this Order under the power conferred by section 357BB(1)(c) and (7) of the Corporation Tax Act 2010:

1 Citation and commencement

(1) This Order may be cited as the Profits from Patents (EEA Rights) Order 2013.
(2) This Order comes into force on 1st April 2013.

2 Rights to which Part 8A of CTA 2010 applies

(1) A right corresponding to a right within section 357BB(1)(a) or (b) of the Corporation Tax Act 2010 which is granted under the law of a qualifying EEA state under the standard process applicable in the state is a right to which Part 8A of that Act applies.
(2) The following are qualifying EEA states—

Austria
Bulgaria
Czech Republic
Denmark
Estonia
Finland
Germany
Hungary
Poland
Portugal
Romania
Slovakia
Sweden.

(3) A right is taken to be granted under the standard process applicable in a state in any case unless—

(a) there is more than one process for determining applications for the right under the law of the state, and

(b) the right in question is granted under a process which is less rigorous than another process.

(4) A process is less rigorous than another if it requires—

(a) a less rigorous examination of the application than the other, or

(b) fewer conditions to be met than the other.

2013/460

BUILDING SOCIETIES (CORE CAPITAL DEFERRED SHARES) REGULATIONS 2013

Made . . . . .28th February 2013

Coming into force in accordance with regulation 1(1)

The Treasury make the following Regulations in exercise of the powers conferred by section 221 of the Finance Act 2012.

A draft of this instrument was laid before and approved by a resolution of the House of Commons in accordance with section 221(6) of the Finance Act 2012.

1 Citation, commencement and effect

(1) These Regulations may be cited as the Building Societies (Core Capital Deferred Shares) Regulations 2013 and come into force on the day after the day on which they are made.

(2) These Regulations have effect in relation to shares issued, and securities converted into shares, on or after that date.

2 Core capital deferred shares

(1) In these Regulations, "core capital deferred shares" are deferred shares that form part of the core tier one capital of a building society.

(2) For the purposes of this regulation—

(a) "building society" and "deferred shares" have the same meanings as in the Building Societies Act 1986, and

(b) the reference to "core tier one capital" is to be read in accordance with the Handbook of Rules and Guidance made by the Financial Services Authority (as that Handbook has effect from time to time).

3 Disapplication of provisions

(1) The following provisions do not apply in relation to core capital deferred shares—

(a) section 109 of the Building Societies Act 1986 (exemption from stamp duty),

(b) section 372 of ITTOIA 2005 (building society dividends),

(c) section 889 of ITA 2007 (payments in respect of building society securities),

(d) the exclusion of a share in a building society in the definition of "share" in section 476(1) of CTA 2009 (other definitions),

(e) section 498 of CTA 2009 (building society dividends and interest),

(f) section 1054 of CTA 2010 (building society payments) (and accordingly any interest, dividend or other distribution payable in respect of core capital deferred shares is a distribution of the society for corporation tax purposes).

(2) Core capital deferred shares are not—

(a) loan capital under section 78(7) of FA 1986,

(b) qualifying corporate bonds under section 117 of TCGA 1992, or

(c) restricted preference shares under section 160 of CTA 2010.

2013/489

NATURAL RESOURCES BODY FOR WALES (TAX CONSEQUENCES) ORDER 2013

Made . . . . .6th March 2013
Laid before the House of Commons . . . . .7th March 2013
Coming into force . . . . .1st April 2013

The Treasury make this Order in exercise of the powers conferred by section 25 of the Public Bodies Act 2011.

1 Citation and Commencement

This Order may be cited as the Natural Resources Body for Wales (Tax Consequences) Order 2013 and comes into force on 1st April 2013.

2 Transfers from the Countryside Council for Wales to the Natural Resources Body for Wales

(1) This article applies in the case of any transfer of property, rights or liabilities from the Countryside Council for Wales to the Natural Resources Body for Wales as a result of a transfer scheme made by the Welsh Ministers under section 23 of the Public Bodies Act 2011.

(2) For the purposes of the Tax Acts those bodies are to be treated as the same person.

(3) In particular, the transfer is to be disregarded for those purposes.

2013/938

SMALL CHARITABLE DONATIONS REGULATIONS 2013

Made . . . . .18 April 2013
Coming into force in accordance with regulation 1

The Commissioners for Her Majesty's Revenue and Customs make the following Regulations in exercise of the powers conferred by sections 11, 12(6), 13(7) and 17(3) of the Small Charitable Donations Act 2012.

In accordance with section 17(2) of that Act, a draft of this instrument was laid before the House of Commons and approved by a resolution of the House of Commons.

1 Citation and commencement

These Regulations may be cited as the Small Charitable Donations Regulations 2013 and come into force on the day after the day on which they are made.

2 Interpretation

In these Regulations—

"the 2012 Act" means the Small Charitable Donations Act 2012;

"overpayment" means an amount paid to a charity under section 1 of the 2012 Act to which the charity was not, or has ceased to be, entitled;

"TMA 1970" means the Taxes Management Act 1970.

3 Making and giving effect to top-up claims

(1) Subject to the modifications in paragraph (2), and to paragraph (3), Schedule 1A to TMA 1970 (claims etc not included in returns) applies in relation to—

(a) making and amending top-up claims and giving effect to top-up claims and amendments;

(b) enquiring into top-up claims and completing an enquiry by issue of a closure notice;

(c) amending a top-up claim in a closure notice and appealing against any such amendment,

as it applies to a claim or election under the Tax Acts made otherwise than in a return.

(2) The modifications are—

(a) a reference to an amount of tax to be discharged or repaid is to be treated as a reference to an amount of top-up payment to be made;

(b) a reference to the discharge or repayment of tax is to be treated as a reference to the making of a top-up payment;

(c) a reference to a year of assessment or accounting period is to be treated as a reference to a tax year;

(d) in paragraph 4(1), for "Subject to sub-paragraphs (1A), (3) to (5)" substitute "Subject to sub-paragraph (3)".

(3) In applying Schedule 1A to TMA 1970 for the purposes of this regulation, omit—

(a) paragraph 2(2);

(b) in paragraph 2A—

(i) sub-paragraph (2A);

(ii) in sub-paragraph (3), "sub-paragraph (3A) and";

(iii) sub-paragraph (3A);
(iv) in sub-paragraph (4), "Subject to sub-paragraph (5) below,";
(v) sub-paragraphs (5) and (7);

(c) in paragraph 4—
(i) sub-paragraphs (1A) and (2);
(ii) in sub-paragraph (3), "or (2)";
(iii) sub-paragraphs (4) and (5);

(d) in paragraph 5—
(i) in sub-paragraph (1), "or, in the case of a partnership claim, any successor of that person";
(ii) in sub-paragraph (3), paragraph (b) and the "or" immediately preceding it;

(e) paragraph 7(3) and (8);

(f) in paragraph 8—
(i) in sub-paragraph (1), the words from "whether—" to the end;
(ii) sub-paragraphs (2) and (3);

(g) in paragraph 9—
(i) in sub-paragraph (1), paragraph (b) and the "or" immediately preceding it;
(ii) sub-paragraphs (2) and (5).

(4) No top-up claim may be made more than 2 years after the end of the tax year to which the claim relates.

[3A Notices under section 9A(1) of the 2012 Act

(1) A notice under section 9A(1) of the 2012 Act is to be in such form, contain such particulars, and be accompanied by such information as HMRC may determine.

(2) HMRC may in particular—

(*a*) require or permit a notice to be given by each connected eligible charity separately, or by all of the connected eligible charities jointly;

(*b*) permit a notice to be given by two or more of the connected eligible charities jointly.

(3) A notice in relation to a tax year may not be given—

(*a*) more than 2 years after the end of that tax year;

(*b*) after the end of the period of 12 months beginning with the day on which a top-up claim in respect of small donations made in that tax year is first made by any of the connected eligible charities.][1]

Amendments—[1] Regulation 3A inserted by the Small Charitable Donations and Childcare Payments Act 2017 s 4(1), (6) with effect for the tax year 2017–18 and subsequent tax years. This regulation may be amended or revoked as if it had been inserted by regulations under the Small Charitable Donations Act 2012 s 11 (Small Charitable Donations and Childcare Payments Act 2017 s 4(7)).

4 Information powers: orders for delivery of documents

The following provisions of TMA 1970 apply to an offence involving serious fraud in connection with, or in relation to, the making of a top-up claim as they apply to such an offence in connection with, or in relation to, tax—

(a) section 20BA (orders for the delivery of documents);

(b) section 20BB (falsification etc of documents);

(c) section 20D (interpretation of sections 20 to 20CC);

(d) Schedule 1AA (orders for production of documents).

5 Information and inspection powers

(1) Subject to the modifications in paragraph (2), and to paragraph (3), Schedule 36 to the Finance Act 2008 (information and inspection powers) applies to checking a charity's position in relation to a top-up claim or an overpayment as it applies to checking a person's tax position.

(2) The modifications are—

(a) a reference to checking a person's tax position is to be treated as a reference to checking a charity's position in relation to a top-up claim or an overpayment;

(b) a reference to a taxpayer is to be treated as a reference to a charity;

(c) a reference to prejudice to the assessment or collection of tax is to be treated as a reference to prejudice to the assessment or collection of an overpayment;

(d) in paragraph 5(4)(b), for "tax" substitute "top-up claims";

(e) in paragraph 19(1)(a), for "tax" substitute "a top-up claim or an overpayment";

(f) in paragraph 25, a reference to a tax adviser is to be treated as a reference to a person appointed to give advice to a charity in relation to a top-up claim or an overpayment;

(g) in paragraph 50—
(i) in sub-paragraph (1)(c), for "the amount of tax that the person has paid, or is likely to pay, is significantly less" substitute "the amount of overpayment made, or likely to be made, to a charity, is significantly more";

(ii) in sub-paragraph (3), for "the amount of tax which has not been, or is not likely to be, paid by the person" substitute "the amount of overpayment which has been, or is likely to be, made to a charity";

(h) in paragraph 62(1), after "the Taxes Acts," omit the "or" and insert—

"(aa) the Small Charitable Donations Act 2012, or".

(3) In applying Schedule 36 to the Finance Act 2008 for the purposes of this regulation, omit—

(a) paragraphs 10A and 11;

(b) in the heading to paragraph 12 and in sub-paragraph (1) of that paragraph, "10A or 11";

(c) paragraphs 12A and 12B;

(d) in paragraph 13—

(i) in sub-paragraph (1A), "(except as required under sub-paragraph (2A))";

(ii) in sub-paragraph (2), "10A or 11";

(iii) sub-paragraphs (2A) and (2B);

(e) paragraph 17;

(f) paragraphs 21 to 22;

(g) paragraphs 33 to 38;

(h) paragraph 41;

(i) in paragraph 50(6)—

(i) paragraph (a);

(ii) paragraph (c) and the "and" immediately preceding it;

(j) paragraphs 56 and 57;

(k) paragraph 60(3);

(l) paragraphs 61 and 61A;

(m) paragraphs 63 to 92.

6 Agents of the charity: information powers and penalties

(1) Subject to the modifications in paragraph (2), and to paragraph (3), Parts 1 to 6 of Schedule 38 to the Finance Act 2012 (tax agents: dishonest conduct) apply to an individual who, in the course of business, assists a charity in connection with a top-up claim, a top-up payment or an overpayment as they apply to tax agents.

(2) The modifications are—

(a) a reference to a tax agent is to be treated as a reference to an individual who, in the course of business, assists a charity in connection with a top-up claim, a top-up payment or an overpayment;

(b) a reference to a client's tax affairs or tax position is to be treated as a reference to the affairs or position of a charity in relation to a top-up claim, a top-up payment or an overpayment;

(c) a reference to a loss of tax revenue or to the tax revenue lost is to be treated as a reference to an overpayment, and a loss of tax revenue is brought about for the purposes of paragraph 3(1) and (4) if an eligible charity obtains a top-up payment to which it is not, or has ceased to be, entitled;

(d) in paragraph 7(3)(a), the reference to an offence relating to tax is to be treated as including a reference to an offence committed in connection with a top-up claim, a top-up payment or an overpayment;

(e) in paragraph 15(1)(a), for "tax" substitute "a top-up claim or an overpayment";

(f) in paragraph 27(3)(b), for "a loss of tax revenue from a client is balanced by an overpayment" substitute "an overpayment to a client charity is balanced by an amount paid to HMRC".

(3) In applying Schedule 38 to the Finance Act 2012 for the purposes of this regulation, omit paragraphs 36 and 37.

7 Overpayments: making and notifying assessment

(1) Where an officer of Revenue and Customs discovers that an overpayment has been made, the officer may make an assessment in the amount to be repaid to HMRC by the charity.

(2) Notice of an assessment under this regulation—

(a) shall be served on the charity assessed;

(b) shall state the amount of overpayment and the reason why, in the officer's view, the charity is not, or has ceased to be, entitled to it;

(c) shall state the date of issue of the assessment and the time within which an appeal against it may be made;

(d) may contain an assessment of overpayments relating to more than one tax year.

(3) In the case of a charity which is a trust, an assessment under this regulation may be made on, and in the name of, any one or more of the trustees in the tax year in which the assessment is made.

8 Overpayments: time limit for assessment

(1) Subject to paragraphs (2) and (3), an assessment of an overpayment may be made at any time not more than 4 years after the end of the tax year to which it relates.

(2) An assessment involving an overpayment brought about carelessly by a charity, or by a person acting on its behalf, may be made at any time not more than 6 years after the end of the tax year to which it relates.
(3) An assessment involving an overpayment brought about deliberately by a charity, or by a person acting on its behalf, may be made at any time not more than 20 years after the end of the tax year to which it relates.
(4) An assessment of an overpayment shall not be out of time if it is made before the relevant date.
(5) The relevant date for the purposes of paragraph (4) is the later of—
- (a) the last day of the tax year following that in which an officer of Revenue and Customs discovered the overpayment; or
- (b) where a top-up claim made by a charity is enquired into by an officer of Revenue and Customs, the day on which, by virtue of paragraph 7(1) of Schedule 1A to TMA 1970 as applied by regulation 3, the enquiry is completed.

(6) An objection to the making of an assessment of an overpayment on the ground that it is out of time shall only be made on an appeal against the assessment.

9 Overpayments: altering an assessment and payment of amount assessed

(1) After the notice of an assessment of an overpayment has been served on a charity, the assessment shall not be altered except in accordance with the provisions of TMA 1970 applied to it by regulation 11(1).
(2) Subject to section 55 of TMA 1970 as applied by regulation 11(2), an amount assessed as an overpayment must be paid to HMRC within 30 days of the date of service on the charity of the notice of assessment.

10 Overpayments: appeal against assessment

(1) An appeal may be brought against an assessment of an overpayment.
(2) Notice of an appeal under paragraph (1) must—
- (a) specify the grounds of appeal, and
- (b) be given—
  - (i) in writing to the officer of Revenue and Customs by whom the notice of assessment was given;
  - (ii) within 30 days of the date of service on the charity of the notice of assessment.

11 Overpayments: application of TMA 1970 to appeals against assessments

(1) The following provisions of TMA 1970 apply to an appeal against an assessment of an overpayment as they apply to an appeal against an assessment to tax—
- (a) section 49 (late notice of appeal);
- (b) sections 49A to 49I (appeal: HMRC review or determination by tribunal);
- (c) section 50(6), (7), (10) and (11)(a) and (b) (procedure);
- (d) section 54 (settling of appeals by agreement).

(2) Subject to the modification in paragraph (4), section 55 (recovery of tax not postponed) of TMA 1970 applies to an appeal against an assessment of an overpayment as it applies to an appeal to the tribunal against an assessment to tax other than a self-assessment.
(3) Subject to the modification in paragraph (4), section 56 (payment of tax where there is a further appeal) of TMA 1970 applies for the purposes of payment of an amount determined as an overpayment as it applies to an amount of tax determined as payable or repayable.
(4) The modification is that a reference to tax is to be treated as a reference to an overpayment.

12 Collection and recovery

Part 6 of TMA 1970 (collection and recovery) applies to overpayments, interest and penalties which have become due and payable under these Regulations as it applies to income tax, interest charged and penalties imposed under that Act.

13 Persons chargeable in a representative capacity

Sections 71 (bodies of persons) and 75 (receivers appointed by a court) of TMA 1970 apply to overpayments as they apply to income tax chargeable to any person.

14 Interest

Sections 101 (late payment interest on sums due to HMRC) and 103 (rates of interest) of, and paragraphs 3 and 4 of Schedule 53 (late payment interest) to, the Finance Act 2009 together with any regulations made by the Treasury under section 103 of that Act, apply to overpayments which have become due and payable under these Regulations as they apply for the purposes of any amount payable by a person to HMRC under or by virtue of an enactment.

15 Penalties

(1) Subject to the modifications in paragraph (2), and to paragraph (3), Schedule 24 to the Finance Act 2007 (penalties for errors) applies in connection with a top-up claim as it applies to income tax for the purposes of—
- (a) liability for penalties;

(b) the calculation and assessment of penalties; and
(c) appeals against the assessment of penalties.

(2) The modifications are—

(a) in paragraphs 1(1) and 1A(1), the reference to a document of a kind listed in the Table includes a reference to a document containing a top-up claim;
(b) in paragraphs 1(2) and 1A(2), the reference to a false or inflated claim to repayment of tax is to be treated as a reference to a false or inflated top-up claim;
(c) in paragraph 5(1), the reference to an additional amount due or payable in respect of tax is to be treated as a reference to an amount of overpayment due or payable;
(d) in paragraph 18, a reference to tax is to be treated as a reference to a top-up claim.

(3) In applying Schedule 24 to the Finance Act 2007 for the purposes of this regulation, omit—

(a) paragraph 2 and references to that paragraph or to the failure to notify or disclose an under-assessment in paragraphs 5, 9, 11, 13, 18 and 21;
(b) paragraph 4(3) to (5);
(c) paragraph 4A(1)(b) and the "or" immediately preceding it, (2), (3) and (7);
(d) paragraph 4C;
(e) paragraph 5(2) to (4);
(f) paragraphs 6 to 8;
(g) paragraph 12;
(h) paragraph 13(4) and (7);
(i) paragraphs 19 and 20;
(j) paragraphs 21A and 21B;
(k) paragraphs 24 to 27;
(l) paragraphs 29 to 31.

16 Penalties: publishing details of defaulters

(1) Subject to the modifications in paragraph (2), and to paragraph (3), section 94 of the Finance Act 2009 (publishing details of deliberate tax defaulters) applies to a charity and its managers where they have incurred one or more penalties in relation to a top-up claim as it applies to a person who has incurred a tax penalty.

(2) The modifications are—

(a) a reference to a relevant tax penalty is to be treated as a reference to a penalty under paragraph 1(1) or 1A(1) of Schedule 24 to the Finance Act 2007 as applied by regulation 15;
(b) a reference to potential lost revenue is to be treated as a reference to the amount of overpayment to be repaid to HMRC as a result of correcting the inaccuracy to which the penalty relates;
(c) all references to Schedule 41 to the Finance Act 2008 (penalties: failure to notify and certain VAT and excise wrongdoing) are omitted.

(3) In applying section 94 of the Finance Act 2009 for the purposes of this regulation, omit subsections (12) to (15).

(4) In this regulation, "managers", in relation to a charity, means the persons having the general control and management of the administration of the charity and includes the trustees of a charity which is a trust.

17 Charity mergers: applications

(1) This regulation applies to an application by the new charity under section 12(1) or 13(1) of the 2012 Act (charity mergers: new charity taking over activities of one charity or several charities).

(2) An application must be made—

(a) *in writing to an officer of Revenue and Customs;*
(b) *before the relevant date.*

(3) An application must contain—

(a) *the information specified in paragraph (4);*
(b) *the consent to the application of each old charity that is in existence at the time of the application, signed by two old charity managers of each consenting charity;*
(c) *if the application is made under section 13(1), notification of which of the old charities is the relevant old charity for the purposes of the application.*

(4) The information specified in this paragraph is, in relation to each old charity and the new charity—

(a) *the name and address of the charity and any reference number given by HMRC;*
(b) *the charitable instruments or other governing documents of the charity;*
(c) *the names and addresses of the managers of the new charity and of the old charity managers;*
(d) *a full description of the charitable activities;*
(e) *any other information which HMRC may reasonably require in order to reach its decision on the application.*

(5) Subject to paragraph (6), the relevant date for the purposes of this regulation and regulation 18 is the earlier of—

(a) *60 days before the new charity makes its first gift aid exemption claim; or*
(b) *90 days after the new charity began to carry on the activities of the old charity or the relevant old charity.*

(6) Where an application relates to a merger which occurred before the date these Regulations come into force, the relevant date for the purposes of this regulation and regulation 18 is the earlier of—
(a) *90 days before the new charity makes its first top-up claim; or*
(b) *5th April 2014.*

Amendments—Regulations 17–19 repealed by the Small Charitable Donations and Childcare Payments Act 2017 s 1(1), (5) with effect for the tax year 2017–18 and subsequent tax years, but will continue to have effect in relation to cases where the time of the merger is before the tax year 2017–18 (Small Charitable Donations and Childcare Payments Act 2017 s 8(1)).

18 Charity mergers: elections as to relevant old charity under section 13(4)(d)

(1) An election under section 13(4)(d) of the 2012 Act must be made by the new charity—
(a) *in writing to an officer of Revenue and Customs;*
(b) *before the relevant date.*

(2) For the relevant date, see regulation 17(5) and (6).

(3) Once notified to an officer of Revenue and Customs, an election under section 13(4)(d) cannot be withdrawn or varied.

Amendments—Regulations 17–19 repealed by the Small Charitable Donations and Childcare Payments Act 2017 s 1(1), (5) with effect for the tax year 2017–18 and subsequent tax years, but will continue to have effect in relation to cases where the time of the merger is before the tax year 2017–18 (Small Charitable Donations and Childcare Payments Act 2017 s 8(1)).

19 Charity mergers: HMRC decisions and appeals

(1) Where an application has been made in accordance with regulation 17, an officer of Revenue and Customs must notify the new charity of a decision by HMRC to—
(a) *certify under section 12(1) or 13(1); or*
(b) *refuse to so certify.*

(2) An appeal may be brought against the refusal by HMRC to certify.

(3) Notice of an appeal under paragraph (2) must—
(a) *specify the grounds of appeal;*
(b) *be given—*
(i) *in writing to the officer of Revenue and Customs by whom the notification under paragraph (1)(b) was given;*
(ii) *within 30 days of the date of service on the charity of the notification under paragraph (1)(b).*

(4) On an appeal to the tribunal under this regulation, the tribunal may—
(a) *direct that the new charity is to be treated as if HMRC had certified under section 12(1) or 13(1) with effect from a specified date;*
(b) *send the matter back to any officer of Revenue and Customs for reconsideration; or*
(c) *dismiss the appeal.*

Amendments—Regulations 17–19 repealed by the Small Charitable Donations and Childcare Payments Act 2017 s 1(1), (5) with effect for the tax year 2017–18 and subsequent tax years, but will continue to have effect in relation to cases where the time of the merger is before the tax year 2017–18 (Small Charitable Donations and Childcare Payments Act 2017 s 8(1)).

20 Documents: form, delivery, service and lodgement

Sections 108(1) and 113 to 115A of, and Schedule 3A to, TMA 1970 (documents) apply to claims, assessments, applications, elections and other documents made, required, issued, served, sent or lodged for the purposes of or in connection with a top-up claim, top-up payment or overpayment as they apply to documents for the purposes of or in connection with income tax.

2013/1741

REGISTERED PENSION SCHEMES AND RELIEVED NON-UK PENSION SCHEMES (LIFETIME ALLOWANCE TRANSITIONAL PROTECTION) (NOTIFICATION) REGULATIONS 2013

Made . . . . 11.06 am on 19th July 2013
Laid before the House of Commons . . . . 22nd July 2013
Coming into force . . . . 12th August 2013

The Commissioners for Her Majesty's Revenue and Customs make the following Regulations in exercise of the powers conferred by section 251(1) of the Finance Act 2004 and now exercisable by them, and paragraphs 3 and 4(1) of Schedule 22 to the Finance Act 2013.

1 Citation, commencement and interpretation

These Regulations may be cited as the Registered Pension Schemes and Relieved Non-UK Pension Schemes (Lifetime Allowance Transitional Protection) (Notification) Regulations 2013 and come into force on 12th August 2013.

2 In these Regulations—

"HMRC" means Her Majesty's Revenue and Customs;

"paragraph 1" means paragraph 1 of Schedule 22 to the Finance Act 2013;

"paragraph 1(3) event" means an event described in sub-paragraph (3) of paragraph 1 (fixed protection 2014);

"paragraph 1 notice" means a notice of intention to rely upon paragraph 1; and

"tribunal" means the First-tier Tribunal or, where determined in accordance with the Tribunal Procedure (First-tier Tribunal) (Tax Chamber) Rules 2009, the Upper Tribunal.

3 Reliance on paragraph 1

(1) Subject to paragraph (2), an individual may rely on paragraph 1 if—

(a) the individual has given a paragraph 1 notice to HMRC, and

(b) HMRC have accepted that notice by issuing a certificate to the individual.

(2) An individual may not rely on paragraph 1 if—

(a) HMRC have refused to accept a paragraph 1 notice in accordance with regulation 6,

(b) HMRC have revoked the certificate in accordance with regulation 11, or

(c) a paragraph 1(3) event has occurred.

4 The paragraph 1 notice

(1) A paragraph 1 notice must include the following information—

(a) the title, full name, address (including post code, if applicable) and date of birth of the individual submitting the paragraph 1 notice,

(b) the national insurance number of the individual or, where the individual does not qualify for a national insurance number, the reasons for this,

(c) a declaration that paragraph 7 of Schedule 36 to the Finance Act 2004 (primary protection) does not make provision for a lifetime allowance enhancement factor in the case of the individual,

(d) a declaration that paragraph 12 of that Schedule (enhanced protection) will not apply in relation to the individual on and after 6th April 2014, and

(e) a declaration that paragraph 14 of Schedule 18 to the Finance Act 2011 (transitional provision relating to new standard lifetime allowance for the tax year 2012–13) will not apply in relation to the individual on and after 6th April 2014.

(2) A paragraph 1 notice must—

(a) be in a form prescribed by HMRC,

(b) contain a declaration that the information provided in the notice is true and complete to the best of the knowledge and belief of the person completing the form, and

(c) be received by HMRC on or before 5th April 2014.

5 Issue of certificate by HMRC

(1) If HMRC accept the paragraph 1 notice, they must issue a certificate to the individual.

(2) The certificate must have a unique reference number.

6 Refusal by HMRC to accept notice

(1) HMRC may refuse to accept the paragraph 1 notice if it does not satisfy the requirements in regulation 4.

(2) If HMRC refuse to accept the paragraph 1 notice the individual may require that HMRC provide reasons for the refusal.

7 Appeal against refusal to accept notice

(1) The individual may appeal against a refusal by HMRC to accept the paragraph 1 notice.

(2) The notice of appeal must be given to HMRC before the end of the period of 30 days beginning with the day on which the refusal to accept the paragraph 1 notice was given.

(3) Where an appeal under this regulation is notified to the tribunal, the tribunal must determine whether HMRC were entitled to take the view that the notice did not satisfy the requirements in regulation 4.

(4) If the tribunal allows the appeal, the tribunal may direct HMRC to accept the paragraph 1 notice and issue a certificate to the individual.

8 Incorrect information given in, or in connection with, the paragraph 1 notice

If the individual realises that any information given in the paragraph 1 notice or given to HMRC in connection with that notice was incorrect or has become incorrect, the individual must provide HMRC with the correct information without undue delay.

9 Requirement to inform HMRC of a paragraph 1(3) event

Where HMRC have issued a certificate the individual must—

(a) inform HMRC when a paragraph 1(3) event occurs, and

(b) provide that information before the end of the period of 90 days beginning with the day on which the individual could first reasonably be expected to have known that a paragraph 1(3) event had occurred.

10 Replacement of a certificate by HMRC

(1) HMRC may issue a certificate, replacing the previous certificate, if they have reason to believe that information given in, or in connection with, the paragraph 1 notice was incorrect or has become incorrect.

(2) A certificate issued in accordance with regulation 10(1) must have a unique reference number.

11 Revocation of a certificate by HMRC

HMRC may revoke a certificate if they—

(a) have reason to believe that a paragraph 1(3) event has occurred,

(b) have reason to believe that any of the conditions in paragraph 1(1) of Schedule 22 to the Finance Act 2013 have not been met, or

(c) have given a taxpayer notice to the individual under Part 1 of Schedule 36 to the Finance Act 2008 (power to obtain information and documents from taxpayer) in connection with paragraph 1 and the individual does not reply to that notice within the time specified in the notice.

12 Appeal against replacement or revocation of a certificate

(1) The individual may require HMRC to provide reasons for replacing or revoking the certificate.

(2) Paragraphs (1) and (2) of regulation 7 apply to a decision to replace or revoke the certificate as they apply to a refusal to accept the paragraph 1 notice.

(3) Where an appeal under this regulation is notified to the tribunal, the tribunal must determine whether HMRC replaced or revoked the certificate in accordance with regulations 10(1) or 11.

(4) If the tribunal allows the appeal, the tribunal may direct HMRC to issue a certificate to the individual.

13 Preservation of documents

(1) Where HMRC have issued a certificate the individual must preserve the certificate until no further benefit crystallisation event can occur in relation to the individual.

(2) The requirement to preserve the certificate ceases where the certificate has been revoked.

2013/1820

LIFE INSURANCE QUALIFYING POLICIES (STATEMENT AND REPORTING REQUIREMENTS) REGULATIONS 2013

Made . . . . *19th July 2013*
Laid before the House of Commons . . . . *22nd July 2013*
Coming into force . . . . *12th August 2013*

The Commissioners for Her Majesty's Revenue and Customs make the following Regulations in exercise of the powers conferred by section 552ZB(1) of, and paragraph B3(2), (7) and (9)(c) of Schedule 15 to, the Income and Corporation Taxes Act 1988.

1 Citation and commencement and interpretation

(1) These Regulations may be cited as the Life Insurance Qualifying Policies (Statement and Reporting Requirements) Regulations 2013 and come into force on 12 August 2013.

(2) In these Regulations, "Schedule 15" means Schedule 15 to the Income and Corporation Taxes Act 1988.

2 Statement by beneficiary

(1) In relation to a statement made under paragraph B3(2) of Schedule 15, the prescribed matters are set out in paragraphs (2) to (6).

(2) The following information must be given in the statement in all cases—

(a) the beneficiary's full name;

(b) the beneficiary's date of birth;

(c) the beneficiary's address including postcode;

(d) the beneficiary's National Insurance number (if any);

(e) whether the beneficiary is a beneficiary under any other qualifying policy—

(i) issued on or after 6 April 2013, or

(ii) issued before that date but in relation to which a premium limit event has occurred;

(f) a statement that the beneficiary is—

(i) not in breach of the premium limit for qualifying policies at the date the statement is made; or

(ii) in breach of the premium limit for qualifying policies at the date the statement is made but the policy in respect of which the statement is made is a restricted relief qualifying policy;

(g) whether the event giving rise to the statement is an event within paragraph B3(1)(d) of Schedule 15 (protected policies within paragraph A2(12) of Schedule 15 - endowment policies);

(h) the date the statement is made; and

(i) confirmation that the statement is correct and complete to the best of the beneficiary's knowledge and belief.

(3) Where the beneficiary is not the sole beneficiary under the policy in respect of which the statement is made, the statement must include details of the beneficiary's proportionate share of the rights under the policy.

(4) Where there has been a variation of a policy within paragraph B3(1)(b) or (c) of Schedule 15, the statement must also include the following information—

(a) the date of the variation; and

(b) details of any variation in relation to the period over which premiums are payable under the policy.

(5) Where there has been an assignment within paragraph B3(1)(e) of Schedule 15, the statement must also include the following information—

(a) the date of the assignment; and

(b) if the policy was issued on or after 6 April 2013, the name and address of the previous beneficiary.

(6) For the purpose of paragraph (2)(f), whether a beneficiary is in breach of the premium limit for qualifying policies is determined in accordance with paragraph A3(1) of Schedule 15.

3 Exceptions to the requirement to make a statement

A beneficiary is not required to make a statement under paragraph B3(2) of Schedule 15 in the following circumstances—

(a) on the issue of a policy, if—

(i) the information that must be included in a statement has been provided to the issuer in connection with the application for the issue of that policy, and

(ii) that information has not changed since making the application;

(b) on an assignment of a share in any rights under a policy, if—

(i) the beneficiary has previously made a statement under paragraph B3(2) of Schedule 15 in respect of that policy, and

(ii) that information has not changed since making that statement;

(c) on a deceased beneficiary event, if before the event the beneficiary is a beneficiary under the policy in relation to which the event [occurs;

(d) on the occurrence of an event within paragraph B3(1)(e) or (f) of Schedule 15 in respect of a policy, if—

(i) the policy is a protected policy within paragraph A4 of Schedule 15, and

(ii) the policy is a paid-up policy.][1]

Amendments—[1] In para (c), words substituted by the Life Insurance Qualifying Policies (Statement and Reporting Requirements) (Amendment) Regulations, SI 2015/544 reg 2 with effect from 26 March 2015.

4 Applications and statements not in writing

Where an application for the issue of a qualifying policy or a statement made under paragraph B3(2) of Schedule 15 is not in writing—

(a) the relevant person must, within 3 business days of receiving the application or statement, make a written record of the information given in the application or statement;

(b) the relevant person must send a copy of the written record to the applicant or beneficiary within 20 business days of making it; and

(c) the applicant or beneficiary must notify the relevant person of any errors in the written record within 30 days of receiving it and the relevant person must amend the application or statement accordingly.

5 Reporting requirements of relevant person

(1) A relevant person must provide the following information to an officer of Revenue and Customs within 3 months of the end of a tax year—

(a) where in relation to a policy a statement has been made under paragraph B3(2) of Schedule 15 in that year, the information given in the statement;

(b) where a policy has been issued in that year and regulation 3(a) applied in relation to the issue of that policy, the information given on the application for the issue of the policy;

(c) in relation to any policy within sub-paragraphs (a) or (b) and any policy which ceased, terminated, matured or in relation to which the premiums payable have reduced in that year—

(i) the date the policy was issued;

(ii) the policy identification reference;

(iii) the premiums payable under the policy.

(2) This regulation does not apply to qualifying policies issued before 6 April 2013 or to pure protection policies.

6 Amendment to the Life Assurance and Other Policies (Keeping of Information and Duties of Insurers) Regulations 1997

(1) The Life Assurance and Other Policies (Keeping of Information and Duties of Insurers) Regulations 1997 are amended as follows.

(2) In regulation 2 (interpretation), in paragraph (3)—

(a) for the words "if, on" substitute—

"if—

(a) on"; and

(b) at the end insert—

", or

(b) it is a qualifying policy".

(3) In regulation 3 (general keeping of records)—

(a) at the end of sub-paragraph (b) omit "and";

(b) at the end of sub-paragraph (c) insert—

"(d) to ascertain whether there has been or is likely to be any contravention of the requirements of the regulations made under section 552ZB(1), and

(e) to verify any information provided to an officer of Revenue and Customs as required by the regulations made under section 552ZB(1)".

(4) In regulation 9 (inspection of records by officers of the Board) at the end of paragraph 1 after "regulation 8" insert "or required by regulation 3(d) and (e).".

2013/1831

CULTURAL TEST (TELEVISION PROGRAMMES) REGULATIONS 2013

Made . . . . *18th July 2013*
Laid before the House of Commons . . . . *22nd July 2013*
Coming into force . . . . *13th August 2013*

The Secretary of State makes the following Regulations in exercise of the powers conferred by sections 1216CB and 1216CC(7) of the Corporation Tax Act 2009.

Regulations 3 to 5 of, and Schedule 1 to, these Regulations are made with the approval of the Treasury in accordance with section 1216CB(2) of that Act.

PART 1
INTRODUCTORY

1 Citation and commencement

(1) These Regulations may be cited as the Cultural Test (Television Programmes) Regulations 2013.

(2) These Regulations come into force on 13th August 2013.

2 Interpretation

(1) In these Regulations—

"the Act" means the Corporation Tax Act 2009;

"cast" means the actors and performers in a drama or animation, but not any extras;

"heads of department" has the meaning given by paragraph (2);

"participant" means a presenter, narrator, subject, or any other person who both participates and appears in a documentary [or a children's programme][1]

"production crew" means all the persons directly involved in the production of a programme who do not appear in the programme;

"programme" means a drama, a documentary[, an animation or a children's programme][1] which is a relevant programme;

"qualifying person" means a national of, or a person ordinarily resident in, an EEA state;
"recognised regional or minority language" means Welsh, Scottish-Gaelic, Irish, Scots, Ulster Scots, Cornish or British Sign Language;
"special effects" means artificial techniques or processes, which are not visual effects, used to create an illusion in a programme; and
"visual effects" means digital alterations to a programme's images.

(2) "Heads of department" means—
- (a) in relation to a drama, lead cinematographer, lead production designer, lead costume designer, lead editor, lead sound designer, lead visual effects supervisor and lead hair and makeup supervisor;
- (b) in relation to a documentary, lead camera operator, lead sound recordist, lead editor and lead researcher;
- (c) in relation to an animation, lead layout supervisor, lead production designer, lead character designer, lead editor, lead sound designer, lead visual effects supervisor and lead modelling supervisor[; and
- (d) in relation to a children's programme, lead cinematographer, lead production designer, lead costume designer, lead editor, lead sound designer, lead visual effects supervisor, lead hair and makeup supervisor and lead researcher][1].

Amendments—[1] In definition of "participant", words inserted, in definition of "programme" words substituted for words "or an animation", and sub-para (2)(d) and preceding word inserted, by the Cultural Test (Television Programmes) (Amendment) Regulations, SI 2015/1449 reg 4 with effect from 23 July 2015. Note that these amendments have effect in relation to any television programme other than an "excepted programme" (for which, see SI 2015/1449 reg 2).

PART 2
THE CULTURAL TESTS

3 Cultural test: dramas and documentaries

(1) A drama or documentary will be certified by the Secretary of State as a British programme under section 1216CB(1) of the Act only if it passes the following cultural test.

(2) A drama or documentary passes the cultural test if it meets either of the following conditions—
- (a) subject to paragraph (3), it is awarded at least [18 points][1] in total under paragraphs (4) to (7); or
- (b) it is a qualifying co-production made in accordance with an international agreement specified in Schedule 1.

(3) A drama or documentary that is awarded all the points available under paragraphs (4)(d) (language), (6) (where work carried out) and (7) (personnel) will not pass the cultural test unless it is awarded—
- (a) at least 2 points under paragraph (4)(a) (setting);
- (b) at least 2 points under paragraph (4)(b) (characters); or
- (c) 4 points under paragraph (4)(c) (story).

(4) Up to [18 points][1] will be awarded in respect of the content of the drama or documentary as follows—
- (a) up to 4 points depending on the percentage of the drama or documentary that is set in the United Kingdom or another EEA state as follows—
  - (i) 4 points for at least 75%;
  - (ii) 3 points for at least 66%;
  - (iii) 2 points for at least 50%;
  - (iv) 1 point for at least 25%;
- (b) up to 4 points depending on the number of the characters depicted in the drama or documentary that are from the United Kingdom or another EEA state as follows—
  - (i) if there are more than three characters depicted in the drama or documentary—
    - (aa) if two or three of the three lead characters are from the United Kingdom or another EEA state, 4 points;
    - (bb) if only one of the three lead characters is from the United Kingdom or another EEA state, 2 points if that character is the first or second lead, or 1 point if that character is the third lead;
  - (ii) if there are only three characters depicted in the drama or documentary—
    - (aa) if two or three of the characters are from the United Kingdom or another EEA state, 4 points;
    - (bb) if only one of the characters is from the United Kingdom or another EEA state, 2 points if that character is the first or second lead, or 1 point if that character is the third lead;
  - (iii) if there are only two characters depicted in the drama or documentary—
    - (aa) if both of the characters are from the United Kingdom or another EEA state, 4 points;

(bb) if one of the characters is from the United Kingdom or another EEA state, 2 points;

(iv) if there is only one character depicted in the drama or documentary, 4 points if that character is from the United Kingdom or another EEA state;

(c) 4 points if the drama or documentary depicts a British story or a story which relates to another EEA state;

(d) up to [6 points][1] depending on the percentage of the original dialogue that is recorded in [a language recognised for official purposes in the United Kingdom or another EEA state][1] as follows—

(i) [6 points][1] for at least 75%;

(ii) [4 points][1] for at least 66%;

(iii) 2 points for at least 50%;

(iv) 1 point for at least 25%.

(5) Up to 4 points will be awarded in respect of the contribution of the drama or documentary to the promotion, development and enhancement of [one or more of the following—

(a) British creativity;

(b) British heritage; or

(c) diversity][1].

[(6) Up to 5 points will be awarded in respect of work carried out in the making of the drama or documentary as follows—

(a) 4 points if at least 80% of the work carried out on any of the following is carried out in the United Kingdom (unless points are awarded under sub-paragraphs (b) or (c) below, in which case nil)—

(i) in relation to a drama—

(aa) principal photography;

(bb) visual effects;

(cc) special effects;

(ii) in relation to a documentary—

(aa) shooting;

(bb) visual effects;

(cc) research and development;

(dd) special effects;

(b) 2 points if at least 50% of the work carried out on any of the following is carried out in the United Kingdom—

(i) in relation to a drama—

(aa) principal photography;

(bb) special effects;

(ii) in relation to a documentary—

(aa) shooting;

(bb) research and development;

(cc) special effects;

(c) 2 points if at least 50% of the work carried out on visual effects is carried out in the United Kingdom;

(d) 1 point if at least 50% of the work carried out on any of the following is carried out in the United Kingdom—

(i) performing and recording the music score created for the drama or documentary;

(ii) audio post production;

(iii) picture post production.][1]

(7) Up to 8 points will be awarded in respect of the personnel involved in the making of the drama or documentary as follows—

(a) 1 point if a director (or, if there are more than three, one of the three lead directors) is a qualifying person;

(b) 1 point if at least one of the scriptwriters (or, if there are more than three, one of the three lead scriptwriters) is a qualifying person;

(c) 1 point if at least one of the producers (or, if there are more than three, one of the three lead producers) is a qualifying person;

(d) 1 point if a composer (or, if there are more than three, one of the three lead composers) is a qualifying person;

(e) 1 point if at least one of the actors or participants (as the case may be) (or, if there are more than three, one of the three lead actors or participants) is a qualifying person;

(f) 1 point if at least 50% of the cast or participants (as the case may be) are qualifying persons;

(g) 1 point if at least one of the heads of department is a qualifying person;

(h) 1 point if at least 50% of the production crew are qualifying persons.

Amendments—[1] In paras (2)(a), (4), "18 points" substituted for "16 points"; in para (4)(d), "6 points" substituted for "4 points" in both places, words substituted for words "the English language or a recognised regional or minority language", and "4 points" substituted for "3 points"; in para (5), words substituted for words "British culture"; and para (6) substituted; by the Cultural Test (Television Programmes) (Amendment) Regulations, SI 2015/1449 reg 5(1), (2) with effect from 23 July 2015. Note that these amendments have effect in relation to any television programme other than an "excepted programme" (for which, see SI 2015/1449 reg 2).

4 Cultural test: animation

(1) An animation will be certified by the Secretary of State as a British programme under section 1216CB(1) of the Act only if it passes the following cultural test.

(2) An animation passes the cultural test if it meets either of the following conditions—

- (a) subject to paragraph (3), it is awarded at least 16 points in total under paragraphs (4) to (7); or
- (b) it is a qualifying co-production made in accordance with an international agreement specified in Schedule 1.

(3) An animation that is awarded all the points available under paragraphs (4)(d) (language), (6) (where work carried out) and (7) (personnel) will not pass the cultural test unless it is awarded—

- (a) at least 2 points under paragraph (4)(a) (setting);
- (b) at least 2 points under paragraph (4)(b) (characters); or
- (c) 4 points under paragraph (4)(c) (story).

(4) Up to 16 points will be awarded in respect of the content of the animation as follows—

- (a) up to 4 points depending on the percentage of the animation that is set in the United Kingdom or another EEA state as follows—
  - (i) 4 points for at least 75%;
  - (ii) 3 points for at least 66%;
  - (iii) 2 points for at least 50%;
  - (iv) 1 point for at least 25%;
- (b) up to 4 points depending on the number of the characters depicted in the animation that are from the United Kingdom or another EEA state as follows—
  - (i) if there are more than three characters depicted in the animation—
    - (aa) if two or three of the three lead characters are from the United Kingdom or another EEA state, 4 points;
    - (bb) if only one of the three lead characters is from the United Kingdom or another EEA state, 2 points if that character is the first or second lead, or 1 point if that character is the third lead;
  - (ii) if there are only three characters depicted in the animation—
    - (aa) if two or three of the characters are from the United Kingdom or another EEA state, 4 points;
    - (bb) if only one of the characters is from the United Kingdom or another EEA state, 2 points if that character is the first or second lead, or 1 point if that character is the third lead;
  - (iii) if there are only two characters depicted in the animation—
    - (aa) if both of the characters are from the United Kingdom or another EEA state, 4 points;
    - (bb) if one of the characters is from the United Kingdom or another EEA state, 2 points;
  - (iv) if there is only one character depicted in the animation, 4 points if that character is from the United Kingdom or another EEA state;
- (c) 4 points if the animation depicts a British story or a story which relates to another EEA state;
- (d) up to 4 points depending on the percentage of the original dialogue that is recorded in the English language or a recognised regional or minority language as follows—
  - (i) 4 points for at least 75%;
  - (ii) 3 points for at least 66%;
  - (iii) 2 points for at least 50%;
  - (iv) 1 point for at least 25%.

(5) Up to 4 points will be awarded in respect of the contribution of the animation to the promotion, development and enhancement of British culture.

(6) Up to 3 points will be awarded in respect of work carried out in the making of the animation as follows—

- (a) 2 points if at least 50% of the work carried out on any of the following is carried out in the United Kingdom—
  - (i) shooting;
  - (ii) visual design;
  - (iii) layout and storyboarding;
  - (iv) visual effects;

(v) special effects;

(b) 1 point if at least 50% of the work carried out on any of the following is carried out in the United Kingdom—

(i) performing and recording the music score created for the animation;

(ii) voice recording;

(iii) audio post production;

(iv) picture post production.

(7) Up to 8 points will be awarded in respect of the personnel involved in the making of the animation as follows—

(a) 1 point if a director (or, if there are more than three, one of the three lead directors) is a qualifying person;

(b) 1 point if at least one of the scriptwriters (or, if there are more than three, one of the three lead scriptwriters) is a qualifying person;

(c) 1 point if at least one of the producers (or, if there are more than three, one of the three lead producers) is a qualifying person;

(d) 1 point if a composer (or, if there are more than three, one of the three lead composers) is a qualifying person;

(e) 1 point if at least one of the actors (or, if there are more than three, one of the three lead actors) is a qualifying person;

(f) 1 point if at least 50% of the cast are qualifying persons;

(g) 1 point if at least one of the heads of department is a qualifying person;

(h) 1 point if at least 50% of the production crew are qualifying persons.

(8) An animation which is set in, or in which any character is from, an undetermined location is eligible to be awarded points under paragraphs (4)(a)(ii)-(iv) (setting) and (4)(b) (characters) as if that location were in the UK or another EEA state, provided it complies with the following condition.

(9) The condition is that that animation is awarded at least one point under any of—

(a) paragraph (4)(c) (story);

(b) paragraph (4)(d) (language); or

(c) paragraph (5) (culture).

[4A Cultural test: children's programme

(1) A children's programme will be certified by the Secretary of State as a British programme under section 1216CB(1) of the Act only if it passes the following cultural test.

(2) A children's programme passes the cultural test if it meets either of the following conditions—

(a) subject to paragraph (3), it is awarded at least 18 points in total under paragraphs (4) to (7); or

(b) it is a qualifying co-production made in accordance with an international agreement specified in Schedule 1.

(3) A children's programme that is awarded all the points available under paragraphs (4)(d) (language), (6) (where work carried out) and (7) (personnel) will not pass the cultural test unless it is awarded—

(a) at least 2 points under paragraph (4)(a) (setting);

(b) at least 2 points under paragraph (4)(b) (characters); or

(c) 4 points under paragraph (4)(c) (story).

(4) Up to 18 points will be awarded in respect of the content of the children's programme as follows—

(a) up to 4 points depending on the percentage of the children's programme that is set in the United Kingdom or another EEA state as follows—

(i) 4 points for at least 75%;

(ii) 3 points for at least 66%;

(iii) 2 points for at least 50%;

(iv) 1 point for at least 25%;

(b) up to 4 points depending on the number of the characters or participants in the children's programme that are from the United Kingdom or another EEA state as follows—

(i) if there are more than three characters or participants in the children's programme—

(aa) if two or three of the three lead characters or participants are from the United Kingdom or another EEA state, 4 points;

(bb) if only one of the three lead characters or participants is from the United Kingdom or another EEA state, 2 points if that character or participant is the first or second lead, or 1 point if that character or participant is the third lead;

(ii) if there are only three characters or participants in the children's programme—

(aa) if two or three of the characters or participants are from the United Kingdom or another EEA state, 4 points;

(bb) if only one of the characters or participants is from the United Kingdom or another EEA state, 2 points if that character or participant is the first or second lead, or 1 point if that character or participant is the third lead;

(iii) if there are only two characters or participants in the children's programme—

(aa) if both of the characters or participants are from the United Kingdom or another EEA state, 4 points;

(bb) if one of the characters or participants is from the United Kingdom or another EEA state, 2 points;

(iv) if there is only one character or participant in the children's programme, 4 points if that character is from the United Kingdom or another EEA state.

(c) 4 points if the children's programme depicts a British story or a story which relates to another EEA state;

(d) up to 6 points depending on the percentage of the original dialogue that is recorded in a language recognised for official purposes in the United Kingdom or another EEA state as follows—

(i) 6 points for at least 75%;

(ii) 4 points for at least 66%;

(iii) 2 points for at least 50%;

(iv) 1 point for at least 25%.

(5) Up to 4 points will be awarded in respect of the contribution of the children's programme to the promotion, development and enhancement of one or more of the following—

(a) British creativity;

(b) British heritage; or

(c) diversity.

(6) Up to 5 points will be awarded in respect of the work carried out in the making of the children's programme as follows—

(a) 4 points if at least 80% of the work carried out on any of the following is carried out in the United Kingdom (unless points are awarded under sub-paragraphs (b) or (c) below, in which case nil)—

(i) principal photography;

(ii) animation shooting;

(iii) visual design;

(iv) layout and storyboarding;

(v) research and development;

(vi) visual effects;

(vii) special effects;

(b) 2 points if at least 50% of the work carried out on any of the following is carried out in the United Kingdom—

(i) principal photography;

(ii) animation shooting;

(iii) visual design;

(iv) layout and storyboarding;

(v) research and development;

(vi) special effects;

(c) 2 points if at least 50% of the work carried out on visual effects is carried out in the United Kingdom;

(d) 1 point if at least 50% of the work carried out on any of the following is carried out in the United Kingdom—

(i) performing and recording the music score for the children's programme;

(ii) voice recording;

(iii) audio post production;

(iv) picture post production.

(7) Up to 8 points will be awarded in respect of the personnel involved in the making of the children's programme as follows—

(a) 1 point if a director (or, if there are more than three, one of the three lead directors) is a qualifying person;

(b) 1 point if at least one of the scriptwriters (or, if there are more than three, one of the three lead scriptwriters) is a qualifying person;

(c) 1 point if at least one of the producers (or, if there are more than three, one of the three lead producers) is a qualifying person;

(d) 1 point if a composer (or, if there are more than three, one of the three lead composers) is a qualifying person;

(e) 1 point if at least one of the actors or participants (or, if there are more than three, one of the three lead actors or participants) is a qualifying person;
(f) 1 point if at least 50% of the cast are qualifying persons;
(g) 1 point if at least one of the heads of department is a qualifying person;
(h) 1 point if at least 50% of the production crew are qualifying persons.

(8) A children's programme which is set in, or in which any character or participant is from, an undetermined location is eligible to be awarded points under paragraphs (4)(a)(ii)-(iv) (setting) and (4)(b) (characters or participants) as if that location were in the UK or another EEA state, provided that it complies with the following condition.

(9) The condition is that that children's programme is awarded at least one point under any of—
(a) paragraph (4)(c) (story);
(b) paragraph (4)(d) (language); or
(c) paragraph (5) (culture).][1]

Amendments—[1] Reg 4A inserted by the Cultural Test (Television Programmes) (Amendment) Regulations, SI 2015/1449 reg 5(1), (3) with effect from 23 July 2015. Note that this amendment has effect in relation to any television programme other than an "excepted programme" (for which, see SI 2015/1449 reg 2).

5 Excluded programmes

(1) A programme must not be certified as a British programme under these Regulations if parts of the programme whose playing time exceeds 10% of the total playing time are derived from a previous programme, unless—
(a) the two programmes have the same television production company or producer; and
(b) the previous programme has not been certified under these Regulations.

(2) The Secretary of State may direct that paragraph (1) does not apply in relation to a programme if in the opinion of the Secretary of State—
(a) it is a documentary within the meaning of section 1216AB(3)(b) of the Act; and
(b) its subject matter makes it appropriate for paragraph (1) not to be applied.

(3) For the purposes of this regulation—
(a) no account may be taken of the programme soundtrack;
(b) "producer" means the person by whom the arrangements necessary for the making of a programme are undertaken.

PART 3
APPLICATIONS FOR CERTIFICATION

6 Applications

(1) An application under section 1216CC(1) for the certification of a relevant programme (other than a co-production) as a British programme must be made in writing to the Secretary of State.

(2) For the purposes of this regulation—
(a) "in writing" includes text which is—
(i) transmitted by electronic means;
(ii) received in legible form; and
(iii) capable of being used for subsequent reference;
(b) "co-production" means a programme which passes the cultural test by satisfying the condition in [regulation 3(2)(b), 4(2)(b) or 4A(2)(b)][1].

Amendments—[1] In para (2)(b), words substituted for words "regulation 3(2)(b) or 4(2)(b)" by the Cultural Test (Television Programmes) (Amendment) Regulations, SI 2015/1449 reg 6(1), (2) with effect from 23 July 2015. Note that this amendment has effect in relation to any television programme other than an "excepted programme" (for which, see SI 2015/1449 reg 2).

7 Particulars

An application in relation to a programme must set out the particulars (where applicable) described in Schedule 2 for that programme.

8 Evidence

(1) An application must be accompanied by a statutory declaration made by the applicant as to the truth of the particulars given in the application.

(2) A statutory declaration will be deemed to be properly made by the applicant if it has been made on behalf of the company by the secretary or one of the directors of the company or by any person duly authorised by the company to make the declaration on its behalf.

9 (1) Where an application for final certification seeks to rely on any point that may be awarded under [any of regulations 3(6), 3(7), 4(6), 4(7), 4A(6) or 4A(7)][1], the application must be accompanied by a report prepared by a person referred to in paragraph (2) verifying (where applicable) the particulars in paragraphs 17 to 19 of Schedule 2.

(2) The person referred to in this paragraph is a person who is eligible for appointment as a statutory auditor under section 1212 of the Companies Act 2006 and is not and was not at any time while the programme was being made—

(a) in partnership with the applicant or any officer or servant of the applicant;
(b) in the employment of the applicant or any officer or servant of the applicant; or
(c) an officer or servant of the applicant or, if the applicant is a member of a group of companies, of any other company in that group.

(3) In this regulation, "group of companies" means a company and all other companies which are its subsidiaries within the meaning of section 1159 of the Companies Act 2006.

Amendments—[1] In para (1), words substituted for words "regulation 3(6) or (7), or 4(6) or (7)" by the Cultural Test (Television Programmes) (Amendment) Regulations, SI 2015/1449 reg 6(1), (3) with effect from 23 July 2015. Note that this amendment has effect in relation to any television programme other than an "excepted programme" (for which, see SI 2015/1449 reg 2).

PART 4
GENERAL

10 For the purposes of these Regulations—

(a) a programme is set in the United Kingdom or another EEA state to the extent that it is set in a country which is now part of the United Kingdom or another EEA state;
(b) a programme depicts a British story or a story which relates to another EEA state if the subject matter of the programme or the underlying material on which the programme is based is British or relates to another EEA state;
(c) a person or a character in a programme is from the United Kingdom or another EEA state if the person or character is a national or resident of the United Kingdom or another EEA state (or was a national or resident of a country which is now part of the United Kingdom or another EEA state).

11 The amount of work that is carried out in the United Kingdom or elsewhere is determined—

(a) for the purposes of [regulations 3(6)(a)(i)(aa), 3(6)(b)(i)(aa), 4A(6)(a)(i), or 4A(6)(b)(i)][1] (principal photography), by reference to the number of days spent on the work;
(b) for the purposes of the rest of [regulations 3(6), 4(6) and 4A(6)][1](where work carried out), by reference to the amount of expenditure on the work.

Amendments—[1] In para (a), words substituted for words "regulation 3(6)(a)(i)(aa)", and in para (b), words substituted for words "regulation 3(6) and regulation 4(6)", by the Cultural Test (Television Programmes) (Amendment) Regulations, SI 2015/1449 reg 6(1), (4), (5) with effect from 23 July 2015. Note that these amendments have effect in relation to any television programme other than an "excepted programme" (for which, see SI 2015/1449 reg 2).

12 No points will be awarded under any provision of [regulations 3(6), 4(6) or 4A(6)][1] (where work carried out) in respect of work the expenditure on which is, in the opinion of the Secretary of State, insignificant in relation to the expenditure on all the work carried out in the making of the programme.

Amendments—[1] Words substituted for words "regulation 3(6) or regulation 4(6)", by the Cultural Test (Television Programmes) (Amendment) Regulations, SI 2015/1449 reg 6(1), (6) with effect from 23 July 2015. Note that this amendment has effect in relation to any television programme other than an "excepted programme" (for which, see SI 2015/1449 reg 2).

SCHEDULE 1
INTERNATIONAL AGREEMENTS

[Regulations 3(2)(b), 4(2)(b), 4A(2)(b)]

The international agreements specified in this Schedule for the purposes of [regulations 3(2)(b), 4(2)(b) and 4A(2)(b)][1] are the agreements made between the UK Government and the Governments of the countries, or the international organisations or authorities, referred to in the first column of the Table on the dates in the second column of the Table and as referred to by the Command Paper numbers in the third column.

[Country/International Organisation/Authority	*Date of Agreement*	*Command Paper*
Australia	12th June 1990	Cm 1758
Brazil	28th September 2012	Cm 9075
Canada	12th September 1975	Cmnd 6380
	9th July 1985	Cmnd 9887
	5th July 1991	Cm 1807

SIs

Israel	3rd November 2010	Cm 7994
New Zealand	14th April 1993	Cm 2638
Palestine Liberation Organisation for the benefit of the Palestinian Authority	3rd November 2010	Cm 7995
South Africa	24th May 2006	Cm 6866
	28th October 2015	Cm 9158]

Amendments—[1] In words following heading, words substituted for words "Regulation 3(2)(b), 4(2)(b)", and in sentence preceding table words substituted for words "regulations 3(2)(b) and 4(2)(b)", by the Cultural Test (Television Programmes) (Amendment) Regulations, SI 2015/1449 reg 7 with effect from 23 July 2015. Note that these amendments have effect in relation to any television programme other than an "excepted programme" (for which, see SI 2015/1449 reg 2).

[2] Table substituted by the Cultural Test (Television Programmes) (Amendment) (No 2) Regulations, SI 2015/1941 with effect from 21 December 2015. Before this substitution, the table read as above but with the omission of entries for Brazil and South Africa.

SCHEDULE 2
PARTICULARS

Regulation 7

1 Title of the programme.

2 Whether the application relates to a drama, a documentary, [an animation, or a children's programme][1].

Amendments—[1] Words substituted for words "or an animation" by the Cultural Test (Television Programmes) (Amendment) Regulations, SI 2015/1449 reg 8(1), (2) with effect from 23 July 2015. Note that this amendment has effect in relation to any television programme other than an "excepted programme" (for which, see SI 2015/1449 reg 2).

3 Total playing time in minutes and seconds of the programme, including credits and titles.

4 Whether the application is for interim or final certification.

5 Whether the programme is intended for broadcast or supply to the general public (as the case may be).

6 Name of the applicant.

7 Address of the applicant's principal place of business.

8 Address of the applicant's registered office.

9 Registered number of the applicant.

10 Date of registration of the applicant.

11 In relation to a drama [or a children's programme][1], the date of the first day of principal photography.

Amendments—[1] Words inserted by the Cultural Test (Television Programmes) (Amendment) Regulations, SI 2015/1449 reg 8(1), (3) with effect from 23 July 2015. Note that this amendment has effect in relation to any television programme other than an "excepted programme" (for which, see SI 2015/1449 reg 2).

12 Date on which the programme was completed for the purposes of section 1216AA(5) of the Act.

13 A copy of the commissioning agreement.

14 The reasons why it should be considered to be a drama, documentary[, animation, or children's programme][1] (as the case may be).

Amendments—[1] Words substituted for words "or animation" by the Cultural Test (Television Programmes) (Amendment) Regulations, SI 2015/1449 reg 8(1), (4) with effect from 23 July 2015. Note that this amendment has effect in relation to any television programme other than an "excepted programme" (for which, see SI 2015/1449 reg 2).

15 [The reasons why any point should be awarded under regulation 3(4) (drama or documentary), 4(4) (animation) or 4A(4) (children's programme) (as the case may be)][1]

Amendments—[1] Para 15 substituted by the Cultural Test (Television Programmes) (Amendment) Regulations, SI 2015/1449 reg 8(1), (5) with effect from 23 July 2015. Note that this amendment has effect in relation to any television programme other than an "excepted programme" (for which, see SI 2015/1449 reg 2).

16 [The reasons why any point should be awarded under regulation 3(5) (drama or documentary), 4(5) (animation) or 4A(5) (children's programme) (as the case may be).][1]

Amendments—[1] Para 16 substituted by the Cultural Test (Television Programmes) (Amendment) Regulations, SI 2015/1449 reg 8(1), (6) with effect from 23 July 2015. Note that this amendment has effect in relation to any television programme other than an "excepted programme" (for which, see SI 2015/1449 reg 2).

17 If the applicant seeks to rely on regulation 3(6)(a)(i)(aa)[, 3(6)(b)(i)(aa), 4A(6)(a)(i) or 4A(6)(b)(i)][1], the total number of days of principal photography and the number of days of principal photography carried out in the United Kingdom.

Amendments—[1] Words inserted by the Cultural Test (Television Programmes) (Amendment) Regulations, SI 2015/1449 reg 8(1), (7) with effect from 23 July 2015. Note that this amendment has effect in relation to any television programme other than an "excepted programme" (for which, see SI 2015/1449 reg 2).

18 If the applicant seeks to rely on any other part of [regulation 3(6), 4(6) or 4A(6)][1], the total expenditure on such other work and the expenditure on such work as was carried out in the United Kingdom.

Amendments—[1] Words substituted for words "regulation 3(6) or 4(6)" by the Cultural Test (Television Programmes) (Amendment) Regulations, SI 2015/1449 reg 8(1), (8) with effect from 23 July 2015. Note that this amendment has effect in relation to any television programme other than an "excepted programme" (for which, see SI 2015/1449 reg 2).

19 The nationality or ordinary residence of all the persons mentioned in [regulation 3(7), 4(7) or 4A(7)][1] in relation to whom the applicant is applying for a point to be awarded.

Amendments—[1] Words substituted for words "regulation 3(7) or 4(7)" by the Cultural Test (Television Programmes) (Amendment) Regulations, SI 2015/1449 reg 8(1), (9) with effect from 23 July 2015. Note that this amendment has effect in relation to any television programme other than an "excepted programme" (for which, see SI 2015/1449 reg 2).

20 Total core expenditure.

21 Total UK expenditure.

22 Total non-UK expenditure by each country the expenditure is carried out in.

23 Other expenditure, meaning all the expenditure on the work carried out in the making of the programme which is not core expenditure.

24 Shooting script in the English language.

25 A complete synopsis or treatment of the screenplay in the English language.

26 Shooting schedule.

27 Production budget.

28 Copy of the chain of title in the programme.

29 The following particulars—

(a) if any part of the programme that is the subject of the application is derived from any previous programme, the playing time in minutes and seconds of that part (the "derived part") and the combined playing time in minutes and seconds of all derived parts;

(b) the particulars in paragraph (a) are only required in relation to any derived parts which—

(i) do not have the same television production company or producer as the programme that is the subject of the application; or

(ii) are derived from a previous programme that has been certified under these Regulations;

(c) if the applicant seeks to rely on regulation 5(2), the reasons why the subject matter of the documentary makes it appropriate for the Secretary of State to direct that regulation 5(1) does not apply;

(d) for the purposes of sub-paragraph (b)(i), "producer" has the same meaning as in regulation 5(3)(b).

2013/1844

ANNUAL TAX ON ENVELOPED DWELLINGS (RETURNS) REGULATIONS 2013

Made . . . . *22nd July 2013*
Laid before the House of Commons . . . . *22nd July 2013*
Coming into force . . . . *12th August 2013*

The Commissioners for Her Majesty's Revenue and Customs, in exercise of the powers conferred on them by paragraphs 1(1) and 1(2) of Schedule 33 to the Finance Act 2013 and section 133 of the Finance Act 1999 , make the following Regulations:

1 Citation and commencement

These Regulations may be cited as the Annual Tax on Enveloped Dwellings (Returns) Regulations 2013 and come into force on 12th August 2013.

2 Interpretation

In these Regulations—

"ATED" means the annual tax on enveloped dwellings;

"the Commissioners" means the Commissioners for Her Majesty's Revenue and Customs;

"prescribed" means prescribed by the Commissioners in a published Notice as revised or replaced from time to time.

3 ATED returns

(1) A return must be made in the manner prescribed.

(2) The return may require the chargeable person to provide the information (or any part of the information) listed in the Schedule.

(3) The Commissioners may modify or dispense with any particular requirement under this regulation where it appears to them to be reasonable to do so in an individual case.

4 Delivery of Returns

(1) A return must be delivered in the prescribed manner.

(2) The Commissioners may in particular prescribe the form in which a return or related communication in relation to that return may be delivered electronically (an "electronic communication").

(3) Where provision is made for an electronic communication, the Commissioners may prescribe the method of delivery (a "prescribed electronic method").

(4) If a chargeable person has communicated with the Commissioners by means of a prescribed electronic method in respect of a return, the Commissioners must issue an electronic acknowledgement of the communication.

(5) If a person has communicated with the Commissioners by a prescribed electronic method, the Commissioners may communicate electronically with the chargeable person in respect of a return, unless they are notified by a prescribed method that the person is not, or is no longer willing to receive such communications electronically.

(6) The Commissioners may treat any information within a return as not having been provided unless it is provided in accordance with this regulation.

5 Validation of electronic communication

(1) A prescribed electronic method must incorporate an electronic validation process.

(2) Unless the contrary is proved—

(a) the use of a prescribed electronic method will be presumed to have resulted in the making of an electronic communication to the Commissioners only if this has been successfully recorded as such by the relevant electronic validation process; and

(b) the time of making an electronic communication to the Commissioners using a prescribed electronic method will be presumed to be the time recorded as such by the relevant electronic validation process.

SCHEDULE

INFORMATION TO BE CONTAINED IN AN ATED RETURN

Regulation 3(3)

Information which the Commissioners may require a chargeable person to include in a return—

(a)	the name and correspondence address of the chargeable person;
(b)	the contact telephone number of the chargeable person;
(c)	an email address;

(d)	the business unique identifier (if any); NOTES: (a) where the chargeable person is a company, the business unique identifier is HMRC's Corporation Tax Unique Taxpayer Reference number . If such a reference is not held then one of the following may be used: Company Registration Number—allocated by the Registrar of Companies where the company is incorporated; VAT Registration Number; Employer PAYE Reference (b) where the chargeable person is not a company, for example a partnership, a UK tax reference number should be entered as the business unique identifier. For example: VAT Registration Number; Employer PAYE Reference; Self Assessment Unique Taxpayer Reference.
(e)	the origin and type of business unique identifier (if any); NOTE: The origin and type of business unique identifier is the name and country of the organisation that allocated the reference, plus the type of tax reference quoted, for example HMRC UK VAT Registration Number.
(f)	the scheme reference number (if any); NOTE: If using an avoidance scheme which is intended to produce an ATED advantage and the scheme promoter has disclosed it to the Commissioners as required by law, this is the Scheme Reference Number (SRN) that the promoter has been given by HMRC.
(g)	confirmation if this is the first time the chargeable person will be required to make an ATED payment to HMRC for this property;
(h)	to confirm whether this is an amended return; NOTE: An amended return changes the information on a return that has already been sent to HMRC.
(i)	to confirm whether this is a further return; NOTE: A further return may be required by law in certain circumstances, in particular where a claim to relief is no longer available, or an acquisition of a further interest in the single dwelling interest has increased its value, so that it is now chargeable in a different band.
(j)	the period start date for the return; NOTE: This is the period start date the return relates to. The ATED period commences on 1 April annually.
(k)	the period end date for the return; NOTE: The ATED period ends on 31 March annually, however, if the taxpayer is making a return where the period of ownership is for a part year, then the period end date would be the last day of ownership.
(l)	whether this return must be filed within 90 days; NOTE: The filing date is normally 30 days after the taxpayer first comes within the charge to ATED. So, for example, if the taxpayer has newly purchased a dwelling the return must be filed within 30 days of acquisition. However, there are two exceptions to the 30 day rule and these are: (i) where a dwelling comes within the charge as a result of being newly built (section 124 of the Finance Act 2013) or (ii) it is a new dwelling produced from other dwellings (section 125 of the Finance Act 2013) In either of these two circumstances the return must be made within 90 days of the defined 'completion date' or occupation if earlier.

(m)	the ATED liability in pounds sterling (if there is an amount to pay);
(n)	the ATED relief code; NOTE: The list of ATED relief codes is: 1 Property rental businesses (to include the special conditions: sale, demolition, and, conversion) 2 Dwellings opened to the public 3 Property developers (including qualifying exchange of dwellings interests) 4 Property traders carrying on a property trading business 5 Financial institutions acquiring dwellings in the course of lending 6 Dwellings used for trade purposes (occupation by qualifying employees and partners) 7 Farmhouses (occupation for the purposes of carrying on a trade of farming) 8 Charitable companies (property held for qualifying charitable purposes) 9 Registered providers of Social Housing
(o)	if submitting an amended return under paragraph 3 of Schedule 33 to the Finance Act 2013 which results in a repayment, the charge reference number and reason for the repayment; NOTE: The charge reference number is the reference number from the original ATED payment.
(p)	the property title number;
(q)	the property address, postcode and date of acquisition;
(r)	the actual value of the dwelling in pounds sterling and date of valuation;
(s)	whether there has been a professional valuation in the period covered by the return;
(t)	whether a pre-return banding check has been requested and if so, the reference number; NOTES: (1) A request may be made to an officer of HMRC for a Pre-Return Banding Check (PRBC) where the valuation was within a ten per cent variance of a banding threshold. (2) If a PRBC was requested, a PRBC reference number is given by HMRC as part of that check.
(u)	additional address information must be provided where relief is being claimed for more than one dwelling;
(v)	total amount to be repaid;
(w)	agent details (if form is being completed by an agent of behalf of a client);
(x)	declaration—signed and dated and stating the capacity in which the person signing the declaration is completing the form.

2013/1962

INTERNATIONAL TAX COMPLIANCE (UNITED STATES OF AMERICA) REGULATIONS 2013

Made . . . . *6th August 2013*
Laid before the House of Commons . . . . *7th August 2013*
Coming into force . . . . *1st September 2013*

The Treasury make these Regulations in exercise of the powers conferred by section 222(1), (2) and (3) of the Finance Act 2013:

Revocation—These Regulations revoked by the International Tax Compliance (United States of America) Regulations, SI 2014/1506 reg 29 with effect from 30 June 2014.

2013/2242

BRB (RESIDUARY) LIMITED (TAX CONSEQUENCES) ORDER 2013

Made . . . . *5th September 2013*
Laid before the House of Commons . . . . *9th September 2013*
Coming into force . . . . *30th September 2013*

The Treasury, in exercise of the powers conferred by section 25 of the Public Bodies Act 2011, makes the following Order.

1 Citation and commencement

This Order may be cited as the BRB (Residuary) Limited (Tax Consequences) Order 2013 and comes into force on 30th September 2013.

2 Interpretation

In this Order—

"BRB Residuary" means BRB (Residuary) Limited (company registration number 4146505),

"LCR" means London & Continental Railways Limited (company registration number 2966054),

"Network Rail" means Network Rail Infrastructure Limited (company registration number 2904587),

"relevant transfer" means a transfer under a transfer scheme made by the Secretary of State for Transport under section 23 of the Public Bodies Act 2011 transferring property, rights or liabilities from BRB Residuary to the Secretary of State for Transport, LCR, Network Rail or the Rail Safety and Standards Board Limited (company registration number 04655675).

3 Chargeable gains: no gain or loss on disposal

For the purposes of the Taxation of Chargeable Gains Act 1992—

(*a*) in relation to a disposal constituted by a relevant transfer to LCR or the Secretary of State for Transport—

(i) the disposal is to be treated in relation to BRB Residuary and LCR as made for a consideration such that no gain or loss accrues to BRB Residuary, and

(ii) for the purposes of any tax provision, sub-paragraph (i) is to be treated as one of the no gain/no loss provisions in section 288(3A) of that Act (meaning of "no gain/no loss provisions"), and

(*b*) in relation to a disposal constituted by a relevant transfer to Network Rail, section 17 of that Act (disposals and acquisitions treated as made at market value) is not to have effect and the disposal is to be treated as made—

(i) in a case where consideration in money or money's worth is given by Network Rail or on its behalf, for a consideration equal to the amount or value of that consideration, or

(ii) in a case where no such consideration is given, for a consideration of nil.

4 Capital allowances

(1) For the purposes of allowances and charges provided for by the Capital Allowances Act 2001, where as a result of a relevant transfer part of a property business ("the transferred part") ceases to be carried on by BRB Residuary and is begun to be carried on by LCR—

(*a*) any allowances that could have been claimed by, or charges that would have been made on, BRB Residuary in relation to the transferred part if BRB Residuary had continued to carry on that part of the business may be claimed by, or will be made on, LCR in relation to the transferred part, and

(*b*) the amount of any such allowance or charge is to be calculated as if everything done to or by BRB Residuary had been done to or by LCR,

but the relevant transfer to LCR is not to be treated as giving rise to any such allowance or charge.

(2) For the purposes of paragraph (1)—

(*a*) the transferred part of the property business is to be treated as a separate property business carried on by LCR and any apportionments of receipts, expenses, assets and liabilities between that business and any other property business of LCR are to be made as may be just and reasonable, and

(*b*) the proportion of any allowances or charges of BRB Residuary's property business which relate to the transferred part of the property business is to be determined on a just and reasonable basis.

5 Corporation Tax: losses

(1) For the purposes of computing the profits of a property business under Part 4 of the Corporation Tax Act 2009 (property income), where as a result of a relevant transfer part of a property business ("the transferred part") ceases to be carried on by BRB Residuary and is begun to be carried on by LCR—

(*a*) any unrelieved loss relating to the transferred part of BRB Residuary's property business is treated as a loss ("the transferred loss") made by LCR in the first accounting period in which it carries on that business, and

(*b*) the transferred loss is not a "UK property loss" for the purposes of Part 5 of the Corporation Tax Act 2010 (group relief).

(2) For the purposes of paragraph (1)—

(*a*) an unrelieved loss is the amount of any loss which—

(i) cannot be deducted from the total profits of BRB Residuary for the last accounting period in which it carries on the transferred part of the business, and

(ii) would be available for carry forward to the next accounting period of BRBR under section 62 of the Corporation Tax Act 2010 if BRB Residuary continued to carry on the business, and

(*b*) the proportion of any loss of BRB Residuary's property business which relates to the transferred part of the property business is to be determined on a just and reasonable basis.

6 Corporation Tax: provisions

For the purposes of corporation tax, where in accordance with generally accepted accounting practice a provision has been recognised in the accounts of BRB Residuary in relation to property, rights or liabilities transferred by a relevant transfer to LCR or the Secretary of State for Transport—

(*a*) in computing the profits of BRB Residuary, no amount is brought into account in respect of the removal or adjustment of that provision in the accounts as a consequence of the relevant transfer, and

(*b*) in computing the profits of LCR, no amount is brought into account in respect of a provision recognised in the accounts of LCR in accordance with generally accepted accounting practice in relation to the property, rights or liabilities transferred by the relevant transfer to the extent that an amount has been brought into account as a debit in computing the profits of BRB Residuary in any accounting period in respect of a liability or charge transferred by the relevant transfer.

7 Corporation tax: loan relationships

For the purposes of Part 5 of the Corporation Tax Act 2009 (loan relationships), in relation to a relevant transfer to LCR, BRB Residuary and LCR are to be treated as if they were members of the same group.

8 Stamp duty

Stamp duty is not chargeable on an instrument making or executing a relevant transfer to LCR.

2013/2571

ANNUAL TAX ON ENVELOPED DWELLINGS AVOIDANCE SCHEMES (PRESCRIBED DESCRIPTIONS OF ARRANGEMENTS) REGULATIONS 2013

Made . . . . *9th October 2013*
Laid before the House of Commons . . . . *10th October 2013*
Coming into force . . . . *4th November 2013*

The Treasury in exercise of the powers conferred upon them by sections 306(1)(*a*) and 317(2) of the Finance Act 2004 make the following Regulations:

1 Citation, commencement and interpretation

These Regulations may be cited as the Annual Tax on Enveloped Dwellings Avoidance Schemes (Prescribed Descriptions of Arrangements) Regulations 2013 and come into force on 4th November 2013.

2 In these Regulations—

"chargeable interest" has the meaning given by section 107 of the Finance Act 2013;

"company" has the meaning given by section 166(1) of the Finance Act 2013;

"collective investment scheme" refers to a scheme as described by section 235(1) of the Financial Services and Markets Act 2000; and

"partnership" has the meaning given by section 167(1) of the Finance Act 2013.

3 In regulation 4(2)(*a*) and the Schedule reference to meeting the "ownership condition" is to be read in accordance with section 94(4) to (7) of the Finance Act 2013.

4 Prescribed description of arrangements in relation to annual tax on enveloped dwellings

(1) For the purposes of Part 7 of the Finance Act 2004 (disclosure of tax avoidance schemes) the arrangements specified in paragraph (2) are prescribed in relation to annual tax on enveloped dwellings.

(2) Arrangements are prescribed if they are not excluded arrangements under the Schedule and as a result of any element of the arrangements—

(*a*) a company, partnership or collective investment scheme ceases to meet the ownership condition in respect of the chargeable interest;

(*b*) the taxable value of the chargeable interest is reduced to [the lowest taxable value shown in the right hand column of the table in section 99(4) of the Finance Act 2013][1] ; or

(*c*) the taxable value of the chargeable interest is reduced with the consequence that a lower annual chargeable amount applies than that which otherwise would have applied.

(3) In this regulation—

(*a*) reference to a lower annual chargeable amount applying is to be read in accordance with the table at section 99(4) of the Finance Act 2013; and

(*b*) reference to "taxable value" is to be read in accordance with section 102 of the Finance Act 2013.

Amendments—[1] In para (2)(*b*), words substituted by the Annual Tax on Enveloped Dwellings Avoidance Schemes (Prescribed Descriptions of Arrangements) (Amendment) Regulations, SI 2015/464 reg 2 with effect from 1 April 2015. It is the Publisher's belief that the intention was to make the substitution for the words "£2 milllion or less" rather than "£2 million", and the amendment has been shown accordingly.

SCHEDULE

EXCLUDED ARRANGEMENTS

Regulation 4(2)

Arrangements are excluded arrangements if they comprise a transfer of the chargeable interest from a company, partnership or collective investment scheme (a "transferor") to a transferee where one or more of the following applies.

1 The transfer is on such terms as would reasonably be expected to be agreed between unconnected persons.

2 The transferor and the transferee are members of the same group of companies and the transferee meets the ownership condition.

3 The transfer constitutes a distribution out of the assets of the transferor, and the transferee is an individual, a corporation sole, a trustee or a person who meets the ownership condition.

4 The transfer constitutes a settlement.

In paragraph 1 reference to being "unconnected persons" is to be read in accordance with section 1122 of the Corporation Tax Act 2010.

In paragraph 2 reference to companies being "members of the same group of companies" is to be read in accordance with section 152 of the Corporation Tax Act 2010.

In paragraph 4 "settlement" has the meaning given by section 43 of the Inheritance Tax Act 1984.

2013/2819

UNAUTHORISED UNIT TRUSTS (TAX) REGULATIONS 2013

Made . . . . 31st October 2013

Coming into force in accordance with regulation 1(2) and (3)

The Treasury make the following Regulations in exercise of the powers conferred by section 217 of the Finance Act 2013.

In accordance with section 217(3) of that Act, a draft of this instrument was laid before the House of Commons and approved by a resolution of that House.

PART 1

INTRODUCTORY AND GENERAL PROVISIONS

1 Citation, commencement and effect

(1) These Regulations may be cited as the Unauthorised Unit Trusts (Tax) Regulations 2013.

(2) Chapters 1 and 2 of Part 2 and Chapter 1 of Part 4 (and this Part so far as applying to those Chapters) come into force on the day after the day on which these Regulations are made.

(3) Apart from that, these Regulations come into force on 6th April 2014.

2 Interpretation

In these Regulations—

"the AIF Regulations" means the Authorised Investment Funds (Tax) Regulations 2006,

"the Commissioners" means the Commissioners for Her Majesty's Revenue and Customs,

"eligible investor" has the meaning given by regulation 3(2),

"exempt unauthorised unit trust" has the meaning given by regulation 3(1),

"friendly society" has the same meaning it has for the purposes of Part 3 of FA 2012 (friendly societies carrying on long-term business),

"insurance company" has the same meaning as it has for the purposes of Part 2 of FA 2012 (insurance companies carrying on long-term business),

"non-reporting fund" has the same meaning as it has for the purposes of the Offshore Funds Regulations,

"notice" means notice in writing,

"the Offshore Funds Regulations" means the Offshore Funds (Tax) Regulations 2009,

"prospectus" means a prospectus or similar document made available to investors,

"UK resident" means resident in the United Kingdom (and references to a UK resident company are to a company which is resident there).

PART 2
EXEMPT UNAUTHORISED UNIT TRUSTS

CHAPTER 1

MEANING OF "EXEMPT UNAUTHORISED UNIT TRUST"

3 Meaning of "exempt unauthorised unit trust"

(1) For the purposes of these Regulations an unauthorised unit trust is an "exempt unauthorised unit trust" with respect to a period of account if—

(*a*) its trustees are UK resident for the period,

(*b*) throughout the period all of its unit holders are eligible investors, . . . [1]

(*c*) it is approved under these Regulations for the period[, and

(*d*) it is not treated by regulations made in exercise of the powers conferred by section 1007(2) of ITA 2007 as not being a unit trust scheme for the purposes of the definition of "unauthorised unit trust" in section 989 of that Act.][1]

(2) For the purposes of these Regulations a unit holder is an "eligible investor" if—

(*a*) any gain accruing in the event of a disposal of its units would be wholly exempt from capital gains tax or corporation tax (otherwise than by reason of residence), or

(*b*) it holds all of its units pending disposal in the capacity of manager of the unauthorised unit trust.

(3) In determining whether paragraph (2)(*a*) applies no account is to be taken of the possibility of a charge to corporation tax on income in respect of a gain accruing on a disposal by an insurance company or a friendly society.

(4) An unauthorised unit trust is not to be regarded as failing to meet the condition in paragraph (1)(*b*) in relation to any unit holder if—

(*a*) the managers or trustees of the unit trust become aware at any time that the unit holder is not an eligible investor,

(*b*) they could not reasonably have been expected to have become aware of that fact before that time, and

(*c*) the unit holder disposes of its units before the end of the period of 28 days beginning with that time.

(5) Paragraph (4) may not be relied on more than twice in any period of ten years.

Amendments—[1] In para (1), word "and" at end of sub-para (b) revoked, and sub-para (d) and preceding word "and" inserted, by the Unauthorised Unit Trusts (Tax) (Amendment) Regulations, SI 2014/585 regs 2, 3 with effect from 6 April 2014.

CHAPTER 2

APPROVAL: EXEMPT UNAUTHORISED UNIT TRUST

4 Application for approval as an exempt unauthorised unit trust

(1) The managers or trustees of an unauthorised unit trust may make an application in writing to the Commissioners for the trust ("the applicant") to be approved.

(2) An application must be made on or before the last day of the first period of account for which approval is sought (or such later date as the Commissioners may allow).

(3) If accepted, an approval has effect for the period of account the first day of which is specified in the application and all subsequent periods (unless withdrawn under regulation 8).

(4) The Commissioners may not approve an unauthorised unit trust unless they are satisfied that the unit trust has, or will have, in place appropriate arrangements for the purpose of securing that the condition in regulation 3(1)(*b*) is met.

5 Contents of application

(1) An application under this Chapter must contain the following—

(*a*) a statement specifying the first day of the first period of account for which approval is sought (such period ending no earlier than 6 April 2014),

(*b*) a copy of the applicant's current trust deed,

(*c*) a copy of the applicant's most recent prospectus,

(*d*) a statement specifying the appropriate arrangements which are or will be in place for the purpose of securing that the condition in regulation 3(1)(*b*) is and will be met for the first period for which approval is sought and all subsequent periods,

(*e*) a statement whether or not the applicant is or will be operating equalisation arrangements.

(2) A day specified in the application in paragraph (1)(*a*) may be provisional.

(3) If a provisional day is specified in the application, any approval by the Commissioners of the application has no effect unless the managers or trustees of the applicant give notice to the Commissioners either—

(*a*) confirming that day is the first day of the first period of account for which approval is sought, or

(*b*) specifying a different day as the first day of the first period of account for which approval is sought.

(4) The notice must be given no later than the date on or before which a return made under section 8A of TMA 1970 relating to the first period must be delivered.

(5) If a different day is specified under paragraph (3)(*b*), the application is to be treated for the purposes of regulation 4(3) as if that day had always been specified in the application.

6 Response by the Commissioners to application

(1) The Commissioners may by notice require the managers or trustees of the applicant to provide further particulars in order to enable them to determine an application.

(2) A requirement may be imposed under paragraph (1) within 28 days of the receipt of the application or of any further particulars required under that paragraph.

(3) If a notice under paragraph (1) is not complied with within 28 days or such longer period as the Commissioners may allow, they need not proceed further on the application.

(4) The Commissioners must give notice to the applicant of their decision to accept or reject an application—

(*a*) within 28 days of receiving the application, or

(*b*) if they give a notice under paragraph (2), within 28 days of that notice being complied with.

(5) A notice of a decision to reject an application must give reasons for that decision.

7 Continuing requirements for approval

(1) Approval under this Chapter is conditional on the requirements in this regulation being met by the unauthorised unit trust with respect to a period of account.

(2) Appropriate arrangements must be in place for the purpose of securing that the condition in regulation 3(1)(b) is met for the period.

(3) The period of account of the unauthorised unit trust must not exceed 18 months.

(4) The accounts for the period—

(*a*) must be prepared in accordance with the IMA SORP or its principles so far as relating to determining revenue and capital, and

(*b*) must be audited by a qualified independent auditor as being so prepared.

(5) In the following provisions of this Part references to accounts of an exempt unauthorised unit trust are to accounts meeting the conditions in paragraph (4).

(6) The managers or trustees of the trust must deliver with a return made under section 8A of TMA 1970—

(*a*) a statement from the managers or the trustees that the condition in regulation 3(1)(*b*) has been met throughout the period, and

(*b*) a copy of the trust's accounts.

(7) In this regulation—

(*a*) "the IMA SORP" means the Investment Management Association's Statement of Recommended Practice for the Financial Statements of Authorised Funds published in October 2010 as amended from time to time (or any successor statement of recommended practice), and

(*b*) "qualified independent auditor" means a person who—

(i) is eligible for appointment as a statutory auditor under Part 42 of the Companies Act 2006, and

(ii) if the appointment were an appointment as a statutory auditor, would not be prohibited from acting by section 1214 of that Act (independence requirement).

8 Withdrawal of approval

(1) The Commissioners may withdraw approval of an exempt unauthorised unit trust if they are satisfied that the requirements in regulation 7 are not met.

(2) The Commissioners may withdraw approval of an exempt unauthorised unit trust if the managers or trustees of an exempt unauthorised unit trust request them to do so.

(3) Withdrawal of an approval of an unauthorised unit trust is to be given by the Commissioners by notice to the managers or trustees of the trust.

(4) Withdrawal of approval has effect as from the date specified in the notice withdrawing the approval.

9 Appeal against rejection of application or withdrawal of approval

(1) An unauthorised unit trust may appeal if an application is rejected or the Commissioners withdraw approval.

(2) The notice of appeal must be given to the Commissioners within a period of 42 days beginning with the day on which the notice of rejection or withdrawal is given.

(3) On an appeal, the tribunal may make a decision to uphold or quash the rejection or withdrawal.

(4) If the tribunal decides to quash a rejection of an application, these Regulations apply as if the Commissioners had accepted the application in the form in which it was considered by the tribunal.

(5) If the tribunal decides to quash the withdrawal of approval, these Regulations apply as if the Commissioners had not withdrawn their approval.

CHAPTER 3

GAINS ACCRUING TO AN EXEMPT UNAUTHORISED UNIT TRUST

10 Exemption for gains accruing to an exempt unauthorised unit trust

Gains accruing to an exempt unauthorised unit trust are not chargeable gains for the purposes of TCGA 1992.

CHAPTER 4

TAXATION OF INCOME OF EXEMPT UNAUTHORISED UNIT TRUSTS

11 Basis periods

(1) The income of an exempt unauthorised unit trust for a tax year is taken to be the income of the exempt unauthorised unit trust arising in a basis period for the tax year.

(2) The general rule is that the basis period for a tax year [(the current year)][1] for an exempt unauthorised unit trust is the period [beginning immediately after the end of the basis period for the previous tax year and ending with the accounting date in the current year][2].

(3) The accounting date, in relation to a tax year, means—

(*a*) the date in the tax year to which accounts are drawn up, or

(*b*) if there are two or more such dates, the latest of them.

[(3A) In the first tax year that a trust is an exempt unauthorised unit trust the basis period for the tax year is the period—

(*a*) beginning on the first day of the first period of account in respect of which the trust is approved under these Regulations as an exempt unauthorised unit trust, and

(*b*) ending with the accounting date in that year.][1]

(4) If there is no accounting date in the first tax year that the trust is an exempt unauthorised unit trust but there is an accounting date in the following tax year—

(*a*) there is no basis period for the first tax year (so that the trust has no income for that year), but

(*b*) the basis period for the following year is the period [beginning on the first day of the first period of account in respect of which the trust is approved under these Regulations as an exempt unauthorised trust and][1] ending with the accounting date in that year.

(5) If there is no accounting date in the first two tax years that the trust is an exempt unauthorised unit trust—

(*a*) there is no basis period for [those years][1] (so that the trust has no income for [those years][1]), but

[(*b*) the basis period for the third tax year that the trust is an exempt unauthorised unit trust is the period—

(i) beginning on the first day of the first period of account in respect of which the trust is approved under these Regulations as an exempt unauthorised unit trust, and

(ii) ending with the accounting date in that year.][1]

(6) Otherwise, if there is no accounting date in the tax year, the basis period is the period of 12 months beginning immediately after the end of the basis period for the previous tax year.

(7) If the basis period for a tax year does not coincide with a period of account of an exempt unauthorised unit trust, either of the steps in paragraph (8) must be taken if necessary in order to arrive at the amount of the income of the trust treated under regulation 14 as if it were accrued income profits arising in a basis period.

(8) The steps are—

(*a*) apportioning the income of a period of account to the parts of that period falling in different basis periods, and

(*b*) adding the income of a period of account (or part of a period) to the income of other periods of account (or parts),

and the steps must be taken by reference to the number of days in the periods concerned.

Amendments—[1] In para (2), words inserted and substituted, para (3A) inserted, in paras (4)(*b*), (5)(*a*), words substituted, and para (5)(*b*) substituted by the Unauthorised Unit Trusts (Tax) (Amendment) Regulations, SI 2015/463 reg 2 with effect from 6 April 2015.

12 Treatment of income of an exempt unauthorised unit trust

(1) If income arises to the trustees of an exempt unauthorised unit trust, the income is treated as the income of the trustees and not of the unit holders.

(2) If income tax on any part of the income arising to the trustees of an exempt unauthorised unit trust would apart from this paragraph be charged at the dividend ordinary rate, income tax on that part of the income is instead charged at the basic rate.

(3) None of the following applies in relation to the income—

(*a*) sections 397(1) and 397A(1) of ITTOIA 2005 (tax credits for qualifying distributions),

(*b*) section 399(2) and (6) of ITTOIA 2005 (person not entitled to tax credits treated as having paid income tax),

(*c*) section 400(2) and (3) of ITTOIA 2005 (person whose income includes non-qualifying distribution treated as having paid income tax), and

(*d*) section 479 of ITA 2007 (trustees' accumulated or discretionary income to be charged at special rates).

[(3A) Subsections (1) to (4) of section 272A of ITTOIA 2005 (restricting deductions for finance costs related to residential property) do not apply in relation to calculating the profits of a UK property business, or overseas property business, for the purposes of charging the trustees of an exempt unauthorised unit trust to income tax on those profits.][1]

(4) Sections 494, 495 and 496B of ITA 2007 (discretionary payments) do not apply in relation to payments made by the trustees.

Amendments—[1] Para (3A) inserted by the Unauthorised Unit Trusts (Tax) (Amendment No 2) Regulations, SI 2015/2053 regs 2, 3 with effect from 7 January 2016.

13 Treatment of capital expenditure of an exempt unauthorised unit trust

The trustees (and not the unit holders) of an exempt unauthorised unit trust are treated as the persons to or on whom an allowance or charge is to be made under any provision relating to relief for capital expenditure.

14 Special provision for accrued income profits

(1) This regulation applies to income of an exempt unauthorised unit trust which—

(*a*) arises from its investments in securities within the meaning of Chapter 2 of Part 12 of ITA 2007 (accrued income profits), and

(*b*) is shown in its accounts.

(2) The income is charged to tax under Chapter 2 of Part 12 of ITA 2007—

(*a*) as if it were accrued income profits, and

(*b*) as if those profits were treated as made in the tax year in which the last day of the period of account in which the income is accounted for falls.

(3) None of the income is charged to income tax under Chapter 2 of Part 4 of ITTOIA 2005 (interest).

CHAPTER 5

CHARGE TO TAX ON UNIT HOLDERS OF EXEMPT UNAUTHORISED UNIT TRUSTS

15 Charge to tax on unit holders

(1) Tax is charged on income treated as received by a unit holder from an exempt unauthorised unit trust in the tax year.

(2) For the purposes of this regulation, unit holders are treated as receiving income if an amount is shown in the trust's accounts for a period of account as income available for payment to them or for investment.

(3) The income is treated as received by a unit holder for a distribution period.

(4) To calculate the amount of the income treated as received by a unit holder for a distribution period, calculate the unit holder's share of the trust's available income by applying the formula—

TAI x (R / TR)

where—

TAI is the total amount shown in the trust's accounts as income available for payment to unit holders or for investment,

R is the unit holder's rights, and

TR is all the unit holders' rights.

(5) The income for a distribution period is treated as received on the date or latest date provided by the terms of the trust for any distribution for the period, unless that date is more than 12 months after it ends.

(6) If—

(*a*) that date is more than 12 months after the distribution period ends, or

(*b*) no date is so provided,

the income for the period is treated as received on the last day of the period.

(7) If the terms of the trust provide for a period over which income from the investments subject to the trust is aggregated to ascertain the amount available for distribution to unit holders, the "distribution period" means—

(*a*) if the period is 12 months or less, that period, or

(*b*) if the period is more than 12 months, each successive period of 12 months within that period and any remaining period of less than 12 months.

(8) In any other case, the "distribution period" means successive periods of 12 months, the first of which begins with the day on which the trust was established.

16 Person liable

The person liable for any tax charged under this Chapter is the unit holder treated as receiving the income.

17 Priority rules

(1) Any income, so far as it falls within—

(*a*) regulation 15, and

(*b*) Chapter 2 of Part 2 of ITTOIA 2005 or Chapter 2 of Part 3 of CTA 2009 (income taxed as trade profits),

is dealt with under Part 2 of ITTOIA 2005 or Part 3 of CTA 2009.

(2) Any income, so far as it falls within—

(*a*) regulation 15, and

(*b*) Chapter 3 of Part 3 of ITTOIA 2005, or Chapter 3 of Part 4 of CTA 2009, so far as relating to a UK property business,

is dealt with under Part 3 of ITTOIA 2005 or Part 4 of CTA 2009.

CHAPTER 6

RELIEF FOR TRUSTEES OF AN EXEMPT UNAUTHORISED UNIT TRUST

18 Relief for deemed payments by trustees of an exempt unauthorised unit trust

(1) If the unit holders of an exempt unauthorised unit trust are treated as receiving income under regulation 15(2), the trustees are treated as making a deemed payment of the same amount on the final day of the period of account referred to in regulation 15(2).

(2) The trustees are entitled to relief for a tax year equal to the amount of the deemed payments treated as made in that year.

(3) The relief is given by deducting that amount in calculating the trustees' net income for the tax year (see Step 2 of the calculation in section 23 of ITA 2007 (calculation of income tax liability)).

(4) The total amount of the relief for a tax year must not exceed the amount of the trustees' modified net income for the tax year.

(5) If there is an excess, that excess is to be treated as if it were a deemed payment in the basis period for the following tax year.

(6) In this regulation "modified net income" has the meaning given by section 1025 of ITA 2007 but as if for subsection (2)(*c*) there were substituted—

"(*c*) any relief to which the person may be entitled under regulation 18 of the Unauthorised Unit Trusts (Tax) Regulations 2013,".

Cross references—See FA 2016 Sch 18 para 20(15) (serial tax avoidance regime: no deduction to be made under this regulation during restricted relief period).

19 Amounts ineligible for relief under regulation 18

(1) Relief is not to be given under regulation 18 for any part of a deemed payment so far as it is ineligible for relief.

(2) In determining the extent (if any) to which the payment is ineligible for relief section 450 of ITA 2007 (payments ineligible for relief) applies in relation to the payment as that section applies in relation to a payment to which section 449 of that Act applies.

20 Amounts ineligible for relief under regulation 18: payments to certain unit holders where regulation 3(4) applies

Relief is not to be given under regulation 18 for any part of a deemed payment so far as it is attributable to income treated as received by a unit holder under regulation 15 where the unit holder—

(*a*) disposed of its units in the circumstances described in regulation 3(4)(*c*), and

(*b*) was not UK resident at the time the income is treated as received.

21 Effect of equalisation arrangements on relief for trustees

(1) This regulation applies to an exempt unauthorised unit trust which operates equalisation arrangements in the case of a disposal of units by way of either cancellation or acquisition by the managers of the trust.

(2) The amount of the deemed payment for which the trustees are entitled to relief for a tax year under regulation 18 includes any amount paid to unit holders (in the basis period for the year) on a disposal of some or all of their units so far as attributable to the income of the trust which has accrued up to the date of the disposal (but has not otherwise been received, or treated as received, by unit holders).

CHAPTER 7
MISCELLANEOUS PROVISIONS

22 No tax charge for disposal of interests in offshore non-reporting funds: reporting condition

(1) No tax is charged on the trustees of an exempt unauthorised unit trust under regulation 17 of the Offshore Funds Regulations on the disposal of an interest in a non-reporting fund if the reporting condition is met.

(2) The reporting condition is met if—

(*a*) the trustees prepare computations of reportable income for the fund for all accounting periods which, if the fund were a reporting fund, would be reporting periods ending on or before the day of disposal, and

(*b*) any excess of the trustees' share of the reportable income of the non-reporting fund over their share of the distributions made by the non-reporting fund is included in the amount mentioned in regulation 15(2) for each period of account ending on or before that day.

(3) Nothing in paragraph (2) applies in relation to any time before the date on which the trustees acquire or re-acquire the interest.

(4) The trustees are treated for all purposes as if they had disposed of and immediately reacquired an interest in a non-reporting fund on a date they specify if in the event of a subsequent disposal of the interest—

(a) the reporting condition would not be met in relation to times before the date, but

(*b*) the trustees reasonably expect the reporting condition will be met in relation to times on and after the date.

(5) The date the trustees specify must be included in an appropriate entry in their return made under section 8A of TMA 1970 for the period of account in which the date falls but the date must not be earlier than 6 April 2014.

(6) The deemed disposal and reacquisition of the interest is taken to be for a consideration equal to its market value on the specified date.

(7) In this regulation—

"market value" has the meaning given by regulation 10 of the Offshore Funds Regulations,

"reporting fund" has the meaning given by regulation 50 of those Regulations, and

"reporting period" has the meaning given by regulation 91 of those Regulations.

(8) If a non-reporting fund is a UCITS fund for the purposes of regulation 12 of the Offshore Funds Regulations, regulation 80 of those regulations (treatment of investment transactions carried out by diversely owned funds) applies for the purposes of the computations mentioned in paragraph (2)(*a*).

23 No tax charge for disposal of interests in offshore non-reporting funds: qualifying index

(1) No tax is charged on the trustees of an exempt unauthorised unit trust under regulation 17 of the Offshore Funds Regulations on the disposal of an interest in a non-reporting fund if—

(*a*) in accordance with the trust's investment strategy contained in its prospectus, the aim of the trust throughout the period during which the trustees held the interest has been to replicate the performance of a qualifying index,

(*b*) the main purpose of the investment in the non-reporting fund throughout that period is to represent the composition of the qualifying index, and

(*c*) the capital and income returns of the trust throughout that period replicated as closely as practicable the returns of the investment comprised in the qualifying index.

(2) For the purposes of this regulation an index is a "qualifying index" if—

(*a*) it is based solely on the value of securities listed on a recognised stock exchange or admitted to trading on a regulated market, (*b*) an authority (whether in the United Kingdom or elsewhere) recognises the index on the basis that—

(i) its composition is sufficiently diverse,

(ii) it represents an adequate benchmark for the market to which it refers, and

(iii) it is published in such a way that it is widely available, and

(*c*) it is calculated and published by a body which is managed independently from the management of the exempt unauthorised unit trust.

(3) In this regulation "regulated market" has the same meaning as in Directive 2004/39/EC of the European Parliament and of the Council on markets in financial instruments.

24 Treatment of investment transactions carried out by exempt unauthorised unit trusts

(1) An investment transaction entered into by the trustees of an exempt unauthorised unit trust is treated for the purposes of the Income Tax Acts as entered into otherwise than in the course of a trade.

[(2) For the purposes of paragraph (1) an "investment transaction" is an investment transaction specified by regulation 2 of the Investment Transactions (Tax) Regulations 2014.][1]

Amendments—[1] Para 2 substituted by the Investment Transactions (Tax) Regulations, SI 2014/685 reg 10 with effect from 8 April 2014.

25 Authorised investment funds investing in exempt unauthorised unit trusts

If an authorised investment fund (within the meaning given by the AIF Regulations) is at any time in a period of account a unit holder of an exempt unauthorised unit trust, the following provisions of CTA 2010 do not apply in relation to the fund for any financial year in which that period (or any part of it) falls—

(*a*) Part 3 (relief for companies with small profits), and

(*b*) sections 614 and 618 (applicable corporation tax rate),

(and, accordingly, the rate of corporation tax which applies in relation to the fund is the main rate within the meaning of section 3 of CTA 2010).

26 Statements about income treated as received by unit holders

A unit holder of an exempt unauthorised unit trust is entitled by notice to require the trustees of the trust to provide the unit holder with a statement in writing showing the amount of income treated as received by the unit holder for a distribution period under regulation 15.

PART 3
NON-EXEMPT UNAUTHORISED UNIT TRUSTS

CHAPTER 1
DEFINITION OF NON-EXEMPT UNAUTHORISED UNIT TRUST

27 Definition of non-exempt unauthorised unit trust

An unauthorised unit trust is a "non-exempt unauthorised unit trust" if it is [not—

(*a*) an exempt unauthorised unit trust, or

(*b*) treated by regulations made in exercise of the powers conferred by section 1007(2) of ITA 2007 as not being a unit trust scheme for the purposes of the definition of "unauthorised unit trust" in section 989 of that Act.][1]

Amendments—[1] Words substituted for words "not an exempt unauthorised unit trust", by the Unauthorised Unit Trusts (Tax) (Amendment) Regulations, SI 2014/585 regs 2, 4 with effect from 6 April 2014.

CHAPTER 2
TAX TREATMENT OF NON-EXEMPT UNAUTHORISED UNIT TRUSTS

28 Non-exempt unauthorised unit trust treated as UK resident company

(1) In respect of income arising and chargeable gains accruing to UK resident trustees of a non-exempt unauthorised unit trust, and for the purposes of the provisions relating to relief for capital expenditure, the Tax Acts have effect as if—

(*a*) the trustees were a UK resident company, and

(*b*) the rights of the unit holders were shares in the company.

(2) References in the Corporation Tax Acts to a body corporate are to be read in accordance with paragraph (1); and sections 1104 and 1107 of CTA 2010 (companies and nominees required to provide tax certificates) apply with any necessary modifications.

29 Part 3 of CTA 2010 not to apply to non-exempt unauthorised unit trusts

Part 3 of CTA 2010 (relief for companies with small profits) does not apply in relation to a non-exempt unauthorised unit trust.

[29A Application of section 490 of CTA 2009 to non-exempt unauthorised unit trusts
Section 490 of CTA 2009 does not apply to any rights held by a company under a non-exempt unauthorised unit trust scheme.][1]

Amendments—[1] Reg 29A inserted by the Unauthorised Unit Trusts (Tax) (Amendment) Regulations, SI 2014/585 regs 2, 5 with effect from 6 April 2014.

PART 4
TRANSITIONAL PROVISIONS

CHAPTER 1
TRANSITIONAL PROVISIONS FOR EXEMPT UNAUTHORISED UNIT TRUSTS

30 Transitional year for exempt unauthorised unit trusts
(1) This regulation applies in the case of a trust—
(*a*) which was an unauthorised unit trust immediately before 6 April 2014, and
(*b*) which is approved as an exempt unauthorised unit trust for a period including 6 April 2014.
(2) For the purposes of this regulation a trust's "transitional year" is—
(*a*) the tax year 2013–14, where the trust has an accounting date in the tax year 2013–14 on or after the day after these Regulations are made, or
(*b*) the tax year 2014–15, where the trust either has an accounting date in the tax year 2013–14 before the day after these Regulations are made or has no accounting date in the tax year 2013–14.
(3) In a tax year which is a trust's transitional year, the income of the trust for that tax year is taken to be the income arising in the period beginning with 6 April and ending with the accounting date in that year.
(4) If a trust's transitional year is the tax year 2014–15, regulation 7(4), Chapters 3 to 7 of Part 2 and Parts 3 and 5 do not apply in relation to the trust for that year.
(5) A transitional year does not count for the purposes of determining the first or second tax year that a trust is an exempt unauthorised unit trust under regulation 11(4) or (5).
(6) Any deemed payment or deemed deduction which would (but for this regulation) have been treated as made by the trustees under section 941 of ITA 2007 after the accounting date of the transitional year of the trust is treated as made on that accounting date.
(7) Any income of the trust which—
(*a*) is shown in the trust's accounts for its transitional year as available for payment to unit holders or for investment, and
(*b*) would (but for this regulation) arise to the trustees in a tax year later than the transitional year,
is treated as arising to the trustees in the trust's transitional year.
(8) For the purposes of this regulation, the accounting date, in relation to a tax year, means—
(*a*) the date in the tax year to which accounts are drawn up, or
(*b*) if there are two or more such dates, the latest of them.

CHAPTER 2
TRANSITIONAL PROVISIONS FOR NON-EXEMPT UNAUTHORISED UNIT TRUSTS

31 Unauthorised unit trusts coming within charge to corporation tax: final deemed payments and accrued income profits
(1) In the case of an unauthorised unit trust which comes within the charge to corporation tax on 6 April 2014 or a later date, any amount of income which would (but for this regulation) have been treated under—
(*a*) Chapter 10 of Part 4 of ITTOIA 2005, or
(*b*) Chapter 5 of Part 10 of CTA 2009,
as received by its unit holders on or after 6 April 2014 or that later date is treated as received on 5 April 2014 or, as the case may be, the day before that later date (and, accordingly, the trustees are treated as making a deemed payment under section 941 of ITA 2007 in respect of that income on the same day).
(2) Any income of the trust which would (but for this regulation) be included in the amount of accrued income profits treated under Part 12 of ITA 2007 as made on or after 6 April 2014 or a later date, is included in the amount of accrued income profits treated under that Part as made on 5 April 2014 or, as the case may be, the day before that later date.

32 Part 5 not to apply to mixed unauthorised unit trusts

(1) An unauthorised unit trust is not a non-exempt unauthorised unit trust, and Part 5 does not apply in relation to the trust, if at all times in the period beginning with 24 May 2012 and ending with 5 April 2014 it had at least one unit holder which was, and at least one unit holder which was not, an eligible investor.

(2) But paragraph (1) ceases to apply in relation to the trust if subsequently it no longer has any unit holders which are eligible investors.

[(3) Where paragraph (1) applies, section 504 of ITA 2007 shall be read as if it included after subsection (4)—

"(4A) Subsections (1) to (4) of section 272A of ITTOIA 2005 (restricting deductions for finance costs related to residential property) do not apply in relation to calculating the profits of a UK property business, or overseas property business, for the purposes of charging the trustees to income tax on those profits."][2]

Amendments—[1] Para (3) inserted by the Unauthorised Unit Trusts (Tax) (Amendment No 2) Regulations, SI 2015/2053 regs 2, 4 with effect from 7 January 2016.

PART 5

REPEALS AND CONSEQUENTIAL AMENDMENTS

33 Chevening Estate Act 1959

(*inserts* the Chevening Estate Act 1959 s 2(1)(*d*) and *revokes* s 2(1A)(*c*))

34 TCGA 1992

(*revokes* TCGA 1992s 100(2)–(2B))

35 Finance Act 2000

In paragraph 51(3) of Schedule 22 to the Finance Act 2000 (tonnage tax: general exclusion of investment income)—

(*a*) (*revokes* FA 2000 Sch 22 para 51(3)(*c*))
(*b*) *amends* FA 2000 Sch 22 para 51(3)(*d*))
(*c*) *inserts* FA 2000 Sch 22 para 51(3)(*e*))

36 ITTOIA 2005

(1) ITTOIA 2005 is amended as follows.
(2) (*revokes* ITTOIA 2005 s 365(1)(*i*))
(3) (*amends* ITTOIA 2005 s 397(6))
(4) (*amends* ITTOIA 2005 s 397A(6))
(5) (*amends* ITTOIA 2005 s 399(7))
(6) (*revokes* ITTOIA 2005 s 400(7))
(7) (*amends* ITTOIA 2005 s 410(3))
(8) (*revokes* ITTOIA 2005 Pt 4 Ch 10)
(9) (*amends* ITTOIA 2005 s 839(3), (3A)(*b*))

37 ITA 2007

(1) ITA 2007 is amended as follows.
(2) (*revokes* ITA 2007 s 2(9)(*e*))
(3) (*amends* ITA 2007 s 14(2))
(4) (*amends* ITA 2007 s 24(2)(*b*))
(5) (*revokes* ITA 2007 s 462(9))
(6) (*revokes* ITA 2007 ss 504–505)
(7) (*amends* ITA 2007 s 532(2)(*f*))
(8) (*amends* ITA 2007 s 809CZB(1)(*b*))
(9) (*revokes* ITA 2007 s 825(2)(*d*) and inserts s 825(2)(*f*))
(10) (*revokes* ITA 2007 s 847(5)(b))
(11) (*revokes* ITA 2007 s 848(4))
(12) (*amends* ITA 2007 s 873(2)(*a*))
(13) (*amends* ITA 2007 s 899(4)(*b*)(ii))
(14) (*amends* ITA 2007 s 904(2)(*b*)(ii))
(15) (*revokes* ITA 2007 Pt 15 Ch 13)
(16) (*revokes* ITA 2007 s 964(2))
(17) In section 975 (statements about deduction of income tax)—

(*a*), (*c*) (*revoke* ITA 2007 s 975(3), (4), (7))
(*b*) (*amends* ITA 2007 s 975(6))

(18) (*revokes* ITA 2007 s 1025(4))
(19) (*revokes* ITA 2007 Sch 2 paras 167, 168)
(20) (*amends* ITA 2007 Sch 4)

38 CTA 2009

(1) CTA 2009 is amended as follows.

(2) (*revokes* CTA 2009 s 932(1)(*d*))

(3) (*revokes* CTA 2009 Pt 10 Ch 5 of Part 10)

(4) (*amends* CTA 2009 s 982(1)(*a*), (2)(*a*))

39 CTA 2010

(1) CTA 2010 is amended as follows.

(2) (*revokes* CTA 2010 s 1(3)(*h*))

(3) (*amends* CTA 2010 s 486(2)(*c*), (4))

(4) (*revokes* CTA 2010 Pt 13 Ch 3)

(5) (*amends* CTA 2010 s 778(1)(*b*))

40 FA 2012

(*amends* FA 2012 s 74(1))

41 Consequential repeals of other enactments

In consequence of the amendments made by the above provisions of this Part, omit the following provisions—

(*a*) in ITA 2007, paragraphs 541 and 542 of Schedule 1,

(*b*) in FA 2008, paragraph 23 of Schedule 1 and paragraph 25 of Schedule 12,

(*c*) in CTA 2009, paragraph 713 of Schedule 1,

(*d*) in FA 2009, paragraph 13(*a*) of Schedule 19,

(*e*) in CTA 2010, paragraph 663 of Schedule 1, and

(*f*) in FA 2010, section 40 and Schedule 13.

42 AIF Regulations

(*amends* the AIF regulations reg 17(2))

43 Offshore Funds Regulations

(*amends* the Offshore Funds Regulations reg 18(6))

2013/2892

TAX TREATMENT OF FINANCING COSTS AND INCOME (EXCLUDED SCHEMES) REGULATIONS 2013

Made . . . .*11 November 2013*

Laid before the House of Commons . . . .*13 November 2013*

Coming into force . . . .*4 December 2013*

The Commissioners for Her Majesty's Revenue and Customs make the following Regulations in exercise of the powers conferred by section 312(2) and (3) of the Taxation (International and Other Provisions) Act 2010.

Revocation—These Regulations revoked by F(No 2)A 2017 s 20, Sch 5 para 11(3)(*h*) with effect in relation to periods of account of the worldwide group that begin on or after 1 April 2017. In relation to periods of account that straddle 1 April 2017 see Sch 5 para 26(2)–(10). **Please note** that Part 2A of the Yellow Book was sent to print before the Act had received Royal Assent. This amendment is therefore based on the 8 September 2017 Finance Bill. Please check F(No 2)A 2017 for confirmation of this amendment.

Introductory provisions

1 Citation, commencement, effect and interpretation

(1) These Regulations may be cited as the Tax Treatment of Financing Costs and Income (Excluded Schemes) Regulations 2013 and come into force on 4th December 2013.

(2) These Regulations have effect in relation to schemes entered into on or after that date.

(3) In these Regulations—

"finance arrangement" has the meaning given by section 328 of TIOPA;

"group treasury company" has the same meaning as in section 316(2) of TIOPA;

"relevant liability" shall be construed in accordance with section 263(3) of TIOPA;

"TIOPA" means the Taxation (International and Other Provisions) Act 2010.[1]

Amendments—[1] These Regulations revoked by F(No 2)A 2017 s 20, Sch 5 para 11(3)(*h*) with effect in relation to periods of account of the worldwide group that begin on or after 1 April 2017. In relation to periods of account that straddle 1 April 2017 see Sch 5 para 26(2)–(10). **Please note** that Part 2A of the Yellow Book was sent to print before the Act had received Royal Assent. This amendment is therefore based on the 8 September 2017 Finance Bill. Please check F(No 2)A 2017 for confirmation of this amendment.

Excluded schemes in relation to a large group

2 *Excluded schemes for the purposes of the application of Part 7 of TIOPA to a large group*

(1) A scheme is an excluded scheme for the purposes of section 305A of TIOPA (schemes preventing Part 7 applying to a large group) if it is a relevant event as a result of which subsection (2) of section 348A (financial statements: business combinations to which the worldwide group is a party) of TIOPA applies.

But this is subject to regulation 12.

(2) In paragraph (1), "relevant event" has the same meaning as in section 348A of TIOPA.[1]

Amendments—[1] These Regulations revoked by F(No 2)A 2017 s 20, Sch 5 para 11(3)(*h*) with effect in relation to periods of account of the worldwide group that begin on or after 1 April 2017. In relation to periods of account that straddle 1 April 2017 see Sch 5 para 26(2)–(10). **Please note** that Part 2A of the Yellow Book was sent to print before the Act had received Royal Assent. This amendment is therefore based on the 8 September 2017 Finance Bill. Please check F(No 2)A 2017 for confirmation of this amendment.

Excluded schemes for the purposes of the gateway test

3 *Excluded schemes for the purposes of the application Chapter 2 of Part 7 of TIOPA*

A scheme of a description within any of regulations 4 to 5 is an excluded scheme for the purposes of section 306 of TIOPA (schemes involving the manipulation of rules in Chapter 2).

But this is subject to regulation 12.[1]

Amendments—[1] These Regulations revoked by F(No 2)A 2017 s 20, Sch 5 para 11(3)(*h*) with effect in relation to periods of account of the worldwide group that begin on or after 1 April 2017. In relation to periods of account that straddle 1 April 2017 see Sch 5 para 26(2)–(10). **Please note** that Part 2A of the Yellow Book was sent to print before the Act had received Royal Assent. This amendment is therefore based on the 8 September 2017 Finance Bill. Please check F(No 2)A 2017 for confirmation of this amendment.

4 *Repayment of relevant liability*

A scheme is within this regulation if it is a transaction for the repayment of a relevant liability by a relevant group company or group securitisation company using—

(*a*) *funds derived directly from the company's trading or investment activity,*

(*b*) *proceeds from the repayment of a relevant asset of the company within section 263(4)(b) or (d) of TIOPA,*

(*c*) *proceeds from the issue of ordinary shares or preference shares in the company, or*

(*d*) *where the relevant liability is owed to a subsidiary of the company (or a subsidiary of that subsidiary), dividend income received from that subsidiary.*[1]

Amendments—[1] These Regulations revoked by F(No 2)A 2017 s 20, Sch 5 para 11(3)(*h*) with effect in relation to periods of account of the worldwide group that begin on or after 1 April 2017. In relation to periods of account that straddle 1 April 2017 see Sch 5 para 26(2)–(10). **Please note** that Part 2A of the Yellow Book was sent to print before the Act had received Royal Assent. This amendment is therefore based on the 8 September 2017 Finance Bill. Please check F(No 2)A 2017 for confirmation of this amendment.

5 *Release of relevant liability*

A scheme is within this regulation if it is a transaction for the release of a relevant group company or group securitisation company from a relevant liability on terms which would have been entered into between knowledgeable and willing parties dealing at arm's length.[1]

Amendments—[1] These Regulations revoked by F(No 2)A 2017 s 20, Sch 5 para 11(3)(*h*) with effect in relation to periods of account of the worldwide group that begin on or after 1 April 2017. In relation to periods of account that straddle 1 April 2017 see Sch 5 para 26(2)–(10). **Please note** that Part 2A of the Yellow Book was sent to print before the Act had received Royal Assent. This amendment is therefore based on the 8 September 2017 Finance Bill. Please check F(No 2)A 2017 for confirmation of this amendment.

Excluded Schemes for the purposes of the main rules

6 *Excluded Schemes for the purposes of the application Chapters 3 and 4 of Part 7 of TIOPA*

A scheme of a description within any of regulations 7 to 11 is an excluded scheme for the purposes of section 307 of TIOPA (schemes involving the manipulation of rules in Chapters 3 and 4).

But this is subject to regulation 12.[1]

Amendments—[1] These Regulations revoked by F(No 2)A 2017 s 20, Sch 5 para 11(3)(*h*) with effect in relation to periods of account of the worldwide group that begin on or after 1 April 2017. In relation to periods of account that straddle 1 April 2017 see Sch 5 para 26(2)–(10). **Please note** that Part 2A of the Yellow Book was sent to print before the Act had received Royal Assent. This amendment is therefore based on the 8 September 2017 Finance Bill. Please check F(No 2)A 2017 for confirmation of this amendment.

7 *Repayment of finance arrangement*

A scheme is within this regulation if it is a transaction—

(*a*) *for the repayment of a finance arrangement by a relevant group company using—*

(i) *funds derived directly from the company's trading or investment activity,*

(ii) *proceeds from the repayment of a finance arrangement which gives rise to a financing income amount,*

(iii) *proceeds from the issue of ordinary shares or preference shares in the company, or*

(iv) *where the relevant liability is owed to a subsidiary of the company (or a subsidiary of that subsidiary), dividend income received from that subsidiary, and*

(*b*) *which gives rise to a financing expense amount.*[1]

Amendments—[1] These Regulations revoked by F(No 2)A 2017 s 20, Sch 5 para 11(3)(*h*) with effect in relation to periods of account of the worldwide group that begin on or after 1 April 2017. In relation to periods of account that straddle 1 April 2017 see Sch 5 para 26(2)–(10). **Please note** that Part 2A of the Yellow Book was sent to print before the Act had received Royal Assent. This amendment is therefore based on the 8 September 2017 Finance Bill. Please check F(No 2)A 2017 for confirmation of this amendment.

8 Release from finance arrangement

A scheme is within this regulation if it is a transaction—

(*a*) *for the release of a relevant group company from a finance arrangement on terms which would have been entered into between knowledgeable and willing parties dealing at arm's length, and*

(*b*) *which gives rise to a financing expense amount.*[1]

Amendments—[1] These Regulations revoked by F(No 2)A 2017 s 20, Sch 5 para 11(3)(*h*) with effect in relation to periods of account of the worldwide group that begin on or after 1 April 2017. In relation to periods of account that straddle 1 April 2017 see Sch 5 para 26(2)–(10). **Please note** that Part 2A of the Yellow Book was sent to print before the Act had received Royal Assent. This amendment is therefore based on the 8 September 2017 Finance Bill. Please check F(No 2)A 2017 for confirmation of this amendment.

9 Transfer to group treasury company

A scheme is within this regulation if it is a transaction—

(*a*) *for the transfer of a finance arrangement from a relevant group company to a group treasury company which is a relevant group company, and*

(*b*) *which gives rise to a financing expense amount.*[1]

Amendments—[1] These Regulations revoked by F(No 2)A 2017 s 20, Sch 5 para 11(3)(*h*) with effect in relation to periods of account of the worldwide group that begin on or after 1 April 2017. In relation to periods of account that straddle 1 April 2017 see Sch 5 para 26(2)–(10). **Please note** that Part 2A of the Yellow Book was sent to print before the Act had received Royal Assent. This amendment is therefore based on the 8 September 2017 Finance Bill. Please check F(No 2)A 2017 for confirmation of this amendment.

10 Liability owed to UK group treasury company

A scheme is within this regulation if it comprises—

(*a*) *a transaction for the repayment of a finance arrangement by a relevant group company, and*

(*b*) *a transaction for the replacement of that arrangement by an equivalent finance arrangement owed to a group treasury company which is a relevant group company.*[1]

Amendments—[1] These Regulations revoked by F(No 2)A 2017 s 20, Sch 5 para 11(3)(*h*) with effect in relation to periods of account of the worldwide group that begin on or after 1 April 2017. In relation to periods of account that straddle 1 April 2017 see Sch 5 para 26(2)–(10). **Please note** that Part 2A of the Yellow Book was sent to print before the Act had received Royal Assent. This amendment is therefore based on the 8 September 2017 Finance Bill. Please check F(No 2)A 2017 for confirmation of this amendment.

11 Transfer to companies with net financing deduction or net financing income that is small

(*1*) A scheme is within this regulation if—

(*a*) *under or in relation to the scheme, a finance arrangement is transferred to a relevant group company or a UK group company, and*

(*b*) *before the transfer the net financing deduction of the relevant group company, or the net financing income of the UK group company, is small and as a result of the transfer the net financing deduction or net financing income is not small.*

(*2*) In paragraph (1)(*b*), "small" has the same meaning as in section 331(1) of TIOPA.[1]

Amendments—[1] These Regulations revoked by F(No 2)A 2017 s 20, Sch 5 para 11(3)(*h*) with effect in relation to periods of account of the worldwide group that begin on or after 1 April 2017. In relation to periods of account that straddle 1 April 2017 see Sch 5 para 26(2)–(10). **Please note** that Part 2A of the Yellow Book was sent to print before the Act had received Royal Assent. This amendment is therefore based on the 8 September 2017 Finance Bill. Please check F(No 2)A 2017 for confirmation of this amendment.

Tax Avoidance

12 Tax avoidance schemes

(*1*) A scheme is not an excluded scheme if the scheme is, or forms part of, a notifiable arrangement, or involves a notifiable proposal, in relation to which a member of the worldwide group is under a duty to provide HMRC with information under Part 7 of the Finance Act 2004 (disclosure of tax avoidance schemes).

(*2*) In paragraph (1), "notifiable arrangement" and "notifiable proposal" have the meanings given by section 306 of the Finance Act 2004.[1]

Amendments—[1] These Regulations revoked by F(No 2)A 2017 s 20, Sch 5 para 11(3)(*h*) with effect in relation to periods of account of the worldwide group that begin on or after 1 April 2017. In relation to periods of account that straddle 1 April 2017 see Sch 5 para 26(2)–(10). **Please note** that Part 2A of the Yellow Book was sent to print before the Act had received Royal Assent. This amendment is therefore based on the 8 September 2017 Finance Bill. Please check F(No 2)A 2017 for confirmation of this amendment.

2013/2910

ADDITIONALLY-DEVELOPED OIL FIELDS ORDER 2013

Made . . . . .15 November 2013

Coming into force in accordance with article 1

The Commissioners for Her Majesty's Revenue and Customs make the following Order, in exercise of the powers conferred by sections 349 and 349A of the Corporation Tax Act 2010 and paragraph 22 of Schedule 22 to the Finance Act 2012.

In accordance with sections 349 and 349A of the Corporation Tax Act 2010, a draft of this Order was laid before the House of Commons and approved by a resolution of that House.

1 Citation, commencement and interpretation

(1) This Order may be cited as the Additionally-developed Oil Fields Order 2013 and is treated as having come into force on 1st April 2013.

(2) In this Order "CTA 2010" means the Corporation Tax Act 2010.

2 Additionally-developed oil field

(1) The conditions which a project that is described in a consent for development of an oil field must meet for the purposes of section 349A(1)(*b*) of CTA 2010 are as follows.

(2) Condition A is that the project was authorised as mentioned in section 349A(1)(*a*) of CTA 2010 on or after 7th September 2012.

(3) Condition B is that the cost per tonne of the project is more than £60.

(4) Condition C is that the additional reserves of oil which the field has as a result of the project have not been taken into account in calculating the cost per tonne of any qualifying project that has previously been authorised in relation to the field.

(5) A project authorised in relation to an oil field is a "qualifying project" for the purposes of paragraph (4) if a field allowance has at any time been held for the field as a result of the project.

(6) Condition D is that, as at the authorisation day, the whole of the oil field lies on the seaward side of the baselines from which the territorial sea is measured.

(7) Condition E is that the project does not involve enhanced oil recovery using carbon dioxide.

(8) For the purposes of this article the "cost per tonne" of a project authorised in relation to an oil field means the amount given by—

E/*R*

where—

E is the expected capital expenditure of the project (see paragraph (9)), and

R is the sum of the amounts of additional reserves of oil (in tonnes) which the field and any other oil fields have as a result of the project.

(9) The expected capital expenditure of a project is to be determined as follows—

Step 1

Calculate the amount of capital expenditure which it is reasonably expected, as at the authorisation day, will be incurred in carrying out the project.

In calculating that amount, ignore any expenditure incurred before the authorisation day which, if the project had not been authorised, would have been wasted expenditure.

Step 2

Calculate the amount of any capital expenditure which it is reasonably expected, as at the authorisation day, would have been incurred on or after that day if the project had not been authorised.

In calculating that amount, ignore any expenditure which—

(*a*) would have been incurred under an agreement entered into before the authorisation day, and

(*b*) would not have been wasted expenditure.

Step 3

Deduct the amount given by step 2 from the amount given by step 1.

But if the amount given by step 2 is greater than the amount given by step 1, the expected capital expenditure of the project is nil.

(10) In determining the expected capital expenditure of a project—

(*a*) where an amount attributed to an item of expenditure includes an amount for contingencies, the amount so included may not exceed 20% of the amount that would be attributed to that item of expenditure in the absence of any amount for contingencies,

(*b*) expenditure is not to be treated as wasted expenditure to the extent that it is recoverable, and

(*c*) the following are to be disregarded—

(i) any decommissioning expenditure (within the meaning of section 330C of CTA 2010), and

(ii) any payments of interest.

(11) For the purposes of this article—

(*a*) the amount of additional reserves of oil which a field has is to be determined on the authorisation day,
(*b*) 1,100 cubic metres of gas at a temperature of 15 degrees celsius and pressure of one atmosphere is to be counted as equivalent to one tonne,
(*c*) "authorisation day", in relation to a project, means the day when the project is authorised as mentioned in section 349A(1)(*a*) of CTA 2010, and
(*d*) "territorial sea" means the territorial sea of the United Kingdom.

3–12 Amendments of CTA 2010

(the amendments to CTA 2010 are already in force and are therefore not reproduced here)

2013/2983

TAXATION OF CHARGEABLE GAINS (GILT-EDGED SECURITIES) (NO 2) ORDER 2013

Made . . . .*25 November 2013*

The Treasury make the following Order in exercise of the powers conferred by paragraph 1 of Schedule 9 to the Taxation of Chargeable Gains Act 1992.

1 Citation

This Order may be cited as the Taxation of Chargeable Gains (Gilt-edged Securities) (No 2) Order 2013.

2 Securities specified as gilt-edged securities

For the purpose of the Taxation of Chargeable Gains Act 1992 the following securities are specified as "gilt-edged securities"—

01/8% Index-linked Treasury Gilt 2068
01/8% Index-linked Treasury Gilt 2019
3½% Treasury Gilt 2068
2¼% Treasury Gilt 2023
1¼% Treasury Gilt 2018.

2013/3118

CAPITAL REQUIREMENTS (COUNTRY-BY-COUNTRY REPORTING) REGULATIONS 2013

Made . . . .*9 December 2013*
Laid before Parliament . . . .*10 December 2013*
Coming into force . . . .*1 January 2014*

The Treasury are designated for the purposes of section 2(2) of the European Communities Act 1972 in relation to financial services.

The Treasury, in exercise of the powers conferred by section 2(2) of the European Communities Act 1972, make the following Regulations:

1 Citation, commencement and interpretation

(1) These Regulations may be cited as the Capital Requirements (Country-by-Country Reporting) Regulations 2013 and come into force on 1st January 2014.

(2) In these Regulations—

"the 2000 Act" means the Financial Services and Markets Act 2000;

"accepted accounting standards" means "international accounting standards" as defined in Article 2 of Regulation (EC) No 1606/2002 of the European Parliament and the Council of 19 July 2002 on the application of international accounting standards or "generally accepted accounting practice" as defined in section 1127 of the Corporation Tax Act 2010;

"branch" has the same meaning as in Article 4(1)(17) of the capital requirements regulation;

"corporation tax" means the tax charged on profits by section 2(1) of the Corporation Tax Act 2009 and any similar tax charged on profits in any jurisdiction outside the United Kingdom;

"capital requirements directive" means Directive 2013/36/EU of the European Parliament and of the Council of 26 June 2013 on access to the activity of credit institutions and the prudential supervision of credit institutions and investment firms, amending Directive 2002/87/EC and repealing Directives 2006/48/EC and 2006/49/EC;

"capital requirements regulation" means Regulation (EU) No 575/2013 of the European Parliament and of the Council of 26 June 2013 on prudential requirements for credit institutions and investment firms and amending Regulation (EU) No 648/2012;

"Directive 2006/43/EC" means Directive 2006/43/EC of the European Parliament and of the Council of 17 May 2006 on statutory audits of annual accounts and consolidated accounts, amending Council Directives 78/660/EEC and 83/349/EEC and repealing Council Directive 84/253/EEC;

"global systemically important institution" means a group identified as a global systemically important bank by the Financial Stability Board in Annex 1 to the "2013 update of group of global systemically important banks" published by the Financial Stability Board on 11 November 2013;

"institution" means an institution as defined in Article 4(1)(3) of the capital requirements regulation;

"period of account" has the same meaning as in section 1119 of the Corporation Tax Act 2010;

"subsidiary" has the same meaning as in Article 4(1)(16) of the capital requirements regulation.

2 Ongoing reporting obligation

(1) Institutions shall publish information in accordance with paragraphs (2) to (7) on or before 31st December 2015 and on or before 31st December each year thereafter.

(2) The information shall be published in accordance with accepted accounting standards on a consolidated basis for each country in which the institution has a subsidiary or branch, or both.

(3) The information shall relate to the institution's period of account ending immediately prior to the date of publication.

(4) The information in relation to the institution is—

(*a*) the name, nature of activities and geographical location of the institution and any subsidiaries and branches;

(*b*) turnover;

(*c*) the average number of employees on a full time equivalent basis;

(*d*) profit or loss before tax;

(*e*) corporation tax paid; and

(*f*) public subsidies received.

(5) For the purposes of paragraph (4)(*c*) the average number is determined by dividing the relevant annual number by the number of months in the period of account.

(6) For the purposes of paragraph (5) the relevant annual number is determined by ascertaining for each month in the period of account the number of persons employed on a full time equivalent basis in that month (whether throughout the month or not) and adding together all the monthly totals.

(7) The information shall be audited in accordance with the standards required by Directive 2006/43/EC.

(8) An institution shall publish in its annual report how it has complied, or how it will comply, with this regulation.

3 Interim reporting obligation

(1) Institutions shall publish information in accordance with regulation 2(2) to (6) on or before 1st July 2014 with the exception of the information in regulation 2(4)(d) to (f).

(2) Global systemically important institutions incorporated in the United Kingdom shall submit the information specified in regulation 2(4)(d) to (f) to the European Commission and to Her Majesty's Revenue and Customs on or before 1st July 2014.

(3) The information referred to in paragraph (2) shall be submitted in accordance with accepted accounting standards on a consolidated basis for each country in which the global systemically important institution has a subsidiary or branch or both and shall relate to that institution's period of account ending immediately prior to the date the information is submitted.

4 Group disclosure

(1) Where an institution is a member of a group whose members include undertakings which are not subject to the obligations in regulations 2(1) or 3(1) it shall be treated as having met those obligations if the parent undertaking has published the information required by regulations 2(1) or 3(1) in accordance with accepted accounting standards on a consolidated basis for each country in which an undertaking which is a member of the group is situated, in respect of all the undertakings which are members of the group.

(2) For the purposes of this regulation "group", in relation to an institution, has the same meaning as "immediate group" in section 421ZA of the 2000 Act and "parent undertaking" has the same meaning as it has for the purposes of that section.

5 Prior disclosure: prevention of duplication

(1) Where the information referred to in Article 89(1) of the capital requirements directive relating to an institution has already been published in another EEA State in accordance with that State's implementation of Article 89(1) of the capital requirements directive the institution shall be treated as having met the obligation in regulation 2(1) provided the institution publishes where that information can be obtained.

(2) Where the information referred to in Article 89(2) of the capital requirements directive relating to an institution has already been published in another EEA State in accordance with that State's implementation of Article 89(2) of the capital requirements directive the institution shall be treated as having met the obligation in regulation 3(1) provided the institution publishes where that information can be obtained.

(3) Where the information referred to in regulation 2(4) relating to an institution has already been published in the United Kingdom in accordance with regulation 2(2), (3) and (5) to (7) the institution shall be treated as having met the obligation in regulation 2(1) provided the institution publishes where that information can be obtained.

(4) Where the information referred to in regulation 2(4)(a) to (c) relating to an institution has already been published in the United Kingdom in accordance with regulation 2(2), (3), (5) and (6) the institution shall be treated as having met the obligation in regulation 3(1) provided the institution publishes where that information can be obtained.

6 Enforcement

(1) Any obligation imposed under these regulations is to be treated as a relevant requirement under Part 14 of the 2000 Act (disciplinary measures).

(2) For the purposes of paragraph (1) the appropriate regulator for the purposes of Part 14 of the 2000 Act is—

- (*a*) the Prudential Regulation Authority in relation to an institution which is a PRA-authorised person within the meaning of section 2B(5) of the 2000 Act;
- (*b*) The Financial Conduct Authority in relation to any other institution.

2013/3209

TAXATION OF REGULATORY CAPITAL SECURITIES REGULATIONS 2013

Made . . . . *18 December 2013*
Coming into force . . . . *1 January 2014*

The Treasury make the following Regulations in exercise of the powers conferred by section 221 of the Finance Act 2012.

A draft of this instrument was laid before and approved by a resolution of the House of Commons in accordance with section 221(6) of the Finance Act 2012.

1 Citation, commencement and effect

(1) These Regulations may be cited as the Taxation of Regulatory Capital Securities Regulations 2013 and shall come into force on 1st January 2014.

(2) These Regulations have effect—

- (*a*) for the purposes of income tax, for payments made on or after 1st January 2014;
- (*b*) for the purposes of corporation tax, for accounting periods beginning on or after that date (this is subject to paragraph (3) and regulation 11);
- (*c*) for the purposes of capital gains tax, in relation to disposals made on or after that date;
- (*d*) for the purposes of stamp duty, in relation to instruments executed on or after that date;
- (*e*) for the purposes of stamp duty reserve tax—
  - (i) in the case of agreements to transfer securities which are not conditional, in relation to agreements made on or after that date, and
  - (ii) in the case of agreements to transfer securities which are conditional, in relation to agreements where the condition is satisfied on or after that date.

(3) For the purposes of paragraph (2)(*b*), an accounting period beginning before and ending on or after 1st January 2014 is to be treated for the purposes of these Regulations as if so much of the period as falls before that date, and so much of the period as falls on or after that date, were separate accounting periods.

2 Regulatory capital securities

(1) For the purposes of these Regulations, "regulatory capital security" means a security which qualifies, or has qualified, as—

- (*a*) an Additional Tier 1 instrument and forms, or formed, a component of Additional Tier 1 capital for the purposes of CRR, . . . [1]
- (*b*) a Tier 2 instrument and forms, or formed, a component of Tier 2 capital for the purposes of CRR.
- ([*c*) an item listed in point (a)(iii) or (b) of Article 69 of CDR which is a Tier 1 item under—
  - (i) Article 69 or 79 of CDR, or
  - (ii) rule 4.1 in the Annex to the PRA Rulebook: Solvency II Firms: Transitional Measures Instrument 2015(c) ("the Transitional Instrument"), or
- (*d*) an item listed in point (*a*)(iii) or (*b*) of Article 72 of CDR which is a Tier 2 item under—
  - (i) Article 72 or 79 of CDR, or

(ii) rule 4.2 in the Annex to the Transitional Instrument.][1]

(2) In paragraph (1), "security" does not include shares other than deferred shares issued by a building society within paragraph (1)(*a*).

(3) For the purposes of this regulation—

"Additional Tier 1 instrument" means a security which qualifies as an Additional Tier 1 instrument under Article 52 of CRR,

"building society" and "deferred shares" have the same meanings as in the Building Societies Act 1986,

"Tier 2 instrument" means a security which qualifies as a Tier 2 instrument under Article 63 of CRR.

(4) [In these Regulations—

"CDR" means the Commission Delegated Regulation (EU) 2015/35 (as amended from time to time),

"CRR"] means the Commission Regulation (EU) No 575/2013 (as amended from time to time).

Amendments—[1] In para (1)(*b*), word "or" revoked, para (1)(*c*), (*d*) inserted and in para (4), words substituted for words "In these Regulations, "CRR"", by the Taxation of Regulatory Capital Securities (Amendment) Regulations, SI 2015/2056 reg 2(1), (2) with effect–

- for the purposes of income tax, for payments made on or after 1 January 2016;
- for the purposes of corporation tax, for accounting periods beginning on or after that date, subject to transitional provisions in relation to —
  - instruments issued by a company in an accounting period beginning before 1 January 2016; and
  - the first accounting period beginning on or after 1 January 2016 in respect of specified securities (see SI 2015/2016 regs 1(3), (3);
- for the purposes of capital gains tax, in relation to disposals made on or after that date;
- for the purposes of stamp duty, in relation to instruments executed on or after that date; and
- for the purposes of stamp duty reserve tax—
  - in the case of agreements to transfer securities which are not conditional, in relation to agreements made on or after that date; and
  - in the case of agreements to transfer securities which are conditional, in relation to agreements where the condition is satisfied on or after that date.

3 Regulatory capital securities treated as loan relationships

(1) For the purposes of the Corporation Tax Acts, a regulatory capital security represents a loan relationship.

(2) But in relation to the issuer of a regulatory capital security and any connected creditor—

(*a*) sections 415, 416 and 585 of CTA 2009 (loan relationships with embedded derivatives) do not apply in relation to the security,

(*b*) the credits and debits to be brought into account in respect of the security are determined as if [measuring the whole or part of the security at fair value were not generally accepted accounting practice (but see paragraph (3A)), and][1]

(*c*) no credit or debit is to be brought into account under Part 5 of CTA 2009—

(i) in respect of the principal amount of the security being written down on a permanent or temporary basis or the security being converted to a Common Equity Tier 1 instrument [or an item listed in point (*a*)(i) or (ii) of Article 69 of CDR][1] in accordance with any regulatory requirements or the provisions governing the security, or

(ii) in respect of the principal amount of the security being written up, following a write down of the principal amount on a temporary basis, in accordance with any regulatory requirements or the provisions governing the security.

(3) Paragraph (2) applies for the purposes of determining the profits and losses to be recognised in determining the [tax-adjusted carrying value][1] of a regulatory capital security for the purposes of [section 465B][1] of CTA 2009 as it applies for the purposes of determining the credits and debits to be brought into account under Part 5 of CTA 2009.

[(3A) Paragraph (2)(*b*) does not prevent the carrying value of the security being adjusted as necessary where the security is the hedged item under a designated fair value hedge.][1]

(4) In this regulation—

"Common Equity Tier 1 instrument" means a capital instrument which qualifies as a Common Equity Tier 1 instrument under Article 28 or 29 of CRR,

"connected creditor" means a company standing in the position of creditor as respects a regulatory capital security where the creditor relationship is a connected companies relationship for the purposes of Part 5 of CTA 2009,

"fair value accounting" have the same meanings as in Part 5 of CTA 2009.

Amendments—[1] In para (2)(*b*), words substituted for words "fair value accounting were not generally accepted accounting practice in relation to the security or part of the security (including a hedged component), and", in para (2)(*c*)(i), words inserted, in para (3), words substituted for words "carrying value" and "section 317", para (3A) inserted, and in para (4), definition of "fair value accounting" revoked, by the Taxation of Regulatory Capital Securities (Amendment) Regulations, SI 2015/2056 reg 2(1), (3) with effect–

- for the purposes of income tax, for payments made on or after 1 January 2016;

– for the purposes of corporation tax, for accounting periods beginning on or after that date, subject to transitional provisions in relation to —
  – instruments issued by a company in an accounting period beginning before 1 January 2016; and
  – the first accounting period beginning on or after 1 January 2016 in respect of specified securities (see SI 2015/2016 regs 1(3), (3);
– for the purposes of capital gains tax, in relation to disposals made on or after that date;
– for the purposes of stamp duty, in relation to instruments executed on or after that date; and
– for the purposes of stamp duty reserve tax—
  – in the case of agreements to transfer securities which are not conditional, in relation to agreements made on or after that date; and
  – in the case of agreements to transfer securities which are conditional, in relation to agreements where the condition is satisfied on or after that date.

[3A Amounts recognised in equity

(1) This regulation applies if in accordance with generally accepted accounting practice, an amount in respect of a regulatory capital security relating to any of the matters in section 306A(1) of CTA 2009—

(*a*) is recognised in equity or shareholders' funds for a period, and

(*b*) is not recognised in the company's accounts for the period as an item of profit or loss or as an item of other comprehensive income.

(2) The amount is to be brought into account for the period for the purposes of Part 5 of CTA 2009 in the same way as an amount which is brought into account as a credit or debit in determining the company's profit or loss for the period in accordance with generally accepted accounting practice.

(3) But this regulation does not bring into account for the purposes of Part 5 of CTA 2009 any exchange gain or loss of the company so far as it is recognised in the company's statement of total recognised gains and losses, statement of recognised income and expense, statement of changes in equity or statement of income and retained earnings.

(4) In this regulation "item of profit or loss", "item of other comprehensive income", "statement of total recognised gains and losses", "statement of recognised income and expense", "statement of changes in equity" and "statement of income and retained earnings" each has the meaning that it has for accounting purposes.][1]

Amendments—[1] Regulation 3A inserted by the Taxation of Regulatory Capital Securities (Amendment) Regulations, SI 2015/2056 reg 2(1), (4) with effect–

– for the purposes of income tax, for payments made on or after 1 January 2016;
– for the purposes of corporation tax, for accounting periods beginning on or after that date, subject to transitional provisions in relation to —
  – instruments issued by a company in an accounting period beginning before 1 January 2016; and
  – the first accounting period beginning on or after 1 January 2016 in respect of specified securities (see SI 2015/2016 regs 1(3), (3);
– for the purposes of capital gains tax, in relation to disposals made on or after that date;
– for the purposes of stamp duty, in relation to instruments executed on or after that date; and
– for the purposes of stamp duty reserve tax—
  – in the case of agreements to transfer securities which are not conditional, in relation to agreements made on or after that date; and
  – in the case of agreements to transfer securities which are conditional, in relation to agreements where the condition is satisfied on or after that date.

4 Regulatory capital securities treated as normal commercial loans

For the purposes of sections 158(1)(*b*) and 159(4)(*b*) of CTA 2010 and section 117(1)(*a*) of TCGA 1992, a regulatory capital security represents a normal commercial loan.

5 Treatment of payments

(1) A payment in respect of a regulatory capital security is—

(*a*) not a distribution for the purposes of the Tax Acts, but

(*b*) is income chargeable under Chapter 2 of Part 4 of ITTOIA 2005 (interest) for the purposes of income tax.

(2) In paragraph (1), "payment" does not include a repayment of the principal amount of the security.

6 Exception from duty to deduct income tax

The duty to deduct a sum representing income tax under section 874 (duty to deduct from certain payments of yearly interest) or section 889 (payments in respect of building society securities) of ITA 2007 does not apply to a payment in respect of a regulatory capital security.

7 Exemption from stamp duties

A transfer of a regulatory capital security is exempt from all stamp duties.

8 Anti-avoidance

(1) Regulations 3 to 7 do not apply in the case of a regulatory capital security if there are arrangements the main purpose, or one of the main purposes, of which is to obtain a tax advantage for any person as a result of the application of these Regulations in respect of that security.

(2) In paragraph (1), "tax advantage" has the meaning given in section 1139 of CTA 2010.

9 Duty to deduct from payments in respect of regulatory capital security

The following sections of ITA 2007 do not apply to a payment in respect of a regulatory capital security—

(*a*) section 878 (interest paid by banks), and

(*b*) section 885 (authorised persons dealing in financial instruments).

10 Amendment of the Loan Relationship and Derivative Contracts (Disregard and Bringing into Account of Profits and Losses) Regulations 2004

(1) The Loan Relationship and Derivative Contracts (Disregard and Bringing into Account of Profits and Losses) Regulations 2004 are amended as follows.

(2) In regulation 2(1)—

(*a*) omit the definition of "Additional Tier 1 instrument", and

(*b*) in the appropriate place insert—

""regulatory capital security" has the meaning given in regulation 2 of the Taxation of Regulatory Capital Securities Regulations 2013;".

(3) In regulations 3(5)(*c*) and 4(4A)(*c*) for "an Additional Tier 1 instrument" substitute "a regulatory capital security".

(4) In regulation 6, in paragraphs (5A) and (5C)—

(*a*) at the end of sub-paragraph (*a*), in both cases, omit "or", and

(*b*) at the end of both paragraphs insert—

"; or

(*c*) where the hedged item is a regulatory capital security in relation to which the company uses fair value accounting.".

11 Transitional provisions

(1) This regulation applies for the purposes of corporation tax in relation to the first accounting period beginning, or treated as beginning, on or after 1st January 2014 in respect of a security—

(*a*) issued before that date,

(*b*) to which Part 5 of CTA 2009 applied in the accounting period ending, or treated as ending, on 31st December 2013, and

(*c*) which is a regulatory capital security for the purposes of these Regulations.

(2) In this regulation—

(*a*) an accounting period ending, or treated as ending, on 31st December 2013 is referred to as "the earlier period", and

(*b*) an accounting period beginning, or treated as beginning, on 1st January 2014 is referred to as "the later period".

(3) If there is an increase in the carrying value of a security which is an asset of the company between—

(*a*) the end of the earlier period, and

(*b*) the beginning of the later period,

a credit equal to the increase must be brought into account for the purposes of Part 5 of CTA 2009 in the later period.

(4) If there is an decrease in the carrying value of such a security between—

(*a*) the end of earlier period, and

(*b*) the beginning of the later period,

a debit equal to the decrease must be brought into account for the purposes of Part 5 of CTA 2009 in the later period.

(5) If there is an increase in the carrying value of a security which is a liability of the company between—

(*a*) the end of the earlier period, and

(*b*) the beginning of the later period,

a debit equal to the increase must be brought into account for the purposes of Part 5 of CTA 2009 in the later period.

(6) If there is an decrease in the carrying value of such a security between—

(*a*) the end of earlier period, and

(*b*) the beginning of the later period,

a credit equal to the decrease must be brought into account for the purposes of Part 5 of CTA 2009 in the later period.

(7) But this regulation does not apply so far as any debit or credit as is mentioned in this regulation falls to be brought into account apart from this regulation.

(8) For the purposes of this regulation, where in the earlier period, in accordance with generally accepted accounting practice, the rights and liabilities under a security have been treated as divided between a loan relationship and one or more derivative financial instruments or equity instruments, the reference to the carrying value of the security means the sum of the carrying values for each of those component instruments.

(9) For the purposes of this regulation, "carrying value" must be construed in accordance with section 317 (subject to regulation 3(3) in the later period) and section 702 of CTA 2009.

12 Repeals

The following provisions are repealed—

(*a*) in CTA 2010—

(i) section 162(1A) (meaning of "normal commercial loan"),

(ii) section 164A (loan forming part of tier two capital),

(iii) section 1029(1)(ca) (overview), and

(iv) section 1032A (payment in respect of tier two capital), and the heading "tier two capital" immediately before that section, and

(*b*) in the Finance Act 2013, section 43 (tier two capital).

2014/520

INTERNATIONAL TAX COMPLIANCE (CROWN DEPENDENCIES AND GIBRALTAR) REGULATIONS 2014

Made . . . . *6 March 2014*

Laid before the House of Commons . . . . *7 March 2014*

Coming into force . . . . *31 March 2014*

The Treasury make these Regulations in exercise of the powers conferred by section 222(1)(c), (2) and (3) of the Finance Act 2013:

Introductory

1 Citation and commencement

(1) These Regulations may be cited as the International Tax Compliance (Crown Dependencies and Gibraltar) Regulations 2014.

(2) These Regulations come into force on 31st March 2014.

2 Implementation of the agreements etc

(1) These Regulations have effect for and in connection with the implementation of obligations arising under each of the Isle of Man agreement, the Guernsey agreement, the Jersey agreement and the Gibraltar agreement and apply separately in relation to each of those agreements.

(2) In these Regulations—

(a) "the Isle of Man agreement" means the agreement between the Government of the United Kingdom of Great Britain and Northern Ireland and the Government of the Isle of Man to improve international tax compliance, signed on 10th October 2013,

(b) "the Guernsey agreement" means the agreement between the Government of the United Kingdom of Great Britain and Northern Ireland and the States of Guernsey to improve international tax compliance, signed on 22nd October 2013,

(c) "the Jersey agreement" means the agreement between the Government of the United Kingdom of Great Britain and Northern Ireland and the Government of Jersey to improve international tax compliance, signed on 22nd October 2013, and

(d) "the Gibraltar agreement" means the agreement between the Government of the United Kingdom of Great Britain and Northern Ireland and the Government of Gibraltar to improve international tax compliance, signed on 21st November 2013,

as each of those agreements has effect from time to time.

(3) In these Regulations, "the relevant agreement" means—

(a) the Isle of Man agreement,

(b) the Guernsey agreement,

(c) the Jersey agreement, or

(d) the Gibraltar agreement,

as the context may require.

(4) Any expression which is not defined in section 222 or 235 of FA 2013 or in these Regulations has the same meaning in these Regulations as it has in the relevant agreement.

Scope

3 Scope: definition of "reporting financial institution"

(1) In these Regulations "reporting financial institution" means a person who carries on business in the United Kingdom as—

(a) a depository institution,

(b) an investment entity,

(c) a custodial institution, or

(d) a specified insurance company.

(2) But a person is not a reporting financial institution for the purposes of these Regulations if that person is a non-reporting financial institution.

(3) For the purposes of these Regulations "depository institution" means—

(a) a person carrying on a regulated activity for the purposes of the Financial Services and Markets Act 2000 by virtue of article 5 of the Financial Services and Markets Act 2000 (Regulated Activities) Order 2001, or

(b) a person who is within paragraphs (a) to (e) or (h) to (j) of the definition of "electronic money issuer" in regulation 2(1) of the Electronic Money Regulations 2011.

(4) For the purposes of these Regulations a person (person A) carries on business in the United Kingdom as an investment entity if—

(a) person A undertakes any of the activities referred to in sub-paragraph 1.j(1) to (3) of Article 1 of the relevant agreement in the course of carrying on business in the United Kingdom, and the gross amount of person A's income of that business for the applicable period wholly or mainly derives from those activities, or

(b) on behalf of person A, a financial institution (person B) undertakes any of the activities referred to in sub-paragraph 1.j(1) to (3) of Article 1 of the relevant agreement in the course of carrying on business in the United Kingdom, and the gross amount of person A's income . . . [1] for the applicable period wholly or mainly derives from investing or dealing in financial assets.

(5) For the purposes of these Regulations—

(a) if a collective investment scheme is constituted by a person (other than a trustee), who carries on business in the United Kingdom, that person (and no-one else) is a reporting financial institution in the case of the scheme and is to be regarded as the investment entity, and

(b) if a collective investment scheme is constituted otherwise than as described in sub-paragraph (a) and the manager, operator or trustee of the scheme is a person who carries on business in the United Kingdom, the manager, operator or trustee of the scheme (and no-one else) is a reporting financial institution in the case of the scheme and is to be regarded as the investment entity.

(6) In paragraph (5) "collective investment scheme" means—

(a) an investment trust within the meaning of the Corporation Tax Acts,

(b) a venture capital trust within the meaning of Part 6 of ITA 2007, or

(c) any arrangements that are a "collective investment scheme" within the meaning of Part 17 of the Financial Services and Markets Act 2000.

(7) For the purposes of these Regulations a person carries on a business in the United Kingdom as a custodial institution if—

(a) more than 20% of the gross amount of the income of that business as is carried on in the United Kingdom for the applicable period derives from any of—

(i) holding financial assets for the account of another person, and

(ii) performing related financial services, or

(b) the person holds [financial][1] assets in the United Kingdom as a nominee for another person who is a connected person within the meaning of section 1122 of CTA 2010.

(8) In paragraph (7)(a)(ii) "related financial services" means financial services provided by the person that directly relate to that person holding financial assets on behalf of the other person.

(9) In paragraphs (7) . . . [1] and (8) "financial assets" means—

(a) assets capable of being the subject-matter of a transaction that is an "investment transaction" within the meaning of regulation 14F of Part 2B of the Authorised Investment Funds (Tax) Regulations 2006,

(b) insurance or annuity contracts,

(c) commodities, or

(d) derivative contracts within the meaning of Part 7 of CTA 2009.

(10) In paragraph (4) and sub-paragraph (7)(a) the "applicable period" is the shorter of—

(a) the three year period—

(i) ending with the person's most recent accounting date if that date is no more than twelve months earlier than the next reporting date, or

(ii) in any other case, the 31st December immediately before the next reporting date, and

(b) the period—

(i) starting on the later of the first day of the period determined under sub-paragraph (a) and the date that the person commenced the business, and

(ii) ending on the earlier of the last day of the period determined under sub-paragraph (a) and the last day that the person carried on the business,

and "accounting date" here has the same meaning as is given to it by section 1119 CTA 2010.

Amendments—[1] In para (4)(*b*) words revoked, in para (7)(*b*) word inserted, and in para (9) reference revoked, by SI 2015/873, reg 2(1), (2) with effect from 15 April 2015.

4 Scope: definition of "reportable account"

(1) In these Regulations a "reportable account" means—

(a) an account which is a reportable account for the relevant agreement maintained in the United Kingdom by a reporting financial institution for the purposes of its business as described in regulation 3(1), and

(b) an account that is—

(i) a preexisting individual account meeting the description at paragraph II.A of Annex I,

(ii) a new individual account meeting the description at paragraph III.A of that Annex,

(iii) a preexisting entity account meeting the description at paragraph IV.A of that Annex, or

(iv) a new entity account meeting the description at paragraph V.A of that Annex.

(2) But an account in any of paragraphs (i) to (iv) of paragraph (1)(b) is not a reportable account for a calendar year if—

(a) there is an election by the reporting financial institution in force for that year to treat such accounts as not being a reportable account, and

(b) the account meets any further description specified by the institution in its election.

(3) An election under paragraph (2)—

(a) is to be made by being given to the Commissioners,

(b) must specify the description of accounts in relation to which the election is to have effect, and

(c) must be made in the return required by regulation 8.

(4) For the purposes of these Regulations—

(a) any reference to an entity account is to a financial account which is not an account the account holder of which (or, if more than one, each account holder of which) is an individual holding the account otherwise than as a partner of a partnership, and

(b) any reference to an individual account is to a financial account held in the name of an individual (whether solely or jointly with another) but not as a partner or a partnership.

(5) For the purposes of determining—

(a) whether or not a financial account maintained by an institution meets any of the descriptions in paragraph (1)(b), and

(b) which case in regulation 6(4) applies to an account,

the institution must apply the account balance aggregation and currency translation rules at paragraph VI.C of Annex I.

But, in determining the balance or value of an account denominated in a currency other than US dollars, instead of applying the currency translation rule in sub-paragraph VI.C.4 of Annex I, the institution may translate the relevant dollar threshold amounts referred to in Annex 1 and regulation 6(4) into the other currency by reference to the spot rate of exchange on the date for which the institution is determining the threshold amounts.

5 Scope: non-resident reporting financial institution's UK representative

(1) If a reporting financial institution is not resident in the United Kingdom, the obligations of the institution under these Regulations are to be treated as if they were also the obligations of any UK representative of the institution.

(2) "UK representative" has the same meaning as it has in—

(a) Chapter 6 of Part 22 of CTA 2010, in relation to a reporting financial institution that is within the charge to corporation tax, and

(b) Chapter 2C of Part 14 of ITA 2007, in relation to any other reporting financial institution.

(3) For the purposes of this regulation—

(a) a reporting financial institution which is a partnership is resident in the United Kingdom if the control and management of the business of the partnership as a reporting financial institution takes place there, and

(b) a reporting financial institution which is not a partnership is resident in the United Kingdom if it is resident in the United Kingdom for corporation tax or income tax purposes.

Obligations in relation to financial accounts

6 Identification obligations

(1) A reporting financial institution must establish and maintain arrangements that are designed to identify reportable accounts.

(2) Such arrangements must identify the territory in which either of the following persons is resident for income tax or corporation tax purposes or for the purposes of any tax imposed by the law of that territory that is of a similar character to either of those taxes—

(a) the account holder, and

(b) any controlling person of the account holder, unless the account holder is either

(i) a financial institution, or

(ii) an active NFFE.

(3) The institution is taken to comply with the obligation to establish and maintain arrangements within paragraph (1) only if—

(a) the arrangements meet the applicable due diligence requirements as set out in this regulation (as modified by regulation 7 where an election under that regulation is in force), and

(b) the arrangements secure that the evidence used in accordance with this regulation or regulation 7, or a record of the steps taken in accordance with this regulation or regulation 7, is kept for a period of six years beginning with the end of the year in which the arrangements applied to the financial accounts.

(4) The due diligence requirements for a calendar year are set out in the following cases.

Preexisting individual accounts

Case 1

In the case of preexisting individual accounts with a balance or value that does not exceed $1,000,000 as of 30 June 2014, the procedures described at paragraphs II.B and II.C of Annex I.

But this does not apply in relation to any preexisting individual account meeting the description at paragraph II.A of Annex I in relation to which an election under regulation 4(2) is in place.

Case 2

In the case of preexisting individual accounts with a balance or value that exceeds $1,000,000 as of 30 June 2014, or 31 December 2015 or 31 December in any subsequent year, the procedures described at paragraphs II.D and II.E of Annex I.

New individual accounts

Case 3

In the case of new individual accounts, the procedures described at paragraphs III.B to III.D of Annex I.

But this does not apply in relation to any new individual account meeting the description at paragraph III.A of Annex I in relation to which an election under regulation 4(2) is in place.

Preexisting entity accounts

Case 4

In the case of preexisting entity accounts, the procedures described at paragraphs IV.D and IV.E (1) and (3) of Annex I.

But this does not apply in relation to any preexisting entity account meeting the description at paragraph IV.A of Annex I in relation to which an election under regulation 4(2) is in place.

Case 5

In the case of preexisting entity accounts with a balance or value that does not exceed $250,000 as of 30 June 2014, but with a balance or value that exceeds $1,000,000 as of 31 December 2015 or 31 December in any subsequent year, the procedures at paragraphs IV.D and IV.E (2) and (3) of Annex I.

New entity accounts

Case 6

In the case of new entity accounts, the procedures described at paragraphs V.B to V.D of Annex I.

But this does not apply in relation to any new entity account meeting the description at paragraph V.A of Annex I in relation to which an election under regulation 4(2) is in place.

(5) If in the case of an account within Case 1—

(a) an institution has established the account holder's relevant tax status from documentary evidence mentioned in paragraph VI.D (4) of Annex I, and

(b) it has done so in order to meet its obligations under a Qualifying Intermediary agreement as mentioned in that paragraph,

the due diligence requirements in the case of that account do not include the requirement to carry out the electronic search described in paragraph II.B (1) of Annex I.

(6) If in the case of an account within Case 2—

(a) an institution has established the account holder's relevant tax status from documentary evidence mentioned in paragraph VI.D (4) of Annex I, and
(b) it has done so in order to meet its obligations under a Qualifying Intermediary agreement as mentioned in that paragraph,

the due diligence requirements in the case of that account do not include the requirement to carry out the electronic searches described in paragraph II.B (1) or II.D (1) of Annex I or the requirement to carry out the paper record search described in paragraph II.D (2) of that Annex.

(7) If, as a result of this regulation, a person's relevant tax status is required to be certified, a reporting financial institution may require the person to supply to the institution such documentary evidence mentioned in paragraph VI.D of Annex I as the institution considers appropriate in support of the certification.

(8) The due diligence requirements in this regulation must be applied in relation to each category of reportable account by reference to the special rules and definitions at paragraph I.D (1) to (3) and section VI of Annex I.

(9) For the purposes of this regulation references to the documentary evidence set out in paragraph VI.D of Annex I are to be treated as if the words "other than a Form W-8 or W-9" were omitted.

7 Modification of due diligence requirements

(1) This regulation modifies the due diligence requirements set out in regulation 6 in the case of a reporting financial institution but only if it makes an election applying those modifications.

(2) If the institution obtains, or is in the process of obtaining, evidence of a person's relevant tax status in relation to any preexisting account, it is entitled to rely on the evidence in relation to any account opened after 30 June 2014 unless it has reasonable cause to believe that the person's relevant tax status has subsequently changed.

(3) Paragraph (2) has effect in the case of preexisting individual accounts maintained by the institution for an account holder only if, for the purpose of establishing which of the cases in regulation 6(4) are applicable to those accounts, the institution treats all those accounts as a single preexisting individual account.

(4) If the institution or a related entity obtains, or is in the process of obtaining, evidence of a person's relevant tax status in relation to a financial account, the institution is entitled to rely on the evidence in relation to all financial accounts maintained by the institution for the account holder unless the institution has reasonable cause to believe that the person's relevant tax status has subsequently changed.

(5) The due diligence requirements set out in regulation 6 do not need to be met in relation to a financial account if—

(a) the institution maintains the account as a result of a merger with, or acquisition of, a qualifying financial institution which had established the relevant tax status of the account holder and any controlling person, and
(b) the institution has no reasonable cause to believe that the relevant tax status of the account holder or any controlling person has changed.

(6) For this purpose "qualifying financial institution", in relation to a financial institution, means another financial institution—

(a) which has not previously been a related entity of the institution, and
(b) which immediately before the merger or acquisition was either a reporting financial institution for the purposes of these Regulations or a financial institution described under sub-paragraph 1(p) of Article 1 of the relevant agreement.

(7) An election under this regulation—

(a) is to be made by being given to the Commissioners,
(b) must be made in the return required under regulation 8, and
(c) has effect in relation to the calendar year in respect of which the return is made and all later calendar years (unless subsequently withdrawn).

8 Reporting obligations

(1) A reporting financial institution must, in respect of 2014 and every following calendar year, prepare a return setting out—

(a) the required information in relation to every reportable account of that category that is maintained by the institution at any time during the calendar year in question, and
(b) the institution's Global Intermediary Identification Number (or, if it has not been allocated such a number, the Unique Taxpayer Reference number allocated to the institution by HMRC).

(2) . . . [1]

(3) [The return must be submitted electronically in accordance with regulation 8A][1] on or before 31st May of the year following the calendar year to which the return relates ("the reporting date").

(4) The required information is—

(a) the name and address of the account holder,
(b) the account holder's social security number,

(c) if an account is identifiable by an account number, that number or, if not, any functional equivalents,

(d) the balance or value of the account (including, in the case of a cash value insurance contract or annuity contract, the cash value or surrender value) as of the end of the calendar year or, if the account was closed during the year, the balance or value on the date that the reporting financial institution closed the account,

(e) the relevant total gross credits, or if there are none, a statement of that fact,

(f) if the account holder is an individual, that person's date of birth, and

(g) if the account holder is a passive NFFE that has a controlling person who is a specified person, the name and address of that specified person, and, if that person is an individual, that person's—

(i) social security number, and

(ii) date of birth.

(5) The "relevant total gross credits" means—

(a) in the case of a custodial account—

(i) the total gross amount of interest, the total gross amount of dividends and the total gross amount of other income generated with respect to assets held in the account which is paid into, or with respect to, the account during the calendar year, and

(ii) the total gross proceeds from the sale or redemption of property paid into the account during the calendar year if the institution acted as a custodian, broker, nominee or otherwise as an agent for the account holder,

(b) in the case of a depository account, the total gross amount of interest paid to the account during the calendar year, and

(c) in the case of any other account, the total gross amount of sums paid by the institution under a legal obligation to the account holder with respect to the account during the calendar year,

and "interest" here includes any amount that is chargeable as interest under Part 4 of ITTOIA 2005.

(6) For the purposes of this regulation—

(a) references to the balance or value of an account include a nil balance or value,

(b) references to paying an amount include crediting an amount,

(c) "social security number" means—

(i) in relation to the Isle of Man agreement, either the number allocated to a person for the social security purposes or a person's United Kingdom National insurance number,

(ii) in relation to any other relevant agreement, the number allocated to a person for the social security purposes of Guernsey, Jersey or Gibraltar as the case may be.

(7) If a reporting financial institution has an established practice for the periodic valuation of accounts of a particular description otherwise than at the end of a calendar year, the institution may report under paragraph (5)(a) or (c) by reference to a period of 12 months ending with the date (or, if more than one, the latest date) in the calendar year on which the institution values accounts of that description (instead of by reference to the calendar year).

(8) If a reporting financial institution does not hold the information that it is required to report under paragraph (4)(b), (f) and (g), the institution must obtain that information from the account holder.

Amendments—[1] Para (2) revoked, and words in para (3) substituted, by SI 2015/873, reg 2(1), (3) with effect from 15 April 2015.

[8A Electronic return system

(1) The return must be made electronically using an electronic return system.

(2) An electronic return system is the form and manner specified in specific or general directions given by the Commissioners for Her Majesty's Revenue and Customs.

(3) A return which is made in a form or manner otherwise than by an electronic return system is treated as not having been made.

(4) An electronic return system must incorporate an electronic validation process.

(5) Unless the contrary is proved—

(a) the use of an electronic return system is presumed to have resulted in the making of the return only if this has been successfully recorded as such by the relevant electronic validation process,

(b) the time of making the return using an electronic return system is presumed to be the time recorded as such by the relevant electronic validation process, and

(c) the person delivering the return is presumed to be the person identified as such by any relevant feature of the electronic return system.

(6) A return made using an electronic return system on behalf of a reporting financial institution is taken to have been made by that institution, unless the institution proves that the return was made without the institution's authority.][1]

Amendments—[1] Reg 8A inserted by SI 2015/873, reg 2(1), (4) with effect from 15 April 2015.

9 Modifications for calendar years 2014 to 2016

(1) In relation to any reportable account—

(a) there is no requirement to include in the return for the calendar year 2014 information about relevant total gross credits, and
(b) there is no requirement to include in the return for the calendar year 2015 any information set out in regulation 8(5)(a)(ii).

(2) In the case of preexisting accounts there is no requirement to include in the return for calendar years before 2017 any information set out in regulation 8(4)(b), (f) and (g) if the reporting financial institution does not hold that information.

(3) In the case of the calendar year 2014 the reporting date is 31st May 2016.

Penalties for breach of obligations

10 Penalties for failure to comply

A person is liable to a penalty of £300 if the person fails to comply with any obligation under these Regulations.

[10A Daily default penalty

If—
(a) a penalty under regulation 10 is assessed, and
(b) the failure in question continues after the person has been notified of the assessment,

the person is liable to a further penalty, for each subsequent day on which the failure continues, of an amount not exceeding £60 for each such day.][1]

Amendments—[1] Reg 10A inserted by SI 2015/873, reg 2(1), (5) with effect from 15 April 2015.

11 Penalties for inaccurate information

(1) A person is liable to a penalty not exceeding £3,000 if—
(a) in complying with an obligation under regulation 8 the person provides inaccurate information, and
(b) condition A, B or C is met.

(2) Condition A is that the inaccuracy is—
(a) due to a failure to comply with regulation 6, or
(b) deliberate on the part of the person.

(3) Condition B is that the person knows of the inaccuracy at the time the information is provided but does not inform HMRC at that time.

(4) Condition C is that the person—
(a) discovers the inaccuracy some time later, and
(b) fails to take reasonable steps to inform HMRC.

12 Matters to be disregarded in relation to liability to penalties

(1) Liability to a penalty under regulation 10[, 10A][1] or 11 does not arise if the person satisfies HMRC or (on an appeal notified to the tribunal) the tribunal that there is a reasonable excuse for the failure.

(2) For the purposes of this regulation neither of the following is a reasonable excuse—
(a) that there is an insufficiency of funds to do something, or
(b) that a person relies upon another person to do something.

(3) If a person had a reasonable excuse for a failure but the excuse has ceased, the person is to be treated as having continued to have the excuse if the failure is remedied without unreasonable delay after the excuse ceased.

Amendments—[1] Reference in para (1) inserted by SI 2015/873, reg 2(1), (6) with effect from 15 April 2015.

13 Assessment of penalties

(1) If the reporting financial institution becomes liable to a penalty under regulation 10[, 10A][1] or 11, an officer of Revenue and Customs may assess the penalty.

(2) If an officer does so, the officer must notify the institution.

(3) An assessment of a penalty under regulation 10 [or 10A][1] must be made within the period of 12 months beginning with the date on which the person became liable to the penalty.

(4) An assessment of a penalty under regulation 11 must be made—
(a) within the period of 12 months beginning with the date on which the inaccuracy first came to the attention of an officer of Revenue and Customs, and
(b) within the period of 6 years beginning with the date on which the person became liable to the penalty.

Amendments—[1] Words in paras (1), (3) inserted by SI 2015/873, reg 2(1), (7) with effect from 15 April 2015.

14 Right to appeal against penalty

A person may appeal against a decision by an officer of Revenue and Customs—
(a) that a penalty is payable under regulation 10[, 10A][1] or 11, or
(b) as to the amount of such a penalty.

Amendments—[1] Reference in para (a) inserted by SI 2015/873, reg 2(1), (8) with effect from 15 April 2015.

15 Procedure on appeal against penalty

(1) Notice of an appeal under regulation 14 must be given—

(a) in writing,

(b) before the end of the period of 30 days beginning with the date on which notification under regulation 13 was given, and

(c) to HMRC.

(2) It must state the grounds of appeal.

(3) On an appeal under regulation 14(a) that is notified to the tribunal, the tribunal may confirm or cancel the decision.

(4) On an appeal under regulation 14(b) that is notified to the tribunal, the tribunal may—

(a) confirm the decision, or

(b) substitute for the decision another decision that the officer of Revenue and Customs had power to make.

(5) Subject to this regulation and regulation 16, the provisions of Part 5 of TMA 1970 relating to appeals have effect in relation to appeals under regulation 14 as they have effect in relation to an appeal against an assessment to income tax.

[15A Increased daily default penalty

(1) This paragraph applies if—

(a) a penalty under regulation 10A is assessed under regulation 13,

(b) the failure in respect of which that assessment is made continues for more than 30 days beginning with the date on which notification of that assessment is given, and

(c) the person has been told that an application may be made under this paragraph for an increased daily penalty to be imposed.

(2) If this regulation applies, an officer of Revenue and Customs may make an application to the tribunal for an increased daily penalty to be imposed on the person.

(3) If the tribunal decides that an increased daily penalty should be imposed then for each applicable day on which the failure continues—

(a) the person is not liable to a penalty under regulation 10A in respect of the failure, and

(b) the person is liable instead to a penalty under this regulation of an amount determined by the tribunal.

(4) The tribunal may not determine an amount exceeding £1000 for each applicable day.

(5) If a person becomes liable to a penalty under this regulation, HMRC must notify the person.

(6) The notification must specify the day from which the increased penalty is to apply.

(7) That day and any subsequent day is an "applicable day" for the purposes of this regulation.][1]

Amendments—[1] Para 15A inserted by SI 2015/873, reg 2(1), (9) with effect from 15 April 2015.

16 Enforcement of penalties

(1) A penalty under these Regulations must be paid before the end of the period of 30 days beginning with the date mentioned in paragraph (2).

(2) That date is—

(a) the date on which notification under regulation 13 is given in respect of the penalty, or

(b) if a notice of appeal under regulation 14 is given, the date on which the appeal is finally determined or withdrawn.

(3) A penalty under these Regulations may be enforced as if it were income tax charged in an assessment and due and payable.

Miscellaneous

17 Accounts with a negative value

For the purpose of applying paragraph VI.C of Annex I as required by these Regulations, an account balance that has a negative value is treated as having a nil value.

18 Anti-avoidance

If a person does things wholly or mainly for the purpose of avoiding any obligation under these Regulations, these Regulations are to have effect as if those things had not been done.

Supplementary

19 Definitions

(1) In these Regulations—

"Annex 1" means Annex 1 of the relevant agreement,

"the Commissioners" means the Commissioners for her Majesty's Revenue and Customs,

"Global Intermediary Identification Number" means a number allocated to a Financial Institution by the Internal Revenue Service in the United States of America for the purposes of the part of the law of that territory commonly known as the Foreign Account Tax Compliance Act, and

"the tribunal" means the first tier Tribunal or, where determined by or under Tribunal Procedure Rules, the Upper Tribunal.

(2) In these Regulations references to a person's relevant tax status are to whether or not that person is—

(a) in relation to the Isle of Man agreement, a specified Isle of Man person,

(b) in relation to the Guernsey agreement, a specified Guernsey person,

(c) in relation to the Jersey agreement, a specified Jersey person, and

(d) in relation to the Gibraltar agreement, a specified Gibraltar person.

(3) In these Regulations references to a value in dollars are references to a value in the currency of the United States of America.

(4) The following table lists the places where expressions that apply for the purposes of these Regulations are defined or otherwise explained—

Expression	*Reference*
account holder	regulation 2(4) and sub-paragraph 1(dd) of Article 1 of the relevant agreement
Active NFFE	regulation 2(4) and paragraph VI.B (6) of Annex 1
Annex 1	regulation 19(1)
annuity contract	regulation 2(4) and sub-paragraph 1(w) of Article 1 of the relevant agreement
the Commissioners	regulation 19(1)
cash value insurance contract	regulation 2(4) and sub-paragraph 1(x) of Article 1 of the relevant agreement
controlling person	regulation 2(4) and sub-paragraph 1(ll) of Article 1 of the relevant agreement
custodial account	regulation 2(4) and sub-paragraph 1(t) of Article 1 of the relevant agreement
custodial institution	regulation 3(7)
depository account	regulation 2(4) and sub-paragraph 1(s) of Article 1 of the relevant agreement
depository institution	regulation 3(3)
entity account	regulation 4(4)(a)
financial account	regulation 2(4) and sub-paragraph 1(r) of Article 1 of the relevant agreement
financial institution	regulation 2(4) and sub-paragraph 1(g) of Article 1 of the relevant agreement
the Gibraltar agreement	regulation 2(2)
Global Intermediary Identification Number	regulation 19(1)
the Guernsey agreement	regulation 2(2)
HMRC	section 222(4) FA 2013
individual account	regulation 4(4)(b)

insurance contract	regulation 2(4) and sub-paragraph 1(v) of Article 1 of the relevant agreement
investment entity	regulation 3(4)
the Isle of Man agreement	regulation 2(2)
the Jersey agreement	regulation 2(2)
new entity account	regulation 2(4) and paragraph V of Annex 1
new individual account	regulation 2(4) and paragraph III of Annex 1
non-reporting financial institution	regulation 2(4) and sub-paragraph 1(q) of Article 1 of the relevant agreement
passive NFFE	regulation 2(4) and sub-paragraph VI.B.5 of Annex 1 of the relevant agreement
preexisting account	regulation 2(4) and sub-paragraph 1(z) of Article 1 of the relevant agreement
preexisting entity account	regulation 2(4) and paragraph IV of Annex 1
preexisting individual account	regulation 2(4) and paragraph II of Annex 1
related entity	regulation 2(4) and sub-paragraph 1(kk) of Article 1 of the relevant agreement
the relevant agreement	regulation 2(3)
relevant tax status	regulation 19(2)
relevant total gross credits	regulation 8(5)
reportable account	regulation 4
reporting date	regulations 8(3) and 9(3)
reporting financial institution	regulation 3
specified Gibraltar person	regulation 2(4) and sub-paragraph 1(gg) of Article 1 of the Gibraltar agreement
specified Guernsey person	regulation 2(4) and sub-paragraph 1(gg) of Article 1 of the Guernsey agreement
specified insurance company	regulation 2(4) and sub-paragraph 1(k) of Article 1 of the relevant agreement
specified Isle of Man person	regulation 2(4) and sub-paragraph 1(gg) of Article 1 of the Isle of Man agreement

specified Jersey person	regulation 2(4) and sub-paragraph 1(gg) of Article 1 of the Jersey agreement
specified person	regulation 2(4) and sub-paragraph 1(ee) of Article 1 of the relevant agreement
the tribunal	regulation 19(1)
United Kingdom financial institution	regulation 2(4) and sub-paragraph 1(l) of Article 1 of the relevant agreement

2014/685

INVESTMENT TRANSACTIONS (TAX) REGULATIONS 2014

Made . . . .*17 March 2014*

Laid before the House of Commons . . . .*18 March 2014*

Coming into force . . . .*8 April 2014*

The Treasury make the following Regulations in exercise of the powers conferred by sections 17(3) and 18 of the Finance (No 2) Act 2005, section 622A of the Corporation Tax Act 2010, section 354 of the Taxation (International and Other Provisions) Act 2010 and section 217 of the Finance Act 2013.

1 Citation, commencement and effect

(1) These Regulations may be cited as the Investment Transactions (Tax) Regulations 2014 and come into force on 8th April 2014.

(2) The Regulations have effect in relation to transactions entered into on or after that date.

2 Investment transactions

(1) These Regulations specify certain kinds of transactions as investment transactions for the purposes of—

- (*a*) the Authorised Investment Funds (Tax) Regulations 2006,
- (*b*) the Offshore Funds (Tax) Regulations 2009,
- (*c*) the Investment Trust (Approved Company) (Tax) Regulations 2011, and
- (*d*) the Unauthorised Unit Trusts (Tax) Regulations 2013.

(2) An investment transaction means—

- (*a*) any transaction in stocks and shares,
- (*b*) any transaction in a relevant contract,
- (*c*) any transaction which results in a fund becoming a party to a loan relationship or a related transaction in respect of a loan relationship,
- (*d*) any transaction in units in a collective investment scheme,
- (*e*) any transaction in securities of any description not falling within paragraphs (*a*) to (*d*),
- (*f*) any transaction consisting in the buying or selling of any foreign currency,
- (*g*) any transaction in a carbon emission trading product,
- (*h*) any transaction in rights under a life insurance policy.

(3) For the purposes of these Regulations, "fund" means an authorised investment fund, an offshore fund, an investment trust or an exempt unauthorised unit trust, as the case may be.

3 "Relevant contract"

(1) For the purposes of regulation 2(2)(*b*), "relevant contract" has the same meaning as in Part 7 of the Corporation Tax Act 2009.

This is subject to paragraphs (2) to (4).

(2) A transaction which relates to land can only be a relevant contract if it uses an index which is—

- (*a*) publicly accessible,
- (*b*) comprised of a significant number of properties, and
- (*c*) not maintained by—
  - (i) the fund,
  - (ii) the manager of the fund, or
  - (iii) a person connected with the fund or the manager of the fund.

(3) A contract the terms of which provide for the delivery of any property other than property a transaction in which would fall within regulation 2(2) where the property is delivered is not a relevant contract.

(4) The reference to a loan relationship in the definition of "warrant" in section 710 of the Corporation Tax Act 2009 is to be construed in accordance with regulation 4 but with references to "fund" in that regulation being treated as references to "company".

(5) For the purposes of this regulation—

(*a*) sections 993 and 994 of the Income Tax Act 2007 (connected persons) apply where the manager is a person other than a company, and

(*b*) sections 1122 and 1123 of CTA 2010 (connected persons) apply in the case of a fund or where the manager is a person which is a company.

(6) For the purposes of the Unauthorised Unit Trusts (Tax) Regulations 2013, references in this regulation to the manager of the fund are to treated as references to the manager or trustee of the fund.

4 Loan relationships and related transactions

(1) For the purposes of regulation 2(2)(*c*), a fund has a loan relationship where the fund stands (whether by reference to a security or otherwise) in the position of a creditor or debtor as respects any money debt and either—

(*a*) that debt is one arising from a transaction for the lending of money, or

(*b*) that debt is not one which arose from a transaction for the lending of money but is one—

(i) on which interest is payable to or by the fund,

(ii) in relation to which the exchange gains or losses arise to the fund, or

(iii) as respects which the conditions in paragraph (2) are satisfied.

(2) The conditions mentioned in paragraph (1)(*b*)(iii) are that—

(*a*) the fund stands in the position of creditor in relation to the money debt, and

(*b*) the money debt is one from which a discount (whether of an income or capital nature) arises to the fund.

(3) For the purposes of this regulation—

"exchange gains or losses" means profits or gains or losses which arise as a result of comparing at different times the expression in one currency of the whole or some part of the valuation put by the fund in another currency on an asset or liability of the fund,

"money debt" has the same meaning as it has for the purposes of Part 5 of the Corporation Tax Act 2009.

(4) For the purposes of regulation 2(2)(*c*), a "related transaction" in relation to a loan relationship means any disposal or acquisition (in whole or in part) of rights or liabilities under that relationship.

5 "Units in a collective investment scheme"

(1) For the purposes of regulation 2(2)(*d*)—

"collective investment scheme" has the meaning given by section 235 of the Financial Services and Markets Act 2000,

"units" means the rights or interests (however described) of the investors in a collective investment scheme.

(2) In paragraph (1) an "investor", in relation to a collective investment scheme, means a beneficial owner of units in the scheme, except where the units are held on trust (other than a bare trust) or are comprised in the estate of a deceased person, and in such a case the investor, in relation to the scheme, means the trustees of the trust or, as the case may be, the deceased's personal representatives.

6 "Transaction in a carbon emission trading product"

(1) For the purposes of regulation 2(2)(*g*), a "transaction in a carbon emission trading product" means a transaction—

(*a*) in transferable units issued pursuant to the Kyoto Protocol, or

(*b*) in any similar transferable units relating to emissions of greenhouse gases,

where the transaction does not otherwise fall within any other sub-paragraph of regulation 2(2).

(2) For the purposes of this regulation—

"the Kyoto Protocol" means the Kyoto Protocol to the United Nations Framework Convention on Climate Change signed at Kyoto on 11th December 1997,

"units" includes assigned amount units, certified emission reductions, emission reduction units and removal units.

7 Consequential amendments

(1) The Authorised Investment Funds (Tax) Regulations 2006 are amended as follows.

(2) In regulation 14E (tax treatment of diversely owned AIFs), in paragraph (5), for "regulation 14F" substitute "regulation 2 of the Investment Transactions (Tax) Regulations 2014".

(3) Omit regulations 14F to 14N.

(4) In Part 2 of the Schedule, omit the definition of "investment transaction".

8 (1) The Offshore Funds (Tax) Regulations 2009 are amended as follows.

(2) In regulation 80 (treatment of investment transactions carried out by diversely owned funds), at the end insert—

"(3) For the purposes of these Regulations an "investment transaction" is an investment transaction specified by regulation 2 of the Investment Transactions (Tax) Regulations 2014."

(3) Omit regulations 81 to 89.

(4) In Part 2 of Schedule 3, omit the definition of "investment transaction".

9 (1) The Investment Trust (Approved Company) (Tax) Regulations 2011 are amended as follows.

(2) In regulation 32 (treatment of transactions carried out by investment trusts), at the end insert—

"(3) For the purposes of this Part an "investment transaction" is an investment transaction specified by regulation 2 of the Investment Transactions (Tax) Regulations 2014."

(3) Omit regulations 33 to 41.

10 In the Unauthorised Unit Trusts (Tax) Regulations 2013, in regulation 24 (treatment of investment transactions carried out by exempt unauthorised unit trusts) for paragraph (2) substitute—

"(2) For the purposes of paragraph (1) an "investment transaction" is an investment transaction specified by regulation 2 of the Investment Transactions (Tax) Regulations 2014."

2014/834

PUBLIC BODIES (MERGER OF THE DIRECTOR OF PUBLIC PROSECUTIONS AND THE DIRECTOR OF REVENUE AND CUSTOMS PROSECUTIONS) ORDER 2014

Made . . . . 26 March 2014

Coming into force in accordance with article 1

The Secretary of State makes the following Order in exercise of the powers conferred by sections 2(1), 6(1) and (2), 23(1), (2), (5) and (6), 24(1) and 35(2) of the Public Bodies Act 2011 ("the Act").

In accordance with section 8 of the Act, the Secretary of State—

(*a*) having had regard to the factors set out in section 8(1) of the Act, considers that this Order serves the purpose of improving the exercise of public functions; and

(*b*) considers that this Order does not remove any necessary protection or prevent any person from continuing to exercise any right or freedom which that person might reasonably expect to continue to exercise.

The Secretary of State has consulted in accordance with section 10 of the Act.

A draft of this Order and an explanatory document containing the information required by section 11(2) of the Act have been laid before Parliament in accordance with section 11(1) after the end of the period of twelve weeks mentioned in section 11(3). In accordance with section 11(4) of the Act, the draft of this Order has been approved by a resolution of each House of Parliament after the expiry of the 40-day period referred to in that provision.

1 1 Citation, commencement and extent

(1) This Order may be cited as the Public Bodies (Merger of the Director of Public Prosecutions and the Director of Revenue and Customs Prosecutions) Order 2014 and comes into force on the day after the day on which it is made.

(2) Any amendment, repeal or revocation made by this Order has the same extent as the enactment to which it relates.

2 Interpretation

In this Order—

"the CPS" means the Crown Prosecution Service;

"the CRCA 2005" means the Commissioners for Revenue and Customs Act 2005;

"the DPP" means the Director of Public Prosecutions;

"the DRCP" means the Director of Revenue and Customs Prosecutions;

"the POA 1985" means the Prosecution of Offences Act 1985;

"the RCPO" means the Revenue and Customs Prosecutions Office.

3 Abolition of the DRCP and transfer of statutory functions to the DPP: merger of offices

(1) The office of the DRCP is abolished.

(2) Subject to provision made by Schedules 1 to 3 to this Order, the functions of the DRCP are transferred to the DPP.

(3) The following Schedules have effect—

(*a*) Schedule 1 (amendments of the POA 1985 and the CRCA 2005);

(*b*) Schedule 2 (amendments of other Acts);
(*c*) Schedule 3 (amendments of secondary legislation).

4 Transfer of property, rights and liabilities

(1) All property, rights and liabilities to which the DRCP or the RCPO is entitled or subject at the coming into force of this Order are transferred to the DPP or, as the case may be, the CPS.
(2) Paragraph (1) has effect in relation to property, rights and liabilities—
(*a*) whether or not they would otherwise be capable of being transferred;
(*b*) without any instrument or other formality being required;
(*c*) irrespective of any requirement for consent that would otherwise apply.

5 The abolition of the office of the DRCP: supplementary

(1) This Order does not affect the validity of anything done (or having effect as if done) by or in relation to the DRCP before the coming into force of this Order.
(2) Anything done (or having effect as if done) by or in relation to the DRCP has effect, so far as is necessary for continuing its effect after the coming into force of this Order, as if done by or in relation to the DPP.
(3) Anything (including legal proceedings) which at the coming into force of this Order is in the process of being done by or in relation to the DRCP may be continued by or in relation to the DPP.
(4) So far as is necessary or appropriate, after the coming into force of this Order, a reference to the DRCP in an enactment, agreement (whether written or not), instrument or other document is to be treated as a reference to the DPP.
(5) In this article—
(*a*) a reference to the DRCP includes a reference to the RCPO, a Revenue and Customs Prosecutor, a member of the staff of the RCPO other than a Revenue and Customs Prosecutor and a person appointed under section 38 of the CRCA 2005, and
(*b*) a reference to the DPP is to be read, so far as is necessary or appropriate, as being a reference to the CPS, a Crown Prosecutor, a member of the staff of the CPS other than a Crown Prosecutor or a person appointed under section 5 of the POA 1985.

6 Saving of powers to conduct proceedings

(1) Where the DPP has conduct of proceedings by virtue of article 5(3), the DPP is to be treated, notwithstanding the repeals and amendments made by this Order—
(*a*) as acting under the enactment under which the DRCP was acting at the coming into force of this Order, and
(*b*) as having the same powers to take steps in relation to those proceedings as the DRCP would have had.
(2) In this article—
(*a*) a reference to the DRCP includes a reference to a Revenue and Customs Prosecutor and a person appointed under section 38 of the CRCA 2005, and
(*b*) a reference to the DPP is to be read, so far as is necessary or appropriate, as being a reference to a Crown Prosecutor or a person appointed under section 5 of the POA 1985.

7 Transfer of appointments, etc

An appointment of a person under section 38 of the CRCA 2005 (appointment of person to conduct proceedings on behalf of the RCPO) relating to—
(*a*) specified proceedings, or
(*b*) a specified class or description of proceedings,
is to be treated after the coming into force of this Order as if it were an appointment of a person by the DPP under section 5 of the POA 1985 relating to the same proceedings or the same class or description of proceedings.

8 Assignment of functions

An assignment of a function to the DRCP by order under section 31(1) of the Borders, Citizenship and Immigration Act 2009 (power to assign prosecution functions relating to criminal investigations by designated customs officials etc) is to be treated after the coming into force of this Order as if it were an assignment to the DPP under section 3(2)(*g*) of the POA 1985.

9 Confidentiality of information

Information held by the CPS by reason of a transfer of property, rights and liabilities to the DPP or the CPS under article 4 is to be treated for the purposes of section 40 of the CRCA 2005 (as amended by this Order) as if it were information disclosed to the DPP by Her Majesty's Revenue and Customs for use in connection with a Revenue and Customs function of the DPP (within the meaning of section 40(6A) of the CRCA 2005).

10 Superintendence of the Attorney General

Functions exercisable by the DPP by virtue of this Order are to be discharged under the superintendence of the Attorney General.

SCHEDULE 1

AMENDMENTS OF THE POA 1985 AND THE CRCA 2005

Article 3(3)

Note—*The amendments made by this Schedule are already in force and have therefore been omitted*

SCHEDULE 2

AMENDMENTS OF OTHER ACTS

Article 3(3)

Note—*The amendments made by this Schedule are already in force and have therefore been omitted*

SCHEDULE 3

AMENDMENTS OF SECONDARY LEGISLATION

Article 3(3)

Note—*The amendments made by this Schedule are already in force and have therefore been omitted*

2014/854

ANNUAL TAX ON ENVELOPED DWELLINGS (INDEXATION OF ANNUAL CHARGEABLE AMOUNTS) ORDER 2014

Made .... *26 March 2014*

The Treasury make the following Order in exercise of the powers conferred by section 101(5) of the Finance Act 2013.

1 Citation

This Order may be cited as the Annual Tax on Enveloped Dwellings (Indexation of Annual Chargeable Amounts) Order 2014.

2 Chargeable amounts

The amounts that by virtue of section 101 (indexation of annual chargeable amounts) of the Finance Act 2013 are to be the annual chargeable amounts for the chargeable period beginning on 1st April 2014 are determined in accordance with the following table, by reference to the taxable value of the interest on the relevant day.

Annual chargeable amount	*Taxable value of the interest on the relevant day*
£15,400	More than £2 million but not more than £5 million.
£35,900	More than £5 million but not more than £10 million.
£71,850	More than £10 million but not more than £20 million.
£143,750	More than £20 million.

2014/April

INVESTMENT MANAGER (INVESTMENT TRANSACTIONS) REGULATIONS 2014

The Commissioners for Her Majesty's Revenue and Customs make the following Regulations in exercise of the powers conferred by sections 827(2) and 835S(4) of the Income Tax Act 2007 (a) and section 1150 of the Corporation Tax Act 2010

1 Citation, commencement and effect

(1) These Regulations may be cited as the Investment Manager (Investment Transactions) Regulations 2014 and come into force on 8 April 2014.

(2) These Regulations have effect in relation to transactions entered into on or after that date.

2 Investment transactions

(1) Any transaction which falls within the meaning of investment transaction in the Investment Transactions (Tax) Regulations 2014 set out in the Schedule to these Regulations is specified for the purposes of—

(*a*) section 827 of the Income Tax Act 2007,

(*b*) section 835S of the Income Tax Act 2007, and

(*c*) section 1150 of the Corporation Tax Act 2010.

This is subject to paragraphs (2) to (5).

(2) References in the Investment Transactions (Tax) Regulations 2014 to "fund" are to be treated as references to "non-UK resident" (and the definition of "fund" in regulation 2(3) of those Regulations is to be ignored).

(3) References in the Investment Transactions (Tax) Regulations 2014 to "manager" are to be treated as references to "investment manager".

(4) "Non-UK resident" has the meaning given in section 989 of the Income Tax Act 2007 or section 1119 of the Corporation Tax Act 2010, as the case may be.

(5) A transaction in a carbon emissions trading product within regulation 6 of the Investment Transactions (Tax) Regulations 2014 is not specified for the purposes in paragraph (1) if it gives rise to a chargeable gain within either—

(*a*) section 10 of the Taxation of Chargeable Gains Act 1992 (non-resident with United Kingdom branch or agency), or

(*b*) section 10B of that Act (non-resident company with United Kingdom permanent establishment).

2014/1120

TAXATION OF CHARGEABLE GAINS (GILT-EDGED SECURITIES) ORDER 2014

Made . . . . *28 April 2014*

The Treasury make the following Order in exercise of the powers conferred by paragraph 1 of Schedule 9 to the Taxation of Chargeable Gains Act 1992:

1 Citation

This Order may be cited as the Taxation of Chargeable Gains (Gilt-edged Securities) Order 2014.

2 Securities specified as gilt-edged securities

For the purposes of the Taxation of Chargeable Gains Act 1992 the following securities are specified as "gilt-edged securities"—

1¾% Treasury Gilt 2019

2¾% Treasury Gilt 2024.

2014/1327

GOVERNMENT ALTERNATIVE FINANCE ARRANGEMENTS REGULATIONS 2014

Made . . . . *22 May 2014*

Laid before the House of Commons . . . . *23 May 2014*

Coming into force . . . . *16 June 2014*

The Treasury, in exercise of the powers conferred by section 157 of, and paragraphs 3, 5, 6, 7, 9, 10, 11 and 12 of Schedule 46 to, the Finance Act 2008, make the following Regulations:

1 Citation and commencement

These Regulations may be cited as the Government Alternative Finance Arrangements Regulations 2014 and come into force on 16th June 2014.

2 Interpretation

In these Regulations—

"available arrangements" means alternative finance arrangements which, by virtue of regulation 3, are available to the Treasury for raising money;

"bond" means arrangements to which section 564G (investment bond arrangements) of the Income Tax Act 2007 or section 151N (investment bond arrangements) of the Taxation of Chargeable Gains Act 1992 applies;

"money" means sterling or any other currency or medium of exchange, whether national or international;

"raising money" includes raising money outside the United Kingdom; and
"relevant person" means the Treasury or the Secretary of State.

3 Available arrangements

(1) Alternative finance arrangements which comply with the conditions specified in this regulation are available to the Treasury for raising money.

(2) Condition 1 is that a relevant person and a company enter into arrangements under which—

(*a*) the relevant person transfers to the company a qualifying interest in land; and

(*b*) the relevant person and the company agree that when the interest ceases to be held by the company as mentioned in paragraph (3)(b), the company will transfer the interest to the relevant person.

(3) Condition 2 is that—

(*a*) the company, as bond-issuer, enters into a bond (whether before or after entering into the arrangements mentioned in paragraph (2)); and

(*b*) the interest in land to which the arrangements mentioned in paragraph (2) relate is held by the company as a bond asset.

(4) Condition 3 is that, for the purpose of generating income or gains for the bond, the company and a relevant person enter into a leaseback agreement.

(5) For the purposes of condition 3, the company and a relevant person enter into a leaseback agreement if the company grants to the relevant person out of the interest transferred to the company—

(*a*) a lease (if the interest transferred is freehold), or

(*b*) a sub-lease (if the interest transferred is leasehold).

(6) Condition 4 is that the company agrees to hold the interest in the land as a bond asset until the termination of the bond.

(7) Alternative finance arrangements may make provision for all or part of the interest transferred to the company to be substituted by another qualifying interest in land ("the substituted interest") in such circumstances as are specified in those arrangements.

(8) If all or part of an interest in land is substituted in accordance with provision made under paragraph (7), the alternative finance arrangements continue to comply with the conditions specified in this regulation if at the time the substitution takes place those conditions are met in relation to the substituted interest.

(9) In assessing whether condition 2 is met for the purposes of paragraph (8), it is irrelevant that the company has entered into the bond mentioned in paragraph (3)(a) before the substitution takes place.

(10) Terms used in this regulation which are also used in paragraph 5 of Schedule 61 to the Finance Act 2009, unless otherwise defined in these Regulations, have the same meaning as in that paragraph.

(11) For the purposes of this regulation—

(*a*) "company" means a company formed under the Companies Acts, and

(*b*) it does not matter whether the company—

(i) is formed specially in connection with raising money through available arrangements,

(ii) is formed by the Treasury, or

(iii) is independent of the Treasury.

4 Purposes for which money may be raised through available arrangements

The Treasury may raise money through available arrangements for any of the following purposes—

(*a*) promoting sound monetary conditions in the United Kingdom,

(*b*) providing the sums required to meet any excess of payments out of the National Loans Fund, or

(*c*) providing any necessary working balance in the National Loans Fund.

5 Considerations in deciding to raise money through available arrangements

In deciding whether to raise money through available arrangements, the Treasury—

(*a*) must take into account the purpose or purposes for which money is to be raised; and

(*b*) may take into account the effect which, in the Treasury's opinion, those arrangements are likely to have on the general availability of alternative finance arrangements within the United Kingdom.

6 Power to enter into arrangements

A relevant person may enter into—

(*a*) any arrangements which, alone or together with other arrangements, constitute available arrangements; and

(*b*) any other arrangements which facilitate or enable money to be raised through available arrangements.

7 Power to give financial assistance

(1) The Treasury may give financial assistance to a company which has entered into available arrangements.

(2) The financial assistance must be for expenditure incurred, or to be incurred, in connection with any of the company's functions relating to the arrangements.

(3) Financial assistance may be given on such terms and conditions as the Treasury consider appropriate.

(4) A company which receives assistance under this regulation must comply with the terms and conditions on which it is given.

(5) Any financial assistance given under this regulation shall be charged on and paid out of the Consolidated Fund.

(6) In this regulation, "financial assistance" includes grants, loans and incurring expenditure for the benefit of the company.

8 National Loans Fund

(1) Any money raised through available arrangements shall be paid into the National Loans Fund.

(2) Any—

(*a*) sums to be paid by, or on behalf of, a relevant person under or in connection with available arrangements; or

(*b*) expenses incurred in connection with raising money or the issue, repayment or redemption of securities under available arrangements;

shall be charged on and paid out of the National Loans Fund with recourse to the Consolidated Fund.

9 Modification of the application of Schedule 5A of the National Loans Act 1968

For the purposes of the provisions of Schedule 5A (the debt management account) to the National Loans Act 1968, except paragraph 14, a security issued under available arrangements shall be treated as a security issued under section 12 of that Act.

2014/1506

INTERNATIONAL TAX COMPLIANCE (UNITED STATES OF AMERICA) REGULATIONS 2014

Made . . . . *9 June 2014*

Laid before the House of Commons . . . . *9 June 2014*

Coming into force . . . . *30 June 2014*

The Treasury make these Regulations in exercise of the powers conferred by section 222(1), (2) and (3) of the Finance Act 2013:

Revocation—These Regulations revoked by the International Tax Compliance Regulations, SI 2015/878 reg 25 with effect from 15 April 2015 in relation to the FATCA agreement and 1 January 2016 in relation to Council Directive 2011/16/EU (DAC) and the Multilateral Competent Authority Agreement on the Automatic Exchange of Financial Account Information (CRS).

2014/1842

REGISTERED PENSION SCHEMES AND RELIEVED NON-UK PENSION SCHEMES (LIFETIME ALLOWANCE TRANSITIONAL PROTECTION) (INDIVIDUAL PROTECTION 2014 NOTIFICATION) REGULATIONS 2014

Made . . . . *15.47 pm on 21 July 2014*

Laid before the House of Commons . . . . *22 July 2014*

Coming into force . . . . *18 August 2014*

The Commissioners for Her Majesty's Revenue and Customs make the following Regulations in exercise of the powers conferred by section 251(1) of the Finance Act 2004 and now exercisable by them, and paragraphs 8 and 9(1) of Schedule 6 to the Finance Act 2014.

1 Citation, commencement and interpretation

These Regulations may be cited as the Registered Pension Schemes and Relieved Non-UK Pension Schemes (Lifetime Allowance Transitional Protection) (Individual Protection 2014 Notification) Regulations 2014 and come into force on 18th August 2014.

2 In these Regulations—

"amounts A, B, C and D" means the amounts calculated in accordance with paragraphs 2 to 5 of Schedule 6 to the Finance Act 2014 (individual protection 2014);

"HMRC" means Her Majesty's Revenue and Customs;

"net appropriate amount" means the amount calculated in accordance with paragraph 1(7) of Schedule 6 to the Finance Act 2014;

"paragraph 1" means paragraph 1 of Schedule 6 to the Finance Act 2014;

"paragraph 1 notice" means a notice of intention to rely upon paragraph 1;

"the date" in relation to a pension debit means the date on which the notice of discharge of liability is issued under regulation 8(1) of the Pensions on Divorce etc (Provision of Information) Regulations 2000; and

"tribunal" means the First-tier Tribunal or, where determined in accordance with the Tribunal Procedure (First-tier Tribunal) (Tax Chamber) Rules 2009, the Upper Tribunal.

3 Reliance on paragraph 1

(1) Subject to paragraph (2), an individual may rely on paragraph 1 if—

(*a*) the individual has given a paragraph 1 notice to HMRC, and

(*b*) HMRC have accepted that notice and issued a certificate to the individual in accordance with regulation 5.

(2) An individual may not rely on paragraph 1 if—

(*a*) HMRC have refused to accept a paragraph 1 notice in accordance with regulation 6, or

(*b*) HMRC have revoked the certificate in accordance with regulation 11.

4 The paragraph 1 notice

(1) A paragraph 1 notice must include the following information—

(*a*) the title, full name, address (including post code, if applicable) and date of birth of the individual giving the paragraph 1 notice,

(*b*) the national insurance number of the individual or, where the individual does not qualify for a national insurance number, the reasons for this,

(*c*) the individual's relevant amount,

(*d*) amounts A, B, C and D for the individual,

(*e*) the date, the appropriate amount and (if relevant) the net appropriate amount of any pension debit to which a relevant arrangement in relation to the individual became subject on or after 6th April 2014, and

(*f*) a declaration that paragraph 7 of Schedule 36 to the Finance Act 2004 (primary protection) does not make provision for a lifetime allowance enhancement factor in the case of the individual.

(2) A paragraph 1 notice must—

(*a*) be in a form prescribed by HMRC, and

(*b*) contain a declaration that the information provided in the notice is true and complete to the best of the knowledge and belief of the person completing the form.

5 Issue of certificate by HMRC

(1) If HMRC accept the paragraph 1 notice, subject to paragraph (2) they must issue a certificate to the individual that includes the individual's relevant amount and has a unique reference number.

(2) Paragraph (1) does not apply at any time when any of the provisions in paragraph 1(3) of Schedule 6 to the Finance Act 2014 applies in the case of the individual.

6 Refusal by HMRC to accept notice

(1) HMRC may refuse to accept the paragraph 1 notice if it does not satisfy the requirements in regulation 4.

(2) If HMRC refuse to accept the paragraph 1 notice the individual may require that HMRC provide reasons for the refusal.

7 Appeal against refusal to accept notice

(1) The individual may appeal against a refusal by HMRC to accept the paragraph 1 notice.

(2) The notice of appeal must be given to HMRC before the end of the period of 30 days beginning with the day on which the refusal to accept the paragraph 1 notice was given.

(3) Where an appeal under this regulation is notified to the tribunal, the tribunal must determine whether HMRC were entitled to take the view that the notice did not satisfy the requirements in regulation 4.

(4) If the tribunal allows the appeal, the tribunal may direct HMRC to accept the paragraph 1 notice and issue a certificate to the individual.

8 Incorrect information given in, or in connection with, the paragraph 1 notice

If the individual realises that any information given in the paragraph 1 notice or given to HMRC in connection with that notice was incorrect or has become incorrect, the individual must provide HMRC with the correct information without undue delay.

9 Requirement to notify HMRC of a pension debit

If HMRC accept the paragraph 1 notice the individual must—

(a) inform HMRC of the date, the appropriate amount and (if relevant) the net appropriate amount of any pension debit to which their rights under a relevant arrangement become subject, and

(b) provide that information before the end of the period of 60 days beginning with the date of the pension debit.

10 Replacement of a certificate by HMRC

(1) HMRC may issue a certificate, replacing the previous certificate, if they have reason to believe that—

(a) information given in, or in connection with, the paragraph 1 notice was incorrect or has become incorrect, or

(b) the individual's rights under a relevant arrangement have become subject to a pension debit.

(2) A certificate issued in accordance with regulation 10(1) must include the individual's relevant amount and have a unique reference number.

11 Revocation of a certificate by HMRC

HMRC may revoke a certificate if they—

(a) have reason to believe that any of the conditions in paragraph 1(1) of Schedule 6 to the Finance Act 2014 have not been met,

(b) have reason to believe that by virtue of a pension debit paragraph 1(2) of that Schedule has ceased to apply in the case of the individual as a consequence of paragraph 1(8) of that Schedule, or

(c) have given a taxpayer notice to the individual under Part 1 of Schedule 36 to the Finance Act 2008 (power to obtain information and documents from taxpayer) in connection with paragraph 1 and the individual does not reply to that notice within the time specified in the notice.

12 Appeal against replacement or revocation of a certificate

(1) The individual may require HMRC to provide reasons for replacing or revoking the certificate.

(2) Paragraphs (1) and (2) of regulation 7 apply to a decision to replace or revoke the certificate as they apply to a refusal to accept the paragraph 1 notice.

(3) Where an appeal under this regulation is notified to the tribunal, the tribunal must determine whether HMRC replaced or revoked the certificate in accordance with regulations 10(1) or 11.

(4) If the tribunal allows the appeal, the tribunal may direct HMRC to issue a certificate to the individual.

13 Preservation of documents

(1) If HMRC accept the paragraph 1 notice, the individual must preserve all documents relating to the calculation of the individual's relevant amount and amounts A, B, C and D for a period of six years beginning with the day on which the individual gives notification to HMRC.

(2) Where HMRC have issued a certificate the individual must preserve the certificate until no further benefit crystallisation event can occur in relation to the individual. The requirement to preserve the certificate ceases where the certificate has been replaced or revoked.

14 Personal representatives

If an individual dies, anything under these Regulations which could have been done by the individual may be done by the individual's personal representatives.

2014/1958

CULTURAL TEST (VIDEO GAMES) REGULATIONS 2014

Made . . . . *22 July 2014*

Laid before the House of Commons . . . . *24 July 2014*

Coming into force . . . . *19 August 2014*

The Secretary of State makes the following Regulations in exercise of the powers conferred by sections 1217CB and 1217CC(7) of the Corporation Tax Act 2009.

Regulations 4 to 11 of these Regulations are made with the approval of the Treasury in accordance with section 1217CB(2) of that Act.

1 Citation and commencement

(1) These Regulations may be cited as the Cultural Test (Video Games) Regulations 2014.

(2) They come into force on 19th August 2014.

2 Interpretation

In these Regulations—

"the Act" means the Corporation Tax Act 2009;

"development team" means all the persons directly involved in the development of the video game;

"heads of department" means the lead gameplay programmer, the lead gameplay designer, the lead level designer, the lead character artist, the lead sound designer, the lead graphics programmer and the lead level artist;

"qualifying person" means a national of, or a person ordinarily resident in, an EEA state; and

"recognised regional or minority language" means Welsh, Scottish-Gaelic, Irish, Scots, Ulster Scots, Cornish or British Sign Language.

3 For the purposes of these Regulations—

(*a*) a video game is set in the United Kingdom or another EEA state to the extent that it is set in a country which is now part of the United Kingdom or another EEA state;

(*b*) a person or character in a video game is from the United Kingdom or another EEA state if the person or character is a national or resident of the United Kingdom or another EEA state (or was a national or resident of a country which is now part of the United Kingdom or another EEA state);

(*c*) a video game depicts a British story or a story which relates to another EEA state if the subject matter of the video game (or the underlying material on which the video game is based) is British or relates to another EEA state; and

(*d*) the amount of work for the purposes of regulation 9 (where work carried out) is determined by reference to the amount of expenditure on the work.

4 Cultural test: video games

A video game will be certified by the Secretary of State as a British video game under section 1217CB(1) of the Act only if it passes the following cultural test.

5 Subject to regulation 6, a video game passes the cultural test if it is awarded at least 16 points in total under regulations 7 to 10.

6 A video game that is awarded all the points available under regulations 7(*d*) (language), 9 (where work carried out) and 10 (personnel) will not pass the cultural test unless it is awarded—

(*a*) at least 2 points under regulation 7(*a*) (setting);

(*b*) at least 2 points under regulation 7(*b*) (characters); or

(*c*) 4 points under regulation 7(*c*) (story).

7 Up to 16 points will be awarded in respect of the content of the video game as follows—

(*a*) up to 4 points depending on the percentage of the video game that is set in the United Kingdom or another EEA state as follows—

(i) 4 points for at least 75%;

(ii) 3 points for at least 66%;

(iii) 2 points for at least 50%;

(iv) 1 point for at least 25;

(*b*) up to 4 points depending on the number of the characters depicted in the video game that are from the United Kingdom or another EEA state as follows—

(i) if there are more than three characters depicted in the video game—

(*aa*) if two or three of the three lead characters are from the United Kingdom or another EEA state, 4 points;

(*bb*) if only one of the three lead characters is from the United Kingdom or another EEA state, 2 points if that character is the first or second lead, or 1 point if that character is the third lead;

(ii) if there are only three characters depicted in the video game—

(*aa*) if two or three of the characters are from the United Kingdom or another EEA state, 4 points;

(*bb*) if only one of the characters is from the United Kingdom or another EEA state, 2 points if that character is the first or second lead, or 1 point if that character is the third lead;

(iii) if there are only two characters depicted in the video game—

(*aa*) if both of the characters are from the United Kingdom or another EEA state, 4 points;

(*bb*) if one of the characters is from the United Kingdom or another EEA state, 2 points; and

(iv) if there is only one character depicted in the video game, 4 points if that character is from the United Kingdom or another EEA state;

(*c*) 4 points if the video game depicts a British story or a story which relates to another EEA state;

(*d*) Up to 4 points depending on the percentage of the original dialogue that is recorded in the English language or a recognised regional or minority language as follows—

(i) 4 points for at least 75%;

(ii) 3 points for at least 66%;

(iii) 2 points for at least 50%;

(iv) 1 point for at least 25%.

8 Up to 4 points will be awarded in respect of the contribution of the video game to the promotion, development and enhancement of British culture.

9 (1) Subject to paragraph (2), up to 3 points will be awarded in respect of work carried out in the making of the video game as follows—

(*a*) 2 points if at least 50% of the work carried out on any of the following is carried out in the United Kingdom—

(i) conceptual development;

(ii) storyboarding;

(iii) programming;

(iv) design;

(*b*) 1 point if at least 50% of the work carried out on any of the following is carried out in the United Kingdom—

(i) performing and recording the music score created for the video game;

(ii) voice recording;

(iii) audio production.

(2) No points will be awarded in respect of work the expenditure on which is, in the opinion of the Secretary of State, insignificant in relation to all the expenditure on all the work carried out in the making of the video game.

10 Up to 8 points will be awarded in respect of the personnel involved in the making of the video game as follows—

(*a*) 1 point if the project leader (or, if there is more than one, the main project leader) is a qualifying person;

(*b*) 1 point if at least one of the scriptwriters (or, if there are more than three, one of the three lead scriptwriters) is a qualifying person;

(*c*) 1 point if the composer (or, if there is more than one, the lead composer) is a qualifying person;

(*d*) 1 point if the artist (or if there is more than one, the lead artist) is a qualifying person;

(*e*) 1 point if the programmer (or, if there is more than one, the lead programmer) is a qualifying person;

(*f*) 1 point if the designer (or, if there is more than one, the lead designer) is a qualifying person;

(*g*) 1 point if at least one of the heads of department is a qualifying person;

(*h*) 1 point if at least 50% of the development team are qualifying persons.

11 (1) A video game which is set in, or in which any character is from, an undetermined location is eligible to be awarded points under paragraphs 7(*a*)(ii)-(iv) (setting) and 7(*b*) (characters) of regulation 7 as if that location were in the United Kingdom or another EEA state, provided it complies with the following condition.

(2) The condition is that the video game is awarded at least one point under any of—

(a) regulation 7(*c*) (story);

(b) regulation 7(*d*) (language); or

(c) regulation 8 (culture).

12 Applications and particulars

(1) An application under section 1217CC(1) of the Act for certification of a video game as a British video game must—

(*a*) be made in writing to the Secretary of State; and

(*b*) set out (where applicable) the particulars described in the Schedule for that video game.

(2) For the purposes of this regulation, "in writing" includes text which is—

(*a*) transmitted by electronic means;

(*b*) received in legible form; and

(*c*) capable of being used for subsequent reference.

13 Evidence

(1) An application must be accompanied by a statutory declaration made by the applicant as to the truth of the particulars given in the application.

(2) A statutory declaration will be deemed to be properly made by the applicant if it has been made on behalf of the company by the secretary or one of the directors of the company or by any person duly authorised by the company to make the declaration on its behalf.

14 (1) If an application for final certification seeks the award of any point under—

(*a*) regulation 9 (where work carried out); or

(*b*) regulation 10 (personnel),

the application must be accompanied by a report prepared by a person referred to in paragraph (2) verifying (where applicable) the particulars in paragraphs 12 and 13 of the Schedule.

(2) The person referred to in this paragraph is a person who is eligible for appointment as a statutory auditor under section 1212 of the Companies Act 2006 and is not and was not at any time while the video game was being made—

(*a*) in partnership with the applicant or any officer or servant of the applicant;

(*b*) in the employment of the applicant or any officer or servant of the applicant; or

(*c*) an officer or servant of the applicant or, if the applicant is a member of a group of companies, of any other company in that group.

(3) In this regulation, "group of companies" means a company and all other companies which are its subsidiaries within the meaning of section 1159 of the Companies Act 2006.

SCHEDULE

PARTICULARS

Regulation 12(1)(*b*)

1 Title of video game.

2 Whether the application is for interim or final certification.

3 Whether the video game is intended for supply to the general public.

4 Name of the applicant.

5 Address of the applicant's principal place of business.

6 Address of the applicant's registered office.

7 Registered number of the applicant.

8 Date of registration of the applicant.

9 Date on which the video game was completed within the meaning of section 1217AA(4) of the Act.

10 The reasons why any point should be awarded under regulation 7 (cultural content).

11 The reasons why any point should be awarded under regulation 8 (culture).

12 In respect of any point claimed under regulation 9 (where work carried out)—

(*a*) the total expenditure on that work; and

(*b*) the expenditure on such work as was carried out in the United Kingdom.

13 The nationality or ordinary residence of all the persons mentioned in regulation 10 (personnel) in relation to whom the applicant is applying for a point to be awarded.

14 Total core expenditure.

15 Total EEA expenditure.

16 Total UK expenditure.

17 Total non-EEA expenditure by reference to each country in which the expenditure is carried out.

18 Other expenditure, meaning all the expenditure on the work varied out in the making of the video game which is not core expenditure.

19 Script in the English language.

20 A complete synopsis of the video game in the English language.

21 Game design documents.

22 Production schedule.

23 Production budget.

24 Copy of the chain of title in the video game.

25 For the purposes of this Schedule, "UK expenditure" means expenditure on goods or services that are provided from within the United Kingdom.

2014/2336

ARMED FORCES PENSION REGULATIONS 2014

Made . . . . *31 August 2014*
Laid before Parliament . . . . *4 September 2014*
Coming into force . . . . *1 April 2015*

The Secretary of State for Defence makes these Regulations in exercise of the powers conferred by sections 1(1), (2)(h), (3) and (4), 2, 3(1), (2), (3)(a) and (c) and (4), 4(1) to (3) and (5), 5(1) to (6) and (8), 7(1), (2)(a) and (3) to (6), 8(1)(a), (2)(a) and (4), 11(1) and (2), 12(1) to (3), (6) and (7), 13(1) to (3), 14, 18(1), (2), (4)(b) and (5) to (9), 25, paragraph (c) of the definition of "employer" in section 37, paragraph 1 of Schedules 1 and 2, Schedule 3, paragraph 1 of Schedules 5 and 6, and paragraphs 1(2) and 2(2) of Schedule 7 to the Public Service Pensions Act 2013. In accordance with section 21 of that Act, the Secretary of State for Defence has consulted the representatives of such persons as appear to the Secretary of State likely to be affected by these Regulations.

In accordance with section 3(5) of that Act, these Regulations are made with the consent of the Treasury.

PART 10
SUPPLEMENTARY

CHAPTER 2

PAYMENT AND DEDUCTION OF TAX

117 Scheme administrator for purposes of the Finance Act 2004

(1) The scheme manager is appointed to be responsible for all functions that are functions conferred or imposed on a scheme administrator by or under Part 4 of the FA 2004.

(2) In this regulation 'scheme administrator' has the meaning given in Part 4 of the FA 2004.

118 Reduction of benefits where lifetime allowance charge payable

(1) This regulation applies if—

(*a*) an event that is a benefit crystallisation event listed in the table in section 216(1) of the FA 2004 ("the table") occurs in relation to a member;

(*b*) the member and scheme manager are jointly and severally liable in relation to that event.

(2) If this regulation applies—

(*a*) the scheme manager must pay the lifetime allowance charge payable on the event;

(*b*) if the event is benefit crystallisation event 8 in the table (transfer to qualifying recognised overseas pension scheme), the amount or value of the sums or assets transferred must be reduced; and

(*c*) in the case of any other event in that table, the amount or value of the benefits payable to or in respect of the member must be reduced.

(3) The amount or value of the reduction must be such that in the opinion of the scheme manager, having consulted the scheme actuary, fully reflects the amount of the lifetime allowance charge so paid and is consistent with normal actuarial practice.

119 Payment on behalf of members of annual allowance charge

(1) The scheme manager must provide a member with information about the payment of an annual allowance charge under section 227 of FA 2004 if the member's total pension input amount for that tax year exceeds the amount of the annual allowance for that tax year.

(2) The member may request the scheme manager to pay the charge in respect of this scheme on the member's behalf.

(3) Such a request must be made by notice in writing in such form and subject to such conditions as the scheme manager requires.

120 Reduction of benefits where annual allowance charge paid by scheme manager

(1) If the scheme manager pays the annual allowance charge on a member's behalf, the amount or value of the benefits payable to or in respect of the member must be reduced.

(2) The amount or value of the reduction of benefits must be such that in the opinion of the scheme manager, having consulted with the scheme actuary, it fully reflects the amount of the charge so paid and is consistent with normal actuarial practice.

2014/2395

FINANCE ACT 2009, SCHEDULE 55 (PENALTIES FOR FAILURE TO MAKE RETURNS) (APPOINTED DAYS AND CONSEQUENTIAL PROVISION) ORDER 2014

Made . . . . *10 September 2014*

The Treasury make the following Order in exercise of the powers conferred by section 106(2) to (6) of the Finance Act 2009.

1 Citation

This Order may be cited as the Finance Act 2009, Schedule 55 (Penalties for failure to make returns) (Appointed Days and Consequential Provision) Order 2014.

2 Appointed Days

(1) The days appointed for the coming into force of Schedule 55 to the Finance Act 2009 (penalty for failure to make returns etc) in relation to a return falling within item 4 of the Table in paragraph 1 of that Schedule are—

(*a*) for paragraph 6C(5), (7), (8), (9) and (11) (amount of penalty: real time information for PAYE), 11th September 2014; and

(*b*) for paragraphs 1, 6B, 6C(1) to (4), (6) and (10), 6D, 16 to 24, 26 and 27—

(i) 6th October 2014 in respect of returns which are required to be delivered to HMRC on or after that date by a Real Time Information employer which at 6th October 2014 is a large existing employer; and

(ii) 6th March 2015 in respect of returns which are required to be delivered to HMRC on or after that date where—

(*aa*) the Real Time Information employer is, at 6th October 2014, a small existing employer; or

(*bb*) a person becomes a new Real Time Information employer after 6th October 2014.

(2) For the purposes of this article—

"HMRC" means Her Majesty's Revenue and Customs;

"large existing employer" means a Real Time Information employer who employs at least 50 employees;

"new Real Time Information employer" means a Real Time Information employer to which HMRC issues an employer's PAYE reference after 6th October 2014;

"Real Time Information employer" means a person who is within regulation 2A (real time information employer) of the Income Tax (Pay As You Earn) Regulations 2003, or who is treated by regulation 10 (application to agencies and agency workers), regulation 11 (application to pension payers and pensioners) or regulation 12 (application to other payers and payees) as an employer for the purposes of those Regulations;

"small existing employer" means a Real Time Information employer who employs no more than 49 employees.

(3) For the purposes of paragraph (2) "employer's PAYE reference" in relation to a Real Time Information employer means the combination of letters, numbers, or both, used by HMRC to identify a Real Time Information employer for the purposes of the Income Tax (Pay As You Earn) Regulations 2003 and the number which identifies that employer's HMRC office.

3 Consequential provision

Regulation 67EA(5) (failure to make a return under regulation 67B or 67D) of the Income Tax (Pay As You Earn) Regulations 2003 is amended by inserting at the end of the text ", but this paragraph does not apply to a return in respect of the tax year 2014-15 or a subsequent tax year".

2014/3066

TAX RELIEF FOR SOCIAL INVESTMENTS (ACCREDITATION OF SOCIAL IMPACT CONTRACTOR) REGULATIONS 2014

Made . . . . *17 November 2014*
Laid before the House of Commons . . . . *18 November 2014*
Coming into force . . . . *10 December 2014*

The Treasury, in exercise of the powers conferred by sections 257JE and 257JF of the Income Tax Act 2007, make the following Regulations.

Commentary—

See *Simon's Taxes* **E3.909**.

1 Citation, commencement and interpretation

These Regulations may be cited as the Tax Relief for Social Investments (Accreditation of Social Impact Contractor) Regulations 2014 and come into force on 10th December 2014.

2 In these Regulations—

"defined outcomes" has the meaning given in [regulation 3(1)(*b*)][1],

"ITA 2007" means the Income Tax Act 2007,

"notice" means notice in writing.

Amendments—[1] In the definition of "defined outcomes", words substituted for words "regulation 3(*b*)" by the Tax Relief for Social Investments (Accreditation of Social Impact Contractor) (Amendment) Regulations, SI 2015/2051 regs 2, 3 with effect from 9 January 2016.

3 Criteria for social impact contracts

(1) The criteria that a contract must meet to be a social impact contract are as follows—

(*a*) a Contracting Authority must be a party to the contract,

(*b*) the contract must set out the outcomes ("the defined outcomes") that are intended to be achieved under the contract,

(*c*) the [Secretary of State][3] must be satisfied that the defined outcomes—

(i) have a social or environmental purpose, and

(ii) satisfy the conditions specified in Part 2B (further conditions for defined outcomes) of the Social Investment Tax Relief—Guidance Concerning the Accreditation of Social Impact Contractors published on behalf of the Minister for the Cabinet Office at the time of the application for accreditation,

(*d*) where services are to be provided under the contract, the contract must distinguish between—

(i) the services to be provided under the contract, and

(ii) the defined outcomes that are intended to be achieved under the contract arising from the provision of those services,

(*e*) the defined outcomes must be capable of being objectively measured, and the method of measurement must be set out in the contract,

(*f*) . . . [2] the progress towards achieving the defined outcomes [must be assessed][2], on the basis of the method of measurement referred to in paragraph (*e*), at intervals which the [Secretary of State][3] is satisfied are appropriate in relation to the contract, and

(*g*) at least 60% of the total amount of the payments that could be made under the contract by the Contracting Authority to the company . . . [2] must be conditional on achieving defined outcomes which the [Secretary of State][3] is satisfied meet the criteria in paragraphs (*c*) and (*e*) above.

(2) For the purposes of this regulation—

(*a*) "Contracting Authority" has the meaning given by [regulation 2(1) of the Public Contracts Regulations 2015][2],

(*b*) a "social or environmental purpose" means one or more of the following purposes—

(i) the relief of those in need by reason of youth, age, ill-health, disability, financial hardship or other disadvantage,

(ii) the relief or prevention of poverty,

(iii) the promotion of employment, culture, heritage or sport,

(iv) the advancement of training and education,

(v) the prevention and reduction of crime,

(vi) environmental protection,

(vii) the provision of social housing and the relief of homelessness,

(viii) the provision of community facilities,

(ix) the promotion of social inclusion and cohesion,

(x) the advancement of citizenship or community development,

(xi) the improvement of physical and mental health,

(xii) the provision of long-term care in relation to any infirmity, or

(xiii) any other areas that may reasonably be regarded as analogous to any areas falling within any of paragraphs (i) to (xii).

Amendments—[1] In para (2)(*a*), words substituted for words "regulation 3(1) of the Public Contracts Regulations 2006" by the Public Contracts Regulations, SI 2015/102 reg 116, Sch 6 para 27 with effect from 26 February 2015. This amendment does not extend to Scotland: SI 2015/102 reg 1(7).

[2] In para (1)(*f*), words "the contract must provide for" repealed, and words substituted for words "to be assessed"; and in para (1)(*g*), words "seeking accreditation" repealed, by the Tax Relief for Social Investments (Accreditation of Social Impact Contractor) (Amendment) Regulations, SI 2015/2051 regs 2, 4 with effect from 9 January 2016.

[3] In para (1)(*c*), (*f*), (*g*), words substituted by the Transfer of Functions (Elections, Referendums, Third Sector and Information) Order, SI 2016/997 art 13, Sch 2 para 38(1), (2)(*a*) with effect from 9 November 2016.

4 Notification of accreditation or refusal

The [Secretary of State][1] must give notice to a company of the grant of an accreditation specifying—

(*a*) the date of the grant of accreditation,
(*b*) the date on which the period of accreditation begins,
(*c*) the requirements of accreditation (if any) to be imposed by virtue of section 257JF(1)(*b*) of ITA 2007, and
(*d*) the length of the period of accreditation or how the length is to be determined.

Amendments—[1] Words substituted by the Transfer of Functions (Elections, Referendums, Third Sector and Information) Order, SI 2016/997 art 13, Sch 2 para 38(1), (2)(*b*) with effect from 9 November 2016.

5 The [Secretary of State][1] must give notice to a company of a refusal to grant an accreditation specifying—
(*a*) the date of the refusal, and
(*b*) the reasons for the refusal.

Amendments—[1] Words substituted by the Transfer of Functions (Elections, Referendums, Third Sector and Information) Order, SI 2016/997 art 13, Sch 2 para 38(1), (2)(*b*) with effect from 9 November 2016.

6 Publication of information

The [Secretary of State][2] may publish from time to time the following information in relation to any accredited social impact contractor—
(*a*) the name of the accredited social impact contractor,
(*b*) the business address of the accredited social impact contractor,
(*c*) the date the accredited social impact contractor was granted accreditation,
(*d*) the length of the period of accreditation, and
(*e*) an outline of—
(i) the defined outcomes, and
[(ii) the services provided, or to be provided, by the contractor in respect of each social impact contract to which the contractor is, or was, a party.][1]

Amendments—[1] Para (*e*)(ii) substituted by the Tax Relief for Social Investments (Accreditation of Social Impact Contractor) (Amendment) Regulations, SI 2015/2051 regs 2, 5 with effect from 9 January 2016.
[2] Words substituted by the Transfer of Functions (Elections, Referendums, Third Sector and Information) Order, SI 2016/997 art 13, Sch 2 para 38(1), (2)(*c*) with effect from 9 November 2016.

[7 Requirements of accreditation

(1) A social impact contractor must comply with the matters in paragraphs (2) and (3) as conditions of its accreditation.
(2) The social impact contractor must ensure that there is no period during the period of its accreditation when it is not a party to at least one social impact contract.
(3) The social impact contractor—
(*a*) must give notice to the [Secretary of State][2] within 30 days of—
(i) any material change in respect of each social impact contract to which it is a party, including the termination of, or an alteration of the defined outcomes set out in, the contract, or
(ii) any change of its name or business address, and
(*b*) must provide a relevant report to the [Secretary of State][2] in respect of—
(i) each period of 12 months since the date of accreditation, within one month of the end of each such period, and
(ii) such other period and by such date after the expiry of that period as the [Secretary of State][2] may by notice reasonably require.
(4) In paragraph (3), "relevant report" means a report setting out such information as the [Secretary of State][2] may by notice specify concerning the performance of the social impact contractor under each social impact contract to which it was a party during the period to which the report relates.][1]

Amendments—[1] Regs 7, 7A substituted for previous reg 7 by the Tax Relief for Social Investments (Accreditation of Social Impact Contractor) (Amendment) Regulations, SI 2015/2051 regs 2, 6 with effect from 9 January 2016.
[2] In para (3)(*a*), (*b*), words substituted, and in paras 7(3)(*b*)(ii), (4), word substituted, by the Transfer of Functions (Elections, Referendums, Third Sector and Information) Order, SI 2016/997 art 13, Sch 2 para 38(1), (2)(*d*), (3) with effect from 9 November 2016.

[7A Provision of information

(1) The [Secretary of State][2] may give notice to an accredited social impact contractor to require that person to provide such information as is specified in the notice.
(2) The information which may be included in the notice is information which the [Secretary of State][2] believes is reasonably required in connection with the discharge of the [Secretary of State's][2] functions under section 257JD or 257JG of ITA 2007.
(3) A notice under paragraph (1) must include the date by which the information must be provided, being a date no earlier than 14 days after the date on which the notice is given.
(4) It is a condition of an accreditation that an accredited social impact contractor must comply with a notice given to it under paragraph (1).][1]

Amendments—[1] Regs 7, 7A substituted for previous reg 7 by the Tax Relief for Social Investments (Accreditation of Social Impact Contractor) (Amendment) Regulations, SI 2015/2051 regs 2, 6 with effect from 9 January 2016.

2 In para (1), words substituted, and in para (2), word substituted, by the Transfer of Functions (Elections, Referendums, Third Sector and Information) Order, SI 2016/997 art 13, Sch 2 para 38(1), (2)(*e*), (3), (4) with effect from 9 November 2016.

8 Notification of changes to contract and breach of conditions for approval

(1) The social impact contractor must as soon as reasonably possible give notice to the [Secretary of State][1] where it fails to comply, or it is likely to fail to comply, with—

(*a*) any requirement of accreditation imposed—

(i) by virtue of section 257JF(1)(*b*) of ITA 2007, or

(ii) by or under these regulations, or

(*b*) a condition in section 257JD(3)(*b*) or (*c*) of ITA 2007.

(2) A notice required under paragraph (1) must—

(*a*) specify the circumstances that caused, or are likely to cause, the requirement or condition to cease to be met, or not to be met,

(*b*) so far as possible, state the extent to which the requirement or condition has ceased or will cease to be met, or has not been met, and

(*c*) where the company considers that the requirement or condition is likely to cease to be met or not to be met by or on a date occurring after the date of the notice, specify (if possible) that future date.

(3) If a notice has been given in respect of circumstances that are likely to cause any requirement or condition to cease to be met or not to be met, no further notice under paragraph (1) is required in relation to those circumstances if any requirement or condition ceases to be met or is not met in, or as a result of, those circumstances.

Amendments—[1] In para (1), words substituted by the Transfer of Functions (Elections, Referendums, Third Sector and Information) Order, SI 2016/997 art 13, Sch 2 para 38(1), (2)(*f*) with effect from 9 November 2016.

9 Withdrawal of accreditation

(1) The [Secretary of State][1] may withdraw an accreditation where there is a failure to comply with any requirement of an accreditation.

(2) A withdrawal of an accreditation must be given by notice to the company which is or has been an accredited social impact contractor by the [Secretary of State][1] specifying the date from which accreditation is withdrawn (which may be the date of the failure or a later date) and the reasons for the withdrawal.

(3) The company must within 30 days of receiving notice under paragraph (2) of withdrawal of accreditation give notice to each of the investors to which it has issued a compliance certificate in respect of investments made within the specified period stating that accreditation has been or will be withdrawn and specifying the date from which accreditation is withdrawn.

(4) For the purpose of paragraph (3), "specified period" means the three years immediately preceding the date from which accreditation is withdrawn.

Amendments—[1] In paras (1), (2), words substituted by the Transfer of Functions (Elections, Referendums, Third Sector and Information) Order, SI 2016/997 art 13, Sch 2 para 38(1), (2)(*g*) with effect from 9 November 2016.

10 Appeals against refusal to grant accreditation or withdrawal of accreditation

(1) An appeal to the tribunal may be brought by a company against—

(*a*) a refusal to grant an accreditation,

(*b*) the imposition of a requirement under section 257JF(1)(*b*) of ITA 2007,

(*c*) the withdrawal of an accreditation (whether under section 257JD(4) of ITA 2007 or under regulation 9).

(2) Notice of an appeal under this regulation must be given to the [Secretary of State][2] within 30 days of the date of the [notice][1] of—

(*a*) the refusal,

(*b*) the imposition of a requirement, or

(*c*) the withdrawal.

(3) The notice of appeal must specify the grounds of appeal.

(4) If the tribunal, on an appeal [made][1] to it, allows the appeal, it may—

(*a*) in an appeal against a refusal to grant accreditation, direct that the [Secretary of State][2] accredit the company within 14 days of its decision,

(*b*) in an appeal against the imposition of a requirement under section 257JF(1)(*b*), direct that the Minister for the Cabinet Office reconsider the decision to impose the requirement, or

(*c*) in an appeal against a withdrawal of accreditation, direct that the withdrawal was ineffective.

Amendments—[1] In para (2), word substituted for word "notification", and in para (4), word substituted for word "notified", by the Tax Relief for Social Investments (Accreditation of Social Impact Contractor) (Amendment) Regulations, SI 2015/2051 regs 2, 7 with effect from 9 January 2016.

1 In paras (2), (4)(*a*), words substituted by the Transfer of Functions (Elections, Referendums, Third Sector and Information) Order, SI 2016/997 art 13, Sch 2 para 38(1), (2)(*h*) with effect from 9 November 2016.

2014/3159

SOCIAL SECURITY CONTRIBUTIONS (LIMITED LIABILITY PARTNERSHIP) REGULATIONS 2014

Made . . . . *4 December 2014*

Coming into force . . . . *5 December 2014*

The Treasury make the following Regulations in exercise of the powers conferred by sections 4AA and 175(3) and (4) of the Social Security Contributions and Benefits Act 1992, 4AA and 171(3) and (4) of the Social Security Contributions and Benefits (Northern Ireland) Act 1992 and, as it appears to the Treasury to be expedient for these Regulations to have retrospective effect in consequence of retrospective tax provisions, namely sections 863A to 863G of the Income Tax (Trading and Other Income) Act 2005, by section 4B of those Acts.

Accordingly, the Treasury, with the concurrence of the Secretary of State and the Department for Social Development in so far as required, make the following Regulations:

A draft of this instrument has been laid before each House of Parliament in accordance with section 176(1) of the Social Security Contributions and Benefits Act 1992 and section 172(11A) of the Social Security Contributions and Benefits (Northern Ireland) Act 1992 and approved by resolution of each House.

1 Citation, commencement, effect and extent

(1) These Regulations may be cited as the Social Security Contributions (Limited Liability Partnership) Regulations 2014.

(2) These Regulations come into force on the day after the day on which they are made, and have effect for the tax year 2014–15 and subsequent tax years.

[(2A) Regulations 2A, 2B and 2C have effect for the tax year 2015-16 and subsequent tax years.][1]

(3) Regulations [2B,][1] 3 and 6 extend only to England and Wales and to Scotland and regulations [2B,][1] 4 and 7 extend only to Northern Ireland.

Amendments—[1] Para (2A) inserted and words in para (3) inserted by the Social Security Contributions (Limited Liability Partnership) (Amendment) Regulations, SI 2015/607 regs 2, 3 with effect from 6 April 2015.

2 Interpretation

In these Regulations—

"employment income" has the meaning given by section 7 of ITEPA 2003;

"ITTOIA 2005" means the Income Tax (Trading and Other Income) Act 2005;

"LLP" means limited liability partnership;

"SSCBA 1992" means the Social Security Contributions and Benefits Act 1992; and

"SSCB(NI)A 1992" means the Social Security Contributions and Benefits (Northern Ireland) Act 1992.

[2A Members of LLPs: employment

(1) The modification in paragraph (2) applies to—

(a) Part 1 and so much of Part 6 of SSCBA 1992 as relates to contributions, and

(b) Part 1 and so much of Part 6 of SSCB(NI)A 1992 as relates to contributions.

(2) The modification is that "employment" includes membership of an LLP which carries on a trade, profession or business with a view to profit.][1]

Amendments—[1] Regulations 2A–2C inserted by the Social Security Contributions (Limited Liability Partnership) (Amendment) Regulations, SI 2015/607 regs 2, 4 with effect from 6 April 2015.

[2B Members of LLPs: Great Britain

A person in employment in Great Britain as a member of an LLP which carries on a trade, profession or business with a view to profit is, unless regulation 3 applies, to be treated as a self-employed earner for the purposes of SSCBA 1992.

Amendments—[1] Regulations 2A–2C inserted by the Social Security Contributions (Limited Liability Partnership) (Amendment) Regulations, SI 2015/607 regs 2, 4 with effect from 6 April 2015.

[2C Members of LLPs: Northern Ireland

A person in employment in Northern Ireland as a member of an LLP which carries on a trade, profession or business with a view to profit is, unless regulation 4 applies, to be treated as a self-employed earner for the purposes of SSCB(NI)A 1992.

Amendments—[1] Regulations 2A–2C inserted by the Social Security Contributions (Limited Liability Partnership) (Amendment) Regulations, SI 2015/607 regs 2, 4 with effect from 6 April 2015.

3 Salaried Members of LLPs: Great Britain

(1) This regulation applies where—

(a) for the purposes of the Income Tax Acts an individual is treated by section 863A of ITTOIA 2005 (limited liability partnerships: salaried members) as being employed by an LLP under a contract of service, including where that is the case by virtue of section 863G of ITTOIA 2005 (anti-avoidance), ("the deemed tax employment"); and

(b) if the services performed, or to be performed, by the individual as a member of the LLP in the relevant period (as defined in section 863B(3) of ITTOIA 2005) were actually performed (or to be performed) under a contract of service with the LLP, the employment under that contract of service would be employment in Great Britain.

(2) For the purposes of SSCBA 1992—

(a) the individual ("the Salaried Member") is to be treated as employed in employed earner's employment by the LLP (being the deemed tax employment);

(b) any amount treated by virtue of section 863A or 863G(4) of ITTOIA 2005 as employment income from the deemed tax employment, other than employment income under Chapters 2 to 11 of Part 3 of ITEPA 2003 (the benefits code), is to be treated as an amount of earnings paid to or for the benefit of the Salaried Member in respect of the Salaried Member's employed earner's employment with the LLP;

(c) the secondary contributor in relation to those earnings is the LLP; and

(d) in the case of an amount of earnings which is an amount of employment income by virtue of section 863G(4) of ITTOIA 2005, the earnings are to be treated as being paid by the LLP to the Salaried Member when the amount mentioned in section 863G(2)(d) of that Act arises.

(3) The reference in paragraph (1)(b) to services performed (or to be performed) by the individual as a member of the LLP includes services personally performed by the individual for the LLP under arrangements by virtue of which section 863G(4) of ITTOIA 2005 applies.

(4) The definitions of "employer" and "employee" in—

(a) section 163 (interpretation of Part 11 and supplementary provisions);

(b) section 171 (interpretation of Part 12 and supplementary provisions);

(c) section 171ZJ (Part 12ZA: supplementary); and

(d) section 171ZS (Part 12ZB: supplementary)

of the SSCBA 1992 have effect as if the Salaried Member were gainfully employed in Great Britain by the LLP under a contract of service with the earnings mentioned in paragraph (2)(b).

4 Salaried Members of LLPs: Northern Ireland

(1) This regulation applies where—

(a) for the purposes of the Income Tax Acts an individual is treated by section 863A of ITTOIA 2005 (limited liability partnerships: salaried members) as being employed by an LLP under a contract of service, including where that is the case by virtue of section 863G of ITTOIA 2005 (anti-avoidance), ("the deemed tax employment"); and

(b) if the services performed, or to be performed, by the individual as a member of the LLP in the relevant period (as defined in section 863B(3) of ITTOIA 2005) were actually performed (or to be performed) under a contract of service, the employment under that contract of service would be employment in Northern Ireland.

(2) For the purposes of SSCB(NI)A 1992—

(a) the individual ("the Salaried Member") is to be treated as employed in employed earner's employment by the LLP (being the deemed tax employment);

(b) any amount treated as employment income by virtue of section 863A or section 863G(4) of ITTOIA 2005 as employment income from the deemed tax employment, other than employment income under Chapters 2 to 11 of Part 3 of ITEPA 2003 (the benefits code), is to be treated as an amount of earnings paid to or for the benefit of the Salaried Member in respect of the Salaried Member's employed earner's employment with the LLP;

(c) the secondary contributor in relation to those earnings is the LLP; and

(d) in the case of an amount of earnings which is an amount of employment income by virtue of section 863G(4) of ITTOIA 2005, the earnings are to be treated as being paid by the LLP to the Salaried Member when the amount mentioned in section 863G(2)(d) of that Act arises.

(3) The reference in paragraph (1)(b) to services performed by the individual as a member of the LLP includes services personally performed by the individual for the LLP under arrangements by virtue of which section 863G(4) of ITTOIA 2005 applies.

(4) The definitions of "employer" and "employee" in—

(a) section 159 (interpretation of Part 11 and supplementary provisions);

(b) section 167 (interpretation of Part 12, etc);

(c) section 167ZJ (Part 12ZA: supplementary); and

(d) section 167ZS (Part 12ZB: supplementary)

of SSCB(NI)A 1992 have effect as if the Salaried Member were gainfully employed in Northern Ireland by the LLP under a contract of service with the earnings mentioned in sub- paragraph (2)(b).

5 Consequential amendment to the Social Security (Contributions) Regulations 2001

(1) The Social Security (Contributions) Regulations 2001 are amended as follows.

(2) (*inserts* SI 2001/1004 reg 40A)

(3) (*inserts* SI 2001/1004 Sch 3 para 25)

6 Consequential amendments to the Social Security Contributions (Intermediaries) Regulations 2000

(1) The Social Security Contributions (Intermediaries) Regulations 2000 are amended as follows.

(2) (*amends* SI 2000/727 reg 7(1))

7 Consequential amendments to the Social Security Contributions (Intermediaries) (Northern Ireland) Regulations 2000

(1) The Social Security Contributions (Intermediaries) (Northern Ireland) Regulations 2000 are amended as follows.

(2) (*amends* SI 2000/728 reg 7(1))

2014/3183

CAPITAL ALLOWANCES (DESIGNATED ASSISTED AREAS) ORDER 2014

Made . . . . *1 December 2014*

Laid before the House of Commons . . . . *2 December 2014*

Coming into force . . . . *23 December 2014*

The Treasury make the following Order in exercise of the powers conferred by section 45K(2)(a), (3) and (4) of the Capital Allowances Act 2001.

1 Citation, commencement, effect and interpretation

(1) This Order may be cited as the Capital Allowances (Designated Assisted Areas) Order 2014.

(2) This Order comes into force on 23rd December 2014 and an area designated by this Order is to be treated as having been designated on 1st April 2012.

(3) In this Order "Capital Allowances Act" means the Capital Allowances Act 2001.

2 Designation of areas

(1) The areas shown enclosed by a red line on the map of a scale of 1:1250 included in the schedule to each memorandum of understanding described in paragraph (2) are designated as designated assisted areas for the purposes of section 45K of the Capital Allowances Act (expenditure on plant and machinery for use in designated assisted areas).

(2) In paragraph (1) references to a "memorandum of understanding" are to a memorandum of understanding entered into for the purposes of section 45K of the Capital Allowances Act by the Treasury with the responsible authority listed in column 1 of the table in the Schedule to this Order on the date listed in column 2 of that table.

(3) Each memorandum of understanding referred to in paragraph (2) is kept at the offices of HM Treasury at 1 Horse Guards Road, London SW1A 2HQ, where they (or a copy of them) may be inspected by members of the public at reasonable hours without charge.

SCHEDULE

Article 2(2)

Table

Name of responsible authority	*Date of memorandum of understanding*	*Area included in the map*	*Enterprise Zone within which area falls*	*Assisted area within which area falls*
Welsh Ministers	19th April 2013	Deeside Enterprise Zone	Deeside Enterprise Zone	Sealand
		Ebbw Vale Enterprise Zone	Ebbw Vale Enterprise Zone	Rassau and Badminton
		Haven Waterway Enterprise Zone	Haven Waterway Enterprise Zone	Milford East and Neyland West
Scottish Ministers	5th June 2013	Dundee Port,	Low Carbon / Renewables East Enterprise Area	East Port
		Dundee Camperdown,	Low Carbon / Renewables East Enterprise Area	East Port

Name of responsible authority	*Date of memorandum of understanding*	*Area included in the map*	*Enterprise Zone within which area falls*	*Assisted area within which area falls*
		Dundee Claverhouse	Low Carbon / Renewables East Enterprise Area	Longhaugh
		Nigg	Low Carbon / Renewables North Enterprise Area	Seaboard
		Irvine	Life Sciences Enterprise Area	Irvine Townhead
East Riding of Yorkshire Council	21st May 2014	Paull	Humber Green Port Corridor	South West Holderness
Hartlepool Borough Council	21st May 2014	Hartlepool Port Estates	Tees Valley	Headland and Harbour
Kingston upon Hull City Council	21st May 2014	Green Port Hull	Humber Renewable Energy Super Cluster	Marfleet
Kingston upon Hull City Council	21st May 2014	Queen Elizabeth Dock South	Humber Renewable Energy Super Cluster	Marfleet
Newcastle City Council	21st May 2014	Neptune Yard	North East	Walkergate
North Lincolnshire Council	21st May 2014	Able Marine Energy Park	Humber Renewable Energy Super Cluster	Ferry
Northumberland County Council	21st May 2014	Port of Blyth - Bates	North East	Cowpen
Northumberland County Council	21st May 2014	Port of Blyth - East Sleekburn	North East	Sleekburn
North Tyneside Council	21st May 2014	North Bank of the Tyne (Port of Tyne)	North East	Riverside
Stockton on Tees Borough Council	21st May 2014	New Energy and Technology Park	Tees Valley	Billingham South

2014/3188

LOAN RELATIONSHIPS AND DERIVATIVE CONTRACTS (DISREGARD AND BRINGING INTO ACCOUNT OF PROFITS AND LOSSES) (AMENDMENT) REGULATIONS 2014

Made . . . . *1 December 2014*

Laid before the House of Commons . . . . *2 December 2014*

Coming into force . . . . *31 December 2014*

The Treasury make the following Regulations in exercise of the powers conferred by sections 310, 328(4) and (7), 598(1)(a) and (4) and 606(4) and (7) of the Corporation Tax Act 2009.

1 Citation, commencement and effect

(1) These Regulations may be cited as the Loan Relationships and Derivative Contracts (Disregard and Bringing into Account of Profits and Losses) (Amendment) Regulations 2014 and come into force on 31st December 2014.

(2) These Regulations have effect from that date, but—

(a) regulations 3, 4 and 5 have effect in relation to accounting periods beginning on or after 1st January 2015,

(b) regulations 6 and 7 have effect in relation to periods of account beginning on or after 1st January 2015.

(3) For the purposes of regulations 3, 4 and 5, an accounting period beginning before and ending on or after 1st January 2015 is to be treated for the purposes of these Regulations as if so much of the period as falls before that date, and so much of the period as falls on or after that date, were separate accounting periods.

2 Amendments to the Loan Relationships and Derivative Contracts (Disregard and Bringing into Account of Profits and Losses) Regulations 2004

The Loan Relationships and Derivative Contracts (Disregard and Bringing into Account of Profits and Losses) Regulations 2004 are amended as follows.

3–8 *(The amendments made by regs 3–8 are already in force and have therefore been omitted)*

9 Transitional provision

(1) This regulation makes transitional provisions in relation to any company which at any time before the start of the first period of account beginning on or after 1st January 2015 uses fair value accounting in relation to a derivative contract which satisfies the conditions in regulation 7(1)(a), 8(1)(a) or 9(1).

(2) At the start of the first period of account beginning on or after 1st January 2015—

(a) the company is treated as having made an election under regulation 6A of the Loan Relationships and Derivative Contracts (Disregard and Bringing into Account of Profits and Losses) Regulations 2004 (as amended by these Regulations) except to the extent that an election under regulation 6 (the "original election") of those Regulations (as they stood before the coming into force of these Regulations) had effect before the coming into force of these Regulations,

(b) the election treated as being made has effect in relation to derivative contracts held by the company in that period and subsequent periods (subject to any amendment or revocation of the election under regulation 6A(4)(b)(ii)), and

(c) the original election, if any, is treated as revoked.

2014/3227

INCOME TAX (RECOMMENDED MEDICAL TREATMENT) REGULATIONS 2014

Made . . . . *9 December 2014*
Laid before the House of Commons . . . . *10 December 2014*
Coming into force . . . . *1 January 2015*

The Treasury make the following Regulations in exercise of the powers conferred by section 320C(3)(c), (4) and (7) of the Income Tax (Earnings and Pensions) Act 2003.

1 Citation and commencement

These Regulations may be cited as the Income Tax (Recommended Medical Treatment) Regulations 2014 and come into force on 1st January 2015.

2 Interpretation

In these Regulations "health care professional" means—

(a) a registered medical practitioner;

(b) a registered nurse; or

(c) an occupational therapist, physiotherapist or psychologist registered with a regulatory body established by an Order in Council under section 60 of the Health Act 1999 (regulation of health professions, social workers, other care workers etc).

3 Specified requirements for purposes of section 320C of the Income Tax (Earnings and Pensions) Act 2003

The requirements set out in regulations 4 and 5 are the other specified requirements that a recommendation for medical treatment is required to meet for the purpose of section 320C of the Income Tax (Earnings and Pensions) Act 2003.

4 Qualifying period of absence

(1) A recommendation for medical treatment can only be given after the employee has been—

(a) assessed by a health care professional as unfit for work for at least 28 consecutive days; or

(b) absent from work due to injury or ill health for at least 28 consecutive days.

(2) For the purpose of sub-paragraph (1)(a), an assessment that an employee is unfit for work includes an assessment that the employee may be fit for work subject to the employer making arrangements to enable the employee to return to work, providing that the employee does not return to work before a recommendation for medical treatment is made.

5 Person making a recommendation and form of a recommendation

A recommendation for medical treatment is required to be made by a health care professional and—

(a) be in writing;
(b) be provided to the employee and employer; and
(c) specify the medical treatment that is recommended.

2014/3294

REVENUE SCOTLAND AND TAX POWERS ACT 2014 (CONSEQUENTIAL PROVISIONS AND MODIFICATIONS) ORDER 2014

Made . . . . 11 December 2014
Coming into force in accordance with article 1(2)

The Secretary of State makes the following Order in exercise of the powers conferred by sections 104, 112(1), 113(2), (4) and (5) and 114(1) of the Scotland Act 1998.

In accordance with paragraphs 1, 2 and 3 of Schedule 7 to that Act a draft of this Order has been laid before and approved by a resolution of each House of Parliament.

1 Citation, commencement and extent

(1) This Order may be cited as the Revenue Scotland and Tax Powers Act 2014 (Consequential Provisions and Modifications) Order 2014.

(2) This Order comes into force on the same day as section 2 (establishment of Revenue Scotland) of the Revenue Scotland and Tax Powers Act 2014 comes into force.

(3) Article 6 extends to Scotland and to England and Wales only.

2 Status of Revenue Scotland as part of the Scottish Administration

Revenue Scotland is part of the Scottish Administration.

3 Construction of references to an office-holder in the Scottish Administration

(1) Unless the context otherwise requires, references in the Scotland Act 1998 and any other enactment to an office-holder in the Scottish Administration are to be taken to include a reference to Revenue Scotland.

(2) Paragraph (1) applies whether or not the enactment defines the expression "office-holder in the Scottish Administration" by reference to the Scotland Act 1998 or any specific provision of that Act.

4 Information sharing

(1) In the Commissioners for Revenue and Customs Act 2005—

(a) in section 18 (confidentiality)—
  (i) in subsection (2)(i), for "the Scottish Ministers" substitute "Revenue Scotland";
  (ii) omit subsection (2A);
(b) in section 19 (wrongful disclosure)—
  (i) in subsection (1), omit "or (2A)";
  (ii) in subsection (8), omit "or (2A)".

(2) In section 24 of the Scotland Act 2012 (amendments relating to the Commissioners for Revenue and Customs), omit subsections (4) and (5).

(3) For the purposes of section 15 of the Revenue Scotland and Tax Powers Act 2014, a disclosure is permitted if it is made to the Commissioners for Her Majesty's Revenue and Customs in connection with the collection and management of revenue within the meaning of section 5 of the Commissioners for Revenue and Customs Act 2005.

5 House of Commons Disqualification Act 1975

In Part 2 of Schedule 1 to the House of Commons Disqualification Act 1975 (bodies of which all members are disqualified), insert the following entry at the appropriate place—

"Revenue Scotland".

6 Public Interest Disclosure (Prescribed Persons) Order 2014

In the Schedule to the Public Interest Disclosure (Prescribed Persons) Order 2014 (prescribed persons)—

(a) insert the entries set out in the following table at the appropriate place—

First Column *Persons and descriptions of people*	*Second Column* *Description of matters*

The Keeper of the Registers of Scotland	Land and buildings transaction tax.
Revenue Scotland	Devolved taxes (within the meaning of section 80A(4) of the Scotland Act 1998).

(b) in the entry for the Scottish Environment Protection Agency, in the second column, at the end, insert—

"Scottish landfill tax.".

2015/80

FINANCE ACT 2004 (REGISTERED PENSION SCHEMES AND ANNUAL ALLOWANCE CHARGE) (AMENDMENT) ORDER 2015

Made . . . . *27 January 2015*

Coming into force . . . . *28 January 2015*

The Treasury make the following Order in exercise of the powers conferred by sections 238A and 282(A1) of the Finance Act 2004:

A draft of this instrument has been laid before the House of Commons in accordance with section 282(1A) of that Act and approved by a resolution of that House.

1 Citation, commencement and effect

This Order may be cited as the Finance Act 2004 (Registered Pension Schemes and Annual Allowance Charge) (Amendment) Order 2015 and comes into force on the day after the day is made.

2 The amendments made by the following articles have effect in relation to pension input periods ending in tax year 2011-12 and subsequent years—

(a) article 12;
(b) article 13(a) to (d);
(c) article 15; and
(d) article 16(a) to (d),

but see article 3.

3 (1) Where the insertion by article 12(b) of subsection (5BC) of section 230 of the Finance Act 2004 (cash balance arrangements) ("the Act") has effect in respect of times before the date on which this Order comes into force, it does so as if that subsection consisted only of the words from "In determining" to "disregarded".

(2) Where the insertion by article 15(b) of subsections (5B) to (5BE) of section 234 of the Act (defined benefits arrangements) has effect in respect of times before the date on which this Order comes into force, it does so as if—

(a) subsection (5BD) were to consist only of the words from "In determining" to "disregarded"; and
(b) subsection (5BE) were omitted.

(3) The amendments made by paragraphs (a) and (b) of article 13 do not have effect in relation to any transfer of sums or assets that occurs before the date on which this Order comes into force if any person's liability to tax would be higher as a result of—

(a) the application of those amendments in relation to that transfer; and
(b) any application in relation to that transfer of the amendments made by article 13(c) and (d),

than it would have been if none of those amendments had effect.

(4) The insertion by article 13(e) of subsection (6D) of section 232 of the Act (cash balance arrangements: adjustments of closing value) does not have effect in relation to transfers of sums or assets that occur before the date on which this Order comes into force.

(5) The amendments made by paragraphs (a) and (b) of article 16 do not have effect in relation to any transfer of sums or assets that occurs before the date on which this Order comes into force if any person's liability to tax would be higher as a result of—

(a) the application of those amendments in relation to that transfer; and
(b) any application in relation to that transfer of the amendments made by article 16(c) and (d),

than it would have been if none of those amendments had effect.

(6) The insertion by article 16(e) of subsection (5D) of section 236 of the Act (defined benefits arrangements: adjustments of closing value) does not have effect in relation to transfers of sums or assets that occur before the date on which this Order comes into force.

4 The amendment made by article 13(f) has effect in relation to benefit crystallisation events that occur on or after the date on which this Order comes into force.

5 The amendment made by article 13(g) has effect in relation to cases where the liability mentioned in section 232(8D) of the Act arose on or after the date on which this Order comes into force and results from a notice under section 237B given on or after that date.

6 The amendment made by article 14 has effect in relation to payments of a refund of excess contributions lump sum made in pension input periods ending in tax year 2014-15 and subsequent tax years.

7 The amendment made by article 16(f) has effect in relation to cases where the liability mentioned in section 236(8D) of the Act arose on or after the date on which this Order comes into force and results from a notice under section 237B given on or after that date.

8 The amendments made by article 17(a) have effect in relation to—

(a) the individual becoming actually entitled to benefits, and

(b) benefit crystallisation events occurring,

after the end of the period of 6 months beginning with the date on which this Order comes into force.

9 The amendment made by article 17(b) has effect in relation to transfers of sums or assets that occur on or after the date on which this Order comes into force.

10 Amendments to the Finance Act 2004

Part 4 of the Act (pension schemes etc) is amended as follows.

11 Carry forward of unused annual allowance

(inserts FA 2004 s 228B)

12 Amendments to section 230

(amends FA 2004 s 230)

13 Amendments to section 232

(amends FA 2004 s 232)

14 Amendment to section 233

(amends FA 2004 s 233)

15 Amendments to section 234

(amends FA 2004 s 234)

16 Amendments to section 236

(amends FA 2004 s 236)

17 Amendments to section 237B

(amends FA 2004 s 237B)

2015/86

FILMS (DEFINITION OF "BRITISH FILM") ORDER 2015

Made . . . . *28 January 2015*

. . . . *29 January 2015*

The Secretary of State, in exercise of the power conferred by paragraph 10(2) of Schedule 1 to the Films Act 1985 and with the consent of the Treasury, makes the following Order.

In accordance with paragraph 10(5) of Schedule 1 to that Act, a draft of this Order was laid before Parliament and approved by a resolution of each House of Parliament.

1 Citation and commencement

This Order may be cited as the Films (Definition of "British Film") Order 2015 and shall come into force on the day after the day on which it is made.

2 Application

(1) The amendments made by this Order have effect in relation to any film other than an excepted film.

(2) A film is an excepted film if—

(a) the amendments made to Schedule 1 to the Films Act 1985 by the Films (Definition of "British Film") (No 2) Order 2006 do not apply in relation to it,

(b) an application for certification of the film was made before the commencement day, or

(c) the film production company has made an election in relation to the film under paragraph (3).

(3) A film production company may make an election under this paragraph in relation to a film if—

(a) the first day of shooting (in relation to a documentary or animation) or principal photography (in the case of a film other than a documentary or animation) was before the commencement day, and

(b) no application for certification of the film was made before the commencement day.

(4) In this article—

"application for certification" means an application for an interim or final certificate under paragraph 2 of Schedule 1 to the Films Act 1985, and

"commencement day" means the day on which this Order comes into force.

3 The cultural test for films other than documentaries and animations

(amends Films Act 1985 Sch 1 para 4A)

4 The cultural test for documentary films

(amends Films Act 1985 Sch 1 para 4B)

5 The cultural test for animation films

(amends Films Act 1985 Sch 1 para 4C)

6 Amendments to paragraph 4D of Schedule 1

(amends Films Act 1985 Sch 1 para 4D)

2015/118

OCCUPATIONAL PENSION SCHEMES (POWER TO AMEND SCHEMES TO REFLECT ABOLITION OF CONTRACTING-OUT) REGULATIONS 2015

Made . . . .*25th February 2015*

Laid before Parliament . . . .*4th March 2015*

Coming into force . . . .*6th April 2015*

The Secretary of State for Work and Pensions, in exercise of the powers conferred by sections 24(5) and 54(5) and (6), of and paragraphs 2(3) and (4), 4, 6, 10(1), 12, 13, and 14(1) and (2) of Schedule 14 to, the Pensions Act 2014, makes the following Regulations:

1 Citation and commencement

(1) These Regulations may be cited as the Occupational Pension Schemes (Power to Amend Schemes to Reflect Abolition of Contracting-out) Regulations 2015.

(2) These Regulations come into force on 6th April 2015.

2 Interpretation

In these Regulations—

"the Act" means the Pensions Act 2014;

"the 2004 Act" means the Pensions Act 2004;

"actuarial valuation" has the meaning given by section 224(2)(a) of the 2004 Act (actuarial valuations and reports);

"the actuary" means the actuary appointed in accordance with regulation 10(2);

"the amendment date" means the date amendments made using the power take effect;

"the calculation date" means the date chosen in accordance with regulation 8(7);

"effective date" means the date referred to in section 224(2)(b) of the 2004 Act;

"the power" means the power under section 24(2) of the Act to amend an occupational pension scheme;

"principal employer" means, in relation to a multi-employer scheme—

(a) a person nominated by the employers, or by rules of the scheme, to act on behalf of the employers for the purposes of section 229 of the 2004 Act (matters requiring agreement of the employer), or

(b) where there is no such nominee, a person nominated by the employers to act on their behalf for the purposes of the use of the power;

"proposed amendments" means the amendments to be certified under paragraph 6(1) of Schedule 14 to the Act;

"segregated scheme" means a multi-employer scheme which is divided into two or more sections where—

(a) any contributions payable to the scheme by an employer in relation to the scheme, or by a member employed by that employer, are allocated to that employer's section, and if more than one section applies to an employer, to the section to which the employment relates, and

(b) a specified proportion of the assets of the scheme is attributable to each section of the scheme and cannot be used for the purposes of any other section; and

"technical provisions" has the meaning given by section 222(2) of the 2004 Act (the statutory funding objective).

3 Protected persons to whom the power does not apply

(1) For the purposes of section 24(4)(a) of the Act (when the power may not be used) a person listed in this regulation is a "protected person in relation to a scheme".

(2) A person who is a "protected employee" as defined by regulation 2(1) of the Electricity (Protected Persons) (England and Wales) Pension Regulations 1990 (interpretation) on or after the amendment date.

(3) A person who is a "protected employee" as defined by regulation 2(1) of the Electricity (Protected Persons) (Scotland) Pension Regulations 1990 (interpretation) on or after the amendment date.

(4) A person who is a "protected employee" as defined by article 1(2) of the Railway Pensions (Protection and Designation of Schemes) Order 1994 (citation, commencement and interpretation) to whom Part II of that Order has effect in relation to relevant pension rights, within the meaning of paragraph 6(3) of Schedule 11 to the Railways Act 1993 (the powers of protection), accruing on or after the amendment date.

(5) A person who is a "protected employee" as defined by regulation 2(1) of the Coal Industry (Protected Persons) Pensions Regulations 1994 (interpretation) on or after the amendment date.

(6) A person who is a "protected person" as defined by article 1(3) of the London Transport Pension Arrangements Order 2000 (citation, commencement and interpretation) to whom that Order has effect on or after the amendment date.

(7) A person who falls within paragraph 9(5) of Schedule 8 to the Energy Act 2004 (persons entitled to pension protection under paragraphs 10 and 11) and to whom paragraph 9(2) of that Schedule applies.

4 Total annual employee contributions of the relevant members

(1) For the purposes of paragraph 2(3)(a) of Schedule 14 to the Act (what can the power be used to do?), the "total annual employee contributions of the relevant members" means the total annual amount of employee contributions for the relevant members calculated using the employee contribution rates shown in the schedule of contributions adopted in relation to the scheme for the purposes of Part 3 of the 2004 Act (scheme funding) as at the calculation date.

(2) The actuary is to calculate the increase, due to the proposed amendments, in the total annual employee contributions of the relevant members—

- (a) estimated to be payable over the period of one year beginning with the calculation date;
- (b) using the earnings data specified in regulation 7; and
- (c) in accordance with the requirements in regulation 8.

5 Annual increase in an employer's national insurance contributions in respect of the relevant members

(1) For the purposes of paragraph 2(3)(b) of Schedule 14 to the Act, the "annual increase in an employer's national insurance contributions in respect of the relevant members" means the increase of 3.4% in the annual amount of national insurance contributions payable by the employer in respect of so much of the earnings of relevant members as exceeds the applicable lower earnings limit but not the upper accrual point (or the prescribed equivalents if the earner is paid otherwise than weekly).

(2) The actuary is to calculate the annual increase in the employer's national insurance contributions in respect of the relevant members—

- (a) estimated to be payable over the period of one year beginning with the calculation date;
- (b) using the earnings data specified in regulation 7; and
- (c) in accordance with the requirements in regulation 8.

(3) In this regulation—

"the 1992 Act" means the Social Security Contributions and Benefits Act 1992;

"applicable" in relation to the lower earnings limit, means the limit or limits in force during the one year after the calculation date;

"lower earnings limit" is to be construed in accordance with section 5 of the 1992 Act (earnings limits and thresholds for class 1 contributions);

"the prescribed equivalents"—

- (a) in the context of the lower earnings limit, means the equivalent prescribed under section 5(4) of the 1992 Act, and
- (b) in the context of the upper accrual point, means the equivalent prescribed under section 122(6A) of that Act (interpretation); and

"the upper accrual point" has the meaning given by section 122(1) of the 1992 Act.

6 Scheme liabilities in respect of the benefits that accrue annually for or in respect of the relevant members

(1) For the purposes of paragraph 2(3)(c) of Schedule 14 to the Act, a "scheme's liabilities in respect of the benefits that accrue annually for or in respect of the relevant members" means any liabilities which arise by virtue of any rights accruing to future benefits under the scheme rules for or in respect of the relevant members.

(2) Where those rights include discretionary benefits, the discretionary benefits are to be taken into account in the same way as in the scheme's technical provisions—

(a) where the calculation date is the same date as the effective date of an actuarial valuation, calculated by reference to that date, or

(b) where the calculation date is not the same date as that date, calculated by reference to the date of the most recent actuarial valuation before the calculation date.

(3) Where those rights include money purchase benefits, the money purchase benefits are not to be taken into account.

(4) The actuary is to calculate the reduction, due to the proposed amendments, in the scheme's liabilities in respect of the benefits that accrue annually for or in respect of the relevant members—

(a) estimated for the period of one year beginning with the calculation date;

(b) using the earnings data specified in regulation 7; and

(c) in accordance with the requirements of regulation 8.

(5) In this regulation, "money purchase benefits" have the meaning given by section 181 of the Pension Schemes Act 1993 (general interpretation) .

7 Earnings data

(1) The actuary must use earnings data which, except where paragraph (3) applies, is for the period of one year ending with the calculation date.

(2) Where paragraph (3) applies, calculations may be made using earnings data which refers to the period of three years ending with the calculation date.

(3) This paragraph applies where—

(a) the actuary is satisfied that the earnings data for some or all of the relevant members for the period of one year ending with the calculation date is significantly abnormal; and

(b) the—

(i) principal employer in a case falling within regulation 14 or 15, or

(ii) employer in any other case;

writes to the actuary stating that it is also so satisfied.

8 General calculation requirements

(1) The actuary must comply with the following requirements in carrying out the calculations under regulations 4(2), 5(2) and 6(4).

(2) The calculations are to be carried out—

(a) as if the proposed amendments took effect on the calculation date;

(b) taking account only of the effect of the proposed amendments;

(c) at the present value at the calculation date; and

(d) where an assumption is used in more than one calculation, using the same assumption for each calculation in which it is used.

(3) Any data used in the calculations, other than earnings data, must be data—

(a) the actuary considers is relevant; and

(b) which—

(i) is as at the calculation date, or

(ii) refers to the period of one year ending with the calculation date,

as the actuary considers appropriate.

(4) Calculations must be made using—

(a) the methods and assumptions used to calculate the scheme's technical provisions—

(i) where the calculation date is the same date as the effective date of an actuarial valuation, calculated by reference to that date, or

(ii) where the calculation date is not the same date as that date, calculated by reference to the date of the most recent actuarial valuation before the calculation date, updated if necessary to reflect market conditions at the calculation date; and

(b) any other assumptions which the actuary considers necessary and which are consistent with the assumptions used to calculate the scheme's technical provisions, updated if necessary to reflect market conditions at the calculation date.

(5) Where paragraph (6) applies, the actuary must adjust the requested assumptions to a best estimate basis by removing any margin for prudence provided the actuary is satisfied such adjustments are consistent with the principles that would be used by the trustees or managers of the scheme in

calculating an initial cash equivalent under regulation 7B of the Occupational Pension Schemes (Transfer Values) Regulations 1996 (initial cash equivalents for salary related benefits other than cash balance benefits not calculated by reference to final salary) at the calculation date.

(6) This paragraph applies where the—

(a) principal employer in a case falling within regulation 14 or 15; or

(b) employer in any other case,

writes to the actuary instructing the actuary to adjust any assumptions ("the requested assumptions") to remove any margin for prudence.

(7) Subject to regulation 8(8), the—

(a) principal employer in a case falling within regulation 14 or 15; or

(b) employer in any other case,

must choose a calculation date which may be any date after 31st December 2011.

(8) Where the power is used in relation to the same members in the same scheme on a second or subsequent occasion the calculation date must be the same date as on the first occasion the power was used.

(9) In this regulation, "any margin for prudence" means any margin for adverse deviation allowed for in accordance with regulation 5(4)(a) of the Occupational Pension Schemes (Scheme Funding) Regulations 2005 (calculation of technical provisions).

9 Further restrictions on the use of the power

(1) The power may not be used to make amendments which would remove a power to determine any matter from the trustees or managers of a scheme.

10 Actuary

(1) For the purposes of paragraph 6(2)(a) of Schedule 14 to the Act (requirement for actuary's certificate), "actuary" means a Fellow of the Institute and Faculty of Actuaries.

(2) The—

(a) principal employer in a case falling within regulation 14 or 15; or

(b) employer in any other case,

must appoint an actuary.

11 Requirement for actuary's certificate

(1) Except in a case where regulation 8(8) applies, the actuary must certify whether, in the actuary's opinion—

(a) the proposed amendments comply with paragraph 2(2) of Schedule 14 to the Act; and

(b) the calculations have been made in accordance with the requirements of regulations 4(2), 5(2), 6(2) to (4), 7 and 8(2) to (6).

(2) In a case where regulation 8(8) applies, the actuary must certify whether, in the actuary's opinion—

(a) all the amendments comply with the requirement in paragraph (1)(a) as if all the amendments are being made on this second or subsequent (as appropriate) occasion; and

(b) the calculations have been made in accordance with the requirements in paragraph (1)(b) and regulation 8(8).

(3) For the purposes of this regulation, "all the amendments" means the proposed amendments and the amendments made by the previous use, or uses, of the power in relation to the same members in the same scheme as covered by the proposed amendments.

(4) The actuary must provide a certificate under this regulation that includes the information specified in the Schedule.

(5) The actuary must issue a certificate under this regulation to the trustees or managers of the scheme and—

(a) the principal employer in a case falling within regulation 14 or 15; or

(b) in any other case, the employer,

before any amendments are made.

12 Information

(1) The trustees or managers of an occupational pension scheme must provide any information reasonably requested by—

(a) the principal employer in a case falling within regulation 14 or 15; or

(b) in any other case, the employer,

in connection with the use of the power.

(2) The information must be provided in writing within such reasonable period as agreed with the principal employer or employer as applicable.

(3) Where the trustees or managers of a scheme have failed to take all reasonable steps to comply with any requirement imposed on them by this regulation, section 10 of the Pensions Act 1995 (civil penalties) applies.

13 Segregated schemes with single employer sections

(1) This regulation applies to a section of a segregated scheme where there is one employer in relation to that section of the scheme.

(2) Section 24 of the Act (abolition of contracting-out for salary related schemes etc) and Schedule 14 to the Act (power to amend schemes to reflect abolition of contracting-out) apply with the following modifications.

(3) In section 24(2) the reference to—

(a) "an employer" is to be read as a reference to "an employer in relation to a section of an occupational pension scheme"; and

(b) "an occupational pension scheme" is to be read as a reference to "that section of an occupational pension scheme".

(4) In Schedule 14 in paragraphs 2(2), 3(1), 9 and 15, references to a "scheme" are to be read as references to a "section of a scheme".

(5) Where these Regulations (apart from this regulation) apply to a section of a segregated scheme where there is one employer in relation to that section of the scheme, they shall apply to that section as if the section were a separate scheme.

14 Non-segregated multi-employer schemes

(1) This regulation applies to multi-employer schemes which are not segregated schemes.

(2) Section 24 of the Act and Schedule 14 to the Act apply with the following modifications.

(3) In section 24(2) the reference to—

(a) "an employer" is to be read as a reference to "the principal employer"; and

(b) "the employer's national insurance contributions" is to be read as a reference to "the employers' national insurance contributions".

(4) In Schedule 14—

(a) in paragraph 2(2), references to "the employer's national insurance contributions" are to be read as references to "the employers' national insurance contributions"; and

(b) in paragraph 2(5), the reference to "the employer is" is to be read as a reference to "the employers are".

15 Segregated schemes with multi-employer sections

(1) This regulation applies to a section of a segregated scheme where there is more than one employer in relation to that section of the scheme.

(2) Section 24 of the Act and Schedule 14 to the Act apply with the following modifications.

(3) In section 24(2) the reference to—

(a) "an employer" is to be read as a reference to "the principal employer in relation to a section of an occupational pension scheme";

(b) "an occupational pension scheme" is to be read as a reference to "that section of an occupational pension scheme"; and

(c) "the employer's national insurance contributions" is to be read as a reference to "the employers' national insurance contributions".

(4) In Schedule 14—

(a) in paragraph 2(2), references to "the employer's national insurance contributions" are to be read as references to "the employers' national insurance contributions"; and

(b) in paragraphs 2(2), 3(1), 9 and 15, references to a "scheme" are to be read as references to a "section of a scheme".

(5) Where these Regulations (apart from this regulation) apply to a section of a segregated scheme where there is more than one employer in relation to that section of the scheme, they shall apply to that section as if the section were a separate scheme.

16 Notification of amendment date

(1) Following the issue of a certificate by the actuary in accordance with regulation 11(5), the—

(a) principal employer in a case falling within regulation 14 or 15; or

(b) employer in any other case,

must consult the trustees or managers of the scheme about an appropriate amendment date.

(2) The principal employer or employer as applicable, must, as soon as reasonably practicable after consultation, notify the trustees or managers of the scheme of the amendment date.

(3) The notification required by paragraph (2) must be in writing.

(4) Amendments may not have effect before 6th April 2016.

SCHEDULE

INFORMATION TO BE INCLUDED IN ACTUARY'S CERTIFICATE

Regulation 11

Name and address of employer/principal employer

Name and Scheme Contracted-out Number (SCON(s)) of scheme/section

The amendments proposed to be made.

Data and assumptions used

Calculation date

Date of scheme actuarial valuation

Any additional assumptions used

Any assumptions which the employer requested were adjusted to remove the margin for prudence

What earnings data used: 1 year to calculation date or 3 years to calculation date

Other data sources used

Estimates of values of scheme amendments

A statement that the Actuary's estimate of the following values is for the proposed amendments as set out in the certificate and on the basis of the data referred to, the methods and assumptions used to calculate the scheme's technical provisions and the additional assumptions set out in the certificate.

The values for—

the annual increase in the employer's national insurance contributions in respect of the earnings of relevant members as exceeds the lower earnings limit but not the upper accrual point

the increase in the total annual employee contributions of the relevant members (if applicable)

the reduction in the scheme's liabilities in respect of the benefits that accrue annually for or in respect of the relevant members (if applicable)

the sum of the increase in the total annual employee contributions and the reduction in the scheme's liabilities in respect of the benefits that accrue annually for or in respect of the relevant members (if applicable).

Note: In a case where the power is being used on a second or subsequent occasion, estimates should be for the changes due to all the amendments, those proposed and the amendments made by the previous use or uses of the power.

Certification

A statement that, in the actuary's opinion—

The proposed amendments to the scheme/section set out in this certificate comply with paragraph 2(2) of Schedule 14 to the Pensions Act 2014.

The calculations have been made in accordance with the requirements of regulations 4(2), 5(2), 6(2) to (4), 7 and 8(2) to (6) of the Occupational Pension Schemes (Power to Amend Schemes to Reflect Abolition of Contracting-out) Regulations 2015.

Alternative certification where the power is being used on a second or subsequent occasion

A statement that, in the actuary's opinion—

All the amendments to the scheme/section, those proposed and set out in this certificate and those made by the previous use or uses of the power and set out in resolutions (give dates) comply with paragraph 2(2) of Schedule 14 to the Pensions Act 2014.

The calculations have been made in accordance with the requirements of regulations 4(2), 5(2), 6(2) to (4), 7, 8(2) to (6) and 8(8) of the Occupational Pension Schemes (Power to Amend Schemes to Reflect Abolition of Contracting-out) Regulations 2015.

Signature:

Date:

Name:

Qualification:

Address:

2015/130

PROMOTERS OF TAX AVOIDANCE SCHEMES (PRESCRIBED CIRCUMSTANCES UNDER SECTION 235) REGULATIONS 2015

Made . . . .*6 February 2015*

Laid before the House of Commons . . . .*9 February 2015*

Coming into force . . . .*2 March 2015*

The Commissioners for Her Majesty's Revenue and Customs make the following Regulations in exercise of the powers conferred by sections 235(6) and (7) and 283(1) of the Finance Act 2014.

1 Citation, commencement and effect

(1) These Regulations may be cited as the Promoters of Tax Avoidance Schemes (Prescribed Circumstances under Section 235) Regulations 2015 and come into force on 2nd March 2015.

(2) Regulations 2 and 3 have effect from 17th July 2014.

2 Company in same group not promoter

(1) A company ("C") is not a promoter to the extent that—

(a) C carries on a business within the meaning of section 235(1);

(b) the other person (or each of the other persons) to whom C provides services in connection with the relevant proposal or relevant arrangements is a company in the same group as C; and

(c) C has not during the previous three years provided services of that kind to a person other than a company which is in the same group as C.

(2) If C at any subsequent time provides services of that kind to a person other than a company which is in the same group as C, paragraph (1) will be deemed not to have applied during the previous three years.

(3) A company cannot rely on paragraph (1) whilst a conduct notice or a monitoring notice has effect in relation to it.

(4) For the purposes of this regulation companies are members of the same group if one is the 51% subsidiary of the other, or both are 51% subsidiaries of a third company.

(5) In this regulation "51% subsidiary" has the same meaning as it does for the purposes of the Corporation Tax Acts.

3 Persons not promoters—special cases

(1) A person ("P") is not a promoter on account of section 235(2)(a), or by virtue of being responsible to any extent for the design of arrangements within the meaning of section 235(3)(b), where any of the following conditions are met.

(2) P does not provide any tax advice in connection with the respective proposed arrangements or arrangements.

(3) P could not reasonably be expected to know that the proposed arrangements, or arrangements, are a relevant proposal or relevant arrangements respectively.

2015/131

FINANCE ACT 2014 (SCHEDULE 34 PRESCRIBED MATTERS) REGULATIONS 2015

Made . . . .*6 February 2015*

Laid before the House of Commons . . . .*9 February 2015*

Coming into force . . . .*2 March 2015*

The Commissioners for Her Majesty's Revenue and Customs in exercise of the powers conferred by section 283(1) of, and paragraphs 8(1), 8(3) and 9(2) of Schedule 34 to, the Finance Act 2014, make the following Regulations:

1 Citation and commencement

These Regulations may be cited as the Finance Act 2014 (Schedule 34 Prescribed Matters) Regulations 2015 and come into force on 2nd March 2015.

2 Prescribed misconduct

(1) Prescribed misconduct for the purposes of paragraph 8(1)(a) of Schedule 34 to the Finance Act 2014 means any conduct by a person—

(a) which a professional body describes as misconduct, or

(b) which is a breach of a rule or condition imposed by a professional body,

and is relevant to the provision of tax advice or tax related services.

3 Prescribed action

Prescribed action for the purposes of paragraph 8(1)(b) of Schedule 34 to the Finance Act 2014 means any action by a professional body which results in any claim of misconduct being referred to—

(a) a disciplinary process which determines—

(i) the seriousness of the misconduct, and

(ii) the level of any penalty to be imposed; or

(b) a conciliation, arbitration or similar settlement process (however described) which determines the seriousness of the misconduct and the level of any penalty to be imposed.

4 Prescribed penalty

A penalty is prescribed for the purposes of paragraph 8(1)(c) of Schedule 34 to the Finance Act 2014 where it is imposed by a professional body and results in one or more of the following in relation to a person—

(a) a fine or financial penalty greater than £5,000;

(b) a condition or restriction on, or attached to, a certificate or licence required to practice under the professional body;

(c) suspension, withdrawal or non-renewal of a certificate or licence required to practice under the professional body;

(d) suspension, expulsion or exclusion from membership of the professional body, however described (including removal from a membership register, striking off), whether temporary or permanent.

5 Prescribed professional bodies

The following are prescribed professional bodies for the purposes of paragraph 8(3)(l) of Schedule 34 to the Finance Act 2014—

(a) the Chartered Institute of Taxation;

(b) Chartered Accountants Ireland.

6 Prescribed relevant sanction

(1) In paragraph 9 of Schedule 34 to the Finance Act 2014 a sanction is prescribed under sub-paragraph (2)(b) if a regulatory authority imposes one or more of the following in relation to a person—

(a) a fine or financial penalty;

(b) a suspension of an approval issued by the regulatory authority to perform any function to which the approval relates;

(c) the imposition of limitations or other restrictions in relation to the performance of any function to which any approval issued by the regulatory authority relates;

(d) the imposition of any conditions in relation to any approval issued by the regulatory authority.

(2) A sanction is also prescribed in relation to a person if a regulatory authority publishes a statement of misconduct by that person.

2015/344

BANK LEVY (DOUBLE TAXATION ARRANGEMENTS) (NETHERLANDS) REGULATIONS 2015

Made . . . . *23rd February 2015*

Laid before the House of Commons . . . . *24th February 2015*

Coming into force . . . . *17th March 2015*

The Treasury make the following Regulations in exercise of the powers conferred by paragraphs 66(8) to (9A) of Schedule 19 to the Finance Act 2011.

Introduction

1 Citation, commencement and effect

(1) These Regulations may be cited as the Bank Levy (Double Taxation Arrangements) (Netherlands) Regulations 2015 and come into force on 17th March 2015.

(2) These Regulations have effect in relation to periods of account ending on or after 1st January 2011.

2 Interpretation

In these Regulations—

"double taxation arrangements" means the Convention between the Government of the United Kingdom of Great Britain and Northern Ireland and the Government of the Kingdom of the Netherlands for the avoidance of double taxation and the prevention of fiscal evasion with respect to bank taxes signed on 12th June 2013 in London and the Protocol attached to the Convention;

"Netherlands bank tax" means the equivalent foreign levy imposed by the Kingdom of the Netherlands.

3 Application of these Regulations

These Regulations apply in relation to the provision of relief from the bank levy provided by the double taxation arrangements where the bank levy and the Netherlands bank tax are charged in relation to—

(a) a relevant group which is a foreign banking group or a relevant non-banking group, or

(b) a relevant entity which is a relevant foreign bank

Double taxation relief by way of credit

4 Double taxation relief

(1) Where these Regulations apply, an amount of the Netherlands bank tax imposed on a relevant group or relevant entity in relation to a period or part of a period which falls within a chargeable period is allowed as a credit against the bank levy for that chargeable period.
(2) Subject to the provisions of these Regulations, the amount of the bank levy for the chargeable period is reduced by the amount of the credit.
(3) But the amount of the bank levy shall not be reduced to below nil.
(4) The credit under paragraph (2) requires a claim.

5 Calculation of the credit

(1) Take steps 1 to 4 to determine how much of the Netherlands bank tax is available as a credit against the bank levy.

Step 1

Determine the amount ("A") of the taxable base of the relevant group or the relevant entity as at the end of the chargeable period shown in the group's or entity's Netherlands bank tax return, before deduction of the efficiency exemption in Article 9 of the Wet bankenbelasting, by reference to which the Netherlands bank tax is calculated.

Step 2

Determine the amount ("B") of the UK taxable base as at the end of the chargeable period by reference to which the Netherlands bank tax is calculated.

Step 3

Determine the amount of the Netherlands bank tax paid ("C") in relation to the chargeable period.
If a proportion (Z%) of the period in relation to which the Netherlands bank tax is calculated falls in any other chargeable period, Z% of the Netherlands bank tax shall be attributable to that other period.

Step 4

The amount of the Netherlands bank tax available as a credit against the bank levy is (B/A)×C.
(2) If the period in relation to which the Netherlands bank tax is calculated ("the Netherlands period") and the chargeable period end on different dates, the amount of the credit is determined as follows—

(a) take of steps 1 to 4 in relation to each Netherlands period which falls wholly or partly within the chargeable period,
(b) the references to the chargeable period in steps 1 to 3 are to be read as references to the Netherlands period,
(c) for the purposes of step 2, to determine the UK taxable base at the end of the Netherlands period, regulation 6 applies as though references to the chargeable period in paragraphs (2) and (3) of that regulation were references to the Netherlands period,
(d) the amount of the credit determined at step 4 in relation to each Netherlands period must be apportioned on a time basis to each of the chargeable periods wholly or partly within the Netherlands period.

6 Determining the UK taxable base

(1) The amount of the UK taxable base of the relevant group or relevant entity is—
EL - (T + PD + I)
where—

EL is the amount of equity and liabilities of the specified members of the relevant group or the relevant entity,
T is the amount of tier one capital equity and liabilities and tier two capital liabilities of the specified members of the relevant group or the relevant entity,
PD is the amount of liabilities representing protected deposits of the specified members of the relevant group or relevant entity, and
I is the amount of relevant insurance liabilities of the specified members of the relevant group or the relevant entity.

(2) In the case of a relevant group, the amounts referred to in paragraph (1) are determined by reference to—

(a) the amounts recognised in the group's consolidated financial statements for the chargeable period as prepared under international accounting standards, or
(b) if no such financial statements are prepared, the amounts which would have been so recognised had consolidated financial statements for the group been prepared for the chargeable period under international accounting standards.

(3) In the case of a relevant entity, the amounts referred to in paragraph (1) are determined by reference to—

(a) the amounts recognised in the entity's financial statements for the chargeable period as prepared under international accounting standards or UK GAAP, or

(b) if no such financial statements are prepared, the amounts which would have been so recognised had such financial statements been prepared for the chargeable period under international accounting standards or under UK GAAP if that is what the entity prepares its financial statements under.

(4) The specified members are—

(a) in relation to a relevant group, any member of the group which has type A, type B, type C or type D equity and liabilities within paragraph 17 or 19 of Schedule 19 to FA 2011; and

(b) in relation to a relevant entity, any permanent establishment through which the entity carries on a trade in the UK.

(5) In relation to a permanent establishment, the amounts in paragraph (1) are X% (as determined at step 2 of paragraph 24(1) of Schedule 19 to FA 2011 in relation to the relevant foreign bank) of each of the amounts of EL, T, PD and I of the relevant foreign bank carrying on trade through the permanent establishment.

(6) For the purposes of this regulation—

"relevant insurance liabilities" has the same meaning as in paragraph 33 of Schedule 19 to FA 2011;

"tier one capital equity and liabilities", in relation to a relevant group or relevant entity, has the same meaning as in paragraph 30 of Schedule 19 to FA 2011;

"tier two capital liabilities", in relation to a relevant group or relevant entity—

(a) in relation to chargeable periods ending before 1st January 2014, has the same meaning as "tier one capital equity and liabilities" in paragraph 30 of Schedule 19 to FA 2011 but the references to "tier one" are to be read as references to "tier two" and the reference to equity is to be ignored, and

(b) in relation to chargeable periods ending on or after 1st January 2014, means so much of the group's or entity's liabilities as is Tier 2 capital within the meaning of Article 71 of the Capital Requirements Regulation (taking account of the transitional provisions in Part Ten of that Regulation).

(7) For the purposes of sub-paragraph (b) of the definition of tier two capital liabilities, the Capital Requirements Regulation is to be treated as applying, in relation to all entities and groups of entities, as if—

(a) to the extent it would not otherwise be the case, the Prudential Regulation Authority were the competent authority in relation to those entities and groups,

(b) the only determinations made, and discretions exercised, by the Prudential Regulation Authority for the purposes of the Capital Requirement Regulation were those published by it in accordance with that Regulation, and

(c) those entities and groups (to the extent that it would not otherwise be the case) were subject to the provisions of the PRA Handbook immediately before 1st January 2014.

(8) "The Capital Requirements Regulation" means Regulation (EU) No 575/2013 of the European Parliament and of the Council of 26 June 2013 on prudential requirements for credit institutions and investment firms.

(9) The amount of liabilities representing protected deposits is determined in accordance with paragraph 29(2) to (10) of Schedule 19 to FA 2011.

7 Exchange rates

For the purposes of regulation 4, the amount of Netherlands bank tax is to be translated into its sterling equivalent by reference to the spot rate of exchange for the last day of the chargeable period in relation to which the credit is claimed.

Claim for double taxation relief

8 General time limit for making a claim

(1) A claim for credit under regulation 4(1) must be made not more than—

(a) four years after the end of the accounting period in relation to which the bank levy is treated as an amount of corporation tax chargeable on the responsible member or the relevant entity, or

(b) if later, one year after the end of the accounting period in which the Netherlands bank tax is paid.

(2) If the chargeable period in relation to which the bank levy is charged falls in more than one accounting period, the accounting period referred to in paragraph (1)(a) shall be the latest of those periods.

9 Relevant groups: responsible member to make claim

Where the bank levy is charged as provided for by paragraph 4 of Schedule 19 to FA 2011 (bank levy to be charged in relation to certain groups of entities) any claim for credit under regulation 4(1) must be made by the responsible member.

Limits on credit

10 Restriction of credit

(1) Where the bank levy is charged in relation to a relevant group, if the parent entity is not resident in the Netherlands, the credit under regulation 4(1) is only available to reduce the amount of the bank levy charged in relation to relevant chargeable equity and liabilities of the relevant group.

(2) In paragraph (1), "relevant chargeable equity and liabilities" means chargeable equity and liabilities that would be recognised in relevant accounts for the chargeable period had such accounts been prepared for the member or members of the group ("the relevant member or members") resident in the Netherlands.

(3) In paragraph (2), "relevant accounts" mean a consolidated financial statement or financial statement—

(a) prepared under international accounting standards if that is what the relevant member or members prepare financial statements under, and

(b) in which the UK taxable base subject to the Netherlands bank tax in respect of which the credit is given would be recognised.

11 Reduction in credit: payment by reference to Netherlands bank tax

(1) Paragraph (2) applies if—

(a) credit for the Netherlands bank tax is to be allowed to an entity under these Regulations, and

(b) a payment is made by a tax authority to that entity, or to any other person, by reference to the Netherlands bank tax.

(2) The amount of the credit must be recalculated under regulation 4 reducing the amount of the Netherlands bank tax by reference to the payment referred to in paragraph (1)(b).

12 Priority of credits

(1) Where credits are allowed in relation to the Netherlands bank tax under these Regulations and any other equivalent foreign levy under any Regulations made under paragraph 66 (arrangements affording double taxation relief) or paragraph 67 (power to provide for double taxation relief) of Schedule 19 to the Finance Act 2011, the credits apply to reduce the bank levy in the order specified in paragraph (2), subject to paragraphs (3) and (4).

(2) The order is—

First, any credit allowed in relation to the equivalent foreign levy imposed by the law of the foreign territory in which the parent entity is resident.

Second, any credit allowed in relation to the equivalent foreign levy imposed by the law of the foreign territory in which a direct subsidiary ("the first subsidiary") is resident or a permanent establishment of the parent entity is located.

Third, any credit allowed in relation to an equivalent foreign levy imposed by the law of the foreign territory in which a direct subsidiary ("the second subsidiary") is resident or a permanent establishment of the first subsidiary is located.

Fourth, any credit allowed in relation to an equivalent foreign levy imposed by the law of the foreign territory in which a direct subsidiary of the second subsidiary is resident or a permanent establishment of the second subsidiary is located, and so on in relation to any fourth and further subsidiaries.

(3) If an entity has direct subsidiaries ("the elected subsidiaries") in more than one foreign territory which imposes an equivalent foreign levy, the responsible member shall elect as to the order ("the elected order") in which the credits allowed in relation to the equivalent foreign levies shall be applied.

(4) If any of the elected subsidiaries themselves have direct subsidiaries in more than one foreign territory which imposes an equivalent foreign levy, paragraphs (2) and (3) shall apply to those direct subsidiaries in the elected order and paragraph (1) shall apply as if each elected subsidiary were a parent entity.

(5) For the purposes of this regulation, where an equivalent foreign levy is not imposed by the law of the foreign territory in which an entity ("E") is resident, any direct subsidiary of E shall be treated as the direct subsidiary of the entity which is the parent entity of E.

Action after adjustment of amount payable by way of bank levy or Netherlands bank tax

13 Consequences of adjustment of the bank levy or Netherlands bank tax

(1) Paragraph (2) applies to a claim or assessment if—

(a) the amount of credit given under regulation 4 is reduced under regulation 11, or becomes excessive or insufficient by reason of any adjustment of the amount of any bank levy or Netherlands bank tax,

(b) the reduction or adjustment gives rise to the claim or assessment, and

(c) the claim or assessment is made not later than 6 years from the time when all material determinations have been made, whether in the UK or elsewhere.

(2) Nothing in the Tax Acts limiting the time for the making of assessments, or limiting the time for the making of claims for relief, applies to the assessment or claim.
(3) In paragraph (1)(c) "material determination" means an assessment, reduction, adjustment or other determination that is material in determining whether any, and (if so) what, credit is to be given.

14 Duty to give notice that adjustment has rendered credit excessive

(1) This regulation applies if—
(a) any credit has been allowed under regulation 4, and
(b) later, the amount of that credit is reduced under regulation 11, or becomes excessive as a result of an adjustment of the amount of the Netherlands bank tax.
(2) The relevant entity or, in the case of a relevant group, the responsible member must give notice that a reduction has been made or that the amount of the credit has become excessive as a result of the making of an adjustment.
(3) Notice under paragraph (2) is to be given—
(a) to an officer of Revenue and Customs, and
(b) within one year from when the reduction or adjustment is made.

Cases about being taxed otherwise than in accordance with the Convention

15 Giving effect to solutions to cases and mutual agreements resolving cases

(1) Paragraphs (2) and (4) apply if under, and for the purposes of, the double taxation arrangements—
(a) an entity presents, to the Commissioners for Her Majesty's Revenue and Customs or to a competent authority in the Netherlands, a case concerning the entity being taxed (whether in the United Kingdom or the Netherlands) otherwise than in accordance with the double taxation arrangements, and
(b) the Commissioners arrive at a solution to the case or make a mutual agreement with a competent authority in the Netherlands for the resolution of the case.
(2) The Commissioners are to give effect to the solution or mutual agreement despite anything in any enactment, and any such adjustment as is appropriate in consequence may be made.
(3) An adjustment under paragraph (2) may be made by way of discharge or repayment of tax, the allowance of credit against tax payable in the United Kingdom, the making of an assessment or otherwise.
(4) A claim for relief under any provision of the Tax Acts or the enactments relating to capital gains tax may be made in pursuance of the solution or mutual agreement at any time before the end of the period of 12 months following the notification of the solution or mutual agreement to the entity affected, even if that involves making the claim after a deadline imposed by another enactment.
(5) In this regulation "competent authority in the Netherlands" means the Minister of Finance in the Netherlands or his authorised representative.

16 Effect of, and deadline for, presenting a case

(1) This regulation applies to the presentation of a case concerning an entity's being taxed (whether in the United Kingdom or the Netherlands) otherwise than in accordance with the double taxation arrangements.
(2) The presentation of any such case under and in accordance with the double taxation arrangements—
(a) does not constitute a claim for relief under the Tax Acts or the enactments relating to capital gains tax, and
(b) is accordingly not subject to section 42 of the Taxes Management Act 1970 or any other enactment relating to the making of such claims.
(3) Any such claim must be presented before the end of the later of—
(a) the period of 3 years following the first notification of the action resulting in the entity being charged otherwise than in accordance with the double taxation arrangements, and
(b) the period of 6 years following the end of the chargeable period to which the case relates.

2015/448

CHILDCARE PAYMENTS (ELIGIBILITY) REGULATIONS 2015

Made . . . . 4 March 2015
Coming into force in accordance with regulation 1

The Treasury make the following Regulations, in exercise of the powers conferred by sections 2(3)(b) to (d), 3(4) and (5), 7(3), 8(2), 9(2) and (3), 10(2), (3) and (4), 14, 32(5), 33(5) and 69(2) and (4) of the Childcare Payments Act 2014.

In accordance with section 70(3) of that Act, a draft of this instrument was laid before Parliament and approved by resolution of each House of Parliament.

1 Citation and commencement

These Regulations may be cited as the Childcare Payments (Eligibility) Regulations 2015 and come into force on the day after the day on which they are made.

2 Interpretation

In these Regulations—

"the Act" means the Childcare Payments Act 2014, and a reference without more to a numbered section is a reference to the section of the Act bearing that number;

"another EEA state" means any EEA state apart from the United Kingdom;

"armed forces independence payment" means armed forces independence payment under the Armed Forces and Reserve Forces (Compensation Scheme) Order 2011;

"disability living allowance" means disability living allowance under sections 71 to 76 of the Social Security Contributions and Benefits Act 1992 or sections 71 to 76 of the Social Security Contributions and Benefits (Northern Ireland) Act 1992;

"employed", except in the expression "self-employed", means engaged under a contract of service or in an office (including an elected office) or so engaged as a United Kingdom resident working overseas;

"minimum weekly income" means the amount a person would be paid for 8 hours of work a week at the hourly rate set out in regulation 11 or 13 of the National Minimum Wage Regulations 1999;

"paid work" means work done for payment or in expectation of payment and does not include being engaged by a charitable or voluntary organisation, or as a volunteer, in circumstances in which the payment received by or due to be paid to the person is in respect of expenses;

"partner" has the meaning given in regulation 3;

"personal independence payment" means a personal independence payment under Part 4 of the Welfare Reform Act 2012;

"prisoner" means—

(a) a person who is detained in custody pending trial or sentence upon conviction or under a sentence imposed by a court; or

(b) a person who is on temporary release in accordance with the provisions of the Prison Act 1952, the Prisons (Scotland) Act 1989 or the Prison Act (Northern Ireland) 1953,

other than a person who is detained in hospital under the provisions of the Mental Health Act 1983, in Scotland under the provisions of the Mental Health (Care and Treatment) (Scotland) Act 2003 or the Criminal Procedure (Scotland) Act 1995 or, in Northern Ireland, under articles 12 to 17 of the Mental Health (Northern Ireland) Order 1986;

"self-employed" means engaged in carrying on a trade, profession or vocation on a commercial basis and with a view to profit, either on one's own account or as a member of a business partnership;

"week" means a period of seven days starting with midnight between Saturday and Sunday.

10 Calculation of expected income

(1) An employed person's expected income comprises the amount of earnings the person expects to receive from—

(a) any employment under a contract of service;

(b) any office, including an elected office.

(2) In paragraph (1), "earnings" has the meaning given by section 62 of ITEPA 2003 (general definition of earnings).

(3) A self-employed person's expected income comprises—

(a) the amount of receipts the person expects to derive from a trade, profession or vocation less the amount of expenses the person expects to incur wholly and exclusively for the purposes of the trade, profession or vocation; or

(b) if the person carries on a trade, profession or vocation in a business partnership, the share expected to be allocated to the person of the partnership's receipts less the share expected to be allocated to that person of the partnership's expenses incurred wholly and exclusively for the purposes of the trade, profession or vocation.

(4) In calculating a self-employed person's income, receipts and expenses of a capital nature are to be disregarded.

(5) A person's expected income may include income from a person's employment and self-employment taken together.

15 Income not to exceed a certain level

(1) A person is treated as meeting the condition of eligibility in section 10 (the income of the person and his or her partner must not exceed limit) if the person does not expect to pay income tax at the additional rate or the dividend additional rate for the relevant tax year.

(2) A resident of another EEA state who is in paid work in the United Kingdom is treated as meeting the condition of eligibility in section 10 if that person would not expect to pay income tax at the additional rate or the dividend additional rate on the hypothetical net income of that person for the relevant tax year.

(3) A person is treated as not meeting the condition of eligibility in section 10 if—

(a) the person has made, or expects to make, a claim under section 809B of the Income Tax Act 2007 (claim for remittance basis to apply) for the relevant tax year; or

(b) the person expects section 809E of that Act (application of remittance basis in certain cases without claim) to apply to the person for the relevant tax year.

(4) In this regulation—

"hypothetical net income" has the meaning given in section 55C(3) of the Income Tax Act 2007 (election to reduce personal allowance);

"the relevant tax year" has the meaning given in section 10(5).

18 Disqualifying tax credit and universal credit claimants from obtaining top-up payments: change of circumstances

(1) The following are to be regarded as changes of circumstances in relation to a person for the purposes of sections 32 and 33 (power to disqualify tax credit or universal credit claimants from obtaining top-up payments)—

(a) a person no longer meets the conditions of eligibility in sections 7 to 9, or a person's partner no longer meets the condition in section 9;

(b) the composition of a person's household changes, including where—

(i) a person's partner joins the person's household or the person joins the partner's household;

(ii) a person or a person's partner takes responsibility for another child or qualifying young person;

(iii) a person's partner or a child leaves the household; or

(iv) a person's partner or child dies;

(c) a person or the person's partner is absent from the household for at least one month;

(d) a person's child or the person's partner's child is awarded, or ceases to be entitled to, disability living allowance, personal independence payment or armed forces independence payment;

(e) the principal employment of a person or a person's partner changes;

(f) the employment status of a person or a person's partner changes;

(g) a person becomes liable to pay HMRC an amount under section 35(2), 36(2), 37(2) or 38(3) (recovery of top-up payment where award of tax credit or universal credit made on review, revision or appeal); or

(h) any other change entitles a person or a person's partner to make a claim that results in either—

(i) a first award of a tax credit; or

(ii) a first award of universal credit.

(2) For the purposes of paragraph (1)(b)(ii)—

(a) in a case within section 32—

(i) a person takes responsibility for a child or qualifying young person where the person takes such responsibility in accordance with the rules in regulation 3 of the Child Tax Credit Regulations 2002; and

(ii) "qualifying young person" has the meaning given in regulations 2 and 5(3) and (4) of those Regulations;

(b) in a case within section 33—

(i) a person takes responsibility for a child or qualifying young person where the person takes such responsibility as determined by regulations 4 and 4A of the Universal Credit Regulations 2013; and

(ii) "qualifying young person" has the meaning given in regulation 5 of those Regulations;

(c) "child" means a person under the age of 16.

(3) In paragraph (1)(b)(iii) and (iv) and (1)(d) "child" means a qualifying child for the purposes of the Act.

(4) In paragraph (1)(e), a person's "principal employment" is the employment in which the greater part of the person's working time is spent.

2015/522

CHILDCARE PAYMENTS REGULATIONS 2015

Made . . . . 4th March 2015
Laid before Parliament . . . . 5th March 2015
Coming into force . . . . 1st June 2015

The Commissioners for Her Majesty's Revenue and Customs make the following Regulations, in exercise of the powers conferred by sections 2(3)(a) and (4), 4(6), 5(3), 15(3), (4) and (5), 17(4), 19(6), 24(1), (3) and (4), 25, 26(1) and (3), 49(6), 62(1), (2), (3) and (5) and 69(3) and (4) of the Childcare Payments Act 2014.

1 Citation and commencement

These Regulations may be cited as the Childcare Payments Regulations 2015 and come into force on 1st June 2015.

2 Interpretation

In these Regulations—

"the Act" means the Childcare Payments Act 2014, and a reference without more to a numbered section is a reference to the section of the Act bearing that number;

"another EEA state" means any EEA state apart from the United Kingdom;

"armed forces independence payment" means an armed forces independence payment under the Armed Forces and Reserve Forces (Compensation Scheme) Order 2011;

"disability living allowance" means disability living allowance under sections 71 to 76 of the Social Security Contributions and Benefits Act 1992 or sections 71 to 76 of the Social Security Contributions and Benefits (Northern Ireland) Act 1992;

"disabled child" is to be read in accordance with regulations made under section 14 (qualifying child);

"personal independence payment" means a personal independence payment under Part 4 of the Welfare Reform Act 2012;

"relevant maximum" for an entitlement period is to be read in accordance with section 19 (payments into childcare accounts).

3 Qualifying childcare: registered or approved childcare

(1) For the purposes of section 2 (qualifying childcare), childcare described in paragraphs (2) to (6) is to be regarded as registered or approved childcare.

(2) Care provided in England for a child—

(a) by a person registered under Part 3 of the Childcare Act 2006;

(b) by or under the direction of the proprietor of a school as part of the school activities—

(i) out of school hours, where a child has reached compulsory school age; or

(ii) at any time, where a child has not yet reached compulsory school age; or

(c) by a domiciliary care provider registered with the Care Quality Commission in accordance with the requirements of the Health and Social Care Act 2008.

(3) Care provided in Wales for a child—

(a) by a person registered under Part 2 of the Children and Families (Wales) Measure 2010;

(b) by a person in circumstances where, but for article 11, 12 or 14 of the Child Minding and Day Care Exceptions (Wales) Order 2010, the care would be day care for the purposes of Part 2 of the Children and Families (Wales) Measure 2010;

(c) out of school hours, by a school as part of the school activities or by a local authority;

(d) by a domiciliary care worker under the Domiciliary Care Agencies (Wales) Regulations 2004;

(e) by a foster parent in relation to a child (other than one whom the foster parent is fostering) in circumstances where the care would be child minding or day care for the purposes of Part 2 of the Children and Families (Wales) Measure 2010 but for the fact that the child is over the age of the children to whom that Measure applies; or

(f) by a childcare provider approved in accordance with a scheme made by the National Assembly for Wales or the Welsh Ministers under section 12(5) of the Tax Credit Act 2002.

(4) Care provided in Scotland for a child—

(a) by a person in circumstances where the care service provided by the person consists of child minding or of day care of children within the meaning of paragraph 12 or 13 of Schedule 12 to the Public Services Reform (Scotland) Act 2010 and is registered under Part 5 of that Act;

(b) by a local authority in circumstances where the care service provided by the local authority consists of child minding or of day care of children within the meaning of paragraph 12 or 13 of Schedule 12 to the Public Services Reform (Scotland) Act 2010 and is registered under Part 5 of that Act; or

(c) by a childcare agency where the care service consists of or includes supplying, or introducing to persons who use the service, childcarers within the meaning of paragraph 5 of Schedule 12 to the Public Services Reform (Scotland) Act 2010.

(5) Care provided in Northern Ireland for a child—

(a) by a person registered under Part 11 of the Children (Northern Ireland) Order 1995;

(b) out of school hours by a school as part of the school activities; or

(c) by a childcare provider approved in accordance with a scheme under the Tax Credits (Approval of Home Child Care Providers) Scheme (Northern Ireland) 2006.

(6) Care provided for a child outside the United Kingdom by a childcare provider approved by an organisation accredited by the Secretary of State under the Tax Credits (New Category of Child Care Provider) Regulations 2002.

(7) The following are not registered or approved childcare—

(a) care provided for a child by the child's parent, step-parent or the parent's partner;

(b) care provided for a child by a relative of the child, wholly or mainly in the child's home;

(c) care provided by a person with parental responsibility for the child; and

(d) care provided by a person who is a foster parent of the child.

(8) Care is not within paragraph (2)(a) if it is provided in breach of a requirement to register under Part 3 of the Childcare Act 2006.

(9) Care is not within paragraph (5)(a) if it is provided in breach of a requirement to register under Part 11 of the Children (Northern Ireland) Order 1995.

(10) In this regulation—

"compulsory school age" is determined in accordance with section 8 of the Education Act 1996;

"foster parent" includes, in Scotland, a foster carer or kinship carer as defined by regulation 2 of the Looked After Children (Scotland) Regulations 2009;

"local authority" means—

(a) in relation to Wales, a county council, a county borough council or a community council;

(b) in relation to Scotland, a council constituted under section 2 of the Local Government etc (Scotland) Act 1994;

"proprietor", in relation to a school, means—

(a) the governing body incorporated under section 19 of the Education Act 2002; or

(b) if there is no such body, the person or body of persons responsible for the management of the school;

"relative" means grandparent, aunt, uncle, brother or sister, whether of the full blood or half blood or by marriage or civil partnership;

"school"—

(a) in England and Wales, has the same meaning as in the Education Act 1996;

(b) in Northern Ireland, means a school as defined by article 2(2) of the Education and Libraries (Northern Ireland) Order 1986.

4 Entitlement periods

(1) A person's first entitlement period begins on the day on which HMRC confirm that the person is an eligible person for the entitlement period.

(2) Each subsequent entitlement period begins on the day after the previous entitlement period ends.

(3) Each entitlement period begins on the same day of a month except as follows—

(a) if the first entitlement period begins or ends on the 31st day of a month, each subsequent entitlement period shall begin or end on the last day of the month; and

(b) if the first entitlement period begins or ends on the 29th or 30th day of a month, each subsequent entitlement period shall begin or end on the 29th or 30th day of the month, except in February where it begins or ends on the 27th day or, in a leap year, the 28th day.

5 Variation of entitlement periods

(1) HMRC may vary the length of an entitlement period—

(a) on the opening of a childcare account in relation to a person's first entitlement period;

(b) on the opening of a childcare account for a person's second or subsequent child; or

(c) in order to align the entitlement periods of two account-holders.

(2) The relevant maximum for the entitlement period varied under paragraph (1) is determined by the formula—

$X \times A \div 91$

where—

X is, in the case of a disabled child, £4,000, or in the case of any other child, £2,000; and

A is the number of days in the varied entitlement period.

6 Declarations of eligibility

(1) A declaration of eligibility must—

(a) be in the form specified by HMRC;

(b) be made to HMRC in accordance with regulation 22; and

(c) contain information specified by HMRC—

(i) to identify the person making the declaration, the person's partner (if any) and the child in respect of whom the childcare account is, or is to be, held; and

(ii) to determine whether the person is an eligible person.

(2) A declaration of eligibility made for the purposes of opening a childcare account must be made on the day the person applies to open the account.

(3) Subject to paragraph (4) and regulation 7, any other declaration of eligibility (a "reconfirming declaration") must be made during the period beginning 28 days before the beginning of the entitlement period for which the reconfirming declaration is made and ending when that entitlement period ends.

(4) If a person makes a reconfirming declaration during the period of 7 days immediately preceding the beginning of the entitlement period for which that declaration is made, HMRC may not determine whether the declaration is valid for the purposes of the Act until—

(a) 7 days after the reconfirming declaration was made; or

(b) such earlier time as HMRC allow.

7 Late declarations of eligibility

(1) If a person makes a declaration of eligibility during the entitlement period for which it is made (a "late declaration of eligibility"), HMRC may not determine whether the declaration is valid for the purposes of the Act until—

(a) 7 days after the declaration was made; or

(b) such earlier time as HMRC allow.

(2) If a person ("P") makes a late declaration of eligibility—

(a) P may make qualifying payments into the childcare account only for the remainder of the entitlement period after the day on which HMRC determine the declaration is valid; and

(b) the relevant maximum for the entitlement period is reduced to an amount determined by the formula—

$$X \times A \div B$$

where—

X is, in the case of a disabled child, £4,000, or in the case of any other child, £2,000;

A is the number of days remaining in the entitlement period after the day on which HMRC determine that the declaration is valid; and

B is the total number of days in the entitlement period.

(3) The relevant maximum for an entitlement period is not reduced under paragraph (2)(b) if P satisfies HMRC that—

(a) P has met the conditions of eligibility in sections 6 to 13 (conditions of eligibility) continuously since the beginning of the entitlement period; and

(b) in a case where P has a partner, P's partner has met the conditions of eligibility in sections 9 to 13 continuously since the beginning of the entitlement period.

(4) In paragraph (3), in relation to a resident of another EEA state, "conditions of eligibility" includes those conditions applied as modified by regulations made under section 8(2)(c) (the person must be in the UK).

(5) Paragraph (3) does not apply if the late declaration of eligibility was made by P in circumstances where section 30(2) (termination of tax credit awards) applies.

8 Circumstances where eligible person unable to act—receivers etc

(1) In the circumstances specified in paragraph (2) a person mentioned in sub-paragraph (b) of that paragraph may act for the person mentioned in sub-paragraph (a) of that paragraph for the purposes of—

(a) making a declaration of eligibility;

(b) opening a childcare account;

(c) managing a childcare account.

(2) The circumstances specified in this paragraph are where—

(a) a person is, or is alleged to be, an eligible person but is unable for the time being to open and manage a childcare account; and

(b) there are any of the following—

(i) a receiver appointed by the Court of Protection with power to open and manage a childcare account on behalf of the person;

(ii) in Scotland, a tutor, curator or other guardian acting or appointed in terms of law who is administering the estate of the person; or

(iii) in Northern Ireland, a controller appointed by the High Court, with power to open and manage a childcare account on behalf of the person.

9 Circumstances where eligible person unable to act—other appointed persons

(1) In the circumstances specified in paragraph (2) a person mentioned in sub-paragraph (b) of that paragraph may act for the person mentioned in sub-paragraph (a) of that paragraph for the purposes of—

(a) making a declaration of eligibility;

(b) opening a childcare account;

(c) managing a childcare account.

(2) The circumstances specified in this paragraph are where—

(a) a person is, or is alleged to be, an eligible person but is unable for the time being to open and manage a childcare account; and

(b) in relation to that person, there is a person appointed under—

(i) regulation 33(1) of the Social Security (Claims and Payments) Regulations 1987;

(ii) regulation 33(1) of the Social Security (Claims and Payments) Regulations (Northern Ireland) 1987; or

(iii) paragraph (3).

(3) Where no person mentioned in regulation 8(2)(b) has been appointed in relation to the person who is unable to act, HMRC may appoint under this paragraph a person who—

(a) if a natural person, is aged 18 years or more; and

(b) has applied in writing to HMRC to be appointed to act on behalf of the person who is unable to act.

(4) A person's appointment under paragraph (3) ends—

(a) when HMRC terminate it;

(b) when the person appointed has resigned from the appointment having given one month's notice in writing to HMRC of that person's resignation; or

(c) when HMRC are notified that a receiver or other person mentioned in regulation 8(2)(b) has been appointed in relation to the person who is unable to open or manage a childcare account.

10 Appointment by account-holder of person to manage childcare account

(1) An account-holder may appoint a person to manage a childcare account on behalf of the account-holder.

(2) The person appointed under paragraph (1) must be an individual whose name is notified to HMRC before any function is performed on behalf of the account-holder.

(3) Except where HMRC otherwise allow, an account-holder cannot appoint under paragraph (1)—

(a) an individual who is an account provider or is an owner of an account provider;

(b) an individual who provides services to an account provider in connection with the provision or management of a childcare account—

(i) as an employee of the account provider;

(ii) as an employee of a person providing such services to the account provider; or

(iii) as a self-employed person; or

(c) an individual who provides qualifying childcare for a child of the account-holder.

(4) A person may be appointed under paragraph (1) to manage not more than 5 childcare accounts at any time (whether or not on behalf of the same account-holder).

(5) A person appointed under paragraph (1) may not make a declaration of eligibility on behalf of the account-holder.

(6) Paragraphs (3), (4) and (5) do not apply to an account-holder's partner appointed under paragraph (1) to manage all the childcare accounts of that account-holder.

11 Opening a childcare account

(1) An application to open a childcare account must—

(a) be in the form specified by HMRC;

(b) be made to HMRC in accordance with regulation 22;

(c) contain information specified by HMRC to identify the applicant, the applicant's partner (if any) and the child in respect of whom the account is to be held; and

(d) contain the child benefit number, if the child has been the subject of an award of that benefit—

(i) to the applicant; or

(ii) to a person other than the applicant, but the applicant knows or can reasonably ascertain the child benefit number.

(2) If the applicant or the applicant's partner is self-employed (the "self-employed person"), in the application to open a childcare account the applicant must—

(a) provide any unique taxpayer's reference of the self-employed person; or

(b) confirm that the self-employed person has, for the tax year in which the application is made, given notice to HMRC under section 7 of the Taxes Management Act 1970 in respect of the self-employment but has not yet received a unique tax reference.

(3) An applicant whose partner is self-employed in another EEA state must, in the course of applying to open a childcare account, provide information specified by HMRC to confirm that the partner is carrying out self-employed work in that other EEA state.

12 Variation of relevant maximum: child ceasing to be qualifying child etc

(1) If a child ceases to be a qualifying child during an entitlement period, the relevant maximum for that entitlement period is determined in accordance with paragraph (3).

(2) If an award of tax credit terminates in accordance with section 30(3) (termination of tax credit awards) in a case within section 30(1)(b), the relevant maximum for an entitlement period is determined in accordance with paragraph (3) for the entitlement period in which the relevant day falls.

(3) The relevant maximum is determined by the formula—

$X \times A \div B$

where—

- (a) X is, in the case of a disabled child, £4,000, or in the case of any other child, £2,000;
- (b) in a case within paragraph (1), A is the number of days beginning on the first day of the entitlement period and ending on the day after the day on which the child ceases to be a qualifying child; or
- (c) in a case within paragraph (2), A is the number of days beginning on the relevant day and ending on the last day of the entitlement period; and
- (d) B is the total number of days in the entitlement period.

(4) In this regulation, "relevant day" has the meaning given in section 30.

13 Variation of relevant maximum: appealable decisions

(1) This regulation applies where an appealable decision under section 56(3)(a), (b), (c), (e) or (h) (appealable decisions) is either—

- (a) varied or cancelled on a review under section 57 (review of decisions); or
- (b) quashed (wholly or partly) under section 60 (powers of tribunal).

(2) Where this regulation applies, the relevant maximum for an entitlement period beginning after the variation, cancellation or quashing of the appealable decision is increased by an amount equal to the relevant maximum that would (but for the decision) have been available to an active childcare account.

(3) Where a person has received compensation under section 62 (compensatory payments)—

- (a) no award of an increased relevant maximum may be made in respect of a variation or quashing of a decision for which the compensation was paid; and
- (b) any award of an increased relevant maximum that has been made in respect of such a variation or quashing is cancelled.

14 Variation of relevant maximum: delay in payment of allowances

(1) This regulation applies where—

- (a) a person has applied to open a childcare account but HMRC are unable to confirm eligibility solely because of a delay in the payment to the person, or to the person's partner, of—
  - (i) carer's allowance under section 70 of the Social Security Contributions and Benefits Act 1992 or section 70 of the Social Security Contributions and Benefits (Northern Ireland) Act 1992; or
  - (ii) contributory employment and support allowance under section 1 of the Welfare Reform Act 2007 or section 1 of the Welfare Reform Act (Northern Ireland) 2007; or
- (b) in relation to a disabled child, a person has applied to open a childcare account but, solely because of a delay in the payment to the child of—
  - (i) disability living allowance;
  - (ii) personal independence payment; or
  - (iii) armed forces independence payment,

  HMRC is unable to grant the application, or is able to grant it but subject to a relevant maximum less than the relevant maximum which applies in respect of a disabled child.

(2) Where this regulation applies, the relevant maximum for an entitlement period beginning after the delay is increased by an amount equal to the relevant maximum that would, but for the delay, have been available to an active childcare account held—

- (a) in a case within paragraph (1)(a), by that person; or
- (b) in a case within paragraph (1)(b), in respect of that child.

(3) Where a person has received compensation under section 62—

- (a) no award of an increased relevant maximum may be made in respect of a delay in payment for which the compensation was paid; and
- (b) any award of increased relevant maximum that has been made in respect of such a delay in payment is cancelled.

(4) In this regulation references to carer's allowance, contributory employment and support allowance, disability living allowance, personal independence payment and armed forces independence payment include references to allowances and payments made under the law of another EEA state which are substantially similar in character to those allowances and payments.

15 Variation of relevant maximum: death of account-holder

(1) This regulation applies where—

(a) an account-holder dies leaving funds in the childcare account ("account A");

(b) a person ("P") has an active childcare account ("account B") at the time account A is closed; and

(c) account A was, and account B is, held in respect of the same qualifying child.

(2) Where this regulation applies, the relevant maximum for P's next entitlement period beginning after the closure of account A is increased by an amount equal to the amount paid to the deceased account-holder's personal representatives under regulation 19(2)(b) and (3) (closure of a childcare account).

16 Variation of relevant maximum: infrastructure failure

(1) This regulation applies where a payment is prevented from being made into a childcare account by a serious technical failure affecting—

(a) HMRC;

(b) the account provider; or

(c) a bank or provider of banking services.

(2) Where this regulation applies, the relevant maximum for the next entitlement period beginning after the failure is increased by—

X-Q

where—

X is, in the case of a disabled child, £4,000, or in the case of any other child, £2,000; and

Q is the sum of qualifying payments made into the childcare account during the entitlement period in which the failure occurred.

17 Compensatory payments

(1) Subject to paragraphs (5) and (6), the circumstances specified in paragraphs (2) and (3) are specified for the purposes of section 62.

(2) The circumstances specified in this paragraph are—

(a) an appealable decision under section 56(3)(a), (b), (c), (e) or (h) is—

(i) varied or cancelled on a review under section 57; or

(ii) quashed (wholly or partly) under section 60;

(b) a person has applied to open a childcare account but HMRC are unable to confirm eligibility solely because of a delay in the payment to the person, or to the person's partner, of—

(i) carer's allowance under section 70 of the Social Security Contributions and Benefits Act 1992 or section 70 of the Social Security Contributions and Benefits (Northern Ireland) Act 1992; or

(ii) contributory employment and support allowance under section 1 of the Welfare Reform Act 2007 or section 1 of the Welfare Reform Act (Northern Ireland) 2007; or

(c) in relation to a disabled child, an application is made to open a childcare account but, solely because of a delay in the payment to the child of—

(i) disability living allowance;

(ii) personal independence payment; or

(iii) armed forces independence payment,

HMRC is unable to grant the application, or is able to grant it but subject to a relevant maximum less than the relevant maximum which applies in respect of a disabled child.

(3) The circumstances specified in this paragraph are—

(a) the circumstances are as specified in paragraph (2)(b) but, at the time the payment is made, the person is no longer an eligible person for a reason unrelated to the delay in payment;

(b) the circumstances are as specified in paragraph (2)(b) but, at the time the payment is made, the child in relation to whom the application was made has died; or

(c) the circumstances are as specified in paragraph (2)(c) but the child dies during the period of delay in payment.

(4) The amount paid to a person under section 62 in respect of a child for a period (the "compensation period") may not exceed the amount of top-up payments that person could have received if—

(a) the circumstances specified in paragraph (2) or (3) had not arisen; and

(b) the person had held an active childcare account in respect of the child throughout the compensation period.

(5) Circumstances specified in paragraph (2)(b) or (c) or (3) are not specified for the purposes of section 62 for any period of delay in payment in respect of which an award of tax credits is or has been made to the person claiming a compensatory payment.

(6) Circumstances specified in paragraph (2) are not specified for the purposes of section 62 to the extent that a person has received, in respect of those circumstances, additional top-up payments by using an increased amount of relevant maximum awarded under regulation 13 or 14.

(7) A person claiming a compensatory payment must provide to HMRC evidence of payment of the costs incurred on qualifying childcare.

(8) In this regulation references to carer's allowance, contributory employment and support allowance, disability living allowance, personal independence payment and armed forces independence payment include references to allowances and payments made under the law of another EEA state which are substantially similar in character to those allowances and payments.

18 Account restriction orders

(1) HMRC may make an account restriction order—

(a) imposing a restriction under section 24(2)(a), if the condition specified in paragraph (2), (3) or (4) is met; or

(b) imposing a restriction under section 24(2)(b), if the condition specified in paragraph (5) is met.

(2) The condition specified in this paragraph is—

(a) an amount has been assessed and notified to a person under section 41 or 47 (assessment and enforcement of recoverable amounts or penalties); and

(b) some or all of the amount assessed has not been paid to HMRC by the time specified in section 41(5) or 47(4).

(3) The condition specified in this paragraph is—

(a) a person ("P") wishes—

(i) to open a childcare account in respect of a child; or

(ii) to make a declaration of eligibility in relation to a childcare account held in respect of a child; and

(b) P is prevented from so doing because another person holds an active childcare account in respect of the child.

(4) The condition specified in this paragraph is that section 35(1), 36(1), 37(1) or 38(1) (recovery of top-up payments) applies in relation to an account-holder or the partner of an account-holder.

(5) The condition specified in this paragraph is—

(a) HMRC have reasonable grounds to suspect that fraudulent payments are to be made from a childcare account; and

(b) HMRC have reasonable grounds to believe that it will not be possible to recover top-up payments if the order is not made.

(6) In a case within paragraph (3), the person who wishes to open a childcare account may apply to HMRC for an account restriction order to be made in relation to the active childcare account.

(7) An account restriction order—

(a) may impose a restriction on the account for the period specified in the order;

(b) may provide that the restriction does not apply in circumstances specified in the order.

(8) HMRC may revoke an account restriction order if they consider it is no longer required, either on their own initiative or on an application by the account-holder.

(9) An account-holder may make such an application if—

(a) the period for applying for a review of, or for bringing an appeal against, the order has elapsed; and

(b) the circumstances of the account-holder have changed since that period elapsed.

19 Closure of a childcare account

(1) A childcare account must be closed if—

(a) two years have elapsed since the end of the last entitlement period for which there was a valid declaration of eligibility; or

(b) one year has elapsed since the end of the entitlement period during which the child ceased to be a qualifying child.

(2) At the time a childcare account is closed, whether under paragraph (1) or otherwise—

(a) the top-up element of the funds remaining in the account at that time, calculated in accordance with section 21 (calculating the top-up element of payments etc), must be paid to HMRC; and

(b) the relevant percentage of the total funds in the account at that time, calculated in accordance with section 22 (withdrawals), must be returned to the account-holder.

(3) Where an account-holder has died, the relevant percentage to be returned under paragraph (2)(b) must be paid to the account-holder's personal representatives.

20 Power to obtain information or documents

(1) A notice (an "information notice") under section 26(1) (power to obtain information or documents) may be addressed to, and may require information or documents from, any of the following persons—

(a) an account-holder or a person who has applied to open a childcare account (the "applicant");
(b) a person named in a declaration of eligibility or application as the partner of an account-holder or applicant;
(c) an agent of a person specified in sub-paragraph (a) or (b);
(d) a person who provides, or has provided, childcare to an account-holder or has received a payment from a childcare account;
(e) an employer or former employer of an account-holder or applicant;
(f) an employer who provides, or has provided, a relevant childcare scheme within the meaning of section 12(2) and any person who provides, or has provided, services to the employer in connection with the provision to employees of such a scheme;
(g) a person or body of persons who HMRC reasonably expect can provide information or documents relevant to an allegation of, or an inquiry into, non-compliance with the Act.

(2) An information notice must—

(a) specify the information or documents required and the form and manner in which they are to be provided;
(b) set out the reason why HMRC are requesting the information or documents; and
(c) specify the period within which the person must provide the information or documents.

(3) The period in paragraph (2)(c) must be at least 30 days beginning with the day on which the notice is issued.

21 Disqualification orders: meaning of "relevant benefit"

For the purposes of section 49 (disqualification orders), a "relevant benefit" is—

(a) any "disqualifying benefit" within the meaning given in section 6A(1) of the Social Security Fraud Act 2001; or
(b) any benefit, payment, allowance, pension or credit made under the law of another EEA state which is substantially similar in character to those specified in paragraph (a).

22 Use of electronic communications

(1) Except as provided by paragraphs (3) and (4), an application to open a childcare account (an "application") or a declaration of eligibility (a "declaration") must be made to HMRC by electronic communications.

(2) Payments made from a childcare account by an account provider in respect of qualifying childcare must be made by electronic communications.

(3) Paragraph (1) does not apply if HMRC are satisfied that the person making the application or declaration—

(a) is prevented, by a court order, from sending information by electronic communications;
(b) holds beliefs which are incompatible with the use of electronic communications; or
(c) is unable to send information by electronic communications by reason of—
  (i) age;
  (ii) disability;
  (iii) inability to operate a computer effectively in a manner that cannot be remedied by the use of assisted digital support; or
  (iv) living in a remote location so that it is not reasonably practicable to use electronic communications.

(4) An application or declaration made by a person to whom paragraph (3) applies must be made to HMRC in the manner specified by HMRC.

(5) If an application or declaration is made by electronic communications, it shall be treated for the purposes of the Act and these Regulations as having been made, and received by HMRC, on the date on which it is recorded on an official computer system.

(6) In this regulation—

(a) "assisted digital support" includes advice and assistance on how to make an application or declaration by means of electronic communications and entering a person's information into the service on that person's behalf;
(b) "electronic communications" includes any communications by means of an electronic communications service;
(c) "electronic communications service" has the meaning given by section 32 of the Communications Act 2003;
(d) "official computer system" means a computer system maintained by or on behalf of HMRC—
  (i) to send or store information; or
  (ii) to process or store information.

2015/549

FINANCE ACT 2014 (HIGH RISK PROMOTERS PRESCRIBED INFORMATION) REGULATIONS 2015

Made . . . . *5 March 2015*

Laid before the House of Commons . . . . *6 March 2015*

Coming into force . . . . *27 March 2015*

The Commissioners for Her Majesty's Revenue and Customs in exercise of the powers conferred by sections 249(3), (10) and (11), 253(2) and (4), 257(2), 259(9), 260(7), 261(2), 268(1), 282(4) and 283(1) of the Finance Act 2014 make the following Regulations:

Commentary—*Simon's Taxes* **A7.254**.

1 Citation, commencement and interpretation

(1) These Regulations may be cited as the Finance Act 2014 (High Risk Promoters Prescribed Information) Regulations 2015 and come into force on 27th March 2015.

(2) In these Regulations—

"accounting period" for the purposes of corporation tax has the same meaning as that given in sections 9 to 12 of the Corporation Tax Act 2009 and "beginning of accounting period" and "end of accounting period" shall be construed accordingly;

"the Act" means the Finance Act 2014;

"audiovisual formats" means any method of presenting information that uses an audible and visible format including broadcasting by electronic means or transmission over, or publication on, the internet; "chargeable period" shall be construed—

(a) for the purposes of annual tax on enveloped dwellings, in accordance with section 94(8) of the Finance Act 2013;

(b) for the purposes of petroleum revenue tax, in accordance with section 1(3) of the Oil Taxation Act 1975;

"effective date" has the meaning given by section 119 of the Finance Act 2003;

"tax year" means a year beginning on 6th April and ending on the following 5th April;

2 Prescribed publication or correspondence

(1) The following publications and correspondence are prescribed for the purposes of subsection (10) of section 249 of the Act (publication by monitored promoter)—

(a) any publication or correspondence that—

(i) with the exception of correspondence with HMRC, contains information about any relevant arrangements or any relevant proposal offered or promoted by the monitored promoter;

(ii) is shown, given or sent to clients or prospective clients in relation to any relevant arrangements or any relevant proposal (whether or not the relevant arrangements or relevant proposal is provided by the monitored promoter);

(iii) is shown, given or sent to intermediaries or prospective intermediaries in relation to any relevant arrangements or any relevant proposal (whether or not the relevant arrangements or relevant proposal is provided by the monitored promoter);

(b) any correspondence with—

(i) a professional body referred to in paragraph 8(3) of Schedule 34 to the Act of which the monitored promoter is a member, prospective member or former member and which concerns any relevant arrangements or any relevant proposal;

(ii) a regulatory authority referred to in paragraph 9(3) of Schedule 34 to the Act which the monitored promoter is regulated by and which concerns the monitored promoter's conduct in respect of any relevant arrangements or any relevant proposal.

(2) In paragraph (1)—

(a) "correspondence" includes correspondence in writing or by electronic means;

(b) "publication" means publication in any format (including audiovisual formats).

3 Information publicised by a monitored promoter

(1) For the purposes of subsection (11) of section 249 of the Act (publication by monitored promoter), the prescribed form and manner is as set out in paragraphs (2), (3) and (4).

(2) Notification given under subsection (1) of section 249 must—

(a) be in writing;

(b) set out clearly and precisely the information required to be stated under paragraphs (a) and (b) of section 249(1) of the Act so that—

(i) in respect of the information required by section 249(1)(a) of the Act, it is clear that the promoter is being monitored by HMRC because it breached a condition or conditions of a conduct notice identified under section 249(1)(b) of the Act, and

(ii) in respect of the information required by section 249(1)(b) of the Act, the specific details of each of the conditions which it has been determined that the person has failed to comply with.

(3) In respect of subsection (3) of section 249 of the Act, the monitored promoter shall publish on the internet the information mentioned in paragraph (a) and (b) of section 249(1) of the Act. The published information must—

(a) appear in a prominent position on the monitored promoter's or other websites promoting, or providing information on, the activities of the promoter;

(b) if in writing, be legible;

(c) if in an audiovisual format, be clearly audible or visible;

(d) not in any way be concealed;

(e) be specifically referred to or included in any promotional material (of whatever kind or format);

(f) not be presented in a way that it promotes the activity of tax avoidance.

(4) The information to be provided under subsection (10) of section 249 of the Act and regulation 2 to these Regulations (prescribed publication or correspondence) must—

(a) be prominent and not in any way be concealed;

(b) if in writing, be legible;

(c) if in an audiovisual format, be clearly audible or visible;

(d) not be presented in a way that promotes the activity of tax avoidance.

4 Duty of persons to notify the Commissioners: prescribed information

(1) The following information is prescribed for the purposes of paragraphs 2(b) and 4(b) of section 253 of the Act (duty of persons to notify the Commissioners)—

(a) the full name and address (including postcode) of the person reporting the promoter reference number;

(b) the promoter reference number which is the subject of the report;

(c) the type of tax in respect of which the person expects to obtain a tax advantage;

(d) the unique identifier (as to the meaning of which see paragraph (3)(a));

(e) the relevant date of the transaction(s) (as to the meaning of which see paragraph (3)(b));

(f) a declaration that the information provided is correct and complete to the best of the knowledge and belief of the person making the report;

(g) the signature of the person making the report;

(h) the full name of the person signing the report;

(i) the date on which the report is made.

(2) For relevant arrangements involving annual tax on enveloped dwellings, stamp duty land tax or stamp duty reserve tax transactions under regulation 4 of the Stamp Duty Reserve Tax Regulations 1986 (notice of charge and payment), the unique identifier in sub-paragraph (1)(d) is to be replaced by the following additional prescribed information—

(a) for annual tax on enveloped dwellings—

(i) title number or numbers of the dwelling associated with the relevant arrangements;

(ii) full address of the dwelling including the postcode sufficient to be able to identify it;

(b) for stamp duty land tax—

(i) the unique transaction reference number (if a land transaction return has been submitted to HMRC at the time the prescribed information is provided);

(ii) title number or numbers of the land associated with the relevant arrangements;

(iii) full address or situation of the land including (where available) the postcode, or information sufficient that the land can be uniquely identified;

(c) for stamp duty reserve tax transactions a full description of the shares or securities associated with the relevant arrangements, including the—

(i) number of shares or securities;

(ii) class or classes of the shares;

(iii) name of the company or other body to which the shares relate;

(iv) nominal value;

(v) consideration paid.

(3) For the purposes of paragraph (1)—

(a) "unique identifier" is to be construed as follows—

(i) where the promoter reference number is not reported in a tax return for an individual, the national insurance number and unique tax reference number of the person making the report;

(ii) where the promoter reference number is not reported in a tax return for a trust or company, the unique tax reference number for the trust or company (as the case may be);

(iii) for inheritance tax purposes, the unique tax reference number and any inheritance tax reference previously allocated by HMRC to the person making the report;

(iv) for stamp duty reserve tax transactions authorised by different arrangements under regulation 4A of the Stamp Duty Reserve Tax Regulations 1986, the unique transaction reference provided by the reporting system under the authorised arrangements;

(b) "relevant date of the transaction(s)" means—

(i) in respect of capital gains tax or income tax, the date on which the tax year, in which the relevant arrangements enable or seek to enable a tax advantage to be obtained, ends;

(ii) in respect of corporation tax, with the exception of partnerships where one or more of the partners is a company, either the date on which the accounting period, in which the relevant arrangements enable or seek to enable a tax advantage to be obtained, ends, or, where the company does not have an accounting period, the date of the first transaction forming part of the relevant arrangements;

(iii) in respect of corporation tax in relation to partnerships, including where one or more of the partners is a company, the date on which the tax year in which the relevant arrangements enable or seek to enable a tax advantage to be obtained, ends;

(iv) in respect of annual tax on enveloped dwellings, the date on which the chargeable period, in which the relevant arrangements enable or seek to enable a tax advantage to be obtained, ends;

(v) in respect of inheritance tax, the date of the first transaction forming part of the relevant arrangements;

(vi) in respect of stamp duty land tax, the effective date of the land transaction that forms part of the relevant arrangements that enable a tax advantage to be obtained;

(vii) in respect of stamp duty reserve tax, the date of the transaction that forms part of the relevant arrangements that enable a tax advantage to be obtained;

(viii) in respect of petroleum revenue tax, the end of each chargeable period within which a tax advantage may arise.

5 Report of promoter reference number: prescribed form and manner

(1) The report made under paragraphs 2(b) and 4(b) of section 253 of the Act (duty of persons to notify the Commissioners) must be made in the form prescribed in Schedule 1 to these Regulations. A separate report must be made for each tax which the relevant arrangements enable or seek to enable an advantage to be obtained.

(2) The completed report must be sent by post to one of the addresses listed in Schedule 2 to these Regulations.

6 Report of promoter reference number: prescribed time

(1) A report under section 253 of the Act (duty of persons to notify the Commissioners) must be made by the deadlines set out in paragraphs (2), (3) and (4).

(2) Where a tax return for an individual, partnership, trustee, company or a return for the purposes of the annual tax on enveloped dwellings is not submitted by the date in section 253(3)(a) or (b) of the Act in relation to the period within which a tax advantage may arise, the report must be made by the end of the fifth working day following the date on which the return was required to be submitted.

(3) Where there is no tax return covering the period within which a tax advantage may arise, then the report must be made—

(a) in the case of an individual, partnership or trustee, by 31st January following the end of each tax year within which a tax advantage may arise;

(b) in the case of a company, not later than 12 months from the end of each accounting period within which a tax advantage may arise;

(c) in the case of an annual tax on enveloped dwellings return, not later than 30 days from the first day of the chargeable period in which the person is within the charge or would have been within the charge but for the relevant arrangements, for each period within which a tax advantage may arise.

(4) For the purposes of inheritance tax, stamp duty land tax, stamp duty reserve tax, and petroleum revenue tax, the report must be made—

(a) for inheritance tax, not later than the sixth month after the end of the month which the first transaction under the relevant arrangements was entered into;

(b) for stamp duty land tax, not later than 30 days from the effective date of each land transaction which forms part of the relevant arrangements within which a tax advantage may arise;

(c) for stamp duty reserve tax—

(i) in respect of transactions under regulation 4 of the Stamp Duty Reserve Tax Regulations 1986, not later than the time that the notice of the charge to tax is due to be made to HMRC (the accountable date), or

(ii) where a transaction is authorised by different arrangements under regulation 4A of the Stamp Duty Reserve Tax Regulations 1986, not later than the seventh day of the month after the month in which the charge to tax occurred or would have occurred but for the relevant arrangements;

(d) for petroleum revenue tax, not later than 7 days from the end of each chargeable period within which a tax advantage may arise.

(5) Where a company does not have an accounting period, the report must be made not later than 24 months from the date of the first transaction which forms part of the relevant arrangements and annually thereafter for any period within which a tax advantage arises.

(6) For the purposes of paragraph (2), "working day" means a day that is not a Saturday or Sunday, Christmas Day, Good Friday or any day that is a bank holiday under the Banking and Finance Dealings Act 1971.

7 Ongoing duty to provide information: prescribed information and documents

(1) The following information is prescribed for the purposes of section 257(2) of the Act (ongoing duty to provide information following HMRC notice)—

(a) the name or names by which the monitored promoter refers to the monitored arrangements or monitored proposal;

(b) a summary description of the monitored arrangements or monitored proposal and how they are intended to result in a tax advantage;

(c) a detailed description of each part of the monitored arrangements or monitored proposal and the details of how they are intended to result in a tax advantage;

(d) the legislative provisions (whether in primary legislation, secondary legislation or both) that the person identified in section 257(1) contends provide the basis for the intended tax advantage under the monitored arrangements or monitored proposal;

(e) any reference number allocated under section 311 of the Finance Act 2004 (arrangements to be given reference number);

(f) if the monitored arrangements or monitored proposal have not been disclosed under Part 7 of the Finance Act 2004 (disclosure of tax avoidance schemes), an explanation as to why the monitored arrangements or monitored proposal have not been disclosed;

(g) if the monitored arrangements or monitored proposal are funded by or will require funding from third parties, the names and addresses of the third parties, the level of funding required and the date on which the third parties agreed to provide funding;

(h) the name and address of any person (including any legal advisers) consulted in respect of the monitored arrangements or monitored proposal;

(i) the name and address of any person otherwise involved in planning, organising or operating the monitored arrangements and detailed information on the involvement and role of that person;

(j) a list of each and every fee paid or to be paid by clients to use or participate in the monitored arrangements with a description of what each fee is charged for or will be charged for;

(k) if not included in (b), (c) or (d) above, a list of all taxes in respect of which it is expected to obtain a tax advantage.

(2) The following are prescribed documents for the purposes of section 257(2) of the Act—

(a) standard letters and templates of documents to be sent to clients regarding the monitored arrangements and monitored proposals;

(b) documentation which is designed or intended to be used in the operation of the monitored arrangements and monitored proposals;

(c) copies of all documents used to market, promote or advertise the monitored arrangements and monitored proposals;

(d) all correspondence which has been sent to, or received from, a client or prospective client or other person involved in the monitored arrangements and monitored proposals and which concerns the arrangements or the proposal;

(e) all correspondence which has been sent to, or received from, any other person which concerns the monitored arrangements and monitored proposals or matters related to the monitored arrangements and monitored proposals;

(f) any agreement signed or otherwise entered into by each client in respect of the monitored arrangements and monitored proposals.

(3) "Prescribed documents" in paragraph (2) includes documents produced in writing or by electronic means.

8 Monitored promoters: prescribed client information

The following information is prescribed for the purposes of section 259(9)(b) of the Act (monitored promoters: duty to provide information about clients)—

(a) where C is an individual, the national insurance number and unique tax reference number identifying C;

(b) where C is a trust, partnership or company, the unique tax reference number identifying C;

(c) in compliance with subsection (3) of section 265 of the Act (duty to provide information to monitored promoter), where C has not provided the information in sub-paragraph (a) or (b), whether or not C has informed the monitored promoter that C has neither a national insurance number nor a unique tax reference number;

(d) the date on which C became a client of the monitored promoter within the meaning of section 259(5) of the Act;

(e) the date on which C entered into transactions referred to in subsection (7) of section 259 of the Act;

(f) the date on which C informed the monitored promoter of the information required by section 265(2) or 265(3) of the Act or, if provided to the monitored promoter earlier, the earlier date;

(g) whether C was a direct client of the monitored promoter, or was acting through an intermediary ("I") and the name and address of I;

(h) the fee or commission paid or payable by C to I in respect of the monitored arrangements or monitored proposals.

9 Intermediaries: prescribed client information

The following information about the person ("C") is prescribed for the purposes of section 260(7)(b) of the Act (intermediaries: duty to provide information about clients)—

(a) where the intermediary knows the national insurance number, unique tax reference number or both which identify C, those numbers;

(b) the name, address and the promoter reference number of the monitored promoter in respect of the monitored proposals referred to in section 260(1);

(c) the name and address of any other intermediary from which, or to which, C has been referred in relation to the monitored proposals;

(d) the date on which the information referred to in section 260(5) was communicated;

(e) any fee or commission paid or payable to I in respect of the monitored proposals.

10 Enquiry following provision of client information: prescribed information

(1) The information set out in paragraphs (2), (3) and (4) is prescribed for the purposes of section 261(2) of the Act (enquiry following provision of client information).

(2) Where the authorised officer's suspicion referred to in section 261(1)(b) of the Act is that information has not been provided in respect of a person under section 259 of the Act, the prescribed information under section 261(2) of the Act is—

(i) the information prescribed by regulation 8;

(ii) the reason or reasons why the prescribed information in regulation 8 was not provided as required by section 259.

(3) Where the authorised officer's suspicion referred to in section 261(1)(b) of the Act is that information has not been provided in respect of a person under section 260 of the Act, the prescribed information under section 261(2) of the Act is—

(a) the information prescribed by regulation 9;

(b) the date of any transaction under section 261(2) of the Act implementing the relevant arrangements or relevant proposal;

(c) the reason or reasons why the prescribed information in regulation 9 was not provided as required by section 260 of the Act.

11 Copy documents: prescribed conditions or exceptions

(1) The following conditions are prescribed for the purposes of section 268(1) of the Act (production of documents: compliance)—

(a) the copy document must be an exact copy of the original document, without any amendments, corrections or deletions;

(b) the original document must be retained by the person as required;

(c) the person required to produce the document must not alter the original document or allow it to be altered.

(2) Subject to other provisions in the Tax Acts on the retention of records and documents, the original document under paragraph (1)(b) shall be retained—

(i) for the purposes of sections 255 and 257 of the Act until such time as the monitoring notice or replacement monitoring is withdrawn under section 245 of the Act;

(ii) for the purposes of section 262 of the Act, until such time as the conduct notice or replacement conduct notice is withdrawn under section 240 of the Act or expires at the end of the period under section 241(2) of the Act.

(3) Nothing in paragraph (1)(a) prevents a person from redacting information in a copy document which is privileged information within the meaning given in section 271 of the Act.

SCHEDULE 1

REPORT OF PROMOTER REFERENCE NUMBERS

Regulation 5(1)

HM Revenue & Customs

Report of promoter reference number

When to use this form

Please fill in this form if you have been given a promoter reference number (PRN) and you expect to get a tax advantage from one of the promoter's tax avoidance schemes. It is important that you report the PRN to HM Revenue & Customs (HMRC). If you fail to report a PRN to HMRC we will ask you to pay a penalty.

Details about the promoter reference number

If you complete a personal, trust partnership, company or Annual Tax on Enveloped Dwellings (ATED) tax return, you usually have to report the PRN in your tax return.

If your tax return is late you will need to report the PRN on this form within 5 working days of the date the return was due.

If there is no return covering the period, you will need to make the report by:

- 31 January following the end of the tax year for which you expect to get a tax advantage
- 12 months after the end of the accounting period for which you expect to get a tax advantage
- 30 days of the first day in the chargeable period for which you expect to get a tax advantage on which you were within the charge to the ATED

If exceptionally, you are a company and do not have an accounting period, you will need to report the PRN within 24 months of the first transaction forming part of the tax avoidance scheme (and annually thereafter).

When to report the PRN

You will need to use this form to report the PRN if the tax advantage is expected to arise for:

- Inheritance Tax – within 6 months of the end of the month in which the first transaction forming part of the tax avoidance scheme took place
- Petroleum Revenue Tax – within 7 days of the end of the half-year chargeable period in which you expect to get a tax advantage
- Stamp Duty Land Tax – within 30 days of the transaction forming part of the tax avoidance scheme or for which you expect to get a tax advantage
- Stamp Duty Reserve Tax – where the transaction is not settled through CREST, with the notice of the charge to tax but no later than 7 days from the end of the month in which the transaction took place
- Stamp Duty Reserve Tax – within 7 days of the end of the month in which the transaction took place where the transaction is settled through CREST

For details on where to submit this form, please read 'Where to send this form' on page 3.

Your details

1 **Full name** use capital letters

2 **Full address**

Postcode

Your promoter reference number

3 **Promoter reference number (PRN)**

About the tax advantage

4 Which tax do you expect to get a tax advantage?
Please tick 1 box and provide the relevant details in box 5 below. Enter:

Annual Tax on Enveloped Dwellings	the title number or numbers and the full address of the property (if the property does not have a postcode you must provide sufficient detail to allow us to identify the property)
Capital Gains Tax	your Unique Taxpayer Reference (UTR) and National Insurance number (for trustees or partnerships, enter the UTR for the trust or partnership)
Corporation Tax	the UTR of the company (or if the form is being sent by a partnership the UTR of the partnership)
Income Tax	your UTR and National Insurance number (for trustees or partnerships, enter the UTR for the trust or partnership)
Inheritance Tax	your UTR and any Inheritance Tax reference previously allocated to you by HM Revenue & Customs
Petroleum Revenue Tax	the name of the oil field for which you expect to get a tax advantage and your participator's reference for that field
Stamp Duty Land Tax	the title number or numbers, full address of the property (if the property does not have a postcode you must provide sufficient detail to allow us to identify the property) and the Unique Transaction Reference number
Stamp Duty Reserve Tax	(if the transaction is **not** settled through CREST) a full description of the shares or securities, including number, class, nominal value, the name of the company to which the shares relate and consideration paid (if the transaction is settled through CREST) the CREST transaction reference ID

5 Unique identifier details - include reference number(s), names and addresses as explained in question 4 above

Details of transaction

Consider when you expect to get a tax advantage and enter the end of the accounting period or transaction date for:

- Annual Tax on Enveloped Dwellings – the end of the chargeable period
- Capital Gains Tax, Income Tax and trustees and partnerships – the end of the tax year
- Corporation Tax – the end of the accounting period unless exceptionally there is no accounting period – then enter the date of the first transaction
- Inheritance Tax – the date of the first transaction
- Petroleum Revenue Tax – the end of the half-year chargeable period
- Stamp Duty Land Tax or Stamp Duty Reserve Tax – the date of the transaction

6 **Date of transaction** DD MM YYYY or **End of period** DD MM YYYY

Declaration

The information I have given on this form is correct and complete to the best of my knowledge and belief.

Full name of signatory use capital letters

Signature

Date DD MM YYYY

Where to send this form

Please return your completed form to:

HM Revenue & Customs
Counter Avoidance Directorate
CA Intelligence S0528
PO Box 194
BOOTLE
L69 9AA

In the case of Stamp Duty Reserve Tax where the transaction is not settled through CREST, send this form to:

HM Revenue & Customs
SDRT Compliance Team
9th Floor, City Centre House
30 Union Street
BIRMINGHAM
B2 4AR

Page 3

SCHEDULE 2

ADDRESSES TO SEND THE PROMOTER REFERENCE NUMBER REPORTS

Regulation 5(2)

In respect of arrangements involving stamp duty reserve tax transactions under regulation 4 of the Stamp Duty Reserve Tax Regulations (1986), the completed report under section 253 must be sent to—

HM Revenue and Customs
SDRT Compliance Team

9th Floor, City Centre House
30 Union Street
BIRMINGHAM
B2 4AR

For all other reports made under section 253 (including those involving stamp duty reserve tax transactions under regulation 4A of the Stamp Duty Reserve Tax Regulations (1986)), the completed report must be sent to—

HM Revenue and Customs
Counter Avoidance Directorate
CA Intelligence S0528
PO Box 194
BOOTLE
L69 9AA

2015/616

MARKET VALUE OF SHARES, SECURITIES AND STRIPS REGULATIONS 2015

Made . . . . *9 March 2015*
Laid before the House of Commons . . . . *10 March 2015*
Coming into force . . . . *6 April 2015*

The Treasury make the following Regulations in exercise of the powers conferred by section 272(3) and (4) of the Taxation of Chargeable Gains Act 1992 and section 450 of the Income Tax (Trading and Other Income) Act 2005.

1 Citation, commencement, effect and interpretation

(1) These Regulations may be cited as the Market Value of Shares, Securities and Strips Regulations 2015 and come into force on 6th April 2015.
(2) These Regulations have effect where the date of valuation falls on or after that date.
(3) These Regulations apply—
(*a*) subject to regulation 2(2), for the purposes of the Taxation of Chargeable Gains Act 1992, to determine the market value of shares or securities which are included in the official UK list,
(*b*) for the purposes of Chapter 8 of Part 4 of the Income Tax (Trading and Other Income) Act 2005 (profits from deeply discounted securities), to determine the market value of a strip, and
(*c*) for the purposes of section 445(1) the Income Tax (Trading and Other Income) Act 2005 (strips of government securities), to determine the market value of a security exchanged for strips of that security.

2 Shares, securities or strips included in the official UK list

(1) The market value at any time of shares, securities or strips which are included in the official UK list is—
(*a*) on any day the Stock Exchange is open, the lower of the two prices shown in the Stock Exchange Daily Official List for that day as the closing price for the shares, securities or strips on that day plus one-half of the difference between those two figures, and
(b) on any day the Stock Exchange is closed, that value on the latest previous day on which it was open.
(2) But these Regulations do not apply to determine the market value of shares or securities for the purposes of the Taxation of Chargeable Gains Act 1992 where in consequence of special circumstances the closing prices quoted in the Stock Exchange Daily Official List are by themselves not a proper measure of market value of the shares or securities.

3 Securities or strips listed on recognised stock exchange outside the United Kingdom

(1) The market value at any time of securities or strips which are not included in the official UK list but are listed on a foreign stock exchange is—
(*a*) on any day the exchange is open, the price shown in the foreign exchange list for that day as the closing price for the securities or strips on that day (or if more than one price is shown the lower price plus one-half of the difference between those two figures), and
(*b*) on any day the exchange is closed, that value on the latest previous day on which it was open.
(2) If securities are quoted in more than one foreign exchange list—
(*a*) any foreign exchange list published for a foreign stock exchange which is regarded as the major exchange for such securities is to be used for those purposes in preference to any other such list, but

(*b*) if no exchange is regarded as the major exchange, any such list published for a foreign stock exchange in the territory in which the issuing company is resident is to be used for the purposes of these Regulations in preference to any other such list.

(3) If a strip or a security exchanged for strips of that security is quoted in more than one foreign exchange list—

(*a*) any such list published for a foreign stock exchange in the territory of the issuing government is to be used for the purposes of these Regulations in preference to any other such list, and

(*b*) any such list published for a foreign stock exchange which is regarded as the major exchange in that territory for such strips or securities is to be used for those purposes in preference to any other such list.

(4) In this regulation—

"foreign exchange list" means any publication which performs in the case of a foreign stock exchange a function equivalent, or broadly similar, to that performed by the Stock Exchange Daily Official List,

"foreign stock exchange" means a recognised stock exchange in a territory outside the United Kingdom on which securities or strips are traded.

4 Consequential amendments

(*revokes* SI 2006/964 reg 108(2))

2015/725

COMMUNITY AMATEUR SPORTS CLUBS REGULATIONS 2015

Made . . . . *16 March 2015*

Coming into force . . . . *1 April 2015*

The Treasury make the following Regulations in exercise of the powers conferred by sections 659(2A), (2B) and (2C), 660(5A)(d), (5B), (8), (9)(a) and (b), (10) and (12) and 660A(1), (3) and (4) of the Corporation Tax Act 2010 and paragraph 8(1), (2)(a) and (3) of Schedule 21 to the Finance Act 2013.

A draft of this instrument was laid before, and approved by a resolution of, the House of Commons in accordance with section 660(11) of the Corporation Tax Act 2010 and paragraph 8(4) of Schedule 21 to the Finance Act 2013.

PART 1
PRELIMINARY

1 Citation, commencement, effect and interpretation

(1) These Regulations may be cited as the Community Amateur Sports Clubs Regulations 2015 and come into force on 1st April 2015.

(2) Regulations 6, 10 and 14 have effect on and after 1st April 2015.

(3) Regulations 2 to 5, 7 to 9, 11 to 13 and 15 to 19 are to be treated as having effect on and after 1st April 2010.

(4) In these Regulations "CTA 2010" means the Corporation Tax Act 2010.

PART 2
MEANING OF "COMMUNITY AMATEUR SPORTS CLUB" AND "REGISTERED CLUB"

2 Amendment of CTA 2010

Regulations 3 and 4 amend Chapter 9 of Part 13 of CTA 2010 (community amateur sports clubs).

3 Meaning of community amateur sports club

(*amends* CTA 2010 658)

4 Income condition

(*inserts* CTA 2010 661CA)

PART 3
COSTS ASSOCIATED WITH MEMBERSHIP OF A CLUB AND MEMBERSHIP FEES

5 Costs associated with membership of a club

(1) The amount specified for a year for the purposes of section 659(2A) of CTA 2010 (costs associated with membership of a club) is £520.

(2) The costs associated with membership of a club for a given year consist of amounts A and B together.

(3) Amount A is the membership fees for a member for that year (see regulation 8).

(4) Amount B is the sporting activity costs for that year (see regulation 9).

6 Limit on membership fees

A club is not entitled to be registered as a community amateur sports club under section 658 of CTA 2010 if it receives membership fees exceeding £1,612 in respect of any member in respect of any year.

7 Apportionment of limits in regulations 5(1) and 6

(1) Where—

(a) the membership fees charged by the club vary by reference to duration of the membership, or

(b) the club offers memberships for periods of greater or less than one year,

the limits specified in regulations 5(1) (costs associated with membership of a club) and 6 (limit on membership fees) are proportionately reduced or increased accordingly.

(2) If a club chooses to reduce the participation threshold (see regulation 19), the limits specified in regulations 5(1) (costs associated with membership of a club) and 6 (limit on membership fees) are proportionally reduced by reference to the number of weeks the club is open.

8 Membership fees

(1) "Membership fees" means—

(a) any joining fees, and

(b) any supplementary fees, subscriptions or other costs,

charged by the club as a condition of membership.

(2) In calculating the costs associated with membership—

(a) where a club charges a membership fee which relates to more than one member, that fee is to be divided the number of members to which it relates, and

(b) where a club charges membership fees which vary, whether by reference to the duration of the membership or otherwise, the highest fee is to be used.

9 Sporting activity costs

(1) "Sporting activity costs", for a year, means charges, fees or other costs that a member would be required to pay or incur to participate fully in the club's activities for the year (other than membership fees).

(2) Sporting activity costs include, in particular—

(a) any fee that a member is required to pay to use the club's facilities for the purpose of playing an eligible sport;

(b) any fee charged to play an eligible sport in a match;

(c) any fee charged by the club for the use of specialist equipment required to play an eligible sport;

(d) where it is not provided free of charge—

(i) the cost of hiring or purchasing any specialist equipment required to play an eligible sport; and

(ii) the cost of hiring or purchasing any clothing required by the club to play an eligible sport; and

(e) the cost of insurance cover required by the club to play an eligible sport.

(3) For the purposes of paragraph (2)(c) and (d)(i) specialist equipment includes equipment required for the purposes of health and safety.

(4) Sporting activity costs paid or incurred—

(a) under paragraph (2)(a), (b) or (c); and

(b) where equipment is hired rather than purchased, under paragraph (2)(d),

are calculated by reference to a member participating fully in the club's activities.

(5) For the purposes of this regulation, a member is not to be treated as participating fully in the club's activities unless the member has the opportunity to participate—

(a) where a club chooses to apportion the participation threshold in accordance with regulation 19(1) (apportionment of days of participation: seasonal sports), on at least one occasion in each week the club is open; or

(b) where a club chooses not to apportion the participation threshold in accordance with regulation 19(1), on at least 52 occasions.

PART 4

MEANING OF "ORGANISED ON AN AMATEUR BASIS"

10 Meaning of "organised on an amateur basis"

(*amends* CTA 2010 660)

11 Limit on paid players

(1) For the purposes of section 660(1)(ba) of CTA 2010 (limit on paid players), a club does not exceed the limit on paid players if the total amount paid to persons paid to play for the club in any year, in respect of activities undertaken for the club, does not exceed £10,000.

(2) For the purposes of this regulation, "year" means an accounting period of the club.
(3) But where the club's accounting period is shorter than 12 months the limit in paragraph (1) is proportionately reduced.
(4) If a club is a registered club for only part of an accounting period, this regulation has effect as if that part were a separate accounting period.
(5) An individual is only regarded as a person paid to play for a club ("a paid player") if conditions A to E (see regulation 12) are met.
(6) The amounts paid to paid players are to be calculated in accordance with regulation 13.

12 Paid players

(1) Condition A is that the individual is paid to play an eligible sport for the club.
(2) Condition B is that all amounts paid to the player to play for the club—
- (a) are agreed on an arm's length basis, or
- (b) if not agreed on an arm's length basis, are agreed in circumstances where the features of the agreement which cause it to be otherwise than on an arm's length basis, when taken together, are more advantageous to the club than if the agreement had been on an arm's length basis.

(3) Condition C is that the individual is not—
- (a) a manager (within the meaning of section 661B(2) of CTA 2010) or an officer of the club, or
- (b) connected with a manager or an officer of the club.

(4) Condition D is that the individual is not paid by one registered club to play for another registered club.
(5) Condition E is that the individual is not paid by a person other than the club, or a person connected to the club, to play for the club.

13 Calculating amounts paid to a player

(1) This regulation makes provision in relation to the calculation of the total amount paid to paid players in any year for the purposes of the limit specified in regulation 11(1).
(2) Amounts paid to a paid player means any amounts paid to the player for playing for the club which would be—
- (a) earnings within Chapter 1 of Part 3 of ITEPA 2003, or
- (b) treated as earnings under Chapters 2 to 11 of Part 3 of ITEPA 2003 (the benefits code).

(3) Amounts paid to a paid player to play for the club include payments made in respect of the following—
- (a) training for the purposes of playing an eligible sport, and
- (b) travel for the purposes of playing or training for an eligible sport.

(4) But amounts paid to a player do not include the reimbursement of reasonable and necessary travel or subsistence expenses referred to in section 660(4)(g) of CTA 2010.
(5) Amounts paid to a paid player include any payments made pursuant to an agreement or understanding (whether or not legally enforceable).
(6) For the purposes of this regulation the paid player is to be treated as employed to play for the club and the provisions of ITEPA 2003 referred to in paragraph (2) are to apply accordingly.

14 Travel and subsistence

(1) Subsistence expenses are neither necessary nor reasonable for the purposes of section 660(4)(g) of CTA 2010 if the journey is a reasonable daily journey.
(2) In this regulation, a "reasonable daily journey" means one where the total travel time to and from the match from the club base is no more than four hours.
(3) In paragraph (2), the "club base" is the address for the club registered with Her Majesty's Revenue and Customs under section 658 of CTA 2010.
(4) Travel and subsistence expenses incurred in connection with away matches are neither necessary nor reasonable for the purposes of section 660(4)(g) of CTA 2010 unless the main purpose of the match or matches is the promotion of, and participation in, an eligible sport.

PART 5

CLUBS CONSISTING MAINLY OF SOCIAL MEMBERS

15 Clubs not to be regarded as meeting the main purpose test

For the purposes of section 660A(1) of CTA 2010 (clubs consisting mainly of social members), the percentage specified is 50%.

16 Participating in the sporting activities of the club

(1) For the purposes of section 660A(2) (definition of social member) of CTA 2010, "participating in the sporting activities of the club" means—
- (a) participating in an eligible sport organised by the club;
- (b) being a match official for an eligible sport for the club;
- (c) coaching club members in an eligible sport;
- (d) providing first aid to persons playing an eligible sport for the club;
- (e) being an accompanying individual (within the meaning of section 660(4A)(b) of CTA 2010) for the club;

(f) driving a club vehicle, or a vehicle hired by the club, to transport persons listed in sub-paragraphs (a) to (e) or equipment on behalf of the club for the purposes of the participation in activities referred to in those sub-paragraphs;

(g) preparing or maintaining club sporting facilities or equipment for use in an eligible sport;

(h) being an officer, or a committee member, of the club; or

(i) undertaking a relevant training course for the purposes of sub-paragraphs (a) to (d), (g) or (h).

(2) Where an event planned by the club is cancelled due to extreme circumstances outside the club's control then planned participation in that event is deemed to be participation.

17 Occasional participation in the sporting activities of the club

(1) For the purposes of section 660A(2) of CTA 2010, a member participates only occasionally in the sporting activities of the club in an accounting period if that member does not meet the participation threshold for that accounting period.

(2) For the purposes of this regulation, the participation threshold is participation in the sporting activities of the club on the required number of days in the accounting period of the club.

(3) The required number of days is determined in accordance with table 1.

Table 1

Number of weeks in the club's accounting period	Participation threshold (number of days)
4 or fewer	1
5 to 8	2
9 to 12	3
13 to 16	4
17 to 20	5
21 to 24	6
25 to 28	7
29 to 31	8
32 to 35	9
36 to 39	10
40 to 43	11
44 or more	12

(4) If the club is registered for only part of an accounting period, that part is to be treated as a separate accounting period for the purposes of this regulation.

18 Apportionment of days of participation: duration of membership

(1) Where a person is a member of a club for only part of an accounting period, the participation threshold in regulation 17 is determined by using table 2 in place of table 1 for the purposes of that regulation.

(2) For the purposes of calculating weeks of membership for table 2, a person is a member during any given week if that person is a member for any part of that week.

Table 2

Number of weeks of membership	Participation threshold (number of days)
4 or fewer	1
5 to 8	2
9 to 12	3
13 to 16	4
17 to 20	5
21 to 24	6
25 to 28	7
29 to 31	8
32 to 35	9
36 to 39	10

Number of weeks of membership	Participation threshold (number of days)
40 to 43	11
44 or more	12

19 Apportionment of days of participation: seasonal sports

(1) Where a club is only open for part of the accounting period, that club may choose to reduce the participation threshold in regulation 17 for all members and use table 3 for the purposes of that regulation in place of table 1.

(2) If a club chooses to reduce the participation threshold under paragraph (1) and a person is a member of a club for only part of an accounting period, then regulation 18 applies to determine the participation threshold for that person and table 2 in regulation 18 is used in place of table 3.

(3) A club is open during any given week if any of the facilities provided by the club are made available to members for any part of that week.

Table 3

Number of weeks the club is open	Participation threshold (number of days)
4 or fewer	1
5 to 8	2
9 to 12	3
13 to 16	4
17 to 20	5
21 to 24	6
25 to 28	7
29 to 31	8
32 to 35	9
36 to 39	10
40 to 43	11
44 or more	12

2015/866

OFFSHORE ASSET MOVES PENALTY (SPECIFIED TERRITORIES) REGULATIONS 2015

Made . . . . at 5.20 pm on 26 March 2015
Coming into force . . . . 27 March 2015
Laid before the House of Commons . . . . . . at 12.30 pm on 27 March 2015

The Treasury make the following Regulations in exercise of the powers conferred by paragraph 4(5) of Schedule 21 to the Finance Act 2015.

1 Citation and commencement

These Regulations may be cited as the Offshore Asset Moves Penalty (Specified Territories) Regulations 2015 and come into force on 27th March 2015.

2 Territories specified

The territories listed in the Schedule to these Regulations are specified for the purposes of Schedule 21 to the Finance Act 2015.

SCHEDULE

Regulation 2

Territories specified

. . . [1], Andorra, Anguilla, Antigua and Barbuda, Argentina, Aruba, Australia, Austria, The Bahamas, [Bahrain,][1] Barbados, Belgium, Belize, Bermuda, Brazil, British Virgin Islands, Brunei Darussalam, Bulgaria, Canada, Cayman Islands, Chile, China, Colombia, [Cook Islands,][1] Costa Rica, Croatia, Curaçao, Cyprus, Czech Republic, Denmark, Dominica, Estonia, Faroe Islands,

Finland, France, Germany, [Ghana,][1] Gibraltar, Greece, Greenland, Grenada, Guernsey, Hong Kong, Hungary, Iceland, India, Indonesia, Ireland, Isle of Man, Israel, Italy, Japan, Jersey, Korea (South), [Kuwait,][1] Latvia, [Lebanon,][1] Liechtenstein, Lithuania, Luxembourg, Macau, Malaysia, Malta, Marshall Islands, Mauritius, Mexico, Monaco, Montserrat, [Nauru,][1] Netherlands (including Bonaire, Sint Eustatius and Saba) New Zealand (not including Tokelau), Niue, Norway, [Panama,][1] Poland, Portugal, Qatar, Romania, Russia, Saint Kitts and Nevis, Saint Lucia, Saint Vincent and the Grenadines, Samoa, San Marino, Saudi Arabia, Seychelles, Singapore, Sint Maarten, Slovak Republic, Slovenia, South Africa, Spain, Sweden, Switzerland, Trinidad and Tobago, Turkey, Turks and Caicos Islands, United Arab Emirates, . . .[1], Uruguay[, Vanuatu][1].

Amendments—[1] Entries for "Albania," and "United States of America (not including overseas territories and possessions)," revoked, and entries inserted, by the Offshore Asset Moves Penalty (Specified Territories) (Amendment) Regulations, SI 2017/989 reg 3 with effect from 3 November 2017.

2015/878

INTERNATIONAL TAX COMPLIANCE REGULATIONS 2015

Made . . . . *24 March 2015*
Laid before the House of Commons . . . . *25 March 2015*
Coming into force . . . . *15 April 2015*

The Treasury make these Regulations in exercise of the powers conferred by section 136 of the Finance Act 2002 and section 222(1), (2) and (3) of the Finance Act 2013:

Introductory

1 Citation, commencement, effect and interpretation

(1) These Regulations may be cited as the International Tax Compliance Regulations 2015 and come into force on 15th April 2015.

(2) These Regulations have effect for and in connection with the implementation of obligations arising under the agreements and arrangements listed in paragraph (3) and apply separately in relation to each of those agreements or arrangements except where the context otherwise requires.

(3) The agreements and arrangements are—

(*a*) Council Directive 2011/16/EU ("the DAC"),

[(*b*) the following arrangements relating to the CRS—

(i) the arrangements entered into, at the date these Regulations come into force, by the United Kingdom with another territory for the exchange of tax information for the purposes of the adoption and implementation of the CRS; and

(ii) the arrangements for the exchange of information arising from the agreements entered into by the EU at the date these Regulations come into force, regarding the adoption and implementation of the CRS as between member States and other territories,][2]

[(3A) In these Regulations, "the CRS" means the common reporting standard for automatic exchange of financial account information developed by the Organisation for Economic Co-operation and Development.][2]

(*c*) the agreement reached between the Government of the United Kingdom of Great Britain and Northern Ireland and the Government of the United States of America to improve international tax compliance and to implement FATCA, signed on 12th September 2012 ("the FATCA agreement").

(4) These Regulations have effect from—

(*a*) 1st January 2016 in relation to the DAC and the CRS, and

(*b*) 15th April 2015 in relation to the FATCA agreement.

(5) In these Regulations, a reference to "relevant agreement" means such agreement or arrangement referred to in paragraph (3) as the context requires, as that agreement or arrangement has effect from time to time.

[(5A) For the purposes of these Regulations—

(*a*) "financial institution" has the same meaning in relation to the FATCA agreement as it does in section 1.1471–5(*e*)(1)(i)-(iv) of the US Treasury Regulations, and

(*b*) "investment entity" has the same meaning in relation to the FATCA agreement as it does in the US Treasury Regulations.][1]

(6) Any expression which is defined in a relevant agreement but not in section 222 or 235 of FA 2013 or in these Regulations has the same meaning in these Regulations as in the relevant agreement.

Amendments—[1] Para (5A) inserted by the International Tax Compliance (Amendment) Regulations, SI 2015/1839 reg 2(1), (2) with effect from 20 November 2015.

[2] Para (3)(*b*) substituted, and para (3A) inserted, by the International Tax Compliance (Amendment) Regulations, SI 2017/598 regs 2, 3 with effect from 17 May 2017. Para (3)(*b*) previously read as follows—

"(*b*) the Multilateral Competent Authority Agreement on the Automatic Exchange of Financial Account Information signed by the Government of the United Kingdom of Great Britain and Northern Ireland on 29th October 2014 in relation to agreements with the participating jurisdictions listed in the table in Schedule 1 to improve international tax compliance based on the standard for automatic exchange of financial account information developed by the Organisation for Economic Co-Operation and Development ("the CRS"),".

2 Meaning of "reportable account"

(1) In these Regulations, a "reportable account" means—

(*a*) an account which is a reportable account within the meaning of the relevant agreement,

(*b*) in relation to a reporting financial institution under the DAC or the CRS, an account that is a pre-existing entity account with an account balance or value that does not exceed US$250,000 as of 31st December 2015, and

(*c*) in relation to a reporting financial institution under the FATCA agreement, an account meeting the description at paragraph II.A, III.A or IV.A of Annex I of the agreement.

(2) But—

(*a*) in relation to a reporting financial institution under the DAC or the CRS, an account listed as an excluded account in Schedule 2 is not a reportable account,

(*b*) in relation to a reporting financial institution under the FATCA agreement, an account is not a reportable account if—

(i) the account holder is deceased or is a personal representative (within the meaning of section 989 of ITA 2007),

(ii) the account is held to comply with an order or judgment made or given in legal proceedings, or

(iii) the funds held in the account are held solely as security for the performance of a party's obligation under a contract for the disposal of an estate or interest in land or of tangible moveable property, . . . [2]

[(*ba*) in relation to a reporting financial institution under the CRS, an account meeting the description at Section III(A) of the CRS, and][2]

[(*c*) in relation to a reporting financial institution—

(i) for the purposes of the DAC or the CRS, a dormant account (other than an annuity contract) with a balance that does not exceed US$1,000, or

(ii) an account within [paragraph (1)(*b*), (*ba*) or (*c*)][2],

is not a reportable account for a calendar year if there is an election by the institution which has effect for that year to treat all such accounts, or a clearly identified group of such accounts, as not being reportable accounts.][1]

(3) An election under paragraph (2)(*c*) must be made for each calendar year for which the election is to have effect in the return required by regulation 6 for that year.

(4) The reporting financial institution must apply the account balance aggregation and currency rules in the relevant agreement for the purposes of determining whether an account maintained by the institution is within paragraph (1)(*b*) or (*c*).

(5) The account balance aggregation and currency rules are—

(*a*) in Section VII.C of Annex I to the DAC,

(*b*) in Section VII.C of the CRS, and

(*c*) in paragraph VI.C of Annex I to the FATCA agreement.

(6) In applying the account balance aggregation and currency rules for the purposes of a relevant agreement and these Regulations, an account balance that has a negative value is treated as having a nil value.

(7) In determining the balance or value of an account denominated in a currency other than US dollars for the purposes of a relevant agreement and for the purposes of paragraph (1)(*b*) or (*c*), the institution must translate the relevant dollar threshold amounts into the other currency by reference to the spot rate of exchange on the date for which the institution is determining the threshold amounts.

(8) For the purposes of a relevant agreement and these Regulations, an account held by an individual as a partner of a partnership is treated as an entity account and is not treated as an individual account.

[(9) An account is a dormant account if—

(*a*) the account holder has not initiated a transaction with regard to the account or any other account held by the account holder with the reporting financial institution in the previous three years,

(*b*) the account holder has not communicated with the reporting financial institution regarding the account or any other account held by the account holder with the reporting financial institution in the previous six years,

(*c*) the account is treated as a dormant account under the reporting financial institution's normal operating procedures, and

(*d*) in the case of a cash value insurance contract, the reporting financial institution has not communicated with the account holder regarding the account or any other account held by the account holder with the reporting financial institution in the previous six years.][1]

Amendments—[1] Para (2)(*c*) substituted and para (9) inserted by the International Tax Compliance (Amendment) Regulations, SI 2015/1839 reg 2(1), (3), (4) with effect from 20 November 2015.

[2] In para (1)(*b*), word "and" at the end revoked, para (1)(*ba*) inserted, and in para (2)(*c*)(ii), words substituted for words "paragraph (1)(*b*) or (*c*)", by the International Tax Compliance (Amendment) Regulations, SI 2017/598 regs 2, 4 with effect from 17 May 2017.

Obligations in relation to financial accounts

3 Due diligence requirements

[(1) A reporting financial institution must establish and maintain arrangements that are designed to identify in respect of a financial account—

(*a*) the territory in which an account holder or a controlling person is resident for the purposes of—

(i) income tax,

(ii) corporation tax, or

(iii) any tax imposed by the law of that territory that is of a similar character to either of those taxes, and

(*b*) whether it is a reportable account.

(2) A reporting financial institution must comply with paragraph (1) by applying the due diligence procedures set out in the relevant agreement.

(2A) A reporting financial institution must keep a record of—

(*a*) the steps taken to comply with this regulation, and

(*b*) the information collected in the course of identifying the matters referred to in paragraph (1).

(2B) A reporting financial institution must keep the records required by paragraph (2A) for a period of—

(*a*) in respect of an account identified as a reportable account, five years beginning with the end of the year in which the account is last included in a return made under regulation 6(1), or

(*b*) in respect of an account which is not a reportable account, five years beginning with the end of the last year in which the reporting financial institution relied upon the due diligence procedures to treat the account as not being a reportable account.][1]

(3) The due diligence procedures are—

(*a*) in relation to a reporting financial institution under the DAC, set out in Annexes I and II to the DAC,

[(*b*) in relation to a reporting financial institution under the CRS, set out in Sections II to VII of the CRS,][2]

(*c*) in relation to a reporting financial institution under the FATCA agreement, set out in Annex I to that agreement.

[(4) A reporting financial institution under the CRS must—

(*a*) apply the rules in Section VII(B) of Annex I of the DAC instead of the equivalent rules in the CRS treating the reference to "each Member State" in that Section as a reference to "the United Kingdom", and

(*b*) also apply the rules in Annex II of the DAC treating the references to "Member State" in that Annex as references to "participating jurisdiction" as defined in the CRS.

(4A) A reporting financial institution under the CRS must in respect of the following terms in the CRS—

(*a*) "pre-existing account", and

(*b*) "related entity",

apply to those terms the definitions as they appear in Annex I of the DAC instead of the definitions as they appear in the CRS.

(4B) Where a provision of the CRS does not specify a deadline for the requirements of that provision to be satisfied but there is an equivalent provision in Annex I of the DAC which does specify a deadline, then that deadline applies for the purposes of the provision in the CRS.][1]

(5) In applying the due diligence procedures, accounts within [regulation 2(1)(*b*), (*ba*) and (*c*)][1] in respect of which no election under regulation 2(2)(*c*) has been made are treated as new accounts or pre-existing accounts as the case may be.

Amendments—[1] Paras (1)–(2B) substituted for previous paras (1), (2), para (3)(*b*) substituted, paras (4)–(4B) substituted for previous para 4, and in para (5), words substituted for words "regulation 2(1)(*b*) and (*c*)", by the International Tax Compliance (Amendment) Regulations, SI 2017/598 regs 2, 5 with effect from 17 May 2017. Paras (1), (2) previously read as follows—

"(1) A reporting financial institution must establish and maintain arrangements that are designed to identify reportable accounts.

(2) Such arrangements must—

(*a*) identify the territory in which an account holder or a controlling person is resident for income tax or corporation tax purposes or for the purposes of any tax imposed by the law of that territory that is of a similar character to either of those taxes,

(*b*) apply the due diligence procedures set out in the relevant agreement, (*c*) secure that the information obtained in accordance with this regulation, or a record of the steps taken to comply with this regulation, in relation to any financial account is kept for a period of six years beginning with the end of the year in which the arrangements applied to the financial accounts.".

Para (3)(*b*) previously read as follows—

"(*b*) in relation a reporting financial institution under to the CRS, set out in Sections 2 to 7 of the CRS,".

Para (4) previously read as follows—

"(4) A reporting financial institution under the CRS must also apply the rules in Annex II of the DAC treating references to "Member State" in that Annex as references to "Participating Jurisdiction".".

4 Modification of due diligence requirements: the DAC and the CRS

A reporting financial institution under the DAC and the CRS may—

(*a*) apply the due diligence procedures for new accounts to pre-existing accounts, and

(*b*) apply the due diligence procedures for high value accounts to low value accounts.

5 Modifications of due diligence requirements: FATCA agreement

(1) A reporting financial institution under the FATCA agreement may modify the due diligence requirements as follows.

(2) In the case of an account within paragraph II.B or II.C of Annex I to the FATCA agreement, the due diligence requirements do not include the requirement to carry out the electronic search described in paragraph II.B (1) of that Annex if—

(*a*) the institution has established that the account holder is a specified U.S. person from documentary evidence mentioned in paragraph VI.D of Annex I of the agreement, and

(*b*) it has done so in order to meet its obligations under a Qualifying Intermediary agreement as mentioned in that paragraph.

(3) In the case of an account with paragraph II.D or II.E of Annex I to the FATCA agreement, the due diligence requirements do not include the requirement to carry out the electronic searches described in paragraph II.B (1) or II.D (1) of that Annex or the requirement to carry out the paper record search described in paragraph II.D (2) of that Annex if—

(*a*) the institution has established the account holder is a specified U.S. person from documentary evidence mentioned in paragraph VI.D of that Annex, and

(*b*) it has done so in order to meet its obligations under a Qualifying Intermediary agreement as mentioned in that paragraph.

(4) The reporting financial institution may rely on evidence that a person is a specified U.S. person obtained in relation to another financial account if the due diligence procedures in the relevant U.S. Treasury Regulations would allow such reliance.

(5) For the purposes of this regulation references to the documentary evidence set out in paragraph VI.D of Annex I of the FATCA agreement are to be treated as if the words "other than a Form W-8 or W-9" were omitted.

6 Reporting obligation

[(1) A reporting financial institution must, in respect of the first reporting year and every following calendar year, make a return setting out the information required to be reported under the relevant agreement in relation to—

(*a*) each reportable account that is maintained by the institution at any time during the calendar year in question, and

(*b*) each pre-existing account identified as a reportable account by the institution at any time during the calendar year in question.][1]

(2) The first reporting year is—

(*a*) the calendar year 2014 in relation to an account identified as a reportable account for the purposes of the FATCA agreement,

(*b*) the calendar year 2016 in relation to an account identified as a reportable account for the purposes of the DAC or the CRS.

(3) The information required to be reported is—

(*a*) in relation to an account identified as a reportable account for the purposes of the DAC, set out in Section I of the Annex I to the DAC,

[(*b*) in relation to an account identified as a reportable account for the purposes of the CRS, set out in Section I of the CRS (ignoring paragraph F of Section I),][1]

(*c*) in relation to an account identified as a reportable account for the purposes of the FATCA agreement, set out in Article 2(2) of that agreement.

(4) The return must be submitted electronically in accordance with regulation 7 on or before 31stMay of the year following the calendar year to which the return relates.

(5) For the purposes of the information required to be reported under the relevant agreement—

(*a*) interest includes any amount that is chargeable as interest under Part 4 of ITTOIA 2005,

(*b*) references to the balance or value of an account include a nil balance or value, and (*c*) references to paying an amount include crediting an amount.

Amendments—[1] Paras (1), (3)(*b*) substituted by the International Tax Compliance (Amendment) Regulations, SI 2017/598 regs 2, 6 with effect from 17 May 2017. The substitution of para (1) applies in respect of the calendar year 2016 and subsequent calendar years for the purposes of the FATCA agreement (SI 2017/598 reg 1(2)). Para (1) previously read as follows—

"(1) A reporting financial institution must, in respect of the first reporting year and every following calendar year, make a return setting out the information required to be reported under the relevant agreement in relation to every reportable account that is maintained by the institution at any time during the calendar year in question.".

Para (3)(*b*) previously read as follows—

"(*b*) in relation to an account identified as a reportable account for the purposes of the CRS, set out in Section I of the CRS,".

7 Electronic return system

(1) The return must be made electronically using an electronic return system.

(2) The form and manner of an electronic return system is specified in specific or general directions given by the Commissioners for Her Majesty's Revenue and Customs.

(3) A return which is made otherwise than in accordance with paragraphs (1) and (2) is treated as not having been made.

(4) An electronic return system must incorporate an electronic validation process.

(5) Unless the contrary is proved—

(*a*) the use of an electronic return system is presumed to have resulted in the making of the return only if this has been successfully recorded as such by the relevant electronic validation process,

(*b*) the time of making the return is presumed to be the time recorded as such by the relevant electronic validation process, and

(*c*) the person delivering the return is presumed to be the person identified as such by any relevant feature of the electronic return system.

(6) A return made behalf of a reporting financial institution is taken to have been made by that institution, unless the institution proves that the return was made without the institution's authority.

Directions—HMRC have issued the following Directions outlined how reporting financial institutions must make an electronic return as part of the international tax compliance systems.

Directions concerning the form and manner of the electronic return system by which an electronic return is made

1 The Commissioners for Her Majesty's Revenue and Customs make these Directions in accordance with—

(a) regulation 7 of the International Tax Compliance Regulations 2015 (SI 2015/878) (electronic return system); and

(b) regulation 8A of the International Tax Compliance (Crown Dependencies and Gibraltar) Regulations 2014 (SI 2014/520) (electronic return system).

2 In these Directions "reporting financial institution" has the same meaning as in the International Tax Compliance Regulations 2015 or the International Tax Compliance (Crown Dependencies and Gibraltar) Regulations 20142, as the case may be.

3 A reporting financial institution, or a person making a return on behalf of a reporting financial institution, must register and then submit the return required to satisfy the reporting obligations of the institution under regulation 6 or 9 of the International Tax Compliance Regulations 2015 or regulation 8 of the International Tax Compliance (Crown Dependencies and Gibraltar) Regulations 2014 under the electronic return system at www.gateway.gov.uk.

4 These Directions have effect in relation to returns made on or after 1 July 2015.

Commentary—*Simon's Taxes* **A6.1205A.**

8 Modifications of reporting requirements: FATCA

(1) In relation to an account identified as a reportable account for the purposes of the FATCA agreement, the information required to be reported is modified as follows.

(2) In the case of all reportable accounts for the calendar year 2014, the information required to be reported is provided in Article 3(3)(*a*)(1) of the FATCA agreement.

(3) In the case of custodial accounts for the calendar year 2015, the information required to be reported is provided in Article 3(3)(*a*)(2) of the FATCA agreement.

(4) In the case of pre-existing accounts—

(*a*) for calendar years before 2017—

(i) there is no requirement to include a U.S. federal taxpayer identifying number if the reporting financial institution does not hold that number, but

(ii) if the account holder is an individual whose date of birth the institution does hold, the institution must include the account holder's date of birth instead, and

(*b*) for the calendar year 2017 and subsequent years, if a reporting financial institution does not hold a U.S. federal taxpayer identifying number that it is required to report, the institution must obtain that number from the account holder.

9 Additional due diligence and reporting obligations in relation to payments to a non-participating financial institution: FATCA

(1) In relation to a reporting financial institution under the FATCA agreement, the due diligence requirements and the information required to be reported are modified as follows in relation to payments to a non-participating financial institution.

(2) A reporting financial institution must establish and maintain arrangements that are designed to identify payments made by the institution to a non-participating financial institution in the calendar year 2015 or 2016,

(3) "Payment" here does not include consideration given by the reporting financial institution for the provision of goods or services to it.

(4) A reporting financial institution must apply the due diligence procedures set out in paragraph IV.D (3) of Annex I of the FATCA agreement to identify whether a financial institution is a non-participating financial institution.

(5) In respect of any case in the calendar years 2015 and 2016 when a reporting financial institution is within the terms of sub-paragraph 1(*e*) of Article 4 of the FATCA agreement, the institution must make a disclosure of information in accordance with the requirements of that sub-paragraph.

(6) A reporting financial institution must in respect of each of the calendar years 2015 and 2016 prepare a return setting out the information set out in Article 4(1)(*b*) of the FATCA agreement.

(7) The return must be submitted electronically in accordance with regulation 7 on or before 31st May of the year following the calendar year to which the return relates.

(8) For the purposes of this regulation, "non-participating financial institution" includes anyone who is treated as a non-participating financial institution as a result of sub-paragraph 5(*a*) of Article 4 of the FATCA agreement.

10 Notification to individual reportable persons

(1) A reporting financial institution must notify each individual reportable person or individual specified U.S. person that information relating to that person which is required to be reported under regulation 6 will be reported to HMRC and may be transferred to the government of another territory in accordance with a relevant agreement.

(2) The notification must be made by 31st January in the calendar year following the first year in which the account held by the individual is a reportable account maintained by the reporting financial institution.

11 Non-resident reporting financial institution's UK representative

(1) If a reporting financial institution is not resident in the United Kingdom, the obligations of the institution under these Regulations are to be treated as if they were also the obligations of any UK representative of the institution.

(2) "UK representative" has the same meaning as it has in—

(*a*) Chapter 6 of Part 22 of CTA 2010, in relation to a reporting financial institution that is within the charge to corporation tax, and

(*b*) Chapter 2C of Part 14 of ITA 2007, in relation to any other reporting financial institution.

(3) For the purposes of this regulation—

(*a*) a reporting financial institution which is a partnership is resident in the United Kingdom if the control and management of the business of the partnership as a reporting financial institution takes place there, and

(*b*) a reporting financial institution which is not a partnership is resident in the United Kingdom if it is resident in the United Kingdom for corporation tax or income tax purposes.

12 Use of service providers

A reporting financial institution may use a service provider to undertake the due diligence requirements under regulations 3 to 5 and the reporting obligations under regulations 6 and 9, but in such cases those obligations continue to be the obligations of the institution.

[*Client notification obligations*

12A Interpretation of regulations 12A to 12F

(1) In this regulation and regulations 12B to 12F—

"connected person" means a person connected with the specified financial institution, specified relevant person or relevant person in question within the meaning of "connected" given in section 1122 of CTA 2010;

"officer", in relation to a specified relevant person or a connected person, includes—

(i) where a person is a body corporate, a director, manager or secretary;

(ii) where a person is a partnership, a partner.

"offshore advice or services" has the meaning given in paragraph (2);

"overseas person" means a person who would be a specified financial institution or specified relevant person if they carried on business in the United Kingdom;

"relevant period" means the period of one year ending with 30th September 2016;

"specified client" means an individual who is identified—

(i) as a specified client of a specified financial institution under regulation 12B, or

(ii) as a specified client of a specified relevant person under regulation 12C;

. . . [2]

. . . [2]

(2) "Offshore advice or services" means advice or services relating to—

(*a*) a financial account in a participating jurisdiction or the United States of America;

(*b*) a source of relevant foreign income, as defined by section 830 of ITTOIA 2005, arising from a participating jurisdiction or the United States of America;

(*c*) a source of employment income, as defined by section 7(2) of ITEPA 2003, arising from a participating jurisdiction or the United States of America;

(*d*) an asset, as defined by section 21 of TCGA 1992, which is held or situated in a participating jurisdiction or the United States of America.

(3) [In these Regulations][2] "specified financial institution" means a financial institution under the DAC or the CRS, unless that financial institution is—

(*a*) a non-reporting financial institution under the DAC or the CRS, or

(*b*) a financial institution that, if it was an NFE, would be an active NFE under Section VIII(D)(8)(*h*) of Annex I to the DAC or Section VIII(D)(9)(*h*) of the CRS (organisations with charitable or other non-profit purposes).

(4) [In these Regulations][2] "specified relevant person" means a relevant person who, in the relevant period, has—

(*a*) provided offshore advice or services in the course of business, or

(*b*) referred an individual to a connected person outside the United Kingdom for the provision of advice or services relating to the individual's personal tax affairs.

(5) For the purpose of determining whether a person is a specified relevant person—

(*a*) offshore advice or services must be disregarded if—

(i) they were provided to an individual by the relevant person only in connection with the preparation and delivery on behalf of that individual of returns and accounts, statements and documents required under section 8 of TMA 1970,

(ii) they were provided to an employee or officer of the relevant person, or

(iii) they were provided to an employee or officer of a connected person;

(*b*) a referral must be disregarded if—

(i) the individual was an employee or officer of the relevant person, or

(ii) the individual was an employee or officer of a connected person.

(6) Where a specified financial institution is also a specified relevant person, regulations 12B to 12F apply as if it were only a specified financial institution.][1]

Amendments—[1] Regulations 12A–12F and preceding crosshead inserted by the International Tax Compliance (Amendment) Regulations, SI 2016/899 regs 2, 3 with effect from 30 September 2016.

[2] In para (1), definitions of "specified financial institution", "specified relevant person" revoked, and in paras (3), (4), words inserted, by the International Tax Compliance (Amendment) Regulations, SI 2017/598 regs 2, 7 with effect from 17 May 2017. Definitions previously read as follows—

""specified financial institution" has the meaning given in paragraph (3);".

""specified relevant person" has the meaning given in paragraph (4).".

[12B Identifying specified clients: specified financial institution

(1) A specified financial institution must identify all of its specified clients.

(2) In order to identify its specified clients, a specified financial institution must use either—

(*a*) the services approach set out in paragraphs (3) and (4), or

(*b*) the high value approach set out in paragraph (5).

(3) An individual is a specified client of a specified financial institution under the services approach if—

(*a*) the specified financial institution reasonably believes that the individual was resident in the United Kingdom for income tax purposes for the tax year 2015–16 or will be so resident for the tax year 2016–17,

(*b*) the individual is an account holder with the specified financial institution on 30th September 2016, and

(*c*) in any part of the relevant period, the specified financial institution has—

(i) maintained a financial account in a participating jurisdiction or the United States of America in relation to which the individual is an account holder, or

(ii) referred the individual to another specified financial institution (wherever located) for the other specified financial institution to provide a financial account for the individual in a participating jurisdiction or the United States of America.

(4) In paragraph (3)(*c*)(i), "financial account" does not include a financial account which the specified financial institution is prevented by legal or regulatory obligations in force on 30th September 2016 from providing as a new account.

(5) An individual is a specified client of a specified financial institution under the high value approach if—

(*a*) the specified financial institution reasonably believes that the individual was resident in the United Kingdom for income tax purposes for the tax year 2015–16 or will be so resident for the tax year 2016–17, and

(*b*) the individual is an account holder of a high value account maintained by the specified financial institution on 30th September 2016.][1]

Amendments—[1] Regulations 12A–12F and preceding crosshead inserted by the International Tax Compliance (Amendment) Regulations, SI 2016/899 regs 2, 3 with effect from 30 September 2016.

[12C Identifying specified clients: specified relevant person

(1) A specified relevant person must identify all of that person's specified clients.

(2) In order to identify its specified clients, a specified relevant person must use either—

(*a*) the specific approach set out in paragraphs (3) and (4), or

(*b*) the general approach set out in paragraphs (5) and (6).

(3) An individual is a specified client of a specified relevant person under the specific approach if—

(*a*) at any time in the relevant period, the specified relevant person has—

(i) provided the individual with offshore advice or services relating to the individual's personal tax affairs, or

(ii) referred the individual to a connected person outside the United Kingdom for the provision of such advice or services, and

(*b*) paragraph (4) does not apply to the individual.

(4) This paragraph applies to an individual if—

(*a*) the specified relevant person reasonably believes that the individual was not resident in the United Kingdom for income tax purposes for the tax year 2015–16 and will not be so resident for the tax year 2016–17,

(*b*) on 30th September 2016 the specified relevant person has no reasonable expectation of providing further advice or services to the individual, or

(*c*) the specified relevant person has prepared and delivered, or reasonably expects to prepare and deliver, a return under section 8 of TMA 1970 on behalf of the individual disclosing the effect of the offshore advice or services referred to in paragraph (3)(*a*).

(5) An individual is a specified client of a specified relevant person under the general approach if—

(*a*) the specified relevant person has provided the individual with any advice or services relating to the individual's personal tax affairs in the relevant period, and

(*b*) paragraph (6) does not apply to the individual.

(6) This paragraph applies to an individual if—

(*a*) the specified relevant person reasonably believes that the individual was not resident in the United Kingdom for income tax purposes for the tax year 2015–16 and will not be so resident for the tax year 2016–17, or

(b) on 30th September 2016 the specified relevant person has no reasonable expectation of providing further advice or services to the individual.

(7) A specified relevant person may choose to exclude an individual from being a specified client under the general approach if the specified relevant person has prepared and delivered, or reasonably expects to prepare and deliver, a return under section 8 of TMA 1970 on behalf of the individual in respect of the tax year to which the advice or services relate.][1]

Amendments—[1] Regulations 12A–12F and preceding crosshead inserted by the International Tax Compliance (Amendment) Regulations, SI 2016/899 regs 2, 3 with effect from 30 September 2016.

[12D Client exchange of tax information notifications

(1) A specified financial institution or specified relevant person must make client exchange of tax information notifications to all of its specified clients on or before 31st August 2017.

(2) Paragraph (1) does not apply in relation to a specified client if—

(*a*) a specified financial institution or specified relevant person is aware that a connected person, who is not an overseas person, has already made a client exchange of tax information notification to that specified client, or

(*b*) despite maintaining proper records, a specified financial institution or specified relevant person holds insufficient information on 30th September 2016 to be able to contact the specified client.][1]

Amendments—[1] Regulations 12A–12F and preceding crosshead inserted by the International Tax Compliance (Amendment) Regulations, SI 2016/899 regs 2, 3 with effect from 30 September 2016.

[12E Client exchange of tax information notifications: overseas persons

(1) A specified financial institution or specified relevant person having control of an overseas person must take all such steps as are reasonably open to it to ensure that the overseas person makes a client exchange of tax information notification on or before 31st August 2017 to all individuals to whom paragraph (2) applies.

(2) This paragraph applies to an individual who—

(*a*) the overseas person reasonably believes to have been resident in the United Kingdom for income tax purposes at any time in the relevant period, and

(*b*) either—

(i) was an account holder in relation to a financial account maintained by the overseas person in a participating jurisdiction or the United States of America in the relevant period, or

(ii) was provided with offshore advice or services relating to the individual's personal tax affairs by the overseas person in the relevant period.][1]

Amendments—[1] Regulations 12A–12F and preceding crosshead inserted by the International Tax Compliance (Amendment) Regulations, SI 2016/899 regs 2, 3 with effect from 30 September 2016.

[12F Making client exchange of tax information client notifications

(1) A client exchange of tax information notification is made to a specified client or an individual to whom regulation 12E(2) applies if—

(*a*) it is in the form set out in Part 1 of Schedule 3,

(*b*) it is accompanied by a covering message which includes—

(i) the name of the specified client, and

(ii) the statement set out in the relevant paragraph of Part 2 of that Schedule, and

(*c*) it is given in accordance with paragraph (3) or (4).

(2) The relevant paragraph in Part 2 of Schedule 3 is—

(*a*) paragraph 2 in the case of a client exchange of tax information notification made by a specified financial institution or an overseas person who would be a specified financial institution if they carried on business in the United Kingdom, or

(*b*) paragraph 3 in the case of a client exchange of tax information notification made by a specified relevant person or an overseas person who would be a specified relevant person if they carried on business in the United Kingdom.

(3) A client exchange of tax information notification is given in accordance with this paragraph if it is sent or supplied in a paper copy.

(4) A client exchange of tax information notification is given in accordance with this paragraph if it is given by email by a specified relevant person who—

(*a*) wholly or mainly communicated with individuals by e-mail when providing advice or services to them in the relevant period, and

(*b*) reasonably believes that the specified client will become aware of the content of a client exchange of tax information notification given to them by e-mail.

(5) If it appears appropriate to a specified financial institution, a specified relevant person or an overseas person, the client exchange of tax information notification and covering message set out in Schedule 3 may be translated into a language other than English or produced in a Braille or audible form.][1]

Amendments—[1] Regulations 12A–12F and preceding crosshead inserted by the International Tax Compliance (Amendment) Regulations, SI 2016/899 regs 2, 3 with effect from 30 September 2016.

[12G Provision of information

(1) In order to determine whether or not the obligations arising under these Regulations have been complied with, an officer of Revenue and Customs may require a reporting financial institution, UK representative, specified financial institution or specified relevant person to provide such information as the officer reasonably requires as specified by written notice.

(2) The information required by notice under paragraph (1) must be provided—

(*a*) within such period, being no less than 14 days, and

(*b*) by such means and in such form,

as is reasonably required by the officer of Revenue and Customs.][1]

Amendments—[1] Regulation 12G inserted by the International Tax Compliance (Amendment) Regulations, SI 2017/598 regs 2, 8 with effect from 17 May 2017.

[12H Liable persons

(1) Where in regulations 13, 14, 15 and 16—

(*a*) a reporting financial institution, UK representative or specified financial institution is made liable to a penalty, and

(*b*) the institution or representative is a partnership or trust,

the liability to the penalty falls upon a liable person of the institution or representative.

(2) In paragraph (1), "liable person" means, in relation to—

(*a*) a partnership, a partner of the partnership,

(*b*) a trust which is not a collective investment scheme, a trustee of the trust, or

(*c*) a trust which is a collective investment scheme, a trustee, manager or operator of the scheme.

(3) In this regulation "collective investment scheme" means—

(*a*) an investment trust within the meaning of the Corporation Tax Acts,

(*b*) a venture capital trust within the meaning of Part 6 of ITA 2007, or

(c) any arrangements that are a "collective investment scheme" within the meaning of the Financial Services and Markets Act 2000.][1]

Amendments—[1] Regulation 12H inserted by the International Tax Compliance (Amendment) Regulations, SI 2017/598 regs 2, 9 with effect from 17 May 2017.

Penalties for breach of obligations

[13 Penalties for failure to comply with Regulations

(1) If a reporting financial institution or UK representative fails to comply with any obligation under regulations 2 to 11 or regulation 12G, the institution or representative is liable to a penalty of £300.

(2) If a specified financial institution or specified relevant person fails to comply with any obligation under regulations 12B to 12E, the institution or person is liable to a penalty of £3,000.

(3) If a specified financial institution or specified relevant person fails to comply with any obligation under regulation 12G, the institution or person is liable to a penalty of £300.][1]

Amendments—[1] Regulation 13 substituted by the International Tax Compliance (Amendment) Regulations, SI 2017/598 regs 2, 10 with effect from 17 May 2017. Regulation 13 previously read as follows—

> "**13 Penalties for failure to comply with Regulations**(1) A person is liable to a penalty of £3,000 if the person fails to comply with any obligation under regulations 12B to 12E.
>
> (2) A person is liable to a penalty of £300 if the person fails to comply with any other obligation under these Regulations.".

14 Daily default penalty

[Subject to regulation 21][1] if—

(a) a penalty under regulation 13 is assessed, and

(b) the failure in question continues after the person [liable to the penalty][1] has been notified of the assessment,

[that person is liable][1] to a further penalty, for each subsequent day on which the failure continues, of an amount not exceeding £60 for each such day.

Amendments—[1] Words at the beginning inserted, and words substituted for words "the person has been notified" and words "the person is liable", by the International Tax Compliance (Amendment) Regulations, SI 2017/598 regs 2, 11 with effect from 17 May 2017.

15 Penalties for inaccurate information

(1) [A reporting financial institution or UK representative][1] is liable to a penalty not exceeding £3,000 if—

(a) in complying with an obligation under regulation 6 [the institution or representative][1] provides inaccurate information, and

(b) condition A, B or C is met.

(2) Condition A is that the inaccuracy is—

(a) due to a failure to comply with the due diligence requirements in regulation 3 (as modified by regulations 4 or 5 where those regulations apply), or

(b) deliberate . . . [1].

(3) Condition B is that the [reporting financial institution or UK representative][1] knows of the inaccuracy at the time the information is provided but does not inform HMRC at that time.

(4) Condition C is that the [reporting financial institution or UK representative][1]—

(a) discovers the inaccuracy some time later, and

(b) fails to take reasonable steps to inform HMRC.

Amendments—[1] In para (1), words substituted for words "a person" and words "the person", in para (2)(b), words "on the part of the person" revoked, and in paras (3), (4), words substituted for word "person", by the International Tax Compliance (Amendment) Regulations, SI 2017/598 regs 2, 12 with effect from 17 May 2017.

16 FATCA agreement penalty: non-participating financial institutions

(1) In relation to payments that are required to be identified under regulation 9(2), [a reporting financial institution or UK representative][1] is liable to—

(a) a penalty of £300 for each failure to report a payment, and

(b) a penalty of £300 for each failure to set out a payment accurately in a report made under regulation 9.

(2) But in relation to a calendar year, [a reporting financial institution or UK representative][1] liability for penalties under this regulation is subject to a limit of £3000.

Amendments—[1] In para (1), words substituted for words "a person", and in para (2), words substituted for words "a person's", by the International Tax Compliance (Amendment) Regulations, SI 2017/598 regs 2, 13 with effect from 17 May 2017.

17 Matters to be disregarded in relation to liability to penalties

(1) Liability to a penalty under regulation 13, 14 or 16 does not arise if the person satisfies HMRC or (on an appeal notified to the tribunal) the tribunal that there is a reasonable excuse for the failure.

(2) For the purposes of this regulation neither of the following is a reasonable excuse—

(a) that there is an insufficiency of funds to do something,

(b) that a person relies upon another person to do something.

(3) If a person had a reasonable excuse for a failure but the excuse has ceased, the person is to be treated as having continued to have the excuse if the failure is remedied without unreasonable delay after the excuse ceased.

18 Assessment of penalties

(1) If a person becomes liable to a penalty under any of regulations [13(2)][1] to 16, an officer of Revenue and Customs may assess the penalty.

(2) If an officer does so, the officer must notify the person [of the assessment][2].

(3) An assessment of a penalty under regulation 13, 14 or 16(1)(*a*) must be made within the period of 12 months beginning with the date on which the person became liable to the penalty.

(4) An assessment of a penalty under regulation [13(1),][1] 15 or 16(1)(*b*) must be made—

(*a*) within the period of 12 months beginning with the date on which the inaccuracy [or failure][1] first came to the attention of an officer of Revenue and Customs, and

(*b*) within the period of 6 years beginning with the date on which the person became liable to the penalty.

Amendments—[1] In para (1), reference substituted for reference "13", in para (4), reference inserted, and in para (4)(*a*), words inserted by the International Tax Compliance (Amendment) Regulations, SI 2016/899 regs 2, 5 with effect from 30 September 2016.

[2] In para (2), words inserted by the International Tax Compliance (Amendment) Regulations, SI 2017/598 regs 2, 14 with effect from 17 May 2017.

19 Right to appeal against penalty

A person may appeal against a penalty assessment—

(*a*) on the grounds that liability to a penalty under any of regulations 13 to 16 does not arise, or

(*b*) as to the amount of [a penalty under regulation 14 or 15][1].

Amendments—[1] In para (*b*), words substituted for words "such a penalty" by the International Tax Compliance (Amendment) Regulations, SI 2017/598 regs 2, 15 with effect from 17 May 2017.

20 Procedure on appeal against penalty

(1) Notice of an appeal under regulation 19 must be given—

(*a*) in writing,

(*b*) before the end of the period of 30 days beginning with the date on which notification under regulation 18 was given,

(*c*) to HMRC.

(2) It must state the grounds of appeal.

(3) On an appeal under regulation 19(*a*) that is notified to the tribunal, the tribunal may confirm or cancel the assessment.

(4) On an appeal under regulation 19(*b*) that is notified to the tribunal, the tribunal may—

(*a*) confirm the assessment, or

(*b*) substitute another assessment that the officer of Revenue and Customs had power to make.

(5) Subject to this regulation and regulation 22, the provisions of Part 5 of TMA 1970 relating to appeals have effect in relation to appeals under regulation 19 as they have effect in relation to an appeal against an assessment to income tax.

21 Increased daily default penalty

[(1) Paragraph (2) applies if—

(*a*) a person is liable to a penalty under regulation 14 and a penalty is assessed under regulation 18, and

(*b*) the failure in respect of which that assessment is made continues for more than 30 days beginning with the date on which notification of that assessment is given.

(2) Where this paragraph applies, an officer of Revenue and Customs may make an application to the tribunal for permission to assess an increased daily penalty under regulation 14.

(3) An officer of Revenue and Customs must notify the person liable to the penalty of an application under paragraph (2) at the time of making it.

(4) If the tribunal determines that an increased daily penalty may be assessed then for each applicable day on which the failure continues, the person's liability to a penalty under regulation 14 shall be for that increased amount.

(5) The tribunal may not determine that an increased daily penalty may be assessed for an amount exceeding £1000 for each applicable day.

(6) If the tribunal determines that an increased daily penalty may be assessed, HMRC must notify the person liable to the penalty.

(7) The notification under paragraph (6) must specify the future day from which the increased penalty is to apply.

(8) That day and any subsequent day is an "applicable day" for the purposes of paragraph (4) and (5).][1]

Amendments—[1] Regulation 21 substituted by the International Tax Compliance (Amendment) Regulations, SI 2017/598 regs 2, 16 with effect from 17 May 2017. Regulation 21 previously read as follows—

"(1) This paragraph applies if—

(*a*) a penalty under regulation 14 is assessed under regulation 18,
(*b*) the failure in respect of which that assessment is made continues for more than 30 days beginning with the date on which notification of that assessment is given, and
(*c*) the person has been told that an application may be made under this paragraph for an increased daily penalty to be imposed.

(2) If this regulation applies, an officer of Revenue and Customs may make an application to the tribunal for an increased daily penalty to be imposed on the person.

(3) If the tribunal decides that an increased daily penalty should be imposed then for each applicable day on which the failure continues—
(*a*) the person is not liable to a penalty under regulation 14 in respect of the failure, and
(*b*) the person is liable instead to a penalty under this regulation of an amount determined by the tribunal.

(4) The tribunal may not determine an amount exceeding £1000 for each applicable day.

(5) If a person becomes liable to a penalty under this regulation, HMRC must notify the person.

(6) The notification must specify the day from which the increased penalty is to apply.

(7) That day and any subsequent day is an "applicable day" for the purposes of this regulation.".

22 Enforcement of penalties

(1) A penalty under these Regulations must be paid before the end of the period of 30 days beginning with the date mentioned in paragraph (2).

(2) That date is—
[(*a*) the date on which the assessment of the penalty under regulation 18 is notified in respect of the penalty, or][1]
(*b*) if a notice of appeal under regulation 20 is given, the date on which the appeal is finally determined or withdrawn.

(3) A penalty under these Regulations may be enforced as if it were income tax charged in an assessment and due and payable.

Amendments—[1] Para (2)(*a*), substituted by the International Tax Compliance (Amendment) Regulations, SI 2017/598 regs 2, 17 with effect from 17 May 2017.

Supplementary

23 Anti-avoidance

If—
(*a*) [a reporting financial institution, UK representative, specified financial institution or specified relevant person][1] enters into any arrangements, and
(*b*) the main purpose, or one of the main purposes, of [the institution or representative][1] in entering into the arrangements is to avoid any obligation under these Regulations,

these Regulations are to have effect as if the arrangements had not been entered into.

Amendments—[1] In para (*a*), words substituted for words "a person", and in para (*b*), words substituted for words "the person", by the International Tax Compliance (Amendment) Regulations, SI 2017/598 regs 2, 18 with effect from 17 May 2017.

24 Definitions

(1) In these Regulations—

"the Commissioners" means the Commissioners for Her Majesty's Revenue and Customs,

"the tribunal" means the First-tier Tribunal or, where determined by or under Tribunal Procedure Rules, the Upper Tribunal,

"US Treasury Regulations" mean the US Regulations Relating to Information Reporting by Foreign Financial Institutions and Other Foreign Entities.

(2) The following table lists the places where expressions that apply for the purposes of these Regulations are defined or otherwise explained—

Expression	*Regulations*	*The DAC*	*The CRS*	*The FATCA agreement*
account holder		Section VIII(E)(1) of Annex I	Section VIII(E)(1) of the CRS	Article 1(1)(*ee*)
annuity contract		Section VIII(C)(6) of Annex I	Section VIII(C)(6) of the CRS	
[CRS	regulation 1(3A)][3]			
cash value insurance contract		Section VIII(C)(7) of Annex I	Section VIII(C)(7) of the CRS	

Expression	*Regulations*	*The DAC*	*The CRS*	*The FATCA agreement*
the Commissioners	regulation 24(1)			
controlling person		Section VIII(D)(5) of Annex I	Section VIII(D)(6) of the CRS	Article 1(1)(*mm*)
[custodial account		Section VIII(C)(3) of Annex I	Section VIII(C)(3) of the CRS	Article 1(1)(*u*)][3]
the DAC	regulations 1(3)(*a*)			
entity		Section VIII(E)(3) of Annex I	Section VIII(E)(3) of the CRS	Article 1(1)(*hh*)
excluded accounts	Schedule 2	Section VIII(C)(17) of Annex I	Section VIII(C)(17) of the CRS	
the FATCA agreement	regulation 1(3)(*c*)			
financial account		Section VIII(C) of Annex I	Section VIII(C) of the CRS	Article 1(1)(*s*)
[financial institution	Regulation 1(5A)	Section VIII(A)(3) of Annex I	Section VIII(A)(3) of the CRS][1]	
[high value account		Section VIII(B)(1) of Annex I	Section VIII(B)(1) of the CRS	Section II(D) of Annex I][2]
[investment entity	regulation 1(5A)	Section VIII(A)(6) of Annex I	Section VIII(A)(6) of the CRS][1]	
new account		Section VIII(C)(10) of Annex I	Section VIII(C)(10) of the CRS	
[NFE		Section VIII(D)(6) of Annex I	Section VIII(D)(7) of the CRS][2]	
non-participating financial institution				Article 1(1)(*r*)
[non-reporting financial institution		Section VIII(B)(1) of Annex I	Section VIII(B)(1) of the CRS	
participating jurisdiction	Schedule 1	Section VIII(D)(4) of Annex I	Section VIII(D)(5) of the CRS][2]	
[pre-existing account	regulation 3(4A)	Section VIII(C)(9) of Annex I	Section VIII(C)(9) of the CRS	Article 1(1)(*aa*)][3]
[pre-existing entity account		Section VIII(C)(13) of Annex I	Section VIII(C)(13) of the CRS	Section IV of Annex I][3]
[related entity	regulation 3(4A)	Section VIII(E)(4) of Annex I	Section VIII(E)(4) of the CRS][3]	
reportable account	regulation 2	Section VIII(D)(1) of Annex I	Section VIII(D)(1) of the CRS	Article 1(1)(*bb*)
[reportable jurisdiction			Section VIII(D)(4) of the CRS][3]	

Expression	*Regulations*	*The DAC*	*The CRS*	*The FATCA agreement*
[reportable person		Section VIII(D)(2) of Annex I	Section VIII(D)(2) of the CRS][1]	
reporting financial institution		Section VIII(A)(1) of Annex I	Section VIII(A)(1) of the CRS	Article 1(1)(*n*)
relevant agreement	regulation 1(5)			
[specified financial institution	regulation 12A(3)][3]			
[specified relevant person	regulation 12A(4)][3]			
specified U.S. person				Article 1(1)(*gg*)
the tribunal	regulation 24(1)			
[UK representative	regulation 11(2)][3]			
US reportable account				Article 1(1)(*dd*) and paragraph I.B of Annex I
US Treasury Regulations	regulation 24(1)			

Amendments—[1] In para (2), entries for "financial institution" and "reportable person" substituted, and entry for "investment entity" inserted by the International Tax Compliance (Amendment) Regulations, SI 2015/1839 reg 2(1), (5) with effect from 20 November 2015.

[2] In para (2), entries for "high value account", "NFE" and "non-reporting financial institution" inserted by the International Tax Compliance (Amendment) Regulations, SI 2016/899 regs 2, 6 with effect from 30 September 2016.

[3] In para (2), entries for "CRS", "custodial account", "pre-existing account" and "pre-existing entity account" substituted, and entries for "related entity", "reportable jurisdiction", "specified financial institution", "specified relevant person" and "UK representative" inserted, by the International Tax Compliance (Amendment) Regulations, SI 2017/598 regs 2, 19 with effect from 17 May 2017. Substituted entries previously read as follows—

"CRS	regulation 1(3)(*b*)".			
"custodial account		Section VIII(A)(3) of Annex I	Section VIII(A)(3) of the CRS	Article 1(1)(*u*)".
"pre-existing account		Section VIII(C)(9) of Annex I	Section VIII(C)(9) of the CRS".	
"pre-existing entity account	regulation 2(3)	Section VIII(C)(13) of Annex I	Section VIII(C)(13) of the CRS	Section IV of Annex I".

25 Revocation

The International Tax Compliance (United States of America) Regulations 2014 are revoked.

SCHEDULE 1
PARTICIPATING JURISDICTIONS

Regulation 1(3)(*b*)

Amendments—[1] Schedule 1 revoked by the International Tax Compliance (Amendment) Regulations, SI 2017/598 regs 2, 20 with effect from 17 May 2017.

The participating jurisdictions for the purposes of the CRS are set out in the following list.

Albania
Andorra
Anguilla

Antigua and Barbuda
Argentina
Aruba
Austria
Australia
The Bahamas
Barbados
Belgium
Belize
Bermuda
Brazil
British Virgin Islands
Brunei Darussalam
Bulgaria
Canada
Cayman Islands
Chile
China
Colombia
Costa Rica
Croatia
Curacao
Cyprus
Czech Republic
Denmark
Dominica
Estonia
Faroe Islands
Finland
France
Germany
[Ghana][1]
Gibraltar
Greece
Greenland
Grenada
Guernsey
Hong Kong (China)
Hungary
Iceland
India
Indonesia
Ireland
Isle of Man
Israel
Italy
Japan
Jersey
Korea
Latvia
Liechtenstein
Lithuania

Luxembourg
Macao (China)
Malaysia
Malta
Marshall Islands
Mauritius
Mexico
Monaco
Montserrat
Netherlands
New Zealand
Niue
Norway
Poland
Portugal
Qatar
Romania
Russian Federation
Saint Kitts and Nevis
Saint Lucia
Saint Vincent and the Grenadines
Samoa
San Marino
Saudi Arabia
Seychelles
Singapore
Sint Maarten
Slovak Republic
Slovenia
South Africa
Spain
Sweden
Switzerland
Trinidad and Tobago
Turkey
Turks and Caicos Islands
United Arab Emirates
Uruguay[2]

Amendments—[1] Entry for "Ghana" inserted by the International Tax Compliance (Amendment) Regulations, SI 2015/1839 reg 2(1), (6) with effect from 20 November 2015.

[2] Schedule 1 revoked by the International Tax Compliance (Amendment) Regulations, SI 2017/598 regs 2, 20 with effect from 17 May 2017.

SCHEDULE 2

EXCLUDED ACCOUNTS

Regulation 2(2)(*a*)

For the purposes of the DAC and the CRS the following are excluded accounts.

1 Certain Retirement Accounts or Products

Pension schemes registered with HMRC under Part 4 of FA 2004.

2 Non-registered pension arrangements where the annual contributions are limited to £50,000 and funds contributed cannot be accessed before the age of 55 except in circumstances of serious ill health.

3 Immediate needs annuities within section 725 ITTOIA 2005.

4 Certain Tax-favoured Accounts and Products
An account within the meaning of the Individual Savings Account Regulations 1998.

5 A child trust fund within the meaning of the Child Trust Funds Act 2004.

6 Premium Bonds issued by the UK National Savings and Investments.

7 Children's Bonds issued by the UK National Savings and Investments.

8 Fixed Interest Savings Certificates issued by UK National Savings and Investments.

9 Index Linked Savings Certificates issued by UK National Savings and Investments.

10 Tax Exempt Savings Plans issued by a friendly society within the meaning of the Friendly Societies Act 1992.

11 A share incentive plan approved by HMRC under Schedule 2 to ITEPA 2003.

12 A SAYE option scheme approved by HMRC under Schedule 3 to ITEPA 2003.

13 A CSOP scheme approved by HMRC under Schedule 4 to ITEPA 2003.

14 *A venture capital trust approved for the purposes of Part 6 of ITA 2007 by the Commissioners.*[1]

Amendments—[1] Paras 14, 15 revoked by the International Tax Compliance (Amendment) Regulations, SI 2015/1839 reg 2(1), (7) with effect from 20 November 2015.

15 (1) A dormant account (other than an annuity contract) with a balance that does not exceed US$1,000.

(2) An account is a dormant account if—

(*a*) the account holder has not initiated a transaction with regard to the account or any other account held by the account holder with the reporting financial institution in the previous three years,

(*b*) the account holder has not communicated with the reporting financial institution regarding the account or any other account held by the account holder with the reporting financial institution in the previous six years,

(*c*) the account is treated as a dormant account under the reporting financial institutions normal operating procedures, and

(*d*) in the case of a cash value insurance contract, the reporting financial institution has not communicated with the account holder regarding the account or any other account held by the account holder with the reporting financial institution in the previous six years.[1]

Amendments—[1] Paras 14, 15 revoked by the International Tax Compliance (Amendment) Regulations, SI 2015/1839 reg 2(1), (7) with effect from 20 November 2015.

[SCHEDULE 3

Regulation 12F

Part 1

1. The form of a client exchange of tax information notification is—

HM Revenue
& Customs

If you have money or other assets abroad, you could owe tax in the UK

Things are changing – the tax world is becoming more transparent

- HM Revenue and Customs (HMRC) is getting tougher on those not paying the right amount of tax across their offshore tax affairs.
- From 2016, HMRC is getting new financial information about our customers from more than 100 jurisdictions – including details about overseas accounts, structures, trusts, and investments.
- HMRC is already using information, supplied by overseas banks, insurers, and wealth and assets managers, to identify the minority who are not paying what they owe.

Are you confident that your UK tax affairs are up-to-date?

You need to regularly check that you have declared all of your UK tax liabilities and, if needed, bring your tax affairs up-to-date. This is your responsibility.

Personal circumstances change. For example, you may have recently inherited assets overseas. Tax laws change too. All of this means that previous advice can be out-of-date, with costly consequences.

- If you are confident that your tax affairs are up-to-date and complete, then you don't need to do anything further.
- If you are unsure, we recommend that you speak to a tax adviser to find out if you need to take action now.
- If you find that you need to bring your tax affairs up-to-date, it can be easier than you think. You can choose to do this now using HMRC's straightforward online disclosure facility at www.gov.uk/guidance/worldwide-disclosure-facility-make-a-disclosure

If you have not paid the right amount of tax and choose not to take action now, you need to know that:

- HMRC will find out about your money and assets overseas through new information from more than 100 jurisdictions.
- Penalties are increasing for those who are not paying the right amount of tax on their offshore assets, and you can even face criminal prosecution. Under new rules, you could face further penalties based on the value of the asset as well as the tax due, resulting in potentially life-changing consequences.

If you choose to delay in coming forward, it's very likely to cost you more and there is also more chance that HMRC will come for you.

Come to us before we come for you

Remember

- If you are confident that your tax affairs are up-to-date, and you have declared all of your UK tax liabilities, then you don't need to do anything further.

We are already using early financial information to identify the minority who are not paying what they owe.
If you need to bring your tax affairs up-to-date, it is your responsibility to do so – act now at www.gov.uk/guidance/worldwide-disclosure-facility-make-a-disclosure

Part 2

2. The statement in this paragraph is—

"Financial institutions in more than 100 jurisdictions around the world are being legally required to find out the tax residence of their account holders and report details of their accounts, structures, trusts, and investments to be exchanged with the appropriate tax authorities. As a UK tax resident, any overseas accounts you have will be sent to HM Revenue & Customs (HMRC). This gives HMRC unprecedented levels of information to check that, as in most cases, the right tax has been paid.

If you have already declared all of your past and present income or gains to HMRC, including from overseas, you do not need to worry. But if you are in any doubt, HMRC recommends that you read the factsheet attached to help you decide now what to do next.".

3. The statement in this paragraph is—

"From 2016, HM Revenue & Customs (HMRC) is getting an unprecedented amount of information about people's overseas accounts, structures, trusts, and investments from more than 100 jurisdictions worldwide, thanks to agreements to increase global tax transparency. This gives HMRC unprecedented levels of information to check that, as in most cases, the right tax has been paid.

If you have already declared all of your past and present income or gains to HMRC, including from overseas, you do not need to worry. But if you are in any doubt, HMRC recommends that you read the factsheet attached to help you decide now what to do next.][1]

Amendments—[1] Schedule 3 inserted by the International Tax Compliance (Amendment) Regulations, SI 2016/899 regs 2, 7 with effect from 30 September 2016.

2015/1449

CULTURAL TEST (TELEVISION PROGRAMMES) (AMENDMENT) REGULATIONS 2015

Made . . . . *29 June 2015*
Laid before Parliament . . . . *1 July 2015*
Coming into force . . . . *23 July 2015*

The Secretary of State, in exercise of the powers conferred by sections 1216CB(2) and 1216CC(7) of the Corporation Tax Act 2009, makes the following Regulations.

Regulations 2, 4, 5 and 7 are made with the approval of the Treasury in accordance with section 1216CB(2) of that Act.

1 Citation and commencement

These Regulations may be cited as the Cultural Test (Television Programmes) (Amendment) Regulations 2015 and come into force on 23rd July 2015.

2 Application

(1) These Regulations have effect in relation to any television programme other than an excepted programme.

(2) A television programme is an excepted programme if—

(*a*) an application for certification of the programme was made before the commencement day, or

(*b*) the television production company has made an election in relation to the programme under paragraph (3).

(3) A television production company may make an election under this regulation in relation to a television programme if—

(*a*) the first day of principal photography (in relation to dramas) or shooting (in relation to documentaries or animations) was before the commencement day, and

(*b*) no application for certification of the programme was made before the commencement day.

(4) In this regulation—

"application for certification" means an application for an interim or final certificate under section 1216CC of the Corporation Tax Act 2009, and

"commencement day" means 23rd July 2015.

3 Interpretation

In these Regulations "the 2013 Regulations" means the Cultural Test (Television Programmes) Regulations 2013.

4 Amendments to Part 1 of the 2013 Regulations

(*amends* SI 2013/1831 reg 2)

5 Amendments to Part 2 of the 2013 Regulations

(*amends* SI 2013/1831 reg 3 and *inserts* reg 4A)

6 Amendments to Part 3 of the 2013 Regulations

(*amends* SI 2013/1831 regs 6, 9, 11, 12)

7 Amendments to Schedule 1 to the 2013 Regulations

(*amends* SI 2013/1831 Sch 1)

8 Amendments to Schedule 2 to the 2013 Regulations

(*amends* SI 2013/1831 Sch 2

2015/1540

HOUSING AND REGENERATION TRANSFER SCHEMES (TAX CONSEQUENCES) REGULATIONS 2015

Made . . . . *16 July 2015*
Laid before Parliament . . . . *17 July 2015*
Coming into force . . . . *7 August 2015*

The Treasury make the following Regulations in exercise of the powers conferred by section 333DC of the Greater London Authority Act 1999 and section 53B of the Housing and Regeneration Act 2008.

1 Citation and commencement

These Regulations may be cited as the Housing and Regeneration Transfer Schemes (Tax Consequences) Regulations 2015 and come into force on 7th August 2015.

2 Interpretation

(1) In these Regulations—

"CAA 2001" means the Capital Allowances Act 2001;

"public body" means a person which is a public body for the purposes of section 66 of the Finance Act 2003;

"TCGA 1992" means the Taxation of Chargeable Gains Act 1992;

"taxable public body" means a public body which is within the charge to corporation tax;

"transfer scheme" means a transfer scheme made under—

(*a*) section 333DA of the Greater London Authority Act 1999, or

(*b*) section 53A of the Housing and Regeneration Act 2008;

"trading stock" has the meaning given by section 163 of the Corporation Tax Act 2009;

"transferee", in relation to a transfer scheme, means the person to whom the transfer is made;

"transferor", in relation to a transfer scheme, means the person from whom the transfer is made.

(2) Expressions used in regulations 7 and 8 and in Part 2 of CAA 2001 have the same meanings in those regulations as in that Part.

3 Application of Regulations to transfers between taxable public bodies

These Regulations apply to any transfer, in accordance with a transfer scheme, from a taxable public body to another taxable public body.

4 Corporation tax: transfers of trading stock

(1) This regulation applies if there is a transfer of trading stock of the transferor.

(2) Paragraphs (3) and (4) have effect in calculating for any corporation tax purpose both—

(*a*) the profits of the transferor's trade in relation to which the stock is trading stock immediately before the transfer takes effect, and

(*b*) the consideration given, or the expenditure incurred, by the transferee for the acquisition of the stock (whether acquired as trading stock or not).

(3) The stock is to be treated as having been—

(*a*) disposed of by the transferor in the course of the transferor's trade, and

(*b*) disposed of and acquired when the transfer takes effect.

(4) The stock is to be valued as if the disposal and acquisition had been for a consideration which in relation to the transferor would have resulted in neither a profit nor a loss being brought into account in respect of the disposal in the accounting period of the transferor which ends with, or is current at, the time when the transfer takes effect.

5 Corporation tax: transfers of assets that will be trading stock of the transferee

(1) This regulation applies if—

(*a*) a transfer constitutes a disposal of an asset for the purposes of TCGA 1992,

(*b*) at the time of the disposal, the asset is not trading stock of the transferor, and

(*c*) immediately after the disposal, the asset will be trading stock of the transferee.

(2) For any corporation tax purpose, the trading stock—

(*a*) is to be treated as having been acquired by the transferee in the course of the transferee's trade, and

(*b*) is to be valued as if it had been acquired by the transferee for a consideration such that no gain or loss would accrue to the transferor for the purposes of TCGA 1992.

6 Chargeable gains: disposal on transfer to be treated as no gain/no loss disposal

(1) For the purposes of TCGA 1992, a disposal constituted by a transfer is to be taken in relation to the transferor and transferee to be for a consideration such that no gain or loss accrues to the transferor.

(2) For the purposes of any provision about a relevant tax, paragraph (1) is to be treated as one of the no gain/no loss provisions in section 288(3A) of that Act (meaning of "the no gain/no loss provisions").

7 Capital allowances: determination of disposal value of plant or machinery

(1) This regulation applies if—

(*a*) there is a transfer of plant or machinery, and

(*b*) the plant or machinery would be treated for the purposes of CAA 2001 as disposed of by the transferor to the transferee on the transfer taking effect.

(2) If the plant or machinery will be used by the transferee for the purposes of a qualifying activity, the disposal value of the plant or machinery is to be treated for the purposes of CAA 2001 as such amount as is determined by the Secretary of State.

(3) The consent of the Treasury is required for the making of a determination under paragraph (2).

(4) If an amount is determined under paragraph (2) then for the purposes of CAA 2001—

(*a*) the transferee is to be treated as having incurred capital expenditure of that amount on the provision of the plant or machinery for the purposes for which it is used by the transferee on and after the taking effect of the transfer, and

(*b*) the property is to be treated as belonging to the transferee as a result of the transferee having incurred that expenditure.

(5) The expenditure treated as incurred under paragraph (4)(*a*) is to be treated as not being AIA qualifying expenditure for the purposes of CAA 2001.

(6) If the plant or machinery will not be used by the transferee for the purposes of a qualifying activity, the disposal value of the plant or machinery is to be treated for the purposes of CAA 2001—

(*a*) if a capital sum is received by the transferor by way of consideration or compensation in respect of the transfer, as an amount equal to that sum, or

(*b*) if no such sum is received, as nil.

(7) For the purposes of paragraph (5) a sum received by a person connected with the transferor is to be treated as received by the transferor.

(8) Section 88 of CAA 2001 (sales at an undervalue) is to be disregarded.

(9) This regulation is subject to sections 63(5) and 68 of CAA 2001 (cases in which disposal value is nil and disposal value on cessation of notional ownership).

8 Capital allowances: determination of disposal value of fixtures

(1) This regulation applies if—

(*a*) there is a transfer of a fixture, and

(*b*) by virtue of the transfer a person is treated by section 188 of CAA 2001 (cessation of ownership when person ceases to have qualifying interest) as ceasing to own the fixture.

(2) For the purposes of the application of section 196 of CAA 2001 (disposal values in relation to fixtures) in relation to the transferor, the disposal value of the fixture is to be treated as such amount as is determined by the Secretary of State.

(3) An amount determined under paragraph (2) must not exceed the qualifying expenditure brought into account by the transferor for the purposes of CAA 2001 on its acquisition of the fixture.

(4) If an amount is determined under paragraph (2) then—

(*a*) the transferee is to be treated for the purposes of CAA 2001 as having incurred capital expenditure of that amount on acquiring an interest in the relevant land, and

(*b*) the expenditure which falls to be treated as incurred by the transferee is to be treated for the purposes of sections 181(1) and 182(1) of CAA 2001 (purchaser of land giving consideration for fixture or discharging obligations of equipment lessee) as being incurred by the giving of a consideration consisting in a capital sum of that amount.

(5) The expenditure treated as incurred under paragraph (4)(a) is to be treated as not being AIA qualifying expenditure for the purposes of CAA 2001.

(6) This regulation is subject to section 63(5) of CAA 2001 (cases in which disposal value is nil).

2015/1783

POLICE AND CRIMINAL EVIDENCE ACT 1984 (APPLICATION TO REVENUE AND CUSTOMS) ORDER 2015

Made . . . .*13 October 2015*
Laid before Parliament. . . . .*14 October 2015*
Coming into force . . . .*4 November 2015*

The Treasury, in exercise of the powers conferred by sections 114(2) and (3) of the Police and Criminal Evidence Act 1984, makes the following Order:

1 Citation and commencement

This Order may be cited as the Police and Criminal Evidence Act 1984 (Application to Revenue and Customs) Order 2015 and shall come into force on 4th November 2015

2 Interpretation

(1) In this Order—

"the Act" means the Police and Criminal Evidence Act 1984;

"the Commissioners" means the Commissioners for Her Majesty's Revenue and Customs;

"the customs and excise Acts" has the meaning given to it by section 1 of the Customs and Excise Management Act 1979;

"designated customs official" has the meaning given to it by section 14(6) of the Borders, Citizenship and Immigration Act 2009;

"Home Office custody suite" means premises wholly or partly used for the detention of persons by designated customs officials;

"office of Revenue and Customs" means premises wholly or partly occupied by Her Majesty's Revenue and Customs;

"relevant indictable offence" means an indictable offence which relates to a matter in relation to which Her Majesty's Revenue and Customs have functions;

"relevant investigation" means a criminal investigation conducted by officers of Revenue and Customs which relates to a matter in relation to which Her Majesty's Revenue and Customs have functions.

(2) A person is in Revenue and Customs detention for the purpose of this Order if—

(*a*) he has been taken to an office of Revenue and Customs after being arrested for an offence; or

(*b*) he is arrested at an office of Revenue and Customs after attending voluntarily at the office or accompanying an officer of Revenue and Customs to it,

and is detained there or detained elsewhere in the charge of an officer of Revenue and Customs.

(3) A person is in Home Office detention for the purpose of this Order if—

(*a*) he has been taken to a Home Office custody suite after being arrested for an offence; or

(*b*) he is arrested at a Home Office custody suite after attending voluntarily at that suite or accompanying a designated customs official to it,

and is detained there or detained elsewhere in the charge of a designated customs official.

3 Application

(1) The provisions of the Act contained in Schedule 1 to this Order, which relate to investigations of offences conducted by police officers or to persons detained by the police, shall apply to relevant investigations conducted by officers of Revenue and Customs and to persons detained by such officers.

This is subject to the modifications in paragraphs (2) and (3) and articles 4 to 19 and Schedule 2.

(2) The Act shall have effect as if the words and phrases in Column 1 of Part 1 of Schedule 2 to this Order were replaced by the substitute words and phrases in Column 2 of that Part.

(3) Where in the Act any act or thing is to be done by a constable of a specific rank, that act or thing shall be done by an officer of Revenue and Customs of at least the grade specified in Column 2 of Part 2 of Schedule 2 to this Order, and the Act shall be construed accordingly.

4 Exceptions

Nothing in the application of the Act to Revenue and Customs confers on an officer of Revenue and Customs any power—

(*a*) to charge a person with any offence;

(*b*) to release a person on bail; or

(*c*) to detain a person for an offence after he has been charged with that offence.

5 Seizure and retention of things found upon search

(1) Where in the Act a constable is given power to seize and retain any thing found upon a lawful search of person or premises, an officer of Revenue and Customs shall have the same power, notwithstanding that the thing found is not evidence of an offence which relates to a matter in relation to which Her Majesty's Revenue and Customs have functions.

(2) Nothing in the application of the Act to Revenue and Customs prevents any thing lawfully seized by a person under any enactment from being accepted and retained by an officer of Revenue and Customs.

(3) Section 21 of the Act (access and copying) shall not apply to any thing seized as liable to forfeiture under the customs and excise Acts.

6 Excluded and special procedure material

In its application by virtue of article 3 above the Act shall have effect as if the following section were inserted after section 14—

"14A Exception for Revenue and Customs

Material in the possession of a person who acquired or created it in the course of any trade, business, profession or other occupation or for the purpose of any paid or unpaid office and which relates to a matter in relation to which Her Majesty's Revenue and Customs have functions, is neither excluded material nor special procedure material for the purposes of any enactment such as is mentioned in subsection 9(2) above.".

7 Restriction on other powers to apply for production of documents

In its application by virtue of article 3 above the Act shall have effect as if the following section were inserted after section 14A—

"14B Revenue and Customs: restriction on other powers to apply for production of documents

(1) An officer of Revenue and Customs may make an application for the delivery of, or access to, documents under a provision specified in subsection (3) only if the condition in subsection (2) is satisfied.

(2) The condition is that the officer thinks that an application under Schedule 1 would not succeed because the material required does not consist of or include special procedure material.

(3) The provisions are—

(*a*) section 20BA and Schedule 1AA of the Taxes Management Act 1970 (serious tax fraud);

(*b*) paragraph 11 of Schedule 11 to the Value Added Tax Act 1994 (VAT);

(*c*) paragraph 4A of Schedule 7 to the Finance Act 1994 (insurance premium tax);

(*d*) paragraph 7 of Schedule 5 to the Finance Act 1996 (landfill tax);

(*e*) paragraph 131 of Schedule 6 to the Finance Act 2000 (climate change levy);

(*f*) paragraph 8 of Schedule 7 to the Finance Act 2001 (aggregates levy);

(*g*) Part 6 of Schedule 13 to the Finance Act 2003 (stamp duty land tax).".

8 Modification of section 18 of the Act (Entry and search after arrest)

(1) Section 18 of the Act (entry and search after arrest) is modified as follows.

(2) For subsection 18(1) substitute—

"(1) Subject to the following provisions of this section, an officer of Revenue and Customs may enter and search any premises occupied or controlled by a person who is under arrest for any relevant indictable offence if he has reasonable grounds for suspecting that there is on the premises evidence, other than items subject to legal privilege, that relates—

(*a*) to that offence; or

(*b*) to some other indictable offence which is connected with or similar to that offence.

(3) In sub-sections (5) and (5A), after "police station", insert ", office of Revenue and Customs or Home Office custody suite".

(4) In sub-section (8), after "police detention", insert ", Revenue and Customs detention or Home Office detention"."

9 Modification of section 30 of the Act (Arrest elsewhere than at police station)

(1) Section 30 of the Act (arrest elsewhere than at police station) is modified as follows.

(2) In subsections (1A), (2), (3), subsection (4)(a), and subsections (5), (6), (7), (7A), (10), (10A) and (11), after "police station", wherever that expression occurs, insert ", office of Revenue and Customs or Home Office custody suite".

(3) In subsection (2), sub-sections (4)(*a*) and (5)(*b*), and subsection (6), after "designated police station", wherever that expression occurs, insert ", designated office of Revenue and Customs or designated Home Office custody suite".

(4) In subsection (3), before "detention", delete "police".

(5) In its application by virtue of article 3 above the Act shall have effect as if the following subsection were inserted after subsection 30(6)—

"(6A) An arrested person may be transferred between Revenue and Customs detention and Home Office detention, and between Revenue and Customs detention and police detention".

10 Modification of section 35 of the Act (Designated police stations)

(1) Section 35 of the Act (designated police stations) is modified as follows.

(2) For subsection 35(1) substitute—

"(1) The Commissioners shall designate offices of Revenue and Customs which, subject to subsections 30(3) and (5), are to be the offices to be used for the purposes of detaining arrested persons.".

(3) For subsection 35(2) substitute—

"(2) The Commissioners' duty under subsection (1) above is to designate offices of Revenue and Customs appearing to them to provide enough accommodation for that purpose.".

(4) For subsection 35(3) substitute—

"(3) Without prejudice to section 12 of the Interpretation Act 1978 (continuity of duties) the Commissioners—

(*a*) may designate an office which was not previously designated; and

(*b*) may direct that a designation of an office previously made shall cease to operate.".

11 Modification of section 36 of the Act (Custody officers at police stations)

(1) Section 36 of the Act (custody officers at police stations) is modified as follows.

(2) For subsection (2) substitute—

"(2) A custody officer for an office of Revenue and Customs designated under subsection 35(1) above shall be appointed—

(*a*) by the Commissioners; or

(*b*) by such officer of Revenue and Customs as the Commissioners may direct.".

12 Modification of section 41 of the Act (Limits on period of detention without charge)

(1) Section 41 of the Act (limits on period of detention without charge) is modified as follows.

(2) For paragraph (2)(*b*) substitute—

"(*b*) in the case of a person arrested outside England and Wales, shall be—

(i) the time at which that person arrives at the office of Revenue and Customs in England and Wales in which the offence for which he was arrested is being investigated; or

(ii) the time 24 hours after the time of that person's entry into England and Wales.".

13 Modification of section 50 of the Act (Records of detention)

(1) Section 50 of the Act (records of detention) is modified as follows.

(2) For subsection (1) substitute—

"(1) The Commissioners shall keep written records showing on an annual basis—

(*a*) the number of persons kept in Revenue and Customs detention for more than 24 hours and subsequently released without charge;

(*b*) the number of applications for warrants of further detention and the results of the applications; and

(*c*) in relation to each warrant of further detention—

(i) the period of further detention authorised by it;

(ii) the period which the person named in it spent in Revenue and Customs detention on its authority; and

(iii) whether he was charged or released without charge.".

(3) For subsection (2) substitute—

"(2) Every annual report made by the Commissioners shall contain information about the matters mentioned in subsection (1) above in respect of the period to which the report relates.".

14 Modification of section 55 of the Act (Intimate searches)

(1) Section 55 of the Act (intimate searches) shall have effect as if it related only to things such as are mentioned in paragraph (1)(*a*) of that section.

(2) The annual report of the Commissioners shall contain information about searches under section 55 which have been carried out during the period to which the report relates.

15 Modification of section 77 of the Act (Definition of independent person)

Subsection 77(3) of the Act (definition of independent person) shall be modified to the extent that the definition of "independent person" shall, in addition to the persons mentioned therein, also include an officer of Revenue and Customs or any other person acting under the authority of the Commissioners.

16 Use of reasonable force

Where any provision of the Act as applied to Revenue and Customs—

(*a*) confers a power on an officer of Revenue and Customs, and

(*b*) does not provide that the power may only be exercised with the consent of some person other than that officer,

the officer may use reasonable force, if necessary, in the exercise of the power.

17 Arrest without warrant

Subsection 24(2) of the Act (arrest without warrant) does not limit—

(*a*) subsection 138(1) of the Customs and Excise Management Act 1979;

(*b*) section 20 and paragraph 4 of Schedule 3 to the Criminal Justice (International Co-operation) Act 1990;

(*c*) any other enactment, including any enactment contained in subordinate legislation, for the time being in force which confers upon officers of Revenue and Customs the power to arrest or detain persons.

18 Search of persons

Where an officer of Revenue and Customs searches premises in reliance on a warrant under section 8 of, or paragraph 12 of Schedule 1 to, the Act (power of justice of the peace to authorise entry and search of premises), he may search any person found on the premises—

(*a*) where he has reasonable cause to believe that person to be in possession of material which is likely to be of substantial value (whether by itself or together with other material) to the investigation of the offence;

(*b*) but no person should be searched except by a person of the same sex.

19 Authorisation

Powers and functions in the provisions of the Act contained in Schedule 1 to this Order may be exercised only by officers of Revenue and Customs acting with the authority (which may be general or specific) of the Commissioners.

20 Revocation

The following instruments are revoked—

(*a*) the Police and Criminal Evidence Act 1984 (Application to Revenue and Customs) Order 2007;

(*b*) the Police and Criminal Evidence Act 1984 (Application to Revenue and Customs) Order 2007 (Amendment) Order 2010;

(*c*) the Police and Criminal Evidence Act 1984 (Application to Revenue and Customs) (Amendment) Order 2014.

SCHEDULE 1

PROVISIONS OF THE ACT APPLIED TO REVENUE AND CUSTOMS

Article 3(1)

Section 8 (power of justice of the peace to authorise entry and search of premises)
Section 9 (special provisions as to access) and Schedule 1 (special procedure)
Section 15 (search warrants—safeguards)
Section 16 (execution of warrants)
Section 17(1)(*a*)(i), (1)(*b*), [(1)(*cab*)(ii),][1] (1)(*cb*), (1)(*d*), (2), (4) (entry for purpose of arrest etc)
Section 18 (entry and search after arrest) (subject to the modification in article 8)
Section 19 (general power of seizure etc)
Section 20 (extension of powers of seizure to computerised information)
Section 21 (access and copying) (subject to the modification in article 5)
Section 22(1) to (4) and (7) (retention)
Section 24(2), (4), (5) (arrest without warrant: constables) (subject to the modification in article 17)
Section 28 (information to be given on arrest)
Section 29 (voluntary attendance at police station etc)
Section 30(1) to (4)(*a*) and (5) to (11) (arrest elsewhere than at police station) (subject to the modification in article 9)
Section 31 (arrest for further offence)
Section 32(1) to (9) (search upon arrest) (subject to the modifications in article 5)
Section 34(1) to (5) (limitations on police detention)
Section 35(1), (2), (3) and (4) (designated police stations) (subject to the modification in article 10)
Section 36(1), (2), (3), (4), (5), (6), (7), (8), (9) and (10) (custody officers at police stations) (subject to the modification in article 11)
Section 37 (duties of custody officer before charge)
Section 39 (responsibilities in relation to persons detained)
Section 40 (review of police detention)
Section 41(1), (2), (4) and (6) to (9) (limits on period of detention without charge) (subject to the modification in article 12)
Section 42(1), (2) and (4) to (11) (authorisation of continued detention)
Section 43(1) to (12) and (14) to (19) (warrants of further detention)
Section 44 (extension of warrants of further detention)

Section 46A(1), (1A) (power of arrest for failure to answer to police bail)
[Section 47ZF
Section 47ZG
Section 47ZH][1]
Section 50 (records of detention) (subject to the modification in article 13)
Section 51(*d*) (savings)
Section 54 (searches of detained persons)
Section 55 (intimate searches) (subject to the modifications in articles 5 and 14)
Section 56(1) to (9) (right to have someone informed when arrested)
Section 57 (additional rights of children and young persons)
Section 58(1) to (11) (access to legal advice)
Section 62 (intimate samples)
Section 63 (other samples)
Section 63D (destruction of fingerprints and DNA profiles)
Section 63E (retention of section 63D material pending investigation or proceeding)
Section 63G (retention of section 63D material by virtue of section 63F(5): consent of Commissioner)
Section 63H (retention of section 63D material: persons arrested for or charged with a minor offence)
Section 63I (retention of material: persons convicted of a recordable offence)
Section 63J (retention of material: persons convicted of an offence outside England and Wales)
Section 63K (retention of section 63D material: exception for persons under 18 convicted of first minor offence)
Section 63L (retention of section 63D material: persons given a penalty notice)
Section 63M (retention of section 63D material for purposes of national security)
Section 63N (retention of section 63D material given voluntarily)
Section 63O (retention of section 63D material with consent)
Section 63P (section 63D material obtained for one purpose and used for another)
Section 63Q (destruction of copies of section 63D material)
Section 63R (destruction of samples)
Section 63S (destruction of impressions of footwear)
Section 63T (use of retained material)
Section 63U (exclusions for certain regimes)
Section 66 (codes of practice)
Section 67 (codes of practice—supplementary)
Section 77 (confessions by mentally handicapped persons) (subject to the modification in article 15)
Section 107 (police officers performing duties of higher rank)

Amendments—[1] In entry for s 17, words inserted, and entries for s 47ZF–47ZH inserted by the Police and Criminal Evidence Act 1984 (Application to Revenue and Customs) (Amendment) Order, SI 2017/736 art 2 with effect from 2 August 2017.

SCHEDULE 2

PART 1
SUBSTITUTION OF EQUIVALENT WORDS AND PHRASES IN THE ACT

Article 3(2)

Where in the Act a word or phrase specified in Column 1 is used, in the application of the Act to Revenue and Customs, there shall be substituted the equivalent word or phrase in Column 2—

Column 1	*Column 2*
WORDS AND PHRASES USED IN THE ACT	***SUBSTITUTED WORDS AND PHRASES***
chief officer of police	director
constable	officer of Revenue and Customs
designated police station (except in section 30)	designated office of Revenue and Customs
officer of a force maintained by a police authority	officer of Revenue and Customs

police detention (except in section 118 and in section 39(1)(*a*) the second time the words occur)	Revenue and Customs detention
police officer	officer of Revenue and Customs
police station (except in sections 30 and 46A(1))	office of Revenue and Customs
rank	grade
station	office of Revenue and Customs
The police	Her Majesty's Revenue and Customs

PART 2
EQUIVALENT TITLES OF OFFICERS

Article 3(3)

Where in the Act an act or thing is to be done by a constable of the rank specified in Column 1, that same act or thing shall, in the application of the Act to Revenue and Customs, be done by an officer of Revenue and Customs of at least an equivalent grade specified in Column 2—

Column 1	***Column 2***
RANK OF CONSTABLE	***GRADE OF OFFICER***
Sergeant	Officer
Inspector	Higher officer
Chief Inspector	Higher officer
Superintendent	Senior officer

Modifications—Crime and Courts Act 2013 (Application and Modification of Enactments) Order, SI 2016/1143 art 4 (modification of the Table, Pt 2, col 2 in its application to designated persons).

2015/1790

1

TAXATION OF CHARGEABLE GAINS (GILT-EDGED SECURITIES) ORDER 2015

Made . . . . *12 October 2015*

The Treasury make the following Order in exercise of the powers conferred by paragraph 1 of Schedule 9 to the Taxation of Chargeable Gains Act 1992:

1 Citation

This Order may be cited as the Taxation of Chargeable Gains (Gilt-edged Securities) Order 2015.

2 Securities specified as gilt-edged securities

For the purposes of the Taxation of Chargeable Gains Act 1992 the following securities are specified as "gilt-edged securities"—

3 1/2 % Treasury Gilt 2045
0 1/8 % Index-linked Treasury Gilt 2058
2% Treasury Gilt 2020
2% Treasury Gilt 2025
0 1/8 % Index-linked Treasury Gilt 2026
0 1/8 % Index-linked Treasury Gilt 2046
1 1/2 % Treasury Gilt 2021.

2015/1948

INCOME TAX (APPROVED EXPENSES) REGULATIONS 2015

Made . . . . *27 November 2015*
Laid before the House of Commons . . . . *30 November 2015*
Coming into force . . . . *21 December 2015*

The Commissioners for Her Majesty's Revenue and Customs, in exercise of the power conferred by section 289A(6)(*a*) and (7) of the Income Tax (Earnings and Pensions) Act 2003, make the following Regulations:

1 Citation, commencement, interpretation and effect

(1) These Regulations may be cited as the Income Tax (Approved Expenses) Regulations 2015 and come into force on 21st December 2015

(2) These Regulations have effect in relation to payments made in the tax year 2016–17 and subsequent tax years.

(3) In these Regulations "qualifying travel" means travel for which a deduction from the employee's earnings would be allowed under Chapter 2 or 5 of Part 5 of the Income Tax (Earnings and Pensions) Act 2003 ("ITEPA 2003").

2 Approved way of calculating and paying or reimbursing standard meal allowances

(1) For the purposes of section 289A of ITEPA 2003, a sum is calculated and paid or reimbursed in an approved way if it is paid or reimbursed to an employee in respect of meals purchased by the employee in the course of qualifying travel ("a meal allowance") and falls within paragraph (2) or (3).

(2) One meal allowance per day paid in respect of one instance of qualifying travel, the amount of which does not exceed—

(*a*) £5 where the duration of the qualifying travel in that day is 5 hours or more;

(*b*) £10 where the duration of the qualifying travel in that day is 10 hours or more; or

(*c*) £25 where the duration of the qualifying travel in that day is 15 hours or more and is ongoing at 8pm.

(3) An additional meal allowance not exceeding £10 per day paid where a meal allowance in sub-paragraph (2)(*a*) or (*b*) is paid and the qualifying travel in respect of which that allowance is paid is ongoing at 8pm.

2015/1983

LLOYD'S UNDERWRITERS (TRANSITIONAL EQUALISATION RESERVES) (TAX) REGULATIONS 2015

Made . . . . *7 December 2015*

Laid before the House of Commons . . . . *8 December 2015*

Coming into force . . . . *1 January 2016*

The Treasury make the following Regulations in exercise of the powers conferred by section 47 of the Finance Act 2009 and section 30(1) of the Finance Act 2012.

1 Citation and commencement

These Regulations may be cited as the Lloyd's Underwriters (Transitional Equalisation Reserves) (Tax) Regulations 2015 and come into force on 1st January 2016.

2 Interpretation

In these Regulations—

"the 2009 Regulations" means the Lloyd's Underwriters (Equalisation Reserves) (Tax) Regulations 2009;

"relevant accounting period" is any accounting period ending on or after 31st December 2008 but ending before 1st January 2016;

"relevant deduction" is an amount deducted by a corporate member or a partnership member in computing the member's profits or losses in a relevant accounting period as a result of the application of section 444BA(2)(*a*) of ICTA under regulation 3(3) (reserves maintained by Lloyd's members which are equivalent to equalisation reserves) of the 2009 Regulations;

"relevant receipt" is an amount treated as a receipt of the underwriting business of a corporate member or a partnership member in a relevant accounting period as a result of the application of section 444BA(2)(*b*) of ICTA under regulation 3(3) of the 2009 Regulations; and

"underwriting business" means, in relation to a corporate member or a partnership member, the member's underwriting business as a member of Lloyd's.

3 Application of sections 26(4) to (8) and 27 of FA 2012 to Lloyd's members

Where a corporate member or partnership member has taken into account a relevant deduction in making any computation of the member's profits or losses for any relevant accounting period, section 26(4) to (8) and section 27 of FA 2012 apply in relation to the member, subject to the modifications specified in regulation 4, in relation to accounting periods ending on or after 1st January 2016.

4 Modified application of sections 26(4) to (8) and 27 of FA 2012

(1) The modifications to sections 26(4) to (8) and 27 of FA 2012 referred to in regulation 3 are as follows.

(2) References in those sections to—

"business" are to be treated as references to the part of the underwriting business of the corporate member or partnership member which relates to insurance business other than life assurance business; and

"an insurance company" or "a company" are to be treated as references to the corporate member or the partnership member (as the case may be).

(3) In section 26(4), "transitional equivalent reserve" is to be treated as substituted for "existing equalisation or equivalent reserve".

(4) Sections 26(7) and (8) and 27(3) are to be treated as omitted.

(5) In paragraph (3), "transitional equivalent reserve" means the amount determined by the sum A - B, where—

"A" means the total of all relevant deductions for all relevant accounting periods; and

"B" means the total of all relevant receipts for all relevant accounting periods.

5 Revocation

The following are revoked—

(*a*) the Insurance Companies (Reserves) (Tax) Regulations 1996; and

(*b*) the 2009 Regulations.

2015/1986

ENFORCEMENT BY DEDUCTION FROM ACCOUNTS (PRESCRIBED INFORMATION) REGULATIONS 2015

Made . . . . *8 December 2015*

Laid before the House of Commons . . . . *9 December 2015*

Coming into force . . . . *25 January 2016*

The Commissioners for Her Majesty's Revenue and Customs make the following Regulations in exercise of the powers conferred by paragraphs 3(2), 8(2)(*a*), 8(2)(*c*), 8(2)(*d*), 8(4)(*b*) and 23(1) of Schedule 8 to the Finance (No 2) Act 2015 .

1 Citation, commencement and extent

(1) These Regulations may be cited as the Enforcement by Deduction from Accounts (Prescribed Information) Regulations 2015 and come into force on 25th January 2016.

(2) These Regulations extend to England and Wales and Northern Ireland only.

2 Interpretation

In these Regulations—

"account details" in respect of an account held by P means—

(*a*) any account number;

(*b*) any roll number;

(*c*) any sort code;

(*d*) the type of account, including whether or not it is a joint account;

(*e*) the account balance (in the currency in which the account is held);

(*f*) whether interest is payable in respect of amounts standing to the credit of the account and, if so, the rate of interest payable;

(*g*) any minimum balance required to keep the account open;

(*h*) any contractual term by virtue of which an account holder or interested third party may suffer economic loss where a hold notice or deduction notice is, or has been, given;

(*i*) specified information about—

(i) any account holder other than P;

(ii) any person (not falling within paragraph (i)) who is an interested third party in relation to the account;

(iii) any person who, in respect of the account, has power of attorney;

"P" means the person in respect of whom HMRC has given an information notice or, as the case may be, hold notice;

"Schedule 8" means Schedule 8 to the Finance (No 2) Act 2015;

"specified information" in respect of a person means—

(*a*) name and address;

(*b*) national insurance number;

(*c*) all email addresses;

(*d*) all telephone numbers;

(*e*) in respect of an account which is a joint account, the proportion of the balance of that joint account to which the person is entitled.

3 Information

(1) Information is only prescribed under these Regulations if it—

(*a*) is in the possession of, or immediately available to, a deposit-taker at the time the deposit-taker is given an information notice or, as the case may be, a hold notice, and

(*b*) describes the account, or, as the case may be, person, at the relevant time.

(2) The relevant time for the purposes of regulation 3(1)(*b*) is—

(*a*) in the case of the information prescribed by regulations 5(1)(*f*) and 5(1)(*g*), immediately after the deposit-taker has complied with the hold notice, and

(*b*) in any other case, immediately before the deposit-taker complies with the information notice, or, as the case may be, hold notice.

4 Prescribed information in respect of an information notice

The following information is prescribed for the purposes of paragraph 3(2) of Schedule 8 (information notice)—

(*a*) account details for each account P holds with the deposit-taker;

(*b*) specified information in relation to P.

5 Prescribed information in respect of a hold notice where an account is an affected account

(1) The following information is prescribed for the purposes of paragraph 8(2) of Schedule 8 (duty to notify HMRC and account-holders etc)—

(*a*) account details for each account P holds with the deposit-taker;

(*b*) specified information in relation to P;

(*c*) confirmation of which of the accounts that P holds with the deposit-taker is an affected account;

(*d*) the date on which the deposit-taker complied with paragraph 6(1) of Schedule 8 (effect of hold notice);

(*e*) confirmation that the deposit-taker understands the effect of paragraph 14(1)(*g*) of Schedule 8 (penalties);

(*f*) the total of all held amounts notified by the deposit-taker under paragraph 8(2)(*b*) of Schedule 8 in response to a hold notice;

(*g*) in respect of each account which P holds with the deposit-taker, the amount standing to the credit of the account which is not subject to action taken by the deposit-taker under paragraph 6(3) of Schedule 8;

(*h*) a description of any economic loss suffered by an account holder or interested third party as a result of any contractual term specified in the definition of "account details" in regulation 2 at sub-paragraph (*h*).

(2) In this regulation "held amounts" is to be read in accordance with paragraph 7 of Schedule 8.

6 Prescribed information in respect of a hold notice where an account is not affected account

(1) The following information is prescribed for the purposes of paragraph 8(4)(b) of Schedule 8.

(2) The information which the deposit-taker has taken into account to determine that there are no affected accounts.

2015/2002

QUALIFYING PRIVATE PLACEMENT REGULATIONS 2015

Made . . . . .9 December 2015

Laid before the House of Commons . . . . .10 December 2015

Coming into force . . . . .1 January 2016

The Treasury make the following Regulations in exercise of the powers conferred by section 888A of the Income Tax Act 2007.

1 Citation and commencement

These Regulations may be cited as the Qualifying Private Placement Regulations 2015 and come into force on 1st January 2016.

2 Interpretation

(1) In these Regulations—

"ITA 2007" means the Income Tax Act 2007;

"cancelled certificate" has the meaning given by regulation 7(7);

"creditor" means, in respect of a payment of interest on a relevant security, the person who is beneficially entitled to that interest;

"creditor certificate" has the meaning given by regulation 5(1);

"notification" means a notification in writing;

"relevant debtor" means the company which stands in the position of debtor in relation to a relevant security;

"relevant security" means a security or a loan relationship entered into before, on or after the date on which these Regulations come into force;

"scheme" includes any scheme, arrangements or understanding of any kind whatever, whether or not legally enforceable, involving a single transaction or two or more transactions;

"tax advantage scheme" means a scheme the main purpose, or one of the main purposes, of which is to obtain a tax advantage within the meaning given by section 1139 of CTA 2010, other than a negligible tax advantage;

"withdrawn certificate" has the meaning given by regulation 6(4).

(2) Reference in these Regulations to a relevant security being entered into includes a relevant security being issued.

3 Relevant securities which are qualifying private placements

(1) A relevant security which meets the debtor and listing conditions is a qualifying private placement if—

(*a*) the conditions specified in regulation 4 are met;

(*b*) subject to paragraph (2), the relevant debtor holds a creditor certificate for each creditor;

(*c*) the relevant security was entered into by the relevant debtor for genuine commercial reasons, and not as part of a tax advantage scheme; and

(*d*) the relevant debtor reasonably believes that the relevant debtor is not a connected person in respect of each creditor.

(2) Paragraph (1)(*b*) does not include a creditor certificate which is a cancelled or a withdrawn certificate.

(3) In this regulation—

(*a*) "connected person" is to be determined in accordance with section 993 of ITA 2007 but any rights that a person has as a loan creditor are to be disregarded for the purposes of section 450(3)(*d*) of CTA 2010; and

(*b*) "the debtor and listing conditions" are the conditions specified in paragraphs (*a*) and (*b*) of section 888A(2) of ITA 2007.

4 Conditions in relation to relevant securities

(1) Conditions A and B are specified in relation to the relevant security.

(2) Condition A is that the term of the relevant security does not exceed 50 years.

(3) Condition B is that—

(*a*) at the time the relevant security was entered into, it had a minimum value of £10 million; or

(*b*) where the relevant security had a lower value at the time it was entered into but it was comprised in a single placement with other relevant securities to the same debtor, the placement had a minimum value of £10 million.

5 Creditor certificates

(1) A "creditor certificate" means a written statement in which a confirmation is made by or on behalf of the creditor that conditions A and B are met in respect of the creditor.

(2) Condition A is that the creditor is a resident of a qualifying territory.

(3) Condition B is that the creditor is beneficially entitled to the interest on the relevant security for genuine commercial reasons, and not as part of a tax advantage scheme.

(4) For the purposes of condition A—

"qualifying territory" has the meaning given by section 173 of the Taxation (International and Other Provisions) Act 2010 ("TIOPA"); and

"resident" has the meaning given by section 167(5) of TIOPA, subject to paragraph (5).

(5) Where—

(*a*) the creditor ("C") is the State or any part of the State (including any local authority) of a qualifying territory; and

(*b*) C would not by virtue of section 167(5) of TIOPA be a resident of that territory,

C is to be treated as a resident of the qualifying territory.

6 Withdrawn certificates

(1) This regulation applies to a creditor certificate other than a cancelled certificate.

(2) As soon as practicable after a creditor becomes aware that the confirmation given in a creditor certificate has ceased to apply, the creditor (or a person on the creditor's behalf) must give a notification to the relevant debtor to that effect.

(3) Where a notification is given under paragraph (2), the creditor certificate is of no effect on and from the day after the date on which the notification is received.
(4) A creditor certificate which is of no effect further to this regulation is a "withdrawn certificate".

7 Production of creditor certificates to HMRC and cancelled certificates

(1) An officer of Her Majesty's Revenue and Customs ("a relevant officer") may by a notification given to a debtor ("D"), require D to produce a creditor certificate to the officer.
(2) A notification under paragraph (1) must—
(*a*) describe the certificate to be produced; and
(*b*) state the date ("the compliance date") required for compliance (being a date not earlier than 28 days after the date on which the notification is given).
(3) D must by the compliance date produce the certificate to the relevant officer.
(4) Paragraph (5) applies where—
(*a*) D fails to comply with paragraph (3); or
(*b*) the relevant officer reasonably believes that a certificate produced by D is inaccurate in a material particular.
(5) Where this paragraph applies, the relevant officer may by a notification given to D determine that a creditor certificate identified in the notification has no effect.
(6) Where a notification is given under paragraph (5), the creditor certificate is of no effect on and from the date the notification is received by D.
(7) A creditor certificate which is of no effect further to this regulation is a "cancelled certificate".

2015/2047

CAPITAL ALLOWANCES (DESIGNATED ASSISTED AREAS) ORDER 2015

Made . . . . *16 December 2015*
Laid before the House of Commons . . . . *17 December 2015*
Coming into force . . . . *7 January 2016*

The Treasury make the following Order in exercise of the powers conferred by section 45K(2)(*a*), (3) and (4) of the Capital Allowances Act 2001.

1 Citation, commencement, effect and interpretation

(1) This Order may be cited as the Capital Allowances (Designated Assisted Areas) Order 2015.
(2) This Order comes into force on 7th January 2016.
(3) An area designated by virtue of Schedule 1 to this Order is to be treated as having been designated on 1st April 2012.
(4) An area designated by virtue of Schedule 2 to this Order is to be treated as having been designated on 1st April 2015.
(5) In this Order "CAA 2001" means the Capital Allowances Act 2001.

2 Designation of areas

(1) The area shown enclosed by a red line on the map of a scale of 1:1250 included in the schedule to each memorandum of understanding described in paragraph (2) are designated as designated assisted areas for the purposes of section 45K of CAA 2001 (expenditure on plant and machinery for use in designated assisted areas).
(2) In paragraph (1) references to a "memorandum of understanding" are to a memorandum of understanding entered into for the purposes of section 45K of CAA 2001 by the Treasury with the responsible authority listed in column 1 of the tables in Schedule 1 or Schedule 2 to this Order on the date listed in column 2 of those tables.
(3) Each memorandum of understanding referred to in paragraph (2) is kept at the offices of HM Treasury at 1 Horse Guards Road, London SW1A 2HQ, where they (or a copy of them) may be inspected by members of the public at reasonable hours without charge.

SCHEDULE 1

Articles 1(3) and 2(2)

Table 1

Name of responsible authority	*Date of memorandum of understanding*	*Area included in the map*	*Enterprise Zone within which area falls*	*Assisted area within which area falls*
Redcar and Cleveland Borough Council	16th July 2013	South Bank Wharf site	Tees Valley Enterprise Zone	North East

Redcar and Cleveland Borough Council	16th July 2013	Wilton site	Tees Valley Enterprise Zone	North East
Wirral Metropolitan Borough Council	9th March 2015	Wirral Waters site	Mersey Waters Enterprise Zone	North West
Walsall Metropolitan Borough Council	2nd March 2015	George Dyke site	Black Country Enterprise Zone	West Midlands
Walsall Metropolitan Borough Council	2nd March 2015	Gasholder site	Black Country Enterprise Zone	West Midlands
Walsall Metropolitan Borough Council	2nd March 2015	Phoenix 10 site	Black Country Enterprise Zone	West Midlands

Note—An area designated by virtue of Schedule 1 is to be treated as having been designated on 1 April 2012 (see art 1(3) above).

SCHEDULE 2

Articles 1(4) and 2(2)

Table 2

Name of responsible authority	*Date of memorandum of understanding*	*Area included in the map*	*Enterprise Zone within which area falls*	*Assisted area within which area falls*
Redcar and Cleveland Borough Council	16th June 2015	Prairie site	Tees Valley Enterprise Zone	North East

Note—An area designated by virtue of Schedule 2 is to be treated as having been designated on 1 April 2015 (see art 1(4) above).

2016/44

ENFORCEMENT BY DEDUCTION FROM ACCOUNTS (IMPOSITION OF CHARGES BY DEPOSIT-TAKERS) REGULATIONS 2016

Made . . . . *18 January 2016*
Laid before the House of Commons . . . . *20 January 2016*
Coming into force . . . . *10 February 2016*

The Commissioners for Her Majesty's Revenue and Customs make the following Regulations in exercise of the powers conferred by paragraph 20(2)(*e*) of Schedule 8 to the Finance (No 2) Act 2015.

1 Citation, commencement and extent

(1) These Regulations may be cited as the Enforcement by Deduction from Accounts (Imposition of Charges by Deposit-takers) Regulations 2016 and come into force on 10th February 2016.

(2) These Regulations extend to England and Wales and Northern Ireland only.

2 Interpretation

In these Regulations "administrative costs" means the administrative costs incurred by a deposit-taker in complying with an obligation under Schedule 8 to the Finance (No 2) Act 2015 to which a final payment required under paragraph 13(11)(*b*)(ii) of that Schedule relates.

3 Imposition of charges

A deposit-taker may impose a charge upon an account holder in respect of administrative costs only where—

(*a*) there is an agreement between it and the account holder (or, as the case may be, account holders), which provides that the deposit-taker may charge a fee in respect of those costs,

(*b*) the deposit taker—

(i) has made the final payment required by paragraph 13(11)(*b*)(ii), and

(ii) has not previously imposed a charge in respect of those costs, and

(*c*) the amount of the charge imposed does not exceed the amount specified in regulation 4.

4 Amount that can be charged for administrative costs

The amount specified in this regulation is the lesser of—

(*a*) the amount of those administrative costs reasonably incurred by the deposit-taker, and

(*b*) £55.

2016/208

PROCEEDS OF CRIME ACT 2002 (CASH SEARCHES: CODE OF PRACTICE) ORDER 2016

Made . . . . *23 February 2016*

Coming into force . . . . *1 March 2016*

The Secretary of State makes this Order in exercise of the powers conferred by sections 292(4) and (5) of the Proceeds of Crime Act 2002 ("the Act").

The Secretary of State—

(*a*) in accordance with section 292(5) of the Act, has revised the code of practice made under section 292(1) of the Act in connection with the exercise of the powers conferred by virtue of section 289 of the Act ("the revised code of practice");

(*b*) in accordance with section 292(2) of the Act, has published a draft of the revised code of practice, considered any representations made about the draft by the Scottish Ministers, the Department of Justice and any other person and, as she thought appropriate, modified the draft accordingly; and

(*c*) in accordance with section 292(3) of the Act, has laid a draft of the revised code of practice before Parliament.

In accordance with section 459(6)(*a*) of the Act, a draft of this instrument has been laid before and approved by a resolution of each House of Parliament.

1 Citation and commencement

(1) This Order may be cited as the Proceeds of Crime Act 2002 (Cash Searches: Code of Practice) Order 2016.

(2) This Order comes into force on 1st March 2016.

2 Revised Code of Practice

The revised code of practice entitled "Code of Practice issued under section 292 of the Proceeds of Crime Act 2002 Recovery of Cash: Search Powers" laid in draft before Parliament on 16th December 2015 comes into operation on 1st March 2016.

3 Revocations

The following instruments are revoked—

(*a*) the Proceeds of Crime Act 2002 (Cash Searches: Code of Practice) Order 2002;

(*b*) the Proceeds of Crime Act 2002 (Cash Searches: Code of Practice) Order 2008;

(*c*) the Proceeds of Crime Act 2002 (Cash Searches: Code of Practice) (England and Wales and Scotland) Order 2015.

2016/209

PROCEEDS OF CRIME ACT 2002 (INVESTIGATIONS: CODE OF PRACTICE) (ENGLAND AND WALES AND NORTHERN IRELAND) ORDER 2016

Made . . . . *23 February 2016*

Coming into force . . . . *1 March 2016*

The Secretary of State makes this Order in exercise of the powers conferred by section 377(4) and (8) of the Proceeds of Crime Act 2002 ("the Act").

The Secretary of State has—

(*a*) in accordance with section 377(8) of the Act, revised the code of practice prepared under section 377(1) of the Act in connection with the exercise of functions under Chapter 2 of Part 8 of the Act by—

(*b*) in accordance with section 377(2) of the Act, published a draft of the revised code of practice, considered any representations made to her about the draft and amended the draft accordingly; and

(*c*) in accordance with section 377(3) of the Act, laid a draft of the revised code of practice before Parliament.

In accordance with section 459(6)(*a*) of the Act, a draft of this instrument has been laid before and approved by a resolution of each House of Parliament.

1 Citation and commencement

(1) This Order may be cited as the Proceeds of Crime Act 2002 (Investigations: Code of Practice) (England and Wales and Northern Ireland) Order 2016.

(2) This Order comes into force on 1st March 2016.

2 Revised Code of Practice

The revised code of practice entitled "Code of Practice issued under section 377 of the Proceeds of Crime Act 2002 Investigations" laid in draft before Parliament on 16th December 2015 comes into operation on 1st March 2016.

3 Revocations

The following instruments are revoked—

(*a*) the Proceeds of Crime Act 2002 (Investigations in England, Wales and Northern Ireland: Code of Practice) Order 2003;

(*b*) the Proceeds of Crime Act 2002 (Investigations in England, Wales and Northern Ireland: Code of Practice) Order 2008; and

(*c*) the Proceeds of Crime Act 2002 (Investigations: Code of Practice) (England and Wales) Order 2015.

2016/222

PROCEEDS OF CRIME ACT 2002 (INVESTIGATIVE POWERS OF PROSECUTORS: CODE OF PRACTICE) (ENGLAND AND WALES AND NORTHERN IRELAND) ORDER 2016

Made . . . . *24 February 2016*

Coming into force . . . . *1 March 2016*

The Attorney General and the Advocate General for Northern Ireland (the "Attorney General") make this Order in exercise of the powers conferred by section 377A(5) and (9) of the Proceeds of Crime Act 2002 ("the Act").

The Attorney General has—

(*a*) in accordance with section 377A(9) of the Act, revised the codes of practice prepared under section 377A(1) and (2) of the Act in connection with the exercise of functions under Chapter 2 of Part 8 of the Act by—

(*b*) in accordance with section 377A(3) of the Act, published a draft of the revised code of practice, considered any representations made to him about the draft and, as he thought appropriate, amended the draft accordingly; and

(*c*) in accordance with section 377A(4) of the Act, laid a draft of the revised code of practice before Parliament.

In accordance with section 459(6)(*aa*) of the Act a draft of this instrument has been laid before and approved by a resolution of each House of Parliament.

1 Citation, commencement and extent

(1) This Order may be cited as the Proceeds of Crime Act 2002 (Investigative Powers of Prosecutors: Code of Practice) (England and Wales and Northern Ireland) Order 2016.

(2) This Order comes into force on 1st March 2016.

2 Revised Code of Practice

The revised code of practice entitled "Code of Practice issued under section 377A of the Proceeds of Crime Act 2002 (England and Wales and Northern Ireland) Investigative Powers of Prosecutors" laid in draft before Parliament on 16th December 2015 comes into operation on 1st March 2016.

3 Revocations

The following instruments are revoked—

(*a*) The Proceeds of Crime Act 2002 (Investigative Powers of Prosecutors in England, Wales and Northern Ireland: Code of Practice) Order 2008; and

(*b*) The Proceeds of Crime Act 2002 (Investigative Powers of Prosecutors: Code of Practice) (England and Wales) Order 2015.

2016/237

TAXES (BASE EROSION AND PROFIT SHIFTING) (COUNTRY-BY-COUNTRY REPORTING) REGULATIONS 2016

Made . . . . *26 February 2016*
Laid before the House of Commons . . . . *26 February 2016*
Coming into force . . . . *18 March 2016*

The Treasury make these Regulations in exercise of the powers conferred by section 136 of the Finance Act 2002 and section 122 of the Finance Act 2015:

1 Citation and commencement

These Regulations may be cited as the Taxes (Base Erosion and Profit Shifting) (Country-by-Country) Reporting Regulations 2016 and come into force on 18th March 2016.

2 Interpretation

(1) In these Regulations—

"CBC report" means a country-by-country report or a United Kingdom country-by-country report;

"the Commissioners" means the Commissioners for Her Majesty's Revenue and Customs;

"country-by-country report" means a report about an MNE Group and its Constituent Entities containing the information specified in specific or general directions given by the Commissioners;

"exchange arrangements" means arrangements to exchange country-by-country reports or their equivalent;

"file", except in relation to filing outside the United Kingdom, means file with Revenue and Customs;

"filing deadline" means 12 months after the end of the . . . [1] period to which the CBC report relates;

"OECD model legislation" means the model legislation in the OECD Transfer Pricing Documentation and Country-by-Country Reporting, Action 13–2015 Final Report;

["partnership" means a partnership governed by the Partnership Act 1890, the Limited Partnerships Act 1907 or the Limited Liability Partnerships Act 2000;][1]

"reporting entity" has the meaning given by regulation 10;

["threshold requirement" has the meaning given by paragraphs (2) to (4) of regulation 3;][1]

"the tribunal" means the First-tier Tribunal or, where determined by or under Tribunal Procedure Rules, the Upper Tribunal;

"United Kingdom country-by-country report" has the meaning given by regulation 5; and

"United Kingdom Entity" has the meaning given by regulation 5.

(2) The following expressions have the same meaning in these Regulations as they do in the OECD model legislation—

"Consolidated Financial Statements" if they are prepared in accordance with generally accepted accounting practice or international accounting standards, which expressions have the meaning given to them in section 1127 of the Corporation Tax Act 2010; . . . [1]

"Constituent Entity"[; and

"International Agreement"][1]

(3) "MNE Group" has the same meaning in these Regulations as it does in Article 1(2) of the OECD model legislation except that Article 1(2)(ii) (Excluded MNE Group) does not apply.

[(4) "Ultimate Parent Entity" has the same meaning in these Regulations as it does in Article 1(6) of the OECD model legislation except with the following modifications to that Article—

(*a*) where an Ultimate Parent Entity is not a partnership, for the purposes of regulations 3A and 10(1)(*a*) for "a Constituent Entity of an MNE Group that meets the following criteria" there is treated as substituted "a Constituent Entity of an MNE Group resident in the United Kingdom for tax purposes that meets the following criteria"; and

(*b*) where an Ultimate Parent Entity is a partnership, for the purposes of regulations 3A and 10(1)(*b*) for "its jurisdiction of tax residence" there is treated as substituted "the jurisdiction under whose laws it is formed or organised" in both places where it occurs.][1]

Amendments—[1] The following amendments made by the Taxes (Base Erosion and Profit Shifting) (Country-by-Country Reporting) (Amendment) Regulations, SI 2017/497 regs 2, 3 with effect from 20 April 2017—

– in para (1), in definition of "filing deadline", word "accounting" revoked, definition of "partnership" inserted, and definition of "threshold requirement" substituted;

– in para (2), word "and" revoked and words inserted; and
– para (4) substituted.

In para (1), definition of "threshold requirement" previously read as follows—

""threshold requirement" has the meaning given by regulation 4;".

Para (4) previously read as follows—

"(4) "Ultimate Parent Entity" has the same meaning as it does in the OECD model legislation except that in regulations 3(3) and 10(1)(a) the entity must be resident in the United Kingdom for tax purposes.".

[3 Filing of CBC reports: general provisions

(1) Regulations 3A, 3B, 3C and 3D apply where the Consolidated Financial Statements of an MNE Group ("G") meet the threshold requirement for a period ("P") where P—

(*a*) commences before and ends on or after 31st December 2015; or

(*b*) commences on or after 1st January 2016.

(2) In paragraph (1) the "threshold requirement" means G has a total consolidated group revenue of €750 million—

(*a*) as shown in its Consolidated Financial Statements for P; or

(*b*) as would have been shown in its Consolidated Financial Statements for P had G been required to produce them by reason of the trading of equity interests in any of the enterprises in G on a public securities exchange.

(3) Where G draws up, or would draw up, its Consolidated Financial Statements in a currency other than euros, the reference to €750 million in paragraph (2) has effect as if it were a reference to the equivalent in that currency at the average exchange rate for P.

(4) When P is a period of more or less than 12 months, the amount of €750million in paragraph (2) (or the equivalent under paragraph (3)) is increased or decreased proportionately.

(5) In regulations 3A, 3B, 3C and 3D, "G" is the MNE Group.

(6) In regulations 3A, 3B, 3C and 3D, "P+1" is the period immediately following P in respect of which G prepares, or would prepare Consolidated Financial Statements.][1]

Amendments—[1] Regs 3–3D substituted for previous reg 3 by the Taxes (Base Erosion and Profit Shifting) (Country-by- Country Reporting) (Amendment) Regulations, SI 2017/497 regs 2, 4 with effect from 20 April 2017. Reg 3 previously read as follows—

"**3 Filing of CBC reports**(1) This regulation applies where an MNE Group ("G") meets the threshold requirement in respect of an accounting period ("AP") where AP—

(*a*) commences before and ends on or after 31st December 2015; or

(*b*) commences on or after 1st January 2016.

(2) The accounting period immediately following AP is "AP+1".

(3) The Ultimate Parent Entity of G must file a country-by-country report in respect of AP+1 by the filing deadline.

(4) Subject to paragraph (5), a United Kingdom Entity of G ("UKEG") must file a United Kingdom country-by-country report in respect of AP+1 by the filing deadline if—

(*a*) the UKEG is not required to file a country-by-country report under paragraph (3); and

(*b*) one of the conditions in regulation 6 is met.

(5) The duty in paragraph (4) does not apply if exception A or exception B applies.

(6) Exception A applies where before the filing deadline—

(*a*) a Constituent Entity of G has filed a country-by-country report further to paragraph (8) in respect of AP+1 and that report includes the information required to be contained in the United Kingdom country-by-country report otherwise required to be filed by the UKEG; and

(*b*) the UKEG provides details to Revenue and Customs of—

(i) the identity of the Constituent Entity which has filed the report; and

(ii) the date the report was filed.

(7) Exception B applies where before the filing deadline—

(*a*) a Constituent Entity of G has filed in a jurisdiction other than the United Kingdom the equivalent of a country-by-country report in respect of AP+1 and that report includes the information required to be contained in the United Kingdom country-by-country report otherwise required to be filed by the UKEG;

(*b*) the appropriate authority of that jurisdiction has entered into exchange arrangements with Revenue and Customs which apply to the report filed and Revenue and Customs has not notified the UKEG that the arrangements are not operating effectively; and

(*c*) the UKEG provides details to Revenue and Customs of—

(i) the identity of the Constituent Entity which has filed the report and where it is resident for tax purposes;

(ii) the jurisdiction in which the report was filed; and

(iii) the date the report was filed.

(8) A Constituent Entity of G ("CEG") may file a country-by-country report on behalf of G in respect of AP+1 by the filing deadline if—

(*a*) CEG or another Constituent Entity of G is resident for tax purposes in the United Kingdom or has a permanent establishment in the United Kingdom;

(*b*) CEG—

(i) is not required to file a country-by-country report under paragraph (3); and

(ii) is authorised by the Ultimate Parent Entity of G to file a country-by-country report on behalf of G in respect of AP+1 and the Ultimate Parent Entity has notified Revenue and Customs of that authority in writing on or before the filing deadline; and

(*c*) one of the conditions in regulation 6 is met.".

[3A Filing of country-by-country reports and notification by Ultimate Parent Entities

(1) Each Ultimate Parent Entity of G must file a country-by-country report in respect of P+1 by the filing deadline.

(2) Subject to paragraph (4) each Ultimate Parent Entity of G must notify to Revenue and Customs—

(*a*) that it is an Ultimate Parent Entity of G responsible for filing a country-by-county report in respect of P+1; and

(*b*) the names and unique taxpayer references of all of its Constituent Entities—

(i) which are resident in the United Kingdom for tax purposes;

(ii) which have a permanent establishment in the United Kingdom; or

(iii) which are partnerships.

(3) The notification required by paragraph (2) must be made by whichever is the later of the last day of P+1 or 1st September 2017 ("the deadline date").

(4) An Ultimate Parent Entity of G ("UPEG1") is not required to comply with paragraph (2) if before the deadline date—

(*a*) another Ultimate Parent Entity of G ("UPEG2") has provided a notification in accordance with paragraph (2) and that notification includes the information required to be contained in the notification otherwise to be provided by UPEG1; and

(*b*) UPEG1 provides details to Revenue and Customs of—

(i) the name of UPEG2; and

(ii) the date the notification by UPEG2 was provided.

(5) Where an Ultimate Parent Entity of G is a partnership the requirements imposed on it by this regulation must be complied with by the partner of the Ultimate Parent Entity of G who is required to deliver a return under section 12AA of TMA 1970.][1]

Amendments—[1] Regs 3–3D substituted for previous reg 3 by the Taxes (Base Erosion and Profit Shifting) (Country-by-Country Reporting) (Amendment) Regulations, SI 2017/497 regs 2, 4 with effect from 20 April 2017. For text of former reg 3, see above.

[3B Filing of CBC reports by United Kingdom Entities

(1) This regulation applies to each United Kingdom Entity of G ("UKEG") if—

(*a*) regulation 3A does not apply to the UKEG; and

(*b*) one of the conditions in regulation 6 is met.

(2) The requirements in paragraphs (3) and (4) do not apply if exception A or exception B applies.

(3) A UKEG must—

(*a*) request from its Ultimate Parent Entity all the information ("filing information") that the UKEG would need in order to file a country-by-country report in respect of P+1 before the filing deadline; and

(**b**) if the UKEG receives the filing information, file a country-by-country report in respect of P+1 by the filing deadline.

(4) If a UKEG does not receive the filing information before the filing deadline, it must by the filing deadline—

(*a*) notify Revenue and Customs in writing that its Ultimate Parent Entity has not provided the filing information; and

(*b*) file a United Kingdom country-by-country report in respect of P+1.

(5) Exception A applies where before the filing deadline—

(*a*) a Constituent Entity of G has filed a country-by-country report in accordance with paragraph (3)(*b*) or regulation 3D in respect of P+1 and that report includes the information required to be contained in the CBC report otherwise to be filed by the UKEG; and

(*b*) the UKEG provides details to Revenue and Customs of—

(i) the name of the Constituent Entity which has filed the report; and

(ii) the date the report was filed.

(6) Exception B applies where before the filing deadline—

(*a*) a Constituent Entity of G has filed in a jurisdiction other than the United Kingdom the equivalent of a country-by-country report in respect of P+1 and that report includes the information required to be contained in the CBC report otherwise required to be filed by the UKEG;

(*b*) the appropriate authority of that jurisdiction has entered into exchange arrangements with Revenue and Customs which apply to the report filed and Revenue and Customs has not notified the UKEG that the arrangements are not operating effectively; and

(*c*) the UKEG provides details to Revenue and Customs of—

(i) the identity of the Constituent Entity which has filed the report and where the Constituent Entity is resident for tax purposes;

(ii) the jurisdiction in which the report was filed; and

(iii) the date the report was filed.][1]

Amendments—[1] Regs 3–3D substituted for previous reg 3 by the Taxes (Base Erosion and Profit Shifting) (Country-by-Country Reporting) (Amendment) Regulations, SI 2017/497 regs 2, 4 with effect from 20 April 2017. For text of former reg 3, see above.

[3C Notification by United Kingdom Entities

(1) This regulation applies to each United Kingdom Entity of G ("UKEG") if regulation 3A does not apply to the UKEG.

(2) Subject to paragraph (4), a United Kingdom Entity of G ("UKEG") must notify to Revenue and Customs—

(*a*) whether or not the UKEG believes exception A or exception B will apply to it in respect of P+1; and

(*b*) if the UKEG does believe exception A or exception B will so apply—

(i) the name and unique taxpayer reference (or equivalent) of the Constituent Entity of G which the UKEG believes will file a CBC report or an equivalent report; and

(ii) the jurisdiction in which the UKEG believes the Constituent Entity will file the report; and

(*c*) the names and unique taxpayer references of all of G's Constituent Entities:

(i) which are resident in the United Kingdom for tax purposes;

(ii) which have a permanent establishment in the United Kingdom; or

(iii) which are partnerships.

(3) The notification required by paragraph (2) must be made by whichever is the later of the last day of P+1 or 1st September 2017 ("the deadline date").

(4) A United Kingdom Entity of G ("UKEG1") is not required to comply with paragraph (2) if before the deadline date—

(*a*) another United Kingdom Entity of G ("UKEG2") has provided a notification in accordance with paragraph (2) and that notification includes the information required to be contained in the notification otherwise to be provided by UKEG1; and

(*b*) UKEG1 provides details to Revenue and Customs of—

(i) the name of UKEG2; and

(ii) the date the notification by UKEG2 was provided.

(5) In this regulation exception A and exception B has the same meaning as in regulation 3B.][1]

Amendments—[1] Regs 3–3D substituted for previous reg 3 by the Taxes (Base Erosion and Profit Shifting) (Country-by-Country Reporting) (Amendment) Regulations, SI 2017/497 regs 2, 4 with effect from 20 April 2017. For text of former reg 3, see above.

[3D Voluntary filing of country-by-country reports by Constituent Entities

A Constituent Entity of G ("CEG") may file a country-by-country report on behalf of G in respect of P+1 by the filing deadline if—

(*a*) the CEG or another Constituent Entity of G is resident for tax purposes in the United Kingdom or has a permanent establishment in the United Kingdom;

(*b*) the CEG—

(i) is not required to file a country-by-country report under regulation 3A; and

(ii) is authorised by the Ultimate Parent Entity of G to file a country-by-country report on behalf of G in respect of P+1 and the Ultimate Parent Entity has notified Revenue and Customs of that authority in writing on or before the filing deadline; and

(*c*) one of the conditions in regulation 6 is met.][1]

Amendments—[1] Regs 3–3D substituted for previous reg 3 by the Taxes (Base Erosion and Profit Shifting) (Country-by-Country Reporting) (Amendment) Regulations, SI 2017/497 regs 2, 4 with effect from 20 April 2017. For text of former reg 3, see above.

4 Threshold requirement

(1) In regulation 3, the "threshold requirement" means that the MNE Group has a total consolidated group revenue of €750 million or more for an accounting period—

(*a*) *as shown in its Consolidated Financial Statements; or*

(*b*) *as would have been shown in its Consolidated Financial Statements had the Group been required to produce them by reason of the trading of equity interests in any of the enterprises in the MNE Group on a public securities exchange.*

(2) Where an MNE Group draws up, or would draw up, its Consolidated Financial Statements for an accounting period in a currency other than euros, the reference to €750 million in paragraph (1) has effect as if it referred to the equivalent in that currency at the average exchange rate for the accounting period.
(3) When the accounting period of an MNE Group is a period of less than 12 months, the amount of €750 million in paragraph (1) (or the equivalent under paragraph (2)) is reduced proportionately.

Amendments—[1] Reg 4 revoked by the Taxes (Base Erosion and Profit Shifting) (Country-by-Country Reporting) (Amendment) Regulations, SI 2017/497 regs 2, 5 with effect from 20 April 2017.

5 United Kingdom country-by-country report and United Kingdom Entity

(1) "United Kingdom country-by-country report" means a report which—

(*a*) relates to—

(i) a United Kingdom Entity; and

(ii) where applicable, the Constituent Entities in respect of which the United Kingdom Entity is required to prepare Consolidated Financial Statements or would be so required if its equity interests were traded on a public securities exchange; and

(*b*) contains the information specified in specific or general directions given by the Commissioners.

(2) "United Kingdom Entity" means a Constituent Entity ("UKE") in respect of which conditions A and B are satisfied.
(3) Condition A is satisfied where UKE is resident in the United Kingdom for tax purposes or has a permanent establishment in the United Kingdom.
(4) Condition B is satisfied where there is no other Constituent Entity of the MNE Group—

(*a*) resident in the United Kingdom for tax purposes; or

(*b*) which has a permanent establishment in the United Kingdom,

and which is required to prepare Consolidated Financial Statements or would be so required if its equity interests were traded on a public securities exchange and such statements include or would include UKE.

6 Conditions that apply for the purposes of [regulation 3B(1)(*b*) and 3D(*c*)]

The conditions referred to in [regulations 3B(1)(*b*) and 3D(*c*)][1] are—

(*a*) the Ultimate Parent Entity is not required to file the equivalent of a country-by-country report in the jurisdiction in which it is resident for tax purposes in respect of the . . . [1] period to which the report relates (or where the Ultimate Parent Entity is resident for tax purposes in more than one jurisdiction, no such requirement to file applies in any of those jurisdictions);

[(*b*) the appropriate authority of the jurisdiction in which the Ultimate Parent Entity is resident for tax purposes has entered into an International Agreement but has not entered into exchange arrangements with Revenue and Customs in respect of the period to which the report relates (or where the Ultimate Parent Entity is resident for tax purposes in more than one jurisdiction, none of the appropriate authorities of those jurisdictions has entered into such arrangements);][1]

(*c*) the appropriate authority of the jurisdiction in which the Ultimate Parent Entity has filed the equivalent of a country-by-country report has entered into exchange arrangements with Revenue and Customs but—

(i) in respect of the obligation on a UKEG in [regulation 3B][1], Revenue and Customs has notified the UKEG that the arrangements are not operating effectively; or

(ii) in respect of a CEG intending to file a county-by-country report further to [regulation 3D][1], the CEG has requested Revenue and Customs to confirm whether or not the arrangements are operating effectively and Revenue and Customs has notified the CEG that they are not.

Amendments—[1] The following amendments made by the Taxes (Base Erosion and Profit Shifting) (Country-by-Country Reporting) (Amendment) Regulations, SI 2017/497 regs 2, 6 with effect from 20 April 2017—

- in heading and opening words, words substituted for words "regulation 3(4)(*b*) and 3(8)(*c*)";
- in para (*a*), word "accounting" revoked;
- para (*b*) substituted; and
- in para (*c*), words substituted for words "regulation 3B" and "regulation 3D".

Para (*b*) previously read as follows—

"(*b*) the appropriate authority of the jurisdiction in which the Ultimate Parent Entity is resident for tax purposes has not entered into exchange arrangements with Revenue and Customs in respect of the accounting period to which the report relates (or where the Ultimate Parent Entity is resident for tax purposes in more than one jurisdiction, none of the appropriate authorities of those jurisdictions has entered into such arrangements);".

7 Commissioners' directions

(1) The Commissioners must give specific or general directions in respect of—

[(*a*) the content and form of presentation of—

(i) a CBC report; and

(ii) a notification required by regulation 3A(2), 3B(4)(*a*) or 3C(3); and

(*b*) the method for filing a report and providing a notification.][1]

(2) If the Commissioners direct an electronic method for filing a CBC report the directions referred to in paragraph (1) must provide for an electronic validation process.

Amendments—[1] Para (1)(*a*), (*b*) substituted by the Taxes (Base Erosion and Profit Shifting) (Country-by-Country Reporting) (Amendment) Regulations, SI 2017/497 regs 2, 7 with effect from 20 April 2017.

Para (1)(*a*), (*b*) previously read as follows—

"(*a*) the content and form of presentation of a CBC report; and

(*b*) the method for filing a report.".

8 Form and method of filing of CBC reports

A CBC report which must or may be filed under [regulations 3A(1), 3B(3)(*b*), 3B(4)(*b*) or 3D][1] must—

(*a*) be presented in the form; and

(*b*) be filed in accordance with the method,

directed by the Commissioners.

Amendments—[1] Words substituted for words "regulation 3" by the Taxes (Base Erosion and Profit Shifting) (Country-by-Country Reporting) (Amendment) Regulations, SI 2017/497 regs 2, 8 with effect from 20 April 2017.

[8A Form and method of notifications

A notification required by regulation 3A(2), 3B(4)(*a*) or 3C(2) must—

(*a*) be presented in the form; and

(*b*) be filed in accordance with the method,

directed by the Commissioners.][1]

Amendments—[1] Regulation 8A inserted by the Taxes (Base Erosion and Profit Shifting) (Country-by-Country Reporting) (Amendment) Regulations, SI 2017/497 regs 2, 9 with effect from 20 April 2017.

9 CBC report filing presumptions

(1) A CBC report which is purported to be filed otherwise than in accordance with regulation 8 is to be treated as not having been filed.

(2) Where Commissioners direct an electronic method for filing, unless the contrary is proved—

(*a*) the use of an electronic system is presumed to have resulted in the filing of the CBC report only if this has been successfully recorded as such by the relevant electronic validation process,

(*b*) the time of filing the CBC report is presumed to be the time recorded as such by the relevant electronic validation process, and

(*c*) the person delivering the CBC report is presumed to be the person identified as such by any relevant feature of the electronic system.

10 Reporting entities

[(1) For the purposes of section 122(4)(*a*) of FA 2015, the following are reporting entities—

(*a*) an Ultimate Parent Entity required to file a country-by-country report and provide a notification by regulation 3A or, where that Ultimate Parent Entity is a partnership, the partner of the Ultimate Parent Entity who is required to deliver a return under section 12AA of TMA 1970;

(*b*) a United Kingdom Entity required to file a CBC report by regulation 3B;

(*c*) a United Kingdom Entity required to provide a notification by regulation 3C; and

(*d*) a Constituent Entity which has filed a country-by-country report in accordance with regulation 3D.][1]

(2) A CBC report purporting to be filed on behalf of a reporting entity is taken to have been filed by that entity, unless the entity proves that the report was filed without the entity's authority.

Amendments—[1] Para 1 substituted by the Taxes (Base Erosion and Profit Shifting) (Country-by-Country Reporting) (Amendment) Regulations, SI 2017/497 regs 2, 10 with effect from 20 April 2017. Paragraph 1 previously read as follows—

"(1) For the purposes of section 122(4)(*a*) of FA 2015, the following are reporting entities—

(*a*) an Ultimate Parent Entity required to file a country-by-country report by regulation 3(3);

(*b*) a United Kingdom Entity required to file a United Kingdom country-by-country report by regulation 3(4); and

(*c*) a Constituent Entity which has filed a country-by-country report further to regulation 3(8).".

11 Provision of information

(1) The Commissioners may give a general or specific direction to a reporting entity requiring it to provide Revenue and Customs with such information (including copies of any relevant books, documents or other records) as may be specified in the direction for the purposes of determining whether information contained in a CBC report filed by that entity is accurate.

(2) Where a person is directed to provide information, the person must do so—

(*a*) within such period, being no less than 14 days; and

(*b*) at such time, by such means and in such form (if any),

as may be specified in the direction.

12 Penalties for failure to comply with Regulations

A person is liable to a penalty of £300 if the person fails to comply with [regulations 3A(1), 3A(2), 3B(3), 3B(4), 3C(3) or 11][1].

Amendments—[1] Words substituted for words "regulation 3(3), regulation 3(4), or regulation 11" by the Taxes (Base Erosion and Profit Shifting) (Country-by-Country Reporting) (Amendment) Regulations, SI 2017/497 regs 2, 11 with effect from 20 April 2017.

13 Daily default penalty

If—

(*a*) a penalty under regulation 12 is assessed; and

(*b*) the failure in question continues after the person has been notified of the assessment,

the person is liable to a further penalty, for each subsequent day on which the failure continues, of an amount (subject to regulation 19) not exceeding £60 for each such day.

14 Penalties for inaccurate information

(1) Where—

(*a*) a person provides inaccurate information when filing a CBC report; and

(*b*) condition A or B is met,

the person is liable to a penalty not exceeding £3,000 in respect of the report to which the inaccuracy relates.

(2) Where—

(*a*) a person provides inaccurate information when responding to a direction under regulation 11; and

(*b*) condition A or B is met,

the person is liable to a penalty not exceeding £3,000 in respect of each CBC report to which the inaccuracy relates.

(3) Condition A is that the person knows of the inaccuracy at the time information is provided but does not inform Revenue and Customs at that time.

(4) Condition B is that the person—

(*a*) discovers the inaccuracy after the information is provided; and

(*b*) fails to take reasonable steps to inform Revenue and Customs of that discovery.

15 Matters to be disregarded in relation to liability to penalties

(1) Liability to a penalty under regulation 12, 13 or 14 does not arise if the person otherwise liable to the penalty satisfies Revenue and Customs (or on an appeal notified to the tribunal, the tribunal) that there is a reasonable excuse for the failure or the provision of inaccurate information.

(2) For the purposes of this regulation it is not a reasonable excuse—

(*a*) that there is an insufficiency of funds to do something; or

(*b*) that a person relies on another person to do something.

(3) If a person has a reasonable excuse for a failure but the excuse ceases, the person is to be treated as continuing to have the excuse if the failure is remedied without unreasonable delay after the excuse ceases.

16 Assessment of penalties

(1) If a person becomes liable to a penalty under regulation 12, 13 or 14, an officer of Revenue and Customs may assess the penalty.

(2) If an officer does so, the officer must notify the person of the assessment.

(3) An assessment of a penalty under regulation 12 or 13 must be made within the period of—

(*a*) 6 years in respect of a failure to comply with [regulations 3A(1), 3A(2), 3B(3), 3B(4) or 3C(3)][1]; or

(*b*) 12 months in respect of a failure to comply with regulation 11,

beginning with the date on which the person became liable to the penalty.

(4) An assessment of a penalty under regulation 14 must be made within the earlier of—

(*a*) 12 months beginning with the date on which the inaccuracy first came to the attention of an officer of Revenue and Customs; or

(*b*) 6 years beginning with the date on which the person became liable to the penalty.

Amendments—[1] In para (3)(*a*), words substituted for words "regulation 3(3) or 3(4)" by the Taxes (Base Erosion and Profit Shifting) (Country-by-Country Reporting) (Amendment) Regulations, SI 2017/497 regs 2, 12 with effect from 20 April 2017.

17 Right to appeal against penalty

A person may by notice appeal against the assessment of a penalty notified to that person—

(*a*) on the grounds that liability to the penalty under any of regulations 12, 13 or 14 does not arise; or

(*b*) as to the amount of a penalty under regulation 13 or 14 .

18 Procedure on appeal against penalty

(1) Notice of an appeal under regulation 17 must be given—

(*a*) in writing;

(*b*) before the end of the period of 30 days beginning with the date on which notification under regulation 16 was given; and

(*c*) to Revenue and Customs.

(2) It must state the grounds of appeal.

(3) On an appeal under regulation 17(a) that is notified to the tribunal, the tribunal may confirm or cancel the assessment.

(4) On an appeal under regulation 17(b) that is notified to the tribunal, the tribunal may

(*a*) confirm the assessment; or

(*b*) substitute another assessment that the officer of Revenue and Customs had power to make.

(5) Subject to this regulation and regulation 20, the provisions of Part 5 of TMA 1970 relating to appeals have effect in relation to appeals under regulation 17 as they have effect in relation to an appeal against an assessment to income tax.

19 Application for increased daily default penalty

(1) Paragraph (2) applies if—

(*a*) a person is liable to a penalty under regulation 13 and a penalty is assessed under regulation 16; and

(*b*) the failure in respect of which that assessment is made continues for more than 30 days beginning with the date on which notification of that assessment is given.

(2) Where this paragraph applies, an officer of Revenue and Customs may make an application to the tribunal for permission to assess an increased daily penalty under regulation 12 but must notify the person liable to the penalty of the application at the time of making it.

(3) If the tribunal determines that an increased daily penalty may be assessed then for each applicable day on which the failure continues, the person's liability to a penalty under regulation 13 shall be for the increased amount determined by the tribunal.

(4) The tribunal may not determine an amount exceeding £1000 for each applicable day.

(5) If the tribunal determines an increased daily penalty, Revenue and Customs must notify the person.

(6) The notification under paragraph (5) must specify the future day from which the increased penalty is to apply.

(7) That day and any subsequent day is an "applicable day" for the purposes of paragraph (3) and (4).

20 Payment and enforcement of penalties

(1) A penalty under these Regulations must be paid before the end of the period of 30 days beginning with the date mentioned in paragraph (2).

(2) That date is—

(*a*) the date on which the assessment of the penalty under regulation 16 is notified in respect of the penalty; or

(*b*) if a notice of appeal under regulation 17 is given, the date on which—

(i) the appeal is finally determined (but the penalty is not cancelled or withdrawn); or;

(ii) the appeal is withdrawn.

(3) A penalty under these Regulations may be enforced as if it were income tax charged in an assessment and due and payable.

21 Anti-avoidance

If—

(*a*) a person enters into any arrangements; and

(*b*) the main purpose, or one of the main purposes, of the person in entering into the arrangements is to avoid any obligation under these Regulations,

these Regulations are to have effect as if the arrangements had not been entered into.

2016/333

FEES FOR PAYMENT OF TAXES, ETC BY CREDIT CARD REGULATIONS 2016

Made . . . . *9 March 2016*
Laid before the House of Commons . . . . *11 March 2016*
Coming into force . . . . *1 April 2016*

The Commissioners for Her Majesty's Revenue and Customs make the following Regulations in exercise of the powers conferred by section 136(1) to (3) of the Finance Act 2008.

In accordance with section 136(2) of that Act, the Commissioners expect that they, or a person authorised by them, will be required to pay a fee in connection with amounts paid by credit card.

1 Citation, commencement and interpretation

(1) These Regulations may be cited as the Fees for Payment of Taxes, etc by Credit Card Regulations 2016.

(2) These Regulations come into force on 1st April 2016.

(3) In these Regulations "relevant credit card" means a card which—

(*a*) is a credit-token within section 14(1)(*b*) of the Consumer Credit Act 1974 or, were the card to be given to an individual, would be such a credit-token, and

(*b*) is listed in Table 1 or Table 2 in the Schedule.

2 Fee payable where a payment is made by a relevant credit card

(1) A person making a payment by a relevant credit card to the Commissioners or a person authorised by them must pay a fee with the payment.

(2) The fee is the amount of the payment multiplied by the rate applicable to the relevant credit card as set out in Table 1 or Table 2 in the Schedule, as the case may be.

3 Revocation

The following are revoked—

(*a*) the Taxes, etc (Fees for Payment by Internet) Regulations 2011,

(*b*) the Taxes, etc (Fees for Payment by Telephone) Regulations 2012, and

(*c*) the Taxes, etc (Fees for Payment by Internet) (Amendment) Regulations 2015.

SCHEDULE

Regulations 1 and 2

Table 1

Personal credit cards

Type of card	*Rate*
VISA Personal Credit Card	0.415%
MasterCard Personal Credit Card	0.386%
MasterCard World Premium Credit Card	0.374%
MasterCard Signia Premium Credit Card	0.606%
MasterCard Elite Premium Credit Card	0.606%

Table 2

Corporate credit cards

Type of card	*Rate*
VISA Business Credit Card	1.508%
VISA Corporate Credit Card	1.744%
VISA Purchasing Credit Card	1.755%
MasterCard Business Credit Card	1.973%
MasterCard Corporate Credit Card	2.248%
MasterCard Purchasing Credit Card	2.406%
MasterCard Fleet Credit Card	2.134%

2016/350

INCOME TAX (TRAVEL EXPENSES OF MEMBERS OF LOCAL AUTHORITIES ETC) REGULATIONS 2016

Made . . . . *11 March 2016*

Laid before the House of Commons . . . . *14 March 2016*

Coming into force . . . .*6 April 2016*

The Treasury make the following Regulations in exercise of the powers conferred by sections 235A(6) and 295A(4) of the Income Tax (Earnings and Pensions) Act 2003.

1 Citation and commencement

These Regulations may be cited as the Income Tax (Travel Expenses of Members of Local Authorities etc) Regulations 2016 and come into force on 6th April 2016.

2 Relevant authority

For the purposes of sections 235A and 295A of the Income Tax (Earnings and Pensions) Act 2003, a body is a relevant authority if it is—

(*a*) in England—

(i) a county council,

(ii) a district council,

(iii) a London borough council,

(iv) the Council of the Isles of Scilly, or

(v) a parish council,

(*b*) in Wales—

(i) a county council,

(ii) a county borough council, or

(iii) a community council,

(*c*) in Scotland, a council constituted under section 2 of the Local Government etc (Scotland) Act 1994, or

(*d*) in Northern Ireland, a district council.

3 Qualifying payment

(1) For the purposes of sections 235A and 295A of the Income Tax (Earnings and Pensions) Act 2003, "qualifying payment" means a payment falling within paragraph (2) which is made—

(*a*) to a member of a relevant authority by a relevant authority, and

(*b*) in connection with activities undertaken by the member as a member of that authority.

(2) A payment falls within this paragraph if it is made—

(*a*) under a scheme made under regulation 8 of the Local Authorities (Members' Allowances) (England) Regulations 2003,

(*b*) under regulation 26 of those Regulations,

(*c*) in accordance with a requirement or authorisation under section 142 of the Local Government (Wales) Measure 2011,

(*d*) under regulation 4 or 5 of the Local Government (Allowances and Expenses) (Scotland) Regulations 2007, or

(*e*) under regulation 7 of the Local Government (Payments to Councillors) Regulations (Northern Ireland) 2012.

2016/566

BANKING SURCHARGE (INFORMATION) REGULATIONS 2016

Made . . . .*9 May 2016*

Laid before the House of Commons . . . .*10 May 2016*

Coming into force . . . .*1 June 2016*

The Treasury, in exercise of the powers conferred by section 59E of the Taxes Management Act 1970, make the following Regulations:

1 Citation and commencement

These Regulations may be cited as the Banking Surcharge (Information) Regulations 2016 and come into force on 1st June 2016.

2 Interpretation

In these Regulations—

"banking surcharge" means a sum—

(*a*) chargeable under section 269DA of CTA 2010 (surcharge on banking companies), as if it were an amount of corporation tax; or

(*b*) charged on a chargeable company at step 5 in section 371BC(1) of TIOPA 2010 (charging the CFC charge);

"surcharge payment" means payment to discharge (wholly or partly) the liability of a company in respect of banking surcharge;

"written notification" means a notification required under—

(*a*) section 269DM(2) of CTA 2010 (payments in respect of the surcharge: information to be provided); or

(*b*) section 371UBA(2) of TIOPA 2010 (payments in respect of a charge on a banking company: information to be provided).

3 Application

These Regulations apply where a surcharge payment is made or is to be made.

4 Additional information to be provided with written notifications

(1) The company providing the written notification must also provide with the notification—

(*a*) details of the accounting period to which the surcharge payment relates;

(*b*) the unique tax reference (if provided by Revenue and Customs) under which the surcharge payment is made; and

(*c*) where the written notification is provided before the surcharge payment is made, the date on which the company intends to make the payment.

(2) Where a reallocation request is made, the company providing the written notification must also provide with the notification—

(*a*) details of the amount (if any) of the surcharge payment which is to be met otherwise than by a reallocation sum;

(*b*) details of the amount of each reallocation sum;

(*c*) details of each tax in respect of which each reallocation sum was paid or allocated as payment;

(*d*) the date on which each reallocation sum was paid or allocated as payment and details of the accounting period to which the payment or allocation related;

(*e*) details of the company which paid or requested allocation as payment of each reallocation sum; and

(*f*) the unique tax reference (if provided by Revenue and Customs) under which each reallocation sum was paid or allocated as payment.

(3) In this regulation—

"reallocation request" means a request to Revenue and Customs to treat a reallocation sum as a sum paid or allocated as payment in respect of a surcharge payment; and

"reallocation sum" means a sum already paid or allocated in or towards the discharge of a liability in respect of any tax.

5 Compliance

The information required to be provided by regulation 4 is to be treated as a requirement to comply with an information notice for the purposes of Part 7 of Schedule 36 to the Finance Act 2008 (information and inspection powers).

2016/751

CAPITAL ALLOWANCES (DESIGNATED ASSISTED AREAS) ORDER 2016

Made .... *14 July 2016*

Laid before the House of Commons .... *14 July 2016*

Coming into force .... *5 August 2016*

The Treasury make the following Order in exercise of the powers conferred by section 45K(2)(*a*), (3) and (4) of the Capital Allowances Act 2001.

1 Citation, commencement, effect and interpretation

(1) This Order may be cited as the Capital Allowances (Designated Assisted Areas) Order 2016.

(2) This Order comes into force on 5th August 2016.

(3) An area designated by virtue of Schedule 1 to this Order is to be treated as having been designated on 18th March 2015.

(4) An area designated by virtue of Schedule 2 to this Order is to be treated as having been designated on 16th March 2016.

(5) In this Order "CAA 2001" means the Capital Allowances Act 2001.

2 Designation of areas

(1) The areas shown enclosed by a line on the map of a scale of 1:1250 included in the schedule to each memorandum of understanding described in paragraph (2) are designated as designated assisted areas for the purposes of section 45K of CAA 2001 (expenditure on plant and machinery for use in designated assisted areas).

(2) In paragraph (1) references to a "memorandum of understanding" are to a memorandum of understanding entered into for the purposes of section 45K of CAA 2001 by the Treasury with the responsible authority listed in column 1 of the tables in Schedule 1 or Schedule 2 to this Order on the date listed in column 2 of those tables.

(3) Each memorandum of understanding referred to in paragraph (2) is kept at the offices of HM Treasury at 1 Horse Guards Road, London SW1A 2HQ, where they (or a copy of them) may be inspected by members of the public at reasonable hours without charge.

SCHEDULE 1

Articles 1(3) and 2(2)

Table 1

Name of responsible authority	*Date of memorandum of understanding*	*Area included in the map*	*Enterprise Zone within which area falls*	*Assisted area within which area falls*
England				
Leeds City Council	12th June 2015	Logic Leeds	Leeds City Region Enterprise Zone	Yorkshire and the Humber
East Riding of Yorkshire Council and North Lincolnshire Council and North East Lincolnshire Council	20th January 2016	Great Coates	Humber Enterprise Zone	North East
Wyre Borough Council	27th January 2016	Hillhouse	Hillhouse International Business Park Enterprise Zone	North West
Blackpool Council	28th January 2016	Blackpool Airport	Blackpool Airport Enterprise Zone	North West
Cumbria County Council and Carlisle City Council	29th January 2016	Kingmoor Park	Kingmoor Park Enterprise Zone	North West
Cheshire West and Chester Borough Council	29th January 2016	South Road Former Simms Recycling Ellesmere Port	Cheshire Science Corridor Enterprise Zone	North West
		Thornton Science Park	Cheshire Science Corridor Enterprise Zone	North West
		South Road Former Simms Recycling Ellesmere Port	Cheshire Science Corridor Enterprise Zone	North West

Cheshire West and Chester Borough Council	29th January 2016	Ince Park (Phase 1) Ellesmere Port	Cheshire Science Corridor Enterprise Zone	North West
Stock-on-Trent City Council	29th January 2016	Chatterley Valley East	Ceramic Valley Enterprise Zone	West Midlands
		Etruria Valley	Ceramic Valley Enterprise Zone	West Midlands
		Temple Green	Ceramic Valley Enterprise Zone	West Midlands
Luton Borough Council	29th January 2016	Luton Airport Business Park	Luton Airport Enterprise Zone	East of England
Derby City Council	23rd June 2016	Infinity Park	Nottingham and Derby Enterprise Zone	East Midlands
Cornwall Council	12th June 2015	Newquay	Aerohub Enterprise Zone	Cornwall and the Isles of Scilly
		Goonhilly Earth Station	Aerohub Enterprise Zone	Cornwall and the Isles of Scilly

SCHEDULE 2

Articles 1(4) and 2(2)

Table 2

Name of responsible authority	*Date of memorandum of understanding*	*Area included in the map*	*Enterprise Zone within which area falls*	*Assisted area within which area falls*
Northern Ireland				
The Department for the Economy	23rd June 2016	Coleraine Industrial Area	Coleraine	Northern Ireland
		Dundooan Road	Coleraine	Northern Ireland
Wales				
Welsh Ministers	29th June 2016	Baglan Energy Park	Port Talbot	Wales
		Industrial Estate	Port Talbot	Wales
		Port Talbot Docks	Port Talbot	Wales

2016/771

MAJOR SPORTING EVENTS (INCOME TAX EXEMPTION) REGULATIONS 2016

Made . . . .*14 July 2016*
Coming into force . . . .*19 July 2016*

The Treasury make the following Regulations in exercise of the powers conferred by section 48 of the Finance Act 2014.

1 Citation, commencement and interpretation
These Regulations may be cited as the Major Sporting Events (Income Tax Exemption) Regulations 2016 and shall come into force on 19th July 2016.

2 In these Regulations—
(*a*) "Championships Period" means the period—
(i) beginning with 12th July 2017; and
(ii) ending with 15th August 2017;
(*b*) "duly accredited competitor" means—
(i) in relation to the London Anniversary Games, a competitor who has been accredited to compete at those Games by the International Association of Athletics Federations, the International Paralympic Committee, UK Athletics Limited (Company number 03686940) or any other official event organiser;
(ii) in relation to the World Athletics Championships, a competitor who has been accredited to compete in either or both of the events making up those Championships by the International Association of Athletics Federations, the International Paralympic Committee, London 2017 Limited (Company number 08492880) or any other official event organiser;
(*c*) "Games Period" means the period—
(i) beginning with 20th July 2016; and
(ii) ending with 25th July 2016;
(*d*) "income" means employment income or profits of a trade, profession or vocation (including profits treated as arising as a result of section 13 of the Income Tax (Trading and Other Income) Act 2005;
(*e*) "London Anniversary Games" means the athletics event planned to be held at the Queen Elizabeth Olympic Park in London on 22nd and 23rd July 2016;
(*f*) "World Athletics Championships" means these events—
(i) the International Paralympic Committee Athletics World Championships event planned to be held at the Queen Elizabeth Olympic Park in London from 14th to 23rd July 2017 inclusive; and
(ii) the International Association of Athletics Federations World Championships event planned to be held at the Queen Elizabeth Olympic Park in London from 4th to 13th August 2017 inclusive.

3 London Anniversary Games
A duly accredited competitor who performs a London Anniversary Games activity is not liable to income tax in respect of any income arising from the activity if the Games non-residence condition is met.

4 The following are London Anniversary Games activities—
(*a*) competing at the London Anniversary Games,
(*b*) any activity that is performed during the Games Period the main purpose of which is to support or promote the London Anniversary Games.

5 The Games non-residence condition is that—
(*a*) the duly accredited competitor is non-UK resident for the tax year 2016–17, or
(*b*) the duly accredited competitor is UK resident for the tax year 2016–17 but the year is a split year as respects the competitor and the activity is performed during the overseas part of the year.

6 Section 966 of the Income Tax Act 2007 (deduction of sums representing income tax) does not apply to any payment or transfer which gives rise to income benefitting from the exemption in regulation 3.

7 World Athletics Championships
A duly accredited competitor who performs a World Athletics Championships activity is not liable to income tax in respect of any income arising from the activity if the Championships non-residence condition is met.

8 The following are World Athletics Championships activities—
(*a*) competing at either or both of the events making up the World Athletics Championships,
(*b*) any activity that is performed during the Championships Period the main purpose of which is to support or promote either or both of the events making up the World Athletics Championships.

9 The Championships non-residence condition is that—
(*a*) the duly accredited competitor is non-UK resident for the tax year 2017–18, or
(*b*) the duly accredited competitor is UK resident for the tax year 2017–18 but the year is a split year as respects the competitor and the activity is performed during the overseas part of the year.

10 Section 966 of the Income Tax Act 2007 does not apply to any payment or transfer which gives rise to income benefitting from the exemption in regulation 7.

2016/1005

REGISTERED PENSION SCHEMES (BRIDGING PENSIONS) AND APPOINTED DAY REGULATIONS 2016

Made .... *17 October 2016*
Laid before House of Commons .... *18 October 2016*
Coming into force .... *8 November 2016*

The Commissioners for Her Majesty's Revenue and Customs make the following Regulations in exercise of the powers conferred by paragraph 2(4)(*h*) and (8) of Schedule 28 to the Finance Act 2004 , and section 20(6) of the Finance Act 2016 and now exercisable by them.

1 Citation, commencement and effect
(1) These Regulations may be cited as the Registered Pension Schemes (Bridging Pensions) and Appointed Day Regulations 2016 and come into force on 8th November 2016
(2) These Regulations have effect in relation to reductions in payments of scheme pensions made on or after 6th April 2016.

2 Appointed day in respect of amendments made to Part 1 of Schedule 28 to the Finance Act 2004
The appointed day for the coming into force of section 20(2) to (5) of the Finance Act 2016 is 6th April 2016.

3 Pensions bridging: Pensionable age on or before 5th April 2016
(1) This regulation applies to a member who reached pensionable age on or before 5th April 2016.
(2) The following are prescribed circumstances for the purposes of paragraph 2(4) of Schedule 28 to the Finance Act 2004—
(*a*) a reduction in the rate of the scheme pension, taking effect at a time during the permitted period, which together with any previous reductions of the kind referred to in this paragraph does not exceed the relevant state retirement pension rate at that time, or
(*b*) the pension ceasing to be payable at a time during the permitted period if at that time that rate is greater than the rate of the pension.
(3) In paragraph (2)
(*a*) "the permitted period" means the period beginning with the day on which the member reaches the age of 60 and ending with the day on which the member reaches the age of 65,
(*b*) "relevant state retirement pension rate" at any time means—
(i) where no employment of the member to which the pension scheme relates is or has been other than contracted-out employment by reference to the pension scheme, 125% of the rate of the basic pension at that time,
(ii) where no such employment of the member is or has been contracted-out employment by reference to the pension scheme, 250% of the rate of the basic pension at that time, and
(iii) otherwise, the percentage of the rate of the basic pension is that found by the formula set out below—

125 + ((125)(A / B))

Where—

A is the total number of years of a member's employment to which the pension scheme relates which is not or has not been contracted-out, and

B is the total number of years of a member's employment to which the pension scheme relates.

(4) For the purposes of paragraph (3)(*b*)—

(*a*) "contracted-out employment" has the meaning given in section 8(1) and (1A) of the Pension Schemes Act 1993 or section 4(1) of the Pension Schemes (Northern Ireland) Act 1993, and

(*b*) "the basic pension" means the basic pension specified in section 44(4) of the Social Security Contributions and Benefits Act 1992 or section 44(4) of the Social Security Contributions and Benefits (Northern Ireland) Act 1992.

4 Pensions bridging: Pensionable age on or after 6th April 2016

(1) This regulation applies to a member who reached pensionable age on or after 6th April 2016.

(2) The following are prescribed circumstances for the purposes of paragraph 2(4) of Schedule 28 to the Finance Act 2004—

(*a*) a reduction in the rate of the scheme pension, taking effect at a time during the permitted period, which together with any previous reductions of the kind referred to in this paragraph does not exceed the relevant state retirement pension rate at that time, or

(*b*) the pension ceasing to be payable at a time during the permitted period if at that time that rate is greater than the rate of the pension.

(3) In paragraph (2)—

(*a*) "the permitted period" means the period beginning with the day on which the member reaches the age of 60 and ending with the day on which the member reaches the age of 65 or, if later, reaches pensionable age,

(*b*) "the relevant state retirement pension rate" at any time is 200% of the full rate of the state pension at that time.

(4) In paragraph (3) "the full rate of the state pension" has the meaning given in section 3(1) of the Pensions Act 2014.

2016/1181

CORPORATION TAX ACT 2010 (PROFITS ARISING FROM THE EXPLOITATION OF PATENTS) FOREIGN TAXES DESIGNATION REGULATIONS 2016

Made . . . . *6 December 2016*
Laid before the House of Commons . . . . . . *7 December 2016*
Coming into force . . . . *31 December 2016*

In accordance with section 357BP(9) of the Corporation Tax Act 2010 it appears to the Treasury that the taxes designated in these Regulations may be charged at a reduced rate under provisions of the law of the country or territory concerned which correspond to the provisions of Part 8A of the Corporation Tax Act 2010.

The Treasury, in exercise of the powers conferred by section 375BP(8)(*d*) of the Corporation Tax Act 2010, make the following Regulations.

1 Citation and commencement

(1) These Regulations may be cited as the Corporation Tax Act 2010 (Profits Arising from the Exploitation of Patents) Foreign Taxes Designation Regulations 2016.

(2) These Regulations come into force on 31st December 2016.

2 Designation of foreign taxes

The following foreign taxes are designated for the purposes of section 357BP of the Corporation Tax Act 2010—

(*a*) in the Kingdom of Belgium, Corporate Income Tax,
(*b*) in the People's Republic of China, Corporate Income Tax,
(*c*) in the Republic of Colombia, Corporate Income Tax,
(*d*) in the Republic of Cyprus, Corporate Income Tax,
(*e*) in the French Republic, Corporation Tax,
(*f*) in the Republic of Hungary, Corporate Income Tax,
(*g*) in the State of Israel, Company Tax,
(*h*) in the Italian Republic, Corporate Income Tax,
(*i*) in the Republic of Korea, Corporate Income Tax,
(*j*) in the Principality of Liechtenstein, Corporate Income Tax,
(*k*) in the Grand Duchy of Luxembourg, Corporation Tax,
(*l*) in the Republic of Malta, Corporate Income Tax,
(*m*) in the Kingdom of the Netherlands, Corporate Income Tax,
(*n*) in the Portuguese Republic, Corporate Income Tax,

(*o*) in the Kingdom of Spain, Corporation Tax,
(*p*) in the Swiss Confederation, in the canton of Nidwalden, Cantonal Income Tax, and
(*q*) in the Republic of Turkey, Corporation Tax.

2016/1195

DONATIONS TO CHARITY (GIFT AID DECLARATIONS) REGULATIONS 2016

Made . . . . *7 December 2016*
Laid before the House of Commons . . . . *8 December 2016*
Coming into force . . . . *6 April 2017*

The Commissioners for Her Majesty's Revenue and Customs make the following Regulations in exercise of the powers conferred by sections 132 and 133 of the Finance Act 1999 and now exercisable by them, and section 428 of the Income Tax Act 2007.

PART 1
GENERAL AND INTERPRETATION

1 Citation, commencement and effect

(1) These Regulations may be cited as the Donations to Charity (Gift Aid Declarations) Regulations 2016 and come into force on 6th April 2017.
(2) These Regulations have effect in relation to gifts made on or after 6th April 2017.

2 Interpretation

In these Regulations—
"the 2000 Regulations" means the Donations to Charity by Individuals (Appropriate Declarations) Regulations 2000,
"HMRC" means the Commissioners for Her Majesty's Revenue and Customs,
"donor" means an individual who makes a gift to a charity,
"donor intermediary" means a person who is or was authorised by a donor to give a gift aid declaration on behalf of that donor to a charity,
"ITA 2007" means the Income Tax Act 2007, and
"tribunal" means the First-tier Tribunal or, where determined in accordance with the Tribunal Procedure (First-tier Tribunal) (Tax Chamber) Rules 2009, the Upper Tribunal.

PART 2
GIFT AID DECLARATION

3 Amendment of the Donations to Charity by Individuals (Appropriate Declarations) Regulations 2000

(1) In regulation 1(2) of the 2000 Regulations (effect)—
(*a*) in sub-paragraph (*a*) after "6th April 2000" insert "and on or before 5th April 2017", and
(*b*) in sub-paragraph (*b*) for "that date" substitute "6th April 2000".
(2) The amendment made by paragraph (1)(*a*) shall not prevent an appropriate declaration, given under regulation 4 of the 2000 Regulations on or before 5th April 2017 and which is capable of relating to gifts made after that date, from applying to such gifts. This is subject to paragraph (3).
(3) Regulations 5, 6 and 7 of the 2000 Regulations continue to apply to a declaration referred to in paragraph (2) on and after 6th April 2017. Regulations 9, 10 and 11 of these Regulations do not apply to such a declaration.

4 Manner in which a gift aid declaration may be given

(1) A gift aid declaration may be given—
(*a*) by a donor to a charity, or
(*b*) by a donor intermediary to a charity,
(2) A gift aid declaration may be given in writing or orally, including the use of written or oral methods of electronic communications.

5 Gift aid declaration given by a donor

(1) A gift aid declaration given by a donor under regulation 4(1)(*a*) must—
(*a*) contain the name and home address of the donor,
(*b*) name the charity (or be made in circumstances where the charity is identified),
(*c*) identify the gift or gifts to which the gift aid declaration relates, and
(*d*) confirm that the identified gift or gifts are to be qualifying donations for the purposes of section 416 of ITA 2007 (meaning of qualifying donation).

(2) An explanation of the effect of section 424 of ITA 2007 (charge to tax) must be given to the donor at the time the gift aid declaration in paragraph (1) is given in order for the gift aid declaration to have effect for the purposes of the Income Tax Acts (subject to paragraph (3) and regulations 10 and 11).
(3) A donor is entitled to cancel the gift aid declaration referred to in paragraph (1) by giving notice to the charity.
(4) The notification under paragraph (3) may be given in writing or orally, including the use of written or oral methods of electronic communications.

6 Gift aid declaration given by a donor intermediary

(1) A gift aid declaration given by a donor intermediary on behalf of a donor under regulation 4(1)(*b*) must—

(*a*) contain the name and home address of the donor,
(*b*) name the charity (or be made in circumstances where the charity is identified),
(*c*) identify the gift to which the gift aid declaration relates, and
(*d*) confirm that the identified gift is to be a qualifying donation for the purposes of section 416 of ITA 2007.

(2) Before giving a gift aid declaration a donor intermediary must have—

(*a*) been authorised by the donor to give a gift aid declaration on behalf of the donor, and
(*b*) given an explanation of the effect of section 424 of ITA 2007 to the donor,

in order for the gift aid declaration to have effect for the purposes of the Income Tax Acts (subject to paragraph (5) and regulation 10).
(3) A donor intermediary must obtain the authorisation referred to in paragraph (2)(*a*) and provide the explanation referred to in paragraph (2)(*b*) in every tax year in which it gives a gift aid declaration on behalf of the donor. This is subject to paragraph (4).
(4) Paragraph (3) does not apply in respect of a tax year if the donor intermediary obtained the authorisation referred to in paragraph (2)(*a*) and gave the explanation referred to in paragraph 2(*b*) on or after 1st March in the immediately preceding tax year.
(5) A donor is entitled to cancel the authorisation referred to in paragraph (2)(*a*) by giving notice to the donor intermediary.
(6) The notification under paragraph (5) may be given in writing or orally, including the use of written or oral methods of electronic communications.
(7) Where a donor notifies a donor intermediary under paragraph (5), the authorisation ceases to have effect from the date on which the donor intermediary receives that notification, or if the notice specifies a later date, from that date.

7 Record keeping by donor intermediaries

(1) For each authorisation given by a donor under regulation 6(2)(*a*), a donor intermediary must maintain a record of—

(*a*) the name and address of the donor, and
(*b*) the date on which the authorisation was received,

in a form, and to a standard, which can be inspected and audited by HMRC.
(2) The donor intermediary must preserve that record for six years from the end of the tax year, or where regulation 6(4) is relied upon from the end of the final tax year, to which the authorisation applies.
(3) For each gift aid declaration given on behalf of a donor under regulation 6, a donor intermediary must maintain a record of the date on which the explanation of the effect of section 424 of ITA 2007 was given to the donor in accordance with regulation 6(2)(*b*), in a form, and to a standard, which can be inspected and audited by HMRC.
(4) The donor intermediary must preserve that record for six years from the end of the tax year in which the gift aid declaration is given.
(5) For each notice of cancellation of authorisation received from a donor under regulation 6(5), a donor intermediary must maintain a record of—

(*a*) the name and home address of the donor, and
(*b*) the date on which notice of cancellation was received,

in a form, and to a standard, which can be inspected and audited by HMRC.
(6) The donor intermediary must preserve that record for six years from the end of the tax year in which the notice of cancellation is received.
(7) An officer of Revenue and Customs may by notice in writing require a donor intermediary to produce a record referred to in paragraph (1), (3) or (5) for inspection.
(8) Where a donor intermediary is required by a notice under paragraph (7) to produce a record for inspection, the donor intermediary must do so—

(*a*) within such period,
(*b*) at such time, by such means and in such form (if any), and
(*c*) at such place, other than a place used solely as a dwelling,

as is reasonably specified in the notice.

8 Annual statement to be provided by donor intermediaries

(1) By the 31st May immediately following the end of a tax year during which a donor intermediary has given a gift aid declaration on behalf of a donor under regulation 6, the donor intermediary must send the donor a statement in writing, or details as to how the donor can access a statement in writing stating—

(*a*) the aggregate value of donations made by the donor which have been subject to a gift aid declaration given by the donor intermediary during that tax year (the "gift aided donations"),

(*b*) the maximum amount of gift aid which charities may claim on the gift aided donations,

(*c*) that the statement does not include any gift aid declarations given by other donor intermediaries on behalf of the donor, or given by the donor directly to a charity, and

(*d*) that if the donor paid less income tax and capital gains tax in that tax year than the amount of gift aid claimed by charities on all the donor's donations in that tax year, it is the donor's responsibility to pay any difference.

This paragraph is subject to paragraph (2).

(2) Paragraph (1) does not apply to a tax year during which—

(*a*) the aggregate value of the gift aided donations is £20 or less, or

(*b*) only one gift aided donation is made.

(3) The donor intermediary must maintain a record of annual statements and details as to how to access annual statements sent under paragraph (1), in a form, and to a standard, which can be inspected and audited by HMRC.

(4) The donor intermediary must preserve that record for six years from the end of the tax year to which the annual statement relates.

9 Record keeping by charities

(1) A charity must either—

(*a*) maintain an auditable record of the gift aid declarations received from a donor or a donor intermediary in respect of which it submits a claim for gift aid relief, or

(*b*) comply with paragraphs (5) to (10) in relation to each such gift aid declaration.

This paragraph is subject to paragraph (4).

(2) The charity must preserve the auditable record for six years from the end of the tax year in which a gift aid declaration is given.

(3) An auditable record is a record of evidence—

(*a*) of gift aid declarations and the giving of them, and

(*b*) that (whether or not separate from the gift aid declarations) statements explaining the effect of section 424 of ITA 2007 were given to donors in accordance with regulation 5(2) or regulation 6(2)(*b*), as the case may be,

in a form, and to a standard, which can be inspected and audited by HMRC.

(4) If HMRC notify a charity that a record relating to a particular gift aid declaration or class of gift aid declarations, in respect of which it submitted a claim to HMRC, does not satisfy HMRC, the charity must comply with paragraphs (5) to (10) in relation to the gift aid declarations in question.

(5) In each case where paragraph (1)(*b*) or (4) applies, the charity must send the donor a written statement containing—

(*a*) the information required by regulation 5(1)(*a*) to (*d*) or 6(1)(*a*) to (*d*), as the case may be,

(*b*) an explanation of the effect of section 424 of ITA 2007,

(*c*) the date on which the charity sends the statement to the donor, and

(*d*) a statement that the donor is entitled to cancel the gift aid declaration by giving notice to the charity within 30 days beginning with the date in sub-paragraph (*c*).

(6) The statement required by paragraph (5) must be sent—

(*a*) within 30 days beginning with the day on which the charity receives—

(i) the gift aid declaration, in a case falling within paragraph (1)(*b*), or

(ii) the notification from HMRC, in a case falling within paragraph (4), or

(*b*) by such other time as may be agreed between an officer of Revenue and Customs and the charity.

(7) Where paragraph (5) applies, the donor is entitled to cancel the gift aid declaration by giving notice of cancellation ("cancellation notice") to the charity.

(8) The cancellation notice may be given in writing or orally, including the use of written or oral methods of electronic communications.

(9) The charity must maintain a record of—

(*a*) statements sent under paragraph (5), and

(*b*) cancellation notices received under paragraph (7),

in a form, and to a standard, which can be inspected and audited by HMRC.

(10) The charity must preserve the record for six years from the end of the tax year in which the statement is sent or the cancellation notice is received, as the case may be.

10 Circumstances in which a gift aid declaration is treated as never having had effect

A gift aid declaration shall be treated for the purposes of the Income Tax Acts as never having had effect where—

(*a*) in a case where it is required to do so by regulation 9(5), the charity does not send a written statement in respect of the gift aid declaration to the donor by the date specified in regulation 9(6)(*a*), or the time agreed under regulation 9(6)(*b*), as the case may be,

(*b*) the donor cancels the gift aid declaration by giving a cancellation notice under regulation 9(7), or

(*c*) in a case where the charity is required by regulation 9(9) and (10) to maintain and preserve a record of statements sent and notices of cancellation received in relation to a gift aid declaration, HMRC notify the charity that the record does not satisfy HMRC.

11 Circumstances in which a gift aid declaration ceases to have effect

Where a donor notifies a charity of the cancellation of a gift aid declaration, other than under regulation 9(7), the gift aid declaration ceases to have effect for the purposes of the Income Tax Acts from the date on which the charity receives that notification, or if the notice specifies a later date, from that date.

PART 3
PENALTIES

12 Penalties for failure to comply with Regulations

(1) A donor intermediary is liable to a penalty of £50 in respect of each failure to—

(*a*) maintain a record of an authorisation, in accordance with regulation 7(1) and (2),

(*b*) maintain a record of the date on which the explanation of the effect of section 424 of ITA 2007 was given, in accordance with regulation 7(3) and (4),

(*c*) maintain a record of a notice of cancellation, in accordance with regulation 7(5) and (6),

(*d*) send an annual statement or details as to how to access an annual statement, in accordance with regulation 8(1), and

(*e*) maintain a record of an annual statement, in accordance with regulation 8(3) and (4).

(2) But in relation to a tax year a donor intermediary's liability for penalties under paragraph (1) attributable to that tax year is subject to a limit of £3,000.

(3) For the purposes of paragraph (2) a failure referred to—

(*a*) in paragraph (1)(*a*) is attributable to the tax year in which the authorisation was obtained,

(*b*) in paragraph (1)(*b*) is attributable to the tax year in which the explanation of the effect of section 424 of ITA 2007 was given,

(*c*) in paragraph (1)(*c*) is attributable to the tax year in which the notice of cancellation was given, and

(*d*) in paragraph (1)(*d*) or (*e*) is attributable to the tax year in respect of which the annual statement was required to be sent.

(4) A donor intermediary who fails to comply with a notice under regulation 7(7) to produce a record for inspection is liable to a penalty of £300.

(5) If the failure mentioned in paragraph (4) continues after the date on which a penalty is imposed under that paragraph in respect of the failure, the donor intermediary is liable to a further penalty or penalties not exceeding £60 for each subsequent day on which the failure continues.

13 Assessment of penalties

(1) If a donor intermediary becomes liable to a penalty under regulation 12, an officer of Revenue and Customs may assess the penalty.

(2) If an officer does so, the officer must notify the donor intermediary.

(3) An assessment of a penalty under regulation 12(1) must be made within the period of 12 months beginning with the date on which the failure first came to the attention of an officer of Revenue and Customs.

(4) An assessment of a penalty under regulation 12(4) or (5) must be made within the period of 12 months beginning with the date on which donor intermediary became liable to the penalty.

14 Suspension of penalties

(1) HMRC may suspend a penalty under regulation 12(1) or (4) by notice in writing to the donor intermediary liable to the penalty.

(2) A notice must specify—

(*a*) that the penalty is to be suspended,

(*b*) a period of suspension not exceeding two years, and

(*c*) conditions of suspension to be complied with by the donor intermediary.

(3) HMRC may suspend a penalty only if compliance with a condition of suspension would help the donor intermediary to avoid becoming liable to further penalties under these Regulations.

(4) A condition of suspension may specify—

(*a*) action to be taken, and

(*b*) a period within which it must be taken.

(5) On the expiry of the period of suspension—

(*a*) if the donor intermediary satisfies HMRC that the conditions of suspension have been complied with, the suspended penalty is cancelled, and

(*b*) otherwise, the suspended penalty becomes payable.

(6) If, during the period of suspension of a penalty under paragraph (1), the donor intermediary becomes liable for another penalty under these Regulations, the suspended penalty becomes payable.

15 Right to appeal in respect of penalties

(1) A donor intermediary may appeal against a decision of HMRC that a penalty is payable under these Regulations.

(2) A donor intermediary may appeal against a decision of HMRC as to the amount of a penalty payable under these Regulations.

(3) A donor intermediary may appeal against a decision of HMRC not to suspend a penalty payable under these Regulations.

(4) A donor intermediary may appeal against a decision of HMRC setting conditions of suspension of a penalty under these Regulations.

16 Procedure on appeal in respect of penalties

(1) Notice of an appeal under regulation 15 must be given—

(*a*) in writing,

(*b*) to HMRC, and

(*c*) before the end of 30 days beginning with the date on which the notification was given—

(i) under regulation 13 in the case of an appeal under regulation 15(1) to (3), or

(ii) under regulation 14 in the case of an appeal under regulation 15(4).

(2) It must state the grounds of appeal.

(3) On an appeal under regulation 15(1) that is notified to the tribunal, the tribunal may confirm or cancel the assessment.

(4) On an appeal under regulation 15(2) that is notified to the tribunal, the tribunal may—

(*a*) confirm the assessment, or

(*b*) substitute another assessment that the officer of Revenue and Customs had power to make.

(5) On an appeal under regulation 15(3) that is notified to the tribunal—

(*a*) the tribunal may order HMRC to suspend the penalty only if it thinks that HMRC's decision not to suspend was flawed, and

(*b*) if the tribunal orders HMRC to suspend the penalty—

(i) the donor intermediary may appeal against a provision of the notice of suspension, and

(ii) the tribunal may order HMRC to amend the notice.

(6) On an appeal under regulation 15(4) that is notified to the tribunal, the tribunal may—

(*a*) affirm the conditions of suspension, or

(*b*) vary the conditions of suspension, but only if the tribunal thinks that HMRC's decision in respect of the conditions was flawed.

(7) In paragraphs (5) and (6) "flawed" means flawed when considered in the light of the principles applicable in proceedings for judicial review.

17 Enforcement of penalties

(1) A penalty under these Regulations must be paid before the end of the period of 30 days beginning with the date mentioned in paragraph (2).

(2) That date is—

(*a*) the date on which the notification under regulation 13 is given in respect of the penalty, or

(*b*) if a penalty is suspended under regulation 14, the date on which the suspended penalty becomes payable, or

(*c*) if a notice of appeal under regulation 16 is given, the date on which the appeal is finally determined in favour of HMRC or withdrawn.

(3) A penalty under these Regulations may be enforced as if it were income tax charged in an assessment and due and payable.

2016/1212

BANK LEVY (DOUBLE TAXATION RELIEF) (SINGLE RESOLUTION FUND LEVY) REGULATIONS 2016

Made . . . . 13 December 2016

Coming into force in accordance with regulation 1(1)

The Treasury make the following Regulations in exercise of the powers conferred by paragraph 67 of Schedule 19 to the Finance Act 2011.

A draft of this instrument was laid before and approved by a resolution of the House of Commons in accordance with paragraph 67(6)(*b*) of Schedule 19 to the Finance Act 2011.

Introduction

1 Citation, commencement and effect

(1) These Regulations may be cited as the Bank Levy (Double Taxation Relief) (Single Resolution Fund Levy) Regulations 2016 and come into force on the day after the day on which they are made.

(2) These Regulations have effect in relation to periods of account ending on or after 1 January 2016.

2 Specified equivalent foreign levy

(1) The equivalent foreign levy in respect of which these Regulations are made is the SRF levy.

(2) In these Regulations, "SRF levy" means the individual contributions within Article 69 or 70 of the SRM Regulation raised from entities by a national resolution authority and transferred to the single resolution fund (established by the SRM Regulation) in accordance with the Agreement.

(3) In this regulation—

"Agreement" has the same meaning as in Article 3(1)(36) of the SRM Regulation;

"entities" means entities within Article 2 of the SRM Regulation;

"national resolution authority" has the same meaning as in Article 3(1)(3) of the SRM Regulation;

"the SRM Regulation" mean Regulation (EU) No 806/2014 of the European Parliament and of the Council establishing uniform rules and a uniform procedure for the resolution of credit institutions and certain investment firms in the framework of a Single Resolution Mechanism and a Single Resolution Fund and amending Regulation (EU) No 1093/2010

3 Application of these Regulations

(1) These Regulations apply where condition 1 or 2 is met.

(2) Condition 1 is that—

(*a*) the bank levy is charged in relation to a UK banking group, a UK sub-group or a UK banking sub-group, and

(*b*) the SRF levy is charged in relation to that UK banking group, UK sub-group or UK banking sub-group.

(3) Condition 2 is that—

(*a*) the bank levy is charged in relation to the relevant entity which is a relevant foreign bank, and

(*b*) the SRF levy is charged in relation to that relevant entity.

(4) These Regulations apply separately in relation to the imposition of the SRF levy by the law of different foreign territories.

Double taxation relief by way of credit

4 Double taxation relief

(1) Subject to the provisions of these Regulations, an amount of the SRF levy paid in relation to a chargeable period in respect of which the SRF levy is calculated is allowed as a credit to reduce the amount of the bank levy arising in that period.

(2) The credit under this regulation requires a claim in accordance with regulations 9 and 10.

(3) The amount of the credit allowed against the bank levy arising in a chargeable period must not exceed the lower of—

(*a*) the amount of the bank levy for that period, and

(*b*) the amount determined under—

(i) regulation 5 in cases where condition 1 in regulation 3 is met, and

(ii) regulation 6 in cases where condition 2 in regulation 3 is met.

5 Calculation of the maximum credit: UK banking group, UK sub-group or UK banking sub-group

(1) The amount of the credit must not exceed the amount of bank levy that would be payable by the entity ("the specified entity") subject to the SRF levy were the specified entity a UK resident bank in relation to which the bank levy would be charged as provided for by paragraph 5 of Schedule 19 to FA 2011 (bank levy to be charged in relation to certain entities which are not members of groups) in the period in relation to which the SRF levy is calculated.

(2) For the purposes of paragraph (1), in determining the amount of bank levy that would be payable, the amount of £20,000,000,000 in Step 5 of paragraph 6 of Schedule 19 to FA 2011 is reduced (in both places) to an amount equal to Y% of £20,000,000,000.

(3) For the purposes of paragraph (2), Y% is the proportion of the chargeable equity and liabilities of the UK banking group, UK sub-group or UK banking sub-group which is chargeable equity and liabilities of the specified entity.

(4) In a case where—

(*a*) the specified entity is subject to the SRF levy and another equivalent foreign levy, and

(*b*) relief is available under arrangements affording double taxation relief under the law of the territory imposing the other equivalent foreign levy,

the credit is limited to an amount equal to the amount of the credit calculated under paragraph (1) less the amount of relief available in relation to the equivalent foreign levy.

6 Calculation of the maximum credit: relevant foreign bank

The amount of the credit must not exceed the amount determined by steps 1 to 4.

Step 1

Determine the amount ("A") of assets of the relevant entity as at the end of the chargeable period by reference to which the SRF levy is calculated.

Step 2

Determine the amount ("B") of UK assets as at the end of the chargeable period by reference to which the SRF levy is calculated.

Step 3

Determine the amount ("C") of the SRF levy paid in relation to the chargeable period.

If a proportion (Z%) of the period in relation to which the SRF levy is calculated falls in any other chargeable period, Z% of the SRF levy is attributable to that other period.

Step 4

The amount of the SRF levy available as a credit against the bank levy must not exceed—

B / A) x C

7 Determining assets and UK assets

(1) This regulation applies for the purposes of regulation 6 to determine the assets and the UK assets of the relevant entity.

(2) In the case of a relevant entity which is part of a relevant group, the amount of the assets and the UK assets are determined by reference to—

(*a*) the amounts recognised in the group's consolidated financial statements for the chargeable period as prepared under international accounting standards or UK GAAP, or

(*b*) if no such financial statements are prepared, the amounts which would have been so recognised had consolidated financial statements for the group been prepared for the chargeable period under international accounting standards.

(3) In the case of a relevant entity which is not part of a relevant group, the assets and UK assets are determined by reference to—

(*a*) the amounts recognised in the entity's financial statements for the chargeable period as prepared under international accounting standards or UK GAAP, or

(*b*) if no such financial statements are prepared, the amounts which would have been so recognised had such financial statements been prepared for the chargeable period under international accounting standards or under UK GAAP.

(4) For the purposes of these Regulations, "UK assets" means the assets of any permanent establishment through which the relevant entity carries on a trade in the United Kingdom.

(5) Paragraph 26 (including sub-paragraph (4)) of Schedule 19 to FA 2011 applies for the purposes of determining the assets of a permanent establishment.

8 Exchange rates

Where the SRF levy is imposed in a currency other than sterling, for the purposes of regulations 5 and 6 the amount of equivalent foreign currency is to be translated into its sterling equivalent by reference to the spot rate of exchange for the last day of the chargeable period in relation to which the credit is claimed.

Claim for double taxation relief

9 General time limit for making a claim

(1) A claim for credit under regulation 4 must be made not more than—

(*a*) four years after the end of the accounting period in relation to which the bank levy is treated as an amount of corporation tax chargeable on the responsible member under paragraph 50 of Schedule 19 to FA 2011 or the relevant entity under paragraph 51 of that Schedule, or

(*b*) if later, one year after the end of the accounting period in which the SRF levy is paid.

(2) If the chargeable period in relation to which the bank levy is charged falls in more than one accounting period, the accounting period referred to in paragraph (1)(*a*) is the latest of those periods.

10 Relevant groups: responsible member to make claim

Where the bank levy is charged as provided for by paragraph 4 of Schedule 19 to FA 2011 (bank levy to be charged in relation to certain groups of entities) any claim for credit under regulation 4 must be made by the responsible member.

Limits on credit

11 Limits on credit in cases where regulation 6 applies

Regulations 12 to 15 apply where the maximum credit against the bank levy is calculated under regulation 6 (cases where the bank levy is charged in relation to a relevant entity which is a relevant foreign bank).

12 Restriction of credit

(1) Where the bank levy is charged in relation to the relevant group, if the parent entity is not resident in the foreign territory ("territory A") the law of which imposes the SRF levy, the credit under regulation 4(1) is only available to reduce the amount of the bank levy charged in relation to relevant chargeable equity and liabilities of the relevant group.

(2) In paragraph (1), "relevant chargeable equity and liabilities" means chargeable equity and liabilities that would be recognised in relevant accounts for the chargeable period had such accounts been prepared for the member or members of the group ("the relevant member or members") resident in territory A.

(3) In paragraph (2), "relevant accounts" mean a consolidated financial statement or financial statement—

(*a*) prepared under international accounting standards or under UK GAAP if that is what the relevant member or members prepare financial statements under, and

(*b*) in which the UK assets subject to the SRF levy in respect of which the credit is given would be recognised.

13(1) Where—

(*a*) there is double taxation in relation to the bank levy and the SRF levy only in relation to a permanent establishment through which a trade is carried on in the United Kingdom by a relevant foreign bank, and

(*b*) that relevant foreign bank is a relevant entity,

the credit under regulation 4(1) is only available to reduce the amount of the bank levy so far as it is attributable to the chargeable equity and liabilities of the permanent establishment.

(2) Subject to paragraph (3), the amount of the bank levy attributable to the chargeable equity and liabilities of the permanent establishment is calculated as follows.

Step 1

Determine the amount ("A") of the chargeable equity and liabilities of the permanent establishment which is long term equity and liabilities and the amount ("B") which is short term liabilities.

Step 2

Determine the amount ("C") of the chargeable equity and liabilities of the relevant group which is long term equity and liabilities and the amount ("D") which is short term liabilities.

Step 3

Determine the weighted average amount ("E") of chargeable equity and liabilities of the permanent establishment as follows—

A + 2B

Step 4

Determine the proportion ("F%") of the weighted average of chargeable equity and liabilities of the relevant group that relates to the weighted average of chargeable equity and liabilities of the permanent establishment (determined at step 3 as E) as follows—

E / (C + 2D)

Step 5

F% of the amount of the bank levy is the amount of the bank levy attributable to the chargeable equity and liabilities of the permanent establishment.

(3) If the basis of attribution in paragraph (2) would work unjustly or unreasonably, the attribution is to be made on another basis that is just and reasonable.

14 Reduction in credit: payment by reference to SRF levy

(1) Paragraph (2) applies if—

(*a*) credit against the bank levy is allowed to an entity under these Regulations, and

(*b*) a payment is made by a tax authority to that entity, or to any other person, by reference to the SRF levy.

(2) The amount of the credit must be recalculated by repeating steps 3 and 4 in regulation 6, reducing the amount of the SRF levy by reference to the payment referred to in paragraph (1)(*b*).

15 Priority of credits

(1) Where credits are allowed in relation to the SRF levy imposed by the law of two or more foreign territories under these Regulations or under these Regulations and any Regulations made under paragraph 66 (arrangements affording double taxation relief) or 67 (power to provide for double taxation relief) of Schedule 19 to FA 2011, the credits apply to reduce the bank levy in the order specified in paragraph (2), subject to paragraphs (3) and (4).

(2) The order is—

First, any credit allowed in relation to the equivalent foreign levy imposed by the law of the foreign territory in which the parent entity is resident.

Second, any credit allowed in relation to the equivalent foreign levy imposed by the law of the foreign territory in which a direct subsidiary ("the first subsidiary") is resident or a permanent establishment of the parent entity is located.

Third, any credit allowed in relation to an equivalent foreign levy imposed by the law of the foreign territory in which a direct subsidiary ("the second subsidiary") is resident or a permanent establishment of the first subsidiary is located.

Fourth, any credit allowed in relation to an equivalent foreign levy imposed by the law of the foreign territory in which a direct subsidiary of the second subsidiary is resident or a permanent establishment of the second subsidiary is located, and so on in relation to any fourth and further subsidiaries.

(3) If an entity has direct subsidiaries ("the elected subsidiaries") in more than one foreign territory which imposes an equivalent foreign levy, the responsible member must elect as to the order ("the elected order") in which the credits allowed in relation to the equivalent foreign levies are to be applied.

(4) If any of the elected subsidiaries themselves have direct subsidiaries in more than one foreign territory which imposes an equivalent foreign levy, paragraphs (2) and (3) apply to those direct subsidiaries in the elected order and paragraph (2) applies as if each elected subsidiary were a parent entity.

(5) For the purposes of this regulation, where an equivalent foreign levy is not imposed by the law of the foreign territory in which an entity ("E") is resident, any direct subsidiary of E is treated as the direct subsidiary of the entity which is the parent entity of E.

Action after adjustment of amount payable by way of bank levy or SRF levy

16 Consequences of adjustment of the bank levy or SRF levy

(1) Paragraph (2) applies to a claim or assessment if—

(*a*) the amount of credit given under regulation 4(1) is reduced under regulation 14, or becomes excessive or insufficient by reason of any adjustment of the amount of any bank levy or SRF levy,

(*b*) the reduction or adjustment gives rise to the claim or assessment, and

(*c*) the claim or assessment is made not later than 6 years from the date on which all material determinations have been made, whether in the UK or elsewhere.

(2) Nothing in the Tax Acts limiting the time for the making of assessments, or limiting the time for the making of claims for relief, applies to the assessment or claim.

(3) In paragraph (1)(*c*), "material determinations" means such assessments, reductions, adjustments or other determinations that are material in determining whether any, and (if so) what, credit is to be given.

17 Notice that adjustment has rendered credit excessive

(1) This regulation applies if—

(*a*) any credit has been allowed under regulation 4(1), and

(*b*) later, the amount of that credit is reduced under regulation 14, or becomes excessive as a result of an adjustment of the amount of the SRF levy.

(2) The relevant entity or, in the case of the relevant group, the responsible member must give notice that a reduction has been made or that the amount of the credit has become excessive as a result of the making of an adjustment.

(3) Notice under paragraph (2) is to be given—

(*a*) to an officer of Revenue and Customs, and

(*b*) within one year from when the reduction or adjustment is made.

2016/1244

ANNUAL TAX ON ENVELOPED DWELLINGS (INDEXATION OF ANNUAL CHARGEABLE AMOUNTS) (NO 2) ORDER 2016

Made . . . . *19 December 2016*

The Treasury make the following Order in discharge of the duty imposed by section 101(5) of the Finance Act 2013.

1 Citation

This order may be cited as the Annual Tax on Enveloped Dwellings (Indexation of Annual Chargeable Amounts) (No 2) Order 2016.

2 Chargeable amounts

The amounts that are to be the annual chargeable amounts for the chargeable period beginning on 1st April 2017 by virtue of section 101 (indexation of annual chargeable amounts) of the Finance Act 2013 are determined in accordance with the following table, by reference to the taxable value of the interest on the relevant day.

Annual chargeable amount	*Taxable value of the interest on the relevant day*
£3,500	More than £500,000 but not more than £1 million.
£7,050	More than £1 million but not more than £2 million.
£23,550	More than £2 million but not more than £5 million.
£54,950	More than £5 million but not more than £10 million.
£110,100	More than £10 million but not more than £20 million.
£220,350	More than £20 million.

2016/1250

SPORTING TESTIMONIAL PAYMENTS (EXCLUDED RELEVANT STEP) REGULATIONS 2016

Made . . . .*19 December 2016*
Laid before the House of Commons . . . .*20 December 2016*
Coming into force . . . .*6 April 2017*

The Commissioners for Her Majesty's Revenue and Customs, in exercise of the powers conferred by section 554Y(1) and (3) of the Income Tax (Earnings and Pensions) Act 2003, make the following Regulations:

1 Citation, commencement and interpretation

(1) These Regulations may be cited as the Sporting Testimonial Payments (Excluded Relevant Step) Regulations 2016 and come into force on 6th April 2017.

(2) Terms used in these Regulations and in section 226E of the Income Tax (Earnings and Pensions) Act 2003 (sporting testimonial payments) have the same meaning as in that section.

2 Disapplication of Chapter 2 of Part 7A: sporting testimonial payments

(1) Chapter 2 of Part 7A of the Income Tax (Earnings and Pensions) Act 2003 (employment income provided through third parties: treatment of relevant step for income tax purposes) does not apply by reason of a relevant step if the relevant step is the making of a sporting testimonial payment.

(2) Paragraph (1) applies in relation to a sporting testimonial payment made out of money raised by a sporting testimonial if—

(*a*) the sporting testimonial was made public on or after 25th November 2015, and

(*b*) the payment is made out of money raised by one or more relevant events or activities which take place on or after 6th April 2017.

2017/10

TAXATION OF CHARGEABLE GAINS (GILT-EDGED SECURITIES) ORDER 2017

Made . . . .*10 January 2017*

The Treasury make the following Order in exercise of the powers conferred by paragraph 1 of Schedule 9 to the Taxation of Chargeable Gains Act 1992:

1 Citation

This Order may be cited as the Taxation of Chargeable Gains (Gilt-edged Securities) Order 2017.

2 Securities specified as gilt-edged securities

For the purposes of the Taxation of Chargeable Gains Act 1992 the following securities are specified as "gilt-edged securities"—

0⅛% Index-linked Treasury Gilt 2036

0⅛% Index-linked Treasury Gilt 2065

0½% Treasury Gilt 2022
1½% Treasury Gilt 2026
1¾% Treasury Gilt 2037
1½% Treasury Gilt 2047
2½% Treasury Gilt 2065.

2017/292

INVESTMENT ALLOWANCE AND CLUSTER AREA ALLOWANCE (INVESTMENT EXPENDITURE) REGULATIONS 2017

Made . . . .*7 March 2017*
Laid before the House of Commons . . . .*8 March 2017*
Coming into force . . . .*29 March 2017*

The Treasury make the following Regulations in exercise of the powers conferred by sections 332BA, 332K, 356JE and 356JN of the Corporation Tax Act 2010.

1 Citation, commencement and effect

(1) These Regulations may be cited as the Investment Allowance and Cluster Area Allowance (Investment Expenditure) Regulations 2017 and come into force on 29th March 2017.
(2) These Regulations have effect in relation to any expenditure that is incurred on or after 8th October 2015.

2 Investment expenditure

(1) Expenditure which is operating expenditure within regulation 3 or leasing expenditure within regulation 4 is investment expenditure for the purposes of Chapter 6A and Chapter 9 of Part 8 of the Corporation Tax Act 2010.
(2) This is subject to regulations 5, 6 and 7.

3 Operating expenditure

(1) Expenditure is "operating expenditure" for the purposes of these Regulations if it satisfies Conditions A, B and C.
(2) Condition A is that the expenditure is incurred by a company for the purpose of increasing—
(*a*) the rate at which oil is extracted from a qualifying oil field or a cluster area;
(*b*) the reserves of oil of a qualifying oil field or a cluster area;
(*c*) the number of years for which it is economically viable to carry out oil extraction activities in relation to a qualifying oil field or a cluster area;
(*d*) the number of years for which a facility can be used for the purposes of oil extraction activities in relation to a qualifying oil field or a cluster area; or
(*e*) the amount of tariff receipts or tax-exempt tariffing receipts that are earned by the company in respect of upstream petroleum infrastructure.
(3) Condition B is that the expenditure is not routine repair or maintenance expenditure.
(4) Condition C is that the expenditure is incurred—
(*a*) in relation to a facility, on—
(i) replacement of a valve, pump, pipeline, power generation plant or compressor that is no longer capable of being used for the purposes of oil extraction activities,
(ii) modifications to increase capacity to carry out oil extraction activities,
(iii) modifications to increase availability to carry out oil extraction activities,
(iv) modifications to enable handling of reduced volumes that arise as a result of reduced operating pressures, or
(v) modifications to enable handling of different fluid compositions, or
(*b*) in relation to an oil well, on—
(i) water shut off,
(ii) gas shut off,
(iii) fracturing, or
(iv) the removal of sand, salt, scale or hydrates.
(5) For the purposes of this regulation, where a company incurs expenditure and part of that expenditure is operating expenditure and part is not, the expenditure is to be apportioned on a just and reasonable basis.
(6) In this regulation—
"facility" means—
(*a*) a platform;
(*b*) a subsea oil well;
(*c*) a platform well;

(*d*) an oil well head; or

(*e*) upstream petroleum infrastructure;

"tariff receipts" has the meaning given by section 6 of the Oil Taxation Act 1983;

"tax-exempt tariffing receipts" has the meaning given by section 6A of the Oil Taxation Act 1983; and

"upstream petroleum infrastructure" has the meaning given by section 9H of the Petroleum Act 1998.

4 Leasing expenditure

(1) Expenditure is "leasing expenditure" for the purposes of these Regulations if it satisfies Conditions A to E.

(2) Condition A is that the expenditure is incurred by a company in relation to the lease of an asset.

(3) Condition B is that the asset is a mobile asset whose main function is the production or storage of oil.

(4) Condition C is that the lease is for a term of 5 years or longer.

(5) Condition D is that the asset is used in—

(*a*) a qualifying oil field whose development was authorised for the first time on or after 8th July 2015;

(*b*) a qualifying oil field in respect of which—

(i) the national authority authorised a project in relation to the oil field after consent for development of the field was first granted,

(ii) the project was described in a further consent for development of the field,

(iii) the project was authorised on or after 8th July 2015, and

(iv) the asset is used for the purposes of the project in respect of which the authorisation was granted; or

(*c*) a cluster area that was determined on or after 3rd December 2014.

(6) Condition E is that on the date that the expenditure is incurred, no company has generated investment allowance or cluster area allowance in respect of the acquisition of the asset.

(7) In paragraph (2) (Condition A)—

(*a*) expenditure is incurred in relation to the lease of an asset only to the extent that it represents payment in return for the asset being made available;

(*b*) expenditure which does not represent payment in return for the asset being made available includes, in particular, any—

(i) charge for the provision of any staff,

(ii) charge for any services,

(iii) amount payable which is, or represents, a profit or premium on the cost of the asset being made available which is paid by a company to an associated company,

(iv) amount which, in accordance with generally accepted accounting practice, falls (or would fall) to be shown in the company's accounts as a finance charge in respect of a lease, or

(v) amount that can be attributed to finance costs by reference to the interest rate implicit in the lease, being the interest rate that would apply to the lease in accordance with normal commercial criteria, including, in particular, generally accepted accounting practice (if applicable).

(8) In paragraph (5) (Condition D)—

(*a*) references to—

(i) authorisation of development of an oil field, and

(ii) consent for development,

are to be interpreted in accordance with section 356IB of the Corporation Tax Act 2010; and

(*b*) "development", and "national authority" have the same meanings as in section 356IB(2) of the Corporation Tax Act 2010.

5 Excluded expenditure: receipt of lease amounts

(1) For the purposes of these Regulations, expenditure is only investment expenditure to the extent that it exceeds the total amount received by the company and its associated companies in respect of any qualifying leases other than—

(*a*) amounts received from the lessee (including a sublessee) where the parties to a qualifying lease are associated companies; or

(*b*) amounts previously set against expenditure under this paragraph which would have been relievable investment expenditure but for this regulation.

(2) In paragraph (1), "qualifying lease" means a lease to which the company or any associated company is, or was, party as lessee (including as sublessee) and in respect of which investment allowance or cluster area allowance has been generated by the company or any associated company by incurring leasing expenditure, or would have been generated but for this regulation.

6 Excluded expenditure: subleases

For the purposes of these Regulations, in relation to a sublease of an asset entered into or modified on or after the date these Regulations come into force, expenditure is not leasing expenditure to the extent it that exceeds the total amount of leasing expenditure incurred in relation to the head lease during the term of the sublease.

7 Excluded expenditure: arrangements

(1) For the purposes of these Regulations, expenditure is not investment expenditure to the extent that it arises in connection with any arrangements in respect of which the main purpose, or one of the main purposes, of entering into the arrangements is to—

(*a*) enable expenditure to qualify as investment expenditure, if it would otherwise not meet the conditions specified in regulation 3 or 4;

(*b*) enable expenditure to be incurred on a date earlier or later than the date on which it would otherwise have been incurred;

(*c*) generate, or increase generation of, investment allowance or cluster area allowance; or

(*d*) generate investment allowance or cluster area allowance earlier than it otherwise would have been generated.

(2) In paragraph (1), "arrangements" includes any transaction, series of transactions, scheme or arrangement, whether or not legally enforceable.

8 When expenditure is incurred

Expenditure that is investment expenditure as a result of these Regulations is treated for the purposes of Chapter 6A and Chapter 9 of Part 8 of the Corporation Tax Act 2010 as incurred on the date when it is paid.

2017/334

ASSET-BASED PENALTY FOR OFFSHORE INACCURACIES AND FAILURES (REDUCTIONS FOR DISCLOSURE AND CO-OPERATION) REGULATIONS 2017

Made . . . . *9 March 2017*
Laid before the House of Commons . . . . *10 March 2017*
Coming into force . . . . *1 April 2017*

The Treasury make the following Regulations in exercise of the powers conferred by paragraph 8(3) and (4) of Schedule 22 to the Finance Act 2016.

1 Citation and commencement

These Regulations may be cited as the Asset-based Penalty for Offshore Inaccuracies and Failures (Reductions for Disclosure and Co-operation) Regulations 2017 and come into force on 1st April 2017.

2 Maximum amount of reduction of the standard amount of the asset-based penalty for disclosure and co-operation

The maximum amount by which the standard amount of the asset-based penalty determined in accordance with paragraph 7 of Schedule 22 to the Finance Act 2016 (standard amount of asset-based penalty) may be reduced as required by paragraph 8 of that Schedule (reductions for disclosure and co-operation) is—

(*a*) 50% of the standard amount in a case involving only unprompted disclosures, and

(*b*) 20% of the standard amount in a case involving prompted disclosures.

2017/345

PENALTIES RELATING TO OFFSHORE MATTERS AND OFFSHORE TRANSFERS (ADDITIONAL INFORMATION) REGULATIONS 2017

Made . . . . *9 March 2017*
Laid before the House of Commons . . . . *10 March 2017*
Coming into force . . . . *1 April 2017*

The Treasury make the following Regulations in exercise of the powers conferred by paragraph 9(1C) of Schedule 24 to the Finance Act 2007, paragraph 12(2C) of Schedule 41 to the Finance Act 2008 and paragraph 14(2C) of Schedule 55 to the Finance Act 2009:

1 Citation and commencement

These Regulations may be cited as the Penalties Relating to Offshore Matters and Offshore Transfers (Additional Information) Regulations 2017 and come into force on 1st April 2017.

2 Interpretation

In these Regulations—

"asset" has the meaning given in section 21(1) of the Taxation of Capital Gains Act 1992, but also includes sterling;

"document" includes part of a document.

3 Additional information for the purposes of paragraph 9(1B)(*d*) of Schedule 24 to the Finance Act 2007, paragraph 12(2B)(*d*) of Schedule 41 to the Finance Act 2008 and paragraph 14(2B)(*d*) of Schedule 55 to the Finance Act 2009

The additional information required for the purposes of paragraph 9(1B)(*d*) of Schedule 24 to the Finance Act 2007, paragraph 12(2B)(*d*) of Schedule 41 to the Finance Act 2008 and paragraph 14(2B)(*d*) of Schedule 55 to the Finance Act 2009, is that a person ("P") must—

(*a*) tell HMRC whether or not regulations 4 or 5 (or both) apply to P; and

(*b*) provide HMRC with the information specified in relation to those regulations set out in regulations 6 and 7 (as appropriate).

4 This regulation applies to P if there is a person ("the enabler") who encouraged, assisted or otherwise facilitated the conduct by P giving rise to the penalty in question.

5 This regulation applies to P if—

(*a*) P is the sole or a joint beneficial owner of an asset ("the asset") situated or held in a territory outside the United Kingdom; and

(*b*) the person holding the asset ("the asset holder") is not P.

6 Additional information to be provided to HMRC where regulation 4 applies to P

The additional information to be provided to HMRC where regulation 4 applies to P is—

(*a*) the name and address of the enabler;

(*b*) a description of the enabler's conduct that encouraged, assisted or otherwise facilitated the conduct by P giving rise to the penalty in question;

(*c*) a description of how the first contact between P and the enabler was made and how the contact was maintained during the times when the enabler's conduct encouraged, assisted or otherwise facilitated the conduct by P giving rise to the penalty in question; and

(*d*) a description of all documents held by P relating to the enabler's conduct that encouraged, assisted or otherwise facilitated the conduct by P giving rise to the penalty in question.

7 Additional information to be provided to HMRC where regulation 5 applies to P

The additional information to be provided to HMRC where regulation 5 applies to P is—

(*a*) the name and address of any other joint beneficial owner of the asset;

(*b*) the extent of P's share of the beneficial ownership of the asset;

(*c*) a description of all documents of title or other documents indicating P's beneficial ownership of the asset;

(*d*) details of where the asset is situated or held;

(*e*) details of when and how P became a beneficial owner of the asset (including a description of all documents held by P relating to the acquisition of P's beneficial ownership of the asset);

(*f*) a description of all changes in the arrangements for the ownership of the asset since P became a beneficial owner of it (including the date of any change in the arrangements and a description of all documents held by P relating to such changes);

(*g*) the names and last known addresses of all persons who have been asset holders of the asset during P's beneficial ownership of it; and

(*h*) in relation to an asset holder who is not an individual, the name and business address (if known) of any director, senior manager, employee or agent of the asset holder who has advised or assisted P in relation to P's beneficial ownership of the asset.

8 (1) A description of a document provided in accordance with regulations 6 or 7 must (as far as it is reasonably practicable to do so) state in relation to the document—

(*a*) the latest of the date when the document was made, prepared or, if appropriate, signed or executed;
(*b*) the person who made or prepared it (and the person on whose behalf it was made or prepared if different);
(*c*) the person who signed or executed the document (if appropriate);
(*d*) the person to whom the document was given or sent (if appropriate);
(*e*) a summary of its contents or the information recorded in the document;
(*f*) the location of the document or where it may be inspected.

(2) The requirement to provide a description of a document in accordance with regulations 6 or 7 may be met by the provision of the document in question to HMRC or a suitable copy of it.

(3) The provision of a document (or a copy of it) to HMRC as described in paragraph (2) is without prejudice to any requirement to produce the document in question to HMRC or power of HMRC to require the production of the document.

2017/377

CAPITAL GAINS TAX (ANNUAL EXEMPT AMOUNT) ORDER 2017

Made . . . . 13th March 2017

The Treasury make the following Order in discharge of the duty imposed by section 3(4) of the Taxation of Chargeable Gains Act 1992:

1 Citation

This Order may be cited as the Capital Gains Tax (Annual Exempt Amount) Order 2017.

2 Exempt amount of capital gains for 2017–18

The amount which is, by virtue of section 3 of the Taxation of Chargeable Gains Act 1992, the exempt amount for the tax year 2017–18 (unless Parliament otherwise determines) is £11,300.

2017/446

SCOTTISH INFECTED BLOOD SUPPORT SCHEME (APPLICATION OF SECTIONS 731, 733 AND 734 OF THE INCOME TAX (TRADING AND OTHER INCOME) ACT 2005) ORDER 2017

Made . . . . 20 March 2017
Laid before the House of Commons . . . . 21 March 2017
Coming into force . . . . 13 April 2017

The Treasury make the following Order in exercise of the power conferred by section 732(2) of the Income Tax (Trading and Other Income) Act 2005.

1 Citation, commencement and interpretation

(1) This Order may be cited as the Scottish Infected Blood Support Scheme (Application of Sections 731, 733 and 734 of the Income Tax (Trading and Other Income) Act 2005) Order 2017 and comes into force on 13th April 2017.

(2) In this Order "Scottish scheme" and "Scheme beneficiary" have the meanings given in section 731(7) and (8) of the Income Tax (Trading and Other Income) Act 2005 (treated as inserted by article 2(2)(*b*)).

2 Application of sections 731, 733 and 734 of the Income Tax (Trading and Other Income) Act 2005

(1) Sections 731, 733 and 734 of the Income Tax (Trading and Other Income) Act 2005 have effect with the following modifications in relation to payments made to a Scheme beneficiary pursuant to the Scottish scheme.

(2) In section 731 (periodical payments of personal injury damages)—
(*a*) in subsection (2)—
(i) the "or" at the end of paragraph (*d*) is treated as omitted; and
(ii) after paragraph (*e*) there is treated as inserted—
" or
(*f*) the Scottish scheme, so far as it relates to a Scheme beneficiary.";
(*b*) after subsection (6) there is treated as inserted—

"(7) In this section, "Scottish scheme" means the "Scheme of Support and Assistance for those Infected with Hepatitis C, HIV, or both, as a result of NHS treatment" made by the Scottish Ministers and dated 21st February 2017.

(8) In this section and sections 733 and 734, "Scheme beneficiary" means a person listed in paragraph 3(1) of the Scottish scheme."

(3) For section 733(*a*) (persons entitled to exemptions for personal injury payments) there is treated as substituted—

"(*a*) the person ("A") who is a Scheme beneficiary or who is entitled to the damages under the order, agreement, undertaking or to the compensation under the award in question,".

(4) In section 734(1)(*a*) (payments from trusts for injured persons) after "who is" there is treated as inserted "a Scheme beneficiary or who is".

2017/614

MAJOR SPORTING EVENTS (INCOME TAX EXEMPTION) REGULATIONS 2017

Made . . . . *26 April 2017*

Coming into force . . . . *31 May 2017*

The Treasury make the following Regulations in exercise of the powers conferred by section 48 of the Finance Act 2014.

A draft of this instrument was laid before, and approved by a resolution of, the House of Commons in accordance with section 48(5) of the Finance Act 2014.

1 Citation and commencement

These Regulations may be cited as the Major Sporting Events (Income Tax Exemption) Regulations 2017 and come into force on 31st May 2017.

2 The UEFA Champions League Final 2017

(1) A relevant person is not liable to income tax in respect of any income arising from duties or services performed during the specified period by the relevant person in the United Kingdom in connection with the final.

(2) The exemption under paragraph (1) does not apply to income that arises as a result of—

(*a*) a contract entered into after the final commences, or

(*b*) an amendment, made after the final commences, to a contract entered into before the final.

(3) Section 966 of the Income Tax Act 2007 (deduction of sums representing income tax) does not apply to any payment or transfer which gives rise to income benefitting from the exemption in paragraph (1).

3 Interpretation

(1) In these Regulations—

"contractor" in relation to a non-UK football club or UEFA means an individual who is neither an employee of the club nor of UEFA but who performs services—

(*a*) under the terms of a contract with the non-UK football club or with UEFA; or

(*b*) under the terms of a contract with a company which is a member of the same group of companies as the non-UK football club or as UEFA (within the meaning given by section 152 of the Corporation Tax Act 2010);

"relevant person" means any person who meets the non-residence condition on the day of the final and who is—

(*a*) an employee or contractor of a non-UK football club that is competing in the final;

(*b*) an individual who is—

(i) named on UEFA's list of delegates for the final; or

(ii) a UEFA official or UEFA employee not named on the list of delegates but who is attending the final in their capacity as a UEFA official or UEFA employee;

(*c*) an individual acting in their capacity as an employee or an official of a national football association which is a member of UEFA; or

(*d*) an individual acting in their capacity as a UEFA contractor;

"income" means employment income, general earnings or specific employment income, or profits of a trade, profession or vocation (including profits treated as arising as a result of section 13 of the Income Tax (Trading and Other Income) Act 2005);

"non-UK football club" means a football club which is not a member of the Football Association, the Scottish Football Association, the Football Association of Wales or the Irish Football Association;

the "specified period" means the period from 1st to 5th June 2017 inclusive;

"the final" means the final of the UEFA Champions League 2016/2017 football competition, to be held at the National Stadium of Wales in Cardiff on 3rd June 2017;

"UEFA" means the Union des Associations Européennes de Football.

(2) The non-residence condition is that the person—

(*a*) is non-UK resident for the tax year 2017–18; or

(*b*) is UK resident for the tax year 2017–18 but the year is a split year as respects the person and the final takes place during the overseas part of the year.

2017/692

MONEY LAUNDERING, TERRORIST FINANCING AND TRANSFER OF FUNDS (INFORMATION ON THE PAYER) REGULATIONS 2017

Made . . . . at 9.20 am on 22nd June 2017
Laid before Parliament . . . . at 4.30 pm on 22nd June 2017
Coming into force . . . . 26th June 2017

The Treasury are designated for the purposes of section 2(2) of the European Communities Act 1972 in relation to the prevention of money laundering and terrorist financing.

The Treasury in exercise of the powers conferred by section 2(2) of that Act and by sections 168(4)(b), 402(1)(b), 417(1) and 428(3) of the Financial Services and Markets Act 2000, make the following Regulations.

PART 1
INTRODUCTION

1 Citation and commencement

(1) These Regulations may be cited as the Money Laundering, Terrorist Financing and Transfer of Funds (Information on the Payer) Regulations 2017.

(2) These Regulations come into force on 26th June 2017.

2 Prescribed regulations

These Regulations are prescribed for the purposes of sections 168(4)(b) (appointment of persons to carry out investigations in particular cases) and 402(1)(b) (power of the FCA to institute proceedings for certain other offences) of the Financial Services and Markets Act 2000.

3 General interpretation

(1) In these Regulations—

"Annex 1 financial institution" has the meaning given by regulation 55(2);

"appropriate body" means any body which regulates or is representative of any trade, profession, business or employment carried on by a relevant person;

"auction platform" has the meaning given by regulation 14(1)(c);

"auditor" (except in regulation 31(4)) has the meaning given by regulation 11(a);

"authorised person" means a person who is authorised for the purposes of FSMA;

"the FCA" means the Financial Conduct Authority;

"beneficial owner"—

(a) in the case of a body corporate or partnership, has the meaning given by regulation 5;

(b) in the case of a trust or similar arrangement, or the estate of a deceased person in the course of administration, has the meaning given by regulation 6;

(c) in any other case, has the meaning given by regulation 6(9);

"body corporate"—

(a) includes—

(i) a body corporate incorporated under the laws of the United Kingdom or any part of the United Kingdom, and

(ii) a body corporate constituted under the law of a country or territory outside the United Kingdom;

(b) but does not include—

(i) a corporation sole, or

(ii) a partnership that, whether or not a legal person, is not regarded as a body corporate under the law by which it is governed;

"bill payment service provider" means an undertaking which provides a payment service enabling the payment of utility and other household bills;

"branch", except where the context otherwise requires, means a place of business that forms a legally dependent part of the entity in question and conducts directly all or some of the operations inherent in its business;

"business relationship" has the meaning given by regulation 4;

"the capital requirements directive" means Directive 2013/36/EU of the European Parliament and of the Council of 26th June 2013 on access to the activity of credit institutions and the prudential supervision of credit institutions and investment firms, amending Directive 2002/87/EC and repealing Directives 2006/48/EC and 2006/49/EC;

"the capital requirements regulation" means Regulation (EU) No 575/2013 of the European Parliament and of the Council of 26th June 2013 on prudential requirements for credit institutions and investment firms and amending Regulation (EU) No 648/2012;

"cash" means notes, coins or travellers' cheques, in any currency;

"casino" has the meaning given by regulation 14(1)(b);

"the Commissioners" means the Commissioners for Her Majesty's Revenue and Customs;

"contract of long-term insurance" means any contract falling within Part 2 of Schedule 1 to the Financial Services and Markets Act 2000 (Regulated Activities) Order 2001;

"correspondent relationship" has the meaning given by regulation 34(4);

"credit institution" has the meaning given by regulation 10(1);

"customer due diligence measures" means the measures required by regulation 28, and where relevant, those required by regulations 29 and 33 to 37;

"Department for the Economy" means the Department for the Economy in Northern Ireland;

"designated supervisory authority" has the meaning given by regulation 76(8);

"document" means anything in which information of any description is recorded;

"electronic money" has the meaning given by regulation 2(1) of the Electronic Money Regulations 2011;

"electronic money institution" has the meaning given by regulation 2(1) of the Electronic Money Regulations 2011;

"electronic money issuer" has the meaning given in regulation 2(1) of the Electronic Money Regulations 2011;

"eligible Scottish partnership" has the meaning given in regulation 3 of the Scottish Partnerships (Register of People with Significant Control) Regulations 2017 (key terms);

"the emission allowance auctioning regulation" means Commission Regulation (EU) No 1031/2010 of 12th November 2010 on the timing, administration and other aspects of auctioning of greenhouse gas emission allowances pursuant to Directive 2003/87/EC of the European Parliament and of the Council establishing a scheme for greenhouse gas emission allowances trading within the Community;

"enactment" includes—

(a) an enactment contained in subordinate legislation;

(b) an enactment contained in, or in an instrument made under, an Act of the Scottish Parliament;

(c) an enactment contained in, or in an instrument made under, a Measure or Act of the National Assembly for Wales; and

(d) an enactment contained in, or in an instrument made under, Northern Ireland legislation;

"enhanced customer due diligence measures" means the customer due diligence measures required under regulations 33 to 35;

"estate agent" has the meaning given by regulation 13(1);

"European Supervisory Authorities" means—

(a) the European Securities and Markets Authority;

(b) the European Banking Authority;

(c) the European Insurance and Occupational Pensions Authority;

"external accountant" (except in regulation 31(4)) has the meaning given by regulation 11(c);

"financial institution" has the meaning given by regulation 10(2);

"firm" means any entity that, whether or not a legal person, is not an individual and includes a body corporate and a partnership or other unincorporated association;

"fourth money laundering directive" means Directive 2015/849/EU of the European Parliament and of the Council of 20th May 2015 on the prevention of the use of the financial system for the purposes of money laundering or terrorist financing;

"FSMA" means the Financial Services and Markets Act 2000;

"funds transfer regulation" means Regulation 2015/847/EU of the European Parliament and of the Council of 20th May 2015 on information accompanying transfers of funds;

"group" has the meaning given by section 421 (group) of FSMA;

"high value dealer" has the meaning given by regulation 14(1)(a);

"independent legal professional" has the meaning given by regulation 12(1);

"insolvency practitioner" has the meaning given by regulation 11(b);

"law enforcement authority" has the meaning given by regulation 44(10);

"local weights and measures authority" has the meaning given by section 69 of the Weights and Measures Act 1985 (local weights and measures authorities);

"manager", in relation to a firm, means a person who has control, authority or responsibility for managing the business of that firm, and includes a nominated officer;

"markets in financial instruments directive" means Directive 2014/65/EU of the European Parliament and of the Council of 15th May 2014 on markets in financial instruments;

"money laundering" has the meaning given by section 340(11) of the Proceeds of Crime Act 2002;

"money service business" means an undertaking which by way of business operates a currency exchange office, transmits money (or any representation of monetary value) by any means or cashes cheques which are made payable to customers;

"the NCA" means the National Crime Agency;

"nominated officer" means a person who is nominated to receive disclosures under Part 3 (terrorist property) of the Terrorism Act 2000 or Part 7 (money laundering) of the Proceeds of Crime Act 2002;

"notice" means a notice in writing;

"occasional transaction" means a transaction which is not carried out as part of a business relationship;

"officer", except in Part 8 and Schedule 5—

(a) in relation to a body corporate, means—

(i) a director, secretary, chief executive, member of the committee of management, or a person purporting to act in such a capacity, or

(ii) an individual who is a controller of the body, or a person purporting to act as a controller;

(b) in relation to an unincorporated association, means any officer of the association or any member of its governing body, or a person purporting to act in such a capacity; and

(c) in relation to a partnership, means a partner, and any manager, secretary or similar officer of the partnership, or a person purporting to act in such a capacity;

"ongoing monitoring" (except where the context otherwise requires) means at least the measures described in regulation 28(11);

"payment services" has the meaning given by regulation 2(1) of the Payment Services Regulations 2009;

"payment service provider" has the meaning given in regulation 2(1) of the Payment Services Regulations 2009;

"politically exposed person" or "PEP" has the meaning given by regulation 35(12);

"the PRA" means the Prudential Regulation Authority;

"PRA-authorised person" has the meaning given by section 2B(5) of FSMA;

"regulated market"—

(a) within the EEA, has the meaning given by Article 4.1(21) of the markets in financial instruments directive; and

(b) outside the EEA, means a regulated financial market which subjects companies whose securities are admitted to trading to disclosure obligations which are equivalent to the specified disclosure obligations;

"relevant parent undertaking" means a relevant person which is a parent undertaking;

"relevant person" means a person to whom, in accordance with regulation 8, Parts 1 to 6 and 8 to 11 of these Regulations apply;

"relevant requirement" has the meaning given by regulation 75;

"self-regulatory organisation" means one of the professional bodies listed in Schedule 1 to these Regulations;

"senior management" means an officer or employee of the relevant person with sufficient knowledge of the relevant person's money laundering and terrorist financing risk exposure, and of sufficient authority, to take decisions affecting its risk exposure;

"the Solvency 2 Directive" means Directive 2009/138/EC of the European Parliament and of the Council of 25th November 2009 on the taking-up and pursuit of the business of Insurance and Reinsurance (Solvency II);

"specified disclosure obligations" means—

(a) disclosure obligations set out in Articles 17 and 19 of Regulation (EU) No 596/2014 of the European Parliament and of the Council of 16th April 2014 on market abuse;

(b) disclosure obligations consistent with Articles 3, 5, 7, 8, 10, 14 and 16 of Directive 2003/71/EC of the European Parliament and of the Council of 4th November 2003 on the prospectuses to be published when securities are offered to the public or admitted to trading;

(c) disclosure obligations consistent with Articles 4 to 6, 14, 16 to 19 and 30 of Directive 2004/109/EC of the European Parliament and of the Council of 15th December 2004 on the harmonisation of transparency requirements in relation to information about issuers whose securities are admitted to trading on a regulated market; and

(d) disclosure requirements consistent with EU legislation made under the provisions mentioned in sub-paragraphs (a) to (c);

"supervisory authority" in relation to—

(a) any relevant person, means the supervisory authority specified for such a person by regulation 7;

(b) any payment service provider, means the transfer of funds supervisory authority;

"supervisory functions" means the functions given to a supervisory authority under these Regulations;

"tax adviser" (except in regulation 31(4)) has the meaning given by regulation 11(d);

"telecommunication, digital and IT payment service provider" has the meaning given by regulation 53;

"terrorist financing" means (except where the context otherwise requires) an act which constitutes an offence under—

(a) section 15 (fund-raising), 16 (use and possession), 17 (funding arrangements), 18 (money laundering) or 63 (terrorist finance: jurisdiction) of the Terrorism Act 2000;

(b) paragraph 7(2) or (3) of Schedule 3 (freezing orders: offences) to the Anti-terrorism, Crime and Security Act 2001;

(c) regulation 10 (contravention and circumvention of prohibitions) of the ISIL (Da'esh) and Al-Qaida (Asset-Freezing) Regulations 2011; or

(d) section 11 (freezing of funds and economic resources), 12 (making funds or financial services available to designated person), 13 (making funds or financial services available for benefit of designated person), 14 (making economic resources available to designated person), 15 (making economic resources available for benefit of designated person) or 18 (circumventing prohibitions etc) of the Terrorist Asset-Freezing etc Act 2010;

"third country" means a state other than an EEA state;

"transfer of funds supervisory authority" means the supervisory authority specified for payment service providers in regulation 62;

"trust or company service provider" has the meaning given in regulation 12(2).

(2) In these Regulations—

(a) references to an amount in euros includes reference to an equivalent amount in any currency;

(b) the equivalent in sterling (or any other currency) on a particular day of a sum expressed in euros is determined by converting the sum in euros into its equivalent in sterling or that other currency using the London closing exchange rate for the euro and the relevant currency for the previous working day;

(c) references to "real property" include, in relation to Scotland, references to heritable property;

(d) references to business being carried on in the United Kingdom, or a person carrying on business in the United Kingdom, are to be read in accordance with regulation 9;

(e) references to a person having a "qualifying relationship" with a PRA-authorised person, or with an authorised person are to be read in accordance with section 415B(4) of FSMA;

(f) "parent undertaking" and "subsidiary undertaking" have the same meaning as in the Companies Acts (see section 1162 of and Schedule 7 to, the Companies Act 2006 (parent and subsidiary undertaking)).

Prospective amendments—In para 1, in definitions of "payment services" and "payment service provider", year "2017" to be substituted for year "2009" by the Payment Services Regulations, SI 2017/752 reg 156, Sch 8 para 26(a) with effect from 13 January 2018.

4 Meaning of business relationship

(1) For the purpose of these Regulations, "business relationship" means a business, professional or commercial relationship between a relevant person and a customer, which—

(a) arises out of the business of the relevant person, and

(b) is expected by the relevant person, at the time when contact is established, to have an element of duration.

(2) A relationship where the relevant person is asked to form a company for its customer is to be treated as a business relationship for the purpose of these Regulations, whether or not the formation of the company is the only transaction carried out for that customer.

(3) For the purposes of these Regulations, an estate agent is to be treated as entering into a business relationship with a purchaser (as well as with a seller), at the point when the purchaser's offer is accepted by the seller.

5 Meaning of beneficial owner: bodies corporate or partnership

(1) In these Regulations, "beneficial owner", in relation to a body corporate which is not a company whose securities are listed on a regulated market, means—

(a) any individual who exercises ultimate control over the management of the body corporate;

(b) any individual who ultimately owns or controls (in each case whether directly or indirectly), including through bearer share holdings or by other means, more than 25% of the shares or voting rights in the body corporate; or

(c) an individual who controls the body corporate.

(2) For the purposes of paragraph (1)(c), an individual controls a body corporate if—

(a) the body corporate is a company or a limited liability partnership and that individual satisfies one or more of the conditions set out in Part 1 of Schedule 1A to the Companies Act 2006 (people with significant control over a company); or

(b) the body corporate would be a subsidiary undertaking of the individual (if the individual was an undertaking) under section 1162 (parent and subsidiary undertakings) of the Companies Act 2006 read with Schedule 7 to that Act.

(3) In these Regulations, "beneficial owner", in relation to a partnership (other than a limited liability partnership), means any individual who—

(a) ultimately is entitled to or controls (in each case whether directly or indirectly) more than 25% share of the capital or profits of the partnership or more than 25% of the voting rights in the partnership;

(b) satisfies one or more the conditions set out in Part 1 of Schedule 1 to the Scottish Partnerships (Register of People with Significant Control) Regulations 2017 (references to people with significant control over an eligible Scottish partnership); or

(c) otherwise exercises ultimate control over the management of the partnership.

(4) In this regulation "limited liability partnership" has the meaning given by the Limited Liability Partnerships Act 2000.

6 Meaning of beneficial owner: trusts, similar arrangements and others

(1) In these Regulations, "beneficial owner", in relation to a trust, means each of the following—

(a) the settlor;

(b) the trustees;

(c) the beneficiaries;

(d) where the individuals (or some of the individuals) benefiting from the trust have not been determined, the class of persons in whose main interest the trust is set up, or operates;

(e) any individual who has control over the trust.

(2) In paragraph (1)(e), "control" means a power (whether exercisable alone, jointly with another person or with the consent of another person) under the trust instrument or by law to—

(a) dispose of, advance, lend, invest, pay or apply trust property;

(b) vary or terminate the trust;

(c) add or remove a person as a beneficiary or to or from a class of beneficiaries;

(d) appoint or remove trustees or give another individual control over the trust;

(e) direct, withhold consent to or veto the exercise of a power mentioned in sub-paragraphs (a) to (d).

(3) In these Regulations, "beneficial owner", in relation to a foundation or other legal arrangement similar to a trust, means those individuals who hold equivalent or similar positions to those set out in paragraph (1).

(4) For the purposes of paragraph (1)—

(a) where an individual is the beneficial owner of a body corporate which is entitled to a specified interest in the capital of the trust property or which has control over the trust, the individual is to be regarded as entitled to the interest or having control over the trust; and

(b) an individual ("P") does not have control solely as a result of—

(i) P's consent being required in accordance with section 32(1)(c) (power of advancement) of the Trustee Act 1925;

(ii) any discretion delegated to P under section 34 (power of investment and delegation) of the Pensions Act 1995;

(iii) the power to give a direction conferred on P by section 19(2) (appointment and retirement of trustee at instance of beneficiaries) of the Trusts of Land and Appointment of Trustees Act 1996; or

(iv) the power exercisable collectively at common law to vary or extinguish a trust where the beneficiaries under the trust are of full age and capacity and (taken together) absolutely entitled to the property subject to the trust (or, in Scotland, have a full and unqualified right to the fee).

(5) For the purposes of paragraph (4), "specified interest" means a vested interest which is—

(a) in possession or in remainder or reversion (or in Scotland, in fee); and

(b) defeasible or indefeasible.

(6) In these Regulations, "beneficial owner", in relation to an estate of a deceased person in the course of administration, means—

(a) in England and Wales and Northern Ireland, the executor, original or by representation, or administrator for the time being of a deceased person;

(b) in Scotland, the executor for the purposes of the Executors (Scotland) Act 1900.

(7) In these Regulations, "beneficial owner", in relation to a legal entity or legal arrangement which does not fall within regulation 5 or paragraphs (1), (3) or (6) of this regulation, means—

(a) any individual who benefits from the property of the entity or arrangement;

(b) where the individuals who benefit from the entity or arrangement have yet to be determined, the class of persons in whose main interest the entity or arrangement is set up or operates;

(c) any individual who exercises control over the property of the entity or arrangement.

(8) For the purposes of paragraph (7), where an individual is the beneficial owner of a body corporate which benefits from or exercises control over the property of the entity or arrangement, the individual is to be regarded as benefiting from or exercising control over the property of the entity or arrangement.

(9) In these Regulations, "beneficial owner", in any other case, means the individual who ultimately owns or controls the entity or arrangement or on whose behalf a transaction is being conducted.

7 Supervisory authorities

(1) Subject to paragraph (2), the following bodies are supervisory authorities in relation to relevant persons—

- (a) the FCA is the supervisory authority for—
  - (i) credit and financial institutions (including money service businesses) which are authorised persons but not excluded money service businesses;
  - (ii) trust or company service providers which are authorised persons;
  - (iii) Annex 1 financial institutions;
  - (iv) electronic money institutions;
  - (v) auction platforms;
  - (vi) credit unions in Northern Ireland;
  - (vii) recognised investment exchanges within the meaning of section 285 of FSMA (exemption for recognised investment exchanges and clearing houses);
- (b) each of the professional bodies listed in Schedule 1 is the supervisory authority for relevant persons who are members of it, or regulated or supervised by it;
- (c) the Commissioners are the supervisory authority for—
  - (i) high value dealers;
  - (ii) money service businesses which are not supervised by the FCA;
  - (iii) trust or company service providers which are not supervised by the FCA or one of the professional bodies listed in Schedule 1;
  - (iv) auditors, external accountants and tax advisers who are not supervised by one of the professional bodies listed in Schedule 1;
  - (v) bill payment service providers which are not supervised by the FCA;
  - (vi) telecommunication, digital and IT payment service providers which are not supervised by the FCA;
  - (vii) estate agents which are not supervised by one of the professional bodies listed in Schedule 1;
- (d) the Gambling Commission is the supervisory authority for casinos

(2) Where under paragraph (1), there is more than one supervisory authority for a relevant person, the supervisory authorities may agree that one of them will act as the supervisory authority for that person.

(3) Where there has been an agreement under paragraph (2), the authority which has agreed to act as the supervisory authority must notify the relevant person or publish the agreement in such manner as it considers appropriate.

(4) Where there has not been an agreement under paragraph (2), the supervisory authorities for a relevant person must co-operate in the performance of their functions under these Regulations.

(5) For the purposes of paragraph (1)(a)(i), a money service business is an "excluded money service business" if it is an authorised person who has permission under FSMA which relates to or is connected with a contract of the kind mentioned in paragraph 23 or 23B of Schedule 2 to that Act (credit agreements and contracts for hire of goods) but does not have permission to carry on any other kind of regulated activity.

(6) Paragraph (5) must be read with—

- (a) section 22 of FSMA (regulated activities);
- (b) any relevant order under that section; and
- (c) Schedule 2 to that Act.

(7) For the purposes of paragraph (1), a credit union in Northern Ireland is a credit union which is—

- (a) registered under regulation 3 of the Credit Unions (Northern Ireland) Order 1985 (registration) and it is an authorised person; or
- (b) registered under Part 2 of the Industrial and Provident Societies Act (Northern Ireland) 1969 (registered societies) as a credit union and it is an authorised person.

PART 2
MONEY LAUNDERING AND TERRORIST FINANCING

CHAPTER 1
APPLICATION

8 Application

(1) Parts 1 to 6 and 8 to 11 apply to the persons ("relevant persons") acting in the course of business carried on by them in the United Kingdom, who—

(a) are listed in paragraph (2); and

(b) do not come within the exclusions set out in regulation 15.

(2) The persons listed in this paragraph are—

(a) credit institutions;

(b) financial institutions;

(c) auditors, insolvency practitioners, external accountants and tax advisers;

(d) independent legal professionals;

(e) trust or company service providers;

(f) estate agents;

(g) high value dealers;

(h) casinos

(3) Regulations 3, 7, 9, 15, 17 to 21, 24, 25, 46, 47, 50 to 52, 65 to 82, 84, 86 to 93, 101, 102 and 106 apply to an auction platform acting in the course of business carried on by it in the United Kingdom, and such an auction platform is a relevant person for the purposes of those provisions.

(4) The definitions in regulations 10 to 14 apply for the purposes of this regulation.

9 Carrying on business in the United Kingdom

(1) For the purposes of these Regulations, a relevant person ("A") is to be regarded as carrying on business in the United Kingdom in the cases described in this regulation even if A would not otherwise be regarded as doing so.

(2) The first case is where—

(a) A's registered office (or if A does not have a registered office, A's head office) is in the United Kingdom;

(b) A is entitled to exercise rights under a single market directive as a UK firm (within the meaning of paragraph 10 of Schedule 3 to FSMA (EEA passport rights)); and

(c) A is carrying on business in an EEA state other than the United Kingdom in the exercise of those rights.

(3) The second case is where—

(a) A's registered office (or if A does not have a registered office, A's head office) is in the United Kingdom; and

(b) the day-to-day management of the carrying on of A's business is the responsibility of—

(i) that office, or

(ii) another establishment maintained by A in the United Kingdom.

(4) The third case is where—

(a) A is a casino which provides facilities for remote gambling (within the meaning of section 4 of the Gambling Act 2005 (remote gambling)) and—

(b) either—

(i) at least one piece of remote gambling equipment (within the meaning of section 36(4) of the Gambling Act 2005 (territorial application)) is situated in Great Britain, or

(ii) no such equipment is situated in Great Britain but the facilities provided by A are used there.

(5) For the purposes of paragraphs (2) and (3)—

(a) "single market directive" means—

(i) a directive referred to in paragraph 1 of Schedule 3 to FSMA;

(ii) Directive 2009/110/EC of the European Parliament and of the Council of 16th September 2009 on the taking up, pursuit and prudential supervision of the business of electronic money institutions;

(iii) Directive 2015/2366/EU of the European Parliament and of the Council of 25th November 2015 on payment services in the internal market;

(b) it is irrelevant where the person with whom the business is carried on is situated.

10 Credit institutions and financial institutions

(1) In these Regulations, "credit institution" means—

(a) a credit institution as defined in Article 4.1(1) of the capital requirements regulation; or

(b) a branch (as defined by Article 4.1(17) of that regulation) located in an EEA state of an institution falling within sub-paragraph (a) (or an equivalent institution whose head office is located in a third country) wherever the institution's head office is located,

when it accepts deposits or other repayable funds from the public or grants credits for its own account (within the meaning of the capital requirements regulation), or when it bids directly in auctions in accordance with the emission allowance auctioning regulation on behalf of its clients.

(2) In these Regulations, "financial institution" means—

(a) an undertaking, including a money service business, other than an institution referred to in paragraph (3), when the undertaking carries out one or more listed activity;

(b) an insurance undertaking duly authorised in accordance with the Solvency 2 Directive, when it carries out any activities or operations referred to in Article 2.3 of that Directive;

(c) a person (other than a person falling within Article 2 of the markets in financial instruments directive), whose regular occupation or business is the provision to other persons of an investment service or the performance of an investment activity on a professional basis, when—

(i) providing investment services or performing investment activities (within the meaning of that directive); or

(ii) bidding directly in auctions in accordance with the emission allowance auctioning regulation on behalf of its clients;

(d) a person falling within Article 2.1(j) of the markets in financial instruments directive, when bidding directly in auctions in accordance with the emission allowance auctioning regulation on behalf of clients of the person's main business;

(e) a collective investment undertaking, when marketing or otherwise offering its units or shares;

(f) an insurance intermediary as defined in Article 2.5 of Directive 2002/92/EC of the European Parliament and of the Council of 9th December 2002 on insurance mediation, with the exception of a tied insurance intermediary as mentioned in Article 2.7 of that Directive, when it acts in respect of contracts of long-term insurance;

(g) a branch located in an EEA state of a person referred to in sub-paragraphs (a) to (f) (or an equivalent person whose head office is located in a third country), wherever the person's head office is located, when carrying out any activity mentioned in sub-paragraphs (a) to (f);

(h) the National Savings Bank;

(i) the Director of Savings, when money is raised under the auspices of the Director under the National Loans Act 1968.

(3) For the purposes of paragraph (2)(a), the institutions referred to are—

(a) a credit institution;

(b) an undertaking whose only listed activity is as a creditor under an agreement which—

(i) falls within section 12(a) of the Consumer Credit Act 1974 (debtor-creditor-supplier agreements);

(ii) provides fixed sum credit (within the meaning given in section 10(1)(b) of the Consumer Credit Act 1974 (running-account credit and fixed-sum credit)) in relation to the provision of services; and

(iii) provides financial accommodation by way of deferred payment or payment by instalments over a period not exceeding 12 months;

(c) an undertaking whose only listed activity is trading for its own account in one or more of the products listed in point 7 of Annex 1 to the capital requirements directive where the undertaking does not have a customer (and, for this purpose, "customer" means a person other than the undertaking which is not a member of the same group as the undertaking).

(4) For the purposes of this regulation, a "listed activity" means an activity listed in points 2 to 12, 14 and 15 of Annex 1 to the capital requirements directive (the relevant text of which is set out in Schedule 2).

11 Auditors and others

In these Regulations—

(a) "auditor" means any firm or individual who is—

(i) a statutory auditor within the meaning of Part 42 of the Companies Act 2006 (statutory auditors), when carrying out statutory audit work within the meaning of section 1210 of that Act (meaning of statutory auditor), or

(ii) a local auditor within the meaning of section 4(1) of the Local Audit and Accountability Act 2014 (general requirements for audit), when carrying out an audit required by that Act.

(b) "insolvency practitioner" means any firm or individual who acts as an insolvency practitioner within the meaning of section 388 of the Insolvency Act 1986 or article 3 of the Insolvency (Northern Ireland) Order 1989 (meaning of "act as insolvency practitioner").

(c) "external accountant" means a firm or sole practitioner who by way of business provides accountancy services to other persons, when providing such services.

(d) "tax adviser" means a firm or sole practitioner who by way of business provides advice about the tax affairs of other persons, when providing such services.

12 Independent legal professionals and trust or company service providers

(1) In these Regulations, "independent legal professional" means a firm or sole practitioner who by way of business provides legal or notarial services to other persons, when participating in financial or real property transactions concerning—

(a) the buying and selling of real property or business entities;
(b) the managing of client money, securities or other assets;
(c) the opening or management of bank, savings or securities accounts;
(d) the organisation of contributions necessary for the creation, operation or management of companies; or
(e) the creation, operation or management of trusts, companies, foundations or similar structures,

and, for this purpose, a person participates in a transaction by assisting in the planning or execution of the transaction or otherwise acting for or on behalf of a client in the transaction.

(2) In these Regulations, "trust or company service provider" means a firm or sole practitioner who by way of business provides any of the following services to other persons, when that firm or practitioner is providing such services—

(a) forming companies or other legal persons;
(b) acting, or arranging for another person to act—
(i) as a director or secretary of a company;
(ii) as a partner of a partnership; or
(iii) in a similar capacity in relation to other legal persons;
(c) providing a registered office, business address, correspondence or administrative address or other related services for a company, partnership or any other legal person or legal arrangement;
(d) acting, or arranging for another person to act, as—
(i) a trustee of an express trust or similar legal arrangement; or
(ii) a nominee shareholder for a person other than a company whose securities are listed on a regulated market.

13 Estate agents

(1) In these Regulations, "estate agent" means a firm or a sole practitioner, who, or whose employees, carry out estate agency work, when the work is being carried out.

(2) For the purposes of paragraph (1) "estate agency work" is to be read in accordance with section 1 of the Estate Agents Act 1979 (estate agency work), but for those purposes references in that section to disposing of or acquiring an interest in land are (despite anything in section 2 of that Act) to be taken to include references to disposing of or acquiring an estate or interest in land outside the United Kingdom where that estate or interest is capable of being owned or held as a separate interest.

14 High value dealers, casinos and auction platforms

(1) In these Regulations—

(a) "high value dealer" means a firm or sole trader who by way of business trades in goods (including an auctioneer dealing in goods), when the trader makes or receives, in respect of any transaction, a payment or payments in cash of at least 10,000 euros in total, whether the transaction is executed in a single operation or in several operations which appear to be linked;
(b) "casino" means the holder of a casino operating licence and, for this purpose, a "casino operating licence" has the meaning given by section 65(2)(a) of the Gambling Act 2005 (nature of licence);
(c) "auction platform" means a platform which auctions two-day spot or five-day futures, within the meanings given by Article 3.4 and 3.5 of the emission allowance auctioning regulation, when it carries out activities covered by that regulation.

(2) A payment does not cease to be a "payment in cash" for the purposes of paragraph (1)(a) if cash is paid by or on behalf of the person making the payment—

(a) to a person other than the other party to the transaction for the benefit of the other party, or
(b) into a bank account for the benefit of the other party to the transaction.

15 Exclusions

(1) Parts 1 to 4, 6 and 8 to 11 do not apply to the following persons when carrying on any of the following activities—

(a) a registered society within the meaning of section 1 of the Co-operative and Community Benefit Societies Act 2014 (meaning of "registered society"), when it—
(i) issues withdrawable share capital within the limit set by section 24 of that Act (maximum shareholding in society); or

(ii) accepts deposits from the public within the limit set by section 67(2) of that Act (carrying on of banking by societies);

(b) a society registered under the Industrial and Provident Societies Act (Northern Ireland) 1969, when it—

(i) issues withdrawable share capital within the limit set by section 6 of that Act (maximum shareholding in society); or

(ii) accepts deposits from the public within the limit set by section 7(3) of that Act (carrying on of banking by societies);

(c) a person who is (or falls within a class of persons) specified in any of paragraphs 2 to 23, 26 to 38 or 40 to 49 of the Schedule to the Financial Services and Markets Act 2000 (Exemption) Order 2001, when carrying out any activity in respect of which that person is exempt;

(d) a local authority within the meaning given in article 3(1) of the Financial Services and Markets Act 2000 (Regulated Activities) Order 2001, when carrying on an activity which would be a regulated activity for the purposes of FSMA but for article 72G of that Order;

(e) a person who was an exempted person for the purposes of section 45 of the Financial Services Act 1986 (miscellaneous exemptions) immediately before its repeal, when exercising the functions specified in that section;

(f) a person whose main activity is that of a high value dealer, when engaging in financial activity on an occasional or very limited basis as set out in paragraph (3); or

(g) a person preparing a home report, which for these purposes means the documents prescribed for the purposes of section 98, 99(1) or 101(2) of the Housing (Scotland) Act 2006 (duties: information and others).

(2) These Regulations do not apply to a person who falls within regulation 8 solely as a result of that person engaging in financial activity on an occasional or very limited basis as set out in paragraph (3).

(3) For the purposes of paragraphs (1)(f) and (2), a person is to be considered as engaging in financial activity on an occasional or very limited basis if all the following conditions are met—

(a) the person's total annual turnover in respect of the financial activity does not exceed £100,000;

(b) the financial activity is limited in relation to any customer to no more than one transaction exceeding 1,000 euros, whether the transaction is carried out in a single operation, or a series of operations which appear to be linked;

(c) the financial activity does not exceed 5% of the person's total annual turnover;

(d) the financial activity is ancillary and directly related to the person's main activity;

(e) the financial activity is not the transmission or remittance of money (or any representation of monetary value) by any means;

(f) the person's main activity is not that of a person falling within regulation 8(2)(a) to (f) or (h);

(g) the financial activity is provided only to customers of the main activity of the person and is not offered to the public.

(4) Chapters 2 and 3 of Part 2, and Parts 3 to 9, do not apply to—

(a) the Auditor General for Scotland;

(b) the Auditor General for Wales;

(c) the Bank of England;

(d) the Comptroller and Auditor General;

(e) the Comptroller and Auditor General for Northern Ireland;

(f) the Official Solicitor to the Supreme Court, when acting as trustee in his or her official capacity;

(g) the Treasury Solicitor.

CHAPTER 2

RISK ASSESSMENT AND CONTROLS

16 Risk assessment by the Treasury and Home Office

(1) The Treasury and the Home Office must make arrangements before 26th June 2018 for a risk assessment to be undertaken to identify, assess, understand and mitigate the risks of money laundering and terrorist financing affecting the United Kingdom ("the risk assessment").

(2) The risk assessment must, among other things—

(a) identify any areas where relevant persons should apply enhanced customer due diligence measures, and where appropriate, specify the measures to be taken;

(b) identify, where appropriate, the sectors or areas of lower and greater risk of money laundering and terrorist financing;

(c) consider whether any rules on money laundering and terrorist financing made by a supervisory authority applying in relation to the sector it supervises are appropriate in the light of the risks of money laundering and terrorist financing applying to that sector;

(d) provide the information and analysis necessary to enable it to be used for the purposes set out in paragraph (3).

(3) The Treasury and the Home Office must ensure that the risk assessment is used to—

(a) consider the appropriate allocation and prioritisation of resources to counter money laundering and terrorist financing;

(b) consider whether the exclusions provided for in regulation 15 are being abused;

(c) consider whether providers of gambling services other than casinos should continue to be excluded from the requirements of these Regulations.

(4) For the purpose of paragraph (3)(c), a "provider of gambling services" means a person who by way of business provides facilities for gambling within the meaning of section 5 of the Gambling Act 2005 (facilities for gambling).

(5) In undertaking the risk assessment, the Treasury and the Home Office must take account of the reports made by the Commission under Article 6.1 of the fourth money laundering directive.

(6) The Treasury and the Home Office must prepare a joint report setting out, as appropriate, the findings of the risk assessment as soon as reasonably practicable after the risk assessment is completed.

(7) A copy of that report must be laid before Parliament, and sent to—

(a) the PRA;

(b) the supervisory authorities;

(c) the European Commission;

(d) the European Supervisory Authorities; and

(e) each of the other EEA states.

(8) If information from the risk assessment would assist the supervisory authorities in carrying out their own money laundering and terrorist financing risk assessment, the Treasury and the Home Office must, where appropriate, make that information available to those supervisory authorities, unless to do so would not be compatible with restrictions on sharing information imposed by or under the Data Protection Act 1998 or any other enactment.

(9) The Treasury and the Home Office must take appropriate steps to ensure that the risk assessment is kept up-to-date.

17 Risk assessment by supervisory authorities

(1) Each supervisory authority must identify and assess the international and domestic risks of money laundering and terrorist financing to which those relevant persons for which it is the supervisory authority ("its own sector") are subject.

(2) In carrying out the risk assessment required under paragraph (1), the supervisory authority must take into account—

(a) reports published by the Commission under Article 6.1 of the fourth money laundering directive;

(b) guidelines issued by the European Supervisory Authorities under Articles 17, 18.4 and 48.10 of the fourth money laundering directive;

(c) the report prepared by the Treasury and the Home Office under regulation 16(6); and

(d) information made available by the Treasury and the Home Office under regulation 16(8).

(3) A supervisory authority must keep an up-to-date record in writing of all the steps it has taken under paragraph (1).

(4) Each supervisory authority must develop and record in writing risk profiles for each relevant person in its own sector.

(5) A supervisory authority may prepare a single risk profile under paragraph (4) in relation to two or more relevant persons in its sector, if—

(a) the relevant persons share similar characteristics; and

(b) the risks of money laundering and terrorist financing affecting those relevant persons do not differ significantly.

(6) Where a supervisory authority has prepared a single risk profile for two or more relevant persons in its sector (a "cluster"), the supervisory authority must keep under review whether an individual risk profile should be prepared in relation to any relevant person in the cluster because sub-paragraph (a) or (b) (or both sub-paragraphs) of paragraph (5) are no longer satisfied in relation to that person.

(7) In developing the risk profiles referred to in paragraph (4), the supervisory authority must take full account of the risks that relevant persons in its own sector will not take appropriate action to identify, understand and mitigate money laundering and terrorist financing risks.

(8) Each supervisory authority must review the risk profiles developed under paragraph (4) at regular intervals and following any significant event or developments which might affect the risks to which its own sector is subject, such as—

(a) significant external events that change the nature of the money laundering or terrorist financing risks;
(b) emerging money laundering or terrorist financing risks;
(c) any findings resulting from measures taken by other supervisory authorities;
(d) any changes in the way in which its own sector is operated;
(e) significant changes in regulation.

(9) If information from the risk assessment carried out under paragraph (1), or from information provided to the supervisory authority under regulation 16(8), would assist relevant persons in carrying out their own money laundering and terrorist financing risk assessment, the supervisory authority must, where appropriate, make that information available to those persons, unless to do so would not be compatible with restrictions on sharing information imposed by or under the Data Protection Act 1998 or any other enactment.

18 Risk assessment by relevant persons

(1) A relevant person must take appropriate steps to identify and assess the risks of money laundering and terrorist financing to which its business is subject.

(2) In carrying out the risk assessment required under paragraph (1), a relevant person must take into account—
(a) information made available to them by the supervisory authority under regulations 17(9) and 47, and
(b) risk factors including factors relating to—
(i) its customers;
(ii) the countries or geographic areas in which it operates;
(iii) its products or services;
(iv) its transactions; and
(v) its delivery channels.

(3) In deciding what steps are appropriate under paragraph (1), the relevant person must take into account the size and nature of its business.

(4) A relevant person must keep an up-to-date record in writing of all the steps it has taken under paragraph (1), unless its supervisory authority notifies it in writing that such a record is not required.

(5) A supervisory authority may not give the notification referred to in paragraph (4) unless it considers that the risks of money laundering and terrorist financing applicable to the sector in which the relevant person operates are clear and understood.

(6) A relevant person must provide the risk assessment it has prepared under paragraph (1), the information on which that risk assessment was based and any record required to be kept under paragraph (4), to its supervisory authority on request.

19 Policies, controls and procedures

(1) A relevant person must—
(a) establish and maintain policies, controls and procedures to mitigate and manage effectively the risks of money laundering and terrorist financing identified in any risk assessment undertaken by the relevant person under regulation 18(1);
(b) regularly review and update the policies, controls and procedures established under sub-paragraph (a);
(c) maintain a record in writing of—
(i) the policies, controls and procedures established under sub-paragraph (a);
(ii) any changes to those policies, controls and procedures made as a result of the review and update required by sub-paragraph (b); and
(iii) the steps taken to communicate those policies, controls and procedures, or any changes to them, within the relevant person's business.

(2) The policies, controls and procedures adopted by a relevant person under paragraph (1) must be—
(a) proportionate with regard to the size and nature of the relevant person's business, and
(b) approved by its senior management.

(3) The policies, controls and procedures referred to in paragraph (1) must include—
(a) risk management practices;
(b) internal controls (see regulations 21 to 24);
(c) customer due diligence (see regulations 27 to 38);
(d) reliance and record keeping (see regulations 39 to 40);
(e) the monitoring and management of compliance with, and the internal communication of, such policies, controls and procedures.

(4) The policies, controls and procedures referred to in paragraph (1) must include policies, controls and procedures—
(a) which provide for the identification and scrutiny of—
(i) any case where—

(aa) a transaction is complex and unusually large, or there is an unusual pattern of transactions, and

(bb) the transaction or transactions have no apparent economic or legal purpose, and

(ii) any other activity or situation which the relevant person regards as particularly likely by its nature to be related to money laundering or terrorist financing;

(b) which specify the taking of additional measures, where appropriate, to prevent the use for money laundering or terrorist financing of products and transactions which might favour anonymity;

(c) which ensure that when new technology is adopted by the relevant person, appropriate measures are taken in preparation for, and during, the adoption of such technology to assess and if necessary mitigate any money laundering or terrorist financing risks this new technology may cause;

(d) under which anyone in the relevant person's organisation who knows or suspects (or has reasonable grounds for knowing or suspecting) that a person is engaged in money laundering or terrorist financing as a result of information received in the course of the business or otherwise through carrying on that business is required to comply with—

(i) Part 3 of the Terrorism Act 2000; or

(ii) Part 7 of the Proceeds of Crime Act 2002;

(e) which, in the case of a money service business that uses agents for the purpose of its business, ensure that appropriate measures are taken by the business to assess—

(i) whether an agent used by the business would satisfy the fit and proper test provided for in regulation 58; and

(ii) the extent of the risk that the agent may be used for money laundering or terrorist financing.

(5) In determining what is appropriate or proportionate with regard to the size and nature of its business, a relevant person may take into account any guidance which has been—

(a) issued by the FCA; or

(b) issued by any other supervisory authority or appropriate body and approved by the Treasury.

(6) A relevant person must, where relevant, communicate the policies, controls and procedures which it establishes and maintains in accordance with this regulation to its branches and subsidiary undertakings which are located outside the United Kingdom.

20 Policies, controls and procedures: group level

(1) A relevant parent undertaking must—

(a) ensure that the policies, controls and procedures referred to in regulation 19(1) apply—

(i) to all its subsidiary undertakings, including subsidiary undertakings located outside the United Kingdom; and

(ii) to any branches it has established outside the United Kingdom;

which is carrying out any activity in respect of which the relevant person is subject to these Regulations;

(b) establish and maintain throughout its group the policies, controls and procedures for data protection and sharing information for the purposes of preventing money laundering and terrorist financing with other members of the group;

(c) regularly review and update the policies, controls and procedures applied and established under sub-paragraphs (a) and (b);

(d) maintain a record in writing of—

(i) the policies, controls and procedures established under sub-paragraphs (a) and (b);

(ii) any changes to those policies, controls and procedures made as a result of the review and update required by sub-paragraph (c); and

(iii) the steps taken to communicate those policies, controls and procedures, or any changes to them, to its subsidiary undertakings and branches.

(2) A relevant parent undertaking must ensure that those of its subsidiary undertakings and branches which are established in an EEA state follow the law of that EEA state that implements the fourth money laundering directive.

(3) If any of the subsidiary undertakings or branches of a relevant parent undertaking are established in a third country which does not impose requirements to counter money laundering and terrorist financing as strict as those of the United Kingdom, the relevant parent undertaking must ensure that those subsidiary undertakings and branches apply measures equivalent to those required by these Regulations, as far as permitted under the law of the third country.

(4) Where the law of a third country does not permit the application of such equivalent measures by the subsidiary undertaking or branch established in that country, the relevant parent undertaking must—

(a) inform its supervisory authority accordingly; and

(b) take additional measures to handle the risk of money laundering and terrorist financing effectively.

(5) A relevant parent undertaking must ensure that information relevant to the prevention of money laundering and terrorist financing is shared as appropriate between members of its group, subject to any restrictions on sharing information imposed by or under any enactment or otherwise.

21 Internal controls

(1) Where appropriate with regard to the size and nature of its business, a relevant person must—

(a) appoint one individual who is a member of the board of directors (or if there is no board, of its equivalent management body) or of its senior management as the officer responsible for the relevant person's compliance with these Regulations;

(b) carry out screening of relevant employees appointed by the relevant person, both before the appointment is made and during the course of the appointment;

(c) establish an independent audit function with the responsibility—

(i) to examine and evaluate the adequacy and effectiveness of the policies, controls and procedures adopted by the relevant person to comply with the requirements of these Regulations;

(ii) to make recommendations in relation to those policies, controls and procedures; and

(iii) to monitor the relevant person's compliance with those recommendations.

(2) For the purposes of paragraph (1)(b)—

(a) "screening" means an assessment of—

(i) the skills, knowledge and expertise of the individual to carry out their functions effectively;

(ii) the conduct and integrity of the individual;

(b) a relevant employee is an employee whose work is—

(i) relevant to the relevant person's compliance with any requirement in these Regulations, or

(ii) otherwise capable of contributing to the—

(aa) identification or mitigation of the risks of money laundering and terrorist financing to which the relevant person's business is subject, or

(bb) prevention or detection of money laundering and terrorist financing in relation to the relevant person's business.

(3) An individual in the relevant person's firm must be appointed as a nominated officer.

(4) A relevant person must, within 14 days of the appointment, inform its supervisory authority of—

(a) the identity of the individual first appointed under paragraph (1)(a);

(b) the identity of the individual first appointed under paragraph (3); and

(c) of any subsequent appointment to either of those positions.

(5) Where a disclosure is made to the nominated officer, that officer must consider it in the light of any relevant information which is available to the relevant person and determine whether it gives rise to knowledge or suspicion or reasonable grounds for knowledge or suspicion that a person is engaged in money laundering or terrorist financing.

(6) Paragraphs (1) and (3) do not apply where the relevant person is an individual who neither employs nor acts in association with any other person.

(7) A relevant person who is an electronic money issuer or a payment service provider must appoint an individual to monitor and manage compliance with, and the internal communication of, the policies, controls and procedures adopted by the relevant person under regulation 19(1), and in particular to—

(a) identify any situations of higher risk of money laundering or terrorist financing;

(b) maintain a record of its policies, controls and procedures, risk assessment and risk management including the application of such policies and procedures;

(c) apply measures to ensure that its policies, controls and procedures are taken into account in all relevant functions including in the development of new products, dealing with new customers and in changes to business activities; and

(d) provide information to senior management about the operation and effectiveness of its policies, controls and procedures whenever appropriate and at least annually.

(8) A relevant person must establish and maintain systems which enable it to respond fully and rapidly to enquiries from any person specified in paragraph (9) as to—

(a) whether it maintains, or has maintained during the previous five years, a business relationship with any person; and

(b) the nature of that relationship.

(9) The persons specified in this paragraph are—

(a) financial investigators accredited under section 3 of the Proceeds of Crime Act 2002 (accreditation and training);

(b) persons acting on behalf of the Scottish Ministers in their capacity as an enforcement authority under that Act; and

(c) constables or equivalent officers of any law enforcement authority.

(10) In determining what is appropriate with regard to the size and nature of its business, a relevant person—

(a) must take into account its risk assessment under regulation 18(1); and

(b) may take into account any guidance which has been—

(i) issued by the FCA; or

(ii) issued by any other supervisory authority or appropriate body and approved by the Treasury.

22 Central contact points: electronic money issuers and payment service providers

(1) An electronic money issuer or a payment service provider to which paragraph (2) applies must, if requested by its supervisory authority, appoint a person to act as a central contact point in the United Kingdom for its supervisory authority on any issue relating to the prevention of money laundering or terrorist financing.

(2) This paragraph applies to any electronic money issuer or payment service provider which—

(a) is established in the United Kingdom otherwise than by a branch; and

(b) has its head office in an EEA state other than the United Kingdom.

23 Requirement on authorised person to inform the FCA

(1) An authorised person whose supervisory authority is the FCA must, before acting as a money service business or a trust or company service provider or within 28 days of so doing, inform the FCA that it intends, or has begun, to act as such.

(2) Paragraph (1) does not apply to an authorised person which—

(a) immediately before the day on which these Regulations come into force ("the relevant date") was acting as a money service business or a trust or company service provider and continues to act as such after that date; and

(b) informs the FCA that it is acting as such within 30 days of the relevant date.

(3) Where an authorised person whose supervisory authority is the FCA ceases to act as a money service business or a trust or company service provider, it must within 28 days inform the FCA.

(4) Any requirement imposed by this regulation is to be treated as if it were a requirement imposed by or under FSMA.

(5) Any information to be provided to the FCA under this regulation must be in such form or verified in such manner as it may specify.

24 Training

(1) A relevant person must—

(a) take appropriate measures to ensure that its relevant employees are—

(i) made aware of the law relating to money laundering and terrorist financing, and to the requirements of data protection, which are relevant to the implementation of these Regulations; and

(ii) regularly given training in how to recognise and deal with transactions and other activities or situations which may be related to money laundering or terrorist financing;

(b) maintain a record in writing of the measures taken under sub-paragraph (a), and in particular, of the training given to its relevant employees.

(2) For the purposes of paragraph (1), a relevant employee is an employee whose work is—

(a) relevant to the relevant person's compliance with any requirement in these Regulations, or

(b) otherwise capable of contributing to the—

(i) identification or mitigation of the risk of money laundering and terrorist financing to which the relevant person's business is subject; or

(ii) prevention or detection of money laundering and terrorist financing in relation to the relevant person's business.

(3) In determining what measures are appropriate under paragraph (1), a relevant person—

(a) must take account of—

(i) the nature of its business;

(ii) its size;

(iii) the nature and extent of the risks of money laundering and terrorist financing to which its business is subject; and

(b) may take into account any guidance which has been—

(i) issued by the FCA; or

(ii) issued by any other supervisory authority or appropriate body and approved by the Treasury.

25 Supervisory action

(1) The supervisory authority must determine whether the additional measures taken under regulation 20(4) by a relevant parent undertaking which is an authorised person or a qualifying parent undertaking (as defined by section 192B of FSMA) are sufficient to handle the risk of money laundering and terrorist financing effectively.

(2) If the supervisory authority does not consider the measures referred to in paragraph (1) to be sufficient, it must consider whether to direct the relevant parent undertaking—

(a) not to enter into a business relationship with a specified person;

(b) not to undertake transactions of a specified description with a specified person;

(c) to terminate an existing business relationship with a specified person;

(d) to cease any operations in the third country.

(e) to ensure that its subsidiary undertaking—

(i) does not enter into a business relationship with a specified person;

(ii) terminates an existing business relationship with a specified person; or

(iii) does not undertake transactions of a specified description with a specified person, or ceases any operations in the third country.

(3) A direction issued under paragraph (2) takes effect—

(a) immediately, if the notice given under paragraph (6) states that that is the case;

(b) on such date as may be specified in the notice; or

(c) if no such date is specified in the notice, when the matter to which the notice relates is no longer open to review.

(4) For the purposes of paragraph (3), a matter to which a notice relates is still open to review if—

(a) the period during which any person may refer the matter to the appropriate tribunal is still running;

(b) the matter has been referred to the appropriate tribunal but has not been dealt with;

(c) the matter has been referred to the appropriate tribunal and dealt with but the period during which an appeal may be brought against the appropriate tribunal's decision is still running; or

(d) such an appeal has been brought but has not been determined.

(5) Where the FCA proposes to issue a direction under paragraph (2) to a PRA-authorised person or to a person who has a qualifying relationship with a PRA-authorised person, it must consult the PRA.

(6) If the supervisory authority issues a direction under paragraph (2) it must give the relevant parent undertaking ("A") a notice in writing.

(7) The notice must—

(a) give details of the direction;

(b) state the supervisory authority's reasons for issuing the direction;

(c) inform A that A may make representations to the supervisory authority within such period as may be specified in the notice (whether or not A has referred the matter to the appropriate tribunal);

(d) inform A of when the direction takes effect; and

(e) inform A of A's right to refer the matter to the appropriate tribunal.

(8) The supervisory authority may extend the period allowed under the notice for making representations.

(9) If, having considered any representations made by A, the supervisory authority decides—

(a) to issue the direction, or

(b) if the direction has been issued, not to rescind the direction,

it must give A notice in writing.

(10) If, having considered any representations made by A, the supervisory authority decides—

(a) not to issue the direction,

(b) to issue a different direction, or

(c) to rescind a direction which has effect,

it must give A notice in writing.

(11) A notice under paragraph (9) must inform A of A's right to refer the matter to the appropriate tribunal.

(12) A notice under paragraph (10)(b) must comply with paragraph (7).

(13) If a notice informs A of A's right to refer a matter to the appropriate tribunal, it must give an indication of the procedure on such a reference.

(14) For the purpose of this regulation—

(a) "appropriate tribunal" means—

(i) the Upper Tribunal, in the case of a direction issued by the FCA;

(ii) the First-tier or Upper Tribunal, as provided for in regulation 99, in the case of a direction issued by the Commissioners;

(b) "specified" means specified in the direction.

CHAPTER 3

OWNERSHIP AND MANAGEMENT RESTRICTIONS

26 Prohibitions and approvals

(1) No person may be the beneficial owner, officer or manager of a firm within paragraph (2) ("a relevant firm"), or a sole practitioner within paragraph (2) ("a relevant sole practitioner"), unless that person has been approved as a beneficial owner, officer or manager of the firm or as a sole practitioner by the supervisory authority of the firm or sole practitioner.

(2) The firms and sole practitioners within this paragraph are—

(a) auditors, insolvency practitioners, external accountants and tax advisors;
(b) independent legal professionals;
(c) estate agents;
(d) high value dealers.

(3) A person does not breach the prohibition in paragraph (1) if that person has before 26th June 2018 applied to the supervisory authority for approval under paragraph (6) and that application has not yet been determined.

(4) A relevant firm must take reasonable care to ensure that no-one is appointed, or continues to act, as an officer or manager of the firm unless—

(a) that person has been approved by the supervisory authority, and the supervisory authority's approval of that person has not ceased to be valid; or
(b) that person has applied for approval of the supervisory authority under paragraph (6) and the application has not yet been determined.

(5) A relevant sole practitioner must not act, or continue to act, as a sole practitioner unless—

(a) that person has been approved by the supervisory authority, and the supervisory authority's approval of that person has not ceased to be valid; or
(b) that person has applied for approval of the supervisory authority under paragraph (6) and the application has not yet been determined.

(6) An application for the approval of the supervisory authority under paragraph (1) may be made by or on behalf of the person concerned.

(7) The application must—

(a) be made in such manner as the supervisory authority may direct;
(b) contain, or be accompanied by, such information as the supervisory authority may reasonably require.

(8) The supervisory authority—

(a) must grant an application for approval under paragraph (6) unless the applicant has been convicted of a relevant offence;
(b) may grant an application so as to give approval only for a limited period.

(9) An approval given by a supervisory authority under paragraph (8)—

(a) is not valid if the person approved under paragraph (1) (the "approved person") has been convicted of a relevant offence;
(b) ceases to be valid if the approved person is subsequently convicted of a relevant offence.

(10) If an approved person ("P") is convicted of a relevant offence—

(a) P must inform the supervisory authority which approved P of the conviction within 30 days of the day on which P was convicted;
(b) the relevant firm for which P was approved must inform its supervisory authority of the conviction within 30 days of the date on which the firm became aware of P's conviction.

(11) If the beneficial owner of a relevant firm is convicted of a relevant offence, the High Court (or in Scotland the Court of Session) may, on the application of the supervisory authority, order the sale of the beneficial owner's interest in that firm.

(12) A person who, in breach of the prohibition in paragraph (1)—

(a) acts as a manager or officer of a relevant firm or as a relevant sole practitioner; or
(b) is knowingly a beneficial owner of a relevant firm,

is guilty of a criminal offence.

(13) A person who is guilty of a criminal offence under paragraph (12) is liable—

(a) on summary conviction—
 (i) in England and Wales, to imprisonment for a term not exceeding three months, to a fine or to both;
 (ii) in Scotland or Northern Ireland, to imprisonment for a term not exceeding three months, to a fine not exceeding the statutory maximum or to both;
(b) on conviction on indictment, to imprisonment for a term not exceeding two years, to a fine or to both.

(14) The offences listed in Schedule 3 are relevant offences for the purposes of this regulation.

PART 3

CUSTOMER DUE DILIGENCE

CHAPTER 1

CUSTOMER DUE DILIGENCE: GENERAL

27 Customer due diligence

(1) A relevant person must apply customer due diligence measures if the person—

(a) establishes a business relationship;

(b) carries out an occasional transaction that amounts to a transfer of funds within the meaning of Article 3.9 of the funds transfer regulation exceeding 1,000 euros;

(c) suspects money laundering or terrorist financing; or

(d) doubts the veracity or adequacy of documents or information previously obtained for the purposes of identification or verification.

(2) A relevant person who is not a high value dealer or a casino must also apply customer due diligence measures if the person carries out an occasional transaction that amounts to 15,000 euros or more, whether the transaction is executed in a single operation or in several operations which appear to be linked.

(3) A high value dealer must also apply customer due diligence measures if that dealer carries out an occasional transaction in cash that amounts to 10,000 euros or more, whether the transaction is executed in a single operation or in several operations which appear to be linked.

(4) A transaction does not cease to be a "transaction in cash" for the purposes of paragraph (3) if cash is paid by or on behalf of a party to the transaction—

(a) to a person other than the other party to the transaction for the benefit of the other party, or

(b) into a bank account for the benefit of the other party to the transaction.

(5) A casino must also apply customer due diligence measures in relation to any transaction within paragraph (6) that amounts to 2,000 euros or more, whether the transaction is executed in a single operation or in several operations which appear to be linked.

(6) A transaction is within this paragraph if it consists of—

(a) the wagering of a stake, including—

(i) the purchase from, or exchange with, the casino of tokens for use in gambling at the casino;

(ii) payment for use of gaming machines (within the meaning of section 235 of the Gambling Act 2005); and

(iii) the deposit of funds required to take part in remote gambling; or

(b) the collection of winnings, including the withdrawal of funds deposited to take part in remote gambling (within the meaning of section 4 of the Gambling Act 2005) or winnings arising from the staking of such funds.

(7) In determining whether a transaction amounts to 2,000 euros or more for the purposes of paragraph (5), no account is to be taken of winnings from a previous transaction which had not been collected from the casino, gaming machine or remote gambling, but are being re-used in the transaction in question.

(8) A relevant person must also apply customer due diligence measures—

(a) at other appropriate times to existing customers on a risk based approach;

(b) when the relevant person becomes aware that the circumstances of an existing customer relevant to its risk assessment for that customer have changed.

(9) For the purposes of paragraph (8), in determining when it is appropriate to take customer due diligence measures in relation to existing customers, a relevant person must take into account, among other things—

(a) any indication that the identity of the customer, or of the customer's beneficial owner, has changed;

(b) any transactions which are not reasonably consistent with the relevant person's knowledge of the customer;

(c) any change in the purpose or intended nature of the relevant person's relationship with the customer;

(d) any other matter which might affect the relevant person's assessment of the money laundering or terrorist financing risk in relation to the customer.

28 Customer due diligence measures

(1) This regulation applies when a relevant person is required by regulation 27 to apply customer due diligence measures.

(2) The relevant person must—

(a) identify the customer unless the identity of that customer is known to, and has been verified by, the relevant person;

(b) verify the customer's identity unless the customer's identity has already been verified by the relevant person; and

(c) assess, and where appropriate obtain information on, the purpose and intended nature of the business relationship or occasional transaction.

(3) Where the customer is a body corporate—

(a) the relevant person must obtain and verify—

(i) the name of the body corporate;

(ii) its company number or other registration number;

(iii) the address of its registered office, and if different, its principal place of business;

(b) subject to paragraph (5), the relevant person must take reasonable measures to determine and verify—

(i) the law to which the body corporate is subject, and its constitution (whether set out in its articles of association or other governing documents);

(ii) the full names of the board of directors (or if there is no board, the members of the equivalent management body) and the senior persons responsible for the operations of the body corporate.

(4) Subject to paragraph (5), where the customer is beneficially owned by another person, the relevant person must—

(a) identify the beneficial owner;

(b) take reasonable measures to verify the identity of the beneficial owner so that the relevant person is satisfied that it knows who the beneficial owner is; and

(c) if the beneficial owner is a legal person, trust, company, foundation or similar legal arrangement take reasonable measures to understand the ownership and control structure of that legal person, trust, company, foundation or similar legal arrangement.

(5) Paragraphs (3)(b) and (4) do not apply where the customer is a company which is listed on a regulated market.

(6) If the customer is a body corporate, and paragraph (7) applies, the relevant person may treat the senior person in that body corporate responsible for managing it as its beneficial owner.

(7) This paragraph applies if (and only if) the relevant person has exhausted all possible means of identifying the beneficial owner of the body corporate and—

(a) has not succeeded in doing so, or

(b) is not satisfied that the individual identified is in fact the beneficial owner.

(8) If paragraph (7) applies, the relevant person must keep records in writing of all the actions it has taken to identify the beneficial owner of the body corporate.

(9) Relevant persons do not satisfy their requirements under paragraph (4) by relying solely on the information—

(a) contained in—

(i) the register of people with significant control kept by a company under section 790M of the Companies Act 2006 (duty to keep register);

(ii) the register of people with significant control kept by a limited liability partnership under section 790M of the Companies Act 2006 as modified by regulation 31E of the Limited Liability Partnerships (Application of Companies Act 2006) Regulations 2009; or

(iii) the register of people with significant control kept by a European Public Limited-Liability Company (within the meaning of the Council Regulation 2157/2001/EC of 8 October 2001 on the Statute for a European Company which is to be, or is, registered in the United Kingdom) under section 790M of the Companies Act 2006 as modified by regulation 5 of the European Public Limited Liability Company (Register of People with Significant Control) Regulations 2016;

(b) referred to in sub-paragraph (a) and delivered to the registrar of companies (within the meaning of section 1060(3) of the Companies Act 2006 (the registrar)) under any enactment; or

(c) contained in required particulars in relation to eligible Scottish partnerships delivered to the registrar of companies under regulation 19 of the Scottish Partnerships (Register of People with Significant Control) Regulations 2017.

(10) Where a person ("A") purports to act on behalf of the customer, the relevant person must—

(a) verify that A is authorised to act on the customer's behalf;

(b) identify A; and

(c) verify A's identity on the basis of documents or information in either case obtained from a reliable source which is independent of both A and the customer.

(11) The relevant person must conduct ongoing monitoring of a business relationship, including—

(a) scrutiny of transactions undertaken throughout the course of the relationship (including, where necessary, the source of funds) to ensure that the transactions are consistent with the relevant person's knowledge of the customer, the customer's business and risk profile;

(b) undertaking reviews of existing records and keeping the documents or information obtained for the purpose of applying customer due diligence measures up-to-date.

(12) The ways in which a relevant person complies with the requirement to take customer due diligence measures, and the extent of the measures taken—

(a) must reflect—

(i) the risk assessment carried out by the relevant person under regulation 18(1);

(ii) its assessment of the level of risk arising in any particular case;

(b) may differ from case to case.

(13) In assessing the level of risk in a particular case, the relevant person must take account of factors including, among other things—

(a) the purpose of an account, transaction or business relationship;

(b) the level of assets to be deposited by a customer or the size of the transactions undertaken by the customer;

(c) the regularity and duration of the business relationship.

(14) If paragraph (15) applies, a relevant person is not required to continue to apply customer due diligence measures under paragraph (2) or (10) in respect of a customer.

(15) This paragraph applies if all the following conditions are met—

(a) a relevant person has taken customer due diligence measures in relation to a customer;

(b) the relevant person makes a disclosure required by—

(i) Part 3 of the Terrorism Act 2000, or

(ii) Part 7 of the Proceeds of Crime Act 2002; and

(c) continuing to apply customer due diligence measures in relation to that customer would result in the commission of an offence by the relevant person under—

(i) section 21D of the Terrorism Act 2000 (tipping off: regulated sector); or

(ii) section 333A of the Proceeds of Crime Act 2002 (tipping off: regulated sector).

(16) The relevant person must be able to demonstrate to its supervisory authority that the extent of the measures it has taken to satisfy its requirements under this regulation are appropriate in view of the risks of money laundering and terrorist financing, including risks—

(a) identified by the risk assessment carried out by the relevant person under regulation 18(1);

(b) identified by its supervisory authority and in information made available to the relevant person under regulations 17(9) and 47.

(17) Paragraph (16) does not apply to the National Savings Bank or the Director of Savings.

(18) For the purposes of this regulation—

(a) except in paragraph (10), "verify" means verify on the basis of documents or information in either case obtained from a reliable source which is independent of the person whose identity is being verified;

(b) documents issued or made available by an official body are to be regarded as being independent of a person even if they are provided or made available to the relevant person by or on behalf of that person.

29 Additional customer due diligence measures: credit institutions and financial institutions

(1) This regulation applies in addition to regulation 28 where a relevant person is a credit institution or a financial institution.

(2) Paragraphs (3) to (5) apply if the relevant person is providing a customer with a contract of long-term insurance ("the insurance policy").

(3) As soon as the beneficiaries of the insurance policy are identified or designated, the relevant person must—

(a) if the beneficiary is a named person or legal arrangement, take the full name of the person or arrangement; or

(b) if the beneficiaries are designated by specified characteristics, as a class or in any other way, obtain sufficient information about the beneficiaries to satisfy itself that it will be able to establish the identity of the beneficiary before any payment is made under the insurance policy.

(4) The relevant person must verify the identity of the beneficiaries (on the basis of documents or information in either case obtained from a reliable source which is independent of the customer and the beneficiaries, and regulation 28(18)(b) applies for the purpose of determining whether a source satisfies this requirement) before any payment is made under the insurance policy.

(5) When the relevant person becomes aware that all or part of the rights under the insurance policy are being, or have been, assigned to an individual, body corporate, trust or other legal arrangement which is receiving the value or part of the value of the insurance policy for its own benefit ("the new beneficiary"), the relevant person must identify the new beneficiary as soon as possible after becoming aware of the assignment, and in any case before a payment is made under the policy.

(6) The relevant person must not set up an anonymous account or an anonymous passbook for any new or existing customer.

(7) The relevant person must apply customer due diligence measures to all anonymous accounts and passbooks in existence on the date on which these Regulations come into force, and in any event before such accounts or passbooks are used in any way.

(8) A relevant person which—

(a) is an open-ended investment company within the meaning of regulation 2(1) of the Open-Ended Investment Companies Regulations 2001; and

(b) is authorised on or after the date on which these Regulations come into force,

may not issue shares evidenced by a share certificate (or any other documentary evidence) indicating that the holder of the certificate or document is entitled to the shares specified in it.

(9) Paragraph (8) does not apply to an open-ended investment company if—

(a) an application for an authorisation order under regulation 12 of the Open-ended Investment Companies Regulations 2001 was made in relation to that open-ended investment company before the date on which these Regulations come into force; and

(b) that application was not determined until a date on or after the date on which these Regulations come into force.

30 Timing of verification

(1) This regulation applies when a relevant person is required to take any measures under regulation 27, 28 or 29.

(2) Subject to paragraph (3) or (4), a relevant person must comply with the requirement to verify the identity of the customer, any person purporting to act on behalf of the customer and any beneficial owner of the customer before the establishment of a business relationship or the carrying out of the transaction.

(3) Provided that the verification is completed as soon as practicable after contact is first established, the verification of the customer, any person purporting to act on behalf of the customer and the customer's beneficial owner, may be completed during the establishment of a business relationship if—

(a) this is necessary not to interrupt the normal conduct of business; and

(b) there is little risk of money laundering and terrorist financing.

(4) The verification by a credit institution or a financial institution of the identity of a customer opening an account, any person purporting to act on behalf of the customer and any beneficial owner of the customer, may take place after the account has been opened provided that there are adequate safeguards in place to ensure that no transactions are carried out by or on behalf of the customer before verification has been completed.

(5) For the purposes of paragraph (4) "account" includes an account which permits transactions in transferable securities.

(6) Paragraph (7) applies if—

(a) the relevant person is required to apply customer due diligence measures in the case of a trust, a legal entity (other than a body corporate) or a legal arrangement (other than a trust); and

(b) the beneficiaries of that trust, entity or arrangement are designated as a class, or by reference to particular characteristics.

(7) If this paragraph applies, the relevant person must establish and verify the identity of any beneficiary before—

(a) any payment is made to the beneficiary; or

(b) the beneficiary exercises its vested rights in the trust, legal entity or legal arrangement.

31 Requirement to cease transactions etc

(1) Where, in relation to any customer, a relevant person is unable to apply customer due diligence measures as required by regulation 28, that person—

(a) must not carry out any transaction through a bank account with the customer or on behalf of the customer;

(b) must not establish a business relationship or carry out a transaction with the customer otherwise than through a bank account;

(c) must terminate any existing business relationship with the customer;

(d) must consider whether the relevant person is required to make a disclosure (or to make further disclosure) by—

(i) Part 3 of the Terrorism Act 2000; or

(ii) Part 7 of the Proceeds of Crime Act 2002.

(2) Paragraph (1)(a) does not prevent money deposited in an account being repaid to the person who deposited it, provided that, in any case where a disclosure is required by the legislation referred in paragraph (1)(d), the relevant person has—

(a) consent (within the meaning of section 21ZA of the Terrorism Act 2000 (arrangements with prior consent)) to the transaction, or

(b) the appropriate consent (within the meaning of section 335 of the Proceeds of Crime Act 2002 (appropriate consent)) to the transaction.

(3) Paragraph (1) does not apply where an independent legal professional or other professional adviser is in the course of ascertaining the legal position for a client or performing the task of defending or representing that client in, or concerning, legal proceedings, including giving advice on the institution or avoidance of proceedings.

(4) In paragraph (3), "other professional adviser" means an auditor, external accountant or tax adviser who is a member of a professional body which is established for any such persons and which makes provision for—

(a) testing the competence of those seeking admission to membership of such a body as a condition for such admission; and

(b) imposing and maintaining professional and ethical standards for its members, as well as imposing sanctions for non-compliance with those standards.

(5) Paragraph (1)(a) to (c) does not apply where an insolvency practitioner has been appointed by the court as administrator or liquidator of a company, provided that—

(a) the insolvency practitioner has taken all reasonable steps to satisfy the requirements set out in regulation 28(2) and (10), and

(b) the resignation of the insolvency practitioner would be prejudicial to the interests of the creditors of the company.

32 Exception for trustees of debt issues

(1) A relevant person—

(a) who is appointed by the issuer of instruments or securities specified in paragraph (2) as trustee of an issue of such instruments or securities; or

(b) whose customer is a trustee of an issue of such instruments or securities,

is not required to apply the customer due diligence measure referred to in regulation 28(3) and (4) in respect of the holders of such instruments or securities.

(2) The specified instruments and securities are—

(a) instruments which fall within article 77 or 77A of the Financial Services and Markets Act 2000 (Regulated Activities) Order 2001; and

(b) securities which fall within article 78 of that Order.

CHAPTER 2

ENHANCED CUSTOMER DUE DILIGENCE

33 Obligation to apply enhanced customer due diligence

(1) A relevant person must apply enhanced customer due diligence measures and enhanced ongoing monitoring, in addition to the customer due diligence measures required under regulation 28 and, if applicable, regulation 29, to manage and mitigate the risks arising—

(a) in any case identified as one where there is a high risk of money laundering or terrorist financing—

(i) by the relevant person under regulation 18(1), or

(ii) in information made available to the relevant person under regulations 17(9) and 47;

(b) in any business relationship or transaction with a person established in a high-risk third country;

(c) in relation to correspondent relationships with a credit institution or a financial institution (in accordance with regulation 34);

(d) if a relevant person has determined that a customer or potential customer is a PEP, or a family member or known close associate of a PEP (in accordance with regulation 35);

(e) in any case where the relevant person discovers that a customer has provided false or stolen identification documentation or information and the relevant person proposes to continue to deal with that customer;

(f) in any case where—

(i) a transaction is complex and unusually large, or there is an unusual pattern of transactions, and

(ii) the transaction or transactions have no apparent economic or legal purpose, and

(g) in any other case which by its nature can present a higher risk of money laundering or terrorist financing.

(2) Paragraph (1)(b) does not apply when the customer is a branch or majority owned subsidiary undertaking of an entity which is established in an EEA state if all the following conditions are satisfied—

(a) the entity is—

(i) subject to the requirements in national legislation implementing the fourth money laundering directive as an obliged entity (within the meaning of that directive), and

(ii) supervised for compliance with those requirements in accordance with section 2 of Chapter VI of the fourth money laundering directive;

(b) the branch or subsidiary complies fully with procedures and policies established for the group under Article 45 of the fourth money laundering directive; and

(c) the relevant person, applying a risk-based approach, does not consider that it is necessary to apply enhanced customer due diligence measures.

(3) For the purposes of paragraph (1)(b), a "high-risk third country" means a country which has been identified by the European Commission in delegated acts adopted under Article 9.2 of the fourth money laundering directive as a high-risk third country.

(4) The enhanced customer due diligence measures taken by a relevant person for the purpose of paragraph (1)(f) must include—

(a) as far as reasonably possible, examining the background and purpose of the transaction, and

(b) increasing the degree and nature of monitoring of the business relationship in which the transaction is made to determine whether that transaction or that relationship appear to be suspicious.

(5) Depending on the requirements of the case, the enhanced customer due diligence measures required under paragraph (1) may also include, among other things—

(a) seeking additional independent, reliable sources to verify information provided or made available to the relevant person;

(b) taking additional measures to understand better the background, ownership and financial situation of the customer, and other parties to the transaction;

(c) taking further steps to be satisfied that the transaction is consistent with the purpose and intended nature of the business relationship;

(d) increasing the monitoring of the business relationship, including greater scrutiny of transactions.

(6) When assessing whether there is a high risk of money laundering or terrorist financing in a particular situation, and the extent of the measures which should be taken to manage and mitigate that risk, relevant persons must take account of risk factors including, among other things—

(a) customer risk factors, including whether—

(i) the business relationship is conducted in unusual circumstances;

(ii) the customer is resident in a geographical area of high risk (see sub-paragraph (c));

(iii) the customer is a legal person or legal arrangement that is a vehicle for holding personal assets;

(iv) the customer is a company that has nominee shareholders or shares in bearer form;

(v) the customer is a business that is cash intensive;

(vi) the corporate structure of the customer is unusual or excessively complex given the nature of the company's business;

(b) product, service, transaction or delivery channel risk factors, including whether—

(i) the product involves private banking;

(ii) the product or transaction is one which might favour anonymity;

(iii) the situation involves non-face-to-face business relationships or transactions, without certain safeguards, such as electronic signatures;

(iv) payments will be received from unknown or unassociated third parties;

(v) new products and new business practices are involved, including new delivery mechanisms, and the use of new or developing technologies for both new and pre-existing products;

(vi) the service involves the provision of nominee directors, nominee shareholders or shadow directors, or the formation of companies in a third country;

(c) geographical risk factors, including—

(i) countries identified by credible sources, such as mutual evaluations, detailed assessment reports or published follow-up reports, as not having effective systems to counter money laundering or terrorist financing;

(ii) countries identified by credible sources as having significant levels of corruption or other criminal activity, such as terrorism (within the meaning of section 1 of the Terrorism Act 2000), money laundering, and the production and supply of illicit drugs;

(iii) countries subject to sanctions, embargos or similar measures issued by, for example, the European Union or the United Nations;

(iv) countries providing funding or support for terrorism;

(v) countries that have organisations operating within their territory which have been designated—

(aa) by the government of the United Kingdom as proscribed organisations under Schedule 2 to the Terrorism Act 2000, or (bb) by other countries, international organisations or the European Union as terrorist organisations;

(vi) countries identified by credible sources, such as evaluations, detailed assessment reports or published follow-up reports published by the Financial Action Task Force, the International Monetary Fund, the World Bank, the Organisation for Economic Co-operation and Development or other international bodies or non-governmental organisations as not implementing requirements to counter money laundering and terrorist financing that are consistent with the recommendations published by the Financial Action Task Force in February 2012 and updated in October 2016.

(7) In making the assessment referred to in paragraph (6), relevant persons must bear in mind that the presence of one or more risk factors may not always indicate that there is a high risk of money laundering or terrorist financing in a particular situation.

(8) In determining what measures to take when paragraph (1) applies, and what the extent of those measures should be, credit institutions and financial institutions must also take account of any guidelines issued by the European Supervisory Authorities under Article 18.4 of the fourth money laundering directive.

34 Enhanced customer due diligence: credit institutions, financial institutions and correspondent relationships

(1) A credit institution or financial institution (the "correspondent") which has or proposes to have a correspondent relationship with another such institution (the "respondent") from a third country must, in addition to the measures required by regulation 33—

(a) gather sufficient information about the respondent to understand fully the nature of its business;

(b) determine from publicly-available information from credible sources the reputation of the respondent and the quality of the supervision to which the respondent is subject;

(c) assess the respondent's controls to counter money laundering and terrorist financing;

(d) obtain approval from senior management before establishing a new correspondent relationship;

(e) document the responsibilities of the respondent and correspondent in the correspondent relationship; and

(f) be satisfied that, in respect of those of the respondent's customers who have direct access to accounts with the correspondent, the respondent—

(i) has verified the identity of, and conducts ongoing customer due diligence measures in relation to, such customers; and

(ii) is able to provide to the correspondent, upon request, the documents or information obtained when applying such customer due diligence measures.

(2) Credit institutions and financial institutions must not enter into, or continue, a correspondent relationship with a shell bank.

(3) Credit institutions and financial institutions must take appropriate enhanced measures to ensure that they do not enter into, or continue, a correspondent relationship with a credit institution or financial institution which is known to allow its accounts to be used by a shell bank.

(4) For the purposes of this regulation—

(a) "correspondent relationship" means—

(i) the provision of banking services by a correspondent to a respondent including providing a current or other liability account and related services, such as cash management, international funds transfers, cheque clearing, providing customers of the respondent with direct access to accounts with the correspondent (and vice versa) and providing foreign exchange services; or

(ii) the relationship between and among credit institutions and financial institutions including where similar services are provided by a correspondent to a respondent, and including relationships established for securities transactions or funds transfers;

(b) a "shell bank" means a credit institution or financial institution, or an institution engaged in equivalent activities to those carried out by credit institutions or financial institutions, incorporated in a jurisdiction in which it has no physical presence involving meaningful decision-making and management, and which is not part of a financial conglomerate or third-country financial conglomerate;

(c) in sub-paragraph (b), "financial conglomerate" and "third-country financial conglomerate" have the meanings given by regulations 1(2) and 7(1) respectively of the Financial Conglomerates and Other Financial Groups Regulations 2004.

35 Enhanced customer due diligence: politically exposed persons

(1) A relevant person must have in place appropriate risk-management systems and procedures to determine whether a customer or the beneficial owner of a customer is—

(a) a politically exposed person (a "PEP"); or

(b) a family member or a known close associate of a PEP,

and to manage the enhanced risks arising from the relevant person's business relationship or transactions with such a customer.

(2) In determining what risk-management systems and procedures are appropriate under paragraph (1), the relevant person must take account of—

(a) the risk assessment it carried out under regulation 18(1);

(b) the level of risk of money laundering and terrorist financing inherent in its business;

(c) the extent to which that risk would be increased by its business relationship or transactions with a PEP, or a family member or known close associate of a PEP, and

(d) any relevant information made available to the relevant person under regulations 17(9) and 47.

(3) If a relevant person has determined that a customer or a potential customer is a PEP, or a family member or known close associate of a PEP, the relevant person must assess—

(a) the level of risk associated with that customer, and

(b) the extent of the enhanced customer due diligence measures to be applied in relation to that customer.

(4) In assessing the extent of the enhanced customer due diligence measures to be taken in relation to any particular person (which may differ from case to case), a relevant person—

(a) must take account of any relevant information made available to the relevant person under regulations 17(9) and 47; and

(b) may take into account any guidance which has been—

(i) issued by the FCA; or

(ii) issued by any other supervisory authority or appropriate body and approved by the Treasury.

(5) A relevant person who proposes to have, or to continue, a business relationship with a PEP, or a family member or a known close associate of a PEP, must, in addition to the measures required by regulation 33—

(a) have approval from senior management for establishing or continuing the business relationship with that person;

(b) take adequate measures to establish the source of wealth and source of funds which are involved in the proposed business relationship or transactions with that person; and

(c) where the business relationship is entered into, conduct enhanced ongoing monitoring of the business relationship with that person.

(6) A relevant person which is providing a customer with a contract of long-term insurance (an "insurance policy") must take reasonable measures to determine whether one or more of the beneficiaries of the insurance policy or the beneficial owner of a beneficiary of such an insurance policy are—

(a) PEPs, or

(b) family members or known close associates of PEPs.

(7) The measures required under paragraph (6) must be taken before—

(a) any payment is made under the insurance policy, or

(b) the benefit of the insurance policy is assigned in whole or in part to another person.

(8) A relevant person must, in addition to the measures required by regulation 33, ensure that—

(a) its senior management is informed before it pays out any sums under an insurance policy the beneficiary of which is a PEP or a person who comes within paragraph (6)(b) in relation to a PEP, and

(b) its entire business relationship with the holder of the insurance policy ("the policy holder") is scrutinised on an ongoing basis in accordance with enhanced procedures, whether or not the policy holder is a PEP or a family member or known close associate of a PEP.

(9) Where a person who was a PEP is no longer entrusted with a prominent public function, a relevant person must continue to apply the requirements in paragraphs (5) and (8) in relation to that person—

(a) for a period of at least 12 months after the date on which that person ceased to be entrusted with that public function; or

(b) for such longer period as the relevant person considers appropriate to address risks of money laundering or terrorist financing in relation to that person.

(10) Paragraph (9) does not apply in relation to a person who—

(a) was not a politically exposed person within the meaning of regulation 14(5) of the Money Laundering Regulations 2007, when those Regulations were in force; and

(b) ceased to be entrusted with a prominent public function before the date on which these Regulations come into force.

(11) When a person who was a PEP is no longer entrusted with a prominent public function, the relevant person is no longer required to apply the requirements in paragraphs (5) and (8) in relation to a family member or known close associate of that PEP (whether or not the period referred to in paragraph (9) has expired).

(12) In this regulation—

(a) "politically exposed person" or "PEP" means an individual who is entrusted with prominent public functions, other than as a middle-ranking or more junior official;

(b) "family member" of a politically exposed person includes—

(i) a spouse or civil partner of the PEP;

(ii) children of the PEP and the spouses or civil partners of the PEP's children;

(iii) parents of the PEP;

(c) "known close associate" of a PEP means—

(i) an individual known to have joint beneficial ownership of a legal entity or a legal arrangement or any other close business relations with a PEP;

(ii) an individual who has sole beneficial ownership of a legal entity or a legal arrangement which is known to have been set up for the benefit of a PEP.

(13) For the purposes of paragraph (5), a reference to a business relationship with an individual includes a reference to a business relationship with a person of which the individual is a beneficial owner.

(14) For the purposes of paragraphs (9), (11) and (12)(a), individuals entrusted with prominent public functions include—

(a) heads of state, heads of government, ministers and deputy or assistant ministers;

(b) members of parliament or of similar legislative bodies;

(c) members of the governing bodies of political parties;

(d) members of supreme courts, of constitutional courts or of any judicial body the decisions of which are not subject to further appeal except in exceptional circumstances;

(e) members of courts of auditors or of the boards of central banks;

(f) ambassadors, charges d'affaires and high-ranking officers in the armed forces;

(g) members of the administrative, management or supervisory bodies of State-owned enterprises;

(h) directors, deputy directors and members of the board or equivalent function of an international organisation.

(15) For the purpose of deciding whether a person is a known close associate of a politically exposed person, a relevant person need only have regard to information which is in its possession, or to credible information which is publicly available.

36 Politically exposed persons: other duties

(1) The duty under section 30(1) of the Bank of England and Financial Services Act 2016 (duty to ensure that regulations or orders implementing the fourth money laundering directive comply with paragraphs (a) to (d) of that subsection) does not apply if, and to the extent that, the duty is otherwise satisfied as a result of any provision contained in these Regulations, or any guidance issued by the FCA under these Regulations.

(2) The duty under section 333U(1) and (2) of FSMA (duty to issue guidance in connection with politically exposed persons) does not apply if, and to the extent that, the duty is otherwise satisfied as a result of guidance issued by the FCA under these Regulations.

CHAPTER 3

SIMPLIFIED CUSTOMER DUE DILIGENCE

37 Application of simplified customer due diligence

(1) A relevant person may apply simplified customer due diligence measures in relation to a particular business relationship or transaction if it determines that the business relationship or transaction presents a low degree of risk of money laundering and terrorist financing, having taken into account—

(a) the risk assessment it carried out under regulation 18(1);

(b) relevant information made available to it under regulations 17(9) and 47; and

(c) the risk factors referred to in paragraph (3).

(2) Where a relevant person applies simplified customer due diligence measures, it must—

(a) continue to comply with the requirements in regulation 28, but it may adjust the extent, timing or type of the measures it undertakes under that regulation to reflect its determination under paragraph (1); and

(b) carry out sufficient monitoring of any business relationships or transactions which are subject to those measures to enable it to detect any unusual or suspicious transactions.

(3) When assessing whether there is a low degree of risk of money laundering and terrorist financing in a particular situation, and the extent to which it is appropriate to apply simplified customer due diligence measures in that situation, the relevant person must take account of risk factors including, among other things—

(a) customer risk factors, including whether the customer—

(i) is a public administration, or a publicly owned enterprise;

(ii) is an individual resident in a geographical area of lower risk (see sub-paragraph (c));

(iii) is a credit institution or a financial institution which is—

(aa) subject to the requirements in national legislation implementing the fourth money laundering directive as an obliged entity (within the meaning of that directive), and

(bb) supervised for compliance with those requirements in accordance with section 2 of Chapter VI of the fourth money laundering directive;

(iv) is a company whose securities are listed on a regulated market, and the location of the regulated market;

(b) product, service, transaction or delivery channel risk factors, including whether the product or service is—

(i) a life insurance policy for which the premium is low;

(ii) an insurance policy for a pension scheme which does not provide for an early surrender option, and cannot be used as collateral;

(iii) a pension, superannuation or similar scheme which satisfies the following conditions—

(aa) the scheme provides retirement benefits to employees;

(bb) contributions to the scheme are made by way of deductions from wages; and

(cc) the scheme rules do not permit the assignment of a member's interest under the scheme;

(iv) a financial product or service that provides appropriately defined and limited services to certain types of customers to increase access for financial inclusion purposes in an EEA state;

(v) a product where the risks of money laundering and terrorist financing are managed by other factors such as purse limits or transparency of ownership;

(vi) a child trust fund within the meaning given by section 1(2) of the Child Trust Funds Act 2004;

(vii) a junior ISA within the meaning given by regulation 2B of the Individual Savings Account Regulations 1998;

(c) geographical risk factors, including whether the country where the customer is resident, established or registered or in which it operates is—

(i) an EEA state;

(ii) a third country which has effective systems to counter money laundering and terrorist financing;

(iii) a third country identified by credible sources as having a low level of corruption or other criminal activity, such as terrorism (within the meaning of section 1 of the Terrorism Act 2000), money laundering, and the production and supply of illicit drugs;

(iv) a third country which, on the basis of credible sources, such as evaluations, detailed assessment reports or published follow-up reports published by the Financial Action Task Force, the International Monetary Fund, the World Bank, the Organisation for Economic Co-operation and Development or other international bodies or non-governmental organisations—

(aa) has requirements to counter money laundering and terrorist financing that are consistent with the revised Recommendations published by the Financial Action Task Force in February 2012 and updated in October 2016; and

(bb) effectively implements those Recommendations.

(4) In making the assessment referred to in paragraph (3), relevant persons must bear in mind that the presence of one or more risk factors may not always indicate that there is a low risk of money laundering and terrorist financing in a particular situation.

(5) A relevant person may apply simplified customer due diligence measures where the customer is a person to whom paragraph (6) applies and the product is an account into which monies are pooled (the "pooled account"), provided that—

(a) the business relationship with the holder of the pooled account presents a low degree of risk of money laundering and terrorist financing; and

(b) information on the identity of the persons on whose behalf monies are held in the pooled account is available, on request to the relevant person where the pooled account is held.

(6) This paragraph applies to—

(a) a relevant person who is subject to these Regulations under regulation 8;

(b) a person who carries on business in an EEA state other than the United Kingdom who is—

(i) subject to the requirements in national legislation implementing the fourth money laundering directive as an obliged entity (within the meaning of that directive), and

(ii) supervised for compliance with those requirements in accordance with section 2 of Chapter VI of the fourth money laundering directive.

(7) In determining what simplified customer due diligence measures to take, and the extent of those measures, when paragraph (1) applies, credit institutions and financial institutions must also take account of any guidelines issued by the European Supervisory Authorities under Article 17 of the fourth money laundering directive.

(8) A relevant person must not continue to apply simplified customer due diligence measures under paragraph (1)—

(a) if it doubts the veracity or accuracy of any documents or information previously obtained for the purposes of identification or verification;

(b) if its risk assessment changes and it no longer considers that there is a low degree of risk of money laundering and terrorist financing;

(c) if it suspects money laundering or terrorist financing; or

(d) if any of the conditions set out in regulation 33(1) apply.

38 Electronic money

(1) Subject to paragraph (3), a relevant person is not required to apply customer due diligence measures in relation to electronic money, and regulations 27, 28, 30 and 33 to 37 do not apply provided that—

(a) the maximum amount which can be stored electronically is 250 euros, or (if the amount stored can only be used in the United Kingdom), 500 euros;

(b) the payment instrument used in connection with the electronic money ("the relevant payment instrument") is—

(i) not reloadable; or

(ii) is subject to a maximum limit on monthly payment transactions of 250 euros which can only be used in the United Kingdom;

(c) the relevant payment instrument is used exclusively to purchase goods or services;

(d) anonymous electronic money cannot be used to fund the relevant payment instrument.

(2) Paragraph (1) does not apply to any transaction which consists of the redemption in cash, or a cash withdrawal, of the monetary value of the electronic money, where the amount redeemed exceeds 100 euros.

(3) The issuer of the relevant payment instrument must carry out sufficient monitoring of its business relationship with the users of electronic money and of transactions made using the relevant payment instrument to enable it to detect any unusual or suspicious transactions.

(4) A relevant person is not prevented from applying simplified customer due diligence measures in relation to electronic money because the conditions set out in paragraph (1) are not satisfied, provided that such measures are permitted under regulation 37.

(5) For the purposes of this regulation "payment instrument" has the meaning given by regulation 2(1) of the Electronic Money Regulations 2011.

PART 4
RELIANCE AND RECORD-KEEPING

39 Reliance

(1) A relevant person may rely on a person who falls within paragraph (3) ("the third party") to apply any of the customer due diligence measures required by regulation 28(2) to (6) and (10) but, notwithstanding the relevant person's reliance on the third party, the relevant person remains liable for any failure to apply such measures.

(2) When a relevant person relies on the third party to apply customer due diligence measures under paragraph (1) it—

(a) must immediately obtain from the third party all the information needed to satisfy the requirements of regulation 28(2) to (6) and (10) in relation to the customer, customer's beneficial owner, or any person acting on behalf of the customer;

(b) must enter into arrangements with the third party which—

(i) enable the relevant person to obtain from the third party immediately on request copies of any identification and verification data and any other relevant documentation on the identity of the customer, customer's beneficial owner, or any person acting on behalf of the customer;

(ii) require the third party to retain copies of the data and documents referred to in paragraph (i) for the period referred to in regulation 40.

(3) The persons within this paragraph are—

(a) another relevant person who is subject to these Regulations under regulation 8;

(b) a person who carries on business in an EEA state other than the United Kingdom who is—

(i) subject to the requirements in national legislation implementing the fourth money laundering directive as an obliged entity (within the meaning of that directive), and

(ii) supervised for compliance with those requirements in accordance with section 2 of Chapter VI of the fourth money laundering directive; or

(c) a person who carries on business in a third country who is—
 (i) subject to requirements in relation to customer due diligence and record keeping which are equivalent to those laid down in the fourth money laundering directive; and
 (ii) supervised for compliance with those requirements in a manner equivalent to section 2 of Chapter VI of the fourth money laundering directive;
(d) organisations whose members consist of persons within sub-paragraph (a), (b) or (c).

(4) A relevant person may not rely on a third party established in a country which has been identified by the European Commission as a high-risk third country in delegated acts adopted under Article 9.2 of the fourth money laundering directive, and for these purposes "high-risk third country" has the meaning given in regulation 33(3).

(5) Paragraph (4) does not apply to a branch or majority owned subsidiary of an entity established in an EEA state if all the following conditions are met—
(a) the entity is—
 (i) subject to requirements in national legislation implementing the fourth money laundering directive as an obliged entity (within the meaning of that directive); and
 (ii) supervised for compliance with those requirements in accordance with section 2 of Chapter VI of the fourth money laundering directive;
(b) the branch or subsidiary complies fully with procedures and policies established for the group under Article 45 of the fourth money laundering directive.

(6) A relevant person is to be treated by a supervisory authority as having complied with the requirements of paragraph (2) if—
(a) the relevant person is relying on information provided by a third party which is a member of the same group as the relevant person;
(b) that group applies customer due diligence measures, rules on record keeping and programmes against money laundering and terrorist financing in accordance with these Regulations, the fourth money laundering directive or rules having equivalent effect; and
(c) the effective implementation of the requirements referred to in sub-paragraph (b) is supervised at group level by—
 (i) an authority of an EEA state other than the United Kingdom with responsibility for the functions provided for in the fourth money laundering directive; or
 (ii) an equivalent authority of a third country.

(7) Nothing in this regulation prevents a relevant person applying customer due diligence measures by means of an agent or an outsourcing service provider provided that the arrangements between the relevant person and the agent or outsourcing service provider provide for the relevant person to remain liable for any failure to apply such measures.

(8) For the purposes of paragraph (7), an "outsourcing service provider" means a person who—
(a) performs a process, a service or an activity that would otherwise be undertaken by the relevant person, and
(b) is not an employee of the relevant person.

40 Record-keeping

(1) Subject to paragraph (5), a relevant person must keep the records specified in paragraph (2) for at least the period specified in paragraph (3).

(2) The records are—
(a) a copy of any documents and information obtained by the relevant person to satisfy the customer due diligence requirements in regulations 28, 29 and 33 to 37;
(b) sufficient supporting records (consisting of the original documents or copies) in respect of a transaction (whether or not the transaction is an occasional transaction) which is the subject of customer due diligence measures or ongoing monitoring to enable the transaction to be reconstructed.

(3) Subject to paragraph (4), the period is five years beginning on the date on which the relevant person knows, or has reasonable grounds to believe—
(a) that the transaction is complete, for records relating to an occasional transaction; or
(b) that the business relationship has come to an end for records relating to—
 (i) any transaction which occurs as part of a business relationship, or
 (ii) customer due diligence measures taken in connection with that relationship.

(4) A relevant person is not required to keep the records referred to in paragraph (3)(b)(i) for more than 10 years.

(5) Once the period referred to in paragraph (3), or if applicable paragraph (4), has expired, the relevant person must delete any personal data obtained for the purposes of these Regulations unless—
(a) the relevant person is required to retain records containing personal data—
 (i) by or under any enactment, or
 (ii) for the purposes of any court proceedings;

(b) the data subject has given consent to the retention of that data; or

(c) the relevant person has reasonable grounds for believing that records containing the personal data need to be retained for the purpose of legal proceedings.

(6) A relevant person who is relied on by another person must keep the records specified in paragraph (2) for the period referred to in paragraph (3) or, if applicable, paragraph (4).

(7) A person referred to in regulation 39(3) ("A") who is relied on by a relevant person ("B") must, if requested by B within the period referred to in paragraph (3) or, if applicable, paragraph (4), immediately—

(a) make available to B any information about the customer, any person purporting to act on behalf of the customer and any beneficial owner of the customer, which A obtained when applying customer due diligence measures; and

(b) forward to B copies of any identification and verification data and other relevant documents on the identity of the customer, any person purporting to act on behalf of the customer and any beneficial owner of the customer, which A obtained when applying those measures.

(8) Paragraph (7) does not apply where a relevant person applies customer due diligence measures by means of an agent or an outsourcing service provider (within the meaning of regulation 39(8)).

(9) For the purposes of this regulation—

(a) B relies on A where B does so in accordance with regulation 39(1);

(b) "copy" means a copy of the original document which would be admissible as evidence of the original document in court proceedings;

(c) "personal data" and "data subject" have the meanings given in section 1 of the Data Protection Act 1998.

41 Data Protection

(1) Any personal data obtained by relevant persons for the purposes of these Regulations may only be processed for the purposes of preventing money laundering or terrorist financing.

(2) Processing personal data for the purposes of preventing money laundering or terrorist financing is to be considered to be necessary for the exercise of—

(a) a function of a public nature in the public interest for the purposes of paragraph 5(d) of Schedule 2 to the Data Protection Act 1998 (conditions relevant for processing personal data); and

(b) a function conferred by or under an enactment for the purposes of paragraph 7(1)(b) of Schedule 3 to the Data Protection Act 1998 (conditions relevant for processing sensitive personal data).

(3) No other use may be made of personal data referred to in paragraph (1), unless—

(a) use of the data is permitted by or under an enactment other than these Regulations; or

(b) the relevant person has obtained the consent of the data subject to the proposed use of the data.

(4) Relevant persons must provide new customers with the following information before establishing a business relationship or entering into an occasional transaction with the customer—

(a) the information specified in paragraph 2(3) in Part 2 of Schedule 1 to the Data Protection Act 1998 (interpretation of data protection principles);

(b) a statement that any personal data received from the customer will be processed only for the purposes of preventing money laundering or terrorist financing, or as permitted under paragraph (3).

(5) For the purposes of this regulation, "personal data", "processing" and "data subject" have the meanings given in section 1 of the Data Protection Act 1998 (basic interpretative provisions).

PART 5

BENEFICIAL OWNERSHIP INFORMATION

42 Application of this Part

(1) This Part applies to UK bodies corporate and relevant trusts.

(2) For the purposes of this Part—

(a) a "UK body corporate" is a body corporate which is incorporated under the law of the United Kingdom or any part of the United Kingdom, and includes an eligible Scottish partnership;

(b) a "relevant trust" is—

(i) a UK trust which is an express trust; or

(ii) a non-UK trust which is an express trust; and

(aa) receives income from a source in the United Kingdom; or

(bb) has assets in the United Kingdom,

on which it is liable to pay one or more of the taxes referred to in regulation 45(14);

(c) a trust is a "UK trust" if—

(i) all the trustees are resident in the United Kingdom; or

(ii) sub-paragraph (d) applies;

(d) this sub-paragraph applies if—
(i) at least one trustee is resident in the United Kingdom, and
(ii) the settlor was resident and domiciled in the United Kingdom at the time when—
(aa) the trust was set up, or
(bb) the settlor added funds to the trust;
(e) a trust is a "non-UK trust" if it is not a UK trust;
(f) a "collective investment scheme" has the meaning given in regulation 12H of the International Tax Compliance Regulations 2015.

(3) A trustee or settlor is resident in the United Kingdom—
(a) in the case of a body corporate, if it is a UK body corporate;
(b) in the case of an individual, if the individual is resident in the United Kingdom for the purposes of one or more of the taxes referred to in regulation 45(14).

43 Corporate bodies: obligations

(1) When a UK body corporate which is not listed on a regulated market enters into a relevant transaction with a relevant person, or forms a business relationship with a relevant person, the body corporate must on request from the relevant person provide the relevant person with—
(a) information identifying—
(i) its name, registered number, registered office and principal place of business;
(ii) its board of directors, or if there is no board, the members of the equivalent management body;
(iii) the senior persons responsible for its operations;
(iv) the law to which it is subject;
(v) its legal owners;
(vi) its beneficial owners; and
(b) its articles of association or other governing documents.

(2) For the purposes of paragraph (1)(a)(v) and (vi), references to the legal owners and beneficial owners of a UK body corporate include a reference to the legal owners and beneficial owners of any body corporate or trust which is directly or indirectly a legal owner or beneficial owner of that body corporate.

(3) Paragraph (1)(a)(vi) does not apply if no person qualifies as a beneficial owner (within the meaning of regulation 5(1)) of—
(a) the UK body corporate; or
(b) any body corporate which is directly or indirectly the owner of that UK body corporate.

(4) If, during the course of a business relationship, there is any change in the identity of the individuals or information falling within paragraph (1), the UK body corporate referred to in paragraph (1) must notify the relevant person of the change and the date on which it occurred within fourteen days from the date on which the body corporate becomes aware of the change.

(5) The UK body corporate must on request provide all or part of the information referred to in paragraph (1) to a law enforcement authority.

(6) Information requested under paragraph (5), must be provided before the end of such reasonable period as may be specified by the law enforcement authority.

(7) The provision of information in accordance with this regulation is not to be taken to breach any restriction, however imposed, on the disclosure of information.

(8) Where a disclosure is made in good faith in accordance with this regulation no civil liability arises in respect of the disclosure on the part of the UK body corporate.

(9) For the purposes of this regulation, a "relevant transaction" means a transaction in relation to which the relevant person is required to apply customer due diligence measures under regulation 27.

44 Trustee obligations

(1) The trustees of a relevant trust must maintain accurate and up-to-date records in writing of all the beneficial owners of the trust, and of any potential beneficiaries referred to in paragraph (5)(b), containing the information required by regulation 45(2)(b) to (d) and (5)(f) and (g).

(2) When a trustee of a relevant trust, acting as trustee, enters into a relevant transaction with a relevant person, or forms a business relationship with a relevant person, the trustee must—
(a) inform the relevant person that it is acting as trustee; and
(b) on request from the relevant person, provide the relevant person with information identifying all the beneficial owners of the trust (which, in the case of a class of beneficiaries, may be done by describing the class of persons who are beneficiaries or potential beneficiaries under the trust).

(3) If, during the course of a business relationship, there is any change in the information provided under paragraph (2), the trustees must notify the relevant person of the change and the date on which it occurred within fourteen days from the date on which any one of the trustees became aware of the change.

(4) For the purposes of this regulation, a "relevant transaction" means a transaction in relation to which the relevant person is required to apply customer due diligence measures under regulation 27.

(5) The trustees of a relevant trust must on request provide information to any law enforcement authority—

(a) about the beneficial owners of the trust; and

(b) about any other individual referred to as a potential beneficiary in a document from the settlor relating to the trust such as a letter of wishes.

(6) Information requested under paragraph (5) must be provided before the end of such reasonable period as may be specified by the law enforcement authority.

(7) The provision of information in accordance with this regulation is not to be taken to breach any restriction, however imposed, on the disclosure of information.

(8) Where a disclosure is made in good faith in accordance with this regulation no civil liability arises in respect of the disclosure on the part of the trustees of a relevant trust.

(9) If the trustees of a relevant trust are relevant persons who are being paid to act as trustees of that trust, they must—

(a) retain the records referred to in paragraph (1) for a period of five years after the date on which the final distribution is made under the trust;

(b) make arrangements for those records to be deleted at the end of that period, unless—

(i) the trustees are required to retain them by or under any enactment or for the purpose of court proceedings;

(ii) any person to whom information in a record relates consents to the retention of that information; or

(iii) the trustees have reasonable grounds for believing that records containing the personal data need to be retained for the purpose of legal proceedings.

(10) For the purposes of this regulation, any of the following authorities is a law enforcement authority—

(a) the Commissioners;

(b) the FCA;

(c) the NCA;

(d) police forces maintained under section 2 of the Police Act 1996;

(e) the Police of the Metropolis;

(f) the Police for the City of London;

(g) the Police Service of Scotland;

(h) the Police Service of Northern Ireland;

(i) the Serious Fraud Office.

(11) For the purposes of this regulation, in the case of a relevant trust which is a collective investment scheme, a reference to the trustees of a relevant trust includes a reference to the manager or operator of the collective investment scheme.

45 Register of beneficial ownership

(1) The Commissioners must maintain a register ("the register") of—

(a) beneficial owners of taxable relevant trusts; and

(b) potential beneficiaries (referred to in regulation 44(5)(b)) of taxable relevant trusts.

(2) The trustees of a taxable relevant trust must within the time specified in paragraph (3) provide the Commissioners with—

(a) the information specified in paragraph (5) in relation to the trust;

(b) the information specified in paragraph (6) in relation to each of the individuals referred to in regulation 44(2)(b) and (5)(b) (but if sub-paragraph (d) applies, this information does not need to be provided in relation to the beneficiaries of the trust);

(c) the information specified in paragraph (7) in relation to each of the legal entities referred to in regulation 44(2)(b);

(d) the information specified in paragraph (8), where the beneficial owners include a class of beneficiaries, not all of whom have been determined.

(3) The information required under paragraph (2) must be provided on or before—

(a) 31st January 2018;

(b) 31st January after the tax year in which the trustees were first liable to pay any of the taxes referred to in paragraph (14) ("UK taxes").

(4) The information required under paragraph (2) must be provided in such form as the Commissioners reasonably require.

(5) The information specified in this paragraph is—

(a) the full name of the trust;

(b) the date on which the trust was set up;

(c) a statement of accounts for the trust, describing the trust assets and identifying the value of each category of the trust assets at the date on which the information is first provided to the Commissioners (including the address of any property held by the trust);

(d) the country where the trust is considered to be resident for tax purposes;

(e) the place where the trust is administered;
(f) a contact address for the trustees;
(g) the full name of any advisers who are being paid to provide legal, financial or tax advice to the trustees in relation to the trust.

(6) The information specified in this paragraph is—
(a) the individual's full name;
(b) the individual's national insurance number or unique taxpayer reference, if any;
(c) if the individual does not have a national insurance number or unique taxpayer reference, the individual's usual residential address;
(d) if the address provided under sub-paragraph (c) is not in the United Kingdom—
(i) the individual's passport number or identification card number, with the country of issue and the expiry date of the passport or identification card; or
(ii) if the individual does not have a passport or identification card, the number, country of issue and expiry date of any equivalent form of identification;
(e) the individual's date of birth;
(f) the nature of the individual's role in relation to the trust.

(7) The information specified in this paragraph is—
(a) the legal entity's corporate or firm name;
(b) the legal entity's unique taxpayer reference, if any;
(c) the registered or principal office of the legal entity;
(d) the legal form of the legal entity and the law by which it is governed;
(e) if applicable, the name of the register of companies in which the legal entity is entered (including details of the EEA state or third country in which it is registered), and its registration number in that register;
(f) the nature of the entity's role in relation to the trust.

(8) The information specified in this paragraph is a description of the class of persons who are beneficiaries or potential beneficiaries under the trust.

(9) The trustees of a taxable relevant trust must—
(a) if a trustee becomes aware that any of the information provided to the Commissioners under paragraph (2) (other than information provided in relation to the value of the trust assets under paragraph (5)(c)) has changed, notify the Commissioners of the change and the date on which it occurred on or before 31st January—
(i) after the tax year in which the change occurred; or
(ii) if the trustees are not liable to pay any UK taxes in that year, after the tax year in which the trustees are liable to pay any UK taxes; or
(b) if the trustees are not aware of any change to any of the information provided under paragraph (2), confirm that fact to the Commissioners on or before 31st January after the tax year in which the trustees are liable to pay any UK taxes.

(10) The register must contain the information referred to in regulation 44(2)(b) and (5)(b) in relation to taxable relevant trusts.

(11) The Commissioners may keep the register in any form they think fit.

(12) The Commissioners must ensure that the information on the register may be inspected by any law enforcement authority.

(13) The Commissioners must make arrangements to ensure that the NCA are able to use information on the register to respond promptly to a request for information about the persons referred to in regulation 44(2)(b) and (5)(b) made by—
(a) an authority responsible for functions provided for in the fourth money laundering directive in an EEA state other than the United Kingdom, or
(b) a financial intelligence unit of an EEA state other than the United Kingdom.

(14) For the purposes of this regulation, a taxable relevant trust is a relevant trust in any year in which its trustees are liable to pay any of the following taxes in the United Kingdom in relation to assets or income of the trust—
(a) income tax;
(b) capital gains tax;
(c) inheritance tax;
(d) stamp duty land tax (within the meaning of section 42 of the Finance Act 2003);
(e) land and buildings transaction tax (within the meaning of section 1 of the Land and Buildings Transaction Tax (Scotland) Act 2013);
(f) stamp duty reserve tax.

(15) For the purpose of this regulation, in the case of a taxable relevant trust which is a collective investment scheme, a reference to the trustees of a taxable relevant trust includes a reference to the manager or operator of the collective investment scheme.

PART 6
MONEY LAUNDERING AND TERRORIST FINANCING: SUPERVISION AND REGISTRATION

CHAPTER 1

DUTIES OF SUPERVISORY AUTHORITIES

46 Duties of supervisory authorities

(1) A supervisory authority must effectively monitor the relevant persons for which it is the supervisory authority ("its own sector") and take necessary measures for the purpose of securing compliance by such persons with the requirements of these Regulations.

(2) Each supervisory authority must—

(a) adopt a risk-based approach to the exercise of its supervisory functions, informed by the risk assessments carried out by the authority under regulation 17;

(b) ensure that its employees and officers have access both at its offices and elsewhere to relevant information on the domestic and international risks of money laundering and terrorist financing which affect its own sector;

(c) base the frequency and intensity of its on-site and off-site supervision on the risk profiles prepared under regulation 17(4);

(d) keep a record in writing of the actions it has taken in the course of its supervision, and of its reasons for deciding not to act in a particular case;

(e) take effective measures to encourage its own sector to report breaches of the provisions of these Regulations to it.

(3) In determining its approach to the exercise of its supervisory functions the supervisory authority must—

(a) take account of any guidelines issued by the European Supervisory Authorities under Articles 17, 18.4 and 48.10 of the fourth money laundering directive;

(b) take account of the degree of discretion permitted to relevant persons in taking measures to counter money laundering and terrorist financing.

(4) In accordance with its risk-based approach, the supervisory authority must take appropriate measures to review—

(a) the risk assessments carried out by relevant persons under regulation 18;

(b) the adequacy of the policies, controls and procedures adopted by relevant persons under regulation 19 to 21 and 24, and the way in which those policies, controls and procedures have been implemented.

(5) A supervisory authority which, in the course of carrying out any of its supervisory functions or otherwise, knows or suspects, or has reasonable grounds for knowing or suspecting, that a person is or has engaged in money laundering or terrorist financing must as soon as practicable inform the NCA.

(6) A disclosure made under paragraph (5) is not to be taken to breach any restriction, however imposed, on the disclosure of information.

(7) Where a disclosure under paragraph (5) is made in good faith, no civil liability arises in respect of the disclosure on the part of the person by whom, or on whose behalf, it is made.

(8) The FCA, when carrying out its supervisory functions in relation to an auction platform—

(a) must effectively monitor the auction platform's compliance with—

(i) the customer due diligence requirements of Articles 19 and 20.6 of the emission allowance auctioning regulation;

(ii) the monitoring and record-keeping requirements of Article 54 of that regulation; and

(iii) the notification requirements of Article 55.2 and 55.3 of that regulation; and

(b) may monitor the auction platform's compliance with regulations 18 to 21 and 24 of these Regulations.

(9) The functions of the FCA under these Regulations shall be treated for the purposes of Parts 1, 2 and 4 of Schedule 1ZA to FSMA (the Financial Conduct Authority) as functions conferred on the FCA under that Act.

47 Duties of supervisory authorities: information

(1) A supervisory authority must, in any way it considers appropriate, make up-to-date information on money laundering and terrorist financing available to those relevant persons which it supervises ("its own sector").

(2) The information referred to in paragraph (1) must include the following—

(a) information on the money laundering and terrorist financing practices considered by the supervisory authority to apply to its own sector;

(b) a description of indications which may suggest that a transfer of criminal funds is taking place in its own sector;

(c) a description of the circumstances in which the supervisory authority considers that there is a high risk of money laundering or terrorist financing.

(3) The information referred to in paragraph (1) must also include information from the following sources which the supervisory authority considers is relevant to its own sector—

(a) reports drawn up by the European Commission under Article 6.1 of the fourth money laundering directive;

(b) recommendations made by the European Commission under Article 6.4 of that directive (unless the Treasury and the Home Office notify the supervisory authority that a recommendation will not be followed);

(c) joint opinions issued by the European Supervisory Authorities under Article 6.5 of that directive;

(d) high-risk third countries identified in delegated acts adopted by the European Commission under Article 9.2 of the fourth money laundering directive;

(e) guidelines issued by the European Supervisory Authorities under Articles 17, 18.4, or 48.10 of that directive;

(f) the report prepared by the Treasury and the Home Office under regulation 16(6);

(g) any relevant information made available by the Treasury and the Home Office under regulation 16(8);

(h) any relevant information published by the Director General of the NCA under section 4(9) (operations) or 6 (duty to publish information) of the Crime and Courts Act 2013.

48 Duties of the FCA: guidance on politically exposed persons

(1) The FCA must give guidance under section 139A of FSMA (power of the FCA to give guidance) to relevant persons, who are subject to rules made by the FCA, in relation to the enhanced customer due diligence measures required under regulation 35 in respect of politically exposed persons ("PEPs"), their family members and known close associates (within the meanings given in regulation 35(12)).

(2) The guidance referred to in paragraph (1) must include guidance on the following matters—

(a) taking into account regulation 35(14), what functions are, and are not, to be taken to be "prominent public functions" for the purposes of determining whether an individual is a PEP;

(b) which persons should be treated as coming within the definitions of—

(i) a family member of a PEP; or

(ii) a known close associate of a PEP;

(c) what constitutes "appropriate risk-management systems and procedures" for the purposes of regulation 35(1);

(d) what account is to be taken of the jurisdiction in which the prominent public function arises (taking into consideration the controls against money-laundering and terrorist financing in different jurisdictions);

(e) how the level of risk associated with a particular individual is to be assessed for the purposes of regulation 35(3), and what approach is to be taken in relation to a PEP, or a family member or known close associate of a PEP, if the PEP, family member or close associate is assessed as presenting a low level of risk;

(f) who should be treated as coming within the meaning of "senior management" for the purposes of regulation 35(5) and (8);

(g) the situations in which it would be appropriate for the senior management approval mentioned in regulation 35(5) to be given by an individual who is not a member of the board of directors (or, if there is no such board, a member of the equivalent management body) of a business;

(h) what constitutes "adequate measures" and "reasonable measures" for the purposes of paragraphs (5) and (6) respectively of regulation 35;

(i) the extent to which information on public registers may be taken into account for the purposes of regulation 35(5) and (6);

(j) what sort of monitoring and scrutiny is required for the purposes of regulation 35(5) and (8);

(k) what measures are required in relation to persons who have ceased to be PEPs to comply with regulation 35(9); and

(l) how to address risks of money laundering or terrorist financing where a PEP, a family member of a PEP or a known close associate of a PEP, is—

(i) the beneficial owner of a customer;

(ii) a beneficiary of a contract of long-term insurance;

(iii) the beneficial owner of a beneficiary of a contract of long-term insurance.

49 Duties of self-regulatory organisations

(1) Self-regulatory organisations must make arrangements to ensure that—

(a) their supervisory functions are exercised independently of any of their other functions which do not relate to disciplinary matters;

(b) sensitive information relating to the supervisory functions is appropriately handled within the organisation;

(c) they employ only persons with appropriate qualifications, integrity and professional skills to carry out the supervisory functions;

(d) contravention of a relevant requirement by a relevant person they are responsible for supervising renders that person liable to effective, proportionate and dissuasive disciplinary measures under their rules.

(2) Self-regulatory organisations must—

(a) provide adequate resources to carry out the supervisory functions;

(b) appoint a person to monitor and manage the organisation's compliance with its duties under these Regulations.

(3) The person appointed under paragraph (2)(b) is to be responsible—

(a) for liaison with—

(i) another supervisory authority or a registering authority (within the meaning of regulation 53);

(ii) any law enforcement authority; and

(iii) any overseas authority (within the meaning of regulation 50(4))

(b) for ensuring that the self-regulatory organisation responds fully and rapidly to any request from an authority referred to in paragraph (a)(i) or (ii) for information about any person it supervises, whether that request concerns an application by that person for registration or any other matter.

50 Duty to co-operate

(1) A supervisory authority must take such steps as it considers appropriate—

(a) to co-operate with other supervisory authorities, the Treasury and law enforcement authorities in relation to the development and implementation of policies to counter money laundering and terrorist financing;

(b) to co-ordinate activities to counter money laundering and terrorist financing with other supervisory authorities and law enforcement authorities;

(c) to co-operate with overseas authorities to ensure the effective supervision of a relevant person to which paragraph (2) applies.

(2) This paragraph applies to a relevant person established—

(a) in the United Kingdom, which has its head office in another country; or

(b) in another country but which has its head office in the United Kingdom.

(3) Co-operation may include the sharing of information which the supervisory authority is not prevented from disclosing.

(4) For the purposes of this regulation "overseas authority" means—

(a) an authority responsible for any of the functions provided for in the fourth money laundering directive in an EEA state other than the United Kingdom in which the relevant person is established or has its head office; and

(b) where the relevant person is established or has its head office in a country which is not an EEA state, an authority in that country which has equivalent functions to any of the functions provided for in the fourth money laundering directive.

(5) A supervisory authority must on request provide a European Supervisory Authority with information reasonably required by the Authority to enable it to carry out its duties under the fourth money laundering directive.

51 Regulatory information

(1) A supervisory authority within regulation 7 must collect such information as it considers necessary for the purpose of performing its supervisory functions, including the information specified in Schedule 4.

(2) A supervisory authority within regulation 7 must on request provide the Treasury with such information collected under paragraph (1) as may be specified by the Treasury, for the purpose of enabling the Treasury to comply with its obligations under Article 6, 7 or 44 of the fourth money laundering directive.

(3) The Treasury must publish an annual consolidated review of the information provided by the supervisory authorities under paragraph (2).

(4) A disclosure made under paragraph (2) is not to be taken to breach any restriction, however imposed, on the disclosure of information.

(5) Where a disclosure under paragraph (2) is made in good faith, no civil liability arises in respect of the disclosure on the part of the person by whom, or on whose behalf, it is made.

52 Disclosure by supervisory authorities

(1) A supervisory authority may disclose to a relevant authority information it holds relevant to its supervisory functions, provided the disclosure is made for purposes connected with the effective exercise of—

(a) the functions of the relevant authority under these Regulations;

(b) the functions of the law enforcement authority; or

(c) in the case of an overseas authority, the functions provided for in the fourth money laundering directive, or equivalent functions.

(2) Information disclosed to a relevant authority under paragraph (1) may not be further disclosed by that authority, except—

(a) in accordance with paragraph (1);

(b) by the FCA to the PRA, where the information concerns a PRA-authorised person or a person who has a qualifying relationship with a PRA-authorised person;

(c) in the case of an overseas authority, in accordance with any conditions imposed on further disclosure of that information by the supervisory authority which disclosed that information to the overseas authority;

(d) with a view to the institution of, or otherwise for the purposes of, any criminal or other enforcement proceedings; or

(e) as otherwise required by law.

(3) A disclosure made under paragraph (1) is not to be taken to breach any restriction, however imposed, on the disclosure of information.

(4) Where a disclosure under paragraph (1) is made in good faith, no civil liability arises in respect of the disclosure on the part of the person by whom, or on whose behalf, it is made.

(5) For the purposes of this regulation, "relevant authority" means—

(a) another supervisory authority;

(b) the Treasury;

(c) any law enforcement authority;

(d) an overseas authority, within the meaning of regulation 50(4).

CHAPTER 2

REGISTRATION

53 Interpretation

For the purposes of this Chapter—

"registering authority" means—

(a) the FCA, in relation to—

(i) those relevant persons which it is required to register under regulation 54(1); and

(ii) those relevant persons it decides to register under regulation 55(1);

(b) the Commissioners, in relation to—

(i) those relevant persons which they are required to register under regulation 54(2); and

(ii) those relevant persons they decide to register under regulation 55(3);

"telecommunication, digital and IT payment service provider" means an undertaking which provides payment services falling within paragraph 1(g) of Schedule 1 to the Payment Services Regulations 2009.

Prospective amendments—In definition of "telecommunication, digital and IT payment service provider", words "consisting of the execution of payment transactions where the consent of the payer to execute a payment transaction is given by means of any telecommunication, digital or IT device and the payment is made to the telecommunication, IT system or network operator acting only as an intermediary between the payment service user and the supplier of the goods and services (and terms used in this definition which are defined in the Payment Services Regulations 2017 have the meanings given in those Regulations)." to be substituted for words "falling within paragraph 1(g) of Schedule 1 to the Payment Services Regulations 2009." by the Payment Services Regulations, SI 2017/752 reg 156, Sch 8 para 26(b) with effect from 13 January 2018.

54 Duty to maintain registers of certain relevant persons

(1) The FCA must maintain a register of those relevant persons who—

(a) are authorised persons, and

(b) have notified the FCA under regulation 23 that they are acting, or intend to act, as a money service business or a trust or company service provider.

(2) The Commissioners must maintain a register of those relevant persons who are not included in the register maintained by the FCA under paragraph (1) and are—

(a) high value dealers;

(b) money service businesses;

(c) trust or company service providers;

(d) bill payment service providers, for which the Commissioners are the supervisory authority;

(e) telecommunication, digital and IT payment service providers, for which the Commissioners are the supervisory authority.

(3) Subject to paragraph (4) the registering authorities may keep the registers required by this regulation in any form they think fit.

(4) The register maintained by the Commissioners must include entries in the registers maintained under regulation 25 of the Money Laundering Regulations 2007 which were current immediately before the date that regulation was revoked.

(5) A registering authority may publish or make available to public inspection all or part of a register maintained by it under this regulation.

55 Power to maintain registers

(1) The FCA may maintain a register of Annex 1 financial institutions.

(2) For the purposes of paragraph (1), an "Annex 1 financial institution" is a financial institution which—

(a) falls within regulation 10(2)(a), and

(b) is not—

(i) a money service business;

(ii) an authorised person;

(iii) a bill payment service provider; or

(iv) a telecommunication, digital and IT payment service provider.

(3) The Commissioners may maintain registers of relevant persons who are not supervised by any of the professional bodies listed in Schedule 1, and who are—

(a) estate agents,

(b) auditors;

(c) external accountants;

(d) tax advisers;

(e) bill payment service providers; or

(f) telecommunication, digital and IT payment service providers.

(4) Where a registering authority decides to maintain a register under this regulation, it must take reasonable steps to bring its decision to the attention of those relevant persons in respect of which the register is to be established.

(5) Subject to paragraph (6) a registering authority may maintain a register under this regulation in any form it thinks fit.

(6) The registers maintained by the registering authorities must include entries in any equivalent registers maintained under regulation 32 of the Money Laundering Regulations 2007 which were current immediately before the date that regulation was revoked.

(7) A registering authority may publish or make available to public inspection all or part of a register maintained by it under this regulation.

56 Requirement to be registered

(1) Unless a person in respect of whom the registering authorities are required to maintain a register under regulation 54 is included in the appropriate register, or paragraph (2) applies, that person must not act as a—

(a) high value dealer;

(b) money service business;

(c) trust or company service provider;

(d) bill payment service provider; or

(e) telecommunication, digital and IT payment service provider.

(2) This paragraph applies if the person concerned has applied for registration in the register, but that application has not yet been determined.

(3) A relevant person which is registered in the register maintained by the Commissioners under regulation 25 or 32 of the Money Laundering Regulations 2007 is to be treated as included in the appropriate registers maintained by the Commissioners under regulation 54 or 55 of these Regulations for the purpose of paragraph (1)—

(a) during the period of 12 months beginning with the date on which these Regulations come into force, and

(b) after that period, if the person concerned has provided the additional information required for registration under regulation 57 within the period referred to in sub-paragraph (a).

(4) A relevant person which is registered in the register maintained by the FCA under regulation 32 of the Money Laundering Regulations 2007 is to be treated as included in the register maintained by the FCA under regulation 55(1) for the purposes of paragraph (1).

(5) Where a registering authority decides to maintain a register under regulation 55(1) or (3) in respect of any description of relevant persons and establishes a register for that purpose, a relevant person of that description must not carry on the business or profession in question for a period of more than 12 months beginning with the date on which the registering authority establishes the register unless—

(a) that person is included in the register, or

(b) that person has applied for registration in the register, but that application has not yet been determined.

57 Applications for registration in a register maintained under regulation 54 or 55

(1) A person applying for registration in a register maintained under regulation 54 or 55 ("an applicant") must make an application in such manner and provide such information as the registering authority may specify.

(2) The information which the registering authority may specify includes, among other things—

- (a) the applicant's full name and where different the name of the business;
- (b) where the applicant is an individual, the applicant's date of birth and residential address;
- (c) the nature of the business;
- (d) the address of the head office of the business with its company number (in the case of a company), and of any branches the business has in the United Kingdom;
- (e) the full name of the nominated officer (if any);
- (f) a risk assessment which satisfies the requirements in regulation 18;
- (g) information as to the way in which the business meets the requirements set out in—
  - (i) these Regulations;
  - (ii) Part 3 of the Terrorism Act 2000 (terrorist property);
  - (iii) Part 7 of the Proceeds of Crime Act 2002 (money laundering); and
  - (iv) Part 8 of the Proceeds of Crime Act 2002 (investigations);
- (h) in relation to a money service business or a trust or company service provider—
  - (i) the full name, date of birth and residential address of any officer, manager or beneficial owner of the business or service provider; and
  - (ii) information needed by the registering authority to decide whether it must refuse the application pursuant to regulation 58;
- (i) in relation to a money service business, the full name and address of any agent it uses for the purposes of its business;
- (j) where the registering authority is not the supervisory authority for the applicant—
  - (i) the name of the applicant's supervisory authority;
  - (ii) confirmation from the applicant's supervisory authority that any person mentioned in regulation 58(1) is a fit and proper person within the meaning of that regulation;
- (k) whether the applicant, or any person named in the application, has been convicted of a criminal offence listed in Schedule 3.

(3) At any time after receiving an application and before determining it, the registering authority may require the applicant to provide, within 21 days beginning with the date on which the requirement is issued, such further information as the registering authority reasonably considers necessary to enable it to determine the application.

(4) If at any time after the applicant has provided the registering authority with any information under paragraph (1) or (3) (whether before or after the applicant is registered)—

- (a) there is a material change affecting any matter contained in that information; or
- (b) it becomes apparent to the applicant that the information contains an inaccuracy,

the applicant must provide the registering authority with details of the change or a correction of the inaccuracy within 30 days beginning with the date of the occurrence of the change (or the discovery of the inaccuracy) or within such later time as may be agreed with the registering authority.

(5) The obligation in paragraph (4) applies also to material changes or inaccuracies affecting any matter contained in any supplementary information provided pursuant to that paragraph.

(6) Any information to be provided to the registering authority under this regulation must be in such form and verified in such manner as the authority may specify.

58 Fit and proper test

(1) The registering authority must refuse to register an applicant for registration in a register maintained under regulation 54 as a money service business or as a trust or company service provider, if it is satisfied that—

- (a) the applicant;
- (b) an officer or manager of the applicant;
- (c) a beneficial owner of the applicant; or
- (d) where the applicant is a money service business—
  - (i) any agent used by the applicant for the purposes of its business; or
  - (ii) any officer, manager or beneficial owner of the agent,

is not a fit and proper person to carry on that business.

(2) Where the FCA has decided to maintain a register of Annex I financial institutions under regulation 55, paragraph (1) applies in relation to those institutions as it applies to a money service business and a trust or company service provider.

(3) A person who has been convicted of a criminal offence listed in Schedule 3 is to be treated as not being a fit and proper person to carry on the business for the purposes of paragraph (1).

(4) If paragraph (3) does not apply, the registering authority must have regard to the following factors in determining the question in paragraph (1)—

- (a) whether the applicant has consistently failed to comply with the requirements of—

(i) these Regulations;
(ii) the Money Laundering Regulations 2001,
(iii) the Money Laundering Regulations 2003, or
(iv) the Money Laundering Regulations 2007; and

(b) the risk that the applicant's business may be used for money laundering or terrorist financing.

(5) Where the applicant is a money service business, the registering authority may, in determining the question in paragraph (1), take account of the opinion of the applicant as to whether any person referred to in paragraph (1)(d) is a fit and proper person to carry on the business.

(6) Where the registering authority is not the supervisory authority of the applicant, the registering authority must consult the supervisory authority and may rely on its opinion as to whether or not the applicant is a fit and proper person to carry on the business referred to in paragraph (1).

59 Determination of applications for registration under regulations 54 and 55

(1) Subject to regulation 58, the registering authority may refuse to register an applicant for registration in a register maintained under regulation 54 or 55 if—

(a) any requirement of, or imposed under, regulation 57 has not been complied with;
(b) it appears to the registering authority that any information provided pursuant to regulation 57 is false or misleading in a material particular;
(c) the applicant has failed to pay—
(i) a penalty imposed by the authority under Part 9;
(ii) a charge imposed by the authority under Part 11; or
(iii) a penalty or charge imposed by the authority under regulation 35(1) or 42(1) of the Money Laundering Regulations 2007;
(d) where the registering authority is not the applicant's supervisory authority, the supervisory authority opposes the application for registration on reasonable grounds; or
(e) the registering authority suspects, on reasonable grounds—
(i) that the applicant will fail to comply with any of its obligations under—
(aa) these Regulations;
(bb) Part 3 of the Terrorism Act 2000; or
(cc) Parts 7 and 8 of the Proceeds of Crime Act 2002;
(the "relevant obligations");
(ii) that any person whom the applicant has identified as one of its officers or managers will fail to comply with any of the relevant obligations.

(2) Where the Commissioners are the registering authority, they must within 45 days beginning either with the date on which they receive the application or, where applicable, with the date on which they receive any further information required under regulation 57(3), give the applicant notice of—

(a) the decision to register the applicant; or
(b) the following matters—
(i) their decision not to register the applicant;
(ii) the reasons for their decision;
(iii) the right to a review under regulation 94; and
(iv) the right to appeal under regulation 99.

(3) Where the FCA is the registering authority, it must within 45 days beginning either with the date on which it receives the application or, where applicable, with the date on which it receives any further information required under regulation 57(3), give the applicant notice of—

(a) its decision to register the applicant; or
(b) the following matters—
(i) that it is minded not to register the applicant;
(ii) the reasons for being minded to refuse to register the applicant; and
(iii) the right to make representations to it within a specified period (which may not be less than 28 days).

(4) After the expiry of the period referred to in paragraph (3)(b)(iii), the FCA must decide, within a reasonable period, whether to register the applicant and it must give the applicant notice of—

(a) its decision to register the applicant; or
(b) the following matters—
(i) its decision not to register the applicant;
(ii) the reasons for its decision; and
(iii) the right to appeal under regulation 93.

(5) The registering authority must, as soon as practicable after deciding to register a person, include that person in the relevant register.

60 Cancellation and suspension of registration in a register under regulation 54 or 55

(1) If paragraph (2) applies, the registering authority may suspend (for such period as it considers appropriate) or cancel—

(a) the registration of a money service business or a trust or company service provider in a register maintained under regulation 54; or

(b) the registration of an Annex 1 financial institution in a register maintained under regulation 55 (including the registration of an Annex 1 financial institution previously included in a register maintained under regulation 32 of the Money Laundering Regulations 2007).

(2) This paragraph applies if, at any time after registration, the registering authority is satisfied that—

(a) the money service business, trust or company service provider, or Annex 1 financial institution (as the case may be); or

(b) any other person mentioned in regulation 58(1) in relation to that business, provider, or financial institution,

is not a fit and proper person for the purposes of regulation 58.

(3) The registering authority may suspend (for such period as it considers appropriate) or cancel a person's registration in a register maintained by it under regulation 54 or 55 if, at any time after registration—

(a) it appears to the authority that any of paragraphs (a) to (e) of regulation 59(1) apply; or

(b) the person has failed to comply with any requirement of a notice given under regulation 66.

(4) The Commissioners may suspend (for such period as they consider appropriate) or cancel the registration of a person who—

(a) was included in a register maintained by the Commissioners under regulation 25 or 32 of the Money Laundering Regulations 2007, and

(b) has not provided the additional information required for registration under regulation 57 within the period of 12 months beginning with the date on which these Regulations come into force.

(5) The Commissioners may suspend (for such period as they consider appropriate) or cancel the registration of a money service business in a register maintained under regulation 54(2)(b) where the money service business is—

(a) providing a payment service in the United Kingdom, or is purporting to do so;

(b) not included in the register of payment service providers maintained by the FCA under regulation 4(1) of the Payment Service Regulations 2009; and

(c) not a person—

(i) mentioned in paragraphs (c) to (h) of the definition of a "payment service provider" in regulation 2(1) of the Payment Services Regulations 2009, or

(ii) to whom regulation 3 or 121 of those Regulations applies.

(6) Where the supervisory authority of a person on the register maintained under regulation 54 or 55 is not the registering authority, the supervisory authority must inform the registering authority as soon as possible if it becomes aware of any grounds on which the registering authority might decide to suspend or cancel that person's registration.

(7) Where the Commissioners decide to suspend or cancel a person's registration they must give that person notice of—

(a) their decision and, subject to paragraph (10), the date from which the suspension or cancellation takes effect;

(b) if appropriate, the period of the suspension;

(c) the reasons for their decision;

(d) the right to a review under regulation 94; and

(e) the right to appeal under regulation 99.

(8) Where the FCA is minded to suspend or cancel a person's registration it must give that person notice—

(a) that it is so minded;

(b) if appropriate, the proposed period of the suspension;

(c) the reasons for being so minded; and

(d) the right to make representations to it within the period specified in the notice (which must not be less than 28 days).

(9) The FCA must then decide, within a reasonable period, whether to suspend or cancel the person's registration and it must give that person notice of—

(a) its decision not to suspend or cancel the person's registration; or

(b) the following matters—

(i) its decision to suspend or cancel the person's registration and, subject to paragraph (10), the date from which the suspension or cancellation takes effect;

(ii) the period of the suspension;

(iii) the reasons for its decision; and

(iv) the right to appeal under regulation 93.

(10) If the registering authority—
 (a) considers that the interests of the public require the suspension or cancellation of a person's registration to have immediate effect; and
 (b) includes a statement to that effect and the reasons for it in the notice given under paragraph (7) or (9),

the suspension or cancellation takes effect when the notice is given to the person.

Prospective amendments—In para (5)(b), (c)(i), year "2017" to be substituted for year "2009", in para (5)(c)(i), words "(d) to (j)" to be substituted for words "(c) to (h)", and in para (5)(c)(ii), reference "154(2)" to be substituted for reference "121", by the Payment Services Regulations, SI 2017/752 reg 156, Sch 8 para 26(c) with effect from 13 January 2018.

PART 7
TRANSFER OF FUNDS (INFORMATION ON THE PAYER) REGULATIONS

61 Interpretation

In this Part "transfer of funds supervisory authority" in relation to a payment service provider means the supervisory authority specified by regulation 62.

62 Transfer of funds supervisory authorities

(1) The FCA is the transfer of funds supervisory authority for payment service providers, who are—
 (a) authorised persons;
 (b) authorised payment institutions under the Payment Services Regulations 2009 which are not included in the register maintained by the Commissioners under regulation 54(2);
 (c) registered small payment institutions under the Payment Services Regulations 2009 which are not included in the register maintained by the Commissioners under regulation 54(2);
 (d) authorised electronic money institutions under the Electronic Money Regulations 2011; or
 (e) registered small electronic money institutions under the Electronic Money Regulations 2011.

(2) The Commissioners are the transfer of funds supervisory authority for payment service providers who do not come within paragraph (1).

Prospective amendments—In para (1)(b), (c), year "2017" to be substituted for year "2009" by the Payment Services Regulations, SI 2017/752 reg 156, Sch 8 para 26(d) with effect from 13 January 2018.

63 Duties of transfer of funds supervisory authorities

(1) A transfer of funds supervisory authority must—
 (a) monitor effectively the payment service providers for whom it is the transfer of funds supervisory authority;
 (b) take the measures necessary to secure compliance by payment service providers with the requirements of the funds transfer regulation;
 (c) take effective measures to encourage the payment service provider to report breaches of the provisions of the funds transfer regulation to the authority;
 (d) take such steps as it considers appropriate—
  (i) to co-operate with other supervisory authorities, the Treasury and law enforcement authorities in relation to the development and implementation of policies to counter money laundering and terrorist financing;
  (ii) to co-ordinate activities to counter money laundering and terrorist financing;
  (iii) to co-operate with overseas authorities to ensure the effective supervision of a payment service provider to which paragraph (2) applies.

(2) This paragraph applies to a payment service provider established—
 (a) in the United Kingdom, which has its head office in another country; or
 (b) in another country but which has its head office in the United Kingdom.

(3) Co-operation may include the sharing of information which the supervisory authority is not prevented from disclosing.

(4) A transfer of funds supervisory authority must take into account any guidelines issued by the European Supervisory Authorities under Article 25 of the funds transfer regulation in determining what measures are required to comply with that regulation.

(5) A transfer of funds supervisory authority which, in the course of carrying out any of its functions under this Part or otherwise, knows or suspects, or has reasonable grounds for knowing or suspecting, that a payment service provider is or has engaged in money laundering or terrorist financing must as soon as practicable inform the NCA.

(6) A disclosure made under paragraph (5) is not to be taken to breach any restriction, however imposed, on the disclosure of information.

(7) Where a disclosure under paragraph (5) is made in good faith, no civil liability arises in respect of the disclosure on the part of the person by whom, or or on whose behalf, it is made.

(8) The functions of the FCA under this Part are to be treated for the purposes of section 1A of, and Parts 1, 2 and 4 of Schedule 1ZA to, FSMA (the Financial Conduct Authority) as functions conferred on the FCA under that Act.

(9) A transfer of funds supervisory authority must on request provide a European Supervisory Authority with information reasonably required by the Authority to enable it to carry out its duties under the funds transfer regulation.

(10) For the purposes of this regulation, "overseas authority" means—

(a) an authority responsible for any of the functions provided for in the funds transfer regulation in an EEA state other than the United Kingdom in which the payment service provider is established or has its head office; and

(b) where the payment service provider is established or has its head office in a country which is not an EEA state, an authority in that country which has equivalent functions to any of the functions provided for in the funds transfer regulation.

64 Obligations of payment service providers

(1) A payment service provider must take into account any guidelines issued by the European Supervisory Authorities under Article 25 of the funds transfer regulation in determining what measures are required to comply with that regulation.

(2) A payment service provider must ensure that it is able (whether by means of the central contact point appointed under regulation 22 or otherwise) to respond fully and rapidly to enquiries from a person specified in paragraph (3) concerning any of the information required by or under the funds transfer regulation.

(3) The persons specified in this paragraph are—

(a) financial investigators accredited under section 3 of the Proceeds of Crime Act 2002 (accreditation and training);

(b) persons acting on behalf of the Scottish Ministers in their capacity as an enforcement authority under that Act; and

(c) constables or equivalent officers of any law enforcement authority.

PART 8

INFORMATION AND INVESTIGATION

65 Interpretation

(1) In this Part—

"premises" means any building or other structure, including a moveable structure, other than premises used only as a dwelling;

"tribunal" means the First-tier Tribunal or, where determined by or under Tribunal Procedure Rules, the Upper Tribunal;

(2) Unless otherwise defined in this Part—

"officer" means—

(a) an officer of the FCA, including a member of the FCA's staff or an agent of the FCA;

(b) an officer of Revenue and Customs; or

(c) an employee or agent of a professional body listed in Schedule 1 who is authorised by the body to act on behalf of the body for the purposes of this Part;

(d) a relevant officer;

"relevant officer" means—

(a) in Great Britain, an officer of a local weights and measures authority;

(b) in Northern Ireland, an officer of the Department for the Economy,

acting pursuant to arrangements made with the FCA or with the Commissioners for the purposes of these Regulations.

(3) For the purposes of this Part, a person is connected to a relevant person or a payment service provider ("a connected person") if that person is a person listed in Schedule 5 in relation to the relevant person or payment service provider.

66 Power to require information

(1) A supervisory authority may, by notice in writing to a person ("P") who is (or was at any time) a relevant person, a payment service provider or a connected person, require P to—

(a) provide specified information, or information of a specified description;

(b) produce specified documents, or documents of a specified description; or

(c) attend before an officer of the supervisory authority (or of a supervisory authority which is acting on behalf of that authority) at a time and place specified in the notice and answer questions.

(2) The information or documents must be provided or produced—

(a) before the end of such reasonable period as may be specified; and

(b) at such place as may be specified.

(3) An officer who has authorisation in writing from a supervisory authority to do so may require P without unreasonable delay to—

(a) provide the officer with specified information or information of a specified description; or

(b) produce to the officer specified documents or documents of a specified description.

(4) The powers in this regulation may only be exercised by a supervisory authority, or by an officer authorised under paragraph (3) to act on behalf of the supervisory authority, in relation to information or documents which are reasonably required by the supervisory authority in connection with the exercise by the authority of any of its supervisory functions.

(5) Where a supervisory authority or an officer requires information to be provided or documents to be produced under paragraph (1) or (3), the notice must set out the reasons why the information is required to be provided or the documents produced, unless the supervisory authority or (as the case may be) the officer is not permitted to disclose this information.

(6) The supervisory authority may require—

(a) information contained in a computer or other storage device, or recorded in any other way otherwise than in legible form to be produced to it in legible form or in a form from which the information can readily be produced in visible and legible form; and

(b) any information provided under this regulation to be provided in such form as it may reasonably require.

(7) The production of a document does not affect any lien which a person has on the document.

(8) If a supervisory authority has power under this regulation to require a person to produce a document but it appears that the document is in the possession of a third person, that power may be exercised by the supervisory authority in relation to the third person.

67 Requests in support of other authorities

(1) On receiving a request to which paragraph (2) applies from a foreign authority, the supervisory authority may exercise the power conferred by regulation 66, and for these purposes, regulation 66 has effect as if it also referred to information and documents reasonably required by the supervisory authority to meet such a request.

(2) This paragraph applies if the request is made by the foreign authority in connection with the exercise by that authority of—

(a) functions provided for in the fourth money laundering directive;

(b) functions provided for in the funds transfer regulation; or

(c) functions provided for in the law of a third country equivalent to those provided for in the fourth money laundering directive or the funds transfer regulation.

(3) In deciding whether or not to exercise its powers under regulation 66 in response to a request, the supervisory authority may take into account in particular—

(a) whether, in the territory of the foreign authority concerned, corresponding assistance would be given to the supervisory authority;

(b) whether the case concerns the breach of a law, or other requirement, which has no close parallel in the United Kingdom or involves the assertion of a jurisdiction not recognised by the United Kingdom;

(c) the seriousness of the case and its importance to persons in the United Kingdom.

(4) The supervisory authority may decide not to exercise its powers under regulation 66 unless the foreign authority undertakes—

(a) to make such contribution towards the cost of doing so as the supervisory authority considers appropriate; and

(b) to comply with such conditions in relation to the information and documents as the supervisory authority considers appropriate.

(5) Paragraphs (3) and (4) do not apply if the supervisory authority considers that the exercise of its powers is necessary to comply with an EU obligation.

(6) "Foreign authority" means an authority in a territory which is not part of the United Kingdom which exercises functions referred to in paragraph (2).

68 Requests to other authorities

(1) This regulation applies if—

(a) documents or information which are reasonably required by a supervisory authority in connection with the exercise by the authority of any of the functions given to it under these Regulations are not (as far as the supervisory authority is aware) available in the United Kingdom; and

(b) the supervisory authority has reason to believe that such documents or information may be held by a person who is within the jurisdiction of a foreign authority.

(2) A supervisory authority may request the assistance of the foreign authority in obtaining specified information or documents which satisfy the conditions in paragraph (1).

(3) The information or documents provided to the supervisory authority pursuant to a request under paragraph (2) must only be used—

(a) for the purpose for which it was provided; or

(b) for the purposes of proceedings arising as a result of contravention of a relevant requirement in these Regulations, or proceedings arising out of such proceedings.

(4) Paragraph (3) does not apply if the foreign authority by which the information or documents were provided consents to its use.

(5) In this regulation, "foreign authority" has the meaning given in regulation 67(6).

69 Entry, inspection of premises without a warrant etc

(1) Paragraph (2) applies where a duly authorised officer of (or acting on behalf of) a supervisory authority in relation to a relevant person or a payment service provider ("P") has reasonable grounds to believe that—

- (a) any premises are being used by P in connection with P's business or professional activities; and
- (b) P may have contravened the requirements of—
  - (i) the fourth money laundering directive,
  - (ii) the funds transfer regulation, or
  - (iii) these Regulations.

(2) The officer may, on producing evidence of the officer's authority, at any reasonable time—

- (a) enter the premises;
- (b) inspect the premises;
- (c) observe the carrying on of business or professional activities by P;
- (d) inspect any documents or other information found on the premises;
- (e) require any person on the premises to provide an explanation of any document or to state where documents or information might be found;
- (f) inspect any cash found on the premises.

(3) The officer may take copies of, or make extracts from, any documents found as a result of the exercise of the power in paragraph (2).

(4) In this regulation, "duly authorised officer" means—

- (a) an officer of the FCA, authorised in writing to exercise the powers under this regulation on behalf of the FCA or another supervisory authority, by a Head of Department working within the enforcement function of the FCA; or
- (b) an officer of Revenue and Customs authorised in writing to exercise the powers under this regulation on behalf of the Commissioners, or another supervisory authority, by an officer of Revenue and Customs of at least the grade of senior officer.

70 Entry of premises under warrant

(1) A justice may issue a warrant under this regulation if satisfied on information given on oath (or in Scotland by evidence on oath) by a duly authorised officer acting on behalf of a supervisory authority that—

- (a) there are reasonable grounds for believing that the first, second, or third set of conditions is satisfied; or
- (b) there are reasonable grounds for suspecting that the fourth set of conditions is satisfied.

(2) The application for the warrant must—

- (a) identify the premises to which the application relates and state that the premises is not used only as a dwelling;
- (b) state that the officer has reasonable grounds to suspect a warrant is necessary in connection with the exercise of the supervisory functions of the supervisory authority for which the officer is acting and the warrant is sought for the purpose of those functions;
- (c) state that the officer executing the warrant—
  - (i) will give to any person on the premises, when entering the premises, evidence of identification and authority to act on behalf of the supervisory authority, and
  - (ii) will give to that person, no later than on entering the premises, a notice identifying and explaining the powers exercisable under this regulation, and
- (d) state that the warrant is sought in relation to material specified in the application, or that there are reasonable grounds for suspecting that there is material falling within regulation 66 on the premises.

(3) The first set of conditions is—

- (a) that a person on whom a requirement has been imposed under regulation 66 has failed (wholly or in part) to comply with it, and
- (b) that on the premises specified in the warrant—
  - (i) there are documents which have been required, or
  - (ii) there is information which has been required.

(4) The second set of conditions is—

- (a) that the premises specified in the warrant are premises of—
  - (i) the relevant person or the payment service provider ("P"),
  - (ii) a member of the same group as P; or
  - (iii) a third person referred to in regulation 66(8);
- (b) that there are on the premises documents or information in relation to which a requirement could be imposed under regulation 66, and
- (c) that if such a requirement were to be imposed—

(i) it would not be complied with, or

(ii) the documents or information to which it related would be removed, tampered with or destroyed.

(5) The third set of conditions is—

(a) that an officer has been obstructed in the exercise of the power under regulation 69; and

(b) that there is on the premises specified in the warrant documents, information or cash which could be inspected under regulation 69(2)(d) or (f).

(6) The fourth set of conditions is—

(a) that an offence under these Regulations has been, is being or is about to be committed by P; and

(b) there is on the premises specified in the warrant information or documents relevant to whether the offence has been, is being or is about to be committed.

(7) A warrant under this regulation authorises the executing officer—

(a) to enter the premises specified in the warrant;

(b) to search the premises and take possession of any documents or information appearing to be documents or information of a kind in respect of which the warrant was issued ("the relevant kind") or to take, in relation to any such documents or information, any other steps which may appear to be necessary for preserving them or preventing interference with them;

(c) to inspect any cash found on the premises;

(d) to take copies of, or extracts from, any documents or information appearing to be of the relevant kind;

(e) to require any person on the premises to provide an explanation of any document or information appearing to be of the relevant kind or to state where it may be found; and

(f) to use such force as may be reasonably necessary.

(8) Where information of the relevant kind is contained in a computer or other storage device, or is recorded in any other way otherwise than in legible form, the warrant authorises the executing officer to take possession of that information in a form in which it can be taken away and in which it is legible.

(9) A warrant under this regulation—

(a) may be exercised by any executing officer;

(b) may authorise persons to accompany any executing officer who is executing it;

(c) may be issued subject to conditions.

(10) The powers in paragraph (7) may be exercised by a person authorised by the warrant to accompany an executing officer; but that person may exercise those powers only in the company of, and under the supervision of, an executing officer.

(11) In England and Wales, sections 15(5) to (8) and 16(3) to (12) of the Police and Criminal Evidence Act 1984 (execution of warrants and safeguards) apply to warrants issued under this regulation.

(12) In Northern Ireland, Articles 17(5) to (8) and 18(3) to (12) of the Police and Criminal Evidence (Northern Ireland) Order 1989 (execution of warrants and safeguards) apply to warrants issued under this regulation.

(13) In this regulation—

"duly authorised officer" means—

(a) where a warrant is issued on the basis of information given on behalf of the FCA or another supervisory authority, an officer of the FCA authorised in writing to exercise the powers under this regulation by a Head of Department working within the enforcement function of the FCA,

(b) where a warrant is issued on the basis of information given on behalf of the Commissioners or another supervisory authority, an officer of Revenue and Customs authorised in writing to exercise the powers under this regulation by an officer of Revenue and Customs of at least the grade of senior officer;

"executing officer" means—

(a) where a warrant is issued on the basis of information given on behalf of the FCA, or of a supervisory authority for which the FCA is acting, a constable,

(b) where a warrant is issued on the basis of information given on behalf of the Commissioners, or of a supervisory authority for which the Commissioners are acting, an officer of Revenue and Customs;

"justice" means—

(a) in England and Wales, a justice of the peace;

(b) in Northern Ireland, a lay magistrate; or

(c) in Scotland, a sheriff or summary sheriff.

71 Retention of documents taken under regulation 66 or 70

(1) Any material possession of which is taken in accordance with a requirement under regulation 66 or under a warrant issued under regulation 70 ("seized material") may be retained for so long as it is necessary to retain it (rather than copies of it) in connection with the exercise of the functions of the supervisory authority under these Regulations for the purposes of which any requirement was imposed or the warrant was issued.

(2) If a duly authorised officer (within the meaning of regulation 70(13)) has reasonable grounds for suspecting that—

(a) the seized material may need to be produced for the purposes of legal proceedings; and

(b) it might otherwise be unavailable for those purposes,

it may be retained until the proceedings are concluded.

(3) A person claiming to be the owner of any seized material may apply to the Crown Court or (in Scotland) the sheriff or the summary sheriff for an order for the delivery of the material to the person appearing to the court, the sheriff or the summary sheriff to be the owner.

(4) If on an application under paragraph (3), the court or (in Scotland) the sheriff or the summary sheriff cannot ascertain who is the owner of the seized material the court, the sheriff or the summary sheriff may make such order as the court, the sheriff or the summary sheriff thinks fit.

(5) An order under paragraph (3) or (4) does not affect the right of any person to take legal proceedings against any person in possession of seized material for the recovery of the material.

72 Provision of information and warrants: safeguards

(1) A person may not be required under regulation 66, 69 or 70 to produce excluded material, or to provide information, produce documents or answer questions which that person would be entitled to refuse to provide, produce or answer on grounds of legal professional privilege in proceedings in the High Court, except that a lawyer may be required to provide the full name and address of the lawyer's client.

(2) The provision of information in accordance with regulation 66, 69 or 70, is not to be taken to breach any restriction, however imposed, on the disclosure of information.

(3) Where a disclosure is made in good faith in accordance with regulations 66, 69 or 70 no civil liability arises in respect of the disclosure on the part of the person making the disclosure.

(4) A warrant issued under regulation 70 does not confer the right to seize privileged material or excluded material.

(5) Privileged material is any material which the person would be entitled to refuse to produce on grounds of legal professional privilege in proceedings in the High Court.

(6) In the application of this regulation to Scotland, the references in paragraphs (1) and (5)—

(a) to proceedings in the High Court are to be read as references to proceedings in the Court of Session; and

(b) to an entitlement on grounds of legal professional privilege are to be read as references to an entitlement on the grounds of confidentiality of communication—

(i) between professional legal advisers and their clients; or

(ii) made in connection with or in contemplation of legal proceedings and for the purposes of those proceedings.

(7) For the purposes of this regulation, "excluded material" means personal records which a person has acquired or created in the course of any trade, business, profession or other occupation or for the purposes of any paid or unpaid office and which is held subject—

(a) to an express or implied undertaking to hold it in confidence; or

(b) to a restriction on disclosure or an obligation of secrecy contained in any enactment, including an enactment contained in, or made under, an Act passed after this Regulation.

73 Admissibility of statements

(1) A statement made by a person in response to a requirement imposed under regulations 66(1)(c), 69(2)(e) or 70(7)(e) may not be used in evidence against the person in criminal proceedings.

(2) Paragraph (1) does not apply—

(a) in the case of proceedings under Parts 2 to 4 of the Proceeds of Crime Act 2002 (confiscation proceedings);

(b) on a prosecution for an offence under section 5 of the Perjury Act 1911 (false statements);

(c) on a prosecution for an offence under Article 10 of the Perjury (Northern Ireland) Order 1979 (false statements);

(d) on a prosecution for an offence under section 44(2) of the Criminal Law (Consolidation) (Scotland) Act 1995 (false statements and declarations);

(e) on a prosecution for an offence under regulation 88; or

(f) for some other offence where, in giving evidence, the person makes a statement inconsistent with the statement mentioned in paragraph (1).

(3) A statement may not be used by virtue of paragraph (2)(f) against a person unless—

(a) evidence relating to it is adduced; or

(b) a question relating to it is asked;

by them or on their behalf in the proceedings arising out of the prosecution.

74 Powers of relevant officers

(1) A relevant officer ("R") may only exercise powers under this Part pursuant to arrangements made with the FCA or with the Commissioners—

(a) by or on behalf of the local weights and measures authority of which R is an officer ("R's authority"); or

(b) by the Department for the Economy.

(2) Anything done or omitted to be done by, or in relation to, R in the exercise or purported exercise of a power in this Part is to be treated for all purposes as having been done or omitted to be done by, or in relation to—

(a) an officer of the FCA, if R is acting pursuant to arrangements made with the FCA, or

(b) an officer of Revenue and Customs, if R is acting pursuant to arrangements made with the Commissioners.

(3) Paragraph (2) does not apply for the purpose of any criminal proceedings brought against R, R's authority, the Department for the Economy, the FCA or the Commissioners, in respect of anything done or omitted to be done by R.

(4) R must not disclose to any person other than the FCA (if R is acting pursuant to arrangements made with the FCA), the Commissioners (if R is acting pursuant to arrangements made with the Commissioners), R's authority or, as the case may be, the Department of the Economy, information obtained by R in the exercise of such powers unless—

(a) R has the approval of the FCA or where appropriate the Commissioners to do so, or

(b) R is under a duty to make the disclosure.

PART 9

ENFORCEMENT

CHAPTER 1

GENERAL

75 Meaning of "relevant requirement"

For the purposes of this Part, "relevant requirement" has the meaning given in Schedule 6.

CHAPTER 2

CIVIL PENALTIES AND NOTICES

76 Power to impose civil penalties: fines and statements

(1) Paragraph (2) applies if a designated supervisory authority is satisfied that any person ("P") has contravened a relevant requirement imposed on that person.

(2) A designated supervisory authority may do one or both of the following—

(a) impose a penalty of such amount as it considers appropriate on P;

(b) publish a statement censuring P.

(3) If a designated supervisory authority considers that another person who was at the material time an officer of P was knowingly concerned in a contravention of a relevant requirement by P, the designated supervisory authority may impose on that person a penalty of such amount as it considers appropriate.

(4) A designated supervisory authority must not impose a penalty on P under this regulation for contravention of a relevant requirement if the authority is satisfied that P took all reasonable steps and exercised all due diligence to ensure that the requirement would be complied with.

(5) Where the FCA proposes to impose a penalty under this regulation on a PRA-authorised person or on a person who has a qualifying relationship with a PRA-authorised person, it must consult the PRA.

(6) In deciding whether P has contravened a relevant requirement, the designated supervisory authority must consider whether at the time P followed—

(a) any relevant guidelines issued by the European Supervisory Authorities in accordance with—

(i) Articles 17, 18.4 or 48.10 of the fourth money laundering directive; or

(ii) Article 25 of the funds transfer regulation;

(b) any relevant guidance which was at the time—

(i) issued by the FCA; or

(ii) issued by any other supervisory authority or appropriate body and approved by the Treasury.

(7) A penalty imposed under this Part is payable to the designated supervisory authority which imposes it.

(8) For the purposes of this regulation—

(a) "appropriate" means (other than in references to an appropriate body) effective, proportionate and dissuasive;
(b) "designated supervisory authority" means the FCA or the Commissioners.

77 Power to impose civil penalties: suspension and removal of authorisation

(1) Paragraph (2) applies if the FCA is satisfied that a relevant person or a payment service provider has—

(a) repeatedly or systematically failed to include the information it is required to include on the payer or the payee under Articles 4, 5 or 6 of the funds transfer regulation;
(b) failed to implement effective risk-based procedures in breach of Articles 8 or 12 of the funds transfer regulation;
(c) failed to comply with Articles 11, 12 or 16 of the funds transfer regulation, where the failure is a serious one;
(d) repeatedly or systematically failed to retain records in breach of Article 16 of the funds transfer regulation; or
(e) failed to comply with a relevant requirement.

(2) The FCA may take one or more of the measures set out in sub-paragraphs (a) and (b)—

(a) to cancel or suspend, for such period as it considers appropriate—
  (i) any permission which an authorised person has to carry on a regulated activity;
  (ii) the authorisation of a payment service provider as an authorised payment institution under the Payment Services Regulations 2009;
  (iii) the registration of a payment service provider as a small payment institution under the Payment Services Regulations 2009;
  (iv) the authorisation of a payment service provider as an authorised electronic money institution under the Electronic Money Regulations 2011; or
  (v) the registration of a payment service provider as a small electronic money institution under the Electronic Money Regulations 2011;
(b) to impose, for such period as it considers appropriate, such limitations or other restrictions as it considers appropriate—
  (i) in relation to the carrying on of a regulated activity by an authorised person;
  (ii) on the authorisation of a payment service provider as a payment institution under the Payment Services Regulations 2009;
  (iii) on the registration of a payment service provider as a small payment institution under the Payment Services Regulations 2009;
  (iv) on the authorisation of a payment service provider as an electronic money institution under the Electronic Money Regulations 2011; or
  (v) on the registration of a payment service provider as a small electronic money institution under the Electronic Money Regulations 2011.

(3) In paragraph (2)—

(a) "permission" means any permission that the authorised person has, whether given (or treated as given) under Part 4A of FSMA;
(b) "regulated activity" has the meaning given by section 22 of FSMA).

(4) The period for which a suspension, limitation or other restriction is to have effect may not exceed 12 months.

(5) A suspension may relate only to the carrying on of an activity in circumstances specified by the FCA when the suspension is imposed.

(6) A restriction may, in particular, be imposed so as to require the person concerned to take, or refrain from taking, specified action.

(7) The FCA may—

(a) withdraw a suspension, limitation or other restriction; or
(b) vary a suspension, limitation or other restriction so as to reduce the period for which it has effect or otherwise to limit its effect.

(8) For the purposes of this regulation, "appropriate" means effective, proportionate and dissuasive.

Prospective amendments—In para (2)(a)(ii), (iii), (b)(ii), (iii), year "2017" to be substituted for year "2009" by the Payment Services Regulations, SI 2017/752 reg 156, Sch 8 para 26(e) with effect from 13 January 2018.

78 Power to impose civil penalties: prohibitions on management

(1) Paragraph (2) applies if a designated supervisory authority considers that another person who was at the material time an officer of P was knowingly concerned in a contravention of a relevant requirement by P.

(2) The designated supervisory authority may impose one of the following measures on the person concerned—

(a) a temporary prohibition on the individual concerned holding an office or position involving responsibility for taking decisions about the management of a relevant person or a payment service provider ("having a management role");

(b) a permanent prohibition on the individual concerned having a management role.

(3) A prohibition may be expressed to expire at the end of such period as the designated supervisory authority may specify, but the imposition of a prohibition under paragraph (2)(a) that expires at the end of a specified period does not affect the designated supervisory authority's power to impose a new prohibition under paragraph (2)(a).

(4) A prohibition imposed under paragraph (2) may be expressed to be a prohibition on an individual having a management role in—

(a) a named relevant person or payment service provider;

(b) a relevant person or payment service provider of a description specified by the designated supervisory authority when the prohibition is imposed; or

(c) any relevant person or payment service provider.

(5) A relevant person or payment service provider must take reasonable care to ensure that no individual who is subject to a prohibition under paragraph (2) on having a management role with that relevant person or payment service provider is given such a role, or continues to act in such a role.

79 Imposition of civil penalties

Any one or more of the powers in regulations 76, 77 and 78 may be exercised by a designated supervisory authority in relation to the same contravention.

80 Injunctions

(1) If, on the application of a designated supervisory authority, the court is satisfied—

(a) that there is a reasonable likelihood that any person will contravene a relevant requirement; or

(b) that any person has contravened a relevant requirement and that there is a reasonable likelihood that the contravention will continue or be repeated,

the court may make an order restraining (or in Scotland an interdict prohibiting) the contravention.

(2) If on the application of a designated supervisory authority the court is satisfied—

(a) that any person has contravened a relevant requirement; and

(b) that there are steps which could be taken for remedying the contravention,

the court may make an order requiring that person, and any other person who appears to have been knowingly concerned in the contravention, to take such steps as the court may direct to remedy it.

(3) If, on the application of a designated supervisory authority, the court is satisfied that any person may have—

(a) contravened a relevant requirement; or

(b) been knowingly concerned in the contravention of a relevant requirement,

the court may make an order restraining (or in Scotland an interdict prohibiting) that person from disposing or otherwise dealing with any assets belonging to that person which it is satisfied that that person is reasonably likely to dispose of or otherwise deal with.

(4) The jurisdiction in this regulation is exercisable by the High Court and the Court of Session.

(5) In paragraph (2), references to remedying a contravention include references to mitigating its effect.

81 The FCA: disciplinary measures (procedure)

(1) When determining the type of sanction, and level of any penalty, to be imposed on a person ("P") under regulation 76, 77 or 78, the FCA must take into account all relevant circumstances, including where appropriate—

(a) the gravity and the duration of the contravention or failure;

(b) the degree of responsibility of P;

(c) the financial strength of P;

(d) the amount of profits gained or losses avoided by P;

(e) the losses for third parties caused by the contravention or failure;

(f) the level of co-operation of P with the FCA;

(g) previous contraventions or failures by P; and

(h) any potential systemic consequences of the contravention or failure.

(2) If the FCA proposes to impose a sanction on P under regulation 76, 77 or 78 it must give P a warning notice.

(3) Where the FCA proposes to impose a penalty on a PRA-authorised person or on a person who has a qualifying relationship with a PRA-authorised person, it must consult the PRA.

(4) Section 387 of FSMA (warning notices) applies in relation to a notice given under paragraph (2) as it applies in relation to a warning notice given by the FCA under that Act, subject to paragraph (5).

(5) In complying with section 387(1)(a), a warning notice must—

(a) if it is about a proposal to publish a statement, set out the terms of the statement;

(b) if it is about a proposal to impose a penalty, specify the amount of the penalty;

(c) if it is about a proposal to impose a suspension, limitation or other restriction—

(i) state the period for which the suspension, limitation or restriction is to have effect,

(ii) sets out the terms of the suspension, limitation or other restriction;

(d) if it is about a proposal to cancel, state the date from which the cancellation is to have effect;

(e) if it is about a proposal to impose a prohibition on an individual, set out the terms of the proposed prohibition.

(6) If the FCA decides to impose a sanction on P under regulation 76, 77 or 78 it must without undue delay give P a decision notice.

(7) If the decision is to publish a statement, the decision notice must set out the terms of the statement.

(8) If the decision is to impose a penalty, the decision notice must specify the amount of the penalty.

(9) If the decision is to impose a suspension, limitation or other restriction, the decision notice must—

(a) state the period for which the suspension, limitation or restriction is to have effect;

(b) sets out the terms of the suspension, limitation or other restriction.

(10) If the decision is to cancel a permission, registration or authorisation, the decision notice must state the date from which the cancellation is to have effect.

(11) If the decision is to impose a prohibition on an individual, the decision notice must set out the terms of the prohibition.

(12) Section 388 of FSMA (decision notices) applies in relation to a decision notice given under paragraph (6) as it applies in relation to a decision notice given by the FCA under FSMA, subject to paragraph (13).

(13) Section 388 of FSMA has effect for the purposes of paragraph (12) as if—

(a) in subsection (1)(e)(i) for "this Act" there were substituted "regulation 93(1) of the Money Laundering, Terrorist Financing and Transfer of Funds (Information on the Payer) Regulations 2017", and

(b) subsections (1A) and (2) were omitted.

82 The FCA: procedure (general)

(1) Sections 389 (notices of discontinuance), 390 (final notices) and 392 (application of sections 393 and 394) to 395 (the FCA's and PRA's procedures) of FSMA apply in relation to a warning notice given under regulation 81(2) and a decision notice given under regulation 81(6) as they apply in relation to a warning notice or decision notice given under FSMA, subject to paragraphs (2) to (3).

(2) Section 390 of FSMA has effect as if—

(a) for subsection (4) there were substituted—

"(4) A final notice about a cancellation, suspension, limitation or other restriction under regulation 77 or 78 of the Money Laundering, Terrorist Financing and Transfer of Funds (Information on the Payer) Regulations 2017 ("the 2017 Regulations") must—

(a) specify the permission, authorisation or registration which is being cancelled, suspended or the terms of the limitation or other restriction being imposed, and

(b) give details of—

(i) the date on which the cancellation, suspension, limitation or other restriction has effect, and

(ii) the period for which the suspension, limitation or other restriction is imposed.

(4A) A final notice about a prohibition under regulation 78 of the 2017 Regulations must—

(a) specify the extent of the prohibition; and

(b) give details of the date on which the prohibition has effect, and if relevant the period for which it has effect.";

(b) subsections (6), (7) and (10) were omitted.

(3) Section 392 of FSMA has effect as if for paragraphs (a) and (b) there were substituted—

"(a) a warning notice given under regulation 81(2) of the Money Laundering, Terrorist Financing and Transfer of Funds (Information on the Payer) Regulations 2017 ("the 2017 Regulations");

(b) a decision notice given under regulation 81(6) of the 2017 Regulations.".

83 The Commissioners: disciplinary measures (procedure)

(1) When determining the type of sanction, and level of any penalty, to be imposed on a person ("P") under regulation 76 or 78, the Commissioners must take into account all relevant circumstances, including where appropriate—

(a) the gravity and the duration of the contravention or failure;

(b) the degree of responsibility of P;

(c) the financial strength of P;

(d) the amount of profits gained or losses avoided by P;

(e) the losses for third parties caused by the contravention or failure;

(f) the level of co-operation of P with the Commissioners;

(g) previous contraventions or failures by P; and

(h) any potential systemic consequences of the contravention or failure.

(2) Where the Commissioners decide to impose a penalty or publish a statement under regulation 76, or impose a prohibition under regulation 78, the Commissioners must give P a notice in accordance with paragraph (3).

(3) A notice must be given of—

(a) the Commissioners' decision—

(i) to impose a penalty, and the amount of the penalty;

(ii) to publish a statement, and the terms of the statement;

(iii) to impose a prohibition, and the terms of the prohibition;

(b) the Commissioners' reasons for imposing a penalty, publishing a statement or imposing a prohibition;

(c) the right to a review under regulation 94; and

(d) the right to appeal under regulation 99.

(4) A notice about a penalty must—

(a) state the manner in which and the period within which, the penalty is to be paid;

(b) give details of the way in which the penalty may be recovered if it is not paid by the date stated in the notice.

84 Publication: the FCA

(1) Where a warning notice is given by the FCA under regulation 81(2), neither the FCA nor any person to whom it is given or copied may publish the notice or any details concerning it.

(2) Where the FCA gives a decision notice under regulation 81(6), the FCA must publish on their official website such information about the matter to which the notice relates as it considers appropriate, subject to paragraphs (3) to (9).

(3) Where the FCA publishes information under paragraph (2) or (4) about a matter to which a decision notice relates and the person to whom the notice is given refers the matter to the Upper Tribunal (see regulation 93), the FCA must, without undue delay, publish on its official website information about the status of the appeal and its outcome.

(4) Subject to paragraph (5), (6) and (9) where the FCA gives a final notice, it must, without undue delay, publish on its official website information on the type and nature of the breach and the identity of the person on whom the sanction or measure is imposed.

(5) Subject to paragraph (8) and (9), information about a matter to which a final notice relates must be published in accordance with paragraph (6) where—

(a) the FCA considers it to be disproportionate to publish the identity of a legal person on whom the sanction or measure is imposed following an assessment by the FCA of the proportionality of publishing the person's identity;

(b) the FCA considers it to be disproportionate to publish the personal data of the individual on whom the sanction or measure is imposed following an assessment by the FCA of the proportionality of publishing the personal data; or

(c) the publication of information under paragraph (4) would jeopardise the stability of the financial markets or an ongoing investigation.

(6) Where paragraph (5) applies, the FCA must—

(a) defer the publication of the information about a matter to which a final notice relates until such time as paragraph (5) ceases to apply; or

(b) publish the information on an anonymous basis if publication on that basis would ensure the effective protection of any anonymised personal data in the information.

(7) Where paragraph (6)(b) applies, the FCA may make such arrangements as to the publication of information (including as to the timing of publication) as are necessary to preserve the anonymity of the person on whom the sanction or measure is imposed.

(8) The FCA may make arrangements for the postponed publication of personal data that is anonymised in information it publishes under paragraph (6)(b) if—

(a) the publication of the data is postponed for a reasonable period of time; and

(b) the FCA considers that paragraphs (5)(b) and (6)(b) will no longer apply in respect of that data at the time of the postponed publication.

(9) Information about a matter to which a final notice relates must not be published if publication in accordance with paragraph under paragraph (6) is considered by the FCA insufficient to ensure—

(a) that the stability of the financial markets would not be put in jeopardy; or

(b) that the publication of the information would be proportionate with regard to sanctions or measures which are considered by the FCA to be of a minor nature.

(10) Where the FCA publishes information in accordance with paragraphs (2) to (8), the FCA must ensure that the information remains on its official website for at least five years, unless the information is personal data and the Data Protection Act 1998 requires the information to be retained for a different period.

(11) For the purposes of this regulation "personal data" has the meaning given in section 1 of the Data Protection Act 1998 (basic interpretative provisions).

85 Publication: the Commissioners

(1) Where the Commissioners give a notice under regulation 83, the Commissioners must publish on their official website such information about the matter to which the notice relates as they consider appropriate, subject to paragraphs (2) to (8).

(2) Where the Commissioners publish information under paragraph (1) or (3) about a matter to which a notice under regulation 83 relates and the person to whom the notice is given refers the matter to the tribunal (see regulation 99), the Commissioners must, without undue delay, publish on their official website information about the status of the appeal and its outcome.

(3) Subject to paragraph (4), (5) and (8) where the Commissioners give a notice under regulation 83, they must, without undue delay, publish on their official website information on the type and nature of the breach and the identity of the person on whom the sanction or measure is imposed.

(4) Subject to paragraph (7) and (8), information about a matter to which a notice under regulation 83 relates must be published in accordance with paragraph (5) where—

- (a) the Commissioners consider it to be disproportionate to publish the identity of a legal person on whom the sanction or measure is imposed following an assessment by the Commissioners of the proportionality of publishing the person's identity;
- (b) the Commissioners consider it to be disproportionate to publish the personal data of the individual on whom the sanction or measure is imposed following an assessment by the Commissioners of the proportionality of publishing the personal data; or
- (c) the publication of information under paragraph (3) would jeopardise the stability of the financial markets or an ongoing investigation.

(5) Where paragraph (4) applies, the Commissioners must—

- (a) defer the publication of the information about a matter to which a notice under regulation 83 relates until such time as paragraph (4) ceases to apply; or
- (b) publish the information on an anonymous basis if publication on that basis would ensure the effective protection of any anonymised personal data in the information.

(6) Where paragraph (5)(b) applies, the Commissioners may make such arrangements as to the publication of information (including as to the timing of publication) as are necessary to preserve the anonymity of the person on whom the sanction or measure is imposed.

(7) The Commissioners may make arrangements for the postponed publication of personal data that is anonymised in information they publish under paragraph (5)(b) if—

- (a) the publication of the data is postponed for a reasonable period of time; and
- (b) the Commissioners consider that paragraphs (4)(b) and (5)(b) will no longer apply in respect of that data at the time of the postponed publication.

(8) Information about a matter to which a notice relates must not be published if publication in accordance with paragraph under paragraph (5) is considered by the Commissioners insufficient to ensure—

- (a) that the stability of the financial markets would not be put in jeopardy; or
- (b) that the publication of the information would be proportionate with regard to sanctions or measures which are considered by the Commissioners to be of a minor nature.

(9) Where the Commissioners publish information in accordance with paragraphs (1) to (7), the Commissioners must ensure that the information remains on their official website for at least five years, unless the information is personal data and the Data Protection Act 1998 requires the information to be retained for a different period.

(10) For the purposes of this regulation "personal data" has the meaning given in section 1 of the Data Protection Act 1998 (basic interpretative provisions).

CHAPTER 3

CRIMINAL OFFENCES, PENALTIES AND PROCEEDINGS ETC

86 Criminal offence

(1) A person who contravenes a relevant requirement imposed on that person is guilty of an offence and liable—

- (a) on summary conviction—
  - (i) in England and Wales, to imprisonment for a term not exceeding three months, to a fine or to both;
  - (ii) in Scotland or Northern Ireland, to imprisonment for a term not exceeding three months, to a fine not exceeding the statutory maximum or to both;
- (b) on conviction on indictment, to imprisonment for a term not exceeding two years, to a fine, or to both.

(2) In deciding whether a person has committed an offence under paragraph (1), the court must decide whether that person followed—

- (a) any guidelines issued by the European Supervisory Authorities in accordance with Article 17, 18.4 and 48.10 of the fourth money laundering directive or Article 25 of the funds transfer regulation; and

(b) any relevant guidance which was at the time—
(i) issued by the FCA; or
(ii) issued by any other supervisory authority or appropriate body and approved by the Treasury.

(3) A person is not guilty of an offence under this regulation if that person took all reasonable steps and exercised all due diligence to avoid committing the offence.

(4) Where a person has been convicted of an offence under this regulation, that person is not also to be liable to a sanction under Chapter 2 of this Part.

87 Offences of prejudicing investigations

(1) This regulation applies if a person ("P") knows or suspects that an appropriate officer is acting (or proposing to act) in connection with an investigation into a potential contravention of a relevant requirement which is being or is about to be conducted.

(2) P commits an offence if—
(a) P makes a disclosure which is likely to prejudice the investigation; or
(b) P falsifies, conceals, destroys or otherwise disposes of, or causes or permits the falsification, concealment, destruction or disposal of, documents which are relevant to the investigation.

(3) P does not commit an offence under paragraph (2)(a) if—
(a) P does not know or suspect that the disclosure is likely to prejudice the investigation;
(b) the disclosure is made in the exercise of a function under these Regulations, or in compliance with a requirement imposed by or under these Regulations;
(c) the disclosure is made in the exercise of a function, or in compliance with a requirement imposed, by or under the Terrorism Act 2000;
(d) the disclosure is made in the exercise of a function, or in compliance with a requirement imposed, by or under the Proceeds of Crime Act 2002;
(e) the disclosure is made in the exercise of a function, or in compliance with a requirement imposed, under any Act relating to criminal conduct or benefit from criminal conduct; or
(f) P is a professional legal adviser and the disclosure falls within paragraph (6).

(4) Criminal conduct is conduct which—
(a) constitutes an offence in any part of the United Kingdom; or
(b) would constitute an offence in any part of the United Kingdom if it occurred there.

(5) A person benefits from conduct if that person obtains property as a result of or in connection with the conduct.

(6) Subject to paragraph (7), a disclosure falls within this paragraph if it is a disclosure—
(a) to (or to a representative of) a client of the professional legal adviser in connection with the giving by the adviser of legal advice to the client; or
(b) to any person in connection with legal proceedings or contemplated legal proceedings.

(7) A disclosure does not fall within paragraph (6) if it is made with the intention of furthering a criminal purpose.

(8) P does not commit an offence under paragraph (2)(b) if—
(a) P does not know or suspect that the documents are relevant in connection with the investigation; or
(b) P does not intend to conceal any facts disclosed by the documents from any appropriate officer acting in connection with the investigation.

(9) A person guilty of an offence under paragraph (2) is liable—
(a) on summary conviction—
(i) in England and Wales, to imprisonment for a term not exceeding three months, to a fine or to both,
(ii) in Scotland or Northern Ireland, to imprisonment for a term not exceeding three months, to a fine not exceeding the statutory maximum or to both;
(b) on conviction on indictment, to imprisonment for a term not exceeding two years or to a fine, or to both.

(10) For the purposes of this regulation—
"appropriate officer" means—
(a) an officer of the FCA, including a member of the FCA's staff or an agent of the FCA;
(b) an officer of Revenue and Customs;
(c) an employee or agent of a professional body listed in Schedule 1 who is authorised by the body to act on behalf of the body for the purposes of this Part; or
(d) a relevant officer;
"relevant officer" means—
(a) in Great Britain, an officer of a local weights and measures authority;
(b) in Northern Ireland, an officer of the Department for the Economy;
acting pursuant to arrangements made with the FCA or with the Commissioners for the purposes of these Regulations.

88 Information offences

(1) A person ("P") commits an offence if, in purported compliance with a requirement imposed on P by or under these Regulations, P provides information to any person which is false or misleading in a material particular, and—

(a) P knows that the information is false or misleading; or

(b) P is reckless as to whether the information is false or misleading.

(2) A person guilty of an offence under paragraph (1) is liable—

(a) on summary conviction—

(i) in England and Wales, to imprisonment for a term not exceeding three months, to a fine or to both,

(ii) in Scotland or Northern Ireland, to imprisonment for a term not exceeding three months, to a fine not exceeding the statutory maximum or to both;

(b) on conviction on indictment, to imprisonment for a term not exceeding two years or to a fine or to both.

(3) A person who discloses information in contravention of a relevant requirement is guilty of an offence and liable—

(a) on summary conviction—

(i) in England and Wales, to imprisonment for a term not exceeding three months, to a fine or to both,

(ii) in Scotland or Northern Ireland, to imprisonment for a term not exceeding three months, to a fine not exceeding the statutory maximum or to both;

(b) on conviction on indictment, to imprisonment for a term not exceeding two years or to a fine or to both.

(4) It is a defence for a person charged with an offence under paragraph (3) of disclosing information to prove that they reasonably believed—

(a) that the disclosure was lawful; or

(b) that the information had already and lawfully been made available to the public.

89 Proceedings: general

(1) Proceedings for an offence under these Regulations may be instituted by—

(a) order of the Commissioners;

(b) a local weights and measures authority;

(c) the Department for the Economy;

(d) the Director of Public Prosecutions; or

(e) the Director of Public Prosecutions for Northern Ireland.

(2) Where proceedings under paragraph (1) are instituted by order of the Commissioners, the proceedings must be brought in the name of an officer of Revenue and Customs.

(3) A local weights and measures authority must, whenever the FCA or (where the authority is acting pursuant to arrangements made with the Commissioners) the Commissioners require, report in such form and with such particulars as the FCA or the Commissioners require on the exercise of its functions under these Regulations.

(4) Where the Commissioners investigate, or propose to investigate, any matter with a view to determining—

(a) whether there are grounds for believing that an offence under these Regulations has been committed by any person; or

(b) whether a person should be prosecuted for such an offence,

that matter is to be treated as an assigned matter within the meaning of section 1(1) of the Customs and Excise Management Act 1979 (interpretation).

(5) Paragraphs (1) and (3) do not extend to Scotland.

(6) In its application to the Commissioners acting in Scotland, paragraph (4)(b) is to be read as referring to the Commissioners determining whether to refer the matter to the Crown Office and Procurator Fiscal Service with a view to the Procurator Fiscal determining whether a person should be prosecuted for such an offence.

90 Proceedings: jurisdiction

(1) Proceedings against any person for an offence under these Regulations may be taken before the appropriate court in the United Kingdom having jurisdiction in the place where that person is for the time being.

(2) Proceedings against any person for an offence under these Regulations which cannot be taken under paragraph (1) may be taken at any appropriate court in the United Kingdom.

(3) An offence falling under these Regulations which is committed wholly or partly outside the United Kingdom may for all incidental purposes be treated as having been committed within the jurisdiction of the court where proceedings were taken.

91 Proceedings: partnership or unincorporated association

(1) Proceedings for an offence alleged to have been committed by—

(a) a partnership must be brought in the name of the partnership; or

(b) an unincorporated association must be brought in the name of the association,

and not in that of its members.

(2) A fine imposed on—

(a) a partnership on its conviction of an offence is to be paid out of the funds of the partnership; and

(b) an unincorporated association on its conviction of an offence is to be paid out of the funds of the association.

(3) Rules of court relating to the service of documents are to have effect as if a partnership or unincorporated association were a body corporate.

(4) In proceedings for an offence brought against a partnership or an unincorporated association—

(a) section 33 of the Criminal Justice Act 1925 (procedure on charge of offence against corporation) and Schedule 3 to the Magistrates' Courts Act 1980 (corporations) apply as they do in relation to a body corporate; and

(b) section 18 of the Criminal Justice (Northern Ireland) Act 1945 (procedure on charge) and Schedule 4 to the Magistrates' Courts (Northern Ireland) Order 1981 (corporations) apply as they do in relation to a body corporate.

92 Offence by bodies corporate, partnership or unincorporated association

(1) If an offence under this Part committed by a body corporate is shown—

(a) to have been committed with the consent or the connivance of an officer of the body corporate; or

(b) to be attributable to any neglect on the part of an officer,

the officer (as well as the body corporate) is guilty of the offence and is liable to be proceeded against and punished accordingly.

(2) If the affairs of a body corporate are managed by its members, paragraph (1) applies in relation to the acts and defaults of a member in connection with their functions of management as if the member was a director of the body.

(3) If an offence under this Part committed by a partnership is shown—

(a) to have been committed with the consent or the connivance of an officer; or

(b) to be attributable to any neglect on the part of an officer,

that officer (as well as the partnership) is guilty of the offence and is liable to be proceeded against and punished accordingly.

(4) If an offence under this Part committed by an unincorporated association (other than a partnership) is shown—

(a) to have been committed with the consent or the connivance of an officer of the association; or

(b) to be attributable to any neglect on the part of an officer,

that officer (as well as the association) is guilty of the offence and is liable to be proceeded against and punished accordingly.

PART 10
APPEALS

CHAPTER 1
DECISIONS OF THE FCA

93 Appeals against decisions of the FCA

(1) A person may appeal from a decision by the FCA under these Regulations to the Upper Tribunal.

(2) The provisions of Part 9 of FSMA (hearings and appeals), apply, subject to the modifications set out in paragraph (3), in respect of appeals to the Upper Tribunal made under this regulation as they apply in respect of references made to that Tribunal under that Act.

(3) Part 9 of FSMA has effect as if—

(a) in section 133 (proceedings before Tribunal: general provision), in subsection (7A), after paragraph (o) there were inserted—

"(p) a decision to take action under any of regulations 76 to 78 of the Money Laundering, Terrorist Financing and Transfer of Funds (Information on the Payer) Regulations 2017."; and

(b) for section 133A there were substituted—

"133A Proceedings before Tribunal: decision notices

(1) The action specified in a decision notice given under regulation 81(6) of the Money Laundering, Terrorist Financing and Transfer of Funds (Information on the Payer) Regulations 2017 must not be taken—

(a) during the period within which the matter to which the notice relates may be referred to the Tribunal under the Money Laundering, Terrorist Financing and Transfer of Funds (Information on the Payer) Regulations 2017; and

(b) if the matter is so referred, until the reference, and any appeal against the Tribunal's determination, has been finally disposed of.

(2) The Tribunal may, on determining a reference under these Regulations in respect of a decision of the FCA, make recommendations as to its regulating provisions or its procedures.".

CHAPTER 2

DECISIONS OF THE COMMISSIONERS

94 Offer of review

(1) The Commissioners must offer a person ("P") a review of a decision that has been notified to P if an appeal lies under this Chapter in respect of the decision.

(2) The offer of a review must be made by notice given to P at the same time as the decision is notified to P.

(3) This regulation does not apply to the notification of the conclusions of a review.

95 Review by the Commissioners

(1) The Commissioners must review a decision if—

(a) they have offered a review of the decision under this Chapter, and

(b) the person concerned ("P") notifies the Commissioners that P accepts the offer within 30 days from the date of the notice of the offer of a review.

(2) P may not notify acceptance of the offer where P has already appealed against the decision to the tribunal under regulation 100.

(3) The Commissioners must not review a decision if P has appealed to the tribunal under regulation 100 in respect of the decision.

96 Extensions of time

(1) If under this Chapter the Commissioners have offered a person ("P") a review of a decision the Commissioners may within the relevant period notify P that the relevant period is extended.

(2) If notice is given, the relevant period is extended to the end of 30 days from—

(a) the date of the notice; or

(b) any other date set out in the notice or a further notice.

(3) More than one notice may be given under paragraph (1).

(4) In this regulation, "relevant period" means—

(a) the period of 30 days referred to in regulation 95(1)(b); or

(b) in the case where one or more notices have already been given under paragraph (1) the period as extended (or as most recently extended) in accordance with paragraph (2).

97 Review out of time

(1) This regulation applies if—

(a) the Commissioners have offered a review of a decision under this Chapter to a person ("P"); and

(b) P does not accept the offer within the time allowed under regulation 95(1)(b) or 96(2).

(2) The Commissioners must review the decision if—

(a) after the time allowed, P notifies the Commissioners in writing requesting a review out of time;

(b) the Commissioners are satisfied that P had a reasonable excuse for not accepting the offer of a review within the time allowed; and

(c) the Commissioners are satisfied that P made the request without unreasonable delay after the excuse had ceased to apply.

98 Nature of review etc

(1) This regulation applies if the Commissioners are required to undertake a review under regulation 95 or 97.

(2) The nature and extent of the review are to be such as appear appropriate to the Commissioners in the circumstances.

(3) For the purpose of paragraph (2), the Commissioners must, in particular, have regard to steps taken before the beginning of the review—

(a) by the Commissioners in reaching the decision; and

(b) by any person in seeking to resolve disagreement about the decision.

(4) The review must take account of any representations made by the person ("P") at a stage which gives the Commissioners a reasonable opportunity to consider them.

(5) The review may conclude that the decision is to be—

(a) upheld;

(b) varied; or

(c) cancelled.

(6) The Commissioners must give P notice of the conclusions of the review and their reasoning within—

(a) a period of 45 days beginning with the relevant date; or

(b) such other period as the Commissioners and P may agree.

(7) In paragraph (6), "relevant date" means—

(a) in a case falling within regulation 95, the date the Commissioners received notification accepting the offer of a review from P; or

(b) in a case falling within regulation 97, the date on which the Commissioners decided to undertake the review.

(8) Where the Commissioners are required to undertake a review but do not give notice of the conclusions within the time period specified in paragraph (6), the review is to be treated as having concluded that the decision is upheld.

(9) If paragraph (8) applies, the Commissioners must notify P of the conclusion which the review is treated as having reached.

99 Appeals against decisions of the Commissioners

(1) Any person who is the subject of a decision by the Commissioners under these Regulations may appeal to the tribunal in accordance with regulation 100.

(2) The provisions of Part 5 of the Value Added Tax Act 1994 (appeals), subject to the modifications set out in paragraph (3), apply in respect of appeals to the tribunal made under this regulation as they apply in respect of appeals made to the tribunal under section 83 of that Act (appeals).

(3) Part 5 of the Value Added Tax Act 1994 has effect as if sections 83A to 84, 85A and 85B (appeals and reviews) were omitted.

(4) The tribunal hearing an appeal under paragraph (1) has the power to—

(a) quash or vary any decision of the Commissioners, including the power to reduce any penalty to such amount (including nil) as the tribunal thinks appropriate; and

(b) substitute the tribunal's own decision for any decision quashed on appeal.

(5) For the purpose of an appeal under this regulation, the meaning of "tribunal" is as defined in section 82 of the Value Added Tax Act 1994 (meaning of tribunal).

100 Appeals against decisions of the Commissioners: procedure

(1) Subject to paragraphs (2) to (4), an appeal under regulation 99 is to be made to the tribunal before—

(a) the end of the period of 30 days beginning with the date of the notice notifying the decision to which the appeal relates; or

(b) if later, the end of the relevant period (within the meaning of regulation 96).

(2) In a case where the Commissioners are required to undertake a review under regulation 95—

(a) an appeal may not be made until the conclusion date; and

(b) any appeal is to be made within the period of 30 days beginning with the conclusion date.

(3) In a case where the Commissioners are requested to undertake a review in accordance with regulation 97—

(a) an appeal may not be made—

(i) unless the Commissioners have notified the person concerned ("P") as to whether or not a review will be undertaken; and

(ii) if the Commissioners have notified P that a review will be undertaken, until the conclusion date;

(b) any appeal where sub-paragraph (a)(ii) applies is to be made within the period of 30 days beginning with the conclusion date; and

(c) if the Commissioners have notified P that a review will not be undertaken, an appeal may be made only if the tribunal gives permission to appeal.

(4) In a case where regulation 98(8) applies, an appeal may be made at any time from the end of the period specified in regulation 98(6) to the date 30 days after the conclusion date.

(5) An appeal may be made after the end of the period specified in paragraph (1), (2)(b), 3(b) or (4) if the tribunal gives permission to appeal.

(6) In this regulation, "conclusion date" means the date of the notice notifying the conclusions of the review.

PART 11
MISCELLANEOUS PROVISIONS

101 Recovery of charges and penalties through the court

Any charge or penalty imposed on a relevant person or on a payment service provider by the FCA or the Commissioners under these Regulations is a debt due from that person to the FCA or the Commissioners respectively, and is recoverable accordingly.

102 Costs of supervision

(1) The FCA and the Commissioners may impose charges on—

- (a) applicants for approval under Chapter 3 of Part 2;
- (b) applicants for registration under Chapter 2 of Part 6;
- (c) relevant persons supervised by them;
- (d) payment service providers supervised by them;
- (e) professional bodies listed in Schedule 1, for which they undertake enforcement action in relation to relevant persons supervised by those professional bodies.

(2) Charges levied under paragraph (1) must not exceed such amount as the FCA or the Commissioners (as the case may be) consider will enable them to meet any expenses reasonably incurred by them in carrying out their functions under these Regulations or for any incidental purpose (including any expenses reasonably incurred by them in undertaking enforcement action on behalf of a self-regulatory organisation).

(3) Without prejudice to the generality of paragraph (2), a charge may be levied in respect of each of the premises at which the relevant person, the provider or a person connected with the relevant person or the provider carries on (or proposes to carry on) business or professional activities.

(4) The FCA must in respect of each of its financial years pay to the Treasury any amounts received by the FCA during the year by way of penalties imposed under Part 9.

(5) The Treasury may give directions to the FCA as to how the FCA is to comply with the duty under paragraph (4).

(6) The directions may in particular—

- (a) specify the time when any payment is required to be made to the Treasury; and
- (b) require the FCA to provide the Treasury at specified times with information relating to penalties that the FCA has imposed under Part 9.

(7) The Treasury must pay into the Consolidated Fund any sums received by them under this regulation.

(8) In paragraph (2), "expenses" includes expenses incurred by a local weights and measures authority or the Department for the Economy pursuant to arrangements made for the purposes of these Regulations with the FCA or with the Commissioners—

- (a) by or on behalf of the authority; or
- (b) by the Department for the Economy.

103 Obligations on public authorities

(1) The following bodies and persons must, if they know or suspect or have reasonable grounds for knowing or suspecting that a person is or has engaged in money laundering or terrorist financing, as soon as practicable, inform the NCA—

- (a) the Auditor General for Scotland;
- (b) the Auditor General for Wales;
- (c) the Bank of England;
- (d) the Comptroller and Auditor General;
- (e) the Comptroller and Auditor General for Northern Ireland;
- (f) the FCA;
- (g) the Gambling Commission;
- (h) the Official Solicitor to the Supreme Court;
- (i) the Pensions Regulator;
- (j) the PRA;
- (k) the Public Trustee;
- (l) the Secretary of State, in the exercise of his or her functions under enactments relating to companies and insolvency;
- (m) the Treasury, in the exercise of their functions under FSMA;
- (n) the Treasury Solicitor;
- (o) a designated professional body for the purposes of Part 20 of FSMA (provision of financial services by members of the professions);
- (p) a person or inspector appointed under section 65 (investigations on behalf of FCA) or 66 (inspections and special meetings) of the Friendly Societies Act 1992;
- (q) an inspector appointed under section 106 of the Co-operative and Community Benefit Societies 2014 (appointment of inspectors) or section 18 of the Credit Unions Act 1979 (power to appoint inspector);
- (r) an inspector appointed under section 431 (investigation of a company on its own application), 432 (other company investigations), 442 (power to investigate company ownership) or 446D (appointment of replacement inspectors) of the Companies Act 1985;
- (s) a person or inspector appointed under section 55 (investigations on behalf of FCA) or 56 (inspections and special meetings) of the Building Societies Act 1986;
- (t) a person appointed under section 167 (appointment of persons to carry out investigations), 168(3) or (5) (appointment of persons to carry out investigations in particular cases),

169(1)(b) (investigations to support overseas regulator) or 284 (power to investigate affairs of a scheme) of FSMA, or under regulations made under section 262(2)(k) (open-ended investment companies) of that Act, to conduct an investigation; and

(u) a person authorised to require the production of documents under section 447 (Secretary of State's power to require production of documents) of the Companies Act 1985, or section 84 of the Companies Act 1989 (exercise of powers by officer).

(2) A disclosure made under paragraph (1) is not to be taken to breach any restriction, however imposed, on the disclosure of information.

(3) Where a disclosure under paragraph (1) is made in good faith, no civil liability arises in respect of the disclosure on the part of the person by whom, or on whose behalf, it is made.

104 Suspicious activity disclosures

(1) The NCA must make arrangements to provide appropriate feedback on the suspicious activity disclosures it has received at least once a year.

(2) The feedback referred to in paragraph (1) may be provided by the NCA jointly with another person, or by another person on behalf of the NCA.

(3) The feedback referred to in paragraph (1) may be provided in any form the NCA thinks fit.

(4) In this regulation, a "suspicious activity disclosure" is a disclosure made to the NCA under—

(a) Part 3 of the Terrorism Act 2000 (terrorist property);

(b) Part 7 of the Proceeds of Crime Act 2002 (money laundering).

105 Disclosure by the Commissioners

(1) The Commissioners may disclose to the FCA information held in connection with their functions under these Regulations if the disclosure is made for the purpose of enabling or assisting the FCA to discharge any of its functions under the Payment Services Regulations 2009 or the Electronic Money Regulations 2011.

(2) Information disclosed to the FCA under paragraph (1) may not be disclosed by the FCA or any person who receives the information directly or indirectly from the FCA except—

(a) to, or in accordance with authority given by, the Commissioners;

(b) with a view to the institution of, or otherwise for the purposes of, any criminal proceedings;

(c) with a view to the institution of any other proceedings by the FCA, for the purposes of any such proceedings, or for the purposes of any reference to the Upper Tribunal under the Payment Services Regulations 2009; or

(d) in the form of a summary or collection of information so framed as not to enable information relating to any particular person to be ascertained from it.

Prospective amendments—In paras (1), (2)(c), year "2017" to be substituted for year "2009" by the Payment Services Regulations, SI 2017/752 reg 156, Sch 8 para 26(f) with effect from 13 January 2018.

106 General restrictions

These Regulations do not authorise or require—

(a) a disclosure, in contravention of any provisions of the Data Protection Act 1998, of personal data which are not exempt from those provisions; or

(b) a disclosure which is prohibited by any of Parts 1 to 3 or 5 to 7 of the Investigatory Powers Act 2016.

107 Transfers between the United Kingdom and the Channel Islands and the Isle of Man

In determining whether a person has failed to comply with any requirement in the funds transfer regulation, any transfer of funds between the United Kingdom and—

(a) the Channel Islands; or

(b) the Isle of Man;

is to be treated as a transfer of funds within the United Kingdom.

108 Review

(1) The Treasury must from time to time—

(a) carry out a review of the regulatory provision contained in these Regulations; and

(b) publish a report setting out the conclusions of the review.

(2) The first report must be published before 26th June 2022.

(3) Subsequent reports must be published at intervals not exceeding 5 years.

(4) Section 30(3) of the Small Business, Enterprise and Employment Act 2015 (provision for review) requires that a review carried out under this regulation must, so far as is reasonable, have regard to how—

(a) the emission allowance auctioning regulation;

(b) the fourth money laundering directive; and

(c) the funds transfer regulation;

are implemented in other member States.

(5) Section 30(4) of the Small Business, Enterprise and Employment Act 2015 requires that a report published under this regulation must, in particular—

(a) set out the objectives intended to be achieved by the regulatory provision referred to in paragraph (1)(a);

(b) assess the extent to which those objectives are achieved;

(c) assess whether those objectives remain appropriate; and

(d) if those objectives remain appropriate, assess the extent to which they could be achieved in another way which involves less onerous regulatory provision.

(6) In this regulation, "regulatory provision" has the same meaning as in sections 28 to 32 of the Small Business, Enterprise and Employment Act 2015 (see section 32 of that Act).

109 Consequential amendments

Schedule 7 makes amendments relating to these Regulations.

110 Revocation and saving provisions

(1) The old money laundering regulations and the old transfer of funds regulations are revoked.

(2) The old money laundering regulations and the old transfer of funds regulations shall continue to have effect where the conduct constituting a contravention of one of those Regulations, or an offence under one of those Regulations began before the date on which these Regulations come into force.

(3) Where the old money laundering regulations or the old transfer of funds regulations continue to have effect, a penalty or an offence under the relevant Part of these Regulations is not to have effect in such circumstances.

(4) Where the conduct is found to have been committed over a period of two or more days, or at some point during a period of two or more days, it is to be taken for the purposes of paragraph (2) to have been begun on the earliest of those days.

(5) The "old money laundering regulations" means—

(a) the Money Laundering Regulations 2007;

(b) the Money Laundering (Amendment) Regulations 2007;

(c) the Money Laundering (Amendment) Regulations 2011;

(d) the Money Laundering (Amendment) Regulations 2012; and

(e) the Money Laundering (Amendment) Regulations 2015.

(6) The "old transfer of funds regulations" means the Transfer of Funds (Information on the Payer) Regulations 2007.

SCHEDULE 1
PROFESSIONAL BODIES

Regulation 7(1)(b)

1 Association of Accounting Technicians

2 Association of Chartered Certified Accountants

3 Association of International Accountants

4 Association of Taxation Technicians

5 Chartered Institute of Legal Executives

6 Chartered Institute of Management Accountants

7 Chartered Institute of Taxation

8 Council for Licensed Conveyancers

9 Faculty of Advocates

10 Faculty Office of the Archbishop of Canterbury

11 General Council of the Bar

12 General Council of the Bar of Northern Ireland

13 Insolvency Practitioners Association

14 Institute of Certified Bookkeepers

15 Institute of Chartered Accountants in England and Wales

16 Institute of Chartered Accountants in Ireland

17 Institute of Chartered Accountants of Scotland

18 Institute of Financial Accountants

19 International Association of Bookkeepers

20 Law Society

21 Law Society of Northern Ireland

22 Law Society of Scotland

SCHEDULE 2

ACTIVITIES LISTED IN POINTS 2 TO 12, 14 AND 15 OF ANNEX I TO THE CAPITAL REQUIREMENTS DIRECTIVE

Regulation 10(4)

The activities listed in points 2 to 12, 14 and 15 of Annex I to the Capital Requirements Directive are—

"2

Lending including, inter alia: consumer credit, credit agreements relating to immovable property, factoring, with or without recourse, financing of commercial transactions (including forfeiting).

3

Financial leasing.

4

Payment services as defined in point (3) of Article 4 of Directive 2015/2366/EU.

5

Issuing and administering other means of payment (eg travellers' cheques and bankers' drafts) insofar as such activity is not covered by point 4.

6

Guarantees and commitments.

7

Trading for own account or for account of customers in any of the following:

(a) money market instruments (cheques, bills, certificates of deposit, etc);
(b) foreign exchange;
(c) financial futures and options;
(d) exchange and interest-rate instruments;
(e) transferable securities.

8

Participation in securities issues and the provision of services relating to such issues.

9

Advice to undertakings on capital structure, industrial strategy and related questions and advice as well as services relating to mergers and the purchase of undertakings.

10

Money broking.

11

Portfolio management and advice.

12

Safekeeping and administration of securities.

14

Safe custody services.

15

Issuing electronic money."

SCHEDULE 3

RELEVANT OFFENCES

Regulation 26(14)

1 An offence under the Perjury Act 1911.

2 An offence under section 89 of the Criminal Justice Act 1967 (false written statements tendered in evidence).

3 An offence under section 20BB of the Taxes Management Act 1970 (falsification of documents).

4 An offence under section 11 of the European Communities Act 1972 (EU offences).

5 An offence under Article 10 of the Perjury (Northern Ireland) Order 1979 (false statutory declarations and other false unsworn statements).

6 An offence under the Customs and Excise Management Act 1979.

7 An offence under the Estate Agency Act 1979, or specified for the purposes of section 3 of that Act in the Estate Agents (Specified Offences) (No 2) Order 1991.

8 An offence under any of sections 1 to 5 of the Forgery and Counterfeiting Act 1981 (counterfeiting offences).

9 An offence under section 35 of the Administration of Justice Act 1985 (penalty for pretending to be a licensed conveyancer or recognised body).

10 An offence under section 11(1) (undischarged bankrupts) or 13 (criminal penalties) of the Company Directors Disqualification Act 1986.

11 An offence under section 1, 2, 3, 3ZA or 3A of the Computer Misuse Act 1990 (computer misuse offences).

12 An offence under section 112 (false representations or obtaining benefit) or 114 (offences relating to contributions) of the Social Security Administration Act 1992.

13 An offence under section 52 of the Criminal Justice Act 1993 (the offence of insider dealing).

14 An offence under the Value Added Tax Act 1994.

15 An offence under section 44(2) of the Criminal Law (Consolidation) (Scotland) Act 1995 (false statement and declarations).

16 An offence under the Data Protection Act 1998.

17 An offence under the Terrorism Act 2000.

18 An offence under paragraph 7(2) or (3) of Schedule 3 to the Anti-Terrorism, Crime and Security Act 2001 (offences).

19 An offence under the Money Laundering Regulations 2001, the Money Laundering Regulations 2003, the Money Laundering Regulations 2007 or under these Regulations.

20 An offence under section 35 of the Tax Credits Act 2002 (offence of fraud).

21 An offence under Part 7 (money laundering) or Part 8 (investigations) of, or listed in Schedule 2 (lifestyle offences: England and Wales), 4 (lifestyle offences: Scotland) or 5 (lifestyle offences: Northern Ireland) to, the Proceeds of Crime Act 2002.

22 An offence under the Commissioners for Revenue and Customs Act 2005.

23 An offence under the Terrorism Act 2006.

24 An offence under section 1, 2, 6 or 7 of the Bribery Act 2010 (bribery).

25 An offence under section 45 of the Serious Crime Act 2015 (offence of participating in activities of organised crime gang).

26 An offence under Parts 1 (general privacy protections); 2 (lawful interception of communications), 3 (authorisations for obtaining communications data), 5 (equipment interference), 6 (bulk warrants) and 7 (bulk personal dataset warrants) of the Investigatory Powers Act 2016.

27 An offence under section 45 (failure to prevent facilitation of UK tax evasion offences) or 46 (failure to prevent facilitation of foreign tax evasion offences) of the Criminal Finances Act 2017.

28 An offence of cheating the public revenue.

29 An offence under the law of any part of the United Kingdom consisting of being knowingly concerned in, or in taking steps with a view to, the fraudulent evasion of tax.

30 Any offence which has deception or dishonesty as one of its components.

31 The common law offences of conspiracy to defraud and perverting the course of justice.

32 An offence of attempting, conspiring or inciting the commission of an offence specified in this Schedule.

33 An offence under section 44 of the Serious Crime Act 2007 of doing an act capable of encouraging or assisting the commission of an offence specified in this Schedule.

34 An offence of aiding, abetting, counselling or procuring the commission of an offence specified in this Schedule.

35 An act which—

(a) constituted an offence under the law of a foreign country, and

(b) would have constituted an offence under any of paragraphs 1 to 34 under the law of any part of the United Kingdom if it had been done—

(i) in that part of the United Kingdom;

(ii) by a person who is linked to part of the United Kingdom (within the meaning of paragraph 5(3) of Schedule 7A to the Proceeds of Crime Act 2002 (connection with relevant part of the United Kingdom)); or

(iii) as regards the United Kingdom.

SCHEDULE 4
SUPERVISORY INFORMATION

Regulation 51(1)

1 The number of persons subject to the supervision of the supervisory authority, or in the case of a self-regulatory organisation, the number of its members ("supervised persons").

2 The number of supervised persons who are individuals.

3 In the case of a self-regulatory organisation, the number of its supervised persons who act as trust or company service providers.

4 In the case of a self-regulatory organisation, the number of applications for membership which the organisation has—

(a) received,

(b) rejected, and

(c) accepted.

5 The services provided by supervised persons.

6 The number of firms subject to the supervision of the supervisory authority which the authority considers to be—

(a) high risk;

(b) medium risk;

(c) low risk;

and for these purposes, "risk" refers to the risk that the firm will be subject to money laundering or terrorist financing.

7 The number of applications for approval received by the supervisory authority under regulation 26, and the number of those that—

(a) were refused;

(b) were accepted;

(c) are to be determined.

8 The number of approvals under regulation 26 which were not valid, or ceased to be valid under paragraph (9) of that regulation.

9 In the case of a self-regulatory organisation, the number, amount and type of disciplinary measures it has imposed in relation to contraventions of these Regulations on supervised persons.

10 The number of times the supervisory authority has—

(a) refused to register an applicant for registration under regulation 59; or

(b) exercised any powers under regulation 60.

11 The number of times the supervisory authority has exercised any powers under Part 8.

12 The number of contraventions of these Regulations committed by supervised persons.

13 The number and amount of penalties or charges which have been imposed under Part 9.

14 The number of times the supervisory authority has exercised the other powers under Part 9.

15 The number of times the supervisory authority or any of its supervised persons has made a suspicious activity disclosure to the NCA, and for these purposes, "suspicious activity disclosure" has the meaning given in regulation 104(4).

16 The number of supervised persons who have contravened requirements imposed by or under—

(a) Part 3 of the Terrorism Act 2000 (terrorist property), or

(b) Part 7 (money laundering) or 8 (investigations) of the Proceeds of Crime Act 2002.

17 Information on the money laundering and terrorist financing practices that the supervisory authority considers apply to its own sector.

18 Indications that the supervisory authority considers to suggest that a transfer of criminal funds takes place in their own sector.

SCHEDULE 5
CONNECTED PERSONS

Regulation 65(3)

Corporate Bodies

1 If the relevant person or payment service provider is a body corporate, any person who is or has been—

(a) an officer or manager of the body corporate;

(b) an officer or manager of a parent undertaking of the body corporate;

(c) an employee of the body corporate;

(d) an agent of the body corporate; or

(e) an agent of a parent undertaking of the body corporate.

Partnerships

2 If the relevant person or payment service provider is a partnership, any person who is or has been a member, manager, employee or agent of the partnership.

Unincorporated Associations

3 If the relevant person or payment service provider is an unincorporated association of persons which is not a partnership, any person who is or has been a member, an officer, manager, employee or agent of the association.

Individuals

4 If the relevant person or payment service provider is an individual, any person who is or has been an employee or agent of that individual.

SCHEDULE 6
MEANING OF "RELEVANT REQUIREMENT"

Regulation 75

1 For the purposes of Part 9 of these Regulations, "relevant requirement" means—

(a) a requirement imposed by the funds transfer regulation specified—

(i) in relation to a payment service provider of a payer, in paragraph 2;

(ii) in relation to a payment service provider of a payee, in paragraph 3;

(iii) in relation to the payment service provider of an intermediary, in paragraph 4.

(b) a requirement imposed (otherwise than on supervisory authorities, registering authorities or auction platforms) in or under the regulations specified in paragraphs 5 to 13;

(c) the following requirements imposed on auction platforms—

(i) the customer due diligence requirements in Article 19 or 20.6 of the emission allowance auctioning regulation;

(ii) the monitoring and record keeping requirements of Article 54 of the emission allowance auctioning regulation; or

(iii) the requirements imposed in regulations 18 to 21 or 24 of these Regulations;

(iv) any requirement imposed under regulations 66, 69(2), 70(7), 77(2) and (6) or 78(2) or (5) of these Regulations.

2 The requirements specified in this paragraph are those imposed in—

(a) Article 4 (information accompanying transfers of funds);

(b) Article 5 (information within the EEA);
(c) Article 6 (transfer of funds outside the EEA);
(d) Article 14 (provision of information);
(e) Article 15 (data protection);
(f) Article 16 (record retention).

3 The requirements specified in this paragraph are those imposed in—
(a) Article 7 (detection of missing information on the payer or the payee);
(b) Article 8 (transfers of funds with missing or incomplete information on the payer or the payee);
(c) Article 9 (assessment and reporting);
(d) Article 14 (provision of information);
(e) Article 15 (data protection);
(f) Article 16 (record retention).

4 The requirements specified in this paragraph are those imposed in—
(a) Article 10 (retention of information on the payer and the payee with the transfer);
(b) Article 11 (detection of missing information on the payer or the payee);
(c) Article 12 (transfer of funds with missing information on the payer or the payee);
(d) Article 13 (assessment and reporting);
(e) Article 14 (provision of information);
(f) Article 15 (data protection);
(g) Article 16 (record retention).

5 The requirements specified in this paragraph are those—
(a) imposed in—
(i) regulation 18 (risk assessment by relevant persons);
(ii) regulation 19 (policies, controls and procedures);
(iii) regulation 20 (policies, controls and procedures: group level);
(iv) regulation 21 (internal controls);
(v) regulation 22 (central contact points: electronic money issuers and payment service providers);
(vi) regulation 23 (requirement on authorised person to inform the FCA);
(vii) regulation 24 (training);
(b) imposed by supervisory authorities under regulation 25 (supervisory action).

6 The requirements specified in this paragraph are those imposed in regulation 26(1), (4), (5) and (10) (prohibition and approvals).

7 The requirements specified in this paragraph are those imposed in—
(a) regulation 27 (customer due diligence);
(b) regulation 28 (customer due diligence measures);
(c) regulation 29 (additional customer due diligence measures: credit institutions and financial institutions),
(d) regulation 30 (timing of verification);
(e) regulation 31(1) (requirement to cease transactions);
(f) regulation 33(1) and (4) to (6) (obligation to apply enhanced customer due diligence);
(g) regulation 34 (enhanced customer due diligence: credit institutions, financial institutions and correspondent relationships);
(h) regulation 35 (enhanced customer due diligence: politically exposed persons);
(i) regulation 37 (application of simplified due diligence);
(j) regulation 38(3) (electronic money).

8 The requirements specified in this paragraph are those imposed in—
(a) regulation 39(2) and (4) (reliance);
(b) regulation 40(1) and (5) to (7) (record keeping);
(c) regulation 41 (data protection).

9 The requirements specified in this paragraph are those imposed in—
(a) regulation 43 (corporate bodies: obligations);
(b) regulation 44 (trustee obligations);
(c) regulation 45(2) and (9) (register of beneficial ownership).

10 The requirements specified in this paragraph are those imposed in—

(a) regulation 56(1) and (5) (requirement to be registered);
(b) regulation 57(1) and (4) (applications for registration in a register maintained under regulations 54 or 55).

11 The requirements specified in this paragraph are those imposed in regulation 64(2) (obligations of payment service providers);

12 The requirements specified in this paragraph are those imposed under—
(a) regulation 66 (power to require information);
(b) regulation 69(2) (entry, inspection of premises without a warrant);
(c) regulation 70(7) (entry of premises under warrant);
(d) regulation 77(2) and (6) (power to impose civil penalties: suspension and removal of authorisation);
(e) regulation 78(2) and (5) (power to prohibit individuals from managing).

13 The requirement specified in this paragraph is the requirement imposed in regulation 84(1).

SCHEDULE 7

CONSEQUENTIAL AMENDMENTS

Regulation 109

PART 1

CONSEQUENTIAL AMENDMENTS TO PRIMARY LEGISLATION

Solicitors (Scotland) Act 1980

1 In section 34 of the Solicitors (Scotland) Act 1980, after subsection (1C), insert—

"(1D) Rules made under this section may make provision as to the way in which solicitors and incorporated practices are to comply with the Money Laundering, Terrorist Financing and Transfer of Funds (Information on the Payer) Regulations 2017.".

Northern Ireland Act 1998

2 In Schedule 3 to the Northern Ireland Act 1998 (reserved matters)—
(a) in paragraph 25, for "the Money Laundering Regulations 2007" substitute "the Money Laundering, Terrorist Financing and Transfer of Funds (Information on the Payer) Regulations 2017";
(b) omit paragraph 25A.

Financial Services and Markets Act 2000

3 (1) FSMA is amended as follows.

(2) In section 226 (complaints: the ombudsman scheme etc) after subsection (7) insert—

"(7A) The rules must provide that a person within subsection (7B) is eligible in relation to a complaint to which subsection (7C) applies.

(7B) A person is within this subsection if he or she has been identified by a respondent, in carrying on an activity to which the rules apply, as—
(a) a politically exposed person;
(b) a family member of a politically exposed person; or
(c) a known close associate of a politically exposed person.

(7C) This subsection applies to a complaint—
(a) that the complainant has been incorrectly identified as a person within subsection (7B); or
(b) relating to an act or omission of the respondent in consequence of the identification of the complainant as a person within subsection (7B).

(7D) In subsection (7B), "politically exposed person", "family member" and "known close associate" have the meanings given in regulation 35(12) of the Money Laundering, Terrorist Financing and Transfer of Funds (Information on the Payer) Regulations 2017.".

(3) For the heading of Part 20C (as inserted by the Bank of England and Financial Services Act 2016), substitute "Politically exposed persons: money laundering and terrorist financing".

(4) In section 333U (guidance relating to money laundering and politically exposed persons)—
(a) in the heading, after "Money laundering" insert "and terrorist financing"; and
(b) in subsection (3)—
(i) for "Secretary of State" substitute "Treasury"; and
(ii) in paragraph (b), after "by the FCA" insert "or under the ombudsman scheme".

Terrorism Act 2000

4 (1) The Terrorism Act 2000 is amended as follows.

(2) In section 21G (other permitted disclosures etc), in subsection (1)(a), for "the Money Laundering Regulations 2007 (SI 2007/2157)" substitute "the Money Laundering, Terrorist Financing and Transfer of Funds (Information on the Payer) Regulations 2017".

(3) In section 21H(4), for the words from "Directive 2005/60/EC" to "2005" substitute "Directive 2015/849/EU of the European Parliament and of the Council of 20th May 2015".

(4) Part 1 of Schedule 3A (business in the regulated sector) is amended in accordance with sub-paragraphs (5) to (10).

(5) In paragraph 1(1)—

(a) in paragraph (b)—

(i) at the end of sub-paragraph (i), omit "or";

(ii) after sub-paragraph (i), insert—

"(ia) an undertaking whose only listed activity is as a creditor under an agreement which—

(aa) falls within section 12(a) of the Consumer Credit Act 1974 (debtor-creditor-supplier agreements);

(bb) provides fixed sum credit (within the meaning given in section 10(1)(b) of the Consumer Credit Act 1974 (running-account credit and fixed-sum credit)) in relation to the provision of services; and

(cc) provides financial accommodation by way of deferred payment or payment by instalments over a period not exceeding 12 months; or";

(b) after paragraph (j), insert—

"(ja) the carrying on of local audit work within the meaning of Schedule 5 to the Local Audit and Accountability Act 2014 (eligibility and regulation of local auditors) by any firm or individual who is a local auditor within the meaning of section 4(1) of that Act (general requirements for audit);";

(c) in paragraph (q)—

(i) after "involves the" insert "making or";

(ii) for "15,000" substitute "10,000".

(6) In paragraph 1(5)(b), omit "contained in international standards and are".

(7) In paragraph 1(6), at the end of paragraph (c) for "or" substitute "and".

(8) In paragraph 2(1)—

(a) in paragraph (c) for "25" substitute "26";

(b) in paragraph (d), at the end, omit "or";

(c) at the end, insert—

"(g) the carrying on by a local authority (within the meaning given in article 3(1) of the Financial Services and Markets Act 2000 (Regulated Activities) Order 2001) of an activity which would be a regulated activity for the purposes of the Financial Services and Markets Act 2000 but for article 72G of that Order; or

(h) the preparation of a home report, which for these purposes means the documents prescribed for the purposes of sections 98, 99(1) or 101(2) of the Housing (Scotland) Act 2006.".

(9) In paragraph 2(3)—

(a) in paragraph (a), for "£64,000" substitute "£100,000;

(b) in paragraph (f), after "(r)" insert "to (t)".

(10) In paragraph 3—

(a) in sub-paragraph (1), at the appropriate place insert—

""the Capital Requirements Directive" means Directive 2013/36/EU of the European Parliament and of the Council of 26th June 2013 on access to the activity of credit institutions and the prudential supervision of credit institutions and investment firms ;";

(b) in sub-paragraph (3)—

(i) after "Capital Requirements Regulation" insert ", the Capital Requirements Directive";

(ii) after "Part as" insert "in that Regulation or".

(11) In Part 2 of Schedule 3A (supervisory authorities), in paragraph 4—

(a) in sub-paragraph (1), omit paragraphs (b), (ea) and (f) (but not the "and" after paragraph (f));

(b) in sub-paragraph (2)—

(i) after paragraph (d), insert—

"(da) the Chartered Institute of Legal Executives;";

(ii) omit paragraph (f).

Criminal Justice and Police Act 2001

5 In the Criminal Justice and Police Act 2001—

(a) in section 68(2) (application to Scotland)—

(i) in paragraph (g), for "regulation 39(6) of the Money Laundering Regulations 2007" substitute "regulation 70(7) of the Money Laundering, Terrorist Financing and Transfer of Funds (Information on the Payer) Regulations 2017";

(ii) omit paragraph (h);

(b) in Part 1 of Schedule 1 (powers of seizure to which section 50 of the 2001 Act applies)—

(i) in the heading above paragraph 73J, for "The Money Laundering Regulations 2007" substitute "The Money Laundering, Terrorist Financing and Transfer of Funds (Information on the Payer) Regulations 2017";

(ii) in paragraph 73J, for "regulation 39(6) of the Money Laundering Regulations 2007" substitute "regulation 70(7) of the Money Laundering, Terrorist Financing and Transfer of Funds (Information on the Payer) Regulations 2017";

(iii) omit paragraph 73K and the heading above it.

Proceeds of Crime Act 2002

6 (1) The Proceeds of Crime Act 2002 is amended as follows.

(2) In section 333D (other permitted disclosures etc), in subsection (1)(a) for "the Money Laundering Regulations 2007 (SI 2007/2157)" substitute "the Money Laundering, Terrorist Financing and Transfer of Funds (Information on the Payer) Regulations 2017".

(3) In section 333E (interpretation), in subsection (4), for the words from "Directive 2005/60/EC" to "2005" substitute "Directive 2015/849/EU of the European Parliament and of the Council of 20th May 2015".

(4) In Part 1 of Schedule 9 (business in the regulated sector), in paragraph 1(1)—

(a) in paragraph (b)—

(i) for "Capital Requirements Regulation", in both places, substitute "Capital Requirements Directive";

(ii) at the end of sub-paragraph (i), omit "or";

(iii) after sub-paragraph (i), insert—

"(ia) an undertaking whose only listed activity is as a creditor under an agreement which—

(aa) falls within section 12(a) of the Consumer Credit Act 1974 (debtor-creditor-supplier agreements);

(bb) provides fixed sum credit (within the meaning given in section 10(1)(b) of the Consumer Credit Act 1974 (running-account credit and fixed-sum credit)) in relation to the provision of services; and

(cc) provides financial accommodation by way of deferred payment or payment by instalments over a period not exceeding 12 months; or";

(b) after paragraph (j), insert—

"(ja) the carrying on of local audit work within the meaning of Schedule 5 to the Local Audit and Accountability Act 2014 (eligibility and regulation of local auditors) by any firm or individual who is a local auditor within the meaning of section 4(1) of that Act (general requirements for audit);";

(c) in paragraph (q)—

(i) after "involves the" insert "making or";

(ii) for "15,000" substitute "10,000".

(5) In paragraph 1(5)(b), omit "contained in international standards and are".

(6) In paragraph 1(6), at the end of paragraph (c) for "or" substitute "and".

(7) In paragraph 2—

(a) in sub-paragraph (1)(c) for "25" substitute "26";

(b) in sub-paragraph (1)(d), at the end, omit "or";

(c) at the end, insert—

"(g) the carrying on by a local authority (within the meaning given in article 3(1) of the Financial Services and Markets Act 2000 (Regulated Activities) Order 2001) of an activity which would be a regulated activity for the purposes of the Financial Services and Markets Act 2000 but for article 72G of that Order; or

(h) the preparation of a home report, which for these purposes means the documents prescribed for the purposes of sections 98, 99(1) or 101(2) of the Housing (Scotland) Act 2006.";

(d) in sub-paragraph (3)—

(i) in paragraph (a), for "£64,000" substitute "£100,000;

(ii) in paragraph (f), after "(r)" insert "to (t)".

(8) In paragraph 3—

(a) in sub-paragraph (1)—

(i) at the appropriate place insert—

""the Capital Requirements Directive" means Directive 2013/36/EU of the European Parliament and of the Council of 26th June 2013 on access to the activity of credit institutions and the prudential supervision of credit institutions and investment firms;";

(ii) at the end of the definition of "the Capital Requirements Regulation insert "of 26th June 2013 on prudential requirements for credit institutions and investment firms"; and

(b) in sub-paragraph (3)—

(i) for "the Banking Consolidation Directive" substitute "the Capital Requirements Regulation, the Capital Requirements Directive";

(ii) after "Part as", insert "in that Regulation or".

(9) In Part 2 of Schedule 9 (supervisory authorities), in paragraph 4—

(a) in sub-paragraph (1), omit paragraphs (b), (ea) and (f) (but not the "and" after paragraph (f));

(b) in sub-paragraph (2)—

(i) after paragraph (d), insert—

"(da) the Chartered Institute of Legal Executives;";

(ii) omit paragraph (f).

Counter-Terrorism Act 2008

7 In Schedule 7 to the Counter-Terrorism Act 2008 (terrorist financing and money laundering), for paragraph 45(3), substitute—

"(3) Unless otherwise defined, expressions used in this Schedule and in Directive 2015/849/EU of the European Parliament and of the Council of 20th May 2015 on the prevention of the use of the financial system for the purpose of money laundering or terrorist financing have the same meaning as in that Directive.".

Borders, Citizenship and Immigration Act 2009

8 In section 1 (general customs functions of the Secretary of State) of the Borders, Citizenship and Immigration Act 2009, in subsection (2)—

(a) in paragraph (d), for "Directive 2005/60/EC on the prevention of the use of the financial system for the purpose of money laundering and terrorist financing" substitute "Directive 2015/849/EU of the European Parliament and of the Council of 20th May 2015 on the prevention of the use of the financial system for the purpose of money laundering or terrorist financing";

(b) in paragraph (e), for "Regulation (EC) No 1781/2006 on information on the payer accompanying transfers of funds" substitute "Regulation (EU) 2015/847 of the European Parliament and of the Council of 20th May 2015 on information accompanying transfers of funds".

Crime and Courts Act 2013

9 In Schedule 17 (offences in relation to which a deferred prosecution arrangement may be entered into) to the Crime and Courts Act 2013, in paragraph 27, for "regulation 45 of the Money Laundering Regulations 2007 (SI 2007/2157)" substitute "regulation 86 of the Money Laundering, Terrorist Financing and Transfer of Funds (Information on the Payer) Regulations 2017".

Finance Act 2014

10 In Schedule 34 to the Finance Act 2014, in paragraph 6(4)(j) (criminal offences) for "regulation 45(1) of the Money Laundering Regulations 2007 (SI 2007/2157)" substitute "regulation 86(1) of the Money Laundering, Terrorist Financing and Transfer of Funds (Information on the Payer) Regulations 2017".

Bank of England and Financial Services Act 2016

11 In the Bank of England and Financial Services Act 2016—

(a) in the italic heading above section 30, after "Money laundering" insert "and terrorist financing";

(b) in section 30 (politically exposed persons: money laundering)—

(i) in the heading, after "Money laundering" insert "and terrorist financing"; and
(ii) in subsection (1) for "Secretary of State" substitute "Treasury".

PART 2
CONSEQUENTIAL AMENDMENTS TO SECONDARY LEGISLATION

Estate Agents (Undesirable Practices) (No 2) Order 1991

12 Schedule 3 (other matters) to the Estate Agents (Undesirable Practices) (No 2) Order 1991 is amended as follows—

(a) at the beginning of paragraph 2, insert "Subject to paragraph 2A";
(b) after paragraph 2, insert—

"2A

Paragraph 2 does not apply if the estate agent does not forward accurate details of the offer because the estate agent is unable to apply the customer due diligence measures required by regulation 28, and where relevant, those required by regulations 33, and 35 to 37 of the Money Laundering, Terrorist Financing and Transfer of Funds (Information on the Payer) Regulations 2017 in relation to the offeror.".

Public Interest Disclosure (Prescribed Persons) Order (Northern Ireland) 1999

13 In the Schedule (description of persons and matters) to the Public Interest Disclosure (Prescribed Persons) Order (Northern Ireland) 1999—

(a) in the entry relating to Her Majesty's Revenue and Customs, in column 2, for "regulation 23(1)(d)(vii) of the Money Laundering Regulations 2007" substitute "regulation 7(1)(c)(vii) of the Money Laundering, Terrorist Financing and Transfer of Funds (Information on the Payer) Regulations 2017";
(b) in the appropriate place, insert the following entry—

"National Crime Agency	Matters relating to compliance with— (a) the Terrorism Act 2000; (b) the Proceeds of Crime Act 2002; or (c) the Money Laundering, Terrorist Financing and Transfer of Funds (Information on the Payer) Regulations 2017"

Terrorism Act 2000 (Crown Servants and Regulators) Regulations 2001

14 In the meaning of "relevant business" in regulation 2 (interpretation) of the Terrorism Act 2000 (Crown Servants and Regulators) Regulations 2001 for "regulation 3(1)(a) to (h) of the Money Laundering Regulations 2007" substitute "regulation 8(2)(a) to (h) of the Money Laundering, Terrorist Financing and Transfer of Funds (Information on the Payer) Regulations 2017".

Representation of the People (England and Wales) Regulations 2001

15 In regulation 114(3)(b) in the Representation of the People (England and Wales) Regulations 2001 (sale of full register to credit reference agencies), for "the Money Laundering Regulations 2007" substitute "the Money Laundering, Terrorist Financing and Transfer of Funds (Information on the Payer) Regulations 2017".

Representation of the People (Scotland) Regulations 2001

16 In regulation 113(3)(b) in the Representation of the People (Scotland) Regulations 2001 (sale of full register to credit reference agencies), for "the Money Laundering Regulations 2007" substitute "Money Laundering, Terrorist Financing and Transfer of Funds (Information on the Payer) Regulations 2017".

Financial Services and Markets Act 2000 (Regulated Activities) Order 2001

17 In article 72E(9) in the Financial Services and Markets Act 2000 (Regulated Activities) Order 2001 (Business and Angel-led Enterprise Capital Funds) for "the Money Laundering Regulations 2007" substitute "the Money Laundering, Terrorist Financing and Transfer of Funds (Information on the Payer) Regulations 2017".

Open-Ended Investment Companies Regulations 2001

18 Regulation 48 (bearer shares) of the Open-Ended Investment Companies Regulations 2001 is amended as follows—

(a) the existing text is renumbered as paragraph (1);

(b) in that paragraph (1), after "investment company" insert "authorised before the day on which the Money Laundering, Terrorist Financing and Transfer of Funds (Information on the Payer) Regulations 2017 came into force ("the relevant date")";

(c) after paragraph (1) insert—

"(2) An open-ended investment company authorised on or after the relevant date may not issue any bearer shares under paragraph (1), and any provision in the instrument of incorporation of such an open-ended investment company purporting to authorise it to do so is void.

(3) Paragraph (2) does not apply to an open-ended investment company if—

(a) an application for an authorisation order was made in relation to that open-ended investment company before the relevant date; and

(b) that application was not determined until a date on or after the relevant date.".

Proceeds of Crime Act 2002 (Disclosure of information to and by Lord Advocate and Scottish Ministers) Order 2003

19 In article 3(d) (disclosure of information by Lord Advocate and by Scottish Ministers) of the Proceeds of Crime Act 2002 (Disclosure of Information to and by Lord Advocate and Scottish Ministers) Order 2003 for "the Money Laundering Regulations 2007" substitute "the Money Laundering, Terrorist Financing and Transfer of Funds (Information on the Payer) Regulations 2017".

Proceeds of Crime Act 2002 (Failure to Disclose Money Laundering: Specified Training) Order 2003

20 In article 2 of the Proceeds of Crime Act 2002 (Failure to Disclose Money Laundering: Specified Training) Order 2003 (training specified), for "regulation 21 of the Money Laundering Regulations 2007" substitute "regulation 24 of the Money Laundering, Terrorist Financing and Transfer of Funds (Information on the Payer) Regulations 2017".

Legislative and Regulatory Reform (Regulatory Functions) Order 2007

21 (1) Part 1 of the Schedule to the Legislative and Regulatory Reform (Regulatory Functions) Order 2007 is amended as follows.

(2) In the reference to "Her Majesty's Revenue and Customs" for "the Money Laundering Regulations 2007" substitute "the Money Laundering, Terrorist Financing and Transfer of Funds (Information on the Payer) Regulations 2017".

(3) In the reference to a "professional body" for "Schedule 3 to the Money Laundering Regulations 2007" substitute "Schedule 1 to the Money Laundering, Terrorist Financing and Transfer of Funds (Information on the Payer) Regulations 2017".

Representation of the People (Northern Ireland) Regulations 2008

22 In regulation 112(3)(b) of the Representation of the People (Northern Ireland) Regulations 2008 (sale of full register etc to credit reference agencies), for paragraph (i), substitute—

"(i) the Money Laundering, Terrorist Financing and Transfer of Funds (Information on the Payer) Regulations 2017;".

Transfer of Tribunal Functions and Revenue and Customs Appeals Order 2009

23 In paragraph 2(6) of Schedule 3 (transitional and saving provisions) to the Transfer of Tribunal Functions and Revenue and Customs Appeals Order 2009, in the definition of "review and appeal provisions"—

(a) in paragraph (i) for "regulations 43 and 44 of the Money Laundering Regulations 2007" substitute "regulations 94 to 100 of the Money Laundering, Terrorist Financing and Transfer of Funds (Information on the Payer) Regulations 2017";

(b) omit paragraph (j).

Payment Services Regulations 2009

24 (1) The Payment Services Regulations 2009 are amended as follows.

(2) In regulation 2(1) (interpretation), in the definition of "the money laundering directive" for "Directive 2005/60/EC of the European Parliament and of the Council of 26th October 2005 on the prevention of the use of the financial system for the purpose of money laundering and terrorist financing" substitute "Directive 2015/849/EU of the European Parliament and of the Council of 20th May 2015 on the prevention of the use of the financial system for the purpose of money laundering or terrorist financing".

(3) In regulation 6(7) (conditions for authorisation as a payment institution) for "the Money Laundering Regulations 2007" substitute "the Money Laundering, Terrorist Financing and Transfer of Funds (Information on the Payer) Regulations 2017".

(4) In regulation 13 (conditions for registration as a small payment institution)—

(a) in sub-paragraph (a) of paragraph (4) for "the Money Laundering Regulations 2007" substitute "the Money Laundering, Terrorist Financing and Transfer of Funds (Information on the Payer) Regulations 2017",

(b) in paragraph (6) for "the Money Laundering Regulations 2007" substitute "the Money Laundering, Terrorist Financing and Transfer of Funds (Information on the Payer) Regulations 2017".

(5) In regulation 25(4)(a) (supervision of firms exercising passport rights) for "the Money Laundering Regulations 2007" substitute "the Money Laundering, Terrorist Financing and Transfer of Funds (Information on the Payer) Regulations 2017".

(6) In regulation 29 (use of agents)—

(a) in sub-paragraph (a)(ii)(aa) of paragraph (3) for "the Money Laundering Regulations 2007" substitute "the Money Laundering, Terrorist Financing and Transfer of Funds (Information on the Payer) Regulations 2017",

(b) in subparagraph (c)(i) of paragraph (6) for "the Money Laundering Regulations 2007" substitute "the Money Laundering, Terrorist Financing and Transfer of Funds (Information on the Payer) Regulations 2017".

(7) In regulation 119(2) (duty to co-operate and exchange of information) for "regulation 49A of the Money Laundering Regulations 2007" substitute "regulation 105 of the Money Laundering, Terrorist Financing and Transfer of Funds (Information on the Payer) Regulations 2017".

(8) In paragraph 6 of Schedule 2 (information to be included in or with an application for authorisation)—

(a) for "the Money Laundering Regulations 2007" substitute "the Money Laundering, Terrorist Financing and Transfer of Funds (Information on the Payer) Regulations 2017";

(b) for "Regulation (EC) No 1781/2006 of the European Parliament and of the Council of 15 November 2006 on information on the payer accompanying transfers of funds" substitute "Regulation 2015/847/EU of the European Parliament and of the Council of 20 May 2015 on information accompanying transfers of funds".

(9) In paragraph 3(d)(ii) in Part 1 of Schedule 5 (application and modification of the Financial Services and Markets Act 2000) for "the Money Laundering Regulations 2007" substitute "the Money Laundering, Terrorist Financing and Transfer of Funds (Information on the Payer) Regulations 2017".

(10) In paragraph 10(h) in Part 2 of Schedule 5 (application and modification of secondary legislation) for "the Money Laundering Regulations 2007" substitute "the Money Laundering, Terrorist Financing and Transfer of Funds (Information on the Payer) Regulations 2017".

Companies (Disclosure of Address) Regulations 2009

25 In paragraph 7(b) of Schedule 2 (disclosure to a credit reference agency) of the Companies (Disclosure of Address) Regulations 2009—

(a) for "the Money Laundering Regulations 2007" substitute "the Money Laundering, Terrorist Financing and Transfer of Funds (Information on the Payer) Regulations 2017";

(b) for "Directive 2005/60/EC of the European Parliament and of the Council of 26 October 2005 on the prevention of the use of the financial system for the purpose of money laundering and terrorist financing" substitute "Directive 2015/849/EU of the European Parliament and of the Council of 20 May 2015 on the prevention of the use of the financial system for the purpose of money laundering or terrorist financing".

Overseas Companies Regulations 2009

26 In paragraph 7(b) of Schedule 2 (disclosure to a credit reference agency) of the Overseas Companies Regulations 2009—

(a) for "the Money Laundering Regulations 2007" substitute "the Money Laundering, Terrorist Financing and Transfer of Funds (Information on the Payer) Regulations 2017";

(b) for "Directive 2005/60/EC of the European Parliament and of the Council of 26 October 2005 on the prevention of the use of the financial system for the purpose of money laundering and terrorist financing" substitute "Directive 2015/849/EU of the European Parliament and of the Council of 20 May 2015 on the prevention of the use of the financial system for the purpose of money laundering or terrorist financing".

Defence and Security Public Contracts Regulations 2011

27 In regulation 23(1)(i) of Part 4 (criteria for the rejection of economic operators) to the Defence and Security Public Contracts Regulations 2011, at the end insert "or of the Money Laundering, Terrorist Financing and Transfer of Funds (Information on the Payer) Regulations 2017".

Electronic Money Regulations 2011

28 (1) The Electronic Money Regulations 2011 are amended as follows.

(2) In regulation 2(1) (interpretation), in the definition of "money laundering directive" for "Directive 2005/60/EC of the European Parliament and of the Council of 26th October 2005 on the prevention of the use of the financial system for the purpose of money laundering and terrorist financing" substitute "Directive 2015/849/EU of the European Parliament and of the Council of 20th May 2015 on the prevention of the use of the financial system for the purpose of money laundering or terrorist financing".

(3) In regulation 6(7) (conditions for authorisation) for "the Money Laundering Regulations 2007" substitute "the Money Laundering, Terrorist Financing and Transfer of Funds (Information on the Payer) Regulations 2017".

(4) In regulation 13 (conditions for registration)—

(a) in subparagraph (a) of paragraph (8) for "the Money Laundering Regulations 2007" substitute "the Money Laundering, Terrorist Financing and Transfer of Funds (Information on the Payer) Regulations 2017";

(b) in paragraph (10) for "the Money Laundering Regulations 2007" substitute "the Money Laundering, Terrorist Financing and Transfer of Funds (Information on the Payer) Regulations 2017".

(5) In regulation 30(4)(a) (supervision of firms exercising passport rights) for "the Money Laundering Regulations 2007" substitute "the Money Laundering, Terrorist Financing and Transfer of Funds (Information on the Payer) Regulations 2017".

(6) In regulation 34 (requirement for agents to be registered)—

(a) in subparagraph (a)(ii)(aa) in paragraph (3) for "the Money Laundering Regulations 2007" substitute "the Money Laundering, Terrorist Financing and Transfer of Funds (Information on the Payer) Regulations 2017";

(b) in subparagraph (c)(i) in paragraph (6) for "the Money Laundering Regulations 2007" substitute "the Money Laundering, Terrorist Financing and Transfer of Funds (Information on the Payer) Regulations 2017".

(7) In regulation 71(2) (duty to cooperate and exchange information), in the words before sub-paragraph (a), for "regulation 49A of the Money Laundering Regulations 2007" substitute "regulation 105 of the Money Laundering, Terrorist Financing and Transfer of Funds (Information on the Payer) Regulations 2017".

(8) In paragraph 6 of Schedule 1 (information to be included in or with an application for authorisation)—

(a) for "the Money Laundering Regulations 2007" substitute "the Money Laundering, Terrorist Financing and Transfer of Funds (Information on the Payer) Regulations 2017";

(b) for "Regulation (EC) No 1781/2006 of the European Parliament and of the Council of 15 November 2006 on information on the payer accompanying transfers of funds" substitute "Regulation 2015/847/EU of the European Parliament and of the Council of 20 May 2015 on information accompanying transfers of funds".

Terrorism Act 2000 and Proceeds of Crime Act 2002 (Business in the Regulated Sector) (No 2) Order 2012

29 (1) Regulation 4 (review) of the Terrorism Act 2000 and Proceeds of Crime Act 2002 (Business in the Regulated Sector) (No 2) Order 2012 is amended as follows.

(2) In paragraph (2) for "Directive 2005/60/EC of the European Parliament and of the Council on the protection of the use of the financial system for the purpose of money laundering and terrorist financing" substitute "Directive 2015/849/EU of the European Parliament and of the Council of 20th May 2015 on the prevention of the use of the financial system for the purpose of money laundering or terrorist financing".

(3) In paragraph (4) for "the end of the period of five years beginning with the day on which this Order comes into force" substitute "26th June 2022".

Payment to Treasury of Penalties (Enforcement Costs) Order 2013

30 In regulation 2(1)(d) (enforcement of powers) of the Payment to Treasury of Penalties (Enforcement Costs) Order 2013 for "regulation 42 of the Money Laundering Regulations 2007" substitute "regulation 76 of the Money Laundering, Terrorist Financing and Transfer of Funds (Information on the Payer) Regulations 2017".

Public Interest Disclosure (Prescribed Persons) Order 2014

31 In the Schedule (description of persons and matters) to the Public Interest Disclosure (Prescribed Persons) Order 2014, in the entry relating to the National Crime Agency, for the words in the second column substitute—

"Matters relating to—

(a) corrupt individuals or companies offering or receiving bribes to secure a benefit for themselves or others;

(b) compliance with—

(i) the Terrorism Act 2000;

(ii) the Proceeds of Crime Act 2002; or

(iii) the Money Laundering, Terrorist Financing and Transfer of Funds (Information on the Payer) Regulations 2017".

Companies (Disclosure of Date of Birth Information) Regulations 2015

32 In paragraph 7(b) of Schedule 2 (disclosure to a credit reference agency) to the Companies (Disclosure of Date of Birth Information) Regulations 2015—

(a) for "the Money Laundering Regulations 2007" substitute "the Money Laundering, Terrorist Financing and Transfer of Funds (Information on the Payer) Regulations 2017";

(b) for "Directive 2005/60/EC of the European Parliament and of the Council of 26 October 2005 on the prevention of the use of the financial system for the purpose of money laundering and terrorist financing" substitute "Directive 2015/849/EU of the European Parliament and of the Council of 20 May 2015 on the prevention of the use of the financial system for the purpose of money laundering or terrorist financing".

Payment Accounts Regulations 2015

33 In regulation 25(1)(b) of Part 4 (refusal of application) in the Payment Accounts Regulation 2015 for "the Money Laundering Regulations 2007" substitute "the Money Laundering, Terrorist Financing and Transfer of Funds (Information on the Payer) Regulations 2017".

Register of People with Significant Control Regulations 2016

34 In paragraph 8(b) of Schedule 4 (disclosure to a credit reference agency) of the Register of People with Significant Control Regulations 2016—

(a) in paragraph (i) for "the Money Laundering Regulations 2007" substitute "the Money Laundering, Terrorist Financing and Transfer of Funds (Information on the Payer) Regulations 2017";

(b) in paragraph (iii) for "Directive 2005/60/EC of the European Parliament and of the Council on the prevention of the use of the financial system for the purpose of money laundering and terrorist financing" substitute "Directive 2015/849/EU of the European Parliament and of the Council on the prevention of the use of the financial system for the purpose of money laundering or terrorist financing".

Economic Growth (Regulatory Functions) Order 2017

35 In Part 1 of the Schedule to the Economic Growth (Regulatory Functions) Order 2017, in the entry for Her Majesty's Revenue and Customs, for "the Money Laundering Regulations 2007" substitute "the Money Laundering, Terrorist Financing and Transfer of Funds (Information on the Payer) Regulations 2017".

2017/876

FACILITATION OF TAX EVASION OFFENCES (GUIDANCE ABOUT PREVENTION) REGULATIONS 2017

Made . . . . *4 September 2017*

Laid before Parliament . . . . .6 *September 2017*

Coming into force . . . . .30 *September 2017*

The Chancellor of the Exchequer, in exercise of the power conferred by section 47(1) and (4) of the Criminal Finances Act 2017 ("the Act"), and having, in accordance with section 47(3) of the Act, consulted the Scottish Ministers, the Welsh Ministers, and the Department of Justice in Northern Ireland in preparing the guidance mentioned in regulation 2, makes the following Regulations:

1 Citation and commencement

These Regulations may be cited as the Facilitation of Tax Evasion Offences (Guidance About Prevention) Regulations 2017 and come into force on 30th September 2017.

2 Guidance about preventing facilitation of tax evasion offences

The guidance titled "Tackling tax evasion: Government guidance for the corporate offence of failure to prevent the criminal facilitation of tax evasion" dated 1st September 2017 comes into operation on 30th September 2017.

Note—The Guidance is reproduced below.

2017/904

INFECTED BLOOD SCHEMES (APPLICATION OF SECTIONS 731, 733 AND 734 OF THE INCOME TAX (TRADING AND OTHER INCOME) ACT 2005) ORDER 2017

Made . . . . .11 *September 2017*

Laid before the House of Commons . . . . .12 *September 2017*

Coming into force . . . . .23 *October 2017*

The Treasury make the following Order in exercise of the power conferred by section 732(2) of the Income Tax (Trading and Other Income) Act 2005.

1 Citation, commencement and interpretation

(1) This Order may be cited as the Infected Blood Schemes (Application of Sections 731, 733 and 734 of the Income Tax (Trading and Other Income) Act 2005) Order 2017 and comes into force on 23rd October 2017.

(2) In this Order "Infected Blood Scheme" has the meaning given in section 731(7) of the Income Tax (Trading and Other Income) Act 2005 (treated as inserted by article 2(2)(b)).

2 Application of sections 731, 733 and 734 of the Income Tax (Trading and Other Income) Act 2005

(1) Sections 731, 733 and 734 of the Income Tax (Trading and Other Income) Act 2005 have effect with the following modifications in relation to payments made pursuant to an Infected Blood Scheme.

(2) In section 731 (periodical payments of personal injury damages)—

(*a*) in subsection (2)—

(i) the "or" at the end of paragraph (*d*) is treated as omitted; and

(ii) after paragraph (*e*) there is treated as inserted—

", or

(*f*) an Infected Blood Scheme."

(*b*) after subsection (6) there is treated as inserted—

"(7) In this section and sections 733 and 734, "Infected Blood Scheme" means a scheme for the purpose of making payments and providing support to, or in respect of, individuals infected with Hepatitis C, HIV or both, through contaminated blood or blood products used by the NHS, which is—

(*a*) in relation to England, established under sections 1 and 2 of the National Health Service Act 2006 and administered by the NHS Business Services Authority,

(*b*) in relation to Wales, established under sections 1 to 3 of the National Health Service (Wales) Act 2006 and administered by the Velindre NHS Trust, or

(*c*) in relation to Northern Ireland, established under sections 2 and 3 of the Health and Social Care (Reform) Act (Northern Ireland) 2009 and administered by the Regional Business Services Organisation.".

(3) For section 733(*a*) (persons entitled to exemptions for personal injury payments), there is treated as substituted—

"(*a*) the person ("A") who is entitled to the damages under the order, agreement, undertaking, to the payments under the Infected Blood Scheme or to the compensation under the award in question,".

(4) In section 734(1)(*a*) (payments from trusts for injured persons) for "or undertaking" there is treated as substituted ", undertaking or Infected Blood Scheme".

2017 No 988

SECTIONS 106B, 106C AND 106D OF THE TAXES MANAGEMENT ACT 1970 (SPECIFIED THRESHOLD AMOUNT) REGULATIONS 2017

Made . . . .*11 October 2017*
Laid before the House of Commons . . . .*13 October 2017*
Coming into force . . . .*3 November 2017*

These Regulations are made by the Treasury in exercise of the powers conferred by sections 106F(2) and (3) and 106H(2) and (3) of the Taxes Management Act 1970.

1 Citation and commencement

These Regulations may be cited as the Sections 106B, 106C and 106D of the Taxes Management Act 1970 (Specified Threshold Amount) Regulations 2017 and come into force on 3rd November 2017.

2 Interpretation

(1) In these Regulations—

(*a*) "CRS" means the common reporting standard for automatic exchange of financial account information in tax matters developed by the Organisation for Economic Co-operation and Development as amended from time to time;

(*b*) "CRS arrangements" means the arrangements relating to the CRS described in paragraph (2).

(*c*) "excluded offshore income tax or capital gains tax" means income tax or capital gains tax chargeable on or by reference to offshore income, assets or activities which, at the relevant time, is reportable to the Commissioners for Her Majesty's Revenue and Customs pursuant to—

(i) CRS arrangements; or

(ii) article 8 of Council Directive 2011/16/EU.

(*d*) "relevant time" means the time when the event giving rise to income tax or capital gains tax chargeable on or by reference to offshore income, assets or activities occurs;

(*e*) "TMA 1970" means the Taxes Management Act 1970.

(2) The arrangements relating to the CRS referred to in paragraph (1)(*b*) are arrangements made to ensure automatic exchange of financial account information between the United Kingdom and the territories specified in the Schedule to these Regulations meeting the CRS.

3 Threshold amount for the purposes of sections 106B to 106D of TMA 1970

The threshold amount for a year of assessment for the purposes of sections 106B to 106D of TMA 1970 (offences relating to certain failures to comply with sections 7 or 8 of TMA 1970 by a taxpayer chargeable to income tax or capital gains tax on or by reference to offshore income, assets or activities) is £25,000.

4 Whether the threshold amount has been exceeded in relation to a person for the purposes of sections 106B to 106D of TMA 1970 must be determined by reference to—

(*a*) regulations 5 and 6 for the purposes of section 106B of TMA 1970 (offence of failure to give notice of being chargeable to tax);

(*b*) regulation 7 for the purposes of section 106C of TMA 1970 (offence of failing to deliver a tax return);

(*c*) regulations 8 and 9 for the purposes of section 106D of TMA 1970 (offence of making an inaccurate return).

5 Calculation of the total amount of income tax and capital gains tax chargeable on or by reference to offshore income, assets or activities for the purposes of section 106B of TMA 1970

The total amount of income and capital gains tax chargeable for a year of assessment on or by reference to offshore income, assets or activities for the purposes of section 106B of TMA 1970 ("the section 106B amount") must be calculated in accordance with the applicable provisions of paragraphs 7 and 11 of Schedule 41 to the Finance Act 2008 (penalty for failure to notify) ("paragraphs 7 and 11") construed as described in regulation 6.

6 Paragraphs 7 and 11 must be construed as if—

(*a*) the purpose of those paragraphs is to calculate the section 106B amount (with references to "potential lost revenue" construed accordingly); and

(*b*) those paragraphs have effect only in relation to income tax or capital gains tax chargeable on or by reference to offshore income, assets or activities (other than excluded offshore income tax or capital gains tax).

7 Calculation of the total amount of income tax and capital gains tax chargeable on or by reference to offshore income, assets or activities for the purposes of section 106C of TMA 1970

The total amount of income and capital gains tax chargeable for a year of assessment for the purposes of section 106C of TMA 1970 is the amount of any liability to income tax or capital gains tax chargeable on or by reference to offshore income, assets or activities (other than excluded offshore income tax or capital gains tax) which would have been shown in the return in question.

8 Calculation of the increase in the amount of income tax and capital gains tax chargeable on or by reference to offshore income, assets or activities for the purposes of section 106D of TMA 1970

The increase in the amount of income and capital gains tax chargeable on or by reference to offshore income, assets or activities for a year of assessment for the purposes of section 106D of TMA 1970 ("the section 106D amount") must be calculated in accordance with the applicable provisions of paragraphs 5, 6 and 7 of Schedule 24 to the Finance Act 2007 (inaccuracy in taxpayer's document) ("paragraphs 5, 6 and 7") construed as described in regulation 9.

9

Paragraphs 5, 6 and 7 must be construed as if—

(*a*) the purpose of those paragraphs is to calculate the section 106D amount (with references to "potential lost revenue" construed accordingly);

(*b*) those paragraphs have effect only in relation to income tax or capital gains tax chargeable on or by reference to offshore income, assets or activities (other than excluded offshore income tax or capital gains tax); and

(*c*) for the purposes of paragraph 6, the inaccuracy were a careless inaccuracy as described in paragraph 3(1)(*a*) of Schedule 24 to the Finance Act 2007.

SCHEDULE

Regulation 2(2)

Arrangements relating to the CRS: specified territories

Andorra, Anguilla, Antigua and Barbuda, Argentina, Aruba, Australia, Austria, The Bahamas, Bahrain, Barbados, Belgium, Belize, Bermuda, Brazil, British Virgin Islands, Brunei Darussalam, Bulgaria, Canada, Cayman Islands, Chile, China, Colombia, Cook Islands, Costa Rica, Croatia, Curaçao, Cyprus, Czech Republic, Denmark, Dominica, Estonia, Faroe Islands, Finland, France, Germany, Ghana, Gibraltar, Greece, Greenland, Grenada, Guernsey, Hong Kong, Hungary, Iceland, India, Indonesia, Ireland, Isle of Man, Israel, Italy, Japan, Jersey, Korea (South), Kuwait, Latvia, Lebanon, Liechtenstein, Lithuania, Luxembourg, Macau, Malaysia, Malta, Marshall Islands, Mauritius, Mexico, Monaco, Montserrat, Nauru, Netherlands (including Bonaire, Sint Eustatius and Saba), New Zealand (not including Tokelau), Niue, Norway, Panama, Poland, Portugal, Qatar, Romania, Russia, Saint Kitts and Nevis, Saint Lucia, Saint Vincent and the Grenadines, Samoa, San Marino, Saudi Arabia, Seychelles, Singapore, Sint Maarten, Slovak Republic, Slovenia, South Africa, Spain, Sweden, Switzerland, Trinidad and Tobago, Turkey, Turks and Caicos Islands, United Arab Emirates, Uruguay, Vanuatu.

2017/1022 (W 260)

TAX COLLECTION AND MANAGEMENT (ADMINISTRATION) (WALES) REGULATIONS 2017

Made . . . . .23 *October 2017*
Laid before the National Assembly for Wales . . . . .26 *October 2017*
Coming into force in accordance with regulation 1(2)

The Welsh Ministers make the following Regulations in exercise of the powers conferred on them by sections 14(1), 27(7)(*a*), 101(3) and (4), 163(1) and (2), and 189(1)(*b*) of the Tax Collection and Management (Wales) Act 2016.

PART 1
GENERAL

1 Title and commencement

(1) The title of these Regulations is the Tax Collection and Management (Administration) (Wales) Regulations 2017.

(2) These Regulations come into force on 1 April 2018 except for regulations contained in Parts 1 and 2 which come into force on 21 November 2017.

2 Interpretation

In these Regulations—

"the TCM Act" ("y *Ddeddf CRhT*") means the Tax Collection and Management (Wales) Act 2016;

"document" ("*dogfen*") means information, a document or part of a document;

"document in dispute" ("*dogfen y mae anghydfod yn ei chylch*") is a document over which there is a dispute between WRA and a person who has been given an information notice as to whether the document is subject to legal professional privilege;

"notice recipient" ("*derbynnydd yr hysbysiad*") means the taxpayer who is given a notice under section 86 of the TCM Act or third party who is given a notice under section 87 or 89 of the TCM Act, or a person authorised to act on their behalf; and

"working day" ("*diwrnod gwaith*") means any day other than a non-business day within the meaning of section 92 of the Bills of Exchange Act 1882.

PART 2

WRA

3 Delegation of functions

The Natural Resources Body for Wales is prescribed as a person to whom WRA may delegate any of its functions in relation to landfill disposals tax under section 14(1) of the TCM Act.

4 Specification of planning period

The period beginning with 1 April 2018 and ending on 31 March 2019 is prescribed as the first planning period for the purposes of section 27(7)(*a*) of the TCM Act.

PART 3

RATES OF INTEREST

5 Meaning of "Bank of England rate"

(1) In this Part, the "Bank of England rate" that applies to a day is the official bank rate as last announced at the meeting of the Bank of England Monetary Policy Committee held prior to that day.

(2) But where a day falls within 3 working days of a meeting at which an announcement referred to in paragraph (1) was made, the "Bank of England rate" for that day means the rate as determined under that paragraph as if that meeting had not taken place.

6 Late payment interest rate

The late payment interest rate for the purposes of section 157 of the TCM Act is the percentage per annum found by applying the following formula—

Bank of England rate + 2.5

7 Repayment interest rate

The repayment interest rate for the purposes of section 161 of the TCM Act is the higher of—

(*a*) 0.5% per annum; and

(*b*) the Bank of England rate.

PART 4

RESOLUTION OF DISPUTES AS TO WHETHER A DOCUMENT IS SUBJECT TO LEGAL PROFESSIONAL PRIVILEGE

8 Application of this Part

This Part applies where—

(*a*) WRA has issued an information notice to a person to provide information or produce a document—

(i) during the course of correspondence; or

(ii) during the course of an inspection under Part 4 of the TCM Act, and

(*b*) there is a dispute between WRA and the notice recipient as to whether a document which has been requested is subject to legal professional privilege.

9 Requirement to provide information and produce documents not in dispute

Nothing in this Part affects—

(*a*) any requirement under an information notice to provide information or produce a document which is not in dispute; or

(*b*) the powers under Part 4 of the TCM Act to inspect premises and other property.

10 Procedure where information notice given in correspondence is in dispute

(1) The following procedure applies where there is a dispute falling within regulation 8(*a*)(i).

(2) On receipt of the information notice, the notice recipient must—

(*a*) specify in a list each document required under the information notice which is in dispute, with a description of the nature and contents of that document; and

(*b*) serve that list on WRA by the date given in the information notice for producing the document.

(3) But no description of a document is required where such a description would itself give rise to a dispute over privilege.

(4) Within 20 working days of receiving the list referred to in paragraph (2), WRA must notify the notice recipient of any document on the list that it requires to be produced and which it considers is not privileged.

(5) On receipt of notification under paragraph (4), the notice recipient must—

(*a*) produce any document which he or she agrees is not privileged; and

(*b*) to the extent that the status of any document remains in dispute, make an application to the tribunal.

(6) An application under paragraph (5)(*b*) must be—

(*a*) accompanied by a copy of the documents which remain in dispute; and

(*b*) made within a reasonable time to be agreed between the notice recipient and WRA, but in any event no later than 20 working days after the date of the notification given by WRA under paragraph (4).

11 Procedure where information notice given during inspection of premises is in dispute

(1) The following procedure applies where there is a dispute falling within regulation 8(*a*)(ii).

(2) On receipt of the information notice, the notice recipient must—

(*a*) indicate to WRA each document required under the information notice which is in dispute; and

(*b*) place any document in dispute in an appropriate container which prevents the contents being visible.

(3) The container must be—

(*a*) sealed, labelled and signed by the notice recipient;

(*b*) countersigned by WRA; and

(*c*) retained by WRA.

(4) Within 42 working days of receiving the container, WRA must—

(*a*) deliver the container to the tribunal with the seal intact together with an application to the tribunal; and

(*b*) send a copy of that application to the notice recipient.

12 Compliance with information notice

Where a notice recipient complies with the procedure set out in this Part, that person is to be treated as having complied with the information notice in relation to any document in dispute until the tribunal determines the status of the document or until an agreement has been reached under regulation 14.

13 Finding of the tribunal

(1) When an application is made under regulation 10(5)(*b*) or 11(4), the tribunal must—

(*a*) resolve the dispute by confirming whether and to what extent the document is or is not privileged; and

(*b*) direct which part or parts of a document (if any) must be disclosed.

(2) The tribunal must ensure that any document in dispute is not inappropriately disclosed to any person pending the tribunal's determination.

14 Resolution of disputes by agreement

A dispute falling within this Part may be resolved at any time by WRA and the notice recipient reaching an agreement, whether in writing or otherwise.

TACKLING TAX EVASION: GOVERNMENT GUIDANCE FOR THE CORPORATE OFFENCES OF FAILURE TO PREVENT THE CRIMINAL FACILITATION OF TAX EVASION.

Government guidance

1st September 2017

Contents

1. INTRODUCTION

1.1 Aim of the legislation

The Government believes that relevant bodies should be criminally liable where they fail to prevent those who act for, or on their behalf from criminally facilitating tax evasion.

The new offences will be committed where a relevant body fails to prevent an associated person *criminally* facilitating the evasion of a tax, and this will be the case whether the tax evaded is owed in the UK or in a foreign country.

Previously, attributing criminal liability to a relevant body required prosecutors to show that the senior members of the relevant body were involved in and aware of the illegal activity, typically those at the Board of Directors level. This had a number of consequences:

- It can be more difficult to hold a large multinational organisation to account. In large multinational organisations decision making is often decentralised and decisions are often taken at a level lower than that of the Board of Directors, with the effect that the relevant body can be shielded from criminal liability. This also created an un-level playing field in comparison to smaller businesses where the Board of Directors will be more actively involved in the day-to-day activities of a business
- The common law method of criminal attribution may have acted as an incentive for the most senior members of an organisation to turn a blind eye to the criminal acts of its representatives in order to shield the relevant body from criminal liability
- The common law may also have acted as a disincentive to internal reporting of suspected illegal tax activity to the most senior members, who would be required to act upon such reporting since otherwise the corporate entity might be criminally liable.

The cumulative effect was an environment that could do more to foster corporate monitoring and self-reporting of criminal activity related to facilitating tax evasion. This meant that bodies that refrained from implementing good corporate governance and strong reporting procedures were harder to prosecute, and in some cases lacked a strong incentive to invest in preventative procedures.

It was those bodies that preserved their ignorance of criminality within their organisation that the earlier criminal law could most advantage.

The new corporate offence therefore aims to overcome the difficulties in attributing criminal liability to relevant bodies for the criminal acts of employees, agents or those that provide services for or on their behalf.

The new offence, however, does not radically alter what is criminal, it simply focuses on who is held to account for acts contrary to the current criminal law. It does this by focussing on the failure to prevent the crimes of those who act for or on behalf of a corporation, rather than trying to attribute criminal acts to that corporation.

The legislation aims to tackle crimes committed by those who act for or on behalf of a relevant body. The legislation does not hold relevant bodies to account for the crimes of their customers, nor does it require them to prevent their customers from committing tax evasion. Nor is the legislation designed to capture the misuse of legitimate products and services that are provided to customers in good faith, where the individual advisor and relevant body did not know that its products were intended to be used for tax evasion purposes.

The Government recognises that any regime that is risk-based and proportionate cannot also be a zero failure regime. If a relevant body can demonstrate that it has put in place a system of reasonable procedures that identifies and mitigates its tax evasion facilitation risks, then prosecution is unlikely as it will be able to raise a defence.

1.2 Purpose of guidance

This guidance explains the policy behind the new offences and is intended to help relevant bodies understand the types of processes and procedures that can be put in place to prevent associated persons from criminally facilitating tax evasion. It will inform the conduct of a risk assessment and the creation of procedures proportionate to that risk.

The guidance is designed to be of general application and is formulated around the following six guiding principles:

- **Risk assessment**
- **Proportionality of risk-based prevention procedures**
- **Top level commitment**
- **Due diligence**
- **Communication (including training)**
- **Monitoring and review**

The Government guidance aims to:

- Provide guidance to relevant bodies on how they might conduct an assessment of the risk of their representatives criminally facilitating tax evasion
- Help relevant bodies adopt a more effective, risk-based and outcomes-focused approach to mitigating the risk of associated persons criminally facilitating tax evasion
- Assist consideration of whether the reasonable procedures defence is available
- Enhance the understanding of Government expectations and help relevant bodies to assess the adequacy of their existing systems and controls, and remedy deficiencies
- Assist trade bodies in the formulation of more detailed sector-specific procedures.

The guidance and examples are intended to be illustrative and cannot cover every form of risk of associated persons criminally facilitating tax evasion that a relevant body may face. The examples present ways, but not the only ways, in which relevant bodies might comply with the requirement of "reasonable procedures". Similarly, there are many examples of poor practices that have not been expressly covered. The examples set out in this guidance are included only to assist with the illustration and explanation of how the key principles operate. It is not possible for illustrative examples to replicate the level of detail to be found in real cases. The factual examples are necessarily simplified and therefore to some extent artificial. It is important to look past, and not place undue reliance upon, superficial similarities between a real case and any of the illustrative examples in this guidance. Instead the principles underpinning the illustrative examples need to be carefully considered and applied.

The guidance is not prescriptive or a one-size-fits-all document. It is not a checklist of things that all relevant bodies must do to reduce their risk of liability under the corporate criminal offences, and should not be used as such.

The guidance should be considered and applied in a risk-based and proportionate way. This includes taking into account the size, nature and complexity of a relevant body when deciding whether a certain example of good or poor practice is appropriate to its business. The guidance therefore needs to be used to inform the creation of bespoke prevention procedures designed to address a relevant body's particular circumstances and the risks arising from them.

Departures from suggested procedures within the guidance will not mean that an organisation does not have reasonable procedures, as different prevention procedures may also be just as reasonable. In addition, a small organisation and a large multi-national organisation may implement the principles in very different ways: what is reasonable for a small business in a low risk sector may be entirely unreasonable for a large business in a high risk sector.

Nor is this guidance intended to provide a safe-harbour: compliance with the guidance will not render a relevant body immune from prosecution. Even strict compliance with this guidance will not necessarily amount to having reasonable procedures where the relevant body faces particular risks arising from the unique facts of its own business that remain unaddressed.

The onus will remain on the relevant organisation, where it seeks to rely on the defence, to prove that it had reasonable prevention procedures in place (or that it was unreasonable to expect it to have such procedures). Ultimately only the courts can determine whether a relevant body has *reasonable prevention procedures* in place to prevent the facilitation of tax evasion in the context of a particular case, taking into account the facts and circumstances of that case.

This guidance is not the only source of guidance on preventing associated persons from criminally facilitating tax evasion. Relevant bodies are reminded that other bodies produce guidance that may also be relevant and useful, for example trade associations and representative bodies.

This Government guidance will also inform trade bodies and sector representatives in the development of more precisely tailored sector-specific guidance for their members which can be put forward for endorsement by the Government.

1.3 Overview of the offences and illustrative examples

There are three stages that apply to both the domestic and foreign tax evasion facilitation offences. There are additional requirements for the foreign offence set out below (including the 'dual criminality' requirement):

Stage one: the **criminal tax evasion** by a **taxpayer** (either an individual or a legal entity) under existing law

Stage two: the criminal facilitation of the tax evasion by an "associated person" of the relevant body acting in that capacity

Stage three: the relevant body failed to prevent its representative from committing the criminal facilitation act

Defence: where the relevant body has put in place 'reasonable prevention procedures' to prevent its associated persons from committing tax evasion facilitation offences (stage two), or where it is unreasonable to expect such procedures, it shall have a defence

"*Relevant body*"

Only a "relevant body" can commit the new offences. This means that only incorporated bodies (typically companies) and partnerships can commit the new offences. The new offences cannot be committed by natural (as opposed to legal) persons. Companies and partnerships, not men and women can commit the new offences.

"*Acting in the Capacity of a Person Associated with a Relevant Body*"

A relevant body can only commit the new offences if a person acting in the capacity of a person associated with it criminally facilitates a tax evasion offence (deliberate and dishonest action).

A person is "associated" with a relevant body if that person is an employee, agent or other person who performs services for or on behalf of the relevant body. The offence is committed where the facilitation offences are committed by someone acting in the capacity of an associated person. The associated person can be an individual or an incorporated body.

The question as to whether a person is performing services for or on behalf of an organisation is to be determined by reference to all the relevant circumstances and not merely by reference to the nature of the relationship between that person and the organisation. The contractual status or label of a person performing services for or on behalf of the organisation does not matter, so, for example, employees, agents and sub-contractors can be associated persons.

The concept of a person who 'performs services for or on behalf of' the organisation is intended to be broad in scope, to embrace the whole range of persons who might be capable of facilitating tax evasion whilst acting on behalf of the relevant body.

For more detail and case studies explaining the terms (and other commonly used terminology please see **Section 3**).

- **UK Tax Evasion Facilitation Offence**

  Where there is a UK tax evasion facilitation offence it does not matter whether the relevant body is UK-based or established under the law of another country, or whether the associated person who performs the criminal act of facilitation is in the UK or overseas. In such cases the new offence will have been committed and can be tried by the courts of the United Kingdom.

Stage one: the **criminal tax evasion** by a **taxpayer** (either an individual or a legal entity) under existing law

For the corporate offence to be committed there must first be a criminal offence at the taxpayer level (stage one). Non-compliance, falling short of fraud, at the taxpayer level will not result in the corporate offence being committed. This offence only relates to the failure to prevent the facilitation of tax evasion.

The domestic offence applies to all categories of taxation in the UK and national insurance contributions except for Scottish Devolved Taxes.

Any fraudulent activity that intends to divert funds from the public revenue constitutes the common law offence of cheating the public revenue. There are also a range of statutory offences of "fraudulently evading" various taxes (for example fraudulently evading VAT, contrary to section 72 of the Value Added Tax Act 1994; or fraudulently evading income tax, contrary to section 106A of the Taxes Management Act 1970).

These provisions make it an offence to dishonestly "take steps with a view to" or "be knowingly concerned in" the evasion of the tax. For these offences to be committed it is not necessary that any tax actually be successfully evaded.

A conviction at the taxpayer level is not a pre-requisite for bringing a prosecution against a relevant body under the legislation. For example, a taxpayer may voluntarily come forward and make a full and honest disclosure to HMRC of their actions and it may not be in the interests of justice to criminally prosecute that individual. Where there is no criminal conviction of the taxpayer (stage 1) the prosecution would still have to prove during the prosecution of the relevant body, to the criminal standard of beyond all reasonable doubt, that the taxpayer level offence had been committed.

Stage two: the **criminal facilitation** of the tax evasion by an **"associated person"** of the relevant body

It is already a crime to deliberately and dishonestly facilitate the commission of revenue fraud by another person. It is already a crime for a person to be knowingly concerned in, or take steps with a view to, another person fraudulently evading tax. It is also a crime to aid and abet another person in committing a revenue fraud.

Therefore if a professional such as a banker, accountant or lawyer, deliberately and dishonestly facilitates the commission of revenue fraud by a client, then that banker, accountant or lawyer also commits a crime. The fact that the crime is committed during the course of their work is no defence.

For the corporate offence to be committed there must be criminal facilitation of the taxpayer evasion by a person acting in the capacity of a person associated with the relevant body (stage two). The associated person must deliberately and dishonestly take action to facilitate the taxpayer-level evasion. If the associated person is only proved to have accidentally, ignorantly or even negligently facilitated tax the evasion offence then the new offence is not committed by the relevant body.

Stage three: the relevant body **failed to prevent** its representative from committing the criminal facilitation act

As the offence is a strict liability offence, if stages one and two offences are committed then the relevant body will have committed the new corporate offence unless it can show it has put in place reasonable preventative procedures.

Defence: where the relevant body has put in place reasonable prevention procedures to prevent the criminal facilitation of tax evasion by an associated person (or where it is unreasonable to expect such procedures) the relevant body shall have a defence. This guidance provides suggestions of the types of processes and procedures that can be put in place to prevent associated persons from criminally facilitating tax evasion.

Below are some illustrative examples of the different types of procedures which would be relevant for companies of varying sizes, complexity, industry focus and risk profile. For all the examples below it should be noted that the precise scale and nature of the tax evasion taking place would influence any decision to prosecute

(1) Low/Medium risk

- A mid-size car parts maker ("UKCO") operating in the UK and Europe, entered into a sub-contracting arrangement with an UK distributor. The senior managers of the UK distributor created a false invoicing scheme with the assistance of a purchaser, allowing the purchaser to evade UK taxes due on its purchase of the car parts in the UK
- UKCO itself undertook a tax evasion focused risk assessment, identifying only low and medium level risks to the organisation, subsequently implementing a number of prevention policies and procedures to mitigate the identified risks. UKCO had a clear policy against tax evasion, including terms and conditions within contracts with all third parties
- UKCO also carried out a due diligence assessment of its sub-contracting partner, but not for the entire supply chain. Nothing abnormal was detected during the due diligence test and consequently, UKCO had no reason to believe that the staff of the distributor were involved in a fraudulent tax scheme
- The UK distributor had no procedures to prevent tax evasion, in part because it is not required to do so in its jurisdiction.

In these circumstances, UKCO had undertaken a tax evasion facilitation risk assessment, had procedures and processes in place, as well as conducting a due diligence assessment of its sub-contracting partner. It is therefore unlikely that this company would have committed the offence as it could advance the defence of having reasonable procedures in place and articulating and evidencing what it had done, even if it did not conduct due diligence for the entire onward supply chain.

Whilst UKCO could have done more, it would not have been reasonable or proportionate to do so, the steps that it did take were proportionate to the risks it identified and faced.

(2) Higher risk

- As part of a large transaction an employee of a UK-based multinational bank knowingly referred a corporate client to an offshore accounting firm with the express intention of assisting the corporate client to set up a structure allowing the client to evade foreign income tax
- The bank, which had rigorous prevention procedures for money laundering and bribery procedures, undertook only a light-touch tax evasion risk assessment, nominally including the word 'tax' into existing procedures and processes, but not effectively implementing them or reviewing tax fraud risks
- The bank undertook no tax evasion focussed due diligence assessment of the accounting firm to which the client was referred.

In these circumstances, although the bank could attempt to mount a defence of having reasonable procedures in place on paper for tackling the facilitation of tax evasion, in reality it had relied on unaltered money laundering and bribery procedures. Despite being in a high risk sector, it had also failed to undertake a thorough risk assessment, or follow Government or sector-focused guidance on the types of processes and procedures needed to mitigate risks. It is therefore likely that the bank would be found to have committed the new offence and would be unable to put forward a successful reasonable procedures defence.

- **Foreign Tax Evasion Facilitation Offence**

  The fraudulent evasion of tax is wrong. It would also be wrong for a UK-based relevant body to escape liability for acts which, if they were in relation to UK tax would be criminal, just because the country suffering the tax loss is unable to bring an action against that relevant body within that jurisdiction's legal system.

  The foreign offence operates in a broadly similar way to the domestic offence, first with a requirement for criminal evasion by a taxpayer (stage one), then the criminal facilitation of tax evasion by an associated person (stage two) and if stages one and two offences are committed then the relevant body is criminally liable (stage three) unless it can show it has put in place reasonable preventative procedures: where the relevant body has put in place reasonable prevention procedures it will have a defence, in the same way as for the domestic offence.

  The foreign offence, however, is slightly narrower in scope, in that only certain relevant bodies with a UK nexus can commit the foreign revenue offence. The prosecution in the UK would also still need to show to the criminal standard that the offences at taxpayer and associated person level had been committed and that there was "dual criminality".

UK Nexus

The foreign tax offence can only be committed by a relevant body:

- incorporated under UK law, for example a limited company incorporated under UK law;
- carrying on a business or part of a business in the UK, for example a company incorporated under the law of France but operating from an office in Manchester; or
- whose associated person is located within the UK at the time of the criminal act that facilitates the evasion of the overseas tax, for example a company incorporated under German law whose employee helps another person to commit a foreign tax evasion offence whilst in London.

These bodies, described above, are considered to be sufficiently connected to the UK and therefore should be subject to the new offence in relation to overseas tax. Further guidance and examples of different scenarios are in Section 3.

"Dual Criminality"

The legislation also requires that there is 'dual criminality' in order to prosecute a foreign tax evasion facilitation offence. There are two stages of dual criminality:

- Firstly, the overseas jurisdiction must have an equivalent tax evasion offence at the taxpayer level and it must be the case that the actions carried out by the taxpayer would constitute a crime if they took place in the UK (an offence of being knowingly concerned in or taking steps with a view to the fraudulent evasion of the tax).
  Therefore, the corporate offence cannot be committed where the acts of the associated person would not be criminal if committed in the UK, regardless of what the foreign criminal law may be.
- Secondly, the overseas jurisdiction must have an equivalent offence covering the associated person's criminal act of facilitation, and it must be the case that the actions of the associated person would constitute a crime had they took place in the UK.
  Even where the foreign criminal law renders inadvertent or negligent facilitation of tax evasion criminal, the corporate offence will not be committed because the requirement for dual criminality will not be met - UK law renders only deliberate and dishonest acts of facilitation criminal.

Therefore, any conduct that contravenes the criminal law of another country relating to tax evasion may give rise to the foreign tax evasion offence where:

- **Stage A** - under UK law the actions of taxpayer (tax evasion) and associated person (facilitation) would be an offence
  AND
- **Stage B** - the overseas jurisdiction has equivalent offences at both the taxpayer and facilitator level and recognises the act(s) of the taxpayer and the act(s) of the facilitator as criminal[1].

Therefore the foreign tax offence cannot be committed by acts that would be lawful in relation to a UK tax. Due to the dual criminality requirement, it is only necessary to have an understanding of the foreign criminal law when doing something that would be illegal if done in the UK. If the actions of the associated person would be lawful in the UK then the "dual-criminality" requirement will not be fulfilled and the new foreign tax offence will not be committed regardless of what the foreign law may be.

The legislation also requires that before proceedings for the foreign offence are commenced in England, Wales or Northern Ireland the personal consent of the Director of Public Prosecutions or the Director of the Serious Fraud Office must be gained[2]. Such consent would only be forthcoming where, having weighed up all factors, the prosecution was in the public interest.

It is highly unlikely that a prosecution would be taken forward where a foreign tax was in some way incompatible with the UK's legal values, such as respect for human rights. It would also be very unlikely to be in the public interest to bring a prosecution where a foreign tax was discriminatory and applied on the basis of race, religion or gender.

Whilst the preference will normally be for the jurisdiction suffering the tax loss to take the appropriate criminal or civil response, if this is not possible (for example due to lack of resources, corruption, or any other reason) the UK Government believes that it should be open to the UK to hold the relevant body to account, should it be in the public interest to do so.

[1] Where the act of facilitation happens outside of the country suffering the tax loss, the country suffering the tax loss must recognise the act(s) of facilitation which occur outside of its borders as criminal under its domestic law.

[2] In relation to Scotland, the decision to prosecute is always taken by the Crown Office and Procurator Fiscal Service and so personal consent is not required in the legislation on the corporate offence. As a public body the Crown Office and Procurator Fiscal Service are bound by the Human Rights Act.

1.4 Initial Implementation Period

The prevention procedures that are considered reasonable will change as time passes. What is *reasonable* on the day that the new offences come into force will not be the same as what is reasonable when the offence has been in effect for a number of years. The Government accepts that some procedures (such as training programmes and new IT systems) will take time to roll out, especially for large multi-national organisations. HMRC will therefore take into consideration the prevention procedures that were in place and planned at the time that the facilitation of tax evasion was committed.

At the same time the Government expects there to be rapid implementation, focusing on the major risks and priorities, with a clear timeframe and implementation plan on entry into force. In addition, HMRC expects reasonable procedures to be kept under regular review and to evolve as a relevant body discovers more about the risks that it faces and lessons are learnt.

1.5 Investigations, Penalties and Sanctions

The UK tax offence will be investigated by HMRC, with prosecutions brought by the local public prosecutor (Crown Prosecution Service (CPS), Crown Office and Procurator Fiscal Service (COPFS) or Public Prosecution Service for Northern Ireland (PPSNI)), whilst the foreign tax offence will be investigated by the Serious Fraud Office (SFO) or National Crime Agency (NCA) and prosecutions will be brought by either the SFO or CPS.

The penalties for this offence will include:
– unlimited financial penalties
– ancillary orders such as confiscation orders or serious crime prevention orders

The mere fact of criminal conviction will also have consequences for a relevant body: it may require disclosure to professional regulators both in the UK and overseas and prevent the body being awarded public contracts.

In order to encourage relevant bodies to disclose wrongdoing, timely self-reporting will be viewed as an indicator that a relevant body has reasonable procedures in place.

A Deferred Prosecution Agreement (DPA) is an agreement reached between a prosecutor and an organisation which could be prosecuted, under the supervision of a judge. As DPAs can be used for fraud, bribery and other economic crimes, they can also be used for this offence.

The agreement allows a prosecution to be suspended for a defined period provided the organisation meets certain specified conditions. The key features of DPAs are:
- They enable a corporate body to make full reparation for criminal behaviour without the collateral damage of a conviction (for example sanctions or reputational damage that could put the company out of business and destroy the jobs and investments of innocent people)
- They are concluded under the supervision of a judge, who must be convinced that the DPA is 'in the interests of justice' and that the terms are 'fair, reasonable and proportionate'
- They avoid lengthy and costly trials

DPAs were introduced in February 2014, under the provisions of Schedule 17 of the Crime and Courts Act 2013[3]. The decision as to when a DPA should be offered is for the Crown Prosecution Service or the Serious Fraud Office. A DPA Code of Practice for Prosecutors[4] was published jointly by the SFO and CPS in February 2014.

[3] Error! Hyperlink reference not valid.
[4] Available at: www.cps.gov.uk/publications/directors_guidance/dpa_cop.pdf

2. THE 6 GUIDING PRINCIPLES

The Government considers that prevention procedures put in place by relevant bodies to prevent tax evasion from being committed on their behalf should be informed by the following six principles.
- **Risk assessment**

- **Proportionality of risk-based prevention procedures**
- **Top level commitment**
- **Due diligence**
- **Communication (including training)**
- **Monitoring and review**

Commentary and guidance on what procedures the application of the principles may produce are set out below.

These principles are not prescriptive, they are intended to be flexible and outcome focussed, allowing for the huge variety of circumstances that relevant bodies find themselves in. As set out in more detail below, procedures to prevent facilitation of tax evasion should be proportionate to risk.

Principle 1 - Risk assessment

The relevant body assesses the nature and extent of its exposure to the risk of those who act in the capacity of a person associated with it criminally facilitating tax evasion offences. The risk assessment is documented and kept under review.

Commentary

Those relevant bodies most affected by the new offence, for example those in the financial services, legal and accounting sectors, may already undertake a range of risk assessments relating to their business activities. The purpose of this principle is to promote the inclusion of tax evasion facilitation risk within the relevant body's wider financial crime risk assessment.

Relevant bodies may wish to consider The Financial Conduct Authority's (FCA) guide for firms on preventing Financial Crime[5] , the Law Society's Anti Money Laundering Guidance, particularly Chapter 2 which considers a risk based approach[6], as well as the Joint Money Steering Group (JMLSG) guidance[7].

Relevant bodies that operate in a regulated sector should also consider any guidance published by their regulator. This would include guidance issued by HMRC as part of its Anti-Money Laundering Supervision[8] to Money Services Businesses[9] and Estate Agency Businesses[10].

Ultimately, relevant bodies need to "sit at the desk" of their employees, agents and those who provide services for them or on their behalf and ask whether they have a motive, the opportunity and the means to criminally facilitate tax evasion offences, and if so how this risk might be managed.

Procedures

Risk assessment procedures that allow a relevant body to accurately identify and prioritise the risks it faces will, whatever its size, activities, customers or markets, usually reflect a few common themes. These are:

- Oversight of the risk assessment by senior management
- Appropriate allocation of resources to the detection and monitoring of risk – this will reflect the size and nature of the relevant body
- Identification of the internal and external information sources that will enable the risk to be assessed and reviewed, as well as any gaps in the information available to the relevant body and how these gaps might be filled
- Due diligence enquiries (see Principle 4)
- Accurate and appropriate documentation of the risk assessment and a clear articulation of tax evasion facilitation risks where this is considered as part of the relevant body's wider risk assessment
- Risk assessments are periodically reviewed and updated in line of changing circumstancesOrganisations should have in place procedures to identify emerging risks and feed these into the organisation's risking
- Internal challenge to risk assessments.

The nature of the risks of facilitating tax evasion faced by a relevant body will evolve as the relevant body's business and customer base evolves. For example, a relevant body may consider that its risk has increased, and thus requires enhanced procedures, where it begins to provide services in jurisdictions not reporting taxpayer information under the Common Reporting Standard[11] or offers a new product which carries a known risk of being misused by those seeking to evade tax.

Commonly encountered risks

An assessment of external risks is intended to help inform how these risks can be mitigated by the relevant body's procedures and the level of due diligence a relevant body may deem it reasonable to apply in relation to a given situation.

Stakeholders may wish to consider the commonly encountered risks based on the Bribery Act guidance[12], which are reproduced below, considered from a tax fraud perspective.

Country risk: this is evidenced by perceived high levels of secrecy or use as a tax shelter. Such countries are also unlikely to subscribe to the Common Reporting Standard and be given a low tax transparency score by the OECD.

(Tax transparency ratings and lists of high risk tax jurisdiction published by organisations like the OECD[13] may also be relevant for tax purposes).

Sectoral risk: some sectors pose a higher risk of facilitating tax evasion than others, such as financial services, tax advisory and legal sectors.

Transaction risk: certain types of transaction give rise to higher risks, for example, complex tax planning structures involving high levels of secrecy, overly complex supply chains, or transactions involving politically exposed persons.

Business opportunity risk: such risks might arise in high value projects or with projects involving many parties, jurisdictions or intermediaries.

Business partnership risk: certain relationships may involve higher risk, for example, the use of intermediaries in transactions, where those intermediaries are based in jurisdictions operating lower levels of transparency and disclosure. Entering into a business partnership with organisations that have either has no fraud prevention procedures, or has known deficiencies in their fraud procedures may involve higher risk. .

In addition, the following risks may also be considered for tax fraud:

Product risk: certain products and services may have a higher risk of misuse by either clients of associated persons.

Customer risk: the identification that a business unit has particular risks related to customers or products is highly likely to indicate that there is a greater risk of the criminal facilitation of tax evasion by an associated person.

In addition, stakeholders may also want to consider the JMLSG guidance on high and low risk factors, although these will need to be considered specifically from a tax fraud perspective:

JMLSG Guidance – high risk factors (4.34-4.36)

Customer risk factors

- The business relationship is conducted in unusual circumstances
- Non-resident customers
- Legal persons or arrangements that are personal asset holding vehicles
- Companies that have nominee shareholders or shares in bearer form
- Business that are cash intensive
- The ownership structure of the company appears unusual or excessively complex

Country or geographic risk factors

- Countries identified by credible sources as not having adequate Anti-Money Laundering and Counter-Terrorism Financing (AML/CTF) approaches
- Countries subject to sanctions, embargoes, or similar measures issued by, for example, the UN
- Countries identified by credible sources as providing support for terrorist activities, or that have designated terrorist organisations operating within their country

Product, service, transaction or delivery channel risk factors

- Private banking
- Anonymous transactions (which may include cash)
- Non face-to-face business relationships or transactions
- Payment received from unknown or un-associated third parties

Firms should examine, as far as reasonably possible, the background and purpose of all complex, unusual large transactions, and all unusual patterns of transactions which have no apparent economic or lawful purpose.

JMLSG Guidance – low risk factors (4.37-4.41)

Customer risk factors

- Other regulated firms and other bodies, where they are subject to requirements to combat money laundering and terrorist financing consistent with the Financial Action Task Force (FATF)[14] Recommendations, have effectively implemented these requirements, and are effectively supervised or monitored to ensure compliance with those requirements
- Public companies listed on a stock exchange and subject to disclosure requirements which impose requirements to ensure adequate transparency of beneficial ownership
- Public administrations or enterprises

Country or geographic risk factors

- Countries identified by credible sources as having effective AML/CTF systems
- Countries identified by credible sources as having a low level of corruption or criminal activity

Product, service, transaction or delivery channel risk factors

- Life assurance policies where the premium is low
- Insurance policies for pension schemes if there is no early surrender option and the policy cannot be used as collateral
- A pension, superannuation or similar scheme that provides retirement benefits to employees, where contributions are made by way of deduction from wages, and the scheme rules do not permit the assignment of a member's interest under the scheme
- Financial products or services that provide appropriately defined and limited services to certain types of customers, so as to increase access for financial inclusion purposes

A risk assessment should also consider the extent to which internal structures or procedures may themselves add to the level of risk. Commonly encountered internal factors may include:

- Deficiencies in employee training, skills and knowledge
- A bonus culture that rewards excessive risk taking
- Lack of clarity on the organisation's policies on, and procedures for, the provision of high risk services and products
- Deficiencies in the organisation's submission of Suspicious Activity Reports (SARs)
- Lack of clear financial controls or whistle-blowing procedures
- Lack of clear messaging from top-level management on refusing to engage in tax fraud.

5 https://www.handbook.fca.org.uk/handbook/document/FC1_FCA_20150427.pdf
6 https://www.handbook.fca.org.uk/handbook/document/FC1_FCA_20150427.pdf
7 https://www.handbook.fca.org.uk/handbook/document/FC1_FCA_20150427.pdf
8 https://www.gov.uk/topic/business-tax/money-laundering-regulations
9 https://www.gov.uk/government/publications/anti-money-laundering-guidance-for-money-service-businesses
10 https://www.gov.uk/guidance/registration-guide-for-estate-agency-businesses
11 Under the standard, jurisdictions obtain financial information from their financial institutions and automatically exchange that information with other jurisdictions on an annual basis. For more information please see: https://www.oecd.org/ctp/exchange-of-tax-information/automatic-exchange-financial-account-information-common-reporting-standard.pdf
12 www.gov.uk/government/publications/bribery-act-2010-guidance
13 http://www.oecd.org/tax/transparency/
14 http://www.fatf-gafi.org/

Principle 2 - Proportionality of risk-based prevention procedures

Reasonable procedures for a relevant body to adopt to prevent persons acting in the capacity of a person associated with it from criminally facilitating tax evasion will be proportionate to the risk the relevant body faces of persons associated with it committing tax evasion facilitation offences. This will depend on the nature, scale and complexity of the relevant body's activities. We recognise that the reasonableness of prevention procedures should take account of the level of control and supervision the organisation is able to exercise over a particular person acting on its behalf, and the proximity of the person to the relevant body. The new offences do not require relevant bodies to undertake excessively burdensome procedures in order to eradicate all risk, but they do demand more than mere lip-service to preventing the criminal facilitation of tax evasion.

Commentary

The term reasonable 'preventative procedures' within this guidance is used to mean both:

- formal policies adopted by a relevant body to prevent criminal facilitation of tax evasion by those acting on its behalf, and
- practical steps taken to implement these policies, enforcement of compliance with the policies, and the monitoring of the policies' effectiveness.

The prevention procedures should outline the relevant body's position on involvement in the criminal facilitation of tax evasion, including the provision of services which pose a high risk of being misused to commit a tax evasion offence. The relevant body should also have a plan of how it will implement and review measures to ensure that persons associated with it are not criminally facilitating tax evasion.

Burdensome procedures designed to perfectly address every conceivable risk, no matter how remote, are **not** required. Procedures need only be reasonable given the risks posed in the circumstances. It is expected that a relevant body will therefore first undertake an assessment of the risks that those who act on its behalf may criminally facilitate tax evasion.

A number of factors (see table below) will be relevant when assessing the risk posed to a relevant body by the services it provides and the manner in which it provides them, including the size of the relevant body, the nature and complexity of its business and the jurisdictions in which it operates.

To be "reasonable", prevention procedures should be proportionate to the risks that the organisation faces. An initial assessment of the risks that those who act in the capacity of a person associated with a relevant body may commit tax evasion facilitation offences is therefore a necessary first step. The size of the organisation will be an important factor, as will the nature and complexity of its business, but size will not be the only determining factor.

When considering the proportionality of reasonable prevention procedures, some suggested risk factors to consider may include the following:

- **Opportunity – could someone facilitate tax evasion?**
  - Do any associated persons have the opportunity to facilitate client tax evasion?
  - Is their work subject to monitoring or scrutiny, for example a second pair of eyes?
  - How likely is detection of any facilitation?
- **Motive – why could it happen?**
  - Does the reward and recognition system and corporate culture (including sanctions and penalties) incentivise or dissuade potential criminal facilitation of tax evasion, or whistle-blowing when tax evasion is uncovered?
  - What are the consequences of wrong-doing?
- **Means – how could it be done?**
  - What means of criminally facilitating tax fraud do your associated persons have?
  - Are there particular products, services or systems that could be open to abuse and used to criminally facilitate tax evasion?
  - Do those in high risk roles receive regular fraud training and how vigorously is compliance with training evaluated or monitored?

Some organisations may face significant risks, and will need more extensive procedures than their counterparts facing limited risks, for example those providing private wealth management services. However, in general small organisations are unlikely to need procedures that are as extensive as those of a large multi-national organisation.

A very small lower risk business, for example, may be able to rely on oral briefings to communicate its policies while a large business may need to rely on more extensive written communications. Larger organisations may also exercise less day-to-day oversight over those providing services on its behalf, and may therefore need to put in place alternative oversight arrangements.

Procedures to prevent the criminal facilitation of tax evasion by a person associated with the relevant body may be independent, standalone procedures; but so long as they properly address the risk of facilitating tax evasion they may form part of a wider package of procedures, for example internal Anti-Money Laundering, Bribery Act or fraud prevention procedures.

What is considered a proportionate timescale for implementing, reviewing and amending procedures to prevent criminal facilitation of tax evasion will depend on the nature, scale and complexity of the relevant body's activities and the resources available to the relevant body. It is expected that a relevant body's procedures will not be static, but will evolve and develop in line with the relevant body's activities and identified risks.

Procedures

The precise prevention procedures that will be reasonable will differ for each organisation, but they are likely to include common elements. For example:

- A clearly articulated risk assessment on which the procedures are based
- A top level commitment to preventing the involvement of those acting on the relevant body's behalf in the criminal facilitation of tax evasion
- An articulation of the approach to mitigating risks of involvement in the criminal facilitation of tax evasion, such as those arising from the nature of its services and areas of operation
- An overview of the strategy and timeframe to implement prevention policies. It is expected that what is reasonable will evolve over time. For example, IT systems which form part of a relevant body's due diligence procedures may take time to develop and subsequently review and amend
- Monitoring and enforcing compliance with procedures
- Reviewing procedures for effectiveness and refining them
- A clear pathway for reporting wrongdoing by persons associated with the relevant body
- Protection for whistle-blowers (with no retribution)
- A commitment to compliance over profit or bonuses.

The procedures put in place to implement a relevant body's preventative policies should be designed to mitigate identified risks as well as address the risk of criminal conduct on the part of those providing services on behalf of the relevant body.

An organisation does not have to publish policies on an external website, but may wish to summarise key principles within corporate materials. The following list is intended as guidance for the topics that preventative procedures may embrace depending on the nature of the particular risks faced:

- The involvement of the relevant body's top level management
- The procedures and methods used to assess the risk to the relevant body posed by its activities
- Due diligence conducted in relation to persons associated with the relevant body
- The contractual terms and conditions of persons associated with the relevant body
- Disciplinary and enforcement action taken against those persons breaching the relevant body's policies
- How the relevant body will communicate its policies to all persons associated with it
- Policies around reporting criminal actions by persons associated with the relevant body
- The process and timeline by which the organisation plans to implement its preventative procedures and training in their application
- The monitoring, review and evaluation of the relevant body's preventative policy and procedures
- Disclosure of client information in line with existing legal requirements, for example reporting under the Common Reporting Standard and the Proceeds of Crime Act.

No Procedures

It is also worth noting that in some limited circumstances it may be unreasonable to expect a relevant body to have prevention procedures in place. For example, where a relevant body has fully assessed all the risks and they are considered to be extremely low and the costs of implementing any prevention procedures are disproportionate or cost-prohibitive in relation to the negligible risks faced. However, it will rarely be reasonable to have not even conducted a risk assessment.

It should be noted that a relevant body should keep the risks under review and be able to articulate the outcome of the risk assessment and the active decision not to implement any procedures, should they be challenged at a later stage.

Principles 3 - Top level commitment

The top-level management of a relevant body should be committed to preventing persons acting in the capacity of a person associated with it from engaging in criminal facilitation of tax evasion. They should foster a culture within the relevant body in which activity intended to facilitate tax evasion is never acceptable.

Commentary

Those at the most senior levels of the organisation are best placed to foster a culture where actions intended to facilitate tax evasion are considered unacceptable. This principle is intended to encourage the involvement of senior management in the creation and implementation of preventative procedures. It is also intended to encourage senior management involvement in the decision making process in relation to the assessment of risk, where this is appropriate.

Procedures

The level and nature of the involvement of senior management of a relevant body will vary depending on the size and structure of the relevant body, but is likely to include:

- communication and endorsement of the relevant body's stance on preventing the criminal facilitation of tax evasion, and
- involvement in the development and review of preventative procedures.

Communication and endorsement of the relevant body's position on preventing the facilitation of tax evasion

The manner and form in which a relevant body chooses to communicate, both internally and externally, its position on ensuring that persons associated with it do not criminally facilitate the evasion of taxes may vary depending on a number of factors including the size of the relevant body, the nature and complexity of its business and the jurisdictions within which it operates.

Communication may vary depending on the target audience, for example communications aimed at the relevant body's clients may be different from those aimed at employees of the relevant body or those to whom it sub-contracts work.

Effective formal statements to demonstrate the commitment by senior managers within the relevant body may include:

- A commitment to zero tolerance towards the criminal facilitation of tax evasion
- he consequences for persons associated with the relevant body for breaching the relevant body's policy on the facilitation of tax evasion
- A commitment not to recommend the services of others who do not have reasonable prevention procedures in place
- Articulation of the benefits of rejecting the provision of services to enable tax evasion (reputational, customer and business partner confidence)
- Articulation of the relevant body's main preventative procedures
- Key individuals and/or departments involved in the development and implementation of the organisation's prevention procedures
- Reference to any membership of collective action against the facilitation of tax evasion, for example, through initiatives undertaken by representative bodies.

Involvement in developing preventative measures

The level and nature of involvement in the creation and implementation of preventative measures will be bespoke to the relevant body involved. It is expected that the level of involvement will be proportionate to the relevant body's size, management structure and business activities.

In smaller relevant bodies, it may be proportionate for the most senior management to be personally involved in the design and implementation of preventative measures. In a large multinational organisation, personal involvement in the design and implementation of preventative measures may not be proportionate, and senior management may instead take responsibility for preventative measures by providing oversight of work delegated to a committee and the publication with positive endorsement for the preventative measures thereby created.

Regardless of the scale of involvement of senior management, it is likely to reflect the following elements:

- Members of the senior management of the relevant body having designated responsibility for preventative measures
- Endorsement of the relevant body's preventative policy and associated publications
- Leadership and designated responsibility for awareness raising of the relevant body's preventative policies
- Engagement with relevant associated persons and external bodies to help articulate the organisation's policies
- Designated responsibility for certifying the assessment of risk
- Designated responsibility at senior level for disciplinary procedures relating to the breach of the relevant body's policies

- Senior management's commitment to whistleblowing processes and rejecting profit by way of facilitating tax evasion.

Principle 4 - Due diligence

The organisation applies due diligence procedures, taking an appropriate and risk based approach, in respect of persons who perform or will perform services on behalf of the organisation, in order to mitigate identified risks.

Commentary

Those organisations in the sectors facing the greatest risks (those providing bespoke financial or tax-related services to clients, for example) are likely already to undertake a wide variety of due diligence procedures, both mandatory and due diligence undertaken in response to risks associated with specific transactions or customers.

It is envisaged that due diligence procedures for this offence will be capable of identifying the risk of criminal facilitation of tax evasion by associated persons. However, it should be noted that merely applying old procedures tailored to a different type of risk (or clients-focused procedures) will not necessarily be an adequate response to tackle the risk of tax evasion facilitation.

Those with exposure to the greatest risk may choose to clearly articulate their due diligence procedures specifically in relation to the corporate offence. In addition, a single relevant body might have differing procedures for different parts of its business reflecting the varying levels of risk across all of its activities.

A relevant body may, upon conducting a risk assessment, decide that services provided to a certain group of its clients pose a higher risk of being misused to perpetrate a tax fraud. As a result they may apply increased scrutiny over those providing services to those clients, or over those who provide those services, to address the specific risks of tax evasion facilitation identified.

Procedures

The due diligence procedures put in place should be proportionate to the identified risk. For example, it may be that the risk identified in given situations is so remote as to justify there being no procedures in place. Alternatively, an organisation may assess the risks as being substantial in relation to a particular associated person, or service, and so apply considerably greater scrutiny in that circumstance.

Organisations may choose to conduct their due diligence internally, or externally, for example by consultants.

We recognise that the reasonableness of prevention procedures should take account of the level of control and supervision the organisation is able to exercise over a particular person acting on its behalf and the relevant body's proximity to that person.

It is expected that the effectiveness of the organisation's procedures will be reviewed and where necessary the procedures will be amended.

Principle 5 - Communication (including training)

The organisation seeks to ensure that its prevention policies and procedures are communicated, embedded and understood throughout the organisation, through internal and external communication, including training. This is proportionate to the risk to which the organisation assesses that it is exposed.

Commentary

A clear articulation of an organisation's policy against engaging in activities to help clients commit tax fraud deters those providing services on behalf of the relevant body from engaging in such activities. Communication should be from all levels within an organisation, i.e. it is not enough for the senior management say that staff should not commit fraud, if middle management then actively ignore this and encourage junior members to circumvent the relevant body's prevention procedures.

It is important that the relevant body ensures awareness and understanding of its policies amongst those who provide services for or on its behalf. The organisation may feel that it is necessary to require its representatives to undertake fraud or potentially tax evasion-specific training, depending on the risks it is exposed to. This would be to ensure that they have the skills needed to identify when they and those around them might be at risk of engaging in an illegal act and what whistle-blowing procedures should be followed if this occurs.

Procedures

The nature of internal and external communication may vary depending on the nature of the risk being addressed, the size, business and operation of the organisation in question.

Internal communications should make clear the relevant body's zero tolerance policy for the facilitation of tax evasion by its representatives and the consequences for anyone found to be complicit in illegal activity. Such communication may focus on high risk areas of operation for the relevant bodies and what is expected of representatives who find themselves being asked to provide a service which they believe will be used to facilitate a tax fraud.

An important aspect of internal communication is an established and confidential means for representatives of the organisation to raise concerns about the provision of services to facilitate tax fraud. It should be clear to those providing services on behalf of the organisation whom they should contact within if they have questions or concerns about the services they are providing. Relevant bodies may wish these communications to form part of their existing communications, for example on money laundering prevention, or to be a standalone communication.

External communication of an organisation's policy on the provision of services to facilitate tax evasion can act as a strong deterrent to those who would seek to use the organisation's services to further illegal activity. Organisations may consider it proportionate and appropriate to convey these messages to partner organisations, particularly those to whom it is making referral, or from whom clients are referred.

Training

The training should be proportionate to the risk faced. Some relevant bodies may wish to incorporate training into their existing financial crime prevention training, other organisations may wish to introduce bespoke training to address specific tax fraud risks.

Consideration should be given to the specific training needs of those in the highest risk posts, and to training required to ensure that the relevant body's representatives understand the process for referring any concerns. The effectiveness of training should be monitored and evaluated.

Relevant bodies may choose either to train third party associated persons, or encourage them to ensure their own arrangements are in place.

Suggested Training Requirements:

In is not envisaged that all associated persons will require a detailed understanding of tax rules in any one country, but instead training should equip them to understand the scope of this offence and the associated risks, without needing to understand the underlying tax law.

Suggested content for tax evasion and general fraud training could include the following:

- the organisation's policies and procedures, which include provisions of the Act and any other sector regulatory rules and principles
- explanation of when and how to seek advice and report any concerns or suspicions of tax evasion or wider financial crime, including whistleblowing procedures
- definition and explanation of the term 'tax evasion' and associated fraud
- explanation of an employee's duty under the law

Principle 6 - Monitoring and review

The organisation monitors and reviews its preventative procedures and makes improvements where necessary.

Commentary

The nature of the risks faced by an organisation will change and evolve over time. This may be as a natural result of external developments, the failure to prevent an incidence of facilitation of tax evasion by an associated person, or as a result of changes in the organisation's activities. The organisation will therefore need to change its procedures in response to the changes in the risks that it faces.

Procedures

There are a range of approaches which an organisation may wish to take when reviewing its monitoring mechanisms. An organisation may wish to have its review conducted by an external party, or may choose to conduct its review internally.

Organisations can review their procedures in a number of ways, for example:

- By seeking internal feedback from staff members and looking to other financial crime prevention procedures
- Through formalised periodic review with documented findings
- Through working with other organisations, such as representative bodies or other organisations facing similar risks.This is not an exhaustive list and it is expected that organisations will choose the approach most suited to their needs. Organisations may change their review process in light of developments, for example an organisation may need to take a more formalised and detailed approach to reviewing its procedures, following criminal activity by persons associated with it.

3. COMMON TERMINOLOGY AND ADDITIONAL CASE STUDIES

3.1 Relevant Body

Only a "relevant body" can commit the new offences. This means that only incorporated bodies (typically companies) and partnerships can commit the new offences. The new offences cannot be committed by natural (as opposed to legal) persons. The new offence can be committed by companies and partnerships, not men and women.

The UK tax offence can be committed by any relevant body regardless of whether it is established under UK law or the law of a foreign jurisdiction. This reflects the fact that under the current law any person can be guilty of a UK tax evasion offence contrary to UK law, regardless of their location, if they assist somebody to evade UK tax with the requisite guilty state of mind.

The fact that an offence is committed against the UK is sufficient to give the criminal courts of the UK jurisdiction over the offence. Thus companies incorporated under the law of France or partnerships formed under German law would be capable of committing the offence in section 2 in relation to taxes owed to the UK.

However, the foreign tax offence can only be committed:

- by a relevant body incorporated under UK law, for example a limited company incorporated under UK law;
- by a relevant body carrying on a business or part of a business from within the UK, for example a company incorporated under the law of France but operating from an office in Manchester; or
- by a relevant body whose associated person is located within the UK at the time of the act that facilitates the evasion of the overseas tax, for example a company incorporated under German law whose employee helps another person to commit a foreign tax evasion offence whilst in London.

These bodies, described above, are considered to be sufficiently connected to the UK and therefore should be subject to the new foreign tax offence.

3.2 Person who acts in the capacity of a person Associated with a relevant body

The tax evasion facilitation offence must be committed by a person acting in the capacity of a person associated with the relevant body. Where an employee criminally facilitates his or her partner's tax evasion in the course of their private life and as a 'frolic of their own', they commit a tax evasion facilitation offence but NOT in the capacity of person associated with their employer. Therefore in this situation the employer does not commit the new offence.

A third-party (e.g. an introducer or agent) may have simultaneous relationships with multiple organisations and perform tasks for several different relevant bodies (or in a personal capacity). Such a person might be associated with various different relevant bodies as he does various tasks. It should therefore be noted that the new offence is only committed where a tax evasion facilitation offence is committed by a person acting in the capacity of a person associated to the relevant body, that is undertaken 'for or on behalf of' the relevant body. Any activity of the associated person beyond that relationship, for example for other relevant bodies or carried out in their private capacity would not lead to liability for the relevant body.

This broad scope means that contractors could be 'associated' persons to the extent that they are performing services for or on behalf of a relevant body. Determining whether a person is associated with a relevant body will always necessitate looking past the contractual form and considering all the relevant factors including contractual proximity, control, and benefit.

The Government recognises that the relevant body will be able to operate greater levels of control and supervision over some categories of representatives (for example those directly employed) than over others (for example those ordinarily employed by another entity but providing services on a temporary basis). We recognise that the reasonableness of procedures should take account of the level of control, proximity and supervision the organisation is able to exercise over a particular person acting on its behalf.

Where a supply chain involves several entities or a project is to be performed by a prime contractor with a series of subcontractors (and even sub-sub-contractors), an organisation is likely only to exercise control over its relationship with its contractual counterparty. Indeed, the organisation may only know the identity of its contractual counterparty.

The principal way in which commercial organisations may decide to approach tax fraud risks which arise as a result of a supply chain is by employing the types of anti-tax evasion facilitation procedures referred to elsewhere in this guidance (e.g. risk-based due diligence and the use of contract terms and conditions) in the relationship with their contractual counterparty, and by requesting that counterparty to adopt a similar approach with the next party in the chain.

3.3 Branches and Subsidiaries

The law does not view branches as separate legal entities (in the way that subsidiaries are): all the branches of a relevant body comprise a single legal entity. This means that any relevant body with a number of branches, including one in the UK, would be subject to these offences. For the UK branch to say "but a different branch did this" is akin to a person's left arm protesting that an assault was committed by the right arm.

Subsidiaries are not automatically presumed to be associated persons of UK relevant bodies, and an examination of the relevant circumstances will be needed to determine whether they are an associated person or not, in the same way as is required for entirely unrelated legal entities or sister companies that that share a parent company. Moreover it is the relevant body, not the UK branch that would commit the offence.

Examples

Branches and the overseas fraud offence

Gladstone Bank is a bank incorporated and headquartered in Switzerland. The bank has branches in a number of jurisdictions, including the UK and Germany. Whilst the bank has several branches across the world, the branches are not separate legal entities (they are branches not subsidiaries): the bank is a single legal entity, a company incorporated under Swiss law. All the bank's branches comprise a single legal person. The Bank chooses not to put in place procedures to prevent persons providing services for or on its behalf facilitating tax evasion. However, the UK branch does its best to put in place UK focused procedures aimed purely at staff working in its UK offices.

UK Branch

The UK Branch consists of a small number of employees whose functions are restricted to:

- attracting and on-boarding clients for Gladstone Bank;
- providing minor administrative services; and
- acting as a first point of contact for UK based customers.

The UK branch attracts and on-boards a number of clients for Gladstone Bank resident in London, including Freya who has UK tax liabilities and Larry who has German tax liabilities. The employees of the UK branch attract the clients in good faith believing that Gladstone Bank is providing routine financial services to its clients. Once the clients have been attracted all financial services are provided by either the bank's headquarters in Switzerland or employees in the German Branch.

German Branch

Employees of the German Branch, deliberately and dishonestly help Larry to evade his German tax liabilities. The employees:

- advise Larry on structures that allow him to hide his assets and income from the German tax authorities;
- provide false certification to hide the true owners of accounts; and
- deliberately fail to comply with the applicable Anti Money Laundering Regulations.

Swiss Head Office

Employees of the Swiss headquarters deliberately and dishonestly help Freya to evade her UK tax liabilities. The employees:

- advise Freya on structures to help her hide overseas income from the UK tax authorities;
- deliberately set up a bank account in Switzerland knowing it is going to be used to hide the overseas income from the UK tax authorities.

A. Liability for the UK fraud offence

Stage 1: Taxpayers

Freya has deliberately and dishonestly failed to declare her taxable income and assets to HMRC with the intention of not paying the tax that she legally owes. She has committed the offence of being knowingly concerned in the fraudulent evasion of income tax contrary to section 106A of the Taxes Management Act 1970.

Stage 2: Associated persons of Gladstone Bank and criminal facilitation

Employees of Gladstone's Swiss Head Office have deliberately and dishonestly provided services to Freya to help her to hide her taxable income and assets in order to help her evade her UK tax liability. They are also guilty of being knowingly concerned in the fraudulent evasion of income tax, an offence contrary to section 106A of the Taxes Management Act 1970.

The associated person was providing services (advice to clients) for or on behalf of the bank when they committed the tax evasion facilitation offence.

Stage 3: Liability for Gladstone Bank for failing to prevent the criminal facilitation of tax evasion

Gladstone Bank is not guilty of the section 106A Taxes Management offence. It is not possible to attribute the requisite guilty mind to the bank itself in respect of the criminal act committed, because none of the people considered to be the bank's directing mind and will (typically the Board of Directors) were involved in the offence.

However, the bank is liable for having failed to prevent its associated persons operating in its Swiss Head Office from criminally facilitating Freya's UK tax liability (the new UK tax offence) unless it is able to establish the reasonable prevention procedures defence.

Gladstone Bank may struggle to mount a reasonable prevention procedures defence, its procedures were arguably not reasonable because it had only implemented procedures for a small number of UK-based staff. It is no defence to claim that it should not be expected to put in place prevention procedures designed to prevent its associated persons from being complicit in fraud resulting in a tax loss outside of Switzerland.

B. Liability for the Overseas Fraud Offence

Stage 1: taxpayers

Larry has deliberately and dishonestly failed to declare his taxable income and assets to the German revenue authorities with the intention of not paying the tax that he legally owes. There is 'dual criminality' as there are equivalent offences at the taxpayer level in the UK and Germany.

Stage 2: Associated persons of Gladstone Bank and criminal facilitation

Employees of Gladstone's German branch have deliberately and dishonestly provided services to Larry to help him hide his taxable income and assets in order to help him evade his German tax liability.

The associated person was providing services (advice to clients) for or on behalf of the bank. There is 'dual criminality' at the facilitator level as there equivalent offences in both the UK and Germany[15].

Stage 3: As Gladstone Bank has a UK branch and the bank is a single legal entity it is within scope of the new foreign tax evasion facilitation offence, because it is a relevant body conducting part of its business in the UK. Gladstone Bank has also failed to prevent its associated person, i.e. employees of its German Branch, from criminally facilitating the evasion of German tax by Larry.

Gladstone Bank is likely to struggle to put forward a defence of having put in place reasonable procedures to prevent the criminal facilitation of tax evasion because its procedures were arguably not reasonable as it decided to only introduce prevention procedures for staff dealing with UK taxpayers. Claiming that it does not believe that it should have to exercise due diligence over employees of its branches in other countries provides no defence to this.

Further examples of branch structures that would be in scope of the overseas offence as there is sufficient UK nexus:

- Any bank incorporated under UK law with overseas branches
- Any bank incorporated under the law of another country that conducts part of its business from the UK, for example a French bank with a London branch
- Any bank incorporated under the law of another country that conducts none of its business from the UK but where its associated person from within the UK, for example any bank incorporated under the law of another country that sends someone to the UK to perform a criminal act of tax evasion facilitation.

[15] See para 3.6 below.

3.4 Joint Ventures

Joint ventures sometimes operate through a separate legal entity, but at other times through contractual arrangements. In the case of a joint venture operating through a separate legal entity, where a tax fraud has been facilitated by the entity this may lead to liability for a participant in the joint venture if the entity is performing services on behalf of that participant.

However, the existence of a joint venture entity will not of itself mean that it is automatically 'associated' with any of the participants. The facilitation of tax evasion by an employee or associated person of the joint venture entity will therefore not always trigger liability for participants in the joint venture simply by virtue of them being connected through their investment in or ownership of the joint venture. The question will always be whether the entity is acting for or on behalf of the participant.

The degree of control that a participant has over the arrangement (for example where the joint venture is conducted through a contractual arrangement) is likely to be one of the 'relevant circumstances' that would be taken into account in deciding whether a person who facilitated tax evasion in the conduct of the joint venture business was 'performing services for or on behalf of' a participant in that arrangement.

The question is always whether the person performing the facilitating act is providing a service for or on behalf of the relevant body. A corporate entity set up to deliver a joint venture may perform services for or on behalf of the participants in that venture, and when it does, it will be an associated person

3.5 Referrals

Where a relevant body makes an introduction in good faith, and believes the external service provider is unlikely to be involved in facilitating tax evasion, and also steps away from the transaction entirely, the company which makes the referral is unlikely to fall within scope of the new offence. This is because in this instance the company to which the referral is made does not provide services for or on behalf of the referrer, it a 'vanilla' referral, not a case of sub-contracting.

However, this would not be the case where the introducing party is aware that either the motive of the client involved is to evade tax or that the external provider to whom a client has been introduced is likely to be involved in facilitating tax evasion. This dishonest referral would itself constitute a deliberate action to facilitate tax evasion at the taxpayer level.

Examples

1) Straight-forward Referral Out

A UK Bank 'B' gets occasional client requests for services in South Africa, where it has neither a branch, nor a subsidiary. It has a relationship with a firm 'F' in that country to which it refers business. This arrangement is a 'pure' or 'vanilla' referral. Once the referral has been made, the client becomes a client of F, and bank B takes no further part in any provision of services in the country in question (although its own separate relationship with the client continues to exist independently). Firm F criminally facilitates the client's tax evasion. It is not a relationship in which services are provided by F for or on behalf of bank B.

Question: Would firm F criminally facilitate the tax evasion whilst acting in the capacity of a person associated with bank B?

Answer: No. Firm F does not, as it was not providing services on behalf of bank B; once the client was introduced, firm F and the customer has their own relationship in which bank B had no role.

2) Inward Referral

A UK bank uses a consultancy firm in India that introduces clients to the bank. The consultancy firm was previously exclusive to the UK bank but now also introduces Indian clients to the UK bank's sister bank in India. The consultancy firm is not used by the UK bank to provide any tax advice to clients of either bank.

The consultancy firm later offers additional services (beyond the contracted services with the banks) and criminally facilitates tax evasion for clients of both the UK and Indian-based banks, including by falsifying documentation. Neither bank was aware of the additional services and illegal activity.

Question: Would the activity of the consultancy firm attract liability for the bank?

Answer: No. The Indian consultancy firm was offering tax services outside of its relationship with the bank. Although the consultancy firm was providing some services on behalf of the bank (introducing clients) the criminal facilitation of tax evasion was outside the contracted service provision and was therefore not provided when acting in the capacity of a person associated with the bank.

3) Holistic Service Provision / Sub-contracting

A UK financial services firm instructs a foreign tax adviser on behalf of a client to give advice on tax and estate planning proposals in a foreign jurisdiction. The UK firm controls the ongoing relationship with the client and the advice sought, passing the advice on to the client. The UK firm takes responsibility for the foreign lawyer's fees and includes those fees as a disbursement in the annual bill to their client.

Question: Would the advice of the foreign tax advisor attract liability for the UK firm?

Answer: Yes. The foreign tax advisor is providing a service for or on behalf of the UK firm; it is doing work that the UK firm sub-contracted to the foreign tax advisor having entered into a contract with its client. The foreign tax advisor is therefore acting in the capacity of a person associated with the UK firm as it is performing services for or on behalf of the UK firm.

3.6 Foreign Tax Evasion Facilitation Offence

– **Dual Criminality**

Below is an example of the dual criminality test to illustrate the types of situation that are in scope of the new offence.

Dual criminality example

Gladstone Bank is a bank incorporated and headquartered in Switzerland. The bank has branches in a number of jurisdictions, including the UK and Germany. Whilst the bank has several branches across the world, the branches are not separate legal entities (they are branches not subsidiaries): the bank is a single legal entity, a company incorporated under Swiss law.. All the bank's branches comprise a single legal person.

UK Branch

The UK Branch consists of a small number of employees whose functions are restricted to:

- attracting and on-boarding clients for Gladstone Bank;

- providing minor administrative services; and
- acting as a first point of contact for UK based customers.

The UK branch attracts and on-boards a number of clients for Gladstone Bank resident in London, including Larry who has German tax liabilities. The employees of the UK branch attract the clients in good faith believing that Gladstone Bank is providing routine financial services to its clients. Once the clients have been attracted all financial services are provided by either the bank's headquarters in Switzerland or employees in the German Branch.

German Branch

Employees of the German Branch, deliberately and dishonestly help Larry to evade his German tax liabilities. The employees:

- advise Larry on structures that allow him to hide his assets and income from the German tax authorities;
- provide false certification to hide the true owners of accounts; and
- deliberately fail to comply with the applicable Anti Money Laundering Regulations.

The German taxpayer, Larry, has committed an offence contrary to section 370 of the German Fiscal Code. He is assisted by an employee of Gladstone Bank who is also based in a branch in Germany.

Section 370 German Fiscal Code

Any person who:

- Furnishes the revenue authorities or other authorities with incorrect or incomplete particulars concerning matters of substantial significance for taxation.
- Fails to inform the revenue authorities of facts of substantial significance for taxation when obliged to do so

There is therefore dual criminality at the taxpayer level as there is an equivalent offence in 106A of the Taxes Management Act 1970 (fraudulent evasion of income tax).

The facilitating acts of the staff of the bank would be an offence if done in the UK and Germany also has the equivalent offence, criminal facilitation of tax evasion, by virtue of sections 26-27 of the German Fiscal Code.

Section 26 Abetting

Any person who intentionally induces another to intentionally commit an unlawful act (abettor) shall be liable to be sentenced as if he were a principal.

Section 27 Aiding

(1) Any person who intentionally assists another in the intentional commission of an unlawful act shall be convicted and sentenced as an aider.

There is therefore dual criminality at the taxpayer (stage 1) and associated person (stage 2) levels.

Stage 3: Liability for Gladstone Bank for failing to prevent the criminal facilitation of tax evasion

Gladstone bank is within scope of the foreign tax evasion offence as it is a relevant body that carries on part of its business in the UK. The fact that the company is incorporated under Swiss law, and that the facilitating acts of its associated person took place outside the UK, does not take it outside the scope of the new offence. It is a legal person that carries out part of its business in the UK and is within scope of the new foreign tax offence.

Gladstone Bank will be guilty of the foreign tax evasion offence unless it can establish the defence of having reasonable prevention procedures.

3.7 Further illustrative case studies

EXAMPLE 1) ACTING AS A BROKER/CONDUIT – ARRANGING ACCESS TO OTHERS IN THE "SUPPLY" CHAIN AND PROVIDING INTRODUCTIONS.

Sarah was referred by her bank to Malus GmbH, a Swiss adviser, to create a tax efficient structure for potential future investment into UK property. Malus was an approved intermediary of a UK high street bank (with the referral made in good faith after they carried out appropriate due diligence on Malus), and Sarah planned to put her post-tax employment earnings into this structure.

Sarah had a relative, Maisie, who was neither resident nor domiciled in the UK. Malus advised Sarah that she should set up a Swiss trust using Maisie as the settlor. This was done, although Maisie was never asked to sign anything and was not aware that a trust was being set up with her named as the settlor. Sarah was advised that she retained beneficial ownership of all the assets despite the trust arrangement.

The trust had bank accounts with Lunar Bank in Monaco. Sarah admitted her actions following initial contact with Malus were deliberate.

Under the new offences: The UK high-street bank did not know that Malus would help Sarah to evade UK tax, and the 'vanilla' referral to Malus was made in good faith. Under these circumstances Malus was not acting as an 'associated person' of the UK high-street bank, so the UK High Street Bank is not liable under the new offences.

Malus's staff, however, by providing advice, as well as professional trustee services to Sarah's trust which they knew was not properly constituted, have deliberately facilitated Sarah's acts to hide her assets and evade tax. In doing so, the staff of Malus were acting in the capacity of persons associated with it. If Malus had not taken reasonable steps to prevent their staff from facilitating Sarah's tax evasion then Malus would be guilty of the new offence. Its compliance with any applicable published guidance, its contractual terms for its staff, the training it provides, and any steps taken to monitor and ensure compliance would all be relevant to the assessment of whether it had reasonable prevention procedures.

Lunar Bank's staff have performed acts that in fact facilitated Sarah's tax evasion. However, they did so without being aware of any tax evasion. They may have been negligent and failed to comply with their anti-money laundering obligations, but they lack the requisite guilty state of mind to commit an offence relating to facilitating Sarah's tax evasion. Therefore, there is no tax evasion facilitation offence that Lunar Bank has failed to prevent.

EXAMPLE 2) PROVIDING PLANNING AND ADVICE ON THE JURISDICTIONS, INVESTMENTS AND STRUCTURES WHICH WILL ENABLE THE TAXPAYER TO HIDE THEIR MONEY.

John ran a UK business. John opened a Channel Islands bank account in which he could hide untaxed business income from HMRC.

John took his untaxed funds on a regular basis to a business contact, Michael, who travels regularly to the Channel Islands. Michael would take the money in a suitcase to the Channel Islands and deposit it in John's bank account.

In 2004, following unsolicited advice from the Channel Island bank to help him continue hiding his untaxed wealth from HMRC, John transferred the bank accounts to a nominee Foundation in Panama thereby avoiding reporting under the EU Savings Directive and retaining secrecy over his funds. The Foundation was operated by other Channel Island professionals to whom the bank subcontracted the work.

Under the new offences: Michael was knowingly helping John to physically move funds offshore for tax evasion purposes. Michael was happy to do this because it fostered continued good business relations with John. Michael is guilty of a tax evasion facilitation offence by virtue of facilitating John's actions but, as he is an individual and not an associated person of a relevant body, no question of his committing the new offence arises.

The Channel Island bank's staff initially opened the account for John knowing that he wanted his activities to remain hidden from HMRC. Many years later the Channel Island bank staff actively advised John on how he could continue to hide his money. This conduct amounts to the criminal facilitation of tax evasion. The Channel Island bank would be guilty of the new offence unless it had taken reasonable steps to prevent its staff facilitating John's tax evasion. Its compliance with any applicable published guidance, its contractual terms for its staff, the training it provides, and any steps taken to monitor and ensure compliance would all be relevant to the assessment of whether it had taken reasonable steps.

The Channel Island bank professionals helped John to maintain a structure which facilitated his evasion activities. These professionals were asked by the bank to assist others in John's position and knew they were assisting people evading UK tax. This conduct amounts to the criminal facilitation of tax evasion. The bank therefore failed to prevent this conduct occurring and would be guilty of the new offence if it could not show that it had taken reasonable steps to prevent its associated persons from facilitating John's tax evasion.

EXAMPLE 3) DELIVERY OF INFRASTRUCTURE – E.G. SETTING UP COMPANIES, TRUSTS AND OTHER VEHICLES WHICH ARE USED TO HIDE BENEFICIAL OWNERSHIP; OPENING BANK ACCOUNTS; PROVIDING LEGAL SERVICES AND DOCUMENTATION WHICH UNDERPIN THE STRUCTURES USED IN THE EVASION SUCH AS NOTARY SERVICES AND POWERS OF ATTORNEY.

Manjit was the owner and Director of a UK-based interior design business. He generated false invoices and drew cheques with fictitious payee details logged in the company records, in order to divert proceeds offshore and reduce taxable profits in the UK. These cheques were in fact made payable to an extensive network of offshore discretionary trusts and corporate vehicles in Gibraltar, Belize, Seychelles, and the British Virgin Islands ("BVI").

In particular, the trustees invested the funds in a portfolio of bank accounts and investment properties held in the name of "off the shelf" corporate vehicles in the Seychelles and BVI. The properties, acquired with the proceeds of tax evasion, were then rented out commercially with UK taxes paid on the rental income under the non-resident landlord scheme ("NRLS") to give the appearance of a genuine offshore ownership arrangement. The NRLS arrangement had been accepted by HMRC, being the only contemporaneous information that was available at the time.

Following an HMRC investigation, Manjit accepted that these transactions were fraudulent. Manjit admitted he deliberately committed offshore tax evasion.

Under the new offences: The trustees claimed that they believed everything they were doing was "above board" - but they also stated that "the affairs of their clients were none of their business". HMRC's view was that the trustees turned a blind eye to the true beneficial ownership of the structure in order to retain Manjit's business. If the trustees in truth had knowledge of, but decided to ignore, Manjit's tax evasion, their conduct would amount to the criminal facilitation of Manjit's tax evasion and any trust company or partnership for which they worked would be guilty of the new offence if it had not taken reasonable steps to prevent the facilitation of Manjit's tax evasion. Their employer's compliance with any applicable published guidance, its contractual terms for its staff, the training it provides, and any steps taken to monitor and ensure compliance would all be relevant to the assessment of whether it had taken reasonable steps.

Of course, if the trustees were truly unaware of the tax evasion (whether out of negligence or otherwise) their assistance would not amount to a tax evasion facilitation offence (as these cannot be committed negligently) and the new offence would not be committed.

EXAMPLE 4) MAINTENANCE OF INFRASTRUCTURE E.G. PROVIDING PROFESSIONAL TRUSTEE OR COMPANY DIRECTOR SERVICES INCLUDING NOMINEE SERVICES; PROVIDING VIRTUAL OFFICES, IT STRUCTURES, LEGAL SERVICES AND DOCUMENTATION WHICH OBSCURES THE TRUE NATURE OF THE ARRANGEMENTS SUCH AS AUDIT CERTIFICATES.

Paula was domiciled in Australia, but had been resident in the UK since the 1970s. In 2017, Paula wanted to regularise her affairs and disclosed to HMRC that she had been hiding substantial UK taxable income for a prolonged period. She had been using companies in Bermuda and the Bahamas to shelter both business and private assets and to facilitate the movement of funds through a variety of jurisdictions.

The network of companies had been set up by Paula's lawyer, a partner in a Guernsey-based legal partnership, in total secrecy, meaning that Paula had never paid UK taxes for more than 30 years of UK residence.

Under the new offences: The lawyer actively assisted Paula in evading UK taxes, knowing that the structures would enable her to evade UK tax. Any company or partnership for which the lawyer was an associated person would be guilty of the new offence if it had not taken reasonable steps to prevent him facilitating Paula's tax evasion. Its compliance with any applicable published guidance, its contractual terms for its staff, the training it provides, and any steps taken to monitor and ensure compliance would all be relevant to the assessment of whether it had taken reasonable steps.

EXAMPLE 5) FINANCIAL ASSISTANCE – HELPING THE EVADER TO MOVE THEIR MONEY OUT OF THE UK, AND/OR KEEP IT HIDDEN BY PROVIDING ONGOING BANKING SERVICES AND PLATFORMS; PROVIDING CLIENT ACCOUNTS AND ESCROW SERVICES; MOVING MONEY THROUGH FINANCIAL INSTRUMENTS, CURRENCY CONVERSIONS ETC.

Christoph was a wealthy non-domiciled individual who was a long-term UK resident. His job entitled him to significant bonus payments, related to duties performed wholly in the UK, on which he did not want to pay UK tax. His UK accountant put him in touch with an adviser in Israel. The Israeli adviser set up a number of bank accounts in Singapore in the names of BVI-registered companies, under the control of a discretionary trust. Christoph arranged for his bonus payments to be lodged in the accounts operated in Singapore. As well as evading income tax on his employment income over a number of years, Christoph's settlements also attracted significant Inheritance Tax liabilities.

Under the new offences: The UK accountant knew what Christoph was trying to achieve, and for many years acted as a conduit through which Christoph contacted the Israeli adviser. This amounts to a tax evasion facilitation offence. The company or partnership that the accountant worked for would be guilty of the new offence if it had not taken reasonable steps to prevent him or her facilitating the tax evasion. Its compliance with any applicable published guidance, its contractual terms for its staff, the training it provides, and any steps taken to monitor and ensure compliance would all be relevant to the assessment of whether it had taken reasonable steps.

The Israeli adviser also knew Christoph's aims, and knew that secrecy was key to achieving those aims. He provided advice, and also set up and maintained the structure. This conduct facilitated Christoph's tax evasion. The company or partnership that the adviser worked for would be guilty of the new offence if it had not taken reasonable steps to prevent the adviser facilitating the tax evasion. Its compliance with any applicable published guidance, its contractual terms for its staff, the training it provides, and any steps taken to monitor and ensure compliance would all be relevant to the assessment of whether it had taken reasonable steps.

The Singapore bank's staff were unaware that the structure was being used to evade UK tax. As such they would not have the requisite state of mind to be guilty of facilitating Christoph's tax evasion. Therefore the Singapore bank could not be guilty of failing to prevent its staff from facilitating tax evasion.

EXAMPLE 6) PAYROLL SERVICES

Bruce is contractually employed by Warrington Ltd and has worked for them for many years. Warrington Ltd provides skilled workers for offshore oil and gas platforms around the United Kingdom.

After many years of working in the oil and gas industry, Bruce becomes disillusioned with his pay and a perceived difference in lifestyle between himself and his colleagues. Bruce airs his grievances with some of his colleagues. Bruce's colleague Nick tells him that the easiest way to take home more pay is to have some of his wages paid into an account in a tax efficient jurisdiction and not to tell the tax man about it. Nick tells Bruce to speak to Sandra who is responsible for payroll and to mention that they have spoken and that he is looking to mitigate his tax liabilities.

Bruce speaks to Sandra in Warrington Ltd's payroll department and Jess agrees that for an administrative fee she can pay a portion of Bruce's pay into an offshore account of his choice and remove that pay from his payslip. Bruce expresses some concerns about losing his job if the company finds out that he is being partially paid "off the books". Sandra reassures Bruce that she helps lots of people in the company to mitigate their taxes and that the company understands that it is just the price that has to be paid to retain long serving employees like Bruce.

With the help of his colleague and friend Nick, Bruce opens an account with a bank in Jersey, falsifying information about his identity and tax residency so that the account is not reportable to the UK, where he has a tax liability. As promised Sandra ensures that 40% of Bruce's pay is kept off the balance sheet, taking a fee for her services before paying the remainder into Bruce's account in Jersey with MJS Bank.

Through a joint investigation with the Jersey authorities HMRC identify the undeclared accounts of Bruce, Nick and other employees of Warrington Ltd at MJS Bank. During an interview under caution Bruce admits everything and fully co-operates with HMRC.

Under the new offences

Sandra knew that Bruce was seeking to evade tax and that in order to achieve this he required her assistance and she provided that assistance. This amounts to a tax evasion facilitation offence. Sandra undertook these activities whilst acting in the capacity of a person associated with Warrington Ltd.

Warrington Ltd would be liable for the new domestic tax evasion offence if it had not taken reasonable steps to prevent Sandra from facilitating the tax evasion. Its compliance with any applicable published guidance, its contractual terms for its staff, the training it provides, and any steps taken to monitor and ensure compliance would all be relevant to the assessment of whether it had taken reasonable steps.

MJS Bank are not liable under the new offence as persons associated with it were acting in good faith when opening bank accounts for Bruce, Nick and other employees of Warrington Ltd. They performed the customer checks required by law and did not know that their provision of financial services were being used to further criminal activity.

4. SUGGESTED REASONABLE PREVENTION PROCEDURES FOR LOWER RISK SMES

An SME should first undertake a risk assessment of the products and services it offers, as well as internal systems and client data that might be used to facilitate tax evasion, including by 'sitting at the desk' of employees and other associated persons, considering the motive, means and opportunity for facilitating tax evasion.

Consider some of the hallmarks of fraud or fraud 'red flags' when undertaking the risk assessment, for example:

- Are there staff who refuse to take leave and do not allow anyone else to review their files, or are overtly defensive over client relationships?
- Do existing processes ensure that for higher risk activity at least a sample of files are routinely reviewed by a second pair of eyes?

Then consider tailoring existing processes and procedures accordingly to prevent and detect potential tax evasion facilitation – this could include:

- Having a commitment to preventing the involvement of those acting on the relevant body's behalf in the criminal facilitation of tax evasion, which might be demonstrated by issuing a prominent message from the board of directors (or the leadership team) against all forms of tax evasion
- Having terms in contracts (with employees and contractors) requiring them not to engage in facilitating tax evasion and to report and concerns immediately
- Providing regular training for staff on preventing the facilitation of tax evasion, which may form part of wider financial crime detection and prevention training.
- Having clear reporting procedures for whistle-blowing of suspected facilitation of tax evasion offences
- Ensure their pay and bonus policy/structure encourages reporting and discourages pursuing profit to the point of condoning tax evasion
- Having regular reviews of the effectiveness of prevention procedures and refining them where necessary
- Monitoring and enforcing compliance with prevention procedures
- An overview of its strategy and timeframe to implement its preventative policies.

5. FUTURE UPDATES TO THE GUIDANCE

The Guidance is intended to be updated as and when required to aid understanding of the offences and the defence of "reasonable procedures". HMRC welcomes comments and contributions from stakeholders which can be submitted via email to: consult.nosafehavens@hmrc.gsi.gov.uk

Note—See the Facilitation of Tax Evasion Offences (Guidance About Prevention) Regulations, SI 2017/876 which bring this Guidance into operation on 30 September 2017.

Scottish Statutory Instruments

Contents

Chronological list of printed Scottish Statutory Instruments

Note—

For a chronological list of current and amending SSIs, *see below*.

Chronological list of Scottish Statutory Instruments

Note—

The following is the list of current and amending SSIs.

SSI 2015/132 Scottish Tax Tribunals (Voting and Offences etc.) Regulations 2015 (revoked)
SSI 2015/184 Scottish Tax Tribunals (Time Limits and Rules of Procedure) Regulations 2015 (revoked)
SSI 2015/187 Scottish Tax Tribunals (Conduct and Fitness Assessment Tribunal) Rules 2015 (revoked)
SSI 2015/247 Courts Reform (Scotland) Act 2014 (Commencement No. 3, Transitional and Saving Provisions) Order 2015
SSI 2015/381 Scottish Tribunals (Eligibility for Appointment) Regulations 2015
SSI 2015/404 Scottish Tribunals (Listed Tribunals) Regulations 2015
SSI 2015/422 Tribunals (Scotland) Act 2014 (Commencement No 3) Order 2015
SSI 2016/196 Inquiries into Fatal Accidents and Sudden Deaths etc. (Scotland) Act 2016 (Commencement No 1 and Transitional Provision) Regulations 2016
SSI 2016/231 The Scottish Tribunals (Time Limits) Regulations 2016
SSI 2016/232 Upper Tribunal for Scotland (Rules of Procedure) Regulations 2016
SSI 2016/333 Upper Tribunal for Scotland (Rules of Procedure) Amendment Regulations 2016
SSI 2016/341 First-tier Tribunal for Scotland (Chambers) Regulations 2016
SSI 2016/342 Scottish Tribunals (Offences in Relation to Proceedings) Regulations 2016
SSI 2017/69 First-tier Tribunal for Scotland Tax Chamber (Procedure) Regulations 2017
SSI 2017/105 Upper Tribunal for Scotland (Transfer of Functions of the Upper Tax Tribunal for Scotland) Regulations 2017
SSI 2017/106 First-tier Tribunal for Scotland (Transfer of Functions of the First-tier Tax Tribunal for Scotland) Regulations 2017
SSI 2017/107 First-tier Tribunal for Scotland Tax Chamber and Upper Tribunal for Scotland (Composition) Regulations 2017
SSI 2017/108 Tribunals (Scotland) Act 2014 (Ancillary Provisions) Regulations 2017
SSI 2017/109 Scottish Tribunals (Listed Tribunals) Regulations 2017
SSI 2017/274 Scottish Tribunals (Eligibility for Appointment) Amendment Regulations 2017

2014/355

SCOTTISH TAX TRIBUNALS (ELIGIBILITY FOR APPOINTMENT) REGULATIONS 2014

Made . . . .*9 December 2014*
Laid before the Scottish Parliament . . . .*11 December 2014*
Coming into force . . . .*1 February 2015*

Revocation—These Regulations revoked by the Tribunals (Scotland) Act 2014 (Ancillary Provisions) Regulations, SSI 2017/108 reg 3, Schedule with effect from 24 April 2017.

The Scottish Ministers make the following Regulations in exercise of the powers conferred by paragraphs 2(3) and 9(1)(*a*) and (*b*) of schedule 2 to the Revenue Scotland and Tax Powers Act 2014.

1 Citation, commencement and interpretation

(1) These Regulations may be cited as the Scottish Tax Tribunals (Eligibility for Appointment) Regulations 2014 and come into force on 1st February 2015.

(2) In these Regulations, "the Act" means the Revenue Scotland and Tax Powers Act 2014.

Revocation—These Regulations revoked by the Tribunals (Scotland) Act 2014 (Ancillary Provisions) Regulations, SSI 2017/108 reg 3, Schedule with effect from 24 April 2017.

2 Eligibility for appointment as ordinary member of the First-tier Tax Tribunal for Scotland

(1) A person is eligible for appointment as an ordinary member of the First-tier Tax Tribunal for Scotland if paragraph (2), (3) or (4) applies.

(2) This paragraph applies to a person who is a member of the Chartered Institute of Taxation.

(3) This paragraph applies to a person who is an accountant who is a member of—

(*a*) the Institute of Chartered Accountants of Scotland;
(*b*) the Institute of Chartered Accountants in England and Wales;
(*c*) the Institute of Chartered Accountants in Ireland;
(*d*) the Institute of Certified Public Accountants in Ireland;
(*e*) the Association of Chartered Certified Accountants;
(*f*) the Chartered Institute of Management Accountants; or
(*g*) the Chartered Institute of Public Finance and Accountancy.

(4) This paragraph applies to a person who has substantial experience in tax matters and related tax procedures (whether obtained in a business, trade, charity or not-for-profit organisation, or in a profession or in academia).

Revocation—These Regulations revoked by the Tribunals (Scotland) Act 2014 (Ancillary Provisions) Regulations, SSI 2017/108 reg 3, Schedule with effect from 24 April 2017.

3 Means of calculating 5-year period of legal practice in connection with eligibility for appointment as legal member of the First-tier Tax Tribunal for Scotland

(1) For the purposes of calculating the 5-year period mentioned paragraph 4(1) of schedule 2 to the Act, the following applies.

(2) The period of 5 years practice need not be continuous.

Revocation—These Regulations revoked by the Tribunals (Scotland) Act 2014 (Ancillary Provisions) Regulations, SSI 2017/108 reg 3, Schedule with effect from 24 April 2017.

4 Means of calculating 10-year period of legal practice in connection with eligibility for appointment as President of the Tax Tribunals or appointment as legal member of the Upper Tax Tribunal for Scotland

(1) For the purposes of calculating the 10-year period mentioned paragraphs 1(2) and 6(1) of schedule 2 to the Act, the following applies.

(2) The period of 10 years practice need not be continuous.

Revocation—These Regulations revoked by the Tribunals (Scotland) Act 2014 (Ancillary Provisions) Regulations, SSI 2017/108 reg 3, Schedule with effect from 24 April 2017.

2015/36

REVENUE SCOTLAND AND TAX POWERS ACT (FEES FOR PAYMENT) REGULATIONS 2015

Made . . . .*29 January 2015*
Laid before the Scottish Parliament . . . .*2 February 2015*
Coming into force . . . .*1 April 2015*

The Scottish Ministers make the following Regulations in exercise of the powers conferred by section 222 of the Revenue Scotland and Tax Powers Act 2014 and all other powers enabling them to do so.

In accordance with section 222(2) of that Act, Revenue Scotland expects that it, or the person authorised by it, will be required to pay a fee in connection with amounts paid where internet authorisation is given for payment by credit card.

1 Citation and commencement

These Regulations may be cited as the Revenue Scotland and Tax Powers Act (Fees for Payment) Regulations 2015 and come into force on 1st April 2015.

2 Interpretation

In these Regulations—

"credit card" means a card which—

(*a*) is a credit-token within section 14(1)(*b*) of the Consumer Credit Act 1974; or

(*b*) would be a credit-token falling within that enactment were the card to be given to an individual; and

"internet authorisation" means authorisation given by a credit card issuer via the internet.

3 Fees for payment by credit card

(1) This regulation shall apply to any payment in respect of tax or interest or penalties to Revenue Scotland where—

(*a*) internet authorisation is given for a person to make a payment by credit card; and

(*b*) that person makes the payment to Revenue Scotland or a person authorised by Revenue Scotland.

(2) Where paragraph 1(1) applies, the person must also pay a fee of 1.4% of the amount of that payment.

(3) The fee must be paid by being added to the payment (so that, accordingly, the person must make a single overall payment, consisting of the payment and the fee).

2015/37

REVENUE SCOTLAND AND TAX POWERS ACT (INVOLVED THIRD PARTY) ORDER 2015

Made . . . . *29 January 2015*

Laid before the Scottish Parliament . . . . *2 February 2015*

Coming into force . . . . *1 April 2015*

The Scottish Ministers make the following Order in exercise of the powers conferred by section 142(3) of the Revenue Scotland and Tax Powers Act 2014 and all other powers enabling them to do so.

1 Citation and commencement

This Order may be cited as the Revenue Scotland and Tax Powers Act (Involved Third Party) Order 2015 and comes into force on 1st April 2015.

2 Involved third parties—Scottish landfill tax

For the purposes of section 142(3) of the Revenue Scotland and Tax Powers Act 2014—

(*a*) an "involved third party" is any person involved (in any capacity) with a taxable disposal as defined in section 3(2) of the Landfill Tax (Scotland) Act 2014;

(*b*) "relevant documents" are documents relating to the taxable disposal mentioned in paragraph (*a*); and

(*c*) a "relevant devolved tax" is Scottish landfill tax within the meaning of section 1(1) of the Landfill Tax (Scotland) Act 2014.

2015/38

REVENUE SCOTLAND AND TAX POWERS ACT (PRIVILEGED COMMUNICATIONS) REGULATIONS 2015

Made . . . . *29 January 2015*

Laid before the Scottish Parliament . . . . *2 February 2015*

Coming into force . . . . *1 April 2015*

The Scottish Ministers make the following Regulations in exercise of the powers conferred by section 138(3) of the Revenue Scotland and Tax Powers Act 2014 and all other powers enabling them to do so.

1 Citation, and commencement

These Regulations may be cited as the Revenue Scotland and Tax Powers Act (Privileged Communications) Regulations 2015 and come into force on 1st April 2015.

2 Interpretation

In these Regulations—

"the Act" means the Revenue Scotland and Tax Powers Act 2014;

"document" means information, a document or part of a document;

"document in dispute" is a document over which there is a dispute between Revenue Scotland and a person who has been given an information notice as to whether the document is privileged;

"person acting on behalf of" a taxpayer or a third party means any person who is acting on behalf of a taxpayer or third party in relation to an information notice;

"taxpayer" means a person who is given a notice under section 123 of the Act;

"third party" means a person who is given a notice under section 124 of the Act;

"working day" means any day except a Saturday, a Sunday, Christmas Day, Good Friday or a bank holiday under section 1 of the Banking and Financial Dealings Act 1971.

3 Application

These Regulations apply where there is a dispute between Revenue Scotland and a person to whom an information notice has been given either—

(*a*) during the course of correspondence; or

(*b*) during the course of an inspection of premises under Part 7 of the Act,

as to whether a document is privileged.

4 Requirement to provide information and produce documents not in dispute

Nothing in these Regulations shall affect—

(*a*) the requirement under an information notice to provide information or produce a document which is not in dispute; or

(*b*) the power under Part 7 of the Act to inspect premises.

5 Procedure where information notice given in correspondence is in dispute

(1) The following procedure applies where there is a dispute falling within regulation 3(*a*).

(2) On receipt of the information notice, the taxpayer, third party or person acting on their behalf shall—

(*a*) by the date given in the notice for providing information or producing documents, specify in a list each document required under the information notice which is in dispute, with a description of the nature and contents of that document; and

(*b*) serve that list on Revenue Scotland.

(3) But no description of a document or type of document is required where such description would itself give rise to a dispute over privilege.

(4) Within twenty working days of receiving the list referred to in sub-paragraph (2), Revenue Scotland must notify the person who served the list of any documents on the list that it requires to be produced and which it considers are not privileged.

(5) On receipt of notification under paragraph (4), the taxpayer, third party or person acting on their behalf (unless he or she agrees that every document notified under paragraph (4) is not privileged) must make an application to the tribunal to consider and resolve the dispute and must include copies of the documents which remain in dispute with that application.

(6) The taxpayer, third party or person acting on their behalf shall provide Revenue Scotland with proof of service under paragraph (2)(*b*).

(7) Service for the purposes of paragraph (2)(*b*) must take place within a reasonable time to be agreed between the taxpayer, third party or person acting on their behalf and Revenue Scotland but in any event no later than twenty working days after the date given in the notice for providing information or producing documents.

(8) An application under paragraph (5) must be made within a reasonable time to be agreed between the taxpayer, third party or person acting on their behalf and Revenue Scotland but in any event no later than twenty working days after the date of the notification required under paragraph (4).

6 Procedure where information notice given during inspection of premises is in dispute

(1) The following procedure applies where there is a dispute falling within regulation 3(b).

(2) On receipt of the information notice, the taxpayer, third party or person acting on their behalf shall indicate to the designated officer carrying out the inspection each document, required under the information notice, which is in dispute.

(3) The taxpayer, third party or person acting on their behalf must place the document or documents in dispute, or a copy of such document or documents, in an appropriate container which prevents the contents being visible.

(4) The container shall be—

(*a*) sealed, labelled and signed by that person;

(*b*) countersigned by the officer; and

(*c*) given into the custody of a designated officer.

(5) The designated officer shall deliver the container to the tribunal with the seal intact within forty working days of having taken custody of it together with an application to the tribunal to consider and resolve the dispute.

(6) The designated officer, at the same time as delivering an application to the tribunal under paragraph (5), must send a copy of that application to the person to whom an information notice has been given that is subject to the dispute falling within regulation 3(*b*).

7 Compliance with information notice

Where a taxpayer or third party who has received an information notice, or a person acting on their behalf, complies with the procedure set out in regulation 5 or, as the case may be, regulation 6, those persons shall be treated as having complied with the information notice in relation to the documents in dispute until the tribunal decides the status of the document or until an agreement has been reached under regulation 9.

8 Finding of the tribunal

(1) When an application is made under regulation 5(5) or 6(5), the tribunal shall—

(*a*) resolve the dispute by confirming whether and to what extent the document is or is not privileged; and

(*b*) direct which part or parts of a document (if any) shall be disclosed.

(2) The tribunal must ensure that any document in dispute, or any copy of such document, is not inappropriately disclosed to any person pending the tribunal's consideration of the status of the document.

9 Resolution of disputes by agreement

A dispute falling within regulation 3 may be resolved at any time by Revenue Scotland and the person to whom an information notice has been given reaching an agreement, whether in writing or otherwise.

2015/128

REVENUE SCOTLAND AND TAX POWERS ACT (INTEREST ON UNPAID TAX AND INTEREST RATES IN GENERAL) REGULATIONS 2015

Made . . . .*17 March 2015*

Coming into force . . . .*1 April 2015*

The Scottish Ministers make the following Regulations in exercise of the powers conferred by sections 217(2) and 220(1) of the Revenue Scotland and Tax Powers Act 2014 and all other powers enabling them to do so.

In accordance with section 254(3)(*m*) of that Act, a draft of this instrument has been laid before and approved by resolution of the Scottish Parliament.

PART 1
GENERAL

1 Citation and commencement

These Regulations may be cited as the Revenue Scotland and Tax Powers Act (Interest on Unpaid Tax and Interest Rates in General) Regulations 2015 and come into force on 1st April 2015.

2 Interpretation

In these Regulations, "the Act" means the Revenue Scotland and Tax Powers Act 2014.

PART 2
INTEREST ON UNPAID TAX

3 Interpretation of Part 2

In this Part—

"disqualifying event" means—

(*a*) in relation to the withdrawal of relief under schedule 4 (relief for certain acquisitions of residential property) to the LBTT(S) Act 2013, an event listed in section 33(4)(*a*) of that Act;

(*b*) in relation to the withdrawal of relief under schedule 5 (relief for transfer of multiple dwellings) to the LBTT(S) Act 2013, an event listed in section 33(4)(*b*) of that Act;

(*c*) in relation to the withdrawal of relief under schedule 8 (relief for alternative finance investment bonds) to the LBTT(S) Act 2013, an event listed in section 33(4)(*c*) of that Act;

(*d*) in relation to the withdrawal of group relief, the buyer ceasing to be a member of the same group as the seller in terms of paragraph 14 of schedule 10 to the LBTT(S) Act 2013;

(*e*) in relation to the withdrawal of relief under schedule 10A (sub-sale development relief) to the LBTT(S) Act 2013, an event listed in section 33(4)(*da*) of that Act;

(*f*) in relation to the withdrawal of reconstruction or acquisition relief, the change of control of the acquiring company in terms of paragraph 13 of schedule 11 to the LBTT(S) Act 2013; or

(*g*) in relation to the withdrawal of charities relief, a disqualifying event as defined in paragraphs 5 and 6 of schedule 13 to the LBTT(S) Act 2013; and

"filing date" means the filing date as defined in section 82 of the Act.

4 Relevant date

(1) The "relevant date" for the purposes of section 217(1) of the Act in respect of the tax or taxes listed in Column 1 of the table below is the date specified in Column 2 corresponding with the taxes listed in Column 1.

	Tax to which unpaid tax relates	'Relevant date'
1	All devolved taxes	(*a*) in relation to an amount, or additional amount, payable following an adjustment made under section 66(1) (counteracting tax advantages) of the Act, the filing date for the return or, if there is no return, the filing date for the return that would have been required to have been made, had the tax avoidance arrangement not been entered into or carried out; (*b*) in relation to an amount, or additional amount, payable following a taxpayer amendment of a return under section 83 of the Act, the filing date for that return; (*c*) in relation to an amount, or additional amount, payable following a Revenue Scotland correction of a return under section 84 of the Act, the filing date for that return; (*d*) in relation to an amount, or additional amount, payable following a Revenue Scotland amendment of a return under section 87 of the Act, the filing date for that return; (*e*) in relation to an amount, or additional amount, payable following a Revenue Scotland amendment of a return made in a closure notice under section 93 of the Act, the filing date for that return; (*f*) in relation to an amount, or additional amount, payable following a Revenue Scotland determination of no return made under section 95 of the Act, the relevant filing date for the return as defined in section 95(2) of that Act; (*g*) in relation to an amount, or additional amount, payable following a Revenue Scotland assessment under section 98 of the Act, the filing date for the return made by the taxpayer where there is a return; otherwise the date when a return should have been made.

	Tax to which unpaid tax relates	'Relevant date'
2	Land and buildings transaction tax	(*a*) in the case of an amount payable because relief is withdrawn under— (i) Part 5 of schedule 4 (relief for certain acquisitions of residential property) to the LBTT(S) Act 2013; (ii) Part 5 of schedule 5 (relief for transfer of multiple dwellings) to the LBTT(S) Act 2013; (iii) Part 4 of schedule 8 (relief for alternative finance investment bonds) to the LBTT(S) Act 2013; (iv) Part 3 of schedule 10 (group relief) to the LBTT(S) Act 2013; (v) Part 3 of schedule 10A (sub-sale development relief) to the LBTT(S) Act 2013; (vi) Part 4 of schedule 11 (reconstruction or acquisition relief) to the LBTT(S) Act 2013; or (vii) schedule 13 (charities relief) to the LBTT(S) Act 2013, 30 days after the date of the disqualifying event unless there is deferral under section 41 of the LBTT(S) Act 2013, in which case paragraph (*b*) below applies; (*b*) in the case of a deferred payment under section 41 of the LBTT(S) Act 2013, the date when the deferred payment is due; (*c*) in a case within sections 18 or 19 (contingent, uncertain or unascertained consideration) of the LBTT(S) Act 2013 where an amount, or additional amount, is payable to Revenue Scotland, the filing date in terms of section 31(3) of that Act; (*d*) in the cases where payment is not deferred following an application under section 41 of that Act, the filing date; (*e*) for any other return under the LBTT(S) Act 2013, the filing date.
3	Scottish landfill tax	In relation to a return made under regulations made under section 25 (accounting for tax and time for payment) of the LT(S) Act 2014, the filing date.

(2) Where a person chargeable to an amount of tax dies before the amount becomes due and payable, and the executor is unable to pay the amount before obtaining confirmation, the relevant date is the later of the date which would be the relevant date apart from this paragraph and the day after the end of the period of 30 days beginning with the grant of confirmation.

PART 3
RATES OF INTEREST IN GENERAL

5 Meaning of "Bank of England rate"

(1) Subject to paragraph (2), in regulations 6 and 7 "Bank of England rate" for a day means the official bank rate as last announced at a meeting of the Bank of England Monetary Policy Committee held prior to that day.

(2) Where a day falls within three working days of a meeting at which an announcement referred to in paragraph (1) was made, the "Bank of England rate" for that day means the rate as determined under that paragraph as if that meeting had not taken place.

(3) In paragraph (2), "working day" means any day other than a non-business day (within the meaning of section 92 of the Bills of Exchange Act 1882).

6 Late payment interest rate

The late payment of tax or penalties interest rate for the purposes of section 217 (interest on unpaid tax) and section 218 (interest on penalties) of the Act is the percentage per annum found by applying the following formula—

Bank of England rate + 2.5.

7 Repayment interest rate

The repayment interest rate for the purposes of section 219 of the Act (interest on repayment of tax overpaid etc) is the higher of—

(*a*) 0.5% per annum; and

(*b*) The Bank of England rate.

2015/129

REVENUE SCOTLAND AND TAX POWERS ACT (POSTPONEMENT OF TAX PENDING A REVIEW OR APPEAL) REGULATIONS 2015

Made . . . . *17 March 2015*

Coming into force . . . . *1 April 2015*

The Scottish Ministers make the following Regulations in exercise of the powers conferred by section 245(2) of the Revenue Scotland and Tax Powers Act 2014 and all other powers enabling them to do so.

In accordance with section 254(3)(*p*) of that Act a draft of this instrument has been laid before and approved by resolution of the Scottish Parliament.

1 Citation and commencement

These Regulations may be cited as the Revenue Scotland and Tax Powers Act (Postponement of Tax Pending a Review or Appeal) Regulations 2015 and come into force on 1st April 2015.

2 Interpretation

In these Regulations, "the Act" means the Revenue Scotland and Tax Powers Act 2014.

3 Postponement of payment of tax pending a review or appeal

(1) Notwithstanding the terms of section 245(1) of the Act (reviews and appeals not to postpone recovery of tax), where there is a review or appeal under Part 11 of the Act, the appellant may make an application to Revenue Scotland for postponement of payment of amounts of tax, penalty and interest due under the Land and Buildings Transaction Tax (Scotland) Act 2013.

(2) Where, on receipt of an application under paragraph (1), Revenue Scotland is satisfied that—

(*a*) there are exceptional circumstances; and

(*b*) these exceptional circumstances are such as to justify postponement,

Revenue Scotland may grant the application in whole or in part and may impose in relation to the granting of the application any further conditions it considers appropriate.

2015/130

REVENUE SCOTLAND AND TAX POWERS ACT (RECORD KEEPING) REGULATIONS 2015

Made . . . . *17 March 2015*

Coming into force . . . . *1 April 2015*

The Scottish Ministers make the following Regulations in exercise of the powers conferred by sections 74(9) to (11) and 81 of, and paragraph 3(3) to (5) of schedule 3 to, the Revenue Scotland and Tax Powers Act 2014 and all other powers enabling them to do so.

In accordance with section 254(3)(*f*) of that Act, a draft of this instrument has been laid before and approved by resolution of the Scottish Parliament.

1 Citation and commencement

These Regulations may be cited as the Revenue Scotland and Tax Powers Act (Record Keeping) Regulations 2015 and come into force on 1st April 2015.

2 Interpretation

In these Regulations—

"the Act" means the Revenue Scotland and Tax Powers Act 2014;

"the Administration Regulations" means the Scottish Landfill Tax (Administration) Regulations 2015;

"landfill invoice" has the meaning given in regulation 2(1) of the Administration Regulations;

"relevant transaction" means a disposal of anything that would be a disposal but for the fact that the material is not disposed of as waste; and

"transfer note" has the meaning given in regulation 2(1) of the Administration Regulations.

3 Records in respect of landfill tax

(1) Every person referred to in section 74(1) and (3) of the Act shall, for the purpose of accounting for landfill tax under the LT(S) Act 2014, preserve the following—

(*a*) the person's business and accounting records;

(*b*) a landfill tax account in such form and containing such particulars as may be specified in a notice published by Revenue Scotland (and not subsequently withdrawn);

(*c*) transfer notes and any other original or copy records in relation to material brought on to or removed from the landfill site;

(*d*) all invoices (including landfill invoices) and similar documents issued to the person and copies of such invoices and similar documents issued by the person;

(*e*) all credit or debit notes or other documents received by the person which evidence an increase or decrease in the amount of any consideration for a relevant transaction, and copies of such documents that are issued by the person;

(*f*) such other records as may be specified in a notice published by Revenue Scotland (and not subsequently withdrawn).

(2) The evidence required in support of a claim detailed in regulation 21 of the Administration Regulations and records required to be kept detailed in regulation 22 of those Regulations are supporting documents specified as required to be kept under section 74 of the Act or, as the case may be, records included in records required to be kept and preserved under that section.

(3) The evidence required in support of a claim detailed in regulation 21 of the Administration Regulations and records required to be kept detailed in regulation 22 of those Regulations are supporting documents specified as required to be kept under paragraph 3 of schedule 3 to the Act or, as the case may be, records included in records required to be kept and preserved under that paragraph.

4 Records in respect of land and buildings transaction tax

(1) The buyer in a land transaction which is not notifiable must keep such records as may be needed to enable the buyer to demonstrate that the transaction is not notifiable.

(2) Subject to paragraph (3), sections 74(2), (5), (7) and (8), and 76 to 79 of the Act apply to a buyer mentioned in paragraph (1) as those sections apply to a person mentioned in section 74(1) of the Act.

(3) In paragraph (2) the reference to section 74(5) of the Act is a reference to that subsection, with the following substituted for paragraph (*a*)—

"(*a*) the fifth anniversary of the day by which a return would have been required to have been made, had the land transaction been notifiable,".

2015/131

REVENUE SCOTLAND AND TAX POWERS ACT (REIMBURSEMENT ARRANGEMENTS) REGULATIONS 2015

Made . . . . *17 March 2015*

Coming into force . . . . *1 April 2015*

The Scottish Ministers make the following Regulations in exercise of the powers conferred by section 111 and 112 of the Revenue Scotland and Tax Powers Act 2014 and all other powers enabling them to do so.

In accordance with section 254(3)(*g*) of that Act, a draft of this instrument has been laid before and approved by resolution of the Scottish Parliament.

1 Citation and commencement
These Regulations may be cited as the Revenue Scotland and Tax Powers Act (Reimbursement Arrangements) Regulations 2015 and come into force on 1st April 2015.

2 Interpretation
In these Regulations—

"the Act" means the Revenue Scotland and Tax Powers Act 2014;

"claim" means a claim made under section 107(2) of the Act for repayment of an amount paid to Revenue Scotland by way of tax which was not chargeable; and "claimed" and "claimant" shall be construed accordingly;

"reimbursement arrangements" means any arrangements for the purposes of a claim which—

(*a*) are made by a claimant for the purpose of securing that the claimant is not unjustly enriched by the repayment of any amount in pursuance of the claim; and

(*b*) provide for the reimbursement of persons ("customers") who have, for practical purposes, borne the whole or any part of the cost of the original payment of that amount to Revenue Scotland;

"relevant amount" means that part (which may be the whole) of the amount of a claim which the claimant has reimbursed or intends to reimburse to customers.

3 Reimbursement arrangements—general
For the purposes of section 109 of the Act (defence to certain claims for relief under section 107 or 108) reimbursement arrangements made by a claimant must be disregarded except where they—

(*a*) include the provisions described in regulation 4; and

(*b*) are supported by the undertakings described in regulation 8.

4 Reimbursement arrangements—provisions to be included
The provisions referred to in regulation 3(a) are that—

(*a*) reimbursement for which the arrangements provide will be completed by no later than 90 days after the repayment to which it relates;

(*b*) no deduction will be made from the relevant amount by way of fee or charge (howsoever expressed or effected);

(*c*) reimbursement will be made only in cash or by cheque or, with the agreement of the claimant, by electronic transfer;

(*d*) any part of the relevant amount that is not reimbursed by the time mentioned in paragraph (*a*) above will be repaid by the claimant to Revenue Scotland;

(*e*) any interest paid by Revenue Scotland on any relevant amount repaid by it will also be treated by the claimant in the same way as the relevant amount falls to be treated under paragraphs (*a*) and (*b*); and

(*f*) the records described in regulation 6 will be kept by the claimant and produced by that person to Revenue Scotland, or to an officer of Revenue Scotland in accordance with regulation 7.

5 Repayments to Revenue Scotland
The claimant must, without prior demand, make any repayment to Revenue Scotland that the claimant is required to make by virtue of regulation 4(*d*) and (*e*) within 30 days of the expiration of the period of 90 days referred to in regulation 4(*a*).

6 Records
The claimant must keep for three years from the date of reimbursement, records of the following matters—

(*a*) the names and addresses of those customers whom the claimant has reimbursed or whom the claimant intends to reimburse;

(*b*) the total amount reimbursed to each such customer, including in all cases receipts from those reimbursed acknowledging how much has been reimbursed and giving the date of reimbursement;

(*c*) the amount of interest included in each total amount reimbursed to each customer;

(*d*) the date that each reimbursement is made.

7 Production of records
(1) Where a claimant is given notice in accordance with paragraph (2), the claimant must in accordance with such notice produce to Revenue Scotland, or to an officer of Revenue Scotland, the records that the claimant is required to keep pursuant to regulation 6.

(2) A notice given for the purposes of paragraph (1) must—

(*a*) be in writing;

(*b*) state the place and time at which, and the date on which the records are to be produced; and

(*c*) be signed and dated by Revenue Scotland, or by an officer of Revenue Scotland,

and may be given before or after, or both before and after, Revenue Scotland has paid the relevant amount to the claimant.

8 Undertakings

(1) The undertakings referred to in regulation 3(*b*) must be given to Revenue Scotland by the claimant no later than the time at which the claimant makes the claim for which the reimbursement arrangements have been made.

(2) The undertakings must be in writing, be signed and dated by the claimant, and be to the effect that—

(*a*) at the date of the undertakings the claimant is able to identify the names and addresses of those customers whom the claimant has reimbursed or whom the claimant intends to reimburse;

(*b*) the claimant will apply the whole of the relevant amount, without any deduction by way of fee or charge or otherwise, to the reimbursement of such customers no later than 90 days after the claimant's receipt of that amount (except insofar as the claimant has already so reimbursed them);

(*c*) the claimant will apply any interest paid to the claimant on the relevant amount wholly to the reimbursement of such customers no later than 90 days after the claimant's receipt of that interest;

(*d*) the claimant will repay to Revenue Scotland without demand the whole or such part of the relevant amount repaid to the claimant or of any interest paid to the claimant as the claimant fails to apply in accordance with the undertakings mentioned in sub-paragraphs (*b*) and (*c*);

(*e*) the claimant will keep the records described in regulation 6; and

(*f*) the claimant will comply with any notice given in accordance with regulation 7 concerning the production of such records.

(3) The claimant must submit to Revenue Scotland an amended undertaking (to reflect the correction or amendment) within 14 days of—

(*a*) the claimant amending a claim under paragraph 10(1) of Schedule 3 to the Act; or

(*b*) Revenue Scotland amending a claim under paragraph 14(3)(*b*) of Schedule 3 to the Act.

9 Penalties

(1) The provisions in paragraphs 5 to 8 of Schedule 3 to the Act (penalties relating to records) apply to a failure to comply with regulation 6 as they apply to a failure to comply with paragraph 3 of Schedule 3 to the Act (duty to keep and preserve records).

(2) The penalty for failure to comply with a notice given under regulation 7(1) is £300 and a further penalty not exceeding £60 for each subsequent day on which the failure continues.

(3) A claimant who fails to comply with regulation 5 is liable to a penalty of 100% of the amount of any repayment to Revenue Scotland that the claimant is required to make by virtue of regulation 4(*d*) and (*e*), but section 218 of the Act (interest on penalties) must not apply to such a penalty.

2015/132

SCOTTISH TAX TRIBUNALS (VOTING AND OFFENCES ETC) REGULATIONS 2015

Made . . . . *17 March 2015*

Coming into force . . . . *1 April 2015*

Revocation—These Regulations revoked by the Tribunals (Scotland) Act 2014 (Ancillary Provisions) Regulations, SSI 2017/108 reg 3, Schedule with effect from 24 April 2017.

The Scottish Ministers make the following Regulations in exercise of the powers conferred by sections 32 and 50(1) of the Revenue Scotland and Tax Powers Act 2014 and all other powers enabling them to do so.

In accordance with section 50(3) of that Act the Scottish Ministers have obtained the approval of the Lord President of the Court of Session in relation to regulations 3 and 4.

In accordance with section 254(3)(*b*) and (*d*) of that Act a draft of these Regulations has been laid before and approved by resolution of the Scottish Parliament.

1 Citation and commencement

These Regulations may be cited as the Scottish Tax Tribunals (Voting and Offences etc) Regulations 2015 and come into force on 1st April 2015.

Revocation—These Regulations revoked by the Tribunals (Scotland) Act 2014 (Ancillary Provisions) Regulations, SSI 2017/108 reg 3, Schedule with effect from 24 April 2017.

2 Tribunal consisting of two or more members—voting

(1) Where a matter is to be decided by two or more members of the First-tier Tax Tribunal for Scotland or of the Upper Tax Tribunal for Scotland, and the decision of the tribunal is not unanimous, the following provisions apply.

(2) The decision of the majority of the members is the decision of the tribunal.

(3) But in the event of a tie the chairing member has a casting vote.

Revocation—These Regulations revoked by the Tribunals (Scotland) Act 2014 (Ancillary Provisions) Regulations, SSI 2017/108 reg 3, Schedule with effect from 24 April 2017.

3 Offences in relation to proceedings before the Scottish Tax Tribunals

(1) In any proceedings before the First-tier Tax Tribunal for Scotland or the Upper Tax Tribunal for Scotland it is an offence for any person to—

(*a*) make a false statement in an application in a case;

(*b*) alter, conceal or destroy, or fail to produce, something that is required to be produced in accordance with tribunal rules; or

(*c*) fail to attend, or give evidence, when required to do so in accordance with tribunal rules.

(2) It is a defence for a person charged with an offence under paragraph (1) to prove that the person had a reasonable excuse for acting in the way charged.

(3) A person who is guilty of an offence under paragraph (1) is liable on summary conviction to imprisonment for a term not exceeding 12 months or a fine not exceeding level 5 on the standard scale (or both).

Revocation—These Regulations revoked by the Tribunals (Scotland) Act 2014 (Ancillary Provisions) Regulations, SSI 2017/108 reg 3, Schedule with effect from 24 April 2017.

4 Circumstances in which a person need not give evidence or produce something to the Scottish Tax Tribunals

In any proceedings before the First-tier Tax Tribunal for Scotland or the Upper Tax Tribunal for Scotland a person need not give evidence or produce something which the person would be entitled to refuse to give or produce in proceedings in a court in Scotland.

Revocation—These Regulations revoked by the Tribunals (Scotland) Act 2014 (Ancillary Provisions) Regulations, SSI 2017/108 reg 3, Schedule with effect from 24 April 2017.

2015/184

SCOTTISH TAX TRIBUNALS (TIME LIMITS AND RULES OF PROCEDURE) REGULATIONS 2015

Made . . . .*29 April 2015*
Laid before the Scottish Parliament . . . .*1 May 2015*
Coming into force . . . .*1 June 2015*

Revocation—These Regulations revoked by the Tribunals (Scotland) Act 2014 (Ancillary Provisions) Regulations, SSI 2017/108 reg 3, Schedule with effect from 24 April 2017.

The Scottish Ministers make the following Regulations in exercise of the powers conferred by sections 39, 51, 52, 53, 54, 55, 56 and 249 of the Revenue Scotland and Tax Powers Act 2014 and all other powers enabling them to do so.

In accordance with section 51(4) of that Act, they have consulted with the President of the Scottish Tax Tribunals and such other persons as they considered appropriate.

1 Citation, commencement and interpretation

(1) These Regulations may be cited as the Scottish Tax Tribunals (Time Limits and Rules of Procedure) Regulations 2015 and the Rules contained in Schedules 1 and 2 may be cited, respectively, as—

(*a*) the First-tier Tax Tribunal for Scotland Rules of Procedure 2015; and

(*b*) the Upper Tax Tribunal for Scotland Rules of Procedure 2015.

(2) These Regulations come into force on 1st June 2015.

(3) In regulations 3 and 4, "RSTPA 2014" means the Revenue Scotland and Tax Powers Act 2014.

Revocation—These Regulations revoked by the Tribunals (Scotland) Act 2014 (Ancillary Provisions) Regulations, SSI 2017/108 reg 3, Schedule with effect from 24 April 2017.

2 Application of Schedules

(1) The Rules in Schedule 1 apply to all proceedings before the First-tier Tax Tribunal for Scotland.

(2) The Rules in Schedule 2 apply to all proceedings before the Upper Tax Tribunal for Scotland.

Revocation—These Regulations revoked by the Tribunals (Scotland) Act 2014 (Ancillary Provisions) Regulations, SSI 2017/108 reg 3, Schedule with effect from 24 April 2017.

3 Time limits for permission to appeal—application to decision making forum

(1) For the purposes of the permissions mentioned in section 34(3)(*a*) of RSTPA 2014 (application for permission to appeal made to the First-tier Tribunal) or section 36(3)(*a*) of RSTPA 2014 (application for permission to appeal made to the Upper Tribunal), the following time limit applies.

(2) An application for permission to appeal must be received by the First-tier Tax Tribunal for Scotland or the Upper Tax Tribunal for Scotland, as appropriate, within the period of 30 days from the relevant date.

(3) The relevant date is the later of—

(*a*) the date on which the decision appealed against was sent to the appellant;

(*b*) the date on which the statement of reasons for the decision was sent to the appellant.

Revocation—These Regulations revoked by the Tribunals (Scotland) Act 2014 (Ancillary Provisions) Regulations, SSI 2017/108 reg 3, Schedule with effect from 24 April 2017.

4 Time limits for permission to appeal—application to appellate forum

(1) For the purposes of the permission mentioned in section 34(3)(*b*) of RSTPA 2014 (application for permission to appeal made to the Upper Tribunal following refusal by the First-tier Tribunal), the following time limit applies.

(2) An application for permission to appeal must be received by the Upper Tax Tribunal for Scotland within the period of 30 days from the relevant date.

(3) The relevant date is the date on which notice of the First-tier Tax Tribunal for Scotland's refusal of permission to appeal was sent to the appellant.

Revocation—These Regulations revoked by the Tribunals (Scotland) Act 2014 (Ancillary Provisions) Regulations, SSI 2017/108 reg 3, Schedule with effect from 24 April 2017.

SCHEDULE 1

THE FIRST-TIER TAX TRIBUNAL FOR SCOTLAND RULES OF PROCEDURE 2015

Regulation 2(1)

Revocation—These Regulations revoked by the Tribunals (Scotland) Act 2014 (Ancillary Provisions) Regulations, SSI 2017/108 reg 3, Schedule with effect from 24 April 2017.

PART 1
INTRODUCTION

Revocation—These Regulations revoked by the Tribunals (Scotland) Act 2014 (Ancillary Provisions) Regulations, SSI 2017/108 reg 3, Schedule with effect from 24 April 2017.

Interpretation

1 In these Rules—

"appellant" means—

(*a*) the person who starts proceedings (whether by notifying an appeal, by making an application, by a reference, or otherwise);

(*b*) in proceedings started jointly by more than one person, such persons acting jointly or each such person, as the context requires;

(*c*) in any case, a person substituted as an appellant under rule 9 (addition, substitution and removal of parties);

"Basic case" means a case allocated to the Basic category under rule 24 (allocation of cases to categories);

"Complex case" means a case allocated to the Complex category under rule 24;

"Default Paper case" means a case allocated to the Default Paper category under rule 24;

"document" means anything in which information is recorded in any form, and an obligation under these Rules to provide or allow access to a document or a copy of a document for any purpose means, unless the First-tier Tribunal directs otherwise, an obligation to provide or allow access to such document or copy in a legible form or in a form which can be readily made into a legible form;

"hearing" means an oral hearing and includes a hearing conducted in whole or in part by video link, telephone or other means of instantaneous two-way electronic communication;

"party" means a person who is (or was at the time that the First-tier Tribunal disposed of the proceedings) an appellant or respondent in proceedings before the First-tier Tribunal;

"practice direction" means a direction given under section 57 of RSTPA 2014;

"President" means the President of the Scottish Tax Tribunals;

"respondent" means—

(*a*) Revenue Scotland, where Revenue Scotland is not an appellant;

(*b*) in proceedings brought by Revenue Scotland alone, a person against whom the proceedings are brought or to whom the proceedings relate;

(*c*) in any case, a person substituted or added as a respondent under rule 9 (addition, substitution and removal of parties);

"RSTPA 2014" means the Revenue Scotland and Tax Powers Act 2014;

"Standard case" means a case allocated to the Standard category under rule 24.

Revocation—These Regulations revoked by the Tribunals (Scotland) Act 2014 (Ancillary Provisions) Regulations, SSI 2017/108 reg 3, Schedule with effect from 24 April 2017.

Overriding objective and parties' obligation to co-operate with the First-tier Tribunal

2 (1) The overriding objective of these Rules is to enable the First-tier Tribunal to deal with cases fairly and justly.

(2) Dealing with a case in accordance with the overriding objective includes—

(*a*) dealing with the case in ways which are proportionate to the importance of the case, the complexity of the issues, the anticipated expenses and the resources of the parties;

(*b*) avoiding unnecessary formality and seeking flexibility in the proceedings;

(*c*) ensuring, so far as practicable, that the parties are able to participate fully in the proceedings;

(*d*) using any special expertise of the First-tier Tribunal effectively; and

(*e*) avoiding delay, so far as compatible with proper consideration of the issues.

(3) The First-tier Tribunal must seek to give effect to the overriding objective when it—

(*a*) exercises any power under these Rules; or

(*b*) interprets any rule or practice direction.

(4) Parties must, insofar as reasonably possible—

(*a*) help the First-tier Tribunal to further the overriding objective; and

(*b*) co-operate with the First-tier Tribunal generally.

Revocation—These Regulations revoked by the Tribunals (Scotland) Act 2014 (Ancillary Provisions) Regulations, SSI 2017/108 reg 3, Schedule with effect from 24 April 2017.

Mediation

3 The First-tier Tribunal should seek, where appropriate—

(*a*) to bring to the attention of the parties the availability of mediation for the resolution of the dispute; and

(*b*) if the parties wish and provided that it is compatible with the overriding objective, to facilitate the use of mediation.

Revocation—These Regulations revoked by the Tribunals (Scotland) Act 2014 (Ancillary Provisions) Regulations, SSI 2017/108 reg 3, Schedule with effect from 24 April 2017.

PART 2
GENERAL POWERS AND PROVISIONS

Revocation—These Regulations revoked by the Tribunals (Scotland) Act 2014 (Ancillary Provisions) Regulations, SSI 2017/108 reg 3, Schedule with effect from 24 April 2017.

Delegation to staff

4 (1) Staff of the Scottish Courts and Tribunals Service may, with the approval of the President, carry out functions of a judicial nature permitted or required to be done by the First-tier Tribunal.

(2) The approval referred to at paragraph (1) may apply generally to the carrying out of specified functions by members of staff of a specified description in specified circumstances.

(3) Within 14 days after the date that the First-tier Tribunal sends notice of a decision made by a member of staff pursuant to an approval under paragraph (1) to a party, that party may make a written application to the First-tier Tribunal for that decision to be considered afresh by a member of the First-tier Tribunal.

Revocation—These Regulations revoked by the Tribunals (Scotland) Act 2014 (Ancillary Provisions) Regulations, SSI 2017/108 reg 3, Schedule with effect from 24 April 2017.

Case management powers

5 (1) Subject to the provisions of RSTPA 2014 and these Rules, the First-tier Tribunal may regulate its own procedure.

(2) The First-tier Tribunal may give a direction in relation to the conduct or disposal of proceedings at any time, including a direction amending, suspending or setting aside an earlier direction.

(3) In particular, and without restricting the general powers in paragraphs (1) and (2), the First-tier Tribunal may by direction—

(*a*) extend or shorten the time for complying with any rule, practice direction or direction, or regulation 3(2) of the Scottish Tax Tribunals (Time Limits and Rules of Procedure) Regulations 2015 (time limit for permission to appeal to the Upper Tax Tribunal for Scotland);

(*b*) conjoin or take concurrently two or more sets of proceedings or parts of proceedings raising common issues, or treat a case as a lead case (whether in accordance with rule 18 (lead cases) or otherwise);
(*c*) permit or require a party to amend a document;
(*d*) permit or require a party or another person to provide documents, information, evidence or submissions to the First-tier Tribunal or a party;
(*e*) deal with an issue in the proceedings as a preliminary issue;
(*f*) hold a hearing to consider any matter, including a case management hearing;
(*g*) decide the form of any hearing;
(*h*) adjourn or postpone a hearing;
(*i*) require a party to produce a file of documents for a hearing;
(*j*) sist proceedings;
(*k*) transfer proceedings to another court or tribunal if that other court or tribunal has jurisdiction in relation to the proceedings and—
(i) because of a change of circumstances since the proceedings were started, the First-tier Tribunal no longer has jurisdiction in relation to the proceedings; or
(ii) the First-tier Tribunal considers that the other court or tribunal is a more appropriate forum for the determination of the case;
(l) suspend the effect of its own decision pending the determination by the First-tier Tribunal or the Upper Tribunal, as the case may be, of an application for permission to appeal or an appeal.

Revocation—These Regulations revoked by the Tribunals (Scotland) Act 2014 (Ancillary Provisions) Regulations, SSI 2017/108 reg 3, Schedule with effect from 24 April 2017.

Procedure for applying for and giving directions

6 (1) The First-tier Tribunal may give a direction on the application of one or more of the parties or on its own initiative.
(2) An application for a direction may be made—
(*a*) by sending or delivering a written application to the First-tier Tribunal; or
(*b*) orally during the course of a hearing.
(3) An application for a direction must include the reasons for making that application.
(4) The First-tier Tribunal must send notice of any direction to every party and to any other person affected by the direction.
(5) If a party or other person sent notice of the direction under paragraph (4) wishes to challenge a direction which the First-tier Tribunal has given, they may do so by applying for another direction which amends, suspends or sets aside the first direction.

Revocation—These Regulations revoked by the Tribunals (Scotland) Act 2014 (Ancillary Provisions) Regulations, SSI 2017/108 reg 3, Schedule with effect from 24 April 2017.

Failure to comply with rules etc

7 (1) An irregularity resulting from a failure to comply with any requirement in these Rules, a practice direction or a direction does not of itself render void the proceedings or any step taken in the proceedings.
(2) If a party has failed to comply with a requirement in these Rules, a practice direction or a direction, the First-tier Tribunal may take such action as it considers just, which may include—
(*a*) waiving the requirement;
(*b*) requiring the failure to be remedied;
(*c*) exercising its power under rule 8 (striking out a party's case); or
(*d*) restricting a party's participation in proceedings.

Revocation—These Regulations revoked by the Tribunals (Scotland) Act 2014 (Ancillary Provisions) Regulations, SSI 2017/108 reg 3, Schedule with effect from 24 April 2017.

Striking out a party's case

8 (1) The proceedings, or the appropriate part of them, will be struck out if the appellant has failed to comply with a direction that stated that failure by a party to comply with the direction would lead to the striking out of the proceedings or that part of them.
(2) The First-tier Tribunal must strike out the whole or a part of the proceedings if the First-tier Tribunal—
(*a*) does not have jurisdiction in relation to the proceedings or that part of them; and
(*b*) does not exercise its power under rule 5(3)(*k*)(i) (transfer to another court or tribunal) in relation to the proceedings or that part of them.
(3) The First-tier Tribunal may strike out the whole or a part of the proceedings if—

(*a*) the appellant has failed to comply with a direction which stated that failure by the appellant to comply with the direction could lead to the striking out of the proceedings or part of them;

(*b*) the appellant has failed to co-operate with the First-tier Tribunal to such an extent that the First-tier Tribunal cannot deal with the proceedings fairly and justly; or

(*c*) the First-tier Tribunal considers there is no reasonable prospect of the appellant's case, or part of it, succeeding.

(4) The First-tier Tribunal may not strike out the whole or a part of the proceedings under paragraph (2) or (3)(*b*) or (*c*) without first giving the appellant an opportunity to make representations in relation to the proposed striking out.

(5) The effect of proceedings being struck out is that all issues are determined against the appellant. The effect of proceedings being partially struck out is that the relevant issues are determined against the appellant.

(6) If the proceedings, or a part of them, have been struck out under paragraph (1) or (3)(*a*), the appellant may make a written application for the proceedings, or a part of them, to be reinstated.

(7) An application under paragraph (6) must be received by the First-tier Tribunal within 30 days after the date that the First-tier Tribunal sent notification of the striking out to the appellant.

(8) This rule applies to a respondent as it applies to an appellant except that—

(*a*) a reference to the striking out of the proceedings is to be read as a reference to the barring of the respondent from taking further part in the proceedings; and

(*b*) a reference to an application for the reinstatement of proceedings which have been struck out is to be read as a reference to an application for the lifting of the bar on the respondent taking further part in the proceedings.

(9) If a respondent has been barred from taking further part in proceedings under this rule and that bar has not been lifted, the First-tier Tribunal need not consider any response or other submissions made by that respondent, and may summarily determine any or all issues against that respondent.

Revocation—These Regulations revoked by the Tribunals (Scotland) Act 2014 (Ancillary Provisions) Regulations, SSI 2017/108 reg 3, Schedule with effect from 24 April 2017.

Addition, substitution and removal of parties

9 (1) The First-tier Tribunal may give a direction adding, substituting or removing a party as an appellant or a respondent including where—

(*a*) the wrong person has been named as a party; or

(*b*) the addition, substitution or removal has become necessary because of a change in circumstances since the start of proceedings.

(2) If the First-tier Tribunal gives a direction under paragraph (1) it may give such consequential directions as it considers appropriate.

(3) A person who is not a party may make a written application to the First-tier Tribunal to be added or substituted as a party under this rule.

(4) If the First-tier Tribunal refuses an application under paragraph (3) it must consider whether to permit the person who made the application to provide submissions or evidence to the First-tier Tribunal.

Revocation—These Regulations revoked by the Tribunals (Scotland) Act 2014 (Ancillary Provisions) Regulations, SSI 2017/108 reg 3, Schedule with effect from 24 April 2017.

Orders for expenses

10 (1) The First-tier Tribunal may only make an order in respect of expenses—

(*a*) in relation to wasted expenses and expenses incurred in applying for such expenses;

(*b*) if the First-tier Tribunal considers that a party or their representative has acted unreasonably in bringing, defending or conducting the proceedings; or

(*c*) if—

(i) the proceedings have been allocated as a Complex case under rule 24 (allocation of cases to categories); and

(ii) the taxpayer (or, where more than one party is a taxpayer, one of them) has not sent or delivered a written request to the First-tier Tribunal, within 30 days of receiving notice that the case had been allocated as a Complex case, that the proceedings be excluded from potential liability for expenses under this sub-paragraph.

(2) The First-tier Tribunal may make an order under paragraph (1) on an application or on its own initiative.

(3) A person making an application for an order under paragraph (1) must—

(*a*) send or deliver a written application to the First-tier Tribunal and to the person against whom it is proposed that the order be made; and

(*b*) send or deliver with the application a schedule of the expenses claimed in sufficient detail to allow the First-tier Tribunal to undertake a summary assessment of such expenses if it decides to do so.

(4) An application for an order under paragraph (1) may be made at any time during the proceedings but may not be made later than 30 days after the date on which the First-tier Tribunal sends—

(*a*) a decision notice recording the decision which finally disposes of all issues in the proceedings; or

(*b*) notice under rule 17(2) of its receipt of a withdrawal which ends the proceedings.

(5) The First-tier Tribunal may not make an order under paragraph (1) against a person (the "paying person") without first—

(*a*) giving that person an opportunity to make representations; and

(*b*) if the paying person is an individual, considering that person's financial means.

(6) The amount of expenses to be paid under an order under this rule may be ascertained by—

(*a*) summary assessment by the First-tier Tribunal;

(*b*) agreement of a specified sum by the paying person and the person entitled to receive the expenses (the "receiving person"); or

(*c*) assessment of the whole or a specified part of the expenses, including the expenses of the assessment, incurred by the receiving person, if not agreed.

(7) Following an order for assessment under paragraph (6)(*c*)—

(*a*) the paying person or the receiving person may apply to the Auditor of the Court of Session (as specified in the order); or

(*b*) the First-tier Tribunal may make a remit to the Auditor of the Court of Session,

for the taxation of the expenses according to the fees payable in that Court.

(8) Upon making an order for the assessment of expenses, the First-tier Tribunal may order an amount to be paid on account before the expenses are assessed.

(9) In this rule—

"taxpayer" means a party who is liable to pay, or has paid, the tax, interest or penalty to which the proceedings relate or part of such tax, interest or penalty, or whose liability to do so is in issue in the proceedings; and

"wasted expenses" means any expenses incurred by a party—

(*a*) as a result of any improper, unreasonable or negligent act or omission on the part of any representative or any employee of such a representative; or

(*b*) which, in the light of any such act or omission occurring after they were incurred, the First-Tier Tribunal considers it is unreasonable to expect that party to pay.

Revocation—These Regulations revoked by the Tribunals (Scotland) Act 2014 (Ancillary Provisions) Regulations, SSI 2017/108 reg 3, Schedule with effect from 24 April 2017.

Representatives

11 (1) A party may appoint a representative to represent that party in the proceedings.

(2) If a party appoints a representative, that party or the representative must send or deliver to the First-tier Tribunal and to each other party to the proceedings notice of the representative's name and address.

(3) Anything permitted or required to be done by a party under these Rules, a practice direction or a direction may be done by the representative of that party, except signing a witness statement.

(4) A person who receives due notice of the appointment of a representative—

(*a*) must provide to the representative any document which is required to be provided to the represented party, and need not provide that document to the represented party; and

(*b*) may assume that the representative is and remains authorised as such until they receive notification that this is not so from the representative or the represented party.

(5) At a hearing a party may be accompanied by another person whose name and address has not been notified under paragraph (2) but who, with the permission of the First-tier Tribunal, may act as a representative or otherwise assist in presenting the party's case at the hearing.

(6) Paragraphs (2) to (4) do not apply to a person who accompanies a party in accordance with paragraph (5).

Revocation—These Regulations revoked by the Tribunals (Scotland) Act 2014 (Ancillary Provisions) Regulations, SSI 2017/108 reg 3, Schedule with effect from 24 April 2017.

Calculating time

12 (1) An act required by these Rules, a practice direction or a direction to be done on or by a particular day must be done before 5pm on that day.

(2) If the time specified by these Rules, a practice direction or a direction for doing any act ends on a day other than a working day, the act is done in time if it is done on the next working day.

(3) In this rule "working day" means any day except a Saturday or Sunday, Christmas Day, Good Friday or a bank holiday in Scotland under section 1 of the Banking and Financial Dealings Act 1971.

Revocation—These Regulations revoked by the Tribunals (Scotland) Act 2014 (Ancillary Provisions) Regulations, SSI 2017/108 reg 3, Schedule with effect from 24 April 2017.

Sending and delivery of documents

13 (1) Any document to be provided to the First-tier Tribunal under these Rules, a practice direction or a direction must be—

(*a*) sent by pre-paid post or document exchange, or delivered by hand, to the address specified for the proceedings; or

(*b*) sent or delivered by such other method as the First-tier Tribunal may permit or direct.

(2) Subject to paragraph (3), if a party or representative provides a fax number, email address or other details for the electronic transmission of documents to them, that party or representative must accept delivery of documents by that method.

(3) If a party informs the First-tier Tribunal and all other parties that a particular form of communication (other than pre-paid post or delivery by hand) should not be used to provide documents to that party, that form of communication must not be so used.

(4) If the First-tier Tribunal or a party sends a document to a party or the First-tier Tribunal by email or any other electronic means of communication, the recipient may request that the sender provide a hard copy of the document to the recipient. The recipient must make such a request as soon as reasonably practicable after receiving the document electronically.

(5) The First-tier Tribunal and each party may assume that the address provided by a party or its representative is and remains the address to which documents should be sent or delivered until receiving notification to the contrary.

Revocation—These Regulations revoked by the Tribunals (Scotland) Act 2014 (Ancillary Provisions) Regulations, SSI 2017/108 reg 3, Schedule with effect from 24 April 2017.

Use of documents and information

14 (1) The First-tier Tribunal may make an order prohibiting the disclosure or publication of-

(*a*) specified documents or information relating to the proceedings; or

(*b*) any matter likely to lead members of the public to identify any person whom the First-tier Tribunal considers should not be identified.

(2) The First-tier Tribunal may give a direction prohibiting the disclosure of a document or information to a person if—

(*a*) the First-tier Tribunal is satisfied that such disclosure would be likely to cause that person or some other person serious harm; and

(*b*) the First-tier Tribunal is satisfied, having regard to the interests of justice, that it is proportionate to give such a direction.

(3) If a party ("the first party") considers that the First-tier Tribunal should give a direction under paragraph (2) prohibiting the disclosure of a document or information to another party ("the second party"), the first party must—

(*a*) exclude the relevant document or information from any documents that will be provided to the second party; and

(*b*) provide to the First-tier Tribunal the excluded document or information, and the reason for its exclusion, so that the First-tier Tribunal may decide whether the document or information should be disclosed to the second party or should be the subject of a direction under paragraph (2).

(4) If the First-tier Tribunal gives a direction under paragraph (2) which prevents disclosure to a party who has appointed a representative, the First-tier Tribunal may give a direction that the documents or information be disclosed to that representative if the First-tier Tribunal is satisfied that—

(*a*) disclosure to the representative would be in the interests of the party; and

(*b*) the representative will act in accordance with paragraph (5).

(5) Documents or information disclosed to a representative in accordance with a direction under paragraph (4) must not be disclosed either directly or indirectly to any other person without the First-tier Tribunal's consent.

(6) The First-tier Tribunal may, on its own initiative or on the application of a party, give a direction that certain documents or information must or may be disclosed to the First-tier Tribunal on the basis that the First-tier Tribunal will not disclose such documents or information to other persons, or specified other persons.

(7) A party making an application for a direction under paragraph (6) may withhold the relevant documents or information from other parties until the First-tier Tribunal has granted or refused the application.

(8) The First-tier Tribunal must conduct proceedings and record its decision and reasons appropriately so as not to undermine the effect of an order made under paragraph (1) or a direction given under paragraph (2) or (6).

Revocation—These Regulations revoked by the Tribunals (Scotland) Act 2014 (Ancillary Provisions) Regulations, SSI 2017/108 reg 3, Schedule with effect from 24 April 2017.

Evidence and submissions

15 (1) Without restriction on the general powers in rule 5(1) and (2) (case management powers), the First-tier Tribunal may give directions as to—

(*a*) issues on which it requires evidence or submissions;

(*b*) the nature of the evidence or submissions it requires;

(*c*) whether the parties are permitted or required to provide expert evidence, and if so whether the parties must jointly appoint a single expert to provide such evidence;

(*d*) any limit on the number of witnesses whose evidence a party may put forward, whether in relation to a particular issue or generally;

(*e*) the manner in which any evidence or submissions are to be provided, which may include a direction for them to be given—

(i) orally at a hearing; or

(ii) by written submissions or witness statement; and

(*f*) the time at which any evidence or submissions are to be provided.

(2) The First-tier Tribunal may—

(*a*) admit evidence whether or not the evidence would be admissible in a court in Scotland; or

(*b*) exclude evidence that would otherwise be admissible where—

(i) the evidence was, without reasonable excuse, not provided within the time allowed by a direction or a practice direction;

(ii) the evidence was, without reasonable excuse, otherwise provided in a manner that did not comply with a direction or a practice direction; or

(iii) it would otherwise be unfair to admit the evidence.

(3) The First-tier Tribunal may consent to a witness giving, or require any witness to give, evidence on oath, and may administer an oath for that purpose.

Revocation—These Regulations revoked by the Tribunals (Scotland) Act 2014 (Ancillary Provisions) Regulations, SSI 2017/108 reg 3, Schedule with effect from 24 April 2017.

Citation of witnesses and orders to answer questions or produce documents

16 (1) On the application of a party or on its own initiative, the First-tier Tribunal may—

(*a*) by citation require any person to attend as a witness at a hearing at the time and place specified in the citation;

(*b*) order any person to answer any questions or produce any documents in that person's possession or control which relate to any issue in the proceedings.

(2) A citation under paragraph (1)(*a*) must—

(*a*) give the person required to attend at least 14 days' notice of the hearing, or such other period as the First-tier Tribunal may direct; and

(*b*) where the person is not a party, make provision for the person's necessary expenses of attendance to be paid, and state who is to pay them.

(3) A person who receives a citation or order may apply to the First-tier Tribunal for it to be varied or set aside if the person did not have an opportunity to object to it before it was made or issued.

(4) A person making an application under paragraph (3) must do so as soon as reasonably practicable after receiving notice of the citation or order.

(5) A citation or order under this rule must—

(*a*) state that the person on whom the requirement is imposed may apply to the First-tier Tribunal to vary or set aside the citation or order, if the person did not have an opportunity to object to it before it was made or issued; and

(*b*) state the consequences of failure to comply with the citation or order.

Revocation—These Regulations revoked by the Tribunals (Scotland) Act 2014 (Ancillary Provisions) Regulations, SSI 2017/108 reg 3, Schedule with effect from 24 April 2017.

Withdrawal

17 (1) Subject to any provision in RSTPA 2014 relating to withdrawal or settlement of particular proceedings, a party may give notice to the First-tier Tribunal of the withdrawal of the case made by it in the First-tier Tribunal proceedings, or any part of that case—

(*a*) by sending or delivering to the First-tier Tribunal a notice of withdrawal; or

(*b*) orally at a hearing.

(2) The First-tier Tribunal must notify each party of its receipt of a withdrawal under this rule.

(3) A party who has withdrawn their case may make a written application to the First-tier Tribunal for the case to be reinstated.

(4) An application under paragraph (3) must be received by the First-tier Tribunal within 30 days after—

(*a*) the date that the First-tier Tribunal received the notice under paragraph (1)(*a*); or

(*b*) the date of the hearing at which the case was withdrawn orally under paragraph (1)(*b*).

Revocation—These Regulations revoked by the Tribunals (Scotland) Act 2014 (Ancillary Provisions) Regulations, SSI 2017/108 reg 3, Schedule with effect from 24 April 2017.

Lead cases

18 (1) This rule applies if—

(*a*) two or more cases have been started before the First-tier Tribunal;

(*b*) in each such case the First-tier Tribunal has not made a decision disposing of the proceedings; and

(*c*) the cases give rise to common or related issues of fact or law.

(2) The First-tier Tribunal may give a direction—

(*a*) specifying one or more cases falling under paragraph (1) as a lead case or lead cases; and

(*b*) sisting the other cases falling under paragraph (1) ("the related cases").

(3) When the First-tier Tribunal makes a decision in respect of the common or related issues—

(*a*) the First-tier Tribunal must send a copy of that decision to each party in each of the related cases; and

(*b*) subject to paragraph (4), that decision shall be binding on each of those parties.

(4) Within 30 days after the date that the First-tier Tribunal sent a copy of the decision to a party under paragraph (3)(*a*), that party may make a written application for a direction that the decision does not apply to, and is not binding on the parties to, that case.

(5) The First-tier Tribunal must give directions in respect of cases which are sisted under paragraph (2)(*b*), providing for the disposal of or further steps in those cases.

(6) If the lead case or cases are withdrawn or disposed of before the First-tier Tribunal makes a decision in respect of the common or related issues, the First-tier Tribunal must give directions as to—

(*a*) whether another case or other cases are to be heard as a lead case or lead cases; and

(*b*) whether any direction affecting the related cases should be set aside or amended.

Revocation—These Regulations revoked by the Tribunals (Scotland) Act 2014 (Ancillary Provisions) Regulations, SSI 2017/108 reg 3, Schedule with effect from 24 April 2017.

Chairing member

19 Where a matter is to be decided by two or more members of the First-tier Tax Tribunal, the President must determine the chairing member.

Revocation—These Regulations revoked by the Tribunals (Scotland) Act 2014 (Ancillary Provisions) Regulations, SSI 2017/108 reg 3, Schedule with effect from 24 April 2017.

Venue for hearings

20 The First-tier Tribunal is to be convened at such time and place in Scotland as the President may determine.

Revocation—These Regulations revoked by the Tribunals (Scotland) Act 2014 (Ancillary Provisions) Regulations, SSI 2017/108 reg 3, Schedule with effect from 24 April 2017.

Enforcement of decisions

21 An order for the payment of a sum payable in pursuance of a decision of the First-tier Tribunal, or a copy of such an order certified by the First-tier Tribunal, may be enforced as if it were an extract registered decree arbitral bearing a warrant for execution issued by the Sheriff Court of any sheriffdom in Scotland.

Revocation—These Regulations revoked by the Tribunals (Scotland) Act 2014 (Ancillary Provisions) Regulations, SSI 2017/108 reg 3, Schedule with effect from 24 April 2017.

PART 3
PROCEDURE FOR CASES IN THE FIRST-TIER TRIBUNAL

Revocation—These Regulations revoked by the Tribunals (Scotland) Act 2014 (Ancillary Provisions) Regulations, SSI 2017/108 reg 3, Schedule with effect from 24 April 2017.

CHAPTER 1

STARTING PROCEEDINGS AND ALLOCATION OF CASES TO CATEGORIES

Proceedings concerning late notice of review

22 (1) A person may apply to the First-tier Tribunal for permission to appeal under section 236(2)(*b*) of RSTPA 2014 (late notice of review) only if—

(*a*) the person has approached Revenue Scotland for agreement under section 236(2)(*a*); and

(*b*) agreement has been refused or has been given only on limited grounds.

(2) Where permission to appeal may be sought under paragraph (1), the notice of review must include a request for the permission referred to in section 236(2)(*b*) of RSTPA 2014 and the reason why the notice of review was not provided in time.

Revocation—These Regulations revoked by the Tribunals (Scotland) Act 2014 (Ancillary Provisions) Regulations, SSI 2017/108 reg 3, Schedule with effect from 24 April 2017.

Notice of appeal to the First-tier Tribunal

23 (1) The notice of appeal referred to in section 242 of RSTPA 2014 must include—

(*a*) the name and address of the appellant;

(*b*) the name and address of the appellant's representative (if any);

(*c*) an address where documents for the appellant may be sent or delivered;

(*d*) details of the decision appealed against;

(*e*) the result the appellant is seeking; and

(*f*) the grounds for making the appeal.

(2) The appellant must provide with the notice of appeal a copy of any written record of any decision appealed against, and any statement of reasons for that decision, that the appellant has or can reasonably obtain.

(3) A person may apply to the First-tier Tribunal for permission to appeal under section 243(2)(*b*) of RSTPA 2014 (late notice of appeal) only if—

(*a*) the person has approached Revenue Scotland for agreement under section 243(2)(*a*); and

(*b*) agreement has been refused or has been given only on limited grounds.

(4) Where permission to appeal may be sought under paragraph (3)—

(*a*) the notice of appeal must include a request for the permission referred to in section 243(2)(*b*) of RSTPA 2014 and the reason why the notice of appeal was not provided in time; and

(*b*) unless the First-tier Tribunal gives such permission, the First-tier Tribunal must not admit the appeal.

(5) When the First-tier Tribunal receives the notice of appeal, it must give notice of the proceedings to the respondent.

Revocation—These Regulations revoked by the Tribunals (Scotland) Act 2014 (Ancillary Provisions) Regulations, SSI 2017/108 reg 3, Schedule with effect from 24 April 2017.

Allocation of cases to categories

24 (1) When the First-tier Tribunal receives a notice of appeal, the First-tier Tribunal must give a direction allocating the case to one of the categories set out in paragraph (2).

(2) The categories referred to in paragraph (1) are—

(*a*) Default Paper cases, which will usually be disposed of without a hearing;

(*b*) Basic cases, which will usually be disposed of after a hearing, with minimal exchange of documents before the hearing;

(*c*) Standard cases, which will usually be subject to more detailed case management and be disposed of after a hearing; and

(*d*) Complex cases, in respect of which see paragraphs (4) and (5) below.

(3) The First-tier Tribunal may give a further direction re-allocating a case to a different category at any time, either on the application of a party or on its own initiative.

(4) The First-tier Tribunal may allocate a case as a Complex case under paragraph (1) or (3) only if the First-tier Tribunal considers that the case—

(*a*) will require lengthy or complex evidence or a lengthy hearing;

(*b*) involves a complex or important principle or issue; or

(*c*) involves a large financial sum.

(5) If a case is allocated as a Complex case—

(*a*) rule 10(1)(*c*) (expenses in Complex cases) applies to the case; and

(*b*) rule 29 (transfer of Complex cases to the Upper Tribunal) applies to the case.

Revocation—These Regulations revoked by the Tribunals (Scotland) Act 2014 (Ancillary Provisions) Regulations, SSI 2017/108 reg 3, Schedule with effect from 24 April 2017.

CHAPTER 2

PROCEDURE AFTER ALLOCATION OF CASES TO CATEGORIES

Basic cases

25 (1) This rule applies to Basic cases.

(2) Rule 26 (respondent's statement of case) does not apply and, subject to paragraph (3) and any direction given by the First-tier Tribunal, the case will proceed directly to a hearing.

(3) If the respondent intends to raise grounds for contesting the proceedings at the hearing which have not previously been communicated to the appellant, the respondent must notify the appellant of such grounds.

(4) If the respondent is required to notify the appellant of any grounds under paragraph (3), the respondent must do so—

(*a*) as soon as reasonably practicable after becoming aware that such is the case; and

(*b*) in sufficient detail to enable the appellant to respond to such grounds at the hearing.

Revocation—These Regulations revoked by the Tribunals (Scotland) Act 2014 (Ancillary Provisions) Regulations, SSI 2017/108 reg 3, Schedule with effect from 24 April 2017.

Respondent's statement of case

26 (1) A respondent must send or deliver a statement of case to the First-tier Tribunal, the appellant and any other respondent so that it is received—

(*a*) in a Default Paper case, within 42 days after the First-tier Tribunal sent the notice of appeal;

(*b*) in a Standard or Complex case, within 60 days after the First-tier Tribunal sent the notice of appeal.

(2) A statement of case must—

(*a*) in an appeal, state the legislative provision under which the decision under appeal was made; and

(*b*) set out the respondent's position in relation to the case.

(3) A statement of case may also contain a request that the case be dealt with at a hearing or without a hearing.

(4) If a respondent provides a statement of case to the First-tier Tribunal later than the time required by paragraph (1) or by any extension allowed under rule 5(3)(*a*) (power to extend time), the statement of case must include a request for an extension of time and the reason why the statement of case was not provided in time.

Revocation—These Regulations revoked by the Tribunals (Scotland) Act 2014 (Ancillary Provisions) Regulations, SSI 2017/108 reg 3, Schedule with effect from 24 April 2017.

Further steps in a Default Paper case

27 (1) This rule applies to Default Paper cases.

(2) The appellant may send or deliver a written reply to the First-tier Tribunal so that it is received within 30 days after the date on which the respondent sent to the appellant the statement of case to which the reply relates.

(3) The appellant's reply may—

(*a*) set out the appellant's response to the respondent's statement of case;

(*b*) provide any further information (including, where appropriate, copies of the documents containing such information) which has not yet been provided to the First-tier Tribunal and is relevant to the case; and

(*c*) contain a request that the case be dealt with at a hearing or without a hearing.

(4) The appellant must send or deliver a copy of any reply provided under paragraph (2) to each respondent at the same time as it is provided to the First-tier Tribunal.

(5) If the appellant provides a reply to the First-tier Tribunal later than the time required by paragraph (2) or by any extension allowed under rule 5(3)(*a*) (power to extend time), the reply must include a request for an extension of time and the reason why the reply was not provided in time.

(6) Following receipt of the appellant's reply, or the expiry of the time for the receipt of the appellant's reply then, unless it directs otherwise and subject in any event to paragraph (7), the First-tier Tribunal must proceed to determine the case without a hearing.

(7) If any party has made a written request to the First-tier Tribunal for a hearing, the First-tier Tribunal must hold a hearing before determining the case.

Revocation—These Regulations revoked by the Tribunals (Scotland) Act 2014 (Ancillary Provisions) Regulations, SSI 2017/108 reg 3, Schedule with effect from 24 April 2017.

Further steps in a Standard or Complex case

28 (1) This rule applies to Standard and Complex cases.

(2) Subject to any direction to the contrary, within 42 days after the date the respondent sent the statement of case (or, where there is more than one respondent, the date of the final statement of case) each party must send or deliver to the First-tier Tribunal and to each other party a list of documents—

(*a*) of which the party providing the list has possession, the right to possession, or the right to take copies; and

(*b*) which the party providing the list intends to rely upon or produce in the proceedings.

(3) A party which has provided a list of documents under paragraph (2) must allow each other party to inspect or take copies of the documents on the list.

Revocation—These Regulations revoked by the Tribunals (Scotland) Act 2014 (Ancillary Provisions) Regulations, SSI 2017/108 reg 3, Schedule with effect from 24 April 2017.

Transfer of Complex cases to the Upper Tribunal

29 (1) If a case has been allocated as a Complex case the First-tier Tribunal may, with the consent of the parties, refer a case or a preliminary issue to the President with a request that the case or issue be considered for transfer to the Upper Tribunal.

(2) If a case or issue has been referred by the First-tier Tribunal under paragraph (1), the President may direct that the case or issue be transferred to and determined by the Upper Tribunal.

Revocation—These Regulations revoked by the Tribunals (Scotland) Act 2014 (Ancillary Provisions) Regulations, SSI 2017/108 reg 3, Schedule with effect from 24 April 2017.

CHAPTER 3

HEARINGS

Decision with or without a hearing

30 (1) Subject to rule 27(6) (determination of a Default Paper case without a hearing) and the following paragraphs in this rule, the First-tier Tribunal must hold a hearing before making a decision which disposes of proceedings, or a part of proceedings, unless—

(*a*) each party has consented to the matter being decided without a hearing; and

(*b*) the First-tier Tribunal considers that it is able to decide the matter without a hearing.

(2) This rule does not apply to decisions under Part 4 (correcting, setting aside and appealing decisions of the First-tier Tribunal).

(3) The First-tier Tribunal may dispose of proceedings, or a part of proceedings, under rule 8 (striking out a party's case) without a hearing.

Revocation—These Regulations revoked by the Tribunals (Scotland) Act 2014 (Ancillary Provisions) Regulations, SSI 2017/108 reg 3, Schedule with effect from 24 April 2017.

Entitlement to attend a hearing

31 Subject to rule 33(4) (exclusion of a person from a hearing), each party is entitled to attend a hearing together with any representative permitted by rule 11.

Revocation—These Regulations revoked by the Tribunals (Scotland) Act 2014 (Ancillary Provisions) Regulations, SSI 2017/108 reg 3, Schedule with effect from 24 April 2017.

Notice of hearings

32 (1) The First-tier Tribunal must give each party entitled to attend a hearing reasonable notice of the time and place of any hearing (including any adjourned or postponed hearing) and any changes to the time and place of any hearing.

(2) In relation to a hearing to consider the disposal of proceedings, the period of notice under paragraph (1) must be at least 14 days except that the First-tier Tribunal may give less than 14 days' notice—

(*a*) with the parties' consent; or

(*b*) in urgent or exceptional circumstances.

Revocation—These Regulations revoked by the Tribunals (Scotland) Act 2014 (Ancillary Provisions) Regulations, SSI 2017/108 reg 3, Schedule with effect from 24 April 2017.

Public and private hearings and power to exclude

33 (1) Subject to the following paragraphs, all hearings must be held in public.

(2) The First-tier Tribunal may give a direction that a hearing, or part of it, is to be held in private if the First-tier Tribunal considers that restricting access to the hearing is justified—

(*a*) in the interests of public order or national security;

(*b*) in order to protect a person's right to respect for their private and family life;

(*c*) in order to maintain the confidentiality of sensitive information;

(*d*) in order to avoid serious harm to the public interest; or

(*e*) because not to do so would prejudice the interests of justice.

(3) Where a hearing, or part of it, is to be held in private, the First-tier Tribunal may determine who is permitted to attend the hearing or part of it.

(4) The First-tier Tribunal may give a direction excluding from any hearing, or part of it—

(*a*) any person whose conduct the First-tier Tribunal considers is disrupting or is likely to disrupt the hearing;

(*b*) any person whose presence the First-tier Tribunal considers is likely to prevent another person from giving evidence or making submissions freely;

(*c*) any person where the purpose of the hearing would be defeated by the attendance of that person; or

(*d*) a person under the age of sixteen years.

(5) The First-tier Tribunal may give a direction excluding a witness from a hearing until that witness gives evidence.

(6) When publishing a decision notice referred to in rule 36(2) resulting from a hearing which was held wholly or partly in private, the First-tier Tribunal must, so far as practicable, ensure that the report does not disclose information which was referred to only in a part of the hearing that was held in private (including such information which enables the identification of any person whose affairs were dealt with in the part of the hearing that was held in private) if to do so would undermine the purpose of holding the hearing in private.

Revocation—These Regulations revoked by the Tribunals (Scotland) Act 2014 (Ancillary Provisions) Regulations, SSI 2017/108 reg 3, Schedule with effect from 24 April 2017.

Hearings in a party's absence

34 If a party fails to attend a hearing the First-tier Tribunal may proceed with the hearing if the First-tier Tribunal—

(*a*) is satisfied that the party has been notified of the hearing or that reasonable steps have been taken to notify the party of the hearing; and

(*b*) considers that it is in the interests of justice to proceed with the hearing.

Revocation—These Regulations revoked by the Tribunals (Scotland) Act 2014 (Ancillary Provisions) Regulations, SSI 2017/108 reg 3, Schedule with effect from 24 April 2017.

CHAPTER 4

DECISIONS

Consent orders

35 (1) The First-tier Tribunal may, at the request of the parties but only if it considers it appropriate, make a consent order disposing of the proceedings and making such other appropriate provision as the parties have agreed.

(2) Notwithstanding any other provision of these Rules, the First-tier Tribunal need not hold a hearing before making an order under paragraph (1) or provide reasons for the order.

Revocation—These Regulations revoked by the Tribunals (Scotland) Act 2014 (Ancillary Provisions) Regulations, SSI 2017/108 reg 3, Schedule with effect from 24 April 2017.

Notice of decisions and reasons

36 (1) Subject to the remainder of this rule, the First-tier Tribunal may give a decision orally at a hearing.

(2) The First-tier Tribunal must provide to each party within 30 days after making a decision (other than a decision under Part 4) which finally disposes of all issues in the proceedings or of a preliminary issue dealt with following a direction under rule 5(3)(*e*), or as soon as practicable thereafter, a decision notice which—

(*a*) states the First-tier Tribunal's decision; and

(*b*) notifies the party of any right of appeal against the decision and the time within which, and the manner in which, the right of appeal may be exercised.

(3) Unless each party agrees that it is unnecessary, and in any event subject to rule 33(6), the decision notice must—

(*a*) include a summary of the findings of fact and reasons for the decision; or

(*b*) be accompanied by full written findings of fact and reasons for the decision.

(4) If the First-tier Tribunal provides no findings and reasons, or summary findings and reasons only, in or with the decision notice, a party to the proceedings may make a written application for full written findings and reasons, and must do so before making an application for permission to appeal under rule 40 (application for permission to appeal).

(5) An application under paragraph (4) must be sent or delivered to the First-tier Tribunal so that it is received within 30 days after the date that the First-tier Tribunal sent or otherwise provided the decision notice under paragraph (2) to the party making the application.

(6) The First-tier Tribunal must send a full written statement of findings and reasons to each party within 30 days after receiving an application for full written reasons made in accordance with paragraphs (4) and (5), or as soon as practicable thereafter.

Revocation—These Regulations revoked by the Tribunals (Scotland) Act 2014 (Ancillary Provisions) Regulations, SSI 2017/108 reg 3, Schedule with effect from 24 April 2017.

PART 4
CORRECTING, SETTING ASIDE AND APPEALING DECISIONS OF THE FIRST-TIER TRIBUNAL

Revocation—These Regulations revoked by the Tribunals (Scotland) Act 2014 (Ancillary Provisions) Regulations, SSI 2017/108 reg 3, Schedule with effect from 24 April 2017.

Interpretation

37 In this Part, "appeal" means the exercise of a right of appeal under section 34 of RSTPA 2014.

Revocation—These Regulations revoked by the Tribunals (Scotland) Act 2014 (Ancillary Provisions) Regulations, SSI 2017/108 reg 3, Schedule with effect from 24 April 2017.

Clerical mistakes and accidental slips or omissions

38 The First-tier Tribunal may at any time correct any clerical mistake or other accidental slip or omission in a decision, a direction or any document produced by it (or record of such a thing), by—

(*a*) sending notification of the amended decision or direction, or a copy of the amended document or record, to all parties; and

(*b*) making any necessary amendment to any information published in relation to the decision, direction, document or record.

Revocation—These Regulations revoked by the Tribunals (Scotland) Act 2014 (Ancillary Provisions) Regulations, SSI 2017/108 reg 3, Schedule with effect from 24 April 2017.

Setting aside a decision which disposes of proceedings

39 (1) The First-tier Tribunal may set aside a decision which disposes of proceedings, or part of such a decision, and re-make the decision, or the relevant part of it, if—

(*a*) the First-tier Tribunal considers that it is in the interests of justice to do so; and

(*b*) one or more of the conditions in paragraph (2) are satisfied.

(2) The conditions are—

(*a*) a document relating to the proceedings was not sent to, or was not received at an appropriate time by, a party or a party's representative;

(*b*) a document relating to the proceedings was not sent to the First-tier Tribunal at an appropriate time;

(*c*) a party, or a party's representative, was not present at a hearing related to the proceedings; or

(*d*) there has been some other procedural irregularity in the proceedings.

(3) A party applying for a decision, or part of a decision, to be set aside under paragraph (1) must make a written application to the First-tier Tribunal so that it is received no later than 30 days after the date on which the First-tier Tribunal sent notice of the decision to the party.

(4) If the First-tier Tribunal sets aside a decision or part of a decision under this rule, the First-tier Tribunal must notify the parties as soon as practicable.

Revocation—These Regulations revoked by the Tribunals (Scotland) Act 2014 (Ancillary Provisions) Regulations, SSI 2017/108 reg 3, Schedule with effect from 24 April 2017.

Application for permission to appeal a decision of the First-tier Tribunal

40 (1) A person seeking permission to appeal must make a written application to the First-tier Tribunal for permission to appeal.

(2) An application under paragraph (1) must—

(*a*) identify the decision of the First-tier Tribunal to which it relates;

(*b*) identify the alleged error or errors in the decision; and

(*c*) state the result the party making the application is seeking.

Revocation—These Regulations revoked by the Tribunals (Scotland) Act 2014 (Ancillary Provisions) Regulations, SSI 2017/108 reg 3, Schedule with effect from 24 April 2017.

First-tier Tribunal's consideration of application for permission to appeal

41 (1) The First-tier Tribunal must send a record of its decision to the parties as soon as practicable.

(2) If the First-tier Tribunal refuses permission to appeal it must send with the record of its decision—

(*a*) a statement of its reasons for such refusal; and

(*b*) notification of the right to make an application to the Upper Tribunal for permission to appeal and the time within which, and the method by which, such an application must be made.

(3) The First-tier Tribunal may give permission to appeal against part only of the decision or on limited grounds, but must comply with paragraph (2) to the extent that permission is refused.

Revocation—These Regulations revoked by the Tribunals (Scotland) Act 2014 (Ancillary Provisions) Regulations, SSI 2017/108 reg 3, Schedule with effect from 24 April 2017.

Power to treat an application as a different type of application

42 The First-tier Tribunal may treat an application for a decision to be corrected or set aside, or for permission to appeal against a decision, as an application for any other one of those things.

Revocation—These Regulations revoked by the Tribunals (Scotland) Act 2014 (Ancillary Provisions) Regulations, SSI 2017/108 reg 3, Schedule with effect from 24 April 2017.

SCHEDULE 2

THE UPPER TAX TRIBUNAL FOR SCOTLAND RULES OF PROCEDURE 2015

Regulation 2(2)

Revocation—These Regulations revoked by the Tribunals (Scotland) Act 2014 (Ancillary Provisions) Regulations, SSI 2017/108 reg 3, Schedule with effect from 24 April 2017.

PART 1
INTRODUCTION

Revocation—These Regulations revoked by the Tribunals (Scotland) Act 2014 (Ancillary Provisions) Regulations, SSI 2017/108 reg 3, Schedule with effect from 24 April 2017.

Interpretation

1 In these Rules—

"appellant" means—

(*a*) a person who makes an appeal or application, or applies for permission to appeal, to the Upper Tribunal;

(*b*) in proceedings transferred or referred to the Upper Tribunal from the First-tier Tribunal, a person who started the proceedings in the First-tier Tribunal; or

(*c*) in any case, a person substituted as an appellant under rule 9(1) (addition, substitution and removal of parties);

"dispose of proceedings" includes, unless indicated otherwise, disposing of a part of the proceedings;

"document" means anything in which information is recorded in any form, and an obligation under these Rules or any practice direction or direction to provide or allow access to a document or a copy of a document for any purpose means, unless the Upper Tribunal directs otherwise, an obligation to provide or allow access to such document or copy in a legible form or in a form which can be readily made into a legible form;

"hearing" means an oral hearing and includes a hearing conducted in whole or in part by video link, telephone or other means of instantaneous two-way electronic communication;

"party" means a person who is (or was at the time that the Upper Tribunal disposed of the proceedings) an appellant or respondent in proceedings before the Upper Tribunal;

"practice direction" means a direction given under section 57 of RSTPA 2014;

"President" means the President of the Scottish Tax Tribunals;

"respondent" means—

(*a*) in an appeal, or application for permission to appeal, against a decision of the First-tier Tribunal, any person other than the appellant who—

(i) was a party before the First-tier Tribunal;

(ii) otherwise has a right of appeal against the decision of the First-tier Tribunal and has given notice to the Upper Tribunal that they wish to be a party to the appeal;

(*b*) in proceedings transferred or referred to the Upper Tribunal from the First-tier Tribunal, a person who was a respondent in the proceedings in the First-tier Tribunal;

(*c*) in any case, a person substituted or added as a respondent under rule 9 (addition, substitution and removal of parties);

"RSTPA 2014" means the Revenue Scotland and Tax Powers Act 2014.

Revocation—These Regulations revoked by the Tribunals (Scotland) Act 2014 (Ancillary Provisions) Regulations, SSI 2017/108 reg 3, Schedule with effect from 24 April 2017.

Overriding objective and parties' obligation to co-operate with the Upper Tribunal

2 (1) The overriding objective of these Rules is to enable the Upper Tribunal to deal with cases fairly and justly.

(2) Dealing with a case in accordance with the overriding objective includes—

(*a*) dealing with the case in ways which are proportionate to the importance of the case, the complexity of the issues, the anticipated expenses and the resources of the parties;

(*b*) avoiding unnecessary formality and seeking flexibility in the proceedings;

(*c*) ensuring, so far as practicable, that the parties are able to participate fully in the proceedings;

(*d*) using any special expertise of the Upper Tribunal effectively; and

(*e*) avoiding delay, so far as compatible with proper consideration of the issues.

(3) The Upper Tribunal must seek to give effect to the overriding objective when it—

(*a*) exercises any power under these Rules; or

(*b*) interprets any rule or practice direction.

(4) Parties must, insofar as reasonably possible—

(*a*) help the Upper Tribunal to further the overriding objective; and

(*b*) co-operate with the Upper Tribunal generally.

Revocation—These Regulations revoked by the Tribunals (Scotland) Act 2014 (Ancillary Provisions) Regulations, SSI 2017/108 reg 3, Schedule with effect from 24 April 2017.

Mediation

3 The Upper Tribunal should seek, where appropriate—

(*a*) to bring to the attention of the parties the availability of mediation for the resolution of the dispute; and

(*b*) if the parties wish and provided that it is compatible with the overriding objective, to facilitate the use of mediation.

Revocation—These Regulations revoked by the Tribunals (Scotland) Act 2014 (Ancillary Provisions) Regulations, SSI 2017/108 reg 3, Schedule with effect from 24 April 2017.

PART 2
GENERAL POWERS AND PROVISIONS

Revocation—These Regulations revoked by the Tribunals (Scotland) Act 2014 (Ancillary Provisions) Regulations, SSI 2017/108 reg 3, Schedule with effect from 24 April 2017.

Delegation to staff

4 (1) Staff of the Scottish Courts and Tribunals Service may, with the approval of the President, carry out functions of a judicial nature permitted or required to be done by the Upper Tribunal.

(2) The approval referred to at paragraph (1) may apply generally to the carrying out of specified functions by members of staff of a specified description in specified circumstances.

(3) Within 14 days after the date on which the Upper Tribunal sends notice of a decision made by a member of staff pursuant to an approval under paragraph (1) to a party, that party may make a written application to the Upper Tribunal for that decision to be considered afresh by a member of the Upper Tribunal.

Revocation—These Regulations revoked by the Tribunals (Scotland) Act 2014 (Ancillary Provisions) Regulations, SSI 2017/108 reg 3, Schedule with effect from 24 April 2017.

Case management powers

5 (1) Subject to the provisions of RSTPA 2014 and these Rules, the Upper Tribunal may regulate its own procedure.

(2) The Upper Tribunal may give a direction in relation to the conduct or disposal of proceedings at any time, including a direction amending, suspending or setting aside an earlier direction.

(3) In particular, and without restricting the general powers in paragraphs (1) and (2), the Upper Tribunal may by direction—

(*a*) extend or shorten the time for complying with any rule, practice direction or direction, or regulation 3(2) or 4(2) of the Scottish Tax Tribunals (Time Limits and Rules of Procedure) Regulations 2015 (time limit for permission to appeal to the Upper Tax Tribunal for Scotland or to the Court of Session);

(*b*) conjoin or take concurrently two or more sets of proceedings or parts of proceedings raising common issues, or treat a case as a lead case (whether in accordance with rule 18 (lead cases) or otherwise);

(*c*) permit or require a party to amend a document;

(*d*) permit or require a party or another person to provide documents, information, evidence or submissions to the Upper Tribunal or a party;

(*e*) deal with an issue in the proceedings as a preliminary issue;

(*f*) hold a hearing to consider any matter, including a case management issue;

(*g*) decide the form of any hearing;

(*h*) adjourn or postpone a hearing;

(*i*) require a party to produce a file of documents for a hearing;

(*j*) sist proceedings;

(*k*) transfer proceedings to another court or tribunal if that other court or tribunal has jurisdiction in relation to the proceedings and—

(i) because of a change of circumstances since the proceedings were started, the Upper Tribunal no longer has jurisdiction in relation to the proceedings; or

(ii) the Upper Tribunal considers that the other court or tribunal is a more appropriate forum for the determination of the case;

(*l*) suspend the effect of its own decision pending an appeal of that decision;

(*m*) in an appeal, or an application for permission to appeal, against the decision of the First-tier Tribunal, suspend the effect of that decision pending the determination of the application for permission to appeal, and any appeal;

(*n*) require the First-tier Tribunal to provide reasons for the decision, or other information or documents in relation to the decision or any proceedings before the First-tier Tribunal.

Revocation—These Regulations revoked by the Tribunals (Scotland) Act 2014 (Ancillary Provisions) Regulations, SSI 2017/108 reg 3, Schedule with effect from 24 April 2017.

Procedure for applying for and giving directions

6 (1) The Upper Tribunal may give a direction on the application of one or more of the parties or on its own initiative.

(2) An application for a direction may be made—

(*a*) by sending or delivering a written application to the Upper Tribunal; or

(*b*) orally during the course of a hearing.

(3) An application for a direction must include the reason for making that application.

(4) The Upper Tribunal must send notice of any direction to every party and to any other person affected by the direction.

(5) If a party or any other person sent notice of the direction under paragraph (4) wishes to challenge a direction which the Upper Tribunal has given, they may do so by applying for another direction which amends, suspends or sets aside the first direction.

Revocation—These Regulations revoked by the Tribunals (Scotland) Act 2014 (Ancillary Provisions) Regulations, SSI 2017/108 reg 3, Schedule with effect from 24 April 2017.

Failure to comply with rules etc

7 (1) An irregularity resulting from a failure to comply with any requirement in these Rules, a practice direction or a direction, does not of itself render void the proceedings or any step taken in the proceedings.

(2) If a party has failed to comply with a requirement in these Rules, a practice direction or a direction, the Upper Tribunal may take such action as it considers just, which may include—

(*a*) waiving the requirement;

(*b*) requiring the failure to be remedied;

(*c*) exercising its power under rule 8 (striking out a party's case); or

(*d*) restricting a party's participation in the proceedings.

Revocation—These Regulations revoked by the Tribunals (Scotland) Act 2014 (Ancillary Provisions) Regulations, SSI 2017/108 reg 3, Schedule with effect from 24 April 2017.

Striking out a party's case

8 (1) The proceedings, or the appropriate part of them, will be struck out if the appellant has failed to comply with a direction that stated that failure by the appellant to comply with the direction would lead to the striking out of the proceedings or part of them.

(2) The Upper Tribunal must strike out the whole or a part of the proceedings if the Upper Tribunal—

(*a*) does not have jurisdiction in relation to the proceedings or that part of them; and

(*b*) does not exercise its power under rule 5(3)(*k*)(i) (transfer to another court or tribunal) in relation to the proceedings or that part of them.

(3) The Upper Tribunal may strike out the whole or a part of the proceedings if—

(*a*) the appellant has failed to comply with a direction which stated that failure by the appellant to comply with the direction could lead to the striking out of the proceedings or part of them;

(*b*) the appellant has failed to co-operate with the Upper Tribunal to such an extent that the Upper Tribunal cannot deal with the proceedings fairly and justly; or

(*c*) in proceedings which have been transferred from the First-tier Tribunal, the Upper Tribunal considers there is no reasonable prospect of the appellant's case, or part of it, succeeding.

(4) The Upper Tribunal may not strike out the whole or a part of the proceedings under paragraph (2) or (3)(*b*) or (*c*) without first giving the appellant an opportunity to make representations in relation to the proposed striking out.

(5) The effect of proceedings being struck out is that all issues are determined against the appellant. The effect of proceedings being partially struck out is that the relevant issues are determined against the appellant.

(6) If the proceedings, or a part of them, have been struck out under paragraph (1) or (3)(*a*), the appellant may make a written application for the proceedings, or a part of them, to be reinstated.

(7) An application under paragraph (6) must be received by the Upper Tribunal within 30 days after the date on which the Upper Tribunal sent notification of the striking out to the appellant.

(8) This rule applies to a respondent as it applies to an appellant except that—

(*a*) a reference to the striking out of the proceedings is to be read as a reference to the barring of the respondent from taking further part in the proceedings; and

(*b*) a reference to an application for the reinstatement of proceedings which have been struck out is to be read as a reference to an application for the lifting of the bar on the respondent taking further part in the proceedings.

(9) If a respondent has been barred from taking further part in proceedings under this rule and that bar has not been lifted, the Upper Tribunal need not consider any response or other submission made by that respondent, and may summarily determine any or all issues against that respondent.

Revocation—These Regulations revoked by the Tribunals (Scotland) Act 2014 (Ancillary Provisions) Regulations, SSI 2017/108 reg 3, Schedule with effect from 24 April 2017.

Addition, substitution and removal of parties

9 (1) The Upper Tribunal may give a direction adding, substituting or removing a party as an appellant or a respondent including where—

(*a*) the wrong person has been named as a party; or

(*b*) the addition, substitution or removal has become necessary because of a change in circumstances since the start of proceedings.

(2) If the Upper Tribunal gives a direction under paragraph (1) it may give such consequential directions as it considers appropriate.

(3) A person who is not a party may make a written application to the Upper Tribunal to be added or substituted as a party under this rule.

(4) If the Upper Tribunal refuses an application under paragraph (3) it must consider whether to permit the person who made the application to provide submissions or evidence to the Upper Tribunal.

Revocation—These Regulations revoked by the Tribunals (Scotland) Act 2014 (Ancillary Provisions) Regulations, SSI 2017/108 reg 3, Schedule with effect from 24 April 2017.

Orders for expenses

10 (1) The Upper Tribunal may not make an order in respect of expenses in proceedings transferred or referred by, or on appeal from, the First-tier Tribunal except to the extent and in the circumstances that the First-tier Tribunal had the power to make an order in respect of expenses.

(2) In other proceedings, the Upper Tribunal may not make an order in respect of expenses except—

(*a*) in relation to wasted expenses and expenses incurred in applying for such expenses; or

(*b*) if the Upper Tribunal considers that a party or its representative has acted unreasonably in bringing, defending or conducting the proceedings.

(3) The Upper Tribunal may make an order for expenses on an application or on its own initiative.

(4) A person making an application for an order for expenses must—

(*a*) send or deliver a written application to the Upper Tribunal and to the person against whom it is proposed that the order be made; and

(*b*) send or deliver with the application a schedule of the expenses claimed in sufficient detail to allow summary assessment of such expenses by the Upper Tribunal.

(5) An application for an order for expenses may be made at any time during the proceedings but may not be made later than 30 days after the date on which the Upper Tribunal sends—

(*a*) a decision notice recording the decision which finally disposes of all issues in the proceedings; or

(*b*) notice under rule 17(2) that a withdrawal which ends the proceedings has taken effect.

(6) The Upper Tribunal may not make an order for expenses against a person (the "paying person") without first—

(*a*) giving that person an opportunity to make representations; and

(*b*) if the paying person is an individual, considering that person's financial means.

(7) The amount of expenses to be paid under an order under this rule may be ascertained by—

(*a*) summary assessment by the Upper Tribunal;

(*b*) agreement of a specified sum by the paying person and the person entitled to receive the expenses (the "receiving person"); or

(*c*) assessment of the whole or a specified part of the expenses, including the expenses of the assessment, incurred by the receiving person, if not agreed.

(8) Following an order for assessment under paragraph (7)(*c*)—

(*a*) the paying person or the receiving person may apply to the Auditor of the Court of Session (as specified in the order); or

(*b*) the Upper Tribunal may make a remit to the Auditor of the Court of Session,

for the taxation of the expenses according to the fees payable in that Court.

(9) Upon making an order for the assessment of expenses, the Upper Tribunal may order an amount to be paid on account before the expenses are assessed.

(10) In this rule, "wasted expenses" means any expenses incurred by a party—

(*a*) as a result of any improper, unreasonable or negligent act or omission on the part of any representative or any employee of such a representative; or

(*b*) which, in the light of any such act or omission occurring after they were incurred, the First-Tier Tribunal considers it is unreasonable to expect that party to pay.

Revocation—These Regulations revoked by the Tribunals (Scotland) Act 2014 (Ancillary Provisions) Regulations, SSI 2017/108 reg 3, Schedule with effect from 24 April 2017.

Representatives

11 (1) A party may appoint a representative to represent that party in the proceedings.

(2) If a party appoints a representative, that party must send or deliver to the Upper Tribunal and to each other party to the proceedings notice of the representative's name and address.

(3) Anything permitted or required to be done by a party under these Rules, a practice direction or a direction may be done by the representative of that party, except signing a witness statement.

(4) A person who receives due notice of the appointment of a representative—

(*a*) must provide to the representative any document which is required to be provided to the represented party, and need not provide that document to the represented party; and

(*b*) may assume that the representative is and remains authorised as such until they receive notification that this is not so from the representative or the represented party.

(5) At a hearing a party may be accompanied by another person whose name and address has not been notified under paragraph (2) but who, subject to the permission of the Upper Tribunal, may act as a representative or otherwise assist in presenting the party's case at the hearing.

(6) Paragraphs (2) to (4) do not apply to a person who accompanies a party under paragraph (5).

Revocation—These Regulations revoked by the Tribunals (Scotland) Act 2014 (Ancillary Provisions) Regulations, SSI 2017/108 reg 3, Schedule with effect from 24 April 2017.

Calculating time

12 (1) An act required by these Rules, a practice direction or a direction to be done on or by a particular day must be done by 5pm on that day.

(2) If the time specified by these Rules, a practice direction or a direction for doing any act ends on a day other than a working day, the act is done in time if it is done on the next working day.

(3) In this rule "working day" means any day except a Saturday or Sunday, Christmas Day, Good Friday or a bank holiday in Scotland under section 1 of the Banking and Financial Dealings Act 1971.

Revocation—These Regulations revoked by the Tribunals (Scotland) Act 2014 (Ancillary Provisions) Regulations, SSI 2017/108 reg 3, Schedule with effect from 24 April 2017.

Sending and delivery of documents

13 (1) Any document to be provided to the Upper Tribunal under these Rules, a practice direction or a direction must be—

(*a*) sent by pre-paid post or by document exchange, or delivered by hand, to the address specified for the proceedings; or

(*b*) sent or delivered by such other method as the Upper Tribunal may permit or direct.

(2) Subject to paragraph (3), if a party provides a fax number, email address or other details for the electronic transmission of documents to them, that party must accept delivery of documents by that method.

(3) If a party informs the Upper Tribunal and all other parties that a particular form of communication, other than pre-paid post or delivery by hand, should not be used to provide documents to that party, that form of communication must not be so used.

(4) If the Upper Tribunal or a party sends a document to a party or the Upper Tribunal by email or any other electronic means of communication, the recipient may request that the sender provide a hard copy of the document to the recipient. The recipient must make such a request as soon as reasonably practicable after receiving the document electronically.

(5) The Upper Tribunal and each party may assume that the address provided by a party or its representative is and remains the address to which documents should be sent or delivered until receiving notification to the contrary.

Revocation—These Regulations revoked by the Tribunals (Scotland) Act 2014 (Ancillary Provisions) Regulations, SSI 2017/108 reg 3, Schedule with effect from 24 April 2017.

Use of documents and information

14 (1) The Upper Tribunal may make an order prohibiting the disclosure or publication of—

(*a*) specified documents or information relating to the proceedings; or

(*b*) any matter likely to lead members of the public to identify any person whom the Upper Tribunal considers should not be identified.

(2) The Upper Tribunal may give a direction prohibiting the disclosure of a document or information to a person if—

(*a*) the Upper Tribunal is satisfied that such disclosure would be likely to cause that person or some other person serious harm; and

(*b*) the Upper Tribunal is satisfied, having regard to the interests of justice, that it is proportionate to give such a direction.

(3) If a party ("the first party") considers that the Upper Tribunal should give a direction under paragraph (2) prohibiting the disclosure of a document or information to another party ("the second party"), the first party must—

(*a*) exclude the relevant document or information from any documents that will be provided to the second party; and

(*b*) provide to the Upper Tribunal the excluded document or information, and the reason for its exclusion, so that the Upper Tribunal may decide whether the document or information should be disclosed to the second party or should be the subject of a direction under paragraph (2).

(4) If the Upper Tribunal gives a direction under paragraph (2) which prevents disclosure to a party who has appointed a representative, the Upper Tribunal may give a direction that the documents or information be disclosed to that representative if the Upper Tribunal is satisfied that—

(*a*) disclosure to the representative would be in the interests of the party; and

(*b*) the representative will act in accordance with paragraph (5).

(5) Documents or information disclosed to a representative in accordance with a direction under paragraph (4) must not be disclosed either directly or indirectly to any other person without the Upper Tribunal's consent.

(6) The Upper Tribunal may, on its own initiative or on the application of a party, give a direction that certain documents or information must or may be disclosed to the Upper Tribunal on the basis that the Upper Tribunal will not disclose such documents or information to other persons, or specified other persons.

(7) A party making an application for a direction under paragraph (6) may withhold the relevant documents or information from other parties until the Upper Tribunal has granted or refused the application.

(8) The Upper Tribunal must conduct proceedings and record its decision and reasons appropriately so as not to undermine the effect of an order made under paragraph (1) or a direction given under paragraph (2) or (6).

Revocation—These Regulations revoked by the Tribunals (Scotland) Act 2014 (Ancillary Provisions) Regulations, SSI 2017/108 reg 3, Schedule with effect from 24 April 2017.

Evidence and submissions

15 (1) Without restriction on the general powers in rule 5(1) and (2) (case management powers), the Upper Tribunal may give directions as to—

(*a*) issues on which it requires evidence or submissions;

(*b*) the nature of the evidence or submissions it requires;

(*c*) whether the parties are permitted or required to provide expert evidence, and if so whether the parties must jointly appoint a single expert to provide such evidence;

(*d*) any limit on the number of witnesses whose evidence a party may put forward, whether in relation to a particular issue or generally;

(*e*) the manner in which any evidence or submissions are to be provided, which may include a direction for them to be given—

(i) orally at a hearing; or

(ii) by written submissions or witness statement; and

(*f*) the time at which any evidence or submissions are to be provided.

(2) The Upper Tribunal may—

(*a*) admit evidence whether or not—

(i) the evidence would be admissible in a court in Scotland; or

(ii) the evidence was available to a previous decision maker; or

(*b*) exclude evidence that would otherwise be admissible where—

(i) the evidence was not, without reasonable excuse, provided within the time allowed by a direction or a practice direction;

(ii) the evidence was, without reasonable excuse, otherwise provided in a manner that did not comply with a direction or a practice direction; or

(iii) it would otherwise be unfair to admit the evidence.

(3) The Upper Tribunal may consent to a witness giving, or require any witness to give, evidence on oath, and may administer an oath for that purpose.

Revocation—These Regulations revoked by the Tribunals (Scotland) Act 2014 (Ancillary Provisions) Regulations, SSI 2017/108 reg 3, Schedule with effect from 24 April 2017.

Citation of witnesses and orders to answer questions or produce documents

16 (1) On the application of a party or on its own initiative, the Upper Tribunal may—

(*a*) by citation require any person to attend as a witness at a hearing at the time and place specified in the citation; or

(*b*) order any person to answer any questions or produce any documents in that person's possession or control which relate to any issue in the proceedings.

(2) A citation under paragraph (1)(*a*) must—

(*a*) give the person required to attend 14 days' notice of the hearing or such other period as the Upper Tribunal may direct; and

(*b*) where the person is not a party, make provision for the person's necessary expenses of attendance to be paid, and state who is to pay them.

(3) A person who receives a citation or order may apply to the Upper Tribunal for it to be varied or set aside if the person did not have an opportunity to object to it before it was made or issued.

(4) A person making an application under paragraph (3) must do so as soon as reasonably practicable after receiving notice of the citation or order.

(5) A citation or order under this rule must—

(*a*) state that the person on whom the requirement is imposed may apply to the Upper Tribunal to vary or set aside the citation or order, if the person did not have an opportunity to object to it before it was made or issued; and

(*b*) state the consequences of failure to comply with the citation or order.

Revocation—These Regulations revoked by the Tribunals (Scotland) Act 2014 (Ancillary Provisions) Regulations, SSI 2017/108 reg 3, Schedule with effect from 24 April 2017.

Withdrawal

17 (1) Subject to any provision in RSTPA 2014 relating to withdrawal or settlement of particular proceedings, a party may give notice to the Upper Tribunal of the withdrawal of the case made by it in the Upper Tribunal proceedings, or any part of that case—

(*a*) by sending or delivering to the Upper Tribunal a notice of withdrawal; or

(*b*) orally at a hearing.

(2) The Upper Tribunal must notify each party of its receipt of a withdrawal under this rule.

(3) A party which has withdrawn its case may make a written application to the Upper Tribunal for the case to be reinstated.

(4) An application under paragraph (3) must be received by the Upper Tribunal within 30 days after—

(*a*) the date on which the Upper Tribunal received the notice under paragraph (1)(*a*); or

(*b*) the date of the hearing at which the case was withdrawn orally under paragraph (1)(*b*).

Revocation—These Regulations revoked by the Tribunals (Scotland) Act 2014 (Ancillary Provisions) Regulations, SSI 2017/108 reg 3, Schedule with effect from 24 April 2017.

Lead cases

18 (1) This rule applies if—

(*a*) two or more cases have been started before the Upper Tribunal;

(*b*) in each such case the Upper Tribunal has not made a decision disposing of the proceedings; and

(*c*) the cases give rise to common or related issues of fact or law.

(2) The Upper Tribunal may give a direction—

(*a*) specifying one or more cases falling under paragraph (1) as a lead case or lead cases; and

(*b*) sisting the other cases falling under paragraph (1) ("the related cases").

(3) When the Upper Tribunal makes a decision in respect of the common or related issues—

(*a*) the Upper Tribunal must send a copy of that decision to each party in each of the related cases; and

(*b*) subject to paragraph (4), that decision shall be binding on each of those parties.

(4) Within 30 days after the date that the Upper Tribunal sent a copy of the decision to a party under paragraph (3)(*a*), that party may make a written application for a direction that the decision does not apply to, and is not binding on the parties to, that case.

(5) The Upper Tribunal must give directions in respect of cases which are sisted under paragraph (2)(*b*), providing for the disposal of or further steps in those cases.

(6) If the lead case or cases are withdrawn or disposed of before the Upper Tribunal makes a decision in respect of the common or related issues, the Upper Tribunal must give directions as to—

(*a*) whether another case or other cases are to be heard as a lead case or lead cases; and

(*b*) whether any direction affecting the related cases should be set aside or amended.

Revocation—These Regulations revoked by the Tribunals (Scotland) Act 2014 (Ancillary Provisions) Regulations, SSI 2017/108 reg 3, Schedule with effect from 24 April 2017.

Chairing member

19 Where a matter is to be decided by two or more members of the Upper Tribunal, the President must determine the chairing member.

Revocation—These Regulations revoked by the Tribunals (Scotland) Act 2014 (Ancillary Provisions) Regulations, SSI 2017/108 reg 3, Schedule with effect from 24 April 2017.

Venue for hearings

20 The Upper Tribunal is to be convened at such time and place in Scotland as the President may determine.

Revocation—These Regulations revoked by the Tribunals (Scotland) Act 2014 (Ancillary Provisions) Regulations, SSI 2017/108 reg 3, Schedule with effect from 24 April 2017.

Enforcement of decisions

21 An order for the payment of a sum payable in pursuance of a decision of the Upper Tribunal, or a copy of such an order certified by the Upper Tribunal, may be enforced as if it were an extract registered decree arbitral bearing a warrant for execution issued by the Sheriff Court of any sheriffdom in Scotland.

Revocation—These Regulations revoked by the Tribunals (Scotland) Act 2014 (Ancillary Provisions) Regulations, SSI 2017/108 reg 3, Schedule with effect from 24 April 2017.

PART 3
PROCEDURE FOR CASES IN THE UPPER TRIBUNAL

Revocation—These Regulations revoked by the Tribunals (Scotland) Act 2014 (Ancillary Provisions) Regulations, SSI 2017/108 reg 3, Schedule with effect from 24 April 2017.

Application to the Upper Tribunal for permission to appeal a decision of the First-tier Tribunal

22 (1) A person may make a written application to the Upper Tribunal for permission to appeal to the Upper Tribunal against a decision of the First-tier Tribunal only if—

(*a*) the person has made an application for permission to appeal to the First-tier Tribunal; and

(*b*) that application has been refused, has not been admitted or has been granted only on limited grounds.

(2) An application for permission to appeal must state—

(*a*) the name and address of the appellant;

(*b*) the name and address of the representative (if any) of the appellant;

(*c*) an address where documents for the appellant may be sent or delivered;

(*d*) details (including the full reference) of the decision challenged;

(*e*) the grounds on which the appellant relies; and

(*f*) whether the appellant wants the application to be dealt with at a hearing.

(3) The appellant must provide with the application a copy of—

(*a*) any written record of the decision being challenged;

(*b*) any separate written statement of reasons for that decision; and

(*c*) if the application is for permission to appeal against a decision of the First-tier Tribunal, the notice of refusal of permission to appeal from the First-tier Tribunal.

(4) If the appellant provides the application to the Upper Tribunal later than the time required by regulation 3(2) or 4(2) of the Scottish Tax Tribunals (Time Limits and Rules of Procedure) Regulations 2015 or by an extension of time allowed under rule 5(3)(*a*) (power to extend time)—

(*a*) the application must include a request for an extension of time and the reason why the application was not provided in time; and

(*b*) unless the Upper Tribunal extends time for the application under rule 5(3)(*a*), the Upper Tribunal must not admit the application.

(5) In this rule, a reference to notice of a refusal of permission to appeal is to be taken to include a reference to notice of a grant of permission to appeal on limited grounds.

Revocation—These Regulations revoked by the Tribunals (Scotland) Act 2014 (Ancillary Provisions) Regulations, SSI 2017/108 reg 3, Schedule with effect from 24 April 2017.

Decision in relation to permission to appeal a decision of the First-tier Tribunal

23 (1) If the Upper Tribunal refuses permission to appeal, it must send notice of the refusal and of the reasons for the refusal to the appellant.

(2) If the Upper Tribunal gives permission to appeal—

(*a*) the Upper Tribunal must send notice of the permission, and of the reasons for any limitations or conditions on such permission, to each party;

(*b*) subject to any direction by the Upper Tribunal, the application for permission to appeal stands as the notice of appeal and the Upper Tribunal must send to each respondent a copy of the application for permission to appeal and any documents provided with it by the appellant; and

(*c*) the Upper Tribunal may, with the consent of the appellant and each respondent, determine the appeal without obtaining any further response.

(3) Where the Upper Tribunal, without a hearing, determines an application for permission to appeal, the appellant may make a written application for the decision to be reconsidered at a hearing if the Upper Tribunal—

(*a*) refuses permission to appeal; or

(*b*) gives permission to appeal on limited grounds or subject to conditions.

(4) An application under paragraph (3) must be received by the Upper Tribunal within 14 days after the date on which the Upper Tribunal sent notice of its decision regarding the application to the appellant.

Revocation—These Regulations revoked by the Tribunals (Scotland) Act 2014 (Ancillary Provisions) Regulations, SSI 2017/108 reg 3, Schedule with effect from 24 April 2017.

Notice of appeal to the Upper Tribunal

24 (1) This rule applies—

(*a*) if the First-tier Tribunal has given permission for a party to appeal to the Upper Tribunal; or

(*b*) subject to any other direction by the Upper Tribunal, if the Upper Tribunal has given permission to appeal and has given a direction that the application for permission to appeal does not stand as the notice of appeal.

(2) The appellant must provide a notice of appeal to the Upper Tribunal so that it is received within 30 days after the date that the First-tier Tribunal or Upper Tribunal (as appropriate) sent notice of such permission to the appellant.

(3) The notice of appeal must include the information listed in rule 22(2)(*a*) to (*f*) (content of the application for permission to appeal) and, where the Upper Tribunal has given permission to appeal, the Upper Tribunal's case reference.

(4) If the First-tier Tribunal has granted permission to appeal, the appellant must provide with the notice of appeal a copy of—

(*a*) any written record of the decision being challenged;

(*b*) any separate written statement of reasons for that decision; and

(*c*) the notice of permission to appeal.

(5) If the appellant provides the notice of appeal to the Upper Tribunal later than the time required by paragraph (2) or by an extension of time allowed under rule 5(3)(*a*) (power to extend time)—

(*a*) the notice of appeal must include a request for an extension of time and the reason why the notice was not provided in time; and

(*b*) unless the Upper Tribunal extends time for the notice of appeal under rule 5(3)(*a*), the Upper Tribunal must not admit the notice of appeal.

(6) When the Upper Tribunal receives the notice of appeal, it must send a copy of the notice and any accompanying documents to each respondent.

Revocation—These Regulations revoked by the Tribunals (Scotland) Act 2014 (Ancillary Provisions) Regulations, SSI 2017/108 reg 3, Schedule with effect from 24 April 2017.

Response to the notice of appeal

25 (1) Subject to any direction given by the Upper Tribunal, a respondent may provide a written response to a notice of appeal.

(2) Any response provided under paragraph (1) must be sent or delivered to the Upper Tribunal so that it is received—

(*a*) if an application for permission to appeal stands as the notice of appeal, no later than 30 days after the date on which the respondent was sent notice that permission to appeal had been granted;

(*b*) in any other case, no later than 30 days after the date on which the Upper Tribunal sent a copy of the notice of appeal to the respondent.

(3) The response must state—

(*a*) the name and address of the respondent;

(*b*) the name and address of the representative (if any) of the respondent;

(*c*) an address where documents for the respondent may be sent or delivered;

(*d*) whether the respondent opposes the appeal;

(*e*) the grounds on which the respondent relies, including (in the case of an appeal against the decision of the First-tier Tribunal) any grounds on which the respondent was unsuccessful in the proceedings which are the subject of the appeal, but intends to rely in the appeal; and

(*f*) whether the respondent wants the case to be dealt with at a hearing.

(4) If the respondent provides the response to the Upper Tribunal later than the time required by paragraph (2) or by an extension of time allowed under rule 5(3)(*a*) (power to extend time), the response must include a request for an extension of time and the reason why the response was not provided in time.

(5) When the Upper Tribunal receives the response, it must send a copy of the response and any accompanying documents to the appellant and each other party.

Revocation—These Regulations revoked by the Tribunals (Scotland) Act 2014 (Ancillary Provisions) Regulations, SSI 2017/108 reg 3, Schedule with effect from 24 April 2017.

Appellant's reply

26 (1) Subject to any direction given by the Upper Tribunal, the appellant may provide a written reply to any response provided under rule 25 (response to the notice of appeal).

(2) Any reply provided under paragraph (1) must be sent or delivered to the Upper Tribunal so that it is received within 30 days after the date on which the Upper Tribunal sent a copy of the response to the appellant.

(3) When the Upper Tribunal receives the reply, it must send a copy of the reply and any accompanying documents to each respondent.

Revocation—These Regulations revoked by the Tribunals (Scotland) Act 2014 (Ancillary Provisions) Regulations, SSI 2017/108 reg 3, Schedule with effect from 24 April 2017.

Cases transferred or referred to the Upper Tribunal, applications made directly to the Upper Tribunal and proceedings without notice to a respondent

27 (1) Paragraphs (2) and (3) apply to—

(*a*) a case transferred or referred to the Upper Tribunal from the First-tier Tribunal; or

(*b*) a case which is started by an application made directly to the Upper Tribunal.

(2) In a case to which this paragraph applies—

(*a*) the Upper Tribunal must give directions as to the procedure to be followed in the consideration and disposal of the proceedings;

(*b*) the preceding rules in this Part will only apply to the proceedings to the extent provided for by such directions.

(3) If a case or matter to which this paragraph applies is to be determined without notice to or the involvement of a respondent—

(*a*) any provision in these Rules requiring a document to be provided by or to a respondent; and

(*b*) any other provision in these Rules permitting a respondent to participate in the proceedings,

does not apply to that case or matter.

Revocation—These Regulations revoked by the Tribunals (Scotland) Act 2014 (Ancillary Provisions) Regulations, SSI 2017/108 reg 3, Schedule with effect from 24 April 2017.

PART 4
HEARINGS

Revocation—These Regulations revoked by the Tribunals (Scotland) Act 2014 (Ancillary Provisions) Regulations, SSI 2017/108 reg 3, Schedule with effect from 24 April 2017.

Decision with or without a hearing

28 (1) Subject to paragraph (2), the Upper Tribunal may make any decision without a hearing.
(2) The Upper Tribunal must have regard to any view expressed by a party when deciding whether to hold a hearing to consider any matter, and the form of any such hearing.

Revocation—These Regulations revoked by the Tribunals (Scotland) Act 2014 (Ancillary Provisions) Regulations, SSI 2017/108 reg 3, Schedule with effect from 24 April 2017.

Entitlement to attend a hearing

29 Subject to rule 31(4) (exclusion of a person from a hearing), each party is entitled to attend a hearing together with any representative permitted by rule 11.

Revocation—These Regulations revoked by the Tribunals (Scotland) Act 2014 (Ancillary Provisions) Regulations, SSI 2017/108 reg 3, Schedule with effect from 24 April 2017.

Notice of hearings

30 (1) The Upper Tribunal must give each party entitled to attend a hearing reasonable notice of the time and place of the hearing (including any adjourned or postponed hearing) and any change to the time and place of the hearing.
(2) The period of notice under paragraph (1) must be at least 14 days except that the Upper Tribunal may give shorter notice—
(*a*) with the parties' consent; or
(*b*) in urgent or exceptional circumstances.

Revocation—These Regulations revoked by the Tribunals (Scotland) Act 2014 (Ancillary Provisions) Regulations, SSI 2017/108 reg 3, Schedule with effect from 24 April 2017.

Public and private hearings and power to exclude

31 (1) Subject to the following paragraphs, all hearings must be held in public.
(2) The Upper Tribunal may give a direction that a hearing, or part of it, is to be held in private if the Upper Tribunal considers that restricting access to the hearing is justified—
(*a*) in the interests of public order or national security;
(*b*) in order to protect a person's right to respect for their private and family life;
(*c*) in order to maintain the confidentiality of sensitive information;
(*d*) in order to avoid serious harm to the public interest; or
(*e*) because not to do so would prejudice the interests of justice.
(3) Where a hearing, or part of it, is to be held in private, the Upper Tribunal may determine who is entitled to attend the hearing or part of it.
(4) The Upper Tribunal may give a direction excluding from any hearing, or part of it—
(*a*) any person whose conduct the Upper Tribunal considers is disrupting or is likely to disrupt the hearing;
(*b*) any person whose presence the Upper Tribunal considers is likely to prevent another person from giving evidence or making submissions freely;
(*c*) any person where the purpose of the hearing would be defeated by the attendance of that person; or
(*d*) a person under the age of sixteen years.
(5) The Upper Tribunal may give a direction excluding a witness from a hearing until that witness gives evidence.
(6) When publishing a decision notice referred to in rule 34(2) resulting from a hearing which was held wholly or partly in private, the Upper Tribunal must, so far as practicable, ensure that the report does not disclose information which was referred to only in a part of the hearing that was held in private (including such information which enables the identification of any person whose affairs were dealt with in the part of the hearing that was held in private) if to do so would undermine the purpose of holding the hearing in private.

Revocation—These Regulations revoked by the Tribunals (Scotland) Act 2014 (Ancillary Provisions) Regulations, SSI 2017/108 reg 3, Schedule with effect from 24 April 2017.

Hearings in a party's absence

32 If a party fails to attend a hearing, the Upper Tribunal may proceed with the hearing if the Upper Tribunal—

(*a*) is satisfied that the party has been notified of the hearing or that reasonable steps have been taken to notify the party of the hearing; and

(*b*) considers that it is in the interests of justice to proceed with the hearing.

Revocation—These Regulations revoked by the Tribunals (Scotland) Act 2014 (Ancillary Provisions) Regulations, SSI 2017/108 reg 3, Schedule with effect from 24 April 2017.

PART 5
DECISIONS

Consent orders

33 (1) The Upper Tribunal may, at the request of the parties but only if it considers it appropriate, make a consent order disposing of the proceedings and making such other appropriate provision as the parties have agreed.

(2) Notwithstanding any other provision of these Rules, the Upper Tribunal need not hold a hearing before making an order under paragraph (1) or provide reasons for the order.

Revocation—These Regulations revoked by the Tribunals (Scotland) Act 2014 (Ancillary Provisions) Regulations, SSI 2017/108 reg 3, Schedule with effect from 24 April 2017.

Notice of decisions and reasons

34 (1) Subject to the remainder of this rule, the Upper Tribunal may give a decision orally at a hearing.

(2) The Upper Tribunal must provide to each party, as soon as reasonably practicable after making a decision (other than a decision under Part 6) which finally disposes of all issues in the proceedings or of a preliminary issue dealt with following a direction under rule 5(3)(*e*), a decision notice which—

(*a*) states the Upper Tribunal's decision; and

(*b*) notifies the party of any right of appeal against the decision and the time within which, and the manner in which, the right of appeal may be exercised.

(3) Unless each party agrees that it is unnecessary, and in any event subject to rule 31(6), the Upper Tribunal must provide written reasons for its decision with a decision notice provided under paragraph (2) unless—

(*a*) the decision was made with the consent of the parties; or

(*b*) the parties have consented to the Upper Tribunal not giving written reasons.

(4) The Upper Tribunal may provide written reasons for any decision to which paragraph (2) does not apply.

(5) The Upper Tribunal must, subject to rule 31(6), publish reports of its decisions, including on a website.

Revocation—These Regulations revoked by the Tribunals (Scotland) Act 2014 (Ancillary Provisions) Regulations, SSI 2017/108 reg 3, Schedule with effect from 24 April 2017.

PART 6
CORRECTING, SETTING ASIDE AND APPEALING DECISIONS OF THE UPPER TRIBUNAL

Revocation—These Regulations revoked by the Tribunals (Scotland) Act 2014 (Ancillary Provisions) Regulations, SSI 2017/108 reg 3, Schedule with effect from 24 April 2017.

Interpretation

35 In this Part, "appeal" means the exercise of a right of appeal under section 36 of RSTPA 2014.

Revocation—These Regulations revoked by the Tribunals (Scotland) Act 2014 (Ancillary Provisions) Regulations, SSI 2017/108 reg 3, Schedule with effect from 24 April 2017.

Clerical mistakes and accidental slips or omissions

36 The Upper Tribunal may at any time correct any clerical mistake or other accidental slip or omission in a decision, a direction or any document produced by it (or record of such a thing) by—

(*a*) sending notification of the amended decision or direction, or a copy of the amended document or record, to all parties; and

(*b*) making any necessary amendment to any information published in relation to the decision, direction, document or record.

Revocation—These Regulations revoked by the Tribunals (Scotland) Act 2014 (Ancillary Provisions) Regulations, SSI 2017/108 reg 3, Schedule with effect from 24 April 2017.

Setting aside a decision which disposes of proceedings

37 (1) The Upper Tribunal may set aside a decision which disposes of proceedings, or part of such a decision, and re-make the decision or the relevant part of it, if—

(*a*) the Upper Tribunal considers that it is in the interests of justice to do so; and

(*b*) one or more of the conditions in paragraph (2) are satisfied.

(2) The conditions are—

(*a*) a document relating to the proceedings was not sent to, or was not received at an appropriate time by, a party or a party's representative;

(*b*) a document relating to the proceedings was not sent to the Upper Tribunal at an appropriate time;

(*c*) a party, or a party's representative, was not present at a hearing related to the proceedings; or

(*d*) there has been some other procedural irregularity in the proceedings.

(3) A party applying for a decision, or part of a decision, to be set aside under paragraph (1) must make a written application to the Upper Tribunal so that it is received no later than 30 days after the date on which the Upper Tribunal sent notice of the decision to the party.

(4) If the Upper Tribunal sets aside a decision or part of a decision under this rule, the Upper Tribunal must notify the parties as soon as practicable.

Revocation—These Regulations revoked by the Tribunals (Scotland) Act 2014 (Ancillary Provisions) Regulations, SSI 2017/108 reg 3, Schedule with effect from 24 April 2017.

Application for permission to appeal a decision of the Upper Tribunal

38 (1) A person seeking permission to appeal must make a written application to the Upper Tribunal for permission to appeal.

(2) An application under paragraph (1) must—

(*a*) identify the decision of the Upper Tribunal to which it relates;

(*b*) identify the alleged error or errors of law in the decision; and

(*c*) state the result the party making the application is seeking.

Revocation—These Regulations revoked by the Tribunals (Scotland) Act 2014 (Ancillary Provisions) Regulations, SSI 2017/108 reg 3, Schedule with effect from 24 April 2017.

Upper Tribunal's consideration of application for permission to appeal

39 (1) The Upper Tribunal must send a record of its decision to the parties as soon as practicable.

(2) If the Upper Tribunal refuses permission to appeal it must send with the record of its decision—

(*a*) a statement of its reasons for such refusal; and

(*b*) notification of the right to make an application to the Court of Session for permission to appeal and the time within which, and the method by which, such an application must be made.

(3) The Upper Tribunal may give permission to appeal against part only of the decision or on limited grounds, but must comply with paragraph (2) to the extent that permission is refused.

Revocation—These Regulations revoked by the Tribunals (Scotland) Act 2014 (Ancillary Provisions) Regulations, SSI 2017/108 reg 3, Schedule with effect from 24 April 2017.

Power to treat an application as a different type of application

40 The Upper Tribunal may treat an application for a decision to be corrected or set aside, or for permission to appeal against a decision, as an application for any other one of those things.

Revocation—These Regulations revoked by the Tribunals (Scotland) Act 2014 (Ancillary Provisions) Regulations, SSI 2017/108 reg 3, Schedule with effect from 24 April 2017.

2015/187

SCOTTISH TAX TRIBUNALS (CONDUCT AND FITNESS ASSESSMENT TRIBUNAL) RULES 2015

Made . . . . *29 April 2015*
Laid before the Scottish Parliament . . . . *1 May 2015*
Coming into force . . . . *1 June 2015*

Revocation—These Regulations revoked by the Tribunals (Scotland) Act 2014 (Ancillary Provisions) Regulations, SSI 2017/108 reg 3, Schedule with effect from 24 April 2017.

The Scottish Ministers make the following Rules in exercise of the powers conferred by paragraphs 22, 23 and 32(1) of Schedule 2 to the Revenue Scotland and Tax Powers Act 2014 and all other powers enabling them to do so.

1 Citation and commencement

(1) These Rules may be cited as the Scottish Tax Tribunals (Conduct and Fitness Assessment Tribunal) Rules 2015 and the Rules contained in Schedules 1 and 2 may be cited, respectively, as—

(*a*) the Scottish Tax Tribunals (Conduct) Rules 2015; and
(*b*) the Scottish Tax Tribunals (Fitness Assessment Tribunal) Rules 2015.

(2) These Rules come into force on 1st June 2015.

Revocation—These Regulations revoked by the Tribunals (Scotland) Act 2014 (Ancillary Provisions) Regulations, SSI 2017/108 reg 3, Schedule with effect from 24 April 2017.

2 Application of Schedules

(1) The Rules in Schedule 1 are made for the purposes of paragraph 22(1) of Schedule 2 to the Revenue Scotland and Tax Powers Act 2014.

(2) The Rules in Schedule 2 are made for the purposes of paragraph 32(1) of Schedule 2 to the Revenue Scotland and Tax Powers Act 2014.

Revocation—These Regulations revoked by the Tribunals (Scotland) Act 2014 (Ancillary Provisions) Regulations, SSI 2017/108 reg 3, Schedule with effect from 24 April 2017.

SCHEDULE 1

THE SCOTTISH TAX TRIBUNALS (CONDUCT) RULES 2015

Regulation 2(1)

Revocation—These Regulations revoked by the Tribunals (Scotland) Act 2014 (Ancillary Provisions) Regulations, SSI 2017/108 reg 3, Schedule with effect from 24 April 2017.

CONTENTS

Interpretation

1 In these Rules—

"President" means the President of the Scottish Tax Tribunals; and

"RSTPA 2014" means the Revenue Scotland and Tax Powers Act 2014.

Revocation—These Regulations revoked by the Tribunals (Scotland) Act 2014 (Ancillary Provisions) Regulations, SSI 2017/108 reg 3, Schedule with effect from 24 April 2017.

Disciplinary judge

2 The Scottish Ministers are to appoint a judge of the Inner House of the Court of Session (to be known as "the disciplinary judge") for the purposes of—

(*a*) supervising the operation generally of these Rules and reporting to the Scottish Ministers about that matter as appropriate; and
(*b*) carrying out the other functions specified by these Rules.

Revocation—These Regulations revoked by the Tribunals (Scotland) Act 2014 (Ancillary Provisions) Regulations, SSI 2017/108 reg 3, Schedule with effect from 24 April 2017.

Making a complaint

3 (1) A complaint is validly made where a complaint document is received by the Scottish Ministers.

(2) A "complaint document" is a document in writing which—

(*a*) is legible;
(*b*) contains an allegation of misconduct on the part of a named or identifiable member of the Scottish Tax Tribunals; and
(*c*) states the name, address and telephone number of the person who is making the complaint.

(3) A complaint document is to be accompanied by all documents within the control of the person complaining upon which the person seeks to rely in making the allegation.
(4) For the purposes of this rule—

(*a*) a document may be sent by any method which the Scottish Ministers have indicated to be an acceptable means of sending it;

(*b*) if sent by an electronic means indicated to be acceptable a document is to be treated as valid only if it is capable of being used for subsequent reference.

(5) A complaint is not validly made where the complaint document (or any communication associated with it) indicates that the person complaining does not want the member of the Scottish Tax Tribunals against whom the complaint is made to see a copy of the complaint document or any document accompanying it.

Revocation—These Regulations revoked by the Tribunals (Scotland) Act 2014 (Ancillary Provisions) Regulations, SSI 2017/108 reg 3, Schedule with effect from 24 April 2017.

Time limit

4 (1) Subject to this rule, the Scottish Ministers are to dismiss any allegation of misconduct in a complaint document which founds on anything occurring more than 3 months before the date on which the complaint was received.
(2) The person complaining may make a case in writing to the Scottish Ministers that there are exceptional circumstances which justify allowing the allegation to proceed.
(3) Where such a case is not made at the time of making the complaint, the Scottish Ministers are to write to the person inviting him or her, by such date as is specified, to make such a case.
(4) Where such a case is made, it is to be put before the disciplinary judge and he or she is to then decide whether the allegation is to be allowed to proceed.
(5) Where an allegation is dismissed under this rule, the Scottish Ministers are to write to the person complaining to that effect.

Revocation—These Regulations revoked by the Tribunals (Scotland) Act 2014 (Ancillary Provisions) Regulations, SSI 2017/108 reg 3, Schedule with effect from 24 April 2017.

Allegations of criminal conduct

5 (1) This rule applies to an allegation which is not dismissed under rule 4.
(2) If it appears to the Scottish Ministers that the allegation is of an act or omission which may constitute a criminal offence—

(*a*) further consideration under these Rules is suspended until—

(i) the relevant prosecutor indicates that no criminal proceedings are to be taken; or

(ii) any such proceedings have been concluded; and

(*b*) the Scottish Ministers are to write to the person complaining to that effect.

Revocation—These Regulations revoked by the Tribunals (Scotland) Act 2014 (Ancillary Provisions) Regulations, SSI 2017/108 reg 3, Schedule with effect from 24 April 2017.

Notification of member of the Scottish Tax Tribunals

6 (1) This rule applies to an allegation—

(*a*) which is not dismissed under rule 4; and

(*b*) whose consideration is not currently suspended under rule 5.

(2) The Scottish Ministers are to send to the member of the Scottish Tax Tribunals—

(*a*) a document (which may be the complaint document) containing the allegation;

(*b*) all information about the allegation which is in or accompanied the complaint document.

Revocation—These Regulations revoked by the Tribunals (Scotland) Act 2014 (Ancillary Provisions) Regulations, SSI 2017/108 reg 3, Schedule with effect from 24 April 2017.

Initial assessment of complaint

7 (1) This rule applies to an allegation once it is sent to the member of the Scottish Tax Tribunals under rule 6.
(2) The Scottish Ministers are to carry out an initial assessment of the allegation.
(3) If the Scottish Ministers consider the allegation falls into paragraph (4), they are to dismiss the allegation.
(4) An allegation falls into this paragraph if—

(*a*) it does not contain sufficient information to enable a proper understanding of the grounds of the allegation to be achieved;

(*b*) it is about a judicial decision;

(*c*) it raises a matter which has already been dealt with (whether under these Rules or otherwise), and does not present any material new evidence; or (*d*) it raises a matter which falls within the functions of the Judicial Complaints Reviewer.

(5) Where a complaint is dismissed under paragraph (3), the Scottish Ministers are to write to the person complaining and the member of the Scottish Tax Tribunals to that effect.

(6) If it appears to the Scottish Ministers that the allegation relates to judicial proceedings which are not concluded, they are to refer the allegation to the disciplinary judge for advice as to whether it would be appropriate for consideration under these Rules to continue before the judicial proceedings are concluded.

(7) Where the disciplinary judge advises that it would be inappropriate for that to occur—

(*a*) no further action is to be taken under these Rules until the proceedings have been concluded; and

(*b*) the Scottish Ministers are to write to the person complaining and to the member of the Scottish Tax Tribunals to that effect.

(8) Where an allegation is not dismissed under paragraph (3) and its consideration is not suspended under paragraph (7), the Scottish Ministers are to write to the person complaining, and to the member of the Scottish Tax Tribunals, to inform them of that fact and of the next step under these Rules.

Revocation—These Regulations revoked by the Tribunals (Scotland) Act 2014 (Ancillary Provisions) Regulations, SSI 2017/108 reg 3, Schedule with effect from 24 April 2017.

Consideration by disciplinary judge

8 (1) This rule applies to an allegation—

(*a*) which is not dismissed under rule 7; and

(*b*) whose consideration is not currently suspended under that rule.

(2) The allegation is to be considered by the disciplinary judge in accordance with the following paragraphs.

(3) If the disciplinary judge is of the view that the allegation falls into paragraph (4), he or she is to dismiss the allegation and is to inform the Scottish Ministers accordingly.

(4) An allegation falls into this paragraph if—

(*a*) it does not contain sufficient information to enable a proper understanding of the grounds of the allegation to be achieved;

(*b*) it is about a judicial decision;

(*c*) it raises a matter which has already been dealt with (whether under these Rules or otherwise) and does not present any material new evidence;

(*d*) it raises a matter which falls within the functions of the Judicial Complaints Reviewer;

(*e*) it is vexatious;

(*f*) it is without substance; or

(*g*) it is insubstantial, that is to say that even if substantiated, it would not require any disciplinary action to be taken.

(5) In forming his or her view as to whether paragraph (4)(*f*) or (*g*) applies, the disciplinary judge is to take due account of the extent to which the conduct concerned complies with any relevant guidance relating to the conduct of members of the Scottish Tax Tribunals issued by the President under section 59 of RSTPA 2014.

(6) Where a complaint is dismissed under paragraph (3), the Scottish Ministers are to write to the person complaining and the member of the Scottish Tax Tribunals to that effect.

(7) If the disciplinary judge is of the view that one or more allegations in a complaint fall outside paragraph (4), he or she is to go on to consider whether paragraph (8) applies and is to inform the Scottish Ministers accordingly.

(8) This paragraph applies where the disciplinary judge thinks that the allegation, if substantiated, would raise a possible question of fitness for office.

(9) Where the Scottish Ministers are informed that paragraph (8) applies, further consideration under these Rules is suspended until the Scottish Ministers decide whether to establish a fitness assessment tribunal to consider the fitness for office of the member of the Scottish Tax Tribunals.

(10) In the event that the Scottish Ministers decide to establish a fitness assessment tribunal, consideration under these Rules is to cease; and the Scottish Ministers are to write to the person complaining, to the member of the Scottish Tax Tribunals and to the President to that effect.

Revocation—These Regulations revoked by the Tribunals (Scotland) Act 2014 (Ancillary Provisions) Regulations, SSI 2017/108 reg 3, Schedule with effect from 24 April 2017.

Referral to a nominated judge

9 (1) This rule applies to an allegation—

(*a*) which is not dismissed under rule 8; and

(*b*) whose consideration is not currently suspended under that rule.

(2) The Scottish Ministers are to refer the allegation to a judge nominated by the disciplinary judge.

(3) The nominated judge is to be a judge of the Court of Session.

(4) Where on initial consideration of the allegation the nominated judge thinks that the matter may be capable of resolution to the satisfaction of the person complaining without further investigation, he or she may communicate with the person complaining and the member of the Scottish Tax Tribunals as he or she thinks fit with a view to securing that outcome.

(5) Where that outcome is achieved, the nominated judge is to write to the Scottish Ministers to that effect and consideration under these Rules is to cease.

Revocation—These Regulations revoked by the Tribunals (Scotland) Act 2014 (Ancillary Provisions) Regulations, SSI 2017/108 reg 3, Schedule with effect from 24 April 2017.

Investigation and report

10 (1) This rule applies to an allegation referred to a nominated judge which is incapable of resolution under rule 9(4).

(2) The nominated judge is to investigate the allegation and to determine—

(*a*) the facts of the matter;

(*b*) whether the allegation is substantiated (or substantiated in part); and if so, to recommend whether the President should exercise a power mentioned in paragraph 24(1) of Schedule 2 to the RSTPA 2014 or take other action.

(3) The report of the nominated judge is to—

(*a*) be in writing;

(*b*) contain reasons for its conclusions; and

(*c*) be submitted to the disciplinary judge.

(4) In deciding whether an allegation is to any extent substantiated and in making any recommendation in consequence the nominated judge is to take due account of the extent to which the conduct concerned complies with any relevant guidance relating to the conduct of member of the Scottish Tax Tribunals issued by the President under section 59 of RSTPA 2014.

Revocation—These Regulations revoked by the Tribunals (Scotland) Act 2014 (Ancillary Provisions) Regulations, SSI 2017/108 reg 3, Schedule with effect from 24 April 2017.

Procedure and conduct of investigation

11 (1) For the purposes of the investigation the nominated judge may—

(*a*) make such inquiries into the allegation as he or she considers appropriate;

(*b*) obtain and consider any documents which appear to be relevant;

(*c*) interview any persons he or she considers appropriate.

(2) The nominated judge is to—

(*a*) give an interviewee reasonable notice of the date and time of the interview;

(*b*) permit an interviewee to be accompanied by a person of his or her choosing for the doing of such of the following for the interviewee as the interviewee requires—

(i) providing moral support;

(ii) helping to manage papers;

(iii) taking notes;

(iv) offering advice.

(3) The nominated judge is to arrange for any interview to be recorded by equipment which records digitally on an appropriate storage medium.

(4) The member of the Scottish Tax Tribunals is to comply with a request that he or she be interviewed.

(5) The procedure and conduct of an investigation is such (consistent with respecting the principles of fairness and natural justice) as the nominated judge thinks fit; but—

(*a*) the member of the Scottish Tax Tribunals is to be afforded the opportunity to submit a written response to the allegation;

(*b*) the person complaining and the member of the Scottish Tax Tribunals are each to be afforded the opportunity to submit written comments on any information obtained by the nominated judge which he or she has not previously seen;

(*c*) so far as the determination of questions of fact is concerned—

(i) the investigation is to be conducted with the aim of ascertaining, so far as reasonably possible, the truth;

(ii) findings of fact are to be made on the balance of probabilities;

(*d*) so far as possible, the investigation is to be conducted without disclosure to third parties of the identity of the person complaining or the member of the Scottish Tax Tribunals.

(6) Before the investigation starts the nominated judge is to prepare and issue to the person complaining and the member of the Scottish Tax Tribunals a statement of the procedure he or she has decided on.

(7) Where, after the investigation starts, the nominated judge wishes to depart from that procedure in a material way, he or she is to inform the person complaining and the member of the Scottish Tax Tribunals in writing before proceeding.
(8) The nominated judge is to make a note of the substance of all conversations in the course of the investigation which are material to it and is to create and maintain a file containing—
(*a*) those notes;
(*b*) all documents relevant to the investigation; and
(*c*) all recordings of interviews carried out in the course of the investigation.

Revocation—These Regulations revoked by the Tribunals (Scotland) Act 2014 (Ancillary Provisions) Regulations, SSI 2017/108 reg 3, Schedule with effect from 24 April 2017.

Review by disciplinary judge

12 (1) This rule applies where the nominated judge has reported under rule 10.
(2) The disciplinary judge is to review the determinations in the report.
(3) Having reviewed the determinations, the disciplinary judge may require that the nominated judge reconsiders any of them.
(4) Such a requirement is to be in writing.
(5) For the purposes of reconsidering a determination, the nominated judge may—
(*a*) make such further inquiries into the allegation as he or she considers appropriate;
(*b*) obtain and consider any further documents which appear to be relevant;
(*c*) interview (or re-interview) any persons he or she considers appropriate.
(6) Paragraphs (2) and (3) of rule 11 apply to an interview under paragraph (5)(*c*) as they apply to an interview conducted under paragraph (1)(*c*) of that rule.
(7) The nominated judge is to make a note of the substance of all conversations in the course of reconsideration of a determination which are material to it and is to update the nominated judge's file with—
(*a*) those notes;
(*b*) all additional documents relevant to the reconsideration;
(*c*) all recordings of interviews carried out in the course of the reconsideration.
(8) Having carried out all reconsiderations required by the disciplinary judge, the nominated judge is to resubmit his or her report.
(9) In relation to any determination which the nominated judge was required to reconsider, the report is to contain statements of—
(*a*) what the nominated judge did in reconsidering the determination;
(*b*) what the outcome of the reconsideration was.

Revocation—These Regulations revoked by the Tribunals (Scotland) Act 2014 (Ancillary Provisions) Regulations, SSI 2017/108 reg 3, Schedule with effect from 24 April 2017.

Substantiated complaint: disciplinary action

13 (1) The disciplinary judge is to send to the Scottish Ministers and the President—
(*a*) where no requirement is imposed under rule 12(3), a copy of the report submitted under rule 10(3)(*c*);
(*b*) in any other case, a copy of the report submitted under rule 12(8).
(2) Paragraph (3) applies where—
(*a*) the report finds the allegation to be substantiated (or substantiated in part);
(*b*) the report recommends that the President should exercise a power mentioned in paragraph 24(1) of Schedule 2 to the RSTPA 2014; and
(*c*) the President proposes to exercise a power mentioned in that provision.
(3) The President is to write to the member of the Scottish Tax Tribunals who is the subject of the report inviting him or her to make written representations.
(4) The President's letter is to contain or be accompanied by such information (including where appropriate the report) as he or she considers to be appropriate for the purpose of giving the member of the Scottish Tax Tribunals a fair opportunity to make any representations.
(5) The member of the Scottish Tax Tribunals who is the subject of the report is to make any representations by such date as is specified in the invitation.
(6) The President is to consider any representations before deciding whether to exercise a power.
(7) Where the member of the Scottish Tax Tribunals who is the subject of the report is the President—
(*a*) paragraph (1) does not require a copy of the report to be sent to the President; and
(*b*) if the report finds the allegation to be substantiated (or substantiated in part) and the Scottish Ministers propose to take the action specified in paragraph (8), paragraphs (3) to (6) apply subject to the modifications that—
(i) references to the President are to be read as references to the Scottish Ministers; and

(ii) the reference in paragraph (6) to "exercise a power" is to be read as a reference to "take the action specified in paragraph (8)".

(8) The action specified is the Scottish Ministers giving the President—

(*a*) formal advice;

(*b*) a formal warning; or

(*c*) a reprimand.

Revocation—These Regulations revoked by the Tribunals (Scotland) Act 2014 (Ancillary Provisions) Regulations, SSI 2017/108 reg 3, Schedule with effect from 24 April 2017.

Notification of outcome, etc

14 (1) This rule applies where—

(*a*) the President has received a report under rule 13(1); and

(*b*) the President has taken all action (if any) which he or she proposes to take in consequence.

(2) The Scottish Ministers are to write to the person complaining to inform the person of—

(*a*) the outcome of the investigation of the complaint; and

(*b*) the action (if any) taken by the President in consequence.

(3) The Scottish Ministers' letter is to contain or be accompanied by such information as the Scottish Ministers consider to be appropriate for the purpose of giving the person complaining a fair understanding of the matters mentioned in paragraph (2)(*a*) and (*b*).

(4) Except where the President has already done so in pursuance of rule 13, he or she is to write to the member of the Scottish Tax Tribunals who is the subject of the report to inform him or her of the matters mentioned in paragraph (2)(*a*) and (*b*).

(5) After paragraphs (2) and (4) have been complied with, the President may publish or disclose to any person such information concerning the whole matter (including the identity of the person complaining or the member of the Scottish Tax Tribunals who is the subject of the report or both) as he or she considers to be appropriate.

(6) Where the member of the Scottish Tax Tribunals who is the subject of the report is the President, this rule does not apply except for paragraphs (2) to (5) which apply subject to the modification that references to the President are to be taken to be references to the Scottish Ministers.

Revocation—These Regulations revoked by the Tribunals (Scotland) Act 2014 (Ancillary Provisions) Regulations, SSI 2017/108 reg 3, Schedule with effect from 24 April 2017.

Withdrawal of complaint

15 (1) A person complaining may, by writing to the Scottish Ministers to that effect, withdraw the complaint at any time before the President has received a report about it under rule 13(1).

(2) Where a complaint is withdrawn before it is referred to a nominated judge under rule 9, the disciplinary judge is to consider whether further consideration of an allegation of misconduct in it is appropriate.

(3) If so, the allegation is to continue to be considered under these Rules as if the complaint had not been withdrawn.

(4) Where a complaint is withdrawn after it is referred to a nominated judge under rule 9, the nominated judge is to consider whether further investigation of an allegation of misconduct in it is appropriate.

(5) If so, the allegation is to continue to be investigated under these Rules as if the complaint had not been withdrawn.

(6) Where an allegation is continuing to be investigated by virtue of paragraph (3) or (5), any requirement in these Rules or in the statement of the procedure decided on under rule 11(6) to communicate a matter to or to seek comments from the person complaining ceases to apply.

Revocation—These Regulations revoked by the Tribunals (Scotland) Act 2014 (Ancillary Provisions) Regulations, SSI 2017/108 reg 3, Schedule with effect from 24 April 2017.

Consideration of matters in absence of a complaint

16 (1) Paragraph (2) applies where no complaint is validly made under these Rules but the disciplinary judge receives information from any source which suggests to him or her that consideration under these Rules of an allegation of misconduct is appropriate.

(2) The allegation is to be considered under these Rules (with the necessary modifications to reflect the lack of a person complaining) as if—

(*a*) a complaint containing it had been made validly under rule 3; and

(*b*) rule 4 did not apply.

Revocation—These Regulations revoked by the Tribunals (Scotland) Act 2014 (Ancillary Provisions) Regulations, SSI 2017/108 reg 3, Schedule with effect from 24 April 2017.

Ceasing to hold office

17 Where a member of the Scottish Tax Tribunals against whom a complaint under these Rules has been made ceases to hold office or dies, consideration of the complaint under these Rules is to cease.

Revocation—These Regulations revoked by the Tribunals (Scotland) Act 2014 (Ancillary Provisions) Regulations, SSI 2017/108 reg 3, Schedule with effect from 24 April 2017.

SCHEDULE 2

THE SCOTTISH TAX TRIBUNALS (FITNESS ASSESSMENT TRIBUNAL) RULES 2015

Regulation 2(2)

Revocation—These Regulations revoked by the Tribunals (Scotland) Act 2014 (Ancillary Provisions) Regulations, SSI 2017/108 reg 3, Schedule with effect from 24 April 2017.

CONTENTS

Interpretation

1 In these Rules—

"clerk to the fitness assessment tribunal" means the person nominated by the Scottish Ministers to act as clerk to a fitness assessment tribunal;

"fitness assessment tribunal" means a fitness assessment tribunal constituted under paragraph 31(1) or (2) of Schedule 2 to the RSTPA 2014;

"fitness case" means the issue of whether the member of the Scottish Tax Tribunals is unfit to hold his or her office;

"investigating officer" means the person appointed in accordance with rule 3(1), and references to an investigating officer are to be read as references to a substitute investigating officer where one has been appointed;

"member of the Scottish Tax Tribunals" means the person with regard to whom a fitness assessment tribunal has been constituted;

"the parties" are the member of the Scottish Tax Tribunals and the presenting officer;

"presenting officer" means the person appointed in accordance with rule 7(1), and references to a presenting officer are to be read as references to a substitute presenting officer where one has been appointed;

"President" means the President of the Scottish Tax Tribunals;

"RSTPA 2014" means the Revenue Scotland and Tax Powers Act 2014; and

"statement of reasons" means a statement of the grounds on which it is alleged that the member of the Scottish Tax Tribunals is unfit to hold office.

Revocation—These Regulations revoked by the Tribunals (Scotland) Act 2014 (Ancillary Provisions) Regulations, SSI 2017/108 reg 3, Schedule with effect from 24 April 2017.

Commencement of investigation

2 When a fitness assessment tribunal is constituted, the clerk to the fitness assessment tribunal must give the member of the Scottish Tax Tribunals written notice of—

(*a*) the decision of the Scottish Ministers to constitute the fitness assessment tribunal;

(*b*) the membership of the fitness assessment tribunal.

Revocation—These Regulations revoked by the Tribunals (Scotland) Act 2014 (Ancillary Provisions) Regulations, SSI 2017/108 reg 3, Schedule with effect from 24 April 2017.

Investigation

3 (1) The chairing member of the fitness assessment tribunal must appoint an investigating officer from a list of persons who have been nominated for that purpose by the Scottish Ministers.
(2) Such an appointment is to be made within two months of the date on which written notice is given in terms of rule 2.
(3) The investigating officer is to investigate the fitness case and in so doing—
(*a*) must consider the existing information relating to the fitness case and make such further enquiries as the investigating officer considers appropriate;
(*b*) may obtain and consider any documents and productions which appear to be relevant; and
(*c*) may interview any person the investigating officer considers appropriate to interview, including the member of the Scottish Tax Tribunals if that person agrees to be interviewed.
(4) If the investigating officer considers that it cannot be established that the member of the Scottish Tax Tribunals is unfit to hold his or her office, the investigating officer must—
(*a*) recommend to the fitness assessment tribunal that no further procedure is required; and
(*b*) give reasons for that recommendation in writing.
(5) The clerk to the fitness assessment tribunal must provide a copy of the recommendation and reasons to the member of the Scottish Tax Tribunals.
(6) If the investigating officer considers that further procedure is required, the investigating officer must—
(*a*) submit a recommendation for further procedure;
(*b*) provide a statement of reasons to the fitness assessment tribunal; and
(*c*) provide a list and copies of any documents and a list of any other productions that are relied on in the statement of reasons.
(7) The clerk to the fitness assessment tribunal must provide the member of the Scottish Tax Tribunals with—
(*a*) written notice of that recommendation;
(*b*) a copy of the statement of reasons; and
(*c*) a list and copies of any documents and a list of any productions that are relied on in the statement of reasons.
(8) If the investigating officer is unable to fulfil his or her duties, the chairing member of the fitness assessment tribunal may appoint a substitute investigating officer from the list of persons referred to in paragraph (1).

Revocation—These Regulations revoked by the Tribunals (Scotland) Act 2014 (Ancillary Provisions) Regulations, SSI 2017/108 reg 3, Schedule with effect from 24 April 2017.

Application for further specification of reasons

4 (1) The member of the Scottish Tax Tribunals may apply to the fitness assessment tribunal for further specification of the information contained in the statement of reasons.
(2) The application must—
(*a*) specify the matters in relation to which further specification is sought; and
(*b*) be made within 21 days of the date on which written notice is given under rule 3(7)(*a*).
(3) Where the fitness assessment tribunal grants the application, it must direct the investigating officer to provide such further specification in writing as the fitness assessment tribunal considers appropriate within 21 days of the decision to grant the application.
(4) Where the fitness assessment tribunal refuses the application, it must notify the member of the Scottish Tax Tribunals in writing within 21 days of the receipt of the application by the fitness assessment tribunal and give reasons for its decision.

Revocation—These Regulations revoked by the Tribunals (Scotland) Act 2014 (Ancillary Provisions) Regulations, SSI 2017/108 reg 3, Schedule with effect from 24 April 2017.

Response to statement of reasons

5 (1) The member of the Scottish Tax Tribunals may lodge a written response to the investigating officer's recommendation and statement of reasons.
(2) Any written response must—
(*a*) be submitted to the clerk to the fitness assessment tribunal within 28 days of—
(i) the date of the written notice provided under rule 3(7)(*a*);
(ii) the date on which the fitness assessment tribunal notifies the member of the Scottish Tax Tribunals that it has refused an application for further specification in terms of rule 4(4); or
(iii) the date on which the investigating officer provides further specification in terms of rule 4(3),
whichever is the latest;

(*b*) state to what extent any facts set out in the statement of reasons are admitted or denied;

(*c*) include any statement of facts that the member of the Scottish Tax Tribunals wishes to make;

(*d*) indicate any issues of law that the member of the Scottish Tax Tribunals intends to raise;

(*e*) provide the names and addresses of any persons that the member of the Scottish Tax Tribunals may wish to provide as witnesses; and

(*f*) provide a list and copies of any documents and a list of any productions to which the member of the Scottish Tax Tribunals may wish to refer at any hearing.

(3) The fitness assessment tribunal may, on cause shown, allow the member of the Scottish Tax Tribunals to lodge a supplementary written response containing further information falling within the scope of paragraph (2)(*b*) to (*f*).

Revocation—These Regulations revoked by the Tribunals (Scotland) Act 2014 (Ancillary Provisions) Regulations, SSI 2017/108 reg 3, Schedule with effect from 24 April 2017.

Consideration of recommendation etc

6 (1) The fitness assessment tribunal must consider the investigating officer's recommendation and statement of reasons and any written response by the member of the Scottish Tax Tribunals, and determine whether—

(*a*) the investigation should proceed to a hearing; or

(*b*) no further procedure is required.

(2) The fitness assessment tribunal must give reasons in writing for its determination.

Revocation—These Regulations revoked by the Tribunals (Scotland) Act 2014 (Ancillary Provisions) Regulations, SSI 2017/108 reg 3, Schedule with effect from 24 April 2017.

Representation at hearings

7 (1) If the fitness assessment tribunal determines that the investigation is to proceed to a hearing, the chairing member of the fitness assessment tribunal must appoint a presenting officer from a list of persons who have been nominated for that purpose by the Scottish Ministers.

(2) The investigating officer must provide to the presenting officer copies of all documents supplied to or by the fitness assessment tribunal and the member of the Scottish Tax Tribunals.

(3) The fitness case is to be presented by the presenting officer.

(4) The presenting officer may instruct the investigating officer to carry out such further investigations as the presenting officer considers necessary.

(5) The member of the Scottish Tax Tribunals may be represented before the fitness assessment tribunal by an advocate or solicitor, or any other person authorised by the fitness assessment tribunal.

(6) If the presenting officer is unable to fulfil his or her duties, the chairing member of the fitness assessment tribunal may appoint a substitute presenting officer from the list of persons referred to in paragraph (1).

Revocation—These Regulations revoked by the Tribunals (Scotland) Act 2014 (Ancillary Provisions) Regulations, SSI 2017/108 reg 3, Schedule with effect from 24 April 2017.

Duty to disclose information

8 (1) The presenting officer and the investigating officer must disclose to the member of the Scottish Tax Tribunals any information not previously disclosed that—

(*a*) is likely to form part of the facts and circumstances placed before the fitness assessment tribunal by the presenting officer;

(*b*) may materially strengthen the member of the Scottish Tax Tribunals' position before the fitness assessment tribunal; or

(*c*) may materially undermine the presenting officer's position before the fitness assessment tribunal.

(2) During the relevant period, the presenting officer must—

(*a*) keep under review all the information that may be relevant to the fitness case of which the presenting officer is aware; and

(*b*) disclose to the member of the Scottish Tax Tribunals any information not previously disclosed in accordance with paragraph (1).

(3) In this rule, "relevant period" means the period which begins when the presenting officer complies with paragraph (1) and ends when the fitness assessment tribunal reports to the Scottish Ministers.

Revocation—These Regulations revoked by the Tribunals (Scotland) Act 2014 (Ancillary Provisions) Regulations, SSI 2017/108 reg 3, Schedule with effect from 24 April 2017.

Preliminary hearing

9 (1) Before proceeding to a hearing under rule 10, the fitness assessment tribunal must hold a preliminary hearing.

(2) The clerk to the fitness assessment tribunal must give the parties written notice of the date, time and place of the preliminary hearing.

(3) At the preliminary hearing, the fitness assessment tribunal may—

(*a*) confirm with the member of the Scottish Tax Tribunals what facts, if any, are in dispute;

(*b*) hear argument from the parties on and decide any legal or other preliminary issue raised in any written response or supplementary written response lodged under rule 5;

(*c*) make any case management directions, including directions as to the lodging of documents or the attendance of witnesses, that it considers necessary for the future conduct of the proceedings; and

(*d*) fix a hearing under rule 10.

Revocation—These Regulations revoked by the Tribunals (Scotland) Act 2014 (Ancillary Provisions) Regulations, SSI 2017/108 reg 3, Schedule with effect from 24 April 2017.

Hearing

10 (1) If the fitness assessment tribunal determines that a hearing is necessary, it may fix—

(*a*) a hearing on legal submissions only; or

(*b*) a hearing at which—

(i) the parties may present oral and documentary evidence and refer to productions;

(ii) witnesses may be examined; and

(iii) the parties may make submissions on fact and law.

(2) The clerk to the fitness assessment tribunal must give the parties written notice of the date, time and place of the hearing.

Revocation—These Regulations revoked by the Tribunals (Scotland) Act 2014 (Ancillary Provisions) Regulations, SSI 2017/108 reg 3, Schedule with effect from 24 April 2017.

Conduct of hearings

11 (1) Subject to paragraph (3), hearings of the fitness assessment tribunal are to be in private.

(2) The fitness assessment tribunal is to deliberate in the absence of any other person.

(3) The fitness assessment tribunal may conduct the hearing or any part of it in public if—

(*a*) the member of the Scottish Tax Tribunals so requests; or

(*b*) for any reason the fitness assessment tribunal considers that the circumstances are such as to make a private hearing inappropriate.

(4) All hearings must be recorded by electronic means or otherwise as approved by the fitness assessment tribunal.

Revocation—These Regulations revoked by the Tribunals (Scotland) Act 2014 (Ancillary Provisions) Regulations, SSI 2017/108 reg 3, Schedule with effect from 24 April 2017.

Powers of fitness assessment tribunal

12 (1) Subject to the provisions of Schedule 2 to the RSTPA 2014 and these Rules, the fitness assessment tribunal may regulate its own procedure.

(2) The fitness assessment tribunal may give a direction in relation to the conduct or disposal of proceedings at any time, including a direction amending, suspending or setting aside an earlier direction.

(3) In particular, and without restricting the general powers in paragraphs (1) and (2), the fitness assessment tribunal may, on cause shown—

(*a*) extend or shorten the time for complying with any rule or direction;

(*b*) permit a party to amend a document;

(*c*) adjourn or postpone a hearing;

(*d*) sist proceedings.

(4) If any hearing is postponed or adjourned, the clerk to the fitness assessment tribunal must give the parties written notice of the date, time and place to which the hearing has been postponed or adjourned.

Revocation—These Regulations revoked by the Tribunals (Scotland) Act 2014 (Ancillary Provisions) Regulations, SSI 2017/108 reg 3, Schedule with effect from 24 April 2017.

Termination of proceedings

13 (1) If the presenting officer considers at any time that it cannot be established that the member of the Scottish Tax Tribunals is unfit to hold his or her office, the presenting officer must—

(*a*) recommend to the fitness assessment tribunal that no further procedure is required; and

(*b*) give reasons for that recommendation in writing.

(2) The clerk to the fitness assessment tribunal must provide a copy of the recommendation and reasons to the member of the Scottish Tax Tribunals.

(3) If the member of the Scottish Tax Tribunals ceases to hold office at any stage in the proceedings, the proceedings are terminated.

(4) At any stage in the proceedings, the fitness assessment tribunal may—

(*a*) on the basis of a recommendation by the investigating officer or the presenting officer;

(*b*) on the basis of a submission by the member of the Scottish Tax Tribunals; or

(*c*) on its own motion,

determine that it cannot be established that the member of the Scottish Tax Tribunals is unfit to hold his or her office.

Revocation—These Regulations revoked by the Tribunals (Scotland) Act 2014 (Ancillary Provisions) Regulations, SSI 2017/108 reg 3, Schedule with effect from 24 April 2017.

Decision and report

14 (1) Where the fitness assessment tribunal, having considered the evidence, proposes to make findings of fact on disputed issues, it must send to the parties a draft of its findings and invite them to comment on the draft by such date as the fitness assessment tribunal specifies.

(2) The fitness assessment tribunal must have regard to any comments made under paragraph (1), but need not give the parties an opportunity to comment on any alterations made to the draft before the submission of its report.

(3) The fitness assessment tribunal must send a copy of its report to the member of the Scottish Tax Tribunals, to the Scottish Ministers and to the President.

Revocation—These Regulations revoked by the Tribunals (Scotland) Act 2014 (Ancillary Provisions) Regulations, SSI 2017/108 reg 3, Schedule with effect from 24 April 2017.

2015/381

SCOTTISH TRIBUNALS (ELIGIBILITY FOR APPOINTMENT) REGULATIONS 2015

Made . . . .*5 November 2015*
Laid before the Scottish Parliament . . . .*9 November 2015*
Coming into force . . . .*1 January 2016*

The Scottish Ministers make the following Regulations in exercise of the powers conferred by section 32(1) and (3) of, paragraphs 1(2), 5(2), 6 and 7(1) of schedule 3 to, and paragraphs 5(2), 6 and 7(1) of schedule 5 to, the Tribunals (Scotland) Act 2014 and all other powers enabling them to do so.

1 Citation, commencement and interpretation

(1) These Regulations may be cited as the Scottish Tribunals (Eligibility for Appointment) Regulations 2015 and come into force on 1st January 2016.

(2) In these Regulations, "the Act" means the Tribunals (Scotland) Act 2014.

2 Eligibility for appointment as an ordinary member of the First-tier Tribunal for Scotland (tax experience)

(1) A person is eligible for appointment as an ordinary member of the First-tier Tribunal for Scotland if paragraph (2), (3) or (4) applies to the person.

(2) This paragraph applies to a person who is a member of the Chartered Institute of Taxation.

(3) This paragraph applies to a person who is a member of—

(*a*) the Institute of Chartered Accountants of Scotland;

(*b*) the Institute of Chartered Accountants in England and Wales;

(*c*) the Institute of Chartered Accountants in Ireland;

(*d*) the Institute of Certified Public Accountants in Ireland;

(*e*) the Association of Chartered Certified Accountants;

(*f*) the Chartered Institute of Management Accountants; or

(*g*) the Chartered Institute of Public Finance and Accountancy.

(4) Subject to paragraph (5), this paragraph applies to a person who has substantial experience in tax matters and related tax procedures (whether obtained in a business, trade, charity or not-for-profit organisation, or in a profession or in academia).

(5) Paragraph (4) does not apply where a person is a former member of any of the professional bodies listed in paragraphs (2) and (3), if the person has been debarred from the person's professional body or if the person has been subject to any sanction that would have led to such debarment had the person not ceased to belong to the professional body.

3 Eligibility for appointment as an ordinary member of the First-tier Tribunal for Scotland (housing, property or surveying experience)

(1) A person is eligible for appointment as an ordinary member of the First-tier Tribunal for Scotland if paragraph (2) or (3) applies to the person.

(2) This paragraph applies to a person who has substantial relevant housing or property experience.
(3) This paragraph applies to a person who has substantial relevant surveying experience.
(4) Paragraph (2) or (3) applies to a person, whether the person has obtained the substantial relevant housing, property or surveying experience in a business, trade, charity or not-for-profit organisation, or in a profession or in academia.
(5) In this regulation—

"relevant housing or property experience" means experience in—

(*a*) matters relating to landlord and tenant relationships;

(*b*) housing matters (including as regards private rented sector, letting agency and factoring matters); or

(*c*) land and property management matters; and

"relevant surveying experience" means experience in surveying related to housing and building conditions as a member or fellow (or former member or fellow) of the Royal Institution of Chartered Surveyors ("RICS"), but such experience does not count as relevant experience where a person is a former member or fellow of RICS, if the person has been debarred from RICS or if the person has been subject to any sanction that would have led to such debarment had the person not ceased to belong to RICS.

[3A Eligibility for appointment as an ordinary member of the First-tier Tribunal for Scotland (health and education experience)

A person is eligible for appointment as an ordinary member of the First-tier Tribunal for Scotland if the person has knowledge and experience of children or young persons with—
(*a*) additional support needs within the meaning of section 1(1) of the Education (Additional Support for Learning) (Scotland) Act 2004; or
(*b*) disability within the meaning of section 6 of the Equality Act 2010.][1]

Amendments—[1] Regulations 3A, 3B inserted by the Scottish Tribunals (Eligibility for Appointment) Amendment Regulations, SSI 2017/274 reg 2 with effect from 2 October 2017.

[3B Eligibility for appointment as an ordinary member of the First-tier Tribunal for Scotland (charity regulatory experience)

person is eligible for appointment as an ordinary member of the First-tier Tribunal for Scotland if the person has knowledge and experience in accounting or governance of public or private bodies or charities.][1]

Amendments—[1] Regulations 3A, 3B inserted by the Scottish Tribunals (Eligibility for Appointment) Amendment Regulations, SSI 2017/274 reg 2 with effect from 2 October 2017.

4 Eligibility for appointment as a legal member of the First-tier Tribunal for Scotland

(1) A person is eligible for appointment as a legal member of the First-tier Tribunal for Scotland under paragraph 5(2) of schedule 3 to the Act if the person qualifies under paragraph (2).
(2) Subject to paragraph (5), a person qualifies under this paragraph, if the person has had—

(*a*) previous engagement in practice for a period of not less than 5 years as a solicitor or advocate in Scotland; and

(*b*) subsequent engagement in any of the activities listed in paragraph (3).

(3) The activities are—

(*a*) exercising judicial functions in any court or tribunal;

(*b*) practice or employment as a lawyer of any kind;

(*c*) teaching or researching law at or for an educational institution.

(4) The 5 year period referred to in paragraph (2)(*a*) (and the 5 year period referred to in paragraph 5(1) of schedule 3 to the Act) may be calculated on a cumulative or a continuous basis.
(5) A person is not to be treated as having satisfied paragraph (2)(*a*), if the person has been debarred from the person's professional body or if the person has been subject to any sanction that would have led to such debarment had the person not ceased to belong to the professional body.

5 Eligibility for appointment as a legal member of the Upper Tribunal for Scotland

(1) A person is eligible for appointment as a legal member of the Upper Tribunal for Scotland under paragraph under paragraph 5(2) of schedule 5 to the Act if the person qualifies under paragraph (2).
(2) Subject to paragraph (5), a person qualifies under this paragraph, if the person has had—

(*a*) previous engagement in practice for a period of not less than 7 years as a solicitor or advocate in Scotland; and

(*b*) subsequent engagement in any of the activities listed in paragraph (3).

(3) The activities are—

(*a*) exercising judicial functions in any court or tribunal;

(*b*) practice or employment as a lawyer of any kind.

(4) The 7 year period referred to in paragraph (2)(*a*) (and the 7 year period referred to in paragraph 5(1) of schedule 5 to the Act) may be calculated on a cumulative or a continuous basis.

(5) A person is not to be treated as having satisfied paragraph (2)(*a*), if the person has been debarred from the person's professional body or if the person has been subject to any sanction that would have led to such debarment had the person not ceased to belong to the professional body.

2016/231

SCOTTISH TRIBUNALS (TIME LIMITS) REGULATIONS 2016

Made . . . .*17 August 2016*
Laid before the Scottish Parliament . . . .*19 August 2016*
Coming into force . . . .*1 December 2016*

The Scottish Ministers make the following Regulations in exercise of the powers conferred by section 55(1), 79(1)(*a*) and paragraph 4(2) of schedule 9 of the Tribunals (Scotland) Act 2014 and all other powers enabling them to do so.

In accordance with paragraph 4(3) of schedule 9 of that Act, the Scottish Ministers have consulted with the President of Tribunals and such other persons as they considered appropriate.

1 Citation, commencement and interpretation

(1) These Regulations may be cited as the Scottish Tribunals (Time Limits) Regulations 2016.

(2) These Regulations come into force on 1st December 2016.

(3) In these Regulations—

"the 2014 Act" means the Tribunals (Scotland) Act 2014;

"appellant" means a party applying for permission to appeal; and

"hearing" means an oral hearing and includes a hearing conducted in whole or in part by video link, telephone or other means of instantaneous two-way electronic communication.

2 Time limits for applying to the First-tier Tribunal or Upper Tribunal for permission to appeal against its own decision

(1) An application for permission under sections 46(3)(*a*) or 48(3)(*a*) of the Act (application for permission to appeal the Tribunal's own decision) must be received by the Tribunal whose decision is being appealed against within the period of 30 days beginning with the relevant date.

(2) The First-tier Tribunal or the Upper Tribunal, as appropriate, may on cause shown extend the period beyond 30 days if it considers such an extension to be in the interests of justice.

(3) Subject to paragraph (4), the relevant date is the later of the date on which—

(*a*) the decision appealed against was sent to the appellant;

(*b*) the statement of reasons for the decision was sent to the appellant.

(4) But where a decision is given orally at a hearing, the relevant date is either—

(*a*) the date on which written reasons were sent to the parties, if—

(i) written reasons were requested at the hearing (or were requested in writing within 14 days beginning with the day after the last day of the hearing); or

(ii) the First-tier Tribunal or the Upper Tribunal, as appropriate, undertook at the hearing to provide written reasons; or

(*b*) the date of the oral decision, if—

(i) written reasons were not requested at the hearing (or were not requested in writing within 14 days beginning with the day after the last day of the hearing); or

(ii) the First-tier Tribunal or the Upper Tribunal, as appropriate, did not undertake at the hearing to provide written reasons.

3 Time limits for applying to the Upper Tribunal for permission to appeal against a decision of the First-tier Tribunal

(1) An application for permission under section 46(3)(*b*) of the 2014 Act (application for permission to appeal to the Upper Tribunal against a decision of the First-tier Tribunal) must be received by the Upper Tribunal within the period of 30 days beginning with the relevant date.

(2) The relevant date is the date on which notice of the First-tier Tribunal's refusal of permission to appeal was sent to the appellant.

(3) The Upper Tribunal may on cause shown extend the period beyond 30 days if it considers such an extension to be in the interests of justice.

2016/232

UPPER TRIBUNAL FOR SCOTLAND (RULES OF PROCEDURE) REGULATIONS 2016

Made . . . .*17 August 2016*
Laid before the Scottish Parliament . . . .*19 August 2016*

Coming into force . . . . *1 December 2016*

The Scottish Ministers make the following Regulations in exercise of the powers conferred by paragraph 4(1)(*b*) and (2) of schedule 9 of the Tribunals (Scotland) Act 2014 and all other powers enabling them to do so.

In accordance with paragraph 4(3) of schedule 9 of that Act, the Scottish Ministers have consulted the President of Tribunals and such other persons as they considered appropriate.

1 Citation and commencement

(1) These Regulations may be cited as the Upper Tribunal for Scotland (Rules of Procedure) Regulations 2016 and the Rules contained in the schedule may be cited as the Upper Tribunal for Scotland Rules of Procedure 2016.

(2) These Regulations come into force on 1st December 2016.

2 Application of Rules in schedule

The Rules in the schedule of these Regulations apply to all proceedings before the Upper Tribunal.

SCHEDULE

THE UPPER TRIBUNAL FOR SCOTLAND RULES OF PROCEDURE 2016

Regulation 2

PART 1

INTERPRETATION

Interpretation

1 In these Rules—

"the 2014 Act" means the Tribunals (Scotland) Act 2014;

"Appeal Appendix" means all the documents and authorities to be relied on for the purpose of the appeal along with an inventory;

"appellant" means—

(*a*) a person who makes an appeal to the Upper Tribunal;

(*b*) a person who has had an application to the First-tier Tribunal transferred to the Upper Tribunal; or

(*c*) in any case, a person substituted as an appellant under rule 11(1) (addition, substitution and removal of parties);

"Convention rights" has the meaning given to it in section 1 of the Human Rights Act 1998;

"document" means anything in which information is recorded in any form;

"excluded decision" means a decision referred to in section 51 of the 2014 Act;

"hearing" means an oral hearing and includes a hearing conducted in whole or in part by video link, telephone or other means of instantaneous two-way electronic communication;

"interested party" means a person other than the appellant or respondent on whom the First-tier Tribunal has ordered the proceedings before it to be served;

"party" means a person who is (or was at the time that the Upper Tribunal disposed of the proceedings) an appellant or respondent in proceedings before the Upper Tribunal;

"practice direction" means a practice direction issued in terms of section 74 of the 2014 Act;

"President" means the President of Tribunals;

"proceedings" includes, unless indicated otherwise, a part of the proceedings;

"respondent" means—

(*a*) in an appeal against a decision of the First-tier Tribunal, that tribunal and any person other than the appellant who—

(i) was a party before the First-tier Tribunal;

(ii) otherwise has a right of appeal against the decision of the First-tier Tribunal and has given notice to the Upper Tribunal that they wish to be a party to the appeal;

(*b*) in proceedings transferred or referred to the Upper Tribunal from the First-tier Tribunal, a person who was a respondent in the proceedings in the First-tier Tribunal; or

(*c*) in any case, a person substituted or added as a respondent under rule 11 (addition, substitution and removal of parties);

"review period" means the time period between an application by a party for a review under rule 30(1), or, as the case may be, the Upper Tribunal's decision to review a decision under that rule, and the receipt by a party of a notification under rule 30(6); and

"witness statement" means a written statement of a witness ordered by the Upper Tribunal to stand for the evidence-in-chief of the witness.

PART 2

ROLE OF THE UPPER TRIBUNAL

Purpose of the Upper Tribunal

2 The Upper Tribunal hears and decides cases transferred or referred to it from the First-tier Tribunal and hears and decides appeals from the First-tier Tribunal.

PART 3

PROCEDURE FOR CASES IN THE UPPER TRIBUNAL

Notice of appeal against a decision of the First-tier Tribunal

3 (1) A person may lodge with the Upper Tribunal a notice of appeal against a decision of the First-tier Tribunal.

(2) A notice of appeal must—

(*a*) identify the decision of the First-tier Tribunal to which it relates; and

(*b*) identify the alleged error or errors of law in the decision.

(3) The appellant must provide with the notice of appeal a copy of—

(*a*) any written record of the decision being challenged;

(*b*) any separate written statement of reasons for that decision; and

(*c*) the notice of permission to appeal or alternatively notice of refusal of permission to appeal from the First-tier Tribunal.

(4) When the Upper Tribunal receives a notice of appeal it must send a copy of the notice and any accompanying documents to each respondent and interested party (if any).

(5) If the appellant lodges the notice of appeal with the Upper Tribunal later than the time required by paragraph (9)—

(*a*) the notice of appeal must:

(i) include a request for an extension of time;

(ii) explain why the notice of appeal was not provided in time; and

(iii) state why it is said to be in the interests of justice that the time be extended; and

(*b*) unless the Upper Tribunal extends the time for lodging a notice of appeal the Upper Tribunal may not admit the notice of appeal.

(6) The Upper Tribunal may, where the First-tier Tribunal has refused permission to appeal—

(*a*) refuse permission to appeal;

(*b*) give permission to appeal; or

(*c*) give permission to appeal on limited grounds or subject to conditions;

and must send a notice of its decision to each party and any interested party including reasons for any refusal of permission or limitations or conditions on any grant of permission.

(7) Where the Upper Tribunal, without a hearing—

(*a*) refuses permission to appeal; or

(*b*) gives permission to appeal on limited grounds or subject to conditions,

the appellant may make a written application (within 14 days after the day of receipt of notice of the decision) to the Upper Tribunal for the decision to be reconsidered at a hearing.

(8) An application under paragraph (7) must be heard and decided by a member or members of the Upper Tribunal different from the member or members who refused permission without a hearing.

(9) Where the First-tier Tribunal sends a notice of permission or refusal of permission to appeal to a person who has sought permission to appeal, that person, if intending to appeal, must provide a notice of appeal to the Upper Tribunal within 30 days after the day of receipt by that person of the notice of permission or refusal of permission to appeal.

Response to the notice of appeal

4 (1) Subject to any order given by the Upper Tribunal, a respondent may provide a written response to a notice of appeal.

(2) Any response provided under paragraph (1) must be sent or delivered to the Upper Tribunal so that it is received no later than 30 days after the day on which the Upper Tribunal sent a copy of the notice of appeal to the respondent.

(3) The response must state—

(*a*) the name and address of the respondent;

(*b*) the name and address of the representative (if any) of the respondent;

(*c*) an address where documents for the respondent may be sent or delivered;

(*d*) whether the respondent opposes the appeal;

(*e*) the grounds on which the respondent relies, including (in the case of an appeal against the decision of the First-tier Tribunal) any grounds on which the respondent was unsuccessful in the proceedings which are the subject of the appeal, but intends to rely in the appeal; and

(*f*) whether the respondent consents to the case being heard without a hearing.

(4) If the respondent provides the response to the Upper Tribunal later than the time required by paragraph (2) or by an extension of time allowed under rule 7(3)(*a*) (power to extend time), the response must include a request for an extension of time and the reason why the response was not provided in time.
(5) When the Upper Tribunal receives the response it must send a copy of the response and any accompanying documents to the appellant and any interested party.

Appellant's reply

5 (1) Subject to any order given by the Upper Tribunal, the appellant may provide a written reply to any response provided under rule 4 (response to the notice of appeal).
(2) Any reply provided under paragraph (1) must be sent or delivered to the Upper Tribunal so that it is received within 30 days after the day on which the Upper Tribunal sent a copy of the response to the appellant.
(3) If the appellant provides the reply to the Upper Tribunal later than the time required by paragraph (2) or by an extension of time allowed under rule 7(3)(*a*) (power to extend time), the reply must include a request for an extension of time and the reason why the reply was not provided in time.
(4) When the Upper Tribunal receives the reply it must send a copy of the reply and any accompanying documents to each respondent and interested party (if any).

Cases transferred or referred to the Upper Tribunal

6 (1) Paragraphs (2) and (3) apply to a case transferred or referred to the Upper Tribunal from the First-tier Tribunal.
(2) In such a case—

(*a*) the Upper Tribunal must give orders as to the procedure to be followed in the consideration and disposal of the proceedings;

(*b*) the preceding rules in this Part will only apply to the proceedings to the extent provided for by such orders.

(3) If a case or matter is to be determined without notice to or the involvement of a respondent—

(*a*) any provision in these Rules requiring a document to be provided by or to a respondent; and

(*b*) any other provision in these Rules permitting a respondent to participate in the proceedings,

does not apply to that case or matter.

PART 4
GENERAL POWERS AND PROVISIONS

Case management

7 (1) Subject to the provisions of the 2014 Act and these Rules, the Upper Tribunal may regulate its own procedure.
(2) The Upper Tribunal may give an order in relation to the conduct of proceedings before it at any time, including an order amending, suspending or setting aside an earlier order.
(3) In particular, and without restricting the general powers in paragraphs (1) and (2), the Upper Tribunal may—

(*a*) extend or shorten the time for complying with any rule or order;

(*b*) conjoin or take concurrently two or more sets of proceedings or parts of proceedings raising common issues;

(*c*) specify one or more cases as a lead case or lead cases where—

(i) two or more cases are before the Upper Tribunal;

(ii) in each such case the proceedings have not been finally determined; and

(iii) the cases give rise to common or related issues of fact or law,

and sist the other cases until the common or related issues have been determined;

(*d*) permit or require a party to amend a document;

(*e*) permit or require a party or another person to provide documents, information, evidence or submissions to the Upper Tribunal or a party;

(*f*) deal with an issue in the proceedings as a preliminary issue;

(*g*) hold a hearing to consider any matter, including a case management issue;

(*h*) decide the form of any hearing;

(*i*) adjourn or postpone a hearing;

(*j*) require a party to produce or lodge documents including but not confined to a note of argument and the Appeal Appendix;

(*k*) sist proceedings;

(*l*) transfer proceedings to another court or tribunal if that other court or tribunal has jurisdiction in relation to the proceedings and—

(i) because of a change of circumstances since the proceedings were started, the Upper Tribunal no longer has jurisdiction in relation to the proceedings; or

(ii) the Upper Tribunal considers that the other court or tribunal is a more appropriate forum for the determination of the case;

(*m*) suspend the effect of its own decision pending an appeal of that decision;

(*n*) in an appeal against the decision of the First-tier Tribunal, suspend the effect of that decision pending the determination of any permission to appeal or any appeal;

(*o*) require the First-tier Tribunal to provide reasons for the decision, or other information or documents in relation to the decision or any proceedings before the First-tier Tribunal.

Procedure for applying for and giving orders

8 (1) The Upper Tribunal may give an order on the application of one or more of the parties or on its own initiative.

(2) An application for an order may be made—

(*a*) by sending or delivering a written application to the Upper Tribunal; or

(*b*) orally during the course of a hearing.

(3) An application for an order must include the reason for making that application.

(4) Before making an order, the Upper Tribunal must afford parties an opportunity to make representations to it concerning whether the order should be imposed and the terms of the order.

Failure to comply with rules etc

9 (1) An irregularity resulting from a failure to comply with any requirement in these Rules, a practice direction or an order, does not of itself render void the proceedings or any step taken in the proceedings.

(2) If a party has failed to comply with a requirement in these Rules, a practice direction or an order, the Upper Tribunal may take such action as it considers just, which may include—

(*a*) waiving the requirement;

(*b*) requiring the failure to be remedied; or

(*c*) exercising its power under rule 10 (dismissal of a party's case).

Dismissal of a party's case

10 (1) The Upper Tribunal must dismiss the whole or a part of the proceedings if the Upper Tribunal—

(*a*) does not have jurisdiction in relation to the proceedings or that part of them; and

(*b*) does not exercise its power under rule 7(3)(*l*)(i) (transfer to another court or tribunal) in relation to the proceedings or that part of them.

(2) The Upper Tribunal may dismiss the whole or a part of the proceedings if—

(*a*) the appellant has failed to comply with an order which stated that failure by the appellant to comply with the order could lead to the dismissal of the proceedings or part of them;

(*b*) the appellant has failed to co-operate with the Upper Tribunal to such an extent that the Upper Tribunal cannot deal with the proceedings fairly; or

(*c*) in proceedings which have been transferred from the First-tier Tribunal, the Upper Tribunal considers there is no reasonable prospect of the appellant's case, or any part of it, succeeding.

(3) The Upper Tribunal may not dismiss the whole or a part of the proceedings under paragraph (1) or (2) without first giving the appellant an opportunity to make representations in relation to the proposed dismissal.

Addition, substitution and removal of parties

11 (1) The Upper Tribunal may give an order adding, substituting or removing a party as an appellant or a respondent including where—

(*a*) the wrong person has been named as a party; or

(*b*) the addition, substitution or removal has become necessary because of a change in circumstances since the start of proceedings.

(2) If the Upper Tribunal gives an order under paragraph (1) it may give such consequential orders as it considers appropriate.

(3) A person who is not a party may make a written application to the Upper Tribunal to be added or substituted as a party under this rule.

(4) If the Upper Tribunal refuses an application under paragraph (3) it must consider whether to permit the person who made the application to provide submissions or evidence to the Upper Tribunal.

Orders for expenses

12 (1) The Upper Tribunal may make an order for expenses as taxed by the Auditor of the Court of Session in proceedings on appeal from the First-tier Tribunal if the First-tier Tribunal had the power to make an order for expenses, and only on the basis on which the First-tier Tribunal had the power to award expenses.

(2) Notwithstanding paragraph (1) and without prejudice to that paragraph, the Upper Tribunal may make an order for expenses as taxed by the Auditor of the Court of Session against a party if that party's act, omission or other conduct has caused any other party to incur expense which it would be unreasonable for that other party to be expected to pay, with the maximum recoverable expenses being the expenses incurred.

(3) The Upper Tribunal, of its own initiative or on the application of a party or the parties, may in exceptional circumstances fix by order a sum payable by a party in discharge of an award of expenses.

Representatives

13 (1) A party may be represented in any proceedings by a legal representative or lay representative whose details must be communicated to the Upper Tribunal prior to any hearing.

(2) A party may show any document or communicate any information about the proceedings to that party's lay representative or legal representative without contravening any prohibition or restriction on disclosure of the document or information.

(3) Where a document or information is disclosed under paragraph (2), the lay representative or legal representative is subject to any prohibition or restriction on disclosure in the same way that the party is.

(4) Anything permitted or required to be done by a party under these Rules, a practice direction or an order may be done by a lay representative, except signing of an affidavit or a precognition.

(5) The Upper Tribunal may order that a lay representative is not to represent a party if—

(*a*) it is of the opinion that the lay representative is an unsuitable person to act as a lay representative (whether generally or in the proceedings concerned); or

(*b*) it is satisfied that to do so would be in the interests of the efficient administration of justice.

Supporters

14 (1) A party who is an individual may be accompanied by another person to act as a supporter.

(2) A supporter may assist the party by—

(*a*) providing moral support;

(*b*) helping to manage tribunal documents and other papers;

(*c*) taking notes of the proceedings;

(*d*) quietly advising on—

(i) points of law and procedure;

(ii) issues which the party might wish to raise with the tribunal.

(3) The party may show any document or communicate any information about the proceedings to that party's supporter without contravening any prohibition or restriction on disclosure of the document or information.

(4) Where a document or information is disclosed under paragraph (3), the supporter is subject to any prohibition or restriction on disclosure in the same way that the party is.

(5) A supporter may not represent the party.

(6) The Upper Tribunal may order that a person is not to act as a supporter of a party if—

(*a*) it is of the opinion that the supporter is an unsuitable person to act as a supporter (whether generally or in the proceedings concerned); or

(*b*) it is satisfied that to do so would be in the interests of the efficient administration of justice.

Calculating time

15 (1) An act required by these Rules, a practice direction or an order to be done on or by a particular day must be done by 5 pm on that day.

(2) If the time specified by these Rules, a practice direction or an order for doing any act ends on a day other than a working day, the act is done in time if it is done on the next working day.

(3) In this rule "working day" means any day except a Saturday, a Sunday, or a bank holiday in Scotland under section 1 of the Banking and Financial Dealings Act 1971.

Sending and delivery of documents

16 (1) Any document to be provided to the Upper Tribunal under these Rules, a practice direction or an order must be—

(*a*) sent by pre-paid post or by document exchange, or delivered by hand, to the address of the Upper Tribunal; or

(*b*) sent or delivered by such other method as the Upper Tribunal may permit or direct.

(2) Subject to paragraph (3), if a party or an interested party provides a fax number, email address or other details for the electronic transmission of documents to them, that party or interested party must accept delivery of documents by that method.

(3) If a party or an interested party informs the Upper Tribunal and all other parties and interested parties that a particular form of communication, other than pre-paid post or delivery by hand, should not be used to provide documents to that party or interested party, that form of communication must not be so used.

(4) If the Upper Tribunal or a party or an interested party sends a document to a party or interested party or the Upper Tribunal by email or any other electronic means of communication, the recipient may request that the sender provide a hard copy of the document to the recipient. The recipient must make such a request as soon as reasonably practicable after receiving the document electronically.
(5) The Upper Tribunal and each party and interested party may assume that the address provided by a party or interested party or its representative is and remains the address to which documents should be sent or delivered until receiving written notification to the contrary.

Disclosure of documents and information

17 The Upper Tribunal may at any stage of the proceedings, on its own initiative or on application by one or more of the parties or any interested party, make an order with a view to preventing or restricting the public disclosure of any aspect of those proceedings so far as it considers necessary in the interests of justice or in order to protect the Convention rights of any person.

Evidence and submissions

18 (1) Without restriction on the general powers in rule 7(1) and (2) (case management powers), the Upper Tribunal may give orders as to—
(*a*) subject to paragraph (4), issues on which parties may lead fresh evidence or make submissions;
(*b*) the nature of any such evidence;
(*c*) whether the parties are permitted or required to provide expert evidence, and if so whether the parties must jointly appoint a single expert to provide such evidence;
(*d*) any limit on the number of witnesses whose evidence a party may put forward, whether in relation to a particular issue or generally;
(*e*) the manner in which any evidence or submissions are to be provided, which may include an order for them to be given—
(i) orally at a hearing; or
(ii) by written submissions or witness statement; and
(*f*) the time at which any evidence or submissions are to be provided.
(2) The Upper Tribunal may exclude evidence that would otherwise be admissible where—
(*a*) the evidence was not, without reasonable excuse, provided within the time allowed by an order or a practice direction;
(*b*) the evidence was otherwise, without reasonable excuse, provided in a manner that did not comply with an order or a practice direction; or
(*c*) it would otherwise be unfair to admit the evidence.
(3) The Upper Tribunal may consent to a witness giving, or require any witness to give, evidence on oath or affirmation, and may administer an oath or affirmation for that purpose.
(4) Fresh evidence may only be led in an appeal if the Upper Tribunal is satisfied—
(*a*) that the evidence—
(i) could not have been obtained with reasonable diligence at the First-tier Tribunal stage;
(ii) is relevant and will probably have an important influence on the hearing; and
(iii) is apparently credible; or
(*b*) that the interests of justice justify the evidence being led.

Citation of witnesses and orders to answer questions or produce documents

19 (1) On the application of a party or on its own initiative, the Upper Tribunal may—
(*a*) by citation require any person to attend as a witness at a hearing at the time and place specified in the citation; or
(*b*) order any person to answer any questions or produce any documents in that person's possession or control which relate to any issue in the proceedings.
(2) A citation under paragraph (1)(*a*) must—
(*a*) give the person required to attend 14 days' notice prior to the day of the hearing or such other period as the Upper Tribunal may order;
(*b*) where the person is not a party, state (if appropriate) how expenses of attendance necessarily incurred may be recovered;
(*c*) state that the person on whom the requirement is imposed may apply to the Upper Tribunal to vary or set aside the citation or order, if the person did not have an opportunity to object to it before it was made or issued; and
(*d*) state the consequences of failure to comply with the citation or order.
(3) A person making an application referred to in sub-paragraph (2)(*c*) must do so as soon as reasonably practicable after receiving notice of the citation or order.

Withdrawal

20 (1) A party may give notice to the Upper Tribunal of the withdrawal of the case made by that party in the Upper Tribunal proceedings, or any part of that case—

(*a*) by sending or delivering to the Upper Tribunal a notice of withdrawal; or
(*b*) orally at a hearing.

(2) Unless satisfied that a party has already been notified, the Upper Tribunal must notify each party of its receipt of a withdrawal under this rule.

Chairing member

21 Where a matter is to be decided by two or more members of the Upper Tribunal, the President must determine the chairing member.

Venue for hearings

22 The Upper Tribunal is to be convened at such time and place in Scotland as the President may determine.

Enforcement of decisions

23 An order for the payment of a sum payable in pursuance of a decision of the Upper Tribunal, or a copy of such an order certified by the Upper Tribunal, may be enforced as if it were an extract registered decree arbitral bearing a warrant for execution issued by the Court of Session.

PART 5

HEARINGS

Decision with or without a hearing

24 The Upper Tribunal may make any decision without a hearing.

Entitlement to attend a hearing

25 Subject to rules 13(5) (representatives), 14(6) (supporters) and 27(4) (public and private hearings), each party and interested party is entitled to participate at a hearing together with any legal or lay representatives and supporters permitted by rules 13 and 14.

Notice of hearings

26 (1) The Upper Tribunal must give each party and interested party entitled to attend a hearing reasonable notice of the time and place of the hearing (including any adjourned or postponed hearing) and any change to the time and place of the hearing.

(2) The period of notice under paragraph (1) must be at least 14 days prior to the day of the hearing except that the Upper Tribunal may give shorter notice—

(a) with the consent of the parties and interested parties; or
(b) in urgent or exceptional circumstances.

Public and private hearings

27 (1) Subject to the following paragraphs, all hearings must be held in public.

(2) The Upper Tribunal may give an order that a hearing, or part of it, is to be held in private if the Upper Tribunal considers that restricting access to the hearing is justified—

(*a*) in the interests of public order;
(*b*) in order to protect a person's right to respect for their private and family life;
(*c*) in order to maintain the confidentiality of sensitive information;
(*d*) in order to avoid serious harm to the public interest; or
(*e*) because to hold it in public would prejudice the interests of justice.

(3) Where a hearing, or part of it, is to be held in private, the Upper Tribunal may determine who is entitled to attend the hearing or part of it.

(4) The Upper Tribunal may give an order excluding from any hearing, or part of it—

(*a*) any person whose conduct the Upper Tribunal considers is disrupting or is likely to disrupt the hearing;
(*b*) any person whose presence the Upper Tribunal considers is likely to prevent another person from giving evidence or making submissions freely; or
(*c*) any person where the purpose of the hearing would be defeated by the attendance of that person.

(5) The Upper Tribunal may give a direction excluding a witness from a hearing until that witness gives evidence.

(6) When publishing a decision in terms of rule 29(4) (notice of decisions and reasons) following a hearing which was held wholly or partly in private, the Upper Tribunal must, so far as practicable, ensure that the decision does not disclose information which was referred to in a part of the hearing that was held in private.

Hearings in a party's absence

28 If a party fails to attend a hearing, the Upper Tribunal may proceed with the hearing if the Upper Tribunal—

(*a*) is satisfied that the party has been notified of the hearing or that reasonable steps have been taken to notify the party of the hearing; and

(*b*) considers that it is in the interests of justice to proceed with the hearing.

PART 6
DECISIONS

Notice of decisions and reasons

29 (1) Subject to the remainder of this rule, the Upper Tribunal may give a decision orally at a hearing.

(2) The Upper Tribunal must provide to each party and interested party as soon as reasonably practicable after making a decision (other than a decision under Part 7) which finally disposes of all issues in the proceedings or on a preliminary issue dealt with following an order under rule 7(3)(*f*)—

(*a*) a decision notice stating the Upper Tribunal's decision; and

(*b*) notification of any rights of appeal against the decision and the time and manner in which such rights of appeal may be exercised.

(3) If the Upper Tribunal does not provide written reasons for a decision, a party or an interested party may request written reasons within 14 days after the day of the decision.

[(3A) A request under paragraph (3) must be made in writing.][1]

(4) The Upper Tribunal may publish any of its decisions if it considers it in the public interest so to do, with the manner of publication also at the discretion of the Upper Tribunal.

Amendments—[1] Para (3A) inserted by the Upper Tribunal for Scotland (Rules of Procedure) Amendment Regulations, SSI 2016/333 reg 2 with effect from 1 December 2016.

Reviews

30 (1) The Upper Tribunal may at its own instance or on the application of a party review a decision (except an excluded decision) made by it if it considers it necessary in the interests of justice to do so and on review it may confirm, set aside, or set aside and redecide the decision.

(2) An application under paragraph (1) shall be made in writing within 14 days after the day of the decision and must state the reasons for making the application.

(3) The Upper Tribunal must send a copy of the application to any other party involved in the proceedings within 10 working days after the day of receipt of the application.

(4) The review must be decided as soon as reasonably practicable by the Upper Tribunal, with insofar as practicable the same members that decided the case, or where this is not practicable with members selected by the President.

(5) A notice of the decision of a review under paragraph (1) must as soon as reasonably practicable be sent by the Upper Tribunal to each party.

(6) The 30 days referred to in regulation 2(2) of the Scottish Tribunals (Time Limits) Regulations 2016 in respect of an application to the Upper Tribunal is extended by any review period.

PART 7
APPEALING DECISIONS OF THE UPPER TRIBUNAL

Interpretation

31 In this Part, "appeal" means the exercise of a right of appeal under section 48(1) of the 2014 Act.

Application for permission to appeal a decision of the Upper Tribunal

32 (1) A party seeking permission to appeal must make a written application to the Upper Tribunal.

(2) An application under paragraph (1) must—

(*a*) identify the decision of the Upper Tribunal to which it relates;

(*b*) identify the alleged error or errors of law in the decision; and

(*c*) state in terms of section 50(4) of the 2014 Act what important point of principle or practice would be raised by a second appeal or what other compelling reason there is that shows the appeal should be allowed to proceed.

Upper Tribunal's consideration of application for permission to appeal

33 (1) The Upper Tribunal must consider whether to give permission to appeal in relation to the decision or part of it.

(2) The Upper Tribunal must provide a record of its decision to the parties and any interested party as soon as practicable.

(3) If the Upper Tribunal refuses permission to appeal it must provide with the record of its decision—

(*a*) a statement of its reasons for such a refusal; and

(*b*) notification of the right to make an application to the Court of Session for permission to appeal and the time within which, and the method by which, such application must be made

(4) The Upper Tribunal may give permission to appeal on limited grounds, but must comply with paragraph (3) in relation to any grounds on which it has refused permission.

PART 8

LEGAL AID

Legal aid

34 If a party is granted legal aid by the Scottish Legal Aid Board in respect of a case before the Upper Tribunal that party must as soon as practicable send a copy of the legal aid certificate to the Upper Tribunal.

2016/341

FIRST-TIER TRIBUNAL FOR SCOTLAND (CHAMBERS) REGULATIONS 2016

Made . . . . *27 October 2016*

Coming into force . . . . *1 December 2016*

The Scottish Ministers make the following Regulations in exercise of the powers conferred by section 20(2) of the Tribunals (Scotland) Act 2014 and all other powers enabling them to do so.

In accordance with section 11(1) of that Act, the Scottish Ministers have obtained the Lord President's approval for the making of these Regulations and have consulted such other persons as they considered appropriate.

In accordance with 79(2)(*a*) of that Act, a draft of this instrument has been laid before and approved by resolution of the Scottish Parliament.

1 Citation and commencement

These Regulations may be cited as the First-tier Tribunal for Scotland (Chambers) Regulations 2016 and come into force on 1st December 2016.

2 Chambers of the First-tier Tribunal for Scotland

The First-tier Tribunal for Scotland is organised into the following chambers—

(*a*) the Mental Health Chamber;

(*b*) the Housing and Property Chamber;

(*c*) the Health and Education Chamber;

(*d*) the General Regulatory Chamber; and

(*e*) the Tax Chamber.

2016/342

SCOTTISH TRIBUNALS (OFFENCES IN RELATION TO PROCEEDINGS) REGULATIONS 2016

Made . . . . *27 October 2016*

Coming into force . . . . *1 December 2016*

The Scottish Ministers make the following Regulations in exercise of the powers conferred by section 67(1) of the Tribunals (Scotland)Act 2014 and all other powers enabling them to do so.

In accordance with section 67(3) of that Act, the Scottish Ministers have obtained the Lord President's approval for the making of these Regulations.

In accordance with section 79(2)(*d*) of that Act, a draft of this instrument has been laid before and approved by resolution of the Scottish Parliament.

1 Citation and commencement

These Regulations may be cited as the Scottish Tribunals (Offences in Relation to Proceedings) Regulations 2016 and come into force on 1st December 2016.

2 Offences in relation to proceedings before the Scottish Tribunals

(1) In any proceedings before the First-tier Tribunal or the Upper Tribunal it is an offence for any person to—

(*a*) make a false statement in an application in a case;

(*b*) alter, conceal or destroy, or fail to produce, something that is required to be produced in accordance with Tribunal Rules; or

(*c*) fail to attend or give evidence, when required to do so in accordance with Tribunal Rules.

(2) It is a defence for a person charged with an offence—

(*a*) under paragraph (1)(*a*), to prove that the false statement was not knowingly made;

(*b*) under paragraph (1)(*b*), to prove that a thing was not knowingly altered, concealed or destroyed;

(*c*) under paragraph (1)(*b*) or (*c*), to prove that there was a reasonable excuse for having acted in the way charged.

(3) A person who commits an offence under paragraph (1) is liable—

(*a*) on summary conviction, to imprisonment for a term not exceeding 12 months or a fine not exceeding level 5 on the standard scale (or both);

(*b*) on conviction on indictment, to imprisonment for a term not exceeding 2 years or a fine not exceeding £5,000 (or both).

3 Circumstances in which a person need not give evidence or produce something to the Scottish Tribunals

In any proceedings before the First-tier Tribunal or the Upper Tribunal a person need not give evidence or produce something which the person would be entitled to refuse to give or produce in proceedings in a court in Scotland.

2017/69

FIRST-TIER TRIBUNAL FOR SCOTLAND TAX CHAMBER (PROCEDURE) REGULATIONS 2017

Made . . . . *8 March 2017*
Laid before the Scottish Parliament . . . . *10 March 2017*
Coming into force . . . . *24 April 2017*

The Scottish Ministers make the following Regulations in exercise of the powers conferred by paragraph 4(2) of schedule 9 of the Tribunals (Scotland) Act 2014 and all other powers enabling them to do so.

In accordance with paragraph 4(3) of schedule 9 of that Act, they have consulted the President of the Scottish Tribunals and such other persons as they have considered appropriate.

1 Citation and commencement

(1) These Regulations may be cited as the First-tier Tribunal for Scotland Tax Chamber (Procedure) Regulations 2017, and the Rules set out in the schedule may be cited as The First-tier Tribunal for Scotland Tax Chamber Rules of Procedure 2017.

(2) These Regulations come into force on 24th April 2017.

2 Application of the Rules set out in the schedule

The Rules in the schedule apply to proceedings before the First-tier Tribunal for Scotland Tax Chamber, when exercising the functions allocated to it by regulation 2(1) of the First-tier Tribunal for Scotland (Transfer of Functions of the First-tier Tax Tribunal for Scotland) Regulations 2017.

SCHEDULE

THE FIRST-TIER TRIBUNAL FOR SCOTLAND TAX CHAMBER RULES OF PROCEDURE 2017

Regulation 2

CONTENTS

PART 1
INTRODUCTION

Interpretation

1 In these Rules—

"the 2014 Act" means the Tribunals (Scotland) Act 2014;

"RSTPA 2014" means the Revenue Scotland and Tax Powers Act 2014;

"appellant" means—

(*a*) the person who starts proceedings (whether by notifying an appeal, by making an application, by a reference, or otherwise);

(*b*) in proceedings started jointly by more than one person, such persons acting jointly or each such person, as the context requires;

(*c*) in any case, a person substituted as an appellant under rule 9 (addition, substitution and removal of parties);

"Basic case" means a case allocated to the Basic category under rule 24 (allocation of cases to categories);

"chairing member" means the chairing member of the First-tier Tribunal, who is the legal member of that tribunal or, as the case may be, the member chosen by the Chamber President in terms of rule 19(1);

"Chamber President" means the Chamber President of the First-tier Tribunal;

"Complex case" means a case allocated to the Complex category under rule 24;

"Convention Rights" has the meaning given to it in section 1 of the Human Rights Act 1998;

"Default Paper case" means a case allocated to the Default Paper category under rule 24;

"document" means anything in which information is recorded in any form, and an obligation under these Rules to provide or allow access to a document or a copy of a document for any purpose means, unless the First-tier Tribunal directs otherwise, an obligation to provide or allow access to such document or copy in a legible form or in a form which can be readily made into a legible form;

"excluded decision" means a decision falling under section 51 of the 2014 Act;

"First-tier Tribunal" means the First-tier Tribunal for Scotland Tax Chamber;

"hearing" means an oral hearing and includes a hearing conducted in whole or in part by video link, telephone or other means of instantaneous two-way electronic communication;

"interested party" means a person other than the appellant or respondent on whom the First-tier Tribunal has ordered the proceedings before it to be served;

"party" means a person who is (or was at the time that the First-tier Tribunal disposed of the proceedings) an appellant or respondent in proceedings before the First-tier Tribunal;

"practice direction" means a direction given under section 74 of the 2014 Act;

"respondent" means—

(*a*) Revenue Scotland, where Revenue Scotland is not an appellant;

(*b*) in proceedings brought by Revenue Scotland alone, a person against whom the proceedings are brought or to whom the proceedings relate;

(*c*) in any case, a person substituted or added as a respondent under rule 9; and

"Standard case" means a case allocated to the Standard category under rule 24.

Overriding objective and parties' obligation to co-operate with the First-tier Tribunal

2 (1) The overriding objective of these Rules is to enable the First-tier Tribunal to deal with cases fairly and justly.

(2) Dealing with a case in accordance with the overriding objective includes—

(*a*) dealing with the case in ways which are proportionate to the importance of the case, the complexity of the issues, the anticipated expenses and the resources of the parties;

(*b*) avoiding unnecessary formality and seeking flexibility in the proceedings;

(*c*) ensuring, so far as practicable, that the parties are able to participate fully in the proceedings;

(*d*) using any special expertise of the First-tier Tribunal effectively; and

(*e*) avoiding delay, so far as compatible with proper consideration of the issues.

(3) The First-tier Tribunal must seek to give effect to the overriding objective when it—

(*a*) exercises any power under these Rules; or

(*b*) interprets any rule or practice direction.

(4) Parties must, insofar as reasonably possible—

(*a*) help the First-tier Tribunal to further the overriding objective; and

(*b*) co-operate with the First-tier Tribunal generally.

Mediation

3 The First-tier Tribunal should seek, where appropriate—

(*a*) to bring to the attention of the parties the availability of mediation for the resolution of the dispute; and

(*b*) if the parties wish, and provided that it is compatible with the overriding objective, to facilitate the use of mediation.

Delegation to staff

4 (1) Staff of the Scottish Courts and Tribunals Service may, with the approval of the Chamber President, carry out functions of a judicial nature permitted or required to be done by the First-tier Tribunal.

(2) The approval referred to at paragraph (1) may apply generally to the carrying out of specified functions by members of staff of a specified description in specified circumstances.

(3) Within 14 days after the date that the First-tier Tribunal sends notice of a decision made by a member of staff pursuant to an approval under paragraph (1) to a party, that party may make a written application to the First-tier Tribunal for that decision to be considered afresh by a member of the First-tier Tribunal.

PART 2
GENERAL POWERS AND PROVISIONS

Case management powers

5 (1) Subject to the provisions of the 2014 Act and these Rules, the First-tier Tribunal may regulate its own procedure.

(2) The First-tier Tribunal may give an order in relation to the conduct or disposal of proceedings at any time, including an order amending, suspending or setting aside an earlier order.

(3) In particular, and without restricting the general powers in paragraphs (1) and (2), the First-tier Tribunal may—

(*a*) extend or shorten the time for complying with any rule or order;

(*b*) conjoin or take concurrently two or more sets of proceedings or parts of proceedings raising common issues;

(*c*) specify one or more cases as a lead case or lead cases where—

(i) two or more cases are before the First-tier Tribunal;

(ii) in each such case the proceedings have not been finally determined; and

(iii) the cases give rise to common or related issues of fact or law;

and sist the other cases until the common or related issues have been determined;

(*d*) permit or require a party to amend a document;

(*e*) permit or require a party or another person to provide documents, information, evidence or submissions to the First-tier Tribunal or a party;

(*f*) deal with an issue in the proceedings as a preliminary issue;

(*g*) hold a hearing to consider any matter, including a case management hearing;

(*h*) decide the form of any hearing;

(*i*) adjourn or postpone a hearing;

(*j*) require a party to produce a file of documents for a hearing;

(*k*) sist proceedings;

(*l*) transfer proceedings to another court or tribunal if that other court or tribunal has jurisdiction in relation to the proceedings and—

(i) because of a change of circumstances since the proceedings were started, the First-tier Tribunal no longer has jurisdiction in relation to the proceedings; or

(ii) the First-tier Tribunal considers that the other court or tribunal is a more appropriate forum for the determination of the case;

(*m*) suspend the effect of its own decision pending the determination by the First-tier Tribunal or the Upper Tribunal, as the case may be, of an application for permission to appeal or an appeal.

Procedure for applying for and giving orders

6 (1) The First-tier Tribunal may give an order on the application of one or more of the parties or on its own initiative.

(2) An application for an order may be made—

(*a*) by sending or delivering a written application to the First-tier Tribunal; or

(*b*) orally during the course of a hearing.

(3) An application for an order must include the reasons for making that application.

(4) Before making an order, the First-tier Tribunal must afford parties an opportunity to make representations to it concerning whether the order should be made and the terms of the order.

Failure to comply with rules etc

7 (1) An irregularity resulting from a failure to comply with any requirement in these Rules, a practice direction or an order does not of itself render void the proceedings or any step taken in the proceedings.

(2) If a party has failed to comply with a requirement in these Rules, a practice direction or an order, the First-tier Tribunal may take such action as it considers just, which may include—

(*a*) waiving the requirement;

(*b*) requiring the failure to be remedied; or

(*c*) exercising its power under rule 8 (dismissal of a party's case).

Dismissal of a party's case

8 (1) The First-tier Tribunal must dismiss the whole or a part of the proceedings if the First-tier Tribunal—

(*a*) does not have jurisdiction in relation to the proceedings or that part of them; and

(*b*) does not exercise its power under rule 5(3)(*l*) (transfer to another court or tribunal) in relation to the proceedings or that part of them.

(2) The First-tier Tribunal may dismiss the whole or a part of the proceedings if—

(*a*) the appellant has failed to comply with an order which stated that failure by the appellant to comply with the order could lead to the dismissal of the proceedings or part of them; or

(*b*) the appellant has failed to co-operate with the First-tier Tribunal to such an extent that the First-tier Tribunal cannot deal with the proceedings fairly and justly.

(3) The First-tier Tribunal may not dismiss the whole or a part of the proceedings under paragraph (1) or (2) without first giving the appellant an opportunity to make representations in relation to the proposed dismissal.

Addition, substitution and removal of parties

9 (1) The First-tier Tribunal may make an order adding, substituting or removing a party as an appellant or a respondent including where—

(*a*) the wrong person has been named as a party; or

(*b*) the addition, substitution or removal has become necessary because of a change in circumstances since the start of proceedings.

(2) If the First-tier Tribunal makes an order under paragraph (1) it may make such consequential orders as it considers appropriate.

(3) A person who is not a party may make a written application to the First-tier Tribunal to be added or substituted as a party under this rule.

(4) If the First-tier Tribunal refuses an application under paragraph (3) it must consider whether to permit the person who made the application to provide submissions or evidence to the First-tier Tribunal.

Orders for expenses

10 (1) The First-tier Tribunal may make an order for expenses as taxed by the Auditor of the Court of Session against a party if that party's act, omission or other conduct has caused any other party to incur expense which it would be unreasonable for that other party to be expected to pay, with the maximum recoverable expenses being the expenses incurred.

(2) The First-tier Tribunal, of its own initiative or on the application of a party or the parties, may in exceptional circumstances fix by order a sum payable by a party in discharge of an award of expenses.

Representatives

11 (1) A party may be represented in any proceedings by a legal representative or lay representative whose details must be communicated to the First-tier Tribunal prior to any hearing.

(2) A party may show any document or communicate any information about the proceedings to that party's lay representative or legal representative without contravening any prohibition or restriction on disclosure of the document or information.

(3) Where a document or information is disclosed under paragraph (2), the lay representative or legal representative is subject to any prohibition or restriction on disclosure in the same way that the party is.

(4) Anything permitted or required to be done by a party under these Rules, a practice direction or an order may be done by a lay representative, except signing of a witness statement.

(5) The First-tier Tribunal may order that a lay representative is not to represent a party if—

(*a*) it is of the opinion that the lay representative is an unsuitable person to act as a lay representative (whether generally or in the proceedings concerned); or

(*b*) it is satisfied that to do so would be in the interests of the efficient administration of justice.

Supporters

12 (1) A party who is an individual may be accompanied by another person to act as a supporter.

(2) A supporter may assist the party by—

(*a*) providing moral support;

(*b*) helping to manage tribunal documents and other papers;

(*c*) taking notes of the proceedings;

(*d*) quietly advising on—

(i) points of law and procedure;

(ii) issues which the party might wish to raise with the tribunal.

(3) The party may show any document or communicate any information about the proceedings to that party's supporter without contravening any prohibition or restriction on disclosure of the document or information.

(4) Where a document or information is disclosed under paragraph (3), the supporter is subject to any prohibition or restriction on disclosure in the same way that the party is.

(5) A supporter may not represent the party.

(6) The First-tier Tribunal may order that a person is not to act as a supporter of a party if—

(*a*) it is of the opinion that the supporter is an unsuitable person to act as a supporter (whether generally or in the proceedings concerned); or

(*b*) it is satisfied that to do so would be in the interests of the efficient administration of justice.

Calculating time

13 (1) An act required by these Rules, a practice direction or an order to be done on or by a particular day must be done before 5pm on that day.

(2) If the time specified by these Rules, a practice direction or an order for doing any act ends on a day other than a working day, the act is done in time if it is done on the next working day.

(3) In this rule "working day" means any day except a Saturday or Sunday or a bank holiday in Scotland under section 1 of the Banking and Financial Dealings Act 1971.

Sending and delivery of documents

14 (1) Any document to be provided to the First-tier Tribunal under these Rules, a practice direction or an order must be—

(*a*) sent by pre-paid post or document exchange, or delivered by hand, to the address of the First-tier Tribunal; or

(*b*) sent or delivered by such other method as the First-tier Tribunal may permit or direct.

(2) Subject to paragraph (3), if a party or representative provides a fax number, email address or other details for the electronic transmission of documents to them, that party or representative must accept delivery of documents by that method.

(3) If a party informs the First-tier Tribunal and all other parties that a particular form of communication (other than pre-paid post or delivery by hand) should not be used to provide documents to that party, that form of communication must not be so used.

(4) If the First-tier Tribunal or a party sends a document to a party or the First-tier Tribunal by email or any other electronic means of communication, the recipient may request that the sender provide a hard copy of the document to the recipient. The recipient must make such a request as soon as reasonably practicable after receiving the document electronically.

(5) The First-tier Tribunal and each party may assume that the address provided by a party or its representative is and remains the address to which documents should be sent or delivered until receiving notification to the contrary.

Disclosure of documents and information

15 The First-tier Tribunal may at any stage of the proceedings, on its own initiative or on application by one or more of the parties, make an order with a view to preventing or restricting the public disclosure of any aspect of those proceedings so far as it considers necessary in the interests of justice or in order to protect the Convention Rights of any person.

Evidence and submissions

16 (1) Without restriction on the general powers in rule 5(1) and (2) (case management powers), the First-tier Tribunal may give orders as to—

(*a*) issues on which it requires evidence or submissions;

(*b*) the nature of any such evidence;

(*c*) whether the parties are permitted or required to provide expert evidence, and if so whether the parties must jointly appoint a single expert to provide such evidence;

(*d*) any limit on the number of witnesses whose evidence a party may put forward, whether in relation to a particular issue or generally;

(*e*) the manner in which any evidence or submissions are to be provided, which may include an order for them to be given—

(i) orally at a hearing; or

(ii) by written submissions or witness statement; and

(f) the time at which any evidence or submissions are to be provided.

(2) The First-tier Tribunal may exclude evidence that would otherwise be admissible where—

(*a*) the evidence was not, without reasonable excuse, provided within the time allowed by an order or a practice direction.

(*b*) the evidence was otherwise, without reasonable excuse, provided in a manner that did not comply with an order or a practice direction; or

(*c*) it would otherwise be unfair to admit the evidence.

(3) The First-tier Tribunal may consent to a witness giving, or require any witness to give, evidence on oath, and may administer an oath for that purpose.

Citation of witnesses and orders to answer questions or produce documents

17 (1) On the application of a party or on its own initiative, the First-tier Tribunal may—

(*a*) by citation require any person to attend as a witness at a hearing at the time and place specified in the citation;

(*b*) order any person to answer any questions or produce any documents in that person's possession or control which relate to any issue in the proceedings.

(2) A citation under paragraph (1)(*a*) must—

(*a*) give the person required to attend at least 14 days' notice of the hearing, or such other period as the First-tier Tribunal may order;

(*b*) where the person is not a party, make provision for the person's necessary expenses of attendance to be paid, and state who is to pay them;

(*c*) state that the person on whom the requirement is imposed may apply to the First-tier Tribunal to vary or set aside the citation or order, if the person did not have an opportunity to object to it before it was made or issued; and

(*d*) state the consequences of failure to comply with the citation or order.

Withdrawal

18 (1) A party may give notice to the First-tier Tribunal of the withdrawal of the case made by it in the First-tier Tribunal proceedings, or any part of that case—

(*a*) by sending or delivering to the First-tier Tribunal a notice of withdrawal; or

(*b*) orally at a hearing.

(2) The First-tier Tribunal must notify each party of its receipt of a withdrawal under this rule.

Chairing member and voting

19 (1) Where a matter is to be decided by two or more members of the First-tier Tribunal, the Chamber President must determine the chairing member.

(2) The decision of the First-tier Tribunal on an application must be made by majority with the chairing member having a casting vote.

Venue for hearings

20 The First-tier Tribunal is to be convened at such time and place in Scotland as the President of Tribunals may determine.

Enforcement of decisions

21 An order for the payment of a sum payable in pursuance of a decision of the First-tier Tribunal, or a copy of such an order certified by the First-tier Tribunal, may be enforced as if it were an extract registered decree arbitral bearing a warrant for execution issued by the sheriff court of any sheriffdom in Scotland.

PART 3
PROCEDURE FOR CASES IN THE FIRST-TIER TRIBUNAL

Proceedings concerning late notice of review

22 (1) A person may apply to the First-tier Tribunal to be allowed a late notice of review under section 236(2)(*b*) of RSTPA 2014 (late notice of review) only if—

(*a*) the person has approached Revenue Scotland for agreement under section 236(2)(*a*); and

(*b*) agreement has been refused or has been given only on limited grounds.

(2) Where permission to be allowed a late notice of review is sought under paragraph (1), the notice of review must include a request for the permission referred to in section 236(2)(*b*) of RSTPA 2014 and the reason why the notice of review was not provided in time.

Notice of appeal to the First-tier Tribunal

23 (1) The notice of appeal referred to in section 242(1) of RSTPA 2014 (notice of appeal) must include—

(*a*) the name and address of the appellant;

(*b*) the name and address of the appellant's representative (if any);

(*c*) an address where documents for the appellant may be sent or delivered;

(*d*) details of the decision appealed against;

(*e*) the result the appellant is seeking; and

(*f*) the grounds for making the appeal.

(2) The appellant must provide with the notice of appeal a copy of any written record of any decision appealed against, and any statement of reasons for that decision, that the appellant has or can reasonably obtain.

(3) A person may apply to the First-tier Tribunal for permission to appeal under section 243(2)(*b*) of RSTPA 2014 (late notice of appeal) only if—

(*a*) the person has approached Revenue Scotland for agreement under section 243(2)(*a*); and

(*b*) agreement has been refused or has been given only on limited grounds.

(4) Where permission to appeal may be sought under paragraph (3)—

(*a*) the notice of appeal must include a request for the permission referred to in section 243(2)(*b*) of RSTPA 2014 and the reason why the notice of appeal was not provided in time; and

(*b*) unless the First-tier Tribunal gives such permission, the First-tier Tribunal must not admit the appeal.

(5) When the First-tier Tribunal receives the notice of appeal, it must give notice of the proceedings to the respondent.

Allocation of cases to categories

24 (1) When the First-tier Tribunal receives a notice of appeal, the First-tier Tribunal must give an order allocating the case to one of the categories set out in paragraph (2).
(2) The categories referred to in paragraph (1) are—
(*a*) Default Paper cases, which will usually be disposed of without a hearing;
(*b*) Basic cases, which will usually be disposed of after a hearing, with minimal exchange of documents before the hearing;
(*c*) Standard cases, which will usually be subject to more detailed case management and be disposed of after a hearing; and
(*d*) Complex cases, in respect of which see paragraphs (4) and (5) below.
(3) The First-tier Tribunal may give a further order re-allocating a case to a different category at any time, either on the application of a party or on its own initiative.
(4) The First-tier Tribunal may allocate a case as a Complex case under paragraph (1) or (3) only if the First-tier Tribunal considers that the case—
(*a*) will require lengthy or complex evidence or a lengthy hearing;
(*b*) involves a complex or important principle or issue; or
(*c*) involves a large financial sum.
(5) If a case is allocated as a Complex case, rule 29 (transfer of Complex cases to the Upper Tribunal) applies to the case.

Basic cases

25 (1) This rule applies to Basic cases.
(2) Rule 26 (respondent's statement of case) does not apply and, subject to paragraph (3) and any direction given by the First-tier Tribunal, the case will proceed directly to a hearing.
(3) If the respondent intends to raise grounds for contesting the proceedings at the hearing which have not previously been communicated to the appellant, the respondent must notify the appellant of such grounds.
(4) If the respondent is required to notify the appellant of any grounds under paragraph (3), the respondent must do so—
(*a*) as soon as reasonably practicable after becoming aware that such is the case; and
(*b*) in sufficient detail to enable the appellant to respond to such grounds at the hearing.

Respondent's statement of case

26 (1) A respondent must send or deliver a statement of case to the First-tier Tribunal, the appellant and any other respondent so that it is received—
(*a*) in a Default Paper case, within 42 days after the day the First-tier Tribunal sent the notice of appeal;
(*b*) in a Standard or Complex case, within 60 days after the day the First-tier Tribunal sent the notice of appeal.
(2) A statement of case must—
(*a*) in an appeal, state the legislative provision under which the decision under appeal was made; and
(*b*) set out the respondent's position in relation to the case.
(3) A statement of case may also contain a request that the case be dealt with at a hearing or without a hearing.
(4) If a respondent provides a statement of case to the First-tier Tribunal later than the time required by paragraph (1) or by any extension allowed under rule 5(3)(*a*) (case management powers), the statement of case must include a request for an extension of time and the reason why the statement of case was not provided in time.

Further steps in a Default Paper case

27 (1) This rule applies to Default Paper cases.
(2) The appellant may send or deliver a written reply to the First-tier Tribunal so that it is received within 30 days after the day on which the respondent sent to the appellant the statement of case to which the reply relates.
(3) The appellant's reply may—
(*a*) set out the appellant's response to the respondent's statement of case;
(*b*) provide any further information (including, where appropriate, copies of the documents containing such information) which has not yet been provided to the First-tier Tribunal and is relevant to the case; and

(*c*) contain a request that the case be dealt with at a hearing or without a hearing.

(4) The appellant must send or deliver a copy of any reply provided under paragraph (2) to each respondent at the same time as it is provided to the First-tier Tribunal.

(5) If the appellant provides a reply to the First-tier Tribunal later than the time required by paragraph (2) or by any extension allowed under rule 5(3)(*a*) (case management powers), the reply must include a request for an extension of time and the reason why the reply was not provided in time.

(6) Following receipt of the appellant's reply, or the expiry of the time for the receipt of the appellant's reply then, unless it orders otherwise and subject in any event to paragraph (7), the First-tier Tribunal must proceed to determine the case without a hearing.

(7) If any party has made a written request to the First-tier Tribunal for a hearing, the First-tier Tribunal must hold a hearing before determining the case.

Further steps in a Standard or Complex case

28 (1) This rule applies to Standard and Complex cases.

(2) Subject to any direction to the contrary, within 42 days after the day the respondent sent the statement of case (or, where there is more than one respondent, the date of the final statement of case) each party must send or deliver to the First-tier Tribunal and to each other party a list of documents—

(*a*) of which the party providing the list has possession, the right to possession, or the right to take copies; and

(*b*) which the party providing the list intends to rely upon or produce in the proceedings.

(3) A party which has provided a list of documents under paragraph (2) must allow each other party to inspect or take copies of the documents on the list.

Transfer of Complex cases to the Upper Tribunal

29 (1) If a case has been allocated as a Complex case the First-tier Tribunal may, with the consent of the parties, refer a case or a preliminary issue to the Chamber President with a request that the case or issue be considered for transfer to the Upper Tribunal.

(2) If a case or issue has been referred by the First-tier Tribunal under paragraph (1), the Chamber President may direct that the case or issue be transferred to and determined by the Upper Tribunal.

Decision with or without a hearing

30 (1) Subject to rule 27(6) (determination of a Default Paper case without a hearing) and the following paragraphs in this rule, the First-tier Tribunal must hold a hearing before making a decision which disposes of proceedings, or a part of proceedings, unless—

(*a*) each party has consented to the matter being decided without a hearing; and

(*b*) the First-tier Tribunal considers that it is able to decide the matter without a hearing.

(2) This rule does not apply to decisions under Part 4 of these Rules (correcting, reviewing and appealing decisions of the First-tier Tribunal).

(3) The First-tier Tribunal may dispose of proceedings, or a part of proceedings, under rule 8 (dismissal of a party's case) without a hearing.

Entitlement to attend a hearing

31 Subject to rules 11(5) (representatives), 12(6)(supporters) and 33(4) (public and private hearings and powers to exclude), each party is entitled to attend a hearing together with any legal or lay representative and supporter permitted respectively by rules 11 and 12.

Notice of hearings

32 (1) The First-tier Tribunal must give each party entitled to attend a hearing reasonable notice of the time and place of any hearing (including any adjourned or postponed hearing) and any changes to the time and place of any hearing.

(2) In relation to a hearing to consider the disposal of proceedings, the period of notice under paragraph (1) must be at least 14 days except that the First-tier Tribunal may give less than 14 days' notice—

(*a*) with the parties' consent; or

(*b*) in urgent or exceptional circumstances.

Public and private hearings

33 (1) Subject to the following paragraphs, all hearings must be held in public.

(2) The First-tier Tribunal may give an order that a hearing, or part of it, is to be held in private if the First-tier Tribunal considers that restricting access to the hearing is justified—

(*a*) in the interests of public order;
(*b*) in order to protect a person's right to respect for their private and family life;
(*c*) in order to maintain the confidentiality of sensitive information;
(*d*) in order to avoid serious harm to the public interest; or
(*e*) because not to do so would prejudice the interests of justice.

(3) Where a hearing, or part of it, is to be held in private, the First-tier Tribunal may determine who is permitted to attend the hearing or part of it.

(4) The First-tier Tribunal may give an order excluding from any hearing, or part of it—
(*a*) any person whose conduct the First-tier Tribunal considers is disrupting or is likely to disrupt the hearing;
(*b*) any person whose presence the First-tier Tribunal considers is likely to prevent another person from giving evidence or making submissions freely;
(*c*) any person where the purpose of the hearing would be defeated by the attendance of that person; or
(*d*) a person under the age of sixteen years.

(5) The First-tier Tribunal may give an order excluding a witness from a hearing until that witness gives evidence.

(6) When publishing a decision notice referred to in rule 35(2) (notice of decisions and reasons) resulting from a hearing which was held wholly or partly in private, the First-tier Tribunal must, so far as practicable, ensure that the report does not disclose information which was referred to only in a part of the hearing that was held in private (including such information which enables the identification of any person whose affairs were dealt with in the part of the hearing that was held in private) if to do so would undermine the purpose of holding the hearing in private.

Hearings in a party's absence

34 If a party fails to attend a hearing the First-tier Tribunal may proceed with the hearing if the First-tier Tribunal—
(*a*) is satisfied that the party has been notified of the hearing or that reasonable steps have been taken to notify the party of the hearing; and
(*b*) considers that it is in the interests of justice to proceed with the hearing.

Notice of decisions and reasons

35 (1) Subject to the remainder of this rule, the First-tier Tribunal may give a decision orally at a hearing.

(2) The First-tier Tribunal must provide to each party within 30 days after the day of making a decision (other than a decision under Part 4 of these Rules) which finally disposes of all issues in the proceedings or of a preliminary issue dealt with following an order under rule 5(3)(*f*) (case management powers), or as soon as practicable thereafter, a decision notice which—
(*a*) states the First-tier Tribunal's decision; and
(*b*) notifies the party of any right of appeal against the decision and the time within which, and the manner in which, the right of appeal may be exercised.

(3) If the First-tier Tribunal does not provide written reasons for a decision, a party or an interested party may by application in writing made within 30 days after the day of the decision notice request such reasons.

(4) The First-tier Tribunal must send a full written statement of findings and reasons to each party within 30 days after the day of receiving an application for written reasons made in accordance with paragraph (3) or as soon as practicable thereafter.

(5) The First-tier Tribunal may publish any of its decisions if it considers it in the public interest so to do, with the manner of publication at the discretion of the First-tier Tribunal.

PART 4
CORRECTING, REVIEWING AND APPEALING DECISIONS OF THE FIRST-TIER TRIBUNAL

Interpretation

36 In this Part—
"appeal" means the exercise of a right of appeal under section 46(1) of the 2014 Act (appeal from the Tribunal); and
"review" means the internal review provided for by section 43(1) of the 2014 Act (review of decisions).

Correction of clerical mistakes or accidental slips or omissions

37 The First-tier Tribunal may at any time correct any clerical mistake or other accidental slip or omission contained in a decision, order or any document produced by it, by—

(*a*) sending notification of the amended decision or order, or a copy of the amended document to all parties; and

(*b*) making any necessary amendment to any information published in relation to the decision, order or document.

Application for permission to appeal a decision of the First-tier Tribunal

38 (1) A person seeking permission to appeal must make a written application to the First-tier Tribunal for permission to appeal.

(2) An application under paragraph (1) must—

(*a*) identify the decision of the First-tier Tribunal to which it relates;

(*b*) identify the alleged point or points of law on which the person making the application wishes to appeal; and

(*c*) state the result the party making the application is seeking.

First-tier Tribunal's consideration of application for permission to appeal

39 (1) The First-tier Tribunal must decide whether to give permission to appeal on any point of law.

(2) The First-tier Tribunal must provide a record of its decision to the parties and any interested party as soon as reasonably practicable.

(3) If the First-tier Tribunal refuses permission on any point of law it must provide with the record of its decision—

(*a*) a statement of its reasons for such a refusal; and

(*b*) notification of the right to make an application to the Upper Tribunal for permission to appeal and the time within which, and the method by which, such an application must be made.

Review of a decision

40 (1) The First-tier Tribunal may either at its own instance or at the request of a party review any decision made by it where it is necessary in the interests of justice to do so.

(2) An application for review under section 43(2)(*b*) of the 2014 Act must—

(*a*) be made in writing (and copied to all other parties);

(*b*) be made within 14 days of the date on which the decision was made or within 14 days of the date that the written reasons were sent to the parties (if later); and

(*c*) set out why a review of the decision is necessary.

(3) If the First-tier Tribunal considers that the application is wholly without merit, the First-tier Tribunal shall refuse the application and shall also inform the parties of the reasons for the refusal.

(4) Except where paragraph (3) applies, the First-tier Tribunal shall send a notice to the parties—

(*a*) setting a time limit for any response to the application by the other parties and seeking the views of the parties on whether the application can be determined without a hearing; and

(*b*) at the discretion of the First-tier Tribunal, setting out the First-tier Tribunal's provisional views on the application.

(5) Except where paragraph (3) applies, the decision shall be reviewed at a hearing unless the First-tier Tribunal considers, having regard to any response to the notice provided under paragraph (4), that a hearing is not necessary in the interests of justice.

(6) Where practicable, the review shall be undertaken by one or more of the members of the First-tier Tribunal who made the decision to which the review relates.

(7) Where the First-tier Tribunal proposes to review a decision at its own instance, it shall inform the parties of the reasons why the decision is being reviewed and the decision shall be reviewed in accordance with paragraph (4) (as if an application had been made and not refused).

(8) A review by the First-tier Tribunal in terms of paragraph (1) either at its own instance or on an application of a party does not affect the time limit of 30 days in regulation 2(1) of the Scottish Tribunals (Time Limits) Regulations 2016 for making an application for permission to appeal.

2017/105

UPPER TRIBUNAL FOR SCOTLAND (TRANSFER OF FUNCTIONS OF THE UPPER TAX TRIBUNAL FOR SCOTLAND) REGULATIONS 2017

Made . . . . *28 March 2017*

Coming into force . . . . *24 April 2017*

The Scottish Ministers make the following Regulations in exercise of the powers conferred by sections 28(2) and 79(1)(*b*) and paragraph 1(1) of schedule 2 of the Tribunals (Scotland) Act 2014 and all other powers enabling them to do so.

In accordance with section 79(2)(*b*) of that Act, a draft of this instrument has been laid before and approved by resolution of the Scottish Parliament.

1 Citation, commencement and interpretation

(1) These Regulations may be cited as the Upper Tribunal for Scotland (Transfer of Functions of the Upper Tax Tribunal for Scotland) Regulations 2017 and come into force on 24th April 2017.

(2) In these Regulations—

the "2014 Act" means the Tribunals (Scotland) Act 2014; and

the "functions of the Upper Tax Tribunal for Scotland" means the functions exercised by the Upper Tax Tribunal for Scotland by virtue of section 21(4) of the Revenue Scotland and Tax Powers Act 2014.

2 Transfer of functions of the Upper Tax Tribunal for Scotland to the Upper Tribunal and abolition of Upper Tax Tribunal for Scotland

(1) The functions of the Upper Tax Tribunal for Scotland are transferred to the Upper Tribunal.

(2) The Upper Tax Tribunal for Scotland is abolished.

3 Transfer of members of the Upper Tax Tribunal for Scotland to the Upper Tribunal

(1) Subject to paragraph (2), the members of the Upper Tax Tribunal for Scotland on the coming into force of these Regulations are transferred to and become legal members of the Upper Tribunal.

(2) Members of the Upper Tax Tribunal for Scotland transferred to the Upper Tribunal under paragraph (1) shall (subject to the provisions of the 2014 Act) be legal members of the Upper Tribunal in accordance with terms and conditions to be offered by the Scottish Ministers on transfer, which will supersede any existing terms and conditions of appointment.

4 Transitional and savings provisions

The schedule of these Regulations contains transitional and savings provisions.

SCHEDULE

TRANSITIONAL AND SAVINGS PROVISIONS

Regulation 4

Appeals, applications, referrals and proceedings in progress before the Upper Tax Tribunal for Scotland immediately before 24th April 2017 to transfer to the Upper Tribunal

1 Any appeal, application and referral to the Upper Tax Tribunal for Scotland in progress immediately before 24th April 2017 but not yet determined and any proceedings of the Upper Tax Tribunal for Scotland in progress immediately before that date shall be transferred to and be completed by the Upper Tribunal as if they were appeals, applications and referrals to the Upper Tribunal or proceedings in the Upper Tribunal but with so far as possible the same persons hearing and determining the case before the Upper Tribunal as members of that tribunal as were prior to 24th April 2017 hearing the case as members of the Upper Tax Tribunal for Scotland.

Decisions, directions and orders of the Upper Tax Tribunal for Scotland to continue in force

2 Any decision (whether or not called a decision), direction or order given or made in appeals, applications and referrals to, and proceedings before, the Upper Tax Tribunal for Scotland which is in force immediately before 24th April 2017 remains in force on and after that date as if it were a decision, direction or order of the Upper Tribunal.

Time limits in respect of appeals, applications, referrals to, and proceedings before, the Upper Tax Tribunal for Scotland to carry over to the Upper Tribunal

3 Any time limit which has started to run before 24th April 2017 in respect of appeals, applications and referrals to, and proceedings before, the Upper Tax Tribunal for Scotland (and which has not expired) shall continue to apply where appeals, applications, referrals and proceedings are transferred to the Upper Tribunal.

Unexercised right of appeal to Court of Session, if exercised, remains as an appeal to the Court of Session

4 Where in respect of a decision of the Upper Tax Tribunal for Scotland before 24th April 2017, there lies a right of appeal to the Court of Session, which has not been exercised before that date but is still exercisable, any appeal on or after 24th April 2017 shall continue to be to the Court of Session as if the decision had been made by the Upper Tribunal and the appeal shall be an appeal from the Upper Tribunal for the purposes of section 48(1) of the 2014 Act

Savings provision

5 Where in respect of a decision of the Upper Tax Tribunal for Scotland before 24th April 2017, there lies a right of appeal to the Court of Session which has been exercised before that date, the appeal shall continue as an appeal from the Upper Tribunal to the Court of Session.

2017/106

FIRST-TIER TRIBUNAL FOR SCOTLAND (TRANSFER OF FUNCTIONS OF THE FIRST-TIER TAX TRIBUNAL FOR SCOTLAND) REGULATIONS 2017

Made . . . .*28 March 2017*
Coming into force . . . .*24 April 2017*

The Scottish Ministers make the following Regulations in exercise of the powers conferred by sections 20(2), 28(2) and 79(1)(*b*) and paragraph 1(1) of schedule 2 of the Tribunals (Scotland) Act 2014 and all other powers enabling them to do so.

In accordance with section 11(1)(*a*) and (*b*) of that Act, the Scottish Ministers have obtained the Lord President's approval and have consulted such other persons as they considered appropriate.

In accordance with section 79(2)(*a*) and (*b*) of that Act, a draft of this instrument has been laid before and approved by resolution of the Scottish Parliament.

1 Citation, commencement and interpretation

(1) These Regulations may be cited as the First-tier Tribunal for Scotland (Transfer of Functions of the First-tier Tax Tribunal for Scotland) Regulations 2017 and come into force on 24th April 2017.

(2) In these Regulations—

the "2014 Act" means the Tribunals (Scotland) Act 2014; and the "functions of the First-tier Tax Tribunal for Scotland" means the functions exercised by the First-tier Tax Tribunal for Scotland by virtue of section 21(2) of the Revenue Scotland and Tax Powers Act 2014.

2 Transfer of functions of the First-tier Tax Tribunal for Scotland to the First-tier Tribunal and abolition of First-tier Tax Tribunal for Scotland

(1) The functions of the First-tier Tax Tribunal for Scotland are transferred to the First-tier Tribunal with allocation to the First-tier Tribunal Tax Chamber.

(2) The First-tier Tax Tribunal for Scotland is abolished.

3 Transfer of members of the First-tier Tax Tribunal for Scotland to the First-tier Tribunal

(1) Subject to paragraphs (2) and (3), the members of the First-tier Tax Tribunal for Scotland on the coming into force of these Regulations are transferred to and become members of the First-tier Tribunal, with—

(a) legal members of the First-tier Tax Tribunal for Scotland becoming legal members of the First-tier Tribunal; and

(b) ordinary members of the First-tier Tax Tribunal for Scotland becoming ordinary members of the First-tier Tribunal.

(2) Members of the First-tier Tax Tribunal transferred to the First-tier Tribunal under paragraph (1) shall (subject to the provisions of the 2014 Act) be members of the First-tier Tribunal in accordance with terms and conditions to be offered by the Scottish Ministers on transfer, which will supersede any existing terms and conditions of appointment.

(3) Paragraph (1) does not apply to any member of the First-tier Tax Tribunal for Scotland if the member has already been transferred to and is a member of the First-tier Tribunal by virtue of regulations made under section 28(2) of the 2014 Act which were in force prior to these Regulations coming into force.

4 Transitional provisions

The schedule of these Regulations contains transitional provisions.

SCHEDULE

TRANSITIONAL PROVISIONS

Regulation 4

Appeals, applications, referrals and proceedings in progress before the First-tier Tax Tribunal for Scotland immediately before 24th April 2017 to transfer to the First-tier Tribunal

1 Any appeal, application and referral to the First-tier Tax Tribunal for Scotland in progress immediately before 24th April 2017 but not yet determined and any proceedings of the First-tier Tax Tribunal for Scotland in progress immediately before that date shall be transferred to and be completed by the First-tier Tribunal but with so far as possible the same persons hearing and determining the case before the First-tier Tribunal as members of that tribunal as were prior to 24th April 2017 hearing the case as members of the First-tier Tax Tribunal for Scotland.

Decisions, directions and orders of the First-tier Tax Tribunal for Scotland to continue in force

2 Any decision (whether or not called a decision), direction or order given or made in appeals, applications and referrals to, and proceedings before, the First-tier Tax Tribunal for Scotland which is in force immediately before 24th April 2017 remains in force on and after that date as if it were a decision, direction or order of the First-tier Tribunal.

Time limits in respect of appeals, applications, referrals to, and proceedings before, the First-tier Tax Tribunal for Scotland to carry over to the First-tier Tribunal

3 Any time limit which has started to run before 24th April 2017 in respect of appeals, applications and referrals to, and proceedings before, the First-tier Tax Tribunal for Scotland (and which has not expired) shall continue to apply where appeals, applications, referrals and proceedings are transferred to the First-tier Tribunal.

Unexercised right of appeal to Upper Tax Tribunal for Scotland, if exercised, is an appeal to the Upper Tribunal

4 Where in respect of a decision of the First-tier Tax Tribunal for Scotland before 24th April 2017, there lies a right of appeal to the Upper Tax Tribunal for Scotland, which has not been exercised before that date but is still exercisable, any appeal on or after 24th April 2017 shall be to the Upper Tribunal as if the decision had been made by the First-tier Tribunal and the appeal shall be an appeal from the First-tier Tribunal for the purposes of section 46(1) of the 2014 Act.

Exercised right of appeal to the Upper Tax Tribunal for Scotland shall be completed by the Upper Tribunal

5 Where in respect of a decision of the First-tier Tax Tribunal for Scotland before 24th April 2017, there lies a right of appeal to the Upper Tax Tribunal for Scotland which has been exercised before that date, the appeal shall transfer to and be completed by the Upper Tribunal in accordance with paragraph 1 of the schedule of the Upper Tribunal for Scotland (Transfer of Functions of the Upper Tax Tribunal for Scotland) Regulations 2017.

2017/107

FIRST-TIER TRIBUNAL FOR SCOTLAND TAX CHAMBER AND UPPER TRIBUNAL FOR SCOTLAND (COMPOSITION) REGULATIONS 2017

Made . . . . *28 March 2017*
Coming into force . . . . *24 April 2017*

The Scottish Ministers make the following Regulations in exercise of the powers conferred by sections 38(1) and 40(1) of the Tribunals (Scotland) Act 2014 and all other powers enabling them to do so.

In accordance with section 11(2) of that Act, they have consulted the President of Tribunals.

In accordance with section 79(2)(*c*) of that Act, a draft of this instrument has been laid before and approved by resolution of the Scottish Parliament.

1 Citation, commencement and interpretation

(1) These Regulations may be cited as the First-tier Tribunal for Scotland Tax Chamber and Upper Tribunal for Scotland (Composition) Regulations 2017 and come into force on 24th April 2017.

(2) In these Regulations—

"the Chamber President" means the Chamber President of the First-tier Tribunal; and
"the First-tier Tribunal" means the First-tier Tribunal for Scotland Tax Chamber.

2 Composition of First-tier Tribunal

The First-tier Tribunal, when convened to decide any matter in a case, shall consist of—

(*a*) a legal member;

(*b*) a legal member and one other member (who may be a legal member or an ordinary member); or

(*c*) a legal member with two or more other members (who may be legal members or ordinary members or a combination of both).

3 Composition of Upper Tribunal hearing appeals or referrals from First-tier Tribunal

(1) The Upper Tribunal, when deciding an appeal or a referral in a case decided by or referred from the First-tier Tribunal to the Upper Tribunal, shall consist of—

(*a*) a legal or judicial member of the Upper Tribunal;

(*b*) the Chamber President (except a temporary Chamber President), acting either alone or with a legal or judicial member of the Upper Tribunal;

(*c*) the President of Tribunals, acting either alone or with the Chamber President or a legal member or another judicial member of the Upper Tribunal; or

(*d*) the Lord President, acting either alone or with the Chamber President or a legal member or another judicial member of the Upper Tribunal.

(2) The Chamber President referred to in paragraph (1) must not have had any involvement in the case prior to the appeal or referral of the case to the Upper Tribunal.

(3) In this regulation "judicial member of the Upper Tribunal" means a judge of the Court of Session.